To Mon,

Congratulations
on your graduation.
Good luck in the
future. Mrs. Larson

Webster's New World™ Encyclopedia

COLLEGE EDITION

Webster's New World™ Encyclopedia

COLLEGE EDITION

Prentice Hall

New York   London   Toronto   Sydney   Tokyo   Singapore

PRENTICE HALL GENERAL REFERENCE
15 Columbus Circle
New York, New York, 10023

Library of Congress Cataloging-in-Publication Data
Webster's new world encyclopedia college edition.
    p.   cm.
Rev. ed. of: *Webster's new world encyclopedia*.
Includes index.
ISBN 0–671–85016–4
1. Encyclopedias and dictionaries. I. Prentice-Hall, inc.
II. Webster's new world encyclopedia.
AG5.W386 1993   93-387
031—dc20   CIP

First Edition

Set in Century Old Style

Pagination and typesetting by Aesthetex, Edinburgh
Manufactured in the United States of America

10   9   8   7   6   5   4   3   2   1

First Prentice Hall Edition

Editors

Contributors

Introduction

The true measure of an encyclopedia's worth must be how useful it is to the general reader at whom it is aimed, not to the expert. Any prospective reader consulting the *Webster's New World College Encyclopedia* is therefore asked to look, not only at a subject they are familiar with, but also at a topic about which they know little or nothing. Does the entry inform? Does it include up-to-date facts and figures? Is it accurate? Does it provide a useful introduction to the subject? Is it easy to understand? If relevant, is there a helpful illustration? If the answer to all these questions is yes, then the encyclopedia can be judged a success. *Webster's New World College Encyclopedia* has been written, edited, and illustrated with these aims in mind.

Arrangement of Entries

Entries are ordered alphabetically, as if there were no spaces between words. Thus entries for words beginning "federal" follow the order:

Federal Bureau of Investigation
Federalism
Federal Reserve System

However, we have avoided a purely mechanical alphabetization in cases where a different order corresponds more with human logic. For example, sovereigns with the same name are grouped according to country and then by number, so that King George II of England is placed before George III of England, and not next to King George II of Greece. Words beginning "Mc" and "Mac" are treated as if they begin "Mac"; "St" and "Saint" are both treated as if they were spelled "Saint."

Cross References

These are shown by a ⟡ symbol immediately preceding the reference. Cross-referencing is selective; a cross reference is shown when another entry contains material directly relevant to the subject matter of any entry, and where the reader may not otherwise think of looking. We do not believe that the existence of a cross reference alone is sufficient for the reader; the encyclopedia should be an aid, not an obstacle course. We have therefore avoided as far as possible entries that consist only of a cross reference; even the shortest cross reference gives some indication of the subject involved.

Foreign Names and Titles

Names of foreign sovereigns and places are usually shown in their English form, except where the foreign name is more familiar; thus, there are entries for Charles V of Spain, but Juan Carlos (not John Charles), and for Florence, not Firenze. Entries for titled people are under the name by which they are best known to the general reader: thus Anthony Eden, not Lord Avon. Cross references have been provided in cases where confusion is possible.

Units

Measurements of distances, temperatures, sizes, and so on show the US unit first, followed by the metric equivalent. SI (metric) units are used throughout for scientific entries. Entries are also included for many weights and measures no longer in common use.

Science and Technology

It would be needlessly pedantic to insist on formally correct terminology for every scientific entry in cases where another name is at present far more familiar. Technical terms and current terminology must of course be included. However, many of these terms are not in common use. Entries are therefore generally placed under the name by which they are better known, with the technical term given as a cross reference. To make it easier for the non-specialist to understand, technical terms are frequently explained when used within the text of an entry, even though they may have their own entry elsewhere.

Systems of Government

Individual countries are identified as one of the following systems: liberal democracy, emergent democracy, communism, nationalistic socialism, authoritarian nationalism, military authoritarianism, and absolutism.

Chinese Names

Pinyin, the preferred system for transcribing Chinese names of people and places, is generally used: thus there is an entry at Mao Zedong, not Mao Tse-tung. An exception is made for a few names that are more familiar in their former (Wade-Giles) form, such as Sun Yat-sen and Chiang Kai-shek. Where confusion is likely, Wade-Giles forms are given as cross references.

Webster's New World Encyclopedia

COLLEGE EDITION

A first letter in nearly all alphabets. The English *a* is derived from the Etruscan *a* through the Latin alphabet, which is the parent of the W European alphabets. The Greeks called the first letter (A, α) *alpha*; the Semites *aleph* or *alph*, which meant "ox," probably because the word began with this sound.

A in music, the reference pitch to which instruments of an orchestra are tuned.

The frequency ("concert pitch") associated with the note A has fluctuated across the centuries from about 370 Hz to about 610 Hz; today it is customarily standardized as 440 Hz although orchestras in Europe are known to favor 442 or 448 Hz.

A in physics, symbol for ◊*ampere*, a unit of electrical current.

A1 abbreviation for *first class* (of ships).

Aachen (French *Aix-la-Chapelle*) German cathedral city and spa in the *Land* of North Rhine–Westphalia, 45 mi/72 km SW of Cologne; population (1988) 239,000. It has thriving electronic, glass, and rubber industries, and is one of Germany's principal railroad junctions.

Aachen was the Roman Aquisgranum, and from the time of Charlemagne until 1531 the German emperors were crowned there. Charlemagne was born and buried in Aachen, and founded the cathedral 796. The 14th-century town hall, containing the hall of the emperors, is built on the site of Charlemagne's palace.

Aalto Alvar 1898–1976. Finnish architect and designer. One of Finland's first Modernists, he had a unique architectural style, characterized by asymmetry, curved walls, and contrast of natural materials. He invented a new form of laminated bent-plywood furniture 1932 and won many design awards for household and industrial items.

Aalto's buildings include the Hall of Residence at the Massachusetts Institute of Technology, Cambridge, Massachusetts, 1947–49; Technical High School, Otaniemi, 1962–65; and Finlandia Hall, Helsinki, 1972.

aardvark (Afrikaans "earth pig") nocturnal mammal *Orycteropus afer*, order Tubulidentata, found in central and southern Africa. A timid, defenseless animal about the size of a pig, it has a long head, piglike snout, and large asinine ears. It feeds on termites, which it licks up with its long sticky tongue.

aardwolf nocturnal mammal *Proteles cristatus* of the ◊hyena family, Hyaenidae. It is found in eastern and southern Africa, usually in the burrows of the aardvark, and feeds on termites.

Aarhus (Danish *Århus*) second-largest city of Denmark, on the east coast overlooking the Kattegat; population (1990) 261,400. It is the capital of Aarhus county in Jylland (Jutland) and a shipping and commercial center.

Aaron *c.* 13th century BC. In the Old Testament, the elder brother of Moses and coleader of the ◊Hebrews in their march from Egypt to the Promised Land of Canaan. He made the Golden Calf for the Hebrews to worship when they despaired of Moses' return from Mount Sinai, but he was allowed to continue as high priest. All his descendants are hereditary high priests, called the *cohanim*, or cohens, and maintain a special place in worship and ceremony in the synagogue. See also ◊Levite.

Aaron Hank (Henry Louis) 1934– . US baseball player and all-time home-run leader. In the course of his career, primarily with the Milwaukee and Atlanta Braves, he won the National League batting title twice, 1955 and 1959. In 1957, as a member of the World Championship team, he was named the National League's most valuable player. His greatest achievement was breaking Babe Ruth's lifetime record of 714 home runs; by the time of his retirement in 1976, Aaron had hit a total of 755 home runs. He was elected to the Baseball Hall of Fame in 1982.

Born in Mobile, Alabama, he played with the Indianapolis team of the Negro National League before joining the Milwaukee Braves 1954.

abacus method of calculating with a handful of stones on "a flat surface" (Latin *abacus*), familiar to the Greeks and Romans, and used by earlier peoples, possibly even in ancient Babylon; it still survives in the more sophisticated bead-frame form of the Russian *schoty* and the Japanese *soroban*. The abacus has been superseded by the electronic calculator.

Abadan Iranian oil port on the E side of the Shatt-al-Arab waterway; population (1986) 294,000. Abadan is the chief refinery and shipping center for Iran's oil industry, nationalized 1951. This measure was the beginning of the worldwide movement by oil-producing countries to assume control of profits from their own resources.

abalone edible marine snail of the worldwide genus *Haliotis*, family Haliotidae. Abalones have flattened, oval, spiraled shells, which have holes around the outer edge and a bluish mother-of-pearl lining. This lining is used in ornamental work.

abb. abbreviation for *abbreviation*.

Abbadid dynasty 11th century. Muslim dynasty based in Seville, Spain, which lasted from 1023 until 1091. The dynasty was founded by Abu-al-Kasim Mohammed Ibn Abbad, who led the townspeople against the Berbers when the Spanish caliphate fell. The dynasty continued under Motadid (1042–1069) and Motamid (1069–1091) when the city was taken by the ◊Almoravids.

Abbado Claudio 1933– . Italian conductor, long associated with the La Scala opera house, Milan. Principal conductor of London Symphony Orchestra from 1979, he also worked with the European Community Youth Orchestra from 1977.

Abbas I *the Great c.* 1557–1629. Shah of Persia from 1588. He expanded Persian territory by conquest, defeating the Uzbeks near Herat 1597 and also the Turks. The port of Bandar-Abbas is named after him. At his death his empire reached from the river Tigris to the Indus. He was a patron of the arts.

Abbas II Hilmi 1874–1944. Last ◊khedive (viceroy) of Egypt, 1892–1914. On the outbreak of war between Britain and Turkey in 1914, he sided with Turkey and was deposed following the establishment of a British protectorate over Egypt.

Abbasid dynasty family of rulers of the Islamic empire, whose ◊caliphs reigned in Baghdad 750–1258. They were descended from Abbas, the prophet Mohammed's uncle, and some of them, such as Harun al-Rashid and Mamun (reigned 813–33), were outstanding patrons of cultural development. Later their power dwindled, and in 1258 Baghdad was burned by the Tatars.

From then until 1517 the Abbasids retained limited power as caliphs of Egypt.

abbey in the Christian church, a monastery (of monks) or a nunnery or convent (of nuns), all dedicated to a life of celibacy and religious seclusion, governed by an abbot or abbess respectively. The word is also applied to a building that was once the church of an abbey, for example, Westminster Abbey, London.

The first abbeys, as established in Syria or Egypt, were mere collections of huts, but later massive and extensive building complexes were constructed throughout Europe. St Benedict's Abbey at Monte Cassino in Italy and Citeaux and Cluny in France set the pattern. In England many abbeys were closed by Henry VIII, who turned from the Roman Catholic Church. In other countries many were closed in the 18th and 19th centuries as a result of political revolutions.

Abbey Edwin Austin 1852–1911. US artist and illustrator. Born in Philadelphia, Abbey was educated by private tutors and later studied at the Pennsylvania Academy of Fine Arts. His illustrations, first published in *Harper's Weekly*, earned him a national reputation and commissions to illustrate many popular books. Living much of his later life in England, he was elected to the Royal Academy and the US National Academy of Design and received the French Legion of Honor. Among his works are the murals he painted for the Boston Public Library depicting the quest for the Holy Grail.

Abbott and Costello adopted names of William Abbott (1895–1974) and Louis Cristillo (1906–1959) US comedy duo. They moved to films from vaudeville, and most, including *Buck Privates* 1941 and *Lost in a Harem* 1944, were showcases for their routines. They also appeared on radio and televison.

Abd al-Malik Ibn Marwan AD 647–705. Caliph who reigned 685–705. Based in Damascus, he waged military campaigns to unite Muslim groups and battled against the Greeks. He instituted a purely Arab coinage and replaced Syriac, Coptic, and Greek with Arabic as the language for his lands. His reign was turbulent but succeeded in extending and strengthening the power of the Omayyad dynasty. He was also a patron of the arts.

Abd el-Krim el-Khettabi 1881–1963. Moroccan chief known as the "Wolf of the ◊Riff."

With his brother Mohammed, he led the *Riff revolt* against the French and Spanish invaders, inflicting disastrous defeat on the Spanish at Anual in 1921, but surrendered to a large French army under Pétain in 1926. Banished to the island of Réunion, he was released in 1947 and died in voluntary exile in Cairo.

abdication crisis in British history, the constitutional upheaval of the period Nov 16, 1936 to Dec 10, 1936, brought about by the English king Edward VIII's decision to marry Wallis Simpson, an American divorcee. The marriage of the "Supreme Governor" of the Church of England to a divorced person was considered unsuitable and the king was finally forced to abdicate on Dec 10 and left for voluntary exile in France. He was created Duke of Windsor and married Mrs Simpson on June 3, 1937.

abdomen in invertebrates, the part of the body below the ⬦thorax, containing the digestive organs; in insects and other arthropods, it is the hind part of the body. In mammals, the abdomen is separated from the thorax by the diaphragm, a sheet of muscular tissue; in arthropods, commonly by a narrow constriction. In insects and spiders, the abdomen is characterized by the absence of limbs.

Abdul-Hamid II 1842–1918. Last sultan of Turkey 1876–1909. In 1908 the ⬦Young Turks under Enver Pasha forced Abdul-Hamid to restore the constitution of 1876 and in 1909 insisted on his deposition. He died in confinement. For his part in the ⬦Armenian massacres suppressing the revolt of 1894–96 he was known as "the Great Assassin"; his actions still motivate Armenian violence against the Turks.

Abdul-Jabbar Kareem 1947– . US basketball player who played for the National Basketball Association's Milwaukee Bucks 1969–75 and the Los Angeles Lakers 1975–89. He held the record for being named professional basketball's most valuable player 6 times over the period between 1971 and 1980. A center at 7 ft 2 in tall, he was noted for his "sky hook" shot. He led the University of California at Los Angeles's (UCLA) to the NCAA championship 1967–69.

Born Ferdinand Lewis Alcindor in New York City, he changed his name in 1971 after converting to the Muslim faith in 1968.

Abdullah ibn Hussein 1882–1951. King of Jordan from 1946. He worked with the British guerrilla leader T E ⬦Lawrence in the Arab revolt of World War I. Abdullah became king of Trans-Jordan 1946; on the incorporation of Arab Palestine (after the 1948–49 Arab–Israeli War) he renamed the country the Hashemite Kingdom of Jordan. He was assassinated.

Abdullah Sheik Mohammed 1905–1982. Indian politician, known as the "Lion of Kashmir." He headed the struggle for constitutional government against the Maharajah of Kashmir, and in 1948, following a coup, became prime minister. He agreed to the accession of the state to India, but was dismissed and imprisoned from 1953 (with brief intervals) until 1966, when he called for Kashmiri self-determination. He became chief minister of Jammu and Kashmir 1975, accepting the sovereignty of India.

Abel in the Old Testament, the second son of Adam and Eve; as a shepherd, he made burned offerings of meat to God which were more acceptable than the fruits offered by his brother Cain; he was killed by the jealous Cain.

Abel John Jacob 1857–1938. US biochemist,

rain falling past window of stationary train   rain falling past window of moving train

direction in which star seems to lie

true position of star

starlight enters telescope

starlight reaches eyepiece

movement of earth

aberration of starlight *The aberration of starlight is an optical illusion caused by the motion of the Earth.*

discoverer of ⬦adrenaline. He studied the chemical composition of body tissues, and this led, in 1898, to the discovery of adrenaline, the first hormone to be identified, which Abel called epinephrine. He later became the first to isolate ⬦amino acids from blood.

Abel Niels Henrik 1802–1829. Norwegian mathematician. He demonstrated that the general quintic equation

$$ax^5 + bx^4 + cx^3 + dx^2 + ex + f = 0$$

could not be solved algebraically. Subsequent work covered elliptic functions, integral equations, infinite series, and the binomial theorem.

He lived a life of poverty and ill health, dying of tuberculosis shortly before the arrival of an offer of a position at the University of Berlin.

Abelard Peter 1079–1142. French scholastic philosopher who worked on logic and theology. His romantic liaison with his pupil ⬦Héloïse caused a medieval scandal. Details of his controversial life are contained in the autobiographical *Historia Calamitatum Mearum/The History of My Misfortunes*.

Abelard, born near Nantes, became canon of Notre Dame in Paris and master of the cathedral school 1115. When his seduction of, and secret marriage to, Héloïse became known, she entered a convent and he was castrated at the instigation of her uncle, Canon Fulbert, and became a monk. Resuming teaching a year later, he was cited for heresy and became a hermit at Nogent, where he built the oratory of the Paraclete, and later abbot of a monastery in Brittany. He died at Châlon-sur-Saône on his way to defend himself against a new charge of heresy. Héloïse was buried beside him at the Paraclete 1164; their remains were taken to Père Lachaise cemetery, Paris, 1817.

He opposed realism in the debate over universals, and propounded "conceptualism" whereby universal terms have only a mental existence. His love letters from Héloïse survive.

Aberdeen city and seaport on the E coast of Scotland, administrative headquarters of

Grampian region; population (1991) 201,100. Industries include agricultural machinery, paper, and textiles; fishing; ship-building; granite-quarrying; and engineering. There are shore-based maintenance and service depots for the North Sea oil rigs. Aberdeen is Scotland's third-largest city.

Aberdeen George Hamilton Gordon, 4th Earl of Aberdeen 1784–1860. British Tory politician, prime minister 1852–55 when he resigned because of the criticism aroused by the miseries and mismanagement of the Crimean War.

aberration of starlight apparent displacement of a star from its true position, due to the combined effects of the speed of light and the speed of the Earth in orbit around the Sun (about 18.5 mi per second/30 km per second).

Aberration, discovered in 1728 by James ⬦Bradley, was the first observational proof that the Earth orbits the Sun.

aberration, optical any of a number of defects that impair the image in an optical instrument. Aberration occurs because of minute variations in lenses and mirrors, and because different parts of the light ⬦spectrum are reflected or refracted by varying amounts.

In *chromatic aberration* the image is surrounded by colored fringes, because light of different colors is brought to different focal points by a lens. In *spherical aberration* the image is blurred because different parts of a spherical lens or mirror have different focal lengths. In *astigmatism* the image appears elliptical or cross-shaped because of an irregularity in the curvature of the lens. In *coma* the

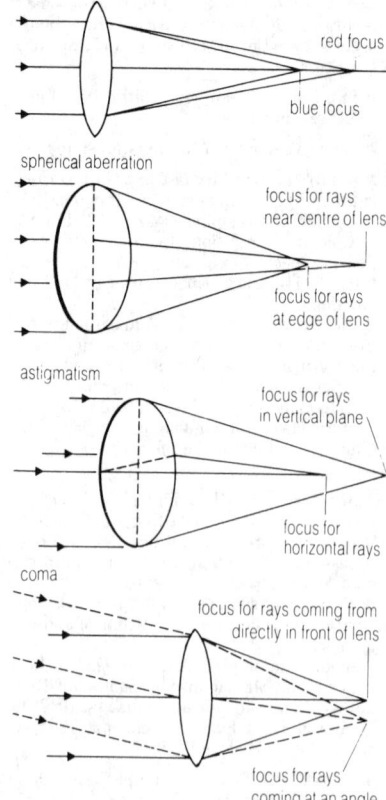

chromatic aberration

red focus

blue focus

spherical aberration

focus for rays near centre of lens

focus for rays at edge of lens

astigmatism

focus for rays in vertical plane

focus for horizontal rays

coma

focus for rays coming from directly in front of lens

focus for rays coming at an angle

aberration, optical *The main defects, or aberrations, of optical systems.*

images appear progressively elongated toward the edge of the field of view.

The term was coined 1737 by French mathematician Alexis Clairaut (1713–1765).

Abidja'n port and former capital (to 1983) of the Republic of Ivory Coast, W Africa; population (1982) 1,850,000. Products include coffee, palm oil, cocoa, and timber (mahogany). It was replaced as capital by Yamoussoukro.

Abilene city in central Texas; SW of Fort Worth; seat of Taylor county. It is a center for oil-drilling equipment; population (1990) 106,650. Abilene was founded 1881 as the terminus for the Texas and Pacific Railroad.

Abilene town in Kansas, on the Smoky Hill River; population (1990) 6,240. In the 1860s Abilene was the northern terminus of the Chisholm Trail cattle drive and the point from which the herds were shipped east by rail. Its economy includes the manufacture of aircraft and missile components and oil-field equipment.

President Eisenhower lived here as a boy and is buried here; the Eisenhower Center, also here, includes a museum and library.

abiotic factor a nonorganic variable within the ecosystem, affecting the life of organisms. Examples include temperature, light, and soil structure. Abiotic factors can be harmful to the environment, as when sulfur dioxide emissions from power stations produce acid rain.

Abkhazia autonomous republic in Georgia, situated on the Black Sea
capital Sukhumi
area 3,320 sq mi/8,600 sq km
products tin, fruit, and tobacco
population (1989) 526,000
history The region has been the scene of secessionist activity on the part of the minority Muslim Abkhazi community since 1989, culminating in the republic's declaration of independence 1992. Georgian troops invaded and took control Aug 1992, but secessionist guerrillas subsequently gained control of the northern half of the republic.

Abkhazia, a Georgian kingdom from the 4th century, was inhabited traditionally by Abkhazis, an ethnic group converted from Christianity to Islam in the 17th century. By the 1980s some 17% of the population were Muslims and two-thirds were of Georgian origin. In March–April and July 1989, Abkhazis demanded secession from Georgia and reinstatement as a full Union republic, conflicting with Georgian nationalists' demands for the republic to be incorporated as part of Georgia. The dispute triggered civil unrest in Abkhazia and nationalist demonstrations throughout Georgia. In July 1992 the local parliament unilaterally declared Abkhazia's independence. The kidnapping of senior Georgian officials in Aug provoked an invasion of Abkhazia by Georgian troops, who seized the capital and set up an interim government. By early Sept Russia's president Boris Yeltsin had successfully brokered a cease-fire, but in a surprise Oct offensive, secessionist guerrillas reclaimed half of Abkhazia, gaining control of all of the region N of the capital, Sukhumi.

ablative in the grammar of certain inflected languages, such as Latin, the ablative case is the form of a noun, pronoun, or adjective used to indicate the agent in passive sentences or the instrument, manner, or place of the action described by the verb.

ABM abbreviation for *anti-ballistic missile*; see ◇nuclear warfare.

Åbo Swedish name for ◇Turku, a port in Finland.

abolitionism in US and UK history, a movement culminating in the late 18th and early 19th centuries that aimed first to end the slave trade, and then to abolish the institution of ◇slavery and emancipate slaves.

In the US, Benjamin ◇Franklin had argued against slavery as early as 1775. It was officially abolished by the Emancipation Proclamation 1863 of President Abraham ◇Lincoln, but it could not be enforced until 1865 after the Union victory in the civil war. The question of whether newly admitted states would allow slavery was a major issue in the breakup of the Union.

abominable snowman or *yeti* legendary creature, said to resemble a human, with long arms and a thickset body covered with reddish-gray hair. Reports of its existence in the Himalayas have been made since 1832, and they gained substance from a published photograph of a huge footprint in the snow in 1951. No further "evidence" has been found.

Aboriginal art art of the Australian Aborigines. Traditionally this was in the main religious and directed toward portraying the stories of the Dreamtime. Perishable materials were used, such as in ◇bark painting and carved trees and logs, and apart from some sheltered cave paintings and rock engravings few early works survive. Abstract patterns and stylized figures predominate.

Rock engravings are found throughout the continent. The earliest, such as those found in Koonalda Cave beneath the Nullarbor Plain and at the Early Man site on Cape York Peninsula, are characterized by stylized designs of circles, animal tracks and meandering patterns, and are between 15,000 and 20,000 years old. In the Hawkesbury River region of New South Wales large figures of animals, birds, fish, and spirit beings have been engraved into the sandstone. Cave walls were painted using natural ochres of red and yellow, white pipeclay, and charcoal. Such paintings are the most common form of Aboriginal fixed art, and include the vast galleries in the Laura district of Cape York, which feature the sticklike *Quinkan* spirit figures, and in the Kimberleys the *Wandjina* figures, towering red and white creatures with halolike headdresses. Stencils, frequently of hands, are found in all rock-painting areas and were produced by placing an object against the rock wall and then blowing a mouthful of paint over it. Trees and logs carved for ceremonial purposes include the burial poles made by the Tiwi people of Bathurst and Melville Islands, which are painted in complex designs using black, white, red, and yellow, and the carved trees (**dendroglyphs**) of the Darling Basin region of New South Wales, which were associated with initiation ceremonies and burial rites.

aborigine (Latin *ab origine* "from the beginning") any indigenous inhabitant of a region or country. The word often refers to the original peoples of areas colonized by Europeans, and especially to ◇Australian Aborigines.

abortion ending of a pregnancy before the fetus is developed sufficiently to survive outside the uterus. Loss of a fetus at a later gestational age is termed premature stillbirth. Abortion may be accidental (miscarriage) or deliberate (termination of pregnancy).

Methods of deliberate abortion vary according to the gestational age of the fetus. Up to 12 weeks, the cervix is dilated and a suction

curette passed into the uterus to remove its contents (*D and C*). Over 12 weeks, a prostaglandin pessary is introduced into the vagina, which induces labor, producing a miscarriage.

Worldwide, an estimated 150,000 unwanted pregnancies are terminated each day by induced abortion. One-third of these abortions are performed outside the law in unsafe conditions, resulting in about 500 deaths a day.

In 1989 an antiprogesterone pill was introduced in France, under the name RU 486. Within 24 hours of ingestion, it leads to the expulsion of the fetus from the uterus, and can be used at an earlier stage in pregnancy. The pill is also an effective contraceptive when taken up to 72 hours after intercourse.

Abortion as a means of birth control has long been the subject of controversy. The argument centers largely upon whether a woman should legally be permitted to have an abortion and, that being so, under what circumstances. Another aspect is whether, and to what extent, the law should protect the fetus. Those who oppose abortion generally believe that human life begins at the moment of conception, when a sperm fertilizes an egg. This is the view held, for example, by the Roman Catholic Church. Those who support unrestricted legal abortion may believe in a woman's right to choose whether she wants a child, and may take into account the large numbers of deaths and injuries from back-street abortions that are thus avoided. Others approve abortion for specific reasons. For example, if a woman's life or health is jeopardized, abortion may be recommended; and if there is a strong likelihood that the child will be born with severe mental or physical handicap. Other grounds for abortion include pregnancy resulting from sexual assault such as rape or incest.

In the US in 1989, a Supreme Court decision gave state legislatures the right to introduce some restrictions on the unconditional right, established by the Supreme Court in an earlier decision (Roe v. Wade), for any woman to decide to have an abortion.

Aboukir Bay, Battle of also known as the *Battle of the Nile*; naval battle between Great Britain and France, in which Admiral Nelson defeated Napoleon's fleet at the Egyptian seaport of Aboukir on Aug 1, 1798.

Abraham c. 2300 BC. In the Old Testament, founder of the Jewish nation. In his early life he was called Abram. God promised him heirs and land for his people in Canaan (Israel), renamed him Abraham ("father of many nations"), and tested his faith by a command (later retracted) to sacrifice his son Isaac.

Abraham was born in Ur, in Sumeria, the son of Terah. With his father, wife Sarah, and nephew Lot, he migrated to Haran, N Mesopotamia, then to Canaan where he received God's promise of land. After visiting Egypt he separated from Lot at Bethel and settled in Hebron (now in Israel). He was still childless at the age of 76, subsequently had a son (Ishmael) with his wife's maidservant Hagar, and then, at the age of 100, a son Isaac with his wife Sarah. God's promise to Abraham that his descendants would be a nation and Canaan their land was fulfilled when the descendants of Abraham's grandson, Jacob, were led out of Egypt by Moses. Abraham was buried in Machpelah Cave, Hebron.

Abraham, Plains of plateau near Québec, where the British commander ◇Wolfe defeated the French under ◇Montcalm, Sept 13,

1759, during the French and Indian War (1754–63). The outcome of the battle established British supremacy in Canada.

Abrams v US a US Supreme Court decision 1919 dealing with First Amendment rights in instances of sedition or espionage. Abrams, convicted of publishing pamphlets criticizing the US role in World War I and encouraging resistance to the war, appealed to the Supreme Court for protection under the right to free speech. The Court upheld the 1918 Sedition Law, ruling that Congress had the right to restrict speech that had a "tendency" toward harmful results. A famous dissent was filed by Justices Holmes and Brandeis.

abrasive substance used for cutting and polishing or for removing small amounts of the surface of hard materials. There are two types: natural and artificial abrasives, and their hardness is measured using the ⊅Mohs' scale. Natural abrasives include quartz, sandstone, pumice, diamond, and corundum; artificial abrasives include rouge, whiting, and carborundum.

Abruzzi mountainous region of S central Italy, comprising the provinces of L'Aquila, Chieti, Pescara, and Teramo; area 4,169 sq mi/10,800 sq km; population (1990) 1,272,000; capital L'Aquila. Gran Sasso d'Italia, 9,564 ft/2,914 m, is the highest point of the ⊅Apennines.

Absalom in the Old Testament, the favorite son of King David; when defeated in a revolt against his father he fled on a mule, but caught his hair in a tree branch and was killed by Joab, one of David's officers.

abscess collection of ⊅pus in the tissues forming in response to infection. Its presence is signaled by pain and inflammation.

abscissa in ⊅coordinate geometry, the *x*-coordinate of a point—that is, the horizontal distance of that point from the vertical or *y*-axis. For example, a point with the coordinates (4, 3) has an abscissa of 3. The *y*-coordinate of a point is known as the ⊅ordinate.

abscission in botany, the controlled separation of part of a plant from the main plant body—most commonly, the falling of leaves or the dropping of fruit. In ⊅deciduous plants the leaves are shed before the winter or dry season, whereas ⊅evergreen plants drop their leaves continually throughout the year. Fruit drop, the abscission of fruit while still immature, is a naturally occurring process.

Abscission occurs after the formation of an abscission zone at the point of separation. Within this, a thin layer of cells, the abscission layer, becomes weakened and breaks down through the conversion of pectic acid to pectin. Consequently the leaf, fruit, or other part can easily be dislodged by wind or rain. The process is thought to be controlled by the amount of ⊅auxin present. Fruit-drop is particularly common in fruit trees such as apples, and orchards are often sprayed with artificial auxin as a preventive measure.

absolute value or *modulus* in mathematics, the value, or magnitude, of a number irrespective of its sign. The absolute value of a number *n* is written |*n*| (or sometimes as mod *n*), and is defined as the positive square root of n^2. For example, the numbers –5 and 5 have the same absolute value: |5| = |–5| = 5.

For a ⊅complex number, the absolute value is its distance to the origin when it is plotted on an Argand diagram, and can be calculated (without plotting) by applying the ⊅Pythagorean theorem. By definition, the absolute value of any complex number $a + bi$ is given by the expression $|a + bi| = \sqrt{(a^2 + b^2)}$.

absolute zero lowest temperature theoretically possible, zero degrees kelvin, equivalent to –459.67°F/–273.16°C, at which molecules are motionless. Although the third law of ⊅thermodynamics indicates the impossibility of reaching absolute zero exactly, a temperature within 3×10^{-8} kelvin of it was produced 1984 by Finnish scientists. Near absolute zero, the physical properties of some materials change substantially (see ⊅cryogenics); for example, some metals lose their electrical resistance and become superconductive.

absolutism or *absolute monarchy* system of government in which the ruler or rulers have unlimited power. The principle of an absolute monarch, given a right to rule by God (see ⊅divine right of kings), was extensively used in Europe during the 17th and 18th centuries. Absolute monarchy is contrasted with limited or constitutional monarchy, in which the sovereign's powers are defined or limited.

absorption in science, the taking up of one substance by another, such as a liquid by a solid (ink by blotting paper) or a gas by a liquid (ammonia by water). In biology, absorption describes the passing of nutrients or medication into and through tissues such as intestinal walls and blood vessels. In physics, absorption is the phenomenon by which a substance retains radiation of particular wavelengths; for example, a piece of blue glass absorbs all visible light except the wavelengths in the blue part of the spectrum; it also refers to the partial loss of energy resulting from light and other electromagnetic waves passing through a medium. In nuclear physics, absorption is the capture by elements, such as boron, of neutrons produced by fission in a reactor.

abstract art nonrepresentational art. Ornamental art without figurative representation occurs in most cultures. The modern abstract movement in sculpture and painting emerged in Europe and North America between 1910 and 1920. Two approaches produce different abstract styles: images that have been "abstracted" from nature to the point where they no longer reflect a conventional reality and nonobjective, or "pure," art forms, supposedly without reference to reality.

Abstract art began in the avant-garde movements of the late 19th century, in Impressionism, Neo-Impressionism, and Post-Impressionism. These styles of painting reduced the importance of the original subject matter and emphasized the creative process of painting itself. In the first decade of the 20th century, some painters in Western Europe began to abandon the established Western convention of imitating nature and storytelling in pictures and developed a new artistic form and expression. Kandinsky is generally regarded as the first abstract artist. His highly colored canvases influenced many younger European artists. In France, the Cubists Picasso and Braque also developed, around 1907, an abstract style; their pictures, some partly collage, were composed mainly of fragmented natural images.

Many variations of abstract art developed in Europe, as shown in the work of Mondrian, Malevich, the Futurists, the Vorticists, and the Dadaists. Sculptors, including Brancusi and Epstein, were inspired by the new freedom in form and content, and Brancusi's *The Kiss* 1910 is one of the earliest abstract sculptures.

Two exhibitions of European art, one in New York in 1913 (the Armory Show), the other in San Francisco in 1917, opened the way for abstraction in US art. Many painters, including the young Georgia O'Keeffe, experimented with new styles. Morgan Russell (1886–1953) and Stanton Macdonald-Wright (1890–1973) invented their own school, Synchronism, a rival to Orphism, a similar style developed in France by Robert Delaunay.

Abstract art has dominated Western art from 1920 and has continued to produce many variations. In the 1940s it gained renewed vigor in the works of the Abstract Expressionists. From the 1950s Minimal art provoked more outraged reactions from critics and the general public alike.

Abstract Expressionism US movement in abstract art that emphasized the act of painting, the expression inherent in paint itself, and the interaction of artist, paint, and canvas. Abstract Expressionism emerged in New York in the early 1940s. Arshile Gorky, Franz Kline, Jackson Pollock, and Mark Rothko are associated with the movement.

Abstract Expressionism may have been inspired by Hans Hofmann and Gorky, who were both working in the US in the 1940s. Hofmann, who emigrated from Germany in the 1930s, had started to use dribbles and blobs of paint to create expressive abstract patterns, while Gorky, a Turkish Armenian refugee, was developing his highly colored abstracts with wild organic forms. Abstract Expressionism was not a distinct school but rather a convergence of artistic personalities, each revolting against restricting conventions in US art. The styles of the movement's exponents varied widely: Pollock's huge dripped and splashed work, Willem de Kooning's grotesque figures, Kline's strong calligraphic style, and Robert Motherwell's and Rothko's calmer large abstract canvases. The movement made a strong impression on European painting in the late 1950s.

Absurd, Theatre of the avant-garde drama originating with a group of playwrights in the 1950s, including Beckett, Ionesco, Genet, and Pinter. Their work expressed the belief that in a godless universe human existence has no meaning or purpose and therefore all communication breaks down. Logical construction and argument gives way to irrational and illogical speech and to its ultimate conclusion, silence, as in Beckett's play *Breath* 1970.

Abu Bakr or *Abu-Bekr* 573–634. "Father of the virgin," name used by Abd-el-Ka'aba from about 618 when the prophet Mohammed married his daughter Ayesha. He was a close adviser to Mohammed in the period 622–32. On the prophet's death, he became the first ⊅caliph, adding Mesopotamia to the Muslim world and instigating expansion into Iraq and Syria.

Traditionally he is supposed to have encouraged some of those who had known Mohammed to memorize his teachings; these words were later written down to form the Koran.

Abu Dhabi sheikdom in SW Asia, on the Arabian Gulf, capital of the ⊅United Arab Emirates. Formerly under British protection, it has been ruled since 1971 by Sheik Sultan Zayed bin al-Nahayan, who is also president of the

Supreme Council of Rulers of the United Arab Emirates.

Abu Simbel former site of two ancient temples cut into the rock on the banks of the Nile in S Egypt during the reign of Ramses II, commemorating him and his wife Nefertari. The temples were moved, in sections, 1966–67 before the site was flooded by the Aswan High Dam.

abutilon any of several ornamental plants of the genus *Abutilon*, family Malvaceae, of which *A. theophrastus*, the Indian mallow or velvet leaf, is one of the more common species. It has bell-shaped yellow flowers and is the source of a jutelike fiber.

Abydos ancient city in Upper Egypt; the Great Temple of Seti I dates from about 1300 BC.

abyssal plain broad expanse of sea floor lying 2–4 mi/3–6 km below sea level. Abyssal plains are found in all the major oceans, and they extend from bordering continental rises to mid-oceanic ridges.

Underlain by outward-spreading, new oceanic crust extruded from ridges, abyssal plains are covered in deep-sea sediments derived from continental slopes and floating microscopic marine organisms. The plains often are interrupted by chains of volcanic islands where plates ride over hot spots in the mantle, and by sea mounts originally formed in mid-oceanic ridge areas. In the Atlantic Ocean, for example, the abyssal plain extends about 930 mi/1,500 km off the E coast of the US.

abyssal zone dark ocean area 6,500–19,500 ft/2,000–6,000 m deep; temperature 39°F/4°C. Three-quarters of the area of the deep ocean floor lies in the abyssal zone, which is too far from the surface for photosynthesis to take place. Some fish and crustaceans living there are blind or have their own light sources. The region above is the bathyal zone; the region below, the hadal zone.

Abyssinia former name of ▷Ethiopia.

AC in physics, abbreviation for ▷*alternating current*.

acacia any of a large group of shrubs and trees of the genus *Acacia* of the legume family Leguminosae. Acacias include the thorn trees of the African savanna and the gum arabic tree *A. senegal* of N Africa, and several North American species of the SW USA and Mexico. Acacias are found in warm regions of the world, particularly Australia.

Academy originally, the school of philosophy founded by ▷Plato in the gardens of Academe, NW of Athens; it was closed by the Byzantine emperor ▷Justinian I, with the other pagan schools, in AD 529. The first academy (in the present-day sense of a recognized society established for the promotion of one or more of the arts and sciences) was the Museum of Alexandria, founded by Ptolemy Soter in the 3rd century BC.

Academy Award annual award in many categories, given since 1927 by the American Academy of Motion Picture Arts and Sciences (founded by Louis B Mayer of Metro-Goldwyn-Mayer 1927). Arguably the film community's most prestigious accolade, the award is a gold-plated statuette, which has been nicknamed "Oscar" since 1931.

Major awards include Best Picture, Best Director, Best Actor and Actress, Best Supporting Actor and Actress, Best Cinematography, Best Visual Effects, Best Screenplay, and Best Music.

Academy, French or *Académie Française* literary society concerned with maintaining the purity of the French language, founded by ▷Richelieu 1635. Membership is limited to 40 "Immortals" at a time.

Acadia (French *Acadie*) name given to ▷Nova Scotia by French settlers 1604, from which the term ▷Cajun derives.

acanthus any herbaceous plant of the genus *Acanthus* with handsome lobed leaves. Twenty species are found in the Mediterranean region and Old World tropics, including bear's breech *A. mollis*, whose leaves were used as a motif in Classical architecture, especially on Corinthian columns.

a cappella (Italian "in the style of the chapel") choral music sung without instrumental accompaniment. It is characteristic of ▷gospel music, ▷doo-wop, and the evangelical Christian church movement.

Acapulco or *Acapulco de Juarez* port and vacation resort in S Mexico; population (1990) 592,200. There is deep-sea fishing, and tropical products are exported. Acapulco was founded 1550 and was Mexico's major Pacific coast port until about 1815.

Sometimes called the Riviera of Mexico, it attracts many tourists to its beaches, luxury hotels, and gambling casinos.

acceleration rate of change of the velocity of a moving body. It is usually measured in feet per second per second (ft s^{-2}) or meters per second per second (m s^{-2}). Because velocity is a ▷vector quantity (possessing both magnitude and direction) a body traveling at constant speed may be said to be accelerating if its direction of motion changes. According to Newton's second law of motion, a body will only accelerate if it is acted upon by an unbalanced, or resultant, ▷force.

Acceleration due to gravity is the acceleration of a body falling freely under the influence of the Earth's gravitational field; it varies slightly at different latitudes and altitudes. The value adopted internationally for gravitational acceleration is 32.174 ft s^{-2}/9.806 m s^{-2}.

The average acceleration a of an object traveling in a straight line over a period of time t may be calculated using the formula:

a = change of velocity/t

or, where u is its initial velocity and v its final velocity:

$a = (v—u)/t$

A negative answer shows that the object is slowing down (decelerating). See also ▷equations of motion.

acceleration, secular in astronomy, the continuous and nonperiodic change in orbital velocity of one body around another, or the axial rotation period of a body.

An example is the axial rotation of the Earth. This is gradually slowing down owing to the gravitational effects of the Moon and the resulting production of tides, which have a frictional effect on the Earth. However, the angular ▷momentum of the Earth—Moon system is maintained, because the momentum lost by the Earth is passed to the Moon. This results in an increase in the Moon's orbital period and a consequential moving away from the Earth. The overall effect is that the Earth's axial rotation period is increasing by about 15-millionths of a second a year, and the Moon is receding from the Earth at about 1.5 in/4 cm a year.

accelerator in physics, a device to bring charged particles (such as protons and electrons) up to high speeds and energies, at which they can be of use in industry, medicine, and pure physics. At low energies, accelerated particles can be used to produce the image on a television screen and generate X-rays (by means of a ▷cathode-ray tube), destroy tumor cells, or kill bacteria. When high-energy particles collide with other particles, the fragments formed reveal the nature of the fundamental forces of nature. For particles to achieve the energies required, successive applications of a high voltage are given to electrodes placed in the path of the particles. During acceleration, the particles are confined within a circular or linear track using a magnetic field.

The first circular accelerator, the *cyclotron*, was built in the early 1930s by US physicist Ernest O Lawrence. The early cyclotrons had circumferences of about 4 in/10 cm, whereas the ▷Large Electron Positron Collider (LEP) at ▷CERN near Geneva, which came into operation 1989, has a circumference of 16.8 mi/

Academy Awards: recent winners

1983	Best Picture: *Terms of Endearment*; Best Director: James L Brooks *Terms of Endearment*; Best Actor: Robert Duvall *Tender Mercies*; Best Actress: Shirley MacLaine *Terms of Endearment*
1984	Best Picture: *Amadeus*; Best Director: Milos Forman *Amadeus*; Best Actor: F Murray Abraham *Amadeus*; Best Actress: Sally Field *Places in the Heart*
1985	Best Picture: *Out of Africa*; Best Director: Sidney Pollack *Out of Africa*; Best Actor: William Hurt *Kiss of the Spiderwoman*; Best Actress: Geraldine Page *The Trip to Bountiful*
1986	Best Picture: *Platoon*; Best Director: Oliver Stone *Platoon*; Best Actor: Paul Newman *The Color of Money*; Best Actress: Marlee Matlin *Children of a Lesser God*
1987	Best Picture: *The Last Emperor*; Best Director: Bernardo Bertolucci *The Last Emperor*; Best Actor: Michael Douglas *Wall Street*; Best Actress: Cher *Moonstruck*
1988	Best Picture: *Rain Man*; Best Director: Barry Levinson *Rain Man*; Best Actor: Dustin Hoffman *Rain Man*; Best Actress: Jodie Foster *The Accused*
1989	Best Picture: *Driving Miss Daisy*; Best Director: Oliver Stone *Born on the 4th of July*; Best Actor: Daniel Day-Lewis *My Left Foot*; Best Actress: Jessica Tandy *Driving Miss Daisy*
1990	Best Picture: *Dances with Wolves*; Best Director: Kevin Costner *Dances with Wolves*; Best Actor: Jeremy Irons *Reversal of Fortune*; Best Actress: Kathy Bates *Misery*
1991	Best Picture: *The Silence of the Lambs*; Best Director: Jonathan Demme *The Silence of the Lambs*; Best Actor: Anthony Hopkins *The Silence of the Lambs*; Best Actress: Jodie Foster *The Silence of the Lambs*
1992	Best Picture: *Unforgiven*; Best Director: Clint Eastwood *Unforgiven*; Best Actor: Al Pacino *Scent of a Woman*; Best Actress: Emma Thompson *Howards End*.

spiral path of charged particles

high frequency alternating voltage applied across here

source of charged particles

accelerated stream

hollow chambers

accelerator *The cyclotron, an early accelerator, consisted of two D-shaped hollow chambers enclosed in a vacuum.*

27 km, around which electrons and positrons (positive electrons) are accelerated before being allowed to collide. In 1988, the US announced the Ronald Reagan Center for High Energy Physics, in Waxahachie, Texas, which will house the Superconducting Super Collider (SSC), an accelerator with a circumference of 53 mi/85 km, to be completed by 1996.

The world's longest *linear accelerator*, or *linac*, is the Stanford Linear Collider, in which electrons and positrons are accelerated along a straight track, 2 mi/3.2 km long, and then steered into a head-on collision with other particles, such as protons and neutrons. Such experiments were instrumental in revealing that protons and neutrons are made up of smaller, elementary particles, called ♢quarks.

accelerometer apparatus, either mechanical or electromechanical, for measuring ♢acceleration or deceleration—that is, the rate of increase or decrease in the ♢velocity of a moving object.

Accelerometers are used to measure the efficiency of the braking systems on road and rail vehicles; those used in aircraft and spacecraft can determine accelerations in several directions simultaneously. There are also accelerometers for detecting vibrations in machinery.

accent way of speaking that identifies a person with a particular country, region, language, social class, linguistic style, or some mixture of these.

People often describe only those who belong to groups other than their own as having accents and may give them special names, for example, an Irish brogue, a Southern accent.

accessory in law, an accessory is a criminal accomplice who aids in commission of a crime that is actually committed by someone else. An accomplice may be either "before the fact" (assisting, ordering, or procuring another to commit a crime) or "after the fact" (giving assistance after the crime). An accomplice present when the crime is committed is an "abettor."

access time or *reaction time* in computing, the time taken by a computer, after an instruction has been given, to read from or write to ♢memory.

acclimation or *acclimatization* the physiological changes induced in an organism by exposure to new environmental conditions. When humans move to higher altitudes, for example, the number of red blood cells rises to increase the oxygen-carrying capacity of the blood in order to compensate for the lower levels of oxygen in the air.

accommodation in biology, the ability of the vertebrate ♢eye to focus on near or far objects by changing the shape of the lens.

For something to be viewed clearly the image must be precisely focused on the retina, the light-sensitive sheet of cells at the rear of the eye. Close objects can be seen when the lens takes up a more spherical shape, far objects when the lens is stretched and made thinner. These changes in shape are directed by the brain and by a ring of ciliary muscles lying beneath the iris.

From about the age of 40, the lens in the human eye becomes less flexible, causing the defect of vision known as *presbyopia* or lack of accommodation. People with this defect need different glasses for reading and distance vision.

accomplice in law, a person who acts with another in the commission or attempted commission of a crime, either as a principal or as an ♢accessory.

accordion musical instrument of the reed organ type comprising left and right wind chests connected by flexible bellows. The right hand plays melody on a piano-style keyboard while the left hand has a system of push buttons for selecting single notes or chord harmonies.

Invented by Cyrill Damien (1772–1847) in Vienna 1829, the accordion spread throughout the world and can be heard in the popular music of France, China, Russia, and the US.

accounting the principles and practice of systematically recording, presenting, and interpreting financial accounts; financial record keeping and management of businesses and other organizations, from balance sheets to policy decisions, for tax or operating purposes. Forms of inflation accounting, such as CCA (current cost accounting) and CCP (current purchasing power) are aimed at providing valid financial comparisons over a period in which money values change.

In the 20th century, especially in the US, the role of accounting has expanded into the realm of decision making, traditionally reserved to the economist. The accountant's role had been one of recording economic events for the purposes of stewardship. The increasing complexity of business organizations has led accountants into the areas of providing information to decision makers and even to prediction and analysis, both historically the function of economists.

accusative in the grammar of some inflected languages, such as Latin, Greek, and Russian, the accusative case is the form of a noun, pronoun, or adjective used when it is the direct object of a verb. The accusative is also used for the object of certain prepositions.

Acer genus of trees and shrubs of the temperate regions of the northern hemisphere with over 115 species, many of them popular garden specimens in Australia. *Acer* includes ♢sycamore and ♢maple.

acetaldehyde common name for ♢ethanal.

acetate common name for ♢ethanoate.

acetic acid common name for ♢ethanoic acid.

acetone common name for ♢propanone.

acetylene common name for ♢ethyne.

acetylsalicylic acid chemical name for the painkilling drug ♢aspirin.

Achaea in ancient Greece, and also today, an area of the N Peloponnese. The *Achaeans*

were the predominant society during the Mycenaean period and are said by Homer to have taken part in the siege of Troy.

Achaean League union in 275 BC of most of the cities of the N Peloponnese, which managed to defeat ♢Sparta, but was itself defeated by the Romans 146 BC.

Achaemenid dynasty family ruling the Persian Empire 550–330 BC, and named after Achaemenes, ancestor of Cyrus the Great, founder of the empire. His successors included Cambyses, Darius I, Xerxes, and Darius III, who, as the last Achaemenid ruler, was killed after defeat in battle against Alexander the Great 330 BC.

Achebe Chinua 1930– . Nigerian novelist whose themes include the social and political impact of European colonialism on African people, and the problems of newly independent African nations. His novels include the widely acclaimed *Things Fall Apart* 1958 and *Anthills of the Savannah* 1987.

achene dry, one-seeded ♢fruit that develops from a single ♢ovary and does not split open to disperse the seed. Achenes commonly occur in groups, for example, the fruiting heads of buttercup *Ranunculus* and clematis. The outer surface may be smooth, spiny, ribbed, or tuberculate, depending on the species.

An achene with part of the fruit wall extended to form a membranous wing is called a *samara*; an example is the pendulous fruit of the elm *Ulmus*. During the development of a ♢*caryopsis*, the ♢carpel wall becomes fused to the seed coat; this type of fruit is typical of grasses and cereals. A *cypsela* is derived from an inferior ovary and is characteristic of the daisy family (Compositae). It often has a ♢pappus of hairs attached, which aids its dispersal by the wind, as in the dandelion.

Achernar or *Alpha Eridani* brightest star in the constellation Eridanus, and the ninth brightest star in the sky. It is a hot, luminous blue star with a true luminosity 250 times that of the Sun. It is 125 light-years away.

Acheron in Greek mythology, one of the rivers of the lower world. The name was taken from a river in S Epirus that flowed through a deep gorge into the Ionian Sea.

Acheson Dean (Gooderham) 1893–1971. US politician. As undersecretary of state 1945–47 in ♢Truman's Democratic administration, he was associated with George C Marshall in preparing the ♢Marshall Plan, and succeeded him as secretary of state 1949–53.

Acheson's foreign policy was widely criticized by Republican members of Congress, especially Senator ♢McCarthy, for an alleged weak response to Communist advances in SE Asia, especially after the outbreak of the Korean War. He advocated containment of the Soviet Union. He survived a vote calling for his resignation, but left the State Department in 1952 following the election of ♢Eisenhower. His books include *Power and Diplomacy* 1958 and *Present at the Creation* 1969, which won the Pulitzer prize for history.

Achilles Greek hero of Homer's ♢*Iliad*. He was the son of Peleus, king of the Myrmidons in Thessaly, and the sea nymph Thetis, who rendered him invulnerable, except for the heel by which she held him, by dipping him in the river Styx. Achilles killed Hector in the Trojan War and was himself killed by Paris who shot a poisoned arrow into Achilles' heel.

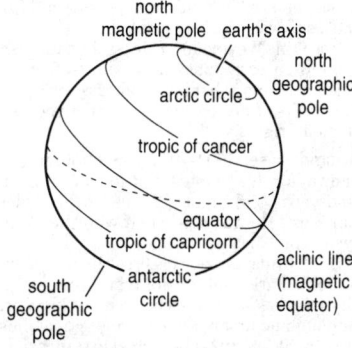

north magnetic pole earth's axis
north geographic pole
arctic circle
tropic of cancer
equator
tropic of capricorn
antarctic circle
aclinic line (magnetic equator)
south geographic pole

aclinic line *The magnetic equator, or the line at which the attraction of both magnetic poles is equal.*

Achilles tendon tendon pinning the calf muscle to the heel bone. It is one of the largest in the human body.

achromatic lens combination of lenses made from materials of different refractive indexes, constructed in such a way as to minimize chromatic aberration (which in a single lens causes colored fringes around images because the lens diffracts the different wavelengths in white light to slightly different extents).

acid compound that, in solution in an ionizing solvent (usually water), gives rise to hydrogen ions (H⁺ or protons). In modern chemistry, acids are defined as substances that are proton donors and accept electrons to form ⬦ionic bonds. Acids react with ⬦bases to form salts, and they act as solvents. Strong acids are corrosive; dilute acids have a sour or sharp taste, although in some organic acids this may be partially masked by other flavor characteristics.
   Acids can be detected by using colored indicators such as ⬦litmus and methyl orange. The strength of an acid is measured by its hydrogen-ion concentration, indicated by the ⬦pH value. Acids are classified as monobasic, dibasic, tribasic, and so forth, according to the number of hydrogen atoms, replaceable by bases, in a molecule. The first known acid was vinegar (ethanoic or acetic acid). Inorganic acids include boric, carbonic, hydrochloric, hydrofluoric, nitric, phosphoric, and sulfuric. Organic acids include acetic, benzoic, citric, formic, lactic, oxalic, and salicylic, as well as complex substances such as ⬦nucleic acids and ⬦amino acids.

acid rain acidic rainfall, thought to be caused principally by the release into the atmosphere of sulfur dioxide (SO_2) and oxides of nitrogen. Sulfur dioxide is formed from the burning of fossil fuels, such as coal, that contain high quantities of sulfur; nitrogen oxides are contributed from various industrial activities and from car exhaust fumes.
   Acid rain is linked with damage to and death of forests and lake organisms in Scandinavia, Europe, and eastern North America. It also results in damage to buildings and statues. US and European power stations burning fossil fuel release some 8 grams of sulfur dioxides and 3 grams of nitrogen oxides per kilowatt-hour. According to the UK Department of the Environment figures, emissions of sulfur dioxide from power stations would have to be decreased by 81% in order to arrest such damage.

aclinic line the magnetic equator, an imaginary line near the equator, where the compass needle balances horizontally, the attraction of the north and south magnetic poles being equal.

acne skin eruption, mainly occurring among adolescents and young adults, caused by inflammation of the sebaceous glands which secrete an oily substance (sebum), the natural lubricant of the skin. Sometimes the openings of the glands become blocked and they swell; the contents decompose and pimples form on the face, back, and chest.

Aconcagua extinct volcano in the Argentine Andes, the highest peak in the Americas; 22,834 ft/6,960 m. It was first climbed by Vines and Zeebruggen 1897.

aconite or **monkshood** herbaceous Eurasian plant *Aconitum napellus* of the buttercup family Ranunculaceae, with hooded blue-mauve flowers. It produces aconitine, a powerful alkaloid with narcotic and analgesic properties.
   There are about 100 species of the genus *Aconitum* throughout the northern temperate regions, all of which contain poison. Summer aconite *A. uncinatum* is a common North American flower. Winter aconite *Eranthus hyemalis* belongs to another genus of the buttercup family; it has yellow buttercuplike flowers with six petals and a ruff of leaves below.

acorn fruit of the oak tree, a ⬦nut growing in a shallow cup.

acouchi any of several small South American rodents, genus *Myoprocta*. They have white-tipped tails, and are smaller relatives of the ⬦agouti.

acoustic in music, describing a performance or instrument sounding without electrical amplification or assistance. In architecture, the sound-reflecting character of a room.

acoustic ohm unit of acoustic impedance (the ratio of the sound pressure on a surface to the sound flux through the surface). It is analogous to the ohm as the unit of electrical ⬦impedance.

acoustics in general, the experimental and theoretical science of sound and its transmission; in particular, that branch of the science that has to do with the phenomena of sound in a particular space such as a room or theater.
   Acoustical engineering is concerned with the technical control of sound, and involves architecture and construction, studying control of vibration, soundproofing, and the elimination of noise. It also includes all forms of sound recording and reinforcement, the hearing and perception of sounds, and hearing aids.

acquired character feature of the body that develops during the lifetime of an individual, usually as a result of repeated use or disuse, such as the enlarged muscles of a weight-lifter.
   ⬦Lamarck's theory of evolution assumed that acquired characters were passed from parent to offspring. Modern evolutionary theory does not recognize the inheritance of acquired characters because there is no reliable scientific evidence that it occurs, and because no mechanism is known whereby bodily changes can influence the genetic material. See also ⬦central dogma.

acquired immune deficiency syndrome full name for the disease ⬦AIDS.

acquittal in law, the setting free of someone charged with a crime after a trial.

It follows a verdict of "not guilty" and prevents retrial of a defendant on the same charges under the US Constitution (see ⬦double jeopardy).

acre traditional English land measure equal to 4,840 square yards (4,047 sq m/0.405 ha). Originally meaning a field, it was the size that a yoke of oxen could plow in a day. It may be subdivided into 160 square rods (one square rod equaling 30.25 sq yd/25.29 sq m).
   As early as Edward I's reign the acre was standardized by statute for official use, although local variations in Ireland, Scotland, and some English counties continued.

Acre or **'Akko** seaport in Israel; population (1983) 37,000. Taken by the Crusaders 1104, it was captured by Saladin 1187 and retaken by Richard I (the Lion-Hearted) 1191. Napoleon failed in a siege 1799. British field marshal Allenby captured the port 1918. From being part of British mandated Palestine, it became part of Israel 1948.

acre-foot unit sometimes used to measure large volumes of water, such as the capacity of a reservoir (equal to its area in acres multiplied by its average depth in feet). One acre-foot equals 43,560 cu ft/1,233.5 cu m or the amount of water covering one acre to a depth of one foot.

acridine $C_{13}H_9N$ organic compound that occurs in coal tar. It is extracted by dilute acids but can also be obtained synthetically. It is used to make dyes and drugs.

acromegaly rare condition in which enlargement of prominent parts of the body, for example, hands, feet, heart, and, conspicuously, the eyebrow ridges and lower jaw, is caused by excessive output of growth hormone in adult life by a nonmalignant tumor of the ⬦pituitary gland.

acronym word formed from the initial letters and/or syllables of other words, intended as a pronounceable abbreviation, for example NATO (**N**orth **A**tlantic **T**reaty **O**rganization), radar (**ra**dio **d**etecting **a**nd **r**anging), and sitrep (**sit**uation **rep**ort).
   Many acronyms are so successfully incorporated into everyday language that their original significance is widely overlooked.

acrophobia ⬦phobia involving fear of heights.

acropolis (Greek "high city") citadel of an ancient Greek town. The Acropolis of Athens contains the ruins of the Parthenon and surrounding complexes, built there during the days of the Athenian empire. The term is also used for analogous structures, as in the massive granite-built ruins of Great ⬦Zimbabwe.

acrostic (Greek "at the extremity of a line or row") a number of lines of writing, usually verse, whose initial letters (read downward) form a word, phrase, or sentence. A **single acrostic** is formed by the initial letters of lines only, while a **double acrostic** is formed by both initial and final letters.

acrylic acid common name for ⬦propenoic acid.

acrylic fiber synthetic fiber often used as a substitute for wool. It was first developed 1947 but not produced in great volumes until the 1950s. Strong and warm, acrylic fiber is often used for casual and athletic wear, and as linings for boots and gloves.

Actaeon in Greek mythology, a hunter,

son of Aristaeus and Autonöe. He surprised ◇Artemis bathing; she changed him into a stag and he was torn to pieces by his own hounds.

ACTH (adrenocorticotropic hormone) ◇hormone secreted by the anterior lobe of the ◇pituitary gland that controls the production of corticosteroid hormones by the ◇adrenal gland. It is commonly produced as a response to stress.

actinide any of a series of 15 radioactive metallic chemical elements with atomic numbers 89 (actinium) to 103 (lawrencium). Elements 89 to 95 occur in nature; the rest of the series are synthesized elements only. Actinides are grouped together because of their chemical similarities (for example, they are all bivalent), the properties differing only slightly with atomic number. The series is set out in a band in the ◇periodic table of the elements, as are the ◇lanthanides.

actinium (Greek *aktis* "ray") white, radioactive, metallic element, the first of the actinide series, symbol Ac, atomic number 89, atomic weight 227; it is a weak emitter of high-energy alpha particles. Actinium occurs with uranium and radium in ◇pitchblende and other ores, and can be synthesized by bombarding radium with neutrons. The longest-lived isotope, Ac-227, has a half-life of 21.8 years (all the other isotopes have very short half-lives). Actinium was discovered in 1899 by the French chemist André Debierne.

action in law, one of the proceedings whereby a person or agency seeks to enforce rights in a civil court.

Actions fall into three principal categories, namely civil (such as the enforcement of a debt), criminal (in which a government agency prosecutes a defendant accused of violation of a criminal law), and penal (violation of a law enacted to preserve public order).

action and reaction in physical mechanics, equal and opposite effects produced by a force acting on an object. For example, the pressure of expanding gases from the burning of fuel in a rocket engine (a force) produces an equal and opposite reaction, which causes the rocket to move.

action painting or **gesture painting** in US art, a dynamic school of Abstract Expressionism. It emphasized the importance of the physical act of painting, sometimes expressed with both inventiveness and aggression, and on occasion performed for the camera. Jackson ◇Pollock was the leading exponent.

The term "action painting" was coined by the US art critic Harold Rosenberg 1952.

Pollock was known to place his canvas on the floor, attacking it with knives and trowels, throwing paint at it, and bicycling over it.

action potential in biology, a change in the potential difference (voltage) across the membrane of a nerve cell when an impulse passes along it. A change in potential (from about –60 to +45 millivolts) accompanies the passage of sodium and potassium ions across the membrane.

Actium, Battle of naval battle in which Octavian defeated the combined fleets of ◇Mark Antony and ◇Cleopatra 31 BC to become the undisputed ruler of the Roman world (as the emperor ◇Augustus). The site is at Akri, a promontory in W Greece.

act of Congress in the US, a bill or resolution passed by both houses of Congress, the Senate

and the House of Representatives, which becomes law with the signature of the president. If vetoed by the president, it may still become law if it returns to Congress again and is passed by a majority of two-thirds in each house.

act of God legal term meaning some sudden and irresistible act of nature that could not reasonably have been foreseen or prevented, such as floods, storms, earthquakes, or sudden death.

Actors Studio theater workshop in New York City, established 1947 by Cheryl Crawford and Elia Kazan. Under Lee Strasberg, who became artistic director 1948, it became known for the study of Konstantin Stanislavsky's ◇Method acting.

Acts of the Apostles book of the New Testament, attributed to ◇Luke, which describes the history of the early Christian church.

actuary mathematician who makes statistical calculations concerning human life expectancy and other risks, on which insurance premiums are based.

The professional body in the US is the Society of Actuaries, formed 1949 by a merger of two earlier bodies.

acupuncture system of inserting long, thin metal needles into the body at predetermined points to relieve pain, as an anesthetic in surgery, and to assist healing. The needles are rotated manually or electrically. The method, developed in ancient China and increasingly popular in the West, is thought to work by somehow stimulating the brain's own painkillers, the ◇endorphins.

acute in medicine, pertaining to a condition that develops and resolves quickly; for example, the common cold and meningitis. In contrast, a **chronic** condition develops and remains over a long period.

acute angle an angle between 0° and 90°.

AD in the Christian calendar, abbreviation for *Anno Domini* (Latin "in the year of the Lord"); used with dates.

ADA high-level computer-programming language, developed and owned by the US Department of Defense, designed for use in situations in which a computer directly controls a process or machine, such as a military aircraft. The language took more than five years to specify, and became commercially available only in the late 1980s. It is named after English mathematician Ada Augusta ◇Byron.

Adam (Hebrew *adham* "man") in the Old Testament, founder of the human race. Formed by God from dust and given the breath of life, Adam was placed in the Garden of Eden, where ◇Eve was created from his rib and given to him as a companion. Because she tempted him, he tasted the forbidden fruit of the Tree of Knowledge of Good and Evil, for which trespass they were expelled from the Garden.

Adam Adolphe Charles 1803–1856. French composer of light operas. Some 50 of his works were staged, including the classic ballet *Giselle*.

Adams Abigail Smith 1744–1818. First lady to US president John Adams and public figure. She married lawyer John Adams of Boston 1764; one of their children, John Quincy Adams, would become the sixth US president. A strong supporter of the cause of American independence, she joined her husband on diplomatic missions to Paris and London after the Revolutionary War. As wife of the US vice-

president 1789–97 and later president 1797–1801, she was widely respected.

Born in Weymouth, Massachusetts, she showed an early interest in public affairs. In detailed letters to her husband, she chronicled the events of her day and was an advocate of women's rights.

Adams Ansel 1902–1984. US photographer known for his printed images of dramatic landscapes and organic forms of the American West. He was associated with the ◇zone system of exposure estimation.

In 1916 Adams made his first trip to Yosemite National Park, and for the rest of his life the High Sierras were a major focus of his work. Although he first became a professional musician, in the late 1920s he turned to professional photography. Light and texture were important elements in his photographs. Adams worked to establish photography as a fine art. He founded the first museum collection of photography, at New York City's Museum of Modern Art 1937. His love of nature also carried over into his work as a conservationist and director of the Sierra Club from 1936.

Adams Charles Francis 1807–1886. US political leader, journalist, and diplomat. Adams was born in Boston, the son of John Quincy Adams. After graduation from Harvard, he studied law with Daniel Webster. As a respected historian and abolitionist, he established the *Boston Whig* and accepted the vice-presidential nomination of the Free Soil party 1848. He later joined the Republican party. After service in the US House of Representatives 1858–61, he was appointed US minister to England by Lincoln. He unsuccessfully sought the 1872 Republican nomination for president.

Adams Franklin Pierce, popularly known as **FPA** 1881–1960. US humorist and social critic. He gained fame as a columnist for the New York *Evening Mail*, *Tribune*, *World*, and *Post*. In addition to publishing books of light verse (*The Melancholy Lute* 1936) and collections of his syndicated newspaper columns (*The Diary of Our Own Samuel Pepys* 1935), he served as a panelist on the popular radio game show *Information Please*.

Born in Chicago, Adams studied briefly at the University of Michigan, worked at a succession of odd jobs, and finally joined the *Chicago Journal* as a feature writer 1903.

Adams Henry Brooks 1838–1918. US historian and novelist, a grandson of President John Quincy Adams. He published the acclaimed nine-volume *A History of the United States During the Administrations of Jefferson and Madison* 1889–91, a study of the evolution of democracy in the US.

Born in Boston, he graduated 1858 from Harvard University and later taught medieval history there 1870–77. He also was editor of the *North American Review* 1870–76. His works include a study of the medieval world *Mont-Saint-Michel and Chartres* 1904, and a classic autobiography *The Education of Henry Adams* 1907, as well as the novels *Democracy, an American Novel* 1880, which reflects his disillusionment with the US political system, and *Esther* 1884, published under a pseudonym, about the conflict between religion and science.

Adams John 1735–1826. 2nd president of the US 1797–1801, and vice-president 1789–97. He was a member of the Continental Congress 1774–78 and signed the Declaration of Independence. In 1779 he went to France and negotiated the treaties that ended the American Revolution. Although suspicious of the French Revolution, he resisted calls for war with France. He became the first US ambassador in London 1785.

He was born in Quincy, Massachusetts.

Adams John Couch 1819–1892. English astronomer who mathematically deduced the existence of the planet Neptune 1845 from the effects of its gravitational pull on the motion of Uranus, although it was not found until 1846 by J G ◊Galle. Adams also studied the Moon's motion, the Leonid meteors, and terrestrial magnetism.

Adams John Quincy 1767–1848. 6th president of the US 1825–29. Eldest son of President John Adams, he was born in Quincy, Massachusetts, and became US minister in The Hague, Berlin, St Petersburg, and London. He negotiated the Treaty of Ghent to end the ◊War of 1812 (fought between Britain and the US) on generous terms for the US. In 1817 he became ◊Monroe's secretary of state, formulated the Monroe Doctrine 1823, and was elected president by the House of Representatives, despite receiving fewer votes than his main rival, Andrew ◊Jackson. As president, Adams was an advocate of strong federal government.

Adams Richard 1920– . English novelist. A civil servant 1948–72, he wrote *Watership Down* 1972, a tale of a rabbit community, which is read by adults and children. Later novels include *Shardik* 1974, *The Plague Dogs* 1977, and *Girl on a Swing* 1980.

Adams Roger 1889–1971. US organic chemist, known for his painstaking analytical work to determine the composition of naturally occurring substances such as complex vegetable oils and plant ◊alkaloids.

Adams Samuel 1722–1803. US politician, second cousin of President John Adams. He was the chief instigator of the Boston Tea Party (see ◊American Revolution). He was also a signatory to the Declaration of Independence, served in the ◊Continental Congress, and anticipated the French emperor Napoleon in calling the British a "nation of shopkeepers."

Adana capital of Adana (Seyhan) province, S Turkey; population (1990) 916,150. It is a major cotton-growing center and Turkey's fourth-largest city.

adaptation in biology, any change in the structure or function of an organism that allows it to survive and reproduce more effectively in its environment. In ◊evolution, adaptation is thought to occur as a result of random variation in the genetic makeup of organisms (produced by ◊mutation and ◊recombination) coupled with ◊natural selection.

adaptive radiation in evolution, the formation of several species, with ◊adaptations to different ways of life, from a single ancestral type. Adaptive radiation is likely to occur whenever members of a species migrate to a new habitat with unoccupied ecological niches. It is thought that the lack of competition in such niches allows sections of the migrant population to develop new adaptations, and eventually to become new species.

The colonization of newly formed volcanic islands has led to the development of many unique species. The 13 species of Darwin's finch on the Galápagos Islands, for example, are probably descended from a single species from the South American mainland. The parent

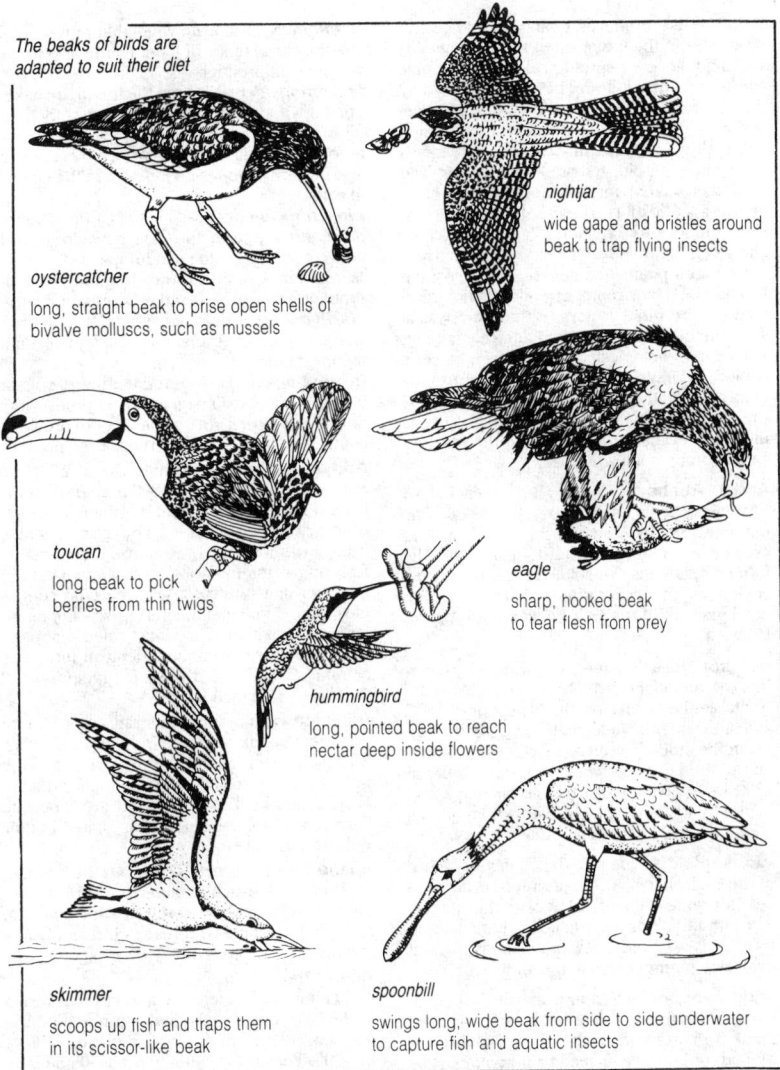

The beaks of birds are adapted to suit their diet

oystercatcher long, straight beak to prise open shells of bivalve molluscs, such as mussels

nightjar wide gape and bristles around beak to trap flying insects

toucan long beak to pick berries from thin twigs

eagle sharp, hooked beak to tear flesh from prey

hummingbird long, pointed beak to reach nectar deep inside flowers

skimmer scoops up fish and traps them in its scissor-like beak

spoonbill swings long, wide beak from side to side underwater to capture fish and aquatic insects

adaptation *The different types of beak found in birds are examples of adaptation.*

stock evolved into different species that now occupy a range of diverse niches.

ADB abbreviation for ◊*Asian Development Bank*.

Addams Charles 1912–1988. US cartoonist, creator of the ghoulish family featured in the *New Yorker* magazine. A successful television comedy series was based on the cartoon in the 1960s.

Addams Jane 1860–1935. US social reformer and feminist, who in 1889 cofounded and led Hull House, a settlement house in the slums of Chicago. It was one of the earliest community centers and served as a model for others throughout the US. Innovative services such as day care were provided. She was vice-president of the National American Women Suffrage Association 1911–14, led the Woman's Peace Party and the first Women's Peace Congress 1915, and was president of the Women's International League for Peace and Freedom 1919. She was a US leader in attempts to reform child-labor laws.

Her publications include *Democracy and Social Ethics, Newer Ideals of Peace* 1907, and *Twenty Years at Hull House* 1910. She was a cowinner of the Nobel Prize 1931 with Nicholas Murray Butler.

addax light-colored ◊antelope *Addax nasomaculatus* of the family Bovidae. It lives in the Sahara desert where it exists on scanty vegetation without drinking. It is about 3.5 ft/1.1 m at the shoulder, and both sexes have spirally twisted horns.

adder European venomous snake, the common ◊viper *Vipera berus*. Growing to about 24 in/60 cm in length, it has a thick body, triangular head, a characteristic V-shaped mark on its head and, often, zigzag markings along the back. It feeds on small mammals and lizards. The puff adder *Bitis arietans* is a large, yellowish, thick-bodied viper up to 5 ft/1.6 m long, living in Africa and Arabia.

addiction state of dependence on drugs, alcohol, or other substances. Symptoms include uncontrolled craving, tolerance, and symptoms of withdrawal when access is denied.

Habitual use produces changes in chemical processes in the brain; when the substance is withheld, severe neurological manifestations, even death, may follow. These are reversed by the administration of the addictive substance, and mitigated by a gradual reduction in dosage.

Initially, only opium and its derivatives (morphine, heroin, codeine) were recognized as addictive, but many other drugs, whether therapeutic (for example, tranquilizers or ergotamine) or recreational (such as cocaine and alcohol), are now known to be addictive.

Research points to a genetic predisposition to addiction; environment and psychological makeup are other factors. Although physical addiction always has a psychological element, not all psychological dependence is accompanied by physical dependence. A carefully controlled withdrawal program can reverse the chemical changes of habituation. Cure is difficult because of the many other factors contributing to addiction.

Addis Ababa or **Adis Abeba** capital of Ethiopia; population (1984) 1,413,000. It was founded 1887 by Menelik, chief of Shoa, who ascended the throne of Ethiopia 1889. His former residence, Menelik Palace, is now occupied by the government. The city is the headquarters of the ⟡Organization of African Unity.

Addison Joseph 1672–1719. English writer. In 1704 he celebrated ⟡Marlborough's victory at Blenheim in a poem, "The Campaign," and subsequently held political appointments, including undersecretary of state and secretary to the Lord-Lieutenant of Ireland 1708. In 1709 he contributed to the *Tatler* magazine, begun by Richard ⟡Steele, with whom he was cofounder 1711 of the *Spectator*.

Addison's disease rare deficiency or failure of the ⟡adrenal glands to produce corticosteroid hormones; it is treated with hormones. The condition, formerly fatal, is characterized by anemia, weakness, low blood pressure, and brownish pigmentation of the skin.

additive in food, any natural or artificial chemical added to prolong the shelf life of processed foods (salt or nitrates), alter the color or flavor of food, or improve its food value (vitamins or minerals). Many chemical additives are used and they are subject to regulation, since individuals may be affected by constant exposure even to traces of certain additives and may suffer side effects ranging from headaches and hyperactivity to cancer.

They must be listed on labels of foods sold in the US so consumers may be aware of those they cannot tolerate. The natural food movement has grown enormously in the 1970s and 1980s, as increasing awareness of the dangers of additives sent consumers looking for additive-free foods.

artificial sweeteners are used in a range of products for diabetics and for weight loss or weight control.

nutrients may be added to replace or enhance food value. Minerals and vitamins are the most common, especially where the diet would otherwise be deficient, leading to diseases such as beriberi and pellagra.

preservatives are primarily antioxidants and antimicrobials that control natural oxidation and the action of microorganisms. See ⟡food technology.

emulsifiers and *surfactants* regulate the consistency of fats in prepared food and on the surface of the food in contact with the air.

thickeners, primarily vegetable gums, regulate the consistency of food. Pectin acts in this way on fruit products.

leavening agents lighten the texture of baked goods without the use of yeasts. Sodium bicarbonate is an example.

acidulants sharpen the taste of foods but may also perform a buffering function in the control of acidity.

bleaching agents assist in the aging of flours.

anticaking agents prevent powdered products coagulating into solid lumps.

humectants control the humidity of the product by absorbing and retaining moisture.

clarifying agents are used in fruit juices, vinegars, and other fermented liquids. Gelatin is the most common.

firming agents restore the texture of vegetables that may be damaged during processing.

foam regulators are used in beer to provide a controlled "head" on top of the poured product.

Addyston Pipe and Steel Co v US a US Supreme Court decision 1899 that granted the federal government certain regulatory powers over private businesses. The case resulted from a number of convictions of pipe-manufacturing firms for price fixing, a violation of the Sherman Antitrust Act. The pipe companies argued that manufacturing was not under federal regulation. The Court ruled that price fixing was a clear impingement on interstate commerce and was therefore under federal regulatory jurisdiction.

Adelaide capital and industrial city of South Australia; population (1990) 1,049,100. Industries include oil refining, shipbuilding, and the manufacture of electrical goods and automobiles. Grain, wool, fruit, and wine are exported. Founded 1836, Adelaide was named after William IV's queen.

Adélie Land (French **Terre Adélie**) region of Antarctica which is about 87 mi/140 km long, mountainous, covered in snow and ice, and inhabited only by a research team. It was claimed for France 1840.

Aden (Arabic *'Adan*) main port and commercial center of Yemen, on a rocky peninsula at the SW corner of Arabia, commanding the entrance to the Red Sea; population (1984) 318,000. The city's economy is based on oil refining, fishing, and shipping. A British territory from 1839, Aden became part of independent South Yemen 1967; it was the capital of South Yemen until 1990.

history After annexation by Britain, Aden and its immediately surrounding area (47 sq mi/121 sq km) were developed as a ship-refueling station following the opening of the Suez Canal 1869. It was a colony 1937–63 and then, after a period of transitional violence among rival nationalist groups and British forces, was combined with the former Aden protectorate (112,000 sq mi/290,000 sq km) to create the Southern Yemen People's Republic 1967, later renamed the People's Democratic Republic of Yemen.

Adenauer Konrad 1876–1967. German Christian Democrat politician, chancellor of West Germany 1949–63. With the French president de Gaulle he achieved the postwar reconciliation of France and Germany and strongly supported all measures designed to strengthen the Western bloc in Europe.

Adenauer was mayor of his native city of Cologne from 1917 until his imprisonment by Hitler in 1933 for opposition to the Nazi regime. After the war he headed the Christian Democratic Union and became chancellor.

adenoids masses of lymphoid tissue, similar to ⟡tonsils, located in the upper part of the throat, behind the nose. They are part of a child's natural defenses against the entry of germs but usually shrink and disappear by the age of ten.

Adenoids may swell and grow, particularly if infected, and block the breathing passages. If they become repeatedly infected, they may be removed surgically (**adenoidectomy**).

adhesion in medicine, the abnormal binding of two tissues as a result of inflammation. The moving surfaces of joints or internal organs may merge together if they have been inflamed.

adhesive substance that sticks two surfaces together. Natural adhesives (glues) include gelatin in its crude industrial form (made from bones, hide fragments, and fish offal) and vegetable gums. Synthetic adhesives include thermoplastic and thermosetting resins, which are often stronger than the substances they join; mixtures of ⟡epoxy resin and hardener that set by chemical reaction; and elastomeric (stretching) adhesives for flexible joints. Superglues are fast-setting adhesives used in very small quantities.

ad infinitum (Latin) to infinity, endlessly.

adipose tissue type of ⟡connective tissue of vertebrates that serves as an energy reserve, and also pads some organs. It is commonly called fat tissue, and consists of large spherical cells filled with fat. In mammals, major layers are in the inner layer of skin and around the kidneys and heart.

Fatty acids are transported to and from it via the blood system.

Adirondacks mountainous area in NE New York, rising to 5,344 ft/1,629 m at Mount Marcy; the source of the Hudson and Ausable rivers; named after an Indian tribe. The Adirondacks area occupies about 25% of the state of New York, and a state park occupies more than 500 million acres/200 million hectares. Thickly wooded, the region is noted for scenery, health resorts such as Saranac Lake, and sports facilities such as those at Lake Placid, where the 1932 and 1980 winter Olympic Games were held.

adit in mining, a horizontal shaft from the surface to reach the mineral seam. It was a common method of mining in hilly districts, and was also used to drain water.

adjective grammatical ⟡part of speech for words that describe nouns (for example, *new* and *beautiful*, as in "a new hat" and "a beautiful day"). Adjectives generally have three degrees (grades or levels for the description of relationships): the positive degree (*new*, *beautiful*), the comparative degree (*newer*, *more beautiful*), and the superlative degree (*newest*, *most beautiful*).

Some adjectives do not normally need comparative and superlative forms; one person cannot be "more asleep" than someone else, a lone action is unlikely to be "the most single-handed action ever seen," and many people dislike the expression "most unique" or "almost unique," because something unique is supposed to be the only one that exists. For purposes of emphasis or style these conventions may be set aside ("I don't know who is more unique; they are both remarkable people"). Double comparatives such as "more bigger" are not grammatical in Standard English, but Shakespeare used a double superlative ("the most unkindest cut of all"). Some adjectives may have both the comparative and superlative forms (*commoner* and *more common*; *commonest* and *most common*), usually shorter words take on the suffixes *-er/-est* but occasionally they may be given the *more/most* forms for emphasis or other reasons ("Which of them is the *most clear?*").

When an adjective comes before a noun it is attributive; a predicate adjective comes after noun and verb (for example, "It looks *good*"). Some adjectives can only be used in the predicate ("The child was asleep," but not "the asleep child"). The participles of verbs are regularly used adjectivally ("a *sleeping* child," "*boiled* milk") and often in compound forms ("a *quick-acting* medicine," "a *glass-making* factory," "a *hard-boiled* egg," "*well-trained* teachers"). Adjectives are often formed by adding suffixes to nouns (sand: sand*y*; nation: nation*al*).

adjutant in military usage, the commanding officer's personal staff officer. The adjutant is responsible for discipline in a military unit.

Adler Alfred 1870–1937. Austrian psychologist. Adler saw the "will to power" as more influential in accounting for human behavior than the sexual drive theory. A dispute over this theory led to the dissolution of his ten-year collaboration with ◊Freud.

Born in Vienna, he was a general practitioner and nerve specialist there 1897–1927, serving as an army doctor in World War I. He joined the circle of Freudian doctors in Vienna about 1900. The concepts of inferiority complex and overcompensation originated with Adler, for example in his books *Organic Inferiority and Psychic Compensation* 1907 and *Understanding Human Nature* 1927.

Adler Cyrus 1863–1940. US educator and public figure. In 1892 he was appointed curator at the Smithsonian Institution and later served as its librarian and assistant secretary. From 1908 until his death, he was president of Dropsie College and a leader of the American Jewish Committee. His appeal for protection of the rights of religious ethnic minorities was adopted in the final text of the Treaty of Versailles after World War I.

Born in Van Buren, Arkansas, Adler studied Semitic languages at the University of Pennsylvania and at Johns Hopkins University, where he received a PhD 1887.

administrative law law concerning the powers and control of government agencies or those agencies granted statutory powers of administration.

These powers include those necessary to operate the agency or to implement its purposes, and making quasi-judicial decisions (such as determining tax liability, granting licenses or permits, or hearing complaints against the agency or its officers). The vast increase in these powers in the 20th century in many countries has been widely criticized.

Depending on legislative mandates, administrative law may or may not be actionable in civil or criminal court or subject to review by executive branch agencies.

admiral highest-ranking naval officer.
In the US Navy, in descending order, the ranks of admiral are: fleet admiral, admiral, vice admiral, and rear admiral.

admiral any of several species of butterfly in the same family (Nymphalidae) as the tortoiseshells. The red admiral *Vanessa atalanta*,

wingspan 2.5 in/6 cm, is found worldwide in the northern hemisphere. It migrates south each year from northern areas to subtropical zones.

Admiralty Islands group of small islands in the SW Pacific, part of Papua New Guinea; population (1980) 25,000. The main island is Manus. The islands became a German protectorate 1884 and an Australian mandate 1920.

adobe in architecture, building with earth bricks. The formation of earth bricks ("adobe") and the construction of walls by enclosing earth within molds (*pisé de terre*) are the two principal methods of earth building. The techniques are commonly found in Spain, Latin America, and the southwestern US.

Jericho is the site of the earliest evidence of building in sun-dried mud bricks, dating from the 8th millennium BC. Firing bricks did not come into practice until the 3rd millennium BC, and then only rarely because it was costly in terms of fuel.

The Great Wall of China is largely constructed of earth; whole cities of mud construction exist throughout the Middle East and North Africa, for example ◊San'a in Yemen and Yazd in Iran. It remains a vigorous vernacular tradition in these areas. A variation of it is found as cob (a mixture of clay and chopped straw) in Devon, England, and in the pueblos of North America.

The most influential contemporary advocate of raw-earth building was Hassan Fathy (1900–1989). In 1945–47 he built the new village of Gourna for 7,000 inhabitants in Egypt, and demonstrated the value of adobe material in helping to solve the housing problems of the Third World. Recent years have seen a revival of interest in the technique and a number of schemes have been built. Examples are La Luz new town by architect Antoine Predock (1967–73); Great Mosque of Niono, Mali, 1955–72 by architect Mason-Lassiné Minta; Wissa Wassef Arts Center, Harrania, Egypt, 1952 by architect Ramses Wissa Wassef (1911–74).

Adonis in Greek mythology, a beautiful youth beloved by the goddess ◊Aphrodite. He was killed while boar-hunting but was allowed to return from the lower world for six months every year to rejoin her. The anemone sprang from his blood.

adoption permanent legal transfer of parental rights and duties in respect of a child from one person to another.

State laws determine processes for adoption, rights of adoptees (such as access to information about natural parents), and inheritance rights.

Adowa alternate form of ◊Aduwa, former capital of Ethiopia.

ADP in biology, abbreviation for *adenosine diphosphate*, a raw material in the manufacture of ◊ATP, the molecule used by all cells to drive their chemical reactions.

Adrastus in Greek mythology, king of Argos, and leader of the expedition of the ◊Seven against Thebes, undertaken to place his son-in-law ◊Polynices on the throne of Thebes.

adrenal gland or *suprarenal gland* gland situated on top of the kidney. The adrenals are soft and yellow, and consist of two parts: the cortex and medulla. The *cortex* (outer part) secretes various steroid hormones, controls salt and water metabolism, and regulates the use of carbohydrates, proteins, and fats. The

medulla (inner part) secretes the hormones adrenaline and noradrenaline which, during times of stress, cause the heart to beat faster and harder, increase blood flow to the heart and muscle cells, and dilate airways in the lungs, thereby delivering more oxygen to cells throughout the body and in general preparing the body for "fight or flight."

adrenaline or *epinephrine* hormone secreted by the medulla of the ◊adrenal glands.

Adrenaline's action on the ◊liver raises blood-sugar levels by stimulating glucose production; it also increases the heart rate, raises blood fatty-acid levels by its action on adipose tissue, and constricts and dilates blood vessels selectively.

adrenocorticotropic hormone hormone secreted by the anterior lobe of the ◊pituitary gland; see ◊ACTH.

Adrian Edgar, 1st Baron Adrian 1889–1977. British physiologist who received the Nobel Prize for Medicine in 1932 for his work with Charles Sherrington in the field of nerve impulses and the function of the nerve cell.

Adrian IV (Nicholas Breakspear) *c.* 1100–1159. Pope 1154–59, the only British pope. He secured the execution of Arnold of Brescia; crowned Frederick I Barbarossa as German emperor; refused Henry II's request that Ireland should be granted to the English crown in absolute ownership; and was at the height of a quarrel with the emperor when he died.

Adrianople older name of the Turkish town Edirne, after the Emperor Hadrian, who rebuilt it about AD 125.

Adriatic Sea large arm of the Mediterranean Sea, lying NW to SE between the Italian and the Balkan peninsulas. The W shore is Italian; the E is Croatian, Yugoslav, and Albanian. The sea is about 500 mi/805 km long, and its area is 52,220 sq mi/135,250 sq km.

adsorption taking up of a gas or liquid at the surface of another substance, usually a solid (for example, activated charcoal adsorbs gases). It involves molecular attraction at the surface, and should be distinguished from ◊absorption (in which a uniform solution results from a gas or liquid being incorporated into the bulk structure of a liquid or solid).

adultery voluntary sexual intercourse between a married person and someone other than his or her legal partner.

It is almost universally recognized as grounds for ◊divorce in the US, and is a punishable offense in some states. The legal definition of adultery varies: in some states both parties have to be married (to other people); in others it is adultery if the woman is married but not if only the man is married, and so on.

Aduwa or *Adwa*, or *Adowa* former capital of Ethiopia, about 110 mi/180 km SW of Massawa at an altitude of 6,270 ft/1,910 m; population (1982) 27,000.

Aduwa, Battle of defeat of the Italians by the Ethiopians at Aduwa in 1896 under Emperor ◊Menelik II. It marked the end of Italian ambitions in this part of Africa until Mussolini's reconquest in 1935.

advanced gas-cooled reactor (AGR) type of ◊nuclear reactor widely used in W Europe. The AGR uses a fuel of enriched uranium dioxide in stainless-steel cladding and a moderator of graphite. Carbon dioxide gas is pumped through the reactor core to extract the heat produced by the ◊fission of the uranium. The heat is transferred to water in a steam generator, and the steam drives a turbogenerator to produce electricity.

Advent in the Christian calendar, the preparatory season for Christmas, including the four Sundays preceding it, beginning with the Sunday that falls nearest (before or after) St Andrew's Day (Nov 30).

Adventist person who believes that Christ will return to make a second appearance on the Earth. Expectation of the Second Coming of Christ is found in New Testament writings generally. Adventist views are held in particular by the ◊Seventh-Day Adventist church (with 1.5 million members in 200 countries), Christadelphians, the Jehovah's Witnesses, the Four Square Gospel Alliance, the Advent Christian church, and the Evangelical Adventist church.

Most American adventists trace their origins to the Millerites of the 1840s, who accepted the calculation of William Miller, a Baptist farmer in New York State, that the Second Coming of Christ would occur on Oct 22, 1844. When it failed to occur, Miller admitted his deductions had been mistaken, but he and his remaining followers continued to expect the imminent return of Christ, and they formed churches that evolved into the contemporary adventist groups.

adventitious root in plants, a root developing in an unusual position, as in ivy, where roots grow sideways out of the stem and cling to trees or walls.

adverb grammatical ◊part of speech for words that modify or describe verbs ("She ran *quickly*"), adjectives ("a *beautifully* clear day"), and adverbs ("They did it *really* well"). Most adverbs are formed from adjectives or past participles by adding *-ly* (quick: quickly) or *-ally* (automatic: automatically).

Sometimes adverbs are formed by adding *-wise* (*likewise* and *clockwise*, as in "moving *clockwise*"; in "a *clockwise* direction," *clockwise* is an adjective). Some adverbs have a distinct form from their partnering adjective; for example, *good/well* ("It was *good* work; they did it *well*"). Others do not derive from adjectives (*very*, in "*very* nice"; *tomorrow*, in "I'll do it *tomorrow*"); and some are unadapted adjectives (*pretty*, as in "It's *pretty* good"). Sentence adverbs modify whole sentences or phrases: "*Generally*, it rains a lot here"; "*Usually*, the town is busy at this time of year." Sometimes there is controversy in such matters. *Hopefully* is universally accepted in sentences like "He looked at them *hopefully*" (= "in a hopeful way"), but some people dislike it in "*Hopefully*, we'll see you again next year" (= "We hope that we'll see you again next year").

advertising any of various methods used by a company to increase the sales of its products or to promote a brand name. Advertising can be seen by economists as either beneficial (since it conveys information about a product and so brings the market closer to a state of perfect competition) or as a hindrance to perfect competition, since it attempts to make illusory distinctions (such as greater sex appeal) between essentially similar products.

advocate (Latin *advocatus*, one summoned to one's aid, especially in a lawcourt) professional pleader in a court of justice.

More common terms are attorney, ◊lawyer, or counsel, but advocate is retained in such countries as Scotland and France, whose legal systems are based on Roman law.

Aegean civilization the cultures of Bronze Age Greece, including the ◊*Minoan civilization* of Crete and the ◊*Mycenaean civilization* of the E Peloponnese.

Aegean Islands islands of the Aegean Sea, but more specifically a region of Greece comprising the Dodecanese islands, the Cyclades islands, Lesvos, Samos, and Chios; population (1991) 460,800; area 3,523 sq mi/ 9,122 sq km.

Aegean Sea branch of the Mediterranean between Greece and Turkey; the Dardanelles connect it with the Sea of Marmara. The numerous islands in the Aegean Sea include Crete, the Cyclades, the Sporades, and the Dodecanese. There is political tension between Greece and Turkey over sea limits claimed by Greece around such islands as Lesvos, Chios, Samos, and Kos.

Aegeus in Greek mythology, king of Athens, and father of ◊Theseus. On his return from Crete, Theseus forgot to substitute white sails for black to indicate his success in killing the ◊Minotaur. Believing his son dead, Aegeus leapt into the Aegean Sea.

Aegina (Greek *Aíyna* or *Aíyina*) Greek island in the Gulf of Aegina about 20 mi/32 km SW of Piraeus; area 32 sq mi/83 sq km; population (1981) 11,100. In 1811 remarkable sculptures were recovered from a Doric temple in the northeast, restored by Thorwaldsen, and taken to Munich.

Aegir in Scandinavian mythology, the god of the sea.

Aegis in Greek mythology, the shield of Zeus, symbolic of the storm cloud associated with him. In representations of deities it is commonly shown as a protective animal skin.

Aelfric c. 955–1020. Anglo-Saxon writer and abbot, author of two collections of *Catholic Homilies* 990–92, sermons, and the *Lives of the Saints* 996–97, written in vernacular Old English prose.

Aeneas in Classical legend, a Trojan prince who became the ancestral hero of the Romans. According to Homer, he was the son of Anchises and the goddess Aphrodite. During the Trojan War he owed his life to the frequent intervention of the gods. The legend on which Virgil's epic poem the ◊*Aeneid* is based describes his escape from Troy and his eventual settlement in Latium, on the Italian peninsula.

Aeneid epic poem by Virgil, written in Latin in 12 books of hexameters and composed during the last 11 years of his life (30–19 BC). It celebrates the founding of Rome through the legend of Aeneas. After the fall of Troy, Aeneas wanders the Mediterranean for seven years and is shipwrecked off North Africa. He is received by Dido, Queen of Carthage, and they fall in love. Aeneas, however, renounces their love and sails on to Italy where he settles as the founder of Latium and the Roman state.

Aeolian harp wind-blown instrument consisting of a shallow soundbox supporting gut strings at low tension and tuned to the same pitch. It produces an eerie harmony that rises and falls with the changing pressure of the wind. It was common in parts of central Europe during the 19th century.

Aeolian Islands another name for the ◊Lipari Islands.

Aeolus in Greek mythology, the god of the winds, who kept them imprisoned in a cave on the ◊Lipari Islands.

Aepyornis genus of large, extinct, flightless birds living in Madagascar until a few thousand years ago. Some stood 10 ft/3 m high and laid eggs with a volume of 2 gallons/9 liters.

Aequi Italian people, originating around the river Velino, who were turned back from their advance on Rome 431 BC and were conquered 304 BC, during the Samnite Wars. Like many other peoples conquered by the Romans, they adopted Roman customs and culture.

aerenchyma plant tissue with numerous air-filled spaces between the cells. It occurs in the stems and roots of many aquatic plants where it aids buoyancy and facilitates transport of oxygen around the plant.

aerial in radio and television broadcasting, a conducting device that radiates or receives electronic waves. The design of an antenna or aerial depends principally on the wavelength of the signal. Long waves (hundreds of yards in wavelength) may employ long wire antennae; short waves (several inches in wavelength) may employ rods and dipoles; microwaves may also use dipoles—often with reflectors arranged like a toast rack—or highly directional parabolic dish antennae. Because microwaves travel in straight lines, giving line-of-sight communication, microwave aerials are usually located at the tops of tall masts or towers.

aerobic in biology, a description of those living organisms that require oxygen (usually dissolved in water) for the efficient release of energy contained in food molecules, such as glucose. They include almost all living organisms (plants as well as animals) with the exception of certain bacteria.

Aerobic reactions occur inside every cell and lead to the formation of energy-rich ◊ATP, subsequently used by the cell for driving its metabolic processes. Oxygen is used to convert glucose to carbon dioxide and water, thereby releasing energy. Most aerobic organisms die in the absence of oxygen, but certain organisms and cells, such as those found in muscle tissue, can function for short periods anaerobically (without oxygen). Other ◊anaerobic organisms can survive without oxygen.

aerobics (Greek "air" and "life") exercises for cardiovascular fitness. A strenuous application of movement to raise the heart rate to 120 beats per minute or more for sessions of 5–20 minutes' duration, 3–5 times per week.

For interest and pleasure, often a combination of dance, stretching exercises, and running aim to improve the performance of the heart and lungs system, but swimming, cycling and race-walking are preferred because they are less punishing to the joints and cause fewer sports-related injuries. Aerobics became a health and fitness pursuit in the 1980s.

aerodynamics branch of fluid physics that studies the forces exerted by air or other gases in motion -for example, the airflow around bodies (such as land vehicles, bullets, rockets, and aircraft) moving at speed through the atmosphere. For maximum efficiency, the aim is usually to design the shape of an object to produce a streamlined flow, with a minimum of turbulence in the moving air.

aerogenerator wind-powered electricity generator. These range from wind farms (see ◊wind turbine) to battery chargers used on yachts.

aeronautics science of travel through the Earth's atmosphere, including aerodynamics, aircraft structures, jet and rocket propulsion, and aerial navigation.

In **subsonic aeronautics** (below the speed of sound), aerodynamic forces increase at the rate of the square of the speed.

Transsonic aeronautics covers the speed range from just below to just above the speed of sound and is crucial to aircraft design. Ordinary sound waves move at about 760 mph/ 1,225 kph at sea level, and air in front of an aircraft moving slower than this is "warned" by the waves so that it can move aside. However, as the flying speed approaches that of the sound waves, the warning is too late for the air to escape, and the aircraft pushes the air aside, creating shock waves, which absorb much power and create design problems. On the ground the shock waves give rise to a ▷sonic boom. It was once thought that the speed of sound was a speed limit to aircraft, and the term ▷sound barrier came into use.

Supersonic aeronautics concerns speeds above that of sound and in one sense may be considered a much older study than aeronautics itself, since the study of the flight of bullets, known as ▷ballistics, was undertaken soon after the introduction of firearms. **Hypersonics** is the study of airflows and forces at speeds above five times that of sound (Mach 5); for example, for guided missiles, space rockets, and advanced concepts such as HOTOL (horizontal takeoff and landing). For all flight speeds streamlining is necessary to reduce the effects of air resistance.

Aeronautics is distinguished from astronautics, which is the science of travel through space. Astronavigation (navigation by reference to the stars) is used in aircraft as well as in ships and is a part of aeronautics.

aerosol particles of liquid or solid suspended in a gas. Fog is a common natural example. Aerosol cans, which contain pressurized gas mixed with a propellant, are used to spray liquid in the form of tiny drops of such products as scents and cleaners. Most aerosols used chlorofluorocarbons (CFCs) as propellants until these were found to cause destruction of the ▷ozone layer in the stratosphere.

The international community has agreed to phase out the use of CFCs, but most so-called "ozone-friendly" aerosols also use ozone-depleting chemicals, although they are not as destructive as CFCs. Some of the products sprayed, such as pesticides, can be directly toxic to humans.

Aeschines lived 4th century BC. Orator of ancient Athens, a rival of ▷Demosthenes.

Aeschylus c. 525–c. 456 BC. Greek dramatist, widely regarded as the founder of Greek tragedy (with ▷Euripides and ▷Sophocles). By the introduction of a second actor he made true dialogue and dramatic action possible. Aeschylus wrote some 90 plays between 499 and 458 BC, of which seven survive. These are *The Suppliant Women* performed about 490 BC, *The Persians* 472 BC, *Seven against Thebes* 467 BC, *Prometheus Bound* c. 460 BC, and the ▷*Oresteia* trilogy 458 BC.

Aeschylus was born at Eleusis, near Athens, of a noble family. He took part in the Persian Wars and fought at Marathon 490 BC. He twice visited the court of Hieron I, king of Syracuse, and died at Gela in Sicily.

Aesculapius in Greek and Roman mythology, the god of medicine; his emblem was a staff with a snake coiled around it, since snakes seemed to renew life by shedding their skin.

Aesir principal gods of Norse mythology—Odin, Thor, Balder, Loki, Freya, and Tyr—whose dwelling place was Asgard.

Aesop traditional writer of Greek fables. According to the historian Herodotus, he lived in the reign of Amasis of Egypt (mid-6th century BC) and was a slave of Iadmon, a Thracian. The fables, for which no evidence of his authorship exists, are anecdotal stories using animal characters to illustrate moral or satirical points.

Aesthetic movement English artistic movement of the late 19th century, dedicated to the doctrine of "art for art's sake"—that is, art as self-sufficient, not needing to justify its existence by serving any particular use. Artists associated with the movement include Aubrey Beardsley and James Whistler. The writer Oscar Wilde was, in his twenties, an exemplary aesthete.

Aetolia district of ancient Greece on the NW of the gulf of Corinth. The **Aetolian League** was a confederation of the cities of Aetolia which, following the death of Alexander the Great, became the chief rival of Macedonian power and the Achaean League.

Afars and the Issas, French Territory of the former French territory that became the Republic of ▷Djibouti 1977.

AFD abbreviation for **accelerated freeze drying**, a common method of food preservation. See ▷food technology.

affidavit legal document, used in court applications and proceedings, in which a person swears that certain facts are true.

affine geometry geometry that preserves parallelism and the ratios between intervals on any line segment.

affinity in chemistry, the force of attraction (see ▷bond) between atoms that helps to keep them in combination in a molecule. The term is also applied to attraction between molecules, such as those of biochemical significance (for example, between ▷enzymes and substrate molecules). This is the basis for affinity ▷chromatography, by which biologically important compounds are separated.

The atoms of a given element may have a greater affinity for the atoms of one element than for another (for example, hydrogen has a great affinity for chlorine, with which it easily and rapidly combines to form hydrochloric acid, but has little or no affinity for argon).

affirmation solemn declaration made instead of taking the oath by a person who has no religious belief or objects to taking an oath on religious grounds.

affirmative action government policy of positive discrimination that favors members of minority ethnic groups and women in such areas as employment and education, designed to counter the effects of long-term discrimination against them. In Europe, Sweden, Belgium, the Netherlands, and Italy actively promote affirmative action through legal and financial incentives.

In the US, the Equal Opportunities Act 1972 set up a commission to enforce the policy in organizations receiving public funds, so many private institutions and employers adopted voluntary affirmative action programs at the same time. In the 1980s the policy was sometimes not rigorously enforced.

The policy has been controversial, and has prompted lawsuits by white males who have been denied jobs or education as a result. Positive discrimination in favor of ethnic-minority construction companies by local government was outlawed Jan 1989.

affluent society society in which most people have money left over after satisfying their basic needs such as food and shelter. They are then able to decide how to spend their excess ("disposable") income, and become "consumers." The term was popularized by the US economist John Kenneth ▷Galbraith.

Galbraith used the term to describe the Western industrialized nations, particularly the US, in his book *The Affluent Society* 1958, in which he advocated using more of the nation's wealth for public spending and less for private consumption.

Afghan native to or an inhabitant of Afghanistan. The dominant group, particularly in Kabul, are the Pathans. The Tajiks, a smaller ethnic group, are predominantly traders and farmers in the province of Herat and around Kabul. The Hazaras, another farming group, are found in the southern mountain ranges of the Hindu Kush. The Uzbeks and Turkomen are farmers and speak Altaic-family languages. The smallest Altaic minority are the Kirghiz, who live in the Pamir. Baluchi nomads live in the south, and Nuristani farmers live in the mountains of the northeast.

The Pathans, Tajiks, and Hazaras are traditionally nomadic horse breeders and speak languages belonging to the Iranian branch of the Indo-European family. The majority of the population are Sunni Muslims, the most recent converts being the Nuristanis.

Afghan hound breed of fast hunting dog resembling the ▷saluki, though more thickly coated, first introduced to the West by British army officers serving on India's North-West Frontier along the Afghanistan border in the late 19th century. The Afghan hound is about 28 in/70 cm tall and has a long, silky coat.

It has an aloof, aristocratic expression, and has become increasingly fashionable since the 1970s.

Afghanistan mountainous, landlocked country in S central Asia, bounded N by Tajikistan, Turkmenistan, and Uzbekistan, W by Iran, and S and E by Pakistan and China.

government In Nov 1987 a grand national assembly (Loya Jirgah) of indirectly elected elders from various ethnic groups approved a new permanent constitution, establishing Islam as the state religion and creating a multiparty, presidential system of government. Under the terms of this constitution, the president, who is elected for a seven-year term by the Loya Jirgah, appoints the prime minister and is empowered to approve the laws and resolutions of the elected two-chamber national assembly (Meli Shura). The constitution was suspended following the withdrawal of Soviet troops Feb 1989 and an emergency military–People's Democratic Party of Afghanistan (PDPA) regime was established.

history Part of the ancient Persian Empire, the region was used by Darius I and Alexander the Great as a path to India; Islamic conquerors arrived in the 7th century, then Genghis Khan and Tamerlane in the 13th and 14th respectively. Afghanistan first became an independent emirate 1747. During the 19th century two ▷Afghan Wars were fought in which imperial Britain checked Russian influence extending toward India. The Anglo-Russian treaty 1907 gave autonomy to Afghanistan, with independence achieved by the Treaty of Rawalpindi 1919 following the third Afghan War. The kingdom was founded 1926 by Emir Amanullah.

During the 1950s, Lt Gen Sardar

Afghanistan
Republic of (*Jamhuria Afghanistan*)

area 251,707 sq mi/652,090 sq km
capital Kabul
cities Kandahar, Herat, Mazar-i-Sharif
physical mountainous in center and NE,
plains in N and SW
environment an estimated 95% of the urban
population is without access to sanitation
services
features Hindu Kush mountain range (Khyber
and Salang passes, Wakhan salient and
Panjshir Valley), Amu Darya (Oxus) River,
Helmand River, Lake Saberi
head of state Burhanuddin Rabbani from 1992
head of government to be announced
political system transitional
political parties Homeland Party (Hezb-i-
Watan, formerly People's Democratic Party
of Afghanistan (PDPA)) Marxist-Leninist;
Hezb-i-Islami and Jamiat-i-Islami, Islamic
fundamentalist mujaheddin; National Liberation
Front, moderate mujaheddin
exports dried fruit, natural gas, fresh fruits,
carpets; small amounts of rare minerals,
karakul lamb skins, and Afghan coats
currency afgháni
population (1989) 15,590,000 (more than 5
million became refugees after 1979); growth
rate 0.6% p.a.
life expectancy (1986) men 43, women 41
languages Pushtu, Dari (Persian)
religion Muslim (80% Sunni, 20% Shiite)
literacy men 39%, women 8% (1985 est)
GNP $3.3 bn (1985); $275 per head
GDP $1,858 million; $111 per head
chronology
1747 Afghanistan became an independent
emirate.
1839–42 and 1878–80 Afghan Wars instigated
by Britain to counter the threat to British
India from expanding Russian influence in
Afghanistan.
1919 Afghanistan recovered full independence
following Third Afghan War.
1953 Lt Gen Daud Khan became prime
minister and introduced reform program.
1963 Daud Khan forced to resign and
constitutional monarchy established.
1973 Monarchy overthrown in coup by Daud
Khan.
1978 Daud Khan ousted by Taraki and the
PDPA.
1979 Taraki replaced by Hafizullah Amin;
Soviet Union entered country to prop up
government; they installed Babrak Karmal
in power. Amin executed.
1986 Replacement of Karmal as leader by
Dr Najibullah Ahmadzai. Partial Soviet troop
withdrawal.
1988 New non-Marxist constitution adopted.
1989 Complete withdrawal of Soviet troops;
state of emergency imposed in response to
intensification of civil war.
1990 PDPA renamed the Homeland Party;
President Najibullah elected its president.
1991 UN peace plan accepted by President
Najibullah but rejected by the mujaheddin.
US and Soviet military aid withdrawn.
Mujaheddin began talks with Russians and
Kabul government.
1992 April: Najibullah regime overthrown.
June: after a succession of short-term
presidents, Burhanuddin Rabbani named
interim head of state; Islamic law introduced.
Sept: Hezb-i-Islami barred from government
participation after shell attacks on Kabul.

Mohammad Daud Khan, cousin of King
Mohammad Zahir Shah (ruled 1933–73), governed as prime minister and introduced a
program of social and economic modernization
with Soviet aid. Opposition to his authoritarian rule forced Daud's resignation 1963; the
king was made a constitutional monarch, but
political parties were outlawed.
republic After a famine 1972, General Daud
Khan overthrew the monarchy in a Soviet-
backed military coup 1973. The king fled to
exile, and a republic was declared. President
Daud was assassinated 1978 in a military coup,
and Nur Mohammad Taraki, the imprisoned
leader of the radical Khalq (masses) faction of
the banned communist People's Democratic
Party of Afghanistan (PDPA), took charge as
president of a revolutionary council. A one-
party constitution was adopted, a Treaty of
Friendship and Mutual Defense signed with
the USSR, and major reforms introduced. Conservative Muslims opposed these initiatives,
and thousands of refugees fled to Iran and
Pakistan. Taraki was replaced 1979 by foreign
minister Hafizullah Amin.
Soviet invasion Internal unrest continued,
and the USSR organized a further coup Dec
1979. Amin was executed and Babrak Karmal
(1929–), the exiled leader of the gradualist

Parcham (banner) faction of the PDPA, was
installed as leader. The numbers of Soviet
forces in Afghanistan grew to over 120,000
by 1985 as Muslim guerrilla resistance by
the "mujaheddin" ("holy warriors") continued.
A war of attrition developed, with the USSR
failing to gain control of rural areas.
Soviet withdrawal Faced with high troop
casualties and a drain on economic resources,
the new Soviet administration of Mikhail
Gorbachev moved toward a compromise settlement 1986. Karmal was replaced as PDPA
leader May 1986 by the Pathan former secret police chief Dr Najibullah Ahmadzai
(1947–), and several noncommunist politicians joined the new government. In Oct
1986, 8,000 Soviet troops were withdrawn as a
good-will gesture, and the Afghan government
announced a six-month unilateral cease-fire
Jan 1987. The mujaheddin rejected this initiative, however, insisting on a full Soviet
withdrawal and replacement of the communist government. The Najibullah government
extended the cease-fire, and a new multiparty
Islamic constitution was ratified Nov 1987 in an
attempt to promote "national reconciliation." A
phased withdrawal of all Soviet forces began
1988. On its completion Feb 1989, the constitution was suspended and a "state of emergency"

imposed by the Najibullah government, which
was faced with a mounting military onslaught
by the mujaheddin. The guerrillas continued
to resist the PDPA regime's "power-sharing"
entreaties, demanding that Najibullah should
first resign.
government in exile formed The
mujaheddin met in Peshawar, Pakistan, Feb
1989 to try to elect a government in exile. The
meeting ended with the election of a prominent
moderate, Prof Sibghatullah Mojadidi (head
of the Afghan National Liberation Front), as
president, and the fundamentalist Prof Abdur-
Rabbur Rasul Sayaf as prime minister of
the Afghan Interim Government (AIG). The
government was not accorded international
recognition.
areas of respective control The ruling PDPA
was renamed the Homeland Party (Hezb-i-
Watan) in June 1990, with President Najibullah
as its chair. The small garrison of Khost, near
the Pakistan border, fell to the mujaheddin
March 1991. It was a significant victory for
the guerrillas, who had reportedly received
logistical support from the US Central Intelligence Agency and Pakistan's Inter Services
Intelligence (ISI) directorate. The mujaheddin,
now in receipt of diminishing amounts of aid
from the US, Saudi Arabia, and Pakistan, also
controlled 90% of the mountainous Afghan
countryside. However, apart from Khost, all
Afghanistan's significant urban centers were
controlled by the Homeland Party.
United Nations peace plan The Najibullah
government accepted a UN peace plan for
Afghanistan in May 1991, but the Hezb-i-Islami
mujaheddin leader, Gulbuddin Hekmatyar,
and AIG both rejected the proposals, refusing
to accept any settlement under the Najibullah
regime. In Sept 1991, the US and the USSR
agreed to halt all weapon supplies to the contending parties in Afghanistan by the end of
the year. In Oct 1991 the USSR also withdrew
its demand to play a key role in any transitional arrangement for President Najibullah. This
encouraged the mujaheddin to enter into peace
talks with the Russians and the Kabul government. In Jan 1992 Pakistan halted military aid
to the mujaheddin and declared support for the
UN peace plan.
Mujaheddin seize power The Najibullah regime collapsed April 1992 when government
troops defected to the mujaheddin forces led
by Ahmad Shah Massoud, and captured Kabul.
Najibullah fled and was placed under UN protection. An attempt by Gulbuddin Hekmatyar
to seize power was thwarted and an interim
government April-June under the moderate
Sibghatullah Mojadidi failed to restore order to
Kabul. Power was transferred to guerrilla leader Burhanuddin Rabbani with Hezb-i-Islami
representative Abdul Sabur Farid as prime minister. Rabbani pledged to seek unity between
the country's warring guerrillas and abolished
all laws contrary to *Sharia* (Islamic law). However, tensions between the government and
the Hekmatyar faction culminated Aug 1992
in indiscriminate and heavy bombardment of
the city by the rebels' forces. In Sept Rabbani
counter-attacked by removing Farid from the
premiership and banning Hezb-i-Islami from
all government activity. *See illustration box.*

Afghan Wars three wars waged between
Britain and Afghanistan to counter the threat to
British India from expanding Russian influence
in Afghanistan.
First Afghan War 1838–42, when the
British garrison at Kabul was wiped out.

Second Afghan War 1878–80, when General Roberts captured Kabul and relieved Kandahar.

Third Afghan War 1919, when peace followed the dispatch by the UK of the first airplane ever seen in Kabul.

AFL–CIO abbreviation for ⟡*American Federation of Labor and Congress of Industrial Organizations*.

Africa second largest of the continents, three times the area of Europe
area 11,620,451 sq mi/30,097,000 sq km
largest cities (population over 1 million) Cairo, Algiers, Lagos, Kinshasa, Abidjan, Cape Town, Nairobi, Casablanca, El Gîza, Addis Ababa, Luanda, Dar es Salaam, Ibadan, Douala, Mogadishu
physical dominated by a uniform central plateau comprising a southern tableland with a mean altitude of 3,000 ft/1,070 m that falls northward to a lower elevated plain with a mean altitude of 1,300 ft/400 m. Although there are no great alpine regions or extensive coastal plains, Africa has a mean altitude of 2,000 ft/610 m, two times greater than Europe. The highest points are Mount Kilimanjaro 19,364 ft/5,900 m, and Mount Kenya 17,058 ft/5,200 m; the lowest point is Lac Assal in Djibouti −471 ft/−144 m. Compared with other continents, Africa has few broad estuaries or inlets and therefore has proportionately the shortest coastline (15,000 mi/24,000 km). The geographical extremities of the continental mainland are Cape Hafun in the E, Cape Almadies in the W, Ras Ben Sekka in the N, and Cape Agulhas in the S. The Sahel is a narrow belt of savanna and scrub forest that covers 1.7 billion acres/700 million hectares of west and central Africa; 75% of the continent lies within the tropics
features Great Rift Valley, containing most of the great lakes of E Africa (except Lake Victoria); Atlas Mountains in NW; Drakensberg mountain range in SE; Sahara Desert (world's largest desert) in N; Namib, Kalahari, and Great Karoo deserts in S; Nile, Zaïre, Niger, Zambezi, Limpopo, Volta, and Orange rivers
products has 30% of the world's minerals including diamonds (51%) and gold (47%); produces 11% of the world's crude petroleum, 58% of the world's cocoa (Ivory Coast, Ghana, Cameroon, Nigeria), 23% of the world's coffee (Uganda, Ivory Coast, Zaire, Ethiopia, Cameroon, Kenya), 20% of the world's groundnuts (Senegal, Nigeria, Sudan, Zaire), and 21% of the world's hardwood timber (Nigeria, Zaire, Tanzania, Kenya)
population (1988) 610 million; more than double the 1960 population of 278 million, and rising to an estimated 900 million by 2000; annual growth rate 3% (10 times greater than Europe); 27% of the world's undernourished people live in sub-Saharan Africa, where an estimated 25 million are facing famine
language over 1,000 languages spoken in Africa; Niger-Kordofanian languages including Mandinke, Kwa, Lingala, Bemba, and Bantu (Zulu, Swahili, Kikuyu), spoken over half of Africa from Mauritania in the W to South Africa; Nilo-Saharan languages, including Dinka, Shilluk, Nuer, and Masai, spoken in Central Africa from the bend of the Niger river to the foothills of Ethiopia; Afro-Asiatic (Hamito-Semitic) languages, including Arabic, Berber, Ethiopian, and Amharic, N of equator; Khoisan languages with "click" consonants spoken in SW by Kung, Khoikhoi, and Nama people of Namibia

Africa: history

14 million BC	Africa, which is considered the "cradle continent," probably produced the first humanlike creatures.
3–5 million	Direct line of descent of modern humans was established in E Africa.
15,000	Agriculture first practiced in Egypt.
10,000–2000	The originally fertile Sahara became a barrier desert between north and south.
5450–2500	Era of Saharan rock and cave paintings.
7th century BC –6th century AD	Assyria, Persia, Greece, Rome, and Byzantium in turn made conquests in N Africa. Meroe: the Egyptian and Negro tradition met in the Nubian kingdom of Kush.
320 BC–AD 50	The kingdom of Axum flourished in Ethiopia and gave rise to the later legend of Prester John.
640	Islamic expansion began in N, E, and Central Africa.
300–1500	Period of the great medieval states: Ghana, Mali, Songhai, Benin, Ife, and the culture of Great Zimbabwe.
12th–15th centuries	Era of the Arab travelers: for example, Ibn Batuta; and of trade, for example, Kilwa.
1488	Diaz rounded the Cape of Good Hope.
15th–16th centuries	European sea trade in gold, ivory, timber, and pepper.
17th–19th centuries	Height of the Atlantic and Indian Ocean slave trade.
18th–19th centuries	European travelers in Africa: Park, Livingstone, Stanley, Speke, Mary Kingsley.
19th century	Colonial wars against well-organized native states: Asante, Dahomey, Zululand.
1880–90	Peak of European colonization in the "scramble for Africa."
1899–1902	South African War, the first large-scale war between whites in Africa.
1920	League of Nations mandate system introduced the idea of European trusteeship.
1936	Italy's conquest of Ethiopia.
1942	World War II reached its turning point in the Battles of Alamein.
1951	Libya became the first independent state to be declared by the United Nations.
1954–62	The fight for independence in Algeria precipitated the end of the French Fourth Republic 1958.
1957	Ghana became independent, the first of the revived black nation states.
1952–60	Mau-Mau movement in Kenya began the ousting of white settlers south of the Sahara.
1963	Organization of African Unity (OAU) founded.
1967–70	Revolt of Biafra within the federation of Nigeria constituted the first civil war in a modern black state.
1975	Mozambique's independence led to the end of dictatorship in Portugal.
1979	Zimbabwe's achievement of independence left South Africa as the last white-ruled state in Africa.
1980	Future of the OAU doubtful due to division over Western Sahara and Libyan aggression toward Chad. Extensive food shortages in many parts of Central and East Africa.
1984	Increasing internal disaster in South Africa leading to violence between black population and minority white groups.
1988	Peace treaty between Angola, South Africa, and Cuba leading to Namibia's independence.
1990	Namibia declared independent. South Africa's African National Congress (ANC) party leader Nelson Mandela freed.
1991	North African states oppose Iraq on Kuwait invasion. Ethiopia's communist regime collapses.
1992	New constitution in South Africa leading to all-races majority rule approved by whites-only referendum. Sout hern Africa experienced t worst drought of the 20th century.

religion Islam in the N and on the E coast as far S as N Mozambique; animism below the Sahara, which survives alongside Christianity (both Catholic and Protestant) in many central and S areas.

Africa, Horn of projection constituted by Somalia and adjacent territories.

African native to or an inhabitant of the continent of Africa, especially of sub-Saharan Africa. The region is culturally heterogeneous with numerous distinctive ethnic and sociolinguistic groups. There are three major language families: Niger-Congo, Afro-Asiatic (Hamito-Semitic), and Chari-Nile (Sudanic).

African art art of sub-Saharan Africa, from prehistory onwards, ranging from the art of ancient civilizations to the new styles of post-imperialist African nations. Examples of historic African art are bronze figures from Benin and Ife (in Nigeria) dating from about 1500 and, also on the west coast, in the same period, bronze or brass figures for weighing gold, made by the Asante.
prehistoric art Rock paintings are found in various regions, notably in the western Sahara, Zimbabwe, South Africa, and, from the end of the period, East Africa. Some of the earliest pictures are of elephants. The images tend to be linear and heavily stylized and sometimes show a geometric style. Terracotta figures from Nigeria, dating from several centuries BC, have stylized features similar to Oceanic art forms and some early South American styles.
Zimbabwe Ruins of ancient stone buildings

from before 300 AD suggest a time of outstanding craft skill in the country's history; sculptures have also been found in the ruins.

Benin and Ife The bronze sculptures from the 13th–16th-century realms of Benin and Ife on the west coast of Africa (examples in the British Museum, London) are distinctive in style and demonstrate technical refinement in casting by the lost-wax method (see ♢sculpture). The Ife heads are naturalistic, while those of Benin are more stylized. The art of Benin includes high-relief bronze plaques with figurative scenes, and ivory carvings. Some of these appear to have been designed for the Portuguese trade.

Asante Metalworkers of the Asante people (in present-day Ghana) made weights, highly inventive forms with comically exaggerated figures.

general Over the centuries, much artistic effort was invested in religious objects and masks, with wooden sculpture playing a large role. Many everyday items, such as bowls, stools, drums, and combs, also display fine craft and a vitality of artistic invention.

Since much of Africa's history up to the late 19th century has not been researched, African art has occupied a meager place in Western art-history studies. In the early 20th century West African art had a profound influence on the work of many European painters and sculptors.

African National Congress (ANC) multiracial nationalist organization formed in South Africa 1912 to extend the franchise to the whole population and end all racial discrimination there. Its president is Nelson ♢Mandela. Although originally nonviolent, the ANC was banned by the government from 1960 to Jan 1990, and in exile in Mozambique developed a military wing, **Umkhonto we Sizwe**, which engaged in sabotage and guerrilla training. The armed struggle was suspended Aug 1990 after the organization's headquarters were moved from Zambia to Johannesburg. Talks between the ANC and the South African government have taken place intermittently since Dec 1991, with the proposed aim of creating a nonracial constitution. In Oct 1992, accusations of inhumane treatment of prisoners held in ANC camps outside South Africa led Mandela to institute an inquiry and promise an end to such abuses.

The ANC is supported by the Organization of African Unity as a movement aimed at introducing majority rule in South Africa. Its vice-president from 1991 is Walter ♢Sisulu. Former ANC leaders include Albert Luthuli and Solomon Plaatje. Several imprisoned leaders were released Oct 1989; Mandela in Feb 1990.

African violet herbaceous plant *Saintpaulia ionantha* from tropical central and E Africa, with velvety green leaves and scentless purple flowers. Different colors and double varieties have been bred.

Afrikaans language an official language (with English) of the Republic of South Africa and Namibia. Spoken mainly by the Afrikaners—descendants of Dutch and other 17th-century colonists—it is a variety of the Dutch language, modified by circumstance and the influence of German, English, French, and other immigrant as well as local languages. It became a standardized written language about 1875.

Afrika Korps German army in the western desert of North Africa 1941–43 during World War II, commanded by Field Marshal Erwin Rommel. They were driven out of N Africa by May 1943.

Afrikaner (formerly known as *Boer*) inhabitant of South Africa descended from the original Dutch, Flemish, and ♢Huguenot settlers of the 17th century. Comprising approximately 60% of the white population in South Africa, they were originally farmers but have now become mainly urbanized. Their language is Afrikaans.

Afro-Caribbean West Indian person of African descent. Afro-Caribbeans are the descendants of W Africans captured or obtained in trade from African procurers. European slave traders then shipped them to the West Indies to English, French, Dutch, Spanish, and Portuguese colonies founded from the 16th century. Since World War II many Afro-Caribbeans have migrated to North America and to Europe, especially to the US, the UK, and the Netherlands.

afterbirth in mammals, the placenta and other material, including blood and membranes, expelled from the uterus soon after birth. In the natural world it is often eaten.

afterburning method of increasing the thrust of a gas turbine (jet) airplane engine by spraying additional fuel into the hot exhaust duct between the turbojet and the the tailpipe where it ignites. Used for short-term increase of power during takeoff, or during combat in military aircraft.

afterimage persistence of an image on the retina of the eye after the object producing it has been removed. This leads to persistence of vision, a necessary phenomenon for the illusion of continuous movement in films and television. The term is also used for the persistence of sensations other than vision.

after-ripening process undergone by the seeds of some plants before germination can occur. The length of the after-ripening period in different species may vary from a few weeks to many months.

It helps seeds to germinate at a time when conditions are most favorable for growth. In some cases the embryo is not fully mature at the time of dispersal and must develop further before germination can take place. Other seeds do not germinate even when the embryo is mature, probably owing to growth inhibitors within the seed that must be leached out or broken down before germination can begin.

AG abbreviation for ***Aktiengesellschaft*** (German "limited company").

aga (Turkish "lord") title of nobility, applied by the Turks to military commanders and, in general, to men of high station in some Muslim countries.

Agadir resort and seaport in S Morocco, near the mouth of the river Sus; population (1984) 110,500. It was rebuilt after being destroyed by an earthquake 1960.

Agadir Incident or the ***Second Moroccan Crisis*** international crisis provoked by Kaiser Wilhelm II of Germany, July–Nov 1911. By sending the gunboat *Panther* to demand territorial concessions from the French, he hoped to drive a wedge into the Anglo-French entente. In fact, German aggression during the second Moroccan crisis merely served to reinforce Anglo-French fears of Germany's intentions. The crisis gave rise to the term "gunboat diplomacy."

Aga Khan IV 1936– . Spiritual head (*imam*) of the ***Ismaili*** Muslim sect (see ♢Islam). He succeeded his grandfather 1957.

agama lizard of the Old World family Agamidae, especially the genus *Agama*. There are about 280 species, found throughout the warmer regions of the Old World. Many are brilliantly colored and all are capable of changing the color of their skin.

Agamemnon in Greek mythology, a Greek hero, son of Atreus, king of Mycenae. He married Clytemnestra, and their children included ♢Electra, ♢Iphigenia, and ♢Orestes. He led the capture of Troy, received Priam's daughter Cassandra as a prize, and was murdered by Clytemnestra and her lover, Aegisthus, on his return home. His children Orestes and Electra later killed the guilty couple.

Agana capital of Guam in the W Pacific; population (1980) 896. It is the administrative center of the island, bordered by residential Agana Heights and Apra Harbor.

agar jellylike carbohydrate, obtained from seaweeds. It is used mainly in microbiological experiments as a culture medium for growing bacteria and other microorganisms. The agar is resistant to breakdown by microorganisms, remaining a solid jelly throughout the course of the experiment.

It is also used as a laxative and in preserved foods.

agaric fungus of typical mushroom shape. Agarics include the field mushroom *Agaricus campestris* and the cultivated edible mushroom *A. brunnesiens*. Closely related is the often poisonous ♢Amanita genus, including the fly agaric *Amanita muscaria*.

Agassiz Jean Louis Rodolphe 1807–1873. Swiss-born US paleontologist and geologist. His interests were comparative zoology and Ice Age geology. In 1832 he accepted a professorship at the University of Neuchâtel; coming to the US 1846, he became a member of the faculty of Harvard. Agassiz, known as a conservative in his opposition to Darwin, conducted many expeditions to the American West. His massive *Contributions to the Natural History of the United States* was published 1857–62.

He earned a PhD at the University of Erlangen 1829 and an MD at Munich 1830.

agate banded or cloudy type of ♢chalcedony, a silica, SiO_2, that forms in rock cavities. Agates are used as ornamental stones and for art objects.

Agate stones, being hard, are also used to burnish and polish gold applied to glass and ceramics.

agave any of several related plants with stiff sword-shaped spiny leaves arranged in a rosette. All species of the genus *Agave* come from the warmer parts of the New World. They include *A. sisalina*, whose fibers are used for rope making, and the Mexican century plant *A. americana*. Alcoholic drinks such as ♢tequila and pulque are made from the sap of agave plants.

Agee James 1909–1955. US journalist, screenwriter, and author. He rose to national prominence as a result of his investigation of the plight of sharecroppers in the South during the Depression. In collaboration with photographer Walker Evans, he published the photo and text essay *Let Us Now Praise Famous Men* 1941. His screenwriting credits include *The African Queen* 1951 and *The Night of the Hunter* 1955. His novel *A Death in the Family* won a Pulitzer Prize 1958.

Born in Knoxville, Tennessee, Agee graduated from Harvard 1932 and embarked on a career as a magazine reporter and feature writer.

ageism discrimination against older people in employment, pensions, housing, and health care.

To combat it the American Association of Retired Persons (AARP) has 30 million members, and the Gray Panthers were formed. They have been responsible for legislation forbidding employers to discriminate; for example, it is illegal in the US to fail to employ people aged 40–69, to dismiss them, or to reduce their working conditions or wages.

Agent Orange selective ◊weedkiller, notorious for its use in the 1960s during the Vietnam War by US forces to eliminate ground cover which could protect enemy forces. It was subsequently discovered to contain highly poisonous ◊dioxin. Thousands of US troops who had handled it later developed cancer or fathered deformed babies.

Agent Orange, named after the distinctive orange stripe on its packaging, combines equal parts of 2,4-D (2,4-trichlorophenoxyacetic acid) and 2,4,5-T (2,4,5-trichlorophenoxyacetic acid), both now banned in the US. Companies that had manufactured the chemicals faced an increasing number of lawsuits in the 1970s. All the suits were settled out of court in a single ◊class action, resulting in the largest ever payment of its kind ($180 million) to claimants.

agglutination in biology, the clumping together of ◊antigens, such as blood cells or bacteria, to form larger, visible masses, under the influence of ◊antibodies. As each antigen clumps only in response to its particular antibody, agglutination provides a way of determining ◊blood groups and the identity of unknown bacteria.

aggression in politics, an unprovoked attack often involving an escalating series of threats aimed at intimidating an opponent. The actions of Nazi Germany, under Adolf Hitler in the 1930s, leading to World War II were considered to be aggressive. The invasion of Kuwait by Iraq in 1990 was condemned as an act of aggression.

aggression in biology, behavior used to intimidate or injure another organism (of the same or of a different species), usually for the purposes of gaining a territory, a mate, or food. Aggression often involves an escalating series of threats aimed at intimidating an opponent without having to engage in potentially dangerous physical contact. Aggressive signals include roaring by wapiti (American Elk), snarling by dogs, the fluffing up of feathers by birds, and the raising of fins by some species of fish.

Agincourt, Battle of battle of the Hundred Years' War in which Henry V of England defeated the French on Oct 25, 1415, mainly through the overwhelming superiority of the English longbow. The French lost more than 6,000 men to about 1,600 English casualties. As a result of the battle, Henry gained France and the French princess, Catherine of Valois, as his wife. The village of Agincourt (modern *Azincourt*) is south of Calais, in N France.

aging in common usage, the period of deterioration of the physical condition of a living organism that leads to death; in biological terms, the entire life process.

Three current theories attempt to account for aging. The first suggests that the process is genetically determined, to remove individuals that can no longer reproduce. The second suggests that it is due to the accumulation of mistakes during the replication of ◊DNA at cell division. The third suggests that aging is actively induced by pieces of DNA that move between cells, or by cancer-causing viruses; these may become abundant in old cells and induce them to produce unwanted ◊proteins or interfere with the control functions of their DNA.

Agnew Spiro 1918– . US vice-president 1969–73. A Republican, he was governor of Maryland 1966–69, and vice-president under ◊Nixon. He took the lead in a campaign against the press and opponents of the ◊Vietnam War. Although he was one of the few administration officials not to be implicated in the ◊Watergate affair, he resigned 1973, shortly before pleading "no contest" to a charge of income-tax evasion.

Agni in Hindu mythology, the god of fire, the guardian of homes, and the protector of humans against the powers of darkness.

Agnon Shmuel Yosef 1888–1970. Israeli novelist. Born in Buczacz, Galicia (now part of W Ukraine), he made it the setting of his most celebrated work, *A Guest for the Night* 1945. He shared a Nobel Prize 1966.

agnosticism belief that the existence of God cannot be proven; that in the nature of things the individual cannot know anything of what lies behind or beyond the world of natural phenomena. The term was coined 1869 by T H ◊Huxley.

Whereas an atheist (see ◊atheism) denies the existence of God or gods, an agnostic asserts that God or a First Cause is one of those concepts—others include the Absolute, infinity, eternity, and immortality—that lie beyond the reach of human intelligence, and therefore can be neither confirmed nor denied.

agoraphobia ◊phobia involving fear of open spaces and crowded places.

The anxiety produced can be so severe that some sufferers are confined to their homes for many years.

agouti small rodent of the genus *Dasyprocta*, family Dasyproctidae. It is found in the forests of Central and South America. The agouti is herbivorous, swift-running, and about the size of a rabbit.

AGR abbreviation for ◊*advanced gas-cooled reactor*, a type of nuclear reactor.

Agra city of Uttar Pradesh, India, on the river Jumna, 100 mi/160 km SE of Delhi; population (1981) 747,318. A commercial and university center, it was the capital of the Mogul empire 1527–1628, from which period the Taj Mahal dates.

history ◊Zahir ud-din Mohammed (known as "Babur"), the first great Mogul ruler, made Agra his capital 1527. His grandson Akbar rebuilt the Red Fort of Salim Shah 1566, and is buried outside the city in the tomb at Sikandra. In the 17th century the buildings of ◊Shah Jahan made Agra one of the most beautiful cities in the world. The Taj Mahal, erected as a tomb for the emperor's wife Mumtaz Mahal, was completed 1650. Agra's political importance dwindled from 1658, when Aurangzeb moved the capital back to Delhi. It was taken from the Marathas by Lord Lake 1803.

agribusiness commercial farming on an industrial scale, often financed by companies whose main interests lie outside agriculture; for example, multinational corporations. Agribusiness farms are mechanized, large in size, highly structured, and reliant on chemicals.

Agricola Gnaeus Julius AD 37–93. Roman general and politician. Born in Provence, he became Consul of the Roman Republic 77 AD, and then governor of Britain AD 78–85. He extended Roman rule to the Firth of Forth in Scotland and won the battle of Mons Graupius. His fleet sailed round the north of Scotland and proved Britain an island.

agriculture the practice of farming, including the cultivation of the soil (for raising crops) and the raising of domesticated animals. Crops are for human nourishment, animal fodder, or commodities such as cotton and sisal. Animals are raised for wool, milk, leather, dung (as fuel), or meat. The units for managing agricultural production vary from small holdings and individually owned farms to corporate-run farms and collective farms run by entire communities.

Agriculture developed in the Middle East and Egypt at least 10,000 years ago. Farming communities soon became the base for society in China, India, Europe, Mexico, and Peru, then spread throughout the world. Reorganization along more scientific and productive lines took place in Europe in the 18th century in response to dramatic population growth.

Mechanization made considerable progress in the US and Europe during the 19th century. After World War II, there was an explosive growth in the use of agricultural chemicals: herbicides, insecticides, fungicides, and fertilizers. In the 1960s there was development of high-yielding species, especially in the ◊green revolution of the Third World, and the industrialized countries began intensive farming of cattle, poultry, and pigs. In the 1980s, hybridization by genetic engineering methods and pest control by the use of chemicals plus ◊pheromones were developed. However, there was also a reaction against some forms of intensive agriculture because of the pollution and habitat destruction caused. One result of this was a growth of alternative methods, including organic agriculture.

plants For plant products, the land must be prepared (plowing, cultivating, harrowing, and rolling). Seed must be planted and the growing plant nurtured. This may involve fertilizers, irrigation, pest control by chemicals, and monitoring of acidity or nutrients. When the crop has grown, it must be harvested and, depending on the crop, processed in a variety of ways before it is stored or sold.

Greenhouses allow cultivation of plants that would otherwise find the climate too harsh. ◊Hydroponics allows commercial cultivation of crops using nutrient-enriched solutions instead of soil. Special methods, such as terracing, may be adopted to allow cultivation in hostile terrain and to retain topsoil in mountainous areas with heavy rainfall.

livestock Animals may be semidomesticated, such as reindeer, or fully domesticated but nomadic (where naturally growing or cultivated food supplies are sparse), or kept in one location. Animal farming involves accommodation (buildings, fencing, or pasture), feeding, breeding, gathering the produce (eggs, milk, or wool), slaughtering, and further processing such as tanning.

organic farming From the 1970s there has been a movement toward more sophisticated natural methods without chemical sprays and fertilizers. These methods are desirable because nitrates have been seeping into the ground water, insecticides are found in lethal concentrations at the top of the ⬦food chain, some herbicides are associated with human birth defects, and hormones fed to animals to promote fast growth have damaging effects on humans.

overproduction The greater efficiency in agriculture achieved since the 19th century, coupled with post–World War II government subsidies for domestic production in the US and the European Community (EC), have led to the development of high stocks, nicknamed "lakes" (wine, milk) and "mountains" (butter, beef, grain). There is no simple solution to this problem, as any large-scale dumping onto the market displaces regular merchandise. Increasing concern about the starving and the cost of storage has led the US and the EC to develop measures for limiting production, such as letting arable land lie fallow to reduce grain crops. The US had some success at selling surplus wheat to the USSR when the Soviet crop was poor, but the overall cost of bulk transport and the potential destabilization of other economies has acted against high producers exporting their excess on a regular basis to needy countries. Intensive farming methods also contribute to soil ⬦erosion and water pollution.

agrimony herbaceous plant *Agrimonia eupatoria* of the rose family Rosaceae, with small yellow flowers on a slender spike.

It grows along hedges and in fields.

Agrippa Marcus Vipsanius 63–12 BC. Roman general. He commanded the victorious fleet at the battle of Actium and married Julia, daughter of the emperor ⬦Augustus.

agrochemical artificially produced chemical used in modern, intensive agricultural systems. Agrochemicals include nitrate and phosphate fertilizers, pesticides, some animal-feed additives, and pharmaceuticals. Many are responsible for pollution and almost all are avoided by organic farmers.

agronomy study of crops and soils, a branch of agricultural science. Agronomy includes such topics as selective breeding (of plants and animals), irrigation, pest control, and soil analysis and modification.

Aguascalientes city in central Mexico, and capital of a state of the same name; population (1990) 506,384. It has hot mineral springs.

AH with reference to the Muslim calendar, abbreviation for *anno hegirae* (Latin "year of the flight" of ⬦Mohammed, from Mecca to Medina).

Ahab *c.* 875–854 BC. King of Israel. His empire included the suzerainty of Moab, and Judah was his subordinate ally, but his kingdom was weakened by constant wars with Syria. By his marriage with Jezebel, princess of Sidon, Ahab introduced into Israel the worship of the Phoenician god Baal, thus provoking the hostility of Elijah and other prophets. Ahab died in battle against the Syrians at Ramoth Gilead.

Ahaggar or *Hoggar* mountainous plateau of the central Sahara, Algeria, whose highest point, Tahat, at 9,576 ft/2,918 m, lies between Algiers and the mouth of the Niger. It is the home of the formerly nomadic Tuareg.

Ahasuerus (Latinized Hebrew form of the Persian **Khshayarsha**, Greek **Xerxes**) name of several Persian kings in the Bible, notably the husband of ⬦Esther. Traditionally it was also the name of the ⬦Wandering Jew.

ahimsa in Hinduism, Buddhism, and Jainism, the doctrine of respect for all life (including the lowest forms and even the elements themselves) and consequently an extreme form of nonviolence. It arises in part from the concept of *karma*, which holds that a person's actions (and thus any injury caused to any form of life) are carried forward from one life to the next, determining each stage of reincarnation.

Ahmadiyya Islamic religious movement founded by Mirza Ghulam Ahmad (1839–1908). His followers reject the doctrine that Mohammed was the last of the prophets and accept Ahmad's claim to be the Mahdi and Promised Messiah. In 1974 the Ahmadis were denounced as non-Muslims by other Muslims.

Ahmad Shah Durrani 1724–1773. Founder and first ruler of Afghanistan. Elected shah in 1747, he had conquered the Punjab by 1751.

Ahmedabad or *Ahmadabad* capital of Gujarat, India; population (1981) 2,515,195. It is a cotton-manufacturing center, and has many sacred buildings of the Hindu, Muslim, and Jain faiths.

Ahriman in Zoroastrianism, the supreme evil spirit, lord of the darkness and death, waging war with his counterpart Ahura Mazda (Ormuzd) until a time when human beings choose to lead good lives and Ahriman is finally destroyed.

Ahura Mazda or *Ormuzd* in Zoroastrianism, the spirit of supreme good. As god of life and light he will finally prevail over his enemy, Ahriman.

Ahváz industrial capital of the province of Khuzestan, on the river Karun, W Iran; population (1986) 590,000. The ancient city was rebuilt in the 3rd century AD; it became a prosperous city in the 20th century after the discovery of oil.

Ahvenanmaa Island island in the Gulf of Bothnia, Finland; largest of the ⬦Åland Islands.

AI abbreviation for ⬦*artificial intelligence*.

Aidan, St *c.* 600–651. Irish monk who converted Northumbria to Christianity and founded Lindisfarne monastery on Holy Island off the NE coast of England. His feast day is Aug 31.

aid, foreign financial and other assistance given by richer, usually industrialized, countries to war-damaged or developing states.

In the US it has become an increasingly contentious domestic issue. With severe budget deficits and a large part of the foreign aid budget allocated by treaty to a very few countries, calls have grown for reform. Aid can be bilateral, by agreement with another country, or through international agencies such as the ⬦International Development Association. Aid is given for political, commercial, or humanitarian reasons or a combination of all three.

AIDS (acronym for *acquired immune deficiency syndrome*) the gravest of the sexually transmitted diseases, or ⬦STDs. It is caused by the human immunodeficiency virus (HIV), now known to be a ⬦retrovirus, an organism first identified 1983. HIV is transmitted in body fluids, mainly blood and sexual secretions.

Sexual transmission of the AIDS virus endangers heterosexual men and women as well as high-risk groups, such as homosexual and bisexual men, prostitutes, intravenous drug-users sharing needles, and haemophiliacs and surgical patients treated with contaminated blood products. The virus itself is not selective, and infection is spreading to the population at large. The virus has a short life outside the body, which makes transmission of the infection by methods other than sexual contact, blood transfusion, and shared syringes extremely unlikely.

Infection with HIV is not synonymous with having AIDS; many people who have the virus in their blood are not ill, and only about half of those infected will develop AIDS within ten years. Some suffer AIDS-related illnesses but not the full-blown disease. However, there is no firm evidence to suggest that the proportion of those developing AIDS from being HIV-positive is less than 100%.

The effect of the virus in those who become ill is the devastation of the immune system, leaving the victim susceptible to (opportunistic) diseases that would not otherwise develop. In fact, diagnosis of AIDS is based on the appearance of rare tumors or opportunistic infections in unexpected candidates. Pneumocystis pneumonia, for instance, normally seen only in the malnourished or those whose immune systems have been deliberately suppressed, is common among AIDS victims and, for them, a leading cause of death.

The estimated incubation period is 9.8 years. Some AIDS victims die within a few months of the outbreak of symptoms, some survive for several years; roughly 50% are dead within three years. There is no cure for the disease, although the new drug zidovudine (⬦AZT) is claimed to delay the onset of AIDS and diminish its effects. The search continues for an effective vaccine. In the US, attempts to carry out clinical trials of HIV vaccines on HIV-positive pregnant women were started 1991 in the hope that they might prevent the transmission of the virus to the fetus.

The HIV virus originated in Africa. In the US, 90,990 cases were reported up to April 1989, with 52,435 deaths; 58% of all cases. One million Americans are thought to be infected with the virus. Recent evidence indicates that the presence of other diseases, especially syphilis, is linked to the full-blown development of AIDS.

Aigun, Treaty of treaty between Russia and China signed 1858 at the port of Aigun in China on the Amur River. The left bank was ceded to Russia, but this has since been repudiated by China.

Aiken Conrad (Potter) 1899–1973. US poet, novelist, and short-story writer whose *Selected Poems* 1929 won the Pulitzer prize. His works were influenced by early psychoanalytic theory and the use of the stream-of-consciousness technique.

Born in Savannah, Georgia, Aiken grew up in New England with relatives after his father, a doctor, killed his mother and then committed suicide. In his autobiography *Ushant* 1952, he confronts this traumatic experience. He graduated from Harvard University 1911 and began to write poetry.

Some of Aiken's poetry is in the form of "symphonies," works that attempt to imitate music in its ability to convey meaning on several levels at once. His poetic works include *The House of Dust* 1920, *Senlin* 1925, *Brownstone Eclogues and Other Poems* 1942, *Collected Poems* 1953, *A Letter from Li Po, and Other Poems* 1955, *Sheepford Hills* 1957, and *A Seizure of Limericks*

1964. His novels include *Great Circle* 1933 and *Conversation* 1940. *The Collected Short Stories of Conrad Aiken* appeared 1960.

Aiken Howard 1900– . US mathematician and computer pioneer. In 1939, in conjunction with engineers from ⬦IBM, he started work on the design of an automatic calculator using standard business-machine components. In 1944 the team completed one of the first computers, the Automatic Sequence Controlled Calculator (known as the Mark 1), a programmable computer controlled by punched paper tape and using ⬦punched cards.

aikido Japanese art of self-defense; one of the ⬦martial arts. Two main systems of aikido are tomiki and uyeshiba.

ailanthus any tree or shrub of the genus *Ailanthus* of the quassia family. All have compound leaves made up of pointed leaflets and clusters of small greenish flowers with an unpleasant smell. The tree of heaven *Ailanthus altissima*, native to E Asia, is grown worldwide as an ornamental. It can grow to 100 ft/30 m in height and 3 ft/1 m in diameter.

Ailey Alvin 1931–1989. US dancer, choreographer, and director whose Alvin Ailey City Center Dance Theater, formed 1958, was the first truly interracial dance company and opened dance to a wider audience. Ailey studied modern, ethnic, jazz, and academic dance, and his highly individual work celebrates rural and urban black America in pieces like *Blues Suite* 1958 and the company signature piece *Revelations* 1960.

Ainu aboriginal people of Japan, driven north in the 4th century AD by ancestors of the Japanese. They now number about 25,000, inhabiting Japanese and Russian territory on Sakhalin, Hokkaido, and the Kuril Islands. Their language has no written form, and is unrelated to any other.

air see ⬦atmosphere.

air conditioning system that controls the state of the air inside a building or vehicle. A complete air-conditioning unit controls the temperature and humidity of the air, removes dust and odors from it, and circulates it by means of a fan. US inventor W H Carrier developed the first effective air-conditioning unit 1902 for a New York printing plant.

The air in an air conditioner is cooled by a type of ⬦refrigeration unit comprising a compressor and a condenser. The air is cleaned by means of filters and activated charcoal. Moisture is extracted by condensation on cool metal plates. The air can also be heated by electrical wires or, in large systems, pipes carrying hot water or steam; and cool, dry air may be humidified by circulating it over pans of water or through a water spray.

A specialized air-conditioning system is installed in spacecraft as part of the life-support system. This includes the provision of oxygen to breathe and the removal of exhaled carbon dioxide.

aircraft any aeronautical vehicle, which may be lighter than air (supported by buoyancy) or heavier than air (supported by the dynamic action of air on its surfaces). ⬦Balloons and ⬦airships are lighter-than-air craft. Heavier-than-air craft include the ⬦airplane, glider, autogyro, and helicopter.

aircraft carrier oceangoing naval vessel with a broad, flat-topped deck for launching and landing military aircraft; an effort to provide a floating military base for warplanes too far from home for refueling, repairing, reconnaissance, escorting, and various attack and defense operations.

Although the first flight from the deck of a ship was in 1910, the first true carrier, the British *Argus* 1918, did not see service in World War I. By World War II, carriers were used extensively, especially in the Pacific, by both the Allies and the Japanese. They were used again in both the Korean and Vietnam wars.

The USS *Enterprise* was the first nuclear-powered carrier 1961; it could go for almost 300,000 mi/480,000 km before refueling. Since aircraft are now capable of long-range flight, and with the possible use of sophisticated missiles, few carriers were built from the 1970s; their enormous cost, low speed, and vulnerability seem to preclude future construction.

air-cushion vehicle (ACV) craft that is supported by a layer, or cushion, of high-pressure air. The ⬦hovercraft is one form of ACV.

Airedale terrier breed of large ⬦terrier dog, about 2 ft/60 cm tall, with a rough red-brown coat. It originated about 1850 in England, as a cross of the otter hound and Irish and Welsh terriers.

air force a nation's fighting aircraft and the organization that maintains them.

history The emergence of the airplane at first brought only limited recognition of its potential value as a means of waging war. Like the balloon, used since the American Civil War, it was considered a way of extending the vision of ground forces. A unified air force was established in the UK 1918, Italy 1923, France 1928, Germany 1935 (after repudiating the arms limitations of the Versailles treaty), and the US 1947 (it began as the Aeronautical Division of the Army Signal Corps in 1907, and evolved into the Army's Air Service Division by 1918; by 1926 it was the Air Corps and in World War II the Army Air Force). The main specialized groupings formed during World War I—such as *combat*, *bombing* (see ⬦bomb), *reconnaissance*, and *transport*—were adapted and modified in World War II; activity was extended, with self-contained tactical air forces to meet the needs of ground commanders in the main theaters of land operations and for the attack on and defense of shipping over narrow seas.

From 1945 to 1960 piston-engine aircraft were superseded by jet aircraft. Computerized guidance systems lessened the difference between missile and aircraft, and flights of unlimited duration became possible with air-to-air refueling. For example, the Strategic Air Command's bombers can patrol 24 hours a day armed with thermonuclear weapons. For some years it was anticipated that the pilot might become obsolete, but the continuation of conventional warfare and the evolution of tactical nuclear weapons led in the 1970s and 1980s to the development of advanced combat aircraft able to fly supersonically beneath an enemy's radar on strike and reconnaissance missions, as well as so-called stealth aircraft that cannot be detected by radar.

airglow faint and variable light in the Earth's atmosphere produced by chemical reactions in the ionosphere.

air lock airtight chamber that allows people to pass between areas of different pressure; also an air bubble in a pipe that impedes fluid flow. An air lock may connect an environment at ordinary pressure and an environment that has high air pressure (such as a submerged caisson used for tunneling or building dams or bridge foundations).

An air lock may also permit someone wearing breathing apparatus to pass into an airless environment (into water from a submerged submarine or into the vacuum of space from a spacecraft).

airplane powered heavier-than-air craft supported in flight by fixed wings. Airplanes can be propelled by the thrust of a jet engine, a rocket engine, or airscrew (propeller), as well as combinations of these. They must be designed aerodynamically, as streamlining ensures maximum flight efficiency. The shape of a plane depends on its use and operating speed—aircraft operating at well below the speed of sound need not be as streamlined as supersonic aircraft. The Wright brothers flew the first powered plane (a biplane) in Kitty Hawk, North Carolina, 1903. For the history of aircraft and aviation, see ⬦flight.

design Efficient streamlining prevents the formation of shock waves over the body surface and wings, which would cause instability and power loss. The wing of an airplane has the cross-sectional shape of an airfoil, being broad and curved at the front, flat underneath, curved on top, and tapered to a sharp point at the rear. It is so shaped that air passing above it is speeded up, reducing pressure below atmospheric pressure. This follows from the ⬦Bernoulli principle and results in a force acting vertically upward, called lift, which counters the plane's weight. In level flight lift equals weight. The wings develop sufficient lift to support the plane when they move quickly through the air. The thrust that causes propulsion comes from the reaction to the air stream accelerated backward by the propeller or the gases shooting backward from the jet exhaust. In flight the engine thrust must overcome the air resistance, or ⬦drag. Drag depends on frontal area (for example, large, airliner; small, fighter plane) and shape (drag coefficient); in level flight, drag equals thrust. The drag is reduced by streamlining the plane, resulting in higher speed and reduced fuel consumption for a given power. Less fuel need be carried for a given distance of travel, so a larger payload (cargo or passengers) can be carried.

The shape of a plane is dictated principally by the speed at which it will operate (see ⬦aeronautics). A low-speed plane operating at well below the speed of sound (about 600 mph/965 kph) need not be particularly well streamlined, and it can have its wings broad and projecting at right angles from the fuselage. An aircraft operating close to the speed of sound must be well streamlined and have swept-back wings. This prevents the formation of shock waves over the body surface and wings, which would result in instability and high power loss. Supersonic planes (faster than sound) need to be severely streamlined, and require a needle nose, extremely swept-back wings, and what is often termed a "Coke-bottle" (narrow-waisted) fuselage, in order to pass through the sound barrier without suffering undue disturbance. To give great flexibility of operation at low as well as high speeds, some supersonic planes are designed with variable geometry, or ⬦swing wings. For low-speed flight the wings are outstretched; for high-speed flight they are swung close to the fuselage to form an efficient ⬦delta wing configuration.

Aircraft designers experiment with different designs in ⬦wind tunnel tests, which indicate

wing
tailfin
tailplane
rudder
elevator
aileron
flaps
spoilers
slats

lift
drag
thrust
weight
lift
airflow
airfoil

airplane *In flight, the forces on an airplane are lift, weight, drag, and thrust.*

at the front, or leading edges, of the wing, called slats, are also extended at these times to improve the airflow. To land, the nose of the plane is brought up so that the angle of attack of the wings exceeds a critical point and the airflow around them breaks down; lift is lost (a condition known as stalling), and the plane drops to the runway. A few planes (for example, the Harrier) have a novel method of takeoff and landing, rising and dropping vertically by swiveling nozzles to direct the exhaust of their jet engines downward. The ⟡helicopter and ⟡convertiplane use rotating propellers (rotors) to obtain lift to take off vertically.

operation The control surfaces of a plane are operated by the pilot on the flight deck, by means of a control stick, or wheel, and by foot pedals (for the rudder). The controls are brought into action by hydraulic power systems. Advanced experimental high-speed craft known as control-configured vehicles use a sophisticated computer-controlled system. The pilot instructs the computer which maneuver the plane must perform, and the computer, informed by a series of sensors around the craft about the altitude, speed, and turning rate of the plane, sends signals to the control surface and throttle to enable the maneuver to be executed.

air pollution contamination of the atmosphere caused by the discharge, accidental or deliberate, of a wide range of toxic airborne substances. Often the amount of the released substance is relatively high in a certain locality, so the harmful effects become more noticeable. The cost of preventing any discharge of pollutants into the air is prohibitive, so attempts are more usually made to reduce gradually the amount of discharge and to disperse this as quickly as possible by using a very tall chimney, or by intermittent release.

air raid aerial attack, usually on a civilian target such as a factory, railroad line, or communications center. In World War II (1939–45), raids were usually made by bomber aircraft, but many thousands were killed in London 1944 by German V1 and V2 rockets. The air raids on Britain 1940–41 became known as **the Blitz**. The Allies made retaliatory raids over European cities 1942–45.

During the ⟡Gulf War 1991 the UN coalition forces made thousands of air raids on Baghdad, Iraq, to destroy the Iraqi infrastructure and communications network (some 250,000 civilians were killed).

air sac in birds, a thin-walled extension of the lungs. There are nine of these and they extend into the abdomen and bones, effectively increasing lung capacity. In mammals, it is

how their designs will behave in practice. Fighter jets in the 1990s are being deliberately designed to be aerodynamically unstable, to ensure greater agility. This is achieved by a main wing of continuously modifiable shape, the airflow over which is controlled by a smaller tilting foreplane. New aircraft are being made lighter and faster (to Mach 3) by the use of heat-resistant materials, some of which are also radar-absorbing, making the aircraft "invisible" to enemy defenses.

construction Planes are constructed using light but strong aluminum alloys such as duralumin (with copper, magnesium, and so on). For supersonic planes special stainless steel and titanium may be used in areas subjected to high heat loads. The structure of the plane, or the airframe (wings, fuselage, and so on) consists of a surface skin of alloy sheets supported at intervals by struts known as ribs and stringers. The structure is bonded together by riveting or by powerful adhesives such as ⟡epoxy resins. In certain critical areas, which have to withstand very high stresses (such as the wing roots), body panels are machined from solid metal for extra strength.

On the ground a plane rests on wheels, usually in a tricycle arrangement, with a nose wheel and two wheels behind, one under each wing. For all except some light planes the landing gear, or undercarriage, is retracted in flight to reduce drag. Seaplanes, which take off and land on water, are fitted with nonretractable hydrofoils.

flight control Wings by themselves are unstable in flight, and a plane requires a tail to provide stability. The tail comprises a horizontal tailplane and vertical tailfin, called the horizontal and vertical stabilizer respectively. The tail plane has hinged flaps at the rear called elevators to control pitch (attitude). Raising the elevators depresses the tail and inclines the

wings upward (increases the angle of attack). This speeds the airflow above the wings until lift exceeds weight and the plane climbs. However, the steeper attitude increases drag, so more power is needed to maintain speed and the engine throttle must be opened up. Moving the elevators in the opposite direction produces the reverse effect. The angle of attack is reduced, and the plane descends. Speed builds up rapidly if the engine is not throttled back. Turning (changing direction) is effected by moving the rudder hinged to the rear of the tailfin, and by banking (rolling) the plane. It is banked by moving the ailerons, interconnected flaps at the rear of the wings which move in opposite directions, one up, the other down.

In planes with a delta wing, such as ⟡Concorde, the ailerons and elevators are combined. Other movable control surfaces, called flaps, are fitted at the rear of the wings closer to the fuselage. They are extended to increase the width and camber (curve) of the wings during takeoff and landing, thereby creating extra lift, while movable sections

air pollution

pollutant	sources	effects
sulfur dioxide SO_2	oil, coal combustion in power stations	acid rain formed, damaging plants, trees, buildings, lakes
oxides of nitrogen NO	high temperature combustion in automobiles, and to some extent power stations	acid rain formed
lead compounds	from leaded gasoline used by cars	nerve poison
carbon dioxide CO_2	oil, coal, gasoline, diesel combustion	greenhouse effect
carbon monoxide CO	limited combustion of oil, coal, gasoline, diesel fuels	poisonous, leads to photochemical smog in some areas
nuclear waste	nuclear power plants, nuclear weapon testing, war	radioactivity, contamination of locality, cancers, mutations, death

another name for the alveoli in the lungs, and in some insects, for widenings of the trachea.

airship or *dirigible* any aircraft that is lighter than air and power-driven, consisting of an elliptical balloon that forms the streamlined envelope or hull and has below it the propulsion system (propellers), steering mechanism, and space for crew, passengers and/or cargo. The balloon section is filled with lighter-than-air gas, either the nonflammable helium or, before helium was industrially available in large enough quantities, the easily ignited and flammable hydrogen. The envelope's form is maintained by internal pressure in the nonrigid (blimp) and semirigid types (in which the nose and tail sections have a metal framework connected by a rigid keel). The rigid type (zeppelin) maintains its form using an internal metal framework. Airships have been used for luxury travel, polar exploration, warfare, and advertising.

Rigid airships predominated from about 1900 until 1940. As the technology developed, the size of the envelope was increased from about 150 ft/45 m to more than 800 ft/245 m for the last two zeppelins built. In 1852 the first successful airship was designed and flown by Henri ⟡Giffard of France. In 1900 the first successful rigid type was designed by Count (Graf) Ferdinand von ⟡Zeppelin of Germany. In 1919 the first nonstop transatlantic roundtrip flight was completed by a rigid airship, the British R34. In the early 1920s a large source of helium was discovered in the USA and was substituted for hydrogen, reducing the danger of fire. The US military attempted to use zeppelins but abandoned the effort early on. In the 1920s and early 1930s luxury zeppelin services took passengers across the Atlantic faster and in greater comfort than the great ocean liners. The successful German airship *Graf Zeppelin*, completed 1927, was used for transatlantic, cruise, and round-the-world trips. In 1929 it traveled 20,000 mi/32,000 km around the world. It was retired and dismantled after years of trouble-free service, and was replaced by the *Hindenburg* in 1936.

Several airship accidents were caused by structural breakup during storms and by fire. The last and best known was the *Hindenburg*, which had been forced to return to the use of flammable hydrogen by a US embargo on helium; it exploded and burned at the mooring mast at Lakehurst, New Jersey, in 1937. The last and largest rigid airship was the German *Graf Zeppelin II*, completed just before World War II; it never saw commercial service but was used as a reconnaissance station off the English coast early in the war (it was the only zeppelin used in the war) and was soon retired and dismantled. Rigid airships, predominant from World War II, are no longer in use but blimps continued in use for coastal and antisubmarine patrol until the 1960s, and advertising blimps can be seen until this day. Recent interest in all types of airship has surfaced (including some with experimental and nontraditional shapes for the envelopes), since they are fuel-efficient, quiet, and capable of lifting enormous loads over great distances.

Aisne river of N France, giving its name to a *département*; length 175 mi/282 km.

Aix-en-Provence town in the *département* of Bouches-du-Rhône, France, 18 mi/29 km N of Marseille; population (1982) 127,000. It is the capital of Provence and dates from Roman times.

Aix-la-Chapelle French name of ⟡Aachen, ancient city in Germany.

Ajaccio capital and second-largest port of Corsica; population (1982) 55,279. Founded by the Genoese 1492, it was the birthplace of Napoleon; it has been French since 1768.

Ajax Greek hero in Homer's ⟡*Iliad*. Son of Telamon, king of Salamis, he was second only to Achilles among the Greek heroes in the Trojan War. When ⟡Agamemnon awarded the armor of the dead Achilles to ⟡Odysseus, Ajax is said to have gone mad with jealousy, and then committed suicide in shame.

Ajman smallest of the seven states that make up the ⟡United Arab Emirates; area 96 sq mi/250 sq km; population (1985) 64,318.

ajolote Mexican reptile of the genus *Bipes*. It and several other tropical burrowing species are placed in the Amphisbaenia, a group separate from lizards and snakes among the Squamata. Unlike the others, however, which have no legs, it has a pair of short but well-developed front legs. In line with its burrowing habits, the skull is very solid, the eyes small, and external ears absent. The scales are arranged in rings, giving the body a wormlike appearance.

AK abbreviation for the state of ⟡*Alaska*.

Akaba alternative transliteration of ⟡Aqaba, a gulf of the Red Sea.

Akbar Jalal ud-Din Mohammed 1542–1605. Mogul emperor of N India from 1556, when he succeeded his father. He gradually established his rule throughout N India. He is considered the greatest of the Mogul emperors, and the firmness and wisdom of his rule won him the title "Guardian of Mankind;" he was a patron of the arts.

à Kempis Thomas see ⟡Thomas à Kempis, religious writer.

Ake v Oklahoma a US Supreme Court decision 1985 dealing with the right of indigent defendants to the "raw materials" needed for an adequate defense. The case was an appeal of the conviction of Glen Ake, a diagnosed paranoid schizophrenic, who had been denied psychiatric assistance by the court during his trial. The Supreme Court ruled that Ake had not been granted due process because his unstable condition, which could have been remedied by treatment, had helped to determine his sentence. The case used the same constitutional grounds to require court-appointed psychiatrists for indigent defendants as an earlier decision had to guarantee court-appointed attorneys.

Akhenaton another name for ⟡Ikhnaton, pharaoh of Egypt.

Akhetaton capital of ancient Egypt established by the monotheistic pharaoh ⟡Ikhnaton as the center for his cult of the Aton, the sun's disk; it is the modern Tell el Amarna 190 mi/300 km S of Cairo. Ikhnaton's palace had formal enclosed gardens. After his death it was abandoned, and the ⟡*Amarna tablets*, found in the ruins, were probably discarded by his officials.

Akhmatova Anna. Adopted name of Anna Andreevna Gorenko 1889–1966. Russian poet. Among her works are the cycle *Requiem* 1963 (written in the 1930s), which deals with the Stalinist terror, and *Poem Without a Hero* 1962 (begun 1940).

Akihito 1933– . Emperor of Japan from 1989, succeeding his father Hirohito (Showa). His reign is called the Heisei ("achievement of universal peace") era.

Unlike previous crown princes, Akihito was educated alongside commoners at the elite Gakushuin school and in 1959 he married Michiko Shoda (1934–), the daughter of a flour-company president. Their three children, the Oxford university-educated Crown Prince Hiro, Prince Aya, and Princess Nori, were raised at Akihito's home instead of being reared by tutors and chamberlains in a separate imperial dormitory.

Akkad northern Semitic people who conquered the Sumerians in 2350 BC and ruled Mesopotamia. The ancient city of Akkad in central Mesopotamia, founded by ⟡Sargon I, was an imperial center in the 3rd millennium BC; the site is unidentified, but it was on the Euphrates.

Akron (Greek "summit") city in Ohio, on the Cuyahoga River, 35 mi/56 km SE of Cleveland; population (1990) 660,000. Known as the "Rubber Capital of the World," it is home to the headquarters of several major tire and rubber companies, although production there ended by 1982.

The city is also a major trucking center and the site of the University of Akron. Akron was first settled 1807. Dr B F Goodrich established a rubber factory 1870, and the industry grew immensely with the rising demand for tires from about 1910.

Aksum ancient Greek-influenced Semitic kingdom that flourished 1st–6th centuries AD and covered a large part of modern Ethiopia as well as the Sudan. The ruins of its capital, also called Aksum, lie NW of Aduwa, but the site has been developed as a modern city.

Aktyubinsk industrial city in the republic of Kazakhstan; population (1987) 248,000. Established 1869, it expanded after the opening of the Trans-Caspian railroad 1905.

al- for Arabic names beginning *al-*, see rest of name; for example, for "al-Fatah," see ⟡Fatah, al-.

AL abbreviation for the state of ⟡*Alabama*.

Alabama Confederate cruiser (1,040 tons) in the ⟡American Civil War. Built in Great Britain, it was allowed to leave port by the British, and sank 68 Union merchant ships before it was itself sunk by a Union warship off the coast of France in 1864. In 1871 the international court awarded damages of $15.5 million to the US, a legal precedent.

The court's ruling requires a neutral country to exercise "due diligence" to prevent the arming within its jurisdiction of a vessel intending to carry out a war against a country with which the neutral is at peace.

Alabama state in S US; nickname Heart of Dixie/Cotton State
area 51,994 sq mi/134,700 sq km
capital Montgomery
cities Birmingham, Mobile, Huntsville, Tuscaloosa
physical the state comprises the Cumberland Plateau in the N; the Black Belt, or Canebrake (excellent cotton-growing country), in the center; S of this, the coastal plain of Piney Woods
features rivers: Alabama, Tennessee; Appalachian mountains, George Washington Carver Museum at the Tuskegee Institute (a college founded for blacks by Booker T Washington); White House of the Confederacy at Montgomery; George C Marshall Space Flight Center at Huntsville; annual Mardi Gras celebration at Mobile, Helen Keller's birthplace at Tuscumbia

Alabama

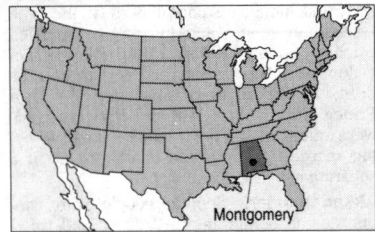

Montgomery

products cotton (no longer the prime crop, but still important), soybeans, peanuts, wood products, coal, livestock, poultry, iron, chemicals, textiles, paper
population (1990) 4,040,600
famous people Hank Aaron, Tallulah Bankhead, Nat King Cole, W C Handy, Helen Keller, Joe Louis, Willie Mays, Jesse Owens, Leroy "Satchel" Paige, George C Wallace, Booker T Washington, Hank Williams
history first settled by the French in the early 18th century; ceded to Britain 1763; passed to the US 1783 and became a state 1819. It was one of the ⟩Confederate States in the American Civil War, and Montgomery was the first capital of the Confederacy. Birmingham became the South's leading industrial center in the late 19th century. Alabama was in the forefront of the civil rights movement in the 1950s and 1960s: Martin Luther ⟩King, Jr, led a successful boycott of segregated Montgomery buses in 1955; school integration began in the early 1960s despite the opposition of Governor George C Wallace; the 1965 Selma march resulted in federal voting-rights legislation.

alabaster naturally occurring fine-grained white or light-colored translucent form of ⟩gypsum, often streaked or mottled. It is a soft material, used for carvings, and ranks second on the ⟩Mohs' scale of hardness.

Aladdin in the ⟩*Arabian Nights*, a poor boy who obtains a magic lamp: when the lamp is rubbed, a jinn (genie, or spirit) appears and fulfills its owner's wishes.

Alain-Fournier adopted name of Henri-Alban Fournier 1886–1914. French novelist. His haunting semiautobiographical fantasy *Le Grand Meaulnes/The Lost Domain* 1913 was a cult novel of the 1920s and 1930s. His life is intimately recorded in his correspondence with his brother-in-law Jacques Rivière. He was killed in action on the Meuse in World War I.

Alamein, El, Battles of in World War II, two decisive battles in the western desert, N Egypt. In the *First Battle of El Alamein* July 1–27, 1942 the British 8th Army under Auchinleck held the German and Italian forces under Rommel. In the *Second Battle of El Alamein* Oct 23–Nov 4, 1942 ⟩Montgomery defeated Rommel.

Alamo, the mission fortress in San Antonio, Texas. It was besieged Feb 23–March 6, 1836 by ⟩Santa Anna and 4,000 Mexicans; they killed the garrison of about 180, including Davy ⟩Crockett and Jim ⟩Bowie.

The struggle against such overwhelming odds made the battle of the Alamo a rallying point for the settlers in the Texas War of Independence from Mexico.

Alanbrooke Alan Francis Brooke, 1st Viscount Alanbrooke 1883–1963. British army officer, Chief of Staff in World War II and largely responsible for the strategy that led to the German defeat.

Åland Islands (Finnish *Ahvenanmaa* "land of waters") group of some 6,000 islands in the Baltic Sea, at the southern extremity of the Gulf of Bothnia; area 572 sq mi/1,481 sq km; population (1990) 24,600. Only 80 are inhabited; the largest island has a small town, Mariehamn. The main sectors of the island economy are tourism, agriculture, and shipping.

Alarcón Pedro Antonio de 1833–1891. Spanish journalist and writer. The acclaimed *Diario/Diary* was based upon his experiences as a soldier in Morocco. His *El Sombrero de tres picos/The Three-Cornered Hat* 1874 was the basis of Manuel de Falla's ballet.

Alaric *c.* 370–410. King of the Visigoths. In 396 he invaded Greece and retired with much booty to Illyria. In 400 and 408 he invaded Italy, and in 410 captured and sacked Rome, but died the same year on his way to invade Sicily. The river Busento was diverted by his soldiers so that he could be buried in its course with his treasures; the laborers were killed to keep the secret.

Alaska largest state of the US, on the NW extremity of North America, separated from the lower 48 states by British Columbia; nickname Last Frontier
total area 591,004 sq mi/1,530,700 sq km
land area 570,833 sq mi/1,478,457 sq km
capital Juneau
cities Anchorage, Fairbanks, Fort Yukon, Holy Cross, Nome
physical much of Alaska is mountainous and includes Mount McKinley (Denali), 20,322 ft/6,194 m, the highest peak in North America, surrounded by Denali National Park. Caribou thrive in the Arctic tundra, and elsewhere there are extensive forests
features Yukon River; Rocky Mountains, including Mount McKinley and Mount Katmai, a volcano that erupted 1912 and formed the Valley of Ten Thousand Smokes (from which smoke and steam still escape and which is now a national monument); Arctic Wild Life Range, with the only large herd of North American caribou; Little Diomede Island, which is only 2.5 mi/4 km from Russian Big Diomede/Ratmanov Island; caribou herds on the tundra. A Congressional act 1980 gave environmental protection to 104 million acres/42 million ha. The chief railroad line runs from Seward to Fairbanks, which is linked by highway (via Canada) with Seattle. Near Fairbanks is the University of Alaska
products oil, natural gas, coal, copper, iron, gold, tin, fur, salmon fisheries and canneries, lumber
population (1990) 550,000; including 9% American Indians, Aleut, and Inuit
history various groups of Indians crossed the Bering land bridge 60,000–15,000 years ago; the Inuit began to settle the Arctic coast from Siberia about 2000 BC; the Aleuts settled the Aleutian archipelago about 1000 BC. The first European to visit Alaska was Vitus Bering 1741. Alaska was a Russian colony from 1744 until purchased by the US 1867 for $7,200,000; gold was discovered five years later. It became a state 1959. Valuable mineral resources have been exploited from 1968, especially in the Prudhoe Bay area to the SE of Point Barrow. An oil pipeline (1977) runs from Prudhoe Bay to the port of Valdez. Oilspill from a tanker in Prince William Sound caused great environmental damage 1989. Under construction is an underground natural-gas pipeline to Chicago and San Francisco.

Alaska Highway road that runs from Dawson Creek, British Columbia, to Fairbanks, Alaska (1,522 mi/2,450 km). It was built 1942 as a supply route for US military forces in Alaska. The highway, which runs along the E edge of the Rocky Mountains, is paved in Alaska but mostly gravel-surfaced in Canada.

Alba Gaelic name for Scotland; also an alternate spelling for ⟩Alva, Ferdinand Alvarez de Toledo, duke of Alva, Spanish politician and general.

albacore name loosely applied to several species of fishes found in warm regions of the Atlantic and Pacific oceans, in particular to a large tuna, *Thunnus alalunga*, and to several other species of the mackerel family.

Alba Iulia (German *Karlsburg*) city on the river Mures, W central Romania, founded by the Romans in the 2nd century AD. The Romanian kings were crowned here, Michael the Brave (1601) and the kings of modern Romania until World War II. Population (1985) 64,300.

Albania country in SE Europe, bounded N and E by Yugoslavia, SE by Greece, and W and SW by the Adriatic Sea.
government Under the 1991 interim constitution, Albania has a single-chamber legislature, the 250-member People's Assembly. It is elected every four years by universal suffrage by means of the two-ballot majority vote system. An executive president, who is also commander in chief of the armed forces and who is debarred from concurrently holding party office, is elected by the People's Assembly. A prime minister and council of ministers (cabinet), drawn from the majority grouping within the assembly, has day-to-day charge of government. Private property, freedom of worship and expression, and political pluralism are endorsed by the interim constitution.
history In the ancient world the area was occupied by the Illyrians, later becoming a Roman province until the end of the 4th century AD. Albania then came under Byzantine rule, which lasted until 1347. There followed about 100 years of invasions by Bulgarians, Serbs, Venetians, and finally Turks, who arrived 1385 and, after the death of the nationalist leader Skanderbeg (George Castriota) (1403–1468), eventually made Albania part of the ⟩Ottoman Empire *c.* 1468.
independence Albania became independent 1912 and a republic 1925. In 1928 President Ahmed Beg Zogu was proclaimed King Zog. Overrun by Italy and Germany 1939–44, Albania became a republic with a communist government 1946 after a guerrilla struggle led by Enver ⟩Hoxha.
the "Hoxha experiment" At first closely allied with Yugoslavia, Albania backed the Soviet dictator Stalin in his 1948 dispute with the Yugoslav ruler Tito and developed close links with the USSR 1949–55, entering the trade organization ⟩Comecon 1949. Hoxha imposed

Alaska

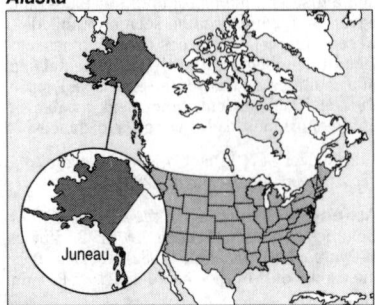

Juneau

a Stalinist system with rural collectivization, industrial nationalization, central planning, and one-party control. Mosques and churches were closed in an effort to create the "first atheist state." Hoxha remained a committed Stalinist and, rejecting the new Soviet leader Khrushchev's denunciations of the Stalin era, broke off diplomatic relations with the USSR 1961 and withdrew from Comecon. Choosing isolation and neutrality, Albania also severed diplomatic relations with China 1978, once Chairman Mao had died and China had made accommodation with the US. The "Hoxha experiment" left Albania with the lowest income per head of population in Europe. After Hoxha's death 1985, there was a widening of external economic contacts and the number of countries with which Albania had formal diplomatic relations increased from 74 in 1978 to 111 in 1988.

open dissent Opposition to the regime began to mount during 1990 around the NW border town of Shkodër. In early July unprecedented antigovernment street demonstrations erupted in Tiranë. Faced with a government crackdown, 5,000 demonstrators sought refuge in foreign embassies and were later allowed to leave the country. Later the same month diplomatic relations with the USSR were restored and embassies re-established.

end of one-party system In Dec 1990, amid continuing protests in Tiranë and economic collapse, the Communist Party leadership announced that the existence of opposition parties had finally been authorized and the ban on religion lifted. An opposition party was immediately formed by the Tiranë intelligentsia: the Democratic Party (DP), led by Sali Berisha.

Elections (secret ballot) to the People's Assembly due to be held Feb 1991 were postponed to give the new party some time to organize, and in return the opposition agreed to a temporary wage freeze and ban on strikes.

civil unrest A huge bronze statue of Hoxha in Tiranë was toppled by demonstrators Feb 1991, and there were riots in several other towns. President Alia replaced the unpopular premier Adil Carçani with Fatos Nano (1951–), a reform economist. Alia also declared the imposition of presidential rule and tanks were moved into the streets of Tiranë. Fears of a right-wing coup prompted a flight of thousands of Albanians to Greece, Yugoslavia, and Italy; the port of Brindisi alone had received more than 20,000 refugees by mid-March 1991. "Nonpolitical" refugees were sent back to Albania.

first multiparty elections Diplomatic relations with the US and the UK, suspended since 1946, were restored March and May 1991 respectively. In Albania's first free multiparty elections, held March–April 1991, the ruling Party of Labor of Albania (PLA) captured 169 of the 250 seats in the new People's Assembly. It secured sufficient seats for the necessary two-thirds majority to make constitutional changes.

PLA support came predominantly from rural areas. In the major towns the DP, which captured 75 seats, polled strongly, convincingly defeating President Alia in the first round in a Tiranë constituency. The frustration of the opposition's supporters was ventilated in anticommunist rioting in Shkodër April 4, 1991, with four persons being shot dead by the police, including the local DP leader. The report

of a commission subsequently blamed the security forces for these deaths and the Siqurimi (secret police) were replaced May 1991 by a new national Security Council.

economic problems An interim constitution was adopted April 1991, with the country renamed the Republic of Albania and the PLA's leading role being abandoned. The new People's Assembly elected Ramiz Alia as both the new executive president of the republic, replacing the presidium, and commander in chief of the armed forces. In May 1991 Fatos Nano was reappointed prime minister, but resigned in June. The economy deteriorated rapidly: agricultural, industrial products, and exports were declining and unemployment stood at almost 40%. Nano was replaced by Ylli Bufi, the former food minister, heading a new, interim "government of national stability" with members from the opposition parties, including Gramoz Pashko (DP leader) as deputy premier. In June 1991 the PLA renamed itself the Socialist Party of Albania, with Fatos Nano elected its chair. In July 1991 a land-privatization bill was passed to restore land to peasants dispossessed under communist rule. From late summer 1991 Albania began to receive emergency aid from the European Community. Between Sept and Dec 1991 there were recurrent anticommunist demonstrations, bread riots, and protest strikes, prompted by deteriorating living conditions and continued attempts by Albanians to leave the country.

first noncommunist leaders The DP withdrew from the coalition government, claiming that it was being manipulated by former communists, and on Dec 6, 1991, prime minister Bufi resigned. On Dec 18, 1991, President Alia appointed Vilson Ahmeti, a former nutrition minister, as Albania's first noncommunist premier. In Jan 1992, 20 former Albanian communist officials were arrested on corruption charges. The newly formed parliament elected Dr Sali Berisha, founder and leader of the DP, as the country's president and granted him increased executive powers. Alexander Meksi succeeded Ahmeti as prime minister. In July 1992 a ban was imposed on all "fascist, antinational, chauvinistic, racist, totalitarian, communist, Marxist-Leninist, Stalinist, or Enverist (following Enver Hoxha)" political organizations.

chaos The economic situation continued to decline, with half the work force unemployed, inflation out of control, and agriculture in a state of paralysis with disagreements over land ownership. In the face of increasing lawlessness, the United Nations intervened to help reorganize the police force and curb drug trafficking. *See illustration box.*

Albania
Republic of (*Republika e Shqipërisë*)

area 11,097 sq mi/28,748 sq km
capital Tiranë
cities Shkodër, Elbasan, Vlorë, chief port Durrës
physical mainly mountainous, with rivers flowing E–W, and a narrow coastal plain
features Dinaric Alps, with wild boar and wolves
head of state Sali Berisha from 1992
head of government Alexander Meksi from 1992
political system emergent democracy
political parties Democratic Party (DP); Amonia (Greek minority party)
exports crude oil, bitumen, chrome, iron ore, nickel, coal, copper wire, tobacco, fruit,

vegetables
currency lek
population (1990 est) 3,270,000; growth rate 1.9% p.a.
life expectancy men 69, women 73
languages Albanian, Greek
religion Muslim 70%, although all religion banned 1967–90
literacy 75% (1986)
GNP $2.8 bn (1986 est); $900 per head
GDP $1,313 million; $543 per head
chronology
c. 1468 Albania made part of the Ottoman Empire.
1912 Independence achieved from Turkey.
1925 Republic proclaimed.
1928–39 Monarchy of King Zog.
1939–44 Under Italian and then German rule.
1946 Communist republic proclaimed under the leadership of Enver Hoxha.
1949 Admitted into Comecon.
1961 Break with Khrushchev's USSR.
1967 Albania declared itself the "first atheist state in the world."
1978 Break with "revisionist" China.
1985 Death of Hoxha.
1987 Normal diplomatic relations restored with Canada, Greece, and West Germany.
1988 Attendance at conference of Balkan states for the first time since the 1930s.
1990 One-party system abandoned; first opposition party formed.
1991 April: PLA won first multiparty elections; Ramiz Alia reelected president; three successive governments formed.
1992 Former communist officials arrested on corruption charges. Presidential elections won by DP; Sali Berisha elected president. Totalitarian and communist parties banned.

Albanian person of Albanian culture from Albania and the surrounding area. The Albanian language belongs to a separate group within the Indo-European family and has 3–4½ million speakers. There are both Christian and Muslim Albanians, the latter having been converted by the Ottoman Turks. Albanians comprise the majority of Kosovo in Yugoslavia and are in conflict with the Serbs, for whom the province is historically and culturally significant.

Alban, St died AD 303. First Christian martyr in England. In 793 King Offa founded a monastery on the site of Alban's martyrdom, around which the city of St Albans grew up.

Albany capital of New York state, situated on the W bank of the Hudson River, about 140 mi/

225 km N of New York City; population (1990) 101,000. With Schenectady and Troy it forms a metropolitan area, population (1980) 794,298.

First reached by Henry Hudson during his 1609 voyage up the river since named for him, Albany, a deepwater port, began as the Dutch trading post Fort Nassau 1614 and was soon the settlement of Fort Orange. It was renamed Albany 1664 when the English took control and incorporated 1686. After the revolution, in 1797, the state capital was moved there from New York City. The completion of the Erie Canal 1825 fostered its economic development. A massive government complex, the Empire State Plaza, was built in the 1960s.

Albany city on the Flint River, Georgia, SE of Columbus; seat of Dougherty county. It is a commercial center for the production of pecans and peanuts, chemicals, lumber, and other industrial products; population (1990) 78,100.

albatross large seabird, genus *Diomedea*, with long narrow wings adapted for gliding and a wingspan of up to 10 ft/3 m, mainly found in the southern hemisphere. It belongs to the order Procellariiformes, the same group as petrels and shearwaters.

Albatrosses cover enormous distances, flying as far as 10,000 miles in 33 days, or up to 600 miles in one day. They continue flying even after dark, at speeds of up to 50 mph, though they may stop for an hour's rest and to feed during the night. They are sometimes called "gooney birds," probably because of their clumsy way of landing. Albatrosses are becoming increasingly rare, and are in danger of extinction.

albedo the fraction of the incoming light reflected by a body such as a planet. A body with a high albedo, near 1, is very bright, while a body with a low albedo, near 0, is dark. The Moon has an average albedo of 0.12, Venus 0.65, Earth 0.37.

Albee Edward 1928– . US playwright. His internationally performed plays are associated with the Theater of the ◊Absurd and include *The Zoo Story* 1960, *The American Dream* 1961, *Who's Afraid of Virginia Woolf?* 1962 (his most successful play; also filmed with Elizabeth Taylor and Richard Burton as the quarreling, alcoholic, academic couple 1966), and *Tiny Alice* 1965. *A Delicate Balance* 1966 and *Seascape* 1975 both won Pulitzer prizes.

Albéniz Isaac 1860–1909. Spanish composer and pianist, born in Catalonia. He composed the suite *Iberia* and other piano pieces, making use of traditional Spanish melodies.

Albert Prince Consort 1819–1861. Husband of British Queen ◊Victoria from 1840; a patron of the arts, science, and industry. Albert was the

Alberta

second son of the Duke of Saxe Coburg-Gotha and first cousin to Queen Victoria, whose chief adviser he became. He planned the Great Exhibition of 1851; the profit was used to buy the sites in London of all the South Kensington museums and colleges and the Royal Albert Hall, built 1871. He died of typhoid.

Albert I 1875–1934. King of the Belgians from 1909, the younger son of Philip, Count of Flanders, and the nephew of Leopold II. In 1900 he married Duchess Elisabeth of Bavaria. In World War I he commanded the Allied army that retook the Belgian coast in 1918.

Alberta province of W Canada
area 255,223 sq mi/661,200 sq km
capital Edmonton
cities Calgary, Lethbridge, Medicine Hat, Red Deer
physical the Rocky Mountains; dry, treeless prairie in the center and S; toward the N this merges into a zone of poplar, then mixed forest. The valley of the Peace River is the northernmost farming land in Canada (except for Inuit pastures), and good grazing lands lie in the foothills of the Rockies
features Banff, Elk Island, Jasper, Waterton Lake, and Wood Buffalo national parks; annual Calgary stampede; extensive dinosaur finds near Drumheller
products coal; wheat, barley, oats, sugar beet in the S; cattle; oil and natural gas
population (1986) 2,375,000
history in the 17th century much of its area was part of a grant to the ◊Hudson's Bay Company for the fur trade, and the first trading posts were established in the late 18th century. The grant was bought by Canada 1869, and Alberta became a province 1905. After an oil strike in 1947, Alberta became a major oil and gas producer.

Alberti Leon Battista 1404–1472. Italian ◊Renaissance architect and theorist who recognized the principles of Classical architecture and their modification for Renaissance practice in *On Architecture* 1452.

Albert, Lake former name of Lake ◊Mobutu in central Africa.

Albertus Magnus, St 1206–1280. German scholar of Christian theology, philosophy (especially Aristotle), natural science, chemistry, and physics. He was known as "doctor universalis" because of the breadth of his knowledge. Feast day Nov 15.

Albertville resort town at the entrance to the Val d'Arly in the *département* of Savoie, SE France; population (1981) 17,500; site of the 1992 Winter Olympics.

Albi chief town in Tarn *département*, Midi-Pyrénées, SW France, on the river Tarn, 45 mi/ 72 km NE of Toulouse; population (1983) 45,000. It was the center of the Albigensian heresy (see ◊Albigenses) and the birthplace of the artist Toulouse-Lautrec. It has a 13th-century cathedral.

Albigenses heretical sect of Christians (associated with the ◊Cathars) who flourished in S France near Albi and Toulouse during the 11th–13th centuries. They adopted the Manichean belief in the duality of good and evil and pictured Jesus as being a rebel against the cruelty of an omnipotent God.

albinism rare hereditary condition in which the body has no tyrosinase, one of the enzymes that form the pigment melanin, normally found in the skin, hair, and eyes. As a result, the hair is

white and the skin and eyes are pink. The skin and eyes are abnormally sensitive to light, and vision is often impaired. The condition occurs among all human and animal groups.

Albinoni Tomaso 1671–1751. Italian Baroque composer and violinist, whose work was studied and adapted by ◊Bach. He composed over 40 operas.

The popular *Adagio* often described as being by Albinoni was actually composed by his biographer Remo Giazotto (1910–   ).

Albion ancient name for Britain used by the Greeks and Romans. It was mentioned by Pytheas of Massilia (4th century BC), and is probably of Celtic origin, but the Romans, having in mind the white cliffs of Dover, assumed it to be derived from *albus* (white).

Alboin 6th century. King of the ◊Lombards about 561–573. At that time the Lombards were settled north of the Alps. Early in his reign he attacked the Gepidae, a Germanic tribe occupying present-day Romania, killing their king and taking his daughter Rosamund to be his wife. About 568 he crossed the Alps to invade Italy, conquering the country as far S as Rome. He was murdered at the instigation of his wife, after he forced her to drink wine from a cup made from her father's skull.

albumin any of a group of sulfur-containing ◊proteins. The best known is in the form of egg white; others occur in milk, and as a major component of serum. Many vegetables and fluids also contain albumins. They are soluble in water and dilute salt solutions, and are coagulated by heat.

The presence of albumin in the urine, termed albuminuria or proteinuria, may be a symptom of a kidney disorder.

Albuquerque largest city of New Mexico, situated E of the Rio Grande, in the Pueblo district; population (1990) 384,750. Founded 1706, it was named after Afonso de Albuquerque. It is a resort and industrial center, specializing in electronic products and aerospace equipment.

Sandia Laboratories here is engaged in high-technology defense and space-related projects. The University of New Mexico was founded here 1889. Kirkland Air Force Base is nearby.

Albuquerque Afonso de 1453–1515. Viceroy and founder of the Portuguese East Indies with strongholds in Ceylon, Goa, and Malacca 1508–15, when the king of Portugal replaced him by his worst enemy. He died at sea on the way home when his ship *Flor del Mar* was lost between Malaysia and India.

Alcaeus *c.* 611–*c.* 580 BC. Greek lyric poet. Born at Mytilene in Lesvos, he was a member of the aristocratic party and went into exile when the popular party triumphed. He wrote odes, and the Alcaic stanza is named after him.

Alcatraz small island in San Francisco Bay, California. Its fortress was a military prison 1886–1934 and then a federal penitentiary until closed 1963. The dangerous tides allowed few successful escapes.

Inmates included the gangster Al Capone and the "Birdman of Alcatraz," a prisoner who used his time in solitary confinement to become an authority on caged birds. American Indian "nationalists" briefly took over the island 1970 as a symbol of their lost heritage.

alcázar (Arabic "fortress") Moorish palace in Spain; one of five in Toledo defended by the Nationalists against the Republicans for 71 days in 1936 during the Spanish ◊Civil War.

Alcazarquivir, Battle of battle on Aug 4, 1578, between the forces of Sebastian, king of Portugal (1554–1578), and those of the Berber kingdom of Fez. Sebastian's death on the field of battle paved the way for the incorporation of Portugal into the Spanish kingdom of Philip II.

Alcestis in Greek mythology, the wife of Admetus, king of Thessaly. At their wedding, the god Apollo secured a promise from the ⟩Fates that Admetus might postpone his death if he could persuade someone else to die for him. Only his wife proved willing, but she was restored to life by ⟩Heracles.

alchemy (Arabic *al-Kimya*) supposed technique of transmuting base metals, such as lead and mercury, into silver and gold by the philosopher's stone, a hypothetical substance, to which was also attributed the power to give eternal life.

This aspect of alchemy constituted much of the chemistry of the Middle Ages. More broadly, however, alchemy was a system of philosophy that dealt both with the mystery of life and the formation of inanimate substances. Alchemy was a complex and indefinite conglomeration of chemistry, astrology, occultism, and magic, blended with obscure and abstruse ideas derived from various religious systems and other sources. It was practiced in Europe from ancient times to the Middle Ages but later fell into disrepute when ⟩chemistry and ⟩physics developed.

Alcibiades 450–404 BC. Athenian general. Handsome and dissolute, he became the archetype of capricious treachery for his military intrigues against his native state with Sparta and Persia; the Persians eventually had him assassinated. He was brought up by ⟩Pericles and was a friend of ⟩Socrates, whose reputation as a teacher suffered from the association.

Alcmaeonidae noble family of ancient Athens; its members included ⟩Pericles and ⟩Alcibiades.

Alcock John William 1892–1919. British aviator. On June 14, 1919, he and Arthur Whitten Brown (1886–1948) made the first nonstop transatlantic flight, from Newfoundland to Ireland.

alcohol any member of a group of organic chemical compounds characterized by the presence of one or more aliphatic OH (hydroxyl) groups in the molecule, and which form ⟩esters with acids. The main uses of alcohols are as solvents for gums, resins, lacquers, and varnishes; in the making of dyes; for essential oils in perfumery; and for medical substances in pharmacy. Alcohol (ethanol) is produced naturally in the ⟩fermentation process and is consumed as part of alcoholic beverages.

Alcohols may be liquids or solids, according to the size and complexity of the molecule. The five simplest alcohols form a series in which the number of carbon and hydrogen atoms increases progressively, each one having an extra CH_2 (methylene) group in the molecule: methanol or wood spirit (methyl alcohol, CH_3OH); ethanol (ethyl alcohol, C_2H_5OH); propanol (propyl alcohol, C_3H_7OH); butanol (butyl alcohol, C_4H_9OH); and pentanol (amyl alcohol, $C_5H_{11}OH$). The lower alcohols are liquids that mix with water; the higher alcohols, such as pentanol, are oily liquids immiscible with water; and the highest are waxy solids—for example, hexadecanol (cetyl alcohol, $C_{16}H_{33}OH$) and melissyl alcohol ($C_{30}H_{61}OH$),

which occur in sperm-whale oil and beeswax respectively. Alcohols containing the CH_2OH group are primary; those containing CHOH are secondary; while those containing COH are tertiary.

alcoholic beverage any drink containing alcohol, often used for its intoxicating effects. Ethyl alcohol, a colorless liquid (C_2H_5OH) is the basis of all common intoxicants. Foods rich in sugars, such as grapes, produce this alcohol as a natural product of decay, called fermentation.

malt liquors are beers, ales, and stouts, in which the starch of the grain is converted to sugar by malting, and the sugar then fermented into alcohol by yeasts. Fermented drinks contain less than 20% alcohol.

liquors are distilled from malt liquors or wines and can contain up to 55% alcohol. Examples are whiskey, rum, and brandy. A concentration of 0.15% alcohol in the blood causes mild intoxication; 0.3% definite drunkenness and partial loss of consciousness; 0.6% endangers life. Alcohol is more rapidly absorbed at higher altitudes, as in, for example, the slightly reduced pressure of an aircraft cabin.

Alcoholics Anonymous (AA) voluntary self-help organization established 1934 in the US to combat alcoholism; branches now exist in many other countries.

alcoholism dependence on alcoholic liquor. It is characterized as an illness when consumption of alcohol interferes with normal physical or emotional health. Excessive alcohol consumption may produce physical and psychological addiction and lead to nutritional and emotional disorders. The direct effect is cirrhosis of the liver, nerve damage, and heart disease, and the condition is now showing genetic predisposition.

Support groups such as Alcoholics Anonymous are helpful.

alcohol strength a measure of the amount of alcohol in an alcoholic beverage. Wine is measured as the percentage volume of alcohol at 68°F/20°C; liquors as a percentage of a mixture of alcohol and water containing by volume 50% ethyl alcohol at 60°F (called a proof spirit). Thus a whiskey labeled 100 proof contains 50% alcohol.

Alcott Louisa May 1832–1888. US author. Her children's classic *Little Women* 1869 drew on her own home circumstances, the heroine Jo being a partial self-portrait.

Born in Germantown, Pennsylvania, she spent most of her life in Concord, Massachusetts, the daughter of transcendentalist and educator Amos Bronson Alcott (1799–1888). She was educated in her home by her father and, occasionally, by family friends Ralph Waldo Emerson and Henry David Thoreau. Alcott began writing to help earn money for the family. Her first book was *Flower Fables* 1848; her first success was *Hospital Sketches* 1863. The publication of *Little Women* was followed by *Little Men* 1871. She also wrote *Eight Cousins* 1875, *Under the Lilacs* 1879, and *A Garland for Girls* 1888.

Alcuin (Flaccus Albinus Alcuinus) 735–804. English scholar. Born in York, he went to Rome 780, and in 782 took up residence at Charlemagne's court in Aachen. From 796 he was abbot of Tours. He disseminated Anglo-Saxon scholarship, organized education and learning in the Frankish empire, gave a strong impulse to the Carolingian Renaissance, and

was a prominent member of Charlemagne's academy.

Aldebaran or *Alpha Tauri* brightest star in the constellation Taurus and the 14th brightest star in the sky; it marks the eye of the "bull." Aldebaran is a red giant 60 light-years away, shining with a true luminosity of about 100 times that of the Sun.

aldehyde any of a group of organic chemical compounds prepared by oxidation of primary alcohols, so that the OH (hydroxyl) group loses its hydrogen to give an oxygen joined by a double bond to a carbon atom (the aldehyde group, with the formula CHO).

The name is made up from *al*cohol *dehyd*rogenation—that is, alcohol from which hydrogen has been removed. Aldehydes are usually liquids and include methanal, ethanal, benzaldehyde, formalehyde, and citral.

alder any tree or shrub of the genus *Alnus*, in the birch family Betulaceae, found mainly in cooler parts of the northern hemisphere and characterized by toothed leaves and catkins.

Sitka alder *A. sinuata* and red alder *A. rubra* are common to W North America.

Alderney third largest of the ⟩Channel Islands, with its capital at St Anne's; area 3 sq mi/8 sq km; population (1980) 2,000. It gives its name to a breed of cattle, better known as the Guernsey.

Aldrin Edwin (Eugene "Buzz") 1930– . US astronaut who landed on the Moon with Neil ⟩Armstrong during the *Apollo 11* mission in July 1969, becoming the second person to set foot on the Moon.

aleatory music (Latin *alea* "dice") method of composition (pioneered by John ⟩Cage) dating from about 1945 in which the elements are assembled by chance by using, for example, dice or computer.

Aleixandre Vicente 1898–1984. Spanish lyric poet, born in Seville. His verse, which influenced younger Spanish writers, had Republican sympathies, and his work was for a time banned by Franco's government. Nobel Prize for Literature 1977.

Alembert Jean le Rond d' 1717–1783. French mathematician and encyclopedist. He was associated with ⟩Diderot in planning the great ⟩*Encyclopédie*.

Born in Paris, he was educated by the Jansenist Catholic sect. He studied law and medicine before devoting himself to mathematics.

Alençon capital of the Orne *département* of France, situated in a rich agricultural plain to the SE of Caen; population (1983) 33,000. Lace, now a declining industry, was once a major product.

Alentejo region of E central Portugal divided into the districts of Alto Alentejo and Baixo Alentejo. The chief towns are Evora, Neja, and Portalegre.

Aleppo (Syrian *Halab*) ancient city in NW Syria; population (1981) 977,000. There has been a settlement on the site for at least 4,000 years.

Aleutian Islands volcanic island chain in the N Pacific, stretching 1,200 mi/1,900 km SW of Alaska, of which it forms part; population 6,000 Aleuts (most of whom belong to the Orthodox Church, plus a large US defense establishment). There are 14 large and more than 100 small islands running along the Aleutian

Trench. The islands are mountainous, barren, and treeless; they are ice-free all year but are often foggy, with only about 25 days of sunshine recorded annually.

The islands were settled by the Aleuts c. 1000 BC and discovered by a Russian expedition 1741; they passed to the US with the purchase of Alaska 1867. The Japanese occupied Attu and Kiska islands 1942–43; Attu was retaken in the only ground fighting on North American soil during World War II.

alewife fish *Alosa pseudoharengus* of the ⬦herring group, up to 1 ft/30 cm long, found in the NW Atlantic and in the Great Lakes of North America.

Alexander Harold Rupert Leofric George, 1st Earl Alexander of Tunis 1891–1969. British field marshal, a commander in World War II in Burma (now Myanmar), N Africa, and the Mediterranean. He was governor-general of Canada 1946–52 and UK minister of defense 1952–54.

Alexander Samuel 1859–1938. Australian philosopher who originated the theory of emergent evolution: that the space-time matrix evolved matter; matter evolved life; life evolved mind; and finally God emerged from mind. His books include *Space, Time and Deity* 1920.

He was professor at Manchester University, England, 1893–1924.

Alexander eight popes, including:

Alexander III (Orlando Barninelli) Pope 1159–81. His authority was opposed by Frederick I Barbarossa, but Alexander eventually compelled him to render homage 1178. He supported Henry II of England in his invasion of Ireland, but imposed penance on him after the murder of Thomas à ⬦Becket.

Alexander VI (Rodrigo Borgia) 1431–1503. Pope 1492–1503. Of Spanish origin, he bribed his way to the papacy, where he furthered the advancement of his illegitimate children, who included Cesare and Lucrezia ⬦Borgia. When ⬦Savonarola preached against his corrupt practices Alexander had him executed.

Alexander was a great patron of the arts in Italy, as were his children. He is said to have died of a poison he had prepared for his cardinals.

Alexander three tsars of Russia:

Alexander I 1777–1825. Tsar from 1801. Defeated by Napoleon at Austerlitz 1805, he made peace at Tilsit 1807, but economic crisis led to a break with Napoleon's ⬦Continental System and the opening of Russian ports to British trade; this led to Napoleon's ill-fated invasion of Russia 1812. After the Congress of Vienna 1815, Alexander hoped through the Holy Alliance with Austria and Prussia to establish a new Christian order in Europe.

After Napoleon's defeat Russia controlled the Congress Kingdom of Poland, for which a constitution was provided.

Alexander II 1818–1881. Tsar from 1855. He embarked on reforms of the army, the government, and education, and is remembered as "the Liberator" for his emancipation of the serfs 1861, but he lacked the personnel to implement his reforms. However, the revolutionary element remained unsatisfied, and Alexander became increasingly autocratic and reactionary. He was assassinated by an anarchistic terrorist group, the ⬦Nihilists.

Alexander III 1845–1894. Tsar from 1881, when he succeeded his father, Alexander II.

He pursued a reactionary policy, promoting Russification and persecuting the Jews. He married Dagmar (1847–1928), daughter of Christian IX of Denmark and sister of Queen Alexandra of Britain, 1866.

Alexander three kings of Scotland:

Alexander I c. 1078–1124. King of Scotland from 1107, known as **the Fierce**. He ruled to the north of the rivers Forth and Clyde while his brother and successor David ruled to the south. He assisted Henry I of England in his campaign against Wales 1114, but defended the independence of the church in Scotland. Several monasteries, including the abbeys of Inchcolm and Scone, were established by him.

Alexander II 1198–1249. King of Scotland from 1214, when he succeeded his father William the Lion. Alexander supported the English barons in their struggle with King John after ⬦Magna Carta.

Alexander III 1241–1285. King of Scotland from 1249, son of Alexander II. In 1263, by military defeat of Norwegian forces, he extended his authority over the Western Isles, which had been dependent on Norway. He strengthened the power of the central Scottish government.

Alexander I Karageorgevich 1888–1934. Regent of Serbia 191–21 and king of Yugoslavia 1921–34, as dictator from 1929. Second son of ⬦Peter I, king of Serbia, he was declared regent for his father 1912 and on his father's death became king of the state of South Slavs—Yugoslavia—that had come into being 1918.

Rivalries with neighboring powers and among the Croats, Serbs, and Slovenes within the country led Alexander to establish a personal dictatorship. He was assassinated on a state visit to France, and Mussolini's government was later declared to have instigated the crime.

Alexander Nevski, St 1220–1263. Russian military leader, son of the grand duke of Novgorod. In 1240 he defeated the Swedes on the banks of the Neva (hence Nevski), and 1242 defeated the Teutonic Knights on the frozen Lake Peipus.

Alexander Obrenovich 1876–1903. King of Serbia from 1889 while still a minor, on the abdication of his father, King Milan. He took power into his own hands 1893 and in 1900 married a widow, Draga Mashin. In 1903 Alexander and his queen were murdered, and ⬦Peter I Karageorgevich was placed on the throne.

Alexander Severus AD 208–235. Roman emperor from 222, when he succeeded his cousin Heliogabalus. He was born in Palestine. His campaign against the Persians 232 achieved some success, but in 235, on his way to defend Gaul against German invaders, he was killed in a mutiny.

Alexander the Great 356–323 BC. King of Macedonia and conqueror of the large Persian empire. As commander of the vast Macedonian army he conquered Greece 336. He defeated the Persian king Darius in Asia Minor 333, then moved on to Egypt, where he founded Alexandria. He defeated the Persians again in Assyria 331, then advanced further east to reach the Indus. He conquered the Punjab before diminished troops forced his retreat.

The son of King Philip of Macedonia and Queen Olympias, Alexander was educated by the philosopher Aristotle. He first saw fighting 340, and at the battle of Chaeronea 338 contributed to the victory by a cavalry charge. At the

age of 20, when his father was murdered, he assumed command of the throne and the army. He secured his northern frontier, suppressed an attempted rising in Greece by his capture of Thebes, and in 334 crossed the Dardanelles for the campaign against the vast Persian empire; at the river Granicus near the Dardanelles he won his first victory. In 333 he routed Darius at Issus, and then set out for Egypt, where he was greeted as Pharaoh. Meanwhile, Darius assembled half a million men for a final battle but at Arbela on the Tigris 331 Alexander, with 47,000 men, drove the Persians into retreat. After the victory he stayed a month in Babylon, then marched to Susa and Persepolis and in 330 to Ecbatana (now Hamadán, Iran). Soon after, he learned that Darius was dead. In Afghanistan he founded colonies at Herat and Kandahar, and in 328 reached the plains of Sogdiana, where he married Roxana, daughter of King Oxyartes. India now lay before him, and he pressed on to the Indus. Near the river Hydaspes (now Jhelum) he fought one of his fiercest battles against the rajah Porus. At the river Hyphasis (now Beas) his men refused to go farther, and reluctantly he turned back down the Indus and along the coast. They reached Susa 324, where Alexander made Darius's daughter his second wife. He died in Babylon of a malarial fever.

Alexandra 1872–1918. Last tsarina of Russia 1894–1917. She was the former Princess Alix of Hessen and granddaughter of Britain's Queen Victoria. She married ⬦Nicholas II and, from 1907, fell under the spell of ⬦Rasputin, a "holy man" brought to the palace to try to cure her son of haemophilia. She was shot with the rest of her family by the Bolsheviks in the Russian Revolution.

Alexandretta former name of ⬦Iskenderun, port in S Turkey.

Alexandria city in central Louisiana, on the Red River, NW of Baton Rouge; seat of Rapides parish. It is a livestock and meatpacking center; population (1990) 49,188.

Alexandria or *El Iskandariya* city, chief port, and second-largest city of Egypt, situated between the Mediterranean and Lake Maryut; population (1986) 5,000,000. It is linked with canal with the Nile and is an industrial city (oil refining, gas processing, and cotton and grain trading). Founded 331 BC by Alexander the Great, Alexandria was the capital of Egypt for over 1,000 years.

history The principal center of Hellenistic culture, Alexandria has since the 4th century AD been the seat of a Christian patriarch. In 641 it was captured by the Muslim Arabs, and after the opening of the Cape route its trade rapidly declined. Early in the 19th century it began to recover its prosperity, and its growth was encouraged by its use as the main British naval base in the Mediterranean during both world wars. Of the large European community, most were expelled after the Suez Crisis 1956 and their property confiscated.

Few relics of antiquity remain. The Pharos, the first lighthouse and one of the seven wonders of the ancient world, has long since disappeared. The library, said to have contained 700,000 volumes, was destroyed by the caliph ⬦Omar in 640. Pompey's Pillar is a column erected, as a landmark visible from the sea, by the emperor Diocletian. Two obelisks that once stood before the Caesarum temple are now in London (Cleopatra's Needle) and New York respectively.

Alexandria, Library of library in Alexandria, Egypt, founded 330 BC by ⚪Ptolemy I Soter. It was the world's first state-funded scientific institution, and comprised a museum, teaching facilities, and a library that contained 700,000 scrolls, including much ancient Greek literature. It was used by ⚪Euclid and ⚪Eratosthenes, and after initial depradations was burned down AD 640 at the time of the Arab conquest.

Alexandria, school of group of writers and scholars of Alexandria who made the city the chief center of culture in the Western world from about 331 BC to AD 642. They include the poets Callimachus, Apollonius Rhodius, and Theocritus; Euclid, pioneer of geometry; Eratosthenes, the geographer; Hipparchus, who developed a system of trigonometry; the astronomer Ptolemy, who gave his name to the Ptolemaic system of astronomy that endured for over 1,000 years; and the Jewish philosopher Philo. The Gnostics and Neoplatonists also flourished in Alexandria.

alexandrite rare gemstone variety of the mineral chrysoberyl (beryllium aluminum oxide $BeAl_2O_4$), which is green in daylight but appears red in artificial light.

Alexeev Vasiliy 1942– . Soviet weight-lifter who broke 80 world records 1970–77, a record for any sport.

He was Olympic super-heavyweight champion twice, world champion seven times. He retired after the 1980 Olympics.

CAREER HIGHLIGHTS

Olympic champion
1972, 1976
World champion
1970–71, 1973–75, 1977
European champion
1970–78

Alexius five emperors of Byzantium, including:

Alexius I (Comnenus) 1048–1118. Byzantine emperor 1081–1118. The Latin (W European) Crusaders helped him repel Norman and Turkish invasions, and he devoted great skill to buttressing the threatened empire. His daughter ⚪Anna Comnena chronicled his reign.

Alexius III (Angelos) died *c.* 1210. Byzantine emperor 1195–1203. He gained power by deposing and blinding his brother Isaac II, but Isaac's Venetian allies enabled him and his son Alexius IV to regain power as coemperors.

Alexius IV (Angelos) 1182–1204. Byzantine emperor from 1203, when, with the aid of the army of the Fourth Crusade, he deposed his uncle Alexius III. He soon lost the support of the Crusaders (by that time occupying Constantinople), and was overthrown and murdered by another Alexius, Alexius Mourtzouphlus (son-in-law of Alexius III) 1204, an act which the Crusaders used as a pretext to sack the city the same year.

alfalfa or *lucerne* perennial tall herbaceous plant *Medicago sativa* of the pea family Leguminosae. It is native to Eurasia and bears spikes of small purple flowers in late summer. It is now a major fodder crop, generally processed into hay, meal, or silage. Alfalfa sprouts, the sprouted seeds, have become a popular salad ingredient.

Alfonsín Foulkes Raúl Ricardo 1927– . Argentine politician, president 1983–89, leader of the moderate Radical Union Party (UCR). As president from the country's return to civilian government, he set up an investigation of the army's human-rights violations. Economic problems caused him to seek help from the International Monetary Fund and introduce austerity measures.

Educated at a military academy and a university law school, Alfonsin joined the UCR at the age of 18 and eventually went on to lead it. He was active in local politics 1951–62, being imprisoned 1953 by the right-wing Perón regime, and was a member of the national congress 1963–66. With the return to civilian government 1983 and the legalization of political activity, Alfonsin and the UCR won convincing victories and he became president. He stepped down 1989 several months before the end of his term to allow his successor, the Perónist Carlos Menem, to institute emergency economic measures.

Alfonso thirteen kings of León, Castile, and Spain, including:

Alfonso VII *c.* 1107–1157. King of León and Castile from 1126 who attempted to unite Spain. Although he protected the Moors, he was killed trying to check a Moorish rising.

Alfonso X *el Sabio* ("the Wise") 1221–1284. King of Castile from 1252. His reign was politically unsuccessful but he contributed to learning: he made Castilian the official language of the country and commissioned a history of Spain and an encyclopedia, as well as several translations from Arabic concerning, among other subjects, astronomy and games.

Alfonso XI *the Avenger* 1311–1350. King of Castile and León from 1312. He ruled cruelly, repressed a rebellion by his nobles, and defeated the last Moorish invasion 1340.

Alfonso XII 1857–1885. King of Spain from 1875, son of ⚪Isabella II. He assumed the throne after a period of republican government following his mother's flight and effective abdication 1868. His rule was peaceful. He ended the civil war started by the Carlists and drafted a constitution, both 1876.

Alfonso XIII 1886–1941. King of Spain 1886–1931. He assumed power 1906 and married Princess Ena, granddaughter of Queen Victoria of the United Kingdom, in the same year. He abdicated 1931 soon after the fall of the Primo de Rivera dictatorship 1923–30 (which he supported), and Spain became a republic. His assassination was attempted several times.

Alfred *the Great c.* 848–c. 900. King of Wessex from 871. He defended England against Danish invasion, founded the first English navy, and put into operation a legal code. He encouraged the translation of works from Latin (some he translated himself), and promoted the development of the ⚪Anglo-Saxon Chronicle.

algae (singular *alga*) diverse group of plants (including those commonly called seaweeds) that shows great variety of form, ranging from single-celled forms to multicellular seaweeds of considerable size and complexity.

Because of their diversity, botanists have established seven separate algae groupings or divisions, belonging to three different kingdoms: Cyanobacteria (blue-green algae) of the kingdom Monerans; Chrysophyta (golden algae ⚪diatoms), Englenophyta (plidosynthetic flagellates) and Pyrrophyta (dinoflagellates) of the kingdom Protists; and Rhodophyta (red algae), Phaeophyta (brown algae), and Chlorophyta (green algae) of the kingdom Plants.

Algarve (Arabic *al-gharb* "the west") ancient kingdom in S Portugal, the modern district of Faro, a popular vacation resort; population (1981) 323,500. Industries include agriculture, fishing, wine, mining, and tourism. The Algarve began to be wrested from the ⚪Moors in the 12th century and was united with Portugal as a kingdom 1253.

It includes the SW extremity of Europe, Cape St Vincent, where the British fleet defeated the Spanish 1797.

algebra system of arithmetic applying to any set of nonnumerical symbols (usually letters), and the axioms and rules by which they are combined or operated upon; sometimes known as *generalized arithmetic*.

The basics of algebra were familiar in Babylon 2000 BC, and were practiced by the Arabs in the Middle Ages. In the 9th century, the Arab mathematician Mohammed ibn-Musa al-⚪Khwa b1rizmi b1 first used the words *hisäb al-jabr* ("calculus of reduction") as part of the title of a treatise. Algebra is used in many branches of mathematics, for example, matrix algebra and Boolean algebra (the latter method was first devised in the 19th century by the British mathematician George Boole and used in working out the logic for computers).

Algeciras port in S Spain, to the W of Gibraltar across the Bay of Algeciras; population (1991) 101,400. Founded by the ⚪Moors 713, it was taken from them by Alfonso XI of Castile 1344.

Algeciras Conference international conference held Jan–April 1906 when France, Germany, Britain, Russia, and Austria–Hungary, together with the US, Spain, the Low Countries, Portugal, and Sweden, met to settle the question of Morocco. The conference was prompted by increased German demands in what had traditionally been seen as a French area of influence, but it resulted in a reassertion of Anglo-French friendship and the increased isolation of Germany. France and Spain gained control of Morocco.

Alger Horatio 1834–1899. US writer of children's books. He wrote over 100 didactic moral tales in which the heroes rise from poverty to riches through hard work, luck, and good deeds, including the series "Ragged Dick" from 1867 and "Tattered Tom" from 1871.

It is estimated that his books sold more than 20 million copies. A "Horatio Alger tale" has now come to mean any rags-to-riches story, often an implausible one.

Algeria country in N Africa, bounded E by Tunisia and Libya, SE by Niger, SW by Mali and Mauritania, NW by Morocco, and N by the Mediterranean Sea.

government The constitution dates from 1989. Algeria is a multiparty state. There is a president and a single-chamber national people's assembly of 295 deputies, elected for a five-year term. Islam is the state religion.

history From the 9th century BC the area now known as Algeria was ruled by ⚪Carthage, and subsequently by Rome 2nd century BC–5th century AD. In the early Christian era, St Augustine was bishop of Hippo (now called Annaba) 396–430. The area was invaded by the ⚪Vandals after the decline of Roman rule and was ruled as part of the ⚪Byzantium Empire from the 6th–8th centuries, after which the Arabs invaded the region, introducing Islam and Arabic. Islamic influence continued to dominate, despite Spain's attempts to take control in the 15th–16th centuries. From the 16th century Algeria was ruled under the ⚪Ottoman Empire and flourished as a center for the slave trade. The sultan's rule was often nominal, and in the 18th

Algeria
Democratic and Popular Republic of
(al-Jumhuriya al-Jazairiya AD-Dimuqratiya ash-Shabiya)

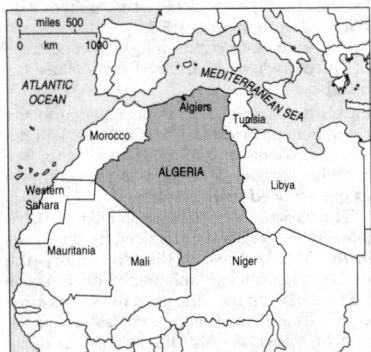

area 919,352 sq mi/2,381,741 sq km
capital al-Jazair (Algiers)
cities Qacentina/Constantine; ports are Ouahran/Oran, Annaba/Bône
physical coastal plains backed by mountains in N; Sahara desert in S
features Atlas mountains, Barbary Coast, Chott Melrhir depression, Hoggar mountains
head of state Ali Kafi from 1992
head of government Belnid Absessalem from 1992
political system semimilitary rule
political parties National Liberation Front (FLN), nationalist socialist
exports oil, natural gas, iron, wine, olive oil
currency dinar

population (1990 est) 25,715,000 (83% Arab, 17% Berber); growth rate 3.0% p.a.
life expectancy men 59, women 62
languages Arabic (official); Berber, French
religion Sunni Muslim (state religion)
literacy men 63%, women 37% (1985 est)
GDP $64.6 bn; $2,796 per head
chronology
1954 War for independence from France led by the FLN.
1962 Independence achieved from France. Republic declared. Ben Bella elected prime minister.
1963 Ben Bella elected Algeria's first president.
1965 Ben Bella deposed by military, led by Colonel Houari Boumédienne.
1976 New constitution approved.
1978 Death of Boumédienne.
1979 Benjedid Chadli elected president. Ben Bella released from house arrest. FLN adopted new party structure.
1981 Algeria helped secure release of US prisoners in Iran.
1983 Chadli reelected.
1988 Riots in protest at government policies; 170 killed. Reform program introduced. Diplomatic relations with Egypt restored.
1989 Constitutional changes proposed, leading to limited political pluralism.
1990 Fundamentalist Islamic Salvation Front (FIS) won Algerian municipal and provincial elections.
1991 Dec: Islamic Salvation Front (FIS) won first round of multiparty elections.
1992 Jan: Chadli resigned; military took control of government; Mohamed Boudiaf became president. March: FIS ordered to disband. June: Boudiaf assassinated; Ali Kafi chosen as new head of state and Belnid Absessalem as prime minister.

century Algeria became a pirate state, preying on Mediterranean shipping. European intervention became inevitable, and an Anglo-Dutch force bombarded Algiers 1816.
French colonization A French army landed 1830 and seized Algiers. By 1847 the north had been brought under French control, and was formed 1848 into the *départements* of Algiers, Oran, and Constantine. Many French colonists settled in these *départements*, which were made part of metropolitan France 1881. The mountainous region inland, inhabited by the Kabyles, was occupied 1850–70, and the Sahara region, subdued 1900–09, remained under military rule.
Struggle for independence After the defeat of France 1940 by Germany in World War II, Algeria came under the control of the Vichy government, which collaborated with the Nazis, until the Allies landed in N Africa 1942. Postwar hopes of integrating Algeria more closely with France were frustrated by opposition in Algeria from both those of non-French and French origin. An embittered struggle for independence from France continued 1954–62, when referenda in Algeria and France resulted 1962 in the recognition of Algeria as an independent one-party republic with ◊Ben Bella as prime minister 1962 and the country's first president from 1963. Colonel Houari ◊Boumédienne deposed Ben Bella in a military coup 1965, suspended the constitution, and ruled through a revolutionary council.
Chadli's presidency A new constitution confirmed Algeria as an Islamic, socialist, one-party state 1976. Boumédienne died 1978, and power was transferred to Benjedid ◊Chadli,

secretary-general of the FLN. During Chadli's presidency, relations with France and the US improved, and there was some progress in achieving greater cooperation with neighboring states, such as Tunisia. Algeria acted as an intermediary in securing the release of the US hostages in Iran 1981. A proposal by Colonel ◊Khaddhafi for political union with Libya received a cool response 1987. Riots and protests at economic austerity measures Oct 1988 prompted reforms and a new constitution, approved by referendum Feb 1989, deleting any reference to socialism, and opening the way for a multiparty system. Islam remained the state religion, and the political reforms were designed, at least in part, to stem the growing fundamentalist movement. Ben Bella returned Sept 1990 after nine years in exile.
military rule In the first round of assembly elections in Dec 1991, the Islamic Salvation Front (FIS) won 188 of the 231 seats contested. Chadli resigned in Jan 1992. The army stepped in and canceled the second round of the elections. It formed a junta headed by a former opponent of the president, Mohamed Boudiaf. The army banned political activity in mosques in an attempt to halt the rise of Islamic fundamentalism, and the FIS was ordered to disband March 1992. Disquiet and potential violence persisted; Boudiaf was assassinated in June and replaced by Ali Kafi. Belnid Absessalem was appointed prime minister. *See illustration box.*

Algiers (Arabic *al-Jazair*; French *Alger*) capital of Algeria, situated on the narrow coastal

plain between the Atlas Mountains and the Mediterranean; population (1984) 2,442,300.
Founded by the Arabs AD 935, Algiers was taken by the Turks 1518 and by the French 1830. The old town is dominated by the Kasbah, the palace and prison of the Turkish rulers. The new town, constructed under French rule, is in European style.
Algiers, Battle of bitter conflict in Algiers 1954–62 between the Algerian nationalist population and the French colonial army and French settlers. The conflict ended with Algerian independence 1962.
alginate salt of alginic acid, $(C_6H_8O_6)_n$, obtained from brown seaweeds and used in textiles, paper, food products, and pharmaceuticals.
ALGOL (abbreviation for *algorithmic language*) in computing, an early high-level programming language, developed in the 1950s and 1960s for scientific applications. A general-purpose language, ALGOL is best suited to mathematical work and has an algebraic style. Although no longer in common use, it has greatly influenced more recent languages, such as ADA and PASCAL.
Algol or *Beta Persei* ◊eclipsing binary, a pair of rotating stars in the constellation Perseus, one of which eclipses the other every 69 hours, causing its brightness to drop by two-thirds.
The brightness changes were first explained 1782 by English amateur astronomer John Goodricke (1764–1786).
Algonquian a group of languages spoken by North American Indians of the Eastern Woodland zone S and E of Hudson Bay. Algonquian includes over 20 languages spoken by American Indians of the NE coast as well as by the Cree, Arapaho, Blackfoot, Cheyenne, Ójibwa, and Fox.
algorithm procedure or series of steps that can be used to solve a problem. In computer science, it describes the logical sequence of operations to be performed by a program. A ◊flow chart is a visual representation of an algorithm.
The word derives from the name of the 9th-century Arab mathematician Mohammed ibn-Mūsā al-◊Khwārizmī.
Alhambra fortified palace in Granada, Spain, built by Moorish kings mainly between 1248 and 1354. It stands on a rocky hill and is the finest example of Moorish architecture.
Ali c. 598–660. 4th caliph of Islam. He was born in Mecca, the son of Abu Talib, uncle to the prophet Mohammed, who gave him his daughter Fatima in marriage. On Mohammed's death 632, Ali had a claim to succeed him, but this was not conceded until 656. After a stormy reign, he was assassinated. Around Ali's name the controversy has raged between the Sunni and the Shiites (see ◊Islam), the former denying his right to the caliphate and the latter supporting it.
Ali (Ali Pasha) 1741–1822. Turkish politician, known as *Arslan* ("the Lion"). An Albanian, he was appointed pasha (governor) of the Janina region 1788 (now Ioánnina, Greece). His court was visited by the British poet Byron. He was assassinated.
Ali Muhammad. Adopted name of Cassius Marcellus Clay, Jr, 1942– . US boxer. Olympic light-heavyweight champion 1960, he went on to become world professional heavyweight champion 1964, and was the only man to regain the title twice. He was known for his fast footwork and extrovert nature.

He had his title stripped from him 1967 for refusing to be drafted into the US Army. He regained his title 1974, lost it Feb 1978, and regained it seven months later.

He had the last of his 61 professional fights 1981 against Trevor Berbick.

CAREER HIGHLIGHTS

fights: 61
wins: 56 (37 knockouts)
draws: 0
defeats: 5
first professional fight: Oct 29, 1960 v. Tunny Hunsaker (USA)
last professional fight: Dec 11, 1981 v. Trevor Berbick (Canada)

Alia Ramiz 1925– . Albanian communist politician, head of state 1982–92. He gradually relaxed the isolationist policies of his predecessor Hoxha and following public unrest introduced political and economic reforms, including free elections 1991, when he was elected executive president.

Born in Shkodër in NW Albania, the son of poor Muslim peasants, Alia joined the National Liberation Army 1944, actively opposing Nazi control. After a period in charge of agitation and propaganda, Alia was inducted into the secretariat and politburo of the ruling Party of Labor of Albania (PLA) 1960–61. On the death of Enver Hoxha he became party leader, soon earning the description of the Albanian Gorbachev. In April 1991, he was elected executive president of the Republic of Albania, following the PLA's victory in multiparty elections. A month later, in conformity with the provisions of the new interim constitution, which debarred the Republic's president from holding party office, he resigned as PLA first secretary and from its politburo and central committee. Sali Berisha replaced Alia as president March 1992.

alibi (Latin "elsewhere") in law, a provable assertion that the accused was at some other place when a crime was committed.

Alice's Adventures in Wonderland children's story by Lewis Carroll, published 1865. Alice dreams she follows the White Rabbit down a rabbit hole and meets fantastic characters such as the Cheshire Cat, the Mad Hatter, and the King and Queen of Hearts.

An Alice-in-Wonderland situation has come to mean an absurd or irrational situation, because of the dreamlike logic of Alice's adventures in the book. With its companion volume *Through the Looking-Glass* 1872. it is one of the most quoted works in the English language.

alien in law, a person who is not a citizen of a particular nation.

In the US, federal legislation determines which aliens may legally enter a country or reside in it; their rights at law, both civil and criminal; and the processes and conditions by which they may become citizens.

Alien and Sedition Acts four laws passed by the US Congress 1798, when war with France seemed likely. The acts lengthened the period of residency required for US citizenship, gave the president the power to expel "dangerous" aliens, and severely restricted criticism of the government. They were controversial because of the degree of power exercised by central government; they are now also seen as an early manifestation of US xenophobia (fear of foreigners).

alienation sense of isolation, powerlessness, and therefore frustration; a feeling of loss of control over one's life; a sense of estrangement from society or even from oneself. As a concept it was developed by the German philosophers Hegel and Marx; the latter used it as a description and criticism of the condition that developed among workers in capitalist society.

The term has also been used by non-Marxist writers and sociologists (in particular Durkheim in his work *Suicide* 1897) to explain unrest in factories and to describe the sense of powerlessness felt by groups such as young people, black people, and women in Western industrial society.

alimentary canal in animals, the tube through which food passes; it extends from the mouth to the anus. It is a complex organ, adapted for ◊digestion. In human adults, it is about 30 ft/ 9 m long, consisting of the mouth cavity, pharynx, esophagus, stomach, and the small and large intestines.

A constant stream of enzymes from the canal wall and from the pancreas assists the breakdown of food molecules into smaller, soluble nutrient molecules, which are absorbed through the canal wall into the bloodstream and carried to individual cells. The muscles of the alimentary canal keep the incoming food moving, mix it with the enzymes and other juices, and slowly push it in the direction of the anus, a process known as ◊peristalsis. The wall of the canal receives an excellent supply of blood and is folded so as to increase its surface area. These two adaptations ensure efficient absorption of nutrient molecules.

alimony in the US, money allowance given by court order to a former spouse after separation or ◊divorce. The right has been extended to relationships outside marriage and is colloquially termed palimony. Alimony is separate and distinct from court orders for child support.

Ali Pasha Mehmed Emin 1815–1871. Grand vizier (chief minister) of the Ottoman empire 1855–56, 1858–59, 1861, and 1867–71, noted for his attempts to westernize the Ottoman Empire.

After a career as ambassador to the UK, minister of foreign affairs 1846, delegate to the Congress of ◊Vienna 1855 and of Paris 1856, he was grand vizier a total of five times. While promoting friendship with Britain and France, he defended the vizier's powers against those of the sultan.

aliphatic compound any organic chemical compound in which the carbon atoms are joined in straight chains, as in hexane (C_6H_{14}), or in branched chains, as in 2-methylpentane ($CH_3CH(CH_3)CH_2CH_2CH_3$).

Aliphatic compounds have bonding electrons localized within the vicinity of the bonded atoms. ◊Cyclic compounds that do not have delocalized electrons are also aliphatic, as in the alicyclic compound cyclohexane (C_6H_{12}) or the heterocyclic piperidine ($C_5H_{11}N$). Compare ◊aromatic compound.

alkali (Arabic *al-qualīy* "ashes") in chemistry, a compound classed as a ◊base that is soluble in water. Alkalis neutralize acids and are soapy to the touch. The hydroxides of metals are alkalis; those of sodium (sodium hydroxide, NaOH) and of potassium (potassium hydroxide, KOH) being chemically powerful; both were derived from the ashes of plants.

alkali metal any of a group of six metallic elements with similar chemical bonding properties: lithium, sodium, potassium, rubidium, cesium, and francium. They form a linked group in the ◊periodic table of the elements. They are univalent (have a valency of one) and of very low density (lithium, sodium, and potassium float on water); in general they are reactive, soft, low-melting-point metals.

Because of their reactivity they are only found as compounds in nature, and are used as chemical reactants rather than as structural metals.

alkaline-earth metal any of a group of six metallic elements with similar bonding properties: beryllium, magnesium, calcium, strontium, barium, and radium. They form a linked group in the ◊periodic table of the elements. They are strongly basic, bivalent (have a valency of two), and occur in nature only in compounds.

alkaloid any of a number of physiologically active and frequently poisonous substances contained in some plants. They are usually organic bases and contain nitrogen. They form salts with acids and, when soluble, give alkaline solutions.

Substances in this group are included by custom rather than by scientific rules. Examples include morphine, cocaine, quinine, caffeine, strychnine, nicotine, and atropine.

alkane member of a group of ◊hydrocarbons having the general formula C_nH_{2n+2}, commonly known as *paraffins*. Lighter alkanes, such as methane, ethane, propane, and butane, are colorless gases; heavier ones are liquids or solids. In nature they are found in natural gas and petroleum. As alkanes contain only single ◊covalent bonds, they are said to be saturated.

alkene member of the group of ◊hydrocarbons having the general formula C_nH_{2n}, formerly known as *olefins*. Lighter alkenes, such as ethene and propene, are gases, obtained from the ◊cracking of oil fractions. Alkenes are unsaturated compounds, characterized by one or more double bonds between adjacent carbon atoms. They react by addition, and many useful compounds, such as poly(ethene) and bromoethane, are made from them.

alkyne member of the group of ◊hydrocarbons with the general formula C_nH_{2n-2}, formerly known as *acetylenes*. They are unsaturated compounds, characterized by one or more triple bonds between adjacent carbon atoms. Lighter alkynes, such as ethyne, are gases; heavier ones are liquids or solids.

Allah (Arabic *al-Ilah* "the God") Islamic name for God.

Allahabad ("city of god") historic city in Uttar Pradesh state, NE India, 360 mi/580 km SE of Delhi, on the Yamuna River where it meets the Ganges and the mythical Seraswati River; population (1981) 642,000. A Hindu religious festival is held here every 12 years with the participants washing away sin and sickness by bathing in the rivers.

Allegheny Mountains range over 500 mi/ 800 km long extending from Pennsylvania to Virginia, rising to more than 4,900 ft/1,500 m and averaging 2,500 ft/750 m. The mountains are a major source of timber, coal, iron, and limestone. They initially hindered western migration, the first settlement to the west being Marietta 1788.

allegory in literature, the description or illustration of one thing in terms of another; a work of poetry or prose in the form of an extended metaphor or parable that makes use of symbolic fictional characters.

An example of the use of symbolic fictional character in allegory is the romantic epic *The Faerie Queene* 1590–96 by Edmund Spenser in homage to Queen Elizabeth I. Allegory is often used for moral purposes, as in John Bunyan's *Pilgrim's Progress* 1678. Medieval allegory often used animals as characters; this tradition survives in such works as *Animal Farm* 1945 by George Orwell.

allele one of two or more alternate forms of a ▷gene at a given position (locus) on a chromosome, caused by a difference in the ▷DNA. Blue and brown eyes in humans are determined by different alleles of the gene for eye color.

Organisms with two sets of chromosomes (diploids) will have two copies of each gene. If the two alleles are identical the individual is said to be ▷homozygous at that locus; if different, the individual is ▷heterozygous at that locus. Some alleles show ▷dominance over others.

Allen Ethan 1738–1789. American Revolutionary War leader. Born in Litchfield, Connecticut, Allen served in the French and Indian War and later obtained large tracts of land in Vermont. A supporter of independence for Vermont (then claimed by both New Hampshire and New York), he organized the "Green Mountain Boys." At the outbreak of the American Revolution, they joined with Benedict Arnold to capture Fort Ticonderoga, the first victory for the American side, but Allen was captured by the British in the subsequent invasion of Canada. Released by the British 1778, Allen continued to campaign for Vermont's autonomy but died before it achieved statehood in 1791.

Allen Hervey 1889–1949. US novelist, poet, and biographer, known for his historical novel *Anthony Adverse* 1933 set in the Napoleonic era. He also wrote a biography of Edgar Allen Poe, *Israfel* 1926.

Allen Woody. Adopted name of Allen Stewart Konigsberg 1935– . US film writer, director, and actor, known for his cynical, witty, often self-deprecating parody and offbeat humor. His film *Annie Hall* 1975 won him three Academy Awards.

His film career began with *What's New Pussycat?* 1965, which he wrote and in which he acted. Other films include *Take the Money and Run* 1969, *Bananas* 1971, *Play It Again, Sam* 1972, *Sleeper* 1973, *Love and Death* 1975, *Interiors* 1978, *Manhattan* 1979, *Stardust Memories* 1982 and *Midsummer Night's Sex Comedy* 1982, *Zelig* 1983, *Broadway Danny Rose* 1984, *Purple Rose of Cairo* 1985, *Hannah and Her Sisters* 1986, and *Radio Days* 1987. His play *Don't Drink the Water* appeared on Broadway 1966.

Allenby Henry Hynman, 1st Viscount Allenby 1861–1936. English field marshal. In World War I he served in France before taking command 1917–19 of the British forces in the Middle East. His defeat of the Turkish forces at Megiddo in Palestine in Sept 1918 was followed almost at once by the capitulation of Turkey. He was high commissioner in Egypt 1919–35.

Allende Gossens Salvador 1908–1973. Chilean Marxist politician, president from 1970 until his death during a military coup in 1973.

Allende, born in Valparaiso, became a Marxist activist in the 1930s. He ran unsuccessfully for the presidency in 1952, 1958, and 1964 but won in 1970, becoming the first Marxist to be elected president of an independent country in the W hemisphere. As president, Allende nationalized the banking and copper industries and instituted land reform, provoking the conservative elements in the country. As Chile's economy declined and strikes and disturbances supported by the US Central Intelligence Agency spread, the military staged a coup, during which Allende either was killed or committed suicide.

Allentown city in E Pennsylvania, on the Lehigh river, just NW of Philadelphia. It is an industrial center for textiles, machinery, and electronic equipment; population (1990) 105,090. Center of munitions production during the American Revolution.

allergy special sensitivity of the body that makes it react, with an exaggerated response of the natural immune defense mechanism, especially with ▷histamines, to the introduction of an otherwise harmless foreign substance (*allergen*).

The person subject to hay fever in summer is allergic to one or more kinds of pollen. Many asthmatics are allergic to certain kinds of dust or to microorganisms in animal fur or feathers. Others react severely to poison ivy or are violently sick if they eat shellfish or eggs. Drugs such as antihistamines and corticosteroids are used to alleviate reactions.

Alliance for Progress program of US assistance to Latin American countries, initiated by President Kennedy 1961 under the auspices of the ▷Organization of American States.

It called for expenditure of $20 billion over ten years, but economic conditions continued to worsen in Latin America and President Nixon effectively dismantled the program.

Allied Coordination Committee or ***Operation Stay Behind*** or ***Gladio*** secret right-wing paramilitary network in W Europe set up in the 1950s to arm guerrillas chosen from the civilian population in the event of Soviet invasion or communist takeover. Initiated and partly funded by the CIA, it is linked to NATO. Its past or present existence was officially acknowledged 1990 by Belgium, France, (West) Germany, Greece, Italy, the Netherlands, Norway, and Portugal; in the UK the matter is covered by the Official Secrets Act. In 1990 those governments that confirmed their countries' participation said that the branches had been or would be closed down; the European Parliament set up a commission of inquiry.

The network was operated by the secret services and armed forces of member countries, and was reported to have links with right-wing extremist groups -at least in Belgium and Italy. Switzerland officially stated 1990 that its secret resistance army, P-26, had no links with the NATO network, although it had cooperated with British secret services.

Allier river in central France, a tributary of the Loire; it is 350 mi/565 km long and gives its name to a *département* (administrative region). Vichy is the chief town on the Allier.

Allies, the in World War I, the 23 countries allied against the Central Powers (Germany, Austria–Hungary, Turkey, and Bulgaria), including France, Italy, Russia, the UK, Australia and other Commonwealth nations, and, in the latter part of the war, the US; and in World War II, the 49 countries allied against the ▷Axis powers (Germany, Italy, and Japan), including France, the UK, Australia and other Commonwealth nations, the US, and the USSR.

In the 1991 Gulf War, there were 28 countries in the Allied coalition.

alligator reptile of the genus *Alligator*, related to the crocodile. There are two species: *A. mississipiensis*, the Mississippi alligator of the southern states of the US, and *A. sinensis* from the swamps of the lower Chang Jiang River in China. The former grows to about 12 ft/4 m, but the latter only to 5 ft/1.5 m. Alligators lay their eggs in sand; they swim well with lashing movements of the tail; they feed on fish and mammals but seldom attack people.

The skin is of value for fancy leather, and alligator farms have been established in the US. Closely related are the caymans of South America; these belong to the genus *Caiman*.

alliteration in poetry and prose, the use, within a line or phrase, of words beginning with the same sound, as in "Two tired toads trotting to Tewkesbury." It was a common device in Old English poetry, and its use survives in many traditional English phrases, such as *kith and kin, hearth and home*.

Allium genus of plants belonging to the lily family Liliaceae. Members of the genus are usually strong-smelling with a sharp taste, but form bulbs in which sugar is stored. Cultivated species include onion, garlic, chive, and leek.

allometry in biology, a regular relationship between a given feature (for example, the size of an organ) and the size of the body as a whole, when this relationship is not a simple proportion of body size. Thus, an organ may increase in size proportionally faster, or slower, than body size does. For example, a human baby's head is much larger in relation to its body than is an adult's.

allopathy the usual contemporary method of treating disease, using therapies designed to counteract the manifestations of the disease. In strict usage, allopathy is the opposite of ▷homeopathy.

allopurinol drug prescribed for the treatment of ▷gout; it is an isomer of hypexanthine $C_5H_4N_4O$, and acts by reducing levels of ▷uric acid in the blood.

Discovered accidentally in the early 1960s in the search for new immunosuppressives, it has no effects on acute gout attacks, and may even provoke them in the initial stages of therapy. In the long term, it prevents the deposit of urate in the joints and the formation of uric-acid kidney stones.

allotropy property whereby an element can exist in two or more forms (allotropes), each possessing different physical properties but the same state of matter (gas, liquid, or solid). The allotropes of carbon are diamond and graphite. Sulfur has several different forms (flowers of sulfur, plastic, rhombic, and monoclinic). These solids have different crystal structures, as do the the white and gray forms of tin and the black, red, and white forms of phosphorus.

Oxygen exists as two gaseous allotropes: "normal" oxygen (O_2) and ozone (O_3), which differ in their molecular configurations.

alloy metal blended with some other metallic or nonmetallic substance to give it special qualities, such as resistance to corrosion, greater hardness, or tensile strength. Useful alloys include bronze, brass, cupronickel, duralumin, German silver, gunmetal, pewter, solder, steel, and stainless steel.

Among the oldest alloys is bronze, whose

widespread use ushered in the Bronze Age. Complex alloys are now common; for example, in dentistry, where a cheaper alternative to gold is made of chromium, cobalt, molybdenum, and titanium. Among the most recent alloys are superplastics: alloys that can stretch to double their length at specific temperatures, permitting, for example, their injection into molds as easily as plastic.

All Saints' Day or *All-Hallows* or *Hallowmas* festival on Nov 1 for all Christian saints and martyrs who have no special day of their own.

All Souls' Day festival in the Roman Catholic church, held on Nov 2 (following All Saints' Day) in the conviction that through prayer and self-denial the faithful can hasten the deliverance of souls expiating their sins in purgatory.

allspice spice prepared from the dried berries of the evergreen pimento tree or West Indian pepper tree *Pimenta dioica* of the myrtle family, cultivated chiefly in Jamaica. It has an aroma similar to that of a mixture of cinnamon, cloves, and nutmeg.

Allston Washington 1779–1843. US painter of sea- and landscapes, a pioneer of the Romantic movement in the US. His handling of light and color earned him the title "the American Titian." He also painted Classical, religious, and historical subjects.

Allston was born in South Carolina and educated at Harvard. He traveled widely in Europe, making contact and sharing ideals with the Romantic set in Britain, including the poets Wordsworth and Coleridge. He apprenticed himself to Benjamin �081West and labored over historical paintings in West's manner without much success. Once settled in the US, he produced poetic, moody and visionary scenes, such as *The Moonlight Landscape* 1819 (Museum of Fine Arts, Boston).

alluvial deposit layer of broken rocky matter, or sediment, formed from material that has been carried in suspension by a river or stream and dropped as the velocity of the current changes. River plains and deltas are made entirely of alluvial deposits, but smaller pockets can be found in the beds of upland torrents.

Alluvial deposits can consist of a whole range of particle sizes, from boulders down through cobbles, pebbles, gravel, sand, silt, and clay. The raw materials are the rocks and soils of upland areas that are loosened by erosion and washed away by mountain streams. Much of the world's richest farmland lies on alluvial deposits. These deposits can also provide an economic source of minerals. River currents produce a sorting action, with particles of heavy material deposited first while lighter materials are washed downstream. Hence heavy minerals such as gold and tin, present in the original rocks in small amounts, can be concentrated and deposited on stream beds in commercial quantities. Such deposits are called "placer ores."

alluvial fan a roughly triangular sedimentary formation found at the base of slopes. An alluvial fan results when a sediment-laden stream or river rapidly deposits its load of gravel and silt as its speed is reduced on entering a plain.

The surface of such a fan slopes outward in a wide arc from an apex at the mouth of the steep valley. A small stream carrying a load of coarse particles builds a shorter, steeper fan than a large stream carrying a load of fine particles.

Over time, the fan tends to become destroyed piecemeal by the continuing headward and downward erosion leveling the slope.

Allyson June. Adopted name of Ella Geisman 1917– . US film actress, popular in musicals and straight drama in the 1940s and 1950s. Her work includes *Music for Millions* 1945, *The Three Musketeers* 1948, and *The Glenn Miller Story* 1954.

Alma-Ata formerly (to 1921) *Vernyi* capital of �081Kazakhstan; population (1991) 1,151,300. Industries include engineering, printing, tobacco processing, textile manufacturing, and leather products.

Established 1854 as a military fortress and trading center, the town was destroyed by an earthquake 1887.

Almagest (Arabic *al* "the" and Greek *majisti* "greatest") book compiled by the Greek astronomer �081Ptolemy during the 2nd century AD, which included the idea of an Earth-centered universe. It survived in an Arabic translation. Some medieval books on astronomy, astrology, and alchemy were given the same title.

Each section of the book deals with a different branch of astronomy. The introduction describes the universe as spherical and contains arguments for the Earth being stationary at the center. From this mistaken assumption, it goes on to describe the motions of the Sun, Moon, and planets; eclipses; and the positions, brightness, and precession of the "fixed stars." The book drew on the work of earlier astronomers such as �081Hipparchus.

Almeida Francisco de *c.* 1450–1510. First viceroy of Portuguese India 1505–08.

He was killed in a skirmish with the Hottentots (present-day Khoikhoi) at Table Bay, S Africa.

He consolidated rule there and sent expeditions out into the Indian Ocean and as far as Madagascar.

Almería Spanish city, chief town of a province of the same name on the Mediterranean; population (1991) 157,800. The province is famous for its white grapes, and in the Sierra Nevada are rich mineral deposits.

Almohad Berber dynasty 1130–1269 founded by the Berber prophet Mohammed ibn Tumart (*c.* 1080–1130). The Almohads ruled much of Morocco and Spain, which they took by defeating the �081Almoravids; they later took the area that today forms Algeria and Tunis. Their policy of religious "purity" involved the forced conversion and massacre of the Jewish population of Spain. The Almohads were themselves defeated by the Christian kings of Spain 1212, and in Morocco 1269.

almond tree *Prunus amygdalus*, family Rosaceae, related to the peach and apricot. Dessert almonds are the kernels of the fruit of the sweet variety *P. amygdalus dulcis*, which is also the source of a low-cholesterol culinary oil. Oil of bitter almonds, from the variety *P. amygdalus amara*, is used in flavoring. Almond oil is also used for cosmetics, perfumes, and fine lubricants.

Almoravid Berber dynasty 1056–1147 founded by the prophet Abdullah ibn Tashfin, ruling much of Morocco and Spain in the 11th-12th centuries. The Almoravids came from the Sahara and in the 11th century began laying the foundations of an empire covering the whole of Morocco and parts of Algeria; their capital was the newly founded Marrakesh. In 1086 *they*

defeated Alfonso VI of Castile to gain much of Spain. They were later overthrown by the �081Almohads.

aloe plant of the genus *Aloe* of African plants, family Liliaceae, distinguished by their long, fleshy, spiny-edged leaves. The drug usually referred to as "bitter aloes" is a powerful cathartic prepared from the juice of the leaves of several of the species.

Aloysius, St 1568–1591. Italian Jesuit who died while nursing plague victims. He is the patron saint of youth. Feast day June 21.

alpaca domesticated South American hoofed mammal *Lama pacos* of the camel family, found in Chile, Peru, and Bolivia, and herded at high elevations in the Andes. It is bred mainly for its long, fine, silky wool, and stands about 3 ft/1 m tall at the shoulder with neck and head another 2 ft/60 cm.

The alpaca is also used for food at the end of its fleece-producing years. Like the �081llama, it was probably bred from the wild �081guanaco and is a close relative of the �081vicuna.

alpha and omega first (α) and last (ω) letters of the Greek alphabet, a phrase hence meaning the beginning and end, or sum total, of anything.

alphabet set of conventional symbols used for writing, based on a correlation between individual symbols and spoken sounds, so called from *alpha* (α) and *beta* (β), the names of the first two letters of the Classical Greek alphabet. The earliest known alphabet is from Palestine, about 1700 BC. Alphabetic writing now takes many forms, for example the Hebrew *aleph-beth* and the Arabic script, both written from right to left; the Devanagari script of the Hindus, in which the symbols "hang" from a line common to all the symbols; and the Greek alphabet, with the first clearly delineated vowel symbols.

Each letter of the alphabets descended from Greek represents a particular sound or sounds, usually grouped into *vowels* (*a, e, i, o, u*, in the English version of the Roman alphabet), *consonants* (*b, p, d, t*, and so on) and *semivowels* (*w, y*). Letters may be combined to produce distinct sounds (for example *a* and *e* in words like *tale* and *take*, or *o* and *i* together to produce a "wa" sound in the French *loi*), or may have no sound whatsoever (for example the silent letters *gh* in *high* and *through*).

Alpha Centauri or *Rigil Kent* brightest star in the constellation Centaurus and the third brightest star in the sky. It is actually a triple star (see �081binary star); the two brighter stars orbit each other every 80 years, and the third, Proxima Centauri, is the closest star to the Sun, 4.2 light-years away, 0.1 light-years closer than the other two.

alpha decay the spontaneous alteration of the nucleus of a radioactive atom, which transmutes the atom from one atomic number to another through the emission of a helium nucleus (known as an alpha particle). As a result, the atomic number decreases by two and the atomic weight decreases by four.

alphanumeric data data made up of any of the letters of the alphabet and any digit from 0 to 9. The classification of data according to the type or types of character contained enables computer validation systems to check the accuracy of data: a computer can be programmed to reject entries that contain the wrong type of character. For example, a person's name would be rejected if it contained any numeric data, and a bank-account number would be rejected if it contained any alphabetic data. A car's registration number, by comparison, would be expected to contain alphanumeric data but no punctuation marks.

alpha particle positively charged, high-energy particle emitted from the nucleus of a radioactive ⟡atom. It is one of the products of the spontaneous disintegration of radioactive elements (see ⟡radioactivity) such as radium and thorium, and is identical with the nucleus of a helium atom—that is, it consists of two protons and two neutrons. The process of emission, **alpha decay**, transforms one element into another, decreasing the atomic (or proton) number by two and the atomic mass (or nucleon number) by four.

Because of their large mass alpha particles have a short range of only a few centimeters in air, and can be stopped by a sheet of paper. They have a strongly ionizing effect (see ⟡ionizing radiation) on the molecules that they strike, and are therefore capable of damaging living cells. Alpha particles traveling in a vacuum are deflected slightly by magnetic and electric fields.

alphorn wind instrument consisting of a straight wooden tube terminating in a conical endpiece with upturned bell, sometimes up to 12 ft/4 m in length. It sounds a harmonic series and is used to summon cattle and serenade tourists in the highlands of central Europe.

Alps mountain chain, the barrier between N Italy and France, Germany and Austria.

Famous peaks include *Mont Blanc*, the highest at 15,777 ft/4,809 m, first climbed by Jacques Balmat and Michel Paccard 1786; *Matterhorn* in the Pennine Alps, 14,694 ft/4,479 m, first climbed by Edward Whymper 1865 (four of the party of seven were killed when a rope broke during their descent); *Eiger* in the Bernese Alps/Oberland, 13,030 ft/3,970 m, with a near-vertical rock wall on the N face, first climbed 1858; *Jungfrau*, 13,673 ft/4,166 m; and *Finsteraarhorn* 14,027 ft/4,275 m.

Famous passes include *Brenner*, the lowest, Austria/Italy; *Great St Bernard*, one of the highest, 8,113 ft/2,472 m, Italy/Switzerland (by which Napoleon marched into Italy 1800); *Little St Bernard*, Italy/France (which Hannibal is thought to have used); and *St Gotthard*, S Switzerland, which Suvorov used when ordered by the tsar to withdraw his troops from Italy. All have been superseded by all-weather road/rail tunnels. The Alps extend into Yugoslavia and N Albania with the Julian and Dinaric Alps.

Alps, Australian highest area of the E Highlands in Victoria/New South Wales, Australia, noted for winter sports. They include the *Snowy mountains* and *Mount Kosciusko*, Australia's highest mountain, 7,316 ft/2,229 m, first noted by Polish-born Paul Strzelecki 1829 and named after a Polish hero.

Alps, Lunar mountain range on the Moon, NE of the Sea of Showers, cut by a valley 93 mi/150 km long.

Alps, Southern range of mountains running the entire length of South Island, New Zealand. They are forested to the west, with scanty scrub to the east. The highest point is Mt Cook, 12,349 ft/3,764 m. Scenic features include gorges, glaciers, lakes, and waterfalls. Among its lakes are those at the southern end of the range: Manapouri, Te Anau, and the largest, Wakatipu, 52 mi/83 km long, which lies about 1,000 ft/300 m above sea level and has a depth of 1,242 ft/378 m.

Alsace region of France; area 3,204 sq mi/8,300 sq km; population (1986) 1,600,000. It consists of the *départements* of Bas-Rhin and Haut-Rhin, and its capital is Strasbourg.

Alsace-Lorraine area of NE France, lying west of the river Rhine. It forms the French regions of ⟡Alsace and ⟡Lorraine. The former iron and steel industries are being replaced by electronics, chemicals, and precision engineering. The German dialect spoken does not have equal rights with French, and there is autonomist sentiment.

Alsace-Lorraine formed part of Celtic Gaul in Caesar's time, was invaded by the Alemanni and other Germanic tribes in the 4th century, and remained part of the German Empire until the 17th century. In 1648 part of the territory was ceded to France; in 1681 Louis XIV seized Strasbourg. The few remaining districts were seized by France after the French Revolution. Conquered by Germany 1870–71 (chiefly for its iron ores), it was regained by France 1919, then again annexed by Germany 1940–44, when it was liberated by the Allies.

Alsatia old name for ⟡Alsace, formerly part of Germany.

Alsatian breed of dog known officially from 1977 as the *German shepherd*. It is about 26 in/63 cm tall and has a wolflike appearance, a thick coat with many varieties of coloring, and a distinctive gait. Alsatians are used as police dogs because of their high intelligence.

They were introduced from Germany into Britain and the US after World War I.

Altai territory of the Russian Federation, in SW Siberia; area 101,043 sq mi/261,700 sq km; capital Barnaul; population (1985) 2,744,000. Industries include mining, light engineering, chemicals, and timber. Altai was colonized by the Russians from the 18th century.

Altai Mountains mountain system of W Siberia and Mongolia. It is divided into two parts, the Russian Altai, which includes the highest peak, Mount Belukha, 14,783 ft/4,506 m, and the Mongolian or Great Altai.

Altair or *Alpha Aquilae* brightest star in the constellation Aquila and the 12th brightest star in the sky. It is a white star 16 light-years away and forms the so-called Summer Triangle with the stars Deneb (in the constellation Cygnus) and Vega (in Lyra).

Altamira caves decorated with Paleolithic wall paintings, the first such to be discovered, 1879. The paintings are realistic depictions of bison, deer, and horses in polychrome (several colors). The caves are near the village of Santillana del Mar in Santander province, N Spain; other well-known Paleolithic cave paintings are in ⟡Lascaux, SW France.

Altamira Amazonian town in the state of Pará, NE Brazil, situated at the junction of the Trans-Amazonian Highway with the Xingu River, 400 mi/700 km SW of Belém; population (1991) 157,884. In 1989 a protest by Brazilian Indians and environmentalists against the building of six dams focused world attention on the devastation of the Amazon rainforest.

Altdorf capital of the Swiss canton Uri at the head of Lake Lucerne, Switzerland; population 9,000. It was the scene of the legendary exploits of William ⟡Tell.

Altdorfer Albrecht *c.* 1480–1538. German painter and printmaker, active in Regensburg, Bavaria. Altdorfer's work, inspired by the linear, Classical style of the Italian Renaissance, often depicts dramatic landscapes that are out of scale with the figures in the paintings. His use of light creates tension and effects of movement. Many of his works are of religious subjects.

With Albrecht Dürer and Lucas Cranach, Altdorfer is regarded as one of the leaders of the German Renaissance. *St George and the Dragon* 1510 (Alte Pinakothek, Munich) is an example of his landscape style; *The Battle of Issus* 1529 (also Munich) is a dramatic panorama.

alternate angles a pair of angles that lie on opposite sides and at opposite ends of a transversal (a line that cuts two or more lines in the same plane). The alternate angles formed by a transversal of two parallel lines are equal.

alternating current (AC) electric current that flows for an interval of time in one direction and then in the opposite direction, that is, a current that flows in alternately reversed directions through or around a circuit. Electric energy is usually generated as alternating current in a power station, and alternating currents may be used for both power and lighting.

The advantage of alternating current over direct current (DC), as from a battery, is that its voltage can be raised or lowered economically by a transformer: high voltage for generation and transmission, and low voltage for safe utilization. Railways, factories, and domestic appliances, for example, use alternating current.

alternation of generations typical life cycle of terrestrial plants and some seaweeds, in which there are two distinct forms occurring alternately: *diploid* (having two sets of chromosomes) and *haploid* (one set of chromosomes). The diploid generation produces haploid spores by ⟡meiosis, and is called the sporophyte, while the haploid generation produces gametes (sex cells), and is called the gametophyte. The gametes fuse to form a diploid ⟡zygote which develops into a new sporophyte; thus the sporophyte and gametophyte alternate.

alternative energy energy from sources that are renewable and ecologically safe, as opposed to sources that are nonrenewable with toxic by-products, such as coal, oil, or gas (fossil fuels), and uranium (for nuclear power). The most important alternative energy source is flowing water, harnessed as ⟡hydroelectric power. Other sources include the oceans' tides and waves, wind (harnessed by windmills and wind turbines), the Sun (⟡solar energy), and the heat trapped in the Earth's crust (⟡geothermal energy).

alternative medicine see ⟡medicine, alternative.

alternator electricity ⟡generator that produces an alternating current.

Altgeld John Peter 1847–1902. US political and social reformer. Born in Prussia, he was taken in infancy to the US. During the Civil War he served in the Union army. He was a judge of the Supreme Court in Chicago 1886–91, and as governor of Illinois 1893–97 was a champion of the worker against the government-backed power of big business.

Althing parliament of Iceland, established

about 930, the oldest in the world. It was dissolved 1800, revived 1843 as an advisory body, and became a legislative body again 1874. It has an upper and a lower house comprising one-third and two-thirds of its members respectively.

altimeter instrument used in aircraft that measures altitude, or height above sea level. The common type is a form of aneroid ⟡barometer, which works by sensing the differences in air pressure at different altitudes. This must continually be recalibrated because of the change in air pressure with changing weather conditions. The ⟡radar altimeter measures the height of the aircraft above the ground, measuring the time it takes for radio pulses emitted by the aircraft to be reflected. Radar altimeters are essential features of automatic and blind-landing systems.

Altiplano densely populated upland plateau of the Andes of South America, stretching from S Peru to NW Argentina. The height of the Altiplano is 10,000–13,000 ft/3,000–4,000 m.

altitude in geometry, the perpendicular distance from a ⟡vertex (corner) of a figure, such as a triangle, to the base (the side opposite the vertex).

Altman Robert 1925– . US maverick film director. His antiwar comedy *M.A.S.H.* 1970 was a critical and commercial success; subsequent films include *McCabe and Mrs Miller* 1971, *The Long Goodbye* 1973, *Nashville* 1975, *Popeye* 1980, and *The Player* 1992.

Alton city in W Illinois, on the Mississippi River, just NE of St Louis, Missouri. It is an industrial center with flour mills and oil refineries; population (1980) 34,171. Site of the Lincoln–Douglas debates 1858.

Altoona city in S central Pennsylvania, in the Allegheny Mountains, NW of Harrisburg. There is coal mining, and it is a railroad manufacturing and repair center; population (1980) 57,078. The first steel railroad tracks in the US were laid from Pittsburgh to Altoona.

altruism in biology, helping another individual of the same species to reproduce more effectively, as a direct result of which the altruist may leave fewer offspring itself. Female honey bees (workers) behave altruistically by rearing sisters in order to help their mother, the queen bee, reproduce, and forego any possibility of reproducing themselves.

ALU abbreviation for ⟡*arithmetic and logic unit.*

alum any double sulfate of a monovalent metal or radical (such as sodium, potassium, or ammonium) and a trivalent metal (such as aluminum or iron). The commonest alum is the double sulfate of potassium and aluminum, $K_2Al_2(SO_4)_4 \cdot 24H_2O$, a white crystalline powder that is readily soluble in water. It is used in curing animal skins. Other alums are used in papermaking and to fix dye in the textile industry.

alumina or *corundum* Al_2O_3 oxide of aluminum, widely distributed in clays, slates, and shales. It is formed by the decomposition of the feldspars in granite and used as an abrasive. Typically it is a white powder, soluble in most strong acids or caustic alkalis but not in water. Impure alumina is called "emery." Rubies and sapphires are corundum gemstones.

aluminum lightweight, silver-white, ductile and malleable, metallic element, symbol Al,

atomic number 13, atomic weight 26.9815. It is the third most abundant element (and the most abundant metal) in the Earth's crust, of which it makes up about 8.1% by mass. It oxidizes rapidly, the layer of oxide on its surface making it highly resistant to tarnish and is an excellent conductor of electricity. In its pure state aluminum is a weak metal, but when combined with elements such as copper, silicon, or magnesium it forms alloys of great strength. In nature it is found only in the combined state in many minerals, and is prepared commercially from the ore bauxite.

The pure metal was not readily obtained until the middle of the 19th century. Because of its light weight (specific gravity 2.70) it is widely used in the shipbuilding and aircraft industries. Consumer uses include food and beverage packaging, foil, outdoor furniture, and homebuilding materials.

The name comes from the Latin for ⟡alumina.

aluminum ore raw material from which aluminum is extracted. The main ore is bauxite, a mixture of minerals, found in economic quantities in Australia, Guinea, West Indies, and several other countries.

Alva or *Alba* Ferdinand Alvarez de Toledo, duke of 1508–1582. Spanish politician and general. He successfully commanded the Spanish armies of the Holy Roman emperor Charles V and his son Philip II of Spain. In 1567 he was appointed governor of the Netherlands, where he set up a reign of terror to suppress Protestantism and the revolt of the Netherlands. In 1573 he was recalled at his own request. He later led a successful expedition against Portugal 1580–81.

Alvarado Pedro de *c.* 1485–1541. Spanish conquistador. In 1519 he accompanied Hernándo Cortés in the conquest of Mexico. In 1523–24 he conquered Guatemala.

Alvarez Luis Walter 1911–1988. US physicist who led the research team that discovered the Xi-zero atomic particle 1959. He had worked on the US atomic bomb project for two years, at Chicago and Los Alamos, New Mexico, during World War II. He was awarded a Nobel Prize 1968.

Alvarez was professor of physics at the University of California from 1945 and an associate director of the Lawrence Livermore Radiation Laboratory 1954–59. In 1980 he was responsible for the theory that dinosaurs disappeared because a meteorite crashed into Earth 70 million years ago, producing a dust cloud that blocked out the Sun for several years, and causing dinosaurs and plants to die.

Alvarez Quintero Serafin 1871–1938 and Joaquin 1873–1945. Spanish dramatists. The brothers, born near Seville, always worked together and from 1897 produced some 200 plays, principally dealing with Andalusia. Among them are *Papá Juan: Centenario* 1909 and *Los Mosquitos* 1928.

alveolus (plural *alveoli*) one of the many thousands of tiny air sacs in the ⟡lungs in which exchange of oxygen and carbon dioxide takes place between air and the bloodstream.

Alzheimer's disease common manifestation of ⟡dementia, thought to afflict one in 20 people over 65. Attacking the brain's "gray matter," it is a disease of mental processes rather than physical function, characterized by memory loss and progressive intellectual impairment.

It was first described by Alois Alzheimer

1906. The cause is unknown, although a link with high levels of aluminum in drinking water was discovered 1989. It has also been suggested that the disease may result from a defective protein circulating in the blood. Under the electron microscope, small plaques of abnormal protein can be seen within the brain, and tiny fibers, called neurofibrils, which are normally aligned with the nerve cells, are seen to form "tangles." There is no treatment, but recent insights into the molecular basis of the disease may aid the search for a drug to counter its effects. For example, one type of early-onset Alzheimer's disease has been shown to be related to a defective gene on chromosome 21.

AM in physics, abbreviation for *amplitude* ⟡*modulation*, one way in which radio waves are altered for the transmission of broadcasting signals. AM is constant in frequency, and varies the amplitude of the transmitting wave in accordance with the signal being broadcast.

a.m. or *A.M.* abbreviation for *ante meridiem* (Latin "before noon").

Amagasaki industrial city on the NW outskirts of Osaka, Honshu island, Japan; population (1989) 493,200.

Amal radical Lebanese ⟡Shiite military force, established by Musa Sadr in the 1970s; its headquarters are in Borj al-Barajneh. The movement split into extremist and moderate groups 1982, but both sides agreed on the aim of increasing Shiite political representation in Lebanon.

Amal guerrillas were responsible for many of the attacks and kidnappings in Lebanon during the 1980s, although subsequently the group came to be considered one of the more mainstream elements on the Lebanese political scene. The Amal militia under Nabih ⟡Berri fought several bloody battles against the Hezbollah (Party of God) in 1988.

Amalekite in the Old Testament, a member of an ancient Semitic people of SW Palestine and the Sinai peninsula. According to Exodus 17 they harried the rear of the Israelites after their crossing of the Red Sea, were defeated by Saul and David, and were destroyed in the reign of Hezekiah.

Amalfi port 24 mi/39 km SE of Naples, Italy, situated at the foot of Monte Cerrato, on the Gulf of Salerno; population 7,000. For 700 years it was an independent republic. It is an ancient archiepiscopal see (seat of an archbishop) and has a Romanesque cathedral.

amalgam any alloy of mercury with other metals. Most metals will form amalgams, except iron and platinum. Amalgam is used in dentistry for filling teeth, and usually contains copper, silver, and zinc as the main alloying ingredients. This amalgam is pliable when first mixed and then sets hard, but the mercury leaches out and may cause a type of heavy-metal poisoning.

Amalgamation, the process of forming an amalgam, is a technique sometimes used to extract gold and silver from their ores. The ores are treated with mercury, which combines with the precious metals.

Amanita genus of fungi (see ⟡fungus), distinguished by a ring, or *volva*, round the stem, warty patches on the cap, and the clear white color of the gills. Many of the species are brightly colored and highly poisonous.

The fly agaric *A. muscaria* is a dangerous,

poisonous toadstool with a white-spotted red cap, which grows under birch or pine. The buff-colored ⟩death cap *A. phalloides* is deadly.

Amarillo town in the Texas panhandle; population (1980) 149,230. The center of the world's largest cattle-producing area, it processes the live animal into frozen supermarket packets in a single continuous operation on an assembly line. It is also a center for assembly of nuclear warheads.

Amarna tablets collection of Egyptian clay tablets with cuneiform inscriptions, found in the ruins of the ancient city of ⟩Akhetaton on the east bank of the Nile. The majority of the tablets, which comprise royal archives and letters of 1411–1375 BC, are in the British Museum.

Amaterasu in Japanese mythology, the sun-goddess, grandmother of Jimmu Tenno, first ruler of Japan, from whom the emperors claimed to be descended.

Amati Italian family of violin-makers, who worked in Cremona, about 1550–1700. *Nicolo Amati* (1596–1684) taught Andrea ⟩Guarneri and Antonio ⟩Stradivari.

Nicolo's grandfather Andrea (*c.* 1520–*c.* 1580) brought the violin to its classic form.

amatol explosive consisting of ammonium nitrate and TNT (trinitrotoluene) in almost any proportions.

Amazon (Indian *Amossona* "destroyer of boats") South American river, the world's second longest, 4,080 mi/6,570 km, and the largest in volume of water. Its main headstreams, the Marañón and the Ucayali, rise in central Peru and unite to flow E across Brazil for about 2,500 mi/4,000 km. It has 30,000 mi/48,280 km of navigable waterways, draining 2,750,000 sq mi/7,000,000 sq km, nearly half the South American land mass. It reaches the Atlantic on the equator, its estuary 50 mi/80 km wide, discharging a volume of water so immense that 40 mi/64 km out to sea, fresh water remains at the surface. The Amazon basin covers 3 million sq mi/7.5 million sq km, of which 2 million sq mi/5 million sq km is tropical forest containing 30% of all known plant and animal species (80,000 known species of trees, 3,000 known species of land vertebrates, 2,000 freshwater fish). It is the wettest region on Earth; average rainfall 8.3 ft/2.54 m a year. Independent estimates and Landsat surveys indicated a deforestation of 12% by 1985 (up from 0.6% in 1975).

The opening up of the Amazon river basin to settlers from the overpopulated east coast has resulted in a massive burning of tropical forest to create both arable and pasture land. Brazil, with one-third of the world's remaining tropical rainforest, has 55,000 species of flowering plant; half of which are only found in Brazilian Amazonia. The problems of soil erosion, the disappearance of potentially useful plant and animal species, and the possible impact of large-scale forest clearance on global warming of the atmosphere have become environmental issues of international concern.

Amazon in Greek mythology, a member of a group of legendary female warriors living near the Black Sea, who cut off their right breasts to use the bow more easily. Their queen, Penthesilea, was killed by Achilles at the siege of Troy. The term Amazon has come to mean a large, strong woman.

The Amazons attacked Theseus and besieged him at Athens, but were defeated, and Theseus took the Amazon Hippolyta captive; she later gave birth to ⟩Hippolytus.

Amazonia those regions of Brazil, Colombia, Ecuador, Peru, and Bolivia lying within the basin of the Amazon River.

Amazonian Indian indigenous inhabitant of the Amazon River Basin in South America. The majority of the societies are kin-based; traditional livelihood includes hunting and gathering, fishing, and shifting cultivation. A wide range of indigenous languages are spoken. Numbering perhaps 2.5 million in the 16th century, they had been reduced to perhaps one-tenth of that number by the 1820s. Their rainforests are being destroyed for mining and ranching, and Indians are being killed, transported, or assimilated.

Amazon Pact treaty signed 1978 by Bolivia, Brazil, Colombia, Ecuador, Guyana, Peru, Suriname, and Venezuela to protect and control the industrial or commercial development of the Amazon River.

ambassador officer of the highest rank in the diplomatic service, who represents the head of one sovereign state at the court or capital of another.

amber fossilized resin from coniferous trees of the Middle Tertiary period. It is often washed ashore on the Baltic coast with plant and animal specimens preserved in it; many extinct species have been found preserved in this way. It ranges in color from red to yellow, and is used to make jewelry.

ambergris fatty substance, resembling wax, found in the stomach and intestines of the sperm ⟩whale. It is found floating in warm seas, and is used in perfumery as a fixative.

Basically intestinal matter, ambergris is not the result of disease, but the product of an otherwise normal intestine. The name derives from the French *ambre gris* (gray amber).

Ambler Eric 1909– . English novelist. He used Balkan/Levant settings in the thrillers *The Mask of Dimitrios* 1939 and *Journey into Fear* 1940.

amblyopia reduced vision without apparent eye disorder.

Amboina or *Ambon* small island in the Moluccas, republic of Indonesia; population (1980) 209,000. The town of Amboina, formerly an historic center of Dutch influence, has shipyards.

Amboise Jacques d' 1934– . US dancer who created roles in many of George ⟩Balanchine's greatest works as a principal dancer with New York City Ballet. He also appeared in films and TV productions, including *Seven Brides for Seven Brothers* 1954.

Ambrose, St *c.* 340–397. One of the early Christian leaders and theologians known as the Fathers of the Church. Feast day Dec 7.

ambrosia (Greek "immortal") food of the gods, which was supposed to confer eternal life upon all who ate it.

Ambrosian chant in Christian church music, reformed chant introduced by St Ambrose in the 4th century. The number of available modes was reduced to four; the interval of the fifth was established as the basis of tonal music, having a lower key note, from which the chant rose and to which it returned; and a higher dominant was established at the fifth, around which the chant was elaborated. Ambrosian chant retains many features of Middle Eastern religious chant.

ameba any of a number of one-celled organisms, especially of the genus *Amoeba*, that move and feed by extensions of their colorless gelatinous protoplasm. They reproduce by ⟩binary fission. Some members of the genus *Entamoeba* are harmful parasites. See also ⟩amebiasis.

amebiasis ongoing infection of the intestines, caused by the ameba *Entamoeba histolytica*, resulting in chronic dysentery and consequent weakness and dehydration. Endemic in the Third World, it is now occurring in North America and Europe.

amen Hebrew word signifying affirmation ("so be it"), commonly used at the close of a Jewish or Christian prayer or hymn. As used by Jesus in the New Testament it was traditionally translated "verily."

Amenhotep four Egyptian pharaohs, including:

Amenhotep III King of Egypt (*c.* 1400 BC) who built great monuments at Thebes, including the temples at Luxor. Two portrait statues at his tomb were known to the Greeks as the colossi of Memnon; one was cracked, and when the temperature changed at dawn it gave out an eerie sound, then thought supernatural. His son *Amenhotep IV* changed his name to ⟩Ikhnaton.

America the W hemisphere of the Earth, containing the continents of North America and

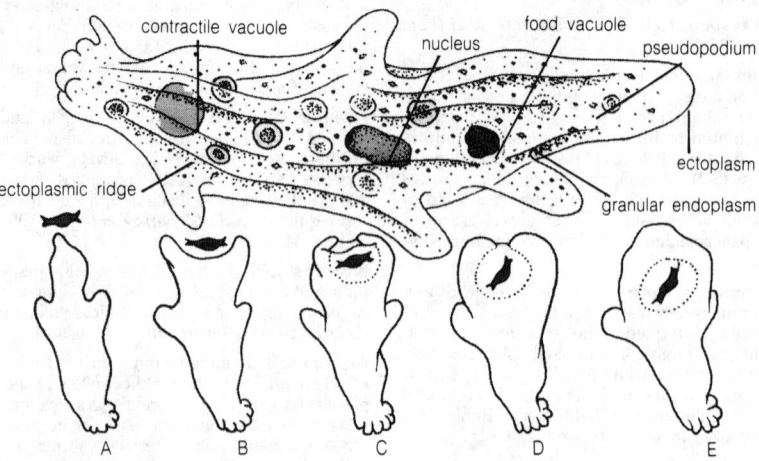

ameba *The amebas are among the simplest living organisms, consisting of a single cell.*

South America. This great land mass extends from the Arctic to the Antarctic, from beyond 75° N to past 55° S. The area is about 16 million sq mi/42 million sq km, and the estimated population is over 500 million. Politically, it consists of 36 nations and US, British, French, and Dutch dependencies.

The name America is derived from Amerigo Vespucci, the Florentine navigator who was erroneously credited with being the first European to reach the (South) American mainland 1497. The name is also popularly used worldwide to refer to the United States of America, a usage that many Canadians, South Americans, and other non-US Americans dislike.

American Ballet Theater (ABT) US company founded 1939 (as Ballet Theater), aiming to present both Classical and contemporary American ballet. ABT has a repertoire of exemplary range and quality with celebrity guest appearances. Based in New York, the company tours annually, and is considered one of the top six ballet companies in the world.

Among ABT's first ballerinas were Alicia Markova and Alicia Alonso. In the 1970s Soviet dancers defecting to the West—Rudolf Nureyev, Natalia Makarova, and Mikhail Baryshnikov (artistic director 1980–89)—enhanced the Classical repertory.

American Civil War 1861–65; see ⟨>Civil War, American.

American Federation of Labor and Congress of Industrial Organizations (AFL–CIO) federation of North American labor unions, currently representing about 20% of the work force in North America.

The AFL was founded 1886, superseding the Federation of Organized Trades and Labor Unions of the US and Canada, and was initially a union of skilled craftworkers. The CIO was known in 1935 as the Committee on Industrial Organization (it adopted its present title 1937 after expulsion from the AFL for its opposition to the AFL policy of including only skilled workers). A merger reunited them 1955, bringing most unions into the national federation.

American Indian any of the aboriginal peoples of the Americas; the Arctic peoples (Inuit and Aleut) are often included, especially by the Bureau of Indian Affairs (BIA) of the Department of the Interior, responsible for overseeing policy on US Indian life, their reservations, education, and social welfare.

Columbus named them Indians in 1492, because he thought he had reached the East Indies. Instead, he had reached the West Indies, inhabited by peoples whose Asian ancestors had migrated, hunting their way from the Old World into the New World on the geological land bridge exposed by lowered sea level between Siberia and Alaska, during the glaciation of the last ⟨>Ice Age, some 65,000 to 30,000 years ago. Several migrations occurred after that time, during emergences of the land bridge, with the last being the Inuit and Aleut of about 3,000 to 1,000 years ago.

Hunting, fishing, and moving camp throughout the Americas, the migrants inhabited both continents, and their nearby islands, and settled all the ecological zones, from the most tropical to the most frozen, including the woodlands, deserts, plains, mountains, and river valleys, from the west coast to the east, and from the Arctic to the Antarctic. As they specialized, many kinds of societies evolved, speaking many languages: hunters and fishers

American Revolution: chronology

1773	A government tax on tea led Massachusetts citizens disguised as North American Indians to board British ships carrying tea and throw it into Boston harbor, the Boston Tea Party.
1774–75	The First Continental Congress was held in Philadelphia to call for civil disobedience in reply to British measures such as the Intolerable Acts, which closed the port of Boston and quartered British troops in private homes.
1775 April 19	Hostilities began at Lexington and Concord, Massachusetts. The first shots were fired when British troops, sent to seize illegal military stores and arrest rebel leaders John Hancock and Samuel Adams, were attacked by the local militia (minutemen).
May 10	Fort Ticonderoga, New York, was captured from the British.
June 17	The colonialists were defeated in the first battle of the Revolution, the Battle of Bunker Hill (which actually took place on Breed's Hill, nearby); George Washington was appointed colonial commander in chief soon afterwards.
1776 July 4	The Second Continental Congress issued the Declaration of Independence, which specified some of the colonists' grievances and called for a new form of government.
Aug 27	Washington was defeated at Long Island and was forced to evacuate New York and retire to Pennsylvania.
Dec 26	Washington recrossed the Delaware River and defeated the British at Trenton, New Jersey.
1777 Jan 3	Washington defeated the British at Princeton, New Jersey.
Sept 11–Oct 4	British general William Howe defeated Washington at Brandywine and Germantown and occupied Philadelphia.
Oct 17	British general John Burgoyne surrendered at Saratoga, New York, and was therefore unable to link up with Howe.
1778–78	Washington wintered at Valley Forge, Pennsylvania, enduring harsh conditions and seeing many of his troops leave to return to their families.
1778	France, with the support of its ally Spain, entered the war on the US side (John Paul Jones led a French-sponsored naval unit).
1780 May 12	The British captured Charleston, South Carolina, one of a series of British victories in the South, but alienated support by enforcing conscription.
1781 Oct 19	British general Charles Cornwallis, besieged in Yorktown, Virginia, by Washington and the French fleet, surrendered.
1782	Peace negotiations opened.
1783 Sept 3	The Treaty of Paris recognized American independence.

(the Inuit, the Athabaskans); specialized fishers (along the Northwest Coast); specialized hunters and gatherers (the Iroquois Nation, the Sioux of the Great Plains); specialized collectors (near the Great Lakes and in the Amazonian rainforests); farmers (the Hopi of the South west); and ancient civilizations (in Mexico—the Olmec, the Maya, the Aztec; in Peru—the Chimú, the Inca). Some of the specialized collectors of plants evolved into farmers, domesticating corn, beans, and squash in

American Indians: major tribes

Area	Tribe
North America	
Arctic	Inuit, Aleut
Sub-Arctic	Algonquin, Cree, Ottawa
NE Woodlands	Huron, Iroquois, Mohican, Shawnee
SE Woodlands	Cherokee, Choctaw, Creek, Hopewell, Natchez, Seminole
Great Plains	Blackfoot, Cheyenne, Comanche, Pawnee, Sioux
NW Coast	Chinook, Tlingit, Tsimshian
Desert West	Apache, Navaho, Pueblo, Hopi, Mohave, Shoshone
Central America	Maya, Aztec, Olmec
South America	
Eastern	Carib, Xingu
Central	Guaraní, Miskito
Western	Araucanian, Aymara, Chimú, Inca, Jivaro, Quechua

Mexico and Central America; potatoes, tomatoes, peppers, lima beans, avocados, peanuts, manioc, sweet potatoes, and tobacco in South America. Farming surpluses led to trade and taxation, which became the basis for the rise of civilizations, where the rulers and the priesthood prized jade, cacao (chocolate), and vanilla beans for ritual purposes; the arts and sciences were pursued—as was writing, astronomy, mathematics, engineering, architecture, and medicine; and crafts flourished—such as pottery, basketry, weaving, and the working of metals, wood, and leather. Militarism became a fact of life in many areas of North, Central, and South America, but political balances were disrupted and destroyed by the Spanish Conquest and subsequent European colonization.

distribution:

Canada 300,000, including the Inuit; the largest group is the Six Nations (Iroquois), with a reserve near Brantford, Ontario, for 7,000; they are members of the National Indian Brotherhood of Canada.

United States 1.6 million, almost 900,000 (including Inuit and Aleuts) living on or near reservations, mainly in Arizona, New Mexico, Utah (where the Navaho have the largest of all reservations), Oklahoma, Texas, Montana, Washington, North and South Dakota, and Wyoming. The rest (700,000) live among the general population. The population level is thought to be about the same as at the time of Columbus, but now includes many people who are of mixed ancestry. Although treaties exist between the US and many Indian nations, Indians were made citizens of the US in 1924. There is an organized American Indian Movement (AIM).

Latin America many mestizo (mixed Indian-

Spanish descent), among them half the 12 million in Bolivia and Peru. Since the 1960s they increasingly stress their Indian inheritance in terms of language and culture. The few Indian groups formerly beyond white contact are being transported and killed while their environment is destroyed with the clearing and industrial development of the Amazon Basin.

American Legion community organization in the US, originally for ex-servicemen of World War I, founded 1919. It has approximately 2.7 million members, and has admitted veterans of World War II, the Korean War, and the Vietnam War.

It has a strong national voice on issues concerning US veterans, and sponsors local welfare programs and essay contests.

American literature see ⇨United States: literature.

American Revolution revolt 1775–83 of the British North American colonies that resulted in the establishment of the United States of America.

It was caused by colonial resentment at the contemporary attitude that commercial or industrial interests of any colony should be subordinate to those of the mother country; and by the unwillingness of the colonists to pay for a standing army. It was also fueled by the colonists' antimonarchist sentiment and a desire to participate in the policies affecting them. *See also p. 35.*

American Samoa see ⇨Samoa, American.

American System, the in US history, a federal legislative program following the ⇨War of 1812 designed to promote an integrated national economy. It introduced tariffs to protect US industry from foreign competition, internal improvements to the transport network, and a national bank to facilitate economic growth.

America's Cup international yacht-racing trophy named after the US schooner *America*, owned by J L Stevens, who won a race around the Isle of Wight 1851.

Offered for a challenge in 1870, it is now contested every three or four years, and is a seven-race series. The US has dominated the race, only twice losing possession, in 1983 to Australia and in 1989 to New Zealand, then regaining it after a court battle. All races were held at Newport, Rhode Island, until 1987 when the Perth Yacht Club, Australia, hosted the series. Yachts are very expensive to produce and only syndicates can afford to provide a yacht capable of winning the trophy.

americium radioactive metallic element of the ⇨actinide series, symbol Am, atomic number 95, atomic weight 243.13; it was first synthesized 1944. It occurs in nature in minute quantities in ⇨pitchblende and other uranium ores, where it is produced from the decay of neutron-bombarded plutonium, and is the element with the highest atomic number that occurs in nature. It is synthesized in quantity only in nuclear reactors by the bombardment of plutonium with neutrons. Its longest-lived isotope is Am-243, with a half-life of 7,650 years.

The element was named by Glenn Seaborg, one of the team who first synthesized it, after the United States of *America*, where transuranics (elements with an atomic number greater than 92) were first produced.

Amerindian contraction of ⇨American Indian.

Ames Adelbert 1880–1955. US scientist who studied optics and the psychology of visual

alanine $CH_3CH \cdot (NH_2) \cdot COOH$

tyrosine $C_6H_4OH \cdot CH_2CH \cdot (NH_2) \cdot COOH$

cysteine $SH \cdot CH_2CH \cdot (NH_2) \cdot COOH$

glycine NH_2CH_2COOH

— covalent bond   ● carbon atom   Ⓝ nitrogen atom
○ hydrogen atom   Ⓞ oxygen atom   Ⓢ sulphur atom

amino acid *Amino acids are natural organic compounds that make up proteins and are considered to be the basic molecules of life.*

perception. He concluded that much of what a person sees depends on what he or she expects to see, based (consciously or unconsciously) on previous experience.

Ames Research Center US space-research (NASA) installation at Mountain View, California, for the study of aeronautics and life sciences. It has managed the Pioneer series of planetary probes and is involved in the search for extraterrestial life.

amethyst variety of ⇨quartz, SiO_2, colored violet by the presence of small quantities of manganese; used as a semiprecious stone. Amethysts are found chiefly in the Ural Mountains, India, the US, Uruguay, and Brazil.

Amhara member of an ethnic group comprising approximately 25% of the population of Ethiopia; 13 million (1987). The Amhara are traditionally farmers. They speak Amharic, a language of the Semitic branch of the Afro-Asiatic family. Most are members of the Ethiopian Christian Church.

amicus curiae (Latin "friend of the court") in law, a lawyer advising the court in a legal case as a neutral person, not representing either side.

Amida Buddha the "Buddha of immeasurable light." Japanese name for *Amitābha*, the Buddha venerated in Pure Land Buddhism. He presides over the Western Paradise (the Buddha-land of his own creation), and through his unlimited compassion and power to save, true believers can achieve enlightenment and be reborn.

Amiens ancient city of NE France at the confluence of the rivers Somme and Avre; capital of Somme *département* and center of a market-gardening region irrigated by canals; population (1982) 154,500. It has a magnificent Gothic cathedral with a spire 370 ft/113 m high and gave its name to the battles of Aug 1918, when British field marshal Douglas Haig launched his victorious offensive in World War I.

Amin (Dada) Idi 1926– . Ugandan politician, president 1971–79. He led the coup that deposed Milton Obote 1971, expelled the Asian community 1972, and exercised a reign of terror over his people. He fled to Libya when insurgent Ugandan and Tanzanian troops invaded the country 1979.

amine any of a class of organic chemical compounds in which one or more of the hydrogen atoms of ammonia (NH_3) have been replaced by other groups of atoms.

Methyl amines have unpleasant ammonia odors and occur in decomposing fish. They are all gases at ordinary temperature. *Aromatic amine compounds* include aniline, which is used in dyeing.

amino acid water-soluble organic ⇨molecule, mainly composed of carbon, oxygen, hydrogen, and nitrogen, containing both a basic amine group (NH_2) and an acidic carboxyl (COOH) group. When two or more amino acids are joined together, they are known as ⇨peptides; ⇨proteins are made up of interacting polypeptides (peptide chains consisting of more than three amino acids) and are folded or twisted in characteristic shapes.

Many different proteins are found in the cells of living organisms, but they are all made up of the same 20 amino acids, joined together in varying combinations (although other types of amino acid do occur infrequently in nature). Eight of these, the *essential amino acids*, cannot be synthesized by humans and must be obtained from the diet. Children need a further two amino acids that are not essential for adults. Other animals also need some preformed amino acids in their diet, but green plants can manufacture all the amino acids they need from simpler molecules, relying on energy from the Sun and minerals (including nitrates) from the soil.

Amis Kingsley 1922– . English novelist and poet. His works include *Lucky Jim* 1954, a comic portrayal of life in a provincial university, and *Take a Girl Like You* 1960. He won the UK's Booker Prize 1986 for *The Old Devils*. He is the father of Martin Amis.

Amis Martin 1949– . English novelist. His works are characterized by their savage wit and include *The Rachel Papers* 1974, *Money* 1984, *London Fields* 1989, and *Time's Arrow* 1991.

Amman capital and chief industrial center of Jordan; population (1986) 1,160,000. It is a major communications center, linking historic trade routes across the Middle East.

ammeter instrument that measures electric current, usually in ⇨amperes.

Ammanati Bartolomeo 1511–1592. Italian

Mannerist sculptor and architect. His best known sculpture is the Fountain of Neptune in the Piazza della Signoria, Florence 1560–75. Ammanati rivaled Vasari as a Mannerist architect. He built the rusticated garden façade of the Palazzo Pitti 1560, Florence, and the graceful bridge of Sta Trinità, also in Florence, completed 1570 (destroyed 1944 but rebuilt).

Ammon in Egyptian mythology, the king of the gods, the equivalent of ⟡Zeus or ⟡Jupiter. The name is also spelled Amen/Amun, as in the name of the pharaoh Tutankh*amen*. In art, he is represented as a ram, as a man with a ram's head, or as a man crowned with feathers. He had temples at Siwa oasis, Libya, and Thebes, Egypt.

ammonia NH_3 colorless pungent-smelling gas, lighter than air and very soluble in water. It is made on an industrial scale by the ⟡Haber process, and used mainly to produce nitrogenous fertilizers, some explosives, and nitric acid.

In aquatic organisms and some insects, nitrogenous waste (from breakdown of amino acids and so on) is excreted in the form of ammonia, rather than urea as in mammals.

Ammonite member of an ancient Semitic people, mentioned in the Old Testament or Jewish Bible, who lived NW of the Dead Sea. Their capital was Amman, in present-day Jordan. They worshiped the god Moloch, to whom they offered human sacrifices. They were frequently at war with the Israelites.

ammonite extinct marine ⟡cephalopod mollusk of the order Ammonoidea, related to the modern nautilus. The shell was curled in a plane spiral and made up of numerous gas-filled chambers, the outermost containing the body of the animal. Many species flourished between 200 million and 65 million years ago, ranging in size from that of a small coin to 6 ft/2 m across.

ammonium chloride or *sal ammoniac* NH_4Cl a volatile salt that forms white crystals around volcanic craters. It is prepared synthetically for use in "dry-cell" batteries, fertilizers, and dyes.

amnesia loss or impairment of memory. As a clinical condition it may be caused by disease or injury to the brain, or by shock; in some cases it may be a symptom of an emotional disorder.

Amnesty International human-rights organization established in the UK 1961 to campaign for the release of political prisoners worldwide; it is politically unaligned. Amnesty International has 700,000 members, and section offices in 43 countries. The organization was awarded the Nobel Peace Prize 1977.

amniocentesis sampling the amniotic fluid surrounding a fetus in the womb for diagnostic purposes. It is used to detect Down's syndrome and other genetic abnormalities.

amnion innermost of three membranes that enclose the embryo within the egg (reptiles and birds) or within the uterus (mammals). It contains the amniotic fluid that helps to cushion the embryo.

Amorites ancient people of Semitic or Indo-European origin who were among the inhabitants of ⟡Canaan at the time of the Israelite invasion. They provided a number of Babylonian kings.

amortization in finance, the ending of a debt by paying it off gradually, over a period of time. The term is used to describe either the paying off of a cash debt or the accounting procedure by which the value of an asset is progressively reduced ("depreciated") over a number of years.

Amos book of the Old Testament written *c.* 750 BC. One of the ⟡prophets, Amos was a shepherd who foretold the destruction of Israel because of the people's abandonment of their faith.

Amoy ancient name for ⟡Xiamen, a port in SE China.

amp in physics, abbreviation for ampere, a unit of electrical current.

ampere SI unit (abbreviation amp, symbol A) of electrical current. Electrical current is measured in a similar way to water current, in terms of an amount per unit time; one ampere represents a flow of about 6.28×10^{18} ⟡electrons per second, or a rate of flow of charge of one coulomb per second.

The ampere is defined as the current that produces a specific magnetic force between two long, straight, parallel conductors placed one meter (3.3 ft) apart in a vacuum. It is named after the French scientist André Ampère.

Ampère André Marie 1775–1836. French physicist and mathematician who made many discoveries in electromagnetism and electrodynamics. He followed up the work of Hans ⟡Oersted on the interaction between magnets and electric currents, developing a rule for determining the direction of the magnetic field associated with an electric current. The ampere is named after him.

Ampère's rule rule developed by André Ampère connecting the direction of an electric current and its associated magnetic currents. It states that if a person were traveling along a current-carrying wire in the direction of conventional current flow (from the positive to the negative terminal), and carrying a magnetic compass, then the north pole of the compass needle would be deflected to the left-hand side.

amphetamine or *speed* powerful synthetic ⟡stimulant. Benzedrine was the earliest amphetamine marketed, used as a pep pill in World War II to help soldiers overcome fatigue, and until the 1970s amphetamines were prescribed by doctors as an appetite suppressant for weight loss; as an antidepressant, to induce euphoria; and as a stimulant, to increase alertness. Indications for its use today are very restricted because of severe side effects, including addiction and distorted behavior. It is a sulfate or phosphate form of $C_9H_{13}N$.

amphibian (Greek "double life") member of the vertebrate class Amphibia, which generally spend their larval (tadpole) stage in fresh water, transferring to land at maturity (after ⟡metamorphosis) and generally returning to water to breed. Like fish and reptiles, they continue to grow throughout life, and cannot maintain a temperature greatly differing from that of their environment. The class includes caecilians (wormlike in appearance), salamanders, frogs, and toads.

amphibole any one of a large group of rock-forming silicate minerals with an internal structure based on double chains of silicon and oxygen, and with a general formula $X_2Y_5Si_8O_{22}(OH)_2$; closely related to ⟡pyroxene. Amphiboles form orthorhombic, monoclinic, and triclinic ⟡crystals.

Amphiboles occur in a wide range of igneous and metamorphic rocks. Common examples are ⟡hornblende (X=Ca, Y=Mg, Fe, Al) and tremolite (*X*=Ca, *Y*=Mg).

Amphion in Greek mythology, one of the two sons of ⟡Zeus and Antiope. He built the walls of Thebes by drawing the stones into place with the music from his lyre, a gift from the god ⟡Hermes.

amphioxus or *lancelet* filter-feeding animal about 2.5 in/6 cm long with a fishlike shape and a notochord, a flexible rod that forms the supporting structure of its body. It lacks organs such as heart or eyes, and lives half-buried on the sea bottom. It is a primitive relative of the vertebrates.

amphitheater large oval or circular building used by the Romans for gladiatorial contests, fights of wild animals, and other similar events; it is a structure with an open space surrounded by rising rows of seats; the arena of an amphitheater is completely surrounded by the seats of the spectators, hence the name (Greek *amphi* "around"). The ⟡Colosseum in Rome, completed AD 80, held 50,000 spectators.

Amphitrite in Greek mythology, one of the daughters of Nereus and wife of the god ⟡Poseidon.

Amphitryon in Greek mythology, the husband of Alcmene, mother of ⟡Heracles.

amphora large two-handled narrow-necked pottery storage jar in the Graeco-Roman world, used for wine, oil, and dry goods.

amphoteric term used to describe the ability of some chemical compounds to behave either as an ⟡acid or as a ⟡base depending on their environment. For example, the metals aluminum and zinc, and their oxides and hydroxides, act as bases in acidic solutions and as acids in alkaline solutions.

Amino acids and proteins are also amphoteric, as they contain both a basic (amino, $-NH_2$) and an acidic (carboxyl, $-COOH$) group.

amplifier electronic device that magnifies the strength of a signal, such as a radio signal. The ratio of output signal strength to input signal strength is called the *gain* of the amplifier. As well as achieving high gain, an amplifier should be free from distortion and able to operate over a range of frequencies. Practical amplifiers are usually complex circuits, although simple amplifiers can be built from single transistors or valves.

amplitude maximum displacement of an oscillation from the equilibrium position. For a wave motion, it is the height of a crest (or the depth of a trough). With a sound wave, for example, amplitude corresponds to the intensity (loudness) of the sound. In AM (amplitude modulation) radio broadcasting, the required audio-frequency signal is made to modulate (vary slightly) the amplitude of a continuously transmitted radio carrier wave.

amplitude or *argument* in mathematics, the angle θ (theta) between the position vector of a ⟡complex number and the real axis. For the complex number z, the amplitude of $z = r(\cos θ + i \sin θ)$, in which r is the radius and $i = \sqrt{-1}$.

The expression $r(\cos θ + i \sin θ)$ is often abbreviated to r cis θ.

amplitude modulation (AM) method by which radio waves are altered for the transmission of broadcasting signals. AM is constant in frequency, and varies the amplitude of the transmitting wave in accordance with the signal being broadcast.

ampulla small vessel with a round body and narrow neck, used by the ancient Greeks and Romans for holding oil, perfumes, and so on; ampullae are used in the Christian church for holding water and wine at the Eucharist.

ampulla in the inner ◌ear, a slight swelling at the end of each semicircular canal, able to sense the motion of the head. The sense of balance largely depends on sensitive hairs within the ampulla responding to movements of fluid within the canal.

amputation loss of part or all of a limb or other body appendage through surgery or accident.

Amritsar industrial city in the Punjab, India; population (1981) 595,000. It is the holy city of ◌Sikhism, with the Guru Nanak University (named after the first Sikh guru) and the Golden Temple from which armed demonstrators were evicted by the Indian army under General Dayal 1984, 325 being killed. Subsequently, Indian prime minister Indira Gandhi was assassinated in reprisal. In 1919 it was the scene of the Amritsar Massacre.

Amritsar Massacre also called *Jallianwallah Bagh massacre* the killing of 379 Indians (and wounding of 1,200) in Amritsar, at the site of a Sikh religious shrine in the Punjab 1919. British troops under General Edward Dyer (1864–1927) opened fire without warning on a crowd of some 10,000, assembled to protest against the arrest of two Indian National Congress leaders.

Amsterdam capital of the Netherlands; population (1991) 1,002,400. Canals cut through the city link it with the North Sea and the Rhine, and as a Dutch port it is second only to Rotterdam. There is shipbuilding, printing, food processing, banking, and insurance.

Art galleries include the Rijksmuseum, Stedelijk, Vincent van Gogh Museum, and the Rembrandt house. Notable also are the Royal Palace 1655 and the Anne Frank house.

Amu Darya (formerly *Oxus*) river in central Asia, flowing 1,578 mi/2,530 km from the ◌Pamirs to the ◌Aral Sea.

Amundsen Roald 1872–1928. Norwegian explorer who in 1903–06 became the first person to navigate the ◌Northwest Passage. Beaten to the North Pole by US explorer Robert Peary 1910, he reached the South Pole ahead of Captain Scott 1911.

In 1918, Amundsen made an unsuccessful attempt to drift across the North Pole in the airship *Maud* and in 1925 tried unsuccessfully to fly from Spitsbergen, in the Arctic Ocean north of Norway, to the Pole by airplane. The following year he joined the Italian explorer Umberto Nobile (1885–1978) in the airship *Norge*, which circled the North Pole twice and landed in Alaska. Amundsen was killed in a plane crash over the Arctic Ocean while searching for Nobile and his airship *Italia*.

Amur river in E Asia. Formed by the Argun and Shilka rivers, the Amur enters the Sea of Okhotsk. At its mouth at Nikolevsk it is 10 mi/16 km wide. For much of its course of over 2,730 mi/4,400 km it forms, together with its tributary, the Ussuri, the boundary between Russia and China.

amylase one of a group of ◌enzymes that break down starches into their component molecules (sugars) for use in the body. It occurs widely in both plants and animals. In humans, it is found in saliva and in pancreatic juices.

Anabaptist (Greek "baptize again") member of any of various 16th-century radical Protestant sects. They believed in adult rather than child baptism, and sought to establish utopian communities. Anabaptist groups spread rapidly in N Europe, particularly in Germany, and were widely persecuted.

Notable Anabaptists included those in Moravia (the Hutterites) and Thomas Müntzer (1489–1525), a peasant leader who was executed for fomenting an uprising in Mühlhausen (now Mulhouse in E France). In Münster, Germany, Anabaptists controlled the city 1534–35. A number of Anabaptist groups, such as the Mennonites, Amish, and Hutterites, emigrated to North America, where they became known for their simple way of life and pacifism.

anabolic steroid any ◌hormone of the ◌steroid group that stimulates tissue growth. Its use in medicine is limited to the treatment of some anemias and breast cancers; it may help to break up blood clots. Side effects include aggressive behavior, masculinization in women, and, in children, reduced height.

It is used in sports, such as weight lifting and track and field, to increase muscle bulk for greater strength and stamina but it is widely condemned because of dangerous side effects. In 1988 the Canadian sprinter Ben Johnson was stripped of an Olympic gold medal for taking anabolic steroids.

anabolism process of building up body tissue, promoted by the influence of certain hormones. It is the constructive side of ◌metabolism, as opposed to catabolism.

anaconda South American snake *Eunectes murinus*, a member of the python and boa family, the Boidae. One of the largest snakes, growing to 30 ft/9 m or more, it is found in and near water, where it lies in wait for the birds and animals on which it feeds. The anaconda is not venomous, but kills its prey by coiling round it and squeezing until the creature suffocates.

Anaconda town in Montana, which had the world's largest copper smelter (closed 1980); population (1990) 10,278. The city was founded as Copperopolis 1883 by the Anaconda Copper Mining Company, and was incorporated as Anaconda 1888. The town is 5,300 ft/1,615 m above sea level and 26 mi/42 km NW of Butte.

anaerobic (of living organisms) not requiring oxygen for the release of energy from food molecules such as glucose. Anaerobic organisms include many bacteria, yeasts, and internal parasites.

Obligate anaerobes such as certain primitive bacteria cannot function in the presence of oxygen; but *facultative anaerobes*, like the fermenting yeasts and most bacteria, can function with or without oxygen. Anaerobic organisms release 19 times less of the available energy from their food than do ◌aerobic organisms.

In some bacteria, instead of oxygen, an inorganic compound, such as sulfate (SO_4), is the final acceptor of electrons stripped from food molecules during their breakdown.

In ◌fermentation (as practiced by yeasts) the final acceptor is an intermediate product of the glucose molecule being degraded.

Anaheim city in SW California, SE of Los Angeles. Its industries produce electronic and farm equipment and processed foods. Disneyland amusement park is here; population (1990) 266,406. Settled by German immigrants 1858 as a wine-producing community.

Analects the most important of the four books that contain the teachings and ideas of ◌Confucianism.

analog (of a quantity or device) changing continuously; by contrast a ◌digital quantity or device varies in series of distinct steps. For example, an analog clock measures time by means of a continuous movement of hands around a dial, whereas a digital clock measures time with a numerical display that changes in a series of discrete steps.

Most computers are digital devices. Therefore, any signals and data from an analog device must be passed through a suitable analog-to-digital converter before they can be received and processed by computer. Similarly, output signals from digital computers must be passed through a digital-to-analog converter before they can be received by an analog device.

analog computer computing device that performs calculations through the interaction of continuously varying physical quantities, such as voltages (as distinct from the more common ◌digital computer, which works with discrete quantities). An analog computer is said to operate in real time (corresponding to time in the real world), and can therefore be used to monitor and control other events as they happen.

Although common in engineering since the 1920s, analog computers are not general-purpose computers, but specialize in solving ◌differential calculus and similar mathematical problems. The earliest analog computing device is thought to be the flat, or planispheric, astrolabe, which originated in about the 8th century.

analysis branch of mathematics concerned with limiting processes on axiomatic number systems; ◌calculus of variations and infinitesimal calculus is now called analysis.

analysis in chemistry, the determination of the composition of substances; see ◌analytical chemistry.

analytic in philosophy, a term derived from ◌Kant: the converse of ◌synthetic. In an analytic judgment, the judgment provides no new knowledge; for example: "All bachelors are unmarried."

analytical chemistry branch of chemistry that deals with the determination of the chemical composition of substances.

Qualitative analysis determines the elements or compounds in a given sample, without necessarily finding their concentrations, using methods such as ◌chromatography and ◌spectroscopy.

Quantitative analysis determines exact composition in terms of concentration, using such techniques as titration (volumetric analysis) and weighing (gravimetric analysis).

analytical engine programmable computing device designed by Charles ◌Babbage 1833. It was based on the ◌difference engine but was intended to automate the whole process of calculation. It introduced many of the concepts of the digital computer but, because of limitations in manufacturing processes, was never built.

Among the concepts introduced were input and output, an arithmetic unit, memory, sequential operation, and the ability to make decisions based on data. It would have required at least 50,000 moving parts. The design was largely forgotten until some of Babbage's writings were rediscovered in 1937.

analytic geometry another name for ⇨coordinate geometry.

Ananda 5th century BC. Favorite disciple of the Buddha. At his plea, a separate order was established for women. He played a major part in collecting the teachings of the Buddha after his death.

anaphylaxis in medicine, a severe allergic response. Typically, the air passages become constricted, the blood pressure falls rapidly, and the victim collapses. A rare condition, anaphylaxis can occur following wasp or bee stings or treatment with some drugs.

anarchism (Greek *anarkhos* "without ruler") political belief that society should have no government, laws, police, or other authority, but should be a free association of all its members. It does not mean "without order;" most theories of anarchism imply an order of a very strict and symmetrical kind, but they maintain that such order can be achieved by cooperation. Anarchism must not be confused with nihilism (a purely negative and destructive activity directed against society); anarchism is essentially a pacifist movement.

Religious anarchism, claimed by many anarchists to be exemplified in the early organization of the Christian church, has found expression in the social philosophy of the Russian writer Tolstoy and the Indian nationalist Gandhi. The growth of political anarchism may be traced through the British Romantic writers William Godwin and Shelley to the 1848 revolutionaries P J ⇨Proudhon in France and the Russian ⇨Bakunin, who had a strong following in Europe.

The theory of anarchism is expressed in the works of the Russian revolutionary ⇨Kropotkin.

Anastasia 1901–1918. Russian Grand Duchess, youngest daughter of ⇨Nicholas II. During the Russian Revolution she was presumed shot with her parents by the Bolsheviks after the Revolution of 1917, but it has been alleged that Anastasia escaped.

Those who claimed her identity included Anna Anderson (1902–1984). Alleged by some detractors to be a Pole, Franziska Schanzkowski, she was rescued from a Berlin canal 1920. The German Federal Supreme Court found no proof of her claim 1970.

anastomosis in medicine, a connection between two vessels (usually blood vessels) in the body. Surgical anastomosis involves the deliberate joining of two vessels or hollow parts of an organ; for example, when part of the intestine has been removed and the remaining free ends are brought together and stitched.

Anatolia (Turkish *Anadolu*) alternate name for Turkey-in-Asia.

anatomy study of the structure of the body and its component parts, especially the ⇨human body, as distinguished from physiology, which is the study of bodily functions.

Herophilus of Chalcedon (*c.* 330–*c.* 260 BC) is regarded as the founder of anatomy. In the 2nd century AD, the Graeco-Roman physician Galen produced an account of anatomy that was the only source of anatomical knowledge until *On the Working of the Human Body* 1543 by Andreas Vesalius. In 1628, William Harvey published his demonstration of the circulation of the blood. Following the invention of the microscope, the Italian Malpighi and the Dutch Leeuwenhoek were able to found the study of ⇨histology. In 1747, Albinus (1697–1770), with

the help of the artist Wandelaar (1691–1759), produced the most exact account of the bones and muscles, and in 1757–65 Albrecht von Haller gave the most complete and exact description of the organs that had yet appeared. Among the anatomical writers of the early 19th century are the surgeon Charles Bell (1774–1842), Jonas Quain (1796–1865), and Henry Gray (1825–1861). Later in the century came stain techniques for microscopic examination, and the method of mechanically cutting very thin sections of stained tissues (using X-rays; see ⇨radiography). Radiographic anatomy has been one of the triumphs of the 20th century, which has also been marked by immense activity in embryological investigation.

Anaximander *c.* 610–*c.* 546 BC. Greek astronomer and philosopher. He claimed that the Earth was a cylinder three times wider than it is deep, motionless at the center of the universe, and he is credited with drawing the first geographical map. He said that the celestial bodies were fire seen through holes in the hollow rims of wheels encircling the Earth. According to Anaximander, the first animals came into being from moisture and the first humans grew inside fish, emerging once fully developed.

ancestor worship religious rituals and beliefs oriented toward deceased members of a family or group, as a symbolic expression of values or in the belief that the souls of the dead remain involved in this world and are capable of influencing current events.

Anchises in Classical mythology, a member of the Trojan royal family, loved by the goddess ⇨Aphrodite. Their son ⇨Aeneas rescued his father on the fall of ⇨Troy and carried him from the burning city on his shoulders. The story forms an episode in ⇨Virgil's *Aeneid*.

Anchorage port and largest city of Alaska, at the head of Cook Inlet; population (1990) 226,340. Established 1918, Anchorage is an important center of administration, communication, and commerce. Oil and gas extraction and fish canning are also important to the local economy.

Two US military bases are nearby—Fort Richardson and Elmendorf Air Force Base. Alaska Pacific University and a branch of the University of Alaska are here. The Fur Rendezvous winter carnival is an annual event. The 1964 earthquake that killed 114 people was the most powerful in North American recorded history—8.4 on the Richter scale.

anchovy small fish *Engraulis encrasicholus* of the ⇨herring family. It is fished extensively, being abundant in the Mediterranean, and is also found on the Atlantic coast of Europe and in the Black Sea. It grows to 8 in/20 cm.

Pungently flavored, it is processed into fish pastes and essences, and used as a garnish, rather than eaten fresh.

ancien régime the old order; the feudal, absolute monarchy in France before the French Revolution 1789.

ancient art art of prehistoric cultures and the ancient civilizations around the Mediterranean that predate the Classical world of Greece and Rome: for example, Sumerian and Aegean art. Artifacts range from simple relics of the Paleolithic period, such as pebbles carved with symbolic figures, to the sophisticated art forms of ancient Egypt and Assyria: for example, mural paintings, sculpture, and jewelry.

Palaeolithic art The earliest surviving artifacts that qualify as art are mainly from Europe,

dating from approximately 30,000 to 10,000 BC. This was a period of hunter-gatherer cultures. Items that survive are small sculptures, such as the *Willendorf Venus* (Kunsthistorisches Museum, Vienna) carved from a small stone and simply painted, and symbolic sculptures carved in ivory. The later cave paintings of Lascaux in France and Altamira in Spain depict animals –bison, bulls, horses, and deer—and a few human figures. The animals are highly colored and painted in profile, sometimes with lively and sinuous outlines.

Neolithic art The Neolithic began in the Near East about 10,000 BC and the earliest art includes ceramic vessels, human and animal figures, and beads used for necklaces. In Europe the period 4000–2400 BC produced great megaliths, such as Carnac in France and Stonehenge in Britain, and decorated ceramics, including pots and figurines—the pots sometimes covered in geometric ornament, heralding the later ornamental art of the Celts.

The Near Eastern tradition developed into three related circummediterranean traditions: Egyptian, Sumerian, and Anatolian/S European, which became Aegean.

Ancient Mariner, The Rime of the poem by Samuel Taylor Coleridge, published 1798, describing the curse that falls upon a mariner and his ship when he shoots an albatross.

Ancona Italian town and naval base on the Adriatic Sea, capital of Marche region; population (1988) 104,000. It has a Romanesque cathedral and a former palace of the popes.

Andalusia (Spanish *Andalucía*) fertile autonomous region of S Spain, including the provinces of Almería, Cádiz, Córdoba, Granada, Huelva, Jaén, Málaga, and Seville; area 33,698 sq mi/87,300 sq km; population (1986) 6,876,000. Málaga, Cádiz, and Algeciras are the chief ports and industrial centers. The *Costa del Sol* on the S coast has many tourist resorts, including Marbella and Torremolinos.

Andalusia has Moorish architecture, having been under Muslim rule from the 8th to the 15th centuries.

andalusite aluminum silicate, Al_2SiO_5, a white to pinkish mineral crystallizing as square- or rhomb-based prisms. It is common in metamorphic rocks formed from clay sediments under low pressure conditions. Andalusite, kyanite, and sillimanite are all polymorphs of Al_2SiO_5.

Andaman and Nicobar Islands two groups of islands in the Bay of Bengal, between India and Myanmar, forming a Union Territory of the Republic of India; capital Port Blair; area 3,204 sq mi/8,300 sq km; population (1991) 278,000. The economy is based on fishing, timber, rubber, fruit, and rice.

Andean Group (Spanish *Grupo Andino*) South American organization aimed at economic and social cooperation between member states. It was established under the Treaty of Cartagena 1969, by Bolivia, Chile, Colombia, Ecuador, and Peru; Venezuela joined 1973, but Chile withdrew 1976. The organization is based in Lima, Peru.

Andean Indian any indigenous inhabitant of the Andes range in South America, stretching from Ecuador to Peru to Chile, and including both the coast and the highlands. Many Andean civilizations developed in this region from local fishing-hunting-farming societies, all of which predated the ⇨Inca, who consolidated the entire region and ruled from about

1200 to the 1530s, when the Spanish arrived and conquered. The earliest pan-Andean civilization was the Chavin, about 1200–800 BC, which was followed by large and important coastal city-states, such as the Mochica, the Chimú, the Nazca, and the Paracas. The region was dominated by the Tiahuanaco when the Inca started to expand, took them and outlying peoples into their empire, and imposed the Quechua language on all. It is now spoken by over 10 million people and is a member of the Andean-Equatorial family.

Andersen Hans Christian 1805–1875. Danish writer of fairy tales, such as "The Ugly Duckling," "The Snow Queen," "The Little Mermaid," and "The Emperor's New Clothes." A gothic inventiveness, strong sense of wonder, and a redemptive evocation of material and spiritual poverty have given these stories perennial and universal appeal; they have been translated into many languages. He also wrote adult novels and travel books.

Andersen was born the son of a shoemaker in Odense, Fyn. His first children's stories were published 1835. Some are based on folklore; others are original. His other works include the novel *The Improvisatore* 1845, romances, and an autobiography *Mit Livs Eventyr* 1855 (translated 1954 as *The Tale of My Life*).

Anderson city in E central Indiana, NE of Indianapolis; seat of Madison county. The city's industries produce automobile accessories and paper products; population (1990) 59,500.

Anderson Carl David 1905–1991. US physicist who discovered the positive electron (positron) in 1932; he shared the Nobel Prize for Physics in 1936.

Carl Anderson was one of the pioneers in cosmic ray physics. He made two of the first discoveries in the field and launched what is now known as "elementary particle physics." The first discovery in 1932 was the positive electron or positron, a particle whose existence had been predicted by British theorist Paul Dirac. Anderson found that positrons were present in cosmic rays, energetic particles reaching Earth from outer space. For this discovery, Anderson shared the 1936 Nobel Prize for Physics with Victor Hess, the discoverer of cosmic rays. In 1937, Anderson discovered a new particle in cosmic rays, one with a mass between that of an electron and a proton. The new particle was first called a mesotron and then a meson muon. The discovery of the muon was a great step forward in physics; the muon was the first elementary particle to be discovered beyond the constituents of ordinary matter (proton, neutron, and electron). This could be said to be the birth of elementary particle physics.

Anderson Marian 1902–   . US contralto whose voice was remarkable for its range and richness. She toured Europe 1930, but in 1939 she was barred from singing at Constitution Hall, Washington, DC, because she was black. In 1955 she sang at the Metropolitan Opera, the first black singer to appear there. In 1958 she was appointed an alternate (deputizing) delegate to the United Nations.

Following her bar from Constitution Hall, Eleanor Roosevelt and others organized a concert at the Lincoln Memorial; it was attended by 75,000 people.

Anderson Maxwell 1888–1959. US playwright, noted for *What Price Glory?* 1924, written with Laurence Stallings, a realistic portrayal of the American soldier in action during

World War I. Anderson followed this with numerous other plays, many in the form of verse tragedies, including *Elizabeth the Queen* 1930, *Winterset* 1935, and *Anne of the Thousand Days* 1948. He won a Pulitzer prize for his comedic prose satire *Both Your Houses*. Most of his plays had moral and social problems as themes.

Anderson Sherwood 1876–1941. US writer, a member of the Chicago Group, who was encouraged by Theodore Dreiser and Carl Sandburg. He was best known for his sensitive, experimental, and poetic novels of the desperation of small-town Midwestern life, such as in his most noted work, *Winesburg, Ohio* 1919.

Born in Camden, Ohio, Anderson joined the army at age 17 and then worked in a factory before leaving his wife and job and going to Chicago. His works include *Windy McPherson's Son* 1916, *Poor White* 1920, *Dark Laughter* 1925, *Hello Towns* 1929, and *Puzzled America* 1935. He also is known for his short-story collections and autobiographical works.

Andes great mountain system or *cordillera* that forms the western fringe of South America, extending through some 67° of latitude and the republics of Colombia, Venezuela, Ecuador, Peru, Bolivia, Chile, and Argentina. The mountains exceed 12,000 ft/3,600 m for half their length of 4,000 mi/6,500 km.

Geologically speaking, the Andes are new mountains, having attained their present height by vertical upheaval of the entire strip of the Earth's crust as recently as the latter part of the Tertiary era and the Quaternary. But they have been greatly affected by weathering; rivers have cut deep gorges, and glaciers have produced characteristic valleys. The majority of the individual mountains are volcanic; some are still active. The whole system may be divided into two almost parallel ranges. The southernmost extremity is Cape Horn, but the range extends into the sea and forms islands. Among the highest peaks are Cotopaxi and Chimborazo in Ecuador, Cerro de Pasco and Misti in Peru, Illampu and Illimani in Bolivia,

Aconcagua (the highest mountain in the New World) in Argentina, and Ojos del Salado in Chile. Andean mineral resources include gold, silver, tin, tungsten, bismuth, vanadium, copper, and lead. Difficult communications make mining expensive. Transport for a long time was chiefly by pack animals, but air transport has greatly reduced difficulties of communications. Three railroads cross the Andes from Valparaiso to Buenos Aires, Antofagasta to Salta, and Antofagasta via Uyuni to Asunción. New roads are being built, including the ⊅Pan-American Highway. The majority of the sparse population is dependent on agriculture, the nature and products of which vary with the natural environment. Newcomers to the Andean plateau, which includes Lake ⊅Titicaca, suffer from *puna*, mountain sickness, but indigenous peoples have hearts and lungs adapted to altitude.

andesite volcanic igneous rock, intermediate in silica content between rhyolite and basalt. It is characterized by a large quantity of the feldspar ⊅minerals, giving it a light color. Andesite erupts from volcanoes at destructive plate margins (where one plate of the Earth's surface moves beneath another; see ⊅plate tectonics), including the Andes, from which it gets its name.

Andhra Pradesh state in E central India
area 106,845 sq mi/276,700 sq km
capital Hyderabad
cities Secunderabad
products rice, sugar cane, tobacco, groundnuts, cotton
population (1991) 66,304,900
languages Telugu, Urdu, Tamil
history formed 1953 from the Telegu-speaking areas of Madras, and enlarged 1956 from the former Hyderabad state.

Andorra landlocked country in the E Pyrenees, bounded N by France and S by Spain.
government Andorra has no formal constitution and the government is based on the

Andorra
Principality of (*Principat d'Andorra*)

area 181 sq mi/468 sq km
capital Andorra-la-Vella
cities Les Escaldes
physical mountainous, with narrow valleys
features the E Pyrenees, Valira River
heads of state Joan Marti i Alanis (bishop of Urgel, Spain) and François Mitterrand (president of France)

head of government Oscar Riba Reig from 1989
political system semifeudal co-principality
political party Democratic Party of Andorra
exports main industries tourism and tobacco
currency French franc and Spanish peseta
population (1990) 51,000 (30% Andorrans, 61% Spanish, 6% French)
languages Catalan (official); Spanish, French
religion Roman Catholic
literacy 100% (1987)
GDP $300 million (1985)
chronology
1278 Treaty signed making Spanish bishop and French count joint rulers of Andorra (through marriage the king of France later inherited the count's right).
1970 Extension of franchise to third-generation women and second-generation men.
1976 First political organization (Democratic Party of Andorra) formed.
1977 Franchise extended to first-generation Andorrans.
1981 First prime minister appointed by General Council.
1982 With the appointment of an Executive Council, executive and legislative powers were separated.
1991 Andorra's first constitution planned; links with European Community (EC) formalized.

country's feudal origins. Although administratively independent, it has no individual international status, its joint heads of state being the bishop of Urgel in Spain and the president of France. They are represented by permanent delegates, the vicar general of the Urgel diocese, and the prefect of the French *département* of Pyrénées–Orientales. There is a General Council of the villages, consisting of four people from each of the seven parishes, elected by Andorran citizens for a four-year term. The Council submits motions and proposals to the permanent delegates for approval.

Until 1982 the General Council elected an official called the First Syndic to act as its chief executive, but in that year an executive council was appointed, headed by a prime minister. This introduced a separation between legislative and executive powers and was an important step toward a more constitutional form of government. For the time being, reforms are dependent on the two co-princes, through their representatives.

history Co-princes have ruled Andorra since 1278. Until 1970 only third-generation Andorran males had the vote; now the franchise extends to all first-generation Andorrans of foreign parentage aged 28 or over. The electorate is small in relation to the total population, up to 70% of which consists of foreign residents, who are demanding political and nationality rights. Immigration, controlled by a quota system, is restricted to French and Spanish nationals intending to work in Andorra. Since 1980 there have been signs of a fragile, but growing, democracy. There are loose political groupings but no direct party representation on the General Council. A technically illegal political organization, the Democratic Party of Andorra, may provide the basis for a future democratic system. Representatives of the co-princes set a timetable April 1991 for writing the state's first constitution. Formal links were established with the European Community (EC) July 1991. *See illustration box.*

Andrássy Gyula, Count Andrássy 1823–1890. Hungarian revolutionary and statesman who supported the Dual Monarchy of Austro-Hungary 1867 and was Hungary's first constitutional prime minister 1867–71. He became foreign minister of the Austro-Hungarian Empire 1871–79 and tried to halt Russian expansion into the Balkans.

André Carl 1935– . US sculptor, a Minimalist, who uses industrial materials to affirm basic formal and aesthetic principles. His *Equivalent VIII* 1976, an arrangement of bricks in Palladian proportion (Tate Gallery, London), was much criticized.

André John 1751–1780. British army major in the American Revolution, with whom Benedict ◊Arnold plotted the surrender of ◊West Point. André was caught by Washington's army, tried, and hanged as a spy.

Andrea del Sarto (Andrea d'Agnola) 1486–1531. Italian Renaissance painter active in Florence, one of the finest portraitists and religious painters of his time. His style is serene and noble, characteristic of High Renaissance art.

He trained under Piero de Cosimo and others but was chiefly influenced by ◊Masaccio and ◊Michelangelo. In 1518 he went to work for Francis I in France and returned to Italy in 1519 with funds to enlarge the royal French

art collection; he spent it on a house for himself and never went back. His pupils included Pontormo and Vasari. Del Sarto was the foremost painter in Florence after about 1510, along with Fra Bartolommeo, although he was gradually superseded by the emerging Mannerists during the 1520s. Apart from portraits, such as *A Young Man* (National Gallery, London), he painted many religious works, including the *Madonna of the Harpies* (Uffizi, Florence), an example of Classical beauty reminiscent of Raphael. He painted frescoes at Sta Annunziata and the Chiostro dello Scalzo, both in Florence.

André le Chapelain 12th century. French priest and author. He wrote *De Arte Honest Amandi/The Art of Virtuous Love*, a seminal work in ◊courtly love literature, at the request of Marie de France, while he was chaplain at her court in Troyes, E France.

Andress Ursula 1936– . Swiss actress specializing in glamor leads. Her international career started with *Dr No* 1962. Other films include *She* 1965, *Casino Royale* 1967, *Red Sun* 1971, and *Clash of the Titans* 1981.

Andrew (full name Andrew Albert Christian Edward) 1960– . Prince of the UK, Duke of York, second son of Queen Elizabeth II. He married Sarah Ferguson 1986; their first daughter, Princess Beatrice, was born 1988, and their second daughter, Princess Eugenie, was born 1990. The couple separated 1992. Prince Andrew is a naval helicopter pilot.

Andrews Julie. Adopted name of Julia Elizabeth Wells 1935– . British-born US singer and actress. A child performer with her mother and stepfather in British music halls, she first appeared in the US in the Broadway production *The Boy Friend* 1954. She was the original Eliza Doolittle in *My Fair Lady* 1956. In 1960 she appeared in Lerner and Loewe's *Camelot* on Broadway. Her films include *Mary Poppins* 1964, *The Americanization of Emily* 1963, *The Sound of Music* 1965, *"10"* 1980, and *Victor/Victoria* 1982.

Andrew, St New Testament apostle. According to tradition, he went with John to Ephesus, preached in Scythia, and was martyred at Patras on an X-shaped cross (**St Andrew's cross**). He is the patron saint of Scotland. Feast day Nov 30.

A native of Bethsaida, he was Simon Peter's brother. With Peter, James, and John, who worked with him as fishermen at Capernaum, he formed the inner circle of Jesus' 12 disciples.

Andreyev Leonid Nicolaievich 1871–1919. Russian author. Many of his works show an obsession with death and madness, including the symbolic drama *Life of Man* 1907, the melodrama *He Who Gets Slapped* 1915, and the novels *Red Laugh* 1904 and *S.O.S.* 1919 published in Finland, where he fled after the Russian Revolution.

Andrić Ivo 1892–1974. Yugoslav novelist and nationalist. He became a diplomat, and was ambassador to Berlin 1940. *Na Drini Ćuprija/The Bridge on the Drina* 1945 is an epic history of a small Bosnian town. Nobel Prize 1961.

Androcles traditionally, a Roman slave who fled from a cruel master into the African desert, where he encountered and withdrew a thorn from the paw of a crippled lion. Recaptured and sentenced to combat a lion in the arena, he found his adversary was his old friend.

The emperor Tiberius was said to have freed them both.

androecium male part of a flower, comprising a number of ◊stamens.

androgen general name for any male sex hormone, of which ◊testosterone is the most important. They are all ◊steroids and are principally involved in the production of male ◊secondary sexual characteristics (such as facial hair in humans).

Andromache in Greek mythology, the faithful wife of Hector and mother of Astyanax. After the fall of Troy she was awarded to Neoptolemus, Achilles' son; she later married a Trojan seer called Helenus. Andromache is the heroine of Homer's ◊*Iliad* and the subject of a play by Euripides.

Andromache tragedy by Euripides, first produced about 426 BC. Hermione, wife of Neoptolemus, seeks revenge on Andromache, her husband's lover, whom she blames for her own childlessness, but fails in her attempt to kill Andromache and her son. Neoptolemus is murdered by Orestes, a former suitor of Hermione.

Andromeda in Greek mythology, an Ethiopian princess chained to a rock as a sacrifice to a sea monster. She was rescued by ◊Perseus, who married her.

Andromeda major constellation of the northern hemisphere, visible in autumn. Its main feature is the Andromeda galaxy. The star Alpha Andromedae forms one corner of the Square of Pegasus. It is named after the princess of Greek mythology.

Andromeda galaxy galaxy 2.2 million light-years away from Earth in the constellation Andromeda, and the most distant object visible to the naked eye. It is the largest member of the ◊Local Group of galaxies. Like the Milky Way, it is a spiral orbited by several companion galaxies but contains about twice as many stars. It is about 200,000 light-years across.

Andropov Yuri 1914–1984. Soviet communist politician, president of the USSR 1983–84. As chief of the KGB 1967–82, he established a reputation for efficiently suppressing dissent.

Andropov was politically active from the 1930s. His part in quelling the Hungarian national uprising 1956, when he was Soviet ambassador, brought him into the Communist Party secretariat 1962 as a specialist on East European affairs. He became a member of the Politburo 1973 and succeeded Brezhnev as party general secretary 1982. Elected president in 1983, he instituted economic reforms.

anechoic chamber room designed to be of high sound absorbency. All surfaces inside the chamber are covered by sound-absorbent materials such as rubber. The walls are often covered with inward-facing pyramids of rubber, to minimize reflections. It is used for experiments in ◊acoustics and for testing audio equipment.

anemia condition caused by a shortage of hemoglobin, the oxygen-carrying component of red blood cells. The main symptoms are fatigue, pallor, breathlessness, palpitations, and poor resistance to infection. Treatment depends on the cause.

Anemia arises either from abnormal loss or defective production of hemoglobin. Excessive loss occurs, for instance, with chronic slow bleeding or with accelerated destruction (◊hemolysis) of red blood cells. Defective production may be due to iron deficiency, vitamin B$_{12}$ deficiency (pernicious anemia), certain blood diseases (sickle-cell disease and thalassemia), chronic infection, kidney disease, or certain kinds of poisoning. Untreated anemia taxes the heart and may prove fatal.

anemometer device for measuring wind speed and liquid flow. The most basic form, the *cup-type anemometer*, consists of cups at the ends of arms, which rotate when the wind blows. The speed of rotation indicates the wind speed.

Vane-type anemometers have vanes, like a small windmill or propeller, that rotate when the wind blows. *Pressure-tube anemometers* use the pressure generated by the wind to indicate speed. The wind blowing into or across a tube develops a pressure, proportional to the wind speed, that is measured by a manometer or pressure gauge. *Hot-wire anemometers* work on the principle that the rate at which heat is transferred from a hot wire to the surrounding air is a measure of the air speed. Wind speed is determined by measuring either the electric current required to maintain a hot wire at a constant temperature, or the variation of resistance while a constant current is maintained.

anemone any plant of the genus *Anemone* of the buttercup family Ranunculaceae. The function of petals is performed by its sepals. The garden anemone *A. coronaria* is white, blue, red, or purple.

The white or lavender-tinged wood anemone *A. quinquefolia* grows in open woods, flowering in spring.

anemophily type of ⬦pollination in which the pollen is carried on the wind. Anemophilous flowers are usually unscented, have either very reduced petals and sepals or lack them altogether, and do not produce nectar. In some species they are borne in ⬦catkins. Male and female reproductive structures are commonly found in separate flowers. The male flowers have numerous exposed stamens, often on long filaments; the female flowers have long, often branched, feathery stigmas.

Many wind-pollinated plants, such as hazel *Corylus americana*, bear their flowers before the leaves to facilitate the free transport of pollen. Since air movements are random, vast amounts of pollen are needed: a single birch catkin, for example, may produce over 5 million pollen grains.

aneroid barometer kind of ⬦barometer.

anesthetic drug that produces loss of sensation or consciousness; the resulting state is anesthesia, in which the patient is insensitive to stimuli. Anesthesia may also happen as a result of nerve disorder.

Ever since the first successful operation in 1846 on a patient rendered unconscious by ether, advances have been aimed at increasing safety and control. Sedatives may be given before the anesthetic to make the process easier. Level and duration of unconsciousness are managed precisely. Where general anesthesia may be inappropriate (for example, in childbirth, for a small procedure, or in the elderly), many other techniques are available. A topical substance may be applied to the skin or tissue surface; a local agent may be injected into the tissues under the skin in the area to be treated; or a regional block of sensation may be achieved by injection into a nerve. Spinal anesthetic, such as epidural, is injected into the tissues surrounding the spinal cord, producing loss of feeling in the lower part of the body.

Less than one in 5,000 patients aged 20–40 may become sensitized to anesthetics as a result of previously having undergone operations. Provided this is noticed promptly by the anesthetist, no ill effects should ensue.

aneurysm weakening in the wall of an artery, causing it to balloon outwards, with the risk of rupture and serious, often fatal, blood loss. If detected in time and accessible, some aneurysms can be excised.

angel (Greek *angelos* "messenger") in Jewish, Christian, and Muslim belief, a supernatural being intermediate between God and humans. The Christian hierarchy has nine orders: **Seraphim**, **Cherubim**, **Thrones** (who contemplate God and reflect his glory), **Dominations**, **Virtues**, **Powers** (who regulate the stars and the universe), **Principalities**, **Archangels**, and **Angels** (who minister to humanity). In traditional Catholic belief every human being has a guardian angel. The existence of angels was reasserted by Pope John Paul II 1986.

angel dust popular name for the anesthetic *phencyclidine*, a depressant drug.

Angel Falls highest waterfalls in the world, on the river Caroni in the tropical rainforest of Bolivar Region, Venezuela; total height 3,210 ft/978 m. They were named after the aviator and prospector James Angel who flew over the falls and crash-landed nearby 1935.

angelfish any of a number of unrelated fishes. The freshwater **angelfish**, genus *Pterophyllum*, of South America, is a tall, side-to-side flattened fish with a striped body, up to 10 in/26 cm long, but usually smaller in captivity. The **angelfish** or **monkfish** of the genus *Squatina* is a bottom-living shark up to 6 ft/1.8 m long with a body flattened from top to bottom. The **marine angelfishes**, *Pomacanthus* and others, are long narrow-bodied fish with spiny fins, often brilliantly colored, up to 2 ft/60 cm long, living around coral reefs in the tropics.

angelica any plant of the genus *Angelica* of the carrot family Umbelliferae. Mostly Eurasian in distribution, they are tall, perennial herbs with divided leaves and clusters of white or greenish flowers. The roots and fruits have long been used in cooking and for medicinal purposes.

Angelico Fra (Guido di Pietro) *c.* 1400–1455. Italian painter of religious scenes, active in Florence. He was a monk and painted a series of frescoes at the monastery of San Marco, Florence, begun after 1436. He also produced several altarpieces in a simple style.

Fra Angelico joined the Dominican order about 1420. After his novitiate, he resumed a career as a painter of religious images and altarpieces, many of which have small predella scenes beneath them, depicting events in the life of a saint. The central images of the paintings are highly decorated with pastel colors and gold-leaf designs, while the predella scenes are often lively and relatively unsophisticated. There is a similar simplicity to his frescoes in the cells at San Marco, which are principally devotional works.

Fra Angelico's later fresco sequences, *Scenes from the Life of Christ* (Orvieto Cathedral) and *Scenes from the Lives of SS Stephen and Lawrence* 1440s (chapel of Nicholas V, Vatican Palace), are more elaborate.

Angell Norman 1874–1967. British writer on politics and economics. In 1910 he acquired

an international reputation with his book *The Great Illusion*, which maintained that any war must prove ruinous to the victors as well as to the vanquished. Nobel Peace Prize 1933.

Angelou Maya (born Marguerite Johnson) 1928– . US novelist, poet, playwright, and short-story writer. Her powerful autobiographical works, *I Know Why the Caged Bird Sings* 1970 and its three sequels, tell of the struggles toward physical and spiritual liberation of a black woman growing up in the South.

Anger Kenneth 1929– . US avant-garde filmmaker, brought up in Hollywood. His films, which dispense with conventional narrative, often use homosexual iconography and a personal form of mysticism. They include *Fireworks* 1947, *Scorpio Rising* 1964, and *Lucifer Rising* 1973.

He wrote the exposé *Hollywood Babylon*, the original version of which was published in France in 1959.

Angers ancient French town, capital of Maine-et-Loire *département*, on the river Maine; population (1982) 196,000. Products include electrical machinery and Cointreau liqueur. It has a 12th–13th century cathedral and castle and was formerly the capital of the duchy and province of Anjou.

Angevin relating to the reigns of the English kings Henry II and Richard I (also known, with the later English kings up to Richard III, as the **Plantagenets**). Angevin derives from Anjou, the region in France controlled by English kings at this time. The **Angevin Empire** comprised the territories (including England) that belonged to the Anjou dynasty.

angina or **angina pectoris** severe pain in the chest due to impaired blood supply to the heart muscle because a coronary artery is narrowed. Faintness and difficulty in breathing accompany the pain. Treatment is by drugs, such as nitroglycerin and amyl nitrite; rest is important.

angiography technique for X-raying major blood vessels. A radiopaque dye is injected into the bloodstream so that the suspect vessel is clearly silhouetted on the X-ray film.

angiosperm flowering plant in which the seeds are enclosed within an ovary, which ripens to a fruit. Angiosperms are divided into ⬦monocotyledons (single seed leaf in the embryo) and ⬦dicotyledons (two seed leaves in the embryo). They include the majority of flowers, herbs, grasses, and trees except conifers.

There are over 250,000 different species of angiosperm, found in a wide range of habitats. Like ⬦gymnosperms, they are seed plants, but differ in that ovules and seeds are protected within the carpel. Fertilization occurs by male gametes passing into the ovary from a pollen tube. After fertilization the ovule develops into the seed while the ovary wall develops into the fruit.

Angkor site of the ancient capital of the Khmer Empire in NW Cambodia, north of Tonle Sap. The remains date mainly from the 10th–12th centuries AD, and comprise temples originally dedicated to the Hindu gods, shrines associated with Theravāda Buddhism, and royal palaces. Many are grouped within the enclosure called **Angkor Thom**, but the great temple of **Angkor Wat** (early 12th century) lies outside. Angkor was abandoned in the 15th century, and the ruins were overgrown by jungle and not adequately described until 1863. Buildings on the site suffered damage during the civil war 1970–75.

Angle member of the Germanic tribe that invaded Britain in the 5th century; see ⬦Anglo-Saxon.

angle pair of rays (half-lines) that share a common endpoint but do not lie on the same line. Angles are measured in ⬦degrees (°) or ⬦radians, and are classified generally by their degree measures. *Acute angles* are less than 90°; *right angles* are exactly 90°; *obtuse angles* are greater than 90° but less than 180°; *reflex angles* are greater than 180° but less than 360°. Angles can be measured by using a protractor.

No angle is classified as having a measure of 180°, as by definition such an "angle" is actually a straight line.

angler any of an order of fishes Lophiiformes, with flattened body and broad head and jaws. Many species have small, plantlike tufts on their skin. These act as camouflage for the fish as it waits, either floating among seaweed or lying on the sea bottom, twitching the enlarged tip of the threadlike first ray of its dorsal fin to entice prey.

There are over 200 species of angler fish, living in both deep and shallow water in temperate and tropical seas. The males of some species have become so small that they live as parasites on the females.

Anglo- combining language form with several related meanings. In *Anglo-Saxon* it refers to the Angles, a Germanic people who invaded Britain in the 5th to 7th centuries. In *Anglo-Welsh* it refers to England or the English. In *Anglo-American* it may refer either to England and the English or, commonly but less accurately, to Britain and the British (as in "*Anglo-American* relations"); it may also refer to the English language (as in "*Anglo-American* speech"); or to the Anglo-Saxon heritage in US society (as in WASP, white *Anglo-Saxon* Protestant).

Anglo-Irish Agreement or *Hillsborough Agreement* concord reached 1985 between the UK premier Margaret Thatcher and Irish premier Garret FitzGerald. One sign of the improved relations between the two countries was increased cooperation between police and security forces across the border with Northern Ireland. The pact also gave the Irish Republic a greater voice in the conduct of Northern Ireland's affairs. However, the agreement was rejected by Northern Ireland Unionists as a step toward renunciation of British sovereignty. In March 1988 talks led to further strengthening of the agreement.

Anglo-Saxon one of the several Germanic invaders (Angles, Saxons, and Jutes) who conquered much of Britain between the 5th and 7th centuries. After the conquest a number of kingdoms were set up, commonly referred to as the *Heptarchy*; these were united in the early 9th century under the overlordship of Wessex. The Norman invasion 1066 brought Anglo-Saxon rule to an end.

The Jutes probably came from the Rhineland and not, as was formerly believed, from Jutland. The Angles and Saxons came from Schleswig–Holstein, and may have united before invading. There was probably considerable intermarriage with the Romanized Celts of ancient Britain, although the latter's language and civilization almost disappeared. The English-speaking peoples of Britain, Australia,

New Zealand, and the US are often referred to today as Anglo-Saxons, but the term is inaccurate, since the Welsh, Scots, and Irish are mainly of Celtic or Norse descent, and by the 1980s fewer than 15% of Americans were of British descent.

Anglo-Saxon art painting and sculpture of England from the 7th century to 1066. Sculpted crosses and ivories, manuscript painting, and gold and enamel jewelry survive. The relics of the Sutton Hoo ship burial, 7th century, and the *Lindisfarne Gospels*, about 690 (both British Museum, London), have typical Celtic ornamental patterns, but in manuscripts of southern England a different style emerged in the 9th century, with delicate, lively pen-and-ink figures and heavily decorative foliage borders.

Anglo-Saxon Chronicle history of England from the Roman invasion to the 11th century, in the form of a series of chronicles written

in Old English by monks, begun in the 9th century (during the reign of King Alfred), and continuing to the 12th century.

The Chronicle, comprising seven different manuscripts, forms a unique record of early English history and of the development of Old English prose up to its final stages in the year 1154, by which date it had been superseded by Middle English.

Anglo-Saxon language group of dialects spoken by the ⬦Anglo-Saxon peoples who, in the 5th to 7th centuries, invaded and settled in Britain (in what became England and Lowland Scotland). Anglo-Saxon is traditionally known as Old English. See ⬦English language.

Angola country in SW Africa, bounded W by the Atlantic ocean, N and NE by Zaire, E by Zambia, and S by Namibia. The Cabinda enclave, a district of Angola, is bounded W by the Atlantic Ocean, N by the river Congo, and E and S by Zaire.

Angola
People's Republic of (*República Popular de Angola*)

area 481,226 sq mi/1,246,700 sq km
capital (and chief port) Luanda
cities Lobito and Benguela, also ports; Huambo, Lubango
physical narrow coastal plain rises to vast interior plateau with rainforest in NW; desert in S
features Cuanza, Cuito, Cubango, and Cunene rivers; Cabinda enclave
head of state and government José Eduardo dos Santos from 1979
political system socialist republic
political parties People's Movement for the Liberation of Angola–Workers' Party (MPLA–PT), Marxist-Leninist; National Union for the Total Independence of Angola (UNITA), backed by South Africa; National Front for the Liberation of Angola (FNLA), backed by 'nonleft' power groups of southern Africa
exports oil, coffee, diamonds, palm oil, sisal, iron ore, fish
currency kwanza
population (1989 est) 9,733,000 (largest ethnic group Ovimbundu); growth rate 2.5% p.a.
life expectancy men 40, women 44
languages Portuguese (official); Bantu dialects
religions Roman Catholic 68%, Protestant 20%, animist 12%
literacy 20%

GDP $2.7 bn; $432 per head
chronology
1951 Angola became an overseas territory of Portugal.
1956 First independence movement formed, the People's Movement for the Liberation of Angola (MPLA).
1961 Unsuccessful independence rebellion.
1962 Second nationalist movement formed, the National Front for the Liberation of Angola (FNLA).
1966 Third nationalist movement formed, the National Union for the Total Independence of Angola (UNITA).
1975 Independence achieved from Portugal. Transitional government of independence formed from representatives of MPLA, FNLA, UNITA, and Portuguese government. MPLA proclaimed People's Republic of Angola under the presidency of Dr Agostinho Neto. FNLA and UNITA proclaimed People's Democratic Republic of Angola.
1976 MPLA gained control of most of the country. South African troops withdrawn, but Cuban units remained.
1977 MPLA restructured to become the People's Movement for the Liberation of Angola–Workers' Party (MPLA—PT).
1979 Death of Neto, succeeded by José Eduardo dos Santos.
1980 Constitution amended to provide for an elected people's assembly. UNITA guerrillas, aided by South Africa, continued raids against the Luanda government and bases of the South West Africa People's Organization (SWAPO) in Angola.
1984 The Lusaka Agreement.
1985 South African forces officially withdrawn.
1986 Further South African raids into Angola. UNITA continuing to receive South African support.
1988 Peace treaty, providing for the withdrawal of all foreign troops, signed with South Africa and Cuba.
1989 Cease-fire agreed with UNITA broke down and guerrilla activity restarted.
1990 Peace offer by rebels. Return to multiparty politics promised.
1991 Peace agreement signed, civil war between MPLA–PT and UNITA officially ended. Amnesty for all political prisoners.
1992 MPLA's general-election victory fiercely disputed by UNITA, threatening renewed civil war.

government The 1975 constitution, amended 1976 and 1980, created a one-party "People's Republic," with political power held by the People's Movement for the Liberation of Angola–Workers' Party (MPLA–PT). The president, elected by the congress of MPLA–PT, chooses and chairs the council of ministers and is commander in chief of the armed forces. There is a 223-member people's assembly, 20 of whom are nominated by MPLA–PT and the rest elected by electoral colleges of "loyal" citizens.

history Angola became a Portuguese colony 1491 and an Overseas Territory of Portugal 1951. A movement for complete independence, the MPLA, was established 1956, based originally in the Congo. This was followed by the formation of two other nationalist movements, the National Front for the Liberation of Angola (FNLA) and the National Union for the Total Independence of Angola (UNITA). War for independence from Portugal broke out 1961, with MPLA supported by socialist and communist states, UNITA helped by the Western powers and FNLA backed by the "nonleft" power groups of southern Africa.

republic Three months of civil war followed the granting of full independence 1975, with MPLA and UNITA the main contestants, and foreign mercenaries and South African forces helping FNLA. By 1975 MPLA, with the help of mainly Cuban forces, controlled most of the country and had established the People's Republic of Angola in Luanda. Agostinho Neto, the MPLA leader, became its first president. FNLA and UNITA had, in the meantime, proclaimed their own People's Democratic Republic of Angola, based in Huambo. President Neto died 1979 and was succeeded by José Eduardo dos Santos, who maintained Neto's links with the Soviet bloc.

Lusaka Agreement UNITA guerrillas, supported by South Africa, continued to operate and combined forces raided Angola 1980–81 to attack bases of the South-West Africa People's Organization (⟁SWAPO), who were fighting for Namibia's independence. South Africa proposed a complete withdrawal of its forces 1983 if Angola could guarantee that the areas vacated would not be filled by Cuban or SWAPO units.

Angola accepted South Africa's proposals 1984, and a settlement was made (the Lusaka Agreement), whereby a Joint Monitoring Commission was set up to oversee South Africa's withdrawal, which was completed 1985. Relations between the two countries deteriorated 1986 when further South African raids into Angola took place. UNITA also continued to receive South African support. Despite the securing of a peace treaty with South Africa and Cuba 1988, guerrilla activity by the UNITA rebels began again 1989.

cease-fire and peace A cease-fire negotiated June 1989 between the Luanda government and UNITA's Jonas ⟁Savimbi collapsed two months later. However, a peace treaty was finally signed on May 31, 1991. President dos Santos promised a return to multiparty politics, and the government proclaimed an amnesty for all political prisoners July 1991. A general election was held Sept 1992, but Savimbi refused to accept the MPLA's victory and accused the party of rigging the vote. The bloody dispute that followed threatened to take the country back to a state of civil war. By Nov 1992 UNITA had increased its strongholds and controlled more than half the country. *See illustration box.*

Angora earlier form of ⟁Ankara, Turkey, which gave its name to the Angora goat (see ⟁mohair), and hence to other species of long-haired animal, such as the Angora rabbit (a native of the island of Madeira) and the Angora cat. Angora "wool" from these animals has long, smooth fibers, and the demand for the fiber has led to wool farming in Europe, Japan, and the US.

Angostura former name of ⟁Ciudad Bolivar; port in Venezuela.

angostura flavoring prepared from oil distilled from the bitter, aromatic bark of either of two South American trees *Galipea officinalis* or *Cusparia trifoliata* of the rue family.

It is blended with herbs and other flavorings to give **angostura bitters**, which was first used as a stomach remedy and is now used to season food and fruit, to make a "pink gin," and to prepare other alcoholic drinks.

Angoulême French town, capital of the *département* of Charente, on the Charente river; population (1982) 104,000. It has a cathedral, and a castle and paper mills dating from the 16th century.

Angry Young Men group of British writers who emerged about 1950 after the creative hiatus that followed World War II. They included Kingsley Amis, John Wain, John Osborne, and Colin Wilson. Also linked to the group were Iris Murdoch and Kenneth Tynan.

angst (German "anxiety") an emotional state of anxiety without a specific cause. In ⟁Existentialism, the term refers to general human anxiety at having free will, that is, of being responsible for one's actions.

angstrom unit (symbol Å) of length equal to 10^{-10} meter or one-ten-millionth of a millimeter, used for atomic measurements and the wavelengths of electromagnetic radiation. It is named after the Swedish scientist A J Ångström.

Ångström Anders Jonas 1814–1874. Swedish astrophysicist who worked in spectroscopy and solar physics. In 1861 Ångström identified the presence of hydrogen in the Sun. His major work *Recherches sur le spectre solaire* 1868, an atlas of solar spectra, presented the measurements of 1,000 spectral lines expressed in units of one-ten-millionth of a millimeter, the unit which later became the angstrom.

Anguilla island in the E Caribbean
area 62 sq mi/160 sq km
capital The Valley
features white coral-sand beaches; 80% of its coral reef has been lost through tourism (pollution and souvenir sales)
exports lobster, salt
currency Eastern Caribbean dollar
population (1988) 7,000
language English, Creole
government from 1982, governor, executive council, and legislative house of assembly (chief minister Emile Gumbs from 1984)
history a British colony from 1650, Anguilla was long associated with St Christopher-Nevis but revolted against alleged domination by the larger island and in 1969 declared itself a republic. A small British force restored order, and Anguilla retained a special position at its own request, since 1980 a separate dependency of the UK.

angular momentum see ⟁momentum.

Anhui or *Anhwei* province of E China, watered by the Chang Jiang (Yangtze River)
area 54,000 sq mi/139,900 sq km
capital Hefei

products cereals in the north; cotton, rice, tea in the south
population (1990) 56,181,000.

Anhwei alternate spelling name of ⟁Anhui.

anhydrous of a chemical compound, containing no water. If the water of crystallization is removed from blue crystals of copper(II) sulfate, a white powder (anhydrous copper sulfate) results. Liquids from which all traces of water have been removed are also described as being anhydrous.

aniline (Portuguese *anil* "indigo") $C_6H_5NH_2$ or *phenylamine* one of the simplest aromatic chemicals (a substance related to benzene, with its carbon atoms joined in a ring). When pure, it is a colorless oily liquid; it has a characteristic odor, and turns brown on contact with air. It occurs in coal tar, and is used in the rubber industry and to make drugs and dyes. It is highly poisonous.

Aniline was discovered in 1826, and was originally prepared by the dry distillation of ⟁indigo, hence its name.

animal or *metazoan* member of the kingdom Animalia, one of the major categories of living things, the science of which is *zoology*. Animals are all ⟁heterotrophs (they obtain their energy from organic substances produced by other organisms); they have cells of the ⟁eukaryote grouping (the genetic material is contained within a distinct nucleus) bounded by a thin cell membrane rather than the thick cell wall of plants. Most animals are capable of moving around for at least part of their life cycle.

In the past, it was common to include the single-celled ⟁protozoa with the animals, but these are now classified as protists, together with single-celled plants. Thus all animals are multicellular. The oldest land animals known date back 440 million years. Their remains were found 1990 in a sandstone deposit near Ludlow, Shropshire, UK and included fragments of two centipedes a few centimeters long and a primitive spider measuring about 1 mm.

animal behavior the scientific study of the behavior of animals, either by comparative psychologists (with an interest mainly in the psychological processes involved in the control of behavior) or by ethologists (with an interest in the biological context and relevance of behavior).

animal, domestic in general, a tame animal. In agriculture, it is an animal brought under human control for exploitation of its labor; use of its feathers, hide, or skin; or consumption of its eggs, milk, or meat. Common domestic animals include poultry, cattle (including buffalo), sheep, goats, and pigs. Starting about 10,000 years ago, the domestication of animals has only since World War II led to intensive ⟁factory farming.

Increasing numbers of formerly wild species have been domesticated, with stress on scientific breeding for desired characteristics. At least 60% of the world's livestock is in developing countries, but the Third World consumes only 20% of all meat and milk produced. Most domestic animals graze plants that are not edible to humans, and 40% of the world's cereal production becomes animal feed; in the US it is 90%.

animism in psychology and physiology, the view of human personality that attributes human life and behavior to a force distinct from matter.

In religious theory, the conception of a

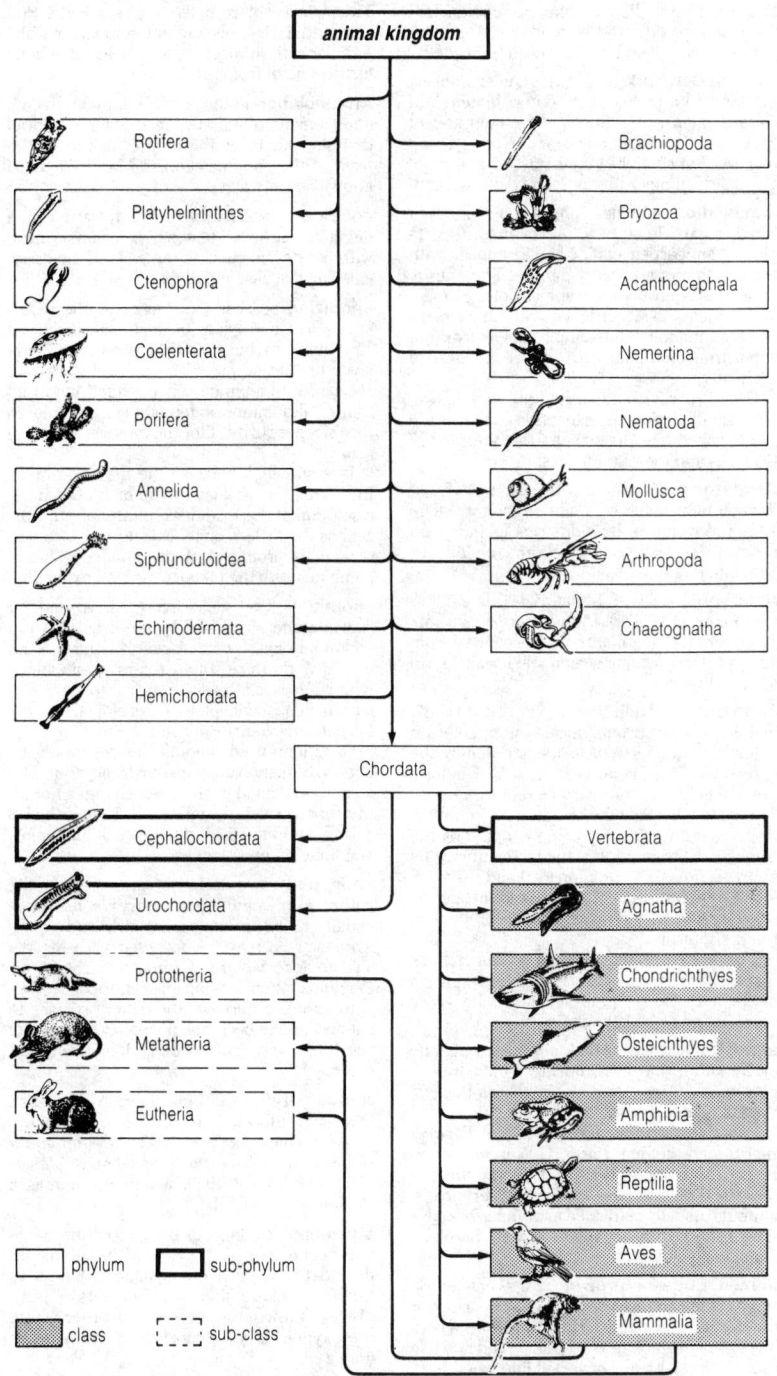

animal *The animal kingdom is divided into 18 major groups or phyla.*

spiritual reality behind the material one: for example, beliefs in the soul as a shadowy duplicate of the body capable of independent activity, both in life and death. In anthropology, the concept of spirits residing in all natural phenomena and objects.

Linked with this is the worship of natural objects such as stones and trees, thought to harbor spirits (naturism); fetishism; and ancestor worship.

anion ion carrying a negative charge. An electrolyte, such as the salt zinc chloride ($ZnCl_2$), is dissociated in aqueous solution or in the molten state into doubly-charged Zn^{2+} zinc ▷cations and singly-charged Cl- anions. During electrolysis, the zinc cations flow to the cathode (to become discharged and liberate zinc metal) and the chloride anions flow to the anode.

anise plant *Pimpinella anisum*, of the carrot family Umbelliferae, whose fragrant seeds are used to flavor foods. Aniseed oil is used in cough medicines.

Anjou old countship and former province in N France; capital Angers. In 1154 the count of Anjou became king of England as Henry II, but the territory was lost by King John 1204. In 1480 the countship was annexed to the French crown. The *départements* of Maine-et-Loire and part of Indre-et-Loire, Mayenne, and Sarthe cover the area. The people are called Angevins -a name also applied by the English to the ▷Plantagenet kings.

Ankara (formerly *Angora*) capital of Turkey; population (1990) 2,559,500. Industries include cement, textiles, and leather products. It replaced Istanbul (then in Allied occupation) as capital 1923.

It has the presidential palace and Grand National Assembly buildings; three universities, including a technical university to serve the whole Middle East; the Atatürk mausoleum on a nearby hilltop; and the largest mosque in Turkey at Kocatepe.

Anna Comnena 1083–after 1148. Byzantine historian, daughter of the emperor ▷Alexius I, who was the historian of her father's reign. After a number of abortive attempts to alter the imperial succession in favor of her husband, Nicephorus Bryennius (*c.* 1062–1137), she retired to a convent to write her major work, the *Alexiad*. It describes the Byzantine view of public office, as well as the religious and intellectual life of the period.

Anna Karenina novel by Leo Tolstoy, published 1873–77. It describes a married woman's love affair with Vronski, a young officer, which ends with her suicide.

Annam former country of SE Asia, incorporated in ▷Vietnam 1946 as Central Vietnam. A Bronze Age civilization was flourishing in the area when China conquered it about 214 BC. The Chinese named their conquest An-Nam, "peaceful south." Independent from 1428, Annam signed a treaty with France 1787 and became a French protectorate, part of Indochina 1884. During World War II, Annam was occupied by Japan.

Annamese member of the majority ethnic group in Vietnam, comprising 90% of the population. The Annamese language is distinct from Vietnamese, though it has been influenced by Chinese and has loan words from Khmer. Their religion combines elements of Buddhism, Confucianism, and Taoism, as well as ancestor worship.

Annapolis seaport and capital of Maryland; population (1984) 31,900. It was named after Princess (later Queen) Anne 1695.

The State House, built 1772–80, is the oldest US state capitol in continuous legislative use. It was in session here Nov 1783–Jun 1784 that ▷Congress received George ▷Washington's resignation as commander in chief 1783 and ratified the peace treaty that ended the Revolutionary War. The US Naval Academy is here, and John Paul ▷Jones is buried in the chapel crypt.

Annapurna mountain 26,502 ft/8,075 m in the Himalayas, Nepal. The north face was first climbed by a French expedition (Maurice Herzog) 1950 and the south by a British team 1970.

Ann Arbor city in SE Michigan, W of Dearborn and Detroit, on the Huron River; seat of

Washtenaw county. It is a center for medical, aeronautical, nuclear, and chemical research. Site of the University of Michigan 1837; population (1990) 109,600.

Anne 1665–1714. Queen of Great Britain and Ireland 1702–14. She was the second daughter of James, Duke of York, who became James II, and Anne Hyde. She succeeded William III 1702. Events of her reign include the War of the Spanish Succession, Marlborough's victories at Blenheim, Ramillies, Oudenarde, and Malplaquet, and the union of the English and Scottish parliaments 1707. Anne was succeeded by George I.

She received a Protestant upbringing, and in 1683 married Prince George of Denmark (1653–1708). Of their many children only one survived infancy, William, Duke of Gloucester (1689–1700). For the greater part of her life Anne was a close friend of Sarah Churchill (1650–1744), wife of John Churchill (1650–1722), afterwards Duke of Marlborough; the Churchills' influence helped lead her to desert her father for her brother-in-law, William of Orange, during the Revolution of 1688, and later to engage in Jacobite intrigues. Her replacement of the Tories by a Whig government 1703–04 was her own act, not due to Churchillian influence. Anne finally broke with the Marlboroughs 1710, when Mrs Masham succeeded the duchess as her favorite, and supported the Tory government of the same year.

Anne (full name Anne Elizabeth Alice Louise) 1950– . Princess of the UK, second child of Queen Elizabeth II, declared Princess Royal 1987. She is an excellent horsewoman, winning a gold medal at the 1976 Olympics, and is actively involved in global charity work, especially for children. In 1973 she married Capt Mark Phillips (1949–); they separated 1989 and were divorced 1992. In Dec 1992 she married Commander Tim Lawrence.

annealing process of heating a material (usually glass or metal) for a given time at a given temperature, followed by slow cooling, to increase ductility and strength. It is a common form of ◊heat treatment.

Annecy capital of the *département* of Haute-Savoie, SE France, at the northern end of Lake Annecy; population (1982) 112,600 (conurbation). It has some light industry, including precision instruments, and is a tourist resort.

annelid any segmented worm of the phylum Annelida. Annelids include earthworms, leeches, and marine worms such as lugworms.

They have a distinct head and soft body, which is divided into a number of similar segments shut off from one another internally by membranous partitions, but there are no jointed appendages.

Anne of Austria 1601–1666. Queen of France from 1615 and regent 1643–61. Daughter of Philip III of Spain, she married Louis XIII of France (whose chief minister, Cardinal Richelieu, worked against her). On her husband's death she became regent for their son, Louis XIV, until his majority.

She chose her lover ◊Mazarin as her chief minister.

Anne of Cleves 1515–1557. Fourth wife of ◊Henry VIII of England 1540. She was the daughter of the Duke of Cleves, and was recommended to Henry as a wife by Thomas ◊Cromwell, who wanted an alliance with German Protestantism against the Holy Roman Empire. Henry did not like her looks, had the marriage declared void after six months, pensioned her, and had Cromwell beheaded.

Anne of Denmark 1574–1619. Queen consort of James VI of Scotland (later James I of Great Britain 1603). She was the daughter of Frederick II of Denmark and Norway, and married James 1589. Anne was suspected of Catholic leanings and was notably extravagant.

annihilation in nuclear physics, a process in which a particle and its "mirror image" particle or ◊antiparticle collide and disappear, with the creation of a burst of energy. The energy created is equivalent to the mass of the colliding particles in accordance with the ◊mass energy equation. For example, an electron and a positron annihilate to produce a burst of high-energy X-rays.

Not all particle-antiparticle interactions result in annihilation; the exception concerns the group called mesons, which are composed of ◊quarks and their antiquarks.

Anniston city in E Alabama, NE of Birmingham; seat of Calhoun county. The site of iron mines, its industries include iron products as well as textiles and chemicals; population (1990) 26,600.

Annobón island in Equatorial Guinea; former name (1973–79) *Pagalu*; area 7 sq mi/ 17 sq km. Its inhabitants are descended from slaves of the Portuguese and still speak a form of that language.

anno Domini (Latin "in the year of our Lord") in the Christian chronological system, refers to dates since the birth of Jesus, denoted by the letters AD. There is no year 0, so AD 1 follows immediately after the year 1 BC (before Christ). The system became the standard reckoning in the Western world after being adopted by the English historian Bede in the 8th century. The abbreviations CE (Common Era) and BCE (before Common Era) are often used instead by scholars and writers as objective, rather than religious, terms.

The system is based on the calculations made 525 by Dionysius Exiguus, a Scythian monk, but the birth of Jesus should more correctly be placed about 4 BC.

annual plant plant that completes its life cycle within one year, during which time it germinates, grows to maturity, bears flowers, produces seed, and then dies.

Examples include the field poppy *Papaver rhoeas* and golden ragwort *Senecio aureus vulgaris*. Among garden plants, some that are described as "annuals" are actually perennials, although usually cultivated as annuals because they cannot survive winter frosts. See also ◊biennial plant.

annual rings or *growth rings* concentric rings visible on the wood of a cut tree trunk or other woody stem. Each ring represents a period of growth when new ◊xylem is laid down to replace tissue being converted into wood (secondary xylem). The wood formed from xylem produced in the spring and early summer has larger and more numerous vessels than the wood formed from xylem produced in autumn when growth is slowing down. The result is a clear boundary between the pale spring wood and the denser, darker autumn wood. Annual rings may be used to estimate the age of the plant (see ◊dendrochronology), although occasionally more than one growth ring is produced in a given year.

annular eclipse solar ◊eclipse in which the Moon does not completely obscure the Sun and a thin ring of sunlight remains visible. Annular eclipses occur when the Moon is at its furthest point from the Earth.

Annunciation in the New Testament, the announcement to Mary by the archangel Gabriel that she was to be the mother of Christ; the feast of the Annunciation is March 25 (also known as Lady Day).

anode the positive electrode toward which negative particles (anions, electrons) move within a device such as the cells of a battery, electrolytic cells, and diodes.

anodizing process that increases the resistance to ◊corrosion of a metal, such as aluminum, by building up a protective oxide layer on the surface. The natural corrosion resistance of aluminum is provided by a thin film of aluminum oxide; anodizing increases the thickness of this film and thus the corrosion protection.

It is so called because the metal becomes the ◊anode in an electrolytic bath containing a solution of, for example, sulfuric or chromic acid as the ◊electrolyte. During ◊electrolysis oxygen is produced at the anode, where it combines with the metal to form an oxide film.

anomie in the social sciences, a state of "normlessness" created by the breakdown of commonly agreed standards of behavior and morality; the term often refers to situations where the social order appears to have collapsed. The concept was developed by the French sociologist Emil Durkheim.

Durkheim used "anomie" to describe societies in transition during industrialization. The term was adapted by the US sociologist Robert Merton to explain deviance and crime in the US as a result of the disparity between high goals and limited opportunities.

anorexia lack of desire to eat, especially the pathological condition of *anorexia nervosa*, usually found in adolescent girls and young women, who may be obsessed with the desire to lose weight. Compulsive eating, or ◊bulimia, often accompanies anorexia.

In anorexia nervosa, the patient refuses to eat and finally becomes unable to do so. The result is severe emaciation and, in rare cases, death.

Anouilh Jean 1910–1987. French dramatist. His plays, influenced by the Neo-Classical tradition, include *Antigone* 1942, *L'Invitation au château/Ring Round the Moon* 1947, *Colombe* 1950, and *Becket* 1959, about St Thomas à Becket and Henry II.

anoxemia shortage of oxygen in the lungs and tissue. It may be due to breathing air deficient in oxygen (for instance, at high altitude or where there are noxious fumes), disease of the lungs, or some disorder where the oxygen-carrying capacity of the blood is impaired.

Anschluss (German "union") the annexation of Austria with Germany, accomplished by the German chancellor Adolf Hitler March 12, 1938.

Austria was occupied jointly by the Allies until 1955, when it declared independence as a republic.

Anselm, St *c.* 1033–1109. Medieval priest and philosopher. As abbot from 1078, he made the abbey of Bec in Normandy, France, a center of scholarship in Europe. He was appointed archbishop of Canterbury by William II of England

1093, but was later forced into exile. He holds an important place in the development of ⬧scholasticism.

In his *Proslogion* he developed the ontological proof of theism, which infers God's existence from our capacity to conceive of a perfect being. His major work, *Cur deus homo?/Why did God become Man?*, treats the subject of the Atonement. He was canonized 1494.

Anshan Chinese city in Liaoning province, 55 mi/89 km SE of Shenyang (Mukden); population (1986) 1,280,000. The iron and steel center started here 1918 was expanded by the Japanese, dismantled by the Russians, and restored by the Communist government of China. It produces 6 million tons of steel annually.

ANSI (abbreviation for *American National Standards Institution*) US national standards body. It sets official procedures in (among other areas) computing and electronics.

ant insect belonging to the family Formicidae, and to the same order (Hymenoptera) as bees and wasps. Ants are characterized by a conspicuous "waist" and elbowed antennae. About 10,000 different species are known; all are social in habit, and all construct nests of various kinds. Ants are found in all parts of the world, except the polar regions. It is estimated that there are about 10 million billion ants.

Ant behavior is complex, and serves the colony rather than the individual. Ants find their way by light patterns, gravity (special sense organs are located in the joints of their legs), and chemical trails between food areas and the nest.

Communities include *workers*, sterile wingless females, often all alike, although in some species large-headed "soldiers" are differentiated; *fertile females*, fewer in number and usually winged; and *males*, also winged and smaller than their consorts, with whom they leave the nest on a nuptial flight at certain times of the year. After aerial mating, the males die, and the fertilized queens lose their wings when they settle, laying eggs to found their own new colonies. The eggs hatch into wormlike larvae, which then pupate in silk cocoons before emerging as adults. *Remarkable species* include army (South American) and driver (African) ants, which march nomadically in huge columns, devouring even tethered animals in their path; leaf-cutter ants, genus *Atta*, which use pieces of leaf to grow edible fungus in underground "gardens;" weaver ants, genus *Oecophylla*, which use their silk-producing larvae as living shuttles to bind the edges of leaves together to form the nest; Eurasian robber ants, *Formica sanguinea*, which raid the nests of another ant species, *Formica fusca*, for pupae, then use the adults as "slaves" when they hatch; and honey ants, in which some workers serve as distended honey stores. In some species, "warfare" is conducted. Others are pastoralists, tending herds of ⬧aphids and collecting a sweet secretion ("honeydew") from them.

Antabuse proprietary name for disulfiram, a synthetic chemical used in the treatment of alcoholism. It produces unpleasant side effects if combined with alcohol, such as nausea, headaches, palpitations, and collapse. The "Antabuse effect" is produced coincidentally by certain antibiotics.

antacid any substance that neutralizes stomach acid, such as sodium bicarbonate or magnesium hydroxide ("milk of magnesia").

Antacids are weak ⬧bases, swallowed as solids or emulsions. They may be taken between meals to relieve symptoms of hyperacidity, such as pain, bloating, nausea, and "heartburn." Excessive or prolonged need for antacids should be investigated medically.

antagonistic muscles in the body, a pair of muscles allowing coordinated movement of the skeletal joints. The extension of the arm, for example, requires one set of muscles to relax, while another set contracts. The individual components of antagonistic pairs can be classified into extensors (muscles that straighten a limb) and flexors (muscles that bend a limb).

Antakya or *Hatay* city in SE Turkey, site of the ancient ⬧Antioch; population (1990) 378,200.

Antananarivo (formerly *Tananarive*) capital of Madagascar, on the interior plateau, with a rail link to Tamatave; population (1986) 703,000. Industries include tobacco, food processing, leather goods, and clothing.

Antarctica continent surrounding the South Pole, arbitrarily defined as the region lying S of the Antarctic Circle. Occupying 10% of the world's surface, Antarctica contains 90% of the world's ice and 70% of its fresh water
area 5,400,000 sq mi/13,900,000 sq km (the size of Europe and the US combined)
physical formed of two blocs of rock with an area of about 3 million sq mi/8 million sq km, Antarctica is covered by a cap of ice that flows slowly toward its 14,000 mi/22,400 km coastline, reaching the sea in high ice cliffs. The most southerly shores are near the 78th parallel in the Ross and Weddell seas. E Antarctica is a massive bloc of ancient rocks that surface in the Transantarctic Mountains of Victoria Land. Separated by a deep channel, W Antarctica is characterized by the mountainous regions of Graham Land, the Antarctic Peninsula, Palmer Land, and Ellsworth Land; the highest peak is Vinson Massif (16,866 ft/5,139 m). Little more than 1% of the land is ice-free. With an estimated volume of 5.9 million cu mi/24 million cu m, the ice-cap has a mean thickness of 6,170 ft/1,880 m and in places reaches depths

of 16,000 ft/5,000 m or more. Each annual layer of snow preserves a record of global conditions, and where no melting at the surface of the bedrock has occurred the ice can be a million years old
climate winds are strong and temperatures are cold, particularly in the interior where temperatures can drop to –100°F/–70°C and below. Precipitation is largely in the form of snow or hoar-frost rather than rain which rarely exceeds 2 in/50 mm per year (less than the Sahara Desert)
flora and fauna the Antarctic ecosystem is characterized by large numbers of relatively few species of higher plants and animals, and a short food chain from tiny marine plants to whales, seals, penguins, and other sea birds. Only two species of vascular plant are known, but there are about 60 species of moss, 100 species of lichen, and 400 species of algae
features Mount Erebus on Ross Island is the world's southernmost active volcano; the Ross Ice Shelf is formed by several glaciers coalescing in the Ross Sea
products cod, Antarctic icefish, and krill are fished in Antarctic waters. Whaling, which began in the early 20th century, ceased during the 1960s as a result of overfishing. Petroleum, coal, and minerals, such as palladium and platinum exist, but their exploitation is prevented by a 50-year ban on commercial mining agreed by 39 nations 1991
population no permanent residents; settlement limited to scientific research stations with maximum population of 2,000 to 3,000 during the summer months. Sectors of Antarctica are claimed by Argentina, Australia, Chile, France, the UK, Norway, and New Zealand.

Antarctic Circle imaginary line that encircles the South Pole at latitude 66° 32′ S. The line encompasses the continent of Antarctica and the Antarctic Ocean.

The region south of this line experiences at least one night during the southern summer during which the Sun never sets, and at least one day during the southern winter during which the Sun never rises.

Antarctic exploration: chronology

1773–74	English explorer James Cook first sailed in Antarctic seas, but exploration was difficult before the development of iron ships able to withstand ice pressure.
1819–21	Antarctica was circumnavigated by Russian explorer Fabian Bellingshausen.
1823	British navigator James Weddell sailed into the sea now named after him.
1841–42	Scottish explorer James Ross sighted the Great Ice Barrier now named after him.
1895	Norwegian explorer Carsten Borchgrevink was one of the first landing party on the continent.
1898	Borchgrevink's British expedition first wintered in Antarctica.
1901–04	English explorer Robert Scott first penetrated the interior of the continent.
1907–08	English explorer Ernest Shackleton came within 113 mi/182 km of the Pole.
1911	Norwegian explorer Roald Amundsen reached the Pole, Dec 14, overland with dogs.
1912	Scott reached the Pole, Jan 18, initially aided by ponies.
1928–29	US naval officer Richard Byrd made the first flight to the Pole.
1935	US explorer Lincoln Ellsworth (1880–1951) first flew across Antarctica.
1946–48	US explorer Finn Ronne's expedition proved the Antarctic to be one continent.
1957–58	English explorer Vivian Fuchs made the first overland crossing.
1959	A Soviet expedition crossed from the West Ice Shelf to the Pole; the International Antarctic Treaty suspended all territorial claims, reserving an area south of 60°S latitude for peaceful purposes.
1961–62	The Bentley Trench was discovered, which suggested that there may be an Atlantic–Pacific link beneath the continent.
1966–67	Specially protected areas were established internationally for animals and plants.
1979	Fossils of apelike humanoids resembling E Africa's Proconsul were found 300 mi/500 km from the Pole.
1980	International Convention on the exploitation of resources—oil, gas, fish, and krill.
1991	The Antarctic Treaty imposing a 50-year ban on mining activity was secured.

Antarctic Ocean popular name for the reaches of the Atlantic, Indian, and Pacific oceans extending S of the Antarctic Circle (66° 32′S). The term is not used by the International Hydrographic Bureau.

Antarctic Peninsula mountainous peninsula of W Antarctica extending 1,200 mi/1,930 km N toward South America; originally named *Palmer Land* after a US navigator, Captain Nathaniel Palmer, who was the first to explore the region 1820. It was claimed by Britain 1832, Argentina 1940, and Chile 1942. Its name was changed to the Antarctic Peninsula 1964.

Antarctic Treaty international agreement aiming to promote scientific research and keep Antarctica free from conflict. It dates from 1961 and in 1991 a 50-year ban on mining activity was secured.

The agreement was signed 1959 between 12 nations with an interest in Antarctica (including Britain), and came into force 1961 for a 30-year period. By 1990 a total of 35 countries were party to it. Its provisions (covering the area south of latitude 60° S) neither accepted nor rejected any nation's territorial claims, but barred any new ones; imposed a ban on military operations and large-scale mineral extraction; and allowed for free exchange of scientific data from bases. In 1980 the treaty was extended to conserve marine resources within the larger area bordered by the Antarctic Convergence.

Antares or *Alpha Scorpii* brightest star in the constellation Scorpius and the 15th brightest star in the sky. It is a red supergiant several hundred times larger than the Sun and perhaps 10,000 times as luminous, lies about 300 light-years away, and fluctuates slightly in brightness.

anteater mammal of the family Myrmecophagidae, order Edentata, native to Mexico, Central America, and tropical South America. An anteater lives almost entirely on ants and termites. It has toothless jaws, an extensile tongue, and claws for breaking into the nests of its prey.

Species include the giant anteater *Myrmecophaga tridactyla*, about 6 ft/1.8 m long including the tail, the tamandua or collared anteater *Tamandua tetradactyla*, about 3.5 ft/90 cm long, and the silky anteater *Cyclopes didactyla*, about 14 in/35 cm long. The name is also incorrectly applied to the aardvark, the echidna, and the pangolin.

antebellum (Latin *ante bellum*, "before the war") in US usage, an adjective referring to the period just before the Civil War (1861–65).

The term "prewar" is used when describing the period before any other war.

antelope any of numerous kinds of even-toed, hoofed mammals belonging to the cow family, Bovidae. Most antelopes are lightly built and good runners. They are grazers or browsers, and chew the cud. They range in size from the dik-diks and duikers, only 1 ft/30 cm high, to the eland, which can be 6 ft/1.8 m at the shoulder.

The majority of antelopes are African, including the eland, gnu, kudu, springbok, and waterbuck, although other species live in Asia, including the deserts of Arabia and the Middle East. The pronghorn antelope *Antilocapra americana* of North America belongs to a different family, the Antilocapridae.

antenna in zoology, an appendage ("feeler") on the head. Insects, centipedes, and millipedes each have one pair of antennae but there are two pairs in crustaceans, such as shrimps. In insects, the antennae are usually involved with the senses of smell and touch; they are frequently complex structures with large surface areas that increase the ability to detect scents.

antenna another name for ◊aerial.

anterior in biology, the front of an organism, usually the part that goes forward first when the animal is moving. The anterior end of the nervous system, over the course of evolution, has developed into a brain with associated receptor organs able to detect stimuli including light and chemicals.

anthelion (Greek "antisun") solar halo caused by a reflection from the atmosphere, snow, or ice, sometimes appearing at the same altitude as the Sun but opposite to it.

anther in a flower, the terminal part of a stamen in which the ◊pollen grains are produced. It is usually borne on a slender stalk or filament, and has two lobes, each containing two chambers, or pollen sacs, within which the pollen is formed.

antheridium organ producing the male gametes, ◊antherozoids, in algae, bryophytes (mosses and liverworts), and pteridophytes (ferns, club mosses, and horsetails). It may be either single-celled, as in most algae, or multicellular, as in bryophytes and pteridophytes.

antherozoid motile (or independently moving) male gamete produced by algae, bryophytes (mosses and liverworts), pteridophytes (ferns, club mosses, and horsetails), and some gymnosperms (notably the cycads). Antherozoids are formed in an antheridium and, after being released, swim by means of one or more ◊flagella, to the female gametes. Higher plants have nonmotile male gametes contained within ◊pollen grains.

Anthony Susan B(rownell) 1820–1906. US pioneering campaigner for women's rights who also worked for the antislavery and temperance movements. Her causes included equality of pay for women teachers, married women's property rights, and women's suffrage. In 1869, with Elizabeth Cady ◊Stanton, she founded the National Woman Suffrage Association.

She edited and published a radical women's newspaper, *The Revolution* 1868–70, and worked on the *History of Woman Suffrage* 1881–86. She organized the International Council of Women and founded the International Woman Suffrage Alliance in Berlin 1904. Her profile appears on the 1979 US dollar coin.

Anthony of Padua, St 1195–1231. Portuguese Franciscan preacher who opposed the relaxations introduced into the order. Born in Lisbon, the son of a nobleman, he became an Augustinian monk, but in 1220 joined the Franciscans. Like St Francis, he is said to have preached to animals. He died in Padua, Italy and was canonized 1232.

Anthony, St *c.* 251–356. Also known as Anthony of Thebes. He was the founder of Christian monasticism. At the age of 20, he renounced all his possessions and began a hermetic life of study and prayer, later seeking further solitude in a cave in the desert.

Anthony was born in Egypt. In 305 he founded the first cenobitic order, a community of Christians following a rule of life under a superior. Late in his life he went to Alexandria and preached against ◊Arianism. He lived to over 100, and a good deal is known about his life since a biography (by St Athanasius) has survived. Anthony's temptations in the desert were a popular subject in art; he is also often depicted with a pig and a bell.

anthracite (from Greek *anthrax*, "coal") hard, dense, shiny variety of ◊coal, containing over 90% carbon and a low percentage of ash and impurities, which causes it to burn without flame, smoke, or smell.

Anthracite gives intense heat, but is slow-burning and slow to light; it is therefore unsuitable for use in open fires. Its characteristic composition is thought to be due to the action of bacteria in disintegrating the coal-forming material when it was laid down during the ◊Carboniferous period.

Among the chief sources of anthracite coal are Pennsylvania in the US; S Wales, UK; the Donbas, Ukraine and Russia; and Shanxi province, China.

anthrax cattle and sheep disease occasionally transmitted to humans, usually via infected hides and fleeces. It may develop as black skin pustules or severe pneumonia. Treatment is with antibiotics.

In the 17th century, some 60,000 cattle died in a European pandemic known as the Black Bane, thought to have been anthrax. The disease is described by the Roman poet Virgil and may have been the cause of the biblical fifth plague of Egypt.

The causative agent is a bacillus (*Bacillus anthracis*).

anthropic principle in science, the idea that "the universe is the way it is because if it were different we would not be here to observe it." The principle arises from the observation that if the laws of science were even slightly different, it would have been impossible for intelligent life to evolve. For example, if the electric charge on the electron were only slightly different, stars would have been unable to burn hydrogen and produce the chemical elements that make up our bodies. Scientists are undecided whether the principle is an insight into the nature of the universe or a piece of circular reasoning.

anthropoid any primate belonging to the suborder Anthropoidea, including monkeys, apes, and humans.

anthropology (Greek *anthropos* "man" and *logos* "discourse") study of humankind, which developed following 19th-century evolutionary theory to investigate the human species, past and present, physically, socially, and culturally.

The four subdisciplines are physical anthropology, linguistics, cultural anthropology, and archeology.

anthropometry science dealing with the measurement of the human body, particularly stature, body weight, cranial capacity, and length of limbs, in samplings of the populations of living peoples, as well as the remains of buried and fossilized humans.

anthropomorphism the attribution of human characteristics to animals, inanimate objects, or deities. It appears in the mythologies of many cultures and as a literary device in fables and allegories.

anthroposophy system of mystical philosophy developed by Rudolf ◊Steiner, who claimed to possess a power of intuition giving him access to knowledge not attainable by scientific means.

Antibes resort, which includes Juan les Pins,

on the French Riviera, in the *département* of Alpes Maritimes; population (1982) 63,248. There is a Picasso collection in the 17th-century castle museum.

antibiotic drug that kills or inhibits the growth of bacteria and fungi. It is derived from living organisms such as fungi or bacteria, which distinguishes it from synthetic antimicrobials.

The earliest antibiotics, the ◊penicillins, came into use from 1941 and were quickly joined by ◊chloramphenicol, the ◊cephalosporins, erythromycins, tetracyclines, and aminoglycosides. A range of broad-spectrum antibiotics, the 4-quinolones, was developed 1989, of which ciprofloxacin was the first. Each class and individual antibiotic acts in a different way and may be effective against either a broad spectrum or a specific type of disease-causing agent. Use of antibiotics has become more selective as side effects, such as toxicity, allergy, and resistance, have become better understood. Bacteria have the ability to develop immunity following repeated or subclinical (insufficient) doses, so more advanced and synthetic antibiotics are continually required to overcome them.

antibody a protein molecule produced in the blood by B-lymphocytes (see ◊lymphocyte). Antibodies bind specific foreign agents that invade the body, tagging them for destruction by phagocytes (white blood cells that engulf and destroy invaders) or activating a chemical system that renders them harmless. Each antibody is specific for a particular ◊antigen (the molecular pattern unique to a foreign substance).

anticholinergic any drug that blocks the passage of certain nerve impulses in the ◊central nervous system by inhibiting the production of acetylcholine, a neurotransmitter.

Its wide range of effects makes it an effective component of premedication: it may be put in the eyes before examination or treatment to dilate the pupil and paralyze the muscles of accommodation, or inhaled to relieve constriction of the airways in bronchitis. Tremor and rigidity can be reduced in mild ◊Parkinson's disease. Bladder muscle tone may also be improved in the treatment of urinary frequency. Its usefulness as an ◊antispasmodic is limited by side effects, such as dry mouth, visual disturbances, and urinary retention.

Antichrist in Christian theology, the opponent of Christ. The appearance of the Antichrist was believed to signal the Second Coming, at which Christ would conquer his opponent. The concept may stem from the idea of conflict between Light and Darkness, which is present in Persian, Babylonian, and Jewish literature and which influenced early Christian thought.

The Antichrist may be a false messiah, or be connected with false teaching, or be identified with an individual, for example Nero at the time of the persecution of Christians, and the pope and Napoleon in later Christian history.

anticline in geology, a fold in the rocks of the Earth's crust in which the layers or beds bulge upward to form an arch (seldom preserved intact).

The fold of an anticline may be undulating or steeply curved. A steplike bend in otherwise gently dipping or horizontal beds is a **monocline**. The opposite of an anticline is a **syncline.**

anticoagulant substance that suppresses the formation of blood clots. Common anticoagulants are heparin, produced by the liver and lungs, and derivatives of coumarin. Anticoagulants are used medically in treating heart attacks, for example. They are also produced by blood-feeding animals, such as mosquitoes, leeches, and vampire bats, to keep the victim's blood flowing.

Most anticoagulants prevent the production of thrombin, an enzyme that induces the formation from blood plasma of fibrinogen, to which blood platelets adhere and form clots.

Anti-Comintern Pact (Anti-Communist Pact) agreement signed between Germany and Japan Nov 25, 1936, opposing communism as a menace to peace and order. The pact was signed by Italy 1937 and by Hungary, Spain, and the Japanese puppet state of Manchukuo in 1939. While directed against the USSR, the agreement also had the effect of giving international recognition to Japanese rule in Manchuria.

anticommunism fierce antagonism toward communism linked particularly with right-wing politician Joseph ◊McCarthy's activities in the US during the 1950s. He made numerous unsubstantiated claims that the State Department had been infiltrated by Communist activity, thus triggering a wave of anticommunist hysteria. He did not succeed in identifying any Communists employed by the government.

anticonvulsant any drug used to prevent epileptic seizures (convulsions or fits); see ◊epilepsy.

In many cases, epilepsy can be controlled completely by careful therapy with one agent. Patients should stop or change treatment only under medical supervision.

anticyclone area of high atmospheric pressure caused by descending air, which becomes warm and dry. Winds radiate from a calm center, taking a clockwise direction in the northern hemisphere and a counterclockwise direction in the southern hemisphere. Anticyclones are characterized by clear weather and the absence of rain and violent winds. In summer they bring hot, sunny days and in winter they bring fine, frosty spells, although fog and low cloud are not uncommon in the UK. *Blocking anticyclones*, which prevent the normal air circulation of an area, can cause summer droughts and severe winters.

antidepressant any drug used to relieve symptoms in depressive illness. The two main groups are the tricyclic antidepressants (TCADs) and the monoamine oxidase inhibitors (MAOIs), which act by altering chemicals available to the central nervous system. Both may produce serious side effects and are restricted.

antidiarrheal any substance that controls diarrhea.

Choice of treatment depends on the underlying cause. One group, including opiates, codeine, and atropine, produces constipation by slowing down motility (muscle activity of the intestine wall). Bulking agents, such as vegetable fibers (for example, methylcellulose), absorb fluid. Antibiotics may be appropriate for certain systemic bacterial infections, such as typhoid, salmonella, and enteritis (caused by *Campylobacter* species). Current therapy of acute diarrhea is based on fluid and ◊electrolyte replacement. Chronic diarrhea, a feature of some bowel disorders (for example, Crohn's disease, colitis, celiac disease) responds to antispasmodics, special diet, and corticosteroids.

antiemetic any substance that counteracts nausea or vomiting.

Antietam, Battle of bloody but indecisive battle of the American Civil War Sept 17, 1862 at Antietam Creek, off the Potomac River. General McClellan of the Union blocked the advance of the Confederates under Robert E Lee on Maryland and Washington, DC. This battle persuaded the British not to recognize the Confederacy.

antifreeze substance added to a water-cooling system (for example, that of a car) to prevent it freezing in cold weather.

The most common types of antifreeze contain the chemical ethylene ◊glycol, or ($HOCH_2CH_2OH$), an organic alcohol with a freezing point of about 5°F/–15°C.

The addition of this chemical depresses the freezing point of water significantly. A solution containing 33.5% by volume of ethylene glycol will not freeze until about –4°F/–20°C. A 50% solution will not freeze until –31°F/–35°C.

antifungal any drug that acts against fungal infection, such as ringworm and athlete's foot.

antigen any substance that causes the production of ◊antibodies by the body's immune system. Common antigens include the proteins carried on the surface of bacteria, viruses, and pollen grains. The proteins of incompatible blood groups or tissues also act as antigens, which has to be taken into account in medical procedures such as blood transfusions and organ transplants.

Antigone in Greek legend, a daughter of Jocasta, by her son ◊Oedipus. She is the subject of a tragedy by Sophocles.

Antigone tragedy by Sophocles, written about 411 BC. Antigone buries her brother Polynices, in defiance of the Theban king Creon, but in accordance with the wishes of the gods. Creon imprisons Antigone in a cave, but after a warning that he has defied the gods, he goes to the cave and finds that Antigone has hanged herself.

Antigonus 382–301 BC. A general of Alexander the Great, after whose death 323 Antigonus made himself master of Asia Minor. He was defeated and slain by ◊Seleucus I at the battle of Ipsus.

Antigua and Barbuda country comprising three islands in the E Caribbean (Antigua, Barbuda, and uninhabited Redonda).

government Antigua and Barbuda constitute an independent sovereign nation within the British ◊Commonwealth, with the British monarch as head of state. The constitution came into effect with independence 1981. The governor-general, representing the British monarch, is appointed on the advice of the Antiguan prime minister, who is chosen by the governor-general as the person most likely to have the support of the legislature. The parliament is similar to Britain's, with a prime minister and cabinet answerable to it. It consists of a senate and a house of representatives, each having 17 members.

Senators are appointed for a five-year term by the governor-general, 11 of them on the advice of the prime minister, four on the advice of the leader of the opposition, one at the governor-general's own discretion, and one on the advice of the Barbuda Council, the main instrument for local government.

Members of the house of representatives are elected by universal suffrage for a similar term.

history The original inhabitants of Antigua and Barbuda were Carib Indians. The first Europeans to visit Antigua were with Christopher Columbus 1493, although they did not go ashore. He named the island after the church of Santa Maria de la Antigua at Seville. Antigua was first colonized by Britain 1632. Charles II leased Barbuda 1685 to the Codrington family, who ran a sugar plantation on Antigua. Barbuda was a source of stock and provisions for the plantation and was inhabited almost entirely by black slaves, who used the relatively barren land cooperatively. The Codringtons finally surrendered the lease 1870. Barbuda reverted to the crown in the later 19th century. The Antiguan slaves were freed 1834 but remained poor, totally dependent on the sugar crop market. Between 1860 and 1959 the islands were administered by Britain within a federal system known as the ⬦Leeward Islands. Antigua and Barbuda was made an associated state of the UK and given full internal independence 1967, with Britain retaining responsibility for defense and foreign affairs. Barbuda, with a population of about 1,200 people, started a separatist movement 1969, fearing that Antigua would sell Barbudan land to foreign developers. Projects approved by the central government against the wishes of Barbudans include sand mining and a plan for a toxic-waste disposal site.

independence from Britain In the 1971 general election, the Progressive Labor Movement (PLM) won a decisive victory, and its leader, George Walter, replaced Vere Bird, leader of the Antigua Labor Party (ALP), as prime minister. The PLM fought the 1976 election on a call for early independence while the ALP urged caution until a firm economic foundation had

been laid. The ALP won and declared 1978 that the country was ready for independence. Opposition from the inhabitants of Barbuda delayed the start of constitutional talks, and the territory eventually became independent as Antigua and Barbuda 1981. Despite its adherence to the ⬦nonaligned movement, the ALP government actively assisted the US invasion of Grenada 1983 and went on to win 16 of the 17 seats in the 1984 general election. In the 1989 general election Bird and the ALP again won a sweeping victory, but in 1990 his government was tarnished by allegations that his son, a cabinet minister, was involved in illegal arms deals. Calls by parliament for Bird's resignation 1991 were unsuccessful. *See illustration box.*

antihistamine any substance that counteracts the effects of ⬦histamine. Antihistamines may be naturally produced (such as vitamin C and epinephrin) or synthesized (pseudepinephrin).

H_1 antihistamines are used to relieve allergies, alleviating symptoms such as runny nose, itching, swelling, or asthma. H_2 antihistamines suppress acid production by the stomach, providing treatment for peptic ulcers that often makes surgery unnecessary.

antihypertensive therapy any treatment that controls ⬦hypertension. The first step is usually exercise and a change in diet to reduce salt and, if necessary, caloric intake. If further measures are required, a drug regimen may be prescribed.

anti-inflammatory any substance that reduces swelling in soft tissues. Antihistamines relieve allergic reactions; aspirin and

⬦NSAIDs are effective in joint and musculoskeletal conditions; rubefacients (counterirritant liniments) ease painful joints, tendons, and muscles.

⬦Steroids, because of their severe side effects, are only prescribed if other therapy is ineffective, or if a condition is life-threatening. A ⬦corticosteroid injection into the affected joint usually gives long-term relief from inflammation.

Anti-Lebanon or *Antilibanus* mountain range on the Lebanese-Syrian border, including Mount Hermon, 9,200 ft/2,800 m. It is separated from the Lebanon mountains by the Bekaa valley.

Antilles whole group of West Indian islands, divided N–S into the *Greater Antilles* (Cuba, Jamaica, Haiti–Dominican Republic, Puerto Rico) and *Lesser Antilles*, subdivided into the Leeward Islands (Virgin Islands, St Kitts–Nevis, Antigua and Barbuda, Anguilla, Montserrat, and Guadeloupe) and the Windward Islands (Dominica, Martinique, St Lucia, St Vincent and the Grenadines, Barbados, and Grenada).

antilogarithm or *antilog* the inverse of ⬦logarithm, or the number whose logarithm to a given base is a given number. If $y = \log_a x$, then $x = \text{antilog}_a y$.

antimatter in physics, a form of matter in which most of the attributes (such as electrical charge, magnetic moment, and spin) of ⬦elementary particles are reversed. Such particles (antiparticles) can be created in particle accelerators, such as those at ⬦CERN in Geneva, Switzerland, and at ⬦Fermilab in the US.

antimony silver-white, brittle, semimetallic element (a metalloid), symbol Sb (from Latin *stibium*), atomic number 51, atomic weight 121.75. It occurs chiefly as the ore stibnite, and is used to make alloys harder; it is also used in photosensitive substances in color photography, optical electronics, fireproofing, pigment, and medicine. It was employed by the ancient Egyptians in a mixture to protect the eyes from flies.

Antioch ancient capital of the Greek kingdom of Syria, founded 300 BC by Seleucus Nicator in memory of his father Antiochus, and famed for its splendor and luxury. Under the Roman and Byzantine empires it was an early center of Christianity. It was captured by the Arabs 637. After a five-month siege 1098 Antioch was taken by the crusaders, who held it until 1268. The site is now occupied by the Turkish town of ⬦Antakya.

Antiochus thirteen kings of Syria of the Seleucid dynasty, including:

Antiochus I c. 324–c. 261 BC. King of Syria from 281 BC, son of Seleucus I, one of the generals of Alexander the Great. He earned the title of Antiochus Soter, or Savior, by his defeat of the Gauls in Galatia 278.

Antiochus II c. 286–c. 246 BC. King of Syria 261–246 BC, son of Antiochus I. He was known as Antiochus Theos, the Divine. During his reign the eastern provinces broke away from the Graeco-Macedonian rule and set up native princes. He made peace with Egypt by marrying the daughter of Ptolemy Philadelphus, but was a tyrant among his own people.

Antiochus III the Great c. 241–187 BC. King of Syria from 223 BC, nephew of Antiochus II. He secured a loose suzerainty over Armenia and Parthia 209, overcame Bactria, received

Antigua and Barbuda
State of

area Antigua 108 sq mi/280 sq km, Barbuda 62 sq mi/161 sq km, plus Redonda 0.4 sq mi/1 sq km
capital (and chief port) St John's
cities Codrington (on Barbuda)
physical low-lying tropical islands of limestone and coral with some higher volcanic outcrops; no rivers and low rainfall result in frequent droughts and deforestation
features Antigua is the largest of the Leeward Islands; Redonda is an uninhabited island of volcanic rock rising to 1,000 ft/305 m
head of state Elizabeth II from 1981 represented by governor-general
head of government Vere C Bird from 1981
political system liberal democracy

political parties Antigua Labor Party (ALP), moderate, left of center; Progressive Labor Movement (PLM), left of center
exports sea-island cotton, rum, lobsters
currency Eastern Caribbean dollar
population (1989) 83,500; growth rate 1.3% p.a.
life expectancy 70 years
language English
media no daily newspaper; weekly papers all owned by political parties
religion Christian (mostly Anglican)
literacy 90% (1985)
GDP $173 million (1985); $2,200 per head
chronology
1493 Antigua visited by Christopher Columbus.
1632 Antigua colonized by English settlers.
1667 Treaty of Breda formally ceded Antigua to Britain.
1871–1956 Antigua and Barbuda administered as part of the Leeward Islands federation.
1967 Antigua and Barbuda became an associated state within the Commonwealth, with full internal independence.
1971 PLM won the general election by defeating the ALP.
1976 PLM called for early independence, but ALP urged caution. ALP won the general election.
1981 Independence from Britain achieved.
1983 Assisted US invasion of Grenada.
1984 ALP won a decisive victory in the general election.
1985 ALP reelected.
1989 Another sweeping general election victory for the ALP under Vere Bird.
1991 Bird remained in power despite calls for his resignation.

the homage of the Indian king of the Kabul valley, and returned by way of the Persian Gulf 204. He took possession of Palestine, entering Jerusalem 198. He crossed into NW Greece, but was decisively defeated by the Romans at Thermopylae 191 and at Magnesia 190. He had to abandon his domains in Anatolia, and was killed by the people of Elymais.

Antiochus IV c. 215–164 BC. King of Syria from 175 BC, known as Antiochus Epiphanes, the Illustrious; second son of Antiochus III. He occupied Jerusalem about 170, seizing much of the Temple treasure, and instituted worship of the Greek type in the Temple in an attempt to eradicate Judaism. This produced the revolt of the Hebrews under the Maccabees; Antiochus died before he could suppress it.

Antiochus VII Sidetes c. 159–129 BC. King of Syria from 138 BC. The last strong ruler of the Seleucid dynasty, he took Jerusalem 134, reducing the Maccabees to subjection, and fought successfully against the Parthians.

Antiochus XIII Asiaticus 1st century BC. King of Syria 69–65 BC, the last of the Seleucid dynasty. During his reign Syria was made a Roman province by Pompey the Great.

antioxidant any substance that prevents deterioration by oxidation in fats, oils, paints, plastics, and rubbers. When used as ⟡food additives, antioxidants prevent fats and oils from becoming rancid when exposed to air, and thus extend their shelf life.

Vegetable oils contain natural antioxidants, such as vitamin E, which prevent spoilage, but antioxidants are nevertheless added to most oils. They are not always listed on food labels because if a food manufacturer buys an oil to make a food product, and the oil has antioxidant already added, it does not have to be listed on the label of the product. Some studies have shown that the antioxidants BHT and BHA cause behavior disorders in animals.

They are limited to 0.02% of the total content by FDA standards.

antiparticle in nuclear physics, a particle corresponding in mass and properties to a given ⟡elementary particle but with the opposite electrical charge, magnetic properties, or coupling to other fundamental forces. For example, an electron carries a negative charge whereas its antiparticle, the positron, carries a positive one. When a particle and its antiparticle collide, they destroy each other, in the process called "annihilation," their total energy being converted to lighter particles and/or photons. A substance consisting entirely of antiparticles is known as ⟡antimatter.

antiphony in music, a form of composition using widely spaced choirs or groups of instruments to create perspectives in sound. It was developed in 17th-century Venice by Giovanni ⟡Gabrieli and his pupil Heinrich Schütz.

antipodes (Greek "opposite feet") places at opposite points on the globe.

The North Pole is antipodal to the South Pole.

antipope rival claimant to the elected pope for the leadership of the Roman Catholic Church, for instance in the Great Schism 1378–1417 when there were rival popes in Rome and Avignon.

antipsychotic or **neuroleptic** any drug used to treat the symptoms of severe mental disorder.

antipyretic any drug, such as aspirin, used to reduce fever.

antiracism and antisexism active opposition to ⟡racism and ⟡sexism; positive action or a set of policies, such as "equal opportunity," can be designed to counteract racism and sexism, often on the part of an official body or an institution, such as a school, a business, or a government agency.

Positive ⟡discrimination is used in some government programs to give preference to those groups who have been victims of long-term sexual or racial prejudice.

antirrhinum or **snapdragon** any of several plants, genus Antirrhinum, in the figwort family Scrophulariaceae. Foxglove and toadflax are relatives. Antirrhinums are native to the Mediterranean region and W North America.

Antirrhinum majus is a common garden flower, native to the Mediterranean.

anti-Semitism literally, prejudice against Semitic people (see ⟡Semite), but in practice it has meant prejudice or discrimination against, and persecution of, the Jews as an ethnic group. Historically this was practiced for almost 2,000 years by European Christians. Anti-Semitism was a tenet of Hitler's Germany, and in the Holocaust 1933–45 about 6 million Jews died in concentration camps and in local extermination ⟡pogroms, such as the siege of the Warsaw ghetto. In eastern Europe, as well as in Islamic nations, anti-Semitism exists and is promulgated by neofascist groups. It is a form of ⟡racism.

The destruction of Jerusalem AD 70 led many Jews to settle in Europe and throughout the Roman Empire. In the 4th century Christianity was adopted as the official religion of the Empire, which reinforced existing prejudice (dating back to pre-Christian times and referred to in the works of Seneca and Tacitus) against Jews who refused to convert. Anti-Semitism increased in the Middle Ages because of the Crusades and the Inquisition, and legislation forbade Jews to own land or be members of a craft guild; to earn a living they had to become moneylenders and traders (and were then resented when they prospered). Britain expelled many Jews 1290, but they were formally readmitted 1655 by Cromwell. From the 16th century Jews were forced by law in many cities to live in a separate area, or **ghetto**.

Late 18th- and early 19th-century liberal thought improved the position of Jews in European society. In the Austro-Hungarian Empire, for example, they were allowed to own land, and after the French Revolution the "rights of man" were extended to French Jews 1790. The rise of 19th-century nationalism and unscientific theories of race instigated new resentments. Anti-Semitism became strong in Austria, France (see ⟡Dreyfus), and Germany, and from 1881 pogroms in Poland and Russia caused refugees to flee to the US (where freedom of religion was enshrined in the constitution), to the UK, and to other European countries as well as Palestine (see ⟡Zionism).

In the 20th century, fascism and the Nazi Party's application of racial theories led to organized persecution and genocide. After World War II, the creation of Israel 1948 provoked Palestinian anti-Zionism, backed by the Arab world. Anti-Semitism is still fostered by extreme right-wing groups, such as the National Front in the UK and France, the Neo-Nazis in the US and Germany, and the Palestine Liberation Organization in the Arab nations.

antiseptic any substance that kills or inhibits the growth of microorganisms. The use of antiseptics was pioneered by Joseph ⟡Lister. He

used carbolic acid (⟡phenol), which is a weak antiseptic; substances such as TCP are derived from this.

antispasmodic any drug that reduces motility, the spontaneous action of the muscle walls. ⟡Anticholinergics are a type of antispasmodic that act indirectly by way of the autonomic nervous system, which controls involuntary movement. Other drugs act directly on the smooth muscle to relieve spasm (contraction).

antitrust laws in economics, regulations preventing or restraining trusts, monopolies, or any business practice considered to be unfair or uncompetitive. In the US, antitrust laws prevent mergers and acquisitions that might create a monopoly situation or ones in which restrictive practices might be stimulated.

antitussive any substance administered to suppress a cough. Coughing, however, is an important reflex in clearing secretions from the airways; its suppression is usually unnecessary and possibly harmful, unless damage is being done to tissue during excessive cough spasms.

antiviral any drug that acts against viruses, usually preventing them from multiplying. Most viral infections are not susceptible to antibiotics. Antivirals have been difficult drugs to develop, and do not necessarily cure viral diseases.

antivivisection opposition to vivisection, that is, experiments on living animals, which is practiced in the pharmaceutical and cosmetics industries on the grounds that it may result in discoveries of importance to medical science. Antivivisectionists argue that it is immoral to inflict pain on helpless creatures, and that it is unscientific because results achieved with animals may not be paralleled with human beings.

Antivivisectionist groups, now joined by animal rights activists, sometimes take illegal action to draw attention to their cause.

antler "horn" of a deer, often branched, and made of bone rather than horn. Antlers, unlike true horns, are shed and regrown each year. Reindeer of both sexes grow them, but in all other types of deer, only the males have antlers.

ant lion larva of one of the insects of the family Myrmeleontidae, order Neuroptera, which traps ants by waiting at the bottom of a pit dug in loose, sandy soil. Ant lions are mainly tropical, but also occur in parts of Europe and in the US, where they are called doodlebugs.

Antofagasta port of N Chile, capital of the region of Antofagasta; population (1990) 218,800. The area of the region is 48,366 sq mi/ 125,300 sq km; its population (1982) 341,000. Nitrates from the Atacama Desert are exported.

Antonello da Messina c. 1430–1479. Italian painter, born in Messina, Sicily, a pioneer of the technique of oil painting, which he is said to have introduced to Italy from N Europe. Flemish influence is reflected in his technique, his use of light, and sometimes in his imagery. Surviving works include bust-length portraits and somber religious paintings.

He visited Venice in the 1470s where his work inspired, among other Venetian painters, the young Giovanni Bellini. St Jerome in His Study about 1460 (National Gallery, London) and A Young Man 1478 (Staatliche Museen, Berlin) are examples of his work.

Antonescu Ion 1882–1946. Romanian general and politician who headed a pro-German government during World War II and was executed for war crimes 1946.

Antonine Wall Roman line of fortification built AD 142–200. It was the Roman Empire's northwest frontier, between the Clyde and Forth rivers, Scotland.

Antoninus Pius AD 86–161. Roman emperor who had been adopted 138 as Hadrian's heir, and succeeded him later that year. He enjoyed a prosperous reign, during which he built the Antonine Wall. His daughter married ▷Marcus Aurelius Antoninus.

Antonioni Michelangelo 1912– . Italian film director, famous for his subtle presentations of neuroses and personal relationships among the leisured classes. His elliptical approach to narrative is best seen in *L'Avventura* 1959.

Beginning his career making documentaries, Antonioni directed his first feature film, *Cronaca di un Amore/Story of a Love Affair* 1950. His other films include *Blow Up* 1966, *Zabriskie Point* 1970, and *The Passenger* 1975.

Antony and Cleopatra tragedy by William Shakespeare, written and first performed 1607–08. Mark Antony falls in love with the Egyptian queen Cleopatra in Alexandria, but returns to Rome when his wife, Fulvia, dies. He then marries Octavia to heal the rift between her brother Augustus Caesar and himself. Antony returns to Egypt and Cleopatra, but is finally defeated by Augustus. Believing Cleopatra dead, Antony kills himself, and Cleopatra takes her own life rather than surrender to Augustus.

antonymy near or precise oppositeness between or among words. *Good* and *evil* are antonyms, and therefore *evil* and *bad* are synonyms in this context.

Antonymy may vary with context and situation: in discussing a color, *dull* and *bright* are antonymous, but when talking about knives and blades, the opposite of *dull* is *sharp* (when it comes to intellect, *bright* and *sharp* are equally used).

Antrim county of Northern Ireland
area 1,092 sq mi/2,830 sq km
cities Belfast (county town), Larne (port)
features Giant's Causeway of natural hexagonal basalt columns, which, in legend, was built to enable the giants to cross between Ireland and Scotland; Antrim borders Lough Neagh, and is separated from Scotland by the 20-mi-/32-km-wide North Channel
products potatoes, oats, linen, synthetic textiles
population (1981) 642,000.

Antwerp (Flemish *Antwerpen*, French *Anvers*) port in Belgium on the river Scheldt, capital of the province of Antwerp; population (1991) 467,500. One of the world's busiest ports, it has shipbuilding, oil-refining, petrochemical, textile, and diamond-cutting industries. The home of the artist Rubens is preserved, and many of his works are in the Gothic cathedral. The province of Antwerp has an area of 1,119 sq mi/2,900 sq km; population (1987) 1,588,000.

It was not until the 15th century that Antwerp rose to prosperity; from 1500 to 1560 it was the richest port in N Europe. After this Antwerp was beset by religious troubles and the Netherlands revolt against Spain. In 1648 the Treaty of Westphalia gave both shores of the Scheldt estuary to the United Provinces, which closed it to Antwerp trade. The Treaty of Paris 1814 opened the estuary to all nations on payment of a small toll to the Dutch, abandoned 1863. During World War I Antwerp was occupied by Germany Oct 1914–Nov 1918; during World War II, May 1940–Sept 1944.

Anu Mesopotamian sky god, commonly joined in a trinity with Enlil and Ea.

Anubis in Egyptian mythology, the jackalheaded god of the dead, son of Osiris. Anubis presided over the funeral cult, including embalming, and led the dead to judgment.

Anuradhapura ancient holy city in Sri Lanka; population (1981) 36,000. It was the capital of the Sinhalese kings of Sri Lanka 5th century BC–8th century AD; rediscovered in the mid-19th century. Sacred in Buddhism, it claims a Bo tree descended from the one under which the Buddha became enlightened.

anus opening at the end of the alimentary canal that allows undigested food and associated materials to pass out of an animal. It is found in all types of multicellular animal except the coelenterates (sponges) and the platyhelminthes (flat worms), which have a mouth only.

Anvers French form of ▷Antwerp, a province in N Belgium.

anxiety emotional state of fear or apprehension. Anxiety is a normal response to potentially dangerous situations. Abnormal anxiety can either be free-floating, experienced in a wide range of situations, or it may be phobic, when the sufferer is excessively afraid of an object or situation.

anxiolytic any drug that reduces an anxiety state.

Anyang city in Henan province, E China; population (1986) 550,000. It was the capital of the Shang dynasty (13th–12th centuries BC). Rich archeological remains have been uncovered since the 1930s.

ANZAC (acronym for *Australian and New Zealand Army Corps*) general term for all troops of both countries serving in World War I and to some extent those in World War II.

Anzio, Battle of in World War II, the beachhead invasion of Italy Jan 22–May 23, 1944, by Allied troops; failure to use information gained by deciphering German codes led to Allied troops being stranded temporarily after German attacks. Anzio is a seaport and resort on the W coast of Italy, 33 mi/53 km SE of Rome; population (1984) 25,000. It is the site of the Roman town of Antium and the birthplace of Emperor Nero.

ANZUS acronym for *Australia, New Zealand, and the United States* (Pacific Security Treaty), a military alliance established 1951. It was replaced 1954 by the ▷Southeast Asia Treaty Organization, (SEATO).

aorta the chief ▷artery, the dorsal blood vessel carrying oxygenated blood from the left ventricle of the heart in birds and mammals. It branches to form smaller arteries, which in turn supply all body organs except the lungs. Loss of elasticity in the aorta provides evidence of ▷atherosclerosis, which may lead to heart disease.

In fish a ventral aorta carries deoxygenated blood from the heart to the ▷gills, and the dorsal aorta carries oxygenated blood from the gills to other parts of the body.

Aouzu Strip disputed territory 60 mi/100 km wide on the Chad–Libya frontier, occupied by Libya 1973. Lying to the N of the Tibesti massif, the area is rich in uranium and other minerals.

a.p. in physics, abbreviation for *a*tmospheric *p*ressure.

Apache member of a group of North ▷American Indian peoples who lived as hunters in the Southwest. They are related to the Navaho, and now number about 10,000, living in reservations in Arizona, SW Oklahoma, and New Mexico. They were known as fierce raiders and horse warriors in the 18th and 19th centuries. Apache also refers to any of several southern Athabaskan languages and dialects spoken by these people.

Apache Point Observatory US observatory in the Sacramento Mountains of New Mexico containing a 3.5-m/138-in reflector, opened 1991, and operated by the Astrophysical Research Consortium (the universities of Washington, Chicago, Princeton, and New Mexico and Washington State universities).

apartheid (Afrikaans "apartness") racial-segregation policy of the government of South Africa, which was legislated 1948, when the Afrikaner National Party gained power. Nonwhites (Bantu, colored or mixed, or Indian) do not share full rights of citizenship with the 4.5 million whites (for example, the 23 million black people cannot vote in parliamentary elections), and many public facilities and institutions were until 1990 (and in some cases remain) restricted to the use of one race only; the establishment of ▷Black National States is another manifestation of apartheid. In 1991 President de Klerk repealed the key elements of apartheid legislation.

The term "apartheid" was coined in the late 1930s by the South African Bureau for Racial Affairs (SABRA), which called for a policy of "separate development" of the races.

Internally, organizations opposed to apartheid were banned, for example the African National Congress and the United Democratic Front, and leading campaigners for its abolition have been, like Steve Biko, killed, or, like Archbishop Tutu, harassed. Anger at the policy has sparked off many uprisings, from ▷Sharpeville 1960 and ▷Soweto 1976 to the Crossroads squatter camps 1986.

Abroad, there are antiapartheid movements in many countries. In 1961 South Africa was forced to withdraw from the Commonwealth because of apartheid; during the 1960s and 1970s there were calls for international ▷sanctions, especially boycotts of sporting and cultural links; and in the 1980s advocates of sanctions extended them into trade and finance.

The South African government's reaction to internal and international pressure was twofold: it abolished some of the more hated apartheid laws (the ban on interracial marriages was lifted 1985 and the pass laws, which restricted the movement of nonwhites, were repealed 1986); and it sought to replace the term "apartheid" with "plural democracy." Under states of emergency 1985 and 1986 it used force to quell internal opposition, and from 1986 there was an official ban on the reporting of it in the media. In Oct 1989 President F W de Klerk permitted antiapartheid demonstrations; the Separate Amenities Act was abolished 1990 and a new constitution promised. In 1990 Nelson Mandela, a leading figure in the African National Congress, was finally released. In 1991 the remaining major discriminating laws embodied in apartheid were repealed, including the Population Registration Act, which had made it obligatory for every citizen to be classified into one of nine racial groups.

The term has also been applied to similar movements and other forms of racial separation, for example social or educational, in other parts of the world.

apastron the point at which an object traveling in an elliptical orbit around a star is at its furthest from the star. The term is usually applied to the position of the minor component of a ◊binary star in relation to the primary. Its opposite is ◊periastron.

apatite common calcium phosphate mineral, $Ca_5(PO_4CO_3)_3(F,OH,Cl)$. Apatite has a hexagonal structure and occurs widely in igneous rocks, such as pegmatite, and in contact metamorphic rocks, such as marbles. It is used in the manufacture of fertilizer and as a source of phosphorus. Apatite is the chief constituent of tooth enamel while hydroxyapatite, $Ca_{10}(PO_4)_6(OH)_2$, is the chief inorganic constituent of bone marrow. Apatite ranks 5 on the ◊Mohs' scale of hardness.

apatosaurus large plant-eating dinosaur, formerly called **brontosaurus**, which flourished about 145 million years ago. Up to 69 ft/21 m long and 30 tons in weight, it stood on four elephantlike legs and had a long tail, long neck, and small head. It probably snipped off low-growing vegetation with peglike front teeth, and swallowed it whole to be ground by pebbles in the stomach.

APC abbreviation for ◊**armored personnel carrier**, a battlefield vehicle.

ape ◊primate of the family Pongidae, closely related to humans, including gibbon, orangutan, chimpanzee, and gorilla.

Ape City Yerkes Regional Primate Center, Atlanta, Georgia, where large numbers of primates are kept for physiological and psychological experiment. A major area of research at Ape City is language.

Apelles 4th century BC. Greek painter, said to have been the greatest in antiquity. He was court painter to Philip of Macedonia and his son Alexander the Great. None of his work survives, only descriptions of his portraits and nude Venuses.

Apennines chain of mountains stretching the length of the Italian peninsula. A continuation of the Maritime Alps, from Genoa it swings across the peninsula to Ancona on the E coast, and then back to the W coast and into the "toe" of Italy. The system is continued over the Strait of Messina along the N Sicilian coast, then across the Mediterranean Sea in a series of islands to the Atlas Mountains of N Africa. The highest peak is Gran Sasso d'Italia at 9,560 ft/2,914 m.

aperture in photography, an opening in the camera that allows light to pass through the lens to strike the film. Controlled by shutter speed and the iris diaphragm, it can be set mechanically or electronically at various diameters.

aphasia difficulty in speaking, writing, and reading, usually caused by damage to the brain.

aphelion the point at which an object, traveling in an elliptical orbit around the Sun, is at its furthest from the Sun.

aphid any of the family of small insects, Aphididae, in the order Homoptera, that live by sucking sap from plants. There are many species, often adapted to particular plants.

In some stages of their life cycle, wingless females rapidly produce large numbers of live young by ◊parthenogenesis, leading to enormous infestations, and numbers can approach 1 billion per acre/2 billion per hectare. They can also cause damage by transmitting viral diseases. An aphid that damages cypress and cedar trees appeared in Malawi in 1985 and by 1991 was attacking millions of trees in central and E Africa. Some research suggests, however, that aphids may help promote fertility in the soil through the waste they secrete, termed "honeydew." Aphids are also known as plant lice, greenflies, or blackflies.

aphrodisiac (from Aphrodite, the Greek goddess of love) any substance that arouses or increases sexual desire.

Sexual activity can be stimulated in humans and animals by drugs affecting the pituitary gland. Preparations commonly sold for the purpose can be dangerous (cantharidin) or useless (rhinoceros horn), and alcohol and marijuana, popularly thought to be effective because they lessen inhibition, often have the opposite effect.

Aphrodite in Greek mythology, the goddess of love (Roman Venus, Phoenician Astarte, Babylonian Ishtar); said to be either a daughter of Zeus (in Homer) or sprung from the foam of the sea (in Hesiod). She was the unfaithful wife of Hephaestus, the god of fire, and the mother of Eros.

Apia capital and port of Western ◊Samoa, on the N coast of Upolu Island, in the W Pacific; population (1981) 33,000. It was the final home of the writer Robert Louis Stevenson from 1888–94.

Apis ancient Egyptian god with a human body and a bull's head, linked with Osiris (and later merged with him into the Ptolemaic god Serapis); his cult centers were Memphis and Heliopolis, where sacred bulls were mummified.

Apocrypha appendix to the Old Testament of the Bible, not included in the final Hebrew canon but recognized by Roman Catholics. There are also disputed New Testament texts known as Apocrypha.

apogee the point at which an object, traveling in an elliptical orbit around the Earth, is at its furthest from the Earth.

Apollinaire Guillaume. Adopted name of Guillaume Apollinaire de Kostrowitsky 1880–1918. French poet of aristocratic Polish descent. He was a leader of the avant-garde in Parisian literary and artistic circles. His novel *Le Poète assassiné/The Poet Assassinated* 1916, followed by the experimental poems *Alcools/Alcohols* 1913 and *Calligrammes/Word Pictures* 1918, show him as a representative of the Cubist and Futurist movements.

Apollinarius of Laodicea Bishop of Laodicea, whose views on the nature of Christ were condemned by the Council of Constantine 381, but who nonetheless laid the foundations for ◊Nestorianism. Rather than seeing the nature of Jesus as a human and divine soul somehow joined in the person of Christ, he saw Christ as having a divine mind only, and not a human one.

Apollo in Greek and Roman mythology, the god of sun, music, poetry, prophecy, agriculture, and pastoral life, and leader of the Muses. He was the twin child (with Artemis) of Zeus and Leto. Ancient statues show Apollo as the embodiment of the Greek ideal of male beauty.

His chief cult centers were his supposed birthplace on the island of Delos, in the Cyclades, and Delphi.

Apollo asteroid member of a group of ◊asteroids whose orbits cross that of the Earth. They are named after the first of their kind, Apollo, discovered 1932 and then lost until 1973. Apollo asteroids are so small and faint that they are difficult to see except when close to Earth (Apollo is about 1.2 mi/2 km across).

Apollo asteroids can collide with the Earth from time to time. In Jan 1991 the Apollo asteroid 1991 BA passed 105,000 mi/170,000 km from Earth, the closest observed approach of any asteroid. A collision with an Apollo asteroid 65 million years ago has been postulated as one of the causes of the extinction of the dinosaurs. A closely related group, the Amor asteroids, come close to Earth but do not cross its orbit.

Apollonius of Perga c. 260–c. 190 BC. Greek mathematician, called "the Great Geometer." In his work *Conic Sections* he showed that a plane intersecting a cone will generate an ellipse, a parabola, or a hyperbola, depending on the angle of intersection. In astronomy, he used a system of circles called epicycles and deferents to explain the motion of the planets; this system, as refined by Ptolemy, was used until the Renaissance.

Apollonius of Rhodes c. 220–180 BC. Greek poet, author of the epic *Argonautica*, which tells the story of Jason and the Argonauts and their quest for the Golden Fleece.

Apollonius of Tyana early 1st century AD. Greek ascetic philosopher of the Neo-Pythagorean school. He traveled in Babylonia and India, where he acquired a wide knowledge of oriental religions and philosophies, and taught at Ephesus. He was said to have had miraculous powers but claimed only that he could see the future.

Apollo of Rhodes Greek statue of Apollo generally known as the ◊Colossus of Rhodes.

Apollo project US space project to land a person on the Moon, achieved July 20, 1969, when Neil Armstrong was the first to set foot there. He was accompanied on the Moon surface by Col Edwin E Aldrin Jr; Michael Collins remained in the orbiting command module.

The program was announced 1961 by President Kennedy. The world's most powerful rocket, *Saturn V*, was built to launch the Apollo spacecraft, which carried three astronauts. When the spacecraft was in orbit around the Moon, two astronauts would descend to the surface in a lunar module to take samples of rock and set up experiments that would send data back to Earth. The first Apollo mission carrying a crew, *Apollo 7*, Oct 1968, was a test flight in orbit around the Earth. After three other preparatory flights, *Apollo 11* made the first lunar landing. Five more crewed landings followed, the last 1972. The total cost of the program was over $24 billion.

Apollo–Soyuz test project joint US-Soviet space mission in which an Apollo and a Soyuz craft docked while in orbit around the Earth on July 17, 1975. The craft remained attached for two days and crew members were able to move from one craft to the other through an air lock attached to the nose of the Apollo. The mission was designed to test rescue procedures as well as having political significance.

In the Apollo craft were Thomas Patten Stafford (commander), Vance DeVoe Brand, and Donald Kent Slayton; the Soyuz vehicle carried Alexei Archipovich Leonov (commander) and Valeri Nikolayevich Kubasov. The project began with the signing of an agreement May 1972 by US president Nixon and Soviet premier Kosygin.

apologetics philosophical writings that attempt to refute attacks on the Christian faith. Apologists include Justin Martyr, Origen, St Augustine, Thomas Aquinas, Blaise Pascal, and Joseph Butler. The questions raised by scientific, historical, and archeological discoveries have widened the field of apologetics.

Apo, Mount active volcano and highest peak in the Philippines, rising to 9,692 ft/2,954 m on the island of Mindanao.

apoplexy alternate name for ⬦stroke.

aposematic coloration in biology, the technical name for ⬦warning coloration markings that make a dangerous, poisonous, or foul-tasting animal particularly conspicuous and recognizable to a predator. Examples include the yellow and black stripes of bees and wasps, and the bright red or yellow colors of many poisonous frogs. See also ⬦mimicry.

a posteriori (Latin "from the latter") in logic, an argument that deduces causes from their effects; inductive reasoning; the converse of ⬦a priori.

apostle (Greek "messenger") in the New Testament, any of the chosen 12 ⬦disciples sent out by Jesus after his resurrection to preach the Gospel. In the earliest days of Christianity the term was extended to include some who had never known Jesus in the flesh, notably St Paul.

Apostles' Creed one of the three ancient ⬦creeds of the Christian church.

Apostolic Age early period in the Christian church dominated by those personally known to Jesus or his disciples.

apostolic succession doctrine in the Christian church that certain spiritual powers were received by the first apostles directly from Jesus, and have been handed down in the ceremony of "laying on of hands" from generation to generation of bishops.

apostrophe mark (') used in written English and some other languages. In English it serves primarily to indicate either a missing letter (*mustn't* for *must not*) or number ('*47* for *1947*), or grammatical possession ("*John's* camera," "*women's* dresses"). It is often omitted in proper names (Publishers Association, Actors Studio, *Collins Dictionary*). Many people otherwise competent in writing have great difficulty with the apostrophe, which has never been stable at any point in its history.

apothecaries' weights obsolete units of mass, formerly used in pharmacy: 20 grains equal one scruple; three scruples equal one dram; eight drams equal an apothecary's ounce (oz apoth.), and 12 such ounces equal an apothecary's pound (lb apoth.). There are 7,000 grains in one pound avoirdupois (0.454 kg).

apothecary person who prepares and dispenses medicines; a pharmacist.

Appalachians mountain system of E North America, stretching about 1,500 mi/2,400 km from Alabama to Québec, composed of ancient eroded rocks and rounded peaks. The chain separates the Mississippi-Missouri lowlands from the Atlantic coastal plain and includes the Allegheny, Catskill, White, and Blue Ridge mountains, the last having the highest peak,

Mount Mitchell, 6,712 ft/2,045 m. The E edge has a fall line to the coastal plain where Philadelphia, Baltimore, and Washington stand. The Appalachians are heavily forested and have deposits of coal and other minerals.

appeal in law, an application for a rehearing of all or part of an issue that has already been dealt with by a lower court or tribunal. The outcome can be a new decision on all or part of the points raised, or the previous decision may be upheld. In criminal cases, an appeal may be against conviction and either the prosecution or the defense may appeal against sentence.

appeasement historically, the conciliatory policy adopted by the British government, in particular under Neville Chamberlain, toward the Nazi and Fascist dictators in Europe in the 1930s in an effort to maintain peace. It was strongly opposed by Winston Churchill, but the ⬦Munich Agreement 1938 was almost universally hailed as its justification. Appeasement ended when Germany occupied Bohemia–Moravia March 1939.

War was declared after Germany attacked Poland Sept 1939, the beginning of World War II.

Appel Karel 1921– . Dutch painter, sculptor, and founder in 1948 of *Cobra*, a group of European abstract artists whose expressive form of painting used thick and lurid colours.

appendicitis inflammation of the appendix, a small, blind extension of the bowel in the lower right abdomen. In an acute attack, the pus-filled appendix may burst, causing a potentially lethal spread of infection. Treatment is by removal (appendectomy).

appendix area of the mammalian gut, associated with the digestion of cellulose. In herbivores it may be large, containing millions of bacteria that secrete enzymes to digest grass. No vertebrate can produce the type of digestive enzyme that will digest cellulose, the main constituent of plant cell walls. Those herbivores that rely on cellulose for their energy have all evolved specialist mechanisms to make use of the correct type of bacteria.

apple fruit of *Malus pumila*, a tree of the family Rosaceae. There are several hundred varieties of cultivated apples, grown all over the world, which may be divided into eating, cooking, and cider apples. All are derived from the wild crab apple.

Apple trees grow best in temperate countries with a cool climate and plenty of rain during the winter. The apple has been an important food plant in Eurasia for thousands of years.

Appleton city in E central Wisconsin, NW of Oshkosh, on the Fox River; seat of Outagamie country. It is a manufacturing center for paper products; population (1990) 65,700. Founded 1847, it claims to have the world's first hydroelectric plant, built 1882.

Appleton Edward Victor 1892–1965. British physicist who worked at Cambridge under Ernest ⬦Rutherford from 1920. He proved the existence of the Kennelly–Heaviside layer (now called the E layer) in the atmosphere, and the Appleton layer beyond it, and was involved in the initial work on the atomic bomb. Nobel Prize 1947.

Appleton layer band containing ionized gases in the Earth's upper atmosphere, above the ⬦E layer (formerly the Kennelly–Heaviside layer). It can act as a reflector of radio signals, although its ionic composition varies with the

sunspot cycle. It is named after the English physicist Edward Appleton.

application a curved line that connects a series of points (or "nodes") in the smoothest possible way. The shape of the curve is governed by a series of complex mathematical formulae. They are used in ⬦computer graphics and ⬦CAD.

applications package in computing, the set of programs and related documentation (such as instruction manuals) used in a particular application. For example, a typical payroll applications package would consist of separate programs for the entry of data, updating the master files, and printing the pay slips, plus documentation in the form of program details and instructions for use.

appliqué embroidery used to create pictures or patterns by "applying" pieces of material onto a background fabric. The pieces are cut into the appropriate shapes and sewn on, providing decoration for wall hangings, furnishing textiles, and clothes.

Appomattox village in Virginia, scene of the surrender April 9, 1865, of the Confederate army under Robert E Lee to the Union army under Ulysses S Grant, which ended the American Civil War.

The courthouse where the surrender was signed is now a museum, 3 mi/5 km from the modern village of Appomattox.

APR abbreviation for ⬦**annual percentage rate**.

apricot fruit of *Prunus armeniaca*, a tree of the rose family Rosaceae, closely related to the almond, peach, plum, and cherry. It has yellow-fleshed fruit. Although native to the Far East, it has long been cultivated in Armenia, from where it was introduced into Europe and the US.

April Fools' Day the first day of April, when it is customary in W Europe and the US to expose people to ridicule by a practical joke, causing them to believe some falsehood or to go on a fruitless errand.

a priori (Latin "from what comes before") in logic, an argument that is known to be true, or false, without reference to experience; the converse of ⬦a posteriori.

Apuleius Lucius lived c. AD 160. Roman lawyer, philosopher, and author of *Metamorphoses*, or *The* ⬦*Golden Ass*.

Apulia English form of ⬦Puglia, region of Italy.

Aqaba, Gulf of gulf extending for 100 mi/160 km between the Negev and the Red Sea; its coastline is uninhabited except at its head, where the frontiers of Israel, Egypt, Jordan, and Saudi Arabia converge. The two ports of Eilat (Israeli "Elath") and Aqaba, Jordan's only port, are situated here.

aquaculture another name for ⬦fish farming.

aqualung or *scuba* underwater breathing apparatus worn by divers, developed in the early 1940s by French diver Jacques Cousteau. Compressed-air cylinders strapped to the diver's back are regulated by a valve system and by a mouth tube to provide air to the diver at the same pressure as that of the surrounding water (which increases with the depth).

aquamarine blue variety of the mineral ⬦beryl. A semiprecious gemstone, it is used in jewelry.

aquaplaning phenomenon in which the tires

of a road vehicle cease to make direct contact with the road surface, owing to the presence of a thin film of water. As a result, the vehicle can go out of control (particularly if the steered wheels are involved).

aquarium tank or similar container used for the study and display of living aquatic plants and animals. The same name is used for institutions that exhibit aquatic life. These have been common since Roman times, but the first modern public aquarium was opened in Regent's Park, London in 1853. A recent development is the oceanarium or seaquarium, a large display of marine life forms.

Aquarius zodiacal constellation a little south of the celestial equator near Pegasus. Aquarius is represented as a man pouring water from a jar. The Sun passes through Aquarius from late Feb to early March. In astrology, the dates for Aquarius are between about Jan 20 and Feb 18 (see ⇨precession).

aquatic living in water. All life on Earth originated in the early oceans, because the aquatic environment has several advantages for organisms. Dehydration is almost impossible, temperatures usually remain stable, and the heaviness of water provides physical support.

aquatint printmaking technique, usually combined with ⇨etching to produce areas of subtle tone as well as more precisely etched lines. Aquatint became common in the late 18th century.

The etching plate is dusted with a fine layer of resin that is fixed to the plate by heating. The plate is then immersed in acid, which bites through the resin, causing tiny pits on the surface of the plate. When printed, this results in a fine, grainy tone. Areas of tone can be controlled by varnishing the plate with acid-resisting material. Denser tones are acquired by longer exposure to the acid.

Gainsborough experimented with aquatint but the first artist to become proficient in the technique was J B Le Prince (1733–1781). Others attracted to it include Goya, Degas, Pissarro, Picasso, and Rouault.

aqueduct any artificial channel or conduit for water, often an elevated structure of stone, wood, or iron built for conducting water across a valley. The Greeks built a tunnel 4,200 ft/ 1,280 m long near Athens, 2,500 years ago. Many Roman aqueducts are still standing, for example the one at Nîmes in S France, built about AD 18 (which is 160 ft/48 m high).

The largest Roman aqueduct is that at Carthage in Tunisia, which is 87 mi/141 km long and was built during the reign of Publius Aelius Hadrianus between AD 117 and 138. A recent aqueduct is the California State Water Project taking water from Lake Oroville in the north, through two power plants and across the Tehachapi mountains, more than 110 mi/ 177 km to S California.

aqueous humour watery fluid found in the space between the cornea and lens of the vertebrate eye. Similar to blood serum in composition, it is renewed every four hours.

aqueous solution solution in which the solvent is water.

aquifer any rock formation containing water. The rock of an aquifer must be porous and permeable (full of interconnected holes) so that it can absorb water. Aquifers supply ⇨artesian wells, and are actively sought in arid areas as sources of drinking and irrigation water.

An aquifer may be underlain, overlain, or sandwiched between impermeable layers, called **aquicludes**, which impede water movement. Sandstones and porous limestones make the best aquifers.

Aquila constellation on the celestial equator (see ⇨celestial sphere). Its brightest star is first-magnitude ⇨Altair, flanked by the stars Beta and Gamma Aquilae. It is represented by an eagle.

Aquinas St Thomas c. 1226–1274. Neapolitan philosopher and theologian, the greatest figure of the school of ⇨scholasticism. He was a Dominican monk, known as the "Angelic Doctor." In 1879 his works were recognized as the basis of Catholic theology. His *Summa contra Gentiles/Against the Errors of the Infidels* 1259–64 argues that reason and faith are compatible. He assimilated the philosophy of Aristotle into Christian doctrine.

Aquino (Maria) Corazon (born Cojuangco) 1933– . President of the Philippines 1986–92. She was instrumental in the nonviolent overthrow of President Ferdinand Marcos 1986. As president, she sought to rule in a conciliatory manner, but encountered opposition from left (communist guerrillas) and right (army coup attempts), and her land reforms were seen as inadequate.

The daughter of a sugar baron, she studied in the US and in 1956 married the politician Benigno Aquino (1933–1983). The chief political opponent of the right-wing president Marcos, he was assassinated by a military guard at Manila airport on his return from exile. Corazon Aquino was drafted by the opposition to contest the Feb 1986 presidential election and claimed victory over Marcos, accusing the government of voting fraud. She led a nonviolent "people's power" campaign, which overthrew Marcos Feb 25. A devout Roman Catholic, Aquino enjoyed strong church backing in her 1986 campaign. The US provided strong support as well and was instrumental in turning back a 1989 coup attempt. In 1991 she announced she would not enter the 1992 presidential elections.

Aquitaine region of SW France; capital Bordeaux; area 15,942 sq mi/41,300 sq km; population (1986) 2,718,000. It comprises the *départements* of Dordogne, Gironde, Landes, Lot-et-Garonne, and Pyrénées-Atlantiques. Red wines (Margaux, St Julien) are produced in the Médoc district, bordering the Gironde. Aquitaine was an English possession 1152–1452.

history early human remains have been found in the Dordogne region. Aquitaine coincides roughly with the Roman province of Aquitania and the ancient French province of Aquitaine. Eleanor of Aquitaine married the future Henry II of England 1152 and brought it to him as her dowry; it remained in English hands until 1452.

AR abbreviation for the state of ⇨*Arkansas*.

Arab any of a Semitic (see ⇨Semite) people native to the Arabian peninsula, but now settled throughout North Africa and the nations of the Middle East.

Arab Common Market organization providing for the abolition of customs duties on agricultural products, and reductions on other items, between the member states: Egypt, Iraq, Jordan, and Syria. It was founded 1965.

Arab Emirates see ⇨United Arab Emirates.

arabesque in ballet, a pose in which the dancer stands on one leg, straight or bent, with the other leg raised behind, fully extended. The arms are held in a harmonious position to give the longest possible line from fingertips to toes.

Arabia peninsula between the Persian Gulf and the Red Sea, in SW Asia; area 1,000,000 sq mi/2,600,000 sq km. The peninsula contains the world's richest oil and gas reserves. It comprises the states of Bahrain, Kuwait, Oman, Qatar, Saudi Arabia, the United Arab Emirates, and Yemen.

physical A sandy coastal plain of varying width borders the Red Sea, behind which a mountain chain rises to about 6,600–8,200 ft/ 2,000–2,500 m. Behind this range is the plateau of the Nejd, averaging 3,300 ft/1,000 m. The interior comprises a vast desert area: part of the Hamad (Syrian) desert in the far N; Nafud in northern Saudi Arabia, and Rub'al Khali in S Saudi Arabia.

history The Arabian civilization was revived by Mohammed during the 7th century, but in the new empire created by militant Islam, Arabia became a subordinate state, and its cities were eclipsed by Damascus, Baghdad, and Cairo. Colonialism only touched the fringe of Arabia in the 19th century, and until the 20th century the interior was unknown to Europeans. Nationalism began actively to emerge at the period of World War I (1914–18), and the oil discoveries from 1953 gave the peninsula significant economic power.

Arabian Gulf another name for the ⇨Persian Gulf.

Arabian Nights tales in oral circulation among Arab storytellers from the 10th century, probably having their roots in India. They are also known as *The Thousand and One Nights* and include "Ali Baba," "Aladdin," "Sinbad the Sailor," and "The Old Man of the Sea."

They were supposed to have been told to the sultan by his bride Scheherazade to avoid the fate of her predecessors, who were all executed following the wedding night to prevent their infidelity. She began a new tale each evening, which she would only agree to finish on the following night. Eventually the "sentence" was rescinded.

The first European translation was by the French writer Antoine Galland (1646–1715) 1704, although the stories were known earlier. The first English translations were by E W Lane 1838–40 and Richard Burton 1885–88.

Arabian Sea NW branch of the ⇨Indian Ocean.

Arabic language major Semitic language of the Hamito-Semitic family of W Asia and North Africa, originating among the Arabs of the Arabian peninsula. It is spoken today by about 120 million people in the Middle East and N Africa. Arabic script is written from right to left.

The language has spread by way of conquest and trade as far west as Morocco and as far east as Malaysia, Indonesia, and the Philippines, and is also spoken in Arab communities scattered across the western hemisphere. Forms of colloquial Arabic vary in the countries where it is the dominant language: Algeria, Bahrain, Egypt, Iraq, Jordan, Kuwait, Lebanon, Libya, Mali, Mauritania, Morocco, Oman, Saudi Arabia, Sudan, Syria, Tunisia, the United Arab Emirates, and Yemen. Arabic is also a language of religious and cultural significance in such other countries as Bangladesh, India, Iran, Israel, Pakistan, and Somalia. Arabic-speaking communities are growing in the US and the West Indies.

A feature of the language is its consonantal

roots. For example, s–l–m is the root for *salaam*, a greeting that implies peace; *Islam*, the creed of submission to God and calm acceptance of his will; and *Muslim*, one who submits to that will (a believer in Islam). The *Koran*, the sacred book of Islam, is "for reading" by a *qari* ("reader") who is engaged in *qaraat* ("reading"). The 7th-century style of the Koran is the basis of Classical Arabic.

Arabic numerals or **Hindu-Arabic numerals** the symbols 0, 1, 2, 3, 4, 5, 6, 7, 8, 9, early forms of which were in use among the Arabs before being adopted by the peoples of Europe during the Middle Ages in place of ⟡Roman numerals.

Arabic numerals include a symbol for zero which can be used as a place holder. Roman numerals do not include a symbol for zero.

They appear to have originated in India and probably reached Europe by way of Spain.

Arab-Israeli Wars series of wars between Israel and various Arab states in the Middle East since the founding of the state of Israel 1948.

First Arab-Israeli War May 15, 1948–Jan 13/March 24, 1949. As soon as the independent state of Israel had been proclaimed by the Jews, it was invaded by combined Arab forces. The Israelis defeated them and went on to annex territory until they controlled 75% of what had been Palestine under British mandate.

Second Arab-Israeli War Oct 29–Nov 4, 1956. After Egypt had taken control of the Suez Canal and blockaded the Straits of Tiran, Israel, with British and French support, invaded and captured Sinai and the Gaza Strip, from which it withdrew under heavy US pressure after the entry of a United Nations force.

Third Arab-Israeli War June 5–10, 1967, the *Six-Day War*. It resulted in the Israeli capture of the Golan Heights from Syria; the eastern half of Jerusalem and the West Bank from Jordan; and, in the south, the Gaza Strip and Sinai peninsula as far as the Suez Canal.

Fourth Arab-Israeli War Oct 6–24, 1973, the "October War" or *Yom Kippur War*, so called because the Israeli forces were taken by surprise on the Day of ⟡Atonement. It started with the recrossing of the Suez Canal by Egyptian forces who made initial gains, though there was some later loss of ground by the Syrians in the north.

Fifth Arab-Israeli War From 1978 the presence of Palestinian guerrillas in Lebanon led to Arab raids on Israel and Israeli retaliatory incursions, but on June 6, 1982 Israel launched a full-scale invasion. By June 14 Beirut was encircled, and ⟡Palestine Liberation Organization (PLO) and Syrian forces were evacuated (mainly to Syria) Aug 21–31, but in Feb 1985 there was a unilateral Israeli withdrawal from the country without any gain or losses incurred. Israel maintains a "security zone" in S Lebanon and supports the South Lebanese Army militia as a buffer against Palestinian guerrilla incursions.

background Arab opposition to an Israeli state began after the Balfour Declaration 1917, which supported the idea of a Jewish national homeland. In the 1920s there were anti-Zionist riots in Palestine, then governed by the UK under a League of Nations mandate. In 1936 an Arab revolt led to a British royal commission that recommended partition (approved by the United Nations 1947, but rejected by the Arabs).

Tension in the Middle East remained high, and the conflict was sharpened and given East–West overtones by Soviet adoption of the Arab cause and US support for Israel. Several wars only increased the confusion over who had a claim to what territory. Particularly in view of the area's strategic sensitivity as an oil producer, pressure grew for a settlement, and in 1978 the ⟡Camp David Agreements brought peace between Egypt and Israel, but this was denounced by other Arab countries. Israel withdrew from Sinai 1979–82, but no final agreement on Jerusalem and the establishment of a Palestinian state on the West Bank was reached. The continuing Israeli occupation of the Gaza Strip and the West Bank in the face of a determined uprising (⟡Intifada) by the residents of these areas has seemingly hardened attitudes on both sides.

Arab League organization of Arab states established in Cairo 1945 to promote Arab unity, primarily in opposition to Israel. The original members were Egypt, Syria, Iraq, Lebanon, Transjordan (Jordan 1949), Saudi Arabia, and Yemen. In 1979 Egypt was suspended and the league's headquarters transferred to Tunis in protest against the Egypt-Israeli peace, but Egypt was readmitted as a full member May 1989, and in March 1990 its headquarters returned to Cairo.

Arab Monetary Fund (AMF) money reserve established 1976 by 20 Arab states plus the Palestine Liberation Organization to provide a mechanism for promoting greater stability in exchange rates and to coordinate Arab economic and monetary policies. It operates mainly by regulating petrodollars within the Arab community to make member countries less dependent on the West for the handling of their surplus money. The fund's headquarters are in Abu Dhabi in the United Arab Emirates.

Arachne (Greek "spider") in Greek mythology, a Lydian woman who was so skillful a weaver that she challenged the goddess Athena to a contest. Athena tore Arachne's beautiful tapestries to pieces and Arachne hanged herself. She was transformed into a spider, and her weaving became a cobweb.

arachnid or *arachnoid* type of arthropod, including spiders, scorpions, and mites. They differ from insects in possessing only two main body regions, the cephalothorax and the abdomen.

Arafat Yassir 1929– . Palestinian nationalist politician, cofounder of al-⟡Fatah 1956 and president of the ⟡Palestine Liberation Organization (PLO) from 1969. His support for Saddam Hussein after Iraq's invasion of Kuwait 1990 weakened his international standing, but he has since been influential in Middle East peace talks.

In the 1970s Arafat's activities in pursuit of an independent homeland for Palestinians made him a prominent figure in world politics, but in the 1980s the growth of factions within the PLO effectively reduced his power. He was forced to evacuate Lebanon 1983, but remained leader of most of the PLO and in 1990 persuaded it to recognize formally the state of Israel. In 1992 he narrowly escaped injury when his aircraft was forced to land in a sand storm.

Arafura Sea area of the Pacific Ocean between N Australia and Indonesia, bounded by the Timor Sea in the W and the Coral Sea in the E. It is 800 mi/1,290 km long and 350 mi/560 km wide.

Arago Dominique 1786–1853. French physicist and astronomer who made major contributions to the early study of electromagnetism.

In 1820 he found that iron enclosed in a wire coil could be magnetized by the passage of an electric current. Later, in 1824, he was the first to observe the ability of a floating copper disk to deflect a magnetic needle, the phenomenon of magnetic rotation.

Aragón autonomous region of NE Spain including the provinces of Huesca, Teruel, and Zaragoza; area 18,412 sq mi/47,700 sq km; population (1986) 1,215,000. Its capital is Zaragoza, and products include almonds, figs, grapes, and olives. Aragón was an independent kingdom 1035–1479.

history A Roman province until taken in the 5th century by the Visigoths, who lost it to the Moors in the 8th century, it became a kingdom 1035. It was united with Castile 1479 under Ferdinand and Isabella.

Aragon Louis 1897–1982. French poet and novelist. Beginning as a Dadaist, he became one of the leaders of Surrealism, published volumes of verse, and in 1930 joined the Communist party. Taken prisoner in World War II, he escaped to join the Resistance; his experiences are reflected in the poetry of *Le Crève-coeur* 1942 and *Les Yeux d'Elsa* 1944.

Arakan state of Myanmar (formerly Burma) on the Bay of Bengal coast, some 400 mi/645 km long and strewn with islands; population (1983) 2,046,000. The chief town is Sittwe. It is bounded along its eastern side by the Arakan Yoma, a mountain range rising to 10,000 ft/3,000 m. The ancient kingdom of Arakan was conquered by Burma 1785.

Aral Sea inland sea divided between Kazakhstan and Uzbekistan, the world's fourth largest lake; former area 24,000 sq mi/62,000 sq km, but decreasing. Water from its tributaries, the Amu Darya and Syr Darya, has been diverted for irrigation and city use, and the sea is disappearing, with long-term consequences for the climate.

Between 1960 and 1990 the water level dropped 40 ft/13 m, reducing the lake to two-thirds of its original area. All native fish species have disappeared, and winds drop 43 million tons of salt a year on the surrounding cropland.

Aramaic language Semitic language of the Hamito-Semitic family of W Asia, the everyday language of Palestine 2,000 years ago, during the Roman occupation and the time of Jesus.

In the 13th century BC Aramaean nomads set up states in Mesopotamia, and during the next 200 years spread into N Syria, where Damascus, Aleppo, and Carchemish were among their chief centers. Aramaic spread throughout Syria and Mesopotamia, becoming one of the official languages of the Persian empire under the Achaemenids and serving as a ⟡lingua franca of the day. Aramaic dialects survive among small Christian communities in various parts of W Asia, although Arabic spread widely with the acceptance of Islam.

Aran Islands three rocky islands (Inishmore, Inishmaan, Inisheer) in the mouth of Galway Bay, Republic of Ireland; population approximately 4,600. The capital is Kilronan. J M ⟡Synge used the language of the islands in his plays.

Ararat double-peaked mountain on the Turkish-Iranian border; the higher, Great Ararat, 16,854 ft/5,137 m, was the reputed resting place of Noah's Ark after the Flood.

Araucanian Indian (Araucanian *Mapuche*) member of a group of South American Indian peoples native to central Chile and the

Argentine pampas. They were agriculturalists and hunters, as well as renowned warriors, defeating the Incas and resisting the Spanish for 200 years. Originally, they lived in small villages; some 200,000 still survive in reserves. Scholars are divided over whether the Araucanian language belongs to the Penutian or the Andean-Equatorial family.

araucaria coniferous tree of the genus *Araucaria*, allied to the firs, with flat, scalelike needles. Once widespread, it is now native only to the southern hemisphere. Some grow to gigantic size. Araucarias include the monkey-puzzle tree *A. araucana*, the Australian bunya bunya pine *A. bidwillii*, and the Norfolk Island pine *A. heterophylla*.

Arawak member of an indigenous American people of the Caribbean and NE Amazon Basin. Arawaks lived mainly by shifting cultivation in tropical forests. They were driven out of many West Indian islands by another American Indian people, the Caribs, shortly before the arrival of the Spanish in the 16th century. Subsequently, their numbers on ◊Hispaniola declined from some 4 million in 1492 to a few thousand after their exploitation by the Spanish in their search for gold; the remaining few were eradicated by disease (smallpox was introduced 1518). Arawakan languages belong to the Andean-Equatorial group.

Arbenz Guzmán Jácobo 1913–1971. Guatemalan social democratic politician and president from 1951 until his overthrow 1954 by rebels operating with the help of the US Central Intelligence Agency.

Guzmán brought in policies to redistribute land, much of which was owned by overseas companies, to landless peasants; he also encouraged labor organization. His last years were spent in exile in Mexico, Uruguay, and Cuba.

Arbil Kurdish town in a province of the same name in N Iraq; population (1985) 334,000. Occupied since Assyrian times, it was the site of a battle 331 BC at which Alexander the Great defeated the Persians under Darius III. In 1974 Arbil became the capital of a Kurdish autonomous region set up by the Iraqi government.

arbitrageur in finance, a person who buys securities (such as currency or commodities) in one country or market for immediate resale in another market, to take advantage of different prices.

Arbitrage became widespread during the 1970s and 1980s with the increasing deregulation of financial markets. The effect of arbitrage is to lessen or eliminate the price differentials among the markets. The term took on additional meaning with the increase in corporate buy-outs in the deregulated atmosphere of the late 1980s. Arbitrageurs speculated on target companies, buying stock and reselling it at the higher buy-out price.

arbitration submission of a dispute to a third, unbiased party for settlement. It may be personal litigation, a labor-union issue, or an international dispute.

The first permanent international court was established in The Hague in the Netherlands 1900, and the League of Nations set up an additional Permanent Court of International Justice 1921 to deal with frontier disputes and the like. The latter was replaced 1945 with the International Court of Justice under the United Nations. Another arbiter is the European Court of Justice, which rules on disputes arising out of the Rome treaties regulating the European Community.

arboretum collection of trees. An arboretum may contain a wide variety of species or just closely related species or varieties—for example, different types of pine tree.

arbor vitae any of several coniferous trees or shrubs of the genus *Thuja* of the cypress family, having flattened branchlets covered in overlapping aromatic green scales. In North America, the northern white cedar *Thuja occidentalis* and the western red cedar *T. plicata* are representatives. The Chinese or Oriental species *T. orientalis*, reaching 60 ft/18 m in height, is grown widely as an ornamental.

Arbuckle Fatty (Roscoe Conkling) 1887–1933. US silent-film comedian; also a writer and director. His successful career in such films as *The Butcher Boy* 1917 and *The Hayseed* 1919 ended in 1921 after a sex-party scandal in which a starlet died. Although acquitted, he was spurned by the public and his films were banned.

arbutus any evergreen shrub of the genus *Arbutus* of the heath family Ericaceae. The strawberry tree *A. unedo* is grown for its ornamental, strawberrylike fruit.

arc in geometry, a section of a curved line or circle. A circle has three types of arc: a *semicircle*, which is exactly half of the circle; *minor arcs*, which are less than the semicircle; and *major arcs*, which are greater than the semicircle.

The arcs of a circle are measured in degrees, according to the angle formed by joining its two ends to the center of the circle. A semicircle is therefore 180°, whereas a minor arc will always be less than 180° (acute or obtuse) and a major arc will always be greater than 180° but less than 360° (reflex).

Arcadia (Greek *Arkadhia*) central plateau of S Greece; area 1,706 sq mi/4,419 sq km; population (1981) 108,000. Tripolis is the capital town.

Arc de Triomphe arch at the head of the Champs Elysées in the Place de l'Etoile, Paris, France, begun by Napoleon 1806 and completed 1836. It was intended to commemorate Napoleon's victories of 1805–06 and commissioned from Jean Chalgrin (1739–1811). Beneath it rests France's "Unknown Soldier."

arch curved structure of masonry that supports the weight of material over an open space, as in a bridge or doorway. The first arches consisted of several wedge-shaped stones supported by their mutual pressure. The term is also applied to any curved structure that is an arch in form only.

The Romans are credited with engineering the earliest round keystone arches, used for aqueducts. Other arches include the pointed Gothic arch and the corbeled arch of the Maya Indians.

Archaean or *Archaeozoic* the earliest period of geological time; the first part of the Precambrian era, from the formation of Earth up to about 2,500 million years ago. It was a time when no life existed, and with every new discovery of ancient life its upper boundary is being pushed further back.

archaebacteria three groups of bacteria whose DNA differs significantly from that of other bacteria (called the "eubacteria"). All are strict anaerobes, that is, they are killed by oxygen. This is thought to be a primitive condition and to indicate that the archaebacteria are related to the earliest life forms, which appeared about 3.5 billion years ago, when there was little oxygen in the Earth's atmosphere.

archaeopteryx extinct primitive bird, known from fossilized remains, about 160 million years old, found in limestone deposits in Bavaria, Germany. It is popularly known as "the first bird," although some earlier bird ancestors are now known. It was about the size of a crow and had feathers and wings, but in many respects its skeleton is reptilian (teeth and a long, bony tail) and very like some small meat-eating dinosaurs of the time. *See illustration on p. 58.*

Archangel (Russian *Arkhangel'sk*) port in N Russia; population (1987) 416,000. It was made an open port by Boris ◊Godunov and was of prime importance until Peter the Great built St Petersburg. It was used 1918–20 by the Allied interventionist armies in collaboration with the White Army in their effort to overthrow the newly established Soviet state. In World War II it was the receiving station for Anglo-American supplies. An open city in a closed area, it can be visited by foreigners only by air and is a center for ICBMs (intercontinental ballistic missiles). Although the port is blocked by ice during half the year, it is the chief timber-exporting port of Russia. Plesetsk, to the south, is a launch site for crewed space flight.

archbishop in the Christian church, a bishop of superior rank who has authority over other bishops in his jurisdiction and often over an ecclesiastical province. The office exists in the Roman Catholic, Eastern Orthodox, and Anglican churches.

archegonium female sex organ found in bryophytes (mosses and liverworts), pteridophytes (ferns, club mosses, and horsetails), and some gymnosperms. It is a multicellular, flask-shaped structure consisting of two parts: the swollen base or venter containing the egg

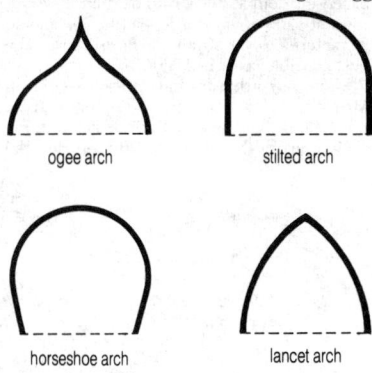

ogee arch   stilted arch

horseshoe arch   lancet arch

keystone

haunch

span

impost

arch *Different types of arch are associated with different architectural styles.*

cell, and the long, narrow neck. When the egg cell is mature, the cells of the neck dissolve, allowing the passage of the male gametes, or ◊antherozoids.

archeology study of history (primarily but not exclusively the prehistoric and ancient periods), based on the examination of physical remains. Principal activities include preliminary field (or site) surveys, excavation (where necessary), and the classification, dating, and interpretation of finds. Since 1958 radiocarbon dating has been used to establish the age of archeological strata and associated materials.

history Interest in the physical remains of the past began in the Renaissance among dealers in and collectors of ancient art. It was further stimulated by discoveries made in Africa, the Americas, and Asia by Europeans during the period of imperialist colonization in the 16th–19th centuries, such as the antiquities discovered during Napoleon's Egyptian campaign in the 1790s. Towards the end of the 19th century archeology became an academic study, making increasing use of scientific techniques and systematic methodologies.

Related disciplines that have been useful in archeological reconstruction include stratigraphy (the study of geological strata), dendrochronology (the establishment of chronological sequences through the study of tree rings), paleobotany (the study of ancient pollens, seeds, and grains), epigraphy (the study of inscriptions), and numismatics (the study of coins).

archerfish surface-living fish of the family Toxotidae, such as the genus *Toxotes*, native to SE Asia and Australia. The archerfish grows to about 10 in/25 cm and is able to shoot down insects up to 5 ft/1.5 m above the water by spitting a jet of water from its mouth.

archery use of the bow and arrow, originally in hunting and warfare, now as a competitive sport. The world governing body is the Fédération Internationale de Tir à l'Arc (FITA) founded 1931. In competitions, results are based on double FITA rounds; that is, 72 arrows at each of four targets at 90, 70, 50, and 30 meters (70, 60, 50, and 30 for women). The best possible score is 2,880.

Stone arrowheads have been found in Mesolithic archeological deposits from *c.* 15,000 BC, and bowmen are depicted in the ancient art of the Americas, Europe, and the

Middle East, as well as later in the art of the early civilizations. Until the introduction of gunpowder in the 14th century, bands of archers were to be found in every European army. By the mid-17th century archery was no longer significant in warfare and interest waned until the 1780s.

Organizations in the US include the National Archery Association 1879 and, for actual hunting with the bow, the National Field Archery Association 1940.

Archimedes *c.* 287–212 BC. Greek mathematician who made major discoveries in geometry, hydrostatics, and mechanics. He formulated a law of fluid displacement (Archimedes' principle), and is credited with the invention of the Archimedes screw, a cylindrical device for raising water.

He was born at Syracuse in Sicily. It is alleged that Archimedes' principle was discovered when he stepped into the public bath and saw the water overflow. He was so delighted that he rushed home naked, crying "Eureka! Eureka!" ("I have found it! I have found it!") He used his discovery to prove that the goldsmith of the king of Syracuse had adulterated a gold crown with silver. Archimedes designed engines of war for the defense of Syracuse, and was killed when the Romans besieged the town.

Archimedes' principle in physics, law stating that an object totally or partly submerged in a fluid displaces a volume of fluid that weighs the same as the apparent loss in weight of the object (which, in turn, equals the upward force, or upthrust, experienced by that object).

If the weight of the object is less than the upthrust exerted by the fluid, it will float partly or completely above the surface; if its weight is equal to the upthrust, the object will come to equilibrium below the surface; if its weight is greater than the upthrust, it will sink.

Archimedes screw one of the earliest kinds of pump, thought to have been invented by Archimedes. It consists of a spiral screw revolving inside a close-fitting cylinder. It is used, for example, to raise water for irrigation.

archipelago group of islands, or an area of sea containing a group of islands. The islands of an archipelago are usually volcanic in origin, and they sometimes represent the tops of peaks in areas around continental margins flooded by the sea.

Volcanic islands are formed either when a hot spot within the Earth's mantle produces a chain of volcanoes on the surface, such as the Hawaiian Archipelago, or at a destructive plate margin (see ◊plate tectonics) where the subduction of one plate beneath another produces an arc-shaped island group, such as the Aleutian Archipelago. Novaya Zemlya in the Arctic Ocean, the northern extension of the Ural Mountains, resulted from continental flooding.

Archipenko Alexander 1887–1964. Ukrainian-born abstract sculptor who lived in France from 1908 and in the US from 1923. He pioneered Cubist works composed of angular forms and spaces and later experimented with clear plastic and sculptures incorporating lights.

architecture art of designing structures. The term covers the design of the visual appearance of structures; their internal arrangements of space; selection of external and internal building materials; design or selection of natural and artificial lighting systems, as well as mechanical, electrical, and plumbing systems; and design or selection of decorations and furnishings. Architectural style may emerge from evolution of techniques and styles particular to a culture in a given time period with or without identifiable individuals as architects, or may be attributed to specific individuals or groups of architects working together on a project.

early architecture Little remains of the earliest forms of architecture, but archeologists have examined remains of prehistoric sites and documented ◊Stone Age villages of wooden post buildings with above-ground construction of organic materials such as mud or wattle and daub from the Upper Paleolithic, Mesolithic, and Neolithic periods in Asia, the Middle East, Europe, and the Americas. More extensive remains of stone-built structures have given clues to later Neolithic farming communities as well as habitations, storehouses, and religious and civic structures of early civilizations. The best documented are those of ancient Egypt, where exhaustive work in the 19th and 20th centuries revealed much about ordinary buildings, the monumental structures such as the pyramid tombs near modern Cairo, and the temple and tomb complexes concentrated at Luxor and Thebes.

Classical The basic forms of Classical architecture evolved in Greece between the 16th and 2nd centuries BC. Its hallmark is its post-and-lintel construction of temples and public structures, classified into the Doric, Ionic, and Corinthian orders, defined by simple, scrolled, and acanthus-leaf capitals for support columns, respectively. The Romans copied and expanded on Greek Classical forms, notably introducing bricks and concrete and inventing the vault, arch, and dome for public buildings and aqueducts.

Byzantine This form of architecture developed primarily in the E Roman Empire from the 4th century, with its center at Byzantium (later named Constantinople, now Istanbul). Its most notable features were construction of churches, some very large, based on the Greek cross plan (Hagia Sophia, Istanbul; St Mark's, Venice), with formalized painted and mosaic decoration.

Islamic This developed from the 8th century, when the Islamic religion spread from its center in the Middle East west to Spain and E to China and parts of the Philippine Islands. Notable features are the development of the

Wing structure of a flying reptile

Wing structure of a bird

archaeopteryx *The archaeopteryx, ancestor of the birds, had features of both reptiles and modern birds.*

archeology: chronology

14th–16th centuries	The Renaissance revived interest in Classical Greek and Roman art and architecture, including ruins and buried art and artifacts.
1748	The buried Roman city of Pompeii was discovered under lava from Vesuvius.
1784	Thomas Jefferson excavated an Indian burial mound on the Rivanna River in Virginia and wrote a report on his finds.
1790	John Frere identified Old Stone Age (Paleolithic) tools together with large extinct animals.
1822	Jean François Champollion deciphered Egyptian hieroglyphics.
1836	Christian Thomsen devised the Stone, Bronze, and Iron Age classification.
1840s	Austen Layard excavated the Assyrian capital of Nineveh.
1868	The Great Zimbabwe ruins in E Africa were first seen by Europeans.
1871	Heinrich Schliemann began excavations at Troy.
1879	Stone Age paintings were first discovered at Altamira, Spain.
1880s	Augustus Pitt-Rivers developed the concept of stratigraphy (identification of successive layers of soil within a site with successive archeological stages; the most recent at the top).
1891	Flinders Petrie began excavating Akhetaton in Egypt.
1899–1935	Arthur Evans excavated Minoan Knossos in Crete.
1900–44	Max Uhle began the systematic study of the civilizations of Peru.
1911	The Inca city of Machu Picchu was discovered by Hiram Bingham in the Andes.
1911–12	The Piltdown skull was "discovered"; it was proved to be a fake 1949.
1914–18	Osbert Crawford developed the technique of aerial survey of sites.
1917–27	John Eric Thompson (1898–1975) discovered the great Mayan sites in Yucatán, Mexico.
1922	Tutankhamen's tomb in Egypt was opened by Howard Carter.
1926	A kill site in Folsom, New Mexico, was found with human-made spearpoints in association with ancient bison.
1935	Dendrochronology (dating events in the distant past by counting tree rings) was developed by A E Douglas.
1939	An Anglo-Saxon ship-burial treasure was found at Sutton Hoo, England.
1947	The first of the Dead Sea Scrolls was discovered.
1948	The *Proconsul* prehistoric ape was discovered by Mary Leakey in Kenya.
1950s–1970s	Several early hominid fossils were found by Louis Leakey in Olduvai Gorge.
1953	Michael Ventris deciphered Minoan Linear B.
1960s	Radiocarbon and thermoluminescence measurement techniques were developed as aids for dating remains.
1961	The Swedish warship *Wasa* was raised at Stockholm.
1963	Walter Emery pioneered rescue archeology at Abu Simbel before the site was flooded by the Aswan Dam.
1969	Human remains found at Lake Mungo, Australia, were dated at 26,000 years; earliest evidence of ritual cremation.
1974	The Tomb of Shi Huangdi was discovered in China. The footprints of a hominid called "Lucy", 3 to 3.7 million years old, were found at Laetoli in Ethiopia.
1978	The tomb of Philip II of Macedon (Alexander the Great's father) was discovered in Greece.
1979	The Aztec capital Tenochtitlán was excavated beneath a zone of Mexico City.
1982	The English king Henry VIII's warship *Mary Rose* of 1545 was raised and studied with new techniques in underwater archeology.
1985	The tomb of Maya, Tutankhamen's treasurer, was discovered at Saqqara, Egypt.
1988	The Turin Shroud was established as being of medieval origin by radiocarbon dating.
1989	The remains of the Globe and Rose Theaters, where many of Shakespeare's plays were originally performed, were discovered in London.
1991	Body of man from 5300 years ago, with clothing, bow, arrows, a copper axe, and other implements, found preserved in Italian Alps.

tower with dome and the pointed arch. Islamic architecture, chiefly through Spanish examples such as the Great Mosque at Córdoba and the Alhambra in Granada, profoundly influenced Christian church architecture—for example, by adoption of the pointed arch into the Gothic arch.

Romanesque This form of architecture is associated with Western European Christianity from the 8th to the 12th centuries. It is marked by churches with massive walls for structural integrity, rounded arches, small windows, and resulting dark volumes of interior space. In England this style is generally referred to as Norman architecture (Durham Cathedral). The style enjoyed a renewal of interest in Europe and the US in the late 19th and early 20th centuries.

Gothic Gothic architecture emerged out of Romanesque, since the pointed arch and flying buttress made it possible to change from thick supporting walls to lighter curtain walls with extensive expansion of window areas (and stained-glass artwork) and resulting increases in interior light. Gothic architecture was developed mainly in France from the 12th to 16th centuries. The style is divided into Early Gothic (Sens Cathedral), High Gothic (Chartres Cathedral), and Late or Flamboyant Gothic. In England the corresponding divisions are Early English (Salisbury Cathedral), Decorated (Wells Cathedral), and Perpendicular (Kings College Chapel, Cambridge). Gothic was also developed extensively in Germany and neighboring countries and in Italy.

Renaissance The 15th and 16th centuries in Europe saw the rebirth of Classical form and motifs in the Italian Neo-Classical movement.

A major source of inspiration for the major Renaissance architects—Palladio, Alberti, Brunelleschi, Bramante, and Michelangelo—was the work of the 1st-century BC Roman engineer Vitruvius. The Palladian style was later used extensively in England by Inigo Jones and the Classical idiom by Christopher Wren. Classical or Neo-Classical style and its elements have been popular in the US from the 18th century, as evidenced in much of the civic and commercial architecture since the time of the early republic (the US Capitol and Supreme Court buildings in Washington; many state capitols).

Baroque European architecture of the 17th and 18th centuries elaborated on Classical models with exuberant and extravagant decoration. In large-scale public buildings, the style is best seen in the innovative work of Giovanni Bernini and Francesco Borromini in Italy and later by John Vanbrugh, Nicholas Hawksmoor, and Christopher Wren in England. There were numerous practitioners in France and the German-speaking countries; Vienna is especially Baroque.

Rococo This architecture extends the Baroque style with an even greater extravagance of design motifs, using a new lightness of detail and naturalistic elements, such as shells, flowers, and trees.

Neo-Classical European architecture of the 18th and 19th centuries again focused on the more severe Classical idiom (inspired by archeological finds), producing, for example, the large-scale rebuilding of London by Robert Adam and John Nash and later of Paris by Georges Haussman.

Neo-Gothic The late 19th century saw a fussy Gothic revival in Europe and the US, particularly evident in churches (Ralph Adams Cram's work in the US—for example, St John the Divine, New York) and public buildings (Charles Barry's work in the Houses of Parliament, London).

Art Nouveau This architecture arising at the end of the 19th century countered Neo-Gothic, using sinuous, flowing shapes for buildings, room plans, and interior design. The style is characterized by the work of Charles Rennie Mackintosh in Scotland (Glasgow Art School) and Antonio Gaudi in Spain (Church of the Holy Family, Barcelona), and design elements were used especially in France but also in England and the US.

Modernist This architecture is also known as Functionalism or the International Style. It began in the 1900s with the Vienna school and

Archimedes screw *The Archimedes screw, a spiral screw turned inside a cylinder, was once commonly used to lift water from canals.*

Gothic arch
moldings
corbel spandrel
spring of arch
capital
column
base

Tuscan

Doric

entablature
capital

the orders of
classical architecture

Corinthian

shaft

base

Ionic

Composite

classical temple

cornice
tympanum
cornice
frieze
architrave triglyph metope
capital
abacus
shaft

entablature pediment

column

architecture *Different types of column and arch are associated with different architectural periods.*

the German Bauhaus but was also seen in the US, Scandinavia, and France. It used spare line and form, an emphasis on rationalism, and the elimination of ornament. It makes great use of technological advances in materials such as glass, steel, and concrete and of construction techniques that allow flexibility of design. Not-

able practitioners include Frank Lloyd Wright, Mies van der Rohe, and Le Corbusier. Modern architecture also furthered the notion of the planning of extensive multibuilding projects and of whole towns or communities.

Post-Modernist This architecture emerged in the US, Japan, and Europe in the 1980s, with one trend toward high-tech forms and another reverting back to using simplified or geometric elements from earlier styles to decorate traditional forms.

archive collection of historically valuable records, ranging from papers and documents to photographs, films, videotapes, and sound recordings.

The **National Archives Hall** in Washington, DC contains the original Declaration of Independence, the Constitution, and the ⟡Bill of Rights. The **National Archives and Records Service** is responsible for preserving federal records and for administration of the presidential libraries, usually established in the incumbent's birthplace.

archon (Greek "ruler") in ancient Greece, title of the chief magistrate in many cities.

In Athens, there were originally three: the king archon, the eponymous archon, and the polemarch. Their numbers were later increased to nine, with the extra six keeping a record of judgments. The king archon was the elected king and religious representative of the state; the eponymous archon, by whose personal name the administrative year was known in Athens, was the head of state and supreme judge; the polemarch was in charge of state security and commanded the army.

arc lamp or **arc light** electric light that uses the illumination of an electric arc maintained between two electrodes. The British scientist Humphry Davy developed an arc lamp 1808, and its main use in recent years has been in cinema projectors. The lamp consists of two carbon electrodes, between which a very high voltage is maintained. Electric current arcs (jumps) between the two, creating a brilliant light.

Arctic, the that part of the northern hemisphere surrounding the North Pole; arbitrarily defined as the region lying N of the Arctic Circle (66° 32′N) or N of the tree line. There is no Arctic continent; the greater part of the region comprises the Arctic Ocean, which is the world's smallest ocean. Arctic climate, fauna, and flora extend over the islands and northern edges of continental land masses that surround the Arctic Ocean (Svalbard, Iceland, Greenland, Siberia, Scandinavia, Alaska, and Canada)

area 14,000,000 sq mi/36,000,000 sq km

physical pack-ice floating on the Arctic Ocean occupies almost the entire region between the North Pole and the coasts of North America and Eurasia, covering an area that ranges in diameter from 1,900 mi/3,000 km to 2,500 mi/ 4,000 km. The pack-ice reaches a maximum extent in Feb when its outer limit (influenced by the cold Labrador Current and the warm Gulf Stream) varies from 50°N along the coast of Labrador to 75°N in the Barents Sea N of Scandinavia. In spring the pack-ice begins to break up into ice floes which are carried by the south-flowing Greenland Current to the Atlantic Ocean. Arctic ice is at its minimum area in Aug. The greatest concentration of icebergs in Arctic regions is found in Baffin Bay. They are derived from the glaciers of W Greenland, then carried along Baffin Bay and down into the N Atlantic where they

melt off Labrador and Newfoundland. The Bering Straits are icebound for more than six months each year, but the Barents Sea between Scandinavia and Svalbard is free of ice and is navigable throughout the year. Arctic coastlines, which have emerged from the sea since the last Ice Age, are characterized by deposits of gravel and disintegrated rock. The area covered by the Arctic icecap shrank 2% 1978–87

climate permanent ice sheets and year-round snow cover are found in regions where average monthly temperatures remain below 32°F/ 0°C, but on land areas where one or more summer months have average temperatures between freezing point and 50°F/10°C, a stunted, treeless tundra vegetation is found. Mean annual temperatures range from –23°C at the North Pole to –12°C on the coast of Alaska. In winter the Sun disappears below the horizon for a time, but the cold is less severe than in parts of inland Siberia or Antartica. During the short summer season there is a maximum of 24 hours of daylight at the summer solstice on the Arctic Circle and six months' constant light at the North Pole. Countries with Arctic coastlines established the International Arctic Sciences Committee in 1987 to study ozone depletion and climatic change

flora and fauna the plants of the relatively infertile Arctic tundra (lichens, mosses, grasses, cushion plants, and low shrubs) spring to life during the short summer season and remain dormant for the remaining ten months of the year. There are no annual plants, only perennials. Animal species include reindeer, caribou, musk ox, fox, hare, lemming, wolf, polar bear, seal, and walrus. There are few birds except in summer when insects, such as mosquitoes, are plentiful

natural resources the Arctic is rich in coal (Svalbard, Russia), oil and natural gas (Alaska, Canadian Arctic, Russia), and mineral resources including gold, silver, copper, uranium, lead, zinc, nickel, and bauxite. Because of climatic conditions, the Arctic is not suited to navigation and the exploitation of these resources. Murmansk naval base on the Kola Peninsula is the largest in the world

population there are about 1 million aboriginal people including the Aleuts of Alaska, North American Indians, the Lapps of Scandinavia and N Russia, the Yakuts, Samoyeds, Komi, Chukchi, Tungus, and Dolgany of Russia, and the Inuit of Siberian Russia, the Canadian Arctic and Greenland.

Arctic Circle imaginary line that encircles the North Pole at latitude 66° 32′ N. Within this line there is at least one day in the summer during which the Sun never sets, and at least one day in the winter during which the Sun never rises.

Arctic Ocean ocean surrounding the North Pole; area 5,400,000 sq mi/14,000,000 sq km. Because of the Siberian and North American rivers flowing into it, it has comparatively low salinity and freezes readily.

It comprises:

Beaufort Sea off Canada/Alaska coast, named after British admiral Francis ⟡Beaufort; oil drilling allowed only in winter because the sea is the breeding and migration route of the bowhead whales, staple diet of the local Inuit people;

Greenland Sea between Greenland and Svalbard;

Norwegian Sea between Greenland and Norway.

From west to east along the N coast of Russia:

Arctic exploration: chronology

60,000 –35,000 BC	Ancestors of the Inuit and American Indians began migration from Siberia to North America by the "lost" landbridge of Beringia.
320 BC	Pytheas, a Greek sailor contemporary with Alexander the Great, possibly reached Iceland.
9th–10th centuries AD	Vikings colonized Iceland and Greenland, which then had a much warmer climate.
c. 1000	Norwegian sailor Leif Ericsson reached Baffin Island (NE of Canada) and Labrador.
1497	Genoese pilot Giovanni Caboto first sought the Northwest Passage as a trade route around North America for Henry VII of England.
1553	English navigator Richard Chancellor tried to find the Northeast Passage around Siberia and first established direct English trade with Russia.
1576	English sailor Martin Frobisher reached Frobisher Bay, but found only "fools' gold" (iron pyrites) for Elizabeth I of England.
1594–97	Dutch navigator Willem Barents made three expeditions in search of the Northeast Passage.
1607	English navigator Henry Hudson failed to cross the Arctic Ocean, but his reports of whales started the northern whaling industry.
1670	Hudson's Bay Company started the fur trade in Canada.
1728	Danish navigator Vitus Bering passed the Bering Strait.
1829–33	Scottish explorer John Ross discovered the North Magnetic Pole.
1845	The mysterious disappearance of English explorer John Franklin's expedition to the Northwest Passage stimulated further exploration.
1878–79	Swedish navigator Nils Nordensköld was the first European to discover the Northeast Passage.
1893–96	Norwegian explorer Fridtjof Nansen's ship *Fram* drifted across the Arctic while locked in the ice, proving that no Arctic continent existed.
1903–06	Norwegian explorer Roald Amundsen sailed through the Northwest Passage.
1909	US explorers Robert Peary, Matt Henson, and four Inuit reached the North Pole on April 2.
1926	US explorers Richard Byrd and Floyd Bennett flew to the Pole on May 9.
1926	Italian aviator Umberto Nobile and Amundsen crossed the Pole (Spitzbergen –Alaska) in the airship *Norge on 12 May*.
1954	Scandinavian Airlines launched the first regular commercial flights over the short-cut polar route.
1958	The US submarine *Nautilus* crossed the Pole beneath the ice.
1960	From this date a Soviet nuclear-powered icebreaker kept open a 2,500 mi/4,000 km Asia–Europe passage along the north coast of Siberia for 150 days a year.
1969	Wally Herbert of the British Transarctic Expedition made the first surface crossing, by dog sled, of the Arctic Ocean (Alaska–Spitzbergen).
1977	The Soviet icebreaker *Arktika* made the first surface voyage to the Pole.
1990	Of the four teams (Canadian, Russian, British, and Norwegian) who attempted to reach the North Pole "unsupported" (without aid of dogs or airplane supplies), only the Norwegians arrived. Their claim was contested.

Barents Sea named after Willem ♢Barents, which has oil and gas reserves and was strategically significant as the meeting point of the NATO and Warsaw Pact forces. The ♢White Sea is its southernmost gulf;
Kara Sea renowned for bad weather and known as the "great ice cellar;"
Laptev Sea between Taimyr Peninsula and New Siberian Island;
East Siberian Sea and **Chukchi Sea** between Russia and the US; the seminomadic Chukchi people of NE Siberia finally accepted Soviet rule in the 1930s.
The Arctic Ocean has the world's greatest concentration of nuclear submarines, but at the same time there is much scientific cooperation on exploration, especially since Russia needs Western aid to develop oil and gas in its areas.

Arcturus or **Alpha Boötis** brightest star in the constellation Boötes and the fourth-brightest star in the sky. Arcturus is a red giant about 28 times larger than the Sun and 70 times more luminous, 34 light-years away from Earth.

Ardabil town in NW Iran, near the frontier with Azerbaijan; population (1986) 281,973. Ardabil exports dried fruits, carpets, and rugs.

Ardèche river in SE France, a tributary of the Rhône. Near Vallon it flows under the Pont d'Arc, a natural bridge. It gives its name to a *département*.

Arden Elizabeth. Adopted name of Florence Nightingale Graham. 1884–1966. Canadian-born US beauty expert and mass merchandiser. Born in Woodbridge, Ontario, she moved to New York 1908. Possessing an extraordinary business sense, she opened a beauty salon 1910 and expanded the firm in 1914 under the corporate name of "Elizabeth Arden," a name she soon adopted herself. She developed and merchandised a line of cosmetic products and also utilized new techniques of mass advertising to introduce her products to the public. She later opened a chain of beauty salons and spas throughout the US.

Ardennes wooded plateau in NE France, SE Belgium, and N Luxembourg, cut through by the river Meuse; also a *département* of ♢Champagne-Ardenne. There was heavy fighting here in World Wars I and II (see ♢Bulge, Battle of the).

are metric unit of area, equal to 100 square meters (119.6 sq yd); 100 ares make one ♢hectare.

areca any palm tree of the genus *Areca*, native to Asia and Australia. The ♢betel nut comes from the species *A. catechu*.

Arecibo site in Puerto Rico of the world's largest single-dish ♢radio telescope, 1,000 ft/ 305 m in diameter. It is built in a natural hollow and uses the rotation of the Earth to scan the sky. It has been used both for radar work on the planets and for conventional radio astronomy, and is operated by Cornell University.

Arendt Hannah 1906–1975. German-born US scholar and political scientist. With the rise of the Nazis, she moved to Paris and emigrated to the US 1940. Her works include *The Origins of Modern Totalitarianism* 1951, *The Human Condition* 1958, *On Revolution* 1963, *Eichmann in Jerusalem* 1963, and *On Violence* 1972.
Arendt received her PhD from Heidelberg University 1928. During World War II she was research director for the Conference on Jewish Relations.

Arequipa city in Peru at the base of the volcano El Misti; population (1990 est) 965,000. Founded by Pizarro 1540, it is the cultural focus of S Peru and a busy commercial center (soap, textiles).

Ares in Greek mythology, the god of war (Roman ♢Mars). The son of Zeus and Hera, he was worshiped chiefly in Thrace.

arête (German *grat*; North American **combe-ridge**) sharp narrow ridge separating two ♢glacial troughs, or valleys. The typical U-shaped cross sections of glacial troughs give arêtes very steep sides. Arêtes are common in glaciated mountain regions such as the Rockies, the Himalayas, and the Alps.

Aretino Pietro 1492–1556. Italian writer. He earned his living, both in Rome and Venice, by publishing satirical pamphlets while under the protection of a highly placed family. His *Letters* 1537–57 are a unique record of the cultural and political events of his time, and illustrate his vivacious, exuberant character. He also wrote poems and comedies.

Arevalo Bermejo Juan José 1904–1990. Guatemalan president 1945–51, elected to head a civilian government after a popular revolt ended a 14-year period of military rule. However, many of his liberal reforms were later undone by subsequent military rulers.

Arezzo town in the Tuscan region of Italy; 50 mi/80 km SE of Florence; population (1981) 92,100. The writers Petrarch and Aretino were born here. It is a mining town and also trades in textiles, olive oil, and antiques.

argali wild sheep *Ovis ammon* of Central Asia. The male can grow to 4 ft/1.2 m at the shoulder, and has massive spiral horns.

Argand diagram in mathematics, a method for representing complex numbers by Cartesian coordinates (x, y). Along the x-axis (horizontal axis) are plotted the real numbers, and along the y-axis (vertical axis) the nonreal, or ♢imaginary numbers.

Argentina country in South America, bounded W and S by Chile, N by Bolivia, and E by Paraguay, Brazil, Uruguay, and the Atlantic Ocean.

government The return of civilian rule 1983 brought a return of the 1853 constitution, with some changes in the electoral system. The constitution created a federal system with a president elected by popular vote through an electoral college, serving a six-year term. The president is head of both state and government and chooses the cabinet.
Argentina is a federal union of 22 provinces, one national territory, and the Federal District. The two-chamber Congress consists of a 46-member senate chosen by provincial legislatures for a nine-year term, and a directly

Argentina
Republic of (*República Argentina*)

area 1,073,116 sq mi/2,780,092 sq km
capital Buenos Aires (to move to Viedma)
cities Rosario, Córdoba, Tucumán, Mendoza, Santa Fe; ports are La Plata and Bahía Blanca
physical mountains in W, forest and savanna in N, pampas (treeless plains) in E central area, Patagonian plateau in S; rivers Colorado, Salado, Paraná, Uruguay, Río de la Plata estuary
territories part of Tierra del Fuego; disputed claims to S Atlantic islands and part of Antarctica
environment an estimated 7,700 sq mi/20,000 sq km of land has been swamped with salt water
features Andes mountains, with Aconcagua the highest peak in the W hemisphere; Iguaçú Falls
head of state and government Carlos Menem from 1989
political system emergent democratic federal republic
political parties Radical Civic Union Party (UCR), moderate centrist; Justicialist Party, right-wing Peronist
exports livestock products, cereals, wool, tannin, peanuts, linseed oil, minerals (coal, copper, molybdenum, gold, silver, lead, zinc, barium, uranium); the country has huge resources of oil, natural gas, hydroelectric power
currency peso = 10,000 australs (which it replaced 1992)
population (1990 est) 32,686,000 (mainly of Spanish or Italian origin, only about 30,000 American Indians surviving); growth rate 1.5% p.a.
life expectancy men 66, women 73
languages Spanish (official); English, Italian, German, French
religion Roman Catholic (state-supported)
literacy men 96%, women 95% (1985 est)
GDP $70.1 bn (1990); $2,162 per head
chronology
1816 Independence achieved from Spain, followed by civil wars.
1946 Juan Perón elected president, supported by his wife "Evita."
1952 "Evita" Perón died.
1955 Perón overthrown and civilian administration restored.
1966 Coup brought back military rule.
1973 A Peronist party won the presidential and congressional elections. Perón returned from exile in Spain as president, with his third wife, Isabel, as vice-president.
1974 Perón died, succeeded by Isabel.
1976 Coup resulted in rule by a military junta led by Lt Gen Jorge Videla. Congress dissolved, and hundreds of people, including Isabel Perón, detained.
1976–83 Ferocious campaign against left-wing elements, the "dirty war."
1978 Videla retired. Succeeded by General Roberto Viola, who promised a return to democracy.
1981 Viola died suddenly. Replaced by General Leopoldo Galtieri.
1982 With a deteriorating economy, Galtieri sought popular support by ordering an invasion of the British-held Falkland Islands. After losing the short war, Galtieri was removed and replaced by General Reynaldo Bignone.
1983 Amnesty law passed and 1853 democratic constitution revived. General elections won by Raúl Alfonsín and his party. Armed forces under scrutiny.
1984 National Commission on the Disappearance of Persons (CONADEP) reported on over 8,000 people who had disappeared during the "dirty war" of 1976–83.
1985 A deteriorating economy forced Alfonsín to seek help from the International Monetary Fund and introduce an austerity program.
1986 Unsuccessful attempt on Alfonsín's life.
1988 Unsuccessful army coup attempt.
1989 Carlos Menem, of the Justicialist Party, elected president.
1990 Full diplomatic relations with the UK restored. Menem elected Justicialist Party leader. Revolt by army officers thwarted.
1992 New currency introduced.

elected chamber of 254 deputies serving a four-year term. Each province has its own elected governor and legislature that deal with matters not assigned to the federal government.
history Originally inhabited by South American Indian peoples, Argentina was first visited by Europeans in the early 16th century. Buenos Aires was founded first 1536 and again 1580 after being abandoned because of Indian attacks. Argentina was made a Spanish viceroyalty 1776, and the population rose against Spanish rule 1810. Full independence was achieved 1816. After a period of civil wars a stable government was established 1853 and the country developed as a democracy with active political parties.
rise of Perón Since 1930 Argentina has been subject to alternate civilian and military rule.

The Radical Civic Union (UCR) held power from 1916 until the first military coup 1930. Civilian government returned 1932, and a second military coup 1943 paved the way for the rise of Lt Gen Juan Domingo ◊Perón. Strengthened by the popularity of his wife, María Eva Duarte de ◊Perón (the legendary "Evita"), Perón created the Peronista party, based on extreme nationalism and social improvement. Evita Perón died 1952, and her husband was overthrown and civilian rule restored 1955. Perón continued to direct the Peronista movement from exile in Spain. A coup 1966 restored military rule, and the success of a later Peronist party, Frente Justicialista de Liberación, brought Héctor Cámpora to the presidency 1973. After three months he resigned to make way for Perón, with his third wife, María Estela Martínez de Perón ("Isabel"), as vice-president. Perón died 1974 and was succeeded by his widow.
Videla and the "dirty war" Two years later, because of concern about the economy, a military coup ousted Isabel and a three-man junta, led by Lt Gen Jorge Videla, was installed. The constitution was amended, and political and labor-union activity banned. The years 1976–83 witnessed a ferocious campaign by the junta against left-wing elements, the "dirty war," during which it is believed that between 6,000 and 15,000 people "disappeared." Although confirmed in office until 1981, Videla retired 1978, to be succeeded by General Roberto Viola, who promised a return to democracy. Viola died 1981 and was replaced by General Leopoldo ◊Galtieri.
Falklands conflict Galtieri, seeking popular support and wishing to distract attention from the deteriorating economy, ordered 1982 the invasion of the *Islas Malvinas*, the ◊Falkland Islands, over which the UK's claim to sovereignty had long been disputed. After a short war, during which 750 Argentinians were killed, the islands were reoccupied by the UK. With the failure of the Falklands invasion, Galtieri was replaced in a bloodless coup by General Reynaldo Bignone. A military inquiry reported 1983 that Galtieri's junta was to blame for the defeat. Several officers were tried, and some, including Galtieri, given prison sentences, while an amnesty was granted to all those convicted of political crimes during the previous ten years. The ban on political and labor-union activity was lifted and general elections were held Oct 1983. The main parties were the UCR, led by Raúl ◊Alfonsín Foulkes, and the Peronist Justicialist Party, led by Italo Lúder.
Alfonsín's reforms and investigations Having won the election, Alfonsín announced radical reforms in the armed forces (leading to the retirement of more than half the senior officers) and the trial of the first three military juntas that had ruled Argentina since 1976. He set up the National Commission on the Disappearance of Persons (CONADEP) to investigate the "dirty war." A report by CONADEP 1984 listed over 8,000 people who had disappeared and 1,300 army officers who had been involved in the campaign of repression. Alfonsín's government was soon faced with enormous economic problems, resulting in recourse to help from the ◊International Monetary Fund and an austerity program.
Menem tackles high inflation The presidential election of May 1989 was won by the Justicialist candidate, Carlos ◊Menem. Alfonsín handed over power July 1989, five months before his term of office formally ended, to allow Menem to come to grips with the high inflation (more than 1,000% a year) that threatened to bring about increasing social unrest. The new government soon established a rapport with the UK authorities and full diplomatic relations were restored Feb 1990 (the issue of sovereignty over the Falklands was skirted). President Menem was elected leader of the Justicialist Party in Aug, and in Dec 1990 a rebellion by junior army officers was put down.

A financial scandal involving Menem's relatives and aides threatened the Justicialist Party's success in mid-term elections; but support for Menem's economic policies secured a victory. In 1991 inflation was, at 84%, the lowest it had been since 1986. In a visit to the US Nov 1991 Menem sought closer ties with the US and support for Argentina's economic reforms.

In Jan 1992 the government introduced a new currency, the peso, to replace the austral which had been rendered almost worthless due to inflation. *See illustration box.*

argon (Greek *argos* "idle") colorless, odorless, nonmetallic, gaseous element, symbol Ar, atomic number 18, atomic weight 39.948. It is grouped with the ⬦inert gases, since it was long believed not to react with other substances, but observations now indicate that it can be made to combine with boron fluoride to form compounds. It constitutes almost 1% of the Earth's atmosphere, and was discovered 1894 by British chemists John Rayleigh (1842–1919) and William Ramsay after all oxygen and nitrogen had been removed chemically from a sample of air. It is used in electric discharge tubes and argon lasers.

argonaut or *paper nautilus* octopus living in the open sea, genus *Argonauta*. The female of the common paper nautilus, *A. argo*, is 8 in/20 cm across, and secretes a spiraled papery shell for her eggs from the web of the first pair of arms. The male is a shell-less dwarf, 0.4 in/1 cm across.

Argonauts in Greek legend, the band of heroes who accompanied ⬦Jason when he set sail in the *Argo* to find the ⬦Golden Fleece.

Argonne wooded plateau in NE France, separating Lorraine and Champagne. It was the scene of much fighting in both world wars.

Argos city in ancient Greece, at the head of the Gulf of Nauplia, which was once a cult center of the goddess Hera. In the Homeric age the name "Argives" was sometimes used instead of "Greeks."

argument in mathematics, a specific value of the independent variable of a ⬦function of *x*. It is also another name for ⬦amplitude.

Argus in Greek mythology, a giant with 100 eyes. When he was killed by Hermes, Hera transplanted his eyes into the tail of her favorite bird, the peacock.

Argyll Archibald Campbell, 5th Earl of Argyll 1530–1573. Adherent of the Scottish presbyterian John ⬦Knox. A supporter of Mary Queen of Scots from 1561, he commanded her forces after her escape from Lochleven Castle 1568. He revised his position and became Lord High Chancellor of Scotland 1572.

Århus alternate form of ⬦Aarhus, a port in Denmark.

aria (Italian "air") solo vocal piece in an opera or oratorio, often in three sections, the third repeating the first after a contrasting central section.

Ariadne in Greek mythology, the daughter of Minos, King of Crete. When Theseus came from Athens as one of the sacrificial victims offered to the Minotaur, she fell in love with him and gave him a ball of thread, which enabled him to find his way out of the labyrinth.

Ariane launch vehicle built in a series by the European Space Agency (first flight 1979). The launch site is at Kourou in French Guiana. Ariane is a three-stage rocket using liquid fuels. Small solid-fuel and liquid-fuel boosters can be attached to its first stage to increase carrying power.

Arianism a system of Christian theology that gave God the Father primacy over Christ.

It was founded about 310 by ⬦Arius, and condemned as heretical at the Council of Nicaea 325.

Some 17th- and 18th-century theologians held Arian views akin to those of ⬦Unitarianism (that God is a single being, and that there is no such thing as the Trinity). In the 1970s the question of the heresy arose again for the Vatican in the writings of such theologians as Edouard Schillebeeckx of the Netherlands.

Arias Sanchez Oscar 1940– . Costa Rican politician, president 1986–90, secretary-general of the left-wing National Liberation Party (PLN) from 1979. He advocated a neutralist policy and in 1987 was the leading promoter of the Central American Peace Plan (see ⬦Nicaragua). He lost the presidency to Rafael Angel Cal-déron 1990. He was awarded the Nobel Peace Prize 1987.

Arica port in Chile; population (1990) 177,300. Much of Bolivia's trade passes through it, and there is contention over the use of Arica by Bolivia to allow access to the Pacific Ocean. It is Chile's northernmost city.

arid zone infertile area with a small, infrequent rainfall that rapidly evaporates because of high temperatures. The aridity of a region is defined by its *aridity index*—a function of the rainfall and also of the temperature, and hence the rate of evaporation. There are arid zones in Morocco, Pakistan, Australia, the US, and elsewhere.

Scarcity of water is a problem for the inhabitants of arid zones, and constant research goes into discovering cheap methods of distilling sea water and artificially recharging natural groundwater reservoirs. Another problem is the eradication of salt in irrigation supplies from underground sources or where a surface deposit forms in poorly drained areas.

Ariège river in S France, a tributary of the Garonne, which rises in the Pyrenees; length 106 mi/170 km. It gives its name to a *département*.

Aries zodiacal constellation in the northern hemisphere between Pisces and Taurus, near Auriga, represented as the legendary ram whose golden fleece was sought by Jason and the Argonauts. Its most distinctive feature is a curve of three stars of decreasing brightness. The brightest of these is Hamal or Alpha Arietis, 65 light-years from Earth.

The Sun passes through Aries from late April to mid-May. In astrology, the dates for Aries are between about March 21 and April 19 (see ⬦precession). The spring ⬦equinox once lay in Aries, but has now moved into Pisces through the effect of the Earth's precession (wobble).

aril accessory seed cover other than a ⬦fruit; it may be fleshy and sometimes brightly colored, woody, or hairy. In flowering plants (⬦angiosperms) it is often derived from the stalk that originally attached the ovule to the ovary wall. Examples of arils include the bright-red, fleshy layer surrounding the yew seed (yews are ⬦gymnosperms so they lack true fruits), and the network of hard filaments that partially covers the nutmeg seed and yields the spice known as mace.

Another aril, the horny outgrowth found toward one end of the seed of the castor-oil plant *Ricinus communis*, is called a caruncle. It is formed from the integuments (protective layers enclosing the ovule) and develops after fertilization.

Ariosto Ludovico 1474–1533. Italian poet who wrote Latin poems and comedies on Classical lines, including the poem *Orlando Furioso 1516, published 1532, an epic treatment of the Roland* story, the perfect poetic expression of the Italian Renaissance.

Ariosto was born in Reggio, and joined the household of Cardinal Ippolito d'Este 1503. He was frequently engaged in ambassadorial missions and diplomacy for the Duke of Ferrara. In 1521 he became governor of a province in the Apennines, and after three years retired to Ferrara, where he died.

Aristarchus of Samos c. 280–264 BC. Greek astronomer. The first to argue that the Earth moves around the Sun, he was ridiculed for his beliefs. He was also the first astronomer to estimate the sizes of the Sun and Moon and their distances from the Earth.

Aristide Jean-Bertrand 1953– . President of Haiti Dec 1990–Oct 1991. A left-wing Catholic priest opposed to the right-wing regime of the Duvalier family, he campaigned for the National Front for Change and Democracy, representing a loose coalition of peasants, labor unionists, and clerics, and won 70% of the vote. He was deposed by the military Sept 1991.

Aristides c. 530–468 BC. Athenian politician. He was one of the ten Athenian generals at the battle of ⬦Marathon 490 BC and was elected chief archon, or magistrate. Later he came into conflict with the democratic leader Themistocles, and was exiled about 483 BC. He returned to fight against the Persians at Salamis 480 BC and in the following year commanded the Athenians at Plataea.

Aristippus c. 435–356 BC. Greek philosopher, founder of the ⬦Cyrenaic or hedonist school. A pupil of Socrates, he developed the doctrine that pleasure is the highest good in life. He lived at the court of ⬦Dionysius of Syracuse and then with Laïs, a courtesan, in Corinth.

Aristophanes c. 448–380 BC. Greek comedic dramatist. Of his 11 extant plays (of a total of over 40), the early comedies are remarkable for the violent satire with which he ridiculed the democratic war leaders. He also satirized contemporary issues such as the new learning of Socrates in *The Clouds* 423 BC and the power of women in ⬦*Lysistrata* 411 BC. The chorus plays a prominent role, frequently giving the play its title, as in *The Wasps* 422 BC, *The Birds* 414 BC, and *The Frogs* 405 BC.

Aristotle 384–322 BC. Greek philosopher who advocated reason and moderation. He maintained that sense experience is our only source of knowledge, and that by reasoning we can discover the essences of things, that is, their distinguishing qualities. In his works on ethics and politics, he suggested that human happiness consists in living in conformity with nature. He derived his political theory from the recognition that mutual aid is natural to humankind, and refused to set up any one constitution as universally ideal. Of Aristotle's works some 22 treatises survive, dealing with logic, metaphysics, physics, astronomy, meteorology, biology, psychology, ethics, politics, and literary criticism.

Born in Stagira in Thrace, he studied in Athens, became tutor to ⬦Alexander the Great, and in 335 BC opened a school in the Lyceum (grove sacred to Apollo) in Athens. It became known as the "peripatetic school" because he walked up and down as he talked, and his works are a collection of his lecture notes.

When Alexander died, Aristotle was forced to flee to Chalcis, where he died. Among his many contributions to political thought were the first systematic attempts to distinguish between different forms of government, ideas about the role of law in the state, and the conception of a science of politics.

His works were lost to Europe after the decline of Rome, but they were reintroduced in the Middle Ages by Arab and Jewish scholars and became the basis of medieval ◊scholasticism.

arithmetic branch of mathematics concerned with the study of numbers and their properties. The fundamental operations of arithmetic are addition, subtraction, multiplication, and division. Raising to powers (for example, squaring or cubing a number), the extraction of roots (for example, square roots), percentages, fractions, and ratios are developed from these operations.

Forms of simple arithmetic existed in prehistoric times. In China, Egypt, Babylon, and early civilizations generally, arithmetic was used for commercial purposes, records of taxation, and astronomy. During the Dark Ages in Europe, knowledge of arithmetic was preserved in India and later among the Arabs. European mathematics revived with the development of trade and overseas exploration. Hindu-Arabic numerals replaced Roman numerals, allowing calculations to be made on paper, instead of by the ◊abacus.

The essential feature of this number system was the introduction of zero, which allows us to have a *place–value* system. The decimal numeral system employs ten numerals (0,1,2,3,4,5,6,7,8,9) and is said to operate in "base ten." In a base-ten number, each position has a value ten times that of the position to its immediate right; for example, in the number 23 the numeral 3 represents three units (ones), and the number 2 represents two tens. The Babylonians, however, used a complex base-sixty system, residues of which are found today in the number of minutes in each hour and in angular measurement (6×60 degrees). The Mayas used a base-twenty system.

There have been many inventions and developments to make the manipulation of the arithmetic processes easier, such as the invention of ◊logarithms by ◊Napier 1614 and of the slide rule in the period 1620–30. Since then, many forms of ready reckoners, mechanical and electronic calculators, and computers have been invented.

Modern computers fundamentally operate in base two, using only two numerals (0,1), known as a binary system. In binary, each position has a value twice as great as the position to its immediate right, so that for example binary 111 (111_2) is equal to 7 in the decimal system, and 1111 (1111_2) is equal to 15. Because the main operations of subtraction, multiplication, and division can be reduced mathematically to addition, digital computers carry out calculations by adding, usually in binary numbers in which the numerals 0 and 1 can be represented by off and on pulses of electric current.

Modular or modulo arithmetic, sometimes known as residue arithmetic, can take only a specific number of digits, whatever the value. For example, in modulo 4 (mod 4) the only values any number can take are 0, 1, 2, or 3. In this system, 7 is written as 3 mod 4, and 35 is also 3 mod 4. Notice 3 is the residue, or remainder, when 7 or 35 is divided by 4. This form of arithmetic is often illustrated on a circle. It

deals with events recurring in regular cycles, and is used in describing the functioning of gasoline engines, electrical generators, and so on. For example, in the mod 12, the answer to a question as to what time it will be in five hours if it is now ten o'clock can be expressed $10 + 5 = 3$.

arithmetic and logic unit (ALU) in a computer, the part of the ◊central processing unit (CPU) that performs the basic arithmetic and logic operations on data.

arithmetic mean the average of a set of n numbers, obtained by adding the numbers and dividing by n. For example, the arithmetic mean of the set of 5 numbers 1, 3, 6, 8, and 12 is $(1 + 3 + 6 + 8 + 12)/5 = 30/5 = 6$.

The term "average" is often used to refer only to the arithmetic mean, even though the mean is in fact only one form of average (the others include ◊median and ◊mode).

arithmetic progression or **arithmetic sequence** sequence of numbers or terms that have a common difference between any one term and the next in the sequence. For example, 2, 7, 12, 17, 22, 27, ... is an arithmetic sequence with a common difference of 5.

The nth term in any arithmetic progression can be found using the formula

nth term $= a + (n-1)d$,

where a is the first term and d is the common difference. For example, to find the 7th term of a sequence in which the first term is 2 and the common difference is 3:

$n = 7$, $a = 3$, and $d = 3$,
7th term $= 3 + (7-1) \times 3 = 21$.

An **arithmetic series** is the sum of the terms in an arithmetic sequence.

Arius *c.* 256–336. Egyptian priest whose ideas gave rise to ◊Arianism, a Christian belief which denied the complete divinity of Jesus.

He was born in Libya, and became a priest in Alexandria 311. In 318 he was excommunicated and fled to Palestine, but his theology spread to such an extent that the emperor Constantine called a council at Nicaea 325 to resolve the question. Arius and his adherents were condemned and banished.

Arizona state in the southwestern US; nickname Grand Canyon State
area 113,500 sq mi/294,100 sq km
capital Phoenix
cities Tucson, Scottsdale, Tempe, Mesa, Glendale, Flagstaff
physical Colorado Plateau in the N and E, desert basins and mountains in the S and W, Colorado River, Grand Canyon
features Grand Canyon National Park (the multicolored-rock gorge through which the Colorado River flows, 4–18 mi/6–29 km wide, up to 1.1 mi/1.7 km deep and 217 mi/350 km long); Organ Pipe Cactus National Monument Park; deserts: Painted (including the Petrified Forest of fossil trees), Gila, Sonoran; dams: Roosevelt, Hoover; old London Bridge (transported 1971 to the tourist resort of Lake Havasu City)
products cotton under irrigation, livestock, copper, molybdenum, silver, electronics, aircraft
population (1990) 3,665,000; including 4.5% American Indians (Navaho, Hopi, Apache), who by treaty own 25% of the state
famous people Cochise, Wyatt Earp, Geronimo, Barry Goldwater, Zane Grey, Percival Lowell, Frank Lloyd Wright
history part of New Spain 1715; part of Mexico 1824; passed to the US after Mexican War 1848; territory 1863; statehood achieved 1912.

Arizona is believed to derive its name from

Arizona

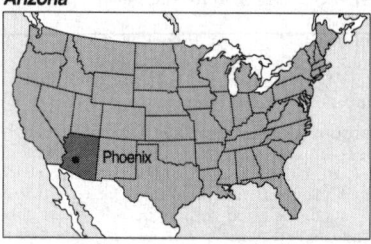

the Spanish *arida-zona* ("dry belt"). The first Spaniard to visit Arizona was the Franciscan Marcos de Niza 1539. After 1863 it developed rapidly as a result of the gold rush in neighboring California. Irrigation has been carried out on a colossal scale since the 1920s. The Roosevelt Dam on Salt River, and Hoover Dam on the Colorado River between Arizona and Nevada, provide the state with both hydroelectric power and irrigation water. At the end of the 19th century, rich copper deposits were found in Arizona and subsequently deposits of many other minerals. The post–World War II era has seen a heavy influx of retired people and a great increase in tourism. The manufacture of electronic equipment has added considerably to the growth of the state economy.

Arjan Indian religious leader, fifth guru (teacher) of Sikhism from 1581. He built the Golden Temple in ◊Amritsar and compiled the *Adi Granth*, the first volume of Sikh scriptures. He died in Muslim custody.

Arkansas state in S central US; nickname Wonder State/Land of Opportunity
area 53,191 sq mi/137,800 sq km
capital Little Rock
cities Fort Smith, Pine Bluff, Fayetteville
physical Ozark Mountains and plateau in the west, lowlands in the east; Arkansas River; many lakes
features Hot Springs National Park
products cotton, soybeans, rice, oil, natural gas, bauxite, timber, processed foods
population (1990) 2,350,700
famous people Bill Clinton, Johnny Cash, J William Fulbright, Douglas MacArthur, Winthrop Rockefeller
history explored by de Soto 1541; European settlers 1648, who traded with local Indians; part of Louisiana Purchase 1803; statehood achieved 1836.

The first European settlement was Arkansas Post, founded by some of the companions of the French explorer La Salle. After seceding from the Union 1861 (see ◊Confederacy), it was readmitted 1868.

In 1957 President Eisenhower sent US troops to enforce a court order to desegregate Central High School in Little Rock after Governor Orval Faubus had called up the National Guard to block integration.

Arkansas

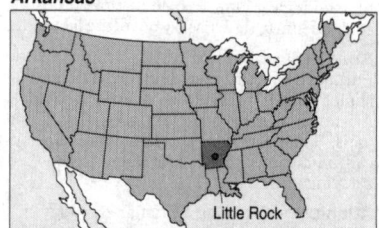

Ark of the Covenant in the Old Testament, the chest that contained the Tablets of the Law as given to Moses. It is now the cupboard in a synagogue in which the ⟡Torah scrolls are kept.

Arkwright Richard 1732–1792. English inventor and manufacturing pioneer who developed a machine for spinning cotton (he called it a "spinning frame") 1768. He set up a water-powered spinning factory 1771 and installed steam power in another factory 1790.

Arles town in Bouches-du-Rhône *département*, SE France, on the left bank of the Rhône; population (1982) 50,772. It is an important fruit- and vine-growing district. Roman relics include an amphitheater for 25,000 spectators. The cathedral of St Trophime is a notable Romanesque structure. The painter Van Gogh lived here 1888–89, a period during which he painted some of his major works.

Arlington county in Virginia, and suburb of Washington, DC; population (1990) 170,900. It is the site of the National Cemetery for the dead of the US wars. The grounds were first used as a military cemetery 1864 during the American Civil War. By 1975, 165,142 military, naval, and civilian persons had been buried there and numbered, including the ⟡Unknown Soldier of both world wars, President John F Kennedy, and his brother Robert Kennedy.

Arlington city in N Texas, located between Dallas and Fort Worth. Industries include machinery, paper products, steel, automobile assembly, rubber, and chemicals; population (1990) 261,700.

Armada fleet sent by Philip II of Spain against England 1588. See ⟡Spanish Armada.

armadillo mammal of the family Dasypodidae, with an armor of bony plates on its back. Some 20 species live between Texas and Patagonia and range in size from the fairy armadillo at 5 in/13 cm to the giant armadillo, 4.5 ft/1.5 m long. Armadillos feed on insects, snakes, fruit, and carrion. Some can roll into an armored ball if attacked; others rely on burrowing for protection.

They belong to the order Edentata ("without teeth") which also includes sloths and anteaters. However, only the latter are toothless. Some species of armadillos can have up to 90 peglike teeth.

Armageddon in the New Testament (Revelation 16), the site of the final battle between the nations that will end the world; it has been identified with ⟡Megiddo in Israel.

Armagh county town of Armagh, Northern Ireland; population (1981) 13,000. It became the religious center of Ireland in the 5th century when St Patrick was made archbishop. For 700 years it was the seat of the kings of Ulster. The Protestant archbishop of Armagh is nominally "Primate of All Ireland."

Armagnac deep-colored brandy named after the district of Armagnac in Gascony, SW France, where it is produced.

Armani Giorgio 1935– . Italian fashion designer. He launched his first menswear collection 1974 and the following year started designing women's clothing. His work is known for understated styles, precise tailoring, and fine fabrics. He designs for young men and women under the Emporio label.

armature in a motor or generator, the wire-wound coil that carries the current and rotates

Armenia
Republic of

area 11,500 sq mi/29,800 sq km
capital Yerevan
cities Kumayri (formerly Leninakan)
physical mainly mountainous (including Mount Ararat), wooded
features State Academia Theater of Opera and Ballet; Yerevan Film Studio
head of state Levon Ter-Petrossian from 1990
head of government Vazguen Manukyan from 1990
political system emergent democracy
products copper, molybdenum, cereals, cotton, silk
population (1991) 3,580,000 (90% Armenian,

5% Azeri, 2% Russian, 2% Kurd)
language Armenian
religion traditionally Armenian Christian
chronology
1918 Became an independent republic.
1920 Occupied by the Red Army.
1936 Became a constituent republic of the USSR.
1988 Feb: demonstrations in Yerevan called for transfer of Nagorno-Karabakh from Azerbaijan to Armenian control. Dec: earthquake claimed around 25,000 lives and caused extensive damage.
1989 Jan-Nov: strife-torn Nagorno-Karabakh placed under "temporary" direct rule from Moscow. Pro-autonomy Armenian National Movement founded. Nov: civil war erupted with Azerbaijan over Nagorno-Karabakh.
1990 March: Armenia boycotted USSR constitutional referendum. Aug: nationalists secured control of Estonian supreme soviet; former dissident Levon Ter-Petrossian indirectly elected president; independence declared. Nakhichevan affected by Nagorno-Karabakh dispute.
1991 March: overwhelming support for independence in referendum. Dec: Armenia joined new Commonwealth of Independent States (CIS); Nagorno-Karabakh declared its independence; Armenia granted diplomatic recognition by US.
1992 Jan: admitted into Conference on Security and Cooperation in Europe (CSCE). March: joined United Nations (UN). Conflict over Nagorno-Karabakh worsened.

in a magnetic field. (In alternating-current machines, the armature is sometimes stationary.) The pole piece of a permanent magnet or electromagnet and the moving, iron part of a ⟡solenoid, especially if the latter acts as a switch, may also be referred to as armatures.

Armenia country in W Asia, bounded E by Azerbaijan, N by Georgia, W by Turkey, and S by Iran.

government There is a 220-member legislature, the supreme soviet, to which deputies are elected by a majority system, and a second ballot "run-off" race in contests in which there is no clear first-round majority. From the majority grouping within the supreme soviet, a prime minister (chair of the cabinet of ministers) is drawn. The state president is directly elected.

history Armenia was in ancient times a kingdom occupying what is now the Van region of Turkey, part of NW Iran, and what is now Armenia. Under King Tigranes II (95–55 BC) the kingdom reached the height of its power, controlling an empire that stretched from the Mediterranean to the Caucasus. Thereafter, it fell under the sway of the ⟡Byzantine Empire, then the Muslim Turks from the late 11th century, the Mongols in the 13th century, and the Ottomans from the 16th century. This domination by foreign powers bred an intense national consciousness and encouraged northward migration of the community.

under Soviet control With the advance of Russia into the Caucasus during the early 19th century, there was a struggle for independence which provoked an Ottoman backlash and growing international concern at Armenian maltreatment. In 1915 an estimated 1,750,000 Armenians were massacred or deported by the Turks. Conquered by Russia 1916, Armenia was briefly independent 1918 until occupied by the Red Army 1920. Along

with Azerbaijan and Georgia, it formed part of the Transcaucasian Soviet Socialist Republic, but became a constituent republic of the USSR 1936.

growth of nationalism As a result of ⟡glasnost, Armenian national identity was reawakened and in 1988 demands for reunion with ⟡Nagorno-Karabakh led to a civil war 1989–91, resulting in the intervention of Soviet troops. The Armenian National Movement, which was formed Nov 1989 by Levon Ter-Petrossian and Vazguen Manukyan, and the militant Karabakh Committee were at the fore of this growing nationalist campaign. The campaign included attempts to secure full control over the Azeri enclave of ⟡Nakhichevan, leading to the flight of almost 200,000 Azeris from the republic. In the 1990 elections to the republic's supreme soviet (parliament) nationalists polled strongly and Ter-Petrossian and Manukyan were chosen as president and prime minister respectively.

struggle for independence On Aug 23, 1990, a declaration of independence was made but ignored by Moscow. The republic boycotted the March 1991 USSR referendum on the preservation of the Soviet Union and in April 1991 the property belonging to the Communist Party of Armenia (CPA) was nationalized. Four months later the CPA dissolved itself. In a referendum held Sept 1991, shortly after the failed anti-Gorbachev coup in Moscow, 94% voted for secession from the USSR. Two days later independence was formally proclaimed by President Ter-Petrossian, but this failed to secure Western recognition. A cease-fire agreement, brokered by the presidents of the Russian Federation and Kazakhstan, was signed by Armenia and Azerbaijan on Sept 24, 1991. It provided the basis for a negotiated settlement to the Nagorno-Karabakh dispute, including the disarming of local militias, the return of refugees, and the holding of free elections in the enclave.

However, the agreement collapsed Nov 1991 when the Azerbaijan parliament, dominated by communists-turned-nationalists, voted to annul Nagorno-Karabakh's autonomous status. Soviet troops were gradually withdrawn from the enclave, leaving it vulnerable to Azeri attacks. In response, after a referendum and elections Dec 1991, Nagorno-Karabakh's parliament declared its "independence", precipitating an intensification of the conflict.

Armenian independence achieved On Oct 16, 1991, Ter-Petrossian was overwhelmingly reelected president, capturing 83% of the vote, in the republic's first direct election. In Dec 1991 Armenia agreed to join the new confederal ◇Commonwealth of Independent States (CIS), which was formed to supersede the Soviet Union. Also in Dec Armenia was accorded diplomatic recognition by the US and in Jan 1992 was admitted into the ◇Conference on Security and Cooperation in Europe (CSCE); in March 1992 it became a member of the United Nations (UN).

During early 1992 Armenia suffered a trade and energy embargo imposed by Azerbaijan in the escalating conflict over Nagorno-Karabakh. Despite capturing the Azerbaijani strategic strongholds of Shusha and Lachin in May, Armenia had by Aug lost much of its newly gained territory in a surprise counteroffensive sprung by Azerbaijani troops.

Armenian member of the largest ethnic group inhabiting Armenia. There are Armenian minorities in Azerbaijan, as well as in Turkey and Iran. Christianity was introduced to the ancient Armenian kingdom in the 3rd century. There are 4–5 million speakers of Armenian, which belongs to the Indo-European family of languages.

Armenian church form of Christianity adopted in Armenia in the 3rd century. The Catholicos, or exarch, is the supreme head, and Echmiadzin (near Yerevan) is his traditional seat.

About 295, Gregory the Illuminator (c. 257–332) was made exarch of the Armenian church, which has developed along national lines. The Seven Sacraments (or Mysteries) are administered, and baptism is immediately followed by confirmation. Believers number about 2 million.

Armenian language one of the main divisions of the Indo-European language family. Old Armenian, the classic literary language, is still used in the liturgy of the Armenian Church. Armenian was not written down until the 5th century AD, when an alphabet of 36 (now 38) letters was evolved. Literature flourished in the 4th to 14th centuries, revived in the 18th and continued throughout the 20th.

Contemporary Armenian, with modified grammar and enriched with words from other languages, is used by a group of 20th-century writers.

Armenian massacres series of massacres of Armenians by Turkish soldiers between 1895 and 1915. Reforms promised to Armenian Christians by Turkish rulers never materialized; unrest broke out and there were massacres by Turkish troops 1895. Again in 1909 and 1915, the Turks massacred altogether more than a million Armenians and deported others into the N Syrian desert, where they died of starvation; those who could flee to Russia or Persia. Only some 100,000 were left.

Armentières town in N France on the Lys River; population about 26,000. The song "Mademoiselle from Armentières" originated during World War I, when the town was held by the British. The town was flattened by German bombardment 1918 and rebuilt.

Arminius 17 BC–AD 21. German chieftain. An ex-soldier of the Roman army, he annihilated a Roman force led by Varus in the Teutoburger Forest area AD 9, and saved Germany from becoming a Roman province. He thus ensured that the empire's frontier did not extend beyond the Rhine.

Arminius Jacobus. Latinized name of Jakob Harmensen 1560–1609. Dutch Protestant priest who founded Arminianism, a school of Christian theology opposed to Calvin's doctrine of predestination. His views were developed by Simon Episcopius (1583–1643). Arminianism is the basis of Wesleyan ◇Methodism.

armistice cessation of hostilities while awaiting a peace settlement. "The Armistice" refers specifically to the end of World War I between Germany and the Allies Nov 11, 1918. On June 22, 1940 French representatives signed an armistice with Germany in the same railroad carriage at Compiègne as in 1918. No armistice was signed with either Germany or Japan 1945; both nations surrendered and there was no provision for the suspension of fighting. The Korean armistice, signed at Panmunjom July 27, 1953, terminated the Korean War 1950–53.

Armistice Day anniversary of the armistice signed Nov 11, 1918, ending World War I.

In the US this holiday is now called Veterans' Day.

armor body protection worn in battle. Body armor is depicted in Greek and Roman art. Chain mail was developed in the Middle Ages but the craft of the armorer in Europe reached its height in design in the 15th century, when knights, and to some extent, their horses, were encased in plate armor that still allowed freedom of movement. Medieval Japanese armor was articulated, made of iron, gilded metal, leather, and silk. Contemporary bulletproof vests and riot gear are forms of armor. The term is used in a modern context to refer to a mechanized armored vehicle, such as a tank.

Since World War II armor for tanks and ships has been developed beyond an increasing thickness of steel plate, becoming an increasingly light, layered composite, including materials such as ceramics. More controversial is "reactive" armor, consisting of "shoeboxes" made of armor containing small, quick-acting explosive charges, which are attached at the most vulnerable points of a tank, in order to break up the force of entry of an enemy warhead. This type is used by, for example, Israel, but the incorporation of explosive material in a tank has potential drawbacks.

The invention of gunpowder led, by degrees, to the virtual abandonment of armor until World War I, when the helmet reappeared as a defense against shrapnel. Suits of armor in the Tower of London were studied by US designers of astronaut wear. Modern armor, used by the army, police, security guards, and people at risk from assassination, uses nylon and fiberglass and is often worn beneath their clothing.

armored personnel carrier (APC) wheeled or tracked military vehicle designed to transport up to ten people. Armored to withstand

small-arms fire and shell splinters, it is used on battlefields.

Armory Show exhibition of Modern European art held Feb 1913 in New York. It marked the arrival of abstract art in the US, and influenced US artists. A rioting crowd threatened to destroy Marcel Duchamp's *Nude Descending a Staircase* (now in the Museum of Art, Philadelphia).

Armstrong Edwin Howard 1890–1954. US radio engineer who developed a system known as superheterodyne tuning for reception over a very wide spectrum of radio frequencies and frequency ◇modulation for static-free reception.

Armstrong Henry. Born Henry Jackson, nicknamed "Homicide Hank" 1912–1988. US boxer. He was the only man to hold world titles at three different weights simultaneously. Between May and Nov 1938 he held the feather-, welter-, and lightweight titles. He retired in 1945 and became a Baptist minister.

Armstrong Louis ("Satchmo") 1901–1971. US jazz cornet and trumpet player and singer. His Chicago recordings in the 1920s with the Hot Five and Hot Seven brought him recognition for his warm and pure trumpet tone, his skill at improvisation, and his quirky, gravelly voice. From the 1930s he also appeared in films.

Armstrong was born in New Orleans. In 1923 he joined the Creole Jazz Band led by the cornet player Joe "King" Oliver (1885–1938) in Chicago, but soon broke away and fronted various bands of his own. In 1947 he formed the Louis Armstrong All-Stars. He firmly established the pre-eminence of the virtuoso jazz soloist. He is also credited with the invention of scat singing (vocalizing meaningless syllables chosen for their sound).

Armstrong Neil Alden 1930– . US astronaut. In 1969, he became the first person to set foot on the Moon, and said, "That's one small step for a man, one giant leap for mankind." The Moon landing was part of the ◇Apollo project.

Born in Ohio, he gained his pilot's license at 16, and served as a naval pilot in Korea 1949–52 before joining NASA as a test pilot. He was selected to be an astronaut 1962 and landed on the Moon July 20, 1969.

army organized military force for fighting on the ground. A national army is used to further a political policy by force either within the state or on the territory of another state. Most countries have a national army, maintained by taxation, and raised either by conscription (compulsory military service) or voluntarily (paid professionals). Private armies may be employed by individuals and groups.

ancient armies (to 1066) Armies were common to all ancient civilizations. The Spartans trained from childhood for compulsory military service from age 21 to 26 in a full-time regular force as a heavily armed infantryman, or *hoplite*. Roman armies subjected all male citizens to military service in *legions* of 6,000 men divided into *cohorts* of 600 men. Cohorts were similarly divided into six *centuries* of 100 men. The concept of duty to military service continued following the collapse of the Roman Empire. For example, the Anglo-Saxon *Fyrd* obliged all able-bodied men to serve in defense of Britain against Danish and then Norman invasion.

armies of knights and mercenaries (1066–1648) Medieval monarchs relied upon mounted men-at-arms, or *chevaliers*, who in turn called on serfs from the land. Feudal armies were thus inherently limited in size and could only fight for limited periods. Free **yeomen** armed with longbows were required by law to practice at the **butts** and provided an early form of indirect fire as **artillery**. In Europe paid troops, or **soldi**, and mounted troops, or **serviertes** (sergeants), made themselves available as **freelances**. By the end of the 15th century, **battles** or **battalions** of pikemen provided defense against the mounted knight. The hard gun, or **arquebus**, heralded the coming of infantrymen as known today. Those who wished to avoid military service could do so by paying **scutage**. For the majority of men, the **conpane**, or **company**, was their home; they were placed under royal command by **ordonnances** and led by crown office holders, or **officiers**. Increased costs led to the formation of the first mercenary armies. For example, the **Great Company** of 10,000 men acted as an international force, employing contractors, or **condottieri**, to serve the highest bidder. By the 16th century the long musket, pikemen, and the use of fortifications combined against the knight. **Sappers** became increasingly important in the creation and breaking of obstacles such as at Metz, a forerunner of the Maginot Line.

professional armies (1648–1792) The emergence of the European nation-state saw the growth of more professional standing armies which trained in drills, used formations to maximize firepower, and introduced service discipline. The invention of the ring bayonet and the flintlock saw the demise of pikemen and the increased capability to fire from three ranks (today still the standard drill formation in the British Army). Artillery was now mobile and fully integrated into the army structure. The defects of raw levies, noble amateurs, and mercenaries led Oliver Cromwell to create the New Model Army for the larger campaigns of the English Civil War. After the Restoration, Charles II established a small standing army, which was expanded under James II and William III. In France, a model regiment was set up under de Martinet which set standards of uniformity for all to follow. State taxation provided for a formal system of army administration (uniforms, pay, ammunition). Nevertheless, recruits remained mainly society's misfits and delinquents. Collectively termed **other ranks**, they were divided from commissioned officers by a rigid hierarchical structure. The sheer cost of such armies forced wars to be fought by maneuver rather than by pitched battle, aiming to starve one's opponent into defeat while protecting one's own logistic chain.

armies of the revolution (1792–1819) Napoleon's organization of his army into autonomous **corps** of two to three **divisions**, in turn comprising two **brigades** of two **regiments** of two **battalions**, was a major step forward in allowing a rapid and flexible deployment of forces. Small-scale skirmishing by **light infantry**, coupled with the increasing devastation created by artillery or densely packed formations, saw the beginnings of the **dispersed battlefield**. Victory in war was now synonymous with the complete destruction of the enemy in battle. Reservists were conscripted to allow the mass army to fight wars through to the bitter end. (Only Britain, by virtue of the English Channel and the Royal Navy, was able to avoid the need to provide such large land forces.) Officers were now required to be professionally trained; the Royal

Military College was set up in Britain 1802, St Cyr in France 1808, the Kriegsakademie in Berlin 1810, and the Russian Imperial Military Academy 1832. **Semaphore telegraph** and **observation balloons** were first steps to increasing the commander's ability to observe enemy movements. The British army, under Wellington, was very strong, but afterwards decreased in numbers and efficiency.

national armies (1792–1819) The defeat of Revolutionary France saw a return to the traditions of the 18th century and a reduction in conscription. Meanwhile the railroad revolutionized the deployment of forces, permitting quick mobilization, continuous resupply to the front, and rapid evacuation of casualties to the rear. The US Civil War has been called the Railway War. By 1870, the limitation of supply inherent to the Napoleonic army had been overcome and once again armies of over 1 million could be deployed. By 1914, continental armies numbered as many as 3 million and were based on conscription. A general staff was now required to manage these. **Breechloading rifles** and **machine guns** ensured a higher casualty rate.

19th-century armies The 19th century saw the great development of rapidly produced missile weapons and the use of railroads to move troops and materials.

technological armies (1918–45) The advent of the internal combustion engine allowed new advances in mobility to overcome the supremacy of the defensive over the offensive. The **tank** and the **radio** were vital to the evolution of armored warfare or **Blitzkrieg**. Armies were able to reorganize into highly mobile formations, such as the German **Panzer Divisions**, which utilized speed, firepower, and surprise to overwhelm static defenses and thereby dislocate the army's rear.

The armies of World War II were very mobile, and were closely coordinated with the navy and air force. The requirement to fuel and maintain such huge fleets of vehicles again increased the need to maintain supplies. The complexity of the mechanized army demanded a wide range of skills not easily found through conscription.

armies of the nuclear age (1945–) The advent of tactical nuclear weapons severely compounded the problems of mass concentration and thus protected mobility assumed greater importance to allow rapid concentration and dispersal of forces in what could be a high chemical threat zone. From the 1960s there were sophisticated developments in tanks and antitank weapons, mortar-locating radar, and heat-seeking missiles.

Arnhem, Battle of in World War II, airborne operation by the Allies, Sept 17–26, 1944, to secure a bridgehead over the Rhine, thereby opening the way for a thrust toward the Ruhr and a possible early end to the war. It was only partially successful, with 7,600 casualties. Arnhem is a city in the Netherlands, on the Rhine SE of Utrecht; population (1991) 131,700. It produces salt, chemicals, and pharmaceuticals.

Arnim Ludwig Achim von 1781–1831. German Romantic poet and novelist. Born in Berlin, he wrote short stories, a romance (*Gräfin Dolores/Countess Dolores* 1810), and plays, but left the historical novel *Die Kronenwächter* 1817 unfinished. With Clemens Brentano he collected the German folk songs in *Des Knaben Wunderhorn/The Boy's Magic Horn* 1805–08.

Arno Italian river 150 mi/240 km long, rising

in the Apennines, and flowing westward to the Mediterranean Sea. Florence and Pisa stand on its banks. A flood in 1966 damaged virtually every Renaissance landmark in Florence.

Arnold Benedict 1741–1801. US soldier and military strategist who, during the American Revolution, won the turning point battle at Saratoga 1777 for the Americans. He is chiefly remembered as a traitor to the American side. A merchant in New Haven, Connecticut, he joined the colonial forces but in 1780 plotted to betray the strategic post at West Point to the British.

Arnold was bitter at having been passed over for promotion, and he contacted Henry Clinton to propose defection. Major André was sent by the British to discuss terms with him, but was caught and hanged as a spy. Arnold escaped to the British, who gave him an army command.

Since the plot failed, he was paid only a fraction of the money promised him.

Arnold Matthew 1822–1888. English poet and critic. His poems, characterized by their elegiac mood and pastoral themes, include *The Forsaken Merman* 1849, *Thyrsis* 1867 (commemorating his friend Arthur Hugh Clough), *Dover Beach* 1867, and *The Scholar Gypsy* 1853. Arnold's critical works include *Essays in Criticism* 1865 and 1888, and *Culture and Anarchy* 1869, which attacks 19th-century philistinism.

aromatic compound organic chemical compound in which some of the bonding electrons are delocalized (shared among several atoms within the molecule and not localized in the vicinity of the atoms involved in bonding). The commonest aromatic compounds have ring structures, the atoms comprising the ring being either all carbon or containing one or more different atoms (usually nitrogen, sulfur, or oxygen). Typical examples are benzene (C_6H_6) and pyridine (C_6H_5N).

Arp Hans or Jean 1887–1966. French abstract painter and sculptor. He was one of the founders of the ♢Dada movement about 1917, and later was associated with the Surrealists. His innovative wood sculptures use organic shapes in bright colors.

In his early experimental works, such as collages, he collaborated with his wife **Sophie Taeuber-Arp** (1889–1943).

Arras French town on the Scarpe River NE of Paris; population (1982) 80,500 (conurbation). It is the capital of Pas-de-Calais *département*, and was formerly known for tapestry. It was the birthplace of the French revolutionary leader Robespierre.

Arras, Congress and Treaty of meeting in N France 1435 between representatives of Henry VI of England, Charles VII of France, and Philip the Good of Burgundy to settle the Hundred Years' War. The outcome was a diplomatic victory for France. Although England refused to compromise on Henry VI's claim to the French crown, France signed a peace treaty with Burgundy, England's former ally.

Arrau Claudio 1903–1991. Chilean pianist. A concert performer from the age of five, he specialized in 19th-century music and was known for his thoughtful interpretation.

arrest deprivation of personal liberty by legal authority to stop commission of a crime or to charge someone with violation of a criminal or civil law.

Federal laws, state laws, and local ordinances define circumstances under which individuals may be detained by law officers acting independently, court-issued warrants, or other individuals (citizen's arrest).

Arrhenius Svante August 1859–1927. Swedish scientist, the founder of physical chemistry. Born near Uppsala, he became a professor at Stockholm in 1895, and made a special study of electrolysis. He wrote *Worlds in the Making* and *Destinies of the Stars*, and in 1903 received the Nobel Prize for Chemistry. In 1905 he predicted global warming as a result of carbon dioxide emission from burning fossil fuels.

arrhythmia disturbance of the natural rhythm of the heart. There are various kinds of arrhythmia, some innocent, some indicative of heart disease.

arrowroot starchy substance derived from the roots and tubers of various tropical plants with thick, clumpy roots. The true arrowroot *Maranta arundinacea* was used by the Indians of South America as an antidote against the effects of poisoned arrows.

The West Indian island of St Vincent is the main source of supply today. The edible starch is easily digested and is good for invalids.

arrowwood any of various North American trees and shrubs, especially of the genus *Viburnum*, named for their long, straight branches, which were used by American Indians to make arrows.

arsenic brittle, grayish-white, semimetallic element (a metalloid), symbol As, atomic number 33, atomic weight 74.92. It occurs in many ores and occasionally in its elemental state, and is widely distributed, being present in minute quantities in the soil, the sea, and the human body. In larger quantities, it is poisonous. The chief source of arsenic compounds is as a by-product from metallurgical processes. It is used in making semiconductors, alloys, and solders.

As it is a cumulative poison, its presence in food and drugs is very dangerous. The symptoms of arsenic poisoning are vomiting, diarrhea, tingling and possibly numbness in the limbs, and collapse. Its name derives from the Latin *arsenicum*.

arson malicious and willful setting fire to property.

Often arson is a crime committed to claim insurance benefits fraudulently.

art in the broadest sense, all the processes and products of human skill, imagination, and invention; the opposite of nature. In contemporary usage, definitions of art usually reflect aesthetic criteria, and the term may encompass literature, music, drama, painting, and sculpture. Popularly, the term is most commonly used to refer to the visual arts. In Western culture, aesthetic criteria introduced by the ancient Greeks still influence our perceptions and judgments of art.

Two currents of thought run through our ideas about art. In one, derived from Aristotle, art is concerned with *mimesis* ("imitation"), the representation of appearances, and gives pleasure through the accuracy and skill with which it depicts the real world. The other view, derived from Plato, holds that the artist is inspired by the Muses (or by God, or by the inner impulses, or by the collective unconscious) to express that which is beyond appearances—inner feelings, eternal truths, or the essence of the age. In the Middle Ages the term "art" was used, chiefly in the plural, to signify a branch of learning which was regarded as an instrument of knowledge. The seven

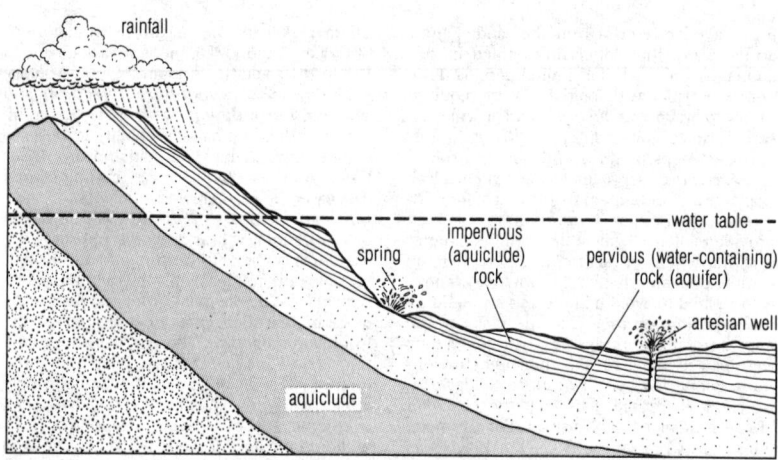

artesian well *In an artesian well, water rises from an underground water-containing rock layer under its own pressure.*

liberal arts consisted of the *trivium*, that is grammar, logic, and rhetoric, and the *quadrivium*, that is arithmetic, music, geometry, and astronomy. In the visual arts of Western civilizations, painting and sculpture have been the dominant forms for many centuries. This has not always been the case in other cultures. Islamic art, for example, is one of ornament, for under the Muslim religion artists were forbidden to usurp the divine right of creation by portraying living creatures. In some cultures masks, tattoos, pottery, and metalwork have been the main forms of visual art. Recent technology has made new art forms possible, such as photography and cinema, and today electronic media have led to entirely new ways of creating and presenting visual images. See also ⟡ancient art, ⟡medieval art, and the arts of individual countries, such as ⟡French art, and individual movements, such as ⟡Romanticism, ⟡Cubism, and ⟡Impressionism.

Artaud Antonin 1896–1948. French theater director. Although his play, *Les Cenci/The Cenci* 1935, was a failure, his concept of the **Theater of ⟡Cruelty**, intended to release feelings usually repressed in the unconscious, has been an important influence on modern dramatists such as Albert Camus and Jean Genet and on directors and producers. Declared insane 1936, Artaud was confined in an asylum.

Art Deco popular and pervasive style in art and architecture named after a 1925 French exhibition of modern art, noted for streamlined shapes and geometric forms. It was popular particularly in France and the US, where it was used extensively in the 1920s and 1930s, in urban architecture such as the Chrysler Building, New York City; in interior design such as in Radio City Music Hall, New York City; and in notable designs for streamlined trains, automobiles, and airplanes. It also influenced industrial design in products such as chinaware, radios, textiles, home furnishings, jewelry, and printed matter. Its use in film sets and costumes helped promote a fascination with Modernism that culminated in the 1939–40 World's Fair in New York City. From the 1970s, a revival of interest in the designs and designers, notably Raymond Loewy, name the style, which in its time was called *moderne*.

Artemis in Greek mythology, the goddess (Roman Diana) of chastity, the Moon, and the hunt. She is the twin sister of ⟡Apollo. Her cult center was at Ephesus.

arteriography method of examining the interior of an artery by injecting into it a radiopaque solution, which is visible on an X-ray photograph. It is used for the arteries of the heart (coronary arteriogram), for example.

arteriosclerosis hardening of the arteries, with thickening and loss of elasticity. It is associated with smoking, aging, and a diet high in saturated fats. The term is used loosely as a synonym for ⟡atherosclerosis.

artery vessel that carries blood from the heart to the rest of the body. It is built to withstand considerable pressure, having thick walls that are impregnated with muscle and elastic fibers. During contraction of the heart muscles, arteries expand in diameter to allow for the sudden increase in pressure that occurs; the resulting ⟡pulse or pressure wave can be felt at the wrist. Not all arteries carry oxygenated (oxygen-rich) blood; the pulmonary arteries convey deoxygenated (oxygen-poor) blood from the heart to the lungs.

Arteries are flexible, elastic tubes, consisting of three layers, the middle of which is muscular; its rhythmic contraction aids the pumping of blood around the body. In middle and old age, the walls degenerate and are vulnerable to damage by the buildup of fatty deposits. These reduce elasticity, hardening the arteries and decreasing the internal bore. This condition, known as ⟡atherosclerosis, can lead to high blood pressure, loss of circulation, heart disease, and death. Research indicates that a typical Western diet, high in saturated fat, increases the chances of arterial disease developing.

artesian well well that is supplied with water rising from an underground water-saturated rock layer (⟡aquifer). The water rises from the aquifer under its own pressure. Such a well may be drilled into an aquifer that is confined by impermeable rocks both above and below. If the water table (the top of the region of water saturation) in that aquifer is above the level of the well head, hydrostatic pressure will force the water to the surface.

The name comes from Artois (Latin *Artesium*), a historical region of N France, on the Strait of Dover, where the phenomenon was first observed.

arthritis inflammation of the joints, with pain, swelling, and restricted motion. Many conditions may cause arthritis, including gout and trauma to the joint.

More common in women, **rheumatoid arthritis** usually begins in middle age in the small joints of the hands and feet, causing a greater or lesser degree of deformity and painfully restricted movement. It is alleviated by drugs, and surgery may be performed to correct deformity.

arthropod member of the phylum Arthropoda; an invertebrate animal with jointed legs and a segmented body with a horny or chitinous casing (exoskeleton), which is shed periodically and replaced as the animal grows. Included are arachnids such as spiders and mites, as well as crustaceans, millipedes, centipedes, and insects.

Arthur 6th century AD. Legendary British king and hero in stories of ⟁Camelot and the quest for the ⟁Holy Grail. Arthur is said to have been born in Tintagel, Cornwall, and buried in Glastonbury, Somerset. He may have been a Romano-Celtic leader against pagan Saxon invaders.

The legends of Arthur and the knights of the Round Table were developed in the 12th century by Geoffrey of Monmouth, Chrétien de Troyes, and the Norman writer Wace. Later writers on the theme include the anonymous author of *Sir Gawayne and the Greene Knight* 1346, Thomas Malory, Tennyson, T H White, and Mark Twain.

Arthur Chester Alan 1830–1886. 21st president of the US 1881–85, a Republican. In 1880 he was chosen as James ⟁Garfield's vice-president, and was his successor when Garfield was assassinated the following year.

He was born in Vermont, the son of a Baptist minister, and became a lawyer and Republican political appointee in New York.

artichoke either of two plants of the composite or sunflower family Compositae. The common or globe artichoke *Cynara scolymus* is native to the Mediterranean, and is a form of thistle. It is tall, with purplish blue flowers; the bracts of the unopened flower are eaten. The Jerusalem artichoke *Helianthus tuberosus* is a sunflower, native to North America. It has edible tubers, and its common name is a corruption of the Italian for sunflower, *girasole*.

article grammatical ⟁part of speech. There are two articles in English: the **definite article** *the*, which serves to specify or identify a noun (as in "This is *the* book I need"), and the **indefinite article** *a* or (before vowels) *an*, which indicates a single unidentified noun ("They gave me *a* piece of paper and *an* envelope").

Some people use the form "an" before *h* ("an historic building"); this practice dates from the 17th century, when an initial *h* was often not pronounced and is nowadays widely considered rather grandiose.

artificial insemination (AI) introduction by instrument of semen from a sperm bank or donor into the female reproductive tract to bring about fertilization. Originally used by animal breeders to improve stock with sperm from high-quality males, in the 20th century it has been developed for use in humans, to help the infertile. In ⟁in vitro fertilization, the egg is fertilized in a test tube and then implanted in the womb. In zygote intrafallopian transfer (ZIFT) the mixed egg and sperm are reintroduced into the fallopian tube.

The sperm for artificial insemination may come from the husband (AIH) or a donor (AID).

artificial intelligence (AI) branch of science concerned with creating computer programs that can perform actions comparable with those of an intelligent human. Current AI research covers such areas as planning (for robot behavior), language understanding, pattern recognition, and knowledge representation.

Early AI programs, developed in the 1960s, attempted simulations of human intelligence or were aimed at general problem-solving techniques. It is now thought that intelligent behavior depends as much on the knowledge a system possesses as on its reasoning power. Present emphasis is on ⟁knowledge-based systems, such as ⟁expert systems. Britain's largest AI laboratory is at the Turing Institute, University of Strathclyde, Glasgow. In May 1990 the first International Robot Olympics was held there, including table-tennis matches between robots of the US and the UK.

artificial limb device to replace a limb that has been removed by surgery or one that is malformed because of genetic defects. It is one form of ⟁prosthesis.

artificial respiration maintenance of breathing when the natural process is suspended. If breathing is permanently suspended, as in paralysis, the whole body is placed inside an airtight metal cylinder, an **iron lung**; in cases of electric shock or apparent drowning, for example, the first choice is the expired-air method, the **kiss of life** by mouth-to-mouth breathing until natural breathing is resumed.

artificial selection in biology, selective breeding of individuals that exhibit particular characteristics that a plant or animal breeder wishes to develop. The development of particular breeds of cattle for improved meat production (such as the Aberdeen Angus) or milk production (such as Holsteins) are examples.

artillery collective term for military ⟁firearms too heavy to be carried. Artillery can be mounted on ships or airplanes and includes cannons and missile launchers.
14th century Cannons came into general use, and were most effective in siege warfare. The term had previously been applied to catapults used for hurling heavy objects.
16th century The howitzer, halfway between a gun and a mortar (muzzle-loading cannon), was first used in sieges.
early 19th century In the Napoleonic period, field artillery became smaller and more mobile.
1914–18 In World War I, howitzers were used to demolish trench systems. Giant cannons were used in the entrenched conditions of the Western Front and at sea against the lumbering, heavily armored battleships, but their accuracy against small or moving targets was poor.
1939–45 In World War II artillery became more mobile, particularly in the form of self-propelled guns.
1980s The introduction of so-called smart munitions meant that artillery rounds could be guided to their target by means of a laser designator.

Art Nouveau art style of about 1890–1910 in Europe, named after a shop in Paris that opened 1895, which makes marked use of sinuous lines, stylized flowers and foliage, and flame shapes. In England, it appears in the illustrations of Aubrey Beardsley; in Spain, in the architecture of Antonio Gaudí; in France, in the architecture of Hector Guimard and the art glass of René Lalique; in Belgium, in the houses and shops of Victor Horta; in the US, in the lamps and metal work of Louis Comfort Tiffany; and in Scotland, in the interior and exterior designs of Charles Rennie Mackintosh. Art Nouveau was also known as *Jugendstil* in Germany and *Stile Liberty* in Italy, after the fashionable London department store.

Artois former province of N France, bounded by Flanders and Picardie and almost corresponding with the modern *département* of Pas-de-Calais. Its capital was Arras. Its Latin name *Artesium* lent its name to the artesian well first sunk at Lillers 1126.

Arts and Crafts movement English social movement, largely antimachine in spirit, based in design and architecture and founded by William Morris in the latter half of the 19th century. It was supported by the architect A W Pugin and by John ⟁Ruskin and stressed the importance of handcrafting. The ⟁Art Nouveau style succeeded it.

Aruba island in the Caribbean, the westernmost of the Lesser Antilles; an overseas part of the Netherlands
area 75 sq mi/193 sq km
population (1989) 62,400
history Aruba obtained separate status from the other Netherlands Antilles 1986 and has full internal autonomy.

arum any plant of the genus *Arum*, family Araceae, especially the Old World genus *Arum*. The arum called the trumpet lily *Zantedeschia aethiopica*, an ornamental plant, is a native of South Africa.

Jack-in-the-pulpit and skunk cabbage are North American arums belonging to related genera.

Arunachal Pradesh state of India, in the Himalayas on the borders of Tibet and Myanmar
area 32,270 sq mi/83,600 sq km
capital Itanagar
products rubber, coffee, spices, fruit, timber
population (1991) 858,400.
languages 50 different dialects
history formerly nominally part of Assam, known as the renamed Arunachal Pradesh ("Hills of the Rising Sun"). It became a state 1986.

Arvand River Iranian name for the ⟁Shatt-al-Arab waterway.

Aryan Indo-European family of languages; also the hypothetical parent language of an ancient people who are believed to have lived between central Asia and E Europe and to have reached Persia and India in one direction and Europe in another, sometime in the 2nd century BC, diversifying into the various Indo-European language speakers of later times. In Nazi Germany Hitler and other theorists erroneously propagated the idea of the Aryans as a white-skinned, blue-eyed, fair-haired master race (see also ⟁Nazism).

Aryana ancient name of ⟁Afghanistan.

Aryan languages 19th-century name for the ⟁Indo-European languages; the languages of the Aryan peoples of India. The name Aryan is no longer used by language scholars because of its association with the Nazi concept of white supremacy.

Arya Samaj Hindu religious sect founded by Dayanand Saraswati (1825–1888) about 1875. He renounced idol worship and urged a return to the purer principles of the Vedas (Hindu scriptures). For its time the movement was quite revolutionary in its social teachings, which included forbidding ◊caste practices, prohibiting child-marriage, and allowing widows to remarry.

ASA abbreviation for ◊*Association of South East Asia* (1961–67), replaced by ASEAN, ◊Association of South East Asian Nations.

ASA in photography, a numbering system for rating the speed of films, devised by the American Standards Association. It has now been superseded by ◊*ISO*, the International Standards Organization.

Asante or *Ashanti* region of Ghana, W Africa; area 9,700 sq mi/25,100 sq km; population (1984) 2,089,683. Kumasi is the capital. Most Asante are cultivators and the main crop is cocoa, but the region is also noted for its metalwork and textiles.

For more than 200 years Asante was an independent kingdom. During the 19th century the Asante and the British fought for control of trade in West Africa. The British sent four expeditions against the Asante and formally annexed their country 1901. Otomfuo Sir Osei Agyeman, nephew of the deposed king, Prempeh I, was made head of the reestablished Ashanti confederation 1935 as Prempeh II. The Golden Stool (actually a chair), symbol of the Asante peoples since the 17th century, was returned to Kumasi in 1935 (the rest of the Asante treasure is in the British Museum). The Asantahene (King of the Asante) still holds ceremonies in which this stool is ceremonially paraded.

a.s.a.p. abbreviation for *as soon as possible*.

ASAT abbreviation for *antisatellite weapon*.

asbestos any of several related minerals of fibrous structure that offer great heat resistance because of their nonflammability and poor conductivity. Commercial asbestos is generally made from olivine, a ◊serpentine mineral, tremolite (a white ◊amphibole), and riebeckite (a blue amphibole, also known as crocidolite when in its fibrous form). Asbestos usage is now strictly controlled because exposure to its dust can cause cancer.

ascariasis infection by the roundworm *Ascaris lumbricoides*, an intestinal parasite in humans and other mammals.

Ascension British island of volcanic origin in the S Atlantic, a dependency of ◊St Helena since 1922; population (1982) 1,625. The chief settlement is Georgetown.

A Portuguese navigator landed there on Ascension Day 1501, but it remained uninhabited until occupied by Britain in 1815. There are sea turtles and sooty terns. It is known for its role as a staging post to the Falkland Islands.

Ascension Day or *Holy Thursday* in the Christian calendar, the feast day commemorating Jesus' ascension to heaven. It is the 40th day after Easter.

asceticism the renunciation of physical pleasure, for example, in eating, drinking, sexuality, and human company. Often for religious reasons, discomfort or pain may be sought.

ASCII (acronym for *American standard code for information interchange*) in computing, a coding system in which numbers are assigned to letters, digits, and punctuation symbols. Although computers work with the ◊binary number system or code, ASCII numbers are usually quoted as decimal or hexadecimal numbers (see ◊hexadecimal number system). For example, the decimal

number 45 (binary 0101101) represents a hyphen, and 65 (binary 1000001) a capital A. The first 32 codes are used for control functions, such as carriage return and backspace.

Strictly speaking, ASCII is a seven-bit binary code, allowing 128 different characters to be represented, but an eighth bit is often used to provide ◊parity or to allow for extra characters. The system is widely used for the storage of text and for the transmission of data between computers.

character	binary code
A	1000001
B	1000010
C	1000011
D	1000100
E	1000101
F	1000110
G	1000111
H	1001000
I	1001001
J	1001010
K	1001011
L	1001100
M	1001101
N	1001110
O	1001111
P	1010000
Q	1010001
R	1010010
S	1010011
T	1010100
U	1010101
V	1010110
W	1010111
X	1011000
Y	1011001
Z	1011010

ascorbic acid $C_6H_8O_6$ or *vitamin C* a relatively simple organic acid found in fresh fruits and vegetables.

It is soluble in water and destroyed by prolonged boiling, so soaking or overcooking of vegetables reduces their vitamin C content. Lack of ascorbic acid results in scurvy.

In the human body, ascorbic acid is necessary for the correct synthesis of collagen. Lack of it causes skin sores or ulcers, tooth and gum problems, and burst capillaries (scurvy symptoms) owing to an abnormal type of collagen replacing the normal type in these tissues.

ASEAN acronym for ◊*Association of South East Asian Nations*.

asepsis practice of ensuring that bacteria are excluded from open sites during surgery, wound dressing, blood sampling, and other medical procedures. Aseptic technique is a first line of defense against infection.

asexual reproduction in biology, reproduction that does not involve the manufacture and fusion of sex cells, nor the necessity for two parents. The process carries a clear advantage in that there is no need to search for a mate nor to develop complex pollinating mechanisms; every asexual organism can reproduce on its own. Asexual reproduction can therefore lead to a rapid population buildup.

In evolutionary terms, the disadvantage of asexual reproduction arises from the fact that only identical individuals, or clones, are produced –there is no variation. In the field of horticulture, where standardized production is needed, this is useful, but in the wild, an asexual population that cannot adapt to a changing environment or evolve defenses against a new disease is at risk of extinction. Many asexually

reproducing organisms are therefore capable of reproducing sexually as well.

Asexual processes include ◊binary fission, in which the parent organism splits into two or more "daughter" organisms, and ◊budding, in which a new organism is formed initially as an outgrowth of the parent organism. The asexual reproduction of spores, as in ferns and mosses, is also common and many plants reproduce asexually by means of runners, rhizomes, bulbs, and corms; see also ◊vegetative reproduction.

Asgard in Scandinavian mythology, the place where the gods lived. It was reached by a bridge called Bifrost, the rainbow.

Ashbery John 1927– . US poet and art critic. His collections of poetry—including *Self-Portrait in a Convex Mirror* 1975, which won a Pulitzer prize—are distinguished by strong visual element and narrative power. Other volumes include *Some Trees* 1956, *As We Know* 1979, and *Shadow Train* 1981.

Ashcan School group of US painters active about 1908–14, also known as *The Eight*. Members included Robert Henri (1865–1929), George Luks (1867–1933), William Glackens (1870–1938), Everett Shinn (1876–1953), and John Sloan (1871–1951). Their style is realist; their subjects on city life, the poor, and the outcast. They organized the ◊Armory Show of 1913, which introduced modern European art to the US.

Ashcroft Peggy 1907–1991. English actress. Her Shakespearean roles included Desdemona in *Othello* (with Paul Robeson) and Juliet in *Romeo and Juliet* 1935 (with Laurence Olivier and John Gielgud), and she appeared in the British TV play *Caught on a Train* 1980 (BAFTA award), the series *The Jewel in the Crown* 1984, and the film *A Passage to India* 1985.

Ashdod deep-water port of Israel, on the Mediterranean 20 mi/32 km S of Tel-Aviv, which it superseded in 1965; population (1982) 66,000. It stands on the site of the ancient Philistine stronghold of Askalon.

Ashe Arthur Robert, Jr 1943–1993. US tennis player and coach. He won the US national men's singles title at Forest Hills and the first US Open 1968. Known for his exceptionally strong serve, Ashe turned professional 1969. He won the Australian men's title 1970 and Wimbledon 1975. Cardiac problems ended his playing career 1979, but he continued his involvement with the sport as captain of the US Davis Cup team.

Born in Richmond, Virginia, Ashe entered the University of California at Los Angeles (UCLA) on a tennis scholarship 1962 and took the National Collegiate Athletic Association (NCAA) men's singles and doubles titles 1966. In 1992 he announced that he had the AIDS virus, contracted from a blood transfusion.

Asheville textile town in the Blue Ridge Mountains of North Carolina; population (1990) 61,600. Showplaces include the 19th-century Biltmore mansion, home of millionaire George W Vanderbilt, and the home of the writer Thomas Wolfe.

Ashikaga in Japanese history, the family who held the office of shogun 1338–1573, a period of civil wars. Nō drama evolved under the patronage of Ashikaga shoguns. Relations with China improved intermittently and there was trade with Korea. The last (15th) Ashikaga shogun was ousted by Oda Nobunaga at the start of the Momoyama period. The Ashikaga belonged to the ◊Minamoto clan.

Ashkenazi (plural **Ashkenazim**) a Jew of German or E European descent, as opposed to a Sephardi, of Spanish, Portuguese, or N African descent.

Ashkenazim developed European customs and the ◊Yiddish language during the centuries they remained outside the influence of the Middle East. They were the ◊Zionists who resettled Palestine and who now run the government of Israel, resettling Jews from anywhere in the world.

Ashkenazy Vladimir 1937– . Russian-born pianist and conductor. His keyboard technique differs slightly from standard Western technique. In 1962 he was joint winner of the Tchaikovsky Competition with John Ogdon, and Liszt. He excels in Rachmaninov, Prokofiev, and Liszt.

After studying in Moscow, he toured the US in 1958. He settled in England in 1963 and moved to Iceland in 1968. He was musical director of the Royal Philharmonic, London, from 1987.

Ashkhabad capital of Turkmenistan; population (1989) 402,000. Industries include glass, carpets ("Bukhara" carpets are made here), cotton; the spectacular natural setting has been used by the film-making industry.

It was established 1881 as a military fort on the Persian frontier, occupying an oasis on the edge of the Kara-Kum Desert.

Ashland city in NE Kentucky on the Ohio River, E of Louisville. Industries include chemicals, coal, oil, limestone, coke, petroleum products, steel, clothing, and leather goods; population (1990) 23,600.

Ashley Laura (born Mountney) 1925–1985. Welsh designer who established and gave her name to a Neo-Victorian country style in clothes and furnishings manufactured by her company from 1953. She founded an international chain of shops.

ashram Indian community whose members lead a simple life of discipline and self-denial and devote themselves to social service. Noted ashrams are those founded by Mahatma Gandhi at Wardha and the poet Rabindranath Tagore at Santiniketan.

Ashton Frederick 1904–1988. British choreographer, director of the Royal Ballet, London, 1963–70. He studied with Marie Rambert before joining the Vic-Wells (now Royal) Ballet 1935 as chief choreographer. His long association with Ninette de Valois and Margot Fonteyn, for whom he created many roles, gave the Royal Ballet a worldwide reputation.

Ashwander v Tennessee Valley Authority (TVA) a US Supreme Court decision 1936 dealing with the government's authority to utilize navigable waterways as public property. The debate arose over the contracted sale of excess electricity produced by the TVA's Wilson Dam. Power companies unaccustomed to government competition in the industry filed suit to have the TVA contracts canceled. The Court ruled that since the government had acquired the electricity legally, through the exercise of its right to dam waterways, it had full right to dispose of its property.

Ash Wednesday first day of Lent, the period in the Christian calendar leading up to Easter; in the Roman Catholic church the foreheads of the congregation are marked with a cross in ash, as a sign of penitence.

Asia largest of the continents, occupying one-third of the total land surface of the world
area 17,000,000 sq mi/44,000,000 sq km
largest cities (population over 5 million) Tokyo, Shanghai, Osaka, Beijing, Seoul, Calcutta, Bombay, Jakarta, Bangkok, Tehran, Hong Kong, Delhi, Tianjin, Karachi
physical lying in the eastern hemisphere, Asia extends from the Arctic Circle to just over 10° S of the equator. The Asian mainland, which forms the greater part of the Eurasian continent, lies entirely in the northern hemisphere and stretches from Cape Chelyubinsk at its N extremity to Cape Piai at the S tip of the Malay Peninsula. From Dezhneva Cape in the E, the mainland extends W over more than 165° longitude to Cape Baba in Turkey. Containing the world's highest mountains and largest inland seas, Asia can be divided into five physical units:
1) at the heart of the continent, a central triangle of plateaus at varying altitudes (Tibetan Plateau, Tarim Basin, Gobi Desert), surrounded by huge mountain chains which spread in all directions (Himalayas, Karakoram, Hindu Kush, Pamirs, Kunlun, Tien Shan, Altai);
2) the W plateaus and ranges (Elburz, Zagros, Taurus, Great Caucasus mountains) of Afghanistan, Iran, N Iraq, Armenia, and Turkey;
3) the lowlands of Turkestan and Siberia which stretch N of the central mountains to the Arctic Ocean and include large areas in which the subsoil is permanently frozen;
4) the fertile and densely populated E lowlands and river plains of Korea, China, and Indochina, and the islands of the East Indies and Japan;
5) the southern plateaus of Arabia, and the Deccan, with the fertile alluvial plains of the Euphrates, Tigris, Indus, Ganges, Brahmaputra, and Irrawaddy rivers.
In Asiatic Russia are the largest areas of coniferous forest (taiga) in the world. The climate shows great extremes and contrasts, the heart

Asia: history

c. 3000 BC	First dynasties of Sumer in Mesopotamia.
2800–2200	Sage kings in China, earliest Chinese dynasty; civilization spreads to all of China.
2500–1500	Indus Valley civilization.
1950–1282	First Babylonian Empire.
625	Chaldeans established second Babylonian Empire.
563	Birth of the Buddha.
551	Birth of Confucius.
538	Cyrus the Great defeated last Babylonian ruler and founded Persian Empire.
334–326	Alexander the Great conquered the Persian Empire.
215	Great Wall of China begun.
AD 166	Tatar invasion of China.
93	Mesopotamia became part of Roman Empire.
320–550	Gupta dynasty in India.
570	Birth of Mohammed.
1192	First Muslim kingdom of India established.
1279	Kublai Khan became emperor of China; Marco Polo visits.
1395	Tamerlane defeated the Golden Horde.
1398	Tamerlane captured Delhi.
1526	Babur established Mogul empire in N India (which lasted until 1857).
1600s	China opened to trade with several European nations despite opposition from the Qing emperors; British East India Company chartered.
1757	Clive defeated the Nawab of Bengal at Plassey.
1839–42	Opium War between Britain and China ended with ceding of Hong Kong to Britain and opening of treaty ports in China.
1854	US Commodore Perry forced Japanese shogun to grant commercial treaty.
1857–58	Indian Mutiny in India.
1904–05	Russo-Japanese War.
1931	Japan invaded China.
1941	Japan attacked US fleet at Pearl Harbor.
1947	India and Pakistan gained independence.
1949	Chiang Kai-shek forced by Chinese communists to flee to Formosa, where he set up Republic of China, a US-backed right-wing government.
1950	Korean War.
1954	End of French colonialism in Indochina: Vietnam was divided into the communist north and the noncommunist south.
1955	US sent to advise South Vietnam against Vietcong communist insurgents, backed by North Vietnam and China.
1965	US troops sent to support South Vietnamese in large numbers.
1971	East Pakistan declared independence as Bangladesh.
1975	Fall of South Vietnam to North Vietnam. Khmer Rouge seized power in Cambodia.
1976	Death of Mao Zedong.
1980	Trial of Gang of Four (including Mao's widow Jiang Qing).
1980s	Japan became world's richest nation.
1986	Agreement between British and Chinese governments on future 1997 administration of Hong Kong.
1989	Pro-democracy demonstrations in China bloodily repressed by government troops.
1991	Peace settlement in Cambodia.
1992	Renewed Hindu-Muslim clashes in India.

of the continent becoming bitterly cold in winter and extremely hot in summer. When the heated air over land rises, moisture-laden air from the surrounding seas flows in, bringing heavy monsoon rains to all SE Asia, China, and Japan between May and Oct.

features Mount Everest at 29,118 ft/8,872 m is the world's highest mountain; Dead Sea at −1,293 ft/−394 m is the world's lowest point below sea level; rivers (over 2,000 mi/3,200 km) include Chiang Jiang (Yangtze), Huang He (Yellow River), Ob-Irtysh, Amur, Lena, Mekong, Yenisei; lakes (over 7,000 sq mi/18,000 sq km) include Caspian Sea (the largest lake in the world), Aral Sea, Baikal (largest freshwater lake in Eurasia), Balkhash; deserts include the Gobi, Takla Makan, Syrian Desert, Arabian Desert, Negev

products 62% of the population are employed in agriculture; Asia produces 46% of the world's cereal crops (91% of the world's rice); other crops include mangoes (India), groundnuts (India, China), 84% of the world's copra (Philippines, Indonesia), 93% of the world's rubber (Indonesia, Malaysia, Thailand), tobacco (China), flax (China, Russia), 95% of the world's jute (India, Bangladesh, China), cotton (China, India, Pakistan), silk (China, India), fish (Japan, China, Korea, Thailand); China produces 55% of the world's tungsten; 45% of the world's tin is produced by Malaysia, China, and Indonesia; Saudi Arabia is the world's largest producer of oil

population (1988) 2,996,000; the world's largest, though not the fastest growing population, amounting to more than half the total number of people in the world; between 1950 and 1990 the death rate and infant mortality were reduced by more than 60%; annual growth rate 1.7%; projected to increase to 3,550,000 by the year 2000

languages predominantly tonal languages (Chinese, Japanese) in the E, Indo-Iranian languages (Hindi, Urdu, Persian) in S Asia, Altaic languages (Mongolian, Turkish) in W and Central Asia, Semitic languages (Arabic, Hebrew) in the SW

religions the major religions of the world had their origins in Asia -Judaism and Christianity in the Middle East, Islam in Arabia, Buddhism, Hinduism, and Sikhism in India, Confucianism in China, and Shintoism in Japan.

Asia Minor historical name for **Anatolia**, the Asian part of Turkey.

Asian native to or an inhabitant of the continent of Asia, which is the contiguous land mass east of the Ural Mountains, the traditional boundary between Europe and Asia. The region is culturally heterogenous with numerous distinctive ethnic and sociolinguistic groups, totaling over half the Earth's human population (including China, India, and Japan). Asians are of three main racial stocks: Mongoloid in the east; Caucasoid in the west; and Negroid in the Philippines and off-shore islands of the Indian Ocean. The Indians of the Americas were Asian migrants to the New World during the last Ice Age.

Asian and Pacific Council (ASPAC) organization established 1966 to encourage cultural and economic cooperation in Oceania and Asia. Its members include Australia, Japan, South Korea, Malaysia, New Zealand, the Philippines, Taiwan, and Thailand.

Asian Development Bank (ADB) bank founded 1966 to stimulate growth in Asia and the Far East by administering direct loans and technical assistance. Members include 30 countries within the region and 14 countries of W Europe and North America. The headquarters are in Manila, Philippines.

Japan played a leading role in the setting-up of the ADB, which was established under the aegis of the United Nations Economic and Social Council for Asia and the Pacific (ESCAP).

Asian Republics, Central see ⬦Central Asian Republics.

Asia-Pacific Economic Cooperation Conference (APEC) trade group comprising 12 Pacific Asian countries, formed Nov 1989 to promote multilateral trade and economic cooperation between member states. Its members are the US, Canada, Japan, Australia, New Zealand, South Korea, Brunei, Indonesia, Malaysia, the Philippines, Singapore, and Thailand.

Asimov Isaac 1920–1992. Russian-born US author and editor of science fiction and nonfiction.

He published more than 400 books including his science fiction *I, Robot* 1950 and the *Foundation* trilogy 1951–53, continued in *Foundation's Edge* 1983.

Asimov immigrated to the US as a child. He graduated from Columbia University with a PhD 1948. Trained as a biochemist, Asimov wrote numerous nonfiction works on scientific subjects. These include *Building Blocks of the Universe* 1957; *Until the Sun Dies* 1977, about black holes; and *The Exploding Suns: The Secrets of the Supernovas* 1985. His science-fiction works include short stories, and he wrote two autobiographical volumes 1981, 1982.

Asmara or **Asmera** capital of Eritrea, Ethiopia; 40 mi/64 km SW of Massawa on the Red Sea; population (1984) 275,385. Products include beer, clothes, and textiles. It has a naval school. In 1974 unrest here precipitated the end of the Ethiopian Empire.

Asoka c. 273–238 BC. Indian emperor, and Buddhist convert from Hinduism. He issued edicts, carved on pillars and rock faces throughout his dominions, promoting wise government and the cultivation of moral virtues according to Buddhist teachings. Many still survive, and are among the oldest deciphered texts in India. In Patna there are the remains of a hall built by him.

asp any of several venomous snakes, including *Vipera aspis* of S Europe, allied to the adder, and the Egyptian cobra *Naja haje*, reputed to have been used by the Egyptian queen Cleopatra for her suicide.

ASPAC abbreviation of ⬦*Asian and Pacific Council.*

asparagus any plant of the genus *Asparagus*, family Liliaceae, with small scalelike leaves and many needlelike branches. Native to Eurasia, *A. officinalis* is cultivated, and the young shoots are eaten as a vegetable.

aspartame noncarbohydrate sweetener used in foods under the tradename Nutrasweet. It is about 200 times as sweet as sugar and, unlike saccharine, has no aftertaste.

The aspartame molecule consists of two amino acids (aspartic acid and phenylalanine) linked by a methylene ($-CH_2-$) group. It breaks down slowly at room temperature and rapidly at higher temperatures. It is not suitable for people who suffer from ⬦phenylketonuria.

Aspasia c. 440 BC. Greek courtesan, the mistress of the Athenian politician ⬦Pericles. As a "foreigner" from Miletus, she could not be recognized as his wife, but their son was later legitimized. The philosopher Socrates visited her salon, a meeting place for the celebrities of Athens. Her free thinking led to a charge of impiety, from which Pericles had to defend her.

aspen any of several species of ⬦poplar tree, genus *Populus*. The European quaking aspen *P. tremula* has flattened leafstalks that cause the leaves to flutter with every breeze. The soft, light-colored wood is used for matches and paper pulp.

Aspen town in W central Colorado, on the Roaring Fork River, lying at an altitude of 7,930 ft/2,417 m; population (1991) 3,700. Established as a silver-mining town in the 1880s, Aspen is now a recreational (winter skiing and summer river rafting) and cultural center.

asphalt mineral mixture containing semisolid brown or black ⬦bitumen, used in the construction industry. Asphalt is mixed with rock chips to form paving material, and the purer varieties are used for insulating material and for waterproofing masonry. It can be produced artificially by the distillation of ⬦petroleum.

The need to recycle colored glass led 1988 to the invention of **glassphalt**, asphalt that is 15% crushed glass. It is used to pave roads in New York.

Considerable natural deposits of asphalt occur around the Dead Sea and in the Philippines, Cuba, Venezuela, and Trinidad. Bituminous limestone occurs at Neufchâtel, France.

asphodel either of two related Old World genera (*Asphodeline* and *Asphodelus*) of plants of the lily family Liliaceae. *Asphodelus albus*, the white asphodel or king's spear, is found in Italy and Greece, sometimes covering large areas, and providing grazing for sheep. *Asphodeline lutea* is the yellow asphodel.

The beautiful plants of *A. lutea* were connected by the Greeks with the dead, and were supposed to grow in the Elysian fields.

asphyxia suffocation; a lack of oxygen that produces a buildup of carbon dioxide waste in the tissues.

Asphyxia may arise from any one of a number of causes, including inhalation of smoke or poisonous gases, obstruction of the windpipe (by water, food, vomit, or foreign object), strangulation, or smothering. If it is not quickly relieved, brain damage or death ensues.

aspidistra Asiatic plant of the genus *Aspidistra* of the lily family Liliaceae. The Chinese *A. elatior* has broad, lanceolate leaves and, like all members of the genus, grows well in warm indoor conditions.

aspirin acetylsalicylic acid, a popular pain-relieving drug (⬦analgesic) developed in the early 20th century for headaches and arthritis. It inhibits ⬦prostaglandins, and is derived from the white willow tree *Salix alba*.

In the long term, even moderate use may cause stomach bleeding, kidney damage, and hearing defects, and aspirin is no longer considered suitable for children under 12, because of a suspected link with a rare disease, Reye's syndrome (consequently, acetaminophen is often substituted). However, recent medical research suggests that an aspirin a day may be of value in preventing heart attack (myocardial infarction) and thrombosis.

Asquith Herbert Henry, 1st Earl of Oxford

assassinations

BC	victim
681	Sennacherib of Assyria
514	Hipparchus, tyrant of Athens
336	Philip II of Macedon
44	Julius Caesar, Roman dictator
AD	**victim**
14	Caligula, Roman emperor
96	Domitian, Roman dictator
1170	Thomas à Becket
1584	William the Silent, Prince of Orange
1589	Henry III of France
1610	Henry IV of France
1634	Prince Wallenstein, German general
1793	Jean Paul Marat, French revolutionary
1801	Paul I of Russia
1865	Abraham Lincoln, US president
1881	James A Garfield, US president
1881	Alexander II of Russia
1882	Lord Frederick Cavendish, chief secretary for Ireland
1894	Marie François Carnot, French president
1900	Umberto I of Italy
1901	William McKinley, US president
1903	Alexander Obrenovich, King of Serbia, and his wife Draga
1914	Archduke Francis Ferdinand
1914	Jean Jaurès, French socialist
1916	Rasputin, Russian monk
1922	Michael Collins, Irish Sinn Fein leader
1934	Dr Engelbert Dollfuss, Austrian chancellor
1934	Alexander I of Yugoslavia
1935	Huey Long, American politician
1940	Leon Trotsky, exiled Russian communist leader
1942	Reinhard Heydrich, second in command of the Nazi secret police
1948	Mahatma Gandhi, Indian nationalist leader
1948	Count Folke Bernadotte, Swedish diplomat
1951	Abdullah I of Jordan
1958	Faisal II of Iraq
1959	Solomon Bandaranaike, Ceylonese premier
1959	Rafael Trujillo Molina, Dominican Republic dictator
1963	John F Kennedy, US president
1963	Malcolm X (Little), US leading representative of the Black Muslims
1966	Hendrik Verwoerd, South African premier
1968	Rev Martin Luther King, US civil rights leader
1968	Robert F Kennedy, US senator
1975	King Faisal of Saudi Arabia
1976	Christopher Ewart Biggs, British ambassador to Republic of Ireland
1978	Aldo Moro, president of Italy's Christian Democrats and five times prime minister
1979	Lord Mountbatten, uncle of Duke of Edinburgh
1979	Park Chung Hee, president of South Korea
1980	John Lennon, singer and songwriter
1981	Anwar al-Sadat, president of Egypt
1984	Indira Gandhi, Indian prime minister
1986	Olof Palme, Swedish prime minister
1991	Rajiv Gandhi, former Indian prime minister
1992	Mohammed Boudiaf, president of Algeria's ruling High State Council

and Asquith 1852–1928. British Liberal politician, prime minister 1908–16. As chancellor of the Exchequer he introduced old-age pensions 1908. He limited the powers of the House of Lords and attempted to give Ireland Home Rule.

During World War I, his attitude of "wait and see" was not adapted to all-out war, and in Dec 1916 he was replaced by Lloyd George. In 1918 the Liberal election defeat led to the eclipse of the party.

ass any of several horselike, odd-toed, hoofed mammals of the genus *Equus*, family Equidae. Species include the African wild ass *E. asinus*, and the Asian wild ass *E. hemionus*. They differ from horses in their smaller size, larger ears, tufted tail, and characteristic bray. Donkeys and burros are domesticated asses.

Assad Hafez al 1930– . Syrian Ba'athist politician, president from 1971. He became prime minister after a bloodless military coup 1970, and the following year was the first president to be elected by popular vote. Having suppressed dissent, he was reelected 1978 and 1985. He is a Shia (Alawite) Muslim.

He has ruthlessly suppressed domestic opposition, and was Iran's only major Arab ally in its war against Iraq. He steadfastly pursued military parity with Israel, and has made himself a key player in any settlement of the Lebanese civil war or Middle East conflict generally. His support for UN action against Iraq following its invasion of Kuwait 1990 raised his international standing.

Assam state of NE India
area 30,262 sq mi/78,400 sq km
capital Dispur
cities Guwahati
products half India's tea is grown and half its oil produced here; rice, jute, sugar, cotton, coal
population (1991) 24,294,600, including 12 million Assamese (Hindus), 5 million Bengalis (chiefly Muslim immigrants from Bangladesh), Nepalis, and 2 million indigenous people (Christian and traditional religions)
language Assamese
history a thriving region from 1000 BC; Assam migrants came from China and Myanmar (Burma). After Burmese invasion 1826, Britain took control and made Assam a separate province 1874; included in the Dominion of India, except for most of the Muslim district of Silhet, which went to Pakistan 1947. Ethnic unrest started in the 1960s when Assamese was declared the official language. After protests, the Gara, Khasi, and Jainitia tribal hill districts became the state of Meghalaya 1971; the Mizo hill district became the Union Territory of Mizoram 1972. There were massacres of Muslim Bengalis by Hindus 1983. In 1987 members of the Bodo ethnic group began fighting for a separate homeland. Direct rule was imposed by the Indian government Nov 1990 following separatist violence from the Marxist-militant United Liberation Front of Assam (ULFA), which had extorted payments from tea-exporting companies. In March 1991 it was reported that the ULFA, operating from the jungles of Myanmar, had been involved in 97 killings, mainly of Congress I politicians, since Nov 27, 1990.

assassination murder, usually of a political, royal, or public person. The term derives from the order of the ◊Assassins, a Muslim sect that, in the 11th and 12th centuries, murdered officials to further its political ends.

Assassins, order of the (Arabic *Assassiyun* "fundamentalists" from *assass* "foundation")

militant offshoot of the Islamic Isma'ili sect 1089–1256, founded by Hassan Sabah (c. 1045–1124). They assassinated high officials in every Muslim town to further their political ends. Their headquarters from 1090 was the Alamut clifftop fortress in the Elburz Mountains, NW Iran.

Having converted to the persecuted, mystic Isma'ili sect, Hassan Sabah became a missionary and rebel against the Seljuk Empire. As grand master of the Assassins, he ran the order with strict asceticism. The assassins were members of a suicide squad: they remained at the scene of the crime to be martyred for their beliefs. Their enemies called them *hashishiyun* "smokers of hashish." Princes, viziers, and also Crusaders were among their victims. Hassan was a scholar and Alamut, built on a peak of 6,000 ft/1,800 m, held one of the largest libraries of the time.

assay in chemistry, the determination of the quantity of a given substance present in a sample. Usually it refers to determining the purity of precious metals.

The assay may be carried out by "wet" methods, when the sample is wholly or partially dissolved in some reagent (often an acid), or by "dry" or "fire" methods, in which the compounds present in the sample are combined with other substances.

assembler in computing, a program that translates a program written in an assembly language into a complete ◊machine code program that can be obeyed by a computer. Each instruction in the assembly language is translated into only one machine code instruction.

assembly language low-level computer-programming language closely related to a computer's internal codes. It consists chiefly of a set of short sequences of letters (mnemonics), which are translated, by a program called an assembler, into ◊machine code for the computer's ◊central processing unit (CPU) to follow directly. In assembly language, for example, "JMP" means "jump" and "LDA" means "load accumulator." Assembly code is used by programmers who need to write very fast or efficient programs.

Because they are much easier to use, high-level languages are normally used in preference to assembly languages. An assembly language may still be used in some cases, however, particularly when no suitable high-level language exists or where a very efficient machine-code program is required.

assembly line method of mass production in which a product is built up step-by-step by successive workers adding one part at a time.

US inventor Eli Whitney pioneered the concept of industrial assembly in the 1790s, when he employed unskilled labor to assemble muskets from sets of identical precision-made parts. In 1901 Ransome Olds in the US began mass-producing motor automobiles on an assembly-line principle, a method further refined by the introduction of the moving conveyor belt by Henry ◊Ford 1913 and the time-and-motion studies of F W ◊Taylor. On the assembly line human workers now stand side by side with ◊robots.

asset in business accounting, a term that covers the land or property of a company or individual, payments due from bills, investments, and anything else owned that can be turned into cash. On a company's balance sheet, total assets must be equal to liabilities (money and services owed).

asset stripping sale or exploitation by other means of the assets of a business, often one that has been taken over for that very purpose. The parts of the business may be potentially more valuable separately than together. Asset stripping is a major force for the more efficient use of assets.

Assisi town in Umbria, Italy, 12 mi/19 km SE of Perugia; population (1981) 25,000. St Francis was born here and is buried in the Franciscan monastery, completed 1253. The churches of St Francis are adorned with frescoes by Giotto, Cimabue, and others.

assize in medieval Europe, the passing of laws, either by the king with the consent of nobles, as in the Constitutions of ▷Clarendon 1164 by Henry II of England, or as a complete system, such as the *Assizes of Jerusalem*, a compilation of the law of the feudal kingdom of Jerusalem in the 13th century.

Association of South East Asian Nations (ASEAN) regional alliance formed in Bangkok 1967; it took over the nonmilitary role of the Southeast Asia Treaty Organization 1975. Its members are Indonesia, Malaysia, the Philippines, Singapore, Thailand, and (from 1984) Brunei; its headquarters are in Jakarta, Indonesia.

The six member states signed an agreement 1992 to establish an ASEAN free trade area (AFTA) by the beginning of 2008.

associative operation in mathematics, an operation in which the outcome is independent of the grouping of the numbers or symbols concerned. For example, multiplication is associative, as $4 \times (3 \times 2) = (4 \times 3) \times 2 = 24$; however, division is not, as $12 \div (4 \div 2) = 6$, but $(12 \div 4) \div 2 = 1.5$. Compare ▷commutative operation and ▷distributive operation.

assortative mating in ▷population genetics, selective mating in a population between individuals that are genetically related or have similar characteristics. If sufficiently consistent, assortative mating can theoretically result in the evolution of new species without geographical isolation (see ▷speciation).

Assy plateau in Haute-Savoie, E France, 3,280 ft/1,000 m above sea level. The area has numerous sanatoriums. The church of Nôtre Dame de Toute Grâce, begun 1937 and consecrated 1950, is adorned with works by Braque, Chagall, Matisse, Derain, Rouault, and other artists.

Assyria empire in the Middle East *c.* 2500–612 BC, in N Mesopotamia (now Iraq); early capital Ashur, later Nineveh. It was initially subject to Sumer and intermittently to Babylon. The Assyrians adopted in the main the Sumerian religion and structure of society. At its greatest extent the empire included Egypt and stretched from the E Mediterranean coast to the head of the Persian Gulf.

The land of Assyria originally consisted of a narrow strip of alluvial soil on each side of the river Tigris. The area was settled about 3500 BC and was dominated by Sumer until about 2350 BC. For nearly 200 years Assyria was subject first to the Babylonian dynasty of Akkad and then to the Gutians, barbarians from the north.

The first Assyrian kings are mentioned during the wars following the decline of the 3rd dynasty of Ur (in Sumer), but Assyria continued under Babylonian and subsequently Egyptian suzerainty until about 1450 BC. Under King Ashur-uballit (reigned about 1380–1340 BC) Assyria became a military power.

His work was continued by Adad-nirari I, Shalmaneser I, and Tukulti-enurta I, who conquered Babylonia and assumed the title of king of Sumer and Akkad.

During the reign of Nebuchadnezzar I (1150–1110 BC), Assyria was again subject to Babylonia, but was liberated by Tiglath-pileser I. In the Aramaean invasions, most of the ground gained was lost. From the accession of Adad-nirari II 911 BC Assyria pursued a course of expansion and conquest, culminating in the mastery over Elam, Mesopotamia, Syria, Palestine, the Arabian marches, and Egypt. Of this period the Old Testament records, and many "documents"—such as the Black Obelisk celebrating the conquest of Shalmaneser III in the 9th century BC—survive.

The reign of Ashur-nazir-pal II (885–860 BC) was spent in unceasing warfare, evidenced by many bas-reliefs. Shalmaneser III warred against the Syrian states. At the battle of Qarqar 854 BC the Assyrian advance received a setback, and there followed a period of decline. The final period of Assyrian ascendancy began with the accession of Tiglath-pileser III (746–728 BC) and continued during the reigns of Sargon II, Sennacherib, Esarhaddon, and Ashurbanipal, culminating in the conquest of Egypt by Esarhaddon 671 BC. From this time the empire seems to have fallen into decay. Nabopolassar of Babylonia and Cyaxares of Media (see ▷Mede) united against it; Nineveh was destroyed 612 BC; and Assyria became a Median province and subsequently a principality of the Persian Empire.

Much of Assyrian religion, law, social structure, and artistic achievement was derived from neighboring sources. The Assyrians adopted the cuneiform script (invented by the Sumerians in 3500 BC) and took over the Sumerian pantheon, although the Assyrian god, Ashur (Assur), assumed the chief place in the cult. The library of Ashurbanipal excavated at Nineveh is evidence of the thoroughness with which Babylonian culture had been assimilated.

Astaire Fred. Adopted name of Frederick Austerlitz 1899–1987. US dancer, actor, singer, and choreographer who starred in numerous films, including *Top Hat* 1935, *Easter Parade* 1948, and *Funny Face* 1957, many containing inventive sequences he designed and choreographed himself. He made ten classic films with the most popular of his dancing partners, Ginger Rogers. He later played straight dramatic roles in such films as *On the Beach* 1959.

Astaire was born in Omaha, Nebraska, and taken to New York in 1904. He danced in partnership with his sister *Adele Astaire* (1897–1981) from 1906 until her marriage in 1932, and they became public favorites on Broadway and in London. He entered films in 1933. Among his many other films are *Roberta* 1935 and *Follow the Fleet* 1936. Astaire was a virtuoso dancer and a perfectionist known for his elegant style.

Astarte alternate name for the Babylonian and Assyrian goddess ▷Ishtar.

astatine (Greek *astatos* "unstable") nonmetallic, radioactive element, symbol At, atomic number 85, atomic weight 210. It is a member of the ▷halogen group, and is very rare in nature. Astatine is highly unstable, with many isotopes; the longest lived has a half-life of about eight hours.

aster any plant of the large genus *Aster*, family Compositae, belonging to the same subfamily as the daisy. All asters have starlike flowers with yellow centers and outer rays (not petals) varying from blue and purple to white and the genus comprises a great variety of size. Many are cultivated as garden flowers, including the Michaelmas daisy *A. nova-belgii*.

The China aster *Callistephus chinensis* belongs to a closely allied genus; it was introduced to Europe and the US from China in the early 18th century.

The white wood aster *A. divaricatus* grows in open woods throughout most of the US.

asterisk starlike punctuation mark (*) used to link the asterisked word with a note at the bottom of a page, and to indicate that certain letters are missing from a word (usually a taboo word such as "f**k").

asteroid or *minor planet* any of many thousands of small bodies, composed of rock and iron, that orbit the Sun. Most lie in a belt between the orbits of Mars and Jupiter, and are thought to be fragments left over from the formation of the Solar System. About 100,000 may exist, but their total mass is only a few hundredths the mass of the Moon.

They include ▷Ceres (the largest asteroid, 584 mi/9,400 km in diameter), Vesta (which has a light-colored surface, and is the brightest as seen from Earth), ▷Eros, and ▷Icarus. Some asteroids are on orbits that bring them close to Earth, and some, such as the ▷Apollo asteroids, even cross Earth's orbit; at least some of these may be former comets that have lost their gas. One group, the Trojans, moves along the same orbit as Jupiter, 60° ahead and behind the planet. One unusual asteroid, ▷Chiron, orbits beyond Saturn. The first asteroid was discovered by the Italian astronomer Guiseppe Piazzi at the Palermo Observatory, Sicily, Jan 1, 1801.

asthenosphere division of the Earth's structure lying beneath the ▷lithosphere, at a depth of approximately 45 mi/70 km to 160 mi/260 km. It is thought to be the soft, partially molten layer of the ▷mantle on which the rigid plates of the Earth's surface move to produce the motions of ▷plate tectonics.

asthma difficulty in breathing due to spasm of the bronchi (air passages) in the lungs. Attacks may be provoked by allergy, infection, stress, or emotional upset. It may also be increasing as a result of air pollution and occupational hazards. Treatment is with ▷bronchodilators to relax the bronchial muscles and thereby ease the breathing, and in severe cases by inhaled ▷steroids that reduce inflammation of the bronchi.

Although the symptoms are similar to those of bronchial asthma, **cardiac asthma** is an unrelated condition and is a symptom of heart deterioration.

Asti town in Piedmont, SE of Turin, Italy; population (1983) 76,439. Asti province is famed for its sparkling wine. Other products include chemicals, textiles, and glass.

astigmatism aberration occurring in lenses, including that in the eye. It results when the curvature of the lens differs in two perpendicular planes, so that rays in one plane may be in focus while rays in the other are not. With astigmatic eyesight, the vertical and horizontal cannot be in focus at the same time; correction is by the use of a cylindrical lens that reduces the overall focal length of one plane so that both planes are seen in sharp focus.

Aston Francis William 1877–1945. English physicist who developed the mass spectrometer, which separates ▷isotopes by projecting their ions (charged atoms) through a magnetic field. He received the Nobel Prize for Chemistry 1922.

Astor John Jacob 1763–1848. German-born US merchant who made his fortune trading in furs and New York City real estate. He came to the US 1784 and worked in small shops before entering the fur trade. When he retired 1834, he was the wealthiest man in the US. His estate endowed the Astor library, now a part of The New York Public Library.

Astor made a farsighted agreement with Canadian merchants to import furs to the US from Montreal. He took advantage of the Louisiana Purchase 1803 and extended his trade to the West, creating the Pacific Fur Company 1811 (founding Astoria, now in Oregon, his trading post at the mouth of the Columbia river), a subsidiary of his monopolistic American Fur Company, founded 1808. He sold some of his furs in China through an agreement with the British East India Company. His profits were systematically invested in New York City real estate. When he died he owned most of the southern half of Manhattan, which his sons inherited and administered.

Astor Mary. Adopted name of Lucille Langhanke 1906–1987. US film actress, renowned for her poise, whose many films included *Don Juan* 1926, *Dodsworth* 1936, and *The Maltese Falcon* 1941. Her memoirs *My Story* 1959 were remarkable for their frankness.

Astrakhan city in Russia, on the delta of the Volga, capital of Astrakhan region; population (1989) 509,000. In ancient times a Tatar capital, it became Russian 1556. It is the chief port for the Caspian fisheries.

astrolabe ancient navigational instrument, forerunner of the sextant. Astrolabes usually consisted of a flat disk with a sighting rod that could be pivoted to point at the Sun or bright stars. From the altitude of the Sun or star above the horizon, the local time could be estimated.

astrology (Greek *astron* "star," *legein* "speak") study of the relative position of the planets and stars in the belief that they influence events on Earth. The astrologer casts a ◊horoscope based on the time and place of the subject's birth. Astrology has no proven scientific basis, but has been widespread since ancient times. Western astrology is based on the 12 signs of the zodiac; Chinese astrology is based on a 60-year cycle and lunar calendar.

history A strongly held belief in ancient Babylon, astrology spread to the Mediterranean world, and was widely used by the Greeks and Romans. In Europe during the Middle Ages it had a powerful influence, since kings and other public figures had their own astrologers; astrological beliefs are reflected in Elizabethan and Jacobean literature.

In the US, horoscopes are syndicated in most newspapers and almost everyone, whether professing belief or not, knows his or her astrological sign.

astrometry measurement of the precise positions of stars, planets, and other bodies in space. Such information is needed for practical purposes including accurate timekeeping, surveying and navigation, and calculating orbits and measuring distances in space. Astrometry is not concerned with the surface features or the physical nature of the body under study.

Before telescopes, astronomical observations were simple astrometry. Precise astrometry has shown that stars are not fixed in

position, but have a ◊proper motion caused as they and the Sun orbit the Milky Way galaxy. The nearest stars also show ◊parallax (apparent change in position), from which their distances can be calculated. Above the distorting effects of the atmosphere, satellites such as *Hipparcos* can make even more precise measurements than ground telescopes, so refining the distance scale of space.

astronaut person making flights into space; the term *cosmonaut* is used in the West for any astronaut from the former Soviet Union.

astronautics science of space travel. See ◊rocket; ◊satellite; ◊space probe.

astronomical unit unit (symbol AU) equal to the mean distance of the Earth from the Sun: 92,955,800 mi/149,597,870 km. It is used to describe planetary distances. Light travels this distance in approximately 8.3 minutes.

astronomy science of the celestial bodies: the Sun, the Moon, and the planets; the stars and galaxies; and all other objects in the universe. It is concerned with their positions, motions, distances, and physical conditions; and with their origins and evolution. Astronomy thus divides into fields such as astrophysics, celestial mechanics, and cosmology. See also ◊gamma-ray astronomy, ◊infrared astronomy, ◊radio astronomy, ◊ultraviolet astronomy, and ◊X-ray astronomy.

Astronomy is perhaps the oldest recorded science; there are observational records from ancient Babylonia, China, Egypt, and Mexico. The first true astronomers, however, were the Greeks, who deduced the Earth to be a sphere, and attempted to measure its size. Ancient Greek astronomers included ◊Thales and ◊Pythagoras. ◊Eratosthenes of Cyrene measured the size of the Earth with considerable accuracy. Star catalogs were drawn up, the most celebrated being that of Hipparchus. The *Almagest*, by ◊Ptolemy of Alexandria, summarized Greek astronomy, and survived in its Arab translation. However, the Greeks still regarded the Earth as the center of the universe, although this was doubted by some philosophers, notably ◊Aristarchus of Samos, who maintained that the Earth moves around the Sun.

Ptolemy, the last famous astronomer of the Greek school, died about AD 180, and little progress was made for some centuries. The Arabs revived the science, carrying out theoretical researches from the 8th and 9th centuries, and producing good star catalogs. Unfortunately a general belief in the pseudoscience of astrology continued until the end of the Middle Ages (and has been revived from time to time).

The dawn of a new era came 1543, when a Polish canon, ◊Copernicus, published a work entitled *De Revolutionibus Orbium Coelestium/ About the Revolutions of the Heavenly Spheres*, in which he demonstrated that the Sun, not the Earth, is the center of our planetary system. (Copernicus was wrong in many respects—for instance, he still believed that all celestial orbits must be perfectly circular.) ◊Brahe, a Dane, increased the accuracy of observations by means of improved instruments allied to his own personal skill, and his observations were used by the German mathematician ◊Kepler to prove the validity of the Copernican system. Considerable opposition existed, however, for removing the Earth from its central position in the universe; the Catholic Church was openly hostile to the idea, and, ironically, Brahe never accepted the idea that the Earth could move around the Sun. Yet before the end of the 17th

century, the theoretical work of Isaac ◊Newton had established celestial mechanics.

The refractor telescope was invented about 1608, by ◊Lippershey in Holland, and was first applied to astronomy by the Italian scientist Galileo in the winter of 1609–10. Immediately, Galileo made a series of spectacular discoveries. He found the four largest satellites of Jupiter, which gave strong support to the Copernican theory; he saw the craters of the Moon, the phases of Venus, and the myriad faint stars of our Galaxy, the Milky Way. Galileo's most powerful telescope magnified only 30 times, but before long, larger telescopes were built, and official observatories were established.

Galileo's telescope was a refractor; that is to say, it collected its light by means of a glass lens or object glass. Difficulties with his design led Newton, in 1671, to construct a reflector, in which the light is collected by means of a curved mirror.

Theoretical researches continued, and astronomy made rapid progress in many directions. New planets were discovered—Uranus 1781 by ◊Herschel, and Neptune 1846, following calculations by ◊Adams and ◊Leverrier. Also significant was the first measurement of the distance of a star, when in 1838 the German astronomer ◊Bessel measured the ◊parallax of the star 61 Cygni, and calculated that it lies at a distance of about 6 light-years (about half the correct value). Astronomical spectroscopy was developed, first by Fraunhofer in Germany and then by people such as ◊Secchi and Huggins, while ◊Kirchhoff successfully interpreted the spectra of the Sun and stars. By the 1860s good photographs of the Moon had been obtained, and by the end of the century photographic methods had started to play a leading role in research.

William Herschel, probably the greatest observer in the history of astronomy, investigated the shape of our Galaxy during the latter part of the 18th century, and concluded that its stars are arranged roughly in the form of a double-convex lens. Basically Herschel was correct, although he placed our Sun near the center of the system; in fact, it is well out toward the edge, and lies 25,000 light-years from the galactic nucleus. Herschel also studied the luminous "clouds" or nebulae, and made the tentative suggestion that those nebulae capable of resolution into stars might be separate galaxies, far outside our own Galaxy. It was not until 1923 that Hubble, using the 100 in/2.5 m reflector at the Mount Wilson Observatory, was able to verify this suggestion. It is now known that the "starry nebulae" are galaxies in their own right, and that they lie at immense distances. The most distant galaxy visible to the naked eye, the Great Spiral in ◊Andromeda, is 2.2 million light-years away; the most remote galaxy so far measured lies over 10 billion light-years away. It was also found that galaxies tended to form groups, and that the groups were apparently receding from each other at speeds proportional to their distances.

This concept of an expanding and evolving universe at first rested largely on ◊Hubble's law, relating the distance of objects to the amount their spectra shift toward red—the ◊red shift. Subsequent evidence derived from objects studied in other parts of the ◊electromagnetic spectrum, at radio and X-ray wavelengths, has provided confirmation. ◊Radio astronomy established its place in probing the structure of the universe by demonstrating in 1954 that an optically visible distant galaxy was identical with a powerful radio source known as Cygnus A. Later analysis of the comparative number, strength, and distance of radio sources suggested that in the distant past these, including the ⬦quasars discovered 1963, had been much more powerful and numerous than today. This fact suggested that the universe has been evolving from an origin, and is not of infinite age as expected under a ⬦steady-state theory. The discovery 1965 of microwave background radiation suggested that residue survived the tremendous thermal power of the giant explosion, or Big Bang, that brought the universe into existence.

In 1986 *Voyager 2* discovered six new moons around Uranus. In 1987 Supernova SN1987A flared up in the Large Magellanic Cloud, the first supernova to reach naked-eye visibility since 1604. Also in 1987, the 165 in/4.2 m William Herschel Telescope on La Palma, Canary Islands, and the James Clerk Maxwell Telescope on Mauna Kea, Hawaii, began operation. In 1988 the most distant individual star was recorded; the supernova in one of the galaxies in the AC118 cluster of galaxies is about 5 billion light-years away. In Aug 1989, *Voyager 2* passed by Neptune. See also ⬦black hole, ⬦cosmology, and ⬦infrared radiation.

astronomy: chronology

2300 BC	Chinese astronomers made their earliest observations.
2000	Babylonian priests made their first observational records.
1900	Stonehenge was constructed: first phase.
365	The Chinese observed the satellites of Jupiter with the naked eye.
3rd century	Aristarchus argued that the Sun is the center of the Solar System.
2nd century AD	Ptolemy's complicated Earth-centered system was promulgated, which dominated the astronomy of the Middle Ages.
1543	Copernicus revived the ideas of Aristarchus in *De Revolutionibus*.
1608	Hans Lippershey invented the telescope, which was first used by Galileo 1609.
1609	Johann Kepler's first two laws of planetary motion were published (the third appeared 1619).
1632	The world's first official observatory was established in Leiden in the Netherlands.
1633	Galileo's theories were condemned by the Inquisition.
1675	The Royal Greenwich Observatory was founded in England.
1687	Isaac Newton's *Principia* was published, including his "law of universal gravitation."
1718	Edmund Halley predicted the return of the comet named after him, observed 1758: its last return was 1986.
1781	William Herschel discovered Uranus and recognized stellar systems beyond our Galaxy.
1796	Pierre Laplace elaborated his theory of the origin of the Solar System.
1801	Giuseppe Piazzi discovered the first asteroid, Ceres.
1814	Joseph von Fraunhofer first studied absorption lines in the solar spectrum.
1846	Neptune was identified by Johann Galle, following predictions by John Adams and Urbain Leverrier.
1859	Gustav Kirchhoff explained dark lines in the Sun's spectrum.
1887	The earliest photographic star charts were produced.
1889	Edward Barnard took the first photographs of the Milky Way.
1908	Fragment of comet fell at Tunguska, Siberia.
1920	Arthur Eddington began the study of interstellar matter.
1923	Edwin Hubble proved that the galaxies are systems independent of the Milky Way, and by 1930 had confirmed the concept of an expanding universe.
1930	The planet Pluto was discovered by Clyde Tombaugh at the Lowell Observatory, Arizona.
1931	Karl Jansky founded radio astronomy.
1945	Radar contact with the Moon was established by Z Bay of Hungary and the US Army Signal Corps Laboratory.
1948	The 5-m/200-in Hale reflector telescope was installed at Mount Palomar, California.
1955	The Jodrell Bank telescope dish in England was completed.
1957	The first Sputnik satellite (USSR) opened the age of space observation.
1962	The first X-ray source was discovered in Scorpius.
1963	The first quasar was discovered.
1967	The first pulsar was discovered by Jocelyn Bell and Antony Hewish.
1969	The first crewed Moon landing was made by US astronauts.
1976	A 6-m/240-in reflector telescope was installed at Mount Semirodniki, USSR.
1977	Uranus was discovered to have rings.
1977	The spacecraft *Voyager 1* and *2* were launched, passing Jupiter and Saturn 1979-81.
1978	The spacecraft *Pioneer Venus 1* and *2* reached Venus.
1978	A satellite of Pluto, Charon, was discovered by James Christy of the US Naval Observatory.
1986	Halley's comet returned.
1986	*Voyager 2* flew by Uranus; Halley's comet returned.
1987	Bright supernovae were visible to the naked eye for the first time since 1604.
1989	*Voyager 2* flew by Neptune and discovered eight moons and three rings.
1990	Hubble Space Telescope was launched into orbit by the US space shuttle.
1991	The space probe *Galileo* flew past the asteroid Gaspra.
1992	COBE satellite detected ripples from the Big Bang that mark the first stage in the formation of galaxies.

Although the practical limit in size and efficiency of optical telescopes has apparently been reached, the siting of these and other types of telescope at new observatories in the previously neglected southern hemisphere has opened fresh areas of the sky to search. Australia has been in the forefront of these developments. The most remarkable recent extension of the powers of astronomy to explore the universe is in the use of rockets, satellites, space stations, and space probes. Even the range and accuracy of the conventional telescope may be greatly improved free from the Earth's atmosphere. The US launched a large optical telescope, called the Hubble Space Telescope, permanently in space in April 1990. It is the most powerful optical telescope yet constructed, with a 94.5 in/2.4 m mirror. It detects celestial phenomena seven times more distant (up to 14 billion light-years) than any land telescope.

astrophotography use of photography in astronomical research. The first successful photograph of a celestial object was the daguerreotype plate of the Moon taken by John W Draper (1811–1882) of the US in March 1840. The first photograph of a star, Vega, was taken by US astronomer William C Bond (1789–1859) in 1850. Modern-day astrophotography uses techniques such as ⬦charge-coupled devices (CCDs).

Before the development of photography, observations were gathered in the form of sketches made at the telescope. Several successful daguerrotypes were obtained prior to the introduction of wet-plate collodion about 1850. The availability of this more covenient method allowed photography to be used on a more systematic basis, including the monitoring of sunspot activity. Dry plates were introduced in the 1870s, and in 1880 Henry Draper (1837–1882) obtained a photograph of the ⬦Orion nebula. The first successful image of a comet was obtained 1882 by the Scottish astronomer David Gill (1843–1914), his plate displaying excellent star images. Following this, Gill and J C Kapteyn (1851–1922) compiled the first photographic atlas of the southern sky, cataloging almost half a million stars.

Modern-day electronic innovations, notably ⬦charge-coupled devices (CCDs), provide a more efficient light-gathering capability than photographic film as well as enabling information to be transferred to a computer for analysis. However, CCD images are expensive and very small in size compared to photographic plates. Photographic plates are better suited to wide-field images, whereas CCDs are used for individual objects, which may be very faint, within a narrow field of sky.

astrophysics study of the physical nature of stars, galaxies, and the universe. It began with the development of spectroscopy in the 19th century, which allowed astronomers to analyze the composition of stars from their light. Astrophysicists view the universe as a vast natural laboratory in which they can study matter under conditions of temperature, pressure, and density that are unattainable on Earth.

Asturias autonomous region of N Spain; area 4,092 sq mi/10,600 sq km; population (1986) 1,114,000. Half of Spain's coal comes from the mines of Asturias. Agricultural produce includes corn, fruit, and livestock. Oviedo and Gijón are the main industrial towns.

It was once a separate kingdom, and the

eldest son of a king of Spain is still called prince of Asturias.

Asturias Miguel Ángel 1899–1974. Guatemalan author and diplomat. He published poetry, Guatemalan legends, and novels, such as *El señor presidente/The President* 1946, *Men of Corn* 1949, and *Strong Wind* 1950, attacking Latin-American dictatorships and "Yankee imperialism." Nobel Prize 1967.

Astyanax in Greek mythology, the son of ◊Hector and ◊Andromache. After the death of all the sons of ◊Priam in battle at the siege of Troy, the child Astyanax was thrown from the city walls by the victorious Greeks.

Asunción capital and port of Paraguay, on the Paraguay River; population (1984) 729,000. It produces textiles, footwear, and food products. Founded 1537, it was the first Spanish settlement in the La Plata region.

Aswan winter resort town in Upper Egypt; population (1985) 183,000. It is near the High Dam, built 1960–70, which keeps the level of the Nile constant throughout the year without flooding. It produces steel and textiles.

asylum, political in international law, refuge granted in another country to a person who, for political reasons, cannot return to his or her own country without putting himself or herself in danger. A person seeking asylum is a type of ◊refugee.

asymptote in ◊coordinate geometry, a straight line that a curve approaches more and more closely but never reaches. The x and y axes are asymptotes to the graph of $xy =$ constant (a rectangular ◊hyperbola).

If a point on a curve approaches a straight line such that its distance from the straight line is d, then the line is an asymptote to the curve if limit d tends to zero as the point moves toward infinity. Among ◊conic sections (curves obtained by the intersection of a plane and a double cone), a hyperbola has two asymptotes, which in the case of a rectangular hyperbola are at right angles to each other.

Asyut commercial center in Upper Egypt, near the Nile, 200 mi/322 km S of Cairo; population (1985) 274,400. An ancient Graeco-Egyptian city, it has many tombs of 11th- and 12th-dynasty nobles.

Atacama Desert desert in N Chile; area about 31,000 sq mi/80,000 sq km. There are mountains inland, and the coastal area is rainless and barren. The Atacama has silver and copper mines, and extensive nitrate deposits.

Atahualpa c. 1502–1533. Last emperor of the Incas of Peru. He was taken prisoner 1532 when the Spaniards arrived, and agreed to pay a substantial ransom, but was accused of plotting against the conquistador Pizarro and sentenced to be burned. On his consenting to Christian baptism, the sentence was commuted to strangulation.

Atalanta in Greek mythology, a woman hunter who challenged all her suitors to a foot race; if they lost they were killed. Aphrodite gave Milanion three golden apples to drop so that when Atalanta stopped to pick them up, she lost the race.

Atatürk Kemal. Name assumed 1934 by Mustafa Kemal Pasha 1881–1938. (Atatürk "Father of the Turks") Turkish politician and general, first president of Turkey from 1923. After World War I he established a provisional rebel government and in 1921–22 the Turkish armies under his leadership expelled the Greeks who were occupying Turkey. He was the founder of the modern republic, which he ruled as virtual dictator, with a policy of consistent and radical westernization.

Kemal, born in Thessaloniki, was banished 1904 for joining a revolutionary society. Later he was pardoned and promoted in the army, and was largely responsible for the successful defense of the Dardanelles against the British 1915. In 1918, after Turkey had been defeated, he was sent into Anatolia to implement the demobilization of the Turkish forces in accordance with the armistice terms, but instead he established a provisional government opposed to that of Constantinople (under Allied control), and in 1921 led the Turkish armies against the Greeks, who had occupied a large part of Anatolia. He checked them at the Battle of the Sakaria, Aug 23–Sept 13, 1921, for which he was granted the title of Ghazi (the Victorious), and within a year had expelled the Greeks from Turkish soil. War with the British was averted by his diplomacy, and Turkey in Europe passed under Kemal's control. On Oct 29, 1923, Turkey was proclaimed a republic with Kemal as first president.

atavism (Latin *atavus* "ancestor") in ◊genetics, the reappearance of a characteristic not apparent in the immediately preceding generations; in psychology, the manifestation of primitive forms of behavior.

ataxia loss of muscular coordination due to neurological damage or disease.

Athabasca lake and river in Alberta and Saskatchewan, with immense tar-sand deposits (source of the hydrocarbon mixture "heavy oil") to the SW of the lake.

Athanasian Creed one of the three ancient ◊creeds of the Christian church. Mainly a definition of the Trinity and Incarnation, it was written many years after the death of Athanasius, but was attributed to him as the chief upholder of Trinitarian doctrine.

Athanasius, St 298–373. Bishop of Alexandria, supporter of the doctrines of the Trinity and Incarnation. He was a disciple of St Anthony the hermit, and an opponent of ◊Arianism in the great Arian controversy. Following the official condemnation of Arianism at the Council of Nicaea 325, Athanasius was appointed bishop of Alexandria 328. The Athanasian creed was not actually written by him, although it reflects his views.

atheism nonbelief in, or the positive denial of, the existence of a God or gods. A related concept is ◊agnosticism.

Dogmatic atheism asserts that there is no God. *Sceptical atheism* maintains that the finite human mind is so constituted as to be incapable of discovering that there is or is not a God. *Critical atheism* holds that the evidence for theism is inadequate. This is akin to *philosophical atheism*, which fails to find evidence of a God manifest in the universe. *Speculative atheism* comprises the beliefs of those who, like the German philosopher Kant, find it impossible to demonstrate the existence of God.

Buddhism has been called an atheistic religion since it does not postulate any supreme being. The Jains are similarly atheistic, and so are those who adopt the Sankhya system of philosophy in Hinduism. Following the revolution of 1917 the USSR and later communist states, such as Albania, adopted an atheist position.

Athelstan c. 895–939. King of the Mercians and West Saxons. Son of Edward the Elder and grandson of Alfred the Great, he was crowned king 925 at Kingston upon Thames. He subdued parts of Cornwall and Wales, and defeated the Welsh, Scots, and Danes at Brunanburh 937.

Athena in Greek mythology, the goddess (Roman Minerva) of war, wisdom, and the arts and crafts, who was supposed to have sprung fully grown from the head of Zeus. Her chief cult center was Athens, where the ◊Parthenon was dedicated to her.

Athens city in NE Georgia, on the Oconee River, NE of Atlanta; seat of Clarke county. The University of Georgia was established here 1801. Industries include cotton and electrical products; population (1980) 42,549.

Athens (Greek *Athinai*) capital city of Greece and of ancient Attica; population (1981) 885,000, metropolitan area (1991) 3,096,800. Situated 5 mi/8 km NE of its port of Piraeus on the Gulf of Aegina, it is built around the rocky hills of the Acropolis 555 ft/169 m and the Areopagus 368 ft/112 m, and is overlooked from the northeast by the hill of Lycabettus, 909 ft/277 m high. It lies in the south of the central plain of Attica, watered by the mountain streams of Cephissus and Ilissus. It has less green space than any other European capital (4%) and severe air and noise pollution.

features The Acropolis dominates the city. Remains of ancient Greece include the Parthenon, the Erechtheum, and the temple of Athena Nike. Near the site of the ancient Agora (marketplace) stands the Theseum, and south of the Acropolis is the theater of Dionysus. To the southeast stand the gate of Hadrian and the columns of the temple of Olympian Zeus. Nearby is the marble stadium built about 330 BC and restored 1896.

history The site was first inhabited about 3000 BC, and Athens became the capital of a united Attica before 700 BC. Captured and sacked by the Persians 480 BC, subsequently under Pericles it was the first city of Greece in power and culture. After the death of Alexander the Great the city fell into comparative decline, but it flourished as an intellectual center until AD 529, when the philosophical schools were closed by Justinian. In 1458 it was captured by the Turks who held it until 1833; it was chosen as the capital of Greece 1834. Among present-day buildings are the royal palace and several museums.

atheroma furring-up of the interior of an artery by deposits, mainly of cholesterol, within its walls.

Associated with atherosclerosis, atheroma has the effect of narrowing the lumen (channel) of the artery, thus restricting blood flow. This predisposes to a number of conditions, including thrombosis, angina, and stroke.

atherosclerosis thickening and hardening of the walls of the arteries, associated with atheroma.

athletics collectively, all the sports, exercises, and contests that utilize and promote such physical skills as speed, agility, and stamina.

Among the Greeks, vase paintings show that competitive athletics were established by at least 1600 BC (see ◊Olympic Games). However, the concept of the unpaid amateur is a recent innovation, ancient athletes having been well paid and sponsored. ◊Aristotle paid the expenses of a boxer contestant at

Olympia, and chariot races were sponsored by the Greek city-states. Athletics have recently become dominated by the desire to set world records. This has led to the use of computer selection for the best potential competitors and the analysis of motion for the greatest speed, distance, and so forth; the specialization of equipment for maximum performance (for example, fiberglass vaulting poles, foam landing pads, aerodynamically designed javelins, composition running tracks); and the unlawful use of drugs such as ⟡anabolic steroids and growth hormones.

Athos mountainous peninsula on the Macedonian coast of Greece. Its peak is 6,672 ft/2,033 m high. The promontory is occupied by a community of 20 Basilian monasteries inhabited by some 3,000 monks and lay brothers.

Atlanta capital and largest city of Georgia; population (1990) 394,000, metropolitan area 2,010,000. It was founded 1837 and was partly destroyed by General ⟡Sherman 1864. There are Ford and Lockheed assembly plants, and it is the headquarters of Coca-Cola. In 1990 it was chosen as the host city for the 1996 summer Olympic Games.

Atlanta is also the financial, trade, and convention center for the SE US and has one of the busiest and most automated US airports. Educational institutions include Atlanta University, Emory University, the Georgia Institute of Technology, and Georgia State University. The city grew considerably in importance after 1900.

Atlantic, Battle of the continuous battle fought in the Atlantic Ocean during World War II by the sea and air forces of the Allies and Germany, to control the supply routes to the UK. The number of U-boats destroyed by the Allies during the war was nearly 800. At least 2,200 convoys of 75,000 merchant ships crossed the Atlantic, protected by US naval forces. Before the US entry into the war 1941, destroyers were supplied to the British under the Lend-Lease Act 1941.

The battle opened on the first night of the war, when on Sept 4, 1939 the ocean liner *Athenia*, sailing from Glasgow to New York, was torpedoed by a German submarine off the Irish coast. Germany tried U-boats, surface-raiders, indiscriminate mine-laying, and aircraft, but every method was successfully countered. The U-boats were the greatest menace, especially after the destruction of the German battleship *Bismarck* by British forces on May 27, 1941.

Atlantic Charter declaration issued during World War II by the British prime minister Churchill and the US president Roosevelt after meetings Aug 1941. It stressed their countries' broad strategy and war aims and was largely a propaganda exercise to demonstrate public solidarity between the Allies.

The Atlantic Charter stated that the US and the UK sought no territorial gains; desired no territorial changes not acceptable to the peoples concerned; respected the rights of all peoples to choose their own form of government; wished to see self-government restored to the occupied countries; would promote access by all states to trade and raw materials; desired international collaboration for the raising of economic standards; hoped to see a peace affording security to all nations, enabling them to cross the seas without hindrance; and proposed the disarmament of the aggressor

states as a preliminary step to general disarmament. This charter was incorporated by reference into the Declaration of the United Nations 1941.

Atlantic City seaside resort in New Jersey; population (1990) 38,000. Formerly a family resort, Atlantic City has become a center for casino gambling, which was legalized in 1978.

It is noted for its "boardwalk" and for being the basis of the Monopoly board game; the Miss America contest has been held here since 1921. It is also a convention center.

Atlantic Ocean ocean lying between Europe and Africa to the E and the Americas to the W, probably named after the legendary island ⟡Atlantis; area of basin 31,500,000 sq mi/81,500,000 sq km; including the Arctic Ocean and Antarctic seas, 41,000,000 sq mi/106,200,000 sq km. The average depth is 2 mi/3 km; greatest depth the Milwaukee Depth in the Puerto Rico Trench 28,374 ft/8,648 m. The Mid-Atlantic Ridge, of which the Azores, Ascension, St Helena, and Tristan da Cunha form part, divides it from N to S. Lava welling up from this central area annually increases the distance between South America and Africa. The N Atlantic is the saltiest of the main oceans, and has the largest tidal range. In the 1960s–80s average wave heights increased by 25%, the largest from 39 ft/12 m to 59 ft/18 m.

Atlantis legendary island continent, said to have sunk around 9600 BC, following underwater convulsions. Although the Atlantic Ocean is probably named after it, the structure of the sea bottom rules out its ever having existed there.

One story told by the Greek philosopher Plato (derived from an account by Egyptian priests) may refer to the volcanic eruption that devastated Santorini in the ⟡Cyclades, north of Crete, c. 1500 BC. The ensuing earthquakes and tidal waves brought about the collapse of the empire of Minoan Crete.

atlas book of maps. The atlas was introduced in the 16th century by ⟡Mercator, who began work on it 1585; it was completed by his son 1594. Early atlases had a frontispiece showing Atlas supporting the globe.

Atlas in Greek mythology, one of the ⟡Titans who revolted against the gods; as a punishment, Atlas was compelled to support the heavens on his head and shoulders. Growing weary, he asked ⟡Perseus to turn him into stone, and he was transformed into Mount Atlas.

Atlas Mountains mountain system of NW Africa, stretching 1,500 mi/2,400 km from the Atlantic coast of Morocco to the Gulf of Gabes, Tunisia, and lying between the Mediterranean on the N and the Sahara on the S. The highest peak is Mount Toubkal 13,670 ft/4,167 m.

Geologically, the Atlas Mountains compare with the ⟡Alps in age, but their structure is much less complex. They are recognized as the continuation of the great Tertiary fold mountain systems of Europe.

Atlas rocket US rocket, originally designed and built as an intercontinental missile, but subsequently adapted for space use. Atlas rockets launched astronauts in the Mercury series into orbit, as well as numerous other satellites and space probes.

atman in Hinduism, the individual soul or the eternal essential self.

atmosphere mixture of gases that surrounds the Earth, prevented from escaping by the pull of the Earth's gravity. Atmospheric pressure decreases with height in the atmosphere. In its lowest layer, the atmosphere consists of nitrogen (78%) and oxygen (21%), both in molecular form (two atoms bounded together). The other 1% is largely argon, with very small quantities of other gases, including water vapor and carbon dioxide. The atmosphere plays a major part in the various cycles of nature (the ⟡water cycle, ⟡carbon cycle, and ⟡nitrogen cycle). It is the principal industrial source of nitrogen, oxygen, and argon, which are obtained by fractional distillation of liquid air.

The lowest level of the atmosphere, the ⟡troposphere, is heated by the Earth, which is warmed by infrared and visible radiation from the Sun. Warm air cools as it rises in the troposphere, causing rain and most other weather phenomena. Infrared and visible radiations form only a part of the Sun's output of electromagnetic radiation. Almost all the shorter-wavelength ultraviolet radiation is filtered out by the upper layers of the atmosphere. The filtering process is an active one: at heights above about 31 mi/50 km ultraviolet photons collide with atoms, knocking out electrons to create a ⟡plasma of electrons and positively charged ions. The resulting *ionosphere* acts as a reflector of radio waves, enabling radio transmissions to "hop" between widely separated points on the Earth's surface. Waves of different wavelengths are reflected best at different heights. The collisions between ultraviolet photons and atoms lead to a

composition of the atmosphere

gas	symbol	volume (%)	role
nitrogen	N_2	78.08	cycled through human activities and through the action of microorganisms on animal and plant waste
oxygen	O_2	20.94	cycled mainly through the respiration of animals and plants and through the action of photosynthesis
carbon dioxide	CO_2	0.03	cycled through respiration and photosynthesis in exchange reactions with oxygen. It is also a product of burning fossil fuels
argon	Ar	0.093	chemically inert and with only a few industrial uses
neon	Ne	0.0018	as argon
helium	He	0.0005	as argon
krypton	Kr	trace	as argon
xenon	Xe	trace	as argon
ozone	O_3	0.00006	a product of oxygen molecules split into single atoms by the Sun's radiation and unaltered oxygen molecules
hydrogen	H_2	0.00005	unimportant

height in km

atmospheric pressure as fraction of pressure at sea level	atmospheric temperature	meteorological phenomena	ionosphere: regions which reflect radio waves

above about 200 km temperature of atmosphere reaches 1500°C during daytime

Appleton F₁ layer

Space shuttle

$$\frac{1}{10\,000\,000\,000}$$

regions of atmosphere classified by temperature

−100°C 0°C +100°C

short waves (nightime)

Appleton F₂ layer

short waves (daytime)

aurorae

Heaviside-Kennelly (E) layer

Thermosphere

Mesopause

$$\frac{1}{1\,000\,000}$$

medium waves

D layer

Mesosphere

Stratopause

meteors

long waves

$$\frac{1}{1\,000}$$

Stratosphere

weather balloons

ozone layer

Tropopause

Concorde

weather

$$\frac{1}{10}$$

Troposphere

Everest: 8.8 km

sea level

atmosphere *All but 1% of the Earth's atmosphere lies in a layer 19 mi/30 km above the ground.*

heating of the upper atmosphere, although the temperature drops from top to bottom within the zone called the **thermosphere** as high-energy photons are progressively absorbed in collisions. Between the thermosphere and the tropopause (at which the warming effect of the Earth starts to be felt) there is a "warm bulge" in the graph of temperature against height, at a level called the **stratopause**. This is due to longer-wavelength ultraviolet photons that have survived their journey through the upper layers; now they encounter molecules and split them apart into atoms. These atoms eventually bond together again, but often in different combinations. In particular, many

◇ozone molecules (oxygen-atom triplets) are formed. Ozone is a better absorber of ultraviolet than ordinary (two-atom) oxygen, and it is the **ozone layer** that prevents lethal amounts of ultraviolet from reaching the Earth's surface. Far above the atmosphere, as so far described, lie the **Van Allen radiation belts**. These are regions in which high-energy charged particles traveling outwards from the Sun (as the so-called solar wind) have been captured by the Earth's magnetic field. The outer belt (at about 1,000 mi/1,600 km) contains mainly protons, the inner belt (at about 1,250 mi/2,000 km) contains mainly electrons. Sometimes electrons spiral down toward the Earth, noticeably

at polar latitudes, where the magnetic field is strongest. When such particles collide with atoms and ions in the thermosphere, light is emitted. This is the origin of the glows visible in the sky as the **aurora borealis** (northern lights) and the **aurora australis** (southern lights). A fainter, more widespread, **airglow** is caused by a similar mechanism.

atmosphere or **standard atmosphere** in physics, a unit (symbol atm) of pressure equal to 760 torr, 1013.25 millibars, or 1.01325×10^5 newtons per square meter. The actual pressure exerted by the atmosphere fluctuates around this value, which is assumed to be standard at sea level and 0°C, and is used when dealing with very high pressures.

atmospheric pollution contamination of the atmosphere with the harmful by-products of human activity; see ◇pollution.

atoll continuous or broken circle of ◇coral reef and low coral islands surrounding a lagoon.

atom smallest unit of matter that can take part in a chemical reaction, and which cannot be broken down chemically into anything simpler. An atom is made up of protons and neutrons in a central nucleus surrounded by electrons (see ◇atomic structure). The atoms of the various elements differ in atomic number, atomic weight, and chemical behavior. There are 109 different types of atom, corresponding with the 109 known elements as listed in the ◇periodic table of the elements.

atomic bomb bomb deriving its explosive force from nuclear fission (see ◇nuclear energy) as a result of a neutron chain reaction, developed in the 1940s in the US into a usable weapon.

Research began in the UK 1940 and was transferred to the US after its entry into World War II the following year. Known as the **Manhattan Project**, the work was carried out under the direction of the US physicist Robert Oppenheimer at Los Alamos, New Mexico. After one test explosion, two atomic bombs were dropped on the Japanese cities of Hiroshima (Aug 6, 1945) and Nagasaki (Aug 9, 1945), each nominally equal to 200,000 tons of TNT. The USSR first detonated an atomic bomb 1949 and the UK 1952.

atomic clock timekeeping device regulated by various periodic processes occurring in atoms and molecules, such as atomic vibration or the frequency of absorbed or emitted radiation.

The first atomic clock was the **ammonia clock**, invented at the US National Bureau of Standards 1948. It was regulated by measuring the speed at which the nitrogen atom in an ammonia molecule vibrated back and forth. The rate of molecular vibration is not affected by temperature, pressure, or other external influences, and can be used to regulate an electronic clock.

A more accurate atomic clock is the **caesium clock**. Because of its internal structure, a cesium atom produces or absorbs radiation of a very precise frequency (9,192,631,770 Hz) that varies by less than one part in 10 billion. This frequency has been used to define the second, and is the basis of atomic clocks used in international timekeeping.

Hydrogen maser clocks, based on the radiation from hydrogen atoms, are the most accurate. The hydrogen maser clock at the US Naval Research Laboratory, Washington, DC, is estimated to lose one second in 1,700,000 years. Cooled hydrogen maser clocks could theoretically be accurate to within one second in 300 million years.

atomic energy former name for ⟩nuclear energy.

atomic force microscope (AFM) microscope developed in the late 1980s that produces a magnified image using a diamond probe, with a tip so fine that it may consist of a single atom, dragged over the surface of a specimen to "feel" the contours of the surface. In effect, the tip acts like the stylus of a phonograph or record player, reading the surface. The tiny up-and-down movements of the probe are converted to an image of the surface by computer, and displayed on a screen. The AFM is useful for examination of biological specimens since, unlike the ⟩scanning tunneling microscope, the specimen does not have to be electrically conducting.

atomicity number of atoms of an ⟩element that combine together to form a molecule. A molecule of oxygen (O_2) has atomicity 2; sulfur (S_8) has atomicity 8.

atomic mass unit or **dalton unit** (symbol amu or u) unit of mass that is used to measure the relative mass of atoms and molecules. It is equal to one-twelfth of the mass of a carbon-12 atom, which is equivalent to the mass of a proton or 1.66×10^{-27} kg. The ⟩atomic weight of an atom has no units; thus oxygen-16 has an atomic mass of 16 daltons, but an atomic weight of 16.

atomic number or **proton number** the number (symbol Z) of protons in the nucleus of an atom. It is equal to the positive charge on the nucleus. In a neutral atom, it is also equal to the number of electrons surrounding the nucleus. The 109 elements are arranged in the ⟩periodic table of the elements according to their atomic number. See also ⟩nuclear notation.

atomic physics former name for ⟩nuclear physics.

atomic radiation energy given out by disintegrating atoms during ⟩radioactive decay, whether natural or synthesized. The energy may be in the form of fast-moving particles, known as ⟩alpha particles and ⟩beta particles, or in the form of high-energy electromagnetic waves known as ⟩gamma radiation. Overlong exposure to atomic radiation can lead to ⟩radiation sickness. Radiation biology studies the effect of radiation on living organisms.

atomic structure internal structure of an ⟩atom. The core of the atom is the **nucleus**, a dense body only one ten-thousandth the diameter of the atom itself. The simplest nucleus, that of hydrogen, comprises a single stable positively charged particle, the **proton**. Nuclei of other elements contain more protons and additional particles, called **neutrons**, of about the same mass as the proton but with no electrical charge. Each element has its own characteristic nucleus with a unique number of protons, the atomic number. The number of neutrons may vary. Where atoms of a single element have different numbers of neutrons, they are called ⟩isotopes. Although some isotopes tend to be unstable and exhibit ⟩radioactivity, they all have identical chemical properties.

The nucleus is surrounded by a number of moving **electrons**, each of which has a negative charge equal to the positive charge on a proton, but which weighs only 1/1,839 times

as much. In a neutral atom, the nucleus is surrounded by the same number of electrons as it contains protons. According to ⟩quantum theory, the position of an electron is uncertain; it may be found at any point. However, it is more likely to be found in some places than others. The region of space in which an electron is most likely to be found is called an orbital (see ⟩orbital, atomic). The chemical properties of an element are determined by the ease with which its atoms can gain or lose electrons from its outer orbitals.

High-energy physics research has discovered the existence of subatomic particles (see ⟩particle physics) other than the proton, neutron, and electron. More than 300 kinds of particle are now known, and these are classified into several classes according to their mass, electric charge, spin, magnetic moment, and interaction. The **elementary particles**, which include the electron, are indivisible and may be regarded as the fundamental units of matter; the **hadrons**, such as the proton and neutron, are composite particles made up of either two or three elementary particles called quarks.

Atoms are held together by the electrical forces of attraction between each negative electron and the positive protons within the nucleus. The latter repel one another with enormous forces; a nucleus holds together only because an even stronger force, called the strong nuclear force, attracts the protons and neutrons to one another. The strong force acts over a very short range—the protons and neutrons must be in virtual contact with one another. If, therefore, a fragment of a complex nucleus, containing some protons, becomes only slightly loosened from the main group of neutrons and protons, the natural repulsion between the protons will cause this fragment to fly apart from the rest of the nucleus at high speed. It is by such fragmentation of atomic nuclei (nuclear ⟩fission) that nuclear energy is released.

atomic time time as given by ⟩atomic clocks, which are regulated by natural resonance frequencies of particular atoms, and display a continuous count of seconds.

In 1967 a new definition of the second was adopted in the SI system of units: the duration of 9,192,631,770 periods of the radiation corresponding to the transition between two hyperfine levels of the ground state of the cesium-133 atom. The International Atomic Time Scale is based on clock data from a number of countries; it is a continuous scale in days, hours, minutes, and seconds from the origin on Jan 1, 1958, when the Atomic Time Scale was made 0 h 0 min 0 sec when Greenwich Mean Time was at 0 h 0 min 0 sec.

atomic weight or **atomic mass** the mass of an atom. It depends on the number of protons and neutrons in the atom, the electrons having negligible mass. It is calculated relative to one-twelfth the mass of an atom of carbon-12. If more than one ⟩isotope of the element is present, the atomic weight is calculated by taking an average that takes account of the relative proportions of each isotope, resulting in values that are not whole numbers.

atomizer device that produces a spray of fine droplets of liquid. A vertical tube connected with a horizontal tube dips into a bottle of liquid, and at one end of the horizontal tube is a nozzle, at the other a rubber bulb. When the bulb is squeezed, air rushes over the top of the

vertical tube and out through the nozzle. Following ⟩Bernoulli's principle, the pressure at the top of the vertical tube is reduced, allowing the liquid to rise. The air stream picks up the liquid, breaks it up into tiny drops, and carries it out of the nozzle as a spray.

Aton in ancient Egypt, the Sun's disk as an emblem of the single deity whose worship was promoted by ⟩Ikhnaton in an attempt to replace the many gods traditionally worshiped.

atonality music in which there is an apparent absence of ⟩key; often associated with an expressionist style.

Atonality is used by film and television composers for situations of mystery or horror; it exploits **dissonance** for its power to disturb. For ⟩Schoenberg, pioneer of atonal music from 1909, the intention was to liberate tonal expression and not primarily to disturb, and he rejected the term as misleading.

atonement in Christian theology, the doctrine that Jesus suffered on the cross to bring about reconciliation and forgiveness between God and humanity.

Atonement is an action that enables a person separated from God by sin to be reconciled ("at one") with him. In ancient Judaism this was achieved through the sacrificial killing of animals.

Atonement, Day of Jewish holy day (**Yom Kippur**) held on the tenth day of Tishri (Sept–Oct), the first month of the Jewish year. It is a day of fasting, penitence, and cleansing from sin, ending the Ten Days of Penitence that follow **Rosh Hashanah**, the Jewish New Year.

ATP abbreviation for **adenosine triphosphate**, a nucleotide molecule found in all cells. It can yield large amounts of energy, and is used to drive the thousands of biological processes needed to sustain life, growth, movement, and reproduction. Green plants use light energy to manufacture ATP as part of the process of ⟩photosynthesis. In animals, ATP is formed by the breakdown of glucose molecules, usually obtained from the carbohydrate component of a diet, in a series of reactions termed ⟩respiration. It is the driving force behind muscle contraction and the synthesis of complex molecules needed by individual cells.

Atreus in Greek mythology, the father of Agamemnon and Menelaus (the Atridae), son of Pelops, and brother of Thyestes, with whom he contested the throne of ⟩Mycenae. As part of the feud, Atreus served the flesh of Thyestes' children to their father at a banquet held to confirm the reconciliation of the two brothers.

atrium in architecture, an open inner courtyard. Originally the central court or main room of an ancient Roman house, open to the sky, often with a shallow pool to catch water.

atrium one of the upper chambers of the heart, receiving blood under low pressure as it returns from the body. Atrium walls are thin and stretch easily to allow blood into the heart. On contraction, the atria force blood into the thick-walled ventricles, which then give a second, more powerful beat.

atrophy in medicine, a diminution in size and function, or output, of a body tissue or organ. It is usually due to nutritional impairment, disease, or disuse (muscle).

atropine alkaloid derived from belladonna, a plant with toxic properties. It acts as an ⟩anticholinergic, inhibiting the passage of certain nerve impulses. As atropine sulfate, it is administered as a mild antispasmodic drug.

Atropine is named after Atropos, one of the three Greek Fates, who cut people's lives short.

attainder, bill of legislative device that allowed the English Parliament to declare guilt and impose a punishment on an individual without bringing the matter before the courts. Such bills were used intermittently from the Wars of the Roses until 1798. Some acts of attainder were also passed by US colonial legislators during the American Revolution to deal with "loyalists" who continued to support the English crown.

Bills of attainder were expressly forbidden by the US Constitution. The use of the device has generally been deplored as it did not require the accusers to prove their case.

attempt in law, a partial or unsuccessful commission of a crime. An attempt must be more than preparation for a crime; it must involve actual efforts to commit a crime.

Attenborough Richard 1923– . English actor, director, and producer. He began his acting career in war films and comedies. His later films include *Brighton Rock* 1947 and *10 Rillington Place* 1970 (as actor), and *Oh! What a Lovely War* 1969, *Gandhi* (which won eight Academy Awards) 1982, *Cry Freedom* 1987, and *Chaplin* 1992 (as director).

Attica (Greek *Attiki*) region of Greece comprising Athens and the district around it; area 1,305 sq mi/3,381 sq km. It is renowned for its language, art, and philosophical thought in Classical times. It is a prefecture of modern Greece with Athens as its capital.

Attila c. 406–453. King of the Huns in an area from the Alps to the Caspian Sea from 434, known to later Christian history as the "Scourge of God." He twice attacked the Eastern Roman Empire to increase the quantity of tribute paid to him, 441–443 and 447–449, and then attacked the Western Roman Empire 450–52.

Attila first ruled jointly with his brother Bleda, whom he murdered in 444. In 450 Honoria, the sister of the western emperor Valentinian III, appealed to him to rescue her from an arranged marriage, and Attila used her appeal to attack the West. He was forced back from Orléans by Aetius and Theodoric, king of the Visigoths, and defeated by them on the ◊Catalaunian Fields in 451. In 452 he led the Huns into Italy, and was induced to withdraw by Pope ◊Leo I.

He died on the night of his marriage to the German Ildico, either by poison, or, as Chaucer represents it in his *Pardoner's Tale*, from a nasal haemorrhage induced by drunkenness.

Attila lived in relative simplicity in his camp close to the Danube, which was described by the Greek historian Priscus after a diplomatic mission. But his advisers included a Greek Orestes, and his control over a large territory required administrative abilities. His conscious aims were to prevent the Huns from serving in the imperial armies, and to use force to exact as much tribute or land from both parts of the empire as he could. His burial place was kept secret.

Attis in Classical mythology, a Phrygian god whose death and resurrection symbolized the end of winter and the arrival of spring. Beloved by the goddess ◊Cybele, who drove him mad as a punishment for his infidelity, he castrated himself and bled to death.

Attleboro city in SE Massachusetts, NW of New Bedford. Manufactures include jewelry, tools, silver products, electronics, and paper goods; population (1990) 38,400.

Attlee Clement (Richard), 1st Earl 1883–1967. British Labour politician. In the coalition government during World War II he was Lord Privy Seal 1940–42, dominions secretary 1942–43, and Lord President of the Council 1943–45, as well as deputy prime minister from 1942. As prime minister 1945–51 he introduced a sweeping program of nationalization and a whole new system of social services.

attorney person who represents another in legal matters. In the US, attorney is the formal title for a lawyer.

See also ◊power of attorney.

Attorney General principal law officer. In the US, the principal officer of the federal government or of a state. Attorneys general act as chief officers for criminal and civil law and as chief legal representatives of their governments in government operations.

Atwood Margaret (Eleanor) 1939– . Canadian novelist, short-story writer, and poet. Her novels, which often treat feminist themes with wit and irony, include *The Edible Woman* 1969, *Life Before Man* 1979, *Bodily Harm* 1981, *The Handmaid's Tale* 1986, and *Cat's Eye* 1989.

Collections of poetry include *Power Politics* 1971, *You are Happy* 1974, and *Interlunar* 1984.

Auber Daniel François Esprit 1782–1871. French operatic composer who studied under the Italian composer and teacher Cherubini. He wrote about 50 operas, including *La Muette de Portici/The Mute Girl of Portici* 1828 and the comic opera *Fra Diavolo* 1830.

aubrieta any spring-flowering dwarf perennial plant of the genus *Aubrieta* of the cress family Cruciferae. All are trailing plants with showy, purple flowers. Native to the Middle East, they are cultivated widely in rock gardens.

Auburn city in SW Maine on the Adroscoggin River, W of Lewiston; seat of Androscoggin county. Industries include shoes, textiles, poultry, livestock, and bricks; population (1990) 24,300.

Auchinleck Sir Claude John Eyre 1884–1981. British commander in World War II. He won the First Battle of El ◊Alamein 1942 in N Egypt. In 1943 he became commander in chief in India and founded the modern Indian and Pakistani armies. In 1946 he was promoted to field marshal; he retired 1947.

Auckland largest city in New Zealand, situated in N North Island; population (1989) 850,900. It fills the isthmus that separates its two harbors (Waitemata and Manukau), and its suburbs spread north across the Harbor Bridge. It is the country's chief port and leading industrial center, having iron and steel plants, engineering, car assembly, textiles, food processing, sugar refining, and brewing.

There was a small whaling settlement on the site in the 1830s, and Auckland was officially founded as New Zealand's capital 1840, remaining so until 1865. The university was founded 1882.

Auckland Islands six uninhabited volcanic islands 300 mi/480 km S of South Island, New Zealand; area 23 sq mi/60 sq km.

auction the sale of goods or property in public to the highest bidder. There are usually conditions of sale by which all bidders are bound. Leading world auctioneers are Christie's and Sotheby's.

A bid may be withdrawn at any time before the auctioneer brings down the hammer, and the seller is likewise entitled to withdraw any lot before the hammer falls. In recent years, auction houses have been increasingly examined for illegal practices. It is illegal for the seller or anyone on their behalf to make a bid for their own goods unless their right to do so has been reserved and notified before the sale. Christie's New York Chairman, Donald Bathurst, resigned after he was found to have falsely stated that some paintings had been sold, a practice known as "buying-in." "Rings" of dealers agreeing to keep prices down are illegal. A reserve price is kept secret, but an upset price (the minimum price fixed for the property offered) is made public before the sale. An auction where property is first offered at a high price and gradually reduced until a bid is received is known as a *"Dutch auction"*.

Aude river in SE France, 130 mi/210 km long, that gives its name to a *département*. Carcassonne is the main town through which it passes.

Auden W(ystan) H(ugh) 1907–1973. English-born US poet. He wrote some of his most original poetry, such as *Look, Stranger!* 1936, in the 1930s when he led the influential left-wing literary group that included Louis MacNeice, Stephen Spender, and Cecil Day Lewis. He moved to the US 1939, became a US citizen 1946, and adopted a more conservative and Christian viewpoint, for example in *The Age of Anxiety* 1947.

audiometer electrical instrument used to test hearing.

audit official inspection of a company's accounts by a qualified accountant as required by law each year to ensure that the company balance sheet reflects the true state of its affairs.

auditory canal tube leading from the outer ◊ear opening to the eardrum. It is found only in animals whose eardrums are located inside the skull, principally mammals and birds.

Audubon John James 1785–1851. US naturalist and artist. In 1827, after extensive travels and observations of birds, he published the first part of his *Birds of North America*, with a remarkable series of color plates. Later he produced a similar work on North American quadrupeds.

He was born in Santo Domingo (now Haiti) and educated in Paris. The National Audubon Society (founded 1886) has branches throughout the US and Canada for the study and protection of birds.

Augean stables in Greek mythology, the stables of Augeas, king of Elis in Greece. One of the labors of ◊Heracles was to clean out the stables, which contained 3,000 cattle and had never been cleaned before. He was given only one day to do the labor and so diverted the river Alpheus through their yard.

Augsburg industrial city in Bavaria, Germany, at the confluence of the Wertach and Lech rivers, 32 mi/52 km NW of Munich; population (1988) 246,000. It is named after the Roman emperor Augustus, who founded it 15 BC.

Augsburg, Confession of statement of the Protestant faith as held by the German Reformers, composed by Philip ◊Melanchthon. Presented to the holy Roman emperor Charles V, at the conference known as the Diet of Augsburg 1530, it is the creed of the modern Lutheran church.

Augsburg, Peace of religious settlement following the Diet of Augsburg 1555, which established the right of princes in the Holy Roman Empire (rather than the emperor himself, Ferdinand I) to impose a religion on their subjects—later summarized by the maxim ◊*cuius regio, eius religio* ("those who live in a country shall adopt the religion of its leader"). It initially applied only to Lutherans and Catholics.

augur member of a college of Roman priests who interpreted the will of the gods from signs or "auspices" such as the flight of birds, the condition of entrails of sacrificed animals, and the direction of thunder and lightning. Their advice was sought before battle and on other important occasions. Consuls and other high officials had the right to consult the auspices themselves, and a campaign was said to be conducted "under the auspices" of the general who had consulted the gods.

Augusta capital of Maine, located in SW part of the state, on the Kennebec River, NE of Lewiston and Auburn. Industries include cotton, timber, and textiles; population (1990) 21,300.

Augusta city in E central Georgia, on the Savannah River on the South Carolina border; seat of Richmond county. It is a manufacturing city and terminal for river barges. Industries include textiles and other cotton products and building materials; population (1990) 44,600. Established 1736 as Fort Augusta, an Indian trading post, it was the site of several battles during the American Revolution and served as Georgia's capital 1786–95.

Augustan Age golden age of the Roman emperor ◊Augustus, during which art and literature flourished. The name is also given to later periods which used Classical ideals, such as that of Queen Anne in England.

Augustine of Hippo, St 354–430. One of the early Christian leaders and writers known as the Fathers of the Church. He was converted to Christianity by Ambrose in Milan and became bishop of Hippo (modern Annaba, Algeria) 396. Among Augustine's many writings are his *Confessions*, a spiritual autobiography, and *De Civitate Dei/The City of God*, vindicating the Christian church and divine providence in 22 books.

Augustine, St first archbishop of Canterbury, England. He was sent from Rome to convert England to Christianity by Pope Gregory I. He landed at Ebbsfleet in Kent 597, and soon after baptized Ethelbert, King of Kent, along with many of his subjects. He was consecrated bishop of the English at Arles in the same year, and appointed archbishop 601, establishing his see at Canterbury. Feast day May 26.

Augustinian member of a religious community that follows the Rule of St ◊Augustine of Hippo. It includes the Canons of St Augustine, Augustinian Friars and Hermits, Premonstratensians, Gilbertines, and Trinitarians.

Augustus 63 BC–AD 14. Title of Octavian (Gaius Julius Caesar Octavianus), first of the Roman emperors. He joined forces with Mark Antony and Lepidus in the Second Triumvirate. Following Mark Antony's liaison with the Egyptian queen Cleopatra, Augustus defeated her troops at Actium 31 BC. As emperor (from 27 BC) he reformed the government of the empire, the army, and Rome's public services, and was a patron of the arts. The period of his rule is known as the ◊Augustan Age.

He was the son of a senator who married a niece of Julius Caesar, and he became his great-uncle's adopted son and principal heir. Following Caesar's murder, Octavian formed with Mark Antony and Lepidus the Triumvirate that divided the Roman world between them and proceeded to eliminate the opposition. Antony's victory 42 BC over Brutus and Cassius had brought the republic to an end. Antony then became enamored of Cleopatra and spent most of his time at Alexandria, while Octavian consolidated his hold on the western part of the Roman dominion. War was declared against Cleopatra, and the naval victory at Actium left Octavian in unchallenged supremacy, since Lepidus had been forced to retire. After his return to Rome 29 BC, Octavian was created *princeps senatus*, and in 27 BC he was given the title of Augustus ("venerable"). He then resigned his extraordinary powers and received from the Senate, in return, the proconsular command, which gave him control of the army, and the tribunician power, whereby he could initiate or veto legislation. In his program of reforms Augustus received the support of three loyal and capable helpers, Agrippa, Maecenas, and his wife, Livia, while Virgil and Horace acted as the poets laureate of the new regime. A firm frontier for the empire was established: to the north, the friendly Batavians held the Rhine delta, and then the line followed the course of the Rhine and Danube; to the east, the Parthians were friendly, and the Euphrates gave the next line; to the south, the African colonies were protected by the desert; to the west were Spain and Gaul. The provinces were governed either by imperial legates responsible to the *princeps* or by proconsuls appointed by the Senate. The army was made a profession, with fixed pay and length of service, and a permanent fleet was established. Finally, Rome itself received an adequate water supply, a fire brigade, a police force, and a large number of public buildings. The years after 12 BC were marked by private and public calamities: the marriage of Augustus' daughter Julia to his stepson Tiberius proved disastrous; a serious revolt occurred in Pannonia AD 6; and in Germany three legions under Varus were annihilated in the Teutoburg Forest AD 9. Augustus died a broken man, but his work remained secure.

auk any member of the family Alcidae, consisting of marine diving birds including razorbills, puffins, murres, and guillemots. Confined to the northern hemisphere, they feed on fish and use their wings to "fly" underwater in pursuit.

The largest was the **great auk** *Pinguinis impennis*, 2.5 ft/75 cm and flightless, the last recorded individual being killed in 1844. The smallest is the least auklet, *Aethia pusilla*, 6 in/15 cm long. It is found along Pacific coasts from Siberia to Alaska.

Aulis anchorage on the eastern coast of Greece, opposite the island of ◊Euboea. In Greek mythology, the point of departure for the Greek expedition against ◊Troy.

Aung San 1916–1947. Burmese politician. He was a founder and leader of the Anti-Fascist People's Freedom League, which led Burma's fight for independence from Great Britain. During World War II he collaborated first with Japan and then with the UK. In 1947 he became head of Burma's provisional government but was assassinated the same year by political opponents; Burma (now Myanmar) became independent 1948.

Aurangzeb or *Aurungzebe* 1618–1707. Mogul emperor of N India from 1658. Third son of Shah Jahan, he made himself master of the court by a palace revolution. His reign was the most brilliant period of the Mogul dynasty, but his despotic tendencies and Muslim fanaticism aroused much opposition. His latter years were spent in war with the princes of Rajputana and Maratha.

Aurelian (Lucius Domitius Aurelianus) *c.* AD 214–275. Roman emperor from 270. A successful soldier, he was chosen emperor by his troops on the death of Claudius II. He defeated the Goths and Vandals, defeated and captured ◊Zenobia of Palmyra, and was planning a campaign against Parthia when he was murdered. The **Aurelian Wall**, a fortification surrounding Rome, was built by Aurelian 271. It was made of concrete, and substantial ruins exist. The **Aurelian Way** ran from Rome through Pisa and Genoa to Antipolis (Antibes) in Gaul.

Aurelius Antoninus Marcus Roman emperor; see ◊Marcus Aurelius Antoninus.

Auric Georges 1899–1983. French composer. He was one of the musical group called ◊*Les Six*. Auric composed a comic opera, several ballets, and incidental music to films of Jean Cocteau.

auricula species of primrose *Primula auricula*, a plant whose leaves are said to resemble bear's ears. It is native to the Alps but popular in cool-climate areas and often cultivated in gardens.

Auriga constellation of the northern hemisphere, represented as a man driving a chariot. Its brightest star is the first-magnitude ◊Capella, about 45 light-years from Earth; Epsilon Aurigae is an ◊eclipsing binary star with a period of 27 years, the longest of its kind (last eclipse 1983).

The charioteer is usually identified as Erichthonius, legendary king of Athens, who invented the four-horse chariot.

Aurignacian in archeology, an Old Stone Age culture that came between the Mousterian and the Solutrian in the Upper Paleolithic. The name is derived from a cave at Aurignac in the Pyrenees of France. The earliest cave paintings are attributed to the Aurignacian peoples of W Europe about 16,000 BC.

Auriol Vincent 1884–1966. French Socialist politician. He was president of the two Constituent Assemblies of 1946 and first president of the Fourth Republic 1947–54.

aurochs (plural **aurochs**) extinct species of long-horned wild cattle *Bos primigenius* that formerly roamed Europe, SW Asia, and N Africa. It survived in Poland until 1627. Black to reddish or gray, it was up to 6 ft/1.8 m at the shoulder. It is depicted in many cave paintings, and is considered the ancestor of domestic cattle.

aurora colored light in the night sky near the Earth's magnetic poles, called **aurora borealis**, "northern lights," in the northern hemisphere and **aurora australis** in the southern hemisphere. An aurora is usually in the form of a luminous arch with its apex toward the magnetic pole followed by arcs, bands, rays, curtains, and coronas, usually green but often showing shades of blue and red, and sometimes yellow or white. Auroras are caused at heights of over 60 mi/100 km by a fast stream of charged particles from solar flares and low-density "holes" in the Sun's corona. These are guided by the Earth's magnetic field toward the north and south magnetic poles, where they enter the upper atmosphere and bombard the gases in the atmosphere, causing them to emit visible light.

The French philosopher Gassendi coined the term "northern dawn" 1621.

Aurora Roman goddess of the dawn. The Greek equivalent is *Eos*.

Aurora city in NE Illinois, on the Fox River, W of Chicago. Manufactures include transportation equipment, glass, and chemicals. It was a pioneer in the use of electric street lights; population (1990) 99,600.

Auschwitz (Polish *Oswiecim*) town near Kraków in Poland, the site of a notorious ◊concentration camp used by the Nazis in World War II to exterminate Jews and other political and social minorities, as part of the "final solution." Each of the four gas chambers could hold 6,000 people.

Austen Jane 1775–1817. English novelist who described her raw material as "three or four families in a Country Village." *Sense and Sensibility* was published 1811, *Pride and Prejudice* 1813, *Mansfield Park* 1814, *Emma* 1816, *Northanger Abbey* and *Persuasion* 1818, all anonymously. She observed speech and manners with wit and precision, revealing her characters' absurdities in relation to high standards of integrity and appropriateness.

She was born at Steventon, Hampshire, where her father was rector, and began writing early; the burlesque *Love and Freindship* (sic), published 1922, was written 1790. In 1801 the family moved to Bath and after the death of her father in 1805, to Southampton, finally settling in Chawton, Hampshire, with her brother Edward. Between 1795 and 1798 she worked on three novels. The first to be published (like its successors, anonymously) was *Sense and Sensibility* (drafted in letter form 1797–98). *Pride and Prejudice* (written 1796–97) followed, but *Northanger Abbey*, a skit on the contemporary Gothic novel (written 1798, sold to a London publisher 1803, and bought back 1816), did not appear until 1818. The fragmentary *Watsons* and *Lady Susan*, written about 1803–05, remained unfinished. The success of her published works, however, stimulated Jane Austen to write in rapid succession *Mansfield Park*, *Emma*, *Persuasion*, and the final fragment *Sanditon* written 1817. She died in Winchester, and is buried in the cathedral.

Auster Paul 1947– . US novelist. His experimental use of detective-story techniques to explore modern urban identity is exemplified in his *New York Trilogy: City of Glass* 1985, *Ghosts* 1986, and *The Locked Room* 1986.

Austerlitz, Battle of battle on Dec 2, 1805 in which the French forces of Emperor Napoleon defeated those of Alexander I of Russia and Francis II of Austria at a small town in Czechoslovakia (formerly in Austria), 12 mi/ 19 km E of Brno.

Austin capital of Texas, on the Colorado River; population (1990) 465,600. It is a center for electronic and scientific research.

It is the home of the University of Texas and the Lyndon B Johnson Library and Museum. The state capitol, 308 ft/94 m high, is the largest of any state. Austin was founded 1838 and developed as a stop on the Chisholm cattle-drive trail in the 1860s.

Austin Herbert, 1st Baron 1866–1941. English industrialist who began manufacturing automobiles 1905 in Northfield, Birmingham, notably the Austin Seven 1921.

Austin Stephen Fuller 1793–1836. American pioneer and political leader. Born in Austinville, Virginia, he grew up in Missouri and followed his father to Texas 1821. Accepting Mexican citizenship, Austin was granted political privileges and encouraged the settlement of Americans in Texas. However, in 1833 he was imprisoned for his support for Texas autonomy. When he was released 1835, the Texas Revolution was already underway, and Austin was dispatched to the US to gain support for the cause. After the war he was appointed secretary of state of the Republic of Texas. The state capital of Austin was named in his honor.

Australasia loosely applied geographical term, usually meaning Australia, New Zealand, and neighboring islands.

Australia country occupying all of the Earth's

Australia
Commonwealth of

area 2,966,136 sq mi/7,682,300 sq km
capital Canberra
cities Adelaide, Alice Springs, Brisbane, Darwin, Melbourne, Perth, Sydney, Hobart, Geelong, Newcastle, Townsville, Wollongong
physical the world's smallest, flattest, and driest continent (40% lies in the tropics, one-third is desert, and one-third is marginal grazing); Great Sandy Desert; Gibson Desert; Great Victoria Desert; Simpson Desert; the Great Barrier Reef (largest coral reef in the world, stretching 1,250 mi/2,000 km off E coast of Queensland); Great Dividing Range and Australian Alps in the E (Mount Kosciusko, 7,136 ft/2,229 m, Australia's highest peak). The fertile SE region is watered by the Darling, Lachlan, Murrumbridgee, and Murray rivers; rivers in the interior are seasonal. Lake Eyre basin and Nullarbor Plain in the S
territories Norfolk Island, Christmas Island, Cocos (Keeling) Islands, Ashmore and Cartier Islands, Coral Sea Islands, Heard Island and McDonald Islands, Australian Antarctic Territory
environment an estimated 75% of Australia's northern tropical rainforest has been cleared for agriculture or urban development since Europeans first settled there in the early 19th century
features Ayers Rock; Arnhem Land; Gulf of Carpentaria; Cape York Peninsula; Great Australian Bight; unique animal species include the kangaroo, koala, platypus, wombat, Tasmanian devil, and spiny anteater; of 800 species of bird, the budgerigar, cassowary, emu, kookaburra, lyre bird, and black swan are also unique as a result of Australia's long isolation from other continents
head of state Elizabeth II from 1952 represented by governor-general
head of government Paul Keating from 1991
political system federal constitutional monarchy
political parties Australian Labor Party (ALP), moderate left of center; Liberal Party of Australia, moderate, liberal, free enterprise; National Party of Australia (formerly Country Party), centrist non-metropolitan

exports world's largest exporter of sheep, wool, diamonds, alumina, coal, lead and refined zinc ores, and mineral sands; other exports include cereals, beef, veal, mutton, lamb, sugar, nickel (world's second largest producer), iron ore; principal trade partners are Japan, the US, and EC member states
currency Australian dollar
population (1990 est) 16,650,000; growth rate 1.5% p.a.
life expectancy men 75, women 80
languages English, Aboriginal languages
religions Anglican 26%, other Protestant 17%, Roman Catholic 26%
literacy 98.5.% (1988)
GDP $220.96 bn (1988); $14,458 per head
chronology
1901 Creation of Commonwealth of Australia.
1911 Site acquired for capital at Canberra.
1927 Seat of government moved to Canberra.
1942 Statute of Westminster Adoption Act gave Australia autonomy from UK in internal and external affairs.
1944 Liberal Party founded by Robert Menzies.
1951 Australia joined New Zealand and the US as a signatory to the ANZUS Pacific security treaty.
1966 Menzies resigned after being Liberal prime minister for 17 years, and was succeeded by Harold Holt.
1967 A referendum was passed giving Aborigines full citizenship rights.
1968 John Gorton became prime minister after Holt's death.
1971 Gorton succeeded by William McMahon, heading a Liberal–Country Party coalition.
1972 Gough Whitlam became prime minister, leading a Labor government.
1975 Senate blocked the government's financial legislation; Whitlam dismissed by the governor-general, who invited Malcolm Fraser to form a Liberal–Country Party caretaker government. The action of the governor-general, John Kerr, was widely criticized.
1977 Kerr resigned.
1978 Northern Territory attained self-government.
1983 Australian Labor Party, returned to power under Bob Hawke, convened meeting of employers and unions to seek consensus on economic policy to deal with growing unemployment.
1986 Australia Act passed by UK government, eliminating last vestiges of British legal authority in Australia.
1988 Labor foreign minister Bill Hayden appointed governor-general designate. Free-trade agreement with New Zealand signed.
1990 Hawke won record fourth election victory, defeating Liberal Party by small majority.
1991 Paul Keating became new Labor Party leader and prime minister.
1992 Keating's popularity in decline as economic problems continued.

smallest continent, situated S of Indonesia, between the Pacific and Indian oceans.

government Australia is an independent sovereign nation within the Commonwealth, retaining the British monarch as head of state and represented by a governor-general. The constitution came into effect Jan 1, 1901. As in the British system, the executive, comprising the prime minister and cabinet, is drawn from the federal parliament and is answerable to it. The parliament consists of two chambers: an elected senate of 76 (12 for each of the six states, two for the Australian Capital Territory, and two for the Northern Territory); and a house of representatives of 148, elected by universal adult suffrage. Senators serve for six years, and members of the house for three years. Voting is compulsory; the senate is elected by proportional representation, but the house of representatives is elected as single-member constituencies with preferential voting. Each state has its own constitution, governor (the monarch's representative), executive (drawn from the parliament), and legislative and judicial system. Each territory has its own legislative assembly. The last relics of UK legislative control over Australia were removed 1986.

history Australia's first inhabitants, the Aborigines, arrived in Australia at least 40,000 years ago, according to present evidence. The first recorded sighting of Australia by Europeans was 1606, when the Dutch ship *Duyfken* sighted the W coast of Cape York and the Spanish ship of Luis Vaez de Torres sailed N of Cape York and through Torres Strait, thus proving that New Guinea was separate from any southern continent. Later voyagers include Dirk Hartog 1616 – who left an inscribed pewter plate (Australia's most famous early European relic, now in Amsterdam) in W Australia—Abel ⭧Tasman, and William ⭧Dampier. A second wave of immigration began 1788, after Capt James ⭧Cook had claimed New South Wales as a British colony 1770.

colonies established The gold rushes of the 1850s and 1880s contributed to the exploration as well as to the economic and constitutional growth of Australia, as did the pioneer work of the overlanders (cattle drivers). The creation of other separate colonies followed the first settlement in New South Wales at Sydney 1788: Tasmania 1825, Western Australia 1829, South Australia 1836, Victoria 1851, and Queensland 1859. The system of transportation of convicts from Britain was never introduced in South Australia and Victoria, and ended in New South Wales 1840, Queensland 1849, Tasmania 1852, and Western Australia 1868. The convicts' contribution to the economic foundation of the country was considerable, and many would not have been convicted under a less harsh and capricious penal system than the one operating in Britain at that time.

inland exploration by Europeans Exploration of the interior began with the crossing of the barrier of the ⭧Blue Mountains 1813. Explorers include Hamilton Hume (1797–1873) and William Hovell (1786–1875) who reached Port Phillip Bay 1824 and were the first Europeans to see the Murray River; Charles ⭧Sturt; Thomas Mitchell (1792–1855), surveyor general for New South Wales 1828–55, who opened up the fertile western area of Victoria; Ludwig Leichhardt, Robert O'Hara ⭧Burke and William Wills (1834–1861), and John ⭧Stuart. In the 1870s the last gaps were filled in by the crossings of W Australia by John ⭧Forrest, (William) Ernest Giles (1835–

1897) 1875–76, and Peter Warburton (1813–1889) 1873.

economic depression and growth In the 1890s there was a halt in the rapid expansion that Australia had enjoyed, and the resulting depression led to the formation of the Australian Labor Party and an increase in labor-union activity, which has characterized Australian politics ever since. State powers waned following the creation of the Commonwealth of Australia 1901. Australia played an important role in both world wars, and after World War II it embarked on a fresh period of expansion, with new mineral finds playing a large part in economic growth. Since 1945 Australia has strengthened its ties with India and other SE Asian countries.

growth of nationalism After heading a Liberal–Country Party coalition government for 17 years, Robert Menzies resigned 1966 and was succeeded by Harold Holt, who died 1967. John Gorton became prime minister 1968 but lost a vote of confidence in the house of representatives and was succeeded by a Liberal–Country Party coalition under William McMahon 1971. At the end of 1972 the Australian Labor Party took office, led by Gough Whitlam. Under the Whitlam government, especially after Britain's entry into the European Community 1973, there was a growth of nationalism. The 1974 general election gave the Labor Party a fresh mandate to govern despite having a reduced majority in the house of representatives.

1975 constitutional crisis The senate blocked the government's financial legislation 1975 and, with Whitlam unwilling to resign, the governor-general took the unprecedented step of dismissing him and his cabinet and inviting Malcolm ⭧Fraser to form a Liberal–Country Party coalition caretaker administration. The wisdom of this action was widely questioned, and eventually governor-general John Kerr resigned 1977. In the 1977 general election the coalition was returned with a reduced majority that was further reduced 1980.

Hawke era In the 1983 general election the coalition was eventually defeated and the Australian Labor Party under Bob ⭧Hawke again took office. Hawke called together employers and unions to a National Economic

Australia, Commonwealth of

state	capital	area in sq km
New South Wales	Sydney	801,600
Queensland	Brisbane	1,727,200
South Australia	Adelaide	984,000
Tasmania	Hobart	67,800
Victoria	Melbourne	227,600
Western Australia	Perth	2,525,500
territories		
Northern Territory	Darwin	1,346,200
Capital Territory	Canberra	2,400
		7,682,300
external territories		
Ashmore and Cartier Islands		5
Australian Antarctic Territory		6,044,000
Christmas Island		135
Cocos (Keeling) Islands		14
Coral Sea Islands		1,000,000
Heard Island and McDonald Islands		410
Norfolk Island		40

Summit to agree to a wage and price policy and to deal with unemployment. In 1984 he called a general election 15 months early and was returned with a reduced majority. Hawke placed even greater emphasis than his predecessors on links with SE Asia and imposed trading sanctions against South Africa as a means of influencing the dismantling of apartheid. In the 1987 general election, Labor marginally increased its majority in the House but did not have an overall majority in the Senate, where the balance was held by the Australian Democrats. The 1990 election was won by Labor, led by Bob Hawke, with a reduced majority in the house of representatives, for a record fourth term in office. The Australian Democrats maintained the balance of power in the senate. In Aug 1991 Hawke announced that agreement had been reached on greater cohesion of the states' economies.

Keating as prime minister In Dec 1991 Hawke's leadership of the Labor Party was successfully challenged by Paul Keating, who became the new party leader and prime minister. Hawke retired from politics Jan 1992. Despite Keating's "kickstart" plan to boost a stagnant economy announced Feb 1992, Australia's unemployment rate reached a record 11.1% in July. Keating's inability to tackle the effects of the recession was seen as the main reason for his waning popularity. An expansionary budget outlined in Aug was criticized by the opposition as an attempt to gain support for the Labor Party in preparation for the 1993 elections.

Australia Day Australian national day and public vacation in Australia, the anniversary of Captain Phillip's arrival on Jan 26, 1788 at Sydney Cove in Port Jackson and the founding of the colony of New South Wales.

Australian Aborigine any of the 500 groups of indigenous inhabitants of the continent of Australia, who migrated to this region from S Asia about 40,000 years ago. They are dark-skinned Caucasoids, with fair hair in childhood and heavy dark beards and body hair in adult males. They were hunters and gatherers, living throughout the continent in small kin-based groups before European settlement. Several hundred different languages developed, including Aranda (Arunta), spoken in central Australia, and Murngin, spoken in Arnhem Land. In recent years a movement for the recognition of Aborigine rights has begun, with campaigns against racial discrimination in housing, education, wages, and medical facilities.

Aborigines make up 1% of Australia's population of 16 million. They live in reserves as well as among the general population. They have an infant mortality four times the national average and an adult life expectancy 20 years below the average 76 years of other Australians.

Australian Antarctic Territory islands and territories S of 60° S, between 160° E and 45° E longitude, excluding Adélie Land; area 2,332,984 sq mi/6,044,000 sq km of land and 29,259 sq mi/75,800 sq km of ice shelf. The population on the Antarctic continent is limited to research personnel.

There are scientific bases at Mawson (1954) in MacRobertson Land, named after the explorer; at Davis (1957) on the coast of Princess Elizabeth Land, named in honor of Mawson's second-in-command; at Casey (1969) in Wilkes Land, named after Lord Casey; and at Macquarie Island (1948). The Australian Antarctic Territory came into being

1933, when established by a British Order in Council.

Australian art art in Australia dates back to early Aboriginal works some 15,000 years ago. These are closely linked with religion and mythology and include rock and bark paintings. True Aboriginal art is now rare. European-style art developed in the 17th century, with landscape painting predominating.

precolonial art Pictures and decorated objects were produced in nearly all settled areas. Subjects included humans, animals, and geometric ornament. The "X-ray style," showing the inner organs in an animal portrait, is unique to Australian Aboriginal art.

17th–18th centuries The first European paintings were topographical scenes of and around Sydney.

late 19th–early 20th century The landscape painters of the Heidelberg School, notably Tom Roberts and later Arthur Streeton (1867–1943), became known outside Australia.

20th century The figurative painters William Dobell, Russell Drysdale, Sidney Nolan, and Albert Namatjira are among Australia's modern artists.

Australian Capital Territory territory ceded to Australia by New South Wales 1911 to provide the site of ⟡Canberra, with its port

Austria
Republic of (*Republik Österreich*)

area 32,374 sq mi/83,500 sq km
capital Vienna
cities Graz, Linz, Salzburg, Innsbruck
physical landlocked mountainous state, with Alps in W and S and low relief in E where most of the population is concentrated
environment Hainburg, the largest primeval forest left in Europe, under threat from a dam project (suspended 1990)
features Austrian Alps (including Grossglockner and Brenner and Semmering passes); Lechtaler and Allgauer Alps N of river Inn; Carnic Alps on Italian border; river Danube
head of state Thomas Klestil from 1992
head of government Franz Vranitzky from 1986
political system democratic federal republic
political parties Socialist Party of Austria (SPÖ), democratic socialist; Austrian People's Party (ÖVP), progressive centrist; Freedom Party of Austria (FPÖ), moderate left of center; United Green Party of Austria (VGÖ),

at Jervis Bay, ceded 1915; area 926 sq mi/ 2,400 sq km; population (1987) 261,000.

Australian literature Australian literature begins with the letters, journals, and memoirs of early settlers and explorers. The first poet of note was Charles Harpur (1813–1868); idioms and rhythms typical of the country were developed by, among others, Henry Kendall (1841–1882) and Andrew Barton (Banjo) Paterson (1864–1941). More recent poets include Christopher Brennan and Judith Wright, Kenneth Slessor (1901–1971), R D (Robert David) Fitzgerald (1902–), A D (Alec Derwent) Hope (1907–), and James McAuley (1917–1976). Among early Australian novelists are Marcus Clarke, Rolfe Boldrewood, and Henry Handel Richardson (1870–1946). Striking a harsh vein in contemporary themes are the dramatist Ray Lawler and novelist Patrick ⟡White; the latter received the Nobel Prize for Literature in 1973. Thomas Keneally won the Booker Prize in 1982 for *Schindler's Ark*.

Austral Islands alternate name for ⟡Tubuai Islands, part of ⟡French Polynesia.

Austria landlocked country in central Europe, bounded E by Hungary, S by Slovenia and Italy, W by Switzerland and Liechtenstein, NW by Germany, and N by Czechoslovakia.

government Austria is a federal republic

conservative ecological; Green Alternative Party (ALV), radical ecological
exports lumber, textiles, clothing, iron and steel, paper, machinery and transport equipment, foodstuffs
currency schilling
population (1990 est) 7,595,000; growth rate 0.1% p.a.
life expectancy men 70, women 77
language German
religions Roman Catholic 85%, Protestant 6%
literacy 98% (1983)
GDP $183.3 bn (1987); $11,337 per head
chronology
1867 Emperor Franz Josef established dual monarchy of Austria-Hungary.
1914 Archduke Franz Ferdinand assassinated by a Serbian nationalist; Austria-Hungary invaded Serbia, precipitating World War I.
1918 Hapsburg empire ended; republic proclaimed.
1938 Austria incorporated into German Third Reich by Hitler (the *Anschluss*).
1945 Under Allied occupation, 1920 constitution reinstated and coalition government formed by the SPÖ and the ÖVP.
1955 Allied occupation ended, and the independence of Austria formally recognized.
1966 ÖVP in power with Josef Klaus as chancellor.
1970 SPÖ formed a minority government, with Dr Bruno Kreisky as chancellor.
1983 Kreisky resigned, was replaced by Dr Fred Sinowatz, leading a coalition.
1986 Dr Kurt Waldheim elected president. Sinowatz resigned, succeeded by Franz Vranitzky. No party won an overall majority; Vranitzky formed a coalition of the SPÖ and the ÖVP, with ÖVP leader, Dr Alois Mock, as vice chancellor.
1989 Austria sought European Community membership.
1990 Vranitzky reelected.
1991 Bid for EC membership endorsed by the Community.
1992 Thomas Klestil elected president, replacing Waldheim.

consisting of nine provinces (*Länder*), each with its own provincial assembly (Landtag), provincial governor, and councillors. The 1920 constitution was amended 1929, suspended during ⟡Hitler's regime, and reinstated 1945. The two-chamber federal assembly consists of a national council (Nationalrat) and a federal council (Bundesrat). The Nationalrat has 183 members, elected by universal suffrage through proportional representation, for a four-year term. The Bundesrat has 63 members elected by the provincial assemblies for varying terms. Each province provides a chair for the Bundesrat for a six-month term. The federal president, elected by popular vote for a six-year term, is formal head of state and chooses the federal chancellor on the basis of support in the Nationalrat. The federal chancellor is head of government and chooses the cabinet.

history Austria was inhabited in prehistoric times by Celtic tribes; the country south of the Danube was conquered by the Romans 14 BC and became part of the Roman Empire. After the fall of the empire in the 5th century AD, the region was occupied by Vandals, Goths, Huns, Lombards, and Avars. Having conquered the Avars 791, ⟡Charlemagne established the East Mark, nucleus of the Austrian empire. Otto II granted the Mark to the House of Babenburg 973, which ruled until 1246. Rudolf of Hapsburg, who became king of the Romans and Holy Roman emperor 1273, seized Austria and invested his son as duke 1282. Until the empire ceased to exist 1806, most of the dukes (from 1453, archdukes) of Austria were elected Holy Roman emperor.

Turks kept at bay Austria, which acquired control of ⟡Bohemia 1526, was throughout the 16th century a bulwark of resistance against the Turks, who besieged Vienna 1529 without success. The ⟡Thirty Years' War (1618–48) did not touch Austria, but it weakened its rulers. A second Turkish siege of Vienna 1683 failed, and by 1697 Hungary was liberated from the ⟡Ottoman Empire and incorporated in the Austrian dominion. As a result of their struggle with Louis XIV, the Hapsburgs secured the Spanish Netherlands and Milan 1713. When Charles VI, last male Hapsburg in the direct line, died 1740, his daughter Maria Theresa became archduchess of Austria and queen of Hungary, but the elector of Bavaria was elected emperor as Charles VII. Frederick II of Prussia seized Silesia, and the War of the ⟡Austrian Succession (1740–48) followed. Charles VII died 1745, and Maria Theresa secured the election of her husband as Francis I, but she did not recover Silesia from Frederick. The archduke Francis who succeeded 1792 was also elected emperor as Francis II; sometimes opposing, sometimes allied with Napoleon, he proclaimed himself emperor of Austria 1804 as Francis I, and the name Holy Roman Empire fell out of use 1806. Under the Treaty of Vienna 1815, Francis failed to recover the Austrian Netherlands (annexed by France 1797) but received Lombardy and Venetia.

Austria–Hungary During the ⟡revolutions of 1848 the grievances of mixed nationalities within the Austrian empire flared into a rebellion; revolutionaries in Vienna called for the resignation of ⟡Metternich, who fled to the UK. By 1851 Austria had crushed all the revolts. As a result of the ⟡Seven Weeks' War 1866 with Prussia, Austria lost Venetia to Italy. In the following year Emperor ⟡Franz Joseph established the dual monarchy of Austria-Hungary. The treaty of Berlin 1878 gave Austria the administration of Bosnia-Herzegovina in the Balkans, though they remained nominally Turkish until Austria annexed them 1908. World War I was precipitated 1914 by an Austrian attack on Serbia, following the assassination of Archduke Franz Ferdinand (Franz Joseph's nephew) and his wife by a Serbian nationalist. Austria-Hungary was defeated 1918, the last Hapsburg emperor overthrown, and Austria became a republic, comprising only Vienna and its immediately surrounding provinces. The Treaty of St Germain, signed 1919 by Austria and the Allies, established Austria's present boundaries. Austria was invaded by Hitler's troops 1938 and incorporated into the German Reich (the ⬦Anschluss).

partition and independence With the conclusion of World War II Austria returned to its 1920 constitution, with a provisional government led by Dr Karl Renner. The Allies divided both the country and Vienna into four zones, occupied by the USSR, the US, Britain, and France. The first postwar elections resulted in a coalition of the Socialist Party of Austria (SPÖ) and the Austrian People's Party (ÖVP). The country was occupied until independence was formally recognized 1955. The first postwar noncoalition government was formed 1966 when the ÖVP came to power with Josef Klaus as chancellor. The SPÖ formed a minority government under Dr Bruno Kreisky 1970 and increased its majority in the 1971 and 1975 general elections. The government was nearly defeated 1978 over proposals to install the first nuclear power plant. The plan was abandoned, but nuclear energy remained a controversial issue. The SPÖ lost its majority 1983. Kreisky resigned, refusing to join a coalition. The SPÖ decline was partly attributed to the emergence of two environmentalist groups, the United Green Party (VGÖ) and the Austrian Alternative List (ALÖ). Dr Fred Sinowatz, the new SPÖ chair, formed a coalition government with the Freedom Party of Austria (FPÖ).

Waldheim controversy When Kurt Waldheim, former UN secretary-general, became president 1986, he was diplomatically isolated by many countries because of controversy over his service in the German army during World War II. Later that year Sinowatz resigned as chancellor and was succeeded by Franz Vranitzky. The SPÖ–FPÖ coalition broke up when an extreme right-winger, Jorg Haider, became FPÖ leader. Vranitzky remained as chancellor with the ÖVP leader, Dr Alois Mock, as vice chancellor. Sinowatz denounced the new coalition as a betrayal of socialist principles and resigned as chair of the SPÖ. In the Oct 1990 general election the Socialists won a clear lead over other parties and Vranitzky began another term as chancellor. Thomas Klestil, the candidate of the People's Party, replaced Waldheim as president in May 1992. In his inaugural speech

he stressed the importance of Austria's application for European Community membership, endorsed 1991.

Austrian Succession, War of the war 1740–48 between Austria (supported by England and Holland) and Prussia (supported by France and Spain).
1740 The Holy Roman emperor Charles VI died and the succession of his daughter Maria Theresa was disputed by a number of European powers. Frederick the Great of Prussia seized Silesia from Austria.
1743 At Dettingen an army of British, Austrians, and Hanoverians under the command of George II was victorious over the French.
1745 An Austro-English army was defeated at ⬦Fontenoy but British naval superiority was confirmed, and there were gains in the Americas and India.
1748 The war was ended by the Treaty of Aix-la-Chapelle.

Austro-Hungarian Empire the Dual Monarchy established by the Hapsburg Franz Joseph 1867 between his empire of Austria and his kingdom of Hungary (including territory that became Czechoslovakia as well as parts of Poland, the Ukraine, Romania, Yugoslavia, and Italy). It collapsed autumn 1918 with the end of World War I. Only two king-emperors ruled: Franz Joseph 1867–1916 and Charles 1916–18.
   The Austro-Hungarian Empire came into being with an agreement known as the Ausgleich. The two countries retained their own legal and administrative systems but shared foreign policy. In 1910 the empire had an area of 100,838 sq mi/261,239 sq km with a population of 51 million.

Austronesian languages (also known as **Malayo-Polynesian**) family of languages spoken in Malaysia, the Indonesian archipelago, parts of the region that was formerly Indochina, Taiwan, Madagascar, Melanesia, and Polynesia (excluding Australia and most of New Guinea). The group contains some 500 distinct languages, including Malay in Malaysia, Bahasa in Indonesia, Fijian, Hawaiian, and Maori.

autarchy national economic policy that aims at achieving self-sufficiency and eliminating the need for imports (by imposing tariffs, for example). Such a goal may be difficult, if not impossible, for a small country. Countries that take protectionist measures and try to prevent free trade are sometimes described as autarchical.

authoritarianism rule of a country by a dominant elite who repress opponents and the press to maintain their own wealth and power. They are frequently indifferent to activities not affecting their security, and rival power centers, such as labor unions and political parties, are often allowed to exist, although under tight control. An extreme form is ⬦totalitarianism.

autism, infantile rare syndrome, generally present from birth, characterized by a withdrawn state and a failure to develop normally in language or social behavior, although the autistic child may, rarely, show signs of high intelligence in other areas, such as music. Many have impaired intellect, however. The cause is unknown, but is thought to involve a number of interacting factors, possibly including an inherent abnormality of the child's brain.

autobiography a person's own biography, or written account of his or her life, distinguished

from the journal or diary by being a connected narrative, and from memoirs by dealing less with contemporary events and personalities. *The Boke of Margery Kempe* about 1432–36 is the oldest extant autobiography in English.

autochrome in photography, a single-plate additive color process devised by the ⬦Lumière brothers 1903. It was the first commercially available process, in use 1907–35.

autoclave pressurized vessel that uses superheated steam to sterilize materials and equipment such as surgical instruments. It is similar in principle to a pressure cooker.

auto-da-fé (Portuguese "act of faith") religious ceremony, including a procession, solemn mass, and sermon, which accompanied the sentencing of heretics by the Spanish ⬦Inquisition before they were handed over to the secular authorities for punishment, usually burning.

autogiro or **autogyro** heavier-than-air craft that supports itself in the air with a rotary wing, or rotor. The Spanish aviator Juan de la ⬦Cierva designed the first successful autogiro 1923. The autogiro's rotor provides only lift and not propulsion; it has been superseded by the helicopter, in which the rotor provides both. The autogiro is propelled by an orthodox propeller.
   The three- or four-bladed rotor on an autogiro spins in a horizontal plane on top of the craft, and is not driven by the engine. The blades have an airfoil cross section, as a plane's wings. When the autogiro moves forward, the rotor starts to rotate by itself, a state known as autorotation. When traveling fast enough, the rotor develops enough lift from its airfoil blades to support the craft.

autoimmunity in medicine, condition where the body's immune responses are mobilized not against "foreign" matter, such as invading germs, but against the body itself. Diseases considered to be of autoimmune origin include ⬦myasthenia gravis, rheumatoid ⬦arthritis, and ⬦lupus erythematosus.
   In autoimmune diseases T-lymphocytes reproduce to excess to home in on a target (properly a foreign disease-causing molecule); however, molecules of the body's own tissue that resemble the target may also be attacked, for example insulin-producing cells, resulting in insulin-dependent diabetes; if certain joint membrane cells are attacked, then rheumatoid arthritis may result; and if myelin, the basic protein of the nervous system, then multiple sclerosis. In 1990 in Israel a T-cell vaccine was produced that arrests the excessive reproduction of T-lymphocytes attacking healthy target tissues.

Autolycus in Greek mythology, an accomplished thief and trickster, son of the god ⬦Hermes, who gave him the power of invisibility.

autolysis in biology, the destruction of a ⬦cell after its death by the action of its own ⬦enzymes, which break down its structural molecules.

automatic pilot control device that keeps an airplane flying automatically on a given course at a given height and speed. Devised by US business executive Lawrence Sperry 1912, the automatic pilot contains a set of ⬦gyroscopes that provide references for the plane's course. Sensors detect when the plane deviates from this course and send signals to the control

Austria: provinces

province	capital	area in sq km
Burgenland	Eisenstadt	4,000
Carinthia	Klagenfurt	9,500
Lower Austria	St Pölten	19,200
Salzburg	Salzburg	7,200
Styria	Graz	16,400
Tirol	Innsbruck	12,600
Upper Austria	Linz	12,000
Vienna	Vienna	420
Vorarlberg	Bregenz	2,600

surfaces—the ailerons, elevators, and rudder –to take the appropriate action. Autopilot is also used in missiles.

automation widespread use of self-regulating machines in industry. Automation involves the addition of control devices, using electronic sensing and computing techniques, which often follow the pattern of human nervous and brain functions, to already mechanized physical processes of production and distribution; for example, steel processing, mining, chemical production, and road, rail, and air control.

automatism performance of actions without awareness or conscious intent. It is seen in sleepwalking and in some (relatively rare) psychotic states.

automaton mechanical figure imitating human or animal performance. Automatons are usually designed for aesthetic appeal as opposed to purely functional robots. The earliest recorded automaton is an Egyptian wooden pigeon of 400 BC.

automobile or *car* a small, driver-guided, passenger-carrying motor vehicle; originally the automated version of the horse-drawn carriage, meant to convey people and their goods over streets and roads. Most are four-wheeled and have water-cooled, piston-type internal-combustion engines fueled by gasoline or diesel. Variations have existed for decades that use ingenious and often nonpolluting power plants, but the automobile industry long ago settled on this general formula for the consumer market. Experimental and sports models are streamlined, energy-efficient, and hand-built.

Although it is recorded that in 1479 Gilles de Dom was paid 25 livres by the treasurer of Antwerp in the Low Countries for supplying a self-propelled vehicle, the ancestor of the automobile is generally agreed to be the cumbersome steam carriage made by Nicolas-Joseph Cugnot (1725–1804) in 1769, still preserved in Paris. In 1808 England's Richard Trevithick built a working steam carriage. Steam was an attractive form of power to the English pioneers, and in the 19th century, practical steam coaches were used for public transport until stifled out of existence by the 4 mph/6.4 kph limit, punitive road tolls, and legislation that required someone to walk in front with a red flag by day and a red lantern by night.

In 1885 ◊Benz built and ran the first gasoline-powered automobile. Panhard 1890 (front radiator, engine under hood, sliding-pinion gearbox, wooden ladder-chassis) and Mercedès 1901 (honeycomb radiator, in-line four-cylinder chassis) set the pattern for the modern car. Emerging with Haynes and Duryea in the early 1890s, US demand was so fervent that 300 makers existed by 1895, but only 109 were left by 1900.

In England in 1896 Frederick Lanchester produced an advanced and reliable vehicle, later much copied. The period 1905–06 inaugurated a world automobile boom continuing to the present day.

Among the legendary automobiles of this century are: De Dion Bouton, with the first practical high-speed engines; Mors, notable first for racing and later as a silent touring car; the incomparable Silver Ghost Rolls-Royce; the enduring Model T ◊Ford; and the many types of Bugatti and Delage, from record-breakers to luxury touring automobiles.

After World War I popular motoring began with the era of inexpensive, light (baby)

automobiles made by Citroën, Peugeot, and Renault (France); Austin 7, Morris, Clyno, and Swift (England); Fiat (Italy); Volkswagen (Germany); and the slightly bigger Ford, Chevrolet, and Dodge (US). During the interwar years a great deal of racing took place, and the experience gained benefited the everyday motorist in improved efficiency, reliability, and safety. There was a divergence between the lighter, economical European car, with its good handling on small winding roads, and the heavier US car, cheap, rugged, and well adapted to long distances on straight roads at high speeds.

After World War II small European automobiles tended to fall into three categories: front engine and rear drive, the classic arrangement; front engine and front-wheel drive; rear engine and rear-wheel drive; in about equal numbers, although US automobiles got longer, lower, more powerful (V8 engines) and "styled" with fins. Big automobiles with soft suspensions and low gasoline mileage became the average family's Dreamcar until the OPEC oil crisis of 1973. Air conditioning was a 1950s new "option." From the 1950s a creative resurgence produced in practical form automatic transmission, rubber suspension, transverse engine mounting, self-leveling ride, disk brakes, and safer wet-weather tires. The drive against pollution from the 1960s and the fuel crisis from the 1970s led to experiments for more ecologically responsible powerplants, with steam automobiles (cumbersome), diesel engines (slow and heavy, although economical), and a more promising development, a hybrid car using both electricity and gasoline. Nevertheless, the auto industry produced for sale the stratified-charge gasoline engine, using fuel injection to achieve 20% improvement in gasoline consumption; weight reduction in the body by the use of aluminum, fiber glass, and plastics; and "slippery" body designs with low air resistance, or drag. Microprocessors were also developed to measure temperature, engine speed, pressure, and oxygen/CO_2 content of exhaust gases, and to readjust engine function accordingly. Japanese and European models led the way for US automakers to follow (see also ◊gasoline engine).

automobile racing competitive racing of motor vehicles. It has forms as diverse as hill-climbing, stock-car racing, rallying, sports-car racing, and Formula One Grand Prix racing. The first organized race was from Paris to Rouen 1894.

Road races such as the *Targa Florio* and *Mille Miglia* were tests of a driver's skill and a machine's durability in the 1920s and 1930s. The 24-hour endurance race at ◊Le Mans is now the foremost race for sports automobiles and prototypes.

In Grand Prix racing (instituted 1906) a world championship for drivers has been in existence since 1950, and for builders since 1958. The first six drivers and automobiles in each race are awarded points from nine to one, and the accumulative total at the end of a season (normally 16 races) decides the winners. Major events include Le Mans Grand Prix d'Endurance, first held in 1923, and the Indianapolis 500, first held 1911.

autonomic nervous system in mammals, the part of the nervous system that controls the involuntary activities of the smooth muscles (of the digestive tract, blood vessels), the heart, and the glands. The **sympathetic** system responds to stress, when it speeds the heart rate, increases blood pressure and generally

prepares the body for action. The **parasympathetic** system is more important when the body is at rest, since it slows the heart rate, decreases blood pressure, and stimulates the digestive system.

At all times, both types of autonomic nerves carry signals that bring about adjustments in visceral organs. The actual rate of heart beat is the net outcome of opposing signals. Today, it is known that the word "autonomic" is not correct—the reflexes managed by this system are actually integrated by commands from the brain and spinal cord (the central nervous system).

autonomy in politics, term used to describe political self-government of a state or, more commonly, a subdivision of a state. Autonomy may be based upon cultural or ethnic differences and often leads eventually to independence.

autopsy or *post-mortem* examination of the internal organs and tissues of a dead body, performed to try to establish the cause of death.

autoradiography in biology, a technique for following the movement of molecules within an organism, especially a plant, by labeling with a radioactive isotope that can be traced on photographs. It is used to study ◊photosynthesis, where the pathway of radioactive carbon dioxide can be traced as it moves through the various chemical stages.

autosome any ◊chromosome in the cell other than a sex chromosome. Autosomes are of the same number and kind in both males and females of a given species.

autosuggestion conscious or unconscious acceptance of an idea as true, without demanding rational proof, but with potential subsequent effect for good or ill. Pioneered by the French psychotherapist Emile Coué (1857–1926) in healing, it is used in modern psychotherapy to conquer nervous habits and dependence on tobacco, alcohol, and so on.

autotroph any living organism that synthesizes organic substances from inorganic molecules by using light or chemical energy. Autotrophs are the **primary producers** in all food chains since the materials they synthesize and store are the energy sources of all other organisms. All green plants and many planktonic organisms are autotrophs, using sunlight to convert carbon dioxide and water into sugars by ◊photosynthesis.

The total ◊biomass of autotrophs is far greater than that of animals, reflecting the dependence of animals on plants, and the ultimate dependence of all life on energy from the sun—green plants convert light energy into a form of chemical energy (food) that animals can exploit. Some bacteria use the chemical energy of sulfur compounds to synthesize organic substances. See also ◊heterotroph.

autumn crocus any member of the genus *Colchicum*, family Liliaceae. One species, the mauve *meadow saffron C. autumnale*, yields *colchicine*, which is used in treating gout and in plant breeding (it causes plants to double the numbers of their chromosomes, forming ◊polyploids).

Auvergne ancient province of central France and a modern region comprising the *départements* Allier, Cantal, Haute-Loire, and Puy-de-Dôme
area 10,036 sq mi/26,000 sq km

population (1986) 1,334,000
capital Clermont-Ferrand
physical mountainous, composed chiefly of volcanic rocks in several masses
products cattle, wheat, wine, and cheese
history named after the ancient Gallic Avenni tribe whose leader, Vercingetorix, led a revolt against the Romans 52 BC. In the 14th century the Auvergne was divided into a duchy, dauphiny, and countship. The duchy and dauphiny were united by the dukes of Bourbon before being confiscated by Francis I 1527. The countship united with France 1615.

Auxerre capital of Yonne *département*, France, 106 mi/170 km SE of Paris, on the river Yonne; population about 40,000. The Gothic cathedral, founded 1215, has exceptional sculptures and stained glass.

auxin plant ◊hormone that promotes stem and root growth in plants. Auxins influence many aspects of plant growth and development, including cell enlargement, inhibition of development of axillary buds, ◊tropisms, and the initiation of roots. **Synthetic auxins** are used in rooting powders for cuttings, and in some weedkillers, where high auxin concentrations cause such rapid growth that the plants die. They are also used to prevent premature fruitdrop in orchards. The most common naturally occurring auxin is known as indoleacetic acid, or IAA. It is produced in the shoot apex and transported to other parts of the plant.

Ava former capital of Burma (now Myanmar), on the river Irrawaddy, founded by Thadomin Payä 1364. Thirty kings reigned there until 1782, when a new capital, Amarapura, was founded by Bodaw Payä. In 1823 the site of the capital was transferred back to Ava by King Baggidaw.

avalanche (from French *avaler* "to swallow") fall of a mass of snow and ice down a steep slope. Avalanches occur because of the unstable nature of snow masses in mountain areas.
Changes of temperature, sudden sound, or earth-borne vibrations may trigger an avalanche, particularly on slopes of more than 35°. The snow compacts into ice as it moves, and rocks may be carried along, adding to the damage caused.

Avalokiteśvara in Mahāyāna Buddhism, one of the most important ◊bodhisattvas, seen as embodying compassion. Known as **Guanyin** in China and **Kannon** in Japan, he is one of the attendants of Amida Buddha.

Avalon in Celtic legend, the island of the blessed, or paradise; and in the legend of King ◊Arthur, the land of heroes, ruled over by ◊Morgan le Fay to which King Arthur is conveyed after his final battle with ◊Mordred. It has been identified since the Middle Ages with Glastonbury in Somerset, SW England.

avant-garde (French "advanced guard") in the arts, those artists or works that are in the forefront of new developments in their media. The term was introduced (as was "reactionary") after the French Revolution, when it was used to describe any socialist political movement.

avant-garde dance experimental dance form that rejects the conventions of modern dance. It is often performed in informal spaces—museums, rooftops, even scaling walls.
In the US, avant-garde dance stemmed mainly from the collaboration between Merce

◊Cunningham in New York and musician Robert Dunn which resulted in the Judson Dance Theater. While retaining technique and rhythm, Cunningham deleted the role of choreographer, thus giving dancers a new freedom. The Judson collective went further, denying even the necessity for technique and concentrating on the use of everyday movements—walking, spinning, jumping.

Avar member of a Central Asian nomadic people who in the 6th century invaded the area of Russia north of the Black Sea previously held by the Huns. They extended their dominion over the Bulgarians and Slavs in the 7th century and were finally defeated by Charlemagne 796.

avatar in Hindu mythology, the descent of a deity to Earth in a visible form, for example the ten avatars of ◊Vishnu.

Avedon Richard 1923– . US photographer. A fashion photographer with *Harper's Bazaar* magazine in New York from the mid-1940s, he moved to *Vogue* 1965. He later became the highest-paid fashion and advertising photographer in the world. Using large-format cameras, his work consists of intensely realistic images, chiefly portraits.
Born in New York City, Avedon was already pursuing an interest in photography by the age of 10. After studying photography in the US merchant marine and at the New School for Social Research, he turned professional. His primary subject, aside from fashion, was portraits. Many of his dramatic portraits were assembled in such books as *Observations* 1959 (text by Truman Capote) and *Nothing Personal* 1974 (text by James Baldwin).

Ave Maria (Latin "Hail, Mary") Christian prayer to the Virgin Mary, which takes its name from the archangel Gabriel's salutation to the Virgin Mary when announcing that she would be the mother of the Messiah (Luke 11:28).

avens any of several low-growing plants of the genus *Geum*, family Rosaceae. Species are distributed throughout Eurasia and N Africa.
Mountain avens *Dryas octopetala* belongs to a different genus and grows in mountain and arctic areas of Eurasia and North America. A creeping perennial, it has white flowers with yellow stamens.

average the typical member of a set of data, technically the ◊arithmetic mean. The term is also used to refer to the middle member of the set when it is sorted in ascending or descending order (the ◊median), and the most commonly occurring item of data (the ◊mode), as in "the average family."

Averroës (Arabic **Ibn Rushd**) 1126–1198. Arabian philosopher who argued for the eternity of matter and against the immortality of the individual soul. His philosophical writings, including commentaries on Aristotle and on Plato's *Republic*, became known to the West through Latin translations. He influenced Christian and Jewish writers into the Renaissance, and reconciled Islamic and Greek thought in that philosophic truth comes through reason. St Thomas Aquinas opposed this position.

Avery Milton 1893–1965. US painter, whose early work was inspired by Henri ◊Matisse, with subjects portrayed in thin, flat, richly colored strokes. His later work, although it remained figurative, shows the influence of Mark ◊Rothko and other experimental US artists.

Born in Altmar, New York, Avery received little formal training.

Avery Tex (Frederick Bean) 1907–1980. US cartoon-film director who used violent, sometimes surreal humor. At Warner Bros he helped develop Bugs Bunny and Daffy Duck, before moving to MGM 1942 where he created, among others, Droopy the dog and Screwball Squirrel.

aviation see ◊flight for the history of aviation and airplanes.

Avicenna (Arabic **Ibn Sina**) 979–1037. Arabian philosopher and physician. He was the most renowned philosopher of medieval Islam. His *Canon Medicinae* was a standard work for many centuries. His philosophical writings were influenced by al-Farabi, Aristotle, and the Neoplatonists, and in turn influenced the scholastics of the 13th century.

Avignon city in Provence, France, capital of Vaucluse *département*, on the river Rhône NW of Marseilles; population (1982) 174,000. An important Gallic and Roman city, it has a 12th-century bridge (only half still standing), a 13th-century cathedral, 14th-century walls, and two palaces built during the residence here of the popes, Le Palais Vieux (1334–42) and Le Palais Nouveau (1342–52). Avignon was papal property 1348–1791.

Ávila town in Spain, 56 mi/90 km NW of Madrid; population (1986) 45,000. It is capital of the province of the same name. It has the remains of a Moorish castle, a Gothic cathedral, and the convent and church of St Teresa, who was born here. The medieval town walls are among the best preserved in Europe.

avocado tree *Persea americana* of the laurel family, native to Central America. Its dark-green, thick-skinned, pear-shaped fruit has buttery-textured flesh and is used in salads.

avocet wading bird, genus *Recurvirostra*, family Recurvirostridae, with a characteristic long, narrow, upturned bill used in sifting water as it feeds in the shallows. It is about 18 in/45 cm long, and has long legs, partly webbed feet, and black and white plumage. There are four species. Stilts belong to the same family.

Avogadro Amedeo Conte di Quaregna 1776–1856. Italian physicist who proposed Avogadro's hypothesis on gases 1811. His work enabled scientists to calculate Avogadro's number, and still has relevance for today's atomic studies.

Avogadro's hypothesis in chemistry, the law stating that equal volumes of all gases, when at the same temperature and pressure, have the same numbers of molecules. It was first propounded by Amedeo Avogadro.

Avogadro's number or **Avogadro's constant** the number of carbon atoms in 12 g of the carbon-12 isotope (6.022137×10^{23}). The atomic weight of any element, expressed in grams, contains this number of atoms. It is named after Amedeo Avogadro.

avoirdupois system of weights based on the pound (0.45 kg), which consists of 16 ounces, each of 16 drams, with each dram equal to 27.34 grains (1.772 g).

Avon any of several rivers in England and Scotland. The Avon in Warwickshire is associated with Shakespeare.
The Upper or Warwickshire Avon, 96 mi/154 km, rises in the Northampton uplands near Naseby and joins the Severn at Tewkesbury.

The Lower, or Bristol, Avon, 75 mi/121 km, rises in the Cotswolds and flows into the Bristol Channel at Avonmouth. The East, or Salisbury, Avon, 65 mi/104 km, rises S of the Marlborough Downs and flows into the English Channel at Christchurch.

AWACS (acronym for *Airborne Warning And Control System*) surveillance system that incorporates a long-range surveillance and detection radar mounted on a Boeing E-3 sentry aircraft. It was used with great success in the 1991 Gulf War.

Axelrod Julius 1912– . US neuropharmacologist who shared the 1970 Nobel Prize for Medicine with the biophysicists Bernard Katz and Ulf von Euler (1905–1983) for his work on neurotransmitters (the chemical messengers of the brain).

Axelrod wanted to know why the messengers, once transmitted, should stop operating. Through his studies he found a number of specific ⟁enzymes that rapidly degraded the neurotransmitters.

axil upper angle between a leaf (or bract) and the stem from which it grows. Organs developing in the axil, such as shoots and buds, are termed axillary, or lateral.

axiom in mathematics, a statement that is assumed to be true and upon which theorems are proved by using logical deduction; for example, two straight lines cannot enclose a space. The Greek mathematician Euclid used a series of axioms that he considered could not be demonstrated in terms of simpler concepts to prove his geometrical theorems.

axis (plural *axes*) in geometry, one of the reference lines by which a point on a graph may be located. The horizontal axis is usually referred to as the x-axis, and the vertical axis as the y-axis. The term is also used to refer to the imaginary line about which an object may be said to be symmetrical (*axis of symmetry*) —for example, the diagonal of a square—or the line about which an object may revolve (*axis of rotation*).

Axis alliance of Nazi Germany and Fascist Italy before and during World War II. The *Rome–Berlin Axis* was formed 1936, when Italy was being threatened with sanctions because of its invasion of Ethiopia (Abyssinia). It became a full military and political alliance May 1939. A ten-year alliance between Germany, Italy, and Japan (*Rome–Berlin–Tokyo Axis*) was signed Sept 1940 and was subsequently joined by Hungary, Bulgaria, Romania, and the puppet states of Slovakia and Croatia. The Axis collapsed with the fall of Mussolini and the surrender of Italy 1943 and Germany and Japan 1945.

axolotl (Aztec "water monster") aquatic larval form ("tadpole") of any of several North American species of salamander, belonging to the family Ambystomatidae. Axolotls are remarkable because they can breed without changing to the adult form and will only metamorphose into adult salamanders in response to the drying-up of their ponds. The adults then migrate to another pond.

Axolotls may be up to 12 in/30 cm long. Species include the Mexican salamander *Ambystomum mexicanum* which lives in mountain lakes near Mexico City, and the tiger salamander *A. tigrinum*, found in North America, from Canada to Mexico. See also ⟁neoteny.

axon long threadlike extension of a ⟁nerve

cell that conducts electrochemical impulses away from the cell body toward other nerve cells, or toward an effector organ such as a muscle. Axons terminate in ⟁synapses with other nerve cells, muscles, or glands.

Axum alternative transliteration of ⟁Aksum, an ancient kingdom in Ethiopia.

Ayacucho capital of a province of the same name in the Andean Mountains of central Peru; population (1988) 94,200. The last great battle against Spanish troops in the war of independence was fought near here Dec 1824.

ayatollah (Arabic "sign of God") honorific title awarded to Shiite Muslims in Iran by popular consent, as, for example, to Ayatollah Ruhollah ⟁Khomeini.

Ayckbourn Alan 1939– . English playwright. His prolific output, characterized by comic dialogue and experiments in dramatic structure, includes the trilogy *The Norman Conquests* 1974, *A Woman in Mind* 1986, *Henceforward* 1987, and *Man of the Moment* 1988.

aye-aye nocturnal tree-climbing prosimian *Daubentonia madagascariensis* of Madagascar, related to the lemurs. It is just over 3 ft/1 m long, including a tail 20 in/50 cm long.

It has an exceptionally long middle finger with which it probes for insects and their larvae under the bark of trees, and gnawing, rodentlike front teeth, with which it tears off the bark to get at its prey. The aye-aye has become rare through loss of its forest habitat, and is now classified as an endangered species.

Ayer A(lfred) J(ules) 1910–1989. English philosopher. He wrote *Language, Truth and Logic* 1936, an exposition of the theory of "logical positivism," presenting a criterion by which meaningful statements (essentially truths of logic, as well as statements derived from experience) could be distinguished from meaningless metaphysical utterances (for example, claims that there is a God or that the world external to our own minds is illusory).

Ayers Rock (Aboriginal *Uluru*) vast ovate mass of pinkish rock in Northern Territory, Australia; 1,110 ft/335 m high and 6 mi/9 km around. It is named after Henry Ayers, a premier of South Australia.

For the Aboriginals, whose paintings decorate its caves, it has magical significance.

Ayesha 611–678. Third and favorite wife of the prophet Mohammed, who married her when she was nine. Her father, Abu Bakr, became ⟁caliph on Mohammed's death 632. She bitterly opposed the later succession to the caliphate of Ali, who had once accused her of infidelity.

Aymara member of an American Indian people of Bolivia and Peru, builders of a great culture, who were conquered first by the Incas and then by the Spaniards. Today 1.4 million Aymara farm and herd llamas and alpacas in the highlands; their language, belonging to the Andean-Equatorial language family, survives and their Roman Catholicism incorporates elements of their old beliefs.

Ayurveda ancient Hindu system of medicine. The main principles are derived from the Vedas of the 1st century AD, and it is still practiced in India, using herbs, purgatives, and liniments, in Ayurvedic hospitals and dispensaries.

AZ abbreviation for the state of ⟁*Arizona*.

azalea any of various deciduous flowering shrubs, genus *Rhododendron*, of the heath family Ericaceae. There are several species na-

tive to Asia and North America, and from these many cultivated varieties have been derived. Azaleas are closely related to the evergreen ⟁rhododendrons of the same genus.

Azaleas, particularly the Japanese varieties, make fine ornamental shrubs. Several species are highly poisonous.

Azaña Manuel 1880–1940. Spanish politician and first prime minister 1931–33 of the second Spanish republic. He was last president of the republic during the Civil War 1936–39, before the establishment of a dictatorship under Franco.

Azerbaijan country in W Asia, bounded S by Iran, E by the Caspian Sea, W by Armenia and Georgia, and N by Russia.

government There is a 360-seat legislature, the supreme soviet, to which deputies are elected by a majority system, and a second ballot runoff race in contests in which there is no clear first-round majority. From the majority grouping within the supreme soviet, a prime minister (chair of the cabinet of ministers) is drawn. The state president is directly elected.

history Azerbaijan shares a common language and culture with Turkey; however, before its conquest by tsarist Russia in the early 19th century, it was a province of Persia, and today 20 million Shiite Azeris live across the border in Iran. In the late 19th century, Baku became the center of a growing oil industry. A member of the Transcaucasian Federation in 1917, Azerbaijan became an independent republic 1918, but was occupied by the Red Army two years later. The republic was secularized under Soviet rule.

growth of nationalism There was a growth in Azeri nationalism from the later 1980s, spearheaded by the Azeri Popular Front, founded in 1989, and fanned by the dispute with neighboring Armenia over ⟁Nagorno-Karabakh and ⟁Nakhichevan. This dispute, which reawakened centuries-old enmities, flared up into full civil war from Dec 1989, prompting Azeri calls for secession from the USSR. In Jan 1990 Soviet troops were sent to Baku to restore order, and a state of emergency was imposed. The Azerbaijan Communist Party (ACP), led by Ayaz Mutalibov, allied itself with the nationalist cause and rejected compromise in the Nagorno-Karabakh dispute.

backlash In the Sept 1990 supreme soviet elections the Popular Front, having been on the verge of power before the Jan 1990 crackdown, was convincingly defeated by the ACP. A new state flag was adopted in Dec 1990 and the words "Soviet Socialist" were dropped from the republic's name. In the March 1991 USSR constitutional referendum, the Azerbaijan population voted overwhelmingly in favor of preserving the Union and the Aug 1991 anti-Gorbachev coup in Moscow was warmly welcomed by President Mutalibov, who ordered the military suppression of demonstrations organized by the Popular Front.

independence declared After the failure of the Moscow coup, Mutalibov resigned from the ACP, which was soon disbanded, and on Aug 30, 1991, independence was declared. The state of emergency, still in force in Baku, was lifted. On Sept 8, 1991, Mutalibov was directly elected state president as the sole candidate in a contest boycotted by the opposition. In Dec 1991 Azerbaijan joined the new ⟁Commonwealth of Independent States, which superseded the Soviet Union. In Jan 1992 Azerbaijan was admitted into the ⟁Conference on Security and Cooperation in Europe

Azerbaijan
Republic of

area 33,400 sq mi/86,600 sq km
capital Baku
cities Gyandzha (formerly Kirovabad), Sumgait
physical Caspian Sea; the country ranges from semidesert to the Caucasus mountains
head of state and government Albufaz Elchibey from 1992
political system emergent democracy
political parties Republican Democratic Party, ex-communist dominated; Popular Front, democratic nationalist; Islamic Party, fundamentalist
products oil, iron, copper, fruit, vines, cotton, silk, carpets
population (1990) 7,145,600 (83% Azeri, 6% Russian, 6% Armenian)

language Turkic
religion traditionally Shiite Muslim
chronology
1917–18 A member of the anti-Bolshevik Transcaucasian Federation.
1918 Became an independent republic.
1920 Occupied by the Red Army.
1922–36 Formed part of the Transcaucasian Federal Republic with Georgia and Armenia.
1936 Became a constituent republic of the USSR.
1988 Riots followed Nagorno-Karabakh's request for transfer to Armenia.
1989 Jan–Nov: strife-torn Nagorno-Karabakh placed under "temporary" direct rule from Moscow. Azerbaijan Popular Front established. Nov: civil war erupted with Armenia.
1990 Jan: Soviet troops dispatched to Baku to restore order. Aug: communists won parliamentary elections. Nakhichevan affected by Nagorno-Karabakh dispute.
1991 Aug: Azeri leadership supported attempted anti-Gorbachev coup in Moscow; independence declared. Sept: former communist Ayaz Mutalibov elected president. Dec: joined new Commonwealth of Independent States (CIS); Nagorno-Karabakh declared independence.
1992 Jan: admitted into Conference on Security and Cooperation in Europe (CSCE); March: Mutalibov resigned; Azerbaijan became a member of the United Nations (UN); accorded diplomatic recognition by the US. June: Albufaz Elchibey, leader of the Popular Front, elected president; renewed campaign against Armenia in the fight for Nagorno-Karabakh.

(CSCE) and in March into the United Nations (UN). Azeri diplomatic and commercial links with Turkey improved and in Feb 1992 the republic joined the Economic Cooperation Organization (ECO), founded by Iran, Pakistan, and Turkey 1975, which aimed to reduce customs tariffs and eventually form a customs union. After independence, the state began to form its own armed forces. In Feb 1992 Azerbaijan switched from the Cyrillic alphabet, imposed by Moscow in 1937, to the Latin alphabet.
unstable leadership The Mutalibov administration and the supreme soviet remained under the domination of former members of the ACP, which was superseded by a new Republican Democratic Party, and much of the old system remained in place. Following Azeri defeats in Nagorno-Karabakh in March 1992, Mutalibov was forced to resign and various factions competed for power. In June 1992 Albufaz Elchibey, leader of the Popular Front, was elected president, pledging withdrawal from the CIS and a renewed campaign against Armenia over Nagorno-Karabakh. By Aug 1992 Azerbaijan had reclaimed much of its lost territory in the disputed enclave.

Azerbaijan, Iranian two provinces of NW Iran, *Eastern Azerbaijan* (capital Tabriz), population (1986) 4,114,000, and *Western Azerbaijan* (capital Orúmiyeh), population 1,972,000. Azerbaijanis in Iran, as in the Republic of Azerbaijan, are mainly Shiite Muslim ethnic Turks, descendants of followers of the Khans from the Mongol Empire.

There are about 5 million in Azerbaijan, and 3 million distributed in the rest of the country, where they form a strong middle class. In 1946, with Soviet backing, they briefly established their own republic. Denied autonomy under the Shah, they rose 1979–80 against the supremacy of Ayatollah Khomeini and were forcibly repressed, although a degree of autonomy was promised.

Azhar, El Muslim university and mosque in Cairo, Egypt. Founded 970 by Jawhar, commander in chief of the army of the Fatimid caliph, it is claimed to be the oldest university in the world. It became the center of Islamic learning, with several subsidiary foundations, and is now primarily a school of Koranic teaching.

Azilian archeological period following the close of the Old Stone (Paleolithic) Age and regarded as one of the cultures of the Mesolithic Age. It was first recognized at Mas d'Azil, a village in Ariège, France.

azimuth in astronomy, the angular distance of an object eastward along the horizon, measured from due north, between the astronomical ◊meridian (the vertical circle passing through the centre of the sky and the north and south points on the horizon) and the vertical circle containing the celestial body whose position is to be measured.

Azores group of nine islands in the N Atlantic, belonging to Portugal; area 867 sq mi/ 2,247 sq km; population (1987) 254,000. They are outlying peaks of the mid-Atlantic Ridge and are volcanic in origin. The capital is Ponta Delgada on the main island, San Miguel.

Portuguese from 1430, the Azores were granted partial autonomy 1976, but remain a Portuguese overseas territory. The islands have a separatist movement. The Azores command the Western shipping lanes.

Azov (Russian *Azovskoye More*) inland sea of Europe forming a gulf in the NE of the Black Sea, between Ukraine and Russia; area 14,500 sq mi/37,555 sq km. Principal ports include Rostov-on-Don, Kerch, and Taganrog. Azov is a good source of freshwater fish.

AZT or *retrovir* or *zidovudine* trademark for azidothymidine, an antiviral drug used in the treatment of ◊AIDS.

Developed in the mid-1980's and approved for used by 1987, it is not a cure for AIDS but is effective in suppressing the causative virus (HIV) for as long as it is administered. Taken every four hours, night and day, it reduces the risk of opportunistic infection and relieves many neurological complications. However, frequent blood monitoring is required to control anemia, a potentially life-threatening side-effect of AZT. Blood transfusions are often necessary, and the drug must be withdrawn if liver damage occurs or bone-marrow function is severely affected.

Aztec member of an ancient Mexican civilization that migrated south into the valley of Mexico in the 12th century, and in 1325 began reclaiming lake marshland to build their capital, Tenochtitlán, on the site of present-day Mexico City. Under Montezuma I (reigned from 1440), the Aztecs created a tribute empire in central Mexico. After the conquistador Cortès landed 1519, Montezuma II (reigned from 1502) was killed and Tenochtitlán subsequently destroyed. Nahuatl is the Aztec language; it belongs to the Uto-Aztecan family of languages.

The Aztecs are known for their architecture, jewelry (gold, jade, and turquoise), sculpture, and textiles. Their form of writing combined hieroglyphs and pictographs, and they used a complex calendar that combined a sacred period of 260 days with the solar year of 365 days. Propitiatory rites were performed at the intersection of the two, called the "dangerous" period, every 52 years, when temples were rebuilt. Their main god in a pantheon of gods was Huitzilopochtli (Hummingbird Wizard), but they also worshiped the feathered serpent ◊Quetzalcoatl, inherited from earlier Mexican civilizations. Religious ritual included human sacrifice on a large scale, the priests tearing the heart from the living victim or flaying people alive. War captives were obtained for this purpose, but their own people were also used. The Aztec state was a theocracy with farmers, artisans, and merchants taxed to support the priestly aristocracy. Tribute was collected from a federation of conquered nearby states.

B the second letter of the English alphabet. It corresponds to the Greek *beta* (B, β) and the Semitic *beth*, and, as written in the current West European alphabet, is derived from Classical Roman block letters. The sound is a voiced bilabial stop, although in some English words (*debt, doubt*) b is silent.

BA in education, abbreviation for *Bachelor of Arts* degree.

Baade Walter 1893–1960. German-born US astronomer who made observations that doubled the distance, scale, and age of the universe. Baade worked at Mount Wilson Observatory, and discovered that stars are in two distinct populations according to their age, known as Population I (the younger) and Population II (the older). Later, he found that ⟳Cepheid variable stars of Population I are brighter than had been supposed, and that distances calculated from them were wrong. Baade's figures showed that the universe was twice as large as previously thought, and twice as old.

Baader-Meinhof gang popular name for the West German left-wing guerrilla group the *Rote Armee Fraktion*/Red Army Faction, active from 1968 against what it perceived as US imperialism. The three main founding members were Andreas Baader (1943–77), Gudrun Ensslin, and Ulrike Meinhof (1934–76).

The group claimed responsibility 1990 for the murder of Detlev Rohwedder, the government agent responsible for selling off state-owned companies of the former East German regime.

A former student activist, Baader was sentenced to life imprisonment in April 1977; he took his own life in Oct, following the failure of the Faction's hostage swap attempt at Mogadishu airport.

Baal (Semitic "lord" or "owner") divine title given to their chief male gods by the Phoenicians, or Canaanites. Their worship as fertility gods, often orgiastic and of a phallic character, was strongly denounced by the Hebrew prophets.

Baalbek city of ancient Syria, now in Lebanon, 36 mi/60 km NE of Beirut, 3,000 ft/1,150 m above sea level. It was originally a center of Baal worship. The Greeks identified Baal with Helios, the Sun, and renamed Baalbek

Heliopolis. Its ruins, including Roman temples, survive; the Temple of Bacchus, built in the 2nd century AD, is still almost intact.

Ba'ath Party ruling political party in Iraq and Syria. Despite public support of pan-Arab unity and its foundations 1943 as a party of Arab nationalism, its ideology has been so vague that it has fostered widely differing (and often opposing) parties in Syria and Iraq.

The Ba'ath party was founded in Damascus, Syria 1943 by three French-educated Syrian intellectuals, in opposition to both French rule and the older generation of Syrian Arab nationalists. Its constitution is an uncertain blend of neo-Marxist socialism and nationalism. The movement split into several factions after 1958 and again in 1966. In Iraq, the Ba'ath party took control briefly in 1963 and again from 1968 although its support here has always been limited. The rise of Saddam Hussein was not so much due to the popularity of the Ba'ath party itself as the exploitation and manipulation of an existing ideology by Hussein for his own purposes.

Bab, the name assumed by Mirza Ali Mohammad 1819–1850. Persian religious leader, born in Shiraz, founder of ⟳Babism, an offshoot of Islam. In 1844 he proclaimed that he was a gateway to the Hidden Imam, a new messenger of Allah who was to come. He gained a large following whose activities caused the Persian authorities to fear a rebellion, and who were therefore persecuted. The Bab was executed for heresy.

Babangida Ibrahim 1941– . Nigerian politician and soldier, president from 1985. He became head of the Nigerian army in 1983 and in 1985 led a coup against President Buhari, assuming the presidency himself. He has promised a return to civilian rule.

Babbage Charles 1792–1871. English mathematician who designed a precursor of the computer. He designed an analytical engine, a general-purpose mechanical computing device for performing different calculations according to a program input on punched cards (an idea borrowed from the Jacquard loom). This device was never built, but it embodied many of the principles on which present digital computers are based.

Babbit metal soft, white metal, an ⟳alloy of tin, lead, copper, and antimony, used to reduce friction in bearings, developed by the US inventor Isaac Babbit 1839.

Babbitt satirical novel 1922 by Sinclair Lewis about a Midwestern businessman obsessed with commerce, clubs, and material values. "Babbittry" came to mean a type of Middle American cultureless innocence.

Babbitt Milton 1916– . US composer. After studying with Roger ⟳Sessions he developed a personal style of ⟳serialism influenced by jazz. He was a leading composer of electronic music using the 1960 RCA Mark II synthesizer, which he helped to design.

babbler bird of the thrush family Muscicapidae with a loud babbling cry. Babblers, subfamily Timaliinae, are found in the Old World, and there are some 250 species in the group.

Babel Hebrew name for the city of ⟳Babylon, chiefly associated with the *Tower of Babel* which, in the Genesis story in the Old Testament, was erected in the plain of Shinar by the descendants of Noah. It was a ziggurat,

or staged temple, seven stories high (300 ft/100 m) with a shrine of Marduk on the summit. It was built by Nabopolassar, father of Nebuchadnezzar, and was destroyed when Sennacherib sacked the city 689 BC.

Bab-el-Mandeb strait that joins the Red Sea and the Gulf of Aden, and separates Arabia and Africa. The name, meaning "gate of tears," refers to its currents.

Babi faith alternate name for ⟳Baha'i faith.

Babington Anthony 1561–1586. English traitor who hatched a plot to assassinate Elizabeth I and replace her with Mary Queen of Scots (1542-1587); its discovery led to Mary's execution and his own.

babirusa wild pig *Babirousa babyrussa*, becoming increasingly rare, found in the moist forests and by the water of Sulawesi, Buru, and nearby Indonesian islands. The male has large upper tusks which grow upward through the skin of the snout and curve back toward the forehead. The babirusa is up to 2.5 ft/80 cm at the shoulder. It is nocturnal, and swims well.

Babism religious movement founded during the 1840s by Mirza Ali Mohammad ("the ⟳Bab"). An offshoot of Islam, its main difference lies in the belief that Mohammed was not the last of the prophets. The movement split into two groups after the death of the Bab; Baha'ullah, the leader of one of these groups, founded the ⟳Baha'i faith.

Babi Yar ravine near Kiev, Ukraine, where more than 100,000 people (80,000 Jews; the others were Poles, Russians, and Ukrainians) were killed by the Nazis in 1941. The site was ignored until the Soviet poet Yevtushenko wrote a poem called "Babi Yar" 1961 in protest at plans for a sports center on the site.

baboon large monkey, genus *Papio*, with a long doglike muzzle and large canine teeth, spending much of its time on the ground in open country. Males, with head and body up to 3.5 ft/1.1 m long, are larger than females and dominant males rule the "troops" in which baboons live. They inhabit Africa and SW Arabia.

Species include the **olive baboon** *Papio anubis* from W Africa to Kenya, the **chacma** *Papio ursinus* from S Africa, and the **sacred baboon** *Papio hamadryas* from NE Africa and SW Arabia. The male sacred baboon has a "cape" of long hair.

Babur (Arabic "lion") title given to ⟳Zahir uddin Mohammed, founder of the Mogul Empire in N India.

Babylon capital of ancient Babylonia, on the bank of the lower Euphrates River. The site is now in Iraq, 55 mi/88 km S of Baghdad and 5 mi/8 km N of Hilla, which is built chiefly of bricks from the ruins of Babylon. The *Hanging Gardens of Babylon*, one of the ⟳Seven Wonders of the World, were probably erected on a vaulted stone base, the only stone construction in the mud-brick city. They formed a series of terraces, irrigated by a hydraulic system.

In 1986–89 President Saddam Hussein constructed a replica of the Southern Palace and citadel of Nebuchadnezzar II, on the plans of the German archeologist Robert Koldeway (1855–1925). In ⟳Rastafarianism, Babylon is the non-African world.

Babylonian captivity exile of Jewish deportees to Babylon after Nebuchadnezzar II's capture of Jerusalem in 586 BC; according to tradition, the captivity lasted 70 years, but Cyrus of Persia, who conquered Babylon, actually allowed her to go home in 536 BC. By analogy, the name has also been applied to the papal exile to Avignon, France, 1309–77.

Bacall Lauren. Adopted name of Betty Joan Perske 1924– . Striking US actress who became an overnight star when cast by Howard Hawks opposite Humphrey Bogart in *To Have and Have Not* 1944. She and Bogart married in 1945, and starred together in *The Big Sleep* 1946 and several other films. She also appeared in *The Cobweb* 1955, *Harper* 1966, and *The Shootist* 1976.

Bacău industrial city in Romania, 155 mi/ 250 km NNE of Bucharest, on the Bistrita; population (1985) 175,300. It is the capital of Bacău county, a leading oil-producing region.

baccarat casino card game with two forms: **chemin de fer** and **baccarat banque**. In the former, each player takes it in turn to hold the bank. In the *banque* variety, all players compete against one banker. Cards are dealt from a wooden holder known as a "shoe."

Bacchus in Greek and Roman mythology, the god of fertility (see ◊Dionysus) and of wine; his rites (the *Bacchanalia*) were orgiastic.

Bach Carl Philip Emmanuel 1714–1788. German composer, third son of J S Bach. He introduced a new "homophonic" style, light and easy to follow, which influenced Mozart, Haydn, and Beethoven.

In the service of Frederick the Great 1740–67, he left to become master of church music at Hamburg in 1768. He wrote over 200 pieces for keyboard instruments, and published a guide to playing the piano. Through his music and concert performances he helped to establish a leading solo role for the piano in Western music.

Bach Johann Christian 1735–1782. German composer, the 11th son of J S Bach, who became celebrated in Italy as a composer of operas. In 1762 he was invited to London, where he became music master to the royal family. He remained in England until his death, enjoying great popularity both as composer and performer.

Bach Johann Sebastian 1685–1750. German composer. He was a master of ◊counterpoint, and his music epitomizes the Baroque polyphonic style. His orchestral music includes the six *Brandenburg Concertos*, other concertos for keyboard instrument and violin, and four orchestral suites. Bach's keyboard music, for ◊clavier and organ, his fugues, and his choral music are of equal importance. He also wrote chamber music and songs.

Born at Eisenach, Bach came from a distinguished musical family. At 15 he became a chorister at Lüneburg, and at 19 he was organist at Arnstadt. His appointments included positions at the courts of Weimar and Anhalt-Köthen, and from 1723 until his death he was musical director at St Thomas's choir school in Leipzig. He married twice and had over 20 children (although several died in infancy). His second wife, Anna Magdalena Wülkens, was a soprano; she also worked for him when his sight failed in later years.

Bach's sacred music includes 200 church cantatas, the Easter and Christmas oratorios, the two great Passions, of St Matthew and St John, and the Mass in B minor. His keyboard music includes a collection of 48 preludes and fugues known as the *Well-Tempered Clavier*, the *Goldberg Variations*, and the *Italian Concerto*. Of his organ music the finest examples are

the chorale preludes. Two works written in his later years illustrate the principles and potential of his polyphonic art—the *Musical Offering* and *The Art of Fugue*.

Bach Wilhelm Friedemann 1710–1784. German composer, who was also an organist, improviser, and master of ◊counterpoint. He was the eldest son of J S Bach.

bacillus member of a group of rodlike ◊bacteria that occur everywhere in the soil and air. Some are responsible for diseases such as anthrax or for causing food spoilage.

bacillus of Calmette and Guérin tuberculosis vaccine ◊BCG.

backgammon board game for two players, often used in gambling. It was known in Mesopotamia, Greece and Rome and in medieval England.

The board is marked out in 24 triangular points of alternating colors, 12 to each side. Throwing two dice, the players move their 15 pieces round the board to the six points that form their own "inner table;" the first player to move all his or her pieces off the board is the winner.

background radiation radiation that is always present in the environment. By far the greater proportion (87%) of it is emitted from natural sources. Alpha and beta particles, and gamma radiation are radiated by the traces of radioactive minerals that occur naturally in the environment and even in the human body, and by radioactive gases such as radon and thoron, which are found in soil and may seep upward into buildings. Radiation from space (◊cosmic radiation) also contributes to the background level.

Because background radiation increases the count rate obtained during any experimental work on radioactive materials, a background count rate is usually subtracted from any data obtained.

backup system in computing, a duplicate computer system that can take over the operation of a main computer system in the event of equipment failure. A large interactive system, such as an airline's ticket-booking system, cannot be out of action for even a few hours without causing considerable disruption. In such cases a complete duplicate computer system may be provided to take over and run the system should the main computer develop a fault or need maintenance. Backup systems include **incremental backup** and **full backup**.

Bacon Francis 1561–1626. English politician, philosopher, and essayist. He became Lord Chancellor 1618, and the same year confessed to bribe-taking, was fined £40,000 (which was later remitted by the king), and spent four days in the Tower of London. His works include *Essays* 1597, characterized by pith and brevity; *The Advancement of Learning* 1605, a seminal work discussing scientific method; the *Novum Organum* 1620, in which he redefined the task of natural science, seeing it as a means of empirical discovery and a method of increasing human power over nature; and *The New Atlantis* 1626, describing a utopian state in which scientific knowledge is systematically sought and exploited.

His writing helped to inspire the founding of the ◊Royal Society.

Bacon Francis 1909–1992. British painter, born in Dublin. He moved to London in 1925 and taught himself to paint. He practiced

abstract art, then developed a distorted Expressionist style with tortured figures presented in loosely defined space. From 1945 he focused on studies of figures, as in his series of screaming popes based on the portrait of Innocent X by Velázquez.

Bacon began to paint about 1930 and held his first show in London in 1949. He destroyed much of his early work. *Three Studies for Figures at the Base of a Crucifixion* 1944 (Tate Gallery, London) is an early example of his mature style.

Bacon Nathaniel 1647–1676. American colonial leader. Born in Suffolk, England, Bacon immigrated to Virginia 1673. As a wealthy planter, he became an opponent of Gov William Berkeley, demanding that frontier settlements be protected against Indian attacks. In 1675 he led a force of colonists on raids against local Indian tribes.

Although denounced as a rebel by Berkeley, Bacon gained wide public support. He was eventually proclaimed "General of Virginia" and forced Berkeley to flee from the capital at Jamestown. Bacon's sudden death 1676 ended the rebellion and enabled Berkeley to regain power.

Bacon Roger 1214–1292. English philosopher, scientist, and a teacher at Oxford University. He was interested in alchemy, the biological and physical sciences, and magic. Many discoveries have been credited to him, including the magnifying lens. He foresaw the extensive use of gunpowder and mechanical automobiles, boats, and planes.

In 1266, at the invitation of his friend Pope Clement IV, he began his *Opus Majus/Great Work*, a compendium of all branches of knowledge. In 1268 he sent this with his *Opus Minus/Lesser Work* and other writings to the pope. In 1277 Bacon was condemned and imprisoned by the church for "certain novelties" (heresy) and not released until 1292.

bacteria (singular **bacterium**) microscopic unicellular organisms with prokaryotic cells (see ◊prokaryote). They usually reproduce by ◊binary fission (dividing into two equal parts), and since this may occur approximately every 20 minutes, a single bacterium is potentially capable of producing 16 million copies of itself in a day. It is thought that 1–10% of the world's bacteria have been identified.

Bacteria are now classified biochemically, but their varying shapes provide a rough classification; for example, *cocci* are round or oval, *bacilli* are rodlike, *spirilla* are spiral, and *vibrios* are shaped like commas. Unlike ◊viruses, bacteria do not necessarily need contact with a live cell to become active.

Bacteria have a large loop of ◊DNA, sometimes called a bacterial chromosome. In addition there are often small, circular pieces of DNA known as ◊plasmids that carry spare genetic information. These plasmids can readily move from one bacterium to another, even though the bacteria may be of different species. In a sense they are parasites within the bacterial cell, but they survive by coding characteristics that promote the survival of their hosts. For example, some plasmids confer antibiotic resistance on the bacteria they inhabit. The rapid and problematic spread of antibiotic resistance among bacteria is due to plasmids, but they are also useful to humans in ◊genetic engineering.

Although generally considered harmful, certain types of bacteria are vital in many food and industrial processes, while others play an essential role in the ⬡nitrogen cycle, which maintains soil fertility. For example, bacteria are used to break down waste products, such as sewage; make butter, cheese, and yogurt; cure tobacco; tan leather; and (by virtue of the ability of certain bacteria to attack metal) clean ships' hulls and de-rust their tanks, and even extract minerals from mines. Bacteria cannot normally survive temperatures above 212°F/100°C, such as those produced in pasteurization; but those in deep sea hot vents in the eastern Pacific are believed to withstand temperatures of 662°F/350°C. *Thermus aquaticus*, or taq, grows freely in the boiling waters of hot springs, and an enzyme derived from it is used in genetic engineering to speed up the production of millions of copies of any DNA sequence, a reaction requiring very high temperatures.

Certain bacteria can influence the growth of others; for example, lactic acid bacteria will make conditions unfavorable for salmonella bacteria. Other strains produce nisin, which inhibits growth of listeria and botulism organisms. Plans in the food industry are underway to produce super strains of lactic acid bacteria to avoid food poisoning. In 1990, a British team of food scientists announced a new, rapid (five-minute) test for contamination of food by listeria or salmonella bacteria. Fluorescent dyes, added to a liquidized sample of food, reveal the presence of bacteria under laser light.

bacteriology the study of ⬡bacteria.

bacteriophage virus that attacks ⬡bacteria. Such viruses are now of use in genetic engineering.

Bactria former region of central Asia (now divided between Afghanistan, Pakistan, and Tajikistan) which was partly conquered by ⬡Alexander the Great. During the 3rd–6th centuries BC it was a center of East-West trade and cultural exchange.

Bactrian species of ⬡camel *Camelus bactrianus* found in the Gobi Desert in Central Asia. Body fat is stored in two humps on the back. It has very long winter fur which is shed in ragged lumps. The head and body length is about 10 ft/3 m, and the camel is up to 6.8 ft/2.1 m tall at the shoulder. Most Bactrian camels are domesticated and are used as beasts of burden in W Asia.

Badajoz city in Extremadura, Spain, on the Portuguese frontier; population (1991) 129,700. It has a 13th-century cathedral and ruins of a Moorish castle. Badajoz has often been besieged and was stormed by the Duke of Wellington 1812 with the loss of 59,000 British troops.

Baden former state of SW Germany, which had Karlsruhe as its capital. Baden was captured from the Romans in 282 by the Alemanni; later it became a margravate and in 1806, a grand duchy. A state of the German empire 1871–1918, then a republic, and under Hitler a *Gau* (province), it was divided between the *Länder* of Württemberg-Baden and Baden in 1945 and in 1952 made part of ⬡Baden-Württemberg.

Baden town in Aargau canton, Switzerland, near Zurich; at an altitude of 1,273 ft/388 m; population (1990) 14,780. Its hot sulfur springs and mineral waters have been visited since Roman times.

Baden-Baden Black Forest spa in Baden-Württemberg, Germany; population (1984) 49,000. Fashionable in the 19th century, it is now a conference center.

Baden-Powell Robert Stephenson Smyth, 1st Baron Baden-Powell 1857–1941. British general, founder of the Scout Association. He fought in defense of Mafeking (now Mafikeng) during the Boer War. After 1907 he devoted his time to developing the Scout movement, which rapidly spread throughout the world. He was created a peer in 1929.

Baden-Württemberg administrative region (German *Land*) of Germany;
area 13,819 sq mi/35,800 sq km
capital Stuttgart
cities Mannheim, Karlsruhe, Freiburg, Heidelberg, Heilbronn, Pforzheim, Ulm
physical Black Forest; Rhine boundary S and W; source of the Danube; see also ⬡Swabia
products wine, jewelry, watches, clocks, musical instruments, textiles, chemicals, iron, steel, electrical equipment, surgical instruments
population (1988) 9,390,000
history formed 1952 (following a plebiscite) by the merger of the *Länder* Baden, Württemberg-Baden, and Württemberg-Hohenzollern.

badger large mammal of the weasel family with molar teeth of a crushing type adapted to a partly vegetable diet, and short strong legs with long claws suitable for digging. The Eurasian **common badger** *Meles meles* is about 3 ft/1 m long, with long, coarse, grayish hair on the back, and a white face with a broad black stripe along each side. Mainly a woodland animal, it is harmless and nocturnal, and spends the day in a system of burrows called a "sett." It feeds on roots, a variety of fruits and nuts, insects, worms, mice, and young rabbits.

The **American badger** *Taxidea taxus* is slightly smaller and lives in open country in North America. Various species of hog badger, ferret badger, and stink badger occur in S and E Asia, the last having the anal scent glands characteristic of the weasel family well developed.

Bad Godesburg SE suburb of ⬡Bonn, Germany, formerly a spa, and the meeting place of Chamberlain and Hitler before the Munich Agreement 1938.

badlands barren landscape cut by erosion into a maze of ravines, pinnacles, gullies and sharp-edged ridges. Areas in South Dakota and Nebraska, are examples.

badminton racket game similar to lawn ⬡tennis but played on a smaller court and with a shuttlecock instead of a ball. The object of the game is to prevent the opponent from being able to return the shuttlecock.

Badminton is played by two or four players. The court measures 20 ft/6.1 m by 44 ft/13.4 m. A net, 2.5 ft/0.8 m deep, is stretched across the middle of the court and at a height of 5 ft/1.52 m above the ground to the top of the net. The shuttlecock must be volleyed.

Only the server can win points. The sport is named after Badminton House, the seat of the duke of Beaufort, where the game was played in the 19th century. The major tournaments are held on indoor courts; they include the **Thomas Cup**, an international team championship for men, first held in 1949, and the **Uber Cup** a women's international team competition, first held in 1957.

Badoglio Pietro 1871–1956. Italian soldier and Fascist politician. A veteran of campaigns against the peoples of Tripoli and Cyrenaica, in 1935 he became commander in chief in Ethiopia, adopting ruthless measures to break patriot resistance. He was created viceroy of Ethiopia and duke of Addis Ababa in 1936. He resigned during the disastrous campaign into Greece 1940 and succeeded Mussolini as prime minister of Italy from July 1943 to June 1944, negotiating the armistice with the Allies.

Baedeker Karl 1801–1859. German editor and publisher of foreign travel guides; the first was for Coblenz 1829. These are now published from Hamburg (before World War II from Leipzig).

Baekeland Leo Hendrik 1863–1944. Belgian-born US chemist. He invented ⬡Bakelite, the first commercial plastic, made from formaldehyde and ⬡phenol. He later made a photographic paper, Velox, which could be developed in artificial light.

Baez Joan 1941– . US folk singer who achieved fame in the early 1960s with versions of traditional English and American folk songs such as "Silver Dagger" and "We Shall Overcome," the latter becoming the anthem of anti-Vietnam War protesters. She was a major influence in the popularization of folk music, helped Bob Dylan at the start of his career, and has also remained active as a pacifist and antiwar campaigner.

Baffin William 1584–1622. English explorer and navigator. In 1616, he and Robert Bylot explored Baffin Bay, NE Canada, and reached latitude 77° 45′ N, which for 236 years remained the "furthest north."

Baffin Island island in the Northwest Territories.
area 195,875 sq mi/507,450 sq km
features largest island in the Canadian Arctic; mountains rise above 6,000 ft/2,000 m, and there are several large lakes. The northernmost part of the strait separating Baffin Island from Greenland forms Baffin Bay, the southern end is Davis Strait. It is named after William Baffin, who carried out research here 1614 during his search for the ⬡Northwest Passage.

bagatelle game resembling billiards but played on a board with numbered cups instead of pockets. The aim is to get the nine balls into the cups.

In **ordinary bagatelle** each player delivers all the balls in turn; in **French bagatelle** two or four players take part alternately.

Baggara member of a Bedouin people of the Nile Basin, principal4ly in Kordofan, Sudan, west of the White Nile. They are Muslims, traditionally occupied in cattle breeding and big-game hunting. Their language is probably Afro-Asiatic.

Baghdad historic city and capital of Iraq, on the river Tigris; population (1985) 4,649,000. Industries include oil refining, distilling, tanning, tobacco processing, and the manufacture of textiles and cement. Founded 762, it became Iraq's capital 1921.

To the SE, on the river Tigris, are the ruins of **Ctesiphon**, capital of Parthia about 250 BC–AD 226 and of the ⬡Sassanian Empire about 226–641; the remains of the Great Palace include the world's largest single-span brick arch 85 ft/26 m wide and 95 ft/29 m high.

A transportation hub from the earliest times, it was developed by the 8th-century caliph Harun al-Rashid, although little of the *Arabian*

Bahamas
Commonwealth of the

area 5,352 sq mi/13,864 sq km
capital Nassau on New Providence
cities Alice Town, Andros Town, Hope
Town, Spanish Wells, Freeport, Moss Town,
George Town
physical comprises 700 tropical coral islands
and about 1,000 cays
features desert islands: only 30 are inhabited;
Blue Holes of Andros, the world's longest
and deepest submarine caves; the Exumas
are a narrow spine of 365 islands
principal islands Andros, Grand Bahama,
Great Abaco, Eleuthera, New Providence,
Berry Islands, Biminis, Great Inagua, Acklins,
Exumas, Mayaguana, Crooked Island, Long
Island, Cat Island, Rum Cay, Watling (San
Salvador) Island
head of state Elizabeth II from 1973
represented by governor-general
head of government Hubert Ingraham
from 1992
political system constitutional monarchy
political parties Progressive Liberal Party
(PLP), centrist; Free National Movement
(FNM), center-left
exports cement, pharmaceuticals, petroleum
products, crawfish, salt, aragonite, rum,
pulpwood; over half the islands' employment
comes from tourism
currency Bahamian dollar
population (1990 est) 251,000; growth rate
1.8% p.a.
languages English and some Creole
media three independent daily newspapers
religions 29% Baptist, 23% Anglican, 22%
Roman Catholic
literacy 95% (1986)
GDP $2.7 bn (1987); $11,261 per head
chronology
1964 Independence achieved from Britain.
1967 First national assembly elections.
1972 Constitutional conference to discuss
full independence.
1973 Full independence achieved.
1983 Allegations of drug trafficking by
government ministers.
1984 Deputy prime minister and two cabinet
ministers resigned. Pindling denied any
personal involvement and was endorsed as
party leader.
1987 Pindling reelected despite claims of
frauds.
1992 FNM led by Hubert Ingraham won
absolute majority in assembly elections.

Nights city remains. It was overrun 1258 by the
Mongols, who destroyed the irrigation system.
In 1639 it was taken by the Turks. During
World War I, Baghdad was captured by General Maude 1917. During the Gulf War 1991, the
UN coalition forces bombed it in repeated air
raids and destroyed much of the city.

Baghdad Pact military treaty of 1955 concluded by the UK, Iran, Iraq, Pakistan, and
Turkey, with the US cooperating; it was replaced by the ◊Central Treaty Organization
(CENTO) when Iraq withdrew in 1958.

bagpipe ancient wind instrument used outdoors and incorporating a number of reed
pipes powered from a single inflated bag.
Known in Roman times, it is found in various
forms throughout Europe including Ireland
and Greece. The most famous, that of the
Highlands, is the Scottish national instrument.

Bagritsky Eduard. Adopted name of Eduard
Dzyubin 1895–1934. Russian poet. One of the
Constructivist group, he published the heroic
poem *Lay About Opanas* 1926, and collections
of verse called *The Victors* 1932 and *The Last
Night* 1932.

Baguio summer resort on Luzon island in
the Philippines, 125 mi/200 km N of Manila,
4,500 ft/1,370 m above sea level; population
(1980) 119,000. It is the official summer
residence of the Philippine president.

Bahadur Shah II 1775–1862. last of the Mogul
emperors of India. He reigned, though in name
only, as king of Delhi 1837–57, when he was
hailed by the mutineers of the ◊Sepoy Rebellion as an independent emperor at Delhi. After
the rebellion he was exiled to Burma with his
family.

Baha'i religion founded in the 19th century
from a Muslim splinter group, ◊Babism, by
the Persian ◊Baha'ullah. His message in essence was that all great religious leaders are
manifestations of the unknowable God and all
scriptures are sacred. There is no priesthood:
all Baha'is are expected to teach, and to work
towards world unification. There are about 4.5
million Baha'is worldwide.

Great stress is laid on equality regardless of
religion, race, or gender. Drugs and alcohol are
forbidden, as is celibacy. Marriage is strongly
encouraged; there is no arranged marriage,
but parental approval must be given. Baha'is
are expected to pray daily, but there is no
set prayer. From March 2–20, adults under 70
fast from sunrise to sunset. Administration is
carried out by an elected body, the Universal
House of Justice.

Bahamas country comprising a group of
about 700 islands and about 2,400 uninhabited
islets and cays in the Caribbean, 50 mi/80 km
from the SE coast of Florida. They extend for
about 760 mi/1,223 km from NW to SE, but
only 22 of the islands are inhabited.
government The Bahamas are an independent sovereign nation within the British
◊Commonwealth, with the British monarch as
head of state and represented by an appointed,
resident governor-general. The constitution,
effective since independence 1973, provides
for a two-chamber parliament with a senate
and house of assembly. The governor-general
appoints a prime minister and cabinet drawn
from and responsible to the legislature. The
governor-general appoints 16 senate members,
nine on the advice of the prime minister, four
on the advice of the leader of the opposition,
and three after consultation with the prime
minister. The house of assembly has 49 members, elected by universal suffrage. Parliament
has a maximum life of five years and may be
dissolved within that period.
history The Bahamas were reached by
Christopher Columbus 1492, who first landed
at San Salvador. The islands were a pirate area
in the early 18th century and became a crown
colony 1717 (although they were disputed by
the Carolina colony until 1787).
independence The Bahamas achieved internal self-government in 1964, and the first
elections for the national assembly on a full
voting register were held 1967. The Progressive Liberal Party (PLP), drawing its support
mainly from voters of African origin, won
the same number of seats as the European-dominated United Bahamian Party (UBP).
Lynden ◊Pindling became prime minister with
support from outside his party. In the 1968
elections the PLP scored a resounding victory, repeated 1972, enabling Pindling to lead
his country to full independence within the
Commonwealth 1973.
Prime minister Pindling The 1977 elections
resulted in an increased majority for the PLP.
The main contestants in the 1982 elections
were the Free National Movement (FNM, consisting of a number of factions that had split
and reunited) and the PLP. Despite allegations
of government complicity in drug trafficking,
the PLP was again successful, and Pindling
was unanimously endorsed as leader at a party
convention in 1984. The 1987 general election
was won by the PLP, led by Pindling, but with
a reduced majority. His time in office came to
an end in Aug 1992, when the FNM wom 33 of
the assembly's 49 seats and its leader Hubert
Ingraham became prime minister.
unequal wealth Whites make up only 10–15%
of the population but control 90% of the the
wealth of the country. *See illustration box.*

Baha'ullah title of Mirza Hosein Ali 1817–
1892. Persian founder of the ◊Baha'i religion.
Baha'ullah, "God's Glory," proclaimed himself
as the prophet the ◊Bab had foretold.

Bahawalpur city in the Punjab, Pakistan;
population (1981) 178,000. Once the capital of
a former state of Bahawalpur, it is now an
industrial town producing textiles and soap. It
has a university, established 1975.

Bahia state of E Brazil
area 216,556 sq mi/561,026 sq km
capital Salvador
industry oil, chemicals, agriculture
population (1986) 10,949,000.

Bahía Blanca port in S Argentina, on the river
Naposta, 3 mi/5 km from its mouth; population
(1991) 271,500. It is a major distribution center
for wool and food processing. The naval base
of Puerto Belgrano is here.

Bahrain country comprising a group of islands
in the Persian Gulf, between Saudi Arabia
and Iran.
government The 1973 constitution provided
for an elected national assembly of 30 members, but was dissolved 1975 after the prime
minister refused to work with it. The emir now
governs Bahrain by decree, through a cabinet
chosen by him. There are no recognizable
political parties.
history Traditionally an Arab monarchy, Bahrain was under Portuguese rule during the
16th century and from 1602 was dominated by
Persia (now Iran). Bahrain became a sheikdom 1783 under the control of the Khalifa

Bahrain
State of (*Dawlat al Bahrayn*)

area 266 sq mi/688 sq km
capital Manama on the largest island (also called Bahrain)
cities Muharraq, Jidd Hafs, Isa Town; oil port Mina Sulman
physical 35 islands, composed largely of sand-covered limestone; generally poor and infertile soil; flat and hot
environment a wildlife park features the oryx on Bahrain; most of the south of the island is preserved for the ruling family's falconry
features causeway linking Bahrain to mainland Saudi Arabia; Sitra island is a communications center for the lower Persian Gulf and has a satellite-tracking station
head of state and government Sheik Isa bin Sulman al-Khalifa (1933–   ) from 1961
political system absolute emirate
political parties none
exports oil, natural gas, aluminum, fish
currency Bahrain dinar
population (1990 est) 512,000 (two-thirds are nationals); growth rate 4.4% p.a.
life expectancy men 67, women 71
languages Arabic (official); Farsi, English, Urdu
religion 85% Muslim (Shiite 60%, Sunni 40%)
literacy men 79%, women 64% (1985 est)
GDP $3.5 bn (1987); $7,772 per head
chronology
1861 Became British protectorate.
1968 Britain announced its intention to withdraw its forces. Bahrain formed, with Qatar and the Trucial States, the Federation of Arab Emirates.
1971 Qatar and the Trucial States withdrew from the federation and Bahrain became an independent state.
1973 New constitution adopted, with an elected national assembly.
1975 Prime minister resigned and national assembly dissolved. Emir and his family assumed virtually absolute power.
1986 Gulf University established in Bahrain. A causeway was opened linking the island with Saudi Arabia.
1988 Bahrain recognized Afghan rebel government.
1991 Bahrain joined United Nations coalition that ousted Iraq from its occupation of Kuwait.

dynasty. British assistance was sought to preserve the country's independence against claims of sovereignty made by Persia and the Ottoman Empire. It became a British protectorate 1861, with government shared between the ruling sheik and a British adviser. Iran (Persia) claimed sovereignty 1928 but accepted a United Nations report 1970 showing that the inhabitants of Bahrain preferred independence.
independence achieved Britain announced the withdrawal of its forces 1968, and Bahrain joined two other territories under British protection, Qatar and the Trucial States (now the ◊United Arab Emirates), to form the Federation of Arab Emirates. Qatar and the Trucial States left the federation 1971, and Bahrain became an independent state. A new constitution 1973 provided for an elected national assembly, but two years later the prime minister, Sheik al-Khalifa, complained of obstruction by the assembly, which was then dissolved.
absolute emirate Since 1975 the emir and his family have ruled with virtually absolute power. Bahrain has become a focal point on the Gulf, being the site of the Gulf University (1986) and an international airport, the center of Gulf aviation. A causeway linking Bahrain with mainland Saudi Arabia was constructed 1986 (at 15.5 mi/25 km it is the longest in the world). Since the Iranian revolution of 1979, relations between the two countries have been uncertain, with fears of Iranian attempts to disturb Bahrain's stability. During the 1991 Gulf War, Bahrain opposed Iraq's invasion of Kuwait. *See illustration box.*

Baikal (Russian *Baykal Ozero*) largest freshwater lake in Asia, and the eighth largest in the world (area 12,150 sq mi/31,500 sq km); also the deepest in the world (up to 5,700 ft/ 1,640 m), in S Siberia, Russia. Fed by more than 300 rivers, it is drained only by the Lower Angara. It has sturgeon fisheries and rich fauna.
The lake has 1,155 species of animals and 1,085 species of plants—more than 1,000 of all these are found nowhere else in the world. The water at the bottom of the lake holds sufficient oxygen to allow animals to live at depths of over 5,200 ft/1,600 m.

bail a security, bonds, or money deposited with the court to obtain the temporary release of an arrested person, on the assurance that the person will obey the court, as by attending a legal proceeding at a stated time and place. If the person does not attend, the bail may be forfeited.
While the US Constitution nominally guarantees individuals right to reasonable bail, in effect availability of bail and amounts of security necessary to secure bail are set by judges, beased on judges' evaluations of the likelihood that a defendant will appear, or likelihood of further criminal acts or danger to the public, on the severity of the charge, and on the economic standing of the accused.

bailiff officer of the court whose job, usually in the county courts, is to serve notices and enforce the court's orders involving seizure of the goods of a debtor.
The term originated in Normandy as the name for a steward of an estate. It retained this meaning in England throughout the Middle Ages, and could also denote a sheriff's assistant. In France, the royal *bailli* or *bayle* was appointed to administer a large area of territory, the *baillage*, and was a leading local official.

Bailly Jean Sylvain 1736–1793. French astronomer who wrote about the satellites of Jupiter and the history of astronomy. Early in the French Revolution, was president of the National Assembly and mayor of Paris, but resigned in 1791; he was guillotined during the Reign of Terror.

Baily's beads bright spots of sunlight seen around the edge of the Moon for a few seconds immediately before and after a total ◊eclipse of the Sun, caused by sunlight shining between mountains at the Moon's edge. Sometimes one bead is much brighter than the others, producing the so-called *diamond ring* effect. The effect was described 1836 by the English astronomer Francis Baily (1774–1844), a wealthy stockbroker who retired in 1825 to devote himself to astronomy.

Bainbridge Beryl 1934–   . English novelist, originally an actress, whose works have the drama and economy of a stage play. They include *The Dressmaker* 1973, *The Bottle Factory Outing* 1974, *Injury Time* 1977, *Young Adolf* 1978, *The Winter Garden* 1980, the collected short stories in *Mum and Mr Armitage* 1985, and *The Birthday Boys* 1991.

Bainbridge Kenneth Tompkins 1904–   . US physicist who was director of the first atomic bomb test at Alamogordo, New Mexico, in 1945.
Bainbridge worked at the Cavendish Laboratory, Cambridge, England, in the 1930s. He also carried out research in radar. From 1961 he was George Vasmer Everett Professor of Physics at Harvard University.

Baird John Logie 1888–1946. Scottish electrical engineer who pioneered television. In 1925 he gave the first public demonstration of television and in 1926 pioneered fiber optics, radar (in advance of Robert ◊Watson-Watt), and "noctovision," a system for seeing at night by using infrared rays.
He also developed video recording on both wax records and magnetic steel disks (1926–27), color TV (1925–28), 3-D color TV (1925–46), and transatlantic TV (1928). In 1944 he developed facsimile television and demonstrated the world's first all-electronic color and 3-D color receiver (500 lines).

Baja California mountainous peninsula that forms the twin NW states of Lower (Spanish *baja*) California, Mexico; area 55,351 sq mi/143,396 sq km; population (1990) 1,736,200.
The northern state, Baja California Norte, includes the cities of Mexicali (its capital) and Tijuana: this area bordering the US now contains many factories. The southern state, Baja California Sur, attracts many US tourists for fishing, whale-watching (gray whales winter here), swimming, and sunbathing: La Paz is the state capital; Cabo San Lucas is a fashionable resort.

Bakelite first synthetic ◊plastic, created by Leo ◊Baekeland in 1909. Bakelite is hard, tough, and heatproof, and is used as an electrical insulator. It is made by the reaction of phenol with formaldehyde, producing a powdery resin that sets solid when heated. Objects are made by subjecting the resin to compression molding (simultaneous heat and pressure in a mold).
It is one of the thermosetting plastics, which do not remelt when heated, and is often used for electrical fittings.

Baker Chet (Chesney) 1929–1988. US jazz trumpeter of the cool school, whose good looks, occasional vocal performances, and romantic interpretations of ballads helped make him a cult figure. He became known with the Gerry Mulligan Quartet in 1952 and formed his own quartet 1953. Recordings include "My Funny Valentine" and "The Thrill Is Gone."

Baker James (Addison), III 1930– . US Republican politician. Under President Reagan, he was White House chief of staff 1981–85 and Treasury secretary 1985–88. After managing George Bush's successful presidential campaign 1988, Baker was appointed secretary of state 1989 and played a prominent role in the 1990–91 Gulf crisis, and the subsequent search for a lasting Middle East peace settlement. In 1992 he left the State Department to become White House chief of staff and to oversee Bush's reelection campaign.

A lawyer from Houston, Texas, Baker entered politics 1970 as one of the managers of his friend George Bush's unsuccessful campaign for the Senate. He served as undersecretary of commerce 1975–76 in the Ford administration and was deputy manager of the 1976 and 1980 Ford and Bush presidential campaigns. Baker joined the Reagan administration 1981. The most powerful member of the Bush team, he was described as an effective "prime minister."

Bakersfield city in S California, NE of Santa Barbara, on the Kern River; the seat of Kern county. It is known for its oil wells and oil products; population (1990) 174,820. Oil was discovered 1899.

Baker v Carr a US Supreme Court decision 1962 dealing with the responsibility of federal courts to hear suits against unconstitutional electoral apportionment. The petitioner filed suit against the Tennessee legislature, which, by neglecting to reapportion the state seats according to demographic changes, had allowed a disparity to develop between the voting powers of urban and rural residents. The Court did not decide whether this constituted an infraction of the 14th Amendment right to equal protection. Instead, it empowered federal courts to rule in state apportionment suits.

Bakhtaran (formerly [until 1980] *Kermanshah*) capital of Bakhtaran province, NW Iran; population (1986) 561,000. The province (area 9,148 sq mi/23,700 sq km; population 1,463,000) is on the Iraqi border and is mainly inhabited by Kurds. Industries include oil refining, carpets, and textiles.

Bakst Leon. Assumed name of Leon Rosenberg 1886–1924. Russian painter and theatrical designer. He used intense colors and fantastic images from Oriental and folk art, with an Art Nouveau tendency to graceful surface pattern. His designs for Diaghilev's touring *Ballets Russes* made a deep impression in Paris 1909–14.

Baku capital city of the Republic of Azerbaijan, industrial port (oil refining) on the Caspian Sea; population (1987) 1,741,000. It is a major oil center and is linked by pipelines with Batumi on the Black Sea. In Jan 1990 there were violent clashes between the Azeri majority and the Armenian minority, and Soviet troops were sent to the region; over 13,000 Armenians subsequently fled from the city. In early March 1992, opposition political forces sponsored protests in the city that led to the resignation of President Mutalibov.

Bakunin Mikhail 1814–1876. Russian anarchist, active in Europe. In 1848 he was expelled from France as a revolutionary agitator. In Switzerland in the 1860s he became recognized as the leader of the anarchist movement.

In 1869 he joined the First International (a coordinating socialist body) but, after stormy conflicts with Karl Marx, was expelled 1872.

Born of a noble family, Bakunin served in the Imperial Guard but, disgusted with tsarist methods in Poland, resigned his commission and traveled abroad. For his share in a brief revolt at Dresden 1849 he was sentenced to death. The sentence was commuted to imprisonment, and he was handed over to the tsar's government and sent to Siberia 1855. In 1861 he managed to escape to Switzerland. He had a large following, mainly in the Latin American countries. He wrote books and pamphlets, including *God and the State*.

Balaclava, Battle of in the Crimean War, an engagement on Oct 25, 1854 near a town in Ukraine, 6 mi/10 km SE of Sevastopol. It was the scene of the ill-timed **Charge of the Light Brigade** of British cavalry against the Russian entrenched artillery. Of the 673 soldiers who took part, there were 272 casualties. **Balaclava helmets** were knitted hoods worn here by soldiers in the bitter weather.

Balakirev Mily Alexeyevich 1837–1910. Russian composer. He wrote orchestral works including the fantasy *Islamey* 1869/1902, piano music, songs, and a symphonic poem *Tamara*, all imbued with the Russian national character and spirit. He was leader of the group known as the Five and taught its members, Mussorgsky, Cui, Rimsky-Korsakov, and Borodin.

balalaika Russian musical instrument, resembling a guitar. It has a triangular sound box, frets, and two, three, or four strings played by strumming with the fingers.

balance apparatus for weighing or measuring mass. The various types include the **beam balance** consisting of a centrally pivoted lever with pans hanging from each end, and the **spring balance**, in which the object to be weighed stretches (or compresses) a vertical coil spring fitted with a pointer that indicates the weight on a scale. Kitchen and bathroom scales are balances.

balance of nature in ecology, the idea that there is an inherent equilibrium in most ⟂ecosystems, with plants and animals interacting so as to produce a stable, continuing system of life on earth. Organisms in the ecosystem are adapted to each other—for example, waste products produced by one species are used by another and resources used by some are replenished by others; the oxygen needed by animals is produced by plants while the waste product of animal respiration, carbon dioxide, is used by plants as a raw material in photosynthesis. The nitrogen cycle, the water cycle, and the control of animal populations by natural predators are other examples. The activities of human beings can, and frequently do, disrupt the balance of nature.

balance of payments in economics, a tabular account of a country's debit and credit transactions with other countries. Items are divided into the *current account*, which includes both visible trade (imports and exports) and invisible trade (such as transport, tourism, interest, and dividends), and the *capital account*, which includes investment in and out of the country, international grants, and loans. Deficits or surpluses on these accounts are brought into balance by buying and selling reserves of foreign currencies.

A *balance of payments crisis* arises when a country's current account deteriorates because the cost of imports exceeds income from exports. In developing countries persistent trade deficits often result in heavy government borrowing overseas, which in turn leads to a ⟂debt crisis.

balance of power in politics, the theory that the best way of ensuring international order is to have power so distributed among states that no single state is able to achieve a dominant position. The term, which may also refer more simply to the actual distribution of power, is one of the most enduring concepts in international relations. Since the development of nuclear weapons, it has been asserted that the balance of power has been replaced by a *balance of terror*.

balance of trade the balance of trade transactions of a country recorded in its current account; it forms one component of the country's ⟂balance of payments.

balance sheet statement of the financial position of a company or individual on a specific date, showing both ⟂assets and ⟂liabilities.

Balanchine George 1904–1983. Russian-born US choreographer. After leaving the USSR in 1924, he worked with ⟂Diaghilev in France. Moving to the US in 1933, he became a major influence on dance, starting the New York City Ballet in 1948. He was the most influential 20th-century choreographer of ballet in the US. He developed an "American Neo-Classic" dance style and made the New York City Ballet one of the world's great companies. He also pioneered choreography in Hollywood films.

His many works include *Apollon Musagète* 1928 and *The Prodigal Son* 1929 for Diaghilev, *Serenade* 1934; several works for music by ⟂Stravinsky, such as *Agon* 1957 and *Duo Concertante* 1972; and Broadway musicals such as *On Your Toes* 1936 and *The Boys from Syracuse* 1938.

Balboa Vasco Núñez de 1475–1519. Spanish ⟂conquistador. He founded a settlement at Darien (now Panama) 1511 and crossed the Isthmus in search of gold, reaching the Pacific Ocean (which he called the South Sea) on Sept 25, 1513, after a 25-day expedition. He was made admiral of the Pacific and governor of Panama but was removed by Spanish court intrigue, imprisoned, and executed.

Balder in Norse mythology, the son of ⟂Odin and ⟂Freya and husband of Nanna, and the best, wisest, and most loved of all the gods. He was killed, at ⟂Loki's instigation, by a twig of mistletoe shot by the blind god Hodur.

Baldwin James 1924–1987. US writer, born in New York City, who portrayed the condition of black Americans in contemporary society. His works include the novels *Go Tell It on the Mountain* 1953, *Another Country* 1962, and *Just Above My Head* 1979; the play *The Amen Corner* 1955; and the autobiographical essays *Notes of a Native Son* 1955 and *The Fire Next Time* 1963. He was active in the civil-rights movement.

Baldwin Stanley, 1st Earl Baldwin of Bewdley 1867–1947. British Conservative politician, prime minister 1923–24, 1924–29, and 1935–37; he weathered the general strike 1926, secured complete adult suffrage 1928, and handled the ⟂abdication crisis of Edward VIII 1936, but failed to prepare Britain for World War II.

Baldwin five kings of the Latin kingdom of Jerusalem, including:

Baldwin I 1058–1118. King of Jerusalem from 1100. A French nobleman, he joined his brother ⟂Godfrey de Bouillon on the First Crusade in 1096 and established the kingdom of Jerusalem in 1100. It was destroyed by Islamic conquest in 1187.

Baldwin II Baldwin du Bourg died 1131. King of the Latin kingdom of Jerusalem from 1118. During his reign Tyre became the seat of a Latin archbishop.

Bâle French form of Basle or ▷Basel, town in Switzerland.

Balearic Islands (Spanish *Baleares*) group of Mediterranean islands forming an autonomous region of Spain; including ▷Majorca, ▷Minorca, ▷Ibiza, Cabrera, and Formentera
area 1,930 sq mi/5,000 sq km
capital Palma de Mallorca
products figs, olives, oranges, wine, brandy, coal, iron, slate; tourism is crucial
population (1986) 755,000
history a Roman colony from 123 BC, the Balearic Islands were an independent Moorish kingdom 1009–1232; they were conquered by Aragón 1343.

Balfour Arthur James, 1st Earl of Balfour 1848–1930. British Conservative politician, prime minister 1902–05 and foreign secretary 1916–19, when he issued the Balfour Declaration 1917 and was involved in peace negotiations after World War I, signing the Treaty of Versailles.

Balfour Declaration letter, dated Nov 2, 1917, from the British foreign secretary A J Balfour to Lord Rothschild (chair, British Zionist Federation) stating: "HM government view with favor the establishment in Palestine of a national home for the Jewish people." It led to the foundation of Israel 1948.

Bali island of Indonesia, E of Java, one of the Sunda Islands;
area 2,240 sq mi/5,800 sq km
capital Denpasar
physical volcanic mountains
features Balinese dancing, music, drama; one million tourists a year (1990)
products gold and silver work, woodcarving, weaving, copra, rice, coffee
population (1989) 2,787,000
history Bali's Hindu culture goes back to the 7th century; the Dutch gained control of the island by 1908.

Baliol John de *c.* 1250–1314. King of Scotland 1292–96. As an heir to the Scottish throne on the death of Margaret, the Maid of Norway, his cause was supported by the English king, Edward I, against 12 other claimants. Having paid homage to Edward, Baliol was proclaimed king but soon rebelled and gave up the kingdom when English forces attacked Scotland.

Bali Strait narrow strait between the two islands of Bali and Java, Indonesia. On Feb 19–20, 1942 it was the scene of a naval action between Japanese and Dutch forces that served to delay slightly the Japanese invasion of Java.

Balkans (Turkish "mountains") peninsula of SE Europe, stretching into the Mediterranean Sea between the Adriatic and Aegean seas, comprising Albania, Bosnia-Herzegovina, Bulgaria, Croatia, Greece, Romania, Slovenia, Turkey-in-Europe, and Yugoslavia. It is joined to the rest of Europe by an isthmus 750 mi/1,200 km wide between Rijeka on the west and the mouth of the Danube on the Black Sea to the east.
The great ethnic diversity resulting from successive waves of invasion has made the

Balkans a byword for political dissension. The Balkans' economy developed comparatively slowly until after World War II, largely because of the predominantly mountainous terrain, apart from the plains of the Save-Danube basin in the north. Political differences have remained strong, for example, the confrontation of Greece and Turkey over Cyprus and the differing types of communism that prevailed until the early 1990s in the rest. More recently civil wars in Croatia and Bosnia-Herzegovina have dominated the peninsula. To "*Balkanize*" is to divide into small warring states.

Balkan Wars two wars 1912–13 and 1913 (preceding World War I) which resulted in the expulsion by the Balkan states of Ottoman Turkey from Europe, except for a small area around Istanbul.
The **First Balkan War**, 1912, of Bulgaria, ▷Serbia, Greece, and Montenegro against Turkey, forced the Turks to ask for an armistice, but the London-held peace negotiations broke down when the Turks, while agreeing to surrender all Turkey-in-Europe W of the city of Edirne (formerly Adrianople), refused to give up the city itself. In Feb 1913 hostilities were resumed. Edirne fell on March 26 and on May 30, by the Treaty of London, Turkey retained in Europe only a small piece of E Thrace and the Gallipoli peninsula.
The **Second Balkan War**, June–July 1913, took place when the victors fought over acquisitions in Macedonia, from most of which Bulgaria was excluded. Bulgaria attacked Greece and Serbia, which were joined by Romania. Bulgaria was defeated, and Turkey retained Thrace.

Balkhash salt lake in the Republic of Kazakhstan; area 6,678 sq mi/17,300 sq km. It is 375 mi/600 km long and receives several rivers, but has no outlet. Very shallow, it is frozen throughout the winter.

Balkhash town on the N shore of Lake Balkhash in the Republic of Kazhakstan; population (1985) 112,000. It was founded 1928. Chief industries include copper mining and salt extraction.

Ball John died 1381. English priest, one of the leaders of the ▷Peasants' Revolt 1381, known as "the mad priest of Kent." A follower of John Wycliffe and a believer in social equality, he was imprisoned for disagreeing with the archbishop of Canterbury. During the revolt he was released from prison, and when in Blackheath, London, incited people against the ruling clases by preaching from the text "When Adam delved and Eve span, who was then the gentleman?" When the revolt collapsed he escaped but was captured near Coventry and executed.

Ball Lucille 1911–1989. US comedy actress, famed as TV's Lucy. She began her film career as a bit player 1933, and appeared in dozens of movies over the next few years, including *Room Service* 1938 (with the Marx Brothers) and *Fancy Pants* 1950 (with Bob Hope). From 1951 to 1957 she starred with her husband, Cuban bandleader Desi Arnaz, in *I Love Lucy*, the first US television show filmed before an audience. It was followed by *The Lucy Show* 1962–68 and *Here's Lucy* 1968–74.
Her TV success limited her film output after 1950; her later films include *Mame* 1974. The television series are still transmitted in many countries.

ballad (Latin *ballare* "to dance") popular poem

that tells a story. Of simple metrical form and dealing with some strongly emotional event, the ballad is halfway between the lyric and the epic. Most English ballads date from the 15th century. Poets of the Romantic movement both in England and in Germany were greatly influenced by the ballad revival, as seen in, for example, the *Lyrical Ballads* 1798 of Wordsworth and Coleridge. Other later forms are the "broadsheets" with a satirical or political motive, and the testamentary "hanging" ballads of the condemned criminal.
Historically, the ballad was primarily intended for singing at the communal ring-dance, the refrains representing the chorus. Opinion is divided as to whether the authorship of the ballads may be attributed to individual poets or to the community. Later ballads tend to center on a popular folk hero, such as Robin Hood or Jesse James.
In 19th-century music the refined drawing-room ballad had a vogue, but a more robust tradition survived in the music hall; folk song played its part in the development of pop music, and in this genre slow songs are often called "ballads" regardless of content.

ballade in music, an instrumental piece based on a story; a form used in piano works by ▷Chopin and ▷Liszt. In literature, a poetic form developed in France in the later Middle Ages from the ballad, generally consisting of one or more groups of three stanzas of seven or eight lines each, followed by a shorter stanza or envoy, the last line being repeated as a chorus.

Ballance John 1839–1893. New Zealand Liberal politician, born in Northern Ireland; prime minister 1891–93. He emigrated to New Zealand, founded and edited the *Wanganui Herald*, and held many cabinet posts. He passed social legislation and opposed federation with Australia.

ball-and-socket joint a joint allowing considerable movement in three dimensions, for instance the joint between the pelvis and the femur. To facilitate movement, such joints are lubricated by cartilage and synovial fluid. The bones are kept in place by ligaments and moved by muscles.

Ballard J(ames) G(raham) 1930– . English novelist whose works include science fiction on the theme of disaster, such as *The Drowned World* 1962 and *High-Rise* 1975; the partly autobiographical *Empire of the Sun* 1984, dealing with his internment in China during World War II; and the autobiographical novel *The Kindness of Women* 1991.

Ballesteros Seve(riano) 1957– . Spanish golfer who came to prominence 1976 and has won several leading tournaments in the US, including the Masters Tournament 1980 and 1983. He has also won the British Open three times: in 1979, 1984, and 1988.
Born in Pedrena, N Spain, he is one of four golf-playing brothers. He has won more than 60 tournaments worldwide.

ballet (Italian *balletto* "a little dance") theatrical representation in dance form in which music also plays a major part in telling a story or conveying a mood. Some such form of entertainment existed in ancient Greece, but Western ballet as we know it today first appeared in Italy. From there it was brought by Catherine de' Medici to France in the form of a spectacle combining singing, dancing, and declamation. In the 20th century Russian ballet has had a vital influence on the Classical tradition in the West, and ballet developed further in the US through the work of George Balanchine and American Ballet Theater, and in the UK through the influence of Marie Rambert. ▷Modern dance is a separate development.

history The first important dramatic ballet, the *Ballet comique de la reine*, was produced 1581 by the Italian Balthasar de Beaujoyeux at the French court and was performed by male courtiers, with ladies of the court forming the *corps de ballet*. In 1661 Louis XIV founded *L'Académie royale de danse*, to which all subsequent ballet activities throughout the world can be traced. Long, flowing court dress was worn by the dancers until the 1720s when Marie-Anne Camargo, the first great ballerina, shortened her skirt to reveal her ankles, thus allowing greater movement *à terre* and the development of dancing *en l'air*. It was not until the early 19th century that a Paris costumier, Maillot, invented tights, thus allowing complete muscular freedom. The first of the great ballet masters was Jean-Georges ▷Noverre, and great contemporary dancers were Teresa Vestris (1726–1808), Anna Friedrike Heinel (1753–1808), Jean Dauberval (1742–1806), and Maximilien Gardel (1741–1787). Carlo Blasis is regarded as the founder of Classical ballet, since he defined the standard conventional steps and accompanying gestures.

Romantic ballet The great Romantic era of ▷Taglioni, Elssler, Grisi, Grahn, and Cerrito began about 1830 but survives today only in the ballets *Giselle* 1841 and *La Sylphide* 1832. Characteristics of this era were the new calf-length Romantic white dress and the introduction of dancing on the toes, *sur les pointes*. The technique of the female dancer was developed, but the role of the male dancer was reduced to that of her partner.

Russian ballet was introduced to the West by Sergei ▷Diaghilev, who set out for Paris 1909, at about the same time that Isadora ▷Duncan, a fervent opponent of Classical ballet, was touring Europe. Associated with Diaghilev were Mikhail Fokine, Vaslav Nijinsky, Anna Pavlova, Léonide Massine, George Balanchine, and Serge Lifar. Ballets presented by his company, before its breakup after his death 1929, included *Les Sylphides*, *Schéhérazade*, *Petrouchka*, and *Blue Train*. Diaghilev and Fokine pioneered a new and exciting combination of the perfect technique of imperial Russian dancers and the appealing naturalism favored by Isadora Duncan. In Russia ballet continues to flourish, the two chief companies being the Kirov and the Bolshoi. Best-known ballerinas are Galina Ulanova and Maya Plisetskaya, and male dancers include the late Rudolf Nureyev, Mikhail Baryshnikov, and Alexander Godunov, now dancing in the West, as are the husband-and-wife team Vyacheslav Gordeyev and Nadezhda Pavlova.

American ballet was firmly established by the founding of Balanchine's School of American Ballet 1934, and by de Basil's Ballets Russes de Monte Carlo and Massine's Ballet Russe de Monte Carlo, which also carried on the Diaghilev tradition. In 1939 Lucia Chase and Richard Pleasant founded American Ballet Theater. From 1948 the New York City Ballet, under the guiding influence of Balanchine, developed a genuine American Neo-Classic style.

British ballet Marie Rambert initiated 1926 the company that developed into the Ballet Rambert, and launched the careers of choreographers such as Frederick Ashton and Anthony Tudor. The national company, the Royal · Ballet (so named 1956), grew from foundations laid by Ninette de Valois and Frederick Ashton 1928. British dancers include Margot Fonteyn, Alicia Markova, Anton Dolin, Antoinette Sibley, Anthony Dowell, David Wall, Merle Park, and Lesley Collier; choreographers include Kenneth MacMillan.

ballet blanc (French "white ballet") ballet, such as *Giselle*, in which the female dancers wear calf-length white dresses. The costume was introduced by Marie ▷Taglioni in *La Sylphide* 1832.

ballet d'action ballet with a plot, developed by ▷Noverre in the 18th century.

ballistics study of the motion and impact of projectiles such as bullets, bombs, and missiles. For projectiles from a gun, relevant exterior factors include temperature, barometric pressure, and wind strength; and for nuclear missiles these extend to such factors as the speed at which the Earth turns.

balloon lighter-than-air craft that consists of a gasbag filled with gas lighter than the surrounding air and an attached basket, or gondola, for carrying passengers and/or instruments. In 1783, the first successful human ascent was in Paris, in a hot-air balloon designed by the ▷Montgolfier brothers. In 1785, a hydrogen-filled balloon designed by J A C Charles traveled across the English Channel.

Coal gas was substituted as a cheap alternative to hydrogen in 1821, and this allowed for voyages by later 19th-century and early 20th-century explorers, scientists, and fairground performers. By the 1920s and 1930s balloons were used for high-altitude scientific research, especially before the development of high-altitude aircraft and Earth-orbiting satellites; for other kinds of research and exploration they were found to be generally unreliable, since they cannot be guided but go where the wind blows. They have become popular for sport and continue in use as instrument-only observers for meteorology, and for monitoring infrared, ultraviolet, and gamma rays.

ballot the process of voting in an election. In political elections in democracies ballots are usually secret: voters indicate their choice of candidate on a voting slip that is placed in a sealed ballot box or by pulling levers on a machine in a voting booth. *Ballot rigging* is a term used to describe elections that are fraudulent because of interference with the voting process or the counting of ▷votes.

ballroom dancing collective term for social dances such as the ▷foxtrot, quickstep, ▷tango, and ▷waltz.

ball valve valve that works by the action of external pressure raising a ball and thereby opening a hole.

An example is the valve used in toilet water tanks to cut off the water supply when it reaches the correct level. It consists of a flat rubber washer at one end of a pivoting arm and a hollow ball at the other. The ball floats on the water surface, rising as the tank fills, and at the correct level the rubber washer is pushed against the water-inlet pipe, cutting off the flow.

Balmer Johann Jakob 1825–1898. Swiss physicist and mathematician who developed a formula in 1884 that gave the wavelengths of the light emitted by the hydrogen atom (the hydrogen spectrum). This simple formula played a central role in the development of spectral and atomic theory.

balsam any of various garden plants of the genus *Impatiens* of the balsam family. They are usually annuals with spurred red or white flowers and pods that burst and scatter their seeds when ripe. In medicine and perfumery, balsam refers to various oily or gummy aromatic plant resins, such as balsam of Peru from the Central American tree *Myroxylon pereirae*.

Baltic Sea large shallow arm of the North Sea, extending NE from the narrow Skagerrak and Kattegat, between Sweden and Denmark, to the Gulf of Bothnia between Sweden and Finland. Its coastline is 5,000 mi/8,000 km long, and its area, including the gulfs of Riga, Finland, and Bothnia, is 163,000 sq mi/422,300 sq km. Its shoreline is shared by Denmark, Germany, Poland, the Baltic States, Russia, Finland, and Sweden.

Many large rivers flow into it, including the Oder, Vistula, Niemen, W Dvina, Narva, and Neva. Tides are hardly perceptible, salt content is low; weather is often stormy and navigation dangerous. Most ports are closed by ice from Dec until May. The Kiel canal links the Baltic and North seas; the Göta canal connects the two seas by way of the S Swedish lakes. Since 1975 the Baltic Sea has been linked by the St Petersburg–Belomorsk seaway with the White Sea.

Baltic States collective name for the states of ▷Estonia, ▷Latvia, and ▷Lithuania, former constituent republics of the USSR (from 1940). They regained independence Sept 1991.

Baltimore industrial port and largest city in Maryland, on the W shore of Chesapeake Bay, NE of Washington, DC; population (1990) 736,000. Industries include shipbuilding, oil refining, food processing, and the manufacture of steel, chemicals, and aerospace equipment.

It is the seat of Johns Hopkins University. The inner harbor area has the National Aquarium, a 30-story World Trade Center, and the first commissioned warship of the US Navy, dating from 1797.

It was named after the founder of Maryland, Lord Baltimore (1606–75). The city of Baltimore dates from 1729 and was incorporated 1797. At Fort McHenry, Francis Scott Key wrote *The Star Spangled Banner*. The writer Edgar Allan Poe and the baseball player Babe Ruth lived here.

Baltistan region in the Karakoram range of NE Kashmir, held by Pakistan since 1949. It is the home of Balti Muslims of Tibetan origin. The chief town is Skardu, but Ghyari is of greater significance to Muslims as the site of a mosque built by Sayyid Ali Hamadani, a Persian who brought the Shia Muslim religion to Baltistan in the 14th century.

Baluchistan mountainous desert area, comprising a province of Pakistan, part of the Iranian province of Sistán and Balúchestan, and a small area of Afghanistan. The Pakistani province has an area of 134,019 sq mi/347,200 sq km and a population (1985) of 4,908,000; its capital is Quetta. Sistán and Balúchestan has an area of 70,098 sq mi/181,600 sq km and a population (1986) of 1,197,000; its capital is Zahedan. The port of Gwadar in Pakistan is strategically important, on the Indian Ocean and the Strait of Hormuz.

The common religion of the Baluch (or Baluchi) people is Islam, and they speak Baluchi, a member of the Iranian branch of the Indo-European language family. In the drier areas they make use of tents, moving when it becomes too arid. Although they practice nomadic pastoralism, many are settled agriculturalists.

The ballet repertory

date	ballet	composer	choreographer	place
1670	Le Bourgeois Gentilhomme	Lully	Beauchamp	Chambord
1735	Les Indes Galantes	Rameau	Blondy	Paris
1828	La Fille Mal Gardée	Hérold	Aumer	Paris
1832	La Sylphide	Schneitzhoeffer	F Taglioni	Paris
1841	Giselle	Coralli	Perrot	Paris
1870	Coppélia	Delibes	Saint-Léon	Paris
1877	La Bayadère	Minkus	M Petipa	St Petersburg
1877	Swan Lake	Tchaikovsky	Reisinger	Moscow
1890	The Sleeping Beauty	Tchaikovsky	M Petipa	St Petersburg
1892	Nutcracker	Tchaikovsky	M Petipa/Ivanov	St Petersburg
1898	Raymonda	Glazunov	M Petipa	St Petersburg
1905	The Dying Swan	Saint-Saëns	Fokine	St Petersburg
1907	Les Sylphides	Chopin	Fokine	St Petersburg
1910	Carnival	Schumann	Fokine	St Petersburg
1910	The Firebird	Stravinsky	Fokine	Paris
1911	Petrushka	Stravinsky	Fokine	Paris
1911	Le Spectre de la Rose	Weber	Fokine	Monte Carlo
1912	L'Après-midi d'un Faune	Debussy	Nijinsky	Paris
1912	Daphnis and Chloe	Ravel	Fokine	Paris
1913	Jeux	Debussy	Nijinsky	Paris
1913	The Rite of Spring	Stravinsky	Nijinsky	Paris
1915	El Amor Brujo	Falla	Imperio	Madrid
1917	Parade	Satie	Massine	Paris
1919	The Three-Cornered Hat	Falla	Massini	London
1923	Les Noces	Stravinsky	Nijinska	Paris
1924	Les Biches	Poulenc	Nijinska	Monte Carlo
1928	Apollon Musagète	Stravinsky	Balanchine	Paris
1928	Le Baiser de la fée	Tchaikovsky	Nijinska	Paris
1928	Bolero	Ravel	Nijinska	Paris
1929	The Prodigal Son	Prokofiev	Balanchine	Paris
1929	La Valse	Ravel	Nijinska	Monte Carlo
1931	Bacchus and Ariadne	Roussel	Lifar	Paris
1931	Façade	Walton	Ashton	London
1937	Checkmate	Bliss	de Valois	Paris
1937	Les Patineurs	Meyerbeer/Lambert	Ashton	London
1938	Billy the Kid	Copland	Loring	Chicago
1938	Romeo and Juliet	Prokofiev	Psota	Moravia
1942	Gayaneh	Khachaturian	Anisimova	Molotov-Perm
1942	The Miraculous Mandarin	Bartók	Milloss	Milan
1942	Rodeo	Copland	de Mille	New York
1944	Appalachian Spring	Copland	Graham	Washington
1945	Cinderella	Prokofiev	Zakharov	Moscow
1949	Carmen	Bizet	Petit	London
1951	Pineapple Poll	Sullivan/Mackerras	Cranko	London
1956	Spartacus	Khachaturian	Jacobson	Leningrad
1957	Agon	Stravinsky	Balanchine	New York
1962	A Midsummer Night's Dream	Mendelssohn	Balanchine	New York
1962	Pierrot Lunaire	Schoenberg	Tetley	New York
1964	The Dream	Mendelssohn/Lanchbery	Ashton	London
1965	The Song of the Earth	Mahler	MacMillan	Stuttgart
1967	Anastasia	Martinu	MacMillan	New York
1968	Enigma Variations	Elgar	Ashton	London
1969	The Taming of the Shrew	Scarlatti/Stolze	Cranko	Stuttgart
1972	Duo Concertant	Stravinsky	Balanchine	New York
1974	Elite Syncopations	Jopolin and others	MacMillan	London
1976	A Month in the Country	Chopin/Lanchbery	Ashton	London
1978	Mayerling	Liszt/Lanchbery	MacMillan	London
1978	Symphony of Psalms	Stravinsky	Kylían	Scheveningen, The Netherlands
1980	Gloria	Poulenc	MacMillan	London
1980	Rhapsody	Rachmaninov	Ashton	London
1981	St Matthew Passion	Bach	Neumeier	Hamburg
1982	The Golden Age	Shostakovich	Grigorovich	Moscow
1984	Different Drummer	Webern/Schoenberg	MacMillan	London
1987	In the Middle, Somewhat Elevated	Willems	Forsythe	Paris
1988	L'allegro, il penseroso ed il moderato	Handel	Morris	Brussels
1989	Falling Angels	Reich	Kylían	Amsterdam
1991	Winter Dreams	Tchaikovsky	MacMillan	London

history Originally a loose tribal confederation, Baluchistan was later divided into four principalities that were sometimes under Persian, sometimes under Afghan suzerainty. In the 19th century British troops tried to subdue the inhabitants until a treaty 1876 gave them autonomy in exchange for British army outposts along the Afghan border and strategic roads. On the partition of India 1947 the khan of Khalat declared Baluchistan independent; the insurrection was crushed by the new Pakistani army after eight months. Three rebellions followed, the last being from 1973 to 1977, when 3,300 Pakistani soldiers and some 6,000 Baluch were killed.

Balzac Honoré de 1799–1850. French novelist. His first success was *Les Chouans/The Chouans* and *La Physiologie du mariage/The Physiology of Marriage* 1829, inspired by Walter Scott. This was the beginning of the long series of novels *La Comédie humaine/The ⟡Human Comedy*. He also wrote the Rabelaisian *Contes drolatiques/Ribald Tales* 1833.

Born in Tours, Balzac studied law and worked as a notary's clerk in Paris before turning to literature. His first attempts included tragedies such as *Cromwell* and novels published pseudonymously with no great success. A venture in printing and publishing 1825–28 involved him in a lifelong web of debt. His patroness, Madame de Berny, figures in *Le Lys dans la vallée/The Lily in the Valley* 1836. Balzac intended his major work *La Comédie humaine/The Human Comedy* to comprise 143 volumes, depicting every aspect of society in 19th-century France, of which he completed 80. The series includes *Eugénie Grandet* 1833, *Le Père Goriot* 1834, and *Cousine Bette* 1846. Balzac corresponded constantly with the Polish countess Evelina Hanska after meeting her 1833, and they married four months before his death in Paris. He was buried in Père Lachaise cemetery.

Bamako capital and port of Mali on the river Niger; population (1976) 400,000. It produces pharmaceuticals, chemicals, textiles, tobacco, and metal products.

Bamberg town in Bavaria, Germany, on the river Regnitz; population (1985) 70,400. The economy is based on engineering and the production of textiles, carpets, and electrical goods. It has an early 13th-century Romanesque cathedral.

bamboo any of numerous plants of the subgroup Bambuseae within the grass family Gramineae, mainly found in tropical and subtropical regions. Some species grow as tall as 120 ft/36 m. The stems are hollow and jointed and can be used in furniture, house, and boat construction. The young shoots are edible; paper is made from the stem.

Bamboo flowers and seeds only once before the plant dies, sometimes after growing for as long as 120 years.

Banaba (formerly *Ocean Island*) island in the Republic of ⟡Kiribati.

banana any of several treelike tropical plants of the genus *Musa*, family Musaceae, which grow up to 25 ft/8 m high. The edible banana is the fruit of a sterile hybrid form.

The curved yellow fruits of the commercial banana, arranged in rows of 'hands,' form cylindrical masses of a hundred or more. They are picked and exported green and ripened aboard refrigerated ships. The plant is destroyed after cropping. The **plantain**, a larger, coarser hybrid variety that is used green as a cooked vegetable, is a dietary staple in many countries. In the wild, bananas depend on bats for pollination.

Banaras alternative transliteration of ⚪Varanasi, holy Hindu city in Uttar Pradesh, India.

Bancroft George 1800–1891. US diplomat and historian. A Democrat, he was secretary of the navy 1845 when he established the US Naval Academy at Annapolis, Maryland, and as acting secretary of war (May 1846) was instrumental in bringing about the occupation of California and the ⚪Mexican war. He wrote a *History of the United States* 1834–76.

band music group, usually falling into a special category: for example, *military*, comprising woodwind, brass, and percussion; *brass*, solely of brass and percussion; *marching*, a variant of brass; *dance and swing*, often like a small orchestra; *jazz*, with no fixed instrumentation; *rock and pop*, generally electric guitar, bass, and drums, variously augmented; and *steel*, from the West Indies, in which percussion instruments made from oildrums sound like marimbas.

Band, the North American rock group 1961–76. They acquired their name when working as Bob Dylan's backing band, and made their solo debut 1968 with *Music from Big Pink*. Their unostentatious ensemble playing and strong original material set a new trend.

Formed in Canada as a backing group for the US rock-and-roll singer Ronnie Hawkins (1935–) and initially known as the Hawks, they took up with Dylan 1965, touring and recording with him intermittently over the next ten years. Their albums include *The Band* 1969, *Stage Fright* 1970, and *Northern Lights—Southern Cross* 1975. In their appearance and mysterious lyrics they often evoked a bygone age, as in the song "The Night They Drove Old Dixie Down." Their farewell concert was filmed by Martin Scorsese as *The Last Waltz* 1978.

Banda Hastings Kamuzu 1902– . Malawi politican, president from 1966. He led his country's independence movement and was prime minister of Nyasaland (the former name of Malawi) from 1963. He became Malawi's first president 1966 and 1971 was named president for life; his rule has been authoritarian. Despite civil unrest during 1992, he has resisted calls for free, multiparty elections.

Bandar Abbas port and winter resort in Iran on the Ormuz strait, Persian Gulf; population (1983) 175,000. Formerly called Gombroon, it was renamed and made prosperous by Shah Abbas I (1571–1629). It is a naval base.

Bandaranaike Sirimavo (born Ratwatte) 1916– . Sri Lankan politician, who succeeded her husband Solomon Bandaranaike to become the world's first female prime minister 1960–65 and 1970–77, but was expelled from parliament 1980 for abuse of her powers while in office. She was largely responsible for the new constitution 1972.

Bandaranaike Solomon West Ridgeway Dias 1899–1959. Sri Lankan nationalist politician. In 1952 he founded the Sri Lanka Freedom party and in 1956 became prime minister, pledged to a socialist program and a neutral foreign policy. He failed to satisfy extremists and was assassinated by a Buddhist monk.

Bandar Seri Begawan formerly *Brunei Town* capital of Brunei; population (1983) 57,600.

bandicoot small marsupial mammal inhabiting Australia and New Guinea. There are about 11 species, family Peramelidae, rat- or rabbit-sized and living in burrows. They have long snouts, eat insects, and are nocturnal. A related group, the rabbit bandicoots or bilbys, is reduced to a single species that is now endangered and protected by law.

Bandung commercial city and capital of Jawa Barat province on the island of Java, Indonesia; population (1980) 1,463,000. Bandung is the third largest city in Indonesia and was the administrative center when the country was the Netherlands East Indies.

Bandung Conference first conference 1955 of the Afro-Asian nations, proclaiming anticolonialism and neutrality between East and West.

bandy-bandy venomous Australian snake *Vermicella annulata* of the cobra family, which grows to about 2.5 ft/75 cm. It is banded in black and white. It is not aggressive toward humans.

Banff resort in Alberta, 62 mi/100 km NW of Calgary; population (1984) 4,250. It is a center for Banff National Park (Canada's first, founded 1885) in the Rocky Mountains.

Bangalore capital of Karnataka state, S India; population (1981) 2,600,000. Industries include electronics, aircraft and machine-tools construction, and coffee.

Bang Ka or *Banka* or *Banca* island in Indonesia off the E coast of Sumatra
area 4,600 sq mi/12,000 sq km
capital Pangkalpinang
cities Mintok (port)
products tin (one of the world's largest producers)
population (1970) 300,000.

Bangkok capital and port of Thailand, on the river Chao Phraya; population (1990) 6,019,000. Products include paper, ceramics, cement, textiles, and aircraft. It is the headquarters of the Southeast Asia Treaty Organization (SEATO).

Bangkok was established as the capital by Phra Chao Tak 1769, after the Burmese had burned down the former capital, Avuthia, about 40 mi/65 km to the N. Features include the temple of the Emerald Buddha and the vast palace complex.

Bangladesh country in southern Asia, bounded N, W, and E by India, SE by Myanmar, and S by the Bay of Bengal.
government The 1972 constitution, which provided for a parliamentary system of government, was suspended in 1982 and replaced by a presidentialist constitution in 1986. It was restored in 1991. It provides for a single-chamber legislature, the Jatiya Sangsad, which consists of 300 members directly elected for five-year terms and 30 women elected by the legislature itself. A prime minister and cabinet is drawn from the grouping which commands a majority within the parliament. The president, who now has a largely ceremonial role, is elected by the parliament.
history For history before 1947 see ⚪India; for history 1947–71 see ⚪Pakistan. Present-day Bangladesh formerly comprised East Bengal province and the Sylhet district of Assam in British India. Predominantly Muslim, it was

formed into the eastern province of Pakistan when India was partitioned 1947. Substantially different in culture, language, and geography from the western provinces of Pakistan 1,000 mi/1,600 km away, and with a larger population, it resented the political and military dominance exerted by West Pakistan during the 1950s and 1960s. A movement for political autonomy grew after 1954, under the Awami League headed by Sheik Mujibur ⚪Rahman. This gained strength as a result of West Pakistan's indifference 1970, when flooding killed 500,000 in East Pakistan.

republic proclaimed In Pakistan's first general elections, in 1970, the Awami League gained an overwhelming victory in East Pakistan and an overall majority in the all-Pakistan National Assembly. Talks on redrawing the constitution broke down, leading to East Pakistan's secession and the establishment of a Bangladesh ("Bengal nation") government in exile in Calcutta, India, 1971. Civil war resulted in the flight of 10 million East Pakistani refugees to India, administrative breakdown, famine, and cholera. The West Pakistani forces in East Pakistan surrendered 1971 after India intervened on the secessionists' side. A republic of Bangladesh was proclaimed and rapidly gained international recognition 1972.

first leader assassinated Sheik Mujibur Rahman became prime minister 1972 under a secular, parliamentary constitution. He introduced a socialist economic program of nationalization but became intolerant of opposition, establishing a one-party presidential system Jan 1975. Rahman, his wife, and close relatives were assassinated in a military coup Aug 1975. The Awami League held power for three months under Khandakar Mushtaq Ahmed before a further military coup Nov 1975 established as president and chief martial-law administrator the nonpolitical chief justice Abu Sadat Mohammed Sayem.

martial law under Zia Maj Gen Zia ur-Rahman (1936–1981) became chief martial-law administrator 1976. President from 1977, he adopted an Islamic constitution, approved by a national referendum in May. In June he won a 4:1 majority in a direct presidential election. Zia's newly formed Bangladesh Nationalist Party (BNP) won a parliamentary majority. A civilian government was installed, and martial law and the state of emergency were lifted 1979. The administration was undermined, however, by charges of corruption and by a guerrilla movement in the Chittagong Hill Tracts 1980. On May 30, 1981 Zia was assassinated in an attempted coup, and interim power was assumed by Vice President Justice Abdus Sattar.

coup led by Ershad With disorder increasing, the civilian administration was overthrown March 1982 by Lt Gen Mohammad Hussain Ershad. Martial law was reimposed and political activity banned. Ershad governed first as chief martial-law administrator and then, from 1983, as president with an appointed council of ministers. The economy improved and a broad opposition coalition, the Movement for the Restoration of Democracy, was formed 1983. A move back to civilian rule began 1983–85 with local elections; Ershad promised presidential and parliamentary elections 1984, but both were canceled after an opposition threat of a boycott and campaign of civil disobedience if martial law was not first lifted.

contentious elections The ban on political activity was removed Jan 1986, and parliamentary elections were held in May. The Awami League agreed to participate in these elections, but the BNP and many other opposition parties boycotted them. With a campaign marked by violence, widespread abstentions, and claims of ballot rigging, Ershad and his Jatiya Dal party gained the two-thirds majority required to pass a law granting retrospective immunity. Ershad was reelected president in a direct election Oct 1986, and martial law was lifted Nov 1986.

opposition to government During 1987 the Awami League, led by Sheika Hasina Wazed (the daughter of Sheik Mujibur Rahman), and the BNP, led by Begum Khaleda Zia (the widow of Maj Gen Zia ur-Rahman), stepped up their campaign against the Ershad government, demanding the president's resignation and free elections. In the wake of a wave of violent strikes and demonstrations, Ershad proclaimed a state of emergency Nov 1987, with urban curfews imposed, the two opposition leaders placed under house arrest, and antigovernment protests banned. A month later, parliament was dissolved and fresh elections called March 1988. As a result of both

ballot rigging and an opposition boycott, the ruling Jatiya Dal gained a sweeping victory. The state of emergency was lifted April 1988, and a bill was passed by parliament June 1988 making Islam the state religion.

floods Bangladesh received Sept 1988 the heaviest monsoon rains in 70 years; in the resulting floods several thousand people died and 30 million became homeless.

Chittagong Hill Tracts The Jatiya Sangsad (parliament) approved legislation 1989 devolving power to directly elected, substantially autonomous councils in three Chittagong Hill Tract districts in SE Bangladesh, where the indigenous people had many grievances and had fought a 14-year resistance struggle led by the Shanti Bahini ("peace force") organization against settlers protected by the army.

Ershad resigns On Dec 4, 1990, after a protracted campaign for the government's removal, Ershad resigned and former prime minister Kazi Zafar Ahmad went into hiding. The state of emergency was lifted, parliament dissolved, and Ershad replaced by Shahabuddin Ahmad, the country's chief justice, as interim executive president. Ahmad

immediately annulled the Special Powers Act (which had allowed the government to detain people without trial and summarily close down newspapers), and set about removing Ershad-installed personnel from key positions in the military and bureaucracy. Police raids on Ershad's residence revealed evidence of corruption. He was charged with illegal possession of firearms and embezzlement of public funds amounting to £3–4 million/$5–7 million in 1990 alone, and eventually found guilty.

free elections When the elections were held Feb 1991, the BNP emerged as the dominant force, capturing 140 of the 300 seats. It was helped by a big turnout from women and young people in the towns. The Awami League, which had been expected to win, obtained less than a third of the seats. Begum Khaleda Zia, leader of the BNP, formed a coalition government with minor parties in preparation for standing for president, and in March 1991 she was sworn in as the first woman prime minister of Bangladesh.

cyclone disaster Around 139,000 people were killed and thousands more threatened by epidemics after the devastating cyclone of April 29–30, 1991, which severely affected the area around Chittagong. Between 4 and 10 million people were made homeless and 500,000 sq mi/1,300,000 sq km was inundated. Overall economic losses were put at $3 billion by the government. By May 1991 emergency aid amounting to $250 million had been provided by the international community, but there were criticisms of the government's management of the relief operation.

parliamentary government restored In late July 1991, the new government introduced a deregulationary New Industrial Policy to boost private enterprise and encourage foreign investment. A nationwide referendum Sept 1991 restored parliamentary government, and in the same month by-elections secured an absolute majority in parliament for the BNP. In Oct 1991 parliament elected its speaker Abdur Rahman Biswas to succeed Shahabuddin Ahmad as state president.

foreign relations Bangladesh has remained a member of the Commonwealth since 1972. It has been heavily dependent on foreign economic aid but has pursued a broader policy of the ◯nonaligned movement. Relations with India have deteriorated since 1975 as a result of disputes over the sharing of Ganges water and the annual influx of 200,000 Bangladeshi refugees in Assam and West Bengal, which has prompted India to threaten to construct a frontier fence. In Jan 1992 Bangladesh became a refuge for around 60,000 Muslims fleeing military crackdowns in Myanmar. The influx caused a further drain on the country's already scanty resources.

living standards Bangladesh is the most densely populated country in the world, with more than 2,255 people per sq mi. Only 15% of the people live in urban areas; 46.6% of the population is under 15, and 75% of women have their first child by the age of 17. There is an estimated one doctor for every 9,000 people and one nurse for every 20,000. *See illustration box.*

Bangladesh
People's Republic of (*Gana Prajatantri Bangladesh*) (formerly **East Pakistan**)

area 55,585 sq mi/144,000 sq km
capital Dhaka (formerly Dacca)
cities ports Chittagong, Khulna
physical flat delta of rivers Ganges (Padma) and Brahmaputra (Jamuna), the largest estuarine delta in the world; annual rainfall of 100 in/2,540 mm; some 75% of the land is less than 10 ft/3 m above sea level and vulnerable to flooding and cyclones; hilly in extreme SE and NE
environment deforestation on the slopes of the Himalayas increases the threat of flooding in the coastal lowlands of Bangladesh, which are also subject to devastating monsoon storms. The building of India's Farakka Barrage has reduced the flow of the Ganges in Bangladesh and permitted salt water to intrude further inland. Increased salinity has destroyed fisheries, contaminated drinking water, and damaged forests
head of state Abdur Rahman Biswas from 1991
head of government Begum Khaleda Zia from 1991
political system emergent democratic republic
political parties Bangladesh Nationalist

Party (BNP), Islamic, right of center; Awami League, secular, moderate socialist; Jatiya Dal (National Party), Islamic nationalist
exports jute, tea, garments, fish products
currency taka
population (1991 est) 107,992,100; growth rate 2.17% p.a.; just over 1 million people live in small ethnic groups in the tropical Chittagong Hill Tracts, Mymensingh, and Sylhet districts
life expectancy men 50, women 52
language Bangla (Bengali)
religion Sunni Muslim 85%, Hindu 14%
literacy men 43%, women 22% (1985 est)
GDP $17.6 bn (1987); $172 per head
chronology
1947 Formed into eastern province of Pakistan on partition of British India.
1970 Half a million killed in flood.
1971 Bangladesh emerged as independent nation, under leadership of Sheik Mujibur Rahman, after civil war.
1975 Mujibur Rahman assassinated. Martial law imposed.
1976–77 Maj Gen Zia ur-Rahman assumed power.
1978–79 Elections held and civilian rule restored.
1981 Assassination of Maj Gen Zia.
1982 Lt Gen Ershad assumed power in army coup. Martial law reimposed.
1986 Elections held but disputed. Martial law ended.
1987 State of emergency declared in response to opposition demonstrations.
1988 Assembly elections boycotted by main opposition parties. State of emergency lifted. Islam made state religion. Monsoon floods left 30 million homeless and thousands dead.
1989 Power devolved to Chittagong Hill Tracts to end 14-year conflict between local people and army-protected settlers.
1990 Following mass antigovernment protests, President Ershad resigned; Shahabuddin Ahmad became interim president.
1991 Feb: elections resulted in coalition government with BNP dominant. April: cyclone killed around 139,000 and left up to 10 million homeless. Sept: parliamentary government restored; Abdur Rahman Biswas elected president.

Bangui capital and port of the Central African Republic, on the River Ubangi; population (1988) 597,000. Industries include beer, cigarettes, office machinery, and timber and metal products.

Banjermasin river port in Indonesia, on Borneo; population (1980) 381,300. It is the capital of Kalimantan Selatan province. It exports rubber, timber, and precious stones.

The university was founded 1960.

banjo resonant stringed musical instrument, with a long fretted neck and circular drum-type sound box covered on the topside only by stretched skin (now usually plastic). It is played with a plectrum.

The banjo originated in the American South among black slaves (based on a similar instrument of African origin).

Banjul capital and chief port of Gambia, on an island at the mouth of the river Gambia; population (1983) 44,536. Established 1816 as a settlement for freed slaves, it was known as Bathurst until 1973.

bank financial institution that uses funds deposited with it to lend money to companies or individuals, and also provides financial services to its customers. In terms of assets, seven of the world's top ten banks were Japanese in 1988.

A *central bank* (in the US, the ⟡Federal Reserve System) issues currency for the government, in order to provide cash for circulation and exchange. A *savings bank* serves personal accounts and is licensed by the state in which it and its branches may operate. A commercial bank may have branches throughout the nation, since it services businesses, and sometimes becomes an international institution. There are also various forms of both public and private savings and loan companies that are called banks.

Bank for International Settlements (BIS) a bank established 1930 to handle German reparations settlements from World War I. The BIS (based in Basel, Switzerland) is today a center for economic and monetary research and assists cooperation of central banks. It also has important trustee duties. Its place in the international financial world was greatly restricted by the ⟡Bretton Woods Conference 1944 and superseded by the ⟡International Monetary Fund.

The BIS role as liaison among central banks is its primary function today and the reason it has survived several attempts to terminate it.

Bankhead Tallulah 1903–1968. US actress, renowned for her wit and flamboyant lifestyle. Her stage appearances include *Dark Victory* 1934, *The Little Foxes* 1939, and *The Skin of Our Teeth* 1942. Her films include Hitchcock's *Lifeboat* 1943.

Bank of Commerce and Credit International (BCCI) international bank, founded 1972. By 1990 BCCI had offices in 69 countries, $15 billion in deposits, and $20 billion in assets. In July 1991 evidence of widespread systematic fraud at BCCI led regulators in seven countries to seize the bank's assets, and its operations in most of the remaining 62 countries were then also shut down. A subsequent investigation resulted in a New York criminal indictment of the institution and four of its units, and the arrest of some 20 BCCI officials in Abu Dhabi for alleged fraud.

BCCI was founded 1972 by Pakistani banker, Agha Hasan Abedi (1922–   ), who remained its chairman until 1989. From March 1990, it was under the control of Sheik Sultan Zayed bin al-Nahayan, the ruler of Abu Dhabi. In July 1990 five former officials of BCCI were convicted in Tampa, Florida, for laundering $32 million in cocaine profits for Colombia's Medellin drug cartel. Despite these convictions and later

evidence of BCCI's fraudulent conduct, regulatory control was hampered by the fact that the bank had no central office under the jurisdiction of an individual government. Its two central offices were located in Luxembourg and the Cayman Islands, both tax havens with secretive banking rules.

Bank of England UK central bank founded by act of Parliament 1694. It was entrusted with the note issue 1844 and nationalized 1946. It is banker to the clearing banks and the UK government. As the government's bank, it manages and arranges the financing of the public-sector borrowing requirement and the national debt, implements monetary policy and exchange-rate policy through intervention in foreign-exchange markets, and supervises the UK banking system.

bankruptcy process by which the property of a person (in legal terms, an individual or corporation) unable to pay debts is taken away under a court order and divided fairly among the person's creditors, after preferential payments such as taxes and wages. Proceedings may be instituted either by the debtor (voluntary bankruptcy) or by any creditor for a substantial sum (involuntary bankruptcy). Until "discharged," a bankrupt is severely restricted in financial activities.

Federal law distinguishes between complete bankruptcy and protection of the assets of a legal person for purposes of financial reorganization. This is commonly referred to as Chapter 11 bankruptcy, since it is provided for under Chapter 11 of the federal bankruptcy law, which allows businesses and individuals to continue to operate while reorganizing to pay debts.

Banks Joseph 1744–1820. British naturalist and explorer. He accompanied Capt James ⟡Cook on his voyage round the world 1768–71 and brought back 3,600 plants, 1,400 of them never before classified. The *Banksia* genus of shrubs is named after him.

A founder and unofficial first director of the Botanical Gardens, Kew, Banks was president of the Royal Society from 1778 to 1819.

Banks Nathaniel Prentiss 1816–1894. US politician and Civil War general. Born in Waltham, Massachusetts, Banks was elected to the state legislature and US House of Representatives, serving as Speaker of the House 1854–57. He resigned to serve as Massachusetts governor 1857–60. At the outbreak of the Civil War, he was appointed major general in command of the Department of Annapolis. Defeated by Stonewall Jackson in the Shenandoah Valley, he was sent to New Orleans 1863 and took command of the Department of the Gulf. He led the ill-fated 1864 Red River expedition. After the war, he served in Congress until 1891.

banksia any shrub or tree of the genus *Banksia*, family Proteaceae, native to Australia and including the honeysuckle tree. The genus is named after Joseph Banks.

Banksias have spiny evergreen leaves and large flower spikes, made up of about 1,000 individual flowers formed around a central axis. The colors of the flower spikes can be gold, red, brown, purple, greenish-yellow, and gray.

Bannister Roger Gilbert 1929–   . English track and field athlete, the first person to run a mile in under four minutes. He achieved this feat at Oxford, England, on May 6, 1954 in a time of 3 min 59.4 sec.

Bannockburn, Battle of battle on June 24,

1314 in which ⟡Robert I of Scotland (known as Robert the Bruce) defeated the English under Edward II, who had come to relieve the besieged Stirling Castle. Named after the town of Bannockburn, S of Stirling.

bantam small variety of domestic chicken. Bantams can either be a small version of one of the large breeds, or a separate type. Some are prolific layers. Bantam cocks have a reputation as spirited fighters.

banteng wild species of cattle *Bos banteng*, now scarce, but formerly ranging from Myanmar (Burma) through SE Asia to Malaysia and Java, inhabiting hilly forests. Its color varies from pale brown to blue-black, usually with white stockings and rump patch, and it is up to 5 ft/1.5 m at the shoulder.

Banting Frederick Grant 1891–1941. Canadian physician who discovered a technique for isolating the hormone insulin 1921 when, experimentally, he and his colleague Charles ⟡Best tied off the ducts of the ⟡pancreas to determine the function of the cells known as the islets of Langerhans. This allowed for the treatment of diabetes. Banting and John J R Macleod (1876–1935), his mentor, shared the 1923 Nobel Prize for Medicine, and Banting divided his prize with Best.

Bantu languages group of related languages belonging to the Niger-Congo family, spoken widely over the greater part of Africa south of the Sahara, including Swahili, Xhosa, and Zulu. Meaning "people" in Zulu, the word Bantu itself illustrates a characteristic use of prefixes: *mu-ntu* "man," *ba-ntu* "people."

The Bantu-speaking peoples probably originated in N Central Africa. Until 1978, the black people of the Republic of South Africa were officially designated Bantu(s).

Bantustan or *homeland* name until 1978 for a ⟡Black National State in the Republic of South Africa.

Banu Musa three brothers, Mohammed (died 873), Ahmad, and al-Hasan, who lived in Baghdad during the reign of the Caliph al-Ma'mun (813–833). They compiled an important mathematical work on the measurement of plane and spherical figures, and one of the earliest works on mechanical engineering *Kitab al-hiyal/The Book of Ingenious Devices*.

banyan tropical Asian fig tree *Ficus benghalensis*, family Moraceae. It produces aerial roots that grow down from its spreading branches, forming supporting pillars that give the appearance of separate trunks.

baobab tree of the genus *Adansonia*, family Bombacaceae. It has rootlike branches, hence its nickname 'upside-down tree,' and a disproportionately thick girth, up to 30 ft/9 m in diameter. The pulp of its fruit is edible and is known as monkey bread.

Baobabs may live for 1,000 years and are found in Africa and Australia.

baptism (Greek "to dip") immersion in or sprinkling with water as a religious rite of initiation. It was practiced long before the beginning of Christianity. In the Christian baptism ceremony, sponsors or godparents make vows on behalf of the child, which are renewed by the child at confirmation. It is one of the seven sacraments. The *amrit* ceremony in Sikhism is sometimes referred to as baptism.

Baptism was universal in the Christian church from the first days, being administered to adults by immersion. The baptism of infants was not practiced until the 2nd century, but became general in the 6th. Baptism by sprinkling (christening) when the child is named is now general among Western Christians, with the exception of some sects (notably the ◊Baptists) where complete immersion of adults is the rule. The Eastern Orthodox Church also practises immersion.

Baptist member of any of several Protestant and evangelical Christian sects that practice baptism by immersion only upon profession of faith. Baptists seek their authority in the Bible. They originated among English Dissenters who took refuge in the Netherlands in the early 17th century, and spread by emigration and, later, missionary activity. Of the world total of approximately 31 million, some 26.5 million are in the US and 265,000 in the UK.

The first Baptist church in America was organized in Rhode Island 1639. Baptism grew rapidly during the Great Awakening religious revival of the 18th century. After the American Revolution, Baptism spread into the South and among blacks, both slave and free. The Southern Baptist Convention remains the largest Protestant denomination in the US. Other Baptists are scattered among the numerous divisions that developed during the last two centuries. In the 19th century Baptism also spread in Europe and to British colonies. Baptists have been among the most active denominations in missionary work.

bar unit of pressure equal to 10^5 pascals or 10^6 dynes/cm^2, approximately 750 mmHg or 0.987 atm. Its diminutive, the **millibar** (one-thousandth of a bar), is commonly used by meteorologists.

bar in music, a modular unit of rhythm, shown in notation by vertical "barring" of the musical continuum into sections of usually constant duration and rhythmic content. The alternative term is "measure."

Bara Theda. Adopted name of Theodosia Goodman 1890–1955. US silent-film actress who became known as the "the vamp," and the first movie sex symbol, after appearing in *A Fool There Was* 1915, based on a poem by Rudyard Kipling, "The Vampire."

She was born in Cincinnati, Ohio. As the most popular star of the Fox studios, Bara made more than 40 films during her relatively brief film career that extended from 1915 to 1920. After unsuccessfully attempting a career on the Broadway stage, she retired from show business and lived the rest of her life in relative obscurity.

Barabbas in the New Testament, a condemned robber released by Pilate at Passover instead of Jesus to appease a mob.

barb general name for fish of the genus *Barbus* and some related genera of the family Cyprinidae. Barbs include many small tropical Old World species, some of which are familiar aquarium species. They are active egg-laying species, usually of "typical" fish shape and with barbels at the corner of the mouth.

Barbados island country in the Caribbean, one of the Lesser Antilles. It is about 300 mi/483 km N of Venezuela.
government The bicameral legislature dates from 1627, when the British settled. The constitution dates from 1966 and provides for a system of parliamentary government on the British model, with a prime minister and cabinet drawn from and responsible to the legislature, which consists of a senate and a house

of assembly. The senate has 21 members appointed by the governor-general, 12 on the advice of the prime minister, two on the advice of the leader of the opposition, and the rest on the basis of wider consultations. The house of assembly has 27 members elected by universal suffrage. The legislature has a maximum life of five years and may be dissolved within this period. The governor-general appoints both the prime minister (on the basis of support in the house of assembly) and the leader of the opposition.
history Originally inhabited by Arawak Indians, who were wiped out soon after the arrival of the first Europeans, Barbados became a British colony 1627 and remained so until independence 1966. Universal adult suffrage was introduced 1951, and the Barbados Labor Party (BLP) won the first general election. Ministerial government was established 1954, and BLP leader Grantley Adams became the first prime minister. A group broke away from the BLP 1955 and formed the Democratic Labor Party (DLP). Six years later full internal self-government was achieved, and in the 1961 general election the DLP was victorious under its leader Errol Barrow.
independence When Barbados attained full independence 1966, Barrow became its first prime minister. The DLP was reelected 1971, but in the 1976 general election the BLP—led now by Grantley Adams's son Tom—ended Barrow's 15-year rule.
foreign relations Both parties were committed to maintaining free enterprise and alignment with the US, although the DLP government established diplomatic relations with Cuba 1972 and the BLP administration supported the US invasion of Grenada 1983.
end of two-party system The BLP was reelected 1981. After Adams's sudden death 1985 he was succeeded by his deputy, Bernard St John, a former BLP leader. In the 1986 general election the DLP, led by Barrow, was returned to power with 24 of the 27 seats in the house of assembly. Errol Barrow died 1987 and was succeeded by Erskine Lloyd Sandiford. Foreign minister James Tudor resigned 1989 in the face of charges that diplomatic staff had been involved in drug smuggling. A new opposition party, the centrist National Democratic Party, was formed 1989. The DLP obtained 18 seats with 49% of the vote in Jan 1991 elections, and the BLP only 10 seats with 44% of the vote. *See illustration box.*

Barbarossa nickname "red beard" given to the Holy Roman emperor ◊Frederick I, and also to two brothers, Horuk and Khair-ed-Din, who were Barbary pirates. Horuk was killed by the Spaniards 1518; Khair-ed-Din took Tunis 1534 and died in Constantinople 1546.

Barbarossa, operation German code name for the plans to invade the USSR in 1941 during World War II.

Barbary ape tailless, yellowish-brown macaque monkey *Macaca sylvanus*, found in the mountains and wilds of Algeria and Morocco. It was introduced to Gibraltar, where legend has it that the British will leave if the ape colony dies out.

Barbary Coast North African coast of the Mediterranean Sea (named after the ◊Berbers) from which pirates operated against US

Barbados

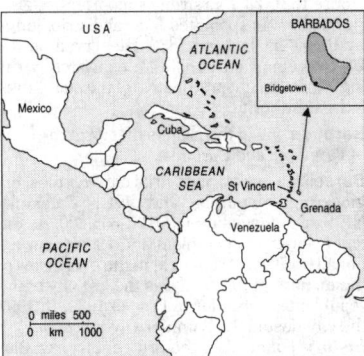

area 166 sq mi/430 sq km
capital Bridgetown
cities Speightstown, Holetown, Oistins
physical most easterly island of the West Indies; surrounded by coral reefs; subject to hurricanes June–Nov
features highest point Mount Hillaby 1,115 ft/340 m
head of state Elizabeth II from 1966 represented by governor-general Hugh Springer from 1984
head of government prime minister Erskine Lloyd Sandiford from 1987
political system constitutional monarchy
political parties Barbados Labor Party (BLP), moderate, left of center; Democratic Labor Party (DLP), moderate, left of center; National Democratic Party (NDP), center
exports sugar, rum, electronic components,

clothing, cement
currency Barbados dollar
population (1990 est) 260,000; growth rate 0.5% p.a.
life expectancy men 70, women 75
languages English and Bajan (Barbadian English dialect)
media two independent daily newspapers
religion 70% Anglican, 9% Methodist, 4% Roman Catholic
literacy 99% (1984)
GDP $1.4 bn (1987); $5,449 per head
chronology
1627 Became British colony; developed as a sugar-plantation economy, initially on basis of slavery.
1834 Slaves freed.
1951 Universal adult suffrage introduced. BLP won general election.
1954 Ministerial government established.
1961 Independence achieved from Britain. DLP, led by Errol Barrow, in power.
1966 Barbados achieved full independence within Commonwealth. Barrow became the new nation's first prime minister.
1972 Diplomatic relations with Cuba established.
1976 BLP, led by Tom Adams, returned to power.
1983 Barbados supported US invasion of Grenada.
1985 Adams died; Bernard St John became prime minister.
1986 DLP, led by Barrow, returned to power.
1987 Barrow died; Erskine Lloyd Sandiford became prime minister.
1989 New NDP opposition formed.
1991 DLP, under Erskine Sandiford, won general election.

and European shipping (taking hostages for ransom) from the 16th up to the 19th century.

President ◊Jefferson took action against them, sending in the US Navy with the Marines who landed on "the shores of Tripoli."

barbastelle insect-eating bat *Barbastella barbastellus* with "frosted" black fur and a wing-span of about 10 in/25 cm, occasionally found in the UK but more common in Europe.

barbed wire cheap fencing material made of strands of galvanized wire (see ◊galvanizing), twisted together with sharp barbs at close intervals. In 1873 an American, Joseph Glidden, devised a machine to mass-produce barbed wire. Its use on the open grasslands of 19th-century America led to range warfare between farmers and cattle ranchers; the latter used to drive their herds cross-country.

Barber Samuel 1910–1981. US composer of a Neo-Classical, later somewhat dissonant style, whose works include *Adagio for Strings* 1936 and the opera *Vanessa* 1958, which won him one of his two Pulitzer prizes. Another Barber opera, *Antony and Cleopatra* 1966, was commissioned for the opening of the new Metropolitan Opera House at Lincoln Center, New York City. Barber's music is lyrical and fastidiously worked. His later works include *The Lovers* 1971.

barberry any spiny shrub of the genus *Berberia* of the barberry family, having sour red berries and yellow flowers. These shrubs are often used as hedges. The barberry family (Berberidaceae) also includes plants such as the May apple *Podophyllum peltatum* of the E North American woodlands.

barbershop in music, a style of unaccompanied close-harmony singing of sentimental ballads, revived in the US during the 19th century. Traditionally sung by four male voices, since the 1970s it has developed as a style of ◊a cappella choral singing for both male and female voices.

Barbershop originated in 17th-century European barber shops, which offered dental and medical services. Waiting customers were provided with a cittern (almond-shaped, flat-backed stringed instrument, popular, cheap, and easy to play) or guitar by managements aware of the benefits of music to those undergoing pain.

barbet small, tropical bird, often brightly colored. There are some 78 species of barbet in the family Capitonidae, about half living in Africa. Barbets eat insects and fruits and, being distant relations of woodpeckers, drill nest holes with their beaks. The name comes from the "little beard" of bristles at the base of the beak.

Barbie Klaus 1913–1991. German Nazi, a member of the ◊SS from 1936. During World War II he was involved in the deportation of Jews from the occupied Netherlands 1940–42 and in tracking down Jews and Resistance workers in France 1942–45. He was arrested 1983 and convicted of crimes against humanity in France 1987.

His work as SS commander, based in Lyon, included the rounding-up of Jewish children from an orphanage at Izieu and the torture of the Resistance leader Jean Moulin. His ruthlessness during this time earned him the epithet "Butcher of Lyon." Having escaped capture 1945, Barbie was employed by the US intelligence services in Germany before moving to Bolivia 1951. Expelled from there in

1983, he was returned to France, where he was tried by a court in Lyon. He died in prison.

Barbirolli John 1899–1970. English conductor. He made his name as a cellist, and in 1937 succeeded Toscanini as conductor of the New York Philharmonic Orchestra. He returned to England 1943, where he remained conductor of the Hallé Orchestra, Manchester, until his death.

barbiturate hypnosedative drug, commonly known as a "sleeping pill," consisting of any salt or ester of barbituric acid $C_4H_4O_3N_2$. They work by depressing brain activity. Most barbiturates, being highly addictive, are no longer prescribed and are listed as controlled substances.

Tolerance develops quickly in the user so that increasingly large doses are required to induce sleep. A barbiturate's action persists for hours or days, causing confused, aggressive behavior or disorientation. Overdosage causes death by inhibiting the breathing center in the brain. Short-acting barbiturates are used as ◊anesthetics to induce general anesthesia.

Barbizon school French school of landscape painters of the mid-19th century, based at Barbizon in the forest of Fontainebleau. Members included Jean-François Millet, Diaz de la Peña (1807–1876), and Théodore Rousseau (1812–1867). They aimed to paint fresh, realistic scenes, sketching and painting their subjects in the open air.

Barbor Philip Pendleton 1783–1841. US jurist and political leader. Born in Barborsville, Virginia, Barbor studied law and briefly practiced in Kentucky before returning to Virginia and beginning a political career. He was elected to the state legislature and the US House of Representatives, serving as Speaker of the House 1821–23. As a strong supporter of states' rights, he was appointed federal district judge by President Jackson 1830. He served on the US Supreme Court 1836–41, consistently ruling in favor of the prerogative of the states over federal authority.

Barbuda one of the islands that form the state of ◊Antigua and Barbuda.

Barcelona capital, industrial city (textiles, engineering, chemicals), and port of Catalonia, NE Spain; population (1991) 1,653,200. As the chief center of anarchism and Catalonian nationalism, it was prominent in the overthrow of the monarchy 1931 and was the last city of the republic to surrender to Franco 1939. In 1992 the city hosted the Summer Olympics.

history Founded in the 3rd century BC, Barcelona's importance grew until, in the 14th century, it had become one of the leading trade cities of the Mediterranean.

features The Ramblas, tree-lined promenades leading from the Plaza de Cataluña, the largest square in Spain; ◊Gaudí's unfinished church of the Holy Family 1883; the Pueblo Español 1929, with specimens of Spanish architecture; a replica of Columbus's flagship the *Santa Maria*, in the Maritime Museum; a large collection of art by Picasso.

bar code pattern of bars and spaces that can be read by a computer. Bar codes are widely used in retailing, industrial distribution, and public libraries. The code is read by a scanning device; the computer determines the code from the widths of the bars and spaces.

The technique was patented 1949 but became popular only in 1973, when the food industry in North America adopted the Universal Product Code system.

Bardeen John 1908–1991. US physicist who won a Nobel Prize 1956, with Walter Brattain and William Shockley, for the development of the transistor 1948. In 1972 he became the first double winner of a Nobel Prize in the same subject (with Leon Cooper and John Schrieffer) for his work on superconductivity.

Bardot Brigitte 1934– . French film actress whose sensual appeal did much to popularize French cinema internationally. Her films include *Et Dieu créa la femme/And God Created Woman* 1950, *Viva Maria* 1965, and *Shalako* 1968.

Bardo Thödol or ***Book of the Dead*** Tibetan Buddhist text giving instructions to the newly dead about the Bardo, or state between death and rebirth.

Bareilly industrial city in Uttar Pradesh, India; population (1981) 438,000. It was a Mogul capital 1657 and at the center of the Indian Mutiny 1857.

Barenboim Daniel 1942– . Israeli pianist and conductor, born in Argentina. Pianist/conductor with the English Chamber Orchestra from 1964, he became conductor of the New York Philharmonic Orchestra 1970 and musical director of the Orchestre de Paris 1975. Appointed artistic and musical director of the Opéra de la Bastille, Paris, July 1987, he was dismissed from his post July 1989, a few months before its opening, for reasons which he claimed were more political than artistic. His dismissal was the subject of a highly publicized and controversial dispute. He is a celebrated interpreter of Mozart and Beethoven.

Barents Willem c. 1550–1597. Dutch explorer and navigator. He made three expeditions to seek the ◊Northeast Passage; he died on the last voyage. The Barents Sea, part of the Arctic Ocean N of Norway, is named after him.

Barents Sea section of the E ◊Arctic Ocean. It has oil and gas reserves.

Bari capital of Puglia region, S Italy, and industrial port on the Adriatic; population (1988) 359,000. It is the site of Italy's first nuclear power station; the part of the town known as Tecnopolis is the Italian equivalent of ◊Silicon Valley.

barium (Greek *barytes* "heavy") soft, silver-white, metallic element, symbol Ba, atomic number 56, atomic weight 137.33. It is one of the alkaline-earth metals, found in nature as barium carbonate and barium sulfate. As the sulfate it is used in medicine: taken as a suspension (a "barium meal"), its progress is followed by using X-rays to reveal abnormalities of the alimentary canal. Barium is also used in alloys, pigments, and safety matches and, with strontium, forms the emissive surface in cathode-ray tubes. It was first discovered in barytes or heavy spar.

bark protective outer layer on the stems and roots of woody plants, composed mainly of dead cells. To allow for expansion of the stem, the bark is continually added to from within, and the outer surface often becomes fissured or is shed as scales. The bark from the cork oak *Quercus suber* is economically important and harvested commercially. The spice ◊cinnamon and the drugs cascara (used as a laxative and stimulant) and ◊quinine all come from bark.

Bark technically includes all the tissues external to the vascular ◊cambium (the ◊phloem, cortex, and periderm). Its thickness may vary from 0.1 in/2.5 mm to 12 in/30 cm or more, as in the giant redwood *Sequoia* where it forms a thick, spongy layer.

Barker Clive 1952– . British writer whose *Books of Blood* 1984–85 are in the sensationalist tradition of ⬦horror.

Barker George 1913–1991. British poet, known for his vivid imagery, as in *Calamiterror* 1937, *The True Confessions of George Barker* 1950, *Collected Poems* 1930–50, and the posthumously published *Street Ballads* 1992.

bark painting technique of painting on the inner side of a strip of tree bark, practiced by Australian Aborigines. In red, yellow, white, brown, and black pigments, the works were often painted with the fingers as the artist lay inside a low bark-roofed shelter.

Barlach Ernst 1870–1938. German Expressionist sculptor, painter, and poet. His simple, evocative figures carved in wood (for example, those in St Catherine's, Lübeck, 1930–32) often express melancholy.

Barletta industrial port on the Adriatic, Italy; population (1981) 83,800. It produces chemicals and soap; as an agriculture center it trades in wine and fruit. There is a Romanesque cathedral built 1150 and a 13th-century castle.

barley cereal belonging to the grass family (Gramineae). Cultivated barley *Hordeum vulgare* comprises three main varieties—six-rowed, four-rowed, and two-rowed. Barley was one of the earliest cereals to be cultivated, about 5000 BC in Egypt, and no other cereal can thrive in so wide a range of climatic conditions; polar barley is sown and reaped well within the Arctic Circle in Europe. Barley is no longer much used in bread-making, but it is used in soups and stews and as a starch. Its high-protein form finds a wide use for animal feeding, and its low-protein form is used in brewing and distilling alcoholic beverages.

Barlow Joel 1754–1812. US poet and diplomat. Born in Redding, Connecticut, Barlow was educated at Yale. As a member of the literary circle known as the "Connecticut Wits," he published an epic entitled *The Vision of Columbus* 1787. Living as an expatriate in Paris and London, Barlow was deeply affected by the philosophical ideals of the Enlightenment and was granted citizenship in revolutionary France.

In 1795–97 he served as US consul in Algiers, gaining the release of American hostages taken by the Barbary pirates. In 1811 he was sent to France on a diplomatic mission and died while accompanying Napoleon in his retreat from Russia.

bar mitzvah (Hebrew "son of the commandment") in Judaism, initiation of a boy, which takes place at the age of 13, into the adult Jewish community; less common is the *bat* or *bas mitzvah* for girls aged 12. The child reads a passage from the Torah in the synagogue on the Sabbath, and is subsequently regarded as a full member of the congregation.

barn farm building traditionally used for the storage and processing of cereal crops and hay. On older farmsteads, the barn is usually the largest building. It is often characterized by ventilation openings rather than windows and has at least one set of big double doors for access. Before mechanization, wheat was threshed by hand on a specially prepared floor inside these doors.

Tithe barns were used in feudal England to

measure to top of meniscus — Torricellian vacuum

atmospheric pressure in mm of mercury — barometer tube — mercury — atmospheric pressure

aneroid barometer

pointer

hairspring — chain — magnifying lever

spring — spindle — pivot

partial vacuum

barometer *(top) The mercury barometer and (bottom) the aneroid barometer.*

store the produce paid as a tax to the parish priest by the local occupants of the land. In the Middle Ages, monasteries often controlled the collection of tithes over a wide area and, as a result, constructed some enormous tithe barns.

Barnabas, St in the New Testament, a "fellow laborer" with St Paul; he went with St Mark on a missionary journey to Cyprus, his birthplace. Feast day June 11.

barnacle marine crustacean of the subclass Cirripedia. The larval form is free-swimming, but when mature, it fixes itself by the head to rock or floating wood. The animal then remains attached, enclosed in a shell through which the cirri (modified legs) protrude to sweep food into the mouth. Barnacles include the stalked *goose barnacle Lepas anatifera* found on ships' bottoms, and the *acorn barnacles*, such as *Balanus balanoides*, common on rocks.

Barnard Christiaan (Neethling) 1922– . South African surgeon who performed the first human heart transplant 1967 in Cape Town. The patient, 54-year-old Louis Washkansky, lived for 18 days.

Barnard's star second closest star to the Sun, six light-years away in the constellation Ophiuchus. It is a faint red dwarf of 10th magnitude, visible only through a telescope. It is named after the US astronomer Edward E Barnard (1857–1923), who discovered 1916 that it has the fastest proper motion of any star, crossing 1 degree of sky every 350 years.

Some observations suggest that Barnard's star may be accompanied by planets.

Barnaul industrial city in S central Siberia, Russia, capital of Altai Territory; population (1987) 596,000. Industries include engineering, textiles, and timber. Founded 1738, it developed alongside the Turkestan-Siberian railroad.

Barnum Phineas T(aylor) 1810–1891. US showman. In 1871, after an adventurous career,

he established the "Greatest Show on Earth" (which included the midget "Tom Thumb") comprising a circus, a menagerie, and an exhibition of "freaks," conveyed in 100 rail automobiles. In 1881, it merged with its chief competitor and has continued to this day as the Ringling Brothers and Barnum and Bailey Circus.

In 1850, in an attempt to change his image to that of an art promoter, Barnum managed the hugely successful US concert tour of Swedish soprano Jenny Lind, whom he dubbed "The Swedish Nightingale."

barograph device for recording variations in atmospheric pressure. A pen, governed by the movements of an aneroid ⬦barometer, makes a continuous line on a paper strip on a cylinder that rotates over a day or week to create a *barogram*, or permanent record of variations in atmospheric pressure.

Baroja Pio 1872–1956. Spanish novelist of Basque extraction whose works include a trilogy dealing with the Madrid underworld, *La lucha por la vida/The Struggle for Life* 1904–05, and the multivolume *Memorias de un hombre de acción/Memoirs of a Man of Action* 1913–28.

barometer instrument that measures atmospheric pressure as an indication of weather. Most often used are the *mercury barometer* and the *aneroid barometer*.

In a mercury barometer a column of mercury in a glass tube, roughly 2.5 ft/0.75 m high (closed at one end, curved upward at the other), is balanced by the pressure of the atmosphere on the open end; any change in the height of the column reflects a change in pressure. In an aneroid barometer, a shallow cylindrical metal box containing a vacuum expands or contracts in response to changes in pressure.

baron rank in the peerage of the UK, above a baronet and below a viscount.

Life peers are always of this rank.

baronet British order of chivalry below the rank of baron, but above that of knight, created 1611 by James I to finance the settlement of Ulster. It is a hereditary honor, although women cannot succeed to a baronetcy. A baronet does not have a seat in the House of Lords, but is entitled to the style *Sir* before his name. The sale of baronetcies was made illegal 1937.

Barons' Wars civil wars in England:
1215–17 between King ⬦John and his barons, over his failure to honor ⬦Magna Carta
1264–67 between ⬦Henry III (and the future ⬦Edward I) and his barons (led by Simon de ⬦Montfort)
1264 May 14 *Battle of Lewes* at which Henry III was defeated and captured
1265 Aug 4 Simon de Montfort was defeated by Edward I at Evesham and killed.

Baroque style of art and architecture characterized by extravagance in ornament, asymmetry of design, and great expressiveness. It dominated European *art* for most of the 17th century, with artists such as the painter Rubens and the sculptor Bernini. In *architecture*, it often involved large-scale designs, such as Bernini's piazza in Rome and the palace of Versailles in France. In *music*, the Baroque period lasted from about 1600 to 1750, and its composers included Monteverdi, Vivaldi, J S Bach, and Handel.

In *painting*, Caravaggio, with his bold use of light and forceful compositions, was an early exponent, but the Carracci family was more typical of the early Baroque style, producing grandiose visions in ceiling paintings that deployed illusionistic displays of florid architectural decoration. In *sculpture*, the master of Baroque was Bernini, whose *Ecstasy of St Theresa* 1645–52 (Sta Maria della Vittoria, Rome) is a fine example of overt emotionalism. Most masterpieces of the new style emerged in churches and palaces in Rome, but the Baroque influence soon spread through Europe. The Swiss art historian Burckhardt was the first to use the term "baroque."

Baroque decorations were applied to building exteriors and interiors including furnishings.

Barquisimeto capital of Lara state, NW Venezuela; population (1989) 764,200.

Barra southernmost of the larger Outer Hebrides, Scotland; area 35 sq mi/90 sq km; population (1981) 1,340. It is separated from South Uist by the Sound of Barra. The main town is Castlebay.

barracuda large predatory fish *Sphyraena barracuda* found in the warmer seas of the world. It can grow over 6 ft/2 m long, and has a superficial resemblance to a pike. Young fish shoal but the older ones are solitary. The barracuda has very sharp shearing teeth, and may attack people.

Barragán Luis 1902–1988. Mexican architect, known for his use of rough wooden beams, cobbles, lava, and adobe.

Barrancabermeja port and oil-refining center on the Magdalena River in the department of Santander, NE Colombia; population (1980 est) 70,000. It is a major outlet for oil from the De Mares fields, which are linked by pipeline to Cartagena on the Caribbean coast.

Barranquilla seaport in N Colombia, on the river Magdalena; population (1985) 1,120,900. Products include chemicals, tobacco, textiles, furniture, and footwear.

It is Colombia's chief port on the Caribbean and the site of Latin America's first air terminal 1919.

Barras Paul François Jean Nicolas, Count 1755–1829. French revolutionary. He was elected to the National Convention 1792 and helped to overthrow Robespierre 1794. In 1795 he became a member of the ruling Directory (see ⇨French Revolution). In 1796 he brought about the marriage of his former mistress, Joséphine de Beauharnais, with Napoleon and assumed dictatorial powers. After Napoleon's coup d'état Nov 19, 1799, Barras fell into disgrace.

Barrault Jean-Louis 1910– . French actor and director. His films include *La Symphonie fantastique* 1942, *Les Enfants du paradis* 1945, and *La Ronde* 1950.

He was producer and director to the ⇨Comédie Française 1940–46, and director of the Théâtre de France (formerly Odéon) from 1959 until his dismissal 1968 because of statements made during the occupation of the theater by student rebels.

barre wooden bar running along the walls of a ballet studio at waist height, designed to help dancers keep their balance while going through the initial daily exercises.

Barre Raymond 1924– . French politician, member of the center-right Union pour la Démocratie Française; prime minister 1976–81, when he also held the Finance Ministry portfolio and gained a reputation as a tough and determined budget cutter.

barrel a unit of liquid capacity, the value of which depends on the liquid being measured. It is used for petroleum, a barrel of which contains 42 gallons/159 liters; a barrel of alcohol contains 49.9 gallons/189 liters.

barrel cylindrical container, tapering at each end, made of thick strips of wood bound together by metal hoops. Barrels are used for the bulk storage of fine wines and spirits.

Barrels were made by craftsmen known as coopers, whose main skill was the shaping and bending of the wooden strips (staves) so that they fitted together without gaps when secured by the hoops. Barrels were widely used for storing liquids and dry goods until the development of plastic containers.

barrel organ portable pipe organ, played by turning a handle. The handle works a pump and drives a replaceable cylinder upon which a pattern of ridges controls the passage of air to certain pipes, producing a variety of tunes.

It is often confused with the barrel or street piano used by buskers, which employed a barrel-and-pin mechanism to control a piano hammer action.

Barren Lands/Grounds ⇨tundra region of Canada, W of Hudson Bay.

Barrett Browning Elizabeth 1806–1861. English poet. In 1844 she published *Poems* (including "The Cry of the Children"), which led to her friendship with and secret marriage to Robert Browning 1846. The *Sonnets from the Portuguese* 1847 were written during their courtship. Later works include *Casa Guidi Windows* 1851 and the poetic novel *Aurora Leigh* 1857.

Barrett Browning was born near Durham. As a child she fell from her pony and injured her spine and was subsequently treated by her father as a confirmed invalid. Freed from her father's oppressive influence, her health improved. She wrote strong verse about social injustice and oppression in Victorian England.

Barrie J(ames) M(atthew) 1860–1937. Scottish playwright and novelist, author of *The Admirable Crichton* 1902 and the children's fantasy *Peter Pan* 1904.

barrier island long island of sand, lying offshore and parallel to the coast. Some are over 60 mi/100 km in length. Most barrier islands are derived from marine sands piled up by shallow longshore currents that sweep sand parallel to the seashore. Others are derived from former spits, connected to land and built up by drifted sand, that were later severed from the mainland.

Often several islands lie in a continuous row offshore. Coney Island and Jones Beach near New York City are well-known examples, as is Padre Island, Texas. The Frisian Islands are barrier islands along the coast of the Netherlands.

barrier reef ⇨coral reef that lies offshore, separated from the mainland by a shallow lagoon.

Barron v Baltimore a US Supreme Court decision 1833 dealing with the responsibilities of state courts under the Fifth Amendment. The plaintiff, a wharf owner who lost money through the municipally engineered reorganization of Baltimore's harbor, sued the city for damages. Although the Fifth Amendment protects citizens from expropriation without proper compensation, the Maryland courts found against Barron. He appealed to the US

Supreme Court, which upheld the Maryland decision, ruling that the intent of the Bill of Rights is protection from the federal government, not from state governments.

barrow burial mound, usually composed of earth but sometimes of stones, examples of which are found in many parts of the world. The two main types are *long*, dating from the New Stone Age, or Neolithic, and *round*, dating from the later Mesolithic peoples of the early Bronze Age.

Barrow northernmost town in the US, at Point Barrow, Alaska; the world's largest Inuit settlement. Population (1990) 3,469. There is oil at nearby Prudhoe Bay, and the US Naval Research Laboratory is in the vicinity. Barrow developed as a whaling center about 1900.

Barrow Clyde 1900–1934. US criminal; see ⇨Bonnie and Clyde.

Barry Comtesse du. See ⇨du Barry, mistress of Louis XV of France.

Barrymore US family of actors, the children of British-born Maurice Barrymore and Georgie Drew, both stage personalities.

Lionel Barrymore (1878–1954) first appeared on the stage with his grandmother, Mrs John Drew, 1893. He played numerous film roles from 1909, including *A Free Soul* 1931 and *Grand Hotel* 1932, but was perhaps best known for his annual radio portrayal of Scrooge in Dickens's *A Christmas Carol*.

John Barrymore (1882–1942), a flamboyant actor who often appeared on stage and screen with his brother and sister. In his early years he was a Shakespearean actor. From 1923 he acted almost entirely in films, including *Dinner at Eight* 1933, and became a screen idol, nicknamed "the Profile."

Ethel Barrymore (1879–1959) played with the British actor Henry Irving in London 1898 and 1928 opened the Ethel Barrymore Theater in New York; she also appeared in many films from 1914, including *None but the Lonely Heart* 1944.

barter exchange of goods or services without the use of money.

Barth Heinrich 1821–1865. German geographer and explorer who in explorations of N Africa between 1844 and 1855 established the exact course of the river Niger.

He studied the coast of N Africa from Tunis to Egypt 1844- -45, traveled in the Middle East 1845–47, crossed the Sahara from Tripoli 1850, and then spent five years exploring the country between Lake Chad and Cameroon which he described in the five-volume *Travels and Discoveries in Central Africa* 1857–58.

Barth John 1930– . US novelist and short-story writer who was influential in the "academic" experimental movement of the 1960s. His works are usually interwoven fictions based on language games, since he is concerned with the relationship of language and reality. They include the novels *The Sot-Weed Factor* 1960, *Giles Goat-Boy* 1966, *Letters* 1979, *Sabbatical: A Romance* 1982, and *The Tidewater Tales* 1987. He also wrote the novella *Chimera* 1972 and *Lost in the Funhouse* 1968, a collection of short stories.

Barth Karl 1886–1968. Swiss Protestant theologian. A socialist in his political views, he attacked the Nazis. His *Church Dogmatics* 1932–62 makes the resurrection of Jesus the focal point of Christianity.

He is generally considered the greatest

Christian theologian of the 20th century. His *Theology of Crisis* rejected liberal theology and stressed scripture and the infinite gulf that separates God from humanity, which can be overcome only by the grace of God.

Barthes Roland 1915–1980. French critic and theorist of ◊semiology, the science of signs and symbols. One of the French "new critics" and an exponent of ◊structuralism, he attacked traditional literary criticism in his early works, including *Le Degré zéro de l'ecriture/ Writing Degree Zero* 1953 and *Sur Racine/On Racine* 1963.

His structuralist approach involved exposing and analyzing the system of signs, patterns, and laws that may be conveyed by a novel or play. He also wrote an autobiographical novel, *Roland Barthes sur Roland Barthes* 1975.

Bartholdi Frédéric Auguste 1834–1904. French sculptor. He designed the Statue of Liberty overlooking New York harbor, 1884.

Bartholomew, Massacre of St see ◊St Bartholomew, Massacre of.

Bartholomew, St in the New Testament, one of the apostles. Some legends relate that after the Crucifixion he took Christianity to India; others that he was a missionary in Anatolia and Armenia, where he suffered martyrdom by being flayed alive. Feast day Aug 24.

Bartók Béla 1881–1945. Hungarian composer who developed a personal musical language, combining folk elements with mathematical concepts of tone and rhythmic proportion. His large output includes six string quartets, concertos, an opera, and graded teaching pieces for piano.

A child prodigy, Bartók studied music at the Budapest Conservatory, later working with Zoltan ◊Kodály in recording and transcribing local folk music for a government project. His ballet *The Miraculous Mandarin* 1919 was banned because of its subject matter (it was set in a brothel). Bartók died in the US, having fled from Hungary 1940.

Bartolommeo Fra, also called *Baccio della Porta* c. 1472–c. 1517. Italian religious painter of the High Renaissance, active in Florence. His painting of *The Last Judgment* 1499 (Museo di San Marco, Florence) influenced Raphael.

Barton Clara 1821–1912. US health worker. Born in Oxford, Massachusetts, Barton was trained as a teacher, and at the outbreak of the US Civil War she became involved in projects for the welfare of Union soldiers. As a volunteer nurse, she tended the casualties in the 1861 Baltimore riot and at the battles of Antietam and Fredericksburg. In 1864 Gen Benjamin Butler named her superintendent of nurses for his forces. In 1870 Barton traveled to Europe to bring medical supplies to troops in the Franco-Prussian War. She founded the American Red Cross 1881 and served as its president until 1904.

Barton Edmund 1849–1920. Australian politician. He was leader of the federation movement from 1896 and first prime minister of Australia 1901–03.

Baruch Bernard (Mannes) 1870–1965. US financier. He was a friend of British prime minister Churchill and a self-appointed, unpaid adviser to US presidents Wilson, F D Roosevelt, and Truman. He strongly advocated international control of nuclear energy.

baryon in nuclear physics, a heavy subatomic particle made up of three indivisible elementary particles called quarks. The baryons form a subclass of the ◊hadrons, and comprise the nucleons (protons and neutrons) and hyperons.

Baryshnikov Mikhail 1948– . Latvian-born dancer, now based in the US. He joined the Kirov Ballet 1967 and became one of their most brilliant soloists. After defecting from the Soviet Union "on artistic, not political grounds" while on tour in Canada 1974, he danced with various companies, and later joined the American Ballet Theater (ABT) as principal dancer, partnering Gelsey Kirkland. He left to join the New York City Ballet 1978–80, but rejoined ABT as director 1980–90. From 1990 he has danced for various companies.

He has created many roles, for example in Twyla Tharp's *Push Comes to Shove* 1976 (music by Haydn/Lamb) and in Jerome Robbins's *Opus 19* 1979 (Prokofiev). He made his film debut in *The Turning Point* 1978 and has since acted in other films, including *White Nights* 1985. He made his dramatic stage debut in *Metamorphosis* 1989.

baryte barium sulfate, $BaSO_4$, the most common mineral of barium. It is white or light-colored, and has a comparatively high density (specific gravity 4.6); the latter property makes it useful in the production of high-density drilling muds. Baryte occurs mainly in ore veins, where it is often found with calcite and with lead and zinc minerals. It crystallizes in the orthorhombic system and can form tabular crystals or radiating fibrous masses.

baryton complex bowed-stringed instrument producing an intense singing tone. It is based on an 18th-century viol and modified by the addition of sympathetic (freely vibrating) strings.

The baryton was a favorite instrument of Prince Nicholas Esterházy, patron of the Austrian composer Joseph Haydn who, to please him, wrote many trios for violin, baryton, and cello.

Barzun Jacques Martin 1907– . French-born US historian and educator. Barzun immigrated to the US with his parents 1919. His specialty was 19th-century European intellectual life. Among his many historical works, he published *Romanticism and the Modern Ego* 1943. His book *The Modern Researcher* 1970 is recognized as a classic study of historical method.

He was educated at Columbia University, earning a PhD in history 1932, and soon afterward joined the faculty there and became a member of the administration.

basal metabolic rate (BMR) amount of energy needed by an animal just to stay alive. It is measured when the animal is awake but resting, and includes the energy required to keep the heart beating, sustain breathing, repair tissues, and keep the brain and nerves functioning. Measuring the animal's consumption of oxygen gives an accurate value for BMR, because oxygen is needed to release energy from food.

A cruder measure of BMR estimates the amount of heat given off, some heat being released when food is used up. BMR varies from one species to another, and from males to females. In humans, it is highest in children and declines with age. Disease, including mental illness, can make it rise or fall. Hormones from the ◊thyroid gland control the BMR.

basalt commonest volcanic ◊igneous rock, and the principal rock type on the ocean floor; it is basic, that is, it contains relatively little silica: under 50%. It is usually dark gray, but can also be green, brown, or black.

The groundmass may be glassy or finely crystalline, sometimes with large ◊crystals embedded. Basaltic lava tends to be runny and flows for great distances before solidifying. Successive eruptions of basalt have formed the great plateaus of Colorado and the Indian Deccan. In some places, such as Fingal's Cave in the Inner Hebrides of Scotland and the Giant's Causeway in Antrim, Northern Ireland, shrinkage during the solidification of the molten lava caused the formation of hexagonal columns.

bascule bridge type of drawbridge in which one or two counterweighted deck members pivot upward to allow shipping to pass underneath. One example is the double bascule Tower Bridge, London.

base in mathematics, the number of different single-digit symbols used in a particular number system. In our usual (decimal) counting system of numbers (with symbols 0, 1, 2, 3, 4, 5, 6, 7, 8, 9) the base is 10. In the ◊binary number system, which has only the symbols 1 and 0, the base is two. A base is also a number that, when raised to a particular power (that is, when multiplied by itself a particular number of times as in $10^2 = 10 \times 10 = 100$), has a ◊logarithm equal to the power. For example, the logarithm of 100 to the base ten is 2.

In geometry, the term is used to denote the line or area on which a polygon or solid stands.

base in chemistry, a substance that accepts protons, such as the hydroxide ion (OH^-) and ammonia (NH_3). Bases react with acids to give a salt. Those that dissolve in water are called ◊alkalis.

Inorganic bases are usually oxides or hydroxides of metals, which react with dilute acids to form a salt and water. A number of carbonates also react with dilute acids, additionally giving off carbon dioxide. Many organic compounds that contain nitrogen are bases.

baseball a bat-and-ball game between two teams, played on a field called a diamond, because of the arrangement of the bases. Bats, balls, and gloves constitute the basic equipment. The game is divided into nine innings. During the "top" half of each inning the home

base

binary (base 2)	octal (base 8)	decimal (base 10)	hexadecimal (base 16)
0	0	0	0
1	1	1	1
10	2	2	2
11	3	3	3
100	4	4	4
101	5	5	5
110	6	6	6
111	7	7	7
1000	10	8	8
1001	11	9	9
1010	12	10	A
1011	13	11	B
1100	14	12	C
1101	15	13	D
1110	16	14	E
1111	17	15	F
10000	20	16	10
11111111	377	255	FF
11111010001	3721	2001	7D1

team plays defense and the visiting team, offense. In the "bottom" half, the roles are reversed. There are nine defensive positions: the pitcher, who stands on a mound 60.5 ft/18.4 m from home plate; the catcher, who crouches behind home plate; the first, second, and third basemen, who stand at or near their respective bases (90 ft/27.4 m apart), which together with home plate form the diamond-shaped infield: the shortstop, who covers the infield between second and third bases; and the right, center, and left fielders, whose domain is the outfield, the dimensions of which vary from stadium to stadium.

Essentially an offensive player attempts to get on base and advance around the bases, to score a run by crossing home plate. Batters appear in an assigned order. Assuming a batting stance in front of the catcher, the batter faces the pitcher, who throws the baseball to home plate to the catcher. Standing behind the catcher is an umpire (major-league games have four umpires at various vantage points), who calls out a "ball" or "strike" ruling for each unhit pitch. A pitch that fails to cross the plate within the batter's "strike zone" is called a ball. However, if such a pitch is swung at and missed, a strike is ruled against the batter. Any unhit pitch that is within the strike zone, whether or not the batter swings, is called a strike. Hit balls that fall outside playing-field bounds are called "foul balls" and are counted as strikes, unless it would be a third strike. A three-strike count is an "out." If the count reaches four balls before the third strike is called, the batter earns a "walk" and proceeds to first base.

When a ball is hit into fair territory, numerous outcomes are possible: among them, the ball could be a "fly ball" caught by a fielder for an out; a "grounder" scooped up and thrown to first base before the batter (now the runner) gets there, also for an out; a "hit," in which the runner reaches a base (first base for a single; second for a double; third for a triple) before the ball; or a "home run," a hit that usually goes beyond the outfield wall, so the batter (and any baserunners) completes the circuit of base paths that leads back to home plate. The object is to advance runners around the bases, and a "run" is scored each time a runner safely crosses home plate.

During each inning, a team's offensive play continues until three outs occur. After nine innings, the team with the most runs wins. If the game is tied after nine innings, extra innings are played until the tie is broken.

history the legend of Abner ⟩Doubleday's invention of baseball in Cooperstown, New York, 1839, was born 1907 when a major-league baseball committee tried to determine the origins of the game. The story was presented as fact, although there was no real evidence to support it, and Doubleday's journals contain no mention of any pastime similar to baseball.

Sports historians vary in their hypotheses, but most agree that baseball was no one person's invention; rather it evolved from numerous ball-and-stick games. Colonial Americans enjoyed several varieties of such English games as rounders and town ball. By the mid-19th century many regional variations of baseball had been developed. The "New York game" became especially popular after 1845, when player A J Cartwright devised such surviving innovations as the nine-man team, the diamond-shaped infield, and the three-outs-per-inning format. Cartwright was a founding member of the New York Knickerbocker Club, which for 13 years exerted its authority over

baseball in the greater New York area. When 25 ball clubs formed the National Association of Base Ball Players 1858, the Knickerbockers lost their arbitership, and the game of baseball entered a new era of standardization and organized competition.

In 1871 the National Association of Professional Base Ball Players was born, becoming baseball's first major league. The more stable National League usurped the Association 1876, and for nearly 40 years watched the rise and fall of several rival leagues. By 1916 the "majors" belonged to just two leagues: the National League (NL) and the American League (AL), and so it remains to this day. In 1916 each league was comprised of 8 teams. Today the NL's 12 teams and the AL's 14 teams are divided into east and west divisions. At the end of the regular playing season (April-Oct), the division-leading teams compete for their league's championship in a best-of-seven "pennant" series. The two pennant winners meet for the best-of-seven World Series.

The exclusivity of US teams in major-league baseball ended 1969 when Canada's Montréal Expos joined the NL. (Another Canadian team, the Toronto Blue Jays, joined the AL 1977.) In 1973 the AL adopted the "designated hitter" rule, which allows a tenth player to assume the batting role of the pitcher without affecting the pitcher's eligibility to continue defensive play.

Professional baseball also includes the "minors," the training leagues for the majors, and has an extensive network across the US. The sport is very popular in Latin America, the Caribbean, and Japan, all of which have baseball leagues similar to those of the US.

Baseball is the quintessential US hometown sport, with American children playing on fields and sandlots from age 3 on. It has been formulated into school leagues and Little League competitions, but most children love to play it for the fun of the game.

Recent World Series Champions

1980	Philadelphia Phillies (NL)
1981	Los Angeles Dodgers (NL)
1982	St Louis Cardinals (NL)
1983	Baltimore Orioles (AL)
1984	Detroit Tigers (AL)
1985	Kansas City Royals (AL)
1986	New York Mets (NL)
1987	Minnesota Twins (AL)
1988	Los Angeles Dodgers (NL)
1989	Oakland Athletics (AL)
1990	Cincinnati Reds (NL)
1991	Minnesota Twins (AL)
1992	Toronto Blue Jays (AL)

Basel or *Basle* (French *Bâle*) financial, commercial, and industrial (dyes, vitamins, agrochemicals, dietary products, genetic products) city in Switzerland; population (1990) 171,000. Basel was a strong military station under the Romans. In 1501 it joined the Swiss confederation and later developed as a center for the Reformation.

It has the chemical firms Hoffman–La Roche, Sandoz, and Ciba–Geigy. There are trade fairs, and it is the headquarters of the Bank for International Settlements. There is an 11th-century cathedral (rebuilt after an earthquake 1356), a 16th-century town hall, and a university dating from the 15th century.

basenji breed of dog originating in Central Africa, where it is used as a hunter. About 1.3 ft/41 cm tall, it has a wrinkled forehead, curled tail, and short glossy coat. It is remarkable because it has no true bark.

base pair in biochemistry, the linkage of two base (purine or pyrimidine) molecules in ⟩DNA. They are found in nucleotides, and form the basis of the genetic code.

One base lies on one strand of the DNA double helix, and one on the other, so that the base pairs link the two strands like the rungs of a ladder. In DNA, there are four bases: adenine and guanine (purines) and cytosine and thymine (pyrimidines). Adenine always pairs with thymine, and cytosine with guanine.

Bashkir autonomous republic of Russia, with the Ural Mountains on the east
area 55,430 sq mi/143,600 sq km
capital Ufa
products minerals, oil, natural gas
population (1982) 3,876,000
languages Russian, Bashkir (about 25%)
history annexed by Russia 1557; became the first Soviet autonomous republic 1919. Since 1989 Bashkirs have demanded greater independence.

Bashkir member of the majority ethnic group of the autonomous republic of Bashkir in Russia. The Bashkirs have been Muslims since the 13th century. The Bashkir language belongs to the Turkic branch of the Altaic family, and has about 1 million speakers.

Bashō Adopted name of Matsuo Munefusa 1644–1694. Japanese poet who was a master of the *haiku*, a 17-syllable poetic form with lines of 5, 7, and 5 syllables, which he infused with subtle allusiveness. His *Oku-no-hosomichi/The Narrow Road to the Deep North* 1694, an account of a visit to northern and western Honshū, consists of haiku interspersed with prose passages.

BASIC (acronym for *beginner's all-purpose symbolic instruction code*) high-level computer-programming language, developed 1964, originally designed to take advantage of ⟩multiuser systems (which can be used by many people at the same time). The language is relatively easy to learn and is popular among microcomputer users.

Most versions make use of an ⟩interpreter, which translates BASIC into ⟩machine code and allows programs to be entered and run

baseball *The dimensions and markings of a baseball field.*

center field
left field
right field
second base
95ft radius
90ft
90ft
pitcher's mound
pitcher's rubber
18ft diameter
foul line
third base
60ft 6in
first base
90ft
90ft
coach's box
coach's box
26ft diameter
a a
b
home plate
60ft backstop
dugout
on-deck circle

a batter's box   b catcher's box

with no intermediate translation. Some more recent versions of BASIC allow a ◇compiler to be used for this process.

Basic English simplified form of English devised and promoted by C K Ogden in the 1920s and 1930s as an international auxiliary language; as a route into Standard English for foreign learners; and as a reminder to the English-speaking world of the virtues of plain language. Its name derives from the initial letters of *B*ritish, *A*merican, *s*cientific, *i*nternational, and *c*ommercial.

Basic has a vocabulary of 850 words (plus names, technical terms, and so on), only 18 of which are verbs or "operators."

basic-oxygen process most widely used method of steelmaking, involving the blasting of oxygen at supersonic speed into molten pig iron.

Pig iron from a blast furnace, together with steel scrap, is poured into a converter, and a jet of oxygen is then projected into the mixture. The excess carbon in the mix and other impurities quickly burn out or form a slag, and the converter is emptied by tilting. It takes only about 45 minutes to refine 400 tons/350 tonnes of steel. The basic-oxygen process was developed 1948 at a steelworks near the Austrian towns of Linz and Donawitz. It is a version of the ◇Bessemer process.

basidiocarp spore-bearing body, or "fruiting body," of all basidiomycete fungi (see ◇fungus), except the rusts and smuts. A well known example is the edible mushroom *Agaricus brunnescens*. Other types include globular basidiocarps (puffballs) or flat ones that project from tree trunks (brackets). They are made up of a mass of tightly packed, intermeshed ◇hyphae.

The tips of these hyphae develop into the reproductive cells, or **basidia**, that form a fertile layer known as the hymenium, or **gills**, of the basidiocarp. Four spores are budded off from the surface of each basidium.

Basie Count (William) 1904–1984. US jazz band leader, pianist, and organist who developed the big-band sound and a simplified, swinging style of music. He led impressive groups of musicians in a career spanning more than 50 years. Basie's compositions include "One O'Clock Jump" and "Jumpin at the Woodside."

His solo piano technique was influenced by the style of Fats Waller. Some consider his the definitive dance band.

basil or *sweet basil* plant *Ocimum basilicum*

basic-oxygen process *The basic-oxygen process is the primary method used to produce steel.*

basidiocarp *The structure of the mushroom, an example of a basidiocarp.*

of the mint family Labiatae. A native of the tropics, it is cultivated in Europe as a culinary herb.

Basil II *c.* 958–1025. Byzantine emperor from 976. His achievement as emperor was to contain, and later decisively defeat, the Bulgarians, earning for himself the title "Bulgar-Slayer" after a victory 1014. After the battle he blinded almost all 15,000 of the defeated, leaving only a few men with one eye to lead their fellows home. The Byzantine empire had reached its largest extent at the time of his death.

basilica Roman public building; a large roofed hall flanked by columns, generally with an aisle on each side, used for judicial or other public business. The earliest known basilica, at Pompeii, dates from the 2nd century BC. This

basilica *The ground plan of an ancient basilica in Rome shows the basilica's characteristic rectangular shape with a curved section (apse) on one of the shorter sides.*

architectural form was adopted by the early Christians for their churches.

Basilicata mountainous region of S Italy, comprising the provinces of Potenza and Matera; area 3,860 sq mi/10,000 sq km; population (1990) 624,500. Its capital is Potenza. It was the Roman province of Lucania.

basilisk South American lizard, genus *Basiliscus*. It is able to run on its hind legs when traveling fast (about 7 mph/11 kph) and may dash a short distance across the surface of water. The male has a well-developed crest on the head, body, and tail.

Basil, St *c.* 330–379. Cappadocian monk, known as "the Great," founder of the Basilian monks. Elected bishop of ◇Caesarea 370, Basil opposed the heresy of ◇Arianism. He wrote many theological works and composed the "Liturgy of St Basil," in use in the Eastern Orthodox Church. His feast day is Jan 2.

Baskerville John 1706–1775. English printer and typographer, who experimented in casting types from 1750 onwards. The Baskerville typeface is named after him.

basketball ball game between two teams of five players, played on both indoor and outdoor rectangular courts. Players move the ball by passing it or by dribbling it (bouncing it on the floor) while running. Basketball is played worldwide by both men and women and, with soccer, is one of the two most popular sports.

In the US the standard court is 94 ft/28.7 m long and 54 ft/16.5 m wide, with a backboard at the center of each end of the court. A circular metal hoop, whose rim is 10 ft/3 m from the floor, is attached to each backboard. The object of the game is to score the most points by throwing the inflated ball through the hoop, also called a basket, with two points scored for each field goal, or basket, shot from the field. Under certain rules, three points are awarded for field goals made beyond a specified distance from the basket. One point is scored for each foul shot (awarded after certain types of rules infractions by the opposing teams). Foul shots, also called free throws, are taken from a line 15 ft/4.6 m from the backboard. The court has lines from the foul line to the court's base line. The lane between the lines cannot be entered by players until the foul shot has been released by the shooter. During regular play, offensive players may remain in the lane for only three consecutive seconds. The court dimensions and markings vary slightly among US amateur, US professional, and international rules. If a regulation game ends in a tie, overtime periods are played until one team wins.

Time limits for games vary: 8-min quarters in high school; 20-min halves in college; 12-min quarters in professional contests. Under some rules the team with possession of the ball must shoot within a certain time period: 24 sec in professional games; 30 sec in international amateur; 45 sec in college. A player must leave the game after accumulating five (high school, college, and international amateur) or six (professional) fouls.

history basketball was invented by James Naismith, a Canadian who was a physical education instructor at what is now Springfield College (Massachusetts). The first game was played 1891, and the first formal rules were set out 1892. It rapidly became popular, especially in the E US, and the first college and professional games were played before 1900. Today, the premier professional league is the National

Basketball Association (NBA), formed 1949. Perhaps the most famous professional team is the Harlem Globetrotters, an independent team composed of black players, founded 1927. Its tours of the world have greatly increased basketball's popularity. Basketball has been played in the Summer Olympic Games since 1936.

Recent NBA Champions

1983	Philadelphia 76ers
1984	Boston Celtics
1985	Los Angeles Lakers
1986	Boston Celtics
1987	Los Angeles Lakers
1988	Los Angeles Lakers
1989	Detroit Pistons
1990	Detroit Pistons
1991	Chicago Bulls
1992	Chicago Bulls

basketry ancient craft (Mesolithic–Neolithic) used to make a wide range of objects (from baskets to furniture) by interweaving or braiding, rushes, cane, or other equally strong, natural fibers. Wickerwork is a more rigid type of basketry worked onto a sturdy frame, usually made from strips of willow.

Basle alternate form of ◊Basel, city in Switzerland.

Basov Nikolai Gennadievich 1912– . Soviet physicist who in 1953, with his compatriot Aleksandr Prokhorov, developed the microwave amplifier called a ◊maser. They were both awarded the Nobel Prize for Physics 1964, which they shared with Charles Townes of the US.

Basque member of a people inhabiting the ◊Basque Country of central N Spain and the extreme SW of France. The Basques are a pre-Indo-European people who largely maintained their independence until the 19th century. During the Spanish Civil War 1936–39, they were on the republican side defeated by Franco. Their language (**Euskara**) is unrelated to any other language. The Basque separatist movement ETA (*Euskadi ta Askatasuna*, "Basque Nation and Liberty") and the French organization Iparretarrak ("ETA fighters from the North Side") have engaged in guerrilla activity from 1968 in an attempt to secure a united Basque state.

Basque Country (Basque *Euskal Herria*) homeland of the Basque people in the W Pyrenees, divided by the Franco-Spanish border. The Spanish Basque Country (Spanish *País Vasco*) is an autonomous region (created 1979) of central N Spain, comprising the provinces of Vizcaya, Alava, and Guipúzcoa (Basque *Bizkaia, Araba,* and *Gipuzkoa*); area 2,818 sq mi/7,300 sq km; population (1988) 2,176,790. The French Basque Country (French *Pays Basque*) comprises the *département* of Pyrénées-Atlantiques, including the arrondissements of Labord, Basse-Navarre, and Soule (Basque *Lapurdi, Nafarroa Beherea,* and *Zuberoa*); area 4770 sq mi/7,633 sq km; population (1981) 555,700. To Basque nationalists *Euskal Herria* also includes the autonomous Spanish province of Navarre.

Basque language language of W Europe known to its speakers, the Basques, as *Euskara,* and apparently unrelated to any other language on Earth. It is spoken by some half a million people in central N Spain and SW France, around the Bay of Biscay, as well as by emigrants in both Europe and the Americas. The language is of central importance to the Basque nationalist movement.

Although previously forbidden in all public places for most of Franco's rule, Basque was permitted in church and primary schools from 1968, and taught in all schools from 1979. The first Basque parliament was elected 1980 and the language officially recognized along with Spanish in the Basque provinces.

Basra (Arabic *al-Basrah*) principal port in Iraq, in the Shatt-al-Arab delta, 60 mi/97 km from the Persian Gulf, founded in the 7th century; population (1977) 1.5 million (1991) 850,000. Exports include wool, oil, cereal, and dates. Aerial bombing during the 1991 Gulf War destroyed bridges, factories, power stations, water-treatment plants, sewage-treatment plants, and the port. A Shiite rebellion March 1991 was crushed by the Iraqi army, causing further death and destruction.

bass long-bodied scaly sea fish *Morone labrax* found in the N Atlantic and Mediterranean. They grow to 3 ft/1 m, and are often seen in shoals.

Other fish of the same family (Serranidae) are also called bass, as are North American freshwater fishes of the family Centrarchidae, such as black bass and small-mouthed bass.

Bass George 1763–c. 1808. English naval surgeon who with Matthew ◊Flinders explored the coast of New South Wales and the strait that bears his name between Tasmania and Australia 1795–98.

Bassein port in Myanmar (Burma), in the Irrawaddy delta, 78 mi/125 km from the sea; population (1983) 355,588. Bassein was founded in the 13th century.

Basse-Normandie or *Lower Normandy* coastal region of NW France lying between Haute-Normandie and Brittany (Bretagne). It includes the *départements* of Calvados, Manche, and Orne; area 6,794 sq mi/17,600 sq km; population (1986) 1,373,000. Its capital is Caen. Apart from stock farming, dairy farming, and textiles, the area produces Calvados (apple brandy).

The invasion of Europe by Allied forces began June 1944 when troops landed on the beaches of Calvados.

basset type of dog with a long low body, wrinkled forehead, and long pendulous ears, originally bred in France for hunting hares.

Basseterre capital and port of St Kitts-Nevis, in the Leeward Islands; population (1980) 14,000. Industries include data processing, rum, clothes, and electrical components.

Basse-Terre port on the Leeward Island Basse-Terre; population (1982) 13,600. It is the capital of the French overseas *département* of Guadeloupe.

Basse-Terre main island of the French West Indian island group of Guadeloupe; area 327 sq mi/848 sq km; population (1982) 141,300. It has an active volcano, Grande Soufrière, rising to 4,870 ft/1,484 m.

basset horn musical ◊woodwind instrument resembling a clarinet, pitched in F and ending in a brass bell. Its range lies between the clarinet and the bass clarinet.

bassoon double-reed ◊woodwind instrument, the bass of the oboe family. It doubles back on itself in a tube about 7.5 ft/2.5 m long. Its tone is rich and deep. It is descended from the **bass pommer**, which was approximately 6 ft/2 m long and perfectly straight.

Bass Strait channel between Australia and Tasmania, named after British explorer George Bass; oil was discovered there in the 1960s.

Bastille castle of St Antoine, built about 1370 as part of the fortifications of Paris. It was made a state prison by Cardinal ◊Richelieu and was stormed by the mob that set the French Revolution in motion July 14, 1789. Only seven prisoners were found in the castle when it was stormed; the governor and most of the garrison were killed, and the Bastille was razed.

Basutoland former name for ◊Lesotho, a kingdom in southern Africa.

bat flying mammal in which the forelimbs are developed as wings capable of rapid and sustained flight. There are two main groups of bats: **megabats**, or **flying foxes**, which eat fruit, and **microbats**, which mainly eat insects. Although by no means blind, many microbats rely largely on echolocation for navigation and finding prey, sending out pulses of high-pitched sound and listening for the echo. Bats are nocturnal, and those native to temperate countries hibernate in winter. There are about 1,000 species of bats forming the order Chiroptera, making this the second-largest mammalian order; bats make up nearly one-fourth of the world's mammals. Although bats are widely distributed, bat populations have declined alarmingly and many species are now endangered.

megabats The Megachiroptera live in the tropical regions of the Old World, Australia, and the Pacific, and feed on fruit, nectar, and pollen. The hind feet have five toes with sharp hooked claws which suspend the animal head downward when resting. Relatively large, up to 2 lb/900 g with a 5 ft/1.5 m wingspan, they have large eyes and a long face earning them the name "flying fox." Many rainforest trees depend on bats for pollination and seed dispersal, and some 300 bat-dependent plant species yield more than 450 economically valuable products. Some bats are keystone species on whose survival whole ecosystems may depend.

microbats Most bats are Microchiroptera, mainly small and insect-eating, though some species feed on blood (◊vampire bats), frogs, or fish. They roost in caves, crevices, and hollow trees. A single bat may eat 3,000 insects in one night.

A bat's wings consist of thin hairless skin stretched between the four fingers of the hand, and from the last finger down to the hindlimb. The thumb is free and has a sharp claw to help in climbing. Some bats live to be over 30 years old. An adult female bat usually rears only one pup a year. The bumblebee bat, inhabiting SE Asian rainforests, is the smallest mammal in the world. In China bats are associated with good luck.

Bataan peninsula in Luzon, the Philippines, which was defended against the Japanese in World War II by US and Filipino troops under General MacArthur Jan 1–April 9, 1942. MacArthur was evacuated, but some 67,000 Allied prisoners died on the *Bataan Death March* to camps in the interior.

Batak member of the several distinct but related peoples of N Sumatra in Indonesia. Numbering approximately 2.5 million, the Batak speak languages belonging to the Austronesian family.

The most numerous and most centrally located are the Toba Batak who live S and W of Lake Toba. Although the Batak possess distinctive traditional beliefs, they were influenced by Hinduism between the 2nd and 15th centuries. The syllabic script of the Batak, which was inscribed on bamboo, horn, bone, and tree bark, is based on Indian scripts. Although the island of Sumatra has many Muslim peoples, most Batak did not adopt Islam. Since 1861 German and other missionaries have been active in N Sumatra and today over 80% of the Batak profess Christianity. Many Batak are rice farmers and produce handicrafts such as dyed textiles.

Batavia former name until 1949 for ◌Jakarta, capital of Indonesia on Java.

Batavian Republic name given to the Netherlands by the French 1795; it lasted until the establishment of the kingdom of the Netherlands 1814 at the end of the Napoleonic Wars.

Bates Alan 1934– . English actor, a versatile male lead in over 60 plays and films. His films include *Zorba the Greek* 1965, *Far from the Madding Crowd* 1967, *Women in Love* 1970, *The Go-Between* 1971, *The Shout* 1978, and *Duet for One* 1986.

Bates H(enry) W(alter) 1825–1892. English naturalist and explorer, who spent 11 years collecting animals and plants in South America and identified 8,000 new species of insects. He made a special study of ◌camouflage in animals, and his observation of insect imitation of species that are unpleasant to predators is known as "Batesian mimicry."

Bates H(erbert) E(rnest) 1906–1974. English author. Of his many novels and short stories, *The Jacaranda Tree* 1949 and *The Darling Buds of May* 1958 demonstrate the fineness of his natural observation and compassionate portrayal of character. *Fair Stood the Wind for France* 1944 was based on his experience as a Squadron Leader in World War II.

Bates eyesight training method developed by US opthalmologist William Bates (1860–1931) to enable people to correct problems of vision without wearing glasses. The method is of proven effectiveness in relieving all refractive conditions, correcting squints, lazy eyes, and similar problems, but does not claim to treat eye disease.

Bath historic city in Avon, England; population (1991) 79,900
features hot springs; the ruins of the baths for which it is named, as well as a great temple, are the finest Roman remains in Britain. Excavations 1979 revealed thousands of coins and "curses," offered at a place which was thought to be the link between the upper and lower worlds. The Gothic Bath Abbey has an unusually decorated west front and fan vaulting. There is much 18th-century architecture, notably the Royal Crescent by John Wood. The Assembly Rooms 1771 were destroyed in an air raid 1942 but reconstructed 1963. The University of Technology was established 1966. The Bath Festival Orchestra is based here.
history the Roman city of Aquae Sulis ("waters of Sul" —the British goddess of wisdom) was built in the first 20 years after the Roman invasion. In medieval times the hot springs were crown property, administered by the church, but the city was transformed in the 18th century to a fashionable spa, presided over by "Beau" Nash. At his home here the astronomer

Herschel discovered Uranus 1781. Visitors included the novelists Smollett, Fielding, and Jane Austen.

batholith large, irregular, deep-seated mass of igneous rock, usually granite, with an exposed surface of more than 40 sq mi/100 sq km. The mass forms by the intrusion or upswelling of magma (molten rock) through the surrounding rock. Batholiths form the core of all major mountain ranges.
According to plate tectonic theory, magma rises in subduction zones along continental margins where one plate sinks beneath another. The solidified magma becomes the central axis of a rising mountain range, resulting in the deformation (folding and overthrusting) of rocks on either side. Gravity measurements indicate that the downward extent or thickness of many batholiths is some 6–9 mi/10–15 km.

Bath, Order of the British order of knighthood, believed to have been founded in the reign of Henry IV (1399–1413). Formally instituted 1815, it included civilians from 1847 and women from 1970.

Báthory Stephen 1533–1586. King of Poland, elected by a diet convened 1575 and crowned 1576. Báthory succeeded in driving the Russian troops of Ivan the Terrible out of his country. His military successes brought potential conflicts with Sweden, but he died before these developed.

bathyal zone upper part of the ocean, which lies on the continental shelf at a depth of between 650 ft/200 m and 6,500 ft/2,000 m.

bathyscaph or *bathyscaphe* or *bathyscape* deep-sea diving apparatus used for exploration at great depths in the ocean. In 1960, Jacques Piccard and Don Walsh took the bathyscaph *Trieste* to a depth of 35,820 ft/10,917 m in the Challenger Deep in the ◌Mariana Trench off the island of Guam in the Pacific Ocean.

bathysphere watertight steel sphere used for observation in deep-sea diving. It is lowered into the ocean by cable to a maximum depth of 3,000 ft/900 m.

batik Javanese technique of hand-applied color design for fabric; areas to be left undyed in a color are sealed with wax. Practiced throughout Indonesia, the craft was introduced to the West by Dutch traders.

Batista Fulgencio 1901–1973. Cuban dictator 1933–44, when he stood down, and again 1952–59, after siezing power in a coup. His authoritarian methods enabled him to jail his opponents and amass a large personal fortune. He was overthrown by rebel forces led by Fidel ◌Castro 1959.

Batman comic-strip character created 1939 by US cartoonist Bob Kane and his collaborator Bill Finger. A crime-busting superhero, disguised by a black batlike mask and cape, Batman is, with his sidekick Robin, a staple of the DC Comics group.
Batman's secret identity is that of millionaire playboy Bruce Wayne. His youthful aide, former circus performer Dick Grayson, is known as Robin the Boy Wonder. Together they zoom around in their "batmobile" and combat the criminal activities of (among others) the Joker, the Penguin, the Riddler, and the Catwoman. Batman films appeared 1943, 1949, and 1989, and there was a Pop-art-inspired *Batman* television series in the 1960s.

Baton Rouge deepwater port on the Mississippi River, the capital of Louisiana; population

(1990) 219,530. Industries include oil refining, petrochemicals, and iron.
The port has become one of the nation's largest. Baton Rouge is the home of Louisiana State and Southern universities. It was settled in 1719 and was, successively, under French, British, Spanish, French, and Spanish rule before the residents rebelled against Spain 1819 and joined it to the US.

battalion or *unit* basic personnel unit in the military system, usually consisting of four or five companies. A battalion is commanded by a lieutenant colonel. Several battalions form a ◌brigade.

Battenberg title (conferred 1851) of German noble family; its members included ◌Louis, Prince of Battenberg, and Louis Alexander, Prince of Battenberg, who anglicized his name to Mountbatten 1917.

battery any energy-storage device allowing release of electricity on demand. It is made up of one or more electrical ◌cells. Primary-cell batteries are disposable; secondary-cell batteries are rechargeable. Primary-cell batteries are an extremely uneconomical form of energy, since they produce only 2% of the power used in their manufacture.
The common *dry cell* is a primary-cell battery based on the ◌Leclanché cell, and consists of a central carbon electrode immersed in a paste of manganese dioxide and ammonium chloride as the electrolyte. The zinc casing forms the other electrode. It is dangerous to try to recharge a primary-cell battery.
The lead-acid *car battery* is a secondary-cell battery. The car's generator continually recharges the battery. It consists of sets of lead (positive) and lead peroxide (negative) plates in an electrolyte of sulfuric acid.
The introduction of rechargeable nickel-cadmium batteries has revolutionized portable electronic newsgathering (sound recording, video) and information processing (computing). These batteries offer a stable, short-term source of power free of noise and other electrical hazards.

Battle Creek city in S Michigan, directly E of Kalamazoo. It became known as the cereal capital of the world after J H Kellogg, W K Kellogg, and C W Post established dry cereal and grain factories here; population (1990) 53,540. Battle Creek was also a station on the ◌Underground Railroad.

battleship class of large warships with the biggest guns and heaviest armor. In 1991, four US battleships were in active service.

battery *The common dry cell relies on chemical changes occurring between the electrodes—the central carbon rod and the outer zinc casing—and the ammonium chloride electrolyte to produce electricity.*

Batumi Black Sea port and capital of the autonomous republic of Adzhar, in the Republic of Georgia; population (1987) 135,000. Main industries include oil refining, food canning, and engineering.

baud in engineering, a unit of telegraph signaling speed equal to one pulse per second; also the number of bits per second that can be transmitted in a computer system.

baud unit that measures the speed of data transmission. One baud represents a transmission rate of one bit per second.

Baudelaire Charles Pierre 1821–1867. French poet whose work combined rhythmical and musical perfection with a morbid romanticism and eroticism, finding beauty in decadence and evil. His first book of verse was *Les Fleurs du mal/Flowers of Evil* 1857.

Baudouin 1930– . King of the Belgians from 1951. In 1950 his father, ◊Leopold III, abdicated and Baudouin was known until his succession July 1951 as *Le Prince Royal*. In 1960 he married Fabiola de Mora y Aragón (1928–), member of a Spanish noble family.

Bauhaus German school of Modern architecture and design founded 1919 by the architect Walter ◊Gropius at Weimar in Germany in an attempt to fuse all arts, design, architecture, and crafts into a unified whole. Moved to Dessau under political pressure 1925, it was closed by the Nazis 1933 because of "decadence." Associated with the Bauhaus were the artists Klee and Kandinsky and the architect Mies van der Rohe.

Gropius and Marcel Breuer worked together in the US 1937–40. The international style of Modern architecture spread worldwide from there and in 1972 the *Bauhaus Archive* was installed in new premises in Berlin.

Baum L(yman) Frank 1856–1919. US writer, author of the children's fantasy *The Wonderful Wizard of Oz* 1900 and its 13 sequels. The series was continued by another author after his death. The film *The Wizard of Oz* 1939 with Judy Garland became a US classic.

Bausch Pina 1940– . German avant-garde dance choreographer and director from 1974 of the Wuppertal Tanztheater. Her works incorporate dialogue, elements of psychoanalysis, comedy, and drama, and have been performed on floors covered with churned earth, rose petals, or water. She never accepts requests to restage her creations.

bauxite principal ore of ◊aluminum, consisting of a mixture of hydrated aluminum oxides and hydroxides, generally contaminated with compounds of iron, which give it a red color. To produce aluminum the ore is processed into a white powder (alumina), which is then smelted by passing a large electric current through it. Chief producers of bauxite are Australia, Guinea, Jamaica, Russia, Kazakhstan, Suriname, and Brazil.

Bavaria (German *Bayern*) administrative region (German *Land*) of Germany;
area 27,252 sq mi/70,600 sq km
capital Munich
cities Nuremberg, Augsburg, Würzburg, Regensburg
features largest of the German *Länder*; forms the Danube basin; festivals at Bayreuth and Oberammergau
products beer, electronics, electrical engineering, optics, automobiles, aerospace, chemicals, plastics, oil refining, textiles, glass, toys

population (1988) 11,000,000
famous people Lucas Cranach, Adolf Hitler, Franz Josef Strauss, Richard Strauss
religion 70% Roman Catholic, 26% Protestant
history the last king, Ludwig III, abdicated 1918, and Bavaria declared itself a republic.

The original Bavarians were Teutonic invaders from Bohemia who occupied the country at the end of the 5th century. From about 555 to 788 Bavaria was ruled by Frankish dukes of the Agilolfing family. In the 7th and 8th centuries the region was christianized by Irish and Scottish monks. In 788 Charlemagne deposed the last of the Agilolfing dukes and incorporated Bavaria into the Carolingian Empire, and in the 10th century it became part of the Holy Roman Empire. The house of Wittelsbach ruled parts or all of Bavaria 1181–1918; Napoleon made the ruler a king 1806. In 1871 Bavaria became a state of the German Empire.

bay various species of ◊laurel, genus *Laurus*. The aromatic evergreen leaves are used for flavoring in cooking. There is also a golden-leaved variety.

Bay City industrial city in Michigan; population (1990) 38,900. Industries include shipbuilding and engineering.

Bayern German name for ◊Bavaria, region of Germany.

Bayes Thomas 1702–1761. English mathematician whose investigations into probability led to what is now known as Bayes' theorem.

Bayesian statistics form of statistics that uses the knowledge of prior probability together with the probability of actual data to determine posterior probabilities, using Bayes' theorem.

Bayes' theorem in statistics, a theorem relating the ◊probability of particular events taking place to the probability that events conditional upon them have occurred.

For example, the probability of picking an ace at random out of a pack of cards is 4/52. If two cards are picked out, the probability of the second card being an ace is conditional on the first card: if the first card was an ace the probability will be 3/51; if not it will be 4/51. Bayes' theorem gives the probability that given that the second card is an ace, the first card is also.

Bayeux town in N France; population (1982) 15,200. Its museum houses the Bayeux Tapestry. There is a 13th-century Gothic cathedral. Bayeux was the first town in W Europe to be liberated by the Allies in World War II, June 8, 1944.

Bayeux Tapestry linen hanging made about 1067–70, which gives a vivid pictorial record of the invasion of England by William I (the Conqueror) 1066. It is an embroidery rather than a true tapestry, sewn with woolen threads in blue, green, red, and yellow, 231 ft/70 m long and 20 in/50 cm wide, and containing 72 separate scenes with descriptive wording in Latin. It is exhibited at the museum of Bayeaux in Normandy, France.

Bayliss William Maddock 1860–1924. English physiologist who discovered the digestive hormone secretin with Ernest Starling 1902. During World War I, Bayliss introduced the use of saline (salt water) injections to help the injured recover from ◊shock.

Bay of Pigs inlet on the S coast of Cuba about 90 mi/145 km SW of Havana. It was the site of an unsuccessful invasion attempt by 1,500

US-sponsored Cuban exiles April 17–20, 1961; 1,173 were taken prisoner.

The creation of this antirevolutionary force by the CIA had been authorized by the Eisenhower administration, and the project was executed under that of J F Kennedy. In 1962 most of the Cuban prisoners were ransomed for $53 million in food and medicine. The incident served to strengthen Cuba's links with the USSR.

bayonet short sword attached to the muzzle of a firearm. The bayonet was placed inside the barrel of the muzzle-loading muskets of the late 17th century. The *sock* or ring bayonet, invented 1700, allowed a weapon to be fired without interruption, leading to the demise of the pike.

Since the 1700s, bayonets have evolved into a variety of types. During World War I, the French used a long needle bayonet, while the Germans attached a bayonet, known as the butcher's knife, to their Mauser 98s. As armies have become more mechanized, bayonets have tended to decrease in length.

Although many military leaders have advocated the use of the bayonet, in practice it has been rarely used. For example, at Inkerman during the Crimean War 1854, only 6% of casualties were attributed to the bayonet. However, the morale effects associated with the fixing of bayonets have generally been considered to outweigh their disadvantages, which include restriction of movement and lack of real utility.

Bayonne river port in SW France; population (1983) 127,000. It trades in timber, steel, fertiliser, and brandy. It is a center of ◊Basque life. The bayonet was invented here.

bayou (corruption of French *boyau* "gut") in the Gulf States, an ◊oxbow lake or marshy offshoot of a river.

Bayous may be formed, as in the lower Mississippi, by a river flowing in wide curves or meanders in flat country, and then cutting a straight course across them in times of flood, leaving loops of isolated water behind.

Bay Psalm Book Puritan rendering of the psalms into meter, printed 1639; it is considered the first work of American literature.

Written by Richard Mather, John Eliot, and 28 other ministers of the Massachusetts Bay Colony, it was published by Stephen Day in Cambridge, with an edition of 1,700 copies.

Bayreuth town in Bavaria, S Germany, where opera festivals are held every summer; population (1983) 71,000. It was the home of composer Richard ◊Wagner, and the Wagner theater was established 1876.

Bazaine Achille François 1811–1888. Marshal of France. From being a private soldier 1831 he rose to command the French troops in Mexico 1862–67 and was made a marshal 1864. In the Franco-Prussian War Bazaine allowed himself to be taken in the fortress of Metz, surrendering Oct 27, 1870 with nearly 180,000 men. For this he was court-martialed 1873 and imprisoned; he escaped to Spain 1874.

BBC abbreviation for ◊*British Broadcasting Corporation*.

BC in the Christian calendar, abbreviation for *before Christ*; used with dates.

BCE abbreviation for *before the Common Era*; used with dates (instead of BC).

B cell or *B* ◊*lymphocyte* immune cell that produces ◊antibodies. Each B cell produces just one type of antibody, specific to a single ⟡antigen. Lymphocytes are related to ⟡T cells.

BCG (abbreviation for *bacillus of Calmette and Guérin*) bacillus used as a vaccine to confer active immunity to ⟡tuberculosis (TB).

BCG was developed by Albert Calmette and Camille Guérin in France 1921 from live bovine TB bacilli. These bacteria were bred in the laboratory over many generations until they became attenuated (weakened). Each inoculation contains just enough live, attenuated bacilli to provoke an immune response: the formation of specific ⟡antibodies. The recipient then has lifelong protection against TB.

beach strip of land bordering the sea, normally consisting of boulders and pebbles on exposed coasts or sand on sheltered coasts. It is usually defined by the high- and low-water marks. A berm, a ridge of sand and pebbles, may be found at the farthest point which the water reaches.

The material of the beach consists of a rocky debris eroded from exposed rocks and headlands. The material is transported to the beach, and along the beach, by waves that hit the coastline at an angle, resulting in a net movement of the material in one particular direction. This movement is known as *longshore drift*. Attempts are often made to halt longshore drift by erecting barriers, or jetties, at right angles to the movement. Pebbles are worn into round shapes by being battered against one another by wave action and the result is called *shingle*. The finer material, the *sand*, may be subsequently moved about by the wind and form sand dunes. Apart from the natural process of longshore drift, a beach may be threatened by the commercial use of sand and aggregate—since the mineral industry—since particles of metal ore are often concentrated into workable deposits by the wave action—and by pollution (for example, by oil spilled or dumped at sea).

Beach Boys, the US pop group formed 1961. They began as exponents of vocal-harmony surf music with Chuck Berry guitar riffs (their hits include "Surfin' USA" 1963 and "Help Me, Rhonda" 1965) but the compositions, arrangements, and production by Brian Wilson (1942–) became highly complex under the influence of psychedelic rock, peaking with "Good Vibrations" 1966. Wilson spent most of the next 20 years in retirement but returned with a solo album 1988.

Beadle George Wells 1903–1989. US biologist. Born in Wahoo, Nebraska, he was professor of biology at the California Institute of Technology 1946–61. In 1958 he shared a Nobel Prize with Edward L Tatum for his work in biochemical genetics, forming the "one-gene–one-enzyme" hypothesis (a single gene codes for a single kind of enzyme).

beagle short-haired hound with pendant ears, sickle tail, and a bell-like voice for hunting hares on foot ("beagling").

Beagle Channel channel to the south of Tierra del Fuego, South America, named after the ship of Charles ⟡Darwin's voyage. Three islands at its eastern end, with krill and oil reserves within their 200 mi/322 km territorial waters, and the dependent sector of the Antarctic with its resources, were disputed between Argentina and Chile and awarded to Chile 1985.

beak horn-covered projecting jaws of a bird, or other horny jaws such as those of the tortoise or octopus. The beaks of birds are adapted by shape and size to specific diets.

Beaker people people thought to be of Iberian origin who spread out over Europe from the 3rd millennium BC. They were skilled in metalworking, and are identified by their use of distinctive earthenware beakers with stamped designs, of which the bell-beaker type was widely distributed throughout Europe. They favored inhumation (burial of the intact body), in a trench or under a round ⟡barrow, or secondary burials in some form of chamber tomb. A beaker accompanied each burial, to hold a drink for the deceased on their final journey.

beam balance instrument for measuring mass (or weight). A simple form consists of a beam pivoted at its midpoint with a pan hanging at each end. The mass to be measured, in one pan, is compared with a variety of standard masses placed in the other. When the beam is balanced, the masses' turning effects or moments under gravity, and hence the masses themselves, are equal.

bean any seed of numerous leguminous plants. Beans are rich in nitrogenous or protein matter and are grown both for human consumption and as food for cattle and horses. Varieties of bean are grown throughout Europe, the US, South America, China, Japan, SE Asia, and Australia.

The broad bean *Vicia faba* has been cultivated in Europe since prehistoric times. The French bean, kidney bean, or haricot *Phaseolus vulgaris* is probably of South American origin; the runner bean *Phaseolus coccineus* is closely allied to it, but differs in its climbing habit. Among beans of warmer countries are the lima or butter bean *Phaseolus lunatus* of South America, the soybean *Glycine max*, extensively used in China and Japan, and the winged bean *Psophocarpus tetragonolobus* of SE Asia. The tuberous root of the winged bean has potential as a main crop in tropical areas where protein deficiency is common. The Asian mung bean *Phaseolus mungo* yields the bean sprouts used in Chinese cooking. Canned baked beans are usually a variety of *Phaseolus vulgaris*, which grows well in the US.

bear large mammal with a heavily built body, short powerful limbs, and a very short tail. Bears breed once a year, producing one to four cubs. In northern regions they hibernate, and the young are born in the winter den. They are found mainly in North America and N Asia. The skin of the polar bear is black to conserve 80–90% of the solar energy trapped and channeled down the hollow hairs of its fur.

Bears walk on the soles of the feet and have long, nonretractable claws. There are seven species of bear, including the *brown bear Ursus arctos*, formerly ranging across most of Europe, N Asia, and North America, but now reduced in number. It varies in size from under 7 ft/2 m long in parts of the Old World to 9 ft/2.8 m long and 1,700 lb/780 kg in Alaska. The *grizzly bear* is a North American variety of this species and another subspecies, the *Kodiak bear* of Alaska, is the largest living land carnivore. The white *polar bear Thalarctos maritimus* is up to 8 ft/2.5 m long, has furry undersides to the feet, and feeds mainly on seals. It is found in the north polar region. The North American *black bear Euarctos americanus* and the *Asian black bear Selenarctos thibetanus* are smaller, only about 5 ft/1.6 m long. The latter has a white V-mark on its chest. The *spectacled bear Tremarctos ornatus* of the Andes is similarly sized, as is the *sloth bear Melursus ursinus* of India and Sri Lanka, which has a shaggy coat and uses its claws and protrusile lips to obtain termites, one of its preferred foods. The smallest bear is the Malaysian *sun bear Helarctos malayanus*, rarely more than 4 ft/ 1.2 m long, a good climber, whose favorite food is honey. The bear family, Ursidae, is related to carnivores such as dogs and weasels, and all are capable of killing prey. The panda is probably related to both bears and raccoons.

bear in business, a speculator who sells stocks or shares on the stock exchange expecting a fall in the price in order to buy them back at a profit, the opposite of a ⟡bull. In a bear market, prices fall, and bears prosper.

bearberry any of several species of evergreen trailing shrub, genus *Arctostaphylos*, of the heath family, found on uplands and rocky places. Most bearberries are North American but *A. uva-ursi* is also found in Asia and Europe in northern mountainous regions. It bears small pink flowers in spring, followed by red berries that are edible but dry.

Beard Charles Austin 1874–1948. US historian. Born near Knightstown, Indiana, Beard earned a PhD from Columbia University 1904. A leading exponent of critical economic history, he published *An Economic Interpretation of the Constitution of the United States* 1913 and *The Economic Origins of Jeffersonian Democracy* 1915. He was a leader of the Progressive

roller bearing
rollers
cage
outer ring
inner ring

journal bearing
journal

ball bearing
outer ring
cage
steel balls
inner ring

bearing *Three types of bearing.*

Movement and resigned from the Columbia faculty 1917 over issues of academic freedom. He helped found the New School for Social Research 1918. With his wife, Mary, he wrote *A Basic History of the United States* 1944, long a standard textbook.

Beardsley Aubrey (Vincent) 1872–1898. British illustrator. His meticulously executed black-and-white work displays the sinuous line and decorative mannerisms of Art Nouveau and was often charged with being grotesque and decadent.

bearing device used in a machine to allow free movement between two parts, typically the rotation of a shaft in a housing. *Ball bearings* consist of two rings, one fixed to a housing, one to the rotating shaft. Between them is a set, or race, of steel balls. They are widely used to support shafts, as in the spindle in the hub of a bicycle wheel.

The *sleeve*, or *journal bearing*, is the simplest bearing. It is a hollow cylinder, split into two halves. It is used for the big-end and main bearings on an automobile ¢crankshaft.

In some machinery the balls of ball bearings are replaced by cylindrical rollers or thinner, *needle bearings*.

In precision equipment such as watches and aircraft instruments, bearings may be made from material such as ruby and are known as *jewel bearings*.

For some applications bearings made from nylon and other plastics are used. They need no lubrication because their surfaces are naturally waxy. *See illustration on p. 113.*

bearing the direction of a fixed point, or the path of a moving object, from a point of observation on the Earth's surface, expressed as an angle from the north. Bearings are taken by ¢compass and are measured in degrees (°), given as three-digit numbers increasing clockwise. For instance, north is 000°, northeast is 045°, south is 180°, and southwest is 225°.

True north differs slightly from magnetic north (the direction in which a compass needle points), hence NE may be denoted as 045M or 045T, depending on whether the reference line is magnetic (M) or true (T) north. True north also differs slightly from grid north since it is impossible to show a spherical Earth on a flat map.

Beas river in Himachal Pradesh, India, an upper tributary of the Sutlej, which in turn joins the Indus. It is one of the five rivers that give the Punjab its name. The ancient Hyphasis, it marked the limit of the invasion of India by Alexander the Great.

beat regular variation in the loudness of the sound when two notes of nearly equal pitch or ¢frequency are heard together. Beats result from the ¢interference between the sound waves of the notes. The frequency of the beats equals the difference in frequency of the notes.

Beat Generation or *Beat movement* beatniks of the 1950s and 1960s, usually in their teens and early twenties, who rejected conventional lifestyles and opted for life on the road, drug experimentation, and antimaterialist values; and the associated literary movement whose members included William S Burroughs, Lawrence Ferlinghetti, Allen ¢Ginsberg, and Jack ¢Kerouac (who is credited with coining the term).

Beat literature has a free, unstructured style; the most important example is Ginsberg's poem *Howl* 1956. Jazz music, Zen, and hallucinogenic visions had a major influence on the attitudes and vocabulary of the Beats, who indicted the "madness" of modern society.

beatification in the Catholic church, the first step toward ¢canonization. Persons who have been beatified can be prayed to, and the title "Blessed" can be put before their names.

Beatitudes in the New Testament, the sayings of Jesus reported in Matthew 6: 1–12 and Luke 6: 20–38, depicting the spiritual qualities that characterize members of the Kingdom of God.

Beatles, the English pop group 1960–70. The members, all born in Liverpool, were John Lennon (1940–80, rhythm guitar, vocals), Paul McCartney (1942– , bass, vocals), George Harrison (1943– , lead guitar, vocals), and Ringo Starr (formerly Richard Starkey, 1940– , drums). Using songs written largely by Lennon and McCartney, the Beatles dominated rock music and pop culture in the 1960s.

In addition to experimenting with a wide range of musical styles, they greatly influenced subsequent bands, made films and toured extensively. Their hit songs include "She Loves You" 1963, "Can't Buy Me Love" 1964, and "Yesterday" 1965. Their films include *A Hard Day's Night* 1964, *Help* 1965, and the animated feature *Yellow Submarine* 1968, for which they provided the soundtrack. The Beatles continued to have an impact on the dress, hair, lifestyle, and thought of young people even after they pursued separate careers.

beat music pop music that evolved in the UK in the early 1960s, known in its purest form as ¢Mersey beat, and as British Invasion in the US. The beat groups characteristically had a simple, guitar-dominated line-up, vocal harmonies, and catchy tunes. They included the Beatles (1960–70), the Hollies (1962–), and the Zombies (1962–67).

Beaton Cecil 1904–1980. English portrait and fashion photographer, designer, illustrator, diarist, and conversationalist. He produced portrait studies and also designed scenery and costumes for ballets, and sets for plays and films.

Beatrix 1936– . Queen of the Netherlands. The eldest daughter of Queen ¢Juliana, she succeeded to the throne on her mother's abdication 1980. In 1966 she married West German diplomat Claus von Amsberg (1926–), who was created Prince of the Netherlands. Her heir is Prince Willem Alexander (1967–).

Beatty Warren. Adopted name of Warren Beaty 1937– . US actor and director, popular for such films as *Splendour in the Grass* 1961, *Bonnie and Clyde* 1967, and *Heaven Can Wait* 1978. His more recent productions include *Reds* 1981 (Academy Award for Best Producer), *Ishtar* 1987, and *Dick Tracy* 1990.

Beaufort Francis 1774–1857. British admiral, hydrographer to the Royal Navy from 1829; the Beaufort scale and the Beaufort Sea in the Arctic Ocean are named after him.

Beaufort Henry 1375–1447. English priest, bishop of Lincoln from 1398, of Winchester from 1405. As chancellor of England, he supported his half brother Henry IV, and made enormous personal loans to Henry V to finance war against France. As a guardian of Henry VI from 1421, he was in effective control of the country until 1426. In the same year he was created a cardinal. In 1431 he crowned Henry VI as king of France in Paris.

Beaufort scale system of recording wind velocity, devised by Francis Beaufort 1806. It is a numerical scale ranging from 0 to 17, calm being indicated by 0 and a hurricane by 12; 13–17 indicate degrees of hurricane force.

In 1874, the scale received international recognition; it was modified 1926. Measurements are made at 33 ft/10 m above ground level.

Beaufort Sea section of the Arctic Ocean off Alaska and Canada, named after Francis Beaufort. Oil drilling is allowed only in the winter months because the sea is the breeding and migration route of bowhead whales, the staple diet of the local Inuit people.

Beauharnais Alexandre, Vicomte de 1760–1794. French liberal aristocrat and general who served in the American Revolution and became a member of the National Convention in the early days of the French Revolution. He was the first husband of Josephine (consort of Napoleon I). Their daughter Hortense (1783–1837) married Louis, a younger brother of Napoleon, and their son became ¢Napoleon III. Beauharnais was guillotined during the Terror for his alleged lack of zeal for the revolutionary cause and his lack of success as Commander of the Republican Army of the North.

Beaufort scale

number and description	features	air speed mi per hr	m per sec
0 calm	smoke rises vertically; water smooth	less than 1	less than 0.3
1 light air	smoke shows wind direction; water ruffled	1–3	0.3–1.5
2 slight breeze	leaves rustle; wind felt on face	4–7	1.6–3.3
3 gentle breeze	loose paper blows around	8–12	3.4–5.4
4 moderate breeze	branches sway	13–18	5.5–7.9
5 fresh breeze	small trees sway, leaves blown off	19–24	8.0–10.7
6 strong breeze	whistling in telephone wires; sea spray from waves	25–31	10.8–13.8
7 moderate gale	large trees sway	32–38	13.9–17.1
8 fresh gale	twigs break from trees	39–46	17.2–20.7
9 strong gale	branches break from trees	47–54	20.8–24.4
10 whole gale	trees uprooted, weak buildings collapse	55–63	24.5–28.4
11 storm	widespread damage	64–72	28.5–32.6
12 hurricane	widespread structural damage	73–82	above 32.7
13		83–92	
14		93–103	
15		104–114	
16		115–125	
17		126–136	

Beaujolais light, fruity red wine produced in the area S of Burgundy in E France. Beaujolais is best drunk while young; the broaching date is the third Thursday in Nov, when the new vintage is rushed to the US, the UK, Japan and other countries, so that the Beaujolais *nouveau* (new Beaujolais) may be marketed.

Beaumarchais Pierre Augustin Caron de 1732–1799. French dramatist. His great comedies *Le Barbier de Seville/The Barber of Seville* 1775 and *Le Mariage de Figaro/The Marriage of Figaro* (1778, but prohibited until 1784) form the basis of operas by ⫗Rossini and ⫗Mozart.

Louis XVI entrusted Beaumarchais with secret missions, notably for the profitable shipment of arms to the American colonies during the War of Independence. Accused of treason 1792, he fled to Holland and England, but in 1799 he returned to Paris.

Beaumont city and port in SE Texas, NE of Houston, on the Neches River; seat of Jefferson county. It is an oil-processing center for the surrounding oil fields and a shipping point via the Sabine–Neches canal to the Gulf of Mexico. Shipbuilding and paper production are also industries; population (1990) 114,320. In 1901, when a successful oil well was drilled at Spindletop Field, the modern oil industry began in the West.

Beaumont Francis 1584–1616. English dramatist and poet. From about 1608 he collaborated with John ⫗Fletcher. Their joint plays include *Philaster* 1610, *The Maid's Tragedy* about 1611, and *A King and No King* about 1611. *The Woman Hater* about 1606 and *The Knight of the Burning Pestle* about 1607 are ascribed to Beaumont alone.

Beaumont William 1785–1853. US surgeon who conducted pioneering experiments on the digestive system. In 1882 he saved the life of a Canadian trapper wounded in the side by a gun blast; the wound only partially healed and, through an opening in the stomach wall, Beaumont was able to observe the workings of the stomach. His *Experiments and Observations on the Gastric Juice and the Physiology of Digestion* was published 1833.

Beauregard Pierre Gustave Toutant 1818–1893. US military leader and Confederate general whose opening fire on ⫗Fort Sumter, South Carolina, started the American Civil War 1861. His military successes were clouded by his conflicts with Confederate President Jefferson Davis.

Beauregard was born in Louisiana and graduated from West Point in 1838. He distinguished himself during the Mexican War and then returned to Louisiana. In 1861 he was appointed superintendent of West Point, but resigned after four days to join the South.

At the outset of the Civil War, Beauregard achieved fame immediately for his attack on Fort Sumter. He played a leading role in the Confederate victory at the 1st Battle of Bull Run and prevented disaster at Shiloh (1862) through an orderly withdrawal. His disagreements with Davis, however, resulted in frequent changes in his commands. In 1865 he helped to delay the Union advance on Petersburg, Virginia. He spent his postwar years in New Orleans, where he was prominent in business and politics.

Beauvais town 47 mi/76 km NW of Paris, France; population (1982) 54,150. It is a market town trading in fruit, dairy produce, and agricultural machinery. Beauvais has a Gothic cathedral, the tallest in France: (223 ft/68 m), and is renowned for tapestries (which are now made at the ⫗Gobelins factory, Paris).

Beauvoir Simone de 1908–1986. French socialist, feminist, and writer who taught philosophy at the Sorbonne university in Paris 1931–43. Her book *Le Deuxième sexe/The Second Sex* 1949 became a seminal work for many feminists.

Her novel of postwar Paris, *Les Mandarins/The Mandarins* 1954, has characters resembling the writers Albert Camus, Arthur Koestler, and Jean-Paul ⫗Sartre. She also published autobiographical volumes.

beaver aquatic rodent *Castor fiber* with webbed hind feet, a broad flat scaly tail, and thick waterproof fur. It has very large incisor teeth and fells trees to feed on the bark and to use the logs to construct the "lodge," in which the young are reared, food is stored, and where much of the winter is spent.

Beavers can construct dams on streams, and thus modify the environment considerably. They once ranged across Europe, N Asia, and North America, but in Europe now only survive where they are protected, and are reduced elsewhere, partly through trapping for their fur.

Beaverbrook (William) Max (well) Aitken, 1st Baron Beaverbrook 1879–1964. British financier, newspaper proprietor, and politician, born in Canada. He bought a majority interest in the *Daily Express* 1919, founded the *Sunday Express* 1921, and bought the London *Evening Standard* 1929. He served in Lloyd George's World War I cabinet and Churchill's World War II cabinet.

bebop or *bop* hot jazz style, rhythmically complex, virtuosic, and highly improvisational, developed in New York 1940–55 by Charlie Parker, Dizzy Gillespie, Thelonius Monk, and other black musicians disaffected with dance bands.

Beccaria Cesare, Marese di Beccaria 1738–1794. Italian philanthropist, born in Milan. He opposed capital punishment and torture; advocated education as a crime preventative; influenced English philosopher Jeremy ⫗Bentham; and coined the phrase "the greatest happiness of the greatest number," the tenet of ⫗utilitarianism.

Bechet Sidney (Joseph) 1897–1959. US jazz musician, born in New Orleans. He played clarinet and was the first to forge an individual style on soprano saxophone. Bechet was based in Paris in the late 1920s and the 1950s, where he was recognized by Classical musicians as a serious artist.

Bechuanaland former name until 1966 of ⫗Botswana.

Becker Boris 1967– . German tennis player. In 1985, at the age of 17, he became the youngest winner of a singles title at Wimbledon. He has won the title three times and helped West Germany to win the Davis Cup 1988 and 1989. He also won the US Open 1989.

Becket St Thomas à 1118–1170. English priest and politician. He was chancellor to ⫗Henry II 1155–62, when he was appointed archbishop of Canterbury. The interests of the church soon conflicted with those of the crown and Becket was assassinated; he was canonized 1172.

He resisted Henry's attempts to regulate relations between church and state, and was murdered by four knights before the altar of Canterbury cathedral.

Beckett Samuel 1906–1989. Irish novelist and dramatist who wrote in French and English. His *En attendant Godot/Waiting for Godot* 1952 is possibly the most universally known example of Theater of the ⫗Absurd, in which life is taken to be meaningless. This genre is taken to further extremes in *Fin de Partie/Endgame* 1957 and *Happy Days* 1961. Nobel Prize for Literature 1969.

Beckmann Max 1884–1950. German Expressionist painter who fled the Nazi regime for the US 1933. After World War I his art was devoted to themes of cruelty in human society, portraying sadists and their victims with a harsh style of realism.

Beckmann was born in Leipzig. He fought in World War I and was discharged following a breakdown, reflected in the agony of his work; pictures include *Carnival* and *The Titanic*. He later painted enormous triptychs, full of symbolic detail. He died in New York.

becquerel SI unit (symbol Bq) of ⫗radioactivity, equal to one radioactive disintegration (change in the nucleus of an atom when a particle or ray is given off) per second.

The becquerel is much smaller than the previous standard unit, the ⫗curie, and so can be used for measuring smaller quantities of radioactivity. It is named after Antoine Becquerel.

Becquerel Antoine Henri 1852–1908. French physicist who discovered penetrating radiation coming from uranium salts, the first indication of ⫗radioactivity, and shared a Nobel Prize with Marie and Pierre ⫗Curie 1903.

bed in geology, a single ⫗sedimentary rock unit with a distinct set of physical characteristics or contained fossils, readily distinguishable from those of beds above and below. Well-defined partings called *bedding planes* separate successive beds or strata.

The depth of a bed can vary from a fraction of a centimeter to several meters or feet, and can extend over any area. The term is also used to indicate the floor beneath a body of water (lake bed) and a layer formed by a fall of particles (lava bed).

bedbug flattened wingless red-brown insect *Cimex lectularius* with piercing mouthparts. It hides by day in crevices or bedclothes, and emerges at night to suck human blood.

Bede c. 673–735. English theologian and historian, known as *the Venerable Bede*, active in Durham and Northumbria. He wrote many scientific, theological, and historical works. His *Historia Ecclesiastica Gentis Anglorum/Ecclesiastical History of the English People* 731 is a seminal source for early English history.

Bedford administrative headquarters of Bedfordshire, England; population (1983) 89,200. Industries include agricultural machinery and airships. John Bunyan wrote *The Pilgrim's Progress* (1678) while imprisoned here.

Bedlam (abbreviation of *Bethlehem*) the earliest mental hospital in Europe. The hospital was opened in the 14th century in London and is now sited in Surrey. It is now used as a slang word meaning chaos.

Bedlington breed of ⫗terrier with a short body, long legs, and curly hair, usually gray, named after a district of Northumberland, England.

Bedouin (Arabic "desert-dweller") Arab of any of the nomadic peoples occupying the desert regions of Arabia and N Africa, now becoming increasingly settled. Their traditional trade was the rearing of horses and camels.

bee four-winged insect of the superfamily Apoidea in the order Hymenoptera, usually with a sting. There are over 12,000 species, of which fewer than 1 in 20 are social in habit. The **hive** or **honey bee** *Apis mellifera* establishes perennial colonies of about 80,000, the majority being infertile females (workers), with a few larger fertile males (drones), and a single very large fertile female (the queen). Worker bees live for no more than a few weeks, while a drone may live a few months, and a queen several years. Queen honey bees lay two kinds of eggs: fertilized, female eggs, which have two sets of chromosomes and develop into workers or queens, and unfertilized, male eggs, which have only one set of chromosomes and develop into drones.

Bees transmit information to each other about food sources by a "dance," each movement giving rise to sound impulses which are picked up by tiny hairs on the back of the bee's head, the orientation of the dance also having significance. They use the Sun in navigation (see also under ⟁migration). Besides their use in crop pollination and production of honey and wax, bees (by a measure of contaminants brought back to their hives) can provide an inexpensive and effective monitor of industrial and other pollution of the atmosphere and soil.

The most familiar species is the **bumblebee**, genus *Bombus*, which is larger and stronger than the hive bee and so is adapted to fertilize plants in which the pollen and nectar lie deep, as in red clover; they can work in colder weather than the hive bee.

Social bees, apart from the bumblebee and the hive bee, include the stingless South American **vulture bee** *Trigona hypogea*, discovered 1982, which is solely carnivorous.

Solitary bees include species useful in pollinating orchards in spring, and may make their nests in tunnels under the ground or in hollow plant stems; 'cuckoo' bees lay their eggs in the nests of bumblebees, which they closely resemble.

Most bees are pacific unless disturbed, but some species are aggressive. One bee sting may be fatal to a person who is allergic to them, but this is comparatively rare (about 1.5% of the population), and most adults can survive 300–500 stings without treatment. A vaccine treatment against bee stings, which uses concentrated venom, has been developed; see ⟁melitin.
The killer bees of South America are a hybrid type, created when an African subspecies of honey bee escaped from a research establishment in Brazil 1957. They mated with, and supplanted, the honey bees of European origin in most of South and Central America, and by 1990 had spread as far north as Texas. As well as being more productive and resistant to disease than European honey bees, they are also more active and aggressive, having killed hundreds of thousands of animals and probably more than 1,000 people.

Beebe Charles 1877–1962. US naturalist, explorer, and writer. He was curator of birds for the New York Zoological Society 1899–1952. He wrote the comprehensive *Monograph of the Pheasants* 1918–22. His interest in deep-sea exploration led to a collaboration with the engineer Otis Barton and the development of a spherical diving vessel, the bathysphere. On August 24, 1934, the two men made a record-breaking dive to 3028 ft/923 m. Beebe's expeditions are described in a series of memoirs.

beech genus of trees *Fagus*, of the family Fagaceae. Of the ten species in this genus only one is native to North America; others grow in Europe. The American beech *F. grandifolia* grows to 100 ft/30 m, with blue-gray bark; a broad, rounded crown; and leaves that are lanceolate, serrate, triangular, and edible.

Beecham Thomas 1879–1961. British conductor and impresario. He established the Royal Philharmonic Orchestra 1946 and fostered the works of composers such as Delius, Sibelius, and Richard Strauss.

Beecher Henry Ward 1813–1887. US Congregational minister and militant opponent of slavery, son of the pulpit orator Lyman ⟁Beecher and brother of the writer Harriet Beecher ⟁Stowe.
He traveled to Britain and did much to turn sentiment against the South.

Beecher Lyman 1775–1863. US Congregational and Presbyterian minister, one of the most popular pulpit orators of his time. He was the father of Harriet Beecher ⟁Stowe and Henry Ward Beecher.
As a pastor in Connecticut and Boston, he preached against Unitarianism and Roman Catholicism and contributed to the development of the New Haven theology of evangelical Calvinism.

bee-eater bird *Merops apiaster* found in Africa, S Europe, and Asia. It feeds on a variety of insects, including bees, which it catches in its long narrow bill. Chestnut, yellow, and blue-green, it is gregarious, and generally nests in river banks and sandpits.

Beelzebub (Hebrew "lord of the flies") in the New Testament, the leader of the devils, sometimes identified with Satan and sometimes with his chief assistant (see ⟁devil). In the Old Testament Beelzebub was a fertility god worshiped by the Philistines and other Semitic groups (Baal).

beer alcoholic drink made from water and malt (fermented barley or other grain), flavored with hops. Beer contains between 1% and 6% alcohol. One of the oldest alcoholic drinks, it was brewed in ancient China, Egypt, and Babylon.
The distinction between beer (containing hops) and ale (without hops) was made in medieval times. Beer is now a generic term including pilsner and lager. Stout is top fermented but is sweet and strongly flavored with roasted grain; lager (German "store") is a light beer, bottom fermented and matured over a longer period. Modern ales are made with hops like beer, but fermented more rapidly at relatively high temperatures. In the US light beers and lite beers are made with more water, fewer calories and less alcohol.

Beerbohm Max 1872–1956. British caricaturist and author, the half brother of actor and manager Herbert Beerbohm Tree. A perfectionist in style, he contributed to *The Yellow Book* 1894; wrote a novel of Oxford undergraduate life *Zuleika Dobson* 1911; and published volumes of caricature, including *Rossetti and His Circle* 1922. He succeeded George Bernard Shaw as critic to the *Saturday Review* 1898.

Beersheba industrial town in Israel; population (1987) 115,000. It is the chief center of the Negev desert and has been a settlement from the Stone Age.

beet plant of the genus *Beta* of the goosefoot family Chenapodiaceae. The common beet *B.*

vulgaris is used in one variety to produce sugar, and another, the mangelwurzel, is grown as cattle fodder. The beetroot, or red beet, *B. rubra* is a salad plant.

Beethoven Ludwig van 1770–1827. German composer and pianist whose mastery of musical expression in every genre made him the dominant influence on 19th-century music. Beethoven's repertoire includes concert overtures; the opera *Fidelio*; five piano concertos and two for violin (one unfinished); 32 piano sonatas, including the *Moonlight* and *Appassionata*; 17 string quartets; the *Mass in D* (*Missa solemnis*); and nine symphonies, as well as many youthful works. He usually played his own piano pieces and conducted his orchestral works until he was hampered by deafness 1801; nevertheless he continued to compose.
Born in Bonn, the son and grandson of musicians, Beethoven became deputy organist at the court of the Elector of Cologne at Bonn before he was 12; later he studied under ⟁Haydn and possibly ⟁Mozart, whose influence dominated his early work. From 1809, he received a small allowance from aristocratic patrons.

beetle common name of insects in the order Coleoptera (Greek "sheath-winged") with leathery forewings folding down in a protective sheath over the membranous hindwings, which are those used for flight. They pass through a complete metamorphosis. They include some of the largest and smallest of all insects: the largest is the **Hercules beetle** *Dynastes hercules* of the South American rainforests, 6 in/15 cm long; the smallest is only 0.02 in/0.05 cm long. Comprising more than 50% of the animal kingdom, beetles number some 370,000 named species, with many not yet described.
Beetles are found in almost every land and freshwater habitat, and feed on almost anything edible. Examples include: **click beetle** or **skipjack** species of the family Elateridae, so called because if they fall on their backs they right themselves with a jump and a loud click; the larvae, known as **wireworms**, feed on the roots of crops. In some tropical species of Elateridae the beetles have luminous organs between the head and abdomen and are known as **fireflies**. The potato pest **Colorado beetle** *Leptinotarsa decemlineata* is striped in black and yellow. The **blister beetle** *Lytta vesicatoria*, a shiny green species from S Europe, was once sold pulverized as an aphrodisiac and contains the toxin cantharidin. The larvae of the **furniture beetle** *Anobium punctatum* and the **death-watch beetle** *Xestobium rufovillosum* and their relatives are serious pests of structural timbers and furniture (see ⟁woodworm).

Begin Menachem 1913–1992. Israeli politician. He was leader of the extremist Irgun Zvai Leumi organization in Palestine from 1942, and prime minister of Israel 1977–83, as head of the right-wing Likud party. In 1978 Begin shared a Nobel Peace Prize with President Sadat of Egypt for work on the ⟁Camp David Agreements for a Middle East peace settlement.
Begin was born in Brest-Litovsk, Poland, studied law in Warsaw, and fled to the USSR 1939. As leader of the Irgun group, he was responsible in 1946 for a bomb attack at the King David Hotel, Jerusalem, which killed 91 people.

begonia any plant of the genus *Begonia* of the tropical and subtropical family Begoniaceae.

Begonias have fleshy and succulent leaves, and some have large, brilliant flowers. There are numerous species native to the tropics, in particular South America and India.

Behan Brendan 1923–1964. Irish dramatist. His early experience of prison and knowledge of the workings of the ◊IRA (recounted in his autobiography *Borstal Boy* 1958) provided him with two recurrent themes in his plays. *The Quare Fellow* 1954 was followed by the tragicomedy *The Hostage* 1958, first written in Gaelic.

behaviorism school of psychology originating in the US, of which the leading exponent was John B ◊Watson. Behaviorists maintain that all human activity can ultimately be explained in terms of conditioned reactions or reflexes and habits formed in consequence. Leading behaviorists include Ivan ◊Pavlov and B F ◊Skinner.

Skinner raised his daughter in a so-called "Skinner Box" so that he could and manipulate the stimuli to which she was exposed.

behavior therapy in psychology, the application of behavioral principles, derived from learning theories, to the treatment of clinical conditions such as ◊phobias, ◊obsessions, sexual and interpersonal problems. For example, in treating a phobia the person is taken into the feared situation in gradual steps. Over time, the fear typically reduces, and the problem becomes less acute.

behemoth (Hebrew "beasts") in the Old Testament (Job 40), an animal cited by God as evidence of his power; usually thought to refer to the hippopotamus. It is used proverbially to mean any giant and powerful creature.

Behn Aphra 1640–1689. English novelist and playwright, the first woman in England to earn her living as a writer. Her writings were criticized for their explicitness; they frequently present events from a woman's point of view. Her novel *Oronooko* 1688 is an attack on slavery.

Between 1670 and 1687 fifteen of her plays were produced, including *The Rover*, which attacked forced and mercenary marriages. She had the patronage of James I and was employed as a government spy in Holland 1666.

Behrens Peter 1868–1940. German architect. He pioneered the adaptation of architecture to industry, and designed the AEG turbine factory in Berlin 1909, a landmark in industrial design. He taught ◊Le Corbusier and Walter ◊Gropius.

Behring Emil von 1854–1917. German physician who discovered that the body produces antitoxins, substances able to counteract poisons released by bacteria. Using this knowledge, he developed new treatments for diseases such as ◊diphtheria.

Educated in Berlin, Behring was Robert ◊Koch's assistant before becoming professor of hygiene at Halle and Marburg. He won the first Nobel Prize for Medicine, in 1901.

Beiderbecke Bix (Leon Bismarck) 1903–1931. US jazz cornetist, composer, and pianist. A romantic soloist with King Oliver, Louis Armstrong, and Paul Whiteman's orchestra, Beiderbecke was the first acknowledged white jazz innovator. He was inspired by the Classical composers Debussy, Ravel, and Stravinsky.

His reputation grew after his early death with the publication of Dorothy Baker's novel *Young Man with a Horn* 1938.

Beijing or *Peking* capital of China; part of its NE border is formed by the Great Wall of China; population (1989) 6,800,000. The municipality of Beijing has an area of 6,871 sq mi/17,800 sq km and a population (1990) of 10,819,000. Industries include textiles, petrochemicals, steel, and engineering.

features Tiananmen Gate (Gate of Heavenly Peace) and Tiananmen Square, where, in 1989, Chinese troops massacred over 1,000 students and civilians demonstrating for greater freedom and democracy; the Forbidden City, built between 1406 and 1420 as Gu Gong (Imperial Palace) of the Ming Emperors, where there were 9,000 ladies-in-waiting and 10,000 eunuchs in service (it is now the seat of the government); the Great Hall of the People 1959 (used for official banquets); museums of Chinese history and of the Chinese revolution; Chairman Mao Memorial Hall 1977 (shared from 1983 with Zhou Enlai, Zhu De, and Liu Shaoqi); the Summer Palace built by the dowager empress Zi Xi (damaged by European powers 1900, but restored 1903); Temple of Heaven (Tiantan); and Ming tombs 30 mi/50 km to the NW.

history Beijing, founded 2,000 years ago, was the 13th-century capital of the Mongol emperor Kublai Khan. Later replaced by Nanking, it was again capital from 1421, except from 1928 to 1949, when it was renamed Peiping. Beijing was held by Japan 1937–45.

Beira port at the mouth of the River Pungwe, Mozambique; population (1986) 270,000. It exports minerals, cotton, and food products. A railroad through the *Beira Corridor* links the port with Zimbabwe.

Beirut or *Beyrouth* capital and port of ◊Lebanon, devastated by civil war in the 1970s and 1980s, when it was occupied by armies of neighboring countries; population (1988 est) 1,500,000. The city is divided into a Christian eastern and a Muslim western sector by the Green Line.

history Beirut dates back to at least 1400 BC. Until the civil war 1975–76, Beirut was an international financial and educational center, with four universities (Lebanese, Arab, French, and US); it was also a center of espionage. Subsequent struggles for power among Christian and Muslim factions caused widespread destruction.

The city was besieged and sections were virtually destroyed by the Israeli army July–Sept 1982 to enforce the withdrawal of the forces of the Palestinian Liberation Organization. After the cease-fire, 500 Palestinians were massacred in the Sabra–Shatila camps Sept 16–18, 1982, by ◊Phalangist and ◊Maronite troops. Civil disturbances continued, characterized by sporadic street fighting and hostage taking. In 1987 Syrian troops entered the city. Intensive fighting broke out between Christian and Syrian troops in Beirut, and by 1990 the strength of Syrian military force in greater Beirut and E Lebanon was estimated at 42,000. In Oct 1990 President Elias Hwari formally invited Syrian troops to remove the Maronite Christian leader General Michel Aoun from his E Beirut stronghold; the troops then went on to dismantle the "Green Line" separating Muslim W and Christian E Beirut. The Syrian-backed "Greater Beirut Security Plan" was subsequently implemented by the Lebanese government, enforcing the withdrawal of all militias from greater Beirut.

Bekka, the or *El Beqa'a* governorate of E

Lebanon separated from Syria by the Anti-Lebanon mountains. The Bekka Valley has been of strategic importance in the Syrian struggle for control of N Lebanon. In the early 1980s the valley was penetrated by Shia Muslims who established an extremist Hezbollah stronghold with the support of Iranian Revolutionary Guards. Zahlé and the ancient city of Baalbek are the chief towns.

Belarus or *Byelorussia* or *Belorussia* country in E central Europe, bounded S by Ukraine, E by Russia, W by Poland, and N by Latvia and Lithuania.

government There is a 360-seat legislature, the supreme soviet, to which deputies are elected by a majority system, and a second ballot runoff race in contests in which there is no clear first-round majority. Out of the constituencies, 310 are organized on a territorial basis, leaving 50 seats to be allocated to associations of the deaf, the blind, invalids, and war veterans. From the majority grouping within the supreme soviet, a prime minister (chair of the cabinet of ministers) is drawn. The state president is directly elected.

history A Byelorussian state developed in the Middle Ages around the town of Polotsk on the river Dvina. From the 13th century it became incorporated within the Slavonic Grand Duchy of Lithunia and from 1569 there was union with Poland.

brief independence Byelorussia was brought into the Russian Empire in the late 18th century and from the later 19th century there was an upsurge in national consciousness. Amid the chaos of the Bolshevik Revolution in Russia, an independent Byelorussian National Republic was declared in 1918, but failed to receive international recognition. Instead, a Byelorussian Soviet Republic was established in 1919, with some loss of territory to Poland.

nationalist revival National culture and language were encouraged until the Soviet dictator Stalin launched a Russification drive, with more than 100,000 people, predominantly writers and intellectuals, being executed between 1937 and 1941. Under the terms of the 1939 Nazi-Soviet pact, Byelorussia was reunified, but then suffered severely under German invasion and occupation 1941–44. Russification resumed in the 1960s and continued into the mid-1980s, when ◊glasnost brought a revival of national culture. A Popular Front, demanding greater autonomy, was established in Feb 1989. In the wake of the April 1986 ◊Chernobyl nuclear disaster, which forced the resettlement of several hundred thousand people, the Byelorussian Ecological Union (BEU) had been formed. Both the Popular Front and BEU contested the March-April 1990 Byelorussian supreme soviet elections under the Democratic Bloc banner, capturing more than a fourth of the seats. In response, Byelorussian was reestablished as the republic's official state language from Sept 1990.

independence achieved Byelorussia's communist president, Nikolai Dementei, expressed support for the Aug 1991 coup attempt against President Gorbachev in Moscow. When it failed, Dementei resigned and the republic's supreme soviet declared Byelorussia's independence on Aug 25, 1991, suspending the activities of the Communist Party. In Sept 1991 the supreme soviet voted to adopt the name of Republic of Belarus and elected Stanislav Shushkevich, an advocate of democratic reform, as its chair, which also made

Belarus
Republic of

area 80,100 sq mi/207,600 sq km
capital Mensk (Minsk)
cities Gomel, Vitebsk, Mogilev, Bobruisk, Grodno, Brest
physical more than 25% forested; rivers W Dvina, Dnieper and its tributaries, including the Pripet and Beresina; the Pripet Marshes in the E; mild and damp climate
environment large areas contaminated by fallout
features Belovezhskaya Pushcha (scenic forest reserve)
head of state Stanislav Shushkevich from 1991
head of government Vyacheslav Kebich from 1990
political system emergent democracy

products peat, agricultural machinery, fertilizers, glass, textiles, leather, salt, electrical goods, meat, dairy produce
currency ruble and dukat
population (1990) 10,200,000 (77% Byelorussian "Eastern Slavs," 13% Russian, 4% Polish, 1% Jewish)
languages Byelorussian, Russian
religions Roman Catholic, Russian Orthodox, with Baptist and Muslim minorities
chronology
1918–19 Briefly independent from Russia.
1937–41 More than 100,000 people were shot in mass executions ordered by Stalin.
1941–44 Occupied by Nazi Germany.
1945 Became a founding member of the United Nations.
1986 April: fallout from the Chernobyl nuclear reactor in Ukraine contaminated a large area.
1989 Byelorussian Popular Front established as well as a more extreme nationalist organization, the Tolaka group.
1990 Sept: Byelorussian established as state language and republican sovereignty declared.
1991 April: Mensk hit by nationalist-backed general strike, calling for disbandment of Communist Party (CP) workplace cells. Aug: declared independence from Soviet Union in wake of failed anti-Gorbachev coup; suspended CP. Sept: Shushkevich elected president. Dec: Commonwealth of Independent States (CIS) formed in Mensk; Belarus accorded diplomatic recognition by US.
1992 Jan: admitted into Conference on Security and Cooperation in Europe (CSCE). May: protocols signed with US agreeing to honor START treaty.

him state president. Shushkevich played an important role in the creation in Dec 1991 of a new ◊Commonwealth of Independent States (CIS), the confederal successor to USSR, with Mensk (Minsk) chosen as the CIS's early center. In the same month Belarus was formally acknowledged as independent by the US and granted diplomatic recognition. In Jan 1992 it was admitted into the ◊Conference on Security and Cooperation in Europe (CSCE). It has been a member of the United Nations since its foundation in 1945.

economy and armed forces Belarus was cautious in its implementation of market-centered economic reform, with privatization and price liberalization introduced very gradually. It remained heavily dependent upon Russia for industrial raw materials. Belarus inherited substantial nuclear arms from the USSR. The Shushkevich administration pledged to gradually remove these to become nuclear-free, but Belarus also planned to establish its own independent armed forces. In May 1992, Belarus and Russia (as a single signatory), along with the the Ukraine and Kazakhstan, signed protocols with the US agreeing to comply with START. It was also agreed to return all tactical nuclear weapons to Russia for destruction.

Belasco David 1859–1931. US playwright and producer. His works include *Madame Butterfly* 1900 and *The Girl of the Golden West* 1905, both of which Puccini used as libretti for operas.

Many of his plays were written in collaboration with others, including J A Herne. As a producer, Belasco was known more for his technical innovations than for the quality of the plays he chose. His name was a big draw for theater audiences, and he made stars out of many unknown performers.

Belaúnde Terry Fernando 1913– . President of Peru from 1963 to 1968 and from 1980 to 1985. He championed land reform and the construction of roads to open up the Amazon valley. He fled to the US 1968 after being deposed by a military junta. After his return, his second term in office was marked by rampant inflation, enormous foreign debts, terrorism, mass killings, and human-rights violations by the armed forces.

Belau, Republic of (formerly *Palau*) self-governing island group in Micronesia
area 193 sq mi/500 sq km
population (1988) 14,000
features 26 larger islands (eight inhabited) and about 300 islets
history Spain held the islands from about 1600, and sold them to Germany 1899. Japan seized them in World War I, administered them by League of Nations mandate, and used them as a naval base during World War II. They were captured by the US 1944, and became part of its Trust Territory three years later. Belau became internally self-governing 1980.

bel canto (Italian "beautiful song") in music, an 18th-century Italian style of singing with emphasis on perfect technique and beautiful tone. The style reached its peak in the operas of Rossini, Donizetti, and Bellini.

Belém port and naval base in N Brazil; population (1991) 1,235,600. The chief trade center of the Amazon Basin, it is also known as Pará, the name of the state of which it is capital. It was founded about 1615 as Santa Maria de Belém do Grãs Pará.

belemnite extinct relative of the squid, with rows of little hooks rather than suckers on the arms. The parts of belemnites most frequently found as fossils are the bullet-shaped shells that were within the body. Like squid, these animals had an ink sac which could be used to produce a smokescreen when attacked.

Belfast industrial port (shipbuilding, engineering, electronics, textiles, tobacco) and capital of Northern Ireland since 1920; population (1985) 300,000. Since 1968 it has been heavily damaged by civil disturbances.
history Belfast grew up around a castle built 1177 by John de Courcy. With the settlement of English and Scots, Belfast became a center of Irish Protestantism in the 17th century. An influx of Huguenots after 1685 extended the linen industry, and the 1800 Act of Union with England resulted in the promotion of Belfast as an industrial center. It was created a city 1888, with a lord mayor from 1892. The former parliament buildings are to the south at Stormont.

Belfort town in NE France; population (1983) 54,500. It is in the strategic **Belfort Gap** between the Vosges and Jura mountains and is the capital of the *département* of Territoire de Belfort. Industries include chemicals, engineering, plastics, and textiles.

Belgae people who lived in Gaul in Roman times, north of the Seine and Marne rivers. They were defeated by Caesar 57 BC. Many of the Belgae settled in SE England during the 2nd century BC.

Belgaum city in Karnataka, S India; population (1981) 300,000. The main industry is cotton manufacture. It is known for its Jain temples.

Belgian Congo former name (1908–60) of ◊Zaire.

Belgium country in W Europe, bounded N by the Netherlands, NW by the North Sea, S and W by France, E by Luxembourg and Germany.
government A parliamentary democracy under a constitutional monarch, with nine provinces, Belgium has a constitution that dates from 1831 and was most recently revised 1971. The prime minister and cabinet are drawn from and answerable to the legislature, which exercises considerable control over the executive. The legislature consists of a senate and a chamber of representatives. The senate has 182 members: 106 nationally elected, 50 representing the provinces, 25 coopted, and, by right, the heir to the throne. Senators are elected for four years. The chamber of representatives has 212 members elected by universal suffrage, through a system of proportional representation, for a four-year term. On the basis of parliamentary support, the monarch appoints the prime minister, who chooses the cabinet.
history The first recorded inhabitants were the Belgae, an ancient Celtic people. Conquered by the Romans, the area was known from 15 BC as the Roman province of Belgica; from the 3rd century AD onwards it was overrun by the Franks. Under ◊Charlemagne, Belgium became the center of the Carolingian dynasty, and the peace and order during this period fostered the growth of such towns as Ghent, Bruges, and Brussels. Following the division of Charlemagne's empire 843 the area became part of Lotharingia.
late Middle Ages By the 11th century seven feudal states had emerged: the counties of Flanders, Hainaut, and Namur, the duchies of

Belgium

Kingdom of (French *Royaume de Belgique*, Flemish *Koninkrijk België*)

area 11,784 sq mi/30,510 sq km
capital Brussels
cities Ghent, Liège, Charleroi, Bruges, Mons, Namur, Leuven; ports are Antwerp, Ostend, Zeebrugge
physical fertile coastal plain in NW, central rolling hills rise eastward, hills and forest in SE
environment a 1989 government report judged the drinking water in Flanders to be "seriously substandard" and more than half the rivers and canals in that region to be in a "very bad" condition
features Ardennes Forest; rivers Scheldt and Meuse
head of state King Baudouin from 1951
head of government Jean-Luc Dehaene from 1992
political system liberal democracy
political parties Flemish Christian Social Party (CVP), center-left; French Social Christian Party (PSC), center-left; Flemish Socialist Party (SP), left of center; French Socialist Party (PS), left of center; Flemish Liberal Party (PVV), moderate centrist; French Liberal Reform Party (PRL), moderate centrist; Flemish People's Party (VU), federalist; Flemish Green Party (Agalev); French Green Party (Ecolo)
exports iron, steel, textiles, manufactured goods, petrochemicals, plastics, vehicles, diamonds
currency Belgian franc
population (1990 est) 9,895,000 (comprising Flemings and Walloons); growth rate 0.1% p.a.
life expectancy men 72, women 78
languages in the N (Flanders) Flemish (a Dutch dialect, known as *Vlaams*) 55%; in the S (Wallonia) Walloon (a French dialect) 32%; bilingual 11%; German (E border) 0.6%; all are official
religion Roman Catholic 75%
literacy 98% (1984)
GDP $111 bn (1986); $9,230 per head
chronology
1830 Belgium became an independent kingdom.
1914 Invaded by Germany.
1940 Again invaded by Germany.
1948 Belgium became founding member of Benelux Customs Union.
1949 Belgium became founding member of Council of Europe and NATO.
1951 Leopold III abdicated in favor of his son Baudouin.
1952 Belgium became founding member of European Coal and Steel Community.
1957 Belgium became founding member of the European Economic Community.
1971 Steps toward regional autonomy taken.
1972 German-speaking members included in the cabinet for the first time.
1973 Linguistic parity achieved in government appointments.
1974 Leo Tindemans became prime minister. Separate regional councils and ministerial committees established.
1978 Wilfried Martens succeeded Tindemans as prime minister.
1980 Open violence over language divisions. Regional assemblies for Flanders and Wallonia and a three-member executive for Brussels created.
1981 Short-lived coalition led by Mark Eyskens was followed by the return of Martens.
1987 Martens head of caretaker government after breakup of coalition.
1988 Following a general election, Martens formed a new CVP–PS–SP–PSC–VU coalition.
1992 Martens-led coalition collapsed; Jean-Luc Dehaene formed a new CVP-led coalition. It was announced that a federal system would be introduced.

overrun by Germany, to whom Leopold III surrendered. His government escaped to London, and Belgium had a strong resistance movement. After Belgium's liberation by the Allies 1944–45, the king's surrender caused acute controversy, ended only by his abdication 1951 in favor of his son Baudouin. Since 1945 Belgium has been a major force for international cooperation in Europe, being a founding member of the ⊳Benelux Economic Union 1948, the Council of Europe, and the European Economic Community. Between 1983 and 1985 there was much debate about the siting of US cruise missiles in Belgium before a majority vote in parliament allowed their installation.

language divisions Belgium's main problems stem from the division between French-and Flemish-speaking members of the population, aggravated by the polarization between the predominantly conservative Flanders in the north, and the mainly socialist French-speaking Wallonia in the south. About 55% of the population speak Flemish, 44% French, and the remainder German. During 1971–73 attempts to close the linguistic and social divisions included the transfer of greater power to the regions, the inclusion of German-speaking members in the cabinet, and linguistic parity in the government. Separate regional councils and ministerial committees were established 1974. The language conflict developed into open violence 1980, and it was eventually agreed that Flanders and Wallonia should be administered by separate regional assemblies, with powers to spend up to 10% of the national budget on cultural facilities, health, roads, and urban projects. Brussels was to be governed by a three-member executive. Linguistic divisions again threatened the government 1983.

political instability Leo Tindemans (Flemish Christian Social Party (CVP)) resigned as prime minister 1978 and was succeeded by Wilfried ⊳Martens. By 1980 Martens had formed no fewer than four coalition governments. A new coalition 1981, led by Mark Eyskens (CVP), lasted less than a year, and Martens again returned to power. Economic difficulties 1981–82 resulted in a series of public-sector strikes, but Martens remained at the head of various coalitions until Jan 1992. With the government on the point of collapse, the king asked Jean-Luc Dehaene (CVP), a deputy prime minister, to form a new coalition government. The coalition, comprising the main center-left parties, was formed March 1992. In Sept 1992 it was announced that the government had agreed, in principle, to move to a federal system of government based on Dutch-speaking Flanders and French-speaking Wallonia. *See illustration box.*

Belgrade (Serbo-Croatian *Beograd*) capital of Yugoslavia and Serbia, and Danube river port linked with the port of Bar on the Adriatic; population (1981) 1,470,000. Industries include light engineering, food processing, textiles, pharmaceuticals, and electrical goods.

Belgrano Manuel 1770–1820. Argentine revolutionary. He was a member of the military group that led the 1810 revolt against Spain. Later, he commanded the revolutionary army until he was replaced by José de ⊳San Martín 1814.

Belisarius c. 505–565. Roman general under Emperor ⊳Justinian I. He won major victories over the Persians in 530 and the Vandals in 533 when he sacked Carthage. Later he invaded Sicily and fought a series of campaigns against the Goths in Italy.

Brabant, Limburg, and Luxembourg, and the bishopric of Liège, all nominally subject to the French kings or the German emperor, but in practice independent. From the 12th century the economy flourished; Bruges, Ghent, and Ypres became centers of the textile industry, while the artisans of Dinant and Liège exploited the copper and tin of the Meuse valley. During the 15th century the states came one by one under the rule of the dukes of Burgundy, and in 1477, by the marriage of Mary (heir of Charles the Bold, duke of Burgundy) to Maximilian (archduke of Austria), passed into the ⊳Habsburg dominions.

under Spanish rule Other dynastic marriages brought all the Low Countries under Spain, and in the 16th century the religious and secular tyranny of Philip II led to revolt in the Netherlands. The independence of the Netherlands as the Dutch Republic was recognized 1648; the south, reconquered by Spain, remained Spanish until the Treaty of ⊳Utrecht 1713 transferred it to Austria. The Austrian Netherlands were annexed 1719 by revolutionary France. The Congress of Vienna 1815 reunited the North and South Netherlands as one kingdom under William, King of Orange-Nassau; but historical differences, and the fact that the language of the wealthy and powerful in the south was (as it remains) French, made the union uneasy.

recognition as an independent kingdom An uprising 1830 of the largely French-speaking people in the south, and continuing disturbances, led to the Great Powers' recognition 1839 of the South Netherlands as the independent and permanently neutral kingdom of Belgium, with Leopold of Saxe-Coburg (widower of Charlotte, daughter of George IV of England) as king, and a parliamentary constitution.

foreign relations Although Prussia had been a party to the treaty 1839 recognizing Belgium's permanent neutrality, Germany invaded Belgium 1914 and occupied a large part of it until 1918. In 1940 Belgium was again

Belize
(formerly **British Honduras**)

area 8,864 sq mi/22,963 sq km
capital Belmopan
cities ports Belize City, Dangriga and Punta Gorda; Orange Walk, Corozal
physical tropical swampy coastal plain, Maya Mountains in S; over 90% forested
environment since 1981 Belize has developed an extensive system of national parks and reserves to protect large areas of tropical forest, coastal mangrove, and offshore islands. Forestry has been replaced by agriculture and ecotourism, which are now the most important sectors of the economy; world's first jaguar reserve created 1986 in the Cockscomb Mountains
features world's second longest barrier reef; Maya ruins
head of state Elizabeth II from 1981 represented by governor-general
head of government George Price from 1989
political system constitutional monarchy
political parties People's United Party

(PUP), left of center; United Democratic Party (UDP), moderate conservative
exports sugar, citrus fruits, rice, fish products, bananas
currency Belize dollar
population (1990 est) 180,400 (including Mayan minority in the interior); growth rate 2.5% p.a.
life expectancy (1988) 60 years
languages English (official); Spanish (widely spoken), native Creole dialects
media no daily newspaper; several independent weekly tabloids
religions Roman Catholic 60%, Protestant 35%
literacy 93% (1988)
GDP $247 million (1988); $1,220 per head
chronology
1862 Belize became a British colony.
1954 Constitution adopted, providing for limited internal self-government. General election won by George Price.
1964 Self-government achieved from the UK (universal adult suffrage introduced).
1965 Two-chamber national assembly introduced, with Price as prime minister.
1970 Capital moved from Belize City to Belmopan.
1973 British Honduras became Belize.
1975 British troops sent to defend the disputed frontier with Guatemala.
1977 Negotiations undertaken with Guatemala but no agreement reached.
1980 United Nations called for full independence.
1981 Full independence achieved. Price became prime minister.
1984 Price defeated in general election. Manuel Esquivel formed the government. The UK reaffirmed its undertaking to defend the frontier.
1989 Price and the PUP won the general election.
1991 Diplomatic relations with Guatemala established.

Belize City chief port of Belize, and capital until 1970; population (1991) 46,000. After the city was destroyed by a hurricane 1961 it was decided to move the capital inland, to Belmopan.

Bell Alexander Graham 1847–1922. Scottish-born US scientist and inventor of the telephone. He patented his invention 1876, and later experimented with a type of phonograph and, in aeronautics, invented the tricycle undercarriage.

Born in Edinburgh, Bell was educated at the universities of Edinburgh and London and studied under his father, who developed a method for teaching the deaf to speak. In 1870 the family moved to Canada and Bell came to the US, where he opened a school 1872 for teachers of the deaf in Boston. In 1873 he began teaching vocal physiology at Boston University. He became a US citizen 1882. Bell also worked on converting seawater to drinking water and on air conditioning and sheep breeding.

belladonna or **deadly nightshade** poisonous plant *Atropa belladonna*, found in Europe and Asia. The dried powdered leaves contain ⟡alkaloids. Belladonna extract acts medicinally as an ⟡anticholinergic (blocking the passage of certain nerve impulses), and is highly toxic in large doses.

Belladonna is of the nightshade family, *Solanaceae*. It grows to 5 ft/1.5 m, with dull green leaves to 8 in/20 cm and solitary greenish flowers that produce deadly black berries. The alkaloids contained are hyoscyamine, atropine, hyoscine, and belladonnine.

Bellamy Edward 1850–1898. US author and social critic. In 1888, deeply concerned with the social problems of the day, he published *Looking Backward: 2000–1887*, a utopian novel. A huge bestseller, it inspired wide public support for Bellamy's political program of state socialism. Bellamy later founded the *New Nation* newspaper and published a second utopian novel, *Equality* 1897.

Born in Chicopee Falls, Massachusetts, Bellamy wrote for the New York *Post* and the Springfield *Union*. In 1880 he founded the Springfield *Daily News* but soon afterward abandoned journalism to become a full-time author.

Bellarmine Roberto Francesco Romolo 1542–1621. Italian Roman Catholic theologian and cardinal. He taught at the Jesuit College in Rome, and became archbishop of Capua 1602. His *Disputationes de controversersiis fidei christianae* 1581–93 was a major defense of Catholicism in the 16th century. He was canonized 1930.

Bellerophon in Greek mythology, a victim of slander who was sent against the monstrous ⟡chimera, which he killed with the help of his winged horse Pegasus. After further trials, he ended his life as a beggar. His story was dramatized by ⟡Euripides.

Belleville city in SW Illinois, SE of East St Louis; seat of St Clair county. Industries include coal, beer, furnaces and boilers, and clothing; population (1990) 42,800.

bellflower general name for many plants of the family Campanulaceae, especially those of the genus *Campanula*. The white, pink, or blue flowers are bell-shaped and showy. The varied leaf bluebell *C. rotundifolia* grows in northern North America and Europe.

Bellingham city and port in NW Washington

As a young man he was a member of Justinian's bodyguard before becoming commander of the eastern army. Although not always favored by the Emperor, it was largely his military skill which preserved the Byzantine Empire from being overthrown.

Belitung alternate name for the Indonesian island of ⟡Billiton.

Belize country in Central America, bounded N by Mexico, W and S by Guatemala, and E by the Caribbean Sea.

government The 1981 constitution provides for a parliamentary government on the British model, with a prime minister and cabinet drawn from the legislature and accountable to it. The national assembly consists of a senate and a house of representatives. The senate has eight members appointed by the governor-general for a five-year term, five on the advice of the prime minister, two on the advice of the leader of the opposition, and one after wider consultations. The house of representatives has 28 members elected by universal suffrage. The governor-general appoints both the prime minister and the leader of the opposition.

history Once part of the ⟡Maya civilization, and colonized in the 17th century, British Honduras (as it was called until 1973) became a recognized British colony 1862. A 1954 constitution provided for internal self-government, with the UK responsible for defense, external affairs, and internal security.

The first general election under the new constitution, and all subsequent elections until 1984, were won by the People's United Party (PUP), led by George Price. Full internal self-government was achieved 1964, and Price became prime minister. The capital was moved 1970 from Belize City to the new town of Belmopan. British troops were sent 1975 to defend the long-disputed frontier with Guatemala. Negotiations begun 1977 were inconclusive.

full independence achieved The United Nations called 1980 for full independence for Belize. A constitutional conference broke up 1981 over Guatemala's demand for territory rather than just access to the Caribbean. Full independence was achieved 1981 with George Price as the first prime minister. The UK agreed to protect the frontier and to assist in the training of Belizean forces. The PUP's uninterrupted 30-year rule ended 1984 when the United Democratic Party (UDP) leader, Manuel Esquivel, became prime minister. The UK reaffirmed its undertaking to protect Belize's disputed frontier. Still led by George Price, the PUP unexpectedly won the Sept 1989 general election by a margin of 15 to 13 seats in the house of representatives.

agreement with Guatemala Diplomatic relations were established with Guatemala Sept 1991 after the latter announced its recognition of Belize's independence and withdrew threats of invasion. *See illustration box.*

just S of the Canadian border, on Bellingham Bay in the Strait of Georgia. A port of entry for the logging and paper industry; shipbuilding and food processing are also carried on; population (1990) 52,180.

Bellingshausen Fabian Gottlieb von 1779–1852. Russian Antarctic explorer, the first to sight and circumnavigate the Antarctic continent 1819–21, although he did not realize what it was.

Bellingshausen Sea section of the S Pacific off the Antarctic coast. It is named after Russian explorer Fabian Gottlieb von Bellingshausen.

Bellini family of Italian Renaissance painters. Jacopo and his sons Gentile and Giovanni were founders of the Venetian school in the fifteenth and early sixteenth centuries.

Jacopo (c. 1400–1470) has left little surviving work, but two of his sketchbooks (now in the British Museum and the Louvre) contain his ideas and designs.

Gentile (c. 1429–1507) assisted in the decoration of the Doge's Palace 1474 and worked in the court of Mohammed II at Constantinople (a portrait of the sultan is in the National Gallery, London). His also painted processional groups (Accademia, Venice).

Giovanni (c.1430–1516), Gentile's younger brother, studied under his father, and painted portraits and various religious subjects. Giovanni Bellini's early works show the influence of his brother-in-law, Mantegna. His style developed from the static manner of mid-15th century Venetian work toward a High Renaissance harmony and grandeur, as in the altarpiece 1505 in Sta Zaccaria, Venice. He introduced softness in tone, harmony in composition, and a use of luminous color that influenced the next generation of painters (including his pupils Giorgione and Titian). He worked in oil rather than tempera, a technique adopted from Antonello da Messina.

Bellini Vincenzo 1801–1835. Italian opera composer whose lyrical, melodic treatments of classic themes include *La Sonnambula* 1831, *Norma* 1831, and *I Puritani* 1835.

Born in Catania, Sicily, Bellini was still a student at the Naples Conservatory when his first opera *Adelson et Salvina* 1825 was performed to great success. Subsequently he was guided by the tenor Giovanni Battista Rubini (1794–1854) to develop a new simplicity of melodic expression which proved irresistible to soloists and concert audiences. His genius for elegaic lyricism found ideal expression in Romantic evocations of classic themes, as in *La Sonnambula*, a great success in Britain, and *Norma*. In *I Puritani*, his last work, he discovered a new boldness and vigor of orchestral effect.

Belloc (Joseph) Hilaire Pierre 1870–1953. English author, remembered primarily for his nonsense verse for children *The Bad Child's Book of Beasts* 1896 and *Cautionary Tales* 1907. Belloc also wrote travel and religious books (he was a devout Catholic). With G K ⬦Chesterton, he advocated a return to the late medieval ⬦guild system of commercial association in place of capitalism or socialism.

Bellona Roman goddess of war, wife or sister of ⬦Mars, with a temple in the Campus Martius, near the altar of Mars.

Bellow Saul 1915– . Canadian-born US novelist. Novels such as *Herzog* 1964, *Humboldt's Gift* 1975, and *The Dean's December* 1982 show his method of inhabiting the consciousness of a central character, frequently a Jewish-American intellectual, to portray an individual's frustration with the ongoing events of an indifferent society. His finely styled works and skilled characterizations won him the Nobel Prize for Literature 1976.

Bellow's sensitivity to mythic dimensions is evident in such novels as *Henderson the Rain King* 1959. His other works include *The Adventures of Augie March* 1953, *Him With His Foot in His Mouth* 1984, and *More Die of Heartbreak* 1987.

Bellow moved 1924 to the US with this family and graduated from Northwestern University 1937. He taught at various colleges, including Princeton, Bard, and the University of Chicago. He won the National Book Award 1954, 1965, and 1971 and a Pulitzer prize 1976.

Bellows George Wesley 1882–1925. US painter. Born in Columbus, Ohio, he painted in the realism of the Ashcan school. Taught by Robert ⬦Henri, he became the youngest academician of his time. Known for his vigorous style, his paintings portray the drama of street life and sport. His most famous works, such as *Stag at Sharkey's* 1909, show the violence and excitement of illegal boxing matches. He was involved in the progressive artists movement and the creation of the Armory Show 1913.

bells nautical term applied to half-hours of watch. A day is divided into seven watches, five of four hours each and two, called dogwatches, of two hours. Each half-hour of each watch is indicated by the striking of a bell, eight bells signaling the end of the watch.

Bell's theorem hypothesis of British physicist John Bell, that an unknown force, of which space, time, and motion are all aspects, continues to link separate parts of the universe that were once united, and that this force travels faster than the speed of light.

Belmondo Jean-Paul 1933– . French film actor who became a star in Jean-Luc Godard's *A bout de souffle/Breathless* 1959. He is best known for his racy personality in French vehicles, many of which he produced. His other films include *Cartouche* 1962, *That Man from Rio* 1964, *The Brain* 1968, *Borsalino* 1970 and *Stavisky* 1974.

Belmont August 1816–1890. German-born US financier. Belmont was employed by the Rothschild banking house and traveled widely throughout Europe. In 1837 he came to New York and established a private bank, becoming the Rothschilds' exclusive representative in the US. Belmont became a naturalized American citizen 1844, was a leading member of New York City society's "400," and was instrumental in financing the costs of the Mexican War.

An active Democrat, he supported the presidential candidacy of Stephen Douglas 1860 but remained a strong unionist after Lincoln's election. He served as the Democratic National Chairman 1872.

Belmopan capital of ⬦Belize from 1970; population (1991) 4,000. It replaced Belize City as administrative center of the country.

Belo Horizonte industrial city (steel, engineering, textiles) in SE Brazil, capital of the fast-developing state of Minas Gerais; population (1991) 2,103,300. Built in the 1890s, it was Brazil's first modern planned city.

Beloit city in SE Wisconsin, on the Rock River, SE of Madison. Industries include electrical machinery, shoes, generators, and diesel engines; population (1990) 35,600.

Belorussia or *Byelorussia* former name 1919–91 of the Republic of ⬦Belarus.

Belsen site of a Nazi ⬦concentration camp in Lower Saxony, Germany.

Belshazzar in the Old Testament, the last king of Babylon, son of Nebuchadnezzar. During a feast (known as *Belshazzar's Feast*) he saw a message, interpreted by Daniel as prophesying the fall of Babylon and death of Belshazzar.

All of this is said to have happened on the same night that the city was invaded by the Medes and Persians (539 BC).

Bemba member of a people native to NE Zambia and neighboring areas of Zaire and Zimbabwe, although many reside in urban areas such as Lusaka and Copperbelt. They number about three million. The Bemba language belongs to the Bantu branch of the Niger–Congo family.

Ben Ali Zine el Abidine 1936– . Tunisian politician, president from 1987. After training in France and the US, he returned to Tunisia and became director-general of national security. He was made minister of the interior and then prime minister under the aging president for life, Habib ⬦Bourguiba, whom he deposed 1987 by a bloodless coup with the aid of ministerial colleagues. He ended the personality cult established by Bourguiba and moved toward a pluralist political system.

Benares alternative transliteration of ⬦Varanasi, holy city in India.

Ben Barka Mehdi 1920–1965. Moroccan politician. He became president of the National Consultative Assembly 1956 on the country's independence from France. He was assassinated by Moroccan agents with the aid of the French secret service.

His assassination followed his alleged involvement in an attempt on King Hassan's life and for supporting Algeria in Algerian-Moroccan border disputes.

Ben Bella Ahmed 1916– . Algerian politician. He was leader of the National Liberation Front (FLN) from 1952, the first prime minister of independent Algeria 1962–63, and its first president 1963–65. In 1965 Ben Bella was overthrown by Col Houari ⬦Boumédienne and detained until 1979. In 1985 he founded a new party, Mouvement pour la Démocratie en Algérie, and returned to Algeria 1990 after nine years in exile.

Benchley Robert 1889–1945. US humorist, actor, and drama critic whose books include *Of All Things* 1921 and *Benchley Beside Himself* 1943. His film skit *How to Sleep* illustrates his ability to extract humor from everyday life.

Born in Massachusetts, he was associated with the writer Dorothy Parker, *The New Yorker* magazine, and the circle of wits at the Algonquin Round Table in New York. He was a master of gentle satire, left New York City for Hollywood, and wrote and appeared in several 1930s and 1940s films.

Benda Julien 1867–1956. French writer and philosopher. He was an outspoken opponent of the philosophy of ⬦Bergson, and in 1927 published a manifesto on the necessity of devotion to the absolute truth, which he felt his contemporaries had betrayed, *La Trahison des clercs/The Treason of the Intellectuals*.

bends popular name for a paralytic affliction of deep-sea divers, arising from too rapid a release of nitrogen from solution in their blood. If a diver surfaces too quickly, nitrogen that had dissolved in the blood under increasing water pressure is suddenly released, forming bubbles in the bloodstream and causing paralysis. Immediate treatment is compression and slow decompression in a special chamber.

Benedict 15 popes, including:

Benedict XV 1854–1922. Pope from 1914. During World War I he endeavored to bring about a peace settlement, and it was during his papacy that British, French, and Dutch official relations were renewed with the Vatican.

Benedictine order religious order of monks and nuns in the Roman Catholic church, founded by St ⟡Benedict at Subiaco, Italy, in the 6th century. It had a strong influence on medieval learning and reached the height of its prosperity early in the 14th century.

There are Benedictine monasteries in the US in Latrobe, Pennsylvania, and St Meinrad, Indiana. In 1985 there were 9,453 monks and 7,911 nuns living in convents.

Benedict, St c. 480–c. 547. Founder of Christian monasticism in the West and of the ⟡Benedictine order. He founded the monastery of Monte Cassino, Italy. Here he wrote out his rule for monastic life, and was visited shortly before his death by the Ostrogothic king Totila, whom he converted to the Christian faith. His feast day is July 11.

benefice in the early Middle Ages, a donation of land or money to the Christian church as an act of devotion; from the 12th century, the term came to mean the income enjoyed by clergy.

Under the ⟡Carolingian dynasty, "benefice" was used to mean a gift of land from a lord to a ⟡vassal, in which sense it is often indistinguishable from a ⟡fief.

Benelux (abbreviation for *Belgium, the Netherlands, and Luxembourg*) customs union agreed by Belgium, the Netherlands, and Luxembourg 1948, fully effective 1960. It was the precursor of the European Community.

Beneš Eduard 1884–1948. Czechoslovak politician. He worked with Tomáš ⟡Masaryk toward Czechoslovak nationalism from 1918 and was foreign minister and representative at the League of Nations. He was president of the republic from 1935 until forced to resign by the Germans; he headed a government in exile in London during World War II. He returned home as president 1945 but resigned again after the Communist coup 1948.

Benét Stephen Vincent 1898–1943. US poet, novelist, and short-story writer who won a Pulitzer prize 1929 for his narrative poem of the Civil War, *John Brown's Body* 1928. One of his short stories, "The Devil and Daniel Webster," became a classic and was made into a play, an opera, and a film (*All That Money Can Buy*). He published more than 17 volumes of verse and prose.

Bengal former province of British India, divided 1947 into ⟡West Bengal, a state of India, and East Bengal, from 1972 ⟡Bangladesh. A famine in 1943, caused by a slump in demand for jute and a bad harvest, resulted in over 3 million deaths.

Bengal, Bay of part of the Indian Ocean lying between the east coast of India and the west coast of Myanmar (Burma) and the Malay Peninsula. The Irrawaddy, Ganges, and Brahmaputra rivers flow into the bay. The principal islands are to be found in the Andaman and Nicobar groups.

Bengali person of Bengali culture from Bangladesh and India (W Bengal, Tripura). There are 80–150 million speakers of Bengali, an Indo-Iranian language belonging to the Indo-European family. It is the official language of Bangladesh and of the state of Bengal, and is also used by emigrant Bangladeshi and Bengali communities in such countries as the US and the UK. Bengalis in Bangladesh are predominantly Muslim, whereas those in India are mainly Hindu.

Between the 8th and 12th centuries the Bengalis were ruled by the Buddhist Pála dynasty. From the 13th century they were governed by semiindependent Muslim princes until their incorporation into the Mogul Empire. In the 18th century Bengal was annexed by the British and on independence the region was partitioned by the successor states of India and E Pakistan (now Bangladesh).

Benghazi or *Banghazi* historic city and industrial port in N Libya on the Gulf of Sirte; population (1982) 650,000. It was controlled by Turkey between the 16th century and 1911, and by Italy 1911–42; a major naval supply base during World War II.

Colonized by the Greeks in the 7th century BC (*Euhesperides*), Benghazi was taken by Rome in the 1st century BC (*Berenice*) and by the Vandals in the 5th century AD. It became Arab in the 7th century. With Tripoli, it was co-capital of Libya 1951–72.

Benguela port in Angola, SW Africa; population (1970) 41,000. It was founded 1617. Its railroad runs inland to the copper mines of Zaire and Zambia.

Benguela current cold ocean current in the S Atlantic Ocean, moving northward along the west coast of Southern Africa and merging with the south equatorial current at a latitude of 15° S. Its rich plankton supports large, commercially exploited fish populations.

Ben-Gurion David. Adopted name of David Gruen 1886–1973. Israeli statesman and socialist politician, one of the founders of the state of Israel, the country's first prime minister 1948–53, and again 1955–63.

He was born in Poland, and went to Palestine 1906 to farm. He was a leader of the Zionist movement, and as defense minister he presided over the development of Israel's armed forces into one of the strongest armies in the Middle East.

Benin country in W Africa, bounded E by Nigeria, N by Niger and Burkina Faso, W by Togo, and S by the Gulf of Guinea.

government The constitution is based on the Fundamental Law (*Loi fondamentale*) of 1977, which established a national revolutionary assembly with 196 members (representing socioprofessional classes rather than geographical constituencies) elected for a five-year term by universal suffrage. The assembly elects the president (head of state) also to serve a five-year term.

history In the 12th–13th centuries the country was settled by the Aja, whose kingdom reached its peak in the 16th century. In the 17th–19th centuries the succeeding Dahomey kingdom (which gave the country its name until 1975) captured and sold its neighbors as slaves to Europeans.

French colonial rule Under French influence from the 1850s, Dahomey formed part of French West Africa from 1899, and became a self-governing dominion within the French Community 1958.

independence Dahomey became fully independent 1960. The country went through a period of political instability 1960–72, with swings from civilian to military rule and disputes between regions.

people's republic The deputy chief of the army, Mathieu Kerekou, established 1972 a military regime pledged to give fair representation to each region. His initial instrument of government was the National Council of the Revolution (CNR). Kerekou announced 1974 that as the People's Republic of Benin the country would follow "scientific socialism," based on Marxist-Leninist principles. From 1975 to 1989 Benin was a one-party state, under the Party of the People's Revolution of Benin. CNR was dissolved 1977 and a "national revolutionary assembly" established, which elected Kerekou 1980 as president and head of state. He was reelected 1984 and, after initial economic and social difficulties, his government grew more stable.

foreign relations Relations with France (Benin's biggest trading partner) improved in the 1980s. President Mitterrand became the first French head of state to visit Benin 1983.

pluralism President Kerekou was reelected Aug 1989 by the assembly for another five-year term. It was announced Dec 1989 that Marxist-Leninism was no longer the official ideology of Benin and that further constitutional reforms—allowing for more private enterprise—would be agreed upon. A preliminary referendum Dec 1990 showed overwhelming support for a multiparty political system, and multiparty elections were held Feb 1991. Kerekou was defeated and Nicéphore Soglo became president. *See illustration box.*

Benin former African kingdom 1200–1897, now part of Nigeria. It reached the height of its power in the 14th–17th centuries when it ruled the area between the Niger Delta and Lagos.

Benin traded in spices, ivory, palm oil, and slaves until its decline and eventual incorporation into Nigeria. The oba (ruler) of Benin continues to rule his people as a divine monarch. The present oba is considered an enlightened leader and one who is helping his people to become part of modern Nigeria.

Artworks honoring the Oba of Benin were looted by a British military expedition 1897. They included cast bronzes and carved ivories and have since found their way into museums and into the hands of collectors worldwide. See ⟡African art.

Benioff zone a seismically active zone dipping beneath a continent or continental margin behind a deep-sea trench. The zone is named after Hugo Benioff, a US seismologist who first described this feature. The zone is equivalent to what is called a subduction zone in plate tectonic theory, where one plate descends beneath another.

Benjamin Judah Philip 1811–1884. US Confederate official. Born in St Thomas, Virgin Islands, Benjamin was raised in South Carolina and was educated at Yale. After entering the legal profession in New Orleans, he served in the state legislature and was elected to the US Senate 1852. As a strong proponent of Southern secession, he resigned from the Senate 1861. Benjamin became one of the leaders of the Confederacy, serving as attorney general, secretary of war, and secretary of state. At the end of the war, he escaped to England, where he spent the rest of his life practicing law.

Bennett (Enoch) Arnold 1867–1931. English novelist. He became a London journalist 1893

Benin
People's Republic of (*République Populaire du Bénin*)

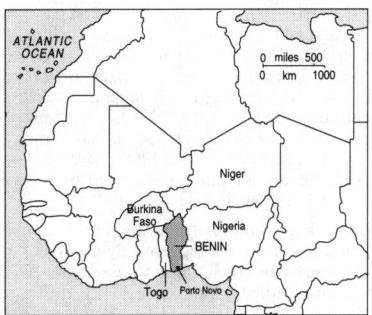

area 43,472 sq mi/112,622 sq km
capital Porto Novo (official), Cotonou (de facto)
cities Abomey, Natitingou, Parakou; chief port Cotonou
physical flat to undulating terrain; hot and humid in S; semiarid in N
features coastal lagoons with fishing villages on stilts; Niger River in NE
head of state and government Nicéphore Soglo from 1991
political system socialist pluralist republic
political parties Party of the People's Revolution of Benin (PRPB); other parties from 1990
exports cocoa, peanuts, cotton, palm oil, petroleum, cement, sea products

currency CFA franc
population (1990 est) 4,840,000; growth rate 3% p.a.
life expectancy men 42, women 46
languages French (official); Fon 47% and Yoruba 9% in south; six major tribal languages in north
religions animist 65%, Christian 17%, Muslim 13%
literacy men 37%, women 16% (1985 est)
GDP $1.6 bn (1987); $365 per head
chronology
1851 Under French control.
1958 Became self-governing dominion within the French Community.
1960 Independence achieved from France.
1960–72 Acute political instability, with switches from civilian to military rule.
1972 Military regime established by General Mathieu Kerekou.
1974 Kerekou announced that the country would follow a path of "scientific socialism."
1975 Name of country changed from Dahomey to Benin.
1977 Return to civilian rule under a new constitution.
1980 Kerekou formally elected president by the national revolutionary assembly.
1989 Marxist-Leninism dropped as official ideology. Strikes and protests against Kerekou's rule mounted; demonstrations banned and army deployed against protesters.
1990 Referendum support for multiparty politics.
1991 Multiparty elections held. Kerekou defeated in presidential elections by Nicéphore Soglo.

and editor of *Woman* 1896. His many novels include *Anna of the Five Towns* 1904, *The Old Wives' Tale* 1908, and the trilogy *Clayhanger, Hilda Lessways,* and *These Twain* 1910–16.

Ben Nevis highest mountain in the British Isles (4,406 ft/1,343 m), in the Grampians, Scotland.

Benny Jack. Adopted name of Benjamin Kubelsky 1894–1974. US comedian notable for his perfect timing and lugubrious manner. Over the years, Benny appeared on the stage, in films, and on radio and television. His radio program, from 1932, made him a national institution. Featuring his wife Mary Livingston, singer Dennis Day, announcer Don Wilson, and valet Eddie "Rochester" Anderson, it was produced for television in the 1950s. His film appearances, mostly in the 1930s and 1940s, included a starring role in *To Be or Not to Be* 1942. He also played in *Charley's Aunt* 1941, *It's In the Bag* 1945, and *A Guide for the Married Man* 1967.

Born in Chicago, he began a musical career in local theater orchestras (playing the violin) and joined a vaudeville troupe. During the 1920s, he turned to comedy, taking the adopted name "Jack Benny" and developing his familiar miserly, yet harmless character.

bent or **bent grass** any grasses of the genus *Agrostris.* Creeping bent grass *A. stolonifera,* also known as fiorin, is common in N North America and Eurasia, including lowland Britain. It spreads by ◊stolons and bears large attractive panicles of yellow or purple flowers on thin stalks. It is often used on lawns and golf courses.

Bentham Jeremy 1748–1832. English philosopher, legal and social reformer, and founder of ◊utilitarianism. The essence of his moral philosophy is found in the pronouncement of his *Principles of Morals and Legislation* (written 1780, published 1789): that the object of all legislation should be "the greatest happiness for the greatest number."

Bentham declared that the "utility" of any law is to be measured by the extent to which it promotes the pleasure, good, and happiness of the people concerned. In 1776 he published *Fragments on Government.* He made suggestions for the reform of the poor law 1798, which formed the basis of the reforms enacted 1834, and in his *Catechism of Parliamentary Reform* 1817 he proposed annual elections, the secret ballot, and universal male suffrage. He was also a pioneer of prison reform.

In economics he was an apostle of *laissez-faire,* and in his *Defence of Usury* 1787 and *Manual of Political Economy* 1798 he contended that his principle of "utility" was best served by allowing every man (sic) to pursue his own interests unhindered by restrictive legislation. He was made a citizen of the French Republic 1792.

Benton Thomas Hart 1782–1858. US political leader. Moving to St Louis 1815, he opened a law practice and published the *Missouri Enquirer* 1818–20. Elected to the US Senate 1820, Benton served in that body for the next 30 years, distinguishing himself as an outspoken opponent of the Bank of the United States and the extension of slavery and as a strong supporter of westward expansion.

Born in Hillsboro (now Hillsborough), North Carolina, Benton moved to Tennessee and was admitted to the bar 1806. During the War of 1812, he served as Gen Andrew Jackson's aide-de-camp, eventually rising to the rank of colonel.

Benton Harbor city in SW Michigan, NE of Chicago, Illinois, which is across Lake Michigan. Industries include iron and other metal products and food processing; population (1990) 12,820. The religious sect, House of David, was established here 1903.

bentonite type of clay, consisting mainly of montmorillonite and resembling ◊fuller's earth, which swells when wet. It is used in papermaking, molding sands, drilling muds for oil wells, and as a decolorant in food processing.

bentwood type of furniture, originally made by steam-heating and then bending rods of wood to form panels. Initially a country style, it was patented in the early 19th century in the US. 20th-century designers such as Marcel ◊Breuer and Alvar ◊Aalto have developed a different form by bending sheets of plywood.

Benue river in Nigeria, largest tributary of the Niger; it is navigable for most of its length of 870 mi/1,400 km.

Benz Karl Friedrich 1844–1929. German automobile engineer who produced the world's first gasoline-driven motor vehicle. He built his first model engine 1878 and the gasoline-driven car 1885.

Benzedrine trade name for ◊amphetamine, a stimulant drug.

benzene C_6H_6 clear liquid hydrocarbon of characteristic odor, occurring in coal tar. It is used as a solvent and in the synthesis of many chemicals.

The benzene molecule consists of a ring of six carbon atoms, all of which are in a single plane, and it is one of the simplest ◊cyclic compounds. Benzene is the simplest of a class of compounds collectively known as **aromatic compounds**. Some are considered carcinogenic (cancer-inducing).

benzodiazepine any of a group of mood-altering drugs (tranquilizers), for example Librium and Valium. They are addictive and interfere with the process by which information is transmitted between brain cells, and various side effects arise from continued use. They were originally developed as a muscle relaxant, and then excessively prescribed in the West as anxiety-relaxing drugs.

Temazepam, a short-acting benzodiazepine, is used for treating insomnia because it has few "hangover" effects.

benzoic acid C_6H_5COOH white crystalline solid, sparingly soluble in water, that is used as a preservative for certain foods and as an antiseptic. It is obtained chemically by the direct oxidation of benzaldehyde and occurs in certain natural resins, some essential oils, and as hippuric acid.

benzoin resin obtained by making incisions in the bark of *Styrax benzoin,* a tree native to the East Indies. Benzoin is used in the preparation of cosmetics, perfumes, and incense.

The name is also used for several bushes of the genus *Lindera* of the laurel family, growing in E North America, especially the common spicebush *L. benzoin.*

Ben Zvi Izhak 1884–1963. Israeli politician, president 1952–63. He was born in Poltava, Russia, and became active in the Zionist movement in Ukraine. In 1907 he went to Palestine but was deported 1915 with ◊Ben-Gurion. They served in the Jewish Legion under Field Marshal Allenby, who commanded the British forces in the Middle East.

Beograd Serbo-Croatian form of ⊅Belgrade, capital of Yugoslavia.

Beowulf Anglo-Saxon poem (composed *c.*700), the only complete surviving example of Germanic folk epic. It exists in a single manuscript copied about 1000 in the Cottonian collection of the British Museum.

Berber member of a non-Semitic Caucasoid people of North Africa who since prehistoric times inhabited Barbary, the Mediterranean coastlands from Egypt to the Atlantic. Their language, present-day Berber (a member of the Afro-Asiatic language family), is spoken by about one-third of Algerians and nearly two-thirds of Moroccans, 10 million people. Berbers are mainly agricultural, but some are still nomadic.

Berbera seaport in Somalia, with the only sheltered harbor on the S side of the Gulf of Aden; population (1982) 55,000. It is in a strategic position on the oil route and has a deep-sea port completed 1969. It was under British control 1884–1960.

Berchtesgaden village in SE Bavaria, Germany, site of Hitler's country residence, the Berghof, which was captured by US troops May 4, 1945, and destroyed.

Berchtold Count Leopold von 1863–1942. Prime minister and foreign minister of Austria–Hungary 1912–15 and a crucial figure in the events that led to World War I, because his indecisive stance caused tension with Serbia.

Berdyaev Nikolai Alexandrovich 1874–1948. Russian philosopher who often challenged official Soviet viewpoints after the Revolution of 1917. Although appointed professor of philosophy in 1919 at Moscow University, he was exiled 1922 for defending Orthodox Christian religion. His books include *The Meaning of History* 1923 and *The Destiny of Man* 1935.

Bérégovoy Pierre 1925– . French socialist politician, prime minister from 1992. A close ally of François ⊅Mitterrand, he was named chief of staff 1981 after managing the successful presidential campaign. He was social affairs minister 1982–84 and finance minister 1984–86 and 1988–92.

The son of a Ukrainian immigrant, he was largely self-educated and his working-class background contrasted sharply with that of the other Socialist Party leaders. As finance minister, he was widely respected by France's financial community. He replaced the unpopular Edith ⊅Cresson as prime minister in April 1992. He pledged to reduce unemployment and cut taxes to stimulate economic growth.

Berengaria of Navarre 1165–1230. Queen of England. The only English queen never to set foot in England, she was the daughter of King Sancho VI of Navarre. She married Richard I of England in Cyprus 1191, and accompanied him on his crusade to the Holy Land.

Berenson Bernard 1865–1959. Lithuanian-born US art historian who was once revered as a leading scholar of Italian Renaissance art. He became wealthy through his advisory work for art galleries, although many of his attributions of anonymous Italian paintings were later questioned.

Berezniki city in Russia, on the Kama river N of Perm; population (1987) 200,000. It was formed 1932 by the amalgamation of several older towns. Industry includes chemicals and paper.

Berg Alban 1885–1935. Austrian composer. He studied under Arnold ⊅Schoenberg and was associated with him as one of the leaders of the serial, or 12-tone, school of composition. His output includes orchestral, chamber, and vocal music as well as two operas, *Wozzeck* 1925, a grim story of working-class life, and the unfinished *Lulu* 1929–35.

His music is emotionally expressive, and sometimes anguished, but can also be lyrical, as in the *Violin Concerto* 1935.

Berg Paul 1926– . US molecular biologist. In 1972, using gene-splicing techniques developed by others, Berg spliced and combined into a single hybrid ⊅DNA from an animal tumor virus (SV40) and DNA from a bacterial virus. Berg's work aroused fears in other workers and excited continuing controversy. For his work on recombinant DNA, he shared the 1980 Nobel Prize for Chemistry with Walter ⊅Gilbert and Frederick ⊅Sanger.

Bergama modern form of ⊅*Pergamum*, ancient city in W Turkey.

Bergamo city in Lombardy, Italy; 30 mi/48 km NE of Milan; population (1989) 117,600. Industries include silk and metal. The Academia Carrara holds a fine collection of paintings.

bergamot small, evergreen tree *Citrus bergamia* of the rue family Rutaceae. From the rind of its fruit a fragrant orange-scented essence used as a perfume is obtained. The sole source of supply is S Calabria, Italy, but the name comes from the town of Bergamo, in Lombardy.

Bergen industrial port (shipbuilding, engineering, fishing) in SW Norway; population (1991) 213,300. Founded 1070, Bergen was a member of the ⊅Hanseatic League.

Bergius Friedrich Karl Rudolph 1884–1949. German research chemist who invented processes for converting coal into oil and wood into sugar. He shared a Nobel Prize 1931 with Carl Bosch for his part in inventing and developing high-pressure industrial methods.

Bergman Ingmar 1918– . Swedish stage producer (from the 1930s) and film director (from the 1950s), regarded by many as one of the great masters of modern cinema. His work deals with complex moral, psychological, and metaphysical problems and is tinged with pessimism. His films include *Wild Strawberries* 1957, *The Seventh Seal* 1957, *Persona* 1966, *Autumn Sonata* 1978 and *Fanny and Alexander* 1982.

Bergman Ingrid 1917–1982. Swedish actress whose films include *Intermezzo* 1939, *Casablanca*, *For Whom the Bell Tolls* both 1943, and *Gaslight* 1944, for which she won an Academy Award.

By leaving her husband to have a child with director Roberto Rossellini, she broke an unofficial moral code of Hollywood star behavior and was ostracized for many years. During her "exile," she made films in Europe such as *Stromboli* 1949 (directed by Rossellini). Later films include *Anastasia* 1956, for which she won an Academy Award.

Her last film, *Autumn Sonata* 1978, was made by Ingmar Bergman. She also did stage plays and received an Emmy for the television film *A Woman Called Golda* 1982, portraying the Israeli prime minister.

Bergson Henri 1859–1941. French philosopher who believed that time, change, and development were the essence of reality. He

thought that time was not a succession of distinct and separate instants but a continuous process in which one period merged imperceptibly into the next. Nobel Prize for Literature 1928.

Beria Lavrenti 1899–1953. Soviet politician who in 1938 became minister of the interior and head of the Soviet police force that imprisoned, liquidated, and transported millions of Soviet citizens. On Stalin's death 1953, he attempted to seize power but was foiled and shot after a secret trial. Apologists for Stalin have blamed Beria for the atrocities committed by Soviet police during Stalin's dictatorship.

beriberi endemic polyneuritis, an inflammation of the nerve endings, mostly occurring in the tropics and resulting from a deficiency of vitamin B_1 (thiamine).

Bering Vitus 1681–1741. Danish explorer, the first European to sight Alaska. He died on Bering Island in the Bering Sea, both named after him, as is the Bering Strait, which separates Asia (Russia) from North America (Alaska).

Beringia or *Bering Land Bridge* former land bridge 1,000 mi/1,600 km wide between Asia and North America; it existed during the ice ages that occurred before 35000 BC and during the period 2400–9000 BC. It is now covered by the Bering Strait and Chukchi Sea.

Bering Sea section of the N Pacific between Alaska and Siberia, from the Aleutian Islands north to the Bering Strait.

Bering Strait strait between Alaska and Siberia, linking the N Pacific and Arctic oceans.

Berio Luciano 1925– . Italian composer. His style has been described as graceful ⊅serialism, and he has frequently experimented with electronic music and taped sound. His works include nine *Sequenzas/Sequences* 1957–75 for various solo instruments or voice, *Sinfonia* 1969 for voices and orchestra, *Points on the curve to find ...* 1974, and a number of dramatic works, including the opera *Un re in ascolto/A King Listens* 1984, loosely based on Shakespeare's *The Tempest*.

Berkeley city on San Francisco Bay in California; population (1990) 102,700. It is the site of an acclaimed branch of the University of California, noted for its nuclear research at the Lawrence Berkeley Laboratory.

Berkeley was settled 1853.

Berkeley Busby. Adopted name of William Berkeley Enos 1895–1976. US choreographer and film director who used ingenious and extravagant sets and teams of female dancers to create large-scale kaleidoscopic patterns through movement and costume when filmed from above, as in *Gold Diggers of 1933* and *Footlight Parade* 1933.

After Berkeley had choreographed more than 20 Broadway shows, producer Samuel Goldwyn engaged him for the musical film *Whoopee* 1930.

Berkeley George 1685–1753. Irish philosopher and cleric who believed that nothing exists apart from perception, and that the all-seeing mind of God makes possible the continued apparent existence of things. For Berkeley, everyday objects are collections of ideas or sensations, hence the dictum *esse est percipi* ("to exist is to be perceived"). He became bishop of Cloyne 1734.

Berkeley Sir William 1606–1677. British colonial administrator. Born in Bruton, England,

and educated at Oxford, Berkeley was knighted by Charles I 1639 and appointed governor of Virginia 1641. Although at first an able administrator, he was drawn into English political struggles. Taking the side of the Royalists in the English Civil War, he was removed from office by Cromwell 1652. With the Restoration 1660, Berkeley was reappointed by Charles II, but he faced the growing opposition that culminated in Bacon's Rebellion 1676. In 1677, Berkeley was removed from office for his brutal repression of that uprising.

berkelium synthesized, radioactive, metallic element of the actinide series, symbol Bk, atomic number 97, atomic weight 247.

It was first produced 1949 by Glenn Seaborg and his team, at the University of California at Berkeley, after which it is named.

Berlin industrial city (machine tools, electrical goods, paper, printing) and capital of the Federal Republic of Germany; population (1990) 3,102,500. The Berlin Wall divided the city from 1961 to 1989, but in Oct 1990 Berlin became the capital of a unified Germany once more with East and West Berlin reunited as the 16th *Land* (state) of the Federal Republic.

Unter den Linden, the tree-lined avenue once the whole city's focal point, has been restored in what was formerly East Berlin. The fashionable Kurfürstendamm and the residential Hansa quarter form part of what was once West Berlin. Prominent buildings include the Reichstag (former parliament building); Schloss Bellevue (Berlin residence of the president); Schloss Charlottenburg (housing several museums); Congress Hall; restored 18th-century State Opera; Dahlem picture gallery. The environs of Berlin include the Grünewald forest and Wannsee lake.

First mentioned about 1230, the city grew out of a fishing village, joined the Hanseatic League in the 15th century, became the permanent seat of the Hohenzollerns, and was capital of the Brandenburg electorate 1486–1701, of the kingdom of Prussia 1701–1871, and of united Germany 1871–1945. From the middle of the 18th century it developed into a commercial and cultural center. In World War II air raids and conquest by the Soviet army April 23–May 2, 1945, destroyed much of the city. After the war, Berlin was divided into four sectors—British, US, French, and Soviet—and until 1948 was under quadripartite government by the Allies. Following the ⟡Berlin blockade the city was divided, with the USSR creating a separate municipal government in its sector. The other three sectors (West Berlin) were made a *Land* of the Federal Republic May 1949, and in Oct 1949 East Berlin was proclaimed capital of East Germany.

Berlin Irving. Adopted name of Israel Baline 1888–1989. Russian-born US composer who wrote over 1,500 songs including such hits as "Alexander's Ragtime Band" 1911, "Always" 1925, "God Bless America" 1939, and "White Christmas" 1942, and the musicals *Top Hat* 1935, *Annie Get Your Gun* 1950, and *Call Me Madam* 1953. He also wrote film scores such as *Blue Skies* and *Easter Parade*.

The son of a poor Jewish cantor, Berlin learned music by ear. He was instrumental in the development of the popular song, taking it from jazz and ragtime to swing and romantic ballads.

Many of his songs are "standards," the most popular and enduring of all time.

Berlin Isaiah 1909– . Latvian-born British philosopher. He emigrated to England with his family 1920, and was professor of social and political theory at Oxford 1957–67. He wrote about Tolstoy's theory of irresistible historical forces and about Marxism; his books include *Historical Inevitability* 1954 and *Four Essays on Liberty* 1969.

Berlin blockade in June 1948, the closing of entry to Berlin from the west by Soviet forces. It was an attempt to prevent the other Allies (the US, France, and the UK) unifying the western part of Germany. The British and US forces responded by sending supplies to the city by air for over a year (the *Berlin airlift*). In May 1949 the blockade was lifted; the airlift continued until Sept. The blockade marked the formal division of the city into Eastern and Western sectors.

Berlin, Conference of conference 1884–85 of the major European powers (France, Germany, the UK, Belgium and Portugal) called by Chancellor Otto von Bismarck to decide on the colonial partition of Africa.

Also discussed were a neutral Congo Basin with free trade, and an independent Congo Free State; the slave trade was forbidden.

Berlin, Congress of congress of the European powers (Russia, Turkey, Austria—Hungary, the UK, France, Italy, and Germany) held in Berlin 1878 to determine the boundaries of the Balkan states after the Russo-Turkish war.

Berlinguer Enrico 1922–1984. Italian Communist who freed the party from Soviet influence. Secretary general of the Italian Communist Party, by 1976 he was near to the premiership, but the murder of Aldo Moro, the prime minister, by Red Brigade guerrillas, prompted a move toward support for the socialists.

Berlin Wall dividing barrier between East and West Berlin 1961–89, erected by East Germany to prevent East Germans from leaving for West Germany. Escapers were shot on sight.

From Aug 13, 1961, the East German security forces sealed off all but 12 of the 80 crossing points to West Berlin with a barbed wire barrier. It was reinforced with concrete by the Russians to prevent the escape of unwilling inhabitants of East Berlin to the rival political and economic system of West Berlin. The interconnecting link between East and West Berlin was *Checkpoint Charlie*, where both sides exchanged captured spies. On Nov 9, 1989 the East German government opened its borders to try to halt the mass exodus of its citizens to the West via other Eastern bloc countries, and the wall was gradually dismantled, with portions of it sold off as souvenirs.

Berlioz (Louis) Hector 1803–1869. French romantic composer, the founder of modern orchestration.

Much of his music was inspired by drama and literature and has a theatrical quality. He wrote symphonic works, such as *Symphonie fantastique* 1830–31 and *Roméo et Juliette* 1839; dramatic cantatas including *La Damnation de Faust* 1846 and *L'Enfance du Christ* 1854; sacred music; and three operas.

Berlioz studied music at the Paris Conservatoire. He won the Prix de Rome 1830, and spent two years in Italy. In 1833 he married Harriet Smithson, an Irish actress playing Shakespearean parts in Paris, but they separated 1842. After some years of poverty and public neglect, he went to Germany 1842 and conducted his own works. He subsequently visited Russia and England. In 1854 he married Marie Recio, a singer. His operas are *Benvenuto Cellini* 1838, *Les Troyens* 1856–58, and *Béatrice et Bénédict* 1862.

Bermuda British colony in the NW Atlantic
area 21 sq mi/54 sq km
capital (and chief port) Hamilton
features consists of about 150 small islands, of which 20 are inhabited, linked by bridges and causeways; Britain's oldest colony
products Easter lilies, pharmaceuticals; tourism and banking are important
currency Bermuda dollar
population (1988) 58,100
language English
religion Christian
government under the constitution of 1968, Bermuda is a fully self-governing British colony, with a governor, senate, and elected House of Assembly (premier from 1982 John Swan, United Bermuda Party)
history the islands were named after Juan de Bermudez, who visited them in 1515, and were settled by British colonists in 1609. Indian and African slaves were transported from 1616, and soon outnumbered the white settlers. Racial violence 1977 led to intervention, at the request of the government, by British troops.

Bermuda Triangle sea area bounded by Bermuda, Florida, and Puerto Rico, which gained the nickname "Deadly Bermuda Triangle" in 1964 when it was suggested that unexplained disappearances of ships and aircraft were exceptionally frequent there; analysis of the data has not confirmed the idea.

Bern (French **Berne**) capital of Switzerland and of Bern canton, in W Switzerland on the Aare River; population (1990) 134,600; canton 945,600. It joined the Swiss confederation 1353 and became the capital 1848. Industries include textiles, chocolate, pharmaceuticals, light metal and electrical goods.

It was founded 1191 and made a free imperial city by Frederick II 1218. Its name is derived from the bear in its coat of arms, and there has been a bear pit in the city since the 16th century. The minster was begun 1421, the town hall 1406, and the university 1834. It is the seat of the Universal Postal Union.

Bernadette, St 1844–1879. French saint, born in Lourdes in the French Pyrenees. In Feb 1858 she had a vision of the Virgin Mary in a grotto, and it became a center of pilgrimage. Many sick people who were dipped in the water of a spring there were said to have been cured. Her feast day is April 16.

Bernadotte Count Folke 1895–1948. Swedish diplomat and president of the Swedish Red Cross. In 1945 he conveyed Nazi commander Himmler's offer of capitulation to the British and US governments, and in 1948 was United Nations mediator in Palestine, where he was assassinated by Israeli Stern Gang guerrillas. He was a nephew of Gustaf VI of Sweden.

Bernadotte Jean-Baptiste Jules 1764–1844. Marshal in Napoleon's army who in 1818 became ⟡Charles XIV of Sweden. Hence, Bernadotte is the family name of the present royal house of Sweden.

Bernard Claude 1813–1878. French physiologist and founder of experimental medicine. Bernard first demonstrated that digestion is not restricted to the stomach, but takes place throughout the small intestine. He discovered the digestive input of the pancreas, several functions of the liver, and the vasomotor nerves which dilate and contract the blood vessels and thus regulate body temperature. This led him to the concept of the *milieu intérieur* ("internal environment") whose stability is essential to good health.

Bernard of Clairvaux, St 1090–1153. Christian founder in 1115 of Clairvaux monastery in Champagne, France. He reinvigorated the ◊Cistercian order, preached in support of the Second Crusade in 1146, and had the scholastic philosopher Abelard condemned for heresy. He is often depicted with a beehive. His feast day is Aug 20.

Bernard of Menthon, St or *Bernard of Montjoux* 923–1008. Christian priest, founder of the hospices for travelers on the Alpine passes that bear his name. The large, heavily built *St Bernard* dogs, formerly employed to find travelers lost in the snow, were also named after him. He is the patron saint of mountaineers. His feast day is May 28.

Bernese Oberland or *Bernese Alps* mountainous area in the S of Berne canton. It includes the Jungfrau, Eiger, and Finsteraarhorn peaks. Interlaken is the chief town.

Bernhard Prince of the Netherlands 1911– . Formerly Prince Bernhard of Lippe-Biesterfeld, he married Princess ◊Juliana in 1937. When Germany invaded the Netherlands in 1940, he escaped to England and became liaison officer for the Dutch and British forces, playing a part in the organization of the Dutch Resistance.

Bernhardt Sarah. Adopted name of Rosine Bernard 1845–1923. French actress who dominated the stage of her day, frequently performing at the Comédie-Française in Paris. She excelled in tragic roles, including Cordelia in Shakespeare's *King Lear*, the title role in Racine's *Phèdre*, and the male roles of Hamlet and of Napoleon's son in Edmond ◊Rostand's *L'Aiglon*.

Bernini Giovanni Lorenzo 1598–1680. Italian sculptor, architect, and painter, a leading figure in the development of the Baroque style. His work in Rome includes the colonnaded piazza in front of St Peter's Basilica (1656), fountains (as in the Piazza Navona), and papal monuments. His sculpture includes *The Ecstasy of St Theresa* 1645–52 (Sta Maria della Vittoria, Rome) and numerous portrait busts.

Bernoulli Swiss family that produced many mathematicians and scientists in the 17th, 18th, and 19th centuries, in particular the brothers *Jakob* (1654–1705) and *Johann* (1667–1748).

Jakob and Johann were pioneers of ◊Leibniz's calculus. Jakob used calculus to study the forms of many curves arising in practical situations, and studied mathematical probability (*Ars conjectandi* 1713); *Bernoulli numbers* are named after him. Johann developed exponential calculus and contributed to many areas of applied mathematics, including the problem of a particle moving in a gravitational field. His son, *Daniel* (1700–82) worked on calculus and probability, and in physics proposed *Bernoulli's principle*, which states that the pressure of a moving fluid decreases the faster it flows (which explains the origin of lift on the airfoil of an aircraft's wing). This and other work on hydrodynamics was published in *Hydrodynamica* 1738.

Bernoulli's principle law stating that the speed of a fluid varies inversely with pressure, an increase in speed producing a decrease in pressure (such as a drop in hydraulic pressure as the fluid speeds up flowing through a constriction in a pipe) and vice versa. The principle also explains the pressure differences on each surface of an airfoil, which gives lift to the wing of an aircraft. The principle was named after Swiss mathematician and physicist Daniel Bernoulli.

Bernstein Leonard 1918–1990. US composer, conductor, and pianist, one of the most energetic and versatile of US musicians in the 20th century. His works, which established a vogue for realistic, contemporary themes, include symphonies such as *The Age of Anxiety* 1949, ballets such as *Fancy Free* 1944, and scores for musicals, including *Wonderful Town* 1953, *West Side Story* 1957, and *Mass* 1971 in memory of President J F Kennedy.

Born in Lawrence, Massachusetts, he educated at Harvard University and the Curtis Institute of Music. From 1958 to 1970 he was musical director of the New York Philharmonic. Among his other works are *Jeremiah* 1944, *Facsimile* 1946, *Candide* 1956, and the *Chichester Psalms* 1965.

Berrigan Daniel 1921– and Philip 1924– . US Roman Catholic priests. The brothers, opponents of the Vietnam War, broke into the draft-records offices at Catonsville, Maryland, to burn the files with napalm. They were sentenced in 1968 to three and six years' imprisonment respectively, but went underground. Subsequently Philip Berrigan was tried with others in 1972 for allegedly conspiring to kidnap President Nixon's adviser Henry Kissinger and blow up government offices in Washington, DC; he was then sentenced to two years' imprisonment.

berry fleshy, many-seeded ◊fruit that does not split open to release the seeds. The outer layer of tissue, the exocarp, forms an outer skin that is often brightly colored to attract birds to eat the fruit and thus disperse the seeds. Examples of berries are the tomato and the grape.

A *pepo* is a type of berry that has developed a hard exterior, such as the cucumber fruit. Another is the *hesperidium*, which has a thick, leathery outer layer, such as that found in citrus fruits, and fluid-containing vesicles within, which form the segments.

Berry Chuck (Charles) 1926– . US musician. He made his first recording, of the song "Maybellene," at Chess Records in Chicago 1955. Widely promoted by New York disk jockey Alan Freed, it became an early rock-and-roll classic. Recognized as one of the fathers of rock and roll, Berry enjoyed a revival of popularity in the 1970s and 1980s.

Born in St Louis, Missouri, Berry began his musical career as a blues guitarist in local clubs. Berry's other early tunes, among them "Roll over Beethoven," "Rock 'n' Roll Music," "Sweet Little Sixteen," and "Johnny B. Goode," featured his trademark guitar solos.

Berryman John 1914–1972. US poet whose somber, complex, and personal works include *Homage to Mistress Bradstreet* 1956, *77 Dream Songs* 1964 (Pulitzer Prize 1965), *His Toy, His Dream, His Rest* 1968, and *Delusions, etc.* 1972.

His poetry has much in common with that of the "confessional" poets, but his use of humor sets it apart. He also wrote short stories and a biography of Stephen Crane 1950. Berryman, an alcoholic, committed suicide.

Berthelot Pierre Eugène Marcellin 1827–1907. French chemist and politician who carried out research into dyes and explosives proving that hydrocarbons and other organic compounds can be synthesized from inorganic materials.

Bertholet Claude Louis 1748–1822. French chemist who carried out research into dyes and bleaches (introducing the use of ◊chlorine as a bleach) and determined the composition of ◊ammonia. Modern chemical nomenclature is based on a system worked out by Bertholet and Antoine ◊Lavoisier.

Bertolucci Bernardo 1940– . Italian film director whose work combines political and historical perspectives with an elegant and lyrical visual appeal. His films include *The Spider's Stratagem* 1970, *Last Tango in Paris* 1972, *1900* 1976, *The Last Emperor* 1987, for which he received an Academy Award, and *The Sheltering Sky* 1990.

He is regarded as one of the most talented of the younger generation of Italian film directors. Among his other films are *The Conformist* 1970.

beryl mineral, beryllium aluminum silicate, $Be_3Al_2Si_6O_{18}$, which forms crystals chiefly in granite. It is the chief ore of beryllium. Two of its gem forms are aquamarine (light-blue crystals) and emerald (dark-green crystals).

Well-formed crystals of up to 200 tons have been found.

beryllium hard, light-weight, silver-white, metallic element, symbol Be, atomic number 4, atomic weight 9.012. It is one of the ◊alkaline-earth metals, with chemical properties similar to those of magnesium; in nature it is found only in combination with other elements. It is used to make sturdy, light alloys and to control the speed of neutrons in nuclear reactors. Beryllium oxide was discovered in 1798 by French chemist Louis-Nicolas Vauquelin (1763–1829), but the element was not isolated until 1828, by Friedrich Wöhler and Antoine-Alexandre-Brutus Bussy independently.

The name comes from Latin *beryllus*.

Berzelius Jöns Jakob 1779–1848. Swedish chemist who accurately determined more than 2,000 relative atomic and molecular masses. He devised (1813–14) the system of chemical symbols and formulae now in use and proposed oxygen as a reference standard for atomic masses. His discoveries include the elements cerium (1804), selenium (1817), and thorium (1828); he was the first to prepare silicon in its amorphous form and to isolate zirconium. The words *isomerism*, *allotropy*, and *protein* were coined by him.

Besançon town on the river Doubs, France; population (1983) 120,000. It is the capital of Franche-Comté. The first factory to produce artificial fibers was established here 1890. Industries include textiles and clock-making. It has fortifications by ◊Vauban, Roman remains, and a Gothic cathedral. The writer Victor Hugo and the Lumière brothers, inventors of cinematography, were born here.

Besant Annie 1847–1933. English socialist and feminist activist. Separated from her clerical husband in 1873 because of her freethinking views, she was associated with the radical atheist Charles Bradlaugh and the socialist ◊Fabian Society. She and Bradlaugh published a treatise advocating birth control and were prosecuted; as a result she lost custody of her daughter. In 1889 she became a disciple of Madame ▷Blavatsky. She thereafter preached theosophy and went to India. As a supporter of Indian independence, she founded the Central Hindu College 1898 and the Indian Home Rule League 1916, and became president of the Indian National Congress in 1917. Her *Theosophy and the New Psychology* was published 1904.

Bessarabia region in SE Europe, divided between Moldova and Ukraine. Bessarabia was annexed by Russia 1812, but broke away at the Russian Revolution to join Romania. The cession was confirmed by the Allies, but not by Russia, in a Paris treaty of 1920; the USSR reoccupied it 1940 and divided it between the Moldavian and Ukrainian republics (now independent Moldova and Ukraine). Romania recognized the position in the 1947 peace treaty.

Bessel Friedrich Wilhelm 1784–1846. German astronomer and mathematician, the first person to find the approximate distance to a star by direct methods when he measured the ▷parallax (annual displacement) of the star 61 Cygni in 1838. In mathematics, he introduced the series of functions now known as *Bessel functions*.

Bessemer Henry 1813–1898. British engineer and inventor who developed a method of converting molten pig iron into steel (the *Bessemer process*).

Bessemer process the first cheap method of making ▷steel, invented by Henry Bessemer in England 1856. It has since been superseded by more efficient steelmaking processes, such as the ▷basic-oxygen process. In the Bessemer process compressed air is blown into the bottom of a converter, a furnace shaped like a cement mixer, containing molten pig iron. The excess carbon in the iron burns out, other impurities form a slag, and the furnace is emptied by tilting.

Best Charles Herbert 1899–1978. Canadian physiologist, one of the team of Canadian scientists including Frederick ▷Banting whose research resulted in 1922 in the discovery of insulin as a treatment for diabetes.

A Banting–Best Department of Medical Research was founded in Toronto, and Best was its director 1941–67.

bestiary in medieval times, a book with stories and illustrations which depicted real and mythical animals or plants to illustrate a (usually Christian) moral. The stories were initially derived from the Greek *Physiologus*, a collection of 48 such stories, written in Alexandria around the 2nd century AD.

Translations of the *Physiologus* into vernacular languages (French, Italian, and English) date from the 13th century; illustrated versions are known from the 9th century. Much of later and contemporary folklore about animals derives from the bestiary, such as the myth of the phoenix burning itself to be born again.

beta-blocker any of a class of drugs that block impulses that stimulate certain nerve endings (beta receptors) serving the heart muscles. This reduces the heart rate and the force of contraction, which in turn reduces the amount of oxygen (and therefore the blood supply) required by the heart. Beta-blockers are banned from use in competitive sports. They may be useful in the treatment of angina, arrhythmia, and raised blood pressure, and following myocardial infarctions. They must be withdrawn from use gradually.

beta decay the spontaneous alteration of the nucleus of a radioactive atom, which transmutes the atom from one atomic number to another through the emission of either an electron (beta-minus decay) or a positron (beta-plus decay). In the more commonly occurring of the two, beta-minus decay, the atomic number increases by one (through the decay of a neutron, which converts to a proton emitting an electron and an antineutrino); in the less commonly occurring beta-plus decay, the atomic number decreases by one (the proton converts to a neutron, emitting a positron and a neutrino). The symbol used for the electron in beta-minus decay is β−; the symbol for the positron in beta-plus decay is β+.

beta particle electron or positron ejected with great velocity from a radioactive atom that is undergoing spontaneous disintegration. Beta particles do not exist in the nucleus but are created on disintegration, beta decay, when a neutron converts to a proton to emit an electron.

Betelgeuse or *Alpha Orionis* red supergiant star in the constellation of Orion and the tenth brightest star in the sky, although its brightness varies. It is over 300 times the diameter of the Sun, about the same size as the orbit of Mars, is over 10,000 times as luminous as the Sun, and lies 650 light-years from Earth.

betel nut fruit of the areca palm *Areca catechu*, used together with lime and betel pepper as a masticatory stimulant by peoples of the East and Papua New Guinea. Chewing it results in blackened teeth and a mouth stained deep red.

Bethe Hans Albrecht 1906– . German-born US physicist who worked on the first atomic bomb. He was awarded a Nobel Prize 1967 for his discoveries concerning energy production in stars.

Bethe left Germany for England in 1933, and worked at Manchester and Bristol universities. In 1935 he moved to the US where he became professor of theoretical physics at Cornell University; his research was interrupted by the war and by his appointment as head of the theoretical division of the Los Alamos atomic bomb project. He has since become a leading peace campaigner, and opposed the US government's Strategic Defense Initiative (Star Wars) program.

Bethlehem city in E Pennsylvania; population (1990) 71,428. Its former steel industry has been replaced by high technology.

Lehigh University is here. Bethlehem was founded 1741 by German immigrants.

Bethlehem (Hebrew *Beit-Lahm*) town on the W bank of the river Jordan, S of Jerusalem. Occupied by Israel in 1967; population (1980) 14,000. In the Bible it is mentioned as the birthplace of King David and Jesus.

Bethmann Hollweg Theobald von 1856–1921. German politician, imperial chancellor 1909–17, largely responsible for engineering popular support for World War I in Germany, but his power was overthrown by a military dictatorship under ▷Ludendorff and ▷Hindenburg.

Béthune city in N France, W of Lille; population (1982) 258,400. Industries include textiles, machinery, and tires.

Bettelheim Bruno 1903–1990. Austrian-born US child psychologist. At the University of Chicago he founded a treatment center for emotionally disturbed children based on the principle of a supportive home environment. Among his most influential books are *Love is Not Enough* 1950, *Truants from Life* 1954, and *Children of the Dream* 1962.

He received his PhD from the University of Vienna 1938. With the Nazi occupation of Austria, he was arrested and sent to the concentration camps at Dachau and Buchenwald, where he began a long-term study of the psychological effects of totalitarianism. He fled Europe 1939 and came to the US, where he joined the faculty of the University of Chicago.

Bevan Aneurin (Nye) 1897–1960. British Labor politician. Son of a Welsh miner, and himself a miner at 13, he became member of Parliament for Ebbw Vale 1929–60. As minister of health 1945–51, he inaugurated the National Health Service (NHS); he was minister of labor Jan—April 1951, when he resigned (with Harold Wilson) on the introduction of NHS charges and led a Bevanite faction against the government. In 1956 he became chief Labor spokesperson on foreign affairs, and deputy leader of the Labor party 1959. He was an outstanding speaker.

beverage any liquid for drinking other than pure water. Beverages are made with plant products to impart pleasant flavors, nutrients, and stimulants to people's fluid intake. Examples include juices, tea, coffee, cocoa, cola drinks, and alcoholic beverages.

The juices of grapes and other fruits are fermented to produce wines, while fermented cereals form the basis of beers and liquors. See also ▷alcoholic beverage.

Beverly Hills residential city and a part of greater Los Angeles, California, known as the home of Hollywood film stars. Population (1990) 31,900.

Rodeo Drive is a popular shopping area for prestige goods.

Beza Théodore (properly *De Bèsze*) 1519–1605. French church reformer. He settled in Geneva, Switzerland, where he worked with the Protestant leader John Calvin and succeeded him as head of the reformed church there 1564. He wrote in defense of the burning of ▷Servetus (1554) and translated the New Testament into Latin.

Bezier curve curved line that connects a series of points (or "nodes") in the smoothest possible way. The shape of the curve is governed by a series of complex mathematical formulae. They are used in ▷computer graphics and ▷CAD.

Béziers city in Languedoc-Roussillon, S France; population (1983) 84,000. It is a center of the wine trade. It was once a Roman station and was the site of a massacre 1209 in the Albigensian Crusade.

Bhagavad-Gītā (Hindu "the Song of the Blessed") religious and philosophical Sanskrit poem, dating from around 300 BC, forming an episode in the sixth book of the *Mahābhārata*, one of the two great Hindu epics. It is the supreme religious work of Hinduism.

bhakti (Sanskrit "devotion") in Hinduism, a tradition of worship that emphasizes love and devotion rather than ritual, sacrifice, or study.

Bhavnagar port in Gujarat, NW India, in the Kathiawar peninsula; population (1981) 308,000. It is a center for textile industry. It was capital of the former Rajput princely state of Bhavnagar.

bhikku Buddhist monk who is totally dependent on alms and the monastic community (*sangha*) for support.

Bhutan
Kingdom of (*Druk-yul*)

area 17,954 sq mi/46,500 sq km
capital Thimbu (Thimphu)
cities Paro, Punakha, Mongar
physical occupies southern slopes of the Himalayas; cut by valleys formed by tributaries of the Brahmaputra; thick forests in S
features Gangkar Punsum (24,700 ft/7,529 m) is one of the world's highest unclimbed peaks
head of state and government Jigme Singye Wangchuk from 1972
political system absolute monarchy
political parties none officially; illegal Bhutan People's Party (BPP)
exports timber, talc, fruit and vegetables, cement, distilled spirits, calcium carbide
currency ngultrum; also Indian currency
population (1990 est) 1,566,000; growth rate 2% p.a. (75% Ngalops and Sharchops, 25% Nepalese)
life expectancy men 44, women 43
languages Dzongkha (official, a Tibetan dialect), Sharchop, Bumthap, Nepali, and English
religions 75% Lamaistic Buddhist (state religion), 25% Hindu
literacy 5%
GDP $250 million (1987); $170 per head
chronology
1865 Trade treaty with Britain signed.
1907 First hereditary monarch installed.
1910 Anglo-Bhutanese Treaty signed.
1949 Indo-Bhutan Treaty of Friendship signed.
1952 King Jigme Dorji Wangchuk installed.
1953 National assembly established.
1959 4,000 Tibetan refugees given asylum.
1968 King established first cabinet.
1972 King died and was succeeded by his son Jigme Singye Wangchuk.
1979 Tibetan refugees told to take Bhutanese citizenship or leave; most stayed.
1983 Bhutan became a founding member of the South Asian Regional Association for Cooperation organization (SAARC).
1988 King imposed "code of conduct" suppressing Nepalese customs.
1990 Hundreds of people allegedly killed during prodemocracy demonstrations.

Bhil member of a seminomadic people of Dravidian origin, living in NW India and numbering about 4 million. They are hunter-gatherers and also practice shifting cultivation. The Bhili language belongs to the Indo-European family, as does Gujarati, which is also spoken by the Bhil. Their religion is Hinduism.

Bhindranwale Sant Jarnail Singh 1947–1984. Indian Sikh fundamentalist leader who campaigned for the creation of a separate state of Khalistan during the early 1980s, precipitating a bloody Hindu–Sikh conflict in the Punjab. Having taken refuge in the Golden Temple complex in Amritsar and built up an arms cache for guerrilla activities, Bhindranwale, along with around 500 followers, died at the hands of Indian security forces who stormed the temple in "Operation Blue Star" June 1984.

Bhopal industrial city (textiles, chemicals, electrical goods, jewelry); capital of Madhya Pradesh, central India; population (1981) 672,000. Nearby Bhimbetka Caves, discovered 1973, have the world's largest collection of prehistoric paintings, about 10,000 years old. In 1984 some 2,600 people died from an escape of the poisonous gas methyl isocyanate from a factory owned by US company Union Carbide; another 300,000 suffer from long-term health problems.

The city was capital of the former princely state of Bhopal, founded 1723, which became allied to Britain in 1817. It was merged with Madhya Pradesh in 1956.

Bhubaneswar city in NE India; population (1981) 219,200. It is the capital of Orissa state. Utkal University was founded 1843. A place of pilgrimage and center of Siva worship, it has temples of the 6th–12th centuries.

Bhumibol Adulyadej 1927– . King of Thailand from 1946. Born in the US and educated in Bangkok and Switzerland, he succeeded to the throne on the assassination of his brother. In 1973 he was active, with popular support, in overthrowing the military government of Marshal Thanom Kittikachorn and thus ended a sequence of army-dominated regimes in power from 1932.

Bhutan mountainous, landlocked country in the eastern Himalayas (SE Asia), bounded N and W by Tibet (China) and to the S and E by India.

government Bhutan is a hereditary limited monarchy in which the king (assisted by the royal council) consults the council of ministers, national assembly (Tsogdu), and the monastic head of Bhutan's Buddhist priesthood. The 151-member Tsogdu, which includes 106 representatives directly elected for three-year terms, is required to pass a vote of confidence in the king by a two-thirds majority every three years and has the power to replace the monarch. In the absence of a written constitution or political parties it is in effect an absolute monarchy. There are, however, certain written rules governing the methods of electing members of the royal council and Tsogdu.

history Bhutan was ruled by Tibet from the 16th century and by China from 1720. In 1774 the British East India Company concluded a treaty with the ruler of Bhutan, and British influence grew during the 19th century. A short border war in 1863 ended with a treaty in 1865, under which an annual subsidy was paid by Britain to Bhutan. In 1907 the first hereditary monarch was installed, and under the Anglo-Bhutanese Treaty, signed three years later, Bhutan was granted internal autonomy while foreign relations were placed under the control of the British government in India.

foreign relations After India's independence 1947, an Indo-Bhutan Treaty of Friendship was signed 1949, under which Bhutan agreed to seek Indian advice on foreign relations but not necessarily to accept it. There is no formal defense treaty, but India would regard an attack on Bhutan as an act of aggression against itself. In 1959, after the Chinese annexation of Tibet, Bhutan gave asylum to some 4,000 Tibetan refugees, who in 1979 were given the choice of taking Bhutanese citizenship or returning to Tibet. Most became citizens, and the rest went to India. In 1983 Bhutan became a founding member of the South Asian Association for Regional Cooperation (SAARC), and in 1985 the first meeting of SAARC foreign ministers was held in Bhutan.

towards democracy In 1952 King Jigme Dorji Wangchuk came to power, and in 1953 a national assembly was established. In 1968 the king appointed his first cabinet. He died 1972 and was succeeded by his Western-educated son Jigme Singye Wangchuk.

ethnic tensions In 1988 the Buddhist Drukpa ethnic minority, headed by King Jigme Singye Wangchuk, imposed its own language, religious practices, and national dress on the divided (although principally Hindu-Nepali) majority community and suppressed the Nepalese language and customs. As a result tension between the Drukpa and Hindu Nepalese communities increased after 1990 and the Nepalese illegally formed a number of political parties to protest against Drukpa policies. Several hundred people were reported to have been killed during security crackdowns on prodemocracy demonstrations. *See illustration box.*

Bhutto Benazir 1953– . Pakistani politician, leader of the Pakistan People's Party (PPP) from 1984 (in exile until 1986), and prime minister of Pakistan 1988–90, when the opposition maneuvered her from office and charged her with corruption. In May 1991 new charges were brought against her. She was the first female leader of a Muslim state.

Benazir Bhutto was educated at Harvard and Oxford universities. She returned to Pakistan 1977 but was placed under house arrest after General ◊Zia ul-Haq seized power from her father, Prime Minister Zulfiqar Ali Bhutto. On her release she moved to the UK and became, with her mother Nusrat (1934–), the joint leader in exile of the opposition PPP. When martial law had been lifted, she returned to Pakistan April 1986 to launch a campaign for open elections. In her first year in office she struck an uneasy balance with the military establishment and improved Pakistan's relations with India.

She led her country back into the Commonwealth 1989. In Aug 1990, she was removed from office by presidential decree, and a caretaker government installed. Charges of corruption and abuse of power were leveled against her and her husband Asif Ali Zardari (who was also accused of mass murder, kidnapping, and extortion), and her party was defeated in the subsequent general election. Bhutto and her husband claimed that the charges were fabrications, with the government's intention being to strike a deal whereby they would receive pardons on condition that they left the country and effectively abandoned politics. In May 1991 new charges (eight in all), alleging misuse of secret service funds, were brought against Benazir Bhutto. She denied all charges. Her husband, who was acquitted on

May 5, 1991 of fraudulently obtaining a bank loan, was charged on May 13 with criminal conspiracy leading to the death of political opponents.

Bhutto Zulfikar Ali 1928–1979. Pakistani politician, president 1971–73; prime minister from 1973 until the 1977 military coup led by General ⌂Zia ul-Haq. In 1978 Bhutto was sentenced to death for conspiring to murder a political opponent and was hanged the following year.

Biafra, Bight of name until 1975 of the Bight of ⌂Bonny, W Africa.

Biafra, Republic of African state proclaimed in 1967 when fears that Nigerian central government was increasingly in the hands of the rival Hausa tribe led the predominantly Ibo Eastern Region of Nigeria to secede under Lt Col Odumegwu Ojukwu. On the proclamation of Biafra, civil war ensued with the rest of the federation. In a bitterly fought campaign federal forces confined the Biafrans to a shrinking area of the interior by 1968, and by 1970 Biafra ceased to exist.

Białystok city in E Poland; population (1990) 270,600. It is the capital city of Białystok region. Industries include textiles, chemicals, and tools. Founded 1310, the city belonged to Prussia 1795–1807 and to Russia 1807–1919.

Biarritz town on the Bay of Biscay, France, near the Spanish border; population (1982) 28,000. A seaside resort and spa town, it was popularized by Queen Victoria and Edward VII.

biathlon an athletic competition that combines cross-country skiing with rifle marksmanship. Basic equipment consists of cross-country skis, poles, and boots, and bolt-action (nonautomatic) rifles.

The course (defined in metric terms) is usually 12.5 mi/20 km long and follows terrain that is uphill, downhill, and level (with approximately equal distances of each). Between the 3rd mi/5th km and the 11th mi/18th km there are 4 stations, at which the biathlete must fire 5 shots at targets that vary from 110 yd/100 m to 275 yd/250 m away. Firing positions alternate between prone and standing.

In standard team competition, a team's score is the total corrected time (penalties are imposed for missed targets) of the team's 3 leading entrants. The typical biathlon relay is a 4-person, 4.7-mi/7.5-km event, in which a 220-yd/200-m penalty loop must be skied for each missed target.

The biathlon can be traced to Sweden, where it began as informal competition among hunters. By 1908 the sport had become organized enough to inspire international military ski races in Europe. The first modern biathlon event in the US was at Camp Hale, Colorado, 1956. In 1960, at the Winter Games in Squaw Valley, California, the sport became an Olympic event. Relay competition was added 1968.

Bible (Greek *ta biblia* "the books") the sacred book of the Jewish and Christian religions. The Hebrew Bible, recognized by both Jews and Christians, is called the ⌂*Old Testament* by Christians. The ⌂*New Testament* comprises books recognized by the Christian church from the 4th century as canonical. The Roman Catholic Bible also includes the ⌂*Apocrypha*.

The first English translation of the entire Bible was by a priest, Miles Coverdale, 1535; the **Authorized Version** or **King James Bible** 1611, was long influential for the clarity and beauty of its language. A revision of the King James Version carried out 1959 by the

the Bible

The Books of the Old Testament

name of book	chapters	date written
The Pentateuch or the Five Books of Moses		
Genesis	50	mid 8th-century BC
Exodus	40	950–586 BC
Leviticus	27	mid 7th-century BC
Numbers	36	850–650 BC
Deuteronomy	34	mid-7th century BC
Joshua	24	c. 550 BC
Judges	21	c. 550 BC
Ruth	4	end 3rd century BC
1 Samuel	31	c. 900 BC
2 Samuel	24	c. 900 BC
1 Kings	22	550–600 BC
2 Kings	25	550–600 BC
1 Chronicles	29	c. 300 BC
2 Chronicles	36	c. 300 BC
Ezra	10	c. 450 BC
Nehemiah	13	c. 450 BC
Esther	10	c. 200 BC
Job	42	600–400 BC
Psalms	150	6th–2nd century BC
Proverbs	31	350–150 BC
Ecclesiastes	12	c. 200 BC
Song of Solomon	8	3rd century BC
Isaiah	66	end 3rd century BC
Jeremiah	52	604 BC
Lamentations	5	586–536 BC
Ezekiel	48	6th century BC
Daniel	12	c. 166 BC
Hosea	14	c. 732 BC
Joel	3	c. 500 BC
Amos	9	775–750 BC
Obadiah	1	6th–3rd century BC
Jonah	4	600–200 BC
Micah	7	end 3rd century BC
Nahum	3	c. 626 BC
Habakkuk	3	c. 600 BC
Zephaniah	3	3rd century BC
Haggai	2	c. 520 BC
Zechariah	14	c. 520 BC
Malachi	4	c. 430 BC

The Books of the New Testament

name of book	chapters	date written
The Gospels		
Matthew	28	before AD 70
Mark	16	before AD 70
Luke	24	AD 70–80
John	21	AD 90–100
The Acts	28	AD 70–80
Romans	16	AD 120
1 Corinthians	16	AD 57
2 Corinthians	13	AD 57
Galatians	6	AD 53
Ephesians	6	AD 140
Philippians	4	AD 63
Colossians	4	AD 140
1 Thessalonians	5	AD 50–54
2 Thessalonians	3	AD 50–54
1 Timothy	6	before AD 64
2 Timothy	4	before AD 64
Titus	3	before AD 64
Philemon	1	AD 60–62
Hebrews	13	AD 80–90
James	5	before AD 52
1 Peter	5	before AD 64
2 Peter	3	before AD 64
1 John	5	AD 90–100
2 John	1	AD 90–100
3 John	1	AD 90–100
Jude	1	AD 75–80
Revelation	22	AD 81–96

British and Foreign Bible Society produced the widely used American translation, the Revised Standard Version. A conference of British churches 1946 recommended a completely new translation into English from the original Hebrew and Greek texts; work on this was carried out over the following two decades, resulting in the publication of the New English Bible (New Testament 1961, Old Testament and Apocrypha 1970). Another recent translation is the Jerusalem Bible, completed by Catholic scholars in 1966.

Missionary activity led to the translation of the Bible into the languages of people they were trying to convert, and by 1975 parts of the Bible had been translated into over 1,500 different languages, with 261 complete translations.

Bible society society founded for the promotion of translation and distribution of the Scriptures. The four largest branches are the British and Foreign Bible Society, founded in 1804, the American Bible Society, the National Bible Society of Scotland, and the Netherlands Bible Society.

Biblical criticism study of the content and origin of the Bible. *Lower* or *textual criticism* is directed toward the recovery of the original text; *higher* or *documentary criticism* is concerned with questions of authorship, date, and literary sources; *historical criticism* seeks to ascertain the actual historical content of the Bible, aided by archeological discoveries and the ancient history of neighboring peoples.

bicarbonate of soda or *baking soda* (technical name *sodium hydrogencarbonate*) $NaHCO_3$ white crystalline solid that neutralizes acids and is used in medicine to treat acid indigestion. It is also used in baking powders and effervescent drinks.

Bichat Marie François Xavier 1771–1802. French physician and founder of ⌂histology, the study of tissues. He studied the organs of the body, their structure, and the ways in which they are affected by disease. This led to his discovery and naming of "tissue," a basic biological and medical concept; he identified 21 types. He argued that disease does not affect the whole organ but only certain of its constituent tissues.

bichir African fish, genus *Polypterus*, found in tropical swamps and rivers. Cylindrical in shape, some species grow to 2.3 ft/70 cm or more. They show many "primitive" features, such as breathing air by using the swimbladder, having a spiral valve in the intestine, having heavy bony scales, and having larvae with external gills. These, and the fleshy fins, lead some scientists to think they are related to lungfish and coelacanths.

bicycle pedal-driven two-wheeled vehicle used in ⌂cycling. It consists of a metal frame mounted on two large wire-spoked wheels, with handlebars in front and a seat between the front and back wheels. The bicycle is an energy-efficient, nonpolluting form of transport, and it is estimated that 800 million bicycles are in use throughout the world—outnumbering automobiles three to one. China, India, Denmark, and the Netherlands are countries with a high use of bicycles. More than 10% of road spending in the Netherlands is on cycleways and bicycle parking.

The first bicycle was seen in Paris 1791 and was a form of hobby-horse. The first treadle-propelled cycle was designed by Kirkpatrick Macmillan (Scotland) 1839. By the end of the 19th century wire wheels, metal frames (replacing wood), and pneumatic tires (invented by J B Dunlop 1888) had been added. Among the bicycles of that time was the front-wheel-driven "Penny Farthing" with a large front wheel.

Bidault Georges 1899–1983. French politician, prime minister 1946, 1949–50. He was a leader of the French resistance during World War II and foreign minister and president in de Gaulle's provisional government. He left the Gaullists over Algerian independence and in 1962 he became head of the ◊Organisation de l'Armée Secrète (OAS), formed 1961 by French settlers devoted to perpetuating their own rule in Algeria. He was charged with treason in 1963 and left the country, but was allowed to return in 1968.

Biddle Nicholas 1786–1844. US financier and public figure. Born in Philadelphia, Biddle was admitted to the Pennsylvania bar 1809 and elected to the state legislature 1814. As an acknowledged expert in international commerce, he was appointed a director of the Bank of the United States by President Monroe 1819. He became president of the bank 1822, but as an extreme fiscal conservative, Biddle became the focus of Andrew ◊Jackson's antibank campaigns in 1828 and 1832. After the withdrawal of the bank's federal charter 1836, he remained its president under a state charter.

Bielefeld city in North Rhine-Westphalia, Germany, 34 mi/55 km E of Münster; population (1988) 299,000. Industries include textiles, drinks, chemicals, machinery, and motorcycles.

Bielostok Russian form of ◊Białystok, city in Poland.

biennial plant plant that completes its life cycle in two years. During the first year it grows vegetatively and the surplus food produced is stored in its ◊perennating organ, usually the root. In the following year these food reserves are used for the production of leaves, flowers, and seeds, after which the plant dies. Many root vegetables are biennials, including the carrot *Daucus carota* and parsnip *Pastinaca sativa*. Some garden plants that are grown as biennials are actually perennials, for example, the wallflower *Cheiranthus cheiri*.

Bienville Jean Baptiste Le Moyne, Sieur de 1680–1768. French colonial administrator. Born in Ville-Marie (now Montreal), Quebec, Bienville saw service in the French navy and in 1698 accompanied ◊Iberville on a mission to establish a French colony at the mouth of the Mississippi river. Serving his first term as governor of Louisiana 1706–13, he founded the settlement at Mobile. In his second term 1717–23, he established the colonial capital at New Orleans. During Bienville's third and final term 1733–43, he was drawn into a costly and ultimately unsuccessful war with the Indians of the lower Mississippi Valley.

Bierce Ambrose (Gwinett) 1842–c. 1914. US author. He established his reputation as a master of supernatural and psychological horror with *Tales of Soldiers and Civilians* 1891 and *Can Such Things Be?* 1893. He also wrote *The Devil's Dictionary* 1911 (first published as *The Cynic's Word Book* 1906), a collection of ironic definitions. He disappeared in Mexico 1913.

He was writer-editor of the *San Francisco Newsletter*, publisher of short stories by Mark Twain and Bret Harte, and the satirical columnist known as "The Prattler" 1887–1906.

Bierstadt Albert 1830–1902. German-born US landscape painter. His spectacular panoramas of the American wilderness fell out of favor after his death until interest in the Hudson River School rekindled late in the century. A classic work is *Thunderstorm in the Rocky Mountains* 1859 (Museum of Fine Arts, Boston).

His *Discovery of the Hudson* hangs in the Capitol in Washington, DC.

bigamy in law, the offense of marrying a person while already lawfully married to another. In some countries marriage to more than one wife or husband is lawful; see also ◊polygamy.

big-band jazz ◊swing music created in the late 1930s and 1940s by bands of 13 or more players, such as those of Duke ◊Ellington and Benny ◊Goodman. Big-band jazz relied on fixed arrangements, where there is more than one instrument to some of the parts, rather than improvisation. Big bands were mainly dance bands, and they ceased to be economically viable in the 1950s.

Big Bang in astronomy, the hypothetical "explosive" event that marked the origin of the universe as we know it. At the time of the Big Bang, the entire universe was squeezed into a hot, superdense state. The Big Bang explosion threw this compacted material outwards, producing the expanding universe (see ◊red shift). The cause of the Big Bang is unknown; observations of the current rate of expansion of the universe suggest that it took place about 10 to 20 billion years ago. The Big Bang theory began modern ◊cosmology.

Big Dipper American name for the seven brightest and most prominent stars in the constellation ◊Ursa Major, which in outline resemble a large dipper.

bight coastal indentation, such as the Bight of ◊Bonny in W Africa and the Great Australian Bight.

Bihar or **Behar** state of NE India
area 67,125 sq mi/173,900 sq km
capital Patna
features river Ganges in the N, Rajmahal Hills in the south
products copper, iron, coal, rice, jute, sugar cane, grain, oilseed
population (1991) 86,338,900
language Hindi, Bihari
famous people Chandragupta, Asoka
history the ancient kingdom of Magadha roughly corresponded to central and S Bihar. Many Bihari people were massacred as a result of their protest at the establishment of Bangladesh 1971.

Bihari member of a N Indian people, also living in Bangladesh, Nepal, and Pakistan, and numbering over 40 million. The Bihari are mainly Muslim. The Bihari language is related to Hindi and has several widely varying dialects. It belongs to the Indic branch of the Indo-European family. Many Bihari were massacred during the formation of Bangladesh, which they opposed.

Bijapur ancient city in Karnataka, Republic of India. It was founded around AD 1489 Yusuf Adil Shah (died 1511), the son of Murad II, as the capital of the Muslim kingdom of Biafra. The city and kingdom was annexed by the Mogul emperor Aurangzeb in 1686.

Bikaner city in Rajasthan, N India; population (1981) 280,000. Once capital of the Rajput state of Bikaner, it is now a center for carpet-weaving.

Bikini atoll in the ◊Marshall Islands, W Pacific, where the US carried out 23 atomic- and hydrogen-bomb tests (some underwater) 1946–58.

The islanders were relocated by the US before 1946. Some returned after Bikini was declared safe for habitation in 1969, but they were again removed in the late 1970s because of continuing harmful levels of radiation. In 1990 a US plan was announced to remove radioactive topsoil, allowing 800 islanders to return home.

Biko Steve (Stephen) 1946–1977. South African civil-rights leader. An active opponent of ◊apartheid, he was arrested in Sept 1977; he died in detention six days later. Since his death in the custody of South African police, he has been a symbol of the anti apartheid movement.

bilateralism in economics, a trade agreement between two countries or groups of countries in which they give each other preferential treatment. Usually the terms agreed result in balanced trade and are favored by countries with limited foreign exchange reserves. Bilateralism is incompatible with free trade.

Bilbao industrial port (iron and steel, chemicals, cement, food) in N Spain, capital of Biscay province; population (1991) 372,200.

bilberry several species of shrubs of the genus *Vaccinium* of the heath family Ericaceae, closely related to North American blueberries.

bilby rabbit-eared bandicoot *Macrotis lagotis*, a lightly built marsupial with big ears and long nose. This burrowing animal is mainly carnivorous, and its pouch opens backward.

Bildungsroman (German "education novel") novel that deals with the psychological and emotional development of its protagonist, tracing his or her life from inexperienced youth to maturity. The first example of the type is generally considered to be Wieland's *Agathon* 1765–66, but it was ◊Goethe's *Wilhelm Meisters Lehrjahr/Wilhelm Meister's Apprenticeship* 1795–96 that established the genre. Although taken up by writers in other languages, it remained chiefly a German form; later examples include Thomas ◊Mann's *Der Zauberberg/The Magic Mountain* 1924.

bile brownish fluid produced by the liver. In most vertebrates, it is stored in the gall bladder and emptied into the small intestine as food passes through. Bile consists of bile salts, bile pigments, cholesterol, and lecithin. *Bile salts* assist in the breakdown and absorption of fats; *bile pigments* are the breakdown products of old red blood cells that are passed into the gut to be eliminated with the feces.

bilharzia or **schistosomiasis** disease that causes anemia, inflammation, formation of scar tissue, dysentery, enlargement of the spleen and liver, cancer of the bladder, and cirrhosis of the liver. It is contracted by bathing in water contaminated with human sewage. Some 300 million people are thought to suffer from this disease in the tropics.

Freshwater snails that live in this water act as host to the first larval stage of flukes of the genus *Schistosoma*; when these larvae leave the snail in their second stage of development, they are able to pass through human skin, become sexually mature, and produce quantities of eggs, which pass to the intestine or bladder. The human host eventually dies of the infestation, but before then numerous eggs have passed from the body in urine or feces to continue the cycle. Treatment is by means of drugs, usually containing antimony, to kill the parasites.

billiards indoor game played, normally by two players, with tapered poles (called cues) and composition balls (one red, two white) on a rectangular table covered with a green, feltlike cloth (baize) without pockets. A variation popular in England is played on a table with six pockets, one at each corner and one in each of the long sides at the middle. Scoring strokes are made by sinking the red ball, sinking the opponent's ball, or sinking another ball off one of these two. The cannon (when the cue ball hits the two other balls on the table) is another scoring stroke.

Billings city in S central Montana on the N shore of the Yellowstone River; seat of Yellowstone county. It is a center for transporting livestock and animal products and for vegetable and grain processing; population (1990) 81,100. Nearby, to the SE, is Big Horn Indian reservation where the Battle of Little Big Horn took place 1876.

billion the cardinal number represented by a 1 followed by nine zeros (1,000,000,000), equivalent to a thousand million.

Billiton Indonesian island in the Java Sea, between Borneo and Sumatra, one of the Sunda Islands; area 1,860 sq mi/4,830 sq km. The chief port is Tanjungpandan. Tin mining is the chief industry.

bill of exchange or **bank draft** a written order in which a *drawer* orders a *drawee* to pay a specified sum to a *payee*. For example, a check is a bill of exchange drawn on a bank or banker. Once signed and endorsed, it becomes negotiable and can be discounted (sold for cash before the maturity date under face value) at current short-term interest rates.

In the US, major corporations make use of short-term "paper" to meet general financial obligations as well as foreign trade transactions.

bill of lading document giving proof of particular goods having been loaded on a ship. The person to whom the goods are being sent normally needs to show the bill of lading in order to obtain the release of the goods. For air freight, there is an *air waybill*.

Bill of Rights in the US, the first ten amendments to the US Constitution:
1 guarantees freedom of worship, of speech, of the press, of assembly, and to petition the government;
2 grants the right to keep and bear arms;
3 prohibits billeting of soldiers in private homes in peacetime;
4 forbids unreasonable search and seizure;
5 guarantees none be "deprived of life, liberty or property without due process of law" or compelled in any criminal case to be a witness against himself or herself;
6 grants the right to speedy trial, to call witnesses, and to have defense counsel;
7 grants the right to trial by jury of one's peers;
8 prevents the infliction of excessive bail or fines, or "cruel and unusual punishment";
9, 10 provide a safeguard to the states and people for all rights not specifically delegated to the central government.

Not originally part of the draft of the Constitution, the Bill of Rights was mooted during the period of ratification. Twelve amendments were proposed by Congress in 1789; the ten now called the Bill of Rights were ratified 1791.

Billy the Kid nickname of William H Bonney 1859–1881. US outlaw, a leader in the 1878 Lincoln County cattle war in New Mexico, who allegedly killed his first victim at 12 and was reputed to have killed 21 men by age 22, when he died.

Born in Brooklyn, New York, Bonney moved west with his family to Kansas and then New Mexico. He was sentenced to death for murdering a sheriff, but escaped (killing two guards), and was finally shot by Sheriff Pat Garrett while trying to avoid recapture.

Biloxi port in Mississippi; population (1990) 46,300. Chief occupations include tourism and seafood canning. Named after a local Indian people, Biloxi was founded 1719 by the French.

The city suffered heavy damage from Hurricane Camille 1969, but rebuilding was rapid.

bimetallic strip strip made from two metals each having a different coefficient of ⏢thermal expansion; it therefore bends when subjected to a change in temperature. Such strips are used widely for temperature measurement and control.

bimetallism monetary system in which two metals, traditionally gold and silver, both circulate at a ratio fixed by the state, are coined by the ⏢mint on equal terms, and are legal tender to any amount. The system was in use in the 19th century.

bimodal in statistics, having two distinct peaks of ⏢frequency distribution.

binary fission in biology, a form of ⏢asexual reproduction, whereby a single-celled organism, such as the ameba, divides into two smaller "daughter" cells. It can also occur in a few simple multicellular organisms, such as sea anemones, producing two smaller sea anemones of equal size.

binary number system or **binary number code** system of numbers to ⏢base two, using combinations of the digits 1 and 0. Binary numbers play a key role in digital computers, in which they form the basis of the internal coding of information, the values of ⏢bits (short for "binary digits") being represented as on/off (1 and 0) states of switches and high/low voltages in circuits.

The value of any position in a binary number increases by powers of 2 (doubles) with each move from right to left (1, 2, 4, 8, 16, and so on). For example, 1011 in the binary number system means $(1 \times 8) + (0 \times 4) + (1 \times 2) + (1 \times 1)$, which adds up to 11 in the decimal system.

binary search in computing, a rapid technique used to find any particular record in a list of records held in sequential order. The computer is programmed to compare the record sought with the record in the middle of the ordered list. This being done, the computer discards the half of the list in which the record does not appear, thereby reducing the number of records left to search by half. This process of selecting the middle record and discarding the unwanted half of the list is repeated until the required record is found.

binary star pair of stars moving in orbit around their common center of mass. Observations show that most stars are binary, or even multiple—for example, the nearest star system to the Sun, ⏢Alpha Centauri.

A *spectroscopic binary* is a binary in which two stars are so close together that they cannot be seen separately, but their separate light spectra can be distinguished by a spectroscope. Another type is the ⏢eclipsing binary.

binary weapon in chemical warfare, weapon consisting of two substances that in isolation are harmless but when mixed together form a poisonous nerve gas. They are loaded into the delivery system separately and combine after launch.

With conventional chemical weapons, chemical stockpiles deteriorate, unstable compounds break down, and the handling and security of such deadly compounds present serious problems to any country possessing them. The development of binary chemical weapons in the US served to minimize these risks, since the principle on which they are based is the combination of two individually harmless compounds into a deadly chemical agent only in the shell or bomb they are housed in, and then only when the projectile is armed or fired. This greatly reduces storage and handling problems.

binding energy in physics, the amount of energy needed to break the nucleus of an atom into the neutrons and protons of which it is made.

Bingham George Caleb 1811–1879. US painter. Born near Charlottesville, Virginia, he grew up in Missouri and studied at the Pennsylvania Academy of the Fine Arts 1837. After painting in New York and Washington, he returned to Missouri. The influence of the Hudson River School is evident in such frontier landscapes as *Fur Traders Descending the Missouri* 1845.

Bingham Hiram 1875–1919. US explorer and politician who from 1907 visited Latin America, discovering ⏢Machu Picchu, Vitcos, and other Inca settlements in Peru. He later entered politics, becoming a senator.

Binghamton city in S central New York where the Chenango River meets the Susquehanna River. Its industries include electronic, computer, and camera equipment and textiles. Johnson City and Endicott, directly to the W on the Susquehanna River, form the Triple Cities with Binghamton; population (1990) 53,000.

binoculars optical instrument for viewing an object in magnification with both eyes;

binoculars *The essential components of binoculars are objective lenses, eye pieces, and a system of prisms to invert and reverse the image.*

for example, field glasses and opera glasses. Binoculars consist of two telescopes containing lenses and prisms, which produce a stereoscopic effect as well as magnifying the image. Use of prisms has the effect of "folding" the light path, allowing for a compact design.

The first binocular telescope was constructed by the Dutch inventor Hans Lippershey (c. 1570–c. 1619), in 1608. Later development was largely due to the German Ernst Abbé (1840–1905) of Jena, who at the end of the 19th century designed prism binoculars that foreshadowed the instruments of today, in which not only magnification but also stereoscopic effect is obtained.

binomial in mathematics, an expression consisting of two terms, such as $a + b$ or $a - b$.

binomial system of nomenclature in biology, the system in which all organisms are identified by a two-part Latinized name. Devised by the biologist ◇Linnaeus, it is also known as the Linnaean system. The first name is capitalized and identifies the ◇genus; the second identifies the ◇species within that genus.

binturong shaggy-coated mammal *Arctitis binturong*, the largest member of the mongoose family, nearly 3 ft/1 m long excluding a long muscular tail with a prehensile tip. Mainly nocturnal and tree-dwelling, the binturong is found in the forests of SE Asia, feeding on fruit, eggs, and small animals.

biochemistry science concerned with the chemistry of living organisms: the structure and reactions of proteins (such as enzymes), nucleic acids, carbohydrates, and lipids.

Its study has led to an increased understanding of life processes, such as those by which organisms synthesize essential chemicals from food materials, store and generate energy, and pass on their characteristics through their genetic material. A great deal of medical research is concerned with the ways in which these processes are disrupted. Biochemistry also has applications in agriculture and in the food industry (for instance, in the use of enzymes).

biodegradable capable of being broken down by living organisms, principally bacteria and fungi. In biodegradable substances, such as food and sewage, the natural processes of decay lead to compaction and liquefaction, and to the release of nutrients that are then recycled by the ecosystem. Nonbiodegradable substances, such as glass, heavy metals, and most types of plastic, present serious problems of disposal.

bioeconomics theory put forward in 1979 by Chicago economist Gary Becker that the concepts of sociobiology apply also in economics. The competitiveness and self-interest built into human genes are said to make capitalism an effective economic system, whereas the selflessness and collectivism proclaimed as the socialist ideal are held to be contrary to human genetic makeup and to produce an ineffective system.

bioengineering the application of engineering to biology and medicine. Common applications include the design and use of artificial limbs, joints, and organs, including hip joints and heart valves.

biofeedback modification or control of a biological system by its results or effects. For example, a change in the position of ◇trophic level of one species affects all levels above it.

Many biological systems are controlled by negative feedback. When enough of the hormone thyroxine has been released into the blood, the hormone adjusts its own level by "switching off" the gland that produces it. In ecology, as the numbers in a species rise, the food supply available to each individual is reduced. This acts to reduce the population to a sustainable level.

biofeedback in medicine, the use of electrophysiological monitoring devices to "feed back" information about internal processes and thus facilitate conscious control. Developed in the US in the 1960s, independently by neurophysiologist Barbara Brown and neuropsychiatrist Joseph Kamiya, the technique is effective in alleviating hypertension and preventing associated organic and physiological dysfunctions.

biofuel any solid, liquid, or gaseous fuel produced from organic (once living) matter, either directly from plants or indirectly from industrial, commercial, domestic, or agricultural wastes. There are three main ways for the development of biofuels: the burning of dry organic wastes (such as household refuse, industrial and agricultural wastes, straw, wood, and peat); the fermentation of wet wastes (such as animal dung) in the absence of oxygen to produce biogas (containing up to 60% methane), or the fermentation of sugar cane or corn to produce alcohol; and energy forestry (producing fast-growing wood for fuel).

biogenesis biological term coined 1870 by T H Huxley to express the hypothesis that living matter always arises out of other similar forms of living matter. It superseded the opposite idea of ◇spontaneous generation or abiogenesis (that is, that living things may arise out of nonliving matter).

biogeography study of how and why plants and animals are distributed around the world, in the past as well as in the present; more specifically, a theory describing the geographical distribution of ◇species developed by Robert MacArthur and E O ◇Wilson. The theory argues that for many species, ecological specializations mean that suitable habitats are patchy in their occurrence. Thus for a dragonfly, ponds in which to breed are separated by large tracts of land, and for edelweiss adapted to alpine peaks the deep valleys between cannot be colonized.

biography account of a person's life. When it is written by that person, it is an ◇autobiography. Biography can be simply a factual narrative, but it was also established as a literary form in the 18th and 19th centuries. Among ancient biographers are Xenophon, Plutarch, Tacitus, Suetonius, and the authors of the Gospels of the New Testament. In the English language Lytton Strachey's *Eminent Victorians* opened the new era of frankness; 20th-century biographers include Richard Ellmann (James Joyce and Oscar Wilde), Michael Holroyd (1935–) (Lytton Strachey and George Bernard Shaw) and Elizabeth Longford (Queen Victoria and Wellington).

Medieval biography was mostly devoted to religious edification and produced chronicles of saints and martyrs; among the biographies of laymen are Einhard's *Charlemagne* and Asser's *Alfred*. In England true biography begins with the early Tudor period and such works as *Sir Thomas More* 1626, written by his son-in-law William Roper (1498–1578). By the 18th century it became a literary form

in its own right through Johnson's *Lives of the Most Eminent English Poets* 1779–81 and Boswell's biography of Johnson 1791. 19th-century biographers include Robert Southey, Elizabeth Gaskell, G H Lewes, J Morley, and Thomas Carlyle. The general tendency was to provide irrelevant detail and suppress the more personal facts.

The earliest **biographical dictionary** in the accepted sense was that of Pierre Bayle 1696, followed during the 19th century by the development of national biographies in Europe, and the foundation of the *English Dictionary of National Biography* 1882 and the *Dictionary of American Biography* 1928.

In the US, notable biographers include William Manchester (John F Kennedy and Douglas MacArthur), Leon Edel (Henry James), and Joseph Lash (Franklin and Eleanor Roosevelt and Helen Keller).

Bioko island in the Bight of Bonny, W Africa, part of Equatorial Guinea; area 786 sq mi/2,017 sq km; products include coffee, cacao, and copra; population (1983) 57,190. Formerly a Spanish possession, as *Fernando Po*, it was known 1973–79 as *Macías Nguema Bijogo*.

biological clock regular internal rhythm of activity, produced by unknown mechanisms, and not dependent on external time signals. Such clocks are known to exist in almost all animals, and also in many plants, fungi, and unicellular organisms. In higher organisms, there appears to be a series of clocks of graded importance. For example, although body temperature and activity cycles in human beings are normally "set" to 24 hours, the two cycles may vary independently, showing that two clock mechanisms are involved.

Exposing humans to bright light can change the biological clock and help, for example, people suffering from ◇seasonal affective disorder.

biological control control of pests such as insects and fungi through biological means, rather than the use of chemicals. This can include breeding resistant crop strains; inducing sterility in the pest; infecting the pest species with disease organisms; or introducing the pest's natural predator. Biological control tends to be naturally self-regulating, but as ecosystems are so complex, it is difficult to predict all the consequences of introducing a biological controlling agent.

The introduction of the cane toad to Australia 50 years ago to eradicate a beetle that was destroying sugar beet provides an example of the unpredictability of biological control. Since the cane toad is poisonous there are few Australian predators and it is now a pest, spreading throughout eastern and northern Australia at a rate of 22 mi/35 km a year.

biological oxygen demand (BOD) the amount of dissolved oxygen taken up by microorganisms in a sample of water. Since these microorganisms live by decomposing organic matter, and the amount of oxygen used is proportional to their number and metabolic rate, BOD can be used as a measure of the extent to which the water is polluted with organic compounds.

biological warfare the use of living organisms, or of infectious material derived from them, to bring about death or disease in humans, animals, or plants. At least ten countries have this capability.

biology: chronology

c. 500 BC	First studies of the structure and behavior of animals, by the Greek Alcmaeon of Creton.
c. 450	Hippocrates of Cos undertook the first detailed studies of human anatomy.
c. 350	Aristotle laid down the basic philosophy of the biological sciences and outlined a theory of evolution.
c. 300	Theophrastus carried out the first detailed studies of plants.
c. AD 175	Galen established the basic principles of anatomy and physiology.
c. 1500	Leonardo da Vinci studied human anatomy to improve his drawing ability and produced detailed anatomical drawings.
1628	William Harvey described the circulation of the blood and the function of the heart as a pump.
1665	Robert Hooke used a microscope to describe the cellular structure of plants.
1672	Marcelle Malphigi undertook the first studies in embryology by describing the development of a chicken egg.
1677	Anthony van Leeuwenhoek greatly improved the microscope and used it to describe spermatozoa as well as many microorganisms.
1682	Nehemiah Grew published the first textbook in botany.
1736	Carolus (Carl) Linnaeus published his systematic classification of plants, so establishing taxonomy.
1768–79	James Cook's voyages of discovery in the Pacific revealed an undreamed-of diversity of living species, prompting the development of theories to explain their origin.
1796	Edward Jenner established the practice of vaccination against smallpox, laying the foundations for theories of antibodies and immune reactions.
1809	Jean-Baptiste Lamarck advocated a theory of evolution through inheritance of acquired characters.
1839	Theodor Schwann proposed that all living matter is made up of cells.
1857	Louis Pasteur established that microorganisms are responsible for fermentation, creating the discipline of microbiology.
1859	Charles Darwin published *On the Origin of Species*, expounding his theory of the evolution of species by natural selection.
1866	Gregor Mendel pioneered the study of inheritance with his experiments on peas, but achieved little recognition.
1883	August Weismann proposed his theory of the continuity of the germ plasm.
1900	Mendel's work was rediscovered and the science of genetics founded.
1935	Konrad Lorenz published the first of many major studies of animal behavior, which founded the discipline of ethology.
1953	James Watson and Francis Crick described the molecular structure of the genetic material, DNA.
1964	William Hamilton recognized the importance of inclusive fitness, so paving the way for the development of sociobiology.
1975	Discovery of endogenous opiates (the brain's own painkillers) opened up a new phase in the study of brain chemistry.
1976	Har Gobind Khorana and his colleagues constructed the first artificial gene to function naturally when inserted into a bacterial cell, a major step in genetic engineering.
1982	Gene databases were established at Heidelberg, Germany, for the European Molecular Biology Laboratory, and at Los Alamos, for the US National Laboratories.
1985	The first human cancer gene, retinoblastoma, was isolated by researchers at the Massachusetts Eye and Ear Infirmary and the Whitehead Institute, Massachusetts.
1988	The Human Genome Organization (HUGO) was established in Washington, DC with the aim of mapping the complete sequence of DNA.

Biological warfare, together with ♢chemical warfare, was originally prohibited by the Geneva Protocol 1925, to which the United Nations has urged all states to adhere. Nevertheless research in this area continues; the Biological Weapons Convention 1972 permits research for defense purposes but does not define how this differs from offensive weapons development. In 1990 the US Department of Defense allocated $60 million to research, develop, and test defense systems. Advances in genetic engineering make the development of new varieties of potentially offensive biological weapons more likely.

biology science of life. Strictly speaking, biology includes all the life sciences—for example, anatomy and physiology, cytology, zoology and botany, ecology, genetics, biochemistry and biophysics, animal behavior, embryology, and plant breeding. During the 1990s an important focus of biological research will be the international Human Genome Project, which will attempt to map the entire genetic code contained in the 23 pairs of human chromosomes.

bioluminescence production of light by living organisms. It is a feature of many deep-sea fishes, crustaceans, and other marine animals. On land, bioluminescence is seen in some nocturnal insects such as glow-worms and fireflies, and in certain bacteria and fungi. Light is usually produced by the oxidation of luciferin, a reaction catalyzed by the ♢enzyme luciferase. This reaction is unique, being the only known biological oxidation that does not produce heat. Animal luminescence is involved in communication, camouflage, or the luring of prey, but its function in other organisms is unclear.

biomass the total mass of living organisms present in a given area. It may be specified for a particular species (such as earthworm biomass) or for a general category (such as herbivore biomass). Estimates also exist for the entire global plant biomass. Measurements of biomass can be used to study interactions between organisms, the stability of those interactions, and variations in population numbers.

biome broad natural assemblage of plants and animals shaped by common patterns of vegetation and climate. Examples include the tundra biome and the desert biome.

biomechanics study of natural structures to improve those produced by humans. For example, mother-of-pearl is structurally superior to fiberglass, and deer antlers have outstanding durability because they are composed of microscopic fibers. Such natural structures may form the basis of high-tech composites.

biometry literally, the measurement of living things, but generally used to mean the application of mathematics to biology. The term is now largely obsolete, since mathematical or statistical work is an integral part of most biological disciplines.

bionics (from "biological electronics") design and development of electronic or mechanical artificial systems that imitate those of living things. The bionic arm, for example, is an artificial limb (♢prosthesis) that uses electronics to amplify minute electrical signals generated in body muscles to work electric motors, which operate the joints of the fingers and wrist.

The first person to receive two bionic ears was Peter Stewart, an Australian journalist, 1989. His left ear was fitted with an array of 22 electrodes, replacing the hairs that naturally convert sounds into electrical impulses. Five years previously he had been fitted with a similar device in his right ear.

biophysics application of physical laws to the properties of living organisms. Examples include using the principles of ♢mechanics to calculate the strength of bones and muscles, and ♢thermodynamics to study plant and animal energetics.

biopsy removal of a living tissue sample from the body for diagnostic examination.

biorhythm rhythmic change, mediated by ♢hormones, in the physical state and activity patterns of certain plants and animals that have seasonal activities. Examples include winter hibernation, spring flowering or breeding, and periodic migration. The hormonal changes themselves are often a response to changes in day length (♢photoperiodism); they signal the time of year to the animal or plant. Other biorhythms are innate and continue even if external stimuli such as day length are removed. These include a 24-hour or ♢circadian rhythm, a 28-day or circalunar rhythm (corresponding to the phases of the Moon), and even a year-long rhythm in some organisms.

Such innate biorhythms are linked to an internal or ♢biological clock, whose mechanism is still poorly understood. Often both types of rhythm operate; thus many birds have a circalunar rhythm that prepares them for the breeding season, and a photoperiodic response. There is also a nonscientific and unproven theory that human activity is governed by three biorhythms: the *intellectual* (33 days), the *emotional* (28 days), and the *physical* (23 days). Certain days in each cycle are regarded as "critical," even more so if one such day coincides with that of another cycle.

biosensor device based on microelectronic

circuits that can directly measure medically significant variables for the purpose of diagnosis or monitoring treatment. One such device measures the blood sugar level of diabetics using a single drop of blood, and shows the result on a liquid crystal display within a few minutes.

biosphere the narrow zone that supports life on our planet. It is limited to the waters of the Earth, a fraction of its crust, and the lower regions of the atmosphere.

BioSphere 2 (BS2) ecological test project, a "planet in a bottle," in Arizona. Under a glass dome, several different habitats are recreated, with representatives of nearly 4,000 species, including eight humans, sealed in the biosphere for two years from summer 1991 to see how effectively recycling of air, water, and waste can work in an enclosed environment and whether a stable ecosystem can be created; ultimately BS2 is a prototype space colony.

BS2 is in fact not the second in a series: Earth itself is regarded as BioSphere 1. Experiments with biospheres that hold only relatively simple life forms have been carried out for decades, and a 21-day trial period 1989 that included humans preceded the construction of BS2. The sealed area covers a total of 3.5 acres. Habitats represented in it are tropical rainforest, salt marsh, desert, coral reef, and savanna, as well as a section for intensive agriculture. The people within will be entirely self-sufficient, except for electricity: solar panels to provide energy for cooling, heating, pumping, and lighting would have been too expensive, so there is a 3.7-megawatt power station on the outside. The biospherians also have a computer link with the outside world.

The cost of setting up and maintaining the project has been estimated at $100 million, some of which will be covered by paying visitors, who can view the inhabitants through the geodesic glass dome. It is run by a private company, Space Biospheres Ventures, with funding from an ecology-minded oil millionaire, Edward P Bass (1945–   ), and other investors who expect to find commercial applications for the techniques that are developed in the course of the project. The US space agency, NASA, is also monitoring BS2, hoping to acquire knowledge that can be utilized in building a base on Mars.

biosynthesis synthesis of organic chemicals from simple inorganic ones by living cells—for example, the conversion of carbon dioxide and water to glucose by plants during ♢photosynthesis. Other biosynthetic reactions produce cell constituents including proteins and fats.

biotechnology industrial use of living organisms to manufacture food, drugs, or other products. The brewing and baking industries have long relied on the yeast microorganism for ♢fermentation purposes, while the dairy industry employs a range of bacteria and fungi to convert milk into cheeses and yogurts. ♢Enzymes, whether extracted from cells or produced artificially, are central to most biotechnological applications.

Recent advances include ♢genetic engineering, in which single-celled organisms with modified ♢DNA are used to produce insulin and other drugs.

biotic factor organic variable affecting an ecosystem—for example, the changing population of elephants and its effect on the African savanna.

biotin or **vitamin H** vitamin of the B complex,

found in many different kinds of food; egg yolk, liver, legumes, and yeast contain large amounts.

biotite dark mica, $K(Mg, Fe)_3Al Si_3O_{10}(OH, F)_2$, a common silicate mineral It is colorless to silvery white with shiny surfaces, and like all micas, it splits into very thin flakes along its one perfect cleavage. Biotite is a mineral of igneous rocks such as granites, and metamorphic rocks such as schists and gneisses.

birch any tree of the genus *Betula*, including about 40 species found in cool temperate parts of the northern hemisphere. Birches grow rapidly, and their hard, beautiful wood is used for veneers and cabinet work.

Paper birch *B. papyrifera* is native to the N half of North America.

Birch John M 1918–1945. American Baptist missionary, commissioned by the US Air Force to carry out intelligence work behind the Chinese lines where he was killed by the communists; the US extreme right-wing *John Birch Society* 1958 is named after him.

bird backboned animal of the class Aves, the biggest group of land vertebrates, characterized by warm blood, feathers, wings, breathing through lungs, and egg-laying by the female. There are nearly 8,500 species of birds.

Birds are bipedal, with the front limb modified to form a wing and retaining only three digits. The heart has four chambers, and the body is maintained at a high temperature (about 106°F/41°C). Most birds fly, but some groups (such as ostriches) are flightless, and others include flightless members. Many communicate by sounds, or by visual displays, in connection with which many species are brightly colored, usually the males. Birds have highly developed patterns of instinctive behavior. Hearing and eyesight are well developed, but the sense of smell is usually poor. Typically the eggs are brooded in a nest and, on hatching, the young receive a period of parental care. The study of birds is called ♢ornithology.

Bird Isabella 1832–1904. British traveler and writer who wrote extensively of her journeys in the US, Persia, Tibet, Kurdistan, China, Japan, and Korea.

Her published works include *The Englishwoman in America* 1856, *A Lady's Life in the Rocky Mountains* 1874, *Unbeaten Tracks in Japan* 1880, *Among the Tibetans* 1894, and *Pictures from China* 1900. Her last great journey was made 1901 when she traveled over 1,000 mi/1,600 km in Morocco.

bird of paradise one of 40 species of crowlike birds, family Paradiseidae, native to New Guinea and neighboring islands. Females are drably colored, but the males have bright and elaborate plumage used in courtship display. Hunted almost to extinction for their plumage, they are now subject to conservation.

Birdseye Clarence 1886–1956. US inventor who pioneered food refrigeration processes. While working as a fur trader in Labrador 1912–16 he was struck by the ease with which food could be preserved in an Arctic climate. Back in the US he found that the same effect could be obtained by rapidly freezing prepared food between two refrigerated metal plates. To market his products he founded the General Sea Foods Co. 1924, which he sold to General Foods 1929.

Birendra Bir Bikram Shah Dev 1945–   . King of Nepal from 1972, when he succeeded his

father Mahendra; he was formally crowned 1975. King Birendra has overseen Nepal's return to multiparty politics and introduced a new constitution 1990.

Birmingham industrial city in the West Midlands, second largest city of the UK; population (1991 est) 934,900, metropolitan area 2,632,000. Industries include motor vehicles, machine tools, aerospace control systems, plastics, chemicals, and food.

features It is the site of the National Exhibition Center and Sports Arena. Aston University is linked to a ♢science park; a school of music and symphony orchestra; the art gallery has a Pre-Raphaelite collection; the repertory theater was founded 1913 by Sir Barry Jackson (1897–1961); since 1990 it has been the home of the ♢Royal Ballet; Symphony Hall (holding over 4,000) opened 1991.

history Lawn tennis was invented here. Sutton Park, in the residential suburb of Sutton Coldfield, has been a public country recreational area since the 16th century. As mayor, Joseph ♢Chamberlain carried out reforms in the 1870s.

Birmingham commercial and industrial city (iron, steel, chemicals, building materials, computers, cotton textiles) and largest city in Alabama; population (1990) 266,000.

Although the 55 ft/17 m statue of Vulcan (Roman god of the forge) still dominates the city from a nearby summit, US Steel shut down its works in what used to be the steelmaking center of the South. Settled 1813, Birmingham became notorious in the early 1960s for its enforcement of segregation, and the 1963 bombing of a church in which four black girls were killed aroused international attention. In 1979 the city, with a black majority population, elected a black mayor.

birth act of producing live young from within the body of female animals. Both viviparous and ovoviviparous animals give birth to young. In viviparous animals, embryos obtain nourishment from the mother via a ♢placenta or other means. In ovoviviparous animals, fertilized eggs develop and hatch in the oviduct of the mother and gain little or no nourishment from maternal tissues. See also ♢pregnancy.

birth control another name for ♢family planning; see also ♢contraceptive.

Birth of a Nation, The epic silent film about Reconstruction, the period after the American Civil War during which the US South was assimilated into the Union. Directed 1915 by D W ♢Griffith, it is widely considered the first cinematic masterpiece.

birth rate the number of live births per year per thousand of the population. Birth rate is a factor in ♢demographic transition. It is sometimes called *crude birth rate* because it takes in the whole population, including men and women who are too old to bear children.

Biscay, Bay of bay of the Atlantic Ocean between N Spain and W France, known for rough seas and exceptionally high tides.

Bishkek formerly *Pishpek* (until 1926) and *Frunze* (1926–92), capital of Kyrgyzstan; population (1987) 632,000. It produces textiles, farm machinery, metal goods, and tobacco.

bishop (Greek "overseer") priest next in rank to an archbishop in the Roman Catholic, Eastern Orthodox, Anglican or episcopal churches. A bishop has charge of a district called a *diocese*.

Originally bishops were chosen by the congregation, but in the Roman Catholic church they are appointed by the pope, although in some countries, such as Spain, the political authority nominates appointees. In the Eastern Orthodox church bishops are always monks. In the Church of England the prime minister selects bishops on the advice of the archbishop of Canterbury; when a diocese is very large, assistant (suffragan) bishops are appointed. Bishops are responsible for meeting to settle matters of belief or discipline; they ordain priests and administer confirmation (as well as baptism in the Orthodox church). In the Methodist and Lutheran churches the bishop's role is mostly that of a supervisory official. In 1989 Barbara Harris of the US Episcopalian church was elected the first woman bishop in the Anglican Communion.

Bishops with more limited authority have the highest rank in certain Lutheran denominations and in the Methodist church.

Bismarck capital of North Dakota, on the Missouri River in Burleigh county, in the S part of the state. It is a shipping point for the region's agricultural and livestock products from surrounding farms and for oil products from nearby oil wells; population (1990) 49,200. Serving as the capital of the Dakota Territory from 1883, it remained the capital when North Dakota became a state 1889. Named for German chancellor Otto von Bismarck, it was the terminus of the heavily German-funded Northern Pacific Railroad.

Bismarck Otto Eduard Leopold, Prince von 1815–1898. German politician, prime minister of Prussia 1862–90 and chancellor of the German Empire 1871–90. He pursued an aggressively expansionist policy, waging wars against Denmark 1863–64, Austria 1866, and France 1870–71, which brought about the unification of Germany.

Bismarck was ambitious to establish Prussia's leadership within Germany and eliminate the influence of Austria. He secured Austria's support for his successful war against Denmark then, in 1866, went to war against Austria and its allies (the ⟡Seven Weeks' War), his victory forcing Austria out of the German Bund and unifying the N German states into the North German Confederation under his own chancellorship 1867. He then defeated France, under Napoleon III, in the Franco-Prussian War 1870–71, proclaimed the German Empire 1871, and annexed Alsace-Lorraine. He tried to secure his work by the ⟡Triple Alliance 1881 with Austria and Italy but ran into difficulties at home with the Roman Catholic church and the socialist movement and was forced to resign by Wilhelm II March 18, 1890.

Bismarck Archipelago group of over 200 islands in SW Pacific Ocean, part of ⟡Papua New Guinea; area 19,200 sq mi/49,660 sq km. The largest island is New Britain.

bismuth hard, brittle, pinkish-white, metallic element, symbol Bi, atomic number 83, atomic weight 208.98. It has the highest atomic number of all the stable elements (the elements from atomic number 84 up are radioactive). Bismuth occurs in ores and occasionally as a free metal (⟡native metal). It is a poor conductor of heat and electricity, and is used in alloys of low melting point and in medical compounds to soothe gastric ulcers.

The name comes from the Latin *besemutum*, from the earlier German *Wismut*.

bison large, hoofed mammal of the bovine family. There are two species, both brown. The *European bison* or *wisent Bison bonasus*, of which only a few protected herds survive, is about 7 ft/2 m high and weighs up to 2,500 lb/1,100 kg. The *North American bison* (often known as "buffalo") *Bison bison* is slightly smaller, with a heavier mane and more sloping hindquarters. Formerly roaming the prairies in vast numbers, it was almost exterminated in the 19th century, but survives in protected areas.

Crossed with domestic cattle, the latter has produced a hardy hybrid, the "beefalo," producing a lean carcass on an economical grass diet.

Bissau capital and chief port of Guinea-Bissau, on an island at the mouth of the Geba river; population (1988) 125,000. Originally a fortified slave-trading center, Bissau became a free port 1869.

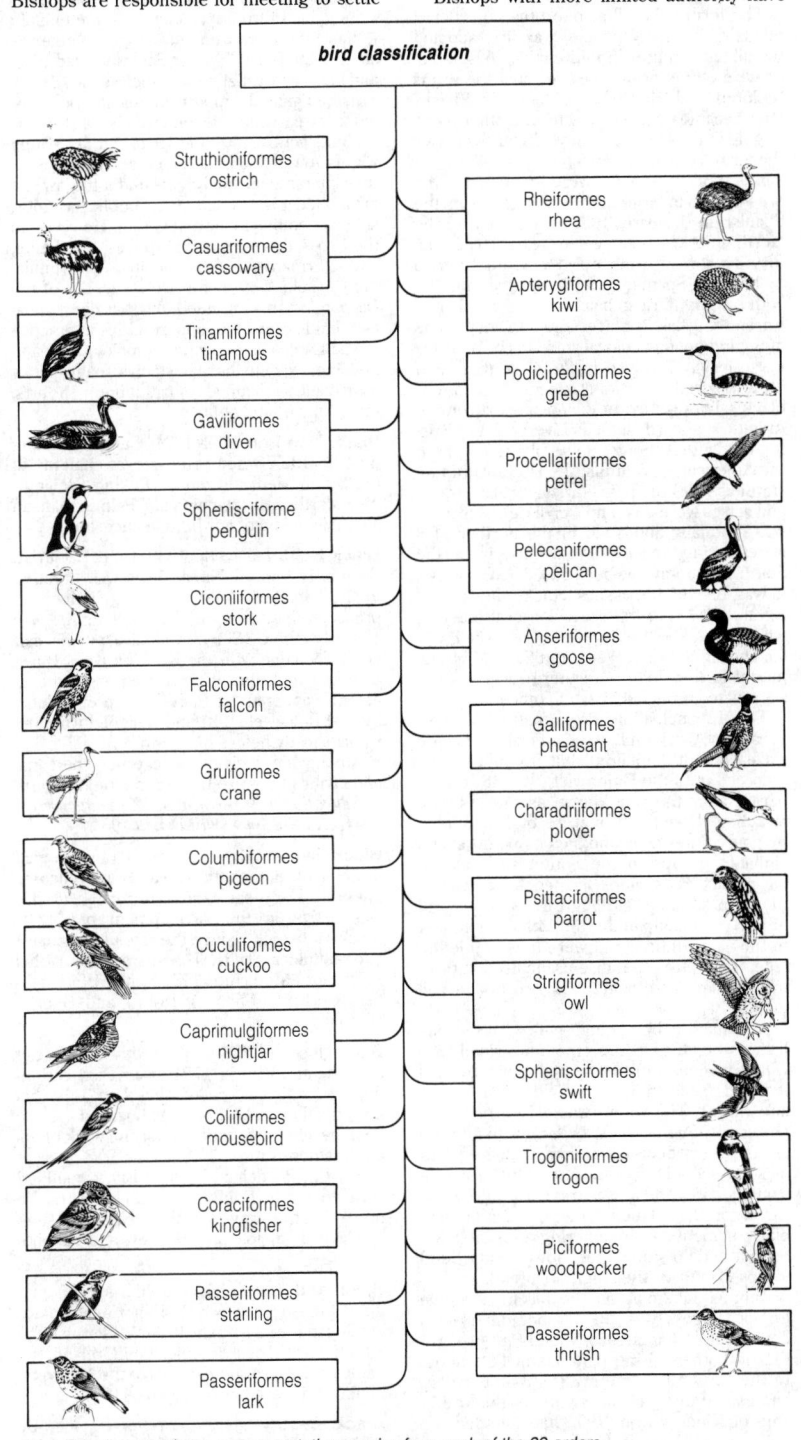

bird classification

Struthioniformes — ostrich	Rheiformes — rhea
Casuariiformes — cassowary	Apterygiformes — kiwi
Tinamiformes — tinamous	Podicipediformes — grebe
Gaviiformes — diver	Procellariiformes — petrel
Sphenisciforme — penguin	Pelecaniformes — pelican
Ciconiiformes — stork	Anseriformes — goose
Falconiformes — falcon	Galliformes — pheasant
Gruiformes — crane	Charadriiformes — plover
Columbiformes — pigeon	Psittaciformes — parrot
Cuculiformes — cuckoo	Strigiformes — owl
Caprimulgiformes — nightjar	Sphenisciformes — swift
Coliiformes — mousebird	Trogoniformes — trogon
Coraciformes — kingfisher	Piciformes — woodpecker
Passeriformes — starling	Passeriformes — thrush
Passeriformes — lark	

bird This diagram shows a representative species from each of the 29 orders.

bit in computing, the smallest unit of information; a binary digit or place in a binary number. A ⏵byte contains eight bits (four bits is sometimes called a nybble).

Microcomputers are often described according to how many bits of information they can handle at once—for instance, the Intel 8088 microprocessor used in the original IBM PC had an 8-bit data bus (it fetched one byte at a time from memory) and 16-bit internal registers (it could store and work on 2-byte numbers). The maximum number of bits that a computer normally processes is called a **word**.

The first microprocessor, the Intel 4004 launched 1971, was a 4-bit device. Business micros of the 1980s used 32-bit processors such as the Intel 80386 and Motorola 68030. In the 1990s 64-bit microprocessors first went into production.

Bithynia district of NW Asia that became a Roman province 74 BC.

bittern any of several small herons, in particular the common bittern *Botaurus stellaris* of Europe and Asia. It is shy, stoutly built, has a streaked camouflage pattern and a loud, booming call. An inhabitant of marshy country, it is now quite rare in Britain.

bitumen impure mixture of hydrocarbons, including such deposits as petroleum, asphalt, and natural gas, although sometimes the term is restricted to a soft kind of pitch resembling asphalt.

Solid bitumen may have arisen as a residue from the evaporation of petroleum. If evaporation took place from a pool or lake of petroleum, the residue might form a pitch or asphalt lake, such as Pitch Lake in Trinidad. Bitumen was used in ancient times as a mortar, and by the Egyptians for embalming.

bivalent in biology, a name given to the pair of homologous chromosomes during reduction division (⏵meiosis). In chemistry, the term is sometimes used to describe an element or group with a ⏵valency of two, although the term "divalent" is more common.

bivalve marine or freshwater mollusk whose body is enclosed between two shells hinged together by a ligament on the dorsal side of the body.

The shell is closed by strong "adductor" muscles. Ventrally, a retractile "foot" can be put out to assist movement in mud or sand. Two large platelike gills are used for breathing and also, with the ⏵cilia present on them, make a mechanism for collecting the small particles of food on which bivalves depend. The bivalves form one of the five classes of mollusks, the Lamellibranchiata, otherwise known as Bivalvia or Pelycypoda, containing about 8,000 species.

Bizet Georges (Alexandre César Léopold) 1838–1875. French composer of operas, among them *Les Pêcheurs de perles/The Pearl Fishers* 1863, and *La jolie Fille de Perth/The Fair Maid of Perth* 1866. He also wrote the concert overture *Patrie* and incidental music to Daudet's *L'Arlésienne*. His operatic masterpiece *Carmen* was produced a few months before his death 1875.

Björnson Björnstjerne 1832–1910. Norwegian novelist, playwright, poet, and journalist. His plays include *The Newly Married Couple* 1865 and *Beyond Human Power* 1883, dealing with politics and sexual morality. Among his novels is *In God's Way* 1889. Nobel Prize for Literature 1903.

black English term first used 1625 to describe West Africans, now used to refer to Africans south of the Sahara and to people of African descent living outside Africa. In some countries such as the UK (but not in North America) the term is sometimes also used for people originally from the Indian subcontinent, for Australian Aborigines, and peoples of Melanesia.

The term "black," at one time considered offensive by many people, was first adopted by militants in the US in the mid-1960s to emphasize ethnic pride; they rejected the terms "colored" and "Negro" as euphemistic. "Black" later became the preferred term in the US and largely in the UK. Currently, US blacks prefer the term "African American."

history Black Africans were first taken to the West Indies in large numbers as slaves by the Spanish in the early 16th century and to the North American mainland in the early 17th century. They were transported to South America by both the Spanish and Portuguese from the 16th century. African blacks were also taken to Europe to work as slaves and servants. Some of the indigenous coastal societies in W Africa were heavily involved in the slave trade and became wealthy on its proceeds. Sometimes, black sailors settled in European ports on the Atlantic seaboard, such as Liverpool and Bristol, England. Although some blacks fought in the American Revolution, the US Constitution (ratified 1788) did not redress the slave trade, and slaves were given no ⏵civil rights. Slavery was gradually abolished in the northern US states during the early 19th century, but as the South's economy had been based upon slavery, it was one of the issues concerning states' rights that led to the secession of the South, which provoked the American Civil War 1861–65. During the Civil War about 200,000 blacks fought in the Union (Northern) army, but in segregated units led by white officers.

The Emancipation Proclamation 1863 of President Abraham Lincoln officially freed the slaves (about 4 million), but it could not be enforced until the Union victory 1865 and the period after the war known as the ⏵Reconstruction. Freed slaves were often resented by poor whites as economic competitors, and vigilante groups in the South, such as the ⏵Ku Klux Klan were formed to intimidate them. In addition, although freed slaves had full US citizenship under the 14th Amendment to the Constitution, and were thus entitled to vote, they were often disenfranchised in practice by state and local literacy tests and poll taxes.

A "separate but equal" policy was established when the US Supreme Court ruled 1896 (*Plessy v. Ferguson*) that segregation was legal if equal facilities were provided for blacks and whites. The ruling was overturned 1954 (*Brown v. Board of Education*) with the Supreme Court decision outlawing segregation in state schools. This led to a historic confrontation in Little Rock, Arkansas, 1957 when Governor Orval Faubus attempted to prevent black students from entering Central High School, and President Eisenhower sent federal troops to enforce their right to attend.

Another landmark in the blacks' struggle for civil rights was the ⏵Montgomery bus boycott in Alabama 1955, which first brought Martin Luther ⏵King Jr to national attention. In the early 1960s the civil-rights movement had gained impetus, largely under the leadership of King, who in 1957 had founded the ⏵Southern Christian Leadership Conference

(SCLC), a coalition group advocating nonviolence. Moderate groups such as the National Association for the Advancement of Colored People (NAACP) had been active since early in the century; for the first time they were joined in large numbers by whites, in particular students, as in the historic march converging on Washington, DC 1963 from all over the US. At about this time, impatient with the lack of results gained through moderation, the militant ⏵Black Power movements began to emerge, such as the Black Panther Party founded 1966, and black separatist groups such as the ⏵Black Muslims gained support. Increasing pressure led to the passage of federal legislation, the Civil Rights acts of 1964 and 1968, and the Voting Rights Act of 1965, under President Johnson; they guaranteed equal rights under the law and prohibited discrimination in public facilities, schools, employment and voting. However, in the 1980s, despite some advances, legislation, and affirmative action (positive discrimination), blacks, who comprise some 12% of the US population, continued to suffer discrimination and inequality of opportunities in practice in such areas as education, employment, and housing. Despite these obstacles, many blacks have made substantial contributions in the arts, the sciences, and politics.

Black Davidson 1884–1934. Canadian anatomist. In 1927, when professor of anatomy at the Union Medical College, Peking (Beijing), he unearthed the remains of ⏵Peking man, an example of one of our human ancestors.

Black Hugo LaFayette 1886–1971. US jurist. Born in Harlan, Alabama, Black was admitted to the bar 1906. After serving as judge and prosecuting attorney in Birmingham, he was elected to the US Senate 1926. Despite his earlier association with the Ku Klux Klan, Black distinguished himself as a progressive populist. He was appointed to the US Supreme Court by F D Roosevelt 1937 and resigned from the Court shortly before his death.

Among his decisions concerning personal and civil rights were those rendered in *Board of Education v Barnette* 1943, *Korematsu v US* 1944, and *Gideon v Wainwright* 1963.

Black James 1924– . British physiologist, director of therapeutic research at Wellcome Laboratories (near London) from 1978. He was active in the development of ⏵beta-blockers (which reduce the rate of heartbeat) and antiulcer drugs. He shared the Nobel Prize for Medicine 1988 with US scientists Gertrude Elion (1918–) and George Hitchings (1905–).

Black Joseph 1728–1799. Scottish physicist and chemist who in 1754 discovered carbon dioxide (which he called "fixed air"). By his investigations in 1761 of latent heat and specific heat, he laid the foundation for the work of his pupil James Watt.

Born in Bordeaux, France, Black qualified as a doctor in Edinburgh. In chemistry, he prepared the way for the scientists Henry Cavendish, Joseph Priestley, and Antoine Lavoisier.

Black and Tans nickname of a special auxiliary force of the Royal Irish Constabulary employed by the British 1920–21 to combat the Sinn Féiners (Irish nationalists) in Ireland; the name derives from the colors of the uniforms, khaki with black hats and belts.

Black Beauty story of a horse's life, by Anna Sewell, published 1877. The book, which describes the experiences of the horse, Black Beauty, under many different owners, revived the genre of "animal autobiography" popular in the late 18th and early 19th centuries.

blackberry prickly shrub *Rubus fruticosus* of the rose family, closely allied to raspberries and dewberries, that is native to northern parts of Europe. It produces pink or white blossoms and edible, black, compound fruits.

The North American blackberry *R. allegheniensis* has white blossoms and grows wild in Canada and E US.

blackbird bird *Turdus merula* of the thrush family. The male is black with a yellow bill and eyelids, the female dark brown with a dark beak. About 10 in/25 cm long, it lays three to five blue-green eggs with brown spots. Its song is rich and flutelike.

Found across Europe and Asia, the blackbird adapts well to human presence and gardens, and is one of the most common British birds. North American "blackbirds" belong to a different family of birds, the Icteridae.

black body in physics, a hypothetical object that completely absorbs all thermal (heat) radiation striking it. It is also a perfect emitter of thermal radiation.

Although a black body is hypothetical, a practical approximation can be made by using a small hole in the wall of a constant-temperature enclosure. The radiation emitted by a black body is of all wavelengths, but with maximum radiation at a particular wavelength that depends on the body's temperature. As the temperature increases, the wavelength of maximum intensity becomes shorter (see ⟡Wien's law). The total energy emitted at all wavelengths is proportional to the fourth power of the temperature (see ⟡Stefan–Boltzmann law). Attempts to explain these facts failed until the development of ⟡quantum theory 1900.

black box popular name for the unit containing an airplane's flight and voice recorders. These monitor the plane's behavior and the crew's conversation, thus providing valuable clues to the cause of a disaster. The box is nearly indestructible and usually painted orange for easy recovery. The name also refers to any compact electronic device that can be quickly connected or disconnected as a unit.

The maritime equivalent is the *voyage recorder*, installed in ships from 1989. It has 350 sensors to record the performance of engines, pumps, navigation lights, alarms, radar, and hull stress.

Black Boy autobiography of the US left-wing writer Richard Wright, published 1945, that summarizes the black person's experience of growing up in the US.

blackbuck antelope *Antilope cervicapra* found in central and NW India. It is related to the gazelle, from which it differs in having spirally-twisted horns. The male is black above and white beneath, whereas the female and young are fawn-colored above. It is about 2.5 ft/76 cm in height.

blackcock large grouse *Lyrurus tetrix* found on moors and in open woods in N Europe and Asia. The male is mainly black with a lyre-shaped tail, and grows up to 1.7 ft/54 cm in height. The female is speckled brown and only 1.3 ft/40 cm tall.

Black Country central area of England, around and to the N of Birmingham. Heavily industrialized, it gained its name in the 19th century from its belching chimneys, but antipollution laws have changed its aspect.

blackcurrant variety of ⟡currant.

Black Death great epidemic of bubonic ⟡plague that ravaged Europe in the 14th century, killing between one-third and half of the population. The cause of the plague was the bacterium *Pasteurella pestis*, transmitted by fleas borne by migrating Asian black rats. The name Black Death was first used in England in the early 19th century.

black earth exceedingly fertile soil that covers a belt of land in NE North America, Europe, and Asia.

In Europe and Asia it extends from Bohemia through Hungary, Romania, S Russia, and Siberia, as far as Manchuria, having been deposited when the great inland ice sheets melted at the close of the last ⟡ice age. In North America, it extends from the Great Lakes E through New York State, having been deposited when the last glaciers melted from the terminal moraine.

black economy See ⟡underground economy.

Blackett Patrick Maynard Stuart, Baron Blackett 1897–1974. British physicist. He was awarded a Nobel Prize 1948 for work in cosmic radiation and his perfection of the Wilson cloud chamber.

blackfly plant-sucking insect, a type of ⟡aphid.

It is especially hungry for human blood in the NE of the US and attacks in May–July, during Blackfly Season.

Blackfoot member of a Plains ⟡American Indian people, some 10,000 in number and consisting of three subtribes: the Blackfoot proper, the Blood, and the Piegan, who live in Montana, and Saskatchewan and Alberta. They were skilled, horse-riding buffalo hunters until their territories were settled by Europeans. Their name derives from their black moccasins. Their language belongs to the Algonquian family.

Black Forest (German *Schwarzwald*) mountainous region of coniferous forest in Baden-Württemberg, W Germany. Bounded W and S by the Rhine, which separates it from the Vosges, it has an area of 1,800 sq mi/4,660 sq km and rises to 4,905 ft/1,493 m in the Feldberg. Parts of the forest have recently been affected by ⟡acid rain.

Black Friday day, Sept 24, 1869, on which Jay Gould (1836–1892) and James Fisk (1834–1872) stock manipulators, attempted to corner the gold market by trying to prevent the government from selling gold. President Grant refused to agree, but they spread the rumor that the president was opposed to the sales. George S Boutwell (1818–1905) with Grant's approval ordered the sale of $4 million in gold. The gold price plunged and many speculators were ruined. The two men made about $11 million.

Black Hawk or *Black Sparrow Hawk*; (Sauk name *Makataimeshekiakiak*). 1767–1838. Sauk Indian leader. He was born on the Rock River near present-day Rock Island, Illinois, and became a leading opponent of the cession of Indian lands to the US government. During the War of 1812, Black Hawk sided with the British and served under the Shawnee leader Tecumseh. After the war, he accompanied his people in their removal to Iowa. In 1832 he led a large contingent back to Illinois to resettle the Sauk homeland. Defeated by Illinois militia in the bloody "Black Hawk War," he was captured by the Illinois forces and permanently exiled to Iowa.

Black Hills mountains in the Dakotas and Wyoming. They occupy about 6,000 sq mi/15,500 sq km and rise to 7,242 ft/2,207 m at Harney Peak, South Dakota.

The Black Hills include a national forest and Mt Rushmore, which has the visages of four presidents (Washington, Jefferson, Lincoln, T Roosevelt) carved on a cliff face. Gold, discovered in 1874, is still mined here.

black hole object in space whose gravity is so great that nothing can escape from it, not even light. Thought to form when massive stars shrink at the ends of their lives, a black hole sucks in more matter, including other stars, from the space around it. Matter that falls into a black hole is squeezed to infinite density at the center of the hole. Black holes can be detected because gas falling toward them becomes so hot that it emits X-rays.

Satellites above the Earth's atmosphere have detected X-rays from a number of objects in our Galaxy that might be black holes. Massive black holes containing the mass of millions of stars are thought to lie at the centers of ⟡quasars. Microscopic black holes may have been formed in the chaotic conditions of the ⟡Big Bang. The English physicist Stephen ⟡Hawking has shown that such tiny black holes could "evaporate" and explode in a flash of energy.

Black Hole of Calcutta incident in Anglo-Indian history: according to tradition, the nawab (ruler) of Bengal confined 146 British prisoners on the night of June 20, 1756 in one small room, of whom only 23 allegedly survived. Later research reduced the death count to 43, assigning negligence rather than intention.

blackmail criminal offense of extorting money with menaces or threats of detrimental action, such as exposure of some misconduct on the part of the victim.

black market illegal trade in rationed or otherwise scarce goods (for example, food, gasoline, and clothing, during World War II and after).

Black Monday worldwide stockmarket crash that began Oct 19, 1987, prompted by the announcement of worse-than-expected US trade figures and the response by US Secretary of the Treasury, James Baker, who indicated that the sliding dollar needed to decline further. This caused a world panic as fears of the likely impact of a US recession were voiced by the major industrialized countries. Between Oct 19 and 23, the New York Stock Exchange fell by 33%, the London Stock Exchange Financial Times 100 Index by 25%, the European index by 17%, and Tokyo by 12%. The expected world recession did not occur; by the end of 1988 it was clear that the main effect had been a steadying in stock market activity and only a slight slowdown in world economic growth.

Black Mountain poets group of experimental US poets of the 1950s who were linked with Black Mountain College, a liberal arts college in North Carolina. They rejected the formalistic constraints of rhyme and meter. Leading members included Charles Olson (1910–1970) and Robert Creeley (1926–).

Blackmun Harry Andrew 1908– . US Supreme Court associate justice 1970– . A conservative in his early years on the Court, he became more moderate during the later part of his tenure.

Born in Nashville, Illinois, he received his law degree from Harvard Law School 1932, practiced law, taught at the University of Minnesota Law School 1945–47, and was judge of the US Court of Appeals of the 8th Circuit 1959–70. President Richard Nixon appointed him to the Supreme Court.

Black Muslim member of a religious group founded 1929 in the US and led, from 1934, by Elijah Mohammed (then Elijah Poole) (1897–1975) after he had a vision of ▷Allah. Its growth from 1946 as a black separatist organization was due to Malcolm X (1926–1965), the son of a Baptist minister who, in 1964, broke away and founded his own Organization for African-American Unity, preaching "active self-defense." Under the leadership of Louis Farrakhan, the movement underwent a recent revival.

black nationalism movement toward black separatism in the US during the 1960s; see ▷Black Power.

Black National State area in the Republic of South Africa set aside for development toward self-government by black Africans in accordance with ▷apartheid. Before 1980 these areas were known as *black homelands* or *bantustans*. They make up less than 14% of the country and tend to be in arid areas (though some have mineral wealth), and may be in scattered blocks. Those that achieved nominal independence are Transkei 1976, Bophuthatswana 1977, Venda 1979, and Ciskei 1981. They are not recognized outside South Africa because of their racial basis.

The repeal of the Land Acts and Group Areas Acts 1991 promises progressively to change the status of Black National States. Since the accession of President de Klerk, outbreaks of violence have resulted in the overthrow of the governments in Ciskei and Venda, and calls for reintegration within South Africa in all four states. Some 11 million blacks live permanently in the country's white-designated areas.

Blackpool seaside resort in Lancashire, England, 28 mi/45 km N of Liverpool; population (1981) 148,000. The largest vacation resort in N England, the amusement facilities include 7 mi/11 km of promenades, known for their "illuminations" of colored lights, funfairs, and a tower 500 ft/152 m high. Political party conferences are often held here.

Black Power movement toward black separatism in the US during the 1960s, embodied in the *Black Panther Party* founded 1966 by Huey Newton and Bobby Seale. Its declared aim was the establishment of a separate black state in the US established by a black plebiscite under the aegis of the United Nations. Following a National Black Political Convention 1972, a National Black Assembly was established to exercise pressure on the Democratic and Republican parties.

The Black Power concept arose when existing ▷civil rights organizations such as the National Association for Advancement of Colored People and the Southern Christian Leadership Conference were perceived to be ineffective in producing major change in the status of black people. Stokely Carmichael then advocated the exploitation of political and economic power and abandonment of nonviolence, with a move toward the type of separatism first developed by the ▷Black Muslims. Leaders such as Martin Luther King rejected this approach, but the Black Panther Party (so named because the panther, though

not generally aggressive, will fight to the death under attack) adopted it fully and, for a time, achieved nationwide influence.

Black Prince nickname of ▷Edward, Prince of Wales, eldest son of Edward III of England.

Black Sea (Russian **Chernoye More**) inland sea in SE Europe, linked with the seas of Azov and Marmara, and via the Dardanelles with the Mediterranean. Uranium deposits beneath it are among the world's largest. It is heavily polluted by agricultural fertilizers.

Black September guerrilla splinter group of the ▷Palestine Liberation Organization formed 1970. Operating from bases in Syria and Lebanon, it was responsible for the kidnappings at the Munich Olympics 1972 that led to the deaths of 11 Israelis, and more recent hijack and bomb attempts. The group is named after the month in which Palestinian guerrillas were expelled from Jordan by King Hussein.

Blackshirts term widely used to describe fascist paramilitary organizations. Originating with Mussolini's fascist Squadristi in the 1920s, it was also applied to the Nazi SS (*Schutzstaffel*) and to the followers of Oswald Mosley's British Union of Fascists.

blacksnake any of several species of snake. The blacksnake *Pseudechis porphyriacus* is a venomous snake of the cobra family found in damp forests and swamps in E Australia. The blacksnake *Coluber constrictor* from E US, is a relative of the European grass snake, growing up to 4 ft/1.2 m long, and without venom.

Blackstone William 1723–1780. English jurist who published his *Commentaries on the Laws of England* 1765–70. A lawyer from 1746, he became professor of law at Oxford 1758, and a justice of the Court of Common Pleas 1770.

Black Stone in Islam, the sacred stone built into the east corner of the ▷Kaaba which is a focal point of the *hajj*, or pilgrimage, to Mecca. There are a number of stories concerning its origin, one of which states that it was sent to Earth at the time of the first man, Adam; Mohammed declared that it was given to Abraham by Gabriel. It has been suggested that it is of meteoric origin.

blackthorn densely branched spiny European bush *Prunus spinosa*, family Rosaceae. It produces white blossom on black and leafless branches in early spring. Its sour, plumlike, blue-black fruit, the sloe, is used to make sloe gin.

Black Thursday day of the Wall Street stock market crash Oct 29, 1929, which precipitated the ▷Depression in the US and throughout the world.

Blackwell Elizabeth 1821–1910. English-born US physician, the first woman to qualify in medicine in the US 1849, and the first woman to be recognized as a qualified physician in the UK 1869.

Elizabeth Blackwell was taken to the US as a child. She studied at Geneva Medical School in New York State and then opened a private clinic in New York City. On her return to the UK 1869, she became the first woman to appear in the Medical Register. She was professor of gynecology at the London School of Medicine for Women 1875–1907.

Her example inspired many other aspiring female doctors.

black widow North American spider *Latrodectus mactans*. The male is small and

harmless, but the female is 0.5 in/1.3 cm long with a red patch below the abdomen and a powerful venomous bite. The bite causes pain and fever in human victims, but they usually recover.

bladder hollow elastic-walled organ in the ▷urinary systems of some fishes, most amphibians, some reptiles, and all mammals. Urine enters the bladder through two ureters, one leading from each kidney, and leaves it through the urethra.

bladderwort any of a large genus *Utricularia* of carnivorous aquatic plants of the family Lentibulariaceae. They have leaves with bladders that entrap small aquatic animals.

Blaine James Gillespie 1830–1893. US politician and diplomat. Born in West Brownsville, Pennsylvania, Blaine moved to Maine 1854. After serving in the state legislature 1858–62, he was elected to the US House of Representatives and became Speaker of the House 1868. He unsuccessfully sought the Republican presidential nomination 1876 and 1880 and served briefly as James Garfield's secretary of state. Gaining the Republican presidential nomination 1884, he was defeated by Democrat Grover Cleveland. During the Benjamin Harrison administration 1889–93, Blaine again served as secretary of state.

Blake William 1757–1827. English poet, artist, engraver, and visionary. His lyrics, as in *Songs of Innocence* 1789 and *Songs of Experience* 1794 express spiritual wisdom in radiant imagery and symbolism. Prophetic books like *The Marriage of Heaven and Hell* 1790, *America* 1793, and *Milton* 1804 yield their meaning to careful study. He created a new composite art form in engraving and hand-coloring his own works.

Blake was born in Soho, London, and apprenticed to an engraver 1771–78. He illustrated the Bible, works by Dante and Shakespeare, and his own poems. His figures are heavily muscled, with elongated proportions. In his later years he attracted a group of followers, including Samuel Palmer, who called themselves the Ancients. Henry Fuseli was another admirer. Blake's poem *Jerusalem* 1820 was set to music by Charles Parry (1848–1918).

Blakey Art. Muslim name Abdullah Ibn Buhaina 1919–1990. US jazz drummer and bandleader whose dynamic, innovative style made him one of the jazz greats. He contributed to the development of bebop in the 1940s and subsequently to hard bop, and formed the Jazz Messengers in the mid-1950s, continuing to lead the band for most of his life and discovering many talented musicians.

Blanche of Castile 1188–1252. Queen of France, wife of ▷Louis VIII of France, and regent for her son Louis IX (St Louis of France) from the death of her husband 1226 until Louis IX's majority 1234, and again from 1247 while he was on a Crusade.

She quelled a series of revolts by the barons and in 1229 negotiated the Treaty of Paris, by which Toulouse came under control of the monarchy.

blank verse in literature, the unrhymed iambic pentameter or ten-syllable line of five stresses. First used by the Italian Gian Giorgio Trissino in his tragedy *Sofonisba* 1514–15, it was introduced to England about 1540 by the Earl of Surrey, and developed by Christopher Marlowe. More recent exponents of blank verse in English include Thomas Hardy, T S Eliot, and Robert Frost.

After its introduction from Italy, blank verse was used with increasing freedom by Shakespeare, John Fletcher, John Webster, and Thomas Middleton. It was remodeled by Milton, who was imitated in the 18th century by James Thomson, Edward Young, and William Cowper; and revived in the early 19th century by Wordsworth, Shelley, and Keats, and later by Tennyson, Robert Browning, and Algernon Charles Swinburne.

Blanqui Louis Auguste 1805–1881. French revolutionary politician. He formulated the theory of the "dictatorship of the proletariat," used by Karl Marx, and spent a total of 33 years in prison for insurrection. Although in prison, he was elected president of the Commune of Paris 1871. His followers, the Blanquists, joined with the Marxists 1881.

Blantyre-Limbe chief industrial and commercial center of Malawi, in the Shire highlands; population (1987) 331,600. It produces tea, coffee, rubber, tobacco, and textiles.

It was formed by the union of the towns of Blantyre (named after the explorer Livingstone's birthplace) and Limbe 1959.

Blarney small town in County Cork, Republic of Ireland, possessing, inset in the wall of the 15th-century castle, the *Blarney Stone*, reputed to give persuasive speech to those kissing it.

blasphemy (Greek "evil-speaking") written or spoken insult directed against religious belief or sacred things with deliberate intent to outrage believers.

There are numerous laws in the US against blasphemy, but they are rarely, if ever, enforced.

blast furnace smelting furnace in which temperature is raised by the injection of an air blast. It is used to extract metals from their ores, chiefly pig iron from iron ore.

The principle has been known for thousands of years, but the present blast furnace is a heavy engineering development combining a number of special techniques.

blastocyst in mammals, a stage in the development of the ◊embryo that is roughly equivalent to the ◊blastula of other animal groups.

blastomere in biology, a cell formed in the first stages of embryonic development, after the splitting of the fertilized ovum, but before the formation of the ◊blastula or blastocyst.

blastula early stage in the development of a fertilized egg, when the egg changes from a solid mass of cells (the morula) to a hollow ball of cells (the blastula), containing a fluid-filled cavity (the blastocoel). See also ◊embryology.

Blaue Reiter, der ("the Blue Rider") group of German Expressionist painters based in Munich, some of whom had left *die ◊Brücke*. They were interested in the value of colors, in folk art, and in the necessity of painting "the inner, spiritual side of nature," but styles were highly varied. Wassily Kandinsky and Franz Marc published a book of their views 1912, and there were two exhibitions 1911, 1912.

Blavatsky Helena Petrovna (born Hahn) 1831–1891. Russian spiritualist and mystic, cofounder of the Theosophical Society (see ◊theosophy) 1875, which has its headquarters near Madras, India. In Tibet she underwent spiritual training and later became a Buddhist. Her books include *Isis Unveiled* 1877 and *The Secret Doctrine* 1888. She was declared

a fraud by the London Society for Psychical Research 1885.

bleaching decolorization of colored materials. The two main types of bleaching agent are the *oxidizing bleaches*, which bring about the ◊oxidation of pigments, and include the ultraviolet rays in sunshine, hydrogen peroxide, and chlorine in household bleaches; and the *reducing bleaches* including sulfur dioxide.

Bleaching processes have been known from antiquity, mainly those acting through sunlight. Both natural and synthetic pigments usually possess highly complex molecules, the color property often being due only to a part of the molecule. Bleaches usually attack only that small part, yielding another substance similar in chemical structure but colorless.

bleeding loss of blood from the circulation; see ◊hemorrhage.

blenny any fish of the family Blenniidae, mostly small fishes found near rocky shores, with elongated slimy bodies tapering from head to tail, no scales, and long pelvic fins set far forward.

Blériot Louis 1872–1936. French aviator who, in a 24-horsepower monoplane of his own construction, made the first flight across the English Channel on July 25, 1909.

blesbok African antelope *Damaliscus albifrons*, about 3 ft/1 m high, with curved horns, brownish body, and a white blaze on the face. It was seriously depleted in the wild at the end of the 19th century. A few protected herds survive in South Africa. It is farmed for meat.

Bligh William 1754–1817. English sailor who accompanied Captain James ◊Cook on his second voyage around the world 1772–74, and in 1787 commanded HMS *Bounty* on an expedition to the Pacific. On the return voyage the crew mutinied 1789, and Bligh was cast adrift in a boat with 18 men. He was appointed governor of New South Wales 1805, where his discipline again provoked a mutiny 1808 (the Rum Rebellion). He returned to Britain, and was made an admiral 1811.

Bligh went to Tahiti with the *Bounty* to collect breadfruit-tree specimens shortly before the mutiny, and gained the nickname "Breadfruit Bligh." In protest against harsh treatment, he and those of the crew who supported him were put in a small craft with no map and few provisions. They survived, after many weeks reaching Timor, near Java, having drifted 3,618 mi/5,822 km. Many of the crew members settled in the ◊Pitcairn Islands.

blight any of a number of plant diseases caused mainly by parasitic species of ◊fungus, which produce a whitish appearance on leaf and stem surfaces—for instance *potato blight* *Phytophthora infestans*. General damage caused by aphids or pollution is sometimes known as blight.

blimp airship: any self-propelled, lighter-than-air craft that can be steered. A blimp with a soft frame is also called a *dirigible*; a ◊*Zeppelin* is rigid-framed.

blindness complete absence or impairment of sight. It may be caused by heredity, accident, disease, or deterioration with age.

Education of the blind was begun by Valentin Haüy, who published a book with raised lettering 1784, and founded a school. Aids to the blind include the use of the ◊Braille and Moon alphabets in reading and writing. Guide dogs for the blind were first trained in Germany for soldiers blinded in World War 1.

Other aids now under development are electronic devices that convert print to recognizable mechanical speech; guide dogs; and flashlights.

blind spot area where the optic nerve and blood vessels pass through the retina of the ◊eye. No visual image can be formed as there are no light-sensitive cells in this part of the retina.

Blitzkrieg (German "lightning war") swift military campaign, as used by Germany at the beginning of World War II 1939–41. The abbreviated *Blitz* was applied to the attempted saturation bombing of London by the German air force between Sept 1940 and May 1941.

Blitzstein Marc 1905–1964. US composer. Born in Philadelphia, he was a child prodigy as a pianist at the age of six. He served with the US Army 8th Air Force 1942–45, for which he wrote *The Airborne* 1946, a choral symphony. His operas include *The Cradle Will Rock* 1937.

Blixen Karen, born Karen Dinesen 1885–1962. Danish writer. Her autobiography *Out of Africa* 1937 is based on her experience of running a coffee plantation in Kenya. She wrote fiction, mainly in English, under the adopted name Isak Dinesen.

BL Lacertae object starlike object that forms the center of a distant galaxy, with a prodigious energy output. BL Lac objects, as they are called, seem to be related to ◊quasars and are thought to be the brilliant nuclei of elliptical galaxies. They are so named because the first to be discovered lies in the small constellation Lacerta.

bloc (French) group, generally used to describe politically allied countries, as in the former "Soviet bloc."

Bloch Ernest 1880–1959. Swiss-born US composer. Among his works are the lyrical drama *Macbeth* 1910, *Schelomo* for cello and orchestra 1916, five string quartets, and *Suite Hébraique*, for viola and orchestra 1953. He often used themes based on Jewish liturgical music and folk song.

Born in Geneva, Switzerland, he went to the US in 1916 and became founder-director of the Cleveland Institute of Music 1920–25.

Bloch Felix 1905–1983. Swiss-US physicist who invented the analytical technique of nuclear magnetic resonance (NMR) ◊spectroscopy 1946. For this work he shared the Nobel Prize for Physics 1952 with US physicist Edward Purcell (1912–).

He was born in Zürich, and was professor of physics at Stanford University, 1934–71.

Bloch Konrad 1912– . German-born US chemist whose research concerned cholesterol. Making use of the ◊radioisotope carbon-14 (the radioactive form of carbon), Bloch was able to follow the complex steps by which the body chemically transforms acetic acid into cholesterol. For his work in this field Bloch shared the 1964 Nobel Prize for Medicine with Feodor Lynen (1911–1979).

blockade cutting-off of a place by hostile forces by land, sea, or air so as to prevent any movement to or fro, in order to compel a surrender without attack or to achieve some other political aim (for example, the ◊Berlin blockade 1948).

During World War I Germany attempted to blockade Britain with intensive submarine warfare, and Britain attempted to blockade Germany. In 1990 a blockade by United Nations member countries was agreed in an attempt to force Iraq to withdraw from the invaded territory of Kuwait, but was superseded by open war.

No nation has the right to declare a blockade unless it has the power to enforce it, according to international law. The Declaration of London 1909 laid down that a blockade must not be extended beyond the coasts and ports belonging to or occupied by an enemy.

block and tackle type of ⟡pulley.

Bloemfontein capital of the Orange Free State and judicial capital of the Republic of South Africa; population (1985) 204,000. Founded 1846, the city produces canned fruit, glassware, furniture, and plastics.

Blois town on the river Loire in central France; population (1983) 49,500. It has a château partly dating from the 13th century.

Blok Alexander Alexandrovich 1880–1921. Russian poet who, as a follower of the French Symbolist movement, used words for their symbolic rather than actual meaning. He backed the 1917 Revolution, as in his poems *The Twelve* 1918, and *The Scythians* 1918, the latter appealing to the West to join in the revolution.

blood liquid circulating in the arteries, veins, and capillaries of vertebrate animals; the term also refers to the corresponding fluid in those invertebrates that possess a closed ⟡circulatory system. Blood carries nutrients and oxygen to individual cells and removes waste products, such as carbon dioxide. It is also important in the immune response and, in many animals, in the distribution of heat throughout the body.

In humans it makes up 5% of the body weight, occupying a volume of 10 pt/5.5 l in the average adult. It consists of a colorless, transparent liquid called *plasma*, containing microscopic cells of three main varieties. **Red cells** (erythrocytes) form nearly half the volume of the blood, with 5 billion cells per liter. Their red color is caused by ⟡hemoglobin. **White cells** (leukocytes) are of various kinds. Some (phagocytes) ingest invading bacteria and so protect the body from disease; these also help to repair injured tissues. Others (lymphocytes) produce antibodies, which help provide immunity. Blood **platelets** (thrombocytes) assist in the clotting of blood.

Blood cells constantly wear out and die, and are replaced from the bone marrow. Dissolved in the plasma are salts, proteins, sugars, fats, hormones, and fibrinogen, which are transported around the body, the last having a role in clotting.

Blood and Iron (German *Blut und Eisen*) description of the methods used by German chancellor ⟡Bismarck to unify Germany 1862–1871. The phrase came from Bismarck's speech in which he declared that "the great questions of the day will be decided, not by speeches and majority votes ... but by iron and blood."

blood–brain barrier theoretical term for the defense mechanism that prevents many substances circulating in the bloodstream (including some germs) from invading the brain.

The blood–brain barrier is not a single entity, but a defensive complex comprising various physical features and chemical reactions to do with the permeability of cells. It ensures that "foreign" proteins, carried in the blood vessels supplying the brain, do not breach the vessel walls and enter the brain tissue. Many drugs are unable to cross the blood–brain barrier.

blood group any of the blood groups into which blood is classified according to antigenic activity. Red blood cells of one individual may carry molecules on their surface that act as ⟡antigens in another individual whose red blood cells lack these molecules. The two main antigens are designated A and B. These give rise to four blood groups: having A only (A), having B only (B), having both (AB), and having neither (O). Each of these groups may or may not contain the ⟡rhesus factor. Correct typing of blood groups is vital in transfusion, since incompatible types of donor and recipient blood will result in blood clotting, with possible death of the recipient.

These ABO blood groups were first described by Karl ⟡Landsteiner 1902. Subsequent research revealed at least 14 main types of blood groupings, 11 of which are involved with induced ⟡antibody production. Blood typing is also of importance in forensic medicine, cases of disputed paternity, and in anthropological studies.

bloodhound ancient breed of dog. Black and tan in color, it has long, pendulous ears and distinctive wrinkled head and face. It grows to a height of about 26 in/65 cm at the shoulder. The breed originated as a hunting dog in Belgium in the Middle Ages, and its excellent powers of scent have been employed in tracking and criminal detection from very early times.

blood poisoning condition in which poisons are spread throughout the body by ⟡pathogens in the bloodstream.

blood pressure pressure, or tension, of the blood against the inner walls of blood vessels, especially the arteries, due to the muscular pumping activity of the heart. Abnormally high blood pressure (see ⟡hypertension) may be associated with various conditions or arise with no obvious cause; abnormally low blood pressure (hypotension) occurs in ⟡shock and after excessive fluid or blood loss from any cause.

In mammals, the left ventricle of the ⟡heart pumps blood into the arterial system. This pumping is assisted by waves of muscular contraction by the arteries themselves, but resisted by the elasticity of the inner and outer walls of the same arteries. Pressure is greatest when the heart ventricle contracts (*systolic pressure*) and least when the ventricle is filling up with blood and pressure is solely maintained by the elasticity of the arteries (*diastolic pressure*). Blood pressure is measured in millimeters of mercury (the height of a column on the measuring instrument, a sphygmomanometer). Normal human blood pressure is around 120/80 mm Hg; the first number represents the systolic pressure and the second the diastolic. Large deviations from this figure usually indicate ill health.

blood test laboratory evaluation of a blood sample. There are numerous blood tests, from simple typing to establish the ⟡blood group to sophisticated biochemical assays of substances, such as hormones, present in the blood only in minute quantities.

The majority of tests fall into one of three categories: *haematology* (testing the state of the blood itself), *microbiology* (identifying infection), and *blood chemistry* (reflecting chemical events elsewhere in the body). Before operations, a common test is haemoglobin estimation to determine how well a patient might tolerate blood loss during surgery.

blood transfusion see ⟡transfusion.

blood vessel specialized tube that carries blood around the body of multicellular animals. Blood vessels are highly evolved in vertebrates, where the three main types–the arteries, veins, and capillaries–are all adapted for their particular role within the body.

bloom whitish powdery or waxlike coating over the surface of certain fruits that easily rubs off when handled. It often contains ⟡yeasts that live on the sugars in the fruit. The term bloom is also used to describe a rapid increase in number of certain species of algae found in lakes, ponds, and oceans.

Such blooms may be natural but are often the result of nitrate pollution, in which artificial fertilizers, applied to surrounding fields, leach out into the waterways. This type of bloom can lead to the death of almost every other organism in the water; because light cannot penetrate the algal growth, the plants beneath can no longer photosynthesize and therefore do not release oxygen into the water. Only those organisms that are adapted to very low levels of oxygen survive.

Bloom Claire 1931– . British film actress, who first made her reputation on the stage in Shakespearean roles. Her films include *Richard III* 1956 and *The Brothers Karamazov* 1958; television appearances include *Brideshead Revisited* 1980.

Bloomer Amelia Jenks 1818–1894. US campaigner for women's rights. In 1849, when unwieldy crinolines were the fashion, she introduced a knee-length skirt combined with loose trousers gathered at the ankles, which became known as *bloomers* (also called "rational dress"). She published the magazine *The Lily* 1849–54, which campaigned for women's rights and dress reform, and lectured with Susan B ⟡Anthony in New York.

Bloomington city in S central Indiana SW of Indianapolis; seat of Monroe county. It is an exporter of limestone from nearby quarries. It is also a center for the manufacture of electrical products and elevators. Indiana University 1820 is located here; population (1990) 42,100.

Bloomington city in central Illinois, SE of Peoria; seat of McLean county. It is in the middle of a rich farming and livestock raising area. Illinois Wesleyan University 1850 is located here; population (1990) 42,200.

Bloomsbury Group group of writers and artists based in Bloomsbury, London, UK. The group included the artists Duncan ⟡Grant and Vanessa Bell, and the writers Lytton ⟡Strachey and Leonard (1880–1969) and Virginia ⟡Woolf.

blowfly any fly of the genus *Calliphora*, also known as bluebottle, or of the related genus *Lucilia*, when it is greenbottle. It lays its eggs in dead flesh, on which the maggots feed.

blubber thick layer of ⟡fat under the skin of marine mammals, which provides an energy store and an effective insulating layer, preventing the loss of body heat to the surrounding water. Blubber has been used (when boiled down) in engineering, food processing, cosmetics, and printing, but all of these products can now be produced synthetically, thus saving the lives of animals.

Blücher Gebhard Leberecht von 1742–1819. Prussian general and field marshal, popularly known as "Marshal Forward." He took an active part in the patriotic movement, and in the War of German Liberation defeated the French as commander in chief at Leipzig 1813, crossed the Rhine to Paris 1814, and was made prince of Wahlstadt (Silesia).

In 1815 he was defeated by Napoleon at Ligny but came to the aid of British commander Wellington at ▷Waterloo.

Bluebeard folktale character, popularized by the writer Charles Perrault in France about 1697, and historically identified with Gilles de ▷Rais. Bluebeard murdered six wives for disobeying his command not to enter a locked room, but was himself killed before he could murder the seventh.

blueberry any of various North American acid-soil shrubs of the genus *Vaccinium* of the heath family. The genus also includes huckleberries, bilberries, deerberries, and cranberries, many of which resemble each other and are difficult to distinguish from blueberries. All have small, elliptical short-stalked leaves, slender green or reddish twigs, and whitish bell-like blossoms. Only true blueberries, however, have tiny granular speckles on their twigs. Blueberries have black or blue edible fruits, often covered with a white powder.

bluebird three species of a North American bird, genus *Sialia*, belonging to the thrush subfamily, Turdinae. The eastern bluebird *Sialia sialis* is regarded as the herald of spring. About 7 in/18 cm long, it has a reddish breast, the upper plumage being sky-blue, and a distinctive song.

bluebuck any of several species of antelope, including the blue ▷duiker *Cephalophus monticola* of South Africa, about 13 in/33 cm high. The male of the Indian ▷nilgai antelope is also known as the bluebuck.

The bluebuck or blaubok, *Hippotragus leucophaeus*, was a large blue-gray South African antelope. Once abundant, it was hunted to extinction, the last being shot 1800.

bluegrass dense, spreading grass of the genus *Poa*, which is blue tinted and grows in clumps. Various species are known from the northern hemisphere. Kentucky bluegrass *P. pratensis*, introduced to the US from Europe, provides pasture for horses.

blue-green algae or *cyanobacteria* single-celled, primitive organisms that resemble bacteria in their internal cell organization, sometimes joined together in colonies or filaments. Blue-green algae are among the oldest known living organisms and, with bacteria, belong to the kingdom Monera; remains have been found in rocks up to 3.5 billion years old. They are widely distributed in aquatic habitats, on the damp surfaces of rocks and trees, and in the soil.

Blue-green algae and bacteria are prokaryotic organisms. Some can fix nitrogen and thus are necessary to the nitrogen cycle, while others follow a symbiotic existence—for example, living in association with fungi to form lichens. Fresh water can become polluted by nitrates and phosphates from fertilizers and detergents. This eutrophication, or overenrichment, of the water causes multiplication of the algae in the form of algae blooms. The algae multiply and cover the water's surface, remaining harmless until they give off toxins as they decay. These toxins kill fish and other wildlife and can be harmful to domestic animals, cattle, and people.

blue gum either of two Australian trees: Tasmanian blue gum *Eucalyptus globulus* of the myrtle family, with bluish bark, a chief source of eucalyptus oil; or Sydney blue gum *E. saligna*, a tall, straight tree. The former is cultivated extensively in California and has also been planted in South America, India, parts of Africa, and S Europe.

Blue Mountains part of the ▷Great Dividing Range, New South Wales, Australia, ranging 2,000–3,600 ft/600–1,100 m and blocking Sydney from the interior until the crossing 1813 by surveyor William Lawson, Gregory Blaxland, and William Wentworth.

Blue Nile (Arabic *Bahr el Azraq*) river rising in the mountains of Ethiopia. Flowing W then N for 1,250 mi/2,000 km, it eventually meets the White Nile at Khartoum. The river is dammed at Roseires where a hydroelectric scheme produces 70% of Sudan's electricity.

blueprint photographic process used for copying engineering drawings and architectural plans, so called because it produces a white copy of the original against a blue background.

The plan to be copied is made on transparent tracing paper, which is placed in contact with paper sensitized with a mixture of iron ammonium citrate and potassium hexacyanoferrate. The paper is exposed to ▷ultraviolet radiation and then washed in water. Where the light reaches the paper, it turns blue (Prussian blue). The paper underneath the lines of the drawing is unaffected, so remains white.

Blue Ridge Mountains range extending from West Virginia to Georgia, and including Mount Mitchell 6,712 ft/2,045 m; part of the ▷Appalachians.

blues African-American music that originated in the rural American South in the late 19th century, characterized by a 12-bar construction and frequently melancholy lyrics. Blues guitar and vocal styles have played a vital part in the development of jazz and pop music in general.

1920s–1930s The *rural* or *delta blues* was usually performed solo with guitar or harmonica, by such artists as Robert Johnson (1911–1938) and Bukka White (1906–1977), but the earliest recorded style, *classic blues*, by such musicians as W C Handy (1873–1958) and Bessie Smith (1894–1937), was sung with a small band.

1940s–1950s The *urban blues*, using electric amplification, emerged in the northern cities, chiefly Chicago. As exemplified by Howlin' Wolf (adopted name of Chester Burnett, 1910–1976), Muddy Waters (adopted name of McKinley Morganfield, 1915–1983), and John Lee Hooker (1917–   ), urban blues became *rhythm and blues*.

1960s The jazz-influenced guitar style of B B King (1925–   ) inspired many musicians of the *British blues boom*, including Eric Clapton (1945–   ).

1980s The "blues *noir*" of Robert Cray (1953–   ) found a wide audience.

blue shift in astronomy, a manifestation of the ▷Doppler effect in which an object appears bluer when it is moving toward the observer or the observer is moving toward it (blue light is of a higher frequency than other colors in the spectrum). The blue shift is the opposite of the ▷red shift.

Blum Léon 1872–1950. French politician. He was converted to socialism by the ▷Dreyfus affair 1899 and in 1936 became the first socialist prime minister of France. He was again premier for a few weeks 1938. Imprisoned under the ▷Vichy government 1942 as a danger to French security, he was released by the Allies 1945. He again became premier for a few weeks 1946.

Blunt Anthony 1907–1983. British art historian and double agent. As a Cambridge lecturer, he recruited for the Soviet secret service and, as a member of the British secret service 1940–45, passed information to the USSR. In 1951 he assisted the defection to the USSR of the British agents Guy ▷Burgess and Donald Maclean (1913–1983). He was the author of many respected works on French and Italian art. Unmasked 1964, he was given immunity after his confession.

boa any of various nonvenomous snakes of the family Boidae, found mainly in tropical and subtropical parts of the New World. Boas feed mainly on small mammals and birds. They catch these in their teeth or kill them by constriction (crushing the creature within their coils until it suffocates). The boa constrictor *Constrictor constrictor* can grow up to 18.5 ft/5.5 m long, but rarely reaches more than 12 ft/4 m. Other boas include the anaconda and the emerald tree boa *Boa canina*, about 6 ft/2 m long and bright green.

Some small burrowing boas live in N Africa and W Asia, while other species live on Madagascar and some Pacific islands, but the majority of boas live in South and Central America. The name boa is sometimes used loosely to include the pythons of the Old World, which also belong to the Boidae family, and which share with boas vestiges of hind limbs and constricting habits.

Boadicea alternate spelling of British queen ▷Boudicca.

boar wild member of the pig family, such as the Eurasian wild boar *Sus scrofa*, from which domestic pig breeds derive. The wild boar is sturdily built, being 4.5 ft/1.5 m long and 3 ft/1 m high, and possesses formidable tusks. Of gregarious nature and mainly woodland-dwelling, it feeds on roots, nuts, insects, and some carrion.

The dark coat of the adult boar is made up of coarse bristles with varying amounts of underfur, but the young are striped. The male domestic pig is also known as a boar, the female as a sow.

Boas Franz 1858–1942. German-born US anthropologist. Joining the faculty of Clark University 1888, Boas became one of America's first academic anthropologists; he stressed the need to study "four fields"—ethnology, linguistics, physical anthropology, and archeology—before generalizations might be made about any one culture or comparisons about any number of cultures.

boat people illegal emigrants traveling by sea, especially those Vietnamese who left their country after the takeover of South Vietnam 1975 by North Vietnam. Some 160,000 Vietnamese fled to Hong Kong, many being attacked at sea by Thai pirates, and in 1989 50,000 remained there in cramped, squalid refugee camps. The UK government began forced repatriation 1990.

Some 500,000 SE Asians became refugees in this way 1975–82 with an estimated 10%–15% mortality rate. Only 10% of those who have arrived in Hong Kong since the policy of "screening" (questioning about reasons for leaving Vietnam) began 1988 have been given refugee status; the others are classified as "economic migrants." In 1990 the total number of boat people in SE Asia was about 90,000, an increase of 30,000 from 1988.

The term "boat people" has also been used for Cuban and Haitian refugees who reach Florida, by boat. More than 2,400 entered the US from Cuba in 1991.

bobcat cat *Felis rufa* living in a variety of habitats from S Canada through to S Mexico. It is similar to the lynx, but only 2.5 ft/75 cm long, with reddish fur and less well-developed ear tufts.

bobolink North American songbird *Dolichonyx oryzivorus*, which takes its common name from the distinctive call of the male. Breeding males are mostly black, with a white rump. Breeding females are buff-colored with dark streaks. Bobolinks are about 7 in/18 cm long, and build their nests on the ground in hayfields and weedy meadows.

Bobruisk town in the Republic of Belarus, on the Beresina River; population (1987) 232,000. Industries include timber, machinery, tires, and chemicals.

bobsledding the sport of racing steel-bodied, steerable toboggans, crewed by two or four people, down mountain ice-chutes at speeds of up to 80 mph/130 kph. It was introduced as an Olympic event in 1924, and world championships have been held every year since 1931. Included among the major bobsledding events are the Olympic Championships (the four-crew event was introduced at the 1924 Winter Olympics and the two-crew in 1932); also the World Championships, the four-crew championship introduced in 1924 and the two-crew in 1931; in Olympic years winners automatically become world champions.

Boca Raton city in SE Florida on the Atlantic Ocean, N of Miami. Although it is mainly a resort and residential area, there is some light industry; population (1990) 61,500.

Boccaccio Giovanni 1313–1375. Italian poet, chiefly known for the collection of tales called the ⟨⟩*Decameron* 1348–53.

Son of a Florentine merchant, he lived in Naples 1328–41, where he fell in love with the unfaithful "Fiammetta" who inspired his early poetry. Before returning to Florence 1341 he had written *Filostrato* and *Teseide* (used by Chaucer in his *Troilus and Criseyde* and *Knight's Tale*). He was much influenced by ⟨⟩Petrarch, whom he met 1350.

Boccherini (Ridolfo) Luigi 1743–1805. Italian composer and cellist. He studied in Rome, made his mark in Paris 1768, and was court composer in Prussia and Spain. Boccherini composed some 350 instrumental works, an opera, and oratorios.

Boccioni Umberto 1882–1916. Italian painter and sculptor. One of the founders of ⟨⟩Futurism, he was a pioneer of abstract art.

Bochum town in the Ruhr district, Germany; population (1988) 381,000. Industries include metallurgy, vehicles, and chemicals.

Böcklin Arnold 1827–1901. Swiss Romantic painter. His mainly imaginary landscapes have a dreamlike atmosphere: for example, *Island of the Dead* 1880 (Metropolitan Museum of Art, New York).

He was strongly attracted to Italy and lived for years in Rome. Many of his paintings are peopled with mythical beings, such as nymphs and naiads.

Bode Johann Elert 1747–1826. German astronomer, director of the Berlin observatory. He published the first atlas of all stars visible to

the naked eye, *Uranographia* 1801, and devised Bode's Law.

Bodensee German name for Lake ⟨⟩Constance, N of the Alps.

Bode's law numerical sequence that gives the approximate distances, in astronomical units (distance between Earth and Sun = one astronomical unit), of the planets from the Sun by adding 4 to each term of the series 0, 3, 6, 12, 24, ... and then dividing by 10. Bode's law predicted the existence of a planet between ⟨⟩Mars and ⟨⟩Jupiter, which led to the discovery of the asteroids.

The "law" breaks down for ⟨⟩Neptune and ⟨⟩Pluto. The relationship was first noted 1772 by the German mathematician Johann Titius (1729–1796) 1772 (it is also known as the Titius-Bode law).

Bodhidharma 6th century AD. Indian Buddhist and teacher. He entered China from S India about 520, and was the founder of the Ch'an school (⟨⟩Zen is the Japanese derivation). Ch'an focuses on contemplation leading to intuitive meditation, a direct pointing to and stilling of the human mind. In the 20th century, the Japanese variation, Zen, has attracted many followers in the west.

bodhisattva in Mahāyāna Buddhism, someone who seeks ⟨⟩enlightenment in order to help other living beings. A bodhisattva is free to enter ⟨⟩nirvana but voluntarily chooses to be reborn until all other beings have attained that state. Bodhisattvas are seen as intercessors to whom believers may pray for redemption.

Bodin Jean 1530–1596. French political philosopher whose six-volume *De la République* 1576 is considered the first work on political economy.

Boeing US military and commercial aircraft manufacturer. Among the models Boeing has produced are the B-17 Flying Fortress, 1935; the B-52 Stratofortress, 1952; the Chinook helicopter, 1961; the first jetliner, the Boeing 707, 1957; the jumbo jet or Boeing 747, 1970; and the ⟨⟩jetfoil, 1975.

The company was founded 1916 near Seattle, Washington, by William E Boeing (1881–1956) as the Pacific Aero Products Company. Renamed the following year, the company built its first seaplane and in 1919 set up an airmail service between Seattle and Victoria, British Columbia.

Boeotia ancient district of central Greece, of which ⟨⟩Thebes was the chief city. The *Boeotian League* (formed by 10 city-states in the 6th century BC) superseded ⟨⟩Sparta in the leadership of Greece in the 4th century BC.

Boer Dutch settler or descendant of Dutch and Huguenot settlers in South Africa; see also ⟨⟩Afrikaner.

Boer War the second of the ⟨⟩South African Wars 1899–1902, waged between the Dutch settlers in South Africa and the British.

Boethius Anicius Manilus Severinus AD 480–524. Roman philosopher. While imprisoned on suspicion of treason by the emperor ⟨⟩Theodoric the Great, he wrote treatises on music and mathematics and *De Consolatione Philosophiae/The Consolation of Philosophy*, a dialogue in prose. It was translated into European languages during the Middle Ages; English translations by Alfred the Great, Geoffrey Chaucer, and Queen Elizabeth I.

bog type of wetland where decomposition is

slowed down and dead plant matter accumulates as ⟨⟩peat. Bogs develop under conditions of low temperature, high acidity, low nutrient supply, stagnant water, and oxygen deficiency. Typical bog plants are sphagnum moss, rushes and cotton grass; insectivorous plants such as sundews and bladderworts are common in bogs (insect prey make up for the lack of nutrients).

Bogarde Dirk. Adopted name of Derek van den Bogaerde 1921– . English actor who appeared in comedies and adventure films such as *Doctor in the House* 1954 and *Campbell's Kingdom* 1957, before acquiring international recognition for complex roles in Joseph Losey's *The Servant* 1963 and *Accident* 1967, and Luchino Visconti's *Death in Venice* 1971.

He has also written autobiographical books and novels: *A Postillion Struck by Lightning* 1977, *Snakes and Ladders* 1978, *Orderly Man* 1983, and *Backcloth* 1986.

Bogart Humphrey 1899–1957. US film actor who achieved fame as the gangster in *The Petrified Forest* 1936. He became an international cult figure as the tough, romantic "loner" in such films as *The Maltese Falcon* 1941 and *Casablanca* 1943, a status resurrected in the 1960s and still celebrated today. He won an Academy Award for his role in *The African Queen* 1952.

He co-starred in *To Have and Have Not* 1944 and *The Big Sleep* 1946 with Lauren Bacall, who became his fourth wife.

bog asphodel any swamp-growing herbaceous plant of the genus *Narthecium* of the lily family. There are three species in North America, of which the grasslike yellow asphodel (*Narthecium americanum*) of the E coastal plain is the best known.

bogbean or **buckbean** aquatic or bog plant *Menyanthes trifoliata* of the gentian family, with a creeping rhizome and leaves and pink flower spikes held above water. It is found over much of the northern hemisphere.

Bogdanovich Peter 1939– . US film director, screenwriter, and producer, formerly a critic. *The Last Picture Show* 1971, a nostalgic look at a small Texas town in the 1950s, was followed by two films that attempted to capture the style of old Hollywood, *What's Up Doc?* 1972 and *Paper Moon* 1973.

Both made money but neither was a critical success. In 1990 he made *Texasville*, a follow-up to *The Last Picture Show*.

Bogomils Christian heretics who originated in 10th-century Bulgaria and spread throughout the Byzantine empire. Their name derives from Bogomilus, or Theophilus, who taught in Bulgaria 927–950. Despite persecution, they were expunged by the Ottomans only after the fall of Constantinople 1453.

Bogotá capital of Colombia, South America; 8,660 ft/2,640 m above sea level on the edge of the plateau of the E Cordillera; population (1985) 4,185,000. It was founded 1538.

Bohemia area of W Czechoslovakia, a kingdom of central Europe from the 9th century. It was under Hapsburg rule 1526–1918, when it was included in Czechoslovakia. The name Bohemia derives from the Celtic Boii, its earliest known inhabitants.

It became part of the Holy Roman Empire as the result of Charlemagne's establishment of a protectorate over the Celtic, Germanic, and Slav tribes settled in this area. Christianity was introduced in the 9th century, the See of Prague being established 975, and feudalism was introduced by King Ottaker I of Bohemia (1197–1230). From the 12th century onwards, mining attracted large numbers of German settlers, leading to a strong Germanic influence in culture and society. In 1310, John of Luxemburg (died 1346) founded a German-Czech royal dynasty that lasted until 1437. His son, Charles IV, became Holy Roman Emperor 1355, and during his reign the See of Prague was elevated to an archbishopric and a university was founded there. During the 15th century, divisions within the nobility and religious conflicts culminating in the Hussite Wars (1420–36) led to decline.

Böhm Karl 1894–1981. Austrian conductor, known for his interpretation of Beethoven, and of the Mozart and Strauss operas.

Bohr Aage 1922– . Danish physicist who produced a new model of the nucleus 1952, known as the collective model. For this work, he shared the 1975 Nobel Prize for Physics. He was the son of Niels Bohr.

Bohr Niels Henrik David 1885–1962. Danish physicist. His theoretic work produced a new model of atomic structure, now called the Bohr model, and helped establish the validity of ⟡quantum theory.

After work with Ernest ⟡Rutherford at Manchester, UK, he became professor at Copenhagen 1916, and founded there the Institute of Theoretical Physics of which he became director 1920. He was awarded the Nobel Prize for Physics 1922. Bohr fled from the Nazis in World War II and took part in work on the atomic bomb in the US. In 1952, he helped to set up ⟡CERN, the European nuclear research organization in Geneva.

boil small abscess originating around a hair follicle or in a sweat gland, most likely to form if resistance is low or diet inadequate.

Boileau Nicolas 1636–1711. French poet and critic. After a series of contemporary satires, his *Epîtres/Epistles* 1669–77 led to his joint appointment with Racine as royal historiographer 1677. Later works include *L'Art poétique/The Art of Poetry* 1674 and the mock-heroic *Le Lutrin/The Lectern* 1674–83.

boiler any vessel that converts water into steam. Boilers are used in conventional power stations to generate steam to feed steam ⟡turbines, which drive the electricity generators. They are also used in steamships, which are propelled by steam turbines, and in steam locomotives. Every boiler has a furnace in which fuel (coal, oil, or gas) is burned to produce hot gases, and a system of tubes in which heat is transferred from the gases to the water.

The common kind of boiler used in ships and power stations is the **water-tube** type, in which the water circulates in tubes surrounded by the hot furnace gases. The water-tube boilers at power stations produce steam at a pressure of up to 300 atmospheres and a temperature of up to 1,100°F/600°C to feed to the steam turbines. It is more efficient than the **fire-tube** type that is used in steam locomotives. In this boiler the hot furnace gases are drawn through tubes surrounded by water.

boiling point for any given liquid, the temperature at which the application of heat raises the temperature of the liquid no further, but converts it into vapor.

The boiling point of water under normal

pressure is 212°F/100°C. The lower the pressure, the lower the boiling point and vice versa.

Boise capital of Idaho, located in the W part of the state, on the Boise River in the W foothills of the Rocky mountains. It serves as a center for the farm and livestock products of the region and has meatpacking and food-processing industries. Steel and lumber products are also manufactured; population (1990) 125,700. It was founded during the Idaho gold rush of 1862 and served as territorial capital 1864–90, when Idaho became a state.

Bokassa Jean-Bédel 1921– . President of the Central African Republic 1966–79 and later self-proclaimed emperor 1977–79. Commander in chief from 1963, in Dec 1965 he led the military coup that gave him the presidency. On Dec 4, 1976 he proclaimed the Central African Empire and one year later crowned himself as emperor for life.

His regime was characterized by arbitrary state violence and cruelty. Overthrown in 1979, Bokassa was in exile until 1986. Upon his return he was sentenced to death, but this was commuted to life imprisonment 1988.

Bokhara another form of ⟡Bukhara, city in Uzbekistan.

bolero Spanish dance in triple time for a solo dancer or a couple, usually with castanet accompaniment. It was used as the title of a one-act ballet score by Ravel, choreographed by Nijinsky for Ida Rubinstein 1928.

boletus genus of fleshy fungi belonging to the class Basidiomycetes, with thick stems and caps of various colors. The European *Boletus edulis* is edible, but some species are poisonous.

Boleyn Anne 1507–1536. Queen of England, the woman for whom Henry VIII broke with the pope and founded the Church of England (see ⟡Reformation). Second wife of Henry, she was married to him 1533 and gave birth to the future Queen Elizabeth I in the same year. Accused of adultery and incest with her half brother (a charge invented by Thomas ⟡Cromwell), she was beheaded.

Bolger Jim (James) Brendan 1935– . New Zealand politician and prime minister from 1990. A successful sheep and cattle farmer, Bolger was elected to Parliament 1972. He held a variety of cabinet posts under Robert Muldoon's leadership 1977–84, and was an effective, if uncharismatic, leader of the opposition from March 1986, taking the National Party to electoral victory Oct 1990. His subsequent failure to honor election pledges, leading to cuts in welfare provision, led to a sharp fall in his popularity.

Bolingbroke title of Henry of Bolingbroke, ⟡Henry IV of England.

Bolívar Simón 1783–1830. South American nationalist, leader of revolutionary armies, known as *the Liberator*. He fought the Spanish colonial forces in several uprisings and eventually liberated his native Venezuela 1821, Colombia and Ecuador 1822, Peru 1824, and Bolivia (a new state named after him, formerly Upper Peru) 1825.

Born in Venezuela, he joined that country's revolution against Spain in 1810, and in the following year he declared Venezuela independent. His army was soon defeated by the Spanish, however, and he was forced to flee. Many battles and defeats followed, and it was

not until 1819 that Bolívar won his first major victory, defeating the Spanish in Colombia and winning independence for that country. He went on to liberate Venezuela 1821 and (along with Antonio ⟡Sucre) Ecuador 1822. These three countries were united into the republic of Gran Colombia with Bolívar as its president. In 1824 Bolívar helped bring about the defeat of Spanish forces in Peru, and the area known as Upper Peru was renamed "Bolivia" in Bolívar's honor. Within the next few years, Venezuela and Ecuador seceded from the union, and in 1830 Bolívar resigned as president. He died the same year, despised by many for his dictatorial ways but since revered as South America's greatest liberator.

Bolivia landlocked country in central Andes mountains in South America, bounded N and E by Brazil, SE by Paraguay, S by Argentina, and W by Chile and Peru.

government Achieving independence 1825 after nearly 300 years of Spanish rule, Bolivia adopted its first constitution 1826, and since then a number of variations have been produced. The present one provides for a congress consisting of a 27-member senate and a 130-member chamber of deputies, both elected for four years by universal suffrage. The president, directly elected for a four-year term, is head of both state and government and chooses the cabinet. For administrative purposes, the country is divided into nine departments, each governed by a prefect appointed by the president.

history Once part of the ⟡Inca civilization, Bolivia was conquered by Spain 1538 and remained under Spanish rule until liberated by Simón Bolívar 1825 (after whom the country took its name). Bolivia formed a Peruvian-Bolivian Confederation 1836–39 under Bolivian president Andrés Santa Cruz, a former president of Peru. Chile declared war on the confederation, Santa Cruz was defeated, and the confederation dissolved. Bolivia was again at war with Chile 1879–84, when it lost its coastal territory and land containing valuable mineral deposits, and with Paraguay (the Chaco War) 1932–35, again losing valuable territory.

army v reformers In the 1951 election, Dr Victor Paz Estenssoro, the National Revolutionary Movement (MNR) candidate exiled in Argentina since 1946, failed to win an absolute majority, and an army junta took over. A popular uprising, supported by MNR and a section of the army, demanded the return of Paz, who became president and began a program of social reform. He lost the 1956 election but returned to power 1960. In 1964 a coup, led by Vice President General René Barrientos, overthrew Paz and installed a military junta. Two years later Barrientos won the presidency. He was opposed by left-wing groups and in 1967 a guerrilla uprising led by Dr Ernesto "Che" ⟡Guevara was put down with US help.

frequent coups In 1969 President Barrientos died in an airplane crash and was replaced by the vice-president. He was later replaced by General Alfredo Ovando, who was ousted by General Juan Torres, who in turn was ousted by Col Hugo Banzer Suárez 1971. Banzer announced a return to constitutional government, but another attempted coup 1974 prompted him to postpone elections, ban all labor union and political activity, and proclaim that military government would last until at least 1980. Banzer agreed to elections 1978, but they were declared invalid after allegations of fraud, and, in that year, two more military coups.

In the 1979 elections Dr Siles and Dr Paz received virtually equal votes, and an interim administration was installed. An election 1980 proved equally inconclusive and was followed by the 189th military coup in Bolivia's 154 years of independence. General Luis García became president but resigned the following year after allegations of drug trafficking. He was replaced by General Celso Torrelio, who promised to fight corruption and return the country to democracy within three years. In 1982 a mainly civilian cabinet was appointed, but rumors of an impending coup resulted in Torrelio's resignation. A military junta led by the hard-line General Guido Vildoso was installed.

economy deteriorates With the economy deteriorating, the junta asked congress to elect a president, and Dr Siles Zuazo was chosen to head a coalition cabinet. Economic aid from Europe and the US, cut off in 1980, was resumed, but the economy continued to deteriorate. The government's austerity measures proved unpopular, and in June the president was temporarily abducted by a group of right-wing army officers. In an attempt to secure national unity, President Siles embarked on a five-day hunger strike. Siles resigned 1985 and an election was held. No candidate won an absolute majority and Dr Victor Paz Estenssoro, aged 77, was chosen by congress. Austerity measures imposed by Estenssoro's administration reduced inflation from 24,000% in 1985 to 3% in the first half of 1989.

power-sharing In the 1989 congressional elections the MNR won marginally more votes than the Nationalist Democratic Action Party (ADN), but did not obtain a clear majority. After an indecisive presidential contest, Jaime Paz Zamora of the Movement of the Revolutionary Left (MIR) was elected president by the congress after he negotiated a power-sharing arrangement with former military dictator Hugo Banzer Suárez. Zamora pledged to maintain fiscal and monetary discipline and preserve free-market policies. A new, radical, free-market party, the Solidarity Civil Union (UCS), was gaining popular support in 1992. *See illustration box.*

Bolkiah Hassanal 1946– . Sultan of Brunei from 1967, following the abdication of his father, Omar Ali Saifuddin (1916–1986). As absolute ruler, Bolkiah also assumed the posts of prime minister and defense minister on independence 1984.

As head of an oil-and gas-rich microstate, the sultan is reputedly the world's richest individual, with an estimated total wealth of $22 billion, which includes the Dorchester and Beverly Hills hotels in London and Los Angeles, and, at a cost of $40 million, the world's largest palace. He was educated at a British military academy.

Böll Heinrich 1917–1985. German novelist. A radical Catholic and anti-Nazi, he attacked Germany's political past and the materialism of its contemporary society. His many publications include poems, short stories, and novels which satirized West German society, for example *Billard um Halbzehn/Billiards at Half-Past Nine* 1959 and *Gruppenbild mit Dame/Group Portrait with Lady* 1971. Nobel Prize for Literature 1972.

boll weevil small American beetle *Anthonomus grandis* of the weevil group. The female lays her eggs in the unripe pods or "bolls" of the cotton plant, and on these the larvae feed, causing great destruction.

Bologna industrial city and capital of Emilia-Romagna, Italy, 50 mi/80 km north of Florence; population (1988) 427,000. It was the site of an Etruscan town, later of a Roman colony, and became a republic in the 12th century. It came under papal rule 1506 and was united with Italy 1860.

The city has a cathedral and medieval towers, and the university, which dates from the 11th century, laid the foundations of the study of anatomy and was attended by the poets Dante, Petrarch, and Tasso, and the astronomer Copernicus.

bolometer sensitive ◊thermometer that measures the energy of radiation by registering the change in electrical resistance of a fine wire when it is exposed to heat or light. The US astronomer Samuel Langley devised it 1880 for measuring radiation from stars.

Bolshevik (from Russian *bolshinstvo* "a majority") member of the majority of the Russian Social Democratic Party who split from the ◊Mensheviks 1903. The Bolsheviks, under ◊Lenin, advocated the destruction of capitalist political and economic institutions, and the setting-up of a socialist state with power in the hands of the workers. The Bolsheviks set the ◊Russian Revolution 1917 in motion. They changed their name to the Russian Communist Party 1918.

They maintained power after the Civil War 1918–1921.

bolson a basin without outlet, found in desert regions. Bolsons often contain temporary lakes, called playa lakes, and become

Bolivia
Republic of (*República de Bolivia*)

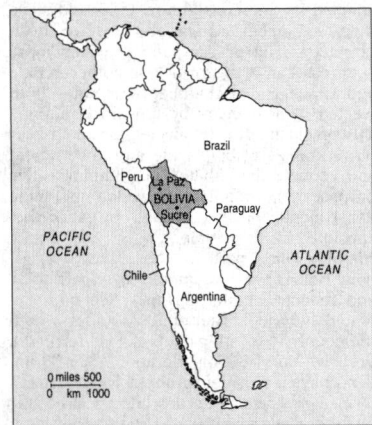

area 424,052 sq mi/1,098,581 sq km
capital La Paz (seat of government), Sucre (legal capital and seat of judiciary)
cities Santa Cruz, Cochabamba, Oruro, Potosí
physical high plateau (Altiplano) between mountain ridges (cordilleras); forest and lowlands (llano) in the E
features Andes, lakes Titicaca (the world's highest navigable lake, 12,500 ft/3,800 m) and Poopó; La Paz is world's highest capital city (11,800 ft/3,600 m)
head of state and government Jaime Paz Zamora from 1989
political system emergent democratic republic
political parties National Revolutionary Movement (MNR), center-right; Nationalist Democratic Action Party (ADN), extreme right-wing; Movement of the Revolutionary Left (MIR), left of center; Solidarity Civil Union (UCS), radical free market
exports tin, antimony (second largest world producer), other nonferrous metals, oil, gas (piped to Argentina), agricultural products, coffee, sugar, cotton
currency boliviano
population (1990 est) 6,730,000; (Quechua 25%, Aymara 17%, mestizo (mixed) 30%, European 14%); growth rate 2.7% p.a.
life expectancy men 51, women 54
languages Spanish, Aymara, Quechua (all official)
religion Roman Catholic 95% (state-recognized)
literacy men 84%, women 65% (1985 est)
GDP $4.2 bn (1987); $617 per head
chronology
1825 Liberated from Spanish rule by Simón Bolívar; independence achieved (formerly known as Upper Peru).
1952 Dr Víctor Paz Estenssoro elected president.
1956 Dr Hernán Siles Zuazo became president.
1960 Estenssoro returned to power.
1964 Army coup led by vice-president.
1966 Gen René Barrientos became president.
1967 Uprising, led by "Che" Guevara, put down with US help.
1969 Barrientos killed in plane crash, replaced by Vice President Siles Salinas. Army coup deposed him.
1970 Army coup put General Juan Torres González in power.
1971 Torres replaced by Col Hugo Banzer Suárez.
1973 Banzer promised a return to democratic government.
1974 Attempted coup prompted Banzer to postpone elections and ban political and labor-union activity.
1978 Elections declared invalid after allegations of fraud.
1980 More inconclusive elections followed by another coup, led by General Luis García. Allegations of corruption and drug trafficking led to cancellation of US and EC aid.
1981 García forced to resign. Replaced by General Celso Torrelio Villa.
1982 Torrelio resigned. Replaced by military junta led by General Guido Vildoso. Because of worsening economy, Vildoso asked congress to install a civilian administration. Dr Siles Zuazo chosen as president.
1983 Economic aid from USA and Europe resumed.
1984 New coalition government formed by Siles. Abduction of president by right-wing officers. The president undertook a five-day hunger strike as an example to the nation.
1985 President Siles resigned. Election result inconclusive; Dr Paz Estenssoro, at the age of 77, chosen by congress as president.
1989 Jaime Paz Zamora (MIR) elected president in power-sharing arrangement with Hugo Banzer Suárez, pledged to maintain fiscal and monetary discipline and preserve free-market policies.
1992 New, free-market party, the Solidarity Civil Union (UCS), gained support.

filled with alluvial deposits from inflowing intermittent streams.

Bolt Robert (Oxton) 1924– . British dramatist, known for his historical plays, such as *A Man for All Seasons* 1960 (filmed 1967) about Thomas More, and for his screenplays, including *Lawrence of Arabia* 1962 and *Dr Zhivago* 1965.

Bolton city in Greater Manchester, England, 11 mi/18 km NW of Manchester; population (1991) 253,300. Industries include chemicals and textiles.

Boltzmann Ludwig 1844–1906. Austrian physicist who studied the kinetic theory of gases, which explains the properties of gases by reference to the motion of their constituent atoms and molecules.

He derived a formula, the *Boltzmann distribution*, which gives the number of atoms or molecules with a given energy at a specific temperature. The constant in the formula is called the *Boltzmann constant*.

Boltzmann constant in physics, the constant (symbol k) that relates the kinetic energy (energy of motion) of a gas atom or molecule to temperature. Its value is 1.380662×10^{-23} joules per Kelvin. It is equal to the gas constant R, divided by ⃝Avogadro's number.

bomb container filled with explosive or chemical material and generally used in warfare. There are also ⃝incendiary bombs and nuclear bombs and missiles (see ⃝nuclear warfare). Any object designed to cause damage by explosion can be called a bomb (car bombs, letter bombs). Initially dropped from airplanes (from World War I), bombs were in World War II also launched by rocket (⃝V1, V2). The 1960s saw the development of missiles that could be launched from aircraft, land sites, or submarines. In the 1970s laser guidance systems were developed to hit small targets with accuracy.

Bombay industrial port (textiles, engineering, pharmaceuticals, diamonds), commercial center, and capital of Maharashtra, W India; population (1981) 8,227,000. It is the center of the Hindi film industry.
features World Trade Center 1975, National Center for the Performing Arts 1969
history Bombay was founded in the 13th century, came under Mogul rule, was occupied by Portugal 1530, and passed to Britain 1662 as part of Catherine of Braganza's dowry. It was the headquarters of the East India Company 1685–1708. The city expanded rapidly with the development of the cotton trade and the railroad in the 1860s.

Bombay duck or **bummalow** small fish *Harpodon nehereus* found in the Indian Ocean. It has a thin body, up to 16 in/40 cm long, and sharp, pointed teeth. It feeds on shellfish and other small fish. It is valuable as a food fish, and is eaten, salted and dried, with dishes such as curry.

bona fide (Latin "in good faith") legal phrase used to signify that a contract is undertaken without intentional misrepresentation.

Bonampak site of a Classic ⃝Mayan city, on the river Usumacinta near the Mexico and Guatemala border, with extensive remains of wall paintings depicting battles, torture, and sacrifices. Rediscovered 1948, the paintings shed new light on Mayan society, which to that date had been considered peaceful.

Bonaparte Corsican family of Italian origin that gave rise to the Napoleonic dynasty: see ⃝Napoleon I, ⃝Napoleon II, and ⃝Napoleon III. Others were the brothers and sister of Napoleon I:
Joseph (1768–1844) whom Napoleon made king of Naples 1806 and Spain 1808;
Lucien (1775–1840) whose handling of the Council of Five Hundred on Nov 10, 1799 ensured Napoleon's future;
Louis (1778–1846) the father of Napoleon III, who was made king of Holland 1806–10;
Caroline (1782–1839) who married Joachim ⃝Murat 1800;
Jerome (1784–1860) made king of Westphalia 1807.

Bonaventura, St (John of Fidanza) 1221–1274. Italian Roman Catholic theologian. He entered the Franciscan order 1243, became professor of theology in Paris, and in 1256 general of his order. In 1273 he was created cardinal and bishop of Albano. Feast day July 15.

bond in chemistry, the result of the forces of attraction that hold together atoms of an element or elements to form a molecule. The principal types of bonding are ⃝ionic , ⃝covalent bonding, ⃝metallic, and intermolecular (such as hydrogen bonding).

bond in commerce, a security issued by a government, local authority, company, bank, or other institution on fixed interest. Usually a long-term security, a bond may be irredeemable (with no date of redemption), secured (giving the investor a claim on the company's property or on a part of its assets), or unsecured (not protected by a lien). Property bonds are nonfixed securities with the yield fixed to property investment. See also ⃝Eurobond.

Bondi Hermann 1919– . Viennese-born British cosmologist. In 1948 he joined with Fred ⃝Hoyle and Thomas Gold (1920–) in developing the steady-state theory of cosmology, which suggested that matter is continuously created in the universe.

bondservant another term for a slave or serf used in the Caribbean in the 18th and 19th centuries; a person who was offered a few acres of land in return for some years of compulsory service. The system was a means of obtaining labor from Europe.

bone hard connective tissue comprising the ⃝skeleton of most vertebrate animals. It consists of a network of collagen fibers impregnated with inorganic salts, especially calcium phosphate. Enclosed within this solid matrix are bone cells, blood vessels, and nerves.

There are two types of bone: those that develop by replacing ⃝cartilage and those that form directly from connective tissue. The latter are usually platelike in shape, and form in the skin of the developing embryo. In strength, the toughest bone is comparable with reinforced concrete. The interior of long bones consists of a spongy matrix filled with a soft marrow that produces blood cells. Humans have about 206 distinct bones in the skeleton.

bone china or **softpaste** semiporcelain made of 5% bone ash added to 95% kaolin; first made in the West in imitation of Chinese porcelain, whose formula was kept secret by the Chinese.

bone marrow substance found inside the cavity of bones. In early life it produces red blood cells but later on lipids (fat) accumulate and its color changes from red to yellow.

Bone marrow may be transplanted using immunosuppressive drugs in the recipient to prevent rejection. Transplants to adult monkeys from early aborted monkey fetuses have successfully bypassed rejection.

bongo Central African antelope *Boocercus eurycerus*, living in dense humid forests. Up to 4.5 ft/1.4 m at the shoulder, it has spiral horns which may be 2.6 ft/80 cm or more in length. The body is rich chestnut, with narrow white stripes running vertically down the sides, and a black belly.

Bonheur Rosa (Marie Rosalie) 1822–1899. French animal painter. Her realistic animal portraits include *Horse Fair* 1853 (Metropolitan Museum of Art, New York).

She exhibited at the Paris Salon every year from 1841, and received international awards. In 1894 she became the first woman Officer of the Légion d'Honneur.

Bonhoeffer Dietrich 1906–1945. German Lutheran theologian and opponent of Nazism. Involved in a plot against Hitler, he was executed by the Nazis in Flossenburg concentration camp. His *Letters and Papers from Prison* 1953 became the textbook of modern radical theology, advocating the idea of a "religionless" Christianity.

Boniface name of nine popes, including:

Boniface VIII Benedict Caetani *c.* 1228–1303. Pope from 1294. He clashed unsuccessfully with Philip IV of France over his taxation of the clergy, and also with Henry III of England.

Boniface exempted the clergy from taxation by the secular government in a bull (edict) 1296, but was forced to give way when the clergy were excluded from certain lay privileges. His bull of 1302 *Unam sanctam*, asserting the complete temporal and spiritual power of the papacy, was equally ineffective.

Boniface, St 680–754. English Benedictine

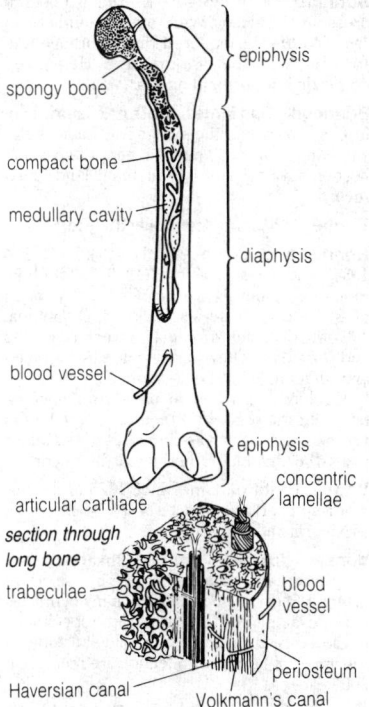

section through long bone

bone *Bone is a network of fibrous material impregnated with mineral salts and as strong as reinforced concrete.*

monk, known as the "Apostle of Germany;" originally named Wynfrith. After a missionary journey to Frisia 716, he was given the task of bringing Christianity to Germany 718 by Pope Gregory II, and was appointed archbishop of Mainz 746. He returned to Frisia 754 and was martyred near Dockum. His feast day is June 5.

Bonin and Volcano islands Japanese islands in the Pacific, N of the Marianas and 800 mi/1,300 km E of the Ryukyu islands. They were under US control 1945–68. The **Bonin Islands** (Japanese *Ogasawara Gunto*) number 27 (in three groups), the largest being Chichijima: area 40 sq mi/104 sq km, population (1991) 2,430. The **Volcano Islands** (Japanese *Kazan Retto*) number three, including ◊Iwo Jima, scene of some of the fiercest fighting of World War II; total area 11 sq mi/28 sq km. They have no civilian population, but a 200-strong maritime self-defense force and 100-strong air self-defense force are stationed there.

bonito any of various species of medium-sized tuna, predatory fish of the genus *Sarda*, in the mackerel family. The ocean bonito *Katsuwonus pelamis* grows to 3 ft/1 m and is common in tropical seas. The Atlantic bonito *Sarda sarda* is found in the Mediterranean and tropical Atlantic and grows to the same length but has a narrower body.

Bonn industrial city (chemicals, textiles, plastics, aluminum) and seat of government of the Federal Republic of Germany, 15 mi/18 km SSE of Cologne, on the left bank of the Rhine; population (1988) 292,000.

Once a Roman outpost, Bonn was captured by the French 1794, annexed 1801, and was allotted to Prussia 1815. Beethoven was born here. It was capital of West Germany 1949–90.

Bonnard Pierre 1867–1947. French Post-Impressionist painter. With other members of **les ◊Nabis**, he explored the decorative arts (posters, stained glass, furniture). He painted domestic interiors and nudes.

Bonneville Salt Flats bed of a prehistoric lake in Utah, of which the Great Salt Lake is the surviving remnant. The flats, near the Nevada border, have been used to set many land speed records.

Bonney William H see ◊Billy the Kid.

Bonnie and Clyde Bonnie Parker (1911–1934) and Clyde Barrow (1900–1934). Infamous US criminals who carried out a series of small-scale robberies in Texas, Oklahoma, New Mexico, and Missouri between Aug 1932 and May 1934. They were eventually betrayed and then killed in a police ambush.

Much of their fame emanated from encounters with the police and their coverage by the press. Their story was filmed as *Bonnie and Clyde* 1967 by the US director Arthur Penn.

Bonny, Bight of name since 1975 of the former Bight of Biafra, an area of sea off the coasts of Nigeria and Cameroon.

bonsai (Japanese "bowl cultivation") art of producing miniature trees by selective pruning. It originated in China many centuries ago and later spread to Japan. Some specimens in China are about 1,000 years old and some in the imperial Japanese collection are more than 300 years old.

Bonus Army or **Bonus Expeditionary Force** in US history, a march on Washington, DC by unemployed ex-servicemen during the great ◊Depression to lobby Congress for immediate cash payment of a promised war veterans' bonus.

During the spring of 1932, some 15,000 veterans camped by the river Potomac or squatted in disused government buildings. They were eventually dispersed by troops.

boobook owl *Ninox novaeseelandiae* found in Australia, so named because of its call.

booby tropical seabird of the genus *Sula*, in the same family, Sulidae, as the northern ◊gannet. There are six species, including the circumtropical brown booby *Sula leucogaster*. They inhabit coastal waters, and dive to catch fish. The name was given by sailors who saw the bird's tameness as stupidity.

One species, **Abbott's booby**, breeds only on Christmas Island, in the western Indian Ocean. Unlike most boobies and gannets it nests high up in trees. Large parts of its breeding ground have been destroyed by phosphate mining, but conservation measures now protect the site.

boogie-woogie jazz played on the piano, using a repeated motif for the left hand. It was common in the US from around 1900 to the 1950s. Boogie-woogie players included Pinetop Smith (1904–1929), Meade "Lux" Lewis (1905–1964), and Jimmy Yancey (1898–1951). Rock-and-roll pianists such as Jerry Lee Lewis adapted the style.

book portable written record. Substances used to make early books included leaves, bark, linen, silk, clay, leather, and papyrus. In about AD 100–150, the codex or paged book, as opposed to the roll or scroll, began to be adopted. Vellum (parchment of calfskin, lambskin, or kidskin) was generally used for book pages by the beginning of the 4th century, and its use lasted until the 15th. It was superseded by paper, which came to Europe from China (where it was made as early as AD 105, a mixture of bark and hemp fibers). Books only became widely available after the invention of the ◊printing press in the 15th century. Printed text is also reproduced and stored in ◊microform.

bookbinding securing of the pages of a book between protective covers by sewing and/or gluing. Cloth binding was first introduced 1822, but from the mid-20th century synthetic bindings were increasingly employed, and most hardcover books are bound by machine.

Bookbinding did not emerge as a distinct craft until ◊printing was introduced to Europe in the 15th century. Until that time scrolls and (from around 1200) codices (see ◊codex) were usual. Gold tooling, the principal ornament of leather bookbinding, was probably introduced to Europe from the East by the Venetian Aldus Manutius (1450–1515).

Booker Prize British literary prize of £20,000 awarded annually (from 1969) by the Booker company (formerly Booker McConnell) to a novel published in the UK during the previous year.

bookkeeping process of recording commercial transactions in a systematic and established procedure. These records provide the basis for the preparation of accounts.

booklouse any of numerous species of tiny wingless insects of the order Psocoptera, especially *Atropus pulsatoria*, which lives in books and papers, feeding on starches and molds.

Most of the other species live in bark, leaves, and lichens. They thrive in dark, damp conditions.

Book of Hours see ◊Hours, Book of.

Book of the Dead ancient Egyptian book, known as the *Book of Coming Forth by Day*, buried with the dead as a guide to reaching the kingdom of Osiris, the god of the underworld. Similar practices were observed by Orphic communities (6th to 1st century BC) in S Italy and Crete, who deposited gold laminae, inscribed with directions about the next world, in the graves of their dead. An ancient Buddhist example is the ◊Bardo Thödol from Tibet. In medieval times, Christians could obtain advice about dying from a book entitled *Ars Morendi/The Art of Dying*.

Boole George 1815–1864. English mathematician whose work *The Mathematical Analysis of Logic* 1847 established the basis of modern mathematical logic, and whose **Boolean algebra** can be used in designing computers.

boomerang hand-thrown, flat wooden hunting missile shaped in a curved angle, formerly used throughout the world but developed by the Australian Aborigines to a great degree of diversity and elaboration. It is used to kill game and as a weapon or, in the case of the returning boomerang, as recreation.

boomslang rear-fanged venomous African snake *Dispholidus typus*, often green but sometimes brown or blackish, and growing to a length of 6 ft/2 m. It lives in trees, and feeds on tree-dwelling lizards such as chameleons. Its venom can be fatal to humans; however, boomslangs rarely attack people.

Boone Daniel 1734–1820. US pioneer who explored the Wilderness Road (East Virginia–Kentucky) 1775 and paved the way for the first westward migration of settlers.

Boone was born in Pennsylvania and spent most of his youth in North Carolina. During the American Revolution, he led militias against Indians allied with the British. He was captured by a Shawnee war party and so impressed the chief that he was adopted by the tribe. He left the Indians and continued to explore westward.

booster first-stage rocket of a space-launching vehicle, or an additional rocket strapped to the main rocket to assist takeoff.

The US Delta rocket, for example, has a cluster of nine strap-on boosters that fire on lift off. Europe's Ariane 3 rocket uses twin strap-on boosters, as does the US space shuttle.

Boötes constellation of the northern hemisphere represented by a herder driving a bear (Ursa Major) around the pole. Its brightest star is ◊Arcturus (or Alpha Bootis) about 36 light-years from Earth.

Booth Edwin Thomas 1833–1893. US actor. Born near Bel Air, Maryland, elder brother of John Wilkes ◊Booth, and member of a distinguished theatrical family, he was one of America's most acclaimed Shakespearean actors. As lead performer, theater manager, and producer, he successfully brought to the New York stage numerous Shakespearean tragedies, becoming famous for his portrayal of Hamlet.

After the public disgrace of his brother's assassination of Lincoln, Booth suffered a series of financial reverses and spent his later years in performance tours of Europe, the British Isles, and the US.

Booth John Wilkes 1839–1865. US actor and fanatical Confederate sympathizer who assassinated President Abraham ◊Lincoln April 14,

1865; he escaped with a broken leg and was later shot in a barn in Virginia when he refused to surrender.

He had earlier conceived a plan to kidnap Lincoln and decided to kill him in vengeance when the plan failed.

Booth William 1829–1912. British founder of the ⬦Salvation Army 1878, and its first "general."

Boothe Claire see ⬦Luce, Claire Boothe.

bootlegging illegal manufacture, distribution, or sale of a product. The term originated in the US, when the sale of alcohol to American Indians was illegal and bottles were hidden for sale in the legs of the jackboots of unscrupulous traders. The term was later used for all illegal liquor sales during the period of ⬦Prohibition in the US 1920–33, and is often applied to unauthorized commercial tape recordings and the copying of computer software.

bop short for ⬦*bebop*, a style of jazz.

Bophuthatswana Republic of; self-governing black "homeland" within South Africa
area 15,571 sq mi/40,330 sq km
capital Mmbatho or Sun City, a casino resort frequented by many white South Africans
features divided into six "blocks"
exports platinum, chromium, vanadium, asbestos, manganese
currency South African rand
population (1985) 1,627,000
language Setswana, English
religion Christian
government executive president elected by the Assembly: Chief Lucas Mangope
recent history first "independent" Black National State from 1977, but not recognized by any country other than South Africa.

Bora-Bora one of the 14 Society Islands of French Polynesia; situated 140 mi/225 km NW of Tahiti; area 15 sq mi/39 sq km. Exports include mother-of-pearl, fruit, and tobacco.

Borah William Edgar 1865–1940. US Republican politician. Born in Illinois, he was a senator from Idaho from 1906. An archisolationist, he was chiefly responsible for the US's repudiation of the League of Nations following World War I.

He also resisted US participation in the World Court (see ⬦International Court of Justice; and the ⬦United Nations).

borax hydrous sodium borate, $Na_2B_4O_7.10H_2O$, found as soft, whitish crystals or encrustations on the shores of hot springs and in the dry beds of salt lakes in arid regions, where it occurs with other borates, halite, and ⬦gypsum. It is used in bleaches and washing powders.

A large industrial source is Borax Lake, California. Borax is also used in glazing pottery, in soldering, as a mild antiseptic, and as a metallurgical flux.

Bordeaux port on the Garonne, capital of Aquitaine, SW France, a center for the wine trade, oil refining, and aeronautics and space industries; population (1982) 640,000. Bordeaux was under the English crown for three centuries until 1453. In 1870, 1914, and 1940 the French government was moved here because of German invasion.

Bordet Jules 1870–1961. Belgian bacteriologist and immunologist who researched the role of blood serum in the human immune response. He was the first to isolate 1906 the whooping cough bacillus.

bore surge of tidal water up an estuary or a river, caused by the funnelling of the rising tide by a narrowing river mouth. A very high tide, possibly fanned by wind, may build up when it is held back by a river current in the river mouth. The result is a broken wave, a meter or a few feet high, that rushes upstream.

Famous bores are found in the rivers Severn (England), Seine (France), Hooghly (India), and Chiang Jiang (China), where bores of over 13 ft/4 m have been reported.

Borelli Giovanni Alfonso 1608–1679. Italian scientist who explored the links between physics and medicine and showed how mechanical principles could be applied to animal ⬦physiology. This approach, known as iatrophysics, has proved basic to understanding how the mammalian body works.

Borg Björn (Rune) 1956– . Swedish tennis player who won the men's singles title at Wimbledon five times 1976–80, a record since the abolition of the challenge system 1922. He also won six French Open singles titles 1974–75 and 1978–81 inclusive. In 1990 Borg announced plans to return to professional tennis, but he enjoyed little competitive success 1991–92.

Borges Jorge Luis 1899–1986. Argentine poet and short-story writer, an exponent of ⬦magic realism. In 1961 he became director of the National Library, Buenos Aires, and was professor of English literature at the university there. He is known for his fantastic and paradoxical work *Ficciones/Fictions* 1944.

Borges explored metaphysical themes in early works such as *Ficciones* and *El Aleph/The Aleph, and other Stories* 1949. In a later collection of tales *El informe de Brodie/Dr Brodie's Report* 1972, he adopted a more realistic style, reminiscent of the work of the young Rudyard ⬦Kipling, of whom he was a great admirer. *El libro de arena/The Book of Sand* 1975 marked a return to more fantastic themes.

Borgia Cesare 1476–1507. Italian general, illegitimate son of Pope ⬦Alexander VI. Made a cardinal at 17 by his father, he resigned to become captain-general of the papacy, campaigning successfully against the city republics of Italy. Ruthless and treacherous in war, he was an able ruler (the model for Machiavelli's *The Prince*), but his power crumbled on the death of his father. He was a patron of artists, including Leonardo da Vinci.

Borgia Lucrezia 1480–1519. Duchess of Ferrara from 1501. She was the illegitimate daughter of Pope ⬦Alexander VI and sister of Cesare Borgia. She was married at 12 and again at 13 to further her father's ambitions, both marriages being annulled by him. At 18 she was married again, but her husband was murdered 1500 on the order of her brother, with whom (as well as with her father) she was said to have committed incest. Her final marriage was to the duke of Este, the son and heir of the duke of Ferrara. She made the court a center of culture and was a patron of authors and artists such as Ariosto and Titian.

Borglum Gutzon 1871–1941. US sculptor. He created a six-ton marble head of Lincoln in Washington, DC, and the series of giant heads of presidents Washington, Jefferson, Lincoln, and Theodore Roosevelt carved on Mount Rushmore, South Dakota (begun 1930).

boric acid or **boracic acid** H_3BO_3, acid formed by the combination of hydrogen and oxygen with nonmetallic boron. It is a weak

antiseptic and is used in the manufacture of glass and enamels. It is also an efficient insecticide against ants and cockroaches.

Boris III 1894–1943. Tsar of Bulgaria from 1918, when he succeeded his father, Ferdinand I. From 1934 he was virtual dictator until his sudden and mysterious death following a visit to Hitler. His son Simeon II was tsar until deposed 1946.

Boris Godunov 1552–1605. See Boris ⬦Godunov, tsar of Russia from 1598.

Borlaug Norman Ernest 1914– . US microbiologist and agronomist. He developed high-yielding varieties of wheat and other grain crops to be grown in Third World countries, and was the first to use the term "Green Revolution." Nobel Prize for Peace 1970.

Bormann Martin 1900–1945. German Nazi leader. He took part in the abortive Munich ⬦putsch (uprising) 1923 and rose to high positions in the Nazi (National Socialist) Party, becoming party chancellor May 1941.

Bormann was believed to have escaped the fall of Berlin May 1945 and was tried in his absence and sentenced to death at the ⬦Nuremberg trials 1945–46, but a skeleton uncovered by a mechanical excavator in Berlin 1972 was officially recognized as his by forensic experts 1973.

Born Max 1882–1970. German physicist who received a Nobel Prize 1954 for fundamental work on the ⬦quantum theory. He left Germany for the UK during the Nazi era.

Borneo third largest island in the world, one of the Sunda Islands in the W Pacific; area 290,000 sq mi/754,000 sq km. It comprises the Malaysian territories of ⬦Sabah and ⬦Sarawak; ⬦Brunei; and, occupying by far the largest part, the Indonesian territory of ⬦Kalimantan. It is mountainous and densely forested. In coastal areas the people of Borneo are mainly of Malaysian origin, with a few Chinese, and the interior is inhabited by the indigenous Dyaks. It was formerly under both Dutch and British colonial influence until Sarawak was formed 1841.

Bornholm Danish island in the Baltic Sea, 22 mi/35 km SE of the nearest point of the Swedish coast. It constitutes a county of the same name
area 227 sq mi/587 sq km
capital Rönne
population (1985) 46,000.

Bornu kingdom of the 9th–19th centuries to the west and south of Lake Chad, W central Africa. Converted to Islam in the 11th century, Bornu reached its greatest strength in the 15th–18th centuries. From 1901 it was absorbed in the British, French, and German colonies in this area, which became the states of Niger, Cameroon, and Nigeria. The largest section of ancient Bornu is now the **state of Bornu** in Nigeria.

Borodin Alexander Porfir'yevich 1833–1887. Russian composer. Born in St Petersburg, the illegitimate son of a Russian prince, he became by profession an expert in medical chemistry, but in his spare time devoted himself to music. His principal work is the opera *Prince Igor*, left unfinished; it was completed by Rimsky-Korsakov and Glazunov and includes the Polovtsian Dances.

Borodino, Battle of battle Sept 7, 1812 where French troops under Napoleon defeated the Russians under Kutusov. Named after the village of Borodino, 110km/70 mi NW of Moscow.

boron nonmetallic element, symbol B, atomic number 5, atomic weight 10.811. In nature it is found only in compounds, as with sodium and oxygen in borax. It exists in two allotropic forms (see ◊allotropy): brown amorphous powder and very hard, brilliant crystals. Its compounds are used in the preparation of boric acid, water softeners, soaps, enamels, glass, and pottery glazes. In alloys it is used to harden steel. Because it absorbs slow neutrons, it is used to make boron carbide control rods for nuclear reactors. It is a necessary trace element in the human diet. The element was named by Humphry Davy, who isolated it 1808, from *borax* + *-on*, as in carb*on*.

Borromeo, St Carlo 1538–1584. Italian Roman Catholic saint and cardinal. He was instrumental in bringing the Council of Trent (1562–3) to a successful conclusion, and in drawing up the catechism that contained its findings. Feast day Nov 4.

Born at Arona of a noble Italian family, Borromeo was created a cardinal and archbishop of Milan by his uncle Pope Pius IV 1560. He lived the life of an ascetic, and 1578 founded the community later called the Oblate Fathers of St Charles. He was canonized 1610.

Borromini Francesco 1599–1667. Italian Baroque architect, one of the two most important (with ◊Bernini, his main rival) in 17th-century Rome. Whereas Bernini designed in a florid, expansive style, his pupil Borromini developed a highly idiosyncratic and austere use of the Classical language of architecture. His genius may be seen in the cathedrals of San Carlo 1641 and San Ivo 1660, and the oratorio of St Filippo Neri 1650.

borzoi (Russian "swift") large breed of dog originating in Russia, 2.5 ft/75 cm or more at the shoulder. It is of the grayhound type, white with darker markings, with a thick, silky coat.

Bosch Carl 1874–1940. German metallurgist and chemist. He developed Fritz Haber's small-scale technique for the production of ammonia into an industrial high-pressure process that made use of water gas as a source of hydrogen; see ◊Haber process. He shared the Nobel Prize for Chemistry 1931 with Friedrich Bergius.

Bosch Hieronymus (Jerome) 1460–1516. Early Netherlandish painter. His fantastic visions of weird and hellish creatures, as shown in *The Garden of Earthly Delights* about 1505–10 (Prado, Madrid), show astonishing imagination and a complex imagery. His religious subjects focused not on the holy figures but on the mass of ordinary witnesses, placing the religious event in a contemporary Netherlandish context and creating cruel caricatures of human sinfulness.

Bosch is named after his birthplace, 'sHertogenbosch, in North Brabant, the Netherlands. His work foreshadowed Surrealism and was probably inspired by a local religious brotherhood. However, he was an orthodox Catholic and a prosperous painter, not a heretic, as was once believed. After his death, his work was collected by Philip II of Spain.

Bosch Juan 1909– . President of the Dominican Republic 1963. His left-wing Partido Revolucionario Dominicano won a landslide victory in the 1962 elections. In office, he attempted agrarian reform and labor legislation. He was opposed by the US, and

overthrown by the army. His achievement was to establish a democratic political party after three decades of dictatorship.

Boscovich Ruggiero 1711–1787. Italian scientist. An early supporter of Newton, he developed a theory, popular in the 19th century, of the atom as a single point with surrounding fields of repulsive and attractive forces.

Bose Jagadis Chunder 1858–1937. Indian physicist and plant physiologist. Born near Dakha, he was professor of physical science at Calcutta 1885–1915, and studied the growth and minute movements of plants, and their reaction to electrical stimuli. He founded the Bose Research Institute, Calcutta.

Bose Satyendra Nath 1894–1974. Indian physicist who formulated the Bose–Einstein law of quantum mechanics with ◊Einstein. He was professor of physics at the University of Calcutta 1945–58.

Bosnia-Herzegovina Serbo-Croatian *Bosna-Hercegovina* country in central Europe, bounded N and W by Croatia, E by the Yugoslavian republic of Serbia, and E and S by the Yugoslavian republic of Montenegro.

government There is a 240-seat bicameral assembly, and a directly elected seven-member state presidency. Election contests are by a majority system, there being a second-round runoff race if no candidate secures a majority of the vote in the first round.

history Once the Roman province of ◊Illyria, the area enjoyed brief periods of independence in medieval times, then was ruled by the Ottoman Empire 1463–1878 and Austria 1878–

1918, when it was incorporated in the future Yugoslavia. It came under Nazi German rule 1941, and Marshal ◊Tito established his provisional government at liberated Jajce in Nov 1943. Bosnia-Herzegovina, kept undivided because of its ethnic and religious compound of Serbs (Orthodox Christians), Croats (Catholic Christians) and Serbo-Croatian-speaking Slavs (Muslims), became a republic within the Yugoslav Socialist Federal Republic in Nov 1945, after the expulsion of remaining German forces.

communist rule The republic's communist leadership became notorious for its corruption, racketeering, and authoritarianism, and from 1980 there was an upsurge in Islamic nationalism. Ethnic violence between Muslims and Serbs worsened 1989–90. In the Nov–Dec 1990 elections nationalist parties routed the ruling communists; subsequent divisions within the Bosnian ruling coalition, formed by the three leading Serb, Muslim, and Croatian parties, complicated the republic's dealings with Serbia.

civil unrest From the spring of 1991 the conflict between Serbia and Croatia and civil war in the latter spread disorder into Bosnia-Herzegovina, with Croats setting up barricades in an attempt to stop the predominantly Serb Yugoslav National Army (JNA) moving through into Croatia. In Aug 1991, the republic's president, Alija Izetbegović, a devout Muslim, expressed concern that Serbia intended to divide up Bosnia-Herzegovina between Serbia and Croatia, with a reduced Muslim buffer state in between, and appealed for support from Turkey and the European Community (EC). From Sept 1991 border areas

Bosnia-Herzegovina
Republic of

area 19,745 sq mi/51,129 sq km
capital Sarajevo
cities Banja Luka, Mostar, Prijedor, Tuzla, Zenica
physical barren, mountainous country
features part of the Dinaric Alps, limestone gorges,
population (1990) 4,300,000 including 44% Muslims, 33% Serbs, 17% Croats; a complex patchwork of ethnically mixed communities
head of state Alija Izetbegović from 1990
head of government to be decided
political system emergent democracy
political parties Party of Democratic Action (SDA), Muslim-oriented; Serbian Democratic Party (SDS); Christian Democratic Union (HDS); League of Communists

products citrus fruits and vegetables; iron, steel, and leather goods; textiles
language Serbian variant of Serbo-Croatian
religions Sunni Muslim, Serbian Orthodox, Roman Catholic
chronology
1918 Incorporated in the future Yugoslavia.
1941 Occupied by Nazi Germany.
1945 Became republic within Yugoslav Socialist Federation.
1980 Upsurge in Islamic nationalism.
1990 Ethnic violence erupted between Muslims and Serbs. Nov–Dec: communists defeated in multiparty elections; coalition formed by Serb, Muslim, and Croatian parties.
1991 May: Serbia–Croatia conflict spread disorder into Bosnia-Herzegovina. Aug: Serbia revealed plans to annex the SE part of the republic. Oct: "sovereignty" declared. Nov: plebiscite by Serbs favored remaining within Yugoslavia; Serbs and Croats established autonomous communities.
1992 Feb–March: Muslims and Croats voted overwhelmingly in favor of independence; referendum boycotted by Serbs. April: US and EC recognized Bosnian independence. Ethnic hostilities escalated, with Serb forces occupying E and Croatian forces much of W; state of emergency declared; all-out civil war ensued. May: admitted into United Nations (UN). June: Canadian–French UN forces drafted into Sarajevo to break three-month siege by Serbs. Cease-fire broken intermittently by both sides; UN and EC mediators vainly sought truce. Fighting continued; Serbs accused of "ethnic cleansing". Oct: UN Security Council voted to create a war crimes commission and banned military flights over Bosnia-Herzegovina.

began to fall into Serbian hands and Serbs began to form autonomous enclaves within the republic.

independence achieved In Oct 1991 the republic's "sovereignty" was declared by its parliament, but was rejected by Serbs, who established an alternative assembly and held a referendum Nov 1991 on remaining in the rump Yugoslav federation. Muslims and Croats, in alliance in the republic's parliament, voted Jan 1992 to seek recognition of independence by the EC. A subsequent referendum Feb 1992, requested by the EC, voted overwhelmingly in favor of independence. The referendum was boycotted by Bosnian Serbs who fiercely opposed independence. Violent ethnic clashes ensued, with bombings in several Bosnian cities. Despite the worsening situation, the EC and the US gave their official recognition of the country's independence in April. In May 1992 Bosnia-Herzegovina became a full member of the United Nations, and the UN called for the withdrawal of the JNA. Both UN and EC mediators vainly sought a solution to the conflict.

continued fighting Serb militia units, allegedly backed by Serbia, took control of border towns in E Bosnia and also launched attacks on the capital, Sarajevo. As Croats and Muslims also struggled to gain disputed territory, a state of emergency was declared. A number of cease-fires were quickly broken. By the end of May hundreds had been killed and hundreds of thousands were homeless. Bosnian Serbs established control over an area stretching from NW to the SE, comprising almost two-thirds of the country, and declared it independent. Croats dominated large portions of the western part of the country, and subsequently declared an independent Croatian state.

UN relief efforts placed in jeopardy From June 1992 Canadian/French UN forces were drafted into Sarajevo in an attempt to relieve a three-month Serbian siege of the capital. Continued Serbian offensives put the relief effort at risk, causing it to be temporarily abandoned Sept after relief workers were killed and a UN plane shot down. In Aug 1992 UN/EC-sponsored peace talks between all parties took place in London. Despite the reaching of an accord, the conflict continued to escalate.

war crimes reported From mid-1992 there was increased evidence of atrocities being perpetrated, particularly by Serbs, to enforce what was described as "ethnic cleansing," and reports of "death camps" and group slaughter of internees. In Oct 1992 the UN Security Council voted to create a war crimes commission and imposed a ban on all military flights over Bosnia-Herzegovina.

Bosnian Crisis period of international tension 1908 when Austria attempted to capitalize on Turkish weakness after the ⟡Young Turk revolt by annexing the provinces of Bosnia and Herzegovina. Austria obtained Russian approval in exchange for conceding Russian access to the Bosporus straits.

The speed of Austrian action took Russia by surprise, and domestic opposition led to the resignation of Russian foreign minister Izvolsky. Russia also failed to obtain necessary French and British agreements on the straits.

boson in physics, an elementary particle whose spin can only take values that are whole numbers or zero. Bosons may be classified as ⟡gauge bosons (carriers of the four fundamental forces) or ⟡mesons. All elementary particles are either bosons or ⟡fermions.

Unlike fermions, more than one boson in a system (such as an atom) can possess the same energy state. When developed mathematically, this statement is known as the Bose–Einstein law, after its discoverers Satyendra Bose and Albert Einstein.

Bosporus (Turkish ***Karadeniz Boğazi***) strait 17 mi/27 km long, joining the Black Sea with the Sea of Marmara and forming part of the water division between Europe and Asia; its name may be derived from the Greek legend of ⟡Io. Istanbul stands on its W side. The ***Bosporus Bridge*** 1973, 5,320 ft/1,621 m, links Istanbul and Turkey-in-Asia. In 1988 a second bridge across the straits was opened, linking Asia and Europe.

Boston industrial and commercial center, capital of Massachusetts; population (1990) 574,300; metropolitan area 4,171,600. It is a publishing center and industrial port on Massachusetts Bay, but the economy is dominated by financial and health services and government. Boston and Northeastern universities are here; Harvard University and the Massachusetts Institute of Technology are in neighboring Cambridge, across the Charles River.

features Faneuil Hall, Old North Church, Paul Revere house, USS *Constitution* ("Old Ironsides"), New England Aquarium, Museum of Science, J F Kennedy National Historic Site.

history founded by Puritans 1630, Boston was a center of opposition to British trade restrictions, culminating in the Boston Tea Party 1773. After the first shots of the American Revolution in 1775 at nearby Lexington and Concord, the Battle of Bunker Hill was fought outside the city. The British withdrew from the city 1776. In the 19th century, Boston became the metropolis of New England. Urban redevelopment and the growth of service industries have compensated for the city's industrial decline.

Boston Tea Party protest 1773 by colonists against the tea tax imposed on them by the British in Massachusetts, America, before the ⟡American Revolution.

When a valuable consignment of tea (belonging to the East India Company and intended for sale in the American colonies) arrived in Boston Harbor aboard three ships from England, it was thrown overboard by a group of Bostonians disguised as Indians during the night of Dec 16, 1773. The British government, angered by this and other colonial protests against British policy, took retaliatory measures 1774, including the closing of the port of Boston.

Boswell James 1740–1795. Scottish biographer and diarist. He was a member of Samuel ⟡Johnson's London Literary Club and the two men traveled to Scotland together 1773, as recorded in Boswell's *Journal of the Tour to the Hebrides* 1785. His classic English biography *Life of Samuel Johnson* was published 1791.

Born in Edinburgh, Boswell studied law but centered his ambitions on literature and politics. He first met Johnson 1763, before setting out on a European tour during which he met the French thinkers Rousseau and Voltaire, and the Corsican nationalist general Paoli (1726–1807), whom he commemorated in his popular *Account of Corsica* 1768. In 1766 he became a lawyer, and in 1772 renewed his acquaintance with Johnson in London. Boswell's long-lost personal papers were acquired for

publication by Yale University 1949, and the *Journals* are of exceptional interest.

Bosworth, Battle of last battle of the Wars of the ⟡Roses, fought on Aug 22, 1485. Richard III, the Yorkist king, was defeated and slain by Henry of Richmond, who became Henry VII. The battlefield is near the village of Market Bosworth, 12 mi/19 km W of Leicester, England.

botanical garden place where a wide range of plants is grown, providing the opportunity to see a botanical diversity not likely to be encountered naturally. Among the earliest forms of botanical garden was the ***physic garden***, devoted to the study and growth of medicinal plants; an example is the Chelsea Physic Garden in London, established 1673 and still in existence. Following increased botanical exploration, botanical gardens were used to test the commercial potential of new plants being sent back from all parts of the world.

Today a botanical garden serves many purposes: education, science, and conservation. Many are associated with universities and also maintain large collections of preserved specimens (see ⟡herbarium), libraries, research laboratories, and gene banks.

In the US, there are both publicly and privately funded botanical gardens. Some botanical gardens and arboretums are devoted to local or New World plants while others preserve, protect, and propagate specialties, such as ornamentals. Most botanical gardens are open year round, with greenhouses and conservatories as well as extensive landscaped grounds and an exhibit hall that sells plants and offers an advisory service. The New York Botanical Society runs the botanical garden at the Bronx Zoo in this way. Winterhur, the former du Pont estate, and Mount Vernon, the former home of George Washington, are now run as private historical sites and botanical gardens.

botany the study of plants. It is subdivided into a number of specialized studies, such as the identification and classification of plants (taxonomy), their external formation (plant morphology), their internal arrangement (plant anatomy), their microscopic examination (plant histology), their functioning and life history (plant physiology), and their distribution over the Earth's surface in relation to their surroundings (plant ecology). Paleobotany concerns the study of fossil plants, while economic botany deals with the utility of plants. Horticulture, agriculture, and forestry are branches of botany.

history The most ancient botanical record was carved on the walls of the temple at Karnak, Egypt, about 1500 BC. The Greeks in the 5th and 4th centuries BC used many plants for medicinal purposes, the first Greek *Herbal* being drawn up about 350 BC by Diocles of Carystus. Botanical information was collected into the works of Theophrastus of Eresus (380–287 BC), a pupil of Aristotle, who founded technical plant nomenclature. Cesalpino in the 16th century sketched out a system of classification based on flowers, fruits, and seeds, while Joachim Jungius (1587–1657) used flowers only as his criterion. John Ray (1627–1705) arranged plants systematically, based on his findings on fruit, leaf, and flower, and described about 18,600 plants.

The Swedish botanist Carl von Linné, or ⟡Linnaeus, who founded systematics in the 18th century, included in his classification all known plants and animals, giving each a

Botswana
Republic of

area 225,000 sq mi/582,000 sq km
capital Gaborone
cities Mahalpye, Serowe, Tutume, Francistown
physical desert in SW, plains in E, fertile
lands and swamp in N
environment the Okavango Swamp is
threatened by plans to develop the area for
mining and agriculture
features Kalahari Desert in SW; Okavango
Swamp in N, remarkable for its wildlife;
Makgadikgadi salt pans in E; diamonds
mined at Orapa and Jwaneng in partnership
with De Beers of South Africa
head of state and government Quett
Ketamile Joni Masire from 1980

political system democratic republic
political parties Botswana Democratic
Party (BDP), moderate centrist; Botswana
National Front (BNF), moderate, left of center
exports diamonds (third largest producer
in world), copper, nickel, meat products,
textiles
currency pula
population (1990 est) 1,218,000 (80%
Bamangwato, 20% Bangwaketse); growth
rate 3.5% p.a.
life expectancy (1988) 59 years
languages English (official), Setswana
(national)
religions Christian 50%, animist 50%
literacy (1988) 84%
GDP $2.0 bn (1988); $1,611 per head
chronology
1885 Became a British protectorate.
1960 New constitution created a legislative
council.
1963 End of rule by High Commission.
1965 Capital transferred from Mafeking
to Gaborone. Internal self-government
achieved. Sir Seretse Khama elected head
of government.
1966 Independence achieved from Britain.
New constitution came into effect; name
changed from Bechuanaland to Botswana;
Seretse Khama elected president.
1980 Seretse Khama died; succeeded by
Vice President Quett Masire.
1984 Masire reelected.
1985 South African raid on Gaborone.
1987 Joint permanent commission with
Mozambique established, to improve
relations.
1989 The BDP and Masire reelected.

○binomial descriptive label. His work greatly
aided the future study of plants, as botanists
found that all plants could be fitted into a systematic classification based on Linnaeus' work.
Linnaeus was also the first to recognize the
sexual nature of flowers. This was followed up
by Charles ○Darwin and others.

Later work revealed the detailed cellular
structure of plant tissues and the exact nature
of ○photosynthesis. Julius von Sachs (1832–
1897) defined the function of ○chlorophyll
and the significance of plant ○stomata. In the
second half of the 20th century, much has
been learned about cell function, repair, and
growth by the hybridization of plant cells (the
combination of the nucleus of one cell with the
cytoplasm of another).

Botany Bay inlet on the E coast of Australia,
5 mi/8 km S of Sydney, New South Wales. Chosen 1787 as the site for a penal colony, it proved
unsuitable. Sydney now stands on the site of
the former settlement. The name Botany Bay
continued to be popularly used for any convict
settlement in Australia.

Botero Fernando 1932– . Colombian painter.
He studied in Spain and gained an international
reputation for his paintings of fat, vulgar figures, often of women, parodies of conventional
sensuality.

botfly any fly of the family Oestridae. The
larvae are parasites that feed on the skin
(warblefly of cattle) or in the nasal cavity (nostrilflies of sheep and deer). The
horse botfly belongs to another family, the
Gasterophilidae. It has a parasitic larva that
feeds in the horse's stomach.

Botha P(ieter) W(illem) 1916– . South

African politician, prime minister from 1978.
Botha initiated a modification of ○apartheid,
which later slowed in the face of Afrikaner
(Boer) opposition. In 1984 he became the
first executive state president. In 1989 he unwillingly resigned both party leadership and
presidency after suffering a stroke, and was
succeeded by F W de Klerk.

Bothe Walther 1891–1957. German physicist
who showed 1929 that the cosmic rays bombarding the Earth are composed not of photons
but of more massive particles. Nobel Prize for
Physics 1954.

Bothwell James Hepburn, 4th Earl of Bothwell
c. 1536–1578. Scottish nobleman, third husband of Mary Queen of Scots, 1567–70, alleged
to have arranged the explosion that killed
Darnley, her previous husband, 1567.

Tried and acquitted a few weeks after the
assassination, he abducted Mary and married
her on May 15th. A revolt ensued, and Bothwell
fled. In 1570 Mary obtained a divorce, and
Bothwell was confined in a castle in mainland
Europe, where he died insane.

bo tree or **peepul** Indian ○fig tree *Ficus
religiosa*, said to be the tree under which the
Buddha became enlightened.

Botswana landlocked country in central
southern Africa, bounded S and SE by South
Africa, W and N by Namibia, and NE by
Zimbabwe.
government The 1966 constitution blends the
British system of parliamentary accountability
with representation for each of Botswana's
major ethnic groups. It provides for a national
assembly of 40 members—34 elected by universal suffrage, four by the assembly itself, plus

the speaker and the attorney general—and has
a life of five years. The president is elected
by the assembly for its duration and is an ex
officio member of that body and answerable to
it. There is also a 15-member house of chiefs,
consisting of the chiefs of Botswana's eight
principal ethnic groups, four members elected
by the chiefs themselves, and three elected by
the house in general. The president may delay
a bill for up to six months and then either sign
it or dissolve the assembly and call a general
election. The house of chiefs is consulted by
the president and the assembly in matters affecting it. The president appoints a cabinet that
is answerable to the assembly.
history The first inhabitants were the ○Kung,
the hunter-gatherer groups living chiefly in
the Kalahari Desert; from the 17th century the
Tswana people became the principal inhabitants of the area, followed by the arrival of
Bantu peoples in the early 19th century. Fearing an invasion by Boer farmers, the local
rulers appealed to Britain and Bechuanaland
(as it was originally called) became a British
protectorate 1885.

On passing the Union of South Africa Act
1910, making South Africa independent, the
British Parliament provided for the possibility of Bechuanaland becoming part of South
Africa, but stipulated that this would not happen without popular consent. Successive South
African governments requested the transfer,
but Botswana preferred full independence.

The 1960 constitution provided for a legislative council, although remaining under
British High Commission control. In 1963
High Commission rule ended, and in the legislative assembly elections the newly formed
Bechuanaland Democratic Party (BDP) won a
majority. Its leader, Seretse ○Khama, had been
deposed as chief of the Bamangwato tribe 1950
and had since lived in exile.
achieved independence In 1966 the country,
renamed Botswana, became an independent
state within the British ○Commonwealth with
Sir Seretse Khama, as he had now become, as
president. He continued to be reelected until
his death 1980, when he was succeeded by
the vice-president, Dr Quett Masire, who was
reelected 1984. In the Oct 1989 elections the
BDP won 31 of the 34 national assembly seats
and Quett Masire was again reelected.
relations with South Africa Since independence Botswana has earned a reputation for
stability. It is a member of the ○nonaligned
movement. South Africa accused it of providing
bases for the African National Congress (ANC)
and Botswana was the target of several cross-
border raids by South African forces. The
presence of ANC bases was always denied by
both Botswana and the ANC. Tension in this
respect was dissipated by the legalization of the
ANC by South Africa 1990. *See illustration box.*

Botta Mario 1943– . Swiss architect. Most
of his work is in Ticino—the Italian canton of
Switzerland. He is a key figure of the Ticinese
school. His work shows a strong regionalist
interpretation of modernism, close attention to
topography, and a very formal geometry. These
aspects are expressed in a striking series of
single family houses including Riva San Vitale
1972–73 and Ligometo 1975–76.

Other works include a school at Morbio
Inferiore 1972–77 and the Staatsbank, Fribor
1977–82.

Botticelli Sandro 1445–1510. Florentine painter of religious and mythological subjects. He
was patronized by the ruling ○Medici family,

for whom he painted *Primavera* 1478 and *The Birth of Venus* about 1482–84 (both in the Uffizi, Florence). From the 1490s he was influenced by the religious fanatic ⟡Savonarola and developed a harshly expressive and emotional style.

His real name was Filipepi, but his elder brother's nickname Botticelli "little barrel" was passed on to him. His work for the Medicis was designed to cater to the educated Classical tastes of the day. As well as his sentimental, beautiful young Madonnas, he produced a series of inventive compositions, including *tondi*, circular paintings. He broke with the Medicis after their execution of Savonarola.

bottlebrush any of several trees or shrubs common in Australia, belonging to the genus *Callistemon* of the myrtle family, with characteristic cylindrical, composite flower heads in green, yellow, white, various shades of red, and violet.

botulism rare, often fatal type of ⟡food poisoning. Symptoms include muscular paralysis and disturbed breathing and vision. It is caused by a toxin produced by the bacterium *Clostridium botulinum*, sometimes found in improperly canned food.

Thorough cooking destroys the toxin, which otherwise suppresses the cardiac and respiratory centers of the brain.

Boucher François 1703–1770. French Rococo painter, court painter from 1765. He was much patronized for his light-hearted, decorative scenes: for example *Diana Bathing* 1742 (Louvre, Paris).

He also painted portraits and decorative chinoiserie for Parisian palaces. He became director of the Gobelins tapestry works, Paris, 1755.

Boudicca Queen of the Iceni (native Britons), often referred to by the Latin form *Boadicea*. Her husband, King Prasutagus, had been a tributary of the Romans, but on his death AD 60 the territory of the Iceni was violently annexed. Boudicca was scourged and her daughters raped. Boudicca raised the whole of SE England in revolt, and before the main Roman armies could return from campaigning in Wales she burned Londinium (London), Verulamium (St Albans), and Camolodunum (Colchester). Later the Romans under governor Suetonius Paulinus defeated the British between London and Chester; they were virtually annihilated and Boudicca poisoned herself.

Boudin Eugène 1824–1898. French artist, a forerunner of the Impressionists, known for his fresh seaside scenes painted in the open air.

Bougainville island province of Papua New Guinea; largest of the Solomon Islands archipelago
area 4,100 sq mi/10,620 sq km
capital Kieta
products copper, gold and silver; in 1992 Bougainville's rebel government claimed that waste from one of the world's largest copper mines (owned by Australian company CRA Minerals) had devastated the island's environment, silting up the streams of the Jaba River system and contaminating the water with dangerous heavy metals
population (1989) 128,000
history named after the French navigator Bougainville who arrived 1768. In 1976 Bougainville became a province (with substantial autonomy) of Papua New Guinea. A state of emergency was declared 1989 after secessionist violence.

Bougainville Louis Antoine de 1729–1811. French navigator. After service with the French in Canada during the Seven Years' War, he made the first French circumnavigation of the world 1766–69 and the first systematic observations of longitude.

Several Pacific islands are named after him, as is the climbing plant *bougainvillea*.

bougainvillea any plant of the genus of South American tropical vines *Bougainvillea*, of the four o'clock family Nyctaginaceae, now cultivated in warm countries throughout the world for the red and purple bracts that cover the flowers. They are named after the French navigator Louis Bougainville.

Bouguer anomaly in geophysics, an increase in the Earth's gravity observed near a mountain or dense rock mass. This is due to the gravitational force exerted by the rock mass. It is named after its discoverer, the French mathematician Pierre Bouguer (1698–1758), who first observed it 1735.

Boulanger George Ernest Jean Marie 1837–1891. French general. He became minister of war 1886, and his anti-German speeches nearly provoked war with Germany 1887. In 1889 he was suspected of aspiring to dictatorship by a coup d'état. Accused of treason, he fled into exile and committed suicide on the grave of his mistress.

Boulanger Nadia (Juliette) 1887–1979. French music teacher and conductor. A pupil of Fauré, and admirer of Stravinsky, she include among her composition pupils at the American Conservatory in Fontainebleau (from 1921) Aaron Copland, Roy Harris, Walter Piston, and Philip Glass.

She was the first woman to conduct the Royal Philharmonic, London 1937, and the Boston Symphony, the New York Philharmonic, and the Philadelphia Orchestra 1938.

Boulder city in N central Colorado, NW of Denver, in the E foothills of the Rocky mountains. A center of scientific research, especially that of space, it is the site of the University of Colorado 1876. Other industries include agriculture, mining, and tourism; population (1990) 83,300.

boules (French "balls") French game (also called *boccie* and *pétanque*) between two players or teams; it is similar to bowls.

Boules is derived from the ancient French game *jeu provençal*. The object is to deliver a boule (or boules) from a standing position to land as near the jack (target) as possible. The boule is approximately 3 in/8 cm in diameter and weighs 22–28 oz/620–800 g. The standard length of the court, normally with a sand base, is 90 ft/27.5 m.

Boulez Pierre 1925– . French composer and conductor. He studied with ⟡Messiaen and promoted contemporary music with a series of innovative *Domaine Musical* concerts and recordings in the 1950s, as conductor of the BBC Symphony and New York Philharmonic orchestras during the 1970s, and as founder and director of IRCAM, a music research studio in Paris opened 1977.

His music, strictly serial and expressionistic in style, includes the cantatas *Le Visage nuptial* 1946–52 and *Le Marteau sans maître* 1955, both to texts by René Char; *Pli selon pli* 1962 for soprano and orchestra; and *Répons* 1981 for soloists, orchestra, tapes, and computer-generated sounds.

Boulogne-sur-Mer town on the English Channel, Pas-de-Calais *département*, France; population (1983) 99,000. Industries include oil refining, food processing, and fishing. It is also a ferry port (connecting with Dover and Folkestone) and seaside resort. Boulogne was a medieval countship, but became part of France 1477.

Boult Adrian (Cedric) 1889–1983. British conductor of the BBC Symphony Orchestra 1930–50 and the London Philharmonic 1950–57. He promoted the work of Holst and Vaughan Williams, and was a celebrated interpreter of Elgar.

Boumédienne Houari. Adopted name of Mohammed Boukharouba 1925–1978. Algerian politician who brought the nationalist leader Ben Bella to power by a revolt 1962, and superseded him as president in 1965 by a further coup.

Boundary Peak highest mountain in Nevada, rising to 13,143 ft/4,006 m on the Nevada-California frontier.

Bounty, Mutiny on the. Naval mutiny in the Pacific 1789 against British captain William ⟡Bligh.

Bourbon, duchy of originally a seigneury (feudal domain) created in the 10th century in the county of Bourges, central France, held by the Bourbon family. It became a duchy 1327.

The lands passed to the Capetian dynasty (see ⟡Capet) as a result of the marriage of the Bourbon heiress Beatrix to Robert of Clermont, son of Louis IX. Their son Pierre became the first duke of Bourbon 1327. The direct line ended with the death of Charles, Duke of Bourbon, in 1527.

Bourbon dynasty French royal house (succeeding that of ⟡Valois) beginning with Henry IV, and ending with Louis XVI, with a brief revival under Louis XVIII, Charles X, and Louis Philippe. The Bourbons also ruled Spain almost uninterruptedly from Philip V to Alfonso XIII and were restored in 1975 (⟡Juan Carlos); at one point they also ruled Naples and several Italian duchies. The Grand Duke of Luxembourg is also a Bourbon by male descent.

Bourdon Eugène 1808–1884. French engineer and instrument maker who invented the pressure gauge that bears his name.

Bourdon gauge instrument for measuring pressure, invented by Eugène Bourdon 1849. The gauge contains a C-shaped tube, closed at one end. When the pressure inside the tube increases, the tube uncurls slightly causing a small movement at its closed end. A system of levers and gears magnifies this movement and turns a pointer, which indicates the pressure on a circular scale. Bourdon gauges are often fitted to cylinders of compressed gas used in industry and hospitals.

bourgeois (French) a member of the middle class, implying that a person is unimaginative, conservative, and materialistic.

Bourgeois Léon Victor Auguste 1851–1925. French politician. Entering politics as a Radical, he was prime minister in 1895, and later served in many cabinets. He was one of the pioneer advocates of the League of Nations. He was awarded the Nobel Peace Prize 1920.

bourgeoisie (French) the middle classes. The

French word originally meant "the freemen of a borough." It came to mean the whole class above the workers and peasants, and below the nobility. Bourgeoisie (and *bourgeois*) has also acquired a contemptuous sense, implying commonplace, philistine respectability. By socialists it is applied to the whole propertied class, as distinct from the proletariat.

Bourges city in central France, 125 mi/200 km S of Paris; population (1982) 92,000. Industries include aircraft, engineering, and tires. It has a 13th-century Gothic cathedral and notable art collections.

Bourgogne region of France that includes the *départements* of Côte-d'Or, Nièvre, Sâone-et-Loire, and Yonne; area 12,198 sq mi/ 31,600 sq km; population (1986) 1,607,000. Its capital is Dijon.

It is renowned for its wines, such as Chablis and Nuits-Saint-Georges, and for its cattle (the Charolais herd-book is maintained at Nevers). A former independent kingdom and duchy (English name ⟩Burgundy), it was incorporated into France 1477.

Bourguiba Habib ben Ali 1903– . Tunisian politician, first president of Tunisia 1957–87. Educated at the University of Paris, he became a journalist and was frequently imprisoned by the French for his nationalist aims as leader of the Néo-Destour party. He became prime minister 1956, president (for life from 1974) and prime minister of the Tunisian republic 1957; he was overthrown in a bloodless coup 1987.

Bourke-White Margaret 1906–1971. US photographer. As an editor of *Fortune* magazine 1929–33, she traveled extensively in the USSR, publishing several collections of photographs. Later, with husband Erskine Caldwell, she also published photo collections of American and European subjects. She began working for *Life* magazine 1936, and covered combat in World War II and documented India's struggle for independence.

Born in New York and educated at Cornell Univeristy, Bourke-White began her career as a freelance industrial and architectural photographer.

Bournonville August 1805–1879. Danish dancer and choreographer. He worked with the Royal Danish ballet for most of his life, giving Danish ballet a worldwide importance. His ballets, many of which have been revived in the last 50 years, include *La Sylphide* 1836 (music by Lövenskjöld) and *Napoli* 1842.

Boutros-Ghali Boutros 1922– . Egyptian diplomat and politician, deputy prime minister 1991–92. He worked toward peace in the Middle East in the foreign ministry posts he held 1977–91. He became secretary-general of the United Nations Jan 1992, and during his first year of office had to deal with the war in Bosnia-Herzegovina and famine in Somalia.

Bouts Dierick *c.* 1420–1475. Early Netherlandish painter. Born in Haarlem, he settled in Louvain, painting portraits and religious scenes influenced by Rogier van der Weyden. *The Last Supper* 1464–68 (St Pierre, Louvain) is one of his finest works.

Bouvet Island uninhabited island in the S Atlantic Ocean, a dependency of Norway since 1930; area 19 sq mi/48 sq km. Discovered by the French captain Jacques Bouvet in 1738, it was made the subject of a claim by Britain in 1825, but this was waived in Norway's favor in 1928.

Bouvines, Battle of victory for Philip II (Philip Augustus) of France in 1214, near the village of Bouvines in Flanders, over the Holy Roman emperor Otto IV and his allies. The battle, one of the most decisive in medieval Europe, ensured the succession of Frederick II as emperor and confirmed Philip as ruler of the whole of N France and Flanders; it led to the renunciation of all English claims to the region.

Bovet Daniel 1907–1992. Swiss physiologist. He pioneered research into antihistamine drugs used in the treatment of nettle rash and hay fever, and was awarded a Nobel Prize for Medicine 1957 for his production of a synthetic form of curare, used as a muscle relaxant in anesthesia.

bovine spongiform encephalopathy (BSE) disease of cattle, allied to ⟩scrapie, that renders the brain spongy and may drive an animal mad. It has been identified only in the UK, where more than 26,000 cases were confirmed between the first diagnosis Nov 1986 and April 1991. The organism causing it is unknown; it is not a conventional virus because it is more resistant to chemicals and heat, cannot be seen even under an electron microscope, cannot be grown in tissue culture, and does not appear to provoke an immune response in the body. BSE is very similar to, and may be related to, Creutzfeld-Jakob disease and kuru, which affect humans.

Bow Clara 1905–1965. US film actress known as a Jazz Baby and the "It Girl" after her portrayal of a glamorous flapper in the silent film *It* 1927.

She made a smooth transition to sound with *The Wild Party* 1929. Earlier films included *Down to the Sea in Ships* 1925 and *The Plastic Age, Kid Boots, Mantrap,* and *Dancing Mothers,* all 1926. Later films include *Rough House Rosie* 1927, *Red Hair* 1928, and *Three Weekends* 1928, and *The Saturday Night Kid* 1929. She made her last film *Hoopla* 1933 and retired to her husband's ranch in Nevada.

Bowditch Nathaniel 1773–1838. US astronomer. Having discovered many inaccuracies in the standard navigation guide of the day, he published his own guide, *The New American Practical Navigator* 1802. Later, as a maritime insurance actuary, Bowditch continued his private study and published works on astronomical observations—among them, *Celestial Mechanics* 1829–39, a translation of the first four volumes of Laplace's *Mécanique céleste*. In 1829 he became president of the American Academy of Arts and Sciences.

Born in Salem, Massachusetts, Bowditch had little formal education but read widely as a merchant seaman during the years 1795–1803.

Bowdler Thomas 1754–1825. British editor whose prudishly expurgated versions of Shakespeare and other authors gave rise to the verb *bowdlerize*.

Bowdoin James 1726–1790. American public official. Born in Boston, Bowdoin was educated at Harvard and began his public career with election to the Massachusetts General Court 1753. Chosen as a member of the Governor's Council 1757, he became a strong supporter of the cause of American independence, serving on the Massachusetts Executive Council 1775–76. Bowdoin later served as president of the state constitutional convention 1779–80 and as governor 1785–87. He was also the first president of the American Academy of Arts and Sciences. Bowdoin College in Brunswick, Maine, is named in his honor.

bower bird New Guinean and N Australian bird of the family Ptilonorhynchidae, related to the ⟩birds of paradise. The males are dull-colored, and build elaborate bowers of sticks and grass, decorated with shells, feathers, or flowers, and even painted with the juice of berries, to attract the females. There are 17 species.

bowfin North American fish *Amia calva* with a swim bladder highly developed as an air sac, enabling it to breathe air. It is the only surviving member of a primitive group of bony fishes.

bowhead Arctic whale *Balaena mysticetus* with strongly curving upper jawbones supporting the plates of baleen with which it sifts planktonic crustaceans from the water. Averaging 50 ft/15 m long and 100 tons/90 tonnes in weight, these slow-moving, placid whales were once extremely common, but by the 17th century were already becoming scarce through hunting. Only an estimated 3,000 remain, and continued hunting by the Inuit may result in extinction.

Bowie David. Adopted name of David Jones 1947– . English pop singer, songwriter, and actor. He became a rock star with the release of the album *The Rise and Fall of Ziggy Stardust and the Spiders from Mars* 1972, and collaborated in the mid-1970s with the electronic virtuoso Brian Eno (1948–) and Iggy Pop. He has also acted in plays and films, including Nicolas Roeg's *The Man Who Fell to Earth* 1976.

Among his albums are *Aladdin Sane* 1973, *Station to Station* 1976, *Low, Heroes* both 1977, *Lodger* 1979, and *Let's Dance* 1983. In 1989 he formed and recorded with Tin Machine.

Bowie James "Jim" 1796–1836. US frontiersman and folk hero. A colonel in the Texan forces during the Mexican War, he is said to have invented the single-edge, guarded hunting and throwing knife known as a *Bowie knife*. He was killed in the Battle of the ⟩Alamo.

Bowles Paul 1910– . US novelist and composer. Born in New York City, he studied with Aaron Copland and Virgil Thomson, writing scores for ballets, films, and an opera, *The Wind Remains* 1943, as well as incidental music for plays. He settled in Morocco, the setting of his novels *The Sheltering Sky* 1949 and *Let It Come Down* 1952. His autobiography, *Without Stopping*, was published in 1972.

bowling indoor sport in which a ball is rolled into a target of standing pins. There are many forms of the sport, but the term "bowling" usually refers to the most popular variety, tenpin. The ball used in tenpin bowling is sometimes plastic but more commonly hard rubber. An official ball (one allowed in league play) must weigh 10–16 lb/4.5–7.3 kg and may not exceed 8.6 in/21.8 cm in diameter. Finger holes are drilled into each ball. Methods of gripping differ from bowler to bowler but most common is the underhand three-finger grip (thumb, middle finger, and ring finger).

Each of the bottle-shaped maple pins is 15 in/38 cm high, at least 5.25 in/13.34 cm in circumference at the neck, and at most 15 in/ 38 cm in circumference at the widest part. Pins are arranged in a triangular pattern at the end of a wooden lane 60 ft/18.3 m long from the headpin to the foul line. A bowler makes an approach toward the foul line, which may not be crossed, bringing the ball into a backswing and then swinging it forward for release. The ball travels down the lane, the object being to "bowl over" as many pins as possible. A game of tenpins is divided into ten frames. In each frame, the bowler has two attempts to knock down all ten pins. Each toppled pin is scored as one point. If all ten pins go down on a first roll, it is called a "strike" and counts ten points plus the number of pins knocked down by the bowler's next two rolls. When all ten pins are toppled by two rolls, it is a "spare" and counts ten points plus the number of pins knocked down by the bowler's first roll of the next frame. A perfect game is 12 consecutive strikes, for a score of 300.

Whereas tenpin is called big-pin bowling, several other forms of the game are classified as small-pin bowling, the most popular being duckpin and candlepin. Both use a much smaller ball than tenpin. The stubby duckpins are 9.4 in/23.9 cm high; the narrow, tapered candlepins are 15.75 in/40.00 cm high and can stand upright on either end.

history bowling in its most rudimentary form can be traced to ancient Egypt. Bowling-type equipment was found in the tomb of an Egyptian boy who died about 5200 BC. Other ancient cultures enjoyed their own variations of the sport, but what is considered the precursor of modern bowling generally is dated to medieval Europe, where *kegels* (the pins) were knocked down by thrown or rolled rocks.

Ninepins, a Dutch version of bowling, was introduced to the Americas in the 17th century. By the 1800s it not only had become very popular in New England but it had evolved into a major gambling activity. When Connecticut put a ban on "bowling at nine pins" in 1841, enterprising bowlers overstepped the law by adding a pin to the game—hence, tenpin bowling.

In 1895 the American Bowling Congress was organized, and under its authority the rules and equipment specifications of bowling in the US became standardized. In 1916 the Women's International Bowling Congress was founded; today it is the largest women's sports organization in the world. Professional bowling is a lucrative occupation for top contenders. The Professional Bowlers Association and the Ladies Pro Bowlers Tour sponsor high-stake tournaments throughout the US and in several other countries as well (Canada, Japan, and Latin America have shown particular interest in the game). Bowling "alleys" are businesses run to attract recreational bowlers; often leagues are formed and competitions or league events are held at them.

bowls a lawn bowling game played on a bowling green and indoors.

Bowman's capsule in the vertebrate kidney, a microscopic filtering device used in the initial stages of waste-removal and urine formation.

There are approximately a million of these capsules in a human kidney, each made up of a tight knot of capillaries and each leading into a kidney tubule or nephron. Blood at high pressure passes into the capillaries where water, dissolved nutrients, and urea move through the capillary wall into the tubule.

box any of several small evergreen trees and shrubs, genus *Buxus*, of the family Buxaceae, with small, leathery leaves. Some species are used as hedge plants and for shaping into garden ornaments.

boxer breed of dog, about 2 ft/60 cm tall, with a smooth coat and a set-back nose. The tail is usually docked. Boxers are usually brown but may be brindled or white.

Boxer member of the *I ho ch'üan* ("Righteous Harmonious Fists"), a society of Chinese nationalists dedicated to fighting European influence. The **Boxer Rebellion** or **Uprising** 1900 was instigated by the Dowager Empress Tzu Hsi (1834–1908). European and US legations in Beijing were besieged and thousands of Chinese Christian converts and missionaries murdered. An international punitive force was dispatched, Beijing was captured Aug 14, 1900, and China agreed to pay a large indemnity.

boxfish or **trunkfish,** any fish of the family Ostraciodontidae, with scales that are hexagonal bony plates fused to form a box covering the body, only the mouth and fins being free of the armor. Boxfishes swim slowly. The cowfish, genus *Lactophrys*, with two "horns" above the eyes, is a member of this group.

boxing fighting with gloved fists, almost entirely a male sport. The sport dates from the 18th century, when fights were fought with bare knuckles and untimed rounds. Each round ended with a knockdown. Fighting with gloves became the accepted form in the latter part of the 19th century after the formulation of the Queensberry Rules 1867.

Jack Broughton (1704–1789) was one of the early champions and in 1743 drew up the first set of boxing rules. The last bare-knuckle championship fight was between John L Sullivan and Jake Kilrain 1899. Today all boxing follows the original Queensberry Rules, but with modifications. Contests take place in a roped ring 14–20 ft/4.3–6.1 m square. All rounds last three minutes. Amateur bouts last three rounds; professional championship bouts last as many as 12 or 15 rounds. Boxers are classified according to weight and may not fight in a division lighter than their own. The weight divisions in professional boxing range from **straw-weight** (also known as paperweight and mini-flyweight), under 108 lb/49 kg, to **heavyweight**, over 195 lb/88 kg.

Boxing has school, amateur, semiprofessional, and professional matches.

boxing: recent winners

World Champions
(WBC = World Boxing Council; WBA = World Boxing Association; IBF = International Boxing Federation; WBO = World Boxing Organization)
heavyweight

1986	Tim Witherspoon *US* (WBA)
1986	Trevor Berbick *Canada* (WBC)
1986	Mike Tyson *US* (WBC)
1986	James Smith *US* (WBA)
1987	Mike Tyson *US* (WBA)
1987	Tony Tucker *US* (IBF)
1987	Mike Tyson *US* (undisputed)
1989	Francesco Damiani *Italy* (WBO)
1990	James Douglas *US* (undisputed)
1990	Evander Holyfield *US* (undisputed)
1992	Riddick Bowe *US* (WBA, IBF)

great heavyweight champions include:
John L Sullivan (bare-knuckle champion) 1882–92
Jim Corbett (first Marquess of Queensberry champion) 1892–97
Jack Dempsey 1919–26
Joe Louis 1937–49
Rocky Marciano 1952–56
Mohammed Ali 1964–67, 1974–78, 1978–79
Larry Holmes 1978–85
Mike Tyson 1986–1990

boyar landowner in the Russian aristocracy. During the 16th century boyars formed a powerful interest group threatening the tsar's power, until their influence was decisively broken in 1565 when Ivan the Terrible confiscated much of their land.

Boycott Charles Cunningham 1832–1897. English land agent in County Mayo, Ireland, who strongly opposed the demands for agrarian reform by the Irish Land League 1879–81, with the result that the peasants refused to work for him; hence the word **boycott**.

Boyd-Orr John 1880–1971. British nutritionist and health campaigner. He was awarded the Nobel Prize for Peace in 1949 in recognition of his work toward alleviating world hunger.

Boyle Charles, 4th Earl of Orrery 1676–1731. Irish soldier and diplomat. The *orrery*, a mechanical model of the Solar System in which the planets move at the correct relative velocities, is named after him.

Boyle Robert 1627–1691. Irish physicist and chemist who published the seminal *The Sceptical Chymist* 1661. He formulated **Boyle's law** 1662.

Boyle's law law stating that the volume of a given mass of gas at a constant temperature is inversely proportional to its pressure. For example, if the pressure of a gas doubles, its volume will be reduced by a half, and vice versa. The law was discovered in 1662 by Robert Boyle. See also ⟩gas laws.

Boyne river in the Irish Republic. Rising in the Bog of Allen in County Kildare, it flows 69 mi/110 km NE to the Irish Sea near Drogheda. The Battle of the Boyne was fought at Oldbridge near the mouth of the river in 1690.

Boyne, Battle of the battle fought July 1, 1690 in E Ireland, in which James II was defeated by William III and fled to France. It was the decisive battle of the War of English Succession, confirming a Protestant monarch. It took its name from the river Boyne which rises in County Kildare and flows 69 mi/110 km NE to the Irish Sea.

Bo Zhu Yi or **Po Chü-i** 772–846. Chinese poet. President from 841 of the imperial war department, he criticized government policy. He is said to have checked his work with an old peasant woman for clarity of expression.

Brabant (Flemish *Braband*) former duchy of W Europe, comprising the Dutch province of ⟩North Brabant and the Belgian provinces of Brabant and Antwerp. They were divided when Belgium became independent 1830. The present-day Belgian province of Brabant has an area of 1,312 sq mi/3,400 sq km and a population (1987) of 2,245,900.

During the Middle Ages Brabant was an independent duchy, and after passing to Burgundy, and thence to the Spanish crown, was divided during the Dutch War of Independence. The southern portion was Spanish until 1713, then Austrian until 1815, when the whole area was included in the Netherlands. In 1830 the French-speaking part of the population in the S Netherlands rebelled, and when Belgium was recognized 1839, S Brabant was included in it.

Brachiopod any member of the phylum Brachiopoda, marine invertebrates with two shells, resembling but totally unrelated to bivalves. There are about 300 living species; they were much more numerous in past geological ages. They are suspension feeders, ingesting minute food particles from water. A single internal organ, the iophophore, handles feeding, aspiration, and excretion.

bracken large fern, especially *Pteridium aquilinum*, abundant in the northern hemisphere. A perennial rootstock throws up coarse fronds.

bracket fungus any ◊fungus of the class Basidiomycetes, with fruiting bodies that grow like shelves from trees.

bract leaflike structure in whose ◊axil a flower or inflorescence develops. Bracts are generally green and smaller than the true leaves. However, in some plants they may be brightly colored and conspicuous, taking over the role of attracting pollinating insects to the flowers, whose own petals are small; examples include poinsettia *Euphorbia pulcherrima* and bougainvillea.

A whorl of bracts surrounding an ◊inflorescence is termed an **involucre**. A **bracteole** is a leaflike organ that arises on an individual flower stalk, between the true bract and the ◊calyx.

Bradbury Ray 1920– . US science-fiction writer, responsible for making the genre "respectable" to a wider readership. His work shows nostalgia for small-town Midwestern life, and includes *The Martian Chronicles* 1950, *Fahrenheit 451* 1953, *R is for Rocket* 1962, and *Something Wicked This Way Comes* 1962.

Some of his short stories are collected in *The Stories of Ray Bradbury* 1980. He also has written several volumes of poetry, television and motion-picture screenplays, radio dramas, and children's stories.

Bradenton city in W Florida on the S shores of Tampa Bay, SW of Tampa; seat of Manatee county. It is a resort center during the winter months. Some travertine, a sparkling sheet of calcium carbonate formed on cave walls and floors, is quarried here; population (1990) 43,800.

Bradford William 1590–1657. First governor of Plymouth Colony. In 1620 he sailed for America aboard the *Mayflower*. Bradford was among the signers of the Mayflower Compact, the first written constitution in the New World. In the spring of 1621 he was chosen as governor of Plymouth and served in that office almost continuously for the next 35 years. His memoirs, *History of Plimoth Plantation*, are an important source for the colony's early history.

Born in Yorkshire, England, Bradford joined the Puritan Separatists (later known as the ◊Pilgrims) at an early age and lived with them in exile in Leiden, Holland, 1609–20.

Bradley James 1693–1762. English astronomer who in 1728 discovered the ◊aberration of starlight. From the amount of aberration in star positions, he was able to calculate the speed of light. In 1748, he announced the discovery of ◊nutation (variation in the Earth's axial tilt).

Bradley Omar Nelson 1893–1981. US general in World War II. In 1943 he commanded the 2nd US Corps in their victories in Tunisia and Sicily, leading to the surrender of 250,000 Axis troops, and in 1944 led the US troops in the invasion of France. His command, as the 12th Army Group, grew to 1.3 million troops, the largest US force ever assembled.

Born in Clark, Missouri, Bradley graduated from West Point 1915 and served in World War I. After World War II, he headed the Veterans Administration 1945–47, was chief of staff of the US Army 1948–49, and was the first chairman of the joint chiefs of staff 1949–53. He was appointed general of the army 1950 and retired from the army 1953. He wrote his memoirs in *A Soldier's Story* 1951.

Brady Mathew B *c.* 1823–1896. US photographer. Famed for his skill in photographic portraiture, he published *The Gallery of Illustrious Americans* 1850. With the outbreak of the US Civil War 1861, Brady and his staff became the foremost photographers of battle scenes and military life. Although his war photos were widely reproduced, Brady later suffered a series of financial reverses and died in poverty.

Born in Warren County, New York, Brady served as an apprentice to a portrait painter. Learning the rudiments of photography from Samuel ◊Morse, Brady established his own ◊daguerreotype studio in New York 1844.

Braga city in N Portugal 30 mi/48 km NNE of Oporto; population (1981) 63,800. Industries include textiles, electrical goods, and vehicle manufacture. It has a 12th-century cathedral, and the archbishop is primate of the Iberian peninsula. As Bracara Augusta it was capital of the Roman province Lusitania.

Bragança capital of a province of the same name in NE Portugal, 110 mi/176 km NE of Oporto. Population (1981) 13,900. It was the original family seat of the House of Braganza which ruled Portugal 1640–1910.

Braganza the royal house of Portugal whose members reigned 1640–1910; another branch were emperors of Brazil 1822–89.

Bragg William Henry 1862–1942. British physicist. In 1915 he shared with his son **(William) Lawrence Bragg** (1890–1971) the Nobel Prize for Physics for their research work on X-rays and crystals.

Brahe Tycho 1546–1601. Danish astronomer who made accurate observations of the planets from which the German astronomer and mathematician Johann ◊Kepler proved that planets orbit the Sun in ellipses. His discovery and report of the 1572 supernova brought him recognition, and his observations of the comet of 1577 proved that it moved on an orbit among the planets, thus disproving the Greek view that comets were in the Earth's atmosphere.

Brahe was a colorful figure who wore a false nose after his own was cut off in a duel, and who took an interest in alchemy. In 1576 Frederick II of Denmark gave him the island of Hven, where he set up an observatory. Brahe was the greatest observer in the days before telescopes, making the most accurate measurements of the positions of stars and planets. He moved to Prague as imperial mathematician in 1599, where he was joined by Kepler, who inherited his observations when he died.

Brahma in Hinduism, the creator of the cosmos, who forms with Vishnu and Siva the Trimurti, or three aspects of the absolute spirit.

In the Hindu creation myth, Brahma, the demiurge, is born from the unfolding lotus flower that grows out of Vishnu's navel; after Brahma creates the world, Vishnu wakes and governs it for the duration of the cosmic cycle *kalpa*, the "day of Brahma," which lasts for 4,200 million earthly years. Unlike Brahman, which is an impersonal principle and of neuter gender, Brahma is a personified god and of masculine gender.

Brahman in Hinduism, the supreme being, an abstract, impersonal world-soul into whom the *atman*, or individual soul, will eventually be absorbed when its cycle of rebirth is ended.

Brahmanism earliest stage in the development of ◊Hinduism. Its sacred scriptures are the ◊Vedas, with their accompanying literature of comment and explanation known as Brahmanas, Aranyakas, and Upanishads.

Brahmaputra river in Asia 1,800 mi/2,900 km long, a tributary of the Ganges.

It rises in the Himalayan glaciers as Zangbo and runs eastward through Tibet, to the mountain mass of Namcha Barwa. Turning south, as the Dihang, it enters India and flows into the Assam valley near Sadiya, where it is now known as the Brahmaputra. It flows generally westward until, shortly after reaching Bangladesh, it turns south and divides into the Brahmaputra proper, without much water, and the main stream, the Jamuna, which joins the Padma arm of the Ganges. The river is navigable for 800 mi/1,285 km from the sea.

Brahma Samaj Indian monotheistic religious movement, founded in 1830 in Calcutta by Ram Mohun Roy who attempted to recover the simple worship of the Vedas and purify Hinduism. The movement had split into a number of sects by the end of the 19th century and is now almost defunct.

Brahms Johannes 1833–1897. German composer, pianist, and conductor. Considered one of the greatest composers of symphonic music and of songs, his works include four symphonies; ◊lieder (songs); concertos for piano and for violin; chamber music; sonatas; and the choral *A German Requiem* 1868. He performed and conducted his own works.

In 1853 the violinist Joachim introduced him to Liszt and Schumann, who encouraged him. From 1868 Brahms made his home in Vienna. Although his music belongs to a reflective strain of Romanticism, similar to Wordsworth in poetry, Brahms saw himself as continuing the Classical tradition from the point to which Beethoven had brought it. To his contemporaries, he was a strict formalist, in opposition to the romantic sensuality of Wagner. His influence on Mahler and Schoenberg was profound.

Brǎila port in Romania on the river Danube; 106 mi/170 km from its mouth; population (1983) 226,000. It is a naval base. Industries include the manufacture of artificial fibers, iron and steel, machinery, and paper. It was controlled by the Ottoman Empire 1544–1828.

Braille system of writing for the blind. Letters are represented by a combination of raised dots on paper or other materials, which are then read by touch. It was invented in 1829 by **Louis Braille** (1809–1852), who became blind at the age of three.

brain in higher animals, a mass of interconnected ◊nerve cells, forming the anterior part of the ◊central nervous system, whose activities it coordinates and controls. In ◊vertebrates, the brain is contained by the skull. An enlarged portion of the upper spinal cord, the **medulla oblongata**, contains centers for the control of respiration, heartbeat rate and strength, and blood pressure. Overlying this is the **cerebellum**, which is concerned with coordinating complex muscular processes such as maintaining posture and moving limbs. The cerebral hemispheres (**cerebrum**) are paired outgrowths of the front end of the forebrain, in early vertebrates mainly concerned with the senses, but in higher vertebrates greatly developed and involved in the integration of all sensory input and motor output, and in intelligent behavior.

In vertebrates, many of the nerve fibers from the two sides of the body cross over as they enter the brain, so that the left cerebral hemisphere is associated with the right side of the body and vice versa. In humans, a certain asymmetry develops in the two halves of

brain *The structure of the human brain.*

into contact with a drum rotating with the wheels. The brake pads and shoes have a tough ◊friction lining that grips well and withstands wear.

Many trucks and trains have **air brakes**, which work by compressed air. On landing, jet planes reverse the thrust of their engines to reduce their speed quickly. Space vehicles use retrorockets for braking in space, and use the air resistance, or drag of the atmosphere, to slow down when they return to Earth.

Bramante Donato c. 1444–1514. Italian Renaissance architect and artist. Inspired by Classical designs, he was employed by Pope Julius II in rebuilding part of the Vatican and St Peter's in Rome.

bramble any prickly bush of a genus *Rubus* belonging to the rose family Rosaceae. Examples are ◊blackberry, raspberry, and dewberry.

Brancusi Constantin 1876–1957. Romanian sculptor, active in Paris from 1904, a pioneer of abstract forms and conceptual art. He developed increasingly simplified natural or organic forms, such as the sculpted head that gradually came to resemble an egg (*Sleeping Muse* 1910, Musée National d'Art Moderne, Paris).

In 1904 he walked from Romania to Paris, where he worked briefly in Rodin's studio. He began to explore direct carving in marble (producing many versions of Rodin's *The Kiss*), and was one of the first sculptors in the 20th century to carve directly from his material, working

the cerebrum. In right-handed people, the left hemisphere seems to play a greater role in controlling verbal and some mathematical skills, whereas the right hemisphere is more involved in spatial perception. In general, however, skills and abilities are not closely localized. In the brain, nerve impulses are passed across ◊synapses by neurotransmitters, in the same way as in other parts of the nervous system.

In mammals the cerebrum is the largest part of the brain, carrying the **cerebral cortex**. This consists of a thick surface layer of cell bodies (gray matter), below which fiber tracts (white matter) connect various parts of the cortex to each other and to other points in the central nervous system. As cerebral complexity grows, the surface of the brain becomes convoluted into deep folds. In higher mammals, there are large unassigned areas of the brain that seem to be connected with intelligence, personality, and higher mental faculties. Language is controlled in two special regions usually in the left side of the brain: **Broca's area** governs the ability to talk, and **Wernicke's area** is responsible for the comprehension of spoken and written words. In 1990, scientists at Johns Hopkins University, Baltimore, succeeded in culturing human brain cells.

brain damage impairment which can be caused by trauma (for example, accidents) or disease (such as encephalitis), or which may be present at birth. Depending on the area of the brain that is affected, language, movement, sensation, judgment, or other abilities may be impaired.

Braine John 1922–1986. English novelist. His novel *Room at the Top* 1957 created the character of Joe Lampton, one of the first of the northern working-class antiheroes.

brainstem central core of the brain, where the top of the spinal cord merges with the undersurface of the brain.

The oldest part of the brain in evolutionary terms, the brainstem is the body's life-support center, containing regulatory mechanisms for vital functions such as breathing, heart rate, and blood pressure. It is also involved in controlling the level of consciousness by acting as a relay station for nerve connections to and from the higher centers of the brain.

In many countries, death of the brainstem is now formally recognized as death of the person as a whole. Such cases are the principal donors of organs for transplant. So-called "beating-heart donors" can be maintained for a limited period by life-support equipment.

Brain Trust nickname of an informal group of experts who advised US president F D Roosevelt on his **New Deal** policy.

brake device used to slow down or stop the movement of a moving body or vehicle. The mechanically applied caliper brake used on bicycles uses a scissor action to press hard rubber blocks against the wheel rim. The main braking system of an automobile works hydraulically: when the driver depresses the brake pedal, liquid pressure forces pistons to apply brakes on each wheel.

Two types of car brakes are used. **Disc brakes** are used on the front wheels of some automobiles and on all wheels of sports and performance automobiles, since they are the more efficient and less prone to fading (losing their braking power) when they get hot. Braking pressure forces brake pads against both sides of a steel disk that rotates with the wheel. **Drum brakes** are fitted on the rear wheels of some automobiles and on all wheels of some passenger automobiles. Braking pressure forces brake shoes to expand outwards

brake *Two common braking systems: the disc brake (top) and the drum brake (bottom).*

with granite, wood, and other materials. By the 1930s he had achieved monumental simplicity with structures of simple repeated forms (*Endless Column* and other works in Tirgu Jiu public park, Romania). Brancusi was revered by his contemporaries and remains a seminal figure in 20th-century sculpture.

Brandeis Louis Dembitz 1856–1941. US jurist. As a crusader for progressive causes, he helped draft social-welfare and labor legislation. In 1916, with his appointment to the US Supreme Court by President Wilson, he became the first Jewish justice and maintained his support of individual rights in his opposition to the 1917 Espionage Act and in his dissenting opinion in the first wiretap case, *Olmstead v US* 1928.

Born in Louisville, Kentucky, Brandeis was educated at Harvard and was admitted to the bar 1877. Brandeis University in Waltham, Massachusetts, is named in his honor.

Brandenburg administrative *Land* (state) of Germany
area 10,000 sq mi/25,000 sq km
capital Potsdam
cities Cottbus, Brandenburg, Frankfurt-on-Oder
products iron and steel, paper, pulp, metal products, semiconductors
population (1990) 2,700,000
history the Hohenzollern rulers who took control of Brandenburg in 1415 later acquired the powerful duchy of Prussia and became emperors of Germany. At the end of World War II, Brandenburg lost over 5,000 sq mi/12,950 sq km of territory when Poland advanced its frontier to the line of the Oder and Neisse rivers. The remainder, which became a region of East Germany, was divided 1952 into the districts of Frankfurt-on-Oder, Potsdam, and Cottbus. When Germany was reunited 1990, Brandenburg reappeared as a state of the Federal Republic.

Brandenburg town in Germany, on the river Havel; 36 mi/60 km W of Berlin; population (1981) 94,700. Industries include textiles, automobiles, and aircraft. It has a 12th-century cathedral.

Brando Marlon 1924– . US actor whose casual style, mumbling speech, and use of ◇Method acting earned him a place as a distinctive actor. He won best-actor Academy Awards for *On the Waterfront* 1954 and *The Godfather* 1972.

He made his Broadway debut in *I Remember Mama* 1944, appeared in *Candida* 1946, and achieved fame in *A Streetcar Named Desire* 1947. His films include *The Men* 1950, *A Streetcar Named Desire* 1951, *Julius Caesar* 1953, *The Wild One* 1954, *Mutiny on the Bounty* 1962, *Last Tango in Paris* 1973, *Apocalypse Now* 1979, and *The Freshman* 1990.

Brandt Willy. Adopted name of Karl Herbert Frahm 1913–1992. German socialist politician, federal chancellor (premier) of West Germany 1969–74. He played a key role in the remolding of the Social Democratic Party (SPD) as a moderate socialist force (leader 1964–87). As mayor of West Berlin 1957–66, Brandt became internationally known during the Berlin Wall crisis 1961. Nobel Peace Prize 1971.

Brandt, born in Lübeck, changed his name when he fled to Norway 1933 and became active in the anti-Nazi resistance. He returned 1945 and entered the Bundestag (federal parliament) 1949. In the "grand coalition" 1966–69 he served as foreign minister and introduced

Ostpolitik, a policy of reconciliation between East and West Europe, which was continued when he became federal chancellor 1969, and culminated in the 1972 signing of the Basic Treaty with East Germany.

He resigned from the chancellorship 1974 following the discovery that an aide had been an East German spy. Brandt continued to wield considerable influence in the SPD, in particular over the party's new radical left wing. He chaired the ◇Brandt Commission on Third World problems 1977–83 and was a member of the European Parliament 1979–83.

Brandt Commission officially the Independent Commission on International Development Issues, established in 1977 and chaired by the former West German chancellor Willy ◇Brandt. Consisting of 18 eminent persons acting independently of governments, the commission examined the problems of developing countries and sought to identify corrective measures that would command international support. It was disbanded in 1983.

Its main report, published in 1980 under the title *North–South: A Program for Survival*, made detailed recommendations for accelerating the development of poorer countries (involving the transfer of resources to the latter from the rich countries).

brandy (Dutch *brandewijn* "burnt wine") alcoholic drink distilled from fermented grape juice (wine). The best-known examples are produced in France, notably Armagnac and Cognac. Brandy can also be prepared from other fruits, for example, apples (Calvados) and cherries (Kirschwasser). Brandies contain up to 55% alcohol.

Braque Georges 1882–1963. French painter who, with Picasso, founded the Cubist movement around 1907–10. They worked together at L'Estaque in the south of France and in Paris. Braque began to experiment in collages and invented a technique of gluing paper, wood, and other materials to canvas. His later work became more decorative.

Brasília capital of Brazil from 1960, 3,000 ft/1,000 m above sea level; population (1991) 1,841,000. It was designed by Lucio Costa (1902–1963), with Oscar Niemeyer as chief architect, as a completely new city to bring life to the interior.

Braşov (Hungarian *Brassó*, German *Krondstadt*) industrial city (machine tools, industrial equipment, chemicals, cement, woolens) in central Romania at the foot of the Transylvanian Alps; population (1985) 347,000. It belonged to Hungary until 1920.

brass metal ◇alloy of copper and zinc, with not more than 5% or 6% of other metals. The zinc content ranges from 20% to 45%, and the color of brass varies accordingly from coppery to whitish yellow. Brasses are characterized by the ease with which they may be shaped and machined; they are strong and ductile, resist many forms of corrosion, and are used for electrical fittings, ammunition cases, screws, household fittings, and ornaments.

Brasses are usually classed into those that can be worked cold (up to 25% zinc) and those that are better worked hot (about 40% zinc).

Brassaï adopted name of Gyula Halesz 1899–1986. French photographer of Hungarian origin. From the early 1930s on he documented, mainly by flash, the nightlife of Paris, before turning to more abstract work.

Brassica genus of plants of the family

Cruciferae. The most familiar species is the common cabbage *Brassica oleracea*, with its varieties broccoli, cauliflower, kale, and brussels sprouts.

In 1990 US experiments in cross-pollinating the wild cabbage *B. campestris* with related varieties of cultivated cabbage, turnip, and rutabaga produced a new plant having a life cycle of only five weeks. It is now being used in US schools to enable pupils to carry out plant-breeding experiments that can produce ten generations in one year.

brass instrument in music, any instrument made of brass or other metal, which is directly blown through a "cup" or "funnel" mouthpiece.

In the symphony orchestra they comprise: the *French horn*, a descendant of the natural hunting horn, valved, and curved into a circular loop, with a wide bell; the *trumpet*, a cylindrical tube curved into an oblong, with a narrow bell and three valves (the state *fanfare trumpet* has no valves); the *trombone*, an instrument with a "slide" to vary the effective length of the tube (the *sackbut*, common from the 14th century, was its forerunner); the *tuba*, normally the lowest toned instrument of the orchestra, which is valved and a very wide bore to give sonority, and a bell that points upward.

In the brass band (in descending order of pitch) they comprise: the *cornet*, three-valved instrument, looking like a shorter, broader trumpet, and with a wider bore; the *flugelhorn*, valved instrument, rather similar in range to the cornet; the *tenor horn*; *B-flat baritone*; *euphonium*; *trombone*; and *bombardon* (bass tuba). A brass band normally also includes bass and side drums, triangle, and cymbals.

Bratislava (German *Pressburg*) industrial port (engineering, chemicals, oil refining) in Czechoslovakia, on the river Danube; population (1991) 441,500. It was the capital of Hungary 1526–1784 and is now capital of the Slovak Socialist Republic and second largest city in Czechoslovakia.

Brattain Walter Houser 1902–1987. US physicist. In 1956 he was awarded a Nobel Prize jointly with William Shockley and John Bardeen for their work on the development of the transistor, which replaced the comparatively costly and clumsy vacuum tube in electronics.

He was born in Amoy, China, the son of a teacher. From 1929 to 1967 he was on the staff of Bell Telephone Laboratories.

Brauchitsch Walther von 1881–1948. German field marshal. A staff officer in World War I, he became in 1938 commander in chief of the army and a member of Hitler's secret cabinet council. He was dismissed after his failure to invade Moscow 1941. Captured in 1945, he died before being tried in the ◇Nuremburg trials.

Braun Eva 1910–1945. German mistress of Adolf Hitler. Secretary to Hitler's photographer and personal friend, Heinrich Hoffmann, she became Hitler's mistress in the 1930s and married him in the air-raid shelter of the Chancellery in Berlin on April 29, 1945. The next day they committed suicide together.

Braunschweig German form of ◇Brunswick.

Brautigan Richard 1935–1984. US novelist, author of playful fictions set in California, such as *Trout Fishing in America* 1967, and Gothic works like *The Hawkline Monster* 1974.

Brazil largest country in South America (almost half the continent), bounded SW by

Brazil
Federative Republic of (*República Federativa do Brasil*)

area 3,285,618 sq mi/8,511,965 sq km
capital Brasília
cities São Paulo, Belo Horizonte, Curitiba, Manaus, Fortaleza; ports are Rio de Janeiro, Belém, Recife, Pôrto Alegre, Salvador
physical the densely forested Amazon basin covers the northern half of the country with a network of rivers; the south is fertile; enormous energy resources, both hydroelectric (Itaipú dam on the Paraná, and Tucuruí on the Tocantins) and nuclear (uranium ores)
environment Brazil has one-third of the world's tropical rainforest. It contains 55,000 species of flowering plants (the greatest variety in the world) and 20% of all the world's bird species. During the 1980s at least 7% of the Amazon rainforest was destroyed by settlers who cleared the land for cultivation and grazing
features Mount Roraima, Xingu National Park; Amazon delta; Rio harbor
head of state and government Itamar Franco from 1992
political system emergent democratic federal republic
political parties Social Democratic Party (PDS), moderate, left of center; Brazilian Democratic Movement Party (PMDB), center-left; Liberal Front Party (PFL), moderate, left of center; Workers' Party (PT), left of center; National Reconstruction Party (PRN), center-right
exports coffee, sugar, soybeans, cotton, textiles, timber, motor vehicles, iron, chrome, manganese, tungsten and other ores, as well as quartz crystals, industrial diamonds, gemstones; the world's sixth largest arms exporter

currency cruzado (introduced 1986; value = 100 cruzeiros, the former unit); inflation 1990 was 1,795%
population (1990 est) 153,770,000 (including 200,000 Indians, survivors of 5 million, especially in Rondônia and Mato Grosso, mostly living on reservations); growth rate 2.2% p.a.
life expectancy men 61, women 66
languages Portuguese (official); 120 Indian languages
religions Roman Catholic 89%; Indian faiths
literacy men 79%, women 76% (1985 est)
GDP $352 bn (1988); $2,434 per head
chronology
1822 Independence achieved from Portugal; ruled by Dom Pedro, son of the refugee King John VI of Portugal.
1889 Monarchy abolished and republic established.
1891 Constitution for a federal state adopted.
1930 Dr Getúlio Vargas became president.
1945 Vargas deposed by the military.
1946 New constitution adopted.
1951 Vargas returned to office.
1954 Vargas committed suicide.
1956 Juscelino Kubitschek became president.
1960 Capital moved to Brasília.
1961 João Goulart became president.
1964 Bloodless coup made General Castelo Branco president; he assumed dictatorial powers, abolishing free political parties.
1967 New constitution adopted. Branco succeeded by Marshal da Costa e Silva.
1969 Da Costa e Silva resigned and a military junta took over.
1974 General Ernesto Geisel became president.
1978 General Baptista de Figueiredo became president.
1979 Political parties legalized again.
1984 Mass calls for a return to fully democratic government.
1985 Tancredo Neves became first civilian president in 21 years. Neves died and was succeeded by the vice-president, José Sarney.
1988 New constitution approved, transferring power from the president to the congress. Measures announced to halt large-scale burning of Amazonian rainforest for cattle grazing.
1989 Forest Protection Service and Ministry for Land Reform abolished. International concern over how much of the Amazon has been burned. Fernando Collor (PRN) elected president Dec, pledging free-market economic policies.
1990 Government won the general election offset by mass abstentions.
1992 Earth Summit, global conference on the environment, held in Rio de Janeiro. Collor forced to resign, facing impeachment on corruption charges. Replaced by vice-president Itamar Franco.

King John VI moved his capital from Lisbon to Rio de Janeiro. In 1821 he returned to Lisbon, leaving his son, Crown Prince Pedro, as regent. In 1822 Pedro declared Brazil an independent kingdom, and took the title Emperor Pedro I. His son Pedro II persuaded large numbers of Portuguese to emigrate, and the center of Brazil developed quickly, largely on the basis of slavery. In 1888 slavery was abolished and in 1889 a republic was founded, followed by the adoption of a constitution for a federated nation 1891.

After social unrest in the 1920s, the world economic crisis of 1930 produced a revolt that brought Dr Getúlio Vargas to the presidency. He held office, as a benevolent dictator, until the army forced him to resign 1945 and General Eurico Dutra became president. In 1951 Vargas returned to power but committed suicide 1954 and was succeeded by Dr Juscelino Kubitschek.

In 1961 Dr Janio Quadros became president but resigned after seven months, to be succeeded by Vice President João Goulart. Suspecting him of left-wing leanings, the army forced a restriction of presidential powers and created the office of prime minister. A referendum brought back the presidential system 1963, with Goulart choosing his own cabinet.
free political parties banned In a bloodless coup 1964, General Castelo Branco assumed dictatorial powers and banned all political groupings except for two artificially created parties, the progovernment National Renewal Alliance (ARENA) and the opposition Brazilian Democratic Movement Party (PMBD). In 1967 Branco named Marshal da Costa e Silva as his successor, and a new constitution was adopted. In 1969 da Costa e Silva resigned because of ill health, and a military junta took over. In 1974 General Ernesto Geisel became president until succeeded by General Baptista de Figueiredo 1978. The ban on opposition parties was lifted 1979.
civilian presidency restored President Figueiredo held office until 1985, his last few years as president witnessing economic decline, strikes, and calls for the return of democracy. In 1985 Tancredo Neves became the first civilian president in 21 years, but died within months of taking office. He was succeeded by Vice President José ◊Sarney, who continued to work with Neves's cabinet and policies. The constitution was again amended to allow direct presidential elections.
Collor impeached on corruption charges In the Dec 1989 presidential election, Fernando Collor of the National Reconstruction Party (PRN) narrowly defeated Luis Inácio da Silva of the Workers' Party (PT). He advocated free-market economic policies and a crackdown on government corruption. In Oct 1990 general elections, despite wins for the PRN, widespread abstentions showed disillusionment with President Collor's policies. In Sept 1992, facing impeachment on corruption charges, Collor was removed from his post by the national congress and replaced by Vice President Itamar Franco. *See illustration box.*
Brazil nut seed, rich in oil and highly nutritious, of the gigantic South American tree *Bertholletia excelsa*. The seeds are enclosed in a hard outer casing, each fruit containing 10–20 seeds arranged like the segments of an orange. The timber of the tree is also valuable.
brazing method of joining two metals by melting an ◊alloy into the joint. It is similar to soldering but takes place at a much higher temperature. Copper and silver alloys are widely

---

Uruguay, Argentina, Paraguay and Bolivia; W by Peru and Colombia; N by Venezuela, Guyana, Suriname, and French Guiana; and NE and SE by the Atlantic Ocean.
government Brazil is a federal republic of 23 states, three territories, and a federal district (Brasília). The two-chamber national congress consists of a senate of 69 members (on the basis of one senator per state) elected for an eight-year term, and a chamber of deputies, whose numbers vary, elected for a four-year term. The number of deputies is determined by

the population of each state, and each territory is represented by one deputy. Elections to both chambers are by universal suffrage. The cabinet is chosen by the president, who is elected by universal adult suffrage for a five-year term and is not eligible for reelection. The states and the federal district each have an elected governor.
history Inhabited by various South ◊American Indians, Brazil was colonized by the Portuguese from 1500. In 1808, after the French emperor Napoleon invaded Portugal,

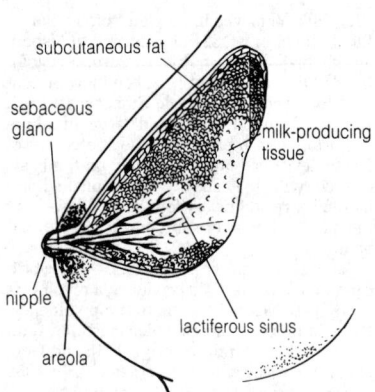

breast *The human breast or mammary gland.*

used for brazing, at temperatures up to about 1,650°F/900°C.

Brazzaville capital of the Congo, industrial port (foundries, railroad repairs, shipbuilding, shoes, soap, furniture, bricks) on the river Zaïre, opposite Kinshasa; population (1984) 595,000. There is a cathedral 1892 and the Pasteur Institute 1908. It stands on Pool Malebo (Stanley Pool).

Brazzaville was founded by the Italian Count Pierre Savorgnan de Brazza (1852–1905), employed in African expeditions by the French government. It was the African headquarters of the Free (later Fighting) French during World War II.

bread food baked from a kneaded dough or batter made with ground cereals, usually wheat, and water; many other ingredients may be added. The dough may be unleavened or raised (usually with yeast).

Bread has been a staple of human diet in many civilizations as long as agriculture has been practiced, and some hunter-gatherer peoples made it from crushed acorns or beech nuts. Potato, banana, and cassava bread are among some local varieties, but most breads are made from fermented cereals which form glutens when mixed with water.

The earliest bread was unleavened and was made from a mixture of flour and water and dried in the sun on flat stones. Leavened bread was first made in the ancient Near East and Egypt in brick ovens similar to ceramic kilns. The yeast creates gas, making the dough rise. Traditionally bread has been made from whole grains: wheat, barley, rye and oats, ground into a meal which varied in quality. Modern manufacturing processes have changed this to optimize the profit and shorten the manufacturing time. Fermentation is speeded up using ascorbic acid and potassium bromide with fast-acting flour improvers. White bread was developed by the end of the 19th century by roller-milling, which removed the wheat germ to satisfy fashionable consumer demand. Today, some of the nutrients, such as vitamins, removed in the processing of bread are synthetically replaced.

breadfruit fruit of the tropical trees *Artocarpus communis* and *A. altilis* of the mulberry family Moraceae. It is highly nutritious and when baked is said to taste like bread. It is native to many South Pacific islands.

Breakspear Nicholas. Original name of ⬦Adrian IV, the only English pope.

bream deep-bodied, flattened fish *Abramis brama* of the carp family, growing to about 1.6 ft/50 cm, typically found in lowland rivers across Europe.

The name bream is also applied to porgies, small-mouthed, deep-bodied marine fishes of the family Sparidae. The pinfish bream *Lagodon rhomboides* is found from Cape Cod S to the Gulf of Mexico. Several members of the North American sunfish family are also popularly referred to as bream.

breast one of a pair of organs on the upper front of the human female, also known as a ⬦mammary gland. Each of the two breasts contains milk-producing cells, and a network of tubes or ducts that lead to an opening in the nipple.

Milk-producing cells in the breast do not become active until a woman has given birth to a baby. Breast milk is made from substances extracted from the mother's blood as it passes through the breasts. It contains all the nourishment a baby needs, including antibodies to help fight infection.

Breasted James Henry 1865–1935. US Orientalist. Born in Rockford, Illinois, Breasted was first trained as a pharmacist but later pursued studies in Egyptology at Yale University and the University of Berlin. He joined the faculty of the University of Chicago 1896, published *A History of Egypt* 1905, and directed the Chicago expedition to Egypt and Sudan 1905–07. Well known as the author of textbooks and popular works on the history of the ancient Near East, Breasted was the founder of the University of Chicago Oriental Institute, funded by John D Rockefeller, as a center of American archeological research.

Breathalyzer trademark for an instrument for on-the-spot checking by police of the amount of alcohol consumed by a suspect driver. The driver breathes into a plastic bag connected to a tube containing a chemical (such as a diluted solution of potassium dichromate in 50% sulfuric acid) that changes color in the presence of alcohol. Another method is to use a gas chromatograph, again from a breath sample.

breathing in terrestrial animals, the muscular movements whereby air is taken into the lungs and then expelled, a form of ⬦gas exchange. Breathing is sometimes referred to as external respiration, for true respiration is a cellular (internal) process.

Lungs are specialized for gas exchange but are not themselves muscular, consisting of spongy material. In order for oxygen to be passed to the blood and carbon dioxide removed, air is forced in and out of the chest region by the ribs and accompanying intercostal muscles, the rate of breathing being controlled by the brain. High levels of activity lead to a greater demand for oxygen and a subsequent higher rate of breathing.

breccia coarse clastic ⬦sedimentary rock, made up of broken fragments (clasts) of pre-existing rocks. It is similar to ⬦conglomerate but the fragments in breccia are large and jagged.

Brecht Bertolt 1898–1956. German dramatist and poet who aimed to destroy the "suspension of disbelief" usual in the theater and to express Marxist ideas. He adapted John Gay's *Beggar's Opera* as *Die Dreigroschenoper/The Threepenny Opera* 1928, set to music by Kurt Weill. Later plays include *Mutter Courage/Mother Courage* 1941, set during the Thirty Years' War, and *Der*

kaukasische Kreidekreis/The Caucasian Chalk Circle 1949.

As an anti-Nazi, he left Germany in 1933 for Scandinavia and the US. He became an Austrian citizen after World War II; in 1949 he established the Berliner Ensemble theater group in East Germany.

Breda town in North Brabant, the Netherlands; population (1991) 124,800. It was here that Charles II of England made the declaration that paved the way for his restoration 1660.

Breda, Treaty of 1667 treaty that ended the Second Anglo-Dutch War (1664–67). By the terms of the treaty, England gained New Amsterdam, which was renamed New York.

breed recognizable group of domestic animals, within a species, with distinctive characteristics that have been produced by ⬦artificial selection.

breeder reactor in nuclear physics, a reactor in which more fissionable material is produced (breeding) than is consumed in running it. Breeder reactors are typically operated by and for the military to produce plutonium-239, the fissile material used in the nuclear weapons industry. Although uranium-235 is fissile, it comprises less than 1% of uranium ore, an amount too small to supply the weapons industry. Therefore, nonfissile uranium-238, which is plentiful, comprising 99% of uranium ore, is used instead, in breeder reactors, to manufacture fissile plutonium-239.

This is done by wrapping a blanket of U-238 around the core of a nuclear reactor. The fission process of the reactor-core material (usually U-235) produces excess neutrons that are captured by the U-238, which transmutes by beta decay into the highly unstable isotope U-239, which in turn through beta decay transmutes into the highly unstable isotope neptunium-239, which in turn undergoes beta decay to transmute into fissile Pu-239.

breeding in biology, the crossing and selection of animals and plants to change the characteristics of an existing ⬦breed or ⬦cultivar (variety), or to produce a new one.

Bremen industrial port (iron, steel, oil refining, chemicals, aircraft, shipbuilding, cars) in Germany, on the Weser 43 mi/69 km from the open sea; population (1988) 522,000.

Bremen was a member of the ⬦Hanseatic League, and a free imperial city from 1646. It became a member of the North German Confederation 1867 and of the German Empire 1871.

Bremen administrative region (German *Land*) of Germany, consisting of the cities of Bremen and Bremerhaven; area 154 sq mi/400 sq km; population (1988) 652,000.

Bremerton city in W Washington, SW of Seattle and NW of Tacoma, on an inlet of Puget Sound. It serves as a port for the area's fish, dairy, and lumber products. Tourism is also important to the economy; population (1990) 38,100.

Brendel Alfred 1931– . Austrian pianist, known for his fastidious and searching interpretations of Beethoven, Schubert, and Liszt. He is the author of *Musical Thoughts and Afterthoughts* 1976 and *Music Sounded Out* 1990.

Brennan Walter 1894–1974. US actor, often seen in Westerns as the hero's sidekick. His work includes *The Westerner* 1940, *Bad Day at Black Rock* 1955, and *Rio Bravo* 1959.

Brennan William Joseph, Jr 1906– . US jurist and associate justice of the US Supreme Court 1956–90. He wrote many important Supreme Court majority decisions that assured the freedoms set forth in the First Amendment and established the rights of minority groups. He is especially noted for writing the majority opinion in *Baker* v *Carr* 1962, in which state voting reapportionment ensured "one person, one vote," and in *US* v *Eichman* 1990, which ruled that the law banning desecration of the flag was a violation of the right to free speech as provided for in the First Amendment.

Born in Newark, New Jersey, Brennan graduated from the University of Pennsylvania and Harvard Law School. A New Jersey superior court 1949–52 and supreme court 1952–56 judge, he was appointed to the US Supreme Court by President Eisenhower. Considered a moderate liberal, his vote was usually cast with the majority during the years of the Court under Chief Justice Earl ⟩Warren, but he became a key liberal influence when the court majority, under chief justices Burger and ⟩Rehnquist, shifted to the conservative side in the 1980s. He retired from the Court 1990, citing health reasons.

Brenner Sidney 1927– . South African scientist, one of the pioneers of genetic engineering. Brenner discovered messenger ⟩RNA (a link between ⟩DNA and the ⟩ribosomes in which proteins are synthesized) 1960.

Brenner first studied medicine, but then moved into molecular biology at Oxford University. He worked for many years with Francis Crick, doing much research on nematode worms.

Brenner Pass lowest of the Alpine passes, 4,495 ft/1,370 m; it leads from Trentino–Alto Adige, Italy, to the Austrian Tirol, and is 12 mi/19 km long.

Brentano Klemens 1778–1842. German writer, leader of the Young Romantics. He published a seminal collection of folk-tales and songs with Ludwig von ⟩Arnim (*Des Knaben Wunderhorn*) 1805–08, and popularized the legend of the Lorelei (a rock in the river ⟩Rhine). He also wrote mystic religious verse, as in *Romanzen vom Rosenkranz* 1852.

Brescia (ancient *Brixia*) historic and industrial city (textiles, engineering, firearms, metal products) in N Italy, 52 mi/84 km E of Milan; population (1988) 199,000. It has medieval walls and two cathedrals (12th and 17th century).

Breslau German name of ⟩Wroclaw, town in Poland.

Brest naval base and industrial port (electronics, engineering, chemicals) on *Rade de Brest* (Brest Roads), a great bay at the western extremity of Bretagne, France; population (1983) 201,000. Occupied as a U-boat base by the Germans 1940–44, the town was destroyed by Allied bombing and rebuilt.

Brest town in Belarus, on the river Bug and the Polish frontier; population (1987) 238,000. It was in Poland (*Brześć nad Bugiem*) until 1795 and again 1921–39. The *Treaty of* ⟩*Brest-Litovsk* (an older Russian name of the town) was signed here.

Brest-Litovsk, Treaty of bilateral treaty signed March 3, 1918 between Russia and Germany, Austria–Hungary, and their allies. Under its terms, Russia agreed to recognize the independence of Georgia, Ukraine, Poland and the Baltic States, and pay heavy compensation. Under the Nov 1918 Armistice that ended World War I, it was annulled, since Russia was one of the winning allies.

Brétigny, Treaty of treaty made between Edward III of England and John II of France in 1360 at the end of the first phase of the Hundred Years' War, under which Edward received Aquitaine and its dependencies in exchange for renunciation of his claim to the French throne.

Breton André 1896–1966. French author, among the leaders of the ⟩Dada art movement. *Les Champs magnétiques/Magnetic Fields* 1921, an experiment in automatic writing, was one of the products of the movement. He was also a founder of ⟩Surrealism, publishing *Le Manifeste de surréalisme/Surrealist Manifesto* 1924. Other works include *Najda* 1928, the story of his love affair with a medium.

Breton language member of the Celtic branch of the Indo-European language family; the language of Brittany in France, related to Welsh and Cornish, and descended from the speech of Celts who left Britain as a consequence of the Anglo-Saxon invasions of the 5th and 6th centuries. Officially neglected for centuries, Breton is now a recognized language of France.

Since 1985 Breton has received some encouragement from the central government. The Breton Liberation Movement claims equal status in Brittany for Breton and French.

Bretton Woods township in New Hampshire, where the United Nations Monetary and Financial Conference was held in 1944 to discuss postwar international payments problems. The agreements reached on financial assistance and measures to stabilize exchange rates led to the creation of the International Bank for Reconstruction and Development in 1945 and the International Monetary Fund (IMF).

There were 44 nations represented at the conference, which considered proposals by the US, UK, and Canadian governments. The IMF became a specialized agency of the UN 1947. The "Bretton Woods" system was based on a policy of fixed exchange rates, the elimination of exchange restrictions, currency convertibility, and a multilateral system of international payments.

Breuer Josef 1842–1925. Viennese physician, one of the pioneers of psychoanalysis. He applied it successfully to cases of hysteria, and collaborated with Freud in *Studien über Hysterie/Studies in Hysteria* 1895.

Breuer Marcel 1902–1981. Hungarian-born architect and designer who studied and taught at the ⟩Bauhaus school in Germany. His tubular steel chair 1925 was the first of its kind. He moved to England, then to the US, where he was in partnership with Walter Gropius 1937–40. His buildings show an affinity with natural materials; the best known is the Bijenkorf, Rotterdam, the Netherlands (with Elzas) 1953.

Breuil Henri 1877–1961. French prehistorian, professor of historic ethnography and director of research at the Institute of Human Paleontology, Paris, from 1910. He established the genuine antiquity of Paleolithic cave art and stressed the anthropological approach to human prehistory.

breviary (Latin, "a summary or abridgement") in the Roman Catholic church, the book of instructions for reciting the daily services. It is usually in four volumes, one for each season.

brewing making of beer, ale, or other alcoholic beverage from ⟩malt and ⟩barley by steeping (mashing), boiling, and fermenting.

Mashing the barley releases its sugars. Yeast is then added, which contains the enzymes needed to convert the sugars into ethanol (alcohol) and carbon dioxide. Hops are added to give a bitter taste.

The term is also used to describe the industry that makes all alcoholic drinks.

brewster unit (symbol B) for measuring the reaction of optical materials to stress, defined in terms of the slowing down of light passing through the material when it is stretched or compressed.

Brezhnev Leonid Ilyich 1906–1982. Soviet leader. A protégé of Stalin and Khrushchev, he came to power (after he and ⟩Kosygin forced Khrushchev to resign) as general secretary of the Soviet Communist Party (CPSU) 1964–82 and was president 1977–82. Domestically he was conservative; abroad the USSR was established as a military and political superpower during the Brezhnev era, extending its influence in Africa and Asia.

Brezhnev, born in the Ukraine, joined the CPSU in the 1920s. In 1938 he was made head of propaganda by the new Ukrainian party chief Khrushchev and ascended in the local party hierarchy. After World War II he caught the attention of the CPSU leader Stalin, who inducted Brezhnev into the secretariat and Politburo 1952. Brezhnev was removed from these posts after Stalin's death 1953, but returned 1956 with Khrushchev's patronage. In 1960, as criticism of Khrushchev mounted, Brezhnev was moved to the ceremonial post of state president and began to criticize Khrushchev's policies.

Brezhnev stepped down as president 1963 and returned to the Politburo and secretariat. He was elected CPSU general secretary 1964, when Khrushchev was ousted, and gradually came to dominate the conservative and consensual coalition. In 1977 he regained the additional title of state president under the new constitution. He suffered an illness (thought to have been a stroke or heart attack) March–April 1976 that was believed to have affected his thought and speech so severely that he was not able to make decisions. These were made by his entourage, for example committing troops to Afghanistan to prop up the government. Within the USSR, economic difficulties mounted; the Brezhnev era was a period of caution and stagnation, although outwardly imperialist.

Brezhnev Doctrine Soviet doctrine 1968 designed to justify the invasion of Czechoslovakia. It laid down for the USSR as a duty the direct maintenance of "correct" socialism in countries within the Soviet sphere of influence. In 1979 it was extended, by the invasion of Afghanistan, to the direct establishment of "correct" socialism in countries not already within its sphere. The doctrine was renounced by Mikhail ⟩Gorbachev in 1989. Soviet troops were withdrawn from Afghanistan and the satellite states of E Europe were allowed to decide their own forms of government, with noncommunist and "reform communist" governments being established from Sept 1989.

Brian Havergal 1876–1972. English composer of 32 symphonies in visionary Romantic style, including the *Gothic* 1919–27 for large choral and orchestral forces.

Brian known as *Brian Boru* ("Brian of

the Tribute") 926–1014. High king of Ireland from 976, who took Munster, Leinster, and Connacht to become ruler of all Ireland. He defeated the Norse at Clontarf, thus ending Norse control of Dublin, although he was himself killed. He was the last high king with jurisdiction over most of Scotland. His exploits were celebrated in several chronicles.

Briand Aristide 1862–1932. French radical socialist politician. He was prime minister 1909–11, 1913, 1915–17, 1921–22, 1925–26 and 1929, and foreign minister 1925–32. In 1925 he concluded the ◊Locarno Pact (settling Germany's western frontier) and in 1928 the ◊Kellogg–Briand Pact renouncing war; in 1930 he outlined a scheme for a United States of Europe.

bribery corruptly receiving or agreeing to receive, giving or promising to give, any gift, loan, fee, reward, or advantage as an inducement or reward to persons in certain positions of trust. For example, it is an offense to improperly influence in this way judges or other judicial officers, members and officers of public bodies, or voters at public elections.

brick common building material, rectangular in shape, made of clay that has been fired in a kiln. Bricks are made by kneading a mixture of crushed clay and other materials into a stiff mud and extruding it into a ribbon. The ribbon is cut into individual bricks, which are fired at a temperature of up to about 1,800°F/1,000°C. Bricks may alternatively be pressed into shape in molds.

concrete arch

cantilever

suspension

steel arch

truss

bridge *Modern materials and engineering techniques have made possible the building of bridges to span ever-greater distances.*

Refractory bricks used to line furnaces are made from heat-resistant materials such as silica and dolomite. They must withstand operating temperatures of 2,700°F/1,500°C or more. Sun-dried bricks of mud reinforced with straw were first used in Mesopotamia some 8,000 years ago. Similar mud bricks, called adobe, are still used today in Mexico and other areas where the climate is warm and dry.

bridewealth or *brideprice* goods or property presented by a man's family to his prospective wife's as part of the marriage agreement. It was the usual practice among many societies in Africa, Asia, and the Pacific, and among many American Indian groups. In most European and S Asian countries the alternative custom was ◊dowry.

Bridewealth is regarded as compensation to the woman's family for giving her away in marriage, and it usually means that the children she bears will belong to her husband's family group rather than her own. It may require a large amount of valuables such as livestock, shell items, or cash.

bridge structure that provides a continuous path or road over water, valleys, ravines, or above other roads. The basic designs and composites of these are based on the way they bear the weight of the structure and its load. *Beam*, or *girder*, bridges are supported at each end by the ground with the weight thrusting downward. *Cantilever* bridges are a complex form of girder. *Arch* bridges thrust outwards but downward at their ends; they are in compression. *Suspension* bridges use cables under tension to pull inwards against anchorages on either side of the span, so that the roadway hangs from the main cables by the network of vertical cables. Some bridges are too low to allow traffic to pass beneath easily, so they are designed with movable parts, like swing and draw bridges.

history In prehistory, people used logs or wove vines into ropes that were thrown across the obstacle. By 4000 BC arched structures of stone and/or brick were used in the Middle East, and the Romans built long arched spans, many of which are still standing. Wooden bridges proved vulnerable to fire and rot and many were replaced with cast and wrought iron, but these were disadvantaged by low tensile strength. The ◊Bessemer process produced steel that made it possible to build long-lived framed structures that support great weight over long spans.

Today the longest spans are suspension bridges, with the measurement referring only to that part of the bridge actually suspended by cables.

bridge card game derived from whist. First played among members of the Indian Civil Service about 1900, bridge was brought to England in 1903 and played at the Portland Club in 1908. It is played in two forms: auction bridge and ◊contract bridge.

Bridgeport city in Connecticut, on Long Island Sound; population (1990) 141,700. Industries include metal goods, electrical appliances, and aircraft, but many factories closed in the 1970s. The university was established 1927.

The P T Barnum Museum and Tom Thumb statues are here. Bridgeport was settled 1639.

Bridges Harry 1901–1990. US labor leader. Born in Australia, he ran away to sea and settled in San Francisco. In 1931 he formed a labor union of clockworkers, and in 1934, after police opened fire on a picket line, killing two strikers,

he organized a successful general strike. He remained head of the International Longshoremen's and Warehousemen's Union for many years, despite Federal Bureau of Investigation objections (later proved false) that he had concealed membership in the Communist Party on his immigration papers.

Bridgeton city in SW New Jersey at the head of the Cohansey River; seat of Cumberland county. Industries include food processing, glassmaking, clothing, and dairy products; population (1990) 18,900.

Bridgetown port and capital of Barbados, founded 1628; population (1987) 8,000. Sugar is exported through the nearby deep-water port.

Bridget, St 453–523. A patron saint of Ireland, also known as *St Brigit* or *St Bride*. She founded a church and monastery at Kildare, and is said to have been the daughter of a prince of Ulster. Feast day Feb 1.

Bridgman Percy Williams 1882–1961. US physicist. His research into machinery producing high pressure led in 1955 to the creation of synthetic diamonds by General Electric. He was awarded the Nobel Prize for Physics 1946.

Born in Cambridge, Massachusetts, he was educated at Harvard, where he was Hollis Professor of Mathematics and Natural Philosophy 1926–50 and Higgins university professor 1950–54.

brief in law, the written instructions sent by a lawyer to a lawyer before a court hearing.

Brieux Eugène 1858–1932. French dramatist, an exponent of the naturalistic problem play attacking social evils. His most powerful plays are *Les trois filles de M Dupont/Mr Dupont's Three Daughters* 1897; *Les Avariés/Damaged Goods* 1901, long banned for its outspoken treatment of syphilis; and *Maternité/Maternity* 1903.

brigade military formation consisting of a minimum of two battalions, but more usually three or more, as well as supporting arms. There are typically about 5,000 soldiers in a brigade, which is commanded by a brigadier general. Two or more brigades form a ◊division.

An infantry brigade is one that contains more infantry than armor; it is said to be "infantry-heavy." A typical armored brigade ("armor-heavy") consists of two armored battalions and one infantry battalion supported by an artillery battalion and a field-engineer battalion as well as other logistic support.

Bright Richard 1789–1858. British physician who described many conditions and linked edema to kidney disease. *Bright's disease*, an inflammation of the kidneys, is named after him; see ◊nephritis.

Brighton resort on the E Sussex coast, England; population (1981) 146,000. It has Regency architecture and The Royal Pavilion 1782 in Oriental style. There are two piers and an aquarium. The University of Sussex was founded 1963.

history Originally a fishing village called Brighthelmstone, it became known as Brighton at the beginning of the 19th century, when it was already a fashionable health resort patronized by the Prince Regent, afterwards George IV. In 1990 the Royal Pavilion reopened after nine years of restoration.

brill flatfish *Scophthalmus laevis*, living in shallow water over sandy bottoms in the NE Atlantic and Mediterranean. It is a freckled sandy brown, and grows to 2 ft/60 cm.

Brindisi (ancient *Brundisium*) port and naval base on the Adriatic, in Puglia, on the heel of Italy; population (1981) 90,000. Industries include food processing and petrochemicals. It is one of the oldest Mediterranean ports, at the end of the Appian Way from Rome. The poet Virgil died here 19 BC.

brine common name for a solution of sodium chloride (NaCl) in water. Brines are used extensively in the food-manufacturing industry for canning vegetables, pickling vegetables (sauerkraut manufacture), and curing meat. Industrially, brine is the source from which chlorine, caustic soda (sodium hydroxide), and sodium carbonate are made.

Brinell hardness test test of the hardness of a substance according to the area of indentation made by a 0.4 in/10 mm hardened steel or sintered tungsten carbide ball under standard loading conditions in a test machine. The resulting Brinell number is equal to the load (kg) divided by the surface area (mm²) and is named after its inventor Johann Brinell.

Brisbane industrial port (brewing, engineering, tanning, tobacco, shoes; oil pipeline from Moonie), capital of Queensland, E Australia, near the mouth of Brisbane River, dredged to carry oceangoing ships; population (1990) 1,301,700.

brisling processed form of sprat *Sprattus sprattus* a small herring, fished in Norwegian fjords, then seasoned and canned.

Brissot Jacques Pierre 1754–1793. French revolutionary leader, born in Chartres. He became a member of the legislative assembly and the National Convention, but his party of moderate republicans, the ⟐Girondins, or Brissotins, fell foul of Robespierre, and Brissot was guillotined.

bristlecone pine The oldest living species of ⟐pine.

bristletail primitive wingless insect of the order Thysanura. Up to 0.8 in/2 cm long, bristletails have a body tapering from front to back, two long antennae, and three "tails" at the rear end. They include the *silverfish Lepisma saccharina* and the *firebrat Thermobia domestica*. Two-tailed bristletails constitute another insect order, the Diplura. They live under stones and fallen branches, feeding on decaying material.

Bristol industrial port (aircraft engines, engineering, microelectronics, tobacco, chemicals, paper, printing), administrative headquarters of Avon, SW England; population (1991 est) 370,300. The old docks have been redeveloped for housing, industry, yachting facilities, and the National Lifeboat Museum. Further developments include a new city center, with Brunel's Temple Meads railroad station at its focus, and a weir across the Avon nearby to improve the waterside environment.

features 12th-century cathedral; 14th-century St Mary Redcliffe; 16th-century Acton Court, built by Sir Nicholas Poynz, a courtier of Henry VIII; Georgian residential area of Clifton; the Clifton Suspension Bridge designed by Brunel, and his *SS Great Britain*, which is being restored in dry dock.

history John Cabot sailed from here 1497 to Newfoundland, and there was a great trade with the American colonies and the West Indies in the 17th–18th centuries, including slaves. The poet Chatterton was born here.

Bristol city located in Virginia and Tennessee

British Columbia

(the states' border runs through the center of the city), NE of Knoxville. This dual city is divided politically, but one unit economically. Manufactures include lumber, steel, office machines, pharmaceuticals, missile parts, and textiles; population (1990) 23,400 (Tennessee), 18,400 (Virginia).

Bristol city in central Connecticut, SW of Hartford. Known as the clock-making capital of the US, its manufactures also include tools and machinery parts; population (1990) 60,600.

Britain or *Great Britain* island off the NW coast of Europe, one of the British Isles. It consists of ⟐England, ⟐Scotland, and ⟐Wales, and is part of the ⟐United Kingdom. The name is derived from the Roman name Britannia, which in turn is derived from ancient Celtic name of the inhabitants, *Bryttas*.

Britain, ancient period in the history of the British Isles (excluding Ireland) from prehistory to the Roman occupation. After the last glacial retreat of the Ice Age about 15,000 BC, Britain was inhabited by hunters who became neolithic farming villagers. They built stone circles and buried their chiefs in ⟐barrow mounds. Around 400 BC Britain was conquered by the ⟐Celts and 54 BC by the Romans under Julius Caesar; ⟐Boudicca led an uprising against their occupation.

Britain, Battle of World War II air battle between German and British air forces over Britain lasting July 10–Oct 31, 1940.

At the outset the Germans had the advantage because they had seized airfields in the Netherlands, Belgium, and France, which were basically safe from attack and from which SE England was within easy range. On Aug 1, 1940 the Luftwaffe had about 4,500 aircraft of all kinds, compared to about 3,000 for the RAF. The Battle of Britain had been intended as a preliminary to the German invasion plan *Seelöwe* (Sea Lion), which Hitler indefinitely postponed Sept 17 and abandoned Oct 10, choosing instead to invade the USSR.

Britannicus Tiberius Claudius *c.* AD 41–55. Roman prince, son of the Emperor Claudius and Messalina; so-called from his father's expedition to Britain. He was poisoned by Nero.

British Antarctic Territory colony created in 1962 and comprising all British territories S of latitude 60° S: the South Orkney Islands, the South Shetland Islands, the Antarctic Peninsula and all adjacent lands, and Coats Land, extending to the South Pole; total land area 170,874 sq mi/660,000 sq km. Population (exclusively scientific personnel): about 300.

British Broadcasting Corporation (BBC) the UK state-owned broadcasting network. It operates television and national and local radio stations, and is financed solely by the sale of television viewing licenses; it is not allowed to carry advertisements. Overseas radio broadcasts (World Service) have a government subsidy.

The BBC was converted from a private company (established 1922) to a public body 1927.

British Columbia province of Canada on the Pacific
area 365,851 sq mi/947,800 sq km
capital Victoria
cities Vancouver, Prince George, Kamloops, Kelowna
physical Rocky Mountains and Coast Range; deeply indented coast; rivers include the Fraser and Columbia; over 80 lakes; more than half the land is forested
products fruit and vegetables; timber and wood products; fish; coal, copper, iron, lead; oil and natural gas; hydroelectricity
population (1991) 3,185,900
history Captain Cook explored the coast in 1778; a British colony was founded on Vancouver Island in 1849, and the gold rush of 1858 extended settlement to the mainland; it became a province in 1871. In 1885 the Canadian Pacific Railroad linking British Columbia to the E coast was completed.

British Commonwealth of Nations former official name of the British ⟐Commonwealth.

British East India Company a commercial company 1600–1858 chartered by Queen Elizabeth I and given a monopoly of trade between England and the Far East. In the 18th century it became, in effect, the ruler of a large part of India, and a form of dual control by the company and a committee responsible to Parliament in London was introduced by Pitt's India Act 1784. The end of the monopoly of China trade came 1834, and after the ⟐Sepoy Rebellion 1857 the crown took complete control of the government of British India; the India Act 1858 abolished the company.

British Empire various territories all over the world conquered or colonized by Britain from about 1600, most now independent or ruled by other powers; the British Empire was at its largest at the end of World War I, with over 25% of the world's population and area. The British ⟐Commonwealth is composed of former and remaining territories of the British Empire.

The first successful British colony was Jamestown, Virginia, founded 1607. British settlement spread up and down the east coast of North America and by 1664, when the British secured New Amsterdam (New York) from the Dutch, continuous colonies existed from the present South Carolina to what is now New Hampshire. The attempt of George III and his minister Lord North to coerce the colonists into paying special taxes to Britain roused them to resistance, which came to a head in the ⟐American Revolution 1775–81 and led to the creation of the United States of America from the 13 English colonies then lost.

Colonies and trading posts were set up in many parts of the world by the British, who also captured them from other European empire builders. Settlements were made in Gambia and on the Gold Coast of Africa 1618; in Bermuda 1609 and other islands of the West Indies; Jamaica was taken from Spain 1655; in Canada, Acadia (Nova Scotia) was secured from France by the Treaty of Utrecht 1713, which recognized Newfoundland and Hudson Bay (as well as Gibraltar in Europe) as British. New France (Québec), Cape Breton Island,

and Prince Edward Island became British as a result of the Seven Years' War 1756–63.

In the Far East, the ⚬British East India Company, chartered 1600, set up trading posts. The company steadily increased its possessions up to the eve of the ⚬Sepoy Rebellion 1857. Although this revolt was put down, it resulted in the taking over of the government of British India by the crown 1858; Queen Victoria was proclaimed empress of India Jan 1, 1877. Ceylon (now Sri Lanka) had also been annexed to the British East India Company 1796, and Burma (now Myanmar), after a series of Anglo-Burmese Wars from 1824, became a province of British India 1886. Burma and Ceylon became independent 1948 and the republic of Sri Lanka dates from 1972. British India, as the two dominions of India and Pakistan, was given independence in 1947. In 1950 India became a republic but remained a member of the Commonwealth.

Constitutional development in Canada started with an act of 1791 which set up Lower Canada (Québec), mainly French-speaking, and Upper Canada (Ontario), mainly English-speaking. Discontent led to rebellion in both Canadas 1837. After the suppression of these uprisings, Lord Durham was sent out to advise on the affairs of British North America. In accordance with his recommendations, the two Canadas were united 1840 and given a representative legislative council. With the British North America Act 1867, the self-governing dominion of Canada came into existence.

In New Zealand and Australia, colonization began with the need for a penal settlement after the loss of the original American colonies. The first shipload of British convicts landed in Australia 1788 on the site of the future city of Sydney. New South Wales was opened to free settlers 1819, and in 1853 transportation of convicts was abolished. An act of Parliament created the federal commonwealth of Australia, an independent dominion, 1901. New Zealand was created a dominion 1907.

The Cape of Good Hope in South Africa was occupied by two English captains 1620, but neither the home government nor the East India Company was interested. The Dutch occupied it from 1650 until 1795 when, French revolutionary armies having occupied the Dutch Republic, the British seized it to keep it from the French. Under the Treaty of Paris 1814 Britain bought it from the Netherlands. It was proclaimed a British colony 1843.

The need to find new farmland and establish independence from British rule led a body of Boers (Dutch "farmers") from the Cape to make the Great Trek northeast 1836, to found Transvaal and Orange Free State. Conflict between the British government and the Boers culminated in the Boer War 1899–1902, which brought Transvaal and Orange Free State under British sovereignty. Given self-government 1907, they were formed, with Cape Colony and Natal, into the Union of South Africa 1910. The British South Africa Company, chartered 1889, extended British influence over Southern Rhodesia and Northern Rhodesia; with Nyasaland, the Rhodesias were formed into a federation 1953–63 with representative government. Uganda was made a British protectorate 1894. Kenya became a colony 1920.

In W Africa, Sierra Leone colony was founded 1788 with the cession of a strip of land to provide a home for liberated slaves; a protectorate was established over the hinterland 1896. British influence in Nigeria began through the activities of the National Africa

British Empire

current name	independent
India	1947
Pakistan	1947
Sri Lanka	1948
Ghana	1957
Nigeria	1960
Cyprus	1960
Sierra Leone	1961
Tanzania	1961
Jamaica	1962
Trinidad & Tobago	1962
Uganda	1962
Kenya	1963
Malaysia	1963
Malawi	1964
Malta	1964
Zambia	1964
The Gambia	1965
Singapore	1965
Guyana	1966
Botswana	1966
Lesotho	1966
Bangladesh	1971
Zimbabwe	1980

Company (the Royal Niger Company from 1886) which bought Lagos from an African chief 1861; in 1900 the two protectorates of N and S Nigeria were proclaimed. In 1921–22, under League of Nations mandate, some German colonies were ceded to Britain: Tanganyika was transferred to British administration, SW Africa to South Africa; and Cameroons and Togoland were divided between Britain and France.

The establishment of the greater part of Ireland as the Irish Free State, with dominion status, occurred 1922. A new constitution 1937 dropped the name and declared Ireland (Eire) to be a "sovereign independent state;" in 1949 Ireland became a republic outside the Commonwealth, though remaining in a special relationship with Britain.

British Expeditionary Force (BEF) British army serving in France in World War I 1914–18. Also the 1939–40 army in Europe in World War II, which was evacuated from Dunkirk, France.

British Honduras former name (until 1973) of ⚬Belize.

British Indian Ocean Territory British colony in the Indian Ocean directly administered by the Foreign and Commonwealth Office. It consists of the Chagos Archipelago some 1,200 mi/1,900 km NE of Mauritius
area 23 sq mi/60 sq km
features lagoons; US naval and air base on Diego Garcia
products copra, salt fish, tortoiseshell
population (1982) 3,000
history purchased in 1965 for $3 million by Britain from Mauritius to provide a joint US/UK base. The islands of Aldabra, Farquhar, and Desroches, some 300 mi/485 km N of Madagascar, originally formed part of the British Indian Ocean Territory but were returned to the administration of the Seychelles in 1976.

British Isles group of islands off the NW coast of Europe, consisting of Great Britain (England, Wales, and Scotland), Ireland, the Channel Islands, the Orkney and Shetland islands, the Isle of Man, and many other islands that are included in various counties, such as the Isle of Wight, Scilly Isles, Lundy Island, and

the Inner and Outer Hebrides. The islands are divided from Europe by the North Sea, Strait of Dover, and the English Channel, and face the Atlantic to the west.

British Museum largest museum of the UK. Founded in 1753, it opened in London in 1759. Rapid additions led to the constuction of the present buildings (1823–47). In 1881 the Natural History Museum was transferred to South Kensington.

British Somaliland British protectorate comprising over 67,980 sq mi/176,000 sq km of territory on the Somali coast of E Africa from 1884 until the independence of Somalia in 1960. British authorities were harassed by Somali nationalists under the leadership of Mohammed bin Abdullah Hassan.

British thermal unit imperial unit (symbol Btu) of heat, now replaced in the SI system by the ⚬joule (one British thermal unit is approximately 1,055 joules). Burning one cubic foot of natural gas releases about 1,000 Btu of heat.

One British thermal unit is defined as the amount of heat required to raise the temperature of 1 lb/0.45 kg of water by 1°F. The exact value depends on the original temperature of the water.

British Virgin Islands part of the ⚬Virgin Islands group in the West Indies.

Brittany (French **Bretagne**, Breton **Breiz**) region of NW France in the Breton peninsula between the Bay of Biscay and the English Channel; area 10,499 sq mi/27,200 sq km; population (1987) 2,767,000; capital Rennes. A farming region, it includes the *départements* of Côtes-du-Nord, Finistère, Ille-et-Vilaine, and Morbihan.

history Brittany was the Gallo-Roman province of Armorica after being conquered by Julius Caesar 56 BC. It was devastated by Norsemen after the Roman withdrawal. In the 5th century AD the region was established under the name of Brittany by Celts fleeing the Anglo-Saxon invasion of Britain. It became a strong, expansionist state that maintained its cultural and political independence, despite pressure from the Carolingians, Normans, and Capetians. In 1171, the duchy of Brittany was inherited by Geoffrey, son of Henry II of England, and remained in the Angevin dynasty's possession until 1203, when Geoffrey's son Arthur was murdered by King ⚬John, and the title passed to the Capetian Peter of Dreux. Under the Angevins, feudalism was introduced, and French influence increased under the Capetians. By 1547 Brittany had been formally annexed by France, and the ⚬Breton language was banned in education. A separatist movement developed after World War II, and there has been guerrilla activity.

Britten (Edward) Benjamin 1913–1976. English composer. He often wrote for the individual voice; for example, the role in the opera *Peter Grimes* 1945, based on verses by George Crabbe, was created for Peter ⚬Pears. Among his many works are the *Young Person's Guide to the Orchestra* 1946; the chamber opera *The Rape of Lucretia* 1946; *Billy Budd* 1951; *A Midsummer Night's Dream* 1960; and *Death in Venice* 1973.

He studied at the Royal College of Music. From 1939 to 1942 he worked in the US, then returned to England and devoted himself to composing at his home in Aldeburgh, Suffolk, where he established an annual music festival. His oratorio *War Requiem* 1962 was written for the rededication of Coventry Cathedral.

brittle-star any member of the echinoderm class Ophiuroidea. A brittle-star resembles a starfish, and has a small, central, rounded body and long, flexible, spiny arms used for walking. The small brittle-star *Amphipholis squamata* is grayish, about 2 in/4.5 cm across, and found on sea bottoms worldwide. It broods its young, and its arms can be luminous.

About 2,000 species of brittle-stars and basket-stars, whose arms are tangled and rootlike, are included in this group.

Brno industrial city in central Czechoslovakia (chemicals, arms, textiles, machinery); population (1991) 388,000. The third largest city in Czechoslovakia, Brno was formerly the capital of the Austrian crown land of Moravia.

broadbill primitive perching bird of the family Eurylaimidae, found in Africa and S Asia. Broadbills are forest birds and are often found near water. They are gregarious and noisy, have brilliant coloration and wide bills, and feed largely on insects.

broadcasting the transmission of sound and vision programs by ◊radio and ◊television. In the US, broadcasting licenses are issued to public organizations and competing commercial companies by the Federal Communications Commission.

Television broadcasting entered a new era with the introduction of high-powered communications satellites in the 1980s. The signals broadcast by these satellites are sufficiently strong to be picked up by a small dish aerial located, for example, on the roof of a house. Direct broadcast by satellite thus became a feasible alternative to land-based television services. See also ◊cable television.

broad-leaved tree another name for a tree belonging to the ◊angiosperms, such as ash, beech, oak, maple, or birch. The leaves are generally broad and flat, in contrast to the needlelike leaves of most ◊conifers. See also ◊deciduous tree.

Broadway major avenue in New York running from the tip of Manhattan NW and crossing Times Square at 42nd Street, at the heart of the theater district, where Broadway is known as "the Great White Way." New York theaters situated outside this area are described as *off-Broadway*; those even smaller and farther away are *off-off-Broadway*.

broccoli variety of ◊cabbage.

Broch Hermann 1886–1951. Austrian novelist, who used experimental techniques in *Die Schlafwandler/The Sleepwalkers* 1932, *Der Tod des Vergil/The Death of Virgil* 1945, and *Die Schuldlosen/The Guiltless*, a novel in 11 stories. He moved to the US 1938 after being persecuted by the Nazis.

brocket name for a male European red deer in its second year, when it has short, straight, pointed antlers. Brocket deer, genus *Mazama*, include a number of species of small, shy, solitary deer found in Central and South America. They are up to 4 ft/1.3 m in body length and 2 ft/65 cm at the shoulder, and have similar small, straight antlers even when adult.

Brockton city in SW Massachusetts, S of Boston. Industries include footwear, tools, and electronic equipment; population (1990) 92,800.

broderie anglaise (French "English embroidery") embroidered fabric, usually white cotton, in which holes are cut in patterns and oversewn, often to decorate lingerie, shirts, and skirts.

Brodsky Joseph 1940– . Russian poet who emigrated to the US in 1972. His work, often dealing with themes of exile, is admired for its wit and economy of language, particularly in its use of understatement. Many of his poems, written in Russian, have been translated into English (*A Part of Speech* 1980). More recently he has also written in English. He was awarded the Nobel Prize for Literature in 1987 and became US poet laureate 1991.

Broglie Louis de, 7th Duc de Broglie 1892–1987. French theoretical physicist. He established that all subatomic particles can be described either by particle equations or by wave equations, thus laying the foundations of wave mechanics. He was awarded the 1929 Nobel Prize for Physics.

Broglie Maurice de, 6th Duc de Broglie 1875–1960. French physicist. He worked on X-rays and gamma rays, and helped to establish the Einsteinian description of light in terms of photons. He was the brother of Louis de Broglie.

Broken Hill mining town in New South Wales, Australia; population (1981) 27,000. It is the base of the Royal Flying Doctor Service.

brolga or *native companion*, Australian crane *Grus rubicunda*, about 5 ft/1.5 m tall, mainly gray with a red patch on the head.

Bromberg German name of ◊Bydgoszcz, port in Poland.

brome grass any annual grasses of the genus *Bromus* of the temperate zone; some are used for forage, but many are weeds.

bromeliad any tropical or subtropical plant of the pineapple family Bromeliaceae, usually with stiff leathery leaves and bright flower spikes.

Many tropical species are epiphytes on rainforest trees. The pineapple plant *Ananas comosus* is widely cultivated for its fleshy collective fruit, resembling a pine cone, developed from a flower spike. Spanish moss *Tillandsia usneoides*, another bromeliad, grows in long strands from the branches of trees in the SE US and tropical America.

Bromfield Louis 1896–1956. US novelist. Among his books are *The Strange Case of Miss Annie Spragg* 1928, *The Rains Came* 1937, and *Mrs Parkington* 1943, dealing with the golden age of New York society.

bromine (Greek *bromos* "stench") dark, reddishbrown, nonmetallic element, a volatile liquid at room temperature, symbol Br, atomic number 35, atomic weight 79.904. It is a member of the ◊halogen group, has an unpleasant odor, and is very irritating to mucous membranes. Its salts are known as bromides.

Bromine was formerly extracted from salt beds but is now mostly obtained from sea water, where it occurs in small quantities. Its compounds are used in photography and in the chemical and pharmaceutical industries.

bromocriptine drug that mimics the actions of the naturally occurring biochemical substance dopamine, a neurotransmitter. Bromocriptine acts on the pituitary gland to inhibit the release of prolactin, the hormone that regulates lactation, and thus reduces or suppresses milk production. It is also used in the treatment of ◊Parkinson's disease.

Bromocriptine may also be given to control excessive prolactin secretion and to treat prolactinoma (a hormone-producing tumor). Recent research has established its effectiveness in reversing some cases of infertility.

bronchiole small-bore air tube found in the vertebrate lung responsible for delivering air to the main respiratory surfaces. Bronchioles lead off from the larger bronchus and branch extensively before terminating in the many thousand alveoli that form the bulk of lung tissue.

bronchitis inflammation of the bronchi (air passages) of the lungs, usually caused initially by a viral infection, such as a cold or flu. It is aggravated by environmental pollutants, especially smoking, and results in a persistent cough, irritated mucus-secreting glands, and large amounts of sputum.

bronchodilator drug that relieves obstruction of the airways by causing the bronchi and bronchioles to relax and widen. It is most useful in the treatment of ◊asthma.

bronchus one of a pair of large tubes (bronchii) branching off from the windpipe and passing into the vertebrate lung. Apart from their size, bronchii differ from the bronchioles in possessing cartilaginous rings, which give rigidity and prevent collapse during breathing movements.

Numerous glands secrete a slimy mucus, which traps dust and other particles; the mucus is constantly being propelled upward to the mouth by thousands of tiny hairs or cilia. The bronchus is adversely effected by several respiratory diseases and by smoking, which damages the cilia and therefore the lung-cleaning mechanism.

Bronson Charles. Adopted name of Charles Bunchinsky 1921– . US film actor. His films are mainly violent thrillers such as *Death Wish* 1974. He was one of *The Magnificent Seven* 1960.

Brontë three English novelists, daughters of a Yorkshire parson. *Charlotte* (1816–1855), notably with *Jane Eyre* 1847 and *Villette* 1853, reshaped autobiographical material into vivid narrative. *Emily* (1818–1848) in *Wuthering Heights* 1847 expressed the intensity and nature mysticism which also pervades her poetry (*Poems* 1846). The more modest talent of *Anne* (1820–1849) produced *Agnes Grey* 1847 and *The Tenant of Wildfell Hall* 1848.

The Brontës were brought up by an aunt at Haworth rectory (now a museum) in Yorkshire. In 1846 the sisters published a volume of poems under the adopted names Currer (Charlotte), Ellis (Emily) and Acton (Anne) Bell. In 1847 (using the same names), they published the novels *Jane Eyre*, *Wuthering Heights*, and *Agnes Grey*, Anne's much weaker work. During 1848–49 Emily, Anne, and their brother Patrick Branwell all died of tuberculosis, aided in Branwell's case by alcohol and opium addiction; he is remembered for his portrait of the sisters. Charlotte married her father's curate, A B Nicholls, in 1854, and died during pregnancy.

brontosaurus former name of a type of large, plant-eating dinosaur, now better known as ◊apatosaurus.

Bronx, the borough of New York City, NE of Harlem River; area 42 sq mi/109 sq km; population (1990) 1,169,000. Largely residential, it is named after an early Dutch settler, James Bronck. The New York Zoological Society and Gardens are here, popularly called the Bronx Zoo and the Bronx Botanical Gardens.

bronze alloy of copper and tin, yellow or brown

in color. It is harder than pure copper, more suitable for ◊casting, and also resists ◊corrosion. Bronze may contain as much as 25% tin, together with small amounts of other metals, mainly lead.

Bronze is one of the first metallic alloys known and used widely by early peoples during the period of history known as the ◊Bronze Age.

Bell metal, the bronze used for casting bells, contains 15% or more tin. **Phosphor bronze** is hardened by the addition of a small percentage of phosphorus. **Silicon bronze** (for telegraph wires) and **aluminium bronze** are similar alloys of copper with silicon or aluminum and small amounts of iron, nickel, or manganese, but usually no tin.

Bronze Age stage of prehistory and early history when bronze became the first metal worked extensively and used for tools and weapons. It developed out of the Stone Age, preceded the Iron Age and may be dated 5000–1200 BC in the Middle East and about 2000–500 BC in Europe. Recent discoveries in Thailand suggest that the Far East, rather than the Middle East, was the cradle of the Bronze Age.

Mining and metalworking were the first specialized industries, and the invention of the wheel during this time revolutionized transport.

Agricultural productivity (which began during the New Stone Age, or Neolithic period, about 10,000 BC) and hence the size of the population that could be supported, was transformed by the ox-drawn plow.

Bronzino Agnolo 1503–1572. Italian painter active in Florence, court painter to Cosimo I, Duke of Tuscany. He painted in an elegant, Mannerist style and is best known for portraits and the allegory *Venus, Cupid, Folly and Time* about 1545 (National Gallery, London).

Brooke Rupert (Chawner) 1887–1915. English poet, symbol of the World War I "lost generation." His five war sonnets, the best known of which is "The Patriot," were published posthumously. Other notable works include "Grantchester" and "The Great Lover."

Brook Farm farm in W Roxbury, near Boston, Massachusetts, which was the scene of an idealistic experiment in communal living in 1841–47, led by George Ripley (1802–1880), a former Unitarian minister. Financial difficulties and a fire led to the community's dissolution.

Brooklyn borough of New York City, occupying the SW end of Long Island. It is linked to Manhattan Island by the Brooklyn-Battery Tunnel, the Brooklyn Bridge 1883, the Williamsburg and the Manhattan bridges, and to Staten Island by the Verrazano-Narrows Bridge 1964. There are more than 60 parks of which Prospect is the largest. There is also a museum, botanical garden, and a beach and amusement area at Coney Island.

Brooks Louise 1906–1985. US actress, known for her roles in silent films such as *A Girl in Every Port* 1928, *Die Büchse der Pandora/ Pandora's Box*, and *Das Tagebuch einer Verlorenen/Diary of a Lost Girl* both 1929 and both directed by G W ◊Pabst. At 25 she had appeared in 17 films. She retired from the screen 1938.

Brooks Mel. Adopted name of Melvin Kaminsky 1926– . US film director and comedian, known for madcap and slapstick verbal humor. He became well known with his record

album *The 2,000-Year-Old Man* 1960. His films include *The Producers* 1968, *Blazing Saddles* 1974, *Young Frankenstein* 1975, *History of the World Part I* 1981, and *To Be or Not to Be* 1983.

Brooks Van Wyck 1886–1963. US literary critic and biographer. His five-volume *Makers and Finders: A History of the Writer in America, 1800–1915* 1936–52 was an influential series of critical works on US literature. The first volume *The Flowering of New England* 1936 won a Pulitzer prize.

An earlier work, *America's Coming-of-Age* 1915, concerned the Puritan heritage and its effects on American literature. His other works include studies of Mark Twain, Henry James, and Ralph Waldo Emerson.

broom any shrub of the family Leguminosae, especially species of the *Cytisus* and *Spartium*, often cultivated for their bright yellow flowers.

Brothers Karamazov, The novel by Dostoevsky, published 1879–80. It describes the reactions and emotions of four brothers after their father's murder. One of them is falsely convicted of the crime, although his illegitimate brother is guilty.

Brown Capability (Lancelot) 1715–1783. English landscape gardener. He acquired his nickname because of his continual enthusiasm for the "capabilities" of natural landscapes.

Brown Charles Brockden 1771–1810. US novelist and magazine editor. He introduced the American Indian into fiction and is called the "father of the American novel" for his *Wieland* 1798, *Ormond* 1799, *Edgar Huntly* 1799, and *Arthur Mervyn* 1800. His works also pioneered the Gothic and fantastic traditions in US fiction.

Brown Ford Madox 1821–1893. British painter associated with the ◊Pre-Raphaelite Brotherhood. His pictures include *The Last of England* 1855 (Birmingham Art Gallery) and *Work* 1852–65 (City Art Gallery, Manchester), packed with realistic detail and symbolic incident.

Brown James 1928– . US rhythm-and-blues and soul singer, a pioneer of funk. Staccato horn arrangements and shouted vocals characterize his hits, which include "Please, Please, Please" 1956, "Papa's Got a Brand New Bag" 1965, and "Say It Loud, I'm Black and I'm Proud" 1968.

In 1988 he was arrested, convicted, and sent to prison for attempted assault, returning to performing after serving his sentence.

Brown John 1800–1859. US slavery abolitionist. With 18 men, on the night of Oct 16, 1859, he seized the government arsenal at Harper's Ferry in W Virginia, apparently intending to distribute weapons to runaway slaves who would then defend the mountain stronghold, which Brown hoped would become a republic of former slaves. On Oct 18 the arsenal was stormed by US Marines under Col Robert E ◊Lee. Brown was tried and hanged on Dec 2, becoming a martyr and the hero of the popular song "John Brown's Body" about 1860.

Born in Connecticut, he settled as a farmer in Kansas in 1855. In 1856 he was responsible for the "Pottawatomie massacre" when five proslavery farmers were killed. In 1858 he formed the plan for a refuge for runaway slaves in the mountains of Virginia.

brown dwarf hypothetical object less massive than a star, but heavier than a planet. Brown dwarfs would not have enough mass to ignite nuclear reactions at their centers, but would

shine by heat released during their contraction from a gas cloud. Because of the difficulty of detection, no brown dwarfs have been spotted with certainty, but some astronomers believe that vast numbers of them may exist throughout the Galaxy.

Browne Robert 1550–1633. English Puritan leader, founder of the Brownists. He founded communities in Norwich, East Anglia, and in the Netherlands which developed into present-day ◊Congregationalism.

Brownian movement the continuous random motion of particles in a fluid medium (gas or liquid) as they are subjected to impact from the molecules of the medium. The phenomenon was explained by Albert Einstein in 1905 but was observed as long ago as 1827 by the Scottish botanist Robert Brown.

Browning Robert 1812–1889. English poet, married to Elizabeth Barrett Browning. His work is characterized by the use of dramatic monologue and an interest in obscure literary and historical figures. It includes the play *Pippa Passes* 1841 and the poems "The Pied Piper of Hamelin" 1842, "My Last Duchess" 1842, "Home Thoughts from Abroad" 1845, and "Rabbi Ben Ezra" 1864.

Browning, born in Camberwell, London, wrote his first poem "Pauline" 1833 under the influence of Shelley; it was followed by "Paracelsus" 1835 and "Sordello" 1840. From 1837 he achieved moderate success with his play *Strafford* and several other works. In the pamphlet series of *Bells and Pomegranates* 1841–46, which contained *Pippa Passes*, *Dramatic Lyrics* 1842 and *Dramatic Romances* 1845, he included the dramas *King Victor and King Charles*, *Return of the Druses*, and *Colombe's Birthday*.

In 1846 he met Elizabeth Barrett; they married the same year and went to Italy. There he wrote *Christmas Eve and Easter Day* 1850 and *Men and Women* 1855, the latter containing some of his finest love poems and dramatic monologues, which were followed by *Dramatis Personae* 1864 and *The Ring and the Book* 1868–69, based on an Italian murder story. After his wife's death in 1861 Browning settled in England and enjoyed an established reputation, although his later works, such as *Red-Cotton Night-Cap Country* 1873, *Dramatic Idylls* 1879–80, and *Asolando* 1889, prompted opposition by their rugged obscurity of style.

Brownshirts the SA (*Sturmabteilung*), or Storm Troops, the private army of the German Nazi party, who derived their name from the color of their uniform.

Brownsville city in S Texas on the Rio Grande just before it flows into the Gulf of Mexico, S of Corpus Christi and N of Matamoros, Mexico; seat of Cameron county. It is a port of entry to the US. Industries include chemicals and food products. Tourism is also important; population (1990) 99,000. Originally Fort Taylor 1846, it was an important Confederate port during the Civil War.

Brown v Board of Education (of Topeka, Kansas) US Supreme Court decision 1954 that consolidated several suits challenging segregation laws in four states and the District of Columbia. The petitioner, Brown, was the father of a schoolgirl who lived near a school but was forced to travel across town to attend class in an all-black school. In a landmark decision the Court did away with the long-standing "separate but equal" doctrine of ◊Plessy v

Ferguson, ruling that segregated educational facilities are intrinsically unequal and are therefore in violation of the 14th Amendment. Lower courts were directed to desegregate schools with all deliberate speed.

Brubeck Dave (David Warren) 1920– . US jazz pianist, a student of the French composer Milhaud and Arnold Schoenberg, inventor of the 12-tone composition system. The Dave Brubeck Quartet (formed 1951) combined improvisation with Classical discipline. Included in his large body of compositions is the internationally popular "Take Five."

Bruce one of the chief Scottish noble houses. ▷Robert I (Robert the Bruce) and his son, David II, were both kings of Scotland descended from Robert de Bruis (died 1094), a Norman knight who arrived in England with William the Conqueror 1066.

Bruce James 1730–1794. Scottish explorer, the first European to reach the source of the Blue Nile 1770, and to follow the river downstream to Cairo 1773.

He was British consul at Algiers 1763–65.

Bruce Robert. King of Scotland; see ▷Robert I.

Bruce Stanley Melbourne, 1st Viscount Bruce of Melbourne 1883–1967. Australian National Party politician, prime minister 1923–29. He was elected to parliament in 1918. As prime minister he introduced a number of social welfare measures.

brucellosis disease of cattle, goats, and pigs, also known when transmitted to humans as **undulant fever** since it remains in the body and recurs. It was named after Australian doctor David Bruce (1855–1931), and is caused by bacteria (genus *Brucella*) present in the milk of infected cattle.

It has largely been eradicated in the West through vaccination of the animals and pasteurization of milk. Brucellosis is especially prevalent in the Mediterranean and in Central and South America.

Bruch Max 1838–1920. German composer, professor at the Berlin Academy 1891. He wrote three operas including *Hermione* 1872. Among the most celebrated of his works are the *Kol Nidrei* for cello and orchestra, violin concertos, and many choral pieces.

Brücke, die (German "the bridge") German Expressionist art movement 1905–13, formed in Dresden. Ernst Ludwig Kirchner was one of its founders, and Emil Nolde was a member 1906–07. Influenced by African art, they strove for spiritual significance, using raw colors to express different emotions. In 1911 the ▷*Blaue Reiter* took over as the leading group in German art.

Bruckner (Joseph) Anton 1824–1896. Austrian Romantic composer. He was cathedral organist at Linz 1856–68, and from 1868 he was professor at the Vienna Conservatoire. His works include many choral pieces and 11 symphonies, the last unfinished. His compositions were influenced by Richard ▷Wagner and Beethoven.

Brüderhof (German "Society of Brothers") Christian Protestant sect with beliefs similar to the ▷Mennonites. They live in groups of families (single persons are assigned to a family), marry only within the sect (divorce is not allowed), and retain a "modest" dress for women (cap or headscarf, and long skirts). In the US they are known as Hutterites.

They originated as an Anabaptist sect in Moravia in 1529. Jacob Hutter, a Swiss minister, was their leader until martyred 1536. They survived relentless persecution in the 16th and 17th centuries.

Brueghel family of Flemish painters. *Pieter Brueghel the Elder* (*c.* 1525–69) was one of the greatest artists of his time. He painted satirical and humorous pictures of peasant life, many of which include symbolic details illustrating folly and inhumanity, and a series of Months (five survive), including *Hunters in the Snow* (Kunsthistorisches Museum, Vienna).

The elder Pieter was nicknamed "Peasant" Brueghel. Two of his sons were painters. *Pieter Brueghel the Younger* (1564–1638), called "Hell" Brueghel, specialized in religious subjects, and another son, *Jan Brueghel* (1568–1625), called "Velvet" Brueghel, painted flowers, landscapes, and seascapes.

Bruges (Flemish *Brugge*) historic city in NW Belgium; capital of W Flanders province, 10 mi/16 km from the North Sea, with which it is connected by canal; population (1991) 117,100. Bruges was the capital of medieval ▷Flanders and was the chief European wool manufacturing town as well as its chief market. *features* Among many fine buildings are the 14th-century cathedral, the church of Nôtre Dame with a Michelangelo statue of the Virgin and Child, the Gothic town hall and market hall; there are remarkable art collections. It was named for its many bridges. The College of Europe is the oldest center of European studies. The contemporary port handles coal, iron ore, oil, and fish. Local manufactures include lace, textiles, paint, steel, beer, furniture, and motors.

Brulé Étienne *c.* 1592–1632. French adventurer and explorer. He traveled with ▷Champlain to the New World in 1608 and settled in Québec, where he lived with the Algonquin Indians. He explored the Great Lakes and traveled as far south as Chesapeake Bay. Returning north, he was killed by Huron Indians.

Brummell Beau (George Bryan) 1778–1840. British dandy and leader of fashion. He introduced long trousers as conventional day and evening wear for men. A friend of the Prince of Wales, the future George IV, he later quarrelled with him. Gambling losses drove him in 1816 to exile in France, where he died in an asylum.

Brundtland Gro Harlem 1939– . Norwegian Labor politician. Environment minister 1974–76, she briefly took over as prime minister 1981, and was elected prime minister 1986 and again 1990. She chaired the World Commission on Environment and Development which produced the Brundtland Report, published as *Our Common Future* 1987.

Brunei country comprising two enclaves on the NW coast of the island of Borneo, bounded to the landward side by Sarawak and to the NW by the South China Sea.
government The 1959 constitution gives supreme authority to the sultan, advised by various councils. Since the constitution was suspended after a revolution 1962, the sultan rules by decree.
history An independent Islamic sultanate from the 15th century, Brunei was a powerful state by the early 16th century, with dominion over all of Borneo, its neighboring islands, and parts of the Philippines. With the growing presence of the Portuguese and Dutch in the region, its influence declined in the late 16th century.

Brunei
Islamic Sultanate of (*Negara Brunei Darussalam*)

area 2,225 sq mi/5,765 sq km
capital Bandar Seri Begawan
cities Tutong, Seria, Kuala Belait
physical flat coastal plain with hilly lowland in W and mountains in E; 75% of the area is forested; the Limbang valley splits Brunei in two, and its cession to Sarawak 1890 is disputed by Brunei
features Temburong, Tutong, and Belait rivers; Mount Pagon (6,070 ft/1,850 m)
head of state and of government HM Muda Hassanal Bolkiah Mu'izzaddin Waddaulah, Sultan of Brunei, from 1968

political system absolute monarchy
political parties Brunei National United Party (BNUP)
exports liquefied natural gas (world's largest producer) and oil, both expected to be exhausted by the year 2000
currency Brunei dollar
population (1990 est) 372,000 (65% Malay, 20% Chinese -few Chinese granted citizenship); growth rate 12% p.a.
life expectancy 74 years
languages Malay (official), Chinese (Hokkien), English
religion 60% Muslim (official)
literacy 95%
GDP $3.4 bn (1985); $20,000 per head
chronology
1888 Brunei became a British protectorate.
1941–45 Occupied by Japan.
1959 Written constitution made Britain responsible for defense and external affairs.
1962 Sultan began rule by decree.
1963 Proposal to join Malaysia abandoned.
1967 Sultan abdicated in favor of his son, Hassanal Bolkiah.
1971 Brunei given internal self-government.
1975 United Nations resolution called for independence for Brunei.
1984 Independence achieved from Britain, with Britain maintaining a small force to protect the oil-and gasfields.
1985 A "loyal and reliable" political party, the Brunei National Democratic Party (BNDP), legalized.
1986 Death of former sultan, Sir Omar. Formation of multiethnic BNUP.
1988 BNDP banned.

In 1888 Brunei became a British protectorate, and under an agreement of 1906 accepted the appointment of a British Resident as adviser to the sultan. The discovery of large oil fields in the 1920s brought economic prosperity to Brunei. The country was occupied by the Japanese 1941 and liberated by the Australians 1945, when it was returned to Britain. In 1950 Sir Muda Omar Ali Saiffuddin Saadul Khairi Waddien (1916–1986), popularly known as Sir Omar, became sultan. In 1959, a new constitution gave Brunei internal self-government but made Britain responsible for defense and external affairs; a proposal in 1962 that Brunei should join the Federation of Malaysia was opposed by a revolution, which was put down with British help. As a result the sultan decided to rule by decree. In 1967, he abdicated in favor of his son, Hassanal Bolkiah, but continued to be his chief adviser. In 1971 Brunei gained full internal self-government.

independence achieved In 1984 full independence was achieved, the sultan becoming prime minister and minister of finance and home affairs, presiding over a cabinet of six, three of whom were close relatives. Britain agreed to maintain a small force to protect the gas-and oil fields that make Brunei the wealthiest nation, per head, in Asia.

In 1985, the sultan cautiously allowed the formation of the loyal and reliable Brunei National Democratic Party (BNDP), an organization dominated by business people. A year later, ethnic Chinese and government employees (who were debarred from joining the BNDP) formed, with breakaway members of the other party, the Brunei National United Party (BNUP), which became the country's only political party after the dissolution by the sultan of the BNDP 1988. While loyal to the sultan, the BNUP favors the establishment of an elected prime-ministerial system.

Islamic nationalism Since the death of Sir Omar 1986, the pace of political reform has quickened, with key cabinet portfolios being assigned to nonmembers of the royal family. A more nationalist socioeconomic policy has also begun, with preferential treatment given to native Malays in the commercial sphere rather than the traditional Chinese, and an Islamic state is being constructed.

support for Contras During the US-Iranian arms scandal 1987, it was revealed that the sultan of Brunei donated $10 million to the Nicaraguan Contras (antigovernment guerrillas).*See illustration box.*

Brunei Town former name (until 1970) of ◊Bandar Seri Begawan, Brunei.

Brunel Isambard Kingdom 1806–1859. British engineer and inventor. In 1833 he became engineer to the Great Western Railway, which adopted the 7 ft/2.1 m gauge on his advice. He built the Clifton Suspension Bridge over the river Avon at Bristol and the Saltash Bridge over the river Tamar near Plymouth. His shipbuilding designs include the *Great Western* 1838, the first steamship to cross the Atlantic regularly; the *Great Britain* 1845, the first large iron ship to have a screw propeller; and the *Great Eastern* 1858, which laid the first transatlantic telegraph cable.

Brunelleschi Filippo 1377–1446. Italian Renaissance architect. One of the earliest and greatest Renaissance architects, he pioneered the scientific use of perspective. He was responsible for the construction of the dome of Florence Cathedral (completed 1438), a

feat deemed impossible by many of his contemporaries.

Bruning Heinrich 1885–1970. German politician. Elected to the Reichstag (parliament) 1924, he led the Catholic Center Party from 1929 and was federal chancellor 1930–32 when political and economic crisis forced his resignation.

Brünn German form of ◊Brno, town in Czechoslovakia.

Bruno, St 1030–1101. German founder of the monastic Catholic ◊Carthusian order. He was born in Cologne, became a priest, and controlled the cathedral school of Rheims 1057–76. Withdrawing to the mountains near Grenoble after an ecclesiastical controversy, he founded the monastery at Chartreuse in 1084. Feast day Oct 6.

Brunswick (German *Braunschweig*) former independent duchy, a republic from 1918, which is now part of ◊Lower Saxony, Germany.

Brunswick (German *Braunschweig*) industrial city (chemical engineering, precision engineering, food processing) in Lower Saxony, Germany; population (1988) 248,000. It was one of the chief cities of N Germany in the Middle Ages and a member of the ◊Hanseatic League. It was capital of the duchy of Brunswick from 1671.

Brussels (Flemish *Brussel*; French *Bruxelles*) capital of Belgium, industrial city (lace, textiles, machinery, chemicals); population (1987) 974,000 (80% French-speaking, the suburbs Flemish-speaking). It is the headquarters of the European Economic Community and since 1967 of the international secretariat of ◊NATO. First settled in the 6th century, a city from 1312, Brussels became the capital of the Spanish Netherlands 1530 and of Belgium 1830.

features It has fine buildings including the 13th-century church of Sainte Gudule; the Hôtel de Ville, Maison du Roi, and others in the Grande Place; the royal palace. The Musées Royaux des Beaux-Arts de Belgique hold a large art collection. The bronze fountain statue of a tiny naked boy urinating, the Manneken Pis (1388) is to be found here. Brussels is also the site of the world's largest cinema complex, with 24 film theaters.

Brussels sprout one of the small edible buds along the stem of a variety (*Brassica oleracea* var. *gemmifera*) of ◊cabbage.

Brussels, Treaty of pact of economic, political, cultural, and military alliance established March 17, 1948, for 50 years, by the UK, France, and the Benelux countries, joined by West Germany and Italy 1955. It was the forerunner of the North Atlantic Treaty Organization and the European Community.

Brussilov Aleksei Alekseevich 1853–1926. Russian general, military leader in World War I who achieved major successes against the Austro-Hungarian forces in 1916. Later he was commander of the Red Army 1920, which drove the Poles to within a few miles of Warsaw before being repulsed by them.

Brutus Marcus Junius *c.* 78–42 BC. Roman soldier, a supporter of ◊Pompey (against ◊Caesar) in the civil war. Pardoned by Caesar and raised to high office by him, he nevertheless plotted Caesar's assassination to restore the purity of the Republic. Brutus committed suicide when he was defeated (with ◊Cassius) by ◊Mark Antony, Caesar's lieutenant, at Philippi 42 BC.

Bryan city in E Texas, NW of Houston; seat of Brazos county. Its industries include the manufacture of cotton gins; population (1990) 55,000.

Bryan William Jennings 1860–1925. US politician who campaigned unsuccessfully for the presidency three times: as the Populist and Democratic nominee 1896, as an antiimperialist Democrat 1900, and as a Democratic tariff reformer 1908. He served as President Wilson's secretary of state 1913–15. In the early 1920s he was a leading fundamentalist and opponent of Clarence Darrow in the ◊Scopes monkey trial.

He died shortly after from the strain.

Bryansk city in W central Russia, SW of Moscow on the Desna; population (1987) 445,000. Industries include lumber mills, textiles, and steel.

Bryant William Cullen 1794–1878. US poet and literary figure. His most famous poem, "Thanatopsis," was published 1817. He was co-owner and co-editor of the *New York Evening Post* 1829–78 and was involved in Democratic party politics. However, his resolute opposition to slavery eventually caused him to become a supporter of the Republican party from its inception 1856.

Born in Cummington, Massachusetts, Bryant briefly attended Williams College and was trained as a lawyer but throughout his life maintained a deep personal interest in poetry.

Brynner Yul 1915–1985. Actor, in the US from 1940, who made a shaven head his trademark. He played the king in *The King and I* both on stage 1951 and on film 1956 (Academy Award), and was the leader of *The Magnificent Seven* 1960.

Although his origins were deliberately shrouded in mystery he is believed to have been born in Sakhalin, an island east of Siberia and north of Japan. He later acknowledged a gypsy background. He made his film debut in a B picture *Port of New York* 1949. His other films include *Taras Bulba* 1962, and *Westworld* 1973.

bryophyte member of the Bryophyta, a division of the plant kingdom containing three classes: the Hepaticae (◊liverwort), Musci (◊moss), and Anthocerotae (◊hornwort). Bryophytes are generally small, low-growing, terrestrial plants with no vascular (water-conducting) system as in higher plants. Their life cycle shows a marked ◊alternation of generations. Bryophytes chiefly occur in damp habitats and require water for the dispersal of the male gametes (◊antherozoids).

In bryophytes, the ◊sporophyte, consisting only of a spore-bearing capsule on a slender stalk, is wholly or partially dependent on the ◊gametophyte for water and nutrients. In some liverworts the plant body is a simple ◊thallus, but in the majority of bryophytes it is differentiated into stem, leaves, and ◊rhizoids.

Bryusov Valery 1873–1924. Russian Symbolist poet, novelist and critic, author of *The Fiery Angel* 1908.

Brzezinski Zbigniew 1928– . US Democrat politician, born in Poland; he taught at Harvard University, and became a US citizen 1949. He was national security adviser to President Carter 1977–81 and chief architect of Carter's human-rights policy.

Btu symbol for ◊*British thermal unit*.

bubble chamber in physics, a device for observing the nature and movement of atomic particles, and their interaction with radiations. It is a vessel filled with a superheated liquid through which ionizing particles move and collide. The paths of these particles are shown by strings of bubbles, which can be photographed and studied. By using a pressurized liquid medium instead of a gas, it overcomes drawbacks inherent in the earlier ▷cloud chamber. It was invented by Donald ▷Glaser 1952.

bubble memory in computing, a memory device based on the creation of small "bubbles" on a magnetic surface. Bubble memories typically store up to 4 megabits (4 million ▷bits) of information. They are not sensitive to shock and vibration, unlike other memory devices such as disk drives, yet, like magnetic disks, they are nonvolatile and do not lose their information when the computer is switched off.

Buber Martin 1878–1965. Austrian-born Israeli philosopher, a Zionist and advocate of the reappraisal of ancient Jewish thought in contemporary terms. His book *I and Thou* 1923 posited a direct dialogue between the individual and God; it had great impact on Christian and Jewish theology. When forced by the Nazis to abandon a professorship in comparative religion at Frankfurt, he went to Jerusalem and taught social philosophy at the Hebrew University 1937–51.

Bubiyan island off Kuwait, occupied by Iraq 1990. On Feb 28, 1991, following Allied success in the ▷Gulf War, Iraqi troops were withdrawn.

bubonic plague epidemic disease of the Middle Ages; see ▷plague and ▷Black Death.

Bucaramanga industrial (coffee, tobacco, cacao, cotton) and commercial city in N central Colombia; population (1985) 493,929. It was founded by the Spanish 1622.

buccaneer member of any of various groups of seafarers who plundered Spanish ships and colonies on the Spanish American coast in the 17th century. Unlike true pirates, they were acting on (sometimes spurious) commission.

Buchanan James 1791–1868. 15th president of the US 1857–61. Born near Mercersburg, Pennsylvania, Buchanan was trained as a lawyer and was admitted to the bar 1812. He served as a member of the state legislature 1814–16 and the US House of Representatives 1821–31. He was US minister to Russia 1832–34 before being elected to the Senate 1834. An accommodationist on the issue of slavery, he left his Senate seat to serve as US secretary of state during the Mexican War. Nominated by the Democrats and elected president 1856, Buchanan could do little to avert the secession of the South over the issue of slavery.

Bucharest (Romanian *Bucureşti*) capital and largest city of Romania; population (1985) 1,976,000, the conurbation of Bucharest district having an area of 587 sq mi/1,520 sq km and a population of 2,273,000. It was originally a citadel built by Vlad the Impaler (see ▷Dracula) to stop the advance of the Ottoman invasion in the 14th century. Bucharest became the capital of the princes of Wallachia 1698 and of Romania 1861. Savage fighting took place in the city during Romania's 1989 revolution.

Buchenwald site of a Nazi ▷concentration camp 1937–45 at a village NE of Weimar, E Germany.

Buchner Eduard 1860–1917. German chemist who researched the process of fermentation. In 1897 he observed that fermentation could be

produced mechanically, by cell-free extracts. Buchner argued that it was not the whole yeast cell that produced fermentation, but only the presence of the enzyme he named zymase. Nobel Prize 1907.

Buck Pearl S(ydenstricker) 1892–1973. US novelist. Daughter of missionaries to China, she spent much of her life there and wrote novels about Chinese life, such as *East Wind–West Wind* 1930 and *The Good Earth* 1931, for which she received a Pulitzer prize 1932. She received the Nobel Prize for Literature 1938.

She wanted to make the East understandable to the West.

Buckingham George Villiers, 1st Duke of Buckingham 1592–1628. English courtier, adviser to James I and later Charles I. After Charles's accession, Buckingham attempted to form a Protestant coalition in Europe, which led to war with France, but he failed to relieve the Protestants (▷Huguenots) besieged in La Rochelle 1627. This added to his unpopularity with Parliament, and he was assassinated.

Buckingham Palace London home of the British sovereign, built 1703 for the duke of Buckingham, but bought by George III 1762 and reconstructed by John Nash 1821–36; a new front was added 1913.

Buckley William F(rank) 1925– . US conservative political writer, novelist, and founder-editor of the *National Review* 1955. In such books as *Up from Liberalism* 1959, and in a weekly television debate *Firing Line*, he represented the "intellectual" right-wing, antiliberal stance in US political thought.

buckminsterfullerene form of carbon, made up of molecules (buckyballs) consisting of 60 carbon atoms arranged in 12 pentagons and 20 hexagons to form a perfect sphere. It was named after the US architect and engineer Buckminster ▷Fuller because of its structural similarity to the geodesic dome that he designed. See ▷fullerene.

buckwheat any of several plants of the genus *Fagopyrum*, family Polygonaceae. The name usually refers to *F. esculentum*, which grows to about 3 ft/1 m and can grow on poor soil in a short summer. The highly nutritious black, triangular seeds (groats) are consumed by both animals and humans. They can be eaten either cooked whole or or as a cracked meal (kasha) or ground into flour, often made into pancakes.

buckyballs popular name for molecules of ▷buckminsterfullerene.

bud undeveloped shoot usually enclosed by protective scales; inside is a very short stem and numerous undeveloped leaves, or flower parts, or both. Terminal buds are found at the tips of shoots, while axillary buds develop in the ▷axils of the leaves, often remaining dormant unless the terminal bud is removed or damaged. Adventitious buds may be produced anywhere on the plant, their formation sometimes stimulated by an injury, such as that caused by pruning.

Budaeus Latin form of the name of Guillaume Budé 1467–1540. French scholar. He persuaded Francis I to found the Collège de France, and also the library that formed the nucleus of the French national library, the Bibliothèque Nationale.

Budapest capital of Hungary, industrial city (chemicals, textiles) on the river Danube; population (1989) 2,115,000. Buda, on the right bank of the Danube, became the Hungarian

capital 1867 and was joined with Pest, on the left bank, 1872.

Budapest saw fighting between German and Soviet troops in World War II 1944–45 and between the Hungarians and Soviet troops in the uprising of 1956.

Buddenbrooks novel by the German writer Thomas Mann, published 1901. Set in N Germany during the 19th century, it describes the decline of a family.

Buddha "enlightened one," title of Prince *Gautama Siddhārtha c.* 563–483 BC. Religious leader, founder of Buddhism, born at Lumbini in Nepal. At the age of 29 he left his wife and son and a life of luxury, to escape from the material burdens of existence. After six years of austerity he realized that asceticism, like overindulgence, was futile, and chose the middle way of meditation. He became enlightened under a bo, or bodhi, tree near Buddh Gaya in Bihar, India. He began teaching at Varanasi, and founded the Sangha, or order of monks. He spent the rest of his life traveling around N India, and died at Kusinagara in Uttar Pradesh.

The Buddha's teaching consisted of the Four Noble Truths: the fact of frustration or suffering; that suffering has a cause; that it can be ended; and that it can be ended by following the Noble Eightfold Path –right views, right intention, right speech, right action, right livelihood, right effort, right mindfulness, and right concentration –eventually arriving at nirvana, the extinction of all craving for things of the senses and release from the cycle of rebirth.

Buddh Gaya village in Bihar, India, where Gautama became the Buddha while sitting beneath a bo (*bodhi* "wisdom") tree; a descendant of the original tree is preserved.

Buddhism one of the great world religions, which originated in India about 500 BC. It derives from the teaching of the Buddha, who is regarded as one of a series of such enlightened beings; there are no gods. The chief doctrine is that of *karma*, good or evil deeds meeting an appropriate reward or punishment either in this life or (through reincarnation) a long succession of lives. The main divisions in Buddhism are *Theravāda* (or *Hīnayāna*) in SE Asia and *Mahāyāna* in N Asia; *Lamaism* in Tibet and *Zen* in Japan are among the many Mahāyāna sects. Its symbol is the lotus. There are over 247.5 million Buddhists worldwide.

scriptures The only complete canon of the Buddhist scriptures is that of the Sinhalese (Sri Lanka) Buddhists, in Pāli, but other schools have essentially the same canon in Sanskrit. The scriptures, known as *pitaka*s (baskets), date from the 2nd to 6th centuries AD. There are three divisions: *vinaya* (discipline), listing offenses and rules of life; the *sūtras* (discourse), or *dharma* (doctrine), the exposition of Buddhism by the Buddha and his disciples; and *abhidharma* (further doctrine), later discussions on doctrine.

beliefs The self is not regarded as permanent, as it is subject to change and decay. It is attachment to the things that are essentially impermanent that causes delusion, suffering, greed, and aversion, the origin of karma, and they in turn create further karma and the sense of self is reinforced. Actions which incline toward selflessness are called "skillful karma" and they are on the path leading to enlightenment. In the *Four Noble Truths* the Buddha acknowledged the existence and source of suffering, and showed the way of deliverance from it through the **Eightfold Path**. The aim of following the Eightfold Path is to break the chain of karma and achieve dissociation from the body by attaining **nirvana** ('blowing out')—the eradication of all desires, either in annihilation or by absorption of the self in the infinite. Supreme reverence is accorded to the historical Buddha (Śākyamuni, or, when referred to by his clan name, Gautama), who is seen as one in a long and ongoing line of Buddhas, the next one (Maitreya) being due *c.* AD 3000.

Theravāda Buddhism, the School of the Elders, also known as **Hīnayāna** or Lesser Vehicle, prevails in SE Asia (Sri Lanka, Thailand, and Myanmar), and emphasizes the mendicant, meditative life as the way to break the cycle of **samsāra**, or death and rebirth. Its three alternative goals are *arahat*: one who has gained insight into the true nature of things; *Paccekabuddha*, an enlightened one who lives alone and does not teach; and fully awakened *Buddha*. Its scriptures are written in Pāli, an Indo-Aryan language with its roots in N India. In India itself Buddhism had virtually died out by the 13th century, and was replaced by Hinduism. However, it has 5 million devotees in the 20th century and is growing.

Mahāyāna Buddhism, or Greater Vehicle arose at the beginning of the Christian era. This tradition emphasized the eternal, formless principle of the Buddha as the essence of all things. It exhorts the individual not merely to attain personal nirvana, but to become a trainee Buddha, or **bodhisattva**, and so save others; this meant the faithful could be brought to enlightenment by a bodhisattva without following the austerities of Theravāda, and the cults of various Buddhas and bodhisattvas arose. Mahāyāna Buddhism also emphasizes **shunyata**, or the experiential understanding of the emptiness of all things, even Buddhist doctrine.

Mahāyāna Buddhism prevails in N Asia (China, Korea, Japan, and Tibet). In the 6th century AD Mahāyāna spread to China with the teachings of Bodhidharma and formed Ch'an, which became established in Japan from the 12th century as **Zen Buddhism**. Zen emphasizes silent meditation with sudden interruptions from a master to encourage awakening of the mind. Japan also has the lay organization **Sōka Gakkai** (Value Creation Society), founded 1930, which equates absolute faith with immediate material benefit; by the 1980s it was followed by more than 7 million households.

Esoteric, **Tantric**, or **Diamond Buddhism** became popular in Tibet and Japan, and holds that enlightenment is already within the disciple and with the proper guidance (that is privately passed on by a master) can be realised. Buddhist believers worldwide are estimated at 350 million.

budding type of ⟩asexual reproduction in which an outgrowth develops from a cell to form a new individual. Most yeasts reproduce in this way.

In a suitable environment, yeasts grow rapidly, forming long chains of cells as the buds themselves produce further buds before being separated from the parent. Simple invertebrates, such as ⟩hydra, can also reproduce by budding.

In horticulture, the term is used for a technique of plant propagation whereby a bud (or scion) and a sliver of bark from one plant are transferred to an incision made in the bark of another plant (the stock). This method of ⟩grafting is often used for roses.

buddleia any shrub or tree of the tropical genus **Buddleia**, family Buddleiaceae. The purple or white flower heads of the butterfly bush *B. davidii* attract large numbers of butterflies.

Budge Donald 1915– . US tennis player. He was the first to perform the Grand Slam when he won the Wimbledon, French, US, and Australian championships all in 1938.

He won 14 Grand Slam events.

budgerigar small Australian parakeet *Melopsittacus undulatus* that feeds mainly on grass seeds. Normally it is bright green, but yellow, white, blue, and mauve varieties have been bred for the pet market.

budget estimate of income and expenditure for some future period, used in financial planning. National budgets set out estimates of government income and expenditure and generally include projected changes in taxation and growth. Interim budgets are not uncommon, in particular, when dramatic changes in economic conditions occur. Governments will sometimes construct a budget deficit or surplus as part of macroeconomic policy.

budget deficit the amount of shortfall that occurs when expenditures exceed revenues. While individuals and private enterprises can have budget deficits, the most economically significant deficit is the federal budget deficit. The deficit must be covered through the sale of government securities on the financial market or through the printing of money. Since printing money would be unacceptably inflationary, the government sells bonds and other financial instruments, promising to repay the face value plus interest in a specified time. The accumulation of obligations constitutes the ⟩national debt.

In the US during the Reagan administrations, tax cuts and increased defense spending combined to create massive budget deficits. Because there is a limited amount of investment capital available, the debt has been sold increasingly to foreigners. Debt service now consumes 15% of the federal budget, and federal borrowing has distorted financial markets, squeezing out private borrowers. Interest on the debt is the fourth largest component of the budget. Public debt is the total net government debt, including net federal and net state and local government debt.

Buenos Aires capital and industrial city of Argentina, on the S bank of the Río de la Plata; population (1991) 2,961,000, metropolitan area 7,950,400. It was founded 1536, and became the capital 1853.

features Congress building; the cathedral and presidential palace (known as the Pink House), both on the Plaza de Mayo; university 1821.

buffalo either of two species of wild cattle. The Asiatic water buffalo *Bubalis bubalis* is found domesticated throughout S Asia and wild in parts of India and Nepal. It likes moist conditions. Usually gray or black, up to 6 ft/1.8 m high, both sexes carry large horns. The African buffalo *Syncerus caffer* is found in Africa, south of the Sahara, where there is grass, water, and cover in which to retreat. There are a number of subspecies, the biggest up to 5 ft/1.6 m high, and black, with massive horns set close together over the head. The name is also commonly applied to the American ⟩bison.

Buffalo industrial port in New York State, at the E end of Lake Erie; population (1990) 328,100. It is linked with New York City by the New York State Barge Canal.

Grain from Buffalo's elevators is shipped overseas via the St Lawrence Seaway. An industrial city, Buffalo was hard hit by the closing of steel mills and auto factories in the late 1970s and early 1980s. The State University of New York at Buffalo and Canisius College are here. Settled in 1780, Buffalo was burned by the British during the War of 1812 but was soon rebuilt and flourished with the completion of the Erie Canal 1825.

buffer in computing, a part of the ⟩memory used to store data temporarily while it is waiting to be used. For example, a program might store data in a printer buffer until the printer is ready to print it.

buffer mixture of chemical compounds chosen to maintain a steady ⟩pH. The commonest buffers consist of a mixture of a weak organic acid and one of its salts or a mixture of acid salts of phosphoric acid. The addition of either an acid or a base causes a shift in the ⟩chemical equilibrium, thus keeping the pH constant.

Buffet Bernard 1928– . French figurative painter who created distinctive, thin, spiky forms with bold, dark outlines. He was a precocious talent in the late 1940s.

Buffon George Louis Leclerc, Comte de 1707–1778. French naturalist and author of the 18th century's most significant work of natural history, the 44-volume *Histoire naturelle* (1749–67). In *The Epochs of Nature*, one of the volumes, he questioned biblical chronology for the first time, and raised the Earth's age from the traditional figure of 6,000 years to the seemingly colossal estimate of 75,000 years.

bug in computing, an error in a program. It can be an error in the logical structure of a program or a syntax error, such as a spelling mistake. Some bugs cause a program to fail immediately; others remain dormant, causing problems only when a particular combination of events occurs. The process of finding and removing errors from a program is called **debugging**.

bug in entomology, an insect belonging to the order Hemiptera. All these have two pairs of wings with forewings partly thickened. They also have piercing mouthparts adapted for sucking the juices of plants or animals, the "beak" being tucked under the body when not in use.

They include: the bedbug, which sucks human blood; the shieldbug, or stinkbug, which has a strong odor and feeds on plants; the water boatman and other water bugs.

Bug name of two rivers in E Europe: the **West Bug** rises in SW Ukraine and flows to the Vistula, and the **South Bug** rises in W Ukraine and flows to the Black Sea.

Buganda two provinces (North and South Buganda) of Uganda, home of the Baganda people and formerly a kingdom from the 17th century. The *kabaka* or king, Edward Mutesa II (1924–1969), was the first president of independent Uganda 1962–66, and his son Ronald Mutebi (1955–) is *sabataka* (head of the Baganda clans).

bugle in music, a valveless brass instrument with a shorter tube and less flared bell than the trumpet. Constructed of copper plated with brass, it has long been used as a military instrument for giving a range of signals based on the tones of a harmonic series. The bugle is conical whereas the trumpet is cylindrical.

bugle any of a genus *Ajuga* of low-growing plants of the mint family Labiatae, with spikes of white, pink, or blue flowers. They are often grown as ground cover.

Bugs Bunny cartoon-film character created by US cartoonist Bob Clampett for *Porky's Hare Hunt* 1938. The cynical, carrot-crunching rabbit with its goofy incisors and catchphrase "Eh, what's up, Doc?" starred again in *A Wild Hare* 1940. By 1962 he had appeared in 159 films, and won an Academy Award for *Knighty Knight Bugs* 1958.

Bujumbura capital of Burundi; population (1986) 272,600. Formerly called **Usumbura** (until 1962), it was founded 1899 by German colonists. The university was established 1960.

Bukavu port in E Zaire, on Lake Kivu; population (1984) 171,100. Mining is the chief industry. Called **Costermansville** until 1966, it is the capital of Itivu region.

Bukhara or **Bokhara** central city in Uzbekistan; population (1987) 220,000. It is the capital of Bukhara region, which has given its name to carpets (made in Ashkhabad). It is an Islamic center, with a Muslim theological training center. An ancient city in central Asia, it was formerly the capital of the independent emirate of Bukhara, annexed to Russia 1868.

Bukharin Nikolai Ivanovich 1888–1938. Soviet politician and theorist. A moderate, he was the chief Bolshevik thinker after Lenin. Executed on Stalin's orders for treason 1938, he was posthumously rehabilitated 1988.

He wrote the major defense of war communism in his *Economics of the Transition Period* 1920. He drafted the Soviet constitution of 1936 but in 1938 was imprisoned and tried for treason in one of Stalin's "show trials." He pleaded guilty to treason, but defended his moderate policies and denied criminal charges. Nevertheless, he was executed, as were all other former members of Lenin's Politburo except Trotsky, who was murdered, and Stalin himself.

Bukovina region in SE Europe, divided between the Ukraine and Romania. It covers 4,050 sq mi/10,500 sq km.
history Part of Moldavia during the Turkish regime, it was ceded by the Ottoman Empire to Austria 1777, becoming a duchy of the Dual Monarchy 1867–1918; then it was included in Romania. N Bukovina was ceded to the USSR 1940 and included in Ukraine as the region of Chernovtsy; the cession was confirmed by the peace treaty 1947, but the question of its return has been raised by Romania. The part of Bukovina remaining in Romania became the district of Suceava.

Bulawayo industrial city and railroad junction in Zimbabwe; population (1982) 415,000. It lies at an altitude of 4,450 ft/1,355 m on the river Matsheumlope, a tributary of the Zambezi, and was founded on the site of the kraal (enclosed village), burned down 1893, of the Matabele chief, Lobenguela. It produces agricultural and electrical equipment. The former capital of Matabeleland, Bulawayo developed with the exploitation of gold mines in the neighborhood.

bulb underground bud with fleshy leaves containing a reserve food supply and with roots growing from its base. Bulbs function in vegetative reproduction and are characteristic of many monocotyledonous plants such as the daffodil, snowdrop, and onion. Bulbs are grown

Bulgaria
Republic of (*Republika Bulgaria***)**

area 42,812 sq mi/110,912 sq km
capital Sofia
cities Plovdiv, Ruse; Black Sea ports Burgas and Varna
physical lowland plains in N and SE separated by mountains that cover three-quarters of the country
environment pollution has virtually eliminated all species of fish once caught in the Black Sea. Vehicle-exhaust emissions in Sofia have led to dust concentrations more than twice the medically accepted level
features key position on land route from Europe to Asia; Black Sea coast; Balkan and Rhodope mountains; Danube River in N
head of state Zhelyu Zhelev from 1990
head of government to be announced
political system emergent democratic republic
political parties Union of Democratic Forces (UDF), right of center; Bulgarian Socialist Party (BSP), the former communist party (BCP); the Movement for Rights and Freedoms (MRF), representing the Turkish-speaking minority in Bulgaria
exports textiles, leather, chemicals, nonferrous metals, timber, machinery, tobacco,

cigarettes (world's largest exporter)
currency lev
population (1990 est) 8,978,000 (including 900,000–1,500,000 ethnic Turks, concentrated in S and NE); growth rate 0.1% p.a.
life expectancy men 69, women 74
languages Bulgarian, Turkish
religions Eastern Orthodox Christian 90%, Sunni Muslim 10%
literacy 98%
GDP $25.4 bn (1987); $2,836 per head
chronology
1908 Bulgaria became a kingdom independent of Turkish rule.
1944 Soviet invasion of German-occupied Bulgaria.
1946 Monarchy abolished and communist-dominated people's republic proclaimed.
1947 Soviet-style constitution adopted.
1949 Death of Georgi Dimitrov, the communist government leader.
1954 Election of Todor Zhivkov as Communist Party general secretary; made nation a loyal satellite of USSR.
1971 Constitution modified; Zhivkov elected president.
1985–89 Large administrative and personnel changes made haphazardly under Soviet stimulus.
1987 New electoral law introduced multicandidate elections.
1989 Program of "Bulgarianization" resulted in mass exodus of Turks to Turkey. Nov: Zhivkov ousted by Petar Mladenov. Dec: opposition parties allowed to form.
1990 April: BCP renamed Bulgarian Socialist Party (BSP). Aug: Dr Zheylyu Zhelev elected president. Nov: government headed by Andrei Lukanov resigned, replaced Dec by coalition led by Dimitur Popov.
1991 July: new constitution adopted. Oct: UDF beat BSP in general election by narrow margin; formation of first noncommunist, UDF-minority government under Filip Dimitrov.
1992 Zhelev became Bulgaria's first directly elected president. Relations with West greatly improved. Dimitrov resigned after vote of no confidence.

on a commercial scale in temperate countries, such as England and the Netherlands.

bulbil small bulb that develops above ground from a bud. Bulbils may be formed on the stem from axillary buds, or in the place of flowers, as in members of the saxifrage family, or in the place of flowers, as seen in many species of onion *Allium*. They drop off the parent plant and develop into new individuals, providing a means of ◊vegetative reproduction and dispersal.

bulbul small fruit-eating passerine bird of the family Pycnonotidae. There are about 120 species, mainly in the forests of the Old World tropics.

Bulfinch Charles 1763–1844. US architect. Born in Boston, Bulfinch was educated at Harvard and traveled widely in Europe. In 1787 his design for the Massachusetts State House was accepted, and he went on to become one of New England's leading architects, planning such important structures as the Hollis Street Church, Harvard's University Hall, the Massachusetts General Hospital, and the Connecticut State House. Deeply involved in the municipal affairs of Boston, Bulfinch served on its board of selectmen 1791–1817.

In 1817 he was appointed architect of the US Capitol by President Monroe.

Bulgakov Mikhail Afanasyevich 1891–1940. Russian novelist and playwright. His novel *The White Guard* 1924, dramatized as *The Days of the Turbins* 1926, deals with the Revolution and the civil war.

Bulganin Nikolai 1895–1975. Soviet politician and military leader. His career began in 1918 when he joined the Cheka, the Soviet secret police. He helped to organize Moscow's defense in World War II, became a marshal of the USSR 1947, and was minister of defense 1947–49 and 1953–55. On the fall of Malenkov he became prime minister (chair of Council of Ministers) 1955–58 until ousted by Khrushchev.

Bulgaria country in SE Europe, bounded N by Romania, W by Yugoslavia, S by Greece, SE by Turkey, and E by the Black Sea.
government Under the 1991 constitution, Bulgaria is a parliamentary republic. It has a single-chamber legislature, the 240-member National Assembly, elected every five years by universal suffrage, with a 4% threshold for party representation. The prime minister and cabinet is drawn from the grouping able to command a majority within the parliament. A

state president, who is also commander in chief of the armed forces, is popularly elected for a five-year term in a two-round election, but the president's powers are largely ceremonial. There is a separation of powers, monitored by a constitutional court.

history In the ancient world Bulgaria comprised ◊Thrace and Moesia and was the Roman province of Moesia Inferior. It was occupied in the 6th century AD by the Slavs (from whom the language derives), followed by Bulgars from Asia in the 7th century. In 865 Khan Boris adopted Eastern Orthodox Christianity, and under his son Simeon (893–927), who assumed the title of tsar, Bulgaria became a leading power. It was ruled by ◊Byzantium from the 11th century and, although a second Bulgarian empire was founded after the 14th century, Bulgaria formed part of the ◊Ottoman Empire for almost 500 years, becoming an independent kingdom 1908.

fascism Bulgaria allied itself with Germany during World War I. From 1919 a government of the leftist Agrarian Party introduced land reforms, but was overthrown 1923 by a fascist coup. A monarchical-fascist dictatorship was established 1934 under King ◊Boris III. During World War II Bulgaria again allied itself with Germany, being occupied 1944 by the USSR.

republic In 1946 the monarchy was abolished, and a republic was proclaimed under a communist-leaning alliance, the Fatherland Front, led by Georgi ◊Dimitrov (1882–1949). Bulgaria reverted largely to its 1919 frontiers. The new republic adopted a Soviet-style constitution 1947, with nationalized industries and cooperative farming introduced. Vulko Chervenkov, Dimitrov's brother-in-law, became the dominant political figure 1950–54, introducing a Stalinist regime. He was succeeded by the more moderate Todor ◊Zhivkov, under whom Bulgaria became one of the Soviet Union's most loyal satellites.

haphazard reforms During the 1980s the country faced mounting economic problems, chiefly caused by the rising cost of energy imports. During 1985–89, under the promptings of the Soviet leader Mikhail Gorbachev, a haphazard series of administrative and economic reforms was instituted. This proved insufficient to placate reformists either inside or outside the BCP. In Nov 1989, influenced by the democratization movements sweeping other East European countries and backed by the army and the USSR, the foreign secretary Petar ◊Mladenov ousted Zhivkov. Mladenov became leader of the BCP and president of the state council, and quickly promoted genuine political pluralism. In Dec 1989 legislation was passed to end the BCP's "leading role" in the state and allow the formation of free opposition parties and labor unions; political prisoners were freed; the secret police wing responsible for dissident surveillance was abolished; and free elections were promised for 1990.

relations with Turkey Bulgaria's relations with neighboring Turkey deteriorated during 1989, following the flight of 300,000 ethnic Turks from Bulgaria to Turkey after the Bulgarian government's violent suppression of their protests at the program of "Bulgarianization" (forcing them to adopt Slavic names and resettle elsewhere). The new Mladenov government announced Dec 1989 that the forced assimilation program would be abandoned; this provoked demonstrations by anti-Turk nationalists (abetted by BCP conservatives) but encouraged more than 100,000

refugees to return from Turkey. Most Turkish refugees gradually returned to Bulgaria, which greatly improved relations with Turkey.

market economy In Feb 1990 Alexander Lilov, a reformer, was elected party chief, and Andrei Lukanov became prime minister. A special commission was established to investigate allegations of nepotism and high-level embezzlement of state funds under Zhivkov. Zhivkov was placed under house arrest and later imprisoned, pending trial on charges of corruption and abuse of power. A government decree Feb 1990 relegalized private farming and a phased lifting of price controls commenced April 1990 as part of a drive toward a market economy. Huge price rises and food shortages were the result. Also in April, the BCP renamed itself the Bulgarian Socialist Party (BSP). Petar Mladenov resigned as president July 1990, and in Aug the opposition leader Dr Zhelyu Zhelev was elected in his place. In Nov 1990, following mass demonstrations in Sofia, a general strike, and a boycott of parliament by opposition deputies, the government of Andrei Lukanov resigned. He was replaced in Dec 1990 by a nonparty politician, Dimitur Popov, heading a caretaker coalition government, and the strikes by workers and students were called off.

end of communist rule A new constitution was adopted in July 1991 which defined the country as a parliamentary republic with a "democratic, constitutional, and welfare state." By Oct 1991 prices had increased tenfold and unemployment reached 300,000. The October 1991 general election resulted in a hung parliament when the right-of-center Union of Democratic Forces (UDF) edged out the BSP, but fell short of an outright majority. On Nov 8, 1991 a minority UDF government, headed by Filip Dimitrov, was formed, becoming Bulgaria's first wholly noncommunist government for 46 years. Western economic aid increased significantly and talks on an association agreement with the Economic Community began. In Nov 1991 the US reduced tariffs on goods imported from Bulgaria. Zhan Videnov replaced Lilov as leader of the BSP Dec 1991. In Jan 1992, Zhelyu Zhelev became Bulgaria's first directly elected president, capturing 53% of the vote. Dimitrov resigned Oct 1992 after a vote of confidence failed to pass in parliament. *See illustration box.*

Bulgarian member of an ethnic group living mainly in Bulgaria. There are 8–8.5 million speakers of Bulgarian, a Slavic language belonging to the Indo-European family. The Bulgarians use the Cyrillic alphabet and are known for their folk arts.

Known in E Europe since the 6th century AD, the Bulgarians were unified under Kurt or Kubrat in the 7th century. In 864 Boris I adopted the Eastern Orthodox faith. Between 1018 and 1185 the Bulgarians were ruled by the Byzantines, and between 1396 and 1878 by the Ottomans.

Bulge, Battle of the or *Ardennes offensive* in World War II, Hitler's plan, code-named "Watch on the Rhine," for a breakthrough by his field marshal ◊Rundstedt aimed at the US line in the Ardennes Dec 16, 1944–Jan 28, 1945. There were 77,000 Allied casualties and 130,000 German, including Hitler's last powerful reserve, his Panzer elite. Although US troops were encircled for some weeks at Bastogne, the German counteroffensive failed.

bulimia (Greek "ox hunger") condition of continuous, uncontrolled hunger. Considered a

counteraction to stress or depression, this eating disorder is found chiefly in young women. When compensated for by forced vomiting or overdoses of laxatives, the condition is called *bulimia nervosa*. It is sometimes associated with ◊anorexia.

bull speculator who buys stocks or shares on the stock exchange expecting a rise in the price in order to sell them later at a profit, the opposite of a ◊bear. In a bull market, prices rise and bulls profit.

bull or *papal bull* document or edict issued by the pope; so called from the circular seals (medieval Latin *bulla*) attached to them. Some of the most celebrated bulls include Leo X's condemnation of Luther 1520 and Pius IX's proclamation of papal infallibility 1870.

Bull John. Imaginary figure personifying England; see ◊John Bull.

bulldog British dog of ancient but uncertain origin. The head is broad and square, with deeply wrinkled cheeks, small folded ears, and the nose laid back between the eyes. The bulldog grows to about 18 in/45 cm at the shoulder.

It was bred for bull-baiting, the peculiar set of the lower jaw making it difficult for the dog to release its grip.

bulldozer earth-moving machine widely used in construction work for clearing rocks and tree stumps and leveling a site. The bulldozer is a kind of ◊tractor with a powerful engine and a curved, shovellike blade at the front, which can be lifted and forced down by hydraulic rams. It usually has ◊caterpillar tracks so that it can move easily over rough ground.

bullfighting the national sport of Spain (where there are more than 400 bullrings), which is also popular in Mexico, Portugal, and much of Latin America. It involves the ritualized taunting of a bull in a circular ring, until its eventual death at the hands of the matador. Originally popular in Greece and Rome, it was introduced into Spain by the Moors in the 11th century.

Picadores on horseback first taunt the bull and wound it with lances before the *banderillos* pierce the bull's neck with darts. The final act, the kill, is performed by the *matador*, who is armed with a red cape and sword. He teases the bull further with the cape and then kills it by plunging the sword between its shoulder blades. In some parts of France and in Portugal it is illegal to kill the bulls. Opponents of the sport criticize its cruelty, and efforts have been made to outlaw it.

bullfinch Eurasian finch *Pyrrhula pyrrhula*, with a thick head and neck, and short heavy bill. It is small and blue-gray or black, the males being reddish and the females brown on the breast. Bullfinches are 6 in/15 cm long, and usually seen in pairs. They feed on tree buds as well as seeds and berries, and are usually seen in woodland. They also live in the Aleutians and on the Alaska mainland.

bullhead any of a North American family, Ictaluridae, of small freshwater catfish, for example, the black bullhead *Ictalurus melas*. Also, another name for the sculpin or other members of the family Cottidae.

bullroarer musical instrument used by Australian Aborigines during religious rites. It consists of a piece of wood or stone, fastened to a cord, and is twirled around the head to make a whirring noise. It is a highly sacred object carved with mythical designs.

Bull Run, Battles of in the American Civil War, two victories for the Confederate army under General Robert E Lee at *Manassas* Junction, NE Virginia: *First Battle of Bull Run* July 21, 1861; *Second Battle of Bull Run* 29–Aug 30, 1862.

In the First Battle of Bull Run 34,000 Confederate troops routed 30,000 Union troops and challenged the North's complacent expectation of quick victory. In the Second Battle of Bull Run, Lee led 54,000 soldiers in a victory over Union forces, routing 63,000 Northern troops and opening an invasion route to the North.

bull terrier heavily built, smooth-coated breed of dog, usually white, originating as a cross between a terrier and a bulldog. It grows to about 16 in/40 cm tall, and was formerly used in ▷bull-baiting. Pit bull terriers are used in illegal dog fights.

Bülow Bernhard, Prince von 1849–1929. German diplomat and politician. He was chancellor of the German Empire 1900–09 under Kaiser Wilhelm II and, holding that self-interest was the only rule for any state, adopted attitudes to France and Russia that unintentionally reinforced the trend toward opposing European power groups: the ▷Triple Entente (Britain, France, Russia) and ▷Triple Alliance (Germany, Austria—Hungary, Italy).

He resigned after losing the confidence of Emperor William II and the Reichstag.

Bülow Hans (Guido) Freiherr von 1830–1894. German conductor and pianist. He studied with Richard ▷Wagner and Franz ▷Liszt, and in 1857 married Cosima, daughter of Liszt. From 1864 he served Ludwig II of Bavaria, conducting first performances of Wagner's *Tristan und Isolde* and *Die Meistersinger*. His wife left him and married Wagner 1870.

bulrush any of a number of marsh plants (especially of the genus *Scirpus*) belonging to the ▷sedge family, having long, slender, solid stems tipped with brown spikelets of tiny flowers. Bulrushes are used in basket-making and thatching.

bumblebee any large ▷bee, 1–2 in/2–5 cm, usually dark-colored but banded with yellow, orange, or white, belonging to the genus *Bombus*.

Most species live in small colonies, usually underground, often in an old mousehole. The queen lays her eggs in a hollow nest of moss or grass at the beginning of the season. The larvae are fed on pollen and honey, and develop into workers. All the bees die at the end of the season except fertilized females, which hibernate and produce fresh colonies in the spring. Bumblebees are found naturally all over the world, with the exception of Australia, where they have been introduced to facilitate the pollination of some cultivated varieties of clover.

Bunche Ralph 1904–1971. US diplomat. Grandson of a slave, he was principal director of the UN Department of Trusteeship 1947–54, and UN undersecretary acting as mediator in Palestine 1948–49 and as special representative in the Congo 1960. He taught at Harvard and Howard universities and was involved in the planning of the ▷United Nations. In 1950 he was awarded the Nobel Prize for Peace, the first awarded to a black man.

Bunin Ivan Alexeyevich 1870–1953. Russian writer, author of *Derevnya/The Village* 1910, which tells of the passing of peasant life;

and *Gospodin iz San Frantsisko/The Gentleman from San Francisco* 1916 (about the death of a millionaire on Capri), for which he received a Nobel Prize 1933. He was also a poet and translated Byron into Russian.

Bunker Hill, Battle of the first significant engagement in the ▷American Revolution, June 17, 1775, near a small hill in Charlestown (now part of Boston), Massachusetts; the battle actually took place on Breed's Hill. Although the colonists were defeated they were able to retreat to Boston and suffered fewer casualties than the British.

The failure to defeat the rebels soundly resulted in the replacement of General Thomas Gage as British commander.

Bunsen Robert Wilhelm von 1811–1899. German chemist credited with the invention of the *Bunsen burner*. His name is also given to the carbon–zinc electric cell, which he invented 1841 for use in arc lamps. In 1859 he discovered two new elements, cesium and rubidium.

Bunshaft Gordon 1909–1990. US architect whose Modernist buildings include the first to be completely enclosed in curtain walling (walls which hang from a rigid steel frame), the Lever Building 1952 in New York. He also designed the Heinz Company's UK headquarters 1965 at Hayes Park, London.

bunting any of a number of sturdy, finchlike, passerine birds with short, thick bills, of the family Emberizidae, especially the genera *Passerim* and *Emberiza*. Most of these brightly colored birds are native to the New World.

Buntline Ned. Adopted name of US author Edward Z C ▷Judson.

Buñuel Luis 1900–1983. Spanish Surrealist film director. He collaborated with Salvador Dali on *Un Chien andalou* 1928 and *L'Age d'or/The Golden Age* 1930, and established his solo career with *Los olvidados/The Young and the Damned* 1950. His works are often anticlerical, with black humor and erotic imagery.

Later films include *Le Charme discret de la bourgeoisie/The Discreet Charm of the Bourgeoisie* 1972 and *Cet Obscur Objet du désir/That Obscure Object of Desire* 1977.

Bunyan John 1628–1688. English author. A Baptist, he was imprisoned in Bedford 1660–72 for unlicensed preaching. During a second jail sentence 1675 he started to write *The Pilgrim's Progress*, the first part of which was published 1678. Other works include *Grace Abounding* 1666, *The Life and Death of Mr Badman* 1680, and *The Holy War* 1682.

buoy floating object used to mark channels for shipping or warn of hazards to navigation. Buoys come in different shapes, such as a pole (spar buoy), cylinder (car buoy), and cone (nun buoy). Light buoys carry a small tower surmounted by a flashing lantern, and bell buoys house a bell, which rings as the buoy moves up and down with the waves. Mooring buoys are heavy and have a ring on top to which a ship can be tied.

buoyancy lifting effect of a fluid on a body wholly or partly immersed in it. This was studied by ▷Archimedes in the 3rd century BC.

bur or *burr* in botany, a type of "false fruit" or ▷pseudocarp, surrounded by numerous hooks; for instance, that of burdock *Arctium*, where the hooks are formed from bracts surrounding the flowerhead. Burs catch in the feathers or fur of passing animals, and thus may be dispersed over considerable distances.

The term is also used to include any type of fruit or seed with hooks, such as that of sandbur *Cenchrus*, a grass, and white avens *Geum canadese*.

Burbage Richard *c.* 1567–1619. English actor, thought to have been ▷Shakespeare's original Hamlet, Othello, and Lear. He also appeared in first productions of works by Ben Jonson, Thomas Kyd, and John Webster. His father *James Burbage* (*c.* 1530–1597) built the first English playhouse, known as "the Theater;" his brother *Cuthbert Burbage* (*c.* 1566–1636) built the original ▷Globe Theatre 1599 in London.

burbot long, rounded fish *Lota lota* of the cod family, the only one living entirely in fresh water. Up to 3 ft/1 m long, it lives on the bottom of clear lakes and rivers, often in holes or under rocks, throughout Europe, Asia, and North America.

Burckhardt Jacob 1818–1897. Swiss art historian, professor of history at Basel University 1858–93. His *The Civilization of the Renaissance in Italy* 1860, intended as part of a study of world cultural history, influenced thought on the significance of this period.

Burckhardt Johann Ludwig 1784–1817. Swiss traveler whose knowledge of Arabic enabled him to travel throughout the Middle East, visiting Mecca disguised as a Muslim pilgrim 1814. In 1817 he discovered the ruins of Petra.

burden of proof in court proceedings, the duty of a party to produce sufficient evidence to prove that his case is true.

In English and US law a higher standard of proof is required in criminal cases (beyond all reasonable doubt), than in civil cases (on the balance of probabilities).

In the US, the burden of proof is on the court, since the accused is presumed innocent; in many other countries, the accused is presumed guilty until cleared, thus putting the burden of proof on the defense.

burdock any of the bushy herbs belonging to the genus *Arctium* of the family Compositae, characterized by hairy leaves and ripe fruit enclosed in ▷burs with strong hooks.

bureaucracy organization whose structure and operations are governed to a high degree by written rules and a hierarchy of offices; in its broadest sense, all forms of administration, and in its narrowest, rule by officials.

The early civilizations of Mesopotamia, Egypt, China, and India were organized hierarchically, thus forming the bureaucratic tradition of government. The German sociologist Max Weber saw the growth of bureaucracy in industrial societies as an inevitable reflection of the underlying shift from traditional authority to a rational and legal system of organization and control. In Weber's view, bureaucracy established a relation between legally enstated authorities and their subordinate officials. This relationship is characterized by defined rights and duties prescribed in written regulations.

Contemporary writers have highlighted the problems of bureaucracy, such as its inflexibility and rigid adherence to rules, so that today the term is often used as a criticism rather than its original neutral sense.

Burgas Black Sea port and resort in Bulgaria; population (1987) 198,000.

Burgenland federal state of SE Austria, extending south from the Danube S along the western border of the Hungarian plain; area

1,544 sq mi/4,000 sq km; population (1989) 267,200. It is a largely agricultural region adjoining the Neusiedler See, and produces timber, fruit, sugar, wine, lignite, antimony, and limestone. Its capital is Eisenstadt.

Burger Warren Earl 1907– . US jurist and chief justice of the United States 1969–86. His term in the US Supreme Court was marked by a conservative turn in civil-rights matters. His majority decision in the Watergate tapes case *US v Nixon* 1974 was instrumental in bringing about Nixon's resignation.

Born in St Paul, Minnesota, Burger was educated at the University of Minnesota and was admitted to the bar 1931. President Eisenhower appointed him judge of the US Court of Appeals 1956. In 1969 Burger was named to the US Supreme Court, succeeding Chief Justice Earl Warren. Burger retired from the Court 1986 and was succeeded by William Rehnquist.

Burgess Anthony. Adopted name of Anthony John Burgess Wilson 1917– . British novelist, critic, and composer. His prolific work includes *A Clockwork Orange* 1962, set in a future London terrorized by teenage gangs, and the panoramic *Earthly Powers* 1980. His vision has been described as bleak and pessimistic, but his work is also comic and satiric, as in his novels featuring the poet Enderby.

Burgess Guy (Francis de Moncy) 1910–1963. British spy, a diplomat recruited by the USSR as an agent. He was linked with Kim ◊Philby, Donald Maclean (1913–1983), and Anthony ◊Blunt.

Burgess Shale Site site of unique fossil-bearing rock formations created 530 million years ago by a mud slide, in Yoho National Park, British Columbia. The shales in this corner of the Rocky Mountains contain more than 120 species of marine invertebrate fossils. Although discovered 1909 by US geologist Charles Walcott, the Burgess Shales have only recently been used as evidence in the debate concerning the evolution of life. In *Wonderful Life* 1990 Stephen Jay Gould drew attention to a body of scientific opinion interpreting the fossil finds as evidence of parallel early evolutionary trends extinguished by chance rather than natural selection.

burgh (burh or borough) term originating in Germanic lands in the 9th–10th centuries referring to a fortified settlement, usually surrounding a monastery or castle. Later, it was used to mean new towns, or towns that enjoyed particular privileges relating to government and taxation and whose citizens were called *burghers*.

Burgh Hubert de died 1243. English ◊justiciar and regent of England. He began his career in the administration of Richard I, and was promoted to the justiciarship by King John; he remained in that position under Henry III from 1216 until his dismissal. He was a supporter of King John against the barons, and ended French intervention in England by his defeat of the French fleet in the Strait of Dover 1217. He reorganized royal administration and the Common Law.

burgher term used from the 11th century to describe citizens of ◊burghs who were freemen of a burgh, and had the right to participate in its government. They usually had to possess a house within the burgh.

Burghley William Cecil, Baron Burghley

Burkina Faso
The People's Democratic Republic of
(formerly **Upper Volta**)

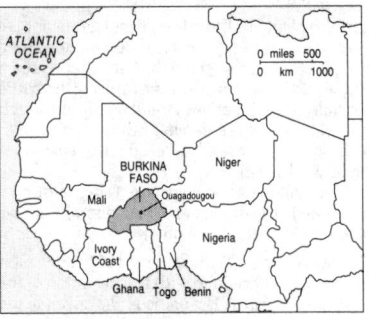

area 105,811 sq mi/274,122 sq km
capital Ouagadougou
cities Bobo-Dioulasso, Koudougou
physical landlocked plateau with hills in W and SE; headwaters of the river Volta; semiarid in N, forest and farmland in S
environment tropical savanna exposed to overgrazing and deforestation
features linked by rail to Abidjan in Ivory Coast, Burkina Faso's only outlet to the sea
head of state and government Blaise Compaoré from 1987
political system transitional
political parties Organization for Popular Democracy–Workers' Movement (ODP–MT), nationalist left-wing; FP–Popular Front
exports cotton, groundnuts, livestock, hides, skins, sesame, cereals
currency CFA franc
population (1990 est) 8,941,000; growth rate 2.4% p.a.
life expectancy men 44, women 47

1520–1598. English politician, chief adviser to Elizabeth I as secretary of state from 1558 and Lord High Treasurer from 1572. He was largely responsible for the religious settlement of 1559, and took a leading role in the events preceding the execution of Mary Queen of Scots 1587.

Burgos city in Castilla-León, Spain, 135 mi/217 km N of Madrid; population (1991) 169,300. It produces textiles, motor parts, and chemicals. It was capital of the old kingdom of Castile, and the national hero El Cid is buried in the Gothic cathedral, built 1221–1567.

Burgoyne John 1722–1792. British general and dramatist. He served in the American War of Independence and surrendered 1777 to the colonists at Saratoga, New York State, in one of the pivotal battles of the war. He wrote comedies, among them *The Maid of the Oaks* 1775 and *The Heiress* 1786. He figures in George Bernard Shaw's play *The Devil's Disciple* 1896.

Burgundy ancient kingdom and duchy in the valleys of the rivers Saône and Rhône, France. The Burgundi were a Teutonic tribe that overran the country about 400. From the 9th century to the death of Duke ◊Charles the Bold 1477, Burgundy was the nucleus of a powerful principality. On Charles's death the duchy was incorporated into France. The capital of Burgundy was Dijon. Today the region to which it corresponds is ◊Bourgogne.

Burke Edmund 1729–1797. British Whig politician and political theorist, born in Dublin,

languages French (official); about 50 native Sudanic languages spoken by 90% of population
religions animist 53%, Sunni Muslim 36%, Roman Catholic 11%
literacy men 21%, women 6% (1985 est)
GDP $1.6 bn (1987); $188 per head
chronology
1958 Became a self-governing republic within the French Community.
1960 Independence from France, with Maurice Yaméogo as the first president.
1966 Military coup led by Col Lamizana. Constitution suspended, political activities banned, and a supreme council of the armed forces established.
1969 Ban on political activities lifted.
1970 Referendum approved a new constitution leading to a return to civilian rule.
1974 After experimenting with a mixture of military and civilian rule, Lamizana reassumed full power.
1977 Ban on political activities removed. Referendum approved a new constitution based on civilian rule.
1978 Lamizana elected president.
1980 Lamizana overthrown in bloodless coup led by Col Zerbo.
1982 Zerbo ousted in a coup by junior officers. Maj Ouédraogo became president and Thomas Sankara prime minister.
1983 Sankara seized complete power.
1984 Upper Volta renamed Burkina Faso, "land of upright men."
1987 Sankara killed in coup led by Blaise Compaoré.
1989 New government party ODP–MT formed by merger of other progovernment parties. Coup against Compaoré foiled.
1991 New constitution approved. Compaoré reelected president.
1992 Multiparty elections won by FP–Popular Front.

Ireland. In Parliament from 1765, he opposed the government's attempts to coerce the American colonists, for example in *Thoughts on the Present Discontents* 1770, and supported the emancipation of Ireland, but denounced the French Revolution, for example in *Reflections on the Revolution in France* 1790.

Burke Martha Jane c. 1852–1903. Real name of US heroine ◊Calamity Jane.

Burkina Faso (formerly Upper Volta) landlocked country in W Africa, bounded E by Niger, NW and W by Mali, S by Ivory Coast, Ghana, Togo, and Benin.

government The 1991 constitution provides for a 107-member National Assembly and popularly elected president, within a multiparty system.

history The area known from 1984 as Burkina Faso was invaded in the 11th to 13th centuries by the Mossi people, whose powerful warrior kingdoms lasted for over 500 years. In the 1890s it became a province of French West Africa, known as Upper Volta.

In 1958 it became a self-governing republic and in 1960 achieved full independence with Maurice Yaméogo as president. A military coup 1966 removed Yaméogo and installed Col Sangoulé Lamizana as president and prime minister. He suspended the constitution, dissolved the national assembly, banned political activity, and set up a supreme council of the armed forces as the instrument of government.

In 1969 the ban on political activity was

lifted, and in 1970 a referendum approved a new constitution, based on civilian rule, which was to come into effect after four years of combined military and civilian government. After disagreements between military and civilian members of the government, General Lamizana announced 1974 a return to army rule and dissolved the national assembly.

Lamizana overthrown In 1977 political activity was allowed again, and a referendum approved a constitution that would create a civilian government. In the 1978 elections the Volta Democratic Union (UDV) won a majority in the national assembly, and Lamizana became president. But a deteriorating economy led to strikes, and a bloodless coup led by Col Zerbo overthrew Lamizana 1980. Zerbo formed a government of national recovery, suspended the constitution, and dissolved the national assembly.

country renamed Burkina Faso In 1982 Zerbo was ousted, and Maj Jean-Baptiste Ouédraogo emerged as leader of a military regime, with Capt Thomas Sankara as prime minister. In 1983 Sankara seized power in another coup, becoming president and ruling through a council of ministers. Opposition members were arrested, the national assembly was dissolved, and a National Revolutionary Council (CNR) set up. In 1984 Sankara announced that the country would be known as Burkina Faso ("land of upright men"), symbolizing a break with its colonial past; his government strengthened ties with Ghana and established links with Benin and Libya. Sankara was killed Oct 1987 in a military coup led by a former close colleague, Capt Blaise Compaoré (1951–). In April 1989 a restructuring of the ruling political groupings took place, and in Sept 1989 a plot to oust Compaoré was discovered and foiled.

Compaoré re-elected Throughout 1991 Compaoré resisted calls for a national conference attended by all political parties, but a new constitution was approved. He was reelected president Dec 1991 but the unusually large number of abstentions in the election reflected his growing unpopularity. In the face of widespread unrest, President Campaoré finally initiated moves Jan 1992 to convene a National Reconciliation Forum to discuss the implementation of the new constitution, which would provide for a multiparty system. The ruling FP–Popular Front won a clear majority in a May 1992 general election, amid opposition claims of electoral fraud. *See illustration box.*

burlesque in the 17th and 18th centuries, a form of satirical comedy parodying a particular play or dramatic genre. For example, John Gay's *The Beggar's Opera* 1728 is a burlesque of 18th-century opera, and Richard Brinsley ○Sheridan's *The Critic* 1777 satirizes the sentimentality in contemporary drama. In the US from the mid-19th century, burlesque referred to a sex and comedy show invented by Michael Bennett Leavitt 1866 with acts including acrobats, singers, and comedians. During the 1920s striptease was introduced in order to counteract the growing popularity of the movies; Gypsy Rose Lee was the most famous stripper. Burlesque was frequently banned in the US.

Burlington city in N central North Carolina, NW of Durham. Industries include textiles, chemicals, furniture, and agricultural products; population (1990) 39,500.

Burlington city in NW Vermont, on the E shore of Lake Champlain; seat of Chittenden county. It is a port of entry and the largest city in Vermont. Industries include computer parts, steel, marble, lumber, dairy products, and tourism. It is the site of the University of Vermont 1791; population (1990) 39,100. It was a naval base during the War of 1812.

Burma former name (to 1989) of ○Myanmar.

Burman member of the largest ethnic group in Myanmar (formerly Burma). The Burmans, speakers of a Sino-Tibetan language, migrated from the hills of Tibet, settling in the areas around Mandalay by the 11th century AD.

From the Mons, a neighboring people, the Burmans acquired Hinayana Buddhism and a written script based on Indian syllables. The Burmans are mainly settled in the valleys where they cultivate rice in irrigated fields.

burn in medicine, destruction of body tissue by extremes of temperature, corrosive chemicals, electricity, or radiation. *First-degree burns* may cause reddening; *second-degree burns* cause blistering and irritation but usually heal spontaneously; *third-degree burns* are disfiguring and may be life-threatening.

Burns cause plasma, the fluid component of the blood, to leak from the blood vessels, and it is this loss of circulating fluid that engenders ○shock. Emergency treatment is needed for third-degree burns in order to replace the fluid volume, prevent infection (a dire threat to the severely burned), and reduce the pain. Plastic, or reconstructive, surgery, including skin grafting, may be required to compensate for damaged tissue and minimize disfigurement.

Burne-Jones Edward Coley 1833–1898. English painter. In 1856 he was apprenticed to the Pre-Raphaelite painter Dante Gabriel ○Rossetti, who remained a dominant influence. His paintings, inspired by legend and myth, were characterized by elongated forms as in *King Cophetua and the Beggar Maid* 1880–84 (Tate Gallery, London). He later moved toward Symbolism. He also designed tapestries and stained glass in association with William ○Morris.

Burnell (Susan) Jocelyn (Bell) 1943– . British astronomer. In 1967 she discovered the first ○pulsar (rapidly flashing star) with Antony ○Hewish and colleagues at Cambridge University, England.

burnet herb *Sanguisorba minor* of the rose family, also known as *salad burnet*. It smells of cucumber and can be used in salads. The term is also used for other members of the genus *Sanguisorba*.

Burnett Frances (Eliza) Hodgson 1849–1924. English writer who emigrated with her family to the US 1865. Her novels for children include the rags-to-riches tale *Little Lord Fauntleroy* 1886 and the sentimental *The Secret Garden* 1909.

Burney Frances (Fanny) 1752–1840. English novelist and diarist, daughter of musician Dr Charles Burney (1726–1814). She achieved success with *Evelina*, published anonymously 1778, became a member of Dr ○Johnson's circle, received a post at court from Queen Charlotte, and in 1793 married the French émigré General d'Arblay. She published three further novels, *Cecilia* 1782, *Camilla* 1796, and *The Wanderer* 1814; her diaries and letters appeared 1842.

Burnham Forbes 1923–1985. Guyanese Marxist-Leninist politician. He was prime minister 1964–80, leading the country to independence 1966 and declaring it the world's first cooperative republic 1970. He was executive president 1980–85. Resistance to the US landing in Grenada 1983 was said to be due to his forewarning the Grenadans of the attack.

Burns Robert 1759–1796. Scottish poet who used the Scots dialect at a time when it was not considered suitably "elevated" for literature. Burns's first volume, *Poems, Chiefly in the Scottish Dialect*, appeared 1786. In addition to his poetry, Burns wrote or adapted many songs, including "Auld Lang Syne."

Burns's fame rests equally on his poems (such as "Holy Willie's Prayer," "Tam o' Shanter," "The Jolly Beggars," and "To a Mouse") and his songs—sometimes wholly original, sometimes adaptations—of which he contributed some 300 to Johnson's *Scots Musical Museum* 1787–1803 and Thomson's *Scottish Airs with Poetry* 1793–1811.

Burnside Ambrose Everett 1824–1881. US military leader and politician. Born in Liberty, Indiana, Burnside attended West Point and was appointed brigadier general in the Union army soon after the outbreak of the Civil War. Named as ○McClellan's successor as commander of the Army of the Potomac, Burnside served briefly in that position before being transferred to the West. Later blamed for the Union defeat at Petersburg 1864, Burnside retired from active service.

Entering politics after the war, he was elected governor of Rhode Island 1866–69 and US Senator 1874–81. His distinctive side whiskers and mustache framing a clean-shaven chin became popularly known as "burnsides," of which "sideburns" is a modification.

Burr Aaron 1756–1836. US politician, Republican vice-president 1800–04, in which year he killed his political rival Alexander ○Hamilton in a duel.

Burr was born in Newark, New Jersey of an eminent Puritan family. He was on George Washington's staff during the ○American Revolution but was critical of the general and was distrusted in turn. He tied with Thomas Jefferson in the presidential election of 1800, but Alexander Hamilton, Burr's longtime adversary, influenced the House of Representatives to vote Jefferson in, Burr becoming vice-president. After killing Hamilton he fled to South Carolina, but returned briefly to Washington to complete his term of office.

In 1807 Burr was tried and acquitted of treason charges, which implicated him variously in a scheme to conquer Mexico, or part of Florida, or to rule over a seceded Louisiana. He spent some years in Europe, seeking British and French aid in overthrowing Jefferson, but reentered the US 1812 under an assumed name. He died in poverty at the age of 80.

Burr Raymond 1917– . Canadian actor who graduated from playing elegant villains to the heroes Perry Mason and Ironside in the long-running television series of the same names. He played the murderer in Alfred Hitchcock's *Rear Window* 1954.

His other films include *The Blue Gardenia*, *The Adventures of Don Juan* 1948, and *Godzilla* (English-language version) 1956.

Burroughs Edgar Rice 1875–1950. US novelist. He wrote *Tarzan of the Apes* 1914, the story of an aristocratic child lost in the jungle and reared by apes, and followed it with over 20 more books about the Tarzan character. He also wrote a series of novels about life on Mars. He was born in Chicago.

Burroughs William S 1914– . US novelist.

He "dropped out" and, as part of the ⊳Beat Generation, wrote *Junkie* 1953, describing his addiction to heroin; *The Naked Lunch* 1959; *The Soft Machine* 1961; and *Dead Fingers Talk* 1963. His later novels include *Queer* and *Mind Wars*, both 1985.

He was born in St Louis, Missouri.

Burroughs William Steward 1857–1898. US industrialist who invented the first hand-operated adding machine to give printed results.

Bursa city in NW Turkey, with a port at Mudania; population (1990) 834,600. It was the capital of the Ottoman Empire 1326–1423.

Burton Richard Francis 1821–1890. British explorer and translator (he knew 35 oriental languages). He traveled mainly in the Middle East and NE Africa, often disguised as a Muslim; made two attempts to find the source of the Nile, 1855 and 1857–58 (on the second, with John ⊳Speke, he reached Lake Tanganyika); and wrote many travel books. He translated oriental erotica and the *Arabian Nights* 1885–88.

After military service in India, Burton explored the Arabian peninsula and Somaliland. In 1853 he visited Mecca and Medina disguised as an Afghan pilgrim; he was then commissioned by the Foreign Office to explore the sources of the Nile. Later travels took him to North and South America. His translations include the *Kama Sutra of Vatsyayana* 1883 and *The Perfumed Garden* 1886. His wife, who had accompanied him on some journeys, burned his unpublished manuscripts and diaries after his death.

Burton Richard. Adopted name of Richard Jenkins 1925–1984. Welsh actor of stage and screen. He had a rich, dramatic voice. Films in which he appeared with his wife, Elizabeth ⊳Taylor, include *Cleopatra* 1962 and *Who's Afraid of Virginia Woolf?* 1966. Among his later films are *Equus* 1977 and *Nineteen Eighty-Four* 1984.

He also won acclaim for his stage performances in both Shakespearian and contemporary dramas throughout his film career.

Burton upon Trent town in Staffordshire, England, NE of Birmingham; population (1983) 57,725. Industries include brewing, tires, and engineering.

Burundi country in E central Africa, bounded N by Rwanda, W by Zaire, SW by Lake Tanganyika, and SE and E by Tanzania.
government Under its 1981 constitution, Burundi's only political party is the Union for National Progress (UPRONA). The president is elected by universal suffrage for a five-year term, and a 65-member national assembly has a five-year tenure, 52 of its members being elected by suffrage and 13 appointed by the president. Ultimate power lies with UPRONA.
history Originally inhabited by the Twa pygmies, Burundi was taken over by Bantu Hutus in the 13th century, and overrun in the 15th century by the Tutsi. In 1890, ruled by a Tutsi king and known as Urundi, it became part of German East Africa and during World War I was occupied by Belgium. Later, as part of Ruanda-Urundi, it was administered by Belgium as a League of Nations (and then United Nations) trust territory.

The 1961 elections, supervised by the UN,

were won by UPRONA, a party formed by Louis, one of the sons of the reigning king, Mwambutsa IV. Louis was assassinated after only two weeks as prime minister and was succeeded by his brother-in-law, André Muhirwa. In 1962 Urundi separated from Ruanda and, as Burundi, attained internal self-government and then full independence.
republic In 1966 King Mwambutsa IV, after a 50-year reign, was deposed by another son, Charles, with army help, and the constitution was suspended. Later that year Charles, now Ntare V, was deposed by his prime minister, Capt Michel Micombero, who declared Burundi a republic. Micombero was a Tutsi, whose main rivals were the numerically superior Hutu. In 1972 the deposed Ntare V was killed, allegedly by the Hutu, giving the Tutsi an excuse to massacre large numbers of Hutu.
one-party state In 1973 amendments to the constitution made Micombero president and prime minister and in the following year UPRONA was declared the only political party. In 1976 Micombero was deposed in an army coup led by Col Jean-Baptiste Bagaza, who became president, with a prime minister and a new council of ministers. In 1977 the prime minister announced a return to civilian rule and a five-year plan to eliminate corruption and secure social justice, including promoting some Hutu to government positions.
army massacre In 1978 the post of prime minister was abolished and a new constitution, providing for a national assembly, was adopted 1981 after a referendum. Bagaza was reelected 1984 (he was the only presidential candidate) but was deposed in a military coup Sept 1987, his government being replaced by a Military Council for National Redemption headed by Maj Pierre Buyoya, believed to be a Tutsi. In Aug 1988 the Tutsi-controlled Burundian army massacred thousands of Hutus in the NE section of the country. Despite Buoya's pledges to end interethnic violence, this massacre was seen by many as a continuation of the strife that began after an abortive Hutu rebellion 1972.

In March 1992 a new constitution, providing for multiparty politics, was approved by referendum by 90% of the electorate in a 97% turnout. *See illustration box.*

Bury town in Greater Manchester, England, on the river Irwell, 10 mi/16 km N of central Manchester; population (1986) 173,650. Industries include cotton, chemicals, and engineering.

Buryat autonomous republic of Russia, in East Siberia
area 135,600 sq mi/351,300 sq km
capital Ulan-Udé
physical bounded on the S by Mongolia, on the W by Lake Baikal; mountainous and forested
products coal, timber, building materials, fish, sheep, cattle
population (1986) 1,014,000
history settled by Russians 17th century; annexed from China by treaties 1689 and 1727.

bus in computing, the electrical pathway through which a computer processor communicates with some of its parts and/or peripherals. Physically, a bus is a set of parallel tracks that can carry digital signals; it may take the form of copper tracks laid down on the computer's ⊳printed circuit boards (PCBs), or of an external cable or connection.

A computer typically has three internal

Burundi
Republic of (*Republika y'Uburundi*)

Rwanda
Bujumbura
Zaire
BURUNDI
Tanzania
INDIAN OCEAN
0 miles 500
0 km 1000

area 10,744 sq mi/27,834 sq km
capital Bujumbura
cities Gitega, Bururi, Ngozi, Muyinga
physical landlocked grassy highland straddling watershed of Nile and Congo
features Lake Tanganyika, Great Rift Valley
head of state and government Pierre Buyoya from 1987
political system one-party military republic
political party Union for National Progress (UPRONA), nationalist socialist
exports coffee, cotton, tea, nickel, hides, livestock, cigarettes, beer, soft drinks; there are 500 million tons of peat reserves in the basin of the Akanyaru River
currency Burundi franc
population (1990 est) 5,647,000 (of whom 15% are the Nilotic Tutsi, still holding most of the land and political power, 1% are Pygmy

Twa, and the remainder Bantu Hutu); growth rate 2.8% p.a.
life expectancy men 45, women 48
languages Kirundi (a Bantu language) and French (both official), Kiswahili
religions Roman Catholic 62%, Protestant 5%, Muslim 1%, animist 32%
literacy men 43%, women 26% (1985)
GDP $1.1 bn (1987); $230 per head
chronology
1962 Separated from Ruanda-Urundi, as Burundi, and given independence as a monarchy under King Mwambutsa IV.
1966 King deposed by his son Charles, who became Ntare V; he was in turn deposed by his prime minister, Capt Michel Micombero, who declared Burundi a republic.
1972 Ntare V killed, allegedly by the Hutu ethnic group. Massacres of 150,000 Hutus by the rival Tutsi ethnic group, of which Micombero was a member.
1973 Micombero made president and prime minister.
1974 UPRONA declared the only legal political party, with the president as its secretary-general.
1976 Army coup deposed Micombero. Col Jean-Baptiste Bagaza appointed president by the Supreme Revolutionary Council.
1981 New constitution adopted, providing for a national assembly.
1984 Bagaza elected president as sole candidate.
1987 Bagaza deposed in coup Sept. Maj Pierre Buyoya headed new Military Council for National Redemption.
1988 Some 24,000 majority Hutu killed by Tutsis.
1992 New constitution approved.

buses laid down on its main circuit board: a **data bus**, which carries data between the components of the computer; an **address bus**, which selects the route to be followed by any particular data item traveling along the data bus; and a **control bus**, which is used to decide whether data is written to or read from the data bus. An external **expansion bus** is used for linking the computer processor to peripheral devices, such as modems and printers.

bus or **omnibus** vehicle that carries fare-paying passengers on a fixed route, with frequent stops where passengers can get on and off.

An omnibus appeared briefly on the streets of Paris in the 1660s, when the mathematician Blaise Pascal introduced the first horse-drawn vehicles for public use. But a successful service, again in Paris, was not established until 1827. Two years later George Shillibeer introduced a horse-drawn bus in London.

Gasoline-engine buses came into general use by the 1910s and provide intracity and nationwide service through both public and private companies.

Bush George Herbert Walker 1924– . 41st president of the US 1989–93. A Republican, he was director of the Central Intelligence Agency (CIA) 1976–81 and US vice-president 1981–89. In 1989, as president, he visited Eastern European countries undergoing reform, held a summit meeting at Malta with Soviet president Gorbachev, and sent US troops to Panama to oust that country's drug-trafficking president, Manuel Noriega. Bush led the UN coalition and sent US forces to Saudi Arabia to prepare for a military strike after Iraq annexed Kuwait 1990. In Jan 1991, he led the coalition war against Iraq that forced Saddam Hussein to remove his troops from Kuwait. He was instrumental in convincing Israel and several of its traditional Arab enemies to convene for a historic face-to-face meeting in Spain in Nov 1991. Domestic economic problems in 1991–92 were followed by his defeat in the 1992 presidential elections by Democrat Bill Clinton.

Born in Milton, Massachusetts, Bush grew up in Connecticut, where his father, Prescott Bush, was a US senator. He graduated from Yale University 1948 and moved to Texas to build up an oil-drilling company. A congressman 1967–70, he was appointed US ambassador to the United Nations 1971–73 and Republican national chairman 1973–74 by President Nixon. During the Ford administration, Bush was a special envoy to China 1974–75. As vice-president during Ronald Reagan's administration he traveled widely and was responsible for overseeing government reform and programs to combat drug smuggling.

bushbuck antelope *Tragelaphus scriptus* found over most of Africa S of the Sahara. Up to 3 ft/1 m high, the males have keeled horns twisted into spirals, and are brown to blackish. The females are generally hornless, lighter, and redder. All have white markings, including stripes or vertical rows of dots down the sides. Rarely far from water, bushbuck live in woods and thick brush.

bushel dry measure used for grain and fruit, equal to eight gallons (2,219.36 cu in/36.37 l) in the UK; some US states have different standards according to the goods measured. One bushel equals four pecks.

bushido chivalric code of honor of the Japanese military caste, the ⟡samurai. Bushido means "the way of the warrior;" the code

stresses simple living, self-discipline, and bravery.

Bushman former name for the ⟡Kung, ⟡San, and other hunter-gatherer groups (for example, the Gikwe, Heikom, and Sekhoin) living in and around the Kalahari Desert in southern Africa. They number approximately 50,000 and speak San and other languages of the ⟡Khoisan family. They are characteristically small-statured and brown-skinned.

They once occupied a large area, but were driven into the Kalahari Desert in the 18th century by Bantu peoples (Sotho and Nguni). Their early art survives in cave paintings.

bushmaster large snake *Lachesis muta*. It is a type of pit viper, and is related to the rattlesnakes. Up to 12 ft/4 m long, it is found in wooded areas of South and Central America, and is the largest venomous snake in the New World. When alarmed, it produces a noise by vibrating its tail among dry leaves.

bushranger Australian armed robber of the 19th century. The first bushrangers were escaped convicts. The last gang was led by Ned ⟡Kelly and his brother Dan in 1878–80. They form the subject of many Australian ballads.

business cycle period of time that includes a peak and trough of economic activity, as measured by a country's national income. In Keynesian economics, one of the main roles of the government is to smooth out the peaks and troughs of the business cycle by intervening in the economy, thus minimizing "overheating" and "stagnation."

business school institution for training in management and marketing. In recent years, the emphasis has shifted to include study of such issues as environmental policy, corporate responsibility, business ethics, and internationalism. The master's in business administration has become a highly prized degree in many professions.

The major business schools are the London Business School (LBS), Harvard in the US, and Insead in France.

Busoni Ferruccio (Dante Benvenuto) 1866–1924. Italian pianist, composer, and music critic. Much of his music was for the piano, but he also composed several operas including *Doktor Faust*, completed by a pupil after his death. An apostle of Futurism, he encouraged the French composer ⟡Varèse.

Bustamante (William) Alexander (born Clarke) 1884–1977. Jamaican socialist politician. As leader of the Labor Party, he was the first prime minister of independent Jamaica 1962–67.

bustard bird of the family Otididae, related to cranes but with a rounder body, a thicker neck, and a relatively short beak. Bustards are found on the ground on open plains and fields.

The great bustard *Otis tarda* is one of the heaviest flying birds at 40 lb/18 kg, and the larger males may have a length of 3 ft/1 m and wingspan of 7.5 ft/2.3 m. It is found in Europe and N Asia.

butane C_4H_{10} one of two gaseous alkanes (paraffin hydrocarbons) having the same formula but differing in structure. Normal butane is derived from natural gas; isobutane is a by-product of petroleum manufacture. Liquefied under pressure, it is used as a fuel for industrial and domestic purposes (for example, in portable cookers).

Bute island and resort in the Firth of Clyde, Scotland; area 46 sq mi/120 sq km. The chief town is Rothesay. It is separated from the mainland in the north by a winding channel, the **Kyles of Bute**. With Arran and the adjacent islands it comprised the former county of Bute, merged 1975 in the region of Strathclyde.

Bute John Stuart, 3rd Earl of Bute 1713–1792. British Tory politician, prime minister 1762–63. On the accession of George III in 1760, he became the chief instrument in the king's policy for breaking the power of the Whigs and establishing the personal rule of the monarch through Parliament.

Buthelezi Chief Gatsha 1928– . Zulu leader and politician, chief minister of KwaZulu, a black "homeland" in the Republic of South Africa from 1970. He is the founder (1975) and president of ⟡Inkatha, a paramilitary organization for attaining a nonracial democratic political system. He has been accused of complicity in the factional violence between Inkatha and ⟡African National Congress supporters that has continued to rack the townships despite his signing of a peace accord with ANC leader, Nelson Mandela, Sept 1991.

Butler Samuel 1835–1902. English author who made his name 1872 with a satiric attack on contemporary utopianism, *Erewhon* (*nowhere* reversed), but is now remembered for his autobiographical *The Way of All Flesh* written 1872–85 and published 1903.

butte steep-sided flat-topped hill, formed in horizontally layered sedimentary rocks, largely in arid areas. A large butte with a pronounced tablelike profile is a ⟡mesa.

Buttes and mesas are characteristic of semiarid areas where remnants of resistant rock layers protect softer rock underneath, as in the plateau regions of Colorado, Utah, and Arizona.

Butte mining town in Montana, in the Rocky Mountains; population (1990) 33,900. Butte was founded in 1864 during a rush for gold, soon exhausted; copper was found some 20 years later on what was called "the richest hill on earth."

The last mine closed 1983. Butte is the seat of the Montana College of Mineral Science and Technology.

butter solid, edible yellowish fat made from whole milk. Making butter by hand, which is done by skimming off the cream and churning it, was traditionally a convenient means of preserving milk.

The transfer of butter making from a farm-based to a factory-based process began in the last quarter of the 19th century, with the introduction of centrifugal separators for the instant separation of cream from milk. It could then be conveyed into large steam-powered churns. Today, most butter is made on a continuous system devised in Germany during World War II. Inside a single machine, the cream is churned, the buttermilk drawn off, and the butter washed, salted, and worked, to achieve an even consistency. Color and flavoring may be added. A continuous stream of finished butter is extruded from the machine ready for wrapping.

Salted butter has a longer shelf-life than sweet butter, salt being added as a preservative.

buttercup plant of the genus *Ranunculus* of the buttercup family with divided leaves and yellow flowers.

Species include the swamp buttercup *R. septentrionaiis* of the US.

butterfly insect belonging, like moths, to the order Lepidoptera, in which the wings are covered with tiny scales, often brightly colored. There are some 15,000 species of butterfly, many of which are under threat throughout the world because of the destruction of habitat.

Butterflies have a tubular proboscis through which they suck up nectar, or, in some species, carrion, dung, or urine. ♢Metamorphosis is complete; the pupa, or chrysalis, is usually without the protection of a cocoon. Adult life span may be only a few weeks, but some species hibernate and lay eggs in the spring.

The largest family, Nymphalidae, has some 6,000 species; it includes the peacock, tortoiseshells, and fritillaries. The family Pieridae includes the **cabbage white**, one of the few butterflies injurious to crops. The Lycaenidae are chiefly small, often with metallic coloration, for example the blues, coppers, and hairstreaks. The **large blue** *Lycaena arion* has a complex life history: it lays its eggs on wild thyme, and the caterpillars are then taken by Myrmica ants to their nests. The ants milk their honey glands, while the caterpillars feed on the ant larvae. In the spring, the caterpillars finally pupate and emerge as butterflies. The mainly tropical Papilionidae, or swallowtails, are large and very beautiful, especially the South American species. The world's largest butterfly is **Queen Alexandra's birdwing** *Ornithoptera alexandrae* of Papua New Guinea, with a body 3 in/7.5 cm long and a wingspan of 10 in/25 cm. The most spectacular migrant is the orange and black **monarch butterfly** *Danaus plexippus*, which may fly from N Canada to Mexico in the autumn.

Butterflies usually differ from moths in having the antennae club-shaped rather than plumed or feathery, no "lock" between the fore and hindwing, and resting with the wings in the vertical position rather than flat or sloping.

butterfly fish any of several fishes, not all related. The freshwater butterfly fish *Pantodon buchholzi* of W Africa can leap from the water and glide for a short distance on its large winglike pectoral fins. Up to 4 in/10 cm long, it lives in stagnant water. The tropical marine butterfly fishes, family Chaetodontidae, are brightly colored with laterally flattened bodies, often with long snouts which they poke into crevices in rocks and coral when feeding.

butterwort insectivorous plant, genus *Pinguicula*, of the bladderwort family, with purplish flowers and a rosette of flat leaves covered with a sticky secretion that traps insects.

Buxtehude Diderik 1637–1707. Danish composer and organist at Lübeck, Germany, who influenced ♢Bach and ♢Handel. He is remembered for his organ works and cantatas, written for his evening concerts or *Abendmusiken*.

buzzard any of a number of species of medium-sized hawks with broad wings, often seen soaring. The **common buzzard** *Buteo buteo* of Europe and Asia is about 1.8 ft/55 cm long with a wingspan of over 4 ft/1.2 m. It preys on a variety of small animals up to the size of a rabbit.

The **rough-legged buzzard** *Buzzard lagopus* lives in the northern tundra and eats lemmings. The **honey buzzard** *Pernis apivora* feeds largely, as its name suggests, on honey and insect larvae. It summers in Europe and W Asia and winters in Africa.

Byatt A(ntonia) S(usan) 1936– . English novelist and critic. Her fifth novel, *Possession*, won the 1990 Booker Prize. *The Virgin in the Garden* 1978 is a confident, zestfully handled account of a varied group of characters putting on a school play during Coronation year, 1953. It has a sequel, *Still Life* 1985.

She was born in Sheffield and educated at a Quaker boarding school (with her sister, novelist Margaret Drabble) and at Newnham College, Cambridge.

Byblos ancient Phoenician city (modern Jebeil), 20 mi/32 km N of Beirut, Lebanon. Known to the Assyrians and Babylonians as *Gubla*, it had a thriving export of cedar and pinewood to Egypt as early as 1500 BC. In Roman times it boasted an amphitheater, baths, and a temple dedicated to an unknown male god, and was known for its celebration of the resurrection of Adonis, worshiped as a god of vegetation.

Bydgoszcz industrial river port in N Poland, 65 mi/105 km NE of Poznań on the Warta; population (1990) 381,500. As *Bromberg* it was under Prussian control 1772–1919.

Byelorussian or *Belorussian* "White Russian" native of Belarus. Byelorussian, a Balto-Slavic language belonging to the Indo-European family, is spoken by about 10 million people, including some in Poland. It is written in the Cyrillic script. Byelorussian literature dates to the 11th century AD.

The Byelorussians are descended from E Slavic tribes who moved into the region between the 6th and 8th centuries AD. They were ruled by Kiev until 1240 when Byelorussian lands went to Lithuania. In the 18th century Catherine the Great acquired Byelorussia, but W Byelorussia was under Polish rule 1921–39.

Byng Julian, 1st Viscount of Vimy 1862–1935. British general in World War I, commanding troops in Turkey and France, where, after a victory at Vimy Ridge, he took command of the Third Army.

Byrd Richard Evelyn 1888–1957. US aviator and explorer. The first to fly over the North Pole (1926), he also flew over the South Pole (1929), and led five overland expeditions in Antarctica.

At the request of President Franklin Roosevelt, he took command of the US Antarctic Service. Byrd maintained that new techniques could be used as supplements to traditional methods, rather than as replacements for them. In holding this view, he disagreed with Norwegian explorer Roald ♢Amundsen.

Byrd William 1543–1623. English composer. His church choral music (set to Latin words, as he was a firm Catholic), notably masses for three, four, and five voices, is among the greatest Renaissance music. He also composed secular vocal and instrumental music.

Byrds, the US pioneering folk-rock group 1964–73. Emulated for their 12-string guitar sound, as on the hits "Mr Tamborine Man" (a 1965 version of Bob Dylan's song) and "Eight Miles High" 1966, they moved toward country rock in the late 1960s.

Byron Augusta Ada 1815–1851. English mathematician, a pioneer in writing programs for Charles ♢Babbage's analytical engine. In 1983 a new, high-level computer language, ADA, was named after her. She was the daughter of the poet Lord Byron.

Byron George Gordon, 6th Baron Byron 1788–1824. English poet who became the symbol of Romanticism and political liberalism throughout Europe in the 19th century. His reputation was established with the first two cantos of *Childe Harold* 1812. Later works include *The Prisoner of Chillon* 1816, *Beppo* 1818, *Mazeppa* 1819, and, most notably, the satirical *Don Juan* 1819–24. He left England in 1816, spending most of his later life in Italy.

Born in London and educated at Harrow and Cambridge, Byron published his first volume *Hours of Idleness* 1807 and attacked its harsh critics in *English Bards and Scotch Reviewers* 1809. Overnight fame came with the first two cantos of *Childe Harold*, romantically describing his tours in Portugal, Spain, and the Balkans (third canto 1816, fourth 1818). In 1815 he married mathematician Anne Milbanke (1792–1860), with whom he had a daughter, Augusta Ada Byron, separating from her a year later amid much scandal. He then went to Europe, where he became friendly with Percy and Mary ♢Shelley. He engaged in Italian revolutionary politics and sailed for Greece in 1823 to further the Greek struggle for independence, but died of fever at Missolonghi. He is remembered for his lyrics, his colloquially easy *Letters*, and as the "patron saint" of Romantic liberalism.

byte in computing, a basic unit of storage of information. A byte contains 8 ♢bits and can specify 256 values, such as the numbers from 0 to 255, or 256 colors at one byte per pixel (picture element). Three bytes (24 bits) can specify 16,777,216 values. Twenty-four-bit color graphics with 16.8 million colors can provide a photo-realistic color display.

The term also refers to a single memory location; large computer memory size is measured in thousands of bytes (kilobytes or KB) or millions of bytes (megabytes or MB).

Byzantine Empire the *Eastern Roman Empire* 395–1453, with its capital at Constantinople (formerly Byzantium, modern Istanbul).

330 Emperor Constantine converted to Christianity and moved his capital to Constantinople.

395 The Roman Empire was divided into eastern and western halves.

476 The Western Empire was overrun by barbarian invaders.

527–565 Emperor Justinian I temporarily recovered Italy, N Africa, and parts of Spain.

7th–8th centuries Syria, Egypt, and N Africa were lost to the Muslims, who twice besieged Constantinople (673–77, 718), but the Christian Byzantines maintained their hold on Anatolia.

8th–11th centuries The ♢Iconoclastic controversy brought the emperors into conflict with the papacy, and in 1054 the Greek Orthodox Church broke with the Roman.

867–1056 Under the Macedonian dynasty the Byzantine Empire reached the height of its prosperity; the Bulgars proved a formidable danger, but after a long struggle were finally crushed in 1018 by ♢Basil II ("the Bulgar-Slayer"). After Basil's death the Byzantine Empire declined because of internal factions.

1071–73 The Seljuk Turks conquered most of Anatolia.

1204 The Fourth Crusade sacked Constantinople and set Baldwin of Flanders (1171–1205) on the throne of the new Latin (W European) Empire.

1261 The Greeks recaptured the Latin (W European) Empire and restored the Byzantine

Empire, but it maintained a precarious existence.

1453 The Turks captured Constantinople and founded the ◊Ottoman Empire.

Byzantine literature written mainly in the Greek *koinē*, a form of Greek accepted as the literary language of the 1st century AD and increasingly separate from the spoken tongue of the people. Byzantine literature is chiefly concerned with theology, history, and commentaries on the Greek classics. Its chief authors are the theologians St Basil, Gregory of Nyssa, Gregory of Nazianzus, Chrysostom (4th century AD) and John of Damascus (8th century); the historians Zosimus (about 500), Procopius (6th century), Bryennius and his wife ◊Anna Comnena (about 1100), and Georgius Acropolita (1220–1282); and the encyclopedist Suidas (about 975). Drama was nonexistent, and poetry, save for the hymns of the 6th–8th centuries, scanty and stilted, but there were many popular works about the lives of the saints.

Byzantine style style in the visual arts and architecture that originated in the 4th–5th centuries in Byzantium (the capital of the Eastern Roman Empire), and spread to Italy, throughout the Balkans, and to Russia, where it survived for many centuries. It is characterized by heavy stylization, strong linear emphasis, the use of rigid artistic stereotypes and rich colors such as gold. Byzantine artists excelled in mosaic work and manuscript painting. In architecture, the dome supported on pendentives was in widespread use.

Classical examples of Byzantine architecture are the churches of Sta Sophia, Constantinople, and St Mark's, Venice. Medieval painting styles were influenced by Byzantine art; a more naturalistic style emerged from the 13th century onwards in the West. See also ◊medieval art.

Byzantium (modern Istanbul) ancient Greek city on the Bosporus, founded as a colony of the Greek city of Megara, near Corinth, about 660 BC. In AD 330 the capital of the Roman Empire was transferred there by Constantine the Great, who renamed it ◊Constantinople.

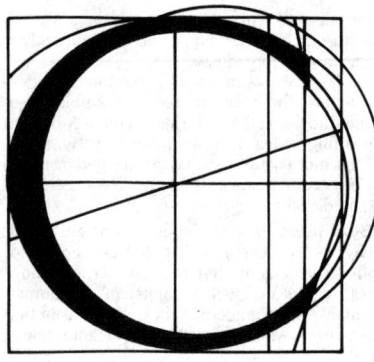

C the third letter of the English alphabet. It corresponds to Hebrew *gimel* and Greek *gamma* (Γ, γ), both derived from the Semitic word for "camel." Originally representing a hard *g*, it was also used by the Romans for *k*. In English it can have the sound of *s* or *k*.

C high-level general-purpose computer-programming language popular on minicomputers andminicomputers. Developed in the early 1970s from an earlier language called BCPL, C was first used as the language of the operating system ⟡Unix, though it has since become widespread beyond Unix. It is useful for writing fast and efficient systems programs, such as operating systems (which control the operations of the computer).

c. abbreviation for *circa* (Latin "about"); used with dates that are uncertain.

C abbreviation for *centum* (Latin "hundred"); *century*; *centigrade*; ⟡*Celsius*.

C °C symbol for ⟡Celsius (temperature scale), formerly called centigrade.

CA abbreviation for the state of ⟡*California*.

Cabal, the (from *kabbala*) group of politicians, the English king Charles II's counselors 1667–73, whose initials made up the word by coincidence—Clifford (Thomas Clifford 1630–1673), Ashley (Anthony Ashley Cooper, 1st Earl of ⟡Shaftesbury), ⟡Buckingham (George Villiers, 2nd Duke of Buckingham), Arlington (Henry Bennett, 1st Earl of Arlington 1618–1685), and ⟡Lauderdale (John Maitland, Duke of Lauderdale).

cabbage plant *Brassica oleracea* of the cress family Cruciferae, allied to the turnip and wild mustard, or charlock. It is a table vegetable, cultivated as early as 2000 BC, and the numerous commercial varieties include kale, Brussels sprouts, common cabbage, savoy, cauliflower, sprouting broccoli, and kohlrabi.

cabbala alternate spelling of ⟡kabbala.

Cabinda or *Kabinda* African coastal enclave, a province of ⟡Angola; area 3,000 sq mi/ 7,770 sq km; population (1980) 81,300. The capital is Cabinda. There are oil reserves. Cabinda, which was attached to Angola in 1886, has made claims to independence.

cabinet in government, a group of ministers that act as advisers to a country's executive.

Cabinet members generally advise on, decide, or administer the government's policy. The US cabinet consists of the secretaries (heads) of the executive departments, appointed by the president and confirmed by the Senate. The secretaries are not members of Congress; they are advisers to the president. In the UK, the cabinet system originated under the Stuart monarchs; under William III it became customary for the king to select his ministers from the party with a parliamentary majority. The chief royal adviser was called the prime minister.

cable car method of transporting passengers up steep slopes by cable. In the *cable railway*, passenger cars are hauled along rails by a cable wound by a powerful winch. A pair of cars usually operate together on the funicular principle, one going up as the other goes down. The other main type is the *aerial cable car*, where the passenger car is suspended from a trolley that runs along an aerial cableway.

A unique form of cable-car system has operated in San Francisco since 1873. The streetcars travel along rails and are hauled by moving cables under the ground.

cable length unit of length, used on ships, originally the length of a ship's anchor cable or 120 fathoms (720 ft/219 m), but in British usage taken as one-tenth of a ⟡nautical mile (608 ft/185 m).

Cable News Network (CNN) international television news channel; the 24-hour service was founded 1980 by US entrepreneur Ted Turner and has its headquarters in Atlanta, Georgia. It established its global reputation 1991 with eyewitness accounts from Baghdad of the beginning of the Gulf War.

cable television distribution of broadcast signals through cable relay systems.

Narrow-band systems were originally used to deliver services to areas with poor regular reception; systems with wider bands, using coaxial and fiberoptic cable, are increasingly used for distribution and development of home-based interactive services.

Cabot Sebastian 1474–1557. Italian navigator and cartographer, the second son of Giovanni ⟡Caboto. He explored the Brazilian coast and the Rio de la Plata for the Holy Roman Emperor Charles V 1526–30.

He was also employed by Henry VIII, Edward VI, and Ferdinand of Spain. He planned a voyage to China by way of the North-East Passage, the sea route along the N Eurasian coast, encouraged the formation of the Company of Merchant Adventurers of London 1551, and in 1553 and 1556 directed the company's expeditions to Russia, where he opened British trade.

the US cabinet

Department of State
Department of the Treasury
Department of the Interior
Department of Agriculture
Department of Justice
Department of Commerce
Department of Labor
Department of Defense
Department of Housing and Urban
  Development
Department of Transportation
Department of Energy
Department of Education
Department of Health and Human Services
Department of Veteran Affairs

Caboto Giovanni or *John Cabot* 1450–1498. Italian navigator. Commissioned, with his three sons, by Henry VII of England to discover unknown lands, he arrived at Cape Breton Island on June 24, 1497, thus becoming the first European to reach the North American mainland (he thought he was in NE Asia). In 1498 he sailed again, touching Greenland, and probably died on the voyage.

Cabral Pedro Alvarez 1460–1526. Portuguese explorer who made Brazil a Portuguese possession in 1500 and negotiated the first commercial treaty between Portugal and India.

Cabrini Frances or Francesca ("Mother Cabrini") 1850–1917. First Roman Catholic US citizen to become a saint. Born in Lombardy, Italy, she founded the Missionary Sisters of the Sacred Heart, and established many schools and hospitals in the care of her nuns. She was canonized 1946. Feast day Dec 22.

cacao tropical American evergreen tree *Theobroma cacao* of the Sterculia family, now also cultivated in W Africa and Sri Lanka. Its seeds are cocoa beans, from which ⟡cocoa and chocolate are prepared.

The trees mature at five to eight years and produce two crops a year. The fruit is 6.5 in/ 17 cm–9.5 in/25 cm long, hard and ridged, with the beans inside. The seeds are called cocoa nibs; when left to ferment, then roasted and separated from the husks, they contain about 50% fat, part of which is removed to make chocolate and cocoa. The Aztecs revered cacao and made a drink for the nobility only from cocoa beans and chillis, which they called chocolatl. In the 16th century Spanish traders brought cacao to Europe. It was used to make a drink, which came to rival coffee and tea in popularity.

cacao beans see ⟡cocoa and chocolate.

cactus (plural *cacti*) plant of the family Cactaceae, although the term is commonly applied to many different succulent and prickly plants. True cacti have a woody axis (central core) overlaid with an enlarged fleshy stem, which assumes various forms and is usually covered with spines (actually reduced leaves). They all have special adaptations to growing in dry areas.

Cactus flowers are often large and brightly colored; the fruit is fleshy and often edible, as in the case of the prickly pear. The Cactaceae are a New World family and include the treelike saguaro and the night-blooming cereus with blossoms 12 in/30 cm across.

CAD (acronym for *computer-aided design*) the use of computers in creating and editing design drawings. CAD also allows such things as automatic testing of designs and multiple or animated three-dimensional views of designs. CAD systems are widely used in architecture, electronics, and engineering, for example in the motor-vehicle industry, where automobiles designed with the assistance of computers are now commonplace. A related development is CAM (computer-assisted manufacture).

caddis fly insect of the order Trichoptera. Adults are generally dull brown, mothlike, with wings covered in tiny hairs. Mouthparts are poorly developed, and many caddis flies do not feed as adults. They are usually found near water.

The larvae are aquatic, and many live in cases, open at both ends, which they make out of sand or plant remains. Some species make silk nets among aquatic vegetation to help trap food.

cadenza in music, an unaccompanied bravura passage (requiring elaborate, virtuoso execution) in the style of an improvisation for the soloist during a concerto.

Cadiz Spanish city and naval base, capital and seaport of the province of Cadiz, standing on Cadiz Bay, an inlet of the Atlantic, 64 mi/ 103 km S of Seville; population (1991) 156,600. After the discovery of the Americas 1492, Cadiz became one of Europe's most vital trade ports. The English adventurer Francis ⌂Drake burned a Spanish fleet here 1587 to prevent the sailing of the ⌂Armada.

Probably founded by the Phoenicians about 1100 BC, it was a center for the tin trade with Cornwall, England. It was recaptured from the ⌂Moors by the king of Castile 1262. Development was restricted by its peninsular location until a bridge to the opposite shore of Cadiz Bay was completed 1969.

cadmium soft, silver-white, ductile, and malleable metallic element, symbol Cd, atomic number 48, atomic weight 112.40. Cadmium occurs in nature as a sulfide or carbonate in zinc ores. It is a toxic metal that, because of industrial dumping, has become an environmental pollutant. It is used in batteries, electroplating, and as a constituent of alloys used for bearings with low coefficients of friction; it is also a constituent of an alloy with a very low melting point.

Cadmium is also used in the control rods of nuclear reactors, because of its high absorption of neutrons. It was named in 1817 by the German chemist Friedrich Strohmeyer (1776–1835) after Cadmus, the Greek mythological founder of the city of Thebes, near which ores containing the element were found.

Cadmus in Greek mythology, a Phoenician from Tyre, brother of ⌂Europa. He founded the city of Thebes in Greece. Obeying the oracle of Athena, Cadmus killed the sacred dragon that guarded the spring of Ares. He sowed the teeth of the dragon, from which sprang a multitude of fierce warriors who fought among themselves; the survivors were considered to be the ancestors of the Theban aristocracy.

Cadmus married Harmonia and was credited with the introduction of the (Phoenician) alphabet into Greece.

caecilian tropical amphibian of wormlike appearance. There are about 170 species known, forming the amphibian order Apoda (also known as Caecilia or Gymnophiona). Caecilians have a grooved skin that gives a "segmented" appearance; they have no trace of limbs, and mostly live below ground. Some species bear live young, others lay eggs.

Caen capital of Calvados *département*, France, on the river Orne; population (1982) 183,500. It is a business center, with ironworks and electric and electronic industries. Caen building stone has a fine reputation. The town is linked by canal with the nearby English Channel to the northeast. The church of St Etienne was founded by William the Conqueror, and the university by Henry VI of England in 1432. Caen was captured by British forces in World War II on July 9, 1944 after five weeks' fighting, during which the town was badly damaged.

Caernarvon or **Caernarfon** administrative headquarters of Gwynedd, N Wales, situated on the SW shore of the Menai Strait; population (1981) 10,000. Formerly a Roman station, it is now a market port city.

The first Prince of Wales (later ⌂Edward II)

was born in Caernarvon Castle; Edward VIII was invested here 1911 and Prince Charles 1969.

Caesar powerful family of ancient Rome, which included Gaius Julius Caesar, whose grand-nephew and adopted son ⌂Augustus assumed the name of Caesar and passed it on to his adopted son ⌂Tiberius. From then on, it was used by the successive emperors, becoming a title of the Roman rulers. The titles "tsar" in Russia and "kaiser" in Germany were both derived from the name Caesar.

Caesar Gaius Julius *c.* 100–44 BC. Roman statesman and general. He formed with Pompey and Crassus the First Triumvirate 60 BC. He conquered Gaul 58–50 and invaded Britain 55 and 54. He fought against Pompey 49–48, defeating him at Pharsalus. After a period in Egypt Caesar returned to Rome as dictator from 46. He was assassinated by conspirators on the ⌂Ides of March 44.

A patrician, Caesar allied himself with the popular party, and when elected to the office of aedile 65, nearly ruined himself with lavish amusements for the Roman populace. Although a free thinker, he was elected chief pontiff 63 and appointed governor of Spain 61. Returning to Rome 60, he formed with Pompey and Crassus the First Triumvirate. As governor of Gaul, he was engaged in its subjugation 58–50, defeating the Germans under Ariovistus and selling thousands of the Belgic tribes into slavery. In 55 he crossed into Britain, returning for a further campaigning visit 54. A revolt by the Gauls under Vercingetorix 52 was crushed 51.

His governorship of Spain was to end 49, and, Crassus being dead, Pompey became his rival. Declaring "the die is cast," Caesar crossed the Rubicon (the small river separating Gaul from Italy) to meet the army raised against him by Pompey. In the ensuing civil war, he followed Pompey to Epirus 48, defeated him at Pharsalus, and chased him to Egypt, where he was murdered. Caesar stayed some months in Egypt, where Cleopatra, queen of Egypt, gave birth to his son, Caesarion.

Caesar executed a lightning campaign 47 against King Pharnaces II (ruled 63–47 BC) in Asia Minor, which he summarized: *Veni vidi vici* "I came, I saw, I conquered." With his final victory over the sons of Pompey at Munda in Spain 45, he established his position, having been awarded a ten-year dictatorship 46. On March 15, 44 he was stabbed to death at the foot of Pompey's statue (see ⌂Brutus, ⌂Cassius) in the Senate house. His commentaries on the campaigns and the civil war survive.

Caesarea ancient city in Palestine (now ⌂Qisarya). It was built by Herod the Great 22–12 BC, who also constructed a port (*portus Augusti*). Caesarea was the administrative capital of the province of Judea.

Caesarean section surgical operation to deliver a baby by cutting through the mother's abdominal and intrauterine walls. It may be recommended for almost any obstetric complication implying a threat to mother or baby.

Caesarean section was named after the Roman emperor Julius Caesar, who was born this way. In medieval Europe, it was performed mostly in attempts to save the life of a child whose mother had died in labor. The Christian church forbade cutting open the mother before she was dead.

Caetano Marcello 1906–1980. Portuguese right-wing politician. Professor of administrative law at Lisbon from 1940, he succeeded the dictator Salazar as prime minister from 1968 until his exile after the military coup of 1974. He was granted political asylum in Brazil.

caffeine ⌂alkaloid organic substance found in tea, coffee, and kola nuts; it stimulates the heart and central nervous system. When isolated, it is a bitter crystalline compound, $C_8H_{10}N_4O_2$. Too much caffeine (more than six average cups of tea or coffee a day) can be detrimental to health.

Cage John 1912–1992. US composer. A pupil of Arnold ⌂Schoenberg, he maintained that all sounds should be available for musical purposes; for example, he used 24 radios, tuned to random stations, in *Imaginary Landscape No 4* 1951. He also worked to reduce the control of the composer over the music, introducing randomness (⌂aleatory music) and inexactitude and allowing sounds to "be themselves." Cage's unconventional ideas have had a profound impact on 20th-century music.

Cage reassessed musical aesthetics and defined the role of music as "purposeless play." In one of his most famous pieces, titled *4 Minutes and 33 Seconds* 1952, the pianist sits at the piano reading a score for that length of time but does not play.

Cagliari capital and port of Sardinia, Italy, on the Gulf of Cagliari; population (1988) 222,000.

Cagnes-sur-Mer capital of the *département* of Alpes-Maritimes; SW of Nice, France; population (1986) 35,200. The château (13th–17th century) contains mementos of the Impressionist painter Renoir, who lived here 1900–19.

Cagney James 1899–1986. US actor who moved to films from Broadway. Usually associated with gangster roles (*The Public Enemy* 1931), he was an actor of great versatility, playing Bottom in *A Midsummer Night's Dream* 1935 and singing and dancing in *Yankee Doodle Dandy* 1942.

He starred in *Mr Roberts* 1955, and *One Two Three* was his last film before retirement; but in 1981 he came back for *Ragtime*.

Cain in the Old Testament, the first-born son of Adam and Eve. Motivated by jealousy, he murdered his brother Abel because the latter's sacrifice was more acceptable to God than his own.

Cain James M(allahan) 1892–1977. US novelist. He was the author of *The Postman Always Rings Twice* 1934, *Mildred Pierce* 1941, and *Double Indemnity* 1943, which all became classic motion pictures. These novels epitomized the "hard-boiled" fiction of the 1930s and 1940s.

Caine Michael. Adopted name of Maurice Micklewhite 1933– . English actor, an accomplished performer with an enduring Cockney streak. His films include *Alfie* 1966, *The Man Who Would Be King* 1975, *Educating Rita* 1983, and *Hannah and Her Sisters* 1986.

cairn Scottish breed of ⌂terrier. Shaggy, short-legged, and compact, it can be sandy, grayish brindle, or red. It was formerly used for flushing out foxes and badgers.

Cairo ((Arabic *El Qahira*)) capital of Egypt, on the E bank of the Nile 8 mi/13 km above the apex of the delta and 100 mi/160 km from the Mediterranean; the largest city in Africa and in the Middle East; population (1985) 6,205,000; metropolitan area (1987) 13,300,000. An earthquake in a suburb of the city Oct 1992 left over 500 dead.

history El Fustat (Old Cairo) was founded by Arabs about AD 642, Al Qahira about 1000 by the ◊Fatimid ruler Gowhar. Cairo was the capital of the Ayyubid dynasty, one of whose sultans, Saladin, built the Citadel in the late 1100s.

Under the Mamelukes 1250–1517 the city prospered, but declined in the 16th century after conquest by the Turks. It became the capital of the virtually autonomous kingdom of Egypt established by Mehmet Ali in 1805. During World War II it was the headquarters of the Allied forces in N Africa.

features Cairo is the site of the mosque that houses the El Azhar university (972). The Mosque of Amr dates from 643; the 12th-century Citadel contains the impressive 19th-century Mohammed Ali mosque. The city is 20 mi/32 km N of the site of the ancient Egyptian center of ◊Memphis. The Great Pyramids and Sphinx are at nearby Giza.

The government and business quarters reflect Cairo's position as a leading administrative and commercial center, and the semiofficial newspaper *al Ahram* is an influential voice in the Arab world. Cairo's industries include the manufacture of textiles, cement, vegetable oils, and beer. At Helwan, 15 mi/24 km to the S, an industrial center is developing, with iron and steelworks powered by electricity from the Aswan High Dam. There are two secular universities: Cairo University (1908) and Ein Shams (1950).

caisson hollow cylindrical or boxlike structure, usually of reinforced ◊concrete, sunk into a riverbed to form the foundations of a bridge.

An **open caisson** is open at the top and at the bottom, where there is a wedge-shaped cutting edge. Material is excavated from inside, allowing the caisson to sink. A **pneumatic caisson** has a pressurized chamber at the bottom, in which workers carry out the excavation. The air pressure prevents the surrounding water entering; the workers enter and leave the chamber through an air lock, allowing for a suitable decompression period to prevent ◊decompression sickness (the so-called bends).

Cajun member of a French-speaking community of Louisiana, descended from French-Canadians who, in the 18th century, were driven there from Nova Scotia (then known as Acadia, from which the name Cajun comes). *Cajun music* has a lively rhythm and features steel guitar, fiddle, and accordion.

cal symbol for ◊*calorie*.

CAL (acronym for *computer-assisted learning*) the use of computers in education and training: the computer displays instructional material to a student and asks questions about the information given; the student's answers determine the sequence of the lessons.

Calabar port and capital of Cross River State, SE Nigeria, on the Cross River, 40 mi/64 km from the Atlantic; population (1983) 126,000. Rubber, timber, and vegetable oils are exported. It was a center of the slave trade in the 18th and 19th centuries.

calabash tropical South American evergreen tree *Crescentia cujete*, family Bignoniaceae, with gourds 20 in/50 cm across, which are used as water containers. The Old World tropical vine bottle gourd *Lagenaria siceraria* of the gourd family Cucurbitaceae is sometimes called calabash, and it produces equally large true gourds.

Calabria mountainous earthquake region occupying the "toe" of Italy, comprising the provinces of Catanzaro, Cosenza, and Reggio; capital Catanzaro; area 5,829 sq mi/15,100 sq km; population (1990) 2,153,700. Reggio is the industrial center.

Calais port in N France; population (1982) 101,000. Taken by England's Edward III in 1347, it was saved from destruction by the personal surrender of the Burghers of Calais commemorated in Rodin's sculpture; the French retook it 1558. In World War II, following German occupation May 1940–Oct 1944, it surrendered to the Canadians.

Calais, Pas de French name for the Strait of ◊Dover.

calamine $Zn_4Si_2O_7(OH)_2.H_2O$ native zinc silicate, an ore of zinc. The term also refers to a pink powder of zinc oxide mixed with 0.5% ferric oxide, used in lotions and ointments as a topical astringent.

Calamity Jane nickname of Martha Jane Burke c. 1852–1903. US heroine of Deadwood, South Dakota. She worked as a teamster, transporting supplies to the mining camps, adopted male dress and, as an excellent shot, promised "calamity" to any aggressor. Many fictional accounts of the Wild West featured her exploits.

She was also known as Martha Jane Canary. During a smallpox epidemic 1878, she assisted in caring for the victims who had been abandoned by local citizens.

calceolaria plant of the *Calceolaria* figwort genus, family Scrophulariaceae, with brilliantly colored slipper-shaped flowers. Native to South America, calceolarias were introduced to Europe and the US in the 1830s.

Calchas in Greek mythology, a visionary and interpreter of omens for the Greek expedition against ◊Troy, responsible for recommending the sacrifice of ◊Iphigenia by her father ◊Agamemnon, as an atonement for an offense against the goddess ◊Artemis.

calcination ◊oxidation of metals by burning in air.

calcite colorless, white, or light-colored common rock-forming mineral, calcium carbonate, $CaCO_3$. It is the main constituent of ◊limestone and marble, and forms many types of invertebrate shell.

Calcite often forms ◊stalactites and stalagmites in caves and is also found deposited in veins through many rocks because of the ease with which it is dissolved and transported by groundwater; ◊oolite is its spheroidal form. It rates 3 on the ◊Mohs' scale of hardness. Large crystals up to 3 ft/1 m have been found in Oklahoma and Missouri. ◊Iceland spar is a transparent form of calcite used in the optical industry; as limestone it is used in the building industry.

calcium (Latin *calcis* "lime") soft, silvery-white metallic element, symbol Ca, atomic number 20, atomic weight 40.08. It is one of the ◊alkaline-earth metals. It is the fifth most abundant element (the third most abundant metal) in the Earth's crust. It is found mainly as its carbonate $CaCO_3$, which occurs in a fairly pure condition as chalk and limestone (see ◊calcite). Calcium is an essential component of bones, teeth, shells, milk, and leaves, and it forms 1.5% of the human body by mass.

Calcium ions in animal cells are involved in regulating muscle contraction, hormone secretion, digestion, and glycogen metabolism in the liver.

The element was discovered and named by the English chemist Humphry Davy in 1808. Its compounds include slaked lime (calcium hydroxide, $Ca(OH)_2$); plaster of Paris (calcium sulfate, $CaSO_4.2H_2O$); calcium phosphate ($Ca_3(PO_4)_2$), the main constituent of animal bones; calcium hypochlorite ($CaOCl_2$), a bleaching agent; calcium nitrate ($Ca(NO_3)_2.4H_2O$), a nitrogenous fertilizer; calcium carbide (CaC_2), which reacts with water to give ethyne (acetylene); calcium cyanamide ($CaCN_2$), the basis of many pharmaceuticals, fertilizers, and plastics, including melamine; calcium cyanide ($Ca(CN)_2$), used in the extraction of gold and silver and in electroplating; and others used in baking powders and fillers for paints.

calculator pocket-sized electronic computing device for performing numerical calculations. It can add, subtract, multiply, and divide; many calculators also compute squares and roots, and have advanced trigonometric and statistical functions. Input is by a small keyboard and results are shown on a one-line computer screen, typically a ◊liquid-crystal display (LCD) or a light-emitting diode (LED). The first electronic calculator was manufactured by the Bell Punch Company in the US 1963.

calculus (Latin "pebble") branch of mathematics that permits the manipulation of continuously varying quantities, used in practical problems involving such matters as changing speeds, problems of flight, varying stresses in the framework of a bridge, and alternating current theory. **Integral calculus** deals with the method of summation or adding together the effects of continuously varying quantities. **Differential calculus** deals in a similar way with rates of change. Many of its applications arose from the study of the gradients of the tangents to curves.

There are several other branches of calculus, including calculus of errors and calculus of variation. Differential and integral calculus, each of which deals with small quantities which during manipulation are made smaller and smaller, compose the **infinitesimal calculus**. Differential equations relate to the derivatives of a set of variables and may include the variables. Many give the mathematical models for physical phenomena such as ◊simple harmonic motion. Differential equations are solved generally through integrative means, depending on their degrees. If no known mathematical processes are available, integration can be performed graphically or by computers.

history Calculus originated with Archimedes in the 3rd century BC as a method for finding the areas of curved shapes and for drawing tangents to curves. These ideas were not developed until the 17th century, when the French philosopher Descartes introduced ◊coordinate geometry, showing how geometrical curves can be described and manipulated by means of algebraic expressions. Then the French mathematician Fermat used these algebraic forms in the early stages of the development of differentiation. Later the German philosopher Leibniz and the English scientist Newton advanced the study.

Calcutta largest city of India, on the river Hooghly, the westernmost mouth of the river Ganges, some 80 mi/130 km N of the Bay of Bengal. It is the capital of West Bengal; population (1981) 9,166,000. It is chiefly a commercial and industrial center (engineering, shipbuilding, jute, and other textiles). Calcutta was the seat of government of British India 1773–1912. There is severe air pollution.

Buildings include a magnificent Jain temple, the palaces of former Indian princes; and the Law Courts and Government House, survivals of the British Raj. Across the river is Howrah, and between Calcutta and the sea there is a new bulk cargo port, Haldia, which is the focus of oil refineries, petrochemical plants, and fertilizer factories. There is a fine museum; educational institutions include the University of Calcutta (1857), oldest of several universities; the Visva Bharati at Santiniketan, founded by Rabindranath Tagore; and the Bose Research Institute.

history Calcutta was founded 1686–90 by Job Charnock of the East India Company as a trading post. Captured by Suraj-ud-Dowlah in 1756, during the Anglo-French wars in India, in 1757 it was retaken by Robert Clive.

Caldecott Randolph 1846–1886. British artist and illustrator of books for children, including *John Gilpin* 1848.

The Caldecott medal, given annually by the American Library Association to the artist of the year's best illustrated book, is named for him.

Calder Alexander 1898–1976. US abstract sculptor, the inventor of *mobiles*, suspended shapes that move in the lightest current of air. In the 1920s he began making wire sculptures and *stabiles* (static mobiles), colored abstract shapes attached by lines of wire. Huge versions adorn Lincoln Center in New York City and UNESCO in Paris.

Calder was born in Philadelphia. An important early influence on him was the Ringling Brothers and Barnum and Bailey Circus, which inspired such works as his miniature *Circus* of wire marionettes. About 1930, his friendship with Joan ⟡Miró and Piet ⟡Mondrian influenced him to create abstract works. In 1943 the first retrospective of his work was exhibited at the Museum of Modern Art.

caldera in geology, a very large basin-shaped ⟡crater. Calderas are found at the tops of volcanoes, where the original peak has collapsed into an empty chamber beneath. The basin, many times larger than the original volcanic vent, may be flooded, producing a crater lake, or the flat floor may contain a number of small volcanic cones, produced by volcanic activity after the collapse.

Typical calderas are Kilauea, Hawaii; Crater Lake, Oregon; and the summit of Olympus Mons, on Mars. Some calderas are wrongly referred to as craters, such as Ngorongoro, Tanzania.

Calderón de la Barca Pedro 1600–1681. Spanish dramatist and poet. After the death of Lope de Vega 1635, he was considered to be the leading Spanish dramatist. Most celebrated of the 118 plays is the philosophical *La vida es sueño/Life is a Dream* 1635.

Calderón was born in Madrid and 1613–19 studied law at Salamanca. In 1620 and 1622 he was successful in poetry contests in Madrid; while still writing dramas, he served in the army in Milan and the Netherlands (1625–35). By 1636 his first volume of plays was published and he had been made master of the revels at the court of Philip IV, receiving a knighthood in 1637. In 1640 he assisted in the suppression of the Catalan rebellion. After the death of his mistress he became a Franciscan in 1650, was ordained in 1651, and appointed as a prebendary of Toledo in 1653. As honorary chaplain to

the king in 1663, he produced outdoor religious plays for the festival of the Holy Eucharist. He died in poverty.

His works include the tragedies *El pintor de su deshonra/The Painter of His Own Dishonor* 1645, *El alcalde de Zalamea/The Mayor of Zalamea* 1640, and *El médico de su honra/The Surgeon of His Honor* 1635; the historical *El príncipe constante/The Constant Prince* 1629; and the dashing intrigue *La dama duende/The Phantom Lady* 1629.

Caldwell Erskine (Preston) 1903–1987. US novelist whose *Tobacco Road* 1932 and *God's Little Acre* 1933 are earthy and vivid presentations of poverty-stricken Southern sharecroppers.

Born in White Oak, Georgia, Caldwell traveled with his father, a minister, and worked among poor whites in the South as a cotton picker. His other works include *Trouble in July* 1940 and *Georgia Boy* 1943. He was married to photojournalist Margaret Bourke-White, who collaborated with him on three books, notably *You Have Seen Their Faces* 1937, about the rural South.

calendar division of the ⟡year into months, weeks, and days and the method of ordering the years. From year one, an assumed date of the birth of Jesus, dates are calculated backward (BC "before Christ" or BCE "before common era") and forward (AD, Latin *anno Domini* "in the year of the Lord," or CE "common era"). The *lunar month* (period between one new moon and the next) naturally averages 29.5 days, but the Western calendar uses for convenience a *calendar month* with a complete number of days, 30 or 31 (Feb has 28). For adjustments, since there are slightly fewer than six extra hours a year left over, they are added to Feb as a 29th day every fourth year (*leap year*), century years being excepted unless they are divisible by 400. For example, 1896 was a leap year; 1900 was not. 1996 is the next leap year.

The *month names* in most European languages were probably derived as follows: January from Janus, Roman god; February from *Februar*, Roman festival of purification; March from Mars, Roman god; April from Latin *aperire*, "to open;" May from Maia, Roman goddess; June from Juno, Roman goddess; July from Julius Caesar, Roman general; August from Augustus, Roman emperor; September, October, November, December (originally the seventh–tenth months) from the Latin words meaning seventh, eighth, ninth, and tenth, respectively.

The *days of the week* are Monday named after the Moon; Tuesday from Tiu or Tyr, Anglo-Saxon and Norse god; Wednesday from Woden or Odin, Norse god; Thursday from Thor, Norse god; Friday from Freya, Norse goddess; Saturday from Saturn, Roman god; and Sunday named after the Sun.

All early calendars except the ancient Egyptian were lunar. The word calendar comes from the Latin *Kalendae* or *calendae*, the first day of each month on which, in ancient Rome, solemn proclamation was made of the appearance of the new moon.

The *Western* or *Gregorian calendar* derives from the *Julian calendar* instituted by Julius Caesar 46 BC. It was adjusted by Pope Gregory XIII 1582, who eliminated the accumulated error caused by a faulty calculation of the length of a year and avoided its recurrence by restricting century leap years to those divisible by 400. Other states only gradually changed

from ⟡Old Style to New Style; Britain and its colonies adopted the Gregorian calendar 1752, when the error amounted to 11 days, and Sept 3, 1752 became Sept 14 (at the same time the beginning of the year was put back from March 25 to Jan 1). Russia did not adopt it until the October Revolution of 1917, so that the event (then Oct 25) is currently celebrated Nov 7.

The *Jewish calendar* is a complex combination of lunar and solar cycles, varied by considerations of religious observance. A year may have 12 or 13 months, each of which normally alternates between 29 and 30 days; the New Year (Rosh Hashanah) falls between Sept 5 and Oct 5. The calendar dates from the hypothetical creation of the world (taken as Oct 7, 3761 BC).

The *Chinese calendar* is lunar, with a cycle of 60 years. Both the traditional and, from 1911, the Western calendar are in use in China.

The *Muslim calendar*, also lunar, has 12 months of alternately 30 and 29 days, and a year of 354 days. This results in the calendar rotating around the seasons in a 30-year cycle. The era is counted as beginning on the day Mohammed fled from Mecca AD 622.

Calgary city in Alberta, on the Bow River, in the foothills of the Rockies; at 3,440 ft/1,048 m it is one of the highest Canadian towns; population (1986) 671,000. It is the center of a large agricultural region and is the oil and financial center of Alberta and W Canada. The 1988 Winter Olympic Games were held here.

Founded as Fort Calgary by the North West Mounted Police 1875, it was reached by the Canadian Pacific Railway 1885 and developed rapidly after the discovery of oil 1914. It has oil-linked and agricultural industries, such as fertilizer factories and flour mills, and is also a tourist center; the annual Calgary Exhibition and Stampede is held in July. The University of Calgary became independent of the University of Alberta 1966.

Calhoun John C(aldwell) 1782–1850. US politician; vice-president 1825–29 under John Quincy Adams and 1829–33 under Andrew Jackson. Throughout his vice-presidency, he was a defender of strong *states' rights* versus an overpowerful federal government and of the institution of slavery. He served in the US Senate 1842–43 and 1845–50, where he continued to espouse the right of states to legislate on slavery.

Born near Abbeville, South Carolina, Calhoun was educated at Yale University and studied law in Connecticut. He served in the South Carolina state legislature 1809–11, after which he became a representative to the US Congress. As secretary of war in President Monroe's cabinet, he supported the federal government, but gradually his political philosophy changed as it became evident to him that states' rights had to stay strong to keep slavery in the South, assuming it essential to the cotton industry. As President Tyler's secretary of state 1844–45, he was responsible for effecting the annexation of Texas.

calibration the preparation of a usable scale on a measuring instrument. A mercury ⟡thermometer, for example, can be calibrated with a Celsius scale by noting the heights of the mercury column at two standard temperatures—the freezing point (0°C) and boiling point (100°C) of water—and dividing the distance between them into 100 equal parts and continuing these divisions above and below.

calico cotton fabric: in the US, it is a printed

cotton; in the UK, a plain woven cotton material. The name derives from Calicut, India, an original source of calico.

California Pacific-coast state of the US; nicknamed the Golden State (originally because of its gold mines, more recently because of its orange groves and sunshine)
area 158,685 sq mi/411,100 sq km
capital Sacramento
cities Los Angeles, San Diego, San Francisco, San José, Fresno
physical Sierra Nevada, including Yosemite and Sequoia national parks, Lake Tahoe, Mount Whitney (14,500 ft/4,418 m, the highest mountain in the lower 48 states); the Coast Range; Death Valley (282 ft/86 m below sea level, the lowest point in the western hemisphere); Colorado and Mohave deserts; Monterey Peninsula; Salton Sea; the San Andreas fault; huge, offshore underwater volcanoes with tops 5 mi/8 km across
features California Institute of Technology (Caltech); Lawrence Berkeley and Lawrence Livermore laboratories of the University of California, which share particle physics and nuclear weapons research with Los Alamos; Stanford University, which has the ⊳Silicon Valley; Paul Getty art museum at Malibu, built in the style of a Roman villa; Hollywood
products leading agricultural state with fruit (peaches, citrus, grapes in the valley of the San Joaquin and Sacramento rivers), nuts, wheat, vegetables, cotton, and rice, all mostly grown by irrigation, the water being carried by immense concrete-lined canals to the Central and Imperial valleys; beef cattle; timber; fish; oil; natural gas; aerospace technology; electronics (Silicon Valley); food processing; films and television programs; great reserves of energy (geothermal) in the hot water that lies beneath much of the state
population (1990) 29,760,000, the most populous state of the US (white 69.9%, Hispanic 25.8%, Asian and Pacific islander including many Vietnamese 9.6%, black 7.4%, American Indian 0.8%)
famous people Luther Burbank, Walt Disney, William Randolph Hearst, Jack London, Marilyn Monroe, Richard Nixon, Ronald Reagan, John Steinbeck
history colonized by Spain 1769; ceded to the US after the Mexican War 1848; became a state 1850. The discovery of gold in the Sierra Nevada Jan 1848 was followed by the gold rush 1849–56.

The completion of the first transcontinental railroad 1869 fostered economic development. The Los Angeles area flourished with the growth of the film industry after 1910, oil discoveries in the early 1920s, and the development of aircraft plants and shipyards during World War II. Some 100,000 Californians of Japanese ancestry were interned during the war. California became the nation's most populous

California

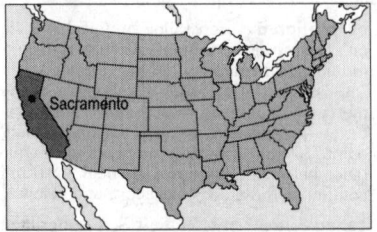

state in 1962. Northern California benefited from the growth of the electronics industry from the 1970s in what came to be called Silicon Valley. The state's economy suffered during the early 1990s as the defense industries declined.

California current cold ocean ⊳current in the E Pacific Ocean flowing southward down the west coast of North America. It is part of the North Pacific ⊳gyre (a vast, circular movement of ocean water).

California, Lower English name for ⊳Baja California.

californium synthesized, radioactive, metallic element of the actinide series, symbol Cf, atomic number 98, atomic weight 251. It is produced in very small quantities and used in nuclear reactors as a neutron source. The longest-lived isotope, Cf-251, has a half-life of 800 years.

It is named after the state of California, where it was first synthesized in 1950 by Glenn Seaborg and his team at the University of California at Berkeley.

Caligula Gaius Caesar AD 12–41. Roman emperor, son of Germanicus and successor to Tiberius AD 37. Caligula was a cruel tyrant and was assassinated by an officer of his guard. Believed to have been mentally unstable, he is remembered for giving a consulship to his horse Incitatus.

calipers instrument used for measuring the thickness or diameter of objects—for example, the internal and external diameter of pipes. Some calipers are made like a drawing compass, having two legs, often curved, pivoting about a screw at one end. The ends of the legs are placed in contact with the object to be measured, and the gap between the ends is then measured against a rule. The slide caliper looks like an adjustable wrench, and carries a scale for direct measuring, usually with a ⊳vernier scale for accuracy.

caliph title of civic and religious heads of the world of Islam. The first caliph was ⊳Abu Bakr. Nominally elective, the office became hereditary, held by the Ummayyad dynasty 661–750 and then by the ⊳Abbasid dynasty. After the death of the last Abbasid (1258), the title was claimed by a number of Muslim chieftains in Egypt, Turkey, and India. The most powerful of these were the Turkish sultans of the Ottoman Empire.

The title was adopted by the prophet Mohammed's successors. During the 10th century the political and military power passed to the leader of the caliph's Turkish bodyguard; about the same time, an independent ⊳Fatimid caliphate sprang up in Egypt. The last of the Turkish caliphs was deposed by Kemal ⊳Atatürk in 1924.

call in finance, a demand for money, especially installments of part-paid securities.

calla alternate name for ⊳arum lily.

Callaghan (Leonard) James, Baron Callaghan 1912– . British Labour politician. As chancellor of the Exchequer 1964–67, he introduced corporation and capital-gains taxes, and resigned following devaluation. He was home secretary 1967–70 and prime minister 1976–79 in a period of increasing economic stress.

Callaghan Morley 1903–1990. Canadian novelist and short-story writer whose realistic novels include *Such is My Beloved* 1934, *More Joy in Heaven* 1937, and *Close to the Sun Again* 1977.

His other works include *They Shall Inherit the Earth* 1935, *The Loved and the Lost* 1951, *Stories* 1959, and *A Passion in Rome* 1961.

Callas Maria. Adopted name of Maria Kalogeropoulos 1923–1977. US lyric soprano, born in New York of Greek parents. With a voice of fine range and a gift for dramatic expression, she excelled in operas including *Norma, La Sonnambula, Madame Butterfly, Aïda, Lucia di Lammermoor,* and *Medea.*

She debuted in Verona, Italy, in 1947 and at New York's Metropolitan Opera in 1956. Although her technique was not considered perfect, she helped to popularize Classical coloratura roles through her expressiveness and charisma.

Callicrates 5th century BC. Athenian architect (with Ictinus) of the ⊳Parthenon on the Acropolis.

calligraphy art of handwriting, regarded in China and Japan as the greatest of the visual arts, and playing a large part in Islamic art because the depiction of the human and animal form is forbidden.

The present letter forms have gradually evolved from originals shaped by the tools used to make them—the flat brush on paper, the chisel on stone, the stylus on wax and clay, and the reed and quill on papyrus and skin.

In Europe during the 4th and 5th centuries books were written in square capitals ("majuscules") derived from Classical Roman inscriptions (Trajan's Column in Rome is the outstanding example). The *rustic* capitals of the same period were written more freely, the pen being held at a severe angle so that the scribe was less frequently inclined to change the angle for special flourishes. *Uncial* capitals, more rounded, were used from the 4th to the 8th centuries. During this period the *cursive* hand was also developing, and the interplay of this with the formal hands, coupled with the need for speedier writing, led to the small letter forms ("minuscules"). During the 7th century the *half-uncial* was developed with ascending and descending strokes and was adopted by all countries under Roman rule. The cursive forms developed differently in different countries. In Italy the italic script was evolved and became the model for italic typefaces.

Printing and the typewriter reduced the need for calligraphy in the West until the 20th-century revival inspired by Edward Johnston (1872–1944).

Calliope in Greek mythology, the ⊳Muse of epic poetry and chief of the Muses.

Callisto in Greek mythology, a ⊳nymph beloved by Zeus (Roman Jupiter) who was changed into a bear by his jealous wife Hera.

Callisto second largest moon of Jupiter, 3,000 mi/4,800 km in diameter, orbiting every 16.7 days at a distance of 1.2 million mi/1.9 million km from the planet. Its surface is covered with large craters.

callus in botany, a tissue that forms at a damaged plant surface. Composed of large, thin-walled ⊳parenchyma cells, it grows over and around the wound, eventually covering the exposed area.

Calmette Albert 1863–1933. French bacteriologist. A student of Pasteur, he developed (with Camille Guérin, 1872–1961) the ⊳BCG vaccine against tuberculosis in 1921.

calorie unit of heat, now replaced by the

◊joule (one calorie is approximately 4.2 joules). It is the heat required to raise the temperature of one gram of water by 1°C. In dietetics, the calorie or kilocalorie is equal to 1,000 calories.

The kilocalorie measures the energy value of food in terms of its heat output: 1 oz/28 g of protein yields 120 kilocalories, of carbohydrate 110, of fat 270, and of alcohol 200.

calorific value the amount of heat generated by a given mass of fuel when it is completely burned. It is measured in joules per kilogram. Calorific values are measured experimentally with a bomb calorimeter.

calorimeter instrument used in physics to measure heat. A simple calorimeter consists of a heavy copper vessel that is polished (to reduce heat losses by radiation) and covered with insulating material (to reduce losses by convection and conduction).

In a typical experiment, such as to measure the heat capacity of a piece of metal, the calorimeter is filled with water, whose temperature rise is measured using a thermometer when a known mass of the heated metal is immersed in it. Chemists use a bomb calorimeter to measure the heat produced by burning a fuel completely in oxygen.

calotype paper-based photograph using a wax paper negative, the first example of the ◊negative/positive process invented by the English photographer Fox Talbot around 1834.

Calvados French brandy distilled from apple cider, named after the *département* in the Basse-Normandie region of NW France where it is produced.

Calvary (Aramaic *Golgotha* "skull") in the New Testament, the site of Jesus' crucifixion at Jerusalem. Two chief locations are suggested: the site where the Church of the Sepulchre now stands, and the hill beyond the Damascus gate.

Calvert George, Baron Baltimore 1579–1632. English politician who founded the American colony of Maryland 1632. A confidant of King James I, Calvert served in Parliament and the Privy Council. He became secretary of state, but was forced to resign from that office because of his conversion to Roman Catholicism 1625. As a supporter of colonization in North America, he was granted land in Newfoundland 1628 but, finding the climate too harsh, obtained a royal charter for Maryland 1632.

Calvert was born in Yorkshire, England, and educated at Oxford. He was knighted in 1617. In 1625, he was named Baron Baltimore by the king.

Calvin John (also known as *Cauvin* or *Chauvin*) 1509–1564. French-born Swiss Protestant church reformer and theologian. He was a leader of the Reformation in Geneva and set up a strict religious community there. His theological system is known as Calvinism, and his church government as ◊Presbyterianism. Calvin wrote (in Latin) *Institutes of the Christian Religion* 1536 and commentaries on the New Testament and much of the Old Testament.

Calvin, born in Noyon, Picardie, studied theology and then law, and about 1533 became prominent in Paris as an evangelical preacher. In 1534 he was obliged to leave Paris and retired to Basel, where he studied Hebrew. In 1536 he accepted an invitation to go to Geneva, Switzerland, and assist in the Reformation, but was expelled 1538 because of public resentment against the numerous and too drastic

changes he introduced. He returned to Geneva 1541 and, in the face of strong opposition, established a rigorous theocracy (government by priests). In 1553 he had the Spanish theologian Servetus burned for heresy. He supported the Huguenots in their struggle in France and the English Protestants persecuted by Queen Mary I.

Calvin Melvin 1911– . US chemist who, using radioactive carbon-14 as a tracer, determined the biochemical processes of ◊photosynthesis, in which green plants use ◊chlorophyll to convert carbon dioxide and water into sugar and oxygen. Nobel Prize 1961.

Calvinism Christian doctrine as interpreted by John Calvin and adopted in Scotland, parts of Switzerland, and the Netherlands; by the ◊Puritans in England and New England; and by the subsequent Congregational and Presbyterian churches in the US. Its central doctrine is predestination, under which certain souls (the elect) are predestined by God through the sacrifice of Jesus to salvation, and the rest to damnation. Although Calvinism is rarely accepted today in its strictest interpretation, the 20th century has seen a Neo-Calvinist revival through the work of Karl ◊Barth.

Calypso in Greek mythology, a sea ◊nymph who waylaid the homeward-bound Odysseus for seven years.

calypso West Indian satirical ballad with a syncopated beat. Calypso is a traditional song form of Trinidad, a feature of its annual carnival, with roots in W African praise singing. It was first popularized in the US by Harry Belafonte (1927–) in 1956. Mighty Sparrow (1935–) is Trinidad's best-known calypso singer.

calyptra in mosses and liverworts, a layer of cells that encloses and protects the young ◊sporophyte (spore capsule), forming a sheathlike hood around the capsule. The term is also used to describe the root cap, a layer of ◊parenchyma cells covering the end of a root that gives protection to the root tip as it grows through the soil. This is constantly being worn away and replaced by new cells from a special ◊meristem, the calyptrogen.

calyx the collective term for the ◊sepals of a flower, forming the outermost whorl of the ◊perianth. It surrounds the other flower parts and protects them while in bud. In some flowers, for example, the catchflies *Silene* of the pink family, the sepals are fused along their sides, forming a sticky tubular calyx.

cam part of a machine that converts circular motion to linear motion or vice versa. The *edge cam* in an automobile engine is in the form of a rounded projection on a shaft, the camshaft. When the camshaft turns, the cams press against linkages (plungers or followers) that open the valves in the cylinders.

A *face cam* is a disk with a groove in its face, in which the follower travels. A *cylindrical cam* carries angled parallel grooves, which impart a to-and-fro motion to the follower when it rotates.

CAM (acronym for *computer-aided manufacture*) the use of computers to control production processes; in particular, the control of machine tools and ◊robots in factories. In some factories, the whole design and production system has been automated by linking ◊CAD (computer-aided design) to CAM.

Linking flexible CAD/CAM manufacture to

computer-based sales and distribution methods makes it possible to produce semicustomized goods cheaply and in large numbers.

Camagüey city in Cuba; population (1989) 283,000. It is the capital of Camagüey province in the center of the island. Founded about 1514, it was the capital of the Spanish West Indies during the 19th century. It has a 17th-century cathedral.

Camargue marshy area of the ◊Rhône delta, S of Arles, France; about 300 sq mi/780 sq km. Bulls and horses are bred here, and the nature preserve, which is known for its bird life, forms the southern part.

cambium in botany, a layer of actively dividing cells (lateral ◊meristem), found within stems and roots, that gives rise to ◊secondary growth in perennial plants, causing an increase in girth. There are two main types of cambium: *vascular cambium*, which gives rise to secondary ◊xylem and ◊phloem tissues, and *cork cambium* (or phellogen), which gives rise to secondary cortex and cork tissues (see ◊bark).

Cambodia (formerly *Khmer Republic* 1970–76, *Democratic Kampuchea* 1976–79, and *People's Republic of Kampuchea* 1979–89) country in SE Asia, bounded N and NW by Thailand, N by Laos, E and SE by Vietnam, and SW by the Gulf of Thailand.

government Under the terms of the 1991 United Nations transitional arrangements, political power is shared between the all-party Supreme National Council (SNC) and the UN Advance Mission/Transitional Authority in Cambodia.

history The area now known as Cambodia was once occupied by the Khmer empire, an ancient civilization that flourished during the 6th–15th centuries. After this, the region was subject to attacks by the neighboring Vietnamese and Thai, and in 1863 became a French protectorate. A nationalist movement began in the 1930s, and anti-French feeling was fueled 1940–41 when the French agreed to Japanese demands for bases in Cambodia, and allowed Thailand to annex Cambodian territory.

During World War II Cambodia was occupied by Japan. France regained control of the country 1946, but it achieved semi autonomy within the French Union 1949 and full independence 1953. Prince Norodom ◊Sihanouk, who had been elected king 1941, abdicated in favor of his parents and became prime minister as leader of the Popular Socialist Community 1955. When his father died 1960, he became head of state.

Khmer Republic Sihanouk remained neutral during the Vietnam War and was overthrown by a right-wing revolt led by pro-USA Lt Gen Lon Nol in 1970. Lon Nol first became prime minister (1971–72) and then president (1972–75) of what was termed the new Khmer Republic. His regime was opposed by the exiled Sihanouk and by the communist Khmer Rouge (backed by North Vietnam and China), who merged to form the National United Front of Cambodia. A civil war developed and, despite substantial military aid from the US during its early stages, Lon Nol's government fell 1975. The country was renamed Kampuchea, with Prince Sihanouk as head of state.

Khmer Rouge regime The Khmer Rouge proceeded ruthlessly to introduce an extreme communist program, forcing urban groups into rural areas, which led to over 2.5 million deaths from famine, disease, and maltreatment. In 1976 a new constitution removed Prince Sihanouk from power, appointed Khieu Samphan (the former deputy prime minister) president, and placed the Communist Party of Kampuchea, led by ⊅Pol Pot, in control. The Khmer Rouge developed close links with China and fell out with its former sponsors, Vietnam and the USSR.

Vietnamese influence In a Vietnamese invasion of Kampuchea launched 1978 in response to border incursions, Pol Pot was overthrown and a pro-Vietnamese puppet government was set up under Heng Samrin. The defeated regime kept up guerrilla resistance under Pol Pot, causing over 300,000 Kampuchean refugees to flee to Thailand in 1979 alone.

resistance movement In 1982 the resistance movement broadened with the formation in Kuala Lumpur, Malaysia, of an anti-Vietnamese coalition and Democratic Kampuchea government in exile with Prince Sihanouk (then living in North Korea) as president, Khieu Samphan (political leader of the now less extreme Khmer Rouge) as vice-president, and Son Sann (an ex-premier and contemporary leader of the noncommunist Khmer People's National Liberation Front [KPNLF]) as prime minister. The coalition received sympathetic support from ⊅ASEAN countries and China. However, its 60,000 troops were outnumbered by the 170,000 Vietnamese who supported the Heng Samrin government, and the resistance coalition's base camps were overrun 1985. During 1982–91 the US aided the KPNLF and the Sihanoukist National Army (ANS)—allies

of the Khmer Rouge—with millions of dollars in "humanitarian" aid and secret "nonlethal" military aid.

Vietnamese troop withdrawal Hopes of a political settlement were improved by the retirement of the reviled Pol Pot as Khmer Rouge military leader 1985 and the appointment of the reformist Hun Sen as prime minister. A mixed-economy domestic approach was adopted and indigenous Khmers promoted to key government posts; at the same time, prompted by the new Soviet leader, Mikhail Gorbachev, the Vietnamese began a phased withdrawal. In spring 1989, after talks with the resistance coalition, the Phnom Penh government agreed to a package of constitutional reforms, including the adoption of Buddhism as the state religion and the readoption of the ideologically neutral name State of Cambodia. Withdrawal of the Vietnamese army was completed Sept 1989.

continued civil war The UN continued to refuse recognition of the Hun Sen government and the civil war intensified, with the Khmer Rouge making advances in the western provinces, capturing the border town of Pailin in Oct 1989. The Phnom Penh government was left with an army of 40,000, backed by a 100,000-strong militia, against the resistance coalition's 45,000 guerrillas, half of whom belonged to the Khmer Rouge. In Sept 1990 the USSR and China reportedly agreed to a mutual cessation of arms supplies to their respective Cambodian clients. In Nov 1990 the five permanent members of the UN Security Council, including the US, USSR, and China, proposed a peace settlement, but the Phnom Penh government

dismissed it, objecting to the establishment of a UN administration within the country.

accord reached Guerrilla fighting intensified Jan 1991 but, for the first time in 12 years, a cease-fire was implemented May–June 1991, and an accord was reached by the all-party Supreme National Council in Pattaya, Thailand, between Prince Sihanouk, the guerrillas' nominal leader, and the Hun Sen government. This breakthrough was brought about, it is believed, by pressure exerted by Vietnam (anxious for Western aid) and China, the respective backers of the Hun Sen regime and the guerrillas. Subsequent meetings in July, Aug, and Sept 1991 added flesh to this accord, including an understanding that the Cambodian government and the Khmer Rouge–led rebel alliance would disband 70% of their armies prior to UN-run elections, which would be held on the basis of proportional representation.

end of civil war On Oct 23, 1991, after nearly four years of intermittent negotiations, Cambodia's four warring factions and 18 interested countries signed a peace agreement in Paris, ending 13 years of civil war. The UN peacekeeping operation provided for a UN Transitional Authority in Cambodia (UNTAC) to be established within six months (preceded by a smaller UN Advance Mission in Cambodia (UNAMIC)). It would administer the country in conjunction with the Supreme National Council (comprising representatives from Cambodia's four warring factions) until the UN-administered general elections in 1993. UNTAC would organize the transportation and resettlement of the 356,000 Cambodian refugees living in camps on the Thai-Cambodian border as well as the 200,000 internally displaced people. It would also attempt the revival of Cambodia's poverty-stricken and moribund economy.

return of Sihanouk and Khmer Rouge The ruling Kampuchean People's Revolutionary Party, anxious to make itself more attractive to voters, formally abandoned its Marxist-Leninist ideology in Oct 1991 and changed its name to the Khmer/Cambodian People's Party. Heng Samrin was replaced as party chair by the powerful Chea Sim and the party endorsed a multiparty democratic system, a free-market economy, and the protection of human rights. It upheld Buddhism as the state religion and declared support for Prince Sihanouk's future candidacy for the state presidency. Prince Sihanouk returned to Phnom Penh on Nov 23, 1991 after a 13-year absence. As the "legitimate head of state" until the presidential elections, he would administer the country in conjunction with Prime Minister Hun Sen and UNAMIC/UNTAC during the transition period. Khieu Samphan, leader of the Khmer Rouge, also returned to Phnom Penh but was forced to fly back to Thailand after being violently attacked by an angry mob.

restoration of human rights begins In Jan 1992 hundreds of political prisoners began to be released from Cambodia's jails and it was announced that freedom of speech and the formation of new political parties would be allowed. Despite promises Aug 1992 that the Khmer Rouge would cooperate in the peace process, they were still refusing to disarm in Oct. *See illustration box.*

Cambodia
State of (formerly **Khmer Republic** 1970–76, **Democratic Kampuchea** 1976–79, **People's Republic of Kampuchea** 1979–89)

area 69,880 sq mi/181,035 sq km
capital Phnom Penh
cities Battambang, the seaport Kompong Som
physical mostly flat forested plains with mountains in SW and N; Mekong River runs N–S
features ruins of ancient capital Angkor; Lake Tonle Sap
head of state Prince Norodom Sihanouk from 1991
head of government Hun Sen from 1985
political system transitional
political parties Cambodian People's Party (CPP), reform socialist (formerly the communist Kampuchean People's Revolutionary Party

(KPRP)); Party of Democratic Kampuchea (Khmer Rouge), ultranationalist communist; Khmer People's National Liberation Front (KPNLF), anticommunist
exports rubber, rice, pepper, wood, cattle
currency Cambodian riel
population (1990 est) 6,993,000; growth rate 2.2% p.a.
life expectancy men 42, women 45
languages Khmer (official), French
religion Theravāda Buddhist 95%
literacy men 78%, women 39% (1980 est)
GDP $592 mn (1987); $83 per head
chronology
1863–1941 French protectorate.
1941–45 Occupied by Japan.
1946 Recaptured by France.
1953 Independence achieved from France.
1970 Prince Sihanouk overthrown by US-backed Lon Nol.
1975 Lon Nol overthrown by Khmer Rouge.
1978–79 Vietnamese invasion and installation of Heng Samrin government.
1982 The three main anti-Vietnamese resistance groups formed an alliance under Prince Sihanouk.
1987 Vietnamese troop withdrawal began.
1989 Sept: completion of Vietnamese withdrawal. Nov: United Nations peace proposal rejected by Phnom Penh government.
1991 Oct: Peace agreement signed in Paris, providing for a UN Transitional Authority in Cambodia (UNTAC) to administer country in transition period in conjunction with all-party Supreme National Council; communism abandoned. Nov: Sihanouk returned as head of state.
1992 Political prisoners released; freedom of speech and party formation restored. Oct: Khmer Rouge refused to disarm in accordance with peace process.

Cambrai chief town of Nord *département*, France, on the river Escaut (Scheldt); population (1982) 36,600. Industries include light textiles (cambric is named after the town) and confectionery. The Peace of Cambrai or

Ladies' Peace (1529) was concluded on behalf of Francis I of France by his mother Louise of Savoy and on behalf of Charles V by his aunt Margaret of Austria.

Cambrai, Battles of two battles in World War I at Cambrai in NE France:
First Battle Nov–Dec 1917, the town was almost captured by the British when large numbers of tanks were used for the first time.
Second Battle Aug 26–Oct 5, 1918, the town was taken during the final British offensive.

Cambrian period of geological time 590–505 million years ago; the first period of the Paleozoic era. All invertebrate animal life appeared, and marine algae were widespread. The earliest fossils with hard shells, such as trilobites, date from this period.

The name comes from Cambria, an old name for Wales, where Cambrian rocks are typically exposed and were first described.

Cambridge city in England, on the river Cam (a river sometimes called by its earlier name, Granta), 50 mi/80 km N of London; population (1989) 101,000. It is the administrative headquarters of Cambridgeshire. The city is centered on Cambridge University (founded 12th century), whose outstanding buildings, including Kings College Chapel, back onto the river.

history As early as 100 BC, a Roman settlement grew up on a slight rise in the low-lying plain, commanding a ford over the river. Apart from those of Cambridge University, fine buildings include St Benet's church, the oldest building in Cambridge, the round church of the Holy Sepulchre, and the Guildhall 1939.

Present-day industries include the manufacture of scientific instruments, radio, electronics, paper, flour milling, and fertilizers.

Cambridge city in Massachusetts, on the river Charles; population (1991) 101,000. Industries include paper and publishing. *Harvard University*, the oldest educational institution in the US, was founded here 1636 and named after John Harvard (1607–1638), who bequeathed his library to it along with half his estate. Massachusetts Institute of Technology 1861 and Harvard's John F Kennedy School of Government are also here, as well as a park named after Kennedy.

Cambridge University English university, one of the earliest in Europe, probably founded in the 12th century, though the earliest of the existing colleges, Peterhouse, was not founded until about 1284.

Famous students of the university include Rupert Brooke, S T Coleridge, Thomas Gray, Christopher Marlowe, John Milton, Samuel Pepys, and William Wordsworth. In 1990, there were 10,000 undergraduate and 3,000 postgraduate students.

Cambyses 6th century BC. Emperor of Persia 529–522 BC. Succeeding his father Cyrus, he assassinated his brother Smerdis and conquered Egypt in 525 BC. There he outraged many of the local religious customs and was said to have become insane. He died in Syria on his journey home, probably by suicide.

Camden industrial city of New Jersey, on the Delaware River; population (1990) 87,500. The city is linked with Philadelphia, Pennsylvania, by the Benjamin Franklin suspension bridge (1926). The Walt ◊Whitman House, where the poet lived 1884–92, is now a museum.

Camden Town Group school of British

painters 1911–13, based in Camden, London, inspired by English artist W R Sickert (1860–1942). The work of Spencer Gore (1878–1914) and Harold Gilman (1876–1919) is typical of the group, rendering everyday town scenes in Post-Impressionist style.

camel large cud-chewing mammal of the even-toed hoofed order Artiodactyla. Unlike typical ruminants, it has a three-chambered stomach. It has two toes which have broad soft soles for walking on sand, and hooves resembling nails. There are two species, the single-humped *Arabian camel Camelus dromedarius* and the twin-humped *Bactrian camel C. bactrianus* from Asia. They carry a food reserve of fatty tissue in the hump, can go without drinking for long periods, can feed on salty vegetation, and withstand extremes of heat and cold, thus being well adapted to desert conditions.

The Arabian camel has long been domesticated, so that its original range is not known. It is used throughout Arabia and N Africa, and has been taken to other places such as North America and Australia, in the latter country playing an crucial part in the development of the interior. The *dromedary* is, strictly speaking, a lightly built, fast, riding variety of the Arabian camel, but often the name is applied to all one-humped camels. Arabian camels can be used as pack animals, for riding, racing, milk production, and for meat.

The Bactrian camel is native to the central Asian deserts, where a small number still live wild, but most are domestic animals. With a head and body length of 10 ft/3 m and shoulder height of about 6 ft/2 m, the Bactrian camel is a large animal, but not so long in the leg as the Arabian. It has a shaggy winter coat.

Smaller, flat-backed members of the camel family include the ◊alpaca, the ◊guanaco, the ◊llama, and the ◊vicuna.

camellia any oriental evergreen shrub with roselike flowers of the genus *Camellia*, tea family Theaceae. Numerous species, including *C. japonica* and *C. reticulata*, have been introduced into Europe, the US, and Australia.

Camelot legendary seat of King ◊Arthur.
A possible site is the Iron Age hill fort of South Cadbury Castle in Somerset, England, where excavations from 1967 have revealed remains dating from 3000 BC to AD 1100, including those of a large 6th-century settlement, the time ascribed to Arthur.

Camembert soft cheese named for a village in Normandy, France, where it originated.

cameo small relief carving of semiprecious stone, shell, or glass. A pale-colored surface layer is carved to reveal a darker ground. Fine cameos were produced in ancient Greece and Rome, during the Renaissance, and in the Victorian era. They were used for decorating goblets and vases, and as jewelry.

camera apparatus used in ◊photography, consisting of a lens system set in a light-proof box inside of which a sensitized film or plate can be placed. The lens collects rays of light reflected from the subject and brings them together as a sharp image on the film; it has marked numbers known as ◊apertures, or f-stops, that reduce or increase the amount of light. Apertures also control depth of field. A shutter controls the amount of time light has to affect the film. There are small-, medium-, and large-format cameras; the format refers to the size of recorded image and the dimensions of the print obtained.

A simple camera has a fixed shutter speed and aperture, chosen so that on a sunny day the correct amount of light is admitted. More complex cameras allow the shutter speed and aperture to be adjusted; most have a built-in exposure meter to help choose the correct combination of shutter speed and aperture for the ambient conditions and subject matter. The most versatile camera is the single lens reflex (◊SLR) which allows the lens to be removed and special lenses attached. A pin-hole camera has a small (pin-sized) hole instead of a lens. It must be left on a firm support during exposures, which are up to ten seconds with slow film, two seconds with fast film and five minutes for paper negatives in daylight. The pin-hole camera gives sharp images from close-up to infinity.

camera obscura darkened box with a tiny hole for projecting the inverted image of the scene outside on to a screen inside. For its development as a device for producing photographs, see ◊photography.

Cameron Simon 1799–1889. US political leader. At the 1860 Republican nominating convention, he threw his support to Lincoln, gaining an appointment as secretary of war. A dismal failure in that position, he was named minister to Russia 1862. After the Civil War he returned to the Senate, serving 1867–77.

Cameron was born in Maytown, Pennsylvania. Trained as a printer, he eventually became a newspaper editor in Harrisburg and embarked on a political career. Gaining wealth through investments in transportation and industry, he served two partial terms in the US Senate 1845–49 and 1857–60.

Cameroon country in W Africa, bounded NW by Nigeria, NE by Chad, E by the Central African Republic, S by Congo, Gabon, and Equatorial Guinea, and W by the Atlantic.

government Cameroon was a federal state until 1972 when a new constitution, revised 1975 and 1991, made it unitary. The constitution provides for a president and a single-chamber national assembly of 180, each elected for a five-year term. The president has the power to choose the cabinet, to lengthen or shorten the life of the assembly, and may run for reelection.

history The area was first visited by Europeans 1472, when the Portuguese began slave trading in the area. In 1884 Cameroon became a German protectorate. After World War I, France governed about 80% of the area under a League of Nations mandate, with Britain administering the remainder. In 1946 both became United Nations trust territories.

independence In 1957 French Cameroon became a state within the French Community and three years later achieved full independence as the Republic of Cameroon. After a plebiscite 1961, the northern part of British Cameroons merged with Nigeria, and the southern part joined the Republic of Cameroon to form the Federal Republic of Cameroon. The French zone became East Cameroon and the British part West Cameroon.

one-party state Ahmadou Ahidjo, who had been the first president of the republic 1960, became president of the federal republic and was reelected 1965. In 1966 Cameroon was made a one-party state when the two government parties and most of the opposition parties merged into the Cameroon National Union (UNC). Extreme left-wing opposition to the UNC was crushed 1971. In 1972 the federal system was abolished, and a new national assembly was elected 1973.

Cameroon
Republic of (*République du Cameroun*)

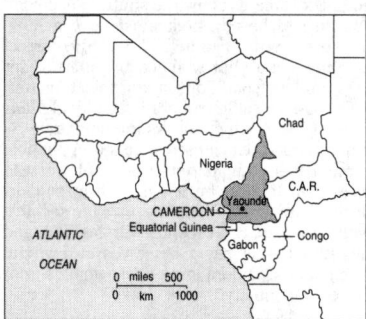

area 183,638 sq mi/475,440 sq km
capital Yaoundé
cities chief port Douala; Nkongsamba,
Garova
physical desert in far north in the Lake
Chad basin, mountains in W, dry savanna
plateau in the intermediate area, and dense
tropical rainforest in the south
environment the Korup National Park
preserves 500 sq mi/1,300 sq km of Africa's fast-
disappearing tropical rainforest. Scientists
have identified nearly 100 potentially useful
chemical substances produced naturally by
the plants of this forest
features Mount Cameroon 13,358 ft/4,070
m, an active volcano on the coast, W of the
Adamawa Mountains
head of state and of government Paul
Biya from 1982
political system emergent democratic
republic
political parties Democratic Assembly of
the Cameroon People (RDPC), nationalist,
left of center; Social Democratic Front
(SDF), center-left; Social Movement for New
Democracy (MSND), left of center; Union
of the Peoples of Cameroon (UPC), left of
center
exports cocoa, coffee, bananas, cotton,
timber, rubber, groundnuts, gold, aluminum,
crude oil
currency CFA franc
population (1990 est) 11,109,000; growth
rate 2.7% p.a.
life expectancy men 49, women 53
languages French and English in pidgin
variations (official); there has been some
discontent with the emphasis on French —
there are 163 indigenous peoples with their
own African languages
media heavy government censorship
religion Roman Catholic 35%, animist 25%,
Muslim 22%, Protestant 18%
literacy men 68%, women 45% (1985 est)
GDP $12.7 bn (1987); $1,170 per head
chronology
1884 Treaty signed establishing German rule.
1916 Captured by Allied forces in World War I.
1922 Divided between Britain and France.
1946 French Cameroon and British Cameroons
made UN trust territories.
1960 French Cameroon became the independent Republic of Cameroon. Ahmadou
Ahidjo elected president.
1961 Northern part of British Cameroon
merged with Nigeria and southern part joined
the Republic of Cameroon to become the
Federal Republic of Cameroon.
1966 One-party regime introduced.
1972 New constitution made Cameroon
a unitary state, the United Republic of
Cameroon.
1973 New national assembly elected.
1982 Ahidjo resigned and was succeeded
by Paul Biya.
1983 Biya began to remove his predecessor's
supporters; accused by Ahidjo of trying to
create a police state. Ahidjo went into exile
in France.
1984 Biya reelected; defeated a plot to
overthrow him. Country's name changed to
Republic of Cameroon.
1988 Biya reelected.
1990 Widespread public disorder. Biya
granted amnesty to political prisoners.
1991 Constitutional changes made.
1992 Ruling RDPC won in first multiparty
elections in 28 years. Biya's presidential
victory challenged by opposition.

Biya's presidency In 1982 Ahidjo resigned,
nominating Paul Biya as his successor. In 1983
Biya began to remove Ahidjo's supporters, and
in protest Ahidjo resigned the presidency of
UNC. Biya was reelected 1984, while Ahidjo
went into exile in France. Biya strengthened
his position by abolishing the post of prime
minister and reshuffling his cabinet. He also
changed the nation's name from the United
Republic of Cameroon to the Republic of
Cameroon. Many of Ahidjo's supporters were
executed after a failed attempt to overthrow
Biya. In 1985 UNC changed its name to the
Democratic Assembly of the Cameroon People (RDPC), and Biya tightened his control
by more cabinet changes. Biya was reelected
president 1988 with 98.75% of the vote.
natural disaster In 1986 a volcanic vent under
Lake Nyos released a vast quantity of carbon dioxide and hydrogen sulfide, which suffocated
large numbers of people and animals.
constitutional reform In 1990 widespread
public disorder resulted from the arrests of
lawyers, lecturers, and students. However,
Biya granted amnesty to political prisoners. In
response to further public unrest, a number
of constitutional changes were introduced in
Dec 1991, including the lowering of the voting
age to 20. Opposition groups complained that
most of the changes were designed to help
Biya win support in the forthcoming assembly
elections. In March 1992 the first multiparty
assembly elections in 28 years were held. The
ruling RDPC won 89 of the 180 assembly seats,
and a coalition of opposition groups 91. A small
element in the coalition, holding 6 seats, supported Biya, thus securing a majority for the
RDPC. Biya also won the Oct 1992 presidential
election, but his victory was challenged by the
opposition. *See illustration box.*

Camoëns or *Camões* Luis Vaz de 1524–1580.
Portuguese poet and soldier. He went on various military expeditions, and was shipwrecked
in 1558. His poem *Os Lusiades/The Lusiads*
1572 tells the story of the explorer Vasco
da Gama and incorporates much Portuguese
history; it has become the country's national
epic. His posthumously published lyric poetry
is also now valued.

Having wounded an equerry of the king
in 1552, he was banished to India. He received a small pension, but died in poverty of
plague.

Camorra Italian secret society formed about
1820 by criminals in the dungeons of Naples
and continued once they were freed. It dominated politics from 1848, was suppressed 1911,
but many members eventually surfaced in the
US ⊅Mafia. The Camorra still operates in the
Naples area.

camouflage colors or structures that allow
an animal to blend with its surroundings to
avoid detection by other animals. Camouflage
can take the form of matching the background
color, of countershading (darker on top, lighter
below, to counteract natural shadows), or of
irregular patterns that break up the outline of
the animal's body. More elaborate camouflage
involves closely resembling a feature of the
natural environment, as with the stick insect;
this is closely akin to ⊅mimicry.

Camp Walter Chauncey 1859–1925. US football coach who initiated the tradition of
selecting an annual All-American football team.
Born in New Britain, Connecticut, Camp was
educated at Yale University. In 1888, after a
brief business career, he returned to Yale as
athletic director. As the Yale football coach and
member of the Intercollegiate Football Rules
Committee, Camp was responsible for instituting some of the most basic rules of the game,
including team size, field dimensions, and the
four-down system.

Campagna Romana lowland stretch of the
Italian peninsula, including and surrounding the city of Rome. Lying between the
Tyrrhenian Sea and the Sabine Hills to the NE,
and the Alban Hills to the SE, it is drained
by the lower course of the river Tiber and
a number of small streams, most of which
dry up in the summer. Prosperous in Roman
times, it later became virtually derelict through
overgrazing, lack of water, and the arrival in
the area of the malaria-carrying *Anopheles* mosquito. Extensive land reclamation and drainage
in the 19th and 20th centuries restored its
usefulness.

Campania agricultural region (wheat, citrus,
wine, vegetables, tobacco) of S Italy, including
the volcano ⊅Vesuvius; capital Naples; industrial centers Benevento, Caserta, and Salerno;
area 5,250 sq mi/13,600 sq km; population
(1990) 5,853,900. There are ancient sites at
Pompeii, Herculaneum, and Paestum.

campanile originally a bell tower erected near,
or attached to, a church or town hall in Italy.
The leaning tower of Pisa is an example; another is the great campanile of Florence, 275 ft/
90 m high.

They were used as components of 19th-
century American factory architecture in New
England.

Campbell Malcolm 1885–1948. British racing
driver who once held both land-and water-
speed records. He set the land-speed record
nine times, pushing it up to 301.1 mph/484.8
kph at Bonneville Flats, Utah, in 1935, and
broke the water-speed record three times, the
best being 141.74 mph/228.2 kph on Coniston
Water, England, in 1939. His car and boat were
both called *Bluebird*.

Campbell Mrs Patrick (born Beatrice Stella
Tanner) 1865–1940. British actress whose
roles included Paula in Pinero's *The Second Mrs
Tanqueray* 1893 and Eliza in *Pygmalion*, written
for her by G B Shaw, with whom she had an
amusing correspondence.

Campbell-Bannerman Henry 1836–1908.
British Liberal politician, prime minister 1905–
08. It was during his term of office that the

South African colonies achieved self-government, and the Trades Disputes Act 1906 was passed.

Camp David official country home of US presidents, situated in the Appalachian mountains, Maryland; it was originally named Shangri-la by F D Roosevelt, but was renamed Camp David by Eisenhower (after his grandson).

It was briefly known (for security reasons) as Camp Number Four after the Kennedy assassination. It is guarded by Marines, and consists of a series of lodges, Aspen Lodge being the presidential residence. It was the site of talks held by President Carter to bring about an Egypt-Israel peace accord (see ⊳Camp David Agreements).

Camp David Agreements two framework agreements signed 1978 by Israeli prime minister Begin and Egyptian president Sadat at Camp David, Maryland, under the guidance of US president Carter, covering an Egypt–Israel peace treaty and phased withdrawal of Israel from Sinai, which was completed 1982, and an overall Middle East settlement including the election by the West Bank and Gaza Strip Palestinians of a "self-governing authority." The latter issue has stalled repeatedly over questions of who should represent the Palestinians and what form the self-governing body should take.

Campeche port on the Bay of ⊳Campeche, Mexico; population (1984) 120,000. It is the capital of Campeche state. Timber and fish are exported, and there is a university, established 1756.

Campeche, Bay of SW area of the Gulf of Mexico, site of a major oil-pollution disaster from the field off Yucatán peninsula in 1979.

camphor $C_{10}H_{16}O$ volatile, aromatic ⊳ketone substance obtained from the camphor tree *Cinnamomum camphora*. It is distilled from chips of the wood, and is used in insect repellents and medicinal inhalants and liniments, and in the manufacture of celluloid.

The camphor tree, a member of the family Lauraceae, is native to China, Taiwan, and Japan.

Campi family of Italian painters practicing in Cremona, N Italy, in the 16th century, the best-known member being *Giulio Campi* (*c.* 1502–1572).

Campin Robert, also known as the *Master of Flémalle c.* 1378–1444. Netherlandish painter of the early Renaissance, active in Tournai from 1406, one of the first northern masters to use oil. Several altarpieces are attributed to him. Rogier van der Weyden was his pupil.

His outstanding work is the *Mérode altarpiece*, about 1425 (Metropolitan Museum of Art, New York), which shows a distinctly naturalistic style, with a new subtlety in modeling and a grasp of pictorial space.

Campinas city of São Paulo, Brazil, situated on the central plateau; population (1980) 566,700. It is a coffee-trading center. There are also metallurgical and food industries.

campion several plants of the genera *Lychnis* and *Silene*, belonging to the pink family (Caryophyllaceae), which include the garden campion *L. coronaria*, introduced from Europe, and the catchflies (genus *Silene*) of E North America.

Campo-Formio, Treaty of peace settlement 1797 during the Revolutionary Wars between Napoleon and Austria, by which France gained the region that is now Belgium and Austria was compensated with Venice and part of an area that now reaches into Slovenia and Croatia.

Cam Ranh port in S Vietnam; population (1989) 114,000. In the Vietnam War it was a US base; it later became a staging complex for the Soviet Pacific fleet.

Camus Albert 1913–1960. Algerian-born French writer. A journalist in France, he was active in the Resistance during World War II. His novels, which owe much to ⊳existentialism, include *L'Etranger/The Outsider* 1942, *La Peste/The Plague* 1948, and *L'Homme révolté/ The Rebel* 1952. He was awarded the Nobel Prize for Literature 1957.

Canaan ancient region between the Mediterranean and the Dead Sea, called in the Bible the "Promised Land" of the Israelites. It was occupied as early as the 3rd millennium BC by the Canaanites, a Semitic-speaking people who were known to the Greeks of the 1st millennium BC as Phoenicians. The capital was Ebla (now Tell Mardikh, Syria).

The Canaanite Empire included Syria, Palestine, and part of Mesopotamia. It was conquered by the Israelites during the 13th to 10th centuries BC. Ebla was excavated 1976–77, revealing an archive of inscribed tablets dating from the 3rd millennium BC, which includes place names such as Gaza and Jerusalem (no excavations at the latter had suggested occupation at so early a date).

Canada country occupying the northern part of the North American continent, bounded S by the US, N by the Arctic Ocean, NW by Alaska, E by the Atlantic Ocean, and W by the Pacific Ocean.

government The Canada Act of 1982 gave Canada power to amend its constitution and added a charter of rights and freedoms. This represented Canada's complete independence, though it remains a member of the British ⊳Commonwealth.

Canada is a federation of ten provinces: Alberta, British Columbia, Manitoba, New Brunswick, Newfoundland, Nova Scotia, Ontario, Prince Edward Island, Québec, and Saskatchewan; and two territories: Northwest Territories and Yukon. Each province has a single-chamber assembly, popularly elected; the premier (the leader of the party with the most seats in the legislature) chooses the cabinet. The two-chamber federal parliament consists of the Senate, whose 104 members are appointed by the government for life or until the age of 75 and must be resident in the provinces they represent; and the House of Commons, which has 295 members, elected by universal suffrage in single-member constituencies.

The federal prime minister is the leader of the best-supported party in the House of Commons and is accountable, with the cabinet, to it. Parliament has a maximum life of five years. Legislation must be passed by both chambers and then signed by the governor-general.

Canada: history

c. 35,000 BC	People arrived in North America from Asia by way of Beringia.
c. 2000 BC	Inuit began settling Arctic coast from Siberia E to Greenland.
c. AD 1000	Vikings, including Leif Ericsson, landed in NE Canada, and started settlements that did not survive.
1497	John Cabot landed on Cape Breton Island.
1534	Jacques Cartier reached the Gulf of St Lawrence.
1603	Samuel Champlain began his exploration of Canada.
1608	Champlain founded Québec.
1759	James Wolfe captured Québec.
1763	France ceded Canada to Britain under the Treaty of Paris.
1775–83	American Revolution caused Loyalist influx to New Brunswick and Ontario.
1791	Canada divided into English-speaking Upper Canada (much of modern Ontario) and French-speaking Lower Canada (much of modern Québec and mainland Newfoundland).
1793	Alexander Mackenzie reached the Pacific by land.
1812–14	War of 1812 between Britain and the US. US invasions repelled by both provinces.
1837	Rebellions led by William Lyon Mackenzie in Upper Canada and Louis Joseph Papineau in Lower Canada.
1840	Upper and Lower Canada united to form the Province of Canada.
1867	British North America Act created the Dominion of Canada (Ontario, Québec, Nova Scotia, and New Brunswick).
1869	Uprising, led by Louis Riel, against the Canadian government and the threat of a flood of white settlers into Rupert's Land.
1870	Manitoba created (from part of Rupert's Land) and joined confederation. North West (later Northwest) Territories created.
1871	British Columbia entered confederation.
1873	Prince Edward Island entered confederation.
1885	Northwest Rebellion crushed and leader Louis Riel hanged. Canadian Pacific Railway completed.
1905	Alberta and Saskatchewan formed from the Northwest Territories and entered confederation.
1914–18	World War I—Canadian troops at 2nd Battle of Ypres, Vimy Ridge, Passchendaele, the Somme, and Cambrai.
1931	Canada became an independent nation. Norway renounced its claim to the Sverdrup Islands, confirming Canadian sovereignty in the entire Arctic Archipelago north of the Canadian mainland.
1939–45	World War II—Canadian participation in all theaters.
1949	Newfoundland joined the confederation.
1950–53	Korean War—Canada participated in United Nations force, and subsequently in almost all UN peacekeeping operations.

For subsequent history see Canada box.

Canada: provinces

province	capital	area in sq km
Alberta	Edmonton	661,200
British Columbia	Victoria	947,800
Manitoba	Winnipeg	650,000
New Brunswick	Fredericton	73,400
Newfoundland	St John's	405,700
Nova Scotia	Halifax	55,500
Ontario	Toronto	1,068,600
Prince Edward Island	Charlottetown	5,700
Québec	Québec	1,540,700
Saskatchewan	Regina	652,300

territory	capital	area in sq km
Northwest Territories	Yellowknife	3,426,300
Yukon Territory	Whitehorse	483,500

history Inhabited by indigenous Indian and Inuit groups, Canada was reached by an English expedition led by John Cabot 1497 and a French expedition under Jacques Cartier 1534. Both countries developed colonies from the 17th century, with hostility between them culminating in the French and Indian Wars (1689–1763), in which France was defeated. Antagonism continued, and in 1791 Canada was divided into English-speaking Upper Canada (much of modern Ontario) and French-speaking Lower Canada (much of modern Québec and all of modern mainland Newfoundland). The two were united as Canada Province 1841, when the self-governing Dominion of Canada was founded.

In 1870 the province of Manitoba was added to the confederation, British Columbia joined 1871, and Prince Edward Island 1873. The new provinces of Alberta and Saskatchewan were created from the Northwest Territories 1905. An improving economy led to vast areas of fertile prairie land being opened up for settlement. The discovery of gold and other metals, the exploitation of forests for lumber and paper, the development of fisheries and tourism, and investment from other countries gradually transformed Canada's economy into one of the most important manufacturing and trading nations in the world. World War II stimulated further rapid industrialization, and in the postwar period discovery and exploitation of mineral resources took place on a vast scale. Newfoundland joined the confederation 1949.

Trudeau's era The Progressive Conservatives returned to power 1957, after 22 years of Liberal Party rule. In 1963 the Liberals were reinstated in office under Lester Pearson, who was succeeded by Pierre Trudeau 1968. Trudeau maintained Canada's defensive alliance with the US but sought to widen its influence internationally. Faced with the problem of Québec's separatist movement, he promised to create equal opportunities for both English-and French-speaking Canadians throughout the country. He won both the 1972 and 1974 elections.

In 1979, with no party having an overall majority in the Commons, the Progressive Conservatives formed a government under Joe Clark. Later that year Trudeau announced his retirement from politics, but when, in Dec 1979, Clark was defeated on his budget proposals, Trudeau reconsidered his decision and won the 1980 general election with a large majority.

Trudeau's third administration was concerned with "patriation," or the extent to which the British Parliament should determine Canada's constitution. The position was resolved with the passing of the Constitution Act 1982, the last piece of UK legislation to have force in Canada.

In 1983 Clark was replaced as leader of the Progressive Conservatives by Brian Mulroney, a corporate lawyer who had never run for public office, and in 1984 Trudeau retired to be replaced as Liberal Party leader and prime minister by John Turner, a former minister of finance. Within nine days of taking office, Turner called a general election, and the Progressive Conservatives, under Mulroney, won 211 seats, the largest majority in Canadian history.

changing direction Soon after taking office, Mulroney began an international realignment, placing less emphasis on links established by Trudeau with Asia, Africa, and Latin America and more on cooperation with Europe and a closer relationship with the US. The election of 1988 was fought on the issue of free trade with the US, and the Conservatives won with a reduced majority. Despite the majority of voters opting for the Liberals or New Democratic Party (NDP), who both opposed free trade, an agreement was signed with the US 1989. Turner and Ed Broadbent, leader of the NDP, both resigned 1989.

Canada

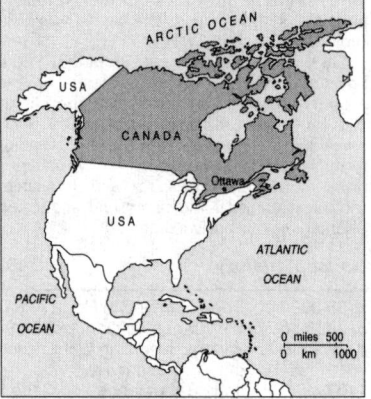

area 3,849,674 sq mi/9,970,610 sq km
capital Ottawa
cities Toronto, Montréal, Vancouver, Edmonton, Calgary, Winnipeg, Quebec, Hamilton, Saskatoon, Halifax
physical mountains in W, with low-lying plains in interior and rolling hills in E. Climate varies from temperate in S to arctic in N
environment sugar maples are dying in E Canada as a result of increasing soil acidification; nine rivers in Nova Scotia are now too acid to support salmon or trout reproduction
features St Lawrence Seaway, Mackenzie River; Great Lakes; Arctic Archipelago; Rocky Mountains; Great Plains or Prairies; Canadian Shield; Niagara Falls; the world's second largest country
head of state Elizabeth II from 1952 represented by governor-general
head of government Brian Mulroney from 1984
political system federal constitutional monarchy
political parties Progressive Conservative Party, free-enterprise, right of center; Liberal Party, nationalist, centrist; New Democratic Party (NDP), moderate, left of center
exports wheat, timber, pulp, newsprint, fish (salmon), furs (ranched fox and mink exceed the value of wild furs), oil, natural gas, aluminum, asbestos (world's second largest producer), coal, copper, iron, zinc, nickel (world's largest producer), uranium (world's largest producer), motor vehicles and parts, industrial and agricultural machinery, fertilizers, chemicals
currency Canadian dollar
population (1990 est) 26,527,000—including 300,000 North American Indians, of whom 75% live on more than 2,000 reservations in Ontario and the four western provinces; some 300,000 Métis (people of mixed race) and 19,000 Inuit of whom 75% live in the Northwest Territories. Over half Canada's population lives in Ontario and Québec. Growth rate 1.1% p.a.
life expectancy men 72, women 79
languages English, French (both official) (about 70% speak English, 20% French, and the rest are bilingual); there are also North American Indian languages and the Inuit Inuktitut
religion Roman Catholic 46%, Protestant 35%
literacy 99%
GDP $412 bn (1987); $15,910 per head
chronology
1867 Dominion of Canada founded.
1949 Newfoundland joined Canada.
1957 Progressive Conservatives returned to power after 22 years in opposition.
1961 NDP formed.
1963 Liberals elected under Lester Pearson.
1968 Pearson succeeded by Pierre Trudeau.
1979 Joe Clark, leader of the Progressive Conservatives, formed a minority government; defeated on budget proposals.
1980 Liberals under Trudeau returned with a large majority. Québec referendum rejected demand for independence.
1982 Canada Act removed Britain's last legal control over Canadian affairs; "patriation" of Canada's constitution.
1983 Clark replaced as leader of the Progressive Conservatives by Brian Mulroney.
1984 Trudeau retired and was succeeded as Liberal leader and prime minister by John Turner. Progressive Conservatives won the federal election with a large majority, and Mulroney became prime minister.
1988 Conservatives reelected with reduced majority on platform of free trade with the US.
1989 Free-trade agreement signed. Turner resigned as Liberal Party leader, and Ed Broadbent as NDP leader.
1990 Collapse of Meech Lake accord. Canada joined the coalition opposing Iraq's invasion of Kuwait.
1991 Constitutional reform package proposed.
1992 Gradual withdrawal of Canadian forces in Europe announced. Self-governing homeland for Inuit approved. Constitutional reform package agreed, devolving power to the provinces; subsequently rejected in national referendum.

Canada: prime ministers

1867	John A Macdonald	(Conservative)
1873	Alexander Mackenzie	(Liberal)
1878	John A Macdonald	(Conservative)
1891	John J Abbott	(Conservative)
1892	John S D Thompson	(Conservative)
1894	Mackenzie Bowell	(Conservative)
1896	Charles Tupper	(Conservative)
1896	Wilfred Laurier	(Liberal)
1911	Robert L Borden	(Conservative)
1920	Arthur Meighen	(Conservative)
1921	William Lyon Mackenzie King	(Liberal)
1926	Arthur Meighen	(Conservative)
1926	William Lyon Mackenzie King	(Liberal)
1930	Richard Bedford Bennett	(Conservative)
1935	William Lyon Mackenzie King	(Liberal)
1948	Louis Stephen St Laurent	(Liberal)
1957	John G Diefenbaker	(Conservative)
1963	Lester Bowles Pearson	(Liberal)
1968	Pierre Elliot Trudeau	(Liberal)
1979	Joseph Clark	(Progressive Conservative)
1980	Pierre Elliot Trudeau	(Liberal)
1984	John Turner	(Liberal)
1984	Brian Mulroney	(Progressive Conservative)

The 1990s began with the collapse of the Meech Lake accord, a 1987 compromise between the Canadian provinces aimed at getting Québec's acceptance of the 1982 constitutional reforms. In 1990–91 Canada joined the coalition opposing Iraq's invasion of Kuwait.

constitutional reform In Sept 1991 Mulroney presented a constitutional reform package to parliament, designed primarily to persuade Québec to remain as part of the Canadian federation. The plan, later called the Charlottestown Accord, was passed Aug 1992, giving greater autonomy to Québec, aboriginal self-government, increased powers to all provinces, and a reformed senate. A subsequent national referendum in Oct 1992, however, rejected the plan.

military cutbacks In Feb 1992 Canada, a key partner in NATO, announced a phased withdrawal of its forces in Europe.

rights granted to Inuit In May 1992 an Inuit self-governing homeland, to be called Nunavut, was approved by voters in Canada's Northwest Territories.

Canadian art painting and sculpture of Canada after colonization. Early painters of Canadian life include Cornelius Krieghoff (1815–1872), who recorded Indian and pioneer life, and Paul Kane (1810–1871), painter of the Plains Indians. In the late 19th century, a Canadian style developed with the landscapes of Tom Thomson (1877–1917) and the 'Group of Seven,' formed 1913, that developed an expressive landscape style. Maurice Cullen (1866–1934), an Impressionist, and James Wilson Morrice (1865–1924), a Fauve, introduced new European trends.

Before World War II Emily Carr (1871–1945) was one of the most original talents, developing eloquent studies of nature. Canadian artists have since joined the international arena. The Automatistes, led by the Surrealist Paul-Emile Borduas (1905-1960), rebelled against the Canadian establishment. Jean-Paul Riopelle (1923–) has made a significant contribution to Abstract Expressionism.

Canadian literature Canadian literature in English began early in the 19th century in the Maritime Provinces with the humorous tales of T C Haliburton (1796–1865); Charles Heavysege (1816–1876), a poet of note, was from Kingston, Ontario. The late 19th century brought the lyrical output of Charles G D Roberts (1860–1943), Bliss Carman (1861–1929), Archibald Lampman (1861–1899), and Duncan Campbell Scott (1862–1944).

Realism in fiction developed with Frederick P Grove (1871–1948), Mazo de la Roche (1885–1961), creator of the "Jalna" series, and Hugh MacLennan (1907–). Humor of worldwide appeal emerged in Stephen Leacock (1869–1944); Brian Moore (1921–), author of *The Luck of Ginger Coffey* 1960; and Mordecai ⟡Richler. Also widely read outside Canada was L M Montgomery (1874–1942), whose *Anne of Green Gables* 1908 became a children's classic. Saul Bellow and Marshall ⟡McLuhan were both Canadian-born, as were contemporary novelists Robertson ⟡Davies and Margaret ⟡Atwood. See also ⟡French Canadian literature.

canal artificial waterway constructed for drainage, irrigation, or navigation. *Irrigation canals* carry water for irrigation from rivers, reservoirs, or wells, and are designed to maintain an even flow of water over the whole length. *Navigation and ship canals* are constructed at one level between ⟡locks, and frequently link with rivers or sea inlets to form a waterway system. The Suez Canal 1869 and the Panama Canal 1914 eliminated long trips around continents and dramatically shortened shipping routes.

Irrigation canals fed from the Nile have maintained life in Egypt since the earliest times; the division of the waters of the Upper Indus and its tributaries form the extensive system in Pakistan and Punjab, India, and was, for more than ten years, a major cause of dispute between India and Pakistan that was settled by a treaty 1960; the Murray basin, Victoria, Australia, and the Imperial and Central Valley projects in California are examples of 19th- and 20th-century irrigation canal development.

Probably the oldest **ship canal** still in use, as well as the longest, is the Grand Canal in China, which links Tianjin and Hangzhou and connects the Huang He (Yellow River) and Chang Jiang. It was originally built in three stages 485 BC– AD 283, reaching a total length of 1,107 mi/1,780 km. Large sections silted up in later years, but the entire system was dredged, widened, and rebuilt 1958–72 in conjunction with work on flood protection, irrigation, and hydroelectric projects. It carries millions of tons of freight every year.

The cost-effectiveness of transporting goods by canal (where speed is not a prime factor) led to a revival and Belgium, France, Germany, and the USSR were among countries that began extending and streamlining their canals. The Baltic–Volga waterway links the Lithuanian port of Klaipeda with Kahovka, at the mouth of the Dnieper on the Black Sea, a distance of 1,510 mi/2,430 km. A further canal cuts across the north Crimea, thus shortening the voyage of ships from the Dnieper through the Black Sea to the Sea of Azov. In Central America, the Panama Canal 1904–14 links the Atlantic and Pacific oceans (40 mi/64 km). In North America, the Erie Canal 1825 linked the Great Lakes with the Hudson River and opened the northeast and Midwest commercially; the St Lawrence Seaway 1954–59 extends from Montréal to Lake Ontario (180 mi/290 km) and, with the deepening of the Welland Canal and some of the river channels, provides a waterway that enables oceangoing vessels to travel (during the ice-free months) between the Atlantic and Duluth, Minnesota, at the western end of Lake Superior, some 2,342 mi/ 3,770 km.

Irrigation canals are the older, dug from ancient times, and provided flood control as well as neolithic farming villages with an expanded area of rich alluvial soil, especially in the Tigris–Euphrates valley and along the Nile, where agricultural surpluses eventually allowed for the rise of ⟡civilizations.

Navigation canals developed after irrigation and drainage canals; often they link two waterways and were at first level and shallow. Soon, those with inclined planes had towpaths along which men and animals towed vessels from one level to the next. Locks were invented to allow passage where great variations in level exist. By the 20th century mechanized tows and self-propelled barges were in use.

Canaletto Antonio (Giovanni Antonio Canale) 1697–1768. Italian painter celebrated for his paintings of views (*vedute*) of Venice (his native city) and of the river Thames and London 1746-56.

Much of his work is very detailed and precise, with a warm light and a sparkling of tiny highlights on the green waters of canals and rivers. His later style became clumsier and more static.

canary bird *Serinus canaria* of the finch family, found wild in the Canary Islands and Madeira. It is greenish with a yellow underside. Canaries have been bred as cage birds in Europe since the 15th century, and many domestic varieties are yellow or orange.

Some canaries are used in mines as detectors of traces of poison gas in the air.

Canary Islands (Spanish *Canarias*) group of volcanic islands 60 mi/100 km off the NW coast of Africa, forming the Spanish provinces of Las Palmas and Santa Cruz de Tenerife; area 2,818 sq mi/7,300 sq km; population (1986) 1,615,000.

features The chief centers are Santa Cruz on Tenerife (which also has the highest peak in extracontinental Spain, Pico de Teide, 12,186 ft/3,713 m), and Las Palmas on Gran Canaria. The province of Santa Cruz comprises Tenerife, Palma, Gomera, and Hierro; the province of Las Palmas comprises Gran Canaria,

Lanzarote, and Fuerteventura. There are also six uninhabited islets. The Northern Hemisphere Observatory (1981) is on the island of La Palma, the first in the world to be controlled remotely. Observation conditions are exceptionally good because there is no moisture, no artificial light pollution, and little natural ⟡airglow.

The Organization of African Unity (OAU) supports an independent Guanch Republic (so called from the indigenous islanders, a branch of the N African Berbers) and revival of the Guanch language.

Canberra capital of Australia (since 1908), situated in the Australian Capital Territory, enclosed within New South Wales, on a tributary of the Murrumbidgee River; area (Australian Capital Territory including the port at Jervis Bay) 939 sq mi/2,432 sq km; population (1988) 297,300.

It contains the Parliament House (first used by the Commonwealth Parliament 1927), the Australian National University 1946, the Canberra School of Music 1965, and the National War Memorial.

cancan high-kicking stage dance for women (solo or line of dancers) originating in Paris about 1830. The music usually associated with the cancan is the *galop* from Offenbach's *Orpheus in the Underworld*.

cancer group of diseases characterized by abnormal proliferation of cells. Cancer (malignant) cells are usually degenerate, capable only of reproducing themselves (tumor formation). Malignant cells tend to spread from their site of origin by traveling through the bloodstream or lymphatic system.

There are more than 100 types of cancer. Some, like lung or bowel cancer, are common; others are rare. The likely cause remains unexplained. Triggering agents (⟡carcinogens) include chemicals such as those found in cigarette smoke, other forms of smoke, asbestos dust, exhaust fumes, and many industrial chemicals. Some viruses can also trigger the cancerous growth of cells (see ⟡oncogenes), as can X-rays and radioactivity. Dietary factors are important in some cancers; for example, lack of fiber in the diet may predispose people to bowel cancer and a diet high in animal fats and low in fresh vegetables and fruit increases the risk of breast cancer. Psychological ⟡stress may increase the risk of cancer, more so if the person concerned is not able to control the source of the stress. In some families there is a genetic tendency toward a particular type of cancer.

Cancer faintest of the zodiacal constellations (its brightest stars are fourth magnitude). It lies in the northern hemisphere, between Leo and Gemini, and is represented as a crab. Cancer's most distinctive feature is the star cluster Praesepe, popularly known as the Beehive. The Sun passes through the constellation during late July and early Aug. In astrology, the dates for Cancer are between about June 22 and July 22 (see ⟡precession).

Cancún Caribbean resort in Mexico where, in 1981, a North–South summit was held to discuss the widening gap between the industrialized countries and the Third World.

candela SI unit (symbol cd) of luminous intensity, which replaced the old units of candle and standard candle. It measures the brightness of a light itself rather than the amount of light falling on an object, which is called *illuminance* and measured in ⟡lux.

One candela is defined as the luminous intensity in a given direction of a source that emits monochromatic radiation of frequency 540×10^{-12} Hz and whose radiant energy in that direction is 1/683 watt per steradian.

Candela Félix 1910– . Spanish-born Mexican architect, originator of the hypar (hyperbolic paraboloid) from 1951, in which doubly curved surfaces are built up on a framework of planks sprayed with cement. Professor at the National School of Architecture, University of Mexico, from 1953.

Candida albicans yeastlike fungus present in the human digestive tract and in the vagina, which causes no harm in most healthy people. However, it can cause problems if it multiplies excessively, as in vaginal candidiasis or ⟡thrush, the main symptom of which is intense itching. The most common form of thrush is oral, which often occurs in those taking steroids or prolonged courses of antibiotics.

Newborn babies may pick up the yeast during birth and suffer an infection of the mouth and throat. There is also some evidence that overgrowth of *Candida* may occur in the intestines, causing diarrhea, bloating, and other symptoms such as headache and fatigue, but this is not yet proven. Occasionally, *Candida* can infect immunocompromised patients, such as those with AIDS. Treatment for candidiasis is based on antifungal drugs.

Candide satire by ⟡Voltaire, published 1759. The hero experiences extremes of fortune in the company of Dr Pangloss, a personification of the popular belief of the time (partly based on a misunderstanding of ⟡Leibniz) that "all is for the best in the best of all possible worlds." Voltaire exuberantly demonstrates that this idea is absurd and inhumane.

cane reedlike stem of various plants such as the sugar cane, bamboo, and, in particular, the group of palms called rattans, consisting of the genus *Calamus* and its allies. Their slender stems are dried and used for making walking sticks, baskets, and furniture.

Canea (Greek **Khaniá**) capital and administrative center of Crete, on the NW coast; population (1981) 47,338. It was founded 1252 by the Venetians and is surrounded by a wall. Vegetable oils, soap, and leather are exported. Heavy fighting took place here during World War II, after the landing of German parachutists in May 1941.

Canes Venatici constellation of the northern hemisphere near Ursa Major, identified with the hunting dogs of ⟡Boötes, the herder. Its stars are faint, and it contains the Whirlpool galaxy (M51), the first spiral galaxy to be recognized.

Canetti Elias 1905– . Bulgarian-born writer. He was exiled from Austria as a Jew 1938 and settled in England 1939. His books, written in German, include *Die Blendung/Auto da Fé* 1935. He was awarded the Nobel Prize for Literature 1981.

He was concerned with crowd behavior and the psychology of power, and wrote the anthropological study *Masse und Machte/Crowds and Power* 1960. His three volumes of memoirs are *Die gerettete Zunge: Geschichte einer Jugend/The Tongue Set Free: Remembrance of a European childhood* 1977, *Die Fackel im Ohr: Lebensgeschichte 1921–31/The Torch in My Ear* 1980, and *Das Augenspeil/The Play of the Eyes* 1985.

canine in mammalian carnivores, any of the

long, often pointed teeth found at the front of the mouth between the incisors and premolars. Canine teeth are used for catching prey, for killing, and for tearing flesh. They are absent in herbivores such as rabbits and sheep, and are much reduced in humans.

Canis Major brilliant constellation of the southern hemisphere, identified with one of the two dogs following at the heel of Orion. Its main star, Sirius, is the brightest star in the sky.

Canis Minor small constellation along the celestial equator, identified with the second of the two dogs of Orion (the other dog is Canis Major). Its brightest star is Procyon.

Cannae village in Puglia, Italy, site of ⟡Hannibal's defeat of the Romans 216 BC.

C Terentius Varro, the Roman commander, fled from the battle. However, he was subsequently praised by the Senate for raising an army from the few survivors.

Cannes resort in Alpes-Maritimes *département*, S France; population (1982) 73,000, conurbation 296,000. A prestigious film festival is held here annually. Formerly only a small seaport, in 1834 it attracted the patronage of British Whig politician Lord Brougham (1778-1868) and other distinguished visitors and soon became a fashionable vacation resort. A new town (La Bocca) grew up facing the Mediterranean.

Cannes Film Festival international film festival held every year in Cannes, France. A number of important prizes are awarded, including the Palme d'Or (Golden Palm) for the best film.

The first festival was held 1946. The main award is the Palme d'Or (known as The Grand Prix prior to 1955); other awards are made for best direction, best actor, and best actress. Awards for supporting performances were introduced 1979.

cannibalism or **anthropophagy** the practice of eating human flesh. The name is derived from the Caribs, a South American and West Indian people, alleged by the conquering Spaniards to eat their captives.

canning food preservation in hermetically sealed containers by the application of heat. Originated by Nicolas Appert in France 1809 with glass containers, it was developed by Peter Durand in England 1810 with cans made of sheet steel thinly coated with tin to delay corrosion. Cans for beer and soft drinks are now generally made of aluminum.

Canneries were established in the US before 1820, but the US canning industry began to grow considerably in the 1870s when the manufacture of cans was mechanized and factory methods of processing were used. The quality and taste of early canned food was frequently dubious but by the end of the 19th century, scientific research made greater understanding possible of the food-preserving process, and standards improved. More than half the aluminum cans used in the US are now recycled.

Canning Charles John, 1st Earl 1812–1862. British administrator, first viceroy of India from 1858. As governor-general of India from 1856, he suppressed the Indian Mutiny with a fair but firm hand which earned him the nickname "Clemency Canning." He was the son of George Canning.

Canning George 1770–1827. British Tory politician, foreign secretary 1807–10 and 1822–27, and prime minister 1827 in coalition with the Whigs. He was largely responsible, during the Napoleonic Wars, for the seizure of the Danish fleet and British intervention in the Spanish peninsula.

Cannizzaro Stanislao 1826–1910. Italian chemist who revived interest in the work of Avogadro that had, in 1811, revealed the difference between ◊atoms and ◊molecules, and so established atomic and molecular weights as the basis of chemical calculations.

Cannizzaro also worked in aromatic organic chemistry. In 1853 he discovered reactions (named after him) that make benzyl alcohol and benzoic acid from benzaldehyde.

Cannon Annie Jump 1863–1941. US astronomer who, from 1896, worked at Harvard College Observatory and carried out revolutionary work on the classification of stars by examining their spectra. Her system, still used today, has spectra arranged according to temperature and runs from O through B, A, F, G, K, and M. O-type stars are the hottest, with surface temperatures of over 25,000 K.

Cano Juan Sebastian del *c.* 1476–1526. Spanish voyager. It is claimed that he was the first sea captain to sail around the world. He sailed with Magellan 1519 and, after the latter's death in the Philippines, brought the *Victoria* safely home to Spain.

canoeing sport of propelling a lightweight, shallow boat, pointed at both ends, by paddles or sails. Currently, canoes are made from fiberglass, but original boats were of wooden construction covered in bark or skin. Canoeing was popularized as a sport in the 19th century.

Two types of canoe are used: the **kayak** and the **Canadian-style** canoe. The kayak, derived from the Eskimo model, has a keel and the canoeist sits. The Canadian-style canoe has no keel and the canoeist kneels. In addition to straightforward racing, there are slalom courses, with up to 30 "gates" to be negotiated through rapids and around artificial rock formations. Penalty seconds are added to course time for touching suspended gate poles or missing a gate. One to four canoeists are carried. The sport was introduced into the Olympic Games 1936.

canon in the Roman Catholic and Anglican churches, a type of priest. Canons, headed by the dean, are attached to a cathedral and constitute the **chapter**.

canon in theology, the collection of writings that is accepted as authoritative in a given religion, such as the *Tripitaka* in Theravāda Buddhism. In the Christian church, it comprises the books of the ◊Bible.

The canon of the Old Testament was drawn up at the assembly of rabbis held at Jamnia in Palestine between AD 90 and 100; certain excluded books were included in the ◊Apocrypha. The earliest list of New Testament books is known as the Muratorian Canon (about 160–70). Bishop Athanasius promulgated a list (*c.* 365) which corresponds with that in modern Bibles.

canon in music, an echo form for two or more parts repeating and following a leading melody at regular time intervals to achieve a harmonious effect. It is often found in Classical music, for example ◊Vivaldi and J S ◊Bach.

canonical hours in the Catholic church, seven set periods of devotion: **matins** and **lauds**, **prime**, **terce**, **sext**, **nones**, **evensong** or **vespers**, and **compline**.

canonization in the Catholic church, the admission of one of its members to the Calendar of Saints. The evidence of the candidate's exceptional piety is contested before the Congregation for the Causes of Saints by the Promotor Fidei, popularly known as the *devil's advocate*. Papal ratification of a favorable verdict results in ◊beatification, and full sainthood (conferred in St Peter's basilica, the Vatican) follows after further proof.

Under a system laid down mainly in the 17th century, the process of investigation was seldom completed in under 50 years, although in the case of a martyr it took less time. Since 1969 the gathering of the proof of the candidate's virtues has been left to the bishop of the birthplace, and miracles being difficult to substantiate, stress is placed on extraordinary "favors" or "graces" that can be proved or attested by serious investigation.

canon law rules and regulations of the Christian church, especially the Greek Orthodox, Roman Catholic, and Anglican churches. Its origin is sought in the declarations of Jesus and the apostles. In 1983 Pope John Paul II issued a new canon law code reducing offenses carrying automatic excommunication, extending the grounds for annulment of marriage, removing the ban on marriage with non-Catholics, and banning labor union and political activity by priests.

The earliest compilations were in the East, and the canon law of the Eastern Orthodox Church is comparatively small. Through the centuries, a great mass of canon law was accumulated in the Western church which, in 1918, was condensed in the *Corpus juris canonici* under Benedict XV. Even so, this is supplemented by many papal decrees.

Canopus or *Alpha Carinae* second brightest star in the sky (after Sirius), lying in the constellation Carina. It is a yellow-white supergiant about 120 light-years from Earth, and thousands of times more luminous than the Sun.

Canova Antonio 1757–1822. Italian Neo-Classical sculptor, based in Rome from 1781. He received commissions from popes, kings, and emperors for his highly finished marble portrait busts and groups. He made several portraits of Napoleon.

Canova was born near Treviso. His reclining marble *Pauline Borghese* 1805–07 (Borghese Gallery, Rome) is a fine example of cool, polished Classicism. He executed the tombs of popes Clement XIII, Pius VII, and Clement XIV. His marble sculptures include *Cupid and Psyche* (Louvre, Paris) and *The Three Graces* (Victoria and Albert Museum, London).

Cánovas del Castillo Antonio 1828–1897. Spanish politician and chief architect of the political system known as the *turno politico* through which his own Conservative party, and that of the Liberals under Práxedes Sagasta, alternated in power. Elections were rigged to ensure the appropriate majorities. Cánovas was assassinated 1897 by anarchists.

Cantabria autonomous region of N Spain; area 2,046 sq mi/5,300 sq km; population (1986) 525,000; capital Santander.

Cantabrian Mountains (Spanish *Cordillera Cantabrica*) mountains running along the N coast of Spain, reaching 8,688 ft/2,648 m in the Picos de Europa massif. The mountains contain coal and iron deposits.

Cantal volcanic mountain range in central France, which gives its name to Cantal *département*. The highest point is the Plomb du Cantal, 6,096 ft/1,858 m.

cantaloupe any of several small varieties of muskmelon *Cucumis melo*, distinguished by their round, ribbed fruits with orange-colored flesh.

cantata in music, an extended work for voices, from the Italian, meaning "sung," as opposed to ◊sonata ("sounded") for instruments. A cantata can be sacred or secular, sometimes uses solo voices, and usually has orchestral accompaniment. The first printed collection of sacred cantata texts dates from 1670.

Canterbury historic cathedral city in Kent, England, on the river Stour, 62 mi/100 km SE of London; population (1984) 39,000. In 597 King Ethelbert welcomed ◊Augustine's mission to England here, and the city has since been the metropolis of the Anglican Communion and seat of the archbishop of Canterbury.

The Roman *Durovernum*, Canterbury was the Saxon capital of Kent. The present name derives from *Cantwarabyrig* (Old English "fortress of the men of Kent").

Canterbury, archbishop of primate of all England, archbishop of the Church of England (Anglican), and first peer of the realm, ranking next to royalty. He crowns the sovereign, has a seat in the House of Lords, and is a member of the Privy Council. He is appointed by the prime minister.

Canterbury Tales, The unfinished collection of stories in prose and verse (*c.* 1387) by Geoffrey ◊Chaucer, told in Middle English by a group of pilgrims on their way to Thomas à ◊Becket's tomb at Canterbury. The tales and preludes are remarkable for their vivid character portrayal and colloquial language.

cantilever beam or structure that is fixed at one end only, though it may be supported at some point along its length; for example, a diving board. The cantilever principle, widely used in construction engineering, eliminates the need for a second main support at the free end of the beam, allowing for more elegant structures and reducing the amount of materials required. Many large-span bridges have been built on the cantilever principle.

A typical cantilever bridge consists of two beams cantilevered out from either bank, each supported part way along, with their free ends meeting in the middle. The multiple-cantilever Forth Rail Bridge (completed 1890) across the Firth of Forth in Scotland has twin main spans of 1,710 ft/521 m.

canton in France, an administrative district, a subdivision of the *arrondissement*; in Switzerland, one of the 23 subdivisions forming the Confederation.

Canton alternate spelling of Kwangchow or Guangzhou in China.

Canton city in NE Ohio, SE of Akron; seat of Stark county. Its products include office equipment, ceramics, and steel; population (1990) 84,161. The home of President William McKinley is here, as is the Football Hall of Fame.

cantor (Latin *cantare* "to sing") in Judaism, the prayer leader and choir master in a synagogue; the cantor is not a rabbi, and the position can be held by any lay person.

Cantor Georg 1845–1918. German mathematician who followed his work on number theory and trigonometry by considering the foundations of mathematics. He defined real numbers and produced a treatment of irrational numbers using a series of transfinite numbers. Cantor's set theory has been used in the development of topology and real function theory.

Canute c. 995–1035. King of England from 1016, Denmark from 1018, and Norway from 1028. Having invaded England 1013 with his father, Sweyn, king of Denmark, he was acclaimed king on his father's death 1014 by his ◊Viking army. Canute defeated ◊Edmund II Ironside at Assandun, Essex, 1016, and became king of all England on Edmund's death. He succeeded his brother Harold as king of Denmark 1018, compelled King Malcolm to pay homage by invading Scotland about 1027, and conquered Norway 1028. He was succeeded by his illegitimate son Harold I.

The legend of Canute disenchanting his flattering courtiers by showing that the sea would not retreat at his command was first told by Henry of Huntingdon 1130.

Canute VI (*Cnut VI*) 1163–1202. King of Denmark from 1182, son and successor of Waldemar Knudsson. With his brother and successor, Waldemar II, he resisted Frederick I's northward expansion, and established Denmark as the dominant power in the Baltic.

canyon (Spanish *cañon* "tube") deep, narrow valley or gorge running through mountains. Canyons are formed by stream down-cutting, usually in arid areas, where the stream or river receives water from outside the area.

There are many canyons in the western USA and in Mexico, for example the Grand Canyon of the Colorado River in Arizona, the canyon in Yellowstone National Park, and the Black Canyon in Colorado.

capacitance, electrical property of a capacitor that determines how much charge can be stored in it for a given potential difference between its terminals. It is equal to the ratio of the electrical charge stored to the potential difference. It is measured in ◊farads.

capacitor or *condenser* device for storing electric charge, used in electronic circuits; it consists of two or more metal plates separated by an insulating layer called a dielectric.

Its *capacitance* is the ratio of the charge stored on either plate to the potential difference between the plates. The SI unit of capacitance is the farad, but most capacitors have much smaller capacitances, and the microfarad (a millionth of a farad) is the commonly used practical unit.

Cape Breton island forming the northern part of the province of Nova Scotia; area 3,970 sq mi/10,282 sq km; population (1988) 170,000. Bisected by a waterway, it has road and rail links with the mainland across the Strait of Canso. It has coal resources and steelworks, and there has been substantial development in the strait area, with docks, oil refineries, and newsprint production from local timber. In the north, the surface rises to 1,800 ft/550 m at North Cape, and the coast has many fine harbors. There are cod fisheries. The climate is mild and very moist. The chief towns are Sydney and Glace Bay.
history The first British colony was established 1629 but was driven out by the French. In 1763 Cape Breton was ceded to Britain and attached to Nova Scotia 1763–84 and from 1820.

Cape Canaveral promontory on the Atlantic coast of Florida, 228 mi/367 km N of Miami, used as a rocket launch site by ◊NASA.

First mentioned 1513, it was known 1963–73 as Cape Kennedy, to honor Pres J F Kennedy after his assassination. The ◊Kennedy Space Center is nearby.

Cape Coast port of Ghana, W Africa, 80 mi/130 km W of Accra; population (1982) 73,000. It has been superseded as the main port since 1962 by Tema. The town, first established by the Portuguese in the 16th century, is built on a natural breakwater, adjoining the castle.

Cape Cod hook-shaped peninsula in SE Massachusetts, 60 mi/100 km long and 1–20 mi/1.6–32 km wide. Its beaches and woods make it a popular tourist area. It is separated from the rest of the state by the Cape Cod Canal. The islands of Martha's Vineyard and Nantucket are just south of the cape.

Basque and Norse fisherfolk are believed to have visited Cape Cod many years before the English Pilgrims landed at Provincetown 1620. It was named after the cod which were caught in the dangerous shoals of the cape. The ◊Kennedy family home is at the resort of Hyannis Port.

Cape Coloured South African term for people of mixed African and European descent, mainly living in Cape Province.

Cape gooseberry plant *Physalis peruviana* of the potato family. Originating in South America, it is grown in South Africa, from where it takes its name. It is cultivated for its fruit, a yellow berry surrounded by a papery ◊calyx.

Cape Horn southernmost point of South America, in the Chilean part of the archipelago of ◊Tierra del Fuego; notorious for gales and heavy seas. It was named 1616 by Dutch explorer Willem Schouten (1580–1625) after his birthplace (Hoorn).

Čapek Karel 1890–1938. Czech writer whose works often deal with social injustice in an imaginative, satirical way. *R.U.R.* 1921 is a play in which robots (a term he coined) rebel against their controllers; the novel *Válka s Mloky/War with the Newts* 1936 is a science-fiction classic.

Capella or *Alpha Aurigae* brightest star in the constellation Auriga and the sixth brightest star in the sky. It consists of a pair of yellow giant stars 41 light-years from Earth, orbiting each other every 104 days.

Cape of Good Hope South African headland forming a peninsula between Table Bay and False Bay, Cape Town. The first European to sail around it was Bartholomew Diaz 1488. Formerly named Cape of Storms, it was given its present name by King John II of Portugal.

Cape Province (Afrikaans *Kaapprovinsie*) largest province of the Republic of South Africa, named after the Cape of Good Hope
area 247,638 sq mi/641,379 sq km, excluding Walvis Bay
capital Cape Town
cities Port Elizabeth, East London, Kimberley, Grahamstown, Stellenbosch
physical Orange River, Drakensberg, Table Mountain (highest point Maclear's Beacon, 3,567 ft/1,087 m); Great Karoo Plateau, Walvis Bay
products fruit, vegetables, wine; meat, ostrich feathers; diamonds, copper, asbestos, manganese
population (1985) 5,041,000; officially including 44% colored; 31% black; 25% white; 0.6% Asian

history Dutch traders established the first European settlement on the Cape 1652, but it was taken by the British 1795, after the French Revolutionary armies had occupied the Netherlands, and was sold to Britain for £6 million 1814. The Cape achieved self-government 1872. It was an original province of the Union 1910.

The Orange River was proclaimed the northern boundary 1825. Griqualand West (1880) and the southern part of Bechuanaland (1895) were later incorporated. Negotiations over Walvis Bay between South Africa and Namibia in March 1991 ended without agreement, and Walvis Bay, although formerly administered with Namibia, remains legally an integral part of Cape Province.

caper trailing shrub *Capparis spinosa*, native to the Mediterranean and belonging to the family Capparidaceae. Its flower buds are preserved in vinegar as a condiment.

capercaillie large bird *Tetrao urogallus* of the grouse type found in coniferous woodland in Europe and N Asia. At nearly 3 ft/1 m long, the male is the biggest gamebird in Europe, with a largely black plumage and rounded tail which is fanned out in courtship. The female is speckled brown and about 2 ft/60 cm long.

Hunted to extinction in Britain in the 18th century, the capercaillie was reintroduced from Sweden in the 1830s and has reestablished itself in Scotland.

Capet Hugh 938–996. King of France from 987, when he claimed the throne on the death of Louis V. He founded the **Capetian dynasty**, of which various branches continued to reign until the French Revolution, for example, ◊Valois and ◊Bourbon.

Cape Town (Afrikaans *Kaapstad*) port and oldest town in South Africa, situated in the SW on Table Bay; population (1985) 776,617. Industries include horticulture and trade in wool, wine, fruit, grain, and oil. It is the legislative capital of the Republic of South Africa and capital of Cape Province; it was founded 1652.

It includes the Houses of Parliament, City Hall, Cape Town Castle 1666, and Groote Schuur ("great barn"), the estate of Cecil Rhodes (he designated the house as the home of the premier, and a university and the National Botanical Gardens occupy part of the grounds). The naval base of **Simonstown** is to the southeast; in 1975 Britain's use of its facilities was ended by the Labour government in disapproval of South Africa's racial policies.

Cape Verde group of islands in the Atlantic, W of Senegal (W Africa).
government The 1980 constitution provides for a national people's assembly of 83, elected by universal suffrage for a five-year term, and a president, elected for a similar term by the assembly.

history The Cape Verde islands were first settled in the 15th century by Portugal, the first black inhabitants being slaves imported from W Africa. Over the next five centuries of Portuguese rule the islands were gradually peopled with Portuguese, African slaves, and people of mixed African-European descent who became the majority. The Cape Verdians kept some African culture but came to speak Portuguese or the Portuguese-derived Creole language, and became Catholics.

A liberation movement developed in the 1950s. The mainland territory to which Cape Verde is linked, Guinea-Bissau, achieved independence 1974, and a process began for their

Cape Verde
Republic of (*República de Cabo Verde*)

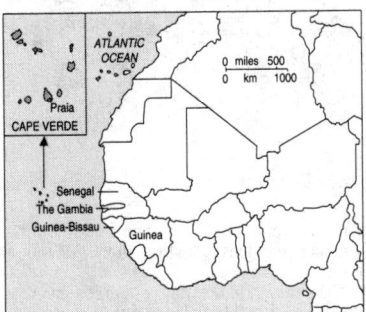

area 1,557 sq mi/4,033 sq km
capital Praia
cities Mindelo, Sal-Rei, Porto Novo
physical archipelago of ten volcanic islands
350 mi/565 km W of Senegal; the windward
(Barlavento) group includes Santo Antão,
São Vicente, Santa Luzia, São Nicolau,
Sal, and Boa Vista; the leeward (Sotovento)
group comprises Maio, São Tiago, Fogo,
and Brava; all but Santa Luzia are inhabited
features strategic importance guaranteed
by its domination of western shipping lanes;
Sal, Boa Vista, and Maio lack water supplies
but have fine beaches
head of state Mascarenhas Monteiro

from 1991
head of government Carlos Viega from 1991
political system socialist pluralist state
political parties African Party for the Independence of Cape Verde (PAICV), African
nationalist; Movement for Democracy (MPD)
exports bananas, salt, fish
currency Cape Verde escudo
population (1990 est) 375,000 (including
100,000 Angolan refugees); growth rate
1.9% p.a.
life expectancy men 57, women 61
language Creole dialect of Portuguese
religion Roman Catholic 80%
literacy men 61%, women 39% (1985)
GDP $158 million (1987); $454 per head
chronology
15th century First settled by Portuguese.
1951–74 Ruled as an overseas territory by
Portugal.
1974 Moved toward independence through
a transitional Portuguese–Cape Verde
government.
1975 Independence achieved from Portugal.
National people's assembly elected. Aristides
Pereira became the first president.
1980 Constitution adopted providing for
eventual union with Guinea-Bissau.
1981 Union with Guinea-Bissau abandoned
and the constitution amended; became
one-party state.
1991 First multiparty elections held. New
party, MPD, won majority in assembly. Pereira
replaced by Mascarenhas Monteiro.

eventual union. A transitional government was set up, composed of Portuguese and members of the African Party for the Independence of Portuguese Guinea and Cape Verde (PAIGC).
after independence In 1975 a national people's assembly was elected, and Aristides Pereira, PAIGC secretary-general, became president and head of government of Cape Verde. The 1980 constitution provided for the union of the two states but in 1981 this aspect was deleted because of insufficient support, and the PAIGC became the African Party for the Independence of Cape Verde (PAICV). From 1981 to 1990 the PAICV was the only permitted political party. Pereira was reelected, and relations with Guinea-Bissau improved. Under President Pereira, Cape Verde adopted a nonaligned policy and achieved considerable respect within the region. An opposition party, the Independent Democratic Union of Cape Verde (UCID), operated from Portugal.
end of one-party system In the first multiparty elections, held Jan 1991, a new party, Movement for Democracy (MPD), won a majority in the assembly. After a very low poll the following month, Mascarenhas Monteiro was elected president in succession to Pereira. *See illustration box.*

capillarity spontaneous movement of liquids up or down narrow tubes, or capillaries. The movement is due to unbalanced molecular attraction at the boundary between the liquid and the tube. If liquid molecules near the boundary are more strongly attracted to molecules in the material of the tube than to other nearby liquid molecules, the liquid will rise in the tube. If liquid molecules are less attracted to the material of the tube than to other liquid molecules, the liquid will fall.

capillary narrowest blood vessel in vertebrates, 0.008–0.02 mm in diameter, barely wider than a red blood cell. Capillaries are

distributed as *beds*, complex networks connecting arteries and veins. Capillary walls are extremely thin, consisting of a single layer of cells, and so nutrients, dissolved gases, and waste products can easily pass through them. This makes the capillaries the main area of exchange between the fluid (⟡lymph) bathing body tissues and the blood.

capillary in physics, a very narrow, thick-walled tube, usually made of glass, such as in a thermometer. Properties of fluids, such as surface tension and viscosity, can be studied using capillary tubes.

capital in architecture, a stone placed on the top of a column, pier, or pilaster, and usually wider on the upper surface than the diameter of the supporting shaft. A capital consists of three parts: the top member, called the *abacus*, a block that acts as the supporting surface to the superstructure; the middle portion, known as the bell or *echinus*; and the lower part, called the necking or *astragal*.

capital in economics, accumulated or inherited wealth held in the form of assets (such as stocks and shares, property, and bank deposits). In stricter terms, capital is defined as the stock of goods used in the production of other goods, and may be *fixed capital* (such as buildings, plant, and machinery) that is durable, or *circulating capital* (raw materials and components) that is used up quickly.

capital expenditure spending on fixed assets such as plant and equipment, trade investments, or the purchase of other businesses.

capital gains tax income tax levied on the change of value of a person's assets after they are sold, including securities and real property.
   It is frequently a politically contentious tax, since if it is set too low, it is seen as a subsidy for the rich who have made large profits on their property. If it is set too high, it can act

as a disincentive for investment, and economic activity can slow.

capitalism economic system in which the principal means of production, distribution, and exchange are in private (individual or corporate) hands and competitively operated for profit. A *mixed economy* combines the private enterprise of capitalism and a degree of state monopoly, as in nationalized industries.

capital punishment punishment by death. Capital punishment is retained in 92 countries and territories (1990), including the US (37 states), China, and Islamic countries. It was abolished in the UK 1965 for all crimes except treason. Methods of execution include electrocution, lethal gas, hanging, shooting, lethal injection, garrotting, and decapitation.
   In the US, the Supreme Court declared capital punishment unconstitutional 1972 (as a cruel and unusual punishment) but decided 1976 that this was not so in all circumstances. It was therefore reintroduced in some states, and in 1990 there were more than 2,000 prisoners on death row (awaiting execution) in the US. The first state to abolish capital punishment was Michigan 1847.

capitulum in botany, a flattened or rounded head (inflorescence) of numerous, small, stalkless flowers. The capitulum is surrounded by a circlet of petallike bracts and has the appearance of a large, single flower. It is characteristic of plants belonging to the daisy family Compositae, such as sunflowers *Helianthus*, goldenrods *Solidago*, and dandelions *Taraxacum*. The individual flowers are known as ⟡florets.

Capone Al (phonse "Scarface") 1898–1947. US gangster. During the ⟡Prohibition period, he built a formidable criminal organization in Chicago. He was brutal in his pursuit of dominance, killing seven members of a rival gang in the St Valentine's Day massacre. He was imprisoned 1931–39 for income-tax evasion, the only charge that could be sustained against him.

Capote Truman. Adopted name of Truman Streckfus Persons 1924–1984. US novelist, journalist, and playwright. He wrote *Breakfast at Tiffany's* 1958; set a trend with the first "nonfiction novel," *In Cold Blood* 1966, reconstructing a Kansas killing; and mingled recollection and fiction in *Music for Chameleons* 1980.
   His other works range from musicals and screenplays to sketches and essays about travel, celebrities, and other topics. He was a prominent figure in the New York social and literary world in his later years.

Cappadocia ancient region of Asia Minor, in E central Turkey. It was conquered by the Persians 584 BC but in the 3rd century BC became an independent kingdom. The region was annexed as a province of the Roman Empire AD 17.
   The area includes over 600 Byzantine cave churches cut into volcanic rock, dating mainly from the 10th and 11th centuries.

Capra Frank 1897–1991. Italian-born US film director. His satirical, populist comedies, which often have the common man pitted against corrupt corporations, were hugely successful in the Depression years of the 1930s. He won Academy Awards for *It Happened One Night* 1934, *Mr Deeds Goes to Town* 1936, and *You Can't Take It With You* 1938. Among his other classic films are *Mr Smith Goes to Washington* 1939, and *It's a Wonderful Life* 1946.

Capri Italian island at the southern entrance of the Bay of Naples; 20 mi/32 km S of Naples; area 5 sq mi/13 sq km. It has two towns, Capri and Anacapri, a profusion of flowers, beautiful scenery, and an ideal climate.

capriccio (Italian "caprice") in music, a short instrumental piece, often humorous or whimsical in character.

Capricornus zodiacal constellation in the southern hemisphere next to Sagittarius. It is represented as a fish-tailed goat, and its brightest stars are third magnitude. The Sun passes through it late Jan to mid-Feb. In astrology, the dates for Capricornus (popularly known as Capricorn) are between about Dec 22 and Jan 19 (see ▷precession).

capsicum any pepper plant of the genus ***Capsicum*** of the nightshade family Solanaceae, native to Central and South America. The differing species produce green to red fruits that vary in size.

capsule in botany, a dry, usually many-seeded fruit formed from an ovary composed of two or more fused ▷carpels, which splits open to release the seeds. The same term is used for the spore-containing structure of mosses and liverworts; this is borne at the top of a long stalk or seta.

Capsules burst open (dehisce) in various ways, including lengthwise, by a transverse lid—for example, scarlet pimpernel *Anagallis arvensis*—or by a number of pores, either toward the top of the capsule, as in the poppy *Papaver*, or near the base, as in certain species of bellflower *Campanula*.

Captain Marvel US comic-book character created 1940 by C(larence) C(harles) Beale (1910–1989). Captain Marvel is a 15-year-old schoolboy, Billy Batson, who transforms himself by saying "Shazam" into a superhuman hero wearing a red-and-yellow caped athletic suit.

capuchin monkey of the genus *Cebus* found in Central and South America, so called because the hairs on the head resemble the cowl of a Capuchin monk. Capuchins live in small groups, feed on fruit and insects, and have a long tail that is semiprehensile and can give support when climbing through the trees.

Capuchin member of the Franciscan order of monks in the Roman Catholic church, instituted by the Italian monk Matteo di Bassi (died 1552), who wished to return to the literal observance of the rule of St Francis. The Capuchin rule was drawn up 1529 and the order recognized by the pope 1619. The name was derived from the French term for the brown habit and pointed hood (*capuche*) that they wore. The order has been involved in missionary activity.

capybara world's largest rodent *Hydrochoerus hydrochaeris*, up to 4 ft/1.3 m long and 110 lb/50 kg in weight. It is found in South America, and belongs to the guinea-pig family. The capybara inhabits marshes and dense vegetation around water. It has thin, yellowish hair, swims well, and can rest underwater with just eyes, ears, and nose above the surface.

car popular name for ▷automobile.

caracal cat *Felis caracal* related to the ▷lynx. It has long black ear tufts, a short tail, and short reddishfawn fur. It lives in bush and desert country in Africa, Arabia, and India, hunting birds and small mammals at night. Head and body length is about 2.5 ft/75 cm.

Caracalla Marcus Aurelius Antoninus AD 186–

carbohydrate *A molecule of the polysaccharide glycogen (animal starch) is formed from linked glucose ($C_6H_{12}O_6$) molecules.*

217. Roman emperor. He succeeded his father Septimus Severus AD 211, ruled with cruelty and extravagance, and was assassinated. He was nicknamed after the Celtic cloak (*caracalla*) that he wore.

With the support of the army he murdered his brother Geta and thousands of his followers to secure sole possession of the throne. During his reign, Roman citizenship was given to all subjects of the empire. He built on a grandiose scale (the Baths of Caracalla in Rome, however, were begun by Septimius AD 206–07 and completed by Caracalla's successors -Caracalla inaugurated them).

Caracas chief city and capital of Venezuela, situated on the Andean slopes, 8 mi/13 km S of its port La Guaira on the Caribbean coast; population of metropolitan area (1989) 3,373,100. Founded 1567, it is now a large industrial and commercial center, notably for oil companies.

It is the birthplace of Simón ▷Bolivar. It has many fine buildings, including Venezuela University. The city has suffered several severe earthquakes.

carambola small evergreen tree *Averrhoa carambola* of SE Asia. The fruits, called **star fruit**, are yellowish, about 4 in/12 cm long, with a five-pointed star-shaped cross-section. They may be eaten raw, cooked, or pickled, and are juicily acidic. The juice is also used to remove stains from hands and clothes.

carat unit for measuring the mass of precious stones, derived from the Arabic word *quirrat*, meaning "seed." Originally, 1 carat was the weight of a carob seed; it is now taken as 0.00705 oz/0.2 g, and is part of the troy system of weights. Also, an alternate spelling of ▷karat.

Caravaggio Michelangelo Merisi da 1573–1610. Italian early Baroque painter, active in Rome 1592–1606, then in Naples, and finally in Malta. His life was as dramatic as his art (he had to leave Rome after killing a man). He created a forceful style, using contrasts of light and shade and focusing closely on the subject figures, sometimes using dramatic foreshortening.

He was born in Caravaggio, near Milan. His compositions were unusual, strong designs in the two-dimensional plane with little extraneous material. He painted from models, making portraits of real Roman people as saints and madonnas, which caused outrage. An example is *The Conversion of St Paul* (Sta Maria del Popolo, Rome).

He had a number of direct imitators (Caravaggisti), and several Dutch and Flemish artists who visited Rome, including Honthorst and Terbrugghen, were inspired by him.

caraway herb *Carum carvi* of the carrot family Umbelliferae. Native to northern temperate Eurasian regions, it is grown for its spicy, aromatic seeds, which are used in cooking, medicine, and perfumery.

carbide compound of carbon and one other chemical element, usually a metal, silicon, or boron.

Calcium carbide (CaC_2) can be used as the starting material for many basic organic chemical syntheses, by the addition of water and generation of ethyne (acetylene). Some metallic carbides are used in engineering because of their extreme hardness and strength. Tungsten carbide is an essential ingredient of carbide tools and high-speed tools. The "carbide process" was used during World War II to make organic chemicals from coal rather than from oil.

carbohydrate chemical compound composed of carbon, hydrogen, and oxygen, with the basic formula $C_m(H_2O)_n$, and related compounds with the same basic structure but modified ▷functional groups. As sugar and starch, carbohydrates form a major energy-providing part of the human diet.

The simplest carbohydrates are sugars (**monosaccharides**, such as glucose and fructose, and **disaccharides**, such as sucrose), which are soluble compounds, some with a sweet taste. When these basic sugar units are joined together in long chains or branching structures they form **polysaccharides**, such as starch and glycogen, which often serve as food stores in living organisms. Even more complex carbohydrates are known, including ▷chitin, which is found in the cell walls of fungi and the hard outer skeletons of insects, and ▷cellulose, which makes up the cell walls of plants. Carbohydrates form the chief foodstuffs of herbivorous animals.

carbolic acid common name for the aromatic compound ▷phenol.

carbon (Latin *carbo* (*carbonaris*) "coal") non-metallic element, symbol C, atomic number 6, atomic weight 12.011. It is one of the most widely distributed elements, both inorganically and organically, and occurs in combination with other elements in all plants and animals. The atoms of carbon can link with one another in rings or chains, giving rise to innumerable complex compounds. It occurs in nature (1) in the pure state in three crystalline forms of graphite, diamond and various fullerenes; (2) as calcium carbonate ($CaCO_3$) in carbonaceous rocks such as chalk and limestone; (3) as carbon dioxide (CO_2) in the atmosphere; and (4) as hydrocarbons in the fossil fuels petroleum, coal, and natural gas. Noncrystalline forms of pure carbon include charcoal and coal.

When added to steel, carbon forms a wide range of alloys. In its elemental form, it is widely used as a moderator in nuclear reactors; as colloidal graphite it is a good lubricant, which, when deposited on a surface in a vacuum, obviates photoelectric and secondary emission of electrons. The radioactive isotope C-14 (half-life 5,730 years) is widely used in archeological dating and as a tracer in biological research.

1. the basic unit of the diamond structure
2. *diamond*, a giant three-dimensional structure
3. *graphite*, a two-dimensional structure

carbon *Molecular structure of diamond and graphite.*

Analysis of interstellar dust has led to the discovery of discrete carbon molecules, each containing 60 carbon atoms. The C_{60} molecules have been named buckminsterfullerenes because of their structural similarity to the geodesic domes designed by US architect and engineer Buckminster Fuller.

Carbonari secret revolutionary society in S Italy in the first half of the 19th century that advocated constitutional government. The movement spread to N Italy but support dwindled after the formation of ◊Mazzini's nationalist Young Italy movement, although it helped prove the way for the unification of Italy (see ◊Risorgimento).

carbonate $CO_3{}^{2-}$ ion formed when carbon dioxide dissolves in water; any salt formed by this ion and another chemical element, usually a metal.

Carbon dioxide (CO_2) dissolves sparingly in water (for example, when rain falls through the air) to form carbonic acid (H_2CO_3), which unites with various basic substances to form carbonates. Calcium carbonate ($CaCO_3$) (chalk, limestone, and marble) is one of the most abundant carbonates known, being a constituent of mollusk shells and the hard outer skeletons of crustaceans.

carbon cycle the sequence by which carbon circulates and is recycled through the natural world. The carbon element from carbon dioxide in the atmosphere is taken up during the process of ◊photosynthesis, and the oxygen component is released back into the atmosphere. Some of this carbon becomes locked up in coal and petroleum and other sediments. Carbon (as carbon dioxide) is released during aerobic respiration of plants and animals. New carbon also enters the atmosphere during volcanic eruptions. Today, the carbon cycle is being altered by the increased consumption of fossil fuels and the burning of large tracts of tropical forests, as a result of which levels of carbon dioxide are building up in the atmosphere and probably contributing to the ◊greenhouse effect.

carbon dating alternate name for ◊radiocarbon dating.

carbon dioxide CO_2 colorless, odorless gas, slightly soluble in water and denser than air. It is formed by the complete oxidation of carbon.

It is produced by living things during the processes of respiration and the decay of organic matter. Its increasing density contributes to the ◊greenhouse effect and ◊global warming.

Britain has 1% of the world's population, yet it produces 3% of CO_2 emissions; the US has 5% of the world's population and produces 25% of CO_2 emissions.

carbon fiber fine, black, silky filament of pure carbon produced by heat treatment from a special grade of Courtelle acrylic fiber, used for reinforcing plastics. The resulting composite is very stiff and, weight for weight, has four times the strength of high-tensile steel. It is used in the aerospace industry, automobiles, and electrical and sports equipment.

Carboniferous period of geological time 360–286 million years ago, the fifth period of the Paleozoic era. In the US it is divided into two periods: the Mississippian (lower) and the Pennsylvanian (upper). Typical of the lower-Carboniferous rocks are shallow-water ◊limestone, while upper-Carboniferous rocks have ◊delta deposits with ◊coal (hence the name). Amphibians were abundant, and reptiles evolved during this period.

carbon monoxide CO colorless, odorless gas formed when carbon is oxidized in a limited supply of air. It is a poisonous constituent of car exhaust fumes, forming a stable compound with haemoglobin in the blood, thus preventing the haemoglobin from transporting oxygen to the body tissues.

In industry, carbon monoxide is used as a reducing agent in metallurgical processes—for example, in the extraction of iron in ◊blast furnaces—and is a constituent of cheap fuels such as water gas.

Carborundum trademark for a very hard, black abrasive, consisting of silicon carbide (SiC), an artificial compound of carbon and silicon. It is harder than ◊corundum but not as hard as ◊diamond.

It was first produced 1891 by US chemist Edward Acheson (1856–1931).

carbuncle in medicine, a bacterial infection of the skin, similar to a ◊boil but deeper and more widespread. It is treated with drawing salves, lancing, or antibiotics.

carburation any process involving chemical combination with carbon, especially the mixing or charging of a gas, such as air, with volatile compounds of carbon (gasoline, kerosene, or fuel oil) in order to increase potential heat energy during combustion. Carburation applies to combustion in the cylinders of reciprocating gasoline engines of the types used in aircraft, road vehicles, or marine vessels. The device by which the liquid fuel is atomized and mixed with air is called a *carburettor*.

Carcassonne city in SW France, capital of Aude *département*, on the river Aude, which divides it into the ancient and modern town; population (1982) 42,450. Its medieval fortifications (restored) are the finest in France.

Carchemish (now *Karkamis*, Turkey) center of the ◊Hittite New Empire (c. 1400–1200 BC) on the river Euphrates, 50 mi/80 km NE of Aleppo, and taken by Sargon II of Assyria 717 BC. Nebuchadnezzar II of Babylon defeated the Egyptians here 605 BC.

carcinogen any agent that increases the chance of a cell becoming cancerous (see ◊cancer), including various chemical compounds, some viruses, X-rays, and other forms of ionizing radiation. The term is often used more narrowly to mean chemical carcinogens only.

carcinoma malignant ◊tumor arising from the skin, the glandular tissues, or the mucous membranes that line the gut and lungs.

Cardano Girolamo 1501–1576. Italian physician, mathematician, philosopher, astrologer, and gambler. He is remembered for his theory of chance, his use of algebra, and many medical publications, notably the first clinical description of typhus fever.

Born in Pavia, he became professor of medicine there 1543, and wrote two works on physics and natural science, *De Subtilitate rerum* 1551 and *De Varietate rerum* 1557.

Cárdenas Lázaro 1895–1970. Mexican center-left politician and general, president 1934–40. A civil servant in early life, Cárdenas took part in the revolutionary campaigns 1915–29 that followed the fall of President Díaz (1830–1915). As president of the republic, he attempted to achieve the goals of the revolution by building schools, distributing land to the peasants, and developing transport and industry. He was minister of defense 1943–45.

cardiac pertaining to the ◊heart.

Cardiff (Welsh *Caerdydd*) capital of Wales (from 1955) and administrative headquarters of South and Mid Glamorgan, at the mouth of the Taff, Rhymney, and Ely rivers; population (1991) 272,600. Besides steelworks, there are car-component, flour-milling, paper, cigar, and other industries.

The city dates from Roman times, the later town being built around a Norman castle. The castle was the residence of the earls and marquesses of Bute from the 18th century and was given to the city 1947 by the fifth marquess. Coal was exported until the 1920s. As coal declined, iron and steel exports continued to grow, and an import trade in timber, grain and flour, tobacco, meat, and citrus fruit developed.

Cardin Pierre 1922– . French pioneering fashion designer whose clothes are bold and fantastic. He was the first to launch menswear (1960) and ready-to-wear collections (1963) and has given his name to a perfume.

Cardin moved to Paris 1944 and worked in the fashion houses of Madame Paquin, Elsa Schiaparelli, and Christian ◊Dior. He began making theatrical costumes 1949, and launched his first couture collection 1957.

cardinal in the Roman Catholic church, the highest rank next to the pope. Cardinals act as an advisory body to the pope and elect him. Their red hat is the badge of office. The number of cardinals has varied; there were 151 in 1989.

Originally a cardinal was any priest in charge of a major parish, but in 1567 the term was confined to the members of the Sacred College, 120 of whom (below the age of 80) elect the pope and are themselves elected by him (since 1973). They advise on all matters of doctrine, canonizations, convocation of councils, liturgy, and temporal business.

cardinal number in mathematics, one of the series of numbers 0, 1, 2, 3, 4, ... Cardinal numbers relate to quantity, whereas ordinal numbers (first, second, third, fourth, . . .) relate to order.

cardioid heart-shaped curve traced out by a point on the circumference of a circle, resulting from the circle rolling around the edge of another circle of the same diameter.

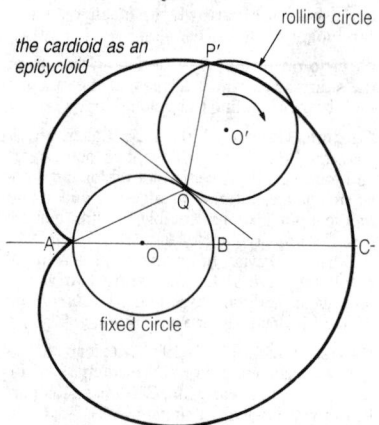

the cardioid as an epicycloid

rolling circle
P'
O'
Q
A   O   B   C
fixed circle

cardioid *The cardioid is the curve formed when one circle rolls around the edge of another circle of the same size.*

The polar equation of the cardioid is of the form $r = a(1 + \cos \theta)$.

Cardozo Benjamin Nathan 1870–1938. US jurist and Supreme Court justice. Cardozo was named to the US Supreme Court by President Hoover 1932. During the F D Roosevelt administration, he upheld the constitutionality of New Deal programs, as in *Ashwander* v *Tennessee Valley Authority* 1936 and the Social Security case *Helvering* v *Davis* 1937.

Born in New York, Cardozo was educated at Columbia University and was admitted to the bar 1891. After a brief career as a corporate counsel, he was elected to the New York Supreme Court 1913. Appointed associate justice of the court of appeals 1917, he became its chief judge 1926.

cards common name for �Dplaying cards.

Carducci Giosuè 1835–1907. Italian poet. Born in Tuscany, he was appointed professor of Italian literature at Bologna 1860, and won distinction through his lecturing, critical work, and poetry. His revolutionary *Inno a Satana/ Hymn to Satan* 1865 was followed by several other volumes of verse, in which his nationalist sympathies are apparent. Nobel Prize 1906.

cargo cult Melanesian religious movement, dating from the 19th century. Adherents believe the arrival of cargo is through the agency of a messianic spirit figure, heralding a new paradise free of white dominance. The movement became active during and after World War II with the apparently miraculous dropping of supplies from airplanes.

Carib member of a group of ⟨⟩American Indian people of the northern coast of South America and the islands of the southern West Indies in the Caribbean. Those who moved north to take the islands from the Arawak Indians were alleged by the conquering Spaniards to be fierce cannibals. In 1796, the English in the West Indies deported most of them to Roatan Island, off Honduras. Carib languages belong to the Ge-Pano-Carib family.

Caribbean Community and Common Market (CARICOM) organization for economic and foreign policy coordination in the Caribbean region, established by the Treaty of Chaguaramas 1973 to replace the former Caribbean Free Trade Association. Its members are Antigua and Barbuda, Bahamas, Barbados, Belize, Dominica, Grenada, Guyana,

Jamaica, Montserrat, St Christopher—Nevis, St Lucia, St Vincent and the Grenadines, and Trinidad and Tobago. The British Virgin Islands and the Turks and Caicos Islands are associate members, and the Dominican Republic, Haiti, Mexico, Puerto Rico, Suriname, and Venezuela are observers. CARICOM headquarters are in Kingston, Jamaica.

Caribbean Sea western part of the Atlantic Ocean between the south coast of North America and the north coasts of South America. Central America is to the west and the West Indies are the islands within the sea, which is about 1,700 mi/2,740 km long and 400–900 mi/650–1,500 km wide. It is from here that the ⟨⟩Gulf Stream turns toward Europe.

The Caribbean Sea was named after the Carib Indians who inhabited the area when it was discovered by Spanish explorers, beginning with Christopher Columbus in 1492. It is a major maritime trade route for oil, other raw materials, seafood, and tropical agricultural products. It is heavily polluted by untreated sewage, which destroys mangrove forests and coral reefs.

A number of continental American nations lie on its shores, and it contains the West Indies archipelago, which consists of independent island nations as well as dependencies of the US, France, the Netherlands, and the UK.

caribou the ⟨⟩reindeer of North America.

caricature exaggerated portrayal of individuals or types, aiming to ridicule or otherwise expose the subject. Classical and medieval examples survive. Artists of the 18th, 19th, and 20th centuries have often used caricature as a way of satirizing society and politics. Notable exponents include the French artist Honoré Daumier and the German George Grosz.

Grotesque drawings have been discovered in Pompeii and Herculaneum, and Pliny refers to a grotesque portrait of the poet Hipponax. Humorous drawings were executed by the ⟨⟩Carracci family and their Bolognese followers (the Italian "eclectic" school of the 16th century). In 1830, Charles Philipon (1800–1862) founded in Paris *La Caricature*, probably the first periodical to specialize in caricature.

CARICOM abbreviation for ⟨⟩*Caribbean Community and Common Market*.

caries decay and disintegration, usually of the substance of teeth (cavity) or bone. It is caused by acids produced when the bacteria that live in the mouth break down sugars in the food. Fluoride, a low sugar intake, and regular brushing are all protective. Caries form mainly in the 45 minutes following an intake of sugary food, so the most dangerous diet for the teeth is one in which frequent sugary snacks and drinks are consumed.

Carina constellation of the southern hemisphere, represented as a ship's keel. Its brightest star is Canopus; it also contains Eta Carinae, a massive and highly luminous star embedded in a gas cloud, perhaps 8,000 light-years away. It has varied unpredictably in the past; some astronomers think it is likely to explode as a supernova within 10,000 years.

Carinthia (German *Kärnten*) federal province of Alpine SE Austria, bordering Italy and Slovenia in the south; capital Klagenfurt; area 3,667 sq mi/9,500 sq km; population (1987) 542,000. It was an independent duchy from 976 and a possession of the Hapsburg dynasty 1276–1918.

Carl XVI Gustaf 1946– . King of Sweden from 1973. He succeeded his grandfather

Gustaf VI, his father having been killed in an airplane crash 1947. Under the new Swedish constitution, which became effective on his grandfather's death, the monarchy was stripped of all power at his accession.

Carlisle city in Cumbria, NW England, situated on the river Eden at the west end of Hadrian's Wall, administrative center of the county; population (1991) 99,800. It is a leading railroad center; textiles, engineering, and cookie making are the chief industries. There is a Norman cathedral and a castle. The bishopric dates from 1133.

Carlisle city in S Pennsylvania, in the Cumberland Valley, SW of Harrisburg; seat of Cumberland county; population (1990) 18,400. Manufactures include electronics and steel products. The US Army War College and Dickinson College are here.

Carlist supporter of the claims of the Spanish pretender Don Carlos de Bourbon (1788–1855), and his descendants, to the Spanish crown. The Carlist revolt continued, primarily in the Basque provinces, until 1839. In 1977 the Carlist political party was legalized and Carlos Hugo de Bourbon Parma (1930–) renounced his claim as pretender and became reconciled with King Juan Carlos. See also ⟨⟩Bourbon.

Carlos I 1863–1908. King of Portugal, of the Braganza-Coburg line, from 1889 until he was assassinated in Lisbon with his elder son Luis. He was succeeded by his younger son Manuel.

Carlos Don 1545–1568. Spanish prince. Son of Philip II, he was recognized as heir to the thrones of Castile and Aragon but became mentally unstable and had to be placed under restraint following a plot to assassinate his father. His story was the subject of plays by Friedrich von Schiller, Vittorio Alfieri, Thomas Otway, and others.

Carlos four kings of Spain; see ⟨⟩Charles.

Carlow county in the Republic of Ireland, in the province of Leinster; county town Carlow; area 347 sq mi/900 sq km; population (1991) 40,900. Mostly flat except for mountains in the south, the land is fertile, and well suited to dairy farming.

Carlson Chester 1906–1968. US scientist who invented ⟨⟩xerography. A research worker at Bell Telephone, he lost his job 1930 during the Depression and set to work on his own to develop an efficient copying machine. By 1938 he had invented the Xerox photocopier.

Carlsson Ingvar (Gösta) 1934– . Swedish socialist politician, leader of the Social Democratic Party, deputy prime minister 1982–86 and prime minister 1986–91.

After studying in Sweden and the US, Carlsson became president of the Swedish Social Democratic Youth League 1961. He was elected to the Riksdag (parliament) 1964 and became a minister 1969. With the return to power of the Social Democrats 1982, Carlsson became deputy to Prime Minister Palme and, on his assassination 1986, succeeded him. He lost his majority Sept 1991 and resigned.

Carlucci Frank (Charles) 1930– . US politician. A former diplomat and deputy director of the CIA, he was national security adviser 1986–87 and defense secretary 1987–89 under Reagan, supporting Soviet–US arms reduction.

Educated at Princeton and Harvard, Carlucci, after fighting in the Korean War, was a career diplomat during the later 1950s and 1960s. He returned to the US 1969 to work under presidents Nixon, Ford, and Carter, his posts including US ambassador to Portugal and deputy director of the CIA. An apolitical Atlanticist, Carlucci found himself out of step with the hawks in the Reagan administration, and left to work in industry after barely a year as deputy secretary of defense. In Dec 1986, after the ⟡Irangate scandal, he replaced John ⟡Poindexter as national security adviser.

Carlyle Thomas 1795–1881. Scottish essayist and social historian. His works include *Sartor Resartus* 1833–34, describing his loss of Christian belief, *The French Revolution* 1837, *Chartism* 1839, and *Past and Present* 1843. His prose style was idiosyncratic, encompassing grand, thunderous rhetoric and deliberate obscurity.

Carlyle was born at Ecclefechan in Dumfriesshire. Leaving Edinburgh University without a degree, he devoted several years to intensive study of German literature, translating Goethe and writing a life of Schiller. In 1821 he passed through the spiritual crisis described in *Sartor Resartus*. He married Jane Baillie Welsh (1801–1866) in 1826 and they moved to her farm at Craigenputtock, where *Sartor Resartus* was written. His reputation was established with *The French Revolution*. The series of lectures he gave 1837–40 included *On Heroes, Hero-Worship and The Heroic in History* (published 1841). He also wrote several pamphlets, including *Chartism*, attacking the doctrine of ⟡laissez-faire; the notable *Letters and Speeches of Cromwell* 1845; and the miniature life of his friend, John Sterling 1851. He was also a friend of J S ⟡Mill and Ralph Waldo ⟡Emerson. Carlyle began his *History of Frederick the Great* 1858–65, and after the death of his wife 1866 edited her letters 1883 and prepared his *Reminiscences* 1881, which shed an unfavorable light on his character and his neglect of her, for which he could not forgive himself. His house in Cheyne Row, Chelsea, London, where they lived from 1834, is a museum.

Carmelite order mendicant order of friars in the Roman Catholic church. The order was founded on Mount Carmel in Palestine by Berthold, a crusader from Calabria, about 1155, and spread to Europe in the 13th century. The Carmelites have devoted themselves largely to missionary work and mystical theology. They are known as *White Friars* because of the white overmantle they wear (over a brown habit).

Traditionally Carmelites originated in the days of Elijah, who according to the Old Testament is supposed to have lived on Mount Carmel. Following the rule which the patriarch of Jerusalem drew up for them about 1210, they lived as hermits in separate huts. About 1240, the Muslim conquests compelled them to move from Palestine and they spread to the west, mostly in France and England, where the order began to live communally. The most momentous reform movement was initiated by St ⟡Teresa. In 1562 she founded a convent in Avila and, with the cooperation of St John of the Cross and others, she established a stricter order of barefoot friars and nuns (the *Discalced Carmelites*).

Carnac Megalithic site in Brittany, France, where remains of tombs and stone alignments of the period 2000–1500 BC have been found. The largest of the latter has 1,000 stones up to 13 ft/4 m high arranged in 11 rows, with a circle at the western end. Named after the village of Carnac; population about 4,000.

Carnap Rudolf 1891–1970. German philosopher, in the US from 1935, an exponent of logical ⟡empiricism. He was a member of the Vienna Circle, who adopted Ernst ⟡Mach as their guide. His books include *The Logical Syntax of Language* 1934 and *Meaning and Necessity* 1956. He was professor of philosophy at the University of California 1954–62.

carnassial tooth powerful scissorlike pair of molars, found in all mammalian carnivores except seals. Carnassials are formed from an upper premolar and lower molar, and are shaped to produce a sharp cutting surface. Carnivores such as dogs transfer meat to the back of the mouth, where the carnassials slice up the food ready for swallowing.

Carnatic region of SE India, in Madras state. It is situated between the Eastern Ghats and the Coromandel Coast and was formerly a leading trading center.

carnation any of numerous double-flowered cultivated varieties of a plant *Dianthus caryophyllus* of the pink family. The flowers smell like cloves; they are divided into flake, bizarre, and picotees, according to whether the petals exhibit one or more colors on their white ground, have the color dispersed in strips, or have a colored border to the petals.

carnauba palm *Copernicia cerifera*, native to South America. It produces fine timber and a hard wax, used for polishes and lipsticks.

Carnegie Andrew 1835–1919. US industrialist and philanthropist, born in Scotland, who developed the Pittsburgh iron and steel industries, making the US the world's leading producer. He endowed public libraries, education, and various research trusts.

Born in Dunfermline, Scotland, he was taken by his parents to the US 1848 and at 14 became a telegraph boy in Pittsburgh. Subsequently he became a railroad employee, rose to be superintendent, introduced sleeping-cars, and invested successfully in oil. He developed the Pittsburgh iron and steel industries, and built up a vast empire that he disposed of to the United States Steel Trust 1901. Then he moved to Skibo castle in Sutherland, Scotland, and used his wealth to endow libraries and universities, the Carnegie Endowment for International Peace, and other good causes. On his death the Carnegie Trusts continued his benevolent activities. *Carnegie Hall* in New York, opened 1891 as the Music Hall, was renamed 1898 because of his large contribution to its construction.

Carnegie was attacked by some as an exploiter of labor and as an unscrupulous business competitor. However, his innovations transformed the US steel industry, and his philanthropies have had lasting effect.

Carnegie Dale 1888–1955. US author and teacher who wrote the best-selling self-help book *How to Win Friends and Influence People* 1937.

His courses in public speaking, which drew huge audiences, first won him fame, and he was asked to publish them as a book. His other books include *Little Known Facts About Well Known People* 1934 and *How to Stop Worrying and Start Living* 1948.

carnelian semiprecious gemstone variety of ⟡chalcedony consisting of quartz (silica) with iron impurities, which give it a translucent red color. It is found mainly in Brazil, India, and Japan.

Carniola former crownland and duchy of Austria, most of which was included in Slovenia, part of the kingdom of the Serbs, Croats, and Slovenes (later Yugoslavia) 1919. The western districts of Idrija and Postojna, then allocated to Italy, were transferred to Yugoslavia 1947.

carnivore animal that eats other animals. Although the term is sometimes confined to those that eat the flesh of ⟡vertebrate prey, it is often used more broadly to include any animal that eats other animals, even microscopic ones. Carrion-eaters may or may not be included.

The mammalian order Carnivora includes civet cats, raccoons, cats, dogs, and bears.

Carnot Lazare Nicolas Marguerite 1753–1823. French general and politician. A member of the National Convention in the French Revolution, he organized the armies of the republic. He was war minister 1800–01 and minister of the interior 1815 under Napoleon. His work on fortification, *De la Défense de places fortes* 1810, became a military textbook. Minister of the interior during the ⟡Hundred Days, he was proscribed at the restoration of the monarchy and retired to Germany.

Carnot (Nicolas Leonard) Sadi 1796–1832. French scientist and military engineer who founded the science of ⟡thermodynamics. His pioneering work was *Réflexions sur la puissance motrice du feu/On the Motive Power of Fire*.

Carnot cycle series of changes in the physical condition of a gas in a reversible heat engine, necessarily in the following order: (1) isothermal expansion (without change of temperature), (2) adiabatic expansion (without change of heat content), (3) isothermal compression, and (4) adiabatic compression.

The principles derived from a study of this cycle are important in the fundamentals of heat and ⟡thermodynamics.

carnotite potassium uranium vanadate, $K_2(UO_2)_2(VO_4)_2 \cdot 3H_2O$, a radioactive ore of vanadium and uranium with traces of radium. A yellow powdery mineral, it is mined chiefly in the Colorado Plateau; Radium Hill, Australia; and Shaba, Zaire.

carob small Mediterranean tree *Ceratonia siliqua* of the legume family Leguminosae. Its pods, 8 in/20 cm long, are used as animal fodder; they are also the source of a chocolate substitute.

carol song that in medieval times was associated with a round dance; now those that are sung at annual festivals, such as Easter and Christmas.

Christmas carols were common as early as the 15th century. The custom of singing carols from house to house, collecting gifts, was called wassailing. Many carols, such as "God Rest You Merry Gentlemen" and "The First Noel," date from the 16th century or earlier.

Carol two kings of Romania:

Carol I 1839–1914. First king of Romania 1881–1914. A prince of the house of Hohenzollern-Sigmaringen, he was invited to become prince of Romania, then part of the Ottoman Empire, 1866. In 1877, in alliance with Russia, he declared war on Turkey, and the Congress of Berlin 1878 recognized Romanian independence.

He promoted economic development and industrial reforms but failed to address rural problems. This led to a peasant rebellion 1907 which he brutally crushed. At the beginning of World War I, King Carol declared Romania's neutrality but his successor (his nephew King Ferdinand I) declared for the Allies.

Carol II 1893–1953. King of Romania 1930–40. Son of King Ferdinand, he married Princess Helen of Greece and they had a son, Michael. In 1925 he renounced the succession because of his affair with Elena Lupescu and went into exile in Paris. Michael succeeded to the throne 1927, but in 1930 Carol returned to Romania and was proclaimed king. In 1938 he introduced a new constitution under which he practically became an absolute ruler. He was forced to abdicate by the pro-Nazi ◊Iron Guard Sept 1940, went to Mexico, and married his mistress 1947.

Caroline of Brunswick 1768–1821. Queen of George IV of Great Britain, who unsuccessfully attempted to divorce her on his accession to the throne 1820.

After they separated 1796, he forbade her access to their daughter Charlotte and kept her from the coronation 1821; her death a few weeks later led to riots.

Carolines scattered archipelago in Micronesia, Pacific Ocean, consisting of over 500 coral islets; area 463 sq mi/1,200 sq km. The chief islands are Ponape, Kusai, and Truk in the eastern group, and Yap and Belau in the western group.

The Carolines are well watered and productive. Occupied by Germany 1899, and Japan 1914, and mandated by the League of Nations to Japan 1919, they were fortified, contrary to the terms of the mandate. Under Allied air attack in World War II they remained unconquered. In 1947 they became part of the US trust territory of the ◊Pacific Islands.

Carolingian dynasty Frankish dynasty descending from Pepin the Short, King of the Franks from 751 (died 768) and named after his son Charlemagne; its last ruler was Louis V of France (reigned 966–87), who was followed by Hugh ◊Capet, first ruler of the Capetian dynasty.

carotene naturally occurring pigment of the ◊carotenoid group. Carotenes produce the orange, yellow, and red colors of carrots, tomatoes, oranges, and crustaceans.

carotenoid any of a group of yellow, orange, red, or brown pigments found in many living organisms, particularly in the ◊chloroplasts of plants. There are two main types, the *carotenes* and the *xanthophylls*. Both types are long-chain lipids (◊fats).

Some carotenoids act as accessory pigments in ◊photosynthesis, and in certain algae they are the principal light-absorbing pigments functioning more efficiently than ◊chlorophyll in low-intensity light. Carotenoids can also occur in organs such as petals, roots, and fruits, giving them their characteristic color, as in the yellow and orange petals of wallflowers *Cheiranthus*. They are also responsible for the autumn colors of leaves, persisting longer than the green chlorophyll, which masks them during the summer.

Carothers Wallace 1896–1937. US chemist who carried out research into polymerization. By 1930 he had discovered that some polymers were fiber-forming, and in 1937 he produced ◊nylon.

carotid artery one of a pair of major blood vessels, one on each side of the neck, supplying blood to the head.

carp fish *Cyprinus carpio* found all over the world. It commonly grows to 1.8 ft/50 cm and 7 lb/3 kg, but may be even larger. It lives in lakes, ponds, and slow rivers. The wild form is drab, but cultivated forms may be golden, or may have few large scales (mirror carp) or be scaleless (leather carp). *Koi* carp are highly prized and can grow up to 3 ft/1 m long with a distinctive pink, red, white, or black coloring.

A large proportion of European freshwater fish belong to the carp family, Cyprinidae, and related fishes are found in Asia, Africa, and North America. The carp's fast growth, large size, and ability to live in still water with little oxygen have made it a good fish to farm, and it has been cultivated for hundreds of years and spread by human agency. Members of this family have a single non-spiny dorsal fin, pelvic fins well back on the body, and toothless jaws, although teeth in the throat form an efficient grinding apparatus. Minnows, roach, rudd, and many others, including goldfish, belong to this family. Chinese *grass carp Ctenopharyngodon idella* have been introduced (one sex only) to European rivers for weed control.

Carpaccio Vittorio 1450/60–1525/26. Italian painter known for scenes of his native Venice. His series *The Legend of St Ursula* 1490–98 (Accademia, Venice) is full of detail of contemporary Venetian life. His other great series is the lives of saints George and Jerome 1502–07 (S Giorgio degli Schiavoni, Venice).

Carpathian Mountains Central European mountain system, forming a semicircle through Czechoslovakia–Poland–Ukraine–Romania, 900 mi/1,450 km long. The central *Tatra mountains* on the Czechoslovakia–Poland frontier include the highest peak, Gerlachovka, 8,737 ft/2,663 m.

carpel female reproductive unit in flowering plants (◊angiosperms). It usually comprises an ◊ovary containing one or more ovules, the stalk or style, and a ◊stigma at its top which receives the pollen. A flower may have one or more carpels, and they may be separate or fused together. Collectively the carpels of a flower are known as the ◊gynoecium.

Carpentaria, Gulf of shallow gulf opening out of the Arafura Sea, north of Australia. It was discovered by Tasman 1606 and named 1623 in honor of Pieter Carpentier, governor-general of the Dutch East Indies.

Carpenter John 1948– . US director of horror and science-fiction films, notable for such films as *Dark Star* 1974 and *Assault on Precinct 13* 1976.

He continued with such films as *Halloween* 1978, *The Thing* 1982, *Christine* 1983 (adapted from a Stephen King story about a vindictive car), the underrated, gentle *Starman* 1984, *They Live* 1988, and *The Fog* 1980. He composes his own film scores, which have often added to the atmosphere of menace that haunt his more scary movies.

carpet thick textile fabric, generally made of wool, used for covering floors and stairs. There is a long tradition of fine handmade carpets in the Middle East, India, Pakistan, and China. Western carpets are machine-made. Carpets and rugs have also often been made in the home as a pastime, cross and tent stitch on canvas being widely used in the 18th and 19th centuries.

history The earliest known carpets date from *c.* 500 BC and were excavated at Passypych in SE Siberia, but it was not until the later Middle Ages that carpets reached W Europe from Turkey. Persian carpets (see ◊Islamic art), which reached a still unrivaled peak of artistry in the 15th and 16th centuries, were rare in Britain until the mid-19th century, reaching North America a little later. The subsequent demand led to a revival of organized carpet-making in Persia. Europe copied oriental technique, but developed Western designs: France produced beautiful work at the Savonnerie and Beauvais establishments under Louis XIV and Louis XV; and Exeter, Axminster, London, and Wilton became British carpet-making centers in the 18th century, though Kidderminster is the biggest center today. The first carpet factory in the US was established in Philadelphia 1791; it is still a large carpet-producing center.

carpetbagger in US history, derogatory name for any of the entrepreneurs and politicians from the North who moved to the Southern states during ◊Reconstruction 1861–65 after the Civil War.

With the votes of newly enfranchised blacks and some local white people (called scalawags), they won posts in newly created Republican state governments, but were resented by many white Southerners as outsiders and opportunists. The term thus came to mean a corrupt outsider who profits from an area's political instability, although some arrivals had good motives. They were so called because they were supposed to own no property except what they carried in their small satchels made of carpeting.

Carracci Italian family of painters in Bologna, whose forte was murals and ceilings. The foremost of them, *Annibale Carracci* (1560–1609), decorated the Farnese Palace, Rome, with a series of mythological paintings united by simulated architectural ornamental surrounds (completed 1604).

Ludovico Carracci (1555–1619), with his cousin *Agostino Carracci* (1557–1602), founded Bologna's Academy of Art. Agostino collaborated with his brother Annibale on the Farnese Palace decorative scheme, which paved the way for a host of elaborate murals in Rome's palaces and churches, ever-more inventive illusions of pictorial depth and architectural ornament. Annibale also painted early landscapes such as *Flight into Egypt* 1603 (Doria Gallery, Rome).

Carradine John (Richmond Reed) 1906–1988. US film actor who often played sinister roles. He appeared in many major Hollywood films, such as *Stagecoach* 1939 and *The Grapes of Wrath* 1940, but was later seen mostly in horror B-movies, including *House of Frankenstein* 1944.

carragheen species of deep-reddish, branched seaweed *Chondrus crispus*. Named after Carragheen in Ireland, it is found on rocky shores on both sides of the Atlantic. It is exploited commercially in food and medicinal preparations and as cattle feed.

Carrara town in Tuscany, Italy, 37 mi/60 km NW of Livorno; population (1981) 66,000. It is known for its quarries of fine white marble, which were worked by the Romans, abandoned in the 5th century, and came into use again with the revival of sculpture and architecture in the 12th century.

Carrel Alexis 1873–1944. US surgeon born in France, whose experiments paved the way for organ transplant. Working at the Rockefeller Institute, New York City, he devised a way of joining blood vessels end to end (anastomosing). This was a key move in the development of transplant surgery, as was his work on keeping organs viable outside the body, for which he was awarded the Nobel Prize for Medicine 1912.

Carrhae, Battle of battle 53 BC in which the invading Roman general Crassus was defeated and killed by the Parthians. The ancient town of Carrhae is near Haran, Turkey.

carrier in medicine, anyone who harbors an infectious organism without ill effects but can pass the infection to others. The term is also applied to those who carry a recessive gene for a disease or defect without manifesting the condition.

Carroll Charles 1737–1832. American public official and signer of the Declaration of Independence.

Born in Annapolis, Maryland, Carroll was educated in France and England, returning to administer Carrollton, the family estate in Maryland. Because of his Catholic faith, he was not allowed to enter political life but was a strong supporter of the cause of American independence. In 1776 he accompanied Benjamin Franklin on a diplomatic mission to Canada and in July of that year, as a member of the Continental Congress, Carroll was one of the signers of the Declaration of Independence. Carroll became one of Maryland's first two US senators 1789–92.

Carroll Lewis. Adopted name of Charles Lutwidge Dodgson 1832–1898. English author of children's classics *Alice's Adventures in Wonderland* 1865 and its sequel *Through the Looking-Glass* 1872. Among later works was the mock-heroic nonsense poem *The Hunting of the Snark* 1876. An Oxford don, he also published mathematical works.

Dodgson, born in Daresbury, Cheshire, was a mathematics lecturer at Oxford 1855–81. There he first told the fantasy stories to Alice Liddell and her sisters, daughters of the dean of Christ Church. He was a prolific letter writer and inventor of games and puzzles, and was one of the pioneers of portrait photography.

carrot hardy European biennial *Daucus carota* of the family Umbelliferae. Cultivated since the 16th century for its edible root, it has a high sugar content and also contains ⟩carotene, which is converted by the human liver to vitamin A.

carrying capacity in ecology, the maximum number of animals of a given species that a particular area can support. When the carrying capacity is exceeded, there is insufficient food (or other resources) for the members of the population. The population may then be reduced by emigration, reproductive failure, or death through starvation.

Carson Kit (Christopher) 1809–68. US frontier settler, guide, and Indian agent, who later fought for the Federal side in the Civil War. Carson City, Nevada, was named after him.

Carson Rachel 1907–1964. US naturalist. An aquatic biologist with the US Fish and Wildlife Service 1936–49, she then became its editor-in-chief until 1952. In 1951 she published *The Sea Around Us* and in 1963 *Silent Spring*, attacking the indiscriminate use of pesticides.

Carson City capital of Nevada; population (1990) 40,400. Settled as a trading post 1851, it was named after the frontier guide Kit Carson 1858. It flourished as a boom town after the discovery of the nearby Comstock silver-ore lode 1859.

Cartagena city in the province of Murcia, Spain, on the Mediterranean; population (1991) 172,200. It is a seaport and naval base. It was founded as **Carthago Nova** about 225 BC by the Carthaginian Hasdrubal, son-in-law of Hamilcar Barca. It continued to flourish under the Romans and the Moors and was conquered by the Spanish 1269. It has a 13th-century cathedral and Roman remains.

Cartagena or **Cartagena de los Indes** port, industrial center, and capital of the department of Bolívar, NW Colombia; population (1985) 531,000. Plastics and chemicals are produced here.

It was founded 1533 and taken by English buccaneer Francis Drake 1586. A pipeline brings petroleum to the city from the De Manes oil fields.

cartel (German *Kartell* "a group") agreement among national or international firms to set mutually acceptable prices for their products. A cartel may restrict supply, or output, or raise prices to prevent entrants to the market and increase member profits. It therefore represents a form of ⟩oligopoly. ⟩OPEC, for example, is an oil cartel.

National laws concerning cartels differ widely, and international agreement is difficult to achieve. Both the Treaty of Rome and the Stockholm Convention, governing respectively the European Community (EC) and the European Free Trade Association (EFTA), contain provisions for control. In Germany, cartels are the most common form of monopolistic organization.

In the US, cartels are generally illegal. The Sherman Antitrust Act 1890 prohibited cartels, but legislation passed during the Great Depression permitted industries to enact "codes of fair competition." These were declared unconstitutional 1935, and public cartels in coal mining, oil production, and agriculture largely ended after World War II.

Carter Elliott (Cook) 1908– . US composer. His early work shows the influence of Igor ⟩Stravinsky, but after 1950 his music became increasingly intricate and densely written in a manner resembling Charles ⟩Ives. He invented "metrical modulation," which allows different instruments or groups to stay in touch while playing at different speeds. He wrote four string quartets, the *Symphony for Three Orchestras* 1967, and the song cycle *A Mirror on Which to Dwell* 1975.

Carter Jimmy (James Earl) 1924– . 39th president of the US 1977–81, a Democrat. In 1976 he narrowly wrested the presidency from Gerald Ford. Features of his presidency were the return of the Panama Canal Zone to Panama, the Camp David Agreements for peace in the Middle East, and the Iranian seizure of US embassy hostages. He was defeated by Ronald Reagan 1980.

Born in Plains, Georgia; he served in the navy, studied nuclear physics, and after a spell as a peanut farmer entered politics 1953.

Carter Doctrine assertion 1980 by President Carter of a vital US interest in the Persian Gulf region (prompted by the Soviet invasion of Afghanistan and instability in Iran): any outside attempt at control would be met by military force if necessary.

Cartesian coordinates in ⟩coordinate geometry, the components of a system used to show the position of a point on a plane (two dimensions) or in space (three dimensions)

with reference to a set of two or more axes. For a plane defined by two axes at right angles (a horizontal x-axis and a vertical y-axis), the coordinates of a point are given by its perpendicular distances from the y-axis and x-axis, written in the form (x,y). For example, a point P that lies three units from the y-axis and four units from the x-axis has Cartesian coordinates (3,4) (see ⟩abscissa). In three-dimensional coordinate geometry, points are located with reference to a third, z-axis.

The Cartesian coordinate system can be extended to any finite number of dimensions (axes), and is used thus in theoretical mathematics. It is named after the French mathematician, Descartes.

The system is useful in creating technical drawings of machines or buildings, and in computer-aided design (⟩CAD).

Carthage ancient Phoenician port in N Africa; it lay 10 mi/16 km N of Tunis, Tunisia. A leading trading center, it was in conflict with Greece from the 6th century BC, and then with Rome, and was destroyed by Roman forces 146 BC at the end of the ⟩**Punic Wars**. About 45 BC, Roman colonists settled in Carthage, and it became the wealthy capital of the province of Africa. After its capture by the Vandals AD 439 it was little more than a pirate stronghold. From 533 it formed part of the Byzantine Empire until its final destruction by Arabs 698, during their conquest in the name of Islam.

Carthage is said to have been founded 814 BC by Phoenician emigrants from Tyre, led by Princess Dido. It developed an extensive commerce throughout the Mediterranean and traded with the Tin Islands, whose location is believed to have been either Cornwall, England, or SW Spain. After the capture of Tyre by the Babylonians in the 6th century BC, it became the natural leader of the Phoenician colonies in N Africa and Spain, and there soon began a prolonged struggle with the Greeks, which centered mainly on Sicily, the east of which was dominated by Greek colonies, while the west was held by Carthaginian trading stations. About 540 BC the Carthaginians defeated a Greek attempt to land in Corsica, and 480 BC a Carthaginian attempt to conquer the whole of Sicily was defeated by the Greeks at Himera.

The population of Carthage before its destruction by the Romans is said to have numbered over 700,000. The constitution was an aristocratic republic with two chief magistrates elected annually and a senate of 300 life members. The religion was Phoenician, including the worship of the Moon goddess Tanit, the great Sun god Baal-Hammon, and the Tyrian Meklarth; human sacrifices were not unknown. The real strength of Carthage lay in its commerce and its powerful navy; its armies were for the most part mercenaries.

Carthusian order Roman Catholic order of monks and, later, nuns, founded by St Bruno 1084 at Chartreuse, near Grenoble, France. Living chiefly in unbroken silence, they ate one vegetarian meal a day and supported themselves by their own labors; the rule is still one of severe austerity.

Cartier Georges Étienne 1814–1873. French-Canadian politician. He fought against the British in the rebellion 1837, was elected to the Canadian parliament 1848, and was joint prime minister with John A Macdonald 1858–62. He brought Québec into the Canadian federation 1867.

Cartier Jacques 1491–1557. French navigator

who was the first European to sail up the St Lawrence River 1534. He named the site of Montréal.

Cartier-Bresson Henri 1908– . French photographer, considered one of the greatest photographic artists. His documentary work was shot in black and white, using a small-format camera. His work is remarkable for its tightly structured composition and his ability to capture the decisive moment.

cartilage flexible bluishwhite connective ◊tissue made up of the protein collagen. In cartilaginous fish it forms the skeleton; in other vertebrates it forms the greater part of the embryonic skeleton, and is replaced by ◊bone in the course of development, except in areas of wear such as bone endings, and the disks between the backbones. It also forms structural tissue in the larynx, nose, and external ear of mammals.

Cartland Barbara 1904– . English romantic novelist. She published her first book, *Jigsaw* 1921 and since then has produced a prolific stream of stories of chastely romantic love, usually in idealized or exotic settings, for a mainly female audience (such as *Love Climbs In* 1978 and *Moments of Love* 1981).

cartography art and practice of drawing maps.

cartoon humorous or satirical drawing or ◊caricature; a cartoon strip or ◊comic strip; traditionally, the base design for a large fresco, mosaic, or tapestry, transferred to wall or canvas by tracing or picking out (pouncing). Surviving examples include Leonardo da Vinci's *Virgin and St Anne* (National Gallery, London).

Cartwright Edmund 1743–1823. British inventor. He patented the power loom 1785, built a weaving mill 1787, and patented a wool-combing machine 1789.

Caruso Enrico 1873–1921. Italian operatic tenor. In 1902 he starred, with Nellie Melba, in Puccini's *La Bohème*. He was one of the first opera singers to profit from phonograph recordings.

Carver George Washington 1864–1943. US agricultural chemist. Born a slave in Missouri, he was kidnapped and raised by his former owner, Moses Carver. He devoted his life to improving the economy of the US South and the condition of blacks. He advocated the diversification of crops, promoted peanut production, and was a pioneer in the field of plastics.

Carver was honored as one of America's most influential and innovative agronomists.

Carver Raymond 1939–1988. US short-story writer and poet, author of vivid tales of contemporary US life, a collection of which were published in *Cathedral* 1983. *Fires* 1985 includes his essays and poems.

Cary (Arthur) Joyce (Lunel) 1888–1957. British novelist. He used his experiences gained in Nigeria in the Colonial Service (which he entered 1918) as a backdrop to such novels as *Mister Johnson* 1939. Other books include *The Horse's Mouth* 1944.

caryatid building support or pillar in the shape of a woman, the name deriving from the Karyatides, who were priestesses at the temple of Artemis at Karyai; the male equivalent is a *telamon* or *atlas*.

caryopsis dry, one-seeded ◊fruit in which the wall of the seed becomes fused to the carpel wall during its development. It is a type of

◊achene, and therefore develops from one ovary and does not split open to release the seed. Caryopses are typical of members of the grass family (Gramineae), including the cereals.

Casablanca (Arabic *Dar el-Beida*) port, commercial and industrial center on the Atlantic coast of Morocco; population (1982) 2,139,000. It trades in fish, phosphates, and manganese. The Great Hassan II Mosque, completed 1989, is the world's largest; it is built on a platform (430,000 sq ft/40,000 sq m) jutting out over the Atlantic, with walls 200 ft/ 60 m high, topped by a hydraulic sliding roof, and a minaret 574 ft/175 m high.

Casablanca was occupied by the French from 1907 until Morocco became independent 1956.

Casablanca Conference World War II meeting of the US and UK leaders Roosevelt and Churchill, Jan 14–24, 1943, at which the Allied demand for the unconditional surrender of Germany, Italy, and Japan was issued.

Casals Pablo 1876–1973. Catalan cellist, composer, and conductor. As a cellist, he was celebrated for his interpretations of J S Bach's unaccompanied suites. He left Spain 1939 to live in Prades, in the French Pyrenees, where he founded an annual music festival. In 1956 he moved to Puerto Rico, where he launched the Casals Festival 1957, and toured extensively in the US. He wrote instrumental and choral works, including the Christmas oratorio *The Manger*.

Casals was born in Tarragona. In 1919 he founded the Barcelona orchestra, which he conducted until leaving Spain at the outbreak of the Spanish Civil War in 1936. He was an outspoken critic of fascism, and a tireless crusader for peace.

He married three times; his first wife was the Portuguese cellist Guilhermina Suggia (1888–1950).

Casanova de Seingalt Giovanni Jacopo 1725–1798. Italian adventurer, spy, violinist, librarian, and, according to his *Memoirs*, one of the world's great lovers. From 1774 he was a spy in the Venetian police service. In 1782 a libel got him into trouble, and after more wanderings he was appointed 1785 librarian to Count Waldstein at his castle of Dûx in Bohemia. Here Casanova wrote his *Memoirs* (published 1826–38, although the complete text did not appear until 1960–61).

Cascade Range volcanic mountains in the western US and Canada, extending 700 mi/ 1,120 km from N California through Oregon and Washington to the Fraser River. They include Mount St Helens and Mount Rainier (the highest peak, 14,408 ft/4,392 m), which is noteworthy for its glaciers. The mountains are the most active in the US, excluding Alaska and Hawaii.

case grammar theory of language that proposes that the underlying structure should contain some sort of functional information about the roles of its components; thus in the sentence "The girl opened the door," the phrase *the girl* would have the role of agent, not merely that of grammatical subject.

casein main protein of milk, from which it can be separated by the action of acid, the enzyme rennin, or bacteria (souring); it is also the main component of cheese. Casein is used commercially in cosmetics, glues, and as a sizing for coating paper.

Casement Roger David 1864–1916. Irish nationalist. While in the British consular service,

he exposed the ruthless exploitation of the people of the Belgian Congo and Peru, for which he was knighted 1911 (degraded 1916). He was hanged for treason by the British for his involvement in the Irish nationalist cause.

Cash Johnny 1932– . US country singer, songwriter, and guitarist. His early hits, recorded for Sun Records in Memphis, Tennessee, include the million-selling "I Walk the Line" 1956. Many of his songs have become classics.

Cash's gruff delivery and storytelling ability distinguish his work. He is widely respected beyond the country-music field for his concern for the underprivileged, expressed in albums like *Bitter Tears* 1964 about American Indians and *Live At Folsom Prison* 1968. He is known as the "Man in Black" because of his penchant for dressing entirely in that color.

cash crop crop grown solely for sale rather than for the farmer's own use, for example, coffee, cotton, or sugar beet. Many Third World countries grow cash crops to meet their debt repayments rather than grow food for their own people. The price for these crops depends on financial interests, such as those of the multinational companies and the International Monetary Fund.

In 1990 Uganda, Rwanda, Nicaragua, and Somalia were the countries most dependent on cash crops for income.

cashew tropical American tree *Anacardium occidentale*, family Anacardiaceae. Extensively cultivated in India and Africa, it produces poisonous kidney-shaped nuts that become edible after being roasted.

cash flow input of cash required to cover all expenses of a business, whether revenue or capital. Alternatively, the actual or prospective balance between the various outgoing and incoming movements which are designated in total, positive or negative according to which is greater.

cashmere natural fiber originating from the wool of the goats of Kashmir, India, used for shawls, scarves, sweaters, and coats.

It can also be made artificially.

Casper city in E central Wyoming, on the North Platte River, NW of Cheyenne; seat of Natrona County; population (1990) 46,700. The largest city in Wyoming, it serves as the marketing center for the region's livestock and petroleum products.

Caspian Sea world's largest inland sea, divided between Iran, Azerbaijan, Russia, Kazakhstan, and Turkmenistan; area about 155,000 sq mi/400,000 sq km, with a maximum depth of 3,250 ft/1,000 m. The chief ports are Astrakhan and Baku. Drainage in the north and damming of the Volga and Ural rivers for hydroelectric power left the sea approximately 90 ft/28 m below sea level. In June 1991 opening of sluices in the dams caused the water level to rise dramatically, threatening towns and industrial areas.

An underwater ridge divides it into two halves, of which the shallow northern half is almost salt-free. There are no tides. The damming has led to shrinkage over the last 50 years, and the growth of industry along its shores has caused pollution and damaged the Russian and Iranian caviar industries. Forty per cent of Russia's polluted waste water flows into the sea.

Cass Lewis 1782–1866. US political leader and diplomat. President Jackson chose him as his secretary of war 1831, and he served as US minister to France 1836–42. In the Buchanan administration, he served as secretary of state 1857–60.

Born in Exeter, New Hampshire, Cass studied law in Ohio and was admitted to the bar 1802. During the War of 1812, he rose to the rank of brigadier general and was appointed governor of the Michigan Territory 1813. After a partial term in the US Senate, Cass was the unsuccessful Democratic presidential candidate in 1848. He returned to the Senate 1849–57.

Cassandra in Greek mythology, the daughter of ⟡Priam, king of Troy.

Her prophecies (for example, of the fall of Troy) were never believed, because she had rejected the love of Apollo. She was murdered with Agamemnon by his wife Clytemnestra.

Cassatt Mary 1845–1926. US Impressionist painter and printmaker. In 1868 she settled in Paris. Her popular, colorful pictures of mothers and children show the then-new influence of Japanese prints, for example *The Bath* 1892 (Art Institute, Chicago).

Born to a wealthy Philadelphia family, in 1868 she settled in Paris and exhibited with the Impressionists 1879–81, 1886, the only American to do so. She also excelled in etching and pastels. Her work, always respected in France, has gained recognition in the US in recent years, the largest collection being on view at the Philadelphia Art Museum.

cassava or **manioc** plant *Manihot utilissima*, belonging to the spurge family Euphorbiaceae. Native to South America, it is now widely grown throughout the tropics for its starch-containing roots, from which tapioca and bread are made.

Cassavetes John 1929–1989. US director and actor whose experimental, apparently improvised films include *Shadows* 1960 and *The Killing of a Chinese Bookie* 1980. He acted in *The Dirty Dozen* 1967 and *Rosemary's Baby* 1968.

Cassel alternate spelling of ⟡Kassel, an industrial town in Germany.

cassia bark of a SE Asian plant *Cinnamomum cassia* of the laurel family Lauraceae. It is aromatic and closely resembles true cinnamon, for which it is a widely used substitute. *Cassia* is also a genus of pod-bearing tropical plants of the family Caesalpiniaceae, many of which have strong purgative properties; *Cassia senna* is the source of the laxative drug senna.

Cassini Giovanni Domenico 1625—1712. Italian-French astronomer who discovered four moons of Saturn and the gap in the rings of Saturn now called the Cassini division.

Cassini joint space probe of the US agency NASA and the European Space Agency to the planet Saturn. *Cassini* is scheduled to be launched Nov 1995 and to go into orbit around Saturn Dec 2003, dropping off a subprobe, *Huygens*, to land on Saturn's largest moon, Titan.

Cassiopeia in Greek mythology, the mother of ⟡Andromeda.

Cassiopeia prominent constellation of the northern hemisphere, named after the mother of Andromeda. It has a distinctive W-shape, and contains one of the most powerful radio sources in the sky, Cassiopeia A, the remains of a ⟡supernova (star explosion).

cassiterite or **tinstone** chief ore of tin, consisting of reddishbrown to black stannic oxide (SnO_2), usually found in granite rocks. When fresh it has a bright ("adamantine") luster. It was formerly extensively mined in Cornwall, England; today Malaysia is the world's main supplier. Other sources of cassiterite are Africa, Indonesia, and South America.

Cassius Gaius died 42 BC. Roman soldier, one of the conspirators who killed Julius ⟡Caesar 44 BC. He fought at Carrhae 53, and with the republicans against Caesar at Pharsalus 48, was pardoned and appointed praetor, but became a leader in the conspiracy of 44, and after Caesar's death joined Brutus. He committed suicide after his defeat at ⟡Philippi 42.

cassowary large flightless bird, genus *Casuarius*, found in New Guinea and N Australia, usually in forests. Related to the emu, the cassowary has a bare head with a horny casque, or helmet, on top, and brightly colored skin on the neck. Its loose plumage is black and its wings tiny, but it can run and leap well and defends itself by kicking. Cassowaries stand up to 5 ft/1.5 m tall.

Castagno Andrea del *c.* 1421–1457. Italian Renaissance painter, active in Florence. In his frescoes in Sta Apollonia, Florence, he adapted the pictorial space to the architectural framework and followed ⟡Masaccio's lead in perspective.

Castagno's work is sculptural and strongly expressive, anticipating the Florentine late 15th-century style, as in his *David*, about 1450–57 (National Gallery, Washington, DC).

castanets Spanish percussion instrument made of two hollowed wooden shells, clapped in the hand to produce a rhythmic accompaniment to dance.

caste (Portuguese *casta* "race") stratification of Hindu society into four main groups: **Brahmans** (priests), **Kshatriyas** (nobles and warriors), **Vaisyas** (traders and farmers), and **Sudras** (servants); plus a fifth group, **Harijan** (untouchables). No upward or downward mobility exists, as in classed societies. The system dates from ancient times, and there are more than 3,000 subdivisions.

In Hindu tradition, the four main castes are said to have originated from the head, arms, thighs, and feet respectively of Brahma, the creator; the members of the fifth were probably the aboriginal inhabitants of the country, known variously as Scheduled Castes, Depressed Classes, Untouchables, or Harijan (name coined by Gandhi, "children of God"). This lowest caste handled animal products, garbage, and human wastes and so was considered to be polluting by touch, or even by sight, to others. Discrimination against them was made illegal 1947 when India became independent, but persists.

Castel Gandolfo castle built by Pope Urban VIII in the 17th century and still used by the pope as a summer residence; it is situated in a village in Italy 15 mi/24 km SE of Rome.

Castello Branco Camillo Ferreira Botelho, Visconde de Corrêa Botelho 1825–1890. Portuguese novelist. His work fluctuates between mysticism and bohemianism, and includes *Amor de perdição/Love of Perdition* 1862, written during his imprisonment for adultery, and *Novelas do Minho* 1875, stories of the rural north.

Castiglione Baldassare, Count Castiglione 1478–1529. Italian author and diplomat who described the perfect Renaissance gentleman in *Il Cortegiano/The Courtier* 1528.

Born near Mantua, Castiglione served the Duke of Milan, and in 1506 was engaged by the Duke of Albino on a mission to Henry VII of England. While in Spain 1524 he was made bishop of Avila.

Castile kingdom founded in the 10th century, occupying the central plateau of Spain. Its union with ⟡Aragon 1479, based on the marriage of ⟡Ferdinand and ⟡Isabella, effected the foundation of the Spanish state, which at the time was occupied and ruled by the ⟡Moors. Castile comprised the two great basins separated by the Sierra de Gredos and the Sierra de Guadarrama, known traditionally as Old and New Castile. The area now forms the regions of ⟡Castilla–León and ⟡Castilla–La Mancha.

The kingdom of Castile grew from a small area in the north. In the 11th century, Old Castile was united with León; the kingdom of Toledo was captured from the Moors 1085 and became New Castile, with Toledo the capital of the whole. Castile was united with Aragon 1479, and in 1492, after routing the Moors, Ferdinand and Isabella established the Catholic kingdom of Spain.

Castilian language member of the Romance branch of the Indo-European language family, originating in NW Spain, in the provinces of Old and New Castile. It is the basis of present-day standard Spanish (see ⟡Spanish language) and is often seen as the same language, the terms *castellano* and *español* being used interchangeably in both Spain and the Spanish-speaking countries of the Americas.

Castilla Ramón 1797–1867. President of Peru 1841–51 and 1855–62. He dominated Peruvian politics for over two decades, bringing political stability. Income from guano exports was used to reduce the national debt and improve transport and educational facilities. He abolished black slavery and the head tax on Indians.

Castilla–La Mancha autonomous region of central Spain; area 30,571 sq mi/79,200 sq km; population (1986) 1,665,000. It includes the provinces of Albacete, Ciudad Real, Cuenca, Guadalajara, and Toledo. Irrigated land produces grain and chickpeas, and merino sheep graze here.

Castilla–León autonomous region of central Spain; area 36,323 sq mi/94,100 sq km; population (1986) 2,600,000. It includes the provinces of Ávila, Burgos, León, Palencia, Salamanca, Segovia, Soria, Valladolid, and Zamora. Irrigated land produces wheat and rye. Cattle, sheep, and fighting bulls are bred in the uplands.

casting process of producing solid objects by pouring molten material into a shaped mold and allowing it to cool. Casting is used to shape such materials as glass and plastics, as well as metals and alloys.

The casting of metals has been practiced for more than 6,000 years, using first copper and bronze, then iron. The traditional method of casting metal is **sand casting**.

Using a model of the object to be produced, a hollow mold is made in a damp sand and clay mix. Molten metal is then poured into the mold, taking its shape when it cools and solidifies.

The sand mold is broken up to release the casting. Permanent metal molds called **dies** are also used for casting, in particular, small items in mass-production processes where molten metal is injected under pressure into cooled dies. **Continuous casting** is a method of shaping bars and slabs that involves pouring molten metal into a hollow, water-cooled mold of the desired cross section.

cast iron cheap but invaluable constructional material, most commonly used for car engine blocks. Cast iron is partly refined pig (crude) ◊iron, which is very fluid when molten and highly suitable for shaping by casting; it contains too many impurities (for example, carbon) to be readily shaped in any other way. Solid cast iron is heavy and can absorb great shock but is very brittle.

castle private fortress of a king or noble. The earliest castles in Britain were built following the Norman Conquest, and the art of castle building reached a peak in the 13th century. By the 15th century, the need for castles for domestic defense had largely disappeared, and the advent of gunpowder made them largely useless against attack. See also ◊château.

structure The main parts of a typical castle are: the **keep**, a large central tower containing store rooms, soldiers' quarters, and a hall for the lord and his family; the **inner bailey** or walled courtyard surrounding the keep; the **outer bailey** or second courtyard, separated from the inner bailey by a wall; crenellated **embattlements** through which missiles were discharged against an attacking enemy; rectangular or round **towers** projecting from the walls; the **portcullis**, a heavy grating which could be let down to close the main gate; and the **drawbridge** crossing the ditch or moat surrounding the castle. Sometimes a tower called a **barbican** was constructed over a gateway as an additional defensive measure.

11th century The **motte and bailey** castle (the motte was a mound of earth, and the bailey a courtyard enclosed by a wall); the earliest example is on the river Loire in France, dated 1010. The first **rectangular keep** dates from this time; an example is the White Tower in the Tower of London.

12th century Development of more substantial defensive systems, based in part on the Crusaders' experiences of sieges during the First Crusade 1096; the first **curtain walls** with projecting towers were built (as at Framlingham, Suffolk).

13th century Introduction of the **round tower**, both for curtain walls (Pembroke, Wales) and for keeps (Conisborough, Yorkshire); **concentric planning** (in the castles of Wales, such as Beaumaris and -Harlech); **fortified town walls**.

14th century First use of gunpowder; inclusion of gunports in curtain walls (Bodiam, Sussex).

15th century Fortified manor houses now adequate for private dwelling.

16th century End of castle as a practical means of defense; fortified coastal defenses, however, continued to be built (Falmouth, Cornwall).

Early castles (11th century) consisted of an earthen hill (motte) surrounded by wooden palisades enclosing a courtyard (bailey). The motte supported a wooden keep. Later developments substituted stone for wood and utilized more elaborate defensive architectural detail. After introduction of gunpowder in the 14th century, castles became less defensible.

Increases in civil order led to their replacement by unfortified manor houses by the 16th century. Large stone fortifications became popular in the 18th century, particularly those modeled after the principles of fortification introduced by the French architect

Vauban, and were built as late as the first half of the 19th century. In the late 19th century, castlelike buildings were built as residences for the wealthy as part of the Romantic revival in Europe and America.

Castlereagh Robert Stewart, Viscount Castlereagh 1769–1822. British Tory politician. As chief secretary for Ireland 1797–1801, he suppressed the rebellion of 1798 and helped the younger Pitt secure the union of England, Scotland, and Ireland 1801. As foreign secretary 1812–22, he coordinated European opposition to Napoleon and represented Britain at the Congress of Vienna 1814–15.

Castor or **Alpha Geminorum** second brightest star in the constellation Gemini and the 23rd brightest star in the sky. Along with ◊Pollux, it forms a prominent pair at the eastern end of Gemini.

Castor is 45 light-years from Earth, and is one of the finest ◊binary stars in the sky for small telescopes. The two main components orbit each other over a period of 467 years. A third, much fainter, star orbits the main pair over a period probably exceeding 10,000 years. Each of the three visible components is a spectroscopic binary, making Castor a sextuple star system.

Castor and Pollux/Polydeuces in Greek mythology, twin sons of Leda (by ◊Zeus), brothers of ◊Helen and ◊Clytemnestra. Protectors of mariners, they were transformed at death into the constellation Gemini.

castor-oil plant tall, tropical and subtropical shrub *Ricinus communis* of the spurge family Euphorbiaceae. The seeds, in North America called castor beans, yield the purgative castor oil and also ricin, one of the most powerful poisons known, which can be targeted to destroy cancer cells, while leaving normal cells untouched.

castration removal of the testicles. Male domestic animals may be castrated to prevent reproduction, to make them larger or more docile, or to remove a disease site.

Castration of humans was used in ancient and medieval times and occasionally later to preserve the treble voice of boy singers or, by Muslims, to provide trustworthy harem guards, called eunuchs. If done in childhood, it greatly modifies the secondary sexual characteristics: for instance, the voice may remain high, and growth of hair on the face and body may become weak or cease, owing to the removal of the hormones normally secreted by the testes.

Male domestic animals, especially stallions and bovine bulls, are castrated to prevent undesirable sires from reproducing, to moderate their aggressive and savage disposition and, for bulls, to improve their value as beef cattle (castrated bovines are called steer). Roosters are castrated (capons) to improve their flavor and increase their size. The effects of castration can also be achieved by chemical means, by administration of hormones, in humans and animals. If done in adulthood, the sexual function may be retained (although infertile) as well as masculine features already established.

castrato in music, a high male voice of unusual brilliance and power achieved by castration before puberty. The practice was outlawed in the mid-19th century.

Castries port and capital of St Lucia, on the NW coast of the island in the Caribbean; population (1988) 53,000. It produces textiles,

chemicals, tobacco, and wood and rubber products.

The town was rebuilt after destruction by fire 1948.

Castro (Ruz) Fidel 1927– . Cuban communist politician, prime minister 1959–76 and president from 1976. He led two unsuccessful coups against the right-wing Batista regime and led the revolution that overthrew the dictator 1959. He raised the standard of living for most Cubans but dealt harshly with dissenters.

Of wealthy parentage, Castro was educated at Jesuit schools and, after studying law at the University of Havana, gained a reputation through his work for poor clients. He opposed the Batista dictatorship, and took part, with his brother Raúl, in an unsuccessful attack on the army barracks at Santiago de Cuba 1953. After some time in exile in the US and Mexico, Castro attempted a secret landing in Cuba 1956 in which all but 11 of his supporters were killed. He eventually gathered an army of over 5,000 which overthrew Batista on Jan 1, 1959 and he became prime minister a few months later. Raúl Castro was appointed minister of armed forces.

Castro's administration introduced a centrally planned economy based on the production for export of sugar, tobacco, and nickel. He nationalized the property of wealthy Cubans, Americans, and other foreigners 1960, resulting in the severance of relations by the US, an economic embargo, and US attempts to subvert Cuba's government (see also ◊Bay of Pigs). This enmity came to a head in the ◊Cuban missile crisis 1962. Aid for development was provided by the USSR, which replaced the US as Cuba's main trading partner, and Castro espoused Marxism-Leninism until, in 1974, he rejected Marx's formula "from each according to his ability and to each according to his need" and decreed that each Cuban should "receive according to his work." He also improved education, housing, and health care for the majority of Cubans but lost the support of the middle class, hundreds of thousands of whom fled the country. Since 1990, events in E Europe and the disintegration of the USSR have left Castro increasingly isolated.

casuarina any tree or shrub of the genus *Casuarina*, family Casuarinaceae, with many species native to Australia and New Guinea but also found in Africa and Asia. Commonly known as she-oaks, casuarinas have taken their Latin name from the resemblance of their long, drooping branchlets to the feathers of the cassowary, whose genus is *Casuarius*.

cat small, domesticated, carnivorous mammal *Felis catus*, often kept as a pet or for catching small pests such as rodents. Found in many color variants, it may have short, long, or no hair, but the general shape and size is constant. All cats walk on the pads of their toes, and have retractile claws. They have strong limbs, large eyes, and acute hearing. The canine teeth are long and well-developed, as are the shearing teeth in the side of the mouth.

Domestic cats have a common ancestor, the **African wild cat** *Felis libyca*, found across Africa and Arabia. This is similar to the **European wild cat** *Felis silvestris*. Domestic cats can interbreed with either of these wild relatives. Various other species of small wild cat live in all continents except Antarctica and Australia. Large cats such as the lion and tiger also belong to the cat family Felidae.

catabolism in biology, the destructive part of ◊metabolism where living tissue is changed into energy and waste products. It is the opposite of ◊anabolism. It occurs continuously in the body, but is accelerated during many disease processes, such as fever, and in starvation.

catacomb underground cemetery, such as the catacombs of the early Christians. Examples include those beneath the basilica of St Sebastian in Rome, where bodies were buried in niches in the walls of the tunnels.

Catalan language member of the Romance branch of the Indo-European language family, an Iberian language closely related to Provençal in France. It is spoken in Catalonia in NE Spain, the Balearic Islands, Andorra, and a corner of SW France.

Since the end of the Franco regime in Spain 1975, Catalan nationalists have vigorously promoted their regional language as being coequal in Catalonia with Castilian Spanish, and it is now accepted as an official language of the European Community. The official languages of the 1992 Olympics in Barcelona were English, French, Spanish, and Catalan.

Catalaunian Fields plain near Troyes, France, scene of the defeat of Attila the Hun by the Romans and Goths under the Roman general Aëtius (died 454) 451.

catalepsy in medicine, an abnormal state in which the patient is apparently or actually unconscious and the muscles become rigid.

There is no response to stimuli, and the rate of heartbeat and breathing is slow. A similar condition can be drug-induced or produced by hypnosis, but catalepsy as ordinarily understood occurs spontaneously in epilepsy, schizophrenia, and other nervous disorders.

Catalonia (Spanish *Cataluña*, Catalan *Catalunya*) autonomous region of NE Spain; area 12,313 sq mi/31,900 sq km; population (1986) 5,977,000. It includes Barcelona (the capital), Gerona, Lérida, and Tarragona. Industries include wool and cotton textiles; hydroelectric power is produced.

The north is mountainous, and the Ebro basin breaks through the Castellón mountains in the south. The soil is fertile, but the climate in the interior is arid. Catalonia leads Spain in industrial development. Tourist resorts have developed along the Costa Brava.

history The region has a long tradition of independence. It enjoyed autonomy 1932–39 but lost its privileges for supporting the republican cause in the ◊Spanish Civil War. Autonomy and official use of the ◊Catalan language were restored 1980.

French Catalonia is the adjacent *département* of Pyrénées-Orientales.

catalpa any tree of the genus *Catalpa* belonging to the trumpet creeper Bignoniaceae family, found in North America, China, and the West Indies. The northern catalpa *C. speciosa* of North America grows to 100 ft/30 m and has heart-shaped, deciduous leaves and tubular white flowers with purple borders.

catalyst substance that alters the speed of, or makes possible, a chemical or biochemical reaction but remains unchanged at the end of the reaction. ◊Enzymes are natural biochemical catalysts. In practice most catalysts are used to speed up reactions.

catalytic converter device for reducing toxic emissions from the ◊internal-combustion engine. It converts harmful exhaust products to relatively harmless ones by passing exhaust gases over a mixture of catalysts. *Oxidation catalysts* convert hydrocarbons into carbon dioxide and water; *three-way catalysts* convert oxides of nitrogen back into nitrogen.

Over the lifetime of a vehicle, a catalytic converter can reduce hydrocarbon emissions by 87%, carbon monoxide emissions by 85%, and nitrogen oxide emissions by 62%, but will cause a slight increase in the amount of carbon dioxide emitted. Catalytic converters are standard in the US, where a 90% reduction in pollution from automobiles was achieved without loss of engine performance or fuel economy.

catamaran (Tamil "tied log") twin-hulled sailing vessel, based on the aboriginal craft of South America and the Indies, made of logs lashed together, with an outrigger. A similar vessel with three hulls is known as a trimaran. Car ferries with a wave-piercing catamaran design are also in use in parts of Europe and North America. They have a pointed main hull and two outriggers and travel at a speed of 35 knots (52.5 mph/84.5 kph).

cataract eye disease in which the crystalline lens or its capsule becomes opaque, causing blindness. Fluid accumulates between the fibers of the lens and gives place to deposits of ◊albumin. These coalesce into rounded bodies, the lens fibers break down, and areas of the lens or the lens capsule become filled with opaque products of degeneration.

The condition nearly always affects both eyes, usually one more than the other. In most cases, the treatment is replacement of the lens with an artificial implant.

catarrh inflammation of any mucous membrane, especially of the nose and throat, with increased production of mucus.

catastrophe theory mathematical theory developed by René Thom in 1972, in which he showed that the growth of an organism proceeds by a series of gradual changes that are triggered by, and in turn trigger, large-scale changes or "catastrophic" jumps. It also has applications in engineering—for example, the gradual strain on the structure of a bridge that can eventually result in a sudden collapse –and has been extended to economic and psychological events.

catastrophism theory that the geological features of the Earth were formed by a series of sudden, violent "catastrophes" beyond the ordinary workings of nature. The theory was largely the work of Georges ◊Cuvier. It was later replaced by the concepts of ◊uniformitarianism and ◊evolution.

Catch-22 black-humor novel by Joseph Heller, published 1961, about a US squadron that is ordered to fly an increased number of bombing missions in Italy in World War II; the crazed military justifications involved were described by the novel's phrase "Catch-22," which has come to represent the dilemma of all false authoritarian logic.

A man "would be crazy to fly more missions and sane if he didn't but if he was sane, he had to fly them. If he flew them he was crazy and didn't have to; but if he didn't, he was sane and had to."

Catcher in the Rye, The 1951 US novel by J D Salinger about a young man's growing up and his fight to maintain his integrity in a "phony" adult world; it has become an international classic.

catchment area area from which water is collected by a river and its tributaries. In the social sciences the term may be used to denote the area from which people travel to obtain a particular service or product, such as the area from which a school draws its pupils.

Cateau-Cambresis, Treaty of treaty that ended the dynastic wars between the Valois of France and the Hapsburg Empire, April 2–3, 1559.

catechism teaching by question and answer on the Socratic method, but chiefly as a means of instructing children in the basics of the Christian creed. A person being instructed in this way in preparation for baptism or confirmation is called a *catechumen*.

A form of catechism was used for the catechumens in the early Christian church. Little books of catechism were written by Luther and Calvin at the Reformation.

catecholamine chemical that functions as a ◊neurotransmitter or a ◊hormone. Dopamine, epinephrine (adrenaline), and norepinephrine (noradrenaline) are catecholamines.

catechu extract of the leaves and shoots of *Acacia catechu*, an East Indian plant. It is rich in tannic acid, which is released slowly, a property that makes it a useful intestinal astringent in diarrhea.

categorical imperative technical term in Immanuel ◊Kant's moral philosophy designating the supreme principle of morality for rational beings. The imperative orders us to act only in such a way that we can wish a maxim, or subjective principle, of our action to be a universal law.

category in philosophy, a fundamental concept applied to being that cannot be reduced to anything more elementary. Aristotle listed ten categories: substance, quantity, quality, relation, place, time, position, state, action, and passion.

catenary curve taken up by a flexible cable suspended between two points, under gravity; for example, the curve of overhead suspension cables that hold the conductor wire of an electric railroad or streetcarway.

caterpillar larval stage of a ◊butterfly or ◊moth. Wormlike in form, the body is segmented, may be hairy, and often has scent glands. The head has strong biting mandibles, silk glands, and a spinneret.

Many caterpillars resemble the plant on which they feed, dry twigs, or rolled leaves. Others are highly colored and rely for their protection on their irritant hairs, disagreeable smell, or on their power to eject a corrosive fluid. Yet others take up a "threat attitude" when attacked.

Caterpillars emerge from eggs that have been laid by the female insect on the food plant and feed greedily, increasing greatly in size and casting their skins several times, until the pupal stage is reached. The abdominal segments bear a varying number of "pro-legs"

catenary *The heavy cables of a suspension bridge demonstrate a catenary curve.*

as well as the six true legs on the thoracic segments.

caterpillar track endless flexible belt of metal plates on which certain vehicles such as tanks and bulldozers run, which takes the place of ordinary tyred wheels and improves performance on wet or uneven surfaces.

A track-laying vehicle has a track on each side, and its engine drives small cogwheels that run along the top of the track in contact with the ground. The advantage of such tracks over wheels is that they distribute the vehicle's weight over a wider area and are thus ideal for use on soft and waterlogged as well as rough and rocky ground.

catfish fish belonging to the order Siluriformes, in which barbels (feelers) on the head are well-developed, so giving a resemblance to the whiskers of a cat. Catfishes are found worldwide, mainly but not exclusively in fresh water, and are plentiful in South America.

The E European **giant catfish** or **wels** *Silurus glanis* grows to 5 ft/1.5 m long or more. It has been introduced to several places in Britain.

The unrelated marine **wolffish** *Anarhicas lupus*, a deep-sea relative of the blenny, growing 4 ft/1.2 m long, is sometimes called a catfish.

cathedral (Latin *cathedra*, "seat" or "throne") Christian church containing the throne of a bishop or archbishop, which is usually situated on the south side of the choir. A cathedral is governed by a dean and chapter.

There are cathedrals in most of the important cities of the world, built in a wide variety of architectural styles.

Cather Willa (Sibert) 1876–1947. US novelist and short-story writer. Born in Virginia, she moved to Nebraska as a child. Her novels frequently explore life in the pioneer West, both in her own time and in past eras; for example, *O Pioneers!* 1913 and *My Antonia* 1918, and *A Lost Lady* 1923. *Death Comes for the Archbishop* 1927 is a celebration of the spiritual pioneering of the Catholic church in New Mexico. She also wrote poetry and essays on fiction.

Catherine I 1684–1727. Empress of Russia from 1725. A Lithuanian peasant, born Martha Skavronsky, she married a Swedish dragoon and eventually became the mistress of Peter the Great. In 1703 she was rechristened Katarina Alexeievna. The tsar divorced his wife 1711 and married Catherine 1712. She accompanied him on his campaigns, and showed tact and shrewdness. In 1724 she was proclaimed empress, and after Peter's death 1725 she ruled capably with the help of her ministers. She allied Russia with Austria and Spain in an anti-English bloc.

Catherine II *the Great* 1729–1796. Empress of Russia from 1762, and daughter of the German prince of Anhalt-Zerbst. In 1745, she married the Russian grand duke Peter. Catherine was able to dominate him; six months after he became Tsar Peter III 1762, he was murdered in a coup and Catherine ruled alone. During her reign Russia extended its boundaries to include territory from wars with the Turks 1768–74, 1787–92, and from the partitions of Poland 1772, 1793, and 1795, as well as establishing hegemony over the Black Sea.

Catherine's private life was notorious throughout Europe, but except for Grigory ▷Potemkin she did not permit her lovers to influence her policy.

She admired and aided the French *Encyclopédistes*.

Catherine de' Medici 1519–1589. French queen consort of Henry II, whom she married 1533; daughter of Lorenzo de' Medici, Duke of Urbino; and mother of Francis II, Charles IX, and Henry III. At first outshone by Henry's mistress Diane de Poitiers (1490–1566), she became regent 1560–63 for Charles IX and remained in power until his death 1574.

During the religious wars of 1562–69, she first supported the Protestant ▷Huguenots against the Roman Catholic **Guises** to ensure her own position as ruler; she later opposed them, and has been traditionally implicated in the Massacre of ▷St Bartholomew 1572.

Catherine of Alexandria, St Christian martyr. According to legend she disputed with 50 scholars, refusing to give up her faith and marry Emperor Maxentius. Her emblem is a wheel, on which her persecutors tried to kill her (the wheel broke and she was beheaded). Feast day Nov 25.

Catherine of Aragon 1485–1536. First queen of Henry VIII of England, 1509–33, and mother of Mary I. Catherine had married Henry's elder brother Prince Arthur 1501 and on his death 1502 was betrothed to Henry, marrying him on his accession. She failed to produce a male heir and Henry divorced her without papal approval, thus beginning the English ▷Reformation.

Of their six children, only Mary lived. Wanting a male heir, Henry sought an annulment 1526 when Catherine was too old to bear children. When the pope demanded that the case be referred to him, Henry married Anne Boleyn, afterwards receiving the desired decree of nullity from Cranmer, the archbishop of Canterbury, in 1533. The Reformation in England followed, and Catherine went into retirement until her death.

Catherine of Braganza 1638–1705. Queen of Charles II of England 1662–85. Her childlessness and practice of her Catholic faith were unpopular, but Charles resisted pressure for divorce. She returned to Lisbon 1692 after his death.

The daughter of John IV of Portugal (1604–1656), she brought the Portuguese possessions of Bombay and Tangier as her dowry and introduced tea drinking and citrus fruits to England.

Catherine of Genoa, St 1447–1510. Italian mystic who devoted herself to the sick and to meditation. Feast day Sept 15.

Catherine of Siena 1347–1380. Italian mystic, born in Siena. She persuaded Pope Gregory XI to return to Rome from Avignon 1376. In 1375 she is said to have received on her body the stigmata, the impression of Jesus' wounds. Her *Dialogue* is a classic mystical work. Feast day April 29.

Catherine of Valois 1401–1437. Queen of Henry V of England, whom she married 1420; the mother of Henry VI. After the death of Henry V, she secretly married Owen Tudor (c. 1400–1461) about 1425, and their son Edmund Tudor became the father of Henry VII.

catheter fine tube inserted into the body to introduce or remove fluids. The original catheter was the urinary one, passed by way of the urethra (the duct that leads urine away from the bladder). In today's practice, catheters

can be inserted into blood vessels, either in the limbs or trunk, to provide blood samples and local pressure measurements, and to deliver drugs and/or nutrients directly into the bloodstream.

cathode in chemistry, the negative electrode of an electrolytic ▷cell, toward which positive particles (cations), usually in solution, are attracted. See ▷electrolysis.

A cathode is given its negative charge by connecting it to the negative side of an external electrical supply. This is in contrast to the negative electrode of an electrical (battery) cell, which acquires its charge in the course of a spontaneous chemical reaction taking place within the cell.

cathode in electronics, the part of an electronic device in which electrons are generated. In a thermionic valve, electrons are produced by the heating effect of an applied current; in a photoelectric cell, they are produced by the interaction of light and a semiconducting material. The cathode is kept at a negative potential relative to the device's other electrodes (anodes) in order to ensure that the liberated electrons stream away from the cathode and toward the anodes.

cathode-ray tube vacuum tube in which a beam of electrons is produced and focused onto a fluorescent screen. It is an essential component of television receivers, computer visual display terminals, and oscilloscopes.

Catholic church whole body of the Christian church, though usually referring to the Roman Catholic Church (see ▷Roman Catholicism).

Catiline (Lucius Sergius Catilina) *c.* 108–62 BC. Roman politician. Twice failing to be elected to the consulship in 64/63 BC, he planned a military coup, but ▷Cicero exposed his conspiracy. He died at the head of the insurgents.

cation ▷ion carrying a positive charge. During electrolysis, cations in the electrolyte move to the cathode (negative electrode).

catkin in flowering plants (▷angiosperms), a pendulous inflorescence, bearing numerous small, usually unisexual flowers. The tiny flowers are stalkless and the petals and sepals are usually absent or much reduced in size. Many types of trees bear catkins, including willows, poplars, and birches. Most plants with catkins are wind-pollinated, so the male catkins produce large quantities of pollen. Some ▷gymnosperms also have catkinlike structures that produce pollen, for example, the swamp cypress *Taxodium*.

Catlin George 1796–1872. US explorer and artist. Born in Wilkes-Barre, Pennsylvania, Catlin briefly practiced law before embarking on a career as a portrait painter. His deep interest in the Indians of the West then led him to travel widely, recording pictorially the lifeways and customs of the tribes of the Rocky Mountains and Great Plains 1832–40.

His *Letters and Notes on the Manners, Customs, and Conditions of the North American Indians* 1841 is among the most important of his published works. After Catlin's death, his collection of paintings and sketches was donated to the Smithsonian Institution.

Cato Marcus Porcius 234–149 BC. Roman politician. Appointed censor (senior magistrate) in 184 BC, he excluded from the Senate those who did not meet his high standards. He was so impressed by the power of ▷Carthage, on a visit 157, that he ended every speech by saying:

"Carthage must be destroyed." His farming manual is the earliest surviving work in Latin prose.

Cato Street Conspiracy in British history, unsuccessful plot hatched in Cato Street, London, to murder the Tory foreign secretary Robert Castlereagh and all his ministers on Feb 20, 1820. The leader, the Radical Arthur Thistlewood (1770–1820), who intended to set up a provisional government, was hanged with four others.

CAT scan or **CT scan** (acronym for **computerized axial tomography**) sophisticated method of X-ray imaging. Quick and noninvasive, CAT scanning is used in medicine as an aid to diagnosis, helping to pinpoint problem areas without the need for exploratory surgery. It is also used in archeology to examine mummies.

The CAT scanner passes a narrow fan of X-rays through successive slices of the suspect body part. These slices are picked up by crystal detectors in a scintillator and converted electronically into cross-sectional images displayed on a viewing screen. Gradually, using views taken from various angles, a three-dimensional picture of the organ or tissue can be built up and suspect irregularities analyzed.

Catskills US mountain range, mainly in SE New York west of the Hudson River. The highest point is Slide mountain 4,204 ft/1,281 m. Long a vacation and resort center for New York City residents, the Catskills offer hiking, skiing, hunting and fishing, and the picturesque trails and scenes of woods, waterfalls, lakes, and streams that have attracted such painters as Frederic Church and Thomas Cole. It is the setting for *Rip Van Winkle*, one of Washington Irving's most popular tales.

cattle any large, ruminant, even-toed, hoofed mammal of the genus *Bos*, family Bovidae, including wild species such as the yak, gaur, gayal, banteng, and kouprey, as well as domestic breeds. Asiatic water buffaloes *Bubalus*, African buffaloes *Syncerus*, and American bison *Bison* are not considered true cattle. Cattle are bred for meat (beef cattle) or milk (dairy cattle).

Cattle were first domesticated in the Middle East during the Neolithic period, about 8000 BC. They were brought north into Europe by migrating Neolithic farmers.

Fermentation in the four-chambered stomach allows cattle to make good use of the grass that is normally the main part of the diet. There are two main types of domesticated cattle: the European breeds, variants of *Bos taurus* descended from the ◊aurochs, and the various breeds of *zebu Bos indicus*, the humped cattle of India, which are useful in the tropics for their ability to withstand the heat and diseases to which European breeds succumb.

The old-established beef breeds are mostly British in origin. The Hereford, for example, is the premier English breed, ideally suited to rich lowland pastures but it will also thrive on poorer land such as that found in the US Midwest and the Argentine pampas. Of the Scottish beef breeds, the Aberdeen Angus, a black and hornless variety, produces high-quality meat through intensive feeding methods. Other breeds include the Devon, a hardy early-maturing type, and the Beef Shorthorn, now less important than formerly, but still valued for an ability to produce good calves when crossed with less promising cattle. In recent years, more interest has been shown

in other European breeds, their tendency to have less fat being more suited to modern tastes. Examples include the Charolais and the Limousin from central France, and the Simmental, originally from Switzerland. In the US, four varieties of zebus, called Brahmans, have been introduced. They interbreed with *B. taurus* varieties and produce valuable hybrids that resist heat, ticks, and insects.

For dairying purposes, a breed raised in many countries is variously known as the Fresian, Holstein, or Black and White. It can give enormous milk yields, up to 3,450 gal/13,000 l in a single lactation, and will produce calves ideally suited for intensive beef production. Other dairying types include the Jersey and Guernsey, whose milk has a high butterfat content, and the Ayrshire, a smaller breed capable of staying outside all year.

Catullus Gaius Valerius *c.* 84–54 BC. Roman lyric poet, born in Verona of a well-to-do family. He moved in the literary and political society of Rome and wrote lyrics describing his unhappy love affair with Clodia, probably the wife of the consul Metellus, calling her Lesbia. His longer poems include two wedding songs. Many of his poems are short verses to his friends.

Caucasoid referring to one of the three major varieties (see ◊race) of humans, *Homo sapiens sapiens*, including the indigenous peoples of Europe, the Near East, North Africa, India, and Australia. Caucasoids exhibit the widest range of variation in physical traits, including straight to curly hair; fair to dark skin; blue, hazel, and brown eyes; blond, red, brown, and black hair; medium to heavy beard and body hair; small to high-bridged noses; medium to thin lips. The term was coined by the German anthropologist J F Blumenbach (1752–1840), who erroneously theorized that they originated in the Caucasus region. See also ◊Mongoloid, ◊Negroid.

Caucasus series of mountain ranges between the Caspian and Black seas, in the republics of Russia, Georgia, Armenia, and Azerbaijan; 750 mi/1,200 km long. The highest peak is Elbruz, 18,480 ft/5,633 m.

Arabian thoroughbreds are raised at Tersk farm in the northern foothills.

Cauchy Augustin Louis 1789–1857. French mathematician who employed rigorous methods of analysis. His prolific output included work on complex functions, determinants, and probability, and on the convergence of infinite series. In calculus, he refined the concepts of the limit and the definite integral.

caucus in the US, a closed meeting of regular party members; for example, to choose a candidate for office. The term was originally used in the 18th century in Boston, Massachusetts.

cauda tail, or taillike appendage; part of the *cauda equina*, a bundle of nerves at the bottom of the spinal cord in vertebrates.

cauliflower variety of ◊cabbage *Brassica oleracea*, distinguished by its large, flattened head of fleshy, aborted flowers. It is similar to broccoli but less hardy.

causality in philosophy, a consideration of the connection between cause and effect, usually referred to as the "causal relationship." If an event is assumed to have a cause, two important questions arise: what is the relationship between cause and effect, and must it follow that every event is caused? The Scottish philosopher David Hume considered these questions to be, in principle, unanswerable.

cauterization in medicine, the use of special instruments to burn or fuse small areas of body tissue to destroy dead cells, prevent the spread of infection, or seal tiny blood vessels to minimize blood loss during surgery.

Cauvery or **Kaveri** river of S India, rising in the W Ghats and flowing 475 mi/765 km SE to meet the Bay of Bengal in a wide delta. It has been a major source of hydroelectric power since 1902 when India's first hydropower plant was built on the river.

Cavaco Silva Anibal 1939– . Portuguese politician, finance minister 1980–81, and prime minister and Social Democratic Party (PSD) leader from 1985. Under his leadership Portugal joined the European Community 1985 and the Western European Union 1988.

Cavaco Silva studied economics in Britain and the US, and was a university teacher and research director in the Bank of Portugal. In 1978, with the return of constitutional government, he entered politics. His first government fell in 1987, but an election later that year gave him Portugal's first absolute majority since democracy was restored. He was reelected in the 1991 elections.

Cavafy Constantinos. Adopted name of Konstantinos Pétrou 1863–1933. Greek poet. An Alexandrian, he shed light on Greek history, recreating the Classical period with zest. He published only one book of poetry and remained almost unknown until translations of his works appeared 1952.

cavalier horseman of noble birth, but mainly used to describe a male supporter of Charles I in the English Civil War (Cavalier), typically with courtly dress and long hair (as distinct from a Roundhead); also a supporter of Charles II after the Restoration.

Cavalier poets poets of Charles I's court, including Thomas Carew, Robert Herrick, Richard Lovelace, and John Suckling. They wrote witty, light-hearted love lyrics.

Cavalli (Pietro) Francesco 1602–1676. Italian composer, organist at St Mark's, Venice, and the first to make opera a popular entertainment with such works as *Xerxes* 1654, later performed in honor of Louis XIV's wedding in Paris. 27 of his operas survive.

cave roofed-over cavity in the Earth's crust usually produced by the action of underground water or by waves on a seacoast. Caves of the former type commonly occur in areas underlain by limestone, such as Kentucky and many Balkan regions, where the rocks are soluble in water. A *pothole* is a vertical hole in rock caused by water descending a crack; it is thus open to the sky.

Cave animals often show loss of pigmentation or sight, and under isolation, specialized species may develop. The scientific study of caves is called *speleology*.

During the ◊Ice Age, humans began living in caves leaving many layers of debris that archeologists have unearthed and dated in the Old World and the New. They also left cave art, paintings of extinct animals often with hunters on their trail. See also ◊Altamira and ◊ancient art.

Celebrated caves include the Mammoth Cave in Kentucky, 4 mi/6.4 km long and 125 ft/38 m high; the Caverns of Adelsberg (Postumia) near Trieste, Italy, which extend for many miles; Carlsbad Cave, New Mexico, the largest in the US; the Cheddar Caves, England; Fingal's Cave, Scotland, which has a range of basalt columns; and Peak Cavern, England.

cavefish cave-dwelling fish, which may belong to one of several quite unrelated groups, independently adapted to life in underground waters. Cavefish have in common a tendency to blindness and atrophy of the eye, enhanced touch-sensitive organs in the skin, and loss of pigment.

The *Kentucky blindfish Amblyopsis spelaea*, which lives underground in limestone caves, has eyes that are vestigial and beneath the skin, and a colorless body. The Mexican *cave characin* is a blind, colorless form of *Astyanax fasciatus* found in surface rivers of Mexico.

Cavendish Henry 1731–1810. English physicist. He discovered hydrogen (which he called "inflammable air") 1766, and determined the compositions of water and of nitric acid.

The ▷Cavendish experiment enabled him to discover the mass and density of the Earth.

Cavendish experiment measurement of the gravitational attraction between lead and gold spheres, which enabled Henry ▷Cavendish to calculate a mean value for the mass and density of Earth, using Newton's law of universal gravitation.

caviar salted roe (eggs) of sturgeon, salmon, and other fishes. Caviar is prepared by beating and straining the egg sacs until the eggs are free from fats and then adding salt. Russia and Iran are the main exporters of the most prized variety of caviar, derived from Caspian Sea sturgeon. Iceland produces various high-quality, lower-priced caviars.

cavitation formation of partial vacuums in fluids at high velocities, produced by propellers or other machine parts in hydraulic engines, in accordance with ▷Bernoulli's principle. When these vacuums collapse, pitting, vibration, and noise can occur in the metal parts in contact with the fluids.

Cavite port city of the Philippine Republic; 8 mi/13 km S of Manila; population (1980) 88,000. It is the capital of Cavite province, Luzon. It was in Japanese hands Dec 1941–Feb 1945. After the Philippines achieved independence in 1946, the US Seventh Fleet continued to use the naval base.

cavity in dentistry, decay of tooth enamel by the acids produced by mouth bacteria. Continuing decay undermines the inner tooth and attacks the nerve, causing toothache. Measures can be taken to save teeth by cleaning out the decay (drilling) and filling the tooth with a plastic substance such as silver amalgam or covering the cavity with a inlay or crown.

Cavour Camillo Benso di, Count 1810–1861. Italian nationalist politician. He was the editor of *Il ▷Risorgimento* from 1847. As prime minister of Piedmont 1852–59 and 1860–61, he enlisted the support of Britain and France for the concept of a united Italy achieved 1861; after expelling the Austrians 1859, he assisted Garibaldi in liberating southern Italy 1860.

Cavour was born in Turin, served in the army in early life and entered politics in 1847. From 1848 he sat in the Piedmontese parliament and held cabinet posts 1850–52. As prime minister, he sought to secure French and British sympathy for the cause of Italian unity by sending Piedmontese troops to fight in the Crimean War. In 1858 he had a secret meeting with Napoleon III at Plombières, where they planned the war of 1859 against Austria, which resulted in the union of Lombardy with Piedmont. Then the central Italian states joined the kingdom of Italy, although Savoy and Nice were to be ceded to France. With Cavour's approval Garibaldi overthrew the Neapolitan monarchy, but Cavour occupied part of the Papal States which, with Naples and Sicily, were annexed to Italy, to prevent Garibaldi from marching on Rome.

cavy short-tailed South American rodent, family Caviidae, of which the guinea-pig *Cavia porcellus* is an example. Wild cavies are grayish or brownish with rather coarse hair. They live in small groups in burrows, and have been kept for food since ancient times.

Caxton William *c.* 1422–1491. The first English printer. He learned the art of printing in Cologne, Germany, 1471 and set up a press in Belgium where he produced the first book printed in English, his own version of a French romance, *Recuyell of the Historyes of Troye* 1474. Returning to England 1476, he established himself in London, where he produced the first book printed in England, *Dictes or Sayengis of the Philosophres* 1477.

Caxton, born in Kent, was apprenticed to a London cloth dealer 1438, and set up his own business in Bruges 1441–70; he became governor of the English merchants there, negotiating on their behalf with the dukes of Burgundy. In 1471 he went to Cologne, where he learned the art of printing, and then set up his own press in Bruges in partnership with Colard Mansion, a calligrapher. The books from Caxton's press in Westminster included editions of the poets Chaucer, John Gower, and John Lydgate (*c.* 1370–1449). He translated many texts from French and Latin and revised some English ones, such as Malory's *Morte d'Arthur*. Altogether he printed about 100 books.

A typeface is named for him.

Cayenne capital and chief port of French Guiana, on Cayenne island at the mouth of the river Cayenne; population (1982) 38,135.

It was founded in 1634, and used as a penal settlement from 1854 to 1946.

cayenne pepper condiment derived from the dried fruits of various species of ▷capsicum (especially *Capsicum frutescens*), a tropical American genus of plants of the family Solanaceae. It is wholly distinct in its origin from black or white pepper, which is derived from an East Indian plant (*Piper nigrum*).

cayman or *caiman* large reptile, resembling the ▷crocodile.

Cayman Islands British island group in the West Indies
area 100 sq mi/260 sq km
features comprises three low-lying islands: Grand Cayman, Cayman Brac, and Little Cayman
government governor, executive council, and legislative assembly
exports seawhip coral, a source of ▷prostaglandins; shrimps; honey; jewelry
currency CI dollar
population (1988) 22,000
language English
history settled by military deserters in the 17th century, the islands became a pirate lair in the 18th century. Administered with Jamaica until 1962, when the Caymans became a separate colony, they are now a tourist resort, international financial center, and tax haven.

CB abbreviation for ▷*citizens' band* (radio).

cc symbol for *cubic centimetre*; abbreviation for *carbon copy/copies*.

CD abbreviation for *Corps Diplomatique* (French "Diplomatic Corps"); ▷*compact disc*; *certificate of deposit*.

CD-ROM (abbreviation for *compact-disc read-only memory*) computer storage device developed from the technology of the audio ▷compact disc. It consists of a plastic-coated metal disk, on which binary digital information is etched in the form of microscopic pits. This can then be read optically by passing a light beam over the disk. CD-ROMs typically hold about 550 ▷megabytes of data, and are used in distributing large amounts of text and graphics, such as encyclopedias, catalogs, and technical manuals.

Standard CD-ROMs cannot have information written onto them by computer, but must be manufactured from a master. Although recordable CDs, called ▷WORMs ("write once, read many times"), have been developed for use as computer disks, they are as yet too expensive for small-scale use. A compact disc that can be overwritten repeatedly by a computer has also been developed; see ▷optical disk. The compact disc, with its enormous storage capability, may eventually replace the magnetic disk as the most common form of backing store for computers.

CE abbreviation for *Common Era* (see ▷calendar); *Church of England* (often *C of E*).

Ceaușescu Nicolae 1918–1989. Romanian politician, leader of the Romanian Communist Party (RCP), in power 1965–89. He pursued a policy line independent of and critical of the USSR. He appointed family members, including his wife *Elena Ceaușescu*, to senior state and party posts, and governed in an increasingly repressive manner, zealously implementing schemes that impoverished the nation. The Ceaușescus were overthrown in a bloody revolutionary coup Dec 1989 and executed.

Ceaușescu joined the underground RCP in 1933 and was imprisoned for antifascist activities 1936–38 and 1940–44. After World War II he was elected to the Grand National Assembly and was soon given ministerial posts. He was inducted into the party secretariat and Politburo in 1954–55. In 1965 Ceaușescu became leader of the RCP and from 1967 chair of the state council. He was elected president in 1974. As revolutionary changes rocked E Europe 1989, protests in Romania escalated until the Ceaușescu regime was toppled. After his execution, the full extent of his repressive rule and personal extravagance became public.

In Aug 1989 a report condemning Ceaușescu for widespread human-rights violations was smuggled out of Romania and presented to a United Nations human-rights conference.

Cebu chief city and port of the island of Cebu in the Philippines; population (1990) 610,400; area of the island 1,964 sq mi/5,086 sq km; population (1980) 1,234,000. The oldest city of the Philippines, Cebu was founded as San Miguel 1565 and became the capital of the Spanish Philippines.

Cecil Robert, 1st Earl of Salisbury 1563–1612. Secretary of state to Elizabeth I of England, succeeding his father, Lord Burghley; he was afterwards chief minister to James I (James VI of Scotland) whose accession to the English throne he secured. He discovered the ▷Gunpowder Plot, the conspiracy to blow up the

King and Parliament 1605. James I created him Earl of Salisbury 1605.

Cecilia, St Christian patron saint of music, martyred in Rome in the 2nd or 3rd century, who is said to have sung hymns while undergoing torture. Feast day Nov 22.

cedar any of an Old World genus *Cedrus* of coniferous trees of the pine family Pinaceae. The **cedar of Lebanon** *C. libani* grows to great heights and age in the mountains of Syria and Asia Minor. Of the historic forests on Mount Lebanon itself, only a few stands of trees remain.

The name cedar is also applied to species of several genera of other coniferous trees in several families—for example, some ▷junipers, ▷cypresses, and ▷redwoods.

Cedar Falls city in NE Iowa, on the Cedar River, W of Waterloo; population (1990) 35,000. Industries include farm and other heavy equipment, rotary pumps, and tools.

Cedar Rapids city in E Iowa; population (1990) 108,800. It produces communications equipment, construction machinery, and processed foods.

Coe College is here. Cedar Rapids was settled 1837.

Cela Camilo José 1916– . Spanish novelist. Among his novels, characterized by their violence and brutal realism, are *La familia de Pascual Duarte/The Family of Pascal Duarte* 1942, and *La colmena/The Hive* 1951. He was awarded the Nobel Prize for Literature 1989.

celandine two plants belonging to different families, and resembling each other only in their bright yellow flowers. The greater celandine *Chelidonium majus* belongs to the poppy family (Papaveraceae) and is a common introduced European weed on wooded slopes in the US. The lesser celandine *Ranunculus ficaria* is a European member of the buttercup family.

Celebes English name for ▷Sulawesi, island of Indonesia.

celeriac variety of garden celery *Apium graveolens* var. *rapaceum* of the carrot family Umbelliferae, with an edible, turniplike root and small, bitter stems.

celery Old World plant *Apium graveolens* of the carrot family Umbelliferae. It grows wild in ditches and salt marshes and has a coarse texture and acrid taste. Cultivated varieties of celery are grown under cover to make them less bitter.

celesta keyboard glockenspiel producing sounds of disembodied purity. It was invented by Auguste Mustel 1886 and first used to effect by Tchaikovsky in *Nutcracker* ballet music.

celestial mechanics the branch of astronomy that deals with the calculation of the orbits of celestial bodies, their gravitational attractions (such as those that produce the Earth's tides), and also the orbits of artificial satellites and space probes. It is based on the laws of motion and gravity laid down by ▷Newton.

Celestial Police group of astronomers in Germany 1800–15, who set out to discover a supposed missing planet thought to be orbiting the Sun between Mars and Jupiter, a region now known to be occupied by types of ▷asteroid. Although they did not discover the first asteroid (found 1801), they discovered the second, Pallas (1802), third, Juno (1804), and fourth, Vesta (1807).

celestial sphere imaginary sphere surrounding the Earth, on which the celestial bodies seem to lie. The positions of bodies such as stars, planets, and galaxies are specified by their coordinates on the celestial sphere. The equivalents of latitude and longitude on the celestial sphere are called ▷declination and ▷right ascension (which is measured in hours from 0 to 24). The *celestial poles* lie directly above the Earth's poles, and the *celestial equator* lies over the Earth's equator. The celestial sphere appears to rotate once around the Earth each day, actually a result of the rotation of the Earth on its axis.

celestine or *celestite* mineral consisting of strontium sulfate, $SrSO_4$, occurring as white or light blue crystals. It is the principal source of strontium.

Celestine is found in small quantities in Germany, Italy, and the US.

celiac disease deficiency disease, usually in young children, due to disorder of the absorptive surface of the small intestine. It is mainly associated with an intolerance to gluten (a constituent of wheat) and characterized by diarrhea and malnutrition.

celibacy way of life involving voluntary abstinence from sexual intercourse. In some religions, such as Christianity and Buddhism, celibacy is a requirement for certain religious roles, such as the priesthood or a monastic life. Other religions, including Judaism, strongly discourage celibacy.

Céline Louis Ferdinand. Adopted name of Louis Destouches 1884–1961. French novelist whose writings (the first of which was *Voyage au bout de la nuit/Journey to the End of the Night* 1932) aroused controversy over their cynicism and misanthropy.

cell in biology, a discrete, membrane-bound portion of living matter, the smallest unit capable of an independent existence. All living organisms consist of one or more cells, with the exception of ▷viruses. Bacteria, protozoa, and many other microorganisms consist of single cells, whereas a human is made up of billions of cells. Essential features of a cell are the membrane, which encloses it and restricts the flow of substances in and out; the jellylike material within, often known as ▷protoplasm; the ▷ribosomes, which carry out protein synthesis; and the ▷DNA, which forms the hereditary material.

cell division the process by which a cell divides, either ▷meiosis, associated with sexual reproduction, or ▷mitosis, associated with growth, cell replacement, or repair. Both forms involve the duplication of DNA and the splitting of the nucleus.

cell, electrical or *voltaic cell* or *galvanic cell* device in which chemical energy is converted into electrical energy; the popular name is ▷"battery," but this actually refers to a collection of cells in one unit. The reactive chemicals of a *primary cell* cannot be replenished, whereas *secondary cells*—such as storage batteries—are rechargeable: their chemical reactions can be reversed and the original condition restored by applying an electric current. It is dangerous to attempt to recharge a primary cell.

Each cell contains two conducting ▷electrodes immersed in an ▷electrolyte, in a container. A spontaneous chemical reaction within the cell generates a negative charge (excess of electrons) on one electrode, and a positive charge (deficiency of electrons) on the other. The accumulation of these equal but opposite charges prevents the reaction from continuing unless an outer connection (external circuit) is made between the electrodes allowing the charges to dissipate. When this occurs, electrons escape from the cell's negative terminal and are replaced at the positive, causing a current to flow. After prolonged

celestial sphere *The main features of the celestial sphere.*

use, the cell will become flat (cease to supply current).

The first cell was made by Alessandro Volta in 1800. Types of primary cells include the Daniell, Lalande, Leclanché, and so-called "dry" cells; secondary cells include Planté, Faure, and Edison. Newer types include the Mallory (mercury depolarizer), which has a very stable discharge curve and can be made in very small units (for example, for hearing aids), and the Venner battery, which can be made substantially solid for some purposes.

Cellini Benvenuto 1500–1571. Italian sculptor and goldsmith working in the Mannerist style; author of an arrogant autobiography (begun 1588). Among his works are a graceful bronze *Perseus* 1545–54 (Loggia dei Lanzi, Florence) and a gold salt cellar made for Francis I of France 1540–43 (Kunsthistorisches Museum, Vienna), topped by nude reclining figures.

cell membrane or *plasma membrane* thin layer of protein and fat surrounding cells that controls substances passing between the cytoplasm and the intercellular space. The cell membrane is semipermeable, allowing some substances to pass through and some not.

Generally, small molecules such as water, glucose, and amino acids can penetrate the membrane, while large molecules such as starch cannot. Membranes also play a part in ⬡active transport, hormonal response, and cell metabolism.

cello abbreviation for *violoncello*, a member of the violin family and fourth member of a string quartet. The cello has been much in demand as a solo instrument because of its exceptional range and brilliance of tone, and its repertoire extends from Bach to Beethoven, Dvořák, and Elgar.

cellophane transparent wrapping film made from wood ⬡cellulose, widely used for packaging, first produced by Swiss chemist Jacques Edwin Brandenberger 1908.

Cellophane is made from wood pulp, in much the same way that the artificial fiber ⬡rayon is made: the pulp is dissolved in chemicals to form a viscose solution, which is then pumped through a long narrow slit into an acid bath where the emergent viscose stream turns into a film of pure cellulose.

cell sap dilute fluid found in the large central vacuole of many plant cells. It is made up of water, amino acids, glucose, and salts. The sap has many functions, including storage of useful materials, and provides mechanical support for non-woody plants.

cellular phone or *cellphone* mobile radio telephone, one of a network connected to the telephone system by a computer-controlled communication system. Service areas are divided into small "cells," about 3 mi/5 km across, each with a separate low-power transmitter.

The cellular system allows the use of the same set of frequencies with the minimum risk of interference. Nevertheless, in crowded city areas, cells can become overloaded. This has led to a move away from analog transmissions to digital methods that allow more calls to be made within a limited frequency range.

cellulite fatty compound alleged by some dietitians to be produced in the body by liver disorder and to cause lumpy deposits on the hips and thighs. Medical opinion generally denies its existence, attributing the lumpy appearance to a type of subcutaneous fat deposit.

cellulitis inflammation of subcutaneous tissue, accompanied by swelling, redness, and pain.

celluloid transparent or translucent, highly flammable, plastic material (a thermoplastic) made from cellulose nitrate and camphor. It was once used for toilet articles, novelties, and photographic film, but has now been replaced by the nonflammable substance cellulose acetate (made by the action of acetic acid on cellulose).

cellulose complex ⬡carbohydrate composed of long chains of glucose units. It is the principal constituent of the cell wall of higher plants, and a vital ingredient in the diet of many ⬡herbivores. Molecules of cellulose are organized into long, unbranched microfibrils that give support to the cell wall. No mammal produces the enzyme (cellulase) necessary for digesting cellulose; mammals such as rabbits and cows are only able to digest grass because the bacteria present in their gut manufacture the appropriate enzyme.

Cellulose is the most abundant substance found in the plant kingdom. It has numerous uses in industry: in rope-making; as a source of textiles (linen, cotton, viscose, and acetate) and plastics (cellophane and celluloid); in the manufacture of nondrip paint; and in such foods as whipped dessert toppings.

Celsius scale of temperature, previously called Centigrade, in which the range from freezing to boiling of water is divided into 100 degrees, freezing point being 0 degrees and boiling point 100 degrees.

The degree centigrade (°) was officially renamed Celsius in 1948 to avoid confusion with the angular measure known as the centigrade (one hundredth of a grade). The Celsius scale is named after the Swedish astronomer Anders Celsius (1701–1744), who devised it in 1742 but in reverse (freezing point was 100°; boiling point 0°).

Celt (Greek *Keltoi*) member of an Indo-European people that originated in Alpine Europe and spread to the Iberian peninsula and beyond. They were ironworkers and farmers. In the 1st century BC they were defeated by the Roman Empire and by Germanic tribes and confined largely to Britain, Ireland, and N France.

The Celts' first known territory was in central Europe about 1200 BC, in the basin of the upper Danube, the Alps, and parts of France and S Germany. In the 6th century they spread into Spain and Portugal. Over the next 300 years, they also spread into the British Isles (see ⬡Britain, ancient), N Italy (sacking Rome 390 BC), Greece, the Balkans, and parts of Asia Minor, although they never established a united empire.

Between the Bronze and Iron Ages, in the 9th–5th centuries BC, they developed a transitional culture (named the **Hallstatt** culture after its archeological site SW of Salzburg). They farmed, raised cattle, and were pioneers of ironworking, reaching their peak in the period from the 5th century to the Roman conquest (the *La Tène* culture). Celtic languages survive in Ireland, Wales, Scotland, the Isle of Man, and Brittany, and have been revived in Cornwall.

Celtic art style of art that originated about 500 BC, probably on the Rhine, and spread as the Celts moved westward to Gaul and the British Isles and southward to Italy and Turkey. Celtic manuscript illumination and sculpture

from Ireland and Anglo-Saxon Britain of the 6th–8th centuries has intricate spiral and geometric ornament, as in *The Book of Kells* (Trinity College, Dublin) and the *Lindisfarne Gospels* (British Museum, London).

Celtic languages branch of the Indo-European family, divided into two groups: the **Brythonic** or *P-Celtic* (Welsh, Cornish, Breton, and Gaulish) and the **Goidelic** or *Q-Celtic* (Irish, Scottish, and Manx Gaelic). Celtic languages once stretched from the Black Sea to Britain, but have been in decline for centuries, limited to the so-called "Celtic fringe" of western Europe.

As their names suggest, a major distinction between the two groups is that where Brythonic has *p* (as in Old Welsh *map*, "son") and Goidelic has a *q* sound (as in Gaelic *mac*, "son"). Gaulish is the long-extinct language of ancient Gaul. Cornish died out as a natural language in the late 18th century and Manx in 1974. All surviving Celtic languages have experienced official neglect in recent centuries and have suffered from emigration; currently, however, governments are more inclined than in the past to encourage their use.

Celtic Sea the sea area bounded by Wales, Ireland, and SW England; the name is commonly used by workers in the oil industry to avoid nationalist significance. The Celtic Sea is separated from the Irish Sea by St George's Channel.

cembalo accompanying keyboard instrument in Classical music.

cement any bonding agent used to unite particles in a single mass or to cause one surface to adhere to another. *Portland cement* is a powder obtained from burning together a mixture of lime (or chalk) and clay, and when mixed with water and sand or gravel, turns into mortar or concrete. In geology, a chemically precipitated material such as carbonate that occupies the interstices of clastic rocks is called cement.

The term "cement" covers a variety of materials, such as fluxes and pastes, and also bituminous products obtained from tar. In 1824 English bricklayer Joseph Aspdin (1779–1855) created and patented the first Portland cement, so named because its color in the hardened state resembled that of Portland stone, a limestone used in building.

cenotaph (Greek "empty tomb") monument to commemorate a person or persons not actually buried at the site, as in the Whitehall Cenotaph, London, designed by Edwin Lutyens to commemorate the dead of both world wars.

Cenozoic or *Caenozoic* era of geological time that began 65 million years ago and is still in process. It is divided into the Tertiary and Quaternary periods. The Cenozoic marks the emergence of mammals as a dominant group, including humans, and the formation of the mountain chains of the Himalayas and the Alps.

censor in ancient Rome, either of two senior magistrates, high officials elected every five years to hold office for 18 months. Their responsibilities included public morality, a census of the citizens, and a revision of the senatorial list.

censor in Freudian psychology, the psychic function that prevents unacceptable unconscious impulses from reaching the conscious mind. This function leads to ⬡repression of intolerable ideas, memories, or impulses.

censorship suppression by authority of material considered immoral, heretical, subversive, libelous, damaging to state security, or otherwise offensive. It is generally more stringent under totalitarian or strongly religious regimes and in wartime.

Despite First Amendment protection of free speech, attempts at censorship are made by government agencies or groups; the question is often tested in the courts, especially with respect to sexually explicit material. Recently, efforts have been made to suppress certain pieces of music and works of art, on such grounds as racial harassment and social depravity.

censorship, film control of the content and presentation of films. Film censorship dates back almost as far as the cinema. In Britain, censorship was established in 1912, in the US 1922. In some countries, self-regulation of the industry has not been regarded as sufficient; in the USSR, for example, state censorship forbade the treatment of certain issues.

In the US, censorship was not established until 1922 with the founding of the Motion Picture Producers and Distributors of America (see ▷Hays Office).

census official count of the population of a country, originally for military call-up and taxation, later for assessment of social trends as other information regarding age, sex, and occupation of each individual was included. They may become unnecessary as computerized databanks are developed.

The first US census was taken in 1790.

centaur in Greek mythology, a creature half-human and half-horse. Centaurs were supposed to live in Thessaly, and be wild and lawless; the mentor of Heracles, Chiron, was an exception.

The earliest representations of centaurs (c. 1800–1000 BC) were excavated near Famagusta, Cyprus, in 1962, and are two-headed. Some female representations also exist.

Centaurus large bright constellation of the southern hemisphere, represented as a centaur. It contains the closest star to the Sun, Proxima Centauri. Omega Centauri, the largest and brightest globular cluster of stars in the sky, is 16,000 light-years away.

Centaurus A, a peculiar galaxy 15 million light-years away, is a strong source of radio waves and X-rays.

center of gravity the point in an object about which its weight is evenly balanced. In a uniform gravitational field, this is the same as the ▷center of mass.

center of mass or **center of gravity** the point in or near an object from which its total weight appears to originate and can be assumed to act. A symmetrical homogeneous object such as a sphere or cube has its center of mass at its physical center; a hollow shape (such as a cup) may have its center of mass in space inside the hollow.

For an object to be in stable equilibrium, a perpendicular line down through its center of mass must run within the boundaries of its base; if tilted until this line falls outside the base, the object becomes unstable and topples over.

centigrade common name for the ▷Celsius temperature scale.

centipede jointed-legged animal of the group

Chilopoda, members of which have a distinct head and a single pair of long antennae. Their bodies are composed of segments (which may number nearly 200), each of similar form and bearing a single pair of legs. Most are small, but the tropical *Scolopendra gigantea* may reach 1 ft/30 cm in length. **Millipedes**, class Diplopoda, have fewer segments (up to 100), but have two pairs of legs on each.

Nocturnal, frequently blind, and all carnivorous, centipedes live in moist, dark places, and protect themselves by a poisonous secretion. They have a pair of poison claws, and strong jaws with poison fangs. The bite of some tropical species is dangerous to humans. Several species live in Britain, *Lithobius forficatus* being the most common.

CENTO abbreviation for ▷*Central Treaty Organization*.

Central African Republic landlocked country in Central Africa, bordered NE and E by Sudan, S by Zaire and the Congo, W by Cameroon, and NW by Chad.

government The president is head of both state and government and presides over the 22-member council of ministers, composed of both military and civilian members. A new constitution was approved by referendum 1986, providing for a 52-member national assembly elected for a five-year term at the summons of

Central African Republic
(*République Centrafricaine*)

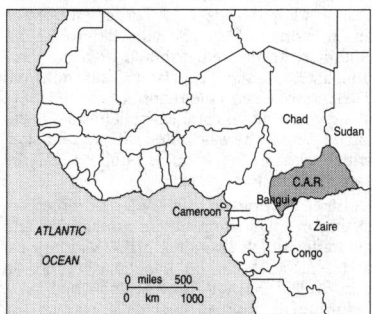

area 240,260 sq mi/622,436 sq km
capital Bangui
cities Berbérati, Bouar, Bossangoa
physical landlocked flat plateau, with rivers flowing N and S, and hills in NE and SW; dry in N, rainforest in SW
environment an est 87% of the urban population is without access to safe drinking water
features Kotto and Mbali river falls; the Oubangui River rises 20 ft/6 m at Bangui during the wet season (June–Nov)
head of state and government André Kolingba from 1981
political system one-party military republic
political parties Central African Democratic Assembly (RDC), nationalist; all political activity has been banned since the 1981 coup, but the main opposition groups, although passive, still exist. They are the Patriotic Front Ubangi Workers' Party (FPO-PT), the Central African Movement for National Liberation (MCLN), and the Movement for the Liberation of the Central African People (MPLC)
exports diamonds, uranium, coffee, cotton, timber, tobacco

the president. Despite this manifesto, however, the country remains under military rule.

history A French colony from the late 19th century, the territory of Ubangi-Shari became self-governing within French Equatorial Africa in 1958 and two years later achieved full independence. Barthélémy Boganda, who had founded the Movement for the Social Evolution of Black Africa (MESAN), had been a leading figure in the campaign for independence and became the country's first prime minister. A year before full independence he was killed in an airplane crash and was succeeded by his nephew, David Dacko, who became president 1960 and 1962 established a one-party state, with MESAN as the only political organization.
Bokassa's rule Dacko was overthrown in a military coup Dec 1965, and the commander in chief of the army, Col Jean-Bédel ▷Bokassa, assumed power. Bokassa annulled the constitution and made himself president for life 1972 and marshal of the republic 1974. An authoritarian regime was established, and in 1976 ex-president Dacko was recalled to be the president's personal adviser. At the end of that year the republic was restyled the Central African Empire, and in 1977 Bokassa was crowned emperor at a lavish ceremony his country could ill afford. His rule became increasingly dictatorial and idiosyncratic, leading to revolts by students and, in April 1979,

currency CFA franc
population (1990 est) 2,879,000 (more than 80 ethnic groups); growth rate 2.3% p.a.
life expectancy men 41, women 45
languages Sangho (national), French (official), Arabic, Hunsa, and Swahili
religions 25% Protestant; 25% Roman Catholic; 10% Muslim; 10% animist
literacy men 53%, women 29% (1985 est)
GDP $1 bn (1987); $374 per head
chronology
1960 Central African Republic achieved independence from France; David Dacko elected president.
1962 The republic made a one-party state.
1965 Dacko ousted in military coup led by Col Bokassa.
1966 Constitution rescinded and national assembly dissolved.
1972 Bokassa declared himself president for life.
1977 Bokassa made himself emperor of the Central African Empire.
1979 Bokassa deposed by Dacko following violent repressive measures by the self-styled emperor, who went into exile.
1981 Dacko deposed in a bloodless coup, led by General André Kolingba, and an all-military government established.
1983 Clandestine opposition movement formed.
1984 Amnesty for all political party leaders announced. President Mitterrand of France paid a state visit.
1985 New constitution promised, with some civilians in the government.
1986 Bokassa returned from France, expecting to return to power; he was imprisoned and his trial started. General Kolingba reelected. New constitution approved by referendum.
1988 Bokassa found guilty and received death sentence, later commuted to life imprisonment.
1991 Government announced that a national conference would be held in response to demands for a return to democracy.

by schoolchildren who objected to the compulsory wearing of school uniforms made by a company owned by the Bokassa family. Many of the children were imprisoned, and it is estimated that at least 100 were killed, with the emperor allegedly personally involved.

Dacko's coup In Sept 1979, while Bokassa was in Libya, Dacko ousted him in a bloodless coup, backed by France. The country became a republic again, with Dacko as president. He initially retained a number of Bokassa's former ministers but, following student unrest, they were dropped, and in Feb 1981 a new constitution was adopted, with an elected national assembly. Dacko was elected president for a six-year term in March, but opposition to him grew and in Sept 1981 he was deposed in another bloodless coup, led by the armed forces' Chief of Staff, General André Kolingba.

military government The constitution and all political organizations were suspended, and a military government was installed. Undercover opposition to the Kolingba regime continued, with some French support, but relations with France were improved by an unofficial visit by President Mitterrand in Oct 1982. The leaders of the banned political parties were granted an amnesty, and at the end of the year the French president paid a state visit. In Jan 1985 proposals for a new constitution were announced and in Sept civilians were included in Kolingba's administration. In 1986 Bokassa returned from exile in France, expecting to be returned to power. Instead, he was tried for his part in the killing of the schoolchildren in 1979 and condemned to death; the sentence was commuted to life imprisonment 1988. In 1991, in response to widespread demonstrations calling for a return to a multiparty system, the government announced that it would convene a national conference to discuss the future of the country. *See illustration box.*

Central America the part of the Americas that links Mexico with the Isthmus of Panama, comprising Belize, Costa Rica, El Salvador, Guatemala, Honduras, Nicaragua, and Panama. It is also an isthmus, crossed by mountains that form part of the Cordilleras, rising to a maximum height of 13,845 ft/4,220 m. There are numerous active volcanoes. Central America is about 200,000 sq mi/523,000 sq km in area and has a population (1980) estimated at 22,700,000, mostly Indians or mestizos (of mixed white-Indian ancestry). Tropical agricultural products and other basic commodities and raw materials are exported.

Much of Central America formed part of the Maya civilization which originated about 2600 BC. It was discovered by Christopher Columbus in 1502. Spanish settlers married indigenous women, and the area remained out of the mainstream of Spanish Empire history. When the Spanish Empire collapsed in the early 1800s, the area formed the Central American Federation, with a constitution based on that of the US. The federation disintegrated 1840, however. Completion of the Panama Canal 1914 enhanced the region's position as a strategic international crossroads. Demand for cash crops (bananas, coffee, cotton), especially from the US, created a strong landowning class controlling a serflike peasantry by military means. There has been US military intervention in the area—for example, in Nicaragua, where the dynasty of General Anastasio Somoza was founded. President Carter officially reversed support for such regimes, but in the 1980s the Reagan and Bush

administrations again favored military and financial aid to selected political groups, including the ⟡Contras in Nicaragua and the ruling regime in El Salvador. Continuing US interest was underscored by its invasion of Panama Dec 1989.

Central American Common Market CACM (**Mercado Común Centroamericana** MCCA) economic alliance established 1960 by El Salvador, Guatemala, Honduras (seceded 1970), and Nicaragua; Costa Rica joined 1962. Formed to encourage economic development and cooperation between the smaller Central American nations and to attract industrial capital, CACM failed to live up to early expectations: nationalist interests remained strong and by the mid-1980s political instability in the region and border conflicts between members were hindering its activities.

Central Asian Republics group of five republics: ⟡Kazakhstan, ⟡Kyrgyzstan, ⟡Tajikistan, ⟡Turkmenistan, and ⟡Uzbekistan. Formerly part of the Soviet Union, their independence was recognized 1991. All five republics belong to the Commonwealth of Independent States (CIS). They comprise a large part of the geographical region of ⟡Turkestan and are the home of large numbers of Muslims.

These were conquered by Russia as recently as 1866–73 and until 1917 were divided into the khanate of Khiva, the emirate of Bokhara, and the governor-generalship of Turkestan. The Soviet government became firmly established 1919, and in 1920 the Khan of Khiva and the Emir of Bokhara were overthrown and People's Republics set up. Turkestan became an Autonomous Soviet Socialist Republic 1921. Boundaries were redistributed 1925 along nationalist lines, and Uzbekistan, Tajikistan, and Turkmenistan became republics of the USSR, along with Bokhara and Khiva. The area populated by Kazakhs was united with Kazakhstan, which became a Union Republic 1936, the same year as Kyrgyzstan.

Central Command military strike force consisting of units from the US army, navy, and air force, which operates in the Middle East and North Africa. Its headquarters are in Fort McDill, Florida. It was established 1979, following the Iranian hostage crisis and the Soviet invasion of Afghanistan, and was known as the Rapid Deployment Force until 1983. It commanded coalition forces in the Gulf War 1991.

Plagued by organizational problems, interservice rivalries, equipment shortages, and lack of access to bases in the Middle East, it was reorganized by President Reagan in 1983 as the US Central Command.

central dogma in genetics and evolution, the fundamental belief that ⟡genes can affect the nature of the physical body, but that changes in the body (for example, through use or accident) cannot be translated into changes in the genes.

central heating system of heating from a central source, typically of a house, larger building, or group of buildings, as opposed to heating each room individually. Steam heat and hot-water heat are the most common systems in use. Water is heated in a furnace burning oil, gas or solid fuel, and, as steam or hot water, is then pumped through radiators in each room. The level of temperature can be selected by adjusting a thermostat or temperature gauge on the burner or in a room.

Central heating has its origins in the hypocaust heating system introduced by the

Romans nearly 2,000 years ago. From the 18th century, steam central heating, usually by pipe, was available in the West and installed in individual houses on an ad hoc basis. The Scottish engineer James ⟡Watt heated his study with a steam pipe connected to a boiler, and Matthew ⟡Boulton installed steam heating in a friend's Birmingham house. Not until the latter half of the 20th century was central heating in general use.

Central heating systems are usually switched on and off by a time switch. Another kind of central heating system uses hot air, which is pumped through ducts (called risers) to grills in the rooms. Underfloor heating (called radiant heat) is used in some houses, the heat coming from electric elements buried in the floor.

Central Intelligence Agency (CIA) US intelligence organization established 1947. It has actively intervened overseas, generally to undermine left-wing regimes or to protect US financial interests; for example, in the Congo (now Zaire) and Nicaragua. From 1980 all covert activity by the CIA has by law to be reported to Congress, preferably beforehand, and must be authorized by the president. In 1990 the CIA's estimated budget was $10–12 billion. Robert Gates became CIA director 1991.

Developed from the wartime Office of Strategic Services and set up by Congress, as part of the National Security Act, on the lines of the British Secret Service, the CIA was intended solely for use overseas in the Cold War. It was involved in, for example, the restoration of the shah of Iran 1953, South Vietnam (during the Vietnam War), Chile (the coup against President Allende), and Cuba (the ⟡Bay of Pigs). On the domestic front, it was illegally involved in the ⟡Watergate political scandal and in the 1970s lost public confidence when US influence collapsed in Iran, Afghanistan, Nicaragua, Yemen, and elsewhere. A fire in the US embassy in Moscow 1991 led to the loss of much sensitive material and, in May, William Webster stepped down as director, following criticisms of the agency's intelligence gathering prior to the 1989 US invasion of Panama and the 1991 Gulf War. Robert Gates (deputy national security adviser 1989–91 and deputy director of the CIA 1986–89) became his successor. CIA headquarters is in Langley, Virginia. Past directors include William Casey, Richard ⟡Helms, and George ⟡Bush. The CIA director is also coordinator of all the US intelligence organizations. Domestic intelligence functions are performed by the ⟡Federal Bureau of Investigation.

The CIA belongs to the executive branch of government and acts on the president's orders. Historically, it runs both covert (secret) and overt (open) operations in the name of national security.

central nervous system (CNS) the part of the nervous system that coordinates various body functions. It has a high concentration of nerve-cell bodies and synapses (junctions between ⟡nerve cells). In ⟡vertebrates, the CNS consists of a brain and a dorsal nerve cord (the spinal cord) enclosed and protected within the spinal column. In worms, insects, and crustaceans, it consists of a paired ventral nerve cord with concentrations of nerve-cell bodies, each known as a ⟡**ganglion**, in each segment, and a small brain in the head.

Some simple invertebrates, such as sponges and jellyfishes, have no CNS but a simple network of nerve cells called a **nerve net**.

CPU

control
unit

external
clock

from
input
devices

input
logic

registers

output
logic

from
RAM
and
ROM

ALU

to
RAM

arithmetic
and logic
unit

central processing unit *The central processing unit is the "brain" of a computer; it is here that all the computer's work is done.*

Central Powers originally the signatories of the ◊Triple Alliance 1882: Germany, Austria-Hungary, and Italy. During the World War I, Italy remained neutral before joining the ◊Allies.

central processing unit (CPU) main component of a computer, the part that executes individual program instructions and controls the operation of other parts. It is sometimes called the central processor or, when contained on a single integrated circuit, a microprocessor.

The CPU has three main components: the *arithmetic and logic unit* (ALU), where all

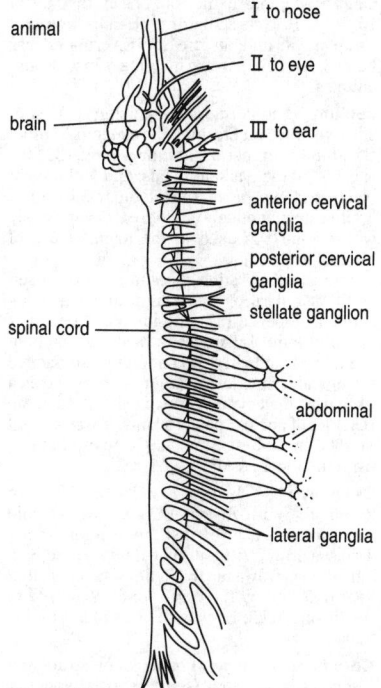

I to nose

animal

II to eye

brain

III to ear

anterior cervical
ganglia

posterior cervical
ganglia

spinal cord

stellate ganglion

abdominal

lateral ganglia

central nervous system *The central nervous system (CNS) with its associated nerves.*

calculations and logical operations are carried out; a *control unit*, which decodes, synchronizes, and executes program instruction; and the *immediate access memory*, which stores the data and programs on which the computer is currently working. All these components contain ◊registers, which are memory locations reserved for specific purposes.

Central Provinces and Berar former British province of India, now part of ◊Madhya Pradesh.

Central Treaty Organization (CENTO) military alliance that replaced the ◊Baghdad Pact 1959; it collapsed when the withdrawal of Iran, Pakistan, and Turkey 1979 left the UK as the only member.

Centre region of N central France; area 15,131 sq mi/39,200 sq km; population (1986) 2,324,000. It includes the *départements* of Cher, Eure-et-Loire, Indre, Indre-et-Loire, Loire-et-Cher, and Loiret. Its capital is Orléans.

centrifugal force useful concept in physics, based on an apparent (but not real) force. It may be regarded as a force that acts radially outwards from a spinning or orbiting object, thus balancing the ◊centripetal force (which is real). For an object of mass m moving with a velocity v in a circle of radius r, the centrifugal force F equals mv^2/r (outwards).

centrifuge apparatus that rotates at high speeds, causing substances inside it to be thrown outwards. One use is for separating mixtures of substances of different densities.

The mixtures are usually spun horizontally in balanced containers ("buckets"), and the rotation sets up centrifugal forces, causing their components to separate according to their densities. A common example is the separation of the lighter plasma from the heavier blood corpuscles in certain blood tests. The *ultra-centrifuge* is a very high-speed centrifuge, used in biochemistry for separating ◊colloids and organic substances; it may operate at several million revolutions per minute. The centrifuges used in the industrial separation of cream from milk, and yeast from fermented wort (infused malt), operate by having mixtures pumped through a continually rotating chamber, the components being tapped off at

different points. Large centrifuges are used for physiological research—for example, in astronaut training where bodily responses to gravitational forces many times the normal level are tested.

centriole structure found in the ◊cells of animals that plays a role in the processes of ◊meiosis and ◊mitosis (cell division).

centripetal force force that acts radially inwards on an object moving in a curved path. For example, with a weight whirled in a circle at the end of a length of string, the centripetal force is the tension in the string. For an object of mass m moving with a velocity v in a circle of radius r, the centripetal force F equals mv^2/r (inwards). The reaction to this force is the ◊centrifugal force.

centromere part of the ◊chromosome where there are no ◊genes. Under the microscope, it usually appears as a constriction in the strand of the chromosome, and is the point at which the spindle fibers are attached during ◊meiosis and ◊mitosis (cell division).

Cephalonia English form of ◊Kefallinia, largest of the Ionian islands, off the W coast of Greece.

cephalopod any predatory marine mollusk of the class Cephalopoda, with the mouth and head surrounded by tentacles. Cephalopods are the most intelligent, the fastest-moving, and the largest of all animals without backbones, and there are remarkable luminescent forms which swim or drift at great depths. They have the most highly developed nervous and sensory systems of all invertebrates, the eye in some closely paralleling that found in vertebrates. Examples include octopus, squid, and cuttlefish. Shells are rudimentary or absent in most cephalopods.

Typically, they move by swimming with the mantle (fold of outer skin) aided by the arms, but can squirt water out of the siphon (funnel) to propel themselves backward by jet propulsion. They grow very rapidly and may be mature in a year. The female common octopus lays 150,000 eggs after copulation, and stays to brood them for as long as six weeks. After they hatch the female dies, and, although reproductive habits of many cephalopods are not known, it is thought that dying after spawning may be typical.

cephalosporin any of a class of broad-spectrum antibiotics derived from a fungus (genus *Cephalosporium*). It is similar to penicillin and is used on penicillin-resistant infections.

The first cephalosporin was extracted from sewage-contaminated water, and other naturally occurring ones have been isolated from molds taken from soil samples. Synthetic cephalosporins can be designed to be effective against a particular ◊pathogen.

Cepheid variable yellow supergiant star that varies regularly in brightness every few days or weeks as a result of pulsations. The time that a Cepheid variable takes to pulsate is directly related to its average brightness; the longer the pulsation period, the brighter the star.

This relationship, the *period luminosity law* (discovered by Henrietta ◊Leavitt), allows astronomers to use Cepheid variables as "standard candles" to measure distances in our Galaxy and to nearby galaxies. They are named after their prototype, Delta Cephei, whose light variations were observed 1784 by English astronomer John Goodricke (1764–1786).

Cepheus constellation of the north polar region, named after King Cepheus of Greek mythology, husband of Cassiopeia and father of Andromeda. It contains the Garnet Star (Mu Cephei), a red supergiant of variable brightness that is one of the reddest-colored stars known, and Delta Cephei, prototype of the ⊳Cepheid variables.

Ceram or **Seram** Indonesian island in the Moluccas; area 6,621 sq mi/17,142 sq km. The principal town is Ambon.

ceramic nonmetallic mineral (clay) used to form articles that are then fired at high temperatures. Ceramics are divided into heavy clay products (bricks, roof tiles, drainpipes, sanitary ware), refractories or high-temperature materials (linings for furnaces used to manufacture steel, fuel elements in nuclear reactors), and pottery, which uses kaolinite, ball clay, china stone, and flint. Superceramics, such as silicon carbide, are lighter, stronger, and more heat-resistant than steel for use in motor and aircraft engines and have to be cast to shape since they are too hard to machine.

The earliest ceramics date back to the beginning of the Neolithic in the Near East, Asia, the Americas, Europe, and Africa.

Cerberus in Greek mythology, the three-headed dog guarding the entrance to ⊳Hades, the underworld.

cereal grass grown for its edible, nutrient-rich, starchy seeds. The term refers primarily to wheat, oats, rye, and barley, but may also refer to corn, millet, and rice. Cereals contain about 75% complex carbohydrates and 10% protein, plus fats and fiber (roughage). They store well. If all the world's cereal crop were consumed as whole-grain products directly by humans, everyone could obtain adequate protein and carbohydrate; however, a large proportion of cereal production in affluent nations is used as animal feed to boost the production of meat, dairy products, and eggs.

The term also refers to breakfast foods prepared from the seeds of cereal crops. Some cereals require cooking (porridge oats), but most are ready to eat. Mass-marketed cereals include refined and sweetened varieties as well as whole cereals such as muesli. Whole cereals are more nutritious and provide more fiber than the refined cereals, which often have vitamins and flavorings added to replace those lost in the refining process.

cerebellum part of the brain of ⊳vertebrate animals which controls muscular movements, balance, and coordination. It is relatively small in lower animals such as newts and lizards, but large in birds since flight demands precise coordination. The human cerebellum is also well developed, because of the need for balance when walking or running, and for coordinated hand movements.

cerebral pertaining to the brain, especially the part known as the cerebrum, concerned with higher brain functions.

cerebral hemisphere one of the two halves of the ⊳cerebrum.

cerebral hemorrhage or **apoplectic fit** in medicine, a ⊳stroke in which a blood vessel bursts in the brain, caused by factors such as high blood pressure combined with hardening of the arteries, or chronic poisoning with lead or alcohol. It may cause death or damage parts of the brain, leading to paralysis or mental impairment. The effects are usually long-term and the condition may recur.

cerebral palsy any nonprogressive abnormality of the brain caused by oxygen deprivation

before birth, injury during birth, haemorrhage, meningitis, viral infection, or faulty development. It is characterized by muscle spasm, weakness, lack of coordination, and impaired movement. Intelligence is not always affected.

cerebrovascular accident (CVA) alternate name for ⊳stroke.

cerebrum part of the vertebrate ⊳brain, formed from the two paired cerebral hemispheres. In birds and mammals it is the largest part of the brain. It is covered with an infolded layer of gray matter, the cerebral cortex, which integrates brain functions.

The cerebrum coordinates the senses, and is responsible for learning and other higher mental faculties.

Ceres the largest asteroid, 584 mi/940 km in diameter, and the first to be discovered (by Giuseppe Piazzi 1801). Ceres orbits the Sun every 4.6 years at an average distance of 257 million mi/414 million km. Its mass is about one-seventieth of that of the Moon.

Ceres in Roman mythology, the goddess of agriculture; see ⊳Demeter.

Cerf Bennett Alfred 1898–1971. US editor and publisher. In 1925 he and a partner purchased the rights to the Modern Library series, and on that base Cerf founded Random House 1927. The company grew to be one of the world's largest publishing houses.

Born in New York, Cerf was educated at Columbia University and briefly worked as a reporter for the *New York Herald Tribune*. He published several collections of humor and appeared as a regular panelist on the popular television show "What's My Line?"

cerium malleable and ductile, gray, metallic element, symbol Ce, atomic number 58, atomic weight 140.12. It is the most abundant member of the lanthanide series, and is used in alloys, electronic components, nuclear fuels, and lighter flints. It was discovered 1804 by the Swedish chemists Jöns Berzelius and Wilhelm Hisinger (1766–1852), and, independently, by Martin Klaproth. The element was named after the then recently discovered asteroid Ceres.

cermet bonded material containing ceramics and metal, widely used in jet engines and nuclear reactors. Cermets behave much like metals but have the great heat resistance of ceramics. Tungsten carbide, molybdenum boride, and aluminum oxide are among the ceramics used; iron, cobalt, nickel, and chromium are among the metals.

CERN nuclear research organization founded 1954 as a cooperative enterprise among European governments. It has laboratories at Meyrin, near Geneva, Switzerland. It was originally known as the *Conseil Européen pour la Recherche Nucléaire* but subsequently renamed *Organisation Européenne pour la Recherche Nucléaire*, although still familiarly known as CERN. It houses the world's largest particle ⊳accelerator, the ⊳Large Electron–Positron Collider (LEP), with which notable advances have been made in ⊳particle physics.

In 1965 the original laboratory was doubled in size by extension across the border from Switzerland into France.

Cervantes Saavedra, Miguel de 1547–1616. Spanish novelist, playwright, and poet whose masterpiece *Don Quixote* (in full *El ingenioso hidalgo Don Quixote de la Mancha*) was published 1605. In 1613, his *Novelas ejemplares/*

Exemplary Novels appeared, followed by *Viaje del Parnaso/The Voyage to Parnassus* 1614. A spurious second part of *Don Quixote* prompted Cervantes to bring out his own second part 1615, often considered superior to the first in construction and characterization.

Born at Alcalá de Henares, he entered the army in Italy, and was wounded in the battle of Lepanto 1571. While on his way back to Spain 1575, he was captured by Barbary pirates and taken to Algiers, where he became a slave until ransomed 1580.

Returning to Spain, he wrote several plays, and in 1585 his pastoral romance *Galatea* was printed. He was employed in Seville 1587 provisioning the Armada. While working as a tax collector, he was imprisoned more than once for deficiencies in his accounts. He sank into poverty, and little is known of him until 1605 when he published *Don Quixote*. The novel was an immediate success and was soon translated into English and French.

cervical cancer ⊳cancer of the cervix (the neck of the womb).

cervical cap see ⊳contraceptive.

cervical smear removal of a small sample of tissue from the cervix (neck of the womb) to screen for changes implying a likelihood of cancer. The procedure is also known as the *Pap test* after its originator, George Papanicolau.

cervix (Latin "neck") abbreviation for *cervix uteri*, the neck of the womb.

Cesalpino, Andrea Andrea 1519–1603. Italian botanist who showed that plants could be and should be classified by their anatomy and structure. In *De plantis* 1583 Cesalpino offered the first remotely modern classification of plants. Before this plants were classed by their location—for example marsh plants, moorland plants, and even foreign plants.

César adopted name of César Baldaccini 1921– . French sculptor who uses iron and scrap metal and, in the 1960s, crushed car bodies. His subjects are imaginary insects and animals.

cesium (Latin *caesius* "bluishgray") soft, silvery-white, ductile, metallic element, symbol Cs, atomic number 55, atomic weight 132.905. It is one of the ⊳alkali metals, and is the most electropositive of all the elements. In air it ignites spontaneously, and it reacts vigorously with water. It is used in the manufacture of photoelectric cells.

The rate of vibration of cesium atoms is used as the standard of measuring time. Its radioactive isotope Cs-137 (half-life 30.17 years) is one of the most dangerous waste products of the nuclear industry; it is a highly radioactive biological analog for potassium, produced as a fission product of nuclear explosions and in the reactors of nuclear power plants. It was named in 1860 by Robert Bunsen, German chemist, from the blueness of its spectral line.

Cetewayo (Cetshwayo) *c.* 1826–1884. King of Zululand, South Africa, 1873–83, whose rule was threatened by British annexation of the Transvaal 1877. Although he defeated the British at Isandhlwana 1879, he was later that year defeated by them at Ulundi. Restored to his throne 1883, he was then expelled by his subjects.

Cetus (Latin "whale") constellation straddling the celestial equator (see ⊳celestial sphere), represented as a sea monster. Cetus contains the long-period variable star ⊳Mira, and ⊳Tau

Ceti, one of the nearest stars visible with the naked eye.

Ceylon former name (until 1972) of ◊Sri Lanka.

Cézanne Paul 1839–1906. French Post-Impressionist painter, a leading figure in the development of modern art. He broke away from the Impressionists' spontaneous vision to develop a style that captured not only light and life, but the structure of natural forms in landscapes, still lifes, portraits, and his series of bathers.

He was born in Aix-en-Provence, where he studied, and was a friend of the novelist Emile Zola. In 1872 Cézanne met Pissarro and lived near him in Pontoise, outside Paris, but soon abandoned Impressionism. His series of paintings of Mont Sainte-Victoire in Provence from the 1880s into the 1900s show an increasing fragmentation of the painting's surface and a movement toward abstraction, with layers of color and square brushstrokes achieving monumental solidity. He was greatly revered by early abstract painters, notably Picasso and Braque.

cf. abbreviation for *confer* (Latin "compare").

CFC abbreviation for ◊*chlorofluorocarbon*.

Chablis white burgundy wine produced near the town of the same name in the Yonne *département* of central France.

Chabrol Claude 1930– . French film director.

Originally a critic, he was one of the New Wave directors. His works of murder and suspense, which owe much to Hitchcock, include *Les Cousins/The Cousins* 1959, *Les Biches/The Girlfriends* 1968, *Le Boucher/The Butcher* 1970, and *Cop au Vin* 1984.

Chaco province of Argentina; area 38,458 sq mi/99,633 sq km; population (1991) 838,300. Its capital is Resistencia, in the SE. The chief crop is cotton, and there is forestry.

Chaco War war between Bolivia and Paraguay 1932–35 over boundaries in the north of Gran Chaco, settled by arbitration 1938.

Chad landlocked country in central N Africa, bounded N by Libya, E by Sudan, S by the Central African Republic, and W by Cameroon, Nigeria, and Niger.

government The 1982 provisional constitution provided for a president assisted by a council of ministers. A new constitution was introduced July 1990, providing for a new national assembly of 123 elective seats to replace the appointed National Consultative Council.

history Called Kanem when settled by Arabs in the 7th–13th centuries, the area later became known as Bornu and in the 19th century was conquered by Sudan. From 1913 a province of French Equatorial Africa, Chad became an autonomous state within the French Community 1958, with François Tombalbaye as prime minister.

independence Full independence was

achieved 1960, and Tombalbaye became president. He soon faced disagreements between the Arabs of the north, who saw Libya as an ally, and the black African Christians of the south, who felt more sympathy for Nigeria. In the north the Chadian National Liberation Front (Frolinat) revolted against the government. In 1975 Tombalbaye was killed in a coup led by former army Chief of Staff Félix Malloum, who became president of a supreme military council and appealed for national unity. Frolinat continued its opposition, however, supported by Libya, which held a strip of land in the north, believed to contain uranium.

Frolinat expansion By 1978 Frolinat, led by General Goukouni Oueddi, had expanded its territory but was halted with French aid. Malloum tried to reach a settlement by making former Frolinat leader, Hissène Habré, prime minister, but disagreements developed between them. In 1979 fighting broke out again between government and Frolinat forces, and Malloum fled the country. Talks resulted in the formation of a provisional government (GUNT), with Goukouni holding the presidency with Libyan support. A proposed merger with Libya was rejected, and Libya withdrew most of its forces.

civil war The Organization for African Unity (OAU) set up a peacekeeping force but civil war broke out and by 1981 Hissène Habré's Armed Forces of the North (FAN) controlled half the country. Goukouni fled and set up a "government in exile." In 1983 a majority of OAU members agreed to recognize Habré's regime, but Goukouni, with Libyan support, fought on.

cease-fire After Libyan bombing, Habré appealed to France for help. Three thousand troops were sent as instructors, with orders to retaliate if attacked. Following a Franco-African summit 1984, a cease-fire was agreed, with latitude 16°N dividing the opposing forces. Libyan president Col Khaddhafi's proposal of a simultaneous withdrawal of French and Libyan troops was accepted. By Dec 1984 all French troops had left, but Libya's withdrawal was doubtful. Habré dissolved the military arm of Frolinat 1984 and formed a new party, the National Union for Independence and Revolution (UNIR), but opposition to his regime grew. In 1987 Goukouni was reported to be under house arrest in Tripoli. Meanwhile Libya intensified its military operations in northern Chad, Habré's government retaliated, and France renewed (if reluctantly) its support.

fall of Habré It was announced March 1989 that France, Chad, and Libya had agreed to observe a cease-fire proposed by the OAU. A meeting July 1989 between Habré and Khaddhafi reflected the improvement in relations between Chad and Libya. Habré was endorsed as president Dec 1989 for another seven-year term under a revised constitution, introduced July 1990. In Dec 1990 the government fell to rebel opposition forces, Hissène Habré was reported killed, and the rebel leader Idriss Deby became president.

toward democracy Between Oct 1991 and Jan 1992, a number of antigovernment coups were foiled, sometimes with the help of French troops. In March 1992 the new government moved nearer to multiparty politics when two opposition groups were approved, the Alliance for Democracy and Progress (RDP) and the Union for Democracy and Progress (UPDT). *See illustration box.*

Chad, Lake lake on the NE boundary of Nigeria. It once varied in extent between

Chad
Republic of (*République du Tchad*)

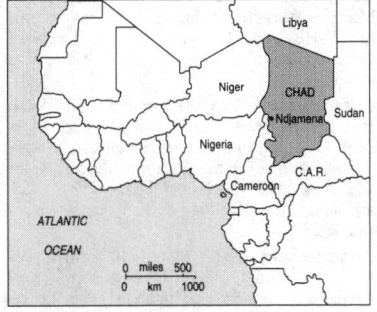

area 495,624 sq mi/1,284,000 sq km
capital Ndjamena (formerly Fort Lamy)
cities Sarh, Moundou, Abéché
physical landlocked state with mountains and part of Sahara Desert in N; moist savanna in S; rivers in S flow NW to Lake Chad
head of state and government Idriss Deby from 1990
political system emergent democratic republic
political parties National Union for Independence and Revolution (UNIR), nationalist; Alliance for Democracy and Progress (RDP), center-left; Union for Democracy and Progress (UPDT), center-left
exports cotton, meat, livestock, hides, skins
currency CFA franc
population (1990 est) 5,064,000; growth rate 2.3% p.a. Nomadic tribes move N–S seasonally in search of water
life expectancy men 42, women 45
languages French, Arabic (both official), over 100 African languages spoken
religion Muslim 44% (N), Christian 33%, animist 23% (S)

literacy men 40%, women 11% (1985 est)
GDP $980 million (1986); $186 per head
chronology
1960 Independence achieved from France, with François Tombalbaye as president.
1963 Violent opposition in the Muslim north, led by the Chadian National Liberation Front (Frolinat), backed by Libya.
1968 Revolt quelled with France's help.
1975 Tombalbaye killed in military coup led by Félix Malloum. Frolinat continued its resistance.
1978 Malloum tried to find a political solution by bringing the former Frolinat leader Hissène Habré into his government but they were unable to work together.
1979 Malloum forced to leave the country; an interim government was set up under General Goukouni. Habré continued his opposition with his Army of the North (FAN).
1981 Habré now in control of half the country. Goukouni fled and set up a "government in exile."
1983 Habré's regime recognized by the Organization for African Unity (OAU), but in the north Goukouni's supporters, with Libya's help, fought on. Eventually a cease-fire was agreed, with latitude 16°N dividing the country.
1984 Libya and France agreed to a withdrawal of forces.
1985 Fighting between Libyan-backed and French-backed forces intensified.
1987 Chad, France, and Libya agreed on cease-fire proposed by OAU.
1988 Full diplomatic relations with Libya restored.
1989 Libyan troop movements reported on border; Habré reelected, amended constitution.
1990 President Habré ousted in coup led by Idriss Deby. New constitution adopted.
1991 Several antigovernment coups foiled.
1992 Anti-government coup foiled. Two new opposition parties approved.

rainy and dry seasons from 20,000 sq mi/ 50,000 sq km to 7,000 sq mi/20,000 sq km, but a series of droughts 1979–89 reduced its area by 80%. The S Chad irrigation project used the lake waters to irrigate the surrounding desert, but the 2,500 mi/4,000 km of canals dug for the project are now permanently dry because of the shrinking size of the lake. The Lake Chad basin is being jointly developed for oil and natron by Cameroon, Chad, Niger, and Nigeria.

The lake was first seen by European explorers 1823.

Chadli Benjedid 1929– . Algerian socialist politician, president 1979–92. An army colonel, he supported Boumédienne in the overthrow of Ben Bella 1965, and succeeded Boumédienne 1979, pursuing more moderate policies. Chadli resigned Jan 1992 following a victory for Islamic fundamentalists in the first round of assembly elections.

chador (Hindi "square of cloth") all-enveloping black garment for women worn by some Muslims and Hindus.

The origin of the chador dates to the 6th century BC under Cyrus the Great and the Achaemenian empire in Persia. Together with the ◊purdah (Persian "veil") and the idea of female seclusion, it persisted under Alexander the Great and the Byzantine Empire, and was adopted by the Arab conquerors of the Byzantines. Its use was revived in Iran in the 1970s by Ayatollah Khomeini in response to the Koranic request for "modesty" in dress.

Chadwick James 1891–1974. British physicist. In 1932 he discovered the particle in the nucleus of an atom that became known as the neutron because it has no electric charge. He received the Nobel Prize for Physics 1935.

chafer beetle of the family Scarabeidae. The adults eat foliage or flowers, and the underground larvae feed on roots, chiefly those of grasses and cereals, and can be very destructive. Examples are the ◊*cockchafer* and the *rose chafer Cetonia aurata*, about 0.8 in/2 cm long and bright green.

chaffinch bird *Fringilla coelebs* of the finch family, common throughout much of Europe and W Asia. About 6 in/15 cm long, the male is olive-brown above, with a bright chestnut breast, a bluishgray cap, and two white bands on the upper part of the wing; the female is duller.

Chagall Marc 1887–1985. Russian-born French painter and designer; much of his highly colored, fantastic imagery was inspired by the village life of his boyhood and by Jewish and Russian folk tradition. He also designed stained glass, mosaics (for Israel's Knesset in the 1960s), the ceiling of the Paris Opera House 1964, tapestries, and stage sets. He was an original figure, often seen as a precursor of Surrealism, as in *The Dream* (Metropolitan Museum of Art, New York).

Chagall lived mainly in France from 1922. His stained glass can be found in, notably, a chapel in Vence, the south of France, 1950s, and a synagogue near Jerusalem 1961. He also produced illustrated books.

Chagas's disease disease common in Central and South America, caused by a trypanosome parasite transmitted by insects; it results in incurable damage to the heart, intestines, and brain. It is named after Brazilian doctor Carlos Chagas (1879–1934).

Chagos Archipelago island group in the Indian Ocean; area 23 sq mi/60 sq km. Formerly a dependency of Mauritius, it now forms the ◊British Indian Ocean Territory. The chief island is Diego Garcia, now a US-British strategic base.

Chain Ernst Boris 1906–1979. German-born British biochemist who worked on the development of ◊penicillin. Chain fled to Britain from the Nazis 1933. After the discovery of penicillin by Alexander Fleming, Chain worked to isolate and purify it. For this work, he shared the 1945 Nobel Prize for Medicine with Fleming and Howard Florey. Chain also discovered penicillinase, an enzyme that destroys penicillin.

chain reaction in chemistry, a succession of reactions, usually involving free radicals, where the products of one stage are the reactants of the next. A chain reaction is characterized by the continual generation of reactive substances.

A chain reaction comprises three separate stages: *initiation*—the initial generation of reactive species; *propagation*—reactions that involve reactive species and generate similar or different reactive species; and *termination*—reactions that involve the reactive species but produce only stable, nonreactive substances. Chain reactions may occur slowly (for example, the oxidation of edible oils) or accelerate as the number of reactive species increases, ultimately resulting in explosion.

chain reaction in nuclear physics, a fission reaction that is maintained because neutrons released by the splitting of some atomic nuclei themselves go on to split others, releasing even more neutrons. Such a reaction can be controlled (as in a nuclear reactor) by using moderators to absorb excess neutrons. Uncontrolled, a chain reaction produces a nuclear explosion (as in an atomic bomb).

Chaka alternate spelling of ◊Shaka, Zulu chief.

Chalatenango department on the N frontier of El Salvador; area 968 sq mi/2,507 sq km; population (1981) 235,700; capital Chalatenango.

Chalcedon, Council of ecumenical council of the early Christian church, convoked 451 by the Roman emperor Marcian, and held at Chalcedon (now Kadiköy, Turkey). The council, attended by over 500 bishops, resulted in the *Definition of Chalcedon*, an agreed doctrine for both the eastern and western churches.

chalcedony form of quartz, SiO_2, in which the crystals are so fine-grained that they are impossible to distinguish with a microscope (cryptocrystalline). Agate, onyx, tiger's eye, and carnelian are ◊gem varieties of chalcedony.

chalcopyrite copper iron sulfide, $CuFeS_2$, the most common ore of copper. It is brassy yellow in color and may have an iridescent surface tarnish. It occurs in many different types of mineral vein, in rocks ranging from basalt to limestone.

Chaldaea ancient region of Babylonia.

Chaliapin Fyodor Ivanovich 1873–1938. Russian bass singer, born in Kazan. His greatest role was that of Boris Godunov in Mussorgsky's opera of the same name. Chaliapin left the USSR 1921 to live and sing in the world's capitals.

chalk soft, fine-grained, whitish rock composed of calcium carbonate, $CaCO_3$, extensively quarried for use in cement, lime, and mortar, and in the manufacture of cosmetics and toothpaste. *Blackboard chalk* in fact consists of ◊gypsum (calcium sulfate, $CaSO_4$).

Chalk was once thought to derive from the remains of microscopic animals or foraminifera. In 1953, however, it was seen under the electron microscope to be composed chiefly of coccolithophores, unicellular lime-secreting algae, and hence primarily of plant origin. It is formed from deposits of deep-sea sediments called oozes.

Châlons-sur-Marne capital of the *département* of Marne, NE France; population (1982) 54,400. It is a market town and trades mainly in champagne. Tradition has it that Attila was defeated in his attempt to invade France, at the *Battle of Châlons* 451 by the Roman general Aëtius and the Visigoth Theodoric.

Chalon-sur-Saône town in the *département* of Saône-et-Loire, France, on the river Saône and the Canal du Center; population (1982) 58,000. It has mechanical and electrical engineering and chemical industries.

Chamberlain (Arthur) Neville 1869–1940. British Conservative politician, son of Joseph Chamberlain. He was prime minister 1937–40; his policy of appeasement toward the fascist dictators Mussolini and Hitler (with whom he concluded the ◊Munich Agreement 1938) failed to prevent the outbreak of World War II. He resigned 1940 following the defeat of the British forces in Norway.

In 1938 Chamberlain went to Munich, Germany, and negotiated with Hitler on the Czechoslovak question. He was ecstatically received on his return and claimed that the Munich Agreement brought "peace in our time." However, Germany advanced against British allies and within a year Britain was at war.

Chamberlain (Joseph) Austen 1863–1937. British Conservative politician, elder son of Joseph Chamberlain; as foreign secretary 1924–29 he negotiated the Pact of ◊Locarno, for which he won the Nobel Peace Prize 1925, and signed the ◊Kellogg–Briand pact to outlaw war 1928.

Chamberlain Joseph 1836–1914. British politician, reformist mayor of and member of Parliament for Birmingham; in 1886, he resigned from the cabinet over Gladstone's policy of home rule for Ireland, and led the revolt of the Liberal-Unionists.

Chamberlain Owen 1920– . US physicist whose graduate studies were interrupted by wartime work on the Manhattan Project at Los Alamos. After World War II, working with Italian physicist Emilio Segrè, he discovered the existence of the antiproton. Both men were awarded the Nobel Prize for Physics 1959.

Chamberlain Wilt (Wilton Norman) 1936– . US basketball player who set a record by averaging 50.4 points a game during the 1962 season, and was the only man to score 100 points in a game.

He played professionally for the Philadelphia Warriors, Philadelphia 76ers, Los Angeles Lakers, and briefly for the ◊Harlem Globetrotters. Playing against the New York Knickerbockers 1962 he became the only man to score 100 points in a National Basketball Association (NBA) game. He was the only center to lead the league in assists. He led the league in scoring 1960–66, was NBA Most Valuable Player 1960, 1966–68, and retired 1973 after a 13-year career.

CAREER HIGHLIGHTS

total games: 1,045
points: 31,419 (average 30.1 per game)
records
most points in a game: 100 (v. New York Knickerbockers 1962)
most points in a season: 4,029 (average 50.4 per game, 1962)
most seasons as NBA top scorer: 7 (1960–66)

chamber music music suitable for performance in a small room or chamber, rather than in the concert hall, and usually written for instrumental combinations, played with one instrument to a part, as in the string quartet.

Chamber music came into use as a reaction to earlier music for voices such as the madrigal, which allowed accompanying instruments little freedom for technical display. At first a purely instrumental style, it developed through Haydn and Beethoven into a private and often experimental medium making unusual demands on players and audiences alike. During the 20th century, the limitations of recording and radio have encouraged many composers to scale down their orchestras to chamber proportions, as in Alban Berg's *Chamber Concerto* and Igor Stravinsky's *Agon.*

Chambéry former capital of Savoy, now capital of Savoie *département*, France; population (1982) 96,000. It is the seat of an archbishopric and has some industry; it is also a vacation and health resort. The town gives its name to a French vermouth.

chameleon any of some 80 or so species of lizard of the family Chameleontidae. Some species have highly developed color-changing abilities, which are caused by changes in the intensity of light, of temperature, and of emotion altering the dispersal of pigment granules in the layers of cells beneath the outer skin.

The tail is long and highly prehensile, assisting the animal when climbing. Most chameleons live in trees and move very slowly. The tongue is very long, protrusile, and covered with a viscous secretion; it can be shot out with great rapidity to 8 in/20 cm for the capture of insects. The eyes are on "turrets," move independently, and can swivel forward to give stereoscopic vision for "shooting." Most live in Africa and Madagascar, but the **common chameleon** *Chameleo chameleon* is found in Mediterranean countries; two species live in SW Arabia, and one species in India and Sri Lanka.

chamois goatlike mammal *Rupicapra rupicapra* found in mountain ranges of S Europe and Asia Minor. It is brown, with dark patches running through the eyes, and can be up to 2.6 ft/80 cm high. Chamois are very sure-footed, and live in herds of up to 30 members.

Both sexes have horns which may be 8 in/20 cm long. These are set close together and go up vertically, forming a hook at the top. Chamois skin is very soft, and excellent for cleaning glass, but the chamois is now comparatively rare and "chamois leather" is often made from the skin of sheep and goats.

Chamonix vacation resort at the foot of Mont Blanc, in the French Alps; population (1982) 9,255. It was the site of the first Winter Olympics 1924.

Chamorro Violeta Barrios de *c.* 1939– . President of Nicaragua from 1990. With strong US support, she was elected to be the candidate for the National Opposition Union (UNO)

1989, winning the presidency from David Ortega Saavedra Feb 1990 and thus ending the period of Sandinista rule.

Her early presidency was marked by rising unemployment, strikes, and continuing skirmishes between ⟂Contra rebels and Sandinista militants in the mountains (despite the official disbanding of the Contras June 1990).

champagne sparkling white wine invented by Dom Pérignon, a Benedictine monk, 1668. It is made from a blend of grapes (*pinot noir* and *pinot chardonnay*) grown in the Marne River region around Reims and Epernay, in Champagne, NE France. After a first fermentation, sugar and yeast are added to the still wine, which, when bottled, undergoes a second fermentation to produce the sparkle. Sugar syrup may be added to make the wine sweet (*sec*) or dry (*brut*).

Champagne has become a symbol of luxurious living and is used worldwide to celebrate special occasions. Increased demand has given rise to the production of similar wines outside France, in the US, for example, and Spain. Although these wines imitate champagnes closely, they are referred to as *méthode champenoise*; only wines produced in the Champagne region of France can be termed "champagne." The pop when a bottle is opened is due to the sudden release of pressure that allows the accumulated carbon dioxide to escape: a bottle may contain up to five times its volume in gas.

Champagne-Ardenne region of NE France; area 9,882 sq mi/25,600 sq km; population (1986) 1,353,000. Its capital is Reims, and it comprises the *départements* of Ardennes, Aube, Marne, and Haute-Marne. It has sheep and dairy farming and vineyards.

Champaign city in E central Illinois, directly W of Urbana, with industries including electronic equipment, academic clothing, and air-conditioning equipment; population (1990) 63,500. Together with Urbana, it is the site of the University of Illinois.

champignon any of a number of edible fungi of the family Agaricaceae. The **fairy ring champignon** *Marasmius oreades* is so called because its fruiting bodies (mushrooms) occur in rings around the outer edge of the underground mycelium (threadlike tubes) of the fungus.

Champion v Ames US Supreme Court decision 1903 that gave judicial sanction to the use of federal police power. Champion, arrested for shipping lottery tickets across state lines, in violation of the Federal Lottery Act 1895, filed suit against the federal government, arguing that the act infringed on the police power of the states. The Court upheld the Lottery Act 5 to 4, ruling that the federal government had the right to use its regulatory and prohibitive powers in the interest of the public good.

Champlain Samuel de 1567–1635. French pioneer, soldier, and explorer in Canada. Having served in the army of Henry IV and on an expedition to the West Indies, he began his exploration of Canada 1603. In a third expedition 1608 he founded and named Québec, and was appointed lieutenant governor of French Canada 1612.

Champlain, Lake lake in NE US (extending some 6 mi/10 km into Canada) on the New York–Vermont border; length 125 mi/201 km; area 430 sq mi/692 sq km. It is linked by canal to the St Lawrence and Hudson rivers.

The largest city on its shores is Burlington, Vermont. Lake Champlain is named after explorer Samuel de ⟂Champlain, who saw it in 1609. It was the scene of a US naval victory over the British in 1814.

Champollion Jean François, le Jeune 1790–1832. French Egyptologist who in 1822 deciphered Egyptian hieroglyphics with the aid of the ⟂Rosetta Stone.

chance likelihood, or ⟂probability, of an event taking place, expressed as a fraction or percentage. For example, the chance that a tossed coin will land heads up is 50%.

As a science, it originated when the Chevalier de Méré consulted ⟂Pascal about how to reduce his gambling losses. In correspondence with another mathematician, ⟂Fermat, Pascal worked out the foundations of the theory of chance. This underlies the science of statistics.

chancel part of a Christian church where the choir and clergy sit, formerly kept separate from the nave.

The term originated in the early Middle Ages, when chancels were raised above the level of the nave, from which they were separated by a rood screen, a pierced partition bearing the image of the Crucifixion. The chancel has usually been considered the preserve and responsibility of the clergy, while the upkeep and repair of the nave was left to the parishioners.

chancroid acute localized, sexually transmitted ulcer on or about the genitals caused by the bacterium *Hemophilus ducreyi*.

The ulcer forms at the point of inoculation from a sexual partner and leads to painful enlargement and suppuration of lymph nodes in the groin area.

Chandigarh city of N India, in the foothills of the Himalayas; population (1981) 421,000. It is also a Union Territory; area 44 sq mi/114 sq km; population (1991) 640,725.

Planned by the architect Le Corbusier, the city was inaugurated 1953 to replace Lahore (capital of British Punjab), which went to Pakistan under partition 1947. Since 1966, when Chandigarh became a Union Territory, it has been the capital city of both Haryana and Punjab, until a new capital is built for the former.

Chandler Happy (Albert Benjamin) 1898–1991. US politician and sports administrator. Born in Corydon, Kentucky, Chandler studied law at the University of Kentucky and was admitted to the bar 1924. Entering politics, he served in the state legislature and was elected governor 1934, resigning from that office 1939 to fill a vacancy in the US Senate. In 1945 Chandler was appointed baseball commissioner but resigned 1951 due in large measure to personality conflicts with several team owners. He again served as governor of Kentucky 1955–59.

Chandler Raymond 1888–1959. US crime writer who created the hard-boiled private eye Philip Marlowe in books that include *The Big Sleep* 1939, *Farewell, My Lovely* 1940, and *The Long Goodbye* 1954.

Many of his books have been made into popular Hollywood films.

He also wrote numerous screenplays, notably *Double Indemnity* 1944 and *Strangers on a Train* 1951.

Chandragupta Maurya ruler of N India *c.* 321–*c.* 297 BC, founder of the Maurya dynasty. He overthrew the Nanda dynasty 325 and then conquered the Punjab 322 after the death of ⟡Alexander the Great, expanding his empire west to Persia. He is credited with having united most of India.

Chandrasekhar Subrahmanyan 1910– . Indian-born US astrophysicist who made pioneering studies of the structure and evolution of stars. The *Chandrasekhar limit* of 1.4 Suns is the maximum mass of a ⟡white dwarf before it turns into a ⟡neutron star. Born in Lahore, he studied in Madras, India, and Cambridge, England, before emigrating to the US. Nobel Prize for Physics 1983.

Chanel Coco (Gabrielle) 1883–1971. French fashion designer, creator of the "little black dress," informal cardigan suit, costume jewelry, and perfumes.

Chaney Lon (Alonso) 1883–1930. US star of silent films, often in grotesque or monstrous roles such as *The Phantom of the Opera* 1925. A master of makeup, he was nicknamed "the Man of a Thousand Faces." He sometimes used extremely painful devices for added effect, as in the title role in *The Hunchback of Notre Dame* 1923, when he carried over 70 lb/30 kg of costume in the form of a heavy hump and harness.

Chaney Lon, Jr (Creighton) 1906–1973. US actor, son of Lon Chaney, who gave an acclaimed performance as Lennie in *Of Mice and Men* 1940. He went on to star in many 1940s horror films, including the title role in *The Wolf Man* 1941. His other work includes *My Favorite Brunette* 1947 and *The Haunted Palace* 1963.

Changchiakow alternative transcription of ⟡Zhangjiakou, trading center in Hesei province, China.

Chang Ch'ien lived 2nd century BC. Chinese explorer who pioneered the ⟡Silk Road.

Changchun industrial city and capital of Jilin province, China; population (1989) 2,020,000. Machinery and motor vehicles are manufactured. It is also the center of an agricultural district.

Chang Jiang or *Yangtze Kiang* longest river of China, flowing about 3,900 mi/6,300 km from Tibet to the Yellow Sea. It is a main commercial waterway.

It has 127 mi/204 km of gorges, below which is Gezhou Ba, the first dam to harness the river. The entire length of the river was first navigated 1986.

Channel, English stretch of water between England and France, leading in the west to the Atlantic Ocean, and in the east via the Strait of Dover to the North Sea; also known as La Manche (French "the sleeve") from its shape.

The English Channel is 280 mi/450 km long W–E; 17 mi/27 km wide at its narrowest (Cap Gris Nez–Dover) and 110 mi/177 km wide at its widest (Ushant–Land's End).

Channel Islands group of islands in the English Channel, off the NW coast of France; they are a possession of the British crown. They comprise the islands of Jersey, Guernsey, Alderney, Great and Little Sark, with the lesser Herm, Brechou, Jethou, and Lihou.

area 75 sq mi/194 sq km
features very mild climate, productive soil; financially the islands are a tax haven
exports flowers, early potatoes, tomatoes, butterflies
currency English pound, also local coinage
population (1981) 128,878
language official language French (⟡Norman French) but English more widely used

religion chiefly Anglican
famous people Lillie Langtry
government the main islands have their own parliaments and laws. Unless specially signified, the Channel Islands are not bound by British acts of Parliament, though the British government is responsible for defense and external relations
history originally under the duchy of Normandy, they are the only part still held by Britain. The islands came under the same rule as England 1066, and are dependent territories of the British crown. Germany occupied the islands during World War II June 1940–May 1945.

Channel Tunnel tunnel built beneath the English Channel, linking Britain with mainland Europe. It comprises twin rail tunnels, 31 mi/50 km long and 24 ft/7.3 m in diameter, located 130 ft/40 m beneath the seabed. Specially designed shuttle trains carrying automobiles and trucks will run between terminals at Folkestone, Kent, England, and Sangatte, W of Calais, France. It was begun 1986 and is scheduled to be operational 1993. The French and English sections were linked Dec 1990.

In the 1880s British financier and railroad promoter Edward Watkin started boring a tunnel near Dover, abandoning it 1894 because of governmental opposition after driving some 1 mi/1.6 km out to sea. In 1973 Britain and France agreed to back a tunnel, but a year later Britain pulled out following a change of government. The anticipated cost has continually been revised upward and is about twice the original estimate.

Channing William Ellery 1780–1842. US minister and theologian. Born in Newport, Rhode Island, Channing was educated at Harvard and was appointed minister of the Federal Street Congregationalist Church in Boston 1803. In 1819, during a theological conflict between liberals and conservatives, he became a leader of the Unitarian movement in its opposition to the strict Calvinism of the New England Congregationalist churches. He was an instrumental figure in the establishment of the American Unitarian Association. In his later years, Channing devoted his energies to the cause of abolitionism.

chanson song type common in France and Italy, often based on a folk tune that originated with the ⟡troubadours. Josquin ⟡Desprez was a chanson composer.

chanson de geste epic poetry of the High Middle Ages in Europe. It probably developed from oral poetry recited in royal or princely courts, and takes as its subject the exploits of heroes, such as those associated with Charlemagne and the crusades. The best known example is the *Chanson de Roland*.

Chanson de Roland early 12th-century epic poem which tells of the real and imaginary deeds of Roland and other knights of Charlemagne, and their last stand against the Basques at Roncesvalles.

It is an example of the *chanson de geste*, a type of epic poem probably originating in the 11th century, and which often took the lives of knights, and their exemplary virtues, as its subject.

chant singing of a formula, usually by a group, for confidence or spiritual improvement. Chants can be secular or religious, both Western and Eastern. Ambrosian and ⟡Gregorian chants are forms of ⟡plainsong melody.

chanterelle edible fungus *Cantharellus cibarius* that is bright yellow and funnel-shaped. It grows in deciduous woodland.

chaos theory or *chaology* branch of mathematics used to deal with chaotic systems —for example, an engineered structure, such as an oil platform, that is subjected to irregular, unpredictable wave stress.

chaparral thick scrub country of the southwestern US. Thorny bushes have replaced what was largely evergreen oak trees.

chapel place of worship used by some Christian denominations; also, a part of a building used for Christian worship. A large church or cathedral may have several chapels.

Chaplin Charlie (Charles Spencer) 1889–1977. English film actor and director. He made his reputation as a ttreetcarp with a smudge moustache, bowler hat, and twirling cane in silent comedies from the mid-1910s, including *The Rink* 1916, *The Kid* 1920, and *The Gold Rush* 1925. His work often contrasts buffoonery with pathos, and his later films combine dialogue with mime and music, as in *The Great Dictator* 1940 and *Limelight* 1952. He was one of cinema's most popular and greatest stars.

Chaplin was born in south London and first appeared on the stage at the age of five. He joined Mack Sennett's Keystone Company in Los Angeles 1913. Along with Mary Pickford, Douglas Fairbanks, and D W ⟡Griffith, Chaplin formed United Artists 1919 as an independent company to distribute their films. His other films include *City Lights* 1931, *Modern Times* 1936, and *Monsieur Verdoux* (in which he spoke for the first time) 1947. *Limelight* 1952 was awarded an Oscar for Chaplin's musical theme. When accused of communist sympathies during the McCarthy witchhunt, he left the US 1952 and moved to Switzerland. He received special Oscars 1928 and 1972.

Until sound films became common, he was the best known and most popular film star of his day. He was married four times, his third wife being actress Paulette Goddard, and his fourth, Oona, was the daughter of the dramatist Eugene O'Neill.

Chapman George 1559–1634. English poet and dramatist. His translations of the Greek epics of Homer (completed 1616) were celebrated; his plays include the comedy *Eastward Ho!* (with Jonson and Marston) 1605 and the tragedy *Bussy d'Amboise* 1607.

Chapman John ("Johnny Appleseed") 1774–1845. US pioneer and folk hero, credited with establishing orchards throughout the Midwest by planting seeds as he traveled.

Chapman was born in Leominster, Massachusetts, and roamed westward from Pennsylvania in the years after 1800, planting apple seeds in Ohio and Indiana. Becoming famous as the subject of local legends and folk tales, Chapman was described as a religious visionary with boundless generosity. However, few specific details about his later life, especially during the War of 1812, can be verified.

char or *charr* fish *Salvelinus alpinus* related to the trout, living in the Arctic coastal waters, and also in Europe and North America in some upland lakes. It is one of Britain's rarest fish, and is at risk from growing acidification.

Numerous variants have been described, but they probably all belong to the same species.

characin freshwater fish belonging to the

family Characidae. There are over 1,300 species, mostly in South and Central America, but also in Africa. Most are carnivores. In typical characins, unlike the somewhat similar carp family, the mouth is toothed, and there is a small dorsal adipose fin just in front of the tail.

Characins are small fishes, often colorful, and they include ⟡tetras and ⟡piranhas.

characteristic in mathematics, the integral part (whole number) of a ⟡logarithm. For example, in base ten, $10^0 = 1$, $10^1 = 10$, $10^2 = 100$, and so on; the powers to which 10 is raised are the characteristics. To determine the power to which 10 must be raised to obtain a number between 10 and 100, say 20, the logarithm for 2 is found (0.3010), and the characteristic 1 added to make 1.3010. The fractional part (in this case 0.3010) is the ⟡mantissa.

charcoal black, porous form of ⟡carbon, produced by heating wood or other organic materials in the absence of air. It is used as a fuel in the smelting of metals such as copper and zinc, and by artists for making black line drawings. **Activated charcoal** has been powdered and dried so that it presents a much increased surface area for adsorption; it is used for filtering and purifying liquids and gases—for example, in drinking-water filters and gas masks.

Charcoal was traditionally produced by burning dried wood in a kiln, a process lasting several days. The kiln was either a simple hole in the ground, or an earth-covered mound. Today kilns are of brick or iron, both of which allow the waste gases to be collected and used.

Charcoal had many uses in earlier centuries. Because of the high temperature at which it burns (1,100°C), it was used in furnaces and blast furnaces before the development of ⟡coke. It was also used in an industrial process for obtaining ethanoic acid (acetic acid), in producing wood tar and the by-product wood pitch, and (when produced from alder or willow trees) as a component of gunpowder.

Charcot Jean-Martin 1825–1893. French neurologist who studied hysteria, sclerosis, locomotor ataxia, and senile diseases. Among his pupils was Sigmund ⟡Freud.

Chardin Jean-Baptiste-Siméon 1699–1779. French painter of naturalistic still lifes and quiet domestic scenes that recall the Dutch tradition. His work is a complete contrast to that of his contemporaries, the Rococo painters. He developed his own technique using successive layers of paint to achieve depth of tone and is generally considered one of the finest exponents of the genre.

Charente French river, rising in Haute-Vienne *département* and flowing past Angoulême and Cognac into the Bay of Biscay below Rochefort. It is 225 mi/360 km long. Its wide estuary is much silted up. It gives its name to two *départements*, Charente and Charente-Maritime (formerly Charente-Inférieure).

charge-coupled device (CCD) device for forming images electronically, using a layer of silicon that releases electrons when struck by incoming light.

The electrons are stored in ⟡pixels and read off into a computer at the end of the exposure. CCDs have now almost entirely replaced photographic film for applications such as astrophotography where extreme sensitivity to light is paramount.

charged particle beam high-energy beam of electrons or protons that does not burn through the surface of its target like a ⟡laser, but cuts through it. Such beams are being developed as weapons.

Charge of the Light Brigade disastrous attack by the British Light Brigade of cavalry against the Russian entrenched artillery on Oct 25, 1854 during the Crimean War at the Battle of ⟡Balaclava.

chariot horse-drawn carriage with two wheels, used in ancient Egypt, Greece, and Rome, for fighting, processions, and races; it is thought to have originated in Asia. Typically, the fighting chariot contained a driver and a warrior, who would fight on foot, with the chariot providing rapid mobility.

Julius Caesar and Tacitus both write of chariots being used by the British against Roman armies in the 1st century AD. The most complete remains of a chariot found in Britain were at Llyn Cerrig Bach in Anglesey, Wales, but many parts of chariots, such as axle caps and harness mounts, have been found.

charismatic movement late 20th-century movement within the Christian church that emphasizes the role of the Holy Spirit in the life of the individual believer and in the life of the church. See ⟡Pentecostal movement.

Charlemagne Charles I *the Great* 742–814. King of the Franks from 768 and Holy Roman emperor from 800. By inheritance (his father was ⟡Pepin the Short) and extensive campaigns of conquest, he united most of W Europe by 804, when after 30 years of war the Saxons came under his control. He reformed the legal, judicial, and military systems; established schools; and promoted Christianity, commerce, agriculture, arts, and literature. In his capital, Aachen, scholars gathered from all over Europe.

Pepin had been mayor of the palace in Merovingian Neustria until he was crowned king by Pope Stephen II (died 757) in 754, and his sons Carl (Charlemagne) and Carloman were crowned as joint heirs. When Pepin died 768, Charlemagne inherited the N Frankish kingdom, and when Carloman died 771, he also took possession of his domains.

He was engaged in his first Saxon campaign when the Pope's call for help against the Lombards reached him; he crossed the Alps, captured Pavia, and took the title of king of the Lombards. The pacification and christianizing of the Saxon peoples occupied the greater part of Charlemagne's reign. From 792 N Saxony was subdued, and in 804 the whole region came under his rule.

In 777 the emir of Zaragoza asked for Charlemagne's help against the emir of Córdoba. Charlemagne crossed the Pyrenees 778 and reached the Ebro but had to turn back from Zaragoza. The rearguard action of Roncesvalles, in which ⟡Roland, warden of the Breton March, and other Frankish nobles were ambushed and killed by Basques, was later glorified in the *Chanson de Roland*. In 801 the district between the Pyrenees and the Llobregat was organized as the Spanish March. The independent duchy of Bavaria was incorporated in the kingdom 788, and the ⟡Avar people were subdued 791–96 and accepted Christianity. Charlemagne's last campaign was against a Danish attack on his northern frontier 810.

The supremacy of the Frankish king in Europe found outward expression in the bestowal of the imperial title: in Rome, during Mass on Christmas Day 800, Pope Leo III crowned Charlemagne emperor. He enjoyed diplomatic relations with Byzantium, Baghdad, Mercia, Northumbria, and other regions. Jury courts were introduced, the laws of the Franks revised, and other peoples' laws written down. A new coinage was introduced, weights and measures were reformed, and communications were improved. Charlemagne also took a lively interest in theology, organized the church in his dominions, and furthered missionary enterprises and monastic reform. The *Carolingian Renaissance* of learning began when he persuaded the Northumbrian scholar Alcuin to enter his service 781. Charlemagne gathered a kind of academy around him. Although he never learned to read, he collected the old heroic sagas, began a Frankish grammar, and promoted religious instruction in the vernacular. He died Jan 28, 814 in Aachen, where he was buried. Soon a cycle of heroic legends and romances developed around him, including epics by Ariosto, Boiardo, and Tasso.

Charlemagne Prize political award established 1949, given annually to those serving European cooperation. Past winners include Winston ⟡Churchill, Konrad ⟡Adenauer, Robert ⟡Schuman, and Edward ⟡Heath.

Charleroi town in Belgium on the river Sambre, Hainault province; population (1991) 206,200. Its coal industry declined in the 1970s.

Charles (Mary) Eugenia 1919– . Dominican politician, prime minister from 1980; cofounder and first leader of the centrist Dominica Freedom Party (DFP). Two years after Dominica's independence the DFP won the 1980 general election and she became the Caribbean's first female prime minister.

Charles Jacques Alexandre César 1746–1823. French physicist who studied gases and made the first ascent in a hydrogen-filled balloon 1783. His work on the expansion of gases led to the formulation of ⟡Charles's law.

Charles Ray 1930– . US singer, songwriter, and pianist whose first hits were "I've Got A Woman" 1955, "What'd I Say" 1959, and "Georgia on My Mind" 1960. He has recorded gospel, blues, rock, soul, country, and rhythm and blues.

Charles two kings of Britain:

Charles I 1600–1649. King of Great Britain and Ireland from 1625, son of James I of England (James VI of Scotland). He accepted the ⟡Petition of Right 1628 but then dissolved Parliament and ruled without a parliament 1629–40. His advisers were Thomas Wentworth, the Ist Earl of Strafford (1593-1641) and ⟡Laud, who persecuted the Puritans and provoked the Scots to revolt. The ⟡Short Parliament, summoned 1640, refused funds, and the ⟡Long Parliament later that year rebelled.

Charles declared war on Parliament 1642 but surrendered 1646 and was beheaded 1649. He was the father of Charles II.

Charles II 1630–1685. King of Great Britain and Ireland from 1660, when Parliament accepted the restoration of the monarchy after the collapse of Cromwell's Commonwealth; son of Charles I. His chief minister Clarendon, who arranged his marriage 1662 with Catherine of Braganza, was replaced 1667 with the so-called Cabal group of advisers (the initials of the ministers in the group made up the word Cabal). His plans to restore Catholicism in Britain led to war with the Netherlands

1672–74 in support of Louis XIV of France and a break with Parliament, which he dissolved 1681. He was succeeded by James II.

When Charles dissolved Parliament, the Whigs fled in terror. He now ruled without a Parliament, financed by Louis XIV. When the Whigs plotted a revolt, their leaders were executed.

Charles (full name Charles Philip Arthur George) 1948– . Prince of the UK, heir to the British throne, and Prince of Wales since 1958 (invested 1969). He is the first-born child of Queen Elizabeth II and the Duke of Edinburgh. He studied at Trinity College, Cambridge, 1967–70, before serving in the Royal Air Force and Royal Navy. He is the first royal heir since 1659 to have an English wife, Lady Diana Spencer, daughter of the 8th Earl Spencer. They have two sons and heirs, William (1982–) and Henry (1984–). Amid much publicity, Charles and Diana separated 1992.

Charles ten kings of France:

Charles I king of France, better known as the Holy Roman emperor ▷Charlemagne.

Charles II *the Bald* king of France, see ▷Charles II, Holy Roman emperor.

Charles III *the Simple* 879–929. King of France 893–922, son of Louis the Stammerer. He was crowned at Reims. In 911 he ceded what later became the duchy of Normandy to the Norman chief Rollo.

Charles IV *the Fair* 1294–1328. King of France from 1322, when he succeeded Philip V as the last of the direct Capetian line.

Charles V *the Wise* 1337–1380. King of France from 1364. He was regent during the captivity of his father, John II, in England 1356–60, and became king on John's death. He reconquered nearly all France from England 1369–80.

Charles VI *the Mad* or *the Well-Beloved* 1368–1422. King of France from 1380, succeeding his father Charles V; he was under the regency of his uncles until 1388. He became mentally unstable 1392, and civil war broke out between the dukes of Orléans and Burgundy. Henry V of England invaded France 1415, conquering Normandy, and in 1420 forced Charles to sign the Treaty of Troyes, recognizing Henry as his successor.

Charles VII 1403–1461. King of France from 1429. Son of Charles VI, he was excluded from the succession by the Treaty of Troyes, but recognized by the south of France. In 1429 Joan of Arc raised the siege of Orléans and had him crowned at Reims. He organized France's first standing army and by 1453 had expelled the English from all of France except Calais.

Charles VIII 1470–1498. King of France from 1483, when he succeeded his father, Louis XI. In 1494 he unsuccessfully tried to claim the Neapolitan crown, and when he entered Naples 1495 was forced to withdraw by a coalition of Milan, Venice, Spain, and the Holy Roman Empire. He defeated them at Fornovo, but lost Naples. He died while preparing a second expedition.

Charles IX 1550–1574. King of France from 1560. Second son of Henry II and Catherine de' Medici, he succeeded his brother Francis II at the age of ten but remained under the domination of his mother's regency for ten years while France was torn by religious wars. In 1570 he fell under the influence of the ▷Huguenot leader Gaspard de Coligny (1517–1572); alarmed

by this, Catherine instigated his order for the Massacre of St ▷Bartholomew, which led to a new religious war.

Charles X 1757–1836. King of France from 1824. Grandson of Louis XV and brother of Louis XVI and Louis XVIII, he was known as the comte d'Artois before his accession. He fled to England at the beginning of the French Revolution, and when he came to the throne on the death of Louis XVIII, he attempted to reverse the achievements of the Revolution. A revolt ensued 1830, and he again fled to England.

Charles seven rulers of the Holy Roman Empire:

Charles I Holy Roman emperor, better known as ▷Charlemagne.

Charles II *the Bald* 823–877. Holy Roman emperor from 875 and (as Charles II) king of France from 843. Younger son of Louis I (the Pious), he warred against his eldest brother, Emperor Lothair I. The Treaty of Verdun 843 made him king of the West Frankish Kingdom (now France and the Spanish Marches).

Charles III *the Fat* 839–888. Holy Roman emperor 881–87; he became king of the West Franks 885, thus uniting for the last time the whole of Charlemagne's dominions, but was deposed.

Charles IV 1316–1378. Holy Roman emperor from 1355 and king of Bohemia from 1346. Son of John of Luxembourg, king of Bohemia, he was elected king of Germany 1346 and ruled all Germany from 1347. He was the founder of the first German university in Prague 1348.

Charles V 1500–1558. Holy Roman emperor 1519–56. Son of Philip of Burgundy and Joanna of Castile, he inherited vast possessions, which led to rivalry from Francis I of France, whose alliance with the Ottoman Empire brought Vienna under siege 1529 and 1532. Charles was also in conflict with the Protestants in Germany until the Treaty of Passau 1552, which allowed the Lutherans religious liberty.

Charles VI 1685–1740. Holy Roman emperor from 1711, father of ▷Maria Theresa, whose succession to his Austrian dominions he tried to ensure, and himself claimant to the Spanish throne 1700, thus causing the War of the ▷Spanish Succession.

Charles VII 1697–1745. Holy Roman emperor from 1742, opponent of ▷Maria Theresa's claim to the Austrian dominions of Charles VI.

Charles (Karl Franz Josef) 1887–1922. Emperor of Austria and king of Hungary from 1916, the last of the Hapsburg emperors. He succeeded his great-uncle Franz Josef 1916 but was forced to withdraw to Switzerland 1918, although he refused to abdicate. In 1921 he attempted unsuccessfully to regain the crown of Hungary and was deported to Madeira, where he died.

Charles (Spanish *Carlos*) four kings of Spain:

Charles I 1500–1558. See ▷Charles V, Holy Roman emperor.

Charles II 1661–1700. King of Spain from 1665. The second son of Philip IV, he was the last of the Spanish Hapsburg kings. Mentally handicapped from birth, he bequeathed his dominions to Philip of Anjou, grandson of Louis XIV, which led to the War of the ▷Spanish Succession.

Charles III 1716–1788. King of Spain from 1759. Son of Philip V, he became duke of Parma

1732 and conquered Naples and Sicily 1734. On the death of his half brother Ferdinand VI (1713–1759), he became king of Spain, handing over Naples and Sicily to his son Ferdinand (1751–1825). During his reign, Spain was twice at war with Britain: during the Seven Years' War, when he sided with France and lost Florida; and when he backed the colonists in the American Revolution and regained it. At home he carried out a program of reforms and expelled the Jesuits.

Charles IV 1748–1819. King of Spain from 1788, when he succeeded his father, Charles III; he left the government in the hands of his wife and her lover, the minister Manuel de Godoy (1767–1851). In 1808 Charles was induced to abdicate by Napoleon's machinations in favor of his son Ferdinand VII (1784–1833), who was subsequently deposed by Napoleon's brother Joseph. Charles was awarded a pension by Napoleon and died in Rome.

Charles (Swedish *Carl*) fifteen kings of Sweden (the first six were local chieftains), including:

Charles VII King of Sweden from about 1161. He helped to establish Christianity in Sweden.

Charles VIII 1408–1470. King of Sweden from 1448. He was elected regent of Sweden 1438, when Sweden broke away from Denmark and Norway. He stepped down 1441 when Christopher III of Bavaria (1418–1448) was elected king, but after his death became king. He was twice expelled by the Danes and twice restored.

Charles IX 1550–1611. King of Sweden from 1604, the youngest son of Gustavus Vasa. In 1568 he and his brother John led the rebellion against Eric XIV (1533–1577); John became king as John III and attempted to Catholicize Sweden, and Charles led the opposition. John's son Sigismund, king of Poland and a Catholic, succeeded to the Swedish throne 1592, and Charles led the Protestants. He was made regent 1595 and deposed Sigismund 1599. Charles was elected king of Sweden 1604 and was involved in unsuccessful wars with Russia, Poland, and Denmark. He was the father of Gustavus Adolphus.

Charles X 1622–1660. King of Sweden from 1654, when he succeeded his cousin Christina. He waged war with Poland and Denmark and in 1657 invaded Denmark by leading his army over the frozen sea.

Charles XI 1655–1697. King of Sweden from 1660, when he succeeded his father Charles X. His mother acted as regent until 1672 when Charles took over the government. He was a remarkable general and reformed the administration.

Charles XII 1682–1718. King of Sweden from 1697, when he succeeded his father, Charles XI. From 1700 he was involved in wars with Denmark, Poland, and Russia.

He won a succession of victories until, in 1709 while invading Russia, he was defeated at Poltava in the Ukraine, and forced to take refuge in Turkey until 1714. He was killed while besieging Fredrikshall, Norway, although it was not known whether he was murdered by his own side or by the enemy.

Charles XIII 1748–1818. King of Sweden from 1809, when he was elected; he became the first king of Sweden and Norway 1814.

Charles XIV (Jean Baptiste Jules ▷Bernadotte) 1763–1844. King of Sweden and

Norway from 1818. A former marshal in the French army, in 1810 he was elected crown prince of Sweden under the name of Charles John (Carl Johan). Loyal to his adopted country, he brought Sweden into the alliance against Napoleon 1813, as a reward for which Sweden received Norway. He was the founder of the present dynasty.

Charles XV 1826–1872. King of Sweden and Norway from 1859, when he succeeded his father Oscar I. A popular and liberal monarch, his main achievement was the reform of the constitution.

Charles Albert 1798–1849. King of Sardinia from 1831. He showed liberal sympathies in early life, and after his accession introduced some reforms. On the outbreak of the 1848 revolution he granted a constitution and declared war on Austria. His troops were defeated at Custozza and Novara. In 1849 he abdicated in favor of his son Victor Emmanuel and retired to a monastery, where he died.

Charles Edward Stuart the *Young Pretender* or *Bonnie Prince Charlie* 1720–1788. British prince, grandson of James II and son of James, the Old Pretender. In the Jacobite rebellion 1745 Charles won the support of the Scottish Highlanders; his army invaded England to claim the throne but was beaten back by the duke of ⧐Cumberland and routed at ⧐Culloden 1746. Charles went into exile.

With a price of £30,000 on his head, Charles Edward fled to France, eventually settling in Italy 1766.

Charles Martel *c.* 688–741. Frankish ruler (Mayor of the Palace) of the E Frankish kingdom from 717 and the whole kingdom from 731. His victory against the Moors at Moussais-la-Bataille near Tours 732 earned him his nickname of Martel, "the Hammer," because he halted the Islamic advance by the ⧐Moors into Europe.

An illegitimate son of Pepin of Heristal (Pepin II, Mayor of the Palace *c.* 640–714), he was a grandfather of Charlemagne.

Charles River Bridge v Warren Bridge US Supreme Court decision 1837 dealing with the interpretation of corporate charters and states' power to regulate corporations. The owners of the Charles River toll bridge, in fear of economic competition, sued for an injunction against the building of the Warren Bridge, which the state of Massachusetts had authorized. They claimed that their 1785 charter implied the exclusive right to bridge the river; the state was impairing that contract by sanctioning a second bridge. The Court ruled implicit rights to be invalid and declared that ambiguous clauses must be interpreted in favor of the public over the corporation.

Charles's law law stating that the volume of a given mass of gas at constant pressure is directly proportional to its absolute temperature (temperature in kelvin). It was discovered by Jacques Charles 1787, and independently by Joseph Gay-Lussac 1802.

The gas increases by 1/273 of its volume at 0°C for each °C rise of temperature. This means that the coefficient of expansion of all gases is the same. The law is only approximately true and the coefficient of expansion is generally taken as 0.003663 per °C.

Charles the Bold Duke of Burgundy 1433–1477. Son of Philip the Good, he inherited Burgundy and the Low Countries from him 1465. He waged wars attempting to free the

duchy from dependence on France and restore it as a kingdom. He was killed in battle.

Charles' ambition was to create a kingdom stretching from the mouth of the Rhine to the mouth of the Rhône. He formed the League of the Public Weal against Louis XI of France, invaded France 1471, and conquered the country as far as Rouen. The Holy Roman emperor, the Swiss, and Lorraine united against him; he captured Nancy, but was defeated at Granson and again at Morat 1476. Nancy was lost, and he was killed while attempting to recapture it. His possessions in the Netherlands passed to the Hapsburgs by the marriage of his daughter Mary to Maximilian I of Austria.

Charleston capital and chief city of West Virginia, on the Kanawha River; population (1990) 57,300. It is the center of a region that produces coal, natural gas, salt, clay, timber, and oil, and it is an important chemical-producing center. Charleston developed from a fort built 1788.

Charleston main port and city of South Carolina; population (1990) 80,400. Industries include textiles, clothing, and paper products. A nuclear-submarine naval base and an air-force base are nearby. The city dates from 1670.

Fort Sumter, in the sheltered harbor of Charleston, was bombarded by Confederate batteries April 12–13, 1861, thus beginning the Civil War. There are many historic houses and fine gardens. Charleston was hard hit by Hurricane Hugo 1989.

Charleston is the setting for George Gershwin's folk opera *Porgy and Bess*. Spoleto Festival USA, dating from 1977, attracts performing-arts groups.

Charleston back-kicking dance of the 1920s that originated in Charleston, South Carolina, and became an American craze.

Charlotte city in North Carolina, on the border with South Carolina; population (1990) 395,900. Industries include data processing, textiles, chemicals, machinery, and food products. It was the gold-mining center of the country until gold was discovered in California 1849.

Charlotte is the birthplace of James K Polk, 11th president of the US. The University of North Carolina–Charlotte is here, and the Mint Museum of Arts has paintings, sculpture, and ceramics. Settled around 1750, Charlotte enjoyed rapid growth in the 1970s and is the largest city in the state.

Charlotte Amalie capital, tourist resort, and free port of the US Virgin Islands; population (1980) 11,756.

Located on the island of St Thomas, Charlotte Amalie was formerly (1921–37) called *St Thomas*. It was founded 1672 by the Danish West India Company. Boatbuilding and rum distilling are among the economic activities. The College of the Virgin Islands and the Museum of the Virgin Islands are here.

Charlottesville city in central Virginia, in the Blue Ridge mountain foothills, NW of Richmond, on the Rivanna River; seat of Albemarle County. Tourism is important, and some textiles are manufactured; population (1990) 40,300. Charlottesville is the site of the University of Virginia, established 1819 by Thomas Jefferson. Jefferson's home, Monticello, is nearby, as is President James Monroe's home, Ash Lawn.

Charlottetown capital of Prince Edward Island; population (1986) 16,000. The city trades

in textiles, fish, timber, vegetables, and dairy produce. It was founded by French settlers in the 1720s.

charm in physics, a property possessed by one type of ⧐quark (very small particles found inside protons and neutrons), called the charm quark. The effects of charm are only seen in experiments with particle ⧐accelerators. See ⧐elementary particles.

Charon in Greek mythology, the boatman who ferried the dead over the rivers Acheron and Styx to Hades, the underworld. A coin placed on the tongue of the dead paid for their passage.

Chartism radical British democratic movement, mainly of the working classes, which flourished around 1838–50. It derived its name from the People's Charter, a six-point program comprising universal male suffrage, equal electoral districts, secret ballot, annual parliaments, and abolition of the property qualification for, and payment of, members of Parliament. Greater prosperity, lack of organization, and rivalry in the leadership led to its demise.

Chartres capital of the *département* of Eure-et-Loir, NW France, 59 mi/96 km SW of Paris, on the river Eure; population (1982) 39,243. The city is an agricultural center for the fertile Plaine de la Beauce. Its cathedral of Nôtre Dame, completed about 1240, is a masterpiece of Gothic architecture.

Chartreuse trademark for a green or yellow liqueur distilled since 1607 by the Carthusian monks at La Grande Chartreuse monastery, France, and also in Tarragona, Spain.

Charybdis in Greek mythology, a whirlpool formed by a monster of the same name on one side of the narrow straits of Messina, Sicily, opposite the monster Scylla.

Chase Salmon Portland 1808–1873. US public official and chief justice of the US. He held a US Senate seat 1849–55 and 1860; helped found the Republican Party 1854–56; was elected governor of Ohio 1855; became Abraham Lincoln's secretary of the treasury 1861; and was appointed chief justice of the US Supreme Court 1864. Chase tempered the abuses of Reconstruction, as in ⧐*Ex parte Milligan* 1866, and presided over the impeachment trial of President A ⧐Johnson 1868.

Born in Cornish, New Hampshire, and educated at Dartmouth, Chase studied law and was admitted to the bar 1829. Moving to Cincinnati, Ohio, he became an abolitionist, often taking the cases of runaway slaves.

chasing indentation of a design on metal by small chisels and hammers. This method of decoration was familiar in ancient Egypt, Assyria, and Greece; it is used today on fine silverware.

château country house or important residence in France. The term originally applied to a French medieval castle, and the château was first used as a domestic building in the late 15th century; by the reign of Louis XIII (1610–43) fortifications such as moats and keeps were no longer used for defensive purposes, but merely as decorative features. The Loire valley contains some fine examples of châteaux.

Chateaubriand François René, vicomte de 1768–1848. French author. In exile from the French Revolution 1794–99, he wrote *Atala* 1801 (after his encounters with North American Indians) and the autobiographical *René*, which formed part of *Le Génie* *du Christianisme*/*The Genius of Christianity* 1802. He later wrote *Mémoires d'outre tombe*/*Memoirs from Beyond the Tomb* 1849–50.

He visited the US 1791 and, on his return to France, fought for the royalist side which was defeated at Thionville 1792. He lived in exile in England until 1800. When he returned to France, he held diplomatic appointments under Louis XVIII.

Châtelet Emilie de Breteuil, Marquise du 1706–1749. French scientific writer and translator into French of Isaac Newton's *Principia*.

Her marriage to the Marquis du Châtelet in 1725 gave her the leisure to study physics and mathematics. She met Voltaire in 1733, and settled with him at her husband's estate at Cirey, in the Duchy of Lorraine. Her study of Newton, with whom she collaborated on various scientific works, influenced Voltaire's work. She independently produced the first (and only) French translation of Newton's *Principia Mathematica* (published posthumously in 1759).

Chattanooga city in Tennessee, on the Tennessee River; population (1990) 152,500. It is the focus of the ⊅Tennessee Valley Authority area. Developed as a salt-trading center after 1835, it now produces chemicals, textiles, and metal products.

The Hunter Museum of Art and a campus of the University of Tennessee are here. Chattanooga was laid out 1838 after Cherokee Indians were removed from the area. Union forces captured it from the Confederacy 1863.

Chatterton Thomas 1752–1770. English poet whose medieval-style poems and brief life were to inspire English Romanticism. Born in Bristol, he studied ancient documents he found in the Church of St Mary Redcliffe and composed poems he ascribed to a 15th-century monk, "Thomas Rowley," which were accepted as genuine. He committed suicide in London, after becoming destitute.

Chatwin Bruce 1940–1989. English writer. His works include *The Songlines* 1987, written after living with Aborigines; the novel *Utz* 1988, a novel about a manic porcelain collector in Prague; and travel pieces and journalism collected in *What Am I Doing Here* 1989.

Chaucer Geoffrey c. 1340–1400. English poet. *The Canterbury Tales*, a collection of stories told by a group of pilgrims on their way to Canterbury, reveals his knowledge of human nature and his stylistic variety, from urbane and ironic to simple and bawdy. Early allegorical poems, including *The Book of the Duchess*, were influenced by French poems like the *Roman de la Rose*. His *Troilus and Criseyde* is a substantial narrative poem about the tragic betrayal of an idealized courtly love.

Chaucer was born in London. Taken prisoner in the French wars, he had to be ransomed by Edward III 1360. He married Philippa Roet 1366, becoming in later life the brother-in-law of ⊅John of Gaunt. He achieved various appointments and was sent on missions to Italy (where he may have met ⊅Boccaccio and ⊅Petrarch), France, and Flanders. His early work showed formal French influence, as in his adaptation of the French allegorical poem on courtly love, *Romance of the Rose*; more mature works reflected the influence of Italian realism, as in his long narrative poem *Troilus and Criseyde*, adapted from Boccaccio. In *The Canterbury Tales* he showed his own genius for meter and characterization. He was the most influential English poet of the Middle Ages.

chauvinism warlike, often unthinking patriotism, as exhibited by Nicholas Chauvin, one of Napoleon I's veterans and his fanatical admirer. In the mid-20th century the expression *male chauvinism* was coined to mean an assumed superiority of the male sex over the female.

Chávez Carlos 1899–1978. Mexican composer. A student of the piano and of the complex rhythms of his country's folk music, he founded the Mexico Symphony Orchestra. He composed a number of ballets, seven symphonies, and concertos for both violin and piano.

Chavez Cesar Estrada 1927– . US labor organizer who founded the National Farm Workers Association 1962 and, with the support of the AFL-CIO and other major unions, embarked on a successful campaign to unionize California grape workers. He led boycotts of citrus fruits, lettuce, and grapes in the early 1970s, but disagreement and exploitation of migrant farm laborers continued despite his successes.

Born near Yuma, Arizona, to a family of migrant farm workers, Chavez was deeply influenced by the organizing efforts of Saul Alinsky among agricultural workers in California in the early 1950s. Chavez devoted himself to the cause of unionization and became director of the Community Service Organization 1958.

Chayefsky (Sidney) Paddy 1923–1981. US writer. He established his reputation with the television plays *Marty* 1955 (for which he won an Oscar when he turned it into a film) and *Bachelor Party* 1957. He also won Oscars for *The Hospital* 1971 and *Network* 1976.

Checheno-Ingush autonomous republic in southern Russia, on the northern slopes of the Caucasus mountains; area 19,000 km/7,350 sq mi; population (1986) 1,230,000. It was conquered in the 1850s, and has a large oil field. The capital is Grozny. The population includes Chechens (53%) and Ingushes (12%). In Oct 1991 the region declared its independence. After a brief, unsuccessful attempt to quell the rebellion, Moscow agreed to enter into negotiations over the republic's future. In March 1992 Checheno-Ingush refused to be party to a federal treaty signed by 18 of Russia's 20 main political subdivisions. By the end of the month at least five people had been killed in clashes between anti and pro-separatist factions, forcing the republic's parliament to declare a state of emergency.

check an order written by the drawer to a commercial or central bank to pay a specific sum on demand.

Usually the check should bear the date on which it is payable, a definite sum of money to be paid, written in words and figures, to a named person or body, or to the bearer, and be signed by the drawer. It is then payable on presentation at the bank on which it is drawn. In the US checks are widely negotiable for retail purchases and other financial transactions.

checkers board game played on a ⊅chess board. Each of the two players has 12 men (disc-shaped pieces), and attempts either to capture all the opponent's men or to block their movements.

Checkpoint Charlie Western-controlled crossing point for non-Germans between West Berlin and East Berlin, opened 1961 as the only crossing point between the Allied and Soviet sectors. Its dismantling in June 1990 was seen as a symbol of the ending of the ⊅Cold War.

cheese food made from the **curds** (solids) of soured milk from cows, sheep, or goats, separated from the **whey** (liquid), then salted, put into molds, and pressed into firm blocks. Cheese is ripened with bacteria or surface fungi, and kept for a time to mature before eating.

There are six main types of cheese. **Soft cheeses** may be ripe or unripe, and include cottage cheese and high-fat soft cheeses such as Bel Paese, Camembert, and Neufchatel. **Semi-hard cheeses** are ripened by bacteria (Munster) or by bacteria and surface fungi (Port Salut, Gouda, St Paulin); they may also have penicillin molds injected into them (Roquefort, Gorgonzola, Blue Stilton, Wensleydale). **Hard cheeses** are ripened by bacteria, and include Cheddar, Cheshire, and Cucciocavallo; some have large cavities within them, such as Swiss Emmental and Gruyère. **Very hard cheeses**, such as Parmesan and Spalen, are made with skimmed milk. **Processed cheese** is made with dried skim-milk powder and additives, and **whey cheese** is made by heat coagulation of the proteins from whey; examples are Mysost and Primost. In France (from 1980) a cheese has the same *appellation controlée* status as wine if it is made only in a special defined area—for example, Cantal and Roquefort are *appellation controlée* cheeses, but not Camembert and Brie, which are made in more than one region.

cheesecloth fine muslin or cotton fabric of very loose weave, originally used to press curds during the cheesemaking process.

cheetah large wild cat *Acinonyx jubatus* native to Africa, Arabia, and SW Asia, but now rare in some areas. Yellowish with black spots, it has a slim lithe build. It is up to 3 ft/1 m tall at the shoulder, and up to 5 ft/1.5 m long. It can reach 70 mph/110 kph, but tires after about 400 meters. Cheetahs live in open country where they hunt small antelopes, hares, and birds.

A cheetah's claws do not retract as fully as in most cats.

Cheever John 1912–1982. US writer whose stories and novels focus on the ironies of upper-middle-class life in suburban America. His short stories were frequently published in *The New Yorker*. His first novel was *The Wapshot Chronicle* 1957, for which he won the National Book Award. Others include *Falconer* 1977.

Cheever was born in Quincy, Massachusetts. His collections of short stories include *The Way Some People Live* 1943, *The Housebreaker of Shady Hill* 1958, *The Brigadier and the Golf Widow* 1964, and *Stories of John Cheever* 1978 (Pulitzer prize). Among his novels are *Bullet Park* 1969 and *Oh What a Paradise It Seems* 1982.

Chefoo former name of ⊅Yantai in China.

Cheka secret police operating in the USSR 1917–23. It originated from the tsarist Okhrana (the security police under the tsar 1881–1917), and became successively the OGPU (GPU) 1923–34, NKVD 1934–46, MVD 1946–53, and the ⊅KGB from 1954.

The name is formed from the initials *che* and *ka* of the two Russian words meaning "extraordinary commission," formed for "the repression of counterrevolutionary activities and of speculation," and extended to cover such matters as espionage and smuggling.

Chekhov Anton (Pavlovich) 1860–1904. Russian dramatist and writer of short stories. His plays concentrate on the creation of atmosphere and delineation of internal development, rather than external action. His first play, *Ivanov* 1887, was a failure, as was *The Seagull* 1896 until revived by Stanislavsky 1898 at the Moscow Art Theater, for which Chekhov went on to write his finest plays: *Uncle Vanya* 1899, *The Three Sisters* 1901, and *The Cherry Orchard* 1904.

Chekhov was born in Taganrog, S Russia. He qualified as a doctor 1884, but devoted himself to writing short stories rather than practicing medicine. The collection *Particoloured Stories* 1886 consolidated his reputation and gave him leisure to develop his style, as seen in "My Life" 1895, "The Lady with the Dog" 1898, and "In the Ravine" 1900.

Chekiang alternative transcription of ⟡Zhejiang, province of SE China.

chelate chemical compound whose molecules consist of one or more metal atoms or charged ions joined to chains of organic residues by coordinate (or dative covalent) chemical ⟡bonds.

The parent organic compound is known as a *chelating agent* –for example, EDTA (ethylene-diaminetetraacetic acid), used in chemical analysis. Chelates are used in analytical chemistry, in agriculture and horticulture as carriers of essential trace metals, in water softening, and in the treatment of thalassemia by removing excess iron, which may build up to toxic levels in the body. Metalloproteins (natural chelates) may influence the performance of enzymes or provide a mechanism for the storage of iron in the spleen and plasma of the human body.

Chelyabinsk industrial town and capital of Chelyabinsk region, W Siberia, Russia; population (1987) 1,119,000. It has iron and engineering works and makes chemicals, motor vehicles, and aircraft.

chemical element alternate name for ⟡element.

chemical equation method of indicating the reactants and products of a chemical reaction by using chemical symbols and formulae. A chemical equation gives two basic pieces of information: (1) the reactants (on the left-hand side) and products (right-hand side); and (2) the reacting proportions (stoichiometry)—that is, how many units of each reactant and product are involved. The equation must balance; that is, the total number of atoms of a particular element on the left-hand side must be the same as the number of atoms of that element on the right-hand side.

$$Na_2CO_3 + 2HCl \rightarrow 2NaCl + CO_2 + H_2O$$
reactants products

This equation states that one molecule of sodium carbonate combines with two molecules of hydrochloric acid to form two molecules of sodium chloride, one of carbon dioxide, and one of water. Double arrows indicate that the reaction is reversible—in the formation of ammonia from hydrogen and nitrogen, the direction depends on the temperature and pressure of the reactants.

$$3H_2 + N_2 \rightleftharpoons 2NH_3$$

chemical warfare use in war of gaseous, liquid, or solid substances intended to have a toxic effect on humans, animals, or plants. Together with ⟡biological warfare, it was banned by the Geneva Protocol 1925 and the United Nations in 1989 also voted for a ban. The total US stockpile 1989 was estimated at 30,000 tons and the Soviet stockpile at 50,000 tons. In June 1990, the US and USSR agreed bilaterally to reduce their stockpile to 5,000 tons each by 2002. The US began replacing its stocks with new nerve-gas ⟡binary weapons.

Some 20 nations currently hold chemical weapons, including Iraq, Iran, Israel, Syria, Libya, South Africa, China, Ethiopia, North Korea, Myanmar, Taiwan, and Vietnam. The Geneva Protocol 1925 remains the only international legal mechanism for the control of chemical weapons, but has not always been observed. In 1989 the 149-nation UN Conference on Disarmament unanimously voted to outlaw chemical weapons, and drew up a draft Convention on Chemical Weapons (CCW), intended as the basis for a new international agreement on chemical warfare. Iraq used chemical weapons during the 1980–88 Iran–Iraq war, inflicting massive casualties on largely unprotected Iranian Revolutionary Guards and on civilians; it threatened the use of chemical weapons during the 1991 Gulf War but did not use them.

There are several types of chemical weapons. *Irritant gases* may cause permanent injury or death. Examples include chlorine, phosgene (Cl_2CO), and mustard gas ($C_4H_8Cl_2S$), used in World War I (1914–18) and allegedly used by Soviet forces in Afghanistan, by Vietnamese forces in Laos, and by Iraq against Iran during their 1980–88 war. *Tear gases*, such as CS gas, used in riot control, affect the lungs and eyes, causing temporary blindness. *Nerve gases* are organophosphorus compounds similar to insecticides, which are taken into the body through the skin and lungs and break down the action of the nervous system. Developed by the Germans for World War II, they were not used.

Incapacitants are drugs designed to put an enemy temporarily out of action by, for example, impairing vision or inducing hallucinations. They have not so far been used. *Toxins* are poisons to be eaten, drunk, or injected; for example, ricin (derived from the castor-oil plant) and the botulism toxin. Ricin has been used in individual cases, and other toxins were allegedly used by Soviet forces in Afghanistan and by Vietnamese forces in Cambodia.

Herbicides are defoliants used to destroy vegetation sheltering troops and the crops of hostile populations. They were used in Vietnam by the US and in Malaya (now Malaysia) by the UK. ⟡Agent Orange became notorious because it caused cancer and birth abnormalities among Vietnam War veterans and US factory staff.

Binary weapons are two chemical components that become toxic in combination, after the shell containing them is fired.

chemisorption the attachment, by chemical means, of a single layer of molecules, atoms, or ions of gas to the surface of a solid or, less frequently, a liquid. It is the basis of catalysis (see ⟡catalyst) and is of great industrial importance.

chemistry science concerned with the composition of matter and of the changes that take place in it under certain conditions.

All matter can exist in three states: gas, liquid, or solid. It is composed of minute particles termed *molecules*, which are constantly moving, and may be further divided into ⟡atoms.

Molecules that contain atoms of one kind only are known as *elements*; those that contain atoms of different kinds are called *compounds*.

Chemical compounds are produced by a chemical· action that alters the arrangement of the atoms in the reacting molecules. Heat, light, vibration, catalytic action, radiation, or pressure, as well as moisture (for ionization), may be necessary to produce a chemical change. Examination and possible breakdown of compounds to determine their components is *analysis*, and the building up of compounds from their components is *synthesis*. When substances are brought together without changing their molecular structures they are said to be *mixtures*.

Organic chemistry is the branch of chemistry that deals with carbon compounds. *Inorganic chemistry* deals with the description, properties, reactions, and preparation of all the elements and their compounds, with the exception of carbon compounds. *Physical chemistry* is concerned with the quantitative explanation of chemical phenomena and reactions, and the measurement of data required for such explanations. This branch studies in particular the movement of molecules and the effects of temperature and pressure, often with regard to gases and liquids.

Symbols are used to denote the elements. The symbol is usually the first letter or letters of the English or Latin name of the element—for example, C for carbon; Ca for calcium; Fe for iron (*ferrum*). These symbols represent one atom of the element; molecules containing more than one atom of an element are denoted by a subscript figure—for example, water is H_2O. In some substances a group of atoms acts as a single entity, and these are enclosed in parentheses in the symbol—for example $(NH_4)_2SO_4$ denotes ammonium sulfate. The symbolic representation of a molecule is known as a *formula*. A figure placed before a formula represents the number of molecules of a substance taking part in, or being produced by, a reaction—for example, $2H_2O$ indicates two molecules of water. Chemical reactions are expressed by means of *equations* as in:

$$NaCl + H_2SO_4 \rightarrow NaHSO_4 + HCl.$$

This equation states the fact that sodium chloride (NaCl) on being treated with sulfuric acid (H_2SO_4) is converted into sodium bisulfate (sodium hydrogensulfate, $NaHSO_4$) and hydrogen chloride (HCl).

Elements are divided into *metals*, which have luster and conduct heat and electricity, and *nonmetals*, which usually lack these properties. The *periodic system*, developed by John Newlands in 1863 and established by Dmitri Mendeleyev in 1869, classified elements according to their atomic weights. Those elements that resemble each other in general properties were found to bear a relation to one another by weight, and these were placed in groups or families. Certain anomalies in this system were later removed by classifying the elements according to their atomic numbers. The latter is equivalent to the positive charge on the nucleus of the atom.

history Ancient civilizations were familiar with certain chemical processes—for example, extracting metals from their ores, and making alloys. The alchemists endeavored to turn base (nonprecious) metals into gold, and chemistry evolved toward the end of the 17th century from the techniques and insights developed during alchemical experiments. Robert Boyle defined elements as the simplest substances into which matter could be resolved. The alchemical doctrine of the four elements (earth, air, fire, and water) gradually lost its hold, and the theory that all combustible bodies contain a substance called phlogiston (a weightless "fire element" generated during combustion) was discredited in the 18th century by the experimental work of Joseph Black, Antoine Lavoisier, and Joseph Priestley (who discovered the presence of oxygen in air). Henry Cavendish discovered the composition of water, and John Dalton put forward the atomic theory, which ascribed a precise relative weight to the "simple atom" characteristic of each element. Much research then took place leading to the development of ◊biochemistry, ◊chemotherapy, and ◊plastics.

Chemnitz industrial city (engineering, textiles, chemicals) in the state of Saxony, Federal Republic of Germany, on the river Chemnitz, 40 mi/65 km SSE of Leipzig; population (1990) 310,000. As a former district capital of East Germany it was named Karl-Marx-Stadt 1953–90.

chemosynthesis method of making ◊protoplasm (contents of a cell) using the energy from chemical reactions, in contrast to the use of light energy employed for the same purpose in ◊photosynthesis. The process is used by certain bacteria, which can synthesize organic compounds from carbon dioxide and water using the energy from special methods of ◊respiration.

Nitrifying bacteria are a group of chemosynthetic organisms which change free nitrogen into a form that can be taken up by plants; nitrobacteria, for example, oxidize nitrites to nitrates. This is a vital part of the ◊nitrogen cycle. As chemosynthetic bacteria can survive without light energy, they can live in dark and inhospitable regions, including the hydrothermal vents of the Pacific ocean. Around these vents, where temperatures reach up to 662°F/350°C, the chemosynthetic bacteria are the basis of a food web supporting fishes and other marine life.

chemotherapy any medical treatment with chemicals. It usually refers to treatment of cancer with cytotoxic and other drugs. The term was coined by the German bacteriologist Paul Ehrlich for the use of synthetic chemicals against infectious diseases.

chemotropism movement by part of a plant in response to a chemical stimulus. The response by the plant is termed "positive" if the growth is toward the stimulus or "negative" if the growth is away from the stimulus.

Fertilization of flowers by pollen is achieved because the ovary releases chemicals that produce a positive chemotrophic response from the developing pollen tube.

Chengchow alternative transcription of ◊Zhengzhou, capital of Henan province of China.

Chengdu or **Chengtu** ancient city, capital of Sichuan province, China; population (1989) 2,780,000. It is a busy rail junction and has railroad workshops, and textile, electronics, and engineering industries. It has well-preserved temples.

Chengtu alternative transliteration of ◊Chengdu.

Chénier André de 1762–1794. French poet, born in Constantinople. His lyrical poetry was later to inspire the Romantic movement, but he was known in his own time for his uncompromising support of the constitutional royalists after the Revolution. In 1793 he went into hiding, but finally he was arrested and, on July 25, 1794, guillotined. While in prison he wrote *Jeune Captive/Captive Girl* and the political *Iambes*, published after his death.

Cherbourg French port and naval station at the northern end of the Cotentin peninsula, in Manche *département*; population (1982) 85,500 (conurbation). There is an institute for studies in nuclear warfare, and Cherbourg has large shipbuilding yards.

During World War II, Cherbourg was captured June 1944 by the Allies, who thus gained their first large port of entry into France. Cherbourg was severely damaged; restoration of the harbor was completed 1952. There is a nuclear processing plant at nearby Cap la Hague. There are ferry links to England (Southampton, Weymouth, and Rosslare).

Cherenkov Pavel 1904– . Soviet physicist. In 1934 he discovered *Cherenkov radiation*; this occurs as a bluish light when charged atomic particles pass through water or other media at a speed in excess of that of light. He shared a Nobel Prize 1958 with his colleagues Ilya ◊Frank and Igor Tamm for work resulting in a cosmic-ray counter.

Cherenkov discovered that this effect was independent of any medium and depended for its production on the passage of high velocity electrons. The phenomenon has also been claimed as the discovery of the French scientist Lucien Mallet.

Chernenko Konstantin 1911–1985. Soviet politician, leader of the Soviet Communist Party (CPSU) and president 1984–85. He was a protégé of Brezhnev and from 1978 a member of the Politburo.

Chernenko, born in central Siberia, joined the Komsomol (Communist Youth League) 1929 and the CPSU 1931. The future CPSU leader Brezhnev brought him to Moscow to work in the central apparatus 1956 and later sought to establish Chernenko as his successor, but he was passed over in favor of the KGB chief Andropov. When Andropov died Feb 1984 Chernenko was selected as the CPSU's stopgap leader by cautious party colleagues and was also elected president. From July 1984 he gradually retired from public life because of failing health.

Chernobyl town in central Ukraine; site of a nuclear power station. In April 1986 a leak, caused by overheating, occurred in a nonpressurized boiling-water nuclear reactor. The resulting clouds of radioactive isotopes were traced as far away as Sweden; over 250 people were killed, and thousands of square miles contaminated.

Cherokee member of a North ◊American Indian people, formerly living in the S Allegheny Mountains of what is now Alabama, the Carolinas, Georgia, and Tennessee. Their scholarly leader Sequoyah (c. 1770–1843) devised the syllabary used for writing their language. Their language belongs to the Macro-Siouan family.

In 1829 they were transported to a reservation in Oklahoma, by forced march, the Trail of Tears, by order of President Andrew Jackson as a punishment for aiding the British during the American Revolution. In 1984, they were permitted to reestablish a tribal center in North Carolina.

cherry any of various trees of the genus *Prunus*, belonging to the rose family. Cherry trees are distinguished from plums and apricots by their fruits, which are spherical and smooth and not covered with a bloom. They grow best in deep fertile soil.

Most cultivated cherries come from Europe. The common chokecherry *P. virginiana* is a widespread wild cherry tree of the US.

Cherry Orchard, The play by Anton Chekhov, first produced in Moscow 1904. Its theme is the demise of the way of life of a landowning family, symbolized by the felling of a cherry orchard after it has been sold to an entrepreneur.

cherub (Hebrew *kerubh*) type of angel in Christian belief, usually depicted as a young child with wings. Cherubim form the second order of ◊angels.

chervil any of several plants of the carrot family Umbelliferae. The garden chervil *Anthriscus cerefolium* has leaves with a sweetish odor, resembling parsley. It is used as a garnish and in soups. Chervil originated on the borders of Europe and Asia and was introduced to W Europe by the Romans.

Chesapeake Bay largest of the inlets on the Atlantic coast of the US, bordered by Maryland and Virginia. It is about 200 mi/320 km in length and 4–40 mi/6–64 km in width.

Among the rivers that flow into the bay are the James, York, Potomac, Rappahannock, Patuxent, and Susquehanna. Deepwater ports on the bay are Newport News, Norfolk, Portsmouth, and Baltimore. The Chesapeake and Delaware Canal links the bay to the Delaware river and the Wilmington-Philadelphia port area. Pollution has greatly diminished the once plentiful shellfish in the bay.

The Chesapeake Bay Bridge Tunnel connects both Virginia shores; farther north the Chesapeake Bay Bridge links the W Maryland shore near Annapolis to Kent Island.

chess board game originating as early as the 2nd century AD. Two players use 16 pieces each, on a board of 64 squares of alternating color, to try to force the opponent into a position where the main piece (the king) is threatened and cannot move to another position without remaining threatened.

The Fédération Internationale des Echecs (FIDE) was established 1924. Leading players are rated according to the Elo System, and Bobby Fischer (US) is considered to be one of the greatest Grand Masters of all time with a rating of 2,785.

Chess originated in India, and spread to Russia, China, Japan, and Iran, and from there was introduced to the Mediterranean area by

chess: recent winners

world champions

men		
1957	Vassily Smyslov	(USSR)
1958	Mikhail Botvinnik	(USSR)
1960	Mikhail Tal	(USSR)
1961	Mikhail Botvinnik	(USSR)
1963	Tigran Petrosian	(USSR)
1969	Boris Spassky	(USSR)
1972	Bobby Fischer	(US)
1975	Anatoly Karpov	(USSR)
1985	Gary Kasparov	(USSR)
women		
1950	Lyudmila Rudenko	(USSR)
1953	Elizaveta Bykova	(USSR)
1955	Olga Runtsova	(USSR)
1958	Elizaveta Bykova	(USSR)
1962	Nona Gaprindashvili	(USSR)
1978	Maya Chiburdanidze	(USSR)

Arab invaders. It reached Britain in the 12th century via Spain and Italy. The first official world championships were recognized in 1886.

Chesterfield Philip Dormer Stanhope, 4th Earl of Chesterfield 1694–1773. English politician and writer, author of *Letters to his Son* 1774. A member of the literary circle of Swift, Pope, and Bolingbroke, he incurred the wrath of Dr Samuel ◊Johnson by failing to carry out an offer of patronage.

Chesterton G(ilbert) K(eith) 1874–1936. English novelist, essayist, and satirical poet, author of a series of novels featuring as detective a naive priest, Father Brown. Other novels include *The Napoleon of Notting Hill* 1904 and *The Man Who Knew Too Much* 1922.

chestnut tree of the genus *Castanea*, belonging to the beech family Fagaceae. The Spanish or sweet chestnut *C. sativa* produces edible nuts inside husks; its timber is also valuable. ◊Horse chestnuts are quite distinct, belonging to the genus *Aesculus*, family Hippocastanaceae.

Horse chestnuts are also called buckeyes. The American chestnut *C. dentata* was a valued hardwood until it was virtually destroyed by an introduced fungus.

Chetnik member of a Serbian nationalist group that operated underground during the German occupation of Yugoslavia during World War II. Led by Col Draza ◊Mihailovič, the Chetniks initially received aid from the Allies, but this was later transferred to the communist partisans led by Tito. The term has also popularly been applied to Serb militia forces in the 1991–92 Yugoslav civil war.

Chevalier Maurice 1888–1972. French singer and actor. He began as dancing partner to the revue artiste Mistinguett at the Folies-Bergère, and made numerous films including *Innocents of Paris* 1929, which revived his song "Louise," *The Merry Widow* 1934, and *Gigi* 1958.

Cheviots range of hills 35 mi/56 km long, mainly in Northumberland, forming the border between England and Scotland for some 30 mi/48 km. The highest point is the Cheviot, 2,676 ft/816 m. For centuries the area was a battleground between the English and the Scots. It gives its name to a breed of sheep.

Chevreul Michel-Eugène 1786–1889. French chemist who studied the composition of fats and identified a number of fatty acids, including "margaric acid," which became the basis of margarine.

Chevreul was director of dyeing at the Gobelins tapestry factory (1824) and director of the Museum of Natural History (1864–1879).

chewing gum gummy confectionery to be chewed not swallowed. It is composed mainly of chicle (milky juice of the tropical sapodilla tree *Achras zapota* of Central America), usually flavored with mint, sweetened, and pressed flat. The first patent was taken out in the US in 1871. **Bubble gum** is a variety that allows chewers to blow bubbles.

Cheyenne capital of Wyoming, located in the SE part of the state, just north of the Colorado border in the foothills of the Laramie Mountains. An agricultural and transportation center, its industries include oil refining, fertilizers, electronics, restaurant equipment, and ceramics. Tourism is also important to the economy; population (1990) 50,000.

Chiang Ching alternative transliteration of ◊Jiang Qing, Chinese actress, third wife of Mao Zedong.

Chiang Ching-kuo 1910–1988. Taiwanese politician, son of Chiang Kai-shek, prime minister 1971–78, president 1978–88.

Chiang Kai-shek (Pinyin *Jiang Jie Shi*) 1887–1975. Chinese nationalist ◊Guomindang (Kuomintang) general and politician, president of China 1928–31 and 1943–49, and of Taiwan from 1949, where he set up a US-supported right-wing government on his expulsion from the mainland by the Communist forces. He was a commander in the civil war that lasted from the end of imperial rule 1911 to the Second ◊Sino-Japanese War and beyond, having split with the Communist leader Mao Zedong 1927.

Chiang took part in the revolution of 1911 that overthrew the Qing dynasty of the Manchus, and on the death of the nationalist Guomindang leader Sun Yat-sen was made commander in chief of the nationalist armies in S China 1925. Collaboration with the Communists, broken 1927, was resumed after the ◊Xian Incident 1936 when China needed to pool military strength, and Chiang nominally headed the struggle against the Japanese invaders of World War II, receiving the Japanese surrender 1945. The following year, civil war between the nationalists and Communists erupted, and in Dec 1949 Chiang and his followers took refuge on the island of Taiwan, maintaining a large army in the hope of reclaiming the mainland. His authoritarian regime enjoyed US support until his death. His son, Chiang Ching-kuo (1910–1988), then became president.

Chiba industrial city (paper, steel, textiles) in Kanton region, E Honshu island, Japan, 25 mi/40 km W of Tokyo; population (1989) 815,500.

Chibcha member of a South American Indian people of Colombia, whose high chiefdom was conquered by the Spanish in 1538. Their practice of covering their chief with gold dust, during rituals, fostered the legend of the "Lost City" of El Dorado (the Golden), which was responsible for many failed expeditions into the interior of the continent.

Chicago financial and industrial city in Illinois, on Lake Michigan. It is the third largest US city; population (1990) 2,783,700, metropolitan area 8,065,000. Industries include iron, steel, chemicals, electrical goods, machinery, meatpacking and food processing, publishing, and fabricated metals. The once famous stockyards are now closed.

The world's first skyscraper was built here 1885 and some of the world's tallest skyscrapers, including the tallest, the Sears Tower, 1,454 ft/443 m. The Museum of Science and Industry, opened 1893, has "hands-on" exhibits including a coal mine, a World War II U-boat, an Apollo spacecraft and lunar module, and exhibits by industrial firms. The Chicago River cuts the city into three "sides." Chicago is known as the Windy City, so called from the breezes of Lake Michigan, as well as from its citizens' (and, allegedly, politicians') voluble talk; the lake shore ("the Gold Coast") is occupied by luxury apartment blocks. It has a symphony orchestra, an art institute, the University of Chicago (site of the first controlled nuclear reaction), DePaul and Loyola universities, a campus of the University of Illinois, and the Illinois Institute of Technology. Chicago-O'Hare International Airport is the nation's busiest. The Board of Trade, Mercantile Exchange, and Options Exchange are among the world's largest commodity markets.

The site of Chicago was visited by Jesuit missionaries 1673, and Fort Dearborn, then a frontier fort, was built here 1803. The original layout of Chicago was a rectangular grid, but many outer boulevards have been constructed on less rigid lines. As late as 1831 Chicago was still an insignificant village, but railroads from the east coast reached it by 1852, and by 1871, when it suffered a disastrous fire, it was a city of more than 300,000 inhabitants. Rapid development began again in the 1920s, and during the years of Prohibition 1919–33, the city became notorious for the activities of its gangsters. The opening of the St Lawrence Seaway 1959 brought Atlantic shipping to its docks.

Chicago School of Sociology the first university department of sociology, founded in Chicago 1892, under Albion Small. He was succeeded by Robert E Park, who with W I Thomas, Ernest Burgess, Louis Wirth, and R McKenzie created a center for the social sciences in the 1920s and 1930s, studying urban life, including crime and deviance in Chicago, with its variety of urban communities, lifestyles, and ethnic subcultures.

A neo-Chicagoan school emerged in the 1940s under Erving Goffman and Howard Becker.

Chicano citizen or resident of the US of Mexican descent. The term was originally used for those who became US citizens after the ◊Mexican War.

Chichen Itzá Toltec city situated among the Mayan city-states of Yucatán, Mexico. It flourished AD 900–1200 and displays Classic and Post-Classic architecture of the Toltec style. The site has temples with sculptures and color reliefs, an observatory, and a sacred well into which sacrifices, including human beings, were cast.

Chichester city and market town in Sussex; 69 mi/111 km SW of London, near Chichester Harbor; population (1981) 24,000. It is the administrative headquarters of West Sussex. It was a Roman township, and the remains of the Roman palace built around AD 80 at nearby Fishbourne are unique outside Italy. There is a cathedral consecrated 1108, later much rebuilt and restored, and the Chichester Festival Theater (1962).

chicken domestic fowl; see under ◊poultry.

chickenpox or *varicella* common acute disease, caused by a virus of the ◊herpes group and transmitted by airborne droplets. Chickenpox chiefly attacks children under the age of ten. The incubation period is two to three weeks. One attack normally gives immunity for life.

The temperature rises and spots (later inflamed blisters) develop on the torso, then on the face and limbs. The sufferer recovers within a week, but remains infectious until the last scab disappears.

chickpea annual plant *Cicer arietinum*, family Leguminosae, which is grown for food in India and the Middle East. Its short, hairy pods contain edible pealike seeds.

chickweed any of several low-growing plants of the genera *Stellaria* and *Cerastium* of the pink family Caryophyllaceae, with small, white, starlike flowers.

Chiclayo capital of Lambayeque department, NW Peru; population (1988) 395,000.

chicle milky juice from the sapodilla tree *Achras zapota* of Central America; it forms the basis of chewing gum.

Chico city in N California, NW of Sacramento. Situated in the fertile Sacramento Valley, a farming region, its industries include food processing and lumber products; population (1990) 40,000.

chiffchaff bird *Phylloscopus collybita* of the warbler family, found in woodlands and thickets in Europe and N Asia during the summer, migrating south for winter. About 4.3 in/ 11 cm long, olive above, grayish below, with an eyestripe and usually dark legs, it looks similar to a willow warbler but has a distinctive song.

Chifley Ben (Joseph Benedict) 1885–1951. Australian Labor prime minister 1945–49. He united the party in fulfilling a welfare and nationalization program 1945–49 (although he failed in an attempt to nationalize the banks 1947) and initiated an immigration program and the Snowy Mountains hydroelectric project.

chigger or **harvest mite** scarlet or rusty brown ⬦mite of the family Trombiculidae, common in summer and autumn. Their tiny red larvae cause intensely irritating bites.

chihuahua smallest breed of dog, 10 in/15 cm high, developed in the US from Mexican origins. It may weigh only 2.2 lb/1 kg. The domed head and wide-set ears are characteristic, and the skull is large compared to the body. It can be almost any color, and occurs in both smooth (or even hairless) and long-coated varieties.

Chihuahua capital of Chihuahua state, Mexico, 800 mi/1,285 km NW of Mexico City; population (1984) 375,000. Founded 1707, it is the center of a mining district and has textile mills.

The University of Chihuahua is here. The revolutionary leader Pancho Villa had his headquarters here during the early 20th century, and his home is a tourist attraction.

chilblain painful inflammation of the skin of the feet, hands, or ears, due to cold. The parts turn red, swell, itch violently, and are very tender. In bad cases, the skin cracks, blisters, or ulcerates.

Child Lydia Maria 1802–1880. US writer, social critic, and feminist, author of the popular women's guides *The Frugal Housewife* 1829 and *The Mother's Book* 1831. With her husband, David Child, she worked for the abolition of slavery, advocating educational support for black Americans. The Childs also edited the weekly *National Anti-Slavery Standard* 1840–44.

Child, born in Medford, Massachusetts, received little formal education but read widely and published several historical novels about life in colonial New England.

child abuse the molesting of children by parents and other adults. It can give rise to various criminal charges and has become a growing concern since the early 1980s.

childbirth the expulsion of a baby from its mother's body following ⬦pregnancy. In a broader sense, it is the period of time involving labor and delivery of the baby, plus the effort and pain involved.

Child, Convention on the Rights of the United Nations document designed to make the well-being of children an international obligation. It was adopted 1989 and covers children from birth up to 18.

It laid down international standards for:
provision of a name, nationality, health care, education, rest, and play;
protection from commercial or sexual exploitation, physical or mental abuse, and engagement in warfare;

participation in decisions affecting a child's own future.

child prodigy young person who has developed a remarkable talent for one or more subjects or pursuits. Unlike ⬦idiots savants, child prodigies are usually taught by an adult. ⬦Mozart was a child prodigy of musical genius.

Children's Crusade ⬦crusade by some 10,000 children from France, the Low Countries, and Germany, in 1212, to recapture Jerusalem for Christianity. Motivated by religious piety, many of them were sold into slavery or died of disease.

children's literature works specifically written for children. The earliest known illustrated children's book in English is *Goody Two Shoes* 1765, possibly written by Oliver Goldsmith. *Fairy tales* were originally part of a vast range of oral literature, credited only to the writer who first recorded them, such as Charles Perrault. During the 19th century several writers, including Hans Christian Andersen, wrote original stories in the fairy tale genre; others, such as the Grimm brothers, collected (and sometimes adapted) existing stories.

Early children's stories were written with a moral purpose; this was particularly true in the 19th century, apart from the unique case of Lewis Carroll's *Alice* books. The late 19th century was the great era of children's literature in the UK, with Lewis Carroll, Beatrix Potter, Charles Kingsley, and J M Barrie. It was also the golden age of illustrated children's books, with such artists as Kate Greenaway and Randolph Caldecott. In the US, Louise May Alcott's *Little Women* 1868 and its sequels found a wide audience.

Among the most popular 20th-century children's writers in English have been Kenneth Grahame (*The Wind in the Willows* 1908) and A A Milne (*Winnie the Pooh* 1926) in the UK; and, in the US, Laura Ingalls Wilder (*Little House on the Prairie* 1935), E B White (*Stuart Little* 1945, *Charlotte's Web* 1952), and Dr Seuss (*Cat in the Hat* 1957). Canadian Lucy Maud Montgomery's series that began with *Anne of Green Gables* 1908 was widely popular.

Adventure stories have often appealed to children even when these were written for adults; examples include *Robinson Crusoe* by Daniel Defoe; the satirical *Gulliver's Travels* by Jonathan Swift, and *Tom Sawyer* 1876 and *Huckleberry Finn* 1884 by Mark Twain.

Many recent children's writers have been influenced by J R R ⬦Tolkien whose *The Hobbit* 1937 and its sequel, the three-volume *Lord of the Rings* 1954–55, are set in the comprehensively imagined world of "Middle-earth." His friend C S ⬦Lewis produced the allegorical chronicles of Narnia, beginning with *The Lion, the Witch and the Wardrobe* 1950. Rosemary Sutcliff's *The Eagle of the Ninth* 1954, Philippa Pearce's *Tom's Midnight Garden* 1958, and Penelope Lively's *The Wild Hunt of Hagworthy* 1971 are other outstanding books by children's authors who have exploited a perennial fascination with time travel. Writers for younger children combining stories and illustrations of equally high quality include Maurice Sendak (*Where the Wild Things Are* 1963) and Quentin Blake (*Mister Magnolia* 1980). Roald ⬦Dahl's *James and the Giant Peach* 1961 is the first of his popular children's books which summon up primitive emotions and have an imperious morality. More realistic stories for teenagers are written by US authors such as Judy Blume and S E Hinton.

Chile South American country, bounded N by Peru and Bolivia, E by Argentina, and S and W by the Pacific Ocean.

government Since 1973 Chile has been ruled by a military junta. A new constitution took effect 1989. It provides for the election of a president for an eight-year, nonrenewable term and a legislature consisting of a senate with 26 elected and nine appointed members and a chamber of deputies with 120 elected members, all serving four-year terms. Strikes in the public services are not allowed, and the economy is based on "free-market principles."

history The area now known as Chile was originally occupied by the Araucanian Indians and invaded by the ⬦Incas in the 15th century. The first European to reach it was Ferdinand Magellan, who in 1520 sailed through the strait now named after him. A Spanish expedition under Pedro de Valdivia founded Santiago 1541, and Chile was subsequently colonized by Spanish settlers who established an agricultural society, although the Indians continued to rebel until the late 19th century. Becoming independent from Spain 1818, Chile went to war with Peru and Bolivia 1879 and gained considerable territory from them.

"social justice" Most of the 20th century has been characterized by left-versus right-wing struggles. The Christian Democrats under Eduardo Frei held power 1964–70, followed by a left-wing coalition led by Dr Salvador ⬦Allende (Gossens), the first democratically elected Marxist head of state. He promised social justice by constitutional means and began nationalizing industries, including US-owned copper mines.

"authoritarian democracy" The US Central Intelligence Agency painted Allende as a pro-Cuban communist and encouraged opposition to him. In 1973 the army, led by General Augusto ⬦Pinochet, overthrew the government. Allende was killed or, as the new regime claimed, committed suicide. Pinochet became president, and his opponents were tortured, imprisoned, or just "disappeared." In 1976 Pinochet proclaimed an "authoritarian democracy" and in 1977 banned all political parties. His policies were "endorsed" by a referendum 1978.

opposition to government In 1980 a "transition to democracy" by 1989 was announced, but imprisonment and torture continued. By 1983 opposition to Pinochet had increased, with demands for a return to democratic government. He attempted to placate opposition by initiating public works. In 1984 an anti-government bombing campaign began, aimed mainly at electricity installations, resulting in a 90-day state of emergency, followed by a 90-day state of siege. In 1985, as opposition grew in the Catholic church and the army as well as among the public, another state of emergency was declared, but the bombings continued, as did the state terror.

pluralist politics In Oct 1988 Pinochet's proposal to remain in office for another eight-year term was rejected in a plebiscite. Another plebiscite Aug 1989 approved constitutional changes leading to a return to pluralist politics and in Dec the moderate Christian Democratic Party (PDC) candidate, Patricio Aylwin, was elected president, his term of office beginning March 1990.

human rights abuses investigated In Jan 1990, the junta approved the disbanding of the secret police of the National Information Center (CNI), which had replaced the National Information Bureau (DINA) 1977. In Sept 1990

Chile
Republic of (*República de Chile*)

area 292,257 sq mi/756,950 sq km
capital Santiago
cities Concepción, Viña del Mar, Temuco; ports Valparaíso, Antofagasta, Arica, Iquique, Punta Arenas
physical Andes mountains along E border, Atacama Desert in N, fertile central valley, grazing land and forest in S
territories Easter Island, Juan Fernández Islands, part of Tierra del Fuego, claim to part of Antarctica
features Atacama Desert is one of the driest regions in the world
head of state and government Patricio Aylwin from 1990
political system emergent democratic republic
political parties Christian Democratic Party (PDC), moderate centrist; National Renewal Party (RN), right-wing
exports copper (world's leading producer), iron, molybdenum (world's second largest producer), nitrate, pulp and paper, steel products, fishmeal, fruit
currency peso
population (1990 est) 13,000,000 (the majority are of European origin or are mestizos, of mixed American Indian and Spanish descent); growth rate 1.6% p.a.
life expectancy men 64, women 73
language Spanish
religion Roman Catholic 89%
literacy 94% (1988)
GDP $18.9 bn (1987); $6,512 per head
chronology
1818 Achieved independence from Spain.
1964 PDC formed government under Eduardo Frei.
1970 Dr Salvador Allende became the first democratically elected Marxist president; he embarked on an extensive program of nationalization and social reform.
1973 Government overthrown by the CIA-backed military, led by General Augusto Pinochet. Allende killed. Policy of repression began during which all opposition was put down and political activity banned.
1983 Growing opposition to the regime from all sides, with outbreaks of violence.
1988 Referendum on whether Pinochet should serve a further term resulted in a clear "No" vote.
1989 President Pinochet agreed to constitutional changes to allow pluralist politics. Patricio Aylwin (PDC) elected president (his term would begin 1990); Pinochet remained as army commander in chief.
1990 Aylwin reached accord on end to military junta government. Pinochet censured by president.
1992 Future US–Chilean free-trade agreement announced.

a government commission was set up to investigate some 2,000 political executions 1973–78, 500 political murders 1978–90, and 700 disappearances. In the same month the formerly discredited Salvador Allende was officially recognized by being buried in a marked grave, and President Aylwin censured General Pinochet for trying to return to active politics. In 1991 the official report for President Aylwin revealed 2,279 deaths during Pinochet's term, of which over 2,115 were executions carried out by the secret police. In 1992 the US announced that a future US–Chilean free-trade agreement would be negotiated. *See illustration box.*

Chilean Revolution in Chile, the presidency of Salvador ♢Allende (Gossens) 1970–73, the Western hemisphere's first democratically elected Marxist-oriented president of an independent state.

chili the pod, or powder made from the pod, of a variety of ♢capsicum, *Capsicum frutescens*, a hot, red pepper. It is widely used in cooking.

chimaera fish of the group Holocephali. Chimaeras have thick bodies that taper to a long thin tail, large fins, smooth skin, and a cartilaginous skeleton. They can grow to 4.5 ft/1.5 m. Most chimaeras are deep-water fish, and even *Chimaera monstrosa*, a relatively shallow-living form caught around European coasts, lives at a depth of 1,000–1,600 ft/300–500 m.

chimera in biology, an organism composed of tissues that are genetically different. Chimeras can develop naturally if a ♢mutation occurs in a cell of a developing embryo, but are more commonly produced artificially by implanting cells from one organism into the embryo of another.

chimera or **chimaera** in Greek mythology, a fire-breathing animal with a lion's head, a goat's body, and tail in the form of a snake; hence any apparent hybrid of two or more creatures. The chimera was killed by the hero Bellerophon on the winged horse Pegasus.

chimpanzee highly intelligent African ape *Pan troglodytes* that lives mainly in rainforests but sometimes in wooded savanna. Chimpanzees are covered in thin but long black body hair, except for the face, hands, and feet, which may have pink or black skin. They normally walk on all fours, supporting the front of the body on the knuckles of the fingers, but can stand or walk upright for a short distance. They can grow to 4.5 ft/1.4 m tall, and weigh up to 110 lb/50 kg. They are strong and climb well, but spend time on the ground, living in loose social groups. The bulk of the diet is fruit, with some leaves, insects, and occasional meat. Chimpanzees can use "tools," fashioning twigs to extract termites from their nests.

Chimpanzees are found in an area from W Africa to W Uganda and Tanzania in the east. Studies of chromosomes suggest that chimpanzees are the closest apes to humans, perhaps sharing 99% of the same genes. Trained chimpanzees can learn to communicate with humans with the aid of machines or sign language, but are probably precluded from human speech by the position of the voicebox.

Chimu South American civilization that flourished on the coast of Peru from about 1250 to about 1470, when it was conquered by the Incas. The Chimu people produced fine work in gold, realistic portrait pottery, savage fanged feline images in clay, and possibly a system of writing or recording by painting patterns on beans. They built aqueducts carrying water many miles, and the huge, mazelike city of Chan Chan, 14 sq mi/36 sq km, on the coast near Trujillo.

The Chimu people built enormous adobe brick mounds or *huacas* as the base of temples and palaces. Chan Chan consists of nine complexes, probably built by successive kings to form their eventual tombs. Their agricultural system depended on extensive irrigation; the invading Incas ensured victory by cutting the Chimu aqueducts.

China the largest country in E Asia, bounded N by Mongolia; NW by Tajikistan, Kyrgyzstan, Kazakhstan, and Afghanistan; SW by India, Nepal, and Bhutan; S by Myanmar (Burma), Laos, and Vietnam; SE by the South China Sea; E by the East China Sea, North Korea, and Yellow Sea; NE by Russia.

government China is divided into 22 provinces, five autonomous regions, and three municipalities (Beijing, Shanghai, and Tianjin), each with an elected local people's government with policy-making power in defined areas. Ultimate authority resides in the single-chamber National People's Congress (NPC), composed of 2,970 deputies indirectly elected every five years through local people's congresses. Deputies to local people's congresses are directly elected through universal suffrage in constituency contests. The NPC, the "highest organ of state power," meets annually and elects a permanent, 133-member committee to assume its functions between sittings. The committee has an inner body comprising a chair and 19 vice chairs. The NPC also elects for a five-year term a State Central Military Commission (SCMC), leading members of the judiciary, the vice-president, and the state president, who must be at least 45 years old. The president is restricted to two terms in office and performs primarily ceremonial functions. Executive administration is effected by a prime minister and a cabinet (state council) that includes three vice premiers, 31 departmental ministers, eight commission chiefs, an auditor general, and a secretary-general, and is appointed by the NPC.

China's controlling force is the Chinese Communist Party (CCP). It has a parallel hierarchy comprising elected congresses and committees functioning from village level upward and taking orders from above. A national party congress every five years elects a 285-member central committee (175 of whom have full voting powers) that meets twice a year and elects an 18-member Politburo and 5-member secretariat to exercise day-to-day control over the party and to frame state and party policy goals. The Politburo meets weekly and is China's most significant political body.

history For early history see ♢China, history. Imperial rule ended 1911 with the formation of a republic 1912. After several years of civil war the nationalist ♢Guomindang, led by ♢Chiang Kai-shek, was firmly installed in power 1926, with communist aid. In 1927 Chiang Kai-shek began a purge of the communists, who set out on the "Long March" (1934–36) to Shaanxi, which became their base. In 1931 Japan began its penetration of Manchuria and 1937 saw the outbreak of the second ⟡Sino-Japanese War, during which both communists and nationalists fought Japan. Civil war resumed after the Japanese surrender 1945, until in 1949, after their elimination of nationalist resistance on the mainland, the communists inaugurated the People's Republic of China, the nationalists having retired to ⟡Taiwan.

To begin with, the communist regime concentrated on economic reconstruction. A centralized Soviet-style constitution was adopted 1954, industries were nationalized, and central planning and moderate land reform introduced. The USSR provided economic aid, while China intervened in the ⟡Korean War. Development during this period was based on material incentives and industrialization.

Great Leap Forward From 1958, under state president and CCP chair ⟡Mao Zedong, China embarked on a major new policy, the ⟡Great Leap Forward. This created large self-sufficient agricultural and industrial communes in an effort to achieve classless "true communism." The experiment proved unpopular and impossible to coordinate, and over 20 million people died in the floods and famines of 1959–62. The failure of the Great Leap reduced Mao's influence 1962–65, and a successful "recovery program" was begun under President Liu Shaoqi. Private farming plots and markets were reintroduced, communes reduced in size, and income differentials and material incentives restored.

Cultural Revolution Mao struck back against what he saw as a return to capitalism by launching the Great Proletarian Cultural Revolution (1966–69), a "rectification campaign" directed against "rightists" in the CCP and seeking to reestablish the supremacy of (Maoist) ideology over economics. During the chaotic campaign, Mao, supported by People's Liberation Army (PLA) chief ⟡Lin Biao and the Shanghai-based ⟡Gang of Four (comprising Mao's wife Jiang Qing, radical intellectuals Zhang Chunqiao and Yao Wenyuan, and former millworker Wang Hongwen), encouraged student (Red Guard) demonstrations against party and government leaders. The chief targets were Liu Shaoqi, ⟡Deng Xiaoping (head of the CCP secretariat), and Peng Zhen (mayor of Beijing). All were forced out of office. Government institutions fell into abeyance during the Cultural Revolution, and new "Three Part Revolutionary Committees," comprising Maoist party officials, labor unionists, and PLA commanders, took over administration.

By 1970, Mao sided with pragmatic prime minister ⟡Zhou Enlai and began restoring order and a more balanced system. In 1972–73 Deng Xiaoping, finance minister Li Xiannian, and others were rehabilitated, and a policy of détente toward the US began. This reconstruction movement climaxed in the summoning of the NPC in 1975 for the first time in 11 years to ratify a new constitution and approve an economic plan termed the "Four Modernizations" –agriculture, industry, armed forces, and science and technology—that aimed at placing China on a par with the West by the year 2000.

after Mao The deaths of Zhou Enlai and Mao Zedong 1976 unleashed a violent succession struggle between the leftist Gang of Four, led by Jiang Qing, and moderate "rightists," grouped around Vice Premier Deng Xiaoping. Deng was forced into hiding by the Gang; and Mao's moderate protégé ⟡Hua Guofeng became CCP chair and head of government 1976. Hua arrested the Gang on charges of treason and held power 1976–78 as a stop-gap leader, continuing Zhou Enlai's modernization program. His authority was progressively challenged, however, by Deng Xiaoping, who returned to office 1977 after campaigns in Beijing.

Deng in power By 1979, after further popular campaigns, Deng had gained effective charge of the government, controlling a majority in the Politburo. State and judicial bodies began to meet again, Liu Shaoqi was rehabilitated as a party hero, and economic reforms were introduced. These involved the dismantling of the commune system, the introduction of direct farm incentives under a new "responsibility system," and the encouragement of foreign investment in "Special Economic Zones" in coastal enclaves. By June 1981 Deng's supremacy was assured when his protégés ⟡Hu Yaobang and ⟡Zhao Ziyang had become party chair and prime minister and the Gang of Four were sentenced to life imprisonment. In 1982, Hua Guofeng and a number of senior colleagues were ousted from the Politburo, and the NPC adopted a definitive constitution, restoring the post of state president (abolished since 1975) and establishing a new civil rights code.

modernization The new administration was a collective leadership, with Hu Yaobang in

China

People's Republic of (*Zhonghua Renmin Gonghe Guo*)

area 3,599,975 sq mi/9,596,960 sq km
capital Beijing (Peking)
cities Chongqing (Chungking), Shenyang (Mukden), Wuhan, Nanjing (Nanking), Harbin; ports Tianjin (Tientsin), Shanghai, Qingdao (Tsingtao), Lüda (Lü-ta), Guangzhou (Canton)
physical two-thirds of China is mountains or desert (N and W); the low-lying E is irrigated by rivers Huang He (Yellow River), Chang Jiang (Yangtze-Kiang), Xi Jiang (Si Kiang)
features Great Wall of China; Gezhouba Dam; Ming Tombs; Terracotta Warriors (Xi'ain); Gobi Desert; world's most populous country
head of state Yang Shangkun from 1988
head of government Li Peng from 1987
political system communist republic
political party Chinese Communist Party (CCP), Marxist-Leninist-Maoist
exports tea, livestock and animal products, silk, cotton, oil, minerals (China is the world's largest producer of tungsten and antimony), chemicals, light industrial goods
currency yuan
population (1990 est) 1,130,065,000 (the majority are Han or ethnic Chinese; the 67 million of other ethnic groups, including Tibetan, Uigur, and Zhuang, live in border areas). The number of people of Chinese origin outside China, Taiwan, and Hong Kong is estimated at 15–24 million. Growth rate 1.2% p.a.
life expectancy men 67, women 69
languages Chinese, including Mandarin (official), Cantonese, and other dialects
religions officially atheist, but traditionally Taoist, Confucianist, and Buddhist; Muslim 13 million; Catholic 3–6 million (divided between the "patriotic" church established 1958 and the "loyal" church subject to Rome); Protestant 3 million
literacy men 82%, women 66% (1985 est)
GDP $293.4 bn (1987); $274 per head
chronology
1949 People's Republic of China proclaimed by Mao Zedong.
1954 Soviet-style constitution adopted.
1956–57 Hundred Flowers Movement encouraged criticism of the government.
1958–60 Great Leap Forward commune experiment to achieve "true communism."
1960 Withdrawal of Soviet technical advisers.
1962 Sino-Indian border war.
1962–65 Economic recovery program under Liu Shaoqi; Maoist "socialist education movement" rectification campaign.
1966–69 Great Proletarian Cultural Revolution; Liu Shaoqi overthrown.
1969 Ussuri River border clashes with USSR.
1970–76 Reconstruction under Mao and Zhou Enlai.
1971 Entry into United Nations.
1972 US president Nixon visited Beijing.
1975 New state constitution. Unveiling of Zhou's "Four Modernizations" program.
1976 Deaths of Zhou Enlai and Mao Zedong; appointment of Hua Guofeng as prime minister and Communist Party chair. Vice Premier Deng Xiaoping in hiding. Gang of Four arrested.
1977 Rehabilitation of Deng Xiaoping.
1979 Economic reforms introduced. Diplomatic relations opened with USA. Punitive invasion of Vietnam.
1980 Zhao Ziyang appointed prime minister.
1981 Hu Yaobang succeeded Hua Guofeng as party chair. Imprisonment of Gang of Four.
1982 New state constitution adopted.
1984 "Enterprise management" reforms for industrial sector.
1986 Student prodemocracy demonstrations.
1987 Hu was replaced as party leader by Zhao, with Li Peng as prime minister. Deng left Politburo but remained influential.
1988 Yang Shangkun replaced Li Xiannian as state president. Economic reforms encountered increasing problems; inflation rocketed.
1989 Over 2,000 killed in prodemocracy student demonstrations in Tiananmen Square; international sanctions imposed.
1991 March: European Community and Japanese sanctions lifted. May: normal relations with USSR resumed. Sept: UK prime minister John Major visited Beijing. Nov: relations with Vietnam normalized.
1992 China promised to sign 1968 Nuclear Non-Proliferation Treaty. Historic visit by Japan's emperor.

control of party affairs, Zhao Ziyang overseeing state administration, and Deng Xiaoping (a party vice chair and SCMC chair) formulating long-term strategy and supervising the PLA. The triumvirate pursued a three-pronged policy aimed firstly at streamlining the party and state bureaucracies and promoting to power new, younger, and better-educated technocrats. Secondly, they sought to curb PLA influence by retiring senior commanders and reducing personnel numbers from 4.2 to 3 million. Thirdly, they gave priority to economic modernization by extending market incentives and local autonomy and by introducing a new "open door" policy to encourage foreign trade and investment.

prodemocracy movement These economic reforms met with substantial success in the agricultural sector (output more than doubled 1978–85) but had adverse side effects, widening regional and social income differentials and fueling a wave of "mass consumerism" that created balance-of-payments problems. Contact with the West brought demands for full-scale democratization in China. These calls led in 1986 to widespread student demonstrations, and party chief Hu Yaobang was dismissed 1987 for failing to check the disturbances. Hu's departure imperiled the post-Dengist reform program, as conservative forces, grouped around the veteran Politburo members Chen Yun and Peng Zhen, sought to halt the changes and reestablish central party control. Chen Yun, Peng Zhen, and Deng Xiaoping all retired from the Politburo in Oct 1987, and soon after ◊Li Peng took over as prime minister, Zhao Ziyang having become CCP chair.

Tiananmen Square massacre With inflation spiraling, economic reform was halted in the autumn of 1988 and an austerity budget

China: provinces

province	alternative transcription
Anhui	Anhwei
Fujian	Fukien
Gansu	Kansu
Guangdong	Kwantung
Guizhou	Kweichow
Hainan	
Hebei	Hopei
Heilongjiang	Heilungkiang
Henan	Honan
Hubei	Hupei
Hunan	
Jiangsu	Kiangsu
Jiangxi	Kiangsi
Jilin	Kirin
Liaoning	
Qinghai	Tsinghai
Shaanxi	Shensi
Shandong	Shantung
Shanxi	Shansi
Sichuan	Szechwan
Yunnan	
Zhejiang	Chekiang
autonomous region	
Guangxi Zhuang	Kwangsi Chuang
Nei Mongol	Inner Mongolia
Ningxia Hui	Ninghsia-Hui
Xinjiang Uygur	Sinkiang Uighur
Xizang	Tibet
municipality	
Beijing	Peking
Shanghai	
Tianjin	Tientsin

introduced 1989. This provoked urban unrest and a student-led prodemocracy movement, launched in Beijing, rapidly spread to provincial cities. There were mass demonstrations during Soviet leader Mikhail Gorbachev's visit to China in May 1989. Soon after Gorbachev's departure, a brutal crackdown was launched against the demonstrators by Li Peng and President Yang Shangkun, with Deng Xiaoping's support. Martial law was proclaimed and in June 1989 more than 2,000 unarmed protesters were massacred by army troops in the capital's Tiananmen Square. Arrests, executions, martial law, and expulsion of foreign correspondents brought international condemnation and economic sanctions. Communist Party general secretary Zhao Ziyang was ousted and replaced by Jiang Zemin (the Shanghai party chief and new protégé of Deng Xiaoping), a move that consolidated the power of the hard-line faction of President Yang Shangkun and Premier Li Peng. Deng officially retired from the last of his party and army posts but remained a dominant figure. A crackdown on dissidents was launched as the pendulum swung sharply away from reform toward conservatism. Several dozen prodemocracy activists arrested 1989 were tried in early 1991 and received sentences of 2–13 years.

foreign affairs In foreign affairs, China's 1960 rift with ◊Khrushchev's Soviet Union over policy differences became irrevocable 1962 when the USSR sided with India during a brief Sino-Indian border war. Relations with the USSR deteriorated further 1969 after border clashes in the disputed Ussuri River region. China pursued the policy of the ◊nonaligned movement, projecting itself as the voice of Third World nations, although it achieved nuclear capability by 1964. During the early 1970s, concern with Soviet expansionism brought rapprochement with the US, bringing about China's entry to the United Nations 1971 (at ◊Taiwan's expense), and culminating in the establishment of full Sino-American diplomatic relations 1979. In the 1980s there was a partial rapprochement with the USSR, culminating in Gorbachev's visit May 1989. However, a new rift became evident 1990, with the Chinese government denouncing the Soviet leader's "revisionism." Until the Tiananmen Square massacre, relations with the West were warm during the Deng administration, with economic contacts broadening. After the massacre, the US imposed an embargo on sales of military equipment and announced the scaling-back of government contacts. But in Dec 1989 US president Bush sent a surprise mission to China, defending the contact as an effort to prevent dangerous isolation of the Chinese and as a way to engage them in constructive peace proposals for Cambodia. And during the Persian Gulf crisis of 1990–91, China used its UN Security Council vote to back much of the policy of the US-led anti-Iraq alliance, although it abstained in the vote authorizing the war. By March 1991 Japan and the European Community had dropped most of the sanctions imposed in the wake of the Tiananmen massacre. In May 1991 Jiang Zemin visited the USSR for talks with Gorbachev. This was the first visit to the USSR of a Chinese Communist Party leader since Mao Zedong visited Moscow 1957. An agreement on the demarcation of the Sino-Soviet border was signed. In Sept 1991 British prime minister John Major became the first Western leader to pay an official visit to China since the 1989 Tiananmen Square massacre. Vietnam's Communist Party leader and

prime minister visited Beijing Nov 1991, after which relations were normalized and a trade agreement was signed. In contrast, relations with the US remained strained as a result of China's poor human rights record and its indiscriminate sale of weapons technologies around the world. However, China said it intended to join the other major nuclear powers in signing the 1968 Nuclear Non-Proliferation Treaty, which requires signatories to refrain from providing other countries with atomic weapons. In Jan 1992 China established full diplomatic relations with Israel, and in Oct 1992 Beijing received the first ever state visit by a Japanese emperor.

signs of economic reform By Aug 1991 China's economy, after stalling 1989–90, began to expand rapidly once again, with a significant increase in industrial output. From Jan 1992, when Deng Xiaoping returned to the forefront with a tour of southern China, there were signs that the country was entering a new phase of economic reform and improved relations with the West. In Oct Emperor Akihito visited China, the first Japanese emperor ever to do so. *See illustration box.*

China Sea area of the Pacific Ocean bordered by China, Vietnam, Borneo, the Philippines, and Japan. Various groups of small islands and shoals, including the Paracels, 300 mi/500 km E of Vietnam, have been disputed by China and other powers because they lie in oil-rich areas.

North of Taiwan it is known as the **East China Sea** and to the south as the **South China Sea.**

chincherinchee poisonous plant *Ornithogalum thyrsoides* of the lily family Liliaceae. It is native to South Africa, and has spikes of long-lasting, white or yellow, waxlike flowers.

chinchilla South American rodent *Chinchilla laniger* found in high, rather barren areas of the Andes in Bolivia and Chile. About the size of a small rabbit, it has long ears and a long bushy tail, and shelters in rock crevices. These gregarious animals have thick, soft, silver-gray fur, and were hunted almost to extinction for it. They are now farmed and protected in the wild.

Chindit member of an Indian division of the British army in World War II that carried out guerrilla operations against the Japanese in Burma (now Myanmar) under the command of Brigadier General Orde Wingate (1903–44). The name derived from the mythical Chinthay—half lion, half eagle—placed at the entrance of Burmese pagodas to scare away evil spirits.

Chinese native to or an inhabitant of China and Taiwan, or a person of Chinese descent. The Chinese comprise more than 25% of the world's population, and the Chinese language (Mandarin) is the largest member of the Sino-Tibetan family.

Chinese traditions are ancient, many going back to at least 3000 BC. They include a range of philosophies and religions, including Confucianism, Taoism, and Buddhism. The veneration of ancestors was an enduring feature of Chinese culture, as were patrilineal-based villages. The extended family was the traditional unit, the five-generation family being the ideal. Recent attempts by the People's Republic of China have included the restriction of traditions and the limit of one child to a married couple.

The majority of Chinese are engaged in

agriculture, cultivating irrigated rice fields in the south, and growing millet and wheat in the north. Many other Chinese work in commerce, industry, and government. Descendants of Chinese migrants are found throughout SE Asia, the Pacific, Australia, North and South America, and Europe. Within China many minorities speak non-Chinese languages belonging to the Sino-Tibetan family (such as Tibetan, Hmong, and Zhuang). Some peoples speak languages belonging to the Altaic (such as Uigur, Mongol, and Manchu) and Indo-European (such as Russian) families, while in the northeast there are Koreans. The Chinese were governed for long periods by the Mongol (AD 1271–1368) and Manchu (AD 1644–1911) dynasties. See ◊China: history.

Although dialects vary considerably, there is a common written language, a non-phonetic script of characters representing concepts rather than sounds, similar to the way numbers represent quantities but may be pronounced differently in every language.

Chinese architecture style of building in China. Traditionally of timber construction, few existing buildings predated the Ming dynasty (1368–1644), but records such as the *Ying Tsao Fa Shih/Method of Architecture* 1103 show that Chinese architecture changed little throughout the ages, both for the peasants and for the well-to-do. Curved roofs are a characteristic feature; also typical is the pagoda with a number of curved tiled roofs, one above the other. The Great Wall of China was built about 228–210 BC as a northern frontier defense, and Beijing's fine city walls, of which only a small section remains, date from the Ming period.

Chinese buildings usually face south, a convention which can be traced back to the "Hall of Brightness," a building from the Zhou dynasty (1050–221 BC), and is still retained in the functionally Western-style Chinese architecture of the present day. Although some sections of Beijing have been destroyed by modernization it still contains fine examples of buildings from the Ming dynasty, such as the Altar of Heaven, the ancestral temple of the Ming tombs, and the Five Pagoda Temple. The introduction of Buddhism from India exerted considerable influence on Chinese architecture.

Chinese art the painting and sculpture of China. From the Bronze Age to the Cultural Revolution, Chinese art shows a stylistic unity unparalleled in any other culture. From about the 1st century AD Buddhism inspired much sculpture and painting. The *Han dynasty* (206 BC–AD 220) produced outstanding metalwork, ceramics, and sculpture. The *Song dynasty* (960–1278) established standards of idyllic landscape and nature painting in a delicate calligraphic style.

Neolithic art Accomplished pottery dates back to about 2500 BC, already showing a distinctive Chinese approach to form.

Bronze Age art Rich burial goods, with bronzes and jade carvings, survive from the second millennium BC, decorated with hieroglyphs and simple stylized animal forms. Astonishing life-size terracotta figures from the Qin period (about 221–206 BC) guard the tomb of Emperor Shi Huangdi in the old capital of Xian. Bronze horses, naturalistic but displaying the soft curving lines of the Chinese style, are a feature of the Han dynasty.

early Buddhist art Once Buddhism was established in China it inspired a monumental art, with huge rock-cut Buddhas and graceful linear relief sculptures at the monasteries of Yungang, about 460–535, and Longmen. Bronze images show the same curving lines and rounded forms.

Tang dynasty (618–907) art shows increasing sophistication in idealized images and naturalistic portraits, such as the carved figures of Buddhist monks (Luohan). This period also produced brilliant metalwork and delicate ceramics. It is known that the aims and, broadly speaking, the style of Chinese painting were already well established, but few paintings survive, with the exception of some Tang scrolls and silk paintings.

Song dynasty The golden age of painting was the Song dynasty (960–1278). The imperial court created its own workshop, fostering

China: history

500,000 BC	The oldest human remains found in China were those of "Peking man" (*Sinanthropus pekinensis* later known as *Homo erectus*).
25,000 BC	Humans of the Upper Paleolithic modern type (*Homo sapiens sapiens*) inhabited the region.
5000 BC	A simple Neolithic agricultural society was established.
c. **2800–** *c.* **2200** BC	The **Sage kings**, a period of agricultural development, known only from legend.
c. **2200–** *c.* **1500** BC	The **Xia dynasty**, a Bronze Age early civilization, with further agricultural developments, including irrigation, and the first known use of writing in this area.
c. **1500–** *c.* **1066** BC	The **Shang dynasty** is the first of which we have documentary evidence. Writing became well-developed; bronze vases survive in ceremonial burials. The first Chinese calendar was made.
c. **1066–221** BC	During the **Zhou dynasty**, the feudal structure of society broke down in a period of political upheaval, though iron, money, and written laws were all in use, and philosophy flourished (see ◊Confucius). The dynasty ended in the "Warring States" period (403–221 BC), with the country divided into small kingdoms.
221–206 BC	The **Qin** dynasty corresponds to the reign of Shih Huang Ti, who curbed the feudal nobility and introduced orderly bureaucratic government; he had roads and canals built and began the ◊Great Wall of China to keep out invaders from the north.
206 BC–AD **220**	The **Han dynasty** was a long period of peace, during which territory was incorporated, the keeping of historical records was systematized, and an extensive civil service set up. Art and literature flourished, and ◊Buddhism was introduced. The first census was taken in AD 2, registering a population of 57 million. Chinese caravans traded with the Parthians.
220–581	The area was divided into **Three Kingdoms**: the Wei, Shu, and Wu. Confucianism was superseded by Buddhism and Taoism; glass was introduced from the West. After prolonged fighting, the Wei became the most powerful kingdom, eventually founding the **Jin dynasty** (265–304), which expanded to take over from the barbarian invaders who ruled much of China at that time, but from 305 to 580 lost the territory they had gained to the Tatar invaders from the north.
581–618	Reunification came with the **Sui dynasty**: the government was reinstated, the barbarian invasions stopped, and the Great Wall refortified.
618–907	During the **Tang dynasty** the system of government became more highly developed and centralized, and the empire covered most of SE and much of central Asia. Sculpture, painting, and poetry flourished again, and trade relations were established with the Islamic world and the Byzantine Empire.
907–960	The period known as the **Five Dynasties and Ten Kingdoms** was characterized by war, economic depression, and loss of territory in N China, central Asia, and Korea, but printing was developed, including the first use of paper money, and porcelain was traded to Islamic lands.
960–1279	The **Song dynasty** was a period of calm and creativity. Central government was restored, and movable type was invented. At the end of the dynasty, the northern and western frontiers were neglected, and Mongol invasions took place. Marco Polo visited the court of the Great Khan in 1275.
1279–1368	The **Yuan dynasty** saw the beginning of Mongol rule in China, with Kublai Khan on the throne in Beijing 1293; there were widespread revolts. Marco Polo served the Kublai Khan.
1368–1644	The Mongols were expelled by the first of the native Chinese **Ming dynasty**, who expanded the empire. Chinese ships sailed to the Sunda Islands 1403, Ceylon 1408, and the Red Sea 1430. Mongolia was captured by the second Ming emperor. Architecture developed and Beijing flourished as the new capital. Portuguese explorers reached Macao 1516 and Canton 1517; other Europeans followed. Chinese porcelain arrived in Europe 1580. The Jesuits reached Beijing 1600.
1644–1912	The last of the dynasties was the **Manchu** or **Ching**, who were non-Chinese nomads from Manchuria. Initially trade and culture flourished, but during the 19th century it seemed that China would be partitioned among the US and European imperialist nations, since all trade was conducted through treaty ports in their control. The ◊**Boxer Rebellion** 1900 against Western influence was suppressed by European troops.
1911–12	Revolution broke out, and the infant emperor Henry ◊P'u-i was deposed. For history 1911–present, see ◊Chinese Revolution and ◊China.

a fine calligraphic art, mainly devoted to natural subjects—landscape, mountains, trees, flowers, birds, and horses—though genre scenes of court beauties were also popular. Scrolls, albums, and fans of silk or paper were painted with watercolors and ink, using soft brushes that produced many different textures. Painting was associated with literature, and painters added poems or quotations to their work to intensify the effect. Ma Yuan (c. 1190–1224) and Xia Gui (active c. 1180–1230) are among the painters; Muqi (1180–c. 1270) was a monk known for exquisite brushwork. The Song dynasty also produced the first true porcelain, achieving a classic simplicity and delicacy in coloring and form.

Ming dynasty (1368–1644) Painters continued the landscape tradition, setting new standards in idealized visions. The painter Dong Qichang wrote a history and theory of Chinese painting. The Song style of porcelain gradually gave way to increasingly elaborate decorative work, and pale shades were superseded by rich colors, as in Ming blue-and-white patterned ware.

Qing dynasty (1644–1911) The so-called Individualist Spirits emerged, painters who developed bolder, personal styles of brushwork.

20th century The strong spirit that supported traditional art began to fade in the 19th and 20th centuries, but attempts to incorporate modernist ideas have been frowned on by the authorities. Not directly concerned with the representation of political events, Chinese art took some years before responding to the political upheavals of this century. Subsequently, response to offical directives produced a period of Soviet-style realism followed by a reversion to a peasant school of painting, which was the officially favored direction for art during the Cultural Revolution.

influence Chinese art had a great impact on surrounding countries. The art of Korea was almost wholly inspired by Chinese example for many centuries. Along with Buddhism, Chinese styles of art were established in Japan in the 6th–7th centuries BC and continued to exert a profound influence, though Japanese culture soon developed an independent style.

Chinese language language or group of languages of the Sino-Tibetan family, spoken in China, Taiwan, Hong Kong, Singapore, and Chinese communities throughout the world. Varieties of spoken Chinese differ greatly, but all share a written form using thousands of ideographic symbols—characters—which have changed little in 2,000 years. Nowadays, *putonghua* ("common speech"), based on the educated Beijing dialect known as Mandarin Chinese, is promoted throughout China as the national spoken and written language.

Because the writing system has a symbolic form (like numbers and music notes) it can be read and interpreted regardless of the reader's own dialect. The Chinese dialects are tonal; that is, they depend on the tone of a syllable to indicate its meaning: *ma* with one tone means "mother," with another means "horse." The characters of Chinese script were traditionally written down the page from right to left. Today they are commonly written horizontally and read left to right, using 2,000 simplified characters. A variant of the Roman alphabet has been introduced and is used in schools to help with pronunciation. This, called *Pinyin*, is prescribed for international use by the People's Republic of China for personal and place names (as in *Beijing* rather than *Peking*). Pinyin spell-

ings are generally used in this volume, but they are not accepted by the government of Taiwan.

Chinese literature *poetry* Chinese poems, often only four lines long, and written in the ancient literary language understood throughout China, consist of rhymed lines of a fixed number of syllables, ornamented by parallel phrasing and tonal pattern. The oldest poems are contained in the *Book of Songs* (800–600 BC). Some of the most celebrated Chinese poets are the nature poet T'ao Ch'ien (372–427), the master of technique Li Po (701–62), the autobiographical Po Chüi (772–846), and the wide-ranging Su Tung-p'o (1036–1101); and among the moderns using the colloquial language under European influence and ex-perimenting in free verse are Hsu Chih-mo (1895–1931), and Pien Chih-lin (1910–   ).

prose Histories are not so much literary works as collections of edited documents with moral comment, whereas the essay has long been cultivated under strict rules of form and style. An example of the latter genre is *Upon the Original Way* by Han Yü (768–824), recalling the nation to Confucianism. Until the 16th century the short story was confined to the anecdote, startling by its strangeness and written in the literary language -for example, the stories of the poetic Tuan Ch'eng-shih (died 863); but after that time the more novelistic type of short story, written in the colloquial tongue, developed by its side. The Chinese novel evolved from the street storyteller's art and has consequently always used the popular language. The early romances *Three Kingdoms, All Men are Brothers*, and *Golden Lotus* are anonymous, the earliest known author of this genre being Wu Che'ng-en (c. 1505–1580); the most realistic of the great novelists is Ts'ao Chan (died 1763). Twentieth-century Chinese novels have largely adopted European form, and have been influenced by Russia, as have the realistic stories of Lu Hsün. In typical Chinese drama, the stage presentation far surpasses the text in importance (the dialogue was not even preserved in early plays), but there have been experiments in the European manner.

Chinese Revolution series of great political upheavals in China 1911–49 that eventually led to Communist party rule and the establishment of the People's Republic of China. In 1912, a Nationalist revolt overthrew the imperial Manchu (or Ching) dynasty. Led by Sun Yat-sen 1923–25, and by Chiang Kai-shek 1925–49, the Nationalists, or Guomindang, were increasing challenged by the growing Communist movement. The 6,000 mi/10,000 km **Long March** to the NW by the Communists 1934–35 to escape from attacks by the Nationalist forces resulted in Mao Zedong's emergence as Communist leader. During World War II 1939–45, the various Chinese political groups pooled military resources against the Japanese invaders. After World War II, the conflict reignited into open civil war 1946–49, until the Nationalists were defeated at Nanking and forced to flee to Taiwan. Communist rule was established in the People's Republic of China under the leadership of Mao.

The Chinese revolution came about with the collapse of the Manchu (or Ching) dynasty, a result of increasing internal disorders, pressure from foreign governments, and the weakness of central government. A Nationalist revolt led to a provisional republican constitution being proclaimed and a government established in Beijing (Peking). Led by Sun Yat Sen and Chiang Kai-shek, the Nationalists

were faced with the problems of restoring the authority of central government and meeting the challenges from militaristic factions and the growing Communist movement. After 1930, Chiang launched a series of attacks that encircled the Communists in SE China and led to an attempt by Communist army commander Chu Teh to break out. The resulting Long March to NW China from Oct 1934–Oct 1935 reduced the Communists' army from over 100,000 to little more than 8,000, mainly as a result of skirmishes with Chiang's forces and the severity of the conditions. During the march, a power struggle developed between Mao Zedong and Chang Kuo T'ao which eventually split the force. Mao's group finally based itself in Yen'an, where it remained throughout the war with the Japanese, forming an uneasy alliance with the Nationalists to expel the invaders. Mao's troops formed the basis of the Red Army that renewed the civil war against the Nationalists 1946 and emerged victorious after defeating them at Nanking 1949. As a result, Communist rule was established in China under Mao's leadership.

Chinghai alternative transcription of ⟶Qinghai, province of NW China.

chinook (American Indian "snow-eater") warm dry wind that blows downhill on the eastern side of the Rocky Mountains of North America. It often occurs in winter and spring when it produces a rapid thaw, and so is important to the agriculture of the area.

chip or **silicon chip** another name for an ⟶in-tegrated circuit, a complete electronic circuit on a slice of silicon (or other semiconductor) crystal only a few millimeters square.

chipmunk any of several species of small ground squirrel with characteristic stripes along its side. Chipmunks live in North America and E Asia, in a variety of habitats, usually wooded, and take shelter in burrows. They have pouches in their cheeks for carrying food. They climb well but spend most of their time on or near the ground.

The **Siberian chipmunk** *Eutamias sibiricus*, about 5 in/13 cm long, is found in N Russia, N China, and Japan.

integrated circuit on a silicon chip

chip in its DIP (dual in-line pins) packaging   printed circuit board

chip *A chip, or integrated circuit.*

Chippendale Thomas c. 1718–1779. English furniture designer. He set up his workshop in St Martin's Lane, London 1753. His book *The Gentleman and Cabinet Maker's Director* 1754, was a significant contribution to furniture design. He favored Louis XVI, Chinese, Gothic, and Neo-Classical styles, and worked mainly in mahogany.

Chirac Jacques 1932– . French conservative politician, prime minister 1974–76 and 1986–88. He established the neo-Gaullist Rassemblement pour la République (RPR) 1976, and became mayor of Paris 1977.

Chirac held ministerial posts during the Pompidou presidency and gained the nickname "the Bulldozer." In 1974 he became prime minister to President Giscard d'Estaing, but the relationship was uneasy. Chirac contested the 1981 presidential election and emerged as the National Assembly leader for the parties of the right during the Socialist administration of 1981–86. Following the rightist coalition's victory 1986, Chirac was appointed prime minister by President Mitterrand in a "cohabitation" experiment. The term was marked by economic decline, nationality reforms, and student unrest.

Student demonstrations in autumn 1986 forced him to scrap plans for educational reform. He stood in the May 1988 presidential elections and was defeated by Mitterrand, who replaced him with the moderate Socialist Michel Rocard.

Chirico Giorgio de 1888–1978. Italian painter born in Greece, whose style presaged Surrealism in its use of enigmatic imagery and dreamlike settings, for example, *Nostalgia of the Infinite* 1911, Museum of Modern Art, New York.

In 1917, with Carlo Carrà (1881–1966), he founded Metaphysical painting, which aimed to convey a sense of mystery and hallucination. This was achieved by distorted perspective, dramatic lighting, and the use of dummies and statues in place of human figures.

Chiron in Greek mythology, the son of ◇Cronus by a sea nymph. A ◇centaur, he was the wise tutor of ◇Jason and ◇Achilles, among others.

Chiron unusual Solar-System object orbiting between Saturn and Uranus, discovered 1977 by US astronomer Charles T Kowal (1940–). Initially classified as an asteroid, it is now believed to be a giant cometary nucleus about 120 mi/200 km across, composed of ice with a dark crust of carbon dust.

chiropody care and treatment of feet.

Originally, it referred to the treatment of hands as well as feet, but is now synonymous with podiatry.

chiropractic technique of manipulation of the spine and other parts of the body, based on the principle that disorders are attributable to aberrations in the functioning of the nervous system, which manipulation can correct.

Developed in the 1890s by US practitioner Daniel David Palmer, chiropractic is widely practiced today by accredited therapists, although orthodox medicine remains skeptical of its efficacy except for the treatment of back problems.

Chisholm Jesse c. 1806–c. 1868. US pioneer who gained a reputation as a resourceful guide, trader, and military scout during the early 19th century. Ranging over the S Great Plains, he customarily followed a route from the Mexican border to Kansas, ending at the market town of Abilene. This overland route later became one of the main paths of the yearly Texas cattle drive and was known among cowboys as the "Chisholm Trail."

Little is known of Chisholm's early life.

Chisholm v Georgia landmark case 1793 in which the US Supreme Court ruled that states are not immune from suits brought by citizens of other states. Alexander Chisholm, a South Carolinian, sued Georgia for payment on Georgia state bonds that were confiscated during the American Revolution. Georgia ignored the case, claiming it was not in federal jurisdiction, but the Supreme Court ruled that Georgia must appear in court to answer the charges. This decision frightened state governments as the number of similar suits grew across the nation. In response to fears about this economic danger to states' survival, the 11th Amendment, passed in 1798, reversed the Chisholm decision.

Chissano Joaquim 1939– . Mozambique nationalist politician, president from 1986; foreign minister 1975–86.

He was secretary to Samora ◇Machel, who led the National Front for the Liberation of Mozambique (Frelimo) during the campaign for independence in the early 1960s. When Mozambique achieved internal self-government 1974, Chissano was appointed prime minister. After independence he served under Machel as foreign minister and on his death succeeded him as president.

chitin complex long-chain compound, or ◇polymer; a nitrogenous derivative of glucose. Chitin is found principally in the ◇exoskeleton of insects and other arthropods. It combines with protein to form a covering that can be hard and tough, as in beetles, or soft and flexible, as in caterpillars and other insect larvae. In crustaceans such as crabs, it is impregnated with calcium carbonate for extra strength.

Chitin also occurs in some ◇protozoans and coelenterates (such as certain jellyfishes), in the jaws of annelid worms, and as the cell-wall polymer of fungi.

In 1991 scientists discovered that chitin can be converted into carbomethylchitosan, a water-soluble, biodegradable material which is also nontoxic. Its uses include coating apples (still fresh after six months), coating seeds, clearing water of heavy metals, and dressing wounds.

chivalry code of gallantry and honor that medieval knights were pledged to observe. Its principal virtues were piety, honor, valor, courtesy, chastity, and loyalty. The word originally meant the knightly class of the feudal Middle Ages.

Chivalry originated in feudal France and Spain, spreading rapidly to the rest of Europe and reaching its height in the 12th and 13th centuries. It was strengthened by the Crusades. The earliest orders of chivalry were the Knights Hospitallers and Knights Templars, founded to serve pilgrims to the Holy Land. Secular literature of the period takes knighthood and chivalry as its theme.

chive or *chives* bulbous perennial European plant *Allium schoenoprasum* of the lily family Liliaceae. It has long, tubular leaves and dense, round flower heads in blue or lilac, and is used as a garnish for salads.

Chladni Ernst Florens Friedrich 1756–1827. German physicist, a pioneer in the field of ◇acoustics. He developed an experimental technique whereby sand is vibrated on a metal plate, and settles into regular and symmetric patterns (**Chladni's figures**) indicating the nodes of the vibration's wave pattern.

chlamydia single-celled bacterium that can live only parasitically in animal cells. Chlamydiae are thought to be descendants of bacteria that have lost certain metabolic processes. In humans, they cause ◇trachoma, a disease found mainly in the tropics (a leading cause of blindness), and ◇psittacosis, a disease which may be contracted from birds; venereally transmitted chlamydiae cause genital and urinary infections.

chloracne eruption of the skin, symptomatic of direct contact with chlorinated organic chemicals or an environment contaminated by such chemicals.

chloramphenicol the first broad-spectrum antibiotic to be used commercially. It was discovered 1947 in a Venezuelan soil sample containing the bacillus *Streptomyces venezuelae*, which produces the antibiotic substance $C_{11}H_{12}Cl_2N_2O_5$, now synthesized. Because of its toxicity, its use is limited to treatment of life-threatening infections, such as meningitis and typhoid fever.

chlorate any salt derived from an acid containing both chlorine and oxygen and possessing the negative ion ClO^-, ClO_2^{2-}, ClO_3^{3-}, or ClO_4^{4-}. Common chlorates are those of sodium, potassium, and barium. Certain chlorates are used in weedkillers.

chlorella any single-celled, green, freshwater alga of the genus *Chlorella*, 3–10 micrometers in diameter, which can increase its weight by four times in 12 hours. Nutritive content: 50% protein, 20% fat, 20% carbohydrate, 10% phosphate, calcium, and ◇trace elements.

chloride Cl⁻ negative ion formed when hydrogen chloride dissolves in water, and any salt containing this ion, commonly formed by the action of hydrochloric acid (HCl) on various metals or by direct combination of a metal and chlorine. Sodium chloride (NaCl) is common table salt.

chlorine (Greek *chloros* "green") greenish-yellow, gaseous, nonmetallic element with a pungent odor, symbol Cl, atomic number 17, atomic weight 35.453. It is a member of the ◇halogen group and is widely distributed, in combination with the ◇alkali metals, as chlorates or chlorides.

In nature it is always found in the combined form, as in hydrochloric acid, produced in the mammalian stomach for digestion. Chlorine is obtained commercially by the electrolysis of concentrated brine and is an important bleaching agent and germicide, used for both drinking and swimming-pool water. As an oxidizing agent it finds many applications in organic chemistry. The pure gas (Cl_2) is a poison and was used in gas warfare in World War I, where its release seared the membranes of the nose, throat, and lungs, producing pneumonia. Chlorine is a component of chlorofluorocarbons (CFCs) and is partially responsible for the depletion of the ◇ozone layer; it is released from the CFC molecule by the action of ultraviolet light in the upper atmosphere, making it available to react with and destroy the ozone.

Chlorine was discovered 1774 by the German chemist Karl Scheele, but Humphry Davy first proved it to be an element 1810 and named it after its color.

chlorofluorocarbon (CFC) synthetic chemical that is odorless, nontoxic, nonflammable, and chemically inert. CFCs have been used as propellants in ⚪aerosol cans, as refrigerants in refrigerators and air conditioners, and in the manufacture of foam packaging. They are partly responsible for the destruction of the ⚪ozone layer. In June 1990 representatives of 93 nations, including the US and the UK, agreed to phase out production of CFCs and various other ozone-depleting chemicals by the end of the 20th century.

When CFCs are released into the atmosphere, they drift up slowly into the stratosphere, where, under the influence of ultraviolet radiation from the Sun, they break down into chlorine atoms which destroy the ozone layer and allow harmful radiation from the Sun to reach the Earth's surface. CFCs can remain in the atmosphere for more than 100 years.

Replacements for CFCs are being developed, and research into safe methods of destroying existing CFCs is being carried out.

chloroform (technical name *trichloromethane*) CCl_3 clear, colorless, toxic, carcinogenic liquid with a characteristic pungent, sickly sweet smell and taste, formerly used as an anesthetic (now superseded by less harmful substances). It is used as a solvent and in the synthesis of organic chemical compounds.

chlorophyll green pigment present in most plants; it is responsible for the absorption of light energy during ⚪photosynthesis. The pigment absorbs the red and blue-violet parts of sunlight but reflects the green, thus giving plants their characteristic color.

Chlorophyll is found within chloroplasts, present in large numbers in leaves. Cyanobacteria (blue-green algae) and other photosynthetic bacteria also have chlorophyll, though of a slightly different type. Chlorophyll is similar in structure to ⚪hemoglobin, but with magnesium instead of iron as the reactive part of the molecule.

chloroplast structure (⚪organelle) within a plant cell containing the green pigment chlorophyll. Chloroplasts occur in most cells of the green plant that are exposed to light, often in large numbers. Typically, they are flattened and disklike, with a double membrane enclosing the stroma, a gellike matrix. Within the stroma are stacks of fluid-containing cavities, or vesicles, where ⚪photosynthesis occurs.

It is thought that the chloroplasts were originally free-living cyanobacteria (blue-green algae) which invaded larger, non-photosynthetic cells and developed a symbiotic relationship

chloroplast *Green chlorophyll within the chloroplast captures light energy to produce food by photosynthesis.*

with them. Like ⚪mitochondria, they contain a small amount of DNA and divide by fission. Chloroplasts are a type of ⚪plastid.

chlorosis abnormal condition of green plants in which the stems and leaves turn pale green or yellow. The yellowing is due to a reduction in the levels of the green chlorophyll pigments. It may be caused by a deficiency in essential elements (such as magnesium, iron, or manganese), a lack of light, genetic factors, or viral infection.

chocolate powder, syrup, confectionery, or beverage derived from cacao seeds. See ⚪cocoa and chocolate.

choir body of singers, normally divided into two or more parts, and commonly four (soprano, alto, tenor, bass). The words *choir* and *chorus* are frequently interchangeable, although all church groups use the former, while larger groups, which may have several hundred members, invariably use the latter.

Choiseul Étienne François, duc de Choiseul 1719–1785. French politician. Originally a protégé of Madame de Pompadour, the mistress of Louis XV, he became minister for foreign affairs 1758, and held this and other offices until 1770. He banished the Jesuits, and was a supporter of the Enlightenment philosophers Diderot and Voltaire.

cholecystectomy surgical removal of the ⚪gall bladder. It is carried out when gallstones or infection lead to inflammation of the gallbladder, which may then be removed either via a ⚪laparotomy or by ⚪endoscopy; the latter method, which performs the operation without making a large wound, is increasing in popularity.

cholera any of several intestinal diseases, especially *Asiatic cholera*, an infection caused by a bacterium *Vibrio cholerae*, transmitted in contaminated water and characterized by violent diarrhea and vomiting. It is prevalent in many tropical areas.

The formerly high death rate during epidemics has been much reduced by treatments to prevent dehydration and loss of body salts. There is an effective vaccine that must be repeated at frequent intervals for people exposed to continuous risk of infection.

The worst epidemic in the Western hemisphere for 70 years occurred in Peru 1991, with 55,000 confirmed cases and 258 deaths. It was believed to have been spread by the consumption of seafood contaminated by untreated sewage.

cholesterol white, crystalline ⚪sterol found throughout the body, especially in fats, blood, nerve tissue, and bile; it is also provided in the diet by foods such as eggs, meat, and butter. A high level of cholesterol in the blood is thought to contribute to atherosclerosis (hardening of the arteries).

Cholesterol is an integral part of all cell membranes and the starting point for steroid hormones, including the sex hormones. It is broken down by the liver into bile salts, which are involved in fat absorption in the digestive system, and it is an essential component of *lipoproteins*, which transport fats and fatty acids in the blood. *Low-density lipoprotein cholesterol* (LDL-cholesterol), when present in excess, can enter the tissues and become deposited on the surface of the arteries, causing atherosclerosis. *High-density lipoprotein cholesterol* (HDL-cholesterol) acts as a scavenger, transporting fat and cholesterol from the tissues to the liver to be broken

down. Blood cholesterol levels can be altered by reducing the amount of alcohol and fat in the diet and by substituting some of the saturated fat for polyunsaturated fat, which gives a reduction in LDL-cholesterol. HDL-cholesterol can be increased by exercise.

Chomsky Noam 1928– . US professor of linguistics. He proposed a theory of transformational generative grammar, which attracted widespread interest because of the claims it made about the relationship between language and the mind and the universality of an underlying language structure. He has been a leading critic of the imperialist tendencies of the US government.

Chomsky distinguished between knowledge and behavior and maintained that the focus of scientific inquiry should be on knowledge. In order to define and describe linguistic knowledge, he posited a set of abstract principles of grammar that appear to be universal and may have a biological basis.

Chongjin capital of North Hamgyong province on the NE coast of North Korea; population (1984) 754,000.

Chongqing or *Chungking*, also known as *Pahsien* city in Sichuan province, China, that stands at the confluence of the ⚪Chang Jiang and Jialing Jiang rivers; population (1984) 2,733,700. Industries include iron, steel, chemicals, synthetic rubber, and textiles.

For over 4,000 years it has been a major commercial center in one of the most remote and economically deprived regions of China. It was opened to foreign trade 1891, and remains a focal point of road, river, and rail transport. When both Beijing and Nanjing were occupied by the Japanese, it was the capital of China 1938–46.

Chopin Frédéric (François) 1810–1849. Polish composer and pianist. He made his debut as a pianist at the age of eight. As a performer, Chopin revolutionized the technique of pianoforte-playing, turning the hands outwards and favoring a light, responsive touch. His compositions for piano, which include two concertos and other works with orchestra, are characterized by great volatility of mood, and rhythmic fluidity.

From 1831 he lived in Paris, where he became known in the fashionable salons, although he rarely performed in public. In 1836 the composer Liszt introduced him to Madame Dudevant (George ⚪Sand), with whom he had a close relationship 1838–46. During this time she nursed him in Majorca for tuberculosis, while he composed intensively and for a time regained his health. His music was made the basis of the ballet *Les Sylphides* by Fokine 1909 and orchestrated by Alexander Gretchaninov (1864–1956), a pupil of Rimsky-Korsakov.

He died Oct 17, 1849 and was buried in Père Lachaise cemetery in Paris.

Chopin Kate 1851–1904. US novelist and short-story writer. Her novel *The Awakening* 1899, the story of a married New Orleans woman's awakening to her sexuality, is now regarded as a classic of feminist sensibility.

chorale traditional hymn tune of the German Protestant church, usually harmonized in four parts for singing by a congregation.

chord in geometry, a straight line joining any two points on a curve. The chord that passes through the center of a circle (its longest chord) is the diameter. The longest and shortest chords of an ellipse (a regular oval) are called the major and minor axes respectively.

chord in music, a group of three or more notes sounded together. The resulting combination of tones may be either harmonious or dissonant.

chordate animal belonging to the phylum Chordata, which includes vertebrates, sea squirts, amphioxi, and others. All these animals, at some stage of their lives, have a supporting rod of tissue (notochord or backbone) running down their bodies.

chorea disease of the nervous system marked by involuntary movements of the face muscles and limbs, formerly called St Vitus's dance. ◊Huntington's chorea is also characterized by such movements.

choreography art of creating and arranging ballet and dance for performance; originally, in the 18th century, the art of dance notation.

chorion outermost of the three membranes enclosing the embryo of reptiles, birds, and mammals; the ◊amnion is the innermost membrane.

chorion villus sampling (CVS) ◊biopsy of a small sample of placental tissue, carried out in early pregnancy at 10–12 weeks' gestation. Since the placenta forms from embryonic cells, the tissue obtained can be tested to reveal genetic abnormality in the fetus. The advantage of CVS over ◊amniocentesis is that it provides an earlier diagnosis, so that if any abnormality is discovered, and the parents opt for an abortion, it can be carried out more safely.

choroid black layer found at the rear of the ◊eye beneath the retina. By absorbing light that has already passed through the retina, it stops back-reflection and so aids vision.

chorus large group of singers; a smaller church group is called a ◊choir.

Chou En-lai alternative transcription of ◊Zhou Enlai.

chough bird *Pyrrhocorax pyrrhocorax* of the crow family, about 15 in/38 cm long, black-feathered, and with red bill and legs. It lives on sea cliffs and mountains from Europe to E Asia, but is now rare.

The *alpine chough Pyrrhocorax graculus* is similar, but has a yellow bill and is found up to the snowline in mountains from the Pyrenees to Central Asia.

chow chow breed of dog originating in China in ancient times. About 1.5 ft/45 cm tall, it has a broad neck and head, round catlike feet, a soft woolly undercoat with a coarse outer coat, and a mane. Its coat should be of one color, and it has an unusual blue-black tongue.

Chrétien de Troyes lived second half of the 12th century. French poet, born in Champagne. His epics, which introduced the concept of the ◊Holy Grail, include *Lancelot, ou le chevalier de la charrette*; *Perceval, ou le conte du Graal*, written for Philip, Count of Flanders; *Erec*; *Yvain, ou le chevalier au Lion*; and other Arthurian romances.

Christ (Greek *khristos* "anointed one") the ◊Messiah as prophesied in the Hebrew Bible, or Old Testament.

Christchurch city on South Island, New Zealand, 7 mi/11 km from the mouth of the Avon River; population (1989) 301,500. It is the principal city of the Canterbury plains and the seat of the University of Canterbury. Industries include fertilizers and chemicals, canning and meat processing, rail workshops, and shoes.

Christchurch uses as its port a bay in the sheltered Lyttelton Harbor on the northern shore of the Banks Peninsula, which forms a denuded volcanic mass. Land has been reclaimed for service facilities, and rail and road tunnels (1867 and 1964 respectively) link Christchurch with Lyttelton.

Christian follower of ◊Christianity, the religion derived from the teachings of Jesus. In the New Testament (Acts 11:26) it is stated that the first to be called Christians were the disciples in Antioch (now Antakya, Turkey).

Christian ten kings of Denmark and Norway, including:

Christianity: chronology

1st century	The Christian church is traditionally said to have originated at Pentecost, and separated from the parent Jewish religion by the declaration of saints Barnabas and Paul that the distinctive rites of Judaism were not necessary for entry into the Christian church.
3rd century	Christians were persecuted under the Roman emperors Severus, Decius, and Diocletian.
312	Emperor Constantine established Christianity as the religion of the Roman Empire.
4th century	A settled doctrine of Christian belief evolved, with deviating beliefs condemned as heresies. Questions of discipline threatened disruption within the Church; to settle these, Constantine called the Council of Arles 314, followed by the councils of Nicaea 325 and Constantinople 381.
5th century	Councils of Ephesus 431 and Chalcedon 451. Christianity was carried northward by such figures as saints Columba and Augustine.
800	Holy Roman Emperor Charlemagne crowned by the pope. The church assisted the growth of the feudal system of which it formed the apex.
1054	The Eastern Orthodox Church split from the Roman Catholic Church.
11th–12th centuries	Secular and ecclesiastical jurisdiction were often in conflict; for example, Emperor Henry IV and Pope Gregory VII, Henry II of England and his archbishop Becket.
1096–1291	The church supported a series of wars in the Middle East, called the Crusades.
1233	The Inquisition was established to suppress heresy.
14th century	Increasing worldliness (against which the foundation of the Dominican and Franciscan monastic orders was a protest) and ecclesiastical abuses led to dissatisfaction and the appearance of the reformers Wycliffe and Huss.
15th–17th centuries	Thousands of women were accused of witchcraft, tortured, and executed.
early 16th century	The Renaissance brought a re-examination of Christianity in N Europe by the humanists Erasmus, More, and Colet.
1517	The German priest Martin Luther started the Reformation, an attempt to return to a pure form of Christianity, and became leader of the Protestant movement.
1519–64	In Switzerland the Reformation was carried out by Calvin and Zwingli.
1529	Henry VIII renounced papal supremacy and proclaimed himself head of the Church of England.
1545–63	The Counter-Reformation was initiated by the Catholic church at the Council of Trent.
1560	The Church of Scotland was established according to Calvin's Presbyterian system.
17th century	Jesuit missionaries established themselves in China and Japan. Puritans, Quakers, and other sects seeking religious freedom established themselves in North America.
18th century	During the Age of Reason, Christian dogmas were questioned, and intellectuals began to examine society in purely secular terms. In England and America, religious revivals occurred among the working classes in the form of Methodism and the Great Awakening. In England the Church of England suffered the loss of large numbers of Nonconformists.
19th century	The evolutionary theories of Darwin and the historical criticism of the Bible challenged the Book of Genesis. Missionaries converted people in Africa and Asia, suppressing indigenous faiths and cultures.
1948	The World Council of Churches was founded as part of the ecumenical movement to reunite various Protestant sects and, to some extent, the Protestant churches and the Catholic church.
1950s–80s	Protestant evangelicism grew rapidly in the US, spread by television.
1969	A liberation theology of freeing the poor from oppression emerged in South America, and attracted papal disapproval.
1972	The United Reformed Church was formed by the union of the Presbyterian Church in England and the Congregational Church. In the US, the 1960s–70s saw the growth of cults, some of them nominally Christian, which were a source of social concern.
1980s	The Roman Catholic Church played a major role in the liberalization of the Polish government; and in the USSR the Orthodox Church and other sects were tolerated and even encouraged under Gorbachev.
1989	Barbara Harris, first female bishop, ordained in the US.
1992	The Church of England General Synod voted in favor of the ordination of women priests.

Christian I 1426–1481. King of Denmark from 1448, and founder of the Oldenburg dynasty. In 1450 he established the union of Denmark and Norway that lasted until 1814.

Christian III 1503–1559. King of Denmark and Norway from 1535. During his reign the Reformation was introduced.

Christian IV 1577–1648. King of Denmark and Norway from 1588. He sided with the Protestants in the Thirty Years' War (1618–48), and founded Christiania (now Oslo, capital of Norway). He was succeeded by Frederick II 1648.

Christian VIII 1786–1848. King of Denmark 1839–48. He was unpopular because of his opposition to reform. His attempt to encourage the Danish language and culture in Schleswig and Holstein led to an insurrection there shortly after his death. He was succeeded by Frederick VII.

Christian IX 1818–1906. King of Denmark from 1863. His daughter Alexandra married Edward VII of the UK and another, Dagmar, married Tsar Alexander III of Russia; his second son, George, became king of Greece. In 1864 he lost the duchies of Schleswig and Holstein after a war with Austria and Prussia.

Christian X 1870–1947. King of Denmark and Iceland from 1912, when he succeeded his father Frederick VIII. He married Alexandrine, Duchess of Mecklenburg-Schwerin, and was popular for his democratic attitude. During World War II he was held prisoner by the Germans in Copenhagen. He was succeeded by Frederick IX.

Christianity world religion derived from the teaching of Jesus in the first third of the 1st century, with a present-day membership of about 1 billion. It is divided into groups or denominations that differ in some areas of belief and practice. Its main divisions are the ⇨Roman Catholic, ⇨Eastern Orthodox, and ⇨Protestant churches.

beliefs Christians believe in one God with three aspects: God the Father, God the Son (Jesus), and God the Holy Spirit, who is the power of God working in the world. God created everything that exists and showed his love for the world by coming to Earth as Jesus, and suffering and dying in order to be reconciled with humanity. Christians believe that three days after his death by crucifixion Jesus was raised to life by God's power, appearing many times in bodily form to his followers, and that he is now alive in the world through the Holy Spirit. Christians speak of the sufferings they may have to endure because of their faith, and the reward of everlasting life in God's presence which is promised to those who have faith in Jesus Christ and who live according to his teaching.

Christian Science or *the Church of Christ, Scientist* sect established in the US by Mary Baker Eddy 1879. Christian Scientists believe that since God is good and is a spirit, matter and evil are not ultimately real. Consequently they refuse all medical treatment. The church has its own daily newspaper, the *Christian Science Monitor.*

Christian Science is regarded by its adherents as the restatement of primitive Christianity with its full gospel of salvation from all evil, including sickness and disease as well as sin. According to its adherents, Chris-

tian Science healing is brought about by the operation of truth in human conscience. There is no ordained priesthood, but there are public practitioners of Christian Science healing who are officially authorized.

The headquarters of the First Church of Christ, Scientist, is in Boston, Massachusetts, with branches in most parts of the world. The textbook of Christian Science is Eddy's *Science and Health with Key to the Scriptures* 1875.

Christie Agatha (born Miller) 1890–1976. English detective novelist who created the characters Hercule ⇨Poirot and Miss Jane ⇨Marple. She wrote more than 70 novels, including *The Murder of Roger Ackroyd* 1926 and *Ten Little Indians* 1939. Her play *The Mousetrap,* which opened in London 1952, is the longest continuous running show in the world.

She was born in Torquay, married Col Archibald Christie 1914, and served during World War I as a nurse. Her first crime novel, *The Mysterious Affair at Styles* 1920, introduced Hercule Poirot. She often broke "purist" rules, as in *The Murder of Roger Ackroyd* in which the narrator is the murderer. She caused a nationwide sensation 1926 by disappearing for ten days when her husband fell in love with another woman.

Christie Julie 1940– . English film actress who became a star following her award-winning performance in *Darling* 1965. She also appeared in *Doctor Zhivago* 1965, *The Go-Between* and *McCabe and Mrs Miller,* both 1971, *Don't Look Now* 1973, and *Heat and Dust* 1982.

Christina 1626–1689. Queen of Sweden 1632–54. Succeeding her father Gustavus Adolphus at the age of six, she assumed power 1644, but disagreed with the former regent ⇨Oxenstjerna. Refusing to marry, she eventually nominated her cousin Charles Gustavus (Charles X) as her successor. As a secret convert to Roman Catholicism, which was then illegal in Sweden, she had to abdicate 1654, and went to live in Rome, twice returning to Sweden unsuccessfully to claim the throne.

Christmas Christian religious holiday, observed throughout the Western world on Dec 25 and traditionally marked by feasting and gift-giving. In the Christian church, it is the day on which the birth of Jesus is celebrated, although the actual birth date is unknown. Many of its customs have a non-Christian origin and were adapted from celebrations of the winter solstice, when the sun is at its farthest point south of the celestial equator.

The choice of a date near the winter solstice owed much to the missionary desire to facilitate conversion of members of older religions, which traditionally held festivals at that time of year.

Christmas Island island in the Indian Ocean, 224 mi/360 km S of Java; area 54 sq mi/140 sq km; population (1986) 2,000. It has phosphate deposits. Found to be uninhabited when reached by Captain W Mynars on Christmas Day 1643, it was annexed by Britain 1888, occupied by Japan 1942–45, and transferred to Australia 1958. After a referendum 1984, it was included in Northern Territory.

Christmas tree any evergreen tree brought indoors and decorated for Christmas. The custom was a medieval German tradition and is now practiced in many Western countries.

Christo adopted name of Christo Javacheff 1935– . US sculptor, born in Bulgaria, active

in Paris in the 1950s and in New York from 1964. He is known for his wrapped works: structures, such as bridges and buildings, and even areas of coastline are temporarily wrapped in synthetic fabric tied down with rope. The *Running Fence* 1976 across California was another temporary work. In 1991 he simultaneously exhibited a work in both Japan and the US.

Christophe Henri 1767–1820. West Indian slave, one of the leaders of the revolt against the French 1791, who was proclaimed king of Haiti 1811. His government distributed plantations to military leaders. He shot himself when his troops deserted him because of his alleged cruelty.

Christopher, St patron saint of travelers. His feast day, July 25, was dropped from the Roman Catholic liturgical calendar 1969.

Traditionally he was a martyr in Syria in the 3rd century, and legend describes him carrying the child Jesus over the stream; despite his great strength, he found the burden increasingly heavy, and was told that the child was Jesus Christ bearing the sins of all the world.

chromatic scale musical scale proceeding by semitones. All 12 notes in the octave are used rather than the 7 notes of the diatonic scale.

chromatography (Greek *chromos* "color") technique used for separating the components of a mixture. This is brought about by means of two immiscible substances, one of which (**the mobile phase**) transports the sample mixture through the other (**the stationary phase**). The mobile phase may be a gas or a liquid; the stationary phase may be a liquid or a solid, and may be in a column, on paper, or in a thin layer on a glass or plastic support. The components of the mixture are absorbed or impeded by the stationary phase to different extents and therefore become separated.

Preparative chromatography is carried out on a large scale for the purification and collection of one or more of a mixture's constituents; for example, in the recovery of protein from abattoir wastes. *Analytical chromatography* is carried out on far smaller quantities, often as little as one microgram (one-millionth of a gram), in order to identify and quantify the component parts of a mixture. It is used to determine the identities and amounts of amino acids in a protein, and the alcohol content of blood and urine samples.

The technique was first used in the separation of colored mixtures into their component pigments.

chromite $FeCr_2O_4$, iron chromium oxide, the main chromium ore. It is one of the ⇨spinel group of minerals, and crystallizes in dark-colored octahedra of the cubic system. Chromite is usually found in association with ultrabasic and basic rocks; in Cyprus, for example, it occurs with ⇨serpentine, and in South Africa it forms continuous layers in a layered ⇨intrusion.

chromium (Greek *chromos* "color") hard, brittle, gray-white, metallic element, symbol Cr, atomic number 24, atomic weight 51.996. It takes a high polish, has a high melting point, and is very resistant to corrosion. It is used in chromium electroplating, in the manufacture of stainless steel and other alloys, and as a catalyst. Its compounds are used for tanning leather and for ⇨alums. In human nutrition it is a vital trace element. In nature, it occurs chiefly as chrome iron ore or chromite

(FeCr$_2$O$_4$). Kazakhstan, Zimbabwe, and Brazil are sources.

The element was named 1797 by the French chemist Louis Vauquelin (1763–1829) after its brightly colored compounds.

chromium ore essentially chromite, FeCr$_2$O$_4$, from which chromium is extracted. South Africa and Zimbabwe are major producers.

chromosome structure in a cell nucleus that carries the ⭗genes. Each chromosome consists of one very long strand of DNA, coiled and folded to produce a compact body. The point on a chromosome where a particular gene occurs is known as its locus. Most higher organisms have two copies of each chromosome (they are ⭗diploid) but some have only one (they are ⭗haploid). There are 46 chromosomes in a normal human cell. See also ⭗mitosis and ⭗meiosis.

chromosphere (Greek "color" and "sphere") layer of mostly hydrogen gas about 6,000 mi/ 10,000 km deep above the visible surface of the Sun (the photosphere). It appears pinkish red during ⭗eclipses of the Sun.

chronic in medicine, term used to describe a condition that is of slow onset and then runs a prolonged course, such as rheumatoid arthritis or chronic bronchitis. In contrast, an *acute* condition develops quickly and may be of relatively short duration.

chronic fatigue syndrome medical condition characterized by long-term fatigue, irritability, confusion, and, often, inflammation of the brain. It is thought to be caused by a virus, an abnormality of the immune system, or a lack of hormones in the brain and endocrine system. It is called "Yuppie flu" because it is found most often in professional women—and sometimes men—in their thirties.

Chronicles two books of the Old Testament containing genealogy and history.

chronicles, medieval books modeled on the Old Testament Books of Chronicles. Until the later Middle Ages, they were usually written in Latin by clerics, who borrowed extensively from one another.

Two early examples were written by Gregory of Tours in the 6th century and by ⭗Bede. In the later Middle Ages, vernacular chronicles appear, written by lay people, but by then the chronicle tradition was in decline, soon to be supplanted by Renaissance histories.

chronometer instrument for measuring time precisely, originally used at sea. It is designed to remain accurate through all conditions of temperature and pressure. The first accurate marine chronometer, capable of an accuracy of half a minute a year, was made 1761 by John Harrison in England.

The term is now applied to scientific timekeeping devices.

chrysanthemum any plant of the genus *Chrysanthemum* of the family Compositae, with about 200 species. There are hundreds of cultivated varieties, whose exact wild ancestry is uncertain. In the Far East the common chrysanthemum has been cultivated for more than 2,000 years and is the imperial emblem of Japan. Chrysanthemums may be grown from seed, but are more usually propagated by cutting or division.

They were introduced into the West in 1789.

Chrysler Walter Percy 1875–1940. US industrialist. A car manufacturer, he founded

the Chrysler Corporation 1925. By 1928 he had acquired Dodge and Plymouth, making Chrysler Corporation one of the largest US motor-vehicle manufacturers.

Chrysler, born in Wamego, Kansas, worked first as a railroad machinist, rising through the ranks to become manager of the American Locomotive Company in Pittsburgh 1912. Shifting to the auto industry, he was hired by General Motors and was named president of the Buick division 1916. After World War I, he became president of the independent Maxwell Motor Company and went on to found the Chrysler Corporation.

Chuang member of the largest minority group in China, numbering about 15 million. They live in S China, where they cultivate rice fields. Their religion includes elements of ancestor worship. The Chuang language belongs to the Tai family.

chub any of several large minnows of the carp family. Creek chub *Semotelusatromaculatus*, up to 12 in/30 cm, is found widely in North American streams. Also, any of a number of small-mouthed marine fishes of the family Kyphosidae.

Chubu mountainous coastal region of central Honshu island, Japan; area 25,791 sq mi/ 66,774 sq km; population (1986) 20,694,000. The chief city is Nagoya.

Chufu alternative transcription of ⭗Qufu, town in Shandong province, China.

Chugoku SW region of Honshu island, Japan; area 12,314 sq mi/31,881 sq km; population (1986) 7,764,000. The chief city is Hiroshima.

Chukchi member of a people of NE Siberia, Russia, numbering approximately 14,000. Their language belongs to the Paleo-Asiatic family.

Although primarily reindeer herders, individual Chukchi stalk seals, while larger groups hunt whales from boats. Historically, the Chukchi were the predominant people of their region and were known to have raided neighboring groups.

Chukchi Sea part of the Arctic Ocean, situated north of Bering Strait between Asia and North America.

Chun Doo-hwan 1931– . South Korean military ruler who seized power 1979, president 1981–88 as head of the newly formed Democratic Justice Party.

Chun, trained in Korea and the US, served as an army commander from 1967 and was in charge of military intelligence 1979 when President Park was assassinated by the chief of the Korean Central Intelligence Agency (KCIA). General Chun took charge of the KCIA and, in a coup, assumed control of the army and the South Korean government. In 1981 Chun was appointed president, and oversaw a period of rapid economic growth, governing in an authoritarian manner. In 1988 he retired to a Buddhist retreat.

Chungking alternative transcription of ⭗Chongqing, city in Sichuan province, China.

church building designed as a Christian place of worship. Churches were first built in the 3rd century, when persecution ceased under the Holy Roman emperor Constantine. The original church design was based on the Roman ⭗basilica, with a central nave, aisles either side, and an apse at one end.

Church Frederic Edwin 1826–1900. US painter, a student of Thomas Cole and follower

of the Hudson River school's style of grand landscape. During the 1850s he visited South America and the Arctic.

He is known for his portrayal of light, as in *Heart of the Andes* 1855 and *Niagara Falls* 1857.

Churchill town in the province of Manitoba, situated on Hudson Bay; population (1986) 1,217. Although the port is ice-free only three months a year, Churchill handles about 500,000 tonnes of grain annually, as well as fuel oil and bulk cargo.

There is a modern airport, and the community is a major center for Arctic research, health programs, and education. The Hudson's Bay Company established a post here and named it for Lord Churchill (later 1st duke of Marlborough). Railway and harbor facilities were completed 1931. A military base was established in World War II, and it continued as a rocket-launching site until the early 1960s.

Churchill Randolph (Henry Spencer) 1849–1895. British Conservative politician, chancellor of the Exchequer and leader of the House of Commons 1886; father of Winston Churchill.

He married Jennie Jerome (1854–1921), daughter of a wealthy New Yorker, 1874.

Churchill Winston (Leonard Spencer) 1874–1965. British Conservative politician, prime minister 1940–45 and 1951–55. In Parliament from 1900, as a Liberal until 1923, he held a number of ministerial offices, including First Lord of the Admiralty 1911–15 and chancellor of the Exchequer 1924–29. Absent from the cabinet in the 1930s, he returned Sept 1939 to lead a coalition government 1940–45, negotiating with Allied leaders in World War II to achieve the unconditional surrender of Germany 1945; he led a Conservative government 1951–55. He received the Nobel Prize for Literature 1953.

He was born at Blenheim Palace, the elder son of Lord Randolph Churchill. During the Boer War he was a war correspondent and made a dramatic escape from imprisonment in Pretoria. In 1900 he was elected Conservative member of Parliament for Oldham, but he disagreed with Chamberlain's tariff-reform policy and joined the Liberals.

In 1911 he was appointed First Lord of the Admiralty. In 1915–16 he served in the

church The ground plan of a typical large cathedral church is in the shape of an elongated cross.

trenches in France but then resumed his parliamentary duties and was minister of munitions under Lloyd George 1917, when he was concerned with the development of the tank. After the armistice he was secretary for war 1918–21 and then as colonial secretary played a leading part in the establishment of the Irish Free State. During the postwar years he was active in support of the Whites (anti-Bolsheviks) in Russia. From 1929 to 1939 he was out of office as he disagreed with the Conservatives on India, rearmament, and Chamberlain's policy of appeasement.

On the first day of World War II he went back to his old post at the Admiralty. In May 1940 he was called to the premiership as head of an all-party administration and made a much quoted "blood, tears, toil, and sweat" speech to the House of Commons. He had a close relationship with US president Roosevelt and in Aug 1941 concluded the ▷Atlantic Charter with him. In Feb 1945 he met Stalin and Roosevelt at Yalta and agreed on the final plans for victory. On May 8 he announced the unconditional surrender of Germany. On May 23, 1945 the coalition was dissolved, and Churchill formed a caretaker government drawn mainly from the Conservatives. Defeated in the general election in July, he became leader of the opposition until the election Oct 1951, in which he again became prime minister. In April 1955 he resigned and retired to paint. After he died his paintings were exhibited in several shows, including a major retrospective in New York City in the 1980s.

Church of England established form of Christianity in England, a member of the Anglican Communion. It was dissociated from the Roman Catholic Church 1534. There were approximately 1,100,000 regular worshipers in 1988.

history
2nd century Christianity arrived in England during the Roman occupation.
597 St Augustine became the first archbishop of Canterbury.
1529–34 At the *Reformation* the chief change was political: the sovereign (Henry VIII) replaced the pope as head of the church and assumed the right to appoint archbishops and bishops.
1536–40 The monasteries were closed down.
1549 First publication of the *Book of Common Prayer*, the basis of worship throughout the Anglican Church.
1563–1604 The *Thirty-Nine Articles*, the Church's doctrinal basis, were drawn up, enforced by Parliament, and revised.
17th–18th centuries Colonizers took the Church of England to North America (where three US bishops were consecrated after the American Revolution, and whose successors still lead the Episcopal Church in the US), Australia, New Zealand, and India.
19th century Missionaries were active in Africa. The *Oxford Movement* eventually developed into Anglo-Catholicism.
20th century There were moves toward reunion with the Methodist and Roman Catholic churches. The *ordination of women* was accepted by some overseas Anglican churches, for example the US Episcopal Church 1976.

Chuvash autonomous republic of Russia, lying west of the Volga, 350 mi/560 km E of Moscow; area 7,100 sq mi/18,300 sq km; population (1986) 1,320,000. The capital is Cheboksary, population (1985) 389,000. The economy is based on lumbering and grain growing and there are phosphate and limestone deposits and electrical and engineering industries.

Chuvash member of the majority ethnic group inhabiting the autonomous republic of Chuvash, Russia. The Chuvash have lived in the middle Volga region since the 8th century. Their language belongs to the Altaic family, although whether it is a member of the Turkic branch or constitutes a branch on its own is not certain.

CIA abbreviation for the US ▷*Central Intelligence Agency*.

cicada any of several insects of the family Cicadidae. Most species are tropical, but a few occur in Europe and North America. Young cicadas live underground, for up to 17 years in some species. The adults live on trees, whose juices they suck. The males produce a loud, almost continuous, chirping by vibrating membranes in resonating cavities in the abdomen.

Cicero Marcus Tullius 106–43 BC. Roman orator, writer, and politician. His speeches and philosophical and rhetorical works are models of Latin prose, and his letters provide a picture of contemporary Roman life. As consul 63 BC he exposed the Roman politician Catiline's conspiracy in four major orations.

Born in Arpinium, Cicero became an advocate in Rome, spent three years in Greece studying oratory, and after the dictator Sulla's death distinguished himself in Rome on the side of the popular party. When the First Triumvirate was formed 59 BC, Cicero was exiled and devoted himself to literature. He sided with Pompey during the civil war (49–48) but was pardoned by Julius Caesar and returned to Rome. After Caesar's assassination 44 BC he supported Octavian (the future emperor Augustus) and violently attacked Antony in speeches known as the *Philippics*. On the reconciliation of Antony and Octavian he was executed by Antony's agents.

cichlid any freshwater fish of the family Cichlidae. Cichlids are somewhat perchlike, but have a single nostril on each side instead of two. They are mostly predatory, and have deep, colorful bodies, flattened from side to side so that some are almost disc-shaped. Many are territorial in the breeding season and may show care of the young. There are more than 1,000 species found in South and Central America, Africa, and India.

The *discus fish Symphysodon* produces a skin secretion on which the young feed. Other cichlids, such as those of the genus *Tilapia*, brood their young in the mouth.

Cid, El Rodrigo Díaz de Bivar 1040–1099. Spanish soldier, nicknamed *El Cid* ("the lord") by the ▷Moors. Born in Castile of a noble family, he fought against the king of Navarre and won his nickname *el Campeador* ("the Champion") by killing the Navarrese champion in single combat. Essentially a mercenary, fighting both with and against the Moors, he died while defending Valencia against them, and in subsequent romances became Spain's national hero.

Much of the Cid's present-day reputation is the result of the exploitation of the legendary character as a model Christian military hero by the Nationalists during the Civil War, with Franco presented as a modern equivalent in his reconquest of Spain.

cider juice pressed from apples as a beverage or for making vinegar. In the US, hard cider refers to fermented apple juice drunk as an alcoholic beverage. Alcoholic cider is produced in large quantities in the Americas, France, and England.

cigar compact roll of cured tobacco leaves, contained in a binder leaf, which in turn is surrounded by a wrapper leaf. The cigar was originally a sheath of palm leaves filled with tobacco, smoked by the Indians of Central America. Cigar smoking was introduced into Spain soon after 1492 and spread all over Europe in the next few centuries. From about 1890 cigar smoking was gradually supplanted in popularity by cigarette smoking.

The first cigar factory was opened in Hamburg, Germany, 1788, and about that time cigar smoking became popular in Britain and the US. The first cigars were made by hand—as the more expensive cigars still are. From about the 1850s various machine methods have been employed.

The best cigars are still hand-rolled in Cuba, hence Havanas.

cigarette (French "little cigar") thin paper tube stuffed with shredded tobacco for smoking, now usually plugged with a filter. The first cigarettes were the *papelitos* smoked in South America about 1750. The habit spread to Spain and then throughout the world; today it is the most general form of tobacco smoking, although it is dangerous to the health of both smokers and nonsmokers who breathe in the smoke.

Since the 1960s warnings from the US Surgeon General have been added to packages and cartons, about the dangers of smoking and cancer, lung disease, heart disease, and the effects on the developing fetus.

cilia (singular *cilium*) small threadlike organs on the surface of some cells, composed of contractile fibers that produce rhythmic waving movements. Some single-celled organisms move by means of cilia. In multicellular animals, they keep lubricated surfaces clear of debris. They also move food in the digestive tracts of some invertebrates.

ciliary muscle ring of muscle surrounding and controlling the lens inside the vertebrate eye, used in ▷accommodation (focusing). Suspensory ligaments, resembling spokes of a wheel, connect the lens to the ciliary muscle and pull the lens into a flatter shape when the muscle relaxes. On contraction, the lens returns to its normal spherical state.

Cilicia ancient region of Asia Minor, now forming part of Turkey, situated between the Taurus Mountains and the Mediterranean.

Successively conquered by the Persians, Alexander the Great, and the Romans under Pompey, Cilicia became an independent Armenian principality 1080 and a kingdom 1198. Sometimes referred to as Lesser Armenia, it was absorbed into the Ottoman Empire during the 15th century. Access from the north across the Taurus range is through the *Cilician Gates*, a strategic pass that has been used for centuries as part of a trade route linking Europe and the Middle East.

Cimabue Giovanni (Cenni de Peppi) *c.* 1240–1302. Italian painter, active in Florence, traditionally styled the "father of Italian painting." His paintings retain the golden background of Byzantine art but the figures have a new naturalism. Among the works attributed to him are *Madonna and Child* (Uffizi, Florence), a huge Gothic image of the Virgin that nevertheless has a novel softness and solidity that points forward to Giotto.

cimbalom in music, a type of ◊dulcimer.

Cimino Michael 1943– . US film director whose reputation was made by *The Deer Hunter* 1978, a moral epic set against the Vietnam War (five Academy Awards). A later film, the Western *Heaven's Gate* 1980, lost its backers, United Artists, some $30 million, and subsequently became a byword for commercial disaster in the industry.

He also made *The Year of the Dragon* 1986.

cinchona any shrub or tree of the tropical American genus *Chinchona* of the madder family Rubiaceae. ◊Quinine is produced from the bark of some species, and these are now cultivated in India, Sri Lanka, the Philippines, and Indonesia.

Cincinnati city and port in Ohio, on the Ohio River; population (1990) 364,000. Chief industries include machinery, clothing, furniture making, wine, chemicals, and meatpacking. Founded in 1788, Cincinnati became a city 1819. It attracted large numbers of European immigrants, particularly Germans, during the 19th century.

Procter and Gamble, a household-products manufacturer, has its headquarters here. Xavier University and the University of Cincinnati are here, and it has a major symphony orchestra. William Howard Taft, 27th president of the US, was born in Cincinnati.

Cincinnatus Lucius Quintus 5th century BC. Roman general. Appointed dictator 458 BC, he defeated the Aequi (an Italian people) in a brief campaign, then resumed life as a yeoman farmer.

"Cinderella" traditional European fairy tale, of which about 700 versions exist, including one by Charles ◊Perrault. Cinderella is an ill-treated youngest daughter who is enabled by a fairy godmother to attend the royal ball. She captivates Prince Charming but must flee at midnight, losing a tiny glass slipper by which the prince later identifies her.

cinema 20th-century form of art and entertainment consisting of "moving pictures" in either black and white or color, projected onto a screen. Cinema borrows from the other arts, such as music, drama, and literature, but is entirely dependent for its origins on technological developments, including the technology of action photography, projection, sound reproduction, and film processing and printing (see ◊photography).

cinema: chronology

1826–34	Various machines invented to show moving images: the stroboscope, zoetrope, and thaumatrope.
1872	Eadweard Muybridge demonstrated movement of horses' legs by using 24 cameras.
1877	Invention of Praxinoscope; developed as a projector of successive images on screen 1879 in France.
1878–95	Marey, a French physiologist, developed various types of camera for recording human and animal movements.
1887	Augustin le Prince produced the first series of images on a perforated film; Thomas A Edison, having developed the phonograph, took the first steps in developing a motion-picture recording and reproducing device to accompany recorded sound.
1888	William Friese-Greene (1855–1921) showed the first celluloid film and patented a movie camera.
1889	Edison invented 35-mm film.
1890–94	Edison, using perforated film, developed his Kinetograph camera and Kinetoscope individual viewer; developed commercially in New York, London, and Paris.
1895	The Lumière brothers projected, to a paying audience, a film of an oncoming train arriving at a station. Some of the audience fled in terror.
1896	Charles Pathé introduced the Berliner phonograph, using disks in synchronization with film. Lack of amplification, however, made the performances ineffective.
1899	Edison tried to improve amplification by using banks of phonographs.
1900	Attempts to synchronize film and disk were made by Leon Gaumont (1863–1946) in France and Goldschmidt in Germany, leading later to the Vitaphone system of the US.
1902	Georges Méliès made *Le Voyage dans la Lune/A Trip to the Moon*.
1903	The first Western was made in the US: *The Great Train Robbery* by Edwin Porter.
1906	The earliest color film (Kinemacolor) was patented in Britain by George Albert Smith (1864–1959).
1907–11	The first films shot in the Los Angeles area called Hollywood. In France, Emile Cohl (1857–1938) experimented with film animation.
1910	With the influence of US studios and fan magazines, film actors and actresses began to be recognized as international stars.
1911	The first Hollywood studio, Horsley's Centaur Film Company, was established, followed in 1915 by Carl Laemmle's Universal City and Thomas Ince's studio.
1912	In Britain, Eugene Lauste designed experimental "sound on film" systems.
1914–18	Full newsreel coverage of World War I.
1915	*The Birth of a Nation*, D W Griffith's epic on the American Civil War, was released in the US.
1917	35 mm was officially adopted as the standard format for motion picture film by the Society of Motion Picture Engineers of America.
1918–19	A sound system called Tri-Ergon was developed in Germany, which led to sound being recorded on film photographically. Photography with sound was also developed in the US by Lee De Forest in his Phonofilm system.
1923	First sound film (as Phonofilm) demonstrated.
1926	*Don Juan*, a silent film with a synchronized music score, was released.
1927	Release of the first major sound film, *The Jazz Singer*, consisting of some songs and a few moments of dialogue, by Warner Brothers, New York City. The first Academy Awards (Oscars) were presented.
1928	Walt Disney released his first Mickey Mouse cartoon, *Steamboat Willie*. The first all-talking film, *Lights of New York*, was released.
1930	*The Big Trail*, a Western filmed and shown in 70-mm rather than the standard 35-mm format, was released. 70 mm is still used, mainly for big-budget epics such as *Lawrence of Arabia*.
1932	Technicolor (three-color) process introduced and used for a Walt Disney cartoon film.
1935	*Becky Sharp*, the first film in three-color Technicolor was released.
1937	Walt Disney released the first feature-length (82 minutes) cartoon, *Snow White and the Seven Dwarfs*.
1939	*Gone With the Wind*, regarded as one of Hollywood's greatest achievements, was released.
1952	Cinerama, a wide-screen presentation using three cameras and three projectors, was introduced in New York.
1953	Commercial 3-D (three-dimensional) cinema and wide-screen CinemaScope were launched in the US. CinemaScope used a single camera and projector to produce a wide-screen effect with an anamorphic lens. The 3-D cameras were clumsy and the audiences disliked wearing the obligatory glasses. The new wide-screen cinema was accompanied by the introduction of Stereographic sound, which eventually became standard.
1959	The first film in Smell-O-Vision, *The Scent of Mystery*, was released. The process did not catch on.
1980	Most major films were released in Dolby stereo.
1981	Designated "the Year of Color Film" by director Martin Scorsese in a campaign to draw attention to, and arrest, the deterioration of color film shot since 1950.
1982	One of the first and most effective attempts at feature-length, computer-generated animation was *Tron*, Walt Disney's $20-million bid to break into the booming fantasy market. 3-D made a brief comeback; some of the films released that used the process, such as *Jaws 3-D* and *Friday the 13th Part 3*, were commercial successes, but the revival was short-lived.
1987	US House Judiciary Committee petitioned by leading Hollywood filmmakers to protect their work from electronic "colorization," the new process by which black-and-white films were tinted for television transmission.
1988	Robert Zemeckis's (1952–) *Who Framed Roger Rabbit* set new technical standards in combining live action with cartoon animation.

film history The first moving pictures were shown in the 1890s. Thomas A Edison persuaded James J Corbett (1866–1933), the world boxing champion 1892–97, to act a boxing match for a film. The Lumière brothers in France, Latham in the US, R W Paul (1869–1943) in England, and others were making moving pictures of actual events (for example, *The Derby* 1896, shown in London on the evening of the race), and of simple scenes such as a train coming into a station. In 1902 Georges Méliès of France made the fantasy story film *A Trip to the Moon*, and in 1903 Edwin Porter directed *The Great Train Robbery* for Edison. This was a story in a contemporary setting, and cost about $100 to make. The film was shown all over the world, and earned more than $20,000.

film technique For a number of years, films of indoor happenings were shot out of doors by daylight in Hollywood. The fairly constant sunny climate was the basis of its success as a center of film production. The first film studio was Edison's at Fort Lee, New Jersey, but the Astoria Studios in New York City turned out many popular silents and early "talkies," since it was near Broadway and could therefore make use of the theater stars on its doorstep. In England, the pioneer company of Cricks and Martin set up a studio at Mitcham (where a romantic domestic drama, *For Baby's Sake*, was made 1908).

D W Griffith, the US director, revolutionized film technique, introducing the close-up, the flashback, the fade-out, and the fade-in. His first epic was *The Birth of a Nation* 1915, and his second, *Intolerance*, with spectacular scenes in the Babylonian section, followed 1916.

film personalities At first, players' names were of no importance, although one who appeared nameless in *The Great Train Robbery*, G M Anderson (1882–1971), afterwards became famous as "Bronco Billy" in a series of cowboy films, the first Westerns. The first movie performer to become a name was Mary Pickford; cinemagoers found her so attractive that they insisted on knowing who she was. World War I virtually stopped film production in Europe, but Hollywood continued to flourish in the 1920s, creating such stars as Rudolph Valentino, Douglas Fairbanks Sr, Lillian Gish, Gloria Swanson, Richard Barthelmess (1895–1963), and Greta Garbo (dramatic actors); and Charlie Chaplin, Buster Keaton, and Harold Lloyd (comedians).

The introduction of sound from the late 1920s ended the careers of silent stars with unsuitable voices, and changed the style of acting to one more natural than mimetic. British stage stars who made the transition to film include Edith Evans, Alec Guinness, Laurence Olivier, and Ralph Richardson. US stars of the golden Hollywood era include Clark Gable, the Marx Brothers, Judy Garland, Greta Garbo, and Joan Crawford. Although many Hollywood stars were "made" by the studios, American stage actors such as Humphrey Bogart, Henry Fonda, Spencer Tracy, Katharine Hepburn, and Bette Davis also became stars in 1930s Hollywood and continued to act in films for many years.

artistic development Concern for artistry began with Griffith, but also developed in Europe, particularly in the USSR and Germany, where directors exploited film's artistic possibilities during both the silent and the sound eras. Silent films were never completely silent; there was usually a musical background, integral to the film, whether played by a solo pianist in a suburban cinema or a 100-piece orchestra in a big city theater. (In Japan there was always a narrator.) The arrival of sound films (John Barrymore as *Don Juan* 1926 and Al Jolson as *The Jazz Singer* 1927), seen at first as having only novelty value, soon brought about a wider perspective and greater artistic possibilities through the combination of sight and sound. Successful directors of early sound films included Jean Renoir in France, Fritz Lang and F W Murnau in Germany, Mauritz Stiller in Sweden, Alfred Hitchcock in Britain, David Selznick, John Ford, and Frank Capra in the US, and Vsevolod Pudovkin and Sergei Eisenstein in the USSR. After World War II, Japanese films were first seen in the West (although the industry dates back to the silent days), and India developed a thriving cinema industry.

Apart from story films, the industry produced newsreels of current events and documentaries depicting factual life, of which the pioneers were US filmmaker Robert Flaherty (*Nanook of the North* 1920, *Man of Aran* 1932–34) and the Scot John Grierson (*Drifters* 1929, *Night Mail* 1936); animated cartoon films, which achieved their first success with Patrick Sullivan's (1887–1933) *Felix the Cat* 1917, were later surpassed in popularity by Walt Disney's Mickey Mouse character, who first appeared in *Steamboat Willie* 1928, and the feature-length *Snow White and the Seven Dwarfs* 1937 and others. During the 1930s classic dramas and screwball comedies were made; during the 1940s war films predominated; and during the 1950s *film noir* and Technicolor musicals competed with early television.

the influence of television By the 1960s, increasing competition from television, perceived at the time as a threat to the studio system of film production and distribution, led the film industry to concentrate on special effects (CinemaScope, Cinerama, Todd AO) and wide-screen spectaculars dealing with historical and biblical themes, for example, *Cleopatra* 1963. Also exploited were the horror genre and areas of sexuality and violence considered unsuitable for family television viewing. Other popular genres were the Chinese Western or kung-fu film, which had a vogue in the 1970s; other films controversial for their potential glorification of violence, epitomized by the character Rambo, a loner who takes the law into his own hands, as played by Sylvester Stallone; and science fiction, such as *Star Wars* 1977, *Close Encounters of the Third Kind* 1977, and *ET* 1982, with expensive special effects.

Throughout the 1980s cinema production was affected by the growth during the preceding decade of the video industry, which made films available for viewing on home television screens (see ▷video cassette recorder).

CinemaScope trade name for a wide-screen process using anamorphic lenses, in which images are compressed during filming and then extended during projection over a wide curved screen. The first film to be made in CinemaScope was *The Robe* 1953.

cinéma vérité (French "cinema truth") filmmaking that aims to capture truth on film by observing, recording, and presenting real events and situations as they occur without major directorial, editorial, or technical control.

Cinerama wide-screen process devised 1937 by Fred Waller of Paramount's special-effects department. Originally three 35-mm cameras and three projectors were used to record and project a single image. Three aspects of the image were recorded and then projected on a large curved screen with the result that the images blended together to produce an illusion of vastness. The first Cinerama film was *How the West Was Won* 1962. It was eventually abandoned in favor of a single-lens 70-mm process.

cinnabar mercuric sulfide, HgS, the only commercially useful ore of mercury. It is deposited in veins and impregnations near recent volcanic rocks and hot springs. The mineral itself is used as a red pigment, commonly known as **vermilion**. Cinnabar is found in the US (California), Spain (Almadén), Peru, Italy, and Slovenia.

cinnamon dried inner bark of a tree *Cinnamomum zeylanicum* of the laurel family, grown in India and Sri Lanka. The bark is ground to make the spice used in curries and confectionery. Oil of cinnamon is obtained from waste bark and is used as flavoring in food and medicine.

cinquefoil any plant of the genus *Potentilla* of the rose family, usually with five-lobed leaves and brightly colored flowers. It is widespread in northern temperate regions.

Field cinquefoil *P. canadensis* is a low-growing perennial with yellow flowers native to E North America in dry grasslands and barrens.

Cinque Ports group of ports in S England, originally five, Sandwich, Dover, Hythe, Romney, and Hastings, later including Rye, Winchelsea, and others. Probably founded in Roman times, they rose to importance after the Norman conquest and until the end of the 15th century were bound to supply the ships and men necessary against invasion.

circadian rhythm metabolic rhythm found in most organisms, which generally coincides with the 24-hour day. Its most obvious manifestation is the regular cycle of sleeping and waking, but body temperature and the concentration of ▷hormones that influence mood and behavior also vary over the day. In humans, alteration of habits (such as rapid air travel round the world) may result in the circadian rhythm being out of phase with actual activity patterns, causing malaise until it has had time to adjust.

Circassia former name of an area of the N Caucasus, ceded to Russia by Turkey 1829 and now part of the Karachai-Cherkess region of Russia.

Circe in Greek mythology, an enchantress living on the island of Aeaea. In Homer's *Odyssey*, she turned the followers of Odysseus into pigs. Odysseus, bearing the herb moly provided by Hermes to protect him from the same fate, forced her to release his men.

circle perfectly round shape. Each circle comprises a **center**, a **radius** (distance from center to boundary), a **circumference** (the boundary), **diameters** (lines crossing the circle through the center), **chords** (lines joining two points on the circumference), **tangents** (lines that touch the circumference at one point only), **sectors** (regions inside the circle between two radii), and **segments** (regions between a chord and the circumference).

circle *Technical terms used in the geometry of the circle; the area of a circle can be seen to equal πr² by dividing the circle into segments which form a rectangle.*

The ratio of the distance all around the circle (the circumference) to the diameter is an ◇irrational number called π (**pi**), roughly equal to 3.1416. A circle of radius r and diameter d has a circumference $C = \pi d$, or $C = 2\pi r$, and an area $A = \pi r^2$.

The area of a circle can be shown by dividing it into very thin sectors and reassembling them to make an approximate rectangle. The proof of $A = \pi r^2$ can be done only by using ◇integral calculus.

circuit in law, the geographic district that constitutes a particular area of jurisdiction.

In the US the Court of Appeals sits in ten judicial areas or circuits—hence circuit courts—and Washington, DC.

circuit in physics or electrical engineering, an arrangement of electrical components through which a current can flow. There are two basic circuits, series and parallel. In a **series circuit**, the components are connected end to end so that the current flows through all components one after the other. In a **parallel circuit**, components are connected side by side so that part of the current passes through each component. A circuit diagram shows in graphical form how components are connected together, using standard symbols for the components.

circuit breaker switching device designed to protect an electric circuit from excessive current. It has the same action as a ◇fuse, and many houses now have a circuit breaker between the incoming main supply and the domestic circuits. Circuit breakers usually work by means of ◇solenoids. Those at electricity-generating stations have to be specially designed to prevent dangerous arcing (the release of luminous discharge) when the

high-voltage supply is switched off. They may use an air blast or oil immersion to quench the arc.

circulatory system system of vessels in an animal's body that transports essential substances (blood or other circulatory fluid) to and from the different parts of the body. Except for simple animals such as sponges and coelenterates (jellyfishes, sea anemones, corals), all animals have a circulatory system.

In fishes, blood passes once around the body before returning to a two-chambered heart (single circulation). In birds and mammals, blood passes to the lungs and back to the heart before circulating around the remainder of the body (double circulation). In all vertebrates, blood flows in one direction. Valves in the heart, large arteries, and veins prevent backflow, and the muscular walls of the arteries assist in pushing the blood around the body.

Although most animals have a heart or hearts to pump the blood, normal body movements circulate the fluid in some small invertebrates. In the **open system**, found in snails and other mollusks, the blood (more correctly called ◇hemolymph) passes from the arteries into a body cavity (haemocoel), and from here is gradually returned to the heart, via the gills, by other blood vessels. Insects and other arthropods have an open system with a heart. In the **closed system** of earthworms, blood flows directly from the main artery to the main vein, via smaller lateral vessels in each body segment. Vertebrates, too, have a closed system with a network of tiny ◇capillaries carrying the blood from arteries to veins.

circumcision surgical removal of all or part of the foreskin (prepuce) of the penis, usually performed on the newborn; it is practiced among Jews and Muslims. In some societies in Africa and the Middle East, female circumcision or clitoridectomy (removal of the labia minora and/or clitoris) is practiced on adolescents as well as babies; it is illegal in the West.

Female circumcision has no medical benefit and often causes disease and complications in childbirth; in 1982 an estimated 84 million women had been circumcised. Male circumcision too is usually carried out for cultural reasons, not as a medical necessity. Some evidence indicates that it protects against the development of cancer of the penis later in life and that women with circumcised partners are at less risk from cancer of the cervix, although these theories have not been proved.

circumference in geometry, the curved line that encloses a plane figure, for example a ◇circle or an ellipse. Its length varies according to the nature of the curve, and may be ascertained by the appropriate formula. The circumference of a circle is $2\pi r$, where r is the radius and π is the constant pi, approximately equal to 3.1416.

circumnavigation sailing around the world. The first ship to sail around the world was the *Victoria*, one of a Spanish squadron of five vessels that sailed from Seville Aug 1519 under the Portuguese navigator Ferdinand Magellan.

Four vessels were lost on the way, but the *Victoria* returned to Spain in Sept 1522 under Juan Cano. Magellan himself did not complete the voyage, but died in the Philippines 1521. The first English circumnavigator was Francis Drake 1577–80 in the *Golden Hind*.

circus (Latin "circle") entertainment, often held in a large tent ("big top"), involving performing animals, acrobats, and clowns. In 1871 Phineas T ◇Barnum created the "Greatest

circulatory system *The circulatory systems of the fish, the bird, and the rabbit.*

Show on Earth" in the US. The popularity of animal acts decreased in the 1980s. Originally, in Roman times, a circus was an arena for chariot races and gladiatorial combats.

cire perdue or **lost-wax technique** bronzecasting method. A model is made of wax and enclosed in an envelope of clay and plaster, with a small hole in the bottom. The whole is baked, the wax melts and runs away through the hole, and the clay and plaster becomes a hard mold. Molten bronze is poured in and allowed to cool; then the clay envelope is cut away.

The result is a bronze cast that exactly reproduces the original and is formed in a single piece. The bronze will be hollow if the original wax model was made around a core of burned clay.

cirrhosis any degenerative disease in an organ of the body, especially the liver, characterized by excessive development of connective tissue, causing scarring and painful swelling. Cirrhosis of the liver may be caused by an infection such as viral hepatitis, by chronic alcoholism or drug use, blood disorder, or malnutrition. If cirrhosis is diagnosed early, it can be arrested by treating the cause; otherwise it will progress to jaundice, edema, vomiting of blood, coma, and death.

CIS abbreviation for ◇**Commonwealth of Independent States**, established 1992 by 11 former Soviet republics.

Cisalpine Gaul region of the Roman province of Gallia (N Italy) south of the Alps; **Transalpine Gaul**, the region north of the Alps, comprised what is now Belgium, France, the Netherlands, and Switzerland.

The **Cisalpine Republic** in N Italy was the creation of Napoleon 1797, known as the Italian Republic 1802–04 and the Kingdom of Italy 1804–15.

Ciskei, Republic of Bantu homeland in South Africa, which became independent 1981, al-

Africa, which became independent 1981, although this is not recognized by any other country

area 2,974 sq mi/7,700 sq km

capital Bisho

features one of the two homelands of the Xhosa people created by South Africa (the other is Transkei)

products wheat, sorghum, sunflower, vegetables, timber, metal products, leather, textiles

population (1985) 925,000

language Xhosa

government president (Brig Oupa Gqozo from 1990), with legislative and executive councils

recent history In Sept 1992 Ciskei troops fired on African National Congress (ANC) demonstrators demanding the ousting of the territory's military leader, Brig Gqozo; 28 people were slain and about 200 injured. Brig Gqozo had assumed power in a military takeover 1990. Initially sympathetic to the aims of the ANC, he had pledged to restore civilian rule and called for the reincorporation of Ciskei into South Africa. Subsequently, he turned against the organization and had been accused of repressing its supporters.

Cistercian order Roman Catholic monastic order established at Cîteaux 1098 by St Robert de Champagne, abbot of Molesme, as a stricter form of the Benedictine order. Living mainly by agricultural labor, the Cistercians made many advances in farming methods in the Middle Ages. The ◊*Trappists*, so called from the original house at La Trappe in Normandy (founded by Dominique de Rancé 1664), followed a particularly strict version of the rule.

cistron in genetics, the segment of ◊DNA that is required to synthesize a complete polypeptide chain. It is the molecular equivalent of a ◊gene.

CITES (abbreviation for *Convention on International Trade in Endangered Species*) international agreement under the auspices of the ◊IUCN with the aim of regulating trade in ◊endangered species of animals and plants. The agreement came into force 1975 and by 1991 had been signed by 110 states. It prohibits any trade in a category of 8,000 highly endangered species and controls trade in a further 30,000 species.

citizens' band (CB) short-range radio communication facility (around 27 MHz) used by members of the public in the US and many European countries to talk to one another or call for emergency assistance.

citizenship status as a member of a state. In most countries citizenship may be acquired either by birth or by naturalization. The status confers rights such as voting and the protection of the law and also imposes responsibilities such as military service, in some countries.

Citlaltépetl (Aztec "star mountain") dormant volcano, the highest mountain in Mexico at 18,700 ft/5,700 m, north of the city of Orizaba (after which it is sometimes named). It last erupted 1687.

citric acid $HOOCCH_2C(OH)(COOH)$ CH_2COOH organic acid widely distributed in the plant kingdom; it is found in high concentrations in citrus fruits and has a sharp, sour taste. At one time it was commercially prepared from concentrated lemon juice, but now the main source is the fermentation of sugar with certain molds.

citronella lemon-scented oil used in cosmetics and insect repellents, obtained from the S Asian grass *Cymbopogon nardus*.

citrus any tree or shrub of the genus *Citrus*, family Rutaceae. Citruses are found in Asia and other warm parts of the world. They are evergreen and aromatic, and several species—the orange, lemon, lime, citron, and grapefruit—are cultivated for fruit.

city generally, a large and important town. In the Middle East and ancient Europe, and in the ancient civilizations of Mexico and Peru, cities were states in themselves. In the early Middle Ages, European cities were usually those towns that were episcopal sees (seats of bishops).

In the US, a city is an incorporated municipality whose boundaries and powers of self-government are defined by charter from the state in which it is located.

City of Akron v Akron Center for Reproductive Health US Supreme Court decision 1983 that reaffirmed the right to privacy in reproduction. The petitioner, an Ohio clinic, challenged a state law that set certain procedural restrictions on second-and third-trimester abortions. The Court found that the Ohio measures, requiring parental consent for minors, a 24-hour waiting period, and "humane disposal" of the fetus, were unconstitutional. The ruling reaffirmed women's constitutional "personal liberty" and the right to abortion.

Ciudad Bolívar former name (1824–49) *Angostura*, city in SE Venezuela, on the river Orinoco, 250 mi/400 km from its mouth; capital of Bolívar state; population (1989) 277,000. Gold is mined in the vicinity. The city is linked with Soledad across the river by the Angostura bridge 1967, the first to span the Orinoco.

civet small to medium-sized carnivorous mammal found in Africa and Asia, belonging to the family Viverridae, which also includes ◊*mongooses* and ◊*genet*s. Distant relations of cats, they generally have longer jaws and more teeth. All have a scent gland in the inguinal (groin) region. Extracts from this gland are taken from the *African civet Civettictis civetta* and used in perfumery.

As well as eating animal matter, many species, for example, the SE Asian *palm civet Arctogalidia trivirgata*, are fond of fruit.

civil aviation the operation of passenger and freight transport by air. With increasing traffic, control of air space is a major problem. The Federal Aviation Agency (FAA) is responsible for regulating development of aircraft, air navigation, traffic control, and communications in the US. The Civil Aeronautics Board is the US authority prescribing safety regulations and investigating accidents. The world's largest airline was the Soviet Union's government-owned Aeroflot (split between republics 1992), which operated 1,300 aircraft over 620,000 mi/1 million km of routes and carried over 110 million passengers a year.

civil defense or *civil protection* organized activities by the civilian population of a state to mitigate the effects of enemy attack.

During World War II civil-defense efforts were centered on providing adequate warning of air raids to permit the civilian population to reach shelter; then firefighting, food, rescue, communications, and ambulance services were needed. Subsequently, the threat of nuclear weapons led to the building of fallout shelters in the US, the USSR, and elsewhere.

China has networks of tunnels in cities that are meant to enable the population to escape nuclear fallout and reach the countryside, but which do not protect against the actual blast. Sweden and Switzerland have highly developed civil-defense systems.

civil disobedience deliberate breaking of laws considered unjust, a form of nonviolent direct action; the term was coined by the US writer Henry Thoreau in an essay of that name 1849. It was advocated by Mahatma ◊Gandhi to prompt peaceful withdrawal of British power from India. Civil disobedience has since been employed by, for instance, the US civil-rights movement in the 1960s and the peace movement in the 1980s.

civil engineering branch of engineering that is concerned with the construction of roads, bridges, aqueducts, waterworks, tunnels, canals, irrigation works, and harbors.

The term is thought to have been used for the first time by British engineer John Smeaton in about 1750 to distinguish civilian from military engineering projects.

civilization highly developed human society with structured division of labor. The earliest civilizations evolved in the Old World from advanced ◊neolithic farming societies in the Middle East (Sumer in 3500 BC; Egypt in 3000 BC), the Indus Valley (in 2500 BC), and China (in 2200 BC). In the New World, similar communities evolved civilizations in Mesoamerica (the Olmec in 1200 BC) and Peru (the Chavin in 800 BC).

In anthropology, civilization is defined as an advanced sociopolitical stage of cultural evolution, whereby a centralized government (over a city, ceremonial center, or larger region called a state) is supported by the taxation of surplus production, and rules the agricultural and, often, mercantile base. Non-food producers become specialists who govern, lead religious ritual, impose and collect taxes, record the past and present, plan and have executed monumental public works (irrigation systems, roads, bridges, buildings, tombs), and elaborate and formalize the style and traditions of the society. These institutions are based on the use of leisure time to develop writing, mathematics, the sciences, engineering, architecture, philosophy, and the arts. Archeological remains of cities and ceremonial centers usually indicate the civilized state, with all the trappings of both style and content.

civil law legal system based on ◊Roman law. It is one of the two main European legal systems, ◊English law being the other. Civil law may also mean the law relating to matters other than criminal law, such as ◊contract and ◊tort.

civil rights rights of the individual citizen. In many countries they are specified (as in the Bill of Rights of the US constitution) and guaranteed by law to ensure equal treatment for all citizens. In the US, the struggle to obtain civil rights for former slaves and their descendants, both through legislation and in practice, has been a major theme since the Civil War. The *civil-rights movement* is a general term for this aspect of US history; see *history* under ◊black.

Civil Rights Cases five Supreme Court cases 1883 that tested the Civil Rights Act of 1875, which guaranteed protection from racial discrimination by private citizens. Congress considered this protection implicit in the 13th and 14th Amendments, but the Court disagreed. According to an 8–1 ruling, the 13th

Amendment only prohibited forced servitude while the 14th Amendment protected citizens only from discrimination by the state, not by private individuals. The Civil Rights Act was struck down, a decision not reversed until 1964 (see ⟡*Heart of Atlanta Motel Inc* v *US*).

civil service the body of administrative staff appointed to carry out the policy of a government. In the US, federal employees are restricted in the role they may play in political activity, and they retain their posts (except at senior levels) when there is a change in administration.

civil war war between rival groups within the same country.

Civil War, American also called **War Between the States** war 1861–65 between the Southern or Confederate States of America and the Northern or Union States. The former wished to maintain certain "states' rights," in particular the right to determine state law on the institution of slavery, and claimed the right to secede from the Union; the latter fought primarily to maintain the Union, with slave emancipation (proclaimed 1863) a secondary issue.

The war, and in particular its aftermath, when the South was occupied by Northern troops in the period known as the ⟡Reconstruction, left behind bitterness that lasts to the present day. Industry prospered in the North, while the economy of the South, which had been based on slavery, declined.

chronology
1861 Seven Southern states set up the Confederate States of America (president Jefferson Davis) Feb 8; ⟡*Fort Sumter*, Charleston, captured April 12–14; Pierre Beauregard (Confederate) was victorious at the **1st Battle of Bull Run** July 21.
1862 Battle of **Shiloh** April 6–7 was indecisive. General Grant (Union) captured New Orleans in May, but the Confederates, under General Robert E ⟡Lee, were again victorious at the **2nd Battle of Bull Run** Aug 29–30. Lee's northward advance was then checked by General McClellan at **Antietam** Sept 17.
1863 The **Emancipation Proclamation** was issued by President Lincoln Jan 1, freeing the slaves and assuring British and French neutrality; **Battle of Gettysburg** (Union victory) July 1–4 marked the turning point of the war; Grant captured **Vicksburg** July 4.
1864 In the **Battle of Cold Harbor** near Richmond, Virginia, June 1–12, Lee delayed Grant in his advance on Richmond. General Sherman (Union) marched through Georgia to the sea, taking **Atlanta** Sept 1 and Savannah Dec 22, destroying much of the infrastructure as he went.
1865 Lee surrendered to Grant at **Appomattox** courthouse April 9; Lincoln was assassinated April 14; the last Confederate troops surrendered May 26. There were 359,528 Union and 258,000 Confederate dead. The period of ⟡Reconstruction began.

The issue of slavery had brought to a head long-standing social and economic differences between the two oldest sections of the country. A series of political crises was caused by the task of determining whether newly admitted states, such as California, should permit or prohibit slavery in their state constitutions. The political parties in the late 1850s came to represent only sectional interests—Democrats in the South, Republicans in the North. This breakdown of an underlying national political

consensus (which had previously sustained national parties) led to the outbreak of hostilities, only a few weeks after the inauguration of the first Republican president, Abraham Lincoln.

Civil War, English in British history, the conflict between King Charles I and the Royalists (Cavaliers) on one side and the Parliamentarians (also called Roundheads) under Oliver ⟡Cromwell on the other. Hostilities began 1642 and a series of Royalist defeats (Marston Moor 1644, Naseby 1645) culminated in Charles's capture 1647 and execution 1649. The war continued until the final defeat of Royalist forces at Worcester 1651. Cromwell became Protector (ruler) 1651 until his death 1658.

chronology
1642 On Aug 22 Charles I raised his standard at Nottingham. The Battle of Edgehill Oct 23 was indecisive.
1644 The Battle of ⟡Marston Moor July 2 was a victory for the Parliamentarians under Cromwell.
1645 The Battle of ⟡Naseby June 14 was a decisive victory for Cromwell.
1646 Charles surrendered to the Scottish army May 5, 1646.
1648 A Royalist and Presbyterian rising March–Aug was soon crushed by Cromwell and his New Model Army.
1649 Charles was beheaded Jan 30.
1649–50 Cromwell invaded Ireland.
1650 Cromwell defeated the Royalists under the future Charles II at Dunbar, Scotland.
1651 The Battle of Worcester, the last military conflict of the war, was another victory for Cromwell.

Civil War, Spanish war 1936–39 precipitated by a military revolt led by General Franco against the Republican government. Inferior military capability led to the gradual defeat of the Republicans by 1939, and the establishment of Franco's dictatorship.

Franco's insurgents (Nationalists, who were supported by Fascist Italy and Nazi Germany) seized power in the south and northwest, but were suppressed in areas such as Madrid and Barcelona by the workers' militia. The loyalists (Republicans) were aided by the USSR and volunteers of the International Brigade, which included several writers, among them George Orwell.

chronology
1937 Bilbao and the Basque country were bombed into submission by the Nationalists.
1938 Catalonia was cut off from the main Republican territory.
1939 Barcelona fell in Jan and Madrid in April, and Franco established a dictatorship.

cladistics method of biological ⟡classification (taxonomy) that uses a formal step-by-step procedure for objectively assessing the extent to which organisms share particular characters, and for assigning them to taxonomic groups. Taxonomic groups (for example, ⟡species, ⟡genus, family) are termed **clades**.

cladode in botany, a flattened stem that is leaflike in appearance and function. It is an adaptation to dry conditions because a stem contains fewer ⟡stomata than a leaf, and water loss is thus minimized. The true leaves in such plants are usually reduced to spines or small scales. Examples of plants with cladodes are butcher's-broom *Ruscus aculeatus*, asparagus, and certain cacti. Cladodes may bear flowers or fruit on their surface, and this distinguishes them from leaves.

Clair René. Adopted name of René-Lucien Chomette 1898–1981. French filmmaker, originally a poet, novelist, and journalist. His *Sous les toits de Paris/Under the Roofs of Paris* 1930 was one of the first sound films. His other films include *Entr'acte* 1924, *Le Million*, and *A nous la Liberté* both 1931.

clam common name for a ⟡bivalve mollusk. The giant clam *Tridacna gigas* of the Indopacific can grow to 3 ft/1 m across in 50 years and weigh, with the shell, 1,000 lb/500 kg.

The term is usually applied to edible species, such as the North American hard clam *Venus mercenaria*, used in clam chowder, and whose shells were formerly used as money by North American Indians.

clan (Gaelic *clann* "children") social grouping based on ⟡kinship. Some traditional societies are organized by clans, which are either matrilineal or patrilineal, and whose members must marry into another clan in order to avoid in-breeding.

Familiar examples are the Highland clans of Scotland. Theoretically each clan is descended from a single ancestor from whom the name is derived—for example, clan MacGregor ("son of Gregor").

Clapton Eric 1945– . English blues and rock guitarist, singer, and composer, member of the Yardbirds 1963–65 and Cream 1966–68. Originally a blues purist, then one of the pioneers of heavy rock with Cream, he recorded with bands such as Blind Faith 1969, Derek and the Dominos (anonymously, on *Layla and Other Assorted Love Songs* 1970), and Bonnie and Delaney 1970–72. In his solo career he adopted a more laid-back style as on *461 Ocean Boulevard* 1974, *Journeyman* 1989, and the acoustic *Unplugged* 1992.

Clarendon Edward Hyde, 1st Earl of Clarendon 1609–1674. English politician and historian, chief adviser to Charles II 1651–67. A member of Parliament 1640, he joined the Royalist side 1641. The **Clarendon Code** 1661–65, a series of acts passed by the government, was directed at Nonconformists (or Dissenters) and were designed to secure the supremacy of the Church of England.

In retirement he wrote the *History of the Rebellion and Civil Wars in England* 1702–04.

Clare, St c. 1194–1253. Christian saint. Born in Assisi, Italy, at 18 she became a follower of St Francis, who founded for her the convent of San Damiano. Here she gathered the first members of the **Order of Poor Clares**. In 1958 she was proclaimed the patron saint of television by Pius XII, since in 1252 she saw from her convent sickbed the Christmas services being held in the Basilica of St Francis in Assisi. Feast day Aug 12.

claret English term since the 17th century for the dry red wines of Bordeaux, France.

clarinet musical ⟡woodwind instrument, developed in Germany in the 18th century, with a single reed and a cylindrical tube, broadening at the end. At the lower end of its range it has a rich "woody" tone, which becomes increasingly brilliant toward the upper register. Its ability both to blend and to contrast with other instruments make it popular for chamber music and as a solo instrument. It is also heard in military and concert bands and as a jazz instrument.

Equally effective both in fast virtuoso passages and as an expressive melodic instrument, the clarinet's potential was quickly exploited, and it found a place in the orchestra by the late 18th century. Music for the instrument is written in one key, for simplicity, but is played in a different key. There are different types of clarinet, varying in range, including the **bass clarinet**, which has become a regular member of the orchestra.

Clark George Rogers 1752–1818. American military leader and explorer. He was made commander of the Virginia frontier militia at the outbreak of the Revolutionary War. In 1778–79 he led an attack on the Indian allies of the British to the west of the Ohio River and founded a settlement at the site of Louisville, Kentucky.

Born near Charlottesville, Virginia, Clark spent his early adult years surveying and exploring Kentucky. After the war he remained in the Northwest Territory as Indian commissioner, leading an attack on the Wabash 1786. After leaving office, he accepted commissions from the French and Spanish colonial authorities.

Clark Jim (James) 1936–1968. Scottish-born automobile racing driver, one of the finest in the postwar era. He was twice world champion in 1963 and 1965.

Clark Joe (Joseph) Charles 1939– . Canadian Progressive Conservative politician who became party leader 1976, and May 1979 defeated Pierre ♢Trudeau at the polls to become the youngest prime minister in Canada's history. Following the rejection of his government's budget, he was defeated in a second election Feb 1980. He became secretary of state for external affairs (foreign minister) 1984 in the ♢Mulroney government.

Clark Kenneth, Lord Clark 1903–1983. British art historian, director of the National Gallery, London, 1934–45. His books include *Leonardo da Vinci* 1939 and *The Nude* 1956.

Clark Mark (Wayne) 1896–1984. US general in World War II. In 1942 he became Chief of Staff for ground forces, and deputy to General Eisenhower. He led a successful secret mission by submarine to get information in North Africa to prepare for the Allied invasion, and commanded the 5th Army in the invasion of Italy.

Clark, born in New York, fought in France in World War I and between the wars held various military appointments in the US. He was commander in chief of the United Nations forces in the Korean War 1952–53.

Clarksville city in N Tennessee at the confluence of the Cumberland and Red rivers, NW of Nashville. Manufactures include tobacco products, clothing, air-conditioning and heating equipment, rubber, and cheese; population (1980) 54,777.

class in sociology, the main grouping of social stratification in industrial societies, based primarily on economic and occupational factors, but also referring to people's style of living or sense of group identity.

Within the social sciences, class has been used both as a descriptive category and as the basis of theories about industrial society. Theories of class may see such social divisions either as a source of social stability (see ♢Durkheim) or social conflict (see ♢Marx).

In the US, little acknowledgment is given to the notion of class. If asked, most Americans identify themselves as middle class, although social scientists use measurements of education level, income, and occupation to ascribe social strata.

class in biological classification, a group of related ♢orders. For example, all mammals belong to the class Mammalia and all birds to the class Aves. Thus, the class Angiospermae (flowering plants) includes numerous plant orders such as Rosales (currants, acacias, roses, and others). The class Reptilia (reptiles) includes the orders Crocodilia and Chelonia (turtles) among others.

class action in law, a court procedure where one or more claimants represent a larger group of people who are all making the same kind of claim against the same defendant. The court's decision is binding on all the members of the group.

classical economics school of economic thought that dominated 19th-century thinking. It originated with Adam ♢Smith's *The Wealth of Nations* 1776, which embodied many of the basic concepts and principles of the Classical school. Smith's theories were further developed in the writings of John Stuart Mill and David Ricardo. Central to the theory were economic freedom, competition, and *laissez faire* government. The idea that economic growth could best be promoted by free trade, unassisted by government, was in conflict with ♢mercantilism.

The belief that agriculture was the chief determinant of economic health was also rejected in favor of manufacturing development, and the importance of labor productivity was stressed. The theories put forward by the Classical economists still influence economists today.

Classicism in art, music, and literature, a style that emphasizes the qualities traditionally considered characteristic of ancient Greek and Roman art, that is, reason, balance, objectivity, restraint, and strict adherence to form. The term Classicism (also ♢Neo-Classicism) is often used to characterize the culture of 18th-century Europe, and contrasted with 19th-century Romanticism.

classification in biology, the arrangement of organisms into a hierarchy of groups on the basis of their similarities in biochemical, anatomical, or physiological characters. The basic grouping is a ♢species, several of which may constitute a ♢genus, which in turn are grouped into families, and so on up through orders, classes, phyla (in plants, sometimes called divisions), to kingdoms.

clathrate compound formed when the small molecules of one substance fill in the holes in the structural lattice of another, solid, substance—for example, sulfur dioxide molecules in ice crystals. Clathrates are therefore intermediate between mixtures and true compounds (which are held together by ♢ionic or covalent chemical bonds).

clathration in chemistry, a method of removing water from an aqueous solution, and therefore increasing the solution's concentration, by trapping it in a matrix with inert gases such as freons.

Claude Georges 1870–1960. French industrial chemist, responsible for inventing neon signs. He discovered 1896 that acetylene, normally explosive, could be safely transported when dissolved in acetone. He later demonstrated that neon gas could be used to provide a bright red light in signs. These were displayed publicly for the first time at the Paris Motor Show 1910. As an old man, Claude spent the period 1945–49 in prison as a collaborator.

Claudel Paul 1868–1955. French poet and dramatist. A fervent Catholic, he was influenced by the Symbolists and achieved an effect of mystic allegory in such plays as *L'Annonce faite à Marie/Tidings Brought to Mary* 1912 and *Le Soulier de satin/The Satin Slipper* 1929, set in 16th-century Spain. His verse includes *Cinq grandes odes/Five Great Odes* 1910.

Claude Lorrain (Claude Gelée) 1600–1682. French landscape painter, active in Rome from 1627. His distinctive, luminous, Classical style had great impact on late 17th-and 18th-century taste. His subjects are mostly mythological and historical, with insignificant figures lost in great expanses of poetic scenery, as in *The Enchanted Castle* 1664 (National Gallery, London).

Born in Lorraine, he established himself in Rome, where his many patrons included Pope Urban VIII. His *Liber Veritatis*, which contains some 200 drawings after his finished works, was made to prevent forgeries of his work by contemporaries.

Claudian (Claudius Claudianus) *c.* 370–404. Last of the great Latin poets of the Roman Empire, probably born in Alexandria, Egypt. He wrote official panegyrics, epigrams, and the epic *The Rape of Proserpine*.

Claudius Tiberius Claudius Nero 10 BC–AD 54. Nephew of ♢Tiberius, made Roman emperor by his troops AD 41, after the murder of his nephew Caligula. Claudius was a scholar, historian, and able administrator. During his reign the Roman Empire was considerably extended, and in 43 he took part in the invasion of Britain.

Lame and suffering from a speech impediment, he was frequently the object of ridicule. He was dominated by his third wife, ♢Messalina, whom he ultimately had executed, and is thought to have been poisoned by his fourth wife, Agrippina the Younger. His life is described by the novelist Robert Graves in his books *I Claudius* 1934 and *Claudius the God* 1934.

Clausewitz Karl von 1780–1831. Prussian officer and writer on war, born near Magdeburg. His book *Vom Kriege/On War* 1833, translated into English 1873, gave a new philosophical foundation to the art of war and put forward a concept of strategy that was influential until World War I.

clausius in engineering, a unit of ♢entropy (the loss of energy as heat in any physical process). It is defined as the ratio of energy to temperature above absolute zero.

Clausius Rudolf Julius Emanuel 1822–1888. German physicist, one of the founders of the science of thermodynamics. In 1850 he enunciated its second law: heat cannot pass from a colder to a hotter body.

claustrophobia ♢phobia involving fear of enclosed spaces.

claves musical percussion instrument of Latin American origin, consisting of small hardwood batons struck together.

clavichord stringed keyboard instrument, common in Renaissance Europe and in 18th-century Germany. Notes are sounded by a metal blade striking the string. The clavichord was a forerunner of the pianoforte.

clavicle the collar bone of many vertebrates. In humans it is vulnerable to fracture; falls involving a sudden force on the arm may result in excessive stress passing into the chest region by way of the clavicle and other bones.

clavier in music, general term for an early keyboard instrument.

claw hard, hooked, pointed outgrowth of the digits of mammals, birds, and most reptiles. Claws are composed of the protein keratin, and grow continuously from a bundle of cells in the lower skin layer. Hooves and nails are modified structures with the same origin as claws.

clay very fine-grained sedimentary deposit that has undergone a greater or lesser degree of consolidation. When moistened it is plastic, and it hardens on heating, which renders it impermeable. It may be white, gray, red, yellow, blue, or black, depending on its composition. Clay minerals consist largely of hydrous silicates of aluminum and magnesium together with iron, potassium, sodium, and organic substances. The crystals of clay minerals have a layered structure, capable of holding water, and are responsible for its plastic properties. According to international classification, in mechanical analysis of soil, clay has a grain size of less than 0.00008 in/0.002 mm.

Types of clay include adobe, alluvial clay, building clay, brick, cement, kaolinite, ferruginous clay, fireclay, fusible clay, puddle clay, refractory clay, and vitrifiable clay. Clays have a variety of uses, some of which, such as pottery and bricks, date back to prehistoric times.

Clay Henry 1777–1852. US politician. He stood unsuccessfully three times for the presidency: as a Democratic-Republican 1824, as a National Republican 1832, and as a Whig 1844. He supported the war of 1812 against Britain, and tried to hold the Union together on the slavery issue in the Missouri Compromise of 1820, and again in the compromise of 1850. He was secretary of state 1825–29, and is also remembered for his "American system," which favored the national bank, internal improvements to facilitate commercial and industrial development, and the raising of protective tariffs.

A powerful orator, he was a strong leader of the House of Representatives. He fought a duel over the accusation that he had struck a corrupt deal with John Quincy ⟡Adams to ensure the latter would be named president by the House in 1824.

Clay Lucius DuBignon 1897–1978. US commander in chief of the US occupation forces in Germany 1947–49. He broke the Soviet blockade of Berlin 1948 after 327 days, with an airlift—a term he brought into general use—which involved bringing all supplies into West Berlin by air.

clay mineral one of a group of hydrous silicate minerals that form most of the fine-grained particles in clays. Clay minerals are normally formed by weathering or alteration of other silicates. Virtually all have sheet silicate structures similar to the ⟡micas. They exhibit the following useful properties: loss of water on heating, swelling and shrinking in different conditions, cation exchange with other media, and plasticity when wet. Examples are kaolinite, illite, and montmorillonite.

Kaolinite $Al_2Si_2O_5(OH)_4$ is a common white clay mineral derived from alteration of aluminum silicates, especially feldspars. Illite contains the same constituents as kaolinite, plus potassium, and is the main mineral of clay sediments, mudstones, and shales; it is a weathering product of feldspars and other silicates. Montmorillonite contains the constituents of kaolinite plus sodium and magnesium; along with related magnesium-and iron-bearing clay minerals, it is derived from alteration and weathering of basic igneous rocks.

Kaolinite (the mineral name for kaolin or kaolinite) is economically important in the ceramic and paper industries. Illite, along with other clay minerals, may also be used in ceramics. Montmorillonite is the chief constituent of fuller's earth, and is also used in drilling muds. Vermiculite (similar to montmorillonite) will expand on heating to produce a material used in insulation.

cleanliness unit unit for measuring air pollution: the number of particles greater than 0.5 micrometers in diameter per cubic foot of air. A more usual measure is the weight of contaminants per cubic meter of air.

Clearwater city in W central Florida on the Gulf of Mexico, NW of St Petersburg; seat of Pinellas County. Industries include tourism, citrus fruits, fishing, electronics, and flowers; population (1990) 98,800.

cleavage in geology, the tendency of a rock, especially slate, to split along parallel or sub-parallel planes that result from realignment of component minerals during deformation or metamorphism.

Cleese John 1939– . English actor and comedian who has written for and appeared in both television programs and films. On British television, he is particularly associated with the comedy series *Monty Python's Flying Circus* and *Fawlty Towers*. His films include *Monty Python and the Holy Grail* 1974, *Life of Brian* 1979, and *A Fish Called Wanda* 1988.

cleft palate fissure of the roof of the mouth, often accompanied by a harelip, the result of the two halves of the palate failing to join properly during prenatal development.

Cleisthenes lived 6th century BC. Ruler of Athens. Inspired by the statesman Solon, he is credited with the establishment of democracy in Athens 507 BC.

cleistogamy production of flowers that never fully open and that are automatically self-fertilized. Cleistogamous flowers are often formed late in the year, after the production of normal flowers, or during a period of cold weather, as seen in several species of violet *Viola*.

Cleland John 1709–1789. English author. He wrote *Fanny Hill, the Memoirs of a Woman of Pleasure* 1748–49 to try to extricate himself from the grip of his London creditors. The book was considered immoral.

clematis any temperate woody climbing plant of the genus *Clematis* with showy flowers. Clematis is a member of the buttercup family, Ranunculaceae.

Rock clematis *C. verticillaris* grows in woods and thickets in most of shady E North America.

Clemenceau Georges 1841–1929. French politician and journalist (prominent in the defense of Alfred ⟡Dreyfus). He was prime minister 1906–09 and 1917–20. After World War I he presided over the peace conference in Paris that drew up the Treaty of ⟡Versailles, but failed to secure for France the Rhine as a frontier.

Clemenceau was mayor of Montmartre, Paris, in the war of 1870, and 1871 was elected a member of the National Assembly at Bordeaux. He was elected a deputy 1876 after the formation of the Third Republic. An extreme radical, he soon earned the nickname of "the Tiger" on account of his ferocious attacks on politicians whom he disliked. He lost his seat 1893 and spent the next ten years in journalism. In 1902 he was elected senator from the Var, and was soon one of the most powerful politicians in France. When he became prime minister for the second time 1917, he made the decisive appointment of Marshal ⟡Foch as supreme commander.

Clemens Samuel Langhorne. Real name of the US writer Mark ⟡Twain.

Clement VII 1478–1534. Pope 1523–34. He refused to allow the divorce of Henry VIII of England and Catherine of Aragon. Illegitimate son of a brother of Lorenzo de' Medici, the ruler of Florence, he commissioned monuments for the Medici chapel in Florence from the Renaissance artist Michelangelo.

Clemente Roberto (Walker) 1934–1972. US baseball player, born in Carolina, Puerto Rico, who played for the Pittsburgh Pirates 1955–72. He had a career batting average of .317, was the 11th player in history to reach 3,000 hits, and was an outstanding right fielder. He died in a plane crash while flying to aid Nicaraguan earthquake victims.

Clementi Muzio 1752–1832. Italian pianist and composer. He settled in London 1782 as a teacher and then as proprietor of a successful piano and music business. He was the founder of the new technique of piano playing, and his series of studies, *Gradus ad Parnassum* 1817, is still in use.

clementine small orange, thought to be a hybrid between a tangerine and an orange or a variety of tangerine. It has a flowery taste and scent and is in season in winter. It is commonly grown in N Africa and Spain.

Clement of Alexandria c. AD 150–c. 215. Greek theologian who applied Greek philosophical ideas to Christian doctrine. He was the teacher of the theologian Origen.

Clement of Rome, St lived late 1st century AD. One of the early Christian leaders and writers known as the Fathers of the Church. According to tradition he was the third or fourth bishop of Rome, and a disciple of St Peter. He wrote a letter addressed to the church at Corinth (First Epistle of Clement), and many other writings have been attributed to him.

Cleon Athenian demagogue and military leader in the ⟡Peloponnesian War 431–404 BC. After the death of Pericles, to whom he was opposed, he won power as representative of the commercial classes and was for some years the foremost man in Athens. He advocated a vigorous war policy in opposition to the moderates who favored an early peace. He was killed fighting the Spartans at Amphipolis.

Cleopatra c. 68–30 BC. Queen of Egypt 51–48 and 47–30 BC. When the Roman general Julius Caesar arrived in Egypt, he restored her to the throne from which she had been ousted. Cleopatra and Caesar became lovers and she went with him to Rome. After Caesar's assassination 44 BC she returned to Alexandria and resumed her position as queen of Egypt. In 41 BC she was joined there by Mark Antony, one of Rome's rulers. In 31 BC Rome declared war on Egypt and scored a decisive victory in the naval Battle of Actium off the W coast of Greece. Cleopatra fled with her 60 ships to Egypt; Antony abandoned the struggle and followed her. Both he and Cleopatra committed suicide.

Cleopatra was Macedonian, and the last ruler of the Macedonian dynasty, which ruled Egypt from 323 until annexation by Rome 31. She succeeded her father Ptolemy XII jointly with her brother Ptolemy XIII, and they ruled together from 51 to 49 BC, when she was expelled by him. Her reinstatement in 48 BC by Caesar caused a war between Caesar and her brother, who was defeated and killed. The younger brother, Ptolemy XIV, was elevated to the throne and married to her, in the tradition of the pharaohs, although she actually lived with Caesar and they had a son, Ptolemy XV, known as Caesarion (he was later killed by Octavian).

After Caesar's death, Cleopatra and Mark Antony had three sons, and he divorced in 32 BC his wife Octavia. She was the sister of Octavian, the ruler of Rome, who then declared war on Egypt. Shakespeare's play *Antony and Cleopatra* recounts that Cleopatra killed herself with an asp (poisonous snake) after Antony's suicide.

Cleopatra's Needle either of two ancient Egyptian granite obelisks erected at Heliopolis in the 15th century BC by Thothmes III, and removed to Alexandria by the Roman emperor Augustus about 14 BC. They have no connection with Cleopatra's reign. One of the pair was taken to England 1878 and erected on the Victoria Embankment in London. The other was given by the khedive of Egypt to the US and erected in Central Park, New York, in 1881.

clerihew humorous verse form invented by Edmund Clerihew Bentley, characterized by a first line consisting of a person's name.

The four lines rhyme AABB, but the meter is often distorted for comic effect. An example, from Bentley's *Biography for Beginners* 1905, is: "Sir Christopher Wren/ Said, I am going to dine with some men./ If anybody calls/ Say I am designing St Paul's."

Clermont-Ferrand city, capital of Puy-de-Dôme *département*, in the Auvergne region of France; population (1983) 256,000. It is a center for agriculture, and its rubber industry is the largest in France.

Cleveland largest city of Ohio, on Lake Erie at the mouth of the river Cuyahoga; population (1990) 505,600, metropolitan area 2,759,800. Its chief industries are iron and steel and petroleum refining.

Iron ore from the Lake Superior region and coal from Ohio and Pennsylvania mines are brought here. Other manufactured goods include machine tools, auto and airplane parts, hardware, trucks, electronic equipment, and appliances. Cleveland has art and natural-history museums, a world-famous symphony orchestra, and Case Western University. It was surveyed 1796 and grew rapidly after a canal linked Lake Erie to the Ohio River 1832. John D Rockefeller established Standard Oil in Cleveland 1870. After surviving a financial crisis in 1978 that resulted from the decline of its industrial base, Cleveland sought vigorously to broaden its economy.

Cleveland (Stephen) Grover 1837–1908. 22nd and 24th president of the US, 1885–89 and 1893–97; the first Democratic president elected after the Civil War and the only president to hold office for two nonconsecutive terms. He attempted to check corruption in the civil service and reduce tariffs. These policies provoked political opposition, and he was defeated by Republican Benjamin Harrison 1888. He was returned to office 1892 and supported the Sherman Silver Purchase Act, which permitted free silver coinage and may have caused the economic panic of 1893. He was a noninterventionist but in 1895 initiated arbitration that settled a boundary dispute between Britain and Venezuela. An unswerving

conservative, he refused to involve the government in economic affairs but used federal troops to end the Pullman strike 1894. Within a year of his taking office for the second time, 4 million were unemployed and the US was virtually bankrupt.

Cleveland was born in Caldwell, New Jersey, and trained as a lawyer. He served as mayor of Buffalo, New York, 1881–82 and as governor of New York 1882–84.

click beetle ▷beetle that can regain its feet from lying on its back by jumping into the air and turning over, clicking as it does so.

Clift (Edward) Montgomery 1920–1966. US film and theater actor. A star of the late 1940s and 1950s in films such as *Red River* 1948, *A Place in the Sun* 1951, and *From Here to Eternity* 1953, he was disfigured in an automobile accident in 1957 but continued to make films. He played the title role in *Freud* 1962.

climacteric period during the life span when an important physiological change occurs, usually referring to ▷menopause.

climate weather conditions at a particular place over a period of time. Climate encompasses all the meteorological elements and the factors that influence them. The primary factors that determine the variations of climate over the surface of the Earth are: (a) the effect of latitude and the tilt of the Earth's axis to the plane of the orbit about the Sun (66.5°); (b) the large-scale movements of different wind belts over the Earth's surface; (c) the temperature difference between land and sea; (d) contours of the ground; and (e) location of the area in relation to ocean currents. Catastrophic variations to climate may be caused by the impact of another planetary body, or by clouds resulting from volcanic activity. The most important local or global metereological changes brought about by human activity are those linked with ▷ozone depleters and the ▷greenhouse effect.

How much heat the Earth receives from the Sun varies in different latitudes and at different times of the year. In the equatorial region the mean daily temperature of the air near the ground has no large seasonal variation. In the polar regions the temperature in the long winter, when there is no incoming solar radiation, falls far below the summer value. Climate types were first classified by Vladimir Köppen (1846–1940) in 1918.

The temperature of the sea, and of the air above it, varies little in the course of day or night, whereas the surface of the land is rapidly cooled by lack of solar radiation. In the same way the annual change of temperature is relatively small over the sea and great over the land. Continental areas are thus colder than the sea in winter and warmer in summer. Winds that blow from the sea are warm in winter and cool in summer, while winds from the central parts of continents are hot in summer and cold in winter.

On average, air temperature drops with increasing land height at a rate of 1.8°F/1°C per 300 ft/90 m. Thus places situated above mean sea level usually have lower temperatures than places at or near sea level. Even in equatorial regions, high mountains are snow-covered during the whole year.

Rainfall is produced by the condensation of water vapor in air. When winds blow against a range of mountains so that the air is forced to ascend, rain results, the amount depending on the height of the ground and the dampness of the air.

The complexity of the distribution of land and sea, and the consequent complexity of the general circulation of the atmosphere, have a direct effect on the distribution of the climate. Centered on the equator is a belt of tropical rainforest, which may be either constantly wet or monsoonal (seasonal with wet and dry seasons in each year). On each side of this is a belt of savannah, with lighter rainfall and less dense vegetation. Usually there is then a transition through ▷steppe (semiarid) to desert (arid), with a further transition through steppe to ▷Mediterranean climate with dry summer, followed by the moist temperate climate of middle latitudes. Next comes a zone of cold climate with moist winter. Where the desert extends into middle latitudes, however, the zones of Mediterranean and moist temperate climates are missing, and the transition is from desert to a cold climate with moist winter. In the extreme east of Asia a cold climate with dry winters extends from about 70° N to 35° N. The polar caps have ▷tundra and glacial climates, with little or no ▷precipitation (rain or snow).

climatology study of climate, its global variations and causes.

climax community an assemblage of plants and animals that is relatively stable in its environment (for example, beech and maple forest in parts of the US). It is brought about by ecological ▷succession, and represents the final point in a successional series.

climax vegetation the state of equilibrium that is reached after a series of changes have occurred in the vegetation of a particular habitat. It is the final stage in a ▷succession, where the structure and species of a habitat do not develop further, provided conditions remain unaltered.

clinical ecology in medicine, ascertaining environmental factors involved in illnesses, particularly those manifesting nonspecific symptoms such as fatigue, depression, allergic reactions, and immune system malfunctions, and prescribing means of avoiding or minimizing these effects.

clinical psychology discipline dealing with the understanding and treatment of health problems, particularly mental disorders. The main problems dealt with include anxiety, phobias, depression, obsessions, sexual and marital problems, drug and alcohol dependence, childhood behavioral problems, psychoses (such as schizophrenia), mental handicap, and brain damage (such as dementia).

Other areas of work include forensic psychology (concerned with criminal behavior) and health psychology. *Assessment procedures* assess intelligence and cognition (for example, in detecting the effects of brain damage) by using psychometric tests. *Behavioral approaches* are methods of treatment which apply learning theories to clinical problems. *Behavior therapy* helps clients change unwanted behaviors (such as phobias, obsessions, sexual problems) and to develop new skills (such as improving social interactions). *Behavior modification* relies on operant conditioning, making selective use of rewards (such as praise) to change behavior. This is helpful for children, the mentally handicapped, and for patients in institutions, such as mental hospitals. *Cognitive therapy* is a new approach to treating emotional problems, such as anxiety and depression, by teaching clients how to deal with negative thoughts and attitudes. *Counseling*, developed by Rogers, is widely used to help clients solve their own problems. *Psychoanalysis*, as developed by Freud and Jung, is little used by clinical psychologists today. It emphasizes childhood conflicts as a source of adult problems.

clinometer hand-held surveying instrument for measuring angles of slope.

Clinton Bill (William Jefferson) 1946– . 42nd president of the US 1993– . A Democrat, he served as governor of Arkansas 1979–81 and 1983–93, establishing a liberal and progressive reputation. After winning the 1992 nomination for president, he chose Al Gore as his running mate. The 1992 campaign centered on the problems of the US economy, with Clinton successfully challenging the incumbent George Bush while weathering criticism of his avoidance of the military draft and other "character" issues.

Born in Hope, Arkansas, Clinton majored in international affairs at Georgetown University, graduating in 1968. He attended Oxford University as a Rhodes scholar 1968–70 and graduated from Yale University Law School 1973. He served as attorney general of Arkansas 1977–79 and, at age 32, became the country's youngest governor.

Clinton De Witt 1769–1828. American political leader, mayor of New York City 1803–15 and governor of New York from 1817. A strong promoter of the Erie Canal, he was instrumental in the initiation of that project, completed 1825.

Born in Little Britain, New York, Clinton was educated at Columbia University, studied law, and became the personal assistant of his uncle George Clinton, governor of New York. After serving in the state legislature 1797–1802 and the US Senate 1802–03, he was elected mayor of New York City. Clinton simultaneously served in the state senate and as lieutenant governor.

Clio in Greek mythology, the inventor of epic poetry and history; one of the nine ⬦Muses.

Clive Robert, Baron Clive of Plassey 1725–1774. British soldier and administrator who established British rule in India by victories over the French 1751 and over the nawab of Bengal 1757. On his return to Britain his wealth led to allegations that he had abused his power. Although acquitted, he committed suicide.

clo unit of thermal insulation of clothing. Standard clothes have an insulation of about 1 clo; the warmest clothing is about 4 clo per 1 in/ 2.5 cm of thickness. See also ⬦tog.

cloaca the common posterior chamber of most vertebrates into which the digestive, urinary, and reproductive tracts all enter; a cloaca is found in most reptiles, birds, and amphibians; many fishes; and, to a reduced degree, marsupial mammals. Placental mammals, however, have a separate digestive opening (the anus) and urinogenital opening. The cloaca forms a chamber in which products can be stored before being voided from the body via a muscular opening, the cloacal aperture.

clock any device that measures the passage of time, usually shown by means of pointers moving over a dial or by a digital display. Traditionally a timepiece consists of a train of wheels driven by a spring or weight controlled by a balance wheel or pendulum. The watch is a portable clock.

history In ancient Egypt the time during the day was measured by a shadow clock, a primitive form of ⬦sundial, and at night the water

clock was used. Up to the late 16th century the only clock available for use at sea was the sand clock, of which the most familiar form is the hourglass. During the Middle Ages various types of sundial were widely used, and portable sundials were in use from the 16th to the 18th century. Watches were invented in the 16th century—the first were made in Nuremberg, Germany, shortly after 1500—but it was not until the 19th century that they became cheap enough to be widely available.

The first known public clock was set up in Milan, Italy, in 1353. The timekeeping of both clocks and watches was revolutionized in the 17th century by the application of pendulums to clocks and of balance springs to watches.

types of clock The **marine chronometer** is a precision timepiece of special design, used at sea for giving Greenwich mean time (GMT). *Electric timepieces* were made possible by the discovery early in the 19th century of the magnetic effects of electric currents. One of the earliest and most satisfactory methods of electrical control of a clock was invented by Matthaeus Hipp in 1842. In one kind of electric clock, the place of the pendulum or spring-controlled balance wheel is taken by a small synchronous electric motor, which counts up the alternations (frequency) of the incoming electric supply and, by a suitable train of wheels, records the time by means of hands on a dial. The **quartz crystal clock** (made possible by the ⬦piezoelectric effect of certain crystals) has great precision, with a short-term variation in accuracy of about one-thousandth of a second per day. More accurate still is the **atomic clock**. This utilizes the natural resonance of certain atoms (for example, cesium) as a regulator controlling the frequency of a quartz crystal ⬦oscillator. It is accurate to within one-millionth of a second per day.

cloisonné ornamental craft technique in which thin metal strips are soldered in a pattern onto a metal surface, and the resulting compartments (*cloisons*) filled with colored ⬦enamels and fired. The technique was probably developed in the Byzantine Middle East and traded to Asia and Europe. Cloisonné vases and brooches were made in medieval Europe, but the technique was perfected in Japan and China during the 17th, 18th, and 19th centuries.

cloister convent or monastery, and more particularly a covered walk within these, often opening onto a courtyard.

Cloisters, the branch of the Metropolitan Museum of Art in Fort Tryon Park, New York. It consists of several reassembled European medieval buildings, and exhibits include medieval tapestries, sculpture, pictures, and books.

Featured outdoors are period gardens including a medicinal herb garden.

Close Glenn 1948– . US actress who received Academy Award nominations for her roles as the embittered "other woman" in *Fatal Attraction* 1987 and as the scheming antiheroine of *Dangerous Liaisons* 1988. She played Gertrude in Franco Zeffirelli's film of *Hamlet* 1990 and appeared as an opera star in *Meeting Venus* 1991.

She was born in Connecticut, made her New York stage debut on graduating from college, and went on to perform in musicals as well as dramatic productions. Her first film was *The World According to Garp* 1982; other screen appearances include *The Big Chill* 1983 and *Jagged Edge* 1985. More recently on Broadway

she has had roles in Tom Stoppard's *The Real Thing* and Michael Frayn's *Benefactors*.

closed-circuit television (CCTV) localized television system in which programs are sent over relatively short distances, the camera, receiver, and controls being linked by cable. Closed-circuit TV systems are used in department stores and large offices as a means of internal security, monitoring people's movements.

closed shop any company or firm, public corporation, or other body that requires its employees to be members of the appropriate labor union. Usually demanded by unions, the closed shop may be preferred by employers as simplifying negotiation, but it was condemned by the European Court of Human Rights 1981.

In the US the closed shop was made illegal by the Taft-Hartley Act 1947, passed by Congress over Truman's veto.

clothes articles made to cover the human body. Clothes can be worn simply for warmth, but they have almost always had the additional purpose of indicating sex and status or of enhancing the appearance.

The earliest clothes were animal skins, replaced by textiles after the discovery of weaving and spinning. Simple woolen clothing predominated in the northern hemisphere but the ancient Mediterranean civilizations made sophisticated use of linens, cotton, and silk. Apart from changing fashions, the main developments in the history of clothing are the mass-production of textiles from the early 19th century and the invention of synthetic materials in the 20th century.

clothes moth moth whose larvae feed on clothes, upholstery, and carpets. The adults are small golden or silvery moths. The natural habitat of the larvae is in the nests of animals, feeding on remains of hair and feathers, but they have adapted to human households and can cause considerable damage, for example, the common moth clothes moth *Tineola bisselliella*.

cloud water vapor condensed into minute water particles that float in masses in the atmosphere. Clouds, like fogs or mists, which occur at lower levels, are formed by the cooling of air containing water vapor, which generally condenses around tiny dust particles.

Clouds are classified according to the height at which they occur and their shape. *Cirrus* and *cirrostratus* clouds occur at 33,000 ft/ 10,000 m. The former, sometimes called mares'-tails, consist of minute specks of ice and appear as feathery white wisps, while cirrostratus clouds stretch across the sky as a thin white sheet. Three types of cloud are found at 10,000–24,000 ft/3,000–7,500 m: cirrocumulus, altocumulus, and altostratus. *Cirrocumulus* clouds occur in small or large rounded tufts, sometimes arranged in the pattern called mackerel sky. *Altocumulus* clouds are similar, but larger, white clouds, also arranged in lines. *Altostratus* clouds are like heavy cirrostratus clouds and may stretch across the sky as a gray sheet.

The lower clouds, occurring at heights of up to 6,000 ft/1,800 m, may be of two types. *Stratocumulus* clouds are the dull gray clouds that give rise to a leaden sky which may not yield rain. *Nimbus* clouds are dark-gray, shapeless rain clouds.

Two types of clouds, **cumulus** and **cumulonimbus**, are placed in a special category because they are produced by daily ascending air currents, which take moisture into the cooler regions of the atmosphere. Cumulus clouds have a flat base generally at 4,500 ft/1,400 m where condensation begins, while the upper part is dome-shaped and extends to about 1,800 m/6,000ft. Cumulonimbus clouds have their base at much the same level, but extend much higher, often up to over 20,000 ft/6,000 m. Short heavy showers and sometimes thunder may accompany them. *Stratus* clouds, occurring below 3,500 ft/1,000 m, have the appearance of sheets parallel to the horizon and are like high fogs.

cloud chamber apparatus for tracking ionized particles. It consists of a vessel fitted with a piston and filled with air or other gas, supersaturated with water vapor. When the volume of the vessel is suddenly expanded by moving the piston outwards, the vapor cools and a cloud of tiny droplets forms on any nuclei, dust, or ions present. As fast-moving ionizing particles collide with the air or gas molecules, they show as visible tracks.

Much information about interactions between such particles and radiations has been obtained from photographs of these tracks. This system has been improved upon in recent years by the use of liquid hydrogen or helium instead of air or gas (see ▷bubble chamber).

The cloud chamber was devised in 1897 by Charles Thomson Rees Wilson (1869–1959) at Cambridge University.

Clouet François *c.* 1515–1572. French portrait painter who succeeded his father Jean Clouet as court painter. He worked in the Italian style of Mannerism. His half-nude portrait of Diane de Poitiers, *The Lady in Her Bath c.* 1570 (National Gallery, Washington), is also thought to be a likeness of Marie Touchet, mistress of Charles IX.

Clouet Jean (known as *Janet*) 1486–1541. French artist, court painter to Francis I. His portraits and drawings, often compared to Holbein's, show an outstanding naturalism.

clove dried, unopened flower bud of the clove tree *Eugenia caryophyllus*. A member of the myrtle family Myrtaceae, the clove tree is a native of the Moluccas. Cloves are used for flavoring in cooking and confectionery. Oil of cloves, which has tonic and carminative qualities, is employed in medicine. The aromatic quality of cloves is shared to a large degree by the leaves, bark, and fruit of the tree.

clover any of an Old World genus *Trifolium* of low-growing leguminous plants, usually with compound leaves of three leaflets and small flowers in dense heads. Sweet clover refers to various species belonging to the related genus *Melilotus*.

Red clover *T. pratense* and white clover *T. repens* now grow widely in the US. The most common honey is made from clover and the most important source of fodder is red clover.

Clovis 465–511. Merovingian king of the Franks from 481. He succeeded his father Childeric as king of the Salian (northern) Franks; defeated the Gallo-Romans (Romanized Gauls) near Soissons 486, ending their rule in France; and defeated the Alemanni, a confederation of Germanic tribes, near Cologne 496. He embraced Christianity and subsequently proved a powerful defender of orthodoxy against the Arian Visigoths, whom he defeated at Poitiers 507. He made Paris his capital.

club moss or *lycopod* any non-seed-bearing plant of the order Lycopodiales belonging to the Pteridophyta family. Club mosses are allied to the ferns and horsetails and, like them, reproduce by spores.

These plants have a wide distribution, but were far more numerous in Paleozoic times, especially the Carboniferous period, when members of this group were large trees. The living species are all of small size.

Lycopodium is the most common genus, with species mostly growing on forest floors.

clubroot disease affecting cabbages, turnips, and allied plants of the Cruciferae family. It is caused by a ▷slime mold, *Plasmodiophora brassicae*. This attacks the roots of the plant, which send out knotty outgrowths. Eventually the whole plant decays.

Cluj (German *Klausenberg*) city in Transylvania, Romania, located on the river Somes; population (1985) 310,000. It is a communications center for Romania and the Hungarian plain. Industries include machine tools, furniture, and knitwear.

There is a 14th-century cathedral, and Romanian (1872) and Hungarian (1945) universities.

clusec unit for measuring the power of a vacuum pump.

clutch any device for disconnecting rotating shafts, used especially in a car's transmission system. In an automobile with a manual gearbox, the driver depresses the clutch when changing gear, thus disconnecting the engine from the gearbox.

The clutch consists of two main plates, a pressure plate and a driven plate, which is mounted on a shaft leading to the gearbox. When the clutch is engaged, the pressure plate presses the driven plate against the engine ▷flywheel, and drive goes to the gearbox. Depressing the clutch springs the pressure plate away, freeing the driven plate. Cars with *automatic transmission* have no clutch. Drive is transmitted from the flywheel to the automatic gearbox by a liquid coupling or ▷torque converter.

Clutha longest river in South Island, New Zealand, 201 mi/322 km long. It rises in the Southern Alps, has hydroelectric installations, and flows to meet the sea near Kaitangata.

Clyde river in Strathclyde, Scotland; 103 mi/170 km long. The Firth of Clyde and Firth of Forth are linked by the Forth and Clyde canal, 35 mi/56 km long. The shipbuilding yards have declined in recent years.

The nuclear-submarine bases of Faslane (Polaris) and Holy Loch (US Poseidon) are here.

Clytemnestra in Greek mythology, the wife of ▷Agamemnon. With her lover Aegisthus, she murdered her husband on his return from the Trojan War and was in turn killed by her son Orestes.

cm symbol for *centimetre*.

Cnossus alternate form of ▷Knossos, city of ancient Crete.

Cnut alternate spelling of ▷Canute.

CO abbreviation for the state of ▷*Colorado*.

coal black or blackish mineral substance of fossil origin, the result of the transformation of ancient plant matter under progressive compression. It is used as a fuel and in the chemical industry. Coal is classified according to the proportion of carbon and volatiles it contains. The main types are ▷*anthracite* (shiny, with more than 90% carbon), **bituminous coal** (shiny and dull patches, more than 80% carbon), and ▷*lignite* (woody, grading into ▷peat, 70% carbon).

In the second half of the 18th century, coal became the basis of the Industrial Revolution. Coal fields are widely distributed throughout the temperate N hemisphere, the greatest reserves being in Europe, W Siberia, and the US. In the Southern hemisphere, Australia is a major producer.

An increasing use, from 1950–70, of cheap natural gas and oil as fuel and for the production of electricity halted when the energy crisis of the 1970s led to greater exploitation of coal resources.

Coal is becoming a major source of synfuel (synthetic gasoline). In the Fischer–Tropsch process (used in Germany in World War II and today in South Africa), the coal is gasified and then catalysts are used to reconstitute it into diesel and jet fuel. In the degradation process (under development in the US for high-octane motor fuel), a liquid fuel is directly produced by adding hydrogen or removing carbon from the coal.

coal gas gas produced when coal is destructively distilled or heated out of contact with the air. Its main constituents are methane, hydrogen, and carbon monoxide. Coal gas has been superseded by ▷natural gas for domestic purposes.

coalition association of political groups, usually for some limited or short-term purpose, such as fighting an election or forming a government when one party has failed to secure a majority in a legislature.

In 1990 a coalition of UN military forces was formed to free Kuwait from annexation by Iraq.

coal tar black oily material resulting from the destructive distillation of bituminous coal.

Further distillation of coal tar yields a number of fractions: light oil, middle oil, heavy oil, and anthracene oil; the residue is called pitch. On further fractionation a large number of substances are obtained, about 200 of which have been isolated. They are used as dyes and in medicines.

coastal erosion the erosion of the land by the constant battering of the sea's waves. This produces two effects. The first is a hydraulic effect, in which the force of the wave compresses air pockets in coastal rocks and cliffs, and the air then expands explosively. The second is the effect of abrasion, in which rocks and pebbles are flung against the cliffs, wearing them away.

In areas where there are beaches, the waves cause longshore drift, in which sand and stone fragments are carried parallel to the shore, causing buildups (sandspits) in some areas and beach erosion in others.

coast guard governmental organization whose members patrol a nation's seacoast to prevent smuggling, assist distressed vessels, watch for oil slicks, and so on.

The US Coast Guard 1915 has wide duties, including enforcing law and order on the high seas and navigable waters. During peacetime, it is administered under the Department of Transportation; in time of war, the Department of the Navy.

coati or *coatimundi* any of several species of carnivores of the genus *Nasua*, in the same family, Procyonidae, as the raccoons. A coati is a good climber and has long claws, a long tail, a good sense of smell, and a long, flexible piglike snout used for digging. Coatis live in packs in the forests of South and Central America.

The common coati *Nasua nasua* of South America is about 2 ft/60 cm long, with a tail about the same length.

coaxial cable electric cable that consists of a solid or stranded central conductor insulated from and surrounded by a solid or braided conducting tube or sheath. It can transmit the high-frequency signals used in television, telephone, and other telecommunications transmissions.

cobalt (German *Kobalt* "goblin") hard, lustrous, gray, metallic element, symbol Co, atomic number 27, atomic weight 58.933. It is found in various ores and occasionally as a free metal, sometimes in metallic meteorite fragments. It is used in the preparation of magnetic, wear-resistant, and high-strength alloys; its compounds are used in inks, paints, and varnishes.

The isotope Co-60 is radioactive (half-life 5.3 years) and is produced in large amounts for use as a source of gamma rays in industrial radiography, research, and cancer therapy. Cobalt was named in 1730 by Swedish chemist Georg Brandt (1694–1768); the name derives from the fact that miners considered its ore worthless because of its arsenic content.

cobalt ore cobalt is extracted from a number of minerals, the main ones being **smaltite**, $(CoNi)As_3$; **linnaeite**, Co_3S_4; **cobaltite**, CoAsS; and **glaucodot**, $(CoFe)AsS$.

All commercial cobalt is obtained as a byproduct of other metals. Zaire is the largest producer of cobalt, and it is obtained there as a byproduct of the copper industry. Other producers include Canada and Morocco. Cobalt is also found in the manganese nodules that occur on the ocean floor, and was successfully refined in 1988 from the Pacific Ocean nodules, although this process has yet to prove economic.

Cobb Ty(rus Raymond), nicknamed "the Georgia Peach" 1886–1961. US baseball player, one of the greatest batters and base runners of all time. He played for Detroit and Philadelphia 1905–28, and won the American League batting average championship 12 times. He holds the record for runs scored (2,254) and batting average (.367). He had 4,191 hits in his career—a record that stood for almost 60 years.

Coblenz alternate spelling of the German city ▷Koblenz.

COBOL (acronym for **common business-oriented language**) high-level computer-programming language, designed in the late 1950s for commercial data-processing problems; it has become one of the major languages in this field. COBOL features powerful facilities for file handling and business arithmetic. Program instructions written in this language make extensive use of words and look very much like English sentences. This makes COBOL one of the easiest languages to learn and understand.

cobra any of several poisonous snakes, especially the genus *Naja*, of the family Elapidae, found in Africa and S Asia, species of which can grow from 3 ft/1 m to over 14 ft/4.3 m. The neck stretches into a hood when the snake is alarmed. Cobra venom contains nerve toxins powerful enough to kill humans.

The Indian cobra *Naja naja* is about 5 ft/1.5 m long, and found over most of S Asia. Some individuals have "spectacle" markings on the hood. The hamadryad *N. hannah* of S and SE Asia can be 14 ft/4.3 m or more, and eats snakes. The ringhals *Hemachatus*

hemachatus of S Africa and the black-necked cobra *N. nigricollis*, of the African savanna are both about 3 ft/1 m long. Both are able to spray venom toward the eyes of an attacker.

Cobra group of European abstract painters formed by the Dutch artist Karel Appel 1948. Other leading members were the Dane Asgar Jorn and the Belgian Corneille. They developed an expressive and dynamic form of abstract painting, using thick paint and lurid colors.

Coburn James 1928– . US film actor, popular in the 1960s and 1970s. His films include *The Magnificent Seven* 1960, *Pat Garrett and Billy the Kid* 1973, and *Cross of Iron* 1977.

coca South American shrub *Erythroxylon coca* of the coca family Erythroxylaceae, whose dried leaves are the source of cocaine. It was used as a holy drug by the Andean Indians.

Coca-Cola trade name of a sweetened, carbonated drink, originally made with coca leaves and flavored with cola nuts, and containing caramel and caffeine. Invented in 1886, Coca-Cola was sold in every state of the US by 1895 and in 155 countries by 1987.

As a rule, Fanta, an orange-flavored soda made by Coca-Cola, preceded the cola-flavored soda in the third world. With the increased presence of Americans in third-world nations, US imperialism became known as Coca-Colonialism.

cocaine alkaloid $C_{17}H_{21}NO_4$ extracted from the leaves of the coca tree. It has limited medical application, mainly as a local anesthetic agent that is readily absorbed by mucous membranes (lining tissues) of the nose and throat. It is both toxic and addictive. Its use as a stimulant is illegal. ▷Crack is a derivative of cocaine.

Cocaine was first extracted from the coca plant in Germany in the 19th century. Most of the world's cocaine is produced from coca grown in Peru, Bolivia, Colombia, and Ecuador. Estimated annual production totals 215,000 tonnes, with most of the processing done in Colombia. Long-term use may cause mental and physical deterioration.

coccus (plural *cocci*) member of a group of globular bacteria, some of which are harmful to humans. The cocci contain the subgroups *streptococci*, where the bacteria associate in straight chains, and *staphylococci*, where the bacteria associate in branched chains.

Cochabamba city in central Bolivia, SE of La Paz; population (1988) 377,200. Its altitude is 8,370 ft/2,550 m; it is a center of agricultural trading and oil refining.

Its refinery is linked by pipeline with the Camiri oil fields. It is the third-largest city in Bolivia.

Cochin seaport in Kerala state, India, on the Malabar coast; population (1983) 686,000. It is a fishing port, naval training base, and an industrial center with oil refineries; ropes and clothing are also manufactured here. It exports coir, copra, tea, and spices. Vasco da Gama established a Portuguese factory at Cochin 1502, and St Francis Xavier made it a missionary center 1530. The Dutch held Cochin from 1663 to 1795, when it was taken by the English.

Cochin-China region of SE Asia. With Cambodia it formed part of the ancient Khmer empire. In the 17th–18th centuries it was conquered by Annam. Together with Cambodia it became, 1863–67, the first part of

the Indochinese peninsula to be occupied by France. Since 1949 it has been part of Vietnam.

cochineal red dye obtained from the cactus-eating Mexican ▷scale insect *Dactylopius coccus*, used in coloring food and fabrics.

Cochise c. 1812–1874. Apache leader. Born in Arizona as a member of the Chiricahua band of Apache, Cochise was unjustly arrested by US authorities 1850. Escaping from custody, he took, and later executed, some American hostages, leading to a bitter and long-lasting conflict with the US government. In his fight to prevent white settlement in his territory, Cochise and his followers joined forces with the Mimbrëno Apache and conducted repeated raids on American posts. In 1862 he successfully held off a large force of California volunteers. Finally apprehended by General George Crook 1871, Cochise made peace with the US government the following year.

cochlea part of the inner ▷ear. It is equipped with approximately 10,000 hair cells, which move in response to sound waves and thus stimulate nerve cells to send messages to the brain. In this way they turn vibrations of the air into electrical signals.

cockatiel Australian parrot *Nymphicus hollandicus*, about 8 in/20 cm long, with grayish plumage, yellow cheeks, a long tail, and a crest like a cockatoo. Cockatiels are popular as pets and aviary birds.

cockatoo any of several crested parrots, especially of the genus *Cacatua*. They usually have light-colored plumage with tinges of red, yellow, or orange on the face, and an erectile crest on the head. They are native to Australia, New Guinea, and nearby islands.

There are about 17 species, one of the most familiar being the sulfur-crested cockatoo *C. galerita* of Australia and New Guinea, about 20 in/50 cm long, white with a yellow crest and dark beak.

cockchafer or **maybug** European beetle *Melolontha melolontha*, of the scarab family, up to 1.2 in/3 cm long, with clumsy, buzzing flight, seen on early summer evenings. Cockchafers damage trees by feeding on the foliage and flowers.

The larvae live underground for up to four years, feeding on grass and cereal roots.

Cockcroft John Douglas 1897–1967. British physicist. In 1932 he and the Irish physicist Ernest Walton succeeded in splitting the nucleus of an atom for the first time. In 1951 they were jointly awarded a Nobel Prize.

cockfighting the pitting of gamecocks against one another to make sport for onlookers and gamblers. In most countries it is illegal because of its cruelty.

The sport was extremely popular in feudal Europe. Cockfighting is still legal in many countries and continues surreptitiously in others. Fighting cocks are 1–2 years old when matched, and steel spurs are attached to their legs.

cockle any of over 200 species of bivalve mollusk with ribbed, heart-shaped shells. Some are edible and are sold in W European markets.

The Atlantic strawberry cockle *Americardia media*, about 1 in/2.5 cm across, is a common E North American species.

cock-of-the-rock South American bird *Rupicola peruviana* of the family Cotingidae, which also includes the cotingas and umbrella birds. The male cock-of-the-rock has brilliant orange plumage including the head crest, the female is a duller brown. Males clear an area of ground and use it as a communal display ground, spreading wings, tail, and crest to attract mates.

cockroach any of numerous insects of the family Blattidae, distantly related to mantises and grasshoppers. There are 3,500 species, mainly in the tropics. They have long antennae and biting mouthparts. They can fly, but rarely do so.

The common cockroach, or black-beetle *Blatta orientalis*, is found in human dwellings, is nocturnal, omnivorous, and contaminates food. The German cockroach *Blattella germanica* and American cockroach *Periplaneta americana* are pests in kitchens, bakeries, and warehouses. In Britain only two innocuous species are native, but several have been introduced with imported food and have become severe pests. They are very difficult to eradicate. Cockroaches have a very high resistance to radiation, making them the only creatures likely to survive a nuclear holocaust.

cocoa and chocolate (Aztec *xocolatl*) food products made from the ⟡cacao (or cocoa) bean, fruit of a tropical tree *Theobroma cacao*, now cultivated mainly in Africa. Chocolate as a drink was introduced to Europe from the New World by the Spanish in the 16th century; eating chocolate was first produced in the late 18th century. Cocoa and chocolate are widely used in confectionery and drinks.
preparation This takes place in the importing country and consists chiefly of roasting, winnowing, and grinding the nib (the edible portion of the bean). If *cocoa* for drinking is required, a proportion of the cocoa butter is removed by hydraulic pressure and the remaining cocoa is reduced by further grinding and sieving to a fine powder. In *chocolate* all the original cocoa butter remains. Sugar and usually milk are added; in the UK cheaper vegetable fats are widely substituted.
history The cacao tree is indigenous to the forests of the Amazon and Orinoco, and the use of the beans, sacred to the Indians of Mexico, was introduced into Europe after the conquest of Mexico by Cortes. In Mexico cacao was mixed with hot spices, whisked to a froth and drunk cold by the ruling class, during ritual events. A "cocoa-house" was opened in London in 1657; others followed and became fashionable meeting places. In 1828 a press was invented that removed two thirds of the cocoa butter from the beans, leaving a cakelike mass which, when mixed with sugar and spices, made a palatable drink. Joseph Fry (1728–1787) combined the cocoa mass with sugar and cocoa butter to obtain a solid chocolate bar, which was turned into milk chocolate by a Swiss, Daniel Pieter, who added condensed milk developed by Henri Nestlé (1814–1890). Cocoa powder was a later development. The Ivory Coast is the world's top cocoa exporter (32% of the world total in 1986).

coconut fruit of the coconut palm *Cocos nucifera* of the family Arecaceae, which grows throughout the lowland tropics. The fruit has a large outer husk of fibers, which is split off and used for coconut matting and ropes. Inside this is the nut exported to temperate countries. Its hard shell contains white flesh and coconut milk, both of which are nourishing and palatable.

The white meat can be eaten, or dried prior to the extraction of its oil, which makes up nearly two-thirds of it. The oil is used in the making of soap and margarine and in cooking; the residue is used in cattle feed.

Cocos Islands or *Keeling Islands* group of 27 small coral islands in the Indian Ocean, about 1,720 mi/2,770 km NW of Perth, Australia; area 5.5 sq mi/14 sq km; population (1986) 616. They are owned by Australia.

Discovered by William Keeling 1609, they were uninhabited until 1826, annexed by Britain 1857, and transferred to Australia as the Territory of Cocos (Keeling) Islands 1955. The Australian government purchased them from John ⟡Clunies-Ross 1978. In 1984 the islanders voted to become part of Australia.

Cocteau Jean 1889–1963. French poet, dramatist, and film director. A leading figure in European Modernism, he worked with Picasso, Diaghilev, and Stravinsky. He produced many volumes of poetry, ballets such as *Le Boeuf sur le toit/The Ox on the Roof* 1920, plays, for example, *Orphée/Orpheus* 1926, and a mature novel of bourgeois French life, *Les Enfants terribles/Children of the Game* 1929, which he made into a film 1950.

cod any fish of the family Gadoidea, especially the Atlantic cod, *Gadus morhua* found in the N Atlantic and Baltic. It is brown to gray with spots, white below, and can grow to 5 ft/1.5 m.

The main cod fisheries are in the North Sea, and off the coasts of Iceland and Newfoundland. Much of the catch is salted and dried. Formerly one of the cheapest fish, decline in numbers from overfishing has made it one of the most expensive.

coda (Italian "tail") in music, a concluding section of a movement added to indicate finality.

codeine opium derivative that provides pain relief in mild to moderate pain. It also suppresses the cough center of the brain. It is an alkaloid, derived from morphine but less toxic and addictive.

codex (plural *codices*) book from before the invention of printing: in ancient times wax-coated wooden tablets; later, folded sheets of parchment were attached to the boards, then bound together. The name "codex" was used for all large works, collections of history, philosophy, poetry, and during the Roman Empire designated collections of laws. During the 2nd century AD codices began to replace the earlier rolls. They were widely used by the medieval Christian church to keep records, from about 1200 onwards.

Various codices record Mexican Indian civilizations just after the time of the Spanish Conquest about 1520. The *Codex Juris Canonici/Code of Canon Law* is the body of laws governing the Roman Catholic Church since 1918.

cod-liver oil oil obtained by subjecting the fresh livers of cod to pressure at a temperature of about 185°F/85°C. It is highly nutritious, being a valuable source of the vitamins A and D; overdose can be harmful.

Cody resort town in NW Wyoming, on the Shoshone River, situated at the entrance to Yellowstone National Park; population (1990) 7,897. It was founded by William F ⟡Cody ("Buffalo Bill") in 1901. There is a Museum of the Old West and a "Buffalo Bill" Historical Center.

Cody (William Frederick) "Buffalo Bill" 1846–1917. US scout and performer. From 1883 he toured the US and Europe with a Wild West show which featured the re-creation of Indian attacks and, for a time, the cast included Chief ⟡Sitting Bull as well as Annie ⟡Oakley. His nickname derives from a time when he had a contract to supply buffalo carcasses to railroad laborers (over 4,000 in 18 months).

He was a heavy drinker and a trusting investor; he died in poverty after seeing his exploits recounted and exaggerated in novels of the West.

coeducation education of both boys and girls in one institution. In most countries coeducation has become favored over single-sex education, although there is some evidence to suggest that girls perform better in a single-sex institution, particularly in maths and science.

In the US, 90% of schools and colleges are coeducational. In 1954, the USSR returned to its earlier coeducational system, which was partly abolished in 1944. In Islamic countries, coeducation is discouraged beyond the infant stage on religious principles.

coefficient the number part in front of an algebraic term, signifying multiplication. For example, in the expression $4x^2 + 2xy - x$, the coefficient of x^2 is 4 (because $4x^2$ means $4 \times x^2$), that of xy is 2, and that of x is –1 (because $-1 \times x = -x$).

In general algebraic expressions, coefficients are represented by letters that may stand for numbers; for example, in the equation $ax^2 + bx + c = 0$, a, b, and c are coefficients, which can take any number.

coefficient of relationship the probability that any two individuals share a given gene by virtue of being descended from a common ancestor. In sexual reproduction of diploid species, an individual shares half its genes with each parent, with its offspring, and (on average) with each sibling; but only a quarter (on average) with its grandchildren or its siblings' offspring; an eighth with its great-grandchildren, and so on.

coelacanth lobe-finned fish *Latimeria chalumnae* up to 6 ft/2 m long. It has bone and muscle at the base of the fins, and is distantly related to the freshwater lobefins, which were the ancestors of all land animals with backbones. Coelacanths live in deep water (650 ft/200 m) around the Comoros Islands, off the coast of Madagascar. They were believed to be extinct until one was caught in 1938.

Coelacanths are now under threat; a belief that fluid from the spine has a life-extending effect has made them much sought after.

coelenterate any freshwater or marine organism of the phylum Coelenterata, having a body wall composed of two layers of cells. They also possess stinging cells. Examples are jellyfish, hydra, and coral.

coelom in all but the simplest animals, the fluid-filled body cavity that contains the gut and associated organs.

Coetzee J(ohn) M 1940– . South African author whose novel *In the Heart of the Country* 1975 dealt with the rape of a white woman by a black man. In 1983 he won Britain's prestigious ⟡Booker Prize for *The Life and Times of Michael K.*

Other works include *Waiting for the Barbarians* 1982 and *Foe* 1987.

coffee drink made from the roasted and ground beanlike seeds found inside the red berries of any of several species of shrubs of the genus *Coffea*, originally native to Ethiopia and now cultivated throughout the tropics. It contains a stimulant, ⟩caffeine.

cultivation The shrub is naturally about 17 ft/ 5 m high, is pruned to about 7 ft/2 m, is fully fruit-bearing in 5 or 6 years, and lasts for 30 years. Coffee grows best on frost-free hillsides with moderate rainfall. The world's largest producers are Brazil, Colombia, and the Ivory Coast; others include Indonesia (Java), Ethiopia, India, Hawaii, and Jamaica.

history Coffee drinking began in Arab regions in the 14th century but did not become common in Europe until 300 years later, when the first coffee houses were opened in Vienna, and soon after in Paris and London. In the American colonies, coffee became the substitute for tea when tea was taxed by the British.

After the US became an independent nation, coffee remained the national drink and is so popular that "coffee breaks" are negotiated into labor contracts. Coffee is usually drunk hot, black or with cream and sugar; it is drunk cold as iced coffee, especially in summer.

Cognac town in Charente *département*, France, 25 mi/40 km W of Angoulême; population (1982) 21,000. Situated in a vine-growing district, Cognac has given its name to a brandy. Bottles, corks, barrels, and crates are manufactured here.

cognition in psychology, a general term covering the functions involved in synthesizing information—for example, perception (seeing, hearing, and so on), attention, memory, and reasoning.

cognitive therapy treatment for emotional disorders such as ⟩depression and ⟩anxiety, developed by Professor Aaron T Beck in the US. This approach encourages the patient to challenge the distorted and unhelpful thinking that is characteristic of these problems. The treatment includes ⟩behaviour therapy and has been most helpful for people suffering from depression.

Cohan George M(ichael) 1878–1942. US composer mainly for the theater. His 1904 Broadway hit musical *Little Johnny Jones* included his songs "Give My Regards to Broadway" and "Yankee Doodle Boy." His 1906 song "You're a Grand Old Flag" further associated him with popular patriotism, as did his World War I song "Over There" 1917.

Born in Providence, Rhode Island, to a theatrical family, Cohan spent his youth touring, writing songs, and appearing in musical comedies. In 1940 Cohan was honored by Congress. A film version of his life, *Yankee Doodle Dandy*, appeared 1942.

Cohan Robert Paul 1925– . US choreographer and founder of the London Contemporary Dance Theater 1969–87; now artistic director of the Contemporary Dance Theater. He was a student of Martha ⟩Graham and co-director of her company 1966–69. His works include *Waterless Method of Swimming Instruction* 1974 and *Mass for Man* 1985.

coherence in physics, property of two or more waves of a beam of light or other electromagnetic radiation having the same frequency and the same ⟩phase, or a constant phase difference.

cohesion in physics, a phenomenon in which interaction between two surfaces of the same material in contact makes them cling together (with two different materials the similar

phenomenon is called adhesion). According to kinetic theory, cohesion is caused by attraction between particles at the atomic or molecular level. ⟩Surface tension, which causes liquids to form spherical droplets, is caused by cohesion.

coil in medicine, another name for an ⟩intrauterine device.

Coimbra city in Portugal, on the Mondego River, 19 mi/32 km from the sea; population (1981) 71,800. It produces fabrics, paper, pottery, and cookies. There is a 12th-century Romanesque cathedral incorporating part of an older mosque, and a university, founded in Lisbon 1290 and transferred to Coimbra 1537. Coimbra was the capital of Portugal 1139–1385.

coin form of money. The right to make and issue coins is a state monopoly, and the great majority are tokens in that their face value is greater than that of the metal of which they consist.

A milled edge, originally used on gold and silver coins to avoid fraudulent "clipping" of the edges of precious-metal coins, is retained in some present-day token coinage.

The invention of coinage is attributed to the Chinese in the 2nd millennium BC, the earliest types being small-scale bronze reproductions of barter objects such as knives and spades. In the Western world, coinage of stamped, guaranteed weight originated with the Lydians of Asia Minor (early 7th century BC) who used electrum, a local natural mixture of gold and silver; the first to issue gold and silver coins was Croesus of Lydia in the 6th century BC.

coke clean, light fuel produced by the carbonization of certain types of coal. When this coal is strongly heated in airtight ovens (in order to release all volatile constituents), the brittle, silver-gray remains are coke. Coke comprises 90% carbon together with very small quantities of water, hydrogen, and oxygen, and makes a useful industrial and domestic fuel. The process was patented in England 1622, but it was only in 1709 that Abraham Darby devised a commercial method of production.

Coke Edward 1552–1634. Lord Chief Justice of England 1613–17. He was a defender of common law against royal prerogative; against Charles I he drew up the Petition of Right 1628, which defines and protects Parliament's liberties.

cola or *kola* any tropical tree of the genus *Cola*, especially *C. acuminata*, family Sterculiaceae. The nuts are chewed in W Africa for their high caffeine content, and in the West are used to flavor soft drinks.

Colbert Claudette. Adopted name of Claudette Lily Cauchoin 1905– . French-born film actress who lived in Hollywood from childhood. She was ideally cast in sophisticated, romantic roles, but had a natural instinct for comedy and appeared in several of Hollywood's finest, including *It Happened One Night* 1934 and *The Palm Beach Story* 1942.

Colbert Jean-Baptiste 1619–1683. French politician, chief minister to Louis XIV, and controller-general (finance minister) from 1665. He reformed the Treasury, promoted French industry and commerce by protectionist measures, and tried to make France a naval power equal to England or the Netherlands, while favoring a peaceful foreign policy.

Colbert, born in Reims, entered the service of Cardinal Mazarin and succeeded him as

chief minister to Louis XIV. In 1661 he set to work to reform the Treasury. The national debt was largely repaid, and the system of tax collection was drastically reformed. Industry was brought under state control, shipbuilding was encouraged by bounties, companies were established to trade with India and America, and colonies were founded in Louisiana, Guiana, and Madagascar. In his later years Colbert was supplanted in Louis's favor by the war minister Louvois (1641–1691), who supported a policy of conquests.

Colchester town and river port in England, on the river Colne, Essex; 50 mi/80 km NE of London; population (1981) 82,000. In an agricultural area, it is a market center with clothing manufacture and engineering and printing works. The University of Essex (1961) is at Wivenhoe to the southeast.

history Claiming to be the oldest town in England (Latin *Camulodunum*), Colchester dates from the time of ⟩Cymbeline (c. AD 10–43). It became a colony of Roman ex-soldiers in AD 50, and one of the most prosperous towns in Roman Britain despite its burning by Boudicca (Boadicea) in 61. Most of the Roman walls remain, as well as ruins of the Norman castle, and St Botolph's priory. Holly Tree Mansion (1718) is a museum of 18th-and 19th-century social life.

cold, common minor disease of the upper respiratory tract, caused by a variety of viruses. Symptoms are headache, chill, nasal discharge, sore throat, and occasionally cough. Research indicates that the virulence of a cold depends on psychological factors and either a reduction or an increase of social or work activity, as a result of stress, in the previous six months.

There is little immediate hope of an effective cure since the viruses transform themselves so rapidly.

cold-blooded of animals, dependent on the surrounding temperature; see ⟩*poikilothermy*.

cold fusion in nuclear physics, the fusion of atomic nuclei at room temperature. Were cold fusion to become possible it would provide a limitless, cheap, and pollution-free source of energy, and it has therefore been the subject of research around the world. In 1989, Martin Fleischmann (1927–) and Stanley Pons (1943–) of the University of Utah, claimed that they had achieved cold fusion in the laboratory, but their results could not be substantiated.

Cold Harbor, Battle of American Civil War engagement near Richmond, Virginia, June 1–12, 1864, in which the Confederate army under Robert E ⟩Lee repulsed Union attacks under Ulysses S ⟩Grant, inflicting as many as 6,000 casualties in an hour and forcing Grant to adopt a siege of Petersburg. This demonstrated the tenacity of the Confederate forces late in the war and kept Grant's army largely stationary until April 1865.

Colditz town in E Germany, near Leipzig, site of a castle used as a high-security prisoner-of-war camp (Oflag IVC) in World War II. Among daring escapes was that of British Captain Patrick Reid (1910–1990) and others Oct 1942. It became a museum 1989. In 1990 the castle was converted into a hotel.

Cold War ideological, political, and economic tensions 1945–90 between the USSR and Eastern Europe on the one hand and the US

Cold War: chronology

1947	The term "Cold War" was first used by Bernard Baruch in a speech referring to the Truman Doctrine in April.
1950–53	The Korean War.
1956	The USSR intervened in Hungary to put down a revolution.
1962	The Cuban missile crisis.
1964–75	The US participated in the Vietnam War.
1968	The USSR intervened in Czechoslovakia.
1972	SALT I accord on arms limitation signed by US and USSR, beginning a thaw, or détente, in East–West relations.
1979	The USSR invaded Afghanistan.
1980–81	US support for the Solidarity movement in Poland. US president Reagan called the USSR an "evil empire."
1982–1900	US covert and military intervention in Central America increased to aid right-wing groups.
1983	US president Reagan proposed to militarize space (Star Wars).
1986	Soviet leader Gorbachev made a proposal for nuclear disarmament that was turned down by Reagan.
1988	Soviet and US leaders reached accord on medium-range nuclear missiles.
1989	Widespread moves toward the abandonment of communism took place in Eastern European countries, including the opening of the Berlin Wall.
1990	Formal end of the Cold War declared in Nov. Treaty signed between NATO and Warsaw Pact countries on reduction of conventional forces in Europe. US president Bush announced the start of a "new world order."

and Western Europe on the other. The Cold War was exacerbated by propaganda, covert activity by intelligence agencies, and economic sanctions; it intensified at times of conflict anywhere in the world. Arms-reduction agreements between the US and USSR in the late 1980s, and a diminution of Soviet influence in Eastern Europe, symbolized by the opening of the Berlin Wall 1989, led to a reassessment of positions, and the "war" officially ended 1990. *origins* Mistrust between the USSR and the West dated from the Russian Revolution 1917 and contributed to the disagreements during and immediately after World War II over the future structure of Eastern Europe. The ▷Atlantic Charter signed 1941 by the US and the UK favored self-determination, whereas the USSR insisted on keeping the territory obtained as a result of the Hitler–Stalin pact of Aug 1939.

After the war the US was eager to have all of Europe open to Western economic interests, while the USSR, afraid of being encircled and attacked by its former allies, saw Eastern Europe as its own sphere of influence and, in the case of Germany, was looking to extract reparations. As the USSR increased its hold on the countries of Eastern Europe, the US pursued a policy of "containment" that involved offering material aid to Western Europe (the ▷Marshall Plan) and to Nazi-victimized countries such as Greece and Turkey. Berlin became the focal point of East–West tension (since it was zoned for military occupational governments of the US, UK, France, and USSR, yet was situated within what was then Soviet-controlled East Germany). This culminated in the Soviet blockade of the US, British, and French zones of the city 1948, which was relieved by a sustained airlift of supplies (see ▷Berlin blockade).

The increasing divisions between the capitalist and the communist worlds were reinforced by the creation of military alliances, the ▷North Atlantic Treaty Organization (NATO) 1949 in the West, and the ▷Warsaw Pact 1955 in the East.

The formal end of the Cold War was declared in Nov 1990 at the Paris Conference on Security and Cooperation in Europe (CSCE).

Cole Thomas 1801–1848. US painter, founder of the Hudson River school of landscape artists.

Cole wrote *An Essay on American Scenery* in 1835. Apart from panoramic views such as *The Oxbow* 1836 (Metropolitan Museum of Art, New York), he painted a dramatic historical series, *The Course of Empire* 1836 (New York Historical Society), influenced by the European artists Claude, Turner, and John Martin.

Coleman Ornette 1930– . US alto saxophonist and jazz composer. In the late 1950s he rejected the established structural principles of jazz for free avant-garde improvisation. He has worked with small and large groups, ethnic musicians of different traditions, and symphony orchestras.

coleoptile the protective sheath that surrounds the young shoot tip of a grass during its passage through the soil to the surface. Although of relatively simple structure, most coleoptiles are very sensitive to light, ensuring that seedlings grow upward.

Coleridge Samuel Taylor 1772–1834. English poet, one of the founders of the Romantic movement. A friend of Southey and Wordsworth, he collaborated with the latter on *Lyrical Ballads* 1798. His poems include "The Rime of the Ancient Mariner," "Christabel," and "Kubla Khan;" critical works include *Biographia Literaria* 1817.

While at Cambridge University, Coleridge was driven by debt to enlist in the Dragoons, and then in 1795, as part of an abortive plan to found a communist colony in the US with Robert Southey, married Sarah Fricker, from whom he afterwards separated. He became addicted to opium and from 1816 lived in Highgate, London, under medical care. As a philosopher, he argued inferentially that even in registering sense-perceptions the mind was performing acts of creative imagination, rather than being a passive arena in which ideas interact mechanistically.

A brilliant talker and lecturer, he was expected to produce some great work of philosophy or criticism. His *Biographia Literaria* 1817, much of it based on German ideas, is full of insight but its formlessness and the limited extent of his poetic output indicates a partial failure of promise.

Coleridge-Taylor Samuel 1875–1912. English

composer who wrote the cantata *Hiawatha's Wedding Feast* 1898, a setting in three parts of Longfellow's poem. The son of a West African doctor and an English mother, he was a student and champion of traditional black music.

Colette Sidonie-Gabrielle 1873–1954. French writer. At 20 she married Henri Gauthier-Villars, a journalist known as "Willy," under whose name and direction her four "Claudine" novels, based on her own early life, were written. Divorced 1906, she worked as a striptease and mime artist for a while, but continued to write. Works from this later period include *Chéri* 1920, *La Fin de Chéri/The End of Chéri* 1926, and *Gigi* 1944.

Colfax Schuyler 1823–1885. US political leader. Becoming active in Indiana state politics, he was first elected to the US House of Representatives 1854 and served as Speaker of the House 1863–69. A Radical Republican, Colfax was elected vice-president for Grant's first term 1869–73. He was not renominated because of charges of corruption and financial improprieties.

Born in New York, Colfax moved with his family to Indiana 1836 and, although having the benefit of little formal education, worked in a succession of jobs, including county auditor, newspaper reporter, and legal assistant.

colic spasmodic attack of pain in the abdomen, usually in infancy. Colicky pains are caused by the painful muscular contraction and subsequent distension of a hollow organ; for example, the bowels, gall bladder (biliary colic), or ureter (renal colic).

Characteristically the pain is severe during contraction of the muscular wall of the organ, then recedes temporarily as the muscle tires.

colitis inflammation of the colon (large intestine) with diarrhea (often bloody). It may be caused by food poisoning or some types of bacterial dysentery.

collage (French "gluing" or "pasting") technique of pasting paper and other materials to create a picture. Several artists in the early 20th century used collage: Jean (or Hans) Arp, Georges Braque, Max Ernst, and Kurt Schwitters, among others.

Many artists also experimented with *photomontage*, creating compositions from pieces of photographs rearranged with often disturbing effects.

collagen strong, rubbery ▷protein that plays a major structural role in the bodies of ▷vertebrates. Collagen supports the ear flaps and the tip of the nose in humans, as well as being the main constituent of tendons and ligaments. Bones are made up of collagen, with the mineral calcium phosphate providing increased rigidity.

collateral security available in return for a loan. Usually stocks, shares, property, or life insurance policies will be accepted as collateral.

collective bargaining the process whereby management, representing an employer, and a labor union, representing employees, agree to negotiate jointly terms and conditions of employment. Agreements can be company-based or industry-wide.

collective farm (Russian *kolkhoz*) farm in which a group of farmers pool their land, domestic animals, and agricultural implements, retaining as private property enough only for the members' own requirements. The profits of the farm are divided among its members. In cooperative farming, farmers retain private ownership of the land.

Collective farming was first developed in the USSR in 1917, where it became general after 1930. Stalin's collectivization drive 1929–33 wrecked a flourishing agricultural system and alienated the Soviet peasants from the land: 15 million people were left homeless, 1 million of whom were sent to labor camps and some 12 million deported to Siberia. In subsequent years, millions of those peasants forced into collectives died. Collective farming is practiced in other countries; it was adopted from 1953 in China, and Israel has a large number of collective farms (see ⬦kibbutz).

collective security system for achieving international stability by an agreement among all states to unite against any aggressor. Such a commitment was embodied in the post-World War I League of Nations and also in the United Nations, although the League was not, and the UN has not yet been, able to live up to the ideals of its founders.

collective unconscious in psychology, the shared pool of memories inherited from ancestors that Carl Jung suggested coexists with individual ⬦unconscious recollections. He thought it could affect individuals both for ill, in precipitating mental disturbance, and for good, in prompting achievements (for example, in the arts).

collectivization policy pursued by the Soviet leader Stalin in the USSR after 1928 to reorganize agriculture by taking land into state ownership or creating ⬦collective farms. Much of this was achieved during the first two so-called Five-Year Plans but only with much coercion and loss of life among the peasantry.

College Station city in E central Texas, NW of Houston, adjoining the city of Bryan. Texas A & M University is here; population (1990) 52,500.

collenchyma plant tissue composed of relatively elongated cells with thickened cell walls, in particular at the corners where adjacent cells meet. It is a supporting and strengthening tissue found in nonwoody plants, mainly in the stems and leaves.

collie sheepdog originally bred in Britain. The rough and smooth collies are about 2 ft/60 cm tall, and have long narrow heads and muzzles. They may be light to dark brown or silver-gray, with black and white markings. The border collie is a working dog, often black and white, about 20 in/50 cm tall, with a dense coat. The bearded collie is about the same size, and is rather like an Old English sheepdog in appearance.

collimator (1) small telescope attached to a larger optical instrument to fix its line of sight; (2) optical device for producing a nondivergent beam of light; (3) any device for limiting the size and angle of spread of a beam of radiation or particles.

Collingwood Robin George 1889–1943. English philosopher who believed that any philosophical theory or position could be properly understood only within its own historical context and not from the point of view of the present. His aesthetic theory is outlined in *Principles of Art* 1938.

Collins Michael 1890–1922. Irish nationalist. He was a Sinn Féin leader, a founder and director of intelligence of the Irish Republican Army

1919, minister for finance in the provisional government of the Irish Free State 1922 (see ⬦Ireland, Republic of), commander of the Free State forces in the civil war, and for ten days head of state before being killed.

Collins Phil(lip David Charles) 1951– . English pop singer, drummer, and actor. A member of the group Genesis from 1970, he has also pursued a successful middle-of-the-road solo career since 1981, with hits (often new versions of old songs) including "In the Air Tonight" 1981 and "Groovy Kind of Love" 1988.

Collins (William) Wilkie 1824–1889. English author of mystery and suspense novels. He wrote *The Woman in White* 1860 (with its fat villain Count Fosco), often called the first English detective novel, and *The Moonstone* 1868 (with Sergeant Cuff, one of the first detectives in English literature).

collision theory theory that explains how chemical reactions take place and why rates of reaction alter. For a reaction to occur the reactant particles must collide. Only a certain fraction of the total collisions cause chemical change; these are called *fruitful collisions*. The fruitful collisions have sufficient energy (activation energy) at the moment of impact to break the existing bonds and form new bonds, resulting in the products of the reaction. Increasing the concentration of the reactants and raising the temperature bring about more collisions and therefore more fruitful collisions, increasing the rate of reaction.

When a ⬦catalyst undergoes collision with the reactant molecules, less energy is required for the chemical change to take place, and hence more collisions have sufficient energy for reaction to occur. The reaction rate therefore increases.

colloid substance composed of extremely small particles of one material (the dispersed phase) evenly and stably distributed in another material (the continuous phase). The size of the dispersed particles (1–1,000 nanometers across) is less than that of particles in suspension but greater than that of molecules in true solution. Colloids involving gases include *aerosols* (dispersions of liquid or solid particles in a gas, as in fog or smoke) and *foams* (dispersions of gases in liquids). Those involving liquids include *emulsions* (in which both the dispersed and the continuous phases are liquids) and *sols* (solid particles dispersed in a liquid). Sols in which both phases contribute to a molecular three-dimensional network have a jellylike form and are known as *gels*; gelatin, starch "solution," and silica gel are common examples.

Milk is a natural emulsion of liquid fat in a watery liquid; synthetic emulsions such as some paints and cosmetic lotions have chemical emulsifying agents to stabilize the colloid and stop the two phases from separating out.

Colloids were first studied thoroughly by the British chemist Thomas Graham, who defined them as substances that will not diffuse through a semipermeable membrane (as opposed to what he termed crystalloids, solutions of inorganic salts, which will diffuse through).

Collor de Mello Fernando 1949– . Brazilian politician, president 1990–92. He founded the center-right National Reconstruction Party (PRN) 1989 and won that year's presidential election by promising to root out government corruption and entrenched privileges. However, rumors of his misconduct led to his constitutional removal from office by a vote of impeachment 1992.

Colman Ronald 1891–1958. English actor, in Hollywood from 1920, who played suave roles in *Beau Geste* 1924, *The Prisoner of Zenda* 1937, *Lost Horizon* 1937, and *A Double Life* 1947, for which he received an Academy Award.

Colmar capital of Haut-Rhin *département*, France, between the river Rhine and the Vosges mountains; population (1983) 82,500. It is the center of a wine-growing and market-gardening area. Industries include engineering, food processing, and textiles. The church of St Martin is 13th–14th century, and the former Dominican monastery, now the Unterlinden Museum, contains a Grünewald altarpiece.

Cologne (German *Köln*) industrial and commercial port in North Rhine–Westphalia, Germany, on the left bank of the Rhine, 22 mi/35 km from Düsseldorf; population (1988) 914,000. To the north is the Ruhr coalfield, on which many of Cologne's industries are based. They include motor vehicles, freight cars, chemicals, and machine tools. Cologne is an important transshipment center.

Founded by the Romans 38 BC and made a colony AD 50 under the name *Colonia Claudia Arae Agrippinensis* (hence the name Cologne), it became a leading Frankish city and during the Middle Ages was ruled by its archbishops. It was a free imperial city from 1288 until the Napoleonic age. In 1815 it passed to Prussia. The great Gothic cathedral was begun in the 13th century, but its towers were not built until the 19th century (completed 1880). Its university (1388–1797) was refounded 1919. Cologne suffered severely from aerial bombardment during World War II; 85% of the city and its three Rhine bridges were destroyed.

Colombia country in South America, bounded N by the Caribbean Sea, W by the Pacific Ocean, NW corner by Panama, E and NE by Venezuela, SE by Brazil, and SW by Peru and Ecuador.

government The 1991 constitution, with 397 articles, and one of the longest in the world, provides for an elected president and vice-president; a bicameral congress consisting of a senate (100 seats), elected nationally, and a house of representatives (160 seats), elected on a regional, department basis. Although it does not have a fully federal system, Colombia is divided into 32 regions, enjoying considerable autonomy, with governors appointed by the president and locally elected legislatures.
history Until it was conquered by Spain in the 16th century, the area was inhabited by the Chibcha Indians. From 1538 Colombia formed part of a colony known as New Granada, comprising Colombia, Panama, and most of Venezuela. In 1819 the area included Ecuador and became independent as Gran Colombia, a state set up by Simón Bolívar. Colombia became entirely independent 1886.
"La Violencia" In 1948 the left-wing mayor of Bogotá was assassinated, and there followed a decade of near civil war, "La Violencia," during which it is thought that over 250,000 people died. Left-wing guerrilla activity continued. In 1957, in an effort to halt the violence, the Conservative and Liberal parties formed a National Front, alternating the presidency between them. They were challenged 1970 by the National Popular Alliance (ANAPO), with a special appeal to the working classes, but the Conservative–Liberal coalition continued, and when in 1978 the Liberals won majorities in both chambers of congress and the presidency, they kept the National Front accord.

In 1982 the Liberals kept their majorities in congress, but Dr Belisario Betancur won the presidency for the Conservatives. He sought a truce with the left-wing guerrillas by granting them an amnesty and freeing political prisoners. He also embarked on a radical program of public works.

antidrug campaign When the minister of justice, who had been using harsh measures to curb drug dealing, was assassinated 1984, Betancur reacted by strengthening his antidrug campaign. In the 1986 elections Liberal Virgilio Barco Vargas won the presidency by a record margin. Three months after taking office, he announced the end of the National Front accord, despite a provision in the constitution that the opposition party always has the opportunity to participate in government if it wishes to. President Vargas declared a new campaign against cocaine traffickers following the assassination in Aug of Luis Carlos Galan, the leading candidate for the 1990 presidential elections. A bombing campaign was undertaken by the cartels in retaliation for confiscation of property and extradition to the US of leading cartel members, but the Colombian

security forces scored a major victory Dec 1989 with the killing in a shoot-out of drug lord José Rodriguez Gacha. US president Bush attended an antidrug summit in Colombia Feb 1990. Assembly elections were held Dec 1990, giving the Liberal Party a five-seat lead over the April 19th movement (M-19), with the Conservatives scoring lowest.

new constitution Under President Cesar Gaviria Trujillo a new constitution was adopted July 1991 which included a clause prohibiting the extradition of Colombians for trial in other countries. As a result, several leading drug traffickers surrendered or were arrested 1991, including the head of the Medellin cocaine cartel, Pablo Escobar. In the first congressional elections under the new constitution held Oct 1991, the Liberal Party retained its control of the senate.

drug baron escapes In July 1992, Escobar escaped from prison along with several other colleagues, purportedly through an underground tunnel system. *See illustration box.*

Colombo capital and principal seaport of Sri Lanka, on the W coast near the mouth of the

Colombia
Republic of (*República de Colombia*)

area 440,715 sq mi/1,141,748 sq km
capital Bogotá
cities Medellín, Cali, Bucaramanga; ports Barranquilla, Cartagena, Buenaventura
physical the Andes mountains run N–S; flat coastland in W and plains (llanos) in E; Magdalena River runs N to Caribbean Sea; includes islands of Providencia, San Andrés, and Mapelo
features Zipaquira salt mine and underground cathedral; Lake Guatavita, source of the legend of "El Dorado"
head of state and government Cesar Gaviria Trujillo from 1990
political system emergent democratic republic
political parties Liberal Party (PL), centrist; April 19 Movement (M-19); National Salvation Movement; Conservative Party, right-of-center **exports** emeralds (world's largest producer), coffee (world's second largest producer), cocaine (country's largest export), bananas, cotton, meat, sugar, oil, skins, hides, tobacco
currency peso
population (1990 est) 32,598,800 (mestizo 68%, white 20%, Amerindian 1%); growth rate 2.2% p.a.
life expectancy men 61, women 66; Indians 34
language Spanish

religion Roman Catholic 95%
literacy men 89%, women 87% (1987); Indians 40%
GDP $31.9 bn (1987); $1,074 per head
chronology
1886 Full independence achieved from Spain. Conservatives in power.
1930 Liberals in power.
1946 Conservatives in power.
1948 Left-wing mayor of Bogotá assassinated; widespread outcry.
1949 Start of civil war, "La Violencia," during which over 250,000 people died.
1957 Hoping to halt the violence, Conservatives and Liberals agreed to form a National Front, sharing the presidency.
1970 National Popular Alliance (ANAPO) formed as a left-wing opposition to the National Front.
1974 National Front accord temporarily ended.
1975 Civil unrest because of disillusionment with the government.
1978 Liberals, under Julio Turbay, revived the accord and began an intensive fight against drug dealers.
1982 Liberals maintained their control of congress but lost the presidency. The Conservative president, Belisario Betancur, granted guerrillas an amnesty and freed political prisoners.
1984 Minister of justice assassinated by drug dealers; campaign against them stepped up.
1986 Virgilio Barco Vargas, Liberal, elected president by record margin.
1989 Drug cartel assassinated leading presidential candidate; Vargas declared antidrug war; bombing campaign by drug lords killed hundreds; police killed José Rodríguez Gacha, one of the most wanted cartel leaders.
1990 Cesar Gaviria Trujillo elected president. Liberals maintained control of congress.
1991 New constitution prohibited extradition of Colombians wanted for trial in other countries; several leading drug traffickers arrested. Oct: Liberal Party won general election.
1992 One of leading drug barons, Pablo Escobar, escaped from prison.

Kelani River; population (1990) 615,000, Greater Colombo about 1,000,000. It trades in tea, rubber, and cacao. It has iron- and steelworks and an oil refinery.

Colombo was mentioned as **Kalambu** about 1340, but the Portuguese renamed it in honor of the explorer Christopher Columbus. The Dutch seized it 1656 and surrendered it to Britain 1796. Since 1983 the chief government offices have been located at nearby Sri-Jayawardenapura, east of the city.

Colombo Matteo Realdo *c.* 1516–1559. Italian anatomist who discovered pulmonary circulation, the process of blood circulating from the heart to the lungs and back.

This showed that ▷Galen's teachings were wrong, and was of help to William ▷Harvey in his work on the heart and circulation. Colombo was a pupil of Andreas ▷Vesalius and became his successor at the University of Padua.

Colombo Plan plan for cooperative economic and social development in Asia and the Pacific, established 1950. The 26 member countries are Afghanistan, Australia, Bangladesh, Bhutan, Cambodia, Fiji, India, Indonesia, Iran, Japan, South Korea, Laos, Malaysia, Maldives, Myanmar (Burma), Nepal, New Zealand, Pakistan, Papua New Guinea, Philippines, Singapore, Sri Lanka, Thailand, UK, and US. They meet annually to discuss economic and development plans such as irrigation, hydroelectric schemes, and technical training.

The plan has no central fund but technical assistance and financing of development projects are arranged through individual governments or the International Bank for Reconstruction and Development.

Colón second-largest city in Panama, at the Caribbean end of the Panama Canal; population (1990) 140,900. It has a special economic zone created 1948 used by foreign companies to avoid taxes on completed products in their home countries; $2 billion worth of goods passed through the zone in 1987, from dozens of countries and 600 companies. Unemployment in the city of Colón, outside the zone, was over 25% in 1991.

Founded 1850, and named **Aspinwall** 1852, it was renamed Colón 1890 in honor of the explorer Christopher Columbus.

Colón, Archipiélago de official name of the ▷Galápagos Islands.

colon in anatomy, the part of the large intestine between the cecum and rectum, where water and mineral salts are absorbed from digested food, and the residue formed into feces or fecal pellets.

colon in punctuation, a mark (:) intended to direct the reader's attention forward, usually because what follows explains or develops what has just been written (for example, *The farmer owned the following varieties of dogs: a spaniel, a pointer, a terrier, a border collie, and three mongrels*).

colonialism another name for ▷*imperialism*.

Colonna Vittoria *c.* 1492–1547. Italian poet. Many of her Petrarchan sonnets idealize her husband, who was killed at the battle of Pavia 1525. She was a friend of Michelangelo, who addressed sonnets to her.

colophon decorative device on the title page or spine of a book, the trademark of the individual publisher. Originally a colophon was an inscription on the last page of a book giving the writer or printer's name and the place and year of publication.

color quality or wavelength of light emitted or reflected from an object. Visible white light consists of electromagnetic radiation of various wavelengths, and if a beam is refracted through a prism, it can be spread out into a spectrum, in which the various colors correspond to different wavelengths. From long to short wavelengths (from about 700 to 400 nanometers) the colors are red, orange, yellow, green, blue, indigo, and violet.

When a surface is illuminated, some parts of the white light are absorbed, depending on the molecular structure of the material and the dyes applied to it. A surface that looks red absorbs light from the blue end of the spectrum, but reflects light from the red, long-wave end. Colors vary in brightness, hue, and saturation (the extent to which they are mixed with white).

Colorado river in North America, rising in the Rocky Mountains and flowing 1,450 mi/ 2,333 km to the Gulf of California through Colorado, Utah, Arizona (including the Grand Canyon), and N Mexico. The many dams along its course, including Hoover and Glen Canyon, provide power and irrigation water, but have destroyed wildlife and scenery, and very little water now reaches the sea. To the west of the river in SE California is the *Colorado Desert*, an arid area of 2,000 sq mi/5,000 sq km.

Its tributaries include the Gunnison, Green, Little Colorado, and Gila rivers. The Imperial Valley is irrigated by the Colorado River.

Colorado state in W central US; nickname Centennial State
area 104,104 sq mi/269,700 sq km
capital Denver
cities Colorado Springs, Aurora, Lakewood, Fort Collins, Greeley, Pueblo
physical Great Plains in the E; the main ranges of the Rocky Mountains (more than 14,000 ft/4,300 m); high plateaus of the Colorado Basin in the W
features Rocky Mountain National Park; Pike's Peak; prehistoric cliff dwellings of the Mesa Verde National Park; Garden of the Gods (natural sandstone sculptures); Dinosaur and Great Sand Dunes national monuments; mining "ghost" towns; ski resorts, including Aspen, Vail, Steamboat Springs; US Air Force Academy
products cereals, meat and dairy products, oil, coal, molybdenum, uranium, iron, steel, machinery
population (1990) 3,294,400
famous people Jack Dempsey, Douglas Fairbanks
history first visited by Spanish explorers in the 16th century; claimed for Spain 1706; east portion passed to the US 1803 as part of the Louisiana Purchase, the rest in 1845 and 1848 as a result of the Mexican War. It attracted

Colorado

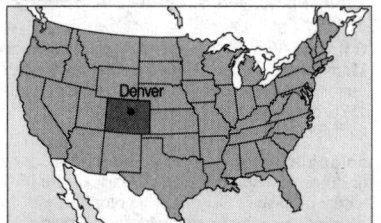

fur traders, and Denver was founded following the discovery of gold 1858. Colorado became a state 1876. Irrigated agriculture, ranching, tourism and outdoor sports, energy development, and the establishment of military bases fueled rapid growth after World War II.

Colorado Springs city in Colorado, 75 mi/ 120 km SE of Denver; population (1990) 281,100. At an altitude of about 6,000 ft/1,800 m, and surrounded by magnificent scenery, it was founded as a health resort 1871. A gold strike at nearby Cripple Creek 1892 aided its growth.

Colorado Springs is the home of the US Air Force Academy and the operations center of the North American Air Defense Command (NORAD).

color blindness hereditary defect of vision that reduces the ability to discriminate certain colors, usually red and green. The condition is sex-linked, affecting men more than women.

coloring food ⬦additive used to alter or improve the color of processed foods. Colorings include artificial colors, such as tartrazine and amaranth, which are made from petrochemicals, and the "natural" colors such as chlorophyll, caramel, and carotene. Some of the natural colors are actually synthetic copies of the naturally occurring substances, and some of these, notably the synthetically produced caramels, may be injurious to health.

Colosseum amphitheater in ancient Rome, begun by the emperor Vespasian to replace the one destroyed by fire during the reign of Nero, and completed by his son Titus AD 80. It was 615 ft/187 m long and 160 ft/49 m high, and seated 50,000 people. Early Christians were martyred there by lions and gladiators. It could be flooded for mock sea battles.

Colossians epistle in the New Testament addressed to the church at Colossae; it is attributed to St Paul.

Colossus of Rhodes bronze statue of Apollo erected at the entrance to the harbor at Rhodes 292–280 BC. Said to have been about 100 ft/ 30 m high, it was counted as one of the Seven Wonders of the World, but in 224 BC fell as a result of an earthquake.

Colt Samuel 1814–1862. US gunsmith, who in 1835 invented the revolver, a handgun that bears his name.

Born in Hartford, Connecticut, Colt developed a gun that had an automatic revolving cylinder. When the US Army ordered a large number of guns during the Mexican War, he established his factory first near New Haven, Connecticut, and then at Hartford, where his business grew into an immense arms-manufacturing establishment.

Coltrane John (William) 1926–1967. US jazz saxophonist who first came to prominence 1955 with the Miles ⬦Davis quintet, later playing with Thelonious Monk 1957. He was a powerful and individual artist, whose performances featured much experimentation. His 1960s quartet was highly regarded for its innovations in melody and harmony.

Like Charlie Parker, Coltrane marked a watershed in jazz and has been deified by his fans. The free-jazz movement of the 1960s owed much to his extended exploratory solos, for example on *Giant Steps* 1959, the year he traded tenor saxophone for soprano. A highly original musician, he has been much imitated, but the deeply emotional tone of his playing, for

example on *A Love Supreme* 1964, is impossible to copy.

coltsfoot perennial plant *Tussilago farfara*, family Compositae. The solitary yellow flower heads have many narrow rays, and the stems have large, purplish scales. The large leaf, up to 9 in/22 cm across, is shaped like a horse's foot and gives the plant its common name. Coltsfoot grows in Europe, N Asia, and N Africa, often on bare ground and in waste places, and has been introduced to North America. It was formerly used in medicine.

colugo SE Asian climbing mammal of the genus *Cynocephalus*, order Dermoptera, about 2 ft/60 cm long including the tail. It glides between forest trees using a flap of skin that extends from head to forelimb to hindlimb to tail. It may glide 425 ft/130 m or more, losing little height. It feeds largely on buds and leaves, and rests hanging upside down under branches.

There are two species, *C. variegatus* of Indochina and Indonesia, and *C. volans* of the Philippines.

Columba, St 521–597. Irish Christian abbot, missionary to Scotland. He was born in County Donegal of royal descent, and founded monasteries and churches in Ireland. In 563 he sailed with 12 companions to Iona, and built a monastery there that was to play a leading part in the conversion of Britain. Feast day June 9.

Columban, St 543–615. Irish Christian abbot. He was born in Leinster, studied at Bangor, and about 585 went to the Vosges, France, with 12 other monks and founded the monastery of Luxeuil. Later, he preached in Switzerland, then went to Italy, where he built the abbey of Bobbio in the Apennines. Feast day Nov 23.

Columbia city in central Missouri, NE of Jefferson City, seat of Boone County. It is the site of the University of Missouri 1853 and Stephens College 1833; population (1990) 69,100.

Columbia river in W North America, 1,215 mi/ 1,950 m in length. It rises in British Columbia and flows through Washington to the Pacific below Astoria, after forming much of the boundary between Washington and Oregon. This fast-running river has enormous hydroelectric potential and is harnessed for irrigation and power by the Grand Coulee and other major dams. Although it is famous for salmon fishing, the catch is now much reduced. The mouth of the Columbia was discovered 1792. The explorer David Thompson followed it from its source to its mouth 1811.

Columbia capital of South Carolina, on the Congaree River; population (1990) 98,100. Manufacturing includes textiles, plastics, electrical goods, fertilizers, and hosiery, but the chief product is fuel assemblies for nuclear reactors.

The main campus of the University of South Carolina is here. Columbia was laid out as the state capital 1786. It was burned by Union troops 1865, near the close of the Civil War.

Columbia Pictures US film production and distribution company founded 1924. It grew out of a smaller company founded 1920 by Harry and Jack Cohn and Joe Brandt. Under Harry Cohn's guidance, Columbia became a major studio by the 1940s, producing such commercial hits as *Gilda* 1946. After Cohn's death 1958 the studio remained successful, producing such international films as *Lawrence of Arabia* 1962.

The company now also produces television films through its subsidiary Screen Gems.

columbine any plant of the genus *Aquilegia* of the buttercup family Ranunculaceae. All are perennial herbs with divided leaves and flowers with spurred petals.

The eastern columbine *A. canadensis*, with red flowers, is native to E North America.

columbium (Cb) former name for the chemical element ◊niobium. The name is still used occasionally in metallurgy.

Columbus capital of Ohio, on the rivers Scioto and Olentangy; population (1990) 632,900. It has coalfield and natural gas resources nearby; its industries include the manufacture of automobiles, planes, missiles, and electrical goods.

Columbus city in W central Georgia, SW of Macon, across the Chattahoochee River from Phenix City, Alabama; seat of Muscogee County; population (1990) 178,700. Industries include processed food, machinery, iron and steel, textiles, cotton, and peanuts. It is a distribution center for surrounding farmlands, and lies just north of the US Army infantry base Fort Benning.

Columbus Christopher (Spanish *Cristóbal Colón*) 1451–1506. Italian navigator and explorer who made four voyages to the New World: 1492 to San Salvador Island, Cuba, and Haiti; 1493–96 to Guadaloupe, Montserrat, Antigua, Puerto Rico, and Jamaica; 1498 to Trinidad and the mainland of South America; 1502–04 to Honduras and Nicaragua.

Believing that Asia could be reached by sailing westward, he eventually won the support of King Ferdinand and Queen Isabella of Spain and set off on his first voyage from Palos Aug 3, 1492 with three small ships, the *Niña*, the *Pinta*, and his flagship the *Santa Maria*. Land was sighted Oct 12, probably Watling Island (now San Salvador Island), and within a few weeks he reached Cuba and Haiti, returning to Spain March 1493.

Born in Genoa, Columbus went to sea at an early age, and settled in Portugal 1478. After his third voyage 1498, he became involved in quarrels among the colonists sent to Haiti, and in 1500 the governor sent him back to Spain in chains. Released and compensated by the king, he made his last voyage 1502–04, during which he hoped to find a strait leading to India. He died in poverty in Valladolid and is buried in Seville cathedral.

In 1968 the site of the wreck of the *Santa Maria*, sunk off Hispaniola Dec 25, 1492, was located.

Columbus Day (Oct 12), a public holiday, is named for him.

column in architecture, a structure, round or polygonal in plan, erected vertically as a support for some part of a building. Cretan paintings reveal the existence of wooden columns in Aegean architecture in about 1500 BC. The Hittites, Assyrians, and Egyptians also used wooden columns, and they are a feature of the monumental architecture of China and Japan. In Classical architecture there are five principal types of column; see ◊order.

The Greeks and Romans used stone, as did later European, Asian, and American builders. Modern architects often design simple but elegant columns.

coma in astronomy, the hazy cloud of gas and dust that surrounds the nucleus of a ◊comet.

coma in medicine, a state of deep unconsciousness from which the subject cannot be roused and in which the subject does not respond to pain. Possible causes include head injury, liver failure, cerebral haemorrhage, and drug overdose.

coma in optics, one of the geometrical aberrations of a lens, whereby skew rays from a point object make a comet-shaped spot on the image plane instead of meeting at a point.

Comaneci Nadia 1961– . Romanian gymnast. She won three gold medals at the 1976 Olympics at the age of 14, and was the first gymnast to record a perfect score of 10 in international competition. Upon retirement she became a coach of the Romanian team, but defected to Canada 1989.

CAREER HIGHLIGHTS

Olympic Games
1976: gold: beam, vault, floor exercise
1980: gold: beam, parallel bars

combine harvester or *combine* machine used for harvesting cereals and other crops, so called because it combines the actions of reaping (cutting the crop) and threshing (beating the ears so that the grain separates).

Combines, drawn by horses, were used in the Californian cornfields in the 1850s. Today's mechanical combine harvesters are capable of cutting a swath of up to 30 ft/9 m or more.

combustion burning, defined in chemical terms as the rapid combination of a substance with oxygen, accompanied by the evolution of heat and usually light. A slow-burning candle flame and the explosion of a mixture of gasoline vapor and air are extreme examples of combustion.

Comecon (acronym for *Council for Mutual Economic Assistance*, or *CMEA*) economic organization 1949–91, linking the USSR with Bulgaria, Czechoslovakia, Hungary, Poland, Romania, East Germany (1950–90), Mongolia (from 1962), Cuba (from 1972), and Vietnam (from 1978), with Yugoslavia as an associated member. Albania also belonged 1949–61. Its establishment was prompted by the ◊Marshall Plan.

It was agreed 1987 that official relations should be established with the European Community, and a free-market approach to trading was adopted 1990. In Jan 1991 it was agreed that Comecon should be effectively disbanded and replaced by a new body, the Organization for International Economic Cooperation (OIEC), to be based probably in Budapest.

The OIEC would act as a "clearinghouse" for mutual E European trade, and would coordinate E European policy toward the European Community. Trade between member countries had been hampered by the lack of a convertible currency, the transferable ruble being merely an accounting device. From Jan 1991, intra-Comecon trade was switched from the transferable ruble to a hard-currency basis, with adverse consequences for E European importers of Soviet oil and gas. Comecon was formally disbanded June 1991.

Comédie Française French national theater (for both comedy and tragedy) in Paris, founded 1680 by Louis XIV. Its base is the Salle Richelieu on the right bank of the river Seine, and the Théâtre de l'Odéon, on the left bank, is a testing ground for avant-garde ideas.

comedy in the simplest terms, a literary work, usually dramatic, with a happy or amusing ending, as opposed to ◊tragedy. The comic tradition has undergone many changes since its Greek and Roman roots; although some comedies are timeless, such as those of Shakespeare and Molière, others are very representative of a particular era, relying upon topical allusion and current fashion.

The comic tradition was established by the Greek dramatists Aristophanes and Menander and the Roman writers Terence and Plautus. In medieval times, the Vices and Devil of the Morality plays developed into the stock comic characters of the Renaissance "Comedy of Humors" with such notable villains as Jonson's Mosca in *Volpone*. The enduring comedies of Shakespeare and Molière were followed during the 17th century in England by the witty "Comedy of Manners" of Restoration writers such as Etherege, Wycherley, and Congreve. Their often coarse but always vital comedy was toned down in the later Restoration dramas of Sheridan and Goldsmith. "Sentimental comedy" dominated most of the 19th century in England and the US, although little of it is remembered or revived today. Its close brought the realistic tradition of Shaw and the elegant social comedy of Wilde.

"Slapstick comedy" went from the stage to silent films from 1900 to 1930. The sophisticated comedy of Coward and Rattigan from the 1920s to the 1940s was performed on stage and in talking films, which also featured "screwball comedy." These were eclipsed during the 1950s and 1960s by a trend toward satire and cynicism, as seen in the works of Samuel Beckett. In the 1970s "black comedy" was dominant in the US and England, but "situation comedy," like Neil Simon's, continued to win audiences of stage, film, and television during the 1970s and 1980s.

comet small, icy body orbiting the Sun, usually on a highly elliptical path. A comet consists of a central nucleus a few miles across, and has been likened to a dirty snowball because it consists mostly of ice mixed with dust. As the comet approaches the Sun the nucleus heats up, releasing gas and dust which form a tenuous coma, up to 60,000 mi/100,000 km wide, around the nucleus. Gas and dust stream away from the coma to form one or more tails, which may extend for millions of miles.

Comets are believed to have been formed at the birth of the Solar System. Billions of them may reside in a halo (the ◊Oort cloud) beyond Pluto. The gravitational effect of passing stars pushes some toward the Sun, when they eventually become visible from Earth. Most comets swing around the Sun and return to distant space, never to be seen again for thousands or millions of years, although some, called *periodic comets*, have their orbits altered by the gravitational pull of the planets so that

major comets

name	first recorded sighting
Halley's comet	240 BC
Comet Tempel-Tuttle	AD 1366
Biela's comet	1772
Encke's comet	1786
Comet Swift-Tuttle	1862
Comet Ikeya-Seki	1965
Comet Kohoutek	1973
Comet West	1975
Comet Bowell	1980
Comet IRAS–Araki–Alcock	1983
Comet Austin	1989

they reappear every 200 years or less. Of the 800 or so comets whose orbits have been calculated, about 160 are periodic. The brightest is ▷Halley's comet. The one with the shortest known period is Encke's comet, which orbits the Sun every 3.3 years. A dozen or more comets are discovered every year, some by amateur astronomers.

comfrey any plant of the genus *Symphytum*, borage family Boraginaceae, with rough, hairy leaves and small bell-shaped flowers (blue, purple-pink, or white), found in Europe and W Asia.

The European species *S. officinale* was once used as a medicinal plant for treating wounds and various ailments, and is still sometimes used as a poultice. Up to 4 ft/1.2 m tall, it has hairy, winged stems, lanceolate (tapering) leaves, and white, yellowish, purple, or pink flowers in drooping clusters.

comic book publication in strip-cartoon form. Comic books are usually aimed at children, although in Japan, Latin America, and Europe millions of adults read them. Artistically sophisticated adult comics and **graphic novels** are produced in the US and several European countries, notably France. Comic books developed from ▷comic strips in newspapers or, like those of Walt ▷Disney, as spinoffs from animated cartoon films.

The first superhero, ▷Superman, created 1938 by Jerome Siegel and Joseph Shuster, soon had his own periodical, and others followed; the Marvel Comics group, formed 1961, was selling 50 million copies a year worldwide by the end of the 1960s and found a cult readership among college students for such titles as *Spiderman* and *The Incredible Hulk*. In Japan 1.9 billion comics were sold in 1987 – a third of all publications there.

comic strip or **strip cartoon** sequence of several frames of drawings in ▷cartoon style.

Strips, which may work independently or form installments of a serial, are usually humorous or satirical in content. Longer stories in comic-strip form are published separately as ▷comic books. Some have been made into animated films.

The first comic strip was "The Yellow Kid" by Richard Felton Outcault, which appeared in the Sunday newspaper *New York World* 1896; it was immediately successful and others soon followed. Some of the most admired early comic strips were the US "Gertie the Dinosaur" and "Happy Hooligan" as well as "Krazy Kat," which began 1910 and ended with the death of its creator, Richard Herriman, 1944. Current comic strips include "Peanuts" by Charles M Schulz (1922–   ), which began 1950 and was read daily by 60 million people by the end of the 1960s; the political "Doonesbury" by Garry Trudeau; the British "Andy Capp" by Reginald Smythe (1917–   ); and the French "Astérix" by Albert Uderzo and René Goscinny, which began in the early 1960s.

The most famous and beloved cartoon characters were devised by Walt ▷Disney from the 1930s; and superheroes such as Superman, Batman, and Flash Gordon have staying power.

Cominform (acronym for **Communist Information Bureau**) organization 1947–56 established by the Soviet politician Andrei Zhdanov (1896–1948) to exchange information between European communist parties. Yugoslavia was expelled 1948.

Comintern acronym from **Communist ▷International**.

comma punctuation mark (,) intended to provide breaks or pauses within a sentence; commas may come at the end of a clause, to set off a phrase, or in lists (for example, *apples, pears, plums, and pineapples*).

Some writers, uncertain where sentences properly end, use a comma instead of a full stop (period), writing *We saw John last night, it was good to see him again*, rather than *We saw John last night. It was good to see him again.* The meaning is entirely clear in both cases. One solution in such situations is to use a **semicolon** (;), which bridges the gap between the close association of the comma and the sharp separation of the period. Commas are also used to indicate parentheses (an explanatory or qualifying phrase not grammatically connected to the text into which it is inserted), as in *They told him—without any explanation—that he must leave immediately.*

command language in computing, a set of commands and the rules governing their use, by which users control a program. For example, an ▷operating system may have commands such as SAVE and DELETE, or a payroll program may have commands for adding and amending staff records.

commando member of a specially trained, highly mobile military unit. The term originated in South Africa in the 19th century, where it referred to Boer military reprisal raids against Africans and, in the South African Wars, against the British. Commando units have often carried out operations behind enemy lines.

commedia dell'arte popular form of Italian improvised comic drama in the 16th and 17th centuries, performed by trained troupes of actors and involving stock characters and situations. It exerted considerable influence on writers such as Molière and Carlo Goldoni, and on the genres of ▷pantomime, harlequinade, and the Punch and Judy show. It laid the foundation for a tradition of mime, strong in France, that has continued with the contemporary mime of Jean-Louis Barrault and Marcel Marceau.

commensalism in biology, a relationship between two ▷species whereby one (the commensal) benefits from the association, whereas the other neither benefits nor suffers. For example, certain species of millipede and silverfish inhabit the nests of army ants and live by scavenging on the refuse of their hosts, but without affecting the ants.

commodity something produced for sale. Commodities may be consumer goods, such as radios, or producer goods, such as copper bars.

Commodity markets deal in raw or semiraw materials that are amenable to grading and that can be stored for considerable periods without deterioration.

Commodity markets developed to their present form in the 19th century, when industrial growth facilitated trading in large, standardized quantities of raw materials. Most markets encompass trading in **commodity futures**—that is, trading for delivery several months ahead. Major commodity markets exist in Chicago, Tokyo, London, and elsewhere. Though specialized markets exist, such as that for silkworm cocoons in Tokyo, most trade relates to cereals and metals. *Softs* is a term used for most materials other than metals.

Commodus Lucius Aelius Aurelius AD 161–192. Roman emperor from 180, son of Marcus Aurelius Antoninus. He was a tyrant, spending lavishly on gladiatorial combats, confiscating the property of the wealthy, persecuting the Senate, and renaming Rome "Colonia Commodia." There were many attempts against his life, and he was finally strangled at the instigation of his mistress and advisers, who had discovered themselves on the emperor's death list.

Common Agricultural Policy (CAP) system that allows the member countries of the European Community (EC) jointly to organize and control agricultural production within their boundaries. The objectives of the CAP were outlined in the Treaty of Rome: to increase agricultural productivity, to provide a fair standard of living for farmers and their employees, to stabilize markets, and to assure the availability of supply at a price that was reasonable to the consumer. The CAP is increasingly criticized for its role in creating overproduction, and consequent environmental damage, and for the high price of food subsidies.

common law that part of the English law not embodied in legislation. It consists of rules of law based on common custom and usage and on judicial decisions. English common law became the basis of law in the US and many other English-speaking countries.

Common law developed after the Norman Conquest 1066 as the law common to the whole of England, rather than local law. As the court system became established (under Henry II), and judges' decisions became recorded in law reports, the doctrine of **precedent** developed. This means that, in deciding a particular case, the court must have regard to the principles of law laid down in earlier reported cases on the same, or similar points, although the law may be extended or varied if the facts of the particular case are sufficiently different. Hence, common law (sometimes called "case law" or "judge-made law") keeps the law in harmony with the needs of the community where no legislation is applicable or where the legislation requires interpretation.

common logarithm another name for a ▷logarithm to the base ten.

Common Market popular name for the **European Economic Community**; see ▷European Community (EC).

Commons, House of the lower but more powerful of the two parts of the British and Canadian ▷parliaments.

commonwealth body politic founded on law for the common "weal" or good. Political philosophers of the 17th century, such as Thomas Hobbes and John Locke, used the term to mean an organized political community. In Britain it was specifically applied to the regime (**the Commonwealth**) of Oliver ▷Cromwell 1649–60.

Commonwealth conference any consultation between the prime ministers (or defense, finance, foreign, or other ministers) of the sovereign independent members of the British Commonwealth. These are informal discussion meetings, and the implementation of policies is decided by individual governments.

The most notable conference occurred in 1926, which defined the relationship of the self-governing members.

Commonwealth Games multisport gathering of competitors from British Commonwealth countries, held every four years. The first meeting (known as the British Empire Games) was in Hamilton, Aug 1930.

Commonwealth of Independent States (CIS) successor body to the ⟡Union of Soviet Socialist Republics, initially formed as a new commonwealth of Slav republics on Dec 8, 1991 by the presidents of the Russian Federation, Belarus, and Ukraine. On Dec 21, eight of the nine remaining non-Slav republics—Moldova, Tajikistan, Armenia, Azerbaijan, Turkmenistan, Kazakhstan, Kyrgyzstan, and Uzbekistan—joined the CIS at a meeting held in Kazakhstan's capital, Alma Ata. The CIS formally came into existence in Jan 1992 when President Gorbachev resigned and the Soviet government voted itself out of existence. It has no real, formal political institutions and its role is uncertain. Its headquarters are in Mensk (Minsk), Belarus.

The main objectives of the CIS were to ensure that some measure of cooperation continued in economic, financial, and monetary matters, in order to avert a collapse in inter-republican trade and to coordinate price liberalization and market reform; to maintain some degree of coordination in foreign (and especially military) policy, and in such areas as transport and communications; and to ensure recognition of borders and thus prevent inter-republican conflicts.

With no formal political institutions, CIS decisions were arrived at through the holding of regular summits of heads of state and through the formation of ministerial committees, with, in theory, all CIS members being equals.

Initially, the inherited Soviet army was placed under a unified command. However, several republics, including Ukraine, made it clear that they would set up their own independent conventional forces, and in March 1992 Russia declared its similar intention. CIS members were also meant to keep a single currency, the *ruble*, but already in Jan 1992 Ukraine began issuing special coupons as a prelude to introducing its own currency.

Commonwealth, the (British) voluntary association of 50 countries and their dependencies that once formed part of the ⟡British Empire and are now independent sovereign states. They are all regarded as "full members of the Commonwealth." Additionally, there are some 20 territories that are not completely sovereign and remain dependencies of the UK or another of the fully sovereign members, and are regarded as "Commonwealth countries." Heads of government meet every two years, apart from those of Nauru and Tuvalu; however, Nauru and Tuvalu have the right to participate in all functional activities. The Commonwealth has no charter or constitution, and is founded more on tradition and sentiment than on political or economic factors.

Queen Elizabeth II was the formal head but not the ruler of 16 member states in 1992; 5 member states had their own monarchs; and 29 were republics. The Commonwealth secretariat, headed from Oct 1989 by Nigerian Emeka Anyaoku (1933–) as secretary-general, is based in London. The secretariat's staff come from a number of member countries, which also pay its operating costs.

On May 15, 1917 Jan Smuts, representing South Africa in the imperial war cabinet of World War I, suggested that "British Commonwealth of Nations" was the right title for the British Empire. The name was recognized in the Statute of Westminster 1931, but after World War II a growing sense of independent

Commonwealth, British

country	date joined
in Africa	
Botswana	1966
British Indian Ocean Territory	1965
Gambia	1965
Ghana	1957
Kenya	1963
Lesotho	1966
Malawi	1964
Mauritius	1968
Namibia	1990
Nigeria	1960
St Helena	1931
Seychelles	1976
Sierra Leone	1961
Swaziland	1968
Tanzania	1961
Uganda	1962
Zambia	1964
Zimbabwe	1980
in the Americas	
Anguilla	1931
Antigua and Barbuda	1981
Bahamas	1973
Barbados	1966
Belize	1982
Bermuda	1931
British Virgin Islands	1931
Canada	1931
Cayman Islands	1931
Dominica	1978
Falkland Islands	1931
Grenada	1974
Guyana	1966
Jamaica	1962
Montserrat	1931
St Christopher–Nevis	1983
St Lucia	1979
St Vincent and the Grenadines	1979
Trinidad and Tobago	1962
Turks and Caicos Islands	1931
Dependencies	
Ross Dependency	1931
in Asia	
Bangladesh	1972
Brunei	1984
Hong Kong	1931
India	1947
Malaysia	1957
Maldives	1982
Pakistan	1947
Singapore	1965
Sri Lanka	1948
in Australasia and the Pacific	
Australia	1931
Cook Islands	1931
Norfolk Island	1931
Kiribati	1979
Nauru	1968
New Zealand	1931
Niue	1931
Papua New Guinea	1975
Pitcairn Islands	1931
Solomon Islands	1978
Tokelau	1931
Tonga	1970
Tuvalu	1978
Vanuata 1980	
Western Samoa	1970
in Europe	
Channel Islands	1931
Cyprus	1961
Gibraltar	1931
Malta	1964
Isle of Man	1931
United Kingdom	1931

nationhood led to the simplification of the title to the Commonwealth.

commune group of people or families living together, sharing resources and responsibilities.

Communes developed from early 17th-century religious communities such as the Rosicrucians and Muggletonians, to more radical groups such as the ⟡Diggers and the ⟡Quakers. Many groups moved to America to found communes, such as the Philadelphia Society (1680s) and the Shakers, which by 1800 had ten groups in North America. The Industrial Revolution saw a new wave of utopian communities associated with the ideas of Robert ⟡Owen and Charles Fourier. Communes had a revival during the 1960s, when many small groups were founded. In 1970 it was estimated there were 2,000 communes in the US, and 100 in England.

The term also refers to a communal division or settlement in a communist country. In China, a policy of Mao Zedong involved the grouping of villages within districts (averaging 30,000 people) and thus, cooperatives were amalgamated into larger units, the communes. 1958 saw the establishment of peoples' communes (workers' combines) with shared living quarters and shared meals. Communes organized workers' brigades and were responsible for their own nurseries, schools, clinics, and other facilities.

The term can also refer to the 11th-century to 12th-century association of ⟡burghers in north and central Italy. The communes of many cities asserted their independence from the overlordship of either the Holy Roman emperor or the pope, only to fall under the domination of oligarchies or despots during the 13th and 14th centuries.

Commune, Paris two separate periods in the history of Paris 1789–94 and March—May 1871; see ⟡Paris Commune.

communication in biology, the signaling of information by one organism to another, usually with the intention of altering the recipient's behavior. Signals used in communication may be *visual* (such as the human smile or the display of colorful plumage in birds), *auditory* (for example, the whines or barks of a dog), *olfactory* (such as the odors released by the scent glands of a deer), *electrical* (as in the pulses emitted by electric fish), or *tactile* (for example, the nuzzling of male and female elephants).

communications satellite relay station in space for sending telephone, television, telex, and other messages around the world. Messages are sent to and from the satellites via ground stations. Most communications satellites are in ⟡geostationary orbit, appearing to hang fixed over one point on the Earth's surface.

The first satellite to carry TV signals across the Atlantic Ocean was *Telstar* in July 1962. The world is now linked by a system of communications satellites called Intelsat. Other satellites are used by individual countries for internal communications, or for business or military use. A new generation of satellites, called *direct broadcast satellites*, are powerful enough to transmit direct to small domestic aerials. The power for such satellites is produced by solar cells (see ⟡solar energy). The total energy requirement of a satellite is small; a typical communications satellite needs about 2 kW of power, the same as an electric heater.

Communion, Holy in the Christian church, another name for the ⟡Eucharist.

communism (French *commun* "common, general") revolutionary socialism based on the theories of the political philosophers Karl Marx and Friedrich Engels, emphasizing common ownership of the means of production and a planned economy. The principle held is that each should work according to their capacity and receive according to their needs. Politically, it seeks the overthrow of capitalism through a proletarian revolution. The first communist state was the USSR after the revolution of 1917. Revolutionary socialist parties and groups united to form communist parties in other countries (in the UK 1920). After World War II, communism was enforced in those countries that came under Soviet occupation. China emerged after 1961 as a rival to the USSR in world communist leadership, and other countries attempted to adapt communism to their own needs. The late 1980s saw a movement for more individual freedoms in many communist countries, culminating in the abolition or overthrow of communist rule in Eastern European countries and Mongolia, and further state repression in China. The failed hard-line coup in the USSR against President Gorbachev 1991 resulted in the effective abandonment of communism there.

Marx and Engels in the *Communist Manifesto* 1848 put forward the theory that human society, having passed through successive stages of slavery, feudalism, and capitalism, must advance to communism. This combines with a belief in economic determinism to form the central communist concept of *dialectical materialism*. Marx believed that capitalism had become a barrier to progress and needed to be replaced by a *dictatorship of the proletariat* (working class), which would build a socialist society.

The Social Democratic parties formed in Europe in the second half of the 19th century professed to be Marxist, but gradually began to aim at reforms of capitalist society rather than at the radical social change envisaged by Marx. The Russian Social Democratic Labor Party, led by Lenin, remained Marxist, and after the Nov 1917 revolution changed its name to Communist Party to emphasize its difference from Social Democratic parties elsewhere. The communal basis of feudalism was still strong in Russia, and Lenin and Stalin were able to impose the communist system.

China's communist revolution was completed 1949 under Mao Zedong. Both China and the USSR took strong measures to maintain or establish their own types of "orthodox" communism in countries on their borders (the USSR in Hungary and Czechoslovakia, and China in North Korea and Vietnam). In more remote areas (the USSR in the Arab world and Cuba, and China in Albania) and (both of them) in the newly emergent African countries, these orthodoxies were installed as the font of doctrine and the source of technological aid.

In 1956 the Soviet premier Nikita Khrushchev denounced *Stalinism*, and there were uprisings in Hungary and Poland. During the late 1960s and the 1970s it was debated whether the state requires to be maintained as "the dictatorship of the proletariat" once revolution on the economic front has been achieved, or whether it may then become the state of the entire people: Engels, Lenin, Khrushchev, and ⟡Liu Shaoqi held the latter view; Stalin and Mao the former.

Many communist parties in capitalist countries, for example, Japan and the *Eurocommunism* of France, Italy, and the

major part of the British Communist Party, have since the 1960s or later rejected Soviet dominance. In the 1980s there was an expansion of political and economic freedom in Eastern Europe: the USSR remained a single-party state, but with a relaxation of strict party orthodoxy and a policy of *perestroika* ("restructuring"), while the other Warsaw Pact countries moved toward an end to communist rule and its replacement by free elections within more democratic political systems.

In the Third World, Libya has attempted to combine revolutionary socialism with Islam; the extreme communist Khmer Rouge devastated Cambodia (then called Kampuchea) 1975–78; Latin America suffers from the US fear of communism in what it regards as its back yard, with the democratically elected Marxist regime in Chile violently overthrown 1973, and the socialist government of Nicaragua (until it fell 1990) involved in a prolonged civil war against US-backed guerrillas (Contras).

Communism Peak alternate form of Pik ⟡Kommunizma, the highest mountain in the ⟡Pamirs.

community in the social sciences, the sense of identity, purpose, and companionship that comes from belonging to a particular place, organization, or social group. The concept dominated sociological thinking in the first half of the 20th century, and inspired the academic discipline of *community studies*.

community in ecology, an assemblage of plants, animals, and other organisms living within a circumscribed area. Communities are

usually named by reference to a dominant feature such as characteristic plant species (for example, oak-hickory community), or a prominent physical feature (for example, a freshwater-pond community).

commutative operation in mathematics, an operation that is independent of the order of the numbers or symbols concerned. For example, addition is commutative: the result of adding $4 + 2$ is the same as that of adding $2 + 4$; subtraction is not: $4 - 2 = 2$, but $2 - 4 = -2$. Compare ⟡associative operation and ⟡distributive operation.

commutator device in a DC (direct-current) electric motor that reverses the current flowing in the armature coils as the armature rotates. A DC generator, or ⟡dynamo, uses a commutator to convert the AC (alternating current) generated in the armature coils into DC. A commutator consists of opposite pairs of conductors insulated from one another, and contact to an external circuit is provided by carbon or metal brushes.

Como city in Lombardy, Italy, on Lake Como at the foot of the Alps; population (1981) 95,500. Motorcycles, glass, silk, and furniture are produced here. The river Adda flows north–south through the lake, and the shores are extremely beautiful. Como has a marble cathedral, built 1396–1732, and is a tourist resort.

Comorin southernmost cape of the Indian subcontinent, in Tamil Nadu, where the Indian Ocean, Bay of Bengal, and Arabian Sea meet.

Comoros group of islands in the Indian Ocean between Madagascar and the east coast of Africa. Three of them—Njazidja, Nzwani,

Comoros
Federal Islamic Republic of (*Jumhurīyat al-Qumur al-Itthādīyah al-Islāmīyah* **)**

area 719 sq mi/1,862 sq km
capital Moroni
cities Mutsamudu, Domoni, Fomboni
physical comprises the volcanic islands of Njazídja, Nzwani, and Mwali (formerly Grande Comore, Anjouan, Moheli); at N end of Mozambique Channel
features active volcano on Njazídja; poor tropical soil
head of state and government Said Mohammad Djohar (interim administration) from 1989
political system authoritarian nationalism
political parties Comoran Union for Progress (Udzima), nationalist Islamic; National Union

for Congolese Democracy (UNDC), left of center; Popular Democratic Movement (MDP), centrist
exports copra, vanilla, cocoa, sisal, coffee, cloves, essential oils
currency CFA franc
population (1990 est) 459,000; growth rate 3.1% p.a.
life expectancy men 48, women 52
languages Arabic (official), Comorian (Swahili and Arabic dialect), Makua, French
religions Muslim (official) 86%, Roman Catholic 14%
literacy 15%
GDP $198 million (1987); $468 per head
chronology
1975 Independence achieved from France, but Mayotte remained part of France. Ahmed Abdallah elected president. The Comoros joined the United Nations.
1976 Abdallah overthrown by Ali Soilih.
1978 Soilih killed by mercenaries working for Abdallah. Islamic republic proclaimed and Abdallah elected president.
1979 The Comoros became a one-party state; powers of the federal government increased.
1985 Constitution amended to make Abdallah head of government as well as head of state.
1989 Abdallah killed by French mercenaries who took control of government; under French and South African pressure, mercenaries left Comoros, turning authority over to French administration and interim president Said Mohammad Djohar.
1990 Antigovernment coup foiled.
1992 Third transitional government appointed. Antigovernment coup foiled.

and Mwali—form the republic of Comoros; the fourth island, Mayotte, is a French dependency.

government Under the 1978 constitution there is a president, elected by universal adult suffrage for a six-year term, with an appointed council of ministers and a single-chamber federal assembly of 42 members elected for five years. Although each of the four main islands has a degree of autonomy, with its own governor and council, the system is a limited form of federalism, since the president appoints the governors and the federal government is responsible for the islands' resources.

history Originally inhabited by Asians, Africans, and Indonesians, the Comoros islands were controlled by Muslim sultans until the French acquired them 1841–1909. The islands became a French colony 1912 and were attached to Madagascar 1914–47, when they were made a French overseas territory. Internal self-government was attained 1961, but full independence not achieved until 1975 because of Mayotte's reluctance to sever links with France. Although the Comoros joined the United Nations 1975, with Ahmed Abdallah as president, Mayotte remained under French administration. Relations with France deteriorated as Ali Soilih, who had overthrown Abdallah, became more powerful as president under a new constitution. In 1978 he was killed by French mercenaries working for Abdallah. Abdallah's use of mercenaries in his return to power led to the Comoros' expulsion from the Organization of African Unity.

one-party state A federal Islamic republic was proclaimed, a new constitution adopted, and Abdallah reconfirmed as president in an election where he was the only candidate. Diplomatic relations with France were restored. In 1979 the Comoros became a one-party state, and government powers were increased. In the same year a plot to overthrow Abdallah was foiled. In 1984 he was reelected president, and in the following year the constitution was amended, abolishing the post of prime minister and making Abdallah head of government as well as head of state.

In Nov 1989 Abdallah was assassinated during an attack on the presidential palace led by a French mercenary, Col Bob Denard. Denard was subsequently arrested by French army units and returned to France. A provisional military administration was set up, with Said Mohammad Djohar as interim president. In Aug 1990 an attempted antigovernment coup was foiled. The third transitional government in a year was appointed July 1992, and in Sept a coup attempt by army officers was thwarted. *See illustration box.*

compact disk disk for storing digital information, about 4.5 in/12 cm across, mainly used for music, when it can have over an hour's playing time. Entirely different from a conventional LP (long-playing) phonograph record, the compact disc is made of aluminum with a transparent plastic coating; the metal disk underneath is etched by a ▷laser beam with microscopic pits that carry a digital code representing the sounds. During playback, a laser beam reads the code and produces signals that are changed into near-exact replicas of the original sounds.

CD-ROM, or compact-disk read-only memory, is used to store written text or pictures rather than music. The disks are ideal for large works, such as catalogs and encyclopedias. CD-I, or compact-disk interactive, is a form

of CD-ROM used with a computerized reader, which responds intelligently to the user's instructions. These disks are used, for example, with audiovisual material, for training. Recordable CDs, called WORMs ('write once, read many times'), are used as computer disks, but are as yet too expensive for home use. Erasable CDs, which can be erased and recorded many times, are also used by the computer industry. These are coated with a compound of cobalt and gadolinium, which alters the polarization of light falling on it. In the reader, the light reflected from the disk is passed through polarizing filters and the changes in polarization are converted into electrical signals.

company see ▷corporation.

company in the army, a subunit of a ▷battalion. It consists of about 120 soldiers, and is commanded by a captain in the US army and by a major in the British army. Four or five companies make a battalion.

comparative advantage law of international trade first elaborated by David Ricardo showing that trade becomes advantageous if the cost of production of particular items differs between one country and another.

At a simple level, if wine is cheaper to produce in country A than in country B, and the reverse is true of cheese, A can specialize in wine and B in cheese and they can trade to mutual benefit.

compass any instrument for finding direction. The most commonly used is a magnetic compass, consisting of a thin piece of magnetic material with the north-seeking pole indicated, free to rotate on a pivot and mounted on a compass card on which the points of the compass are marked. When the compass is properly adjusted and used, the north-seeking pole will point to the magnetic north, from which true north can be found from tables of magnetic corrections.

Compasses not dependent on the magnet are gyrocompasses, dependent on the ▷gyroscope, and radiocompasses, dependent on the

use of radio. These are unaffected by the presence of iron and by magnetic anomalies of the Earth's magnetic field, and are widely used in ships and aircraft.

A compass (or pair of compasses) is also an instrument used for drawing circles or taking measurements, consisting of a pair of pointed legs connected by a central pivot.

compensation point in biology, the point at which there is just enough light for a plant to survive. At this point all the food produced by ▷photosynthesis is used up by ▷respiration. For aquatic plants, the compensation point is the depth of water at which there is just enough light to sustain life (deeper water = less light = less photosynthesis).

competence and performance in linguistics, the potential and actual utterances of a speaker. As formulated by the linguist Noam ▷Chomsky, a person's linguistic competence is the set of internalized rules in his or her brain that makes it possible to understand and produce language—rules that stipulate, for example, the order words take to form a sentence. A person's performance consists of the actual phrases and sentences he or she produces on the basis of these inner rules.

competition in ecology, the interaction between two or more organisms, or groups of organisms (for example, species), that use a common resource which is in short supply. Competition invariably results in a reduction in the numbers of one or both competitors, and in ▷evolution contributes both to the decline of certain species and to the evolution of ▷adaptations.

competition, perfect in economics, a market situation in which there are many potential and actual buyers and sellers, each being too small to be an individual influence on the price; the market is open to all and the products being traded are homogeneous. At the same time, the producers are seeking the maximum profit and consumers the best value for money.

compact disk *The compact disk is a digital storage device; music is recorded as a series of etched pits representing numbers in digital code.*

There are many economic, social, and political barriers to perfect competition, not least because the underlying assumptions are unrealistic and in conflict. Nevertheless some elements are applicable in free trade.

Compiègne town in Oise *département*, France, on the river Oise near its confluence with the river Aisne; population (1983) 37,250. It has an enormous château, built by Louis XV. The armistices of 1918 and 1940 were signed (the latter by Hitler and Pétain) in a railroad coach in the forest of Compiègne.

compiler computer program that translates programs written in a ⟩high-level language into machine code (the form in which they can be run by the computer). The compiler translates each high-level instruction into several machine-code instructions—in a process called *compilation*—and produces a complete independent program that can be run by the computer as often as required, without the original source program being present.

Different compilers are needed for different high-level languages and for different computers. In contrast to using an ⟩interpreter, using a compiler adds slightly to the time needed to develop a new program because the machine-code program must be recompiled after each change or correction. Once compiled, however, the machine-code program will run much faster than an interpreted program.

complement the set of the elements within the universal set that are not contained in the designated set. For example, if the universal set is the set of all positive whole numbers and the designated set S is the set of all even numbers, then the complement of S (denoted S') is the set of all odd numbers.

complementary angles two angles that add up to 90°.

complementary number in number theory, the number obtained by subtracting a number from its base. For example, the complement of 7 in numbers to base 10 is 3. Complementary numbers are necessary in computing, as the only mathematical operation of which digital computers (including pocket calculators) are directly capable is addition. Two numbers can be subtracted by adding one number to the complement of the other; two numbers can be divided by using successive subtraction (which, using complements, becomes successive addition); and multiplication can be performed by using successive addition.

The four main operations of arithmetic can thus all be reduced to various types of addition and made with the capability of a digital computer, using the binary number system.

complementation in genetics, the interaction that can occur between two different mutant alleles of a gene in a ⟩diploid organism, to make up for each other's deficiencies and allow the organism to function normally.

complex in psychology, a group of ideas and feelings that have become repressed because they are distasteful to the person in whose mind they arose, but are still active in the depths of the person's unconscious mind, continuing to affect his or her life and actions, even though he or she is no longer fully aware of their existence. Typical examples include the ⟩Oedipus complex and the inferiority complex.

complex number in mathematics, a number written in the form $a + ib$, where a and b are ⟩real numbers and i is the square root of –1 (that is, $i^2 = -1$); i used to be known as the

Argand diagram

complex number *A complex number can be represented graphically as a line whose end-point coordinates equal the real and imaginary parts of the complex number.*

"imaginary" part of the complex number. Some equations in algebra, such as those of the form $x^2 + 5 = 0$, cannot be solved without recourse to complex numbers, because the real numbers do not include square roots of negative numbers.

The sum of two or more complex numbers is obtained by adding separately their real and imaginary parts, for example, $(a + bi) + (c + di) = (a + c) + (b + d)i$.

Complex numbers can be represented graphically on an Argand diagram, which uses rectangular ⟩Cartesian coordinates in which the x-axis represents the real part of the number and the y-axis the imaginary part. Thus the number $z = a + bi$ is plotted as the point (a, b). Complex numbers have applications in various areas of science, such as the theory of alternating currents in electricity.

component in mathematics, one of the the vectors produced when a single vector is resolved into two or more parts. The perpendicular components add up to the original vector.

componential analysis in linguistics, the analysis of the elements of a word's meaning. The word *boy*, for example, might be said to have three basic meaning elements (or semantic properties): "human," "young," and "male;" and so might the word *murder*. "kill," "intentional," and "illegal."

Compositae daisy family, comprising dicotyledonous flowering plants characterized by flowers borne in composite heads (see ⟩capitulum). It is the largest family of flowering plants, the majority being herbaceous. Birds seem to favor the family for use in nest "decoration," possibly because many species either

repel or kill insects (see ⟩pyrethrum). Species include the daisy and dandelion; food plants such as the artichoke, lettuce, and safflower; and the garden varieties of chrysanthemum, dahlia, and zinnia.

composite in industry, any purpose-designed engineering material created by combining single materials with complementary properties into a composite form. Most composites have a structure in which one component consists of discrete elements, such as fibers, dispersed in a continuous matrix. For example, lengths of asbestos, glass, or carbon steel, or "whiskers" (specially grown crystals a few millimeters long) of substances such as silicon carbide may be dispersed in plastics, concrete, or steel.

Composite in Classical architecture, one of the five types of ⟩column. See ⟩order.

composite function in mathematics, a function made up of two or more other functions carried out in sequence, usually denoted by * or ∘, as in the relation $(f*g) x = f[g(x)]$.

Usually, composition is not commutative: $(f*g)$ is not necessarily the same as $(g*f)$.

compost organic material decomposed by bacteria under controlled conditions to make a nutrient-rich natural fertilizer for use in gardening or farming. A well-made compost heap reaches a high temperature during the composting process, killing most weed seeds that might be present.

As the ⟩decomposers feed, they raise the temperature in the center of the compost as high as 150°F/66°C.

compound chemical substance made up of two or more ⟩elements bonded together, so that they cannot be separated by physical means. Compounds are held together by ionic or covalent bonds.

compound interest interest calculated by computing the rate against the original capital plus reinvested interest each time the interest becomes due. When simple interest is calculated, only the interest on the original capital is added.

Compromise of 1850 in US history, legislative proposals designed to resolve the sectional conflict between North and South over the admission of California to the Union 1850.

computer *A desktop computer is made of a number of connected units.*

Slavery was prohibited in California, but a new fugitive slave law was passed to pacify the slave states. The Senate debate on the compromise lasted nine months: acceptance temporarily revitalized the Union.

Compton Arthur Holly 1892–1962. US physicist known for his work on X-rays. Working at Chicago 1923 he found that X-rays scattered by such light elements as carbon increased their wavelengths. Compton concluded from this unexpected result that the X-rays were displaying both wavelike and particlelike properties, since named the **Compton effect**. He shared a Nobel Prize 1927 with Scottish physicist Charles Wilson (1869–1959).

Compton-Burnett Ivy 1892–1969. English novelist. She used dialogue to show reactions of small groups of characters dominated by the tyranny of family relationships. Her novels, set at the turn of the century, include *Pastors and Masters* 1925, *More Women Than Men* 1933, and *Mother and Son* 1955.

computer programmable electronic device that processes data and performs calculations and other symbol-manipulation tasks. There are three types: the ◊*digital computer*, which manipulates information coded as binary numbers (see ◊binary number system); the ◊*analog computer*, which works with continuously varying quantities; and the **hybrid computer**, which has characteristics of both analog and digital computers.

There are four types of digital computer, corresponding roughly to their size and intended use. *Microcomputers* are the smallest and most common, used in small businesses, at home, and in schools. They are usually single-user machines. *Minicomputers* are found in medium-sized businesses and university departments. They may support from 10 to 200 or so users at once. *Mainframes*, which can often service several hundred users simultaneously, are found in large organizations, such as national companies and government departments. *Supercomputers* are mostly used for highly complex scientific tasks, such as analyzing the results of nuclear physics experiments and weather forecasting.

Microcomputers now come in a range of sizes from battery-powered pocket PCs and electronic organizers, notebook and laptop PCs to floor-standing tower systems that may serve local area ◊networks or work as minicomputers. Indeed, most minicomputers are now built using low-cost microprocessors, and large-scale computers built out of multiple microprocessors are starting to challenge traditional mainframe and supercomputer designs.

history Computers are only one of the many kinds of ◊computing device. The first mechanical computer was conceived by Charles ◊Babbage 1835, but it never went beyond the design stage. In 1943, more than a century later, Thomas Flowers built Colossus, the first electronic computer. Working with him at the time was Alan Turing, a mathematician who seven years earlier had published a paper on the theory of computing machines that had a major impact on subsequent developments. John von Neumann's computer, EDVAC, built 1949, was the first to use binary arithmetic and to store its operating instructions internally. This design still forms the basis of today's computers.

basic components At the heart of a computer is the ◊central processing unit (CPU), which performs all the computations. This is

computing: chronology

1614	John Napier invented logarithms.
1615	William Oughtred invented the slide rule.
1623	Wilhelm Schickard (1592–1635) invented the mechanical calculating machine.
1645	Blaise Pascal produced a calculator.
1672–74	Gottfried Leibniz built his first calculator, the Stepped Reckoner.
1801	Joseph-Marie Jacquard developed an automatic loom controlled by punch cards.
1820	The first mass-produced calculator, the Arithometer, was developed by Charles Thomas de Colmar (1785-1870).
1822	Charles Babbage completed his first model for the difference engine.
1830s	Babbage created the first design for the analytical engine.
1890	Herman Hollerith developed the punched-card ruler for the US census.
1936	Alan Turing published the mathematical theory of computing.
1938	Konrad Zuse constructed the first binary calculator, using Boolean algebra.
1939	US mathematician and physicist J V Atanasoff (1903–) became the first to use electronic means for mechanizing arithmetical operations.
1943	The Colossus electronic code-breaker was developed at Bletchley Park, England. The Harvard University Mark I or Automatic Sequence Controlled Calculator (partly financed by IBM) became the first program-controlled calculator.
1946	ENIAC (acronym for electronic numerator, integrator, analyzer, and computer), the first general purpose, fully electronic digital computer, was completed at the University of Pennsylvania.
1948	Manchester University (England) Mark I, the first stored-program computer, was completed. William Shockley of Bell Laboratories invented the transistor.
1951	Launch of Ferranti Mark I, the first commercially produced computer. Whirlwind, the first real-time computer, was built for the US air-defense system. Grace Murray Hopper of Remington Rand invented the compiler computer program.
1952	EDVAC (acronym for electronic discrete variable computer) was completed at the Institute for Advanced Study, Princeton (by John Von Neumann and others).
1953	Magnetic core memory was developed.
1958	The first integrated circuit was constructed.
1963	The first minicomputer was built by Digital Equipment (DEC). The first electronic calculator was built by Bell Punch Company.
1964	Launch of IBM System/360, the first compatible family of computers. John Kemeny and Thomas Kurtz of Dartmouth College invented BASIC (Beginner's All-purpose Symbolic Instruction Code), a computer language similar to FORTRAN.
1965	The first supercomputer, the Control Data CD6600, was developed.
1971	The first microprocessor, the Intel 4004, was announced.
1974	CLIP–4, the first computer with a parallel architecture, was developed by John Backus at IBM.
1975	Altair 8800, the first personal computer (PC), or microcomputer, was launched.
1981	The Xerox Star system, the first WIMP system (acronym for windows, icons, menus, and pointing devices), was developed. IBM launched the IBM PC.
1984	Apple launched the Macintosh computer.
1985	The Inmos T414 transputer, the first "off-the-shelf" microprocessor for building parallel computers, was announced.
1988	The first optical microprocessor, which uses light instead of electricity, was developed.
1989	Wafer-scale silicon memory chips, able to store 200 million characters, were launched.
1990	Microsoft released Windows 3, a popular windowing environment for PCs.
1991	IBM developed world's fastest high-capacity memory computer chip, SRAM (static random access memory), able to send or receive 8 billion bits of information per second.
1992	Philips launched the CD-I (compact disk-interactive) player, based on CD audio technology, to provide interactive multimedia programs for the home user.

supported by memory, which holds the current program and data, and "logic arrays," which help move information around the system. A main power supply is needed and, for a mainframe or minicomputer, a cooling system. The computer's "device driver" circuits control the ◊peripheral devices that can be attached. These will normally be keyboards and ◊VDTs (visual display terminals) for user input and output, disk drive units for mass memory storage, and printers for printed output.

computer-aided design use of computers to create and modify design drawings; see ◊CAD.

computer-aided manufacture use of computers to regulate production processes in industry; see ◊CAM.

computer-assisted learning use of computers in education and training; see ◊CAL.

computer game or *video game* any

computer-controlled game in which the computer (usually) opposes the human player. Computer games typically employ fast, animated graphics on a ◊VDT (visual display terminal), and synthesized sound.

Commercial computer games became possible with the advent of the ◊microprocessor in the mid-1970s and rapidly became popular as amusement-arcade games, using dedicated chips. Available games range from chess to fighter-plane simulations.

computer generation any of the five broad groups into which computers may be classified:

first generation the earliest computers, developed in the 1940s and 1950s, made from valves and wire circuits;

second generation from the early 1960s, based on transistors and printed circuits;

third generation from the late 1960s, using integrated circuits and often sold as families of computers, such as the IBM 360 series;

fourth generation using ⟡microprocessors, large-scale integration (LSI), and sophisticated programming languages, still in use in the 1990s; and

fifth generation based on parallel processors and very large-scale integration, currently under development.

computer graphics use of computers to display and manipulate information in pictorial form. The output may be as simple as a pie chart, or as complex as an animated sequence in a science-fiction film, or a seemingly three-dimensional engineering blueprint. Input may be achieved by drawing with a mouse or stylus on a graphics tablet, or by drawing directly on the screen with a light pen. The drawing is stored in the computer, often as ⟡vector graphics. Computer graphics are increasingly used in computer-aided design (⟡CAD), and to generate models and simulations in engineering, meteorology, medicine and surgery, and other fields of science.

computer literacy ability to understand and make use of computer technology in an everyday context.

computer simulation representation of a real-life situation in a computer program. For example, the program might simulate the flow of customers arriving at a bank. The user can alter variables, such as the number of cashiers on duty, and see the effect.

computing device any device built to perform or help perform computations, such as the ⟡abacus, ⟡slide rule, or ⟡computer.

The earliest known example is the abacus. Mechanical devices with sliding scales (similar to the slide rule) date from ancient Greece. In 1642, French mathematician Blaise Pascal built a mechanical adding machine and, in 1671, German mathematician Gottfried Leibniz produced a machine to carry out multiplication. The first mechanical computer, the ⟡analytical engine, was designed by Charles Babbage 1835. For the subsequent history of computing, see ⟡computer.

Comte Auguste 1798–1857. French philosopher regarded as the founder of sociology, a term he coined 1830. He sought to establish sociology as an intellectual discipline, using a scientific approach ("positivism") as the basis of a new science of social order and social development.

Comte, born in Montpellier, was expelled from the Paris Ecole Polytechnique for leading a student revolt 1816. In 1818 he became secretary to the socialist Saint-Simon and was much influenced by him. He began lecturing on the "Positive Philosophy" 1826, but almost immediately succumbed to a nervous disorder and once tried to commit suicide in the river Seine. On his recovery he resumed his lectures and mathematical teaching.

In his six-volume *Cours de philosophie positive* 1830–42 he argued that human thought and social development evolve through three stages: the theological, the metaphysical, and the positive or scientific. Although he originally sought to proclaim society's evolution to a new golden age of science, industry, and rational morality, his radical ideas were increasingly tempered by the political and social upheavals of his time. His influence, however, continued in Europe and the US until the early 20th century.

From 1816–18 he taught mathematics. He divided human knowledge into a hierarchy, with sociology at the top of the academic pyramid. Positivism offered a method of logical analysis and provided an ethical and moral basis for predicting and evaluating social progress.

Conakry capital and chief port of the Republic of Guinea; population (1983) 705,300. It is on the island of Tumbo, linked with the mainland by a causeway and by rail with Kankan, 300 mi/480 km to the NE. Bauxite and iron ore are mined nearby.

concave lens converging ⟡lens—a parallel beam of light gets wider as it passes through such a lens. A concave lens is thinner at its center than at the edges.

Common forms include **biconcave** (with both surfaces curved inwards) and **plano-concave** (with one flat surface and one concave). The whole lens may be further curved overall (making a **convexo-concave** or diverging meniscus lens, as in some lenses used for corrective purposes).

concentration camp prison camp for civilians in wartime or under totalitarian rule. The first concentration camps were devised by the British during the Second Boer War in South Africa 1899 for the detention of Afrikaner women and children (with the subsequent deaths of more than 20,000 people). A system of hundreds of concentration camps was developed by the Nazis in Germany and occupied Europe (1933–45) to imprison Jews and political and ideological opponents after Hitler became chancellor Jan 1933. The most infamous camps in World War II were the extermination camps of Auschwitz, Belsen, Dachau, Maidanek, Sobibor, and Treblinka. The total number of people who died at the camps exceeded 6 million, and some inmates were subjected to medical experimentation before being killed.

At Oswiecim (Auschwitz-Birkenau), a vast camp complex was created for imprisonment and slave labor as well as the extermination of over 4 million people in gas chambers or by other means. In addition to Jews, the victims included Gypsies, homosexuals, Romanies and other "misfits" or "unwanted" people. At Maidanek, about 1.5 million people were exterminated, cremated, and their ashes used as fertilizer. Many camp officials and others responsible were tried after 1945 for war crimes, and executed or imprisoned. Foremost was Adolf ⟡Eichmann, the architect of the extermination system, who was tried and executed by the state of Israel 1961.

concentric circles two or more circles that share the same center.

Concepción city in Chile, near the mouth of the river Bió-Bió; population (1990) 306,400. It is the capital of the province of Concepción. It is in a rich agricultural district and is also an industrial center for coal, steel, paper, and textiles.

conceptacle flask-shaped cavities found in the swollen tips of certain brown seaweeds (Phaeophyta), notably rockweed and other large members of the genus *Fucus*. The gametes are formed within them and released into the water via a small pore in the conceptacle, known as an ostiole.

concertina portable reed organ related to the ⟡accordion but smaller in size and rounder in shape, with buttons for keys. It was invented in England in the 19th century.

concert master in music, the leader of an orchestra, usually the principal violinist.

concerto composition, usually in three movements, for solo instrument (or instruments) and orchestra. It developed during the 18th century from the **concerto grosso** form for string orchestra, in which a group of solo instruments is contrasted with a full orchestra.

Corelli and Torelli were early concerto composers, followed by Vivaldi, Handel, and Bach (*Brandenburg Concertos*). Mozart wrote about 40 concertos, mostly for piano. Recent concerto composers include George Gershwin, Erich Korngold, Arnold Schoenberg, Alban Berg, and Béla Bartók, who have developed the form along new lines.

Conchobar in Celtic mythology, king of Ulster whose intended bride, Deirdre, eloped with Noisi. She died of sorrow when Conchobar killed her husband and his brothers.

conciliar movement in the history of the Christian church, a 15th-century attempt to urge the supremacy of church councils over the popes, with regard to the ⟡Great Schism and the reformation of the church. Councils were held in Pisa 1409, Constance 1414–18, Pavia-Siena 1423–24, Basle 1431–49, and Ferrara-Florence-Rome 1438–47.

After ending the Schism 1417 with the removal of John XXIII (1410–15), Gregory XII (1406–15), and Benedict XIII (1394–1423), and the election of Martin V (1417–31), the movement fell into disunity over questions of reform, allowing Eugenius IV (1431–47) to use the Ferrara-Florence-Rome council to reunite the church and reassert papal supremacy.

conclave (Latin "a room locked with a key") secret meeting, in particular the gathering of cardinals in Rome to elect a new pope. They are locked away in the Vatican Palace until they have reached a decision. The result of each ballot is announced by a smoke signal—black for an undecided vote and white when the choice is made.

Concord capital of New Hampshire, in the S central part of the state, on the Merrimack River, N of Manchester. Industries include granite, leather goods, electrical equipment, printed products, and wood products; population (1990) 36,000.

Concord town in Massachusetts, now a suburb of Boston; population (1990) 17,100. Concord was settled 1635 and was the site of the first battle of the American Revolution, April 19, 1775. The writers Ralph Waldo Emerson, Henry Thoreau, Nathaniel Hawthorne, and Louisa May Alcott lived here.

Although electronic equipment, metal products, and leather goods are manufactured, it is mainly a residential suburb of Boston, which lies 18 mi/29 km to the SW. The Minuteman National Historical Park is here.

concordance book containing an alphabetical list of the important words in a major work, with reference to the places in which they occur. The first concordance was one for the Latin Vulgate Bible compiled by a Dominican monk in the 13th century.

Alexander Cruden composed a concordance of the Bible in 1737, of which many editions have appeared. Concordances to Shakespeare, Milton, and other writers also appear in many editions.

concordat agreement regulating relations between the papacy and a secular government, for example, that for France between Pius VII and the emperor Napoleon, which lasted 1801–1905; Mussolini's concordat, which lasted 1929–78 and safeguarded the position of the church in Italy; and one of 1984 in Italy in which Roman Catholicism ceased to be the Italian state religion.

Concorde the only supersonic airliner, which cruises at Mach 2, or twice the speed of sound, about 1,350 mph/2,170 kph. Concorde, the result of Anglo-French cooperation, made its first flight 1969 and entered commercial service seven years later. It is 202 ft/62 m long and has a wing span of nearly 84 ft/26 m.

In 1990 a feasibility study began of providing a replacement for Concorde.

concrete building material composed of cement, stone, sand, and water. It has been used since Egyptian and Roman times. During the 20th century, it has been increasingly employed as an economical alternative to materials such as brick and wood.

history
c. 5600 BC Earliest discovered use of concrete at Lepenski Vir, Yugoslavia (hut floors in Stone Age village).
2500 BC Concrete used in Great Pyramid at Giza by Egyptians.
2nd century BC Romans accidentally discovered the use of lime and silicon/alumina to produce "pozzolanic" cement.
AD 127 Lightweight concrete (using crushed pumice as aggregate) used for walls of Pantheon, Rome.
medieval times Concrete used for castles (infill in walls) and cathedrals (largely foundation work).
1756 John Smeaton produced the first high-quality cement since Roman times (for rebuilding of Eddystone lighthouse, England).
1824 Joseph Aspdin patented Portland cement in Britain.
1854 William Wilkinson patented reinforced concrete in Britain—first successful use in a building.
1880s First continuous-process rotary cement kiln installed (reducing costs of manufacturing cement).
1898 François Hennébique: first multistory reinforced concrete building in Britain (factory in Swansea).
1926 Eugène Freysinnet began experiments on prestressed concrete in France.
1930s US substituted concrete for limestone during federal building projects of the Great Depression; also used extensively for pavements, roadbeds, bridge approaches, dams, and sports facilities (stadiums, swimming pools, tennis courts, playgrounds).
1940s–1950s Much use of poured concrete to rebuild war-torn cities of Europe and the Middle East.
1960s–1990s Widespread use of concrete in industrialized countries as an economical house and office building material instead of traditional materials.

concurrent lines two or more lines passing through a single point; for example, the diameters of a circle are all concurrent at the center of the circle.

concussion impaired functioning of an organ, especially the brain, resulting from a violent blow. Temporary unconsciousness is a symptom.

Condé Louis de Bourbon, Prince of Condé 1530–1569. Prominent French ◊Huguenot leader, founder of the house of Condé and uncle of Henry IV of France. He fought in the wars between Henry II and the Holy Roman emperor Charles V, including the defense of Metz.

Condé Louis II 1621–1686. Prince of Condé called the *Great Condé*. French commander who won brilliant victories during the Thirty Years' War at Rocroi 1643 and Lens 1648, but rebelled 1651 and entered the Spanish service. Pardoned 1660, he commanded Louis XIV's armies against the Spanish and the Dutch.

condensation in physical chemistry, conversion of a vapor to a liquid as it loses heat. This is frequently achieved by letting the vapor come into contact with a cold surface. It is an essential step in ◊distillation processes.

condensation in organic chemistry, a reaction in which two organic compounds combine to form a larger molecule, accompanied by the removal of a smaller molecule (usually water). This is also known as an addition–elimination reaction. Polyamides (such as nylon) and polyesters (such as Terylene) are made by condensation ◊polymerization.

condensation number in physics, the ratio of the number of molecules condensing on a surface to the total number of molecules touching that surface.

condenser in optics, a ◊lens or combination of lenses with a short focal length used for concentrating a light source onto a small area, as used in a slide projector or microscope substage lighting unit. A condenser can also be made using a concave mirror. In electricity, another name for ◊capacitor.

conditioning in psychology, two major principles of behavior modification. In *classical conditioning*, described by Ivan Pavlov, a new stimulus can evoke an automatic response by being repeatedly associated with a stimulus that naturally provokes a response. For example, the sound of a bell repeatedly associated with food will eventually trigger salivation, even if sounded without food being presented. In *operant conditioning*, described by Edward Lee Thorndike (1874–1949) and B F Skinner, the frequency of a voluntary response can be increased by following it with a reinforcer or reward.

condom or *sheath* or *prophylactic* barrier contraceptive, made of rubber, which fits over an erect penis and holds in the sperm produced by ejaculation. It is an effective means of preventing pregnancy if used carefully, preferably with a ◊spermicide. A condom with spermicide is 97% effective; one without spermicide is 85% effective. Condoms also give protection against sexually transmitted diseases, including AIDS.

condominium joint rule of a territory by two or more states, for example, Kanton and Enderbury islands in the South Pacific Phoenix group (under the joint control of Britain and the US for 50 years from 1939).

The term has also come into use in North America to describe a type of joint property ownership of, for example, apartment buildings.

condor large bird, a New World vulture *Vultur gryphus*, with wingspan up to 10 ft/3 m, weight up to 28 lb/13 kg, and length up to 3.8 ft/1.2 m. It is black, with some white on the wings and a white frill at the base of the neck. It lives in the Andes and along the South American coast, and feeds on carrion. The Californian condor *Gymnogyps californianus* is a similar bird, on the verge of extinction.

The Californian condor lays only one egg at a time and may not breed every year. It is the subject of a special conservation effort.

conductance ability of a material to carry an electrical current, usually given the symbol G. For a direct current, it is the reciprocal of resistance: a conductor of resistance R has a conductance of $1/R$. For an alternating current, conductance is the resistance R divided by the impedance Z: $G = R/Z$. Conductance was formerly expressed in reciprocal ohms (or mhos); the SI unit is the siemens (S).

conductor any material that conducts heat or electricity (as opposed to an insulator, or nonconductor). A good conductor has a high electrical or heat conductivity, and is generally a substance rich in free electrons such as a metal. A poor conductor (such as the nonmetals glass and porcelain) has few free electrons. Carbon is exceptional in being nonmetallic and yet (in some of its forms) a relatively good conductor of heat and electricity. Substances such as silicon and germanium, with intermediate conductivities that are improved by heat, light, or voltage, are known as ◊semiconductors.

conductor in music, the member of an orchestra who beats time and controls the overall expression and balance of sound.

cone in geometry, a solid or surface consisting of the set of all straight lines passing through a fixed point (the vertex) and the points of a circle or ellipse whose plane does not contain the vertex.

A circular cone of perpendicular height, with its apex above the center of the circle, is known as a *right circular cone*; it is generated by rotating an isosceles triangle or framework about its line of symmetry. A right circular cone of perpendicular height h and base of radius r has a volume $V = 1/3\pi r^2 h$. The distance from the edge of the base of a cone to the vertex is called the slant height. In a right circular cone of slant height l, the curved surface area is $\pi r l$, and the area of the base is πr^2. Therefore the total surface area $A = \pi r l + \pi r^2 = \pi r (l + r)$.

cone in botany, the reproductive structure of the conifers and cycads; also known as a ◊strobilus. It consists of a central axis surrounded by numerous, overlapping, scalelike, modified leaves (sporophylls) that bear the reproductive organs. Usually there are separate male and female cones, the former bearing pollen sacs containing pollen grains, and the larger female cones bearing the ovules that contain the ova or egg cells. The pollen is carried from male to female cones by the wind (◊anemophily). The seeds develop within the female cone and are released as the scales open in dry atmospheric conditions, which favor seed dispersal.

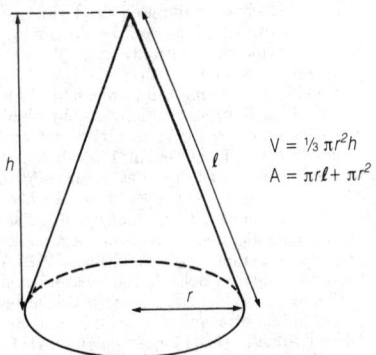

$$V = 1/3 \, \pi r^2 h$$
$$A = \pi r l + \pi r^2$$

cone *The volume and surface area of a cone are given by formulae involving a few simple dimensions.*

In some groups (for example, the pines) the cones take two or even three years to reach maturity. The cones of ▷junipers have fleshy cone scales that fuse to form a berrylike structure. One group of ▷angiosperms, the alders, also bear conelike structures; these are the woody remains of the short female catkins, and they contain the alder ▷fruits.

Coney Island seaside resort on a peninsula in Brooklyn, in the SW of Long Island, New York. It has been popular for ocean bathing and its amusement parks since the 1840s.

Coney Island was named after the wild rabbits (coneys) that inhabited what was originally a small island.

Confederacy in US history, popular name for the ***Confederate States of America***, the government established by 6 (later 11) Southern states Feb 1861 when they seceded from the Union, precipitating the American ▷Civil War. Richmond, Virginia, was the capital, and Jefferson Davis the president. The Confederacy fell after its army was defeated 1865 and General Robert E Lee surrendered.

The Confederacy suffered from a lack of political leadership as well as a deficit of troops and supplies. Still, Southern forces won many significant victories. Confederate leaders had hoped to enlist support from Britain and France, but the slavery issue and the Confederacy's uncertain prospects prompted the Europeans to maintain neutrality, although they provided supplies for a time. The Union's blockade and the grinding weight of superior resources made the outcome virtually inevitable 1865. The states of the Confederacy were South Carolina, Georgia, Florida, Alabama, Louisiana, Mississippi, Texas, Virginia, Tennessee, Arkansas, and North Carolina.

Confederation, Articles of in US history, the initial means by which the 13 former British colonies created a form of national government. Ratified 1781, the articles established a unicameral legislature, Congress, with limited powers of raising revenue, regulating currency, and conducting foreign affairs. But because the individual states retained significant autonomy, the confederation was unmanageable. The articles were superseded by the US Constitution 1788.

Conference on Security and Cooperation in Europe (CSCE) international forum attempting to reach agreement in security, economics, science, technology, and human rights. The CSCE first met at the ▷Helsinki Conference in Finland 1975. By the end of March 1992, having admitted the former republics of the USSR, as well as Croatia and Slovenia, its membership had risen to 51 states.

A second conference in Paris Nov 1990 was hailed as marking the formal end of the ▷Cold War. Reversing a long-standing policy of noninterference in members' internal affairs, the CSCE agreed in 1991 that fact-finding teams could be sent to investigate alleged human-rights abuses in any member country. A ministerial bureaucracy, an Office for Democratic Institutions, and a Conflict Prevention Center were established 1992. A third conference in Helsinki July 1992 debated the Yugoslav problem and gave the CSCE the power to authorize military responses of the ▷North Atlantic Treaty Organization (NATO), the ▷Western European Union (WEU), and the ▷European Community (EC) within Europe. A revised version of the 1990 ▷Conventional Forces in Europe (CFE) treaty was signed at the summit, but awaited ratification by Armenia and Belarus.

confession in religion, the confession of sins practiced in Roman Catholic, Orthodox, and most Far Eastern Christian churches, and since the early 19th century revived in Anglican and Lutheran churches. The Lateran Council of 1215 made auricular confession (self-accusation by the penitent to a priest, who in Catholic doctrine is divinely invested with authority to give absolution) obligatory once a year.

Both John the Baptist's converts and the early Christian church practiced public confession. The Roman Catholic penitent in recent times has always confessed alone to the priest in a confessional box, but from 1977 such individual confession might be preceded by group discussion, or the confession itself might be made openly by members of the group.

confirmation rite practiced by a number of Christian denominations, including Roman Catholic, Anglican, and Orthodox, in which a previously baptized person is admitted to full membership in the church. In Reform Judaism there is often a confirmation service several years after the bar or bat mitzvah (initiation into the congregation).

Christian confirmation is believed to give the participant the gift of the Holy Spirit. In the Anglican church it consists in the laying on of hands by a bishop, while in the Roman Catholic and Orthodox churches the participant is anointed with oil. Except in the Orthodox churches, where infant confirmation is usual, the rite takes place around early adolescence. Until recently a child preparing for confirmation was required to learn by heart a series of questions and answers known as a ▷catechism.

Confucianism body of beliefs and practices based on the Chinese classics and supported by the authority of the philosopher Confucius. The origin of things is seen in the union of ***yin*** and ***yang***, the passive and active principles. Human relationships follow the patriarchal pattern. For more than 2,000 years Chinese political government, social organization, and individual conduct was shaped by Confucian principles. In 1912, Confucian philosophy, as a basis for government, was dropped by the state.

The writings on which Confucianism is based include the ideas of a group of traditional books edited by Confucius, as well as his own works, such as the *Analects*, and those of some of his pupils. The ▷*I Ching* is included among the Confucianist texts.

doctrine Until 1912 the emperor of China was regarded as the father of his people, appointed by heaven to rule. The Superior Man was the ideal human and filial piety was the chief virtue. Accompanying a high morality was a kind of ancestor worship.

practices Under the emperor, sacrifices were offered to heaven and earth, the heavenly bodies, the imperial ancestors, various nature gods, and Confucius himself. These were abolished at the Revolution in 1912, but ancestor worship (better expressed as reverence and remembrance) remained a regular practice in the home.

Under communism Confucianism continued. The defense minister Lin Biao was associated with the religion, and although the communist leader Mao Zedong undertook an anti-Confucius campaign 1974–76, this was not pursued by the succeeding regime.

Confucius (Latinized form of ***Kong Zi***, "Kong the master") 551–479 BC. Chinese sage whose name is given to Confucianism. He devoted his life to relieving suffering among the poor through governmental and administrative reform. His emphasis on tradition and ethics attracted a growing number of pupils during his lifetime. *The Analects of Confucius*, a compilation of his teachings, was published after his death. Within 300 years of the death of Confucius his teaching was adopted by the Chinese state.

Confucius was born in Lu, in what is now the province of Shangdong, and his early years were spent in poverty. Married at 19, he worked as a minor official, then as a teacher. In 517 there was an uprising in Lu, and Confucius spent the next year or two in the adjoining state of Ch'i. As a teacher he was able to place many of his pupils in government posts but a powerful position eluded him. Only in his fifties was he given an office, but he soon resigned because of the lack of power it conveyed. Then for 14 years he wandered from state to state looking for a ruler who could give him a post where he could put his reforms into practice. At the age of 67 he returned to Lu and devoted himself to teaching. At his death five years later he was buried with great pomp, and his grave outside Qufu has remained a center of pilgrimage.

conga Latin American dance, originally from Cuba, in which the participants form a winding line, take three steps forward or backward, and then kick.

congenital disease in medicine, a disease that is present at birth. It is not necessarily genetic in origin; for example, congenital herpes may be acquired by the baby as it passes through the mother's birth canal.

conger any large marine eel of the family Congridae, especially the genus *Conger*. Conger eels live in shallow water, hiding in crevices during the day and active by night, feeding on fish and crabs. They are valued for food and angling.

The American conger *C. oceanicus* grows to 4.5 ft/1.4 m in length.

conglomerate in mineralogy, coarse clastic ▷sedimentary rock, composed of rounded fragments (clasts) of pre-existing rocks cemented in a finer matrix, usually sand.

The fragments in conglomerates are pebble- to boulder-sized, and the rock can be regarded as the lithified equivalent of gravel. A ▷bed of conglomerate is often associated with a break in a sequence of rock beds (an unconformity), where it marks the advance of the sea over an old eroded landscape. An ***oligomict conglomerate*** contains one type of pebble; a ***polymict conglomerate*** has a mixture of pebble types. If the rock fragments are angular, it is called a ▷breccia.

Congo former name (1960–71) of ▷Zaire.

Congo country in W central Africa, bounded N by Cameroon and the Central African Republic, E and S by Zaire, W by the Atlantic Ocean, and NW by Gabon.

government The constitution of 1992 provides for an elected president who appoints a prime minister from the majority party in the assembly. This consists of two elected chambers, the national assembly and the senate. The president and the national assembly are elected for five-year terms and the senate for a six-year term.

Congo
Republic of (*République du Congo*)

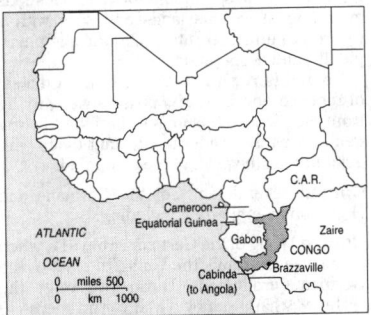

area 132,012 sq mi/342,000 sq km
capital Brazzaville
cities chief port Pointe-Noire; N'Kayi, Loubomo
physical narrow coastal plain rises to central plateau, then falls into northern basin; Zaïre (Congo) River on the border with Zaire; half the country is rainforest
environment an estimated 93% of the rural population is without access to safe drinking water
features 70% of the population lives in Brazzaville, Pointe-Noire, or in towns along the railroad linking these two places
head of state and government Pascal Lissouba from 1992
political system emergent democracy
political parties Pan-African Union for Social Democracy (UPADS), moderate left of center; Congolese Labor Party (PCT), (Marxist-Leninist ideology abandoned 1990) left-wing; Union for Congolese Democracy (UDC), left of center; National Union for Democracy and Progress (UNDP), left of center
exports timber, petroleum, cocoa, sugar
currency CFA franc
population (1990 est) 2,305,000 (chiefly Bantu); growth rate 2.6% p.a.
life expectancy men 45, women 48
languages French (official); many African languages
religion animist 50%, Christian 48%, Muslim 2%
literacy men 79%, women 55% (1985 est)
GDP $2.1 bn (1983); $500 per head
chronology
1910 Became part of French Equatorial Africa.
1960 Achieved independence from France, with Abbé Youlou as the first president.
1963 Youlou forced to resign. New constitution approved, with Alphonse Massamba-Débat as president.
1964 The Congo became a one-party state.
1968 Military coup, led by Capt Marien Ngouabi, ousted Massamba-Débat.
1970 A Marxist state, the People's Republic of the Congo, was announced, with the PCT as the only legal party.
1977 Ngouabi assassinated. Col Yhombi-Opango became president.
1979 Yhombi-Opango handed over the presidency to the PCT, who chose Col Denis Sassou-Nguessou as his successor.
1984 Sassou-Nguessou elected for another five-year term.
1990 The PCT abandoned Marxist-Leninism and promised multiparty politics.
1991 1979 constitution suspended. Country renamed the Republic of Congo.
1992 New constitution approved and multiparty elections held, giving UPADS most assembly seats.

history Occupied from the 15th century by the Bakongo, Bateke, and Sanga, the area was exploited by Portuguese slave traders. From 1889 it came under French administration, becoming part of French Equatorial Africa 1910.

The Congo became an autonomous republic within the French Community 1958, and Abbé Fulbert Youlou, a Roman Catholic priest who involved himself in politics and was suspended by the church, became prime minister and then president when full independence was achieved 1960. Two years later plans were announced for a one-party state, but in 1963, after industrial unrest, Youlou was forced to resign.

one-party state A new constitution was approved, and Alphonse Massamba-Débat, a former finance minister, became president, adopting a policy of "scientific socialism." The National Revolutionary Movement (MNR) was declared the only political party. In 1968 Capt Marien Ngouabi overthrew Massamba-Débat in a military coup, and the national assembly was replaced by a national council of the revolution. Ngouabi proclaimed a Marxist state but kept economic links with France.

In 1970 the nation became the People's Republic of the Congo, with the Congolese Labor Party (PCT) as the only party, and in 1973 a new constitution provided for an assembly chosen from a single party list. In 1977 Ngouabi was assassinated, and Col Joachim Yhombi-Opango took over. He resigned 1979 and was succeeded by Denis Sassou-Nguessou, who moved away from Soviet influence and strengthened links with France, the US, and China.

In 1984 Sassou-Nguessou was elected for another five-year term. He increased his control by combining the posts of head of state, head of government, and president of the central committee of the PCT.

communism abandoned In Aug 1990 the ruling PCT announced political reforms, including the abandonment of Marxist-Leninism, the broadening of its membership, and an eventual end of the one-party system; in 1991 the country was renamed the Republic of Congo. A new constitution was approved by referendum March 1992, and multiparty elections were held in Aug. UPADS won the most assembly seats, though no overall majority, and Pascal Lissouba became the country's first democratically elected president. *See illustration box.*

Congregationalism form of church government adopted by those Protestant Christians known as Congregationalists, who let each congregation manage its own affairs, like the people of the Old Testament. The first Congregationalists established themselves in London and were called the Brownists after Robert Browne, who in 1581 defined the congregational principle. They opposed King James I and were supporters of Oliver ▷Cromwell. They became one of the most important forces in the founding of New England.

During the 17th century they joined with Puritans in opposing the Church of England hierarchy. Many fled to Holland to avoid persecution, and in 1620 Congregationalists who left Holland on the *Mayflower* founded Plymouth Colony in Massachusetts. The early Congregational churches in New England were distinguished for their devotion to education—founding Harvard, Yale, and most of the other older private colleges of the region. During the 19th century, Congregationalists lost their semiestablished status in New England, and many congregations turned to ▷Unitarianism, but Congregationalism spread to the Midwest and elsewhere. In 1959, Congregationalists merged with several other groups to form the United Church of Christ.

Congress national legislature of the US, consisting of the House of Representatives (435 members, apportioned to the states of the Union on the basis of population, and elected for two-year terms) and the Senate (100 senators, two for each state, elected for six years, one-third elected every two years). Both representatives and senators are elected by direct popular vote. Congress meets in Washington, DC, in the Capitol Building. An ▷act of Congress is a bill passed by both houses.

The Congress of the United States met for the first time on March 4, 1789. It was preceded by the Congress of the Confederation representing the several states under the Articles of Confederation from 1781 to 1789.

Congress of Racial Equality (CORE) US nonviolent civil-rights organization, founded in Chicago 1942.

Congreve William 1670–1729. English dramatist and poet. His first success was the comedy *The Old Bachelor* 1693, followed by *The Double Dealer* 1694, *Love for Love* 1695, the tragedy *The Mourning Bride* 1697, and *The Way of the World* 1700. His plays, which satirize the social affectations of the time, are characterized by elegant wit and wordplay.

congruent in geometry, having the same shape and size, as applied to two-dimensional or solid figures. With plane congruent figures, one figure will fit on top of the other exactly, though this may first require rotation of one of the figures.

conic section curve obtained when a conical surface is intersected by a plane. If the intersecting plane cuts both extensions of the cone, it yields a ▷hyperbola; if it is parallel to the side of the cone, it produces a ▷parabola. Other intersecting planes produce ▷circles or ▷ellipses.

The Greek mathematician Apollonius wrote eight books with the title *Conic Sections*, which superseded previous work on the subject by Aristarchus and Euclid.

conidium (plural *conidia*) asexual spore formed by some fungi at the tip of a specialized ▷hypha or conidiophore. The conidiophores grow erect, and cells from their ends round off and separate into conidia, often forming long chains. Conidia easily become detached and are dispersed by air movements.

conifer tree or shrub of the class Coniferales, in the gymnosperm or naked-seed-bearing group of plants. They are often pyramidal in form, with leaves that are either scaled or made up of needles; most are evergreen. Conifers include pines, spruces, firs, yews, junipers, monkey puzzles, and larches.

The reproductive organs are the male and female cones, and pollen is distributed by the wind. The seeds develop in the female cones. The processes of maturation, fertilization, and seed ripening may extend over several years.

conjugate in mathematics, a term indicating that two elements are connected in some way; for example, $(a + ib)$ and $(a − ib)$ are conjugate complex numbers.

conjugate angles two angles that add up to 360°.

conjugation in biology, the bacterial equivalent of sexual reproduction. A fragment of the ◊DNA from one bacterium is passed along a thin tube, the pilus, into the cell of another bacterium.

conjunction grammatical ◊part of speech that serves to connect words, phrases, and clauses; for example *and* in "apples and pears" and *but* in "we're going but they aren't."

conjunction in astronomy, the alignment of two celestial bodies as seen from Earth. A ◊superior planet (or other object) is in conjunction when it lies behind the Sun. An ◊inferior planet (or other object) comes to **inferior conjunction** when it passes between the Earth and the Sun; it is at **superior conjunction** when it passes behind the Sun. **Planetary conjunction** takes place when a planet is closely aligned with another celestial object, such as the Moon, a star, or another planet.

Because the orbital planes of the inferior planets are tilted with respect to that of the Earth, they usually pass either above or below the Sun at inferior conjunction. If they line up exactly, a ◊transit will occur.

conjunctiva membrane covering the vertebrate ◊eye. It is continuous with the epidermis of the eyelids, and lies on the surface of the cornea.

conjunctivitis inflammation of the conjunctiva, the delicate membrane that lines the inside of the eyelids and covers the front of the eye. It may be caused by infection, allergy, or other irritant.

Conkling Roscoe 1829–1888. US political leader, one of the founders of the Republican Party. He served in the US House of Representatives 1859–63 and 1865–67 and in the US Senate 1867–81. A Radical Republican, Conkling was an active prosecutor in Andrew ◊Johnson's impeachment trial.

Born in Albany, New York, the son of a judge, Conkling was admitted to the bar 1850 and soon named district attorney. He served as mayor of Utica 1858. As an opponent of James Garfield, Conkling declined an appointment to the US Supreme Court 1882 and returned to private law practice.

Connecticut state in NE US; nickname Constitution State/Nutmeg State
area 5,018 sq mi/13,000 sq km
capital Hartford
physical highlands in the NW, Connecticut River
features Yale University; Mystic Seaport (reconstruction of 19th-century village, with restored ships)
products dairy, poultry, and market-garden products; tobacco, watches, clocks, silverware, helicopters, jet engines, nuclear submarines, hardware and locks, electrical and electronic equipment, guns and ammunition, optical instruments. Hartford is the center of the nation's insurance industry
population (1990) 3,287,100
famous people Benedict Arnold, Phineas T Barnum, Jonathan Edwards, Nathan Hale, Katharine Hepburn, Charles Ives, Edward H Land, Eugene O'Neill, Wallace Stevens,

Connecticut

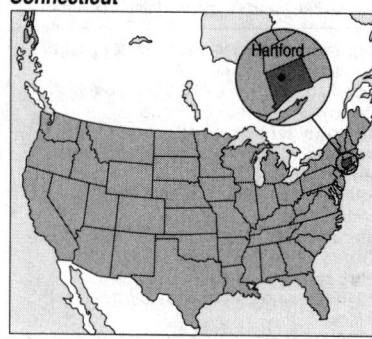

Hartford

Harriet Beecher Stowe, Mark Twain, Eli Whitney
history Dutch navigator Adriaen Block was the first European to record the area 1614, and in 1633 Dutch colonists built a trading post near modern Hartford but it soon was settled by Puritan colonists from Massachusetts 1635. It was one of the original 13 colonies and became a state 1788. It prospered in the 19th century from shipbuilding, whaling, and growing industry. In the 20th century it became an important supplier of military equipment. Connecticut is second to Alaska among states in personal income per capita. Many of New York City's most affluent residential suburbs are in SW Connecticut.

connective tissue in animals, tissue made up of a noncellular substance, the ◊extracellular matrix, in which some cells are embedded. Skin, bones, tendons, cartilage, and adipose tissue (fat) are the main connective tissues. There are also small amounts of connective tissue in organs such as the brain and liver, where they maintain shape and structure.

Connery Sean 1930– . Scottish film actor, the first and best interpreter of James Bond in several films based on the novels of Ian Fleming. His films include *Dr No* 1962, *From Russia with Love* 1963, *Marnie* 1964, *Goldfinger* 1964, *Diamonds Are Forever* 1971, *A Bridge Too Far* 1977, *The Name of the Rose* 1986, and *The Untouchables* 1987 (Academy Award).

Connors Jimmy 1952– . US tennis player who won the Wimbledon title 1974 and 1982, and subsequently won ten Grand Slam events. He was one of the first players to popularize the two-handed backhand.

CAREER HIGHLIGHTS

Wimbledon
singles: 1974, 1982
doubles: 1973
US Open
singles: 1974, 1976, 1978, 1982–83
doubles: 1975
Australian Open
singles: 1974
Grand Prix Masters
1978

conquistador (Spanish "conqueror") any of the early Spanish explorers and adventurers in the Americas, such as Hernán Cortés (Mexico) and Francisco Pizarro (Peru).

Conrad Joseph. Adopted name of Teodor Jozef Conrad Korzeniowski 1857–1924. English novelist, born in the Ukraine of Polish parents. He joined the French merchant marine at the age of 17 and first learned English at 21. His greatest works include the novels *Lord Jim* 1900,

Nostromo 1904, *The Secret Agent* 1907, and *Under Western Eyes* 1911, and the short stories "Heart of Darkness" 1902 and "The Shadow Line" 1917. These combine a vivid sensuous evocation of various lands and seas with a rigorous, humane scrutiny of moral dilemmas, pitfalls, and desperation.

Conrad is regarded as one of the greatest of modern novelists. His prose style, varying from eloquently sensuous to bare and astringent, keeps the reader in constant touch with a mature, truth-seeking, creative mind.

Conrad several kings of the Germans and Holy Roman emperors, including:

Conrad I King of the Germans from 911, when he succeeded Louis the Child, the last of the German Carolingians. During his reign the realm was harassed by ◊Magyar invaders.

Conrad II King of the Germans from 1024, Holy Roman emperor from 1027. He ceded the Sleswick (Schleswig) borderland, south of the Jutland peninsula, to King Canute, but extended his rule into Lombardy and Burgundy.

Conrad III 1093–1152. Holy Roman emperor from 1138, the first king of the Hohenstaufen dynasty. Throughout his reign there was a fierce struggle between his followers, the ◊*Ghibellines*, and the ◊*Guelphs*, the followers of Henry the Proud, duke of Saxony and Bavaria (1108–1139), and later of his son Henry the Lion (1129–1195).

Conrad IV 1228–1254. Elected king of the Germans 1237. Son of the Holy Roman emperor Frederick II, he had to defend his right of succession against Henry Raspe of Thuringia (died 1247) and William of Holland (1227–56).

Conrad V (Conradin) 1252–1268. Son of Conrad IV, recognized as king of the Germans, Sicily, and Jerusalem by German supporters of the ◊Hohenstaufens 1254. He led Ghibelline forces (see ◊Guelph and Ghibelline) against Charles of Anjou at the battle of Tagliacozzo, N Italy 1266, and was captured and executed.

consanguinity relationship by blood, whether lineal (for example by direct descent) or collateral (by virtue of a common ancestor). The degree of consanguinity is significant in laws relating to the inheritance of property and also in relation to marriage, which is forbidden in many cultures between parties closely related by blood. See also ◊affinity.

conscientious objector person refusing compulsory service, usually military, on moral, religious, or political grounds.

The term originally denoted parents who objected to compulsory vaccination of their children.

conscription legislation for all able-bodied male citizens (and female in some countries, such as Israel) to serve with the armed forces. It originated in France 1792, and in the 19th and 20th centuries became the established practice in almost all European states. Modern conscription systems often permit alternative national service for conscientious objectors.

In the US conscription (the *draft*) was introduced during the Civil War—by the Confederates 1862 and by the Union side 1863. In World War I a Selective Service Act was passed 1917, then again 1940 in anticipation of US entry into World War II. It remained in force (except for 15 months 1947–48) until after the US withdrawal from Vietnam 1973, although the system was changed to a lottery based on a registrant's birthday. This was done to rectify the inequities stemming from the deferment system that had allowed college students to delay their service. In 1980 Carter restored registration for a possible military draft for men at 18, but his proposal that it be extended to women was rejected by Congress. The US now has a policy based on all-volunteer armed forces.

consent, age of age at which consent may legally be given to sexual intercourse by a girl or boy.

In the US it varies according to state statutes.

conservation in the life sciences, action taken to protect and preserve the natural world, usually from pollution, overexploitation, and other harmful features of human activity. The late 1980s saw a great increase in public concern for the environment, with membership in conservation groups, such as ⟡Friends of the Earth, rising sharply. Globally the most important issues include the depletion of atmospheric ozone by the action of chlorofluorocarbons (CFCs), the buildup of carbon dioxide in the atmosphere (thought to contribute to an intensification of the ⟡greenhouse effect), and the destruction of the tropical rainforests (see ⟡deforestation).

conservatism approach to government favoring the maintenance of existing institutions and identified with a number of Western political parties, such as the US Republican, British Conservative, German Christian Democratic, and Australian Liberal parties. It tends to be explicitly nondoctrinaire and pragmatic but generally emphasizes free-enterprise capitalism, minimal government intervention in the economy, rigid law and order, and the importance of national traditions.

conservative margin in plate tectonics, a region on the Earth's surface in which one plate slides past another. An example is the San Andreas Fault, California, where the movement of the plates is irregular and sometimes takes the form of sudden jerks, which cause the ⟡earthquakes common in the San Francisco–Los Angeles area.

Conservative Party although there is a Conservative Party in the US, it is generally a minor element in national elections. The term is most often used in reference to the UK political party, one of the two historic British parties; the name replaced "Tory" in general use from 1830 onwards. Traditionally the party of landed interests, it broadened its political base under Disraeli's leadership in the 19th century. The present Conservative Party's free-market capitalism is supported by the world of finance and the management of industry; its economic policies have increased the spending power of the majority, but also the gap between rich and poor; nationalized industries are sold off (see ⟡privatization); military spending and close alliance with the US are favored.

Under the leadership of Margaret ⟡Thatcher, the Conservative Party returned to power May 1979; she was reelected for a third term in 1987 and resigned 1989.

conspicuous consumption selection and purchase of goods for their social rather than their inherent value. These might include items with an obviously expensive brand-name tag. The term was coined by US economist Thorsten Veblen.

Constable John 1776–1837. English landscape painter. He painted scenes of his native Suffolk, including *The Haywain* 1821 (National Gallery, London), as well as castles, cathedrals, landscapes, and coastal scenes in other parts of Britain. Constable inherited the Dutch tradition of somber realism, in particular the style of Jacob Ruisdael, but he aimed to capture the momentary changes of nature as well as to create monumental images of British scenery, such as *The White Horse* 1819 (Frick Collection, New York) and *Flatford Mill* 1825.

Constable's paintings are remarkable for their atmospheric effects and were admired by many French painters including Eugene Delacroix. His many sketches are often considered among his best work.

Constance, Council of council held by the Roman Catholic church 1414–17 in Constance, Germany. It elected Pope Martin V, which ended the Great Schism 1378–1417 when there were rival popes in Rome and Avignon.

constant in mathematics, a fixed quantity or one that does not change its value in relation to ⟡variables. For example, in the algebraic expression $y^2 = 5x - 3$, the numbers 3 and 5 are constants. In physics, certain quantities are regarded as universal constants, such as the speed of light in a vacuum.

Constanţa chief Romanian port on the Black Sea, capital of Constanţa region, and third-largest city of Romania; population (1985) 323,000. It has refineries, shipbuilding yards, and food factories.

constantan or *eureka* high-resistance alloy of approximately 40% nickel and 60% copper with a very low coefficient of ⟡thermal expansion (measure of expansion on heating). It is used in electrical resistors.

Constantine city in Algeria; population (1983) 449,000. It produces carpets and leather goods. It was one of the chief towns of the Roman province of Numidia, but declined and was ruined, then restored 313 by Constantine the Great, whose name it bears. It was subsequently ruled by Vandals, Arabs, and Turks. It was captured by the French 1837.

Constantine II 1940– . King of the Hellenes (Greece). In 1964 he succeeded his father Paul I, went into exile 1967, and was formally deposed 1973.

He married Princess Anne-Marie of Denmark in 1964.

Constantine the Great c. AD 280–337. First Christian emperor of Rome and founder of Constantinople. He defeated Maxentius, joint emperor of Rome AD 312, and in 313 formally recognized Christianity. As sole emperor of the west of the empire, he defeated Licinius, emperor of the east, to become ruler of the Roman world 324. He presided over the church's first council at Nicaea 325. In 330 Constantine moved his capital to Byzantium, renaming it Constantinople.

Constantine was born at Naissus (Niš, Yugoslavia), the son of Constantius. He was already well known as a soldier when his father died in York in 306 and he was acclaimed by the troops there as joint emperor in his father's place. A few years later Maxentius, the joint emperor in Rome (whose sister had married Constantine), challenged his authority and mobilized his armies to invade Gaul. Constantine won a crushing victory outside Rome in 312. During this campaign he was said to have seen a vision of the cross of Jesus superimposed upon the sun, accompanied by the words: "In this sign, conquer." By the Edict of Milan 313 he formally recognized Christianity as one of the religions legally permitted within the Roman Empire and in 314 he summoned the bishops of the Western world to the Council of Arles. However, there has never been agreement on whether Constantine adopted Christianity for reasons of faith or as an act of imperial absolutism to further his power. Sole emperor of the West from 312, by defeating Licinius, the emperor in the East, Constantine became sole Roman emperor 324. He increased the autocratic power of the emperor, issued legislation to tie the farmers and workers to their crafts in a sort of caste system, and enlisted the support of the Christian church. He summoned, and presided over, the first general council of the church in Nicaea 325. Constantine moved his capital to Byzantium on the Bosporus 330 and renamed it Constantinople (now Istanbul).

Constantinople former name (330–1453) of Istanbul, Turkey. It was named after the Roman emperor Constantine the Great when he enlarged the Greek city of Byzantium 328 and declared it the capital of the ⟡Byzantine Empire 330. Its elaborate fortifications enabled it to resist a succession of sieges, but it was captured by crusaders 1204, and was the seat of a Latin (Western European) kingdom until recaptured by the Greeks 1261. An attack by the Turks 1422 proved unsuccessful, but it was taken by another Turkish army May 29, 1453, after nearly a year's siege, and became the capital of the Ottoman Empire.

constant prices a series of prices adjusted to reflect real purchasing power. If wages were to rise by 15% from $100 per week (to $115) and the rate of inflation was 10% (requiring $110 to maintain spending power), the real wage would have risen by 5%. Also an index used to create a constant price series, unlike ⟡current prices.

constellation one of the 88 areas into which the sky is divided for the purposes of identifying and naming celestial objects. The first constellations were simple, arbitrary patterns of stars in which early civilizations visualized gods, sacred beasts, and mythical heroes.

The constellations in use today are derived from a list of 48 known to the ancient Greeks, who inherited some from the Babylonians. The current list of 88 constellations was adopted by the International Astronomical Union, astronomy's governing body, in 1930.

constitution body of fundamental laws of a state, laying down the system of government and defining the relations of the legislature, executive, and judiciary to each other and to the citizens. Since the French Revolution almost all countries (the UK is an exception) have adopted written constitutions; that of the US (1787) is the oldest.

constructive margin in plate tectonics, a region in which two plates are moving away from each other. Magma, or molten rock, escapes to the surface along this margin to form new crust, usually in the form of a ridge. Over time, as more and more magma reaches the surface, the sea floor spreads—for example, the upwelling of magma at the Mid-Atlantic Ridge causes the floor of the Atlantic Ocean to grow at a rate of about 2 in/5 cm a year.

Constructivism revolutionary art movement founded in Moscow 1917 by the Russians Naum ⟡Gabo, his brother Antoine Pevsner (1886–1962), and Vladimir Tatlin (1885–1953). Tatlin's abstract sculptures, using wood, metal, and clear plastic, were hung on walls or suspended from ceilings. Gabo and Pevsner soon left the USSR and joined the European avant-garde.

consul chief magistrate of ancient Rome after the expulsion of the last king 510 BC. The consuls were two annually elected magistrates, both of equal power; they jointly held full civil power in Rome and the chief military command in the field. After the establishment of the Roman Empire the office became purely honorary.

consumer durable any commodity that is required to satisfy personal requirements and that has a long life, such as furniture and electrical goods, as opposed to food and drink, which are **perishables** and have to be replaced frequently.

consumer price index yearly index of the cost of goods and services to the consumer needed for an average standard of living. See also ⟡producer price index.

The US Department of Labor reforms its consumer price index (CPI), the most widely used measure of inflation, periodically, establishing a base year at 100. Prices 20% higher than those in the base year would thus be expressed as 120. The index is calculated on the spending habits of salaried employees, wage earners, and retired and unemployed persons in 85 metropolitan areas. The income of almost half the US population is related to the CPI through collective bargaining agreements, alimony, rent, and Social Security payments, all of which are linked to changes in the cost of living. The items making up the "market basket" of typical consumer purchases are also revised periodically, reflecting changes in consumer spending habits.

consumer protection laws and measures designed to ensure fair trading for buyers. Responsibility for checking goods and services for quality, safety, and suitability has in the past few years moved increasingly away from the consumer to the producer.

In earlier days it was assumed that consumers could safeguard themselves by common sense, testing before purchase, and confronting the seller personally if they were dissatisfied. Today the technical complexities of products, the remoteness of outlets from the original producer, and pressures from advertising require protection for the consumer.

In the US, both federal and state governments make special provisions for consumer protection. In 1962 President Kennedy set out the four basic rights of the consumer: to safety, to be informed, to choose, and to be heard. There are many private consumer associations, and among the most vociferous of crusaders for greater protection has been Ralph ⟡Nader.

Consumers Union private organization formed to protect consumers' interests, usually in terms of quality and safety.

In the US, Consumers Union publishes *Consumer Reports*, a monthly summary of tests and comparisons conducted by independent researchers. The group is part of a growing movement of consumer advocacy that seeks to inform the public and hold manufacturers responsible for their products. See also Ralph ⟡Nader.

consumption in economics, the purchase of goods and services for final use, as opposed to spending by firms on capital goods, known as capital formation.

In national accounting, it means a country's total expenditure over a given period (usually a year) on goods and services, including expenditure on raw materials and defense.

consumption (Latin *consumptio* "wasting") in medicine, former name for the disease ⟡tuberculosis.

contact lens lens, made of soft or hard plastic, that is worn in contact with the cornea and conjunctiva of the eye, beneath the eyelid, to correct defective vision. In special circumstances, contact lenses may be used as protective shells or for cosmetic purposes, such as changing eye color.

The earliest use of contact lenses in the late 19th century was protective, or in the correction of corneal malformation. It was not until the 1930s that simplification of fitting technique by taking eye impressions made general use possible. Recent developments are a type of soft lens that can be worn for lengthy periods without removal, and a disposable soft lens that needs no cleaning but should be discarded after a week of constant wear.

contado in northern and central Italy from the 9th to the 13th century, the territory under a count's jurisdiction. During the 13th century, this jurisdiction passed to the cities, and it came to refer to the rural area over which a city exerted political and economic control.

Contadora Group alliance formed between Colombia, Mexico, Panama, and Venezuela Jan 1983 to establish a general peace treaty for Central America. It was named after Contadora, the island of the Pearl Group in the Gulf of Panama where the first meeting was held.

The process was designed to include the formation of a Central American parliament (similar to the European parliament). Support for the Contadora Group has come from Argentina, Brazil, Peru, and Uruguay, as well as from the Central American states.

containment US policy (adopted from 1947) that was designed to prevent the spread of communism beyond the borders of the USSR.

contempt of court behavior that shows lack of respect for the authority of a court of law, such as disobeying a court order, breach of an injunction, or improper use of legal documents. Behavior that disrupts, prejudices, or interferes with court proceedings either inside or outside the courtroom may also be contempt. The court may punish contempt with a fine or imprisonment.

continent any one of the seven large land masses of the Earth, as distinct from the oceans. They are Asia, Africa, North America, South America, Europe, Australia, and Antarctica. Continents are constantly moving and evolving (see ⟡plate tectonics). A continent does not end at the coastline; its boundary is the edge of the shallow continental shelf, which may extend several hundred kilometers or miles out to sea.

At the center of each continental mass lies a shield or ⟡craton, a deformed mass of old ⟡metamorphic rocks dating from Precambrian times. The shield is thick, compact, and solid (the Canadian Shield is an example), having undergone all the mountain-building activity it is ever likely to, and is usually worn flat. Around the shield is a concentric pattern of fold mountains, with older ranges, such as the Rockies, closest to the shield, and younger ranges, such as the coastal ranges of North America, farther away. This general concentric pattern is modified when two continental masses have drifted together and they become welded with a great mountain range along the join, the way Europe and N Asia are joined along the Urals. If a continent is torn apart, the new continental edges have no fold mountains; for instance, South America has fold mountains (the Andes) along its western flank, but none along the east where it tore away from Africa 200 million years ago.

Continental Congress in US history, the federal legislature of the original 13 states, acting as a provisional revolutionary government during the ⟡American Revolution. It convened in Philadelphia from 1774 until 1789, when the US Constitution was adopted. The Second Continental Congress, convened May 1775, was responsible for drawing up the ⟡Declaration of Independence and, in 1777, the ⟡Articles of Confederation. The Congress authorized an army to resist the British and issued paper money to finance the war effort. It also oversaw the deliberations of the Constitutional Convention.

continental drift in geology, theory proposed by the German meteorologist Alfred Wegener in 1915 that, about 200 million years ago, Earth consisted of a single large continent (⟡Pangaea) that subsequently broke apart to form the continents known today. Such vast continental movements could not be satisfactorily explained until the study of ⟡plate tectonics in the 1960s.

The term "continental drift" is not strictly correct, since land masses do not drift through the oceans. The continents form part of a plate, and the amount of crust created at divergent plate margins must equal the amount of crust destroyed at subduction zones.

continent The North American continent is growing in the west as a result of collision with the Pacific plate.

continental rise the portion of the ocean floor rising gently from the abyssal plain toward the steeper continental slope. The continental rise is a depositional feature formed from sediments transported down the slope mainly by turbidity currents. Much of the continental rise consists of coalescing submarine alluvial fans bordering the continental slope.

continental slope sloping, submarine portion of a continent. It extends downward from the continental margin at the edge of the continental shelf. In some places, such as south of the Aleutian Islands of Alaska, continental slopes extend directly to the ocean deeps or abyssal plain. In others, such as the E coast of North America, they grade into the gentler continental rises that in turn grade into the abyssal plains.

Continental System system of economic preference and protection within Europe created by the French emperor Napoleon in order to exclude British trade. Apart from its function as economic warfare, the system also reinforced the French economy at the expense of other European states. It lasted 1806–13 but failed owing to British naval superiority.

continuity in mathematics, property of functions of a real variable that have an absence of "breaks." A function f is said to be continuous at a point a if $\lim f(x) = f(a)$.

continuo abbreviation for *basso continuo*; in music, the bass line on which a keyboard player, often accompanied by a bass stringed instrument, built up a harmonic accompaniment in 17th-century Baroque music.

continuum in mathematics, a ⟩set that is infinite and everywhere continuous, such as the set of points on a line.

Contra member of a Central American right-wing guerrilla force attempting to overthrow the democratically elected Nicaraguan Sandinista government 1979–90. The Contras, many of them mercenaries or former members of the deposed dictator Somoza's guard (see ⟩Nicaraguan Revolution), operated mainly from bases outside Nicaragua, mostly in Honduras, with covert US funding, as revealed by the ⟩Irangate hearings 1986–87.

In 1989 US president Bush announced an agreement with Congress to provide $41 million in "nonlethal" aid to the Contras until Feb 1990. The Sandinista government was defeated by the National Opposition Union, a US-backed coalition, in the Feb 1990 elections. The Contras were disbanded in the same year but, fearing reprisals, a few hundred formed the Re-Contra (officially the 380 Legion) in Feb 1991.

contrabassoon larger version of the ⟩bassoon, sounding an octave lower.

contraceptive any drug, device, or technique that prevents pregnancy. The contraceptive pill (the ⟩Pill) contains female hormones that interfere with egg production or the first stage of pregnancy. The "morning-after" pill can be taken up to 72 hours after unprotected intercourse. Barrier contraceptives include ⟩condoms (sheaths) and ⟩diaphragms, also called caps or Dutch caps; they prevent the sperm entering the cervix (neck of the womb). ⟩Intrauterine devices, also known as IUDs or coils, cause a slight inflammation of the lining of the womb; this prevents the fertilized egg from becoming implanted. See also ⟩family planning.

Other contraceptive methods include ⟩sterilization (women) and ⟩vasectomy (men); these are usually nonreversible. "Natural" methods include withdrawal of the penis before ejaculation (coitus interruptus), and avoidance of intercourse at the time of ovulation (⟩rhythm method). These methods are unreliable and normally only used on religious grounds. A new development is a sponge impregnated with spermicide that is inserted into the vagina. The use of any contraceptive (birth control) is part of family planning.

The effectiveness of a contraceptive method is often given as a percentage. To say that a method has 95% effectiveness means that, on average, out of 100 healthy couples using that method for a year, 95 will not conceive.

contract agreement between two or more parties that will be enforced by law according to the intention of the parties.

A contract made in the proper form may be unenforceable if it is made under a mistake, misrepresentation, duress, or undue influence, or if one of the parties does not have the capacity to make it (for example, ⟩minors and people who are insane). Illegal contracts are void, including those to commit a crime or civil wrong, those to trade with the enemy, immoral contracts, and contracts in restraint of trade. Contracts by way of gaming and wagering are also void.

In a contract each party mutually obliges himself or herself to the other for exchange of property or performance for a consideration.

contract bridge card game first played 1925. From 1930 it quickly outgrew auction bridge in popularity.

contractile root in botany, a thickened root at the base of a corm, bulb, or other organ that helps position it at an appropriate level in the ground. Contractile roots are found, for example, on the corms of plants of the genus *Crocus*. After they have become anchored in the soil, the upper portion contracts, pulling the plant deeper into the ground.

contractile vacuole tiny organelle found in many single-celled fresh-water organisms. It slowly fills with water, and then contracts, expelling the water from the cell.

Fresh-water protozoa such as *Amoeba* absorb water by the process of ⟩osmosis, and this excess must be eliminated. The rate of vacuole contraction slows as the external salinity is increased, because the osmotic effect weakens; marine protozoa do not have a contractile vacuole.

contrapuntal in music, a work employing ⟩counterpoint.

control experiment essential part of a scientifically valid experiment, designed to show that the factor being tested is actually responsible for the effect observed. In the control experiment all factors, apart from the one under test, are exactly the same as in the test experiments, and all the same measurements are carried out. In drug trials, a placebo (a harmless substance) is given alongside the substance being tested in order to compare effects.

convection heat energy transfer that involves the movement of a fluid (gas or liquid). According to kinetic theory, molecules of fluid in contact with the source of heat expand and tend to rise within the bulk of the fluid. Less energetic, cooler molecules sink to take their place, setting up convection currents. This is

the principle of natural convection in many domestic hot-water systems and space heaters.

convent religious house for ⟩nuns.

conventionalism the view that ⟩a priori truths, logical axioms, or scientific laws have no absolute validity but are disguised conventions representing one of a number of possible alternatives. The French philosopher and mathematician Jules Henri Poincaré introduced this position into philosophy of science.

convergence in mathematics, the property of a series of numbers in which the difference between consecutive terms gradually decreases. The sum of a converging series approaches a limit as the number of terms tends to ⟩infinity.

convergent evolution in biology, the independent evolution of similar structures in species (or other taxonomic groups) that are not closely related, as a result of living in a similar way. Thus, birds and bats have wings, not because they are descended from a common winged ancestor, but because their respective ancestors independently evolved flight.

converse in mathematics, the reversed order of a conditional statement; the converse of the statement "if a, then b" is "if b, then a." The converse does not always hold true; for example, the converse of "if $x = 3$, then $x^2 = 9$" is "if $x^2 = 9$, then $x = 3$," which is not true, as x could also be -3.

convertiplane ⟩vertical takeoff and landing craft (VTOL) with rotors on its wings that spin horizontally for takeoff, but tilt to spin in a vertical plane for forward flight.

At takeoff it looks like a two-rotor helicopter, with both rotors facing skywards. As forward speed is gained, the rotors tilt slowly forward until they are facing directly ahead. There are several different forms of convertiplane. The LTV-Hillier-Ryan XC-142, designed in the US, had wings, carrying the four engines and propellers, that rotated. The German VC-400 had two rotors on each of its wingtips. Neither of these designs went into production. A recent Boeing and Bell design, the Osprey, uses a pair of tilting engines, with propellers 38 ft/11.5 m across, mounted at the end of the wings. It is intended eventually to carry about 50 passengers direct to city centers. The design should also be useful for search and rescue operations and for transport to offshore oil rigs.

convex lens converging ⟩lens—that is, a parallel beam of light passing through it converges and is eventually brought to a focus; it can therefore produce a real image on a screen. Such a lens is wider at its center than at the edges.

Common forms include *biconvex* (with both surfaces curved outwards) and *planoconvex* (with one flat surface and one convex). The whole lens may be further curved overall, making a *concavo-convex* or converging meniscus lens, as in some lenses used in corrective eyewear.

conveyancing administrative process involved in transferring title to land, usually on its sale or purchase.

conveyor device used for transporting materials. Widely used throughout industry is the *conveyor belt*, usually a rubber or fabric belt running on rollers. Trough-shaped belts are used, for example in mines, for transporting ores and coal. *Chain conveyors* are also used in coal mines to remove coal from the cutting machines. Overhead endless chain conveyors are used to carry components and bodies in car-assembly works. Other types include **bucket conveyors** and **screw conveyors**, powered versions of the ⋄Archimedes' screw.

convolvulus or **bindweed** any plant of the genus *Convolvulus* of the morning-glory family Convolvulaceae. They are characterized by their twining stems and by their petals, which are united into a funnel-shaped tube.

The hedge bindweed *C. sepium*, a trailing plant with spear-shaped leaves and large, pinkish-white flowers, is native to N Eurasia and North America.

convoy system grouping of ships to sail together under naval escort in wartime. In World War I (1914–18) navy escort vessels were at first used only to accompany troopships, but the convoy system was adopted for merchant shipping when the unrestricted German submarine campaign began 1917. In World War II (1939–45) the convoy system was widely used by the Allies to keep the Atlantic sea lanes open.

convulsion series of violent contractions of the muscles over which the patient has no control. It may be associated with loss of consciousness. Convulsions may arise from any one of a number of causes, including brain disease (such as ⋄epilepsy), injury, high fever, poisoning, and electrocution.

Cook James 1728–1779. British naval explorer. After surveying the St Lawrence 1759, he made three voyages: 1768–71 to Tahiti, New Zealand, and Australia; 1772–75 to the South Pacific; and 1776–79 to the South and North Pacific, attempting to find the Northwest Passage and charting the Siberian coast. He was killed in Hawaii.

In 1768 Cook was given command of an expedition to the South Pacific to witness Venus eclipsing the Sun. He sailed in the *Endeavour* with Joseph ⋄Banks and other scientists, reaching Tahiti in April 1769. He then sailed around New Zealand and made a detailed survey of the east coast of Australia, naming New South Wales and Botany Bay. He returned to England June 12, 1771.

Now a commander, Cook set out 1772 with the *Resolution* and *Adventure* to search for the Southern Continent. The location of Easter Island was determined, and the Marquesas and Tonga Islands plotted. He also went to New Caledonia and Norfolk Island. Cook returned July 25, 1775, having sailed 60,000 mi in three years.

On June 25, 1776, he began his third and last voyage with the *Resolution* and *Discovery*. On the way to New Zealand, he visited several of the Cook or Hervey Islands and revisited the Hawaiian or Sandwich Islands. The ships sighted the North American coast at latitude 45° N and sailed north hoping to discover the Northwest Passage. He made a continuous survey as far as the Bering Strait, where the way was blocked by ice. Cook then surveyed the opposite coast of the strait (Siberia), and returned to Hawaii early 1779, where he was killed in a scuffle with islanders.

Cook Thomas 1808–1892. Pioneer British travel agent and founder of Thomas Cook & Son. He introduced traveler's checks (then called "circular notes") in the early 1870s.

Cooke Alistair 1908– . British-born US journalist. He is best known for his writings interpreting US history and culture and for

his role as television host of "Omnibus" and "Masterpiece Theatre."

Cooke studied theater at Yale and Harvard universities and returned to the US as a BBC correspondent 1938; he became a US citizen 1941. In 1947 he began his radio broadcast "Letter from America" for the BBC. During the 1970s, he hosted the BBC-produced television series "America" 1972–73 and followed this with the bestselling book *Alistair Cooke's America* 1973, based on the series.

Cooke Sam 1931–1964. US soul singer and songwriter who began his career as a gospel singer and turned to pop music 1956. His hits include "You Send Me" 1957 and "Wonderful World" 1960 (re-released 1986).

cooking heat treatment of food to make it more palatable, digestible, and safe. It breaks down connective tissue in meat, making it tender, and softens the cellulose in plant tissue. Some nutrients may be lost in the process, but this does not affect the overall nutritional value of a balanced diet.

Cookery has been practiced since prehistoric times, becoming fairly sophisticated in the aristocratic societies of ancient civilizations. Professional cooks existed in medieval Europe, but cooking as a recognized art originated in 16th-century Italy and developed in 17th-century France. French pre-eminence in cooking remained unchallenged until the 1940s, when rapidly increasing interest led to the rediscovery and appreciation of traditional cooking styles worldwide.

Cook Islands group of six large and a number of smaller Polynesian islands 1,600 mi/2,600 km NE of Auckland, New Zealand; area 112 sq mi/290 sq km; population (1991) 19,000. Their main products include fruit, copra, and crafts. They became a self-governing overseas territory of New Zealand 1965.

The chief island, Rarotonga, is the site of Avarua, the seat of government. Niue, geographically part of the group, is separately administered. The Cook Islands were visited by Captain Cook 1773, annexed by Britain 1888, and transferred to New Zealand 1901. They have common citizenship with New Zealand.

Cooley's anemia alternate name for ⋄thalassemia.

Coolidge (John) Calvin 1872–1933. 30th president of the US 1923–29, a Republican. As governor of Massachusetts 1919, he was responsible for crushing a Boston police strike. As Warren ⋄Harding's vice-president 1921–23, he succeeded to the presidency on Harding's death (Aug 2, 1923). He won the 1924 presidential election, and his period of office was marked by great economic prosperity.

Coolidge declined to run for reelection in 1928, supporting his secretary of the interior, Herbert ⋄Hoover, who won the presidency.

Cooper Gary 1901–1962. US film actor. He epitomized the lean, true-hearted Yankee, slow of speech but capable of outdoing the "bad guys" in *Lives of a Bengal Lancer* 1935, *Mr Deeds Goes to Town* (Academy Award for best picture 1936), *Sergeant York* 1940 (Academy Award for best actor 1941), and *High Noon* (Academy Award for best actor 1952).

Cooper James Fenimore 1789–1851. US writer, considered the first great US novelist. He wrote about 50 novels, mostly about the frontier, wilderness life, and the sea. He is best remembered for his ⋄Leatherstocking Tales,

a series of five novels: *The Pioneers* 1823, *The Last of the Mohicans* 1826, *The Prairie* 1827, *The Pathfinder* 1840, and *The Deerslayer* 1841. All describe the adventures of the frontier hero Natty Bumppo before and after the American Revolution.

Cooper was born in Burlington, New Jersey, son of the wealthy landowner who founded Cooperstown, New York. He grew up in that frontier settlement and after expulsion from Yale sailed as an apprentice seaman in Europe. In 1811 he married the wealthy Susan DeLancey and became a gentleman farmer, achieving success as a writer with his novel *The Spy* 1821. He then moved to New York City, where he became a member of the Knickerbocker Group of writers. Cooper lived and wrote in Europe for seven years before returning to New York 1833 to live in Cooperstown. His many works include *The Pilot* 1823 (the first American novel of the sea), *The Red Rover* 1828, and *Satanstoe* 1845.

Cooper Leon 1930– . US physicist who in 1955 began work on the puzzling phenomenon of ⋄superconductivity. He proposed that at low temperatures electrons would be bound in pairs (since known as ***Cooper pairs***) and in this state electrical resistance to their flow through solids would disappear. He shared the 1972 Nobel Prize for Physics with John ⋄Bardeen and John Schrieffer (1931-).

Cooperative Council for the Arab States of the Gulf (CCASG) Arab organization for promoting peace in the Persian Gulf area, established 1981. Its declared purpose is "to bring about integration, coordination, and cooperation in economic, social, defense, and political affairs among Arab Gulf states." Its members include Bahrain, Kuwait, Oman, Qatar, Saudi Arabia, and the United Arab Emirates; its headquarters are in Ryiadh, Saudi Arabia.

cooperative movement the banding together of groups of people for mutual assistance in trade, manufacture, the supply of credit, housing, or other services. The original principles of the cooperative movement were laid down 1844 by the Rochdale Pioneers, under the influence of Robert Owen, and by Charles Fourier in France.

In the US, the period from 1915 to 1930 saw the greatest growth in the number of cooperative associations because they were recognized under statute laws rather than simply under common law. By the 1960s, agricultural cooperatives had declined dramatically due to mergers and more technically advanced marketing procedures. The future for cooperative associations is seen in the areas of consumers' associations, workers' groups, and the housing market.

coordinate in geometry, a number that defines the position of a point relative to a point or axis. ⋄Cartesian coordinates define a point by its perpendicular distances from two or more axes drawn through a fixed point at right angles to each other; ⋄polar coordinates define a point in a plane by its distance from a fixed point and direction from a fixed line.

coordinate geometry or ***analytical geometry*** system of geometry in which points, lines, shapes, and surfaces are represented by algebraic expressions. In plane (two-dimensional) coordinate geometry, the plane is usually defined by two axes at right angles to each other, the horizontal x-axis and the vertical y-axis, meeting at O, the origin. A point on the plane can be represented by a pair of ◊Cartesian coordinates, which define its position in terms of its distance along the x-axis and along the y-axis from O. These distances are respectively the x and y coordinates of the point.

Lines are represented as equations; for example, $y = 2x + 1$ gives a straight line, and $y = 3x^2 + 2x$ gives a ◊parabola (a curve). The graphs of varying equations can be drawn by plotting the coordinates of points that satisfy their equations, and joining up the points. One of the advantages of coordinate geometry is that geometrical solutions can be obtained without drawing but by manipulating algebraic expressions. For example, the coordinates of the point of intersection of two straight lines can be determined by finding the unique values of x and y that satisfy both of the equations for the lines, that is, by solving them as a pair of ◊simultaneous equations. The curves studied in simple coordinate geometry are the ◊conic sections (circle, ellipse, parabola, and hyperbola), each of which has a characteristic equation.

coot any of various freshwater birds of the genus *Fulica* in the rail family. Coots are about 1.2 ft/38 cm long, and mainly black. They have a white bill, extending up the forehead in a plate, and big feet with lobed toes.

The American coot *F. americana* is found in North and South America and the Caribbean. It feeds on plants, insects, and small fish.

cope semicircular cape, without sleeves, worn by priests of the Western Christian church in processions and on some other formal occasions, but not when officiating at Mass.

Copenhagen (Danish **København**) capital of Denmark, on the islands of Zealand and Amager; population (1990) 1,337,100 (including suburbs).

To the NE is the royal palace at Amalienborg; the 17th-century Charlottenburg Palace houses the Academy of Arts, and parliament meets in the Christiansborg Palace. The statue of Hans Christian Andersen's *Little Mermaid* (by Edvard Eriksen) is at the harbor entrance. The Tivoli amusement park is on the shore of the Öresund ("the Sound," between Copenhagen and S Sweden).
history Copenhagen was a fishing village until 1167, when the bishop of Roskilde built the castle on the site of the present Christiansborg palace. A settlement grew up, and it became the Danish capital 1443. The university was founded 1479. The city was under German occupation April 1940–May 1945.

copepod ◊crustacean of the subclass Copepoda, mainly microscopic and found in plankton.

Copernicus Nicolaus 1473–1543. Polish astronomer who believed that the Sun, not the Earth, is at the center of the Solar System, thus defying the Christian church doctrine of the time. For 30 years he worked on the hypothesis that the rotation and the orbital motion of the Earth were responsible for the apparent movement of the heavenly bodies. His great work *De Revolutionibus Orbium Coelestium/About the Revolutions of the Heavenly Spheres* was not published until the year of his death.

Born at Torun on the Vistula, then under the Polish king, Copernicus studied at Kraków and in Italy, and lectured on astronomy in Rome. On his return to Pomerania 1505 he became physician to his uncle, the bishop of Ermland, and was made canon at Frauenburg, although he did not take holy orders. Living there until

his death, he interspersed astronomical work with the duties of various civil offices.

Copland Aaron 1900–1990. US composer. His early works, such as his piano concerto 1926, were in the jazz idiom but he gradually developed a gentler style with a regional flavor drawn from American folk music. Among his works are the ballets *Billy the Kid* 1939, *Rodeo* 1942, *Appalachian Spring* 1944 (based on a poem by Hart Crane), and *Inscape for Orchestra* 1967.

Born in New York, Copland studied in France with Nadia Boulanger, and taught from 1940 at the Berkshire Music Center. He took avant-garde European styles and gave them a distinctive American accent. His eight film scores, including *The Heiress* 1949, set new standards for Hollywood.

Copley John Singleton 1738–1815. American painter. He was the leading portraitist of the colonial period, but from 1775 he lived mainly in London, where he painted lively historical scenes such as *The Death of Major Pierson* 1783 (Tate Gallery, London).

Copley was born in Boston, Massachusetts. Some of his history paintings are unusual in that they portray dramatic events of his time, such as *Brook Watson and the Shark* 1778 (National Gallery, Washington, DC).

copper orange-pink, very malleable and ductile, metallic element, symbol Cu (from Latin *cuprum*), atomic number 29, atomic weight 63.54. It is used for its durability, pliability, high thermal and electrical conductivity, and resistance to corrosion.

It was the first metal used systematically for tools by humans; when mined and worked into utensils it formed the technological basis for the Copper Age in prehistory. When alloyed with tin it forms bronze, which strengthens the copper, allowing it to hold a sharp edge; the systematic production and use of this was the basis for the prehistoric Bronze Age. Brass, another hard copper alloy, includes zinc. The element's name comes from the Greek for Cyprus (*Kyprios*), where copper was mined.

copper ore any mineral from which copper is extracted, including native copper, Cu; chalcocite, Cu_2S; chalcopyrite, $CuFeS_2$; bornite, Cu_5FeS_4; azurite, $Cu_3(CO_3)_2(OH)_2$; malachite, $Cu_2CO_3(OH)_2$; and chrysocolla, $CuSiO_3.nH_2O$.

Native copper and the copper sulfides are usually found in veins associated with igneous intrusions. Chrysocolla and the carbonates are products of the weathering of copper-bearing rocks. Copper was one of the first metals to be worked, because it occurred in native form and needed little refining. Today the main producers are the US, Russia, Kazakhstan, Georgia, Uzbekistan, Armenia, Zambia, Chile, Peru, and Zaire.

Coppola Francis Ford 1939– . US film director and screenwriter. He directed *The Godfather* 1972, which became one of the biggest money-making films of all time, and its sequels *The Godfather Part II* 1974, which garnered seven Academy Awards, and *The Godfather Part III* 1990. His other films include *Apocalypse Now* 1979, *One From the Heart* 1982, *Rumblefish* 1983, *The Outsiders* 1983, and *Tucker: The Man and His Dream* 1988.

After working on horror B-films, his first successes were *Finian's Rainbow* 1968 and *Patton* 1969, for which his screenplay won an Academy Award. Among his other films are *The Conversation* 1972, *The Cotton Club* 1984, and *Gardens of Stone* 1987.

copra dried meat from the kernel of the ◊coconut, used to make coconut oil.

Copt descendant of those ancient Egyptians who adopted Christianity in the 1st century and refused to convert to Islam after the Arab conquest. They now form a small minority (about 5%) of Egypt's population. *Coptic* is a member of the Hamito-Semitic language family. It is descended from the language of the ancient Egyptians and is the ritual language of the Coptic Christian church. It is written in the Greek alphabet with some additional characters derived from ◊demotic script.

The head of the Coptic church is the Patriarch of Alexandria, currently Shenouda III (1923–), 117th pope of Alexandria. Imprisoned by President Sadat 1981, he is opposed by Muslim fundamentalists.

Before the Arab conquest a majority of Christian Egyptians had adopted Monophysite views (that Christ had "one nature" rather than being both human and divine). When this was condemned by the Council of Chalcedon 451, they became schismatic and were persecuted by the orthodox party, to which they were opposed on nationalistic as well as religious grounds. They readily accepted Arab rule, but were later subjected to persecution by their new masters. They are mainly town-dwellers, distinguishable in dress and customs from their Muslim compatriots. They rarely marry outside their own sect.

copulation act of mating in animals with internal ◊fertilization. Male mammals have a ◊penis or other organ that is used to introduce spermatozoa into the reproductive tract of the female. Most birds transfer sperm by pressing their cloacas (the openings of their reproductive tracts) together.

copyright law applying to literary, musical, and artistic works (including plays, recordings, films, photographs, radio and television broadcasts, and, in the US and the UK, computer programs), which prevents the reproduction of the work, in whole or in part, without the author's consent.

Copyright applies to a work, not an idea. For example, the basic plots of two novels might be identical, but copyright would be infringed only if it was clear that one author had copied from another. A translation is protected in its own right. The copyright holder may assign the copyright to another or license others to reproduce or adapt the work. In 1991, the US Supreme Court ruled that copyright does not exist in the information in a telephone directory since "copyright rewards originality, not effort."

In the US (since 1989) copyright lasts for a holder's lifetime plus 50 years, or a flat 75 years for a company copyright. It must be registered with the US Copyright Office of the Library of Congress to bring a court action. Works first federally copyrighted before 1978 must still be renewed in the 28th year to receive the second term of 47 years or it will fall into the public domain at the end of the 28th year. Various conditions apply to works published before 1989 and those between Jan 1, 1978, and March 1, 1989. For specific information, contact the Copyright Office, Library of Congress, Washington, DC.

Copyright is internationally enforceable under the Berne Convention 1886 (ratified by the US March 1, 1989) and the Universal Copyright Convention 1952

Computer software is specifically covered in

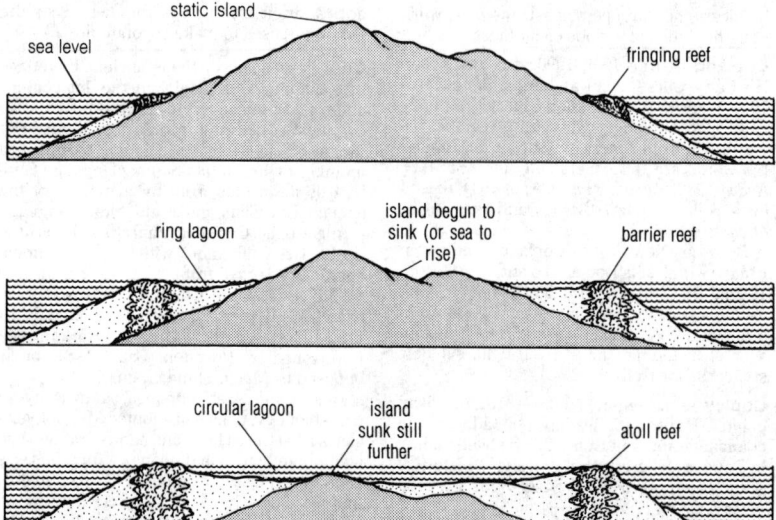

coral *The formation of a coral atoll by the gradual sinking of a volcanic island.*

the US under the Copyright Act 1976 and the Computer Software Act 1980.

coral marine invertebrate of the class Anthozoa in the phylum Cnidaria, which also includes sea anemones and jellyfish. It has a skeleton of lime (calcium carbonate) extracted from the surrounding water. Corals exist in warm seas, at moderate depths with sufficient light. Some coral is valued for decoration or jewelry, for example, Mediterranean red coral *Corallum rubrum.*

Corals live in a symbiotic relationship with microscopic ◊algae (zooxanthellae), which are incorporated into the soft tissue. The algae obtain carbon dioxide from the coral polyps, and the polyps receive nutrients from the algae. Corals also have a relationship to the fish that rest or take refuge within their branches, and which excrete nutrients that make the corals grow faster. The majority of corals form large colonies although there are species that live singly. Their accumulated skeletons make up large coral reefs and atolls. The Great Barrier Reef, to the NE of Australia, is about 1,000 mi/ 1,600 km long, has a total area of 7,700 sq mi/ 20,000 sq km, and adds 50 million tons of calcium to the reef each year. The world's reefs cover an estimated 240,000 sq mi/ 620,000 sq km.

coralroot any leafless orchid of the genus *Corallorhiza*, having branched coral-colored roots and small yellowish or purplish flowers. These orchids are either parasitic on the roots of other plants, or saprophytes, living on decaying organic matter.

Coral Sea or *Solomon Sea* part of the Pacific Ocean bounded by NE Australia, New Guinea, the Solomon Islands, Vanuatu, and New Caledonia. It contains numerous coral islands and reefs. The Coral Sea Islands are a territory of Australia; they comprise scattered reefs and islands over an area of about 386,000 sq mi/ 1,000,000 sq km. They are uninhabited except for a meteorological station on Willis Island. The ◊Great Barrier Reef lies along its western edge, just off the east coast of Australia.

In the World War II Battle of the Coral Sea, May 7–8, 1942, the US fleet prevented the Japanese from landing in SE New Guinea and thus threatening Australia.

cor anglais or *English horn* alto member of the ◊oboe family.

Corbett Gentleman Jim (James John) 1866–1933. US boxer who gained the heavyweight title in his 1892 New Orleans fight with reigning champion John L Sullivan; this was the first title bout to be fought with gloves and according to the Marquess of Queensberry rules. Corbett held the title until his defeat 1897 by Robert Fitzsimmons.

Corbett was born in San Francisco and after a brief career as a bank clerk became a professional boxer 1886. He eventually gained a national reputation for his elegant manner and his dangerous right hook (a punch that he popularized).

Corbusier, Le see ◊Le Corbusier, architect.

cord unit for measuring the volume of wood cut for fuel. One cord equals 128 cubic feet (3.456 cubic meters), or a stack 8 feet (2.4 m) long, 4 feet (1.2 m) wide, and 4 feet high.

Corday Charlotte 1768–1793. French Girondin (right-wing republican during the French Revolution). After the overthrow of the Girondins by the more extreme Jacobins May 1793, she stabbed to death the Jacobin leader, Jean Paul Marat, with a bread knife as he sat in his bath in July of the same year. She was guillotined.

cordierite silicate mineral, $(Mg,Fe)_2Al_4Si_5O_{18}$, blue to purplish in color. It is characteristic of metamorphic rocks formed from clay sediments under conditions of low pressure but moderate temperature; it is the mineral that forms the spots in spotted slate and spotted hornfels.

cordillera group of mountain ranges and their valleys, all running in a specific direction, formed by the continued convergence of two tectonic plates (see ◊tectonics) along a line.

The whole western section of North America, including the Rocky Mountains and the coastal ranges parallel to the contact between the North American and the Pacific plates, is called the Western Cordillera.

Cordilleras, the mountainous western section of North America, with the Rocky mountains and the coastal ranges parallel to the contact

between the North American and the Pacific plates.

Córdoba city in central Argentina, on the Río Primero; population (1991) 1,179,000. It is the capital of Córdoba province. Main industries include cement, glass, textiles, and vehicles. Founded 1573, it has a university founded 1613, a military aviation college, an observatory, and a cathedral.

Córdoba capital of Córdoba province, Spain, on the river Guadalquivir; population (1991) 309,200. Paper, textiles, and copper products are manufactured here. It has many Moorish remains, including the mosque, now a cathedral, founded by 'Abd-ar-Rahman I in 785, which is one of the largest Christian churches in the world. Córdoba was probably founded by the Carthaginians; it was held by the Moors 711–1236.

core in earth science, the innermost part of the Earth. It is divided into an inner core, the upper boundary of which is 1,060 mi/1,700 km from the center, and an outer core, 1,130 mi/ 1,820 km thick. Both parts are thought to consist of iron-nickel alloy, with the inner core being solid and the outer core being semisolid. The temperature may be 5,400°F/3,000°C.

Evidence for the nature of the core comes from seismology (observation of the paths of earthquake waves through the Earth), and calculations of the Earth's density.

CORE (acronym from *Congress of Racial Equality*) US nonviolent civil-rights organization, founded in Chicago 1942.

Corelli Arcangelo 1653–1713. Italian composer and violinist. He was one of the first virtuoso violinists and his music, marked by graceful melody, includes a set of *concerti grossi* and five sets of chamber sonatas.

Born near Milan, he studied in Bologna and in about 1685 settled in Rome, under the patronage of Cardinal Pietro Ottoboni, where he published his first violin sonatas.

Corfu (Greek *Kérkira*) northernmost and second largest of the Ionian islands of Greece, off the coast of Epirus in the Ionian Sea; area 414 sq mi/1,072 sq km; population (1981) 96,500. Its businesses include tourism, fruit, olive oil, and textiles. Its largest town is the port of Corfu (Kérkira), population (1981) 33,560. Corfu was colonized by the Corinthians about 700 BC. Venice held it 1386–1797, Britain 1815–64.

Cori Carl 1896–1984 and Gerty 1896–1957. Husband-and-wife team of US biochemists, both born in Prague, who, together with Argentine physiologist Bernardo Houssay (1887–1971), received a Nobel Prize 1947 for their discovery of how ◊glycogen (animal starch)—a derivative of glucose—is broken down and resynthesized in the body, for use as a store and source of energy.

coriander pungent fresh herb, the Eurasian plant *Coriandrum sativum*, a member of the parsley family Umbelliferae, also a spice: the dried ripe fruit. The spice is used commercially as a flavoring in meat products, bakery goods, tobacco, gin, liqueurs, chilli, and curry powder. Both are much used in cooking in the Middle East, India, Mexico, and China.

Corinth (Greek *Kórinthos*) port in Greece, on the isthmus connecting the Peloponnese with the mainland; population (1981) 22,650. The rocky isthmus is bisected by the 4 mi/ 6.5 km Corinth canal, opened 1893. The site

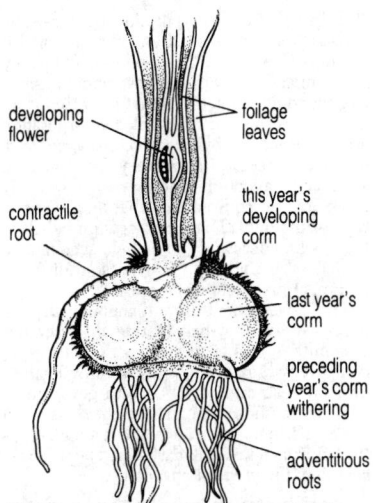

corm *Corms, found in plants such as the gladiolus and crocus, are underground storage organs.*

developing flower

foilage leaves

contractile root

this year's developing corm

last year's corm

preceding year's corm withering

adventitious roots

of the ancient city-state of Corinth lies 4.5 mi/ 7 km SW of the port.

Corinth was already a place of some commercial importance in the 9th century BC. At the end of the 6th century BC it joined the Peloponnesian League, and took a prominent part in the ⟁Persian and the ⟁Peloponnesian wars. In 146 BC it was conquered by the Romans. The emperor Augustus (63 BC– AD 14) made it capital of the Roman province of Achaea. St Paul visited Corinth AD 51 and addressed two epistles to its churches. After many changes of ownership it became part of independent Greece 1822. Corinth's ancient monuments include the ruined temple of Apollo (6th century BC).

Corinthian in Classical architecture, one of the five types of column; see ⟁order.

Corinthians two ⟁epistles (Corinthians I, Corinthians II) in the New Testament to the church at Corinth; attributed to St ⟁Paul.

Coriolis effect the effect of the Earth's west-to-east rotation upon the atmosphere and upon all objects on the Earth's surface. In the northern hemisphere it causes winds, ocean currents, and aircraft to be deflected to the right (clockwise); in the southern hemisphere it causes deflection to the left (counterclockwise).

The effect has to be allowed for in launching guided missiles, but despite popular belief it has negligible effect on the clockwise or counterclockwise direction of water running out of a bath. It is named after its discoverer, French mathematician Gaspard Coriolis (1792–1843).

cork light, waterproof outer layers of the bark of the stems and roots of almost all trees and shrubs. The cork oak *Quercus suber*, a native of S Europe and N Africa, is cultivated in Spain and Portugal; the exceptionally thick outer layers of its bark provide the cork that is used commercially.

Cork city and seaport of County Cork, on the river Lee, at the head of the long inlet of Cork Harbor; population (1991) 127,000. Cork is the second port of the Republic of Ireland. The lower section of the harbor can berth liners, and the town has distilleries, shipyards, and

iron foundries. St Finbarr's 7th-century monastery was the original foundation of Cork. It was eventually settled by Danes who were dispossessed by the English 1172.

corm short, swollen, underground plant stem, surrounded by protective scale leaves, as seen in the genus *Crocus*. It stores food, provides a means of ⟁vegetative reproduction, and acts as a ⟁perennating organ.

During the year, the corm gradually withers as the food reserves are used for the production of leafy, flowering shoots formed from axillary buds.

Several new corms are formed at the base of these shoots, above the old corm.

Corman Roger 1926– . US film director and prolific producer. He made a stylish series of Edgar Allan Poe films starring Vincent Price, beginning with *The House of Usher* 1960.

After 1970 Corman confined himself to production and distribution.

cormorant any of various diving seabirds, mainly of the genus *Phalacrocorax*, about 3 ft/ 90 cm long, with webbed feet, long neck, hooked beak, and glossy black plumage. There are some 30 species of cormorant worldwide, including a flightless form *Nannopterum harrisi* in the Galápagos Islands. Cormorants generally feed on fish and shellfish. Some species breed on inland lakes and rivers.

corn cultivated New World plant *Zea mays* of the grass family, with the grain borne on cobs enclosed in husks. It is also called maize or Indian corn. It was domesticated 6,000 BC in Mesoamerica, where it grew wild. It became the staple crop for the ⟁Neolithic farming villages and ⟁civilizations of Mexico and Peru; it was cultivated throughout most of the New World at the point of European contact. It was brought to Europe, Asia, and Africa by the colonizing powers, but its use is mainly for animal feed in those regions. In the US, a corn monoculture dominates the Midwest, where many hybrids have been developed for both human food and animal feed. Today it is grown extensively in all subtropical and warm temperate regions, and its range has been extended to colder zones by hardy varieties developed in the 1960s.

Corn is eaten fresh (on the cob or creamed), canned (niblets), frozen, and in dried forms (cornmeal, popcorn), and is made into hominy, polenta, cornflour, and corn bread. It is pressed for corn oil and fermented into a mash, which, distilled, is corn liquor (whiskey). Most of the methods of storing, processing, and cooking corn can be traced to American Indian recipes. Popcorn has been found in archeological sites in the SW dating from 4,000 BC. Corn stalks are made into paper and hardboard.

cornea transparent front section of the vertebrate ⟁eye. The cornea is curved and behaves as a fixed lens, so that light entering the eye is partly focused before it reaches the lens.

There are no blood vessels in the cornea and it relies on the fluid in the front chamber of the eye for nourishment. Further protection for the eye is provided by the ⟁conjunctiva. In humans, diseased or opaque parts may be replaced by grafts of corneal tissue from a donor.

Corneille Pierre 1606–1684. French dramatist. His many tragedies, such as *Oedipe* 1659, glorify the strength of will governed by reason, and established the French Classical dramatic tradition for the next two centuries. His first play,

Mélite, was performed 1629, followed by others that gained him a brief period of favor with Cardinal Richelieu. *Le Cid* 1636 was attacked by the Academicians, although it received public acclaim. Later plays were based on Aristotle's unities.

Although Corneille enjoyed public popularity, periodic disfavor with Richelieu marred his career, and it was not until 1639 that Corneille (again in favor) produced plays such as *Horace* 1639, *Polyeucte* 1643, *Le Menteur* 1643, and *Rodogune* 1645, leading to his election to the Académie 1647. His later plays were approved by Louis XIV.

Cornell Katherine 1898–1974. German-born US actress. Her first major success came with an appearance on Broadway in *Nice People* 1921. This debut was followed by a long string of New York stage successes, several of which were directed by her husband, Guthrie McClintic. By 1930 she began to produce her own plays; the most famous of them, *The Barretts of Wimpole Street* 1931, was later taken on tour and produced for television 1956.

Born in Berlin of American parents, Cornell was attracted to the stage at an early age, appearing with the Washington Square Players 1916.

cornet brass band instrument. It is like a shorter, broader trumpet, with a wider bore and mellower tone, and without fixed notes. Notes of different pitch are obtained by overblowing and by means of three pistons.

cornett 17th-century woodwind instrument. It has a cup mouthpiece and produces a trumpetlike tone.

cornflower plant *Centaurea cyanus* of the family Compositae. It is distinguished from the knapweeds by its deep azure-blue flowers. Formerly a common weed in N European wheat fields, it is now commonly grown in gardens as a herbaceous plant.

Cornforth John Warcup 1917– . Australian chemist. Using ⟁radioisotopes as markers, he found out how cholesterol is manufactured in the living cell and how enzymes synthesize chemicals that are mirror images of each other (optical ⟁isomers). He shared a Nobel Prize 1975 with Swiss chemist Vladimir Prelog (1906–).

Corniche (French "mountain ledge") *la Grande* (Great) *Corniche*, a road with superb alpine and coastal scenery, built between Nice and Menton, S France, by Napoleon; it rises to 1,700 ft/520 m. *La Moyenne* (Middle) and *la Petite* (Little) *Corniche* are supplementary parallel roads, the latter being nearest the coast.

Cornish language extinct member of the ⟁Celtic languages, a branch of the Indo-European language family, spoken in Cornwall, England, until 1777. Written Cornish first appeared in 10th-century documents; some religious plays were written in Cornish in the 15th and 16th centuries, but later literature is scanty, consisting mainly of folk tales and verses. In recent years the language has been revived in a somewhat reconstructed form by members of the Cornish nationalist movement.

Corn Laws in Britain until 1846, laws used to regulate the export or import of cereals in order to maintain an adequate supply for consumers and a secure price for producers. For centuries the Corn Laws formed an integral part of the mercantile system in England; they were repealed because they became an unwarranted tax on food and a hindrance to British exports.

Although mentioned as early as the 12th century, the Corn Laws only became significant in the late 18th century. After the Napoleonic wars, with mounting pressure from a growing urban population, the laws aroused strong opposition because of their tendency to drive up prices. They were modified 1828 and 1842 and, partly as a result of the Irish potato famine, repealed by prime minister Robert Peel 1846.

cornstarch purified, fine, powdery starch made from corn, used as a thickener in cooking and to make corn syrup commercially.

cornucopia (Latin "horn of plenty") in Greek mythology, one of the horns of the goat Amaltheia, which was caused by Zeus to refill itself indefinitely with food and drink. In paintings, the cornucopia is depicted as a horn-shaped container spilling over with fruit and flowers.

Cornwall county in SW England including the ⇨Scilly Islands (Scillies)
area (excluding Scillies) 1,370 sq mi/3,550 sq km
cities Truro (administrative headquarters), Camborne, Launceston; resorts of Bude, Falmouth, Newquay, Penzance, St Ives
physical Bodmin Moor (including Brown Willy 1,375 ft/419 m), Land's End peninsula, St Michael's Mount, rivers Tamar, Fowey, Fal, Camel
features Poldhu, site of first transatlantic radio signal 1901. The Stannary or Tinners' Parliament has six members from each of the four Stannary towns: Losthwithiel, Launceston, Helston, and Truro. The flag of St Piran, the patron saint of Cornwall, a white St George's cross on a black ground, is used by separatists
products electronics, spring flowers, tin (mined since Bronze Age, some workings renewed 1960s, though the industry has all but disappeared), kaolin (St Austell), fish
population (1991) 469,300
famous people John Betjeman, Humphry Davy, Daphne Du Maurier, William Golding
history the Stannary, established in the 11th century, ceased to meet 1752 but its powers were never rescinded at Westminster, and it was revived 1974 as a separatist movement.

Cornwallis Charles, 1st Marquess 1738–1805. British general in the ⇨American Revolution until 1781, when his defeat at Yorktown led to final surrender and ended the war. He then served twice as governor-general of India and once as viceroy of Ireland.

corolla a collective name for the petals of a flower. In some plants the petal margins are partially or completely fused to form a **corolla tube**, for example in morning glories *Convolvulus*.

corona faint halo of hot (about 3,600,000°F/2,000,000°C) and tenuous gas around the Sun, which boils from the surface. It is visible at solar ⇨eclipses or through a **coronagraph**, an instrument that blocks light from the Sun's brilliant disk. Gas flows away from the corona to form the ⇨solar wind.

Corona Australis or **Southern Crown** constellation of the southern hemisphere, located near the constellation Sagittarius.

Corona Borealis or **Northern Crown** constellation of the northern hemisphere, between Hercules and Boötes, traditionally identified with the jeweled crown of Ariadne that was cast into the sky by Bacchus (in Greek mythology). Its brightest star is Alphecca (or Gemma), which is 78 light-years from Earth.

Coronado Francisco de *c.* 1500–1554. Spanish explorer who sailed to the New World 1535 in search of gold. In 1540 he set out with several hundred men from the Gulf of California on an exploration of what are today the Southern states. Although he failed to discover any gold, his expedition came across the impressive Grand Canyon of the Colorado and introduced the use of the horse to the indigenous Indians.

coronary artery disease (Latin *corona* "crown," from the arteries' encircling of the heart) condition in which the fatty deposits of ⇨atherosclerosis form in the coronary arteries that supply the heart muscle, making them too narrow.

These arteries may already be hardened (arteriosclerosis). If the heart's oxygen requirements are increased, as during exercise, the blood supply through the narrowed arteries may be inadequate, and the pain of ⇨angina results. A ⇨heart attack occurs if the blood supply to an area of the heart is cut off, for example because a blood clot (thrombus) has blocked one of the coronary arteries. The subsequent lack of oxygen damages the heart muscle (infarct), and if a large area of the heart is affected, the attack may be fatal. Coronary artery disease tends to run in families and is linked to smoking, lack of exercise, and a diet high in saturated (mostly animal) fats, which tends to increase the level of blood ⇨cholesterol. It is a common cause of death in many industrialized countries; older men are the most vulnerable group.

coronation ceremony of investing a sovereign with the emblems of royalty, as a symbol of inauguration in office. Since the coronation of Harold 1066, English sovereigns have been crowned in Westminster Abbey, London.

Corot Jean-Baptiste-Camille 1796–1875. French painter, creator of a distinctive landscape style with cool colors and soft focus. His early work, including Italian scenes in the 1820s, influenced the Barbizon school of painters. Like them, Corot worked outdoors, but he also continued a conventional academic tradition with more romanticized paintings.

Born in Paris, Corot lived in Rome 1825–28, where he learned the tradition of Classical landscape painting, centered around a historical or mythological incident.

corporal punishment physical punishment of wrongdoers—for example, by whipping. It is still used as a punishment for criminals in many countries, especially under Islamic law. Corporal punishment of children by parents is illegal in some countries, including Sweden, Finland, Denmark, and Norway.

corporation a number of people grouped together in a legally constituted joint enterprise, usually for the conduct of business and for tax advantages. Types of corporations include publicly traded corporations, which sell stock to the public to raise capital, and privately held corporations. Corporations are legal entities filed with state governments and distinct from the individuals who manage their affairs or the owners of their stock. Only about 15% of the businesses in the US are corporations, but they produce 80% of sales.

The legal status of a corporation as a unique entity gives the owners and managers freedom from liability for the corporation's actions. The corporation can be sued and can sue, and it can make contracts. This limitation of liability is essential for growth and development, since large amounts of capital must be raised from many sources. The affairs of the corporation are governed by bylaws and managed by a board of directors. Laws vary from state to state and nation to nation as to how many directors are required and whether they must be stockholders. The board acts on behalf of the stockholders and can be held accountable for failure to abide by the bylaws or for faulty judgment that results in losses.

The development of multinational corporations, enterprises that operate in a number of countries, has been a subject of increasing controversy since they operate only in their own interest, often at odds with government policies in those countries. They also can cause disruptions in domestic economies as they shift facilities and marketing operations in search of the greatest advantage.

corporation tax tax levied on a company's profits by public authorities. It is a form of income tax, and rates vary according to country, but there is usually a flat rate. It is a large source of revenue for governments.

corps de ballet dancers in a ballet company who usually dance in groups, in support of the soloists. At the Paris Opéra this is the name given to the whole company.

Corpus Christi feast celebrated in the Roman Catholic and Orthodox churches, and to some extent in the Anglican church, on the Thursday after Trinity Sunday. It was instituted in the 13th century through the devotion of St Juliana, prioress of Mount Cornillon, near Liège, Belgium, in honor of the Real Presence of Christ in the Eucharist.

Corpus Christi city and port in SE Texas, on the Gulf of Mexico at the mouth of the river Nueces, SE of San Antonio; seat of Nueces County; population (1990) 257,500. Its main industries are oil refining and shipping, commercial fishing, and the processing and shipping of agricultural products. Corpus Christi began as a small trading post. It was used as a base by General Zachary Taylor during the Mexican–American War 1845–58 and was captured by Union troops 1864 during the Civil War.

corpuscular theory hypothesis about the nature of light championed by Isaac Newton, who postulated that it consists of a stream of particles or corpuscles. The theory was superseded at the beginning of the 19th century by Thomas ⇨Young's wave theory. ⇨Quantum theory and wave mechanics embody both concepts.

corpus luteum temporary endocrine gland found in the mammalian ⇨ovary. It is formed after ovulation from the Graafian follicle, a group of cells associated with bringing the egg to maturity, and secretes the hormone progesterone.

After the release of an egg the follicle enlarges under the action of luteinizing hormone, released from the pituitary. The corpus luteum secretes the hormone progesterone, which maintains the uterus wall ready for pregnancy. If pregnancy does not occur the corpus luteum breaks down.

Correggio Antonio Allegri da *c.* 1494–1534. Italian painter of the High Renaissance whose style followed the Classical grandeur of

Leonardo and Titian but anticipated the Baroque in its emphasis on movement, softer forms, and contrasts of light and shade.

Based in Parma, he painted splendid illusionistic visions in the cathedral there, including *The Ascenscion of the Virgin*. His religious paintings, including the night scene *Adoration of the Shepherds* about 1527–30 (Gemäldegalerie, Dresden), and mythological scenes, such as *The Loves of Jupiter* (Wallace Collection, London), were much admired in the 18th century.

Corregidor island fortress off the Bataan Peninsula at the mouth of Manila Bay, Luzon, the Philippines. On May 6, 1942, Japanese forces captured Corregidor and its 10,000 US and Filipino defenders, completing their conquest of the Philippines. US forces recaptured Corregidor in Feb 1945.

correlation relation between two sets of information: they correlate when they vary together. If one set of data increases at the same time as the other, the relationship is said to be positive or direct. If one set of data increases as the other decreases, the relationship is negative or inverse. Correlation can be shown by plotting a best-fit line on a ⟳scatter diagram.

In statistics, such relations are measured by the calculation of ⟳coefficients. These generally measure correlation on a scale with 1 indicating perfect positive correlation, 0 no correlation at all, and −1 perfect inverse correlation.

Correlation coefficients for assumed linear relations include the Pearson product moment correlation coefficient (known simply as the correlation coefficient), Kendall's tau correlation coefficient, or Spearman's rho correlation coefficient, which is used in nonparametric statistics (where the data are measured on ordinal rather than interval scales). A high correlation does not always indicate dependence between two variables; it may be that there is a third (unstated) variable upon which both depend.

correspondence in mathematics, the relation between two sets where an operation on the members of one set maps some or all of them onto one or more members of the other. For example, if *A* is the set of members of a family and *B* is the set of months in the year, *A* and *B* are in correspondence if the operation is: "... has a birthday in the month of ... ."

corresponding society in British history, one of the first independent organizations for the working classes, advocating annual parliaments and universal male suffrage. The London Corresponding Society was founded 1792 by politicians Thomas Hardy (1752–1832) and John Horne Tooke (1736–1812). It later established branches in Scotland and the provinces. Many of its activities had to be held in secret and government fears about the spread of revolutionary doctrines led to its banning 1799.

Corrientes city and river port of Argentina, on the Paraná River; population (1991) 267,700. Capital of Corrientes province, it is a stock-raising district. Industries include tanning, lumber milling, and textiles.

corrigendum (Latin) something to be corrected.

corrosion the eating away and eventual destruction of metals and alloys by chemical attack. The rusting of ordinary iron and steel is the most common form of corrosion. Rusting takes place in moist air, when the iron combines with oxygen and water to form a brown-orange deposit of ⟳rust (hydrated iron oxide). The rate of corrosion is increased where the atmosphere is polluted with sulfur dioxide. Salty road and air conditions accelerate the rusting of car bodies.

Corrosion is largely an electrochemical process, and acidic and salty conditions favor the establishment of electrolytic cells on the metal, which cause it to be eaten away. Other examples of corrosion include the green deposit that forms on copper and bronze, called verdigris, a basic copper carbonate. The tarnish on silver is a corrosion product, a film of silver sulfide.

corsair pirate based on the N African Barbary Coast. From the 16th century onwards the corsairs plundered shipping in the Mediterranean and Atlantic, holding hostages for ransom or selling them as slaves. Although many punitive expeditions were sent against them, they were not suppressed until France occupied Algiers 1830.

Most pirates were Turkish or North African, but there were also many Europeans, such as the Englishman Sir Francis Verney, half brother of Edmund Verney.

Corse French name for ⟳Corsica.

Corsica (French *Corse*) island region of France, in the Mediterranean off the W coast of Italy, N of Sardinia; it comprises the *départements* of Haute Corse and Corse du Sud
area 3,358 sq mi/8,700 sq km
capital Ajaccio (port)
physical mountainous; ⟳maquis vegetation
features ⟳maquis vegetation. Corsica's mountain bandits were eradicated 1931, but the tradition of the vendetta or blood feud lingers. The island is the main base of the Foreign Legion
government its special status involves a 61-member regional parliament with the power to scrutinize French National Assembly bills applicable to the island and propose amendments
products wine, olive oil
population (1986) 249,000, including just under 50% native Corsicans. There are about 400,000 *émigrés*, mostly in Mexico and Central America, who return to retire
language French (official); the majority speak Corsican, an Italian dialect
famous people Napoleon
history the Phocaeans of Ionia founded Alalia about 570 BC, and were succeeded in turn by the Etruscans, the Carthaginians, the Romans, the Vandals, and the Arabs. In the 14th century Corsica fell to the Genoese, and in the second half of the 18th century a Corsican nationalist, Pasquale Paoli (1725–1807), led an independence movement. Genoa sold Corsica to France 1768. In World War II Corsica was occupied by Italy 1942–43. From 1962, French *pieds noirs* (refugees from Algeria), mainly vine growers, were settled in Corsica, and their prosperity helped to fan nationalist feeling, which demands an independent Corsica. This fueled the National Liberation Front of Corsica (FNLC), banned 1983, which has engaged in some terrorist bombings (a truce began June 1988 but ended Jan 1991).

Cort Henry 1740–1800. British iron manufacturer. For the manufacture of ⟳wrought iron, he invented the puddling process and developed the rolling mill, both of which were significant in the Industrial Revolution.

Cortázar Julio 1914–1984. Argentine writer whose novels include *The Winners* 1960, *Hopscotch* 1963, and *Sixty-two: A Model Kit* 1968.

One of his several volumes of short stories includes "Blow-up," adapted for a film by the Italian director Michelangelo Antonioni.

Cortés Hernán (Ferdinand) 1485–1547. Spanish conquistador. He conquered the Aztec empire 1519–21, and secured Mexico for Spain.

Cortés went to the West Indies as a young man and in 1518 was given command of an expedition to Mexico. Landing with only 600 men, he was at first received as a god by the Aztec emperor ⟳Montezuma II but was expelled from Tenochtitlán (Mexico City) when he was found not to be "divine." With the aid of Indian allies he recaptured the city 1521, and overthrew the Aztec empire. His conquests eventually included most of Mexico and N Central America.

cortex in biology, the outer layer of a structure such as the brain, kidney, or adrenal gland. In botany the cortex includes non-specialized cells lying just beneath the surface cells of the root and stem.

corticosteroid any of several steroid hormones secreted by the cortex of the ⟳adrenal glands; also synthetic forms with similar properties. Corticosteroids have antiinflammatory and ⟳immunosuppressive effects and may be used to treat a number of conditions including rheumatoid arthritis, severe allergies, asthma, some skin diseases, and some cancers. Side effects can be serious, and therapy must be withdrawn very gradually.

The two main groups of corticosteroids include **glucocorticoids** (⟳cortisone, hydrocortisone, prednisone, and dexamethasone), which affect carbohydrate metabolism, and **mineralocorticoids** (aldosterone, fluorocortisone), which control the balance of water and salt in the body.

cortisone natural corticosteroid produced by the ⟳adrenal gland, now synthesized for its antiinflammatory qualities and used in the treatment of rheumatoid arthritis.

Cortisone was discovered by Tadeus Reichstein of Basel, Switzerland, and put to practical clinical use for rheumatoid arthritis by Philip Hench (1896–1965) and Edward Kendall (1886–1972) in the US (all three shared a Nobel Prize 1950). A product of the adrenal gland, it was first synthesized from a constituent of ox bile, and is now produced commercially from a Mexican yam and from a by-product of the sisal plant. It is used for treating allergies and certain cancers, as well as rheumatoid arthritis. The side effects of cortisone steroids include muscle wasting, fat redistribution, diabetes, bone thinning, and high blood pressure.

corundum native aluminum oxide, Al_2O_3, the hardest naturally occurring mineral known apart from diamond (corundum rates 9 on the Mohs' scale of hardness); lack of ⟳cleavage also increases its durability. Varieties of gem-quality corundum are **ruby** (red) and **sapphire** (any color other than red, usually blue). Poorer-quality and synthetic corundum is used in industry, for example as an ⟳abrasive.

Corundum forms in silica-poor igneous and metamorphic rocks. It is a constituent of emery, which is metamorphosed bauxite.

Its crystals are barrel-shaped prisms of the trigonal system.

Corunna (Spanish *La Coruña*) city in the extreme NW of Spain; population (1991) 251,300.

It is the capital of Corunna province. Industry is centered on the fisheries; tobacco, sugar refining, and textiles are also important. The ◊Armada sailed from Corunna 1588, and the town was sacked by Francis Drake 1589.

corvette small-armed vessel, such as those escorting convoys in World War II. The term, now obsolete, was revived from sailing days.

Cos alternate spelling of ◊Kos, a Greek island.

Cosby Bill (William Henry) 1937– . US comedian and actor. His portrayal of the dashing, handsome secret agent in the television series *I Spy* 1965–68 won him three Emmy awards and revolutionized the way in which blacks were presented on screen. His sardonic humor, based on wry observations of domestic life and parenthood, found its widest audience in *The Cosby Show* 1984–92, which consistently topped the national ratings and provided new role models for young African Americans. It also made him one of the richest performers in showbusiness.

Among his other tv series are *The Bill Cosby Show* 1969–77 and *Fat Albert and the Cosby Kids* 1972–84. He hosted the game show *You Bet Your Life* from 1992.

cosecant in trigonometry, a ◊function of an angle in a right-angled triangle found by dividing the length of the hypotenuse (the longest side) by the length of the side opposite the angle. Thus the cosecant of an angle A, usually shortened to cosec A, is always greater than (or equal to) 1. It is the reciprocal of the sine of the angle, that is, cosec $A = 1/\sin A$.

Cosenza town in Calabria, S Italy, at the junction of the rivers Crati and Busento; population (1989) 105,300. It is the capital of Cosenza province and is an archiepiscopal see. ◊Alaric, king of the Visigoths, is buried here.

Cosgrave Liam 1920– . Irish Fine Gael politician, prime minister of the Republic of Ireland 1973–77. As party leader 1965–77, he headed a Fine Gael–Labor coalition government from 1973. Relations between the Irish and UK governments improved under his premiership.

Cosgrave William Thomas 1880–1965. Irish politician. He took part in the ◊Easter Rising 1916 and sat in the Sinn Féin cabinet of 1919–21. Head of the Free State government 1922–33, he founded and led the Fine Gael opposition 1933–44. His eldest son is Liam Cosgrave.

cosine in trigonometry, a function of an angle in a right triangle found by dividing the length of the side adjacent to the angle by the length of the hypotenuse (the longest side). It is usually shortened to cos.

cosmic background radiation or *3° radiation* electromagnetic radiation left over from the original formation of the universe in the Big Bang around 15 billion years ago. It corresponds to an overall background temperature of 3K (–270°C/–454°F), or 3°C above absolute zero.

Cosmic background radiation was first detected 1965 by US physicists Arno Penzias (1933–) and Robert Wilson (1936–), who in 1978 shared the Nobel Prize for Physics for their discovery.

cosmic radiation streams of high-energy particles from outer space, consisting of protons, alpha particles, and light nuclei, which collide with atomic nuclei in the Earth's atmosphere, and produce secondary nuclear particles (chiefly ◊mesons, such as pions and muons) that shower the Earth.

Those of low energy seem to be galactic in origin, and detectors (such as the water-Cherenkov detector near Leeds, England, with an area of 4.5 sq mi/12 sq km) are in use to detect extragalactic sources of high-energy rays (possibly the rotating disks of infalling matter around black holes).

cosmid fragment of ◊DNA from the human genome inserted into a bacterial cell. The bacterium replicates the fragment along with its own DNA. In this way the fragments are copied for a gene library. Cosmids are characteristically 40,000 base pairs in length. The most commonly used bacterium is *Escherichia coli*. A ◊yeast artificial chromosome works in the same way.

cosmogony (Greek "universe" and "creation") study of the origin and evolution of cosmic objects, especially the Solar System.

cosmology study of the structure of the universe. Modern cosmology began in the 1920s with the discovery that the universe is expanding, which suggested that it began in an explosion, the ◊Big Bang. An alternative view, the ◊steady-state theory, claimed that the universe has no origin, but is expanding because new matter is being continually created.

cosmonaut term used in the West for any astronaut from the former Soviet Union.

Cossack member of any of several, formerly horse-raising groups of S and SW Russia, Ukraine, and Poland, predominantly of Russian or Ukrainian origin, who took in escaped serfs and lived in independent communal settlements (military brotherhoods) from the 15th to the 19th century. Later they held land in return for military service in the cavalry under Russian and Polish rulers. After 1917, the various Cossack communities were incorporated into the Soviet administrative and collective system.

Costa Rica country in Central America, bounded N by Nicaragua, SE by Panama, E by the Caribbean Sea, and W by the Pacific Ocean.
government The 1949 constitution provides for a president elected for a four-year term by compulsory adult suffrage, two elected vice-presidents, and an appointed cabinet. There is a single-chamber legislature, the 57-member assembly, also serving a four-year term.
history Originally occupied by Guaymi Indians, the area was visited by Christopher ◊Columbus 1502 and was colonized by Spanish settlers from the 16th century, becoming independent 1821. Initially part of the ◊Mexican Empire, then—with El Salvador, Guatemala, Honduras, and Nicaragua—part of the Central American Federation from 1824, Costa Rica became a republic 1838. Apart from a military dictatorship 1870-82 and a brief civil war 1948 after a disputed presidential election, it has been one of the most democratically governed states in Latin America.

In 1949 a new constitution abolished the army, leaving defense to the Civil Guard. José Figueres, leader of the antigovernment

Costa Rica
Republic of (*República de Costa Rica*)

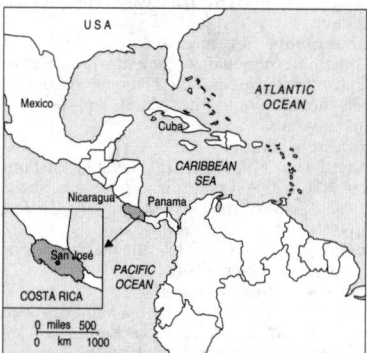

area 19,735 sq mi/51,100 sq km
capital San José
cities ports Limón, Puntarenas
physical high central plateau and tropical coasts; Costa Rica was once entirely forested, containing an estimated 5% of the Earth's flora and fauna. By 1983 only 17% of the forest remained; half of the arable land had been cleared for cattle ranching, which led to landlessness, unemployment (except for 2,000 politically powerful families), and soil erosion; the massive environmental destruction also caused incalculable loss to the gene pool
environment one of the leading centers of conservation in Latin America, with more than 10% of the country protected by national parks, and tree replanting proceeding at a rate of 60 sq mi/150 sq km per year
features Poas Volcano; Guayabo pre-Colombian ceremonial site
head of state and government Rafael

Calderón from 1990
political system liberal democracy
political parties National Liberation Party (PLN), left of center; Christian Socialist Unity Party (PUSC), centrist coalition; ten minor parties
exports coffee, bananas, cocoa, sugar, beef
currency colón
population (1990 est) 3,032,000 (including 1,200 Guaymi Indians); growth rate 2.6% p.a.
life expectancy men 71, women 76
language Spanish (official)
religion Roman Catholic 95%
literacy men 94%, women 93% (1985 est)
GDP $4.3 bn (1986); $1,550 per head
chronology
1821 Independence achieved from Spain.
1949 New constitution adopted. National army abolished. José Figueres, cofounder of the PLN, elected president; he embarked on an ambitious socialist program.
1958–73 Mainly conservative administrations.
1974 PLN regained the presidency and returned to socialist policies.
1978 Rodrigo Carazo, conservative, elected president. Sharp deterioration in the state of the economy.
1982 Luis Alberto Monge (PLN) elected president. Harsh austerity program introduced to rebuild the economy. Pressure from the US to abandon neutral stance and condemn Sandinista regime in Nicaragua.
1983 Policy of neutrality reaffirmed.
1985 Following border clashes with Sandinista forces, a US-trained antiguerrilla guard formed.
1986 Oscar Arias Sánchez won the presidency on a neutralist platform.
1987 Oscar Arias Sánchez won Nobel Prize for Peace for devising a Central American peace plan.
1990 Rafael Calderón (PUSC) elected president.

forces in the previous year, became president. He cofounded the National Liberation Party (PLN), nationalized the banks, and introduced a social security system. He was reelected 1953.

There followed 16 years of mostly conservative rule, with the reversal of some PLN policies. In 1974 Daniel Oduber won the presidency for the PLN. He returned to socialist policies, extended the welfare state, and established friendly relations with communist states. Communist and left-wing parties were legalized.

In 1978 Rodrigo Carazo of the conservative Unity Coalition (CU) became president. His presidency was marked by economic collapse and allegations of his involvement in illegal arms trafficking between Cuba and El Salvador.

In 1982 Luis Alberto Monge, a former labor-union official and cofounder of the PLN, won a convincing victory in the presidential election. To reverse the damage done by the Carazo government, he introduced a 100-day emergency economic program.

relations with Nicaragua The Monge government came under pressure from the US to abandon its neutral stance and condemn the left-wing Sandinista regime in Nicaragua. Costa Rica was also urged to reestablish its army. Monge resisted the pressure and in 1983 reaffirmed his country's neutrality, but relations with Nicaragua deteriorated after border clashes between Sandinista forces and the Costa Rican Civil Guard. In 1985 Monge agreed to create a US-trained antiguerrilla guard, increasing doubts about Costa Rica's neutrality.

In 1986 Oscar Arias Sánchez became president on a neutralist platform, defeating the pro-US candidate, Rafael Angel Calderón, of the Christian Socialist Unity Party (PUSC). Arias worked tirelessly for peace in the region, hosting regional summit meetings and negotiating framework treaties. He won the Nobel Prize for Peace 1987 for his efforts. However, Calderón won the 1990 presidential election.

cost–benefit analysis process whereby a project is assessed for its social and welfare benefits in addition to considering the financial return on investment. For example, this might take into account the environmental impact of an industrial plant or convenience for users of a new railroad.

Costello Elvis. Adopted name of Declan McManus 1954– . English rock singer, songwriter, and guitarist whose intricate yet impassioned lyrics have made him one of Britain's foremost songwriters. The great stylistic range of his work was evident from his 1977 debut *My Aim Is True*.

Coster Laurens Janszoon 1370–1440. Dutch printer. According to some sources, he invented movable type, but after his death an apprentice ran off to Mainz with the blocks and, taking Johann ⚬Gutenberg into his confidence, began a printing business with him.

Costner Kevin 1955– . US film actor. He first achieved top-ranking success with his role as law-enforcer Elliot Ness, in the film version of the 1960s television series *The Untouchables* 1987. Increasingly identified with the embodiment of idealism and high principle, Costner went on to direct and star in *Dances With Wolves* 1990, a Western sympathetic to the

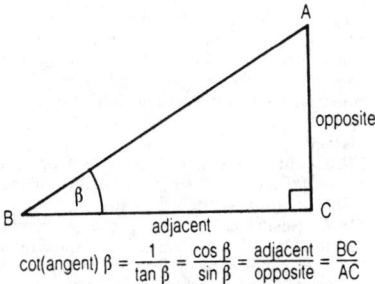

$$\mathrm{cot(angent)}\ \beta = \frac{1}{\tan \beta} = \frac{\cos \beta}{\sin \beta} = \frac{\text{adjacent}}{\text{opposite}} = \frac{BC}{AC}$$

cotangent *The cotangent of angle β is equal to the ratio of the length of the adjacent side to the length of the side opposite.*

native American Indian, which won several Academy Awards. Subsequent films include *Robin Hood—Prince of Thieves* 1991, *JFK* 1991, and *The Bodyguard* 1992.

cost of living see ⚬consumer price index.

cotangent in trigonometry, a ⚬function of an angle in a right-angled triangle found by dividing the length of the side adjacent to the angle by the length of the side opposite it. It is usually written as cotan, or cot and it is the reciprocal of the tangent of the angle, so that cot *A* = 1/tan *A*, where *A* is the angle in question.

Côte d'Azur Mediterranean coast from Menton to St Tropez, France, renowned for its beaches; part of ⚬Provence-Alpes-Côte d'Azur.

cotoneaster any shrub or tree of the Eurasian genus *Cotoneaster*, rose family Rosaceae, closely allied to the hawthorn and medlar. The fruits, though small and unpalatable, are usually bright red and conspicuous, often persisting through the winter. Some of the shrubs are cultivated for their attractive appearance.

Cotonou chief port and largest city of Benin, on the Bight of Benin; population (1982) 487,000. Palm products and timber are exported. Although not the official capital, it is the seat of the president, and the main center of commerce and politics.

Cotopaxi (Quechua "shining peak") active volcano, situated to the S of Quito in Ecuador. It is 19,347 ft/5,897 m high and was first climbed 1872.

cottage industry manufacture undertaken by employees in their homes and often using their own equipment. Cottage industries frequently utilize a traditional craft such as weaving or pottery, but may also use high technology.

Cotten Joseph 1905– . US actor, intelligent and low-keyed, who was brought into films by Orson Welles. Cotten gave outstanding performances in *Citizen Kane* 1941, *The Magnificent Ambersons* 1942, and *The Third Man* 1949.

cotton tropical and subtropical herbaceous plant of the genus *Gossypium* of the mallow family Malvaceae. Fibers surround the seeds inside the ripened fruits, or bolls, and these are spun into yarn for cloth.

Cotton disease (byssinosis), caused by cotton dust, affects the lungs of those working in the industry. The seeds are used to produce cooking oil and livestock feed, and the pigment gossypol has potential as a male contraceptive in a modified form. See also ⚬cotton gin.

Cotton John 1585–1652. American religious leader. Born in Derby, England, and educated at Cambridge University, Cotton was

named vicar in Boston, Lincolnshire, 1612. His extreme Puritan views led to charges of heterodoxy being filed against him in 1633. In the same year, he immigrated to the Massachusetts Bay Colony, where he was named teacher of Boston's First Congregational Church. A leader in the public prosecution of Anne ⚬Hutchinson and Roger ⚬Williams, Cotton was, throughout his career, a powerful conservative force in the colony and published widely circulated sermons and theological works.

cotton gin machine that separates cotton fibers from the seed boll. Production of the gin (then called an en*gin*e) by US inventor Eli Whitney 1793 was a milestone in textile history.

The modern gin consists of a roller carrying a set of circular saws. These project through a metal grill in a hopper containing the seed bolls. As the roller rotates, the saws pick up the cotton fibers, leaving the seeds behind.

cotton grass any grasslike plant of the genus *Eriophorum* of the sedge family Cyperaceae. White tufts cover the fruiting heads in midsummer; these break off and are carried long distances on the wind. Cotton grass is found in wet places throughout the Arctic and temperate regions of the northern hemisphere, most species being found in acid bogs.

cotton spinning creating thread or fine yarn from the cotton plant by spinning the raw fiber contained within the seed-pods. The fiber is separated from the pods by a machine called a ⚬cotton gin. It is then cleaned and the fibers are separated out (carding). Finally the fibers are drawn out to the desired length and twisted together to form strong thread.

cottonwood any of several North American poplars of the genus *Populus*, with seeds topped by a thick tuft of silky hairs. The eastern cottonwood *P. deltoides*, growing to 100 ft/30 m, is native to the eastern US. The name cottonwood is also given to the downy-leaved Australian tree *Bedfordia salaoina*.

cotyledon structure in the embryo of a seed plant that may form a "leaf" after germination and is commonly known as a seed leaf. The number of cotyledons present in an embryo is an important character in the classification of flowering plants (⚬angiosperms).

Monocotyledons (such as grasses, palms, and lilies) have a single cotyledon, whereas dicotyledons (the majority of plant species) have two. In seeds that also contain ⚬endosperm (nutritive tissue), the cotyledons are thin, but where they are the primary food-storing tissue, as in peas and beans, they may be quite large. After germination the cotyledons either remain below ground (hypogeal) or, more commonly, spread out above soil level (epigeal) and become the first green leaves. In gymnosperms there may be up to a dozen cotyledons within each seed.

couch grass European grass *Agropyron repens* of the family Gramineae. It spreads rapidly by underground stems. It is considered a troublesome weed in North America, where it has been introduced.

cougar another name for the ⚬puma, a large North American cat.

coulomb SI unit (symbol C) of electrical charge. One coulomb is the quantity of electricity conveyed by a current of one ⚬ampere in one second.

Coulomb Charles Auguste de 1736–1806.

French scientist, inventor of the torsion balance for measuring the force of electric and magnetic attraction. The coulomb was named after him.

Council for Mutual Economic Assistance (CMEA) full name for ▷Comecon, an organization of Eastern bloc countries 1949–91.

Council of Europe body constituted 1949 in Strasbourg, France (still its headquarters), to secure "a greater measure of unity between the European countries." The widest association of European states, it has a **Committee** of foreign ministers, a **Parliamentary Assembly** (with members from national parliaments), and a **European Commission** investigating violations of human rights.

The first session of the **Consultative Assembly** opened Aug 1949, the members then being the UK, France, Italy, Belgium, the Netherlands, Sweden, Denmark, Norway, the Republic of Ireland, Luxembourg, Greece, and Turkey; Iceland, Germany, Austria, Cyprus, Switzerland, Malta, Portugal, Spain, Liechtenstein, Finland, and San Marino joined subsequently. With the collapse of communism in E Europe, the Council acquired a new role in assisting the establishment of Western-style democratic and accountable political systems in the region, and several countries applied for membership. Hungary joined 1990, Czechoslovakia and Poland 1991; Romania and Yugoslavia applied for membership 1991 and Albania for observer status.

counseling approach to treating problems, usually psychological ones, in which clients are encouraged to solve their own problems with support from a counselor. There is some overlap with ▷psychotherapy although counseling is less concerned with severe psychological disorders.

counterfeiting fraudulent imitation, usually of banknotes. It is countered by special papers, elaborate watermarks, skilled printing, and sometimes the insertion of a metallic strip. ▷Forgery is also a form of counterfeiting.

counterpoint in music, the art of combining different forms of an original melody with apparent freedom and yet to harmonious effect. Giovanni Palestrina and J S ▷Bach were masters of counterpoint.

It originated in ▷plainsong, with two independent vocal lines sung simultaneously (Latin *punctus contra punctum* "note against note").

Counter-Reformation movement initiated by the Catholic church at the Council of Trent 1545–63 to counter the spread of the ▷Reformation. Extending into the 17th century, its dominant forces included the rise of the Jesuits as an educating and missionary group and the deployment of the Spanish ▷Inquisition in other countries.

countervailing power in economics, the belief that too much power held by one group or company can be balanced or neutralized by another, creating a compatible relationship, such as labor unions in the case of strong management in a large company, or an opposition party facing an authoritarian government.

country and western or **country music** popular music of the white US South and West; it evolved from the folk music of the English, Irish, and Scottish settlers and has a strong blues influence. Characteristic instruments are the steel guitar, mandolin, and fiddle.

Lyrics typically extol family values and traditional sex roles, and often have a strong narrative element. Country music encompasses a variety of regional styles, and ranges from mournful ballads to fast and intricate dance music.

history
1920s Jimmie Rodgers (1897–1933) wrote a series of "Blue Yodel" songs that made him the first country-music recording star.
1930s Nashville, Tennessee, became a center for the country-music industry, with the Grand Ole Opry a showcase for performers. The Carter Family arranged and recorded hundreds of traditional songs. Hollywood invented the singing cowboy.
1940s Hank Williams (1923–1953) emerged as the most significant singer and songwriter; *western swing* spread from Texas.
1950s The **honky-tonk** sound; Kentucky *bluegrass*; ballad singers included Jim Reeves (1923-1964) and Patsy Cline (1932–1963).
1960s Songs of the Bakersfield, California, school, dominated by Buck Owens (1929–) and Merle Haggard (1937–), contrasted with lush Nashville productions of such singers as George Jones (1931–) and Tammy Wynette (1942–).
1970s Dolly Parton (1946–) and Emmylou Harris (1947–); the Austin, Texas, **outlaws** Willie Nelson (1933–) and Waylon Jennings (1937–); *country rock* pioneered by Gram Parsons (1946–1973).
1980s Neotraditionalist *new country* represented by Randy Travis (1963–), Dwight Yoakam (1957–), and Nanci Griffith (1954–).

It is played on radio stations throughout the US, and the 1980s saw its popularity spread even into Eastern urban centers like New York City, which had not been part of the country-and-western tradition.

county administrative unit of a country or state. In the US a county is a subdivision of a state; the power of counties differs widely between states. In the UK it is nowadays synonymous with "shire," although historically the two had different origins. Many of the English counties can be traced back to Saxon times. The republic of Ireland has 26 geographical and 27 administrative counties.

coup d'état or *coup* forcible takeover of the government of a country by elements from within that country, generally carried out by violent and illegal means. It differs from a revolution in typically being carried out by a small group (for example, of army officers or opposition politicians) to install its leader as head of government, rather than being a mass uprising by the people.

Early examples include the coup of 1799, in which Napoleon overthrew the Revolutionary Directory and declared himself first consul of France, and the coup of 1851 in which Louis Napoleon (then president) dissolved the French national assembly and a year later declared himself emperor. Coups of more recent times include the overthrow of the socialist government of Chile 1973 by a right-wing junta, the military seizure of power in Suriname Dec 1990, and the short-lived removal of Mikhail Gorbachev from power in the USSR by hard-line communists Aug 19–22, 1991.

Couperin François *le Grand* 1668–1733. French composer. He held various court appointments under Louis XIV and wrote vocal, chamber, and harpsichord music.

couplet in literature, a pair of lines of verse, usually of the same length and rhymed.

The **heroic couplet**, consisting of two rhymed lines in iambic pentameter, was widely adopted for epic poetry, and was a convention of both serious and mock-heroic 18th-century English poetry, as in the work of Alexander ▷Pope. An example, from Pope's *An Essay on Criticism*, is: "A little learning is a dang'rous thing;/Drink deep, or taste not the Pierian spring."

Courbet Gustave 1819–1877. French artist, a portrait, genre, and landscape painter. Reacting against academic trends, both Classicist and Romantic, he sought to establish a new realism based on contemporary life. His *Burial at Ornans* 1850 (Louvre, Paris), showing ordinary working people gathered round a village grave, shocked the public and the critics with its "vulgarity."

His spirit of realism was to be continued by Edouard Manet. In 1871 Courbet was active in the ▷Paris Commune and was later imprisoned for six months for his part in it.

Courrèges André 1923– . French fashion designer who is credited with inventing the miniskirt 1964. His "space-age" designs—square-shaped short skirts and trousers—were copied worldwide in the 1960s.

Courrèges worked for Cristobal Balenciaga 1950–61, and founded his own label 1961. From 1966 he produced both couture and ready-to-wear lines of well-tailored designs, often in pastel shades.

Court Margaret (born Smith) 1942– Australian tennis player. The most prolific winner in the women's game, she won a record 64 Grand Slam titles, including 25 at singles.

Court was the first from her country to win the ladies title at Wimbledon 1963, and the second woman after Maureen Connolly to complete the Grand Slam 1970.

CAREER HIGHLIGHTS

Wimbledon
singles: 1963, 1965, 1970
doubles: 1964, 1969
mixed: 1963, 1965–66, 1968, 1975
US Open
singles: 1962, 1965, 1968–70, 1973
doubles: 1963, 1968–70, 1973, 1975
mixed: 1961–65, 1969–70, 1972
French Open
singles: 1962, 1964, 1969–70, 1973
doubles: 1964–66, 1973
mixed: 1963–65, 1969
Australian Open
singles: 1960–66, 1969–71, 1973
doubles: 1961–63, 1965, 1969–71, 1973
mixed: 1963–64

courtly love medieval European code of amorous conduct between noblemen and noblewomen.

Originating in 11th-century Provence, it was popularized by troubadours under the patronage of Eleanor of Aquitaine, and codified by André le Chapelain. Essentially, it was concerned with the (usually) unconsummated love between a young bachelor knight and his lord's lady. The affair between Lancelot and Guinevere is a classic example. This theme was usually treated in an idealized form, but the relationship did reflect the social realities of noble households, in which the lady of the household might be the only noblewoman among several young unmarried knights. It inspired a great deal of medieval and 16th-century art and literature, including the 14th-century *Romance of the Rose* and Chaucer's *Troilus and Criseyde*, and was closely related to concepts of ⟡chivalry.

court martial court convened for the trial of persons subject to military discipline who are accused of violations of military laws.

The Uniform Code of Military Justice establishes military law and procedures for courts-martial in the US military.

Courtrai, Battle of defeat of French knights July 11, 1302 by the Flemings of Ghent and Bruges. It is also called the **Battle of the Spurs** because about 800 gilt spurs were hung in Courtrai cathedral to commemorate the victory of billmen (soldiers with pikes) over unsupported cavalry.

courtship behavior exhibited by animals as a prelude to mating. The behavior patterns vary considerably from one species to another, but are often ritualized forms of behavior not obviously related to courtship or mating (for example, courtship feeding in birds).

court tennis racket and ball game played in France from about the 12th century, over a central net in an indoor court, but with a sloping roof let into each end and one side of the court, against which the ball may be hit. It is now played in several countries including the US, but there are very few courts. Basic scoring is as for ⟡tennis, but with various modifications. It is the game on which tennis was based.

Cousteau Jacques Yves 1910– . French oceanographer, known for his researches in command of the *Calypso* from 1951, his film and television documentaries, and his many books; he pioneered the invention of the aqualung 1943 and techniques in underwater filming.

couvade custom in some societies of a man behaving as if he were about to give birth when his child is being born, which may include feeling or appearing to feel real pain. It has been observed since antiquity in many cultures and may have begun either as a magic ritual or as a way of asserting paternity.

covalence in chemistry, a form of ⟡valence in which two atoms unite by sharing electrons in pairs, so that each atom provides half the shared electrons (see also ⟡bond).

Covent Garden London square (named after the convent garden once on the site) laid out by Inigo ⟡Jones 1631. The buildings that formerly housed London's fruit and vegetable market (moved to Nine Elms, Wandsworth 1973) were adapted for shops and restaurants. The Royal Opera House, also housing the Royal Ballet, is here; also the London Transport Museum.

Coward Noël 1899–1973. English playwright, actor, producer, director, and composer, who epitomized the witty and sophisticated man of the theater. From his first success with *The Young Idea* 1923, he wrote and appeared in plays and comedies on both sides of the Atlantic such as *Hay Fever* 1925, *Private Lives* 1930 with Gertrude Lawrence, *Design for Living* 1933, and *Blithe Spirit* 1941.

cowfish type of ⟡boxfish.

cowrie marine snail of the family Cypreidae, in which the interior spiral form is concealed by a double outer lip. The shells are hard, shiny, and often colored. Most cowries are shallow-water forms, and are found in many parts of the world, particularly the tropical Indo-Pacific. Cowries have been used as ornaments and for fertility charms, and also as currency, for example the Pacific money cowrie *Cypraea moneta*.

Four species are found in the SE US and one in California.

Cox Jacob Dolson 1828–1900. Canadian-born US educator and public figure. He was elected governor of Ohio 1866 and served as secretary of the interior under Grant. After service in the US Congress 1876–79, Cox was president of the University of Cincinnati 1885–89.

coyote wild dog *Canis latrans*, in appearance like a small wolf, living from Alaska to Central America and east to New York. Its head and body are about 3 ft/90 cm long and brown, flecked with gray or black. Coyotes live in open country and can run at 40 mph/65 kph. Their main foods are rabbits and rodents. Although persecuted by humans for over a century, the species is very successful.

coypu another name for ⟡nutria.

CP/M (abbreviation for **control program/ monitor** or **control program for microcomputers**) one of the earliest ⟡operating systems for microcomputers. It was produced by Digital Research Corporation, and became a standard for microcomputers based on the Intel 8080 and Zilog Z80 8-bit microprocessors. In the 1980s it was superseded by ⟡MS-DOS, written for 16-bit microprocessors.

CPR abbreviation for **cardiopulmonary** ⟡**resuscitation**.

CPU in computing, abbreviation for **central processing unit**.

crab any decapod (ten-legged) crustacean of the division Brachyura, with a broad, rather round, upper body shell (carapace) and a small ⟡abdomen tucked beneath the body. Crabs are related to lobsters and crayfish. Mainly marine, some crabs live in fresh water or on land. They are alert carnivores and scavengers. They have a typical sideways walk, and strong pincers on the first pair of legs, the other four pairs being used for walking. Periodically, the outer shell is cast to allow for growth. The name "crab" is sometimes used for similar arthropods, such as the horseshoe crab, which is neither a true crab nor a crustacean.

There are many species of true crabs worldwide. The North American blue crab *Callinectes sapidus*, called the soft-shelled crab after molting, is about 6 in/15 cm wide. It is extensively fished along the Atlantic and Gulf coasts. Other true crabs include fiddler crabs (Uca), the males of which have one enlarged claw to wave at and attract females, and spider crabs, with small bodies and very long legs, including the Japanese spider crab *Macrocheira kaemperi* with a leg span of 11 ft/3.4 m. Hermit crabs (division Anomura) have a soft, spirally twisted abdomen and make their homes in empty shells of sea snails for protection. Some tropical hermit crabs are found a considerable distance from the sea. The robber crab *Birgus latro* grows large enough to climb palm trees and feed on coconuts.

crab apple any of 25 species of wild ⟡apple trees (genus *Malus*), native to temperate regions of the northern hemisphere. Numerous varieties of cultivated apples have been derived from *M. pumila*, the common native crab apple of SE Europe and central Asia. The fruit of native species is smaller and more bitter than that of cultivated varieties and used in crab-apple jelly.

Crab nebula cloud of gas 6,000 light-years from Earth, in the constellation Taurus. It is the remains of a star that exploded as a ⟡supernova (observed as a brilliant point of light

on Earth 1054). At its center is a ⟡pulsar that flashes 30 times a second. The name comes from its crablike shape.

crack street name for a chemical derivative (bicarbonate) of ⟡cocaine in hard, crystalline lumps; it is heated and inhaled (smoked) as a stimulant. Crack was first used in San Francisco in the early 1980s, and is highly addictive.

Its use has led to numerous deaths but it is the fastest-growing sector of the illegal drug trade, since it is less expensive than cocaine.

cracking reaction in which a large ⟡alkane molecule is broken down by heat into a smaller alkane and a small ⟡alkene molecule. The reaction is carried out at a high temperature (600°C or higher) and often in the presence of a catalyst. Cracking is a commonly used process in the petrochemical industry.

It is the main method of preparation of alkenes and is also used to manufacture gasoline from the higher-boiling-point ⟡fractions that are obtained by fractional ⟡distillation (fractionation) of crude oil.

Cracow alternate form of ⟡Kraków, Polish city.

Cranach Lucas 1472–1553. German painter, etcher, and woodcut artist, a leading light in the German Renaissance. He painted many full-length nudes and precise and polished portraits, such as *Martin Luther* 1521 (Uffizi, Florence).

Born at Kronach in Bavaria, he settled at Wittenberg 1504 to work for the elector of Saxony. He is associated with the artists Albrecht Dürer and Albrecht Altdorfer and was a close friend of the Christian reformer Martin Luther, whose portrait he painted several times. His religious paintings feature splendid landscapes. His second son, **Lucas Cranach the Younger** (1515–1586), had a similar style and succeeded his father as director of the Cranach workshop.

cranberry any of several trailing evergreen plants of the genus *Vaccinium* in the heath family Ericaceae, allied to bilberries and blueberries. They grow in marshy places and bear small, acid, crimson berries, high in vitamin C, used for making sauce and jelly.

crane in engineering, a machine for raising, lowering, or placing in position heavy loads. The three main types are the jib crane, the overhead traveling crane, and the tower crane. Most cranes have the machinery mounted on a revolving turntable. This may be mounted on trucks or be self-propelled, often being fitted with ⟡caterpillar tracks.

The main features of a *jib crane* are a power winch, a rope or cable, and a movable arm or jib. The cable, which carries a pulley block, hangs from the end of the jib and is wound up and down by the winch. The *overhead traveling crane*, chiefly used in workshops, consists of a fixed horizontal arm, along which runs a trolley carrying the pulley block. *Tower cranes*, seen on large building sites, have a long horizontal arm able to revolve on top of a tall tower. The arm carries the trolley.

crane in zoology, a large, wading bird of the family Gruidae, with long legs and neck, and powerful wings. Cranes are marsh- and plains-dwelling birds, feeding on plants as well as insects and small animals. They fly well and are usually migratory. Their courtship includes frenzied, leaping dances. They are found in all parts of the world except South America.

The common crane *Grus grus* is still numerous in many parts of Europe, and winters in Africa and India. It stands over 3ft/1 m high. The plumage of the adult bird is gray, varied with black and white, and a red patch of bare skin on the head and neck. All cranes have suffered through hunting and loss of wetlands; the population of the North American whooping crane *Grus americana* fell to 21 wild birds 1944. Through careful conservation, numbers have now risen to about 200.

The sandhill crane of North America *Grus canadensis* reaches a height of 3.5 ft/1 m and has grayish plumage, with a red patch on the head. It winters in Mexico and breeds in the far north.

Crane (Harold) Hart 1899–1932. US poet. His long mystical poem *The Bridge* 1930 uses the Brooklyn Bridge as a symbol. In his work he attempted to link humanity's present with its past, in an epic continuum. He drowned after jumping overboard from a steamer bringing him back to the US after a visit to Mexico.

Crane Stephen 1871–1900. US writer who introduced grim realism into the US novel. His book *The Red Badge of Courage* 1895 deals vividly with the US Civil War.

Born in Newark, New Jersey, Crane became a journalist. His first novel, self-published, *Maggie: A Girl of the Streets* 1893, was rejected by many editors because of its unpleasant subject of New York slum life. His free-verse poetry is collected in *The Black Riders* 1895. His critically acclaimed short stories include "The Open Boat," based on a true experience of shipwreck during a journalistic assignment to Cuba 1897.

crane fly or **daddy-longlegs** any fly of the family Tipulidae, with long, slender, fragile legs. They look like giant mosquitoes, but the adults are quite harmless. The larvae live in soil or water.

craniotomy operation to remove or turn back a small flap of skull bone to give access to the living brain.

cranium the dome-shaped area of the vertebrate skull, consisting of several fused plates, that protects the brain. Fossil remains of the human cranium have aided the development of theories concerning human evolution.

The cranium has been studied as a possible indicator of intelligence or even of personality. The Victorian argument that a large cranium implies a large brain, which in turn implies a more profound intelligence, has been rejected.

crank handle bent at right angles and connected to the shaft of a machine; it is used to transmit motion or convert reciprocating (back-and-forward or up-and-down) movement into rotary movement, or vice versa.

Although similar devices may have been employed in antiquity and as early as the 1st century in China and the 8th century in Europe, the earliest recorded use of a crank in a water-raising machine is by Arab mathematician al-Jazari in the 12th century. Not until the 15th century, however, did the crank become fully assimilated into developing European technology. -

crankshaft essential component of piston engines that converts the up-and-down (reciprocating) motion of the pistons into useful rotary motion. The car crankshaft carries a number of cranks. The pistons are connected to the cranks by connecting rods and ▷bearings; when the pistons move up and down, the connecting rods force the offset crank pins to describe a circle, thereby rotating the crankshaft.

Cranmer Thomas 1489–1556. English cleric, archbishop of Canterbury from 1533. A Protestant convert, he helped to shape the doctrines of the Church of England under Edward VI. He was responsible for the issue of the Prayer Books of 1549 and 1552, and supported the succession of Lady Jane Grey 1553.

Condemned for heresy under the Catholic Mary Tudor, he at first recanted, but when his life was not spared, resumed his position and was burned at the stake, first holding to the fire the hand which had signed his recantation.

craps casino game adapted from the game of hazard by Bernard de Mandeville in the early 19th century. It is played with two dice: a throw of 7 or 11 wins; a throw of 2, 3, or 12 loses.

If none of the above show on the first toss, the "shooter" tries to repeat the number originally thrown before throwing a 7 or 11.

Crassus Marcus Licinius *c.* 108–53 BC. Roman general who crushed the ▷Spartacus uprising 71 BC. In 60 BC he joined with Caesar and Pompey in the First Triumvirate and obtained command in the east 55 BC. Invading Mesopotamia, he was defeated by the Parthians at the battle of Carrhae, captured, and put to death.

crater bowl-shaped depression, usually round and with steep sides. Craters are formed by explosive events such as the eruption of a volcano or by the impact of a meteorite. A ▷caldera is a much larger feature.

The Moon has more than 300,000 craters over 6 mi/1 km in diameter, formed by meteorite bombardment; similar craters on Earth have mostly been worn away by erosion. Craters are found on many other bodies in the Solar System.

craton or **shield** core of a continent, a vast tract of highly deformed ▷metamorphic rock around which the continent has been built. Intense mountain-building periods shook these shield areas in Precambrian times before stable conditions set in.

Cratons exist in the hearts of all the continents, a typical example being the Canadian Shield.

Crawford Joan. Adopted name of Lucille Le Seur 1908–1977. US film actress who became a star with her performance as a flapper (liberated young woman) in *Our Dancing Daughters* 1928. Later she appeared as a sultry, often suffering, mature woman. Her films include *Mildred Pierce* 1945 (for which she won an Academy Award), *Password* 1947, and *Whatever Happened to Baby Jane?* 1962.

Beginning her career as a chorus girl 1924, Crawford made her first film appearance 1925. In the 1930s she played in many Clark Gable films, and in *Grand Hotel* 1932. *Whatever Happened to Baby Jane?* was her last "great" film, before cameo appearances and *Trog* 1970.

Craxi Bettino 1934– . Italian socialist politician, leader of the Italian Socialist Party (PSI) from 1976, prime minister 1983–87.

Craxi, born in Milan, became a member of the Chamber of Deputies 1968 and general secretary of the PSI 1976. In 1983 he became Italy's first socialist prime minister, successfully leading a broad coalition until 1987.

crayfish freshwater decapod (ten-limbed) crustacean belonging to several families structurally similar to, but smaller than, the lobster. Crayfish are brownish-green scavengers and are found in all parts of the world except Africa. They are edible, and some species are farmed.

The spiny lobster *Palinurus vulgaris*, is sometimes called crayfish; it is actually a marine lobster without pincers, and grows up to 20 in/50 cm long.

Crazy Horse 1849–1877. Sioux Indian chief, one of the Indian leaders at the massacre of ▷Little Bighorn. He was killed when captured.

creationism theory concerned with the origins of matter and life, claiming, as does the Bible in Genesis, that the world and humanity were created by a supernatural Creator, not more than 6,000 years ago. It was developed in response to Darwin's theory of ▷evolution; it is not recognized by most scientists as having a factual basis.

After a trial 1981–82 a US judge ruled unconstitutional an attempt in Arkansas schools to enforce equal treatment of creationism and evolutionary theory.

creation myth legend of the origin of the world. All cultures have ancient stories of the creation of the Earth or its inhabitants. Often this involves the violent death of a primordial being from whose body everything then arises; the giant Ymir in Scandinavian mythology is an example. Marriage between heaven and earth is another common explanation, as in Greek mythology (Uranus and Gaia).

Crécy, Battle of first major battle of the Hundred Years' War 1346. Philip VI of France was defeated by Edward III of England at the village of Crécy-en-Ponthieu, now in Somme *département*, France, 11 mi/18 km NE of Abbeville.

credit in economics, means by which goods or services are obtained without immediate payment, usually by agreeing to pay interest. The three main forms are **consumer credit** (usually extended to individuals by retailers), **bank credit** (such as overdrafts or personal loans), and **trade credit** (common in the commercial world both within countries and internationally).

Consumer credit is increasingly used to pay for goods. In the US 1989 it amounted to $711.8 billion, with about 18.5% of disposable income expended on installment buying and credit-card payments.

credit card card issued by a credit company, retail outlet, or bank, which enables the holder to obtain goods or services on credit (usually to a specified limit), payable on specified terms. The first credit card was introduced 1950 in the US.

Some credit cards also act as bank cards to enable customers to obtain money more easily from various bank branches. "Intelligent" credit cards are now being introduced that contain coded information about the customer and the amount of credit still available. This can be read by a terminal connected with the company's central computer.

Credit cards are usually made of or coated with plastic; using them may be called "paying with plastic."

credit rating measure of the willingness or ability to pay for goods, loans, or services rendered by an individual, company, or country. A country with a good credit rating will attract loans on favorable terms.

Cree member of a North American Indian people whose language belongs to the Algonquian family. The Cree are distributed over a vast area in Canada from Québec to Alberta. In the US the majority of Cree live in the Rocky Boys reservation in Montana. Cree and Ojibwa languages are closely related and are spoken by around 50,000 people.

creed in general, any system of belief; in the Christian church the verbal confessions of faith expressing the accepted doctrines of the church. The different forms are the ◊Apostles' Creed, the ◊Nicene Creed, and the ◊Athanasian Creed. The only creed recognized by the Orthodox Church is the Nicene Creed.

The oldest is the **Apostles' Creed**, which, though not the work of the apostles, was probably first formulated in the 2nd century. The full version of the Apostles' Creed, as now used, first appeared about 750.

The use of creeds as a mode of combating heresy was established by the appearance of the **Nicene Creed**, introduced by the Council of Nicaea 325 when ◊Arianism was widespread, and giving the orthodox doctrine of the Trinity. The Nicene Creed used today is substantially the same as the version adopted at the church council in Constantinople 381, with a ◊filioque clause added during the 5th and 8th centuries in the Western church.

The **Athanasian Creed** is thought to be later in origin than the time of Athanasius (died 373), although it represents his views in a detailed exposition of the doctrines of the Trinity and the incarnation. Some authorities suppose it to have been composed in the 8th or 9th century but others place it as early as the 4th or 5th century.

creep in civil and mechanical engineering, the property of a solid, typically a metal, under continuous stress that causes it to deform below its yield point (the point at which any elastic solid normally stretches without any increase in load or stress). Lead, tin, and zinc, for example, exhibit creep at ordinary temperatures, as seen in the movement of the lead sheeting on the roofs of old buildings.

Copper, iron, nickel, and their alloys also show creep at high temperatures.

creeper any small, short-legged passerine bird of the family Certhidae. They spiral with a mouselike movement up tree trunks, searching for insects and larvae with their thin, down-curved beaks.

The brown creeper *Certhia familiaris* is 5 in/ 12 cm long, brown above, white below, and is found across North America and Eurasia.

cremation disposal of the dead by burning. The custom was universal among ancient Indo-European peoples, for example, the Greeks, Romans, and Teutons. It was discontinued among Christians until the late 19th century because of their belief in the bodily resurrection of the dead. Overcrowded urban cemeteries gave rise to its revival in the West. It has remained the usual method of disposal in the East.

Creole in the West Indies and Spanish America, originally someone of European descent born in the New World; later someone of mixed European and African descent. In Louisiana and other states on the Gulf of Mexico, it applies either to someone of French or Spanish descent or (popularly) to someone of mixed French or Spanish and African descent.

Also, a patois or dialect based on French, Dutch, or English, as spoken in the West Indies.

Creole language any ◊pidgin language that has ceased to be simply a trade jargon in ports and markets and has become the mother tongue of a particular community. Many Creoles have developed into distinct languages with literatures of their own; for example, Jamaican Creole, Haitian Creole, Krio in Sierra Leone, and Tok Pisin, now the official language of Papua New Guinea.

The name *Creole* derives through French from Spanish and Portuguese, in which it originally referred both to children of European background born in tropical colonies and to house slaves on colonial plantations. The implication is that such groups picked up the pidgin forms of colonists' languages (Portuguese, Spanish, Dutch, French, and English) as they were used in and around the Caribbean, in parts of Africa, and in island communities in the Indian and Pacific Oceans. According to circumstance, in such places as Jamaica, Haiti, Mauritius, and W Africa, there may be a "Creole continuum" of usage between the strongest forms of a Creole and the standard version of the language with which the Creole is associated.

Creon in Greek mythology, brother of ◊Jocasta, father of Haemon, and king of Thebes in ◊Sophocles' *Antigone*.

creosote black, oily liquid derived from coal tar, used as a wood preservative. Medicinal creosote, which is transparent and oily, is derived from wood tar.

crescent curved shape of the Moon when it appears less than half-illuminated. It also refers to any object or symbol resembling the crescent Moon. Often associated with Islam, it was first used by the Turks on their standards after the capture of Constantinople 1453, and appears on the flags of many Muslim countries. The **Red Crescent** is the Muslim equivalent of the Red Cross.

cress any of several plants of the Cruciferae family, characterized by a pungent taste. The common European garden cress *Lepidium sativum* is cultivated worldwide.

Cresson Edith 1934– . French politician and founder member of the Socialist Party, prime minister 1991–92. Cresson held successive ministerial portfolios in François Mitterrand's government 1981–86 and 1988–90. Her government was troubled by a struggling economy, a series of strikes, and unrest in many of the country's poor suburban areas, which eventually forced her resignation.

Cretaceous (Latin *creta* "chalk") period of geological time 144–65 million years ago. It is the last period of the Mesozoic era, during which angiosperm (seed-bearing) plants evolved, and dinosaurs and other reptiles reached a peak before almost complete extinction at the end of the period. Chalk is a typical rock type of the second half of the period.

Crete (Greek *Kríti*) largest Greek island in the E Mediterranean Sea, 62 mi/100 km SE of mainland Greece
area 3,234 sq mi/8,378 sq km
capital Khaniá (Canea)
cities Iráklion (Heraklion), Rethymnon, Aghios Nikolaos
products citrus fruit, olives, wine
population (1991) 536,900
language Cretan dialect of Greek
history it has remains of the ◊Minoan civilization 3000–1400 BC (see ◊Knossos) and was

successively under Roman, Byzantine, Venetian, and Turkish rule. The island was annexed by Greece 1913.

In 1941 it was captured by German forces from Allied troops who had retreated from the mainland and was retaken by the Allies 1944.

cribbage card game, invented in the 17th century by the English poet John Suckling, which is played with a holed board for keeping score. It can be played as singles or in pairs, the number of cards per player depending upon the number of players. There is always a "spare hand," which each player takes in turn to "own." Cards are discarded one at a time until the face values of discarded cards total 31. When all players have discarded their cards, the total of each player's hand is calculated according to the cards held, whether they be in pairs, three of a kind, four of a kind, and so on.

crib death death of an apparently healthy baby during sleep, also known as sudden infant death syndrome (SIDS). It is most common in the winter months, and strikes boys more than girls. The cause is not known.

Crick Francis 1916– . British molecular biologist. From 1949 he researched the molecular structure of DNA, and the means whereby characteristics are transmitted from one generation to another. For this work he was awarded a Nobel Prize (with Maurice ◊Wilkins and James ◊Watson) 1962.

cricket in zoology, an insect belonging to any of various families, especially the Grillidae, of the order Orthoptera. Crickets are related to grasshoppers. They have somewhat flattened bodies and long antennae. The males make a chirping noise by rubbing together special areas on the forewings. The females have a long needlelike egglaying organ (ovipositor). There are some 900 species known worldwide.

cricket bat-and-ball game between two teams of 11 players each. It is played with a small solid ball and long flat-sided wooden bats, on a round or oval field, at the center of which is a finely mown pitch, 22 yd/20 m long. At each end of the pitch is a wicket made up of three upright wooden sticks (stumps), surmounted by two smaller sticks (bails). The object of the game is to score more runs than the opposing team. A run is normally scored by the batsman striking the ball and exchanging ends with his or her partner until the ball is returned by a fielder, or by hitting the ball to the boundary line for an automatic four or six runs.

A batsman stands at each wicket and is bowled a stipulated number of balls (usually six), after which another bowler bowls from the other wicket. A batsman can make an "out" in several ways. Games comprise either one or two innings per team.

The exact origins are unknown. The first rules were drawn up in 1774 and modified following the formation of the Marylebone Cricket Club (MCC) in 1787.

Crimea northern peninsula on the Black Sea, an autonomous republic of ◊Ukraine; formerly a region (1954–91)
area 10,425 sq mi/27,000 sq km
capital Simferopol
cities Sevastopol, Yalta
features mainly steppe, but southern coast is a vacation resort
products iron, oil
population 2.5 million (70% Russian, despite return of 150,000 Tatars since 1989)
history Since 1991 the Crimea has sought to gain independence from the Ukraine; the

latter has resisted all secessionist moves, threatening to resort to force if necessary.

Crimea was under Turkish rule 1475–1774; a subsequent brief independence was ended by Russian annexation 1783. Crimea was the republic of Taurida 1917–20 and the Crimean Autonomous Soviet Republic from 1920 until occupied by Germany 1942–1944. It was then reduced to a region, its Tatar people being deported to Uzbekistan for collaboration. Although they were exonerated 1967 and some were allowed to return, others were forcibly re-exiled 1979. A drift back to their former homeland began 1987 and a federal ruling 1988 confirmed their right to residency. In a referendum organized by the regional soviet (council) 1991, citizens of the Crimean peninsula voted overwhelmingly in favor of restoring Crimea as an autonomous republic independent of the Ukraine. This referendum was opposed by representatives of the Tatars, who sought restriction of the voting solely to their community, and by the Ukrainian nationalist group Rukh. In Feb 1991, the Ukrainian Supreme Soviet voted to restore to the Crimea the status of an autonomous Soviet socialist republic within the Ukraine. In Sept 1991, Crimea declared its independence but this was not recognized by Ukraine. In May 1992, the Crimean parliament declared the republic's sovereignty subject to a regional referendum planned for Aug. Ukrainian president Kravchuk responded by authorizing the use of "all necessary means" to prevent Crimea's secession and demanded that the declaration be rescinded. The Crimean parliament acceded but declared itsheir intention to go ahead with the referendum. Also in May, Russia voted to nullify the 1945 transfer of Crimea to the Ukraine and called for bilateral talks on the republic's status.

Crime and Punishment novel by Russian writer Dostoevsky, published 1866. It analyses the motives of a murderer and his reactions to the crime he has committed.

Crimean War war 1853–56 between Russia and the allied powers of England, France, Turkey, and Sardinia. The war arose from British and French mistrust of Russia's ambitions in the Balkans. It began with an allied Anglo-French expedition to the Crimea to attack the Russian Black Sea city of Sevastopol. The battles of the river ▷Alma, ▷Balaclava (including the Charge of the Light Brigade), and Inkerman 1854 led to a siege which, owing to military mismanagement, lasted for a year until Sept 1855. The war was ended by the Treaty of Paris 1856. The scandal surrounding French and British losses through disease led to the organization of proper military nursing services by Florence Nightingale.
1853 Russia invaded the Balkans (from which they were compelled to withdraw by Austrian intervention) and sank the Turkish fleet at Sinope.
1854 Britain and France declared war on Russia, invaded the Crimea, and laid siege to Sevastopol (Sept 1854–Sept 1855). Battles of Alma Sept 20, Balaclava Oct 25, Inkerman Nov 5.
1855 Sardinia declared war on Russia.
1856 The Treaty of Paris in Feb ended the war.

crime, organized illegal operations run like a large business. The best-known such organization is the ▷Mafia. For the history of US organized crime, see ▷gangsterism. Japanese gangsters are called ▷*yakuza*.

criminal law body of law that defines the public wrongs (crimes) that are punishable by the state and establishes methods of prosecution and punishment. It is distinct from ▷civil law, which deals with legal relationships between individuals (including organizations), such as contract law.

The laws of each country specify what actions or omissions are criminal. These include serious moral wrongs, such as murder; wrongs that endanger the security of the state, such as treason; wrongs that disrupt an orderly society, such as evading taxes; and wrongs against the community, such as dropping litter. An action may be considered a crime in one country but not in others, such as homosexuality or drinking alcohol. Some actions, such as assault, are both criminal and civil wrongs; the offender can be both prosecuted and sued for compensation.

Criminal offenses are either ▷felonies or ▷misdemeanors. Felonies are more likely to require a formal charge, called an indictment, by a grand jury. Punishments include imprisonment, fines, suspended terms of imprisonment, probation, and ▷community service.

Crispi Francesco 1819–1907. Italian prime minister 1887–91 and 1893–96. He advocated the ▷Triple Alliance of Italy with Germany and Austria, but was deposed 1896.

crith unit of mass used for weighing gases. One crith is the mass of one liter of hydrogen gas (H_2) at standard temperature and pressure.

critical angle in optics, for a ray of light passing from a denser to a less dense medium (such as from glass to air), the smallest angle of incidence at which the emergent ray grazes the surface of the denser medium—at an angle of refraction of 90°.

When the angle of incidence is less than the critical angle, the ray does not pass out into the less dense medium; when the angle of incidence is greater than the critical angle, the ray is not reflected back into the denser medium.

critical mass in nuclear physics, the minimum mass of fissile material that can undergo a continuous ▷chain reaction. Below this mass, too many ▷neutrons escape from the surface for a chain reaction to carry on; above the critical mass, the reaction may accelerate into a nuclear explosion.

critical path analysis procedure used in the management of complex projects to minimize the amount of time taken. The analysis shows which subprojects can run in parallel with each other, and which have to be completed before other subprojects can follow on. By identifying the time required for each separate subproject and the relationship between the subprojects, it is possible to produce a planning schedule showing when each subproject should be started and finished in order to complete the whole project most efficiently. Complex projects may involve hundreds of subprojects, and computer ▷applications packages for critical path analysis are widely used to help reduce the time and effort involved in their analysis.

critical temperature temperature above which a particular gas cannot be converted into a liquid by pressure alone. It is also the temperature at which a magnetic material loses its magnetism (the Curie temperature or point).

Crivelli Carlo 1435/40–1495/1500. Italian painter in the early Renaissance style, active in Venice. He painted extremely detailed, decorated religious works, sometimes festooned with garlands of fruit. His figure style is

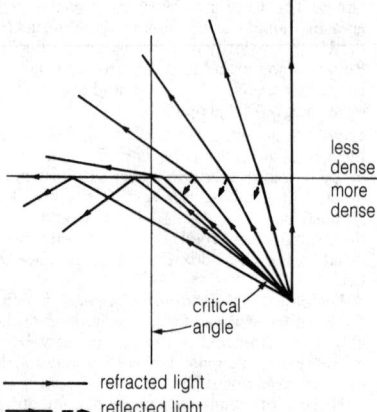

less dense
more dense

critical angle

——▶ refracted light
——▪ - ▶ reflected light

critical angle *The critical angle is the angle at which light from within a transparent medium just grazes the surface of the medium.*

strongly Italian, reflecting the influence of Mantegna.

Croat member of the majority ethnic group in Croatia. Their language is generally considered to be identical to that of the Serbs, hence Serbo-Croatian.

The Croats, who are mainly Roman Catholics, had a long association with the ▷Austro-Hungarian Empire. During World War II they were closely affiliated to the ▷Axis powers and Croatian fascists were involved in attacks on Serbs. Conflicting separatist demands provoked the outbreak of civil war in Yugoslavia 1991 and led to eventual recognition by the EC of Croatia's independence Jan 1992.

Croatia (Serbo-Croatian *Hrvatska*) country in central Europe, bounded N by Slovenia and Hungary, W by the Adriatic Sea, and E by Bosnia-Herzegovina and the Yugoslavian republic of Serbia.
government There is a three-chamber parliament, which elects the executive president. Election contests are majoritarian, and there is a second-round runoff race if no candidate secures a majority of the vote in the first round.
history Part of Pannonia in Roman times, the region was settled by Carpathian Croats in the 7th century. For eight years from 1102 it was an autonomous kingdom under the Hungarian crown. It was briefly an Austrian crownland 1849 and again a Hungarian crownland 1868. It was included in the kingdom of the Serbs, Croats, and Slovenes 1918 (called Yugoslavia from 1929). During World War II a Nazi puppet state, "Greater Croatia," was established from April 1941 under Ante Pavelic (1889–1959). As many as 500,000 Serbs and 55,000 Jews were massacred by this Croatian regime, which sought to establish a "pure" Croatian Catholic republic. In Nov 1945 it became a constituent republic within the Yugoslav Socialist Federal Republic, whose dominant figure was Marshal ▷Tito.
Serb–Croat separatism From the 1970s, resentful of perceived Serb dominance of the Yugoslav Federation, a violent separatist movement began to gain ground, leading to the establishment of a looser federation from 1974. Nationalist agitation continued through the 1980s and there was mounting industrial unrest from 1987 as spiraling inflation caused a sharp fall in living standards. In an effort to court popularity and concerned at the

Serb chauvinism of Slobodan Milosevic, the Croatia League of Socialists (communists), later renamed the Party of Democratic Renewal (PDR), adopted an increasingly anti-Serb line from the mid-1980s. Following Slovenia's lead, it allowed the formation of rival political parties from 1989. In the multiparty republic elections of April–May 1990, the PDR was comprehensively defeated by the right-wing nationalist Croatian Democratic Union (HDZ). Led by Franjo Tudjman, who had been imprisoned in 1972 for his nationalist activities, the HDZ secured almost a two-thirds assembly majority.

secession from Yugoslavia As president, Tudjman was initially conciliatory, declaring that his government's aim was simply greater autonomy. However, in Feb 1991 the Croatian assembly, along with that of neighboring Catholic Slovenia, issued a proclamation calling for secession from Yugoslavia and the establishment of a new confederation that excluded Serbia and Montenegro. It also ordered the creation of an independent Croatian army. Concerned at possible maltreatment in a future independent Croatia, Serb militants announced March 1991 the secession from Croatia of the self-proclaimed "Serbian Autonomous Region of Krajina," containing 250,000 Serbs. In a May 1991 referendum there was 90% support in Krajina for its remaining with Serbia and Montenegro within a residual Yugoslavia. A week later, Croatia's electors voted overwhelmingly (93%) for independence within a loose confederation of Yugoslav sovereign states. On June 26, 1991 the Croatian

government, in concert with Slovenia, issued a unilateral declaration of independence.

civil war From July 1991, despite Croatia's agreeing to suspend implementation of its independence declaration for three months, there was an escalating conflict with the Serb-dominated Yugoslav army and civil war within Croatia. Independent Serbian "governments" were proclaimed in Krajina and in eastern and western Slavonia. A succession of cease-fires ordered by the Yugoslav federal presidency and European Community (EC) observers passed unobserved and by Sept 1991 at least a third of Croatia had fallen under Serb control, with intense fighting taking place around the towns of Osijek and Vukovar in Slavonia, near Croatia's eastern border. Croatia's ports were besieged and at least 500,000 people were made refugees. Rich in oil, Croatia retaliated with an oil-supply blockade on Serbia and announced, in Oct 1991, that it had formally severed all official relations with Yugoslavia. By the close of 1991 the conflict had claimed as many as 10,000 lives. Croatia's assembly passed a law Dec 1991 committing the country to adherence to international conventions on human rights and cultural autonomy in its relations with ethnic minorities.

cease-fire agreed In early Jan 1992 a peace plan was successfully brokered in Sarajevo by United Nations (UN) envoy Cyrus Vance. The agreement provided for an immediate cease-fire, the full withdrawal of the Yugoslav army from Croatia, and the deployment of 10,000 UN troops in contested Krajina and E and W

Slavonia until a political settlement was worked out. This accord was disregarded by the breakaway Serb leader in Krajina, Milan Babic, but recognized by the main Croatian and Serbian forces. Under German pressure, Croatia's and Slovenia's independence was recognized by the European Community (EC) and the US early 1992, and in May by the UN.

UN peacekeeping force established During March and April UN peacekeeping forces began to arrive in Croatia and gradually took control of Krajina, although Croatian forces continued to shell Krajina's capital, Knin. In Sept President Tudjman requested that peacekeeping forces be withdrawn 1993 on expiry of their mandate, claiming that full civil rights had been granted to Serb minorities in Croatian territory.

Croce Benedetto 1866–1952. Italian philosopher, historian, and literary critic; an opponent of fascism. His *Filosofia dello spirito/Philosophy of the Spirit* 1902–17 was a landmark in idealism. Like Hegel, he held that ideas do not represent reality but *are* reality; but unlike Hegel, he rejected every kind of transcendence.

crochet craft technique similar to both knitting and lacemaking, in which one hooked needle is used to produce a loosely looped network of wool or cotton.

Remains of crocheted clothing have been discovered in 4th-century Egyptian tombs. In 19th-century Europe the craft was popular among Victorian ladies, and the availability of fine machine-made thread made it possible to create fine laces. Both garments and trims are still produced by crocheting.

Crockett Davy 1786–1836. US folk hero, born in Tennessee, a Democratic Congressman 1827–31 and 1833–35. A series of books, of which he may have been part-author, made him into a mythical hero of the frontier, but their Whig associations cost him his office. He died in the battle of the ◊Alamo during the War of Texan Independence.

He clashed with Andrew ◊Jackson, claiming Jackson had betrayed his frontier constituency, and left for Texas in bitterness.

crocodile large aquatic carnivorous reptile of the family Crocodiliae, related to alligators and caymans, but distinguished from them by a more pointed snout and a notch in the upper jaw into which the fourth tooth in the lower jaw fits. Crocodiles can grow up to 20 ft/6 m, and have long, powerful tails that propel them when swimming. They can live up to 100 years.

Crocodiles are fierce hunters, larger specimens attacking animals the size of antelopes or, occasionally, people. In some species, the female lays over 100 hard-shelled eggs in holes or nest mounds of vegetation, which she guards until the eggs hatch. When in the sun, crocodiles cool themselves by opening their mouths wide, which also enables scavenging birds to pick their teeth. They can stay underwater for long periods, but must surface to breathe. The nostrils can be closed underwater. They ballast themselves with stones to adjust their buoyancy. They have remained virtually unchanged for 200 million years.

About a dozen species of crocodiles, all of them endangered, are found in tropical parts of Africa, Asia, Australia, and Central America. The largest is the saltwater crocodile *Crocodylus porosus*, which can grow to 20 ft/6 m or more, and is found in E India, Australia, and the W Pacific. The Nile crocodile *C. niloticus* is

Croatia
Republic of

area 21,824 sq mi/56,538 sq km
capital Zagreb
cities chief port: Rijeka (Fiume); other ports: Zadar, Sibenik, Split, Dubrovnik
physical Adriatic coastline with large islands; very mountainous, with part of the Karst region and the Julian and Styrian Alps; some marshland
features popular sea resorts along the extensive Adriatic coastline
head of state Franjo Tudjman from 1990
head of government Franjo Greguric from 1991
political system emergent democracy
political parties Christian Democratic Union (HDZ), right-wing, nationalist; Coalition of National Agreement, centrist; Communist Party, reform-communist
products cereals, potatoes, tobacco, fruit, livestock, metal goods, textiles

currency Croatian dinar
population (1990) 4,760,000 including 75% Croats, 12% Serbs, and 1% Slovenes
language Croatian variant of Serbo-Croatian
religions Roman Catholic (Croats); Orthodox Christian (Serbs)
GNP $7.9 bn (1990); $1,660 per head
chronology
1918 Became part of the kingdom which united the Serbs, Croats, and Slovenes.
1929 The kingdom of Croatia, Serbia, and Slovenia became Yugoslavia. Croatia continued its campaign for autonomy.
1941 Became a Nazi puppet state following German invasion.
1945 Became constituent republic of Yugoslavia.
1970s Separatist demands resurfaced. Crackdown against anti-Serb separatist agitators.
1989 Formation of opposition parties permitted.
1990 April-May: Communists defeated by Tudjman-led Croatian Democratic Union (HDZ) in first free election since 1938. Sept: "sovereignty" declared. Dec: new constitution adopted.
1991 Feb: assembly called for Croatia's secession. March: Serb-dominated Krajina announced secession from Croatia. June: Croatia declared independence; military conflict with Serbia; internal civil war ensued. July onwards: civil war intensified. Oct: Croatia formally seceded from Yugoslavia.
1992 Jan: United Nations (UN) peace accord reached in Sarajevo; independence recognized by the European Community (EC). March–April: UN peacekeeping forces drafted into Croatia. April: independence recognized by US. May: became a member of the UN. Sept: Tudjman requested withdrawal of UN forces on expiry of mandate 1993.

found in Africa and Madagascar. The American crocodile *C. acutus*, about 15 ft/4.6 m long, is found from S Florida to Ecuador. The gharial, or gavial, *Gavialis gangeticus* is sometimes placed in a family of its own. It is an Indian species which grows to 15 ft/4.5 m or more, and has a very long narrow snout specialized for capturing and eating fish.

crocus any plant of the genus *Crocus* of the iris family Iridaceae, native to northern parts of the Old World, especially S Europe and Asia Minor. It has single yellow, purple, or white flowers and narrow, pointed leaves.

During the dry season of the year crocuses remain underground in the form of a corm, and produce fresh shoots and flowers in spring or autumn. At the end of the season of growth fresh corms are produced. Several species are cultivated as garden plants, the familiar mauve, white, and orange forms being varieties of *C. vernus*, *C. versicolor*, and *C. aureus*. To the same genus belongs the saffron *C. sativus*. The so-called ◊autumn crocus or meadow saffron *Colchicum autumnale* is not a true crocus but belongs to the lily family.

Croesus 6th century BC. Last king of Lydia, famed for his wealth. His court included ◊Solon, who warned him that no man could be called happy until his life had ended happily. When Croesus was overthrown by Cyrus the Great 546 BC and condemned to be burned to death, he called out Solon's name. Cyrus, having learned the reason, spared his life.

croft small farm in the Highlands of Scotland, traditionally farming common land cooperatively; the 1886 Crofters Act gave security of tenure to crofters. Today, although grazing land is still shared, arable land is typically enclosed.

Crohn's disease or *regional ileitis* chronic inflammatory bowel disease. It tends to flare up for a few days at a time, causing diarrhea, abdominal cramps, loss of appetite, and mild fever. The cause of Crohn's disease is unknown, although stress may be a factor.

Crohn's disease may occur in any part of the digestive system, from the mouth to the anus, but usually affects the small intestine. It is characterized by ulceration, abscess formation, small perforations, and the development of adhesions binding the loops of the small intestine. Affected segments of intestine may constrict, causing obstruction, or may perforate. It is treated by surgical removal of badly affected segments, and by corticosteroids. Mild cases respond to rest, bland diet, and drug treatment. Crohn's disease first occurs most often in adults of 20–50.

Cro-Magnon prehistoric human *Homo sapiens sapiens* believed to be ancestral to Europeans, the first skeletons of which were found 1868 in the Cro-Magnon cave near Les Eyzies, in the Dordogne region of France. They are thought to have superseded the Neanderthals in the Middle East, Africa, Europe, and Asia about 40,000 years ago. Although modern in skeletal form, they were more robust in build than some present-day humans. They hunted bison, reindeer, and horses, and are associated with Upper Paleolithic cultures, which produced fine flint and bone tools, jewelry, and naturalistic cave paintings.

Cromwell Oliver 1599–1658. English general and politician, Puritan leader of the Parliamentary side in the English ◊Civil War. He raised cavalry forces (later called **Ironsides**)

which aided the victories at Edgehill 1642 and ◊Marston Moor 1644, and organized the New Model Army, which he led (with General Fairfax) to victory at Naseby 1645. He declared Britain a republic ("the Commonwealth") 1649, following the execution of Charles I. As Lord Protector (ruler) from 1653, Cromwell established religious toleration and raised Britain's prestige in Europe on the basis of an alliance with France against Spain.

Cromwell was a critic of Charles I and became active in events leading to the Civil War. He signed the king's death warrant in 1648 and in the power struggle that followed sided with the army and the establishment of the Commonwealth. He expelled parliament and established the Protectorate. His foreign policy was dictated by religious and commercial considerations; he found no constitutional basis for his rule and refused the crown 1657.

Cromwell Richard 1626–1712. Son of Oliver ◊Cromwell, he succeeded his father as Lord Protector but resigned May 1659, having been forced to abdicate by the army. He lived in exile after the Restoration until 1680, when he returned.

Cromwell Thomas, Earl of Essex *c.* 1485–1540. English politician who drafted the legislation making the Church of England independent of Rome. Originally in Lord Chancellor Wolsey's service, he became secretary to Henry VIII 1534 and the real director of government policy; he was executed for treason.

Cromwell had Henry divorced from Catherine of Aragon by a series of acts that proclaimed him head-of the church. From 1536 to 1540 Cromwell suppressed the monasteries, ruthlessly crushed all opposition, and favored Protestantism, which denied the divine right of the pope. His mistake in arranging Henry's marriage to Anne of Cleves (to cement an alliance with the German Protestant princes against France and the Holy Roman Empire) led to his being accused of treason and beheaded.

Cronkite Walter 1916– . US broadcast journalist who was anchorperson of the national evening news program for CBS, a US television network, from 1962 to 1981.

Cronus or *Kronos* in Greek mythology, ruler of the world and one of the ◊Titans. He was the father of Zeus, who overthrew him.

Crookes William 1832–1919. English scientist whose many chemical and physical discoveries included the metallic element thallium 1861, the radiometer 1875, and the Crookes high-vacuum tube used in X-ray techniques.

crop in birds, the thin-walled enlargement of the digestive tract between the esophagus and stomach. It is an effective storage organ especially in seed-eating birds; a pigeon's crop can hold about 500 cereal grains. Digestion begins in the crop, by the moisturizing of food. A crop also occurs in insects and annelid worms.

crop any plant product grown or harvested for human use. Over 80 crops are grown worldwide, providing people with the majority of their food and supplying fibers, rubber, pharmaceuticals, dyes, and other materials. Crops grown for export are ◊cash crops. A catch crop is one grown in the interval between two main crops.

There are four main groups of crops. *Food crops* provide the bulk of people's food worldwide. The main types are cereals, roots,

pulses (peas, beans), vegetables, fruits, oil crops, tree nuts, sugar, and spices. Cereals make the largest contribution to human nutrition. *Forage crops* are those such as grass and clover which are grown to feed livestock. Forage crops cover a greater area of the world than food crops. Grasses, which dominate this group, form the world's most abundant crop, consisting mostly of wild species grown in an unimproved state. *Fibre crops* produce vegetable fibers. Temperate areas produce flax and hemp, but the most valuable fiber crops are cotton, jute, and sisal, which are grown mostly in the tropics. Cotton dominates fiber-crop production. *Miscellaneous crops* include tobacco, rubber, ornamental flowers, and plants that produce perfumes, pharmaceuticals, and dyes.

crop rotation system of regularly changing the crops grown on a piece of land. The crops are grown in a particular order to utilize and add to the nutrients in the soil and to prevent the buildup of insect and fungal pests. Including a legume crop, such as peas or beans, in the rotation helps build up nitrate in the soil because the roots contain bacteria capable of fixing nitrogen from the air.

A simple seven-year rotation, for example, might include a three-year ◊ley followed by two years of wheat and then two years of barley, before returning the land to temporary grass once more. In this way, the cereal crops can take advantage of the buildup of soil fertility that occurs during the period under grass.

In the 18th century, a four-year rotation was widely adopted with autumn-sown cereal, followed by a root crop, then spring cereal, and ending with a leguminous crop. Since then, more elaborate rotations have been devised with two, three, or four successive cereal crops, and with the root crop replaced by a cash crop such as sugar beet or potatoes, or by a legume crop such as peas or beans.

croquet outdoor game played with mallets and balls on a level hooped lawn measuring 90 ft/27 m by 60 ft/18 m. Played in France in the 16th and 17th centuries, it gained popularity in the US and England in the 1850s.

Two or more players can play, and the object is to drive the balls though the hoops (wickets) in rotation. A player's ball may be advanced or retarded by another ball. The headquarters of croquet is the Croquet Association (founded 1897), based at the Hurlingham Club, London.

Crosby Bing (Harry Lillis) 1904–1977. US film actor and singer who achieved world success with his distinctive style of crooning in such songs as "Pennies from Heaven" 1936 (featured in a film of the same name) and "White Christmas" 1942. He won an acting Oscar for *Going My Way* 1944, and made a series of "road" film comedies with Dorothy Lamour and Bob ◊Hope, the last being *Road to Hong Kong* 1962.

cross symbol of the Christian religion, in widespread use since the 3rd century. It is a symbol of the crucifixion of Jesus and the central significance of his suffering, death, and resurrection. The Latin cross is the most commonly used; other types are the Greek cross, St Anthony's cross, and St Andrew's cross. Symbolic crosses were used by pre-Christian cultures, for example the ancient Egyptian ankh (St Anthony's cross with a loop at the top), symbol of life, and the swastika, used by Hindus, Buddhists, Celts, and N American Indians before it was adopted by the Nazis.

crossbill species of bird, a ⟡finch of the genus *Loxia*, in which the hooked tips of the upper and lower beak cross one another, an adaptation for extracting the seeds from conifer cones. The red or common crossbill *Loxia curvirostra* is found in parts of Eurasia and North America.

The parrot crossbill *Loxia pytopsittacus* of Europe, and the white-winged crossbill *Loxia leucoptera* of N Asia and North America feed on pine and larch respectively.

cross-eye alternative term for ⟡squint.

crossing over in biology, a process that occurs during ⟡meiosis. While the chromosomes are lying alongside each other in pairs, each partner may twist around the other and exchange corresponding chromosomal segments. It is a form of genetic ⟡recombination, which increases variation and thus provides the raw material of evolution.

crossword puzzle in which a grid of open and blacked-out squares must be filled with interlocking words, to be read horizontally and vertically, according to numbered clues. The first crossword was devised by Arthur Wynne of Liverpool, England, in the *New York World* 1913.

croup inflammation (usually viral) of a child's larynx and trachea, with croaking breathing and hoarse coughing.

crow any of 35 species of the genus *Corvus*, family Corvidae, which also includes jays and magpies. Ravens belong to the same genus as crows. Crows are usually about 1.5 ft/45 cm long, black, with a strong bill feathered at the base, and omnivorous with a bias toward animal food. They are considered to be very intelligent.

crown official headdress worn by a king or queen. The modern crown originated with the diadem, an embroidered fillet worn by Eastern rulers, for which a golden band was later substituted. A laurel crown was granted by the Greeks to a victor in the games, and by the Romans to a triumphant general. Crowns came into use among the Byzantine emperors and the European kings after the fall of the Western Empire.

Perhaps the oldest crown in Europe is the Iron Crown of Lombardy, made in 591. The crown of Charlemagne, preserved in Vienna, consists of eight gold plates.

crown colony any British colony that is under the direct legislative control of the crown and does not possess its own system of representative government. Crown colonies are administered by a crown-appointed governor or by elected or nominated legislative and executive councils with an official majority. Usually the crown retains rights of veto and of direct legislation by orders in council.

crucifixion death by fastening to a cross, a form of capital punishment used by the ancient Romans, Persians, and Carthaginians, and abolished by the Roman emperor Constantine. Specifically, **the Crucifixion** refers to the execution by the Romans of ⟡Jesus in this manner.

Cruelty, Theater of theory advanced by Antonin ⟡Artaud in his book *Le Théâtre et son double* 1938 and adopted by a number of writers and directors. It aims to shock the audience into an awareness of basic, primitive human nature through the release of feelings usually repressed by conventional behavior.

Cruikshank George 1792–1878. British painter and illustrator, remembered for his political cartoons and illustrations for Charles Dickens's *Oliver Twist* and Daniel Defoe's *Robinson Crusoe*.

cruise missile long-range guided missile that has a terrain-seeking radar system and flies at moderate speed and low altitude. It is descended from the German V-1 of World War II. Initial trials in the 1950s demonstrated the limitations of cruise missiles, which included high fuel consumption and relatively slow speeds (when compared to intercontinental ballistic missiles—ICBMs) as well as inaccuracy and a small warhead. Improvements to guidance systems by the use of terrain-contour matching (TERCOM) ensured pinpoint accuracy on low-level flights after launch from a mobile ground launcher (ground-launched cruise missile—GLCM), from an aircraft (air-launched cruise missile –ALCM), or from a submarine or ship (sea-launched cruise missile –SLCM).

crusade European war against non-Christians and heretics, sanctioned by the pope; in particular, the Crusades, a series of wars 1096–1291 undertaken by European rulers to recover Palestine from the Muslims. Motivated by religious zeal, the desire for land, and the trading ambitions of the major Italian cities, the Crusades were varied in their aims and effects.
1st Crusade 1095–99 led by Baldwin of Boulogne, Godfrey of Bouillon, and Peter the Hermit. Motivated by occupation of Anatolia and Jerusalem by the Seljuk Turks. The crusade succeeded in recapturing Jerusalem and establishing a series of Latin kingdoms on the Syrian coast.
2nd Crusade 1147–49 led by Louis VII of France and Emperor Conrad III; a complete failure.
3rd Crusade 1189–92 led by Philip II Augustus of France and Richard I of England. Failed to recapture Jerusalem, which had been seized by Saladin 1187.
4th Crusade 1202–04 led by William of Montferrata, and Baldwin of Hainault. Directed against Egypt but diverted by the Venetians to sack and divide Constantinople.
Children's Crusade 1212 thousands of children crossed Europe on their way to Palestine but many were sold into slavery in Marseille, or died of disease and hunger.
5th Crusade 1218–21 led by King Andrew of Hungary, Cardinal Pelagius, King John of Jerusalem, and King Hugh of Cyprus. Captured and then lost Damietta, Egypt.
6th Crusade 1228–29 led by the Holy Roman emperor Frederick II. Jerusalem recovered by negotiation with the sultan of Egypt, but the city was finally lost 1244.
7th and 8th Crusades 1249–54, 1270–72 both led by Louis IX of France. Acre, the last Christian fortress in Syria, was lost 1291.

crust the outermost part of the structure of Earth, consisting of two distinct parts, the oceanic crust and the continental crust. The *oceanic* crust is on average about 6.2 mi/10 km thick and consists mostly of basaltic types of rock. By contrast, the *continental* crust is largely made of granite and is more complex in its structure. Because of the movements of ⟡plate tectonics, the oceanic crust is in no place older than about 200 million years. However, parts of the continental crust are over 3 billion years old.

Beneath a layer of surface sediment, the oceanic crust is made up of a layer of basalt, followed by a layer of gabbro. The composition of the oceanic crust overall shows a high proportion of *si*licon and *ma*gnesium oxides, hence named *sima* by geologists. The continental crust varies in thickness from about 25 mi/40 km to 45 mi/70 km, being deeper beneath mountain ranges. The surface layer consists of many kinds of sedimentary and igneous rocks. Beneath lies a zone of metamorphic rocks built on a thick layer of granodiorite. *Si*licon and *al*uminium oxides dominate the composition and the name *sial* is given to continental crustal material.

crustacean one of the class of arthropods that includes crabs, lobsters, shrimps, pillbugs, and barnacles. The external skeleton is made of protein and chitin hardened with lime. Each segment bears a pair of appendages that may be modified as sensory feelers (antennae), as mouthparts, or as swimming, walking, or grasping structures.

Crux constellation of the southern hemisphere, popularly known as the Southern Cross, the smallest of the 88 constellations. Its brightest star, Alpha Crucis (or Acrux), is a ⟡double star about 400 light-years from Earth. Near Beta Crucis lies a glittering star cluster known as the Jewel Box. The constellation also contains the Coalsack, a dark cloud of dust silhouetted against the bright starry background of the Milky Way.

cryogenics science of very low temperatures (approaching ⟡absolute zero), including the production of very low temperatures and the exploitation of special properties associated with them, such as the disappearance of electrical resistance (⟡superconductivity).

Low temperatures can be produced by the Joule-Thomson effect (cooling a gas by making it do work as it expands). Gases such as oxygen, hydrogen, and helium may be liquefied in this way, and temperatures of $0.3K$ can be reached. Further cooling requires magnetic methods; a magnetic material, in contact with the substance to be cooled and with liquid helium, is magnetized by a strong magnetic field. The heat generated by the process is carried away by the helium. When the material is then demagnetized, its temperature falls; temperatures of around $10^{-3}K$ have been achieved in this way. A similar process, called *nuclear adiabatic expansion*, was used to produce the lowest temperature recorded: $3 \times 10^{-8}K$, produced in 1984 by a team of Finnish scientists.

At temperatures near absolute zero, materials can display unusual properties. Some metals, such as mercury and lead, exhibit superconductivity. Liquid helium loses its viscosity and becomes a "superfluid" when cooled to below $2K$; in this state it flows up the sides of its container.

Cryogenics has several practical applications. *Cryotherapy* is a process used in eye surgery, in which a freezing probe is briefly applied to the outside of the eye to repair a break in the retina. Electronic components called ⟡Josephson junctions, which could be used in very fast computers, need low temperatures to function. Magnetic levitation (⟡maglev) systems must be maintained at low temperatures. Food can be frozen for years, and it has been suggested that space travelers could be frozen for long journeys. Freezing people with terminal illnesses, to be revived when a cure has been developed, has also been suggested.

cryolite rare granular crystalline mineral

(sodium aluminum fluoride), Na_3AlF_6, used in the electrolytic reduction of ▷bauxite to aluminum. It is chiefly found in Greenland.

Cryolite also occurs in Colorado at Pike's Peak.

cryonics practice of freezing a body at the moment of clinical death with the aim of enabling eventual resuscitation. The body, drained of blood, is indefinitely preserved in a thermos-type container filled with liquid nitrogen at $-321°F/-196°C$.

The first human treated was James H Bedford, a lung-cancer patient of 74, in the US in 1967.

cryptogam obsolete name applied to the lower plants. It included the algae, liverworts, mosses, and ferns (plus the fungi and bacteria in very early schemes of classification). In such classifications seed plants were known as ▷phanerogams.

cryptography science of creating and reading codes; for example, those produced by the Enigma coding machine used by the Germans in World War II (as in ▷Ultra) and those used in commerce by banks encoding electronic fund-transfer messages, business firms sending computer-conveyed memos between headquarters, and in the growing field of electronic mail. No method of encrypting is completely unbreakable, but decoding can be made extremely complex and time consuming.

cryptorchism or **cryptorchidism** condition marked by undescended testicles; failure of the testes to complete their descent into the scrotum before birth. When only one testicle has descended, the condition is known as monorchism.

About 10% of boys are born with one or both testes undescended. Usually the condition resolves within a few weeks of birth. Otherwise, an operation is needed to bring the testes down and ensure normal sexual development.

cryptosporidium waterborne parasite first discovered 1983. It infects drinking-water supplies, causing diarrhea, abdominal cramps, vomiting, and fever, and can be fatal in people with damaged immune systems, such as AIDS sufferers or those with leukemia.

crystal substance with an orderly three-dimensional arrangement of its atoms or molecules, thereby creating an external surface of clearly defined smooth faces having characteristic angles between them. Examples are table salt and quartz.

Each geometrical form, many of which may be combined in one crystal, consists of two or more faces—for example, dome, prism, and pyramid. A mineral can often be identified by the shape of its crystals and the system of crystallization determined. A single crystal can vary in size from a submicroscopic particle to a mass some 100 ft/30 m in length.

Crystals fall into seven crystal systems or groups, classified on the basis of the relationship of three or four imaginary axes that intersect at the center of any perfect, undistorted crystal.

crystallography the scientific study of crystals. In 1912 it was found that the shape and size of the repeating atomic patterns (unit cells) in a crystal could be determined by passing X-rays through a sample. This method, known as ▷X-ray diffraction, opened up an entirely new way of "seeing" atoms. It has been found that many substances have a unit cell that exhibits all the symmetry of the whole crystal; in table

salt (sodium chloride, NaCl), for instance, the unit cell is an exact cube.

Many materials were not even suspected of being crystals until they were examined by X-ray crystallography. It has been shown that purified biomolecules, such as proteins and DNA, can form crystals, and such compounds may now be studied by this method. Other applications include the study of metals and their alloys, and of rocks and soils.

crystal system all known crystalline substances crystallize in one of the seven crystal systems defined by symmetry. The elements of symmetry used for this purpose are: (1) planes of **mirror symmetry**, across which a mirror image is seen, and (2) axes of **rotational symmetry**, about which, in a 360° rotation of the crystal, equivalent faces are seen twice, three, four, or six times. To be assigned to a particular crystal system, a mineral must possess a certain minimum symmetry, but it may also possess additional symmetry elements. Since crystal symmetry is related to internal structure, a given mineral will always crystallize in the same system, although the crystals may not always grow into precisely the same shape. In cases where two minerals have the same chemical composition (for example graphite and diamond, or quartz and crystobalite), they will generally have different crystal systems because their internal structures are different.

CSCE abbreviation for ▷**Conference on Security and Cooperation in Europe**.

CT abbreviation for the state of ▷**Connecticut**.

Ctesiphon ruined royal city of the Parthians, and later capital of the Sassanian Empire, 12 mi/19 km SE of Baghdad, Iraq. A palace of the 4th century still has its throne room standing, spanned by a single vault of unreinforced brickwork some 80 ft/24 m across.

cu abbreviation for **cubic** (measure).

Cuba island country in the Caribbean Sea, the largest of the West Indies, off the S coast of Florida and to the E of Mexico.

government The 1976 constitution created a socialist state with the National Assembly of People's Power as its supreme organ. It consists of 510 deputies elected by universal suffrage for a five-year term and elects 31 of its members to form the Council of State. It also elects the head of state, who is president of the council, head of government, and first secretary and chair of the political bureau of the only party, the Cuban Communist Party (PCC).

history The first Europeans to visit Cuba were those of the expedition of Christopher Columbus 1492, who found Arawak Indians there. From 1511 Cuba was a Spanish colony, its economy based on sugar plantations worked by slaves, who were first brought from Africa 1523 to replace the decimated Indian population. Slavery was not abolished until 1886. Cuba was ceded to the US 1898, at the end of the ▷Spanish-American War. A republic was proclaimed 1901, but the US retained its naval base and asserted a right to intervene in internal affairs until 1934.

Batista dictatorship In 1933 an army sergeant, Fulgencio ▷Batista, seized and held power until he retired 1944. In 1952 he regained power in a bloodless coup and began another period of rule that many Cubans found oppressive. In 1953 a young lawyer and son of a sugar planter, Dr Fidel Castro, tried to overthrow him but failed. He went into exile to

prepare for another coup in 1956 but was again defeated. He fled to the hills with Dr Ernesto "Che" ▷Guevara and ten others to form a guerrilla force.

revolution In 1959 Castro's force of 5,000 guerrillas deposed Batista, to great popular acclaim. The 1940 constitution was suspended and replaced by a "Fundamental Law," power being vested in a council of ministers with Castro as prime minister, his brother Raúl as his deputy, and Che Guevara, reputedly, as the next in command. In 1960 the US broke off diplomatic relations after all US businesses in Cuba were nationalized without compensation. In 1961 it went further, sponsoring a full-scale (but abortive) invasion, the ▷Bay of Pigs episode. In Dec of that year Castro proclaimed a communist state whose economy would develop along Marxist-Leninist lines.

Cuban missile crisis In 1962 Cuba was expelled from the Organization of American States (OAS), which initiated a full political and economic blockade. Castro responded by tightening relations with the USSR that, in the same year, supplied missiles with atomic warheads for installation in Cuba. The ▷Cuban missile crisis brought the US and the USSR to the brink of nuclear war, but conflict was averted when the USSR agreed to dismantle the missiles at the US president's insistence. With Soviet help, Cuba made substantial economic and social progress 1965–72, in 1972 becoming a member of the Council for Mutual Economic Assistance (CMEA), a Moscow-based organization linking communist states.

foreign policy In 1976 a referendum approved a socialist constitution, and Fidel Castro and his brother were elected president and vice-president. During the following five years Cuba played a larger role in world affairs, particularly in Africa, to the disquiet of the US. Cuban troops played an important role in Angola, supporting the Luanda government against South African–backed rebels.

Re-elected 1981, Castro offered to discuss foreign policy with the US but Cuba's support for Argentina, against Britain, cooled relations and drew it closer to other Latin American countries. The 1983 US invasion of Grenada lowered the diplomatic temperature still further, though Cuba has since adopted a more conciliatory position toward the US. Cuban support of leftist rebels seeking to overthrow the repressive government of El Salvador caused continuing strains with the US. Castro also reaffirmed his communist orthodoxy in the light of events in eastern Europe 1989–90. The advent of Soviet leader ▷Gorbachev and the USSR's abandonment of its policy of supporting Third World revolutions led in 1989 to a curtailment of Cuba's foreign military interventions. In Sept 1991 the Kremlin announced that, against the wishes of Castro, all Soviet troops were to be withdrawn. In 1992 Castro reaffirmed his faith in communism. *See illustration box.*

Cuban missile crisis confrontation in international relations 1962 when Soviet rockets were installed in Cuba and US president Kennedy compelled Soviet leader Khrushchev, by an ultimatum, to remove them. The drive by the USSR to match the US in nuclear weaponry dates from this event.

The US imposed a naval "quarantine" around the island, and the two superpowers came closer to possible nuclear war than at any other time. Soviet inferiority in nuclear weapons forced a humiliating capitulation to

Cuba
Republic of (*República de Cuba*)

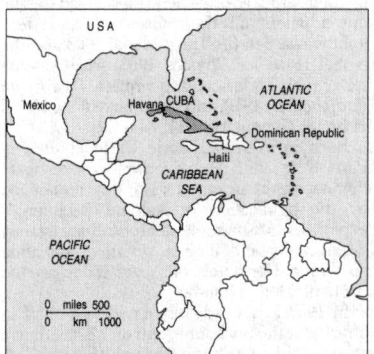

area 42,820 sq mi/110,860 sq km
capital Havana
cities Santiago de Cuba, Camagüey
physical comprises Cuba, the largest and westernmost of the West Indies, and smaller islands including Isle of Youth; low hills; Sierra Maestra mountains in SE
features 2,100 mi/3,380 km of coastline, with deep bays, sandy beaches, coral islands and reefs; more than 1,600 islands surround the Cuban mainland
head of state and government Fidel Castro Ruz from 1959
political system communist republic
political party Communist Party of Cuba (PCC), Marxist-Leninist
exports sugar, tobacco, coffee, nickel, fish
currency Cuban peso
population (1990 est) 10,582,000; 37% are white of Spanish descent, 51% mulatto, and 11% are of African origin; growth rate 0.6% p.a.
life expectancy men 72, women 75
language Spanish
religions Roman Catholic 85%; also Episcopalians and Methodists
literacy men 96%, women 95% (1988)
disposable national income $15.8 bn (1983); $1,590 per head
chronology
1492 Christopher Columbus landed in Cuba and claimed it for Spain.
1898 USA defeated Spain in Spanish-American War; Spain gave up all claims to Cuba.

1901 Cuba achieved independence; Tomás Estrada Palma became first president of the Republic of Cuba.
1933 Fulgencia Batista seized power.
1944 Batista retired.
1952 Batista seized power again to begin an oppressive regime.
1953 Fidel Castro led an unsuccessful coup against Batista.
1956 Second unsuccessful coup by Castro.
1959 Batista overthrown by Castro. Constitution of 1940 replaced by a "Fundamental Law," making Castro prime minister, his brother Raúl Castro his deputy, and Che Guevara his number three.
1960 All US businesses in Cuba appropriated without compensation; US broke off diplomatic relations.
1961 US sponsored an unsuccessful invasion at the Bay of Pigs. Castro announced that Cuba had become a communist state, with a Marxist-Leninist program of economic development.
1962 Cuba expelled from the Organization of American States. Soviet nuclear missiles installed but subsequently removed from Cuba at US insistence.
1965 Cuba's sole political party renamed Cuban Communist Party (PCC). With Soviet help, Cuba began to make considerable economic and social progress.
1972 Cuba became a full member of the Moscow-based Council for Mutual Economic Assistance.
1976 New socialist constitution approved; Castro elected president.
1976–81 Castro became involved in extensive international commitments, sending troops as Soviet surrogates, particularly to Africa.
1982 Cuba joined other Latin American countries in giving moral support to Argentina in its dispute with Britain over the Falklands.
1984 Castro tried to improve US-Cuban relations by discussing exchange of US prisoners in Cuba for Cuban "undesirables" in the US.
1988 Peace accord with South Africa signed, agreeing to withdrawal of Cuban troops from Angola.
1989 Reduction in Cuba's overseas military activities.
1991 Soviet troops withdrawn.
1992 Castro reaffirmed support for communism.

Kennedy's demands. Some historians maintain that Kennedy's lack of resolve during the ◊Bay of Pigs invasion attempt gave Khrushchev reason to believe that the US would not resist the introduction of Soviet missiles into Cuba.

In Aug 1979 there was a lesser crisis when US president Carter discovered a Soviet combat brigade on the island, but failed to enforce its withdrawal.

cube in geometry, a solid figure whose faces are all squares. It has six equal-area faces and 12 equal-length edges. If the length of one edge is l, the volume V of the cube is given by $V = l^3$ and its surface area $A = 6l^2$.

cubic measure measure of volume, indicated either by the word "cubic" followed by a linear measure, as in "cubic foot," or the word "cubed" after a linear measure, as in "meter cubed."

Cubism revolutionary movement in early 20th-century painting, pioneering abstract art.

Its founders, Georges Braque and Pablo Picasso, were admirers of Paul Cézanne and were inspired by his attempt to create a structure on the surface of his canvas. About 1907–10 in France the Cubists began to "abstract" images from nature, gradually releasing themselves from the imitation of reality. Cubism announced that a work of art exists in its own right rather than as a representation of the real world, and it attracted such artists as Juan Gris, Fernand Léger, and Robert Delaunay.

cubit earliest known unit of length, which originated between 2800 and 2300 BC. It is approximately 20.6 in/50.5 cm long, which is about the length of the human forearm measured from the tip of the middle finger to the elbow.

cuboid six-sided three-dimensional prism whose faces are all rectangles. A brick is a cuboid.

Cuchulain in Celtic mythology, a legendary

hero, the chief figure in a cycle of Irish legends. He is associated with his uncle Conchobar, king of Ulster; his most famous exploits are described in *Taín Bó Cuailnge/The Cattle Raid of Cuchulain*.

cuckoo species of bird, any of about 200 members of the family Culidae, especially the Eurasian cuckoo *Cuculus canorus*, whose name derives from its characteristic call.

Somewhat hawklike, it is about 1.1 ft/33 cm long, bluishgray and barred beneath (females sometimes reddish), and has a long, typically rounded tail. Cuckoos feed on insects, including hairy caterpillars that are distasteful to most birds. It is a "brood parasite," laying its eggs singly, at intervals of about 48 hours, in the nests of small insectivorous birds. As soon as the young cuckoo hatches, it ejects all other young birds or eggs from the nest and is tended by its "foster parents" until fledging. American species hatch and rear their own young.

The North American **roadrunner** *Geococcyx californianus* is a member of the cuckoo family.

cucumber trailing annual plant *Cucumis sativus* of the gourd family Cucurbitaceae, producing long, green-skinned fruit with crisp, translucent, edible flesh. Small cucumbers, called gherkins, usually the fruit of *C. anguria*, are often pickled.

Cugnot Nicolas-Joseph 1728–1804. French engineer who produced the first high-pressure steam engine. While serving in the French army, he was asked to design a steam-operated gun carriage. After several years, he produced a three-wheeled, high-pressure carriage capable of carrying 400 gallons/1,800 liters of water and four passengers at a speed of 3 mph/5 kph. Although he worked further on the carriage, the political upheavals of the French revolutionary era obstructed progress and his invention was ignored.

Cukor George 1899–1983. US film director. He moved to the cinema from the theater, and was praised for his skilled handling of such stars as Greta ◊Garbo (in *Camille* 1937) and Katharine Hepburn (in *The Philadelphia Story* 1940). He won an Academy Award for the direction of *My Fair Lady* 1964.

His films were usually sophisticated dramas or light comedies.

Culloden, Battle of defeat 1746 of the ◊Jacobite rebel army of the British prince ◊Charles Edward Stuart by the Duke of Cumberland on a stretch of moorland in Inverness-shire, Scotland. This battle effectively ended the military challenge of the Jacobite rebellion.

cultivar variety of a plant developed by horticultural or agricultural techniques. The term derives from "*culti*vated *var*iety."

cultural anthropology or *social anthropology* subdiscipline of anthropology that analyses human culture and society, the nonbiological and behavioral aspects of humanity. Two principal branches are ethnography (the study at first hand of living cultures) and ethnology (the comparison of cultures using ethnographic evidence).

Cultural Revolution mass movement begun by Chinese Communist Party chair Mao Zedong 1966–69, directed against the upper middle class—bureaucrats, artists, and academics who were killed, imprisoned, humiliated, or "resettled." Intended to "purify"

Chinese communism, it was also an attempt by Mao to renew his political and ideological pre-eminence inside China. Half a million people are estimated to have been killed.

The "revolution" was characterized by the violent activities of the semimilitary Red Guards, most of them students. Many established and learned people were humbled and eventually sent to work on the land, and from 1966 to 1970 universities were closed. Although the revolution was brought to an end in 1969, the resulting bureaucratic and economic chaos had many long-term effects.

culture in biology, the growing of living cells and tissues in laboratory conditions.

culture in sociology and anthropology, the way of life of a particular society or group of people, including patterns of thought, beliefs, behavior, customs, traditions, rituals, dress, and language, as well as art, music, and literature. Sociologists and anthropologists use culture as a key concept in describing and analyzing human societies.

Cuman member of a powerful alliance of Turkic-speaking peoples of the Middle Ages, which dominated the steppes in the 11th and 12th centuries and built an empire reaching from the river Volga to the Danube.

For a generation the Cumans held up the Mongol advance on the Volga, but in 1238 a Cuman and Russian army was defeated near Astrakhan, and 200,000 Cumans took refuge in Hungary, where they settled and where their language died out only about 1775. The Mameluke dynasty of Egypt was founded by Cuman ex-slaves. Most of the so-called Tatars of S Russia were of Cuman origin.

Cumberland city in NW Maryland, in the Allegheny mountains, on the Potomac River, directly S of Johnstown, Pennsylvania; seat of Allegheny County; population (1990) 23,700. Its industries include the mining and shipping of coal, sheet metal, iron products, and tires. It was first an Indian village and then a trading post and fort before it was incorporated 1815.

cumin seedlike fruit of the herb *Cuminum cyminum* of the carrot family Umbelliferae, with a bitter flavor. It is used as a spice in cooking.

cummings e e. Literary signature of Edward Estlin Cummings 1894–1962. US poet and novelist. He made his reputation with collections of poetry such as *Tulips and Chimneys* 1923. At first the poems gained notoriety for their idiosyncratic punctuation and typography (using only lowercase letters, for example), but their lyric power has gradually been recognized.

Born in Cambridge, Massachusetts, Cummings graduated from Harvard University and served in the ambulance corps during World War I. He was imprisoned for a brief period for alleged treasonous statements in his correspondence. Out of this experience came his novel, *The Enormous Room* 1922. Other collections of poetry include *XLI*, 1925, *ViVa* 1931, and *1 x 1* 1944. *Him* 1927 was an expressionist drama. Also notable are his paintings, lectures, and the essays *Eimi* 1933, his impressions of the USSR.

cumulative frequency in statistics, the total frequency of a given value up to and including a certain point in a set of data. It is used to draw the cumulative frequency curve, the ogive.

cuneiform ancient writing system formed of combinations of wedge-shaped strokes, usually impressed on clay. It was probably invented by the Sumerians, and was in use in Mesopotamia as early as the middle of the 4th millennium BC.

It was adopted and modified by the Assyrians, Babylonians, Elamites, Hittites, Persians, and many other peoples with different languages. In the 5th century BC it fell into disuse, but sporadically reappeared in later centuries. The decipherment of cuneiform scripts was pioneered by the German George Grotefend 1802 and the British orientalist Henry Rawlinson 1846.

Cunningham Merce 1919– . US dancer and choreographer. Influenced by Martha ⊳Graham, with whose company he was soloist from 1939–45, he formed his own avant-garde dance company and school in New York in 1953. His works include *The Seasons* 1947, *Antic Meet* 1958, *Squaregame* 1976, and *Arcade* 1985.

Cunningham worked closely with composers and artists when staging his works; among them *Septet* 1953, *Suite for Five* 1956, *Crises* 1960, *Winterbranch* 1964, *Scramble* 1967, *Signals* 1970, and *Sounddance* 1974.

Cupid in Roman mythology, the god of love, identified with the Greek god ⊳Eros.

cuprite Cu_2O ore (copper(I) oxide), found in crystalline form or in earthy masses. It is red to black in color, and is often called ruby copper.

cupronickel copper alloy (75% copper and 25% nickel), used in hardware products and for coinage.

US coins made with cupronickel include the dime, quarter, half-dollar, and dollar.

Curaçao sweet liqueur made by flavoring alcohol (obtained from distillation) with sugar and the dried peels of bitter oranges. Originally from the Caribbean island of Curaçao, it is now made elsewhere. The alcohol content varies between 36% and 40%.

Curaçao island in the West Indies, one of the ⊳Netherlands Antilles; area 171 sq mi/444 sq km; population (1988) 148,500. The principal industry, dating from 1918, is the refining of Venezuelan petroleum. Curaçao was colonized by Spain 1527, annexed by the Dutch West India Company 1634, and gave its name from 1924 to the group of islands renamed Netherlands Antilles in 1948. Its capital is the port of Willemstad.

curare black, resinous poison extracted from the bark and juices of various South American trees and plants. Originally used on arrowheads by Amazonian hunters to paralyze prey, it blocks nerve stimulation of the muscles. Alkaloid derivatives (called curarines) are used in medicine as muscle relaxants during surgery.

Curia Romana the judicial and administrative bodies through which the pope carries on the government of the Roman Catholic Church. It includes certain tribunals; the chancellery, which issues papal bulls; various offices including that of the cardinal secretary of state; and the Congregations, or councils of cardinals, each with a particular department of work.

curie former unit (symbol Ci) of radioactivity, equal to 37×10^9 ⊳becquerels. One gram of radium has a radioactivity of about one curie. It was named after French physicist Pierre Curie.

Curie Marie (born Sklodovska) 1867–1934. Polish scientist. In 1898 she reported the possible existence of a new, powerfully radioactive element in pitchblende ores. Her husband, Pierre (1859–1906) abandoned his own researches to assist her, and in the same year they announced the existence of polonium and radium elements 1902. Both scientists refused to take out a patent on their discovery and were jointly awarded the Davy Medal 1903 and the Nobel Prize for Physics 1903, with Antoine ⊳Becquerel. Marie Curie wrote a *Treatise on Radioactivity* 1910, and was awarded the Nobel Prize for Chemistry 1911.

Born in Warsaw, Marie Curie studied in Paris from 1891. Her decision to investigate the nature of uranium rays was influenced by the publication of Antoine Becquerel's experiments. She took no precautions against radioactivity and died a victim of radiation poisoning. Her notebooks, even today, are too contaminated to handle.

In 1904 Pierre was appointed to a chair in physics at the Sorbonne, and on his death in a street accident was succeeded by his wife.

Curie temperature the temperature above which a magnetic material cannot be strongly magnetized. Above the Curie temperature, the energy of the atoms is too great for them to join together to form the small areas of magnetized material, or ⊳domains, which combine to produce the strength of the overall magnetization.

curium synthesized, radioactive, metallic element of the *actinide* series, symbol Cm, atomic number 96, atomic weight 247. It is produced by bombarding plutonium or americium with neutrons. Its longest-lived isotope has a half-life of 1.7×10^7 years.

Curium is used to generate heat and power in satellites or in remote places. Named in 1946 for Pierre and Marie Curie by Glenn Seaborg, it was first synthesized in 1944 by Seaborg at the University of California at Berkeley, by analogy with the corresponding ⊳lanthanide, gadolinium (see ⊳periodic table of the elements).

curlew wading bird of the genus Numenius of the sandpiper family, Scolopacidae. The curlew is between 14 in/36 cm and 1.8 ft/55 cm in length, and has mottled brown plumage, long legs, and a long, thin, downcurved bill. Several species live in N Europe, Asia, and North America. The name derives from its haunting flutelike call.

One species, the Eskimo curlew, is almost extinct, never having recovered from relentless hunting in the late 19th century.

Curley James Michael 1874–1958. US Democrat politician, several times mayor of Boston between 1914 and 1950. He was a member of the US House of Representatives 1912–14. He served as mayor until 1934, when, having established a powerful political organization, he was elected governor. He lost a bid for the US Senate 1936 and did not hold political office again until elected to the House 1942. His fourth and last mayoral term began 1946, during which time he spent six months in federal prison on a mail-fraud conviction.

Born in Boston, Curley became active in the local Democratic party soon after leaving school. He served in the state legislature 1902–03, on the Boston Board of Aldermen 1904–09, and on the Boston City Council 1910–11.

The flamboyant Curley's political career inspired Edwin O'Connor's *The Last Hurrah* 1956.

curling game played on ice with stones; sometimes described as "bowls on ice." One of the national games of Scotland, it has spread to many countries. It can also be played on artificial (cement or asphalt) ponds.

currant berry of a small seedless variety of cultivated grape *Vitis vinifera*. Currants are grown on a large scale in Greece and California and used dried in cooking and baking. Because of the similarity of the fruit, the name currant is also given to several species of shrubs in the genus *Ribes*, family Grossulariaceae.

The garden red currant *Ribes rubrum* is a native of S Europe and Asia, now also growing in North America. The European black currant *R. nigrum* is widely cultivated. The American black currant *R. americanum* is native to E North America, as is the skunk currant *R. glandulosum*.

currency the type of money in use in a country; for example, the US dollar, the Australian dollar, the UK pound sterling, the German Deutschmark, and the Japanese yen.

current flow of a body of water or air, or of heat, moving in a definite direction. There are three basic types of ◊oceanic current: *drift currents* are broad and slow-moving; *stream currents* are narrow and swift-moving; and *upwelling currents* bring cold, nutrient-rich water from the ocean bottom.

Stream currents include the ◊Gulf Stream and the ◊Japan (or Kuroshio) Current. Upwelling currents, such as the Gulf of Guinea Current and the Peru (Humboldt) current, provide food for plankton, which in turn supports fish and sea birds. At approximate five-to-eight-year intervals, the Peru Current that runs from the Antarctic up the W coast of South America, turns warm, with heavy rain and rough seas, and has disastrous results (as in 1982–83) for Peruvian wildlife and for the anchovy industry. The phenomenon is called *El Niño* (Spanish "the Child") because it occurs toward Christmas.

current account in economics, that part of the balance of payments concerned with current transactions, as opposed to capital movements. It includes trade (visibles) and service transactions, such as investment, insurance, shipping, and tourism (invisibles). The state of the current account is regarded as a barometer of overall economic health.

In some countries, such as Italy, Spain, and Portugal, visibles make a large contribution to the current account and may more than offset trade deficits.

current prices series of prices that express values pertaining to a given time but that do not take account of the changes in purchasing power, unlike ◊constant prices.

curriculum in education, the range of subjects offered within an institution or course.

The term also refers to the specific series of courses required for graduation and to the series of topics taught within any one course during a semester.

Curtin John 1885–1945. Australian Labor politician, prime minister and minister of defense 1941–45. He was elected leader of the Labor Party 1935. As prime minister, he organized the mobilization of Australia's resources to meet the danger of Japanese invasion during World War II.

Curtis Tony. Adopted name of Bernard Schwarz 1925– . US film actor who starred in the 1950s and 1960s in such films as *The Vikings* 1958 and *The Boston Strangler* 1968, as well as specializing in light comedies such as

Some Like it Hot 1959, with Jack Lemmon and Marilyn Monroe.

Curtiss Glenn Hammond 1878–1930. US aeronautical inventor, pioneer aviator, and aircraft designer. He belonged to Alexander Graham Bell's Aerial Experiment Assoc 1907–09 and in 1908 made the first public flights in the US, including the 1-mile flight. It was followed by his sensational flight down the Hudson from Albany to New York City in 1910. Curtiss had established the first flying school in 1909, and in 1916 organized the Curtiss Airplane and Motor Corp, based on his invention of ailerons in 1911, which he designed for the first ◊seaplanes (also 1911). He designed and constructed many planes for the Allied nations during World War I, and after the war continued to make improvements in both plane and motor designs.

Curtiz Michael. Adopted name of Mihaly Kertész 1888–1962. Hungarian-born film director who worked in Austria, Germany, and France before moving to the US in 1926, where he made several films with Errol Flynn, directed *Mildred Pierce* 1945, which revitalized Joan Crawford's career, and *Casablanca* 1942 (Academy Award).

His wide range of films include *Doctor X* 1932, *The Adventures of Robin Hood* 1938, and *White Christmas* 1954.

curve in geometry, the ◊locus of a point moving according to specified conditions. The circle is the locus of all points equidistant from a given point (the center). Other common geometrical curves are the ◊ellipse, ◊parabola, and ◊hyperbola, which are also produced when a cone is cut by a plane at different angles.

Many curves have been invented for the solution of special problems in geometry and mechanics—for example, the cissoid (the inverse of a parabola) and the ◊cycloid.

Curzon George Nathaniel, 1st Marquess Curzon of Kedleston 1859–1925. British Conservative politician, viceroy of India 1899–1905. During World War I, he was a member of the cabinet 1916–19. As foreign secretary 1919–24, he set up a British protectorate over Persia.

Curzon Robert, Lord Zouche 1810–1873. English diplomat and traveler, author of *Monasteries in the Levant* 1849.

Curzon Line Polish-Soviet frontier proposed after the Russo-Polish war 1919–20. It was based on the eastward limit of areas with a predominantly Polish population and acquired its name 1920 after the British foreign secretary, Lord Curzon, suggested that the Poles, who had invaded the USSR, should retire to this line pending a peace conference. The frontier established 1945 in general follows the Curzon Line.

Cushing Harvey Williams 1869–1939. US neurologist who pioneered neurosurgery. He developed a range of techniques for the surgical treatment of brain tumors, and also studied the link between the ◊pituitary gland and conditions such as dwarfism.

Cushing Peter 1913– . British actor who specialized in horror roles in films made at Hammer studios 1957–73, including *Dracula* 1958, *The Mummy* 1959, and *Frankenstein Must Be Destroyed* 1969. Other films include *Doctor Who and the Daleks* 1966, *Star Wars* 1977, and *Top Secret* 1984.

Cushing's syndrome condition in which the body chemistry is upset by excessive production of ◊steroid hormones from the adrenal cortex.

Symptoms include weight gain in the face and trunk, raised blood pressure, excessive growth of facial and body hair (hirsutism), demineralization of bone, and, sometimes, diabeteslike effects. The underlying cause may be an adrenal or pituitary tumor, or prolonged high-dose therapy with ◊corticosteroid drugs.

cusp point where two branches of a curve meet and the tangents to each branch coincide.

custard apple any of numerous, primarily tropical trees and shrubs of the family Annonaceae. Several are cultivated for their large, edible, heart-shaped fruits. The pawpaw *A. simina triloba* of the E US, and the pond-apple *Annona glabra* of the West Indies are representatives.

Custer George A(rmstrong) 1839–1876. US Civil War general, the Union's youngest brigadier general as a result of a brilliant war record. Reduced in rank in the regular army at the end of the Civil War, he campaigned against the Sioux from 1874, and was killed with a detachment of his troops by the forces of Sioux chief Sitting Bull in the Battle of Little Bighorn, Montana: also called *Custer's last stand*, June 25, 1876.

Some historians accuse Custer of a reckless desire to advance his career.

Cuthbert, St died 687. Christian saint. A shepherd in Northumbria, England, he entered the monastery of Melrose, Scotland, after receiving a vision. He traveled widely as a missionary and because of his alleged miracles was known as the "wonderworker of Britain."

cuticle in zoology, the horny noncellular surface layer of many invertebrates such as insects; in botany, the waxy surface layer on those parts of plants that are exposed to the air, continuous except for ◊stomata and ◊lenticels. All types are secreted by the cells of the ◊epidermis. A cuticle reduces water loss and, in arthropods, acts as an ◊exoskeleton.

cuttlefish any of a family, Sepiidae, of squidlike cephalopods with an internal calcareous shell (cuttlebone). The common cuttle *Sepia officinalis* of the Atlantic and Mediterranean is up to 1 ft/30 cm long. It swims actively by means of the fins into which the sides of its oval, flattened body are expanded, and jerks itself backward by shooting a jet of water from its "siphon."

It is capable of rapid changes of color and pattern. The large head has conspicuous eyes, and the ten arms are provided with suckers. Two arms are very much elongated, and with them the cuttle seizes its prey. It has an ink sac from which a dark fluid can be discharged into the water, distracting predators from the cuttle itself. The dark brown pigment sepia is obtained from the ink sacs of cuttlefish.

Cuvier Georges, Baron Cuvier 1769–1832. French comparative anatomist. In 1799 he showed that some species have become extinct by reconstructing extinct giant animals that he believed were destroyed in a series of giant deluges. These ideas are expressed in *Recherches sur les ossiments fossiles de quadrupèdes* 1812 and *Discours sur les révolutions de la surface du globe* 1825.

In 1798 Cuvier produced *Tableau élémentaire de l'histoire naturelle des animaux*, in which his scheme of classification is outlined. He was professor of natural history in the Collège de France from 1799 and at the Jardin des Plantes from 1802; at the Restoration in 1815 he was elected chancellor of the University of Paris. Cuvier was the first to relate the structure of ⌕fossil animals to that of their living relatives. His great work *Le Règne animal/The Animal Kingdom* 1817 is a systematic survey.

Cuyp Aelbert 1620–1691. Dutch painter of countryside scenes, seascapes, and portraits.

His idyllically peaceful landscapes are bathed in golden light; for example, *A Herdsman with Cows by a River* (about 1650, National Gallery, London). His father, **Jacob Gerritsz Cuyp** (1594–1652), was also a landscape and portrait painter.

Cuzco city in S Peru, capital of Cuzco department, in the Andes, over 11,000 ft/3,350 m above sea level and 350 mi/560 km SE of Lima; population (1988) 255,000. It was founded in the 11th century as the ancient capital of the ⌕Inca empire and was captured by Francisco Pizarro 1533.

The university was founded 1598. The city has a Renaissance cathedral and other relics of the early Spanish conquerors. There are many Inca remains and in the 1970s and 1980s the Inca irrigation canals and terracing nearby were being restored to increase cultivation.

CVA abbreviation for **cerebrovascular accident**; see ⌕stroke.

cwt symbol for ⌕**hundredweight**, a unit of weight equal to 100 lb (45.36 kg) in the US and 112 lb (50.8 kg) in the UK and Canada.

cyanide CN- ion derived from hydrogen cyanide (HCN), and any salt containing this ion (produced when hydrogen cyanide is neutralized by alkalis), such as potassium cyanide (KCN). The principal cyanides are potassium, sodium, calcium, mercury, gold, and copper. Certain cyanides are poisons.

cyanocobalamin chemical name for ⌕vitamin B_{12}, which is normally produced by microorganisms in the gut. The richest natural source is raw liver. The deficiency disease, pernicious anemia, is the poor development of red blood cells with possible degeneration of the spinal chord. Sufferers develop extensive bruising and recover slowly from even minor injuries.

cyanosis bluish discoloration of the skin or mucous membranes, usually around the mouth, due to diminished uptake of oxygen. It is most often seen in diseases of the heart, lungs, or blood.

Cybele in Phrygian mythology, an earth goddess, identified by the Greeks with ⌕Rhea and honored in Rome.

cybernetics (Greek *kubernan* "to steer") science concerned with how systems organize, regulate, and reproduce themselves, and also how they evolve and learn. In the laboratory, inanimate objects are created that behave like living systems. Applications range from the creation of electronic artificial limbs to the running of the fully automated factory where decision-making machines operate up to managerial level.

Cybernetics was founded and named in 1947 by US mathematician Norbert Wiener. Originally, it was the study of control systems using feedback to produce automatic processes.

cycad plant of the order Cycadales belonging to the gymnosperms. Some have a superficial resemblance to palms, others to ferns. Their large cones contain fleshy seeds. There are ten genera and about 80–100 species, native to tropical and subtropical countries.

The stems of many species yield an edible starchy substance resembling sago. Cycads were widespread during the Mesozoic era.

Cyclades (Greek *Kikládhes*) group of about 200 Greek islands in the Aegean Sea, lying between mainland Greece and Turkey; area 996 sq mi/2,579 sq km; population (1981) 88,500. They include Andros, Melos, Paros, Naxos, and Siros, on which is the capital Hermoupolis.

cyclamate derivative of cyclohexysulfamic acid, formerly used as an artificial sweetener, 30 times sweeter than sugar. It was first synthesized 1937.

Its use in foods was banned in the US and the UK from 1970, when studies showed that massive doses caused cancer in rats.

cyclamen any plant of the genus *Cyclamen* of perennial plants of the primrose family Primulaceae, with heart-shaped leaves and petals that are twisted at the base and bent back. The flowers are usually white or pink, and several species are cultivated.

cycle in physics, a sequence of changes that moves a system away from, and then back to, its original state. An example is a vibration that moves a particle first in one direction and then in the opposite direction, with the particle returning to its original position at the end of the vibration.

cyclic compound any of a group of organic chemicals that have rings of atoms in their molecules, giving them a closed-chain structure.

cycling riding a ⌕bicycle for sport, pleasure, or transport. Cycle racing can take place on oval artificial tracks, on the road, or across country (cyclo-cross).

Stage races are run over grueling terrain and can last anything from three days to three and a half weeks, as in the ⌕Tour de France, Tour of Italy, and Tour of Spain. *Criteriums* are fast, action-packed races around the closed streets of town or city centers. Each race lasts about an hour. *Road races* are run over a prescribed circuit, which the riders will lap several times. Such a race will normally cover a distance of approximately 100 mi/160 km. *Track racing* takes place on a concrete or wooden banked circuit, either indoors or outdoors. In *time trialing* each rider races against the clock, with all the competitors starting at different intervals.

Among the main events are the Tour de France, first held in 1903; the Tour of Britain (formerly called the Milk Race), first held in 1951; and the World Professional Road Race Championship, first held at the Neuburgring, Germany, in 1927.

cycloid in geometry, a curve resembling a series of arches traced out by a point on the circumference of a circle that rolls along a straight line. Its applications include the study of the motion of wheeled vehicles along roads and tracks.

cyclone alternate name for a ⌕depression, an area of low atmospheric pressure. A severe

cylinder *The volume and area of a cylinder are given by simple formulae relating the dimensions of the cylinder.*

$$V = \pi r^2 h$$
$$A = 2\pi r h + 2\pi r^2$$

cyclone that forms in the tropics is called a tropical cyclone or ⌕hurricane.

Cyclops in Greek mythology, one of a legendary nation of giants who lived in Sicily, had one eye in the middle of the forehead, and lived as shepherds; Odysseus fought and overcame them in Homer's *Odyssey*.

cyclosporin ⌕immunosuppressive drug derived from a fungus (*Tolypocladium inflatum*). In use by 1978, it revolutionized transplant surgery by reducing the incidence and severity of rejection of donor organs.

It suppresses the T-cells (see ⌕lymphocyte) that reject foreign tissue without suppressing other cells that fight infection and cancer.

cyclotron circular type of particle ⌕accelerator.

Cygnus large prominent constellation of the northern hemisphere, named after its shape (Latin "swan"). Its brightest star is first-magnitude ⌕Deneb.

Beta Cygni (Albireo) is a yellow and blue ⌕double star, visible by small telescopes. The constellation contains the North America nebula (named after its shape), the Veil nebula (the remains of a supernova that exploded about 50,000 years ago), Cygnus A (apparently a double galaxy, and a powerful radio source), and the X-ray source Cygnus X-1, thought to mark the position of a black hole.

cylinder in geometry, a tubular solid figure with a circular base. In everyday use, the term applies to a *right cylinder*, the curved surface of which is at right angles to the base.

The volume V of a cylinder is given by the formula $V = \pi r^2 h$, where r is the radius of the base and h is the height of the cylinder. Its total surface area A has the formula $A = 2\pi r(h + r)$, where $2\pi r h$ is the curved surface area, and $2\pi r^2$ is the area of both circular ends.

cymbal ancient musical instrument of percussion, consisting of a shallow circular brass dish held at the center; either used in pairs clashed together or singly, struck with a beater. Smaller finger cymbals or *crotala*, used by Debussy

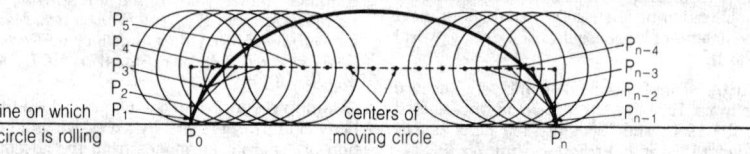

cycloid *The cycloid is the curve traced out by a point on a circle as it rolls along a straight line.*

Cyprus

Greek Republic of Cyprus (*Kypriaki Dimokratía*) in the south, and **Turkish Republic of Northern Cyprus** (*Kibris Cumhuriyeti*) in the north

area 3,571 sq mi/9,251 sq km, 37% in Turkish hands
capital Nicosia (divided between Greeks and Turks)
cities ports Limassol, Larnaca, Paphos (Greek); Morphou, and ports Kyrenia and Famagusta (Turkish)
physical central plain between two E–W mountain ranges
features archeological and historic sites; Mount Olympus 6,406 ft/1,953 m (highest peak); beaches
heads of state and government Georgios Vassiliou (Greek) from 1988, Rauf Denktaş (Turkish) from 1976
political system democratic divided republic
political parties Democratic Front (DIKO), center-left; Progressive Party of the Working People (AKEL), socialist; Democratic Rally (DISY), centrist; Socialist Party (EDEK), socialist; *Turkish zone*: National Unity Party (NUP), Communal Liberation Party (CLP), Republican Turkish Party (RTP), New British Party (NBP)
exports citrus, grapes, raisins, Cyprus sherry, potatoes, clothing, footwear
currency Cyprus pound and Turkish lira
population (1990 est) 708,000 (Greek Cypriot 78%, Turkish Cypriot 18%); growth rate 1.2% p.a.
life expectancy men 72, women 76
languages Greek and Turkish (official), English
religions Greek Orthodox 78%, Sunni Muslim 18%
literacy 99% (1984)
GDP $3.7 bn (1987); $5,497 per head
chronology
1878 Came under British administration.
1955 Guerrilla campaign began against the British for enosis (union with Greece), led by Archbishop Makarios and General Grivas.
1956 Makarios and enosis leaders deported.
1959 Compromise agreed and Makarios returned to be elected president of an independent Greek-Turkish Cyprus.
1960 Independence achieved from Britain, with Britain retaining its military bases.
1963 Turks set up their own government in northern Cyprus. Fighting broke out between the two communities.
1964 United Nations peacekeeping force installed.
1971 Grivas returned to start a guerrilla war against the Makarios government.
1974 Grivas died. Military coup deposed Makarios, who fled to Britain. Nicos Sampson appointed president. Turkish army sent to northern Cyprus to confirm Turkish Cypriots' control; military regime in southern Cyprus collapsed; Makarios returned. Northern Cyprus declared itself the Turkish Federated State of Cyprus (TFSC), with Rauf Denktaş as president.
1977 Makarios died; succeeded by Spyros Kyprianou.
1983 An independent Turkish Republic of Northern Cyprus proclaimed but recognized only by Turkey.
1984 UN peace proposals rejected.
1985 Summit meeting between Kyprianou and Denktaş failed to reach agreement.
1988 Georgios Vassiliou elected president. Talks with Denktaş began, under UN auspices.
1989 Vassiliou and Denktaş agreed to draft an agreement for the future reunification of the island, but peace talks were abandoned Sept.
1991 Turkish offer of peace talks rejected by Cyprus and Greece.
1992 Peace talks resumed.

of the earliest Christian writers, and bishop of Carthage about 249. He wrote a treatise on the unity of the church. Feast day Sept 16.

Cyprus island in the Mediterranean Sea, off the S coast of Turkey and W coast of Syria.
government Under the 1960 constitution, power is shared between Greek and Turkish Cypriots, but in 1963 the Turks ceased participating and in 1964 set up a separate community in northern Cyprus, refusing to acknowledge the Greek government in the south.

The Greek Cypriot government is internationally recognized as the legal government of all Cyprus, except by the Turkish community. There are, therefore, two republics, each with a president, council of ministers, legislature, and judicial system. The "Turkish Republic of Northern Cyprus" has its own representatives overseas.

Greek Cyprus has a president who appoints and heads a council of ministers, elected for five years by universal adult suffrage, and a single-chamber legislature, the 80-member house of representatives, also elected for five years. Under the separate constitution adopted by Turkish Cyprus 1985, there is a president, council of ministers, and legislature similar to that in the south. Turkey is the only country to have recognized this government.
history For early history, see ▷Greece, ancient. The strategic position of Cyprus has long made it a coveted territory, and from the 15th century BC it was colonized by a succession of peoples from the mainland. In the 8th century it was within the Assyrian empire, then the Babylonian, Egyptian, and Persian. As part of Ptolemaic Egypt, it was seized by Rome 58 BC. From AD 395 it was ruled by Byzantium, until taken 1191 by England during the Third ▷Crusade. In 1489 it was annexed by Venice, and became part of the Ottoman empire 1571. It came under British administration 1878 and was annexed by Britain 1914, becoming a crown colony 1925.
enosis In 1955 a guerrilla war against British rule was begun by Greek Cypriots seeking *enosis*, or unification with Greece. The chief organization in this campaign was the National Organization of Cypriot Combatants (EOKA), and its political and military leaders were the head of the Greek Orthodox Church in Cyprus, Archbishop Makarios, and General Grivas. In 1956 Makarios and other enosis leaders were deported by the British government. After years of negotiation, Makarios was allowed to return to become president of a new, independent Greek-Turkish Cyprus, retaining British military and naval bases.
Greek-Turkish conflict In 1963 the Turks withdrew from power-sharing, and fighting began. The following year a United Nations peacekeeping force was set up to keep the two sides apart. After a prolonged period of mutual hostility, relations improved and talks were resumed, with the Turks arguing for a federal state and the Greeks wanting a unitary one. In 1971 General Grivas returned to the island and began a guerrilla campaign against the Makarios government, which he believed had failed the Greek community. Three years later he died, and his supporters were purged by Makarios, who was himself deposed 1974 by Greek officers of the National Guard and an Enosis extremist, Nicos Sampson, who became president. Makarios fled to Britain.

At the request of the Turkish Cypriot leader Rauf Denktaş, Turkey sent troops to the island 1974, taking control of the north and

and Stockhausen, are more solid and pure in tone. Turkish or "buzz" cymbals have loose rivets to extend the sound.

Cymbeline play by Shakespeare, first acted about 1610 and printed 1623. It combines various sources to tell the story of Imogen (derived from Ginevra in Boccaccio's *Decameron*), the daughter of the legendary British king Cymbeline, who proves her virtue and constancy after several ordeals.

Cymbeline or **Cunobelin** 1st century AD. King of the Catuvellauni AD 5–40, who fought unsuccessfully against the Roman invasion of Britain. His capital was at Colchester.

Cynewulf early 8th century. Anglo-Saxon poet. He is thought to have been a Northumbrian monk and is the undoubted author of "Juliana" and part of the "Christ" in the Exeter Book (a collection of poems now in Exeter Cathedral), and of the "Fates of the Apostles" and "Elene" in the Vercelli Book (a collection of Old English manuscripts housed in Vercelli, Italy), in all of which he inserted his name by using runic acrostics.

Cynic school of Greek philosophy (Cynicism), founded in Athens about 400 BC by Antisthenes, a disciple of Socrates, who advocated a stern and simple morality and a complete disregard of pleasure and comfort.

His followers, led by ▷Diogenes, not only showed a contemptuous disregard for pleasure, but despised all human affection as a source of weakness. Their "snarling contempt" for ordinary people earned them the name of Cynic (Greek "doglike").

cypress any coniferous tree or shrub of the genera *Cupressus* and *Chamaecyparis*, family Cupressaceae. There are about 20 species, originating from temperate regions of the northern hemisphere. They have minute, scalelike leaves and small cones made up of woody, wedge-shaped scales and containing an aromatic resin.

All species of cypress native to the US occur in the west. Baldcypresses (genus *Taxodium*) belong to the redwood family and are found only in the S US and Mexico.

Cyprian, St c. 210–258. Christian martyr, one

dividing Cyprus along what became known as the Attila Line, cutting off about a third of the total territory. Sampson resigned, the military regime that had appointed him collapsed, and Makarios returned. The Turkish Cypriots established an independent government for what they called the "Turkish Federated State of Cyprus" (TFSC), with Denktaş as president.

In 1977 Makarios died and was succeeded by Spyros Kyprianou, who had been president of the house of representatives. In 1980 UN-sponsored peace talks were resumed. The Turkish Cypriots offered to hand back about 4% of the 35% of the territory they controlled and to resettle 40,000 of the 200,000 refugees who had fled to the north, but stalemate was reached on a constitutional settlement.

The Turks wanted equal status for the two communities, equal representation in government, and firm links with Turkey. The Greeks, on the other hand, favored an alternating presidency, strong central government, and representation in the legislature on a proportional basis.

seeking a solution Between 1982 and 1985 several attempts by the Greek government in Athens and the UN to find a solution failed, and the Turkish Republic of Northern Cyprus (TRNC), with Denktaş as president, was formally declared, but recognized only by Turkey.

In 1985 a meeting between Denktaş and Kyprianou failed to reach agreement, and the UN secretary-general drew up proposals for a two-zone federal Cyprus, with a Greek president and a Turkish vice-president, but this was not found acceptable. Meanwhile, both Kyprianou and Denktaş had been reelected.

In 1988 Georgios Vassiliou was elected president of the Greek part of Cyprus, and in Sept talks began between him and Denktaş. However, these were abandoned Sept 1989, reportedly because of Denktaş's intransigence. Peace talks were resumed Aug 1992 under UN auspices in New York, but the dispute between the communities remained unresolved. Because of its strategic importance in the Mediterranean, Cyprus is of international concern. *See illustration box.*

Cyrano de Bergerac Savinien 1619–1655. French writer. He joined a corps of guards at 19 and performed heroic feats which brought him fame. He is the hero of a classic play by Edmond ⟡Rostand, in which his excessively long nose is used as a counterpoint to his chivalrous character.

Cyrenaic member of a school of Greek hedonistic philosophy (see ⟡hedonism) founded about 400 BC by Aristippus of Cyrene. He regarded pleasure as the only absolutely worthwhile thing in life but taught that self-control and intelligence were necessary to choose the best pleasures.

Cyrenaica area of E Libya, colonized by the Greeks in the 7th century BC; later held by the Egyptians, Romans, Arabs, Turks, and Italians. Present cities in the region are Benghazi, Derna, and Tobruk.

The Greek colonies passed under the rule of the Ptolemies 322 BC, and in 174 BC Cyrenaica became a Roman province. It was conquered by the Arabs in the AD 7th century, by Turkey in the 16th, and by Italy 1912, when it was developed as a colony. It was captured by the British 1942, and remained under British control until it became a province of the new kingdom of Libya from 1951. In 1963 it was split into a number of smaller divisions under the constitutional reorganization. There are archeological ruins at Cyrene and Apollonia.

Cyril and Methodius, Sts two brothers, both Christian saints: Cyril 826–869 and Methodius 815–885. Born in Thessalonica, they were sent as missionaries to what is today Moravia. They invented a Slavonic alphabet, and translated the Bible and the liturgy from Greek to Slavonic. The language (known as *Old Church Slavonic*) remained in use in churches and for literature among Bulgars, Serbs, and Russians up to the 17th century. The *cyrillic alphabet* is named after Cyril and may also have been invented by him. Feast day Feb 14.

Cyril of Alexandria, St 376–444. Bishop of Alexandria from 412, persecutor of Jews and other non-Christians, and suspected of ordering the murder of Hypatia (*c.* 370–*c.* 415), a philosopher whose influence was increasing at the expense of his. He was violently opposed to ⟡Nestorianism.

Cyrus the Great died 529 BC. Founder of the Persian Empire. As king of Persia, he was originally subject to the ⟡Medes, whose empire he overthrew 550 BC. He captured ⟡Croesus 546 BC, and conquered all Asia Minor, adding Babylonia (including Syria and Palestine) to his empire 539 BC, allowing exiled Jews to return to Jersualem. He died fighting in Afghanistan.

cystic fibrosis hereditary disease involving defects of various tissues, including the sweat glands, the mucous glands of the bronchi (air passages), and the pancreas. The sufferer experiences repeated chest infections and digestive disorders and generally fails to thrive. In 1989 the gene for cystic fibrosis was identified by teams of researchers in Michigan and Toronto. This discovery promises more reliable diagnosis of the disease in babies before birth.

One person in 22 is a carrier of the disease. If two carriers have children, each child has a one-in-four chance of having the disease, so that it occurs in about one in 2,000 pregnancies. Cystic fibrosis was once universally fatal at an early age; now, although there is no definitive cure, treatments have raised both the quality and expectancy of life. Management is by diets and drugs, physiotherapy to keep the chest clear, and use of antibiotics to combat infection and minimize damage to the lungs. Some sufferers have benefited from heart-lung transplants.

cystitis inflammation of the bladder, usually caused by bacterial infection, and resulting in frequent and painful urination. Treatment is by antibiotics and copious fluids with vitamin C.

cytochrome one of a number of iron-containing, red proteins responsible for part of the process of ⟡respiration by which food molecules are broken down in ⟡aerobic organisms. Cytochromes are also used for the part of the process of ⟡photosynthesis by which molecules of water are oxidized to oxygen gas. Cytochromes are part of the electron transport chain, by which energized electrons are passed along to release energy and to make ⟡ATP.

cytokine in biology, chemical messenger that carries information from one cell to another, for example the ⟡lymphokines.

cytokinin ⟡plant hormone that stimulates cell division. Cytokinins affect several different aspects of plant growth and development, but only if ⟡auxin is also present. They may delay the process of senescence, or aging, break the dormancy of certain seeds and buds, and induce flowering.

cytology the study of ⟡cells and their functions. Major advances have been made possible in this field by the development of ⟡electron microscopes.

cytoplasm the part of the cell outside the ⟡nucleus. Strictly speaking, this includes all the ⟡organelles (mitochondria, chloroplasts, and so on), but often cytoplasm refers to the jellylike matter in which the organelles are embedded (correctly termed the cytosol).

In many cells, the cytoplasm is made up of two parts: the *ectoplasm* (or plasmagel), a dense gelatinous outer layer concerned with cell movement, and the *endoplasm* (or plasmasol), a more fluid inner part where most of the organelles are found.

cytoskeleton in a living cell, a matrix of protein filaments and tubules that occurs within the cytosol (the liquid part of the cytoplasm). It gives the cell a definite shape, transports vital substances around the cell, and may also be involved in cell movement.

cytotoxic drug any drug used to kill the cells of a malignant tumor, or as an ⟡immunosuppressive following organ transplant; it may also damage healthy cells. Side effects include nausea, vomiting, hair loss, and bone-marrow damage.

czar alternate form of ⟡*tsar*, an emperor of Russia.

Czechoslovakia landlocked country in E central Europe, bounded NE by Poland, E by Ukraine, S by Hungary and Austria, and W and NW by Germany. On Jan 1, 1993, the country split into two independent nations, the Czech Republic and the Slovak Republic.

government From 1968 Czechoslovakia was a federation of two national republics, Czech and Slovak. The supreme legislative body of the Czech and Slovak Federative Republic (CSFR) was the federal assembly, Federalni Shromazdeni, composed of two chambers having equal rights, the directly elected, 150-deputy chamber of the people and the 150-deputy chamber of nations. The first was elected for five-year terms and had a 2:1 Czech majority. The second was divided equally between members chosen by each of the Czech and Slovak national councils (local parliaments).

The federal assembly elected for a two-year term the president of the republic, who appointed a prime minister and federal government accountable to the federal assembly. The federal government had authority in military and foreign affairs and broad fiscal strategy, but a Dec 1990 amendment devolved considerable economic powers to the two republics, and in other areas, power was shared with the national councils elected by the republics.

history Czechoslovakia came into existence as an independent republic 1918 after the breakup of the ⟡Austro-Hungarian empire at the end of World War I. It consisted originally of the Bohemian crownlands (⟡Bohemia, ⟡Moravia, and part of ⟡Silesia) and ⟡Slovakia, the area of Hungary inhabited by Slavonic peoples; to this was added as a trust, part of Ruthenia when the Allies and associated powers recognized the new republic under the treaty of St Germain-en-Laye. Besides the Czech and Slovak peoples, the country included substantial minorities of German origin, long settled in the north, and of Hungarian (or Magyar) origin in the south. Despite the problems of welding into a nation such a mixed group of people, Czechoslovakia made considerable political and economic progress until the troubled 1930s. It was the only East European state to retain a parliamentary democracy throughout the interwar period, with five coalition governments (dominated by the Agrarian and National Socialist parties), with Thomas ⟡Masaryk serving as president.

Munich Agreement The rise to power of the Nazi leader Hitler in Germany brought a revival of opposition among the German-speaking population, and nationalism among the Magyar speakers. In addition, the Slovak clerical party demanded autonomy for Slovakia. In 1938 the ⟡Munich Agreement was made between Britain, France, Germany, and Italy, without consulting Czechoslovakia, resulting in the Sudetenland being taken from Czechoslovakia and given to Germany. Six months later Hitler occupied all Czechoslovakia. A government in exile was established in London under Eduard ⟡Beneš until the liberation 1945 by Soviet and US troops. In the same year some 2 million Sudeten Germans were expelled, and Czech Ruthenia was transferred to the Ukraine, USSR.

Elections 1946 gave the left a slight majority, and in Feb 1948 the communists seized power, winning an electoral victory in May. Beneš, who had been president since 1945, resigned. The country was divided into 19 and, in 1960, into 10 regions plus Prague and Bratislava. There was a Stalinist regime during the 1950s,

Czechoslovakia
Czech and Slovak Federative Republic
(Česká a Slovenská federativní)

area 49,371 sq mi/127,903 sq km
capital Prague
cities Bratislava, Brno, Ostrava
physical Carpathian Mountains, rivers Morava, Labe (Elbe), Vltava (Moldau); hills and plateau; Danube plain in S
environment Czechoslovakia is the most polluted country in E Europe. Pollution is worst in N Bohemia, which produces 70% of the country's coal and 45% of its coal-generated electricity. Up to 20 times the permissible level of sulfur dioxide is released over Prague, where 75% of the drinking water fails to meet the country's health standards
features divided by valley of the Morava into the densely populated Czech area with good communications in W, and the sparsely populated, mainly agricultural Slovak area in E; summer and winter resort areas in Western Carpathian, Bohemian, and Sudetes mountain ranges
head of state to be decided
head of government Václav Klaus from 1992
political system emergent democratic republic
political parties Civic Democratic Party (CDP), right of center, Czech-based (formerly part of Civic Forum); Civic Movement (CM), left of center, Czech-based (formerly part of Civic Forum); Civic Democratic Union (CDU), Slovakia-based; Movement for Democratic Slovakia (MFDS), Slovak-nationalist; Communist Party of Czechoslovakia (CCP), Marxist-Leninist; Christian Democratic Movement (CDM), centrist

exports machinery, vehicles, timber, ceramics, glass, textiles, lignite, magnesite, mercury
currency koruna
population (1990 est) 15,695,000 (63% Czech, 31% Slovak, with Hungarian, Polish, German, Russian, and other minorities); growth rate 0.4% p.a.
life expectancy men 68, women 75
languages Czech and Slovak (official)
religions Roman Catholic 75%, Protestant 15%
literacy 99% (1981)
GDP $148.5 bn (1987); $3,127 per head
chronology
1918 Independence achieved from Austro-Hungarian Empire; Czechs and Slovaks formed Czechoslovakia as independent nation.
1938 Infamous Munich Agreement gave Sudetenland to Nazi Germany as "appeasement," but six months later Hitler occupied the entire nation. Beneš headed government in exile until 1945.
1945 Liberation of Czechoslovakia from Nazis by USSR and USA.
1948 Communists assumed power in coup and new constitution framed.
1968 "Prague Spring" liberalization ended by Soviet invasion and occupation. Czechoslovakia became a federal state.
1969 Husák elected Communist Party leader.
1977 Emergence and suppression of Charter 77 human-rights movement.
1985–86 Criticism of Husák rule by new Soviet leadership.
1987 Husák resigned as communist leader, remaining president; replaced by Miloš Jakeš.
1988 Personnel overhaul of party and state bodies, including replacement of Prime Minister Štrougal by the technocrat Adamec.
1989 Communist regime overthrown in Nov–Dec bloodless "gentle revolution." Communist monopoly of power ended, with new "grand coalition" government formed. Václav Havel appointed state president.
1990 22,000 prisoners released. Havel announced agreement with USSR for complete withdrawal of Soviet troops. Devolution of more powers to federal republics.
1991 Bill of rights passed. Steps taken toward privatization. Splits appeared in reform coalitions, with the emergence of new parties. Last Soviet troops withdrawn. Increasing Czech and Slovak separatism.
1992 Václav Klaus, leader of the CDP, became prime minister. Havel resigned. Creation of separate states from Jan 1993 agreed: Klaus and Vladimir Meciar, leader of the MFDS, to become the respective presidents.

under presidents Klement Gottwald (1948–53), Antonin Zapotocky (1953–57), and Antonin Novotný (1957–68).

Prague Spring Pressure from students and intellectuals brought about policy changes from 1965. Following Novotný's replacement as the Communist Party (CCP) leader by Alexander ⟡Dubček and as president by war hero General Ludvik Svoboda (1895–1979), and the appointment of Oldřich Černik as prime minister, a liberalization program began 1968. This "Socialist Democratic Revolution," as it was known, promised the return of freedom of assembly, speech, and movement, and the imposition of restrictions on the secret police, all with the goal of creating "socialism with a human face."

Despite assurances that Czechoslovakia would remain within the ⟡Warsaw Pact, the USSR viewed these events with suspicion, and in Aug 1968 sent 600,000 troops from Warsaw Pact countries to restore the orthodox line. Over 70 deaths and some 266 injuries were inflicted by this invasion. After the invasion a purge of liberals began in the CCP, with Dr Gustáv ⟡Husák (a Slovak Brezhnevite) replacing Dubček as CCP leader 1969 and Lubomir Štrougal (a Czech) becoming prime minister 1970. Svoboda remained as president until 1975 and negotiated the Soviet withdrawal. In 1973 an amnesty was extended to some of the 40,000 who had fled after the 1968 invasion, signaling a slackening of repression. But a new crackdown commenced 1977, triggered by a human-rights manifesto ("Charter 77") signed by over 700 intellectuals and former party officials in response to the 1975 Helsinki ⟡Conference on Security and Cooperation in Europe (CSCE).

protest movement Czechoslovakia under Husák emerged as a loyal ally of the USSR during the 1970s and early 1980s. However, after Mikhail Gorbachev's accession to the Soviet leadership 1985, pressure for economic and administrative reform mounted. In 1987 Husák, while remaining president, was replaced as CCP leader by Miloš Jakeš (1923–), a Czech-born economist. Working with prime minister Ladislav Adamec, a reformist, he began to introduce a reform program (*prestavba* "restructuring") on the USSR's perestroika model. His approach was cautious, and dissident activity, which became increasingly widespread 1988–89, was suppressed.

Influenced by events elsewhere in Eastern Europe, a series of initially student-led prodemocracy rallies were held in Prague's Wenceslas Square from Nov 17, 1989. Support for the protest movement rapidly increased after the security forces' brutal suppression of the early rallies; by Nov 20 there were more than 200,000 demonstrators in Prague and a growing number in Bratislava. An umbrella opposition movement, Civic Forum, was swiftly formed under the leadership of playwright and Charter 77 activist Václav ⟡Havel, which attracted the support of prominent members of the small political parties that were members of the ruling CCP-dominated National Front coalition.

With the protest movement continuing to grow, Jakeš resigned as CCP leader Nov 24 and was replaced by Karel Urbanek (1941–), a South Moravian, and the politburo was purged. Less than a week later, following a brief general strike, the national assembly voted to amend the constitution to strip the CCP of its "leading role" in the government, and thus of its monopoly on power. Opposition parties, beginning with Civic Forum and its Slovak counterpart, Public Against Violence (PAV), were legalized. On Dec 7 Adamec resigned as prime minister and was replaced by Marián Čalfa, who formed a "grand coalition" government in which key posts, including the foreign, financial, and labor ministries, were given to former dissidents. Čalfa resigned from the CCP Jan 1990, but remained premier.

reform government On Dec 27, 1989 the rehabilitated Dubček was sworn in as chair of the federal assembly, and on Dec 29 Havel became president of Czechoslovakia. The new reform government immediately extended an amnesty to 22,000 prisoners, secured agreements from the CCP that it would voluntarily give up its existing majorities in the federal and regional assemblies and state agencies, and promised multiparty elections for June 1990. It also announced plans for reducing the size of the armed forces, called on the USSR to pull out its 75,000 troops stationed in the country, and applied for membership in the International Monetary Fund and World Bank. Václav Havel was reelected president, unopposed, for a further two years by the assembly on July 5, 1990.

moves towards privatization Some devolution of power was introduced 1990 to ameliorate friction between the Czech and Slovak republics. A bill of rights was passed Jan 1991, and moves were made toward price liberalization and privatization of small businesses. In Feb 1991 a bill was passed to return property nationalized after Feb 25, 1948 to its original owners, the first such restitution measure in Eastern Europe, and legislation was approved May 1991. The name "Czech and Slovak Federative Republic" was adopted April 1990. In Nov 1990 the Slovak Republic declared Slovak the official language of the republic, a move promoted by the Slovak National Party.

new parties emerge During the opening months of 1991, Civic Forum began to split in two: a center-right faction under the leadership of finance minister Václav Klaus, designated the Civic Democratic Party April 1991; and a social-democratic group, the Civic Forum Liberal Club, renamed the Civic Movement April 1991, led by foreign minister Jiri Dienstbier and deputy prime minister Pavel Rychetsky. The two factions agreed to work together until the next election. In March 1991 PAV also split when Slovak premier Vladimir Meciar formed a splinter grouping pledged to greater autonomy from Prague. In April 1991 he was dismissed as head of the Slovak government by the presidium of the Slovak National Council (parliament) because of policy differences. Protest rallies were held in the Slovak capital of Bratislava by Meciar supporters. Jan Carnogursky, leader of the Christian Democratic Movement, junior partner in the PAV-led ruling coalition, took over as Slovak premier. In Oct 1991, PAV became a liberal-conservative political party, and was renamed the Civic Democratic Union–Public Action Against Violence (PAV), led by Martin Porubjak. The major political parties were becoming divided into separate Czech and Slovak groups.

foreign relations In July 1991, a month after the final withdrawal of Soviet troops, the USSR agreed to pay the equivalent of US$ 160 million to Czechoslovakia in compensation for damage done to the country since the 1968 Soviet invasion. In Aug, the phased privatization of Czech industry commenced, with 50 of its largest businesses put up for sale on international markets. Friendship treaties were signed with France, Germany, and the USSR in Oct 1991.

Czech and Slovak split A general election was held June 1992. Václav Klaus, leader of the CDP, became prime minister, and President Havel resigned. It was agreed that two separate Czech and Slovak states would be created from Jan 1993, Meciar to be the Czech president and Klaus the Slovak, and the separation took place as scheduled. *See illustration box.*

Czerny Carl 1791–1857. Austrian composer and pianist. He wrote an enormous quantity of religious and concert music, but is chiefly remembered for his books of graded studies and technical exercises used in piano teaching.

Częstochowa town in Poland, on the river Vistula, 120 mi/193 km SW of Warsaw; population (1990) 257,900. It produces iron goods, chemicals, paper, and cement. The basilica of Jasna Góra is a center for Catholic pilgrims (it contains the painting known as the Black Madonna).

D fourth letter of the English alphabet; it corresponds to the Semitic *daleth* and the Greek *delta* (Δ, δ). The d sound is a voiced alveolar stop.

D abbreviation for *500* in the Roman numeral system.

DA abbreviation for *district attorney*.

dab small marine flatfish of the flounder family, especially the genus *Limanda*. Dabs live in the N Atlantic and around the coasts of Britain and Scandinavia.

Species include *L. limanda* which grows to about 16 in/40 cm, and the American dab *L. proboscida*, which grows to 12 in/30 cm. Both have both eyes on the right side of their bodies. The left, or blind, side is white, while the rough-scaled right side is light-brown or gray, with dark-brown spots.

Dacca alternate name for ⟡Dhaka, the capital of Bangladesh.

Dachau site of a Nazi ⟡concentration camp during World War II, in Bavaria, Germany.

dachshund (German "badger-dog") small dog of German origin, bred originally for digging out badgers. It has a long body and short legs. Several varieties are bred: standard size (up to 22 lb/10 kg), miniature (11 lb/ 5 kg or less), long-haired, smooth-haired, and wire-haired.

Dacia ancient region forming much of modern Romania. The various Dacian tribes were united around 60 BC, and for many years posed a threat to the Roman Empire; they were finally conquered by the Roman emperor Trajan AD 101–06, and the region became a province of the same name. It was abandoned to the invading Goths about 275.

dacoit historically a member of an armed gang of robbers, formerly active in India and Myanmar.

Dada or *Dadaism* artistic and literary movement founded 1915 in Zürich, Switzerland, by the Romanian poet Tristan Tzara (1896–1963) and others in a spirit of rebellion and disillusionment during World War I. Other Dadaist groups were soon formed by the artists Marcel ⟡Duchamp and ⟡Man Ray in New York and Francis Picabia in Barcelona. Dada had a considerable impact on early 20th-century art, questioning established artistic rules and values.

The Dadaists produced deliberately antiaesthetic images, often using photomontages with worded messages to express their political views, and directly scorned established art, as in Duchamp's *Mona Lisa* 1919, where a moustache and beard were added to Leonardo's classic portrait.

With the German writers Hugo Ball and Richard Huelsenbeck, Tzara founded the Cabaret Voltaire in Zürich 1916, where works by Hans Arp, the pioneer Surrealist Max Ernst, and others were exhibited. In New York in the same period the artist Man Ray met Duchamp and Picabia and began to apply Dadaist ideas to photography. In the 1920s Dada evolved into Surrealism.

Dadra and Nagar Haveli since 1961, a Union Territory of W India; capital Silvassa; area 189 sq mi/490 sq km; population (1991) 138,500. It was formerly part of Portuguese Daman. It produces rice, wheat, millet, and timber.

Daedalus in Greek mythology, an Athenian artisan supposed to have constructed for King Minos of Crete the labyrinth in which the ⟡Minotaur was imprisoned. When Minos became displeased with him, Daedalus fled from Crete with his son ⟡Icarus using wings made by them from feathers fastened with wax.

daffodil any of several Old World species of the genus *Narcissus*, family Amaryllidaceae, distinguished by their trumpet-shaped flowers. The common daffodil of N Europe *N. pseudonarcissus* has large yellow flowers and grows from a large bulb. There are numerous cultivated forms.

Dafydd ap Gwilym c. 1340–c. 1400. Welsh poet. His work is notable for its complex but graceful style, its concern with nature and love rather than with heroic martial deeds, and for its references to Classical and Italian poetry.

Dagestan autonomous republic of S Russia, situated E of the ⟡Caucasus, bordering the Caspian Sea; capital Makhachkala; area 19,421 sq mi/50,300 sq km; population (1982) 1,700,000. It is mountainous, with deep valleys, and its numerous ethnic groups speak a variety of distinct languages. Annexed 1723 from Iran, which strongly resisted Russian conquest, it became an autonomous republic 1921.

Daguerre Louis Jacques Mande 1789–1851. French pioneer of photography. Together with Joseph Niépce, he is credited with the invention of photography (though others were reaching the same point simultaneously). In 1838 he invented the daguerreotype, a single image process superseded ten years later by ⟡Talbot's negative/positive process.

daguerreotype in photography, a single-image process using mercury vapor and an iodine-sensitized silvered plate; it was invented by Louis Daguerre 1838.

Dahl Johann Christian 1788–1857. Norwegian landscape painter in the Romantic style. He trained in Copenhagen but was active chiefly in Dresden from 1818. He was the first great painter of the Norwegian landscape, in a style that recalls the Dutch artist Jacob van Ruisdael.

Dahl Roald 1916–1990. British writer, celebrated for short stories with a twist, for example, *Tales of the Unexpected* 1979, and for children's books, including *Charlie and the Chocolate Factory* 1964. He also wrote the screenplay for the James Bond film *You Only Live Twice* 1967.

His autobiography *Going Solo* 1986 recounted his experiences as a fighter pilot in the RAF.

dahlia any perennial plant of the genus *Dahlia*, family Compositae, comprising 20 species and many cultivated forms. Dahlias are stocky plants with showy flowers that come in a wide range of colors. They are native to Mexico and Central America.

Dahomey former name (until 1975) of the People's Republic of ⟡Benin.

Daimler Gottlieb 1834–1900. German engineer who pioneered the modern car. In 1886 he produced his first motor vehicle and a motorbicycle. He later joined forces with Karl ⟡Benz and was one of the pioneers of the high-speed four-stroke gasoline engine.

Dairen former name for the Chinese port of Dalian, part of ⟡Lüda.

dairying the business of producing ⟡milk and milk products.

In the US and the UK, over 70% of the milk produced is consumed in its liquid form, whereas areas such as the French Alps and New Zealand rely on easily transportable milk products such as butter, cheese, and condensed and dried milk.

It is now usual for dairy farms to concentrate on the production of milk and for factories to take over the handling, processing, and distribution of milk as well as the manufacture of dairy products.

daisy any of numerous species of perennial plants in the family Compositae, especially the field daisy of Europe *Chrysanthemum leucanthemum* and the English common daisy *Bellis perennis*, with a single white or pink flower rising from a rosette of leaves.

daisy bush any of several Australian and New Zealand shrubs of the genus *Olearia*, family Compositae, with flowers like daisies and felted or hollylike leaves.

Dakar capital and chief port (with artificial harbor) of Senegal; population (1984) 1,000,000. It is an industrial center, and there is a university, established 1957.

Dakhla port and capital of Western Sahara; population (1982) 17,800. First established as a Spanish trading port 1476, it was known as *Villa Cisneros*.

Daladier Edouard 1884–1970. French Radical politician. As prime minister April 1938–March 1940, he signed the ⟡Munich Agreement 1938 (by which the Sudeten districts of Czechoslovakia were ceded to Germany) and declared war on Germany 1939. He resigned 1940 because of his unpopularity for failing to assist Finland against Russia. He was arrested on the fall of France 1940 and was a prisoner in Germany 1943–45. Following the end of World War II he was reelected to the Chamber of Deputies 1946–58.

Dalai Lama 14th incarnation 1935– . Spiritual and temporal head of the Tibetan state until 1959, when he went into exile in protest against Chinese annexation and oppression. His people have continued to demand his return.

Tibetan Buddhists believe that each Dalai Lama is a reincarnation of his predecessor and also of Avalokiteśvara.

Enthroned 1940, the Dalai Lama temporarily fled 1950–51 when the Chinese overran Tibet, and in March 1959—when a local uprising against Chinese rule was suppressed—made a dramatic escape from Lhasa to India. He then settled at Dharmsala in the Punjab. The Chinese offered to lift the ban on his living in Tibet, providing he would refrain from calling for Tibet's independence. His deputy, the Panchen Lama, has cooperated with the Chinese but failed to protect the monks. The Dalai Lama was awarded the Nobel Prize for Peace 1989 in recognition of his commitment to the nonviolent liberation of his homeland.

Dalcroze Emile Jaques see ⟡Jaques-Dalcroze, Emile.

Dalen Nils 1869–1937. Swedish industrial engineer who invented the light-controlled valve. This allowed lighthouses to operate automatically and won him the 1912 Nobel Prize for Physics.

Daley Richard Joseph 1902–1976. US politician and controversial mayor of Chicago. He built a formidable political machine and became a force in national Democratic politics, ensuring a Democratic victory 1960 and hosting the turbulent national Democratic convention 1968.

Born in Chicago, Daley became deeply involved in local Democratic politics and attended law school at DePaul University, gaining admission to the bar 1933. He served in the Illinois legislature 1936–46. He became Cook County clerk 1953 and was elected mayor of Chicago 1955, a post that he held until his death.

Dali Salvador 1904–1989. Spanish painter. In 1928 he collaborated with Luis Buñuel on the film *Un chien andalou*. In 1929 he joined the Surrealists and became notorious for his flamboyant eccentricity. Influenced by the psychoanalytic theories of Freud, he developed a repertoire of dramatic images, such as the distorted human body, limp watches, and burning giraffes in such pictures as *The Persistence of Memory* 1931 (Museum of Modern Art, New York). They are painted with a meticulous, polished clarity. He also used religious themes and painted many portraits of his wife Gala.

Dali, born near Barcelona, initially came under the influence of the Italian Futurists. He is credited as co-creator of *Un chien andalou*, but his role is thought to have been subordinate; he abandoned film after collaborating on the script for Buñuel's *L'Age d'or* 1930. He designed ballet costumes, scenery, jewelry, and furniture.

The books *Secret Life of Salvador Dali* 1942 and *Diary of a Genius* 1966 are autobiographical. He was buried beneath a crystal dome in the museum of his work at Figueras on the Costa Brava, Spain.

Dalian one of the two cities comprising the Chinese port of ⟡Lüda.

Dallas commercial city in Texas; population (1990) 1,006,900, metropolitan area (with Fort Worth) 3,885,400. Industries include banking, insurance, oil, aviation, aerospace, and electronics. Dallas—Fort Worth Regional Airport (opened 1973) is one of the world's largest. John F ⟡Kennedy was assassinated here 1963.

Dallas is a cultural center, with a symphony orchestra, opera, ballet, and theater; there is an annual Texas State Fair. Southern Methodist University is here. Founded as a trading post 1844, it developed as the focus of a cotton area and then as a mineral and oil-producing center, with banking and insurance operations. After World War II, growth increased rapidly.

Dalmatia region divided among Croatia, Montenegro in Yugoslavia, and Bosnia-Herzegovina. The capital is Split. It lies along the eastern shore of the Adriatic Sea and includes a number of islands. The interior is mountainous. Important products are wine, olives, and fish. Notable towns in addition to the capital are Zadar, Sibenik, and Dubrovnik.
history Dalmatia became Austrian 1815 and by the treaty of Rapallo 1920 became part of the kingdom of the Serbs, Croats, and Slovenes (Yugoslavia from 1931), except for the town of Zadar (Zara) and the island of Lastovo (Lagosta), which, with neighboring islets, were given to Italy until transferred to Yugoslavia 1947. The part of Dalmatia within Croatia was made a region 1949.

Dalmatian breed of dog, about 2 ft/60 cm tall at the shoulder, white with spots that are black or brown. Dalmatians are born white; the spots appear later. They were formerly used as coach dogs, walking beside horse-drawn carriages to fend off highwaymen.

dalmatic outer liturgical vestment of the deacon in the Roman Catholic Church; a mantle worn at Mass and in solemn processions.

Dalton John 1766–1844. British chemist who proposed the theory of atoms, which he considered to be the smallest parts of matter. He produced the first list of atomic weights in *Absorption of Gases* 1805 and put forward the law of partial pressures of gases (Dalton's law).

He was one of the first scientists to note and record color blindness (he was himself color blind).

Daly Augustin 1838–1899. US theater manager. He began as a drama critic and playwright before building his own theater in New York 1879 and another, Daly's, in Leicester Square, London 1893.

dam structure built to hold back water in order to prevent flooding, provide water for irrigation and storage, and to provide hydroelectric power. The biggest dams are of the earth- and rock-fill type, also called *embankment dams*. Early dams in Britain, built before about 1800, had a core made from puddled clay (clay which has been mixed with water to make it impermeable). Such dams are generally built on broad valley sites. Deep, narrow gorges dictate a *concrete dam*, where the strength of reinforced concrete can withstand the water pressures involved. The first major all-concrete dam in Britain was built at Woodhead in 1876. The first dam in which concrete was used to seal the joints in the rocks below was built at Tunstall 1879.

A valuable development in arid regions, as in parts of Brazil, is the *underground dam*, where water is stored on a solid rock base, with a wall to ground level, so avoiding rapid evaporation.

Many concrete dams are triangular in cross section, with their vertical face pointing upstream. Their sheer weight holds them in position, and they are called *gravity dams*. Other concrete dams are more slightly built in the shape of an arch, with the curve facing upstream: the *arch dam* derives its strength from the arch shape, just as an arch bridge does.

Major dams include: Rogun (Tajikistan), the world's highest at 1,099 ft/335 m; New Cornelia Tailings (US), the world's biggest in volume, 7.4 billion cu ft/209 million cu m; Owen Falls (Uganda), the world's largest reservoir capacity, 7.2 trillion cu ft/204.8 billion

dam *Types of dam.*

cu m; and Itaipu (Brazil/Paraguay), the world's most powerful, producing 12,700 megawatts of electricity.

Dam (Henrik) Carl (Peter) 1895–1976. Danish biochemist who discovered vitamin K. For his success in this field he shared the 1943 Nobel Prize for Medicine with US biochemist Edward Doisy (1893–1986).

In 1928 Dam began a series of experiments to see if chickens could live on a cholesterol-free diet. The birds, it turned out, were able to metabolize their own supply. Yet they continued to die from spontaneous haemorrhages. Dam concluded that their diet lacked an unknown essential ingredient to control coagulation, which he eventually found in abundance in green leaves. Dam named the new compound vitamin K.

damages in law, compensation for a ⟡tort (such as personal injuries caused by negligence) or breach of contract. In the case of breach of contract the complainant can claim all the financial loss he or she has suffered. Damages for personal injuries include compensation for loss of earnings, as well as for the injury itself. The court might reduce the damages if the claimant was partly to blame. In the majority of cases, the parties involved reach an out-of-court settlement (a compromise without going to court).

Daman and Diu Union Territory of W India; area 43 sq mi/112 sq km; capital Daman; population (1981) 79,000. **Daman** has an area of

28 sq mi/72 sq km and a population (1981) of 49,000. The port and capital, Daman, is on the W coast, 100 mi/160 km N of Bombay; population (1981) 21,000. The economy is based on tourism and fishing. *Diu* is an island off the Kathiawar peninsular with an area of 15 sq mi/40 sq km and a population of (1981) 30,000. The main town is also called Diu; population 8,000. The economy is based on tourism, coconuts, pearl millet, and salt.

history Daman was seized by Portugal 1531 and ceded to Portugal by the Shah of Gujarat 1539; Diu was captured by the Portuguese 1534. Both areas were annexed by India 1961 and were part of the Union Territory of ⇩Goa, Daman, and Diu until Goa became a separate state 1987.

Damascus (Arabic *Dimashq*) capital of Syria, on the river Barada, SE of Beirut; population (1981) 1,251,000. It produces silk, wood products, and brass and copper ware. Said to be the oldest continuously inhabited city in the world, Damascus was an ancient city even in Old Testament times; most notable of the old buildings is the Great Mosque, completed as a Christian church in the 5th century.

The Assyrians destroyed Damascus about 733 BC. In 332 BC it fell to one of the generals of Alexander the Great; in 63 BC it came under Roman rule. In AD 635 it was taken by the Arabs, and has since been captured many times, by Egyptians, Mongolians, and Turks. In 1918, during World War I, it was taken from the Turks by the British with Arab aid and in 1920 became the capital of French-mandated Syria.

The "street which is called straight" is associated with St Paul, who was converted while on the road to Damascus. The tomb of ⇩Saladin is here. The fortress dates from 1219.

damask textile of woven linen, cotton, wool, or silk, with a reversible figured pattern. It was first made in the city of Damascus, Syria.

daminozide (trade name *Alar*) chemical used by fruit growers to make apples redder and crisper. In 1989 a report published in the US found the consumption of daminozide to be linked with cancer, and the US Environment Protection Agency (EPA) called for an end to its use.

Damocles lived 4th century BC. In Classical legend, a courtier of the elder Dionysius, ruler of Syracuse, Sicily. Having extolled the happiness of his sovereign, Damocles was invited by him to a feast, during which he saw above his head a sword suspended by a single hair. He recognized this as a symbol of the insecurity of the great.

Damon and Pythias in Greek legend, devoted friends. When Pythias was condemned to death by a tyrant, Damon offered his own life as security to allow Pythias the freedom to go and arrange his affairs. When Pythias returned, they were both pardoned.

Dampier William 1652–1715. English explorer and hydrographic surveyor who circumnavigated the world three times.

damselfly long, slender, colorful dragonfly of the suborder Zygoptera, with two pairs of similar wings that are generally held vertically over the body when at rest, unlike those of other dragonflies.

damson cultivated variety of plum tree *Prunus domestica* var. *institia*, distinguished by its small, oval, edible fruits, which are dark purple or blue to black in color.

Dana Charles Anderson 1819–1897. US journalist who covered the European revolutions of 1848 and earned a reputation as one of America's most able foreign correspondents. During the US Civil War he served as assistant secretary of war 1863–65 and in 1868 purchased the *New York Sun*, with which he pioneered the daily tabloid format.

Born in Hinsdale, New Hampshire, and educated at Harvard, Dana left college before graduating to become manager of Brook Farm, an experimental community in West Roxbury, Massachusetts, 1841–47. After its breakup he embarked on a journalistic career and became city editor of the *New York Tribune* 1847.

Dana Richard Henry 1815–1882. US author and lawyer who went to sea and worked for his passage around Cape Horn to California and back, then wrote an account of the journey *Two Years before the Mast* 1840. He also published *The Seaman's Friend* 1841, a guide to maritime law.

Danaë in Greek mythology, daughter of Acrisius, king of Argos. He shut her up in a bronze tower because of a prophecy that her son would kill his grandfather. Zeus became enamored of her and descended in a shower of gold; she gave birth to ⇩Perseus.

Da Nang port city (formerly Tourane) of southern Vietnam, 50 mi/80 km SE of Hué; population (1989) 370,600. Following the reunion of North and South Vietnam, the major part of the population was dispersed 1976 to rural areas.

Danbury city in SW Connecticut, NW of Bridgeport. Long a center for the manufacturing of hats, Danbury's newer industries include electronics, publishing, chemicals, and furniture; population (1980) 60,470.

Danbury Hatters Case a US Supreme Court case (*Loewe* v *Lawler*) 1908 dealing with the right of the federal government to prohibit certain labor union activities. Dietrich Loewe, owner of the Danbury Hat Co in Connecticut filed suit for damages resulting from a boycott of Danbury Hat products. The boycott was initiated by the United Hatters of North America in support of a strike by the Danbury hatters. The Court ruled unanimously that this sort of secondary boycott was a conspiracy for the restraint of trade, a violation of the Sherman Antitrust act.

dance rhythmic movement of the body, usually performed in time to music. Its primary purpose may be religious, magical, martial, social, or artistic—the last two being characteristic of nontraditional societies. The pre-Christian era had a strong tradition of ritual dance, and ancient Greek dance still exerts an influence on dance movement today. Although Western folk and social dances have a long history, the Eastern dance tradition long predates the Western. The European Classical tradition dates from the 15th century in Italy, the first printed dance text from 16th-century France, and the first dance school in Paris from the 17th century. The 18th century saw the development of European Classical ballet as we know it today, and the 19th century saw the rise of Romantic ballet. In the 20th century Modern dance firmly established itself as a separate dance idiom, not based on Classical ballet, and many divergent styles and ideas have grown from a willingness to explore a variety of techniques and amalgamate different traditions.

history European dance is relatively young in comparison to that of the rest of the world. The first Indian book on dancing, the *Natya Sastra*, existed a thousand years before its European counterpart. The *bugaku* dances of Japan, with orchestra accompaniment, date from the 7th century and are still performed at court. When the Peking (Beijing) Opera dancers first astonished Western audiences during the 1950s, they were representatives of a tradition stretching back to 740, the year in which Emperor Ming Huang established the Pear Garden Academy. The first comparable European institution, *L'Académie Royale de Danse*, was founded by Louis XIV 1661.

In the European tradition social dances have always tended to rise upward through the social scale; for example, the medieval court dances derived from peasant country dances. One form of dance tends to typify a whole period, thus the galliard represents the 16th century, the minuet the 18th, the waltz the 19th, and the quickstep represents ballroom dancing in the first half of the 20th century.

The nine dances of the modern world championships in ⇩ballroom dancing are the standard four (⇩waltz, ⇩foxtrot, ⇩tango, and quickstep), the Latin-American styles (samba, rumba, cha-cha-cha, and paso doble), and the Viennese waltz. A British development since the 1930s, which has spread to some extent abroad, is "formation" dancing in which each team (usually eight couples) performs a series of ballroom steps in strict coordination.

Popular dance crazes have included the Charleston in the 1920s, jitterbug in the 1930s and 1940s, ⇩jive in the 1950s, the twist in the 1960s, disco and jazz dancing in the 1970s, and break dancing in the 1980s. In general, since the 1960s popular dance in the West has moved away from any prescribed sequence of movements and physical contact between participants, the dancers performing as individuals with no distinction between the male and the female role. Dances requiring skilled athletic performance, such as the hustle and the New Yorker, have been developed.

In Classical dance, the second half of the 20th century has seen a great cross-fertilization from dances of other cultures. Troupes visited the West, not only from the USSR and Eastern Europe, but from such places as Indonesia, Japan, South Korea, Nigeria, and Senegal. In the 1970s jazz dance, pioneered in the US by Matt Mattox, became popular; it includes elements of ballet, Modern, tap, Indian Classical, Latin American, and African-American dance. Freestyle dance is loosely based on ballet with elements of jazz, ethnic, and Modern dance. *See chronology on p. 296.*

dandelion plant *Taraxacum officinale* belonging to the Compositae family. The stalk rises from a rosette of leaves that are deeply indented like a lion's teeth, hence the name (from French *dent de lion*). The flower heads are bright yellow. The fruit is surmounted by the hairs of the calyx which constitute the familiar dandelion "puff."

The milky juice of the dandelion has laxative properties, and the young leaves are sometimes eaten in salads. In the Russian species *Taraxacum koksaghyz*, the juice forms an industrially usable latex, relied upon especially during World War II.

Dandelions, introduced from Europe, now grow throughout North America.

Dandie Dinmont breed of ⇩terrier that originated in the Scottish border country. It is

dance: chronology

1000 BC	King David danced "with all his might" before the ark of the Covenant in Jerusalem—one of the earliest known instances of ritual dance.
142	Consul Scipio Aemilianus Africanus closed the burgeoning dance schools of Rome in a drive against hedonism.
AD 774	Pope Zacharias forbade dancing.
1050	The *Ruodlieb*, a poem written by a monk at Tegernsee, Bavaria, contained the first European reference to dancing in couples.
1313	Rabbi Hacén ben Salomo of Zaragoza, in Aragon, like many other Jews in medieval times, was the local dancing master.
1489	A rudimentary allegorical ballet was performed in honor of the marriage of the Duke of Milan, at Tortona, Italy.
1581	In Paris, the first modern-style unified ballet, the *Ballet Comique de la Reine*, was staged at the court of Catherine de' Medici.
1588	Dance and ballet's first basic text, *L'Orchésographie*, by the priest Jehan Tabouret, was printed in Langres, near Dijon.
1661	Louis XIV founded L'Académie Royale de Danse in Paris.
1670	The first classic ballet, *Le Bourgeois Gentilhomme*, was produced in Chambord, France.
1681	La Fontaine, the first professional female ballet dancer, made her debut in *Le Triomphe de L'amour* at the Paris Opéra.
1734	The dancer Marie Sallé adopted the gauze tunic, precursor to the Romantic tutu, and Marie Camargo shortened her skirts.
1738	The Kirov Ballet was established in St Petersburg, Russia.
1760	The great dancer and choreographer Jean-Georges Noverre published in Lyons *Lettres sur la Danse et sur les Ballets*, one of the most influential of all ballet books.
1776	The Bolshoi Ballet was established in Moscow.
late 1700s	The waltz originated in Austria and Germany from a popular folk dance, the *Ländler*.
1820	Carlo Blasis, teacher and choreographer, published his *Traité élémentaire théoretique et pratique de l'arte de la danse* in Milan which, together with his later works of dance theory, codified techniques for future generations of dancers.
1821	The first known picture of a ballerina *sur les pointes*, the French Fanny Bias by F Waldeck, dates from this year.
1832	The first performance of *La Sylphide* at the Paris Opéra opened the Romantic era of ballet and established the central significance of the ballerina. Marie Taglioni, the producer's daughter, who created the title role, wore the new-style Romantic tutu.
1841	Ballet's Romantic masterpiece *Giselle* with Carlotta Grisi in the leading role, was produced in Paris.
1866	*The Black Crook*, the ballet extravaganza from which US vaudeville and musical comedy developed, began its run of 474 performances in New York.
1870	*Coppélia*, 19th-century ballet's comic masterpiece, was presented in Paris.
1877	*La Bayadère* and *Swan Lake* were premiered in Moscow, but the latter failed through poor production and choreography. The Petipa-Ivanov version, in which Pierina Legnani performed 32 *fouettés*, established the work 1895.
1897	Anna Pavlova made her debut in St Petersburg with the Imperial Russian Ballet.
1905	Isadora Duncan appeared in Russia, making an immense impression with her "antiballet" innovations derived from Greek dance.
1906	Vaslav Nijinsky made his debut in St Petersburg.
1909	The first Paris season given by Diaghilev's troupe of Russian dancers, later to become known as the Ballets Russes, marked the beginning of one of the most exciting periods in Western ballet.
1913	The premiere of Stravinsky's *The Rite of Spring* provoked a scandal in Paris.
1914	The foxtrot developed from the two-step in the US.
1915	The Denishawn school of Modern dance was founded in Los Angeles.
1926	Martha Graham, one of the most innovative figures in Modern dance, gave her first recital in New York. In England, students from the Rambert School of Ballet, opened by Marie Rambert in 1920, gave their first public performance in *A Tragedy of Fashion*, the first ballet to be choreographed by Frederick Ashton.
1928	The first performance of George Balanchine's *Apollon Musagète* in Paris, by the Ballets Russes, marked the birth of Neo-Classicism in ballet.
1931	Ninette de Valois's Vic-Wells Ballet gave its first performance in London. In 1956 the company became the Royal Ballet.
1933	The Hollywood musical achieved artistic independence through Busby Berkeley's kaleidoscopic choreography in *Forty-Second Street* and Dave Gould's airborne finale in *Flying Down to Rio*, in which Fred Astaire and Ginger Rogers appeared together for the first time.
1939	The American Ballet Theater was founded in New York.
1940	The Dance Notation Bureau was established in New York for recording ballets and dances.
1948	The New York City Ballet was founded with George Balanchine as artistic director and principal choreographer.
1950	The Festival Ballet, later to become the London Festival Ballet, was created by Alicia Markova and Anton Dolin, who had first danced together with the Ballets Russes de Monte Carlo 1929.
1952	Gene Kelly starred and danced in the film *Singin' in the Rain*.
1953	The US experimental choreographer Merce Cunningham, who often worked with the composer John Cage, formed his own troupe.
1956	The Bolshoi Ballet opened its first season in the West at Covent Garden in London, with Galina Ulanova dancing in *Romeo and Juliet*.
1957	Jerome Robbins conceived and choreographed the musical *West Side Story*, demonstrating his outstanding ability to work in both popular and Classical forms.
1961	Rudolf Nureyev defected from the USSR while dancing with the Kirov Ballet in Paris. He was to have a profound influence on male dancing in the West.
1962	Glen Tetley's ballet *Pierrot Lunaire*, in which he was one of the three dancers, was premiered in New York. In the same year he joined the Nederlands Dans Theater.
1965	US choreographer Twyla Tharp produced her first works.
1966	The School of Contemporary Dance was founded in London, from which Robin Howard and the choreographer Robert Cohan created the London Contemporary Dance Theatre, later to become an internationally renowned company. The choreographer Norman Morrice rejoined the Ballet Rambert as director and the company began to concentrate on contemporary works.
1968	Arthur Mitchell, the first black principal dancer to join the New York City Ballet, founded the Dance Theater of Harlem.
1974	Mikhail Baryshnikov defected from the USSR while dancing with the Kirov Ballet in Toronto, and made his US debut with the American Ballet Theater.
1977	The release of Robert Stigwood's film *Saturday Night Fever* popularized disco dancing worldwide.
1980	Natalia Makarova, who had defected from the USSR 1979, staged the first full-length revival of Petipa's *La Bayadère* in the West with the American Ballet Theater in New York.
1983	Peter Martins, principal dancer with the New York City Ballet, became choreographer and codirector with Jerome Robbins on the death of Balanchine. Break dancing became widely popular in Western inner cities.
1984	The avant-garde group Michael Clark and Company made its debut in London.
1990	*Maple Leaf Rag*, Martha Graham's final work, was premiered in New York City.

about 10 in/25 cm tall, short-legged and long-bodied, with drooping ears and a long tail. Its hair, about 2 in/5 cm long, can be grayish or yellowish. It is named after the character Dandie Dinmont in Walter Scott's novel *Guy Mannering* 1815.

Dandolo Venetian family that produced four doges (rulers), of whom the most outstanding, *Enrico* (c. 1120–1205), became doge in 1193. He greatly increased the dominions of the Venetian republic and accompanied the crusading army that took Constantinople in 1203.

Dane person of Danish culture from Denmark and N Germany. There are approximately 5 million speakers of Danish (including some in the US), a Germanic language belonging to the Indo-European family. The Danes are known for their seafaring culture, which dates back to the Viking age of expansion between the 8th and 10th centuries.

danegeld in English history, a tax imposed from 991 by Anglo-Saxon kings to pay tribute to the Vikings. After the Norman Conquest the tax continued to be levied until 1162, and the Normans used it to finance military operations.

Danelaw 11th-century name for the area of N and E England settled by the Vikings in the 9th century. It occupied about half of England, from the river Tees to the river Thames. Within its bounds, Danish law, customs, and language prevailed. Its linguistic influence is still apparent.

Daniel 6th century BC. Jewish folk hero and prophet at the court of Nebuchadnezzar; also the name of a book of the Old Testament, probably compiled in the 2nd century BC. It includes stories about Daniel and his companions Shadrach, Meshach, and Abednego, set during the Babylonian captivity of the Jews.

One of the best-known stories is that of Daniel in the den of lions, where he was thrown for refusing to compromise his beliefs, and was preserved by divine intervention. The book also contains a prophetic section dealing with the rise and fall of a number of empires.

Daniell John Frederic 1790–1845. British chemist and meteorologist who invented a primary electrical cell 1836. The *Daniell cell* consists of a central zinc cathode dipping into a porous pot containing zinc sulfate solution. The porous pot is, in turn, immersed in a solution of copper sulfate contained in a copper can, which acts as the cell's anode. The use of a porous barrier prevents polarization (the covering of the anode with small bubbles of hydrogen gas) and allows the cell to generate a continuous current of electricity.

Daniell cell

Danish language member of the North Germanic group of the Indo-European language family, spoken in Denmark and Greenland and related to Icelandic, Faroese, Norwegian, and Swedish. It has had a particularly strong influence on Norwegian. As one of the languages of the Vikings, who invaded and settled in parts of Britain during the 9th to 11th centuries, Old Danish had a strong influence on English.

Danish literature Danish writers of international fame emerged in the 19th century: Hans Christian Andersen, the philosopher Søren Kierkegaard, and the critic Georg Brandes (1842–1927), all of whom played a major part in the Scandinavian literary awakening, encouraging Ibsen and others. The novelists Henrik Pontoppidan (1857–1943), Karl Gjellerup (1857–1919), and Johannes Jensen (1873–1950) were all Nobel Prize-winners.

D'Annunzio Gabriele 1863–1938. Italian poet, novelist, and playwright. Marking a departure from 19th-century Italian literary traditions, his use of language and style of writing earned him much criticism in his own time.

His first volume of poetry, *Primo vere/In Early Spring* 1879, was followed by further collections of verse, short stories, novels, and plays (he wrote the play *La Gioconda* for the actress Eleonora Duse 1898). After serving in World War I, he led an expedition of volunteers in 1919 to capture Fiume, which he held until 1921. He became a national hero, and was created Prince of Montenevoso 1924. Influenced by Nietzsche's writings, he later became an ardent exponent of Fascism.

Dante Alighieri 1265–1321. Italian poet. His masterpiece *La divina commedia/The Divine Comedy* 1307–21 is an epic account in three parts of his journey through Hell, Purgatory, and Paradise, during which he is guided part of the way by the poet Virgil; on a metaphorical level the journey is also one of Dante's own spiritual development. Other works include the philosophical prose treatise *Convivio/The Banquet* 1306–08, the first major work of its kind to be written in Italian rather than Latin; *Monarchia/On World Government* 1310–13, expounding his political theories; *De vulgari eloquentia/Concerning the Vulgar Tongue* 1304–06, an original Latin work on Italian, its dialects, and kindred languages; and *Canzoniere/Lyrics*, containing his scattered lyrics.

Dante was born in Florence, where in 1274 he first met and fell in love with Beatrice Portinari (described in *La vita nuova/New Life* 1283–92). His love for her survived her marriage to another and her death 1290 at the age of 24. He married Gemma Donati 1291.

In 1289 Dante fought in the battle of Campaldino, won by Florence against Arezzo, and from 1295 took an active part in Florentine politics. In 1300 he was one of the six Priors of the Republic, favoring the moderate "White" Guelph party rather than the extreme papal "Black" Ghibelline faction (see ○Guelph and Ghibelline); when the Ghibellines seized power 1302, he was convicted in his absence of misapplication of public money, and sentenced first to a fine and then to death. He escaped from Florence and spent the remainder of his life in exile, in central and N Italy.

Danton Georges Jacques 1759–1794. French revolutionary. Originally a lawyer, during the early years of the Revolution he was one of the most influential people in Paris. He organized the uprising Aug 10, 1792 that overthrew Louis XVI and the monarchy, roused the country

to expel the Prussian invaders, and in April 1793 formed the revolutionary tribunal and the *Committee of Public Safety*, of which he was the leader until July of that year. Thereafter he lost power to the ○Jacobins, and, when he attempted to recover it, was arrested and guillotined.

Danube (German *Donau*) second longest of European rivers, rising on the E slopes of the Black Forest, and flowing 1,776 mi/2,858 km across Europe to enter the Black Sea in Romania by a swampy delta.

The head of river navigation is Ulm, in Baden-Württemberg; Braila, Romania, is the limit for oceangoing ships. Cities on the Danube include Linz, Vienna, Bratislava, Budapest, Belgrade, Ruse, Braila, and Galati. A canal connects the Danube with the river Main, and thus with the Rhine river system. Plans to dam the river for hydroelectric power at Nagymaros in Hungary, with participation by Austria and Czechoslovakia, were abandoned on environmental grounds 1989.

Danville city in S Virginia, just above the North Carolina border, on the Dan River, SE of Roanoke; seat of Averett county. Danville is situated in a tobacco-growing area. Industries include tobacco processing and marketing and the manufacture of tools, textiles, and building materials; population (1990) 53,100. The Confederate government moved from Richmond to Danville during the last days of the Civil War 1865.

Danzig German name for the Polish port of ○Gdańsk.

Daphne in Greek mythology, a nymph who was changed into a laurel tree to escape from Apollo's amorous pursuit.

darcy unit (symbol D) of permeability, used mainly in geology to describe the permeability of rock (for example, to oil, gas, or water).

Dardanelles (ancient name Hellespont, Turkish name *Canakkale Boğazi*) Turkish strait connecting the Sea of Marmara with the Aegean Sea; its shores are formed by the ○Gallipoli peninsula on the NW and the mainland of Turkey-in-Asia on the SE. It is 47 mi/75 km long and 3–4 mi/5–6 km wide.

Dare Virginia 1587–?. First English child born in America. Dare was the daughter of settlers to the Roanoke colony (now in North Carolina) and granddaughter of the colony's governor, John White. Soon after her birth, White returned to England, and because of the sea war with Spain, English communication with Roanoke was cut off for nearly four years. An English ship arriving in 1591 found the colony deserted, with only the enigmatic inscription "Croatan" carved in a tree, as a clue that perhaps the settlers, fearful of hostile Indians, had taken refuge with the friendly Croatan.

Dar es Salaam (Arabic "haven of peace") chief seaport in Tanzania, on the Indian Ocean, and capital of Tanzania until its replacement by ○Dodoma 1974; population (1985) 1,394,000.

Darfur province in the W of the Republic of Sudan; area 75,920 sq mi/196,555 sq km; population (1983) 3,093,699. The capital is El Fasher (population 30,000). The area is a vast rolling plain. It produces gum arabic, and there is also some stock raising. Darfur was an independent sultanate until conquered by Egypt 1874.

Darien former name for the Panama isthmus as a whole, and still the name of an eastern province of Panama; area 6,490 sq mi/16,803 sq km; population (1980) 26,500. The

Gulf of Darien, part of the Caribbean Sea, lies between Panama and Colombia. The **Darien Gap** is the complex of swamp, jungle, and ravines, which long prevented the linking of the North and South American sections of the Pan-American Highway, stretching about 200 mi/300 km between Canitas, Panama, and Chigorodo, Colombia. At the Colombian end is the Great Atrato Swamp, 35 mi/60 km across and over 1,000 ft/300 m deep. The **Darien Expedition** was a Scottish attempt to colonize the isthmus 1698–99, which failed disastrously due to the climate and Spanish hostility. The British Trans-Americas Expedition, led by John Blashford-Snell, made the first motorized crossing 1972.

Darío Rubén. Adopted name of Félix Rubén García Sarmiento 1867–1916. Nicaraguan poet. His first major work *Azul/Azure* 1888, a collection of prose and verse influenced by French Symbolism, created a sensation. He went on to establish *modernismo*, the Spanish-American modernist literary movement, distinguished by an idiosyncratic and deliberately frivolous style that broke away from the prevailing Spanish provincialism and adapted French poetic models. His vitality and eclecticism influenced every poet writing in Spanish after him, both in the New World and in Spain.

Darius I *the Great* c. 558–486 BC. King of Persia 521–486 BC. A member of a younger branch of the Achaemenid dynasty, he won the throne from the usurper Gaumata (died 522 BC) and reorganized the government. In 512 BC he marched against the Scythians, a people north of the Black Sea, and subjugated Thrace and Macedonia.

An expedition in 492 BC to crush a rebellion in Greece failed, and the army sent into Attica 490 BC was defeated at the battle of Marathon. Darius had an account of his reign inscribed on the mountain at Behistun, Persia.

Darjeeling town and health resort in West Bengal, India; situated 7,000 ft/2,150 m above sea level, on the southern slopes of the Himalayas; population (1981) 57,600. It is connected by rail with Calcutta, 370 mi/595 km to the S. It is the center of a tea-producing district.

Darling river in SE Australia, a tributary of the river Murray, which it joins at Wentworth. It is 1,910 mi/3,075 km long, and its waters are conserved in Menindee Lake (60 sq mi/155 sq km) and others nearby. The name comes from Sir Ralph Darling (1775–1858), governor of New South Wales 1825–31. The **Darling Range**, a ridge in W Australia, has a highest point of about 1,669 ft/582 m.

Darnley Henry Stewart or Stuart, Lord Darnley 1545–1567. British aristocrat, second husband of Mary Queen of Scots from 1565, and father of James I of England (James VI of Scotland). On the advice of her secretary, David ⊳Rizzio, Mary refused Darnley the crown matrimonial; in revenge, Darnley led a band of nobles who murdered Rizzio in Mary's presence. Darnley was assassinated 1567.

He was killed in an explosion (while ill in bed), probably by James ⊳Bothwell, who became Mary's third husband. Mary's role in the plot remains controversial.

Darrow Clarence (Seward) 1857–1938. US lawyer, born in Ohio, a champion of liberal causes and defender of the underdog. He defended many labor-union leaders, including Eugene ⊳Debs 1894. He was counsel for the

defense in the Nathan Leopold and Richard Loeb murder trial in Chicago 1924, and in the ⊳Scopes monkey trial. Darrow matched wits in the trial with prosecution attorney William Jennings ⊳Bryan. He was an opponent of capital punishment.

Dart Raymond 1893–1988. Australian-born South African paleontologist and anthropologist who in 1924 discovered the first fossil remains of the Australopithecenes, early hominids, near Taungs in Botswana. He named them *Australopithecus africanus*, and spent many years trying to prove to skeptics that they were early humans, since their cranial and dental characteristics were not apelike in any way. In the 1950s and 1960s, the ⊳Leakey family found more fossils of this type and of related types in the Olduvai Gorge of E Africa, establishing that Australopithecines were hominids, walked erect, made tools, and lived as early as 5.5 million years ago. After further discoveries in the 1980s, they are today classified as *Homo sapiens australopithecus*, and Dart's assertions have been validated.

Dartmoor plateau of SW Devon, England, over 400 sq mi/1,000 sq km in extent, of which half is some 1,000 ft/300 m above sea level. Most of Dartmoor is a National Park. The moor is noted for its wild aspect, and rugged blocks of granite, or "tors," crown its higher points.

Dartmouth port in Nova Scotia, on the NE of Halifax harbor; population (1986) 65,300. It is virtually part of the capital city itself. Industries include oil refining and shipbuilding.

Dartmouth College Case US Supreme Court case (officially *Trustees of Dartmouth College v Woodward*) 1819 dealing with the protection of private corporations from state intervention under contract law. After some dissention among the trustees of the college, the New Hampshire legislature revised Dartmouth's original corporate charter 1769, placing the administration under the control of a state-appointed board. The trustees sued the new secretary of the college, William H Woodward, for recovery of the official seal and documents. The Supreme Court voted 4 to 1 to uphold the original royal charter, ruling that corporations have contractual obligations and therefore are protected from impairment by states.

darts indoor game played on a circular board. Darts (like small arrow shafts) about 5 in/13 cm long are thrown at segmented targets and score points according to their landing place.

The game may have derived from target practice with broken arrow shafts in days when archery was a compulsory military exercise. The Pilgrim Fathers are believed to have played darts aboard the *Mayflower* 1620.

Darwin capital and port in Northern Territory, Australia, in NW Arnhem Land; population (1986) 69,000. It serves the uranium mining site at Rum Jungle to the south. Destroyed 1974 by a cyclone, the city was rebuilt on the same site.

Darwin is the north terminus of the rail line from Birdum; commercial fruit and vegetable growing is being developed in the area. Founded 1869, under the name of Palmerston, the city was renamed after Charles Darwin 1911.

Darwin Charles Robert 1809–1882. English scientist who developed the modern theory of ⊳evolution and proposed, with Alfred Russel Wallace, the principle of ⊳natural selection. After research in South America and the

Galápagos Islands as naturalist on HMS *Beagle* 1831–36, Darwin published *On the Origin of Species by Means of Natural Selection or the Preservation of Favoured Races in the Struggle for Life* 1859. This explained the evolutionary process through the principles of natural and sexual selection. It aroused bitter controversy because it disagreed with the literal interpretation of the Book of Genesis in the Bible.

Darwin Erasmus 1731–1802. British poet, physician, naturalist, and grandfather of Charles Darwin. He anticipated aspects of evolutionary theory, but tended to ⊳Lamarck's interpretation.

Darwinism, social in US history, an influential but misleading social theory, based upon the work of Charles Darwin and Herbert Spencer, which claimed to offer a scientific justification for late 19th-century *laissez-faire* capitalism (the principle of unrestricted freedom in commerce).

Popularized by academics and by entrepreneurs such as Andrew ⊳Carnegie, social Darwinism was used to legitimize competitive individualism and a market economy unregulated by government; it argued that only the strong and resourceful businesses and individuals would thrive in a free environment.

Dasam Granth collection of the writings of the tenth Sikh guru (teacher), Gobind Singh, and of poems by a number of other writers. It is written in a script called Gurmukhi, the written form of Punjabi popularized by Guru Angad. It contains a retelling of the Krishna legends, devotional verse, and amusing anecdotes.

Das Kapital Karl Marx's exposition of his theories on economic production, published in three volumes 1867–95. It focuses on the exploitation of the worker and appeals for a classless society where the production process and its rewards are shared equally.

dasyure any ⊳marsupial of the family Dasyuridae, also known as a "native cat," found in Australia and New Guinea. Various species have body lengths from 10 in/25 cm to 2.5 ft/75 cm. Dasyures have long, bushy tails and dark coats with white spots. They are agile, nocturnal carnivores, able to move fast and climb.

DAT abbreviation for ⊳*digital audio tape*.

data facts, figures, and symbols, especially as stored in computers. The term is often used to mean raw, unprocessed facts, as distinct from information, to which a meaning or interpretation has been applied.

database structured collection of data. The database makes data available to the various programs that need it, without the need for those programs to be aware of how the data are stored. There are three main types (or "models"): hierarchical, network, and ⊳relational, of which relational is the most widely used. A **free-text database** is one that holds the unstructured text of articles or books in a form that permits rapid searching.

A collection of databases is known as a **databank**. A database-management system (DBMS) program ensures that the integrity of the data is maintained by controlling the degree of access of the ⊳application programs using the data. Databases are normally used by large organizations with mainframes or minicomputers.

A telephone directory stored as a database

might allow all the people whose names start with the letter B to be selected by one program, and all those living in Chicago by another.

data compression in computing, techniques for reducing the amount of storage needed for a given amount of data. They include word tokenization (in which frequently used words are stored as shorter codes), variable bit lengths (in which common characters are represented by fewer ◊bits than less common ones), and run-length encoding (in which a repeated value is stored once along with a count).

data-flow diagram in computing, a diagram illustrating the route taken by data through the various programs in an application.

data processing (DP) use of computers for performing clerical tasks such as stock control, payroll, and dealing with orders. DP systems are typically batch systems (needing little or no operator intervention), running on mainframe computers. DP is sometimes called EDP (electronic data processing).

A large organization usually has a special department to support its DP activities, which might include the writing and maintenance of software (programs), control and operation of the computers, and an analysis of the organization's information requirements.

date palm tree of the genus *Phoenix*. The female tree produces the fruit, dates, in bunches weighing 20–25 lb/9–11 kg. Dates are an important source of food in the Middle East, being rich in sugar; they are dried for export. The tree also supplies timber, and materials for baskets, rope, and animal feed.

The most important species is *P. dactylifera*; native to N Africa, SW Asia, and parts of India, it grows up to 80 ft/25 m high. A single bunch can contain as many as 1,000 dates. Their juice is made into a kind of wine.

dating science of determining the age of geological structures, rocks, and fossils, and placing them in the context of geological time. Dating can be carried out by identifying fossils of creatures that lived only at certain times (marker fossils), by looking at the physical relationships of rocks to other rocks of a known age, or by measuring how much of a rock's radioactive elements have changed since the rock was formed, using the process of ◊radiometric dating.

dative in the grammar of certain inflected languages (see ◊language) such as Latin, the dative case is the form of a noun, pronoun, or adjective used for the indirect object of a verb. It is also used with some prepositions.

Datura genus of plants *Datura*, family Solanaceae, such as jimson weed, with handsome trumpet-shaped blooms. Species in this genus have narcotic properties.

Daudet Alphonse 1840–1897. French novelist. He wrote about his native Provence in *Lettres de mon moulin/Letters from My Mill* 1866, and created the character Tartarin, a hero epitomizing southern temperament, in *Tartarin de Tarascon* 1872 and two sequels.

Daudet Léon 1867–1942. French writer and journalist, who founded the militant right-wing royalist periodical *Action Française* 1899 after the Dreyfus case. During World War II he was a collaborator with the Germans. He was the son of Alphonse Daudet.

Daumier Honoré 1808–1879. French artist. His sharply dramatic and satirical cartoons

dissected Parisian society. He produced over 4,000 lithographs and, mainly after 1860, powerful satirical oil paintings that were little appreciated in his lifetime.

Daumier drew for *La Caricature, Charivari*, and other periodicals. He created several fictitious stereotypes of contemporary figures and was once imprisoned for an attack on Louis Philippe. His paintings show a fluent technique and a mainly monochrome palette. He also produced sculptures of his caricatures, such as the bronze statuette of *Ratapoil* about 1850 (Louvre, Paris).

dauphin title of the eldest son of the kings of France, derived from the personal name of a count, whose lands, known as the *Dauphiné*, traditionally passed to the heir to the throne from 1349 to 1830.

Dauphiné ancient province of France, comprising the modern *départements* of Isère, Drôme, and Hautes-Alpes.

After the collapse of the Roman Empire it belonged to Burgundy, then was under Frankish domination. Afterwards part of Arles, it was sold by its ruler to France in 1349 and thereafter was used as the personal fief of the heir to the throne (the dauphin) until 1560, when it was absorbed into the French kingdom. The capital was Grenoble.

Davao town in the Philippine Republic, at the mouth of the Davao River on the island of Mindanao; population (1990) 849,900. It is the capital of Davao province. It is the center of a fertile district and trades in pearls, copra, rice, and corn.

Davenport city in SE Iowa, S of Dubuque, directly across from Rock Island, Illinois, on the Mississippi River; seat of Scott county. It forms the "Quad Cities" metropolitan area with the Illinois cities of Rock Island, Moline, and East Moline. Industries include aluminum, agriculture, and machinery parts; population (1990) 95,300.

David c. 1060–970 BC. Second king of Israel. According to the Old Testament he played the harp for King Saul to banish Saul's melancholy; he later slew the Philistine giant Goliath with a sling and stone. After Saul's death David was anointed king at Hebron, took Jerusalem, and made it his capital.

David sent Uriah (a soldier in his army) to his death in the front line of battle so that he might marry his widow, Bathsheba. Their son Solomon became the third king.

David probably wrote a few of the psalms (of the Book of Psalms) and was celebrated as a secular poet. In both Jewish and Christian belief, the messiah would be a descendant of David; Christians hold this prophecy to have been fulfilled by Jesus Christ.

David Jacques Louis 1748–1825. French painter in the Neo-Classical style. He was an active supporter of and unofficial painter to the republic during the French Revolution, for which he was imprisoned 1794–95. In his *Death of Marat* 1793, he turned political murder into a Classical tragedy. Later he devoted himself to the empire in paintings such as the enormous, pompous *Coronation of Napoleon* 1805–07 (Louvre, Paris).

David won the Prix de Rome 1774 and studied in Rome 1776–80. Back in Paris, his strongly Classical themes and polished style soon earned success; a picture from this period is *The Oath of the Horatii* 1784 (Louvre, Paris). During the Revolution he was elected

to the Convention and became a member of the Committee of Public Safety, and narrowly escaped the guillotine. He was later appointed court painter to the emperor Napoleon, of whom he created images such as the horseback figure of *Napoleon Crossing the Alps* 1800 (Louvre, Paris). After Napoleon's fall, David was banished by the Bourbons and settled in Brussels.

David two kings of Scotland:

David I 1084–1153. King of Scotland from 1124. The youngest son of Malcolm III Canmore and St ◊Margaret, he was brought up in the English court of Henry I, and in 1113 married ◊Matilda, widow of the 1st earl of Northampton. He invaded England 1138 in support of Queen Matilda, but was defeated at Northallerton in the Battle of the Standard, and again 1141.

David II 1324–1371. King of Scotland from 1329, son of ◊Robert I (the Bruce). David was married at the age of four to Joanna, daughter of Edward II of England. In 1346 David invaded England, was captured at the battle of Neville's Cross, and imprisoned for 11 years.

David Copperfield novel by Charles Dickens, published 1849–50. The story follows the orphan David Copperfield from his school days and early poverty to eventual fame as an author. Among the characters he encounters are Mr Micawber, Mr Peggotty, and Uriah Heep.

David, St or *Dewi* 5th–6th century. Patron saint of Wales, Christian abbot and bishop. According to legend he was the son of a prince of Dyfed and uncle of King Arthur; he was responsible for the adoption of the leek as the national emblem of Wales, but his own emblem is a dove. Feast day March 1.

Davies Peter Maxwell 1934– . English composer and conductor. His music combines medieval and serial codes of practice with a heightened Expressionism as in his opera *Taverner* 1962–68.

Davies Robertson 1913– . Canadian novelist. He published the first novel of his Deptford trilogy *Fifth Business* 1970, a panoramic work blending philosophy, humor, the occult, and ordinary life. Other works include *A Mixture of Frailties* 1958, *The Rebel Angels* 1981, and *What's Bred in the Bone* 1986.

da Vinci see ◊Leonardo da Vinci, Italian Renaissance artist.

Davis Angela 1944– . US left-wing activist for black rights, prominent in the student movement of the 1960s. In 1970 she went into hiding after being accused of supplying guns used in the murder of a judge who had been seized as a hostage in an attempt to secure the release of three black convicts. She was captured, tried, and acquitted. At the University of California she studied under Herbert ◊Marcuse, and was assistant professor of philosophy at UCLA 1969–70. In 1980 she was the Communist vice-presidential candidate.

Davis Bette 1908–1989. US actress. She entered films in 1930, and established a reputation as a forceful dramatic actress with *Of Human Bondage* 1934. Later films included *Dangerous* 1935 and *Jezebel* 1938, both winning her Academy Awards, *All About Eve* which won the 1950 Academy Award for best picture, and *Whatever Happened to Baby Jane?* 1962. She continued to make films throughout the 1980s such as *How Green Was My Valley* for television, and *The Whales of August* 1987, in which she co-starred with Lillian Gish.

Davis Jefferson 1808–1889. US politician, president of the short-lived Confederate States of America 1861–65. He was a leader of the Southern Democrats in the US Senate from 1857, and a defender of "humane" slavery; in 1860 he issued a declaration in favor of secession from the US. During the Civil War he assumed strong political leadership, but often disagreed with military policy. He was imprisoned for two years after the war, one of the few cases of judicial retribution against Confederate leaders.

Born in Kentucky, he graduated from ◊West Point military academy and served in the US army before becoming a cotton planter in Mississippi. He sat in the US Senate 1847–51, was secretary of war 1853–57, and returned to the Senate 1857. His fiery temper and self-righteousness hindered effort to achieve broad unity among the Southern states. His call for conscription in the South raised protests that he was a military dictator, violating the very ideals of freedom for which the Confederacy was fighting.

Davis John 1550–1605. English navigator and explorer. He sailed in search of the Northwest Passage through the Canadian Arctic to the Pacific Ocean 1585, and in 1587 sailed to Baffin Bay through the straits named after him. He was the first European to see the Falkland Islands 1592.

Davis Miles (Dewey, Jr) 1926–1991. US jazz trumpeter, composer, and bandleader. He recorded bebop with Charlie Parker 1945, pioneered cool jazz in the 1950s and jazz-rock fusion beginning in the late 1960s. His significant albums include *Birth of the Cool* 1957 (recorded 1949 and 1950), *Sketches of Spain* 1959, and *Bitches' Brew* 1970.

Davis Sammy, Jr 1925–1990. US entertainer. His starring role in the Broadway show *Mr Wonderful* 1956, his television work, and his roles in films with Frank Sinatra's "rat pack"—among them, *Ocean's Eleven*1960 and *Robin and the Seven Hoods* 1964—made him a national celebrity. He also appeared in the film version of the opera *Porgy and Bess* 1959. He published two memoirs, *Yes I Can* 1965 and *Why Me?* 1989.

Born in New York City, Davis appeared on stage at age four and became a member of the Will Mastin Trio 1932. Recognized as one of the best tap dancers in the country, Davis served as an army entertainer during World War II and became a nightclub headliner in the 1950s.

Davis Stuart 1894–1964. US abstract painter. He used hard-edged geometric shapes in primary colors and experimented with collage. Much of his work shows the influence of jazz tempos. In the 1920s he produced paintings of commercial packaging, such as *Lucky Strike* 1921 (Museum of Modern Art, New York), that foreshadow Pop art.

His early abstracts reflect the impact of Cubism, and he was deeply influenced by the ◊Armory Show in New York 1913. He often used numbers or letters as the focus for his compositions.

Davis Cup annual lawn tennis tournament for men's international teams, first held 1900 after Dwight Filley Davis (1879–1945) donated the trophy.

The Davis Cup was held on a challenge basis up to 1971. Since then it has been organized on an elimination basis, with countries divided into zonal groups, with a promotion and relegation system.

Davis Cup: recent winners

1983	Australia
1984	Sweden
1985	Sweden
1986	Australia
1987	Sweden
1988	West Germany
1989	West Germany
1990	US
1991	France
1992	US

Davisson Clinton Joseph 1881–1958. US physicist. With Lester Germer (1896–1971), he discovered that electrons can undergo diffraction, so proving Louis de Broglie's theory that electrons, and therefore all matter, can show wavelike structure. George ◊Thomson carried through the same research independently, and in 1937 the two men shared the Nobel Prize for Physics.

Born in Illinois, Davisson worked under Owen ◊Richardson at Princeton before joining Bell Telephone Labs in 1917.

Davitt Michael 1846–1906. Irish nationalist. He joined the Fenians (forerunners of the Irish Republican Army) 1865, and was imprisoned for treason 1870–77. After his release, he and the politician Charles Parnell founded the ◊Land League 1879. Davitt was jailed several times for land-reform agitation. He was a member of Parliament 1895–99, advocating the reconciliation of extreme and constitutional nationalism.

Davy Humphry 1778–1829. English chemist. He discovered, by electrolysis, the metallic elements sodium and potassium in 1807, and calcium, boron, magnesium, strontium, and barium in 1808. In addition, he established that chlorine is an element and proposed that hydrogen is present in all acids. He invented the "safety lamp" for use in mines where methane was present, enabling miners to work in previously unsafe conditions.

As a laboratory assistant in Bristol in 1799, he discovered the respiratory effects of laughing gas (nitrous oxide).

Davy Jones personification of a malevolent spirit of the sea. The phrase "gone to Davy Jones's locker" is used by sailors referring to those drowned at sea.

Dawes Charles Gates 1865–1951. US Republican politician. In 1923 he was appointed by the Allied Reparations Commission president of the committee that produced the **Dawes Plan**, a $200 million loan that enabled Germany to pay enormous war debts after World War I. It reduced tensions temporarily in Europe but was superseded by the ◊Young Plan (which reduced the total reparations bill) 1929. Dawes was elected US vice-president (under Calvin Coolidge) 1924, received the Nobel Peace Prize 1925, and was ambassador to Britain 1929–32.

dawn raid in business, sudden and unexpected buying of a significant proportion of a company's shares, usually as a prelude to a takeover bid. The aim is to prevent the target company from having time to organize opposition to the takeover.

"Corporate raiders" have gotten bolder and more numerous since the deregulation efforts of the Reagan administration. These acquisitions are ostensibly controlled and monitored by the Security and Exchange Commission (SEC) and governed under antitrust laws.

Recent court decisions have made mergers easier in the US. See also ◊leveraged buyout; ◊poison pill; ◊white knight.

Dawson City town in Canada, capital until 1953 of ◊Yukon Territory, at the junction of the Yukon and Klondike rivers; population (1986) 1,700. It was founded 1896, at the time of the Klondike gold rush, when its population was 25,000.

Dawson Creek town in British Columbia; population (1981) 11,500. It is the SE terminus of the Alaska Highway.

day time taken for the Earth to rotate once on its axis. The *solar day* is the time that the Earth takes to rotate once relative to the Sun. It is divided into 24 hours, and is the basis of our civil day. The *sidereal day* is the time that the Earth takes to rotate once relative to the stars. It is 3 minutes 56 seconds shorter than the solar day, because the Sun's position against the background of stars as seen from Earth changes as the Earth orbits it.

Day Clarence Shepard, Jr 1874–1935. US cartoonist and author. His autobiographical memoir *Life with Father* 1935 became a national bestseller, a long-running Broadway play from 1939, and a popular feature film 1947. Day's sequels to that work, *Life with Mother* 1937 and *Father and I* 1940, were published after his death.

Born in New York and educated at Yale, Day joined his father's Wall Street firm after graduation. Poor health forced his retirement from business at an early age, and he devoted himself to freelance cartooning and humor writing for a number of New York-based magazines.

Day Doris. Adopted name of Doris von Kappelhoff 1924– . US film actress and singing star of the 1950s and early 1960s, mostly in musicals and, later, coy sex comedies. Her films include *Tea for Two* 1950, *Calamity Jane* 1953, *Love Me or Leave Me* 1955, and Hitchcock's *The Man Who Knew Too Much* 1956. With *Pillow Talk* 1959, *Lover Come Back* 1962, and other 1960s light sex comedies, she played a self-confident but coy woman who manipulated some of the biggest male stars to capitulate.

Dayan Moshe 1915–1981. Israeli general and politician. As minister of defense 1967 and 1969–74, he was largely responsible for the victory over neighboring Arab states in the 1967 Six-Day War, but he was criticized for Israel's alleged unpreparedness in the 1973 October War and resigned along with Prime Minister Golda Meir. Foreign minister from 1977, Dayan resigned 1979 in protest over the refusal of the Begin government to negotiate with the Palestinians.

daycare all-day care for babies and young children, usually of working mothers. There is controversy among psychologists about the effects on children of spending so much time with their peers when very young. Some early research indicated that daycare for very young children could make them insecure and aggressive, but research in the US in 1990 indicated beneficial effects.

dayflower any plant of the genus *Commelina* of the spiderwort family. All have pointed leaves and creeping stems that form roots. The flowers, usually blue, open in the morning and wither by day's end throughout the summer and fall.

Day Lewis Cecil 1904–1972. Irish poet, British poet laureate 1968–1972. With W H Auden and Stephen Spender, he was one of the influential left-wing poets of the 1930s. He also wrote detective novels under the pseudonym *Nicholas Blake*.

daylight saving time legal time for a given zone that is one hour later than the standard time based on universal coordinated time (see ⋄time). It is used to provide additional daylight during the summer at the end of the usual working day.

Dayton city in Ohio; population (1990) 182,000. It produces precision machinery, household appliances, and electrical equipment. It has an aeronautical research center and a Roman Catholic university and was the home of aviators Wilbur and Orville Wright.

The Aviation Hall of Fame is in the city, and Wright-Patterson Air Force Base, which has an aviation museum, is nearby. Dayton was settled in 1796.

Daytona Beach city on the Atlantic coast of Florida; population (1990) 62,000. Economic activities include printing, commercial fishing, and manufacture of electronic equipment and metal products. It is also a resort. The Daytona International Speedway for automobile racing is here.

Dazai Osamu. Adopted name of Shuji Tsushima 1909–1948. Japanese novelist. The title of his novel *The Setting Sun* 1947 became identified in Japan with the dead of World War II.

dBASE family of microcomputer programs used for manipulating large quantities of data; also, a related ⋄fourth-generation language. The first version, dBASE II, appeared in 1981; it has since become a recognized standard for database applications.

DC in music, abbreviation for *da capo* (Italian "from the beginning"); in physics, abbreviation for *direct current* (electricity); abbreviation for the state of ⋄*District of Columbia*.

DD abbreviation for *Doctor of Divinity*.

D-day June 6, 1944, the day of the Allied invasion of Normandy under the command of General Eisenhower, with the aim of liberating Western Europe from German occupation. The Anglo-American invasion fleet landed on the Normandy beaches on the stretch of coast between the Orne River and St Marcouf. Artificial harbors known as "Mulberries" were constructed and towed across the Channel so that equipment and armaments could be unloaded onto the beaches. After overcoming fierce resistance the allies broke through the German defenses; Paris was liberated on Aug 25, and Brussels on Sept 2.

D-day is also military jargon for any day on which a crucial operation is planned. D+1 indicates the day after the start of the operation.

DDT abbreviation for *dichloro-diphenyl-trichloroethane* $(ClC_6H_4)_2CHCHCl_2)$, an insecticide discovered 1939 by Swiss chemist Paul Müller. It is useful in the control of insects that spread malaria, but resistant strains develop. DDT is highly toxic and persists in the environment and in living tissue. Its use is now banned in most countries, but it continues to be used on food plants in Latin America.

DE abbreviation for the state of ⋄*Delaware*.

deacon in the Roman Catholic and Anglican churches, an ordained minister who ranks immediately below a priest. In the Protestant churches, a deacon is in training to become a minister or is a lay assistant.

deadly nightshade another name for ⋄belladonna, a poisonous plant.

Dead Sea large lake, partly in Israel and partly in Jordan, lying 1,293 ft/394 m below sea level; area 394 sq mi/1,020 sq km. The chief river entering it is the Jordan; it has no outlet and the water is very salty.

Since both Israel and Jordan use the waters of the Jordan River, the Dead Sea is now dried up in the center and divided into two halves, but in 1980 Israel announced a plan to link it by canal with the Mediterranean. The Dead Sea Rift is part of the fault between the African and Arab plates.

Dead Sea Scrolls collection of ancient scrolls (rolls of writing) and fragments of scrolls found 1947–56 in caves on the W side of the Dead Sea, 7 mi/12 km S of Jericho and 2 km/1 mi from the N end of the Dead Sea, at ⋄Qumran. They include copies of Old Testament books a thousand years older than those previously known to be extant. The documents date mainly from about 150 BC–AD 68, when the monastic community that owned them, the Essenes, was destroyed by the Romans because of its support for a revolt against their rule. Some scrolls were found still intact in their storage jars.

The total of 800 manuscripts, containing all the books of the Old Testament except Esther, were publicly available for the first time 1986. Before this, only half the scrolls were published and only fifteen scholars had access to them.

deafness lack or deficiency in the sense of hearing, either inborn or caused by injury or disease of the middle or inner ear. Of assistance are hearing aids, lip-reading, a cochlear implant in the ear in combination with a special electronic processor, sign language (signs for concepts), and "cued speech" (manual clarification of ambiguous lip movement during speech).

Deakin Alfred 1856–1919. Australian politician, prime minister 1903–04, 1905–08, and 1909–10. In his second administration, he enacted legislation on defense and pensions.

Deal port and resort on the E coast of Kent, England; population (1981) 26,000. It was one of the ⋄Cinque Ports. Julius Caesar is said to have landed here 55 BC. The castle was built by Henry VIII and houses the town museum.

deamination removal of the amino group (–NH2) from an unwanted ⋄amino acid. This is the nitrogen-containing part, and it is converted into ammonia, uric acid, or urea (depending on the type of animal) to be excreted in the urine. In vertebrates, deamination occurs in the ⋄liver.

Dean Dizzy (Jay Hanna) 1911–1974. US baseball player. In 1930 he signed with the St Louis Cardinals and made his major-league pitching debut 1932. The offbeat brashness and good-natured arrogance that won him the nickname "Dizzy" are as legendary as his explosive fast-ball pitch. Winning 30 games and leading the Cardinals to a World Series win, he was voted the National League's most valuable player 1934. Following an injury in the 1937 All-Star Game, his pitching suffered. He was traded to the Chicago Cubs, for whom he pitched until his retirement 1941. Dean was elected to the Baseball Hall of Fame 1953.

Born in Lucas, Arkansas, Dean worked as a farmhand until he was old enough to join the army, where his pitching skills were recognized.

Dean James (Byron) 1931–1955. US actor. Killed in an automobile accident after the public showing of his first film, *East of Eden* 1955, he posthumously became a cult hero with *Rebel Without a Cause* 1955 and *Giant* 1956.

He has become a symbol of teenage rebellion against American middle-class values.

Deane Silas 1737–1789. American public leader and diplomat. Dispatched to Paris to obtain aid and support from the French government, Deane recruited Lafayette, Pulaski, and Steuben for the Continental army. Falsely accused of financial improprieties, he was discharged from his post; he was exonerated posthumously by Congress 1842.

Born in Groton, Connecticut, and educated at Yale, Deane was admitted to the bar 1761. A supporter of American independence, he served in the colonial legislature 1772, on the Connecticut Committee of Correspondence 1773, and in the Continental Congress 1774–76.

Dearborn city in Michigan, on the Rouge River 10 mi/16 km SW of Detroit; population (1990) 89,300. Settled in 1795, it was the birthplace and home of Henry ⋄Ford, who built his first car factory here. Car manufacturing is still the main industry. Dearborn also makes aircraft parts, steel, and bricks.

death permanent ending of all the functions that keep an organism alive. Death used to be pronounced when a person's breathing and heartbeat stopped. The advent of mechanical aids has made this point sometimes difficult to determine, and in controversial cases a person is now pronounced dead when the brain ceases to control the vital functions even if breath and heartbeat are maintained.

For removal of vital organs in transplant surgery, the World Health Organization in 1968 set out that the donor should exhibit no brain-body connection, muscular activity, blood pressure, or ability to breathe unaided by machine.

In religious belief death may be seen as the prelude to rebirth (as in Hinduism and Buddhism); under Islam and Christianity, there is the concept of a day of judgment and consignment to heaven or hell; Judaism concentrates not on an afterlife but on survival through descendants who honor tradition.

death cap fungus ⋄*Amanita phalloides*, the most poisonous mushroom known. The fruiting body has a scaly white cap and a collarlike structure near the base of the stalk.

Death of a Salesman 1949 Broadway play by Arthur Miller, the story of the defeated sales representative Willy Loman, which captured the limitations and deceptions of the American dream of success.

death penalty another name for ⋄capital punishment.

Death Valley depression 140 mi/225 km long and 4–16 mi/6–26 km wide, in SE California. At 280 ft/85 m below sea level, it is the lowest point in the W hemisphere. Bordering mountains rise to 10,000 ft/3,000 m. It is one of the world's hottest and driest places, with temperatures sometimes exceeding 125°F/51°C and an annual rainfall of less than 2 in/5.1 cm. Borax, iron ore, tungsten, gypsum, and salts are extracted.

deathwatch beetle any wood-boring beetle of the family Anobiidae, especially *Xestobium rufovillosum*. The larvae live in oaks and willows, and sometimes cause damage by boring in old furniture or structural timbers. To attract the female, the male beetle produces a ticking sound by striking his head on a wooden surface, and this is taken by the superstitious as a warning of approaching death.

Deborah in the Old Testament, a prophet and judge (leader). She helped lead an Israelite army against the Canaanite general Sisera, who was killed trying to flee; her song of triumph at his death is regarded as an excellent example of early Hebrew poetry.

Debrecen third largest city in Hungary, 120 mi/193 km E of Budapest, in the Great Plain (*Alföld*) region; population (1988) 217,000. It produces tobacco, agricultural machinery, and pharmaceuticals. Lajos ◊Kossuth declared Hungary independent of the ◊Habsburgs here in 1849. It is a commercial center and has a university founded 1912.

de Broglie see ◊Broglie, de.

Debs Eugene Victor 1855–1926. US labor leader and socialist who organized the Social Democratic Party 1897. He was the founder and first president of the American Railway Union 1893, and was imprisoned for six months in 1894 for defying a federal injunction to end the Pullman strike in Chicago. He was socialist candidate for the presidency in every election from 1900 to 1920, except that of 1916.

Debs was born in Terre Haute, Indiana. He opposed US intervention in World War I and was imprisoned 1918–21 for allegedly advocating resistance to conscription, but was pardoned by President Harding 1921. In 1920 he polled nearly 1 million votes, the highest socialist vote ever in US presidential elections, despite having to conduct the campaign from a federal penitentiary in Atlanta, Georgia.

His powerful oratory and his evocation of homespun American ideals were the source of his appeal rather than any doctrinaire adherence to socialist theory.

debt something that is owed by a person or organization, usually money, goods, or services, usually as a result of borrowing. Debt servicing is the payment of interest on a debt. The national debt of a country is the total money owed by the national government to private individuals, banks, and so on; international debt, the money owed by one country to another, began on a large scale with the investment in foreign countries by newly industrialized countries in the late 19th–early 20th centuries. International debt became a global problem as a result of the oil crisis of the 1970s.

As a result of the ◊Bretton Woods conference in 1944, the World Bank (officially called the ◊International Bank for Reconstruction and Development) was established 1945 as an agency of the United Nations to finance international development by providing loans where private capital was not forthcoming. Loans were made largely at prevailing market rates ("hard loans") and therefore generally to the developed countries, who could afford them.

In 1960 the International Development Association (IDA) was set up as an offshoot of the World Bank to provide interest-free ("soft") loans over a long period to finance the economies of developing countries and assist their long-term development. The cash surpluses of Middle Eastern oil-producing countries were channeled by Western banks to Third World countries. However, a slump in both the world economy and increases in interest rates have resulted in the debtor countries paying an ever-increasing percentage share of their national output in debt-servicing (paying off the interest on a debt, rather than paying off the debt itself). As a result, many loans had to be rescheduled (renegotiated so that repayments were made over a longer term).

During the early 1980s, Poland and Brazil suspended some payments on their debt, and others threatened to follow suit. With debt-servicing ratios (proportion of export earnings required to pay debt obligations) of more than 50% in some countries, the debt crisis threatened the stability of governments and the international, especially US, banking system. In 1987, one US bank announced that it was writing off $3 billion of international loans. The banks and the borrowing countries both recognized the need for relief, as debtor states could only pay the interest on existing loans by securing new loans. Disagreement over who should bear the cost of debt relief has delayed any real reform. Austerity measures imposed by the International Monetary Fund (IMF) in exchange for loans have provoked riots and an increase in nationalist sentiment, but Brazil began making payments on its debt in 1988, and the US and Mexico have negotiated reduction plans. Poland received substantial loans 1990 from the US and W Europe to assist its transition to a market-based economy.

debt crisis any situation in which an individual, company, or country owes more to others than it can repay or pay interest on; more specifically, the massive indebtedness of many Third World countries that became acute in the 1980s, threatening the stability of the international banking system as many debtor countries became unable to service their debts.

debt-for-nature swap agreement under which a country's debts are written off in exchange for a commitment by the debtor country to undertake projects for environmental protection. Debt-for-nature swaps were set up by environment groups in the 1980s in an attempt to reduce the debt problem of developing countries, while simultaneously promoting conservation.

To date, most debt-for-nature swaps have concentrated on setting aside areas of land, especially tropical rainforest, for protection and have involved private conservation foundations. The first swap took place 1987, when a US conservation group bought $650,000 of Bolivia's national debt from a bank for $100,000, and persuaded the Bolivian government to set aside a large area of rainforest as a nature preserve in exchange for never having to pay back the money owed. Other countries participating in debt-for-nature swaps are the Philippines, Costa Rica, Ecuador, and Poland. However, the debtor country is also expected to ensure that the area of land remains adequately protected, and in practice this does not always happen.

Debussy (Achille-) Claude 1862–1918. French composer. He broke with the dominant tradition of German Romanticism and introduced new qualities of melody and harmony based on the whole-tone scale, evoking oriental music. His work includes *Prélude à l'après-midi d'un faune* 1894 and the opera *Pelléas et Mélisande* 1902.

Among his other works are numerous piano pieces, songs, orchestral pieces such as *La Mer* 1903–05, and the ballet *Jeux* 1910–13. Debussy also wrote with humor about the music of his day, using the fictional character Monsieur Croche "antidilettante" (professional debunker).

Debye Peter 1884–1966. Dutch physicist. A pioneer of X-ray powder crystallography, he also worked on polar molecules, dipole moments, and molecular structure. In 1940, he went to the US where he was professor of chemistry at Cornell University 1940–52. He was awarded the 1936 Nobel Prize for Chemistry.

decagon in geometry, a ten-sided ◊polygon.

Decalogue ten commandments which, according to the Old Testament, were delivered by God to ◊Moses on Mount Sinai, stated in the books Exodus 20:1–17 and Deuteronomy 5:6–21. The Decalogue is recognized as the basis of morality by Jews and Christians.

Decameron, The collection of tales by the Italian writer Giovanni Boccaccio, brought together 1348–53. Ten young people, fleeing plague-stricken Florence, amuse their fellow travelers by each telling a story on the ten days they spend together. The work had a great influence on English literature, particularly on Chaucer's *Canterbury Tales*.

decathlon two-day athletic competition for men consisting of ten events: 100 meters, long jump, shot put, high jump, 400 meters (day one); 110 meters hurdles, discus, pole vault, javelin, 1,500 meters (day two). Points are awarded for performances and the winner is the athlete with the greatest aggregate score. The decathlon is an Olympic event.

Decatur city in central Illinois, on Lake Decatur; population (1990) 83,900. It has engineering, food processing, and plastics industries. It was founded 1829 and named after the US naval hero, Stephen Decatur.

Decatur Stephen 1779–1820. US naval hero, who distinguished himself in the war with the Barbary pirates at Tripoli 1801–05 when he succeeded in boarding and burning the *Philadelphia*, a US frigate captured by the enemy. During the War of 1812, he commanded three vessels, captured the British frigate *Macedonian*, and was blockaded by the British. Then in Jan 1815, unaware that the war was over, he battled four British ships, taking one but surrendering to the three pursuers. In 1815 he was again sent to the Barbary Coast, where he forced the bey of Algiers to sign the treaty ending US tribute to Algeria.

Born in Sinepuxent, Maryland, Decatur was killed in a duel with Commodore James Barron, whose return to duty he had opposed following the Chesapeake-Leopard Incident in 1807, one of the events leading to the ◊War of 1812. Decatur is known for the phrase "Our country, right or wrong," coined while giving a toast.

Deccan triangular tableland in E India, stretching between the Vindhya Hills in the N, and the Western and Eastern Ghats in the S.

decibel unit (symbol dB) of measure used originally to compare sound densities and subsequently electrical or electronic power outputs; now also used to compare voltages. An increase of 10 dB is equivalent to a 10-fold increase in intensity or power, and a 20-fold increase in voltage. A whisper has an intensity of 20 dB; 140 dB (a jet aircraft taking off nearby) is the threshold of pain.

The difference in decibels between two levels of intensity (or power) L_1 and L_2 is 10 $\log_{10}(L_1/L_2)$; a difference of 1 dB thus corresponds to a change of about 25%. For two voltages V_1 and V_2, the difference in decibels is 20 $\log_{10}(V_1/V_2)$; 1 dB corresponding in this case to a change of about 12%. Commonly such differences are given now not as ratios but as absolute values; for example, 10 dBV corresponds to the voltage level V_1 with V_2 set equal to 1 volt. In acoustics, the absolute reference used in the power ratio is 10^{-16} watt per sq cm.

deciduous of trees and shrubs, that shed their leaves at the end of the growing season or during a dry season to reduce ◊transpiration, the loss of water by evaporation.

Most deciduous trees belong to the ◊angiosperms, plants in which the seeds are enclosed within an ovary, and the term "deciduous tree" is sometimes used to mean "angiosperm tree," despite the fact that many angiosperms are evergreen, especially in the tropics, and a few ◊gymnosperms, plants in which the seeds are exposed, are deciduous (for example, larches). The term **broad-leaved** is now preferred to "deciduous" for this reason.

Examples of deciduous trees are oak and maple.

decimal fraction a ◊fraction expressed by the use of the decimal point, that is, a fraction in which the denominator is any higher power of 10. Thus 3/10, 51/100, and 23/1,000 are decimal fractions and are normally expressed as 0.3, 0.51, 0.023. The use of decimals greatly simplifies addition and multiplication of fractions, though not all fractions can be expressed exactly as decimal fractions.

The regular use of the decimal point appears to have been introduced about 1585, but the occasional use of decimal fractions can be traced back as far as the 12th century.

decimal number system or **denary number system** the most commonly used number system, to the base ten. Decimal numbers do not necessarily contain a decimal point; 563, 5.63, and –563 are all decimal numbers. Other systems are mainly used in computing and include the ◊binary number system, ◊octal number system, and ◊hexadecimal number system.

Decimal numbers may be thought of as written under column headings based on the number ten. For example, the number 2,567 stands for:

1,000s 100s 10s 1s
(10^3) (10^2) (10^1) (10^0)
2567.

Large decimal numbers may also be expressed in ◊floating-point notation.

decision table in computing, a method of describing a procedure for a program to follow, based on comparing possible decisions and their consequences. It is often used as an aid in systems design.

The top part of the table contains the conditions for making decisions (for example, if a number is negative rather than positive and is less than 1), and the bottom part describes the outcomes when those conditions are met. The program either ends or repeats the operation.

decision theory system of mathematical techniques for analyzing decision-making problems, for example, over unpredictable factors. The system aims to minimize error. It includes game theory, risk analysis, and utility theory.

Decius Gaius Messius Quintus Traianus 201–251. Roman emperor from 249. He fought a number of campaigns against the ◊Goths but was finally beaten and killed by them near Abritum. He ruthlessly persecuted the Christians.

Declaration of Independence historic US document stating the theory of government on which the US was founded, based on the right "to life, liberty, and the pursuit of happiness." The statement was issued by the American Continental Congress July 4, 1776, renouncing all allegiance to the British crown and ending the political connection with Britain.

Following a resolution moved June 7, by Richard Henry Lee, "that these United Colonies are, and of right ought to be, free and independent States," a committee including Thomas Jefferson and Benjamin Franklin was set up to draft a declaration; most of the work was done by Jefferson. The resolution, coming almost a year after the outbreak of hostilities, was adopted by the representatives of 12 colonies (New York at first abstaining) July 2, and the Declaration July 4; the latter date has ever since been celebrated as Independence Day in the US. The representatives of New York announced their adhesion July 15, and the Declaration was afterwards signed by the members of Congress Aug 2.

The declaration enumerated the grievances the colonists harbored against the king, which included his use of Indians to attack colonists, taxation without representation, and denial of civil liberties.

Declaration of Rights in Britain, the statement issued by the Convention Parliament Feb 1689, laying down the conditions under which the crown was to be offered to ◊William III and Mary. Its clauses were later incorporated in the ◊Bill of Rights.

declination in astronomy, the coordinate on the ◊celestial sphere (imaginary sphere surrounding the Earth) that corresponds to latitude on the Earth's surface. Declination runs from 0° at the celestial equator to 90° at the north and south celestial poles.

Decline and Fall of the Roman Empire, The History of the historical work by Edward Gibbon, published in the UK 1776–88. Arranged in three parts, the work spans 13 centuries and covers the history of the empire from Trajan and the Antonines through to the Turkish seizure of Constantinople 1453.

decolonization gradual achievement of independence by former colonies of the European imperial powers which began after World War I. The process of decolonization accelerated after World War II and the movement affected every continent: India and Pakistan gained independence from Britain 1947; Algeria gained independence from France 1962.

decomposer in biology, any organism that breaks down dead matter. Decomposers play a vital role in the ◊ecosystem by freeing important chemical substances, such as nitrogen compounds, locked up in dead organisms or excrement. They feed on some of the released organic matter, but leave the rest to filter back into the soil or pass in gas form into the atmosphere. The principal decomposers are bacteria and fungi, but earthworms and many other invertebrates are often included in this group. The ◊nitrogen cycle relies on the actions of decomposers.

decomposition process whereby a chemical compound is reduced to its component substances. In biology, it is the destruction of dead organisms either by chemical reduction or by the action of decomposers.

decompression sickness illness brought about by a sudden and substantial change in atmospheric pressure. It is caused by a too rapid release of nitrogen that has been dissolved into the bloodstream under pressure; when the nitrogen bubbles it causes the ◊bends. The condition causes breathing difficulties, joint and muscle pain, and cramps, and is experienced mostly by deep-sea divers who surface too quickly.

After a one-hour dive at 100 ft/30 m, 40 minutes of decompression are needed, according to US Navy tables.

decontamination factor in radiological protection, a measure of the effectiveness of a decontamination process. It is the ratio of the original contamination to the remaining radiation after decontamination: 1,000 and above is excellent; 10 and below is poor.

decretal in medieval Europe, a papal ruling on a disputed point, sent to a bishop or abbot in reply to a request or appeal. The earliest dates from Siricius 385. Later decretals were collected to form a decretum.

decretum collection of papal decrees. The best known is that collected by Gratian (died 1159) about 1140, comprising some 4,000 items. The decretum was used as an authoritative source of canon law (the rules and regulations of the church).

Dedekind Richard 1831–1916. German mathematician, who made contributions to number theory. In 1872 he introduced the **Dedekind cut** (which divides a line of infinite length representing all ◊real numbers) to categorize ◊irrational numbers as fractions and thus increase their usefulness.

dedicated computer computer built into another device for the purpose of controlling or supplying information to it. Its use has increased dramatically since the advent of the ◊microprocessor: washing machines, digital watches, automobiles, and video recorders all now have their own processors.

A dedicated system is a general-purpose computer system confined to performing only one function for reasons of efficiency or convenience. A word processor is an example.

deduction in philosophy, a form of argument in which the conclusion necessarily follows from the premises. It would be inconsistent ◊logic to accept the premises but deny the conclusion.

deed legal document that passes an interest in property or binds a person to perform or abstain from some action. Deeds are of two kinds: indenture and deed poll. **Indentures** bind two or more parties in mutual obligations. A **deed poll** is made by one party only, such as when a person changes his or her name.

Bargain sale deeds convey title to property by contract but do not guarantee title unless they include a specific covenant to that effect; quitclaim deeds convey a grantor's interest but do not guarantee title; warranty deeds convey interest and guarantee title to the subject property.

deep freezing method of preserving food by rapid freezing and storage at 0°F/–18°C. Commercial freezing is usually done by one of the following methods: blast, the circulation of air at –40°F/–40°C; contact, in which a refrigerant is circulated through hollow shelves; immersion, for example, fruit in a solution of sugar and glycerol; or cryogenic means, for example, by liquid nitrogen spray.

Rapid freezing avoids structural change that would affect the taste or appearance of the food, as in the shrinkage and distortion of cells by formation of enlarged ice crystals in the extracellular spaces. Some "quick-frozen" foods require thawing before use, and cooking must then be prompt.

Accelerated freeze drying (AFD) involves rapid freezing followed by heat drying in a vacuum, for example, prawns for later rehydration. The product does not have to be stored in frozen conditions.

Freezing was developed in the late 19th century and found early commercial application in the transportation of large quantities of meat on long sea voyages.

Deep-Sea Drilling Project research project initiated by the US 1968 to sample the rocks of the ocean ⊅crust. The operation became international 1975, when Britain, France, West Germany, Japan, and the USSR also became involved.

Over 800 boreholes were drilled in all the oceans using the ship *Glomar Challenger*, and knowledge of the nature and history of the ocean basins was increased dramatically. The technical difficulty of drilling the seabed to a depth of 6,500 ft/2,000 m was overcome by keeping the ship in position with side-thrusting propellers and satellite navigation, and by guiding the drill using a radiolocation system.

deer any of various ruminant, even-toed, hoofed mammals belonging to the family Cervidae. The male typically has a pair of antlers, shed and regrown each year. Most species of deer are forest-dwellers and are distributed throughout Eurasia and North America, but are absent from Australia and Africa S of the Sahara.

Native to North America are white-tailed deer *Odocoileus viginianus*, mule deer *O. hemionus*, wapiti or elk *Cervus canadensis*, moose *Alces alces*, and caribou or reindeer *Rangifer tarandus*. The last two also occur in Eurasia. Red deer *Cervus elaphus*, roe deer *Capreolus capreolus*, and fallow deer *Dama dama* are typical Eurasian species.

deerhound large, rough-coated dog, formerly used for hunting and killing deer. Slim and long-legged, it grows to 2.5 ft/75 cm or more, usually with a bluishgray coat.

de Falla Manuel Spanish composer. See ⊅Falla, Manuel de.

defamation in law, an attack on a person's reputation by libel (a published, permanent defamation such as in a book or newspaper), or slander (a spoken defamatory statement, except if broadcast on TV or radio, which constitutes libel).

default in commerce, failure to meet an obligation, usually financial.

Defense, Department of US government department presided over by the secretary of defense, with headquarters in the ⊅Pentagon. The secretary holds a seat in the president's cabinet; each of the three military services has a civilian secretary, not of cabinet rank, at its head. It was established when the army, navy, and air force were unified by the National Security Act 1947.

defibrillation use of electrical stimulation to restore a chaotic heartbeat to a rhythmical pattern. In fibrillation, which may occur in most kinds of heart disease, the heart muscle contracts irregularly; the heart is no longer working as an efficient pump. Paddles are applied to the chest wall, and one or more electric shocks are delivered to normalize the beat.

deficit financing in economics, a planned excess of expenditure over income, dictated by government policy, creating a shortfall of public revenue which is met by borrowing. The decision to create a deficit is made to stimulate an economy by increasing consumer purchasing and at the same time to create more jobs.

deflation in economics, a reduction in the level of economic activity, usually caused by an increase in interest rates and reduction in the money supply, increased taxation, or a decline in government expenditure.

Deflation may be chosen as an economic policy to improve the balance of payments, through a reduction in demand and therefore of imports, and lowering inflation to stimulate exports. It can reduce wage increases but may also reduce the level of employment.

Defoe Daniel 1660–1731. English writer. His *Robinson Crusoe* 1719, though purporting to be a factual account of shipwreck and solitary survival, was influential in the development of the novel. The fictional *Moll Flanders* 1722 and the partly factual *A Journal of the Plague Year* 1724 are still read for their concrete realism. A prolific journalist and pamphleteer, he was imprisoned 1702–04 for the ironic *The Shortest Way with Dissenters* 1702.

Defoe wrote numerous pamphlets and first achieved fame with the satire *The True-Born Englishman* 1701. His version of the contemporary short story "True Relation of the Apparition of one Mrs Veal" 1706 first revealed a gift for realistic narrative.

de Forest Lee 1873–1961. US inventor who held more than 300 patents, including the triode tube, precursor to the radio tube and one of the most influential inventions of the century 1906, called by him the audion. It generated, detected, and amplified radio waves. He also developed a movie-sound system and contributed to the phonograph, telephone, television, radar, and diathermy.

deforestation destruction of forest for timber, fuel, charcoal burning, and clearing for agriculture and extractive industries, such as mining, without planting new trees to replace those lost (reforestation) or working on a cycle that allows the natural forest to regenerate. Deforestation causes fertile soil to be blown away or washed into rivers, leading to ⊅soil erosion, drought, flooding, and loss of wildlife.

Deforestation is taking place in both tropical rainforests and temperate forests.

Degas (Hilaire Germain) Edgar 1834–1917. French Impressionist painter and sculptor. He devoted himself to lively, informal studies, often using pastels, of ballet, horse racing, and young women working. From the 1890s he turned increasingly to sculpture, modeling figures in wax in a fluent, naturalistic style.

Degas studied under a pupil of Ingres and worked in Italy in the 1850s, painting Classical themes. In 1861 he met Manet, and they developed Impressionism. Degas' characteristic style soon emerged, showing the influence of Japanese prints and of photography in inventive compositions and unusual viewpoints. An example of his sculpture is *The Little Dancer* 1881 (Tate Gallery, London).

de Gaulle Charles André Joseph Marie 1890–1970. French general and first president of the Fifth Republic 1959–69. He organized the ⊅Free French troops fighting the Nazis 1940–44, was head of the provisional French government 1944–46, and leader of his own Gaullist party. In 1958 the national assembly asked him to form a government during France's economic recovery and to solve the crisis in Algeria. He became president at the end of 1958, having changed the constitution to provide for a presidential system, and served until 1969.

Born in Lille, he graduated from Saint-Cyr 1911 and was severely wounded and captured by the Germans 1916. In June 1940 he refused to accept the new prime minister Pétain's truce with the Germans and became leader of the Free French in England. In 1944 he entered Paris in triumph and was briefly head of the provisional government before resigning over the new constitution of the Fourth Republic 1946. In 1947 he founded the *Rassemblement du Peuple Français*, a nonparty constitutional reform movement, then withdrew from politics 1953. When national bankruptcy and civil war in Algeria loomed 1958, de Gaulle was called to form a government.

As prime minister he promulgated a constitution subordinating the legislature to the presidency and took office as president Dec 1958. Economic recovery followed, as well as Algerian independence after a bloody war. A nationalist, he opposed "Anglo-Saxon" influence in Europe.

Re-elected president 1965, he violently quelled student demonstrations May 1968 when they were joined by workers. The Gaullist party, reorganized as *Union des Democrats pour la Cinquième République*, won an overwhelming majority in the elections of the same year. In 1969 he resigned after the defeat of the government in a referendum on constitutional reform. He retired to the village of Colombey-les-Deux-Eglises in NE France.

degaussing neutralization of the magnetic field around a body by encircling it with a conductor through which a current is maintained. Ships were degaussed in World War II to prevent them from detonating magnetic mines.

degree in mathematics, a unit (symbol °) of measurement of an angle or arc. A circle is divided into 360°; a degree is subdivided into 60 minutes (symbol ′). **Temperature** is also measured in degrees, which are divided on a decimal scale. See also ⊅Celsius, ⊅Fahrenheit, and ⊅circle.

A quarter-turn (90°) is a right angle; a half-turn (180°) is the angle on a straight line. A degree of latitude is the length along a meridian such that the difference between its north and south ends is 1°. A degree of longitude is the length between two meridians making an angle of 1° at the center of the Earth.

De Havilland Geoffrey 1882–1965. British aircraft designer who designed and whose company produced the Moth biplane, the Mosquito fighter-bomber of World War II, and the postwar Comet, the world's first jet-driven airliner to enter commercial service.

De Havilland Olivia 1916– . US actress, a star in Hollywood from the age of 19, when she appeared in *A Midsummer Night's Dream* 1935. She later successfully played more challenging dramatic roles in *Gone With the Wind* 1939, *To Each His Own* (Academy Award) and *Dark*

Mirror 1946, and *The Snake Pit* 1948. She won her second Academy Award for *The Heiress* 1949, and played in *Lady in a Cage* and *Hush, Hush, Sweet Charlotte*, both 1964.

dehydration process to preserve food. Moisture content is reduced to 10–20% in fresh produce, and this provides good protection against molds. Bacteria are not inhibited by drying, so the quality of raw materials is vital.

The process was developed commercially in France about 1795 to preserve sliced vegetables, using a hot-air blast. The earliest large-scale application was to starch products such as pasta, but after 1945 it was extended to milk, potato, soups, instant coffee, and prepared baby and pet foods. A major benefit to food manufacturers is reduction of weight and volume of the food products, lowering distribution cost.

Deianira in Greek mythology, wife of ⷧHeracles, who won her in combat, and mother of his sons, considered ancestors of the ⷧDorian Greeks. She killed Heracles by mistake, giving him poison instead of an aphrodisiac, and in her grief committed suicide. Her story is dramatized in ⷧSophocles' *Women of Trachis*.

Deighton Len 1929– . British author of spy fiction, including *The Ipcress File* 1963 and the trilogy *Berlin Game*, *Mexico Set*, and *London Match* 1983–85, featuring the spy Bernard Samson. Samson was also the main character in Deighton's second trilogy *Spy Hook* 1989, *Spy Line* 1989, and *Spy Sinker* 1990.

Deimos one of the two moons of Mars. It is irregularly shaped, $9 \times 7.5 \times 7$ mi/$15 \times 12 \times 11$ km, orbits at a height of 15,000 mi/24,000 km every 1.26 days, and is not as heavily cratered as the other moon, Phobos. Deimos was discovered 1877 by US astronomer Asaph Hall (1829–1907), and is thought to be an asteroid captured by Mars's gravity.

deindustrialization decline in the share of manufacturing industries in a country's economy. Typically, industrial plants are closed down and not replaced, and service industries increase.

Deirdre in Celtic mythology, the beautiful intended bride of ⷧConchobar. She eloped with Noisi, and died of sorrow when Conchobar killed him and his brothers.

deism belief in a supreme being; but the term usually refers to a movement of religious thought in the 17th and 18th centuries, characterized by the belief in a rational "religion of nature" as opposed to the orthodox beliefs of Christianity. Deists believed that God is the source of natural law but does not intervene directly in the affairs of the world, and that the only religious duty of humanity is to be virtuous.

Deism emerged in England in the writings of Lord Herbert of Cherbury (1583–1648). John Toland (1670–1722) and Matthew Tindal (1657–1733) were among its major exponents. In France, the writer Voltaire was the most prominent advocate of deism. In the US, many of the founding fathers, including Benjamin Franklin and Thomas Jefferson, were essentially deists. See also ⷧtheism.

de Klerk F(rederik) W(illem) 1936– . South African National Party politician, president from 1989. Trained as a lawyer, he entered the South African parliament 1972. He served

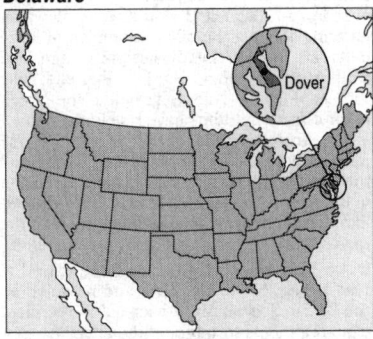

Delaware

in the cabinets of B J Vorster and P W Botha 1978–89, and replaced Botha as National Party leader Feb 1989 and as state president Aug 1989. Projecting himself as a pragmatic conservative who sought gradual reform of the apartheid system, he won the Sept 1989 elections for his party, but with a reduced majority. In Feb 1990 he ended the ban on the ⷧAfrican National Congress opposition movement and released its effective leader, Nelson Mandela. In Feb 1991 de Klerk promised the end of all apartheid legislation and a new multiracial constitution, and by June of the same year had repealed all racially discriminating laws. In March 1992 a nationwide, whites-only referendum gave de Klerk a clear mandate to proceed with plans for major constitutional reform to end white minority rule.

de Kooning Willem 1904– . Dutch-born US painter who immigrated to the US 1926 and worked as a commercial artist. After World War II he became, together with Jackson Pollock, one of the leaders of the Abstract Expressionist movement. His *Women* series, exhibited 1953, was criticized for its grotesque figurative style.

De Kooning joined the faculty of the Yale Art School and became a member of the National Institute of Arts 1960 and received the Presidential Medal of Freedom 1964. His paintings were commissioned for numerous Work Projects Administration (WPA) projects, and he won praise for his mural in the Hall of Pharmacy at the 1939 New York World's Fair.

Delacroix Eugène 1798–1863. French Romantic painter. His prolific output included religious and historical subjects and portraits of friends, among them the musicians Paganini and Chopin. Against French academic tradition, he evolved a highly colored, fluid style, as in *The Death of Sardanapalus* 1827 (Louvre, Paris).

The *Massacre at Chios* 1824 (Louvre, Paris) shows Greeks enslaved by wild Turkish horsemen, a contemporary atrocity (his use of a contemporary theme recalls Géricault's example). His style was influenced by the English landscape painter Constable. Delacroix also produced illustrations for Shakespeare, Dante, and Byron. His *Journal* is a fascinating record of his times.

de la Mare Walter 1873–1956. English poet, known for his verse for children, such as *Songs of Childhood* 1902, and the novels *The Three Royal Monkeys* 1910 for children and, for adults, *The Memoirs of a Midget* 1921.

Delaunay Robert 1885–1941. French painter, a pioneer in abstract art. With his wife Sonia

Delaunay-Terk, he invented Orphism, an early variation on Cubism, focusing on the effects of pure color.

In 1912 he painted several series, notably *Circular Forms* (almost purely abstract) and *Windows* (inspired by Parisian cityscapes).

Delaunay-Terk Sonia 1885–1979. French painter and textile designer born in Russia, active in Paris from 1905. With her husband Robert Delaunay, she was a pioneer of abstract art.

De Laurentiis Dino 1919– . Italian producer. His early films, including Fellini's *La strada/ The Street* 1954, brought more acclaim than later epics such as *Waterloo* 1970. He then produced a series of Hollywood films: *Death Wish* 1974, *King Kong* (remake) 1976, and *Dune* 1984.

Delaware state in NE US; nickname First State/Diamond State
area 2,046 sq mi/5,300 sq km
capital Dover
cities Wilmington, Newark
physical two main divisions: (1) hilly and wooded; (2) gently undulating to the sea
features one of the most industrialized states; headquarters of the Du Pont chemical firm; Rehoboth Beach; Winterthur Museum
products dairy, poultry, and market-garden produce; chemicals; motor vehicles; textiles
population (1990) 666,200
famous people Du Pont family, J P Marquand
history the first settlers were Dutch 1631 and Swedes 1638, but in 1664 the area was captured by the British and transferred to William Penn. A separate colony from 1704, it fought in the American Revolution as a state 1776, was one of the original 13 states, and was the first state to ratify the US Constitution, Dec 7, 1787. In 1802 the Du Pont gunpowder mill was established near Wilmington. Completion of the Philadelphia–Baltimore railroad line 1838, through Wilmington, fostered development. Delaware was famous as a chemical center by the early 1900s. Two auto-assembly plants and an oil refinery were built after World War II.

de la Warr Thomas West, Baron de la Warr 1577–1618. US colonial administrator, known as Delaware. Appointed governor of Virginia 1609, he arrived 1610 just in time to prevent the desertion of the Jamestown colonists, and by 1611 had revitalized the settlement. He fell ill, returned to England, and died during his return voyage to the colony 1618. Both the river and state are named after him.

Delbruck Max 1906–1981. German-born US biologist who pioneered techniques in molecular biology, studying genetic changes occurring when viruses invade bacteria. He was awarded the Nobel Prize for Medicine 1969 which he shared with Salvador Luria (1912–1951) and Alfred Hershey (1908–).

de Lesseps Ferdinand, Vicomte French engineer; see de ⷧLesseps.

Delft town in the Netherlands in the province of South Holland, 9 mi/14 km NW of Rotterdam; population (1991) 89,300. It produces pottery and porcelain. The Dutch nationalist leader William the Silent was murdered here 1584. It is the birthplace of the artist Jan Vermeer.

Delhi Union Territory of the Republic of India from 1956; capital New Delhi; area 579 sq mi/ 1,500 sq km; population (1991) 9,370,400. It produces grain, sugar cane, fruit, and vegetables.

Delibes (Clément Philibert) Léo 1836–1891. French composer. His lightweight, perfectly judged works include the ballet *Coppélia* 1870, *Sylvia* 1876, and the opera *Lakmé* 1883.

Delilah in the Old Testament, the Philistine mistress of ◊Samson. Following instructions from the lords of the Philistines she sought to find the source of Samson's great strength. When Samson eventually revealed that his physical power lay in the length of his hair, she shaved his head while he slept and then delivered him into the hands of the Philistines.

deliquescence phenomenon of a substance absorbing so much moisture from the air that it ultimately dissolves in it to form a solution.

Deliquescent substances make very good drying agents and are used in the bottom chambers of ◊desiccators. Calcium chloride (CaCl₂) is one of the commonest.

delirium in medicine, a state of temporary confusion in which the subject is incoherent, frenzied, and out of touch with reality. It is often accompanied by delusions or hallucinations.

Delirium may occur in feverish illness, some forms of mental illness, and as a result of drug or alcohol intoxication. In chronic alcoholism, attacks of **delirium tremens** (DTs), marked by hallucinations, sweating, trembling, and anxiety, may persist for several days.

Delius Frederick (Theodore Albert) 1862–1934. English composer. His works include the opera *A Village Romeo and Juliet* 1901; the choral pieces *Appalachia* 1903, *Sea Drift* 1904, *A Mass of Life* 1905; orchestral works such as *In a Summer Garden* 1908, *A Song of the High Hills* 1911; chamber music; and songs.

His romantic style of writing was influenced by Grieg.

della Robbia Italian family of artists; see ◊Robbia, della.

Delon Alain 1935– . French actor who appeared in the films *Purple Noon* 1960, *Rocco e i suoi fratelli/Rocco and His Brothers* 1960, *Il gattopardo/The Leopard* 1963, *Texas Across the River* 1966, *Scorpio* 1972, and *Swann in Love* 1984.

Delos Greek island, smallest in the ◊Cyclades group, in the SW Aegean Sea; area about 2 sq mi/5 sq km. The great temple of Apollo (4th century BC) is still standing.

Delphi city of ancient Greece, situated in a rocky valley north of the gulf of Corinth, on the southern slopes of Mount Parnassus, site of a famous ◊oracle in the temple of Apollo. In the same temple was the *Omphalos*, a conical stone supposed to stand at the center of the Earth. The oracle was interpreted by priests from the inspired utterances of the Pythian priestess until it was closed down by the Roman emperor Theodosius AD 390.

delphinium any plant of the genus *Delphinium* belonging to the buttercup family Ranunculaceae. There are some 250 species, including the great flowered larkspur *D.grandiflorum*, an Asian form and one of the ancestors of the garden delphinium. Most species have blue, purple, or white flowers in a long spike.

Delray Beach city in SE Florida on the Atlantic Ocean, N of Fort Lauderdale. A tourist resort, it also relies economically on the cultivation of flowers; population (1990) 47,200.

del Sarto Andrea 1486–1531. Italian Renaissance painter; see ◊Andrea del Sarto.

delta tract of land at a river's mouth, composed of silt deposited as the water slows on entering the sea. Familiar examples of large deltas are those of the Mississippi, Ganges and Brahmaputra, Rhône, Po, Danube, and Nile; the shape of the Nile delta is like the Greek letter *delta* Δ, and thus gave rise to the name.

The **arcuate delta** of the Nile is only one form. Others are **birdfoot deltas**, like that of the Mississippi which is a seaward extension of the river's ◊levee system; and **tidal deltas**, like that of the Mekong, in which most of the material is swept to one side by sea currents.

Delta Force US antiguerrilla force, based at Fort Bragg, North Carolina, and modeled on the British Special Air Service (SAS) recruited from regiments throughout the army.

Delta rocket US rocket used to launch many scientific and communications satellites since 1960, based on the Thor ballistic missile. Several increasingly powerful versions were produced as satellites became larger and heavier. Solid-fuel boosters were attached to the first stage to increase lifting power.

delta wing aircraft wing shaped like the Greek letter *delta* Δ. Its design enables an aircraft to pass through the ◊sound barrier with little effect. The supersonic airliner Concorde and the US space shuttle have delta wings.

demand in economics, the quantity of a product or service that customers want to buy at any given price. Also, the desire for a commodity, together with ability to pay for it.

demarcation in industrial relations, the practice of stipulating that particular workers should perform particular tasks. The practice can be the source of industrial disputes.

dementia mental deterioration as a result of physical changes in the brain. It may be due to degenerative change, circulatory disease, infection, injury, or chronic poisoning. *Senile dementia*, a progressive loss of mental abilities such as memory and orientation, is typically a problem of old age, and can be accompanied by ◊depression.

Dementia is distinguished from amentia, or severe congenital mental insufficiency.

Demerara river in Guyana, 215 mi/346 km long, which gives its name to the country's chief sugar-cane growing area, after which Demerara sugar is named.

demesne in the Middle Ages in Europe, land kept in the lord's possession, not leased out, but, under the system of ◊villeinage, worked by villeins to supply the lord's household.

Demeter in Greek mythology, the goddess of agriculture (identified with Roman ◊Ceres), daughter of Cronus and Rhea, and mother of Persephone by Zeus. She is identified with the Egyptian goddess Isis and had a temple dedicated to her at Eleusis where ◊mystery religions were celebrated.

Demetrius Donskoi ("of the Don") 1350–1389. Grand prince of Moscow from 1363. In 1380 he achieved the first Russian victory over the Tatars on the plain of Kulikovo, next to the river Don (hence his nickname).

De Mille Agnes George 1905–1989. US choreographer. After becoming a member of the Ballet Theater, she choreographed a long string of Broadway hits, including *Oklahoma!* 1943, *Carousel* 1945, *Brigadoon* 1947, *Gentlemen Prefer Blondes* 1949, and *Paint Your Wagon* 1951. She founded the Agnes De Mille Dance Theater 1953.

Born in New York, the niece of film director Cecil B De Mille, she was trained in Classical ballet and made her stage debut 1928. She later concentrated on choreography, directing the dance movements of the stage adaptation of *Romeo and Juliet* 1936.

De Mille Cecil B(lount) 1881–1959. US film director and producer. He entered films 1913 with Jesse L Lasky (with whom he later established Paramount Pictures), and was one of the founders of Hollywood. He specialized in biblical epics, such as *The Sign of the Cross* 1932 and *The Ten Commandments* 1923; remade 1956. He also made the 1952 Academy-Award-winning *The Greatest Show on Earth*.

Demirel Suleyman 1924– . Turkish politician. Leader from 1964 of the Justice Party, he was prime minister 1965–71, 1975–77, and 1979–80. He favored links with the West, full membership in the European Community, and foreign investment in Turkish industry.

democracy (Greek *demos* "the community," *kratos* "sovereign power") government by the people, usually through elected representatives. In the modern world, democracy has developed from the American and French revolutions.

Representative parliamentary government existed in Iceland from the 10th century and in England from the 13th century, but the British working classes were excluded almost entirely from the ◊vote until 1867, and women were admitted and property qualifications abolished only in 1918.

In *direct democracy* the whole people meets for the making of laws or the direction of executive officers, for example in Athens in the 5th century BC (and allegedly in modern Libya). Direct democracy today is represented mainly by the use of the ◊referendum, as in the UK, France, Switzerland, and certain states of the US.

The Western concept of democracy differs from that in communist countries: the former emphasizes the control of the government by the electorate, and freedom of speech and the press; in the latter, both political and economic power rest in the Communist Party.

Democratic Party one of the two main political parties of the US. It tends to be the party of the working person, as opposed to the Republicans, the party of big business, but the divisions between the two are not clear cut. Its stronghold since the Civil War has traditionally been industrial urban centers and the Southern states, but conservative Southern Democrats were largely supportive of Republican positions and helped elect President Reagan.

Originally called Democratic Republicans, the party was founded by Thomas Jefferson 1792 to defend the rights of the individual states against the centralizing policy of the Federalists. The Democratic Party held power almost continuously 1800–60, and later returned with the presidencies of Grover Cleveland, Woodrow Wilson, Franklin D Roosevelt, Harry Truman, John F Kennedy, Lyndon B Johnson, and Jimmy Carter. In the 20th century it has had more liberal social reform policies than the Republicans.

Democritus *c.* 460–361 BC. Greek philosopher and speculative scientist who made a significant contribution to metaphysics with his atomic theory of the universe: all things originate from a vortex of atoms and differ according to the shape and arrangement of their atoms.

His concepts come to us through Aristotle's work in this area. His discussion of the constant motion of atoms to explain the origins of the universe was the most scientific theory proposed in his time.

demodulation in radio, the technique of separating a transmitted audio frequency signal from its modulated radio carrier wave. At the transmitter the audio frequency signal (representing speech or music, for example) may be made to modulate the amplitude (AM broadcasting) or frequency (FM broadcasting) of a continuously transmitted radio-frequency carrier wave. At the receiver, the signal from the aerial is demodulated to extract the required speech or sound component. In early radio systems, this process was called detection.

demographic transition any change in birth and death rates; over time, these generally shift from a situation where both are high to a situation where both are low. This may be caused by a variety of social factors (among them education and the changing role of women) and economic factors (such as higher standard of living and improved diet). The *demographic transition model* suggests that it happens in four stages:
1) high birth rate, fluctuating but high death rate;
2) birth rate stays high, death rate starts to fall, giving maximum population growth;
3) birth rate starts to fall, death rate continues falling;
4) birth rate is low, death rate is low.

In some industrialized countries death rate exceeds birth rate, leading to a declining population. The history of many European countries follows the demographic transition model, but in poorer countries the pattern is far less clear. A ⬦population pyramid illustrates demographic composition, and the ⬦Malthus theory gives a worst-case scenario of demographic change.

demography study of the size, structure, dispersement, and development of human populations to establish reliable statistics on such factors as birth and death rates, marriages and divorces, life expectancy, and migration.

Demography is significant in the social sciences as the basis for industry and for government planning in such areas as education, housing, welfare, transport, and taxation.

demonstration public show of support for, or opposition to, a particular political or social issue, typically by a group of people holding a rally, displaying placards, and making speeches. They usually seek some change in official policy by drawing attention to their cause with a media-worthy event.

Demonstrations can be static or take the form of elementary street theater or processions. A specialized type of demonstration is the *picket*, in which striking or dismissed workers try to dissuade others from using or working in the premises of the employer.

In the US, pickets are closely regulated. Violence and intimidation are beyond the protections of the First Amendment and are illegal. The Supreme Court has also held (1957) that picketing for the purpose of coercing employers as part of a union-organizing campaign is not protected as free speech.

Demosthenes *c.* 384–322 BC. Athenian orator and politician. From 351 BC he led the party that advocated resistance to the growing power of ⬦Philip of Macedon, and in his *Philippics* incited the Athenians to war. This policy resulted in the defeat of Chaeronea 338, and the establishment of Macedonian supremacy. After the death of Alexander he organized a revolt; when it failed, he took poison to avoid capture by the Macedonians.

Demotic Greek common or vernacular variety of the modern ⬦Greek language.

demotic script cursive (joined) writing derived from Egyptian hieratic script, itself a cursive form of ⬦hieroglyphic. Demotic documents are known from the 6th century BC to about AD 470. It was written horizontally, from right to left.

Dempsey Jack (William Harrison) 1895–1983. US heavyweight boxing champion, nicknamed "the Manassa Mauler." He beat Jess Willard 1919 to win the title and held it until 1926, when he lost it to Gene Tunney. He engaged in the "Battle of the Long Count" with Tunney 1927.

denaturation irreversible changes occurring in the structure of proteins such as enzymes, usually caused by changes in pH or temperature. An example is the heating of egg albumen resulting in solid egg white.

The enzymes associated with digestion and metabolism become inactive if given abnormal conditions. Heat will damage their complex structure so that the usual interactions between enzyme and substrate can no longer occur.

dendrite part of a ⬦nerve cell or neuron. The dendrites are slender filaments projecting from the cell body. They receive incoming messages from many other nerve cells and pass them on to the cell body. If the combined effect of these messages is strong enough, the cell body will send an electrical impulse along the axon (the threadlike extension of a nerve cell). The tip of the axon passes its message to the dendrites of other nerve cells.

dendrochronology analysis of the ⬦annual rings of trees to date past events. Samples of wood are obtained by means of a narrow metal tube that is driven into a tree to remove a core extending from the bark to the center. Samples taken from timbers at an archeological site can be compared with a master core on file for that region or by taking cores from old, living trees; the year when they were felled can be determined by locating the point where the rings of the two samples correspond and counting back from the present.

Since annual rings are formed by variations in the water-conducting cells produced by the plant during different seasons of the year, they also provide a means of determining past climatic conditions in a given area (the rings are thin in dry years, thick in moist ones). In North America, sequences of tree rings extending back over 8,000 years have been obtained for the SW and N Mexico by using cores from the bristle-cone pine *Pinus aristata*, which can live for over 4,000 years in that region. Also, the dryness of the area has preserved wood in SW archeological sites; in wet temperate regions the soil acidity usually absorbs wood, so this dating technique cannot be used.

Dene term used in Canada since the 1970s to describe the Native Americans (Athabaskan Indians) in the Northwest Territories. The official body representing them is called the Dene Nation.

Deneb or *Alpha Cygni* brightest star in the constellation Cygnus, and the 19th brightest star in the sky. It is one of the greatest supergiant stars known, with a true luminosity of about 60,000 times that of the Sun. Deneb is about 1,800 light-years from Earth.

Deneuve Catherine 1943– . French actress acclaimed for her poise and her performance in Roman Polanski's film *Repulsion* 1965. She also appeared in *Les Parapluies de Cherbourg/ Umbrellas of Cherbourg* 1964 (with her sister Françoise Dorléac (1942–1967)), *Belle de jour* 1967, *Hustle* 1975, *Le Dernier métro/The Last Metro* 1980 and *The Hunger* 1983.

dengue tropical viral fever transmitted by mosquitoes and accompanied by joint pains, a rash, and glandular swelling. The incubation time is a week and the fever also lasts about a week. A more virulent form, dengue haemorrhagic fever, is thought to be caused by a second infection on top of the first, and causes internal bleeding.

Deng Xiaoping or *Teng Hsiao-ping* 1904– . Chinese political leader. A member of the Chinese Communist Party (CCP) from the 1920s, he took part in the Long March 1934–36. He was in the Politburo from 1955 until ousted in the Cultural Revolution 1966–69. Reinstated in the 1970s, he gradually took power and introduced a radical economic modernization program. He retired from the Politburo 1987 and from his last official position (as chair of State Military Commission) March 1990, but remained influential behind the scenes.

Deng, born in Sichuan province into a middle-class landlord family, joined the CCP as a student in Paris, where he adopted the name Xiaoping ("Little Peace") 1925, and studied in Moscow 1926. After the Long March, he served as a political commissar to the People's Liberation Army during the civil war of 1937–49. He entered the CCP Politburo 1955 and headed the secretariat during the early 1960s, working closely with President Liu Shaoqi. During the Cultural Revolution Deng was dismissed as a "capitalist roader" and sent to work in a tractor factory in Nanchang for "re-education."

Deng was rehabilitated by his patron Zhou Enlai 1973 and served as acting prime minister after Zhou's heart attack 1974. On Zhou's death Jan 1976 he was forced into hiding but returned to office as vice premier July 1977. By Dec 1978, although nominally a CCP vice chair, state vice premier, and Chief of Staff to the PLA, Deng was the controlling force in China. His policy of "socialism with Chinese characteristics," misinterpreted in the West as a drift to capitalism, had success in rural areas. He helped to oust ⬦Hua Guofeng in favor of his protégés ⬦Hu Yaobang (later in turn ousted) and ⬦Zhao Ziyang.

When Deng officially retired from his party and army posts, he claimed to have renounced political involvement. His reputation, both at home and in the West, was tarnished by his sanctioning of the army's massacre of more than 2,000 prodemocracy demonstrators in Tiananmen Square, Beijing, in June 1989.

denier unit used in measuring the fineness of yarns, equal to the mass in grams of 9,000 meters of yarn. Thus 9,000 meters of 15 denier nylon, used in nylon stockings, weighs 0.5 oz/ 15 g, and in this case the thickness of thread would be 0.0017 in/0.00425 mm. The term is derived from the French silk industry; the *denier* was an old French silver coin.

In the US and Canada a unit called the drex, equal to the mass of 10,000 meters is used. The tex, equal to the mass of 1,000 meters, is the most common unit in the textile industry.

Denikin Anton Ivanovich 1872–1947. Russian general. He distinguished himself in the

Denmark
Kingdom of (*Kongeriget Danmark*)

area 16,627 sq mi/43,075 sq km
capital Copenhagen
cities Aarhus, Odense, Aalborg, Esbjerg, all ports
physical comprises the Jutland peninsula and about 500 islands (100 inhabited) including the island of Bornholm in the Baltic Sea; the land is flat and cultivated; sand dunes and lagoons on the W coast and long inlets (fjords) on the E; the main island is Sjælland (Zealand), where most of Copenhagen is located (the rest of it is on the island of Amager)
territories the dependencies of Faeroe Islands and Greenland
features Kronborg Castle in Helsingør (Elsinore); Tivoli Gardens (Copenhagen); Legoland Park in Sillund
head of state Queen Margrethe II from 1972
head of government Poul Schlüter from 1982
political system liberal democracy
political parties Social Democrats (SD), left of center; Conservative People's Party

(KF), moderate center-right; Liberal Party (V), center-left; Socialist People's Party (SF), moderate left-wing; Radical Liberals (RV), radical internationalist, left of center; Center Democrats (CD), moderate centrist; Progress Party (FP), radical antibureaucratic; Christian People's Party (KrF), interdenominational, family values; Left Socialists
exports bacon, dairy produce, eggs, fish, mink pelts, car and aircraft parts, electrical equipment, textiles, chemicals
currency kroner
population (1990 est) 5,134,000; growth rate 0% p.a.
life expectancy men 72, women 78
languages Danish (official); there is a German-speaking minority
religion Lutheran 97%
literacy 99% (1983)
GDP $85.5 bn (1987); $16,673 per head
chronology
1940–45 Occupied by Germany.
1945 Iceland's independence recognized.
1947 Frederik IX succeeded Christian X.
1948 Home rule granted for Faeroe Islands.
1949 Became a founding member of NATO.
1960 Joined European Free Trade Association (EFTA).
1972 Margrethe II became Denmark's first queen in nearly 600 years.
1973 Left EFTA and joined European Economic Community (EEC).
1979 Home rule granted for Greenland.
1985 Strong non-nuclear movement in evidence.
1990 General election; another coalition government formed.
1992 Rejection of Maastricht Treaty in national referendum; government requested modifications prior to second referendum, planned for 1993.

⟡Russo-Japanese War 1904–05 and World War I. After the outbreak of the Bolshevik Revolution 1917 he organized a volunteer army of 60,000 Whites (loyalists) but was routed 1919 and escaped to France. He wrote a history of the Revolution and the Civil War.

De Niro Robert 1943– . US actor. He won Oscars for his performances in *The Godfather Part II* 1974 and *Raging Bull* 1979, for which role he put on weight in the interests of authenticity as the boxer gone to seed, Jake LaMotta. His other films include *Mean Streets* 1973, *Taxi Driver* 1976, *The Deer Hunter* 1978, *The Untouchables* 1987, *Midnight Run* 1988, and *Cape Fear* 1992. He showed his versatility in *The King of Comedy* 1982 and other Martin Scorsese vehicles.

Denison city in NE Texas, near the Red River and the Oklahoma border, N of Dallas. A distribution center for grain and dairy products, its industries include textiles, wood products, and food processing; population (1990) 21,500.

Denis, St 3rd century AD. First bishop of Paris and one of the patron saints of France who was martyred by the Romans. Feast day Oct 9.

denitrification process occurring naturally in soil, where bacteria break down ⟡nitrates to give nitrogen gas, which returns to the atmosphere.

Denktaş Rauf R 1924– . Turkish-Cypriot nationalist politician. In 1975 the Turkish Federated State of Cyprus (TFSC) was formed in the northern third of the island, with Denktaş as its head, and in 1983 he became president of

the breakaway Turkish Republic of Northern Cyprus (TRNC).

Denmark peninsula and islands in N Europe, bounded N by the Skagerrak, E by the Kattegat, S by Germany, and W by the North Sea.
government Under the 1849 constitution (last revised 1953) there is a hereditary monarch with no personal political power and a single-chamber parliament, the Folketing. The prime minister and cabinet are drawn from and responsible to the Folketing, which has 179 members elected by adult franchise—175 representing metropolitan Denmark, two for the Faroe Islands, and two for Greenland. Voting is by proportional representation; the Folketing has a life of four years but may be dissolved within this period if the government is defeated on a vote of confidence. The government need only resign on what it itself defines as a "vital element" of policy.
history The original home of the Danes was Sweden, and they migrated in the 5th and 6th centuries. Ruled by local chieftains, they terrified Europe by their piratical raids during the 8th–10th centuries, until Harald Bluetooth (c. 940–985) unified Denmark and established Christianity. King Canute (ruled 1014–35) founded an empire embracing Denmark, England, and Norway, which fell apart at his death. After a century of confusion Denmark again dominated the Baltic under Valdemar I, Canute VI, and Valdemar II (1157–1241). Domestic conflict then produced anarchy, until

Valdemar IV (1340–1375) restored order. Denmark, Norway, and Sweden were united under one sovereign 1397.
loss of Sweden Sweden broke away 1449 and after a long struggle had its independence recognized 1523. Christian I (1448–1481) secured the duchies of Schleswig and Holstein, fiefs of the Holy Roman Empire, in 1460, and they were held by his descendants until 1863. Christian II (ruled 1513–23) was deposed in favor of his uncle Frederick, whose son Christian III (ruled 1534–59) made Lutheranism the established religion 1536. Attempts to regain Sweden led to disastrous wars with that country 1563–70, 1643–45, and 1657–60; equally disastrous was Christian V's intervention, 1625–29, on the Protestant side of the ⟡Thirty Years' War.
policy of neutrality Frederick III (ruled 1648–70) made himself absolute monarch 1665 and ruled through a burgher bureaucracy. Serfdom was abolished 1788. Denmark's adherence 1780 to armed neutrality against Britain resulted in the naval defeat of Copenhagen 1801, and in 1807 the British bombarded Copenhagen and seized the Danish fleet to keep it from the expansionist French emperor Napoleon. This incident drove Denmark into the arms of France, and the Allies at the Congress of ⟡Vienna took Norway from Denmark and gave it to Sweden 1815. A liberal movement then arose that in 1848–49 compelled Frederick VII (ruled 1848–63) to grant a democratic constitution. The Germans in Schleswig-Holstein revolted with Prussian support 1848–50, and Prussia seized the provinces 1864 after a short war. North Schleswig was recovered after a plebiscite 1920.

Neutral in World War I, Denmark tried to preserve its neutrality 1939 by signing a pact with Hitler, but was occupied by Germany 1940–45. Although traditionally neutral, Denmark joined the North Atlantic Treaty Organization (⟡NATO) 1949 and the ⟡European Free Trade Association (EFTA) 1960 but resigned 1973 to join the European Economic Community (EEC). ⟡Iceland was part of the Danish kingdom until 1945 and the other parts of nonmetropolitan Denmark, the Faroe Islands and Greenland, were given special recognition by a constitution that has been adapted to meet changing circumstances. In 1953 provision was made for a daughter to succeed to the throne in the absence of a male heir, and a system of voting by proportional representation was introduced.

Left-wing policies have dominated Danish politics, and proportional representation (often resulting in minority or coalition governments) has encouraged a moderate approach. In the Dec 1990 general election, the Social Democrats received 37.4% of the vote, the Conservatives 16%, the Liberals 15.8%, Socialist People's Party 8.3%, Progress Party 6.4%. Poul Schlüter continued as prime minister. In a referendum 1992 on European Community policies, the Danish people rejected the Maastricht Treaty, triggering referendums and debates elsewhere in the EC. The Danish government subsequently proposed modifications (codicils) to the treaty prior to a second referendum, planned for 1993. *See illustration box.*

Dennis et al v US a US Supreme Court decision 1951 dealing with the power of Congress to suppress certain political activities by revoking First Amendment rights. The case was brought by Dennis, a Communist Party official, and others to test the Smith Act 1940, which outlawed advocacy of the violent overthrow of the government. The Court upheld the Smith Act, implicitly returning to the "bad tendency" doctrine by defining any teaching that suggests the overthrow of the government as a clear and present danger to society. This definition gave Congress the right to restrict speech and assembly of anyone affiliated with the Communist Party.

Denpasar capital town of Bali in the Lesser Sunda Islands of Indonesia; population (1980) 88,100.

density measure of the compactness of a substance; it is equal to its mass per unit volume and is measured in lb per cubic foot/kg per cubic meter. Density is a ⬦scalar quantity. The density D of a mass m occupying a volume V is given by the formula:

$D = m/V$.

⬦Relative density is the ratio of the density of a substance to that of water at 4°C.

In photography, density refers to the degree of opacity of a negative; in population studies, it is the quantity or number per unit of area; in electricity, current density is the amount of current passing through a cross-sectional area of a conductor in a given amount of time (usually given in amperes per sq in or per sq cm).

dental formula way of showing what an animal's teeth are like. The dental formula consists of eight numbers separated by a line into two rows. The four above the line represent the teeth in one side of the upper jaw, starting at the front. If this reads 2 1 2 3 (as for humans) it means two incisors, one canine, two premolars, and three molars (see ⬦tooth). The numbers below the line represent the lower jaw. The total number of teeth can be calculated by adding up all the numbers and multiplying by two.

dentistry care and treatment of the teeth and gums. **Orthodontics** deals with the straightening of the teeth for aesthetic and clinical reasons, and **periodontics** with care of the supporting tissue (bone and gums).

The bacteria that start the process of dental decay are normal, nonpathogenic members of a large and varied group of microorganisms present in the mouth. They are strains of oral streptococci, and it is only in the presence of sucrose (from refined sugar) in the mouth that they become damaging to the teeth. ⬦Fluoride in the water supply has been one attempted solution, and in 1979 a vaccine was developed from a modified form of the bacterium *Streptococcus mutans*.

The earliest dental school was opened in Baltimore, Maryland, 1839. An International Dental Federation was founded 1900.

dentition type and number of teeth in a species. Different kinds of teeth have different functions; a grass-eating animal will have large molars for grinding its food, whereas a meat-eater will need powerful canines for catching and killing its prey. The teeth that are less useful may be reduced in size or missing altogether. An animal's dentition is represented diagramatically by a ⬦dental formula.

denudation natural loss of soil and rock debris, blown away by wind or washed away by running water, that lays bare the rock below. Over millions of years, denudation causes a general lowering of the landscape.

The landscape is constantly being lifted by ⬦plate tectonic activity and leveled by weathering and erosion. For example, the Himalayas are being formed by the collision between two plates, yet they are being constantly denuded by glacial erosion and frost shattering. As a result, overall uplift is not as great as it might be.

Denver city and capital of Colorado, on the South Platte River, near the foothills of the Rocky Mountains; population (1990) 467,600, Denver–Boulder metropolitan area 1,848,300. It is a processing and distribution center for a large agricultural area and for natural resources (minerals, oil, gas). It was the center of a gold and silver boom in the 1870s and 1880s, and for oil in the 1970s.

Denver was founded 1858 with the discovery of gold, becoming a mining-camp supply center; coal is also mined nearby. There is a university, a mining school, many medical institutions, and a branch of the US mint.

deodar Himalayan ⬦cedar tree *Cedrus deodara*, often planted as a rapid-growing ornamental. It has fragrant, durable wood, valuable as timber.

deontology ethical theory that the rightness of an action consists in its conformity to duty, regardless of the consequences that may result from it. Deontological ethics is thus opposed to any form of utilitarianism or pragmatism.

deoxyribonucleic acid full name of ⬦DNA.

De Palma Brian 1941– . US film director, especially of thrillers. His technical mastery and enthusiasm for spilling blood are shown in films such as *Sisters* 1973, *Carrie* 1976, and *The Untouchables* 1987.

Depardieu Gérard 1948– . French actor renowned for his imposing physique and screen presence. His films include *Deux hommes dans la ville* 1973, *Le camion* 1977, *Mon oncle d'Amérique* 1980, *The Moon in the Gutter* 1983, *Jean de Florette* 1985, *Cyrano de Bergerac* 1990. His English-speaking films include the US romantic comedy *Green Card* 1990 and *1492– Conquest of Paradise* 1992.

depilatory any instrument or substance used to remove growing hair, usually for cosmetic reasons. Permanent eradication is by electrolysis, the destruction of each individual hair root by an electrolytic needle or an electrocautery, but there is a danger of some regrowth as well as scarring.

depreciation in economics, the decline of a currency's value in relation to other currencies. Depreciation also describes the fall in value of an asset (such as factory machinery) resulting from age, wear and tear, or other circumstances. It is an important factor in assessing company profits and tax liabilities.

depression in economics, a period of exceptionally low output and investment, with high unemployment. Specifically, the term describes two periods of crisis in world economy 1873–96 and 1929–39, also known as panics.

The term is most often used to refer to the world economic crisis precipitated by the Wall Street crash of Oct 29, 1929, when millions of (inflated and margined) dollars were wiped off US stock values by panic selling in a matter of hours. This forced the closure of many US banks whose reserves were involved in stock speculation and led to the recall of US overseas investments. This loss of US credit had serious repercussions on the European economy, especially that of Germany (still recovering from World War I), and led to a steep fall in the levels of international trade as countries attempted to protect their own economies.

Despite unprecedented federal government intervention under President Franklin D Roosevelt's New Deal, the economy began a real recovery only after the rearmament programs of the late 1930s and 1940s boosted employment and output.

depression or *cyclone* or *low* in meteorology, a region of low atmospheric pressure. A depression forms as warm, moist air from the tropics mixes with cold, dry polar air, producing warm and cold boundaries (⬦fronts) and unstable weather—low cloud and drizzle, showers, or fierce storms. The warm air, being less dense, rises above the cold air to produce the area of low pressure on the ground. Air spirals in toward the center of the depression in a counterclockwise direction in the northern hemisphere, clockwise in the southern hemisphere, generating winds up to gale force. Depressions tend to travel eastward and can remain active for several days.

A deep depression is one in which the pressure at the center is very much lower than that round about; it produces very strong winds, as opposed to a shallow depression in which the winds are comparatively light. A severe depression in the tropics is called a ⬦hurricane, tropical cyclone, or typhoon, and is a great danger to shipping; a ⬦tornado is a very intense, rapidly swirling depression, with a diameter of only a few hundred feet or so.

depression emotional state characterized by sadness, unhappy thoughts, apathy, and dejection. Sadness is a normal response to major losses such as bereavement or unemployment. After childbirth, postnatal depression is common. However, clinical depression, which is prolonged or unduly severe, often requires treatment, such as antidepressant medication, ⬦cognitive therapy, or, in very rare cases, electroconvulsive therapy (ECT), in which an electrical current is passed through the brain.

Periods of depression may alternate with periods of high optimism, over-enthusiasm, and confidence. This is the manic phase in a disorder known as **manic depression** or **bipolar disorder**. A manic depressive state is one in which a person switches repeatedly from one extreme to the other. Each mood can last for weeks or for months. Typically, the depressive state lasts longer than the manic phase.

De Quincey Thomas 1785–1859. English author whose works include *Confessions of an English Opium-Eater* 1821 and the essays "On the Knocking at the Gate in Macbeth" 1823 and "On Murder Considered as One of the Fine Arts" 1827. He was a friend of the poets Wordsworth and Coleridge.

Born in Manchester, De Quincey ran away from school there to wander and study in Wales. He then went to London, where he lived in extreme poverty but with the constant companionship of the young orphan Ann, of whom he writes in the *Confessions*. In 1803 he was reconciled to his guardians and was sent to university at Oxford, where his opium habit began. In 1809 he settled with the Wordsworths and Coleridge in the Lake District. He moved to Edinburgh 1828, where he eventually died. De Quincey's work had a powerful influence on Charles ⬦Baudelaire and Edgar Allan ⬦Poe among others.

Derain André 1880–1954. French painter. He experimented with the strong, almost primary colors associated with ⬦Fauvism but later developed a more somber landscape style. His work includes costumes and scenery for Diaghilev's Ballets Russes.

Derby Edward (George Geoffrey Smith) Stanley, 14th Earl of Derby 1799–1869. British politician, prime minister 1852, 1858–59, and 1866–68. Originally a Whig, he became secretary for the colonies 1830, and introduced the bill for the abolition of slavery. He joined the Tories 1834, and the split in the Tory Party over Robert Peel's free-trade policy gave Derby the leadership for 20 years.

Derbyshire county in N central England
area 1,015 sq mi/2,630 sq km
cities Matlock (administrative headquarters), Derby, Chesterfield, Ilkeston
features Peak District National Park (including Kinder Scout 2,088 ft/636 m); rivers: Derwent, Dove, Rother, Trent; Chatsworth House, Bakewell (seat of Duke of Devonshire); Haddon Hall
products cereals; dairy and sheep farming.

deregulation action to abolish or reduce government controls and supervision over private economic activities, as with the deregulation of the US airline industry 1978. Its purpose is to improve competition. Increased competition had the effect, in some areas, of driving smaller companies out of business. A tremendous increase in mergers, acquisitions, and bankruptcies followed deregulation as the stronger companies consumed the weaker. A wider array of services and lower prices in some industries also have resulted; see also ⟡monetarism; ⟡privatization.

derivative or *differential coefficient* in mathematics, the limit of the gradient of a chord linking two points on a curve as the distance between the points tends to zero; for a function with a single variable, $y = f(x)$, it is denoted by $f'(x)$, $Df(x)$, or dy/dx, and is equal to the gradient of the curve.

dermatitis inflammation of the skin (see ⟡eczema), usually related to allergy. *Dermatosis* refers to any skin disorder and may be caused by contact or systemic problems.

dermatology science of the skin, its nature and diseases. It is a rapidly expanding field due to the proliferation of industrial chemicals affecting workers, and the universal use of household cleaners, cosmetics, and sun screens.

derrick simple lifting machine consisting of a pole carrying a block and tackle. Derricks are commonly used on ships that carry freight. In the oil industry the tower used for hoisting the drill pipes is known as a derrick.

derris climbing plant of SE Asia *Derris elliptica* of the legume family Fabaceae. Its roots contain rotenone, a strong insecticide.

Derry county of Northern Ireland
area 799 sq mi/2,070 sq km
cities Derry (county town, formerly Londonderry), Coleraine, Portstewart
features rivers Foyle, Bann, and Roe; borders Lough Neagh
products mainly agricultural, but farming is hindered by the very heavy rainfall; flax, cattle, sheep, food processing, textiles, light engineering
population (1981) 187,000
famous people Joyce Cary.

dervish in Iran and Turkey, a religious mendicant; throughout the rest of Islam a member of an Islamic religious brotherhood, not necessarily mendicant in character. The Arabic equivalent is **fakir**. There are various orders of dervishes, each with its rule and special ritual.

The "whirling dervishes" claim close communion with the deity through ecstatic dancing; the "howling dervishes" gash themselves with knives to demonstrate the miraculous feats possible to those who trust in Allah.

Desai Morarji 1896– . Indian politician. An early follower of Mahatma Gandhi, he was prime minister 1977–79, as leader of the ⟡Janata party, after toppling Indira Gandhi. Party infighting led to his resignation of both the premiership and the party leadership.

desalination removal of salt, usually from sea water, to produce fresh water for irrigation or drinking. Distillation has usually been the method adopted, but in the 1970s a cheaper process, using certain polymer materials that filter the molecules of salt from the water by reverse osmosis, was developed.

Desalination plants occur along the shores of the Middle East where fresh water is in short supply.

Descartes René 1596–1650. French philosopher and mathematician. He believed that commonly accepted knowledge was doubtful because of the subjective nature of the senses, and attempted to rebuild human knowledge using as his foundation *cogito ergo sum* ("I think, therefore I am"). He also believed that the entire material universe could be explained in terms of mathematical physics, and founded coordinate geometry as a way of defining and manipulating geometrical shapes by means of algebraic expressions. ⟡Cartesian coordinates, the means by which points are represented in this system, are named after him. Descartes also established the science of optics, and helped to shape contemporary theories of astronomy and animal behavior.

Born near Tours, Descartes served in the army of Prince Maurice of Orange, and in 1619, while traveling through Europe, decided to apply the methods of mathematics to metaphysics and science. He settled in the Netherlands 1628, where he was more likely to be free from interference by the ecclesiastical authorities. In 1649 he visited the court of Queen Christina of Sweden, and shortly thereafter he died in Stockholm.

His works include *Discourse on Method* 1637, *Meditations on the First Philosophy* 1641, and *Principles of Philosophy* 1644, and numerous books on physiology, optics, and geometry.

Descartes identified the "thinking thing" (*res cogitans*) or mind with the human soul or consciousness; the body, though somehow interacting with the soul, was a physical machine, secondary to, and in principle separable from, the soul. He held that everything has a cause; nothing can result from nothing. He believed that, although all matter is in motion, matter does not move of its own accord; the initial impulse comes from God. He also postulated two quite distinct substances —spatial substance, or matter, and thinking substance, or mind. This is called "Cartesian dualism," and it preserved him from serious controversy with the church.

Deschamps Eustache 1346–1406. French poet, born in Champagne. He was the author of more than 1,000 ballades, and the *Miroir de mariage/The Mirror of Marriage*, an attack on women.

desert arid area without sufficient rainfall and, consequently, vegetation to support human life. The term includes the ice areas of the polar regions (known as cold deserts). Almost 33% of Earth's land surface is desert, and this proportion is increasing.

The *tropical desert* belts of latitudes from 5° to 30° are caused by the descent of air that is heated over the warm land and therefore has lost its moisture. Other natural desert types are the *continental deserts*, such as the Gobi, that are too far from the sea to receive any moisture; *rain-shadow deserts*, such as California's Death Valley, that lie in the lee of mountain ranges, where the ascending air drops its rain only on the windward slopes; and *coastal deserts*, such as the Namib, where cold ocean currents cause local dry air masses to descend. Desert surfaces are usually rocky or gravelly, with only a small proportion being covered with sand. Deserts can be created by changes in climate, or by the human-aided process of desertification.

Desert Storm, Operation code name of the military action to eject the Iraqi army from Kuwait 1991. The buildup phase was code named *Operation Desert Shield* and lasted from Aug 1990, when Kuwait was first invaded by Iraq, to Jan 1991 when Operation Desert Storm was unleashed, starting the ⟡Gulf War. Desert Storm ended with the defeat of the Iraqi army in the Kuwaiti theater of operations late Feb 1991. The cost of the operation was $53 billion.

De Sica Vittorio 1901–1974. Italian director and actor. He won his first Oscar with *Bicycle Thieves* 1948, a film of subtle realism. Later films included *Umberto D* 1952, *Two Women* 1960, and *The Garden of the Finzi-Continis* 1971. His considerable acting credits include *Madame de ...* 1953 and *The Millionaires* 1960.

He was born in Sora, Caserta. He won four Oscars for best foreign film with *Shoeshine* 1946, *Bicycle Thieves, Yesterday Today and Tomorrow* 1964, and *The Garden of the Finzi-Continis*.

desiccator airtight vessel, traditionally made of glass, in which materials may be stored either to dry them or to prevent them, once dried, from reabsorbing moisture.

The base of the desiccator is a chamber in which is placed a substance with a strong affinity for water (such as calcium chloride or silica gel), which removes water vapor from the desiccator atmosphere and from substances placed in it.

desktop publishing (DTP) use of microcomputers for small-scale typesetting and page makeup. DTP systems are capable of producing camera-ready pages (pages ready for photographing and printing), made up of text and graphics, with text set in different typefaces and sizes. The page can be previewed on the screen before final printing on a laser printer.

Des Moines capital and largest town in Iowa, on the Des Moines River, a tributary of the Mississippi; population (1990) 193,200. It is a major road, railroad, and air center. Industries include printing, banking, insurance, and food processing.

Drake University is here. The Des Moines Art Center was designed by Eliel Saarinen. Incorporated 1851, Des Moines became the state capital 1857.

Desmoulins Camille 1760–1794. French revolutionary who summoned the mob to arms on July 12, 1789, so precipitating the revolt that culminated in the storming of the Bastille. A prominent left-wing ⟡Jacobin, he was elected to the National Convention 1792. His *Histoire des Brissotins* was largely responsible for the overthrow of the right-wing ⟢Girondins, but shortly after he was sent to the guillotine as too moderate.

de Soto Hernando *c.* 1496–1542. Spanish explorer who sailed with d'Avila (*c.* 1400–1531) to Darien, Central America, 1519, explored the Yucatán Peninsula 1528, and traveled with Francisco Pizarro in Peru 1530–35. In 1538 he was made governor of Cuba and Florida. In his expedition of 1539, he explored Florida, Georgia, and the Mississippi River.

Emperor Charles V appointed de Soto governor of Florida in 1537. His expeditions may have penetrated Missouri and Louisiana. Upon his death on May 21, 1542, his companions buried his body in a river to preserve the local Indians' belief that de Soto had descended from heaven.

Desprez Josquin Franco-Flemish composer; see ⟢Josquin Desprez.

Dessalines Jean Jacques *c.* 1758–1806. Emperor of Haiti 1804–06. Born in Guinea, he was taken to Haiti as a slave, where in 1802 he succeeded ⟢Toussaint L'Ouverture as leader of the black revolt against the French. After defeating the French, he proclaimed Haiti's independence and made himself emperor. He was killed when trying to suppress an uprising provoked by his cruelty.

Dessau Paul 1894–1979. German composer. His work includes incidental music to Bertolt Brecht's theater pieces; an opera, *Der Verurteilung des Lukullus* 1949, also to a libretto by Brecht; and numerous choral works and songs.

He studied in Berlin, becoming a theater conductor until moving to Paris 1933, where he studied Schoenberg's serial method with René Leibowitz. He collaborated with Brecht from 1942, when they met as political exiles in the US, returning with him to East Berlin 1948.

destroyer small, fast warship designed for antisubmarine work. Destroyers played a critical role in the convoy system in World War II.

Modern destroyers often carry guided missiles and displace 3,700–5,650 tons.

destructive margin in plate tectonics, a region on the Earth's crust in which two plates are moving toward one another. Usually one plate (the denser of the two) is forced to dive below the other into what is called the **subduction zone**. The descending plate melts to form a body of magma, which may then rise to the surface through cracks and faults to form volcanoes. If the two plates consist of more buoyant continental crust, subduction does not occur. Instead, the crust crumples gradually to form fold mountains, such as the Himalayas.

detective fiction novel or short story in which a mystery is solved mainly by the action of a professional or amateur detective. Where the mystery to be solved concerns a crime, the work may be called **crime fiction**. The earliest work of detective fiction as understood today was *Murders in the Rue Morgue* 1841 by Edgar Allan Poe, and his detective Dupin became the model for those who solved crimes by deduction from a series of clues. A popular deductive sleuth was Sherlock Holmes in the stories by Arthur Conan Doyle.

The "golden age" of the genre was the period from the 1920s to the 1940s, when the leading writers were women—Agatha Christie, Margery Allingham, and Dorothy L Sayers. Types of detective fiction include the **police**

procedural, where the mystery is solved by detailed police work, as in the work of Swedish writers Maj Sjowall and Per Wahloo; the **inverted novel**, where the identity of the criminal is known from the beginning and only the method or the motive remains to be discovered, as in *Malice Aforethought* by Francis Iles; and the **hard-boiled school** of private investigators begun by Raymond Chandler and Dashiell Hammett, which became known for its social realism and explicit violence. More recently, the form and traditions of the genre have been used as a framework within which to explore other concerns, as in *Innocent Blood* and *A Taste for Death* by P D James, *The Name of the Rose* by Umberto Eco, and the works of many women writers who explore feminist ideas, as in *Murder in the Collective* by Barbara Wilson.

Like most genres, crime fiction has produced its oddities. *Murder in Pastiche* by Marion Mainwaring is written in the styles of nine famous writers. Agatha Christie, Georgette Heyer, and Ellis Peters have all written detective novels with historical settings. *Murder Off Miami* by Dennis Wheatley was a dossier containing real clues such as photographs, ticket stubs, and hairpins for the reader to use in solving the mystery; the solution was in a closed envelope at the back of the book.

détente (French) reduction of political tension and the easing of strained relations between nations, for example, the ending of the Cold War 1989–90, although it was first used in the 1970s to describe the easing East–West relations, trade agreements, and cultural exchanges.

detergent surface-active cleansing agent. The common detergents are made from ⟢fats (hydrocarbons) and sulfuric acid, and their long-chain molecules have a type of structure similar to that of ⟢soap molecules: a salt group at one end attached to a long hydrocarbon "tail." They have the advantage over soap in that they do not produce scum by forming insoluble salts with the calcium and magnesium ions present in hard water.

To remove dirt, which is generally attached to materials by means of oil or grease, the hydrocarbon "tails" (soluble in oil or grease) penetrate the oil or grease drops, while the "heads" (soluble in water but insoluble in grease) remain in the water and, being salts, become ionized. Consequently the oil drops become negatively charged and tend to repel one another; thus they remain in suspension and are washed away with the dirt.

Detergents were first developed from coal tar in Germany during World War I, and synthetic organic detergents came into increasing use after World War II. Domestic powder detergents for use in hot water have alkyl benzene as their main base, and may also include bleaches and fluorescers as whiteners, perborates to free stain-removing oxygen, and water softeners. Environment-friendly detergents contain no phosphates or bleaches. Liquid detergents for washing dishes are based on epoxyethane (ethylene oxide). Cold-water detergents consist of a mixture of various alcohols, plus an ingredient for breaking down the surface tension of the water, so enabling the liquid to penetrate fibers and remove the dirt. When these surface-active agents (surfactants) escape the normal processing of sewage, they cause troublesome foam in rivers; phosphates in some detergents can also cause the excessive enrichment (⟢eutrophication) of rivers and lakes.

determinism in philosophy, the view that denies human freedom of action. Everything is strictly governed by the principle of cause and effect, and human action is no exception. It is the opposite of free will, and rules out moral choice and responsibility.

In antiquity, the theory of determinism was a feature of ⟢stoicism. In Christian theology, the Calvinist doctrine of predestination is deterministic. Quantum mechanics and the ⟢uncertainty principle lend support to free will.

deterrence underlying conception of the nuclear arms race: the belief that a potential aggressor will be discouraged from launching a "first strike" nuclear attack by the knowledge that the adversary is capable of inflicting "unacceptable damage" in a retaliatory strike. This doctrine is widely known as that of **mutual assured destruction (MAD)**. Three essential characteristics of deterrence are: the "capability to act," "credibility," and the "will to act."

de Tocqueville Alexis French politician; see ⟢Tocqueville, Alexis de.

detonator or **blasting cap** or **percussion cap** small explosive charge used to trigger off a main charge of high explosive. The relatively unstable compounds mercury fulminate and lead acid are often used in detonators, being set off by a lighted fuse or, more commonly, an electric current.

detritus in biology, the organic debris produced during the ⟢decomposition of animals and plants.

Detroit city in Michigan, situated on Detroit River; population (1990) 1,028,000, metropolitan area 4,665,200. It is an industrial center with the headquarters of Ford, Chrysler, and General Motors, hence its nickname, Motown (from "motor town"). Other manufactured products include metal products, machine tools, chemicals, office machines, and pharmaceuticals. Detroit is a port on the St Lawrence Seaway and the home of Wayne State University and its Medical Center complex. The University of Detroit and the Detroit Institute of Arts are also here.

Detroit was founded 1701 and is the oldest US city of any size west of the original colonies. It was captured from the French by the British 1760 and passed to the US 1796. In 1805 it was completely destroyed by fire but was soon rebuilt. The opening of the Erie Canal 1825 aided development. Detroit grew rapidly after the building of the first automobile factories, 1899–1903. A recent major development is the waterfront Renaissance Center complex.

There were significant race riots 1943 and 1967; a black mayor was elected 1973. During the 1960s and 1970s Detroit became associated with the "Motown Sound" of rock and soul music.

Detskoe Selo (Russian "children's village") former name (1917–37) of ⟢Pushkin, near St Petersburg, which was renamed after the Russian poet 1937.

Deucalion in Greek mythology, the son of ⟢Prometheus, and an equivalent of ⟢Noah in the Old Testament. Warned by his father of a coming flood, Deucalion and his wife Pyrrha built an ark. After the waters had subsided, the stones they were instructed by a god to throw over their shoulders became men and women.

deus ex machina (Latin "a god from a machine") far-fetched or unlikely event that resolves an intractable difficulty. The phrase was originally used in drama to indicate a god descending from heaven to resolve the plot.

deuterium naturally occurring heavy isotope of hydrogen, mass number 2 (one proton and one neutron), discovered by Harold Urey 1932. It is sometimes given the symbol D. In nature, about one in every 6,500 hydrogen atoms is deuterium. Combined with oxygen, it produces "heavy water" (D_2O), used in the nuclear industry.

deuteron nucleus of an atom of deuterium (heavy hydrogen). It consists of one proton and one neutron, and is used in the bombardment of chemical elements to synthesize other elements.

Deuteronomy book of the Old Testament; fifth book of the ⋄Torah. It contains various laws, including the laws for ⋄kosher and the ten commandments, and gives an account of the death of Moses.

de Valera Eámon 1882–1975. Irish nationalist politician, prime minister of the Irish Free State/Eire/Republic of Ireland 1932–48, 1951–54, and 1957–59, and president 1959–73. Repeatedly imprisoned, he participated in the Easter Rising 1916 and was leader of the nationalist ⋄Sinn Féin party 1917–26, when he formed the republican Fianna Fáil party; he directed negotiations with Britain 1921 but refused to accept the partition of Ireland until 1937.

He was sentenced to death for his part in the Easter Rising, but the sentence was commuted, and he was released under an amnesty 1917. He directed the negotiations of 1921 but refused to accept the ensuing treaty that divided Ireland into the Free State and the North.

Civil war followed. De Valera formed a new party, Fianna Fáil 1926, which secured a majority 1932. De Valera became prime minister and foreign minister of the Free State. Throughout World War II he maintained a strict neutrality, rejecting an offer by Churchill 1940 to recognize the principle of a united Ireland in return for Eire's entry into the war. He resigned after his defeat at the 1948 elections but was again prime minister in the 1950s and then president of the republic.

de Valois Ninette. Adopted name of Edris Stannus 1898– . Irish dancer, choreographer, and teacher. A pioneer of British national ballet, she worked with Sergei Diaghilev in Paris before opening a dance academy in London 1926. Collaborating with Lilian Baylis at the ⋄Old Vic, she founded the Vic-Wells Ballet 1931, which later became the Royal Ballet and Royal Ballet School. Among her works are *Job* 1931 and *Checkmate* 1937.

devaluation in economics, the lowering of the official value of a currency against other currencies, so that exports become cheaper and imports more expensive. Used when a country is badly in deficit in its balance of trade, it results in the goods the country produces being cheaper abroad, so that the economy is stimulated by increased foreign demand.

The increased cost of imported food, raw materials, and manufactured goods as a consequence of devaluation may, however, stimulate an acceleration in inflation, especially when commodities are rising in price because of increased world demand. *Revaluation* is the opposite process.

Devaluation of important currencies upsets

the balance of the world's money markets and encourages speculation. Significant devaluations include that of the German mark in the 1920s and Britain's devaluation of sterling in the 1960s. To promote greater stability, many countries have allowed the value of their currencies to "float," that is, to fluctuate in value.

developing in photography, the process that produces a visible image on exposed photographic film. Developing involves treating the emulsion with chemical developer, a reducing agent that changes the light-altered salts into dark metallic silver. The developed image is a negative: darkest where the strongest light hit the emulsion, lightest where the least light hit it.

development in the social sciences, the acquisition by a society of industrial techniques and technology; hence the common classification of the "developed" nations of the First and Second Worlds and the poorer, "developing" or "underdeveloped" nations of the Third World. The assumption that development in the sense of industrialization is inherently good has been increasingly questioned since the 1960s.

Many universities today have academic departments of *development studies* that address the theoretical questions involved in proposing practical solutions to the problems of development in the Third World.

deviance abnormal behavior; that is, behavior that deviates from the norms or the laws of a society or group, and so invokes social sanctions, controls, or stigma.

Deviance is a relative concept: what is considered deviant in some societies may be normal in others; in a particular society the same act (killing someone, for example) may be either normal or deviant depending on the circumstances (in wartime or for money, for example). Some sociologists, such as Howard Becker, argue that the reaction of others, rather than the act itself, is what determines whether an act is deviant, and that deviance is merely behavior other people so label.

devil in Jewish, Christian, and Muslim theology, the supreme spirit of evil (*Beelzebub, Lucifer, Iblis*), or an evil spirit generally.

The devil, or Satan, is mentioned only in the more recently written books of the Old Testament, but the later Jewish doctrine is that found in the New Testament. The concept of the devil passed into the early Christian church from Judaism, and theology until at least the time of St Anselm represented the Atonement as primarily the deliverance, through Christ's death, of mankind from the bondage of the devil. Jesus recognized as a reality the kingdom of evil, of which Satan or Beelzebub is the prince. In the Middle Ages the devil in popular superstition assumed the attributes of the horned fertility gods of paganism, and was regarded as the god of witches. The belief in a personal devil was strong during the Reformation, and the movement's leader Luther regarded himself as the object of a personal Satanic persecution. With the development of liberal Protestantism in the 19th century came a strong tendency to deny the existence of a positive spirit of evil, and to explain the devil as merely a personification. However, the traditional conception was never abandoned by the Roman Catholic church, and theologians, such as C S Lewis, have maintained the existence of a power of evil.

In Muslim theology, Iblis is one of the *jinn* (beings created by Allah from fire) who

refused to prostrate himself before Adam, and who tempted Adam and his wife Hawwa (Eve) to disobey Allah, an act which led to their expulsion from Paradise. He continues to try to lead people astray, but at the Last Judgment he and his hosts will be consigned to hell.

devil ray any of several large rays of the genera *Manta* and *Mobula*, fish in which two "horns" project forward from the sides of the huge mouth. These flaps of skin guide the plankton on which the fish feed into the mouth. The largest of these rays can be 23 ft/7 m across, and weigh 2,200 lb/1,000 kg. They live in warm seas.

Devil's Island (French *Ile du Diable*) smallest of the Iles du Salut, off French Guiana, 27 mi/43 km NW of Cayenne. The group of islands was collectively and popularly known by the name Devil's Island and formed a penal colony notorious for its terrible conditions.

Alfred ⋄Dreyfus was imprisoned here 1895–99. Political prisoners were held on Devil's Island, and dangerous criminals on St Joseph, where they were subdued by solitary confinement in tiny cells or subterranean cages. The largest island, Royale, now has a tracking station for the French rocket site at Kourou.

devil wind minor form of ⋄tornado, usually occurring in fine weather; formed from rising thermals of warm air (as is a ⋄cyclone). A fire creates a similar updraft.

A *fire devil* or *firestorm* may occur in oil-refinery fires, or in the firebombings of cities, for example Dresden, Germany, in World War II.

Devolution, War of war waged unsuccessfully 1667–68 by Louis XIV of France to gain Spanish territory in the Netherlands, of which ownership had allegedly "devolved" on his wife Maria Theresa.

During the course of the war the French marshal Turenne (1611–1675) conducted a series of sieges. An alliance of England, Sweden, and the Netherlands threatened intervention, so peace was made at Aix-la-Chapelle.

Devon or *Devonshire* county in SW England
area 2,594 sq mi/6,720 sq km
cities Exeter (administrative headquarters), Plymouth; resorts: Paignton, Torquay, Teignmouth, and Ilfracombe
features rivers: Dart, Exe, Tamar; National Parks: Dartmoor, Exmoor; Lundy bird sanctuary and marine nature preserve in the Bristol Channel
products mainly agricultural, with sheep and dairy farming; cider and clotted cream; kaolin in the S; Honiton lace; Dartington glass
population (1991) 1,008,300
famous people Francis Drake, John Hawkins, Charles Kingsley, Robert F Scott.

Devonian period of geological time 408–360 million years ago, the fourth period of the Paleozoic era. Many desert sandstones from North America and Europe date from this time. The first land plants flourished in the Devonian period, corals were abundant in the seas, amphibians evolved from air-breathing fish, and insects developed on land.

The name comes from the county of Devon in SW England, where Devonian rocks were first studied.

De Vries Hugo 1848–1935. Dutch botanist who conducted important research on osmosis in plant cells and was a pioneer in the study of plant evolution. His work led to the rediscovery of ⋄Mendel's laws and the discovery of spontaneously occurring ⋄mutations.

dew precipitation in the form of moisture that collects on the ground. It forms after the temperature of the ground has fallen below the ◊dew point of the air in contact with it. As the temperature falls during the night, the air and its water vapor become chilled, and condensation takes place on the cooled surfaces.

When moisture begins to form, the surrounding air is said to have reached its dew point. If the temperature falls below freezing point during the night, the dew will freeze, or if the temperature is low and the dew point is below freezing point, the water vapor condenses directly into ice; in both cases hoar frost is formed.

Dewar James 1842–1923. Scottish chemist and physicist who invented the ◊vacuum flask (Thermos) 1872 during his research into the properties of matter at extremely low temperatures.

de Wet Christiaan Rudolf 1854–1922. Boer general and politician. He served in the South African Wars 1880 and 1899. When World War I began, he headed a pro-German rising of 12,000 Afrikaners but was defeated, convicted of treason, and imprisoned. He was sentenced to six years' imprisonment for his part in the uprising, but was released 1915.

Dewey George 1837–1917. US naval officer. A specialist in naval administration, he was named chief of the Bureau of Equipment 1889 and of the Board of Inspection and Survey 1895. As commodore, Dewey was dispatched to the Pacific 1896. He destroyed the Spanish fleet in Manila harbor at the outbreak of the Spanish—American War 1898. Dewey was promoted to the rank of admiral of the navy (the highest naval rank ever awarded) 1899 and retired from active service 1900.

Born in Montpelier, Vermont, and educated at the US Naval Academy, Dewey saw action on the Mississippi River and in the blockade of Southern ports during the Civil War.

Dewey John 1859–1952. US philosopher who believed that the exigencies of a democratic and industrial society demanded new educational techniques. He expounded his ideas in numerous writings, including *School and Society* 1899, and founded a progressive school in Chicago. A pragmatist thinker, influenced by William James, Dewey maintained that there is only the reality of experience and made "inquiry" the essence of logic.

He was born in Vermont and from 1904 was professor of philosophy at Columbia University, New York.

Dewey Melvil 1851–1931. US librarian. In 1876, he devised the Dewey decimal system of classification for accessing, storing, and retrieving books, widely used in libraries. The system uses the numbers 000 to 999 to designate the major fields of knowledge, then breaks these down into more specific subjects by the use of decimals.

Dewey founded the American Library Association 1876 and the first school of library science, at Columbia University, 1887.

Dewey Thomas Edmund 1902–1971. US public official. He was Manhattan district attorney 1937–38 and served as governor of New York 1942–54. Dewey was twice the Republican presidential candidate, losing to F D Roosevelt 1944 and to Truman 1948, the latter race being one of the greatest electoral upsets in US history.

Born in Owosso, Michigan, Dewey received a law degree from Columbia University 1925. He was appointed chief assistant to the US attorney in the Southern District of New York 1931. He gained a reputation as a crime fighter while serving as special investigator of organized crime 1935–37.

dew point temperature at which the air becomes saturated with water vapor. At temperatures below the dew point, the water vapor condenses out of the air as droplets. If the droplets are large they become deposited on the ground as dew; if small they remain in suspension in the air and form mist or fog.

Dhaka or *Dacca* capital of Bangladesh from 1971, in Dhaka region, west of the river Meghna; population (1984) 3,600,000. It trades in jute, oilseed, sugar, and tea and produces textiles, chemicals, glass, and metal products. *history* A former French, Dutch, and English trading post, Dhaka became capital of East Pakistan 1947; it was handed over to Indian troops Dec 1971 to become capital of the new country of Bangladesh.

dharma (Sanskrit "justice, order") in Hinduism, the consciousness of forming part of an ordered universe, and hence the moral duty of accepting one's station in life. In Buddhism, dharma is anything that increases generosity and wisdom, and so leads toward enlightenment.

For Hindus, correct performance of dharma has a favorable effect on their ◊karma (fate); this may enable them to be reborn to a higher caste or on a higher plane of existence, thus coming closer to the final goal of liberation from the cycle of reincarnation.

Dhaulagiri mountain in the ◊Himalayas of W central Nepal, rising to 26,811 ft/8,172 m.

Dhofar mountainous western province of ◊Oman, on the border with Yemen; population (1982) 40,000. South Yemen supported guerrilla activity here in the 1970s, while Britain and Iran supported the government's military operations. The capital is Salalah, which has a port at Rasut.

dhole wild dog *Cuon alpinus* found in Asia from Siberia to Java. With head and body up to 3 ft/1 m long, variable in color but often reddish above and lighter below, the dhole lives in groups of from 3 to 30 individuals. The species is becoming rare and is protected in some areas.

Dholes can chase prey for long distances; a pack is capable of pulling down deer and cattle as well as smaller prey. They are even known to have attacked tigers and leopards.

diabase igneous rock formed below the Earth's surface, a form of basalt, containing relatively little silica (basic in composition).

Diabase is a medium-grained (hypabyssal) basalt and forms in minor intrusions, such as dykes which cut across the rock strata, and sills, which push between beds of sedimentary rock. When exposed at the surface, diabase weathers into spherical lumps.

diabetes disease *diabetes mellitus* in which a disorder of the islets of Langerhans in the ◊pancreas prevents the body producing the hormone ◊insulin, so that sugars cannot be used properly. Treatment is by strict dietary control and oral or injected insulin.

Sugar accumulates first in the blood, then in the urine. The patient experiences thirst, weight loss, and copious voiding, along with degenerative changes in the capillary system.

Without treatment, the patient may go blind, ulcerate, lapse into diabetic coma, and die. Early-onset diabetes tends to be more severe than that developing in later years. Before the discovery of insulin by Frederick ◊Banting and Charles ◊Best, severe diabetics did not survive. Today, it is seldom fatal. A continuous infusion of insulin can be provided via a catheter implanted under the skin, which is linked to an electric pump. This more accurately mimics the body's natural secretion of insulin than injections or oral doses, and can provide better control of diabetes. It is, however, very dangerous if the pump should malfunction.

Much rarer, *diabetes insipidus* is due to a deficiency of a hormone secreted by the ◊pituitary gland to regulate the body's water balance. It is controlled by hormone therapy. In 1989, it was estimated that 4% of the world's population had diabetes, and that there were 12 million sufferers in Canada and the US.

diagenesis or *lithification* in geology, the physical and chemical changes by which a sediment becomes a ◊sedimentary rock. The main processes involved include compaction of the grains, and the cementing of the grains together by the growth of new minerals deposited by percolating groundwater.

Diaghilev Sergei Pavlovich 1872–1929. Russian ballet impresario who in 1909 founded the Ballets Russes/Russian Ballet (headquarters in Monaco), which he directed for 20 years. Through this company he brought Russian ballet to the West, introducing and encouraging a dazzling array of dancers, choreographers, and composers, such as Anna Pavlova, Vaslav Nijinsky, Mikhail Fokine, Léonide Massine, George Balanchine, Igor Stravinsky, and Sergey Prokofiev.

dialect variation of a spoken language shared by those in a particular area or a particular social group or both. The term is used both objectively, to indicate a geographical area ("northern dialects") or social group ("black dialect"), and subjectively, in a judgmental and sometimes dismissive way.

In the latter case, the standard language of a community is not seen as a dialect itself, but as the proper form of that language, dialects being considered in some way corrupt. This is a matter of social attitude, not of linguistic study.

dialectic Greek term, originally associated with the philosopher Socrates' method of argument through dialogue and conversation. *Hegelian dialectic*, named after the German philosopher ◊Hegel, refers to an interpretive method in which the contradiction between a thesis and its antithesis is resolved through synthesis.

dialectical materialism political, philosophical, and economic theory of the 19th-century German thinkers Karl Marx and Friedrich Engels, also known as ◊Marxism.

Dial, The US magazine of transcendentalism 1840–44, founded in Boston by several of the transcendentalist group, including Margaret Fuller (1810–1850) and Ralph Waldo Emerson, its first and second editors respectively. Publishing Henry Thoreau and other major essayists and poets, it had great intellectual influence. Several later magazines used the same title. *The Dial* of the 1920s published modern poetry and criticism under Marianne Moore's editorship.

dialysis in medicine, the process used to mimic the effects of the kidneys. It may be life-saving in some types of poisoning. Dialysis is usually performed to compensate for failing kidneys; there are two main methods, haemodialysis and peritoneal dialysis.

In *haemodialysis*, the patient's blood is passed through a pump, where it is separated from sterile dialysis fluid by a semipermeable membrane. This allows any toxic substances which have built up in the bloodstream, and which would normally be secreted by the kidneys, to diffuse out of the blood into the dialysis fluid. The red and white blood cells, however, are maintained in the circulation by the membrane. Haemodialysis is very expensive and requires the patient to attend a specialized unit.

Peritoneal dialysis uses one of the body's natural semipermeable membranes for the same purpose. About two liters of dialysis fluid is slowly instilled into the peritoneal cavity of the abdomen, and drained out again, over about two hours. During that time toxins from the blood diffuse into the peritoneal cavity across the peritoneal membrane. The advantage of peritoneal dialysis is that the patient can walk around while the dialysis is proceeding—this is known as continuous ambulatory peritoneal dialysis (CAPD).

In the long term dialysis is expensive and debilitating, and ◊transplants are now the treatment of choice for patients in chronic kidney failure.

diameter a straight line dividing a circle into two equal halves. Every diameter of a circle passes through the center.

diamond generally colorless, transparent mineral, the hard crystalline form of carbon. It is regarded as a precious gemstone, and is the hardest natural substance known (10 on the ◊Mohs' scale). Industrial diamonds are used for cutting, grinding, and polishing.

Diamond crystallizes in the cubic system as octahedral crystals, some with curved faces and striations. The high refractive index of 2.42 and the high dispersion of light, or "fire," account for the spectral displays seen in cut diamonds.

Diamonds were known before 3000 BC and until their discovery in Brazil 1725, India was the principal source of supply. Present sources are Angola, Ghana, Guyana, Sierra Leone, South Africa, Namibia, Tanzania, and Yakut (Russia); Brazil and Zaire are noted for industrial diamonds. In 1885 there were 42 diamond-mining communities in South Africa, by 1890 only one, De Beers Consolidated.

Diamonds may be found as alluvial diamonds on or close to the Earth's surface in riverbeds or dried watercourses; on the sea bottom (off W Africa); or, more commonly, in volcanic pipes composed of "blue ground" or ◊kimberlite, where the original matrix has penetrated the Earth's crust from great depths. They are sorted from the residue of washed ground by X-ray. Natural diamonds may be exhausted by the year 2000 unless new deposits are found.

There are four chief varieties of diamond: well-crystallized transparent stones, colorless or only slightly tinted, valued as gems; *bort*, poorly crystallized or inferior diamonds; *balas*, an industrial variety, extremely hard and tough; and *carbonado*, or industrial diamond, also called black diamond or carbon, which is opaque, black or gray, and very tough. Industrial diamonds (20 metric tons per annum) are also produced synthetically from graphite. Some synthetic diamonds conduct heat 50% more efficiently than natural diamonds and are

five times greater in strength. This is a great advantage in their use to disperse heat in electronic and telecommunication devices and in the production of laser components.

Because diamonds act as perfectly transparent windows and do not absorb infrared radiation, they were used aboard NASA space probes to Venus 1978. The tungsten-carbide tools used in steel mills are cut with industrial diamond tools.

Rough diamonds are dull or greasy before being cut, and only 20% are suitable as gems. Diamond gemstones are valued by weight (◊carat), cut (highlighting the stone's optical properties), color, and clarity (on a six-point scale from P or "pique," showing a flaw visible to the naked eye, to FL, or "flawless"). They are cut by the use of diamond dust. The two most frequent forms of cut gem diamonds are the brilliant, for thicker stones, and the rose, for shallower ones. By 1980 India was on the way to replacing Antwerp and Tel Aviv as the world's chief cutting and polishing center.

Noted diamonds include the Cullinan, or Star of Africa (3,106 carats, over 17.5 oz/500 g before cutting, South Africa, 1905); Excelsior (995.2 carats, South Africa, 1893); and Star of Sierra Leone (968.9 carats, Yengema, 1972).

Diamond v Chakrabarty a US Supreme Court decision 1980 that defined human-engineered microorganisms as patentable products.

diamorphine technical term for ◊heroin.

Diana in Roman mythology, the goddess of chastity, hunting, and the Moon (Greek ◊Artemis), daughter of Jupiter and twin of Apollo.

Diana Princess of Wales 1961– . The daughter of the 8th Earl Spencer, she married Prince Charles in St Paul's Cathedral, London 1981, the first English bride of a royal heir since 1659. She is descended from the only sovereigns from whom Prince Charles is not descended, Charles II and James II.

DIANE (acronym for *direct information access network for Europe*) collection of information suppliers, or "hosts," for the European computer network.

dianetics form of psychotherapy developed by the US science-fiction writer L Ron Hubbard (1911–1986), which formed the basis for ◊Scientology. Hubbard believed that all mental illness and certain forms of physical illness are caused by "engrams," or incompletely assimilated traumatic experiences, both pre- and postnatal. These engrams can be confronted during therapy with an auditor and thus exorcised. An individual free from engrams would be a "Clear" and perfectly healthy.

Hubbard later expanded this theory: behind each mind is a nonphysical and immortal being, the Thetan, which has forgotten its true nature and is therefore trapped in a cycle of reincarnation, accumulating engrams with each lifetime. If these engrams are cleared, the individual will become an Operating Thetan, with quasi-miraculous powers.

During the 1970s and 80s the Church of Scientology was accused of having taken on a cultlike character and of financial duplicity.

diapause a period of suspended delayed development or growth that occurs in some species of insects and other invertebrates, characterized by greatly reduced metabolism. Periods of diapause are often timed to coincide with the winter months, and improve the animal's chances of surviving adverse conditions.

diaphragm muscular sheet separating the thorax from the abdomen in mammals. Its rhythmical movements affect the size of the thorax and cause the pressure changes within the lungs that result in breathing.

The diaphragm muscle is under both voluntary and involuntary (automatic) control. Skilled divers can voluntarily hold their breath for up to five minutes, overriding the normal breathing cycles that we barely notice in day-to-day living.

diaphragm barrier ◊contraceptive that is inserted into the vagina and fits over the cervix (neck of the uterus), preventing sperm from entering the uterus. For it to be effective, a ◊spermicide must be used and the diaphragm left in place for 6–8 hours after intercourse. This method is 97% effective if practiced correctly.

In the US, diaphragms are prescribed by physicians who fit them for size; they may then be purchased in drug stores or at clinics.

diarrhea excessive action of the bowels so that the feces are fluid or semifluid. It is caused by intestinal irritants (including some drugs and poisons), infection with harmful organisms (as in dysentery, salmonella, or cholera), or allergies.

Diarrhea is the biggest killer of children in the world. The World Health Organization estimates that 4.5 million children die each year from dehydration as a result of diarrheal disease in Third World countries. It can be treated by giving an accurately measured aqueous solution of salt and glucose by mouth in large quantities (salt water with sugar, to restore the electrolyte balance in the blood). Since most diarrhea is viral in origin, antibiotics are ineffective.

diary informal record of day-to-day events, observations, or reflections, usually not intended for a general readership. One of the earliest diaries extant is that of a Japanese noblewoman, the *Kagerō Nikki* 954–974, and the earliest diary extant in English is that of Edward VI (ruled 1547–53). Notable diaries include those of Samuel Pepys, the writer John Evelyn, the Quaker George Fox, and in the 20th century those of Anne Frank and the writers André Gide and Katherine Mansfield.

Diaspora dispersal of the Jews, initially from Palestine after the Babylonian conquest 586 BC, and then following the Roman sack of Jerusalem AD 70 and their crushing of the Jewish revolt of 135. The term has come to refer to all the Jews living outside Israel.

diathermy generation of heat in body tissues by the passage of high-frequency electric currents between two electrodes placed on the body, used in diathermic surgery and to relieve arthritic pain.

In diathermic surgery, one electrode is very much reduced for cutting purposes and the other correspondingly enlarged and placed at a distance on the body. The high-frequency current produces, at the tip of the cutting electrode, sufficient heat to cut tissues, or to coagulate and kill tissue cells, with a minimum of bleeding.

diatom microscopic alga of the division Bacillariophyta found in all parts of the world. Diatoms consist of single cells, sometimes grouped in colonies.

The cell wall is made up of two overlapping valves known as *frustules*, which are usually impregnated with silica, and which fit together like the lid and body of a pillbox. Diatomaceous earths (diatomite) are made up of the valves of fossil diatoms, and are used in the manufacture of dynamite and in the rubber and plastics industries.

diatomic molecule molecule composed of two atoms joined together. In the case of an element such as oxygen (O_2), the atoms are identical.

diatonic in music, a scale consisting of the seven notes of any major or minor key.

Diaz Bartolomeu *c.* 1450–1500. Portuguese explorer, the first European to reach the Cape of Good Hope 1488, and to establish a route around Africa. He drowned during an expedition with Pedro ♢Cabral.

Díaz Porfirio 1830–1915. Dictator of Mexico 1877–80 and 1884–1911. After losing the 1876 election, he overthrew the government and seized power. He was supported by conservative landowners and foreign capitalists, who invested in railroads and mines. He centralized the state at the expense of the peasants and Indians, and dismantled all local and regional leadership. He faced mounting and revolutionary opposition in his final years and was forced into exile 1911.

Dickens Charles 1812–1870. English novelist, popular for his memorable characters and his portrayal of the social evils of Victorian England. In 1836 he published the first number of the *Pickwick Papers*, followed by *Oliver Twist* 1838, the first of his "reforming" novels; *Nicholas Nickleby* 1839; *Barnaby Rudge* 1840; *The Old Curiosity Shop* 1841; and *David Copperfield* 1849. Among his later books are *A Tale of Two Cities* 1859 and *Great Expectations* 1861.

Born in Portsea, Hampshire, the son of a clerk, Dickens received little formal education, although a short period spent working in a blacking factory in S London, while his father was imprisoned for debt in the Marshalsea prison during 1824, was followed by three years in a private school. In 1827 he became a lawyer's clerk, and then after four years a reporter for the *Morning Chronicle*, to which he contributed the *Sketches by Boz*. In 1836 he married Catherine Hogarth, three days after the publication of the first number of the *Pickwick Papers*. Originally intended merely as an accompaniment to a series of sporting illustrations, the adventures of Pickwick outgrew their setting and established Dickens' reputation.

In 1842 he visited the US, where his attack on the pirating of English books by American publishers chilled his welcome; his experiences are reflected in *American Notes* and *Martin Chuzzlewit* 1843. In 1843 he published the first of his Christmas books, *A Christmas Carol*, followed 1844 by *The Chimes*, written in Genoa during his first long sojourn abroad, and in 1845 by the even more successful *Cricket on the Hearth*. A venture as editor of the Liberal *Daily News* 1846 was short-lived, and *Dombey and Son* 1848 was largely written abroad. *David Copperfield*, his most popular novel, appeared 1849 and contains many autobiographical incidents and characters.

Returning to journalism, Dickens inaugurated the weekly magazine *Household Words* 1850, reorganizing it 1859 as *All the Year Round*; many of his later stories were published serially in these periodicals.

In 1857 Dickens met the actress Ellen Ternan and in 1858 agreed with his wife on a separation; his sister-in-law remained with

him to care for his children. In 1858 he began giving public readings from his novels, which proved such a success that he was invited to make a second US tour 1867. Among his later novels are *Bleak House* 1853, *Hard Times* 1854, *Little Dorrit* 1857, and *Our Mutual Friend* 1864. *Edwin Drood*, a mystery story influenced by the style of his friend Wilkie ♢Collins, was left incomplete on his death.

Dickinson Emily Elizabeth 1830–1886. US poet. Dickinson wrote most of her poetry between 1850 and the late 1860s and was particularly prolific during the Civil War years, when she lived at home in Amherst, Massachusetts, in seclusion. She experimented with poetic rhythms, rhymes, and forms, as well as language and syntax. Her work is characterized by a wittiness and boldness that seem to contrast sharply with the quiet, reclusive life she led.

Born in Amherst, she lived in near seclusion there after 1862. Almost none of her many short, mystical poems were published during her lifetime, since many of those who read her poems failed to recognize their greatness, and she was discouraged from publishing. Her concentrated, brilliant work has become well known only in the 20th century. Dickinson also carried on lengthy correspondences with a number of friends and acquaintances, and many of her letters are extraordinary artistic achievements in themselves. The first collection of her poetry, *Poems by Emily Dickinson* was published 1890.

Dick Tracy comic-strip character created by US cartoonist Chester Gould 1931. The strong-jawed detective's battles against the ruthless criminal underworld involved such characters as Flattop, Pruneface, Itchy, and the Stooge, with the help of his incapable crew of law-enforcers: Helmlock Holmes, Jo Jitsu, and Go Go Gomez. Dick Tracy became a television series in the 1950s. The film *Dick Tracy* 1990 starred US pop star Madonna and US actor Warren Beatty.

dicotyledon major subdivision of the ♢angiosperms, containing the great majority of flowering plants. Dicotyledons are characterized by the presence of two seed leaves, or ♢cotyledons, in the embryo, which is usually surrounded by an ♢endosperm. They generally have broad leaves with netlike veins.

Dicotyledons may be small plants such as the daisy and buttercup, shrubs such as the blueberry, or trees such as oak and birch. The other subdivision of the angiosperms is the ♢monocotyledons.

dictatorship term or office of an absolute ruler, overriding the constitution. (In ancient Rome a dictator was a magistrate invested with emergency powers for six months.) Although dictatorships were common in Latin America during the 19th century, the only European example during this period was the rule of Napoleon III. The crises following World War I produced many dictatorships, including the regimes of Atatürk and Piłsudski (nationalist); Mussolini, Hitler, Primo de Rivera, Franco, and Salazar (all right-wing); and Stalin (Communist).

dictatorship of the proletariat Marxist term for a revolutionary dictatorship established during the transition from capitalism to ♢communism after a socialist revolution.

dictionary book that contains a selection of the words of a language, with their pronunciations and meanings, usually arranged

in alphabetical order. The term *dictionary* is also applied to any usually alphabetic work of reference containing specialized information about a particular subject, art, or science; for example, a dictionary of music. Bilingual dictionaries provide translations of one language into another.

The first dictionaries of English (*glossa collectae*), in the 17th century, served to explain difficult words, generally of Latin or Greek origin, in everyday English. Samuel Johnson's *A Dictionary of the English Language* 1755 was one of the first dictionaries of standard English, and the first to give extensive coverage to phrasal verbs. Noah Webster's *An American Dictionary of the English Language* 1828 quickly became a standard work throughout North America. The many-volume *Oxford English Dictionary*, begun 1884 and subject to continuous revision (and now computerization), provides a detailed historical record of each word and, therefore, of the English language.

Diderot Denis 1713–1784. French philosopher. He is closely associated with the Enlightenment, the European intellectual movement for social and scientific progress, and was editor of the enormously influential ♢*Encyclopédie* 1751–80.

An expanded and politicized version of the English encyclopedia 1728 of Ephraim Chambers (*c.* 1680–1740), this work exerted an enormous influence on contemporary social thinking with its materialism and anti-clericalism. Its compilers were known as Encyclopédistes.

Diderot's materialism, most articulately expressed in *D'Alembert's Dream*, published after Diderot's death, sees the natural world as nothing more than matter and motion. His account of the origin and development of life is purely mechanical.

Didion Joan 1934– . US author and journalist. She is known for her terse yet eloquent views of modern American society, especially California, where she grew up. Her works include the essays *Slouching toward Bethlehem* 1968 and *The White Album* 1979 and the novels *Run River* 1963, *Play It As It Lays* 1970, *A Book of Common Prayer* 1977, and *Democracy* 1984, which depict the cultural disintegration of modern life. She reported on current events in *Salvador* 1983 and the state of affairs in the city in *Miami* 1987.

Dido Phoenician princess, legendary founder of Carthage, N Africa, who committed suicide to avoid marrying a local prince. In the Latin epic *Aeneid*, Virgil claims that it was because ♢Aeneas deserted her.

diecasting form of ♢casting in which molten metal is injected into permanent metal molds or dies.

Diefenbaker John George 1895–1979. Canadian Progressive Conservative politician, prime minister 1957–63. In 1958, seeking to increase his majority in the House of Commons, Diefenbaker called for new elections; his party won the largest majority in Canadian history. In 1963, however, Diefenbaker refused to accept atomic warheads for missiles supplied by the US, and the Progressive Conservative Party was ousted after losing a no-confidence vote in parliament.

Diego Garcia island in the ♢Chagos Archipelago, named after its Portuguese discoverer in 1532. See ♢British Indian Ocean Territory.

dielectric substance (an insulator such as ceramic, rubber, or glass) capable of supporting electric stress. The dielectric constant, or relative permittivity, of a substance is the ratio of the capacitance of a capacitor with the substance as dielectric to that of a similar capacitor in which the dielectric is replaced by a vacuum.

Diels Otto 1876–1954. German chemist. In 1950 he and his former assistant, Kurt Alder (1902–1958), were jointly awarded the Nobel Prize for Chemistry for their research into the synthesis of organic chemical compounds.

Diemen Anthony van 1593–1645. Dutch admiral. In 1636 he was appointed governor-general of Dutch settlements in the E Indies, and wrested Ceylon and Malacca from the Portuguese. In 1636 and 1642 he supervised expeditions to Australia, on the second of which the navigator Abel Tasman discovered land not charted by Europeans and named it *Van Diemen's Land*, now Tasmania.

Dien Bien Phu, Battle of decisive battle in the ◊Indochina War at a French fortress in North Vietnam, near the Laotian border. French troops were besieged March 13–May 7, 1954 by the communist Vietminh. The fall of Dien Bien Phu resulted in the end of French control of Indochina.

Dieppe channel port at the mouth of the river Arques, Seine-Maritime *département*, N France; population (1983) 39,500. There are ferry services from its harbor to Newhaven and elsewhere; industries include fishing, shipbuilding, and pharmaceuticals.

Diesel Rudolf 1858–1913. German engineer who patented the diesel engine. He began his career as a refrigerator engineer and, like many engineers of the period, sought to develop a more efficient power source than the conventional steam engine. Able to operate with greater efficiency and economy, the diesel engine soon found a ready market.

diesel engine ◊internal-combustion engine that burns a lightweight fuel oil. The diesel engine operates by compressing air until it becomes sufficiently hot to ignite the fuel. It is a piston-in-cylinder engine, like the ◊gasoline engine, but only air (rather than an air-and-fuel mixture) is taken into the cylinder on the first piston stroke (down). The piston moves up and compresses the air until it is at a very high temperature. The fuel oil is then injected into the hot air, where it burns, driving the piston down on its power stroke. For this reason the engine is called a compression-ignition engine.

The principle of the diesel engine was first explained in England by Herbert Akroyd (1864–1937) in 1890, and was applied practically by Rudolf Diesel in Germany in 1892.

diet the range of foods eaten by an animal. The basic components of a diet are a group of chemicals: proteins, carbohydrates, fats, vitamins, minerals, and water. Different animals require these substances in different proportions, but the necessity of finding and processing an appropriate diet is a very basic drive in animal evolution. For instance, all guts are adapted for digesting and absorbing food, but different guts have adapted to cope with particular diets.

The diet an animal needs may vary over its life span, according to whether it is growing, reproducing, highly active, or approaching death. For instance, an animal may need increased carbohydrate for additional energy, or increased minerals during periods of growth.

diet a particular selection of food, or the overall intake and selection of food for a particular person or people. A special diet may be recommended for medical reasons, to balance, limit, or increase certain nutrients; undertaken to lose weight, by a reduction in calorie intake or selection of specific foods; or observed on religious, moral, or emotional grounds. An adequate diet is one that fulfills the body's nutritional requirements and gives an energy intake proportional to the person's activity level (the average daily requirement is 2,400 calories for men, less for women, more for active children). In the Third World and in famine and poverty areas some 450 million people in the world subsist on fewer than 1,500 calories per day, whereas in the developed countries the average daily intake is 3,300 calories.

diet meeting or convention of the princes and other dignitaries of the Holy Roman (German) Empire, for example, the Diet of Worms 1521 which met to consider the question of Luther's doctrines and the governance of the empire under Charles V.

dietetics specialized branch of human nutrition, dealing with the promotion of health through the proper kinds and quantities of food.

Therapeutic dietetics has a large part to play in the treatment of certain illnesses, such as allergies, arthritis, and diabetes; it is sometimes used alone, but often in conjunction with drugs. The preventative or curative effects of specific diets, such as the "grape cure" or raw vegetable diets sometimes prescribed for cancer patients, are disputed by orthodox medicine.

Dietrich Marlene (Maria Magdalene) 1904–1992. German-born US actress and singer who appeared with Emil Jannings in both the German and American versions of the film *The Blue Angel* 1930, directed by Josef von Sternberg. She stayed in Hollywood, becoming a US citizen 1937. Her husky, sultry singing voice added to her appeal. Her other films include *Blonde Venus* 1932, *Destry Rides Again* 1939, and *Just a Gigolo* 1978.

She also starred in *Judgment at Nuremberg* 1961 and was the subject of Maximilian Schell's documentary *Marlene* 1983.

difference engine mechanical calculating machine designed (and partly built 1822) by the British mathematician, Charles ◊Babbage, to produce reliable tables of life expectancy. A precursor of the ◊analytical engine, it was to calculate mathematical functions by solving the differences between values given to ◊variables within equations. Babbage designed the

calculator so that once the initial values for the variables were set it would produce the next few thousand values without error.

differential arrangement of gears in the final drive of a vehicle's transmission system that allows the driving wheels to turn at different speeds when cornering. The differential consists of sets of bevel gears and pinions within a cage attached to the crown wheel. When cornering, the bevel pinions rotate to allow the outer wheel to turn faster than the inner.

differential calculus branch of ◊calculus involving applications such as the determination of maximum and minimum points and rates of change.

differentiation in mathematics, a procedure for determining the gradient of the tangent to a curve f(x) at any point x.

It may be regarded as the limit of the expression $[f(x + \delta x) - f(x)]/\delta x$ as δx tends to zero. Graphically, this is equivalent to the gradient (slope) of the curve represented by $y = f(x)$ at any point x.

differentiation in embryology, the process whereby cells become increasingly different and specialized, giving rise to more complex structures that have particular functions in the adult organism. For instance, embryonic cells may develop into nerve, muscle, or bone cells.

diffraction spreading of a wave motion (such as light or sound) as it passes an obstacle and expands into a region not exposed directly to incoming waves behind the obstacle. This accounts for interference phenomena observed at the edges of opaque objects, or discontinuities between different media in the path of a wave train. The phenomena give rise to slight spreading of light into colored bands at the shadow of a straight edge.

A diffraction grating is a plate of glass or metal ruled with close, equidistant parallel lines used for separating a wave train such as a beam of incident light into its component frequencies (white light results in a spectrum). The regular spacing of atoms in crystals are used to diffract X-rays, and in this way the structure of many substances has been elucidated, including recently that of proteins.

diffusion spontaneous and random movement of molecules or particles in a fluid (gas or liquid) from a region in which they are at a high concentration to a region in which they are at a low concentration, until a uniform concentration is achieved throughout. No mechanical mixing or stirring is involved. For instance, if a drop of ink is added to water, its molecules will diffuse until their color becomes evenly distributed throughout.

In biological systems, diffusion plays an essential role in the transport, over short distances, of molecules such as nutrients, respiratory gases, and neurotransmitters. It provides the means by which small molecules pass into and out of individual cells and microorganisms, such as amebas, that possess no circulatory system.

One application of diffusion is the separation of isotopes, particularly those of uranium. When uranium hexafluoride diffuses through a porous plate, the ratio of the 235 and 238 isotopes is changed slightly. With sufficient number of passages, the separation is nearly complete. There are large plants in the US and UK for obtaining enriched fuel for fast nuclear reactors and the fissile uranium-235, originally required for the first atomic bombs. Another

differentiation *A mathematical procedure for determining the gradient, or slope, of the tangent to any curve f(x) at any point x.*

application is the diffusion pump, used extensively in vacuum work, in which the gas to be evacuated diffuses into a chamber from which it is carried away by the vapor of a suitable medium, usually oil or mercury.

digestion process whereby food eaten by an animal is broken down physically, and chemically by ◊enzymes, usually in the ◊stomach and ◊intestines, to make the nutrients available for absorption and cell metabolism.

In some single-celled organisms, such as amebas, a food particle is engulfed by the cell and digested in a ◊vacuole within the cell.

digestive system mouth, stomach, intestine, and associated glands of animals, which are responsible for digesting food. The food is broken down by physical and chemical means in the ◊stomach; digestion is completed, and most nutrients are absorbed in the small intestine; what remains is stored and concentrated into feces in the large intestine. In birds, additional digestive organs are the ◊crop and ◊gizzard.

In smaller, simpler animals such as jellyfishes, the digestive system is simply a cavity (coelenteron or enteric cavity) with a "mouth" into which food is taken; the digestible portion is dissolved and absorbed in this cavity, and the remains are ejected back through the mouth.

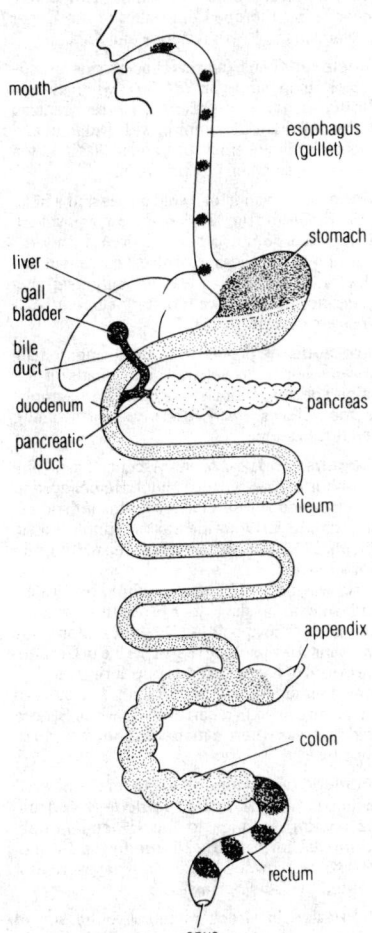

digestive system *The human digestive system.*

Diggers or *true* ◊**Levelers** English 17th-century radical sect that attempted to dig common land. The Diggers became prominent April 1649 when, headed by Gerrard Winstanley (c. 1609–1660), they set up communal colonies near Cobham, Surrey, and elsewhere. These colonies were attacked by mobs and, being pacifists, the Diggers made no resistance. The support they attracted alarmed the government and they were dispersed 1650. Their ideas influenced the early ◊Quakers.

digit in mathematics, any of the numbers from 0 to 9 in the decimal system. Different bases have different ranges of digits. For example, the ◊hexadecimal number system has digits 0 to 9 and A to F, whereas the ◊binary number system has two digits (or ◊bits), 0 and 1.

digital in electronics and computing, a term meaning "coded as numbers." A digital system uses two-state, either on/off or high/low voltage pulses, to encode, receive, and transmit information. A **digital display** shows discrete values as numbers (as opposed to an analog signal, such as the continuous sweep of a pointer on a dial).

Digital electronics is the technology that underlies digital techniques. Low-power, miniature, integrated circuits (chips) provide the means for the coding, storage, transmission, processing, and reconstruction of information of all kinds.

digital audio tape (DAT) digitally recorded audio tape produced in cassettes that can carry two hours of sound on each side and are about half the size of standard cassettes. DAT players/recorders were developed 1987 but not marketed in the UK until 1989. Prerecorded cassettes are copy-protected. The first DAT for computer data was introduced 1988.

DAT machines are constructed like videocassette recorders (though they use metal audio tape), with a movable playback head, the tape winding in a spiral around a rotating drum. The tape can also carry additional information; for example, it can be programmed to skip a particular track and repeat another. The music industry delayed releasing prerecorded DAT cassettes because of fears of bootlegging, but a system has now been internationally agreed whereby it is not possible to make more than one copy of any prerecorded compact disc or DAT. DAT is mainly used in recording studios for making master tapes. The system was developed by Sony.

By 1990, DATs for computer data had been developed to a capacity of around 2.5 gigabytes per tape, achieved by using helical scan recording (in which the tape covers some 90% of the total head area of the rotating drum). This enables data from the tape to be read over 200 times faster than it can be written. Any file can be located within 60 seconds.

digital computer computing device that operates on a two-state system, using symbols that are internally coded as binary numbers (numbers made up of combinations of the digits 0 and 1); see ◊computer.

digital data transmission in computing, a way of sending data by converting all signals (whether pictures, sounds, or words) into numeric (normally binary) codes before transmission, then reconverting them on receipt. This virtually eliminates any distortion or degradation of the signal during transmission, storage, or processing.

digitalis drug that increases the efficiency of

the heart by strengthening its muscle contractions and slowing its rate. It is derived from the leaves of the common European woodland plant *Digitalis purpurea* (foxglove).

It is purified to digoxin, digitoxin, and lanatoside C, which are effective in cardiac regulation but induce the side effects of nausea, vomiting, and pulse irregularities. Pioneered in the late 1700s by William Withering, an English physician and botanist, digitalis was the first cardiac drug.

digitalis plant of the genus *Digitalis* of the figwort family Scrophulariaceae, which includes the ◊foxgloves.

digital recording technique whereby the pressure of sound waves is sampled more than 30,000 times a second and the values converted by computer into precise numerical values. These are recorded and, during playback, are reconverted to sound waves.

This gives very high-quality reproduction. The numerical values converted by computer represent the original sound-wave form exactly and are recorded on compact disc. When this is played back by ◊laser, the exact values are retrieved. When the signal is fed via an amplifier to a loudspeaker, sound waves exactly like the original ones are reproduced.

digital sampling electronic process used in ◊telecommunications for transforming a constantly varying (analog) signal into one composed of discrete units, a digital signal. In the creation of recorded music, sampling enables the composer, producer, or remix engineer to borrow discrete vocal or instrumental parts from other recorded work (it is also possible to sample live sound).

A telephone microphone changes sound waves into an analog signal that fluctuates up and down like a wave. In the digitizing process the waveform is sampled thousands of times a second and each part of the sampled wave is given a binary code number (made up of combinations of the digits 0 and 1) related to the height of the wave at that point, which is transmitted along the telephone line. Using digital signals, messages can be transmitted quickly, accurately, and economically.

Dijon city and capital of Bourgogne (Burgundy), France; population (1983) 216,000. As well as metallurgical, chemical, and other industries, it has a wine trade and is famed for its mustard.

dik-dik any of several species of tiny antelope, genus *Madoqua*, found in Africa south of the Sahara in dry areas with scattered brush. Dik-diks are about 2 ft/60 cm long and 1.1 ft/35 cm tall, and are often seen in pairs. Males have short, pointed horns. The dik-dik is so named because of its alarm call.

dilatation and curettage (D and C) common gynecological procedure in which the cervix (neck of the womb) is widened, or dilated, giving access so that the lining of the womb can be scraped away (curettage). It may be carried out to terminate a pregnancy, treat an incomplete miscarriage, discover the cause of heavy menstrual bleeding, or for biopsy.

dill herb *Anethum graveolens* of the carrot family Umbelliferae, whose bitter seeds and aromatic leaves are used for culinary and medicinal purposes.

Dillinger John 1903–1934. US bank robber and murderer. In 1923 he was convicted of armed robbery and spent the next ten years in state prison. Released in 1933, he led a gang on a robbery spree throughout the Midwest, staging daring raids on police stations to obtain guns. Named "Public Enemy Number One" by the Federal Bureau of Investigation (FBI), Dillinger led the authorities on a long chase. He was finally betrayed by his mistress, the mysterious "Lady in Red," and was killed by FBI agents in Chicago as he left a cinema.

Born in Indianapolis, Dillinger began a life of crime after deserting from the navy 1920.

Dilthey Wilhelm 1833–1911. German philosopher, a major figure in the interpretive tradition of ⟡hermeneutics. He argued that the "human sciences" (*Geisteswissenschaften*) could not employ the same methods as the natural sciences but must use the procedure of "understanding" (*Verstehen*) to grasp the inner life of an alien culture or past historical period. Thus Dilthey extended the significance of hermeneutics far beyond the interpretation of texts to the whole of human history and culture.

DiMaggio Joe 1914– . US baseball player with the New York Yankees 1936–51. In 1941 he set a record by getting hits in 56 consecutive games. He was an outstanding fielder, played center field, hit 361 home runs, and had a career average of .325. DiMaggio was married to the actress Marilyn Monroe. He was elected to the Baseball Hall of Fame.

dime novel melodramatic paperback novel of a series started in the US in the 1850s, published by Beadle and Adams of New York, which frequently dealt with Deadwood Dick and his frontier adventures. Authors included Edward L Wheeler, E Z C Judson, Prentiss Ingraham, and J R Coryell. The "Nick Carter" Library added detective stories to the genre. Like British "penny dreadfuls," dime novels attained massive sales and were popular with troops during the American Civil War and World War I.

Today's mass-market paperbacks continue to serve readers of Westerns, Mystery, Science Fiction, Romance, and Detective fiction that grew out of the dime-novel concept.

dimension in science, any directly measurable physical quantity such as mass (M), length (L), and time (T), and the derived units obtainable by multiplication or division from such quantities. For example, acceleration (the rate of change of velocity) has dimensions (LT^{-2}), and is expressed in such units as km s^{-2}. A quantity that is a ratio, such as relative density or humidity, is dimensionless.

In geometry, the dimensions of a figure are the number of measures needed to specify its size. A point is considered to have zero dimension, a line to have one dimension, a plane figure to have two, and a solid body to have three.

dimethyl sulphoxide (DMSO) $(CH_3)_2SO$ colorless liquid used as an industrial solvent and an antifreeze. It is obtained as a by-product of the processing of wood to paper.

diminishing returns, law of in economics, the principle that additional application of one factor of production, such as an extra machine or employee, at first results in rapidly increasing output but eventually yields declining returns, unless other factors are modified to sustain the increase.

Dimitrov Georgi 1882–1949. Bulgarian communist, prime minister from 1946. He was elected a deputy in 1913 and from 1919 was a member of the executive of the Comintern,

an international communist organization (see the ⟡International). In 1933 he was arrested in Berlin and tried with others in Leipzig for allegedly setting fire to the parliament building (see ⟡Reichstag Fire). Acquitted, he went to the USSR, where he became general secretary of the Comintern until its dissolution in 1943.

Dinant ancient town in Namur province, Belgium, on the river Meuse; population (1991) 12,100. It is a tourist center for the Ardennes.

Dinaric Alps extension of the European ⟡Alps that runs parallel to the E Adriatic coast, stretching from Slovenia along the frontier between Croatia and Bosnia-Herzegovina into W Yugoslavia and N Albania. The highest peak is Durmitor at 8,274 ft/2,522 m.

Dine Jim 1935– . US Pop artist. He experimented with combinations of paintings and objects, such as a sink attached to a canvas.

Dine was a pioneer of happenings (art as live performance) in the 1950s and of environment art (three-dimensional works that attempt active interaction with the spectator, sometimes using sound or movement).

Dinesen Isak 1885–1962. Adopted name of Danish writer Karen ⟡Blixen, born Karen Christentze Dinesen.

Dingaan Zulu chief who obtained the throne in 1828 by murdering his predecessor, Shaka, and became notorious for his cruelty. In warfare with the Boer immigrants into Natal he was defeated on Dec 16, 1838—"Dingaan's Day." He escaped to Swaziland, where he was deposed by his brother Mpande and subsequently assassinated.

dingo wild dog of Australia. Descended from domestic dogs brought from Asia by Aborigines thousands of years ago, it belongs to the same species *Canis familiaris* as other domestic dogs. It is reddish brown with a bushy tail, and often hunts at night. It cannot bark.

dinitrogen oxide alternate name for ⟡nitrous oxide or "laughing gas," one of the nitrogen oxides (chemical compund containing only nitrogen and oxygen).

Dinka member of the Dinka culture from S Sudan. The Dinka, numbering approximately 1 million, are a group of ⟡Negroid tribes, primarily cattle herders, and inhabit the lands around the river system that flows into the White Nile. Their language belongs to the Chari-Nile family.

Dinkins David 1927– . Mayor of New York City from Jan 1990, a Democrat. He won a reputation as a moderate and consensual community politician and was Manhattan borough president before succeeding Edward I Koch to become New York's first black mayor.

dinosaur (Greek *deinos* "terrible," *sauros* "lizard") any of a group (sometimes considered as two separate orders) of extinct reptiles living between 215 million and 65 million years ago. Their closest living relations are crocodiles and birds, the latter perhaps descended from the dinosaurs. Many species of dinosaur evolved over the millions of years during which they were the dominant large land animals. Most were large (up to 90 ft/27 m), but some were as small as birds and lizards, into which some evolved. Most became extinct 65 million years ago for reasons not fully understood, although many paleontological, astronomical, and ecological theories exist. They never coexisted with the human species, which began to evolve only some 6 million years ago.

Brachiosaurus, a long-necked plant-eater of the sauropod group, was about 40 ft/12.6 m to the top of its head, and weighed 80 tons. Compsognathus, a meat-eater, was only the size of a chicken, and ran on its hind legs. Stegosaurus, an armored plant-eater 20 ft/6 m long, had a brain only about 1.25 in/3 cm long. Not all dinosaurs had small brains. At the other extreme, the hunting dinosaur Stenonychosaurus, 6ft/2 m long, had a brain size comparable to that of a mammal or bird of today, stereoscopic vision, and grasping hands. Many dinosaurs appear to have been equipped for a high level of activity.

An almost complete fossil of a dinosaur skeleton was found in 1969 in the Andean foothills, South America; it had been a two-legged carnivore 6 ft/2 m tall and weighing more than 220lb/100 kg. More than 230 million years old, it is the oldest known dinosaur. Eggs are known of some species. In 1982 a number of nests and eggs were found in "colonies" in Montana, suggesting that some bred together like modern seabirds. In 1987 finds were made in China that may add much to the traditional knowledge of dinosaurs, chiefly gleaned from North American specimens. In 1989 and 1990 an articulated *Tyrannosaurus rex* was unearthed by a paleontological team in Montana, with a full skull, one of only six known. **Tyrannosaurs** were huge, two-footed, meat-eating theropod dinosaurs of the Upper Cretaceous in North America and Asia.

Diocletian Gaius Valerius Diocletianus AD 245–313. Roman emperor 284–305, when he abdicated in favor of Galerius. He reorganized and subdivided the empire, with two joint and two subordinate emperors, and in 303 initiated severe persecution of Christians.

diode combination of a cold anode and a heated cathode (or the semiconductor equivalent, which incorporates a p–n junction). Either device allows the passage of direct current in one direction only, and so is commonly used in a ⟡rectifier to convert alternating current (AC) to direct current (DC).

dioecious of plants with male and female flowers borne on separate individuals of the same species. Dioecism occurs, for example, in the willows *Salix*. It is a way of avoiding self-fertilization.

Diogenes c. 412–323 BC. Ascetic Greek philosopher of the ⟡Cynic school. He believed in freedom and self-sufficiency for the individual, and that the virtuous life was the simple life; he did not believe in social mores. His writings do not survive.

He was born at Sinope, captured by pirates, and sold as a slave to a Corinthian named Xeniades, who appointed Diogenes tutor to his two sons. He spent the rest of his life in Corinth. He is said to have carried a lamp during the daytime, looking for one honest man. The story of his having lived in a barrel arose when Seneca said that was where a man so crabbed ought to have lived.

Diomede two islands off the tip of the Seward peninsula, Alaska. **Little Diomede** (2.4 sq mi/6.2 sq km) belongs to the US and is only 2.4 mi/3.9 km from **Big Diomede** (11.3 sq mi/29.3 sq km), owned by Russia. They were first sighted by Vitus Bering 1728.

Diomedes in Greek mythology, the son of Tydeus, and a prominent Greek leader in ⟡Homer's *Iliad*.

Dion Cassius AD 150–235. Roman historian.

He wrote, in Greek, a Roman history in 80 books (of which 26 survive), covering the period from the founding of the city to AD 229, including the only surviving account of the invasion of Britain by Claudius 43 BC.

Dionysia festivals of the god ◊Dionysus (Bacchus) celebrated in ancient Greece, especially in Athens. They included the lesser Dionysia in Dec, chiefly rural festivals, and the greater Dionysia, at the end of March, when new plays were performed.

Dionysius two tyrants of the ancient Greek city of Syracuse in Sicily. *Dionysius the Elder* (432–367 BC) seized power 405 BC. His first two wars with Carthage further extended the power of Syracuse, but in a third (383–378 BC) he was defeated. He was a patron of ◊Plato. He was succeeded by his son, *Dionysius the Younger* (c. 390–344 BC), who was driven out of Syracuse by Dion 356; he was tyrant again 353, but in 343 returned to Corinth.

Dionysus in Greek mythology, the god of wine (son of Semele and Zeus), and also of orgiastic excess, who was attended by women called maenads, who were believed to be capable of tearing animals to pieces with their bare hands when under his influence. He was identified with the Roman ◊Bacchus, whose rites were less savage.

Diophantus lived c. 250. Greek mathematician in Alexandria whose *Arithmetica* is one of the first known works on problem solving by algebra, in which both words and symbols were used.

Dior Christian 1905–1957. French couturier. He established his own Paris salon 1947 and made an impact with the "New Look"—long, cinch-waisted, and full-skirted—after wartime austerity.

diorite igneous rock intermediate in composition; the coarse-grained plutonic equivalent of ◊andesite.

Dioscuri title of ◊Castor and Pollux in Classical mythology, meaning "sons of Zeus."

Diouf Abdou 1935– . Senegalese left-wing politician, president from 1980. He became prime minister 1970 under President Leopold Senghor and, on his retirement, succeeded him, being reelected in 1983 and 1988. His presidency has been characterized by authoritarianism.

dioxin any of a family of over 200 organic chemicals, all of which are heterocyclic hydrocarbons (see ◊cyclic compounds). The term is commonly applied, however, to only one member of the family, 2,3,7,8-tetrachlorodibenzodioxin (2,3,7,8-TCDD), a highly toxic chemical that occurs as an impurity in the defoliant Agent Orange, used in the Vietnam War, and in the weedkiller 2,4,5-T. It has been associated with a disfiguring skin complaint (chloracne), birth defects, miscarriages, and cancer.

Disasters involving accidental release of large amounts of dioxin into the environment have occurred at Seveso, Italy, and Times Beach, Missouri. Small amounts of dioxins are released by the burning of a wide range of chlorinated materials (treated wood, exhaust fumes from fuels treated with chlorinated additives, and plastics). The possibility of food becoming contaminated by dioxins in the environment has led the EC to significantly decrease the allowed levels of dioxin emissions from incinerators. Dioxin may be produced as a by-product in the manufacture of the bactericide ◊hexachlorophene.

dip, magnetic

diphtheria acute infectious disease in which a membrane forms in the throat (threatening death by ◊asphyxia), along with the production of a powerful neurotoxin that poisons the system. The organism responsible is a bacterium (*Corynebacterium diphtheriae*). Its incidence has been reduced greatly by immunization.

diplodocus plant-eating sauropod dinosaur that lived about 145 million years ago, the fossils of which have been found in the W US. Up to 88 ft/27 m long, most of which was neck and tail, it weighed about 11 tons. It walked on four elephantine legs, had nostrils on top of the skull, and peglike teeth at the front of the mouth.

diploid having two sets of ◊chromosomes in each cell. In sexually reproducing species, one set is derived from each parent, the ◊gametes, or sex cells, of each parent being ◊haploid (having only one set of chromosomes) due to ◊meiosis (reduction cell division).

diplomacy process by which states attempt to settle their differences through peaceful means such as negotiation or ◊arbitration. See ◊foreign relations.

dip, magnetic angle at a particular point on the Earth's surface between the direction of the Earth's magnetic field and the horizontal. It is measured using a *dip circle*, which has a magnetized needle suspended so that it can turn freely in the vertical plane of the magnetic field. In the northern hemisphere the needle dips below the horizontal, pointing along the line of the magnetic field toward its north pole. At the magnetic north and south poles, the needle dips vertically and the angle of dip is 90°.

dipole uneven distribution of magnetic or electrical characteristics within a molecule or substance so that it behaves as though it possesses two equal but opposite poles or charges, a finite distance apart. The uneven distribution of electrons within a molecule composed of atoms of different ◊electronegativities may result in an apparent concentration of electrons toward one end of the molecule and a deficiency toward the other, so that it forms a dipole consisting of apparently separated positive and negative charges. A bar magnet behaves as though its magnetism were concentrated in separate north and south magnetic poles because of the uneven distribution of its magnetic field.

dipper any of various passerine birds of the family Cinclidae, found in hilly and mountainous regions across Eurasia and North America, where there are clear, fast-flowing streams. It

can swim, dive, or walk along the bottom, using the pressure of water on its wings and tail to keep it down, while it searches for insect larvae and other small animals.

The American dipper *cinclus mexicanus* of W North America, is about 8 in/20 cm long, sooty-gray overall, and resembles a wren.

Dirac Paul Adrien Maurice 1902–1984. British physicist who worked out a version of quantum mechanics consistent with special ◊relativity. The existence of the positron (positive electron) was one of its predictions. He shared the Nobel Prize for Physics 1933 with Austrian physicist Erwin Schrödinger (1887–1961).

direct current (DC) electric current that flows in one direction, and does not reverse its flow as ◊alternating current does. The electricity produced by a battery is direct current.

directed number an ◊integer with a positive (+) or negative (−) sign attached, for example +5 or −5. On a graph, a positive sign shows a movement to the right or upward; a negative sign indicates movement downward or to the left.

Dirichlet Peter Gustav Lejeune 1805–1859. German mathematician. His most important work was on the convergence of the ◊Fourier analysis, which led him to the modern notion of a generalized function as represented in the form $f(x)$. He also made major contributions to number theory, producing *Dirichlet's theorem*: in every arithmetical sequence a, $a + d$, $a + 2d$, and so on, where a and d are relatively prime (that is, have no common divisors other than 1), there is an infinite number of prime numbers.

Dirichlet applied his mathematical knowledge to various aspects of physics, such as an analysis of vibrating strings, and to astronomy in a critique of the ideas about the stability of the ◊Solar System as proposed by the French mathematician Pierre Laplace.

Dis in Roman mythology, the god of the underworld (Greek Pluto, ruler of Hades), also known as Orcus. Dis is also a synonym for the underworld itself.

disability limitation of a person's ability to carry out the activities of daily living, to the extent that he or she may need help in doing so.

Among adults the commonest disability is in walking. Other common disabilities are in hearing, personal care, dexterity, and continence. Most disabilities arise from debilitating illness such as arthritis or stroke, although injury is also a leading cause. Other forms of disability are recognized in children: *developmental disability* is the failure to achieve a normal level of competence in some aspect of behavior during infancy, childhood, or adolescence; a *learning disability* in a child of normal intelligence is a difficulty in acquiring one of the basic cognitive skills of speaking, reading, writing, or calculation.

disaccharide ◊sugar made up of two monosaccharides or simple sugars, such as glucose or fructose. Sucrose, $C_{12}H_{22}O_{11}$, or table sugar, is a disaccharide.

disarmament reduction of a country's weapons of war. Most disarmament talks since World War II have been concerned with nuclear-arms verification and reduction, but biological, chemical, and conventional weapons have also come under discussion at the United Nations and in other forums. Attempts to limit the arms race between the US and (until its demise) the USSR included the ◊Strategic Arms Limitation Talks (SALT) of the 1970s and the ◊Strategic Arms Reduction Talks (START) of the 1980s–90s. Russia's president, Boris Yeltsin, continued the process of strategic arms reductions into 1992.

1930s League of Nations attempt to achieve disarmament failed.

1968 US president Johnson's proposals for Strategic Arms Limitation Talks (SALT) were delayed by the Soviet invasion of Czechoslovakia.

1972–77 SALT I was in effect.

1979–85 SALT II, signed by the Soviet and US leaders Brezhnev and Carter, was never ratified by the US Senate, but both countries abided by it.

1986 US president Reagan revoked this pledge, against the advice of his European NATO partners.

1987 Reagan and the Soviet leader Gorbachev agreed to reduce their nuclear arsenals by 4% by scrapping intermediate-range nuclear weapons.

1990 Treaty signed between the US and the USSR limiting both NATO and the Warsaw Pact to much reduced conventional weapons systems in Europe.

Jan 1991 President Bush announced decision to halve US military presence in Europe.

July 30–31, 1991 US president Bush and Soviet president Gorbachev signed the Strategic Arms Reduction Treaty (START) which limited both sides to no more than 6,000 nuclear warheads.

Sept-Oct 1991 President Bush announced the unilateral reduction of about 2,400 US nuclear weapons, asking the Soviet Union to respond in kind. President Gorbachev offered a package of unilateral cuts and proposals that surpassed the broad arms-control initiative presented by President Bush.

Jan 1992 President Bush and Russia's president, Boris Yeltsin, promised additional (60–80%) cuts in land-based and sea-based long-range nuclear missiles. In addition, Bush promised an accelerated withdrawal of US troops from Europe and the halting of future production of the advanced B-2 bomber. Yeltsin announced that Russian long-range missiles would no longer be targetted on US cities.

June 1992 President Yeltsin consented to the abandonment of strategic parity (equal balance of arms) and announced, with US president Bush, bilateral cuts in long-term nuclear weapons that far surpassed the terms of the 1991 START treaty. By 2003, it was promised, US warheads would be cut from 9,986 to 3,500, and Russian warheads from 10,237 to 3,000.

discharge tube device in which a gas conducting an electric current emits visible light. It is usually a glass tube from which virtually all the air has been removed (so that it "contains" a near vacuum), with electrodes at each end. When a high-voltage current is passed between the electrodes, the few remaining gas atoms in the tube (or some deliberately introduced ones) ionize and emit colored light as they conduct the current along the tube. The light originates as electrons change energy levels in the ionized atoms.

By coating the inside of the tube with a phosphor, invisible emitted radiation (such as ultraviolet light) can produce visible light; this is the principle of the fluorescent lamp.

disciple follower, especially of a religious leader. The word is used in the Bible for the early followers of Jesus. The 12 disciples closest to him are known as the ◊apostles.

discotheque club for dancing to pop music on records (disks), originating in the 1960s. The shortened form, *disco*, was used for an international style of recorded dance music of the 1970s with a heavily emphasized beat, derived from funk (dance music of black US origin and relying on heavy percussion using polyrhythm patterns).

discount rate the rate that banks are charged to borrow money from the ◊Federal Reserve System. One of the tools of ◊monetary policy, the discount rate allows the Federal Reserve System to govern consumer interest rates and the amount of money in circulation.

discrimination distinction made (social, economic, political, legal) between individuals or groups such that one has the power to treat the other unfavorably. *Negative discrimination*, often based on ◊stereotype, includes anti-Semitism, apartheid, caste, racism, sexism, and slavery. *Positive discrimination*, or "affirmative action," is sometimes practiced in an attempt to counteract the effects of previous long-term discrimination. Minorities and, in some cases, majorities have been targets for discrimination.

Discrimination may be on grounds of difference of color, nationality, religion, politics, culture, class, sex, age, or a combination of such factors. Legislation has been to some degree effective in forbidding *racial discrimination*, against which there is a United Nations convention 1969.

National legislation in the US includes the Civil Rights Acts of 1964 and 1968, the Voting Rights Act 1965, and a movement to add an amendment to the Constitution mandating equal rights for women.

discus circular disk thrown by athletes who rotate the body to gain momentum from within a circle 8 ft/2.5 m in diameter. The men's discus weighs 4.4 lb/2 kg and the women's 2.2 lb/1 kg. Discus throwing was a competition in ancient Greece at gymnastic contests, such as those of the Olympic Games. It is an event in the modern Olympics and athletics meetings.

disease any condition that impairs the normal state of an organism, and usually alters the functioning of one or more of its organs or systems. A disease is usually characterized by a set of specific symptoms and signs, although these may not always be apparent to the sufferer. Diseases may be inborn (see ◊congenital disease) or acquired through infection, injury, or other cause. Many diseases have unknown causes.

disinfectant agent that kills, or prevents the growth of, bacteria and other microorganisms. Chemical disinfectants include carbolic acid (phenol, used by ◊Lister in surgery in the 1870s), ethanal, methanal, chlorine, and iodine.

disinvestment withdrawal of investments in a country for political reasons. The term is also used in economics to describe non-replacement of stock as it wears out.

It is generally applied to the ostensive removal of funds from South Africa in recent years by such multinational companies as General Motors and to the withdrawal of private investment funds (by universities, pension funds, and other organizations) from portfolios doing business in South Africa. Disinvestment may be motivated by fear of loss of business in the home market caused by adverse publicity or by fear of loss of foreign resources if the local government changes.

disk in computing, a common medium for storing large volumes of data (an alternative is ◊magnetic tape.) A magnetic disk is rotated at high speed in a disk-drive unit as a read/write (playback or record) head passes over its surfaces to record or "read" the magnetic variations that encode the data. There are several types, including ◊floppy disks, ◊hard disks, and ◊CD-ROM.

Fixed disks provide the most storage. Up to 600 megabytes (million ◊bytes) is quite common, although the **hard disks** of this type used with microcomputers may hold only 10 or 20 megabytes. Fixed or hard disks are built into the drive unit, occasionally stacked one on top of another.

Removable disks are common in minicomputer systems, hold about 80 megabytes of data, and are contained in a rigid plastic case that can be taken out of the drive unit. A *floppy disk* (also called diskette) is very much smaller in size and capacity. Normally holding less than 1 megabyte of data, it is flexible, mounted in a card envelope or rigid plastic case, and can be removed from the drive unit.

Recently, laser disks and compact disks have been used to store computer data. These have an enormous capacity (about 600 megabytes on a compact disk and billions of bytes on a laser disk) but, once written onto the disk, data cannot be erased.

disk drive mechanical device that reads data from and writes data to a magnetic disk.

disk formatting in computing, preparing a blank magnetic disk so that data can be stored on it. Data are recorded on a disk's surface on circular tracks, each of which is divided into a number of sectors. In formatting a disk the computer's operating system adds control information such as track and sector numbers, which enables the data stored to be accessed correctly by the disk-drive unit.

Some hard disks, called hard-sectored disks, are sold already formatted. However, because different makes of computer use different disk formats, most new disks are sold unformatted, or soft-sectored, and computers are provided with the necessary utility program to format these disks correctly before they are used.

Disney Walt (Walter Elias) 1901–1966. US filmmaker who became a pioneer of family entertainment. He and his brother established an animation studio in Hollywood in 1923, and his first Mickey Mouse animated cartoon (*Plane Crazy*) appeared in black and white 1928. *Steamboat Willie* 1928 was his first Mickey Mouse cartoon in color. He developed the "Silly Symphony," a type of cartoon based on the close association of music with the visual image, such as *Fantasia* 1940. His many feature-length cartoons include *Snow White and the Seven Dwarfs* 1938 (his first), *Pinocchio* 1939, *Dumbo* 1941, *Bambi* 1942, *Cinderella* 1950, *Alice in Wonderland* 1952, and *Peter Pan* 1953. Published materials such as books, magazines, comic books, and records accompanied his films and helped make his animated characters beloved throughout the world.

From 1953, when *The Living Desert* was shown, Disney made some remarkable nature-study films. Wholesome features with human casts began with *Treasure Island* 1950, *Davy Crockett* 1955, *The Swiss Family Robinson* 1960, and *Mary Poppins* 1964. Disney produced the first television series in color 1961. He also originated 1955 the concept of pleasure parks, of which Disneyland, California, was the first.

Walt Disney World, near Orlando, Florida, 1971, includes the Epcot (Experimental Prototype Community of Tomorrow) Center 1982, a cross between a science museum and a theme park. There are also parks in Tokyo, Japan, and near Paris, France.

dispersion in optics, the splitting of white light into a spectrum; for example, when it passes through a prism or a diffraction grating. It occurs because the prism (or grating) bends each component wavelength to a slightly different extent. The natural dispersion of light through raindrops creates a rainbow.

displacement activity in animal behavior, an action that is performed out of its normal context, while the animal is in a state of stress, frustration, or uncertainty. Birds, for example, often peck at grass when uncertain whether to attack or flee from an opponent; similarly, humans scratch their heads when nervous.

displacement reaction chemical reaction in which a less reactive element is replaced in a compound by a more reactive one.

For example, the addition of powdered zinc to a solution of copper(II) sulfate displaces copper metal, which can be detected by its characteristic color. See also ◊electrochemical series.

Disraeli Benjamin, Earl of Beaconsfield 1804–1881. British Conservative politician and novelist. Elected to Parliament 1837, he was chancellor of the Exchequer under Lord ◊Derby 1852, 1858–59, and 1866–68, and prime minister 1868 and 1874–80. His imperialist policies brought India directly under the crown, and he was personally responsible for purchasing control of the Suez Canal. The central Conservative Party organization is his creation. His popular, political novels reflect an interest in social reform and include *Coningsby* 1844 and *Sybil* 1845.

Entering Parliament in 1837 after four unsuccessful attempts, he was laughed at as a dandy; when his maiden speech was shouted down, he said: "The time will come when you will hear me."

Excluded from Peel's government of 1841–46, Disraeli formed his Young England group to keep a critical eye on Peel's Conservatism and gradually came to be recognized as the leader of the Conservative Party in the Commons.

During the next 20 years the Conservatives formed short-lived minority governments in 1852, 1858–59, and 1866–68, with Lord Derby as prime minister and Disraeli as chancellor of the Exchequer and leader of the Commons. On Lord Derby's retirement in 1868 Disraeli became prime minister, but a few months later he was defeated by William Gladstone in a general election. In 1874 Disraeli took office for the second time. Some useful reform measures were carried, but the outstanding feature of the government's policy was its imperialism: Disraeli purchased from the Khedive of Egypt a controlling interest in the Suez Canal; conferred on the Queen the title of Empress of India; and sent the Prince of Wales on the first royal tour of that country.

Dissenter former name for a Protestant refusing to conform to the established Christian church. For example, Baptists, Presbyterians, and Independents (now known as Congregationalists) were Dissenters.

dissident in one-party states, a person intellectually dissenting from the official line. Dissidents have been sent into exile, prison, labor camps, and mental institutions, or deprived of their jobs. In the USSR the number of imprisoned dissidents declined from more than 600 in 1986 to fewer than 100 in 1990, of whom the majority were ethnic nationalists. In China the number of prisoners of conscience increased after the 1989 Tiananmen Square massacre, and in South Africa, despite the release of Nelson Mandela in 1990, numerous political dissidents remained in jail.

In the former USSR before the introduction of ◊glasnost, dissidents comprised communists who advocated a more democratic and humanitarian approach; religious proselytizers; Jews wishing to emigrate; and those who supported ethnic or national separatist movements within the USSR (among them Armenians, Lithuanians, Ukrainians, and Tatars). Their views were expressed through samizdat (clandestinely distributed writings) and sometimes published abroad. In the late 1980s Mikhail Gorbachev lifted censorship, accepted a degree of political pluralism, and extended tolerance to religious believers. Almost 100,000 Jews were allowed to emigrate 1985–90. Some formerly persecuted dissidents, most prominently the physicist Andrei ◊Sakharov, emerged as supporters, albeit impatient, of the new reform program.

distance ratio in a machine, the distance moved by the input force, or effort, divided by the distance moved by the output force, or load. The ratio indicates the movement magnification achieved, and is equivalent to the machine's ◊velocity ratio.

distemper any of several infectious diseases of animals characterized by catarrh, cough, and general weakness. Specifically, it refers to a virus disease in young dogs, also found in wild animals, which can now be prevented by vaccination. In 1988 an allied virus killed over 10,000 common seals in the Baltic and North seas.

distillation technique used to purify liquids or to separate mixtures of liquids possessing different boiling points. **Simple distillation** is used in the purification of liquids (or the separation of substances in solution from their solvents)—for example, in the production of pure water from a salt solution.

The solution is boiled and the vapors of the solvent rise into a separate piece of apparatus (the condenser) where they are cooled and condensed. The liquid produced (the distillate) is the pure solvent; the non-volatile solutes (now in solid form) remain in the distillation vessel to be discarded as impurities or recovered as required.

Mixtures of liquids (such as ◊petroleum or aqueous ethanol) are separated by **fractional distillation**, or fractionation. When the mixture is boiled, the vapors of its most volatile component rise into a vertical ◊fractionating column where they condense to liquid form. However, as this liquid runs back down the column it is reheated to boiling point by the hot rising vapors of the next-most-volatile component and so its vapors ascend the column once more. This boiling-condensing process occurs repeatedly inside the column, eventually bringing about a temperature gradient along its length. The vapors of the more volatile components therefore reach the top of the column and enter the condenser for collection before those of the less volatile components. In the fractional distillation of petroleum, groups of compounds (◊fractions) possessing similar molecular weights and boiling points are tapped off at different points on the column.

The earliest-known reference to the process is to the distillation of wine in the 12th century by Adelard of Bath. The chemical retort used for distillation was invented by Muslims, and was first seen in the West about 1570.

distributive operation in mathematics, an operation, such as multiplication, that bears a relationship to another operation, such as addition, such that $a \times (b + c) = (a \times b) + (a \times c)$. For example, $3 \times (2 + 4) = (3 \times 2) + (3 \times 4) = 18$. Multiplication may be said to be distributive over addition. Addition is not, however, distributive over multiplication because $3 + (2 \times 4) \neq (3 + 2) \times (3 + 4)$.

distributor device in the ignition system of a piston engine that distributes pulses of high-voltage electricity to the ◊spark plugs in the cylinders. The electricity is passed to the plug leads by the tip of a rotor arm, driven by the engine camshaft, and current is fed to the rotor arm from the ignition coil. The distributor also houses the contact point or breaker, which opens and closes to interrupt the battery current to the coil, thus triggering the high-voltage pulses. With electronic ignition it is absent.

District of Columbia seat of the federal government of the US, conterminous with the city of Washington, DC; area 69 sq mi/179 sq km. A rectangle along the Potomac River, donated by Maryland and Virginia, was selected as the federal seat of government 1791. For many years the District of Columbia included other local entities besides Washington. At the request of its residents, the portion donated by Virginia was returned to the state 1846, thus confining the District of Columbia to the eastern shore of the Potomac River. Residents elect a mayor and city council and a nonvoting delegate to the US Congress.

Diu island off the Kathiawar peninsular, NW India, part of the Union Territory of ◊Daman and Diu. V

diuretic any drug that rids the body of fluid accumulated in the tissues by increasing the output of urine by the kidneys. It may be used in the treatment of heart disease, high blood pressure, kidney or liver disease, and some endocrine disorders. A potassium supplement is prescribed where potassium loss would be dangerous.

diverticulitis inflammation of diverticula (pockets of herniation) in the large intestine. It is usually controlled by diet and antibiotics.

divertissement (French "entertainment") dance, or group of dances, within a ballet or opera that has no connection with the plot, such as the character dances in the last act of *Coppélia* by Delibes.

dividend in business, the amount of money that company directors decide should be taken out of profits for distribution to stockholders. It is usually declared as a percentage or fixed amount per share.

Most companies pay dividends quarterly; others once a year.

divination art of ascertaining future events or eliciting other hidden knowledge by supernatural or nonrational means. Divination played a large part in the ancient civilizations of the Egyptians, Greeks (see ◊oracle), Romans, and Chinese (see ◊*I Ching*), and is still practiced throughout the world.

Divination generally involves the intuitive interpretation of the mechanical operations of chance or natural law. Forms of divination have included omens drawn from the behavior of birds and animals; examination of the entrails of sacrificed animals; random opening of such books as the Bible; fortune-telling by cards (see ◊tarot) and palmistry; ◊dowsing; oracular trance-speaking; automatic writing; necromancy, or the supposed raising of the spirits of the dead; and dreams, often specially induced.

Divine Comedy, The epic poem by Dante Alighieri 1307–21, describing a journey through Hell, Purgatory, and Paradise. The poet Virgil is Dante's guide through Hell and Purgatory; to each of the three realms, or circles, Dante assigns historical and contemporary personages according to their moral (and also political) worth. In Paradise Dante finds his lifelong love Beatrice. The poem makes great use of symbolism and allegory, and influenced many English writers including Milton, Byron, Shelley, and T S Eliot.

Divine Light Mission religious movement founded in India in 1960, which gained a prominent following in the US in the 1970s. It proclaims *Guru Maharaj Ji* as the present age's successor to the gods or religious leaders Krishna, Buddha, Jesus, and Mohammed. He is believed to be able to provide his followers with the knowledge required to attain salvation.

divine right of kings Christian political doctrine that hereditary monarchy is the system approved by God, hereditary right cannot be forfeited, monarchs are accountable to God alone for their actions, and rebellion against the lawful sovereign is therefore blasphemous.

The doctrine had its origins in the anointing of Pepin in 751 by the pope after Pepin had usurped the throne of the Franks. It was at its peak in 16th-and 17th-century Europe as a weapon against the claims of the papacy—the court of Louis XIV of France pushed this to the limit—and was in 17th-century England maintained by the supporters of the Stuarts in opposition to the democratic theories of the Puritans and Whigs.

Many of the latter group migrated to the American colonies to avoid persecution.

diving the sport of entering the water either from a springboard (3ft/ 1 m or 10 ft/3 m) above the water, or from a platform (33ft/10 m) above the water. Various differing starts are adopted, facing forward or backward, and somersaults, twists, and other positions or combinations thereof are performed in midair before entering the water. Pool depths of 20 ft/ 6 m are needed for high or platform diving, but 10 ft/3 m-deep pools may accommodate 1 or 3 meter diving. Points are awarded and the level of difficulty of each dive is used as a multiplying factor.

diving apparatus any equipment used to enable a person to spend time underwater. Diving bells were in use in the 18th century, the diver breathing air trapped in a bell-shaped chamber. This was followed by cumbersome diving suits in the early 19th century. Complete freedom of movement came with the ◊aqualung, invented by Jacques ◊Cousteau in the early 1940s. For work at greater depths the technique of saturation diving was developed in the 1970s by which divers live for a week or more breathing a mixture of helium and oxygen at the pressure existing on the seabed where they work (as in tunnel building).

The first diving suit, with a large metal helmet supplied with air through a hose, was

Djibouti
Republic of (*Jumhouriyya Djibouti*)

area 8,955 sq mi/23,200 sq km
capital (and chief port) Djibouti
cities Tadjoura, Obock, Dikhil
physical mountains divide an inland plateau from a coastal plain; hot and arid
features terminus of railroad link with Ethiopia; Lac Assal salt lake is the second lowest point on Earth (−471 ft/−144 m)
head of state and government Hassan Gouled Aptidon from 1977
political system authoritarian nationalism
political party People's Progress Assembly

(RPP), nationalist
exports acts mainly as a transit port for Ethiopia
currency Djibouti franc
population (1990 est) 337,000 (Issa 47%, Afar 37%, European 8%, Arab 6%); growth rate 3.4% p.a.
life expectancy 50
languages French (official), Somali, Afar, Arabic
religion Sunni Muslim
literacy 20% (1988)
GDP $378 million (1987); $1,016 per head
chronology
1884 Annexed by France as part of French Somaliland.
1967 French Somaliland became the French Territory of the Afars and the Issas.
1977 Independence achieved from France; Hassan Gouled elected president.
1979 All political parties combined to form the People's Progress Assembly (RPP).
1981 New constitution made RPP the only legal party. Gouled reelected. Treaties of friendship signed with Ethiopia, Somalia, Kenya, and Sudan.
1984 Policy of neutrality reaffirmed.
1987 Gouled reelected for a final term.
1991 Amnesty International accused secret police of brutality.
1992 Djibouti elected member of United Nations (UN) Security Council 1993-95.

invented in the UK by the brothers John and Charles Deane in 1828.

Saturation diving was developed for working in offshore oil fields. Working divers are ferried down to the work site by a lock-out ◊submersible. By this technique they avoid the need for lengthy periods of decompression after every dive. Slow decompression is necessary to avoid the dangerous consequences of an attack of the bends, or ◊decompression sickness.

division military formation consisting of two or more brigades. A major general at divisional headquarters commands the brigades and also additional artillery, engineers, attack helicopters, and other logistic support. There are 10,000 or more soldiers in a division. Two or more divisions form a corps.

division of labor the separation of tasks in processing or producing goods, especially in industrial or factory settings, but also in traditional societies where males and females perform gender-related tasks (a sexual division of labor). See also ◊factory system.

divorce legal dissolution of a lawful marriage. It is distinct from an annulment, which is a legal declaration that the marriage was invalid. The ease with which a divorce can be obtained in different countries varies considerably and is also affected by different religious practices.

In the US divorce laws differ from state to state. The grounds include adultery (in all states), cruelty, desertion, alcoholism, drug addiction, insanity, and declaration of irreconcilable differences or mutual incompatibility. Quick divorces in states with more liberal laws have been restricted by the imposition of minimum residence periods and by the right to challenge the divorce if one party has not been notified of the proceedings. Couples are increasingly negotiating prenuptial agreements that make an advance settlement of division of property and assets, including maintenance provisions. In some states, so-called no-fault

divorce laws make divorces readily available to couples with no economic quarrels and with agreeable obligations to children.

The Roman Catholic church does not permit divorce among its members, and under Pope John Paul II conditions for annulment have been tightened. Among Muslims a wife cannot divorce her husband, but he may divorce her by repeating the formula "I divorce you" three times (called *talaq*). In Shiite law this must be pronounced either once or three times in the presence of two witnesses; in Sunni law it can be either oral or in writing. No reason need be given, nor does the wife have to be notified (although some Muslim countries, for example Pakistan, have introduced such a requirement). Property settlements by careful parents make this a right infrequently exercised.

Laws introduced in the USSR in the 1960s made divorce easy and cheap. Maintenance for a wife after divorce decreased in importance, but she was likely to benefit by a more equitable division of property.

Dix Dorothea Lynde 1802–1887. US educator and medical reformer. From 1841 she devoted herself to a campaign for the rights of the mentally ill, helping to improve conditions and treatment in public institutions for the insane in the US, and Japan. During the US Civil War, she served as superintendent of nurses.

Born in Hampden, Maine, and raised in Boston, Dix began her career as a teacher at a girls' school in Worcester, Massachusetts, and opened her own school in Boston 1821. Forced by ill health to retire in 1835, she traveled in Europe and published several books.

Dixieland jazz name given to a jazz style that originated in New Orleans in the early 20th century and worked its way up the Mississippi. It is characterized by improvisation and the playing back and forth of the cornet, trumpet, clarinet, and trombone. The steady background beat is supplied by the piano, bass, and percussion instrument players, who also have

Key
S sugars
P phosphates
C cytosine
G guanine
A adenine
T thymine

DNA *How the DNA molecule divides.*

(Figure labels, top to bottom: 1 original double helix; 2 forms ladder; 3 unzips; 4 new bases join onto opened zip teeth; 5 two new identical double strands)

their turns to solo. It is usually played by bands of four to eight members. Noted Dixieland musicians were King Oliver, Jelly Roll ◊Morton, and Louis ◊Armstrong.

Diyarbakir town in Asiatic Turkey, on the river Tigris; population (1990) 381,100. It has a trade in gold and silver filigree work, copper, wool, and mohair, and manufactures textiles and leather goods.

Djakarta variant spelling of ◊Jakarta, capital of Indonesia.

Djibouti country on the E coast of Africa, at the S end of the Red Sea, bounded E by the Gulf of Aden, SE by Somalia, and S, W, and N by Ethiopia.
government The 1981 constitution made Djibouti a one-party state, the only legal party being the People's Progress Assembly (RPP). The constitution also provides for a single-chamber legislature, the 65-member chamber of deputies, elected by universal suffrage for a five-year term, and a president, nominated by the party, who is elected for six years and may not serve more than two terms.
history During the 9th century missionaries from Arabia converted the Afars inhabiting the area to Islam. A series of wars was fought by the Afar Islamic states and Christian Ethiopia from the 13th to 17th centuries. The French arrived 1862, and in 1884 annexed Djibouti and the neighboring region as the colony of French Somaliland. In 1967 it was renamed the French Territory of the Afars and the Issas. Opposition to French rule grew during the 1970s, and calls for independence were frequent, sometimes violent.
independence Independence as the Republic of Djibouti was achieved 1977, with Hassan Gouled as president. In 1979 all political parties combined to form the RPP, and the government embarked on the task of uniting the two main ethnic groups: the Issas, who traditionally had strong links with Somalia, and the Afars, who had been linked with Ethiopia.
amicable neutralism In 1981 a new constitution was adopted, making the RPP the only party. President Gouled was reelected, and in 1982 a chamber of deputies was elected from a list of RPP nominees. Under Gouled, Djibouti pursued a largely successful policy of amicable neutralism with its neighbors, concluding treaties of friendship with Ethiopia, Somalia, Kenya, and Sudan, and tried to assist the peace process in East Africa. Although affected by the 1984-85 droughts, Djibouti managed to maintain stability with European Community aid. Gouled was reelected 1987 for his final term with 98.71% of the popular vote. In 1991 Amnesty International charged Djibouti's security police with brutality in their treatment of political prisoners. In 1992 Djibouti was elected to the United Nations (UN) Security Council for the period 1993-95. *See illustration box.*

Djibouti chief port and capital of the Republic of Djibouti, on a peninsula 149 mi/240 km SW of Aden and 351 mi/565 km NE of Addis Ababa; population (1988) 290,000.
The city succeeded Obock as capital of French Somaliland 1896 and was the official port of Ethiopia 1897–1949.

Djilas Milovan 1911– . Yugoslav political writer and dissident. A former close wartime colleague of Marshal Tito, in 1953 he was dismissed from high office and subsequently imprisoned because of his advocacy of greater political pluralism. He was released 1966 and formally rehabilitated 1989.

DMus abbreviation for *Doctor of Music*.

DNA (*deoxyribonucleic acid*) complex giant molecule that contains, in chemically coded form, all the information needed to build, control, and maintain a living organism. DNA is a ladderlike double-stranded ◊nucleic acid that forms the basis of genetic inheritance in all organisms, except for a few viruses that have only ◊RNA. In organisms other than bacteria it is organized into ◊chromosomes and contained in the cell nucleus.
DNA is made up of two chains of ◊nucleotide sub-units, with each nucleotide containing either a purine (adenine or guanine) or pyrimidine (cytosine or thymine) base. The bases link up with each other (adenine linking with thymine, and cytosine with guanine) to form ◊base pairs that connect the two strands of the DNA molecule like the rungs of a twisted ladder. The specific way in which the pairs form means that the base sequence is preserved from generation to generation.

Hereditary information is stored as a specific sequence of bases. A set of three bases—known as a *codon*—acts as a blueprint for the manufacture of a particular ◊amino acid, the sub-unit of a protein molecule. Geneticists identify the codons by the initial letters of the constituent bases—for example, the base sequence of codon CAG is cytosine–adenine–guanine. The meaning of each of the codons in the ◊genetic code has been worked out by molecular geneticists. There are four different bases, which means that there must be $4 \times 4 \times 4 = 64$ different codons. Proteins are usually made up of only 20 different amino acids, so many amino acids have more than one codon (for example, GGT, GGC, GGA and GGG all code for the same amino acid, glycine).
The information encoded by the codons is transcribed (see ◊transcription) by messenger RNA and is then translated into amino acids in the ribosomes and cytoplasm. The sequence of codons determines the precise order in which amino acids are linked up during manufacture and, therefore, the kind of protein that is to be produced. Because proteins are the chief structural molecules of living matter and, as enzymes, regulate all aspects of metabolism, it may be seen that the genetic code is effectively responsible for building and controlling the whole organism.

Dnepropetrovsk city in Ukraine, on the right bank of the river Dnieper; population (1987) 1,182,000. It is the center of an major industrial region, with iron, steel, chemical, and engineering industries. It is linked with the Dnieper Dam, 37 mi/60 km downstream.

Dnieper or *Dnepr* river rising in the Smolensk region of Russia and flowing south through Belarus, Ukraine to enter the Black Sea east of Odessa; total length 1,400 mi/2,250 km.

do. abbreviation for *ditto*.

Dobermann or *Dobermann pinscher* smooth-coated dog with a docked tail, much used as a guard dog. It stands up to 2.2 ft/70 cm tall, has a long head with a flat, smooth skull, and is often black with brown markings. It takes its name from the man who bred it in 19th-century Germany.

Döblin Alfred 1878–1957. German novelist. His *Berlin-Alexanderplatz* 1929 owes much to James Joyce in its minutely detailed depiction of the inner lives of a city's inhabitants, and is considered by many to be the finest 20th-century German novel. Other works include *November 1918: Eine deutsche Revolution/A German Revolution* 1939–50 (published in four parts) about the formation of the Weimar Republic.

Dobruja district in the Balkans, bounded to the N and W by the Danube and to the E by the Black Sea. It is low-lying, partly marshland, partly fertile steppe land. Constanta is the chief town. Dobruja was divided between Romania and Bulgaria in 1878. In 1913, after the second Balkan War, Bulgaria ceded its part to Romania but received it back in 1940, a cession confirmed by the peace treaty of 1947.

Dobrynin Anataloy Fedorovich 1919– . Soviet diplomat, ambassador to the US 1962-86, emerging during the 1970s as a warm supporter of ◊détente.
Dobrynin joined the Soviet diplomatic service in 1941. He served as counselor at the Soviet embassy in Washington, DC 1952-55,

assistant to the minister for foreign affairs 1955–57, undersecretary at the United Nations 1957–59, and head of the USSR's American department 1959–61, before being appointed Soviet ambassador to Washington in 1962. He remained at this post for 25 years. Brought back to Moscow by the new Soviet leader Mikhail Gorbachev, he was appointed to the Communist Party's Secretariat as head of the International Department, before retiring in 1988.

Dobzhansky Theodosius 1900–1975. US geneticist of Ukrainian origin. A pioneer of modern genetics and evolutionary theory, he showed that genetic variability between individuals of the same species is very high and that this diversity is vital to the process of evolution. His book *Genetics and the Origin of Species* was published in 1937.

dock or **sorrel** in botany, any of a number of plants of the genus *Rumex* of the buckwheat family Polygonaceae. They are tall, annual to perennial herbs, often with lance-shaped leaves and small, greenish flowers. Native to temperate regions, there are 30 North American and several British species.

Doctorow E(dgar) L(awrence) 1931– . US writer. He is noted for novels in which he weaves history and fiction together. His first novel, *The Book of Daniel* 1971, about the ◊Rosenbergs' trial and execution, won him instant fame. His other works include *Ragtime* 1975, *Loon Lake* 1980, *Lives of the Poets* 1984, *World's Fair* 1985, and *Billy Bathgate* 1989.

Doctor Zhivago novel by the Russian writer Boris Pasternak, published (in Italy) 1957. The novel, which describes a doctor's disillusionment with the Russian revolution, was banned in the USSR as a "hostile act" and only published there in magazine form 1988.

document in computing, data associated with a particular application. For example, a **text document** might be produced by a ◊word processor and a **graphics document** might be produced with a ◊CAD package. An ◊OCR document is a paper document containing data that can be directly input to the computer using a document reader.

documentation in computing, the written information associated with a computer program or ◊applications package. Documentation is usually divided into two categories: program documentation and user documentation.

Program documentation is the complete technical description of a program, drawn up as the software is written and intended to support any later maintenance or development of that program. It typically includes details of when, where, and by whom the software was written; a general description of the purpose of the software, including recommended input, output, and storage methods; a detailed description of the way the software functions, including full program listings and ◊flow charts; and details of software testing, including sets of ◊test data with expected results.

User documentation explains how to operate the software. It typically includes a nontechnical explanation of the purpose of the software; instructions for loading, running, and using the software; instructions for preparing any necessary input data; instructions for requesting and interpreting output data; and explanations of any error messages that the program may produce.

dodder parasitic plant, genus *Cuscuta*, of the

morning-glory family Convolvulaceae, without leaves or roots. The thin stem twines around the host, and penetrating suckers withdraw nourishment.

Dodecanese (Greek *Dhodhekánisos* "twelve islands") group of islands in the Aegean Sea; area 1,028 sq mi/2,663 sq km. Once Turkish, the islands were Italian from 1912 to 1947, when they were ceded to Greece. They include ◊Rhodes and ◊Kos. Chief products include fruit, olives, and sponges.

dodecaphonic in music, the ◊twelve-tone system of composition.

Dodge City city in SW Kansas, on the Arkansas River; population (1990) 21,100. It was a noted frontier cattle town in the days of the Wild West.

Founded 1872 with the arrival of the railroad, it became the terminus for cattle drives from the Santa Fe Trail. Wyatt Earp and Bat Masterson were law officials here, and Boot Hill Cemetery has been preserved. Farm and livestock-handling machinery are manufactured here.

Dodgson Charles Lutwidge. Real name of writer Lewis ◊Carroll.

dodo extinct bird *Raphus cucullatus* formerly found on the island of Mauritius, but exterminated before the end of the 17th century. Although related to the pigeons, it was larger than a turkey, with a bulky body and very short wings and tail. Flightless and trusting, it was easy prey to humans.

Dodoma capital (replacing Dar es Salaam 1974) of Tanzania; 3,713 ft/1,132 m above sea level; population (1985) 85,000. It is a center of communications, linked by rail with Dar es Salaam and Kigoma on Lake Tanganyika, and by road with Kenya to the north and Zambia and Malawi to the south.

Doe Samuel Kenyon 1950–1990. Liberian politician and soldier, head of state 1980–90. He seized power in a coup. Having successfully put down an uprising April 1990, Doe was deposed and killed by rebel forces Sept 1990.

Doe joined the army in 1969 and rose to the rank of master sergeant ten years later. He led a coup in which President Tolbert was killed 1980. Doe replaced him as head of state, then had 13 cabinet members shot in front of reporters. In 1981 he made himself general and army commander in chief. In 1985 he was narrowly elected president, as leader of the newly formed National Democratic Party of Liberia. His human-rights record was poor.

dog any carnivorous mammal of the family Canidae, including wild dogs, wolves, jackals, coyotes, and foxes. Specifically, the domestic dog *Canis familiaris*, the earliest animal descended from the wolf or jackal. Dogs were first domesticated over 10,000 years ago, and migrated with humans to all the continents. They have been selectively bred into many different varieties for use as working animals and pets.

Of the wild dogs, some are solitary, such as the long-legged maned wolf *Chrysocyon brachurus* of South America, but others hunt in groups, such as the African hunting dog *Lycaon pictus* (classified as a vulnerable species) and the ◊wolf. ◊Jackals scavenge for food, and the raccoon dog *Nyctereutes procyonoides* of E Asia includes plant food as well as meat in its diet. The Australian wild dog is the ◊dingo.

In the US, the American Kennel Club sets standards for about 200 registered breeds.

dogbane any sometimes poisonous herbaceous North American plant of the genus *Apocynum*, with opposite leaves, small white or pink flowers, and milky juice. The term also is used to designate any member of the dogbane family Apocynaceae, which includes various herbaceous plants, shrubs, and trees such as oleander and periwinkle.

doge chief magistrate in the ancient constitutions of Venice and Genoa. The first doge of Venice was appointed 697 with absolute power (modified 1297), and from his accession dates Venice's prominence in history. The last Venetian doge, Lodovico Manin, retired 1797 and the last Genoese doge 1804.

Dōgen 1200–1253. Japanese Buddhist monk, pupil of Eisai; founder of the Sōtō school of Zen. He did not reject study, but stressed the importance of *zazen*, seated meditation, for its own sake.

dogfish any of several small sharks found in the NE Atlantic, Pacific, and Mediterranean.

The spiny dogfish *Squalus acanthius* of the Pacific and Atlantic grows to about 4 ft/1.2 m long. It is a common subject for dissection in biology laboratories.

Dogger Bank submerged sandbank in the North Sea, about 70 mi/115 km off the coast of Yorkshire, England. In places the water is only 36 ft/11 m deep, but the general depth is 60–120 ft/18–36 m; it is a well-known fishing ground.

Dogon member of the W African Dogon culture from E Mali and NW Burkina Faso. The Dogon number approximately 250,000 and their language belongs to the Voltaic (Gur) branch of the Niger-Congo family.

dogwood any of a genus *Cornus* of trees and shrubs of the dogwood family (Cornaceae), native to temperate regions of North America and Eurasia. The flowering dogwood *Cornus florida* of the E US is often cultivated as an ornamental for its beautiful blooms consisting of clusters of small greenish flowers surrounded by four large white or pink petallike ◊bracts.

Heads of small white flowers, each with four petals joined as a tube, are produced in midsummer, followed by black berries. The dogwood is characteristic of lime soils in the S of England, and is found over much of S Europe. Various other species of dogwood are planted in gardens.

Doha (Arabic *Ad Dawḥah*) capital and chief port of Qatar; population (1986) 217,000. Industries include oil refining, refrigeration plants, engineering, and food processing. It is the center of vocational training for all the Persian Gulf states.

Doi Takako 1929– . Japanese socialist politician, leader of the Japan Socialist Party (JSP) from 1986 and responsible for much of its recent revival. She is the country's first female major party leader.

Doisy Edward 1893–1986. US biochemist. In 1939 he succeeded in synthesizing vitamin K, a compound earlier discovered by Carl ◊Dam, with whom he shared the 1943 Nobel Prize for Medicine.

Dolci Carlo 1616–1686. Italian painter of the late Baroque period, active in Florence. He created intensely emotional versions of religious subjects, such as *The Last Communion of St Jerome*.

Dolci was the foremost painter in Florence in his time and continued to be much admired in the 18th century. He was also a portraitist, and was sent to Austria in 1675 to paint the Medici wife of the emperor Leopold I.

doldrums area of low atmospheric pressure along the equator, in the intertropical convergence zone where the NE and SE trade winds converge. The doldrums are characterized by calm or very light westerly winds, during which there may be sudden squalls and stormy weather. For this reason the areas are avoided as far as possible by sailing ships.

Dolin Anton. Adopted name of Patrick Healey-Kay 1904–1983. British dancer and choreographer, a pioneer of UK ballet. After studying under Vaslav Nijinsky, he was a leading member of Sergei Diaghilev's company 1924–29. He formed the Markova–Dolin Ballet with Alicia Markova 1935–38, and was a guest soloist with the American Ballet Theater 1940–46.

dollar monetary unit of several countries. In the US the dollar, which contains 100 cents, was adopted 1785 and is represented by the symbol "$." US dollars originally were issued as gold or silver coins; today both metal and paper dollars circulate, but paper predominates. Australia, Canada, and Hong Kong are among the other countries that use the dollar unit, but none of these dollars is equivalent in value to the US dollar.

The US dollar emerged from World War II as the standard currency for international trade. Commodities, even if priced in other currencies, were valued at the prevailing dollar exchange rate. Rising US imports, especially of oil, and government spending resulted in large numbers of dollars held in foreign hands with the resultant devaluation of the dollar by the 1980s. The German mark and the Japanese yen are increasingly important as trading currencies. See also ⬦Eurodollar; ⬦petrodollars.

Dollfuss Engelbert 1892–1934. Austrian Christian Socialist politician. He was appointed chancellor in 1932, and in 1933 suppressed parliament and ruled by decree. In Feb 1934 he crushed a protest by the socialist workers by force, and in May Austria was declared a "corporative" state. The Nazis attempted a coup d'état on July 25; the Chancellery was seized and Dollfuss murdered.

Doll's House, The play by Henrik Ibsen, first produced in Norway 1879. It describes the blackmail of Nora, the sheltered wife of a successful lawyer, the revelation of her guilty secret to her husband, and the subsequent marital breakdown.

dolmen prehistoric monument in the form of a chamber built of large stone slabs, roofed over by a flat stone which they support. Dolmens are grave chambers of the Neolithic period, found in Europe and Africa, and occasionally in Asia as far east as Japan.

dolomite white mineral with a hexagonal structure, calcium magnesium carbonate $(CaMg (CO_3)_2)$. The term also applies to a type of limestone rock where the calcite content is replaced by the mineral dolomite. Dolomite rock may be white, gray, brown, or reddish in color, commonly crystalline. It is used as a building material. The region of the Alps known as the Dolomites is a fine example of dolomite formation.

dolomite in geology, a sedimentary rock containing a high proportion of the mineral dolomite; a variety of limestone, or marble (if

metamorphosed). The magnesian limestone of N England is a dolomite.

dolphin any of various highly intelligent aquatic mammals of the family Delphinidae, which also includes porpoises. There are about 60 species. The name "dolphin" is generally applied to species having a beaklike snout and slender body, whereas the name "porpoise" is reserved for the smaller species with a blunt snout and stocky body. Dolphins use sound (echolocation) to navigate, to find prey, and for communication.

The common dolphin *Delphinus delphis* is found in all temperate and tropical seas. It is up to 8 ft/2.5 m long, and is dark above and white below, with bands of gray, white, and yellow on the sides. It has up to 100 teeth in its jaws, which make the 6 in/15 cm "beak" protrude forward from the rounded head. The corners of its mouth are permanently upturned, giving the appearance of a smile, though dolphins cannot actually smile. Dolphins feed on fish and squid.

The river dolphins, of which there are only five species, belong to the family Platanistidae. All river dolphins are threatened by dams and pollution, and some, such as the whitefin dolphin *Lipotes vexillifer* of the Chiang Jiang River, China, are in danger of extinction. As a result of living in muddy water, river dolphins' eyes have become very small. They rely on echolocation to navigate and find food.

Some species of dolphin can swim at up to 35 mph/56 kph, helped by special streamlining modifications of the skin. All power themselves by beating the tail up and down, and use the flippers to steer and stabilize. The flippers betray dolphins' land-mammal ancestry with their typical five-toed limb-bone structure.

Dolphins are popular performers in aquariums. The species most frequently seen is the bottle-nosed dolphin *Tursiops truncatus*, found in all warm seas, mainly gray in color and growing to a maximum 14 ft/4.2 m. The US Navy began training dolphins for military purposes in 1962, and in 1987 six dolphins were sent to detect mines in the Persian Gulf.

Marine dolphins are endangered by fishing nets, speedboats, and pollution. In 1990 the North Sea states agreed to introduce legislation to protect them.

Also known as **dolphin** is the totally unrelated true fish *Coryphaena hippurus*, up to 5 ft/1.5 m long.

Domagk Gerhard 1895–1964. German pathologist, discoverer of antibacterial sulfonamide drugs. He found in 1932 that a coal-tar dye called Prontosil red contains chemicals with powerful antibacterial properties. Sulfanilamide became the first of the sulfonamide drugs, used before ⬦antibiotics were discovered to treat a wide range of conditions, including pneumonia and septic wounds. Domagk was awarded the 1939 Nobel Prize for Physiology and Medicine.

domain small area in a magnetic material that behaves like a tiny magnet. The magnetism of the material is due to the movement of electrons in the atoms of the domain. In an unmagnetized sample of material, the domains point in random directions, or form closed loops, so that there is no overall magnetization of the sample. In a magnetized sample, the domains are aligned so that their magnetic effects combine to produce a strong overall magnetism.

dome a geological feature that is the reverse of a basin. It consists of anticlinally folded rocks

that dip in all directions from a central high point, like an inverted but usually irregular cup.

Such structural domes are the result of pressure acting upward from below to produce an uplifted portion of the crust. Domes are often formed by the upwelling of plastic materials such as salt or magma. The salt domes along the North American Gulf Coast were produced by upwelling ancient sea salt deposits, while the Black Hills of South Dakota are the result of structural domes pushed up by intruding igneous masses.

Domenichino real name Domenico Zampieri 1582–1641. Italian Baroque painter and architect, active in Bologna, Naples, and Rome. He began as an assistant to the ⬦Carracci family of painters and continued the early Baroque style in, for example, frescoes 1624–28 in the choir of S Andrea della Valle, Rome.

This style was superseded by High Baroque, and Domenichino retreated to Naples. He is considered a pioneer of landscape painting in the Baroque period.

Domenico Veneziano c. 1400–1461. Italian painter, active in Florence. His few surviving frescoes and altarpieces show a remarkably delicate use of color and light (which recurs in the work of Piero della Francesca, who worked with him).

He worked in Sta Egidio, Florence, on frescoes now lost. Remaining works include the *Carnesecchi Madonna and Two Saints* and the St Lucy altarpiece, now divided between Florence (Uffizi), Berlin, Cambridge (Fitzwilliam), and Washington, DC (National Gallery).

Dome of the Rock building in Jerusalem dating from the 7th century AD that enshrines the rock from which, in Muslim tradition, Mohammed ascended to heaven on his ⬦Night Journey. It stands on the site of the Jewish national Temple and is visited by pilgrims.

Domesday Book record of the survey of England carried out 1086 by officials of William the Conqueror in order to assess land tax and other dues, ascertain the value of the crown lands, and enable the king to estimate the power of his vassal barons. The name is derived from the belief that its judgment was as final as that of Doomsday.

Northumberland and Durham were omitted, and also London, Winchester, and certain other towns. The Domesday Book is preserved in two volumes at the Public Record Office, London.

dominance in genetics, the masking of one allele (an alternate form of a gene) by another allele. For example, if a ⬦heterozygous person has one allele for blue eyes and one for brown eyes, his or her eye color will be brown. The allele for blue eyes is described as recessive and the allele for brown eyes as dominant.

Domingo Placido 1937– . Spanish tenor who excels in romantic operatic roles. He made his debut 1960 as Alfredo in Verdi's *La Traviata*, then spent four years with the Israel National Opera. He sang at the New York City Opera 1965 and has since performed diverse roles in opera houses worldwide. In 1986 he starred in the film version of *Otello*.

Dominica island in the E Caribbean, between Guadeloupe and Martinique, the largest of the Windward Islands, with the Atlantic Ocean to the E and the Caribbean Sea to the W.
government Dominica is an independent republic within the British Commonwealth. The

constitution dates from independence 1978 and provides for a single-chamber, 30-member house of assembly. Twenty-one are representatives elected by universal suffrage, and nine are appointed senators, five on the advice of the prime minister and four on the advice of the leader of the opposition. The assembly serves a five-year term, as does the president, who is elected by it and acts as constitutional head of state, appointing the prime minister on the basis of assembly support. The prime minister chooses the cabinet, and all are responsible to the assembly.

history The island was inhabited by the Amerindian Caribs at the time Christopher Columbus visited it 1493 (since Columbus arrived at the island on a Sunday, he named it Dominica). It became a British possession in the 18th century and was part of the Leeward Islands federation until 1939. In 1940 it was transferred to the Windward Islands and remained attached to that group until 1960, when it was given separate status, with a chief minister and legislative council.

full independence achieved In 1961 the leader of the Dominica Labor Party (DLP), Edward le Blanc, became chief minister; after 13 years in office he retired and was succeeded as prime minister by Patrick John. The DLP held office until full independence was achieved 1978, at which time its leader, John, became the first prime minister under the new constitution. Opposition to John's increasingly authoritarian style of government soon developed, and in the 1980 elections the Dominica Freedom Party (DFP) won a convincing victory on a free-enterprise program. Its leader, Eugenia Charles, became the Caribbean's first woman prime minister.

antigovernment intrigue In 1981 John was thought to be implicated in a plot against the government, and a state of emergency was imposed. The next year he was tried and acquitted. He was retried 1985, found guilty, and given a 12-year prison sentence. Left-of-center parties regrouped, making the new Labor Party of Dominica (LPD) the main opposition to the DFP. Eugenia Charles was reelected 1985 and, with a reduced majority, 1990.

foreign relations Under Eugenia Charles's leadership, Dominica has developed links with France and the US and in 1983 sent a small force to participate in the US-backed invasion of Grenada. In 1991 representatives of Dominica, St Lucia, St Vincent and the Grenadines, and Grenada proposed that integration with the Windward Islands would benefit the islands politically and economically. Integration would be based on a federal state system, with an elected, executive president and a two-chamber assembly. *See illustration box.*

Dominican order Roman Catholic order of friars founded 1215 by St Dominic. The Dominicans are also known as Friars Preachers, Black Friars, or Jacobins. The order is worldwide and there is also an order of contemplative nuns; the habit is black and white.

The first house was established in Toulouse in 1215; in 1216 the order received papal recognition, and their rule was drawn up in 1220–21. They soon spread all over Europe. Dominicans have included Thomas Aquinas, Savonarola, and Las Casas.

Dominican Republic country in the West Indies (E Caribbean), occupying the eastern two-thirds of the island of Hispaniola, with Haiti covering the western third; the Atlantic Ocean is to the E and the Caribbean Sea to the W.

government Although not a federal state, the Dominican Republic has a highly devolved system of 27 provinces (each administered by an appointed governor), and a national district, which includes the capital, Santo Domingo. The 1966 constitution provides for a popularly elected president and a two-chamber congress, comprising a senate and a chamber of deputies, all elected for a four-year term. The senate has 28 members, one for each province and one for the national district, and the chamber of deputies 120 members, one per 50,000 inhabitants. The president is head of both government and state and chooses the cabinet.

history The island was inhabited by Arawak and Carib Indians when Christopher Columbus arrived 1492, the first European to visit the island. He named it Hispaniola ("Little Spain"). It was divided between France and Spain 1697, and in 1795 the Spanish part (Santo Domingo) was ceded to France. After a revolt it was retaken by Spain 1808. Following a brief period of independence 1821, it was occupied by Haiti until a successful revolt resulted in the establishment of the Dominican Republic 1844.

Spain occupied the country again 1861–65, and after independence was restored, it was in such financial difficulties that in 1904 the US took over its debts and intervened militarily 1916–24.

military coups In 1930 the elected president was overthrown in a military coup, and General Rafael Trujillo Molina became dictator. He was assassinated 1961, and in 1962 Dr Juan Bosch, founder and leader of the left-wing Dominican Revolutionary Party (PRD), who had been in exile for over 30 years, won the country's first free elections. Within a year he was overthrown by the military, who set up their own three-person ruling junta.

democratic constitution An attempt to reestablish Bosch 1965 was defeated with the intervention of US forces, and in 1966 Joaquín Balaguer, a protégé of Trujillo and leader of the Christian Social Reform Party (PRSC), won the presidency. A more democratic constitution was adopted, and Balaguer, despite his links with Trujillo, proved a popular leader, being reelected 1970 and 1974.

The 1978 election was won by the PRD candidate, Silvestre Antonio Guzmán. The PRD was again successful in the 1982 election, and Salvador Jorge Blanco, the party's left-wing nominee, became president-designate. After allegations of fraud by his family, Guzmán committed suicide before he had finished his term, and an interim president was chosen before the start of Blanco's term.

Blanco steered a restrained course in foreign policy, maintaining good relations with the US and avoiding too close an association with Cuba. The economy deteriorated, and in 1985 the Blanco administration was forced to adopt harsh austerity measures in return for help from the ◊International Monetary Fund. The PRD became increasingly unpopular, and the PRSC, under Joaquin Balaguer, returned to power 1986. He was reelected 1990, but by a paper-thin margin, and his party lost its legislative majority. *See illustration box.*

Dominic, St 1170–1221. Founder of the Roman Catholic Dominican order of preaching friars. Feast day Aug 7.

Born in Old Castile, Dominic was sent by Pope Innocent III in 1205 to preach to the heretic Albigensian sect in Provence. In 1208 the Pope instigated the Albigensian crusade to suppress the heretics by force, and this was supported by Dominic. In 1215 the Dominican order was given premises at Toulouse; during the following years Dominic established friaries at Bologna and elsewhere in Italy,

Dominica
Commonwealth of

area 290 sq mi/751 sq km
capital Roseau, with a deepwater port
cities Portsmouth, Marigot
physical second largest of the Windward Islands, mountainous central ridge with tropical rainforest
features of great beauty, it has mountains of volcanic origin rising to 5,317 ft/1,620 m; Boiling Lake (an effect produced by escaping subterranean gas)
head of state Clarence Seignoret from 1983
head of government Eugenia Charles from 1980
political system liberal democracy

political parties Dominica Freedom Party (DFP), centrist; Labor Party of Dominica (LPD), left-of-center coalition
exports bananas, coconuts, citrus, lime, bay oil
currency E Caribbean dollar, pound sterling, French franc
population (1990 est) 94,200 (mainly black African in origin, but with a small Carib reserve of some 500); growth rate 1.3% p.a.
life expectancy men 57, women 59
language English (official), but the Dominican patois reflects earlier periods of French rule
media one independent weekly newspaper
religion Roman Catholic 80%
literacy 80%
GDP $91 million (1985); $1,090 per head
chronology
1763 Became British possession.
1978 Independence achieved from Britain. Patrick John, leader of Dominica Labor Party (DLP), elected prime minister.
1980 Dominica Freedom Party (DFP), led by Eugenia Charles, won convincing victory in general election.
1981 Patrick John implicated in plot to overthrow government.
1982 John tried and acquitted.
1985 John retried and found guilty. Regrouping of left-of-center parties resulted in new Labor Party of Dominica (LPD). DFP, led by Eugenia Charles, reelected.
1990 Charles elected to a third term.
1991 Integration into Windward Islands confederation proposed.

and by the time of his death the order was established all over W Europe.

Domino "Fats" (Antoine) 1928– . US rock-and-roll pianist, singer, and songwriter, exponent of the New Orleans style. His hits include "Ain't That a Shame" 1955 and "Blueberry Hill" 1956.

domino theory idea popularized by US president Eisenhower in 1954 that if one country came under communist rule, adjacent countries were likely to become communist as well.

Initially used to justify US intervention in SE Asia, the domino theory has also been invoked in reference to Central America.

Domitian Titus Flavius Domitianus AD 51–96. Roman emperor from AD 81. He finalized the conquest of Britain (see ◊Agricola), strengthened the Rhine–Danube frontier, and suppressed immorality as well as freedom of thought in philosophy (see ◊Epictetus) and religion (Christians were persecuted). His reign of terror led to his assassination.

Don river in Russia, rising to the S of Moscow and entering the NE extremity of the Sea of Azov; length 1,180 mi/1,900 km. In its lower reaches the Don is 1 mi/1.5 km wide, and for about four months of the year it is closed by ice. Its upper course is linked with the river Volga by a canal.

Donald Ian 1910–1987. English obstetrician who introduced ultrasound (very high-frequency sound wave) scanning. He pioneered its use in obstetrics as a means of scanning the growing fetus without exposure to the danger of X-rays. Donald's experience of using radar in World War II suggested to him the use of ultrasound for medical purposes.

Donald Duck cartoon character created 1934 by US animator Walt Disney. The belligerent, sailor-suited duck first appeared in a supporting role for the "Silly Symphony" short of *The Wise Little Hen*. He rapidly gained popularity and achieved star billing for the first time in *Donald and Pluto* 1936. From 1936 he appeared in a US newspaper comic strip. He won an Academy Award with *Der Fuhrer's Face* 1942.

Donatello (Donato di Niccolo) 1386–1466. Italian sculptor of the early Renaissance, born in Florence. He was instrumental in reviving the Classical style, as in his graceful bronze statue of the youthful *David* (Bargello, Florence) and his equestrian statue of the general *Gattamelata* 1443 (Padua). The course of Florentine art in the 15th century was strongly influenced by his style.

Donatello introduced true perspective in his relief sculptures, such as the panel of *St George Slaying the Dragon* about 1415–17 (Or San Michele, Florence). During a stay in Rome 1430–32 he absorbed Classical influences, and *David* is said to be the first free-standing nude since antiquity. In his later work, such as his wood-carving of the aged *Mary Magdalene* about 1456 (Baptistry, Florence), he sought dramatic expression through a distorted, emaciated figure style.

Donation of Constantine forged 8th-century document purporting to record the Roman emperor Constantine's surrender of temporal sovereignty in W Europe to Pope Sylvester I (314–25).

In the Middle Ages, this document was used as papal propaganda in the struggle between pope and emperor, which was at its most heated during the ◊investiture contest. It was finally exposed as forged by the German philosopher ◊Nicholas of Cusa and Lorenzo Valla in the 15th century.

Donatist member of a puritanical Christian movement in 4th- and 5th-century N Africa, named after Donatus of Casae Nigrae, a 3rd-century bishop, later known as Donatus of Carthage.

The Donatists became for a time the major Christian movement in N Africa; following the tradition of ◊Montanism, their faith stressed the social revolutionary aspects of Christianity, the separation of church from state, and a belief in martyrdom and suffering. Their influence was ended by Bishop Augustine of Hippo; they were formally condemned 412.

Donbas abbreviation for the ◊*Donets Basin*, a coal-rich area in Ukraine.

Donegal mountainous county in Ulster province in the NW of the Republic of Ireland, surrounded on three sides by the Atlantic; area 1,864 sq mi/4,830 sq km; population (1991) 127,900. The county town is Lifford; the market port city of Donegal is at the head of Donegal Bay in the SW. Commercial activities include sheep and cattle raising, tweed and linen manufacture, and some deep-sea fishing. The river Erne hydroelectric project (1952) involved the building of large power stations at Ballyshannon.

Donen Stanley 1924– . US film director, formerly a dancer, who co-directed two of Gene Kelly's best musicals, *On the Town* 1949 and *Singin' in the Rain* 1952. His other films include *Charade* 1963 and *Two for the Road* 1968.

Donets river rising in the Kursk region of Russia and flowing 670 mi/1,080 km through Ukraine to join the river Don 60 mi/100 km E of Rostov; see also ◊Donets Basin.

Donets Basin (abbreviated to *Donbas*) area in Ukraine, situated in the bend formed by the rivers Don and Donets, which holds one of Europe's richest coalfields, together with salt, mercury, and lead.

Donetsk city in Ukraine; capital of Donetsk region, situated in the Donets Basin, a major coal-mining area, 372 mi/600 km SE of Kiev; population (1987) 1,090,000. It has blast furnaces, rolling mills, and other heavy industries.

It developed from 1871 when a Welshman, John Hughes, established a metallurgical factory, and the town was first called Yuzovka after him; it was renamed Stalino 1924, and Donetsk 1961.

Dönitz Karl 1891–1980. German admiral, originator of the wolf-pack submarine technique, which sank 15 million tons of Allied shipping in World War II. He succeeded Hitler in 1945, capitulated, and was imprisoned 1946–56.

Donizetti Gaetano 1797–1848. Italian composer who created more than 60 operas, including *Lucrezia Borgia* 1833, *Lucia di Lammermoor* 1835, *La Fille du régiment* 1840, *La Favorite* 1840, and *Don Pasquale* 1843. They show the influence of Rossini and Bellini, and are characterized by a flow of expressive melodies.

Don Juan character of Spanish legend, Don Juan Tenorio, supposed to have lived in the 14th century and notorious for his debauchery. Tirso de Molina, Molière, Mozart, Byron, and George Bernard Shaw have featured the legend in their works.

donkey another name for ◊ass.

Dominican Republic
(*República Dominicana*)

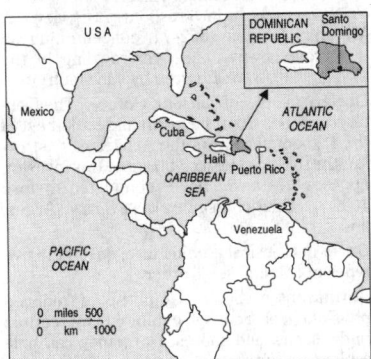

area 18,700 sq mi/48,442 sq km
capital Santo Domingo
cities Santiago de los Caballeros, San Pedro de Macoris
physical comprises eastern two-thirds of island of Hispaniola; central mountain range with fertile valleys
features Pico Duarte 10,417 ft/3,174 m, highest point in Caribbean islands; Santo Domingo is the oldest European city in the western hemisphere
head of state and government Joaquín Ricardo Balaguer from 1986
political system democratic republic
political parties Dominican Revolutionary Party (PRD), moderate, left of center; Christian Social Reform Party (PRSC), independent socialist; Dominican Liberation Party (PLD), nationalist
exports sugar, gold, silver, tobacco, coffee, nickel
currency peso
population (1989 est) 7,307,000; growth rate 2.3% p.a.
life expectancy men 61, women 65
language Spanish (official)
religion Roman Catholic 95%
literacy men 78%, women 77% (1985 est)
GDP $4.9 bn (1987); $731 per head
chronology
1492 Visited by Christopher Columbus.
1844 Dominican Republic established.
1930 Military coup established dictatorship of Rafael Trujillo.
1961 Trujillo assassinated.
1962 First democratic elections resulted in Juan Bosch, founder of the PRD, becoming president.
1963 Bosch overthrown in military coup.
1965 US Marines intervene to restore order and protect foreign nationals.
1966 New constitution adopted. Joaquín Balaguer, leader of PRSC, became president.
1978 PRD returned to power, with Silvestre Antonio Guzmán as president.
1982 PRD reelected, with Jorge Blanco as president.
1985 Blanco forced by International Monetary Fund to adopt austerity measures to save the economy.
1986 PRSC returned to power, with Balaguer reelected president.
1990 Balaguer reelected by a small majority.

Donne John 1571–1631. English metaphysical poet. His work consists of love poems, religious poems, verse satires, and sermons, most of which were first published after his death. His religious poems show the same passion and ingenuity as his love poetry. A Roman Catholic in his youth, he converted to the Church of England and finally became dean of St Paul's Cathedral, where he is buried.

Donne was brought up in the Roman Catholic faith and matriculated early at Oxford to avoid taking the oath of supremacy. Before becoming a law student 1592 he traveled in Europe. During his four years at the law courts he was notorious for his wit and reckless living. In 1596 he sailed as a volunteer in an expedition against Spain with the Earl of Essex and Walter Raleigh, and on his return became private secretary to Sir Thomas Egerton, Keeper of the Seal. This appointment was ended by his secret marriage to Ann More (died 1617), niece of Egerton's wife, and they endured many years of poverty. The more passionate and tender of his love poems were probably written to her.

From 1621 to his death Donne was dean of St Paul's. His sermons rank him with the century's greatest orators, and his fervent poems of love and hate, violent, tender, or abusive, give him a unique position among English poets. His verse was not published in collected form until after his death, and was long out of favor, but he is now recognized as one of the greatest English poets.

Donnybrook former village, now part of Dublin, Republic of Ireland, notorious until 1855 for riotous fairs.

Donovan William Joseph 1883–1959. US military leader and public official. Donovan served as US district attorney 1922–24 and as assistant to the US attorney general 1925–29. He was national security adviser to both presidents Hoover and F D Roosevelt and founded the Office of Strategic Services (OSS) 1942. As OSS director 1942–45, Donovan coordinated US intelligence during World War II. When the OSS became the CIA 1947, President Truman passed over Donovan as its first director. President Eisenhower, however, appointed Donovan ambassador to Thailand 1953–54, calling him America's "last hero."

Born in Buffalo, New York, Donovan was educated at Columbia University and was admitted to the bar 1907. He saw action along the Mexican border 1912 and was decorated for bravery during World War I, gaining the nickname "Wild Bill."

Don Quixote de la Mancha satirical romance by the Spanish novelist Miguel de Cervantes, published in two parts 1605 and 1615. Don Quixote, a self-styled knight, embarks on a series of chivalric adventures accompanied by his servant Sancho Panza. Quixote's imagination leads him to see harmless objects as enemies to be fought, as in his tilting at windmills.

doodlebug another name for ⟩ant lion.

Dooley Thomas Anthony 1927–1961. US medical missionary. As a naval physician, he was sent to Vietnam 1954 to tend to the refugees streaming south after the partition of the country. This assignment aroused Dooley's compassion, and he was involved in medical work in SE Asia for the rest of his life. He founded Medico, an international welfare organization 1957, as well as medical clinics in Cambodia, Laos, and Vietnam.

Born in St Louis, Dooley attended Notre Dame University, joined the navy, and received an MD degree from St Louis University 1953.

Doolittle Hilda. Adopted name *HD* 1886–1961. US poet who went to Europe 1911, and was associated with Ezra Pound and the British writer Richard Aldington (to whom she was married 1913–37) in founding the Imagist school of poetry, advocating simplicity, precision, and brevity. Her work includes the *Sea Garden* 1916 and *Helen in Egypt* 1916.

Doolittle James Harold 1896– . US aviation pioneer. He helped develop new aircraft designs and more efficient aircraft fuel. With the approach of World War II, he returned to active service and in 1942 led a daring bombing raid over Tokyo. Later in the war he participated in the invasion of North Africa and the intensive bombing of Germany.

Born in Alameda, California, Doolittle attended the University of California and served as an army flying instructor during World War I. Later, in the Army Air Corps, he became an aviation specialist, earning an engineering degree from the Massachusetts Institute of Technology (MIT).

Doomsday Book variant spelling of ⟩Domesday Book, the English survey of 1086.

Doors, the US psychedelic rock group formed 1965 in Los Angeles by Jim Morrison (1943–1971, vocals), Ray Manzarek (1935– , keyboards), Robby Krieger (1946– , guitar), and John Densmore (1944– , drums). Their first hit was "Light My Fire" from their debut album *The Doors* 1967. They were noted for Morrison's poetic lyrics and flamboyant performance.

doo-wop US pop-music form of the 1950s, a style of harmony singing without instrumental accompaniment or nearly so, almost exclusively by male groups. The name derives from the practice of having the lead vocalist singing the lyrics against a backing of nonsense syllables from the other members of the group. Many of the doo-wop groups were named after birds; for example, the Ravens and the Orioles.

Doo-wop had roots in the 1930s with rhythm-and-blues groups like the Ink Spots and in gospel music. It was practiced by street-corner groups in the inner cities, some of whom went on to make hit records; for example, "Earth Angel" by the Penguins 1954 and "Why Do Fools Fall in Love" by Frankie Lymon and the Teenagers 1956. The first doo-wop record to be a number-one US pop hit was "The Great Pretender" by the Platters 1955.

dopamine neurotransmitter, hydroxytyramine $C_8H_{11}NO_2$, an intermediate in the formation of adrenaline. There are special nerve cells (neurones) in the brain that use dopamine for the transmission of nervous impulses. One such area of dopamine neurones lies in the basal ganglia, a region that controls movement. Patients suffering from the tremors of Parkinson's disease show nerve degeneration in this region. Another dopamine brain area lies in the limbic system, a region closely involved with emotional responses. It has been found that schizophrenic patients respond well to drugs that act on limbic dopamine receptors in the brain.

doppelgänger (German "double-goer") apparition of a living person, a person's double, or a guardian spirit. The German composer and writer E T A Hoffman wrote a short story called *Die Doppelgänger* in 1821. English novelist Charles Williams used the idea to great effect in his novel *Descent into Hell* 1937.

Doppler Christian Johann 1803–1853.

Austrian physicist. He became professor of experimental physics at Vienna. He described the *Doppler effect*.

Doppler effect change in the observed frequency (or wavelength) of waves due to relative motion between the wave source and the observer. The Doppler effect is responsible for the perceived change in pitch of a siren as it approaches and then recedes, and for the ⟩red shift of light from distant stars. It is named after the Austrian physicist Christian Doppler (1803–1853).

Dorado constellation of the southern hemisphere, represented as a goldfish. It is easy to locate, since the Large ⟩Magellanic Cloud marks its southern border.

Its brightest star is Alpha Doradus, just under 200 light-years from Earth.

Dorati Antál 1906–1988. US conductor, born in Hungary. He toured with ballet companies 1933–45 and went on to conduct orchestras in the US and Europe in a career spanning more than half a century. Dorati gave many first performances of Bartók's music and recorded all Haydn's symphonies with the Philharmonia Hungarica.

Dordogne river in SW France, rising in Puy-de-Dôme *département* and flowing 300 mi/490 km to join the river Garonne, 14 mi/23 km N of Bordeaux. It gives its name to a *département* and is a major source of hydroelectric power.

The valley of the Dordogne is a popular tourist area, and the caves of the wooded valleys of its tributary, the Vézère, have signs of early human occupation. Famous sites include the Cro Magnon, Le Moustier, and Lascaux caves.

Doré Gustave 1832–1883. French artist, chiefly known as a prolific illustrator, and also active as a painter, etcher, and sculptor. He produced closely worked engravings of scenes from, for example, Rabelais, Dante, Cervantes, the Bible, Milton, and Edgar Allan Poe.

Doré was born in Strasbourg. His views of Victorian London 1869–71, concentrating on desperate poverty and overcrowding in the swollen city, were admired by van Gogh.

Dorian people of ancient Greece. They entered Greece from the north and took most of the Peloponnese from the Achaeans, destroying the ⟩Mycenaean civilization; this invasion appears to have been completed before 1000 BC. Their chief cities were Sparta, Argos, and Corinth.

Doric in Classical architecture, one of the five types of column; see ⟩order.

dormancy in botany, a phase of reduced physiological activity exhibited by certain buds, seeds, and spores. Dormancy can help a plant to survive unfavorable conditions, as in annual plants that pass the cold winter season as dormant seeds, and plants that form dormant buds.

For various reasons many seeds exhibit a period of dormancy even when conditions are favorable for growth. Sometimes this dormancy can be broken by artificial methods, such as penetrating the seed coat to facilitate the uptake of water (chitting) or exposing the seed to light. Other seeds require a period of ⟩after-ripening.

dormouse small rodent, of the family Gliridae, with a hairy tail. There are about ten species, living in Europe, Asia, and Africa. They are arboreal (live in trees) and nocturnal, and they hibernate during winter in cold regions.

The fat or edible dormouse *Glis glis* lives in

continental Europe and is 12 in/30 cm long including its tail. It was a delicacy at Roman feasts.

Dorset county in SW England
area 1,023 sq mi/2,650 sq km
cities Dorchester (administrative headquarters), Poole, Shaftesbury, Sherborne; resorts: Bournemouth, Lyme Regis, Weymouth
features Chesil Bank, a shingle bank along the coast 11 mi/19 km long; Isle of Purbeck, a peninsula where kaolinite and Purbeck "marble" are quarried, and which includes Corfe Castle and the vacation resort of Swanage; Dorset Downs; Cranborne Chase; rivers Frome and Stour; Maiden Castle; Tank Museum at Royal Armoured Corps Center, Bovington, where the cottage of T E ◊Lawrence is a museum
products Wytch Farm is the largest onshore oil field in the UK
population (1987) 649,000
famous people Thomas Hardy, the novelist, born at Higher Bockhampton (Dorchester is "Casterbridge," the heart of Hardy country).

Dorsey Jimmy 1904–1957, and Tommy 1905–1956. US bandleaders, musicians, and composers during the ◊swing music era. They worked together in the Dorsey Brothers Orchestra 1934–35 and 1953–56, but led separate bands in the intervening period. The Jimmy Dorsey band was primarily a dance band; the Tommy Dorsey band was more jazz-oriented and featured the singer Frank Sinatra 1940–42. Both Dorsey bands featured in a number of films in the 1940s, and the brothers appeared together in *The Fabulous Dorseys* 1947.

Dortmund industrial center in the ◊Ruhr, Germany, 36 mi/58 km NE of Düsseldorf; population (1988) 568,000. It is the largest mining town of the Westphalian coalfield and the southern terminus of the Dortmund–Ems canal. Industries include iron, steel, construction machinery, engineering, and brewing.

dory any of several marine fishes of the order Zeiformes. The American John Dory *Zenopsis ocellata*, to 2 ft/60 cm long, is deep-bodied with long spines on the dorsal and ventral fins. It lives in depths of 300 ft/90 m to 1,200 ft/365 m.

DOS (acronym for *disk operating system*) computer ◊operating system specifically designed for use with disk storage; also used as an alternate name for a particular operating system, ◊MS-DOS.

Dos Passos John 1896–1970. US author. He made his reputation with the war novels *One Man's Initiation* 1919 and *Three Soldiers* 1921. His major work is the trilogy *U.S.A.* 1930–36, which gives a panoramic view of US life through the device of placing fictitious characters against the setting of real newspaper headlines and contemporary events.

Born in Chicago, Dos Passos was a member of the post-World War I "lost generation," and his writing was shaped by his radical sympathies. He also wrote a second, less ambitious trilogy, *District of Columbia* 1939–49. Other works include *One Man's Initiation—1917* 1919 and *Midcentury* 1961.

Dos Santos José Eduardo 1942– . Angolan left-wing politician, president from 1979, a member of the People's Movement for the Liberation of Angola (MPLA). By 1989, he had negotiated the withdrawal of South African and Cuban forces, and in 1991 a peace agreement to end the civil war. An upsurge of civil strife followed a victory for Dos Santos and the MPLA in Sept 1992 elections.

Dos Santos joined the MPLA in 1961 and went into exile the same year during the struggle for independence and the civil war between nationalist movements—the MPLA and the National Union for the Total Independence of Angola (UNITA)—backed by foreign powers. He returned to Angola 1970 and rejoined the war, which continued after independence 1975. He held key positions under President Agostinho Neto, and succeeded him on his death. Despite the uncertainty of the cease-fire between MPLA and UNITA 1989, Dos Santos confirmed his pledge of substantial political reform, and concluded a peace agreement 1991. In Sept 1992 his victory in multiparty elections was disputed by rebel leader Jonas Savimbi; fighting between government and UNITA supporters ensued.

Dostoevsky Fyodor Mikhailovich 1821–1881. Russian novelist. Remarkable for their profound psychological insight, Dostoevsky's novels have greatly influenced Russian writers, and since the beginning of the 20th century have been increasingly influential abroad. In 1849 he was sentenced to four years' hard labor in Siberia, followed by army service, for printing socialist propaganda. *The House of the Dead* 1861 recalls his prison experiences, followed by his major works *Crime and Punishment* 1866, *The Idiot* 1868–69, and *The Brothers Karamazov* 1880.

Born in Moscow, the son of a physician, Dostoevsky was for a short time an army officer. His first novel, *Poor Folk*, appeared in 1846. In 1849, during a period of intense tsarist censorship, he was arrested as a member of a free-thinking literary circle and sentenced to death. After a last-minute reprieve he was sent to the penal settlement at Omsk for four years, where the terrible conditions increased his epileptic tendency. Finally pardoned in 1859, he published the humorous *Village of Stepanchikovo, The House of the Dead*, and *The Insulted and the Injured* 1862. Meanwhile he had launched two unsuccessful liberal periodicals, in the second of which his *Letters from the Underworld* 1864 appeared. Compelled to work by pressure of debt, he quickly produced *Crime and Punishment* 1866 and *The Gambler* 1867, before fleeing the country to escape from his creditors. He then wrote *The Idiot* (in which the hero is an epileptic like himself), *The Eternal Husband* 1870, and *The Possessed* 1871–72.

Returning to Russia in 1871, he again entered journalism and issued the personal miscellany *Journal of an Author*, in which he discussed contemporary problems. In 1875 he published *A Raw Youth*, but the great work of his last years is *The Brothers Karamazov*.

Dothan city in the SE corner of Alabama, SE of Montgomery; seat of Houston county. Its industries include fertilizer, clothing, furniture, vegetable oils, and hosiery. It is an agricultural and livestock marketing center; population (1990) 53,589.

Douai town in the Nord *département*, France, on the river Scarpe; population (1982) 44,515, conurbation 202,000. It has coal mines, iron foundries, and breweries. An English Roman Catholic college was founded there 1568 by English Catholics in exile. The Douai-Reims Bible, published 1582–1610, influenced the translators of the King James Version.

Douala or *Duala* chief port and industrial center (aluminum, chemicals, textiles, pulp) of Cameroon, on the Wouri River estuary; population (1981) 637,000. Known as Kamerunstadt

until 1907, it was capital of German Cameroon 1885–1901.

double bass large bowed four-stringed musical instrument, the bass of the ◊violin family, tuned in fourths, and descended from the violone of the ◊viol family.

double bond two covalent bonds between adjacent atoms, as in the ◊alkenes (–C=C–) and ◊ketones (–C=O–).

double coconut treelike ◊palm plant *Lodoicea maldivica*, also known as *coco de mer*, of the Seychelles. It produces a two-lobed edible nut, one of the largest known fruits.

Doubleday Abner 1819–1893. Military leader and reputed inventor of baseball. He was present at Fort Sumter at the outbreak of the Civil War and was eventually promoted to the rank of major general, serving in the Shenandoah Valley and at Bull Run, Antietam, and Gettysburg. He retired from active service 1873. In 1907 Doubleday's name surfaced during a baseball committee's investigation into the origins of the major-league sport. According to testimony given at the time, Doubleday invented the game of baseball 1839 in Cooperstown, New York, a claim refuted by sports historians ever since.

Born in Ballston Spa, New York, Doubleday graduated from West Point 1842 and saw action in the Mexican War.

double decomposition reaction between two chemical substances (usually ◊salts in solution) that results in the exchange of a constituent from each compound to create two different compounds.

For example, if silver nitrate solution is added to a solution of sodium chloride, there is an exchange of ions yielding sodium nitrate and silver chloride.

double jeopardy in law, the principle that a person cannot be prosecuted twice for the same offense. It is contained in the Fifth Amendment of the US Constitution.

double star two stars that appear close together. Most double stars attract each other due to gravity, and orbit each other, forming a genuine ◊binary star, but other double stars are at different distances from Earth, and lie in the same line of sight only by chance. Through a telescope both types of double star look the same.

dough mixture consisting primarily of flour, water, and yeast, which is used in the manufacture of bread.

The preparation of dough involves thorough mixing (kneading) and standing in a warm place to "prove" (increase in volume) so that the ◊enzymes in the dough can break down the starch from the flour into smaller sugar molecules, which are then fermented by the yeast. This releases carbon dioxide, which causes the dough to rise.

doughboy nickname for a US infantry soldier in the two world wars, especially World War I.

Douglas Kirk. Adopted name of Issur Danielovitch Demsky 1916– . US film actor. Usually cast as a dynamic and intelligent hero, as in *Spartacus* 1960, he was a major star of the 1950s and 1960s in such films as *Ace in the Hole* 1951, *The Bad and the Beautiful* 1953, *Lust for Life* 1956, *The Vikings* 1958, *Seven Days in May* 1964, and *The War Wagon* 1967. He continues to act and produce, along with his son Michael Douglas.

Douglas Michael 1944– . US film actor and

producer. One of the biggest box-office draws of the late 1980s and 1990s, Douglas won an Academy Award for his portrayal of a ruthless corporate raider in *Wall Street* 1987. His acting range includes both romantic and heroic leads in films such as *Romancing the Stone* 1984 and *Jewel of the Nile* 1985, both of which he produced. Among his other films are *Fatal Attraction* 1987 and *Basic Instinct* 1991.

Douglas first achieved recognition in the television series *The Streets of San Francisco* 1972–76, and as co-producer of *One Flew Over the Cuckoo's Nest* 1975 which won an Academy Award for best picture. He is the son of actor Kirk ⟩Douglas.

Douglas Stephen Arnold 1813–1861. US politician. An active Democrat, he served in the Illinois state legislature 1836, as a judge of the state supreme court 1841, and in the US House of Representatives 1843–47. As a US senator 1847–61, he gained the nickname "Little Giant" for his support for westward expansion. Urging a compromise on slavery, he debated Lincoln during the 1858 Senate race and won that election. After losing the 1860 presidential race to Lincoln, Douglas pledged his loyal support to the Lincoln administration.

Born in Brandon, Vermont, Douglas moved west, settling in Illinois, where he studied law and was admitted to the bar 1834.

Douglas fir any of some six species of coniferous evergreen tree of the family Pinaceae. The most common is *Pseudotsuga menziesii*, native to western North America and E Asia. It grows 200–300 ft/60–90 m, has long, flat, spirally-arranged needles and hanging cones, and produces hard, strong timber. *P. glauca* has shorter, bluish needles and grows to 100 ft/30 m in mountainous areas.

Douglass Frederick 1817–1895. US antislavery campaigner, especially through speeches and his newspaper *North Star*. He issued a call to blacks to take up arms against the South and helped organize two black regiments. After the Civil War, he held several US government posts, including minister to Haiti 1889–91. He published appeals for full civil rights for blacks and also campaigned for women's suffrage.

Born a slave in Maryland, he escaped 1838 and fled to Britain to avoid reenslavement, returning to the US after he had secured sufficient funds to purchase his freedom. His autobiographical *Narrative of the Life of Frederick Douglass* 1845 aroused support for the abolition of slavery.

Doukhobor member of a Christian sect of Russian origin, now mainly found in Canada, also known as "Christians of the Universal Brotherhood."

They were long persecuted, mainly for refusing military service—the writer Tolstoy organized a relief fund for them—but in 1898 were permitted to emigrate and settled in Canada, where they number about 13,000, mainly in British Columbia and Saskatchewan. An extremist group, "the Sons of Freedom," staged demonstrations and guerrilla acts in the 1960s, leading to the imprisonment of about 100 of them.

Some of the Doukhobor teachings resemble those of the Quakers.

Doulton Henry 1820–1897. English ceramicist. He developed special wares for the chemical, electrical, and building industries, and established the world's first stoneware-drainpipe factory 1846. From 1870 he created art pottery and domestic tablewares in

Lambeth, S London, and Burslem, near Stoke-on-Trent.

Douro (Spanish *Duero*) river rising in N central Spain and flowing through N Portugal to the Atlantic at Porto; length 500 mi/800 km. Navigation at the river mouth is hindered by sand bars. There are hydroelectric installations.

Dover market town and seaport on the SE coast of Kent, England; population (1981) 33,000. It is Britain's nearest point to mainland Europe, being only 21 mi/34 km from Calais, France. Dover's development has been chiefly due to the cross-Channel traffic, which includes train, ferry, hovercraft, and other services. It was one of the ⟩Cinque Ports, part of England's defenses against invasion after the Norman Conquest.

Dover city in SE New Hampshire, on the Cocheco River, NW of Portsmouth; seat of Strafford county. Industries include lumber, electronics, rubber, and aluminum products; population (1990) 25,000.

Dover capital of Delaware, located in the central part of the state, on the St Jones River, S of Wilmington. Industries include synthetic materials, adhesives, latex, resins, chemicals, food products, and space equipment; population (1990) 27,600.

Dover, Strait of (French *Pas-de-Calais*) stretch of water separating England from France, and connecting the English Channel with the North Sea. It is about 22 mi/35 km long and 21 mi/34 km wide at its narrowest part. It is one of the world's busiest sea lanes.

Dow Jones average New York Stock Exchange index, the most widely used indicator of US stock market prices. The average (no longer simply an average but today calculated to take into account changes in the constituent companies) is based on prices of 30 major companies, such as IBM and Walt Disney. It was first compiled 1884 by Charles Henry Dow, cofounder of Dow Jones & Co., publishers of the *Wall Street Journal*.

Down county in SE Northern Ireland, facing the Irish Sea on the E; area 953 sq mi/2,470 sq km; population (1981) 53,000. To the S are the Mourne mountains, to the E Strangford sea lough. The county town is Downpatrick; the main industry is dairying.

Down syndrome chromosomal abnormality that manifests itself by slowing the person's mental abilities and motor skills; the leading clinical cause of mental disabilities. The incidence is approximately 1 in every 800 to 1,000 live births, and it has no predetermination to race, sex, or national origin. The extra chromosome material can come from either the mother or the father. With special education, these children can reach a level, in many cases, on a par with their non-disabled peers, but may do so at a slower pace. The syndrome is named after English physician J L H Down (1828–1896).

dowry property or money given by the bride's family to the groom or his family as part of the marriage agreement; the opposite of ⟩bridewealth. In 1961 dowries were made illegal in India; however, in 1992 the Indian government reported more than 15,000 murders or suicides between 1988 and 1991 that were a direct result of insufficient dowries.

dowsing ascertaining the presence of water or minerals beneath the ground with a forked twig or pendulum. Unconscious muscular action by the dowser is thought to move the twig,

usually held with one fork in each hand, possibly in response to a local change in the pattern of electrical forces. The ability has been known since at least the 16th century and, though not widely recognized by science, it has been used commercially and in archeology.

Doxiadis Constantinos 1913–1975. Greek architect and town planner; designer of ⟩Islamabad, the capital of Pakistan.

Doyle Arthur Conan 1859–1930. British writer, creator of the detective Sherlock Holmes and his assistant Dr Watson, who first appeared in *A Study in Scarlet* 1887 and featured in a number of subsequent stories, including *The Hound of the Baskervilles* 1902. Conan Doyle also wrote historical romances (*Micah Clarke* 1889 and *The White Company* 1891) and the scientific romance *The Lost World* 1912.

Born in Edinburgh, Conan Doyle qualified as a doctor, and during the second South African War (or Boer War) was senior physician of a field hospital. His Sherlock Holmes character featured in several books, including *The Sign of Four* 1889 and *The Valley of Fear* 1915, as well as in volumes of short stories, first published in the *Strand Magazine*. In his later years Conan Doyle became a spiritualist.

D'Oyly Carte Richard 1844–1901. British producer of the Gilbert and Sullivan operas at the Savoy Theater, London, which he built. The old D'Oyly Carte Opera Company founded 1876 was disbanded 1982, but a new one opened its first season 1988. Since 1991 the company has moved to the Alexandra Theater in Birmingham.

Drabble Margaret 1939– . British writer. Her novels include *The Millstone* 1966 (filmed as *The Touch of Love*), *The Middle Ground* 1980, *The Radiant Way* 1987, and *A Natural Curiosity* 1989. She edited the 1985 edition of the *Oxford Companion to English Literature*.

Draco 7th century BC. Athenian politician, the first to codify the laws of the Athenian city-state. These were notorious for their severity; hence **draconian**, meaning particularly harsh.

Draco in astronomy, a large but faint constellation, representing a dragon coiled around the north celestial pole. The star Alpha Draconis (Thuban) was the pole star 4,800 years ago.

Dracula in the novel *Dracula* 1897 by Bram ⟩Stoker, the caped count who, as a ⟩vampire, drinks the blood of beautiful women. The original of Dracula is thought to have been Vlad Tepeş, or Vlad the Impaler, ruler of medieval Wallachia, who used to impale his victims and then mock them.

draft compulsory military service; also known as ⟩conscription.

drag resistance to motion a body experiences when passing through a fluid—gas or liquid. The aerodynamic drag aircraft experience when traveling through the air represents a great waste of power, so they must be carefully shaped, or streamlined, to reduce drag to a minimum. Cars benefit from streamlining, and aerodynamic drag is used to slow down spacecraft returning from space. Boats traveling through water experience hydrodynamic drag on their hulls, and the fastest vessels are ⟩hydrofoils, whose hulls lift out of the water while cruising.

dragon Euro-Asian mythical reptilian beast, often portrayed as breathing fire. The name is popularly given to various sorts of lizard. These include the ⟩flying dragon *Draco volans* of SE

Asia; the komodo dragon *Varanus komodoensis* of Indonesia, at over 10 ft/3 m the largest living lizard; and some Australian lizards with bizarre spines or frills.

dragonfly any of numerous insects of the order Odonata, including the ▷damselfly. They all have long narrow bodies, two pairs of almost equal-sized, glassy wings with a network of veins; short, bristlelike antennae; powerful, "toothed" mouthparts; and very large compound eyes which may have up to 30,000 facets. They hunt other insects by sight, both as adults and as aquatic nymphs.

The largest species have a wingspan of 7 in/18 cm, but fossils related to dragonflies with wings up to 2.3 ft/70 cm across have been found.

drag racing motor sport popular in the US. High-powered single-seater automobiles with large rear and small front wheels are timed over a 440 yd/402.2 m strip. Speeds of up to 280 mph/450 kph have been attained.

Drake Francis *c.* 1545–1596. English buccaneer and explorer. Having enriched himself as a pirate against Spanish interests in the Caribbean 1567–72, he was sponsored by Elizabeth I for an expedition to the Pacific, sailing round the world 1577–80 in the *Golden Hind*, robbing Spanish ships as he went. This was the second circumnavigation of the globe (the first was by the Portuguese explorer Ferdinand Magellan). Drake also helped to defeat the Spanish Armada 1588 as a vice admiral in the *Revenge*.

Drake suggested to Queen Elizabeth I an expedition to the Pacific, and it was granted; in Dec 1577 he sailed in the *Pelican* with four other ships and 166 men toward South America. In Aug 1578 the fleet passed through the Straits of Magellan and was then blown south to Cape Horn. The ships became separated and returned to England, all but the *Pelican*, now renamed the *Golden Hind*. Drake sailed north along the coast of Chile and Peru, robbing Spanish ships as far north as California, and then, in July 1579, traveled southwest across the Pacific. He rounded the South African Cape June 1580, and reached England Sept 1580, thus completing the second voyage around the world. When the Spanish ambassador demanded Drake's punishment, the Queen knighted him on the deck of the *Golden Hind* in London.

In a raid on Cádiz 1587 he burned 10,000 tons of shipping and delayed the Spanish Armada for a year. Drake sailed on his last expedition to the West Indies 1595, and in Jan 1596 died on his ship.

Drakensberg (Afrikaans "dragon"s mountain') mountain range in South Africa (Sesuto name *Quathlamba*), on the boundary of Lesotho and the Orange Free State with Natal. Its highest point is Thaban Ntlenyana, 10,988 ft/3,350 m, near which is Natal National Park.

drama in theater, any play performed by actors for an audience. The term is also used collectively to group plays into historical or stylistic periods—for example, Greek drama, Restoration drama—as well as referring to the whole body of work written by a dramatist for performance. Drama is distinct from literature in that it is a performing art open to infinite interpretation, the product not merely of the playwright but also of the collaboration of director, designer, actors, and technical staff. See also ▷comedy, ▷tragedy, and ▷mime.

dramatis personae (Latin) the characters in a play.

Dravidian group of non-Indo-European peoples of the Deccan region of India and in N Sri Lanka. The Dravidian language family is large, with about 20 languages spoken in S India; the main ones are Tamil, which has a literary tradition 2,000 years old; Kanarese; Telugu; Malayalam; and Tulu.

Dreadnought class of battleships built for the British navy after 1905 and far superior in speed and armaments to anything then afloat. The first modern battleship to be built, it was the basis of battleship design for more than 50 years. It was first launched February 18, 1906, with armaments consisting entirely of big guns.

The German Nassau class was begun in 1907, and by 1914, the US, France, Japan and Austria-Hungary all had battleships of a similar class to the Dreadnought. German plans to build similar craft led to the naval race that contributed to Anglo-German antagonism and the origins of World War II.

dream series of events or images perceived through the mind during sleep. Their function is unknown, but by Sigmund ▷Freud saw them as wish fulfillment (nightmares being failed dreams prompted by fears of "repressed" impulses). Dreams occur in periods of rapid eye movement (REM) by the sleeper, when the cortex of the brain is approximately as active as in waking hours. Dreams occupy about a fifth of sleeping time.

If a high level of acetylcholine is present (see under ▷brain), dreams occur too early in sleep, causing wakefulness, confusion, and ▷depression, which suggests that a form of memory search is involved. Prevention of dreaming, by taking sleeping pills, for example, has similar unpleasant results.

For the purposes of (allegedly) foretelling the future, dreams fell into disrepute in the scientific atmosphere of the 18th century.

Dred Scott Decision US Supreme Court decision 1857 dealing with citizenship and legal rights of slaves. Dred Scott (c. 1800–1858), a slave from Missouri, sued for his freedom from his owner John Sanford in the Missouri courts, arguing that he had lived with his owner in Illinois, a free state, and the Wisconsin Territory, where slavery had been outlawed by the Missouri Compromise. After a series of reversals the case reached the Supreme Court, which ruled (1) black people were not US citizens, (2) slaves did not become free by entering a free state; and (3) the Missouri Compromise was illegal as it interfered with the right to own slaves, guaranteed by the Constitution (this was only the second Congressional act overturned by the Supreme Court). The decision heightened regional tensions as the Civil War neared.

Drees Willem 1886–1988. Dutch socialist politician, prime minister 1948–58. Chair of the Socialist Democratic Workers' Party from 1911 until the German invasion of 1940, he returned to politics in 1947, after being active in the resistance movement.

In 1947, as the responsible minister, he introduced a state pension plan.

Dreiser Theodore 1871–1945. US writer who wrote the naturalist novels *Sister Carrie* 1900 and *An American Tragedy* 1925, based on the real-life crime of a young man, who in his drive to "make good," drowns a shop assistant he has

made pregnant. It was filmed as *A Place in the Sun* 1951.

Born in Terre Haute, Indiana, Dreiser was a journalist 1889–90 in Chicago and was editor of several magazines. His other novels include *The Financier* 1912, *The Titan* 1914, and *The Genius* 1915. *An American Tragedy* finally won him great popularity after years of publishing works that had been largely ignored. His other works range from autobiographical pieces to poems and short stories. Although his work is criticized for being technically unpolished, it is praised for its powerful realism and sincerity. In the 1930s he devoted much of his energy to the radical reform movement.

Drenthe low-lying northern province of the Netherlands
area 1,027 sq mi/2,660 sq km
population (1988) 437,000
cities capital Assen; Emmen, Hoogeveen
physical fenland and moors; well-drained clay and peat soils
products livestock, arable crops, horticulture, petroleum
history governed in the Middle Ages by provincial nobles and by bishops of Utrecht, Drenthe was eventually acquired by Charles V of Spain 1536. It developed following land drainage initiated in the mid-18th century and was established as a separate province of the Netherlands 1796.

Dresden capital of the state of Saxony, Germany; population (1990) 520,000. Industries include chemicals, machinery, glassware, and musical instruments. It was one of the most beautiful German cities until its devastation by Allied fire-bombing 1945. Dresden county has an area of 2,602 sq mi/6,740 sq km and a population of 1,772,000.
history Under the elector Augustus II the Strong (1694–1733), it became a center of art and culture. The manufacture of Dresden china, started in Dresden 1709, was transferred to Meissen 1710. The city was bombed by the Allies on the night Feb 13–14, 1945, 6 sq mi/15.5 sq km of the inner town being destroyed, and deaths being estimated at 35,000–135,000. Following the reunification of Germany in 1990 Dresden once again became capital of Saxony.

dressage (French "preparation") method of training a horse to carry out a predetermined routine of specified movements. Points are awarded for discipline and style.

Dreyer Carl Theodor 1889–1968. Danish film director. His wide range of films include the austere silent classic *La Passion de Jeanne d'Arc/The Passion of Joan of Arc* 1928 and the Expressionist horror film *Vampyr* 1932, after the failure of which Dreyer made no full-length films until *Vredens Dag/Day of Wrath* 1943. His two late masterpieces are *Ordet/The Word* 1955 and *Gertrud* 1964.

Dreyfus Alfred 1859–1935. French army officer, victim of miscarriage of justice, anti-Semitism, and cover-up. Employed in the War Ministry, in 1894 he was accused of betraying military secrets to Germany, court-martialed, and sent to the penal colony on ▷Devil's Island, French Guiana. When his innocence was discovered 1896 the military establishment tried to conceal it, and the implications of the Dreyfus affair were passionately discussed in the press until he was exonerated in 1906.

Dreyfus was born in Mulhouse, E France, of a Jewish family. He had been a prisoner in the French Guiana penal colony for two years when it emerged that the real criminal was a

Major Esterhazy; the high command nevertheless attempted to suppress the facts and used forged documents to strengthen their case. After a violent controversy, in which the future prime minister Georges ◊Clemenceau and the novelist Emile ◊Zola championed Dreyfus, he was brought back for a retrial 1899, found guilty with extenuating circumstances, and received a pardon. In 1906 the court of appeal declared him innocent, and he was reinstated in his military rank.

drill large Old World monkey *Mandrillus leucophaeus* similar to a baboon and in the same genus as the ◊mandrill. Drills live in the forests of Cameroon and Nigeria. Brownish-coated, black-faced, and stoutly built, with a very short tail, the male can have a head and body up to 2.5 ft/75 cm long, although females are much smaller.

drilling common woodworking and metal machinery process that involves boring holes with a drill ◊bit. The commonest kind of drill bit is the fluted drill, which has spiral grooves around it to allow the cut material to escape. In the oil industry, rotary drilling is used to bore oil wells. The drill bit usually consists of a number of toothed cutting wheels, which grind their way through the rock as the drill pipe is turned, and mud is pumped through the pipe to lubricate the bit and flush the ground-up rock to the surface.

In rotary drilling, a drill bit is fixed to the end of a length of drill pipe and rotated by a turning mechanism, the rotary table. More lengths of pipe are added as the hole deepens. The long drill pipes are handled by lifting gear in a steel tower or ◊derrick.

driver in computing, a program that controls a peripheral device. Every device connected to the computer needs a driver program.

The driver ensures that communication between the computer and the device is successful.

For example, it is often possible to connect many different types of printer, each with its own special operating codes, to the same type of computer. This is because driver programs are supplied to translate the computer's standard printing commands into the special commands needed for each printer.

dromedary variety of Arabian ◊camel. The dromedary or one-humped camel has been domesticated since 400 BC. During a long period without water, it can lose up to one-fourth of its bodyweight without ill effects.

drug abuse the abuse of narcotic and hallucinogenic substances and stimulants.

They are classified generally as (1) most harmful: heroin, morphine, opium, and other narcotics; cocaine, a powerful, dangerous stimulant and its relative, crack; hallucinogens, such as mescalin and LSD; and injectable amphetamines, such as methedrine; (2) less harmful: narcotics such as codeine and cannabis (marijuana); stimulants of the amphetamine type, such as Benzedrine; and barbiturate sedatives; and (3) least harmful: milder drugs of the amphetamine type. "Designer drugs," for example ecstasy, are usually modifications of the amphetamine molecule, altered in order to evade the law as well as for different effects, and may be many times more powerful and dangerous. Crack, for example, became available to drug users in the 1980s. Sources of traditional drugs include the "Golden Triangle" (where Myanmar, Laos, and Thailand meet), Mexico, Colombia, China, Pakistan, and the Middle East.

drug and alcohol dependence physical or psychological craving for addictive drugs such as alcohol, nicotine (in cigarettes), tranquilizers, heroin, or stimulants (for example, amphetamines). Such substances can alter mood or behavior. When dependence is established, sudden withdrawal from the drug can cause unpleasant physical and/or psychological reactions, which may be dangerous.

drug, generic any drug produced without a brand name that is identical to a branded product. Usually generic drugs are produced when the patent on a branded drug has expired, and are cheaper than their branded equivalents.

Druidism religion of the Celtic peoples of the pre-Christian British Isles and Gaul. The word is derived from Greek *drus* "oak." The Druids regarded this tree as sacred; one of their chief rites was the cutting of mistletoe from it with a golden sickle. They taught the immortality of the soul and a reincarnation doctrine, and were expert in astronomy. The Druids are thought to have offered human sacrifices.

Druidism was stamped out in Gaul and most of Britain after the Roman conquest. They existed in Scotland and Ireland until the coming of the Christian missionaries. What are often termed Druidic monuments—cromlechs and stone circles—are of Neolithic origin, although they may later have been used for religious purposes by the Druids.

drum percussion instrument, essentially a piece of skin (parchment, plastic, or nylon) stretched over a resonator and struck with a stick or the hands, one of the oldest instruments. Electronic drums, first marketed 1980, are highly touch—and force-sensitive and can also be controlled by computer.

drumlin geologically feature formed in formerly glaciated areas. It consists of long, streamlined hills formed from glacial till or unstratified glacial drift of clay, sand, boulders, and gravel. A drumlin's long axis is oriented in the direction of glacial flow, and its blunt nose points upstream, with the gentler slope trailing off downstream.

Drumlins range from 25 ft/8 m to 200 ft/60 m in height. In length, they vary from 0.3 mi/0.5 km to 0.6 mi/1 km and are generally several times narrower than long.

Drummond de Andrade Carlos 1902–1987. Brazilian writer, generally considered the greatest modern Brazilian poet, and a prominent member of the Modernist school. His verse, often seemingly casual, continually confounds the reader's expectations of the "poetical."

drupe fleshy ◊fruit containing one or more seeds which are surrounded by a hard, protective layer—for example cherry, almond, and plum. The wall of the fruit (◊pericarp) is differentiated into the outer skin (exocarp), the fleshy layer of tissues (mesocarp), and the hard layer surrounding the seed (endocarp).

The coconut is a drupe, but here the pericarp becomes dry and fibrous at maturity. Blackberries are an aggregate fruit composed of a cluster of small drupes.

Druse or *Druze* religious sect in the Middle East of some 500,000 people. They are monotheists, preaching that the Fatimid caliph al-Hakim (996–1021) is God; their scriptures are drawn from the Bible, the Koran, and Sufi allegories. Druse militia groups form one of the three main factions involved in the

Lebanese civil war (the others are Amal Shiite Muslims and Christian Maronites). The Druse military leader (from the time of his father's assassination 1977) is Walid Jumblatt.

The Druse sect was founded in Egypt in the 11th century, and then fled to Palestine to avoid persecution; today they occupy areas of Syria, Lebanon, and Israel.

dryad in Greek mythology, a forest nymph or tree spirit.

dryas any arctic or alpine herbaceous plant of the genus *Dryas* of the rose family, with simple leaves and white or yellow flowers. The white-flowered mountain avens *Dryas octopetata* is a common plant of northern regions.

Dryden John 1631–1700. English poet and dramatist, noted for his satirical verse and for his use of the heroic couplet. His poetry includes the verse satire *Absalom and Achitophel* 1681, *Annus Mirabilis* 1667, and "St Cecilia's Day" 1687. Plays include the comedy *Marriage à la Mode* 1672 and *All for Love* 1678, a reworking of Shakespeare's *Antony and Cleopatra*.

dry ice solid carbon dioxide (CO_2), used as a refrigerant. At temperatures above –110.2°F/–79°C, it sublimes (turns into vapor without passing through a liquid stage) to gaseous carbon dioxide.

dry point in printmaking, a technique of engraving on copper, using a hard, sharp tool. The resulting lines tend to be fine and angular, with a strong furry edge created by the metal shavings.

dry rot infection of timber in damp conditions by fungi, such as *Merulius lacrymans*, that form a threadlike surface. Whitish at first, the fungus later reddens as reproductive spores are formed. Fungoid tentacles also enter the fabric of the timber, rendering it dry-looking and brittle. Dry rot spreads rapidly through a building.

Dual Entente alliance between France and Russia that lasted from 1893 until the Bolshevik Revolution of 1917.

dualism in philosophy, the belief that reality is essentially dual in nature. The French philosopher René ◊Descartes, for example, refers to thinking and material substance. These entities interact but are fundamentally separate and distinct.

Dualism is contrasted with ◊monism, the theory that reality is made up of only one substance.

Duarte José Napoleon 1925–1990. El Salvadorean politician, president 1980–82 and 1984–88. He was mayor of San Salvador 1964–70, and was elected president 1972, but exiled by the army 1982. On becoming president again 1984, he sought a negotiated settlement with the left-wing guerrillas 1986, but resigned on health grounds.

Dubai one of the ◊United Arab Emirates.

du Barry Marie Jeanne Bécu, Comtesse 1743–1793. Mistress of ◊Louis XV of France from 1768. At his death 1774 she was banished to a convent, and during the Revolution fled to London. Returning to Paris 1793, she was guillotined.

Dubček Alexander 1921–1992. Czechoslovak politician, chair of the federal assembly 1989–92. He was a member of the Slovak ◊resistance movement during World War II, and became first secretary of the Communist Party 1967–69. He launched a liberalization campaign (called the Prague Spring) that was opposed by the USSR and led to the Soviet invasion of Czechoslovakia 1968. He was arrested by Soviet troops and expelled from the party 1970. In 1989 he gave speeches at prodemocracy rallies, and after the fall of the hard-line regime, he was elected speaker of the National Assembly in Prague, a position to which he was reelected 1990. He was fatally injured in an automobile crash Nov 1992.

Dublin (Gaelic *Baile Atha Cliath*) capital and port on the E coast of the Republic of Ireland, at the mouth of the river Liffey, facing the Irish Sea; population (1981) 526,000, Greater Dublin (including Dun Laoghaire) 921,000. It is the site of one of the world's largest breweries (Guinness); other industries include textiles, pharmaceuticals, electrical goods, and machine tools. It was the center of English rule from 1171 (exercised from Dublin Castle 1220) until 1922.

history The city was founded 840 by the invading Danes, who were finally defeated 1014 at Clontarf, now a northern suburb of the city. In the Georgian period many fine squares were laid out, and the Custom House (damaged in the 1921 uprising but later restored) survives. There is a Roman Catholic procathedral, St Mary's (1816); two Protestant cathedrals; and two universities, the University of Dublin and the National University of Ireland. Trinity College library contains the Book of Kells, a splendidly illuminated 8th-century gospel book produced at the monastery of Kells in County Meath, founded by St Columba. Other buildings are the City Hall (1779), the Four Courts (1796), the National Gallery, Dublin Municipal Gallery, National Museum, Leinster House (where the legislature, Dáil Eireann, sits), and the Abbey and Gate theaters.

Du Bois W(illiam) E(dward) B(urghardt) 1868–1963. US educator and social critic. Du Bois was one of the early leaders of the National Association for the Advancement of Colored People (NAACP), the editor of its journal *Crisis* 1909–32, and organizer of several Pan-African conferences. As an uncompromising advocate of black American rights, he came into conflict with the more accommodationist Booker T ⟡Washington.

Born in Great Barrington, Massachusetts, Du Bois earned a PhD from Harvard 1895 and was appointed to the faculty of Atlanta University. In 1962 he established his home in Accra, Ghana.

Dubos René Jules 1901–1981. French-US microbiologist who studied soil microorganisms and became interested in their antibacterial properties.

The antibacterials he discovered had limited therapeutic use since they were toxic. However, he opened up a new field of research that eventually led to the discovery of such major drugs as ⟡penicillin and ⟡streptomycin.

Dubrovnik (Italian *Ragusa*) city and port in Croatia on the Adriatic Sea; population (1985) 35,000. It manufactures cheese, liqueurs, silk, and leather.

Once a Roman station, Dubrovnik was for a long time an independent republic but passed to Austrian rule 1814–1919. During the 1991 civil war, Dubrovnik was placed under siege by Yugoslav federal forces (as part of its blockade of the Croatian coast) and subjected to frequent artillery barrages and naval shelling. The plight of the city and its residents attracted international concern during the siege; medieval buildings and works of art were destroyed.

Dubuffet Jean 1901–1985. French artist. He originated *l'art brut*, "raw or brutal art," in the 1940s. He used a variety of materials in his paintings and sculptures (plaster, steel wool, straw, and so on) and was inspired by graffiti and children's drawings.

L'art brut emerged 1945 with an exhibition of Dubuffet's own work and of paintings by psychiatric patients and naive or untrained artists. His own paintings and sculptural works have a similar quality, primitive and expressive.

Dubuque city in E central Iowa, NE of Iowa City, just across the Mississippi River from the Wisconsin–Illinois border. An important port, it has shipbuilding and agricultural marketing facilities; industries include meatpacking, lumber, metals, and machinery; population (1990) 57,546.

Duccio di Buoninsegna c. 1255–1319. Italian painter, a major figure in the Sienese school. His greatest work is his altarpiece for Siena Cathedral, the *Maestà* 1308–11; the figure of the Virgin is Byzantine in style, with much gold detail, but Duccio also created a graceful linear harmony in drapery hems, for example, and this proved a lasting characteristic of Sienese style.

Duce (Italian "leader") title bestowed on the fascist dictator Benito ⟡Mussolini by his followers and later adopted as his official title.

Duchamp Marcel 1887–1968. US artist, born in France. He achieved notoriety with his *Nude Descending a Staircase* 1912 (Philadelphia Museum of Art), influenced by Cubism and Futurism. An active exponent of ⟡Dada, he invented "ready-mades," everyday items like a bicycle wheel on a kitchen stool, which he displayed as works of art.

A major early work that focuses on mechanical objects endowed with mysterious significance is *La Mariée mise à nu par ses célibataires, même/The Bride Stripped Bare by Her Bachelors, Even* 1915–23 (Philadelphia Museum of Art). Duchamp continued to experiment with collage, mechanical imagery, and abstract sculpture throughout his career. He lived mostly in New York and became a US citizen 1954.

duck any of several short-legged waterbirds with webbed feet and flattened bills, of the family Anatidae, which also includes the larger geese and swans. Ducks were domesticated for eggs, meat, and feathers by the ancient Chinese and the ancient Maya (see ⟡poultry). Most ducks live in fresh water, feeding on worms and insects as well as vegetable matter. They are generally divided into dabbling ducks and diving ducks.

The three front toes of a duck's foot are webbed and the hind toe is free. The bill is skin-covered with a horny tip provided with little plates (lamellae) through which the duck is able to strain its food from water and mud.

A typical species is the mallard *Anas platyrhynchos*, 1.9 ft/58 cm, found over most of the northern hemisphere. The male (drake) has a glossy green head, brown breast, gray body, and yellow bill. The female (duck) is speckled brown, with a duller bill. The male molts and resembles the female for a while just after the breeding season. There are many other species of duck including ⟡teal, ⟡eider, ⟡merganser, ⟡shelduck, and ⟡shoveler. They have different-shaped bills according to their diet and habitat; for example, the shoveler has a wide spade-shaped bill for scooping insects off the surface of water.

The main threat to the survival of ducks in the wild is hunting by humans. The pink-headed duck of India and Nepal is believed to be extinct, no wild specimens having been seen since 1936.

duckweed any of a family of tiny plants of the family Lemnaceae, especially of the genus *Lemna*, found floating on the surface of still water throughout most of the world, except the polar regions and tropics. Each plant consists of a flat, circular, leaflike structure 0.15 in/0.4 cm or less across, with a single thin root up to 6 in/15 cm long below.

The plants bud off new individuals and soon cover the surface of the water. Flowers rarely appear, but when they do, they are minute and located in a pocket at the edge of the plant.

ductless gland alternate name for an ⟡endocrine gland.

duel fight between two people armed with weapons. A duel is usually fought according to pre-arranged rules with the aim of settling a private quarrel.

In medieval Europe duels were a legal method of settling disputes. By the 16th century the practice had largely ceased but duelling with swords or pistols, often with elaborate ritual, continued unofficially in aristocratic and military circles until the 20th century. In some German universities exclusive duelling clubs continue to this day.

due process of law legal principle, dating from the ⟡Magna Carta, the charter of rights granted by King John of England 1215, and now enshrined in the fifth and fourteenth amendments to the US Constitution, that no person shall be deprived of life, liberty, or property without due process of law (a fair legal procedure). In the US, the provisions have been given a wide interpretation, to include, for example, the right to representation by an attorney.

Dufay Guillaume 1400–1474. Flemish composer. He is recognized as the foremost composer of his time, of both secular songs and sacred music (including 84 songs and eight masses). His work marks a transition between the music of the Middle Ages and that of the Renaissance and is characterized by expressive melodies and rich harmonies.

Dufourspitze second highest of the alpine peaks, 15,203 ft/4,634 m high. It is the highest peak in the Monte Rosa group of the Pennine Alps on the Swiss-Italian frontier.

Du Fu another name for the Chinese poet ⟡Tu Fu.

Dufy Raoul 1877–1953. French painter and designer. He originated a fluent, brightly colored style in watercolor and oils, painting scenes of gaiety and leisure, such as horse racing, yachting, and life on the beach. He also designed tapestries, textiles, and ceramics.

dugong marine mammal *Dugong dugong* of the order Sirenia (sea cows), found in the Red Sea, the Indian Ocean, and W Pacific. It can grow to 11 ft/3.6 m long, and has a tapering body with a notched tail and two fore-flippers.

It is herbivorous, feeding on sea grasses and seaweeds.

It may have given rise to the mermaid myth.

duiker (Afrikaans *diver*) any of several antelopes of the family Bovidae, common in Africa. Duikers are shy and nocturnal, and grow to 12–28 in/30–70 cm tall.

Dukakis Michael 1933– . US Democrat politician, governor of Massachusetts 1974–78 and 1982–90, presiding over a high-tech economic boom, the "Massachusetts miracle." He was a presidential candidate 1988.

Dukakis was born in Boston, Massachusetts, the son of Greek immigrants. After studying law at Harvard and serving in Korea (1955–57), he concentrated on a political career in his home state. Elected as a Democrat to the Massachusetts legislature 1962, he became state governor 1974. After an unsuccessful first term, marred by his unwillingness to compromise, he was defeated 1978. He returned as governor 1982, committed to working in a more consensual manner, was reelected 1986, and captured the Democratic Party's presidential nomination 1988. After a poor campaign, the diligent but uncharismatic Dukakis was defeated by the incumbent vice-president George Bush. His standing in Massachusetts dropped and he announced that he would not seek a new term.

Dukas Paul (Abraham) 1865–1935. French composer. His orchestral scherzo *L'Apprenti sorcier/The Sorcerer's Apprentice* 1897 is full of the color and energy that characterizes much of his work.

He was professor of composition at the Paris Conservatoire and composed the opera *Ariane et Barbe-Bleue/Ariane and Bluebeard* 1907, and the ballet *La Péri* 1912.

duke highest title in the English peerage. It originated in England 1337, when Edward III created his son Edward, Duke of Cornwall.

dulcimer musical instrument consisting of a shallow soundbox strung with many wires that are struck with small wooden hammers. In Hungary it is called a ⬦cimbalom.

Also an oval-shaped stringed instrument of the Appalachian Mountains that is played in the lap or on a surface by plucking the strings with a quill or plectrum.

Dulles Alan 1893–1969. US lawyer, director of the Central Intelligence Agency (CIA) 1953–61. He was the brother of John Foster Dulles.

He helped found the CIA 1950 but was embroiled in the ⬦Bay of Pigs controversy, among others, which forced his resignation.

Dulles John Foster 1888–1959. US lawyer and politician. Senior US adviser at the founding of the United Nations, he largely drafted the Japanese peace treaty of 1951. As secretary of state 1952–59 he was critical of Britain in the ⬦Suez Crisis. He was the architect of US ⬦Cold War foreign policy, securing ⬦SEATO and US intervention in support of South Vietnam following the expulsion of the French in 1954.

Born in Washington, DC, he was educated at Princeton, the University of Paris, and George Washington University. His specialty as a lawyer was international law. He sought to go beyond the "containment" policy of the time, considering communism as a moral evil with which there could be no compromise. Even so, during his term as secretary of state, he was limited to giving moral support to the Hungarians 1956 when they rose against the Soviets, and Cuba and North Vietnam fell to the Communists during his tenure.

dulse any of several edible red seaweeds, especially *Rhodymenia palmata*, found on middle and lower shores of the N Atlantic. They may have a single broad blade up to 12 in/30 cm long rising directly from the holdfast which attaches them to the sea floor, or be palmate or fan-shaped. The frond is tough and dark red, sometimes with additional small leaflets at the edge.

Duluth port on Lake Superior; by the mouth of the St Louis River, Minnesota; population (1990) 85,500. It manufactures steel, flour, timber, and dairy products. The westernmost port on the St Lawrence Seaway, Duluth ships iron ore, grain, coal, oil, and timber. Permanent settlement on what had been a fur-trading post began 1852.

Duma in Russia, before 1917, an elected assembly that met four times following the short-lived 1905 revolution. With progressive demands the government could not accept, the Duma was largely powerless. After the abdication of Nicholas II, the Duma directed the formation of a provisional government.

Dumas Alexandre 1802–1870. French author, known as Dumas *père* (the father). He is remembered for his romances, the reworked output of a "fiction-factory" of collaborators. They include *Les trois mousquetaires/The Three Musketeers* 1844 and its sequels. Dumas *fils* was his son.

His play *Henri III et sa cour/Henry III and His Court* 1829 established French romantic historical drama.

Dumas Alexandre 1824–1895. French author, known as Dumas *fils* (the son of Dumas *père*) and remembered for the play *La Dame aux camélias/The Lady of the Camellias* 1852, based on his own novel and the source of Verdi's opera *La Traviata*.

Du Maurier Daphne 1907–1989. British novelist whose romantic fiction includes *Jamaica Inn* 1936, *Rebecca* 1938, and *My Cousin Rachel* 1951. *Jamaica Inn*, *Rebecca*, and her short story "The Birds" were made into films by the English director Alfred Hitchcock.

She was the granddaughter of British cartoonist and novelist George Du Maurier (1834–1896).

Dumbarton Oaks 18th-century mansion in Washington, DC, used for conferences and seminars. It was the scene of a conference held 1944 that led to the foundation of the United Nations.

Dumouriez Charles François du Périer 1739–1823. French general during the Revolution. In 1792 he was appointed foreign minister, supported the declaration of war against Austria, and after the fall of the monarchy was given command of the army defending Paris. After intriguing with the royalists he had to flee for his life, and from 1804 he lived in England.

dump in computing, the process of rapidly transferring data to external memory or to a printer. It is usually done to help with debugging (see ⬦bug) or as part of an error-recovery procedure.

dumping in international trade, when one country sells goods to another at below marginal cost or at a price below that in its own country. Countries dump to sell off surplus produce or to improve their competitive positions in the recipient country. The practice is deplored by ⬦free trade advocates because of the artificial, unfair advantage it yields. Dumping is

barchans with weak wind

barchans with strong wind

star dunes with irregular winds

seif dunes on bare rock, parallel to wind direction

dune *The shape of a dune indicates the prevailing wind pattern.*

also used by protectionists to justify retaliatory measures.

Dunant Jean Henri 1828–1910. Swiss philanthropist; the originator of the international relief agency, the Red Cross. At the Battle of Solferino 1859 he helped tend the wounded, and in *Un Souvenir de Solferino* 1862 he proposed the establishment of an international body for the aid of the wounded—an idea that was realized in the Geneva Convention 1864. He shared the 1901 Nobel Peace Prize.

Dunaway Faye 1941– . US actress whose first starring role was in *Bonnie and Clyde* 1967. Her subsequent films, including *Network* 1976 (for which she won an Academy Award) and *Mommie Dearest* 1981, received a varying critical reception. She also starred in Roman Polanski's *Chinatown* 1974 and *The Handmaid's Tale* 1990.

Duncan Isadora 1878–1927. US dancer and teacher. An influential pioneer of Modern dance, she adopted an expressive free form, dancing barefoot and wearing a loose tunic, inspired by the ideal of Hellenic beauty. She toured extensively, often returning to Russia after her initial success there 1905.

She died in an accident when her long scarf caught in the wheel of the car in which she was traveling.

dune mound or ridge of wind-drifted sand. Loose sand is blown and bounced along by the wind, up the windward side of a dune. The sand particles then fall to rest on the lee side, while more are blown up from the windward side. In this way a dune moves gradually downwind.

Dunes are features of sandy deserts and beach fronts. The typical crescent-shaped nitroglycerine and diatomaceous earth (diatomite, an absorbent, chalklike material). It was first devised by Alfred Nobel.

dynamo former name for ◇generator.

dyne unit (symbol dyn) of force. 10^5 dynes make one newton. The dyne is defined as the force that will accelerate a mass of one gram by one centimeter per second per second.

dysentery infection of the large intestine causing abdominal cramps and painful ◇diarrhea with blood. There are two kinds of dysentery: **amebic** (caused by a protozoan), common in the tropics, which may lead to liver damage; and **bacterial**, the kind most often seen in the temperate zones.

Both forms are successfully treated with antibacterials and fluids to prevent dehydration.

dyslexia (Greek "bad," "pertaining to words") malfunction in the brain's synthesis and interpretation of sensory information, popularly known as "word blindness." It results in poor ability to read and write, though the person may otherwise excel, for example, in mathematics. A similar disability with figures is called dyscalculus.

dyspepsia synonym for ◇indigestion.

dysphagia difficulty in swallowing. It may be due to infection, obstruction, or spasm in the throat or esophagus (gullet).

dyspnoea difficulty in breathing, or shortness of breath disproportionate to effort. It occurs if the supply of oxygen is inadequate or if carbon dioxide accumulates. It can be caused by circulatory or respiratory diseases.

dysprosium (Greek *dusprositos* "difficult to get near") silver-white, metallic element of the lanthanide series, symbol Dy, atomic number 66, atomic weight 162.50. It is among the most magnetic of all known substances and has a great capacity to absorb neutrons.

It was discovered 1886 by French chemist Paul Lecoq de Boisbaudran (1838–1912).

dystopia imaginary society whose evil qualities are meant to serve as a moral or political warning. The term was coined in the 19th century by the English philosopher John Stuart ◇Mill, and is the opposite of a ◇Utopia. George Orwell's *1984* 1949 and Aldous Huxley's *Brave New World* 1932 are examples of novels about dystopias. Dystopias are common in science fiction.

E second vowel and fifth and most often used letter of the English alphabet.

E abbreviation for *east*.

eagle any of several genera of large birds of prey of the family Accipitridae, including the golden eagle *Aquila chrysaetos* of Eurasia and North America, which has a 6 ft/2 m wingspan and is dark brown.

The white-headed bald eagle *Haliaetus leucocephalus* is the symbol of the US; rendered infertile through the ingestion of agricultural chemicals, it is now very rare, except in Alaska. Another endangered species is the Philippine eagle, sometimes called the Philippine monkey-eating eagle (although its main prey is flying lemurs). Loss of large tracts of forest, coupled with hunting by humans, have greatly reduced its numbers.

In North America the golden eagle is found throughout most of the US, and N Mexico, with the exception of the SE. The larger spotted eagle *A. clanga* lives in Central Europe and Asia. The sea eagles *Haliaetus* include Steller's sea eagle *H. pelagicus*, mainly a carrion-feeder which breeds on sea cliffs.

Eakins Thomas 1844–1916. US painter. A trained observer of human anatomy and a devotee of photography, Eakins attempted to achieve a strong sense of visual realism. His work is characterized by strong contrasts between light and shade, as in *The Gross Clinic* 1875 (Jefferson Medical College, Philadelphia), a group portrait of a surgeon, his assistants, and students.

Born in Philadelphia, Eakins attended the Pennsylvania Academy of the Fine Arts and the Ecole des Beaux-Arts in Paris, later becoming an instructor at the Pennsylvania Academy. He studied with the French academic painter J L Gérôme (1824–1904) in Paris in the 1860s and on a European tour drew inspiration from Rembrandt, Velázquez, and Ribera.

The most memorable motifs for his paintings were medical and sporting scenes. Among his larger-than-life-size sculptures commissioned for public monuments are the war memorials in Trenton, New Jersey, and Brooklyn, New York.

Eames Charles 1907–1978 and Ray 1916–1988. US designers, a husband-and-wife team who worked together in California 1941–78. They created some of the most highly acclaimed furniture designs of the 20th century: a molded plywood chair 1945–46; the Lounge Chair, a black leather-upholstered chair 1956; and a fiberglass armchair 1950–53.

Eanes António dos Santos Ramalho 1935– . Portuguese politician. He helped plan the 1974 coup that ended the Caetano regime, and as army chief of staff put down a left-wing revolt Nov 1975. He was president 1976–86.

ear organ of hearing in animals. It responds to the vibrations that constitute sound, and these are translated into nerve signals and passed to the brain. A mammal's ear consists of three parts: outer ear, middle ear, and inner ear. The *outer ear* is a funnel that collects sound, directing it down a tube to the *ear drum* (tympanic membrane), which separates the outer and *middle ear*. Sounds vibrate this membrane, the mechanical movement of which is transferred to a smaller membrane leading to the *inner ear* by three small bones, the auditory ossicles. Vibrations of the inner ear membrane move fluid contained in the snail-shaped cochlea, which vibrates hair cells that stimulate the auditory nerve connected to the brain. Three fluid-filled canals of the inner ear detect changes of position; this mechanism, with other sensory inputs, is responsible for the sense of balance.

When a loud noise occurs, muscles behind the eardrum contract automatically, suppressing the noise to enhance perception of sound and prevent injury.

Earhart Amelia 1898–1937. US aviation pioneer and author, who in 1928 became the first woman to fly across the Atlantic. With copilot Frederick Noonan, she attempted a round-the-world flight 1937. Somewhere over the Pacific their plane disappeared.

Born in Atchison, Kansas, Earhart worked as an army nurse and social worker, before discovering that her true calling lay in aviation. In 1928 she became the first woman to fly across the Atlantic as a passenger and in 1932 completed a solo transatlantic flight. During a flight over the Pacific 1937, her plane disappeared without trace, although clues found 1989 on Nikumaroro island, SE of Kiribati's main island group, suggest that she and her copilot might have survived a crash only to die of thirst.

earl in the British peerage, the third title in order of rank, coming between marquess and viscount; it is the oldest of British titles, being of Scandinavian origin. An earl's wife is a countess.

Early Jubal Anderson 1816–1894. American Confederate military leader. Born in Franklin County, Virginia, Early graduated from West Point 1837 and saw action in the Seminole War. After studying law, he was admitted to the bar 1840 and later served in the Virginia legislature. Although long in favor of preserving the Union, Early joined the Confederate army at the outbreak of the Civil War. After Bull Run he was named general in the Army of Northern Virginia and led campaigns in the Shenandoah Valley, threatening Washington, DC 1864. After a brief period of exile after the war, he resumed his Virginia law practice.

Earp Wyatt 1848–1929. US frontier law officer. In 1876 Earp was appointed assistant marshal in Dodge City, Kansas. Known also as a gambler and brawler, Earp's closest friends were the legendary Bat Masterson and Doc Holliday. With them and his brothers Virgil and Morgan he participated in the famous gunfight at the OK Corral on Oct 26, 1881, in Tombstone, Arizona. He left Tombstone 1882, traveled, and operated saloons before he settled in Los Angeles.

Born in Monmouth, Illinois, Earp moved with his family to Iowa, finally settling in California 1864. Later gaining fame as a scout and buffalo hunter, he moved to Wichita, Kansas, 1874, where he was occasionally employed by the US marshal.

Earth third planet from the Sun. It is almost spherical, flattened slightly at the poles, and is composed of three concentric layers: the ⬦core, the ⬦mantle, and the ⬦crust. 70% of the surface (including the north and south polar icecaps) is covered with water. The Earth is surrounded by a life-supporting atmosphere and is the only planet on which life is known to exist.

ear *The structure of the ear.*

mean distance from the Sun 92,860,000 mi/149,500,000 km
equatorial diameter 7,923 mi/12,756 km
circumference 24,900 mi/40,070 km
rotation period 23 hr 56 min 4.1 sec
year (complete orbit, or sidereal period) 365 days 5 hr 48 min 46 sec. Earth's average speed around the Sun is 18.5 mps/30 kps; the plane of its orbit is inclined to its equatorial plane at an angle of 23.5°, the reason for the changing seasons
atmosphere nitrogen 78.09%; oxygen 20.95%; argon 0.93%; carbon dioxide 0.03%; and less than 0.0001% neon, helium, krypton, hydrogen, xenon, ozone, radon
surface land surface 57,500,000 sq mi/150,000,000 sq km (greatest height above sea level 29,118 ft/8,872 m Mount Everest); water surface 139,400,000 sq mi/361,000,000 sq km (greatest depth 36,201 ft/11,034 m ◊Mariana Trench in the Pacific). The interior is thought to be an inner core about 1,600 mi/2,600 km in diameter, of solid iron and nickel; an outer core about 1,400 mi/2,250 km thick, of molten iron and nickel; and a mantle of mostly solid rock about 1,800 mi/2,900 km thick, separated by the ◊Mohorovičić discontinuity from the Earth's crust. The crust and the topmost layer of the mantle form about 12 major moving plates, some of which carry the continents. The plates are in constant, slow motion, called tectonic drift
satellite the ◊Moon
age 4.6 billion years. The Earth was formed with the rest of the ◊Solar System by consolidation of interstellar dust. Life began 3.5–4 billion years ago.

earthenware pottery made of porous clay and fired to temperatures of up to 2,101°F/1,150°C. Earthenware may be unglazed (flowerpots, winecoolers) or glazed (most tableware); the glaze and body characteristically form quite separate layers.

earthquake shaking of the Earth's surface as a result of the sudden release of stresses built up in the Earth's crust. The study of earthquakes is called ◊seismology. Most earthquakes occur along ◊faults (fractures or breaks) in the crust. ◊Plate tectonic movements generate the major proportion: as two plates move past each other they can become jammed and deformed, and a series of shock waves (seismic waves) occur when they spring free. Their force is

major 20th-century earthquakes

date	place	number of deaths
1906	San Francisco	3,000
1908	Messina, Italy	83,000
1915	Avezzano, Italy	29,980
1920	Gansu, China	100,000
1923	Tokyo, Japan	99,330
1927	Nan-Shan, China	200,000
1932	Gansu, China	70,000
1935	Quetta, India	30,000
1939	Erzincan, Turkey	30,000
1939	Chillán, Chile	28,000
1948	USSR	110,000
1970	N Peru	66,794
1976	Tangshan, China	242,000
1978	NE Iran	25,000
1980	El Asnam, Algeria	20,000
1985	Mexico	25,000
1988	Armenia, USSR	25,000
1989	San Francisco	300
1990	NW Iran	50,000

measured on the ◊Richter scale, and the effect of an earthquake is measured on the Mercalli scale. The point at which an earthquake originates is the **sesmic focus**; the point on the Earth's surface directly above this is the *epicentre*.

In 1987 a California earthquake was successfully predicted by measurement of underground pressure waves; prediction attempts have also involved the study of such phenomena as the change in gases issuing from the ◊crust, the level of water in wells, and the behavior of animals. The possibility of earthquake prevention is remote. However, rock slippage might be slowed at movement points or promoted at stoppage points by the extraction or injection of large quantities of water underground, since water serves as a lubricant. This would ease overall pressure.

earth sciences scientific study of the planet Earth as a whole, a synthesis of several traditional subjects such as ◊geology, ◊meteorology, ◊oceanography, ◊geophysics, ◊geochemistry, and ◊paleontology.

The mining and extraction of minerals and gems, the prediction of weather and earthquakes, the pollution of the atmosphere, and the forces that shape the physical world all fall within its scope of study. The emergence of the discipline reflects scientists' concern that an understanding of the global aspects of the Earth's structure and its past will hold the key to how humans affect its future, ensuring that its resources are used in a sustainable way.

Earth Summit (official name *United Nations Conference on Environment and Development*) international meeting in Rio de Janeiro, Brazil, June 1992 which drew up measures toward world environmental protection. Treaties were made to combat global warming and protect wildlife ("biodiversity") (the latter was not signed by the US)

earthworm ◊annelid worm of the class Oligochaeta. Earthworms are hermaphroditic, and deposit their eggs in cocoons. They live by burrowing in the soil, feeding on the organic matter it contains. They are vital to the formation of humus, aerating the soil and leveling it by transferring earth from the deeper levels to the surface as castings.

Most North American earthworms belong to the genus *Lumbricus*. These are comparatively small, but some tropical forms reach over 3 ft/1 m in length. *Megascolides australis*, of Queensland, for instance, can be over 11 ft/3 m long.

earwig nocturnal insect of the order Dermaptera. The fore-wings are short and leathery and serve to protect the hind-wings, which are large and are folded like a fan when at rest. Earwigs seldom fly. They have a pincerlike appendage in the rear. The male is distinguished by curved pincers, those of the female are straight. Earwigs are regarded as pests because they feed on flowers and fruit, but they also eat other insects, dead or alive. Eggs are laid beneath the soil, and the female cares for the young even after they have hatched. The male dies before the eggs have hatched.

Forficula is the common genus in North America.

easement in law, rights that a person may have over the land of another. A common example is a right of way; others are the right to bring water over another's land and the right to a sufficient quantity of light.

east one of the four cardinal points of the compass, indicating that part of the horizon where the Sun rises; when facing north, east is to the right.

The Sun, and hence the east, has held a significant place in various religions; ancient temples had their altars at the east end so that sacrifices and other rituals could be made facing the rising Sun. In the 2nd century it became customary for Christians to worship facing the east, and also to bury the dead with their feet toward the east, so that on the morning of the Resurrection they would be facing the direction from which Christ was to come in glory.

East Anglia region of E England, formerly a Saxon kingdom, including Norfolk, Suffolk, and parts of Essex and Cambridgeshire. Norwich is the principal city of East Anglia. The University of East Anglia was founded in Norwich 1962, and includes the Sainsbury Center for the Visual Arts, opened 1978, which has a collection of ethnographic art and sculpture. East Anglian ports such as Harwich and Felixstowe have greatly developed as trade with the rest of Europe increases.

Easter spring feast of the Christian church, commemorating the Resurrection of Jesus. It is a moveable feast, falling on the first Sunday following the full moon after the vernal equinox (March 21), that is, between March 22 and April 25.

The English name derives from Eostre, Anglo-Saxon goddess of spring, who was honored in April.

Dyed easter eggs, and pieces of candy shaped like eggs, young chickens, ducklings, lambs, or rabbits—all symbolizing new life —are given to young children.

Easter Island or *Rapa Nui* Chilean island in the S Pacific Ocean, part of the Polynesian group, about 2,200 mi/3,500 km W of Chile; area about 64 sq mi/166 sq km; population (1985) 2,000. It was first reached by Europeans on Easter Sunday 1722. On it stand over 800 huge carved statues (moai) and the remains of boat-shaped stone houses, the work of neolithic peoples of unknown origin. The chief center is Hanga-Roa.

Eastern Orthodox Church see ◊Orthodox Church.

Easter Rising or *Easter Rebellion* in Irish history, a republican insurrection that began on Easter Monday, April 1916, in Dublin. It was inspired by the Irish Republican Brotherhood (IRB) in an unsuccessful attempt to overthrow British rule in Ireland. It was led by Patrick Pearce of the IRB and James Connolly of Sinn Féin.

East India Company, Dutch (*VOC*, or *Vereenigde Oost-Indische Compagnie*) trading company chartered by the States General (parliament) of the Netherlands, and established in the N Netherlands 1602. It was given a monopoly on Dutch trade in the Indonesian archipelago, and certain sovereign rights such as the creation of an army and a fleet.

In the 17th century some 100 ships were regularly trading between the Netherlands and the East Indies. The company's main base was Batavia in Java (Indonesia); ships sailed there via the Cape of Good Hope, a colony founded by the company 1652 as a staging post. During the 17th and 18th centuries the company used its monopoly of East Indian trade to pay out high dividends, but wars with England and widespread corruption led to a suspension of payments 1781 and a takeover of the company by the Dutch government 1798.

Eastman George 1854–1932. US entrepreneur and inventor who founded the Eastman Kodak photographic company 1892. From 1888 he marketed his patented daylight-loading flexible roll films (to replace the glass plates used previously) and portable cameras. By 1900 his company was selling a pocket camera for as little as one dollar.

The films first worked with chemicals fixed to a paper base 1884 and later on celluloid 1889. In 1928 he perfected a film process for color photography and development, an important service offered on fine papers. He was known for his contributions to education and music.

East Pakistan former province of ⋄Pakistan, now Bangladesh.

East River tidal strait 16 mi/26 km long, between Manhattan and the Bronx, and Long Island, in New York. It links Long Island Sound with New York Bay and is also connected, via the Harlem River, with the Hudson. There are docks; most famous of its many bridges is the Brooklyn.

East Siberian Sea part of the ⋄Arctic Ocean, off the N coast of Russia, between the New Siberian Islands and Chukchi Sea. The world's widest continental shelf, with an average width of nearly 404 mi/650 km, lies in the East Siberian Sea.

East St Louis city in SW Illinois on the Mississippi River, across from St Louis, Missouri. A center for the processing of livestock; its other industries include steel, paint materials, and machinery; population (1990) 40,900.

East Sussex county in SE England
area 695 sq mi/1,800 sq km
cities Lewes (administrative headquarters), Newhaven (cross-channel port), Brighton, Eastbourne, Hastings, Bexhill, Winchelsea, Rye
features Beachy Head, highest headland on the S coast at 590 ft/180 m, the E end of the South Downs, a line of chalk hills running across Sussex to Beachy Head; the Weald (including Ashdown Forest); Friston Forest; rivers: Ouse, Cuckmere, East Rother; Romney Marsh; the "Long Man" chalk hill figure at Wilmington, near Eastbourne; Herstmonceux, with a 15th-century castle (conference and exhibition center) and adjacent modern buildings, site of the Greenwich Royal Observatory 1958–90; other castles at Hastings, Lewes, Pevensey, and Bodiam; Battle Abbey and the site of the Battle of Hastings; Michelham Priory; Sheffield Park garden; University of Sussex at Falmer, near Brighton, founded 1961
products electronics, gypsum, timber
population (1987) 698,000

East Timor disputed territory on the island of ⋄Timor in the Malay Archipelago; prior to 1975, it was a Portuguese colony for almost 460 years
area 5,706 sq mi/14,874 sq km
capital Dili
products coffee
population (1980) 555,000
history Following Portugal's withdrawal 1975, the left-wing Revolutionary Front of Independent East Timor (Fretilin) occupied the capital, Dili, calling for independence. In opposition, troops from neighboring Indonesia invaded the territory, declaring East Timor (**Loro Sae**) the 17th province of Indonesia July 1976. This claim is not recognized by the United Nations. In Nov 1991, at least 19 people were killed and 91 injured when Indonesian troops fired on pro-independence demonstrators.

The Portuguese colonizers left behind a literacy rate of under 10% and no infrastructure. A brief civil war followed their departure and, following calls for independence from Fretilin guerrillas, Indonesian troops invaded, bombed villages, and carried out mass executions of suspected Fretilin sympathizers. The war and its attendant famine are thought to have caused more than 100,000 deaths, but starvation had been alleviated by the mid-1980s, and the Indonesian government had built schools, roads, and hospitals. Fretilin guerrillas remained active, claiming to have the support of the population.

Eastwood Clint 1930– . US film actor and director. As the "Man with No Name" in *A Fistful of Dollars* 1964, he started the vogue for "spaghetti Westerns." Later Westerns include *The Good, the Bad, and the Ugly* 1966, *High Plains Drifter* 1973, *Outlaw Josey Wales* 1976, and *Unforgiven* 1992.

Eastwood starred in the TV series *Rawhide* and in the "Dirty Harry" series of films, and directed *Bird* 1988. He was elected mayor of Carmel, California 1986.

Eau Claire city in W central Wisconsin, N of LaCrosse, on the Chippewa River; seat of Eau Claire county; population (1990) 56,850. It is a processing and marketing center for the region's dairy farmers. Industries include machine parts, electronics, printing, and brewing. Tourism is important to the economy.

eau de cologne refreshing toilet water (weaker than perfume), made of alcohol and aromatic oils. Its invention is ascribed to Giovanni Maria Farina (1685–1766), who moved from Italy to Cologne 1709 to manufacture it.

Eban Abba 1915– . Israeli diplomat and politician, ambassador in Washington 1950–59 and foreign minister 1966–74.

Eban was born in Cape Town, South Africa, and educated in England; he taught at Cambridge University before serving at Allied HQ during World War II. He subsequently settled in Israel.

EBCDIC (abbreviation for *extended binary-coded decimal interchange code*) in computing, a code used for storing and communicating alphabetic and numeric characters. It is an 8-bit code, capable of holding 256 different characters, although only 85 of these are defined in the standard version. It is still used in many mainframe computers, but almost all mini-and microcomputers now use ⋄ASCII code.

ebony any of a group of hardwood trees of the ebony family Ebenaceae, especially some tropical persimmons of the genus *Diospyros*, native to Africa and Asia.

Their very heavy, hard, black timber polishes well and is used in cabinetmaking, inlaying, for piano keys, violin fingerboards, chinrests, and pegs, and for sculpture.

EC abbreviation for ⋄*European Community*.

eccentricity in geometry, a property of a ⋄conic section (circle, ellipse, parabola, or hyperbola). It is the distance of any point on the curve from a fixed point (the focus) divided by the distance of that point from a fixed line (the directrix). A circle has an eccentricity of zero; for an ellipse it is less than one; for a parabola it is equal to one; and for a hyperbola it is greater than one.

Eccles John Carew 1903– . Australian physiologist who shared (with Alan Hodgkin and Andrew Huxley) the 1963 Nobel Prize for Medicine for work on conduction in the central nervous system. In some of his later works, he argued that the mind has an existence independent of the brain.

Ecclesiastes also known as "The Preacher," a book of the Old Testament, traditionally attributed to ⋄Solomon, on the theme of the vanity of human life.

ecdysis periodic shedding of the ⋄exoskeleton by insects and other arthropods to allow growth. Prior to shedding, a new soft and expandable layer is first laid down underneath the existing one. The old layer then splits, the animal moves free of it, and the new layer expands and hardens.

Echegaray José 1832–1916. Spanish dramatist. His dramas include *O locura o santidad/Madman or Saint* 1877, and *El gran Galeoto/The World and his Wife* 1881.

He won a Nobel Prize 1904.

echidna or **spiny anteater** any of several species of toothless, egg-laying, spiny mammals of the genera *Tachyglossus* and *Zaglossus* in the order Monotremata, found in Australia and New Guinea. They feed entirely upon ants and termites, which they dig out with their powerful claws and lick up with their prehensile tongues. When attacked, an echidna rolls itself into a ball, or tries to hide by burrowing in the earth.

echinoderm marine invertebrate of the phylum Echinodermata ("spiny-skinned"), characterized by a five-radial symmetry. Echinoderms have a water-vascular system which transports substances around the body. They include starfishes (or sea stars), brittlestars, sea-lilies, sea-urchins, and sea-cucumbers. The skeleton is external, made of a series of limy plates, and echinoderms generally move by using tube-feet, small water-filled sacs that can be protruded or pulled back to the body.

echo repetition of a sound wave, or of a ⋄radar or ⋄sonar signal, by reflection from a surface. By accurately measuring the time taken for an echo to return to the transmitter, and by knowing the speed of a radar signal (the speed of light) or a sonar signal (the speed of sound in water), it is possible to calculate the range of the object causing the echo (⋄echolocation).

A similar technique is used in echo sounders to estimate the depth of water under a ship's keel or the depth of a school of fish.

Echo in Greek mythology, a nymph who pined away until only her voice remained, after being rejected by Narcissus.

echolocation method used by certain animals, notably bats and dolphins, to detect the positions of objects by using sound. The animal emits a stream of high-pitched sounds, generally at ultrasonic frequencies (beyond the range of human hearing), and listens for the returning echoes reflected off objects to determine their exact location.

The location of an object can be established by the time difference between the emitted sound and its differential return as an echo to the two ears. Echolocation is of particular value under conditions when normal vision is poor (at night in the case of bats, in murky water

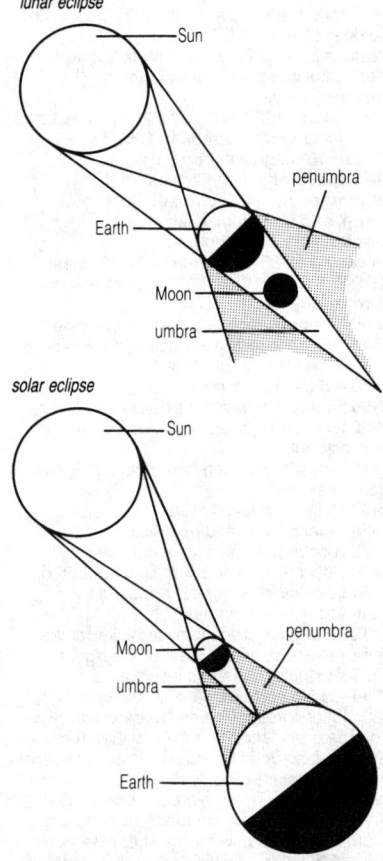

lunar eclipse

Sun — penumbra — Earth — Moon — umbra

solar eclipse

Sun — Moon — penumbra — umbra — Earth

eclipse *The two types of eclipse: lunar and solar.*

for dolphins). A few species of bird can also echolocate.

echo sounder or *sonar device* device that detects objects under water by means of ▷sonar—by using reflected sound waves. Most boats are equipped with echo sounders to measure the water depth beneath them. An echo sounder consists of a transmitter, which emits an ultrasonic pulse (see ▷ultrasound), and a receiver, which detects the pulse after reflection from the seabed. The time between transmission and receipt of the reflected signal is a measure of the depth of water.

Eckert John Presper Jr 1919– . US mathematician who collaborated with John ▷Mauchly on the development of the early ENIAC (1946) and Univac 1 (1951) computers.

Eckhart Johannes, called Meister Eckhart *c.* 1260–1327. German theologian and leader of a popular mystical movement. In 1326 he was accused of heresy, and in 1329 a number of his doctrines were condemned by the pope as heretical. His theology stressed the absolute transcendence of God, and the internal spiritual development through which union with the divine could be attained.

eclipse passage of an astronomical body through the shadow of another. The term is usually employed for solar and lunar eclipses, which may be either partial or total, but also, for example, for eclipses by Jupiter of its satellites. An eclipse of a star by a body in the Solar System is called an occultation.

A *solar eclipse* occurs when the Moon passes in front of the Sun as seen from Earth, and can happen only at new Moon. During a total eclipse the Sun's ▷corona can be seen. A total solar eclipse can last up to 7.5 minutes. When the Moon is at its farthest from Earth it does not completely cover the face of the Sun, leaving a ring of sunlight visible. This is an **annular eclipse** (from the Latin word *annulus* "ring"). Between two and five solar eclipses occur each year.

A *lunar eclipse* occurs when the Moon passes into the shadow of the Earth, becoming dim until emerging from the shadow. Lunar eclipses may be partial or total, and they can happen only at full Moon. Total lunar eclipses last for up to 100 minutes; the maximum number each year is three.

eclipsing binary binary (double) star in which the two stars periodically pass in front of each other as seen from Earth.

When one star crosses in front of the other the total light received on Earth from the two stars declines. The first eclipsing binary to be noticed was ▷Algol.

ecliptic path, against the background of stars, that the Sun appears to follow each year as the Earth orbits the Sun. It can be thought of as the plane of the Earth's orbit projected on to the ▷celestial sphere (imaginary sphere around the Earth).

The ecliptic is tilted at about 23.5° with respect to the celestial equator, a result of the tilt of the Earth's axis relative to the plane of its orbit around the Sun.

Eco Umberto 1932– . Italian writer, semiologist, and literary critic. His works include *The Role of the Reader* 1979, the "philosophical thriller" *The Name of the Rose* 1983, and *Foucault's Pendulum* 1988.

ecology (Greek *oikos* "house") study of the relationship among organisms and the environments in which they live, including all living and nonliving components. The term was coined by the biologist Ernst Haeckel 1866.

Ecology may be concerned with individual organisms (for example, behavioral ecology, feeding strategies), with populations (for example, population dynamics), or with entire communities (for example, competition between species for access to resources in an ecosystem, or predator–prey relationships). Applied ecology is concerned with the management and conservation of habitats and the consequences and control of pollution.

econometrics application of mathematical and statistical analysis to the study of economic relationships, including testing economic theories and making quantitative predictions.

economic community or *common market* organization of autonomous countries formed to promote trade. Examples include the European Community (EC) 1957, Caribbean Community (Caricom) 1973, Latin American Economic System 1975, and Central African Economic Community 1985.

Economic Community of West African States (ECOWAS, *Communauté Economique des Etats de l'Afrique de l'Ouest*) organization for the promotion of economic cooperation and development, established 1975 by the Treaty of Lagos. Its members include Benin, Burkina Faso, Cape Verde, Gambia, Ghana, Guinea, Guinea-Bissau, Ivory Coast, Liberia, Mali, Mauritania, Niger, Nigeria, Senegal, Sierra Leone, and Togo. Its headquarters are in Lagos, Nigeria.

economic growth rate of growth of output of all goods and services in an economy, usually measured as the percentage increase in gross domestic product or gross national product from one year to the next. It is regarded as an indicator of the rate of increase or decrease (if economic growth is negative) in the standard of living.

economics (Greek "household management") social science devoted to studying the production, distribution, and consumption of wealth. It consists of the disciplines of ▷**microeconomics**, the study of individual producers, consumers, or markets, and ▷**macroeconomics**, the study of whole economies or systems (in particular, areas such as taxation and public spending).

Economics is the study of how, in a given society, choices are made in the allocation of resources to produce goods and services for consumption, and the mechanisms and principles that govern this process. Economics seeks to apply scientific method to construct theories about the processes involved and to test them against what actually happens. Its two central concerns are the efficient allocation of available resources and the problem of reconciling finite resources with a virtually infinite desire for goods and services. Economics analyses the ingredients of economic efficiency in the production process, and the implications for practical policies, and examines conflicting demands for resources and the consequences of whatever choices are made, whether by individuals, enterprises, or governments.

Microeconomics and macroeconomics frequently overlap. They include the sub-discipline of *econometrics*, which analyses economic relationships using mathematical and statistical techniques. Increasingly sophisticated econometric methods are today being used for such topics as economic forecasting. Pioneers in this field include ▷Frisch and ▷Kantorovich.

Economics aims to be either *positive*, presenting objective and scientific explanations of how an economy works, or *normative*, offering prescriptions and recommendations on what should be done to cure perceived ills. However, almost inevitably, value judgments are involved in all economists' formulations.

Economics came of age as a separate area of study with the publication of Adam Smith's *The Wealth of Nations* 1776; the economist Alfred Marshall (1842–1924) established the orthodox position of "Neo-Classical" economics, which, as modified by John Maynard Keynes remains the standard today. Major economic thinkers include David Ricardo, Thomas Malthus, J S Mill, Karl Marx, Vilfredo Pareto, and Milton Friedman.

economies of scale in economics, when production capacity is increased at a financial cost that is more than compensated for by the greater volume of output. In a dress factory, for example, a reduction in the unit cost may be possible only by the addition of new machinery, which would be worthwhile only if the volume of dresses produced were increased and there were sufficient market demand for them.

In business, economies of scale are usually considered in relation to specific areas of the production process, which may be technical, managerial, marketing, finance, and risk. In achieving economies of scale, many factors must be considered, not least of which is the demand for a particular product.

ecosystem in ▷ecology, an integrated unit

consisting of the ▷community of living organisms and the physical environment in a particular area. The relationships among species in an ecosystem are usually complex and finely balanced, and removal of any one species may be disastrous. The removal of a major predator, for example, can result in the destruction of the ecosystem through overgrazing by herbivores.

Energy and nutrients pass through organisms in an ecosystem in a particular sequence (see ▷food chain): energy is captured through ▷photosynthesis, and nutrients are taken up from the soil or water by plants; both are passed to herbivores that eat the plants and then to carnivores that feed on herbivores. These nutrients are returned to the soil through the ▷decomposition of excrement and dead organisms, thus completing a cycle that is crucial to the stability and survival of the ecosystem.

ECOWAS acronym from ▷*Economic Community of West African States.*

ecstasy or *MDMA* (3,4-methylenedioxymethamphetamine) illegal drug in increasing use from the 1980s. It is a modified amphetamine with mild psychedelic effects, and works by depleting serotonin (a neurotransmitter) in the brain.

ECT abbreviation for ▷*electroconvulsive therapy.*

ectoparasite ▷parasite that lives on the outer surface of its host.

ectopic in medicine, term applied to an anatomical feature that is displaced or found in an abnormal position. An ectopic pregnancy is one occurring outside the womb, usually in a Fallopian tube.

ectoplasm outer layer of a cell's ▷cytoplasm.

ectotherm "coldblooded" animal (see ▷poikilothermy), such as a lizard, that relies on external warmth (ultimately from the sun) to raise its body temperature so that it can become active. To cool the body, ectotherms seek out a cooler environment.

ECU abbreviation for *European Currency Unit*, the official monetary unit of the European Community. It is based on the value of the different currencies used in the ▷European Monetary System (EMS).

Ecuador country in South America, bounded N by Colombia, E and S by Peru, and W by the Pacific Ocean.

government Ecuador is not a fully federal state but has a devolved system of 20 provinces, each administered by an appointed governor. The 1979 constitution provides for a president and a single-chamber national congress—the 72-member chamber of representatives—both popularly elected for a four-year term. The president is not eligible for reelection.

history The tribes of N highland Ecuador formed the Kingdom of Quito about AD 1000, and it was conquered by the ▷Inca in the 15th century. Ecuador was invaded and colonized by Spain from 1532. It joined Venezuela, Colombia, and Panama in the confederacy of Gran Colombia 1819. After joining other South American colonies in a revolt against Spain, Ecuador was liberated 1822 by Antonio José de ▷Sucre and became fully independent 1830. Since independence, Peru has repeatedly invaded Ecuador because of boundary disputes, which remain unresolved.

political instability From independence onwards the political pendulum has swung from

Ecuador
Republic of (*República del Ecuador*)

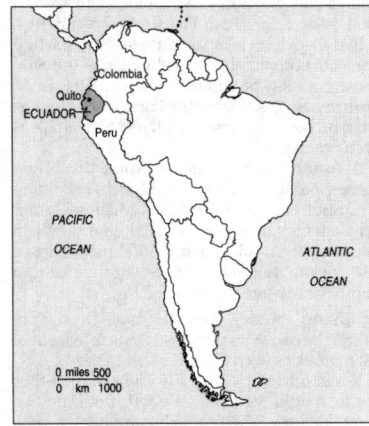

area 104,479 sq mi/270,670 sq km
capital Quito
cities Cuenca; chief port Guayaquil
physical coastal plain rises sharply to Andes Mountains, which are divided into a series of cultivated valleys; flat, low-lying rainforest in E
environment about 25,000 species became extinct 1965–90 as a result of environmental destruction
features Ecuador is crossed by the equator, from which it derives its name; Galápagos Islands; Cotopaxi is world's highest active volcano; rich wildlife in rainforest of Amazon basin
head of state and government Sixto Duran Ballen from 1992
political system emergent democracy
political parties Social Christian Party (PSC), right-wing; United Republican Party (PUR), right-of-center coalition; Ecuadorean Roldosist Party (PRE)
exports bananas, cocoa, coffee, sugar, rice, fruit, balsa wood, fish, petroleum
currency sucre
population (1989 est) 10,490,000; (mestizo 55%, Indian 25%, European 10%, black African 10%); growth rate 2.9% p.a.
life expectancy men 62, women 66
languages Spanish (official), Quechua, Jivaro, and other Indian languages
religion Roman Catholic 95%
literacy men 85%, women 80% (1985 est)
GDP $10.6 bn (1987); $1,069 per head
chronology
1830 Independence achieved from Spain.
1925–48 Great political instability; no president completed his term of office.
1948–55 Liberals in power.
1956 First conservative president in 60 years.
1960 Liberals returned, with José Velasco as president.
1961 Velasco deposed and replaced by the vice-president.
1962 Military junta installed.
1968 Velasco returned as president.
1972 A coup put the military back in power.
1978 New democratic constitution adopted.
1979 Liberals in power but opposed by right-and left-wing parties.
1982 Deteriorating economy provoked strikes, demonstrations, and a state of emergency.
1983 Austerity measures introduced.
1984–85 No party with a clear majority in the national congress; Febres Cordero narrowly won the presidency for the Conservatives.
1988 Rodrigo Borja Cevallos elected president for moderate left-wing coalition.
1989 Guerrilla left-wing group, *Alfaro Vive, Carajo* ("Alfaro lives, Dammit"), numbering about 1,000, laid down arms after nine years.
1992 PUR leader, Sixto Duran Ballen, elected president; PSC became largest party in congress.

the conservatives to the liberals, from civilian to military rule, and from democracy to dictatorship. By 1948 some stability was evident, and eight years of liberal government ensued. In 1956, Dr Camilo Ponce became the first conservative president for 60 years. Four years later a liberal, Dr José Maria Velasco (president 1933–35, 1944–47, and 1952–56), was reelected. He was deposed 1961 by the vice-president, who was himself replaced by a military junta the following year. In 1968 Velasco returned from exile and took up the presidency again. Another coup 1972 put the military back in power until in 1978 a new, democratic constitution was adopted.

Economic deterioration caused strikes, demonstrations, and, in 1982, a state of emergency. In the 1984 elections there was no clear majority in the national congress, and the conservative León Febres Cordero became president on a promise of "bread, roofs, and jobs." In 1985 he won a majority in congress when five opposition members shifted their allegiance to him. In 1988 Rodrigo Borja Cevallos was elected president for a moderate left-wing coalition government. In July 1992 the United Republican Party (PUR) leader Sixto Duran Ballen was elected president. The right-wing Social Christian Party (PSC) became the largest party in congress, but without an overall majority. *See illustration box.*

ecumenical council (Greek *oikoumenikos* "of

the whole world") meeting of church leaders worldwide to determine Christian doctrine; their results are binding on all church members. Seven such councils are accepted as ecumenical by both Eastern and Western churches, while the Roman Catholic Church accepts a further 14 as ecumenical.

ecumenical movement movement for reunification of the various branches of the Christian church. It began in the 19th century with the extension of missionary work to Africa and Asia, where the divisions created in Europe were incomprehensible; the movement gathered momentum from the need for unity in the face of growing secularism in Christian countries and of the challenge posed by such faiths as Islam. The *World Council of Churches* was founded 1948.

ecumenical patriarch head of the Eastern Orthodox Church, the patriarch of Istanbul (Constantinople). The Bishop of Constantinople was recognized as having equal rights with the Bishop of Rome 451, and first termed "patriarch" in the 6th century. The office survives today but with only limited authority, mainly confined to the Greek and Turkish Orthodox churches.

eczema inflammatory skin condition, a form of dermatitis, marked by dryness, rashes, itching, the formation of blisters, and the exudation of fluid. It may be allergic in origin and is sometimes complicated by infection.

Edberg Stefan 1966– . Swedish tennis player. He won the junior Grand Slam 1983 and his first Grand Slam title, the Australian Open, 1985, repeated 1987. Other Grand Slam singles titles include Wimbledon 1988, 1990 and the US Open 1991 and 1992.

Edda two collections of early Icelandic literature that together constitute our chief source for Old Norse mythology. The term strictly applies to the *Younger* or *Prose Edda*, compiled by Snorri Sturluson, a priest, about AD 1230.

The *Elder* or *Poetic Edda* is the collection of poems discovered around 1643 by Brynjólfr Sveinsson, written by unknown Norwegian poets of the 9th to 12th centuries.

Eddington Arthur Stanley 1882–1944. British astrophysicist, who studied the motions, equilibrium, luminosity, and atomic structure of the stars, and became a leading exponent of Einstein's relativity theory. In 1919 his observation of stars during an ⟩eclipse confirmed Einstein's prediction that light is bent when passing near the Sun. His book *The Nature of the Physical World* 1928 is a popularization of science. In *The Expanding Universe* 1933 he expressed the theory that in the spherical universe the outer galaxies or spiral nebulae are receding from one another.

Eddy Mary Baker 1821–1910. US founder of the Christian Science movement.

She was born in New Hampshire and brought up as a Congregationalist. Her pamphlet *Science of Man* 1869 was followed by *Science and Health with Key to the Scriptures* 1875, which systematically set forth the basis of Christian Science. She founded the Christian Science Association 1876. In 1879 the Church of Christ, Scientist, was established, and although living in retirement after 1892 she continued to direct the activities of the movement until her death.

Separated from her husband and in poor health, she discovered in 1862 the work of a faith healer named Phineas Quimby, who decisively influenced her belief in healing through divine grace, a belief enhanced by her own recovery.

eddy current electric current induced, in accordance with ⟩Faraday's laws, in a conductor located in a changing magnetic field. Eddy currents can cause much wasted energy in the cores of transformers and other electrical machines.

Edelman Gerald Maurice 1929– . US biochemist who worked out the sequence of 1330 amino acids that makes up human ⟩immunoglobulin, a task completed 1969. For this work he shared the Nobel Prize for Medicine 1972 with Rodney Porter.

edelweiss perennial alpine plant *Leontopodium alpinum*, family Compositae, with a white, woolly, star-shaped bloom, found in the high mountains of Eurasia.

edema any abnormal accumulation of fluid in tissues or cavities of the body; waterlogging of the tissues due to excessive loss of ⟩plasma through the capillary walls. It may be generalized (the condition once known as dropsy) or confined to one area, such as the ankles.

Edema may be mechanical—the result of obstructed veins or heart failure—or it may be due to increased permeability of the capillary walls, as in liver or kidney disease or malnutrition. Accumulation of fluid in the abdomen, a complication of cirrhosis, is known as ascites.

Eden Anthony, 1st Earl of Avon 1897–1977. British Conservative politician, foreign secretary 1935–38, 1940–45, and 1951–55; prime minister 1955–57, when he resigned after the failure of the Anglo-French military intervention in the ⟩Suez Crisis.

Upset by his prime minister's rejection of a peace plan secretly proposed by Roosevelt Jan 1938, Eden resigned as foreign secretary Feb 1938 in protest against Chamberlain's decision to open conversations with the Fascist dictator Mussolini. He was foreign secretary again in the wartime coalition, formed Dec 1940, and in the Conservative government, elected 1951. With the Soviets, he negotiated an interim peace in Vietnam 1954. In April 1955 he succeeded Churchill as prime minister. His use of force in the Suez Crisis led to his resignation Jan 1957, but he continued to maintain that his action was justified.

Eden, Garden of in the Old Testament book of Genesis and in the Koran, the "garden" in which Adam and Eve lived after their creation, and from which they were expelled for disobedience.

Its location has often been identified with the Fertile Crescent in Mesopotamia (now in Iraq) and two of its rivers with the Euphrates and the Tigris.

Edgar known as the *Atheling* ("of royal blood") c. 1050–c. 1130. English prince, born in Hungary. Grandson of Edmund Ironside, he was supplanted as heir to Edward the Confessor by William the Conqueror. He led two rebellions against William 1068 and 1069, but made peace 1074.

Edgar the Peaceful 944–975. King of all England from 959. He was the younger son of Edmund I, and strove successfully to unite English and Danes as fellow subjects.

Edinburg city in SE Texas, NW of Brownsville; seat of Hidalgo county. It is a shipping center for the area's citrus fruit crops; population (1990) 29,800.

Edinburgh capital of Scotland and administrative center of the region of Lothian, near the southern shores of the Firth of Forth; population (1985) 440,000. A cultural center, it holds an annual festival of music and the arts; the university was established 1583. Industries include printing, publishing, banking, insurance, chemical manufactures, distilling, brewing, and some shipbuilding.

features Edinburgh Castle contains the 12th-century St Margaret's chapel, the oldest building in Edinburgh. The palace of Holyrood House was built in the 15th and 16th centuries on the site of a 12th-century abbey; it is the British sovereign's official Scottish residence. ⟩Rizzio was murdered here 1566 in the apartments of Mary Queen of Scots. The Parliament House, begun 1632, is now the seat of the supreme courts. The Royal Scottish Academy and the National Gallery of Scotland (renovated 1989) in Classical style are by William Henry Playfair (1789–1857). The episcopal cathedral of St Mary, opened 1879, and St Giles parish church (mostly 15th-century) are the principal churches. The Royal Observatory has been at Blackford Hill since 1896. The principal thoroughfares are Princes Street and the Royal Mile. The university has a famous medical school and the Koestler chair of parapsychology (instituted 1985), the only such professorship in the UK. The Heriot-Watt University (established 1885; university status 1966) is mainly a technical institution.

history In Roman times the site was occupied by Celtic peoples and about 617 was captured by Edwin of Northumbria, from whom the town took its name. The early settlement grew up around a castle on Castle Rock, while about a mile to the E another burgh, Canongate, developed around the abbey of Holyrood, founded 1128 by David I. It remained separate from Edinburgh until 1856. Robert Bruce made Edinburgh a burgh 1329, and established its port at Leith. In 1544 the town was destroyed by the English. After the union with England 1707, Edinburgh lost its political importance but remained culturally preeminent. During the 18th century, Edinburgh was known as the "Athens of the North" because of its concentration of intellectual talent, for example, Adam Smith, David Hume, and Joseph Black.

Edison Thomas Alva 1847–1931. US scientist and inventor, with over 1,000 patents. In Menlo Park, New Jersey, 1876–87, he produced his most important inventions, including the electric light bulb 1879. He constructed a system of electric power distribution for consumers, the telephone transmitter, and the phonograph.

In 1869 he invented an automatic vote recorder and the improved stock ticker in 1871, which earned him enough to found his manufacturing plant in Newark, New Jersey. He moved to Menlo Park in 1876 and from there to West Orange, New Jersey, where he invented the movie camera, mimeograph, fluoroscope, and an improved battery. In 1889 he began the Edison Light Co., which became the General Electric Co.

Edmonton capital of Alberta, on the North Saskatchewan River; population (1986) 576,200. It is the center of an oil and mining area to the N and also an agricultural and dairying region. Petroleum pipelines link Edmonton with Superior, Wisconsin, and Vancouver, British Columbia.

The city is on the Alaska Highway. Manufactured goods include processed foods, petrochemicals, plastic and metal products, lumber, and clothing. The University of Alberta, Athabasca University, and the Provincial Museum of Alberta are here. Fort Edmonton, a Hudson's Bay Company fur-trading post, was built in 1795. It was incorporated as a town soon after the arrival of the Canadian Pacific Railroad in 1891. It flourished as an outfitting point for prospectors seeking gold in the Klondike region of the Yukon in the late 1890s. Edmonton grew rapidly as a center for the rapidly growing Alberta oil industry after 1950.

Edmund II Ironside c. 989–1016. King of England 1016, the son of Ethelred II the Unready. He led the resistance to ⟩Canute's invasion 1015, and on Ethelred's death 1016 was chosen king by the citizens of London, whereas the Witan (the king's council) elected Canute. In the struggle for the throne, Edmund was defeated by Canute at Assandun (Ashington), Essex, and they divided the kingdom between them; when Edmund died the same year, Canute ruled the whole kingdom.

Edom in the Old Testament, a mountainous area of S Palestine, which stretched from the Dead Sea to the Gulf of Aqaba. Its people, said to be descendants of Esau, were enemies of the Israelites.

education the process, beginning at birth, of developing intellectual capacity, manual skill, and social awareness, especially through instruction. In its more restricted sense, the term refers to the process of imparting literacy, numeracy, and a generally accepted body of knowledge.

history of education The earliest known European educational systems were those of ancient Greece, based on those of the early civilizations of the Near East and Egypt. In Sparta the process was devoted mainly to the development of military skills; in Athens, to politics, philosophy, and public speaking, but both were accorded only to the privileged few.

In ancient China, formalized education received impetus from the imperial decree of 165 BC, which established open competitive examinations for the recruitment of members of the civil service, based mainly on a detailed study of literature.

Rome adopted the Greek system of education and imposed it on their conquered peoples of Europe. Following the disintegration of the Roman Empire, widespread education vanished from Europe, although Christian monasteries preserved both learning and Latin.

In the Middle Ages, Charlemagne's monastic schools taught the "seven liberal arts:" grammar, logic, rhetoric, arithmetic, geometry, music, and astronomy. These schools produced the theological philosophers of the Scholastic Movement, which in the 11th–13th centuries led to the foundation of the universities of Paris (⟡Sorbonne), Bologna, Padua, ⟡Oxford, and ⟡Cambridge. The capture of Constantinople, capital of the E Roman Empire, by the Turks in 1453 sent the Christian scholars there into exile across Europe, thus reviving European interest in learning and fueling the Renaissance. Compulsory attendance at European primary schools was first established in the mid-18th century, in Prussia, and has since spread almost worldwide.

education today In the US, public education is paid for by property taxes and is mainly the responsibility of the states and local school boards, but the Department of Education, headed by a secretary who is a member of the president's cabinet, is responsible for federal aspects, including the administration of federal monies to state and local school systems. In the US, private schools may be church affiliated or secular, and both must meet minimum local standards to be accredited.

Education is usually divided into optional nursery or kindergarten (to age 6), compulsory elementary or grammar school (grades 1–6), junior high school (grades 7–9) or middle school (grades 6–8), and high school (grades 10–12 or 9–12). Upon graduation, students receive a high-school diploma, awarded by the individual school or local school district on successful completion of a broad secondary school curriculum authorized by the state. High schools give specialized programs to prepare students for technical and commercial careers, as well as academic programs aimed at preparation for college. In their senior year of high school, some students take the ⟡Scholastic Aptitude Test (SAT), since many private colleges and universities require certain minimum SAT scores for admission. A large proportion of US high-school graduates go on to higher education at two-year junior colleges or four-year state-funded or private colleges or universities.

educational psychology the work of psychologists primarily in schools, including the assessment of children with achievement problems and advising on problem behavior in the classroom.

Edward (full name Edward Antony Richard

Louis) 1964–   . Prince of the UK, third son of Queen Elizabeth II. He is seventh in line to the throne after Charles, Charles's two sons, Andrew, and Andrew's two daughters.

Edward the **Black Prince** 1330–1376. Prince of Wales, eldest son of Edward III of England. The epithet (probably posthumous) may refer to his black armor. During the Hundred Years' War he fought at the Battle of Crécy 1346 and captured the French king at Poitiers 1356. He ruled Aquitaine 1360–71; during the revolt that eventually ousted him, he caused the massacre of Limoges 1370.

Edward eight kings of England or the UK:

Edward I 1239–1307. King of England from 1272, son of Henry III. Edward led the royal forces against Simon de Montfort in the ⟡Barons' War 1264–67, and was on a crusade when he succeeded to the throne. He established English rule over all Wales 1282–84, and secured recognition of his overlordship from the Scottish king, although the Scots (under Wallace and Bruce) fiercely resisted actual conquest. In his reign Parliament took its approximate modern form with the ⟡Model Parliament 1295. He was succeeded by his son Edward II.

Edward II 1284–1327. King of England from 1307. Son of Edward I and born at Caernarvon Castle, he was created the first Prince of Wales 1301. His invasion of Scotland 1314 to suppress revolt resulted in defeat at ⟡Bannockburn. He was deposed 1327 by his wife Isabella (1292–1358), daughter of Philip IV of France, and her lover Roger de ⟡Mortimer, and murdered in Berkeley Castle, Gloucestershire. He was succeeded by his son Edward III.

In addition to military disasters, his reign was troubled by his extravagance and the unpopularity of his favorites.

Edward III 1312–1377. King of England from 1327, son of Edward II. He assumed the government 1330 from his mother, through whom in 1337 he laid claim to the French throne and thus began the ⟡Hundred Years' War. He was succeeded by Richard II.

At 18 Edward imprisoned his mother Isabella of France and executed her lover Roger de Mortimer. In 1360 he surrendered his claim to the French throne, but the war resumed 1369, and his son John of Gaunt dominated the government in his later years.

Edward IV 1442–1483. King of England 1461–70 and from 1471. He was the son of Richard, Duke of York, and succeeded Henry VI in the Wars of the ⟡Roses, temporarily losing the throne to Henry when Edward fell out with his adviser ⟡Warwick, but regaining it at the Battle of Barnet 1471. He was succeeded by his son Edward V.

Edward V 1470–1483. King of England 1483. Son of Edward IV, he was deposed three months after his accession in favor of his uncle (⟡Richard III), and is traditionally believed to have been murdered (with his brother) in the Tower of London on Richard's orders.

Edward VI 1537–1553. King of England from 1547, son of Henry VIII and Jane Seymour. The government was entrusted to his uncle the Duke of Somerset (who fell from power 1549), and then to the Earl of Warwick, later created Duke of Northumberland. He was succeeded by his sister, Mary I.

Jane Seymour was Henry VIII's third wife, and Edward was his only son. Edward became

a staunch Protestant and during his reign the Reformation progressed. He died from tuberculosis.

Edward VII 1841–1910. King of Great Britain and Ireland from 1901. As Prince of Wales he was a prominent social figure, but his mother Queen Victoria considered him too frivolous to take part in political life. In 1860 he made the first tour of Canada and the US ever undertaken by a British prince.

He took a close interest in politics and was on good terms with party leaders. He succeeded to the throne 1901 and was crowned 1902. Although he overrated his political influence, he contributed to the Entente Cordiale 1904 with France and the Anglo-Russian agreement 1907.

Edward VIII 1894–1972. King of Great Britain and Northern Ireland Jan–Dec 1936, when he renounced the throne to marry Wallis Warfield ⟡Simpson (see ⟡abdication crisis). He was created Duke of Windsor and was governor of the Bahamas 1940–45, subsequently settling in France.

Edward was extremely popular as prince of Wales, and he made fashion statements that changed the way men dressed throughout the 20th century in the Western world—soft collars, tweed sport jackets, cuffed trousers, low shoes, the Windsor knotted tie, and V-necked sweaters freed men from the starched look that characterized the turn of the century. He succeeded his father George V on Jan 20, 1936, and on Dec 11 he abdicated. A divorcee, Mrs Simpson was not acceptable constitutionally as queen. They were married in France in May 1937.

Edward, Lake lake in Uganda, area 830 sq mi/2,150 sq km, at about 3,000 ft/900 m above sea level in the Albertine rift valley. From 1973 to 1979 it was known as Lake Idi Amin Dada, after President Amin of Uganda.

Edwards Blake. Adopted name of William Blake McEdwards 1922–   . US film director and writer, formerly an actor. Specializing in comedies, he directed the series of *Pink Panther* films 1963–78, starring Peter Sellers. His other work includes *Breakfast at Tiffany's* 1961 and *Blind Date* 1986.

Edward the Confessor c. 1003–1066. King of England from 1042, the son of Ethelred II. He lived in Normandy until shortly before his accession. During his reign power was held by Earl ⟡Godwin and his son ⟡Harold, while the king devoted himself to religion, including the rebuilding of Westminster Abbey (consecrated 1065), where he is buried. His childlessness led ultimately to the Norman Conquest 1066. He was canonized 1161.

Edward the Elder c. 870–924. King of the West Saxons. He succeeded his father ⟡Alfred the Great 899. He reconquered SE England and the Midlands from the Danes, uniting Wessex and ⟡Mercia with the help of his sister, Athelflad. By the time Edward died, his kingdom was the most powerful in the British Isles. He was succeeded by his son ⟡Athelstan.

Edward the Martyr c. 963–978. King of England from 975. Son of King Edgar, he was murdered at Corfe Castle, Dorset, probably at his stepmother Aelfthryth's instigation (she wished to secure the crown for her son, Ethelred). He was canonized 1001.

EEC abbreviation for *European Economic Community*; see ⟡European Community.

egg *Section through a fertilized bird egg.*

EEG abbreviation for ▷*electroencephalogram*.

eel any fish of the order Anguilliformes. Eels are snakelike, with elongated dorsal and anal fins. They include the freshwater eels of Europe and North America (which breed in the Atlantic), the marine conger eels, and the morays of tropical coral reefs.

eelgrass or **tape grass** or **glass wrack** any of several flowering plants of the genus *Zostera*, especially *Zostera marina*, of the pondweed family Zosteraceae. Eelgrass is found in tidal mud flats and is one of the few flowering plants to adapt to marine conditions, being completely submerged at high tide.

EEPROM (acronym for *electrically erasable programmable read-only memory*) computer memory that can record data and retain it indefinitely. The data can be erased with an electrical charge and new data recorded.

Some EEPROM must be removed from the computer and erased and reprogrammed using a special device. Other EEPROM, called **flash memory**, can be erased and reprogrammed without removal from the computer.

efficiency output of a machine (work done by the machine) divided by the input (work put into the machine), usually expressed as a percentage. Because of losses caused by friction, efficiency is always less than 100%, although it can approach this for electrical machines with no moving parts (such as a transformer).

Since the **mechanical advantage**, or force ratio, is the ratio of the load (the output force) to the effort (the input force), and the **velocity ratio** is the distance moved by the effort divided by the distance moved by the load, for certain machines the efficiency can also be defined as the mechanical advantage divided by the velocity ratio.

EFTA acronym for ▷*European Free Trade Association*.

e.g. abbreviation for **exempli gratia** (Latin "for the sake of example").

egalitarianism belief that all citizens in a state should have equal rights and privileges. Interpretations of this can vary, from the notion of equality of opportunity to equality in material welfare and political decision-making. Some states clearly reject any thought of egalitarianism; most accept the concept of equal opportunities but recognize that people's abilities vary widely. Even those states which claim to be socialist find it necessary to have hierarchical structures in the political, social, and economic spheres. Egalitarianism was one of the principles of the French Revolution.

Egbert died 839. King of the West Saxons from 802, the son of Ealhmund, an under-king of Kent. By 829 he had united England for the first time under one king.

egg in animals, the ovum, or female ▷gamete (reproductive cell).

After fertilization by a sperm cell, it begins to divide to form an embryo. Eggs may be deposited by the female (▷oviparity) or they may develop within her body (▷viviparity and ▷ovoviviparity). In the oviparous reptiles and birds, the egg is protected by a shell, and well supplied with nutrients in the form of yolk.

eggplant perennial plant, *Solanum melongena*, a member of the nightshade family (Solanaceae), originally native to tropical Asia. Its purple-skinned fruits are eaten as a vegetable.

ego (Latin "I") in psychology, a general term for the processes concerned with the self and a person's conception of himself or herself, encompassing values and attitudes. In Freudian psychology, the term refers specifically to the element of the human mind that represents the conscious processes concerned with reality, in conflict with the ▷id (the instinctual element) and the ▷superego (the ethically aware element).

egret any of several herons with long feathers on the head or neck.

The snowy egret *Egretta thula* of North America, about 2 ft/60 cm long, was almost hunted to extinction for its graceful plumes before the practice was made illegal. The little egret *E. garzetta* 2 ft/60 cm long, is found in Asia, Africa, S Europe, and Australia.

Egypt country in NE Africa, bounded N by the Mediterranean Sea, E by the Suez Canal and Red Sea, S by Sudan, and W by Libya.

government The 1971 constitution provides for a single-chamber people's assembly of 458, ten nominated by the president and 448 elected for a five-year term by 48 constituencies. The president is nominated by the assembly and then elected by popular referendum for a six-year term, and is eligible for reelection. At least one vice-president and a council of ministers are appointed by the president. There is also a 210-member consultative council (Shura), with advisory powers.

history For early history see ▷Egypt, ancient. After its conquest by ▷Augustus 30 BC, Egypt passed under the rule of Roman, and later Byzantine, governors, and Christianity superseded the ancient religion. The Arabs conquered Egypt AD 639–42, introducing Islam and Arabic to the area, and the country was ruled by successive Arab dynasties until 1250, when the ▷Mamelukes seized power.

Mameluke rule lasted until 1517, when Egypt became part of the Turkish ▷Ottoman Empire.

Contact with Europe began with Napoleon's invasion and the French occupation 1798–1801. A period of anarchy followed, until in 1805 an Albanian officer, Mehemet Ali, was appointed pasha, a title that later became hereditary in his family. Under his successors Egypt met with economic difficulties over the building of the ▷Suez Canal (1859–69), to the extent that an Anglo-French commission was placed in charge of its finances. After subduing a nationalist revolt 1881–82, Britain occupied Egypt, and the government was from then on mainly in the hands of British civilian agents who directed their efforts to the improvement of the Egyptian economy. On the outbreak of World War I in 1914, nominal Turkish suzerainty was abolished, and the country was declared a British protectorate.

independence Postwar agitation by the nationalist Wafd party led to the granting of nominal independence 1922, under King Fuad I. He was succeeded by King Farouk 1936, and Britain agreed to recognize Egypt's full independence, announcing a phased withdrawal of its forces, except from the Suez Canal, Alexandria, and Port Said, where it had naval bases. The start of World War II delayed the British departure, as did the consequent campaign in Libya that ended in the defeat of the German and Italian forces that had threatened the Canal Zone.

republic In 1946 all British troops except the Suez Canal garrison were withdrawn. In the immediate postwar years a radical movement developed, calling for an end to the British presence and opposing Farouk for his extravagant lifestyle and his failure to prevent the creation of Israel. This led, in 1952, to a bloodless coup by a group of army officers, led by Col Gamal ▷Nasser, who replaced Farouk with a military junta. The 1923 constitution was suspended and all political parties banned. The following year Egypt declared itself a republic, with General Mohammad Neguib as president and prime minister. In 1954 Nasser became prime minister, and an agreement was signed for the withdrawal of British troops from the Canal Zone by 1956.

After a dispute with Neguib, Nasser took over as head of state and embarked on a program of social reform. He became a major force for the creation of Arab unity and a leader of the ▷nonaligned movement. In 1956 the presidency was strengthened by a new constitution, and Nasser was elected president, unopposed. Later that year, British forces were withdrawn, in accordance with the 1954 agreement.

Suez crisis When the US and Britain canceled their offers of financial aid for the ▷Aswan High Dam 1956, Nasser responded by nationalizing the Suez Canal. In a contrived operation, Britain, France, and Israel invaded the Sinai Peninsula Oct 31, 1956, and two days later Egypt was attacked. US pressure brought a cease-fire and an Anglo-French withdrawal 1957. The effect of the abortive Anglo-French operation was to push Egypt toward the USSR and to enhance Nasser's reputation in the Arab world.

In 1958 Egypt and Syria merged to become the United Arab Republic (UAR), with Nasser as president, but three years later Syria withdrew, though Egypt retained the title of UAR until 1971. The 1960s saw several unsuccessful attempts to federate Egypt, Syria, and Iraq. Despite these failures Nasser's prestige among his neighbors grew, while at home, in 1962, he founded the Arab Socialist Union (ASU) as Egypt's only recognized political organization.

Six-Day War In 1967 Egypt led an attack on Israel that developed into the Six-Day War, in which Israel defeated all its opponents, including Egypt. One result of the conflict was the blocking of the Suez Canal, which was not reopened until 1975. After Egypt's defeat, Nasser offered to resign but was persuaded to stay on. In 1970, aged 52, he died and was succeeded by Vice President Col Anwar ⬦Sadat.

In 1971 a new constitution was approved, and the title Arab Republic of Egypt adopted. Sadat continued Nasser's policy of promoting Arab unity, but proposals to create a federation of Egypt, Libya, and Syria again failed.

Yom Kippur War In 1973 an attempt was made to regain territory from Israel. After 18 days' fighting, US secretary of state Henry ⬦Kissinger arranged a cease-fire, resulting in Israel's evacuation of parts of Sinai, with a UN buffer zone separating the rival armies. This US intervention strengthened ties between the two countries while relations with the USSR cooled.

Camp David Agreements In 1977 Sadat went to Israel to address the Israeli parliament and plead for peace. Other Arab states were dismayed by this move, and diplomatic relations with Syria, Libya, Algeria, and the Yemen, as well as the Palestine Liberation Organization (PLO), were severed. Despite this opposition, Sadat pursued his peace initiative, and with the Israeli prime minister, Menachem Begin, signed the ⬦Camp David Agreements 1978. The first laid a framework for peace in the Middle East, and the second, a framework for a treaty between the two countries. In 1979 a treaty was signed and Israel began a phased withdrawal from Sinai. As a consequence, Egypt's isolation from the Arab world grew, the country was expelled from the ⬦Arab League, and the economy suffered from the withdrawal of Saudi subsidies. US aid became vital to Egypt's survival, and links between the two governments grew steadily closer.

position in Arab world In 1981 Sadat was assassinated by a group of Muslim fundamentalists who opposed him and was succeeded by Lt Gen Hosni ⬦Mubarak, who had been vice-president since 1975. Just as Sadat had continued the policies of his predecessor, so did Mubarak. In the 1984 elections the National Democratic Party (NDP), formed by Sadat 1948, won an overwhelming victory in the assembly, strengthening Mubarak's position. Although Egypt's treaty with Israel remained intact, relations between the two countries became strained, mainly because of Israel's preemptive activities in Lebanon and the disputed territories. Egypt's relations with other Arab nations improved, and only Libya maintained its trade boycott; the restoration of diplomatic relations with Syria 1989 paved the way for Egypt's resumption of its leadership of the Arab world.

Mubarak has played a growing role in the search for Middle East peace, proposing a ten-point program to bring about elections in the occupied territories. At home, problems with Muslim fundamentalists increased Mubarak's dependence on military support. In Oct 1987 he was reelected by referendum for a second term. In the Dec 1990 general election, despite the success of the ruling party (NDP), with 348 seats, independents did well in many areas. Egypt was a member of the UN coalition forces that sought an economic embargo against

Egypt
Arab Republic of (*Jumhuriyat Misr al-Arabiya*)

area 386,990 sq mi/1,001,450 sq km
capital Cairo
cities Gîza; ports Alexandria, Port Said, Suez, Damietta
physical mostly desert; hills in E; fertile land along Nile valley and delta; cultivated and settled area is about 13,700 sq mi/ 35,500 sq km
environment the building of the Aswan Dam (opened 1970) on the Nile has caused widespread salinization and an increase in waterborne diseases in villages close to Lake Nasser. A dramatic fall in the annual load of silt deposited downstream has reduced the fertility of cropland and has led to coastal erosion and the consequent loss of sardine shoals
features Aswan High Dam and Lake Nasser; Sinai; remains of ancient Egypt (pyramids, Sphinx, Luxor, Karnak, Abu Simbel, El Faiyum)
head of state and government Hosni Mubarak from 1981
political system democratic republic
political parties National Democratic Party (NDP), moderate, left of center; Socialist Labor Party, right of center; Socialist Liberal Party, free-enterprise; New Wafd Party, nationalist
exports cotton and textiles, petroleum, fruit and vegetables
currency Egyptian pound
population (1989 est) 54,779,000; growth rate 2.4% p.a.
life expectancy men 57, women 60
languages Arabic (official); ancient Egyptian survives to some extent in Coptic
media there is no legal censorship, but the largest publishing houses, newspapers, and magazines are owned and controlled by the state, as is all television. Questioning of

prevalent values, ideas, and social practices is discouraged
religions Sunni Muslim 95%, Coptic Christian 5%
literacy men 59%, women 30% (1985 est)
GDP $34.5 bn (1987); $679 per head
chronology
1914 Egypt became a British protectorate.
1936 Independence achieved from Britain. King Fuad succeeded by his son Farouk.
1946 Withdrawal of British troops except from Suez Canal Zone.
1952 Farouk overthrown by army in bloodless coup.
1953 Egypt declared a republic, with General Neguib as president.
1956 Neguib replaced by Col Gamal Nasser. Nasser announced nationalization of Suez Canal; Egypt attacked by Britain, France, and Israel. Cease-fire agreed because of US intervention.
1958 Short-lived merger of Egypt and Syria as United Arab Republic (UAR). Subsequent attempts to federate Egypt, Syria, and Iraq failed.
1967 Six-Day War with Israel ended in Egypt's defeat and Israeli occupation of Sinai and Gaza Strip.
1970 Nasser died suddenly, succeeded by Anwar Sadat.
1973 Attempt to regain territory lost to Israel led to fighting; cease-fire arranged by US secretary of state Henry Kissinger.
1977 Sadat's visit to Israel to address the Israeli parliament was criticized by Egypt's Arab neighbors.
1978–79 Camp David talks in the US resulted in a treaty between Egypt and Israel. Egypt expelled from the Arab League.
1981 Sadat assassinated, succeeded by Hosni Mubarak.
1983 Improved relations between Egypt and the Arab world; only Libya and Syria maintained a trade boycott.
1984 Mubarak's party victorious in the people's assembly elections.
1987 Mubarak reelected. Egypt readmitted to Arab League.
1988 Full diplomatic relations with Algeria restored.
1989 Improved relations with Libya; diplomatic relations with Syria restored. Mubarak proposed a peace plan.
1990 Gains for independents in general election.
1991 Participation in Gulf War on US-led side. Major force in convening Middle East peace conference in Spain.
1992 Outbreaks of violence between Muslims and Christians. Earthquake devastates Cairo.

Iraq 1990 for annexing Kuwait, and its armed forces joined in the military action against Iraq 1991. In Nov 1991, Egypt attended the Middle East peace talks in Spain. From May 1992 outbreaks of violence between Muslim militants and Christians were common. An earthquake in Oct devastated Cairo. *See illustration box.*

Egypt, ancient
5000 BC Egyptian culture already well established in the Nile Valley, with Neolithic farming villages.
3200 Menes united Lower Egypt (the delta) with his own kingdom of Upper Egypt.
2800 The architect Imhotep built the step pyramid at Sakkara.
c. 2600 Old Kingdom reached the height

of its power and the kings of the 4th dynasty built the pyramids at Gîza.
c. 2200–1800 Middle Kingdom, under which the unity lost toward the end of the Old Kingdom was restored.1730 Invading Asian Hyksos people established their kingdom in the Nile Delta.
c. 1580 New Kingdom established by the 18th dynasty following the eviction of the Hyksos, with its capital at Thebes. The high point of ancient Egyptian civilization under the pharaohs Thothmes, Hatshepsut, Amenhotep, Ikhnaton (who moved the capital to Akhetaton), and Tutankhamen.
c. 1321 19th dynasty Ramses I built a temple at Karnak, Ramses II the temple at Abu Simbel.

1191 Ramses III defeated the Indo-European Sea Peoples, but after him there was decline, and power within the country passed from the pharaohs to the priests of Ammon.

1090–663 Late New Kingdom during this period Egypt was often divided between two or more dynasties; the nobles became virtually independent.

8th–7th centuries Brief interlude of rule by kings from Nubia.

666 The Assyrians under Ashurbanipal occupied Thebes.

663–609 Psammetichus I restored Egypt's independence and unity.

525 Egypt was conquered by Cambyses and became a Persian province.

c. 405–340 Period of independence.

332 Conquest by Alexander the Great. On the division of his empire, Egypt went to one of his generals, Ptolemy I, and his descendants, the Macedonian dynasty.

30 Death of Cleopatra, last of the Macedonians, and conquest by the Roman emperor Augustus; Egypt became a province of the Roman and Byzantine empires.

AD 641 Conquest by the Arabs; the Christianity of later Roman rule was for the most part replaced by Islam.

For later history, see ⟩Egypt.

Egyptian art see ⟩ancient art.

Egyptian religion in the civilization of ancient Egypt, totemic animals, believed to be the ancestors of the clan, were worshiped. Totems later developed into gods, represented as having animal heads. One of the main cults was that of ⟩Osiris, the god of the underworld. Immortality, conferred by the magical rite of mummification, was originally the sole prerogative of the king, but was extended under the New Kingdom to all who could afford it; they were buried with the ⟩Book of the Dead.

The hawk was sacred to **Ra** and **Horus**, the ibis to **Thoth**, the jackal to **Anubis**. The story of Osiris, who was murdered, mourned by his sister and wife Isis, and then rose again, was enacted in a fertility ritual similar to that of Tammuz. Under the 18th dynasty a local deity of Thebes, **Ammon**, came to be regarded as supreme, a reflection of rediscovered national unity. The pharaoh Ikhnaton attempted, without success, to establish the monotheistic cult of Aton, the solar disk, as the one national god.

Egyptology the study of ancient Egypt. Interest in the subject was aroused by the Napoleonic expedition's discovery of the ⟩Rosetta Stone 1799. Various excavations continued throughout the 19th century and gradually assumed a more scientific character, largely as a result of the work of the British archeologist Flinders ⟩Petrie from 1880 onwards and the formation of the Egyptian Exploration Fund 1892. In 1922 another British archeologist, Howard Carter, discovered the tomb of Tutankhamen, the only royal tomb with all its treasures intact.

Special branches of Egyptology are the study of prehistoric Egypt and the search for papyri (ancient documents) preserved by the dryness of the climate; besides ancient Egyptian writings, many lost Greek and early Christian works have been recovered.

Ehrlich Paul 1854–1915. German bacteriologist and immunologist who produced the first cure for ⟩syphilis. He developed the arsenic compounds, in particular ⟩Salvarsan, that were used in the treatment of syphilis prior to the discovery of antibiotics. He shared the 1908 Nobel Prize for Medicine with Ilya ⟩Mechnikov for his work on immunity.

Eichmann (Karl) Adolf 1906–1962. Austrian Nazi. As an ⟩SS official during Hitler's regime (1933–1945), he was responsible for atrocities against Jews and others, including the implementation of genocide. He managed to escape at the fall of Germany 1945, but was discovered in Argentina 1960, abducted by Israeli agents, tried in Israel 1961 for ⟩war crimes, and executed.

eider large marine ⟩duck, *Somateria mollissima*, highly valued for its soft down, which is used in quilts and cushions for warmth. The adult male has a black cap and belly and a green nape. The rest of the plumage is white with pink breast and throat while the female is a mottled brown. The bill is large and flattened. It is found on the northern coasts of the Atlantic and Pacific Oceans.

Eiffel (Alexandre) Gustave 1832–1923. French engineer who constructed the **Eiffel Tower** for the 1889 Paris Exhibition. The tower, made of iron, is 1,050 ft/320 m high, and stands in the Champ de Mars, Paris. Sightseers may ride to the top for a view.

Eiffel set up his own business in Paris and quickly established his reputation with the construction of a series of ambitious railroad bridges, of which the 525 ft/160 m span across the Douro at Oporto, Portugal, was the longest. In 1881 he provided the iron skeleton for the Statue of Liberty.

Eigen Manfred 1927– . German chemist who worked on extremely rapid chemical reactions (those taking less than 1 millisecond). From 1954 he developed a technique by which very short bursts of energy could be applied to solutions, disrupting their equilibrium and enabling him to investigate momentary reactions such as the formation and dissociation of water.

For this work he shared the Nobel Prize in Chemistry 1967 with English chemists George Porter and Ronald Norrish.

Eijkman Christiaan 1858–1930. Dutch bacteriologist. He pioneered the recognition of vitamins as essential to health and identified vitamin B_1 deficiency as the cause of the disease beriberi. He shared the 1929 Nobel Prize for Medicine with Frederick Hopkins.

Eilat alternate spelling of ⟩Elat, a port in Israel.

Einstein Albert 1879–1955. German-born US physicist who formulated the theories of ⟩relativity, and worked on radiation physics and thermodynamics. In 1905 he published the special theory of relativity, and in 1915 issued his general theory of relativity. He received the Nobel Prize for Physics 1921. His latest conception of the basic laws governing the universe was outlined in his ⟩unified field theory, made public 1953.

Born at Ulm, in Württemberg, West Germany, he lived with his parents in Munich and then in Italy. After teaching at the polytechnic school at Zürich, he became a Swiss citizen and was appointed an inspector of patents in Berne. In his spare time, he took his PhD at Zürich. In 1909 he became a lecturer in theoretical physics at the university. After holding a similar post at Prague 1911, he returned to teach at Zürich 1912, and in 1913 took up a specially created post as director of the Kaiser Wilhelm Institute for Physics, Berlin. After being deprived of his position at Berlin by the Nazis, he emigrated to the US 1933, and became professor of mathematics and a permanent member of the Institute for Advanced Study at Princeton, New Jersey. During World War II he worked for the US Navy Ordnance Bureau.

einsteinium in chemistry, a synthesized, radioactive, metallic element of the actinide series, symbol Es, atomic number 99, atomic weight 254.

It was produced by the first thermonuclear explosion, in 1952, and discovered in fallout debris in the form of the isotope Es-253 (half-life 20 days). Its longest-lived isotope, Es-254, with a half-life of 276 days, allowed the element to be studied at length. It is now synthesized by bombarding lower-numbered ⟩transuranic elements in particle accelerators. It was first identified by A Ghiorso and his team who named it in 1955 after Albert Einstein, in honor of his theoretical studies of mass and energy.

Einthoven Willem 1860–1927. Dutch physiologist and inventor of the electrocardiograph. He demonstrated that certain disorders of the heart alter its electrical activity in characteristic ways. He was awarded the 1924 Nobel Prize for Medicine.

Eire Gaelic name for the Republic of ⟩Ireland.

Eisai 1141–1215. Japanese Buddhist monk who introduced Zen and tea from China to Japan and founded the ⟩Rinzai school.

Eisenhower Dwight David ("Ike") 1890–1969. 34th president of the US 1953–60, a Republican. A general in World War II, he commanded the Allied forces in Italy 1943, then the Allied invasion of Europe, and from Oct 1944 all the Allied armies in the West. As president he promoted business interests at home and conducted the ⟩Cold War abroad. His vice-president was Richard Nixon.

Eisenhower was born in Texas. A graduate of West Point military academy in 1915, he served in a variety of staff and command posts before World War II. He became commander in chief of the US and British forces for the invasion of North Africa Nov 1942; commanded the Allied invasion of Sicily July 1943; and announced the surrender of Italy Sept 8, 1943. In Dec he became commander of the Allied Expeditionary Force. He served as president of Columbia University and chair of the joint Chiefs of Staff between 1949 and 1950. He resigned from the army 1952 to campaign for the presidency; he was elected, and reelected by a wide margin in 1956. A popular politician, Eisenhower held office during a period of domestic and international tension, with the growing civil rights movement at home and the Cold War dominating international politics, although the US was experiencing an era of postwar prosperity and growth.

He was well-liked and had a talent for administration.

Eisenhower, Mount Rocky Mountain peak in Alberta, Canada, included in Banff National Park, 9,390 ft/2,862 m.

Eisenstein Sergei Mikhailovich 1898–1948. Soviet film director who pioneered film theory and introduced the use of montage (the juxtaposition of shots to create a particular effect) as a means of propaganda, as in *The Battleship Potemkin* 1925.

eisteddfod (Welsh "sitting") traditional Welsh gathering lasting up to a week and dedicated to the encouragement of the bardic arts of music, poetry, and literature; it dates from pre-Christian times.

EKG abbreviation for ⟩*electrocardiogram*.

Ekman spiral effect an application of the ▷Coriolis effect to ocean currents, whereby the currents flow at an angle to the winds that drive them. It derives its name from the Swedish oceanographer Vagn Ekman (1874–1954).

In the northern hemisphere, surface currents are deflected to the right of the wind direction. The surface current then drives the subsurface layer at an angle to its original deflection. Consequent subsurface layers are similarly affected, so that the effect decreases with increasing depth. The result is that most water is transported at about right-angles to the wind direction. Directions are reversed in the southern hemisphere.

eland largest species of ▷antelope, *Taurotragus oryx*. Pale fawn in color, it is about 6 ft/2 m high, and both sexes have spiral horns about 18 in/45 cm long. It is found in central and southern Africa.

elasticity in economics, the measure of response of one variable to changes in another. If the price of butter is reduced by 10% and the demand increases by 20%, the elasticity measure is 2. Such measures are used to test the effects of changes in prices, incomes, and supply and demand. Inelasticity may exist in the demand for necessities such as water, the demand for which will remain the same even if the price changes considerably.

elasticity in physics, the ability of a solid to recover its shape once deforming forces (stresses modifying its dimensions or shape) are removed. An elastic material obeys ▷Hooke's law: that is, its deformation is proportional to the applied stress up to a certain point, called the *elastic limit*, beyond which additional stress will deform it permanently. Elastic materials include metals and rubber; however, all materials have some degree of elasticity.

Elat or *Eilat* port at the head of the Gulf of Aqaba, Israel's only outlet to the Red Sea; population (1982) 19,500. Founded in 1948, on the site of the Biblical Elath, it is linked by road with Beersheba. There are copper mines and granite quarries nearby, and a major geophysical observatory, opened in 1968, is 10 mi/16 km to the N.

E layer (formerly called the Kennelly–Heaviside layer) the lower regions of the ▷ionosphere, which refract radio waves, allowing their reception around the surface of the Earth. The E layer approaches the Earth by day and recedes from it at night.

Elba island in the Mediterranean, 6 mi/10 km off the W coast of Italy; area 86 sq mi/223 sq km; population (1981) 35,000. Iron ore is exported from the capital, Portoferraio, to the Italian mainland, and there is a fishing industry. The small uninhabited island of *Monte Cristo*, 25 mi/40 km to the S, supplied the title of Alexandre Dumas's hero in *The Count of Monte Cristo*. Elba was Napoleon's place of exile 1814–15.

Elbe one of the principal rivers of Germany, 725 mi/1,166 km long, rising on the southern slopes of the Riesengebirge, Czech Republic, and flowing NW across the German plain to the North Sea.

Elbruz or *Elbrus* highest mountain (18,510 ft/5,642 m) on the continent of Europe, in the Caucasus, Georgia.

Elburz volcanic mountain range in NW Iran, close to the southern shore of the Caspian Sea; the highest point is Mount Damavand at 18,602 ft/5,670 m.

Eldem Sedad Hakki 1908– . Turkish architect whose work is inspired by the spatial harmony and regular rhythms of the traditional Turkish house. These qualities are reinterpreted in modern forms with great sensitivity to context, as in the Social Security Agency Complex, Zeyrek, Istanbul (1962–64), and the Ataturk Library, Istanbul (1973).

elder in botany, small tree or shrub of the genus *Sambucus*, of the honeysuckle family (Caprifoliaceae), native to North America, Eurasia, and N Africa. Some are grown as ornamentals for their showy yellow or white flower clusters and their colorful black or scarlet berries. The American elder *Sambucus canadensis* attains tree size and has blue berries.

elder in the Presbyterian church, a lay member who assists the minister (or teaching elder) in running the church.

El Dorado fabled city of gold believed by the 16th-century Spanish and other Europeans to exist somewhere in the area of the Orinoco and Amazon rivers.

Eleanor of Aquitaine *c.* 1122–1204. Queen of France 1137–51 as wife of Louis VII, and of England from 1154 as wife of Henry II. Henry imprisoned her 1174–89 for supporting their sons, the future Richard I and King John, in revolt against him.

She was the daughter of William X, Duke of Aquitaine, and was married 1137–52 to Louis VII of France, but the marriage was annulled. The same year she married Henry of Anjou, who became king of England 1154.

Eleanor of Castile *c.* 1245–1290. Queen of Edward I of England, the daughter of Ferdinand III of Castile. She married Prince Edward 1254, and accompanied him on his crusade 1270. She died at Harby, Nottinghamshire, and Edward erected stone crosses in towns where her body rested on the funeral journey to London. Several *Eleanor Crosses* are still standing, for example at Northampton.

elector (German *Kurfürst*) any of originally seven (later ten) princes of the Holy Roman Empire who had the prerogative of electing the emperor (in effect, the king of Germany). The electors were the archbishops of Mainz, Trier, and Cologne, the court palatine of the Rhine, the Duke of Saxony, the Margrave of Brandenburg, and the king of Bohemia (in force to 1806). Their constitutional status was formalized 1356 in the document known as the *Golden Bull*, which granted them extensive powers within their own domains, to act as judges, issue coins, and impose tolls.

electoral college in the US government, the indirect system of voting for the president and vice-president. The people of each state officially vote not for the presidential candidate, but for a list of electors nominated by each party. The whole electoral-college vote of the state then goes to the winning party (and candidate). A majority is required for election.

The US has as many electors as it has senators and representatives in Congress, so that the electoral college numbers 538 (535 state electors and 3 from the District of Columbia), and a majority of 270 electoral votes is needed to win. The system can lead to a presidential candidate being elected with a minority of the total vote over the whole country (as happened when Benjamin Harrison was elected over Grover Cleveland 1888). It has been proposed, for example by President Carter in 1977, to substitute a direct popular vote. A constitutional amendment to this effect failed in 1979, partly because minority groups argued that this would deprive them of their politically influential block vote in key states.

electoral system see electoral college and ▷vote.

Electra in Greek mythology, daughter of ▷Agamemnon and ▷Clytemnestra, and sister of ▷Orestes and ▷Iphigenia. Her hatred of her mother for murdering her father and her desire for revenge, fulfilled by the return of her brother Orestes, made her the subject of tragedies by Greek dramatists ▷Aeschylus, ▷Sophocles, and ▷Euripides.

Electra plays by Sophocles and Euripides, produced in Greece about 418–410 BC and 417 BC, respectively. Both plays explore Electra's role in the complex family tragedy that involved the deaths of her sister Chrysothemis, her parents Agamemnon and Clytemnestra, and her brother Orestes.

electrical relay an electromagnetic switch; see ▷relay.

electric arc a continuous electric discharge of high current between two electrodes, giving out a brilliant light and heat. The phenomenon is exploited in the carbon-arc lamp, once widely used in film projectors. In the electric-arc furnace an arc struck between very large carbon electrodes and the metal charge provides the heating. In arc ▷welding an electric arc provides the heat to fuse the metal. The discharges in low-pressure gases, as in neon and sodium lights, can also be broadly considered as electric arcs.

electric charge property of some bodies that causes them to exert forces on each other. Two bodies both with positive or both with negative charges repel each other, whereas bodies with opposite or "unlike" charges attract each other, since each is in the ▷electric field of the other. In atoms, ▷electrons possess a negative charge, and ▷protons an equal positive charge. The ▷SI unit of electric charge is the coulomb (symbol C).

Electric charge can be generated by friction induction or chemical change and shows itself as an accumulation of electrons (negative charge) or loss of electrons (positive charge) on an atom or body. Atoms have no charge but can sometimes gain electrons to become negative ions or lose them to become positive ions. So-called ▷static electricity, seen in such phenomena as the charging of nylon shirts when they are pulled on or off, or in brushing hair, is in fact the gain or loss of electrons from the surface atoms. A flow of charge (such as electrons through a copper wire) constitutes an electric current; the flow of current is measured in amperes (symbol A).

electric current the flow of electrically charged particles through a conducting circuit due to the presence of a ▷potential difference. The current at any point in a circuit is the amount of charge flowing per second; its SI unit is the ampere (coulomb per second).

Current carries electrical energy from a power supply, such as a battery of electrical cells, to the components of the circuit, where it is converted into other forms of energy, such as heat, light, or motion. It may be either ▷direct current or ▷alternating current.

electric energy in physics, the ◁energy of a body that is due to its position in an electric field (generated by an electric charge).

electric field in physics, the electrically charged region of space surrounding an electrically charged body. In this region, an electric charge experiences a force owing to the presence of another electric charge.

electric fish any of several unrelated fishes that have electricity-producing powers, including the South American "electric eel." These include *Electrophorus electricus*, which is not a true eel, and in which the lateral tail muscles are modified to form electric organs capable of generating 650 volts; the current passing from tail to head is strong enough to stun another animal. Not all electric fishes produce such strong discharges; most use weak electric fields to navigate and to detect nearby objects.

electricity all phenomena caused by ◁electric charge, whether static or in motion. Electric charge is caused by an excess or deficit of electrons in the charged substance, and an electric current by the movement of electrons around a circuit. Substances may be electrical conductors, such as metals, which allow the passage of electricity through them, or insulators, such as rubber, which are extremely poor conductors. Substances with relatively poor conductivities that can be improved by the addition of heat or light are known as ◁semiconductors.

Electricity generated on a commercial scale was available from the early 1880s and used for electric motors driving all kinds of machinery, and for lighting, first by carbon arc, but later by incandescent filaments (first of carbon and then of tungsten), enclosed in glass bulbs partially filled with inert gas under vacuum. Light is also produced by passing electricity through a gas or metal vapor or a fluorescent lamp. Other practical applications include telephone, radio, television, and X-ray machines.

The fact that amber has the power, after being rubbed, of attracting light objects, such as bits of straw and feathers, is said to have been known to Thales of Miletus and to the Roman naturalist Pliny. William Gilbert, Queen Elizabeth I's physician, found that many substances possessed this power, and he called it "electric" after the Greek word meaning "amber."

In the early 1700s, it was recognized that there are two types of electricity and that unlike kinds attract each other and like kinds repel. The charge on glass rubbed with silk came to be known as positive electricity, and the charge on amber rubbed with wool as negative electricity. These two charges were found to cancel each other when brought together.

In 1800 Alessandro Volta found that a series of cells containing brine, in which were dipped plates of zinc and copper, gave an electric current, which later in the same year was shown to evolve hydrogen and oxygen when passed through water (◁electrolysis). Humphry Davy, in 1807, decomposed soda and potash (both thought to be elements) and isolated the metals sodium and potassium, a discovery that led the way to ◁electroplating. Other properties of electric currents discovered were the heating effect, now used in lighting and central heating, and the deflection of a magnetic needle, described by Hans Oersted 1820 and elaborated by André Ampère 1825. This work made possible the electric telegraph.

For Michael Faraday, the fact that an electric current passing through a wire caused a magnet to move suggested that moving a wire

electricity *Coal-fired power station (highly simplified).*

or coil of wire rapidly between the poles of a magnet would induce an electric current. He demonstrated this 1831, producing the first ◁dynamo, which became the basis of electrical engineering. The characteristics of currents were crystallized about 1827 by Georg Ohm, who showed that the current passing along a wire was equal to the electromotive force (emf) across the wire multiplied by a constant, which was the conductivity of the wire. The unit of resistance (ohm) is named after Ohm, the unit of emf is named after Volta (volt), and the unit of current after Ampère (amp).

The work of the late 1800s indicated the wide interconnections of electricity (with magnetism, heat, and light), and about 1855 James Clerk Maxwell formulated a single electromagnetic theory. The universal importance of electricity was decisively proved by the discovery that the atom, up until then thought to be the ultimate particle of matter, is composed of a positively charged central core, the nucleus, about which negatively charged electrons rotate in various orbits.

Electricity is the most useful and most convenient form of energy, readily convertible into heat and light and used to power machines. Electricity can be generated in one place and distributed anywhere because it readily flows through wires. It is generated at power stations where a suitable energy source is harnessed to drive ◁turbines that spin electricity generators. Current energy sources are coal, oil, water power (hydroelectricity), natural gas, and ◁nuclear energy. Research is under way to increase the contribution of wind, tidal, and geothermal power. Nuclear fuel has proved a more expensive source of electricity than initially anticipated and worldwide concern over radioactivity may limit its future development. Electricity is generated at power stations at a voltage of about 25,000 volts, which is not a suitable voltage for long-distance transmission. For minimal power loss, transmission must take place at very high voltage (400,000 volts or more). The generated voltage is therefore increased ("stepped up") by a ◁transformer. The resulting high-voltage electricity is then fed into the main arteries of the ◁grid system, an interconnected network of power stations and distribution centers covering a large area. After transmission to a local substation, the line voltage is reduced by a step-down transformer and distributed to consumers.

Among specialized power units that convert energy directly to electrical energy without the intervention of any moving mechanisms, the most promising are thermionic converters. These use conventional fuels such as propane gas, as in portable military power packs, or, if refueling is to be avoided, radioactive fuels, as in uncrewed navigational aids and spacecraft.

electric motor a machine that converts electrical energy into mechanical energy. There are various types, including direct-current and induction motors, most of which produce rotary motion. A linear induction motor produces linear (sideways) rather than rotary motion.

A simple ***direct-current motor*** consists of a horseshoe-shaped permanent ◁magnet with a wire-wound coil (◁armature) mounted so that it can rotate between the poles of the magnet. A ◁commutator reverses the current (from a battery) fed to the coil on each half-turn, which rotates because of the mechanical force exerted on a conductor carrying a current in a magnetic field.

An ***induction motor*** employs ◁alternating current. It comprises a stationary current-carrying coil (stator) surrounding another coil (rotor), which rotates because of the current induced in it by the magnetic field created by the stator; it thus requires no commutator.

electric power the rate at which an electrical machine uses electrical ◁energy or converts it into other forms of energy—for example, light, heat, mechanical energy. Usually measured in watts (equivalent to joules per second), it is equal to the product of the voltage and the current flowing.

An electric lamp that passes a current of 0.4 amps at 250 volts uses 100 watts of electrical power and converts it into light—in ordinary terms it is a 100-watt lamp. An electric motor that requires 6 amps at the same voltage consumes 1,500 watts (1.5 kilowatts), equivalent to delivering about 2 horsepower of mechanical energy.

electric ray another name for the ◁torpedo.

electrocardiogram (ECG) or (EKG) graphic recording of the electrical changes in the heart muscle, as detected by electrodes placed on the chest. Electrocardiography is used in the diagnosis of heart disease.

electrochemical series list of chemical elements arranged in descending order of the ease with which they can lose electrons to form cations (positive ions). An element can be displaced (◁displacement reaction) from a compound by any element above it in the series.

electrochemistry the branch of science that studies chemical reactions involving electricity. The use of electricity to produce chemical effects, ▷electrolysis, is employed in many industrial processes, such as the manufacture of chlorine and the extraction of aluminum. The use of chemical reactions to produce electricity is the basis of electrical ▷cells, such as the dry cell and the ▷Leclanché cell.

Since all chemical reactions involve changes to the electronic structure of atoms, all reactions are now recognized as electrochemical in nature. Oxidation, for example, was once defined as a process in which oxygen was combined with a substance, or hydrogen was removed from a compound; it is now defined as a process in which electrons are lost.

electroconvulsive therapy (ECT) or **electroshock therapy** treatment for ▷schizophrenia and ▷depression, given under anesthesia and with a muscle relaxant. An electric current is passed through the brain to induce alterations in the brain's electrical activity. The treatment can cause distress and loss of concentration and memory, and so there is much controversy about its use and effectiveness.

electrocution death caused by electric current. It is used as a method of execution in some US states. The condemned person is strapped into a special chair and a shock of 1,800–2,000 volts is administered. See ▷capital punishment.

electrode any terminal by which an electric current passes in or out of a conducting substance; for example, the anode or cathode in a battery or the carbons in an arc lamp. The terminals that emit and collect the flow of electrons in thermionic ▷valves (electron tubes) are also called electrodes: for example, cathodes, plates, and grids.

electrodynamics the branch of physics dealing with electric currents and associated magnetic forces. ▷Quantum electrodynamics (QED) studies the interaction between charged particles and their emission and absorption of electromagnetic radiation. This field combines quantum theory and relativity theory, making accurate predictions about subatomic processes involving charged particles such as electrons and protons.

electroencephalogram (EEG) graphic record of the electrical discharges of the brain, as detected by electrodes placed on the scalp. The pattern of electrical activity revealed by electroencephalography is helpful in the diagnosis of some brain disorders, such as epilepsy.

electrolysis in chemistry, the production of chemical changes by passing an electric current through a solution or molten salt (the electrolyte), resulting in the migration of ions to the electrodes: positive ions (cations) to the negative electrode (cathode) and negative ions (anions) to the positive electrode (anode).

During electrolysis, the ions react with the electrode, either receiving or giving up electrons. The resultant atoms may be liberated as a gas, or deposited as a solid on the electrode, in amounts that are proportional to the amount of current passed, as discovered by Michael Faraday. For instance, when acidified water is electrolyzed, hydrogen ions (H^+) at the cathode receive electrons to form hydrogen gas; hydroxide ions (OH^-) at the anode give up electrons to form oxygen gas and water.

electrolysis

One application of electrolysis is **electroplating**, in which a solution of a salt, such as silver nitrate ($AgNO_3$), is used and the object to be plated acts as the negative electrode, thus attracting silver ions (Ag^+). Electrolysis is used in many industrial processes, such as coating metals for vehicles and ships, and refining bauxite into aluminum; it also forms the basis of a number of electrochemical analytical techniques, such as polarography.

electrolyte a solution or molten substance in which an electric current is made to flow by the movement and discharge of ions in accordance with Faraday's laws of ▷electrolysis.

The term "electrolyte" is frequently used to denote a substance that, when dissolved in a specified solvent, usually water, produces an electrically conducting medium.

electromagnet an iron bar with coils of wire around it, which acts as a magnet when an electric current flows through the wire. Electromagnets have many uses: in switches, electric bells, solenoids, and metal-lifting cranes.

electromagnetic field in physics, the agency by which a particle with an ▷electric charge experiences a force in a particular region of space. If it does so only when moving, it is in a pure **magnetic field**; if it does so when stationary, it is in an **electric field**. Both can be present simultaneously.

electromagnetic force one of the four fundamental ▷forces of nature, the other three being gravity, the strong nuclear force, and the weak nuclear force. The ▷elementary particle that is the carrier for the electromagnetic (em) force is the photon.

electromagnetic induction in electronics, the production of an ▷electromotive force (emf) in a circuit by a change of magnetic flux through the circuit or by relative motion of the circuit and the magnetic flux. In a closed circuit an induced current will be produced. All dynamos and generators make use of this effect. When magnetic tape is driven past the playback head (a small coil) of a tape-recorder, the moving magnetic field induces an emf in the head, which is then amplified to reproduce the recorded sounds.

If the change of magnetic flux is due to a variation in the current flowing in the same circuit, the phenomenon is known as self-induction; if it is due to a change of current flowing in another circuit it is known as mutual induction.

electromagnetic spectrum the complete range, over all wavelengths from the lowest to the highest, of ▷electromagnetic waves.

electromagnetic system of units former system of absolute electromagnetic units (emu) based on the ▷c.g.s. system and having, as its primary electrical unit, the unit magnetic pole. It was replaced by ▷SI units.

electromagnetic waves oscillating electric and magnetic fields traveling together through space at a speed of nearly 186,000 mi/300,000 km per second. The (limitless) range of possible wavelengths or ▷frequencies of electromagnetic waves, which can be thought of as making up the **electromagnetic spectrum**, includes radio waves, infrared radiation, visible light, ultraviolet radiation, X-rays, and gamma rays.

electromotive force (emf) in physics, the greatest potential difference that can be generated by a source of current. This is always greater than the measured potential difference generated, due to the resistance of the wires and components in the circuit.

electron stable, negatively charged ▷elementary particle; it is a constituent of all atoms, and a member of the class of particles known as ▷leptons. The electrons in each atom surround the nucleus in groupings called shells; in a neutral atom the number of electrons is equal to the number of protons in the nucleus. This electron structure is responsible for the chemical properties of the atom (see ▷atomic structure).

Electrons are the basic particles of electricity. Each carries a charge of 1.602192×10^{-19} coulomb, and all electrical charges are multiples of this quantity. A beam of electrons will undergo ▷diffraction (scattering) and produce interference patterns in the same way as ▷electromagnetic waves such as light; hence they may also be regarded as waves.

electronegativity the ease with which an atom can attract electrons to itself. Electronegative elements attract electrons, so forming negative ions.

Linus Pauling devised an electronegativity scale to indicate the relative power of attraction of elements for electrons. Fluorine, the most nonmetallic element, has a value of 4.0 on this scale; oxygen, the next most nonmetallic, has a value of 3.5.

In a covalent bond between two atoms of different electronegativities, the bonding electrons will be located close to the more electronegative atom, creating a ▷dipole.

electron gun a part in many electronic devices consisting of a series of ▷electrodes, including a cathode for producing an electron beam. It plays an essential role in ▷cathode-ray tubes (television tubes) and ▷electron microscopes.

electronic flash discharge tube that produces a high-intensity flash of light, used for photography in dim conditions. The tube contains an inert gas such as krypton. The flash lasts only a few thousandths of a second.

electronic mail ▷telecommunications system that sends messages to people or machines (such as computers) via computers and the telephone network rather than by letter.

Subscribers to an electronic mail system type messages in ordinary letter form on a word processor, or microcomputer, and "drop" the letters into a central computer's memory bank by means of a computer/telephone connector (a modem). The recipient "collects" the letter by calling up the central computer and feeding a unique password into the system.

electron microscope instrument that produces a magnified image by using a beam of ▷electrons instead of light rays, as in an optical ▷microscope. An **electron lens** is an arrangement of electromagnetic coils that control and focus the beam. Electrons are not visible to the eye, so instead of an eyepiece there is a fluorescent screen or a photographic plate on which the electrons form an image. The wavelength of the electron beam is much shorter than that of light, so much greater magnification and resolution (ability to distinguish detail) can be achieved.

A **high-resolution electron microscope** (HREM) can produce a magnification of 7 million times (7,000,000 ×). The development of the electron microscope has made possible the observation of very minute organisms, viruses, and even large molecules. A **transmission electron microscope** passes the electron beam through a very thin slice of a specimen. A **scanning electron microscope** looks at the exterior of a specimen.

electrons, delocalized electrons that are not associated with individual atoms or identifiable chemical bonds, but are shared collectively by all the constituent atoms or ions of some chemical substances (such as metals, graphite, and ▷aromatic compounds).

A metallic solid consists of a three-dimensional arrangement of metal ions through which the delocalized electrons are free to travel. Aromatic compounds are characterized by the sharing of delocalized electrons by several atoms within the molecule.

electrons, localized a pair of electrons in a covalent bond (see ▷covalence) that are located in the vicinity of the nuclei of the two contributing atoms. Such electrons cannot move beyond this area.

electron volt unit (symbol eV) for measuring the energy of a charged particle (▷ion or ▷electron) in terms of the energy of motion an electron would gain from a potential difference of one volt. Because it is so small, more usual units are mega-(million) and giga-(billion) electron volts (MeV and GeV).

electron microscope The transmission electron microscope.

Electromagnetic spectrum diagram

gamma rays — 10^{20}, 10^{19} (10^{-11}, 10^{-10}): gamma rays; certain cancer therapies; nuclear de-excitations

X-rays — 10^{18}, 10^{17} (10^{-9}, 10^{-8}): X-rays; seeing through non-dense materials, studying crystal structure; rapidly decelerating electrons

ultraviolet — 10^{16}, 10^{15} (10^{-7}): ultraviolet; sun tanning

visible light — violet indigo blue green yellow orange red; visible

infrared — 10^{14}, 10^{13}, 10^{12} (10^{-5}, 10^{-4}, 10^{-3}): infrared; carrying heat, 'seeing' in the dark with special detectors; electrons changing energy levels, as in hot solids and liquids

microwaves — 10^{11}, 10^{10} (10^{-2}, 10^{-1}): super high frequency; ultra high frequency; microwave ovens, radar; electrons made to vibrate by electronic circuits

radio waves — 10^{9}, 10^{8}, 10^{7}, 10^{6}, 10^{5}, 10^{4} (1, 10^{1}, 10^{2}, 10^{3}): very high frequency; high frequency (short wave); medium frequency; low frequency (long wave); TV; radio communication

wavelength in metres
frequency in hertz

uses

usual source

electromagnetic waves *Radio waves have the lowest frequency. Infrared radiation, visible light, ultraviolet radiation, X-rays, and gamma rays have progressively higher frequencies.*

electronic music a form of studio-based serial music composed entirely of electronically generated and modified tones, as opposed to **concrete music**, which arranges prerecorded sounds by intuition. The term was later broadened to include pre-recorded vocal and instrumental sounds, although always implying a serial basis. ▷Maderna, ▷Stockhausen, and ▷Babbitt were among the pioneers of electronic music in the 1950s.

After 1960, with the arrival of the purpose-built synthesizer developed by Robert Moog, Peter Zinovieff, and others, interest switched to computer-aided synthesis, culminating in the 4X system installed at ▷IRCAM.

electronics branch of science that deals with the emission of ▷electrons from conductors and ▷semiconductors, with the subsequent manipulation of these electrons, and with the construction of electronic devices. The first electronic device was the thermionic ▷valve, or vacuum tube, in which electrons moved in a vacuum, and led to such inventions as ▷radio, ▷television, ▷radar, and the digital ▷computer. Replacement of valves with the comparatively tiny and reliable transistor in 1948 revolutionized electronic development. Modern electronic devices are based on minute integrated circuits (silicon chips), wafer-thin crystal slices holding tens of thousands of electronic components.

By using solid-state devices such as integrated circuits, extremely complex electronic circuits can be constructed, leading to the development of ▷digital watches, pocket ▷calculators, powerful ▷microcomputers, and ▷word processors.

electrophoresis the ▷diffusion of charged particles through a fluid under the influence of an electric field. It can be used in the biological sciences to separate ▷molecules of different sizes, which diffuse at different rates. In industry, electrophoresis is used in paint-dipping operations to ensure that paint reaches awkward corners.

electroplating deposition of metals upon metallic surfaces by electrolysis for decorative and/or protective purposes. It is used in the preparation of printers' blocks, "master" audio discs, and in many other processes.

A current is passed through a bath containing a solution of a salt of the plating metal, the object to be plated being the cathode (negative terminal); the anode (positive terminal) is either an inert substance or the plating metal. Among the metals most commonly used for plating are zinc, nickel, chromium, cadmium, copper, silver, and gold.

In *electropolishing*, the object to be polished is made the anode in an electrolytic solution and by carefully controlling conditions the high spots on the surface are dissolved away, leaving a high-quality stain-free surface. This technique is useful in polishing irregular stainless-steel articles.

electropositivity in chemistry, a measure of the ability of elements (mainly metals) to donate electrons to form positive ions. The greater the metallic character, the more electropositive the element.

electroscope an apparatus for detecting ▷electric charge. The simple gold-leaf electroscope consists of a vertical conducting (metal) rod ending in a pair of rectangular pieces of gold foil, mounted inside and insulated from an earthed metal case. An electric charge applied to the end of the metal rod makes the gold leaves diverge, because they each receive a similar charge (positive or negative) and so repel each other.

The polarity of the charge can be found by bringing up another charge of known polarity and applying it to the metal rod. A like charge has no effect on the gold leaves, whereas an opposite charge neutralizes the charge on the leaves and causes them to collapse.

electrostatics the study of electric charges from stationary sources (not currents). See ▷static electricity.

electrovalent bond another name for an ▷ionic bond, a chemical bond in which the combining atoms lose or gain electrons to form ions.

electrum naturally occurring alloy of gold and

metal sphere
insulator
foil leaves

electroscope *The electroscope, a simple means of detecting electric charge.*

silver used by early civilizations to make the first coins, about the 6th century BC.

element substance that cannot be split chemically into simpler substances. The atoms of a particular element all have the same number of protons in their nuclei (their atomic number). Elements are classified in the periodic table (see ▷periodic table of the elements). Of the 109 known elements, 95 are known to occur in nature (those with atomic numbers 1–95). Those from 96 to 109 do not occur in nature and are synthesized only, produced in particle accelerators. Eighty-one of the elements are stable; all the others, which include atomic numbers 43, 61, and from 84 up, are radioactive.

Elements are classified as metals, nonmetals, or metalloids (weakly metallic elements) depending on a combination of their physical and chemical properties; about 75% are metallic. Some elements occur abundantly (oxygen, aluminum); others occur moderately or rarely (chromium, neon); some, in particular the radioactive ones, are found in minute (neptunium, plutonium) or very minute (technetium) amounts.

Symbols (devised by Jöns Berzelius) are used to denote the elements; the symbol is usually the first letter or letters of the English or Latin name (for example, C for carbon, Ca for calcium, Fe for iron, *ferrum*). The symbol represents one atom of the element.

According to current theories, hydrogen and helium were produced in the ▷Big Bang at the beginning of the universe. Of the other elements, those up to atomic number 26 (iron) are made by nuclear fusion within the stars. The more massive elements such as lead and uranium, are produced when an old star explodes; as its center collapses, the gravitational energy squashes nuclei together to make new elements.

elementary particle or **fundamental particle** any of those particles that combine to form ▷atoms and all ▷matter, the most familiar being the electron, proton, and neutron. More than 200 particles have now been identified by physicists, categorized into several classes as characterized by their mass, electric charge, spin, magnetic moment, and interaction. Although many particles were thought to be nondivisible and permanent, now most are known to be combinations of a small number of basic particles.

Since the 1890s, inquiry has progressed from the atom to its nucleus to the ▷hadrons that make up the nucleus to the ▷quarks that make up the hadrons. Since the 1960s, the main interest of particle physicists has been the elucidation of hadron structure. Only a small number of the 200 known particles are nondivisible—basic and stable—those that cannot be subdivided. They include eight of the 12 ▷leptons (the electron, the positron, and six kinds of neutrinos); the quarks (36 varieties); and the ▷gauge bosons—the particles that carry the four fundamental forces (the photon, the graviton, eight kinds of gluons, and three kinds of weakons). All matter in the universe is now seen as being made up of various combinations and interactions of these particles.

elephant mammal belonging to either of two surviving species of the order Proboscidea: the Asian elephant *Elephas maximus* and the African elephant *Loxodonta africana*. Elephants can grow to 13 ft/4 m and weigh up to

8 tons; they have a thick, gray, wrinkled skin, a large head, a long trunk used to obtain food and water, and upper incisors or tusks, which grow to a considerable length. The African elephant has very large ears and a flattened forehead, and the Asian species has smaller ears and a convex forehead. In India, Myanmar (Burma), and Thailand, Asiatic elephants are widely used for transport and logging.

Elephants are herbivorous, highly intelligent, and extremely social, living in matriarchal herds. The period of gestation is about 19–22 months (the longest among mammals), and the life span is about 60–70 years. Elephants have one of the lowest metabolic rates among placental mammals. They are slaughtered needlessly for the ivory of their tusks, and this, coupled with the fact that they reproduce slowly and do not breed readily in captivity, is leading to their extinction. In Africa there were 1.3 million in 1981; fewer than 700,000 in 1988, and about 600,000 in 1990. They were placed on the list of most endangered species in 1989, and a world ban on trade in ivory was imposed.

Elephanta island in Bombay harbor, Maharashtra, India, some 5 mi/8 km from Bombay. The Temple Caves (6th century), cut out of solid rock, have sculptures of many Hindu deities executed 450–740. There was formerly a large stone elephant near the island's landing place.

elephant bird another name for extinct members of the genus ▷Aepyornis.

elephantiasis in the human body, a condition of local enlargement and deformity, most often of a leg, the scrotum, a labium of the vulva, or a breast, caused by the blocking of lymph channels.

The commonest form of elephantiasis is the tropical variety (filariasis) caused by infestation by parasitic roundworms (filaria); the enlargement is due to chronic blocking of the lymph channels by the worms and consequent overgrowth of the skin and tissues.

Eleusinian Mysteries ceremonies in honor of the Greek deities ▷Demeter, ▷Persephone, and ▷Dionysus, celebrated in the remains of the temple of Demeter at Eleusis, Greece. Worshipers saw visions in the darkened temple, supposedly connected with the underworld.

elevator any mechanical device for raising or lowering people or materials. It usually consists of a platform or boxlike structure suspended by motor-driven cables with safety ratchets along the sides of the shaft. US inventor Elisha Graves ▷Otis developed the first passenger safety elevator 1852, installed 1857. This invention permitted the development of skyscrapers from the 1880s. At first steam powered the movement, but hydraulic and then electric elevators were common from the early 1900s. Elevator operators worked controls and gates within the cab until the automatic, or self-starter, was introduced.

El Faiyûm city in N Egypt, 56 mi/90 km SW of Cairo; population (1985) 218,500. It was a center of prehistoric culture; the crocodile god Sobek was worshiped nearby, and realistic mummy portraits dating from the 1st–4th centuries AD were found in the area.

Elgar Edward (William) 1857–1934. English composer. His *Enigma Variations* appeared 1899, and although his celebrated choral work, the oratorio setting of John Henry Newman's *The Dream of Gerontius*, was initially a failure, it was well received at Düsseldorf in 1902. Many of his earlier works were then performed, including the *Pomp and Circumstance* marches.

Among his later works are oratorios, two symphonies, a violin concerto, a cello concerto, chamber music, songs, and the tone-poem *Falstaff* 1913.

Elgin city in NE Illinois, NW of Chicago, on the Fox River. Industries include electrical machinery and dairy products; population (1990) 77,000. The city was once the home of Elgin watches.

Elgin marbles collection of ancient Greek sculptures mainly from the Parthenon at Athens, assembled by the 7th Earl of Elgin. Sent to England 1812, and bought for the nation 1816 for £35,000, they are now in the British Museum. Greece has repeatedly asked for them to be returned to Athens.

Eli in the Old Testament, a priest and childhood teacher of the first prophet, Samuel.

Elijah c. mid-9th century BC. In the Old Testament, a Hebrew prophet during the reigns of the Israelite kings Ahab and Ahaziah. He came from Gilead. He defeated the prophets of ◊Baal, and was said to have been carried up to heaven in a fiery chariot in a whirlwind. In Jewish belief, Elijah will return to Earth to herald the coming of the Messiah.

Eliot Charles William 1834–1926. US educator. Born in Boston and educated at Harvard, Eliot specialized in mathematics and chemistry, teaching briefly at Harvard and being appointed professor at the Massachusetts Institute of Technology (MIT) 1865. After extended travel in Europe, he took up the cause of educational reform and was named president of Harvard 1869. Under Eliot's administration, the college and its graduate and professional schools were reorganized and the curriculum and admission requirements standardized. Eliot, credited with having established the standards of modern American higher education, retired 1909.

Eliot George. Adopted name of Mary Ann Evans 1819–1880. English novelist whose works include the pastoral *Adam Bede* 1859, *The Mill on the Floss* 1860, with its autobiographical elements, *Silas Marner* 1861, which contains elements of the folktale, and *Daniel Deronda* 1876. *Middlemarch*, published serially in 1871–2, is considered her greatest novel for its confident handling of numerous characters and central social and moral issues. Her work is pervaded by a penetrating and compassionate intelligence.

Born at Chilvers Coton, Warwickshire, George Eliot had a strict evangelical upbringing. In 1841 she was converted to ◊free thought. As assistant editor of the *Westminster Review* under John Chapman 1851–53, she made the acquaintance of Thomas Carlyle, Harriet Martineau, Herbert Spencer, and the philosopher and critic George Henry Lewes (1817–1878). Lewes was married but separated from his wife, and from 1854 he and Eliot lived together in a relationship that she regarded as a true marriage and that continued until his death. In 1880 she married John Cross (1840–1924).

Eliot T(homas) S(tearns) 1888–1965. US poet, playwright, and critic who lived in London from 1915. His first volume of poetry, *Prufrock and Other Observations* 1917, introduced new verse forms and rhythms; further collections include *The Waste Land* 1922, *The Hollow Men* 1925, and *Old Possum's Book of Practical Cats* 1939. His plays include *Murder in the Cathedral* 1935 and *The Cocktail Party* 1949. His critical works include *The Sacred Wood* 1920. He was awarded the Nobel Prize for Literature 1948.

Eliot was born in St Louis, Missouri, and was educated at Harvard, the Sorbonne, and Oxford. He settled in London 1915 and became a British subject 1927. He was for a time a bank clerk, later lecturing and entering publishing at Faber & Faber. As editor of *The Criterion* 1922–39, he influenced the thought of his generation.

Prufrock and Other Observations expressed the disillusionment of the generation affected by World War I and caused a sensation with its experimental form and rhythms. His reputation was established by the desolate modernity of *The Waste Land*. *The Hollow Men* continued on the same note, but *Ash Wednesday* 1930 revealed the change in religious attitude that led him to become a Catholic. Among his other works are *Four Quartets* 1943, a religious sequence in which he seeks the eternal reality, and the poetic dramas *Murder in the Cathedral* (about Thomas à Becket); *The Cocktail Party*; *The Confidential Clerk* 1953; and *The Elder Statesman* 1958. His collection *Old Possum's Book of Practical Cats* was used for the popular British composer Andrew Lloyd Webber's musical *Cats* 1981. His critical works include *Notes toward the Definition of Culture* 1949.

Elisabethville former name of ◊Lubumbashi, a town in Zaire.

Elisha mid-9th century BC. In the Old Testament, a Hebrew prophet, successor to Elijah.

elite a small group with power in a society, having privileges, and status above others. An elite may be cultural, educational, religious, political (also called "the establishment" or "the governing circles"), or social. Sociological interest has centered on how such minorities get, use, and hold onto power, and on what distinguishes elites from the rest of society.

Elizabeth city in NE New Jersey; population (1990) 110,000. Established 1664, it was the first English settlement in New Jersey. It has automobile, sewing-machine, and tool factories, oil refineries, and chemical works.

Elizabeth in the New Testament, mother of John the Baptist. She was a cousin of Jesus' mother Mary, who came to see her shortly after the Annunciation; on this visit (called the Visitation), Mary sang the hymn of praise later to be known as the "Magnificat."

Elizabeth two queens of England or the UK:

Elizabeth I 1533–1603. Queen of England 1558–1603, the daughter of Henry VIII and Anne Boleyn. Through her Religious Settlement of 1559 she enforced the Protestant religion by law. She had ◊Mary, Queen of Scots, executed 1587. Her conflict with Roman Catholic Spain led to the defeat of the ◊Spanish Armada 1588. The Elizabethan age was expansionist in commerce and geographical exploration, and arts and literature flourished. The rulers of many European states made unsuccessful bids to marry Elizabeth, and she used these bids to strengthen her power. She was succeeded by James I.

Her mother was Henry VIII's second wife, the woman for whom he started the ◊Reformation. On the death of his Catholic half sister Mary I, Elizabeth became queen. Mary Queen of Scots, also a Catholic, was her cousin.

The colonization of the New World began during Elizabeth's reign. Although the courtiers ◊Leicester, Sir Walter ◊Raleigh, and ◊Essex were favored, Elizabeth was known as the Virgin Queen and never married. She was astute, well-educated, and shrewd in both personal and political affairs; she is considered one of England's greatest monarchs.

Elizabeth II Queen of Great Britain and Northern Ireland from 1952, the elder daughter of George VI. She married her third cousin, Philip, the Duke of Edinburgh, 1947. They have four children: Charles, Anne, Andrew, and Edward.

Princess Elizabeth Alexandra Mary was born in London April 21, 1926; she was educated privately, and assumed official duties at 16. During World War II she served in the Auxiliary Territorial Service, and by an amendment to the Regency Act she became a state counselor on her 18th birthday. On the death of George VI in 1952 she succeeded to the throne while in Kenya with her husband and was crowned on June 2, 1953.

Elizabeth 1709–1762. Empress of Russia from 1741, daughter of Peter the Great. She carried through a palace revolution and supplanted her cousin, the infant Ivan VI (1730–1764), on the throne. She continued the policy of westernization begun by Peter and allied herself with Austria against Prussia.

Elizabethan literature literature produced during the reign of Elizabeth I of England (1558–1603). This period saw a remarkable florescence of the arts in England, and the literature of the time is characterized by a new energy, richness, and confidence. Renaissance humanism, Protestant zeal, and geographical discovery all contributed to this upsurge of creative power. Drama was the dominant form of the age, and ◊Shakespeare and ◊Marlowe were popular with all levels of society. Other writers of the period include Edmund Spenser, Sir Philip Sidney, Francis Bacon, Thomas Lodge, Robert Greene, and John Lyly.

During this period, the resources of English were increased by the free adoption of words from Latin. This was accompanied by a growing belief that English was capable of all the requirements of great literature. There was a balance between the university and courtly elements and the coarse gusto of popular culture. Music was closely related to literature, and competence in singing and musical composition was seen as a normal social skill. Successive editions of the Bible were produced during these years, written with dignity, vividness, and the deliberate intention of reaching a universal audience.

Elizavetpol former name of ◊Kirovabad, industrial town in Azerbaijan.

elk or **wapiti** North American deer *Cervus canadensis*, closely related to the red ◊deer of Eurasia. Head and body length is about 8 ft/ 2.5 m, and shoulder height is about 5 ft/1.5 m. They are grayish-brown with a yellow rump patch. Males carry magnificent antlers up to 5.8 ft/1.8 m along the beam. In Europe, moose are called elk.

Elkhart city in N Indiana, E of South Bend, where the Elkhart River meets the St Joseph River. Its factories produce mobile homes, firefighting apparatus, recreational vehicles, pharmaceuticals, and musical instruments; population (1990) 43,600.

Ellesmere second largest island of the

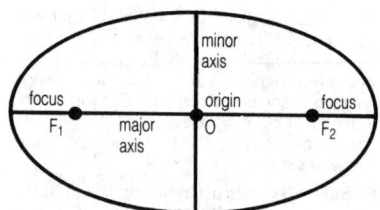

ellipse *Technical terms used to describe the ellipse; for all points on the ellipse, the sum of the distances from the two foci, F₁ and F₂, is the same.*

Canadian Arctic archipelago, Northwest Territories; area 82,097 sq mi/212,687 sq km. It is for the most part barren or glacier-covered.

Ellice Islands former name of ◊Tuvalu, a group of islands in the W Pacific Ocean.

Ellington Duke (Edward Kennedy) 1899–1974. US pianist who had an outstanding career as a composer and arranger of jazz. He wrote numerous pieces for his own jazz orchestra, accentuating the strengths of individual virtuoso instrumentalists, and became one of the leading figures in jazz over a 55-year period. Some of his most popular compositions include "Mood Indigo," "Sophisticated Lady," "Solitude," and "Black and Tan Fantasy." He was one of the founders of big band jazz.

ellipse curve joining all points (loci) around two fixed points (foci) such that the sum of the distances from those points is always constant. The diameter passing through the foci is the major axis, and the diameter bisecting this at right angles is the minor axis. An ellipse is one of a series of curves known as ◊conic sections. A slice across a cone that is not made parallel to, and does not pass through, the base will produce an ellipse.

Ellis (Henry) Havelock 1859–1939. English psychologist and writer of many works on the psychology of sex, including *Studies in the Psychology of Sex* (seven volumes) 1898–1928.

Ellis Island island in New York Harbor; area 27 acres/11 hectares. A former reception center for steerage-class immigrants during the immigration waves between 1892–1943 (12 million people passed through it 1892–1924), it was later used as a detention center for nonresidents without documentation, or for those who were being deported. It was declared a National Historic Site 1964 by President Lyndon Johnson.

In 1989 the Museum of Immigration was established on Ellis Island.

Ellison Ralph 1914– . US novelist. His *Invisible Man* 1952 portrays with humor and energy the plight of a black man whom postwar American society cannot acknowledge; it is regarded as one of the most impressive novels published in the US in the 1950s.

Its success encouraged the development of black literature in the 1950s and 1960s.

Ellsworth Oliver 1745–1807. US jurist and chief justice of the US Supreme Court 1796–1800. He was a Connecticut delegate 1787 to the Constitutional Convention, where he was instrumental in effecting the "Connecticut Compromise," which balanced large and small state interests. He was selected to be a US senator from Connecticut in 1787. He was appointed chief justice 1796 by President Washington. His opinions as chief justice shaped admiralty law and treaty law.

Born in Windsor, Connecticut, he attended Yale College and graduated from Princeton 1766. After establishing himself as a lawyer, he became a delegate from Connecticut to the Continental Congress in 1787, serving for seven years. He served concurrently in a number of political posts in Connecticut, becoming a judge of the new state court of appeals in 1785, and then moved to the new state superior court as a judge the same year.

elm tree of the genus *Ulmus* of the family Ulmaceae, found in temperate regions of the N hemisphere and in mountainous parts of the tropics. All have double-toothed leaf margins and bear clusters of small flowers. The American elm *U. americana* and slippery elm *U. rubra* are native to E North America.

Other species are the wych elm *Ulmacaeae glabra*, indigenous to Britain, the North American white elm *Ulmacaeae americana*, and the red or slippery elm *Ulmacaeae fulva*. Most elms (apart from the wych elm) reproduce not by seed but by suckering (new shoots arising from the root system). This nonsexual reproduction results in an enormous variety of forms.

The fungus disease *Ceratocystis ulmi*, known as Dutch elm disease because of a severe outbreak in the Netherlands 1924, has reduced the numbers of elm trees in Europe and North America. It is carried from tree to tree by beetles. Elms were widespread throughout Europe to about 4,000 BC, when they suddenly disappeared and were not again common until the 12th century. This may have been the fault of an earlier epidemic of Dutch elm disease.

Elmira city in S central New York, on the Chemung River, W of Binghamton, just below the Finger Lakes region; seat of Chemung county. It is the processing and marketing center for the area's dairy and poultry farms. Other industries include business machinery, machine parts, airplanes, and fire engines. Elmira College 1853 is located here; population (1990) 33,700.

El Niño (Spanish "the child") warm ocean surge of the ◊Peru Current, so called because it tends to occur at Christmas, recurring every 5–8 years or so in the E Pacific off South America. It warms the nutrient-rich waters along the coast of Ecuador and Peru, killing coldwater fishes and plants, and is an important factor in global weather.

El Niño is believed to be caused by the failure of the trade winds and, consequently, of the cool ocean currents normally driven by these winds. Warm surface waters then flow in from the east. It can disrupt the climate of the area disastrously, and has played a part in causing famine in Indonesia 1983, bush fires in Australia because of drought, rainstorms in California and South America, and the destruction of Peru's anchovy harvest and wildlife 1982–83.

elongation in astronomy, the angular distance between the Sun and a planet or other solar-system object. This angle is 0° at ◊conjunction, 90° at quadrature (where two celestial bodies, usually the Sun and the Moon, form the angle with a third body, usually the Earth), and 180° at ◊opposition.

El Paso city in Texas, situated at the base of the Franklin Mountains, on the Rio Grande, opposite the Mexican city of Ciudad Juárez; population (1990) 515,000. It is the center of an agricultural and cattle-raising area, and there are electronics, food processing, packing, and

leather industries, as well as oil refineries and industries based on local iron and copper mines.

There are several military installations in the area.

El Salvador country in Central America, bounded N and E by Honduras, S and SW by the Pacific Ocean, and NW by Guatemala.

government The 1983 constitution, amended 1985, provides for a president elected by universal suffrage for a five-year term, assisted by an appointed vice-president and a council of ministers. There is a single-chamber national assembly of 60, elected by universal suffrage for a three-year term.

history The original inhabitants of the area were Indians, who arrived from Mexico around 3000 BC. From the period of the Maya Indians AD 100 to 1000 remain huge limestone pyramids built by them in western El Salvador. The Pipil Indians were in control of the area at the time of the Spanish conquest 1525. El Salvador and other Central American Spanish colonies broke away from Spanish rule 1821, and became part of the federation of Central American states until 1838. Since then there have been frequent coups and episodes of political violence.

After a coup 1961 the conservative National Conciliation Party (PCN) was established, winning all the seats in the national assembly. The PCN stayed in power, with reports of widespread human-rights violations, until challenged 1979 by a socialist guerrilla movement, the Farabundo Marti Liberation Front (FMLN). A civilian-military junta deposed the president.

internal conflict In 1980 the archbishop of San Salvador, Oscar Romero, a champion of human rights, was shot dead in his cathedral. The murder of three US nuns and a social worker prompted US president Jimmy Carter to suspend economic and military aid. In 1980 José Napoleón Duarte, leader of a moderately left-of-center coalition, returned from exile and became president. The conservative US administration of Ronald Reagan supported him, as an anticommunist, and encouraged him to call elections 1982. The left-wing parties refused to participate, and the elections were held amid great violence, at least 40 people being killed on election day. Although Duarte's Christian Democrats (PDC) won the largest number of assembly seats, a coalition of right-wing parties blocked his continuation as president. A provisional chief executive was selected from a list of candidates acceptable to the military, serving until the 1984 elections, which Duarte won in a runoff against Roberto d'Aubuisson, a rightist suspected of involvement in the death of Archbishop Romero.

guerrilla war In 1984 the president's daughter was abducted by guerrillas, forcing him to negotiate with them, in the face of criticism from opposition parties and the military. In 1985 the antiimperialist PDC won a convincing victory in the assembly, with 33 seats. The right-wing National Republic Alliance (ARENA) and PCN won 13 and 12 seats respectively, fighting the election on a joint platform. The guerrilla war continued, Duarte again attempting 1986 to negotiate a settlement with the rebels. In Aug 1987 they agreed to meet and discuss the Regional Peace Plan of the Contadora group with him. The peace initiative collapsed and in 1989, the election of Alfredo Cristiani of D'Aubuisson's ARENA party (amid allegations of ballot rigging) appeared to herald a return

El Salvador
Republic of (*República de El Salvador*)

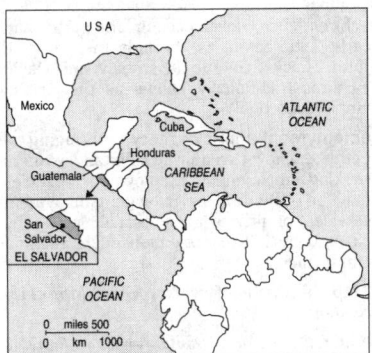

area 8,258 sq mi/21,393 sq km
capital San Salvador
cities Santa Ana, San Miguel
physical narrow coastal plain, rising to mountains in N with central plateau
features smallest and most densely populated Central American country; Mayan archeological remains
head of state and government Alfredo Cristiani from 1989
political system emergent democracy
political parties Christian Democrats (PDC), antiimperialist; National Republican Alliance (ARENA), right-wing; National Conciliation Party (PCN), right-wing; Farabundo Marti Liberation Front (FMLN), left-wing
exports coffee, cotton, sugar
currency colón

population (1989 est) 5,900,000 (mainly of mixed Spanish and Indian ancestry; 10% Indian); growth rate 2.9% p.a.
life expectancy men 63, women 66
languages Spanish, Nahuatl
religion Roman Catholic 97%
literacy men 75%, women 69% (1985 est)
GDP $4.7 bn (1987); $790 per head
chronology
1821 Independence achieved from Spain.
1931 Peasant unrest followed by a military coup.
1961 Following a coup, PCN established and in power.
1969 "Soccer" war with Honduras.
1972 Allegations of human-rights violations and growth of left-wing guerrilla activities. General Carlos Romero elected president.
1979 A coup replaced Romero with a military-civilian junta.
1980 Archbishop Oscar Romero assassinated; country on verge of civil war. José Duarte became first civilian president since 1931.
1981 Mexico and France recognized the guerrillas as a legitimate political force but the US actively assisted the government in its battle against them.
1982 Assembly elections boycotted by left-wing parties and held amid considerable violence.
1986 Duarte sought a negotiated settlement with the guerrillas.
1988 Duarte resigned.
1989 Alfredo Cristiani (ARENA) became president in rigged elections; rebel attacks intensified.
1991 United Nations-sponsored peace accord signed by representatives of the government and the socialist guerrilla group, the FMLN.
1992 Peace accord validated; FMLN became political party.

to a hard line against the FMLN rebels. Following the rigged right-wing victory in the 1989 elections, many activists in labor-union, cooperative, and human-rights organizations were arrested. The guerrillas mounted a surprisingly effective offensive in the wealthy suburbs of San Salvador but in Sept 1989 agreed to peace talks. In 1990 a consistently high level of "disappearances" was denounced by the country's Human Rights Commission. In the 1991 general election ARENA claimed 43 assembly seats and continued in power.
peace accord signed A peace accord initiated by the United Nations, signed by representatives of the government and the FMLN Dec 1991, came into effect Feb 1992. The FMLN subsequently became a political party. It was estimated that the civil war 1980–90 had claimed some 70,000 lives. *See illustration box.*

Elsinore another form of ▷Helsingør, a port on the NE coast of Denmark.

Elton Charles 1900–1991. British ecologist, a pioneer of the study of animal and plant forms in their natural environments, and of animal behavior as part of the complex pattern of life. He defined the concept of ▷food chains and was an early conservationist, instrumental in establishing (1949) the Nature Conservancy Council of which he was a member 1949–56, and much concerned with the impact of introduced species on natural systems.

His books include *Animal Ecology and Evolution* 1930 and *The Pattern of Animal Communities* 1966.

Eluard Paul. Adopted name of Eugène Grindel 1895–1952. French poet, born in Paris. He expressed the suffering of poverty in his verse, and was a leader of the Surrealists. He fought in World War I, which inspired his *Poèmes pour la paix/Poems for Peace* 1918, and was a member of the Resistance in World War II. His books include *Poésie et vérité/Poetry and Truth* 1942 and *Au Rendezvous allemand/To the German Rendezvous* 1944.

Ely Richard Theodore 1854–1943. US economist. Born in Ripley, New York, he was educated at Columbia University and received his PhD from the University of Heidelberg 1879. Appointed professor of political economy at Johns Hopkins University 1881, Ely was an early advocate of government economic intervention, central planning, and the organization of the labor force. In 1885 he founded the American Economic Association and in 1892 became chair of the department of economics at the University of Wisconsin. He joined the faculty of Northwestern University 1925 and retired from teaching 1933.

Elyria city in N Ohio, on the Black River, W of Cleveland; seat of Lorain county. Industries include tools, electric motors, chromium hardware, chemicals, and automotive parts; population (1990) 56,700.

Elysium in Greek mythology, the Islands of the Blessed, situated at the western end of the Earth, near the river Oceanus, to which favored heroes are sent by the gods to enjoy a life after death. Later a region in ▷Hades.

Elytis Odysseus. Adopted name of Odysseus Alepoudelis 1911– . Greek poet, born in Crete. His verse celebrates the importance of the people's attempts to shape an individual existence in freedom. His major work *To Axion Esti/Worthy It Is* 1959 is a lyric cycle, parts of which have been set to music by Theodorakis. He was awarded the Nobel Prize for Literature in 1979.

emancipation being liberated, being set free from servitude or subjection of any kind. The changing role of women in social, economic, and particularly in political terms in the 19th and 20th centuries, is sometimes referred to as the "emancipation of women" (see ▷women's movement).

In the UK, the 1829 Catholic Emancipation Act freed Roman Catholics from the civil disabilities imposed on them by English law. In 1861 the emancipation of Russian serfs was proclaimed. In 1862 President Abraham Lincoln issued an edict freeing all slaves, known as the Emancipation Proclamation; the Thirteenth Amendment of the Constitution declared the abolition of slavery throughout the US.

Emancipation Proclamation, The in US history, President Lincoln's Civil War announcement, Sept 22, 1862, stating that from the beginning of 1863 all black slaves in states still engaged in rebellion against the federal government would be emancipated. Slaves in border states still remaining loyal to the Union were excluded.

Lincoln had read a preliminary proclamation to his cabinet, who urged him to wait until a major Union victory before delivering it publicly.

embargo the legal prohibition by a government of trade with another country, forbidding foreign ships to leave or enter its ports. Trade embargoes may be imposed on a country seen to be violating international laws.

They may be used as a tool of bilateral (political) policy, such as the embargo of sensitive technology that existed between the US and the USSR.

embezzlement in law, theft by an employee of property entrusted to him or her by an employer.

embolism blockage of a blood vessel by an obstruction called an embolus (usually a blood clot, fat particle, or bubble of air).

embossing relief decoration on metals, which can be cast, chased, or repoussé, and executed by hand or machine. In the 16th century the term was also used for carved decorations on wood. Embossed bindings for books were developed from the early 19th century; the leather is embossed before binding.

embroidery the art of decorating cloth with a needle and thread. It includes ▷broderie anglaise, ▷gros point, and ▷petit point, all of which have been used for the adornment of costumes, gloves, book covers, furnishings, and ecclesiastical vestments.

embryo early development stage of an animal or a plant following fertilization of an ovum (egg cell), or activation of an ovum by ▷parthenogenesis. In humans, the term embryo describes the fertilized egg during its first seven weeks of existence; from the eighth week onwards it is referred to as a fetus.

In animals the embryo exists either within an egg (where it is nourished by food contained in the yolk), or in mammals, in the ▷uterus of the mother. In mammals (except marsupials) the embryo is fed through the ⟐placenta. The plant embryo is found within the seed in higher plants. It sometimes consists of only a few cells, but usually includes a root, a shoot (or primary bud), and one or two ⟐cotyledons, which nourish the growing seedling.

embryology study of the changes undergone by an organism from its conception as a fertilized ovum (egg) to its emergence into the world at hatching or birth. It is mainly concerned with the changes in cell organization in the embryo and the way in which these lead to the structures and organs of the adult (the process of ⟐differentiation).

Applications of embryology include embryo transplants, both commercial (for example, in building up a prize dairy-cow herd quickly at low cost) and in obstetric medicine (as a method for helping couples with fertility problems to have children). This usually involves the surgical removal of eggs from a female, their fertilization under laboratory conditions, and, once normal development is under way, their replacement in the womb.

embryo sac large cell within the ovule of flowering plants that represents the female ⟐gametophyte when fully developed. It typically contains eight nuclei. Fertilization occurs when one of these nuclei, the egg nucleus, fuses with a male ⟐gamete.

emerald a clear, green gemstone variety of the mineral ⟐beryl. It occurs naturally in Colombia, the Ural Mountains, in Russia, Zimbabwe, and Australia.

emergent properties features of a system that are due to the way in which its components are structured in relation to each other, rather than to the individual properties of those components. Thus the distinctive characteristics of chemical ⟐compounds are emergent properties of the way in which the constituent elements are organized, and cannot be explained by the particular properties of those elements taken in isolation. In biology, ⟐ecosystem stability is an emergent property of the interaction between the constituent species, and not a property of the species themselves.

Emerson Ralph Waldo 1803–1882. US philosopher, essayist, and poet. He settled in Concord, Massachusetts, which he made a center of ⟐transcendentalism, and wrote *Nature* 1836, which states the movement's main principles emphasizing the value of self-reliance and the Godlike nature of human souls. His two volumes of *Essays* (1841, 1844) made his reputation: "Self-Reliance" and "Compensation" are among the best known.

Born in Boston, Massachusetts, and educated at Harvard, Emerson became a Unitarian minister. In 1832 he resigned and traveled to Europe, meeting the British writers Carlyle, Coleridge, and Wordsworth. On his return to Massachusetts in 1833 he settled in Concord. He made a second visit to England 1847 and incorporated his impressions in *English Traits* 1856. Much of his verse was published in the literary magazine *The Dial*. His poems include "The Rhodora," "Threnody," and "Brahma." His later works include *Representative Men* 1850 and *The Conduct of Life* 1870.

emery grayish-black opaque metamorphic rock consisting of ⟐corundum and magnetite, together with other minerals such as hematite. It is used as an ⟐abrasive.

emetic any substance administered to induce vomiting. Emetics are used to empty the stomach in many cases of deliberate or accidental

ingestion of a poison. The most frequently used is ipecacuanha.

emf in physics, abbreviation for ⟐*electromotive force*.

Emilia-Romagna region of N central Italy including much of the Po valley; area 8,531 sq mi/22,100 sq km; population (1988) 3,924,000. The capital is Bologna; other towns include Reggio, Rimini, Parma, Ferrara, and Ravenna. Agricultural produce includes fruit, wine, sugar beet, beef, and dairy products; oil and natural-gas resources have been developed in the Po valley.

eminent domain in the US, the right of federal and state government and other authorized bodies to compulsorily purchase land that is needed for public purposes. The owner is entitled to receive a fair price for the land.

Emin Pasha Mehmed. Adopted name of Eduard Schnitzer 1849–1892. German explorer, doctor, and linguist. Appointed by General Gordon as chief medical officer and then governor of the Equatorial province of S Sudan, he carried out extensive research in anthropology, botany, zoology, and meteorology.

Isolated by his remote location and cut off from the outside world by Arab slave traders, he was "rescued" by an expedition led by H M Stanley in 1889. He traveled with Stanley as far as Zanzibar but returned to continue his work near Lake Victoria. Three years later he was killed by Arabs while leading an expedition to the W coast of Africa.

emission spectroscopy in analytical chemistry, a technique for determining the identity or amount present of a chemical substance by measuring the amount of electromagnetic radiation it emits at specific wavelengths; see ⟐spectroscopy.

Emmet Robert 1778–1803. Irish nationalist leader. In 1803 he led an unsuccessful revolt in Dublin against British rule and was captured, tried, and hanged. His youth and courage made him an Irish hero.

emotivism a philosophical position in the theory of ethics. Emotivists deny that moral judgments can be true or false, maintaining that they merely express an attitude or an emotional response.

The concept came to prominence during the 1930s, largely under the influence of *Language, Truth and Logic* 1936 by A J ⟐Ayer.

Empedocles *c.* 490–430 BC. Greek philosopher and scientist. He lived at Acragas (Agrigentum) in Sicily, and proposed that the universe is composed of four elements—fire, air, earth, and water—which through the action of love and discord are eternally constructed, destroyed, and constructed anew. According to tradition, he committed suicide by throwing himself into the crater of Mount Etna.

emphysema incurable lung condition characterized by disabling breathlessness. Progressive loss of the thin walls dividing the air spaces (alveoli) in the lungs reduces the area available for the exchange of oxygen and carbon dioxide, causing the lung tissue to expand. The term "emphysema" can also refer to any abnormal swelling of body tissues caused by the accumulation of air.

empiricism (Greek *empeiria* "experience" or "experiment") in philosophy, the belief that all knowledge is ultimately derived from sense experience. It is suspicious of metaphysical

schemes based on ⟐a priori propositions, which are claimed to be true irrespective of experience. It is frequently contrasted with ⟐rationalism.

Empiricism developed in the 17th and early 18th centuries through the work of John ⟐Locke, George ⟐Berkeley, and David ⟐Hume, traditionally known as the British empiricist school.

employment agency agency for bringing together employers requiring labor and workers seeking employment. Employment agencies may be state run, as in state employment services, or private agencies paid either by client companies or by individuals seeking employment.

EMS abbreviation for ⟐*European Monetary System*.

emu flightless bird *Dromaius novaehollandiae* native to Australia. It stands about 6 ft/1.8 m high and has coarse brown plumage, small rudimentary wings, short feathers on the head and neck, and powerful legs, well adapted for running and kicking. The female has a curious bag or pouch in the windpipe that enables her to emit the characteristic loud booming note.

In Western Australia emus are farmed for their meat, skins, feathers, and oil.

emulsifier food ⟐additive used to keep oils dispersed and in suspension, in products such as mayonnaise and peanut butter. Egg yolk is a naturally occurring emulsifier, but most of the emulsifiers in commercial use today are synthetic chemicals.

emulsion a stable dispersion of a liquid in another liquid—for example, oil and water in some cosmetic lotions.

enamel vitrified (glasslike) coating of various colors used for decorative purposes on a metallic or porcelain surface. In ⟐*cloisonné* the various sections of the design are separated by thin metal wires or strips. In *champlevé* the enamel is poured into engraved cavities in the metal surface.

The ancient art of enameling is believed to be of Near Eastern origin. The Egyptians, Greeks, and Romans enameled their jewelry, and Byzantium was famed for enamels from about the 9th to 11th centuries. The enameled altarpiece at St Mark's, Venice, which was brought from Constantinople, still survives. Byzantine work was emulated in Europe, particularly in Saxony, Brunswick, and in the Rhine valley. German enamelers were later employed in France, and during the 13th and 14th centuries the art was introduced into Italy and China. The chief centers of enameling during the 15th and 16th centuries were the cities of Lorraine and Limoges, France.

encaustic painting an ancient technique of painting, commonly used by the Egyptians, Greeks, and Romans, in which colored pigments were mixed with molten wax and painted on panels.

encephalin a naturally occurring chemical produced by nerve cells in the brain that has the same effect as morphine or other derivatives of opium, acting as a natural painkiller. Unlike morphine, encephalins are quickly degraded by the body, so there is no buildup of tolerance to them, and hence no "addiction." Encephalins are a variety of ⟐peptides, as are ⟐endorphins, which have similar effects.

encephalitis inflammation of the brain, nearly always due to virus infection but also to parasites, fungi, or malaria. It varies widely in severity, from short-lived, relatively slight effects of headache, drowsiness, and fever to paralysis, coma, and death. One such type of viral infection is also sometimes called "sleeping sickness."

Encke's comet comet with the shortest known orbital period, 3.3 years. It is named after German mathematician and astronomer Johann Franz Encke (1791–1865) who calculated the orbit in 1819 from earlier sightings.

It was first seen in 1786 by the French astronomer Pierre Méchain (1744–1804). It is the parent body of the Taurid meteor shower and a fragment of it may have hit the Earth in the ▷Tunguska event 1908.

In 1913, it became the first comet to be observed throughout its entire orbit when it was photographed near ▷aphelion (the point in its orbit furthest from the Sun) by astronomers at Mount Wilson Observatory in California.

encyclical letter addressed by the Pope to Roman Catholic bishops for the benefit of the people. The first was issued by Benedict XIV in 1740, but encyclicals became common only in the 19th century. They may be doctrinal (condemning errors), exhortative (recommending devotional activities), or commemorative.

Recent encyclicals include *Pacem in terris* (Pope John XXIII, 1963), *Sacerdotalis celibatus* (on the celibacy of the clergy, Pope Paul VI, 1967), and *Humanae vitae* (Pope Paul VI, 1967, on methods of contraception).

encyclopedia work of reference covering either all fields of knowledge or one specific subject. Although most encyclopedias are alphabetical, with cross-references, some are organized thematically with indexes, to keep related subjects together.

The earliest extant encyclopedia is the *Historia Naturalis/Natural History* AD 23–79 of ▷Pliny the Elder. The first alphabetical encyclopedia in English was the *Lexicon Technicum/Technical Lexicon* 1704, compiled by John Harris. In 1728 Ephraim Chambers published his *Cyclopaedia*, which coordinated scattered articles by a system of cross-references and was translated into French 1743–45. This translation formed the basis of the *Encyclopédie* edited by Diderot and d'Alembert, published 1751–72. By this time the system of engaging a body of expert compilers and editors was established, and in 1768–71 the *Encyclopaedia Britannica* first appeared.

American encyclopedias include the *Encyclopedia Americana* and *Collier's Encyclopedia*, both prepared with attention to cultural and stylistic interpretations appropriate to the US.

Encyclopédie encyclopedia in 35 volumes written 1751–77 by a group of French scholars (Encyclopédistes) including D'Alembert and Diderot, inspired by the English encyclopedia produced by Ephraim Chambers 1728. Religious skepticism and ▷Enlightenment social and political views were a feature of the work.

The first 28 volumes 1751–72 were edited by Diderot. A further five volumes were produced by other editors 1776–77 and the two-volume index was completed 1780.

endangered species plant or animal species whose numbers are so few that it is at risk of becoming extinct. Officially designated endangered species are listed by the International Union for the Conservation of Nature (▷IUCN).

An example of an endangered species is the Javan rhinoceros. There are only about 50 alive today and, unless active steps are taken to promote this species' survival, it will probably be extinct within a few decades.

A fourth of the world's plants are in danger of becoming extinct by the year 2020.

endemic of a disease, more or less prevalent in a given region or country all the time. It refers most often to tropical diseases, such as ▷malaria, which are hard to eradicate.

Enders John Franklin 1897–1985. US virologist. With Thomas Weller (1915–) and Frederick Robbins (1916–), he discovered the ability of the polio virus to grow in cultures of various tissues, which led to the perfection of an effective vaccine. The three were awarded the Nobel Prize for Medicine 1954. Enders also succeeded in isolating the measles virus.

endive cultivated annual plant *Cichorium endivia*, family Compositae, the leaves of which are used in salads and cooking. One variety has narrow, curled leaves; another has wide, smooth leaves. It is related to ▷chicory.

endocrine gland gland that secretes hormones into the bloodstream to regulate body processes. Endocrine glands are most highly developed in vertebrates, but are also found in other animals, notably insects. In humans the main endocrine glands are the pituitary, thyroid, parathyroid, adrenal, pancreas, ovary, and testis.

endolymph fluid found in the inner ▷ear, filling the central passage of the cochlea as well as the semicircular canals.

Sound waves traveling into the ear pass eventually through the three small bones of the middle ear and set up vibrations in the endolymph. These are detected by receptors in the cochlea, which send nerve impulses to the hearing centers of the brain.

endometriosis common gynecological complaint in which patches of endometrium (the

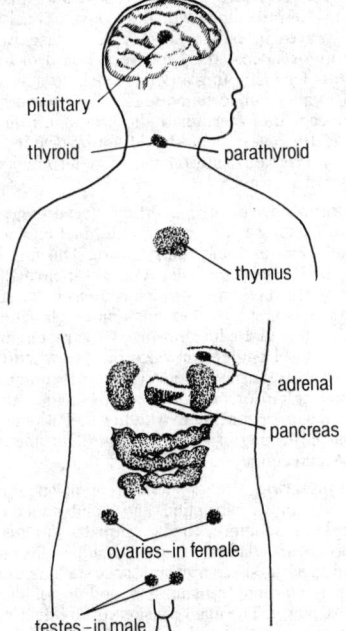

endocrine gland *The main human endocrine glands.*

pituitary

thyroid

parathyroid

thymus

adrenal

pancreas

ovaries –in female

testes –in male

lining of the womb) are found outside the uterus.

This ectopic (abnormally positioned) tissue is present most often in the ovaries, although it may invade any pelvic or abdominal site, as well as the vagina and rectum. Endometriosis may be treated with analgesics, hormone preparations, or surgery.

endoparasite ▷parasite that lives inside the body of its host.

endoplasm inner, liquid part of a cell's ▷cytoplasm.

endoplasmic reticulum (ER) a membranous system of tubes, channels, and flattened sacs that form compartments within ▷eukaryotic cells. It stores and transports proteins within cells and also carries various enzymes needed for the synthesis of ▷fats. The ▷ribosomes, or the organelles that carry out protein synthesis, are attached to parts of the ER.

Under the electron microscope, ER looks like a series of channels and vesicles, but it is in fact a large, sealed, baglike structure crumpled and folded into a convoluted mass. The interior of the "bag," the ER lumen, stores various proteins needed elsewhere in the cell, then organizes them into transport vesicles formed by a small piece of ER membrane budding from the main membrane.

endorphin natural substance (a polypeptide) that modifies the action of nerve cells. Endorphins are produced by the pituitary gland and hypothalamus of vertebrates. They lower the perception of pain by reducing the transmission of signals between nerve cells.

Endorphins not only regulate pain and hunger, but are also involved in the release of sex hormones from the pituitary gland. Opiates act in a similar way to endorphins, but are not rapidly degraded by the body, as natural endorphins are, and thus have a long-lasting effect on pain perception and mood. Endorphin release is stimulated by exercise.

endoscopy examination of internal organs or tissues by an instrument allowing direct vision. An endoscope is equipped with an eyepiece, lenses, and its own light source to illuminate the field of vision. The endoscope that examines the alimentary canal is a flexible fiberoptic instrument swallowed by the patient.

There are various types of endoscope in use—some rigid, some flexible—with individual names prefixed by their site of application (for example, bronchoscope and laryngoscope). The value of endoscopy is in permitting diagnosis without the need for exploratory surgery. Biopsies (tissue samples) and photographs may be taken by way of the endoscope as an aid to diagnosis, or to monitor the effects of treatment. In some cases, treatment can be given during the course of an examination, using fine instruments introduced through the endoscope.

endoskeleton the internal supporting structure of vertebrates, made up of cartilage or bone. It provides support, and acts as a system of levers to which muscles are attached to provide movement. Certain parts of the skeleton (the skull and ribs) give protection to vital body organs.

Sponges are supported by a network of rigid, or semirigid, spiky structures called spicules; a bath sponge is the proteinaceous skeleton of a sponge.

endosperm nutritive tissue in the seeds of most flowering plants. It surrounds the embryo and is produced by an unusual process that parallels the ⇨fertilization of the ovum by a male gamete. A second male gamete from the pollen grain fuses with two female nuclei within the ⇨embryo sac. Thus endosperm cells are triploid (having three sets of chromosomes); they contain food reserves such as starch, fat, and protein that are utilized by the developing seedling.

In "non-endospermic" seeds, absorption of these food molecules by the embryo is completed early, so that the endosperm has disappeared by the time of germination.

endotherm "warm-blooded," or homeothermic, animal. Endotherms have internal mechanisms for regulating their body temperatures to levels different from the environmental temperature. See ⇨homeothermy.

Endymion in Greek mythology, a beautiful young man loved by Selene, the Moon goddess. He was granted eternal sleep in order to remain forever young. Keats's poem *Endymion* 1818 is an allegory of searching for perfection.

Energiya most powerful Soviet space rocket, first launched May 15, 1987. Used to launch the Soviet space shuttle, the Energiya ⇨booster is capable, with the use of strap-on boosters, of launching payloads of up to 190 tons into Earth orbit.

energy capacity for doing ⇨work. Potential energy (PE) is energy deriving from position; thus a stretched spring has elastic PE, and an object raised to a height above the Earth's surface, or the water in an elevated reservoir, has gravitational PE. A lump of coal and a tank of gasoline, together with the oxygen needed for their combustion, have chemical energy. Other sorts of energy include electrical and nuclear energy, and light and sound. Moving bodies possess kinetic energy (KE). Energy can be converted from one form to another, but the total quantity stays the same (the **conservation of energy** principle that governs many natural phenomena). For example, as an apple falls, it loses gravitational PE but gains KE.

So-called energy resources are stores of convertible energy. Nonrenewable resources include the fossil fuels (coal, oil, and gas) and nuclear-fission "fuels"—for example, uranium-235. Renewable resources, such as wind, tidal, and geothermal power, have so far been less exploited. Hydroelectric projects are well established, and wind turbines and tidal systems are being developed. All energy sources depend ultimately on the Sun's energy.

Einstein's special theory of ⇨relativity 1905 correlates any gain, E, in energy with a gain, m, in mass, by the equation $E = mc^2$, in which c is the speed of light. The equation applies universally, not just to nuclear reactions, although it is only for these that the percentage change in mass is large enough to detect. Although energy is never lost, after a number of conversions it tends to finish up as the kinetic energy of random motion of molecules (of the air, for example) at relatively low temperatures. This is "degraded" energy in that it is difficult to convert it back to other forms.

energy of reaction energy released or absorbed during a chemical reaction, also called **enthalpy of reaction** or **heat of reaction**. In a chemical reaction, the energy stored in the reacting molecules is rarely the same as that stored in the product molecules. Depending on which is the greater, energy is either released (an exothermic reaction) or absorbed (an endothermic reaction) from the surroundings.

The amount of energy released or absorbed by the quantities of substances represented by the chemical equation is the energy of reaction.

Engadine the upper valley of the river Inn in Switzerland, a winter sports resort.

Engels Friedrich 1820–1895. German social and political philosopher, a friend of, and collaborator with, Karl ⇨Marx on *The Communist Manifesto* 1848 and other key works. His later interpretations of Marxism, and his own philosophical and historical studies such as *Origins of the Family, Private Property, and the State* 1884 (which linked patriarchy with the development of private property), developed such concepts as historical materialism. His use of positivism and Darwinian ideas gave Marxism a scientific and deterministic flavor which was to influence Soviet thinking.

In 1842 Engels's father sent him to work in the cotton factory owned by his family in Manchester, England, where he became involved with ⇨Chartism. In 1844 his lifelong friendship with Karl Marx began, and together they worked out the materialist interpretation of history and in 1847–48 wrote the *Communist Manifesto*. Returning to Germany during the 1848–49 revolution, Engels worked with Marx on the *Neue Rheinische Zeitung/New Rhineland Newspaper* and fought on the barricades in Baden. After the defeat of the revolution he returned to Manchester, and for the rest of his life largely supported the Marx family.

Engels's first book was *The Condition of the Working Classes in England* 1845. He summed up the lessons of 1848 in *The Peasants' War in Germany* 1850 and *Revolution and Counter-Revolution in Germany* 1851. After Marx's death Engels was largely responsible for the wider dissemination of his ideas; he edited the second and third volumes of Marx's *Das Kapital* 1885 and 1894. Although Engels himself regarded his ideas as identical with those of Marx, discrepancies between their works are the basis of many Marxist debates.

Engel v Vitale US Supreme Court decision 1962 dealing with the constitutionality of prayer in public schools. The case was brought against the New York Board of Regents for instituting an official daily prayer in the state's public schools. The Court ordered the regents to terminate the program, ruling that the government should not involve itself in the creation of any official religious practice, sectarian or not.

engine device for converting stored energy into useful work or movement. Most engines use a fuel as their energy store. The fuel is burned to produce heat energy—hence the name "heat engine"—which is then converted into movement. Heat engines can be classified according to the fuel they use (⇨petrol engine or ⇨diesel engine), or according to whether the fuel is burned inside (⇨internal-combustion engine) or outside (⇨steam engine) the engine, or according to whether they produce a reciprocating or rotary motion (⇨turbine or ⇨Wankel engine).

engineering the application of science to the design, construction, and maintenance of works, machinery, roads, railroads, bridges, harbor installations, engines, ships, aircraft and airports, spacecraft and space stations, and the generation, transmission, and use of electrical power. The main divisions of engineering are aerospace, chemical, civil, electrical, electronic, gas, marine, materials, mechanical, mining, production, radio, and structural.

English sovereigns from 900

name	date of accession
West Saxon Kings	
Edward the Elder	901
Athelstan	925
Edmund	940
Edred	946
Edwy	955
Edgar	959
Edward the Martyr	975
Ethelred II	978
Edmund Ironside	1016
Danish Kings	
Canute	1016
Hardicanute	1040
Harold I	1035
West Saxon Kings (restored)	
Edward the Confessor	1042
Harold II	1066
Norman Kings	
William I	1066
William II	1087
Henry I	1100
Stephen	1135
House of Plantagenet	
Henry II	1154
Richard I	1189
John	1199
Henry III	1216
Edward I	1272
Edward II	1307
Edward III	1327
Richard II	1377
House of Lancaster	
Henry IV	1399
Henry V	1413
Henry VI	1422
House of York	
Edward IV	1461
Edward V	1483
Richard III	1483
House of Tudor	
Henry VII	1485
Henry VIII	1509
Edward VI	1547
Mary I	1553
Elizabeth I	1558
House of Stuart	
James I	1603
Charles I	1625
The Commonwealth	
House of Stuart (restored)	
Charles II	1660
James II	1685
William III and Mary	1689
Anne	1702
House of Hanover	
George I	1714
George II	1727
George III	1760
George IV	1820
William IV	1830
Victoria	1837
House of Saxe Coburg	
Edward VII	1901
House of Windsor	
George V	1910
Edward VIII	1936
George VI	1936
Elizabeth II	1952

engineering drawing technical drawing that forms the plans for the design and construction of engineering components and structures. Engineering drawings show different projections, or views of objects, with the relevant dimensions, and show how all the separate parts fit together.

England largest division of the United Kingdom.
area 50,318 sq mi/130,357 sq km
capital London
cities Birmingham, Coventry, Leeds, Leicester, Manchester, Newcastle-upon-Tyne, Nottingham, Sheffield; ports Bristol, Dover, Liverpool, Portsmouth, Southampton
features variability of climate and diversity of scenery; among European countries, only the Netherlands is more densely populated
exports agricultural (cereals, rape, sugar beet, potatoes); meat and meat products; electronic (software), and telecommunications equipment; scientific instruments; textiles and fashion goods; North Sea oil and gas, petrochemicals, and pharmaceuticals; film and television programs; sound recordings. Tourism is important. There are worldwide banking and insurance interests
currency pound sterling
population (1986) 47,255,000
language English, with more than 100 minority languages
religion Christian, with the Church of England as the established church; Jewish; Muslim
For *government* and *history*, see ♢Britain, ancient; ♢England: history; ♢United Kingdom.

England: history for pre-Roman history, see ♢Britain, ancient.
5th–7th centuries Anglo-Saxons overran all England except Cornwall and Cumberland, forming independent kingdoms including Northumbria, Mercia, Kent, and Wessex.
c. 597 England converted to Christianity by St Augustine.
829 Egbert of Wessex accepted as overlord of all England.
878 Alfred ceded N and E England to the Danish invaders but kept them out of Wessex.
1066 Norman Conquest; England passed into French hands under William the Conqueror.
1172 Henry II became king of Ireland and established a colony there.
1215 King John forced to sign Magna Carta.
1284 Conquest of Wales, begun by the Normans, completed by Edward I.
1295 Model Parliament set up.
1338–1453 Hundred Years' War with France enabled Parliament to secure control of taxation and, by impeachment, of the king's choice of ministers.
1348–49 Black Death killed about 30% of the population.
1381 Social upheaval led to the ♢Peasants' Revolt, which was brutally repressed.
1399 Richard II deposed by Parliament for absolutism.
1414 Lollard revolt repressed.
1455–85 Wars of the Roses.
1497 Henry VII ended the power of the feudal nobility with the suppression of the Yorkist revolts.
1529 Henry VIII became head of the Church of England after breaking with Rome.
1536–43 Acts of Union united England and Wales after conquest.
1547 Edward VI adopted Protestant doctrines.

1553 Reversion to Roman Catholicism under Mary I.
1558 Elizabeth I adopted a religious compromise.
1588 Attempted invasion of England by the Spanish Armada.
1603 James I united the English and Scottish crowns; parliamentary dissidence increased.
1642–52 Civil War between royalists and parliamentarians, resulting in victory for Parliament.
1649 Charles I executed and the Commonwealth set up.
1653 Oliver Cromwell appointed Lord Protector.
1660 Restoration of Charles II.
1685 Monmouth rebellion.
1688 William of Orange invited to take the throne; flight of James II.
1707 Act of Union between England and Scotland under Queen Anne, after which the countries became known as Great Britain.
For further history, see ♢United Kingdom.

English native to or an inhabitant of England, part of Britain, as well as their descendants, culture, and language. The English have a mixed cultural heritage combining Celtic, Anglo-Saxon, Norman, and Scandinavian elements.

English architecture the main styles in English architecture are: Saxon, Norman, Early English (of which Westminster Abbey is an example), Decorated, Perpendicular (15th century), Tudor (a name chiefly applied to domestic buildings of about 1485–1558), Jacobean, Stuart (including the Renaissance and Queen Anne styles), Georgian, the Gothic revival of the 19th century, Modern, and Postmodern. Notable architects include Christopher Wren, Inigo Jones, John Vanbrugh, Nicholas Hawksmoor, Charles Barry, Edwin Lutyens, Hugh Casson, Basil Spence, Frederick Gibberd, Denys Lasdun, and Richard Rogers.
Roman period (55 BC–AD 410) Stretches of Hadrian's Wall remain, and excavations continue to reveal the forums, basilicas, baths, villas, and mosaic pavements spread across the country.
Anglo-Saxon period (449–1066) Much of the architecture of this period, being of timber, has disappeared. The stone church towers that remain, such as at Earls Barton, appear to imitate timber techniques with their "long and short work" and triangular arches.
Norman period (1066–1189) William the Conqueror inaugurated an enormous building program. He brought the *Romanesque style* of round arches, massive cylindrical columns, and thick walls. At Durham Cathedral, the rib vaults (1093) were an invention of European importance in the development of the Gothic style.
Gothic architecture Early English (1189–1307) began with the very French east end of Canterbury cathedral designed 1175 by William of Sens (died *c.* 1180), and attained its English flowering in the cathedrals of Wells, Lincoln, and Salisbury. A simple elegant style of lancet arches, deeply carved moldings and slender, contrasting shafts of Purbeck marble.
Decorated (1307–77) is characterized by a growing richness in carving and a fascination with line. The double curves of the ogee arch, elaborate window tracery, and vault ribs woven into star patterns may be seen in such buildings as the Lady Chapel at Ely and the Angel Choir at Lincoln. The gridded and panelled cages of light of the *Perpendicular* (1377–1485)

style are a dramatic contrast to the Decorated period. Although they lack the richness and invention of the 14th century, they often convey an impressive sense of unity, space, and power. The chancel of Gloucester cathedral is early Perpendicular whereas Kings College chapel, Cambridge, is late Perpendicular.
Tudor and Elizabethan period (1485–1603) This period saw the Perpendicular style interwoven with growing Renaissance influence. Buildings develop a conscious symmetry elaborated with continental Patternbrook details. Hybrid and exotic works result such as Burghley House and Hardwick Hall (1591–97).
Jacobean (1603–25) This period showed scarcely more sophistication.
English Renaissance Stuart period The provincial scene was revolutionized by Inigo ♢Jones with the Queens House, Greenwich 1616 and the Banqueting House, Whitehall 1619. Strict Palladianism appeared among the half-timber and turrets of Jacobean London. With Christopher ♢Wren a more mannered classicism evolved showing French Renaissance influence, for example St Paul's cathedral (1675–1710). Under Wren's pupil Nicholas Hawksmoor (1661–1736) and John Vanbrugh (1664–1726) theatrical Baroque style emerged, as in Blenheim Palace 1705–20.
Georgian architecture Lord ♢Burlington, reacting against the Baroque, inspired a revival of the pure Palladian style of Inigo Jones. William Kent, also a Palladian, invented the picturesque garden as at Rousham, Oxfordshire. Alongside the great country houses, an urban architecture evolved of plain, well-proportioned houses, defining elegant streets and squares. The second half of the century mingled Antiquarian and Neo-Classical influences, exquisitely balanced in the works of Robert Adam at Kedleston Hall (1757–70). John Nash carried Neo-Classicism into the new century. By the dawn of the Victorian era this had become a rather bookish Greek Revival, for example the British Museum (1823–47).
19th century Throughout the century Classic and Gothic engaged with Victorian earnestness in the "Battle of the Styles:" Gothic for the Houses of Parliament (1840–60), Renaissance for the Foreign Office (1860–75). Meanwhile, the great developments in engineering and the needs of new types of buildings, such as railroad stations, transformed the debate. Joseph Paxton's prefabricated Crystal Palace (1850–51) was the most remarkable building of the era. The Arts and Crafts architects, Philip Webb (1831–1915) and Norman Shaw (1831–1912), brought renewal and simplicity inspired by William Morris.
20th century The early work of Lutyens and the white rendered houses of Charles Voysey (1857–1941) such as Broadleys, Windermere (1898–99), maintained the Arts and Crafts spirit of natural materials and simplicity. Norman Shaw, however, developed an Imperial Baroque style.

After World War I classicism again dominated, grandly in Lutyens' New Delhi government buildings (1912–31). There was often a clean Scandinavian influence as in the RIBA building, London (1932–34), which shows growing Modernist tendencies. Modernism arrived fully with continental refugees such as Lubetkin (1901–   ), the founder of the Tecton architectural team that designed London Zoo (1934–38).

The strong social dimension of English 20th-century architecture is best seen in the New Town movement. Welwyn Garden City was begun 1919 and developed after World War II. The latest of the New Towns, Milton Keynes, was designated 1967. Recently English architects have again achieved international recognition, for example Norman �◊Foster and Richard ◊Rogers for their High-Tech innovative Lloyds Building (1979–84). James Stirling (1926–   ) maintains a Modernist technique and planning while absorbing historical and contextural concerns.

English art painting and sculpture of England.
painting Medieval English painting was chiefly religious and included wall paintings and illuminated manuscripts.
portrait painting portrait painting was taken to new levels at the court of Henry VIII by the German artist Hans Holbein. At the court of Queen Elizabeth I, Nicholas Hilliard established a tradition of miniature painting. The Flemish Anthony van Dyck, employed as a court painter by Charles I from 1632, greatly influenced English portrait painters. Joshua Reynolds, Thomas Gainsborough, and Thomas Lawrence are among the best known of the late 18th and early 19th centuries. In the 20th century, Graham Sutherland, Lucian Freud, and David Hockney painted many portraits.
social satire in the 18th century William Hogarth and Thomas Rowlandson used art as a way of criticizing the customs and behavior of contemporary society in styles suggesting political cartoons.
animal painting an indigenous form is the sporting picture, George Stubbs being the great 18th-century exponent.
landscape painting among painters specializing in landscape were Richard Wilson in the 18th century and, in the 19th, the watercolorist Samuel Palmer, John Constable, and J M W Turner. The 20th century is reflected in the war-ravaged landscapes of Paul Nash and the multifigure townscapes of L S Lowry.
the Pre-Raphaelites Millais, Holman Hunt, and Rossetti were founding members, painting literary and genre scenes in the mid-19th century.
Impressionism J M Whistler, the American who settled in London and introduced the doctrine of "art for art's sake," had as his disciple W R Sickert, who helped introduce Impressionism to England.
Modernism this style ranges from the scenes of British work and village life by Stanley Spencer to the tortured figures of Francis Bacon.
Pop art a movement influenced by mass media images, pop art began in the mid-1950s with the work of Richard Hamilton and Peter Blake.
sculpture
ancient early Celtic and Roman work predominate.
medieval some ecclesiastical stone, wood, and ivory sculptures survived the destruction of the churches and monasteries during the ◊Reformation.
17th-18th centuries the woodcarvings of Grinling Gibbons are found in stately homes and St Paul's cathedral. One of the first widely known English sculptors was the Neo-Classicist John Flaxman.
19th century academic portraits were produced by Francis Chantrey and Frederick Leighton.
20th century the stylized stone figures of Jacob Epstein and Eric Gill led toward the abstract forms of Henry Moore and Barbara Hepworth. Anthony Caro and Eduardo Paolozzi have used industrial metals and machine components to create their diverse and dramatic styles since the 1960s.

English Channel stretch of water between England and France, leading in the west to the Atlantic Ocean, and in the east via the Strait of Dover to the North Sea; also known as *La Manche* (French "the sleeve") from its shape.
The English Channel is 280 mi/450 km long W–E; 17 mi/27 km wide at its narrowest (Cap Gris Nez-Dover) and 110 mi/117 km wide at its widest (Ushant–Land's End).
In 1986 work began on the construction of the ◊Channel Tunnel, a railroad link between Britain and France, running beneath the sea floor; it is due to be operational by mid 1993.

English horn alternate name for ◊cor anglais, musical instrument of the oboe family.

English language member of the Germanic branch of the Indo-European language family. It is traditionally described as having passed through four main stages over about 1,500 years: *Old English* or *Anglo-Saxon* (*c.* 500–1050), rooted in the dialects of invading settlers (Jutes, Saxons, Angles, and Frisians); *Middle English* (*c.* 1050–1550), influenced by Norman French after the Conquest 1066 and by ecclesiastical Latin; *Early Modern English* (*c.* 1550–1700), including a standardization of the diverse influences of Middle English; and *Late Modern English* (*c.* 1700 onward), including in particular the development and spread of current Standard English. Through extensive exploration, colonization, and trade, English spread worldwide from the 17th century onward and remains the most important international language of trade and technology. It is used in many variations, for example, British, American, Canadian, West Indian, Indian, Singaporean, and Nigerian English, and many pidgins and Creoles.
historical roots The ancestral forms of English were dialects brought from the NW coastlands of Europe to Britain by Angle, Saxon, and Jutish invaders who gained footholds in the SE in the 5th century and over the next 200 years extended and consolidated their settlements from S England to the middle of Scotland. Scholars distinguish four main early dialects: of the Jutes in Kent, the Saxons in the south, the Mercians or S Angles in the Midlands, and the Northumbrians or N Angles north of the Humber. Until the Danish invasions 9th–11th centuries, Old English was a highly inflected language but appears to have lost many of its grammatical endings in the interaction with Danish, creating a more open or analytic style of language that was further changed by the influence of Norman French after the Conquest 1066. For several centuries English was in competition with other languages: first the various Celtic languages of Britain, then Danish, then French as the language of Plantagenet England and Latin as the language of the Church. In Scotland, English was in competition with Gaelic and Welsh as well as French and Latin (see ◊Scots language).
In 1362 English replaced French as the language of the law courts of England, although the records continued for some time to be kept in Latin. Geoffrey Chaucer was a court poet at this time and strongly influenced the literary style of the London dialect. When William Caxton set up his printing press in London 1477 the new hybrid language (vernacular English mixed with courtly French and scholarly Latin) became increasingly standardized, and by 1611, when the Authorized (King James) Version of the Bible was published, the educated English of the Home Counties and London had become the core of what is now called Standard English. Great dialect variation remained, and still remains, throughout Britain.
By the end of the 16th century, English was firmly established in four countries: England, Scotland, Wales, and Ireland, and with the establishment of the colonies in North America in the early 17th century was spoken in what are now the US, and the West Indies. Seafaring, exploration, commerce, and colonial expansion in due course took both the standard language and other varieties throughout the world. By the time of Johnson's dictionary 1755 and the American Declaration of Independence 1776, English was international and recognizable as the language we use today.
current usage The orthography of English was more or less established by 1650, and, in England in particular, a form of standard educated speech (known as Received Pronunciation) spread from the major public (private) schools in the 19th century. This accent was adopted in the early 20th century by the BBC for its announcers and readers, and is variously known as RP, BBC English, Oxford English, and the King's or Queen's English. It was the socially dominant accent of the British Empire and retains prestige as a model for those learning the language. In the UK, however, it is no longer as sought after as it once was.
Generally, Standard English today does not depend on accent but rather on shared educational experience, mainly of the printed language. Present-day English is an immensely varied language, having absorbed material from many other tongues. It is spoken by more than 300 million native speakers, and between 400 and 800 million foreign users. It is the official language of air transport and shipping; the leading language of science, technology, computers, and commerce; and a major medium of education, publishing, and international negotiation. For this reason scholars frequently refer to its latest phase as World English.

English law one of the major European legal systems, ◊Roman law being the other. English law has spread to many other countries, including former English colonies such as the US, Australia, and New Zealand.
English law has a continuous history dating from the local customs of the Anglo-Saxons, traces of which survived until 1925. After the Norman Conquest there grew up, side by side with the Saxon shire courts, the feudal courts of the barons and the ecclesiastical courts. From the king's council developed the royal courts, presided over by professional judges, which gradually absorbed the jurisdictions of the baronial and ecclesiastical courts. By 1250 the royal judges had amalgamated the various local customs into the system of ◊common law—that is, law common to the whole country. A second system known as ◊equity developed in the Court of Chancery, in which the Lord Chancellor considered petitions.
In the 17th–18th centuries, common law absorbed the Law Merchant, the international code of mercantile customs. During the 19th century virtually the whole of English law was reformed by legislation; for example, the number of capital offenses was greatly reduced.
A unique feature of English law is the doctrine of judicial precedents, whereby the

reported decisions of the courts form a binding source of law for future decisions. A judge is bound by decisions of courts of superior jurisdiction but not necessarily by those of inferior courts.

English literature the earliest surviving English literature is in the form of Old English poems—*Beowulf* and the epic fragments *Finesburh, Waldhere, Deor,* and *Widsith*—that reflect the heroic age and Germanic legends of the 4th–6th centuries, although they were probably not written down until the 7th century. Heroic elements survive in elegiac lyrics, for example, *The Wanderer, The Seafarer,* and in many poems with a specifically Christian content, such as *The Dream of the Rood*; and the Saints' Lives, for example, *Elene,* by the 8th-century poet Cynewulf. These poems are all written in unrhymed alliterative meter. The great prose writers of the early period were the Latin scholars Bede, Aldhelm, and Alcuin. King Alfred founded the tradition of English prose with his translations and his establishment of the Anglo-Saxon Chronicle.

With the arrival of a Norman ruling class at the end of the 11th century, the ascendancy of Norman-French in cultural life began, and it was not until the 13th century that the native literature regained its strength. Prose was concerned chiefly with popular devotional use, but verse emerged typically in the metrical chronicles, such as Layamon's *Brut,* and the numerous romances based on the stories of Charlemagne, the Arthurian legends, and the Classical episodes of Troy. First of the great English poets was Chaucer, whose early work reflected the predominant French influence, but later that of Renaissance Italy. Of purely native inspiration was *The Vision of Piers Plowman* of Langland in the old alliterative verse, and the anonymous *Pearl, Patience,* and *Gawayne and the Grene Knight.*

Chaucer's mastery of versification was not shared by his successors, the most original of whom was Skelton. More successful were the anonymous authors of songs and carols, and of the ballads, which (for example those concerned with Robin Hood) often formed a complete cycle. Drama flowered in the form of ◊miracle and ◊morality plays, and prose, although still awkwardly handled by Wycliffe in his translation of the Bible, rose to a great height with Malory in the 15th century. The Renaissance, which had first touched the English language through Chaucer, came to delayed fruition in the 16th century. Wyatt and Surrey used the sonnet and blank verse in typically Elizabethan forms and prepared the way for Spenser, Sidney, Daniel, Campion, and others. With Kyd and Marlowe, drama emerged into theatrical form; it reached the highest level in Shakespeare and Jonson. Elizabethan prose is represented by Hooker, North, Ascham, Holinshed, Lyly, and others, but English prose achieved full richness in the 17th century, with the King James Version of the Bible 1611, Bacon, Milton, Bunyan, Taylor, Browne, Walton, and Pepys. Most renowned of the 17th-century poets were Milton and Donne; others include the religious writers Herbert, Crashaw, Vaughan, and Traherne, and the Cavalier poets Herrick, Carew, Suckling, and Lovelace. In the Restoration period Butler and Dryden stand out as poets. Dramatists include Otway and Lee in tragedy. Comedy flourished with Congreve, Vanbrugh, and Farquhar.

The 18th century is known as the Augustan Age in English literature. Pope developed the poetic technique of Dryden; in prose Steele and Addison evolved the polite essay, Swift used satire, and Defoe exploited his journalistic ability. This century saw the development of the ◊novel, through the epistolary style of Richardson to the robust narrative of Fielding and Smollett, the comic genius of Sterne, and the Gothic "horror" of Horace Walpole. The Neo-Classical standards established by the Augustans were maintained by Johnson and his circle—Goldsmith, Burke, Reynolds, Sheridan, and others—but the romantic element present in the work of poets Thomson, Gray, Young, and Collins was soon to overturn them.

The *Lyrical Ballads* 1798 of Wordsworth and Coleridge were the manifesto of the new Romantic age. Byron, Shelley, and Keats form a second generation of Romantic poets. In fiction Scott took over the Gothic tradition from Mrs Radcliffe, to create the ◊historical novel, and Jane Austen established the novel of the comedy of manners. Criticism gained new prominence with Coleridge, Lamb, Hazlitt, and De Quincey.

During the 19th century the novel was further developed by Dickens, Thackeray, the Brontës, George Eliot, Trollope, and others. The principal poets of the reign of Victoria were Tennyson, Robert and Elizabeth Browning, Arnold, the Rossettis, Morris, and Swinburne. Among the prose writers of the era are Macaulay, Newman, Mill, Carlyle, Ruskin, and Pater. The transition period at the end of the century saw the poetry and novels of Meredith and Hardy; the work of Butler and Gissing; and the plays of Pinero and Wilde.

Although a Victorian, Gerald Manley Hopkins anticipated the 20th century with the experimentation of his verse forms. Poets of World War I include Sassoon, Brooke, Owen, and Graves. A middle-class realism developed in the novels of Wells, Bennett, Forster, and Galsworthy while the novel's break with traditional narrative and exposition came through the Modernists James Joyce, D H Lawrence, Virginia Woolf, Somerset Maugham, Aldous Huxley, Christopher Isherwood, Evelyn Waugh, and Graham Greene. Writers for the stage include Shaw, Galsworthy, J B Priestley, Coward, and Rattigan, and the writers of poetic drama, such as T S Eliot, Fry, Auden, Isherwood, and Dylan Thomas. The 1950s and 1960s produced the "kitchen sink" dramatists, including Osborne and Wesker. The following decade saw the rise of Harold Pinter, John Arden, Tom Stoppard, Peter Shaffer, Joe Orton, and Alan Ayckbourn. Poets since 1945 include Thom Gunn, Roy Fuller, Philip Larkin, Ted Hughes, and John Betjeman; novelists include William Golding, Iris Murdoch, Angus Wilson, Muriel Spark, Margaret Drabble, Kingsley Amis, Anthony Powell, Alan Sillitoe, Anthony Burgess, John Fowles, Ian McEwan, Martin Amis, Angela Carter, and Doris Lessing.

English-Speaking Union society for promoting the fellowship of the English-speaking peoples of the world, founded 1918 by Evelyn Wrench.

engraving art of creating a design by means of inscribing blocks of metal, wood, or some other hard material with a point. **Intaglio prints** are made mainly on metal by ◊dry point, and ◊etching.

enhanced radiation weapon another name for the ◊neutron bomb.

Enid city in N central Oklahoma, N of Oklahoma City, seat of Garfield county. It is a processing and marketing center for the surrounding region's poultry, cattle, dairy farms, and oil wells; population (1990) 45,300. Enid was founded 1893, when land in the Cherokee Strip region, which was originally put aside for Indian tribes, was opened to white settlement.

Eniwetok atoll in the ◊Marshall Islands, in the central Pacific Ocean; population (1980) 453. It was taken from Japan by the US 1944, which made the island a naval base; 43 atomic tests were conducted there from 1947. The inhabitants were resettled at Ujelang, but insisted on returning home 1980. Despite the clearance of nuclear debris and radioactive soil to the islet of Runit, high radiation levels persisted.

enlightenment in Buddhism, the term used to translate the Sanskrit *bodhi,* awakening: perceiving the reality of the world, or the unreality of the self, and becoming liberated from suffering (Sanskrit *dukkha*). It is the gateway to nirvana.

Enlightenment European intellectual movement that reached its high point in the 18th century. Enlightenment thinkers were believers in social progress and in the liberating possibilities of rational and scientific knowledge. They were often critical of existing society and were hostile to religion, which they saw as keeping the human mind chained down by superstition.

The American and French revolutions were justified by Enlightenment principles of human natural rights. Leading representatives of the Enlightenment were ◊Voltaire, ◊Lessing, and ◊Diderot.

enosis (Greek "union") movement, developed from 1930, for the union of ◊Cyprus with Greece. The campaign (led by ◊EOKA and supported by Archbishop Makarios) intensified from the 1950s. In 1960 independence from Britain, without union, was granted, and increased demands for union led to its proclamation 1974. As a result, Turkey invaded Cyprus, ostensibly to protect the Turkish community, and the island was effectively partitioned.

ENT in medicine, an abbreviation for *ear, nose, and throat.* It is usually applied to a specialist clinic or hospital department.

entail in law, the settlement of land or other property on a successive line of people, usually succeeding generations of the original owner's family. An entail can be either *general,* in which case it simply descends to the heirs, or *special,* when it descends according to a specific arrangement—for example, to children by a named wife.

Entails are increasingly rare and the power to make them has often been destroyed by legislation—for example, restrictions in certain states of the US. In England entails can be easily terminated.

Entebbe town in Uganda, on the NW shore of Lake Victoria, 12 mi/20 km SW of Kampala, the capital; 3,728 ft/1,136 m above sea level; population (1983) 21,000. Founded 1893, it was the administrative center of Uganda 1894–1962.

In 1976, a French aircraft was hijacked by a Palestinian liberation group. It was flown to Entebbe airport, where the hostages on board were rescued six days later by Israeli troops.

Entente Cordiale (French "friendly understanding") agreement reached by Britain and France 1904 recognizing British interests in

Egypt and French interests in Morocco. It formed the basis for Anglo-French cooperation before the outbreak of World War I 1914.

enteric in medicine, of the intestine, an old term used to qualify infective fevers such as ⇨typhoid fever.

enterprise zone special zone designated by government to encourage industrial and commercial activity, usually in economically depressed areas. Investment is attracted by means of tax reduction and other financial incentives.

In the US, the creation of enterprise zones was an important part of the early Reagan administration's plan to encourage private investment in inner-city and other economically depressed areas. It was also a step in the process of reducing government involvement in the economy. The plan called for the creation of up to 25 zones a year for a three-year period. Tax incentives would reduce by as much as 75% the corporate income taxes, and capital-gains taxes would be eliminated entirely for participating businesses.

entomology study of ⇨insects.

entrepreneur in business, a person who successfully manages and develops an enterprise through personal skill and initiative. Examples include John D ⇨Rockefeller and Henry ⇨Ford.

entropy in ⇨thermodynamics, a parameter representing the state of disorder of a system at the atomic, ionic, or molecular level; the greater the disorder, the higher the entropy. Thus the fast-moving disordered molecules of water vapor have higher entropy than those of more ordered liquid water, which in turn have more entropy than the molecules in solid crystalline ice.

In a closed system undergoing change, entropy is a measure of the amount of energy unavailable for useful work. At ⇨absolute zero (−459.67°F/−273°C/0K), when all molecular motion ceases and order is assumed to be complete, entropy is zero.

enucleation in medicine, surgical removal of a complete organ or tumor; for example, the eye from its socket.

Enugu town in Nigeria, capital of Anambra state; population (1983) 228,400. It is a coal-mining center, with steel and cement works, and is linked by rail with Port Harcourt.

envelope in geometry, a curve that touches all the members of a family of lines or curves. For example, a family of three equal circles all touching each other and forming a triangular pattern (like a clover leaf) has two envelopes: a small circle that fits in the space in the middle, and a large circle that encompasses all three circles.

Enver Pasha 1881–1922. Turkish politician and soldier. He led the military revolt 1908 that resulted in the Young Turks' revolution (see ⇨Turkey). He was killed fighting the Bolsheviks in Turkestan.

environment in ecology, the sum of conditions affecting a particular organism, including physical surroundings, climate, and influences of other living organisms. See also ⇨biosphere and ⇨habitat.

In common usage, "the environment" often means the total global environment, without reference to any particular organism. In genetics, it is the external influences that affect an organism's development, and thus its ⇨phenotype.

environmentalism theory emphasising the primary influence of the environment on the development of groups or individuals. It stresses the importance of the physical, biological, psychological, or cultural environment as a factor influencing the structure or behavior of animals, including humans.

In politics this has given rise in many countries to ⇨Green parties, which aim to "preserve the planet and its people."

Environmental Protection Agency (EPA) US agency set up 1970 to control water and air quality, industrial and commercial wastes, pesticides, noise, and radiation. In its own words, it aims to protect "the country from being degraded, and its health threatened, by a multitude of human activities initiated without regard to long-ranging effects upon the life-supporting properties, the economic uses, and the recreational value of air, land, and water."

environment art large sculptural or spatial works that create environments that the spectator may enter. The US artists Jim ⇨Dine and Claes ⇨Oldenburg were early exponents in the 1960s.

environment–heredity controversy see ⇨*nature–nurture controversy*.

enzyme biological ⇨catalyst produced in cells, and capable of speeding up the chemical reactions necessary for life by converting one molecule (substrate) into another. Enzymes are not themselves destroyed by this process. They are large, complex ⇨proteins, and are highly specific, each chemical reaction requiring its own particular enzyme. The enzyme fits into a "slot" (active site) in the substrate molecule, forming an enzyme–substrate complex that lasts until the substrate is altered or split, after which the enzyme can fall away. The substrate may therefore be compared to a lock, and the enzyme to the key required to open it.

The activity and efficiency of enzymes are influenced by various factors, including temperature and pH conditions. Temperatures above 140°F/60°C damage (denature) the intricate structure of enzymes, causing reactions to cease. Each enzyme operates best within a specific pH range, and is denatured by excessive acidity or alkalinity.

Digestive enzymes include ⇨amylases (which digest starch), ⇨lipases (which digest fats), and ⇨proteases (which digest protein). Other enzymes play a part in the conversion of food energy into ⇨ATP; the manufacture of all the molecular components of the body; the replication of ⇨DNA when a cell divides; the production of hormones; and the control of movement of substances into and out of cells.

Enzymes have many medical and industrial uses, from washing powders to drug production, and as research tools in molecular biology. They can be extracted from bacteria and molds, and ⇨genetic engineering now makes it possible to tailor an enzyme for a specific purpose.

Eocene second epoch of the Tertiary period of geological time, 55–38 million years ago. Originally considered the earliest division of the Tertiary, the name means "early recent," referring to the early forms of mammals evolving at the time, following the extinction of the dinosaurs.

EOKA acronym for *Ethniki Organósis Kipriakóu Agónos* (National Organization of Cypriot Struggle) an underground organization formed by General George ⇨Grivas 1955

to fight for the independence of Cyprus from Britain and ultimately its union (*enosis*) with Greece. In 1971, 11 years after the independence of Cyprus, Grivas returned to the island to form EOKA B and to resume the fight for *enosis*, which had not been achieved by the Cypriot government.

eolian referring to sediments carried, formed, eroded, or deposited by the wind. Such sediments include desert sands and dunes as well as deposits of windblown silt, called loess, carried long distances from deserts and from stream sediments derived from the melting of glaciers.

Eos in Greek mythology, the goddess of the dawn, equivalent to the Roman Aurora.

eotvos unit unit (symbol E) for measuring small changes in the intensity of the Earth's ⇨gravity with horizontal distance.

Epaminondas *c.* 420–362 BC. Theban general and politician who won a decisive victory over the Spartans at Leuctra 371. He was killed at the moment of victory at Mantinea.

ephedrine drug that acts like adrenaline on the sympathetic ⇨nervous system (sympatho-mimetic). Once used to relieve bronchospasm in ⇨asthma, it has been superseded by safer, more specific drugs. It is contained in some cold remedies as a decongestant. Side effects include rapid heartbeat, tremor, dry mouth, and anxiety.

Ephedrine is an alkaloid, $C_{10}H_{15}NO_1$, derived from Asian gymnosperms (genus *Ephedra*) or synthesized. It is sometimes misused; in 1990 an Australian truck driver collided with a bus after taking ephedrine to stay awake. Excess leads to mental confusion and increased confidence in one's own capabilities as they actually decline.

Ephesians ⇨epistle in the New Testament attributed to ⇨Paul but possibly written after his death; the earliest versions are not addressed specifically to the church at Ephesus.

Ephesus ancient Greek seaport in Asia Minor, a center of the ⇨Ionian Greeks, with a temple of Artemis destroyed by the Goths AD 262. Now in Turkey, it is one of the world's largest archeological sites. St Paul is said to have visited the city, and addressed a letter (⇨epistle) to the Christians there.

In the 2nd century AD Ephesus had a population of 300,000.

epic narrative poem or cycle of poems dealing with some great deed—often the founding of a nation or the forging of national unity—and often using religious or cosmological themes. The two major epic poems in the Western tradition are *The Iliad* and *The Odyssey*, attributed to Homer, and which were probably intended to be chanted in sections at feasts.

Greek and later criticism, which considered the Homeric epic the highest form of poetry, produced the genre of **secondary epic**—such as the *Aeneid* of Virgil, Tasso's *Jerusalem Delivered*, and Milton's *Paradise Lost*—which attempted to emulate Homer, often for a patron or a political cause. The term is also applied to narrative poems of other traditions: the Anglo-Saxon *Beowulf* and the Finnish *Kalevala*; in India the *Ramayana* and *Mahabharata*; and the Babylonian *Gilgamesh*. All of these evolved in different societies to suit similar social needs and used similar literary techniques.

epicenter the point on the Earth's surface immediately above the seismic focus of an

⊃earthquake. Most damage usually takes place at an earthquake's epicenter. The term sometimes refers to a point directly above or below a nuclear explosion ("at ground zero").

Epictetus c. AD 55–135. Greek Stoic philosopher who encouraged people to refrain from self-interest and to promote the common good of humanity. He believed that people were in the hands of an all-wise providence and that they should endeavor to do their duty in the position to which they were called.

Born at Hierapolis in Phrygia, he lived for many years in Rome as a slave but eventually secured his freedom. He was banished by the emperor ⊃Domitian from Rome in AD 89.

Epicureanism system of philosophy that claims soundly based human happiness is the highest good, so that its rational pursuit should be adopted. It was named after the Greek philosopher Epicurus. The most distinguished Roman Epicurean was ⊃Lucretius.

Epicurus 341–270 BC. Greek philosopher, founder of Epicureanism, who taught at Athens from 306 BC.

epicyclic gear or **sun-and-planet gear** gear system that consists of one or more gear wheels moving around another. Epicyclic gears are found in bicycle hub gears and in automatic gearboxes.

epicycloid in geometry, a curve resembling a series of arches traced out by a point on the circumference of a circle that rolls around another circle of a different diameter. If the two circles have the same diameter, the curve is a ⊃cardioid.

Epidaurus or **Epidavros** ancient Greek city and port on the E coast of Argolis, in the NE Peloponnese. The site contains a well-preserved theater of the 4th century BC; nearby are the ruins of the temple of Aesculapius, the god of healing.

epidemic outbreak of infectious disease affecting large numbers of people at the same time. A widespread epidemic that sweeps across many countries (such as the ⊃Black Death in the late Middle Ages) is known as a **pandemic**.

epidermis outermost layer of ⊃cells on an organism's body. In plants and many invertebrates such as insects, it consists of a single layer of cells. In vertebrates, it consists of several layers of cells.

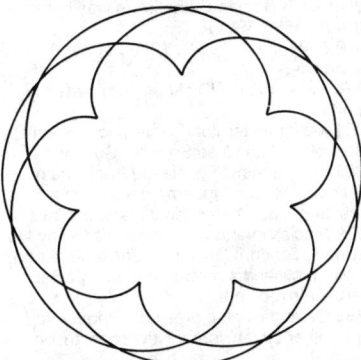

epicycloid A seven-cusped epicycloid, formed by a point on the circumference of a circle (of diameter d) that rolls around another circle (of diameter 7d/3).

The epidermis of plants and invertebrates often has an outer noncellular ⊃cuticle that protects the organism from desiccation.

In vertebrates, such as reptiles, birds, and mammals, the outermost layer of cells is dead, forming a tough, waterproof layer, which is sloughed off continuously or shed periodically.

epigeal seed germination in which the ⊃cotyledons (seed leaves) are borne above the soil.

epiglottis small flap found in the throats of mammals. It moves during swallowing to prevent food from passing into the windpipe and causing choking.

The action of the epiglottis is a highly complex reflex process involving two phases. During the first stage a mouthful of chewed food is lifted by the tongue toward the top and back of the mouth. This is accompanied by the cessation of breathing and by the blocking of the nasal areas from the mouth. The second phase involves the epiglottis moving over the larynx while the food passes down into the esophagus.

epigram short poem, originally a religious inscription but later a short, witty, and pithy saying.

The form was common among writers of ancient Rome, including Catullus and Martial. In English, the epigram has been employed by Ben Jonson, Herrick, Pope, Swift, Yeats, and Ogden Nash.

epigraphy (Greek *epigráphein* "to write on") art of writing with a sharp instrument on hard, durable materials such as stone; also the scientific study of epigraphical writings or inscriptions.

epilepsy medical disorder characterized by a tendency to develop fits, which are convulsions or abnormal feelings caused by abnormal electrical discharges in the cerebral hemispheres of the ⊃brain. Epilepsy can be controlled with a number of ⊃anticonvulsant drugs.

Epileptic fits can be classified into four categories. The first two are generalized, where the abnormal discharges affect the whole of the cerebrum; the second two are focal in nature, involving a particular area of the cortex. In **grand mal**, a vague feeling of uneasiness leads to a phase of generalized stiffening (the tonic phase), followed by a phase of generalized jerking (the clonic phase). A brief period of unconsciousness follows, and finally drowsiness that may last several hours. **Petit mal** occurs almost exclusively in school-age children; the child stops, stares, and pales slightly. The attack lasts only a few seconds. About 5% of children will have a fit at some time in their lives, but most of these are isolated instances caused by feverish illnesses. **Jacksonian** fits begin with jerking in a small area of the body, for example the angle of the mouth or the thumb. They may spread to involve the whole of one side of the body. After the fit, the affected limbs may be paralyzed for several hours. **Temporal-lobe** fits result in hallucinations and feelings of unreality. They may also cause disordered speech and impaired consciousness.

Epilepsy is more common in the Third World, with up to 30 sufferers per 1,000 people in some areas; in industrialized countries the figure is 3–5 per 1,000.

Most epileptics have infrequent fits that have little impact on their daily lives. Epilepsy does not imply that the sufferer has any impairment of intellect, behavior, or personality.

Epinal capital of Vosges *département*, on the river Moselle, France; population (1982) 40,954. A cotton-textile center, it dates from the 10th century.

Epiphany festival of the Christian church, held Jan 6, celebrating the coming of the Magi (the three Wise Men) to Bethlehem with gifts for the infant Jesus, and symbolizing the manifestation of Jesus to the world. It is the 12th day after Christmas, and marks the end of the Christmas festivities.

In many countries the night before Epiphany, called **Twelfth Night**, is marked by the giving of gifts. In the Eastern Orthodox Church, the festival celebrated on this day is known as the **theophany** and commemorates the baptism of Jesus.

epiphyte any plant that grows on another plant or object above the surface of the ground, and has no roots in the soil. An epiphyte does not parasitize the plant it grows on but merely uses it for support. Its nutrients are obtained from rainwater, organic debris such as leaf litter, or from the air.

The greatest diversity of epiphytes is found in tropical areas and includes many orchids.

Epirus (Greek "mainland") country of ancient Greece; the N part was in Albania; the remainder, in NW Greece, was divided into four provinces—Arta, Thesprotia, Yannina, and Preveza.

Epirus (Greek **Ipiros**) region of NW Greece; area 3,551 sq mi/9,200 sq km; population (1981) 325,000. Its capital is Yannina, and it consists of the provinces (nomes) of Arta, Thesprotia, Yannina, and Preveza. There is livestock farming.

episcopacy in the Christian church, a system of government in which administrative and spiritual power over a district (diocese) is held by a bishop.

The Roman Catholic, Eastern Orthodox, Anglican, and Episcopal churches are episcopalian; episcopacy also exists in the Lutheran Church of Scandinavia and of the US, where bishops are elected for districts called "synods," and in most branches of the American Methodist Church, where bishops are supervisory officials.

Episcopalianism US term for the Anglican Communion.

episiotomy incision made in the perineum (the tissue bridging the vagina and rectum) to facilitate childbirth and prevent tearing of the vagina.

Episiotomy may be necessary, mainly for women giving birth for the first time, to widen the birth outlet and prevent perineal tearing. The incision is made in the second stage of labor, as the largest part of the baby's head begins to emerge from the birth canal. An episiotomy is quickly repaired using absorbable stitches under regional anesthetic using 1% lignocaine. Approximately 40% of patients find intercourse painful subsequently, but this is usually temporary.

epistemology branch of philosophy that examines the nature of knowledge and attempts to determine the limits of human understanding. Central issues include how knowledge is derived and how it is to be validated and tested.

epistle in the New Testament, any of the 21 letters to individuals or to the members of various churches written by Christian leaders, including the 13 written by St ⊃Paul. The term also describes a letter with a suggestion of pomposity and literary affectation, and a letter addressed to someone in the form of a poem, as in the epistles of ◇Horace and ◇Pope.

The **epistolary novel**, a story told as a series of (fictitious) letters, was popularized by Samuel ◇Richardson in the 18th century.

EPNS abbreviation for **electroplated nickel silver**; see ◇electroplating.

epoch subdivision of a geological period in the geological time scale. Epochs are sometimes given their own names (such as the Paleocene, Eocene, Oligocene, Miocene, and Pliocene epochs comprising the Tertiary period), or they are referred to as the late, early, or middle portions of a given period (as the Late Cretaceous or the Middle Triassic epoch).

epoxy resin synthetic ◇resin used as an ◇adhesive and as an ingredient in paints. Household epoxy resin adhesives come in component form as two separate tubes of chemical, one tube containing resin, the other a curing agent (hardener). The two chemicals are mixed just before application, and the mix soon sets hard.

EPROM (acronym for **erasable programmable read-only memory**) computer memory device in the form of an ◇integrated circuit (chip) that can record data and retain it indefinitely. The data can be erased by exposure to ultraviolet light, and new data recorded. Other kinds of computer memory chips are ◇ROM (read-only memory), ◇PROM (programmable read-only memory), and ◇RAM (random-access memory).

Epsom salts $MgSO_4.7H_2O$ hydrated magnesium sulfate, used as a relaxant and laxative and added to baths to soothe the skin. The name is derived from a bitter saline spring at Epsom, Surrey, England, which contains the salt in solution.

Epstein Jacob 1880–1959. British sculptor, born in New York. He experimented with abstract forms, but is chiefly known for his controversial muscular nude figures such as **Genesis** 1931 (Whitworth Art Gallery, Manchester). He was better appreciated as a portraitist (bust of Einstein, 1933), and in later years executed several monumental figures, notably the expressive bronze of *St Michael and the Devil* 1959 (Coventry Cathedral).

equal opportunities the right to be employed or considered for employment without discrimination on the grounds of race, gender, physical or mental handicap.

equation in mathematics, expression that represents the equality of two expressions involving constants and/or variables, and thus usually includes an equals sign (=). For example, the equation $A = \pi r^2$ equates the area A of a circle of radius r to the product πr^2. The algebraic equation $y = mx + c$ is the general one in coordinate geometry for a straight line.

If a mathematical equation is true for all variables in a given domain, it is sometimes called an identity and denoted by ≡. Thus $(x + y)^2 \equiv x^2 + 2xy + y^2$ for all $x, y \in R$.

An **indeterminate equation** is an equation for which there is an infinite set of solutions—for example, $2x = y$. A **diophantine equation** is an indeterminate equation in which the solution and terms must be whole numbers (after Diophantus of Alexandria, c. AD 250).

equations of motion mathematical equations that give the position and velocity of a moving object at any time. Given the mass of an object, the forces acting on it, and its initial position and velocity, the equations of motion are used to calculate its position and velocity at any later time. The equations must be based on ◇Newton's laws of motion or, if speeds near that of light are involved, on the theory of ◇relativity.

equator the **terrestrial equator** is the ◇great circle whose plane is perpendicular to the Earth's axis (the line joining the poles). Its length is 24,901.8 mi/40,092 km, divided into 360 degrees of longitude. The **celestial equator** is the circle in which the plane of the Earth's equator intersects the ◇celestial sphere.

Equatorial Guinea country in W central Africa, bounded N by Cameroon, E and S by Gabon, and W by the Atlantic Ocean; also five offshore islands including Bioko, off the coast of Cameroon.

government The constitution of 1982, approved by referendum, provides for a president and a house of 41 representatives of the people, elected by universal suffrage for a five-year term. The president governs with the supreme military council. Political parties have been banned.

history The area was inhabited by Pygmies before the 1200s, followed by various ethnic groups settling the mainland and islands. Reached by Portuguese explorers 1472, the islands came under Spanish rule in the mid-1800s and the mainland territory of Río Muni (now Mbini) 1885, the whole colony being known as Spanish Guinea. From 1959 the territory was a Spanish Overseas Province, with internal autonomy from 1963.

dictatorship After 190 years of Spanish rule, Equatorial Guinea became fully independent 1968, with Francisco Macias Nguema as president with a coalition government. In 1970 he banned all political parties and replaced them with one, the United National Party (PUN). Two years later he declared himself president for life and established a dictatorship, controlling press and radio and forbidding citizens to leave the country. There were many arrests and executions 1976–77. He also established close relations with the Soviet bloc.

military regime In 1979 he was overthrown in a coup by his nephew, Lt-Col Teodoro Obiang Nguema Mbasogo, with at least the tacit approval of Spain. Macias was tried and executed. Obiang expelled the Soviet advisers and technicians and renewed economic and political ties with Spain. He banned the PUN and other political parties and ruled through a supreme military council. Coups against him 1981 and 1983 were unsuccessful, and he was reelected 1982 and 1989. In 1992 a new constitution was introduced and elections held, but the members of the house of representatives were all nominated by the president and elected unopposed. *See illustration box.*

equestrianism skill in horse riding, as practiced under International Equestrian Federation rules. An Olympic sport, there are three main branches of equestrianism: showjumping, dressage, and three-day eventing.

Showjumping is horse-jumping over a course of fences. The winner is usually the competitor with fewest "faults" (penalty marks given for knocking down or refusing fences), but in timed competitions it is the competitor completing the course most quickly, additional seconds being added for mistakes.

Dressage tests the horse's obedience skills and the rider's control. Tests consist of a series of movements at walk, trot, and canter, with each movement marked by judges who look for suppleness, balance, and a special harmony between rider and horse. The term is derived from the French "dresser," which means training. It became an Olympic sport 1960.

Equatorial Guinea
Republic of (*República de Guinea Ecuatorial*)

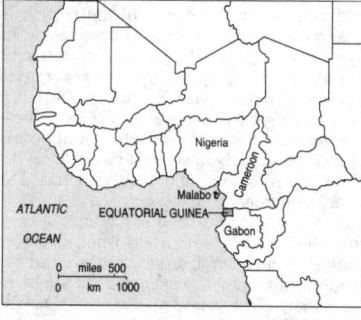

area 10,828 sq mi/28,051 sq km
capital Malabo (Bioko)
cities Bata, Mbini (Río Muni)
physical comprises mainland Río Muni, plus the small islands of Corisco, Elobey Grande and Elobey Chico, and Bioko (formerly Fernando Po) together with Annobón (formerly Pagalu)
features volcanic mountains on Bioko
head of state and government Teodoro Obiang Nguema Mbasogo from 1979
political system one-party military republic
political party Democratic Party of Equatorial Guinea (PDGE), militarily controlled
exports cocoa, coffee, timber
currency ekuele; CFA franc
population (1988 est) 336,000 (plus 110,000 estimated to live in exile abroad); growth rate 2.2% p.a.
life expectancy men 44, women 48
languages Spanish (official); pidgin English is widely spoken, and on Annobón (whose people were formerly slaves of the Portuguese) a Portuguese dialect; Fang and other African dialects spoken on Río Muni
religions nominally Christian, mainly Catholic, but in 1978 Roman Catholicism was banned
literacy 55% (1984)
GDP $90 million (1987); $220 per head
chronology
1778 Fernando Po (Bioko Island) ceded to Spain.
1885 Mainland territory came under Spanish rule; colony known as Spanish Guinea.
1968 Independence achieved from Spain. Francisco Macias Nguema became first president, soon assuming dictatorial powers.
1979 Macias overthrown and replaced by his nephew, Teodoro Obiang Nguema Mbasogo, who established a military regime. Macias tried and executed.
1982 Obiang elected president unopposed for another seven years. New constitution adopted.
1989 Obiang reelected president.
1992 New constitution adopted; elections held, but president continued to nominate those for top government posts.

Three-Day Eventing tests the all-round abilities of a horse and rider in dressage, cross-country, and showjumping.

The major showjumping events include the World Championship, first held 1953 for men, and 1965 for women (since 1978 men and women have competed together).

equilateral of a geometrical figure, having all sides of equal length.

For example, a rhombus is an equilateral parallelogram. An equilateral triangle is also equiangular, which means that all three angles are equal as well.

equilibrium in physics, an unchanging condition in which the forces acting on a particle or system of particles (a body) cancel out, or in which energy is distributed among the particles of a system in the most probable way; or the state in which a body is at rest or moving at constant velocity. A body is in *thermal equilibrium* with its surroundings if no heat enters or leaves it, so that all its parts are at the same temperature as the surroundings.

equinox the points in spring and autumn at which the Sun's path, the ◊ecliptic, crosses the celestial equator, so that the day and night are of approximately equal length. The *vernal equinox* occurs about March 21 and the *autumnal equinox*, Sept 23.

equity a company's assets, less its liabilities, which are the property of the owner or stockholders. Popularly, equities are stocks and shares which do not pay interest at fixed rates but pay dividends based on the company's performance. The value of equities tends to rise over the long term, but in the short term they are a risk investment because of fluctuating values. Equity is also used to refer to the paid value of mortgaged real property, most commonly a house.

With changes in US tax regulations, from the late 1980s, home-equity loans (second mortgages) have become a very popular financial tool, since the interest is, like mortgage interest, tax deductible.

Equity a shortened term for the American Actors' Equity Association, the labor union for professional actors in the theater.

era any of the major divisions of geological time, each including several periods, but smaller than an eon. The currently recognized eras all fall within the Phanerozoic eon—or the vast span of time, starting about 590 million years ago, when fossils are found to become abundant. The eras in ascending order are the Paleozoic, Mesozoic, and Cenozoic. We are living in the Recent epoch of the Quaternary period of the Cenozoic era.

Erasmus Desiderius *c.* 1466–1536. Dutch scholar and leading humanist of the Renaissance era, who taught and studied all over Europe and was a prolific writer. His pioneer translation of the Greek New Testament 1516 exposed the Vulgate as a second-hand document. Although opposed to dogmatism and abuse of church power, he remained impartial during Martin ◊Luther's conflict with the pope.

Erasmus was born in Rotterdam, and as a youth he was a monk in an Augustinian monastery near Gouda. After becoming a priest, he went to study in Paris 1495. He paid the first of a number of visits to England 1499, where he met the physician Thomas Linacre, the politician Thomas More, and the Bible interpreter John Colet, and for a time was professor of

divinity and Greek at Cambridge University. He edited the writings of St Jerome, and published *Colloquia* (dialogues on contemporary subjects) 1519. In 1521 he went to Basel, Switzerland, where he edited the writings of the early Christian leaders.

Erasmus Prize prize awarded annually since 1958 to outstanding contributors to international understanding, usually in social or cultural fields. Previous winners include Martin Buber, Herbert Read, Robert Schuman, and Jan Tinbergen.

Erastianism belief that the church should be subordinated to the state. The name is derived from Thomas Erastus (1534–83), a German-Swiss theologian and opponent of Calvinism, who maintained in his writings that the church should not have the power of excluding people as a punishment for sin.

Eratosthenes *c.* 276–194 BC. Greek geographer and mathematician whose map of the ancient world was the first to contain lines of latitude and longitude, and who calculated the Earth's circumference with an error of about 10%. His mathematical achievements include a method for duplicating the cube, and for finding ◊prime numbers (Eratosthenes' sieve).

erbium soft, lustrous, grayish, metallic element of the lanthanide series, symbol Er, atomic number 68, atomic weight 167.26. It occurs with the element yttrium or as a minute part of various minerals. It was discovered 1843 by Carl Mosander (1797–1858), and named after the town of Ytterby, Sweden, where the lanthanides (rare-earth elements) were first found.

Erebus, Mount the world's southernmost active volcano, 12,452 ft/3,794 m high, on Ross Island, Antarctica.

It contains a lake of molten lava, that scientists are investigating in the belief that it can provide a "window" onto the magma beneath the Earth's crust.

Erebus in Greek mythology, the god of darkness and the intermediate region between upper Earth and ◊Hades.

ergonomics study of the relationship between people and the furniture, tools, and machinery they use at work. The object is to improve work performance by removing sources of muscular stress and general fatigue: for example, by presenting data and control panels in easy-to-view form, making office furniture comfortable, and creating a generally pleasant environment.

ergosterol substance that, under the action of the sun's ultraviolet rays on the skin, gives rise to the production of vitamin D—a vitamin that helps in calcium and phosphorus metabolism, promotes bone-formation, and in children prevents ◊rickets.

Ergosterol $C_{28}H_{43}OH$ is a ◊sterol that occurs in ergot (hence the name), yeast and other fungi, and some animal fats. The principal source of commercial ergosterol is yeast.

ergot certain parasitic fungi (especially of the genus *Claviceps*), whose brown or black grainlike masses replace the kernels of rye or other cereals. *C. purpurea* attacks the rye plant. Ergot poisoning is caused by eating infected bread, resulting in burning pains, gangrene, and convulsions.

The large grains of the fungus contain the alkaloid ergotamine.

ergotamine ◊alkaloid $C_{33}H_{35}O_5N_5$ administered to treat migraine. Isolated from ergot, a

fungus that colonizes rye, it relieves symptoms by causing the cranial arteries to constrict. Its use is limited by severe side effects, including nausea and abdominal pain.

Erhard Ludwig 1897–1977. West German Christian Democrat politician, chancellor of the Federal Republic 1963–66. The "economic miracle" of West Germany's recovery after World War II is largely attributed to Erhard's policy of social free enterprise (German *Marktwirtschaft*), which he initiated during his period as federal economics minister (1949–63).

erica in botany, any plant of the genus *Erica*, family Ericaceae, including the heathers. There are about 500 species, distributed mainly in South Africa with some in Europe.

Ericsson John 1803–1889. Swedish-born US engineer who took out a patent to produce screw-propeller powered paddle-wheel ships 1836. He built a number of such ships, including the *Monitor*, which was successfully deployed during the American Civil War.

Ericsson Leif *c.* AD 1000. Norse explorer, son of Eric the Red, who sailed west from Greenland about 1000 to find a country first sighted by Norsemen 986. Landing with 35 companions in North America, he called it Vinland, because he discovered grape vines growing there.

The story was confirmed 1963 when a Norwegian expedition, led by Helge Ingstad, discovered remains of a Viking settlement (dated about 1000) near the fishing village of L'Anse-aux-Meadows at the northern tip of Newfoundland.

Eric the Red 940–1010. Allegedly the first European to find Greenland. According to a 13th-century saga, he was the son of a Norwegian chieftain, and was banished from Iceland about 982 for murder. He then sailed westward and discovered a land that he called Greenland.

Eridanus in astronomy, the sixth largest constellation, which meanders from the celestial equator deep into the southern hemisphere of the sky. Its brightest star is ◊Achernar. Eridanus is represented as a river.

Erie city and port on the Pennsylvania bank of Lake Erie; population (1981) 120,000. It has heavy industries and a trade in iron, grain, and freshwater fish. A French fort was built on the site 1753, and a permanent settlement was laid out 1795.

Erie, Lake fourth largest of the Great Lakes of North America, connected to Lake Ontario by the Niagara River and bypassed by the Welland Canal; area 9,930 sq mi/25,720 sq km.

It is linked to Lake Huron by Lake St Clair and the St Clair and Detroit rivers and to the Hudson River by the New York State Barge Canal. It is an important component of the St Lawrence Seaway. Lake Erie ports include Cleveland and Toledo, Ohio; Erie, Pennsylvania; and Buffalo, New York. A US naval victory near the W end of the lake on Sept 9, 1813 forced the British to evacuate Detroit. The shallowest of the Great Lakes, Lake Erie has become severely polluted from industrial and municipal waste.

Erin poetic name for Ireland, derived from the dative case Érinn of the Gaelic name Ériu, possibly derived from Sanskrit "western."

Eritrea province of N Ethiopia
area 45,394 sq mi/117,600 sq km

capital Asmara

cities Assab and Massawa (Ethiopia's outlets to the sea)

physical coastline on the Red Sea 620 mi/ 1,000 km; narrow coastal plain that rises to an inland plateau

products coffee, salt, citrus fruits, grains, cotton

currency birr

population (1984) 2,615,000

language Amharic (official)

religion Muslim

history part of an ancient Ethiopian kingdom until the 7th century; under Ethiopian influence until it fell to the Turks mid-16th century; Italian colony 1889–1941, when it was the base for Italian invasion of Ethiopia; under British administration from 1941 to 1952, when it became an autonomous part of Ethiopia. Since 1962, when it became a region, various secessionist movements have risen. During the civil war in the 1970s, guerrillas held most of Eritrea; the Ethiopian government, backed by Soviet and Cuban forces, recaptured most towns 1978. Resistance continued throughout the 1980s, aided by conservative Gulf states, and some cooperation with guerrillas in Tigré province. The collapse of Ethiopia's government 1991 led to the recognition of Eritrea's right to seek independence.

Erivan alternative transliteration of ◊Yerevan, capital of Armenia.

ermine short-tailed weasel *Mustela erminea*, of the N hemisphere, whose winter coat becomes white. In N latitudes the coat becomes completely white, except for a black tip to the tail, but in warmer regions the back may remain brownish. The alternate Eurasian name "stoat" is used especially during the summer, when the coat is brown. The fur is used commercially.

Ernst Max 1891–1976. German artist who worked in France 1922–38 and in the US from 1941. He was an active Dadaist, experimenting with collage, photomontage, and surreal images, and helped found the Surrealist movement 1924. His paintings are highly diverse.

Ernst first exhibited in Berlin 1916. He produced a "collage novel," *La Femme cent têtes* 1929, worked on films with Salvador Dali and Luis Buñuel, and designed sets and costumes for Sergei Diaghilev and the Ballets Russes. His pictures range from smooth Surrealist images to highly textured emotive abstracts, from 1925 making use of frottage (rubbing over textured materials).

Eros in Greek mythology, boy-god of love, traditionally armed with bow and arrows. He was the son of Aphrodite (Roman, Venus), and fell in love with ◊Psyche. He is identified with the Roman Cupid.

Eros in astronomy, an asteroid, discovered 1898, that can pass 14 million mi/22 million km from the Earth, as observed in 1975. Eros was the first asteroid to be discovered that has an orbit coming within that of Mars. It is elongated, measures about 22 × 7 mi/36 × 12 km, rotates around its shortest axis every 5.3 hours, and orbits the Sun every 1.8 years.

erosion wearing away of the Earth's surface, caused by the breakdown and transportation of particles of rock or soil (by contrast, ◊weathering does not involve transportation). Agents of erosion include the sea, rivers, glaciers, and wind. Water, consisting of sea waves and currents, rivers, and rain; ice, in the form of glaciers; and wind, hurling sand fragments against exposed rocks and moving dunes along, are the most potent forces of erosion. People also contribute to erosion by bad farming practices and the cutting down of forests, which can lead to the formation of dust bowls.

error detection in computing, the techniques that enable a program to detect incorrect data. A common method is to add a check digit to important codes, such as account numbers and product codes. The digit is chosen so that the code conforms to a rule that the program can verify. Another technique involves calculating the sum (called the hash total) of each instance of a particular item of data, and storing it at the end of the data.

Ershad Hussain Mohammad 1930– . Military ruler of Bangladesh 1982–90. He became chief of staff of the Bangladeshi army 1979 and assumed power in a military coup 1982. As president from 1983, Ershad introduced a successful rural-oriented economic program. He was re-elected 1986 and lifted martial law, but faced continuing political opposition, which forced him to resign Dec 1990. In 1991 he was formally charged with the illegal possession of arms, convicted, and sentenced to ten years' imprisonment. He received a further sentence of three years' imprisonment Feb 1992 after being convicted of corruption.

erysipelas in medicine, an acute disease of the skin or mucous membranes due to infection by a streptococcus bacterium. Starting at some point where the skin is broken or injured, the infection spreads, producing a swollen red patch with small blisters and generalized fever. The condition is now rare.

erythromycin an antibiotic with the chemical formula $C_{37}H_{67}NO_{13}$, isolated from a red-pigmented soil bacterium, *Streptomyces erythreus*. It is used in the treatment of a wide range of bacterial diseases and usually administered orally in the form of various salts and esters.

Erzurum capital of Erzurum province, NE Turkey; population (1985) 253,000. It is a center of agricultural trade and mining, and has a military base.

Esaki Leo 1925– . Japanese physicist who in 1957 noticed that electrons could sometimes "tunnel" through the barrier formed at the junctions of certain semiconductors. The effect is now widely used in the electronics industry. For this early discovery Esaki shared the 1973 Nobel Prize for Physics with British physicist Brian Josephson and Norwegian-born US physicist Ivar Giaever (1929–).

Esarhaddon King of Assyria from 680 BC, when he succeeded his father ◊Sennacherib. He conquered Egypt 674–71 BC.

Esau in the Old Testament, the son of Isaac and Rebekah, and the hirsute elder twin brother of Jacob. Jacob tricked the blind Isaac into giving him the blessing intended for Esau by putting on goatskins for Isaac to feel. Earlier Esau had sold his birthright to Jacob for a "mess of red pottage." Esau was the ancestor of the Edomites.

escalator automatic moving staircase that carries people between floors or levels. It consists of treads linked in an endless belt arranged to form strips (steps), powered by an electric motor that moves both steps and handrails at the same speed. Towards the top and bottom the steps flatten out for ease of passage. The first escalator was exhibited in Paris 1900.

escape velocity in physics, minimum velocity with which an object must be projected for it to escape from the gravitational pull of a planetary body. In the case of the Earth, the escape velocity is 6.9 mps/11.2 kps; the Moon 1.5 mps/2.4 kps; Mars 3.1 mps/5 kps; and Jupiter 37 mps/59.6 kps.

escheat (Old French *escheir* "to fall") in feudal society, the reversion of lands to the lord in the event of the tenant dying without heirs or being convicted for treason. By the late Middle Ages in W Europe, tenants had insured against their lands escheating by granting them to trustees, or feoffees, who would pass them on to the grantor nominated in the will. Lands held directly by the king could not legally be disposed of in this way.

Escher M(aurits) C(ornelis) 1902–1972. Dutch graphic artist. His prints are often based on mathematical concepts and contain paradoxes and illusions. The lithograph *Ascending and Descending* 1960, with interlocking staircases creating a perspective puzzle, is a typical work.

escrow (Old French *escroe*, "scroll") in law, a document sealed and delivered to a third party and not released or coming into effect until some condition has been fulfilled or performed, whereupon the document takes full effect.

Money deposited with a neutral third party to be delivered when conditions of a contract are fulfilled, as in real estate transactions, is commonly referred to as escrow.

esker geological feature of formerly glaciated areas consisting of a long, steep-walled narrow ridge, often sinuous and sometimes branching. Eskers consist of stratified glacial drift and are thought to form by the deposits of streams running through tunnels underneath melting stagnant ice. When the glacier finally disappeared, the old stream deposits were left standing as a high ridge. Eskers vary in height 10–100 ft/3–30 m and can run to about 100 mi/160 km in length.

Eskimo (Algonquian "eater of raw meat") member of a group of Asian, North American, and Greenland Arctic peoples who migrated east from Siberia about 2,000 years ago, exploiting the marine coastal environment and the tundra.

Eskimo languages belong to the Eskimo–Aleut family and form a continuum of dialects from Siberia east to Greenland. Some Arctic peoples, for example the ◊Inuit, consider the term Eskimo offensive.

esophagus the passage by which food travels from mouth to stomach. The human esophagus is about 9 in/23 cm long. Its upper end is at the bottom of the ◊pharynx, immediately behind the windpipe.

ESP abbreviation for ◊*extrasensory perception*.

esparto grass *Stipa tenacissima*, native to S Spain, S Portugal, and the Balearics, but now widely grown in dry, sandy locations throughout the world. The plant is just over 3 ft/1 m high, producing grayish-green leaves, which are used for making paper, ropes, baskets, mats, and cables.

A similar grass *Lygeum spartum* from the same area and used for the same purposes is also called esparto.

Esperanto language devised 1887 by Polish

philologist Ludwig L Zamenhof (1859–1917) as an international auxiliary language. For its structure and vocabulary it draws on Latin, the Romance languages, English, and German.

Esperanto spread from Europe to Japan, Brazil, and, especially, China. Its structure is completely regular, with consistent endings for nouns and adjectives. The spelling is phonetic, but the accent varies according to the regional background of its users.

espionage the practice of spying; a way to gather ⍟intelligence.

Esquipulas pilgrimage town in Chiquimula department, SE Guatemala; seat of the "Black Christ" which is a symbol of peace throughout Central America. In May 1986 five Central American presidents met here to discuss a plan for peace in the region.

Esquivel Adolfo 1932– . Argentinian sculptor and architect. As leader of the Servicio de Paz y Justicia (Peace and Justice Service), a Catholic-Protestant human-rights organization, he was awarded the 1980 Nobel Peace Prize.

essay short piece of nonfiction, often dealing from a personal point of view with some particular subject. The essay became a recognized genre with the French writer Montaigne's *Essais* 1580. Francis Bacon's *Essays* 1597 are among the most famous in English. From the 19th century the essay was increasingly used in Europe and the US as a vehicle for literary criticism.

Abraham Cowley, whose essays appeared 1668, brought a greater ease and freedom to the genre than it had possessed before in England, but it was with the development of periodical literature in the 18th century that the essay became a widely used form. The great names are Addison and Steele, with their *Tatler* and *Spectator* papers, and later Johnson and Goldsmith. In North America Benjamin Franklin was noted for his style. A new era was inaugurated by Lamb's *Essays of Elia* 1820; to the same period belong Leigh Hunt, Hazlitt, and De Quincey in England, Sainte-Beuve in France, and Emerson and Thoreau in the US. Hazlitt may be regarded as the originator of the critical essay, and his successors include Arnold and Gosse. Macaulay, whose essays began to appear shortly after those of Lamb, presents a strong contrast to Lamb with his vigorous but less personal tone. There was a revival of the form during the closing years of the 19th and beginning of the 20th centuries, in the work of R L Stevenson, Oliver Wendell Holmes, Anatole France, Théophile Gautier, and Max Beerbohm. The literary journalistic tradition of the essay was continued by James Thurber, Mark Twain, H L Mencken, Edmund Wilson, Desmond MacCarthy, and others, and the critical essay by George Orwell, Cyril Connolly, F R Leavis, T S Eliot, Norman Mailer, John Updike, and others. However, its leisured approach made it a less often used form by the mid-20th century, although its spirit survived in the radio "essays" of Alistair Cooke, and in the "opinion pieces" of newspapers and magazines.

Essen city in North Rhine–Westphalia, Germany; population (1988) 615,000. It is the administrative center of the Ruhr, with textile, chemical, and electrical industries.

Essene member of an ancient Jewish religious sect located in the area near the Dead Sea *c.* 200 BC–AD 200, whose members lived a life of denial and asceticism, as they believed that the day of judgment was imminent.

The ⍟Dead Sea Scrolls, discovered in 1947, are believed by some scholars to be the library of the community. John the Baptist may have been a member of the Essenes.

Essex county in SE England
area 1,417 sq mi/3,670 sq km
cities Chelmsford (administrative headquarters), Colchester; ports: Harwich, Tilbury; resorts: Southend, Clacton
features former royal hunting ground of Epping Forest (controlled from 1882 by the City of London); the marshy coastal headland of the Naze; since 1111 at Great Dunmow the Dunmow flitch (side of cured pork) can be claimed every four years by any couple proving to a jury they have not regretted their marriage within the year (winners are few); Stansted, London's third airport
products dairying, cereals, fruit
population (1987) 1,522,000.

Essex Robert Devereux, 2nd Earl of Essex 1566–1601. English soldier and politician. He became a favorite with Queen Elizabeth I from 1587, but was executed because of his policies in Ireland.

In 1599 he led an army unsuccessfully against Irish rebels under the Earl of Tyrone in Ulster, made an unauthorized truce with Tyrone, and returned without permission to England. Forbidden to return to court, he marched into the City of London at the head of a body of supporters, was promptly arrested, tried for treason, and beheaded on Tower Green.

estate in law, the rights that a person has in relation to any property. *Real estate* is an interest in any land; *personal estate* is an interest in any other kind of property.

Estate property refers to the assets of a deceased person.

estate in European history, an order of society that enjoyed a specified share in government. In medieval theory, there were usually three estates—the **nobility**, the **clergy**, and the **commons**—with the functions of, respectively, defending society from foreign aggression and internal disorder, attending to its spiritual needs, and working to produce the base with which to support the other two orders.

When parliaments and representative assemblies developed from the 13th century, their organization reflected this theory, with separate houses for the nobility, the commons (usually burghers and gentry), and the clergy.

ester organic compound formed by the reaction between an alcohol and an acid, with the elimination of water. Unlike ⍟salts, esters are covalent compounds.

Esther in the Old Testament, the wife of the Persian king Ahasuerus (Xerxes I), who prevented the extermination of her people by the king's vizier Haman. Their deliverance is celebrated in the Jewish festival of Purim. Her story is told in the Old Testament Book of Esther.

estivation in zoology, a state of inactivity and reduced metabolic activity, similar to ⍟hibernation, that occurs during the dry season in species such as lungfishes and snails. In botany, the term is used to describe the way in which flower petals and sepals are folded in the buds. It is an important feature in ⍟plant classification.

Estonia country in N Europe, bounded E by Russia, S by Latvia, and N and W by the Baltic Sea.

government There is a 105-deputy, popularly elected Ülemnõukogu (parliament), whose members elect a chair to serve as state president, and a prime minister.

history Independent states were formed in the area now known as Estonia during the 1st century AD. In the 13th century southern Estonia came under the control of the ⍟Teutonic Knights, German crusaders, who converted the inhabitants to Christianity. The Danes, who had taken control of northern Estonia, sold this area to the Teutonic Knights 1324. By the 16th century German nobles owned much of the land. In 1561 Sweden took control of the north, with Poland governing the south; Sweden ruled the whole country 1625–1710. Estonia came under Russian control 1710, but it was not until the 19th century that the Estonians started their movement for independence.

struggle for independence Estonia was occupied by German troops during World War I. The Soviet forces, who tried to regain power 1917, were overthrown by Germany in March 1918, restored Nov 1918, and again overthrown with the help of the British navy May 1919, when Estonia, having declared independence 1918, was established as a democratic republic. A fascist coup 1934 replaced the government.

Soviet republic In 1939 Germany and the USSR secretly agreed that Estonia should come under Russian influence and the country was incorporated into the USSR as the Estonian Soviet Socialist Republic 1940. During World War II Estonia was again occupied by Germany 1941–44, but the USSR subsequently regained control.

renewed nationalism Nationalist dissent grew from 1980. In 1988 Estonia adopted its own constitution, with a power of veto on all Soviet legislation. The new constitution allowed private property and placed land and natural resources under Estonian control. An Estonian popular front (Rahvarinne) was established Oct 1988 to campaign for democratization, increased autonomy, and eventual independence, and held mass rallies. In Nov of the same year Estonia's supreme soviet (state assembly) voted to declare the republic "sovereign" and thus autonomous in all matters except military and foreign affairs, although the presidium of the USSR's supreme soviet rejected this as unconstitutional. In 1989 a law was passed replacing Russian with Estonian as the main language and in Nov of that year Estonia's assembly denounced the 1940 incorporation of the republic into the USSR as "forced annexation."

multiparty elections Several parties had sprung up by the elections of March 1990—the Popular Front, the Association for a Free Estonia, and the Russian-oriented International Movement—and a coalition government was formed. A plebiscite in the spring of 1991 voted 77.8% in favor of independence. By the summer the republic had embarked on a program of privatization. The prices of agricultural products were freed in July 1991.

independence On Aug 20, 1991, in the midst of the attempted anti-Gorbachev coup in the USSR, during which Red Army troops were moved into Tallinn to seize the television transmitter and the republic's main port was blocked by the Soviet navy, Estonia declared its full independence (it had previously been in a "period of transition") and outlawed the Communist Party. In Sept 1991 this declaration was recognized by the Soviet government and Western nations and the new state was granted membership in the United Nations and

Estonia
Republic of

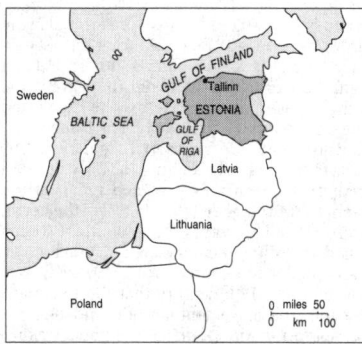

area 17,000 sq mi/45,000 sq km
capital Tallinn
cities Tartu, Narva, Kohtla-Järve, Pärnu
physical lakes and marshes in a partly forested plain; 481 mi/774 km of coastline; mild climate
features Lake Peipus and Narva River forming boundary with Russian Federation; Baltic islands, the largest of which is Saaremaa Island
head of state Arnold Rüütel from 1988
head of government Tiit Vahl from 1992
political system emergent democracy
political parties Estonian Popular Front (Rahvarinne), nationalist; Association for a Free Estonia, nationalist; Fatherland Group, right-wing; International Movement, ethnic Russian; Estonian Green Party, environmentalist
products oil and gas (from shale), wood products, flax, dairy and pig products
currency kroon
population (1989) 1,573,000 (Estonian 62%, Russian 30%, Ukrainian 3%, Byelorussian 2%)
language Estonian, allied to Finnish
religion traditionally Lutheran
chronology
1918 Estonia declared its independence.

March: Soviet forces, who had tried to regain control from occupying German forces during World War I, were overthrown by German troops. Nov: Soviet troops took control after German withdrawal.
1919 Soviet rule overthrown with help of British navy; Estonia declared a democratic republic.
1934 Fascist coup replaced government.
1940 Estonia incorporated into USSR.
1941–44 German occupation during World War II.
1944 USSR regained control.
1980 Beginnings of nationalist dissent.
1988 Adopted own constitution, with power of veto on all centralized Soviet legislation. Popular Front (Rahvarinne) established to campaign for democracy. Estonia's supreme soviet (state assembly) voted to declare the republic "sovereign" and autonomous in all matters except military and foreign affairs; rejected by USSR as unconstitutional.
1989 Estonian replaced Russian as main language.
1990 Feb: Communist Party (CP) monopoly of power abolished; multiparty system established. March: pro-independence candidates secured majority after republic elections; coalition government formed with Popular Front leader Edgar Savisaar as prime minister; Arnold Rüütel became president. May: prewar constitution partially restored.
1991 March: independence plebiscite overwhelmingly approved. Aug: full independence declared after abortive anti-Gorbachev coup; CP outlawed. Sept: independence recognized by Soviet government and Western nations; admitted into United Nations (UN) and Conference on Security and Cooperation in Europe (CSCE).
1992 Jan: Savisaar resigned owing to his government's inability to alleviate food and energy shortages; new government formed by Tiit Vahl. June: New constitution approved. Sept: presidential election inconclusive; right-wing Fatherland Group did well in general election.

also entered the ⟡Conference on Security and Cooperation in Europe.
economic problems Prime minister Edgar Savisaar and his cabinet resigned Jan 1992 after failing to alleviate food and energy shortages. Tiit Vahl, the former transport minister, formed a new government which included five key ministers unchanged from the previous cabinet. He proposed the lifting of the state of economic emergency which had recently been imposed by Savisaar. In June a new constitution was approved in a nationwide referendum, but the Sept 1992 presidential election failed to produce a clear winner, putting the onus on the parliament to elect a new head of state. In the parliamentary elections no single party won an overall majority but the right-wing Fatherland Group emerged with the largest number of seats. *See illustration box.*

Estonian member of the largest ethnic group in Estonia. There are 1 million speakers of the Estonian language, a member of the Finno-Ugric branch of the Uralic family. Most live in Estonia.

Estoril fashionable resort on the coast 13 mi/20 km W of Lisbon, Portugal; population (1981) 16,000. There is a Grand Prix motor-racing circuit.

estradiol type of ⟡estrogen (female sex hormone).

estrogen any of a group of hormones produced by the ⟡ovaries of vertebrates; the term is also used for various synthetic hormones that mimic their effects. (Some estrogens are also secreted by the cortex of the ⟡adrenal glands.) The principal estrogen in mammals is estradiol. Estrogens promote the development of female secondary sexual characteristics; stimulate egg production; and, in mammals, prepare the lining of the uterus for pregnancy.

estrus in mammals, the period during a female's reproductive cycle (also known as the estrous cycle) when mating is most likely to occur. It usually coincides with ovulation.

estuary river mouth widening into the sea, where fresh water mixes with salt water and tidal effects are felt.
    Estuaries are extremely rich in life forms and are breeding grounds for thousands of species. Water pollution threatens these ⟡ecosystems.

et al. abbreviation for *et alii* (Latin "and others"); used in bibliography.

etc. abbreviation for *et cetera* (Latin "and the rest").

etching a ⟡printmaking technique in which

the design is made from a metal plate (usually copper or zinc), which is covered with a waxy overlayer (ground) and then drawn on with an etching needle. The exposed areas are then "etched," or bitten into, by a corrosive agent (acid), so that they will hold ink for printing.
    The method was developed in Germany about 1500, the earliest dated etched print being of 1513. Among the earliest etchers were Dürer, van Dyck, Hollar, and Rembrandt. Some artists combine etching with ⟡aquatint.

Eteocles in Greek mythology, son of the incestuous union of ⟡Oedipus and ⟡Jocasta and brother of ⟡Polynices. He denied his brother a share in the kingship of Thebes, thus provoking the expedition of the ⟡Seven against Thebes, in which he and his brother died by each other's hands.

ethanal common name *acetaldehyde* CH_3CHO one of the chief members of the group of organic compounds known as ⟡aldehydes. It is a colorless inflammable liquid boiling at 69.6°F/20.8°C. Ethanal is formed by the oxidation of ethanol or ethene and is used to make many other organic chemical compounds.

ethane CH_3CH_3 colorless, odorless gas, the second member of the ⟡alkane series of hydrocarbons (paraffins).

ethane-1,2-diol technical name for ⟡glycol.

ethanoate common name *acetate* $CH_3CO_2^-$ negative ion derived from ethanoic (acetic) acid; any salt containing this ion. In textiles, acetate rayon is a synthetic fabric made from modified cellulose (wood pulp) treated with ethanoic acid; in photography, acetate film is a non-flammable film made of cellulose ethanoate.

ethanoic acid common name *acetic acid* CH_3CO_2H one of the simplest fatty acids (a series of organic acids). In the pure state it is a colorless liquid with an unpleasant pungent odor; it solidifies to an icelike mass of crystals at 62.4°F/16.7°C, and hence is often called glacial ethanoic acid. Vinegar contains 5% or more ethanoic acid, produced by fermentation.
    Cellulose (derived from wood or other sources) may be treated with ethanoic acid to produce a cellulose ethanoate (acetate) solution, which can be used to make plastic items by injection molding or extruded to form synthetic textile fibers.

ethanol common name *ethyl alcohol* C_2H_5OH alcohol found in beer, wine, cider, spirits, and other alcoholic drinks. When pure, it is a colorless liquid with a pleasant odor, miscible with water or ether; it burns in air with a pale blue flame. The vapor forms an explosive mixture with air and may be used in high-compression internal combustion engines. It is produced naturally by the fermentation of carbohydrates by yeast cells. Industrially, it can be made by absorption of ethene and subsequent reaction with water, or by the reduction of ethanal in the presence of a catalyst, and is widely used as a solvent.
    Ethanol is used as a raw material in the manufacture of ether, chloral, and iodoform. It can also be added to gasoline, where it improves the performance of the engine, or be used as a fuel in its own right (as in Brazil). Crops such as sugar cane may be grown to provide ethanol (by fermentation) for this purpose.

Ethelred II *the Unready c.* 968–1016. King

of England from 978. He tried to buy off the Danish raiders by paying Danegeld. In 1002, he ordered the massacre of the Danish settlers, provoking an invasion by Sweyn I of Denmark. War with Sweyn and Sweyn's son, Canute, occupied the rest of Ethelred's reign. He was nicknamed the "Unready" because of his apparent lack of foresight.

The son of King Edgar, Ethelred became king after the murder of his half brother, Edward the Martyr.

ethene common name *ethylene* C_2H_4 colorless, flammable gas, the first member of the ◊alkene series of hydrocarbons. It is the most widely used synthetic organic chemical and is used to produce the plastics polyethene (polyethylene), polychloroethene, and polyvinyl chloride (PVC). It is obtained from natural gas or coal gas, or by the dehydration of ethanol.

Ethene is produced during plant metabolism and is classified as a plant hormone. It is important in the ripening of fruit and in ◊abscission. Small amounts of ethene are often added to the air surrounding fruit to artificially promote ripening.

ether in chemistry, any of a series of organic chemical compounds having an oxygen atom linking the carbon atoms of two hydrocarbon radical groups (general formula R-O-R'); also the common name for ethoxyethane $C_2H_5OC_2H_5$ (also called diethyl ether). This is used as an anesthetic and as an external cleansing agent before surgical operations. It is also used as a solvent, and in the extraction of oils, fats, waxes, resins, and alkaloids.

Ethoxyethane is a colorless, volatile, inflammable liquid, slightly soluble in water, and miscible with ethanol. It is prepared by treatment of ethanol with excess concentrated sulfuric acid at 284°F/140°C.

ether or *aether* in the history of science, a hypothetical medium permeating all of space. The concept originated with the Greeks, and has been revived on several occasions to explain the properties and propagation of light. It was supposed that light and other electromagnetic radiation—even in outer space—needed a medium, the ether, in which to travel. The idea was abandoned with the acceptance of ◊relativity.

Its existence was disproved in 1887 by the classic Michelson–Morley experiment, which showed that light travels at the same speed in the direction of the Earth's motion through space as it does at right angles to the motion. This later led ◊Einstein to formulate his special theory of relativity.

Ethical Culture Movement movement during the late 19th and early 20th centuries designed to further the moral or ethical factor as the real substance and fundamental part of religion.

It originated in the New York Society for Ethical Culture founded by Felix Adler in 1876. Mainly Jewish at first, it soon attracted adherents of Christian and skeptical backgrounds. It had spread to England (where the first Ethical Society was founded 1888 by Dr Stanton Colt), Germany, and other countries by the turn of the century. In 1952 the International Humanist and Ethical Union was formed, with headquarters in Utrecht, the Netherlands.

ethics area of ◊philosophy concerned with human values, which studies the meanings of moral terms and theories of conduct and goodness; also called *moral philosophy*. It is one of the three main branches of contemporary philosophy.

The study of ethics began in ancient India and China, and began to be systematized by the Greek philosopher Socrates in the 5th century BC. Plato's *Republic* is an exposition of the nature of justice or righteousness, and ethical theory was advanced by Aristotle's *Nicomachean Ethics* and similar writings. The Cyrenaics, Epicureans, and Stoics advanced theories that have been many times revived.

The "Christian ethic" is mainly a combination of New Testament moral teaching with ideas drawn from Plato and Aristotle, combining hedonism and rationalism. Medieval ◊scholasticism saw God's will as the ethical standard but tempered it with Aristotelian ethics.

In the 17th and 18th centuries, Thomas Hobbes and David Hume were notable British ethical philosophers. One of the greatest contributors to ethical theory was the German Immanuel Kant, an idealist, with his "categorical imperative" (the obligation to obey absolute moral law), since conscience is to ethics as intelligence is to logic.

The utilitarian ethic (for the good of society rather than the individual) was expounded in the UK during the 18th and 19th centuries by Jeremy Bentham, J S Mill, and Herbert Spencer, and opposed by F H Bradley and T H Green, who linked ethics with metaphysics and emphasized the place of the individual in organized society. Utilitarianism has become the ostensible basis for law, politics, commerce, and social ethics, while conscience guides the individual.

Ethicists of the 20th century include G E Moore and C D Broad in the UK and John Dewey in the US.

◊Medical ethics concerns the provision of guidelines for doctors.

Ethiopia
People's Democratic Republic of
(*Hebretesebawit Ityopia*, formerly also known as **Abyssinia**)

area 471,653 sq mi/1,221,900 sq km
capital Addis Ababa
cities Asmara (capital of Eritrea), Dire Dawa; ports Massawa, Assab
physical a high plateau with central mountain range divided by Rift Valley; plains in E; source of Blue Nile River
environment more than 90% of the forests of the Ethiopian highlands have been destroyed since 1900
features Danakil and Ogaden deserts; ancient remains (in Aksum, Gondar, Lalibela, among others); only African country to retain its independence during the colonial period
head of state and government Meles Zenawi from 1991
political system transition to democratic socialist republic
political parties Ethiopian People's Revolutionary Democratic Front (EPRDF), nationalist, left of center; Tigré People's Liberation Front (TPLF); Eritrean People's Liberation Front (EPLF); Ethiopian People's Democratic Movement (EPDM); Oromo People's Democratic Organization (OPDO)
exports coffee, pulses, oilseeds, hides, skins
currency birr
population (1989 est) 47,709,000 (Oromo 40%, Amhara 25%, Tigré 12%, Sidamo 9%); growth rate 2.5% p.a.
life expectancy 38
languages Amharic (official), Tigrinya, Orominga, Arabic
religions Sunni Muslim 45%, Christian (Ethiopian Orthodox Church, which has had its own patriarch since 1976) 40%
literacy 35% (1988)
GDP $4.8 bn (1987); $104 per head
chronology
1889 Abyssinia reunited by Menelik II.
1930 Haile Selassie became emperor.
1962 Eritrea annexed by Haile Selassie; resistance movement began.
1974 Haile Selassie deposed and replaced by a military government led by General Teferi Benti. Ethiopia declared a socialist state.
1977 Teferi Benti killed and replaced by Col Mengistu Haile Mariam.
1977–79 "Red Terror" period in which Mengistu's regime killed thousands of innocent people.
1981–85 Ethiopia spent at least $2 billion on arms.
1984 WPE declared the only legal political party.
1985 Worst famine in more than a decade; Western aid sent and forcible internal resettlement programs undertaken.
1987 New constitution adopted, Mengistu Mariam elected president. New famine; food aid hindered by guerrillas.
1988 Mengistu agreed to adjust his economic policies in order to secure IMF assistance. Influx of refugees from Sudan.
1989 Coup attempt against Mengistu foiled. Peace talks with Eritrean rebels mediated by former US president Carter reported some progress.
1990 Rebels captured port of Massawa. Mengistu announced new reforms.
1991 Mengistu overthrown; transitional government set up by EPRDF. EPLF secured Eritrea; Eritrea's right to secede recognized. Meles Zenawi elected Ethiopia's new head of state and government. Isaias Afwerki became secretary-general of provisional government in Eritrea.

Ethiopia country in E Africa, bounded NE by Djibouti and the Red Sea, E and SE by Somalia, S by Kenya, and W and NW by Sudan.
government The constitution of 1987 provided for an 835-member national assembly, elected from nominees of political parties and other economic and social organizations. An interim representative government came into force 1991.
history Long subject to Egypt, the area became independent about the 11th century BC. The kingdom of ◊Aksum flourished 1st–10th centuries AD, reaching its peak about the 4th century with the introduction of Coptic Christianity from Egypt, and declining from

the 7th century as Islam expanded. The Arab conquests isolated Aksum from the rest of the Christian world.

During the 10th century there emerged a kingdom that formed the basis of Abyssinia, reinforced 1270 with the founding of a new dynasty. Although it remained independent throughout the period of European colonization of Africa, Abyssinia suffered civil unrest and several invasions from the 16th century, and was eventually reunited 1889 under ◊Menelik II, with Italian support. In 1896 Menelik put down an invasion by Italy, which claimed he had agreed to make the country an Italian protectorate, and annexed Ogaden in the southeast and several provinces to the west.

Ethiopian empire Ethiopia was ruled for over 50 years by ◊Haile Selassie, who became regent 1916, king 1928, and emperor 1930. The country was occupied by Italy 1935–41, and Haile Selassie went into exile in Britain. Ogaden was returned to Somalia, which was also under Italian control. Haile Selassie returned from exile 1941 and ruled until 1974, when he was deposed by the armed forces after famine, high inflation, growing unemployment, and demands for greater democracy. His palace and estates were nationalized, parliament dissolved, and the constitution suspended. Ethiopia was proclaimed a socialist state and rule was established by a Provisional Military Administrative Council (PMAC). Haile Selassie died 1975, aged 83, detained in an apartment in his former palace in Addis Ababa.

secessionist movements General Teferi Benti, who had led the uprising and been made head of state, was killed 1977 by fellow officers and replaced by Col Mengistu Haile Mariam. The Ethiopian empire had been built up by Haile Selassie and Menelik, and annexed regions had made frequent attempts to secede. The 1974 revolution encouraged secessionist movements to increase their efforts, and the military government had to fight to keep Eritrea and Ogaden, where Somalian troops were assisting local guerrillas.

The USSR, having adopted Ethiopia as a new ally, threatened to cut off aid to Somalia, and Cuban troops assisted Mengistu in ending the fighting there. Eritrea and its neighbor, Tigré, continued their struggle for independence.

famine Amid this confusion there was acute famine in the north, including Eritrea, when the rains failed for three successive seasons. In addition to a massive emergency aid program from many Western nations, the Ethiopian government tried to alleviate the problem by resettling people from the north in the more fertile south. By 1986 more than 500,000 had been forcibly resettled.

Tigré breaks free Meanwhile, the military regime had reestablished normal relations with most of its neighbors. In 1987 a new constitution was adopted and Col Mengistu Mariam was elected the country's first president. Tigré province was captured by the Eritrean People's Liberation Front (EPLF) and the Tigré People's Liberation Front (TPLF) Feb 1989, the first time the government had lost control of the entire province. A coup against Mengistu in May 1989 was put down and the military high command subsequently purged. Following a mediation offer by the former US president Jimmy ◊Carter, peace talks with the Eritrean rebels began Aug 1989. At the same time, droughts in the north threatened another widespread famine.

Mengistu ousted Rebel pressure on the Mengistu government increased steadily during early 1991; in May Mengistu fled the country when the Ethiopian People's Revolutionary Democratic Front (EPRDF) occupied Addis Ababa. The EPLF gained virtually complete control of Eritrea and secured the province's capital, Asmara, after 30 years of fighting.

transition period Peace and stability commissions were set up to monitor the end of the civil war. In July 1991 delegates from Ethiopia's political and ethnic groups met to organize a transitional government to administer the country until the elections planned for 1993. The conference also gave regional and ethnic groups the right to form their own countries, and agreed Eritrea's right to seek independence. On July 21, Meles Zenawi, leader of the EPRDF (which held a majority in Ethiopia's transitional legislature), was elected head of state. In Sept 1991 Isaias Afwerki, leader of the EPLF, became secretary-general of the provisional government of Eritrea. *See illustration box.*

ethnicity (from Greek *ethnos* "a people") people's own sense of cultural identity; a social term that overlaps with such concepts as race, nation, class, and religion.

Social scientists use the term **ethnic group** to refer to groups or societies who feel a common sense of identity, often based on a traditional shared culture, language, religion, and customs. It may or may not include common territory, skin color, or common descent. The US, for example, is often described as a **multiethnic society** because many members would describe themselves as members of an ethnic group (Jewish, black, or Irish, for example) as well as their national one (American).

ethnology the branch of anthropology that deals with the comparative study of contemporary cultures, acculturation, and human ecology.

ethology comparative study of animal behavior in its natural setting. Ethology is concerned with the causal mechanisms (both the stimuli that elicit behavior and the physiological mechanisms controlling it), as well as the development of behavior, its function, and its evolutionary history.

Ethology was pioneered during the 1930s by Konrad Lorenz and Karl von Frisch who, with Nikolaas Tinbergen, received the Nobel Prize in 1973. Ethologists believe that the significance of an animal's behavior can be understood only in its natural context, and emphasize the importance of field studies and an evolutionary perspective. A recent development within ethology is sociobiology, the study of the evolutionary function of ◊social behavior.

ethyl alcohol common name for ◊ethanol.

ethylene common name for ◊ethene.

ethylene glycol alternate name for ◊glycol.

ethyne common name **acetylene** CHCH colorless inflammable gas produced by mixing calcium carbide and water. It is the simplest member of the ◊alkyne series of hydrocarbons. It is used in the manufacture of the synthetic rubber neoprene, and in oxyacetylene welding and cutting.

Ethyne was discovered by Edmund Davy 1836 and was used in early gas lamps, where it was produced by the reaction between water and calcium carbide. Its combustion provides more heat, relatively, than almost any other

fuel known (its calorific value is five times that of hydrogen). This means that the gas gives an intensely hot flame; hence its use in oxyacetylene torches.

etiolation in botany, a form of growth seen in plants receiving insufficient light. It is characterized by long, weak stems, small leaves, and a pale yellowish color (◊chlorosis) owing to a lack of chlorophyll. The rapid increase in height enables a plant that is surrounded by others to quickly reach a source of light, after which a return to normal growth usually occurs.

Etna volcano on the east coast of Sicily, 10,906 ft/3,323 m, the highest in Europe. About 90 eruptions have been recorded since 1800 BC, yet because of the rich soil, the cultivated zone on the lower slopes is densely populated, including the coastal town of Catania. The most recent eruption was in Dec 1985.

Tours of this smoking volcano are conducted.

Etruscan member of an ancient people inhabiting Etruria, Italy (modern-day Tuscany and part of Umbria) from the 8th to 4th centuries BC. The Etruscan dynasty of the Tarquins ruled Rome 616–509 BC. At the height of their civilization, in the 6th century BC, the Etruscans achieved great wealth and power from their maritime strength. They were driven out of Rome 509 BC and eventually dominated by the Romans.

Etruscan art sculpture, painting, pottery, metalwork, jewelry, and design of the first known Italian civilization. Etruscan terracotta coffins (*sarcophagi*), carved with reliefs and topped with portraits of the dead reclining on one elbow, were to influence the later Romans and early Christians.

Most examples of Etruscan painting come from excavated tombs, whose frescos depict scenes of everyday life, mythology, and mortuary rites, typically in bright colors and a vigorous, animated style. Scenes of feasting, dancing, swimming, fishing, and playing evoke a confident people who enjoyed life to the full, and who even in death depicted themselves in a joyous and festive manner (as on their *sarcophagi*). The decline of their civilization, in the shadow of Rome's expansion, is reflected in their later art, which loses its original *joie de vivre* and whose figures assume a more somber appearance.

Influences from archaic Greece and the Middle East are evident, as are those from the preceding Iron Age Villanovan culture, but the full flowering of Etruscan art represents a unique synthesis of existing traditions and artistic innovation, which was to have a profound influence on the development of Western art.

etymology study of the origin and history of words within and across languages. It has two major aspects: the study of the phonetic and written forms of words, and of the semantics or meanings of those words.

Etymological research has been particularly successful in tracing the development of words and word elements within the Indo-European language family. Since languages are always changing and usage differs among cultures, it is important to trace words to their original sources. Standard dictionaries of a language such as English typically contain etymological information within square brackets at the end of each entry.

Euboea (Greek *Evvoia*) mountainous island off the east coast of Greece, in the Aegean sea;

area 1,450 sq mi/3,755 sq km; about 110 mi/177 km long; population (1981) 188,410. Mount Delphi reaches 5,721 ft/1,743 m. The chief town, Chalcis, is connected by a bridge to the mainland.

eucalyptus any tree of the genus *Eucalyptus* of the myrtle family Myrtaceae, native to Australia and Tasmania, where they are commonly known as gum trees. About 90% of Australian timber belongs to the eucalyptus genus, which comprises about 500 species. The trees have dark hardwood timber which is used principally for heavy construction as in railroad and bridge building. They are tall, aromatic, evergreen trees with pendant leaves and white, pink, or red flowers.

Eucharist chief Christian sacrament, in which bread is eaten and wine drunk in memory of the death of Jesus. Other names for it are the **Lord's Supper**, **Holy Communion**, and (among Roman Catholics, who believe that the bread and wine are transubstantiated, that is, converted to the body and blood of Christ) the **Mass**. The doctrine of transubstantiation was rejected by Protestant churches during the Reformation.

The word comes from the Greek for "thanksgiving," and refers to the statement in the Gospel narrative that Jesus gave thanks over the bread and the cup.

Euclid *c.* 330–*c.* 260 BC. Greek mathematician, who lived in Alexandria and wrote the *Stoicheia/Elements* in 13 books, of which nine deal with plane and solid geometry and four with number theory. His great achievement lay in the systematic arrangement of previous discoveries, based on axioms, definitions, and theorems.

Euclid's geometry texts remained in common usage for over 2,000 years.

Eudoxus of Cnidus *c.* 390–*c.* 340 BC. Greek mathematician and astronomer. He devised the first system to account for the motions of celestial bodies, believing them to be carried around the Earth on sets of spheres. Probably Eudoxus regarded these spheres as a mathematical device for ease of computation rather than as physically real, but the idea of celestial spheres was taken up by ◊Aristotle and became entrenched in astronomical thought until the time of Tycho ◊Brahe. Eudoxus also described the constellations in a work called *Phaenomena*, providing the basis of the constellation system still in use today.

Eugene city in W central Oregon, S of Portland, on the Willamette River; processing and shipping center for agricultural products from the surrounding region; wood products are also manufactured; population (1990) 112,700. The University of Oregon 1872 is here.

Eugène Prince of Savoy 1663–1736. Austrian general who had many victories against the Turkish invaders (whom he expelled from Hungary 1697 in the Battle of Zenta) and against France in the War of the ◊Spanish Succession (battles of Blenheim, Oudenaarde, and Malplaquet).

eugenics (Greek "well-born") study of ways in which the physical and mental quality of a people can be controlled and improved by selective breeding, and the belief that this should be done. The idea was abused by the Nazi Party in Germany during the 1930s to justify the attempted extermination of entire groups of people. Eugenics can try to control the spread of inherited genetic abnormalities by counseling prospective parents.

The term was coined by Francis ◊Galton in 1883, and the concept was originally developed in the late 19th century with a view to improving human intelligence and behavior.

In 1986 Singapore became the first democratic country to adopt an openly eugenic policy by guaranteeing pay increases to female university graduates when they give birth to a child, while offering grants toward house purchases for nongraduate married women on condition that they are sterilized after the first or second child.

Eugénie Marie Ignace Augustine de Montijo 1826–1920. Empress of France, daughter of the Spanish count of Montijo. In 1853 she married Louis Napoleon, who had become emperor as ◊Napoleon III. She encouraged court extravagance, Napoleon III's intervention in Mexico, and urged him to fight the Prussians. After his surrender to the Germans at Sedan, NE France, 1870 she fled to England.

eukaryote in biology, one of the two major groupings into which all organisms are divided. Included are all organisms, except bacteria and cyanobacteria (◊blue-green algae), which belong to the ◊prokaryote grouping.

The cells of eukaryotes possess a clearly defined nucleus, bounded by a membrane, within which DNA is formed into distinct chromosomes. Eukaryotic cells also contain mitochondria, chloroplasts, and other structures (organelles) that, together with a defined nucleus, are lacking in the cells of prokaryotes.

Euler Leonhard 1707–1783. Swiss mathematician. He developed the theory of differential equations and the calculus of variations, and worked in astronomy and optics. He was a pupil of Johann ◊Bernoulli.

Euler became professor of physics at the University of St Petersburg in 1730. In 1741 he was invited to Berlin by Frederick the Great, where he spent 25 years before returning to Russia.

Eumenides ("kindly ones") in Greek mythology, appeasing name for the ◊Furies.

eunuch (Greek *eunoukhos* "one in charge of a bed") castrated man. Originally eunuchs were bedchamber attendants in harems in the East, but as they were usually castrated to keep them from taking too great an interest in their charges, the term became applied more generally. In China, eunuchs were employed within the imperial harem from some 4,000 years ago and by medieval times wielded considerable political power. Eunuchs often filled high offices of state in India and Persia.

Italian *castrati* were singers castrated as boys to preserve their soprano voices, a practice that ended with the accession of Pope Leo XIII 1878.

Eupen-et-Malmédy region of Belgium around the towns of Eupen and Malmédy. It was Prussian from 1814 until it became Belgian 1920 after a plebiscite; there was fierce fighting here in the German Ardennes offensive Dec 1944.

Euphrates (Arabic *Furat*) river, rising in E Turkey, flowing through Syria and Iraq and joining the river Tigris above Basra to form the river Shatt-al-Arab, at the head of the Persian/Arabian Gulf; 2,240 mi/3,600 km in length. The ancient cities of Babylon, Eridu, and Ur were situated along its course.

Eurasian a person of mixed European and Asian parentage; also, native to or an inhabitant of both Europe and Asia.

Euratom acronym for ◊*European Atomic Energy Commission*, forming part of the ◊European Community organization.

eureka in chemistry, alternate name for the copper–nickel alloy ◊constantan, which is used in electrical equipment.

eurhythmics practice of coordinated bodily movement as an aid to musical development. It was founded about 1900 by the Swiss musician Emil ◊Jaques-Dalcroze, professor of harmony at the Geneva conservatoire. He devised a series of "gesture" songs, to be sung simultaneously with certain bodily actions.

Euripides *c.* 484–407 BC. Greek dramatist whose plays deal with the emotions and reactions of ordinary people and social issues rather than with deities and the grandiose themes of his contemporaries. He wrote more than 80 plays, of which 18 survive, including *Alcestis* 438 BC, *Medea* 431 BC, *Andromache* 426 BC, *The Trojan Women* 415 BC, *Electra* 417 BC, *Iphigenia in Tauris* 413 BC, *Iphigenia in Aulis* 405 BC, and *Bacchae* 405 BC. His influence on later drama was probably greater than that of the other two accomplished tragedians, Aeschylus and Sophocles.

A realist, he was bitterly attacked for his unorthodox "impiety" and sympathy for the despised: slaves, beggars, and women. He went into voluntary exile from Athens to Macedonia at the end of his life.

Eurobond in finance, a bond underwritten by an international syndicate and sold in countries other than the country of the currency in which the issue is denominated. It provides longer-term financing than is possible with loans in Eurodollars.

Eurocommunism policy followed by communist parties in Western Europe to seek power within the framework of national political initiative rather than by revolutionary means. In addition, Eurocommunism enabled these parties to free themselves from total reliance on the USSR.

Eurodollar in finance, US currency deposited outside the US and held by individuals and institutions, not necessarily in Europe. Eurodollars originated in the 1960s when East European countries deposited their US dollars in West European banks. Banks holding Eurodollar deposits may lend in dollars, usually to finance trade, and often redeposit with other foreign banks. The practice is a means of avoiding credit controls and exploiting interest rate differentials.

Europa in astronomy, the fourth largest moon of the planet Jupiter, diameter 1,950 mi/3,140 km, orbiting 417,000 mi/671,000 km from the planet every 3.55 days. It is covered by ice and criss-crossed by thousands of thin cracks, each some 30,000 mi/50,000 km long.

Europa in Greek mythology, the daughter of the king of Tyre, carried off by Zeus (in the form of a bull); she personifies the continent of Europe.

Europe second smallest continent, occupying 8% of the Earth's surface
area 4,000,000 sq mi/10,400,000 sq km
largest cities (population over 1.5 million) Athens, Barcelona, Berlin, Birmingham, Bucharest, Budapest, Hamburg, Istanbul, Kharkov, Kiev, Lisbon, London, Madrid, Manchester, Milan, Moscow, Paris, Rome, St Petersburg, Vienna, Warsaw
physical conventionally occupying that part of Eurasia to the west of the Ural Mountains,

north of the Caucasus Mountains and north of the Sea of Marmara; Europe lies entirely in the northern hemisphere between 36° N and the Arctic Ocean. About two-thirds of the continent is a great plain which covers the whole of European Russia and spreads westward through Poland to the Low Countries and the Bay of Biscay. To the north lie the Scandinavian highlands rising to 8,110 ft/ 2,470 m at Glittertind in the Jotenheim Range of Norway. To the south, a series of mountain ranges stretch from east to west (Caucasus, Balkans, Carpathians, Apennines, Alps, Pyrenees, and Sierra Nevada). The most westerly point of the mainland is Cape Roca in Portugal; the most southerly location is Tarifa Point in Spain; the most northerly point on the mainland is Nordkynn in Norway. A line from the Baltic to the Black Sea divides Europe between an eastern continental region and a western region characterized by a series of peninsulas that include Scandinavia (Norway, Sweden, and Finland), Jutland (Denmark and Germany), Iberia (Spain and Portugal), and Italy and the Balkans (Greece, Albania, Yugoslavia, Bulgaria, and European Turkey). Because of the large number of bays, inlets, and peninsulas, the coastline is longer in proportion to its size than that of any other continent. The largest islands adjacent to continental Europe are the British Isles, Novaya Zemlya, Sicily, Sardinia, Crete, Corsica, Gotland (in the Baltic Sea) and the Balearic Islands; other more distant islands associated with Europe include Iceland, Svalbard, Franz Josef Land, Madeira, the Azores, and the Canary Islands. The greater part of Europe falls within the northern temperate zone which is modified by the Gulf Stream in the northwest; Central Europe has warm summers and cold winters; the Mediterranean coast has comparatively mild winters and hot summers

features Mount Elbruz 18,517 ft/5,642 m in the Caucasus mountains is the highest peak in Europe; Mont Blanc 15,772 ft/4,807 m is the highest peak in the Alps; lakes (over 2,000 sq mi/5,100 sq km) include Ladoga, Onega, Vänern; rivers (over 500 mi/800 km) include the Volga, Danube, Dnieper Ural, Don, Pechora, Dneister, Rhine, Loire, Tagus, Ebro, Oder, Prut, Rhône

products nearly 50% of the world's automobiles are produced in Europe (Germany, France, Italy, Spain, Russia, Georgia, Ukraine, Latvia, Belarus, UK); the rate of fertilizer consumption on agricultural land is four times greater than that in any other continent; Europe produces 43% of the world's barley (Germany, Spain, France, UK), 41% of its rye (Poland, Germany), 31% of its oats (Poland, Germany, Sweden, France), and 24% of its wheat (France, Germany, UK, Romania); Italy, Spain, and Greece produce more than 70% of the world's olive oil

population (1985) 496 million (excluding Turkey and the ex-Soviet republics); annual growth rate 0.3%, projected population of 512 million by 2000

language mostly Indo-European, with a few exceptions, including Finno-Ugrian (Finnish and Hungarian), Basque and Altaic (Turkish); apart from a fringe of Celtic, the NW is Germanic; Letto-Lithuanian languages separate the Germanic from the Slavonic tongues of E Europe; Romance languages spread E-W from Romania through Italy and France to Spain and Portugal

religion Christianity (Protestant, Roman Catholic, Eastern Orthodox), Muslim (Turkey, Albania, Yugoslavia, Bulgaria), Judaism.

European native to or an inhabitant of the continent of Europe and their descendants. Europe is multicultural and, although most of its languages belong to the Indo-European family, there are also speakers of Uralic (such as Hungarian) and Altaic (such as Turkish) languages, as well as Basque.

European Atomic Energy Commission (Euratom) organization established by the second Treaty of Rome 1957, which seeks the cooperation of member states of the European Community in nuclear research and the rapid and large-scale development of nonmilitary nuclear energy.

Europe: history

BC
3000	Bronze Age civilizations: Minoan, Mycenaean.
1000	Iron Age.
6th–4th centuries	Greek civilization at its height; Alexander the Great advances E to India.
3rd century	Rome in control of the Italian peninsula.
146	Greece a Roman province, and Carthage destroyed.
1st century	Augustus made the Rhine and Danube the Roman Empire's northern frontiers; see ▷Celts.

AD
1st century	Britain brought within the Roman Empire.
2nd century	Roman Empire ceased to expand.
4th century	Christianity the established religion of the Roman Empire, which halved into E and W empires (see ▷Byzantine empires).
4th–6th centuries	W Europe overrun by Anglo Saxons, Franks, Goths, Lombards. W Roman empire fell 476. Middle Ages begin; feudalism prevails.
7th–8th centuries	Christendom threatened by the Moors (Muslim Arabs) via the Mediterranean countries.
800	Charlemagne given title of emperor by the Pope; Holy Roman empire begins.
1073	Gregory VII began 200 years of conflict between the powers of the empire and papacy.
1096–1272	Crusades to take Jerusalem.
12th century	Setting up of German, Flemish, and Italian city-states, which in the 14th-15th centuries fostered the Renaissance.
1453	Byzantine empire falls to the Turks.
16th–17th centuries	Dominated by rivalry of France and the Hapsburgs, the Protestant Reformation, and the Catholic Counter Reformation.
17th century	Absolute monarchy came to prevail (Louis XIV) in Europe, although in Britain supremacy of Parliament established by Civil War.
18th century	War of the Austrian Succession and Seven Years' War ended in the loss of the French colonial empire to Britain and the establishment of Prussia as Europe's military power.
1789–95	French Revolution led to the Revolutionary and Napoleonic wars.
1821–29	Greek War of Independence marked the end of Turkish control of the Balkans.
1848	Year of revolutions (see ▷Louis Philippe, ▷Metternich, ▷Risorgimento).
1914–1918	World War I arose from the Balkan question, Franco–German rivalry, and colonial differences; it destroyed the Austrian, Russian, and Turkish empires and paved the way for the Russian Revolution and the formation of the USSR.
1933	Hitler came to power in a defeated, impoverished Germany. His geopolitical aggression caused World War II.
1939–45	World War II resulted in decline of European colonial rule in Africa and Asia; emergence of Soviet power, and most of Western Europe under the military aegis of the US (NATO); the Cold War begins.
1957	Establishment of the European Economic Community, the "Common Market."
1973	Enlargement of the European Community to include Britain, Denmark, and the Irish Republic.
1979	First direct elections to the European Parliament.
1989–90	Beginning of democratization of Eastern bloc, including USSR, Poland, Romania, Czechoslovakia, East Germany, Lithuania. Unification of Germany.
1991	Baltic republics of Estonia, Latvia, and Lithuania regain independence; other Soviet republics follow.
1992	Civil war in Yugoslavia. Division of Czechoslovakia into two states. Confusion within EC over future of Maastricht Treaty.

European Bank for Reconstruction and Development (EBRD) international bank established 1991, with an initial capital of 10 billion ECUs, to assist the economic reconstruction of central and E Europe. Its headquarters are in London.

European Coal and Steel Community (ECSC) former organization established by the treaty of Paris 1951 (ratified 1952) as a single authority for the coal and steel industries of France, West Germany, Italy, Belgium, Holland, and Luxembourg, eliminating tariffs and other restrictions; in 1967 it became part of the European Community.

The ECSC arose out of the ▷Schuman plan 1950, which proposed a union of the French and German coal and steel industries so as to make future war between the two countries impossible. The ECSC was, in effect, a prototype institution for the European Community itself, under whose authority it came 1967. Subsequent members of the EC automatically became ECSC members also.

European Community political and economic alliance consisting of the European Coal and Steel Community (1952), European Economic Community (EEC, popularly called the Common Market, 1957), and the European Atomic Energy Commission (Euratom, 1957). The original six members—Belgium, France, West Germany, Italy, Luxembourg, and the Netherlands—were joined by the UK, Denmark, and the Republic of Ireland 1973, Greece 1981, and Spain and Portugal 1986. In 1991 association agreements—providing for free trade within ten years and the possibility of full EC membership—were signed between the EC and Czechoslovakia, Hungary, and Poland, subject to ratification. The aims of the EC include the expansion of trade, reduction of competition, the abolition of restrictive trading practices, the encouragement of free movement of capital and labor within the community, and the establishment of a closer union among European people. The Maastricht Treaty 1992 provides the framework for closer economic and political union but delays over its ratification have put the future of the EC itself in doubt.

The EC has the following institutions: the *Commission* of 17 members pledged to independence of national interests, who initiate Community action (two members each from France, Germany, Italy, Spain, and the UK; and one each from Belgium, Denmark, Greece, Ireland, Luxembourg, Netherlands, and Portugal); the *Council of Ministers*, which makes decisions on the Commission's proposals; the ⟂*European Parliament*, directly elected from 1979; the *Economic and Social Committee*, a consultative body; the *Committee of Permanent Representatives* (COMEPER), consisting of civil servants temporarily seconded by member states to work for the Commission; and the ⟂*European Court of Justice*, to safeguard interpretation of the Rome Treaties (1957) that established the Community.

In 1992 there were more than 340 million people in the EC countries. A single market with free movement of goods and capital was established Jan 1993. A European Charter of Social Rights was approved at the Maastricht summit Dec 1991 by all members except the UK. The same meeting secured agreement on a treaty framework for European union, including political and monetary union, with a timetable for implementation, and for a new system of police and military EC cooperation. In May 1992 the bill to ratify the treaty was given a second reading. In June the Danish people voted narrowly against ratification in a national referendum, throwing the future of the treaty into doubt, but compromises agreed between all 12 nations at an Edinburgh Summit Dec 1992 appeared to guarantee its survival.

Almost 60% of the EC's budget in 1990 was spent on supporting farmers (about 4 million people); of this, almost $7 billion a year went to dairy farmers, because the dairy quotas, which were introduced 1984, were 14% greater than EC consumption. The EC sheep policy cost approximately $3 billion in 1990, and 30 million metric tons of excess grain were exported annually at a subsidized price. Altogether it

cost member countries' taxpayers around $15 billion in 1989–90 to maintain the international competitiveness of the EC's overpriced produce under the ⟂*Common Agricultural Policy*.

European Court of Justice the court of the European Community (EC), which is responsible for interpreting ⟂Community law and ruling on breaches by member states and others of such law. It sits in Luxembourg with judges from the member states.

European Economic Community (EEC) popularly called the *Common Market* organization established 1957 with the aim of creating a single European market for the products of member states by the abolition of tariffs and other restrictions on trade.

European Free Trade Association (EFTA) organization established 1960 consisting of Austria, Finland, Iceland, Norway, Sweden, Switzerland, and (from 1991) Liechtenstein, previously a nonvoting associate member. There are no import duties between members. Of the original members, Britain and Denmark left (1972) to join the ⟂European Community, as did Portugal (1985). In 1973 the EC signed agreements with EFTA members, setting up a free-trade area of over 300 million consumers. Trade between the two groups amounted to over half of total EFTA trade. A further pact signed Oct 1991 between the EC and EFTA provided for a European Economic Area (EEA) to be set up, allowing EFTA greater access to the EC market by ending many of the restrictions. The area would span 19 nations and 380 million people.

European Monetary System (EMS) attempt by the European Community to bring financial cooperation and monetary stability to Europe. It was established 1979 in the wake of the 1974 oil crisis, which brought growing economic disruption to European economies because of floating exchange rates. Central to the EMS is the *Exchange Rate Mechanism* (ERM), a voluntary system of semifixed exchange rates based on the European Currency Unit (ECU).

European Monetary Union (EMU) the proposed European Community policy for a single currency and common economic policies. The proposal was announced by a European Community committee headed by EC Commission president Jacques Delors April 1989.

Three stages are envisaged for EMU. In the first stage, all controls on individual nations' capital flow would be ended, and the *European System of Central Banks* (ESCB) created. In stage two, the ESCB would begin to regulate money supply. Finally, exchange rates between member states would be fixed, and a single European currency created, and the ESCB would take over the function of all the nations' ⟂central banks.

European Parliament the parliament of the European Community, which meets in Strasbourg to comment on the legislative proposals of the Commission of the European Communities. Members are elected for a five-year term. The European Parliament has 518 seats, apportioned on the basis of population, of which the UK, France, Germany, and Italy have 81 each, Spain 60, the Netherlands 25, Belgium, Greece, and Portugal 24 each, Denmark 16, the Republic of Ireland 15, and Luxembourg 6.

Originally merely consultative, the European Parliament became directly elected 1979,

and assumed increased powers. Though still not a true legislative body, it can dismiss the whole Commission and reject the Community budget in its entirety. Full sittings are in Strasbourg; most committees meet in Brussels, and the seat of the secretariat is in Luxembourg. After the 1989 elections the Left held 260 seats (Socialist 180, Communist 41, Green 39); the Center 203 (Christian Democrats 123, Liberals 44); Independents 16; Gaullists (with Fianna Fáil and SNP) 20; and the Right 55 (Conservatives 34, Right 21). Egon Klepsch (Germany) became president 1992.

European Space Agency (ESA) an organization of European countries (Austria, Belgium, Denmark, France, Germany, Ireland, Italy, the Netherlands, Norway, Spain, Sweden, Switzerland, and the UK) that engages in space research and technology. It was founded 1975, with headquarters in Paris.

ESA developed various scientific and communications satellites, the ⟂*Giotto* space probe, and the ⟂*Ariane* rockets. ESA built ⟂*Spacelab*, plans to build its own space station, *Columbus*, for attachment to a US space station, and is working on its own shuttle project, Hermes.

europium soft, grayish, metallic element of the lanthanide series, symbol Eu, atomic number 63, atomic weight 151.96. It is used in lasers and as the red phosphor in color televisions; its compounds are used to make control rods for nuclear reactors.

It was named in 1901 by French chemist Eugène Demarçay (1852–1904) after the continent of Europe, where it was first found.

Eurydice in Greek mythology, the wife of ⟂Orpheus. She was a dryad, or forest nymph, and died from a snake bite. Orpheus attempted unsuccessfully to fetch her back from the realm of the dead.

Eusebius *c.* 260–340. Bishop of Caesarea (modern Qisarya, Israel); author of a history of the Christian church to 324.

eusociality form of social life found in insects such as honey bees and termites, in which the colony is made up of special castes (for example, workers, drones, and reproductives) whose membership is biologically determined. The worker castes do not usually reproduce. Only one mammal, the naked mole rat, has a social organization of this type. See also ⟂social behavior.

eustachian tube small air-filled canal connecting the middle ⟂ear with the back of the throat. It is found in all land vertebrates and equalizes the pressure on both sides of the ear drum.

euthanasia in medicine, mercy killing of someone with a severe and incurable condition or illness. The Netherlands legalized voluntary euthanasia 1983, but is the only country to have done so.

eutrophication excessive enrichment of rivers, lakes, and shallow sea areas, primarily by nitrate fertilizers washed from the soil by rain, and by phosphates from fertilizers and detergents in municipal sewage. These encourage the growth of algae and bacteria which use up the oxygen in the water, thereby making it uninhabitable for fishes and other animal life.

Eutyches *c.* 384–456. Christian theologian. An archimandrite (monastic head) in Constantinople, he held that Jesus had only one nature, the human nature being subsumed in the divine (a belief which became known as ⟂Monophysitism). He was exiled after his ideas were condemned as heretical by the Council of ⟁Chalcedon 451.

evangelicalism the beliefs of some Protestant Christian movements that stress biblical authority, faith, and the personal commitment of the "born again" experience.

Evangelical groups constituted the fastest-growing part of American Christianity during the 1970s and 1980s; their influence was spread through Bible colleges, Christian publishing houses and bookstores, television evangelism, and missionary efforts.

evangelist person traveling to spread the Christian gospel, in particular the authors of the four Gospels in the New Testament: Matthew, Mark, Luke, and John. See also ⟁televangelist.

Evans Arthur John 1851–1941. English archeologist. His excavation of ⟁Knossos on Crete resulted in the discovery of pre-Phoenician Minoan script and proved the existence of the legendary Minoan civilization.

Evans Edith 1888–1976. English character actress who performed on the London stage and on Broadway. Her many imposing performances include the film role of Lady Bracknell in Oscar Wilde's comedy *The Importance of Being Earnest* 1952. Among her other films are *Tom Jones* 1963 and *Crooks and Coronets* 1969.

Evans Walker 1903–1975. US photographer best known for his documentary photographs of people in the rural American South during the Great Depression. Many of his photographs appeared in James Agee's book *Let Us Now Praise Famous Men* 1941.

Born in St Louis, Evans was in 1938 the first photographer to have an exhibit at the Museum of Modern Art in New York City. From 1945 to 1965 he served as an associate editor of *Fortune* magazine, in which he published several photo essays. Throughout his career, he devoted much attention to photographing architecture. He also did a renowned series of photographs of people in the New York City subways.

Evansville industrial city in SW Indiana, on the Ohio River; industries include pharmaceuticals and plastics; population (1990) 126,200. The University of Evansville is here.

The community, which dates to 1812, grew after the 1853 completion of the Wabash and Erie canal linking the Ohio at Evansville with Lake Erie.

evaporation process in which a liquid turns to a vapor without its temperature reaching boiling point. A liquid left to stand in a saucer eventually evaporates because, at any time, a proportion of its molecules will be fast enough (have enough kinetic energy) to escape through the attractive intermolecular forces at the liquid surface into the atmosphere. The temperature of the liquid tends to fall because the evaporating molecules remove energy from the liquid. The rate of evaporation rises with increased temperature because as the mean kinetic energy of the liquid's molecules rises, so will the number possessing enough energy to escape.

A fall in the temperature of the liquid, known as the *cooling effect*, accompanies evaporation because as the faster proportion of the molecules escapes through the surface the mean energy of the remaining molecules falls. The effect may be noticed when wet clothes are worn, or as perspiration evaporates. ⟁Refrigeration makes use of the cooling effect to extract heat from foodstuffs.

evaporite sedimentary deposit precipitated on evaporation of salt water. With a progressive evaporation of seawater, the most common salts are deposited in a definite sequence: calcite (calcium carbonate), gypsum (hydrous calcium sulfate), halite (sodium chloride), and finally salts of potassium and magnesium.

Calcite precipitates when seawater is reduced to half its original volume, gypsum precipitates when the seawater body is reduced to one-fifth, and halite when the volume is reduced to one-tenth. Thus the natural occurrence of chemically precipitated calcium carbonate is common, of gypsum fairly common, and of halite less common. Because of the concentrations of different dissolved salts in seawater, halite accounts for about 95% of the chlorides precipitated if evaporation is complete. More unusual evaporite minerals include borates (for example borax, hydrous sodium borate) and sulfates (for example glauberite, a combined sulfate of sodium and calcium).

Eve in the Old Testament, the first woman, wife of ⟁Adam. She was tempted by Satan (in the form of a snake) to eat the fruit of the Tree of Knowledge of Good and Evil, and then tempted Adam to eat of the fruit as well, thus bringing about their expulsion from the Garden of Eden.

There are two versions of the creation myth in the Bible: in one of them, Eve was created simultaneously with Adam; in the other, she was created from his rib. In the Hebrew writings known as the "Midrash," ⟁Lilith was the first woman (and her children were the wives available to Eve's sons Cain and Abel).

evening primrose any plant of the genus *Oenothera*, family Onagraceae. Some 50 species are native to North America, several of which now also grow in Europe. Some are cultivated for their oil, which is used in treating eczema, premenstrual tension, and chronic fatigue syndrome.

Everest, Mount (Chinese *Qomolungma* "goddess mother of the snows/world;" Nepalese *Sagarmatha* "head of the earth") the world's highest mountain above sea level, in the Himalayas, on the China–Nepal frontier; height 29,118 ft/8,872 m (recently measured by satellite to this new height from the former official height of 29,028 ft/8,848 m). It was first climbed by Edmund Hillary and Tenzing Norgay 1953. More than 360 climbers have reached the summit; over 100 have died during the ascent.

The English name comes from George Everest (1790–1866), surveyor general of India. In 1987 a US expedition obtained measurements of ⟁K2 that disputed Everest's "highest mountain" status, but the recent satellite measurements have established Mount Everest as the highest.

Everett Edward 1794–1865. US religious leader, educator, and public figure. Born in Dorchester, Massachusetts, and educated at Harvard, Everett was named pastor of Boston's Brattle Street Church 1814. After gaining his PhD at Göttingen 1817 and teaching at Harvard, he served in the US House of Representatives 1825–35, as Massachusetts governor 1835–39, as US minister to England 1841–45, and as president of Harvard 1846–49. His four-month role as President Fillmore's secretary of state 1852–53 was followed by a short tenure in the US Senate 1853–54. Thereafter, he spoke out as a private citizen for abolitionism and the preservation of the Union.

Everglades area of swamps, marsh, and lakes in S ⟁Florida; area 5,000 sq mi/12,950 sq km. A national park covers the southern tip.

Formed by overflow of Lake Okeechobee after heavy rains, it is one of the wildest areas in the US, noted for its distinctive plant and animal life. The only human residents are several hundred Seminole, a North American Indian people. Large drainage programs have reduced the flow of water from the lake southward, threatening the region's ecological balance.

evergreen in botany, a plant such as pine, spruce, or holly, that bears its leaves all year round. Most ⟁conifers are evergreen. Plants that shed their leaves in autumn or during a dry season are described as ⟁deciduous.

everlasting flower any flower head with colored bracts that retains its color when cut and dried.

They are mostly of the composite family, including some species of *Ammobium*, *Helichrysum*, and *Xeranthemum*. The strawflower of Australia *Helichrysum bracteatum* is a popular example.

Evert Chris(tine) 1954– . US tennis player. She won her first Wimbledon title 1974, and has since won 21 Grand Slam titles. She became the first woman tennis player to win $1 million in prize money. She has an outstanding two-handed backhand and is a great exponent of baseline technique. Evert retired from competitive tennis 1989.

From 1974 to 1989 she never failed to reach the quarter-finals at Wimbledon. She married British Davis Cup player John Lloyd 1979 but subsequently divorced him.

CAREER HIGHLIGHTS

Wimbledon
singles: 1974, 1976, 1981
doubles: 1976
US Open
singles: 1975–78, 1980, 1982
French Open
singles: 1974–75, 1979–80, 1983, 1985–86
doubles: 1974–75
Australian Open
singles: 1982, 1984

evidence in law, the testimony of witnesses and production of documents and other material in court proceedings, in order to prove or disprove facts at issue in the case. Witnesses must swear or affirm that their evidence is true. In English law, giving false evidence is the crime of ⟁perjury.

Documentary evidence has a wide scope including maps, soundtracks, and films, in addition to documents in writing. Objects such as weapons used in crimes may serve as evidence. Evidence obtained illegally, such as a confession under duress, may be excluded from the court.

evolution slow process of change from one form to another, as in the evolution of the universe from its formation in the ⟁Big Bang to its present state, or in the evolution of life on Earth. Some Christians and Muslims deny the theory of evolution as conflicting with the belief that God created all things (see ⟁creationism).

The idea of continuous evolution in the living world can be traced as far back as ⟁Lucretius in the 1st century BC, but it did not gain wide acceptance until the 19th century, following the work of Charles ⟁Lyell, J B ⟁Lamarck, Charles ⟁Darwin, and T H ⟁Huxley. Darwin assigned the major role in evolutionary change to ◊natural selection acting on randomly occurring variations. Natural selection occurs because those individuals better adapted to their particular environments reproduce more effectively, thus contributing their characteristics to future generations. The current theory of evolution, called ◊Neo-Darwinism, combines Darwin's theory with Gregor ◊Mendel's theories on genetics and Hugo de Vries' discovery of genetic mutation. Although neither the general concept of evolution nor the importance of natural selection is doubted by the vast majority of biologists, there remains dispute over other possible processes involved in evolutionary change. Besides natural selection and ◊sexual selection, chance may play a large part in deciding which genes become characteristic of a population, a phenomenon called "genetic drift." It is now also clear that evolutionary change does not always occur at a constant rate, but that the process can have long periods of relative stability interspersed with periods of rapid change. This has led to new theories, such as ◊punctuated equilibrium model, developed by Stephen J ◊Gould and Niles Eldridge 1972 based partly on the stability–change theory. See also ◊adaptive radiation.

evolutionary stable strategy (ESS) in sociobiology (the study of ◊social behavior), an assemblage of behavioral or physical characters (collectively termed a"strategy") of a population that is resistant to replacement by any forms bearing new traits, because the new traits will not be capable of successful reproduction.

ESS analysis is based on ◊game theory and can be applied both to genetically determined physical characters (such as horn length), and to learned behavioral responses (for example, whether to fight or retreat from an opponent). An ESS may be conditional on the context, as in the rule "fight if the opponent is smaller, but retreat if the opponent is larger."

Evvoia Greek name for the island of ◊Euboea.

evzone member of a Greek infantry regiment whose soldiers wear distinctive white, short-skirted uniform.

Ewe member of a group of people inhabiting Ghana and Togo, and numbering about 2.5 million. The Ewe live by fishing and farming, and practice an animist religion. Their language belongs to the Kwa branch of the Niger-Congo family.

ex cathedra (Latin "from the throne") term describing a statement by the pope, taken to be indisputably true, and which must be accepted by Catholics.

excavator machine designed for digging in the ground, or for earth-moving in general. Diggers with hydraulically powered digging arms are widely used on building sites. They may run on wheels or on ◊caterpillar tracks. The largest excavators are the draglines used in mining to strip away earth covering the coal or mineral deposit.

exchange rate the price at which one currency is bought or sold in terms of other currencies, gold, or accounting units such as the special drawing right (SDR) of the ◊International Monetary Fund. Exchange rates may be fixed by international agreement or by government policy; or they may be wholly or partly allowed to "float" (that is, find their own level) in world currency markets.

Central banks, as large holders of foreign currency, often intervene to buy or sell particular currencies in an effort to maintain some stability in exchange rates.

Under the Reagan administration, the US dollar was allowed, even encouraged, to drop in relation to other currencies, especially the Japanese yen.

excise taxes imposed on goods, usually considered luxury items or those items quickly consumed. The taxes are paid prior to sale, the cost being passed on to the consumer.

Among the most common excise taxes in the US are those on cigarettes, gasoline, and alcohol.

exclamation point punctuation mark (!) used to indicate emphasis or strong emotion ("That's terrible!"). It is appropriate after interjections ("Rats!"), emphatic greetings ("Yo!"), and orders ("Shut up!"), as well as those sentences beginning *How* or *What* that are not questions ("How embarrassing!," "What a surprise!").

exclusion principle in physics, a principle of atomic structure originated by Wolfgang ◊Pauli. It states that no two electrons in a single atom may have the same set of ◊quantum numbers. Hence, it is impossible to pack together certain elementary particles, such as electrons, beyond a certain critical density, otherwise they would share the same location and quantum number. A white dwarf star is thus prevented from contracting further by the exclusion principle and never collapses.

excommunication in religion, exclusion of an offender from the rights and privileges of the Roman Catholic Church; King John, Henry VIII, and Elizabeth I were all excommunicated.

excretion in biology, the removal of waste products from the cells of living organisms. In plants and simple animals, waste products are removed by diffusion, but in higher animals they are removed by specialized organs. In mammals, for example, carbon dioxide and water are removed via the lungs, and nitrogenous compounds and water via the liver, the kidneys, and the rest of the urinary system.

executor in law, a person appointed in a will to carry out the instructions of the deceased. A person so named has the right to refuse to act. The executor also has a duty to bury the deceased, prove the will, and obtain a grant of probate (that is, establish that the will is genuine and obtain official approval of his or her actions).

The executor must also pay the liens, fees, and taxes on the estate before distributing the estate property to the heirs.

Exeter city, administrative headquarters of Devon, England, on the river Exe; population (1981) 96,000. It has medieval, Georgian, and Regency architecture, including a cathedral (1280–1369), a market center, and a university (1955). It manufactures agricultural machinery, pharmaceuticals, and textiles.

existentialism branch of philosophy based on the concept of an absurd universe where humans have free will. Existentialists argue that philosophy must begin from the concrete situation of the individual in such a world, and that humans are responsible for and the sole judge of their actions as they affect others, though no one else's existence is real to the individual. The origin of existentialism is usually traced back to the Danish philosopher ◊Kierkegaard; among its proponents were Martin Heidegger in Germany and Jean-Paul ◊Sartre in France.

exobiology study of life forms that may possibly exist elsewhere in the universe, and of the effects of extraterrestrial environments on Earth organisms.

exocrine gland gland that discharges secretions, usually through a tube or a duct, onto a surface. Examples include sweat glands which release sweat onto the skin, and digestive glands which release digestive juices onto the walls of the intestine. Some animals also have ◊endocrine glands (ductless glands) that release hormones directly into the bloodstream.

Exodus second book of the Old Testament, which relates the departure of the Israelites from slavery in Egypt, under the leadership of ◊Moses, for the Promised Land of Canaan. The journey included the miraculous parting of the Red Sea, with the Pharaoh's pursuing forces being drowned as the waters returned.

The Exodus is also recorded in the *Hagadda*, which is read at the Seder (during the Jewish festival of Passover) to commemorate the deliverance. During the 40 years of wandering in the wilderness, Moses brought the Ten Commandments down from Mt. Sinai.

exorcism rite used in a number of religions for the expulsion of so-called evil spirits. In Christianity it is employed, for example, in the Roman Catholic and Pentecostal churches.

exoskeleton the hardened external skeleton of insects, spiders, crabs, and other arthropods. It provides attachment for muscles and protection for the internal organs, as well as support. To permit growth it is periodically shed in a process called ◊ecdysis.

exosphere the uppermost layer of the ◊atmosphere. It is an ill-defined zone above the thermosphere, beginning at about 435 mi/ 700 km and fading off into the vacuum of space. The gases are extremely thin, with hydrogen as the main constituent.

exothermic reaction a chemical reaction during which heat is given out (see ◊energy of reaction).

Ex parte McCardle US Supreme Court decision 1869 dealing with the power of Congress to deprive the Supreme Court of jurisdiction over appeals. William McCardle, a Mississippi journalist convicted of sedition by a military court and refused a writ of habeas corpus by the federal circuit court, appealed his case to the Supreme Court. Afraid that the military Reconstruction governments would be found unconstitutional, Congress revoked the Court's jurisdiction over appeals. The Court ruled unanimously that this was fully within the constitutional right of Congress to make exceptions to the Supreme Court's right to hear appeals; furthermore, it was not the Court's job to discern the political motives of restrictions imposed by Congress.

Ex parte Merryman circuit court decision 1861 dealing with the right of the US president to restrict the civilian court under martial law for secessionist activities. Merryman, a Baltimore citizen, received a writ of habeas corpus from the acting circuit court judge, Chief Justice Taney. Taney ordered that Merryman be brought to trial or released and found the military in contempt of court when, under the authority of President Lincoln, it refused to comply. Taney declared that Lincoln was in violation of the Constitution, saying only Congress had the right to suspend habeas corpus. The case never reached the US Supreme Court.

Ex parte Milligan US Supreme Court decision 1866 that attended to the issue of the jurisdiction of military tribunals in areas where civilian courts are operating. Milligan, an Indiana citizen sentenced by a military tribunal to hang for secessionist activities, petitioned for a writ of habeas corpus on the grounds that as a civilian he was not subject to military law. The Court ruled 5–4 in favor of Milligan, holding that neither the US president nor Congress had the right to impose martial law outside of a war zone.

expectorant any substance, often added to cough mixture, intended to help expel mucus from the airways. It is debatable whether expectorants have an effect on lung secretions.

experiment in science, a practical test designed with the intention that its results will be relevant to a particular theory or set of theories. Although some experiments may be used merely for gathering more information about a topic that is already well understood, others may be of crucial importance in confirming a new theory or in undermining long-held beliefs.

The manner in which experiments are performed, and the relation between the design of an experiment and its value, are therefore of central importance. In general an experiment is of most value when the factors that might affect the results (variables) are carefully controlled; for this reason most experiments take place in a well-managed environment such as a laboratory or clinic.

experimental psychology application of scientific methods to the study of mental processes and behavior.

This covers a wide range of fields of study including: *human and animal learning* in which learning theories describe how new behaviors are acquired and modified; *cognition*, the study of a number of functions, such as perception, attention, memory, and language; *physiological psychology*, which relates the study of cognition to different regions of the brain. *Artificial intelligence* refers to the computer simulation of cognitive processes, such as language and problem-solving.

expert system computer program for giving advice (such as diagnosing an illness or interpreting the law) that incorporates knowledge derived from human expertise. It is a kind of ◊knowledge-based system containing rules that can be applied to find the solution to a problem. It is a form of ◊artificial intelligence.

explanation in science, an attempt to make clear the cause of any natural event, by reference to physical laws and to observations.

The extent to which any explanation can be said to be true is one of the chief concerns of philosophy, partly because observations may be wrongly interpreted, partly because explanations should help us predict how nature will behave. Although it may be reasonable to expect that a physical law will hold in the future, that expectation is problematic in that it relies on ◊induction, a much-criticized feature of human thought; in fact no explanation, however "scientific," can be held to be true for all time, and thus the difference between a scientific and a common-sense explanation remains the subject of intense philosophical debate.

Explorer series of US scientific satellites. *Explorer 1*, launched Jan 1958, was the first US satellite in orbit and discovered the Van Allen radiation belts around the Earth.

explosive any material capable of a sudden release of energy and the rapid formation of a large volume of gas, leading when compressed to the development of a high-pressure wave (blast).

exponent or *index* in mathematics, a number that indicates the number of times a term is multiplied by itself; for example $x^2 = x \times x$, $4^3 = 4 \times 4 \times 4$.

Exponents obey certain rules. Terms that contain them are multiplied together by adding the exponents; for example, $x^2 \times x^5 = x^7$. Division of such terms is done by subtracting the exponents; for example, $y^5 \div y^3 = y^2$. Any number with the exponent 0 is equal to 1; for example, $x^0 = 1$ and $99^0 = 1$.

exponential in mathematics, descriptive of a ◊function in which the variable quantity is an exponent (a number indicating the power to which another number or expression is raised).

Exponential functions and series involve the constant $e = 2.71828...$. Napier devised natural ◊logarithms in 1614 with e as the base.

Exponential functions are basic mathematical functions, written as e^x or exp x. The expression e^x has five definitions, two of which are: (i) e^x is the solution of the differential equation $dx/dt = x$ ($x = 1$ if $t = 0$); (ii) e^x is the limiting sum of the infinite series $1 + x + (x^2/2!) + (x^3/3!) + ... + (x^n/n!)$.

Exponential growth is not constant. It applies, for example, to population growth, where the population doubles in a short time period. A graph of population number against time is an exponential growth function and produces a curve that is characteristically rather flat at first but then shoots almost directly upward.

export goods or service produced in one country and sold to another. Exports may be visible (goods physically exported) or invisible (services provided in the exporting country but paid for by residents of another country).

export credit loan, finance, or guarantee provided by a government or a financial institution enabling companies to export goods and services in situations where payment for them may be delayed or subject to risk.

exposure meter instrument used in photography for indicating the correct exposure—the length of time the camera shutter should be open under given light conditions. Meters use substances such as cadmium sulfide and selenium as light sensors. These materials change electrically when light strikes them, the change being proportional to the intensity of the incident light. Many cameras have a built-in exposure meter that sets the camera controls automatically as the light conditions change.

expressionism in music, atonal music that uses dissonance for disturbing effect.

Expressionism style of painting, sculpture, and literature that expresses inner emotions; in particular, a movement in early 20th-century art in northern and central Europe. Expressionists tended to distort or exaggerate natural appearance in order to create a reflection of an inner world; the Norwegian painter Edvard Munch's *Skriket/The Scream* 1893 (National Gallery, Oslo) is perhaps the most celebrated example. Expressionist writers include August Strindberg and Frank Wedekind.

Other leading Expressionist artists were James Ensor, Oskar Kokoschka, and Chaïm Soutine. The Blaue Reiter group was associated with this movement, and the Expressionist trend in German art emerged even more strongly after World War I in the work of Max Beckmann and Georg Grosz.

extensor a muscle that straightens a limb.

extinction in biology, the complete disappearance of a species. In the past, extinctions are believed to have occurred because species were unable to adapt quickly enough to a naturally changing environment. Today, most extinctions are due to human activity. Some species, such as the ◊dodo of Mauritius, the ◊moas of New Zealand, and the passenger ◊pigeon of North America, were exterminated by hunting. Others became extinct when their habitat was destroyed. See also ◊endangered species.

Mass extinctions are episodes during which whole groups of species have become extinct, the best known being that of the dinosaurs, other large reptiles, and various marine invertebrates about 65 million years ago. Another mass extinction occurred about 10,000 years ago when many giant species of mammal died out. This is known as the "Pleistocene overkill" because their disappearance was probably hastened by the hunting activities of prehistoric humans. The current mass extinction is largely due to human destruction of habitats, as in the tropical forests and coral reefs; it is far more serious and damaging than mass extinctions of the past because of the speed at which it occurs. Man-made climatic changes and pollution also make it less likely that the biosphere can recover and evolve new species to suit a changed environment. The rate of extinction is difficult to estimate, since most losses occur in the rich environment of the tropical rainforest, where the total number of existent species is not known. Conservative estimates put the rate of loss due to deforestation alone at 4,000 to 6,000 species a year. Overall, the rate could be as high as one species an hour, with the loss of one species putting those dependent on it at risk. Australia has the worst record for extinction: 18 mammals have disappeared since Europeans settled there, and 40 more are threatened.

extracellular matrix strong material naturally occurring in animals and plants, made up of protein and long-chain sugars (polysaccharides) in which cells are embedded. It is often called a "biological glue," and forms part of ◊connective tissues such as bone and skin.

The cell walls of plants and bacteria, and the ◊exoskeletons of insects and other arthropods, are also formed by types of extracellular matrix.

extradition surrender, by one state or country to another, of a person accused of a criminal offense in the state or country to which that person is extradited.

When two nations are involved, extradition is usually governed by a treaty between the two countries concerned. A country usually will not allow extradition for political offenses or an offense that it does not treat as a crime, even though it is a crime in the requesting country.

extrasensory perception (ESP) form of perception beyond and distinct from the known sensory processes. The main forms of ESP are clairvoyance (intuitive perception or vision of events and situations without using the senses); precognition (the ability to foresee events); and telepathy or thought transference (communication between people without using any known visible, tangible, or audible medium). Verification by scientific study has yet to be achieved.

Extremadura autonomous region of W Spain including the provinces of Badajoz and Cáceres; area 16,058 sq mi/41,600 sq km; population (1986) 1,089,000. Irrigated land is used for growing wheat; the remainder is either oak forest or used for pig or sheep grazing.

extroversion or *extraversion* personality dimension described by ◊Jung and later by Eysenck. The typical extrovert is sociable, impulsive, and carefree. The opposite of extroversion is introversion; the typical introvert is quiet and inward-looking.

extrusion common method of shaping metals, plastics, and other materials. The materials, usually hot, are forced through the hole in a metal die and take its cross-sectional shape. Rods, tubes, and sheets may be made in this way.

Eyck Jan van *c.* 1390–1441. Flemish painter of the early northern Renaissance, one of the first to work in oils. His paintings are technically brilliant and sumptuously rich in detail and color. In his *Arnolfini Wedding* 1434 (National Gallery, London) the bride and groom appear in a domestic interior crammed with disguised symbols, as a kind of pictorial marriage certificate.

Little is known of his brother **Hubert van Eyck** (died 1426), who is supposed to have begun the massive and complex altarpiece in St Bavo's cathedral, Ghent, *The Adoration of the Mystical Lamb*, completed by Jan 1432.

Jan van Eyck is known to have worked in The Hague 1422–24 for John of Bavaria, Count of Holland. He served as court painter to Philip the Good, Duke of Burgundy, from 1425, and worked in Bruges from 1430. Philip the Good valued him not only as a painter but also as a diplomatic representative, sending him to Spain and Portugal in 1427 and 1428, and he remained in the duke's employ after he settled in Bruges.

Oil painting allowed for subtler effects of tone and color and greater command of detail than the egg-tempera technique then in common use, and van Eyck took full advantage of this.

eye the organ of vision. In the human eye, the light is focused by the combined action of the curved *cornea*, the internal fluids, and the *lens*. The insect eye is compound—made up of many separate facets—known as ommatidia, each of which collects light and directs it separately to a receptor to build up an image. Invertebrates have much simpler eyes, with no lens. Among mollusks, cephalopods have complex eyes similar to those of vertebrates. The mantis shrimp's eyes contain ten color pigments with which to perceive color; some flies and fishes have five, while the human eye has only three.

human eye This is a roughly spherical structure contained in a bony socket. Light enters it through the cornea, and passes through the circular opening (*pupil*) in the iris (the colored part of the eye). The ciliary muscles act on the lens (the rounded transparent structure behind the iris) to change its shape, so that images of objects at different distances can be focused on the *retina*. This is at the back of the eye, and is packed with light-sensitive cells (rods and cones), connected to the brain by the optic nerve.

eyebright any wild flower of the genus *Euphrasia* of the figwort family (Scrophulariaceae). *E americana* of the SE US, with pale lavender flowers in clusters, is an example.

eyeglasses pair of lenses fitted in a frame and worn in front of the eyes to correct or assist defective vision. Common defects of the eye corrected by such lenses are near-sightedness (myopia), corrected by using concave (spherical) lenses, far-sightedness (hypermetropia), corrected by using convex (spherical) lenses, and astigmatism, corrected by using cylindrical lenses. Spherical and cylindrical lenses may be combined in one lens. Bifocal glasses correct vision both at a distance and for reading by combining two lenses of different curvatures in one piece of glass. Today, lightweight plastic lenses are common instead of glass.

Eyeglasses are said to have been invented in the 13th century by a Florentine monk. Few people found the need for eyeglasses until printing was invented, when the demand for them increased rapidly. Using photosensitive glass, lenses can be produced that darken in glare and lighten in ordinary light conditions. See also ◊contact lenses.

Eyre, Lake Australia's largest lake, in central South Australia, which frequently runs dry, becoming a salt marsh in dry seasons; area up to 3,500 sq mi/9,000 sq km. It is the continent's lowest point, 39 ft/12 m below sea level.

Ezekiel lived *c.* 600 BC. In the Old Testament, a Hebrew prophet. Carried into captivity in Babylon by ◊Nebuchadnezzar 597, he preached that Jerusalem's fall was due to the sins of Israel. The book of Ezekiel begins with a description of a vision of supernatural beings.

Ezra in the Old Testament, a Hebrew scribe who was allowed by Artaxerxes, king of Persia (probably Artaxerxes I, 464–423 BC), to lead his people back to Jerusalem from Babylon 458 BC. He reestablished the Mosaic law (laid down by Moses) and forbade intermarriage.

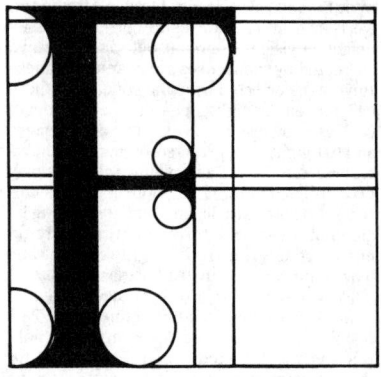

F the sixth letter of the English alphabet. Its capital form has changed little from that of the earlier Semitic alphabets. The sound f is an unvoiced lip-biting fricative.

°F symbol for degrees ⟡*Fahrenheit*.

Fabergé Peter Carl 1846–1920. Russian goldsmith and jeweler. Among his masterpieces was a series of jeweled Easter eggs, the first of which was commissioned by Alexander III for the tsarina 1884.

His workshops in St Petersburg and Moscow were celebrated for the exquisite delicacy of their products, especially the use of gold in various shades. Fabergé died in exile in Switzerland.

Fabian Society UK socialist organization for research, discussion, and publication, founded in London 1884. Its name is derived from the Roman commander Fabius Maximus, and refers to the evolutionary methods by which it hopes to attain socialism by a succession of gradual reforms. Early members included the playwright George Bernard Shaw and Beatrice and Sidney ⟡Webb. The society helped to found the Labour Representation Committee in 1900, which became the Labour Party in 1906.

Fabius Laurent 1946– . French politician, leader of the Socialist Party from 1992. As prime minister 1984–86, he introduced a liberal, free-market economic program, but his career was damaged by the 1985 ⟡Greenpeace sabotage scandal.

Fabius Maximus, Quintus c. 260–203 BC. Roman general, known as *Cunctator* or "Delayer" because of his cautious tactics against Hannibal 217–214 BC, when he continually harassed Hannibal's armies but never risked a set battle.

fable story, either in verse or prose, in which animals or inanimate objects are endowed with the mentality and speech of human beings to point out a moral. Fabulists include Aesop, Babrius, Phaedrus, Avianus, and La Fontaine.

Fabre Jean Henri Casimir 1823–1915. French entomologist, celebrated for his vivid and intimate descriptions and paintings of the life of wasps, bees, and other insects.

Fabricius Geronimo 1537–1619. Italian anatomist and embryologist. He made a detailed study of the veins and discovered the valves that direct the blood flow toward the heart. He also studied the development of chick embryos.

Fabricius was a professor of surgery and anatomy at Padua, where his work greatly influenced and helped his pupil William ⟡Harvey. Despite many errors, he raised anatomy and embryology to a higher scientific level.

facies in geology, any assemblage of mineral, rock, or fossil features that reflect the environment in which rock was formed.

The set of characters that distinguish one facies from another in a given time stratigraphic unit is used to interpret local changes in simultaneously existing environments. Thus one facies in a body of rock might consist of porous limestone containing fossil reef-building organisms in their living positions. This facies might pass on the side into a reef-flank facies of steeply dipping deposits of rubble from the reef, which in turn might grade into an interreef basin composed of fine, clayey limestone.

Ancient floods and migrations of the seashore up or down can also be traced by changes in facies.

facsimile transmission full name for ⟡*fax* or *telefax*.

factor a number that divides into another number exactly. For example, the factors of 64 are 1, 2, 4, 8, 16, 32, and 64. In algebra, certain kinds of polynomials (expressions consisting of several or many terms) can be factorized. For example, the factors of $x^2 + 3x + 2$ are $x + 1$ and $x + 2$, since $x^2 + 3x + 2 = (x + 1) (x + 2)$. This is called factorization. See also ⟡prime number.

factorial of a positive number, the product of all the whole numbers (integers) inclusive between 1 and the number itself. A factorial is indicated by the symbol "!." Thus $6! = 1 \times 2 \times 3 \times 4 \times 5 \times 6 = 720$. Factorial zero, 0!, is defined as 1.

factoring lending money to a company on the security of money owed to that company; this is often done on the basis of collecting those debts. The lender is known as the factor. Factoring may also describe acting as a commission agent for the sale of goods.

factory farming intensive rearing of poultry or animals for food, usually on high-protein foodstuffs in confined quarters. Chickens for eggs and meat, and calves for veal are commonly factory farmed. Some countries restrict the use of antibiotics and growth hormones as aids to factory farming, because they can persist in the flesh of the animals after they are slaughtered. Many people object to factory farming for moral as well as health reasons.

Egg-laying hens are housed in "batteries" of cages arranged in long rows. If caged singly, they lay fewer eggs, so there are often four to a cage with a floor area of only 372 sq in/ 2,400 sq cm. In the course of a year, battery hens average 261 eggs each, whereas for free-range chickens the figure is 199.

factory system the basis of manufacturing in the modern world. In the factory system workers are employed at a place where they carry out specific tasks, which together result in a product. This is called the division of labor. Usually these workers will perform their tasks with the aid of machinery. Such ⟡mechanization is another feature of the factory system, which leads to ⟡mass production.

Fadiman Clifton Paul 1904– . US editor.

From 1938 to 1948 Fadiman served as moderator of the national radio program "Information Please." In 1944 he was appointed to the editorial board of the Book of the Month Club. From the 1950s, he published literary anthologies and continued to be a popular radio and television personality.

Born in Brooklyn, New York, and educated at Columbia University, Fadiman began his career as a teacher at the New York Ethical Culture School. He was hired as an editor for Simon and Schuster 1927 and published his own work as a freelance writer. In 1933 he became book reviewer for the *New Yorker*.

Faerie Queene, The a poem by Edmund Spenser, published 1590–96, dedicated to Elizabeth I. The poem, in six books, describes the adventures of six knights. Spenser used a new stanza form, later adopted by Keats, Shelley, and Byron.

Faeroe Islands or *Faeroes* alternate spelling of the ⟡Faroe Islands, in the N Atlantic.

Fagatogo capital of American ⟡Samoa, situated on Pago Pago Harbor, Tutuila Island, population (1980) 30,124.

Fahd 1921– . King of Saudi Arabia from 1982, when he succeeded his half brother Khalid. As head of government, he has been active in trying to bring about a solution to the Middle East conflicts.

Fahrenheit Gabriel Daniel 1686–1736. German physicist who lived mainly in England and Holland. He devised the Fahrenheit temperature scale.

Fahrenheit scale a temperature scale invented 1714 by Gabriel Fahrenheit which was commonly used in English-speaking countries up until the 1970s, after which the ⟡Celsius scale was generally adopted, in line with the rest of the world. In the Fahrenheit scale, intervals are measured in degrees (°F);
$$°F = (°C \times 9/5) + 32.$$

Fahrenheit took as the zero point the lowest temperature he could achieve anywhere in the laboratory, and, as the other fixed point, body temperature, which he set at 96°F. On this scale, water freezes at 32°F and boils at 212°F.

fainting sudden, temporary loss of consciousness caused by reduced blood supply to the brain. It may be due to emotional shock or physical factors, such as pooling of blood in the legs from standing still for long periods.

Fairbanks town in central Alaska, situated on the Chena Slough, a tributary of the Tanana River; population (1990) 30,800. Founded 1902, it became a gold-mining and fur-trading center and the terminus of the Alaska Railroad and the Pan-American Highway.

It functions as a service center for the mineral development of central and N Alaska. Fort Wainwright, Eielson Air Force Base, and the main campus of the University of Alaska are outside the city limits.

Fairbanks Douglas, Sr. Adopted name of Douglas Elton Ulman 1883–1939. US actor. He played acrobatic swashbuckling heroes in silent films such as *The Mark of Zorro* 1920, *The Three Musketeers* 1921, *Robin Hood* 1922, *The Thief of Bagdad* 1924, and *Don Quixote* 1925. He was married to film star Mary Pickford ("America's Sweetheart") 1920–33. In 1919 founded United Artists with Charlie Chaplin and D W Griffith.

Fairbanks Douglas, Jr 1909– . US actor who appeared in the same type of swashbuckling film roles as his father, Douglas Fairbanks; for example, in *Catherine the Great* 1934 and *The Prisoner of Zenda* 1937.

Fair Deal the policy of social improvement advocated by Harry S Truman, President of the US 1945–53. The Fair Deal proposals, first mooted in 1945 after the end of World War II, aimed to extend the ⟡New Deal on health insurance, housing development, and the laws to maintain farming prices. Although some bills became law—for example a Housing Act, a higher minimum wage, and wider social security benefits—the main proposals were blocked by a hostile Congress.

Fairfax Thomas, 3rd Baron Fairfax of Cameron 1612–1671. English general, commander in chief of the Parliamentary army in the English Civil War. With Oliver Cromwell he formed the ⟡New Model Army and defeated Charles I at Naseby. He opposed the king's execution, resigned in protest 1650 against the invasion of Scotland, and participated in the restoration of Charles II after Cromwell's death.

Fairfield city in W central California, SW of Sacramento; seat of Solano County. It is a trading center for the area's fruits, grains, and dairy products; population (1990) 77,200.

fairy tale magical story, usually a folk tale in origin. Typically in European fairy tales, a poor, brave, and resourceful hero or heroine goes through testing adventures to eventual good fortune.

The Germanic tales, such as "Hansel and Gretel" and "Rumpelstiltskin" were gathered by fairy tale collectors Jakob and Wilhelm Grimm (1785–1863) and (1786–1859) and have been retold in many variants. The form may also be adapted for more individual moral and literary purposes, as was done by Danish writer Hans Christian ⟡Andersen.

Faisal Ibn Abdul Aziz 1905–1975. King of Saudi Arabia from 1964. He was the younger brother of King Saud, on whose accession 1953 he was declared crown prince. He was prime minister from 1953–60 and from 1962–75. In 1964 he emerged victorious from a lengthy conflict with his brother and adopted a policy of steady modernization of his country. He was assassinated by his nephew.

Faisal I 1885–1933. King of Iraq 1921–33. An Arab nationalist leader during World War I, he was instrumental in liberating the Near East from Ottoman control and was declared king of Syria in 1918 but deposed by the French in 1920. The British then installed him as king in Iraq, where he continued to foster pan-Arabism.

fakir originally a Muslim mendicant of some religious order, but in India a general term for an ascetic.

Falange Española (Spanish Phalanx) former Spanish Fascist Party, founded 1933 by José Antonio Primo de Rivera (1903–1936), son of military ruler Miguel ⟡Primo de Rivera. It was closely modeled in program and organization on the Italian fascists and on the Nazis. In 1937, when ⟡Franco assumed leadership, it was declared the only legal party, and altered its name to Traditionalist Spanish Phalanx.

Falasha member of a small community of black Jews in Ethiopia. They suffered discrimination there, and, after being accorded Jewish status by Israel 1975, began a gradual process of resettlement in Israel. In the early 1980s only about 30,000 Falashim remained in Ethiopia.

falcon any bird of prey of the genus *Falco*, family Falconidae, order Falconiformes. Falcons are the smallest of the hawks (6–24 in/15–60 cm). They nest in high places and kill their prey by "stooping" (swooping down at high speed). They include the peregrine and kestrel.

The peregrine falcon *F. peregrinus*, up to about 1.8 ft/50 cm long, has become reestablished in North America and Britain after near extinction (by pesticides, gamekeepers, and egg collectors). When stooping on its intended prey, it is the fastest creature in the world, timed at 150 mph/240 kph.

Other hawks include the worldwide merlin or pigeon hawk *F. columbarius* and the Eurasian kestrel *F. tinnunculus*. Merlins are about 1 ft/30 cm in length, steel-blue above and reddish below, and nest on moors. Kestrels are just over 1 ft/30 cm long, with gray head and tail, light chestnut back with black spots, and an unmistakeable quivering hover.

Falconet Etienne-Maurice 1716–1791. French sculptor whose works range from formal Baroque to gentle Rococo in style. He directed sculpture at the Sèvres porcelain factory 1757–66. His bronze equestrian statue *Peter the Great* in Leningrad was commissioned 1766 by Catherine II.

falconry the use of specially trained falcons and hawks to capture birds or small mammals. Practiced since ancient times in the Middle East, falconry was introduced from continental Europe to Britain in Saxon times.

In recent times there has been a revival of interest in the West.

Faldo Nick 1957– . English golfer who was the first Briton in 54 years to win three British Open titles, and the only person after Jack ⟡Nicklaus to win two successive US Masters titles (1989 and 1990). He is one of only six golfers to win the Masters and British Open in the same year.

Since turning professional in 1976 he has won more than 25 tournaments worldwide.

CAREER HIGHLIGHTS

British Open
1987, 1989, 1992
US Masters
1989, 1990
US PGA Championship
1978, 1980–81, 1989

Falkland Islands British crown colony in the S Atlantic
area 4,700 sq mi/12,173 sq km, made up of two main islands: East Falkland 2,610 sq mi/6,760 sq km, and West Falkland 2,090 sq mi/5,413 sq km
capital Stanley; new port facilities opened 1984, Mount Pleasant airport 1985
features in addition to the two main islands, there are about 200 small islands, all with wild scenery and rich bird life
products wool, alginates (used as dyes and as a food additive) from seaweed beds
population (1986) 1,916
government a governor (Gordon Jewkes from Oct 1985) is advised by an executive council, and a mainly elected legislative council. Administered with the Falklands, but separate dependencies of the UK, are South Georgia and the South ⟡Sandwich Islands; see also ⟡British Antarctic Territory.
history the first European to visit the islands was Englishman John Davis 1592, and at the end of the 17th century they were named after Lord Falkland, treasurer of the British navy. West Falkland was settled by the French in 1764. The first British settlers arrived 1765; Spain bought out a French settlement 1766, and the British were ejected 1770–71, but British sovereignty was never ceded, and from 1833, when a few Argentines were expelled, British settlement was continuous. Argentina asserts its succession to the Spanish claim to the "Islas Malvinas," but the inhabitants oppose cession. Occupied by Argentina April 1982, the islands were recaptured by British military forces in May–June of the same year.

In April 1990 Argentina's congress declared the Falkland Islands and other British-held South Atlantic islands part of the new Argentine province of Tierra del Fuego.

Falkland Islands, Battle of the British naval victory (under Admiral Sturdee) Dec 8, 1914 over the German admiral von Spee.

Falklands War war between Argentina and Britain over disputed sovereignty of the Falkland Islands initiated when Argentina invaded and occupied the islands April 2, 1982. On the following day, the United Nations Security Council passed a resolution calling for Argentina to withdraw. A British task force was immediately dispatched and, after a fierce conflict in which over 1,000 Argentine and British lives were lost, 12,000 Argentine troops surrendered and the islands were returned to British rule June 14–15, 1982.

Falla Manuel de 1876–1946. Spanish composer. His opera *La vida breve/Brief Life* 1905 (performed 1913) was followed by the ballets *El amor brujo/Love the Magician* 1915 and *El sombrero de tres picos/The Three-Cornered Hat* 1919, and his most ambitious concert work, *Noches en los jardines de España/Nights in the Gardens of Spain* 1916. The folk idiom of southern Spain is an integral part of his compositions. He also wrote songs and pieces for piano and guitar.

Born in Cádiz, he lived in France, where he was influenced by the Impressionist composers Claude Debussy and Maurice Ravel. In 1939 he moved to Argentina.

Fallopian tube or *oviduct* in mammals, one of two tubes that carry eggs from the ovary to the uterus. An egg is fertilized by sperm in the Fallopian tubes, which are lined with cells whose ⟡cilia move the egg toward the uterus.

Fallopius Gabriel. Latinized name of Gabriello Fallopio 1523–1562. Italian anatomist who discovered the ⟡Fallopian tubes, which he described as "trumpets of the uterus," and named the vagina. As well as the reproductive system, he studied the anatomy of the brain and eyes, and gave the first accurate description of the inner ear.

Fallopius studied at Padua under Andreas ⟡Vesalius, and later taught there and at Ferrara and Pisa.

fallout harmful radioactive material released into the atmosphere in the debris of a nuclear explosion (see ⟡nuclear weapons) and descending to the surface of the Earth. Such material can enter the food chain, cause ⟡radiation sickness, and last for hundreds of thousands of years (see ⟡half-life).

Fall River city and port in Massachusetts; population (1990) 92,700. It stands at the mouth of the Taunton River, over the Little Fall River, which gave it its name. Textiles and clothing, rubber, paper, and plastics are among the goods produced.

It was founded 1656 and was one of the nation's most important textile-mill centers in the 19th century. Lizzie Borden was acquitted here of murdering her father and stepmother 1892.

false-color imagery graphic technique that displays images in false (not true-to-life) colors so as to enhance certain features. It is widely used in displaying electronic images taken by spacecraft; for example, Earth-survey satellites such as *Landsat*. Any colors can be selected by a computer processing the received data.

falsificationism in philosophy of science, the belief that a scientific theory must be under constant scrutiny and that its merit lies only in how well it stands up to rigorous testing. It was first expounded by philosopher Karl ♢Popper in his *Logic of Scientific Discovery* 1934.

Such thinking also implies that a theory can only be held to be scientific if it makes predictions that are clearly testable. Critics of this belief acknowledge the strict logic of this process, but doubt whether the whole of scientific method can be subsumed into so narrow a program. Philosophers and historians such as Thomas ♢Kuhn and Paul ♢Feyerabend have attempted to use the history of science to show that scientific progress has resulted from a more complicated methodology than Popper suggests.

family in biological classification, a group of related genera (see ♢genus). Family names are not printed in italic (unlike genus and species names), and by convention they all have the ending -idae (animals) or -aceae (plants and fungi). For example, the genera of hummingbirds are grouped in the hummingbird family, Trochilidae. Related families are grouped together in an ♢order.

family group of people related to each other by blood or by marriage.

Families are usually described as either "extended" (a large group of relations living together or in close contact with each other) or "nuclear" (a family consisting of two parents and their children).

In some societies an extended family consists of a large group of people of different generations closely or distantly related, depending on each other for economic support and security. In other societies the extended family is split into small units, with members living alone or in nuclear families. The "one-parent" family has recently emerged in the West following the divorce or separation of parents or as a result of a child born to a single woman.

family planning spacing or preventing the birth of children. Access to family-planning services (see ♢contraceptive) is a significant factor in women's health as well as in limiting population growth. If all those women who wished to avoid further childbirth were able to do so, the number of births would be reduced by 27% in Africa, 33% in Asia, and 35% in Latin America; and the number of women who die during pregnancy or childbirth would be reduced by about 50%.

The average number of pregnancies per woman is two in the industrialized countries, where 71% use family planning, as compared to six or seven pregnancies per woman in the Third World. According to a World Bank estimate, doubling the annual $2 billion spent on family planning would avert the deaths of 5.6 million infants and 250,000 mothers each year.

In the face of increased populations and decreased food supplies and natural resources,

family planning has become a priority for some nations.

famine severe shortage of food affecting a large number of people. Almost 750 million people (equivalent to double the population of Europe) worldwide suffer from hunger and malnutrition. The *food availability deficit* (FAD) theory explains famines as being caused by insufficient food supplies. A more recent theory is that famines arise when one group in a society loses its opportunity to exchange its labor or possessions for food.

Most Western famine-relief agencies, such as the International ♢Red Cross, set out to supply food or to increase its local production, rather than becoming involved in local politics. The FAD theory was challenged in the 1980s. Crop failures do not inevitably lead to famine; nor is it always the case that adequate food supplies are not available nearby. In 1990, for example, the Ethiopian air force bombed grain depots in a rebel-held area.

Fang member of a W African people living in the rainforests of Cameroon, Equatorial Guinea, and NW Gabon, numbering about 2.5 million. They live by farming, as well as by hunting and fishing.

In the colonial period the Fang were involved in trading, and used coins made of copper and iron. The Fang language belongs to the Bantu branch of the Niger-Congo family.

fan-jet another name for ♢turbofan, the jet engine used by most airliners.

fantasia *fantasy* or *fancy* in music, a free-form instrumental composition of improvised character.

fantasy fiction nonrealistic fiction. Much of the world's fictional literature could be classified under this term but, as a commercial and literary genre, fantasy started to thrive after the success of J R R Tolkien's *Lord of the Rings* 1954–55. Earlier works by such writers as Lord Dunsany, Hope Mirrlees, E R Eddison, and Mervyn Peake, which are not classifiable in fantasy subgenres such as ♢science fiction, ♢horror, or ghost story, could be labeled fantasy.

Much fantasy is pseudomedieval in subject matter and tone. Recent works include Ursula K LeGuin's *Earthsea* series 1968–91, Stephen Donaldson's *Chronicles of Thomas Covenant* 1978–83, and, in the more urban tradition, John Crowley's *Little Big* 1980, Michael Moorcock's *Gloriana* 1978, and Gene Wolfe's *Free, Live Free* 1985. Such books largely overlap in content with the ♢magic realism of writers such as Gabriel García Márquez, Angela Carter, and Isabel Allende.

Well-known US fantasy authors include Thomas Pynchon (as, for example, in *V*), and Ray Bradbury, whose works are often in the science fiction genre.

Fantin-Latour (Ignace) Henri (Joseph Théodore) 1836–1904. French painter excelling in delicate still lifes, flower paintings, and portraits. *Homage à Delacroix* 1864 (Musée d'Orsay, Paris) is a portrait group with many poets, authors, and painters, including Charles Baudelaire and James Whistler.

FAO abbreviation for ♢*Food and Agriculture Organization*.

farad SI unit (symbol F) of electrical capacitance (how much electricity a ♢capacitor can store for a given voltage). One farad is a capacitance of one ♢coulomb per volt. For practical

purposes the microfarad (one millionth of a farad) is more commonly used.

The farad is named after the English scientist Michael Faraday, and replaced the now obsolete unit the jar (so called because it represented the charge stored in a Leiden jar, the earliest electrical circuit). One farad = 9×10^8 jars.

Faraday Michael 1791–1867. English chemist and physicist. In 1821 he began experimenting with electromagnetism, and ten years later discovered the induction of electric currents and made the first dynamo. He subsequently found that a magnetic field will rotate the plane of polarization of light (see ♢polarized light). Faraday also investigated electrolysis.

Faraday's constant constant (symbol F) representing the electric charge carried on one mole of electrons. It is found by multiplying Avogadro's constant by the charge carried on a single electron, and is equal to 9.648×10^4 coulombs per mole. One *faraday* is this constant used as a unit. The constant is used to calculate the electric charge needed to discharge a particular quantity of ions during ♢electrolysis.

Faraday's laws three laws of electromagnetic induction, and two laws of electrolysis, all proposed originally by Michael Faraday:

induction (1) a changing magnetic field induces an electromagnetic force in a conductor; (2) the electromagnetic force is proportional to the rate of change of the field; (3) the direction of the induced electromagnetic force depends on the orientation of the field.

electrolysis (1) the amount of chemical change during electrolysis is proportional to the charge passing through the liquid; (2) the amount of chemical change produced in a substance by a given amount of electricity is proportional to the electrochemical equivalent of that substance.

farce a broad form of comedy involving stereotyped characters in complex, often improbable situations frequently revolving around extramarital relationships (hence the term "bedroom farce").

Originating in the physical knockabout comedy of Greek satyr plays and the broad humor of medieval religious drama, the farce was developed and perfected during the 19th century by Eugène Labiche (1815–1888) and Georges Feydeau (1862–1921) in France and Arthur Pinero in England.

Far East geographical term for all Asia E of the Indian subcontinent.

Fargo city in SE North Dakota, across the Red River from Moorhead, Minnesota; seat of Cass County. The largest city in the state, it is a center for processing and distributing agricultural products and farm machinery. Chemicals and building materials are also manufactured; population (1990) 74,100.

Fargo William George 1818–1881. US long-distance transport pioneer. In 1844 he established with Henry Wells (1805–1878) and Daniel Dunning the first express company to carry freight west of Buffalo. Its success led to his appointment 1850 as secretary of the newly established American Express Company, of which he was president 1868–81. He also established *Wells, Fargo & Company* 1851, carrying goods express between New York and San Francisco via Panama.

Farmer Frances 1913–1970. US actress who

starred in such films as *Come and Get It* 1936, *The Toast of New York* 1937, and *Son of Fury* 1942, before her career was ended by alcoholism and mental illness.

She published an autobiography *Will There Really Be a Morning?*.

Farnese an Italian family, originating in upper Lazio, who held the duchy of Parma 1545–1731. Among the family's most notable members were Alessandro Farnese (1468–1549), who became Pope Paul III in 1534 and granted his duchy to his illegitimate son Pier Luigi (1503–1547); Elizabeth (1692–1766), niece of the last Farnese duke, married Philip V of Spain and was a force in European politics of the time.

Faroe Islands or **Faeroe Islands** or **Faeroes** (Danish **Faerøerne**, "Sheep Islands") island group (18 out of 22 inhabited) in the N Atlantic, between the Shetland Islands and Iceland, forming an outlying part of ⟡Denmark
area 540 sq mi/1,399 sq km; largest islands are Strømø, Østerø, Vagø, Suderø, Sandø, and Bordø
capital Thorshavn on Strømø, population (1986) 15,287
products fish, crafted goods
currency Danish krone
population (1986) 46,000
language Faerøese, Danish
government since 1948 the islands have had full self-government; they do not belong to the EC
history first settled by Norsemen in the 9th century, the Faroes were a Norwegian province 1380–1709. Their parliament was restored 1852. They withdrew from the European Free Trade Association 1972.

Farouk 1920–1965. King of Egypt 1936–52. He succeeded his father ⟡Fuad I. In 1952 a coup headed by General Muhammed Neguib and Colonel Gamal Nasser compelled him to abdicate, and his son Fuad II was temporarily proclaimed in his place.

Farquhar George 1677–1707. Irish dramatist. His plays *The Recruiting Officer* 1706 and *The Beaux' Stratagem* 1707 are in the tradition of the Restoration comedy of manners, although less robust.

Farragut David (Glasgow) 1801–1870. US admiral, born near Knoxville, Tennessee. During the US Civil War he took New Orleans 1862, after destroying the Confederate fleet, and in 1864 effectively put an end to blockade-running at Mobile. The ranks of vice admiral (1864) and admiral (1866) were created for him by Congress.

It was at Mobile Bay that Farragut rallied his fleet in the face of Confederate mines (then called torpedoes) with the cry, "Damn the torpedoes: Full speed ahead!"

Farrell James T(homas) 1904–1979. US novelist and short-story writer. His naturalistic *Studs Lonigan* trilogy 1932–35, comprising *Young Lonigan*, *The Young Manhood of Studs Lonigan*, and *Judgment Day*, describes the development of a young Catholic man in Chicago after World War I, and was written from his own experience. *The Face of Time* 1953 is one of his finest works.

Farrow Mia 1945– . US film and television actress. Popular since the late 1960s, she was associated with the director Woody Allen, both on and off screen 1982–92. She starred in his films *Zelig* 1983, *Hannah and Her Sisters* 1986, and *Crimes and Misdemeanors* 1990, as well as in Roman Polanski's *Rosemary's Baby* 1968.

Fars province of SW Iran, comprising fertile valleys among mountain ranges running NW–SE; population (1982) 2,035,600; area 51,487 sq mi/133,300 sq km. The capital is Shiraz, and there are imposing ruins of Cyrus the Great's city of Parargardae and of ⟡Persepolis.

Farsi or **Persian** language belonging to the Indo-Iranian branch of the Indo-European family, and the official language of Iran (formerly Persia). It is also spoken in Afghanistan, Iraq, and Tajikistan.

Farsi is the language of the province of Fars (Persia proper).

It is written in Arabic script, from right to left, and has a large mixture of Arabic religious, philosophical, and technical vocabulary.

fasces in ancient Rome, bundles of rods carried in procession by the lictors (minor officials) in front of the chief magistrates, as a symbol of the latter's power over the lives and liberties of the people. An axe was included in the bundle. The fasces were revived in the 20th century as the symbol of ⟡fascism.

Fasching period preceding Lent in German-speaking towns, particularly Munich, Cologne, and Vienna, devoted to masquerades, formal balls, and street parades.

fascism political ideology that denies all rights to individuals in their relations with the state; specifically, the totalitarian nationalist movement founded in Italy 1919 by ⟡Mussolini and followed by Hitler's Germany 1933.

Fascism was essentially a product of the economic and political crisis of the years after World War I. Units called *fasci di combattimento* (combat groups), from the Latin ⟡fasces, were originally established to oppose communism. The fascist party, the *Partitio Nazionale Fascista*, controlled Italy 1922–43. Fascism protected the existing social order by forcible suppression of the working-class movement and by providing scapegoats for popular anger such as minorities who lived within the state: Jews, foreigners, or blacks; it also prepared the citizenry for the economic and psychological mobilization of war.

The atrocities committed by Nazi Germany and other fascist countries discredited fascism, but neo-fascist groups exist today in the US, Latin America, and many W European countries.

Fashoda Incident dispute 1898 in the town of Fashoda (now Kodok) situated on the White Nile in SE Sudan, in which a clash between French and British forces nearly led the two countries into war.

Fassbinder Rainer Werner 1946–1982. West German film director who began as a fringe actor and founded his own "antitheater" before moving into films. His works are mainly stylized indictments of contemporary German society. He made more than 40 films, including *Die bitteren Tränen der Petra von Kant/The Bitter Tears of Petra von Kant* 1972, *Angst essen Seele auf/Fear Eats the Soul* 1974, and *Die Ehe von Maria Braun/The Marriage of Maria Braun* 1979.

fasting the practice of voluntarily going without food. It can be undertaken as a religious observance, a sign of mourning, a political protest (hunger strike), or for slimming purposes.

Fasting or abstinence from certain types of food or beverages occurs in most religious traditions. It is seen as an act of self-discipline that increases spiritual awareness by lessening dependence on the material world. In the Roman Catholic church, fasting is seen as a penitential rite, a means to express repentance for sin. The most commonly observed Christian fasting is in Lent, from Ash Wednesday to Easter Sunday and recalls the 40 days Christ spent in the wilderness. Roman Catholics and Orthodox usually fast before taking communion and monastic communities observe regular weekly fasts. Devout Muslims go without food or water between sunrise and sunset during the month of Ramadan.

Total abstinence from food for a limited period is prescribed by some ⟡naturopaths to eliminate body toxins or make available for recuperative purposes the energy normally used by the digestive system. Prolonged fasting can be dangerous. The liver breaks up its fat stores, releasing harmful by-products called ketones, which results in a condition called ketosis, which develops within three days, an early symptom of which is a smell of pear drops on the breath. Other symptoms include nausea, vomiting, fatigue, dizziness, severe depression, and irritability. Eventually the muscles and other body tissues become wasted, and death results.

fat in the broadest sense, a mixture of ⟡lipids—chiefly triglycerides (lipids containing three ⟡fatty acid molecules linked to a molecule of glycerol). More specifically, the term refers to a lipid mixture that is solid at room temperature (20°C); lipid mixtures that are liquid at room temperature are called *oils*. The higher the proportion of saturated fatty acids in a mixture, the harder the fat.

Boiling fats in strong alkali forms soaps (saponification). Fats are essential constituents of food for many animals, with a calorific value twice that of carbohydrates; however, eating too much fat, especially fat of animal origin, has been linked with heart disease in humans. In many animals and plants, excess carbohydrates and proteins are converted into fats for storage. Mammals and other vertebrates store fats in specialized connective tissues (⟡adipose tissues), which not only act as energy reserves but also insulate the body and cushion its organs.

As a nutrient fat serves five purposes: it is a source of energy (9 kcal/g); makes the diet palatable; provides basic building blocks for cell structure; provides essential fatty acids (linoleic and linolenic); and acts as a carrier for fat-soluble vitamins (A, D, E, and K). Foods rich in fat are butter, lard, margarine, and cooking oils.

Fatah, al- Palestinian nationalist organization founded 1956 to bring about an independent state of Palestine. Also called the Palestine National Liberation Movement, it is the main component of the ⟡Palestine Liberation Organization. Its leader is Yassir ⟡Arafat.

fata morgana (Italian "Morgan the Fairy") a mirage, often seen in the Strait of Messina and traditionally attributed to the sorcery of ⟡Morgan le Fay. She was believed to reside in Calabria, a region of S Italy.

Fates in Greek mythology, the three female figures who determined the destiny of human lives. They were envisaged as spinners; Clotho spun the thread of life, Lachesis twisted the thread, and Atropos cut it off. They are analogous to the Roman Parcae and Norse ⟡Norns.

Father of the Church any of certain teachers and writers of the early Christian church, eminent for their learning and orthodoxy, experience, and sanctity of life. They lived between the end of the 1st and the end of the 7th century, a period divided by the Council of Nicaea 325 into the Ante-Nicene and Post-Nicene Fathers.

The Ante-Nicene Fathers include the Apostolic Fathers: Clement of Rome, Ignatius of Antioch, Polycarp of Smyrna, Barnabas, Justin Martyr, Clement of Alexandria, Origen, Tertullian, and Cyprian. Among the Post-Nicene Fathers are Cyril of Alexandria, Athanasius, John Chrysostom, Eusebius of Caesarea, Basil the Great, Ambrose of Milan, Augustine, Pope Leo I, Boethius, Jerome, Gregory of Tours, Pope Gregory the Great, and Bede.

Father's Day a day set apart in many countries for honoring fathers, observed on the third Sunday in June in the US, UK, and Canada. The idea for a father's day originated with Sonora Louise Smart Dodd of Spokane, Washington, in 1909 (after hearing a sermon on Mother's Day), and through her efforts the first Father's Day was celebrated there in 1910.

fathom (Anglo-Saxon *faethm* "to embrace") in mining, seafaring, and handling timber, a unit of depth measurement (6 ft/1.83 m) used prior to metrication; it approximates to the distance between an adult man's hands when the arms are outstretched.

Fatimid dynasty of Muslim Shiite caliphs founded 909 by Obaidallah, who claimed to be a descendant of Fatima (the prophet Mohammed's daughter) and her husband Ali, in N Africa. In 969 the Fatimids conquered Egypt, and the dynasty continued until overthrown by Saladin 1171.

fatty acid or **carboxylic acid** organic compound consisting of a hydrocarbon chain, up to 24 carbon atoms long, with a carboxyl group (–COOH) at one end. The covalent bonds between the carbon atoms may be single or double; where a double bond occurs the carbon atoms concerned carry one instead of two hydrogen atoms. Chains with only single bonds have all the hydrogen they can carry, so they are said to be **saturated** with hydrogen. Chains with one or more double bonds are said to be **unsaturated** (see ◊polyunsaturate).

Saturated fatty acids include palmitic and stearic acids; unsaturated fatty acids include oleic (one double bond), linoleic (two double bonds) and linolenic (three double bonds). Fatty acids are generally found combined with glycerol in ◊lipids such as tryglycerides.

fatwa in Islamic law, an authoritative legal opinion on a point of doctrine. In 1989 a fatwa calling for the death of English novelist Salman ◊Rushdie was made by the Ayatollah ◊Khomeini of Iran, following publication of Rushdie's controversial and allegedly blasphemous book *The Satanic Verses*.

Faulkner William 1897–1962. US novelist who wrote in an experimental stream-of-consciousness style, often considered the finest 20th-century American writer. His works include *The Sound and the Fury* 1929, dealing with a favorite topic—the Southern family in decline; *As I Lay Dying* 1930; and *The Hamlet* 1940, *The Town* 1957, and *The Mansion* 1959, a trilogy covering the rise of the materialistic Snopes family. He was awarded the Nobel Prize for Literature in 1949.

Faulkner served in World War I and his first novel, *Soldier's Pay* 1929, is about a war veteran. After the war he returned to Oxford,

Mississippi, on which he was to model the town of Jefferson in the county of Yoknapatawpha, the setting of his major novels. Other works include *Light in August* 1932, a study of segregation; *The Unvanquished* 1938, stories of the Civil War; and *The Wild Palms* 1939.

Further notable novels are *Sartoris* 1929, *Intruder in the Dust* 1948, *Requiem for a Nun* 1953, dramatized 1955, and *The Reivers* 1962. He also published short stories including "A Rose for Emily" and "Barn Burning," poems, and essays.

fault in geology, a fracture in the Earth's crust along which the two sides have moved as a result of differing strains in the adjacent rock bodies. Displacement of rock masses horizontally or vertically along a fault may be microscopic, or it may be massive, causing major ◊earthquakes.

If the movement has a major vertical component, the fault is termed a **normal fault**, where rocks on each side have moved apart, or a **reverse fault**, where one side has overridden the other (a low angle reverse fault is called a **thrust**). A particular kind of fault found only in ocean ridges is the **transform fault** (a term coined by Canadian geophysicist J Tuzo Wilson 1965). On a map an ocean ridge has a stepped appearance. The ridge crest is broken into sections, each section offset from the next. Between each section of the ridge crest the newly generated plates are moving past one another, forming a transform fault.

Faunus in Roman mythology, god of fertility and prophecy, with goat's ears, horns, tail and hind legs, identified with the Greek Pan.

Fauré Gabriel (Urbain) 1845–1924. French composer of songs, chamber music, and a choral *Requiem* 1888. He was a pupil of Saint-Saëns, became professor of composition at the Paris Conservatoire 1896 and was director from 1905 to 1920.

Faust legendary magician who sold his soul to the Devil. The historical Georg Faust appears to have been a wandering scholar and conjurer in Germany at the start of the 16th century. Goethe, Heine, Thomas Mann, and Paul Valéry all used the legend, and it inspired musical works by Schumann, Berlioz, Gounod, Boito, and Busoni.

Earlier figures such as Simon Magus (1st century AD, Middle Eastern practitioner of magic arts) contributed to the Faust legend. In 1587 the first of a series of Faust books appeared. Marlowe's tragedy, *Dr Faustus*, was acted in 1594. In the 18th century the story was a subject for pantomime in England and puppet plays in Germany.

Faust play by Goethe, completed in two parts 1808 and 1832. Mephistopheles attempts to win over the soul of world-weary Faust but ultimately fails after helping Faust in the pursuit of good.

Fauvism style of painting with a bold use of vivid colors inspired by van Gogh, Cézanne, and Gaugin. A short-lived but influential art movement, Fauvism originated in Paris 1905 with the founding of the Salon d'Automne by Henri ◊Matisse and others, when the critic Louis Vauxcelles called their gallery *"une cage aux fauves"* (a cage of wild beasts).

Rouault, Dufy, Marquet, Derain, and Signac were early Fauves.

Fawkes Guy 1570–1606. English conspirator in the ◊Gunpowder Plot to blow up King James I and the members of both Houses of Parliament. Fawkes, a Roman Catholic convert, was arrested in the cellar underneath the House Nov 4, 1605, tortured, and executed. The event is still commemorated in Britain and elsewhere every Nov 5 with bonfires, fireworks, and the burning of the "guy," an effigy.

fax (common name for **facsimile transmission** or **telefax**) the transmission of images over a ◊telecommunications link, usually the telephone network. When placed on a fax machine, the original image is scanned by a transmitting device and converted into coded signals, which travel via the telephone lines to the receiving fax machine, where an image is created that is a copy of the original. Photographs as well as printed text and drawings can be sent.

The world's first fax machine, the pantélégraphe, was invented by Italian physicist Giovanni Caselli 1866, over a century before the first electronic model came on the market. Standing over 6.5 ft/2 m high, it transmitted by telegraph nearly 5,000 handwritten documents and drawings between Paris and Lyon in its first year.

Fayetteville city in the NW corner of Arkansas, SE of Fort Smith; seat of Washington County. Its main industry is poultry processing; others include lumber, clothing, and tools. The University of Arkansas 1871 is here; population (1990) 42,100.

Fayetteville city in S central North Carolina, on the Cape Fear river, S of Durham and Chapel Hill and SW of Raleigh. Its industries include processing of the area's agricultural products, tools, textiles, and lumber; population (1990) 75,700. It was named for the Marquis de Lafayette.

FBI abbreviation for ◊*Federal Bureau of Investigation*, agency of the US Department of Justice.

fealty in feudalism, the loyalty and duties owed by a vassal to his lord. In the 9th century fealty obliged the vassal not to take part in any action that would endanger the lord or his property, but by the 11th century the specific duties of

← Tension →   → Compression ←

Normal fault   Reverse fault

fault *Faults are caused by the movement of rock layers, producing such features as block mountains and rift valleys.*

communication satellite

antenna

antenna

audio coupler (modem)

input signal

scanning device in fax machine

output signal

fax image

fax machine

fax *The fax machine scans a document to produce a digital (dot-by-dot) signal.*

fraud against the government, and conducts security clearances. Field divisions are maintained in more than 60 US cities. The FBI's special agents are qualified in law, accounting, or auditing.

In 1964 the agency was criticized by the Warren Commission concerning the assassination of President Kennedy. In 1973 L Patrick Gray, the acting director, resigned when it was revealed that he had destroyed relevant material in the ◊Watergate investigation. Through the Freedom of Information Act it became known that the FBI had kept files on many eminent citizens and that Hoover had abused his power, for example, in investigating the civil rights leader Martin Luther King.

Federal Deposit Insurance Corporation (FDIC) US government authority established 1933 to regulate US banks and insure them against loss.

The body was set up following the collapse of the banking sector early 1933. All members of the Federal Reserve System are required to belong to the FDIC, and many other US banks that are prepared to conform to certain regulations are also members.

federalism system of government in which two or more separate states unite under a common central government while retaining a considerable degree of local autonomy. A federation should be distinguished from a *confederation*, a looser union of states for mutual assistance. Switzerland, the US, Australia, and Malaysia are all examples of federal government, and many supporters of the European Community see it as the forerunner of a federal Europe.

The US federal government is organized with an executive branch, a ◊legislature, and a judiciary; each has means to control both of the other branches, thus creating a system of checks and balances, which was considered necessary for fair governing by the framers of the US Constitution. Each of the 50 states retains rights and privileges that overlap with those of the branches of the federal government. When jurisdiction is challenged, cases are decided by the US Supreme Court of the judiciary branch, thus creating constitutional law.

Federalist in US history, one who advocated the ratification of the US Constitution 1787–88 in place of the Articles of ◊Confederation. The Federalists became in effect the ruling political party during the presidencies of George Washington and John Adams 1789–1801, legislating to strengthen the authority of the newly created federal government.

The Federalists advocated reconciliation with Britain and were urban, educated, and vaguely antidemocratic.

Federalist Papers, the in US politics, a series of 85 letters published in the newly independent US in 1788, attempting to define the relation of the states to the nation, and making the case for a federal government. The papers were signed "Publius," which proved to be the joint pseudonym of three leading political figures, Alexander Hamilton, John Jay, and James Madison.

Federal Reserve System (the "Fed") US central banking system and note-issuing authority, established 1913 to regulate the country's credit and ◊monetary policy. The Fed consists of the 12 federal reserve banks, their 25 branches and other facilities throughout the country; it is headed by a board of governors in Washington,

fealty were established and included financial obligations and military service. Following an oath of fealty, an act of allegiance and respect (homage) was made by the vassal; when a ◊fief was granted by the lord, it was formalized in the process of investiture.

feather rigid outgrowth of the outer layer of the skin of birds, made of the protein keratin. Feathers provide insulation and facilitate flight. There are several types, including long quill feathers on the wings and tail, fluffy down feathers for retaining body heat, and contour feathers covering the body. The coloring of feathers is often important in camouflage or in courtship and other displays. Feathers are replaced at least once a year.

feather star any of an unattached, free-swimming group of sea-lilies, order Comatulida. The arms are branched into numerous projections (hence "feather" star), and grow from a small cup-shaped body. Below the body are appendages that can hold onto a surface, but the feather star is not permanently attached.

February Revolution the first of the two political uprisings of the ◊Russian revolution in 1917 that led to the overthrow of the tsar and the end of the ◊Romanov dynasty.

The immediate cause of the revolution was the inability of the tsardom to manage World War I. On March 8 (dating by the Western calendar, not adopted at that time in Russia) strikes and bread riots broke out in Petrograd (formerly St Petersburg), where the troops later mutinied and joined the rioters. A provisional government under Prince Lvov was appointed by the ◊Duma (assembly) and Tsar Nicholas II abdicated on March 15 (Feb 27 Julian calendar).

The Petrograd Soviet of Workers, Peasants and Soldiers (formed originally during the Russian revolution of 1905) was revived by the Bolsheviks and opposed the provisional government, especially when Lenin returned from Switzerland in April. On July 16–18 the Bolsheviks made an unsuccessful attempt to

seize power and Lenin was forced into hiding in Finland. The provisional government tried to continue the war, but was weakened by serious misunderstandings between the prime minister, Kerensky, and the commander in chief, General Kornilov, who tried unsuccessfully to gain power in Sept 1917. Shortly afterwards the Bolsheviks seized power in the ◊October Revolution.

feces remains of food and other debris passed out of the digestive tract of animals. Feces consist of quantities of fibrous material, bacteria and other microorganisms, rubbed-off lining of the digestive tract, bile fluids, undigested food, minerals, and water.

fecundity the rate at which an organism reproduces, as distinct from its ability to reproduce (◊fertility). In vertebrates, it is usually measured as the number of offspring produced by a female each year.

Federal Aviation Administration (FAA) agency of the US Department of Transportation that controls air traffic. Its responsibilities include regulating air transportation, aviation safety, developing and operating a system of air traffic control, requiring airports and airlines to provide antihijacking security, and conducting aviation research. The agency is also responsible for investigating airplane accidents. It was established in 1958 as the Federal Aviation Agency and was renamed upon its assignment to Transportation in 1967. It is directed by an administrator appointed directly by the President.

Federal Bureau of Investigation (FBI) agency of the US Department of Justice that investigates violations of federal law not specifically assigned to other agencies, being particularly concerned with internal security. The FBI was established 1908 and built up a position of powerful autonomy during the autocratic directorship of J Edgar Hoover 1924–72. William Sessions, a former judge, has been director since 1987.

The FBI reports to the US Attorney General, and investigates espionage, sabotage, kidnapping, bank robbery, civil-rights violations, and

DC, appointed by the president with Senate approval.

The Fed plays a major role in the formulation and implementation of monetary policy. It is independent and autonomous in its decisions. Inflation, interest rates, and overall economic activity can be governed by the Fed's decision to expand or restrict the supply of money to the economy. The ◇discount rate is the rate the Fed charges member banks to borrow money. By raising or lowering that rate, the Fed regulates credit. By requiring member banks to keep larger or smaller amounts of their deposits on hand as reserves, the Fed can apply another control. For these reasons, the chairman of the Federal Reserve is one of the most powerful figures in government. The decisions of the board of governors concerning discount and other rates are reached under exceptionally tight security and are eagerly awaited.

Federal Theater Project US arts employment scheme 1935–39 founded as part of Roosevelt's New Deal by the Works Progress Administration; it organized cheap popular theater all over the US and had long-term influence on modern US drama.

The project was directed by Hallie Flanagan, head of drama at Vassar college, and included the "Living Theater" presenting current social and economic issues, the Negro Theater (initially under John Houseman), and an experimental theater. It created many new groups and works before it was halted by Congress.

Federal Writers' Project US arts project founded in 1934 by the Works Progress Administration (WPA) to encourage and employ writers during the Depression, generate compilations of regional records and folklore, and develop a series of guides to states and regions.

feedback general principle whereby the results produced in an ongoing reaction become factors in modifying or changing the reaction; it is the principle used in self-regulating control systems, from a simple thermostat or temperature gauge and steam-engine ◇governor to automatic computer-controlled machine tools. A fully computerized control system, in which there is no operator intervention, is called a **closed-loop feedback** system. A system that also responds to control signals from an operator is called an **open-loop feedback** system.

In self-regulating systems, information about what *is* happening in a system (such as level of temperature, engine speed, or size of workpiece) is fed back to a controlling device, which compares it with what *should* be happening. If the two are different, the device takes suitable action (such as switching a heater, allowing more steam to the engine, or resetting the tools).

feedback in biology, another term for ◇biofeedback.

feedback in music, a continuous tone, usually a high-pitched squeal, caused by the overloading of circuits between electric guitar and amplifier as the sound of the speakers is fed back through the guitar pickup. Deliberate feedback is much used in rock music.

The electric-guitar innovator Les Paul used feedback in recording ("How High the Moon" 1954) but it was generally regarded by producers as an unwanted noise until the Beatles introduced it on "I Feel Fine" 1964. Both live and in recording, feedback was employed especially by the Who, Jimi Hendrix, and the Velvet

Underground in the 1960s, and by hardcore bands in the 1980s.

Fehling's test chemical test to determine whether an organic substance is a reducing agent (substance that donates electrons to other substances in a chemical reaction).

If the test substance is heated with a freshly prepared solution containing copper(II) sulfate, sodium hydroxide and sodium potassium tartrate, the production of a brick-red precipitate indicates the presence of a reducing agent.

Feininger Lyonel 1871–1956. US abstract artist, an early Cubist. He worked at the Bauhaus, a key center of design in Germany 1919–33, and later helped to found the Bauhaus in Chicago.

Feininger was born in New York, the son of German immigrants. While in Germany, he formed the *Blaue Vier* (Blue Four) in 1924 with the painters Alexei von Jawlensky (1864–1941), Wassily Kandinsky, and Paul Klee. He returned to the US after the rise of the Nazis.

feldspar one of a group of rock-forming minerals; the chief constituents of ◇igneous rock. Feldspars all contain silicon, aluminum, and oxygen, linked together to form a framework; spaces within this structure are occupied by sodium, potassium, calcium, or occasionally barium, in various proportions. Feldspars form white, gray, or pink crystals and rank 6 on the ◇Mohs' scale of hardness.

The four components of feldspar are **orthoclase**, $KAlSi_3O_8$; **albite**, $NaAlSi_3O_8$; **anorthite**, $CaAl_2Si_2O_8$; and **celsian**, $BaAl_2Si_2O_8$. These are subdivided into **plagioclase feldspars**, which range from pure sodium feldspar (albite) through pure calcium feldspar (anorthite) with a negligible potassium content; and **alkali feldspars**, (including orthoclase), which have a high potassium content, less sodium, and little calcium.

The type known as ◇**moonstone** has a pearllike effect and is used in jewelry. Approximately 4,000 tons of feldspar are used in the ◇ceramics industry annually.

feldspathoid any of a group of silicate minerals resembling feldspars but containing less silica. Examples are nepheline ($NaAlSiO_4$) with a little potassium and leucite ($KAlSi_2O_6$). Feldspathoids occur in igneous rocks that have relatively high proportions of sodium and potassium. Such rocks may also contain alkali feldspar, but they do not generally contain quartz because any free silica would have combined with the feldspathoid to produce more feldspar instead.

felicific calculus or **hedonic calculus** in ethics, a technique for establishing the rightness and wrongness of an action. Using the calculus, one can attempt to work out the likely consequences of an action in terms of the pain or pleasure of those affected by the action. The calculus is attributed to English utilitarian philosopher Jeremy Bentham.

Feller Bob (Robert William Andrew) 1918– . US baseball pitcher. Born in Van Meter, Iowa, Feller was signed by the Cleveland Indians organization while he was still in high school. He made his major-league debut 1936 and went on to a brilliant pitching career that lasted for the next 20 years, interrupted by service in the navy during World War II. Six times he led the American League by winning 20 or more games in a season; he pitched 3 no-hitters and 12 one-hitters and posted 266 career wins.

Feller was famed for his powerful fastball and pinpoint control. He was elected to the Baseball Hall of Fame 1962.

Fellini Federico 1920– . Italian film director and script writer whose films combine dream and fantasy sequences with satire and autobiographical details. His films include *I vitelloni/ The Young and the Passionate* 1953, *La Strada/ The Street* 1954, *La dolce vita* 1960, *Otto e mezzo/8 1/2* 1963, *Giulietta degli spiriti/Juliet of the Spirits* 1965, *Satyricon* 1969, and *La città delle donne/City of Women* 1980.

felony in ◇criminal law, former term for an offense that is more serious than a ◇misdemeanor; in the US, a felony is a crime generally punishable by imprisonment for a year or more.

felt matted fabric of hair fibers and/or wool, made by joining them together using pressure, heat, or chemical action.

The origin of felt is in the steppes of Central Asia, where ◇yurts, shoes, hats, blankets, and other items were made by nomadic herding peoples.

fem. in grammar, abbreviation for **feminine**; see ◇gender.

feminism an active belief in equal rights and opportunities for women; see ◇women's movement.

femur the **thigh-bone**; also the upper bone in the hind limb of a four-limbed vertebrate.

fencing sport of fighting with swords including the foil, derived from the light weapon used in practice duels; the épée, a heavier weapon derived from the duelling sword proper; and the **saber**, with a curved handle and narrow V-shaped blade. In saber fighting, cuts count as well as thrusts. Masks and protective jackets are worn, and hits are registered electronically in competitions. Men's fencing has been part of every Olympic program since 1896; women's fencing was included from 1924 but only using the foil.

Fénelon François de Salignac de la Mothe 1651–1715. French writer and ecclesiastic. He entered the priesthood 1675 and in 1689 was appointed tutor to the duke of Burgundy, grandson of Louis XIV. For him he wrote his *Fables* and *Dialogues des morts/Dialogues of the Dead* 1690, *Télémaque/Telemachus* 1699, and *Plans de gouvernement/Plans of Government*.

Fenian movement Irish-American republican secret society, founded 1858 and named after the ancient Irish legendary warrior band of the Fianna. The collapse of the movement began when an attempt to establish an independent Irish republic by an uprising in Ireland 1867 failed, as did raids into Canada 1866 and 1870, and England 1867.

fennec small nocturnal desert ◇fox *Fennecus zerda* found in N Africa and Arabia. It has a head and body only 1.3 ft/40 cm long, and its enormous ears act as radiators to lose excess heat. It eats insects and small animals.

fennel any of several varieties of a perennial plant *Foeniculum vulgare* with feathery green leaves, of the carrot family Umbelliferae. Fennels have an aniseed flavor, and the leaves and seeds are used in seasoning. The thickened leafstalks of sweet fennel *F. vulgare dulce* are eaten.

Ferber Edna 1887–1968. US novelist and playwright. Her novel *Show Boat* 1926 was adapted as an operetta 1927 by Jerome Kern and Oscar

Hammerstein II, and her plays, in which she collaborated with George S Kaufmann, include *The Royal Family* 1927, about the Barrymore theatrical family, *Dinner at Eight* 1932, and *Stage Door* 1936.

Her novels include *The Girls* 1921, *So Big* 1924, *Cimarron* 1930, *Giant* 1952, about Texas, and *Ice Palace* 1959, about Alaska.

Ferdinand 1861–1948. King of Bulgaria 1908–18. Son of Prince Augustus of Saxe-Coburg-Gotha, he was elected prince of Bulgaria 1887 and, in 1908, proclaimed Bulgaria's independence of Turkey and assumed the title of tsar. In 1915 he entered World War I as Germany's ally, and in 1918 abdicated.

Ferdinand five kings of Castile, including:

Ferdinand I *the Great* c. 1016–1065. King of Castile from 1035. He began the reconquest of Spain from the Moors and united all NW Spain under his and his brothers' rule.

Ferdinand V 1452–1516. King of Castile from 1474, **Ferdinand II** of Aragon from 1479, and **Ferdinand III** of Naples from 1504; first king of all Spain. In 1469 he married his cousin ♢Isabella I, who succeeded to the throne of Castile 1474; they were known as **the Catholic Monarchs** because after 700 years of rule by the ♢Moors, they Catholicized Spain. When Ferdinand inherited the throne of Aragon 1479, the two great Spanish kingdoms were brought under a single government for the first time. They introduced the ♢Inquisition 1480; expelled the Jews, forced the final surrender of the Moors at Granada, and financed Columbus' expedition to the Americas, 1492.

Ferdinand conquered Naples 1500–03 and Navarre 1512, completing the unification of Spain and making it one of the chief powers in Europe.

Ferdinand three Holy Roman emperors:

Ferdinand I 1503–1564. Holy Roman emperor who succeeded his brother Charles V 1558; king of Bohemia and Hungary from 1526, king of the Germans from 1531. He reformed the German monetary system and reorganized the judicial Aulic council (*Reichshofrat*). He was the son of Philip the Handsome and grandson of Maximilian I.

Ferdinand II 1578–1637. Holy Roman emperor from 1619, when he succeeded his uncle Matthias; king of Bohemia from 1617 and of Hungary from 1618. A zealous Catholic, he provoked the Bohemian revolt that led to the Thirty Years' War. He was a grandson of Ferdinand I.

Ferdinand III 1608–1657. Holy Roman emperor from 1637 when he succeeded his father Ferdinand II; king of Hungary from 1625. Although anxious to conclude the Thirty Years' War, he did not give religious liberty to Protestants.

Ferdinand 1865–1927. King of Romania from 1914, when he succeeded his uncle Charles I. In 1916 he declared war on Austria. After the Allied victory in World War I, Ferdinand acquired Transylvania and Bukovina from Austria-Hungary, and Bessarabia from Russia. In 1922 he became king of this Greater Romania. His reign saw agrarian reform and the introduction of universal suffrage.

Ferghana town in Uzbekistan, in the fertile *Ferghana Valley*; population (1987) 203,000. It is the capital of the major cotton- and fruit-growing Ferghana region; nearby are petroleum fields. The Ferghana Valley

is divided between Uzbekistan, Kyrgyzstan, and Tajikistan, causing interethnic violence between Uzbek, Meskhetian, and Kyrgyz communities.

Fermanagh county in the southern part of Northern Ireland
area 648 sq mi/1,680 sq km
cities Enniskillen (county town), Lisnaskea, Irvinestown
physical in the center is a broad trough of low-lying land, in which lie Upper and Lower Lough Erne
products mainly agricultural; livestock, tweeds, clothing
population (1981) 52,000.

Fermat Pierre de 1601–1665. French mathematician, who with Blaise Pascal founded the theory of ♢probability and the modern theory of numbers and who made contributions to analytical geometry.

Fermat's last theorem states that equations of the form $x^n + y^n = z^n$ where $x, y, z,$ and n are all ♢integers have no solutions if $n>2$. There is no general proof of this, although it has never yet been disproved, so it constitutes a conjecture rather than a theorem.

fermentation the breakdown of sugars by bacteria and yeasts using a method of respiration without oxygen (♢anaerobic). Fermentation processes have long been utilized in baking bread, making beer and wine, and producing cheese, yogurt, soy sauce, and many other foodstuffs.

In baking and brewing, yeasts ferment sugars to produce ♢ethanol and carbon dioxide; the latter makes bread rise and puts bubbles into beers and champagne. Many antibiotics are produced by fermentation; it is one of the processes that can cause food spoilage.

Fermi Enrico 1901–1954. Italian-born US physicist who proved the existence of new radioactive elements produced by bombardment with neutrons, and discovered nuclear reactions produced by low-energy neutrons. His theoretical work included study of the weak nuclear force, one of the fundamental forces of nature, and (with Paul Dirac) of the quantum statistics of fermion particles. He was awarded a Nobel Prize 1938.

Born in Rome, he was professor of theoretical physics there 1926–38. Upon receiving the Nobel Prize he and his family immigrated to the US. He was professor at Columbia University in New York 1939–42 and from 1946 at the University of Chicago, where he had built the first US nuclear reactor 1942. This was the basis for studies leading to the atomic bomb and ♢nuclear energy.

In 1954, the US Atomic Energy Commission made a special award to Fermi in recognition of his outstanding work in nuclear physics; these annual awards subsequently were known as Fermi awards.

Fermilab (shortened form of *Fermi National Accelerator Laboratory*) US center for ♢particle physics at Batavia, Illinois, near Chicago.

It is named after Enrico Fermi. Fermilab was opened in 1972, and is the home of the Tevatron, the world's most powerful particle ♢accelerator. It is capable of boosting protons and antiprotons to speeds near that of light (to energies of 20 TeV).

fermion in physics, a subatomic particle whose spin can only take values that are half-integers, such as 1/2 or 11/2. Fermions may

be classified as leptons, such as the electron, and baryons, such as the proton and neutron. All elementary particles are either fermions or ♢bosons.

The exclusion principle, formulated by Wolfgang Pauli 1925, asserts that no two fermions in the same system (such as an atom) can possess the same position, energy state, spin, or other quantized property.

fermium synthesized, radioactive, metallic element of the ♢actinide series, symbol Fm, atomic number 100, atomic weight 257. Ten isotopes are known, the longest-lived of which, Fm-257, has a half-life of 80 days. Fermium has been produced only in minute quantities in particle accelerators.

It was discovered in 1952 in the debris of the first thermonuclear explosion. The element was named 1955 in honor of US physicist Enrico ♢Fermi.

fern plant of the class Filicineae, related to ♢gymnosperms and ♢angiosperms; however, ferns reproduce by spores and not seed. Most are perennial, spreading by low-growing roots. The leaves, known as fronds, vary widely in size and shape. Some taller types, such as tree-ferns, grow in the tropics. There are over 7,000 species.

Common forms include polypody (*Polypodium*); shield fern (*Polystichum*); maidenhair (*Adiantum capillus-veneris*); and bracken (*Pteridium*), a common weed.

Fernández Juan c. 1536–c. 1604. Spanish explorer and navigator. As a pilot on the Pacific coast of South America 1563, he reached the islands off the coast of Chile that now bear his name. Alexander ♢Selkirk was later marooned on one of these islands, and his life story formed the basis of Daniel Defoe's *Robinson Crusoe*.

Fernandez de Quirós Pedro 1565–1614. Spanish navigator, one of the first Europeans to search for the great southern continent that Ferdinand ♢Magellan believed lay to the south of the Magellan Strait. Despite a series of disastrous expeditions, he took part in the discovery of the Marquesas Islands and the main island of Espiritu Santo in the New Hebrides.

Fernando Pó former name (until 1973) of ♢Bioko, Equatorial Guinea.

Ferrara industrial city and archbishopric in Emilia-Romagna region, N Italy, on a branch of the Po delta 32 mi/52 km W of the Adriatic Sea; population (1988) 143,000. There are chemical industries and textile manufacturers.

It has the Gothic castle of its medieval rulers, the House of Este, palaces, museums, and a cathedral, consecrated 1135. The university was founded 1391. Italian religious reformer Girolamo Savonarola was born here, and the poet Torquato Tasso was confined in the asylum from 1579 to 1586.

Ferrari Enzo 1898–1988. Italian founder of the Ferrari car manufacturing company, which specializes in Grand Prix racing automobiles and high-quality sports automobiles. He was a racing driver for Alfa Romeo in the 1920s, went on to become one of their designers and in 1929 took over their racing division. In 1947 the first "true" Ferrari was seen. The Ferrari car has won more world championship Grands Prix than any other car.

Ferraro Geraldine 1935– . US Democrat politician, vice-presidential candidate in the 1984 election.

Ferraro, a lawyer, was elected to Congress in 1981 and was selected in 1984 by Walter Mondale to be the US's first female vice-presidential candidate from one of the major parties. The Democrats were defeated by the incumbent president Reagan, and Ferraro, damaged by investigations of her husband's business affairs, retired temporarily from politics.

ferret domesticated variety of the Old World ⬠polecat. About 1.2 ft/35 cm long, it usually has yellowish-white fur and pink eyes, but may be the dark brown color of a wild polecat. Ferrets may breed with wild polecats. They have been used since ancient times to hunt rabbits and rats.

ferro-alloy alloy of iron with a high proportion of elements such as manganese, silicon, chromium, and molybdenum. Ferro-alloys are used in the manufacture of alloy steels. Each alloy is generally named after the added metal—for example, ferrochromium.

Ferry Jules François Camille 1832–1893. French republican politician, mayor of Paris during the siege of 1870–71. As a member of the republican governments of 1879–85 (prime minister 1880–81 and 1883–85) he was responsible for the 1882 law making primary education free, compulsory, and secular. He directed French colonial expansion in Tunisia 1881 and Indochina (the acquisition of Tonkin in 1885).

fertility an organism's ability to reproduce, as distinct from the rate at which it reproduces (see ⬠fecundity). Individuals become infertile (unable to reproduce) when they cannot generate gametes (eggs or sperm) or when their gametes cannot yield a viable ⬠embryo after fertilization.

fertility drug any of a range of drugs taken to increase a female's fertility, developed in Sweden in the mid-1950s. They increase the chances of a multiple birth.

The most familiar is gonadotropin, which is made from hormone extracts taken from the human pituitary gland: follicle-stimulating hormone and lutenizing hormone. It stimulates ovulation in women. As a result of a fertility drug, in 1974 the first sextuplets to survive were born to Susan Rosenkowitz of South Africa.

fertilization in ⬠sexual reproduction, the union of two ⬠gametes (sex cells, often called egg and sperm) to produce a ⬠zygote, which combines the genetic material contributed by each parent. In self-fertilization the male and female gametes come from the same plant; in cross-fertilization they come from different plants. Self-fertilization rarely occurs in animals; usually even ⬠hermaphrodite animals cross-fertilize each other.

In terrestrial insects, mammals, reptiles, and birds, fertilization occurs within the female's body; in the majority of fishes and amphibians, and most aquatic invertebrates, it occurs externally, when both sexes release their gametes into the water. In most fungi, gametes are not released, but the hyphae of the two parents grow toward each other and fuse to achieve fertilization. In higher plants, ⬠pollination precedes fertilization.

fertilizer substance containing some or all of a range of about 20 chemical elements necessary for healthy plant growth, used to compensate for the deficiencies of poor or depleted soil. Fertilizers may be **organic**, for example farmyard manure, composts, bonemeal, blood, and

fishmeal; or **inorganic**, in the form of compounds, mainly of nitrogen, phosphate, and potash, which have been used on a very much increased scale since 1945.

Because externally applied fertilizers tend to be in excess of plant requirements and drain away to affect lakes and rivers (see ⬠eutrophication), attention has turned to the modification of crop plants themselves. Plants of the legume family, including the bean, clover, and lupin, live in symbiosis with bacteria located in root nodules, which fix nitrogen from the atmosphere. Research is now directed to producing a similar relationship between such bacteria and crops such as wheat.

Fès or **Fez** former capital of Morocco 808–1062, 1296–1548, and 1662–1912, in a valley N of the Great Atlas mountains, 100 mi/160 km E of Rabat; population (1982) 563,000. Textiles, carpets, and leather are manufactured, and the **fez**, a brimless hat worn in S and E Mediterranean countries, is traditionally said to have originated here. Kairwan Islamic University dates from 859; a second university was founded 1961.

fescue any grass of the widely distributed genus *Festuca*. Many are used in temperate regions for lawns and pasture. Many upland species are viviparous.

Fessenden Reginald Aubrey 1866–1932. Canadian physicist who worked in the US, first for Thomas Edison and then for George Westinghouse. Fessenden patented the modulation of radio waves (transmission of a signal using a carrier wave), an essential technique for voice transmission. At the time of his death, he held 500 patents.

Early radio communications relied on telegraphy by using bursts of single-frequency signals in Morse code. In 1900 Fessenden devised a method of making audio-frequency speech (or music) signals modulate the amplitude of a transmitted radio-frequency carrier wave—the basis of AM radio broadcasting.

fetal surgery any operation on the fetus to correct a congenital condition (for example, ⬠hydrocephalus). Fetal surgery was pioneered in the US 1981. It leaves no scar tissue.

fetishism in anthropology, belief in the supernormal power of some inanimate object that is known as a fetish. Fetishism in some form is common to most cultures, and often has religio-magical significance.

fetus stage in mammalian ⬠embryo development. The human embryo is usually termed a fetus after the eighth week of development, when the limbs and external features of the head are recognizable.

feudalism (Latin *feudem* "fief," coined 1839) main form of social organization in medieval Europe. A system based primarily on land, it involved a hierarchy of authority, rights, and power that extended from the monarch downward. An intricate network of duties and obligations linked royalty, nobility, lesser gentry, free tenants, villeins, and serfs. Feudalism was reinforced by a complex legal system and supported by the Christian church. With the growth of commerce and industry from the 13th century, feudalism gradually gave way to the class system as the dominant form of social ranking.

In return for military service the monarch allowed powerful vassals to hold land, and often also to administer justice and levy taxes. They in turn "sublet" such rights. At the bottom of

the system were the serfs, who worked on their lord's manor lands in return for being allowed to cultivate some for themselves, and so underpinned the system. They could not be sold as if they were slaves, but they could not leave the estate to live or work elsewhere without permission. The system declined from the 13th century, partly because of the growth of a money economy, with commerce, trade, and industry, and partly because of the many peasants' revolts 1350–1550. Serfdom ended in England in the 16th century, but lasted in France until 1789 and in the rest of Western Europe until the early 19th century. In Russia it continued until 1861.

fever condition of raised body temperature, usually due to infection but also normally caused by exercise and ovulation.

The body temperature may rise up to 106°F/41.11°C, with daily fluctuations of several degrees occurring, peaking in the late afternoon.

Feyerabend Paul K 1924– . US philosopher of science, who rejected the attempt by certain philosophers (for instance ⬠Popper) to find a methodology applicable to all scientific research. His works include *Against Method* 1975.

Although his work relies on historical evidence, Feyerabend argues that successive theories that apparently concern the same subject (for instance the motion of the planets) cannot in principle be subjected to any comparison that would aim at finding the truer explanation. According to his notion of incommensurability, there is no neutral or objective standpoint and therefore no rational way in which one theory can be chosen over another. Instead, scientific progress is claimed to be the result of a range of sociological factors working to promote politically convenient notions of how nature operates.

Feynman Richard Phillips 1918–1988. US physicist whose work laid the foundations of quantum electrodynamics. As a member of the committee investigating the *Challenger* space-shuttle disaster 1986, he demonstrated the lethal faults in rubber seals on the shuttle's booster rocket. For his work on the theory of radiation he shared the Nobel Prize for Physics 1965 with Julian Schwinger and Sin-Itiro Tomonaga (1906–1979).

Feynman was professor of physics at Caltech (California Institute of Technology) from 1950 until his death. In the course of his work he developed his remarkably simple and elegant system of Feynman diagrams to represent interactions between particles. He also contributed to many aspects of particle physics including the nature of the weak nuclear force, and quark theory. Towards the end of his life he became widely known for his revealing autobiographies *Surely You're Joking, Mr Feynman!* 1985 and *What Do You Care What Other People Think?* 1988.

Fez alternate spelling of ⬠Fès, a city in Morocco.

Fezzan former province of Libya, a desert region, with many oases, and with rock paintings from about 3000 BC. It was captured from Italy 1942, and placed under French control until 1951 when it became a province of the newly independent United Kingdom of Libya. It was split into smaller divisions 1963.

ff abbreviation for **folios**; and **the following**; used in reference citation and bibliography.

fiber, dietary or *roughage* plant material that cannot be digested by human digestive enzymes; it consists largely of cellulose, a carbohydrate found in plant cell walls. Fiber adds bulk to the gut contents, assisting the muscular contractions that force food along the intestine. A diet low in fiber causes constipation and is believed to increase the risk of developing diverticulitis, diabetes, gall-bladder disease, and cancer of the large bowel—conditions that are rare in nonindustrialized countries, where the diet contains a high proportion of unrefined cereals.

Soluble fiber consists of indigestible plant carbohydrates (such as pectins, hemicelluloses, and gums) that dissolve in water. A high proportion of the fiber in such foods as oat bran, pulses, and vegetables is of this sort. Its presence in the diet has been found to reduce the amount of cholesterol in blood over the short term, although the mechanism for its effect is disputed.

fiberglass glass that has been formed into fine fibers, either as long continuous filaments or as a fluffy, shortfibered glass wool. Fiberglass is heat- and fire-resistant and a good electrical insulator. It has applications in the field of fiber optics and as a strengthener for plastics in ▷GRP (glass-reinforced plastics).

The long filament form is made by forcing molten glass through the holes of a spinneret, and is woven into textiles. Glass wool is made by blowing streams of molten glass in a jet of high-pressure steam, and is used for electrical, sound, and thermal insulation, especially for the roof space in houses.

fiber optics branch of physics dealing with the transmission of images through glass or plastic fibers known as ▷optical fibers.

Fibonacci Leonardo, also known as *Leonardo of Pisa* c. 1175–c. 1250. Italian mathematician. He published *Liber abaci* in Pisa 1202, which was instrumental in the introduction of Arabic notation into Europe. From 1960, interest increased in *Fibonacci numbers*, in their simplest form a sequence in which each number is the sum of its two predecessors (1, 1, 2, 3, 5, 8, 13,..). They have unusual characteristics with possible applications in botany, psychology, and astronomy (for example, a more exact correspondence than is given by ▷Bode's law to the distances between the planets and the Sun).

fibrin an insoluble blood protein used by the body to stop bleeding. When an injury occurs fibrin is deposited around the wound in the form of a mesh, which dries and hardens, so that bleeding stops. Fibrin is developed in the blood from a soluble protein, fibrinogen.

The conversion of fibrinogen to fibrin is the final stage in blood clotting. Platelets, a type of cell found in blood, release the enzyme thrombin when they come into contact with damaged tissue, and the formation of fibrin then occurs. Calcium, vitamin K, and a variety of enzymes called factors are also necessary for efficient blood clotting.

fibrositis inflammation and overgrowth of fibrous tissue, mainly of the muscle sheaths. It is also known as muscular rheumatism. Symptoms are sudden pain and stiffness, usually relieved by analgesics and rest.

fibula the rear lower bone in the hind leg of a vertebrate. It is paired and often fused with a smaller front bone, the tibia.

Fichte Johann Gottlieb 1762–1814. German philosopher who developed a comprehensive form of subjective idealism, expounded in *The Science of Knowledge* 1794. He was an admirer of Immanuel ▷Kant.

In 1792, Fichte published *Critique of Religious Revelation*, a critical study of Kant's doctrine of the "thing-in-itself." For Fichte, the absolute ego posits both the external world (the non-ego) and finite self. Morality consists in the striving of this finite self to rejoin the absolute. In 1799 he was accused of atheism, and was forced to resign his post as professor of philosophy at Jena. He moved to Berlin, where he devoted himself to public affairs and delivered lectures, including *Reden an die deutsche Nation/Addresses to the German People* 1807–08, which influenced contemporary liberal nationalism.

fiction in literature, any work in which the content is completely or largely invented. The term describes imaginative works of narrative prose (such as the novel or the short story), and is distinguished from **nonfiction** (such as history, biography, or works on practical subjects), and *poetry*.

This usage reflects the dominance in contemporary Western literature of the novel as a vehicle for imaginative literature: strictly speaking, poems can also be fictional (as opposed to factual). Genres such as the historical novel often combine a fictional plot with real events; biography may also be "fictionalized" through the use of imagined conversations or events.

Fiedler Arthur 1894–1979. US orchestra conductor. Born in Boston and trained at the Academy of Music in Berlin, Fiedler joined the Boston Symphony Orchestra 1916. Always interested in the promotion of music among the general public, he founded the Boston Sinfonetta chamber-music group 1924. He reached an even wider audience with the Esplanade concerts along the Charles River from 1929. Fiedler's greatest fame came as founder and conductor of the Boston Pops Orchestra, dedicated to popularizing light Classical music through live and televised concert appearances.

fief an estate of lands held by a ▷vassal from his lord, given after the former had sworn homage, or ▷fealty, promising to serve the lord. As a noble tenure, it carried with it rights of jurisdiction.

In the later Middle Ages, it could also refer to a grant of money, given in return for service, as part of bastard feudalism.

field in physics, a region of space in which an object exerts a force on another separate object because of certain properties they both possess. For example, there is a force of attraction between any two objects that have mass when one is in the gravitational field of the other.

Other fields of force include ▷electric fields (caused by electric charges) and ▷magnetic fields (caused by magnetic poles), either of which can involve attractive or repulsive forces.

Field Sally 1946– . US film and television actress. She won an Academy Award for *Norma Rae* 1979 and again for *Places in the Heart* 1984. Her other films include *Hooper* 1978, *Absence of Malice* 1981, and *Murphy's Romance* 1985.

Prior to her movie career, she first became known as TV's *Flying Nun*, a role she played for several years.

fieldfare thrush *Turdus pilaris* of the family Muscicapidae; it has a pale-gray lower back and neck and a dark tail.

It breeds in Scandinavia and N Russia, and is a casual visitor to N North America.

field hockey a game played with hooked sticks and a ball, the object being to hit the ball into the goal. It is played between two teams, each of not more than 11 players. Hockey has been an Olympic sport for men since 1908 and for women since 1980.

The playing field is 100 yd/91.5 m long and 60 yd/54.9 m wide.

Goals, 7 ft/2.1 m high and 12 ft/3.7 m wide, are placed within a striking circle of 48 ft/14.6 m radius, from which all shots at goal must be made. The white ball weighs about 5.5 oz/156 g, circumference about 9 in/123 cm. Most sticks are about 3 ft/91 cm long. The game is started by a "push-back." The ball may be stopped with the hand but not held, picked up, thrown, or kicked, except by the goalkeeper in his or her own striking circle. If the ball is sent into touch, it is returned to play by a "push-in." The game is divided into two 35-minute periods; it is controlled by two umpires, one for each half of the field.

A game using hooked sticks, not unlike the modern ones, was played by the ancient Greeks.

Fielding Henry 1707–1754. English novelist. His greatest work, *The History of Tom Jones, a Foundling* 1749 (which he described as "a comic epic in prose"), realized for the first time in English the novel's potential for memorable characterization, coherent plotting, and perceptive analysis. In youth a prolific playwright, he began writing novels with *An Apology for the Life of Mrs Shamela Andrews* 1741, a merciless parody of Samuel ▷Richardson's *Pamela*.

field marshal the highest rank in many European armies. A British field marshal is equivalent to a US ▷general (of the army).

Field of the Cloth of Gold site between Guines and Ardres near Calais, France, where a meeting took place between Henry VIII of England and Francis I of France in June 1520, remarkable for the lavish clothes worn and tent pavilions erected. Francis hoped to gain England's support in opposing the Holy Roman emperor, Charles V, but failed.

Fields W C. Adopted name of William Claude Dukenfield 1879–1946. US actor and screenwriter. His distinctive speech and professed attitudes such as hatred of children and dogs gained him enormous popularity in such films as *David Copperfield* 1935, *My Little Chickadee* (co-written with Mae West) and *The Bank Dick* both 1940, and *Never Give a Sucker an Even Break* 1941.

Originally a vaudeville performer, he incorporated his former stage routines, such as juggling and pool playing, into his films. He was also a popular radio performer.

field studies study of ecology, geography, geology, history, archeology, and allied subjects, in the natural environment as opposed to the laboratory.

Fiesole resort town 4 mi/6 km NE of Florence, Italy, with many Etruscan and Roman relics; population (1971) 14,400. The Romanesque cathedral was completed 1028.

fife a type of small flute. Originally from Switzerland, it was known as the Swiss pipe and has long been played by military bands.

Fife region of E Scotland (formerly the county of Fife), facing the North Sea and Firth of Forth

area 502 sq mi/1,300 sq km

cities administrative headquarters Glenrothes; Dunfermline, St Andrews, Kirkcaldy, Cupar

physical the only high land is the Lomond Hills, in the NW; chief rivers Eden and Leven

features Rosyth naval base and dockyard (used for nuclear submarine refits) on N shore of the Firth of Forth; Tentsmuir, possibly the earliest settled site in Scotland. The ancient palace of the Stuarts was at Falkland, and eight Scottish kings are buried at Dunfermline

products potatoes, cereals, electronics, petrochemicals (Mossmorran), light engineering

population (1991) 339,200.

Fifteen, the ⟡Jacobite rebellion of 1715, led by the "Old Pretender" ⟡James Edward Stuart and the Earl of Mar, in order to place the former on the English throne. Mar was checked at Sheriffmuir, Scotland, and the revolt collapsed.

fifth column group within a country secretly aiding an enemy attacking from without. The term originated 1936 during the Spanish Civil War, when General Mola boasted that Franco supporters were attacking Madrid with four columns and that they had a "fifth column" inside the city.

fifth-generation computer anticipated new type of computer based on emerging microelectronic technologies with high computing speeds and ⟡parallel processing. The development of very large-scale integration (⟡VLSI) technology, which can put many more circuits on to an integrated circuit (chip) than is currently possible, and developments in computer hardware and software design may produce computers far more powerful that those in current use.

It has been predicted that such a computer will be able to communicate in natural spoken language with its user; store vast knowledge databases; search rapidly through these databases, making intelligent inferences and drawing logical conclusions; and process images and "see" objects in the way that humans do.

In 1981 Japan's Ministry of International Trade and Industry launched a ten-year project to build the first fifth-generation computer, the "parallel inference machine," consisting of over a thousand microprocessors operating in parallel with each other. By 1992, however, the project was behind schedule and had only produced 256-processor modules. It has since been suggested that research into other technologies, such as neural networks (modelled on the network of neurons in the human brain) may present more promising approaches to artificial intelligence. See also ⟡computer generations.

fig any tree of the genus *Ficus* of the mulberry family Moraceae, including the many cultivated varieties of *F. carica*, originally from W Asia. They produce two or three crops of fruit a year. Eaten fresh or dried, figs have a high sugar content and laxative properties.

In the wild, *F. carica* is dependent on the fig wasp for pollination, and the wasp in turn is parasitic on the flowers. The tropical ***banyan*** *F. benghalensis* has less attractive edible fruit, and roots that grow down from its branches. The ***bo tree*** under which Buddha became enlightened is the Indian peepul or wild fig *F. religiosa*.

The only native US fig is the Florida strangler fig *F. aurea*, which starts off as an ⟡epiphyte before developing its own root system.

fighting fish any of a SE Asian genus *Betta* of fishes of the gourami family, especially *B. splendens*, about 2 in/6 cm long and a popular aquarium fish. It can breathe air, using an accessory breathing organ above the gill, and can live in poorly oxygenated water. The male has large fins and various colors, including shining greens, reds, and blues. The female is yellowish brown with short fins.

The male builds a nest of bubbles at the water's surface and displays to a female to induce her to lay. Rival males are attacked, and in a confined space, fights may occur. In Thailand, public contests are held.

figwort any Old World plant of the genus *Scrophularia* of the figwort family, which also includes foxgloves and snapdragons. Members of the genus have square stems, opposite leaves, and open two-lipped flowers in a cluster at the top of the stem.

Fiji country comprising 844 islands and islets in the SW Pacific Ocean, about 100 of which are inhabited.

government The constitution in existence from independence 1970 was replaced by a new constitution 1990. It gave indigenous Fijians the right to hold the premiership, and a guaranteed 37 seats in the 70-seat House of Representatives (parliament). Fijian citizens of Indian descent were given 27 seats, other races 5, and the Polynesian island of Rotuma, 1. The Upper House has 24 seats for Fijians, 9 for other races and 1 for Rotuma.

history Originally inhabited by ⟡Melanesian and ⟡Polynesian peoples, Fiji's first European visitor was Abel ⟡Tasman 1643. Fiji became a British possession 1874 and achieved full independence within the Commonwealth 1970.

Before independence there had been racial tension between Indians, descended from workers brought from India in the late 19th century, and Fijians, so the constitution incorporated an electoral system that would ensure racial balance in the house of representatives.

ethnic divisions Traditionally the Fijians support the Alliance Party (AP), whose leader, Ratu Sir Kamisese Mara, became prime minister at the time of independence and has held office ever since. The Indians support the National Federation Party (NFP), led by Siddiq Koya. The main divisions between the two have centerd on land ownership, with the Fijians owning more than 80% of the land and defending their traditional rights, and the Indians demanding greater security of land tenure. The Fijian Labor Party (FLP) was formed 1985 but has so far made little impact at the polls.

republic An attempted coup May 1987, led by Col Sitiveni Rabuka, was abandoned after intervention by the governor-general and the Great Council of Chiefs. Another coup by Rabuka in Sept seemed, despite indecision by its leader, more likely to succeed. On this occasion Queen Elizabeth II, at the instigation of the governor-general, condemned the coup in an unprecedented fashion. Nevertheless, the coup went ahead and in Oct 1987 the Queen accepted the resignation of the governor-general, thereby relinquishing her role as head of state and making Fiji a republic. A new constitution, first drafted Aug 1989, was introduced 1990. It guaranteed indigenous Fijians 37 seats in the new 70-seat parliament; the rest were reserved for native Indians and other national groups. The electoral law of the new constitution would also prevent the army from taking control.

Fiji
Republic of

area 7,078 sq mi/18,333 sq km

capital Suva

cities ports Lautoka and Levuka

physical comprises 844 Melanesian and Polynesian islands and islets (about 110 inhabited), the largest being Viti Levu (4,028 sq mi/10,429 sq km) and Vanua Levu (2,146 sq mi/5,550 sq km); mountainous, volcanic, with tropical rainforest and grasslands

features almost all islands surrounded by coral reefs; high volcanic peaks; crossroads of air and sea services between N America and Australia

head of state Ratu Sir Penaia Ganilau from 1987

head of government Col Sitiveni Rabuka from 1992

political system democratic republic

political parties Alliance Party (AP), moderate centrist Fijian; National Federation Party (NFP), moderate left-of-center Indian; Fijian Labor Party (FLP), left-of-center Indian; United Front, Fijian

exports sugar, coconut oil, ginger, timber, canned fish, gold; tourism is important

currency Fiji dollar

population (1989 est) 758,000 (46% Fijian, holding 80% of the land communally, and 49% Indian, introduced in the 19th century to work the sugar crop); growth rate 2.1% p.a.

life expectancy men 67, women 71

languages English (official), Fijian, Hindi

religions Hindu 50%, Methodist 44%

literacy men 88%, women 77% (1980 est)

GDP $1.2 bn (1987); $1,604 per head

chronology

1874 Fiji became a British crown colony.

1970 Independence achieved from Britain; Ratu Sir Kamisese Mara elected as first prime minister.

1987 April: general election brought to power an Indian-dominated coalition led by Dr Timoci Bavadra. May: military coup by Col Sitiveni Rabuka removed new government at gunpoint; Governor General Ratu Sir Penaia Ganilau regained control within weeks. Sept: second military coup by Rabuka proclaimed Fiji a republic and suspended the constitution. Oct: Fiji ceased to be a member of the Commonwealth. Dec: civilian government restored with Rabuka retaining control of security as minister for home affairs.

1990 New constitution, favoring indigenous Fijians, introduced.

1992 General election produced coalition government; Col Rabuka named as president.

The May 1992 general election resulted in a coalition government. The president named former coup leader Rabuka as prime minister in June. *See illustration box.*

filariasis collective term for several diseases, prevalent in tropical areas, caused by certain roundworm (nematode) parasites.

Symptoms include blocked and swollen lymph vessels leading to grotesque swellings of the legs and genitals (Bancroftian filariasis, ▷elephantiasis), blindness, and dry, scaly skin (▷onchocerciasis). The disease-causing worms are spread mainly by insects, notably mosquitoes and blackflies.

file in computing, a collection of data or a program stored in a computer's external memory (for example, on ▷disk). It might include anything from information on a company's employees to a program for an adventure game. *Serial files* hold information as a sequence of characters, so that, to read any particular item of data, the program must read all those that precede it. *Random-access files* allow the required data to be reached directly.

Files usually consist of a set of records, each having a number of fields for specific items of data. For example, the file for a class of schoolchildren might have a record for each child, with five fields of data in each record, storing: (1) family name; (2) first name; (3) house name or number; (4) street name; (5) town. To find out, for example, which children live on the same street, one would look in field 4.

Filene Edward Albert 1860–1937. US businessman. Born in Salem, Massachusetts, Filene took over his father's dry goods store in Boston, expanding it dramatically through the introduction of retailing innovations. The concern was incorporated as William Filene's Sons 1891. One of Filene's most imaginative merchandising ideas was the concept of the "bargain basement," where prices were dramatically lowered on certain goods. Filene was also committed to employee profit-sharing and for that reason was removed by his partners 1928. A political progressive, he was active in public welfare programs in Boston.

Fillmore Millard 1800–1874. 13th president of the US 1850–53, a Whig. Born into a poor farming family in New Cayuga County, New York State, he was Zachary Taylor's vice-president from 1849, and succeeded him on Taylor's death, July 9, 1850. Fillmore supported a compromise on slavery 1850 to reconcile North and South.

This compromise pleased neither side, and it contained a harsh fugitive slave act requiring escaped slaves to be returned to their owners. He threatened to enforce this act with troops, if necessary, earning the wrath of the ▷abolitionists. Fillmore failed to be nominated for another term.

film, art of see ▷cinema.

film noir (French "dark film") a term originally used by French critics to describe films characterized by pessimism, cynicism, and a dark, somber tone. It has been used to describe black-and-white Hollywood films of the 1940s and 1950s that portrayed the seedy side of life.

Typically, the *film noir* is shot with lighting that emphasizes shadow and stark contrasts, abounds in night scenes, and contains a cynical antihero—for example, Philip Marlowe as played by Humphrey Bogart in *The Big Sleep* 1946.

film, photographic strip of transparent material (usually cellulose acetate) coated with a light-sensitive emulsion, used in cameras to take pictures. The emulsion contains a mixture of light-sensitive silver halide salts (for example, bromide or iodide) in gelatin. When the emulsion is exposed to light, the silver salts are invisibly altered, giving a latent image, which is then made visible by the process of ▷developing. Films differ in their sensitivities to light, this being indicated by their speeds. Color film consists of several layers of emulsion, each of which records a different color in the light falling on it.

In *color film* the front emulsion records blue light, then comes a yellow filter, followed by layers that record green and red light respectively. In the developing process the various images in the layers are dyed yellow, magenta (red), and cyan (blue), respectively. When they are viewed, either as a transparency or as a color print, the colors merge to produce the true color of the original scene photographed.

film score music specially written to accompany a film on the soundtrack. Scores were also written for some silent films and performed live as the film was shown. Films, with or without sound, have used the potential power of musical scores to change the mood of a scene or enhance the emotional impact.

As early as 1908 the French composer Saint-Saëns was commissioned to write a special score for the first production of Film d'Art company, *The Assassination of the Duke de Guise*. D W ▷Griffith collaborated on scoring his own epics such as *Birth of a Nation* 1915 and *Intolerance* 1916.

filter in chemistry, a porous substance, such as blotting paper, through which a mixture can be passed to separate out its solid constituents. In optics, a filter is a piece of glass or transparent material that passes light of one color only.

filter in electronics, a circuit that transmits a signal of some frequencies better than others. A low-pass filter transmits signals of low frequency and direct current; a high-pass filter transmits high-frequency signals; a band-pass filter transmits signals in a band of frequencies.

filtration technique by which suspended solid particles in a fluid are removed by passing the mixture through a porous barrier, usually paper or cloth. The particles are retained by the paper or cloth to form a residue and the fluid passes through to make up the filtrate. Soot is filtered from air while suspended solids are filtered from water.

final solution (to the Jewish question; German *Endlosung der Judenfrage*) phrase used by the Nazis to describe the extermination of Jews before and during World War II. See ▷Holocaust.

finch any of various songbirds of the family Fringillidae, in the order Passeriformes (perching birds).

They are seed-eaters with stout conical beaks and include goldfinches, crossbills, redpolls, and canaries.

Finch Peter 1916–1977. Australian-born English cinema actor who began his career in Australia before moving to London in 1949 to start on an international career with such roles as those in *A Town Like Alice* 1956, *The Trials of Oscar Wilde* 1960, *Sunday, Bloody Sunday* 1971, and *Network* 1976, for which he won an Academy Award.

fin de siècle (French "end of century") the art and literature of the 1890s; decadent.

Fingal's Cave cave on the island of Staffa, Inner Hebrides, Scotland. It is lined with natural basalt columns, and is 200 ft/60 m long and 65 ft/20 m high. Fingal, based on the Irish hero Finn Mac Cumhaill, was the leading character in Macpherson's Ossianic forgeries. Visited by Mendelssohn in 1829, the cave was the inspiration of his *Hebrides* overture, otherwise known as *Fingal's Cave*.

fingerprint ridge pattern of the skin on a person's fingertips; this is constant through life and no two are exactly alike. Fingerprinting was first used as a means of identifying crime suspects in India, and was adopted by the English police 1901; it is now widely employed in police and security work.

Finistère *département* of ▷Brittany, NW France; area 7,030 sq km/2,714 mi; population (1982) 828,500. The administrative center is Quimper.

Finland country in Scandinavia, bounded N by Norway, E by Russia, S and W by the Baltic Sea, and NW by Sweden.

government Finland is a republic that combines a parliamentary system with a strong presidency. The single-chamber parliament, the Eduskunta, has 200 members, elected by universal suffrage through a system of proportional representation, for a four-year term. The president is elected for six years by a 301-member electoral college, chosen by popular vote in the same way as the parliament. The president appoints a prime minister and a cabinet (called a council of state), whose members are collectively responsible to the Eduskunta.

The relationship between the president, prime minister, and council of state is unusual, with the nearest equivalent to be found in France. The president has supreme executive power and can ignore even a unanimous decision reached in the council of state, but the prime minister is concerned with the day-to-day operation of the government, so that to some extent they can, at times, both act as heads of government. Both the president and the Eduskunta can initiate legislation and the president has a right of veto, though this can be overruled by a newly appointed parliament.

Because of the system of proportional representation, there is a multiplicity of parties, and the prime minister invariably heads a coalition council of state, typically among four parties.

history The nomadic Saami, or Lapps, were the earliest known inhabitants; from about the 1st century BC they were gradually driven north by Finnic nomads from Asia into the far northern region they occupy today. The area was conquered in the 12th–13th centuries by Sweden, and for much of the next 200 years the country was the scene of wars between Sweden and Russia. As a duchy of Sweden, Finland was allowed a measure of autonomy, becoming a grand duchy 1581. In 1809, during the Napoleonic Wars, Finland was invaded and annexed by Russia; nationalist feeling grew, and the country proclaimed its independence during the 1917 Russian revolution. The Soviet regime initially tried to regain control but acknowledged Finland's independence 1920.

Winter War In 1939 the USSR's request for military bases in Finland was rejected, and the USSR invaded Finland. The resulting ▷Winter War lasted for 15 weeks. Finland was defeated and forced to cede territory. In the hope of regaining it, in 1941 it joined Nazi Germany in attacking the USSR, but agreed to a separate armistice 1944. It was again forced to cede

Finland
Republic of (*Suomen Tasavalta*)

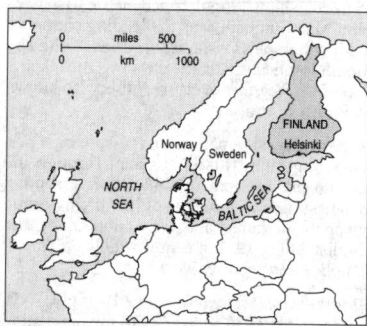

area 130,608 sq mi/338,145 sq km
capital Helsinki
cities Tampere, Rovaniemi, Lahti; ports Turku, Oulu
physical most of the country is forest, with low hills and about 60,000 lakes; one-third is within the Arctic Circle; archipelago in S; includes Åland Islands
features Helsinki is the most northerly national capital on the European continent; at the 70th parallel there is constant daylight for 73 days in summer and 51 days of uninterrupted night in winter
head of state Mauno Koivisto from 1982
head of government Esko Aho from 1991
political system democratic republic
political parties Social Democratic Party (SDP), moderate, left of center; National Coalition Party (KOK), moderate, right of center; Center Party (KP), centrist, rural-oriented; Finnish People's Democratic League (SKDL), left-wing; Swedish People's Party (SFP), independent Swedish-oriented; Finnish Rural Party (SMP), farmers and small businesses; Democratic Alternative, left-wing; Green Party
exports metal, chemical, and engineering products (icebreakers and oil rigs), paper, sawn wood, clothing, fine ceramics, glass, furniture
currency markka
population (1989 est) 4,990,000; growth rate 0.5% p.a.
life expectancy men 70, women 78
languages Finnish 93%, Swedish 6% (both official), small Saami and Russian-speaking minorities
religions Lutheran 97%, Eastern Orthodox 1.2%
literacy 99%
GDP $77.9 bn (1987); $15,795 per head
chronology
1809 Finland annexed by Russia.
1917 Independence declared from Russia.
1920 Soviet regime acknowledged independence.
1939 Defeated by USSR in Winter War.
1941 Allowed Germany to station troops in Finland to attack USSR; USSR bombed Finland.
1944 Concluded separate armistice with USSR.
1948 Finno-Soviet Pact of Friendship, Cooperation, and Mutual Assistance signed.
1955 Finland joined the United Nations and the Nordic Council.
1956 Urho Kekkonen elected president; reelected 1962, 1968, 1978.
1973 Trade treaty with European Economic Community signed.
1977 Trade agreement with USSR signed.
1982 Koivisto elected president; reelected 1988.
1989 Finland joined Council of Europe.
1991 Big swing to the center in general election. New coalition government formed.
1992 Formal application for European Community (EC) membership.

territory (12% of its total area) and agree to huge war reparations; in 1948 it signed the Finno-Soviet Pact of Friendship, Co-operation, and Mutual Assistance (the YYA Treaty). War reparations to the USSR were paid off 1952 (amounting to 5% of the gross domestic product 1945–48). In 1955 Finland joined the United Nations and the Nordic Council (which includes Denmark, Iceland, Norway, and Sweden).
neutrality The YYA Treaty was extended 1955, 1970, and 1983. Although the Treaty requires it to repel any attack on the USSR through Finnish territory by Germany or its allies, Finland maintained a policy of strict neutrality. It signed a trade treaty with the EC 1973 and a 15-year trade agreement with the USSR 1977. In 1989 it was admitted into the Council of Europe.
short-term governments Finnish politics have been characterized by instability in governments, over 60 having been formed since independence, including many minority coalitions. The presidency, on the other hand, has been very stable, with only two presidents in over 30 years. Urho Kekkonen was elected president 1956 and reelected 1962, 1968, and 1978. In 1981 he resigned from office on health grounds and Mauno Koivisto became president Jan 1982; he was reelected 1988.

The Social Democratic and Center parties dominated Finland's coalition politics for many years, but the 1987 general election resulted in the Social Democrats entering the government in coalition with their archenemies, the Conservatives (KOK), while the Center Party was forced into opposition. In the 1991 elections the Center Party emerged with 55 seats, the Social Democrats 48, the Conservatives 40, the Alliance of the Left 19, and the Greens 10.

In March 1992 the Finnish government agreed to apply formally for membership in the European Community. The economy was hit by the world recession and the disruption of trade with the former USSR; the markka was devalued and cutbacks made in the extensive welfare system. *See illustration box.*

Finland, Gulf of eastern arm of the ◊Baltic Sea, separating Finland from Estonia.

Finlandization political term for the tendency of a small state to shape its foreign policy so as to accommodate a much more powerful neighbor, taken from the example of Finland's foreign policy with respect to the USSR.

Finney Albert 1936– . English stage and film actor. He created the title roles in Keith Waterhouse's stage play *Billy Liar* 1960 and John Osborne's *Luther* 1961, and was artistic director of the Royal Court Theater from 1972 to 1975. His films include *Saturday Night and Sunday Morning* 1960, *Tom Jones* 1963, *Murder on the Orient Express* 1974, and *The Dresser* 1984.

Finnish language member of the Finno-Ugric language family, the national language of Finland and closely related to neighboring Estonian, Livonian, Karelian, and Ingrian languages. At the beginning of the 19th century Finnish had no official status, since Swedish was the language of education, government, and literature in Finland. The publication of the *Kalevala*, a national epic poem, in 1835, contributed greatly to the arousal of Finnish national and linguistic feeling.

Finn Mac Cumhaill legendary Irish hero, identified with a general who organized an Irish regular army in the 3rd century. James Macpherson (1736–96) featured him (as Fingal) and his followers in the verse of his popular epics 1762–63, which were supposedly written by a 3rd-century bard, ◊Ossian. Although challenged by the critic Dr Johnson, the poems were influential in the Romantic movement.

Finno-Ugric group or family of more than 20 languages spoken by some 22 million people in scattered communities from Norway in the west to Siberia in the east and to the Carpathian mountains in the south. Members of the family include Finnish, Lapp, and Hungarian.

Finsen Niels Ryberg 1860–1904. Danish physician, the first to use ultraviolet light treatment for skin diseases. Nobel Prize for Medicine 1903.

finsen unit unit (symbol FU) for measuring the intensity of ultraviolet (UV) light; for instance, UV light of 2 FUs causes sunburn in 15 minutes.

fiord alternate spelling of ◊fjord.

fir any ◊conifer of the genus *Abies* in the pine family Pinaceae. The true firs include the balsam fir of N North America and the Eurasian silver fir *A. alba*. Douglas firs of the genus *Pseudotsuga* are native to W North America and the Far East.

Firdausi Abdul Qasim Mansur *c*. 935–1020. Persian poet, whose epic *Shahnama/The Book of Kings* relates the history of Persia in 60,000 verses.

firearm weapon from which projectiles are discharged by the combustion of an explosive. Firearms are generally divided into two main sections: ◊artillery (ordnance or cannon), with a bore greater than 1 in/2.54 cm, and ◊small arms, with a bore of less than 1 in/2.54 cm. Although gunpowder was known in Europe 60 years previously, the invention of guns dates from 1300–25, and is attributed to Berthold Schwartz, a German monk.

firebrat any insect of the order Thysanura (◊bristletail).

fire clay a ◊clay with refractory characteristics (resistant to high temperatures), and hence suitable for lining furnaces (firebrick). Its chemical composition consists of a high percentage of silicon and aluminum oxides, and a low percentage of the oxides of sodium, potassium, iron, and calcium.

fire extinguisher device for putting out a fire. Fire extinguishers work by removing one of the three conditions necessary for fire to continue (heat, oxygen, and fuel), either by cooling the fire or by excluding oxygen.

The simplest fire extinguishers contain water, which when propelled onto the fire cools it down. Water extinguishers cannot be used on electrical fires, as there is a danger of electrocution, or on burning oil, as the oil will float on the water and spread the blaze.

Many domestic extinguishers contain liquid carbon dioxide under pressure. When the handle is pressed, carbon dioxide is released as a gas that blankets the burning material and prevents oxygen from reaching it. Dry extinguishers spray powder, which then releases carbon dioxide gas. Wet extinguishers are often of the soda-acid type; when activated, sulfuric acid mixes with sodium bicarbonate, producing carbon dioxide. The gas pressure forces the solution out of a nozzle, and a foaming agent may be added.

Some extinguishers contain halons (hydrocarbons with one or more hydrogens substituted by a halogen such as chlorine, bromine, or fluorine). These are very effective at smothering fires, but cause damage to the ◊ozone layer.

firefly any winged nocturnal beetle of the family Lampyridae. They all emit light through the process of ◊bioluminescence.

Firenze Italian form of ◊Florence.

fire protection methods available for fighting fires. Industrial and commercial buildings are often protected by an automatic sprinkler system: heat or smoke opens the sprinkler heads on a network of water pipes which spray the source of the fire. In circumstances where water is ineffective and may be dangerous; for example, for oil and gasoline storage-tank fires, foam systems are used; for industrial plants containing flammable vapors, carbon dioxide is used; where electricity is involved, vaporizing liquids create a nonflammable barrier; for some chemicals only various dry powders can be used.

Public fire-fighting services are usually maintained by local authorities, and similiar services operate in other countries. In small communities, volunteer fire departments and local government work together.

Firestone Harvey Samuel 1868–1938. US industrialist. Born in Columbiana, Ohio, and educated at local schools, Firestone entered the family buggy business and quickly recognized the advantages of rubber for wheel rims. He founded a retail tire outlet in Chicago 1896 and in 1900 established a tire-manufacturing firm, the Firestone Tire and Rubber Co., in Akron, Ohio. Firestone pioneered the principle of the detachable rim and, from 1906, was the major supplier of tires to the Ford Motor Co. A strong opponent of organized labor, he long resisted the unionization of his work force.

Firestone Shulamith 1945– . Canadian feminist writer and editor, whose book *The Dialectic of Sex: the Case for Feminist Revolution* 1970, which analyzed the limited future of feminism under Marxist and Freudian theories, exerted considerable influence on feminist thought.

She was one of the early organizers of the women's liberation movement in the US. Her other works include *Notes from the Second Year* 1970.

firework a device, originating in China, for producing a display of colored sparks (and sometimes noises) by burning chemicals. A firework consists of a container, usually cylindrical in shape and of rolled paper, enclosing a mixture capable of burning independently of the oxygen in the air. One of the ingredients holds a separate supply of oxygen that is readily given up to the other combustible ingredients.

Fireworks are often used in China and Japan.

In Britain they are traditionally used on Nov 5, Guy Fawkes Day, and in the US on July 4, Independence Day.

first aid action taken immediately in a medical emergency in order to save a sick or injured person's life, prevent further damage, or facilitate later treatment. See also ◊resuscitation.

First Legal Tender Case a US Supreme Court case (*Hepburn* v *Griswold*) 1870 that reviewed Congress's right to pay its debts with unbacked paper money. The case was one of numerous suits protesting the use of $450 million issued under the Legal Tender Acts (1862, 1863) to repay loans. The Court found the acts unconstitutional because they made the paper money legal tender for the payment of all debts, including ones contracted before the passage of the acts, a violation of the obligation of contracts. The Court also noted that the Constitution prohibits payment of public debts with anything but gold and silver.

First World War another name for ◊World War I, 1914–18.

fiscal policy that part of government policy devoted to achieving the desired level of revenue, notably through taxation, and deciding the priorities and purposes governing its expenditure.

US fiscal policy has been directed largely at achieving or maintaining full employment while avoiding high inflation. Raising or lowering income taxes or corporate taxes can govern the level of economic activity, and government spending can sustain activity when private funds are unavailable. The tax cuts of the early Reagan administration helped to generate a long economic boom and brought an end to a severe recession with inflation (called a ◊stagflation), but the budget deficits incurred remain a critical economic problem.

fiscal year the financial year, which does not necessarily coincide with the calendar year.

For the US government, the budget year runs from Oct 1 to Sept 30. For businesses and financial institutions, it generally runs July 1 to June 30.

Fischer Bobby (Robert James) 1943– . US chess champion. In 1958, after proving himself in international competition, he became the youngest grand master in history. He was the author of *Games of Chess* 1959, and was also celebrated for his unorthodox psychological tactics. He won the world title from Boris Spassky in Reykjavik, Iceland, 1972 but retired the same year without defending his title. He returned to competitive chess 1992.

Born in Chicago, Fischer was raised in New York and began serious involvement with chess at an early age. By 1956 he had won the US junior chess title and, within two years, had also won the US Chess Federation championship for adults.

Fischer Emil Hermann 1852–1919. German chemist who produced synthetic sugars and from these various enzymes. His descriptions of the chemistry of the carbohydrates and peptides laid the foundations for the science of biochemistry. Nobel Prize 1902.

Fischer Hans 1881–1945. German chemist awarded a Nobel Prize 1930 for his discovery of haemoglobin in blood.

Fischer-Dieskau Dietrich 1925– . German baritone, renowned for his interpretation of Franz Schubert's *lieder* (songs).

fish aquatic vertebrate that uses gills for obtaining oxygen from fresh or sea water. There are three main groups, not closely related: the bony fishes or Osteichthyes (goldfish, cod, tuna); the cartilaginous fishes or Chondrichthyes (sharks, rays); and the jawless fishes or Agnatha (hagfishes, lampreys).

The **bony fishes** constitute the majority of living fishes (about 20,000 species). The skeleton is bone, movement is controlled by mobile fins, and the body is usually covered with scales. The gills are covered by a single flap. Many have a swim bladder with which the fish adjusts its buoyancy. Most lay eggs, sometimes in vast numbers; some ◊cod can produce as many as 28 million. These are laid in the open sea, and probably no more than 28 of them will survive to become adults. Those species that produce small numbers of eggs very often protect them in nests, or brood them in their mouths. Some fishes are internally fertilized and retain eggs until hatching inside the body, then giving birth to live young. Most bony fishes are ray-finned fishes, but a few, including lungfishes and coelacanths, are fleshy-finned.

The **cartilaginous fishes** are efficient hunters. There are fewer than 600 known species of sharks and rays. The skeleton is cartilage, the mouth is generally beneath the head, the nose is large and sensitive, and there is a series of open gill slits along the neck region. They may lay eggs ("mermaid's purses") or bear live young. Some types of cartilaginous fishes, such as sharks, retain the shape they had millions of years ago.

Jawless fishes have a body plan like that of some of the earliest vertebrates that existed before true fishes with jaws evolved. There is no true backbone but a ◊notochord. The lamprey attaches itself to the fishes on which it feeds by a suckerlike rasping mouth. Hagfishes are entirely marine, very slimy, and feed on carrion and injured fishes.

The nutrient composition of fish is similar to that of meat, except that there are no obvious deposits of fat. Examples of fish comparatively high in fat are salmon, mackerel, and herring. White fish such as cod, haddock, and whiting contain only 0.4–4% fat. Fish are good sources of B vitamins and iodine, and the fatty fish livers are good sources of A and D vitamins. Calcium can be obtained from fish with soft skeletons, such as sardines. Roe and caviar have a high protein content (20–25%). *See table on p. 392.*

Fish Hamilton 1808–1893. US public figure and diplomat. In 1851 he was elected to the US Senate, serving until 1857, by which time he had become a member of the Republican party. Fish was appointed secretary of state by President Grant 1869. His eight years in that office were marked by moderation in his pursuit of US claims against the UK in the *Alabama* case and in averting war with Spain over Cuba.

Born in New York and educated at Columbia University, Fish was admitted to the bar 1830. Active in Whig politics, he served as governor of New York 1849–50.

fisher North American ◊marten *Martes pennanti*, dark brown with grayish foreparts and blackish rump and tail. It is less arboreal than the smaller American marten *A. americana*.

Fisher Andrew 1862–1928. Australian Labor politician. Born in Scotland, he went to Australia 1885, and entered the Australian parliament 1901. He was prime minister

1908–09, 1910–13, and 1914–15, and Australian high commissioner to the UK 1916–21.

Fisher John, St c. 1469–1535. English bishop, created bishop of Rochester 1504. He was an enthusiastic supporter of the revival in the study of Greek, and a friend of the humanists Thomas More and Desiderius Erasmus. In 1535 he was tried on a charge of denying the royal supremacy of Henry VIII and beheaded.

Fisher Ronald Aylmer 1890–1962. English statistician and geneticist. He modernized Charles Darwin's theory of evolution, thus securing the key biological concept of genetic change by natural selection. Fisher developed several new statistical techniques and, applying his methods to genetics, published *The Genetical Theory of Natural Selection* 1930.

fish farming or *aquaculture* raising fish (including mollusks and crustaceans) under controlled conditions in tanks and ponds, sometimes in offshore pens. It has been practiced for centuries in the Far East, where Japan today produces some 100,000 tons of fish a year; the US, Norway, and Canada are also big producers. In the 1980s 10% of the world's consumption of fish was farmed, notably trout, Atlantic salmon, turbot, eel, mussels, and oysters.

fishing and fisheries fisheries can be classified by (1) type of water: freshwater (lake, river, pond); marine (inshore, midwater, deep sea); (2) catch: for example salmon fishing, (3) fishing method: diving, stunning or poisoning, harpooning, trawling, drifting.

marine fishing The greatest proportion of the world's catch comes from the oceans. The primary production area is the photic zone, the relatively thin surface layer (164 ft/50 m) of water that can be penetrated by light, allowing photosynthesis by plant ⟡plankton to take place. Plankton-eating fish tend to be small in size and include herrings and sardines. Demersal fishes, such as haddock, halibut, and cod, live primarily near the ocean floor, and feed on various invertebrate marine animals. Over 20 million of them are caught each year by trawling. Pelagic fish, such as tuna, live in the open sea, near the surface, and purse seine nets are used to catch them; the annual catch is over 30 million tons a year.

freshwater fishing There is large demand for salmon, trout, carp, eel, bass, pike, perch, and catfish. These inhabit ponds, lakes, rivers, or swamps, and some species have been successfully cultivated (⟡fish farming).

methods Lines, seine nets, and lift nets are the common commercial methods used. Purse seine nets, which close like a purse and may be as long as 30 nautical miles, have caused a crisis in the S Pacific where Japan, Taiwan, and South Korea fish illegally in other countries' fishing zones.

history Until the introduction of refrigeration, fish was too perishable to be exported, and fishing met local needs only. Between 1950 and 1970, the global fish catch increased by an average of 7% each year. On refrigerated factory ships, filleting and processing can be done at sea. Japan evolved new techniques for locating shoals (by sonar and radar) and catching them (for example, with electrical charges and chemical baits). By the 1970s, indiscriminate overfishing had led to serious depletion of stocks, and heated confrontations between countries using the same fishing grounds. A partial solution was the extension of fishing limits to 200 mi/320 km. The North Sea countries have experimented with the artificial breeding of fish eggs and release of small fry into the sea. In 1988, overfishing of the NE Atlantic led to hundreds of thousands of starving seals on the N coast of Norway. Marine pollution is blamed for the increasing number (up to 30%) of diseased fish in the North Sea. A United Nations resolution was passed 1989 to end drift-net fishing by June 1992.

ancillary industries These include the manufacture of nets, the processing of oil and fishmeal (nearly 25% of the fish caught annually are turned into meal for animal feed), pet food, glue, manure, and drugs such as insulin and other pharmaceutical products.

fission in physics, the splitting of a heavy atomic nucleus into two or more major fragments. It is accompanied by the emission of two or three neutrons and the release of large amounts of energy (see ⟡nuclear energy).
Fission occurs spontaneously in nuclei of

fish classification

superclass Agnatha (jawless fishes)

order	no of species	examples
Petromyzoniformes	30	lamprey
Myxiniformes	15	hagfish

superclass Gnathostomata (jawed fishes)
class Chondrichthyes (cartilaginous fishes)
subclass Elasmobranchii (sharks and rays)

order	no of species	examples
Hexanchiformes		frilled shark, comb-toothed shark
Heterodontiformes	10	Port Jackson shark
Lamniformes	200	"typical" shark
Rajiformes	300	skate, ray

subclass Holocephali (rabbitfishes)

order	no of species	examples
Chimaeriformes	20	chimaera, rabbitfish

class Osteichthyes (bony fishes)
subclass Sarcopterygii (fleshy finned fishes)
coelacanths

order	no of species	examples
Coelacanthiformes	1	coelacanth

lungfishes

order	no of species	examples
Ceratodontiformes	1	Australian lungfish
Lepidosireniformes	4	S American and African lungfish

subclass Actinopterygii (ray-finned fishes)
superorder Chondrostei

order	no of species	examples
Polypteriformes	11	bichir, reedfish
Acipensiformes	25	paddlefish, sturgeon

superorder Holostei

order	no of species	examples
Amiiformes	8	bowfin, garpike

superorder Teleostei

order	no of species	examples
Elopiformes	12	tarpon, tenpounder
Anguilliformes	300	eel
Notacanthiformes	20	spiny eel
Clupeiformes	350	herring, anchovy
Osteoglossiformes	16	arapaima, African butterfly fish
Mormyriformes	150	elephant-trunk fish, featherback
Salmoniformes	500	salmon, trout, smelt, pike
Gonorhynchiformes	15	milkfish
Cypriniformes	350	carp, barb, characin, loache
Siluriformes	200	catfish
Myctophiformes	300	deep-sea lantern fish, Bombay duck
Percopsiformes	10	pirate perch, cave-dwelling amblyopsid
Batrachoidiformes	10	toadfish
Gobiesociformes	100	clingfish
Lophiiformes	150	anglerfish
Gadiformes	450	cod, pollack, pearlfish, eelpout
Atheriniformes	600	flying fish, toothcarp, halfbeak
Lampridiformes	50	opah, ribbonfish
Beryciformes	150	squirrelfish
Zeiformes	60	John Dory, boarfish
Gasterosteiformes	150	stickleback, pipefish, seahorse
Channiformes	5	snakeshead
Synbranchiformes	7	cuchia
Scorpaeniformes	700	gurnard, miller's thumb, stonefish
Dactylopteriformes	6	flying gurnard
Pegasiformes	4	sea-moth
Pleuronectiformes	500	flatfish
Tetraodontiformes	250	puffer fish, triggerfish, sunfish
Perciformes	6500	perch, cichlid, damsel fish, gobie, wrass, parrotfish, gourami, marlin, mackerel, tuna, swordfish, spiny eel, mullet, barracuda, sea bream, croaker, ice fish, butterfish

uranium-235, the main fuel used in nuclear reactors. However, the process can also be induced by bombarding nuclei with neutrons because a nucleus that has absorbed a neutron becomes unstable and soon splits. The neutrons released spontaneously by the fission of uranium nuclei may therefore be used in turn to induce further fissions, setting up a ▷chain reaction that must be controlled if it is not to result in a nuclear explosion.

fission-track dating in geology, a dating method based on the natural and spontaneous nuclear fission of uranium-238 and its physical product, linear atomic displacements (tracks) created along the trajectory of released energized fission fragments. Knowing the rate of fission (a constant), the uranium content of the material and by counting the number of fission tracks, the age of the material can be determined. The method is most widely used to date volcanic deposits adjacent to archeological material.

fistula in medicine, an abnormal pathway developing between adjoining organs or tissues, or leading to the exterior of the body. A fistula developing between the bowels and the bladder, for instance, may give rise to urinary-tract infection by intestinal organisms.

Fitch John 1743–1798. US inventor and early experimenter with steam engines and steamships, designing in 1786 the first steamboat to serve the Delaware River. His venture failed, so Robert ▷Fulton is erroneously considered the inventor of the steamship.

Fitchburg city in N Massachusetts, on the Nashua river, N of Worcester. Industries include paper, textiles, furniture, clothing, and foundry products; population (1990) 41,200.

fitness in genetic theory, a measure of the success with which a genetically determined character can spread in future generations. By convention, the normal character is assigned a fitness of one, and variants (determined by other ▷alleles) are then assigned fitness values relative to this. Those with fitness greater than one will spread more rapidly and will ultimately replace the normal allele; those with fitness less than one will gradually die out.

Fitzgerald Edward 1809–1883. English poet and translator. In 1859 he published his poetic version of the *Rubaiyat of Omar Khayyam*, which is generally considered more an original creation than a translation.

Fitzgerald Ella 1918– . US jazz singer, recognized as one of the finest, most lyrical voices in jazz, both in solo work and with big bands. She is celebrated for her smooth interpretations of Gershwin and Cole Porter songs.

Fitzgerald mastered the "scat" technique and was widely imitated in the 1950s and 1960s. She is among the best-selling recording artists in the history of jazz.

Fitzgerald F(rancis) Scott (Key) 1896–1940. US novelist and short-story writer. His early autobiographical novel *This Side of Paradise* 1920 made him known in the postwar society of the East Coast, and *The Great Gatsby* 1925 epitomizes the Jazz Age.

Fitzgerald was born in Minnesota. His first book, *This Side of Paradise*, reflected his experiences at Princeton University. In 1920 he married Zelda Sayre (1900–1948). His second novel, *The Beautiful and the Damned* 1922, tells of a glamorous couple (resembling the Fitzgeralds) and of their unhappy decline. In

1924 the Fitzgeralds moved to the French Riviera, where they became members of a fashionable group of expatriates. In *The Great Gatsby* 1925 the narrator resembles the author, and Gatsby, the self-made millionaire, is lost in the soulless society he enters. Zelda Fitzgerald, a schizophrenic, entered an asylum in 1930. Her descent into mental illness forms the subject of *Tender is the Night* 1934. After her confinement Fitzgerald went to Hollywood to write screenplays and earn enough to pay Zelda's medical bills. He fell in love with Sheilah Graham but declined into alcoholism. His other works include numerous short stories and his novel *The Last Tycoon*, about the film business, which was unfinished at his death but was made into a major motion picture 1976.

Fitzsimmons Robert Prometheus 1862–1917. English prizefighter best known for his US fights. Born in England and raised in New Zealand, Fitzsimmons began boxing at an early age. Having won the New Zealand championship, he traveled to the US and won the middleweight title in New Orleans 1891. Although he weighed only 160 lb/73 kg, he also competed in the heavyweight division, winning the title from James J ("Gentleman Jim") Corbett in Carson City, Nevada, 1897. He lost that title to James J Jeffries in New York 1899. Fitzsimmons held the lightheavyweight title briefly and continued to fight professionally until 1914.

five pillars of Islam the five duties required of every Muslim: repeating the **creed**, which affirms that Allah is the one God and Mohammed is his prophet; daily **prayer** or ▷salat; giving **alms**; **fasting** during the month of Ramadan; and, if not prevented by ill health or poverty, the hajj, or **pilgrimage** to Mecca, once in a lifetime.

fixed point temperature that can be accurately reproduced and used as the basis of a temperature scale. In the Celsius scale, the fixed points are the temperature of melting ice, which is 0°C (32°F), and the temperature of boiling water (at standard atmospheric pressure), which is 100°C (212°F).

fixed-point arithmetic form of arithmetic in which the decimal point is always in its correct position in relation to the digits. In computing, it is faster than ▷floating-point arithmetic. Fixed-point arithmetic is a system of representing numbers by a single set of digits with the decimal point in its correct position (for example, 97.8, 0.978). For very large and very small numbers this requires a lot of digits. In computing, the numbers that can be handled in this form are limited by the capacity of a computer, so the slower floating-point arithmetic is often preferred.

Fixx James 1932–1984. US popularizer of jogging for cardiovascular fitness with his book *The Complete Book of Running* 1978. He died of a heart attack while jogging.

fjord or **fiord** narrow sea inlet enclosed by high cliffs. Fjords are found in Norway, New Zealand, and western parts of Scotland. They are formed when an overdeepened glacial valley is drowned by a rise in sea-level. At the mouth of the fjord there is a characteristic lip causing a shallowing of the water. This is due to reduced glacial erosion at this point.

Fiordland is the deeply indented SW coast of South Island, New Zealand; one of the most beautiful inlets is Milford Sound.

FL abbreviation for the State of ▷*Florida*.

flaccidity in botany, the loss of rigidity (turgor) in plant cells, caused by loss of water from the central vacuole so that the cytoplasm no longer pushes against the cellulose cell wall. If this condition occurs throughout the plant then wilting is seen.

Flaccidity can be induced in the laboratory by immersing the plant cell in a strong saline solution. Water leaves the cell by ▷osmosis causing the vacuole to shrink. In extreme cases the actual cytoplasm pulls away from the cell wall, a phenomenon known as plasmolysis.

flag piece of cloth used as an emblem or symbol for nationalistic, religious, or military displays, or as a means of signaling. Flags have been used since ancient times. Many localities and public bodies, as well as shipping lines, schools, and yacht clubs, have their own distinguishing flags.

symbolism The *Stars and Stripes*, also called Old Glory, is the flag of the US; the 50 stars on a field of blue represent the 50 states now in the Union, and the 13 red and white stripes represent the 13 original colonies. Each state also has its own flag. The US presidential standard displays the American eagle, surrounded by 50 stars.

The British national flag, the **Union Jack**, unites the crosses of St George, St Andrew, and St Patrick, representing England, Scotland, and Ireland. The flags of Australia and New Zealand both incorporate the Union Jack, together with symbols of the Southern Cross constellation.

The flags of the Scandinavian countries bear crosses; the Danish *Dannebrog* ("strength of Denmark") is the oldest national flag, used for 700 years. The Swiss flag inspired the Red Cross flag with colors reversed. Muslim states often incorporate in their flags the crescent emblem of Islam and the color green, also associated with their faith. Similarly Israel uses the Star of David and the color blue.

The flag of the former USSR placed the crossed hammer and sickle that represented the workers of town and country, on a red field, the emblem of revolution.

The Canadian flag has a maple-leaf design and that of Japan a red disk symbolising the sun.

signals a flag is flown upside down to indicate distress; is dipped as a salute; and is flown at half-mast to show mourning. The "Blue Peter," blue with a white center, announces that a vessel is about to sail; a flag half red and half white, that a pilot is on board. A yellow flag means "plague."

flag in botany, another name for ▷iris especially yellow flag *Iris pseudacorus*, which grows wild in damp places throughout Europe; it is a true water plant but adapts to border conditions. It has a thick rhizome, stiff, bladelike, monocotyledonous leaves, and stems up to 5 ft/150 cm high. The flowers are large and yellow.

flagellant religious person who uses a whip on him- or herself as a means of penance. Flagellation was practiced in many religions from ancient times; notable outbreaks of this type of extremist devotion occurred in Christian Europe in the 11th–16th centuries.

flagellum small hairlike organ on the surface of certain cells. Flagella are the motile organs of certain protozoa and single-celled algae, and of the sperm cells of higher animals. Unlike ▷cilia, flagella usually occur singly or in pairs;

they are also longer and have a more complex whiplike action.

Each flagellum consists of contractile filaments producing snakelike movements that propel cells through fluids, or fluids past cells. Water movement inside sponges is also produced by flagella.

Flagg James Montgomery 1877–1960. US illustrator. His World War I recruiting poster "I Want You," features a haggard image of Uncle Sam modeled on Flagg himself.

In addition to collections of humor writing, Flagg wrote numerous plays and an autobiography, *Roses and Buckshot* 1946. Born in Pelham Manor, New York, Flagg trained at the Art Students League in New York and at private studios in Paris and London. In his teens he contributed illustrations to national magazines; after his return from Europe he became a portraiturist.

Flagler Henry Morrison 1830–1913. US entrepreneur. Born in Hopewell, New York, Flagler left home at age 14, settling in Ohio, where he worked as a clerk and grain merchant. In 1862 he established a salt factory in Saginaw, Michigan, but with the failure of that concern, moved to Cleveland and entered the oil-refining business with John D Rockefeller 1867. Flagler served as a director of Standard Oil 1870–1911 and invested in the Florida tourist industry, establishing the Florida East Coast Railroad 1886 and building a string of luxury hotels.

flag of convenience national flag flown by a ship that has registered in that country in order to avoid legal or tax commitments. Flags of convenience are common in the merchant fleets of Liberia and Panama; ships registered in these countries avoid legislation governing, for example, employment of sailors and minimum rates of pay. In the 1980s more than 12,500 ships were registered in Panama, making it the world's largest merchant fleet.

Flaherty Robert 1884–1951. US film director, the father of documentary filmmaking. He exerted great influence through his pioneer documentary of Inuit life, *Nanook of the North* 1922, a critical and commercial success.

Later films include *Moana* 1926, a South Seas documentary; *Man of Aran* 1934, *Elephant Boy* 1936, *The Lands* 1942, and the Standard Oil-sponsored *Louisiana Story* 1948. Critics subsequently raised questions about the truthfulness of his documentary method.

flamenco music and dance of the Andalusian gypsies of S Spain, evolved from Andalusian and Arabic folk music. The *cante* (song) is sometimes performed as a solo but more often accompanied by guitar music and passionate improvised dance. Hand clapping, finger clicking (castanets are a more recent addition), and enthusiastic shouts are all features. Male flamenco dancers excel in powerful, rhythmic footwork while the female dancers place emphasis on the graceful and erotic movements of their hands and bodies.

flame test in chemistry, the use of a flame to identify metal ⟡cations present in a solid.

A nichrome or platinum wire is moistened with acid, dipped in a compound of the element, either powdered or in solution, and then held in a hot flame. The color produced in the flame is characteristic of metals present; for example, sodium burns with a yellow flame, and potassium with a lilac one.

flame tree any of various trees with brilliant red flowers, including the smooth-stemmed semideciduous tree *Brachychiton acerifolium* with scarlet bell-shaped flowers, native to Australia, but spread throughout the tropics.

flamingo long-legged and long-necked wading bird, family Phoenicopteridae, of the stork order Ciconiiformes. Largest of the family is the greater or roseate flamingo *Phoenicopterus ruber*, found in Africa, the Caribbean, and South America, with delicate pink plumage and 4 ft/1.25 m tall. They sift the mud for food with their downbent bills, and build colonies of high, conelike mud nests, with a little hollow for the eggs at the top.

Flaminius Gaius died 217 BC. Roman consul and general. He constructed the Flaminian Way northward from Rome to Rimini 220 BC, and was killed at the battle of Lake Trasimene fighting ⟡Hannibal.

Flamsteed John 1646–1719. English astronomer, who began systematic observations of the positions of the stars, Moon, and planets at the Royal Observatory he founded at Greenwich, London, 1676. His observations were published 1725.

Flanders region of the Low Countries that in the 8th and 9th centuries extended from Calais to the Scheldt and is now covered by the Belgian provinces of Oost Vlaanderen and West Vlaanderen (East and West Flanders), the French *département* of Nord, and part of the Dutch province of Zeeland. The language is Flemish. East Flanders, capital Ghent, has an area of 1,158 sq mi/3,000 sq km and a population (1991) of 1,335,700. West Flanders, capital Bruges, has an area of 1,197 sq mi/3,100 sq km and a population (1991) of 1,106,800.

history It was settled by Salian Franks as Roman allies 358, and in the 6th century, became a province of the Frankish kingdom. Baldwin I (died 879), the son-in-law of Charles the Bald, became its first count 862. During the following 300 years, the county resisted Norman encroachment, expanded its territory, and became a leading center of the wool industry. In 1194, Philip II married the niece of Count Philip of Alsace (1143–1191), and so began a period of active French involvement in the county. There was friction within Flemish society between the pro-French bourgeoisie and nobility and the craftworkers in the towns who supported the English, their major partners in the wool trade. In 1302, the craftworkers seized power in Bruges and Ghent and defeated the French at Courtrai, but the pro-French faction regained control of the county 1328. During the Hundred Years' War, Edward III of England put a trade embargo on Flemish wool, which caused serious economic depression, and led to further popular revolts, which were finally put down at the battle of Roosebeke 1382 by the French. The last count, Louis de Male, died 1384, and the county was inherited by his son-in-law, Philip the Bold of Burgundy (1342–1404), to become part of the Burgundian domains.

It underwent a decline under Austrian rule in the 17th to 19th centuries. Fierce battles were fought here in World War I. In World War II the **Battle of Flanders** began with the German breakthrough May 10, 1940 and ended with the British amphibious retreat from Dunkirk May 27–June 4.

flare, solar brilliant eruption on the Sun above a ⟡sunspot, thought to be caused by release of magnetic energy. Flares reach maximum brightness within a few minutes, then fade away over about an hour. They eject a burst of atomic particles into space at up to 600 mps/1,000 kps. When these particles reach Earth they can cause radio blackouts, disruptions of the Earth's magnetic field, and ⟡auroras.

flash point in physics, the lowest temperature at which a liquid or volatile solid heated under standard conditions gives off sufficient vapor to ignite on the application of a small flame.

The *fire point* of a material is the temperature at which full combustion occurs. For safe storage of materials such as fuel or oil, conditions must be well below the flash and fire points to reduce fire risks to a minimum.

flatfish bony fishes of the order Pleuronectiformes, having a characteristically flat, asymmetrical body with both eyes (in adults) on the upper side. Species include flounders, turbots, halibuts, plaice, and the European soles.

flatworm invertebrate of the phylum Platyhelminthes. Some are free-living, but many are parasitic (for example, tapeworms and flukes). The body is simple and bilaterally symmetrical, with one opening to the intestine. Many are hermaphroditic (with both male and female sex organs), and practice self-fertilization.

Flaubert Gustave 1821–1880. French novelist, author of *Madame Bovary* 1857, *Salammbô* 1862, *L'Education sentimentale/Sentimental Education* 1869, and *La Tentation de Saint Antoine/The Temptation of St Anthony* 1874. Flaubert also wrote the short stories *Trois contes/Three Tales* 1877. His dedication to art resulted in a meticulous prose style, realistic detail, and psychological depth, which is often revealed through interior monologue.

flax any plant of the genus *Linum*, family Linaceae. The species *L. usitatissimum* is the cultivated strain; **linen** is produced from the fiber in its stems. The seeds yield **linseed oil**, used in paints and varnishes. The plant, of almost worldwide distribution, has a stem up to 24 in/60 cm high, small leaves, and bright blue flowers.

The residue of the seeds is fed to cattle. The stems are retted (soaked) in water after harvesting, and then dried, rolled, and scutched (pounded), separating the fiber from the central core of woody tissue. The long fibers are spun into linen thread, twice as strong as cotton, yet more delicate, and suitable for lace; shorter fibers are used to make twine or paper.

Annual world production of flax fiber amounts to approximately 60,000 tons, with Russia, Ukraine, Belarus, and Latvia accounting for half of the total. Other producers are Belgium, the Netherlands, and N Ireland.

flea wingless insect of the order Siphonaptera, with blood-sucking mouthparts. Fleas are parasitic on warm-blooded animals. Some fleas can jump 130 times their own height.

Species include the human flea *Pulex irritans*; the rat flea *Xenopsylla cheopis*, the transmitter of plague and typhus; and (fostered by central heating) the cat and dog fleas *Ctenocephalides felis* and *C. canis*.

fleabane any of several plants of the genera *Erigeron* and *Pulicaria*, of the daisy or composite family. Poor Robin's plantain *E. pulchellus* has lavender-rayed flowers on tall, slender stalks and is native to E North America.

Fleming Alexander 1881–1955. Scottish bacteriologist who discovered the first antibiotic drug, ⟡penicillin, in 1928. In 1922 he had discovered lysozyme, an antibacterial enzyme present in saliva, nasal secretions, and tears. While studying this, he found an unusual mold growing on a neglected culture dish, which he isolated and grew into a pure culture; this led to his discovery of penicillin. It came into use in 1941. In 1945 he won the Nobel Prize for Physiology and Medicine with Howard W Florey and Ernst B Chain, whose research had brought widespread realization of the value of penicillin.

Fleming Ian 1908–1964. English author of suspense novels featuring the ruthless, laconic James Bond, British Secret Service agent No. 007. Most of the novels were made into successful films.

Fleming's rules memory aids used to recall the relative directions of the magnetic field, current, and motion in an electric generator or motor, using one's fingers. The three directions are represented by the thumb (for motion), forefinger (for field) and second finger (current), all held at right angles to each other. The right hand is used for generators and the left for motors. The rules were devised by the English physicist John Fleming.

Flemish member of the W Germanic branch of the Indo-European language family, spoken in N Belgium and the Nord *département* of France. It is closely related to Dutch.

In opposition to the introduction of French as the official language in the Flemish provinces of Belgium after 1830, a strong Flemish movement arose. Although equality of French and Flemish was not achieved until 1898, it brought about a cultural and political revival of Flemish.

Flemish art the style of painting developed and practiced in ◊Flanders. A Flemish style emerged in the early 15th century. Paintings are distinguished by keen observation, minute attention to detail, bright colors, and superb technique—oil painting was a Flemish invention. Apart from portraits, they depict religious scenes, often placed in contemporary Flemish landscapes, townscapes, and interiors. Flemish sculpture shows German and French influence.

15th century Jan van Eyck made Bruges the first center of Flemish art; other schools arose in Tournai, Ghent, and Louvain. The great

Fleming's rules *Fleming's rules give the direction of the magnetic field, motion, and current in electrical machines.*

names of the early period were Rogier van der Weyden, Dierick Bouts, Hugo van der Goes, Hans Memling, and Gerard David.

16th century Italian influences were strongly felt, and the center shifted to Antwerp, where Quentin Massys worked. Hieronymus Bosch painted creatures of his own wild imagination, but the pictures of Pieter Brueghel are realistic reflections of Flemish life.

17th century Peter Paul Rubens and his school created a new powerful style, which was continued by van Dyck and others. Teniers and many minor artists continued the tradition of genre painting.

Flemish literature in Belgium, Flemish literature in its written form was the same as Dutch and was stimulated by the declaration, following the revolution of 1830–39, that French was the only official language in Belgium (it remained so until 1898). J F Willems (1793–1846) brought out a magazine that revived medieval Flemish works; H Conscience (1812–1883) and J T van Ryswyck (1811–1849) published novels in Flemish; K L Ledeganck (1805–1847), Prudens van Du (1804–1859), and Jan de Beers

(1821–1888) wrote poetry. Later writers include Albrecht Rodenbach (1856–1880), Pol de Mont (1857–1931), and Cyriel Buysse (1859–1932).

Fletcher John 1579–1625. English dramatist. He collaborated with ◊Beaumont, producing, most notably, *Philaster* 1609 and *The Maid's Tragedy* 1610–11. He is alleged to have collaborated with Shakespeare on *The Two Noble Kinsmen* and *Henry VIII* in 1612.

Fletcher v Peck a US Supreme Court decision 1810 dealing with the right of states to impair contracts. A complaint was filed against the Georgia state legislature, which had revoked land claims of settlers who had bought land from fraudulent land companies that had been granted the land by the corrupt legislature. In the Yazoo Land Fraud the Court ruled that the judiciary could not judge the motives of the state legislature and that Georgia could not pass a law impairing what was therefore a valid contract.

fleur-de-lis (French "flower of the lily") heraldic device in the form of a stylized iris flower,

flight: chronology

1783	First human flight, by Jean F Pilâtre de Rozier and the Marquis d'Arlandes, in Paris, using a hot-air balloon made by Joseph and Etienne Montgolfier; first ascent in a hydrogen-filled balloon by Jacques Charles and M N Robert in Paris.
1785	Jean-Pierre Blanchard and John J Jeffries made the first balloon crossing of the English Channel.
1804	George Cayley flew the first true airplane, a model glider 5 ft/1.5 m long.
1852	Henri Giffard flew the first steam-powered airship over Paris.
1891–96	Otto Lilienthal piloted a glider in flight.
1903	First powered and controlled flight of a heavier-than-air craft (airplane) by Orville Wright, at Kitty Hawk, North Carolina.
1909	Louis Blériot flew across the English Channel from France to England by plane in 36 minutes.
1919	First E–W flight across the Atlantic by Albert C Read, using a flying boat; first nonstop flight across the Atlantic E–W by John William Alcock and Arthur Whitten Brown in 16 hours 27 minutes; first complete flight from Britain to Australia by Ross Smith and Keith Smith.
1923	Juan de la Cieva flew the first autogiro with a rotating wing.
1927	Charles Lindbergh made the first W–E solo, nonstop flight across the Atlantic from New York to Paris.
1928	First trans-Pacific flight, from San Francisco to Brisbane, by Charles Kinsford Smith and C T P Ulm.
1930	Frank Whittle patented the jet engine; Amy Johnson became the first woman to fly solo from England to Australia.
1937	The first fully pressurized aircraft, the Lockheed XC-35, came into service.
1939	Erich Warsitz flew the first Heinkel jet plane, in Germany; Igor Sikorsky designed the first helicopter, with a large main rotor and a smaller tail rotor.
1947	A rocket-powered plane, the Bell X-1, was the first aircraft to fly faster than the speed of sound.
1949	The de Havilland Comet, the first jet airliner, entered service; James Gallagher made the first nonstop round-the-world flight, in a Boeing Superfortress.
1953	The first vertical takeoff aircraft, the Rolls-Royce "Flying Bedstead," was tested.
1968	The world's first supersonic airliner, the Russian TU-144, flew for the first time.
1970	The Boeing 747 jumbo jet entered service, carrying 500 passengers.
1976	A Lockheed SR-17A, piloted by Eldon W Joersz and George T Morgan, set the world air-speed record of 2,193.167 mph over Beale Air Force Base, California.
1979	First crossing of the English Channel by a human-powered aircraft, *Gossamer Albatross*, piloted by Bryan Allen.
1981	The solar-powered *Solar Challenger* flew across the English Channel, from Paris to Kent, taking 5 hours for the 163 mi journey.
1986	Dick Rutan and Jeana Yeager made the first nonstop flight around the world without refueling, piloting *Voyager*, which completed the flight in 9 days 3 minutes 44 seconds.
1987	Richard Branson made the first transatlantic crossing by hot-air balloon.
1988	*Daedalus*, a human-powered craft piloted by Kanellos Kanellopoulos, flew 74 mi/118 km across the Aegean Sea.
1991	Richard Branson and Per Lindstrand crossed the Pacific Ocean in the hot-air balloon *Virgin Otsouka Pacific Flyer* from the southern tip of Japan to NW Canada in 46 hours 15 minutes.
1992	US engineers demonstrated a model radio-controlled ornithopter, the first aircraft to be successfully propelled and maneuvered by flapping wings.

borne on coats of arms since the 12th century and adopted by the French royal house of Bourbon.

Flevoland formerly *IJsselmeerpolders* low-lying province of the Netherlands established 1986
area 544 sq mi/1,410 sq km
population (1988) 194,000
cities capital Lelystad, Dronten, Almere *history* created in 1986 out of land reclaimed from the IJsselmeer 1950–68.

flexor any muscle that bends a limb. Flexors usually work in opposition to other muscles, the extensors, an arrangement known as antagonistic.

flight or *aviation* people first took to the air in lighter-than-air craft such as balloons 1783 and began powered flight in 1852 in airships, but the history of aviation focuses on heavier-than-air craft called ◇airplanes. Developed from glider design, with wings, a tail, and a fuselage, the first successful flight of a powered, heavier-than-air craft was in 1896 by S P ◇Langley's unmanned plane (*Model No 5*), for 3/4 of a mile near the Potomac River; then, in 1903, the ◇Wright brothers flew the first piloted plane at Kitty Hawk. In 1903, Glenn ◇Curtiss publicized flight in the US and began the first flying school in 1909. A competition for the development of airplanes was inspired by a series of flights and air races in the US and Europe, and planes came into their own during World War I, being used by both sides. Biplanes were generally succeeded by monoplanes in the 1920s and 1930s, and they used runways or water (seaplanes and flying boats) for takeoffs and landings at airfields that soon became airports. In these decades airlines were formed for international travel, airmail, and cargo. The first jet plane was produced in Germany in 1939, the Heinkel He-178, but conventional prop planes were used for most of the destruction and transport of World War II. The 1950s brought economical passenger air travel on turboprops and jet airliners, which by the 1970s flew transatlantic in about 6 hours. The Concorde, a supersonic jetliner, flies passengers over that route in about 3 hours.

The early development of aircraft took place in the US and Europe. In the US, after the Wright brothers' Kitty Hawk flight, Glenn Curtiss made publicity flights and founded a flight school 1909, then designed and developed 1911 planes with modern ailerons and stabilizers, for guidance control and stability; in France, Louis ◇Blériot brought aviation much publicity by flying the Channel 1909; as did the Reims air races of that year. The flight experience of World War I (1914–18) and the subsequent rapid development of powerful gasoline engines led to planes that could maneuver at speeds of 200 mph/320 kph. Streamlining became imperative; the body, wings, and exposed parts were shaped to reduce drag and the biplane was mostly replaced by the internally braced monoplane structure. Probably the most successful plane of this type ever produced was the Douglas DC-3 and all its variants—with about 10,000 built, used for passengers and cargo in the 1930s and war duty in World War II—about 3,000 are still in daily use. Although by the 1930s planes had acquired the range for long distance flights needed in cargo, mail, and passenger service, by the 1940s new design concepts were developed especially for warplanes that later became important to peacetime aviation, such as the jet engine.

The first flight of a jet-powered aircraft was the German Heinkel He-178 in 1939, and German jets were in use during World War II by 1943; British jet fighters went into action during the last year of the war. Turboprop planes were also developed by the end of the war, and became very successful in commercial service during the interim years between propeller and jet service; in the 1960s turboprops found new operational life when they were needed for fuel economy in flying heavy loads over the short distances into small airports with difficult terrain, as in the third world. Jet airliners such as the Comet were introduced in the 1950s. The late 1960s introduced jumbo jets and the supersonic airliner, notably the Anglo-French Concorde; the former brought economical air travel and the latter a transatlantic crossing of under 3 hours with ideal conditions. Today, jet planes dominate both civilian and military aviation, although many light planes—for sport and business—use piston engines and propellers. Clubs now restore old and antique planes, which are flown in demonstrations, displayed and flown in airshows, and donated to museums. Prop planes still see use in agricultural crop dusting, in bush piloting (especially in Alaska), and for sky writing. *See chronology p.395.*

Flinders Matthew 1774–1814. English navigator who explored the Australian coasts 1795–99 and 1801–03.

Named after him are *Flinders Island*, NE of Tasmania, Australia; the *Flinders Range* in S Australia; and *Flinders River* in Queensland, Australia.

Flint city in Michigan, on the Flint river, 56 mi/90 km NW of Detroit. Automobile manufacturing is the chief industry but it is declining; population (1990) 140,800.

flint compact, hard, brittle mineral (a variety of chert), brown, black, or gray in color, found in nodules in limestone or shale deposits. It consists of fine-grained silica, SiO_2, in cryptocrystalline form (usually ◇quartz). Flint implements were widely used in prehistory and constitute the basis of all human technology.

When chipped, the flint nodules show a shell-like fracture and a sharp cutting edge. The earliest flint implements, belonging to Palaeolithic cultures and made by striking one flint against another, are simple, while those of the Neolithic are expertly chipped and formed, and are often ground or polished. The best flint, used for Neolithic tools, is *floorstone*, a shiny black flint that occurs deep within the chalk.

Because of their hardness (7 on the ◇Mohs' scale), flint splinters are used for abrasive purposes and, when ground into powder, added to clay during pottery manufacture. Flints have been used for making fire by striking the flint against steel, which produces a spark, and for discharging guns. Flints in cigarette lighters are made from cerium alloy.

floating-point arithmetic form of arithmetic in which numbers are represented as a fraction and exponent. For example, 123.45 would be represented as 0.12345 (the fraction) and 3 (because the fraction must be multiplied by 10 to the power of 3), assuming a base-10 system. In computing, it enables programs to work with very large and very small numbers, but is slower than ◇fixed-point arithmetic and suffers from small rounding errors. Floating-point arithmetic is a system representing numbers as multiples of the appropriate base

raised to some power; for example, 97.8 can be expressed as 0.0978×10^3 or 9780×10^{-2}. In computing the number is expressed as a decimal fraction, so 97.8 becomes 0.978×10^2. See ◇fixed-point arithmetic.

In a computer, the numbers are represented by pairs: 97.8 = (.978, + 2). The first number of the pair is called the mantissa and the second the exponent. The definition applies equally to numbers expressed to a different base (for example, binary fractions multiplied by 2 raised to some power).

The advantage of floating-point arithmetic is that very large and very small numbers can be expressed with a few digits. Thus (.978 + 18) written out in full would require 18 digits (978 followed by 15 zeros).

flocculation in soils, the artificially induced coupling together of particles to improve aeration and drainage. Clay soils, which have very tiny particles and are difficult to work, are often treated in this way. The method involves adding more lime to the soil.

Flodden, Battle of the defeat of the Scots by the English under the Earl of Surrey Sept 9, 1513 on a site 3 mi/5 km SE of Coldstream, Northumberland, England; many Scots, including King James IV, were killed.

Flood, the in the Old Testament, the Koran, and *The Epic of Gilgamesh* (an ancient Sumerian legend), a deluge lasting 40 days and nights, a disaster alleged to have obliterated all humanity except a chosen few (in the Old Testament, the survivors were the family of ◇Noah and the pairs of animals sheltered on his ark).

The story may represent legends of a major local flood; for example, excavations at Ur in Iraq revealed 8 ft/2.5 m of water-laid clay dating before 4000 BC, over an area of about 400 mi/645 km by 100 mi/160 km.

flood plain area of periodic flooding along the course of river valleys. When river discharge exceeds the capacity of the channel, water rises over the channel banks and floods the adjacent low-lying lands. As water spills out of the channel some alluvium (silty material) will be deposited on the banks to form ◇levees (raised river banks). This water will slowly seep into the flood plain, depositing a new layer of rich fertile alluvium as it does so. Many important floodplains, such as the inner Niger delta in Mali, occur in arid areas where their exceptional productivity has great importance for the local economy.

A flood plain (often called inner ◇delta) can be regarded as part of a river's natural domain, statistically to be claimed by the river at repeated intervals. By plotting floods that have occurred and extrapolating from these data we can speak of ten-year floods, 100-year floods, 500-year floods, and so forth, based on the statistical probability of flooding across certain parts of the flood plain.

Even the most energetic flood-control plans (such as dams, dredging, and channel modification) will sometimes fail, and using flood plains as the site of towns and villages is always laden with risk. It is more judicious to use flood plains in ways compatible with flooding, such as for agriculture or parks.

Floodplain features include ◇meanders and ◇oxbow lakes.

floppy disk in computing, a storage device consisting of a light, flexible disk enclosed in a cardboard or plastic jacket. The disk is placed in a disk drive, where it rotates at high speed. Data are recorded magnetically on one or both surfaces.

Floppy disks were invented by IBM in 1971 as a means of loading programs into the computer. They were originally 8 in/20 cm in diameter and typically held about 240 kilobytes of data. Present-day floppy disks, widely used on ⇨microcomputers, are usually either 5.25 in/13.13 cm or 3.5 in/8.8 cm in diameter, and generally hold 0.5–2 ⇨megabytes, depending on the disk size, recording method, and whether one or both sides are used.

Flora in Roman mythology, goddess of flowers, youth, and spring. Festivals were held in her name.

floral diagram diagram showing the arrangement and number of parts in a flower, drawn in cross section. An ovary is drawn in the center, surrounded by representations of the other floral parts, indicating the position of each at its base. If any parts such as the petals or sepals are fused, this is also indicated. Floral diagrams allow the structure of different flowers to be compared, and are usually shown with the floral formula.

floral formula symbolic representation of the structure of a flower. Each kind of floral part is represented by a letter (K for calyx, C for corolla, P for perianth, A for androecium, G for gynoecium) and a number to indicate the quantity of the part present, for example, C5 for a flower with five petals. The number is in brackets if the parts are fused. If the parts are arranged in distinct whorls within the flower, this is shown by two separate figures, such as A5 + 5, indicating two whorls of five stamens each.

Florence city in NW Alabama, on the

floral diagram *a floral diagram shows how the parts of a flower are arranged. The diagram is a ground plan showing the relative position and number of sepals, petals, stamens, and carpels of a flower. A floral diagram and a drawing of half a flower are both needed to fully describe a flower.*

Florida

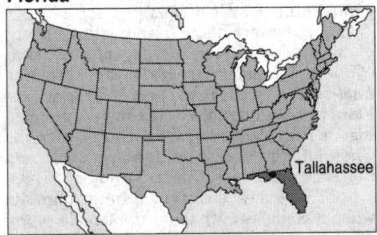

Tennessee River near the Tennessee Valley Authority's Wilson Dam, NW of Birmingham; seat of Lauderdale County. Industries include agricultural and poultry products, building materials, lumber, and fertilizers; population (1990) 36,400.

Florence city in NE South Carolina, NW of Myrtle Beach; seat of Florence County. It is a center of the trucking industry, serving as a terminus for many companies. Other industries include dairy products, fertilizers, film, furniture, machined goods, and clothing; population (1990) 29,800.

Florence (Italian *Firenze*) capital of ⇨Tuscany, N Italy, 55 mi/88 km from the mouth of the river Arno; population (1988) 421,000. It has printing, engineering, and optical industries; many crafts, including leather, gold and silver work, and embroidery; and its art and architecture attract large numbers of tourists. Notable medieval and Renaissance citizens included the writers Dante and Boccaccio, and the artists Giotto, Leonardo da Vinci, and Michelangelo.

history The Roman town of Florentia was founded in the 1st century BC on the site of the Etruscan town of Faesulae. It was besieged by the Goths AD 405 and visited by Charlemagne 786.

In 1052, Florence passed to Countess Matilda of Tuscany (1046–1115), and from the 11th century onwards gained increasing autonomy. In 1198 it became an independent republic, with new city walls, and governed by a body of 12 citizens. In the 13th–14th centuries, the city was the center of the struggle between the Guelphs (papal supporters) and Ghibellines (supporters of the Holy Roman emperor). Despite this, Florence became immensely prosperous and went on to reach its cultural peak during the 14th–16th centuries.

From the 15th to the 18th century, the ⇨Medici family, originally bankers, were the predominant power, in spite of their having been twice expelled by revolutions. In the first of these, in 1493, a year after Lorenzo de' Medici's death, a republic was proclaimed (with ⇨Machiavelli as secretary) that lasted until 1512. From 1494 to 1498, the city was under the control of religious reformer ⇨Savonarola. In 1527, the Medicis again proclaimed a republic, which lasted through many years of gradual decline until 1737, when the city passed to Maria Theresa of Austria. From 1737 the city was ruled by the Hapsburg imperial dynasty. The city was badly damaged in World War II and by floods 1966.

features Florence's architectural treasures include the Ponte Vecchio, 1345; the Pitti and Vecchio palaces; the churches of Santa Croce and Santa Maria Novella; the cathedral of Santa Maria del Fiore, 1314; and the Uffizi Gallery, which has one of Europe's finest art collections, based on that of the Medici.

floret small flower, usually making up part of a

larger, composite flower head. There are often two different types present on one flower head: disk florets in the central area, and ray florets around the edge which usually have a single petal known as the ligule. In the common daisy, for example, the disk florets are yellow, while the ligules are white.

Florey Howard Walter, Baron Florey 1898–1968. Australian pathologist whose research into lysozyme, an antibacterial enzyme discovered by Alexander ⇨Fleming, led him to study penicillin (another of Fleming's discoveries), which he and Ernst ⇨Chain isolated and prepared for widespread use. With Fleming, they were awarded the Nobel Prize for Physiology or Medicine 1945.

Florida southeasternmost state of the US; mainly a peninsula jutting into the Atlantic, which it separates from the Gulf of Mexico; nickname Sunshine State
area 58,672 sq mi/152,000 sq km
capital Tallahassee
cities Miami, Tampa, Jacksonville
population (1990) 12,937,900, one of the fastest-growing of the states; including 15% nonwhite; 10% Hispanic, (especially Cuban)
physical 50% forested; lakes (including Okeechobee 695 sq mi/1,800 sq km/; Everglades National Park (1,930 sq mi/5,000 sq km), with birdlife, cypresses, alligators
features Palm Beach island resort, between the lagoon of Lake Worth and the Atlantic; Florida Keys; John F Kennedy Space Center at Cape Canaveral; Disney World theme park; beach resorts on Gulf and on Atlantic; Daytona International Speedway
products citrus fruits, melons, vegetables, fish, shellfish, phosphates, chemicals, electrical and electronic equipment, aircraft, fabricated metals
famous people Chris Evert, Henry Flagler, James Weldon Johnson, Sidney Poitier, Philip Randolph, Joseph Stilwell
history discovered by Ponce de Leon and under Spanish rule from 1513 until its cession to England 1763; was returned to Spain 1783 and purchased by the US 1819, becoming a state 1845.

It grew rapidly in the early 1920s, stimulated by feverish land speculation. Despite the 1926 collapse of the boom, migration continued, especially of retirees from the North. After World War II, resorts, agriculture, and industry grew in importance. The space center at Cape Canaveral also contributed to the state economy. More recently, Florida has become a banking center, a development often partially attributed to the sizable inflow of cash derived from the traffic in illegal drugs from Latin America. Because of its proximity to Caribbean nations, the state became a haven for refugees from such countries as Cuba and Haiti.

Florida Keys series of small coral islands that curve over 150 mi/240 km SW from the southern tip of Florida. The most important are Key Largo and Key West (with a US naval and air station); they depend on fishing and tourism.

A causeway links the keys to the mainland. Key West is the largest settlement.

flotation process common method of preparing mineral ores for subsequent processing by making use of the different wetting properties of various components. The ore is finely ground and then mixed with water and a specially selected wetting agent. Air is bubbled through the mixture, forming a froth; the

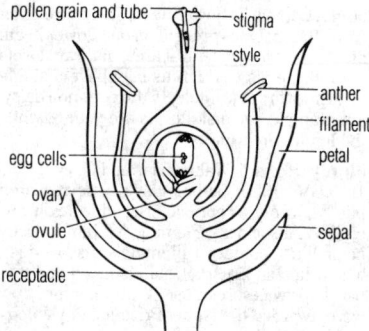

flower

desired ore particles attach themselves to the bubbles and are skimmed off, while unwanted dirt or other ores remain behind.

flotsam, jetsam, and lagan in law, terminology referring to goods cast from ships at sea, due usually to the event or prevention of shipwreck. *Flotsam* is the debris or cargo found floating; *jetsam* is what has been thrown overboard to lighten a sinking vessel; *lagan* is cargo secured, as to a buoy, for future recovery.

flounder any of a number of ⊳flatfishes of several genera. A common North American species is the southern flounder *Paralichthys lethostigma*, a valuable food fish about 20 in/50 cm long.

flow chart diagram, often used in computing, to show the possible paths that data can take through a system or program.

A *system flow chart*, or *data flow chart*, is used to describe the flow of data through a complete data-processing system. Different graphic symbols represent the clerical operations involved and the different input, storage, and output equipment required. Although the flow chart may indicate the specific programs used, no details are given of how the programs process the data.

A *program flow chart* is used to describe the flow of data through a particular computer program, showing the exact sequence of operations performed by that program in order to process the data. Different graphic symbols are used to represent data input and output, decisions, branches, and ⊳subroutines.

flower the reproductive unit of an ⊳angiosperm or flowering plant, typically consisting of four whorls of modified leaves: ⊳sepals, ⊳petals, ⊳stamens, and ⊳carpels. These are borne on a central axis or ⊳receptacle. The many variations in size, color, number, and arrangement of parts are closely related to the method of pollination. Flowers adapted for wind pollination typically have reduced or absent petals and sepals and long, feathery ⊳stigmas that hang outside the flower to trap airborne pollen. In contrast, the petals of insect-pollinated flowers are usually conspicuous and brightly colored.

The sepals and petals form the **calyx** and **corolla** respectively and together comprise the perianth with the function of protecting the reproductive organs and attracting pollinators. The stamens lie within the corolla, each having a slender stalk, or filament, bearing the pollen-containing anther at the top. Collectively they are known as the **androecium** (male organs). The inner whorl of the flower comprises the carpels, each usually consisting of an ⊳ovary in which are borne the ⊳ovules, and a stigma borne at the top of a slender stalk, or style.

Collectively the carpels are known as the **gynoecium** (female organs).

In size, flowers range from the tiny blooms of duckweeds scarcely visible with the naked eye to the gigantic flowers of the Malaysian *Rafflesia*, which can reach over 3 ft/1 m across. Flowers may either be borne singly or grouped together in ⊳inflorescences. The stalk of the whole inflorescence is termed a peduncle, and the stalk of an individual flower is termed a pedicel. A flower is termed hermaphrodite when it contains both male and female reproductive organs. When male and female organs are carried in separate flowers, they are termed monoecious; when male and female flowers are on separate plants, the term dioecious is used.

flowering plant term generally used for ⊳angiosperms, which bear flowers with various parts, including sepals, petals, stamens, and carpels. Sometimes the term is used more broadly, to include both angiosperms and ⊳gymnosperms, in which case the ⊳cones of conifers and cycads are referred to as "flowers." Usually, however, the angiosperms and gymnosperms are referred to collectively as ⊳seed plants, or spermatophytes.

flower power youth movement of the 1960s; see ⊳hippie.

flugelhorn alto brass instrument, similar in appearance to the ⊳cornet.

fluid any substance, either liquid or gas, in which the molecules are relatively mobile and can "flow."

fluid mechanics the study of the behavior of fluids (liquids and gases) at rest and in motion. Fluid mechanics is important in the study of the weather, the design of aircraft and road vehicles, and in industries, such as the chemical industry, which deal with flowing liquids or gases.

fluid, supercritical fluid brought by a combination of heat and pressure to the point at which, as a near vapor, it combines the properties of a gas and a liquid. Supercritical fluids are used as solvents in chemical processes, such as the extraction of lubricating oil from refinery residues or the decaffeination of coffee, because they avoid the energy-expensive need for phase changes (from liquid to gas and back again) required in conventional distillation processes.

fluke any of various parasitic flatworms of the classes Monogenea and Digenea, that as adults live in and destroy the lives of sheep, cattle, horses, dogs, and humans. Monogenetic flukes can complete their life cycle in one host; digenetic flukes require two or more hosts, for example a snail and a human being, to complete their life cycle.

fluorescence in scientific usage, very short-lived ⊳luminescence (a glow not caused by high temperature). Generally, the term is used for any luminescence regardless of the persistence. See ⊳phosphorescence.

Fluorescence is used in strip and other lighting, and was developed rapidly during World War II because it was a more efficient means of illumination than the incandescent lamp. Other important applications are in fluorescent screens for television and cathode-ray tubes.

fluoridation addition of small amounts of fluoride salts to drinking water by certain water authorities to help prevent tooth decay. Experiments in Britain, the US, and elsewhere have indicated that a concentration of fluoride of 1 part per million in tap water retards the decay of teeth in children by more than 50%.

fluoride negative ion (Fl-) formed when hydrogen fluoride dissolves in water; compound formed between fluorine and another element in which the fluorine is the more electronegative element (see ⊳electronegativity, ⊳halide).

fluorine pale yellow, gaseous, nonmetallic element, symbol F, atomic number 9, atomic weight 19. It is the first member of the halogen group of elements, and is pungent, poisonous, and highly reactive, uniting directly with nearly all the elements. It occurs naturally as the minerals fluorite (CaF_2) and cryolite (Na_3AlF_6). Hydrogen fluoride is used in etching glass, and the freons, which all contain fluorine, are widely used as refrigerants.

Fluorine was discovered by the Swedish chemist Karl Scheele in 1771 and isolated by the French chemist Henri Moissan in 1886. Combined with uranium as UF_6, it is used in the separation of uranium isotopes.

fluorite or **fluorspar** a glassy, brittle mineral, calcium fluoride CaF_2, forming cubes and octahedra; colorless when pure, otherwise violet.

Fluorite is used as a flux in iron and steel making; colorless fluorite is used in the manufacture of microscope lenses. It is also used for the glaze on pottery, and as a source of fluorine in the manufacture of hydrofluoric acid.

fluorocarbon compound formed by replacing the hydrogen atoms of a hydrocarbon with fluorine. Fluorocarbons are used as inert coatings, refrigerants, synthetic resins, and as propellants in aerosols.

There is concern that the release of fluorocarbons—particularly those containing chlorine (chlorofluorocarbons, CFCs)—depletes the ⊳ozone layer, allowing more ultraviolet light from the Sun to penetrate the Earth's atmosphere, and increasing the incidence of skin cancer in humans.

flute member of a group of ⊳woodwind musical instruments (although usually made of metal), including the piccolo, the concert flute, and the bass or alto flute. Flutes are cylindrical in shape, with a narrowed end, containing a shaped aperture, across which the player blows. The air vibrations produce the note, which can be altered by placing fingers over lateral holes. Certain keys can be depressed to extend the range of the flute to three octaves.

The orchestral flute is at concert pitch—middle C to C sharp three octaves higher. The alto (sometimes known as the "bass") flute has a range the same as that of the concert flute, but a fourth lower. The bass flute in B flat is usually only played in fife and drum bands.

flux in smelting, a substance that combines with the unwanted components of the ore to produce a fusible slag, which can be separated from the molten metal. For example, the mineral fluorite, CaF_2, is used as a flux in iron smelting; it has a low melting point and will form a fusible mixture with substances of higher melting point such as silicates and oxides.

flux in soldering, a substance that improves the bonding properties of solder by removing contamination from metal surfaces and preventing their oxidation, and by reducing the surface tension of the molten solder alloy. For example, with solder made of lead-tin alloys, the flux may be resin, borax, or zinc chloride.

fly any insect of the order Diptera. A fly has a single pair of wings, antennae, and compound eyes; the hind wings have become modified into knoblike projections (halteres) used to maintain equilibrium in flight. There are over 90,000 species.

The mouthparts project from the head as a proboscis used for sucking fluids, modified in some species, such as mosquitoes, to pierce a victim's skin and suck blood. Discs at the ends of hairs on their feet secrete a fluid enabling them to walk up walls and across ceilings. Flies undergo complete metamorphosis; their larvae (maggots) are without true legs, and the pupae are rarely enclosed in a cocoon. The sexes are similar and coloration is rarely vivid, though some are metallic green or blue. The fruitfly, genus *Drosophila*, is much used in genetic experiments as it is easy to keep, fast-breeding, and has easily visible chromosomes.

flying dragon lizard *Draco volans* of the family Agamidae. It lives in SE Asia, and can glide on flaps of skin spread and supported by its ribs. This small (3 in/7.5 cm head and body) arboreal lizard can glide between trees for 6m/20 ft or more.

flying fish any of a family, Exocoetidae, of marine bony fishes of the order Beloniformes, best represented in tropical waters. They have winglike pectoral fins that can be spread to glide over the water.

flying fox fruit-eating ⟡bat of the suborder Megachiroptera.

flying gurnard any of various marine fishes of the order Dactylopteriformes (especially the genus *Dactylopterus*), having winglike pectoral fins and capable of gliding for short distances. They are not related to ⟡flying fishes.

flying lemur commonly used, but incorrect, name for ⟡colugo. It cannot fly, and it is not a lemur.

flying lizard another name for ⟡flying dragon.

flying squirrel any of numerous species of squirrel, not closely related to the true squirrels. They are characterized by a membrane along the side of the body from forelimb to hindlimb (in some species running to neck and tail) which allows them to glide through the air. Several genera of flying squirrel are found in the Old World; the New World has the genus *Glaucomys*. Most species are E Asian.

The giant flying squirrel *Petaurista* grows up to 3.5 ft/1.1 m including tail, and can glide 210 ft/65 m.

Flynn Errol. Adopted name of Leslie Thompson 1909–1959. Australian-born US film actor. He is renowned for his portrayal of swashbuckling heroes in such films as *Captain Blood* 1935, *Robin Hood* 1938, *The Charge of the Light Brigade* 1938, *The Private Lives of Elizabeth and Essex* 1939, *The Sea Hawk* 1940, and *The Master of Ballantrae* 1953.

In *The Sun Also Rises* 1957 he portrayed a middle-aged Hemingway roué, and in *Too Much Too Soon* 1958 he portrayed his friend, actor John Barrymore. Flynn wrote an autobiography, *My Wicked, Wicked Ways* 1959. He became a US citizen 1942.

flywheel heavy wheel that helps keep an engine running and smooths its motion. The ⟡crankshaft in a gasoline engine has a flywheel at one end, which keeps the crankshaft turning in between the intermittent power strokes of the pistons. It also comes into contact with the ⟡clutch, serving as the connection between the engine and the car's transmission system.

C = centre of curvature   P = pole
F = focus   f = focal length

focal length *The distance from the pole (P), or optical center, of a lens or spherical mirror to its principal focus (F).*

M in physics, symbol for *frequency ⟡modulation*, or the variation of the frequency of a carrier wave in accordance with the signal to be transmitted. Used in radio, FM is constant in amplitude and has much better signal-to-noise ratio than AM (amplitude modulation).

FNLA abbreviation for *Front National de Libération de l'Angola* (French "National Front for the Liberation of Angola").

f-number measure of the relative aperture of a telescope or camera lens; it indicates the light-gathering power of the lens. In photography, each successive f-number represents a halving of exposure speed.

Fo Dario 1926–   . Italian playwright. His plays are predominantly political satires combining black humor with slapstick. They include *Morte accidentale di un anarchico/Accidental Death of an Anarchist* 1970, and *Non si paga non si paga/Can't Pay? Won't Pay!* 1975/1981.

focal length or *focal distance* the distance from the center of a lens or curved mirror to the focal point. For a concave mirror or convex lens, it is the distance at which parallel rays of light are brought to a focus to form a real image (for a mirror, this is half the radius of curvature). For a convex mirror or concave lens, it is the distance from the center to the point at which a virtual image (an image produced by diverging rays of light) is formed.

With lenses, the greater the power (measured in dioptres) of the lens the shorter its focal length.

Foch Ferdinand 1851–1929. Marshal of France during World War I. He was largely responsible for the Allied victory at the first battle of the ⟡Marne Sept 1914, and commanded on the NW front Oct 1914–Sept 1916. He was appointed commander in chief of the Allied armies in the spring of 1918, and launched the Allied counter-offensive in July that brought about the negotiation of an armistice to end the war.

fog cloud that collects at the surface of the Earth, composed of water vapor that has condensed on particles of dust in the atmosphere. Cloud and fog are both caused by the air temperature falling below ⟡dew point. The thickness of fog depends on the number of water particles it contains. Usually, fog is formed by the meeting of two currents of air, one cooler than the other, or by warm air flowing over a cold surface. Sea fogs commonly occur where warm and cold currents meet and the air above them mixes.

Fog frequently forms on calm nights as the land surface cools more rapidly than the air immediately above it. In drought areas, for example, Baja California, Canary Islands, Cape Verde islands, Namib Desert, Peru, and Chile, coastal fogs enable plant and animal life to survive without rain and are a potential source of water for human use (by means of water collectors exploiting the effect of condensation).

Officially, fog refers to a condition when visibility is reduced to 0.62 mi/1 km or less, and mist or haze to that giving a visibility of 0.62–1.24 mi/1–2 km. A mist is produced by condensed water particles, and a haze by smoke or dust. Industrial areas uncontrolled by pollution laws have a continual haze of smoke over them, and if the temperature falls suddenly, a dense yellow smog forms. At some airports since 1975 it has been possible for certain aircraft to land and take off blind in fog, using radar navigation.

föhn or *foehn* warm dry wind that blows down the leeward slopes of mountains.

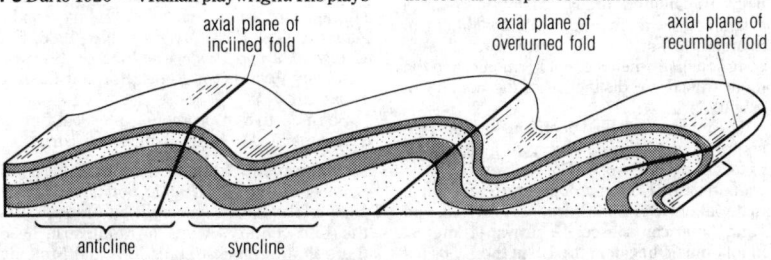

fold *The folding of rock strata occurs where compression causes them to buckle.*

The air heats up as it descends because of the increase in pressure, and it is dry because all the moisture was dropped on the windward side of the mountain. In the valleys of Switzerland it is regarded as a health hazard, producing migraine and high blood pressure. A similar wind, the chinook, is found on the eastern slopes of the Rocky Mountains in North America.

Fokine Mikhail 1880–1942. Russian dancer and choreographer, born in St Petersburg. He was chief choreographer to the Ballets Russes 1909–14, and with ◊Diaghilev revitalized and reformed the art of ballet, promoting the idea of artistic unity among dramatic, musical, and stylistic elements.

fold in geology, a bend in ◊beds or layers of rock. If the bend is arched in the middle it is called an **anticline**; if it sags downward in the middle it is called a **syncline**. The line along which a bed of rock folds is called its axis. The axial plane is the plane joining the axes of successive beds. *See illustration on p. 399.*

folic acid a ◊vitamin of the B complex. It is found in legumes, green leafy vegetables, and whole grains, and is also synthesized by intestinal bacteria. It is essential for growth, and plays many other roles in the body. Lack of folic acid causes anemia, diarrhea, and a red tongue.

folk dance dance characteristic of a particular people, nation, or region. Many European folk dances are derived from the dances accompanying the customs and ceremonies of pre-Christian times. Some later became ballroom dances (for example, the minuet and waltz). Once an important part of many rituals, folk dance has tended to die out in industrialized countries. Examples of folk dance are Morris dance, farandole, and jota.

folklore the oral traditions and culture of a people, expressed in legends, riddles, songs, tales, and proverbs. The term was coined 1846 by W J Thoms (1803–85), but the founder of the systematic study of the subject was German collector of fairy tails Jacob Grimm (1785-1863); see also ◊oral literature.

The approach to folklore has varied greatly: the German scholar Max Müller (1823–1900) interpreted it as evidence of nature myths; Scottish anthropologist James Frazer (1854-1941) was the exponent of the comparative study of early and popular folklore as mutually explanatory; Laurence Gomme (1853–1916) adopted a historical analysis; and Bronislaw ◊Malinowski and Alfred Radcliffe-Brown (1881–1955) examined the material as an integral element of a given living culture. Folklore overlaps with cultural anthropology but their roots and theoretical concerns are not the same.

folk music body of traditional music, originally transmitted orally. Many folk songs originated as a rhythmic accompaniment to manual work or to mark a specific ritual. Folk song is usually melodic, not harmonic, and the modes used are distinctive of the country of origin.

The interest in ballad poetry in the later 18th century led to the discovery of a rich body of folk song in Europe. The multiethnic background of the US has brought forth a wealth of material derived from European, African, and Latin American sources. A revival of interest in folk music began in the US in the 1950s led by the researcher Alan Lomax (1915–) and

the singers Henry Belafonte (1927–), Odetta (1930–), Pete Seeger, Woody Guthrie, and Joan Baez, and Bob Dylan who wrote new material in folk-song style, dealing with contemporary topics such as nuclear weapons and racial prejudice.

follicle in botany, a dry, usually many-seeded fruit that splits along one side only to release the seeds within. It is derived from a single ◊carpel, examples include the fruits of the larkspurs *Delphinium* and columbine *Aquilegia*. It differs from a pod, which always splits open (dehisces) along both sides.

follicle in zoology, a small group of cells that surround and nourish a structure such as a hair (hair follicle) or a cell such as an egg (Graafian follicle; see ◊menstrual cycle).

follicle-stimulating hormone (FSH) a ◊hormone produced by the pituitary gland. It affects the ovaries in women, triggering off the production of an egg cell. Luteinizing hormone is needed to complete the process. In men, FSH stimulates the testes to produce sperm.

Folsom site in New Mexico, where in 1926 a flint point was found embedded among the bones of an extinct type of bison, thus proving that humans had existed in the Americas in the Pleistocene period.

Fomalhaut or *Alpha Piscis Austrini* the brightest star in the southern constellation Piscis Austrinus and the 18th brightest star in the sky. It is 22 light-years from Earth, with a true luminosity 13 times that of the Sun.

Fomalhaut is one of a number of stars around which the Infra-Red Astronomy Satellite (see ◊infrared astronomy) detected excess infrared radiation, presumably from a region of solid particles around the star. This material may be a planetary system in the process of formation.

Fon member of a people living mainly in Benin, and also in Nigeria, numbering about 2.5 million. The Fon language belongs to the Kwa branch of the Niger-Congo family. The Fon founded a kingdom which became powerful in the 18th and 19th centuries through the slave trade, and the region became known as the Slave Coast.

Fonda Henry 1905–1982. US actor whose engaging style made him ideal in the role of the American pioneer and honorable man. His many films include the Academy Award-winning *The Grapes of Wrath* 1940, *My Darling Clementine* 1946, and *On Golden Pond* 1981, for which he won the Academy Award for best actor. He was the father of actress Jane Fonda and actor and director Peter Fonda (1939–).

Fonda Jane 1937– . US actress. Her early films include *Cat Ballou* 1965, *Barefoot in the Park* 1967, *Barbarella* 1968, *They Shoot Horses, Don't They?* 1969, *Julia*, 1977, *The China Syndrome* 1979, *On Golden Pond* 1981, in which she appeared with her father, Henry Fonda, *Agnes of God* 1985, *Morning After* 1986, *Old Gringo* 1989, and *Stanley and Iris* 1990. She won Academy Awards for *Klute* 1971 and *Coming Home* 1979.

She is active in promoting physical fitness and is married to businessman Ted Turner.

Fontainebleau town to the SE of Paris, in Seine-et-Marne *département*; population (1982) 18,753. The palace was built by François I in the 16th century. Mme de Montespan lived there in the reign of Louis XIV, and Mme du Barry in that of Louis XV. Napoleon signed his

abdication there in 1814. Nearby is the village of Barbizon, the haunt of several 19th-century painters (known as the ◊Barbizon school).

Fontainebleau school French school of Mannerist painting and sculpture. It was established at the court of Francis I, who brought Italian artists to Fontainebleau near Paris to decorate his hunting lodge: Rosso Fiorentino (1494–1540) arrived 1530, Francesco Primaticcio (1504/5–1570) came 1532. They evolved a distinctive decorative style using a combination of stucco sculpture and painting.

Their work, with its exuberant ornament and figure style, had a lasting impact on French art in the 16th century. Others associated with the school include Benvenuto ◊Cellini.

Fontana Domenico 1543–1607. Italian architect. He was employed by Pope Sixtus V to build the Lateran Palace, Rome 1586–88, the Vatican library 1587–90, and the completion of the dome of St Peter's in Rome 1588–90, as well as the royal palace in Naples 1600–02.

Fontanne Lynn 1887–1983. US actress, one-half of the husband-and-wife acting partnership known as the "Lunts" with her husband Alfred ◊Lunt.

Fontenoy, Battle of battle in the War of the ◊Austrian Succession 1745. Marshal Saxe and the French defeated the British, Dutch, and Hanoverians under the duke of Cumberland at a village in Hainaut province, Belgium, SE of Tournai.

Fonteyn Margot. Adopted name of Margaret Hookham 1919–1991. English ballet dancer. She made her debut with the Vic-Wells Ballet in *Nutcracker* 1934 and first appeared as Giselle 1937, eventually becoming prima ballerina of the Royal Ballet, London. Renowned for her perfect physique, musicality, and interpretive powers, she created many roles in Frederick ◊Ashton's ballets and formed a legendary partnership with Rudolf ◊Nureyev. She did not retire from dancing until 1979.

food anything eaten by human beings and other animals to sustain life and health. The building blocks of food are nutrients, and humans can utilize the following nutrients: *carbohydrates*, as starches found in bread, potatoes, and pasta; as simple sugars in sucrose and honey; as fibers in cereals, fruit, and vegetables; *proteins* as from nuts, fish, meat, eggs, milk, and some vegetables; *fats* as found in most animal products (meat, lard, dairy products, fish), also in margarine, nuts and seeds, olives, and edible oils; vitamins are found in a wide variety of foods, except for vitamin B_{12}, which is mainly found in animal foods; minerals are found in a wide variety of foods; good sources of calcium are milk and broccoli, for example; iodine from seafood; iron from liver and green vegetables; water is ubiquitous in nature; alcohol is found in fermented distilled beverages, from more than 40% in liquor to 0.01% in low-alcohol beers.

Food is needed both for energy, measured in calories or kilojoules, and nutrients, which are converted to body tissues. Some nutrients, such as fat, carbohydrate, and alcohol, provide mainly energy; other nutrients are important in other ways; for example, fiber is an aid to metabolism. Proteins provide energy and are necessary for building cell and tissue structure.

Food and Agriculture Organization (FAO) United Nations agency that coordinates activities to improve food and timber production and levels of nutrition throughout the world.

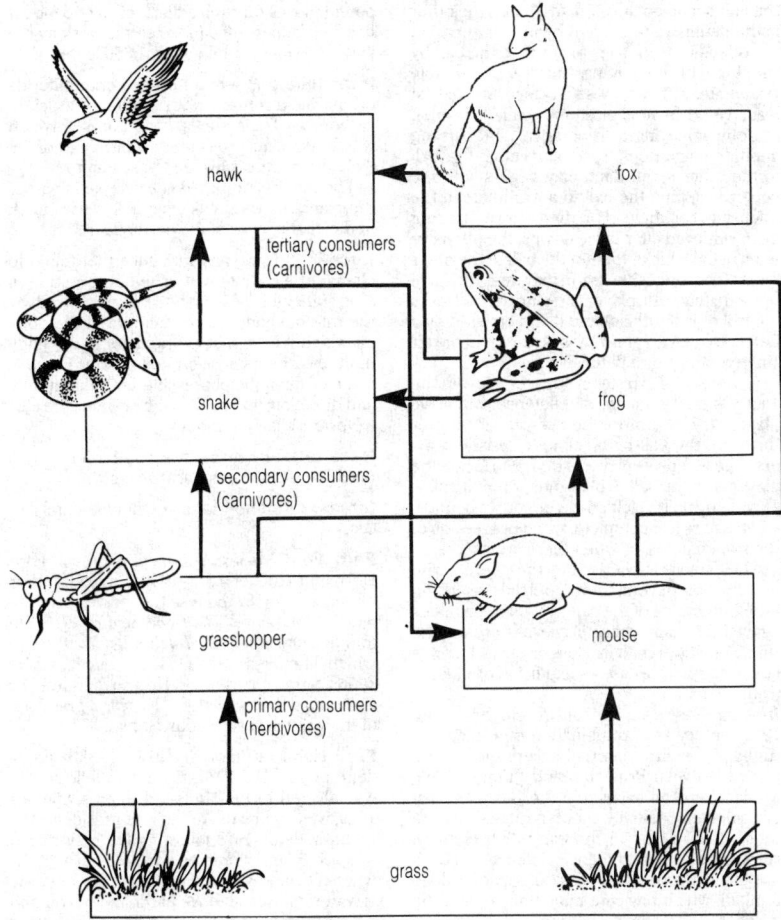

hawk

fox

tertiary consumers
(carnivores)

snake

frog

secondary consumers
(carnivores)

grasshopper

mouse

primary consumers
(herbivores)

grass

food chain *The complex inter-relationship between animals and plants in a food chain. Food chains are normally only three or four links long. This is because the major part of the energy stored within the chain is wasted. For food chains to be longer, large areas of vegetation would be needed at the lowest level. A chain of 20 links would require an area of vegetation the size of a continent.*

It is also concerned with investment in agriculture and dispersal of emergency food supplies. It has headquarters in Rome and was founded 1945.

The US cut its FAO funding in 1990 from $61.4 million to $18 million because of its alleged politicization.

food chain or **food web** in ecology, the sequence of organisms through which energy and other nutrients are successively transferred. Since many organisms feed at several different levels (for example, omnivores feed on both fruit and meat), the relationships often form a complex web rather than a simple chain. See also ⟩ecosystem.

The sequence of the food chain comprises ⟩autotrophs, or producers, which are principally plants and photosynthetic microorganisms, and a series of ⟩heterotrophs, or consumers, which are ⟩herbivores that feed on the producers; ⟩carnivores that feed on the herbivores; and ⟩decomposers that break down the dead bodies and waste products of all four groups (including their own), ready for recycling.

food irradiation the exposure of food to low-level ⟩irradiation to kill microorganisms; a

technique used in ⟩food technology. Irradiation is highly effective, and does not make the food any more radioactive than it is naturally. Irradiated food is used for astronauts and immunocompromised patients in hospitals. Some vitamins are partially destroyed, such as vitamin C, and it would be unwise to eat only irradiated fruit and vegetables.

The main cause for concern is that it may be used by unscrupulous traders to "clean up" consignments of food, particularly shellfish, with high bacterial counts. Bacterial toxins would remain in the food, so that it could still cause illness, although irradiation would have removed signs of live bacteria. Stringent regulations would be needed to prevent this happening. Other damaging changes may take place in the food, such as the creation of ⟩free radicals, but research so far suggests that the process is relatively safe.

food poisoning any acute illness characterized by vomiting and diarrhea and caused by eating food contaminated with harmful bacteria (for example, ⟩listeriosis), poisonous food (for example, certain mushrooms, puffer fish), or poisoned food (such as lead or arsenic introduced accidentally during processing). A

frequent cause of food poisoning is ⟩Salmonella bacteria. These come in many forms, and strains are found in cattle, pigs, poultry, and eggs.

Deep freezing of poultry before the birds are properly cooked is a common cause of food poisoning. Attacks of salmonella also come from contaminated eggs that have been eaten raw or cooked only lightly. Pork may carry the roundworm *Trichinella*, and rye the parasitic fungus ergot. The most dangerous food poison is the bacillus that causes ⟩botulism. This is rare but leads to muscle paralysis and, often, death. ⟩Food irradiation is intended to prevent food poisoning.

food technology the application of science to the commercial processing of foodstuffs. Food is processed to make it more palatable or digestible, for which the traditional methods include boiling, frying, flour-milling, breadmaking, yogurt- and cheese-making, brewing, or to preserve it from spoilage caused by the action of ⟩enzymes within the food that change its chemical composition, or the growth of bacteria, molds, yeasts, and other microorganisms. Fatty or oily foods also suffer oxidation of the fats, which makes them rancid. Traditional forms of **food preservation**, include salting, smoking, pickling, drying, bottling, and preserving in sugar. Modern food technology also uses many novel processes and ⟩additives, which allow a wider range of foodstuffs to be preserved.

Refrigeration below 41°F/5°C (or below 37°F/3°C for cooked foods) slows the processes of spoilage, but is less effective for foods with a high water content. This process cannot kill microorganisms, nor stop their growth completely, and a failure to realize its limitations causes many cases of food poisoning. Refrigerator temperatures should be checked as the efficiency of the machinery (see ⟩refrigeration) can decline with age, and higher temperatures are dangerous.

Deep freezing (−1°F/−18°C or below) stops almost all spoilage processes, except residual enzyme activity in uncooked vegetables, which are blanched (dipped in hot water to destroy the enzymes) before freezing. Microorganisms cannot grow or divide while frozen, but most remain alive and can resume activity once defrosted. Some foods are damaged by freezing, notably soft fruits and salad vegetables, the cells of which are punctured by ice crystals, leading to loss of crispness. Fatty foods such as cow's milk and cream tend to separate. Various processes are used for ⟩deep freezing foods commercially.

Pasteurization is used mainly for milk. By holding the milk at 161.6°F/72°C for 15 seconds, all disease-causing bacteria can be destroyed. Less harmful bacteria survive, so the milk will still go sour within a few days.

Ultra-heat treatment is used to produce UHT milk. This process uses higher temperatures than pasteurization, and kills all bacteria present, giving the milk a long shelf life but altering the flavor.

Drying is effective because both microorganisms and enzymes need water to be active. Products such as dried milk and instant coffee are made by spraying the liquid into a rising column of dry, heated air.

Freeze-drying is carried out under vacuum. It is less damaging to food than straight dehydration in the sense that foods reconstitute better, and is used for quality instant coffee and dried vegetables.

Canning relies on high temperatures to destroy microorganisms and enzymes. The food is sealed into a can to prevent recontamination. Drinks may be canned to preserve the carbon dioxide that makes them fizzy.

Pickling utilizes the effect of acetic acid, found in vinegar, in stopping the growth of molds. In sauerkraut, lactic acid, produced by bacteria, has the same effect. Similar types of non-harmful, acid-generating bacteria are used to make yogurt and cheese.

Curing of meat involves soaking in salt (sodium chloride) solution, with saltpeter (sodium nitrate) added to give the meat its pink color and characteristic taste. Bacteria convert the nitrates in cured meats to nitrites and nitrosamines, which are potentially carcinogenic to humans.

Irradiation is a method of preserving food by subjecting it to low-level radiation (see ▷food irradiation).

Puffing is a method of processing cereal grains. They are subjected to high pressures, then suddenly ejected into a normal atmospheric pressure, causing the grain to expand sharply. This is used to make puffed wheat cereals and puffed rice cakes.

Chemical treatments are widely used, for example in margarine manufacture, in which hydrogen is bubbled through vegetable oils in the presence of a ▷catalyst to produce a more solid, spreadable fat. The catalyst is later removed. Chemicals introduced in processing that remain in the food are known as **food additives** and include flavorings, preservatives, antioxidants, emulsifiers, and colorings.

foot imperial unit of length (symbol ft), equivalent to 0.3048 m, in use in Britain since Anglo-Saxon times. It originally represented the length of a human foot. One foot contains 12 inches and is one-third of a yard.

foot-and-mouth disease contagious eruptive viral disease of cloven-hoofed mammals, characterized by blisters in the mouth and around the hooves. In cattle it causes deterioration of milk yield and abortions. It is an airborne virus which makes its eradication extremely difficult.

Inoculation with a vaccine is practiced in the US as a preventive measure.

football a contact sport played between two teams of 11 players with an inflated, pointed-oval ball. It is played on a field 100 yd/91 m long from goal line to goal line, with a goal posts on each of these lines, followed by a 10-yd/9-m end zone. The field is 53.3 yd/48.8 m wide. The team that scores the most points wins. Points are scored by running or passing the ball across the goal line (touchdown), by kicking it over the goal's crossbar after a touchdown (conversion or point after touchdown) or from the field during regular play (field goal), or by tackling an offensive player who has the ball in the end zone or blocking an offensive team's kick so it goes out of bounds from the end zone (safety). A touchdown counts 6 points, a field goal 3, a safety 2, and a conversion 1. Except in professional football, teams may attempt a 2-point conversion after a touchdown by running or passing the ball into the end zone. College and professional games consist of four 15-min quarters; high-school quarters are 12 min long. Players wear padded uniforms and helmets.

A game begins with one team kicking off to the other. Kickoffs also take place after each touchdown and field goal and to start the second half of the game. The team that receives the ball becomes the offensive team; the other is the defensive team. Led by its quarterback, the offensive team tries to advance the ball by running with it or by passing it to an eligible teammate. A team must advance the ball at least 10 yd in four attempts (called downs), thereby achieving a "first down" and earning another four attempts, or surrender the ball to the other team. Each play begins with the center snapping the ball to a teammate in the offensive backfield. If a first down has not been achieved after three downs, the offensive team usually kicks (punts) the ball to the other team. The offensive team may lose the ball immediately if the player carrying the ball loses control of it (fumbles) and it is recovered by a defensive player, or if a pass is caught in the air (interception) by a defensive player.

Generally, separate groups of players on each team play offense and defense. Offensive players try to protect the person carrying or throwing the ball by blocking defensive players. The defensive players attempt to tackle the player with the ball. A play ends when the player with the ball is tackled or goes out of bounds, when a pass is incomplete, when possession of the ball changes, or when there is a score.

The game is supervised by the referee, who usually has several other officials assisting him. Infractions of the rules result in penalties against the team whose player has broken the rule. Penalties result in a loss of yards, loss of a down, or—in rare cases—expulsion of a player from the game.

history American football developed in the 19th century as a combination of soccer and rugby. The first intercollegiate game was played between Princeton and Rutgers 1869. Modern football evolved in the 1880s as eastern colleges gradually adopted rules similar to those now in use. In the early 20th century, rules were passed to reduce violence and to allow the forward pass. The popularity of college football, which has continued unabated to the present, led to the formation of professional teams from the 1890s on. What is now the National Football League (NFL) was founded 1920. Although there have been other professional leagues, the NFL has remained dominant. The NFL struggled for many years but gradually established itself in large cities; explosive growth occurred after World War II as attendance rose and television broadcasts added millions of fans. Another surge of popularity followed the merger of the American Football League (AFL) into the NFL, completed 1970. There are now 28 teams in the NFL, divided into the American and National conferences. The champions of the two conferences meet in a title game called the Super Bowl.

Recent Super Bowl Winners

1984	Los Angeles Raiders
1985	San Francisco 49ers
1986	Chicago Bears
1987	New York Giants
1988	Washington Redskins
1989	San Francisco 49ers
1990	San Francisco 49ers
1991	New York Giants
1992	Washington Redskins
1993	Dallas Cowboys

foot-candle unit of illuminance, now replaced by the lux. One foot-candle is the illumination received at a distance of one foot from an international candle. It is equal to 10.764 lux.

foot-pound imperial unit of energy (ft-lb), defined as the work done when a force of one pound moves through a distance of one foot. It has been superseded for scientific work by the joule: one foot-pound equals 1.356 joule.

foraminifera any of an order Foraminiferida of marine protozoa with shells of calcium carbonate. Their shells have pores through which filaments project. Some form part of the ▷plankton, others live on the sea bottom.

The many-chambered *Globigerina* is part of the plankton. Its shells eventually form much of the chalky ooze of the ocean floor.

force in physics, any influence that tends to change the state of rest or uniform motion in a straight line of a body. It is measured by the rate of change of momentum of the body on which it acts, that is, the mass of the body multiplied by its acceleration: $F=ma$. Force is a vector quantity, possessing both magnitude and direction; its SI unit is the newton. See also ▷Newton's laws of motion.

force ratio the magnification of a force by a machine; see ▷mechanical advantage.

forces, fundamental see ▷fundamental forces.

Ford Ford Madox. Adopted name of Ford Hermann Hueffer 1873–1939. English author of more than 82 books, the best known of which is the novel *The Good Soldier* 1915. He founded and edited the *English Review* 1909, to which Thomas Hardy, D H Lawrence, and Joseph Conrad contributed. He also founded *The Transatlantic Review* 1924. He was a grandson of the painter Ford Madox Brown.

Ford Gerald R(udolph) 1913– . 38th president of the US 1974–77, a Republican. He was elected to the House of Representatives 1949, was nominated to the vice-presidency by Richard Nixon 1973 following the resignation of Spiro ▷Agnew, and became president 1974, when Nixon was forced to resign following the ▷Watergate scandal. He pardoned Nixon and gave amnesty to those who had resisted the draft for the Vietnam War.

Ford was born in Omaha, Nebraska, was an All-American football player in college, and graduated from Yale Law School. He was appointed vice-president Dec 1973, at a time when Nixon's reelection campaign was already being investigated for "dirty tricks," and became president the following Aug. Ford's visit to Vladivostok 1974 resulted in agreement with the USSR on strategic arms limitation. He was defeated by Carter in the 1976 election by a narrow margin.

Ford Glenn (Gwyllym Samuel Newton) 1916– . Canadian-born US actor, active in Hollywood from the 1940s to the 1960s. Usually cast as the tough but good-natured hero, he was equally at home in Westerns, thrillers, and comedies. His films include *Gilda* 1946, *The Big Heat* 1953, and *Dear Heart* 1965.

Ford Henry 1863–1947. US automobile manufacturer, who built his first car 1896 and founded the Ford Motor Company 1903. His Model T (1908–27) was the first car to be constructed solely by assembly-line methods and to be mass marketed; 15 million of these automobiles were made and sold.

Born in Dearborn, Michigan, Ford was apprenticed to a Detroit machinist 1878 before he started his own company. His innovative policies, such as a $5 daily minimum wage and a 5-day work week, revolutionized employment practices. In 1928 he introduced the Model A, a stepped-up version of the Model T.

Ford was politically active and a pacifist; he opposed US intervention in both world wars and promoted his own anti-Semitic views. In 1936 he founded, with his son Edsel Ford (1893–1943), the philanthropic Ford Foundation; he retired in 1945 from the Ford Motor Co, then valued at over $1 billion.

Ford John 1586–c. 1640. English poet and dramatist. His play *'Tis Pity She's a Whore* (performed about 1626, printed 1633) is a study of incest between brother and sister.

Ford John. Adopted name of Sean O'Feeney 1895–1973. US film director. Active from the silent film era, he was one of the original creators of the "Western," directing *The Iron Horse* 1924; *Stagecoach* 1939 became his masterpiece. He won Academy Awards for *The Informer* 1935, *The Grapes of Wrath* 1940, *How Green Was My Valley* 1941, and *The Quiet Man* 1952.

Other films include *Rio Grande* 1950, *Mr Roberts* 1955, *The Last Hurrah* 1958, and *The Man Who Shot Liberty Valance* 1962.

foreclosure in law, the transfer of title of a mortgaged property from the mortgagor (borrower, usually a home owner) to the mortgagee (loaner, for example a bank) if the mortgagor is in breach of the mortgage agreement, usually by failing to make a number of payments on the mortgage (loan).

The mortgagor may keep or sell the mortgaged property, often by auction. If the selling price is less than the mortgage, the mortgagee is responsible to the mortgagor for the difference. If the selling price is more than the worth of the mortgage, the mortgagor must give the mortgagee the difference. If the mortgage calls for installment payments, foreclosure may be warded off if the mortgagee pays all back payments and expenses incurred. Otherwise, foreclosure can be canceled only by the payment of the mortgage in full.

foredeep in earth science, an elongate structural basin lying inland from an active mountain system and receiving sediment from the rising mountains. According to plate tectonic theory, a mountain chain forming behind a subduction zone along a continental margin develops a foredeep or gently sloping trough parallel to it on the landward side. Foredeeps form rapidly and usually are so deep initially that the sea floods them through gaps in the mountain range. As the mountain system evolves, sediments choke the foredeep, pushing out marine water. As marine sedimentation stops, only nonmarine deposits from the rapidly eroding mountains are formed. These consist of alluvial fans and also rivers, flood plains, and related environments inland.

Before the advent of plate tectonic theory, such foredeep deposits and changes in sediments had been interpreted as sedimentary troughs, called geosynclines, that were supposed ultimately to build upward into mountains.

foreign aid see ⬙aid, foreign

Foreign Legion volunteer corps of foreigners within a country's army. The French *Légion Etrangère*, 1831, is one of a number of such forces. Enlisted volunteers are of any nationality (about half are now French), but the officers are usually French. Headquarters until 1962 was in Sidi Bel Abbès, Algeria; the main base is now Corsica, with reception headquarters at Aubagne, near Marseille, France.

The French foreign legion was founded by Louis-Philippe "to clear France of foreigners" and since then has always taken cast-offs and undesirables, including those from the French army itself. Levels of desertion are relatively high, around 6%.

foreign relations a country's dealings with other countries. Specialized diplomatic bodies first appeared in Europe during the 18th century. After 1818 diplomatic agents were divided into: **ambassadors**, papal legates, and nuncios; **envoys** extraordinary, **ministers** plenipotentiary, and other ministers accredited to the head of state; ministers resident; and **chargés d'affaires**, who may deputize for an ambassador or minister, or be themselves the representative accredited to a minor country. Other diplomatic staff may include counselors and attachés (military, labor, cultural, press). **Consuls** are state agents with commercial and political responsibilities in foreign towns.

After World War II there was an increase in the number of countries represented by a diplomat of ambassadorial rather than lower rank, although in recent years improved communications have lessened the importance of the career diplomat as the person on the spot. Professional spies (see ⬙intelligence) often inflate the number of "diplomats" accredited to a country. In the US foreign relations are handled by the ⬙State Department.

Foreman George 1948– . US heavyweight boxer who was the undisputed world heavyweight champion 1973–74. After 11 years out of the ring, he made an amazing comeback, fighting in the 1991 world title at the age of 42, the oldest fighter for the heavyweight championship in the world.

forensic science the use of scientific techniques to solve criminal cases. A multidisciplinary field embracing chemistry, physics, botany, zoology, and medicine, forensic science includes the identification of human bodies or traces. Traditional methods such as fingerprinting (see ⬙fingerprint) are still used, assisted by computers; in addition, blood analysis, forensic dentistry, voice and speech spectograms, and ⬙genetic fingerprinting are increasingly applied. Chemicals, such as poisons and drugs, are analyzed by ⬙chromatography. Ballistics (the study of projectiles, such as bullets), another traditional forensic field, makes use of tools such as the comparison microscope and the ⬙electron microscope.

The first forensic laboratory was supposedly founded in Lyons, France in 1910 by Edmond Locard, although it is claimed that Locard's teacher, Alphonse Bertillon, had established one earlier, and that the laboratory in Lyons was founded by Jean Lacassagne. The science developed as a systematic discipline in the 1930s. In 1932 the US Federal Bureau of Investigation established a forensic science laboratory in Washington, DC, and in the UK the first such laboratory was founded in London in 1935.

Forester C(ecil) S(cott) 1899–1966. English novelist, born in Egypt. He wrote a series of historical novels set in the Napoleonic era that, beginning with *The Happy Return* 1937, cover the career—from midshipman to admiral—of Horatio Hornblower.

He also wrote *Payment Deferred* 1926, a subtle crime novel, and *The African Queen* 1938, later filmed with Humphrey Bogart.

forestry the science of forest management. Recommended forestry practice aims at multipurpose crops, allowing the preservation of varied plant and animal species as well as human uses (lumbering, recreation). Forestry has often been confined to the planting of a single species, such as a rapid-growing conifer providing softwood for paper pulp and construction timber, for which world demand is greatest. In tropical countries, logging contributes to the destruction of ⬙rainforests, causing global environmental problems. Small unplanned forests are ⬙woodland.

The earliest planned forest dates from 1368 at Nuremberg, Germany; in Britain, planning of forests began in the 16th century. In the UK, Japan, and other countries, forestry practices have been criticized for concentration on softwood conifers to the neglect of native hardwoods.

forgery the making of a false document, painting, or object with deliberate intention to deceive or defraud. The most common forgeries involve financial instruments such as checks or credit-card transactions or money (counterfeiting). There are also literary forgeries, forged coins, and forged antiques.

Financial gain is not the only motive for forgery. Han van Meegeren probably began painting in the style of Vermeer to make fools of the critics, but found such a ready market for his creations that he became a rich man before he was forced to confess. The archeological ⬙Piltdown Man hoax in England in 1912 also appears to have been a practical joke.

forget-me-not any marsh plant of the genus *Myosotis* of the borage family. These plants have hairy leaves; bear clusters of small blue, white, or red flowers; and are considered a symbol of fidelity and friendship. The European true forget-me-not *Myosotis scorpioides*, 12–28 in/30–70 cm in height, now grows widely in North America.

forging one of the main methods of shaping metals, which involves hammering or a more gradual application of pressure. A blacksmith hammers red-hot metal into shape on an anvil, and the traditional place of work is called a forge. The blacksmith's mechanical equivalent is the drop forge. The metal is shaped by the blows from a falling hammer or ram, which is usually accelerated by steam or air pressure. Hydraulic presses forge by applying pressure gradually in a squeezing action.

formaldehyde common name for ⬙methanal.

formalin aqueous solution of formaldehyde (methanal) used to preserve animal specimens.

Formosa alternate name for ⬙Taiwan.

formula in chemistry, a representation of a molecule, radical, or ion, in which the component chemical elements are represented by their symbols. An **empirical formula** indicates the simplest ratio of the elements in a compound, without indicating how many of them there are or how they are combined. A **molecular formula** gives the number of each type of element present in one molecule. A **structural formula** shows the relative positions of the atoms and the bonds between them. For example, for ethanoic acid, the empirical formula is CH_2O, the molecular formula is $C_2H_4O_2$, and the structural formula is CH_3COOH.

Formula is also another name for ⬙chemical equation.

Forrest Nathan Bedford 1821–1877. American Confederate military leader and founder of the ⬦Ku Klux Klan. Born in Chapel Hill, Tennessee, Forrest had little formal schooling but accumulated enough wealth through slave dealing to buy land in Mississippi and establish a cotton plantation. At the outbreak of the Civil War, Forrest led a Confederate cavalry troop and escaped from Union troops before the fall of Fort Donelson in Tennessee 1862. After the Battle of Shiloh 1862, he was promoted to the rank of brigadier general and led raids on Union forces throughout the South. After the war, while a civilian railroad executive, he founded the Klan.

Forrestal James Vincent 1892–1949. US Democratic politician. As under secretary from 1940 and secretary of the navy from 1944, he organized its war effort, accompanying the US landings on the Japanese island Iwo Jima. He was the first secretary of the Department of Defense 1947–49, a post created to unify the three armed forces at the end of World War II.

He committed suicide after exhaustion and illness forced him to resign 1949. He wrote *The Forrestal Diaries*, which were published posthumously 1951.

Forssmann Werner 1904–1979. German heart surgeon. In 1929 he originated, by experiment on himself, the technique of cardiac catheterization (passing a thin tube from an arm artery up into the heart itself for diagnostic purposes). He shared the 1956 Nobel Prize for Physiology or Medicine.

Forster E(dward) M(organ) 1879–1970. English novelist, concerned with the interplay of personality and the conflict between convention and instinct. His novels include *A Room with a View* 1908, *Howard's End* 1910, and *A Passage to India* 1924. He also wrote short stories, for example, "The Eternal Omnibus" 1914; criticism, including *Aspects of the Novel* 1927; and essays, including *Abinger Harvest* 1936.

Forster published his first novel, *Where Angels Fear to Tread*, 1905. He enhances the superficial situations of his plots with unexpected insights in *The Longest Journey* 1907, *A Room with a View*, and *Howard's End*. His many years spent in India and as secretary to the Maharajah of Dewas in 1921 provided him with the material for *A Passage to India*, which explores the relationship between the English and the Indians. *Maurice*, published 1971, has a homosexual theme.

Forsyth Frederick 1938– . English thriller writer. His books include *The Day of the Jackal* 1970, *The Dogs of War* 1974, and *The Fourth Protocol* 1984.

forsythia any temperate E Asian shrub of the genus *Forsythia* of the olive family Oleaceae, which bear yellow bell-shaped flowers in early spring before the leaves appear.

Fort Collins city in N Colorado, on the Cache de la Poudre river, NE of Boulder; seat of Larimer County. It is the processing and marketing center for the surrounding agricultural area. Industries include engines, cement, plastics, film, and prefabricated metal buildings; population (1990) 87,800. The city was established as a fort 1864 for the protection of travelers on the Overland Trail.

Fort-de-France capital, chief commercial center, and port of Martinique, West Indies; population (1982) 99,844.

fortepiano an alternate name for pianoforte, used to specify early pianos of the 18th and early 19th centuries (see ⬦piano).

Fort Knox US army post and gold depository in Kentucky, established 1917 as a training camp. The US Treasury gold-bullion vaults were built 1937.

Fort Lamy former name of ⬦N'djamena, capital of Chad.

Fort Lauderdale city in SE coastal Florida, just N of Miami; seat of Broward County, the city's main industry is tourism. Channels for boating cross the city, Atlantic Ocean beaches line it on the E, and deep-water Port Everglades to the S allows oceangoing vessels to dock; population (1990) 149,400. A fort was built here 1837 during the Seminole War.

Fort Myers city in SW Florida, on the Caloosahatchee River, SE of St Petersburg; seat of Lee County. It is a shipping center for its fish, fruit, and vegetable products. Tourism is also an important industry; population (1990) 45,200. The surrender of Holatto-Micco, the last Seminole chief, took place here 1858.

Fort Pierce city in E central Florida, where the Indian River flows into the Atlantic Ocean; seat of St Lucie County. It is an important transportation center for the fruit and vegetable crops of the surrounding area. Fishing and tourism are significant industries; population (1990) 36,800.

FORTRAN (acronym for *formula translation*) high-level computer-programming language suited to mathematical and scientific computations. Developed in the mid-1950s, it is one of the earliest languages still in use. ⬦BASIC was strongly influenced by FORTRAN and is similar in many ways.

Fort Smith city in W Arkansas, on the Arkansas River where it crosses the Oklahoma—Arkansas border, SW of Fayetteville. The site of coal and natural-gas mines, the city's industries include furniture, automobiles, paper, plastics, and metals. Fort Smith national historic site is here; population (1990) 72,800.

Fort Sumter fort in ⬦Charleston Harbor, South Carolina, 4 mi/6.5 km SE of Charleston. The first shots of the US Civil War were fired here April 12, 1861, after its commander had refused the call to surrender made by the Confederate General Beauregard.

The attack was successful, with the South holding the fort until 1865; it had been prompted by President Lincoln's refusal to evacuate the fort and his decision instead to send reinforcements. Southern leaders felt they must attack to lend weight to their claims of independence.

Fort Ticonderoga fort in New York State, near Lake Champlain. It was the site of battles between the British and the French 1758–59, and was captured from the British May 10, 1775 by Benedict ⬦Arnold and Ethan Allen (leading the ⬦Green Mountain Boys).

Fortuna in Roman mythology, goddess of chance and good fortune (Greek *Tyche*).

Fortune 500 the 500 largest publicly owned US industrial corporations, a list compiled by the US business magazine *Fortune*. An industrial corporation is defined as one that derives at least 50% of its revenue from manufacturing or mining.

Fort Walton Beach city in NW panhandle of Florida, on the Gulf of Mexico, E of Pensacola. It is a tourist and fishing center; population (1990) 21,500.

Fort Wayne town in NE Indiana; population (1990) 173,100. Industries include electrical goods, electronics, and farm machinery. A fort was built here against the North American Indians in 1794 by General Anthony Wayne (1745–96), hero of a surprise attack on a British force at Stony Point, New York, in 1779, which earned him the nickname "Mad Anthony."

Fort Worth city in NE Texas; population (1990) 447,600. Formerly an important cattle area, it is now a grain, petroleum, aerospace, and railroad center serving the S US.

Manufactured products include aerospace equipment, motor vehicles, and refined petroleum. Carswell Air Force Base, Texas Christian University, and the Kimbell Art Museum are here. Fort Worth developed from an army post 1849 and was a stop on the Chisholm cattle trail. The arrival of the railroad 1876 fostered economic development that was furthered by the discovery of oil nearby in 1920.

Forty-Five, the ⬦Jacobite rebellion 1745, led by Prince ⬦Charles Edward Stuart. With his army of Highlanders "Bonnie Prince Charlie" occupied Edinburgh and advanced into England as far as Derby, but then turned back. The rising was crushed by the Duke of Cumberland at Culloden 1746.

Foss Lukas 1922– . US composer and conductor. He wrote the cantata *The Prairie* 1942 and *Time Cycle* for soprano and orchestra 1960.

Born in Germany, he studied in Europe before settling in the US in 1937. A student of ⬦Hindemith, his vocal music is composed in Neo-Classical style; in the mid-1950s he began increasingly to employ improvisation. Foss has also written chamber and orchestral music in which the players reproduce tape-recorded effects.

Fosse Bob (Robert) 1927–1987. US film director who entered films as a dancer and choreographer from Broadway, making his directorial debut with *Sweet Charity* 1968. He received an Academy Award for his second film as director, *Cabaret* 1972. Other films includes *All That Jazz* 1979 and several musical productions, including *Pippin* 1975.

fossil (Latin *fossilis* "dug up") remains of an animal or plant preserved in rocks. Fossils may be formed by refrigeration (for example, Arctic ⬦mammoths in ice); carbonization (leaves in coal); formation of a cast (dinosaur or human footprints in mud); or mineralization of bones, more generally teeth or shells. The study of fossils is called ⬦paleontology.

fossil fuel fuel, such as coal, oil, and natural gas, formed from the fossilized remains of plants that lived hundreds of millions of years ago. Fossil fuels are a ⬦nonrenewable resource and will eventually run out. Extraction of coal (mining) causes considerable environmental pollution, and burning coal contributes to problems of ⬦acid rain and the ⬦greenhouse effect.

Foster Jodie. Adopted name of Alicia Christian Foster 1962– . US film actress and director who began as a child in a great variety of roles. She starred in *Taxi Driver* and *Bugsy Malone* both 1976, when only 14. Subsequent films include *The Accused* 1988 and *The Silence of the Lambs* 1991, for both of which she won the Academy Award for best actress.

Foster Stephen Collins 1826–1864. US songwriter, composer of "The Old Folks at Home" 1851, "My Old Kentucky Home" 1853, and others, which mostly drew from the black minstrel style.

Born in Lawrenceville, Pennsylvania, he had no formal training in music but began to write early. He also wrote sentimental popular music. Although many of his songs became very popular and profitable, he mismanaged his career and died in debt.

Foucault Jean Bernard Léon 1819–1868. French physicist who used a pendulum to demonstrate the rotation of the Earth on its axis, and invented the gyroscope.

He investigated heat and light, discovered eddy currents induced in a copper disk moving in a magnetic field, invented a polarizer, and made improvements in the electric arc.

Foucault Michel 1926–1984. French philosopher who rejected phenomenology and existentialism. He was concerned with how forms of knowledge and forms of human subjectivity are constructed by specific institutions and practices.

Foucault was deeply influenced by ◊Nietzsche, and developed an analysis of the operation of power in society using Nietzschean concepts.

Fouché Joseph, duke of Otranto 1759–1820. French politician. He was elected to the National Convention (the post-Revolutionary legislature), and organized the conspiracy that overthrew the ◊Jacobin leader ◊Robespierre. Napoleon employed him as police minister.

Fouquet Jean *c.* 1420–1481. French painter. He became court painter to Charles VIII in 1448 and to Louis XI in 1475. His *Melun diptych* about 1450 (Musées Royaux, Antwerp, and Staatliche Museen, Berlin) shows Italian Renaissance influence.

Fouquet Nicolas 1615–1680. French politician, a rival to Louis XIV's minister ◊Colbert. Fouquet became *procureur général* of the Paris *parlement* 1650 and *surintendant des finances* 1651, responsible for raising funds for the long war against Spain, a post he held until arrested and imprisoned for embezzlement (at the instigation of Colbert, who succeeded him).

four-color process color ◊printing using four printing plates, based on the principle that any color is made up of differing proportions of the primary colors blue, red, and green. The first stage in preparing a color picture for printing is to produce separate films, one each for the blue, red, and green respectively in the picture (color separations). From these separations three printing plates are made, with a fourth plate for black (for shading or outlines). Ink colors complementary to those represented on the plates are used for printing—yellow for the blue plate, cyan for the red, and magenta for the green.

Four Freedoms, the four kinds of liberty essential to human dignity as defined in an address to the US Congress by President F D ◊Roosevelt Jan 6, 1941: freedom of speech and expression, freedom of worship, freedom from want, freedom from fear.

Before US entry into World War II, Roosevelt urged support of the democracies fighting to defend freedom, and two months later Congress passed the ◊Lend-Lease Act. The Four Freedoms were the basis for the ◊Atlantic Charter specifying Allied war aims 1941.

Fourier François Charles Marie 1772–1837. French socialist. In *Le Nouveau monde industriel/The New Industrial World* 1829–30, he advocated that society should be organized in self-sufficient cooperative units of

about 1,500 people, and marriage should be abandoned.

Fourier Jean Baptiste Joseph 1768–1830. French applied mathematician whose formulation of heat flow 1807 contains the proposal that, with certain constraints, any mathematical function can be represented by trigonometrical series. This principle forms the basis of *Fourier analysis*, used today in many different fields of physics. His idea, not immediately well received, gained currency and is embodied in his *Théorie analytique de la chaleur/The Analytical Theory of Heat* 1822.

Four Noble Truths in Buddhism, a summary of the basic concepts: life is suffering (Sanskrit *duhkha*); suffering has its roots in desire (*tanha*, clinging or grasping); the cessation of desire is the end of suffering, *nirvana*; and this can be reached by the Noble Eightfold Path of *dharma* (truth).

four-stroke cycle the engine-operating cycle of most gasoline and ◊diesel engines. The "stroke" is an upward or downward movement of a piston in a cylinder. In a gasoline engine the cycle begins with the induction of a fuel mixture as the piston goes down on its first stroke. On the second stroke (up) the piston compresses the mixture in the top of the cylinder. An electric spark then ignites the mixture, and the gases produced force the piston down on its third, power, stroke. On the fourth stroke (up) the piston expels the burned gases from the cylinder into the exhaust.

Fourteen Points the terms proposed by President Wilson of the US in his address to Congress Jan 8, 1918, as a basis for the settlement of World War I. The creation of the League of Nations was one of the points.

The terms included: open diplomacy; freedom of the seas; removal of economic barriers; international disarmament; adjustment of colonial claims; German evacuation of Russian, Belgian, French, and Balkan territories; the restoration of Alsace-Lorraine to France; autonomy for the various ethnic groups in Austria, Hungary and the Ottoman Empire; an independent Poland; and a general association of nations (which was to become the League of Nations).

Wilson was obliged to compromise on many of the points in light of secret agreements concluded by several of the Allies. The Germans, having agreed to the armistice largely on the

basis of the Fourteen Points, felt betrayed by subsequent decisions imposed upon them by the Treaty of ◊Versailles.

fourth estate another name for the press. The term was coined by the British politician Edmund Burke in analogy with the traditional three ◊estates.

fourth-generation language in computing, a type of programming language designed for the rapid programming of ◊applications but often lacking the ability to control the individual parts of the computer. Such a language typically provides easy ways of designing screens and reports, and of using databases. Other "generations" (the term implies a class of language rather than a chronological sequence) are ◊machine code (first generation); assembly code or low-level languages (second); and conventional high-level languages such as ◊BASIC and ◊PASCAL (third).

Fourth of July in the US, the anniversary of the day in 1776 when the ◊Declaration of Independence was adopted by the Continental Congress. It is a public holiday, officially called *Independence Day*, commemorating independence from Britain.

Fourth Republic the French constitutional regime that was established between 1944 and 1946 and lasted until Oct 4, 1958: from liberation after Nazi occupation during World War II to the introduction of a new constitution by General de Gaulle.

fowl chicken or chickenlike bird. Sometimes the term is also used for ducks and geese. The red jungle fowl *Gallus gallus* is the ancestor of all domestic chickens. It is a forest bird of Asia, without the size or egg-laying ability of many domestic strains. ◊Guinea fowl are of African origin.

Fowler William 1911– . US astrophysicist. In 1983 he and Subrahmanyan Chandrasekhar were awarded the Nobel Prize for Physics for their work on the life cycle of stars and the origin of chemical elements.

Fowles John 1926– . English writer whose novels, often concerned with illusion and reality and with the creative process, include *The Collector* 1963, *The Magus* 1965, *The French Lieutenant's Woman* 1969, *Daniel Martin* 1977, *Mantissa* 1982, and *A Maggot* 1985.

fox member of the smaller species of wild dog of the family Canidae, which live in Africa, Asia, Europe, North America, and South

four-stroke cycle *The four-stroke cycle of a modern gasoline engine.*

America. Foxes feed on a wide range of animals from worms to rabbits, scavenge for food, and also eat berries. They are very adaptable, maintaining high populations close to urban areas.

Most foxes are nocturnal, and make an underground den, or "earth." The common or red fox *Vulpes vulpes* is about 2 ft/60 cm long plus a tail ("brush") 1.3 ft/40 cm long. The fur is reddish with black patches behind the ears and a light tip to the tail. Other foxes include the Arctic fox *Alopex lagopus*, the ▷fennec, the gray foxes genus *Urocyon* of North and Central America, and the South American genus *Dusicyon*, to which the extinct Falkland Islands dog belonged.

Fox George 1624–1691. English founder of the Society of ▷Friends. After developing his belief in a mystical "inner light," he became a traveling preacher 1647, and in 1650 was imprisoned for blasphemy at Derby, where the name Quakers was first applied derogatorily to him and his followers, supposedly because he enjoined Judge Bennet to "quake at the word of the Lord."

He suffered further imprisonments, made a missionary journey to America in 1671–72, and wrote many evangelical and meditative works, including a *Journal*, published 1694.

Fox James 1939– . English film actor, usually cast in upper-class, refined roles but celebrated for his portrayal of a psychotic gangster in Nicolas Roeg's *Performance* 1970, which was followed by an eight-year break from acting. Fox appeared in *The Servant* 1963 and *Isadora* 1968. He returned to acting in *No Longer Alone* 1978. His other films include *Runners* 1984, *A Passage to India* 1984, and *The Russia House* 1990.

Fox Margaret 1833–1893. Canadian-born US spiritual medium. Raised in New York State, Fox and her younger sister Katherine claimed unusual psychic powers from an early age. Becoming famous for their ability to communicate with departed spirits, the Fox girls began to hold public demonstrations of their powers.

Moving to New York City 1850, they received much favorable publicity and sparked a widespread public interest in spiritualism as a modern religious movement. In 1888, however, Margaret publicly confessed that her "psychic powers" were a hoax.

foxglove any flowering plant of the genus *Digitalis*, family Scrophulariaceae, found in Europe and the Mediterranean region. It bears showy spikes of bell-like flowers, and grows up to 5 ft/ 1.5 m high.

The wild species *D. purpurea*, native to Britain, produces purple to reddish flowers. Its leaves were the original source of digitalis, a drug used for some heart problems.

foxhound small, keen-nosed hound, up to 2 ft/ 60 cm tall and black, tan, and white in color. There are two recognized breeds: the English foxhound, bred for some 300 years to hunt foxes, and the American foxhound, not quite as stocky, used for foxes and other game.

fox-hunting the pursuit of a fox across country on horseback, aided by a pack of foxhounds, specially trained to track the fox's scent. The aim is to catch and kill the fox. In draghunting, hounds pursue a prepared trail rather than a fox.

Described by the playwright Oscar Wilde as "the unspeakable in pursuit of the uneatable," fox-hunting has met with increasing opposition. Animal-rights activists condemn it

as involving excessive cruelty, and in Britain groups such as the Hunt Saboteurs disrupt it.

Fox-hunting dates from the late 17th century, when it arose as a practical method of limiting the fox population which endangered poultry farming, but by the early 19th century it was indulged in as a sport by the British aristocracy and gentry who ceremonialized it. Fox-hunting was introduced into the US by early settlers from England and continues in the S and middle Atlantic regions.

foxtrot ballroom dance originating in the US about 1914. It has alternating long and short steps, supposedly like the movements of the fox.

fraction (from Latin *fractus* "broken") in mathematics, a number that indicates one or more equal parts of a whole. Usually, the number of equal parts into which the unit is divided (denominator) is written below a horizontal line, and the number of parts comprising the fraction (numerator) is written above; thus $\frac{2}{3}$ or $\frac{3}{4}$. Such fractions are called **vulgar** or **simple** fractions. The denominator can never be zero.

A **proper fraction** is one in which the numerator is less than the denominator. An **improper fraction** has a numerator that is larger than the denominator, for example $\frac{3}{2}$. It can therefore be expressed as a mixed number, for example, $1\frac{1}{2}$. A combination such as $\frac{5}{0}$ is not regarded as a fraction (an object cannot be divided into zero equal parts), and mathematically any number divided by 0 is equal to infinity. A **decimal fraction** has as its denominator a power of 10, and these are omitted by use of the decimal point and notation, for example 0.04, which is $\frac{4}{100}$. The digits to the right of the decimal point indicate the numerators of vulgar fractions whose denominators are 10, 100, 1,000, and so on. Most fractions can be expressed exactly as decimal fractions ($\frac{1}{3} = 0.333...$). Fractions are also known as the **rational numbers**, that is numbers formed by a ratio. **Integers** may be expressed as fractions with a denominator of 1.

fraction in chemistry, a group of similar compounds, the boiling points of which fall within a particular range and which are separated during fractional ▷distillation (fractionation).

fractionating column device in which many separate ▷distillations can occur so that a liquid mixture can be separated into its components.

Various designs exist but the primary aim is to allow maximum contact between the hot rising vapors and the cooling descending liquid. As the mixture of vapors ascends the column it becomes progressively enriched in the lower-boiling-point components, so these separate out first.

fractionation or **fractional distillation** process used to split complex mixtures (such as crude oil) into their components, usually by repeated heating, boiling, and condensation; see ▷distillation.

Fragonard Jean Honoré 1732–1806. French painter, the leading exponent of the Rococo style (along with his master Boucher). His light-hearted subjects include *The Swing* about 1766 (Wallace Collection, London).

franc French coin, so called from 1360 when it was a gold coin inscribed *Francorum Rex*, "King of the Franks." The **franc CFA** (*Communauté française d'Afrique*) is the currency of the former French territories in Africa; in France's Pacific territories the **franc CFP**

France: regions and départements

region and département
Alsace
Bas-Rhin
Haut-Rhin
Aquitaine
Dordogne
Gironde
Landes
Lot-et-Garonne
Pyrénées-Atlantiques
Auvergne
Allier
Cantal
Haute-Loire
Puy-de-Dôme
Basse-Normandie
Calvados
Manche
Orne
Bourgogne
Côte-d'Or
Nièvre
Saône-et-Loire
Yonne
Bretagne
Côtes-du-Nord
Finistère
Ille-et-Vilaine
Morbihan
Center
Cher
Eure-et-Loire
Indre
Indre-et-Loire
Loire-et-Cher
Loiret
Champagne-Ardenne
Ardenne
Aube
Marne
Haute-Marne
Corsica
Haute Corse
Corse du Sud
Franche-Comté
Doubs
Jura
Haute Saône
Terre de Belfort
Haute-Normandie
Eure
Seine-Maritime
Ile de France
Essonne
Val-de-Marne
Val d'Oise
Ville de Paris
Seine-et-Marne
Hauts-de-Seine
Seine-Saint-Denis
Yvelines
Languedoc-Roussillon
Aude
Gard
Hérault
Lozère
Pyrénées-Orientales
Limousin
Corrèze
Creuse
Haute-Vienne
Lorraine
Meurthe-et-Moselle
Meuse
Moselle
Vosges

(*Communauté française du pacifique*) is used. The currency units of Belgium, Luxembourg, and Switzerland are also called francs.

France country in W Europe, bounded NE by Belgium and Germany, E by Germany, Switzerland, and Italy, S by the Mediterranean Sea, SW by Spain and Andorra, and W by the Atlantic Ocean.

government Under the 1958 Fifth Republic constitution, amended 1962, France has a two-chamber legislature and a "shared executive" government. The legislature comprises a National Assembly, with 577 deputies elected for five-year terms from single-member constituencies following a two-ballot, runoff majority system, and a Senate, whose 321 members are indirectly elected, a third at a time, triennially for nine-year terms from groups of local councillors.

Twenty-two National Assembly and 13 Senate seats are elected by overseas *départements* (administrative regions) and territories, and 12 Senate seats by French nationals abroad. The National Assembly is the dominant chamber. The Senate can temporarily veto legislation, but its vetoes can be overridden by the National Assembly.

France's executive is functionally divided between the president and prime minister. The

France
French Republic (*République Française*)

area (including Corsica) 209,970 sq mi/ 543,965 sq km
capital Paris
cities Lyons, Lille, Bordeaux, Toulouse, Nantes, Strasbourg; ports Marseille, Nice, Le Havre
physical rivers Seine, Loire, Garonne, Rhône, Rhine; mountain ranges Alps, Massif Central, Pyrenees, Jura, Vosges, Cévennes; the island of Corsica
territories Guadeloupe, French Guiana, Martinique, Réunion, St Pierre and Miquelon, Southern and Antarctic Territories, New Caledonia, French Polynesia, Wallis and Futuna
features Ardennes forest, Auvergne mountain region, Riviera, Mont Blanc (15,781 ft/4,810 m), caves of Dordogne with relics of early humans; largest W European nation
head of state François Mitterrand from 1981
head of government Pierre Bérégovoy from 1992
political system liberal democracy
political parties Socialist Party (PS), left of center; Rally for the Republic (RPR), neo-Gaullist conservative; Union for French Democracy (UDF), center-right; Republican Party (RP), center-right; French Communist Party (PCF), Marxist-Leninist; National Front, far right; Greens, environmentalist
exports fruit (especially apples), wine,

cheese, wheat, automobiles, aircraft, iron and steel, petroleum products, chemicals, jewelry, silk, lace; tourism is very important
currency franc
population (1990 est) 56,184,000 (including 4,500,000 immigrants, chiefly from Portugal, Algeria, Morocco, and Tunisia); growth rate 0.3% p.a.
life expectancy men 71, women 79
language French (regional languages include Basque, Breton, Catalan, and the Provençal dialect)
religions Roman Catholic 90%, Protestant 2%, Muslim 1%
literacy 99% (1984)
GNP $568 bn (1983); $7,179 per head
chronology
1944–46 De Gaulle provisional government; start of Fourth Republic.
1954 Indochina achieved independence.
1956 Morocco and Tunisia achieved independence.
1957 Entry into EEC.
1958 Recall of de Gaulle after Algerian crisis; start of Fifth Republic.
1959 De Gaulle became president.
1962 Algeria achieved independence.
1966 France withdrew from military wing of NATO.
1968 "May events" crisis.
1969 De Gaulle resigned after referendum defeat; Pompidou became president.
1974 Giscard d'Estaing elected president.
1981 Mitterrand elected Fifth Republic's first socialist president.
1986 "Cohabitation" experiment, with the conservative Jacques Chirac as prime minister.
1988 Mitterrand reelected. Moderate socialist Michel Rocard became prime minister. Matignon Accord on future of New Caledonia approved by referendum.
1989 Greens gained 11% of vote in elections to European Parliament.
1991 French forces were part of the US-led coalition in the Gulf War. Edith Cresson became France's first woman prime minister. Mitterrand's popularity rating fell rapidly.
1992 March: Socialist Party humiliated in regional and local elections; Greens and National Front polled strongly. April: Cresson replaced by Pierre Bérégovoy. Sept: referendum narrowly endorsed Maastricht Treaty.

president, elected for a seven-year term by direct universal suffrage after gaining a majority in either a first or second runoff ballot, functions as head of state, commander in chief of the armed forces, and guardian of the constitution. The president selects the prime minister, presides over cabinet meetings, countersigns government bills, negotiates foreign treaties, and can call referendums and dissolve the National Assembly.

The prime minister is selected from the ranks of the National Assembly. According to the constitution, ultimate control over policy-making rests with the prime minister and council of ministers.

The president and prime minister work with ministers from political and technocratic backgrounds, assisted by a skilled and powerful civil service. A nine-member constitutional council (selected every three years in a staggered manner by the state president and the presidents of the Senate and National Assembly) and a *Conseil d'Etat*, staffed by senior

civil servants, rule on the legality of legislation passed.

At the local level there are 21 regional councils concerned with economic planning. Below these are 96 *département* councils and almost 36,000 town and village councils. Corsica has its own directly elected 61-seat parliament with powers to propose amendments to National Assembly legislation.

There are four overseas *départements* (⇨French Guiana, ⇨Guadeloupe, ⇨Martinique, and ⇨Réunion) with their own elected general and regional councils, two overseas "collective territories" (⇨Mayotte and ⇨St Pierre and Miquelon) administered by appointed commissioners, and four overseas territories (⇨French Polynesia, the French ⇨Southern and Antarctic Territories, ⇨New Caledonia, and the ⇨Wallis and Futuna Islands) governed by appointed high commissioners, which form constituent parts of the French Republic, returning deputies to the national legislature.

history For history before 1945, see ⬦France, history. A "united front" provisional government headed by de Gaulle, and including communists, assumed power in the reestablished republic before a new constitution was framed and adopted for a Fourth Republic Jan 1946. This provided for a weak executive and powerful National Assembly that, being elected under a generous system of proportional representation, was to be divided between numerous small party groupings. With 26 impermanent governments being formed 1946–58, real power passed to the civil service, which, by introducing a new system of "indicative economic planning," engineered rapid economic reconstruction. Decolonization of French ⬦Indochina 1954, Morocco and Tunisia 1956, and entry into the European Economic Community 1957 were also effected. The Fourth Republic was overthrown 1958 by a political and military crisis over Algerian independence, which threatened to lead to a French army revolt. De Gaulle was recalled from retirement to head a government of national unity and supervised the framing of the new Fifth Republic constitution, which strengthened the president and prime minister.

Fifth Republic De Gaulle, who became president 1959, restored domestic stability and presided over the decolonization of Francophone Africa, including Algerian independence 1962. Close economic links were maintained with former colonies. De Gaulle also initiated a new foreign policy, withdrawing France from military cooperation in the North Atlantic Treaty Organization (⬦NATO) 1966 and developing an autonomous nuclear deterrent force. The de Gaulle era was one of economic growth and large-scale rural—urban migration. Politically, however, there was tight censorship and strong centralization, and in 1967 the public reacted against de Gaulle's paternalism by voting the "right coalition" a reduced majority.

"May events" In 1968, the nation was paralyzed by students' and workers' demonstrations in Paris that spread to the provinces and briefly threatened the government. De Gaulle called elections and won a landslide victory. In 1969, however, he was defeated in a referendum over proposed Senate and local-government reforms, and resigned. De Gaulle's former prime minister Georges ⬦Pompidou was elected president and pursued Gaullist policies until his death 1974.

Pompidou's successor as president, Valéry Giscard d'Estaing, leader of the center-right Independent Republicans, introduced domestic reforms and played a more active and cooperative role in the EC. Giscard faced opposition, however, from his "right coalition" partner, Jacques ⬦Chirac, who was prime minister 1974–76, and deteriorating international economic conditions. France performed better than many of its European competitors 1974–81, with the president launching a major nuclear power program to save on energy imports and, while Raymond ⬦Barre was prime minister 1976–81, a new liberal "freer market" economic strategy. During this period the Union for French Democracy party (UDF) was formed to unite several center-right parties. However, with 1.7 million unemployed, Giscard was defeated by Socialist Party leader François ⬦Mitterrand in the 1981 presidential election.

"left coalition" Mitterrand's victory was the first presidential success for the "left coalition"

France: rulers

title of ruler	name	date of accession	title of ruler	name	date of accession
kings	Pepin III/Childerich III	751	**kings**	Louis XIII	1610
	Pepin III	752		Louis XIV	1643
	Charlemagne/Carloman	768		Louis XV	1715
	Louis I	814		Louis XVI	1774
	Lothair I	840		National Convention	1792
	Charles II (the Bald)	843		Directory (five members)	1795
	Louis II	877	**first consul**	Napoléon Bonaparte	1799
	Louis III	879	**emperor**	Napoléon I	1804
	Charles III (the Fat)	882	**king**	Louis XVIII	1814
	Odo	888	**emperor**	Napoléon I	1815
	Charles III (the Simple)	893	**kings**	Louis XVIII	1815
	Robert I	922		Charles X	1824
	Rudolf	923		Louis XIX	1830
	Louis IV	936		Henri V	1830
	Lothair II	954		Louis-Philippe	1830
	Louis V	986	**heads of**	Philippe Buchez	1848
	Hugues Capet	987	**state**	Louis Cavaignac	1848
	Robert II	996	**president**	Louis Napoléon Bonaparte	1848
	Henri I	1031	**emperor**	Napoléon III	1852
	Philippe I	1060	**presidents**	Adolphe Thiers	1871
	Louis VI	1108		Patrice MacMahon	1873
	Louis VII	1137		Jules Grevy	1879
	Philippe II	1180		François Sadui-Carnot	1887
	Louis VIII	1223		Jean Casimir-Périer	1894
	Louis IX	1226		François Faure	1895
	Philippe III	1270		Emile Loubet	1899
	Philippe IV	1285		Armand Fallières	1913
	Louis X	1314		Raymond Poincaré	1913
	Jean I	1316		Paul Deschanel	1920
	Philippe V	1328		Alexandre Millerand	1920
	Charles IV	1322		Gaston Doumergue	1924
	Philippe VI	1328		Paul Doumer	1931
	Jean II	1350		Albert Le Brun	1932
	Charles V	1356		Philippe Pétain (Vichy	
	Charles VI	1380		government)	1940
	Charles VII	1422		provisional government	1944
	Louis XI	1461		Vincent Auriol	1947
	Charles VIII	1483		René Coty	1954
	Louis XII	1498		Charles de Gaulle	1959
	François I	1515		Alain Poher	1969
	Henri II	1547		Georges Pompidou	1969
	François II	1559		Alain Poher	1974
	Charles IX	1560		Valéry Giscard	
	Henri III	1574		d'Estaing	1974
	Henri IV	1574		François Mitterrand	1981

during the Fifth Republic and was immediately succeeded by a landslide victory for the Socialist Party (PS) and French Communist Party (PCF) in elections to the National Assembly 1981. The new administration introduced a radical program of social reform, decentralization, and nationalization, and passed a series of reflationary budgets aimed at reducing unemployment.

Financial constraints forced a switch toward a more conservative policy of *"rigueur"* (austerity) 1983. A U-turn in economic policy was completed 1984 when Prime Minister Pierre Mauroy was replaced by Laurent ⬦Fabius, prompting the resignation of communist members of the cabinet. Unemployment rose to over 2.5 million 1985–86, increasing racial tension in urban areas. The extreme right-wing National Front, led by Jean-Marie ⬦Le Pen, benefited from this and gained seats in the March 1986 National Assembly elections. The "left coalition" lost its majority, the PCF having been in decline in recent years. The PS, however, had emerged as France's single most popular party.

From 1958 to 1986 the president and prime minister had been drawn from the same party

coalition, and the president had been allowed to dominate in both home and foreign affairs. In 1986 Mitterrand was obliged to appoint as prime minister the leader of the opposition, Jacques Chirac, who emerged as the dominant force in the "shared executive." Chirac introduced a radical "new conservative" program of denationalization, deregulation, and "desocialization," using the executive's decree powers and the parliamentary guillotine to steamroller measures through. His educational and economic reforms encountered serious opposition from militant students and striking workers, necessitating embarrassing policy concessions. With his national standing tarnished, Chirac was defeated by Mitterrand in the May 1988 presidential election.

progressive program In the National Assembly elections June 1988, the socialists emerged as the largest single political party. Mitterrand duly appointed Michel ⬦Rocard, a moderate social democrat, as prime minister heading a minority PS government that included several center-party representatives. Rocard implemented a progressive program, aimed at protecting the underprivileged and improving the quality of life. In June 1988 he negotiated the Matignon Accord, designed to solve the New Caledonia problem, which was later approved by referendum. Between 1988 and 1990 France enjoyed a strong economic upturn and attention focused increasingly on quality of life, with the Green Party gaining 11% of the national vote in the European Parliament elections of June 1989.

racial tensions The extreme right National Front continued to do well in municipal elections, forcing the government to adopt a hard line against illegal immigration and to announce new programs for the integration of Muslim immigrants into mainstream French society. Religious and cultural tensions increased with the influx of Muslims from Algeria, Tunisia, and other areas with French colonial ties. The Rocard government narrowly survived a censure vote in the National Assembly Nov 1990. This followed an outbreak of serious student violence in Paris and earlier antipolice race riots in the Lyons suburbs. A commission set up to look at the problems of immigrant integration reported 1991 that France's foreign population was 3.7 million (6.8% of the population), the same as in 1982. However, 10 million citizens were of "recent foreign origin."

Gulf War In Sept 1990, after Iraqi violation of the French ambassador's residence in Kuwait, the French government dispatched 5,000 troops to Saudi Arabia. Despite France's previously close ties with Iraq (including arms sales), French military forces played a prominent role within the US-led coalition in the 1991 Gulf War. Defense minister Jean-Pierre Chevenement resigned Feb 1991 in opposition to this strategy, but the majority of people in the country—which has the largest Muslim population in W Europe—supported the government's stance.

Mitterrand's popularity wanes In April 1991 the neo-Gaullist Rally for the Republic (RPR) and the Union for French Democracy (UDF), France's main, usually fractious, right-of-center opposition parties, signed a formal election pact. In May, after disagreements over economic policy, Mitterrand replaced Rocard with Edith Cresson, citing her experience as a former member of the European Parliament and minister for European affairs as important for France's future in Europe. The government announced July 1991 that its armed forces would be cut by up 70,000 personnel within five or six years, with 48,000 troops being withdrawn from Germany. In Sept 1991 Mitterrand became the Fifth Republic's longest-serving president. However, with the economy in recession, racial tensions increasing, discontented farmers, militancy among public-sector workers, and the reputation of the SP tarnished by a number of financial scandals, Mitterrand's popularity fell from over 50% in Sept 1991 to barely 35% in Jan 1992. By the close of 1991 the popularity rating of Cresson was the lowest ever for a premier in the Fifth Republic and national support for the SP was only 21%. Public confidence in the administration was eroded further in Feb 1992 when George Habash, the leader of the Popular Front for the Liberation of Palestine and a man with a terrorist past, was granted entry to France for medical treatment. In March 1992 the Socialist Party captured only 18% share of the national vote in regional council elections.

Mitterrand appointed Pierre Bérégovoy to replace Cresson as prime minister April 1992. As finance minister, he was blamed by Cresson for the nation's economic troubles but was

France: history

5th century BC	France, then called *Gaul* (*Gallia* by the Romans) was invaded by Celtic peoples.
57–51 BC	Conquest by the Roman general Julius Caesar.
1st–5th century AD	During Roman rule the inhabitants of France accepted Roman civilization and the Latin language. As the empire declined, Germanic tribes overran the country and settled.
481–511	A Frankish chief, Clovis, brought the other tribes under his rule, accepted Christianity, and made Paris the capital.
511–751	Under Clovis' successors, the Merovingians, the country sank into anarchy.
741–68	Unity was restored by Pepin, founder of the Carolingian dynasty.
768–814	Charlemagne made France the center of the Holy Roman Empire.
912	The province of Normandy was granted as a duchy to the Viking leader Rollo, whose invading Norsemen had settled here.
987	The first king of the House of Capet assumed the crown. Under Charlemagne's weak successors the great nobles had become semiindependent. The Capets established rule in the district around Paris but were surrounded by vassals stronger than themselves.
11th–13th centuries	The power of the Capets was gradually extended, with the support of the church and the townspeople.
1337–1453	In the Hundred Years' War Charles VII expelled the English from France, aided by Joan of Arc.
1483	Burgundy and Brittany were annexed. Through the policies of Louis XI the restoration of the royal power was achieved.
1503–1697	Charles VIII's Italian wars initiated a struggle with Spain for supremacy in W Europe that lasted for two centuries.
1592–98	Protestantism (Huguenot) was adopted by a party of the nobles for political reasons; the result was a succession of civil wars, fought under religious slogans.
1589–1610	Henri IV restored peace, established religious toleration, and made the monarchy absolute.
1634–48	The ministers Richelieu and Mazarin, by their intervention in the Thirty Years' War, secured Alsace and made France the leading power in Europe.
1643–1763	Louis XIV embarked on an aggressive policy that united Europe against him; in his reign began the conflict with Britain that lost France its colonies in Canada and India in the War of the Spanish Succession (1701–14), War of the Austrian Succession (1756–58), and Seven Years' War (1756–63).
1789–99	The French Revolution abolished feudalism and absolute monarchy, but failed to establish democracy.
1799–1815	Napoleon's military dictatorship was aided by foreign wars (1792–1802, 1803–15). The Bourbon monarchy was restored 1814 with Louis XVIII.
1830	Charles X's attempt to substitute absolute for limited monarchy provoked a revolution, which placed his cousin, Louis Philippe, on the throne.
1848	In the Feb revolution Louis Philippe was overthrown and the Second Republic set up.
1852–70	The president of the republic, Louis Napoleon, Napoleon I's nephew, restored the empire 1852, with the title of Napoleon III. His expansionist foreign policy ended in defeat in the Franco-Prussian War and the foundation of the Third Republic.
1863–1946	France colonized Indochina, parts of N Africa, and the S Pacific.
1914	France entered World War I.
1936–38	A radical-socialist-communist alliance introduced many social reform
1939	France entered World War II.
1940	The German invasion allowed the extreme right to set up a puppet dictatorship under Pétain in Vichy, but resistance was maintained by the *maquis* and the Free French under de Gaulle.
1944	Liberation from the Nazis.

For postwar history see ⇪France.

respected by the country's financial community. The opposition Gaullist party attacked the Maastricht Treaty on European union, but in a referendum in Sept 1992 the treaty was narrowly endorsed. *See illustration box.*

France Anatole. Adopted name of Jacques Anatole Thibault 1844–1924. French writer renowned for the wit, urbanity, and style of his works. His earliest novel was *Le Crime de Sylvestre Bonnard/The Crime of Sylvester Bonnard* 1881; later books include the autobiographical series beginning with *Le Livre de mon ami/My Friend's Book* 1885, the satiric *L'Île des pingouins/Penguin Island* 1908, and *Les Dieux ont soif/The Gods Are Athirst*

1912. He was awarded the Nobel Prize for Literature 1921.

France was born in Paris. He published a critical study of Alfred de Vigny 1868, which was followed by several volumes of poetry and short stories. He was elected to the French Academy 1896. His other books include *Thaïs* 1890 and *Crainquebille* 1905. He was a socialist and supporter of ⇪Dreyfus.

Francesca Piero della See ⇪Piero della Francesca, Italian painter.

Franche-Comté region of E France; area 6,253 sq mi/16,200 sq km; population (1987) 1,086,000. Its capital is Besançon, and it includes the *départements* of Doubs, Jura, Haute

Saône, and Territoire de Belfort. In the mountainous Jura, there is farming and forestry, and elsewhere there are engineering and plastics industries.

Once independent and ruled by its own count, it was disputed by France, Burgundy, Austria, and Spain from the 9th century until it became a French province under the Treaty of ▷Nijmegen 1678.

franchise in business, the right given by a manufacturer to a distributor to market the manufacturer's product.

Examples of franchise operations in the US include fast-food restaurants, auto-repair shops, and specialty stores, where the owner/managers have purchased the right to operate a brand-name business using materials supplied by the manufacturer for a percentage of the profits.

Francis or *François* two kings of France:

Francis I 1494–1547. King of France from 1515. He succeeded his cousin Louis XII, and from 1519 European politics turned on the rivalry between him and the Holy Roman emperor Charles V, which led to war 1521–29, 1536–38, and 1542–44. In 1525 Francis was defeated and captured at Pavia and released only after signing a humiliating treaty. At home, he developed absolute monarchy.

Francis II 1544–1560. King of France from 1559 when he succeeded his father, Henri II. He married Mary Queen of Scots 1558. He was completely under the influence of his mother, ▷Catherine de' Medici.

Francis II 1768–1835. Holy Roman emperor 1792–1806. He became Francis I, Emperor of Austria 1804, and abandoned the title of Holy Roman emperor 1806. During his reign Austria was five times involved in war with France, 1792–97, 1798–1801, 1805, 1809, and 1813–14. He succeeded his father Leopold II.

Franciscan order Catholic order of friars, *Friars Minor* or *Gray Friars*, founded 1209 by Francis of Assisi. Subdivisions were the strict Observants; the Conventuals, who were allowed to own property corporately; and the ▷Capuchins, founded 1529.

The Franciscan order included such scholars as the English scientist Roger Bacon. A female order, the *Poor Clares*, was founded by St ▷Clare 1215, and lay people who adopt a Franciscan regime without abandoning the world form a third order, *Tertiaries*.

Francis Ferdinand English form of ▷Franz Ferdinand, archduke of Austria.

Francis Joseph English form of ▷Franz Joseph, emperor of Austria-Hungary.

Francis of Assisi, St 1182–1226. Italian founder of the Roman Catholic Franciscan order of friars 1209 and, with St Clare, of the Poor Clares 1212. In 1224 he is said to have undergone a mystical experience during which he received the *stigmata* (five wounds of Jesus). Many stories are told of his ability to charm wild animals, and he is the patron saint of ecologists. His feast day is Oct 4.

The son of a wealthy merchant, Francis changed his life after two dreams he had during an illness following spells of military service when he was in his early twenties. He resolved to follow literally the behests of the New Testament and live a life of poverty and service while preaching a simple form of the Christian gospel. In 1219 he went to Egypt to convert the sultan, and lived for a month in

his camp. Returning to Italy, he resigned his leadership of the friars.

Francis of Sales, St 1567–1622. French bishop and theologian. He became bishop of Geneva 1602, and in 1610 founded the order of the Visitation, an order of nuns. He is the patron saint of journalists and other writers. His feast day is Jan 24.

Francis de Sales was born in Savoy. His writings include *Introduction à la vie dévote/Introduction to a Devout Life* 1609, written to reconcile the Christian life with living in the real world.

francium radioactive metallic element, symbol Fr, atomic number 87, atomic weight 223. It is one of the ▷alkali metals and occurs in nature in small amounts as a decay product of actinium. Its longest-lived isotope has a half-life of only 21 minutes. Francium was discovered and named in 1939 by Marguérite Perey to honor her country.

Franck César Auguste 1822–1890. Belgian composer. His music, mainly religious and Romantic in style, includes the Symphony in D minor 1866–68, *Symphonic Variations* 1885 for piano and orchestra, the *Violin Sonata* 1886, the oratorio *Les Béatitudes/The Beatitudes* 1879, and many organ pieces.

Franck James 1882–1964. US physicist. He was awarded a Nobel Prize 1925 for his experiments of 1914 on the energy transferred by colliding electrons to mercury atoms, showing that the transfer was governed by the rules of ▷quantum theory.

Born and educated in Germany, he emigrated to the US after publicly protesting against Hitler's racial policies. Franck participated in the wartime atomic-bomb project at Los Alamos but organized the "Franck petition" 1945, which argued that the bomb should not be used against Japanese cities. After World War II he turned his research to photosynthesis.

Franco Francisco (Paulino Hermenegildo Teódulo Bahamonde) 1892–1975. Spanish dictator from 1939. As a general, he led the insurgent Nationalists to victory in the Spanish ▷Civil War 1936–39, supported by Fascist Italy and Nazi Germany, and established a dictatorship. In 1942 Franco reinstated the Cortes (Spanish parliament), which in 1947 passed an act by which he became head of state for life.

Franco was born in Galicia, NW Spain. He entered the army 1910, served in Morocco 1920–26, and was appointed Chief of Staff 1935, but demoted to governor of the Canary Islands 1936. Dismissed from this post by the Popular Front (Republican) government, he plotted an uprising with German and Italian assistance, and on the outbreak of the Civil War organized the invasion of Spain by N African troops and foreign legionaries. After the death of General Sanjurjo, he took command of the Nationalists, proclaiming himself *Caudillo* (leader) of Spain. The defeat of the Republic with the surrender of Madrid 1939 brought all Spain under his government. On the outbreak of World War II, in spite of Spain's official attitude of "strictest neutrality," his pro-Axis sympathies led him to send aid, later withdrawn, to the German side.

At home, he curbed the growing power of the Falange Española (fascist party), and in later years slightly liberalized his regime. In 1969 he nominated ▷Juan Carlos as his successor and future king of Spain. He relinquished the premiership 1973, but remained head of state until his death.

François French form of ▷Francis, two kings of France.

Franco-Prussian War 1870–71. The Prussian chancellor Bismarck put forward a German candidate for the vacant Spanish throne with the deliberate, and successful, intention of provoking the French emperor Napoleon III into declaring war. The Prussians defeated the French at ▷Sedan, then besieged Paris. The Treaty of Frankfurt May 1871 gave Alsace, Lorraine, and a large French indemnity to Prussia. The war established Prussia, at the head of a newly established German empire, as Europe's leading power.

frangipani any tropical American tree of the genus *Plumeria*, especially *P. rubra*, of the dogbane family Apocynaceae. Perfume is made from the strongly scented flowers.

Frank member of a group of Germanic peoples prominent in Europe in the 3rd to 9th centuries. Believed to have originated in Pomerania on the Black Sea, they had settled on the Rhine by the 3rd century, spread into the Roman Empire by the 4th century, and gradually conquered most of Gaul, Italy, and Germany under the ▷Merovingian and ▷Carolingian dynasties. The kingdom of the W Franks became France, the kingdom of the E Franks became Germany.

The Salian (western) Franks conquered Roman Gaul during the 4th–5th centuries. Their ruler, Clovis, united the Salians with the Ripuarian (eastern) Franks, and they were converted to Christianity. The agriculture of the Merovingian dynasty (named after Clovis's grandfather, Merovech) was more advanced than that of the Romans, and they introduced the three-field system (see ▷field). The Merovingians conquered most of western and central Europe, and lasted until the 8th century when the Carolingian dynasty was founded under Charlemagne. The kingdom of the W Franks was fused by the 9th century into a single people with the Gallo-Romans, speaking the modified form of Latin that became modern French.

Frank Anne 1929–1945. German diarist who fled to the Netherlands with her family 1933 to escape Nazi anti-Semitism (the ▷Holocaust). During the German occupation of Amsterdam, they and two other families remained in a sealed-off room, protected by Dutch sympathizers 1942–44, when betrayal resulted in their deportation and Anne's death in Belsen concentration camp. Her diary of her time in hiding was published 1947.

Previously suppressed portions of her diary were published 1989. The house in which the family took refuge is preserved as a museum. Her diary has sold 20 million copies in more than 50 languages and has been made into a play and a film publicizing the fate of millions.

Frank Ilya 1908– . Russian physicist known for his work on radiation. In 1934 ▷Cherenkov had noted a peculiar blue radiation sometimes emitted as electrons passed through water. It was left to Frank and his colleague at Moscow University, Igor Tamm (1895–1971), to realize that this form of radiation was produced by charged particles traveling faster through the medium than the speed of light in the same medium. Frank shared the 1958 Nobel Prize for Physics with Cherenkov and Tamm.

Frankenstein or *The Modern Prometheus* Gothic horror story by Mary Shelley, published in England 1818. Frankenstein, a scientist, discovers how to bring inanimate matter to life, and creates a man-monster. When Frankenstein fails to provide a mate to satisfy the creature's human emotions, it seeks revenge by killing Frankenstein's brother and bride. Frankenstein dies in an attempt to destroy his creation.

Frankenthaler Helen 1928– . US Abstract Expressionist painter, inventor of the color-staining technique whereby the unprimed, absorbent canvas is stained or soaked with thinned-out paint, creating deep, soft veils of translucent color.

Frankfort capital of Kentucky, located in the N central part of the state, on the Kentucky River, E of Louisville. Industries include bourbon, electronic equipment, furniture, footwear; population (1990) 26,000. Frankfort became the capital of Kentucky 1786.

Frankfurt-am-Main city in Hessen, Germany, 45 mi/72 km NE of Mannheim; population (1988) 592,000. It is a commercial and banking center, with electrical and machine industries, and an inland port on the river Main. An international book fair is held here annually.

history Frankfurt was a free imperial city from 1372 to 1806, when it was incorporated into ◊Prussia. It is the birthplace of the poet Goethe. It was the headquarters of the US zone of occupation in World War II and of the Anglo-US zone 1947–49.

Frankfurter Felix 1882–1965. Austrian-born US jurist and Supreme Court justice. After law school he served as assistant to the US attorney for the southern district of New York and joined the faculty of Harvard Law School 1914. As a supporter of liberal causes, Frankfurter was one of the founders of the American Civil Liberties Union 1920. Appointed to the US Supreme Court 1939 by F D Roosevelt, he remained liberal yet opposed the use of the judicial veto to advance political ends. Frankfurter received the Presidential Medal of Freedom 1963.

Born in Vienna, Frankfurter immigrated with his family to the US 1894, attended the City College of New York, and received a law degree from Harvard 1906.

Frankfurt Parliament an assembly of liberal politicians and intellectuals that met for a few months in 1848 in the aftermath of the ◊revolutions of 1848 and the overthrow of monarchies in most of the German states. They discussed a constitution for a united Germany, but the restoration of the old order and the suppression of the revolutions ended the parliament.

Frankfurt School the members of the *Institute of Social Research*, set up at Frankfurt University, Germany, 1923 as the first Marxist research center. With the rise of Hitler, many of its members went to the US and set up the institute at Columbia University, New York. In 1969 the institute was dissolved.

In the 1930s, under its second director Max Horkheimer (1895–1973), a group that included Erich Fromm, Herbert Marcuse, and T W Adorno (1903–1969) attempted to update Marxism and create a coherent and viable social theory. Drawing on a variety of disciplines as well as the writings of Marx and Freud, they produced works such as *Authority and the Family* 1936 and developed a Marxist perspective known as *critical theory*. After World War II the institute returned to Frankfurt, although Marcuse and some others remained in the US. The German and US branches diverged in the 1950s, and the institute was dissolved after Adorno's death, although Jurgen

Habermas (1929–) and others have since attempted to revive its theory and research program.

frankincense resin of various African and Asian trees of the genus *Boswellia*, family Burseraceae, burned as incense. Costly in ancient times, it is traditionally believed to be one of the three gifts brought by the Magi to the infant Jesus.

Franklin district of ◊Northwest Territories; area 549,250 sq mi/1,422,550 sq km.

Franklin Benjamin 1706–1790. US printer, publisher, author, scientist, and statesman. He proved that lightning is a form of electricity, distinguished between positive and negative electricity, and invented the lightning conductor. He was the first US ambassador to France 1776–85, and negotiated peace with Britain 1783. As a delegate to the Continental Congress from Pennsylvania 1785–88, he helped to draft the ◊Declaration of Independence and the US Constitution.

Born in Boston, Franklin moved to Philadelphia as a young man and combined a successful printing business with scientific experiment and inventions; he authored and published the popular *Poor Richard's Almanac* 1733–58. A member of the Pennsylvania Assembly 1751–64, he was sent to Britain to lobby Parliament about tax grievances and achieved the repeal of the ◊Stamp Act; on his return to the US he was prominent in the deliberations leading up to independence. As ambassador in Paris he enlisted French help for the ◊American Revolution.

Franklin was one of the most well-traveled of the colonial leaders, and he brought an internationalist perspective to the ◊Constitutional Convention.

He organized an effective postal system; taught himself Spanish, French, Italian, and Latin; and created a discussion group 1743 that would become the American Philosophical Society. His autobiography first appeared 1781 (in complete form, 1868).

Franklin John 1786–1847. English naval explorer who took part in expeditions to Australia, the Arctic, and N Canada, and in 1845 commanded an expedition to look for the Northwest Passage from the Atlantic to the Pacific, during which he and his crew perished.

Franz Ferdinand or Francis Ferdinand 1863–1914. Archduke of Austria. He became heir to his uncle, Emperor Franz Joseph, in 1884 but while visiting Sarajevo June 28, 1914, he and his wife were assassinated by a Serbian nationalist. Austria used the episode to make unreasonable demands on Serbia that ultimately precipitated World War I.

Franz Josef Land (Russian *Zemlya Frantsa Iosifa*) archipelago of over 85 islands in the Arctic Ocean, E of Spitsbergen and NW of Novaya Zemlya, Russia. Area 8,000 sq mi/20,250 sq km. There are scientific stations on the islands.

Franz Joseph or Francis Joseph 1830–1916. Emperor of Austria-Hungary from 1848, when his uncle, Ferdinand I, abdicated. After the suppression of the 1848 revolution, Franz Joseph tried to establish an absolute monarchy but had to grant Austria a parliamentary constitution 1861 and Hungary equality with Austria 1867. He was defeated in the Italian War 1859 and the Prussian War 1866. In 1914 he made the assassination of his heir and nephew Franz Ferdinand the excuse for attacking Serbia, thus precipitating World War I.

Frasch process process used to extract underground deposits of sulfur. Superheated steam is piped into the sulfur deposit and melts it. Compressed air is then pumped down to force the molten sulfur to the surface. The process was developed in the US 1891 by German-born Herman Frasch (1851–1914).

Fraser river in British Columbia. It rises in the Yellowhead Pass of the Rockies and flows NW, then S, then W to the Strait of Georgia. It is 850 mi/1,370 km long and rich in salmon.

Fraser Antonia 1932– . English author of biographies, including *Mary Queen of Scots* 1969; historical works, such as *The Weaker Vessel* 1984; and a series of detective novels featuring investigator Jemima Shore.

She is married to the playwright Harold Pinter, and is the daughter of Lord Longford.

Fraser Dawn 1937– . Australian swimmer. The only person to win the same swimming event at three consecutive Olympic Games: 100 meters freestyle in 1956, 1960, and 1964. The holder of 27 world records, she was the first woman to break the one-minute barrier for the 100 meters.

Fraser Simon 1776–1862. Canadian explorer and surveyor for the Hudson Bay Company who crossed the Rockies and traveled most of the way down the river that bears his name 1805–07.

fraternity and sorority student societies (fraternity for men; sorority for women) in some US and Canadian universities and colleges. Although mainly social and residential, some are purely honorary, membership being on the basis of scholastic distinction; Phi Beta Kappa, the earliest of the fraternities, was founded at the College of William and Mary, Virginia in 1776.

Usually named with Greek letters, they are nominally secret, with badge, dues, passwords, motto, and initiation rites. They have a central governing body and a "chapter" at participating colleges.

fraud in law, an act of deception resulting in injury to another. To establish fraud it has to be demonstrated that (1) a false representation (for example, a factually untrue statement) has been made, with the intention that it should be acted upon; (2) the person making the representation knows it is false or does not attempt to find out whether it is true or not; and (3) the person to whom the representation is made acts upon it to his or her detriment.

A contract based on fraud can be declared void, and the injured party can sue for damages.

Fraunhofer Joseph von 1787–1826. German physicist who did important work in optics. The dark lines in the solar spectrum (*Fraunhofer lines*), which reveal the chemical composition of the Sun's atmosphere, were accurately mapped by him.

Born in Bavaria, he was apprenticed to a glass cutter, and in 1807 founded an optical institute.

Frazer James George 1854–1941. Scottish anthropologist, author of *The Golden Bough* 1890, a pioneer study of the origins of religion and sociology on a comparative basis. It exerted considerable influence on writers such as TS Eliot and D H Lawrence, but by the standards of modern anthroppology, many of its methods and findings are unsound.

Frederick V known as *the Winter King* 1596–

1632. Elector palatine of the Rhine 1610–23 and king of Bohemia 1619–20 (for one winter, hence the name), having been chosen by the Protestant Bohemians as ruler after the deposition of Catholic emperor ⟡Ferdinand II. His selection was the cause of the Thirty Years' War. Frederick was defeated at the Battle of the White Mountain, near Prague, in Nov 1620, by the army of the Catholic League and fled to Holland.

Frederick IX 1899–1972. King of Denmark from 1947. He was succeeded by his daughter who became Queen ⟡Margrethe II.

Frederick two Holy Roman emperors:

Frederick I *Barbarossa* ("red-beard") c. 1123–1190. Holy Roman emperor from 1152. Originally duke of Swabia, he was elected emperor 1152, and was engaged in a struggle with Pope Alexander III 1159–77, which ended in his submission; the Lombard cities, headed by Milan, took advantage of this to establish their independence of imperial control. Frederick joined the Third Crusade, and was drowned while crossing a river in Anatolia.

Frederick II 1194–1250. Holy Roman emperor from 1212, called "the Wonder of the World." He led a crusade 1228–29 that recovered Jerusalem by treaty, without fighting. He quarrelled with the pope, who excommunicated him three times, and a feud began that lasted with intervals until the end of his reign. Frederick, who was a religious skeptic, is often considered the most cultured man of his age. He was the son of Henry VI.

Frederick three kings of Prussia:

Frederick I 1657–1713. King of Prussia from 1701. He became elector of Brandenburg 1688.

Frederick II *the Great* 1712–1786. King of Prussia from 1740, when he succeeded his father Frederick William I. In that year he started the War of the ⟡Austrian Succession by his attack on Austria. In the peace of 1745 he secured Silesia. The struggle was renewed in the ⟡Seven Years' War 1756–63. He acquired West Prussia in the first partition of Poland 1772 and left Prussia as Germany's foremost state. He was an efficient and just ruler in the spirit of the Enlightenment and a patron of the arts.

In his domestic policy he encouraged industry and agriculture, reformed the judicial system, fostered education, and established religious toleration. He corresponded with the French writer Voltaire, and was a talented musician.

Frederick III 1831–1888. King of Prussia and emperor of Germany 1888. The son of Wilhelm I, he married the eldest daughter (Victoria) of Queen Victoria of the UK 1858 and, as a liberal, frequently opposed Chancellor Bismarck. He died three months after his accession.

Frederick William 1620–1688. Elector of Brandenburg from 1640, "the Great Elector." By successful wars against Sweden and Poland, he prepared the way for Prussian power in the 18th century.

Frederick William four kings of Prussia:

Frederick William I 1688–1740. King of Prussia from 1713, who developed Prussia's military might and commerce.

Frederick William II 1744–1797. King of Prussia from 1786. He was a nephew of Frederick II but had little of his relative's military skill. He was unsuccessful in waging war

on the French 1792–95 and lost all Prussia west of the Rhine.

Frederick William III 1770–1840. King of Prussia from 1797. He was defeated by Napoleon 1806, but contributed to his final overthrow 1813–15 and profited by being allotted territory at the Congress of Vienna.

Frederick William IV 1795–1861. King of Prussia from 1840. He upheld the principle of the ⟡divine right of kings, but was forced to grant a constitution 1850 after the Prussian revolution 1848. He suffered two strokes 1857 and became mentally debilitated. His brother William (later emperor) took over his duties.

Fredericton capital of New Brunswick, on the St John River; population (1986) 44,000. It was known as *St Anne's Point* until 1785 when it was named after Prince Frederick, second son of George III.

Freedom, Presidential Medal of the highest peacetime civilian honor in the US. Instituted by President Kennedy 1963, it is awarded to those "who contribute significantly to the quality of American life." A list of recipients is published each Independence Day and often includes unknown individuals as well as artists, performers, and politicians.

It replaced the *Medal of Freedom*, instituted 1945, which had been conferred 24 times on an irregular basis.

free enterprise or *free market* economic system where private capital is used in business with profits going to private companies and individuals. The term has much the same meaning as ⟡capitalism.

free fall the state in which a body is falling freely under the influence of ⟡gravity, as in free-fall parachuting. The term *weightless* is normally used to describe a body in free fall in space.

In orbit, astronauts and spacecraft are still held by gravity and are in fact falling toward the Earth. Because of their speed (orbital velocity), the amount they fall toward the Earth just equals the amount the Earth's surface curves away; in effect they remain at the same height, apparently weightless.

free-falling another name for ⟡skydiving.

Free French in World War II, movement formed by General Charles ⟡de Gaulle in the UK June 1940, consisting of French soldiers who continued to fight against the Axis after the Franco-German armistice. They took the name *Fighting France* 1942 and served in many campaigns, among them General Leclerc's advance from Chad to Tripolitania 1942, the Syrian campaigns 1941, the campaigns in the Western Desert, the Italian campaign, the liberation of France, and the invasion of Germany. Their emblem was the Cross of Lorraine, a cross with two bars.

freeman one who enjoys the freedom of a borough. Since the early Middle Ages, a freeman has been allowed to carry out his craft or trade within the jurisdiction of the borough and to participate in municipal government, but since the development of modern local government, such privileges have become largely honorary.

There have generally been four ways of becoming a freeman: by apprenticeship to an existing freeman; by patrimony, or being the son of a freeman; by redemption, that is, buying the privilege; or, by gift from the borough, the usual method today, when the privilege is granted in recognition of some achievement,

benefaction, or special status on the part of the recipient.

Freemasonry the beliefs and practices of a group of linked national organizations open to men over the age of 21, united by a common code of morals and certain traditional "secrets." Modern Freemasonry began in 18th-century Europe. Freemasons do much charitable work, but have been criticized in recent years for their secrecy, their male exclusivity, and their alleged use of influence within and between organizations (for example, the police or local government) to further each other's interests. There are approximately 6 million members.

beliefs Freemasons believe in God, whom they call the "Great Architect of the Universe."

history Freemasonry is descended from a medieval guild of itinerant masons, which existed in the 14th century and by the 16th was admitting men unconnected with the building trade. The term "freemason" may have meant a full member of the guild or one working in free-stone, that is, a mason of the highest class. There were some 25 lodges in 17th-century Scotland, of which 16 were in centers of masonic skills such as stonemasonry.

The present order of *Free and Accepted Masons* originated with the formation in London of the first Grand Lodge, or governing body, in 1717, and during the 18th century spread from Britain to the US, continental Europe, and elsewhere. In France and other European countries, freemasonry assumed a political and anticlerical character; it has been condemned by the papacy, and in some countries was suppressed by the state.

free port port or sometimes a zone within a port, where cargo may be accepted for handling, processing, and reshipment without the imposition of tariffs or taxes. Duties and tax become payable only if the products are for consumption in the country to which the free port belongs.

Free ports are established to take advantage of a location with good trade links. They facilitate the quick entry and departure of ships, unhampered by lengthy customs regulations. Important free ports include Singapore, Copenhagen, New York, Gdańsk, Macao, San Francisco, and Seattle.

free radical in chemistry, an atom or molecule that has an unpaired electron and is therefore highly reactive. Most free radicals are very short-lived. If free radicals are produced in living organisms they can be very damaging.

Free radicals are often produced by high temperatures and are found in flames and explosions.

A very simple free radical is the methyl radical CH_3 produced by the splitting of the covalent carbon-to-carbon bond in ethane.

$$CH_3CH_3 \rightleftharpoons 2CH_3$$

freesia any plant of the South African genus *Freesia* of the iris family Iridaceae, commercially grown for their scented, funnel-shaped flowers.

Freetown capital of Sierra Leone, W Africa; population (1988) 470,000. It has a naval station and a harbor. Industries include cement, plastics, footwear, and oil refining. Platinum, chromite, diamonds, and gold are traded. It was founded as a settlement for freed slaves in the 1790s.

free trade economic system where governments do not interfere in the movement of goods between countries; there are thus no taxes on imports. In the modern economy, free trade tends to hold within economic groups such as the European Community (EC), but not generally, despite such treaties as ⊅GATT 1948 and subsequent agreements to reduce tariffs. The opposite of free trade is ⊅protectionism.

The case for free trade, first put forward in the 17th century, received its classic statement in Adam Smith's *Wealth of Nations* 1776. According to traditional economic theory, free trade allows nations to specialize in those commodities that can be produced most efficiently. The Ottawa Agreements 1932 marked the end of free trade until in 1948 GATT came into operation. A series of drastic international tariff reductions was agreed in the Kennedy Round Conference 1964–67, and the Tokyo Round 1974–79 gave substantial incentives to developing countries.

The 1980s recession, prompted by increased world oil prices and unemployment, swung the pendulum back toward protectionism, which discourages foreign imports by heavy duties, thus protecting home products.

Economists generally favor a system closer to free trade than now exists but recognize that developing countries might need some protection in establishing new industries and that there are health and national security reasons for some controls on trade. Among the damaging impediments to free trade, economists would cite ⊅dumping of products at an unrealistically low price, subsidy by governments of export-related industries, overly strict environmental standards for imported products, and other subtle restrictions in addition to tariffs and quotas. It is feared that the EC will erect barriers against external competition after it eliminates trade restrictions within the EC in 1992.

free verse poetry without metrical form. At the beginning of the 20th century, under the very different influences of Whitman and Mallarmé, many poets believed that the 19th century had accomplished most of what could be done with regular meter, and rejected it, in much the same spirit as Milton had rejected rhyme, preferring irregular meters that made it possible to express thought clearly and without distortion.

This was true of T S ⊅Eliot and the Imagists; it was also true of poets who, like the Russians Esenin and Mayakovsky, placed emphasis on public performance.

Poets including Robert Graves and Auden have criticized free verse on the ground that it lacks the difficulty of true accomplishment, but their own metrics would have been considered loose by earlier critics. The freeness of free verse is largely relative.

free will the doctrine that human beings are free to control their own actions, and that these actions are not fixed in advance by God or fate. Some Jewish and Christian theologians assert that God gave humanity free will to choose between good and evil; others that God has decided in advance the outcome of all human choices (⊅predestination), as in Calvinism.

freeze-drying method of preserving food; see ⊅food technology. The product to be dried is frozen and then put in a vacuum chamber that forces out the ice as water vapor, a process known as sublimation.

Many of the substances that give products such as coffee their typical flavor are volatile,

and would be lost in a normal drying process because they would evaporate along with the water. In the freeze-drying process these volatile compounds do not pass into the ice that is to be sublimed, and are therefore largely retained.

freezing change from liquid to solid state, as when water becomes ice. For a given substance, freezing occurs at a definite temperature, known as the ***freezing point***, that is invariable under similar conditions of pressure, and the temperature remains at this point until all the liquid is frozen. The amount of heat per unit mass that has to be removed to freeze a substance is a constant for any given substance, and is known as the latent heat of fusion.

Ice is less dense than water since water expands just before its freezing point is reached. If pressure is applied, expansion is retarded and the freezing point will be lowered. The presence of dissolved substances in a liquid also lowers the freezing point (⊅depression of freezing point), the amount of lowering being proportional to the molecular concentration of the solution. Antifreeze mixtures for car radiators and the use of salt to melt ice on roads are common applications of this principle.

Animals in arctic conditions, for example insects or fish, cope with the extreme cold either by manufacturing natural "antifreeze" and staying active, or by allowing themselves to freeze in a controlled fashion, that is, they manufacture proteins to act as nuclei for the formation of ice crystals in areas that will not produce cellular damage, and so enable themselves to thaw back to life again.

freezing point, depression of lowering of a solution's freezing point below that of the pure solvent; it depends on the number of molecules of solute dissolved in it. For a single solvent, such as pure water, all solute substances in the same molar concentration produce the same lowering of freezing point. The depression d produced by the presence of a solute of molar concentration C is given by the equation $d = KC$, where K is a constant (called the cryoscopic constant) for the solvent concerned.

Measurement of freezing-point depression is a useful method of determining the molecular weights of solutes. It is also used to detect the illicit addition of water to milk.

Frege Friedrich Ludwig Gottlob 1848–1925. German philosopher, the founder of modern mathematical logic. He created symbols for concepts like "or" and "if ... then," which are now in standard use in mathematics. His *Die Grundlagen der Arithmetik/The Foundations of Arithmetic* 1884 influenced Bertrand ⊅Russell and ⊅Wittgenstein. His major work is *Berggriftsschrift/Conceptual Notation* 1879.

Frelimo (acronym for ***Front for the Liberation of Mozambique***) nationalist group aimed at gaining independence for Mozambique from the occupying Portuguese. It began operating from S Tanzania 1963 and continued until independence 1975.

Fremantle chief port of Western Australia, at the mouth of the Swan river, SW of ⊅Perth; population (1981) 23,780. It has shipbuilding yards, lumber mills, and iron foundries and exports wheat, fruit, wool, and timber. It was founded as a penal settlement 1829.

Frémont John Charles 1813–1890. US soldier and politician who explored much of the Far West, was influential in the US acquisition of California, and ultimately saw his

military career overshadowed by his political ambitions.

Born in Savannah, Georgia, he became a US Army engineer and led three exploration expeditions in the West that brought him fame. He also gained political influence through his marriage to Sen. Thomas Hart Benton's daughter. Frémont came into conflict with General Kearney in California, which led to a court martial, and he resigned from the army. After a brief term representing California in the US Senate and an expedition to chart a southern railroad route, he was the Republican Party's first presidential candidate 1856, losing to Buchanan. In the Civil War, he had disagreements with Lincoln and then resigned rather than serve under General John Pope. His postwar career was disappointing; railroad endeavors failed, and he was relegated to being territorial governor of Arizona 1878–83.

French native to or an inhabitant of France, as well as their descendents, culture, or primary language, which is one of the Romance languages (see ⊅French language). There are also some sociolinguistic minorities within France who speak Catalan, Breton, Flemish, German, Corsican, or Basque.

French is also spoken in the former colonies, such as in Africa and Québec, and in overseas territories such as Martinique and French Guiana.

French Daniel Chester 1850–1931. US sculptor, whose most famous works include *The Minute Man* 1875 in Concord, Massachusetts, *John Harvard* 1884 at Harvard College, *Alma Mater* at Columbia University, and the imposing seated *Abraham Lincoln* 1922 in the Lincoln Memorial, Washington, DC.

Born in Exeter, New Hampshire, French briefly attended the Massachusetts Institute of Technology (MIT) before embarking on an artistic career.

Trained in anatomy and sculpture in private studios in Boston, New York, and Europe, he was by far the most noted American sculptor of public monuments in the late 19th century.

French Antarctica *French Southern and Antarctic Territories* territory created 1955; area 3,900 sq mi/10,100 sq km; population about 200 research scientists. It includes Adélie Land on the Antarctic continent, the Kerguelen and Crozet archipelagos, and St Paul and Nouvelle Amsterdam islands in the southern seas. It is administered from Paris.

Port-aux-Français on Kerguelen is the chief center, with several research stations. There are also research stations on Nouvelle Amsterdam and in Adélie Land and a meteorological station on Possession Island in the Crozet archipelago. St Paul is uninhabited. In 1988 French workers, who were illegally building an airstrip, thus violating a United Nations treaty on Antarctica, attacked ⊅Greenpeace workers.

French art painting and sculpture of France. A number of styles have emerged in France over the centuries, from Gothic in the Middle Ages to Impressionism, Cubism, Surrealism, and others.

11th–14th centuries The main forms of artistic expression were manuscript painting, architecture, and sculpture. France played the leading role in creating the Gothic style.

15th century The miniatures of Jean Fouquet and the *Très riches heures* (a prayer book) of the Limbourg brothers, manuscript illuminators, show remarkable naturalism.

16th century Artists were influenced by the Italians, but the miniature tradition was kept up by the court painters such as Jean Clouet.

17th century Landscape painting became increasingly popular. Two exceptional artists in the genre were Poussin and Claude Lorrain.

18th century French painting and sculpture became dominant throughout Europe. Popular Rococo painters were Watteau, Fragonard, and Boucher. The still lifes of Chardin show Dutch influence. The Neo-Classical French school was founded by David.

early 19th century Ingres was the most widely admired painter. Delacroix was the leader of the Romantic movement. Géricault excelled as a history and animal painter.

mid-19th century Courbet and Manet were the great rebels in art, breaking with age-old conventions. The Barbizon school of landscape painting was followed by the Impressionists: Monet, Renoir, Degas, and others.

late 19th century The Pointillist Seurat took the Impressionists' ideas further. The individual styles of Cézanne and Gauguin helped prepare the way for Modernism. Rodin's powerful, realistic sculptures had great influence.

1900s Fauvism, showing the influence of Gauguin with his emphasis on pure color, was introduced by Matisse and others. Cubism, deriving from Cézanne, was begun by Picasso and Braque.

1920s Paris was a center of the Surrealist movement.

1930s Abstraction-création movement started in Paris to develop a form of abstract art constructed from non-figurative, usually geometrical elements.

1945–90 After World War II the center of the art world shifted from France to the US.

French Canadian literature F-X Garneau's *Histoire du Canada* (1845–48) inspired a school of patriotic verse led by Octave Crémazie (1827–79) and continued by Louis Fréchette (1838–1908). A new movement began after 1900 with such poets as André Lozeau (1878–1924), Paul Morin, Robert Choquette (1862–1941), Alain Grandbois, St Denys Garneau, Eloi de Grandmont, and Pierre Trottier. Fiction reached a high point with Louis Hémon (1880–1914) whose *Maria Chapdelaine* inspired many genre works. Outstanding later novelists are Germaine Guèvremont, Gabrielle Roy, "Ringuet" (Philippe Panneton), Robert Elie, Roger Lemelin, and Yves Thériault.

French Community former association consisting of France and those overseas territories joined with it by the constitution of the Fifth Republic, following the 1958 referendum. Many of the constituent states withdrew during the 1960s, and it no longer formally exists, but in practice all former French colonies have close economic and cultural as well as linguistic links with France.

French Guiana (French *Guyane Française*) French overseas *département* from 1946, and administrative region from 1974, on the N coast of South America, bounded to the W by Suriname and to the E and S by Brazil.

area 32,230 sq mi/83,500 sq km
capital Cayenne
cities St Laurent
features Eurospace rocket launch pad at Kourou; Îles du Salut, which include ⫿Devil's Island
products timber, shrimps, gold
currency franc
population (1987) 89,000

language 90% Creole, French, Amerindian
famous people Alfred ⫿Dreyfus
history first settled by France 1604, the territory became a French possession 1817; penal colonies, including Devil's Island, were established from 1852; by 1945 the shipments of convicts from France ceased.

French horn musical ⫿brass instrument.

French India former French possessions in India: Pondicherry, Chandernagore, Karaikal, Mahé, and Yanam (Yanaon). They were all transferred to India by 1954.

French language member of the Romance branch of the Indo-European language family, spoken in France, Belgium, Luxembourg, Monaco, and Switzerland in Europe; also in Canada (principally in the province of Québec), various Caribbean and Pacific Islands (including overseas territories such as Martinique and French Guiana), and certain N and W African countries (for example, Mali and Senegal).

French developed from Latin as spoken in Gaul and was established as a distinct language by the 9th century. Varieties used north of the river Loire formed the *Langue d'oil* (*oui*) while those to the south formed the *Langue d'oc*, according to their word for "yes." By the 13th century the dialect of the Île de France was supreme and became the official medium of the courts and administration of France 1539. Its literary form still serves as the basis of *le bon français* ("correct French"), which is officially protected by the Academie Française (founded 1635 at the behest of Cardinal Richelieu) and by occasional legislation in both France and Québec. From 1991 a government-approved commission has approved changes to the language, such as the abolition of the circumflex accent in many words, and some simplified spellings.

French literature
The Middle Ages The *Chanson de Roland* (c. 1080) is one of the early *chansons de geste* (epic poems about deeds of chivalry), which were superseded by the Arthurian romances (seen at their finest in the work of Chrétien de Troyes in the 12th century), and by the Classical themes of Alexander, Troy, and Thebes. Other aspects of French medieval literature are represented by the anonymous *Aucassin et Nicolette* of the early 13th century; the allegorical *Roman de la Rose/Romance of the Rose*, the first part of which was written by Guillaume de Lorris (c. 1230) and the second by Jean de Meung (c. 1275); and the satiric *Roman de Renart/Story of Renard* of the late 12th century. The period also produced the historians Villehardouin, Joinville, Froissart, and Comines, and the first great French poet, François Villon.

Renaissance to the 18th century One of the most celebrated poets of the Renaissance was Ronsard, leader of La ⫿Pléiade (a group of seven writers); others included ⫿Marot at the beginning of the 16th century and Mathurin Régnier (1573–1613) at its close. In prose the period produced the broad genius of Rabelais and the essayist Montaigne. In the 17th century came the triumph of form with the great Classical dramatists Corneille, Racine, and Molière, the graceful brilliance of La Fontaine, and the poet and critic Boileau. Masters of prose in the same period include the philosophers Pascal and Descartes; the preacher Bossuet; the critics La Bruyère, Fénelon, and Malebranche; and La Rochefoucauld, Cardinal de Retz, Mme de Sévigné, and Le Sage.

The 18th century was the age of the

⫿Enlightenment and an era of prose, with Montesquieu, Voltaire, and Rousseau; the scientist Buffon; the encyclopedist Diderot; the ethical writer Vauvenargues; the novelists Prévost and Marivaux; and the memoir writer Saint-Simon.

19th and 20th centuries In the 19th century poetry came to the fore again with the Romantics Lamartine, Hugo, Vigny, Musset, Leconte de Lisle, and Gautier; novelists of the same school were George Sand, Stendhal, and Dumas *père*, while criticism is represented by Sainte-Beuve, and history by Thiers, Michelet, and Taine. The realist novelist Balzac was followed by the school of Naturalism, whose representatives were Flaubert, Zola, the Goncourt brothers, Alphonse Daudet, Maupassant, and Huysmans. Nineteenth-century dramatists include Hugo, Musset, and Dumas *fils*. Symbolism, a movement of experimentation and revolt against Classical verse and materialist attitudes, with the philosopher Bergson as one of its main exponents, found its first expression in the work of Gérard de Nerval, followed by Baudelaire, Verlaine, Mallarmé, Rimbaud, Corbière, and the prose writer Villiers de l'Isle Adam; later writers in the same tradition were Henri de Régnier and Laforgue.

In the late 19th and early 20th centuries drama and poetry revived with Valéry, Claudel, and Paul Fort, who advocated "pure poetry"; other writers were the novelists Gide and Proust, and the critics Thibaudet (1874–1936) and later St John Perse, also a poet. The Surrealist movement, which developed from "pure poetry" through the work of Eluard and Apollinaire, influenced writers as diverse as Giraudoux, Louis Aragon, and Cocteau. The literary reaction against the Symbolists was seen in the work of Charles Péguy, Rostand, de Noailles, and Romain Rolland. Twentieth-century novelists in the Naturalist tradition were Henri Barbusse, Jules Romains, Julian Green, François Mauriac, Francis Carco, and Georges Duhamel. Other prose writers were Maurois, Malraux, Montherlant, Anatole France, Saint-Exupéry, Alain-Fournier, Pierre Hamp, and J R Bloch, while the theater flourished with plays by J J Bernard, Anouilh, Beckett, and Ionesco. World War II had a profound effect on French writing, and distinguished postwar writers include the Existentialists Sartre and Camus, "Vercors" (adopted name of Jean Bruller), Simone de Beauvoir, Alain Robbe-Grillet, Romain Gary, Nathalie Sarraute, and Marguerite Duras.

French Polynesia French Overseas Territory in the S Pacific, consisting of five archipelagos: Windward Islands, Leeward Islands (the two island groups comprising the ⫿Society Islands), ⫿Tuamotu Archipelago (including ⫿Gambier Islands), ⫿Tubuai Islands, and ⫿Marquesas Islands

total area 1,521 sq mi/3,940 sq km
capital Papeete on Tahiti
products cultivated pearls, coconut oil, vanilla; tourism is important
population (1990) 199,100
language Tahitian (official), French
government a high commissioner (Jean Montpezat) and Council of Government; two deputies are returned to the National Assembly in France
history first visited by Europeans 1595; French Protectorate 1843; annexed to France 1880–82; became an Overseas Territory, changing its name from French Oceania 1958;

French revolutionary calendar

revolutionary month (date 1–30)	meaning	time period
Vendémiaire	vintage	Sept 22–Oct 21
Brumaire	fog	Oct 22–Nov 20
Frimaire	frost	Nov 21–Dec 20
Nivôse	snow	Dec 21–Jan 19
Pluviôse	rain	Jan 20–Feb 18
Ventôse	wind	Feb 19–March 20
Germinal	budding	March 21–April 19
Floréal	flowers	April 20–May 19
Prairial	meadows	May 20–June 18
Messidor	harvest	June 19–July 18
Thermidor	heat	July 19–Aug 17
Fructidor	fruit	Aug 18–Sept 16
Sanculottides	festival	Sept 17–Sept 21

self-governing 1977. Following demands for independence in ◊New Caledonia 1984–85, agitation increased also in Polynesia.

French Revolution the period 1789–1799 that saw the end of the French monarchy. Although the revolution began as an attempt to create a constitutional monarchy, by late 1792 demands for long-overdue reforms resulted in the proclamation of the First Republic. The violence of the revolution, attacks by other nations, and bitter factional struggles, riots, and counterrevolutionary uprisings consumed the republic. This helped bring the extremists to power, and the bloody Reign of Terror followed. French armies then succeeded in holding off their foreign enemies and one of the generals, ◊Napoleon Bonaparte, seized power 1799.

On May 5, 1789, after the monarchy had attempted to increase taxation and control of affairs, the ◊States General (three "estates" of nobles, clergy, and commons) met at Versailles to try to establish some constitutional controls. Divisions within the States General led to the formation of a National Assembly by the third (commons) estate June 17. Repressive measures by ◊Louis XVI led to the storming of the ◊Bastille by the Paris mob July 14, 1789.

On June 20, 1791 the royal family attempted to escape from the control of the Assembly, but Louis XVI was brought back a prisoner from Varennes and forced to accept a new constitution. War with Austria after April 20, 1792 threatened to undermine the revolution, but on Aug 10 the mob stormed the royal palace, and on Sept 21 the First French Republic was proclaimed.

On Jan 21, 1793 Louis XVI was executed. The moderate ◊Girondins were overthrown June 2 by the ◊Jacobins, and control of the country was passed to the infamous Committee of Public Safety, and ◊Robespierre. The mass executions of the Reign of Terror (see ◊Terror, Reign of) began Sept 5, and the excesses led to the overthrow of the Committee and Robespierre July 27, 1794. The Directory was established to hold a middle course between royalism and Jacobinism. It ruled until Napoleon seized power 1799 as dictator.

French revolutionary calendar the French Revolution 1789 was initially known as the 1st Year of Liberty. When the monarchy was abolished on Sept 21, 1792, the 4th year became 1st Year of the Republic. This calendar was formally adopted in Oct 1793 but its usage was backdated to Sept 22, 1793, which became 1 Vendémiaire. The calendar was discarded from Jan 1, 1806.

French Somaliland former name, until 1967, of ◊Djibouti, in E Africa.

French Sudan former name (1898–1959) of ◊Mali.

French West Africa group of French colonies administered from Dakar 1895–1958. They are now Senegal, Mauritania, Sudan, Burkina Faso, Guinea, Niger, Ivory Coast, and Benin.

Freneau Philip Morin 1752–1832. US poet whose *A Political Litany* 1775 was a mock prayer for deliverance from British tyranny.

His other works include *The British Prison-Ship* 1781, about his experiences as a British prisoner. He was a professional journalist, the first in the US.

frequency in physics, the number of periodic oscillations, vibrations, or waves occurring per unit of time. The unit of frequency is the hertz (Hz), one hertz being equivalent to one cycle per second. Human beings can hear sounds from objects vibrating in the range 20–15,000 Hz. Ultrasonic frequencies well above 15,000 Hz can be detected by mammals such as bats.

frequency modulation see ◊FM.

Frere John 1740–1807. English archeologist, a pioneering discoverer of Old Stone Age (Paleolithic) tools in association with large extinct animals at Hoxne, Suffolk, in 1790. He suggested (long before Charles Darwin) that they predated the conventional biblical timescale. Frere was high sheriff of Suffolk and member of Parliament for Norwich.

fresco mural painting technique using water-based paint on wet plaster. Some of the earliest frescoes (about 1750–1400 BC) were found in Knossos, Crete (now preserved in the Heraklion Museum). Fresco reached its finest expression in Italy from the 13th to the 17th centuries. Giotto, Masaccio, Michelangelo, and many other artists worked in the medium.

Fresnel Augustin 1788–1827. French physicist who refined the theory of ◊polarized light. Fresnel realized in 1821 that light waves do not vibrate like sound waves longitudinally, in the direction of their motion, but transversely, at right angles to the direction of the propagated wave.

Fresno city in central California, SE of San Jose, seat of Fresno County. It is the processing and marketing center for the fruits and vegetables of the San Joaquin valley. Industries include glass, machinery, fertilizers, and vending machines; population (1990) 354,200. Fresno was originally a stop on the Central Pacific Railroad.

Freud Anna 1895–1982. Austrian-born founder of child psychoanalysis in the UK. Her work was influenced by the theories of her father, Sigmund Freud. She held that understanding of the stages of psychological development was essential to the treatment of children, and that this knowledge could only be obtained through observation of the child.

Anna Freud and her father left Nazi-controlled Vienna in 1938 and settled in London. There she began working in a Hampstead nursery. In 1947 she founded the Hampstead Child Therapy Course and Clinic, which specialized in the treatment of children and the training of child therapists.

Freud Sigmund 1865–1939. Austrian physician who pioneered the study of the unconscious mind. He developed the methods of free association and interpretation of dreams that are basic techniques of ◊psychoanalysis, and formulated the concepts of the ◊id, ◊ego, and ◊superego. His books include *Die Traumdeutung/The Interpretation of Dreams* 1900, *Totem and Taboo* 1913, and *Das Unbehagen in der Kultur/Civilization and its Discontents* 1930.

Freud studied medicine in Vienna and was a member of the research team that discovered the local anesthetic effects of cocaine. From 1885 to 1886 he studied hypnosis in Paris under the French physiologist ◊Charcot and 1889 in Nancy under two of Charcot's opponents. From 1886 to 1938 he had a private practice in Vienna, and his theories and writings drew largely on case studies of his own patients, who were mainly upper-middle class, middle-aged women. He was also influenced by the research into hysteria of the Viennese physician ◊Breuer. In the early 1900s a group of psychoanalysts gathered around Freud. Some of these later broke away and formed their own schools: Alfred ◊Adler in 1911 and Carl ◊Jung in 1913. Following the Nazi occupation of Austria in 1938, Freud left for London, where he died.

The word "psychoanalysis" was, like much of its terminology, coined by Freud, and many terms have passed into popular usage, not without distortion. The way that unconscious forces influence people's thoughts and actions was Freud's discovery, and his theory of the repression of infantile sexuality as the root of neuroses in the adult (as in the ◊Oedipus complex) was controversial. Later he also stressed the significance of aggressive drives. His work has changed the way people think about human nature. His theories have brought about a more open approach to sexual matters; antisocial behavior is now understood to result in many cases from unconscious forces, and these new concepts have led to wider expression of the human condition in art and literature. Nevertheless, Freud's theories have caused disagreement among psychologists and psychiatrists, and his methods of psychoanalysis cannot be applied in every case.

Freya or *Frigga* in Scandinavian mythology, wife of Odin and mother of Thor, goddess of married love and the hearth. Friday is named after her.

friar a monk of any order, but originally the title of members of the mendicant (begging) orders, the chief of which were the Franciscans or Minors (Gray Friars), the Dominicans or Preachers (Black Friars), the Carmelites (White Friars), and Augustinians (Austin Friars).

friction in physics, the force that opposes the relative motion of two bodies in contact. The *coefficient of friction* is the ratio of the force required to achieve this relative motion to the force pressing the two bodies together.

Friction is greatly reduced by the use of lubricants such as oil, grease, and graphite. Air bearings are now used to minimize friction in high-speed rotational machinery. In other instances friction is deliberately increased by making the surfaces rough—for example, brake linings, driving belts, soles of shoes, and tires.

Friedan Betty 1921– . US liberal feminist. Her book *The Feminine Mystique* 1963 started the contemporary women's movement, both in the US and the UK. She was a founder of the National Organization for Women (NOW)

1966 (and its president 1966–70), the National Women's Political Caucus 1971, and the First Women's Bank 1973. Friedan also helped to organize the Women's Strike for Equality 1970 and called the First International Feminist Congress 1973.

Born in Peoria, Illinois, her other works include *It Changed My Life* 1976 and *The Second Stage* 1981, a call for a change of direction in the movement.

Friedman Milton 1912– . US economist. The foremost exponent of ⊅monetarism, he argued that a country's economy, and hence inflation, can be controlled through its money supply, although most governments lack the "political will" to control inflation by cutting government spending and thereby increasing unemployment. He was awarded the Nobel Prize for Economics 1976.

Friedman argued for extending private choice among competing businesses into virtually all spheres of economic life. He suggested, for example, that the public school system be abolished and that parents pay to send their children to the school of their choosing. He was an influential adviser to presidents Nixon and Reagan and wrote several books.

Friedrich German form of ⊅Frederick.

Friedrich Caspar David 1774–1840. German Romantic landscape painter, active mainly in Dresden. He imbued his subjects—mountain scenes and moonlit seas—with poetic melancholy and was later admired by Symbolist painters.

Friendly Islands another name for ⊅Tonga.

Friends of the Earth (FoE or FOE) environmental pressure group, established in the UK 1971, that aims to protect the environment and to promote rational and sustainable use of the Earth's resources. It campaigns on issues such as acid rain; air, sea, river, and land pollution; recycling; disposal of toxic wastes; nuclear power and renewable energy; the destruction of rainforests; pesticides; and agriculture. FoE has branches in 30 countries.

Friends, Society of or *Quakers* Christian Protestant sect founded by George ⊅Fox in England in the 17th century. They were persecuted for their nonviolent activism, and many emigrated to form communities elsewhere, for example in Pennsylvania and New England. They now form a worldwide movement of about 200,000. Their worship stresses meditation and the freedom of all to take an active part in the service (called a meeting, held in a meeting house). They have no priests or ministers.

The name "Quakers" may originate in Fox's injunction to "quake at the word of the Lord." Originally marked out by their sober dress and use of "thee" and "thou" to all as a sign of equality, they incurred penalties by their pacifism and refusal to take oaths or pay tithes. In the 19th century many Friends were prominent in social reform, for example, Elizabeth ⊅Fry.

Quakers have exerted a profound influence on American life through their pacifism and belief in social equality, education, and prison reform.

Friesland maritime province of the N Netherlands, which includes the Frisian Islands and land that is still being reclaimed from the former Zuyder Zee; the inhabitants of the province are called ⊅Frisians
area 1,312 sq mi/3,400 sq km
population (1990) 600,000

cities capital Leeuwarden; Drachten, Harlingen, Sneek, Heerenveen
products livestock (Fresian cattle originated here), dairy products, small boats
history ruled as a county of the Holy Roman Empire during the Middle Ages, Friesland passed to Saxony in 1498 and, after a revolt, to Charles V of Spain. In 1579 it subscribed to the Treaty of Utrecht, opposing Spanish rule. In 1748 its stadholder, Prince William IV of Orange, became stadholder of all the United Provinces of the Netherlands.

frigate escort warship smaller than a destroyer. Before 1975 the term referred to a warship larger than a destroyer but smaller than a light cruiser. In the 18th and 19th centuries a frigate was a small, fast sailing warship.

fringe benefit in employment, payment in kind over and above wages and salaries. These may include a pension, subsidized lunches, company car, favorable loan facilities, and health insurance. Fringe benefits may, in part, be subject to income tax.

fringing reef ⊅coral reef that is attached to the coast without an intervening lagoon.

Frisch Karl von 1886–1982. Austrian zoologist, founder with Konrad ⊅Lorenz of ⊅ethology, the study of animal behavior. He specialized in bees, discovering how they communicate the location of sources of nectar by movements called "dances." He was awarded the Nobel Prize for Medicine 1973 together with Lorenz and Nikolaas ⊅Tinbergen.

Frisch Otto 1904–1979. Austrian physicist who coined the term "nuclear fission." A refugee from Nazi Germany, he worked from 1943 on the atomic bomb at Los Alamos, New Mexico, and later at Cambridge, England. He was the nephew of Lise ⊅Meitner.

Frisch Ragnar 1895–1973. Norwegian economist, pioneer of ⊅econometrics (the application of mathematical and statistical methods in economics). He shared the first Nobel Prize for Economics in 1969 with Jan ⊅Tinbergen.

Frisch–Peierls memorandum a document revealing, for the first time, how small the critical mass (the minimum quantity of substance required for a nuclear chain reaction to begin) of uranium needed to be if the isotope uranium-235 was separated from naturally occurring uranium; the memo thus implied the feasibility of using this isotope to make an atomic bomb. It was written by Otto Frisch and Rudolf Peierls (1907–) at the University of Birmingham 1940.

Frisian or *Friesian* member of a Germanic people of NW Europe (Friesland and the Frisian Islands). In Roman times they occupied the coast of Holland and may have taken part in the Anglo-Saxon invasions of Britain. Their language is closely akin to Anglo-Saxon, with which it forms the Anglo-Frisian branch of the West Germanic languages, part of the Indo-European family.

The Frisian language is almost extinct in the German districts of East Friesland, but it has attained some literary importance in the North Frisian Islands and Schleswig and developed a considerable literature in the West Frisian dialect of the Dutch province of Friesland.

Frisian Islands chain of low-lying islands 3–20 mi/5–32 km off the NW coasts of the Netherlands and Germany, with a northerly extension off the W coast of Denmark. They were formed by the sinking of the intervening land. *Texel* is the largest and westernmost island.

fritillary in botany, any plant of the genus *Fritillaria* of the lily family Liliaceae. The snake's head fritillary *F. meleagris* has bell-shaped flowers with purple-checkered markings.

fritillary in zoology, any of a large grouping of butterflies of the family Nymphalidae. Mostly medium-sized, fritillaries are usually orange and reddish with a black criss-cross pattern or spots above and with silvery spots on the underside of the hindwings. They take their name from the Latin word *fritillus* ("dice box") because of their spotted markings.

Friuli-Venezia Giulia autonomous agricultural and wine-growing region of NE Italy, bordered to the E by Slovenia; area 3,011 sq mi/ 7,800 sq km; population (1990) 1,201,000. Cities includes Udine (the capital), Gorizia, Pordenone, and Trieste.

Formed 1947 from the province of Venetian Friuli and part of Eastern Friuli, to which Trieste was added after its cession to Italy 1954, it was granted autonomy 1963. A Slav minority numbers about 100,000, and in Friuli there is a movement for complete independence.

Frobisher Martin 1535–1594. English navigator. He made his first voyage to Guinea, West Africa, 1554. In 1576 he set out in search of the Northwest Passage, and visited Labrador, and Frobisher Bay, Baffin Island. Second and third expeditions sailed 1577 and 1578.

Froebel Friedrich August Wilhelm 1782–1852. German educationist. He evolved a new system of education using instructive play, described in *Education of Man* 1826 and other works. In 1836 he founded the first kindergarten (German "garden for children") in Blankenburg, Germany. He was influenced by ⊅Pestalozzi.

frog any amphibian of the order Anura (Greek "tailless"). There are no clear rules for distinguishing between frogs and toads. Frogs usually have squat bodies, hind legs specialized for jumping, and webbed feet for swimming. Many frogs use their long, extensible tongues to capture insects. Frogs vary in size from the tiny North American little grass frog *Limnaoedus ocularis*, 0.5 in/12 mm long, to the giant aquatic frog *Telmatobius culeus*, 20 in/50 cm long, of Lake Titicaca, South America.

In many species the males attract the females in great gatherings, usually by croaking. In some tropical species, the male's inflated vocal sac may exceed the rest of his body in size. Other courtship "lures" include thumping on the ground and "dances." Some lay eggs in large masses (spawn) in water. The jelly surrounding the eggs provides support and protection and retains warmth. Some South American frogs build little mud-pool "nests," and African tree frogs make foam nests from secreted mucus. In other species, the eggs may be carried in "pockets" on the mother's back, or brooded by the male in his vocal sac, or, as with the Eurasian midwife toad *Alytes obstetricans*, carried by the male, wrapped round his hind legs until hatching. Certain species of frog have powerful skin poisons (alkaloids) to deter predators.

"True frogs" are placed in the worldwide family Ranidae, of which the genus *Rana* is the best known. The North American bullfrog *Rana catesbeiana*, with a croak that carries for miles, is able to jump nine times its own length (annual jumping competitions are held at Calaveras, California). The flying frogs, genus

Rhacophorus, of Malaysia, using webbed fore and hind feet, can achieve a 40 ft/12 m glide.

froghopper or *spittlebug* leaping plant-bug, of the family Cercopidae, in the same order (Homoptera) as leafhoppers and aphids. Froghoppers live by sucking the juice from plants. The pale green larvae protect themselves (from drying out and from predators) by secreting froth ("cuckoo spit") from their anuses.

frogmouth nocturnal bird, related to the nightjar, of which the commonest species, the tawny frogmouth *Podargus strigoides*, is found throughout Australia, including Tasmania. Well camouflaged, it sits and awaits its prey.

Fromm Erich 1900–1980. German psychoanalyst who moved to the US 1933 to escape the Nazis. Hiis *The Fear of Freedom* 1941 and *The Sane Society* 1955 were source books for alternative lifestyles.

Fromm stressed the role of culture in the formation of personality, a view that distinguished him from traditional psychoanalysts. He also described the authoritarian personality, an important concept in the study of personality.

frond large leaf or leaflike structure; in ferns it is often pinnately divided. The term is also applied to the leaves of palms and less commonly to the plant bodies of certain seaweeds, liverworts, and lichens.

Fronde French revolts 1648–53 against the administration of the chief minister ◊Mazarin during Louis XIV's minority. In 1648–49 the Paris *parlement* attempted to limit the royal power, its leaders were arrested, Paris revolted, and the rising was suppressed by the royal army under Louis II Condé. In 1650 Condé led a new revolt of the nobility, but this was suppressed by 1653. The defeat of the Fronde enabled Louis to establish an absolutist monarchy in the later 17th century.

front in meteorology, the boundary between two air masses of different temperature or humidity. A *cold front* marks the line of advance of a cold air mass from below, as it displaces a warm air mass; a *warm front* marks the advance of a warm air mass as it rises up over a cold one.

Warm air, being lighter, tends to rise above the cold; its moisture is carried upward and usually falls as rain or snow, hence the changeable weather conditions at fronts. Fronts are rarely stable and move with the air mass. An *occluded front* is a composite form, where a cold front overtakes a warm front, lifting warm air above the Earth's surface. An *inversion* occurs when the normal properties get reversed; this happens when a layer of air traps another near the surface, preventing the normal rising of surface air. Warm temperatures and pollution result from inversions.

frontal lobotomy an operation on the brain. See ◊lobotomy.

Frontenac et Palluau Louis de Buade, Comte de Frontenac et Palluau 1622–1698. French colonial governor. He began his military career 1635, and was appointed governor of the French possessions in North America 1672. Although efficient, he quarrelled with the local bishop and his followers and was recalled 1682. After the Iroquois, supported by the English, won several military victories, Frontenac was reinstated 1689. He defended Québec against the English 1690 and defeated the Iroquois 1696.

frontier literature writing reflecting the US experience of frontier and pioneer life, long central to US literature. The category includes James Fenimore Cooper's *Leatherstocking Tales*; the frontier humor writing of Artemus Ward, Bret Harte, and Mark Twain; dime novels; westerns; the travel records of Francis Parkman; and the pioneer romances of Willa Cather. Much modern American writing has been influenced by the frontier theme.

front-line states the black nations of southern Africa in the "front line" of the struggle against the segregationist policies of South Africa: Mozambique, Tanzania, and Zambia, as well as Botswana and Zimbabwe.

frost condition of the weather that occurs when the air temperature is below freezing, 32°F/0°C. Water in the atmosphere is deposited as ice crystals on the ground or exposed objects. As cold air is heavier than warm, ground frost is more common than hoar frost, which is formed by the condensation of water particles in the same way that ◊dew collects.

Frost Robert (Lee) 1874–1963. US poet whose verse, in traditional form, is written with an individual voice and penetrating vision. His poems include "Mending Wall" ("Something there is that does not love a wall"), "The Road Not Taken," and "Stopping by Woods on a Snowy Evening" and are collected in *A Boy's Will* 1913, *North of Boston* 1914, *New Hampshire* 1924, *Collected Poems* 1930, *A Further Range* 1936, and *A Witness Tree* 1942.

Born in San Francisco, Frost was raised in New England, where he attended Dartmouth College and Harvard University for brief periods. He was awarded four Pulitzer prizes (1924, 1931, 1937, 1943) and in 1961 read his "The Gift Outright" at the inauguration of J F Kennedy.

frostbite the freezing of skin or flesh, with formation of ice crystals leading to tissue damage. The treatment is slow warming of the affected area; for example, by skin-to-skin contact or with lukewarm water. Frostbitten parts are extremely vulnerable to infection, with the risk of gangrene.

fructose $C_6H_{12}O_6$ a sugar that occurs naturally in honey, the nectar of flowers, and many sweet fruits; it is commercially prepared from glucose.

It is a monosaccharide, whereas the more familiar cane or beet sugar is a disaccharide, made up of two monosaccharide units: fructose and glucose. It is sweeter than cane sugar.

fruit (from Latin *frui* "to enjoy") in botany, the ripened ovary in flowering plants that develops from one or more seeds or carpels and encloses one or more seeds. Its function is to protect the seeds during their development and to aid in their dispersal. Fruits are often edible, sweet, juicy, and colorful. When eaten they provide vitamins, minerals, and enzymes, but little protein. Most fruits are borne by perennial plants. When fruits are eaten by animals the seeds pass through the alimentary canal unharmed, and are passed out with the feces.

Fruits are divided into three agricultural categories on the basis of the climate in which they grow. *Temperate fruits* require a cold season for satisfactory growth; the principal temperate fruits are apples, pears, plums, peaches, apricots, cherries, and soft fruits, such as strawberries. *Subtropical fruits* require warm conditions but can survive light frosts; they include oranges and other citrus fruits, dates, pomegranates, and avocados.

Tropical fruits cannot tolerate temperatures that drop close to freezing point; they include bananas, mangoes, pineapples, papayas, and litchis.

Fruits can also be divided botanically into *dry* (such as the ◊capsule, ◊follicle, ◊schizocarp, ◊nut, ◊caryopsis, pod or legume, ◊lomentum, and ◊achene) and those that become *fleshy* (such as the ◊drupe and the ◊berry).

The fruit structure consists of the ◊pericarp or fruit wall, which is usually divided into a number of distinct layers. Sometimes parts other than the ovary are incorporated into the fruit structure, resulting in a false fruit or ◊pseudocarp, such as the apple and strawberry. Fruits may be dehiscent, which open to shed their seeds, or indehiscent, which remain unopened and are dispersed as a single unit.

Simple fruits (for example, peaches) are derived from a single ovary, whereas compositae or multiple fruits (for example, blackberries) are formed from the ovaries of a number of flowers.

In ordinary usage, "fruit" includes only sweet, fleshy items; it excludes many botanical fruits such as acorns, bean pods, thistledown, and cucumbers (see ◊vegetable).

Recorded world fruit production in the mid-1980s was approximately 300 million tons per year. Technical advances in storage and transport have made tropical fruits available to consumers in temperate areas, and fresh temperate fruits available all year in major markets.

Frunze (formerly *Pishpek*) former name (1926–92) of ◊Bishkek in Kyrgyzstan.

frustule the cell wall of a ◊diatom (microscopic alga). Frustules are intricately patterned on the surface with spots, ridges, and furrows, each pattern being characteristic of a particular species.

frustum (from Latin for "a piece cut off") in geometry, a "slice" taken out of a solid figure by a pair of parallel planes. A conical frustum, for example, resembles a cone with the top cut off. The volume and area of a frustum are calculated by subtracting the volume or area

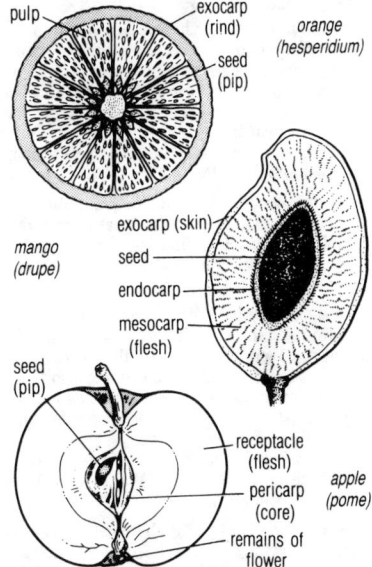

fruit *A fruit contains the seeds of a plant.*

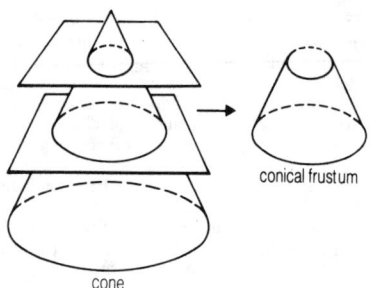

frustum *The frustum, a slice of a cone.*

of the "missing" piece from those of the whole figure.

Fry Christopher 1907– . English dramatist. He was a leader of the revival of verse drama after World War II with *The Lady's Not for Burning* 1948, *Venus Observed* 1950, and *A Sleep of Prisoners* 1951.

FSH abbreviation for ⟡*follicle-stimulating hormone*.

f-stop in photography, one of a series of numbers on the lens barrel designating the size of the variable aperture; it stands for the focal length and follows an internationally accepted scale.

ft symbol for ⟡*foot*, a measure of distance.

Fuad two kings of Egypt:

Fuad I 1868–1936. King of Egypt from 1922. Son of the Khedive Ismail, he succeeded his elder brother Hussein Kiamil as sultan of Egypt 1917; when Egypt was declared independent 1922 he assumed the title of king.

Fuad II 1952– . King of Egypt 1952–53, between the abdication of his father ⟡Farouk and the establishment of the republic. He was a grandson of Fuad I.

Fuchs Klaus (Emil Julius) 1911–1988. German spy who worked on atom-bomb research in the US in World War II, and subsequently in the UK. He was imprisoned 1950–59 for passing information to the USSR and resettled in eastern Germany.

fuchsia any shrub or herbaceous plant of the genus *Fuchsia* of the evening-primrose family Onagraceae. Species are native to South and Central America and New Zealand, and bear red, purple, or pink bell-shaped flowers that hang downward.

The genus was named in 1703 after German botanist Leonhard Fuchs (1501–66).

fuel any source of heat or energy, embracing the entire range of materials that burn (combustibles). A *nuclear fuel* is any material that produces energy by nuclear fission in a nuclear reactor.

fuel-air explosive warhead containing a highly flammable petroleum and oxygen mixture; when released over a target, this mixes with the oxygen in the atmosphere and produces a vapor which, when ignited, causes a blast approximately five times more powerful than conventional high explosives.

Fuel-air explosives were used by the US Air Force in the 1991 Gulf War against Iraqi defensive positions.

fuel cell cell converting chemical energy directly to electrical energy. It works on the same principle as a battery but is continually fed with fuel, usually hydrogen. Fuel cells are silent and reliable (no moving parts) but expensive to produce.

Hydrogen is passed over an ⟡electrode (usually nickel or platinum) containing a ⟡catalyst, which strips electrons off the atoms. These pass through an external circuit while hydrogen ions (charged atoms) pass through an ⟡electrolyte to another electrode, over which oxygen is passed. Water is formed at this electrode (as a by-product) in a chemical reaction involving electrons, hydrogen ions, and oxygen atoms. If the spare heat also produced is used for hot water and space heating, 80% efficiency in fuel is achieved.

fuel injection injecting fuel directly into the cylinders of an internal combustion engine, instead of by way of a carburetor. It is the standard method used in ⟡diesel engines, and is now becoming standard for gasoline engines. In the diesel engine oil is injected into the hot compressed air at the top of the second piston stroke and explodes to drive the piston down on its power stroke. In the gasoline engine, fuel is injected into the cylinder at the start of the first induction stroke of the ⟡four-stroke cycle.

Fuentes Carlos 1928– . Mexican novelist, lawyer, and diplomat whose first novel *La región más transparente/Where the Air Is Clear* 1958 encompasses the history of the country from the Aztecs to the present day.

More than other Mexican novelists he presents the frustrated social philosophy of the failed Mexican revolution. He received international attention for *The Death of Artemeo Cruz* 1962, *Terra nostra* 1975, and *El Gringo veijo/The Old Gringo* 1985. *The Campaign* 1991 is set during the revolutionary wars leading to independence in Latin America.

fugue (Latin "flight") in music, a contrapuntal form (with two or more melodies) for a number of parts or "voices," which enter successively in imitation of each other. It was raised to a high art by J S ⟡Bach.

Führer or *Fuehrer* title adopted by Adolf ⟡Hitler as leader of the Nazi Party.

Fujairah or *Fujayrah* one of the seven constituent member states of the ⟡United Arab Emirates; area 450 sq mi/1,150 sq km; population (1985) 54,000.

Fujian or *Fukien* province of SE China, bordering Taiwan Strait, opposite Taiwan
area 47,517 sq mi/123,100 sq km
capital Fuzhou
physical dramatic mountainous coastline
features being developed for tourists; designated as a pace-setting province for modernization 1980
products sugar, rice, special aromatic teas, tobacco, timber, fruit
population (1990) 30,048,000

Fujimori Alberto 1939– . President of Peru from July 1990. As leader of the newly formed Cambio 90 (Change 90) he campaigned on a reformist ticket and defeated his more experienced Democratic Front opponent. With no assembly majority, and faced with increasing opposition to his policies, he imposed military rule early in 1992.

Fujiwara in Japanese history, the ruling clan 858–1185. During that period, the office of emperor became merely ceremonial, with power exercised by chancellors and regents, who were all Fujiwara and whose daughters in every generation married into the imperial family. There was a Fujiwara in Japanese government as recently as during World War II.

The name Fujiwara dates from 669; the family claimed divine descent. The son of the first Fujiwara became a minister and the grandfather of an emperor, and as this pattern repeated itself for centuries, the clan accumulated wealth and power through the control of government appointments. The reigning emperors were often under age, since it was common to retire from office after a few years; those emperors who were interested in politics then operated from behind the throne ("cloistered emperors") and these to some extent countered the Fujiwara dominance. Many Fujiwara were also prominent in literature and scholarship.

In 1868, when the last shogun had been ousted, it was a Fujiwara that the Meiji emperor appointed to the highest government post.

Fujiyama or *Mount Fuji* Japanese volcano and highest peak, on Honshu Island, near Tokyo; height 12,400 ft/3,778 m. Extinct since 1707, it has a ⟡Shinto shrine and a weather station on its summit. Fuji has long been revered for its picturesque cone-shaped crater peak, and figures prominently in Japanese art, literature, and religion.

Fukien alternative transcription of ⟡Fujian, a province of SE China.

Fula W African empire founded by people of predominantly Fulani extraction. The Fula conquered the Hausa states in the 19th century.

Fulani member of a W African culture from the southern Sahara and Sahel. Traditionally nomadic pastoralists and traders, Fulani groups are found in Senegal, Guinea, Mali, Burkina Faso, Niger, Nigeria, Chad, and Cameroon. The Fulani language is divided into four dialects and belongs to the W Atlantic branch of the Niger-Congo family; it has more than 10 million speakers.

Fulbright (James) William 1905– . US Democratic politician. A US senator 1945–75, he was responsible for the *Fulbright Act* 1946, which provided grants for thousands of Americans to study abroad and for overseas students to study in the US. Fulbright chaired the Senate Foreign Relations Committee 1959–74, and was a strong internationalist and supporter of the ⟡United Nations.

Born in Sumner, Missouri, Fulbright studied abroad at Oxford University on a Rhodes scholarship. He served in the US House of Representatives 1942–45 before becoming a senator. He anticipated the creation of the ⟡United Nations, calling for US membership in an international peacekeeping body. He was an advocate of military and economic aid to Western nations but a powerful critic of US involvement in the ⟡Vietnam War.

Fuller (Richard) Buckminster 1895–1983. US architect, engineer, and futurist social philosopher who embarked on an unorthodox career in an attempt to maximize energy resources through improved technology. In 1947 he invented the lightweight geodesic dome, a half-sphere of triangular components independent of buttress or vault.

He also invented a Dymaxion (a combination of the words "dynamics" and "maximum") house 1928 and car 1933 that was inexpensive and utilized his concept of using the least amount of energy output to gain maximum interior space and efficiency, respectively.

Among his books are *Ideas and Integrities* 1963, *Utopia or Oblivion* 1969, and *Critical Path* 1981.

Fuller Margaret 1810–1850. US author and reformer. Born in Cambridge, Massachusetts, and tutored by her father, Fuller began adult life as a teacher and writer. From 1839 to 1844, she held public "conversations" for the edification of the women of Boston; during the same period, she became the editor of *The Dial*, the Transcendentalist magazine. Fuller was hired as the literary critic for the *New York Tribune* 1844; later, while on assignment in Italy, she met and married the Marchese Angelo Ossoli and joined Mazzini's doomed nationalist revolt. She was lost at sea while returning to the US 1850.

Fuller Melville Weston 1833–1910. US jurist and chief justice of the US Supreme Court 1888–1910. As chief justice, Fuller generally supported a conservative approach, endorsing court options that limited state and federal strengths to regulate private business, limiting the jurisdiction of the Supreme Court, and in *United States* v *E C Knight Co* 1895, the application of the new Sherman Antitrust Act. He sided with the majority of the Court in *Pollack* v *Farmers Loan and Trust Co* 1895, which held invalid a flat-rate US income tax and led to passage of the 16th Amendment to the Constitution in 1913, authorizing an income tax.

Fuller was born in Augusta, Maine. He followed an early career in law and Democratic politics in Maine and then continued his activities in Chicago 1856. He was a supporter of Stephen Douglas in his 1858 election as US senator and in his bid for the presidency 1860. Fuller supported Grover Cleveland in the 1884 presidential election and was appointed chief justice by Cleveland in 1888.

fullerene form of carbon, discovered 1985, based on closed cages of carbon atoms. The molecules of the most symmetrical of the fullerenes are called buckminsterfullerenes. They are perfect spheres made up of 60 carbon atoms linked together in 12 pentagons and 20 hexagons fitted together like those of a spherical football. Other fullerenes are C_{28}, C_{32}, C_{50}, and C_{70}.

Fullerenes can be made by arcing electricity between carbon rods. They may also occur in candle flames, and in clouds of interstellar gas. Fullerene chemistry may turn out to be as important as organic chemistry based on the benzene ring. Already, new molecules based on the buckyball enclosing a metal atom, and "buckytubes" (cylinders of carbon atoms arranged in hexagons), have been made. Applications envisaged include using the new molecules as lubricants, semiconductors, superconductors and as the starting point for making new drugs.

fuller's earth a soft, greenish-gray rock resembling clay, but without clay's plasticity. It is formed largely of clay minerals, rich in montmorillonite, but a great deal of silica is also present. Its absorbent properties make it suitable for removing oil and grease, and it was formerly used for cleaning fleeces ("fulling"). It is still used in the textile industry, but its chief application is in the purification of oils. Beds of fuller's earth are found in the southern USA, Germany, Japan, and the UK.

Fullilove v Klutznick a US Supreme Court decision 1980 dealing with the constitutionality of Congressional legislation allocating a certain percentage of public works contracts to minority-owned businesses. Fullilove, a

white business owner, filed suit against the government, arguing that the Public Works Employment Act, a bill that required states to use at least 10% of federal public works funds to hire minority businesses, was racially discriminatory. The Court found that the act was not a violation of the 14th Amendment but a remedial measure intended to enforce the equal protection clause. Congress, according to a 6–3 decision, was within its rights to use control over federal funds for the legitimate goal of reversing racial discrimination.

fulmar any of several species of petrels of the family Procellariidae, which are similar in size and color to herring gulls. The northern fulmar *Fulmarus glacialis* is found in the N Atlantic and visits land only to nest, laying a single egg.

Fulton Robert 1745–1815. US gunsmith, artist, engineer, and inventor who designed steamships based on those invented by James Rumsey 1787 and John Fitch 1790. He managed to acquire British steam engines to power his first vessels, although at the time the British were not selling to the newly independent US. Fulton had lived 20 years in Europe, 1786–1805, and was well known as a painter and as an engineer of naval technology and canals; with the support of the new French government 1801, he built the first submarine, the *Nautilus*. He returned to the US with a commission from Robert Livingston, who had a license to serve the Hudson by steamboat, and combined the British-built steam engine with his own design of riverboat, a sidewheeler, and registered it as the *North River Steam Boat* 1807 (now erroneously known as the *Clermont*, a stop on the river). It and others were established and maintained by Fulton, going from New York City to Albany. Fulton also designed and oversaw the building of the first steam-powered warship, the USS *Fulton*, for the new US Navy.

fumitory any plant of the genus *Fumeria*, family Fumariaceae, native to Europe and Asia. The common fumitory *F. officinalis* grows to 20 in/ 50 cm tall, and produces pink flowers tipped with blackish red; it has been used in medicine for stomach and liver complaints.

Funafuti atoll consisting of 30 islets in the W Pacific and capital of the state of ◊Tuvalu; area 1.1 sq mi/2.8 sq km; population 900.

Funchal capital and chief port of the Portuguese island of Madeira, on the south coast; population (1980) 100,000. Tourism and wine are the main industries.

function in computing, a small part of a program that supplies a specific value–for example, the square root of a specified number, or the current date. Most programming languages incorporate a number of built-in functions; some allow programmers to write their own. A function may have one or more arguments (the values on which the function operates). A *function key* on a keyboard is one that, when pressed, performs a designated task, such as ending a program.

function in mathematics, a function *f* is a nonempty set of ordered pairs $(x, f(x))$ of which no two can have the same first element. Hence, if $f(x) = x^2$, two ordered pairs are (–2,4) and (2,4). The set of all first elements in a function's ordered pairs is called the *domain*; the set of all second elements is the *range*. In the algebraic expression $y = 4x^3 + 2$, the dependent variable *y* is a function of the independent variable *x*, generally written as $f(x)$.

Functions are used in all branches of mathematics, physics, and science generally; for

example, the formula $t = 2\pi\sqrt{(l/g)}$ shows that for a simple pendulum the time of swing *t* is a function of its length *l* and of no other variable quantity (π and *g*, the acceleration due to gravity, are ◊constants).

functional group in chemistry, a small number of atoms in an arrangement that determines the chemical properties of the group and of the molecule to which it is attached (for example, the carboxyl group COOH, or the amine group NH_2). Organic compounds can be considered as structural skeletons, with a high carbon content, with functional groups attached.

functionalism in the social sciences, the view of society as a system made up of a number of interrelated parts, all interacting on the basis of a common value system or consensus about basic values and common goals. Every social custom and institution is seen as having a function in ensuring that society works efficiently; deviance and crime are seen as forms of social sickness.

Functionalists often describe society as an organism with a life of its own, above and beyond the sum of its members. The French sociologists Comte and ◊Durkheim and the American ◊Parsons assumed functionalist approaches for their studies.

Functionalism in architecture and design, a 20th-century school, also called Modernism or International Style, characterized by the ideal of excluding everything that serves no practical purpose. It developed as a reaction against the 19th-century practice of imitating and combining earlier styles, and its finest achievements are in the realm of industrial architecture and office furnishings.

Its leading exponents were the German ◊Bauhaus school, the Dutch group de ◊Stijl, and the Scandinavians, especially the Swedish and Finnish designers. Prominent architects in the field were Le Corbusier and Walter ◊Gropius.

fundamental constant physical quantity that is constant in all circumstances throughout the whole universe. Examples are the electric charge of an electron, the speed of light, Planck's constant, and the gravitational constant.

fundamental forces in physics, the four fundamental interactions believed to be at work in the physical universe. There are two long-range forces: *gravity*, which keeps the planets in orbit around the Sun, and acts between all ◊particles that have mass; and the *electromagnetic force*, which stops solids from falling apart, and acts between all particles with ◊electric charge. There are two very short-range forces: the *weak force*, responsible for radioactive decay and for other subatomic reactions; and the *strong force*, which binds together the protons and neutrons in the nuclei of atoms.

By 1971, Steven Weinberg and Sheldon Glashow (US), Abdus Salam (UK), and others developed a theory that suggested that the weak and electromagnetic forces were linked; experimental support came from observation at ◊CERN in the 1980s. Physicists are now working on theories to unify all four forces. See ◊supersymmetry.

fundamentalism in religion, an emphasis on basic principles or articles of faith. *Christian fundamentalism* emerged in the US just after World War I (as a reaction to theological

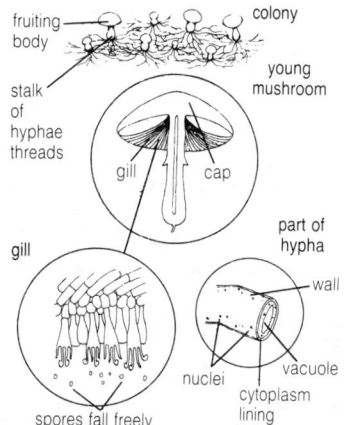

fruiting body / colony / young mushroom / stalk of hyphae threads / gill / cap / gill / part of hypha / wall / nuclei / vacuole / cytoplasm lining / spores fall freely

fungus

modernism and the historical criticism of the Bible) and insisted on belief in the literal truth of everything in the Bible. *Islamic fundamentalism* insists on strict observance of Muslim Shari'a law.

Christian adherents see the virgin birth, the physical resurrection of Jesus, the atonement, and the Bible miracles as fundamental to their faith. The movement soon became more belligerent, attempting to outlaw the teaching of evolution (as in Dayton, Tennessee, 1925) and replace it with ▷creationism.

In the 1950s a more moderate tendency broke off to form the evangelical movement, which claims to carry on the original intentions of Fundamentalism.

fundamental particle another term for ▷*elementary particle*.

Fundy, Bay of Canadian Atlantic inlet between New Brunswick and Nova Scotia, with a rapid tidal rise and fall of 60 ft/18 m (harnessed for electricity since 1984). In summer, fog increases the dangers to shipping.

fungicide any chemical ▷pesticide used to prevent fungus diseases in plants and animals. Inorganic and organic compounds containing sulfur are widely used.

fungus (plural *fungi*) any of a group of organisms in the kingdom Fungi. Fungi are not considered plants; they lack leaves and roots; they contain no chlorophyll and reproduce by spores. Molds, yeasts, rusts, smuts, mildews, and mushrooms are all types of fungi.

Because fungi have no chlorophyll, they must get food from organic substances. They are either ▷parasites, existing on living plants or animals, or ▷saprotrophs, living on dead matter. Some 50,000 different species have been identified. Some are edible, but many are highly poisonous.

Before the classification Fungi came into use, they were included within the division Thallophyta, along with algae and bacteria.

In 1992 an individual honey fungus, *Armallaria ostoyae*, in Washington State, was identified as the world's largest living thing—estimated to be between 500 and 1,000 years old, its underground network of hyphae covers 1,480 acres/600 hectares.

Funk Casimir 1884–1967. US biochemist, born in Poland, who pioneered research into vitamins.

Funk proposed that certain diseases are caused by dietary deficiencies. In 1912 he demonstrated that rice extracts cure beriberi in pigeons. As the extract contains an ▷amine, he mistakenly concluded that he had discovered a class of "vital amines," a phrase soon reduced to "vitamins."

fur pelts of certain animals. Fur is used as clothing, although this is vociferously criticized by environmental groups on humane grounds, because the methods of breeding or trapping animals are often cruel. Mink, chinchilla, and sable are among the most valuable, the wild furs being finer than the farmed. Fur such as mink is made up of a soft, thick, insulating layer called underfur and a top layer of longer, lustrous guard hairs.

Furs have been worn since prehistoric times and have long been associated with status and luxury (ermine traditionally worn by royalty, for example), except by certain ethnic groups like the Inuit. The fur trade had its origin in North America, exploited by the Hudson's Bay Company from the late 17th century. The chief centers of the fur trade are New York, London, St Petersburg, and Kastoria in Greece. It is illegal to import furs or skins of endangered species listed by ▷CITES, for example the leopard. Many synthetic fibers are widely used as substitutes.

Furies in Greek mythology, the Erinyes, appeasingly called the Eumenides ("kindly ones"). They were the daughters of Earth or of Night, represented as winged maidens with serpents twisted in their hair. They punished such crimes as filial disobedience, murder, and inhospitality.

furlong unit of measurement, originating in Anglo-Saxon England, equivalent to 220 yd (201.168 m).

A furlong consists of 40 rods, poles, or perches; 8 furlongs equal one statute ▷mile. Its literal meaning is "furrow-long," and refers to the length of a furrow in the common field characteristic of medieval farming.

Furman v Georgia (Jackson v Georgia; Branch v Texas) a US Supreme Court decision 1972 consolidating several challenges to the constitutionality of the death penalty. Three men, condemned to death by the states of Georgia and Texas, appealed against their sentences, arguing that their 8th Amendment protection against cruel and unusual punishment had been violated. The Court voted 5–4 to invalidate the sentences, ruling that the death penalty not only violated the 8th Amendment but the 14th as well, since it was meted out unequally to the "poor and despised." The decision affected 600 persons already on death row.

furnace structure in which fuel such as coal, coke, gas, or oil is burned to produce heat for various purposes. Furnaces are used in conjunction with ▷boilers for heating, to produce hot water, or steam for driving turbines—in ships for propulsion and in power stations for generating electricity. The largest furnaces are those used for smelting and refining metals, such as the ▷blast furnace, electric furnace, and ▷open-hearth furnace.

furze another name for ▷gorse, a shrub.

fuse in electricity, a wire or strip of metal designed to melt when excessive current passes

through. It is a safety device to stop at that point in the circuit when surges of current would otherwise damage equipment and cause fires. In explosives, a fuse is a cord impregnated with chemicals so that it burns slowly at a predetermined rate. It is used to set off a main explosive charge, sufficient length of fuse being left to allow the person lighting it to get away to safety.

fusel oil liquid with a characteristic unpleasant smell, obtained as a by-product of the distillation of the product of any alcoholic fermentation, and used in paints, varnishes, essential oils, and plastics. It is a mixture of fatty acids, alcohols, and esters.

fusion in physics, the fusing of the nuclei of light elements, such as hydrogen, into those of a heavier element, such as helium. The resultant loss in their combined mass is converted into energy. Stars and thermonuclear weapons work on the principle of ▷nuclear fusion.

So far no successful fusion reactor—one able to produce the required energy and contain the reaction—has been built. See ▷energy and ▷cold fusion.

future in business, a contract to buy or sell a specific quantity of a particular commodity or currency (or even a purely notional sum, such as the value of a particular stock index) at a particular date in the future. There is usually no physical exchange between buyer and seller. It is only the difference between the ground value and the market value that changes hands. Such transactions are a function of the *futures market*.

futures trading buying and selling commodities (usually cereals and metals) at an agreed price for delivery several months ahead.

Futurism literary and artistic movement 1909–14, originating in Paris. The Italian poet ▷Marinetti published the *Futurist Manifesto* 1909 urging Italian artists to join him in Futurism. In their works the Futurists eulogized the modern world and the "beauty of speed and energy," trying to capture the dynamism of a speeding car or train by combining the shifting geometric planes of ▷Cubism with vibrant colors. As a movement Futurism died out during World War I, but the Futurists' exultation in war and violence was seen as an early manifestation of ▷fascism.

Gino Severini (1883–1966) painted a topsy-turvy landscape as if seen from the window of a moving train, in *Suburban Train Arriving at Paris* 1915 (Tate Gallery, London), and Giacomo Balla (1871–1958) represented the abstract idea of speed by the moving object in such pictures as *Abstract Speed-wake of a Speeding Car* 1919 (Tate Gallery, London). Umberto Boccioni, a sculptor, froze his figures as if they were several frames of a film moving at once.

Fuzhou or *Foochow* industrial port and capital of Fujian province, SE China; population (1989) 1,270,000. It is a center for shipbuilding and steel production; rice, sugar, tea, and fruit pass through the port. There are joint foreign and Chinese factories.

The Mazu (Matsu) island group, occupied by the Nationalist Chinese, is offshore.

Fyn (German *Fünen*) island forming part of Denmark and lying between the mainland and Zealand; capital Odense; area 1,149 sq mi/2,976 sq km; population (1984) 454,000.

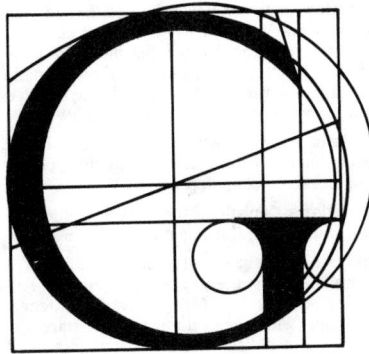

G the seventh letter of the English alphabet. It was formed by the Romans by adding a "tail" to the letter C, which represented the *k* sound.

g symbol for ◇*gram*.

G7 or **Group of Seven** the seven wealthiest nations in the world: the US, Japan, Germany, France, the UK, Italy, and Canada. Since 1975 their heads of government have met once a year to discuss economic and, increasingly, political matters.

GA abbreviation for the state of ◇*Georgia*.

gabbro basic (low-silica) igneous rock formed deep in the Earth's crust. It contains pyroxene and calcium-rich feldspar, and may contain small amounts of olivine and amphibole. Its coarse crystals of dull minerals give it a speckled appearance.

Gabbro is the plutonic version of basalt (that is, derived from magma that has solidified

below the Earth's surface), and forms in large, slow-cooling intrusions.

gabelle in French history, term that originally referred to a tax on various items but came to be used exclusively for a tax on salt, first levied by Philip the Fair in 1286 and abolished 1790.

Gable (William) Clark 1901–1960. US actor. A star for more than 30 years in 90 films, he played romantic roles such as Rhett Butler in *Gone With the Wind* 1939. His other films include *The Painted Desert* 1931 (his first), *It Happened One Night* 1934 (Academy Award), *Mutiny on the Bounty* 1935, and *The Misfits* 1960. He was nicknamed the "King" of Hollywood.

Gabo Naum. Adopted name of Naum Neemia Pevsner 1890–1977. US abstract sculptor, born in Russia. One of the leading exponents of ◇Constructivism, he left the USSR in 1922 for Germany and taught at the Bauhaus in Berlin (a key center of modern design). He lived in Paris and England in the 1930s, then settled in the US in 1946. He was one of the first artists to make kinetic (moving) sculpture and often used transparent colored plastics.

Gabon country in central Africa, bounded N by Cameroon, E and S by the Congo, W by the Atlantic Ocean, and NW by Equatorial Guinea.
government The 1961 constitution, revised in 1967, 1975, and 1981, provides for a president elected by universal suffrage for a seven-year term. As head of both state and government, the president appoints and presides over a prime minister and council of ministers and is also founder and secretary-general of the Gabonese Democratic Party (PDG). There is a single-chamber legislature, the National Assembly, of 120 members, 111 elected and 9 nominated for a five-year term.
history Gabon was colonized by some of its present inhabitants (the Fang and the Omiéné) between the 16th and 18th centuries. Its first European visitors were the Portuguese in the late 15th century. They began a slave trade that lasted almost 400 years. In 1889 Gabon became

part of the French Congo and was a province of French Equatorial Africa from 1908.

Gabon achieved full independence 1960. There were then two main political parties, the Gabonese Democratic Bloc (BDG), led by Léon M'ba, and the Gabonese Democratic and Social Union (UDSG), led by Jean-Hilaire Aubame. Although the two parties were evenly matched in popular support, on independence M'ba became president, and Aubame foreign minister.

In 1964 the BDG wanted the two parties to merge, but the UDSG resisted, and M'ba called a general election. Before the elections M'ba was deposed in a military coup by supporters of Aubame but was restored to office with French help. Aubame was tried and imprisoned for treason. The UDSG was outlawed, and most of its members joined the BDG.
Bongo's presidency In 1964 M'ba, although in failing health, was reelected. He died later that year and was succeeded by Albert-Bernard Bongo who, the following year, established the Gabonese Democratic Party (PDG) as the only legal party. Bongo was reelected 1973 and was converted to Islam, changing his first name to Omar. In 1979 Bongo, as the sole presidential candidate, was reelected for a further seven years.

Gabon's reserves of uranium, manganese, and iron make it the richest country per head in Black Africa, and both M'ba and Bongo have successfully exploited these resources, gaining control of the iron-ore ventures once half-owned by the Bethlehem Steel Corporation of the US, and concluding economic and technical agreements with China as well as maintaining ties with France. Although President Bongo has operated an authoritarian regime, Gabon's prosperity has diluted any serious opposition to him. He was reelected Nov 1986, and a coup attempt against him 1989 was defeated by loyal troops. In Sept 1990 the first multiparty elections since 1964 were won by PDG despite claims of widespread fraud, with 553 candidates contesting 120 assembly seats. *See illustration box.*

Gabor Dennis 1900–1979. Hungarian-born British physicist. In 1947 he invented the holographic method of three-dimensional photography (see ◇holography). He was awarded a Nobel Prize 1971.

Gaborone capital of Botswana from 1965, mainly an administrative center; population (1989) 120,200. Light industry includes textiles.

Gabriel in the New Testament, the archangel who foretold the birth of John the Baptist to Zacharias and of Jesus to the Virgin Mary. He is also mentioned in the Old Testament in the book of Daniel. In Muslim belief, Gabriel revealed the Koran to Mohammed and escorted him on his ◇Night Journey.

Gabrieli Giovanni *c.* 1555–1612. Italian composer and organist. Although he composed secular music and madrigals, he is best known for his motets, which are frequently dramatic and often use several choirs and groups of instruments. In 1585 he became organist at St Mark's, Venice.

Gaddafi alternate form of ◇Khaddhafi, Libyan leader.

Gaddi family of Italian painters in Florence: *Gaddo Gaddi* (*c.* 1250–1330); his son *Taddeo Gaddi* (*c.* 1300–1366), who was inspired by Giotto and painted the fresco cycle *Life of the*

Gabon
Gabonese Republic (*République Gabonaise*)

area 103,319 sq mi/267,667 sq km
capital Libreville
cities Port-Gentil and Owendo (ports); Masuku (Franceville)
physical virtually the whole country is tropical rainforest; narrow coastal plain rising to hilly interior with savanna in E and S; Ogooué River flows N–W
features Schweitzer hospital at Lambaréné; Trans-Gabonais railroad
head of state and government Omar Bongo from 1967
political system emergent democracy
political parties Gabonese Democratic Party (PDG), nationalist; Morena Movement of National Recovery, left of center **exports** petroleum, manganese, uranium, timber
currency CFA franc
population (1988) 1,226,000 including 40 Bantu groups; growth rate 1.6% p.a.
life expectancy men 47, women 51
languages French (official), Bantu
religions 96% Christian (Roman Catholic 65%), small Muslim minority (1%), animist 3%
literacy men 70%, women 53% (1985 est)
GDP $3.5 bn (1987); $3,308 per head
chronology
1889 Gabon became part of the French Congo.
1960 Independence from France achieved; Léon M'ba became the first president.
1964 Attempted coup by rival party foiled with French help. M'ba died; he was succeeded by his protégé Albert-Bernard Bongo.
1968 One-party state established.
1973 Bongo reelected; converted to Islam, he changed his first name to Omar.
1986 Bongo reelected.
1989 Coup attempt against Bongo defeated.
1990 PDG won first multiparty elections since 1964 amidst allegations of ballot rigging.

Virgin in Santa Croce, Florence; and grandson *Agnolo Gaddi* (active 1369–96), who also painted frescoes in Santa Croce, *The Story of the Cross* 1380s, and produced panel paintings in characteristic pale pastel colors.

Gaddis William 1922– . US novelist. His work is experimental, and his best-known novel *The Recognitions* 1955 is about artistic counterfeiting. His other novels are *JR* 1976 and *Carpenter's Gothic* 1985.

gadfly fly that bites cattle, such as a ▷botfly or ▷horsefly.

gadolinium silvery-white metallic element of the lanthanide series, symbol Gd, atomic number 64, atomic weight 157.25. It is found in the products of nuclear fission and used in electronic components, alloys, and products needing to withstand high temperatures.

Gadsden city in NE Alabama, on the Coosa river, SE of Huntsville; seat of Etowah county. It is a distribution center for the area's livestock, poultry, and dairy products. Industries include manganese, bauxite, coal, timber, steel, rubber products, electrical machinery parts, and farm equipment; population (1990) 42,500.

Gadsden James 1788–1858. US military leader and diplomat who negotiated the Gadsden Purchase for the US 1854. Born in Charleston, South Carolina, and educated at Yale, Gadsden served in the War of 1812 and in the First Seminole War. In 1823 he was appointed by President Monroe to supervise the forced resettlement of the Seminoles to S Florida and held a command in the Second Seminole War. After several years as a railroad executive, Gadsden was named US minister to Mexico 1853. In that post he negotiated for the sale of Mexican territory S of the Gila river, which became part of New Mexico and Arizona, to be used as a route to California. The Gadsden Purchase was approved by the Senate 1854.

Gadsden Purchase, the in US history, the purchase of approximately 30,000 sq mi/ 77,700 sq km in what is now New Mexico and Arizona by the US 1853. The land was bought from Mexico for $10 million in a treaty negotiated by James Gadsden (1788–1858) of South Carolina, to construct a transcontinental railroad route, the Southern Pacific, completed in the 1880s.

Gaelic language member of the Celtic branch of the Indo-European language family, spoken in Ireland, Scotland, and (until 1974) the Isle of Man. Gaelic has been in decline for several centuries, discouraged until recently within the British state. There is a small Gaelic-speaking community in Nova Scotia.

It is, along with English, one of the national languages of the Republic of Ireland, with over half a million speakers, and is known there as both Irish and Irish Gaelic. In Scotland, speakers of Gaelic number around 90,000 and are concentrated in the Western Isles, in parts of the NW coast and in the city of Glasgow.

Gagarin Yuri (Alexeyevich) 1934–1968. Soviet cosmonaut who in 1961 became the first human in space aboard the spacecraft *Vostok 1*.

Born in the Smolensk region, the son of a farmer, he qualified as a foundryman. He became a pilot 1957, and on April 12, 1961 completed one orbit of the Earth, taking 108 minutes from launch to landing. He died in a plane crash while training for the *Soyuz 3* mission.

Gaia or *Ge* in Greek mythology, the goddess of the Earth. She sprang from primordial Chaos and herself produced Uranus, by whom she was the mother of the Cyclopes and Titans.

Gaia hypothesis theory that the Earth's living and nonliving systems form an inseparable whole that is regulated and kept adapted for life by living organisms themselves. The planet therefore functions as a single organism, or a giant cell. Since life and environment are so closely linked, there is a need for humans to understand and maintain the physical environment and living things around them. The Gaia hypothesis was elaborated by British scientist James (Ephraim) Lovelock (1919–) in the 1970s.

Gainesville city in N Florida, SW of Jacksonville; seat of Alachua County.

Its industries include electronic parts, concrete, and wooden products. The University of Florida 1853 is here; population (1990) 84,700.

Gainsborough Thomas 1727–1788. English landscape and portrait painter. In 1760 he settled in Bath and painted society portraits. In 1774 he went to London and became one of the original members of the Royal Academy. He was one of the first British artists to follow the Dutch in painting realistic landscapes rather than imaginative Italianate scenery.

Born in Sudbury, Suffolk, Gainsborough began to paint while still at school. In London he learned etching and studied at the Academy of Arts, but remained largely self taught.

gal or *galileo* unit of acceleration, used in geological surveying. One gal is one centimeter per second per second. The Earth's gravitational field often differs by several milligals (thousandths of a gal) in different places, because of the varying densities of the rocks beneath the surface.

Galahad in Arthurian legend, one of the knights of the Round Table. Galahad succeeded in the quest for the ▷Holy Grail because of his virtue. He was the son of ▷Lancelot of the Lake.

Galápagos Islands (official name *Archipiélago de Colón*) group of 15 islands in the Pacific, belonging to Ecuador; area 3,000 sq mi/7,800 sq km; population (1982) 6,120. The capital is San Cristóbal on the island of the same name. The islands are a nature preserve. Their unique fauna (including giant tortoises, iguanas, penguins, flightless cormorants, and Darwin's finches), which inspired Charles ▷Darwin to formulate the principle of evolution by natural selection, is under threat from introduced species.

Hubble classification of galaxies

Galatea in Greek mythology, a sea nymph who loved Acis, and when he was killed by Polyphemus transformed his blood into the river Acis. Pygmalion, a king of Cyprus, made a statue (later named Galatea) that he married after it was brought to life by Aphrodite.

Galatia ancient province of Asia Minor. It was occupied in the 3rd century BC by the ▷Gauls, and became a Roman province 25 BC.

Galatians ▷epistle in the New Testament to the churches in Galatia; attributed to St Paul.

galaxy congregation of millions or billions of stars, held together by gravity. *Spiral galaxies*, such as the ▷Milky Way, are flattened in shape, with a central bulge of old stars surrounded by a disk of younger stars, arranged in spiral arms like a Catherine wheel. *Barred spirals* are spiral galaxies that have a straight bar of stars across their center, from the ends of which the spiral arms emerge. The arms of spiral galaxies contain gas and dust from which new stars are still forming. *Elliptical galaxies* contain old stars and very little gas. They include the most massive galaxies known, containing a trillion stars. At least some elliptical galaxies are thought to be formed by mergers between spiral galaxies. There are also irregular galaxies. Most galaxies occur in clusters, containing anything from a few to thousands of members.

Our own galaxy, the Milky Way, is about 100,000 light-years in diameter, and contains at least 100 billion stars. It is a member of a small cluster, the ▷Local Group. The Sun lies in one of its spiral arms, about 25,000 light-years from the center.

Galbraith John Kenneth 1908– . Canadian-born US economist; he became a US citizen 1937. His major works include the *Affluent Society* 1958, in which he documents the tendency of the "invisible hand" of free-market capitalism to create private splendor and public squalor, *Economics and the Public Purpose* 1974, and *The Culture of Containment* 1992.

He was a professor of economics at Harvard, worked for the Office of Price Administration during World War II, and served the Kennedy administration as ambassador to India. He was an adviser to presidential candidates Adlai Stevenson, Eugene McCarthy, and George McGovern and believed strongly in a governmental role in economic planning.

Galen *c.* 130–*c.* 200. Greek physician whose ideas dominated Western medicine for almost 1,500 years. Central to his thinking were the theories of ▷humors and the threefold

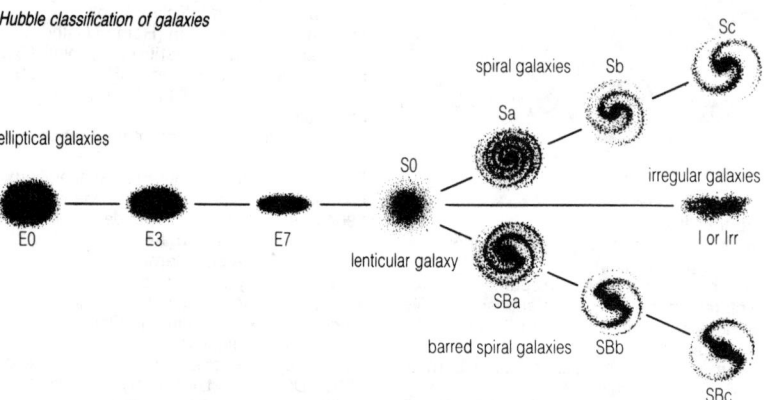

galaxy *Galaxies were classified by US astronomer Edwin Hubble in 1925.*

circulation of the blood. He remained the highest medical authority until Andreas Vesalius and William Harvey exposed the fundamental errors of his system.

Galen was born in Pergamum in Asia Minor. He attended the Roman emperor Marcus Aurelius. Although he made relatively few discoveries and relied heavily on the teachings of ◊Hippocrates, he wrote a large number of books, over 100 of which are known.

galena chief ore of lead, consisting of lead sulfide, PbS. It is lead-gray in color, has a high metallic luster and breaks into cubes because of its perfect cubic cleavage. It may contain up to 1% silver, and so the ore is sometimes mined for both metals. Galena occurs mainly among limestone deposits in Australia, Mexico, Russia, Kazakhstan, the UK, and the US.

Galicia mountainous but fertile autonomous region of NW Spain, formerly an independent kingdom; area 11,348 sq mi/29,400 sq km; population (1986) 2,785,000. It includes La Coruña, Lugo, Orense, and Pontevedra. Industries include fishing and the mining of tungsten and tin. The language is similar to Portuguese.

Galicia former province of central Europe, extending from the northern slopes of the Carpathians to the Czechoslovak-Romanian border. Once part of the Austrian Empire, it was included in Poland after World War I and divided in 1945 between Poland and the USSR.

Galilee region of N Israel (once a Roman province in Palestine) which includes Nazareth and Tiberias, frequently mentioned in the Gospels of the New Testament.

Galilee, Sea of alternate name for Lake ◊Tiberias in N Israel.

Galileo spacecraft launched from the space shuttle *Atlantis* Oct 1989, on a six-year journey to Jupiter. It flew past Venus Feb 1990 and passed within 600 mi/970 km of Earth Dec 1990, using the gravitational fields of these two planets to increase its velocity. The craft is scheduled to fly past Earth Dec 1992 to receive its final boost toward Jupiter.

Galileo properly Galileo Galilei 1564–1642. Italian mathematician, astronomer, and physicist. He developed the astronomical telescope and was the first to see sunspots, the four main satellites of Jupiter, mountains and craters on the Moon, and the appearance of Venus going through "phases," thus proving it was orbiting the Sun. In mechanics, Galileo discovered that freely falling bodies, heavy or light, had the same, constant acceleration (although the story of his dropping cannonballs from the Leaning Tower of Pisa is questionable) and that a body moving on a perfectly smooth horizontal surface would neither speed up nor slow down.

He demonstrated in 1583 that each oscillation of a pendulum takes the same amount of time despite the difference in amplitude. He invented a hydrostatic balance, and discovered that the path of a projectile is a parabola.

Galileo was born in Pisa, and in 1589 became professor of mathematics at the university there; in 1592 he became a professor at Padua, and in 1610 was appointed chief mathematician to the Grand Duke of Tuscany. Galileo's observations and arguments were an unwelcome refutation of the ideas of ◊Aristotle taught at the (church-run) universities, largely because they made plausible for the first time the heliocentric (Sun-centered) theory of ◊Copernicus. Galileo's persuasive *Dialogues on the Two Chief Systems of the World* 1632 was banned by the church authorities in Rome; he was made to recant by the ◊Inquisition and put under house arrest for his last years.

gall abnormal outgrowth on a plant that develops as a result of attack by insects or, less commonly, by bacteria, fungi, mites, or nematodes. The attack causes an increase in the number of cells or an enlargement of existing cells in the plant. Gall-forming insects generally pass the early stages of their life inside the gall. Gall wasps are responsible for the conspicuous bud galls forming on oak trees, 1 – 1.5 in/2.5 – 4 cm across, known as "oak apples."

Gall *c.* 1840–1894. Sioux leader. Born along the Moreau river in the Dakota Territory, Gall became a noted warrior of the Hunkpapa Sioux and a protégé of Sitting Bull.

After participating in raids against the US Army along the Bozeman Trail, he opposed the Treaty of Fort Laramie 1868, which established the reservation system in the N plains. Gall accompanied Sitting Bull to Montana 1876 and led the encirclement and annihilation of Custer's force at the Little Bighorn. Escaping to Canada with Sitting Bull, he later settled on a reservation and became an Indian judge, opposing the Ghost Dance Uprising of 1890.

Gallatin Albert 1761–1849. Swiss-born US political leader and diplomat. He served in the Pennsylvania state legislature 1790–94 and the US House of Representatives 1795–1801. A critic of the Federalists, Gallatin helped establish the fiscal power of the House. He served as secretary of the treasury 1801–13 under presidents Jefferson and Madison and was sent to negotiate the treaty ending the War of 1812. Gallatin served as US Minister to France 1815–22 and to England 1826–27. In later years, he devoted himself to banking and American Indian ethnology.

gall bladder small muscular sac, part of the digestive system of most, but not all, vertebrates. In humans, it is situated on the underside of the liver and connected to the small intestine by the bile duct. It stores bile from the liver.

Galle Johann Gottfried 1812–1910. German astronomer who located the planet Neptune 1846, close to the position predicted by French mathematician Urbain Leverrier.

Gallegos Rómulo 1884–1969. Venezuelan politician and writer. He was Venezuela's first democratically elected president 1948 before being overthrown by a military coup the same year. He was also a professor of philosophy and literature. His novels include *La trepadora/The Climber* 1925 and *Doña Bárbara* 1929.

galley ship powered by oars, and usually also equipped with sails. Galleys typically had a crew of hundreds of oarsmen arranged in rows; they were used in warfare in the Mediterranean from antiquity until the 18th century.

France maintained a fleet of some 40 galleys, crewed by over 10,000 convicts, until 1748. The maximum speed of a galley is estimated to have been only four knots (4.5 mph/7.5 kph), while only 20% of the oarsmen's effort was effective, and galleys could not be used in stormy weather because of their very low waterline.

Gallico Paul (William) 1897–1976. US author. Originally a sports columnist, he began writing fiction in 1936. His many books include *The Snow Goose* 1941.

Gallic Wars series of military campaigns 58–51 BC in which Julius Caesar, as proconsul of Gaul, annexed Transalpine Gaul (the territory that formed the geographical basis of modern-day France). His final victory over the Gauls led by Vercingetorix 52 BC left him in control of the land area from the Rhine to the Pyrenees and from the Alps to the Atlantic.

Gallipoli port in European Turkey, giving its name to the peninsula (ancient name **Chersonesus**) on which it stands. In World War I, at the instigation of Winston Churchill, an unsuccessful attempt was made Feb 1915–Jan 1916 by Allied troops to force their way through the Dardanelles and link up with Russia. The campaign was fought mainly by Australian and New Zealand (◊ANZAC) forces, who suffered heavy losses. An estimated 36,000 Commonwealth troops died during the nine-month campaign.

gallium gray metallic element, symbol Ga, atomic number 31, atomic weight 69.75. It is liquid at room temperature. Gallium arsenide crystals are used in microelectronics, since electrons travel a thousand times faster through them than through silicon. The element was discovered in 1875 by Lecoq de Boisbaudran (1838–1912).

gallon unit of liquid measure, equal to 3.785 liters, and subdivided into four quarts or eight pints. The UK and Canadian imperial gallon is equivalent to 4.546 liters.

gallstone pebblelike, insoluble accretion formed in the human gall bladder or bile ducts from cholesterol or calcium salts present in bile. Gallstones may be symptomless or they may cause pain, indigestion, or jaundice. They can be dissolved with medication or removed, along with the gall bladder, in an operation known as cholecystectomy.

Gallup George Horace 1901–1984. US journalist and statistician, who founded in 1935 the American Institute of Public Opinion and devised the Gallup Poll, in which public opinion is sampled by questioning a number of representative individuals.

Galois Evariste 1811–1832. French mathematician who originated the theory of groups. His attempts to gain recognition for his work were largely thwarted by the French mathematical establishment, critical of his lack of formal qualifications. Galois was killed in a duel before he was 21. The night before, he had hurriedly written out his unpublished discoveries on group theory, the importance of which would come to be appreciated more and more as the 19th century progressed.

Galsworthy John 1867–1933. English novelist and dramatist whose work examines the social issues of the Victorian period. He wrote *The Forsyte Saga* 1922 and its sequel *A Modern Comedy* 1929. His other novels include *The Country House* 1907 and *Fraternity* 1909; plays include *The Silver Box* 1906.

Galsworthy first achieved recognition with *The Man of Property* 1906, the first installment of the *Forsyte* series, which includes *In Chancery* and *To Let*. Soames Forsyte, the central character, is the embodiment of Victorian values and feeling for property, and the wife whom he also "owns"—Irene—was based on Galsworthy's wife. Later additions to the series are *A Modern Comedy* 1929, which contained *The White Monkey, The Silver Spoon*, and *Swan Song*, and the short stories *On Forsyte Change* 1930.

Galtieri Leopoldo 1926– . Argentine general,

president 1981–82. A leading member from 1979 of the ruling right-wing military junta and commander of the army, Galtieri became president in 1981. Under his leadership the junta ordered the seizure 1982 of the Falkland Islands (Malvinas), a British colony in the SW Atlantic claimed by Argentina. After the surrender of his forces he resigned as army commander and was replaced as president. He and his fellow junta members were tried for abuse of human rights and court-martialed for their conduct of the war; he was sentenced to 12 years in prison in 1986.

Galton Francis 1822–1911. English scientist who studied the inheritance of physical and mental attributes in humans, with the aim of improving the human species. He discovered that no two sets of human fingerprints are the same, and is considered the founder of ▷eugenics.

Galvani Luigi 1737–1798. Italian physiologist who discovered galvanic, or voltaic, electricity in 1762, when investigating the contractions produced in the muscles of dead frogs by contact with pairs of different metals. His work led quickly to Alessandro Volta's invention of the electrical ▷cell, and later to an understanding of how nerves control muscles.

galvanizing process for rendering iron rust-proof, by plunging it into molten zinc (the dipping method), or by electroplating it with zinc.

galvanometer instrument for detecting small electric currents by their magnetic effect.

Galveston Gulf of Mexico port on Galveston Island in Texas; population (1990) 59,000. It exports cotton, petroleum, wheat, and timber and has chemical works and petroleum refineries. In 1900, 8,000 people died in one of the hurricanes that periodically hit the region.

The city dates from an 1817 settlement by the pirate Jean Lafitte. Fishing is important, and the city has long been a resort for the island's sandy beaches.

Galway county on the W coast of the Republic of Ireland, in the province of Connacht; area 2,293 sq mi/5,940 sq km; population (1991) 180,300. Towns include Galway (county town), Ballinasloe, Tuam, Clifden, and Loughrea (near which deposits of lead, zinc, and copper were found 1959).

The east is low-lying. In the south are the Slieve Aughty mountains and Galway Bay, with the Aran islands. West of Lough Corrib is Connemara, a wild area of moors, hills, lakes, and bogs. The Shannon is the principal river.

Galway James 1939– . Irish flutist, born in Belfast. He was a member of the Berlin Philharmonic Orchestra 1969–75, before taking up a solo career.

Gama Vasco da c. 1469–1524. Portuguese navigator who commanded an expedition in 1497 to discover the route to India around the Cape of Good Hope in modern South Africa. On Christmas Day 1497 he reached land, which he named Natal. He then crossed the Indian Ocean, arriving at Calicut May 1498, and returning to Portugal Sept 1499.

In 1502 he founded a Portuguese colony at Mozambique.

Gambetta Léon Michel 1838–1882. French politician, organizer of resistance during the Franco-Prussian War, and founder in 1871 of the Third Republic. In 1881–82 he was prime minister for a few weeks.

Gambia
Republic of The

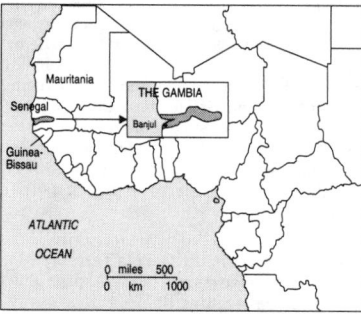

Mauritania

THE GAMBIA

Senegal

Banjul

Guinea-Bissau

ATLANTIC OCEAN

0 miles 500
0 km 1000

area 4,018 sq mi/10,402 sq km
capital Banjul
cities Serekunda, Bakau, Georgetown
physical banks of the river Gambia flanked by low hills
features smallest state in black Africa; stone circles; Karantaba obelisk marking spot where Mungo Park began his journey to the Niger River 1796
head of state and government Dawda Jawara from 1970
political system liberal democracy
political parties Progressive People's Party (PPP), moderate centrist; National Convention Party (NCP), left of center
exports groundnuts, palm oil, fish
currency dalasi
population (1990 est) 820,000; growth rate 1.9% p.a.
life expectancy 42 (1988 est)
languages English (official), Mandinka, Fula and other native tongues
media no daily newspaper; two official weeklies sell about 2,000 copies combined and none of the other independents more than 700
religions Muslim 90%, with animist and Christian minorities
literacy men 36%, women 15% (1985 est)
GDP $189 million (1987); $236 per head
chronology
1843 The Gambia became a crown colony.
1965 Independence achieved from Britain as a constitutional monarchy within the Commonwealth, with Dawda K Jawara as prime minister.
1970 Declared itself a republic, with Jawara as president.
1972 Jawara reelected.
1981 Attempted coup foiled with the help of Senegal.
1982 Formed with Senegal the Confederation of Senegambia; Jawara reelected.
1987 Jawara reelected.
1989 Confederation of Senegambia dissolved.
1990 Gambian troops contributed to the stabilizing force in Liberia.

Gambia river in W Africa, which gives its name to The ▷Gambia; 620 mi/1,000 km long.

Gambia, The country in W Africa, bounded N, E, and S by Senegal and W by the Atlantic Ocean.

government The Gambia is an independent republic within the British Commonwealth. Its constitution dates from 1970 and provides for a single-chamber legislature, the house of representatives, consisting of 49 members, 35 directly elected by universal suffrage, five elected by the chiefs, eight nonvoting nominated members; and the attorney general, ex officio. It serves a five-year term, as does the president, who is elected by direct universal suffrage and appoints a vice-president (who also leads the house of representatives) and a cabinet.

history The Gambia was formerly part of the ▷Mali Empire, a Muslim gold-trading empire that flourished in W Africa between the 7th and 15th centuries, and declined at the time of the Portuguese arrival 1455. In the late 16th century commerce was taken over from Portugal by England, and trading posts established on Gambia River were controlled from Sierra Leone. In 1843 The Gambia was made a crown colony, becoming an independent British colony 1888.

Jawara's presidency Political parties were formed in the 1950s, internal self-government was achieved 1963, and full independence within the Commonwealth 1965, with Dawda Jawara as prime minister. The country declared itself a republic 1970, with Jawara as president, replacing the British monarch as head of state. He was reelected 1972 and 1977.

With the Progressive People's Party (PPP) the dominant political force, there was pressure to make The Gambia a one-party state, but Jawara resisted this. When an attempted coup against him 1981 was thwarted with

Senegalese military aid, ties between the two countries were strengthened to the extent that plans were announced for their merger into a confederation of Senegambia. However, Senegal had doubts about the idea, and in economic terms The Gambia had more to gain. In Sept 1989 it was announced that The Gambia had formally agreed to end the confederation. In 1982 Jawara was reelected; he was again reelected 1987. In 1990, The Gambia contributed troops to the multinational force attempting to stabilize Liberia. *See illustration box.*

Gambier Islands island group, part of ▷French Polynesia, administered with the ▷Tuamotu Archipelago; area 14 sq mi/36 sq km; population (1983) 582. It includes four coral islands and many small islets. The main island is Mangareva, with its town Rikitea.

gambling or *gaming* staking of money or anything else of value on the outcome of a competition. Forms of gambling include betting on sports results, casino games like blackjack and roulette, card games such as poker and bridge, slot machines, or lotteries.

For many years certain forms of gambling were illegal in the US, but revenue needs in state and local governments led to the the legalization of some gambling operations, such as casinos, state-wide lotteries, and off-track betting parlors. Gambling is a multibillion dollar operation worldwide and can be addictive. Gamblers Anonymous was set up in the US 1957 to help compulsive gamblers overcome their addiction.

gamelan Indonesian orchestra employing tuned gongs, xylophones, metallophones (with bars of metal), cymbals, drums, flutes, and fiddles, the music of which has inspired such Western composers as Debussy, Colin

McPhee, John Cage, Benjamin Britten, and Philip Glass.

Originally court music with Hindustan influences, it withdrew under Dutch colonial administration to rural communities, and was played as an accompaniment to ceremonial occasions, dancing, and puppet theater. The music is improvised and based on interlocking tonal and rhythmic patterns. Javanese gamelan music uses a seven-tone *pelog* scale, Balinese preferring a five-tone *slendro* scale. The scale of gongs vary in precise pitch, but incorporate matched pairs that deviate slightly in pitch.

gamete cell that functions in sexual reproduction by merging with another gamete to form a ◊zygote. Examples of gametes include sperm and egg cells. In most organisms, the gametes are haploid (they contain half the number of chromosomes of the parent), owing to reduction division or ◊meiosis.

In higher organisms, gametes are of two distinct types: large immobile ones known as eggs or egg cells (see ◊ovum) and small ones known as ◊sperm. They come together at ◊fertilization. In some lower organisms the gametes are all the same, or they may belong to different mating strains but have no obvious differences in size or appearance.

game theory a group of mathematical theories, developed in 1944 by Oscar Morgenstern (1902–1977) and John von Neumann, that seeks to abstract from invented game-playing scenarios and their outcome the essence of situations of conflict and/or cooperation in the real political, business, and social world.

A feature of such games is that the rationality of a decision by one player will depend on what the others do; hence game theory has particular application to the study of ◊oligopoly (a market largely controlled by a few producers).

gametophyte the ◊haploid generation in the life cycle of a plant that produces gametes; see ◊alternation of generations.

gamma radiation very-high-frequency electromagnetic radiation, similar in nature to X-rays but of shorter wavelength, emitted by the nuclei of radioactive substances during decay or by the interactions of high-energy electrons with matter. Cosmic gamma rays have been identified as coming from pulsars, radio galaxies, and quasars, although they cannot penetrate the Earth's atmosphere.

Gamma rays are stopped only by direct collision with an atom and are therefore very penetrating; they can, however, be stopped by about 1.5 in/4 cm of lead or by a very thick concrete shield. They are less ionizing in their effect than alpha and beta particles, but are dangerous nevertheless because they can penetrate deeply into body tissues such as bone marrow. They are not deflected by either magnetic or electric fields.

Gamma radiation is used to kill bacteria and other microorganisms, sterilize medical devices, and change the molecular structure of plastics to modify their properties (for example, to improve their resistance to heat and abrasion).

gamma-ray astronomy the study of gamma rays from space. Much of the radiation detected comes from collisions between hydrogen gas and cosmic rays in our galaxy. Some sources have been identified, including the Crab nebula and the Vela pulsar (the most powerful gamma-ray source detected). Gamma rays are difficult to detect and are generally studied by use of balloon-borne detectors and artificial satellites. The first gamma-ray satellites were *SAS II* (1972) and *COS B* (1975), although gamma-ray detectors were carried on the *Apollo 15* and *16* missions. *SAS II* failed after only a few months, but *COS B* continued working until 1982, carrying out a complete survey of the galactic disk.

The US Gamma Ray Observatory was launched by US space shuttle *Atlantis* in April 1991 to study the gamma-ray sky for five years. The observatory cost $617 million and at 17 tons was the heaviest payload ever carried by space shuttle.

Gamow George 1904–1968. Russian-born US cosmologist, nuclear physicist, and popularizer of science. His work in astrophysics included a study of the structure and evolution of stars and the creation of the elements. He also explained how the collision of nuclei in the solar interior could produce the nuclear reactions that power the Sun.

Ganda member of the Baganda people, the majority ethnic group in Uganda; the Baganda also live in Kenya. Until the 19th century they formed an independent kingdom, the largest in E Africa. It was a British protectorate 1894–1962, and the monarchy was officially overthrown in 1966. Their language, Luganda, belongs to the Niger-Congo language family and has about 3 million speakers.

Gandhi Indira (born Nehru) 1917–1984. Indian politician, prime minister of India 1966–77 and 1980–84, and leader of the Congress Party 1966–77 and subsequently of the Congress (I) party. She was assassinated 1984 by members of her Sikh bodyguard, resentful of her use of troops to clear malcontents from the Sikh temple at ◊Amritsar.

Her father, Jawaharlat Nehru, was India's first prime minister. She married Feroze Gandhi in 1942 (died 1960, not related to Mahatma Gandhi) and had two sons, Sanjay Gandhi (1946–1980), who died in an airplane crash, and Rajiv ◊Gandhi, who was assassinated May 21, 1991. In 1975 the validity of her reelection to parliament was questioned, and she declared a state of emergency. During this time her son Sanjay was implementing a social and economic program (including an unpopular family-planning policy) which led to her defeat in 1977, although he masterminded her return to power in 1980.

Gandhi Mohandas Karamchand, called **Mahatma** ("Great Soul") 1869–1948. Indian nationalist leader. A pacifist, he led the struggle for Indian independence from the UK by advocating nonviolent noncooperation (*satyagraha*, defense of and by truth) from 1915. He was imprisoned several times by the British authorities and was influential in the nationalist Congress Party and in the independence negotiations 1947. He was assassinated by a Hindu nationalist in the violence that followed the partition of British India into India and Pakistan.

Gandhi was born in Porbandar and studied law in London, later practicing as a lawyer. He settled in South Africa where until 1914 he led the Indian community in opposition to racial discrimination. Returning to India, he emerged as leader of the Indian National Congress. He organized hunger strikes and events of civil disobedience, and campaigned for social reform, including religious tolerance and an end to discrimination against the so-called untouchable ◊caste. In 1947, after World War II, he played a significant role in negotiations for an autonomous Indian state.

Gandhi Rajiv 1944–1991. Indian politician, prime minister from 1984 (following his mother Indira Gandhi's assassination) to Nov 1989. As prime minister, he faced growing discontent with his party's elitism and lack of concern for social issues. He was assassinated by a bomb at an election rally.

Elder son of Indira Gandhi and grandson of Nehru, Rajiv Gandhi was born into the Kashmiri Brahmin family that had governed India for all but four years since 1947. He initially displayed little interest in politics and became a pilot with Indian Airlines. But after the death in a plane crash of his brother **Sanjay** (1946–1980), he was elected to his brother's Amethi parliamentary seat 1981. In the Dec 1984 parliamentary elections he won a record majority. His reputation became tarnished by a scandal concerning alleged kickbacks to senior officials from an arms deal with the Swedish munitions firm Bofors and, following his party's defeat in the general election of Nov 1989, Gandhi was forced to resign as premier. He was killed in the middle of the 1991 election campaign at a rally near Madras, while attempting to regain office.

Ganesh Hindu god, son of Siva and Parvati; he is represented as elephant-headed and is worshiped as a remover of obstacles.

Ganges (Hindi **Ganga**) major river of India and Bangladesh; length 1,560 mi/2,510 km.

It is the most sacred river for Hindus.

Its chief tributary is the Jumna (**Yamuna**, length 860 mi/1,385 km), which joins the Ganges near Allahabad, where there is a sacred bathing place. The Ganges is joined in its delta in Bangladesh by the river ◊Brahmaputra, and its most commercially important and westernmost channel to the Bay of Bengal is the **Hooghly**. It receives untreated sewage and chemical waste from more than 100 cities. The political leaders M K Gandhi, Nehru, and Indira Gandhi were all cremated on the banks of the Jumna at Delhi.

Deforestation of the Ganges watershed has decreased the river's dry-season flow by 20%; the area regularly flooded in the wet season has increased about 40%; the annual cost of flood damage has risen from $120 million to $1 billion.

ganglion (plural **ganglia**) solid cluster of nervous tissue containing many cell bodies and ◊synapses, usually enclosed in a tissue sheath; found in invertebrates and vertebrates.

In many invertebrates, the central nervous system consists mainly of ganglia connected by nerve cords. The ganglia in the head (cerebral ganglia) are usually well developed and are analogous to the brain in vertebrates. In vertebrates, most ganglia occur outside the central nervous system.

Gang of Four chief members of the radical faction that tried to seize power in China after the death of Mao Zedong 1976. It included his widow, ◊Jiang Qing; the other members were Zhang Chunjao, Wang Hungwen, and Yao Wenyuan. The coup failed, and they were soon arrested.

gangrene death and decay of body tissue (often of a limb) due to bacterial action; the affected part gradually turns black and causes blood poisoning.

Gangrene sets in as a result of loss of blood supply to the area. This may be due to disease (diabetes, atherosclerosis), an obstruction of a major blood vessel (as in ◊thrombosis), injury, or frostbite. Bacteria colonize the site unopposed, and a strong risk of blood poisoning often leads to surgical removal of the tissue or the affected part (amputation).

gangue the part of an ore deposit that is not itself economically valuable; for example, calcite may occur as a gangue mineral with galena.

gannet N Atlantic seabird *Sula bassana* in the same family (Sulidae) as the boobies. When fully grown, it is white with black-tipped wings having a span of 5.6 ft/1.7 m. The young are speckled. It breeds on cliffs in nests made of grass and seaweed. Only one (white) egg is laid.

Gannet Peak the highest peak in Wyoming, rising to 13,804 ft/4,207 m.

Gansu or *Kansu* province of NW China
area 204,580 sq mi/530,000 sq km
capital Lanzhou
features subject to earthquakes; the "Silk Road" (now a motor road) passed through it in the Middle Ages, carrying trade to central Asia
products coal, oil, hydroelectric power from the Huang He (Yellow) river
population (1990) 22,371,000, including many Muslims.

Ganymede in Greek mythology, a youth so beautiful he was chosen as cupbearer to Zeus.

Ganymede in astronomy, the largest moon of the planet Jupiter, and the largest moon in the Solar System, 3,270 mi/5,260 km in diameter (larger than the planet Mercury). It orbits Jupiter every 7.2 days at a distance of 1.1 million km/700,000 mi. Its surface is a mixture of cratered and grooved terrain.

gar primitive bony fish of the order Semionotiformes, which also includes ⟡sturgeons. Gar have long, beaklike snouts and elongated bodies covered in heavy, bony scales. All four species of gar inhabit freshwater rivers and lakes of the Mississippi drainage. See also ⟡needlefish.

Garbo Greta. Adopted name of Greta Lovisa Gustafsson 1905–1990. Swedish-born US film actress. She went to the US in 1925, and her captivating beauty and leading role in *The Torrent* 1926 made her one of Hollywood's first stars in silent films. Her later films include *Mata Hari* 1931, *Grand Hotel* 1932, *Queen Christina* 1933, *Anna Karenina* 1935, *Camille* 1936, and *Ninotchka* 1939. Her qualities of ethereality and romantic mystery on the screen intermingled with her seclusion in private life. She retired 1941.

García Lorca Federico, Spanish poet. See ⟡Lorca, Federico García.

García Márquez Gabriel 1928– . Colombian novelist. His sweeping novel *Cien años de soledad/One Hundred Years of Solitude* 1967 (which tells the story of a family over a period of six generations) is an example of magic realism, a technique used to heighten the intensity of realistic portrayal of social and political issues by introducing grotesque or fanciful material. Nobel Prize for Literature 1982.

His other books include *El amor en los tiempos del cólera/Love in the Time of Cholera* 1985 and *The General in His Labyrinth* 1991, which describes the last four months of Simón Bolívar's life.

García Perez Alan 1949– . Peruvian politician, leader of the moderate, left-wing APRA party; president 1985–90. He inherited an ailing economy and was forced to trim his socialist program.

Garcia v San Antonio Metropolitan Transit

Authority a US Supreme Court decision 1985 dealing with the imposition of federal labor regulations on the states as employers. Prior to this decision, the states had enjoyed immunity from the Federal Labor Standards Act under the 10th-Amendment provision that all rights not explicitly reserved for the federal government belong to the states. The Court ruled, however, that state employees are protected by federal minimum-wage and maximum-hours laws, deciding on the grounds that the judiciary is not responsible for safeguarding state sovereignty.

Garcilaso de la Vega 1503–1536. Spanish poet. A soldier, he was a member of Charles V's expedition in 1535 to Tunis; he was killed in battle at Nice. His verse, some of the greatest of the Spanish Renaissance, includes sonnets, songs, and elegies, often on the model of Petrarch.

Garcilaso de la Vega 1539–1616. Spanish writer, called *el Inca*. Son of a Spanish conquistador and an Inca princess, he wrote an account of the conquest of Florida and *Comentarios reales de los Incas* on the history of Peru.

garden plot of land, usually belonging to a householder. It can be cultivated to produce food or to create pleasant surroundings. Pleasure gardens were common in all ancient civilizations. In medieval Europe gardens were devoted to growing medicinal plants and herbs but in the 16th century formal recreational gardens became a feature of larger town and country houses. The taste for formality continued into the 19th century, when a more natural look became fashionable. Most 18th-century rural workers had vegetable gardens and the practice was continued wherever possible in the new industrial towns. The miniature landscaped garden with lawns and flowerbeds became a feature of 20th-century housing estates in Europe and the US.

gardenia subtropical and tropical trees and shrubs of Africa and Asia, genus *Gardenia*, of the madder family Rubiaceae, with evergreen foliage and flattened rosettes of fragrant waxen-looking blooms, often white in color.

garderobe medieval lavatory. Garderobes were often built into the thickness of a castle wall, with an open drop to the moat below.

Gardner Ava 1922–1990. US film actress, a sensuous star in such films as *The Killers* 1946, *Pandora and the Flying Dutchman* 1951, and *The Barefoot Contessa* 1954, a tragically slanted Cinderella tale of a Romany girl who becomes an international celebrity. Her later roles include that of Lillie Langtry in *The Life and Times of Judge Roy Bean* 1972. She remained active in films until the 1980s, when she retired to London.

Gardner Erle Stanley 1889–1970. US author of crime fiction. He created the character of the lawyer-detective Perry Mason, who was later featured in film and on television. Originally a lawyer, Gardner gave up his practice with the success of the first Perry Mason stories.

Gardner Isabella Stewart 1840–1924. US art collector and founder of the Isabella Stewart Gardner Museum in Boston. Born in New York and educated in Paris, she married prominent Boston manufacturer John Gardner 1860. A tireless world traveler, socialite, and local celebrity, she scandalized proper Bostonians with her lavish parties and public appearances. Gardner was a patron of the Boston Symphony

Orchestra and participant in the intellectual life of the city. As an art collector, she specialized in the works of the Renaissance and of the Dutch masters. Her private art gallery in Boston was opened as a public museum 1903.

Garfield James A(bram) 1831–1881. 20th president of the US 1881, a Republican. A compromise candidate for the presidency, he held office for only four months before being assassinated in Washington, DC railroad station by a disappointed office-seeker. His short tenure was marked primarily by struggles within the Republican party over influence and cabinet posts.

He was born in a log cabin in Ohio, and served in the Civil War with the Union forces.

gargoyle spout projecting from the roof gutter of a building with the purpose of directing water away from the wall. The term is usually applied to the ornamental forms found in Gothic architecture; these were carved in stone in the form of fantastic animals, angels, or human heads.

Garibaldi Giuseppe 1807–1882. Italian soldier who played a central role in the unification of Italy by conquering Sicily and Naples 1860. From 1834 a member of the nationalist Mazzini's ⟡Young Italy society, he was forced into exile until 1848 and again 1849–54. He fought against Austria 1848–49, 1859, and 1866, and led two unsuccessful expeditions to liberate Rome from papal rule in 1862 and 1867.

Born in Nice, he became a sailor and then joined the nationalist movement ⟡*Risorgimento*. Condemned to death for treason, he escaped to South America where he became a mercenary. He returned to Italy during the 1848 revolution, served with the Sardinian army against the Austrians, and commanded the army of the Roman republic in its defense of the city against the French. He subsequently lived in exile until 1854, when he settled on the island of Caprera. In 1860, at the head of his 1,000 redshirts, he won Sicily and Naples for the new kingdom of Italy. He served in the Austrian War of 1866 and fought for France in the Franco-Prussian War 1870–71.

Garland Judy. Adopted name of Frances Gumm 1922–1969. US singer and actress whose performances are marked by a compelling intensity. Her films include *The Wizard of Oz* (which featured the tune that was to become her theme song, "Over the Rainbow"), *Babes in Arms* 1939, *Strike Up the Band* 1940, *Meet Me in St Louis* 1944, *Easter Parade* 1948, *A Star is Born* 1954, and *Judgment at Nuremberg* 1961.

She began her acting career 1935 in the Andy Hardy series. She was the mother of actress and singer Liza Minnelli.

garlic perennial plant *Allium sativum* of the lily family Liliaceae, with white flowers. The bulb, made of small segments, or cloves, is used in cooking, and its pungent essence has an active medical ingredient, allyl methyl trisulfide, which prevents blood clotting.

Garner John Nance 1868–1967. US political leader and vice-president of the US. Garner was appointed county judge 1895 and embarked on a career in Democratic party politics, serving in the state legislature 1898–1902 and the US House of Representatives 1903–33. A Democratic leader in the House, he was chosen as Speaker 1931. He later served as vice-president during Franklin Roosevelt's first two terms 1933–41. Opposing Roosevelt's reelection in 1940, Garner retired from public life.

Born in Red River County, Texas, Garner briefly attended Vanderbilt University. After privately studying law in Clarksville, Texas, he was admitted to the bar 1890.

garnet group of silicate minerals with the formula $X_3Y_2(SiO_4)_3$, when X is calcium, magnesium, iron, or manganese, and Y is iron, aluminum, or chromium. Garnets are used as semiprecious gems (usually pink to deep red) and as abrasives. They occur in metamorphic rocks such as gneiss and schist.

Garonne river in SW France, rising on the Spanish side of the Pyrenees and flowing to the ⇨Gironde estuary; length 350 mi/560 km.

Garret Almeida 1799–1854. Portuguese poet, novelist, and dramatist. As a liberal, in 1823 he was forced into 14 years of exile. His works, which he saw as a singlehanded attempt to create a national literature, include the prose *Viagens na Minha Terra/Travels in My Homeland* 1843–46 and the tragedy *Frei Luis de Sousa* 1843.

Garrick David 1717–1779. British actor and theater manager. He was a pupil of Samuel ⇨Johnson. From 1747 he became joint licensee of the Drury Lane theater with his own company, and instituted a number of significant theatrical conventions including concealed stage lighting and banishing spectators from the stage. He played Shakespearean characters such as Richard III, King Lear, Hamlet, and Benedick, and collaborated with George Colman (1732–1794) in writing the play *The Clandestine Marriage* 1766. He retired from the stage 1766, but continued as a manager.

Garrison William Lloyd 1805–1879. US editor and reformer who was an uncompromising opponent of slavery. He founded the abolitionist journal *The Liberator* 1831 and became a leader of the American Anti-Slavery Society. Although initially opposed to violence, he supported the Union cause in the Civil War. After the Emancipation Proclamation, he disbanded the Anti-Slavery Society and devoted his energies to prohibition, feminism, and Indian rights.

Born in Newburyport, Massachusetts, and trained as a printer, Garrison later worked as an editor of various publications in Boston, Vermont, and Baltimore.

Garter, Order of the senior British order of knighthood, founded by Edward III in about 1347. Its distinctive badge is a garter of dark blue velvet, with the motto of the order, *Honi soit qui mal y pense* ("Shame be to him who thinks evil of it") in gold letters.

Garvey Marcus (Moziah) 1887–1940. Jamaican political thinker and activist, an early advocate of black nationalism. He founded the UNIA (Universal Negro Improvement Association) in 1914, and moved to the US in 1916, where he established branches in New York and other northern cities. Aiming to achieve human rights and dignity for black people through black pride and economic self-sufficiency, he was considered one of the first militant black nationalists. He led a Back to Africa movement for black Americans to establish a black-governed country in Africa. The Jamaican cult of ⇨Rastafarianism is based largely on his ideas.

Gary city in NW Indiana; population (1990) 116,000. It contains the steel and cement works of the US Steel Corporation and was named after E H Gary (1846–1927), its chairman. Cutbacks in steel production have left the city economically depressed.

gas in physics, a form of matter, such as air, in which the molecules move randomly in otherwise empty space, filling any size or shape of container into which the gas is put.

A sugar-lump sized cube of air at room temperature contains 30 trillion molecules moving at an average speed of 500 meters per second (1,200 mph/1,800 kph). Gases can be liquefied by cooling, which lowers the speed of the molecules and enables attractive forces between them to bind them together.

gas constant in physics, the constant R that appears in the equation $PV = nRT$, which describes how the pressure P, volume V, and temperature T of an ideal gas are related (n is the amount of gas in the specimen). This equation combines ⇨Boyle's law and ⇨Charles's law.

R has a value of 8.3143 joules per kelvin per mole.

Gascony ancient province of SW France. With Guienne it formed the duchy of Aquitaine in the 12th century; Henry II of England gained possession of it through his marriage to Eleanor of Aquitaine in 1152, and it was often in English hands until 1451. It was then ruled by the king of France until it was united with the French royal domain 1607 under Henry IV.

The area is now divided into several *départements*, including Landes and Pyrénées-Atlantiques.

gas engine internal-combustion engine in which a gas (coal gas, producer gas, natural gas, or gas from a blast furnace) is used as the fuel. The first practical gas engine was built 1860 by Jean Etienne Lenoir, and the type was subsequently developed by Nikolaus August Otto, who introduced the ⇨four-stroke cycle.

gas exchange in biology, the exchange of gases between living organisms and the atmosphere, principally oxygen and carbon dioxide.

In animals, gas exchange is only respiratory (or using oxygen to convert food to energy). In plants, gas exchange is photosynthetic (or using carbon dioxide to make food) as well as respiratory. In humans and other tetrapods (four-limbed vertebrates), gas exchange or respiration is the absorption of oxygen into the blood when air meets blood vessels in the ⇨lungs, and the exhalation of carbon dioxide with water and small quantities of ammonia and waste matter. Many adult amphibia and terrestrial invertebrates can absorb oxygen directly through the skin. The bodies of insects and some spiders contain a system of air-filled tubes known as ⇨tracheae. Fish and most other aquatic organisms have ⇨gills, which exchange gases with the surrounding water. In plants, gas exchange necessary for photosynthesis and respiration generally takes place via the ⇨stomata.

gas laws physical laws concerning the behavior of gases. They include ⇨Boyle's law and ⇨Charles's law, which are concerned with the relationships between the pressure, temperature, and volume of an ideal (hypothetical) gas. These two laws can be combined to give the *general* or *universal gas law*, which may be expressed as:

(pressure × volume)/temperature = constant

Van der Waals' law includes corrections for the nonideal behavior of real gases.

gasohol motor fuel that is 90% gasoline and 10% ethanol (alcohol). The ethanol is usually obtained by fermentation, followed by distillation, using corn, wheat, potatoes, or sugar cane. It was used in early automobiles before gasoline became economical, and its use was revived during the 1940s war shortage and the energy shortage of the 1970s, for example in Brazil.

gasoline mixture of hydrocarbons derived from petroleum, whose main use is as a fuel for internal combustion engines. It is colorless and highly volatile.

gasoline engine or *piston engine* the most commonly used source of power for motor vehicles, introduced by the German engineers Gottlieb Daimler and Karl Benz 1885. The gasoline engine is a complex piece of machinery made up of about 150 moving parts. It is a reciprocating piston engine (see ⇨internal-combustion engine), in which a number of pistons move up and down in cylinders. The motion of the pistons rotates a crankshaft, at the end of which is a heavy flywheel. From the flywheel the power is transferred to the car's driving wheels via the transmission system of clutch, gearbox, and final drive.

The parts of the gasoline engine can be subdivided into a number of systems. The *fuel system* pumps fuel from the gasoline tank into the carburetor. There it mixes with air and is sucked into the engine cylinders. (With electronic fuel injection, it goes directly from the tank into the cylinders by way of an electronic monitor.) The *ignition system* supplies the sparks to ignite the fuel mixture in the cylinders. By means of an ignition coil and contact breaker, it boosts the 12-volt battery voltage to pulses of 18,000 volts or more. These go via a ⇨distributor to the ⇨spark plugs in the cylinders, where they create the sparks. (Electronic ignitions replace these parts.) Ignition of the fuel in the cylinders produces temperatures of 1,300°F/700°C or more, and the engine must be cooled to prevent overheating. Most engines have a *water-cooling system*, in which water circulates through channels in the cylinder block, thus extracting the heat. It flows through pipes in a radiator, which are cooled by fan-blown air. A few automobiles and most motorbikes are air-cooled, the cylinders being surrounded by many fins to present a large surface area to the air. The *lubrication system* also reduces some heat, but its main job is to keep the moving parts coated with oil, which is pumped under pressure to the camshaft, crankshaft, and valve-operating gear.

Gaspé Peninsula mountainous peninsula in SE Québec; area 11,390 sq mi/29,500 sq km. It has fishing and lumbering industries.

Gassendi Pierre 1592–1655. French physicist and philosopher who played a crucial role in the revival of atomism (the theory that the world is made of small, indivisible particles), and the rejection of Aristotelianism so characteristic of the period. He was a propagandist and critic of other views rather than an original thinker.

Gastonia city in SW North Carolina, directly W of Charlotte; seat of Gaston county. Its most important industry is textiles; population (1990) 54,700. It was the site of a violent labor strike 1929.

gastritis inflammation of the lining of the stomach. The term is a vague one, applied to a range of conditions.

gastroenteritis inflammation of the stomach and intestines, giving rise to abdominal pain, vomiting, and diarrhea. It may be caused by food or other poisoning, allergy, or infection, and is dangerous in babies.

gastroenterology medical specialty concerned with disorders of the ▷alimentary canal.

gastropod any member of a very large class (Gastropoda) of ▷mollusks. Gastropods are single-shelled (in a spiral or modified spiral form), have eyes on stalks, and move on a flattened, muscular foot. They have well-developed heads and rough, scraping tongues called radulae. Some are marine, some freshwater, and others land creatures, but all tend to inhabit damp places.

They include land snails, slugs, abalones, conches, coneshells, and cowries.

gas turbine engine in which burning fuel supplies hot gas to spin a ▷turbine. The most widespread application of gas turbines has been in aviation. All jet engines (see under ▷jet propulsion) are modified gas turbines, and some locomotives and ships also use gas turbines as a power source.

They are also used in industry for generating and pumping purposes.

In a typical gas turbine a multivaned compressor draws in and compresses air. The compressed air enters a combustion chamber at high pressure, and fuel is sprayed in and ignited. The hot gases produced escape through the blades of (typically) two turbines and spin them around. One of the turbines drives the compressor; the other provides the external power that can be harnessed.

gas warfare military use of gas to produce a toxic effect on the human body. See ▷chemical warfare.

Gates Horatio *c.* 1727–1806. British-born American military leader who won the first major battle (Saratoga) of the Revolution after several American losses and retreats.

Born in England, Gates joined the British army, serving in Nova Scotia and seeing action in the French and Indian War. After returning to England, he immigrated to America in 1772. A friend of George Washington, he was appointed brigadier general in the Continental army 1775. Gates was placed in command of the Northern Department and won a tide-turning victory against Burgoyne at Saratoga 1777. Later falling out of favor with Washington, he was dispatched to the South, where his defeat at the Battle of Camden in 1780 effectively ended his military career.

Gatling Richard Jordan 1818–1903. US inventor of a rapid-fire gun. Patented in 1862, the Gatling gun had ten barrels arranged as a cylinder rotated by a hand crank. Cartridges from an overhead hopper or drum dropped into the breech mechanism, which loaded, fired, and extracted them at a rate of 320 rounds per minute.

The Gatling gun was used in the US Civil War and in the Indian Wars that followed the settling of the American West. It was the precursor of the ▷machine gun.

GATT acronym for ▷*General Agreement on Tariffs and Trade*.

gaucho part Indian, part Spanish cattle herder of the Argentine and Uruguayan pampas.

Gaudí Antonio 1852–1926. Spanish architect distinguished for his flamboyant Art Nouveau style. Gaudí worked almost exclusively in Barcelona, designing both domestic and industrial buildings. He introduced color, unusual materials, and audacious technical innovations. His spectacular Church of the Holy Family, Barcelona, begun 1883, is still under construction.

gauge any scientific measuring instrument—for example, a wire gauge or a pressure gauge. The term is also applied to the width of a railroad or streetcarway track.

gauge boson or *field particle* any of the particles that carry the four fundamental forces of nature (see ▷forces, fundamental). Gauge bosons are ▷elementary particles that cannot be subdivided, and include the photon, the graviton, the gluons, and the weakons.

Gauguin Paul 1848–1903. French Post-Impressionist painter. Going beyond the Impressionists' notion of reality, he sought a more direct experience of life in the magical rites of the people and rich colors of the South Sea islands. He disliked theories and rules of painting, and his pictures are ▷Expressionist compositions characterized by his use of pure, unmixed colors. Among his paintings is *Le Christe Jaune* 1889 (Albright-Knox Art Gallery, Buffalo, New York).

Born in Paris, Gauguin spent his childhood in Peru. After a few years as a stockbroker, he took up full-time painting in 1881, exhibited with the Impressionists, and spent two months with van ▷Gogh in Arles 1888. On his return to Brittany he concentrated on his new style, Synthetism, based on the use of powerful, expressive colors and boldly outlined areas of flat tone. Influenced by Symbolism, he chose subjects reflecting his interest in the beliefs of other cultures.

After a visit to Martinique 1887, he went to Pont Aven in Brittany, becoming the leading artist in the Synthetic movement, and abandoning conventional perspective. He lived in Tahiti 1891–93 and 1895–1901 and from 1901 in the Marquesas Islands.

Gaul member of the Celtic-speaking peoples who inhabited France and Belgium in Roman times; also their territory. The Romans conquered S Gaul between the Mediterranean and the Cevennes in about 125 BC and the remaining Gauls up to the Rhine were conquered by Julius ▷Caesar 58–51 BC.

Gauls were divided into several groups but were united by a common religion controlled by the Druid priesthood. Certain Gauls invaded Italy around 400 BC, sacked Rome, and settled between the Alps and the Apennines; this district, known as Cisalpine Gaul, was conquered by Rome in about 225 BC.

Gaulle Charles de. French politician, see Charles ▷de Gaulle.

gaur Asiatic wild cattle *Bos gaurus*, dark gray-brown with white "socks," and 6 ft/2 m tall at the shoulders. The original range was from India to SE Asia and Malaysia, but numbers and range are now diminished.

gauss unit (symbol Gs) of magnetic induction or magnetic flux density, replaced by the SI unit, the ▷tesla, but still commonly used. It is equal to one line of magnetic flux per square centimeter. The Earth's magnetic field is about 0.5 Gs, and changes to it over time are measured in gammas (one gamma equals 10^{-5} gauss).

Gauss Karl Friedrich 1777–1855. German mathematician who worked on the theory of numbers, non-Euclidean geometry, and the mathematical development of electric and magnetic theory. A method of neutralizing a magnetic field, that is used to protect ships from magnetic mines, is called "degaussing."

Gautama family name of the historical ▷Buddha.

Gautier Théophile 1811–1872. French Romantic poet whose later works emphasized the perfection of form and the polished beauty of language and imagery (for example, *Emaux et camées/Enamels and Cameos* 1852). He was also a novelist (*Mlle de Maupin* 1835) and later turned to journalism.

gavial large reptile *Gavialis gangeticus* related to the crocodile. It grows to about 23 ft/7 m long, and has a very long snout with about 100 teeth in its jaws. Gavials live in rivers in N India, where they feed on fish and frogs. They have been extensively hunted for their skins, and are now extremely rare.

Gaviria (Trujillo) Cesar 1947– . Colombian Liberal Party politician, president from 1990; he was finance minister 1986–87 and minister of government 1987–89. He has supported the extradition of drug traffickers wanted in the US and has sought more US aid in return for stepping up the drug war.

An economist, Gaviria began his career in local government at the age of 22 and became mayor of his hometown Pereira at 27. He went on to the house of representatives and became a deputy minister at 31. As acting president in 1988, while President Virgilio Barco was out of the country, Gaviria negotiated the freedom of a kidnapped presidential candidate. In 1989 he left the government to manage the campaign of another presidential candidate, who was, however, assassinated later the same year.

Gawain in Arthurian legend, one of the knights of the Round Table who participated in the quest for the ▷Holy Grail. He is the hero of the 14th-century epic poem *Sir Gawayne and the Greene Knight*.

Gaya ancient city in Bihar state, NE India; population (1986) 200,000. It is a center of pilgrimage for Buddhists and Hindus with many temples and shrines. A bo tree at ▷Buddh Gaya is said to be a direct descendant of the original tree under which the Buddha sat.

Gaye Marvin 1939–1984. US soul singer and songwriter whose hits, including "Stubborn Kinda Fellow" 1962, "I Heard It Through the Grapevine" 1968, and "What's Goin' On" 1971, exemplified the Detroit ▷Motown sound.

He was killed by his father.

Gay-Lussac Joseph Louis 1778–1850. French physicist and chemist who investigated the physical properties of gases, and discovered new methods of producing sulfuric and oxalic acids. In 1802 he discovered the approximate rule for the expansion of gases now known as ▷Charles's law; see also ▷gas laws.

Gaza capital of the ▷Gaza Strip, once a Philistine city, and scene of three World War I battles; population (1980 est) 120,000.

Gazankulu ▷Black National State in Transvaal province, South Africa, with self-governing status from 1971; population (1985) 492,700.

Gaza Strip strip of land on the Mediterranean sea, under Israeli administration; capital Gaza; area 140 sq mi/363 sq km; population (1989) 645,000 of which 446,000 are refugees.

Part of the British mandate of Palestine until 1948, it was then occupied by Egypt. It was invaded by Israel 1956, reoccupied 1967, and retained 1973. Clashes between the Israeli authorities and the Arab Palestinian inhabitants escalated to ▷Intifada (uprising) 1988. In April 1992 the UN Security Council issued a statement condemning Israel for allowing "the continued deterioration of the situation in the Gaza Strip," after clashes between Israeli troops and Palestinian demonstrators left five Palestinians dead and more than 60 wounded.

gazelle any of a number of species of lightly built, fast-running antelopes found on the open plains of Africa and S Asia, especially those of the genus *Gazella*.

Gdańsk (German *Danzig*) Polish port; population (1990) 465,100. Oil is refined, and textiles, televisions, and fertilizers are produced. In the 1980s there were repeated antigovernment strikes at the Lenin shipyards.

Formerly a member of the ♦Hanseatic League, it was in almost continuous Prussian possession 1793–1919, when it again became a free city under the protection of the League of Nations. The annexation of the city by Germany marked the beginning of World War II. It reverted to Poland 1945, when the churches and old merchant houses were restored. The Lenin shipyards were the birthplace of Solidarity, the Polish resistance movement to pro-Soviet Communism, 1981.

GDP abbreviation for ♦*gross domestic product*.

GDR abbreviation for *German Democratic Republic*, the former state of East Germany (see ♦Germany, East).

Gdynia port in N Poland; population (1990) 251,500. It was established 1920 to give newly constituted Poland a sea outlet to replace lost ♦Gdańsk. It has a naval base and shipyards and is now part of the "Tri-city," which includes Sopot and Gdańsk.

Ge in Greek mythology, an alternate name for ♦Gaia, goddess of the Earth.

gear a toothed wheel that transmits the turning movement of one shaft to another shaft. Gear wheels may be used in pairs, or in threes if both shafts are to turn in the same direction. The gear ratio—the ratio of the number of teeth on the two wheels—determines the torque ratio, the turning force on the output shaft compared with the turning force on the input shaft. The ratio of the angular velocities of the shafts is the inverse of the gear ratio.

The common type of gear for parallel shafts is the *spur gear*, with straight teeth parallel to the shaft axis. The *helical gear* has teeth cut along sections of a helix or corkscrew shape; the double form of the helix gear is the most efficient for energy transfer. *Bevil gears*, with tapering teeth set on the base of a cone, are used to connect intersecting shafts.

gecko any lizard of the family Gekkonidae. Geckos are common worldwide in warm climates, and have large heads and short, stout bodies. Many have no eyelids. Their adhesive toe pads enable them to climb vertically and walk upside down on smooth surfaces in their search for flies, spiders, and other prey.

The Texas banded gecko *Coleonyx brevis*, 4.5 in/12 cm long, is unusual in that it has no toe pads.

Geddes Patrick 1854–1932. Scottish town planner who established the importance of surveys, research work, and properly planned "diagnoses before treatment." His major work is *City Development* 1904. His protégé was Lewis ♦Mumford.

Gehenna another name for ♦hell; in the Old Testament, a valley S of Jerusalem where children were sacrificed to the Phoenician god Moloch and fires burned constantly.

Gehrig Lou (Henry Louis) 1903–1941. US baseball player. Nicknamed "The Iron Horse" for his incomparable stamina and strength, Gehrig was named the American League's most valuable player 1927, 1931, 1934, and 1936. Born in New York, Gehrig attended Columbia University. He was signed by the New York Yankees 1923 and went on to a 17-year career as the Yankees' first baseman and most consistent hitter.

Among his remarkable achievements as a ballplayer are his lifetime 493 home runs, his .340 lifetime batting average, and his record 2,130 consecutive games played. Diagnosed with a degenerative muscle disease (now known as "Lou Gehrig's disease"), he retired from baseball 1939 and was elected to the Baseball Hall of Fame the same year. A film biography, *Pride of the Yankees*, appeared 1942.

Gehry Frank 1929– . US architect, based in Los Angeles. His architecture approaches abstract art in its use of collage and montage techniques.

His own experimental house in Santa Monica 1977, Edgemar Shopping Center and Museum, Santa Monica 1988, and the Vitra Furniture Museum, Weil am Rhein, Switzerland 1989—his first building in Europe—demonstrate his vitality.

Geiger Hans 1882–1945. German physicist who produced the Geiger counter. After studying in Germany, he spent the period 1907–12 in Manchester, England, working with Ernest Rutherford on radioactivity. In 1908 they designed an instrument to detect and count ♦alpha particles, positively charged ionizing particles produced by radioactive decay.

In 1928 Geiger and Walther Müller produced a more sensitive version of the counter, which could detect all kinds of ionizing radiation.

Geiger counter any of a number of devices used for detecting nuclear radiation and/ or measuring its intensity by counting the number of ionizing particles produced (see ♦radioactivity). It detects the momentary current that passes between ♦electrodes in a suitable gas when a nuclear particle or a radiation pulse causes the ionization of that gas. The electrodes are connected to electronic devices that enable the number of particles passing to be measured. The increased frequency of measured particles indicates the intensity of radiation. It is named after Hans Geiger.

Geiger–Müller, Geiger–Klemperer, and Rutherford–Geiger counters are all devices often referred to loosely as Geiger counters.

Hans Geiger studied under Ernest ♦Rutherford, and was professor of physics at Kiel, Germany.

Geisel Theodor Seuss; better known as *Dr Seuss*. 1904–1991. US author. His first children's book, *And to Think That I Saw It on Mulberry Street*, was published 1937. His classic *Horton Hatches the Egg* appeared 1940. After winning Academy Awards for documentary films in 1946 and 1947, Geisel returned to writing children's books in the 1950s—among them, *Horton Hears a Who* 1954, *How the Grinch Stole Christmas* 1957, *The Cat in the Hat* 1957, and *Yertle the Turtle* 1958. He later wrote books for adults, including *Oh, the Places You'll Go!* 1989.

Born in Springfield, Massachusetts, and educated at Dartmouth, Geisel began his career as a cartoonist and illustrator.

geisha female entertainer (music, singing, dancing, and conversation) in Japanese tea-houses and at private parties. They are apprenticed from childhood and highly skilled in traditional Japanese arts and graces. There are now only approximately 20,000 geishas in Japan compared to 100,000 before World War II.

Geissler tube high-voltage ♦discharge tube in which traces of gas ionize and conduct electricity. Since the electrified gas takes on a luminous color characteristic of the gas, the instrument is also used in ♦spectroscopy. It was developed 1858 by the German physicist Heinrich Geissler (1814–1879).

gel solid produced by the formation of a three-dimensional cage structure, commonly of linked large-molecular-mass polymers, in which a liquid is trapped. It is a form of ♦colloid. A gel may be a jellylike mass (pectin, gelatin) or have a more rigid structure (silica gel).

gelatin water-soluble protein prepared from boiled hide and bone, used in cooking to set jellies, and in glues and photographic emulsions.

Gelderland (English *Guelders*) province of the E Netherlands
area 1,938 sq mi/5,020 sq km
population (1991) 1,817,000
cities capital Arnhem; Apeldoorn, Nijmegen, Ede
products livestock, textiles, electrical goods
history in the Middle Ages Gelderland was divided into Upper Gelderland (Roermond in N Limburg) and Lower Gelderland (Nijmegen, Arnhem, Zutphen). These territories were inherited by Charles V of Spain, but when the revolt against Spanish rule reached a climax 1579, Lower Gelderland joined the United Provinces of the Netherlands.

Geldof Bob 1954– . Irish fundraiser and rock singer, leader of the group the Boomtown Rats 1975–86. In the mid-1980s he instigated the charity Band Aid, which raised large sums of money for famine relief, primarily for Ethiopia.

Gell-Mann Murray 1929– . US physicist. In 1964 he formulated the theory of the ♦quark as one of the fundamental constituents of matter. In 1969 he was awarded a Nobel Prize for his work on elementary particles and their interaction.

He was R A Millikan professor of theoretical physics at the California Institute of Technology from 1967.

gem mineral valuable by virtue of its durability (hardness), rarity, and beauty, cut and polished for ornamental use, or engraved. Of 120 minerals known to have been used as gemstones, only about 25 are in common use in jewelry today; of these, the diamond, emerald, ruby, and sapphire are classified as precious, and all the others semiprecious, for example the topaz, amethyst, opal, and aquamarine.

Among the synthetic precious stones to have been successfully produced are rubies, sapphires, emeralds, and diamonds (first produced by General Electric in the US 1955). Pearls are not technically gems.

Gemara in Judaism, part of the ♦Talmud, the compilation of ancient Jewish law.

Gemayel Amin 1942– . Lebanese politician, a Maronite Christian; president 1982–88.

He succeeded his brother, president-elect *Bechir Gemayel* (1947–1982), on his assassination on Sept 14, 1982. The Lebanese parliament was unable to agree on a successor when his term expired, so separate governments were formed under rival Christian and Muslim leaders.

Gemeinschaft and **Gesellschaft** German terms (roughly, "community" and "association") coined by Ferdinand ◊Tönnies 1887 to contrast social relationships in traditional rural societies with those in modern industrial societies. He saw *Gemeinschaft* (traditional) as intimate and positive, and *Gesellschaft* (modern) as impersonal and negative.

In small-scale societies where everyone knows everyone else, the social order is seen as stable and the culture as homogeneous. In large urban areas life is faster and more competitive, and relationships are seen as more superficial, transitory, and anonymous.

Gemini prominent zodiacal constellation in the northern hemisphere represented as the twins Castor and Pollux. Its brightest star is ◊Pollux; ◊Castor is a system of six stars. The Sun passes through Gemini from late June to late July. Each Dec, the Geminid meteors radiate from Gemini. In astrology, the dates for Gemini are between about May 21 and June 21 (see ◊precession).

Gemini project US space program (1965–66) in which astronauts practiced rendezvous and docking of spacecraft, and working outside their spacecraft, in preparation for the ◊Apollo Moon landings.

Gemini spacecraft carried two astronauts and were launched by Titan rockets.

gemma (plural **gemmae**) unit of ◊vegetative reproduction, consisting of a small group of undifferentiated green cells. Gemmae are found in certain mosses and liverworts, forming on the surface of the plant, often in cup-shaped structures, or gemmae cups. Gemmae are dispersed by splashes of rain and can then develop into new plants. In many species, gemmation is more common than reproduction by ◊spores.

gender in grammar, one of the categories into which nouns are divided in many languages, such as masculine, feminine, and neuter (as in Latin, German, and Russian), masculine and feminine (as in French, Italian, and Spanish), or animate and inanimate (as in some North American Indian languages).

gene unit of inherited material, encoded by a strand of ◊DNA, and transcribed by ◊RNA. In higher organisms, genes are located on the ◊chromosomes. The term "gene," coined 1909 by the Danish geneticist Wilhelm Johannsen (1857–1927), refers to the inherited factor that consistently affects a particular character in an individual—for example, the gene for eye color. Also termed a Mendelian gene, after Gregor ◊Mendel, it occurs at a particular point or ◊locus on a particular chromosome and may have several variants or ◊alleles, each specifying a particular form of that character—for example, the alleles for blue or brown eyes. Some alleles show ◊dominance. These mask the effect of other alleles known as recessive (see ◊recessive gene).

In the 1940s, it was established that a gene could be identified with a particular length of DNA, which coded for a complete protein molecule, leading to the "one-gene-one-enzyme" principle. Later it was realized that proteins can be made up of several ◊polypeptide chains, each with a separate gene, so this principle was modified to "one-gene-one-polypeptide." However, the fundamental idea remains the same, that genes produce their visible effects simply by coding for proteins; they control the structure of those proteins via the genetic code, as well as the amounts produced and the timing of production. In modern genetics, the gene is identified either with the ◊cistron (a set of ◊codons that determines a complete polypeptide) or with the unit of selection (a Mendelian gene that determines a particular character in the organism on which ◊natural selection can act). Genes undergo ◊mutation and ◊recombination to produce the variation on which natural selection operates.

genealogy the study and tracing of family histories.

In the US there are many genealogical societies that trace people's descent and some groups, such as the Daughters of the American Revolution, limit membership to those who can demonstrate a particular lineage.

gene amplification technique by which selected DNA from a single cell can be repeatedly duplicated until there is a sufficient amount to analyze by conventional genetic techniques.

Gene amplification uses a procedure called the polymerase chain reaction. The sample of DNA is mixed with a solution of enzymes called polymerases, which enable it to replicate, and with a plentiful supply of nucleotides, the building blocks of DNA. The mixture is repeatedly heated and cooled. At each warming, the double-stranded DNA present separates into two single strands, and with each cooling the polymerase assembles a new paired strand for each single strand. Each cycle takes approximately 30 minutes to complete, so that after 10 hours there is one million times more DNA present than at the start.

The technique has been used to analyze DNA from a man who died 1959, showing the presence of sequences from the HIV virus in his cells. It can also be used to test for genetic defects in a single cell taken from an embryo, before the embryo is reimplanted in ◊in vitro fertilization.

gene bank collection of seeds or other forms of genetic material, such as tubers, spores, bacterial or yeast cultures, live animals and plants, frozen sperm and eggs, or frozen embryos. These are stored for possible future use in agriculture, plant and animal breeding, or in medicine, genetic engineering, or the restocking of wild habitats where species have become extinct. Gene banks will be increasingly used as the rate of extinction increases, depleting the Earth's genetic variety (biodiversity).

gene pool total sum of ◊alleles (variants of ◊genes) possessed by all the members of a given population or species alive at a particular time.

general senior military rank, the ascending grades being brigadier general, major general, lieutenant general, general and general of the army. The US rank of general of the army is equivalent to the British ◊field marshal.

General Agreement on Tariffs and Trade (GATT) organization within the United Nations founded 1948 with the aim of encouraging ◊free trade between nations through low tariffs, abolitions of quotas, and curbs on subsidies.

During the latest round of talks, begun 1986 in Uruguay and ending 1990 in Geneva, the US opposed EC restrictions on agricultural imports, but argued to maintain restrictions on textile imports to the US. The talks reached a deadlock Dec 1990 after negotiators failed to agree on a plan to reduce farm subsidies. Subsequent bilateral US/EC talks in Geneva and Brussels have repeatedly stalled over this issue.

general strike refusal to work by employees in several key industries, with the intention of paralyzing the economic life of a country. In British history, the General Strike was a nationwide strike called by the Trade Union Congress on May 3, 1926 in support of the miners' union.

The immediate cause of the 1926 General Strike was the report of a royal commission on the coal mining industry (Samuel Report 1926) which, among other things, recommended a cut in wages. The mine-owners wanted longer hours as well as lower wages. The miners' union under the leadership of A J Cook resisted with the slogan "not a penny off the pay, not a minute on the day." A coal strike started in early May 1926 and the miners asked the TUC to bring all major industries out on strike in support of the action; eventually it included more than 2 million workers. The Conservative government under Stanley Baldwin used troops, volunteers, and special constables to maintain food supplies and essential services, and had a monopoly on the information services, including BBC radio. After nine days the TUC ended the general strike, leaving the miners—who felt betrayed by the TUC—to remain on strike, unsuccessfully, until Nov 1926.

The Trades Disputes Act of 1927 made general strikes illegal.

generator machine that produces electrical energy from mechanical energy, as opposed to an ◊electric motor, which does the opposite. A simple generator (dynamo) consists of a wire-wound coil (◊armature) that is rotated between the poles of a permanent magnet. The movement of the wire in the magnetic field induces a current in the coil by ◊electromagnetic induction, which can be fed by means of a ◊commutator as a continuous direct current into an external circuit. Slip rings instead of a commutator produce an alternating current, when the generator is called an alternator.

gene shears new technique in ◊genetic engineering which may have practical applications in the future. The gene shears are pieces of messenger ◊RNA that can bind to other pieces of messenger RNA, recognizing specific sequences, and cut them at that point. If a piece of ◊DNA which codes for the shears can be inserted in the chromosomes of a plant or animal cell, that cell will then destroy all messenger RNA of a particular type. Genetic shears may be used to protect plants against viruses which infect them and cause disease. They might also be useful against ◊AIDS.

Genesis first book of the Old Testament, which includes the stories of the creation of the world, Adam and Eve, the Flood, and the history of the Jewish patriarchs Abraham, Isaac, Jacob, and Joseph (who brought his people to Egypt).

gene-splicing technique for inserting a foreign gene into laboratory cultures of bacteria to generate commercial biological products, such as synthetic insulin, hepatitis-B vaccine, and interferon. It was invented 1973 by the US scientists Stanley Cohen and Herbert Boyer, and patented in the US 1984. See ◊genetic engineering.

Cohen was working at Stanford University

and Boyer at the University of California. Cohen shared a 1989 Nobel Prize for Physiology or Medicine for his work in cell growth.

genet small, nocturnal, meat-eating mammal, genus *Genetta*, in the mongoose and civet family (Viverridae). Most species live in Africa, but *G. genetta* is also found in Europe and the Middle East. It is about 1.6 ft/50 cm long with a 1.5 ft/45 cm tail, and grayish yellow with rows of black spots. It climbs well.

Genet Jean 1910–1986. French dramatist, novelist, and poet, an exponent of the Theater of ♢Cruelty. His turbulent life and early years spent in prison are reflected in his drama, characterized by ritual, role-play, and illusion, in which his characters come to act out their bizarre and violent fantasies. His plays include *Les Bonnes/The Maids* 1947, *Le Balcon/The Balcony* 1957, and two plays dealing with the Algerian situation: *Les Nègres/The Blacks* 1959 and *Les Paravents/The Screens* 1961.

genetic code the way in which instructions for building proteins, the basic structural molecules of living matter, are "written" in the genetic material ♢DNA. This relationship between the sequence of bases (the subunits in a DNA molecule) and the sequence of ♢amino acids (the subunits of a protein molecule) is the basis of heredity. The code employs codons of three bases each, which direct the placement of a particular amino acid during the process of protein synthesis; it is the same in almost all organisms, except for a few minor differences recently discovered in some protozoa.

genetic disease any disorder caused at least partly by defective genes or chromosomes. In humans there are some 3,000 genetic diseases, including cleft palate, cystic fibrosis, Down's syndrome, haemophilia, Huntington's chorea, some forms of anemia, spina bifida, and Tay-Sachs disease.

genetic engineering deliberate manipulation of genetic material by biochemical techniques. It is often achieved by the introduction of new ♢DNA, usually by means of a virus or ♢plasmid. This can be for pure research or to breed functionally specific plants, animals, or bacteria. These organisms with a foreign gene added are said to be transgenic (see ♢transgenic organism).

In genetic engineering, the splicing and reconciliation of genes is used to increase knowledge of cell function and reproduction, but it can also achieve practical ends. For example, plants grown for food could be given the ability to fix nitrogen, found in some bacteria, and so reduce the need for expensive fertilizers, or simple bacteria may be modified to produce rare drugs. Developments in genetic engineering have led to the production of human insulin, human growth hormone, and a number of other bone-marrow stimulating hormones. New strains of animals have also been produced; a new strain of mouse was patented in the US 1989 (the application was rejected in the European patent office). A ♢vaccine against a sheep parasite (a larval tapeworm) has been developed by genetic engineering; most existing vaccines protect against bacteria and viruses. There is a risk that when transplanting genes between different types of bacteria (*Escherichia coli*, which lives in the human intestine, is often used) new and harmful strains might be produced. For this reason strict safety precautions are observed, and the altered bacteria are disabled in some way so they are unable to exist outside the laboratory.

genetic fingerprinting technique used for determining the pattern of certain parts of the genetic material ♢DNA that is unique to each individual. Like skin fingerprinting, it can accurately distinguish humans from one another, with the exception of identical siblings from multiple births.

Genetic fingerprinting involves isolating DNA from cells, then comparing and contrasting the sequences of component chemicals between individuals. The DNA pattern can be ascertained from a sample of skin, hair, or semen. Although differences are minimal (only 0.1% between unrelated people), certain regions of DNA, known as *hypervariable regions*, are unique to individuals.

Genetic fingerprinting is used in paternity testing, forensic medicine, and inbreeding studies.

genetics study of inheritance and of the units of inheritance (♢genes). The founder of genetics was Gregor ♢Mendel, whose experiments with plants, such as peas, showed that inheritance takes place by means of discrete "particles," which later came to be called genes.

Before Mendel, it had been assumed that the characteristics of the two parents were blended during inheritance, but Mendel showed that the genes remain intact, although their combinations change. Since Mendel, genetics has advanced greatly, first through ♢breeding experiments and light-microscope observations (Classical genetics), later by means of biochemical and electron-microscope studies (molecular genetics). An advance was the elucidation of the structure of ♢DNA by James D Watson and Francis Crick, and the subsequent cracking of the ♢genetic code. These discoveries opened up the possibility of deliberately manipulating genes, or ♢genetic engineering. See also ♢genotype, ♢phenotype, and ♢monohybrid inheritance.

Geneva (French *Genève*) Swiss city, capital of Geneva canton, on the shore of Lake Geneva; population (1990) city 167,200; canton 376,000. It is a point of convergence of natural routes and is a cultural and commercial center. Industries include the manufacture of watches, scientific and optical instruments, foodstuffs, jewelry, and musical boxes.

The site on which Geneva now stands was the chief settlement of the Allobroges, a central European tribe who were annexed to Rome 121 BC; Julius Caesar built an entrenched camp here. In the Middle Ages, Geneva was controlled by the prince-bishops of Geneva and the rulers of Savoy. Under the Protestant theologian John ♢Calvin, it became a center of the Reformation 1536–64; the Academy, which he founded 1559, became a university 1892. Geneva was annexed by France 1798; it was freed 1814 and entered the Swiss Confederation 1815. In 1864 the International Red Cross Society was established in Geneva. It was the headquarters of the ♢League of Nations, whose properties in Geneva passed 1946 into the possession of the United Nations.

Geneva Convention international agreement 1864 regulating the treatment of those wounded in war, and later extended to cover the types of weapons allowed, the treatment of prisoners and the sick, and the protection of civilians in wartime. The rules were revised at conventions held 1906, 1929, and 1949, and by the 1977 Additional Protocols.

Geneva, Lake (French *Lac Léman*) largest of the central European lakes, between Switzerland and France; area 225 sq mi/ 580 sq km.

Geneva Protocol international agreement 1925 designed to prohibit the use of poisonous gases, chemical weapons, and bacteriological methods of warfare. It came into force 1928 but was not ratified by the US until 1974.

Genghis Khan *c.* ?1167–1227. Mongol conqueror, ruler of all Mongol peoples from 1206. He began the conquest of N China 1213, overran the empire of the shah of Khiva 1219–25, and invaded N India, while his lieutenants advanced as far as the Crimea. When he died, his empire ranged from the Yellow Sea to the Black Sea; it continued to expand after his death to extend from Hungary to Korea. Genghis Khan controlled probably a larger area than any other individual in history. He was not only a great military leader, but the creator of a stable political system.

The ruins of his capital Karakorum are SW of Ulaanbaatar in Mongolia; his alleged remains are preserved at Ejin Horo, Inner Mongolia.

genitalia reproductive organs of sexually reproducing animals, particularly the external/visible organs of mammals: in males, the penis and the scrotum, which contains the testes, and in females, the clitoris and vulva.

genitive in the grammar of certain inflected languages, the form of a word used to indicate possession for nouns, pronouns, or adjectives.

Genji alternate name for ♢Minamoto, an ancient Japanese clan.

Prince Genji, "the shining prince," is the hero of one of Japan's best-known literary works, *Genji Monogatari/The Tale of Genji*, whose author is known as ♢Murasaki.

Gennesaret, Lake of another name for Lake ♢Tiberias (Sea of Galilee) in N Israel.

Genoa (Italian *Genova*) historic city in NW Italy, capital of Liguria; population (1989) 706,700. It is Italy's largest port; industries include oil-refining, chemicals, engineering, and textiles.

Decline followed its conquest by the Lombards 640, but from the 10th century it established a commercial empire in the W Mediterranean, pushing back the Muslims, and founding trading posts in Corsica, Sardinia, and N Africa; during the period of the Crusades, further colonies were founded in the kingdom of Jerusalem and on the Black Sea, where Genoese merchants enjoyed the protection of the Byzantine empire. At its peak about 1300, the city had a virtual monopoly of European trade with the East. Strife between lower-class Genoese and the ruling mercantile-aristocratic oligarchy led to weakness and domination by a succession of foreign powers, including Pope John XXII (1249–1334), Robert of Anjou, king of Naples (1318–43), and Charles VI of France (1368–1422). During the 15th century, most of its trade and colonies were taken over by Venice or the Ottomans.

Rebuilt after World War II, it became the busiest port on the Mediterranean, and the first to build modern container facilities.

The nationalist Giuseppe Mazzini and the explorer Columbus were born here.

genocide deliberate and systematic destruction of a national, racial, religious, or ethnic group defined by the exterminators as undesirable. The term is commonly applied to the policies of the Nazis during World War II (what they called the "final solution"—the extermination of all Jews in occupied Europe).

In 1948 the United Nations General Assembly adopted a convention on the prevention and punishment of genocide, as well as the Universal Declaration of ◊Human Rights.

genome the full complement of ◊genes carried by a single (haploid) set of ◊chromosomes. The term may be applied to the genetic information carried by an individual or to the range of genes found in a given species.

genotype the particular set of ◊alleles (variants of genes) possessed by a given organism. The term is usually used in conjunction with ◊phenotype, which is the product of the genotype and all environmental effects. See also ◊environment–heredity controversy.

Genova Italian form of ◊Genoa, city in Italy.

genre painting (French *genre* "kind," "type") painting scenes from everyday life. Genre paintings were enormously popular in the Netherlands and Flanders in the 17th century (Vermeer, de Hooch, and Brouwer were great exponents). The term "genre" is also used more broadly to mean a category in the arts, such as landscape painting, or literary forms, such as the detective novel.

Gentile da Fabriano c. 1370–1427. Italian painter of frescoes and altarpieces in the International Gothic style. Gentile was active in Venice, Florence, Siena, Orvieto, and Rome and collaborated with the artists Pisanello and Jacopo Bellini. *The Adoration of the Magi* 1423 (Uffizi, Florence) is typically rich in detail and crammed with courtly figures.

Gentileschi Artemisia 1593–c. 1652. Italian painter, born in Rome. She trained under her father Orazio Gentileschi, but her work is more melodramatic than his. She settled in Naples from about 1630 and focused on macabre and grisly subjects, such as *Judith Decapitating Holofernes* (Museo di Capodimonte, Naples).

Gentili Alberico 1552–1608. Italian jurist. He practiced law in Italy but having adopted Protestantism was compelled to flee to England, where he lectured on Roman law in Oxford. His publications, such as *De Jure Belli libri tres/On the Law of War, Book Three* 1598, made him the first true international law writer and scholar.

genus (plural *genera*) group of ◊species with many characteristics in common. Thus all doglike species (including dogs, wolves, and jackals) belong to the genus *Canis* (Latin "dog"). Species of the same genus are thought to be descended from a common ancestor species. Related genera are grouped into ◊families.

geochemistry science of chemistry as it applies to geology. It deals with the relative and absolute abundances of the chemical elements and their ◊isotopes in the Earth, and also with the chemical changes that accompany geologically processes.

geochronology the branch of geology that deals with the dating of the Earth by studying its rocks and contained fossils. The geologically time chart is a result of these studies, dividing Earth time into eons, eras, periods, and epochs determined on the basis of absolute and relative dating methods. Absolute dating methods involve the measurement of radioactive decay over time in certain chemical elements found in rocks, whereas relative dating methods establish the sequence of deposition of various rock layers by identifying and comparing their contained fossils.

geode in geology, a subspherical cavity into which crystals have grown from the outer wall into the center. Geodes often contain very well-formed crystals of quartz (including amethyst), calcite, or other minerals.

geodesy methods of surveying the Earth for making maps and correlating geological, gravitational, and magnetic measurements. Geodesic surveys, formerly carried out by means of various measuring techniques on the surface, are now commonly made by using radio signals and laser beams from orbiting satellites.

Geoffrey of Monmouth c. 1100–1154. Welsh writer and chronicler. While a canon at Oxford, he wrote *Historia Regum Britanniae/History of the Kings of Britain* c. 1139, which included accounts of the semilegendary kings Lear, Cymbeline, and Arthur, and *Vita Merlini*, a life of the legendary wizard. He was bishop-elect of St Asaph, N Wales, 1151 and ordained a priest 1152.

geography science of the Earth's surface; its topography, climate, and physical conditions, and how these factors affect people and society. It is usually divided into *physical geography*, dealing with landforms and climates; *biogeography*, dealing with the conditions that affect the distribution of animals and plants; and *human geography*, dealing with the distribution and activities of peoples on Earth.

geological time time scale embracing the history of the Earth from its physical origin to the present day. Geological time is divided into eras (Precambrian, Paleozoic, Mesozoic, Cenozoic), which in turn are divided into periods, epochs, ages, and finally chrons.

geology science of the Earth, its origin, composition, structure, and history. It is divided into several branches: *mineralogy* (the minerals of Earth), *petrology* (rocks), *stratigraphy* (the deposition of successive beds of sedimentary rocks), *palaeontology* (fossils), and *tectonics* (the deformation and movement of the Earth's crust).

Geology is regarded as part of earth science, a more widely embracing subject that brings in meteorology, oceanography, geophysics, and geochemistry.

geometric mean in mathematics, the nth root of the product of n positive numbers. The geometric mean m of two numbers p and q is such that $m = \sqrt{p \times q}$. For example, the mean of 2 and 8 is $\sqrt{2} \text{ m} 3 \: 8 = \sqrt{16} = 4$.

geometric progression or *geometric sequence* in mathematics, a sequence of terms (progression) in which each term is a constant multiple (called the common ratio) of the one preceding it. For example, 3, 12, 48, 192, 768, ... is a geometric progression with a common ratio 4, since each term is equal to the previous term multiplied by 4.

The sum of n terms of a *geometric series* $1 + r + r^2 + r^3 + ... + r^{n-1} + r^n$ is given by the formula $S_n = (1 - r^{n+1})/(1 - r)$ for all $r \neq 1$. For $r = 1$, the geometric series can be summed to infinity: $S_\infty = 1/(1 - r)$. See ◊arithmetic progression.

In nature, many single-celled organisms reproduce by splitting in two so that one cell gives rise to 2, then 4, then 8 cells, and so on, forming a geometric sequence 1, 2, 4, 8, 16, 32, ..., in which the common ratio is 2.

geometry branch of mathematics concerned with the properties of space, usually in terms of plane (two-dimensional) and solid (three-dimensional) figures. The subject is usually divided into *pure geometry*, which embraces roughly the plane and solid geometry dealt with in Euclid's *Elements*, and *analytical* or ◊*coordinate geometry*, in which problems are solved using algebraic methods. A third, quite distinct, type includes the non-Euclidean geometries.

Geometry probably originated in ancient Egypt, in land measurements necessitated by the periodic inundations of the river Nile, and was soon extended into surveying and navigation. Early geometers were the Greek mathematicians Thales, Pythagoras, and Euclid. Analytical methods were introduced and developed by the French philosopher René Descartes in the 17th century. From the 19th century, various non-Euclidean geometries were devised by the Germans Karl Gauss and Georg Riemann, the Russian Nikolai Lobachevsky, and others. These proved significant in the development of the theory of relativity and in the formulation of atomic theory.

geomorphology branch of geology that deals with the nature and origin of surface landforms such as mountains, valleys, plains, and plateaus.

At the end of the 19th century, US geologist William Morris Davis (1850–1934) advanced a unifying concept called the geomorphic cycle to this study. He believed that landforms

geological time chart

eon	era	period	epoch	millions of years ago	life forms
			Holocene	0.01	
		Quaternary	Pleistocene	1.8	humans appeared
			Pliocene	5	
	Cenozoic		Miocene	25	
		Tertiary	Oligocene	38	
			Eocene	55	
			Paleocene	65	mammals flourished
Phanerozoic		Cretaceous		144	heyday of dinosaurs
	Mesozoic	Jurassic		213	first birds
		Triassic		248	first mammals and dinosaurs
		Permian		286	reptiles expanded
		Carboniferous		360	first reptiles
	Paleozoic	Devonian		408	first amphibians
		Silurian		438	first land plants
		Ordovician		505	first fish
		Cambrian		590	first fossils
	Precambrian	Proterozoic		2,500	earliest living things
		Archaean		4,600	

progress from a youthful stage of high, rugged mountains to a more mature stage of rounded forms, eventually worn down to an old age of almost level plains. This kind of predictable pattern does not hold up under current insights. Any given landscape can be regarded only as the balance between whatever forces of uplift and erosion are operating at a given time. What a region is like now does not allow us to reconstruct its past or predict its future, necessarily, since mountain building is a long, drawn-out, intermittent, and uneven process. Even if the progression from youth to old age were an uninterrupted sequence, this progression could still produce different landforms, depending on climatic variables.

geophysics branch of geology using physics to study the Earth's surface, interior, and atmosphere. Studies also include winds, weather, tides, earthquakes, volcanoes, and their effects.

George Henry 1839–1897. US economist, born in Philadelphia. His *Progress and Poverty* 1879 suggested a "single tax" on land, to replace all other taxes on earnings and savings. He hoped such a land tax would abolish poverty, by ending speculation on land values. George's ideas have never been implemented thoroughly, although they have influenced taxation policy in many countries.

George six kings of Great Britain:

George I 1660–1727. King of Great Britain and Ireland from 1714. He was the son of the first elector of Hanover, Ernest Augustus (1629–1698), and his wife ♢Sophia, and a great-grandson of James I. He succeeded to the electorate 1698, and became king on the death of Queen Anne. He attached himself to the Whigs, and spent most of his reign in Hanover, never having learned English.

The British Parliament, seeking to ensure a Protestant line of succession to oppose the claim of the Catholic ♢James Edward Stuart, made George third in line after Queen Anne and his mother. He was supported upon his succession by the Whigs, especially Stanhope, Townsend, and Walpole. The king grew more and more dependent upon his advisers as scandal surrounded him; his supporters turned against him, demanding freedom of action as the price of reconciliation.

George II 1683–1760. King of Great Britain from 1727, when he succeeded his father, George I, whom he detested. He married Caroline of Anspach 1705. She supported Robert ♢Walpole's position as adviser, and Walpole rallied support for George during the ♢Jacobite rebellions against him.

George III 1738–1820. King of Great Britain and Ireland from 1760, when he succeeded his grandfather George II. His rule was marked by intransigence resulting in the loss of the American colonies, for which he shared the blame with his chief minister Lord North, and the emancipation of Catholics in England. Possibly suffering from ♢porphyria, he had repeated attacks of insanity, permanent from 1811. He was succeeded by his son George IV.

He was virtually blind in his later years, giving rise to suspicions and misunderstandings concerning documents and decrees for his signature.

George IV 1762–1830. King of Great Britain and Ireland from 1820, when he succeeded his father George III, for whom he had been regent during the king's period of insanity 1811–20.

In 1785 he secretly married a Catholic widow, Maria Fitzherbert, but in 1795 also married Princess ♢Caroline of Brunswick, in return for payment of his debts. His prestige was undermined by his treatment of Caroline (they separated 1796), his dissipation, and his extravagance. He was succeeded by his brother, the duke of Clarence, who became William IV.

George V 1865–1936. King of Great Britain from 1910, when he succeeded his father Edward VII. He was the second son, and became heir 1892 on the death of his elder brother Albert, Duke of Clarence. In 1893, he married Princess Victoria Mary of Teck (Queen Mary), formerly engaged to his brother. During World War I he made several visits to the front. In 1917, he abandoned all German titles for himself and his family. The name of the royal house was changed from Saxe-Coburg-Gotha (popularly known as Brunswick or Hanover) to Windsor.

His mother was Princess Alexandra of Denmark, sister of Empress Marie of Russia.

George VI 1895–1952. King of Great Britain from 1936, when he succeeded after the abdication of his brother Edward VIII, who had succeeded their father George V. Created Duke of York 1920, he married in 1923 Lady Elizabeth Bowes-Lyon (1900–), and their children are Elizabeth II and Princess Margaret. During World War II, he visited the Normandy and Italian battlefields.

George two kings of Greece:

George I 1845–1913. King of Greece 1863–1913. The son of Christian IX of Denmark, he was nominated to the Greek throne and, in spite of early unpopularity, became a highly successful constitutional monarch. He was assassinated by a Greek, Schinas, at Salonika.

George II 1890–1947. King of Greece 1922–23 and 1935–47. He became king on the expulsion of his father Constantine I 1922 but was himself overthrown 1923. Restored by the military 1935, he set up a dictatorship under Joannis ♢Metaxas, and went into exile during the German occupation 1941–45.

George, St patron saint of England. The story of St George rescuing a woman by slaying a dragon, evidently derived from the ♢Perseus legend, first appears in the 6th century. The cult of St George was introduced into W Europe by the Crusaders. His feast day is April 23.

He is said to have been martyred at Lydda in Palestine 303, probably under the Roman emperor Diocletian, but the other elements of his legend are of doubtful historical accuracy.

Georgetown capital and port of Guyana; population (1983) 188,000.

Founded 1781 by the British, it was held 1784–1812 by the Dutch, who renamed it Stabroek, and ceded to Britain 1814.

Georgetown or *Penang* chief port of the Federation of Malaysia, and capital of Penang, on the island of Penang; population (1980) 250,600. It produces textiles and toys.

It is named after King George III of Great Britain.

Georgia country in the Caucasus of SE Europe, bounded N by Russia, E by Azerbaijan, S by Armenia, and W by the Black Sea.

government There is a 250-seat legislature, the supreme soviet, to which deputies are elected by a majority system, and a second ballot runoff race in contests in which there

is no clear first-round majority. The executive state president is directly elected.

history Georgia was converted to Christianity in the 4th century AD. In the 7th century, with the weakening of the Persian and Byzantine empires, an independent Georgian kingdom was created. The kingdom became especially powerful between the late 11th and early 13th centuries. Thereafter the country fell under the sway of Persian, Mongol, and Turkish imperial powers, before being annexed by tsarist Russia in 1801. Tbilisi (Tiflis) developed into an important commercial center under the tsars; however, the Georgian language and church were gradually suppressed.

under Soviet control In May 1918, amid turmoil in the Russian Empire, Georgia reasserted its independence but, denied economic help from the West, its rebellion was crushed by the Red Army in Feb 1921. In 1922 Georgia entered the USSR as part of the Transcaucasian Federation, along with Armenia and Azerbaijan, before becoming a full republic in 1936. There was rapid industrialization between the 1920s and 1950s, but considerable resistance to rural collectivization, and political purges were instituted by police chief Lavrenti Beria during the 1930s. During World War II, the Soviet dictator Stalin ordered the deportation of 200,000 ♢Meskhetians to Central Asia.

growth of nationalism During the 1950s and 1960s, Georgia's administration became notorious for its laxity and corruption. A drive against crime and corruption was launched 1972–85 by Eduard ♢Shevardnadze, leader of the Georgian Communist Party (GCP), and there was accelerated Russification. This provoked a nationalist backlash, witnessed in the form of mass demonstrations and the founding, in 1974, of the Initiative Group for the Defense of Human Rights in Georgia by the university lecturer Zviad Gamsakhurdia. ♢Glasnost produced an intensification of the nationalist campaign in the later 1980s, with a Georgian Popular Front and separatist group, the National Democratic Party of Georgia, established 1988. This fueled anti-Georgian feeling among the republic's ♢Abkhazian and ♢Ossetian minorities. The massacre in Tbilisi of at least 20 peaceful Georgian pro-independence demonstrators by Soviet troops on April 9, 1989 added momentum to the nationalist movement and during 1989–90, with its old-guard leadership purged, the GCP joined the secessionist camp. After the seven-party Round Table–Free Georgia nationalist coalition triumphed in Georgia's Oct–Nov 1990 supreme soviet elections, Zviad Gamsakhurdia was elected state president. The new parliament voted, in Jan 1991, to establish a republican National Guard and end conscription to the Soviet Army.

independence declared In March 1991 Georgia boycotted the all-Union USSR constitutional referendum. Instead, the republic held a plebiscite on independence, which secured 99% approval. Independence was declared on April 9, 1991 and a campaign of civil disobedience against Soviet interests was launched. On May 26, 1991 Gamsakhurdia became the first republic president in the USSR to be directly elected, winning 87% of the vote and defeating five other candidates. President Gamsakhurdia failed to strongly denounce the anti-Gorbachev coup in Moscow in Aug 1991, prompting the resignation in protest of prime minister Tengiz Sigua. However, the GCP was banned in the wake of the failed Moscow coup.

civil unrest From Sept 1991 the increasingly

Georgia, Republic of

area 26,911 sq mi/69,700 sq km
capital Tbilisi
cities Kutaisi, Rustavi, Batumi, Sukhumi
physical largely mountainous with a variety
of landscape from the subtropical Black
Sea shores to the ice and snow of the crest
line of the Caucasus; chief rivers are Kura
and Rioni
features vacation resorts and spas on the
Black Sea; good climate; two autonomous
republics, Abkhazia and Adzharia; one
autonmous region, South Ossetia
interim head of state Eduard Shevardnadze
from 1992
head of government Tengiz Sigua from 1992
political system transitional
political parties over 100 including: Georgian
Popular Front, moderate nationalist; National
Democratic Party of Georgia, radical nationalist; the National Independence Party; the
Monarchist Party
products tea, citrus and orchard fruits, tung
oil, tobacco, vines, silk, hydroelectricity
population (1990) 5,500,000 (70% Georgian,

8% Armenian, 8% Russian, 6% Azeri, 3%
Ossetian, 2% Abkhazian)
language Georgian
religion Georgian Church, independent of
the Russian Orthodox Church since 1917
chronology
1918–21 Independent republic.
1921 Uprising quelled by Red Army and
Soviet republic established.
1922–36 Linked with Armenia and Azerbaijan
as the Transcaucasian Republic.
1936 Became separate republic within USSR.
1981–88 Increasing demands for autonomy,
spearheaded from 1988 by the Georgian
Popular Front.
1989 March-April: Abkhazians demanded
secession from Georgia, provoking inter-
ethnic clashes. April: Georgian Communist
Party (GCP) leadership purged. July: state of
emergency imposed in Abkhazia; inter-ethnic
clashes in South Ossetia. Nov: economic
and political sovereignty declared.
1990 March: GCP monopoly ended. Oct:
nationalist coalition triumphed in supreme
soviet elections. Nov: Zviad Gamsakhurdia
became president. Dec: GCP seceded from
Communist Party of USSR; calls for Georgian
independence.
1991 April: declared independence. May:
Gamsakhurdia popularly elected president.
Aug: GCP outlawed and all relations with
USSR severed. Sept: anti-Gamsakhurdia
demonstrations; state of emergency declared.
Dec: Georgia failed to join new Commonwealth
of Independent States (CIS).
1992 Jan: Gamsakhurdia fled to Armenia;
Sigua appointed prime minister; Georgia
admitted into Conference on Security and
Cooperation in Europe (CSCE). Eduard
Shevardnadze appointed interim president.
July: admitted into United Nations (UN).
Oct: Shevardnadze elected chair of new
parliament. Clashes in South Ossetia and
Abkhazia continued.

dictatorial president, arresting political opponents and ordering the closure of pro-opposition
newspapers, faced a growing popular protest movement, fueled further by government
troops firing on the crowds. With disorder
mounting, Gamsakhurdia declared a state of
emergency on Sept 24, 1991. By late Oct
1991 most of the leadership of the nationalist National Democratic Party (NDP), headed
by Giorgi Chanturia, had been arrested. The
power struggle intensified and Gamsakhurdia
was forced to flee to Armenia on Jan 6, 1992.
Distracted by these events, Georgia failed to
join the new ⬦Commonwealth of Independent States (CIS) which was established in
Dec 1991.
international recognition In Jan 1992
Georgia was admitted into the ⬦Conference
on Security and Cooperation in Europe, and in
July it became a member of the United Nations
(UN).
multiparty elections A military council with
Tengiz Sigua as prime minister, having
crushed a rebellion by Gamsakhurdia supporters, gave way to a new parliament elected Oct
1992, with Shevardnadze as its chair. There
is an exceptionally fragmented multiparty system, riven by clan and regional rivalries, with
more than 100 parties competing for power.
The new government had to deal with violent unrest in South Ossetia and Akhazia,
both of which were seeking autonomy. *See
illustration box.*

Georgia state in SE US; nicknames Empire
State of the South/Peach State
area 58,904 sq mi/152,600 sq km
capital Atlanta
cities Columbus, Savannah, Macon
features Okefenokee National Wildlife Refuge (656 sq mi/1,700 sq km), Sea Islands,
historic Savannah
products poultry, livestock, tobacco, corn,
peanuts, cotton, soybeans, kaolinite, crushed
granite, textiles, carpets, aircraft, paper products
population (1990) 6,480,000
famous people Jim Bowie; Erskine Caldwell;
Jimmy Carter; Ray Charles; Ty Cobb; Bobby Jones; Martin Luther King, Jr; Margaret
Mitchell; James Oglethorpe; Jackie Robinson
history explored 1540 by Hernando de Soto;
claimed by the British and named after
George II of England; founded 1733 as a colony

Georgia

Atlanta

for the industrious poor by James Oglethorpe,
a philanthropist, and was one of the original
13 states of the US. In 1864, during the Civil
War, General W T Sherman's Union troops cut
a wide swath of destruction as they marched
from Atlanta to the sea. The state benefited
after World War II from the growth of Atlanta
as the financial and transportation center of the
SE US.

Georgian period of English architecture,
furniture making, and decorative art between
1714 and 1830. The architecture is mainly
Classical in style, although external details and
interiors were often rich in Rococo carving.
Furniture was frequently made of mahogany
and satinwood, and mass production became
increasingly common; designers included
Thomas Chippendale, George Hepplewhite,
and Thomas Sheraton. The silver of this period
is particularly fine, and ranges from the earlier,
simple forms to the ornate, and from the Neo-
Classical style of Robert Adam to the later,
more decorated pre-Victorian taste.

Georgian or ***Grazinian*** member of any of
a number of related groups which make up
the largest ethnic group in Georgia and the
surrounding area. There are 3–4 million speakers of Georgian, a member of the Caucasian
language family.
"Georgian" is a distortion of *Gurji*, the
name by which these people were known
to the Turks. Distinct Georgian communities
include Khevsurs (E Georgia), Kakhetians (E
Georgia), Meskhians (S Georgia), Imeretians
(W Georgia), Syanians (W Georgia),
Lekhumians (NW Georgia), Rachuelians (NW
Georgia), Gurians (W Georgia), Mengrelians
(W Georgia), and Laz (Turkey).

geostationary orbit circular path 22,300 mi/
35,900 km above the Earth's equator on which
a ⬦satellite takes 24 hours, moving from west
to east, to complete an orbit, thus appearing to
hang stationary over one place on the Earth's
surface. Geostationary orbits are particularly
used for communications satellites and weather satellites. They were first thought of by the
author Arthur C Clarke. A **geosynchronous
orbit** lies at the same distance from Earth but
is inclined to the equator.

geothermal energy energy extracted for
heating and electricity generation from natural
steam, hot water, or hot dry rocks in the Earth's
crust. Water is pumped down through an injection well where it passes through joints in
the hot rocks. It rises to the surface through a
recovery well and may be converted to steam
or run through a heat exchanger. Dry steam
may be directed through turbines to produce
electricity.

ger. in grammar, the abbreviation for ⬦ger-
und.

geranium or cranesbill, plant of the genus
Geranium, family Geraniaceae, which contains
about 400 species. The plants are named after
the long, beaklike process attached to the seed
vessels. When ripe, this splits into coiling spirals, which jerk the seeds out, assisting in their
distribution.

gerbil any of numerous rodents of the family
Cricetidae with elongated back legs and good
hopping or jumping ability. Gerbils range from
mouse-to rat-size, and have hairy tails. Many
of the 13 genera live in dry, sandy, or sparsely
vegetated areas of Africa and Asia.
The Mongolian jird or gerbil *Meriones
unguiculatus* is a popular pet.

gerenuk antelope *Litocranius walleri* about

3 ft/1 m at the shoulder, with a greatly elongated neck. It browses on leaves, often balancing on its hind legs to do so. Sandy brown in color, it is well camouflaged in its E African habitat of dry scrub.

geriatrics branch of medicine concerned with diseases and problems of the elderly.

Géricault Théodore (Jean Louis André) 1791–1824. French Romantic painter. *The Raft of the Medusa* 1819 (Louvre, Paris) was notorious for exposing a relatively recent scandal in which shipwrecked sailors had been cut adrift and left to drown. He painted *The Derby at Epsom* 1821 (Louvre, Paris) and pictures of cavalry. He also painted portraits.

germ colloquial term for a microorganism that causes disease, such as certain ♢bacteria and ♢viruses. Formerly, it was also used to mean something capable of developing into a complete organism (such as a fertilized egg, or the ♢embryo of a seed).

German native to or an inhabitant of Germany and their descendants, as well as their culture and language. In eastern Germany the Sorbs comprise a minority population who, in addition to German, speak a Slavic language. The Austrians and Swiss Germans speak German, although they are ethnically distinct. German-speaking minorities are found in France (Alsace-Lorraine), Romania (Transylvania), Czechoslovakia, Siberian Russia, Central Asia, Poland, Italy (Tyrol), and in areas that once belonged to the German Empire abroad.

German art painting and sculpture in the Germanic north of Europe from the early Middle Ages to the present.

Middle Ages A revival of the arts was fostered by the emperor Charlemagne in the early 9th century. In the late 10th and early 11th centuries under the Ottoman emperors new styles emerged. German artists produced remarkable work in the Romanesque and later Gothic style. Wood carving played a major role in art.

15th century The painter Stefan Lochner, active in Cologne, excelled in the International Gothic style. Sculptors included Hans Mültscher (*c.* 1400–57) and the wood carver Veit Stoss (Wit Stwosz), active in Nuremberg and Poland.

16th century The incarnation of the Renaissance in Germany was Albrecht Dürer; other painters included Hans Baldung Grien, Lucas Cranach, Albrecht Altdorfer, Mathias Grünewald, and Hans Holbein.

17th and 18th centuries Huge wall and ceiling paintings decorated new churches and princely palaces.

19th century Caspar David Friedrich was a pioneer of Romantic landscape painting in the early 19th century. At the turn of the century came Jugendstil (corresponding to French Art Nouveau).

20th century The movement known as die Brücke (the Bridge) was parallel with Fauvism. It was followed by the Munich Expressionist group Blaue Reiter (Blue Rider). After World War I, Otto Dix, George Grosz, and Max Beckmann developed satirical Expressionist styles. The Bauhaus school of design, emphasizing the dependence of form on function, had enormous impact abroad. The painter Max Ernst moved to Paris and became a founding member of Surrealism. Artists since 1945 include Joseph Beuys and Anselm Kiefer.

German expansion aggressive territorial expansion of ♢Germany during the 1930s before the outbreak of World War II.

Germanic languages branch of the Indo-European language family, divided into *East Germanic* (Gothic, now extinct), *North Germanic* (Danish, Faroese, Icelandic, Norwegian, Swedish), and *West Germanic* (Afrikaans, Dutch, English, Flemish, Frisian, German, Yiddish).

The Germanic languages differ from the other Indo-European languages most prominently in the consonant shift known as Grimm's law: the sounds *p, t, k* became either (as in English) *f, th, h* or (as in Old High German) *f, d, h*. Thus, the typical Indo-European of the Latin *pater* is *father* in English and *Fater* in Old High German. In addition, the Indo-European *b, d, g* moved to become *p, t, k* (in English) or (in Old High German) *f, ts, kh*; compare Latin *duo*, English *two*, and German *zwei* (pronounced tsvai).

Germanicus Caesar 15 BC–AD 19. Roman general. He was the adopted son of the emperor ♢Tiberius and married the emperor ♢Augustus' granddaughter Agrippina. Although he refused the suggestion of his troops that he claim the throne on the death of Augustus, his military victories in Germany made Tiberius jealous. Sent to the Middle East, he died near Antioch, possibly murdered at the instigation of Tiberius. He was the father of ♢Caligula and Agrippina, mother of ♢Nero.

germanium brittle, gray-white, weakly metallic (♢metalloid) element, symbol Ge, atomic number 32, atomic weight 72.6. It belongs to the silicon group, and has chemical and physical properties between those of silicon and tin. Germanium is a semiconductor material and is used in the manufacture of transistors and integrated circuits. The oxide is transparent to infrared radiation, and is used in military applications. It was discovered 1886 by German chemist Clemens Winkler (1838–1904).

In parts of Asia, germanium and plants containing it are used to treat a variety of diseases, and it is sold in the West as a food supplement despite fears that it may cause kidney damage.

German language member of the Germanic group of the Indo-European language family, the national language of Germany and Austria, and an official language of Switzerland. There are many spoken varieties of German, including High German (*Hochdeutsch*) and Low German (*Plattdeutsch*).

"High" and "Low" refer to dialects spoken in the highlands or the lowlands rather than to social status. Hochdeutsch originated in the central and southern highlands of Germany, Austria, and Switzerland; Plattdeutsch from the lowlands of N Germany. Standard and literary German is based on High German, in particular on the Middle German dialect used by Martin Luther for his translation of the Bible in the 16th century. Low German is closer to English in its sound system, the verb "to make" being *machen* in High German but *maken* in Low German. Such English words as *angst*, *blitz*, *frankfurter*, *hamburger*, *poltergeist*, and *sauerkraut* are borrowings from High German.

German literature the most substantial relic of the *Old High German* period is the fragmentary alliterative poem the *Hildebrandslied* (about 800). In the *Middle High German* period there was a flowering of the vernacular, which had been forced into subservience to Latin after the early attempts at encouragement by Charlemagne. The court epics of Hartmann von Aue, Gottfried von Strassburg,

and Wolfram von Eschenbach in the early 13th century were modeled on French style and material, but the folk-epic, the *Nibelungenlied*, revived the spirit of the old heroic Germanic sagas. Adopted from France and Provence, the *Minnesang* reached its height in the lyric poetry of Walther von der Vogelweide.

Modern German literature begins in the 16th century with the standard of language set by Martin Luther's Bible. Also in this century came the climax of popular drama in the *Fastnachtsspiel* as handled by the songwriter Hans Sachs. In the later 16th and 17th centuries French influence was renewed and English influence, by troupes of players, was introduced. Martin Opitz's *Buch von der deutschen Poeterey* 1624, in which he advocates the imitation of foreign models, epitomizes the German Renaissance, which was followed by the Thirty Years' War, vividly described in H J C Grimmelshausen's *Simplicissimus*.

In the 18th century French Classicism predominated, but Romanticism was anticipated by the Germanic *Messias* of Klopstock. Both the playwright G E Lessing and the critic J G Herder were admirers of Shakespeare, and Herder's enthusiasm inaugurated the *Sturm und Drang* phase which emphasized individual inspiration. His collection of folk songs was symptomatic of the feeling that inspired Gottfried Bürger's ballad *Lenore*. The greatest representatives of the Classical period at the end of the century were Wolfgang von Goethe and Friedrich Schiller, but their ideals were combated by the new Romantic school that based its theories on the work of J L Teck and the brothers August and Friedrich von Schlegel, and included Novalis, Achim von Arnim, Clemens Brentano, J F von Eichendorff, Adelbert von Chamisso, J L Uhland, and E T A Hoffmann.

With the playwrights Heinrich von Kleist and Franz Grillparzer in the early 19th century, stress on the poetic element in drama ended, and the psychological aspect soon received greater emphasis. Emerging around 1830 was the "Young German" movement, with Heinrich Heine among its leaders, which the authorities tried to suppress. Other 19th-century writers include Jeremias Gotthelf, who recounted stories of peasant life; the psychological novelist Friedrich Spielhagen; poets and novella writers Gottfried Keller and Theodor Storm (1817–1888); and the realist novelists Wilhelm Raabe and Theodor Fontane (1819–1898). Influential in literature, as in politics and economics, were Karl Marx and Friedrich Nietzsche.

Outstanding writers of the early 20th century included the lyric poets Stefan George and Rainer Maria Rilke; the poet and dramatist Hugo von Hofmannsthal; and the novelists Thomas and Heinrich Mann, E M Remarque, and Hermann Hesse. Just before World War I Expressionism emerged in the poetry of Georg Trakl. It dominated the novels of Franz Kafka and the plays of Ernst Toller, Franz Werfel, and Georg Kaiser, and was later to influence Bertolt Brecht. Under Nazism many good writers left the country, while others were silenced or ignored. After World War II came the Swiss dramatists Max Frisch and Friedrich Dürrenmatt, the novelists Heinrich Böll, Christa Wolf, and Siegfried Lenz, the poet Paul Celan, and the poet and novelist Günter Grass.

German measles or *rubella* mild, communicable virus disease, usually caught by children. It is marked by a sore throat, pinkish rash, and

Germany

Federal Republic of (*Bundesrepublik Deutschland***)**

area 137,853 sq mi/357,041 sq km
capital Berlin
cities Cologne, Munich, Essen, Frankfurt-am-Main, Dortmund, Stuttgart, Düsseldorf, Leipzig, Dresden, Chemnitz, Magdeburg; ports Hamburg, Kiel, Cuxhaven, Bremerhaven, Rostock
physical flat in N, mountainous in S with Alps; rivers Rhine, Weser, Elbe flow N, Danube flows SE, Oder, Neisse flow N along Polish frontier; many lakes, including Müritz
environment acid rain causing *Waldsterben* (tree death) affects more than half the country's forests; industrial E Germany has the highest sulfur dioxide emissions in the world per head of population
features Black Forest, Harz Mountains, Erzgebirge (Ore Mountains), Bavarian Alps, Fichtelgebirge, Thüringer Forest
head of state Richard von Weizsäcker from 1984
head of government Helmut Kohl from 1982
political system liberal democratic federal republic
political parties Christian Democratic Union (CDU), right of center; Christian Social Union (CSU), right of center; Social Democratic Party, left of center; Free Democratic Party (FDP), liberal; Greens, environmentalist; Republicans, far right; Party of Democratic Socialism (PDS), reform-communist (formerly Socialist Unity Party: SED)
exports machine tools (world's leading exporter), automobiles, commercial vehicles, electronics, industrial goods, textiles, chemicals, iron, steel, wine, lignite (world's largest producer), uranium, coal, fertilizers, plastics
currency Deutschmark
population (1990) 78,420,000 (including nearly 5,000,000 "guest workers," *Gastarbeiter*,

of whom 1,600,000 are Turks; the rest are Yugoslav, Italian, Greek, Spanish, and Portuguese); growth rate –0.7% p.a.
life expectancy men 68, women 74
languages German, Sorbian
religions Protestant 42%, Roman Catholic 35%
literacy 99% (1985)
GNP $1,250 bn (1989); $16,200 per head
chronology
1945 Germany surrendered; country divided into four occupation zones (US, French, British, Soviet).
1948 Blockade of West Berlin.
1949 Establishment of Federal Republic under the "Basic Law" Constitution with Adenauer as chancellor; establishment of the German Democratic Republic as an independent state.
1953 Uprising in East Berlin suppressed by Soviet troops.
1954 Grant of full sovereignty to both West Germany and East Germany.
1957 West Germany was a founder-member of the European Economic Community; recovery of Saarland.
1961 Construction of Berlin Wall.
1963 Retirement of Chancellor Adenauer.
1964 Treaty of Friendship and Mutual Assistance signed between East Germany and USSR.
1969 Willy Brandt became chancellor of West Germany.
1971 Erich Honecker elected SED leader in East Germany.
1972 Basic Treaty between West Germany and East Germany; treaty ratified 1973, normalizing relations between the two.
1974 Resignation of Brandt; Helmut Schmidt became chancellor.
1975 East German friendship treaty with USSR renewed for 25 years.
1982 Helmut Kohl became West German chancellor.
1987 Official visit of Honecker to the Federal Republic.
1988 Death of West German Bavarian CSU leader Franz-Josef Strauss.
1989 West Germany: rising support for far right in local and European elections, declining support for Kohl. East Germany: mass exodus to West Germany began. Honecker replaced by Egon Krenz. National borders opened in Nov, including Berlin Wall. Reformist Hans Modrow appointed prime minister. Krenz replaced.
1990 March: East German multiparty elections won by a coalition led by the right-wing CDU. Oct 3: official reunification of East and West Germany. Dec 2: first all-German elections since 1932, resulting in a victory for Kohl.
1991 Kohl's popularity declined after tax increase. The CDU lost its Bundesrat majority to the SPD. Racism continued with violent attacks on foreigners.
1992 Neo-Nazi riots against immigrants continued.

marked the turning point of World War I. After winning the battle the Allies advanced steadily, and by Sept, Germany had lost all the territory it had gained during the Spring.

Germany Federal Republic of; country in central Europe, bounded N by the North and Baltic Seas and Denmark, E by Poland and Czechoslovakia, S by Austria and Switzerland, and W by France, Luxembourg, Belgium, and the Netherlands.
government With reunification 1990 the German government remained almost identical to that of former West Germany. It is based on the West German constitution (the Basic Law), drafted 1948–49 by the Allied military governors and German provincial leaders in an effort to create a stable, parliamentary form of government, to diffuse authority, and to safeguard liberties. It borrowed from British, American, and neighboring European constitutional models. It established, firstly, a federal system of government built around ten (16 since reunification) *Länder* (federal states), each with its own constitution, elected parliament, and government headed by a minister-president. The *Länder* have original powers in education, police, and local government, and are responsible for the administration of federal legislation through their own civil services. They have local taxation powers and are assigned shares of federal income tax and VAT revenues, being responsible for 50% of government spending.

The constitution, secondly, created a new federal parliamentary democracy, built around a two-chamber legislature comprising a directly elected 662-member lower house Bundestag (federal assembly), and an indirectly elected 69-member upper house Bundesrat (federal council). Bundestag representatives are elected for four-year terms by universal suffrage under a system of "personalized proportional representation" in which electors have one vote for an ordinary constituency seat and one for a *Land* party list, enabling adjustments in seats gained by each party to be made on a proportional basis.

Political parties must win at least 5% of the national vote to qualify for shares of "list seats." Bundesrat members are nominated and sent in blocs by *Länder* governments, each state being assigned between three and five seats depending on population size. The Bundestag is the dominant parliamentary chamber, electing from the ranks of its majority party or coalition a chancellor (prime minister) and cabinet to form the executive government. Once appointed, the chancellor can only be removed by a "constructive vote of no confidence" in which a majority votes positively in favor of an alternative leader.

Legislation is effected through all-party committees. The Bundesrat has few powers to initiate legislation, but has considerable veto authority. All legislation relating to *Länder* responsibilities requires its approval, constitutional amendments need a two-thirds Bundesrat (and Bundestag) majority, while the Bundesrat can temporarily block bills or force amendments in joint Bundestag–Bundesrat "conciliation committees." Bundestag members also join an equal number of representatives elected by *Länder* parliaments in a special Bundesversammlung (federal convention) every five years to elect a federal president as head of state. The president, however, has few powers and is primarily a titular figure.

The 1949 constitution is a written document.

slight fever, and has an incubation period of two to three weeks. If a woman contracts it in the first three months of pregnancy, it may cause serious damage to the unborn child.

For this reason immunization is recommended for girls.

German Shepherd see ▷Alsatian, a breed of dog.

German silver or **nickel silver** silvery alloy of nickel, copper, and zinc. It is widely used

for cheap jewelry and the base metal for silver plating. The letters EPNS on silverware stand for **e**lectro**p**lated **n**ickel **s**ilver.

German Spring offensive Germany's final offensive on the Western Front during World War I. By early 1918, German forces outnumbered the Allies on the Western Front. Germany staged three separate offensives, which culminated in the Second Battle of the Marne, fought between July 15 and Aug 6. It

Adherence to it is policed by an independent federal constitutional court based at Karlsruhe which is staffed by 16 judges, who serve terms of up to 12 years. All-party committees from the Bundestag and Bundesrat select eight each. The court functions as a guarantor of civil liberties and adjudicator in Federal–*Land* disputes. (Similar courts function at the *Land* level.)

history For history before 1949, see ▷Germany, history. In 1949 Germany was divided by the Allied powers and the Soviet Union, forming the German Democratic Republic in the eastern part of the country (formerly the Soviet zone of occupation), and the Federal Republic of Germany in the west (comprising the British, US, and French occupation zones under Allied military control following Germany's surrender 1945). For the next four and a half decades West and East Germany were divided by the policies of the ▷Cold War, with West Germany becoming the strongest European NATO power, and East Germany a vital member of ▷Comecon and the ▷Warsaw Pact during the era of Soviet leader Brezhnev, stationing Soviet medium-range nuclear missiles on its soil.

West Germany under Adenauer In postwar West Germany, a policy of demilitarization, decentralization, and democratization was instituted by the Allied control powers and a new, intentionally provisional, constitution framed, which included eventual German reunification. West ▷Berlin was blockaded by the Soviet Union 1948–49, but survived to form a constituent *Land* in the Federal Republic, after an airlift operation by the Allied powers. Politics during the Federal Republic's first decade were dominated by the Christian Democratic Union (CDU), led by the popular Konrad ▷Adenauer. Chancellor Adenauer and his economics minister, Ludwig ▷Erhard, established a successful approach to economic management, termed the "social market economy," which combined the encouragement of free market forces with strategic state intervention on the grounds of social justice. This new approach, combined with aid under the ▷Marshall Plan and the enterprise of the labor force (many of whom were refugees from the partitioned East), brought rapid growth and reconstruction during the 1950s and 1960s, an era termed the "miracle years."

During this period, West Germany was also reintegrated into the international community. It gained full sovereignty 1954, entered NATO 1955, emerging as a loyal supporter of the US, and, under Adenauer's lead, was a founder member of the European Economic Community 1957. Close relations with France enabled the ▷Saarland to be transferred to German sovereignty 1957.

East Germany sovietized East Germany dissolved its five *Länder* (Brandenburg, Mecklenburg–West Pomerania, Saxony, Saxony-Anhalt, and Thuringia) 1952, and its Chamber of States, or upper house, 1958, vesting local authority in 15 *Bezirke*, or administrative districts. Under the 1968 constitution the supreme legislative and executive body in the German Democratic Republic was the Volkskammer (people's chamber), whose 500 members (including 66 from East Berlin) were elected every five years by universal suffrage. The years immediately after 1949 saw the rapid establishment of a communist regime on the Soviet model, involving the nationalization of industry, the formation of agricultural collectives, and the creation of a one-party political system. Opposition to such sovietization led,

during food shortages, to demonstrations and an uprising 1953, which was suppressed by Soviet troops. East Germany became a sovereign state 1954, recognized at first only by the communist powers.

Brandt and Ostpolitik In 1961, East Germany's construction of the ▷Berlin Wall to prevent refugees from leaving the East created a political crisis that vaulted West Berlin's mayor, Willy ▷Brandt, to international prominence. Domestically, Brandt played a major role in shifting the Social Democratic Party (SPD) away from its traditional Marxist affiliation toward a more moderate position. Support for the SPD steadily increased after this policy switch and the party joined the CDU in a "grand coalition" 1966–69, before gaining power itself, with the support of the FDP, under Brandt's leadership 1969. As chancellor, Brandt introduced the foreign policy of ▷Ostpolitik, which sought reconciliation with Eastern Europe as a means of improving contacts between East and West Germany.

East Germany saw economic reforms and improved living conditions in the 1960s, and during the next decade a more moderate political stance was adopted, with the replacement of the Stalinist Socialist Unity Party (SED) leader Walter ▷Ulbricht by the pragmatic Erich ▷Honecker. Economic and diplomatic relations with the West were extended.

Schmidt's centrist course West German treaties 1970 normalized relations with the Soviet Union and Poland, and recognized the Oder–Neisse border line, and in 1972 a treaty was effected with East Germany, acknowledging East Germany's borders and separate existence and enabling both countries to enter the United Nations 1973. Brandt resigned as chancellor 1974, after the revelation that his personal assistant had been an East German spy. His successor, the former finance minister, Helmut ▷Schmidt, adhered to Ostpolitik and emerged as a leading advocate of European cooperation.

The CDU is represented in Bavaria by a more right-wing sister party, the Christian Social Union (CSU). A West German SPD–FDP (Free Democratic Party) coalition gained a comfortable victory 1980 when the controversial Franz-Josef ▷Strauss headed the CDU–CSU ticket. Between 1980 and 1982, the left wing of the SPD and the liberal FDP were divided over military policy (in particular the proposed stationing of US nuclear missiles in West Germany) and economic policy.

Kohl's chancellorship Chancellor Schmidt fought to maintain a moderate, centrist course but the FDP eventually withdrew from the federal coalition 1982 and joined forces with the CDU, led by Dr Helmut ▷Kohl, to unseat the chancellor in a "positive vote of no confidence." Helmut Schmidt immediately retired from politics and the SPD, led by Hans-Jochen Vögel, was heavily defeated in the Bundestag elections 1983, losing votes on the left to the new environmentalist Green Party. The new Kohl administration, with the FDP's Hans-Dietrich Genscher remaining as foreign minister, adhered closely to the external policy of the previous chancellorship.

At home, a freer market approach was introduced. With unemployment rising to 2.5 million in 1984, problems of social unrest emerged, while violent demonstrations greeted the installation of US nuclear missiles on German soil 1983–84. Internally, the Kohl administration was rocked by scandals over illegal party funding, which briefly touched

the chancellor himself. However, a strong recovery in the German economy from 1985 enabled the CDU–CSU–FDP coalition to gain reelection in the federal election 1987.

During 1988–89, after the death of the CSU's Franz-Josef Strauss, support for the far-right Republican party began to climb, and it secured 7% of the vote in the European Parliament elections of June 1989. In 1989–90 events in East Germany and elsewhere in Eastern Europe caused half a million economic and political refugees to enter the Federal Republic, as well as reopening the debate on reunification (*Wiedervereinigung*); this resulted in West German politics becoming more highly charged and polarized. The CDU gave strong support to swift, graduated moves toward "confederative" reunification, if desired, following free elections in East Germany.

exodus to West Germany In East Germany Honecker had been urged by the USSR since 1987 to accelerate the pace of domestic economic and political reform; his refusal to do so increased grassroots pressure for liberalization. In Sept 1989, after the violent suppression of a church and civil-rights activists' demonstration in Leipzig, an umbrella dissident organization, Neue Forum (New Forum), was illegally formed. The regime was further destabilized between Aug and Oct 1989 both by the exodus of more than 30,000 of its citizens to West Germany through Hungary (which had opened its borders with Austria in May) and by Honecker's illness during the same period.

reform in East Germany On 6 and Oct 7 the Soviet leader Mikhail Gorbachev visited East Berlin, and made plain his desire to see greater reform. This catalyzed the growing reform movement, and a wave of demonstrations (the first since 1953) swept East Berlin, Dresden, Leipzig, and smaller towns. At first, under Honecker's orders, they were violently broken up by riot police. However, the security chief, Egon ▷Krenz, ordered a softer line and in Dresden the reformist Communist Party leader, Hans Modrow, actually marched with the protesters. Faced with the rising tide of protest and the increasing exodus to West Germany (between 5,000 and 10,000 people a day), which caused grave disruption to the economy, Honecker was replaced as party leader and head of state by Krenz on Oct 18–24, 1991. In an attempt to keep up with the reform movement, Krenz sanctioned far-reaching reforms in Nov 1989 that effectively ended the SED monopoly of power and laid the foundations for a pluralist

Germany: states

state	capital
Baden-Württemberg	Stuttgart
Bavaria	Munich
Berlin	Berlin
Brandenburg	Potsdam
Bremen	Bremen
Hamburg	Hamburg
Hessen	Wiesbaden
Lower Saxony	Hanover
Mecklenburg–West Pomerania	Schwerin
North Rhine–Westphalia	Düsseldorf
Rhineland-Palatinate	Mainz
Saarland	Saarbrücken
Saxony	Dresden
Saxony-Anhalt	Magdeburg
Schleswig-Holstein	Kiel
Thuringia	Erfurt

system. The Politburo was purged of conservative members; Modrow became prime minister and a new cabinet was formed; New Forum was legalized, and opposition parties allowed to form; and borders with the West were opened and free travel allowed, with the Berlin Wall being effectively dismantled.

moves towards reunification In Dec West German Chancellor Kohl announced a ten-point program for reunification of the two Germanys. While the US and USSR both called for a slower assessment of this idea, reunification was rapidly achieved on many administrative and economic levels as the governments cooperated on a number of cross-border issues. By mid-Dec the Communist Party had largely ceased to exist as an effective power in East Germany; following revelations of high-level corruption during the Honecker regime, Krenz was forced to resign as SED leader and head of state, being replaced by Gregor Gysi (1948–) and Manfred Gerlach (1928–) respectively. Honecker was placed under house arrest awaiting trial on charges of treason, corruption, and abuse of power, and the Politburo was again purged.

political crisis in East Germany An interim SED–opposition "government of national responsibility" was formed Feb 1990. The political crisis continued to deepen, with the opposition divided over reunification with West Germany, while the popular reform movement showed signs of running out of control after the storming in Jan of the former security-police (Stasi) headquarters in East Berlin. The East German economy deteriorated further following the exodus of 344,000 people to West Germany in 1989, with a further 1,500 leaving each day, while countrywide work stoppages increased.

East German elections March 1990 were won by the center-right Alliance for Germany, a three-party coalition led by the CDU. Talks were opened with the West German government on monetary union, concluding with a treaty unifying the economic and monetary systems in July 1990.

reunification Official reunification came about on Oct 3, 1990, with Berlin as the capital (though the seat of government remained in Bonn). In mid-Oct new *Länder* elections were held in former East Germany, in which the conservative parties did well. The first all-German elections since 1932 took place Dec 2, 1990, resulting in victory for Chancellor Kohl and a coalition government composed of the CDU, CSU, and FDP, with only three former East German politicians. In Berlin, which became a *Land*, the ruling SPD lost control of the city council to a new coalition government. The former states of East Germany resumed their status as *Länder*.

social conflict During 1991 divisions grew within the newly united nation as the economy continued to boom in the west, while in the east unemployment rose rapidly. More than 90% of Ossis (easterners) said they felt like second-class citizens, and those in work received less than half the average pay of the Wessis (westerners). Hundreds of racist attacks on foreigners took place, mainly in the east. Public support for Kohl slumped, notably after taxes were raised in order to finance both the rebuilding of the east and the German contribution to the cost of the US-led coalition in the Gulf War against Iraq.

economic crisis in the east Eastern Germany's GDP fell by 15% during 1990 and was projected to decline by 20% during 1991, with

Germany: history

BC–4th century AD	The W Germanic peoples, originating in Scandinavia, moved into the region between the rivers Rhine, Elbe, and Danube, where they were confined by the Roman Empire.
496	The Frankish king Clovis conquered the Alemanni.
768–814	The reign of Holy Roman Emperor Charlemagne, who extended his authority over Germany and imposed Christianity on the Saxons.
814–919	After Charlemagne's death Germany was separated from France under its own kings while the local officials or dukes became virtually independent.
919–1002	Central power was restored by the Saxon dynasty. Otto I, who in 962 revived the title of emperor, began colonizing the Slav lands east of the river Elbe.
1075–1250	A feud between emperors and popes enabled the Germanic princes to recover their independence.
1493–1519	A temporary revival of imperial power took place under Maximilian I.
1521	The Diet of Worms at which Charles V confronted the Protestant Martin Luther. The **Reformation** increased Germany's disunity.
1618–48	The **Thirty Years' War** reduced the empire to a mere name and destroyed Germany's economic and cultural life.
1740–86	The rise of Brandenburg-Prussia as a military power, which had begun in the 17th century, reached its height under Frederick II.
1806	The French emperor Napoleon united W Germany in the **Confederation of the Rhine** and introduced the ideas and reforms of the French Revolution: his reforms were subsequently imitated in Prussia. The Holy Roman Empire was abolished.
1848	Ideas of democracy and national unity inspired the unsuccessful revolutions of 1848.
1867	The North German Confederation, under the leadership of Prussia, was formed.
1871	Under Chancellor Bismarck's leadership, the German Empire was formed after victorious wars with Austria and France. William I of Prussia became emperor.
1914–18	World War I: it was caused by Germany's political, industrial, and colonial rivalries with Britain, France, and Russia.
1918	A revolution overthrew the monarchy; the socialists seized power and established the democratic **Weimar Republic**.
1922–24	Rampant inflation. In 1922 one dollar was worth 50 marks; in 1924 one dollar was worth 2.5 trillion marks.
1929–33	The economic crisis brought Germany close to revolution, until in 1933 the reaction maneuvered the **Nazis** into power with Adolf Hitler as chancellor.
1933–39	At home the Nazis solved the unemployment problem by a vast rearmament program; they abolished the democratic constitution and ruthlessly destroyed all opposition. Abroad, the policy of geopolitical aggression led to war.
1939–45	World War II: Germany (from 1940 in an alliance known as the Axis with Italy and Japan) attacked and occupied neighboring countries, but was defeated by the Allies (the UK and Commonwealth, France 1939–40, the USSR and the US from 1941, and China).
1945–52	Germany was divided, within its 1937 frontiers, into British, US, French, and Soviet occupation zones.
1949	Germany was partitioned into the communist **German Democratic Republic** (see ▷Germany, East) and the capitalist **German Federal Republic** (see ▷Germany, West).

For subsequent history see ▷Germany, Federal Republic of.

a third of the work force either unemployed or on short time. There were large anti-Kohl demonstrations and outbreaks of right-wing racist violence in eastern cities March–April 1991 as the economic crisis deepened, and the ruling CDU suffered reverses in state elections in western Germany during the spring of 1991 as Wessi voters reacted against Kohl's backtracking on his Dec 1990 election promise not to raise taxes to finance the east's economic development. Defeat in Kohl's home *Land* of Rhineland-Palatinate April 1991 meant that the CDU lost, to the SPD, the majority it had held in the Bundesrat since Oct 1990. In May 1991 Bjorn Engholm, the minister-president of Schleswig-Holstein since 1988, was elected chair of the SPD. He replaced Hans-Jochen Vögel, who continued as the SPD's leader within the Bundestag. Having previously voted to move from Bonn to Berlin, the Bundesrat voted July 5, 1991 to remain in Bonn, agreeing to reconsider the decision in later years.

racist attacks Throughout 1991 and 1992,

neo-Nazis and other far-right groups continued their nationwide campaign against foreigners. In elections held in Bremen Sept 1991 a shift to the right emerged with support for the CDU and the right-wing, antiforeigner German People's Union (DVU) rising significantly. Pressure mounted for the government to impose tighter restrictions on refugees: during 1991 250,000 asylum seekers entered Germany. The summer and autumn of 1992 saw numerous violent riots against immigrants by neo-Nazis. *See illustration box.*

Germany, East (German Democratic Republic) country 1949–90, formed from the Soviet zone of occupation in the partition of Germany following World War II. East Germany became a sovereign state 1954, and was reunified with West Germany Oct 1990. For history before 1949, see ▷Germany: history; for history after 1949, see ▷Germany, Federal Republic of.

germination in botany, the initial stages of growth in a seed, spore, or pollen grain. Seeds

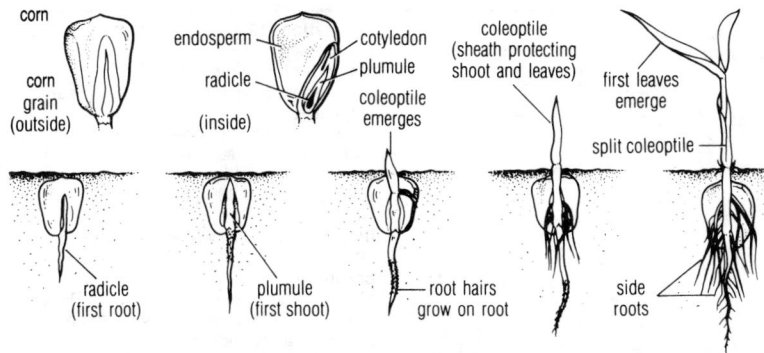

germination *The germination of a corn grain.*

germinate when they are exposed to favorable external conditions of moisture, light, and temperature, and when any factors causing dormancy have been removed.

The process begins with the uptake of water by the seed. The embryonic root, or radicle, is normally the first organ to emerge, followed by the embryonic shoot, or plumule. Food reserves, either within the ▷endosperm or from the ▷cotyledons, are broken down to nourish the rapidly growing seedling. Germination is considered to have ended with the production of the first true leaves.

germ layer in ▷embryology, a layer of cells that can be distinguished during the development of a fertilized egg. Most animals have three such layers: the inner, middle, and outer.

The inner layer (**endoderm**) gives rise to the gut, the middle one (**mesoderm**) develops into most of the other organs, while the outer one (**ectoderm**) gives rise to the skin and nervous system. Simple animals, such as sponges, lack a mesoderm.

Geronimo 1829–1909. Chief of the Chiricahua Apache Indians and war leader. From 1875 to 1885, he fought US federal troops, as well as settlers encroaching on tribal reservations in the Southwest, especially in SE Arizona and New Mexico.

After surrendering to General George Crook March 1886, and agreeing to go to Florida where their families were being held, Geronimo and his followers escaped. Captured again Aug 1886, they were taken to Florida, then to Alabama. The climate proved unhealthy, and they were taken to Fort Sill, Oklahoma, where Geronimo became a farmer. He dictated *Geronimo's Story of His Life* 1906.

Geronimo fell from his horse following a drinking spree and lay on the cold ground overnight, resulting in his death from pneumonia.

gerrymander in politics, the rearranging of constituency boundaries to give an unfair advantage to the ruling party. It is now used more generally to describe various kinds of political trickery.

The term derives from US politician Elbridge Gerry (1744–1814), who, while governor of Massachusetts 1812, reorganized an electoral district (shaped like a salamander) in favor of his party.

Gershwin George 1898–1937. US composer who wrote both "serious" music, such as the tone poem *Rhapsody in Blue* 1924 and *An American in Paris* 1928, and popular musicals and songs, many with lyrics by his brother *Ira Gershwin* (1896–1983), including "I Got Rhythm," "'S Wonderful," and "Embraceable

You." His opera *Porgy and Bess* 1935 was an ambitious work that incorporated jazz rhythms and popular song styles in an operatic format.

Although his scores to musicals made him famous, his "serious" work earned him much critical acclaim. *Of Thee I Sing* 1931, a collaboration between the Gershwin brothers, was the first musical to win a Pulitzer prize.

gerund in the grammar of certain languages, such as Latin, a noun formed from a verb and functioning as a noun to express an action or state. In English, gerunds end in *-ing*.

When the gerund is used as an adjective, it is called a gerundive.

Gesell Arnold Lucius 1880–1961. US psychologist and educator. Born in Alma, Wisconsin, Gesell received his PhD from Clark University 1906. Appointed to the Yale University faculty, he established the Yale Clinic of Child Development which he directed 1911–48. He received a medical degree from Yale 1915. As professor of child hygiene, he was among the first to study the stages of normal development, publishing both scholarly and popular works on child psychology. He became a consultant to The Gesell Institute of Child Development, founded to promote his educational ideas, in New Haven, Connecticut, 1950.

gestalt concept of a unified whole that is greater than, or different from, the sum of its parts; that is, a complete structure whose nature is not explained simply by analyzing its constituent elements. A chair, for example, will generally be recognized as a chair despite great variations between individual chairs in such attributes as size, shape, and color. The term was first used in psychology in Germany about 1910. It has been adopted from German because there is no exact equivalent in English.

Gestalt psychology regards all mental phenomena as being arranged in organized, structured wholes. For example, learning is seen as a reorganizing of a whole situation (often involving insight), as opposed to the behaviorists' view that it consists of associations between stimuli and responses. Gestalt psychologists' experiments show that the brain is not a passive receiver of information, but that it structures all its input in order to make sense of it, a belief that is now generally accepted.

Gestapo (contraction of *Geheime Staatspolizei*) Nazi Germany's secret police, formed 1933, and under the direction of Heinrich Himmler from 1936.

The Gestapo used torture and terrorism to stamp out anti-Nazi resistance. It was declared a criminal organization at the Nuremberg Trials 1946.

gestation in all mammals except the monotremes (duck-billed platypus and spiny anteaters), the period from the time of implantation of the embryo in the uterus to birth. This period varies among species; in humans it is about 266 days, in elephants 18–22 months, in cats about 60 days, and in some species of marsupial (such as opossum) as short as 12 days.

Gethsemane site of the garden where Judas Iscariot, according to the New Testament, betrayed Jesus. It is on the Mount of Olives, E of Jerusalem. When Jerusalem was divided between Israel and Jordan 1948, Gethsemane fell within Jordanian territory.

Getty J (ean) Paul 1892–1976. US oil billionaire, president of the Getty Oil Company from 1947, and founder of the Getty Museum (housing the world's highest-funded art gallery) in Malibu, California.

Gettysburg site in Pennsylvania of a decisive battle of the American ▷Civil War 1863, won by the North. The site is now a national cemetery, at the dedication of which President Lincoln delivered the *Gettysburg Address* Nov 19, 1863, a speech in which he reiterated the principles of freedom, equality, and democracy embodied in the US Constitution.

The South's heavy losses at Gettysburg came in the same week as their defeat at Vicksburg, and the Confederacy remained on the defensive for the rest of the war. The battle ended Robert E ▷Lee's invasion of the North. The address begins with "Fourscore and seven years ago," and ends with an assertion of "government of the people, by the people, and for the people."

Getz Stan (ley) 1927–1991. US tenor saxophonist of the 1950s cool jazz school, closely identified with the Latin American bossa nova sound, which gave him a hit single, "The Girl from Ipanema" 1964. He is regarded as one of the foremost tenor-sax players of his generation.

Getz became a professional musician at 15, working with the big-band leaders of the era: Jack Teagarden, Tommy Dorsey, Stan Kenton, Benny Goodman, Woody Herman. Technically brilliant but never showy, he was influenced by Lester Young, and became a cult hero in the cool-jazz movement with its tendency toward subtlety and restraint, as on the album *West Coast Jazz* 1955. In the early 1960s *Jazz Samba*, *Big Band Bossa Nova*, and other albums brought jazz to a wider public. Later he experimented with jazz-rock fusion. Getz returned to Latin American rhythms on his last LP, *Apasionado* 1990.

geyser natural spring that intermittently discharges an explosive column of steam and hot water into the air. One of the most remarkable geysers is Old Faithful, in Yellowstone National Park, Wyoming. Geysers also occur in New Zealand and Iceland.

G-force force that pilots and astronauts experience when their craft accelerate or decelerate rapidly. One G is the ordinary pull of gravity. Early astronauts were subjected to launch and reentry forces of up to six G or more; in the Space Shuttle, more than three G is experienced on liftoff. Pilots and astronauts wear G-suits that prevent their blood "pooling" too much under severe G-forces, which can lead to unconsciousness.

Ghana country in W Africa, bounded N by Burkina Faso, E by Togo, S by the Gulf of Guinea, and W by the Ivory Coast.

government The 1979 constitution was suspended 1981 when Flight-Lt Jerry Rawlings seized power and set up a Provisional National Defense Council (PNDC), with himself as chair. Parliament and the council of state were abolished, and the government now rules by decree. All political parties were banned, but opposition groups still operate from outside the country.

history The area now known as Ghana was once made up of several separate kingdoms, including those of the Fanti on the coast and the �ØAsante further inland.

The first Europeans to arrive in the region were the Portuguese 1471. Their coastal trading centers, dealing in gold and slaves, flourished alongside Dutch, Danish, British, Swedish, and French traders until about 1800, when the Ashanti, having conquered much of the interior, began to invade the coast. Denmark and the Netherlands abandoned their trading centers, and the Ashanti were defeated by Britain and the Fanti 1874.

the Gold Coast The coastal region became the British colony of the Gold Coast, and after continued fighting, the inland region to the north of Ashanti 1898, and the Ashanti kingdom 1901, were made British protectorates. After 1917 the W part of Togoland, previously governed by Germany, was administered with the Gold Coast. Britain thus controlled both coastal and inland territories, and in 1957 these, together with British Togoland, became independent as Ghana.

Nkrumah's presidency In 1960 Ghana was declared a republic and Dr Kwame ØNkrumah, a former prime minister of the Gold Coast, became president. He embarked on a policy of what he called "African socialism" and established an authoritarian regime. In 1964 he declared Ghana a one-party state, with the Convention People's Party (CPP, which he led) as the only political organization. He then dropped his stance of nonalignment and forged links with the USSR and other communist countries. In 1966, while visiting China, he was deposed in a coup led by General Joseph Ankrah, whose national liberation council released many political prisoners and purged CPP supporters.

In 1969 Ankrah was replaced by General Akwasi Afrifa, who announced plans for a return to civilian government. A new constitution established an elected national assembly and a nonexecutive presidency. The Progress Party (PP) won a big majority in the assembly, and its leader, Kofi Busia, became prime minister. In 1970 Edward Akufo-Addo became the civilian president.

economic problems and coups Following economic problems, the army seized power again 1972. The constitution was suspended and all political institutions replaced by a National Redemption Council under Col Ignatius Acheampong. In 1976 he too promised a return to civilian rule but critics doubted his sincerity and he was replaced by his deputy, Frederick Akuffo, in a bloodless coup 1978. Like his predecessors, he announced a speedy return to civilian government, but before elections could be held he, in turn, was deposed by junior officers led by Flight-Lt Jerry Rawlings, claiming that previous governments had been corrupt and had mismanaged the economy.

Civilian rule was restored 1979, but two years later Rawlings led another coup, again complaining of the government's incompetence. He established a Provisional National Defense Council with himself as chair, again

Ghana
Republic of

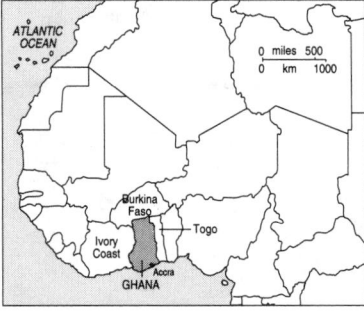

area 91,986 sq mi/238,305 sq km
capital Accra
cities Kumasi, and ports Sekondi-Takoradi, Tema
physical mostly tropical lowland plains; bisected by river Volta
environment forested areas have shrunk from 3.17 million sq mi/8.2 million sq km at the beginning of the 20th century to 730,000 sq mi/1.9 million sq km by 1990
features world's largest artificial lake, Lake Volta; relics of traditional kingdom of Ashanti: 32,000 chiefs and kings
head of state and government Jerry Rawlings from 1981
political system military republic
exports cocoa, coffee, timber, gold, diamonds, manganese, bauxite
currency cedi

suspending the constitution, dissolving parliament, and banning political parties. Although Rawlings's policies were initially supported by workers and students, his failure to revive the economy caused discontent, and he has had to deal with a number of demonstrations and attempted coups, including one in Oct 1989. In 1990 the country contributed troops to the multinational force that attempted to stabilize Liberia. A national referendum April 1992 gave overwhelming approval to a proposal for a new, multiparty constitution. In Nov 1992, in the first presidential elections since 1979, Rawlings was elected by a 58.5% majority to head a new civilian government. *See illustration box.*

Ghana, ancient trading empire that flourished in NW Africa between the 5th and 13th centuries. Founded by the Soninke people, the Ghana Empire was based, like the Mali Empire that superseded it, on the Saharan gold trade. Trade consisted mainly of the exchange of gold from inland deposits for salt from the coast. At its peak in the 11th century, it occupied an area that includes parts of present-day Mali, Senegal, and Mauritania. Wars with the Berber tribes of the Sahara led to its fragmentation and collapse in the 13th century, when much of its territory was absorbed into Mali.

ghat in Hinduism, broad steps leading down to one of the sacred rivers. Some of these, known as "burning ghats," are used for cremation.

Ghats, Eastern and Western twin mountain ranges in S India, E and W of the central plateau; a few peaks reach about 9,800 ft/3,000 m.

population (1990 est) 15,310,000; growth rate 3.2% p.a.
life expectancy men 50, women 54
languages English (official) and African languages
media all media are government-controlled and the two daily newspapers are government-owned
religion animist 38%, Muslim 30%, Christian 24%
literacy men 64%, women 43% (1985 est)
GNP $3.9 bn (1983); $420 per head
chronology
1957 Independence achieved from Britain, within the Commonwealth, with Kwame Nkrumah as president.
1960 Ghana became a republic.
1964 Ghana became a one-party state.
1966 Nkrumah deposed and replaced by General Joseph Ankrah.
1969 Ankrah replaced by General Akwasi Afrifa, who initiated a return to civilian government.
1970 Edward Akufo-Addo elected president.
1972 Another coup placed Col Acheampong at the head of a military government.
1978 Acheampong deposed in a bloodless coup led by Frederick Akuffo; another coup put Flight-Lt Jerry Rawlings in power.
1979 Return to civilian rule under Hilla Limann.
1981 Rawlings seized power again, citing the incompetence of previous governments. All political parties banned.
1989 Coup attempt against Rawlings foiled.
1992 New multiparty constitution approved. Partial lifting of ban on political parties. Nov: Rawlings won presidency in national elections.

The name is a European misnomer, the Indian word *ghat* meaning "pass," not "mountain."

They are connected by the Nilgiri Hills.

Ghent (Flemish **Gent**, French **Gand**) city and port in East Flanders, NW Belgium; population (1991) 230,200. Industries include textiles, chemicals, electronics, and metallurgy. The cathedral of St Bavon (12th–14th centuries) has paintings by van Eyck and Rubens.

Gheorghiu-Dej Gheorge 1901–1965. Romanian communist politician. A member of the Romanian Communist Party from 1930, he played a leading part in establishing a communist regime 1945. He was prime minister 1952–55 and state president 1961–65. Although retaining the support of Moscow, he adopted an increasingly independent line during his final years.

gherkin young or small green Øcucumber, used for pickling.

ghetto (Old Venetian *gèto* "foundry") any deprived area occupied by a minority group, whether voluntarily or not. Originally a ghetto was the area of a town where Jews were compelled to live, decreed by a law enforced by papal bull 1555. The term came into use 1516 when the Jews of Venice were expelled to an island within the city which contained an iron foundry. Ghettos were abolished, except in E Europe, in the 19th century, but the concept and practice were revived by the Germans and Italians 1940–45.

Ghibelline in medieval Germany and Italy, a supporter of the emperor and member of a rival party to the Guelphs (see ØGuelph and Ghibelline).

Ghiberti Lorenzo 1378–1455. Italian sculptor and goldsmith. In 1401 he won the commission for a pair of gilded bronze doors for Florence's baptistry. He produced a second pair (1425–52), the *Gates of Paradise*, one of the masterpieces of the early Italian Renaissance. They show sophisticated composition and use of perspective.

He also wrote *Commentarii/Commentaries* about 1450, a mixture of art history, manual, and autobiography.

Ghirlandaio Domenico c. 1449–1494. Italian fresco painter, head of a large and prosperous workshop in Florence. His fresco cycle 1486–90 in Sta Maria Novella, Florence, includes portraits of many Florentines and much contemporary domestic detail. He also worked in Pisa, Rome, and San Gimignano, and painted portraits.

GI abbreviation for *government issue*; hence (in the US) a common soldier.

Giacometti Alberto 1901–1966. Swiss sculptor and painter who trained in Italy and Paris. In the 1930s, in his Surrealist period, he began to develop his characteristic spindly constructions. His mature style of emaciated single figures, based on wire frames, emerged in the 1940s.

Giambologna (Giovanni da Bologna or Jean de Boulogne) 1529–1608. Flemish-born sculptor active mainly in Florence and Bologna. In 1583 he completed his public commission for the Loggia dei Lanzi in Florence, *The Rape of the Sabine Women*, a dynamic group of muscular figures and a prime example of Mannerist sculpture.

He also produced the *Neptune Fountain* 1563–67 in Bologna and the equestrian statues of the Medici grand dukes Cosimo and Ferdinando. There are several versions of his figure of *Mercury* on tiptoe (the one in Bargello, Florence, for example). His workshop in Florence produced small replicas of his work in bronze.

giant in many mythologies and folklore, one of a race of outsize humanoids, often characterized as stupid and aggressive. In Greek mythology the giants grew from the spilled blood of Uranus and rebelled against the gods. During the Middle Ages in many parts of Europe, wicker effigies of giants were carried in midsummer processions and sometimes burned.

Giant's Causeway stretch of basalt columns forming a headland on the N coast of Antrim, Northern Ireland. It was formed by an outflow of lava in Tertiary times that has solidified in polygonal columns.

gibberellin plant growth substance (see also ⇨auxin) that promotes stem growth and may also affect the breaking of dormancy in certain buds and seeds, and the induction of flowering. Application of gibberellin can stimulate the stems of dwarf plants to additional growth, delay the aging process in leaves, and promote the production of seedless fruit (⇨parthenocarpy).

gibbon any of several small S Asian apes of the genus *Hylobates*, including the subgenus *Symphalangus*. The common or lar gibbon *H. lar* is about 2 ft/60 cm tall, with a body that is hairy except for the buttocks, which distinguishes it from other types of apes. Gibbons have long arms and no tail. They are arboreal in habit, being very agile when swinging from branch to branch. On the ground they

walk upright, and are more easily caught by predators.

The siamang *S. syndactylus* is the largest of the gibbons, growing to 90 cm/36in tall. It is entirely black. Gibbons are found from Assam through the Malay peninsula to Borneo, but are becoming rare, with certain species classified as endangered.

Gibbon Edward 1737–1794. British historian, author of *The History of the Decline and Fall of the Roman Empire* 1776–88.

The work is a continuous narrative from the 2nd century AD to the fall of Constantinople 1453. He began work on it while in Rome 1764. Although immediately successful, he was compelled to reply to attacks on his account of the early development of Christianity by a *Vindication* 1779.

Gibbon John Heysham 1903–1974. US surgeon who invented the heart–lung machine in 1953. It has become indispensable in heart surgery, maintaining the circulation while the heart is temporarily inactivated.

Gibbons v Ogden US Supreme Court decision 1824 dealing with states' intervention in the regulation of interstate commerce. The conflict arose when New York State issued an injunction against Gibbons prohibiting his steamboat operation between New York and New Jersey. Although Gibbons was federally licensed, his business was in violation of a state law that granted to Ogden a monopoly on all steamboat operation in New York. Gibbons appealed to the US Supreme Court, which ruled that the New York law was de facto interference with the federal regulation of interstate commerce and therefore was unconstitutional.

Gibbs Josiah Willard 1839–1903. US theoretical physicist and chemist who developed a mathematical approach to thermodynamics. His book *Vector Analysis* 1881 established vector methods in physics.

In 1863 he gained the first engineering doctorate awarded in the US, and in 1871 he became professor of mathematical physics at Yale University, where he remained until his death.

Gibbs' function in ⇨thermodynamics, an expression representing part of the energy content of a system that is available to do external work, also known as the free energy G. In an equilibrium system at constant temperature and pressure, $G = H - TS$, where H is the enthalpy (heat constant), T the temperature, and S the ⇨entropy (decrease in energy availability). The function was named after US physicist Josiah Willard Gibbs.

Gibraltar British dependency, situated on a narrow rocky promontory in S Spain
area 2.5 sq mi/6.5 sq km
features strategic naval and air base, with NATO underground headquarters and communications center; colony of Barbary apes; the frontier zone is adjoined by the Spanish port of La Línea
exports mainly a trading center for the import and reexport of goods
population (1988) 30,000
history captured from Spain 1704 by English admiral George Rooke (1650–1709), it was ceded to Britain under the Treaty of Utrecht 1713. A referendum 1967 confirmed the wish of the people to remain in association with the UK, but Spain continues to claim sovereignty and closed the border 1969–85. In 1989, the UK government announced it would reduce

the military garrison by half. Ground troop withdrawals began March 1991, but navy and airforce units remained.
currency Gibraltar government notes and UK coinage
language English
religion mainly Roman Catholic
government the governor has executive authority, with the advice of the Gibraltar council, and there is an elected house of assembly (chief minister Joe Bossano from 1988).

Gibraltar, Strait of strait between N Africa and Spain, with the Rock of Gibraltar on the north side and Jebel Musa on the south, the so-called Pillars of Hercules.

Gibson Althea 1927– . US tennis player. As a student at Florida A&M University, she became the first black American woman to compete at the US Championships at Forest Hills 1950 and at Wimbledon 1951. In 1957 she took both the women's singles and doubles titles at Wimbledon and the singles at Forest Hills. In 1958 she successfully defended all three titles. She later played professional golf.

Born in Silver, South Carolina, and raised in New York, Gibson was hindered in her tennis career by racial discrimination and segregation. In 1943 she won the New York State Negro girls' singles title, and in 1948 the national Negro women's title.

Gibson Charles Dana 1867–1944. US illustrator. He portrayed an idealized type of American young woman, known as the "Gibson Girl."

Gibson was born in Roxbury, Massachusetts. He worked for *Life* magazine, eventually becoming its editor. He also illustrated books and later painted in oils.

Gibson Mel 1956– . Australian actor who became an international star following lead roles in *Mad Max* 1979 and *Mad Max II* 1982 which was released in the US as *Road Warrior*. His other films include *The Year of Living Dangerously* 1982, *Mutiny on the Bounty* 1984 as Fletcher Christian, and the *Lethal Weapon* series, in which Danny Glover co-starred.

Gide André 1869–1951. French novelist, born in Paris. His work is largely autobiographical and concerned with the dual themes of self-fulfillment and renunciation. It includes *L'Immoraliste/The Immoralist* 1902, *La Porte étroite/Strait Is the Gate* 1909, *Les Caves du Vatican/The Vatican Cellars* 1914, and *Les Faux-monnayeurs/The Counterfeiters* 1926; and an almost lifelong *Journal*. Nobel Prize for Literature 1947.

Gideon in the Old Testament, one of the Judges of Israel, who led a small band of Israelite warriors which succeeded in routing an invading Midianite army of overwhelming number in a surprise night attack.

Gideon v Wainwright US Supreme Court decision 1963 dealing with the right of accused persons who are unable to afford legal assistance to a court-appointed lawyer. Prior to this case, only those defendants being tried for capital offenses were guaranteed counsel. Clarence Gideon, a Florida man accused only of a felony, was forced by poverty to defend himself. He was convicted but appealed his conviction, arguing that his constitutional right to a lawyer had been denied. The Court ordered a retrial, ruling that states must provide counsel for felony-case defendants who are too poor to provide their own.

Gielgud John 1904– . English actor and

director, renowned as one of the greatest Shakespearean actors of his time. He made his debut at the Old Vic 1921, and his numerous stage appearances ranged from roles in works by Chekhov and Sheridan to those of Alan Bennett, Harold Pinter, and David Storey. Gielgud's films include *Becket* 1964, *Oh! What a Lovely War* 1969, *Providence* 1977, and *Prospero's Books* 1991. He won an Academy Award for his role as a butler in *Arthur* 1981.

Gierek Edward 1913– . Polish Communist politician. He entered the Politburo of the ruling Polish United Workers' Party (PUWP) in 1956 and was party leader 1970–80. His industrialization program plunged the country heavily into debt and sparked a series of ♢Solidarity-led strikes.

Gierek, a miner's son, lived in France and Belgium for much of the period between 1923 and 1948, becoming a member of the Belgian Resistance. He served as party boss in Silesia during the 1960s. After replacing Gomulka as PUWP leader in Dec 1970, he embarked on an ambitious program of industrialization. A wave of strikes in Warsaw and Gdańsk, spearheaded by the Solidarity free labor-union movement, forced Gierek to resign in Sept 1980.

Giffard Henri 1825–1882. French inventor of the first passenger-carrying powered and steerable airship, called a dirigible, built 1852. The hydrogen-filled airship was 144 ft/43 m long, had a 3-hp steam engine that drove a three-bladed propeller, and was steered using a saillike rudder. It flew at an average speed of 3 mph/5 kph.

The first flight was on Sept 24, 1852.

giga- prefix signifying multiplication by 10^9 (1,000,000,000 or 1 billion), as in **gigahertz**, a unit of frequency equivalent to 1 billion hertz.

gigabyte in computing, a measure of ♢memory capacity, equal to 1,024 ♢megabytes. It is also used, less precisely, to mean 1,000 billion ♢bytes.

ginger beer carbonated drink like ginger ale but with fermented ginger and bitters added for a stronger taste.

GIGO (acronym for **garbage in, garbage out**) expression used in computing to emphasize that inaccurate input data will result in inaccurate output data.

gila monster lizard *Heloderma suspectum* of SW USA and Mexico. It is one of the only two existing venomous lizards, the other being the Mexican beaded lizard of the same genus. It has poison glands in its lower jaw, but its bite is not usually fatal to humans.

Gilbert Cass 1859–1934. US architect, major developer of the ♢skyscraper. He designed the Woolworth Building, New York, 1913, the highest building in America (868 ft/265 m) when built and famous for its use of Gothic decorative detail.

He was also architect of the US Supreme Court building in Washington, DC, the Minnesota state capitol in St Paul, and the US Customs House in New York City.

Gilbert Humphrey *c.* 1539–1583. English soldier and navigator who claimed Newfoundland (landing at St John's) for Elizabeth I in 1583. He died when his ship sank on the return voyage.

Gilbert W(illiam) S(chwenk) 1836–1911. British humorist and dramatist who collaborated with composer Arthur ♢Sullivan, providing the libretti for their series of light comic operas from 1871; they include *HMS Pinafore*

1878, *The Pirates of Penzance* 1879, and *The Mikado* 1885.

Born in London, he became a lawyer in 1863, but in 1869 published a collection of his humorous verse and drawings, *Bab Ballads*, which was followed by a second volume in 1873.

Gilbert Walter 1932– . US molecular biologist who studied genetic control, seeking the mechanisms that switch genes on and off. By 1966 he had established the existence of the *lac* repressor, the molecule that suppresses lactose production. Further work on the sequencing of ♢DNA nucleotides won him a share of the 1980 Nobel Prize for Chemistry, with Frederick Sanger and Paul Berg.

Gilbert William 1544–1603. English scientist and physician to Elizabeth I and (briefly) James I. He studied magnetism and static electricity, deducing that the Earth's magnetic field behaves as if a bar magnet joined the North and South poles. His book on magnets, published 1600, is the first printed scientific book based wholly on experimentation and observation.

He erroneously thought that the planets were held in their orbits by magnetic forces.

Gilbert and Ellice Islands former British colony in the Pacific, known since independence 1978 as the countries of ♢Tuvalu and ♢Kiribati.

Gilded Age, the in US history, a derogatory term referring to the opulence displayed in the post-Civil War decades. It borrows the title of an 1873 political satire by Mark Twain and Charles Dudley Warner (1829–1900), which highlights the respectable veneer of public life covering the many scandals of graft and corruption.

Gilgamesh hero of Sumerian, Hittite, Akkadian, and Assyrian legend. The 12 verse "books" of the *Epic of Gilgamesh* were recorded in a standard version on 12 cuneiform tablets by the Assyrian king Ashurbanipal's scholars in the 7th century BC, and the epic itself is older than Homer's *Iliad* by at least 1,500 years. One-third mortal and two-thirds divine, Gilgamesh is lord of the Sumerian city of Uruk.

The *Epic's* incident of the Flood is similar to the Old Testament account, since Abraham had been a citizen of the nearby city of Ur in Sumer.

gill in biology, the main respiratory organ of most fishes and immature amphibians, and of many aquatic invertebrates. In all types, water passes over the gills, and oxygen diffuses across the gill membranes into the circulatory system, while carbon dioxide passes from the system out into the water.

In aquatic insects, these gases diffuse into and out of air-filled canals called tracheae.

gill imperial unit of volume for liquid measure, equal to one-fourth of a pint or four fluid ounces (0.118 liter). It is used in selling alcoholic drinks.

Gillespie Dizzy (John Birks) 1917–1993. US jazz trumpeter who, with Charlie ♢Parker, was the chief creator and exponent of the ♢bebop style. He influenced many modern jazz trumpeters, including Miles Davis.

Although associated mainly with small combos, Gillespie formed his first big band 1945 and toured with a big band in the late 1980s, as well as in the intervening decades.

Gilman Charlotte Perkins 1860–1935. US feminist socialist poet, novelist, and historian, author of *Women and Economics* 1898,

proposing the ending of the division between "men's work" and "women's work" by abolishing housework.

From 1909 to 1916 she wrote and published a magazine *The Forerunner* in which her feminist Utopian novel *Herland* 1915 was serialized.

gin (Dutch *jenever* "juniper") alcoholic drink made by distilling a mash of corn, malt, or rye, with juniper flavoring. It was first produced in the Netherlands.

ginger SE Asian reedlike perennial *Zingiber officinale*, family Zingiberaceae; the hot-tasting underground root is used as a condiment and in preserves.

ginger ale sweetened, carbonated drink containing ginger flavoring, sugar, and syrup.

ginkgo or **maidenhair tree** tree *Ginkgo biloba* of the gymnosperm (or naked-seed-bearing) division of plants. It may reach a height of 100 ft/30 m by the time it is 200 years old.

The only living member of its group (Ginkgophyta), widespread in Mesozoic times, it has been cultivated in China and Japan since ancient times, and is planted in many parts of the world. Its leaves are fan-shaped, and it bears fleshy, yellow, foul-smelling fruit enclosing edible kernels.

Ginsberg Allen 1926– . US poet. His "Howl" 1956, an influential poem of the ♢Beat Generation, criticizes the materialism of contemporary US society. In the 1960s Ginsberg traveled widely in Asia and was a key figure in introducing Eastern thought to students of that decade.

ginseng plant *Panax ginseng*, family Araliaceae, with a thick, forked aromatic root used in medicine as a tonic.

Giolitti Giovanni 1842–1928. Italian liberal politician, born in Mondovi. He was prime minister 1892–93, 1903–05, 1906–09, 1911–14, and 1920–21. He opposed Italian intervention in World War I and pursued a policy of broad coalitions, which proved ineffective in controlling Fascism after 1921.

Giordano Luca 1632–1705. Italian Baroque painter, born in Naples, active in Florence in the 1680s. In 1692 he was summoned to Spain by Charles II and painted ceilings in the Escorial palace for the next ten years.

In Florence Giordano painted a ceiling in the Palazzo Riccardi-Medici 1682–83. He also produced altarpieces and frescoes for churches. His work shows a variety of influences, including Paolo ♢Veronese, and tends to be livelier than that of earlier Baroque ceiling painters.

Giorgione del Castelfranco *c.* 1475–1510. Italian Renaissance painter, active in Venice, probably trained by Giovanni Bellini. His work influenced Titian and other Venetian painters. His subjects are imbued with a sense of mystery and treated with a soft technique, reminiscent of Leonardo da Vinci's later works, as in *The Tempest* 1504 (Accademia, Venice).

Few details of his life are certain, but Giorgione created the Renaissance poetic landscape, with rich colors and a sense of intimacy; an example is the *Madonna and Child Enthroned with Two Saints*, an alterpiece for the church of Castelfranco.

Giotto space probe built by the European Space Agency to study ♢Halley's comet. Launched by an Ariane rocket in July 1985, *Giotto* passed within 375 mi/600 km of the comet's nucleus on March 13, 1986. On July 2,

1990 it flew 14,000 mi/23,000 km from Earth, which diverted its path to encounter another comet, Grigg-Skjellerup, on July 10, 1992.

Giotto di Bondone 1267–1337. Italian painter and architect. He broke away from the conventional Gothic style of the time, and introduced a naturalistic style, painting saints as real people. He painted cycles of frescoes in churches at Assisi, Florence, and Padua.

Giotto was born in Vespignano, N of Florence. The interior of the Arena Chapel, Padua, was covered by him in a fresco cycle (completed by 1306) illustrating the life of Mary and the life of Jesus. Giotto's figures occupy a definite pictorial space, and there is an unusual emotional intensity and dignity in the presentation of the story. In one of the frescoes he made the Star of Bethlehem appear as a comet; ♢Halley's comet had appeared 1303, just two years before.

From 1334 he was official architect to Florence and from 1335 overseer of works at the cathedral; he collaborated with Andrea Pisano in decorating the cathedral façade with statues and designing the campanile, which was completed after his death.

giraffe world's tallest mammal, *Giraffa camelopardalis*, belonging to the ruminant family Giraffidae. It stands over 18 ft/5.5 m tall, the neck accounting for nearly half this amount. The giraffe has two to four small, skincovered, hornlike structures on its head and a long, tufted tail. The skin has a mottled appearance and is reddish brown and cream. Giraffes are found only in Africa, south of the Sahara Desert.

Both members of the Giraffidae, the giraffe and the okapi, are able to use their extremely long tongues for cleaning their eyes and ears.

Giraudoux (Hippolyte) Jean 1882–1944. French playwright and novelist who wrote the plays *Amphitryon 38* 1929 and *La Folle de Chaillot/The Madwoman of Chaillot* 1945, and the novel *Suzanne et la Pacifique/Suzanne and the Pacific* 1921.

His other plays include *La Guerre de Troie n'aura pas lieu/Tiger at the Gates* 1935.

Gironde navigable estuary 50 mi/80 km long, formed by the mouths of the ♢Garonne, length 360 mi/580 km, and ♢Dordogne rivers, in SW France. The Lot, length 300 mi/480 km, is a tributary of the Garonne.

Girondin member of the right-wing republican party in the French Revolution, so called because a number of their leaders came from the Gironde region. They were driven from power by the ♢Jacobins 1793.

Giscard d'Estaing Valéry 1926– . French conservative politician, president 1974–81. He was finance minister to de Gaulle 1962–66 and Pompidou 1969–74. As leader of the Union pour la Démocratie Française, which he formed in 1978, Giscard sought to project himself as leader of a "new center."

Giscard was active in the wartime Resistance. After a distinguished academic career, he worked in the Ministry of Finance and entered the National Assembly for Puy de Dôme in 1956 as an Independent Republican. After Pompidou's death he was narrowly elected president in 1974, in difficult economic circumstances; he was defeated by the socialist Mitterrand in 1981. He returned to the National Assembly in 1984. In 1989 he resigned from the National Assembly to play a leading role in the European Parliament.

Gish Lillian. Adopted name of Lillian de Guiche 1896– . US film and stage actress who worked with the director D W Griffith, playing virtuous heroines in *Way Down East* and *Orphans of the Storm* both 1920. Deceptively fragile, she made a notable Hester in Victor Sjöström's *The Scarlet Letter* (based on the novel by Nathaniel Hawthorne). Her career continued well into the 1980s with movies such as *The Whales of August* 1987. She was the sister of the actress **Dorothy Gish** (1898–1968).

Gitlow v New York US Supreme Court decision 1925 dealing with state legislation that restricts freedom of speech. Benjamin Gitlow, editor of the left-wing *Manifesto*, was convicted, under a New York state law, of advocating the violent overthrow of the government. The Court upheld the law, ruling that First-Amendment rights are secondary to the preservation of the state.

Giulini Carlo Maria 1914– . Italian conductor. Principal conductor at La Scala in Milan 1953–55, and musical director of the Los Angeles Philharmonic 1978–84, he is renowned as an interpreter of Verdi.

Giulio Romano c. 1499–1546. Italian painter and architect. An assistant to Raphael, he developed a Mannerist style, creating effects of exaggerated movement and using rich colors, for example the frescoes in the Palazzo del Tè (1526, Mantua).

Giza, El or *al-Jizah* site of the Great Pyramids and Sphinx; a suburb of ♢Cairo, Egypt; population (1983) 1,500,000. It has textile and film industries.

gizzard muscular grinding organ of the digestive tract, below the ♢crop of birds, earthworms, and some insects, and forming part of the ♢stomach. The gizzard of birds is lined with a hardened horny layer of the protein keratin, preventing damage to the muscle layer during the grinding process. Most birds swallow sharp grit which aids maceration of food in the gizzard.

Glace Bay port on Cape Breton Island, Nova Scotia, center of a coal-mining area; population (1986) 20,500.

glacial trough or *U-shaped valley* steepsided, flat-bottomed valley formed by a glacier. The erosive action of the glacier and of the debris carried by it results in the formation not only of the trough itself but also of a number of associated features, such as truncated spurs (projections of rock that have been sheared off by the ice) and hanging valleys (smaller glacial valleys that enter the trough at a higher level than the trough floor). Features characteristic of glacial deposition, such as drumlins and eskers, are commonly found on the floor of the trough, together with linear lakes called ribbon lakes.

glacier tongue of ice, originating in mountains in snowfields above the snowline, which moves slowly downhill and is constantly replenished from its source. The scenery produced by the erosive action of glaciers is characteristic and includes ♢glacial troughs (U-shaped valleys), corries (steep-walled hollows representing the source of a melted glacier), and ♢arêtes. In lowlands, the laying down of ♢moraine (rocky debris once carried by glaciers) produces a variety of landscape features.

Glaciers form where annual snowfall exceeds annual melting and drainage. The snow compacts to ice under the weight of the layers

above. When a glacier moves over an uneven surface, deep crevasses are formed in the ice mass; if it reaches the sea or a lake, it breaks up to form icebergs. A glacier that is formed by one or several valley glaciers at the base of a mountain is called a **piedmont** glacier. A body of ice that covers a large land surface or continent, for example Greenland or Antarctica, and flows outward in all directions is called an **ice sheet**.

Glackens William James 1870–1938. American painter. Born in Philadelphia, he studied at the Pennsylvania Academy of the Fine Arts under Robert ♢Henri. He was a member of the Ashcan school and one of "The Eight," a group of realists who exhibited at New York's Macbeth Gallery 1908. Glackens's painting eventually evolved into a realism that was strongly influenced by Impressionism. He painted subjects from everyday urban life, as well as those from fashionable society.

gladiator in ancient Rome, a trained fighter, recruited mainly from slaves, criminals, and prisoners of war, who fought to the death in arenas for the entertainment of spectators. The custom, which originated in the practice of slaughtering slaves on a chieftain's grave, was introduced into Rome from Etruria in 264 BC and continued until the 5th century AD.

gladiolus any plant of the genus *Gladiolus* of S European and African cultivated perennials of the iris family Iridaceae, with brightly colored, funnel-shaped flowers, borne in a spike; the swordlike leaves spring from a corm.

Gladstone William Ewart 1809–1898. British Liberal politician, repeatedly prime minister. He entered Parliament as a Tory in 1833 and held ministerial office, but left the party 1846 and after 1859 identified himself with the Liberals. He was chancellor of the Exchequer 1852–55 and 1859–66, and prime minister 1868–74, 1880–85, 1886, and 1892–94. He introduced elementary education 1870 and vote by secret ballot 1872 and many reforms in Ireland, although he failed in his efforts to get a Home Rule Bill passed.

In Gladstone's first term as prime minister he carried through a series of reforms, including the disestablishment of the Church of Ireland, the Irish Land Act, and the abolition of the purchase of army commissions and of religious tests in the universities.

Gladstone strongly resisted Disraeli's imperialist and pro-Turkish policy during his government of 1874–80, not least because of Turkish violence against subject Christians; by his Midlothian campaign of 1879 he helped to overthrow Disraeli. Gladstone's second government carried the second Irish Land Act and the Reform Act 1884. Returning to office in 1886, Gladstone introduced his first Home Rule Bill, which was defeated, and he thereupon resigned. He formed his last government in 1892; his second Home Rule Bill was rejected by the Lords, and in 1894 he resigned.

Glamorgan (Welsh *Morgannwg*) three counties of S Wales—Mid Glamorgan, South Glamorgan, and West Glamorgan—created in 1974 from the former county of Glamorganshire.

All are on the Bristol Channel, and the administrative headquarters of Mid and South Glamorgan is Cardiff; the headquarters of West Glamorgan is Swansea. *Mid Glamorgan*, which also takes in a small area of the former county of Monmouthshire to the east, contains the coal-mining towns of Aberdare and

Merthyr Tydfil, and the Rhondda in the valleys. The mountains are in the northern part of the county; area 394 sq mi/1,019 sq km; population (1991) 526,500. In **South Glamorgan**, there is mixed farming in the fertile Vale of Glamorgan, and towns include Cardiff, Penarth, and Barry; area 161 sq mi/416 sq km; population (1991) 383,300. **West Glamorgan** includes Swansea, with tin-plating and copper industries, Margam, with large steel-rolling mills, Port Talbot, and Neath; area 315 sq mi/815 sq km; population (1991) 357,500.

gland specialized organ of the body that manufactures and secretes enzymes, hormones, or other chemicals. In animals, glands vary in size from small (for example, tear glands) to large (for example, the pancreas), but in plants they are always small, and may consist of a single cell. Some glands discharge their products internally, ▷endocrine glands, and others, ▷exocrine glands, externally. Lymph nodes are sometimes wrongly called glands.

glandular fever or *infectious mononucleosis* viral disease characterized at onset by fever and painfully swollen lymph nodes (in the neck); there may also be digestive upset, sore throat, and skin rashes. Lassitude persists for months and even years, and recovery can be slow. It is caused by the Epstein-Barr virus.

Glaser Donald Arthur 1926– . US physicist who invented the ▷bubble chamber in 1952, for which he received the Nobel Prize for Physics in 1960.

Born in Cleveland, Ohio, he was educated at the Case Institute of Technology, did research at the University of Michigan, and in 1960 became professor at the University of California.

Glasgow city and administrative headquarters of Strathclyde, Scotland; population (1991) 654,500. Industries include engineering, chemicals, printing, and distilling.

Buildings include the 12th-century cathedral of St Mungo; the Cross Steeple (part of the historic Tolbooth); the universities of Glasgow, established 1451 (present buildings constructed 1868–70 to designs by George Gilbert Scott) and Strathclyde, established 1964; the Royal Exchange; the Stock Exchange; Kelvingrove Art Gallery (Impressionist collection); the Glasgow School of Art, designed by C R Mackintosh; the Burrell Collection at Pollock Park, bequeathed by shipping magnate William Burrell (1861–1958); and Mitchell Library.

Glasgow Ellen 1873–1945. US novelist. Her books, set mainly in her native Virginia, often deal with the survival of tough heroines in a world of adversity and include *Barren Ground* 1925, *The Sheltered Life* 1932, and *Vein of Iron* 1935.

Glashow Sheldon Lee 1932– . US particle physicist. In 1964 he proposed the existence of a fourth "charmed" ▷quark, and later argued that quarks must be colored. Insights gained from these theoretical studies enabled Glashow to consider ways in which the weak nuclear force and the electromagnetic force (two of the fundamental forces of nature) could be unified as a single force now called the electroweak force. For this work he shared the Nobel Prize for Physics 1979 with Abdus Salam and Steven Weinberg.

glasnost (Russian "openness") former Soviet leader Mikhail ▷Gorbachev's policy of liberalizing various aspects of Soviet life, such as introducing greater freedom of expression and information and opening up relations with Western countries. *Glasnost* was introduced and adopted by the Soviet government 1986.

Glasnost has involved the lifting of bans on books, plays, and films, the release of political ▷dissidents, the tolerance of religious worship, a reappraisal of Soviet history (destalinization), the encouragement of investigative journalism to uncover political corruption, and the sanctioning of greater candor in the reporting of social problems and disasters (such as ▷Chernobyl). Under legislation introduced 1990, censorship of mass media was abolished; however, publication of state secrets, calls for the overthrow of the state by force, incitement of national or religious hatred, and state interference in people's private lives were prohibited. Journalists' rights to access were enshrined, and the right of reply instituted. Citizens gained the right to receive information from abroad.

glass transparent or translucent substance that is physically neither a solid nor a liquid. Although glass is easily shattered, it is one of the strongest substances known. It is made by fusing certain types of sand (silica); this fusion occurs naturally in volcanic glass (see ▷obsidian).

In the industrial production of common types of glass, the type of sand used, the particular chemicals added to it (for example, lead, potassium, barium), and refinements of technique determine the type of glass produced. Types of glass include: soda glass; flint glass, used in cut-crystal ware; optical glass; stained glass; heat-resistant glass; and glasses that exclude certain ranges of the light spectrum. Blown glass is either blown individually from molten glass (using a tube up to 4.5 ft/1.5 m long), as in the making of expensive crafted glass, or blown automatically into a mold—for example, in the manufacture of light bulbs and bottles; pressed glass is simply pressed into molds, for jam jars, cheap vases, and light fittings; while sheet glass, for windows, is made by putting the molten glass through rollers to form a "ribbon," or by floating molten glass on molten tin in the "float glass" process; ▷fiberglass is made from fine glass fibers. Metallic glass is produced by treating alloys so that they take on the properties of glass while retaining the malleability and conductivity characteristic of metals.

Glass Philip 1937– . US composer. As a student of Nadia ▷Boulanger, he was strongly influenced by Indian music; his work is characterized by repeated rhythmic figures that are continually expanded and modified. His compositions include the operas *Einstein on the Beach* 1975, *Akhnaten* 1984, and *The Making of the Representative for Planet 8* 1988.

glass harmonica or armonica. In music, an instrument based on the principle of playing a wine glass with a wet finger. Devised by Benjamin Franklin, it consists of a graded series of glass bowls mounted on a spindle and resting in a trough part-filled with water. Rotated by a foot-pedal, it emits pure tones of unchanging intensity when touched. Mozart, Beethoven, and Schubert all wrote pieces for it.

glass lizard another name for ▷glass snake.

glass snake or *glass lizard* any of a worldwide genus *Ophisaurus* of legless lizards of the family Anguidae. Their tails are up to three times the head–body length and are easily broken off.

The eastern glass lizard *O. ventralis* grows to 36 in/1.1 m and inhabits wet grasslands in the SE US.

Glauber Johann 1604–1668. German chemist who discovered the salt known variously as "Glauber's salt" and "*sal mirabile.*" He made his living selling patent medicines.

Glauber's salt in chemistry, crystalline sodium sulfate decahydrate $Na_2SO_4.10H_2O$, which melts at 87.8°F/31°C; the latent heat stored as it solidifies makes it a convenient thermal energy store. It is used in medicine.

glaucoma condition in which pressure inside the eye (intraocular pressure) is raised abnormally as excess fluid accumulates. It occurs when the normal flow of intraocular fluid out of the eye is interrupted. As pressure rises, the optic nerve suffers irreversible damage, leading to a reduction in the field of vision and, ultimately, loss of eyesight.

The most common type, *chronic glaucoma*, usually affects people over the age of 40, when the trabecular meshwork (the filtering tissue at the margins of the eye) gradually becomes blocked and drainage slows down. The condition cannot be cured, but, in many cases, it is controlled by drug therapy. Laser treatment to the trabecular meshwork often improves drainage for a time; surgery to create an artificial channel for fluid to leave the eye offers more long-term relief. A tiny window may be cut in the iris during the same operation.

Acute glaucoma is a medical emergency. A precipitous rise in pressure occurs when the trabecular meshwork suddenly becomes occluded (blocked). This is treated surgically to remove the cause of the obstruction. Acute glaucoma is extremely painful. Treatment is required urgently since damage to the optic nerve begins within hours of onset.

glaucophane in geology, a blue amphibole, $Na_2(Mg,Fe,Al)_5Si_8O_{22}(OH)_2$. It occurs in glaucophane schists (blue schists), formed from the ocean floor basalt under metamorphic conditions of high pressure and low temperature; these conditions are believed to exist in subduction systems associated with destructive plate boundaries (see ▷plate tectonics), and so the occurrence of glaucophane schists can indicate the location of such boundaries in geological history.

glaze transparent vitreous coating for pottery and porcelain, which gives the object a shiny, protective finish and helps to keep it from leaking and chipping.

Glazed pottery is first known from the mid- to late-Neolithic in Egypt, where ▷glass was first made.

Glendower Owen c. 1359–c. 1416. (Welsh **Owain Glyndwr**) Welsh nationalist leader of a successful revolt against the English in N Wales, who defeated Henry IV in three campaigns 1400–02, although Wales was reconquered 1405–13. Glendower disappeared 1416 after some years of guerrilla warfare.

Glenn John (Herschel), Jr 1921– . US astronaut and politician. On Feb 20, 1962, he became the first American to orbit the Earth, doing so three times in the Mercury spacecraft *Friendship 7*, in a flight lasting 4 hr 55 min. After retiring from ▷NASA, he was elected to the US Senate as a Democrat from Ohio 1974; reelected 1980 and 1986. He unsuccessfully sought the Democratic presidential nomination 1984.

As a senator, he advocated nuclear-arms-production limitations and increased aid to education and job-skills programs.

Glens Falls city in E central New York, N of Albany and S of lakes George and Champlain. Situated in Warren County by a waterfall in the Hudson River, its industries include clothing, paper, machinery parts, insurance, and tourism; population (1990) 15,000.

gliding the art of using air currents to fly unpowered aircraft. Technically, gliding involves the gradual loss of altitude; gliders designed for soaring flight (utilizing air rising up a cliff face or hill, warm air rising as a "thermal" above sun-heated ground, and so on) are known as sailplanes. The sport of ⟁hang-gliding was developed in the 1970s.

Pioneers include George Cayley, Otto ⟁Lilienthal, Octave Chanute (1832–1910), and the ⟁Wright brothers, the last-named perfecting gliding technique in 1902. Launching may be by rubber catapult from a hilltop by a winch that raises the glider like a kite (in the UK, the only remaining site for catapult launches is Long Mynd in Shropshire); or by aircraft tow. In World War II, towed troop-carrying gliders were used by the Germans in Crete and the Allies at Arnhem.

Glinka Mikhail Ivanovich 1804–1857. Russian composer. He broke away from the prevailing Italian influence and turned to Russian folk music as the inspiration for his opera *A Life for the Tsar* (originally *Ivan Susanin*) 1836. His later works include another opera, *Ruslan and Lyudmila* 1842, and the orchestral *Kamarinskaya* 1848.

global warming projected imminent climate change attributed to the ⟁greenhouse effect.

globefish another name for ⟁puffer fish.

Globe Theatre 17th-century London theater, octagonal and open to the sky, near Bankside, Southwark, where many of Shakespeare's plays were performed by Richard Burbage and his company. Built 1599 by Cuthbert Burbage, it was burned down 1613 after a cannon, fired during a performance of *Henry VIII*, set light to the thatch. It was rebuilt in 1614 but pulled down in 1644. The site was rediscovered Oct 1989 near the remains of the contemporaneous Rose Theater.

globular cluster spherical or near-spherical ⟁star cluster from approximately 10,000 to millions of stars. More than a hundred globular clusters are distributed in a spherical halo around our Galaxy. They consist of old stars, formed early in the Galaxy's history. Globular clusters are also found around other galaxies.

glockenspiel percussion instrument of light metal keys mounted on a carrying frame for use in military bands or on a standing frame for use in an orchestra (in which form it resembles a small xylophone or celesta).

glomerulus in the kidney, the blood capillaries responsible for forming the fluid that passes down the tubules and ultimately becomes urine. In the human kidney there are approximately one million tubules, each possessing its own glomerulus.

The structure of the glomerulus allows a wide range of substances including amino acids and sugar, as well as a large volume of water, to pass out of the blood. As the fluid moves through the tubules, most of the water and all of the sugars are reabsorbed, so that only waste remains, dissolved in a relatively small amount of water. This fluid collects in the bladder as urine.

Glomma river in Norway, 350 mi/570 km long.

The largest river in Scandinavia, it flows into the Skagerrak (an arm of the North Sea) at Frederikstad.

Glorious Revolution in British history, the events surrounding the removal of James II from the throne and his replacement by Mary (daughter of Charles I) and William of Orange as joint sovereigns in 1689. James had become increasingly unpopular on account of his unconstitutional behavior and Catholicism. Various elements in England, including seven prominent politicians, plotted to invite the Protestant William to invade. Arriving at Torbay on Nov 5, 1688, William rapidly gained support and James was allowed to flee to France after the army deserted him. William and Mary then accepted a new constitutional settlement, the Bill of Rights 1689, which assured the ascendency of parliamentary power over sovereign rule.

Gloucester city in NE Massachusetts, on Cape Ann, NE of Boston. A famous fishing port, its industries include tourism and fish processing, especially lobster, whiting, and cod; population (1990) 28,700.

Gloucestershire county in SW England
area 1,019 sq mi/2,640 sq km
cities Gloucester (administrative headquarters), Stroud, Cheltenham, Tewkesbury, Cirencester
features Cotswold Hills; river Severn and tributaries; Berkeley Castle, where Edward II was murdered; Prinknash Abbey, where pottery is made; Cotswold Farm Park, near Stow-on-the-Wold, which has rare and ancient breeds of farm animals
products cereals, fruit, dairy products; engineering, coal in the Forest of Dean
population (1991) 520,600
famous people Edward Jenner, John Keble, Gustav Holst.

glow-worm wingless female of some luminous beetles (fireflies) in the family Lampyridae. The luminous organs situated under the abdomen serve to attract winged males for mating. There are about 2,000 species, distributed worldwide.

Gluck Christoph Willibald von 1714–1787. German composer who settled in Vienna as kapellmeister to Maria Theresa in 1754. In 1762 his *Orfeo ed Euridice/Orpheus and Eurydice* revolutionized the 18th-century conception of opera by giving free scope to dramatic effect. *Orfeo* was followed by *Alceste/Alcestis* 1767 and *Paride ed Elena/Paris and Helen* 1770.

Born in Erasbach, Bavaria, he studied music at Prague, Vienna, and Milan, went to London in 1745 to compose operas for the Haymarket, but returned to Vienna in 1746 where he was knighted by the pope. In 1762 his *Iphigénie en Aulide/Iphigenia in Aulis* 1774, produced in Paris, brought to a head the fierce debate over the future of opera in which Gluck's French style had the support of Marie Antoinette while his Italian rival Nicolò Piccinni (1728–1800) had the support of Madame Du Barry. With *Armide* 1777 and *Iphigénie en Tauride/Iphigenia in Tauris* 1779 Gluck won a complete victory over Piccinni.

glucose or *dextrose* or *grape-sugar* $C_6H_{12}O_6$ sugar present in the blood, and found also in honey and fruit juices. It is a source of energy for the body, being produced from other sugars and starches to form the "energy currency" of many biochemical reactions also involving ⟁ATP.

Glucose is prepared in syrup form by the hydrolysis of cane sugar or starch, and may be purified to a white crystalline powder. Glucose is a monosaccharide sugar (made up of a single sugar unit), unlike the more familiar sucrose (cane or beet sugar), which is a disaccharide (made up of two sugar units: glucose and fructose).

glue type of ⟁adhesive.

glue-sniffing or *solvent misuse* inhalation of the fumes from organic solvents of the type found in paints, lighter fuel, and glue, for their hallucinatory effects. As well as being addictive, solvents are dangerous for their effects on the user's liver, heart, and lungs. It is believed that solvents produce hallucinations by dissolving the cell membrane of brain cells, thus altering the way the cells conduct electrical impulses.

gluon in physics, a ⟁gauge boson that carries the strong nuclear force, responsible for binding quarks together to form the strongly interacting subatomic particles known as ⟁hadrons. There are eight kinds of gluon.

glut excess of goods in a market. A glut of agricultural produce often follows an exceptional harvest, causing prices to fall unless there is some form of intervention in the market.

gluten protein found in cereal grains, especially wheat. Gluten enables dough to stretch during rising. It has to be avoided by sufferers from celiac disease.

glyceride ⟁ester formed between one or more acids and glycerol (propan-1,2,3-triol). A glyceride is termed a mono-, di-, or triglyceride, depending on the number of hydroxyl groups from the glycerol that have reacted with the acids.

Glycerides, chiefly triglycerides, occur naturally as esters of ⟁fatty acids in plant oils and animal fats.

glycerine another name for ⟁glycerol.

glycerol or *glycerine* or *propan-1,2,3-triol* $HOCH_2CH(OH)CH_2OH$ thick, colorless, odorless, sweetish liquid. It is obtained from vegetable and animal oils and fats (by treatment with acid, alkali, superheated steam, or an enzyme), or by fermentation of glucose, and is used in the manufacture of high explosives, in antifreeze solutions, to maintain moist conditions in fruits and tobacco, and in cosmetics.

glycine $CH_2(NH_2)COOH$ the simplest amino acid, and one of the main components of proteins. When purified, it is a sweet, colorless crystalline compound.

glycogen polymer (a polysaccharide) of the sugar ⟁glucose made and retained in the liver as a carbohydrate store, for which reason it is sometimes called animal starch. It is a source of energy when needed by muscles, where it is converted back into glucose by the hormone ⟁insulin and metabolized.

glycol or *ethylene glycol* or *ethane-1,2-diol* $(CH_2OH)_2$ thick, colorless, odorless, sweetish liquid. It is used in antifreeze solutions, in the preparation of ethers and esters (used for explosives), as a solvent, and as a substitute for glycerol.

GMT abbreviation for ⟁*Greenwich Mean Time*.

gnat any of various small flies of the order Diptera, that sometimes suck blood. In Britain, mosquitoes are often called gnats.

gneiss coarse-grained ◊metamorphic rock, formed under conditions of increasing temperature and pressure, and often occurring in association with schists and granites. It has a foliated, laminated structure, consisting of thin bands of micas and amphiboles alternating with granular bands of quartz and feldspar. Gneisses are formed during regional metamorphism; **paragneisses** are derived from sedimentary rocks and **orthogneisses** from igneous rocks. Garnets are often found in gneiss.

gnome in fairy tales, a small, mischievous spirit of the earth. The males are bearded, wear tunics and hoods, and often guard an underground treasure.

Gnosticism esoteric cult of divine knowledge (a synthesis of Christianity, Greek philosophy, Hinduism, Buddhism, and the mystery cults of the Mediterranean), which flourished during the 2nd and 3rd centuries and was a rival to, and influence on, early Christianity. The medieval French Cathar heresy and the modern *Mandean* sect (in S Iraq) descend from Gnosticism.

Gnostic 4th-century codices discovered in Egypt in the 1940s include the *Gospel of St Thomas* (unconnected with the disciple) and the *Gospel of Mary*, probably originating about AD 135. Gnosticism envisaged the world as a series of emanations from the highest of several gods. The lowest emanation was an evil god (the demiurge) who created the material world as a prison for the divine sparks that dwell in human bodies. The Gnostics identified this evil creator with the God of the Old Testament, and saw the Adam and Eve story and the ministry of Jesus as attempts to liberate humanity from his dominion, by imparting divine secret wisdom.

GNP abbreviation for ◊*gross national product.*

gnu or **wildebeest** either of two species of African ◊antelope, genus *Connochaetes*, with a cowlike face, a beard and mane, and heavy curved horns in both sexes. The body is up to 4.2 ft/1.3 m at the shoulder and slopes away to the hindquarters.

The brindled gnu *C. taurinus* is silver-gray with dark face, mane, and tail tuft, and occurs from Kenya southward. Vast herds move together on migration. The white-tailed gnu *C. gnou* of South Africa almost became extinct, but was saved by breeding on farms.

go board game originating in China 3,000 years ago, and now the national game of Japan. It is played by placing small counters on a large grid. The object is to win territory and eventual superiority.

The board, squared off by 19 horizontal and 19 vertical lines, begins empty and gradually fills up with black and white counters (originally flattish, rounded stones) as the players win territory by surrounding areas of the board with "men" and capturing the enemy armies by surrounding them. A handicapping system enables expert and novice to play against each other.

It is far more complex and subtle than chess, the mathematical possibilities being 1×10^{720}.

Goa state of India
area 1,428 sq mi/3,700 sq km
capital Panaji
population (1991) 1,168,600
history captured by the Portuguese 1510; the inland area added in the 18th century. Goa was incorporated into India as a Union Territory with Daman and ◊Diu 1961 and became a state 1987.

goat ruminant mammal of the genus *Capra* in the family Bovidae, closely related to the sheep. Both males and females have horns and beards. They are sure-footed animals, and feed on shoots and leaves more than on grass.

Domestic varieties are kept for milk, or for mohair (the angora and cashmere). Wild species include the ibex *C. ibex* of the Alps, and markhor *C. falconeri* of the Himalayas, 3 ft/1 m high and with long twisted horns. The Rocky Mountain goat *Oreamnos americanus* is a "goat antelope" and is not closely related to true goats.

Gobbi Tito 1913–1984. Italian baritone singer renowned for his opera characterizations of Figaro in *The Marriage of Figaro*, Scarpia in *Tosca*, and Iago in *Otello*.

Gobelins French tapestry factory, originally founded as a dyeworks in Paris by Gilles and Jean Gobelin about 1450. The firm began to produce tapestries in the 16th century, and in 1662 the establishment was bought for Louis XIV by his minister Colbert. With the support of the French government, it continues to make tapestries.

Gobi Asian desert divided between the Mongolian People's Republic and Inner Mongolia, China; 500 mi/800 km N–S, and 1,000 mi/1,600 km E–W. It is rich in fossil remains of extinct species.

Gobind Singh 1666–1708. Indian religious leader, the tenth and last guru (teacher) of Sikhism, 1675–1708, and founder of the Sikh brotherhood known as the ◊Khalsa. On his death, the Sikh holy book, the *Guru Granth Sahib*, replaced the line of human gurus as the teacher and guide of the Sikh community.

During a period of Sikh persecution Gobind Singh asked those who were willing to die for their faith to join him, the first five willing to risk their lives were named the *panj pyares* "the faithful ones" by him and proclaimed the first members of the Khalsa. He also introduced the names Singh (lion) for male Sikhs, and Kaur (princess) for female Sikhs.

God the concept of a supreme being, a unique creative entity, basic to several monotheistic religions (for example, Judaism, Christianity, Islam); in many polytheistic cultures (for example, Norse, Roman, Greek), the term "god" refers to a supernatural being who personifies the force behind an aspect of life (for example, Neptune, Roman god of the sea).

Since the 17th century, advances in science and the belief that the only valid statements were those verifiable by the senses have had a complex influence on the belief in God. (See also ◊monotheism, ◊polytheism, ◊deism, ◊theism, and ◊pantheism.)

Godard Jean-Luc 1930– . French film director, one of the leaders of ◊New Wave cinema. His works are often characterized by experimental editing techniques and an unconventional dramatic form. His films include *A bout de souffle* 1959, *Vivre sa Vie* 1962, *Weekend* 1968, and *Je vous salue, Marie* 1985.

His other films include *Pierrot le fou* 1965.

Goddard Paulette. Adopted name of Marion Levy 1911–1990. US film actress. She starred with comedian Charlie Chaplin in *Modern Times* 1936 and *The Great Dictator* 1940, and her other films include the British-made version of Oscar Wilde's play *An Ideal Husband* 1948.

Goddard Robert Hutchings 1882–1945. US rocket pioneer. His first liquid-fueled rocket was launched at Auburn, Massachusetts in 1926. By 1935 his rockets had gyroscopic control and carried cameras to record instrument readings. Two years later a Goddard rocket gained the world altitude record with an ascent of 1.9 mi/3 km.

Goddard Space Flight Center NASA installation at Greenbelt, Maryland, responsible for the operation of NASA's unmanned scientific satellites, including the ◊Hubble Space Telescope. It is also home of the National Space Science Data center, a repository of data collected by satellites.

Gödel Kurt 1906–1978. Austrian-born US mathematician and philosopher. He proved that a mathematical system always contains statements that can be neither proved nor disproved within the system; in other words, as a science, mathematics can never be totally consistent and totally complete. He worked on relativity, constructing a mathematical model of the universe that made travel back through time theoretically possible.

Godfrey de Bouillon c. 1060–1100. French crusader, second son of Count Eustace II of Boulogne. He and his brothers, ◊Baldwin I and Eustace, led 40,000 Germans in the First Crusade 1096. When Jerusalem was taken 1099, he was elected its ruler, but refused the title of king. After his death, Baldwin was elected king.

Godiva Lady c. 1040–1080. Wife of Leofric, earl of Mercia (died 1057). Legend has it that her husband promised to reduce the heavy taxes on the people of Coventry if she rode naked through the streets at noon. The grateful citizens remained indoors as she did so, but "Peeping Tom" bored a hole in his shutters and was struck blind.

Godkin Edwin Lawrence 1831–1902. Irish-born US editor and writer on political affairs who founded the liberal weekly magazine *The Nation* 1865.

Educated in Ireland, Godkin studied law but chose a journalistic career, covering the Crimean War for the *London Daily News* and *The New York Times*. Immigrating to the US 1856, he studied law and was admitted to the bar 1858. During the American Civil War he again served as a correspondent for the *London Daily News* and in 1865 founded his own political journal, *The Nation*. In it, Godkin crusaded for national reform and progressive causes. After selling *The Nation* 1881 to the *New York Evening Post*, Godkin continued to write on national affairs.

Godthaab (Greenlandic **Nuuk**) capital and largest town of Greenland; population (1982) 9,700. It is a storage center for oil and gas, and the chief industry is fish processing.

Godunov Boris 1552–1605. Tsar of Russia from 1598, elected after the death of Fyodor I, son of Ivan the Terrible. He was assassinated by a pretender to the throne who professed to be Dmitri, a brother of Fyodor and the rightful heir. The legend that has grown up around this forms the basis of Pushkin's play *Boris Godunov* 1831 and Mussorgsky's opera of the same name 1874.

An apocryphal story of Boris killing the true Dmitri in order to gain the throne was fostered by Russian historians anxious to discredit

Boris because he was not descended from the main ruling families.

Godunov's rule was marked by a strengthening of the Russian church. It was also the beginning of the Time of Troubles, a period of instability.

Goebbels Paul Josef 1897–1945. German Nazi leader. As minister of propaganda from 1933, he brought all cultural and educational activities under Nazi control and built up sympathetic movements abroad to carry on the "war of nerves" against Hitler's intended victims. On the capture of Berlin by the Allies, he poisoned himself.

He was born in the Rhineland, became a journalist, joined the Nazi party in its early days, and was given control of its propaganda 1929.

Goeppert-Mayer Maria 1906–1972. German-born US physicist who studied the structure of the atomic nucleus. She shared the 1963 Nobel Prize for Physics with Eugene ¢Wigner and Hans Jensen (1907–1973).

Her explanation of the stability of particular atoms 1948 envisaged atomic nuclei as shell-like layers of protons and neutrons, with the most stable atoms having completely filled outermost shells.

Goering (German *Göring*) Hermann Wilhelm 1893–1946. Nazi leader, German field marshal from 1938. He was part of Hitler's inner circle, and with Hitler's rise to power in 1933, he established the Gestapo and concentration camps. Appointed successor to Hitler in 1939, he built a vast economic empire in occupied Europe, but later lost favor and was expelled from the party in 1945. Tried at Nuremberg for war crimes, he poisoned himself before he could be executed.

Goering was born in Bavaria. He was a renowned fighter pilot in World War I, and joined the Nazi party in 1922. He was elected to the Reichstag in 1928 and became its president in 1932. As commissioner for aviation from 1933 he built up the Luftwaffe (airforce). In 1936 he took charge of the four-year plan for war preparations.

Goes Hugo van der, died 1482. Flemish painter, chiefly active in Ghent. His *Portinari altarpiece* about 1475 (Uffizi, Florence) is a huge oil painting of the Nativity, full of symbolism and naturalistic detail, and the *Death of the Virgin* about 1480 (Musée Communale des Beaux Arts, Bruges) is remarkable for the varied expressions on the faces of the apostles.

Goethe Johann Wolfgang von 1749–1832. German poet, novelist, and dramatist, generally considered the founder of modern German literature, and leader of the Romantic ¢*Sturm und Drang* movement. His works include the autobiographical *Die Leiden des Jungen Werthers/The Sorrows of the Young Werther* 1774 and *Faust* 1808, his masterpiece. A visit to Italy 1786–88 inspired the Classical dramas *Iphigenie auf Tauris/Iphigenia in Tauris* 1787 and *Torquato Tasso* 1790.

Goethe was born in Frankfurt-am-Main, and studied law. Inspired by Shakespeare, to whose work he was introduced by ¢Herder, he wrote the play *Götz von Berlichingen* 1773. His autobiographical *The Sorrows of the Young Werther* 1774 and the poetic play *Faust* 1808, made him known throughout Europe. Other works include the *Wilhelm Meister* novels 1796–1829. Between 1775 and 1785 he served as prime minister at the court of Weimar.

Gogh Vincent van 1853–1890. Dutch Post-Impressionist painter. He tried various careers, including preaching, and began painting in the 1880s. He met Paul ¢Gauguin in Paris, and when he settled in Arles, Provence, 1888, Gauguin joined him there. After a quarrel van Gogh cut off part of his own earlobe, and in 1889 he entered an asylum; the following year he committed suicide. The Arles paintings vividly testify to his intense emotional involvement in his art; among them are *The Yellow Chair* and several *Sunflowers* 1888 (National Gallery, London).

Born in Zundert, van Gogh worked for a time as a schoolmaster in England before he took up painting. He studied under van Mauve at The Hague. One of the leaders of the Post-Impressionist painters, he executed still lifes and landscapes, including *A Cornfield with Cypresses* 1889 (National Gallery, London).

Gogol Nicolai Vasilyevich 1809–1852. Russian writer. His first success was a collection of stories, *Evenings on a Farm near Dikanka* 1831–32, followed by *Mirgorod* 1835. Later works include *Arabesques* 1835, the comedy play *The Inspector General* 1836, and the picaresque novel *Dead Souls* 1842, which satirizes Russian provincial society.

Gogol was born near Poltava. He tried several careers before entering the St Petersburg civil service. From 1835 he traveled in Europe, and it was in Rome that he completed the earlier part of *Dead Souls* 1842. Other works include the short stories "The Overcoat" and "The Nose."

goiter enlargement of the thyroid gland seen as a swelling on the neck. It is most pronounced in simple goiter, which is caused by iodine deficiency. Much more common is toxic goiter or thyrotoxicosis, caused by overactivity of the thyroid gland.

Golan Heights (Arabic *Jawlan*) plateau on the Syrian border with Israel, bitterly contested in the ¢Arab-Israeli Wars and annexed by Israel on Dec 14, 1981.

gold shiny, yellow, ductile and very malleable, metallic element, symbol Au (from Latin *aurum*, "gold"), atomic number 79, atomic weight 197. It occurs in nature frequently as a free metal (see ¢native metal) and is highly resistant to acids, tarnishing, and corrosion. Pure gold is the most malleable of all metals and is used as gold leaf or powder, where small amounts cover vast surfaces, such as gilded domes and statues. The elemental form is so soft that it is alloyed for strength with a number of other metals, such as silver, copper, and platinum. Its purity is then measured in ¢carats on a scale of 24 (24K = pure gold; 18K = 75% gold). It is used mainly for decorative purposes (jewelry, gilding) but also for coinage, dentistry, and conductivity in electronic devices.

Gold has been known and worked from ancient times, and currency systems were based on it in Western civilization, where mining it became an economic and imperialistic goal. In 1988 the three leading gold-producing countries were: South Africa, 563 tons; US, 186 tons; and Australia, 138 tons. In 1989 gold deposits were found in Greenland with an estimated yield of 11 tons per year.

The name is very old and derives from the Germanic form of Indo-European *ghel*, "to shine" or "to gleam."

Goldberg Rube 1883–1970. US cartoonist. Born in San Francisco and trained in engineering at the University of California, Goldberg abandoned that profession for cartooning, joining the staff of the *San Francisco Chronicle* 1904. Moving to New York City 1907, Goldberg produced several popular comic strips that were nationally syndicated from 1915. The most famous and widely read of his strips featured ridiculously complicated inventions. Goldberg also devoted time to political cartooning, winning a Pulitzer Prize 1948.

Gold Coast former name for ¢Ghana, but historically the west coast of Africa from Cape Three Points to the Volta River, where alluvial gold is washed down. Portuguese and French navigators visited this coast in the 14th century, and a British trading settlement developed into the colony of the Gold Coast 1618. With its dependencies of Ashanti and Northern Territories plus the trusteeship territory of Togoland, it became Ghana 1957. The name is also used for many coastal resort areas—for example, in Florida.

Gold Coast resort region on the east coast of Australia, stretching 20 mi/32 km along the coast of Queensland and New South Wales S of Brisbane; population (1986) 219,000.

Golden Ass, The or *Metamorphoses* a ¢picaresque adventure by the Roman writer Lucius Apuleius, written in Latin about AD 160, sometimes called the world's first novel. Lucius, turned into an ass, describes his exploits with a band of robbers, weaving into the narrative several ancient legends, including that of Cupid and Psyche.

Golden Calf in the Old Testament, image made by ¢Aaron in response to the request of the Israelites for a god when they despaired of Moses' return from Mount Sinai.

Golden Fleece in Greek mythology, fleece of the winged ram Chrysomallus, which hung on an oak tree at Colchis and was guarded by a dragon. It was stolen by Jason and the Argonauts.

Golden Gate strait in California, linking ¢San Francisco Bay with the Pacific, spanned by a suspension bridge that was completed 1937. The longest span is 4,200 ft/1,280 m.

Golden Horde the invading Mongol-Tatar army that first terrorized Europe from 1237 under the leadership of Batu Khan, a grandson of Genghis Khan. ¢Tamerlane broke their power 1395, and ¢Ivan III ended Russia's payment of tribute to them 1480.

goldenrod one of several tall, leafy perennials of the North American genus *Solidago*, in the daisy family Compositae. Flower heads are mostly composed of yellow florets.

goldenseal North American plant *Hydrastis canadensis* of the buttercup family whose thick yellow root is used medicinally as an astringent and a tonic. The root contains the alkaloid hydrastine, employed by herbalists to stop uterine bleeding.

golden section visually satisfying ratio, first constructed by the Greek mathematician ¢Euclid and used in art and architecture. It is found by dividing a line AB at a point O such that the rectangle produced by the whole line and one of the segments is equal to the square drawn on the other segment. The ratio of the two segments is about 8:13 or 1:1.26, and a rectangle whose sides are in this ratio is called a *golden rectangle*.

In van Gogh's picture *Mother and Child*, for example, the Madonna's face fits perfectly into a golden rectangle. See p. 448.

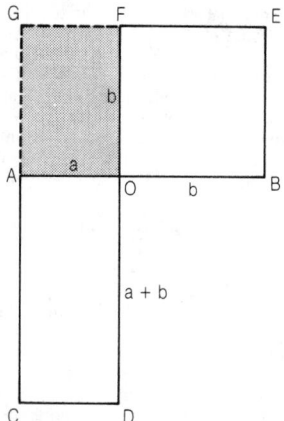

golden section *The golden section is the ratio a/b, equal to 8:13.*

goldfinch songbird of the genus *Carduelis*, found in Eurasia, N Africa, and North America.

The American goldfinch *C. tristis* is about 5 in/13 cm long and golden-brownish on top and underside, with white-barred wings and tail.

goldfish fish *Carassius auratus* of the ◊carp family, found in E Asia. Greenish-brown in its natural state, it has for centuries been bred by the Chinese, taking on highly colored and sometimes freakishly shaped forms. Goldfish can see a greater range of colors than any other animal tested.

Golding William 1911– . English novelist. His first book, *Lord of the Flies* 1954, was about savagery taking over among a group of English schoolboys marooned on a Pacific island. Later novels include *The Spire* 1964, *Rites of Passage* 1980 (Booker prize), and *The Paper Men* 1984. He was awarded the Nobel Prize for Literature in 1983.

Goldman Emma 1869–1940. US political organizer, feminist, and anarchist. In 1893 she was jailed for inciting unemployed workers to riot; after her release she became a well-known political lecturer and was again imprisoned for opposing military conscription during World War I. With Alexander Berkman, she published the anarchist monthly *Mother Earth* 1906–17. In 1908 her citizenship was revoked, and in 1919 she was deported to Russia but broke with the Bolsheviks in 1921. She spent the rest of her life in exile. Her writings include *My Disillusionment in Russia* 1923 and *Living My Life* 1931.

Born in Lithuania and raised in Russia, Goldman immigrated to the US 1885 and worked in a clothing factory in Rochester, New York. There she became attracted to radical socialism and moved to New York City 1889, where she became part of the anarchist movement.

Goldoni Carlo 1707–1793. Italian dramatist, born in Venice. He wrote popular comedies for the Sant'Angelo theater, including *La putta onorata/The Respectable Girl* 1749, *I pettegolezzi delle donne/Women's Gossip* 1750, and *La locandiera/Mine Hostess* 1753. In 1761 he moved to Paris, where he directed the Italian theater and wrote more plays, including *L'Eventail/The Fan* 1763.

gold rush large influx of gold prospectors to an area where gold deposits have recently been discovered. The result is a dramatic increase in population. Cities such as Johannesburg, Melbourne, and San Francisco either originated or were considerably enlarged by gold rushes. Melbourne's population trebled from 77,000 to some 200,000 between 1851–53.

famous gold rushes

1848	Sutter's Mill, California (the "Forty-niners")
1851	New South Wales and Victoria, Australia
1880s	Rhodesia
1886	Fortymile Creek, Yukon; Johannesburg, Transvaal; Kimberley, West Australia
1890s	Klondike River, Yukon

Goldsmith Jerry (Jerrald) 1930– . US composer of film music who originally worked in radio and television. His prolific output includes *Planet of the Apes* 1968, *The Wind and the Lion* 1975, *The Omen* 1976 (Academy Award), and *Gremlins* 1984.

Goldsmith Oliver 1728–1774. Irish writer whose works include the novel *The Vicar of Wakefield* 1766; the poem "The Deserted Village" 1770; and the play *She Stoops to Conquer* 1773. In 1761 Goldsmith met Samuel Johnson, and became a member of his "club." *The Vicar of Wakefield* was sold (according to Johnson's account) to save him from imprisonment for debt.

Goldsmith was the son of a cleric. He was educated at Trinity College, Dublin, and Edinburgh, where he studied medicine 1752. After traveling extensively in Europe, he returned to England and became a hack writer, producing many works, including *History of England* 1764 and *Animated Nature* 1774. One of his early works was *The Citizen of the World* 1762, a series of letters by an imaginary Chinese traveler. In 1764 he published the poem "The Traveller," and followed it with collected essays 1765.

gold standard system under which a country's currency is exchangeable for a fixed weight of gold on demand at the central bank. It was almost universally applied 1870–1914, but by 1937 no single country was on the full gold standard. Britain abandoned the gold standard 1931; the US abandoned it 1971. Holdings of gold are still retained because it is an internationally recognized commodity, which cannot be legislated upon or manipulated by interested countries.

The gold standard broke down in World War I, and attempted revivals were undermined by the Great Depression. After World War II the par values of the currency units of the ◊International Monetary Fund (which included nearly all members of the United Nations not in the Soviet bloc) were fixed in terms of gold and the US dollar, but by 1976 floating exchange rates (already unofficially operating from 1971) were legalized.

Goldwater Barry 1909– . US Republican politician; presidential candidate in the 1964 election, when he was overwhelmingly defeated by Lyndon ◊Johnson. As a US senator 1953–86, he voiced the views of his party's right-wing conservative faction. Many of Goldwater's conservative ideas were later adopted by the Republican right, especially the Reagan administration.

Born in Phoenix, Arizona, he attended military high school in Virginia and served in the Army Air Forces during World War II. He achieved the rank of major general 1962 in the Air Force Reserve. After a stint 1949 on the Phoenix city council, he ran successfully for the US Senate. He wrote *The Conscience of a Conservative* 1960 and *Why Not Victory?* 1962.

Goldwyn Samuel. Adopted name of Samuel Goldfish 1882–1974. US film producer. Born in Poland, he emigrated to the US 1896. He founded the Goldwyn Pictures Corporation 1917, which eventually merged into Metro-Goldwyn-Mayer (MGM) 1924, although he was not part of the deal. He remained a producer for many years, making classics such as *Wuthering Heights* 1939, *The Little Foxes* 1941, *The Best Years of Our Lives* 1946, and *Guys and Dolls* 1955.

He was famed for his illogical aphorisms known as "goldwynisms," for example, "Include me out."

golf outdoor game in which a small rubber-cored ball is hit with a wooden- or iron-faced club into a series of holes using the least number of shots. On the first shot for each hole, the ball is hit from a tee, which elevates the ball slightly off the ground; subsequent strokes are played off the ground. Most courses have 18 holes and are approximately 6,000 yd/5,500 m in length.

Each hole is made up of distinct areas: the *tee*, from where plays start at each hole; the *green*, a finely manicured area where the hole

golf: recent winners

British Open	
1983	Tom Watson *(US)*
1984	Severiano Ballesteros *(Spain)*
1985	Sandy Lyle *(UK)*
1986	Greg Norman *(Australia)*
1987	Nick Faldo *(UK)*
1988	Severiano Ballesteros *(Spain)*
1989	Mark Calcavecchia *(US)*
1990	Nick Faldo *(UK)*
1991	Ian Baker-Finch *(Australia)*
1992	Nick Faldo *(UK)*
US Open	
1983	Larry Nelson *(US)*
1984	Fuzzy Zoeller *(US)*
1985	Andy North *(US)*
1986	Ray Floyd *(US)*
1987	Scott Simpson *(US)*
1988	Curtis Strange *(US)*
1989	Curtis Strange *(US)*
1990	Hale Irwin *(US)*
1991	Payne Stewart *(US)*
1992	Tom Kite *(US)*
US Masters	
1983	Severiano Ballesteros *(Spain)*
1984	Ben Crenshaw *(US)*
1985	Bernhard Langer *(West Germany)*
1986	Jack Nicklaus *(US)*
1987	Larry Mize *(US)*
1988	Sandy Lyle *(UK)*
1989	Nick Faldo *(UK)*
1990	Nick Faldo *(UK)*
1991	Ian Woosnam *(UK)*
1992	Fred Couples *(US)*
US PGA Championship	
1983	Hal Sutton *(US)*
1984	Lee Trevino *(US)*
1985	Hubert Green *(US)*
1986	Bob Tway *(US)*
1987	Larry Nelson *(US)*
1988	Jeff Sluman *(US)*
1989	Payne Stewart *(US)*
1990	Wayne Grady *(Australia)*
1991	John Daly *(US)*
1992	Nick Price *(Zimbabwe)*

is located; the *fairway*, the grassed area between the tee and the green, not cut as finely as the green; and the *rough*, the perimeter of the fairway, which is left to grow naturally. Natural hazards such as trees, bushes, and streams make play more difficult, and there are additional artificial hazards in the form of sand-filled bunkers. The club faces have varying angles and are styled for different types of shot.

Golf is played in two principal forms: *stroke play* (also known as *medal play*) and *match play*. In stroke play the lowest aggregate score for a round determines the winner. Play may be more than one round, in which case the aggregate score for all rounds counts. In match play, the object is to win holes by scoring less than one's opponent(s). Golf's handicap system allows for golfers of all levels to compete on equal terms. There are three types of play (as seen in the ◊Ryder Cup): *singles*, which has one player competing with one other; *foursomes*, where there are two players per side alternately playing a single ball; and *fourball*, again two players per side but each plays his own ball.

Golf was played in Scotland in the 15th century. The Royal & Ancient Golf Club at St Andrews dates from 1754. Major golfing events include the British and US Opens, US Masters, US Professional Golfers Association (PGA), World Match-Play Championship, and British PGA. There are golf tours in North America, Europe, Australia, North Africa, and Japan.

The major golfing events are the British Open, first held in 1860; the US Open, first held in 1895; the US Masters, first held in 1934; and the US PGA, first held in 1916.

Golgi Camillo 1843–1926. Italian cell biologist who with Santiago Ramón y Cajal produced the first detailed knowledge of the fine structure of the nervous system.

Golgi's use of silver salts in staining cells proved so effective in showing up the components and fine processes of nerve cells that even the synapses—tiny gaps between the cells—were visible. The *Golgi apparatus*, a series of flattened membranous cavities found in the cytoplasm of cells, was first described by him in 1898. Golgi and Ramón y Cajal shared the 1906 Nobel Prize for Physiology or Medicine.

Golgi apparatus or *Golgi body* stack of flattened membranous sacs found in the cells of ◊eukaryotes. Many molecules travel through the Golgi apparatus on their way to other organelles or to the endoplasmic reticulum. Some are modified or asssembled inside the sacs. Named after the Italian physician Camillo Golgi (1844–1926).

Goliath in the Old Testament, champion of the ◊Philistines, who was said to have been slain by a stone from a sling by the young ◊David in single combat in front of their opposing armies.

Gómez Juan Vicente 1864–1935. Venezuelan dictator 1908–35. The discovery of oil during his rule attracted US, British, and Dutch oil interests and made Venezuela one of the wealthiest countries in Latin America. Gómez amassed a considerable personal fortune and used his well-equipped army to dominate the civilian population.

Gompers Samuel 1850–1924. US labor leader. His early career in the Cigarmakers' Union led him to found and lead the ◊American Federation of Labor 1882.

Gompers advocated nonpolitical activity within the existing capitalist system to secure improved wages and working conditions for members.

Gomułka Władysław 1905–1982. Polish Communist politician, party leader 1943–48 and 1956–70. He introduced moderate reforms, including private farming and tolerance for Roman Catholicism.

gonad the part of an animal's body that produces the sperm or egg cells (ova) required for sexual reproduction. The sperm-producing gonad is called a ◊testis, and the ovule-producing gonad is called an ◊ovary.

gonadotropin any hormone that supports and stimulates the function of the gonads (sex glands); some gonadotropins are used as ◊fertility drugs.

Goncharov Ivan Alexandrovitch 1812–1891. Russian novelist. His first novel, *A Common Story* 1847, was followed in 1858 by his humorous masterpiece *Oblomov*, which satirized the indolent Russian landed gentry.

From 1852–55 he was secretary on the ship *Pallada*, which was sent to Japan by the Tsar to open it to trade. His wry description of the world cruise was published as *The Frigate "Pallada"* 1858.

Goncourt, de the brothers Edmond 1822–1896 and Jules 1830–1870. French writers. They collaborated in producing a compendium, *L'Art du XVIIIème siècle/18th-Century Art* 1859–75, historical studies, and a *Journal* published 1887–96 that depicts French literary life of their day. Edmond de Goncourt founded the Académie Goncourt, opened 1903, which awards an annual prize, the Prix Goncourt, to the author of the best French novel of the year.

Gond member of a heterogenous people of central India, about half of whom speak unwritten languages belonging to the Dravidian family. The rest speak Indo-European languages. There are over 4 million Gonds, most of whom live in Madhya Pradesh, E Maharashtra, and N Andra Pradesh, although some live in Orissa. Traditionally, many Gonds practiced shifting cultivation; agriculture and livestock remain the basis of the economy.

Gond beliefs embrace Hinduism as well as a range of more ancient gods and spirits, and there are a limited number of clans that coexist within a defined set of social and ritual relationships. The dynasties of one group, the Raj Gonds, rivaled those of neighboring Hindus until the Muslim conquests of the 16th century.

Gondwanaland or *Gondwana* land mass, including the continents of South America, Africa, Australia, and Antarctica, that formed the southern half of ◊Pangaea, the "supercontinent" or world continent that existed between 250 and 200 million years ago. The northern half was ◊Laurasia. The baobab tree of Africa and Australia is a relic of Gondwanaland.

gonorrhea common sexually transmitted disease arising from infection with the bacterium *Neisseria gonorrhoeae*, which causes inflammation of the genito-urinary tract. After an incubation period of two to ten days, infected men experience pain while urinating and a discharge from the penis; infected women often have no external symptoms.

González Márquez Felipe 1942– . Spanish socialist politician, leader of the Socialist Workers' Party (PSOE), prime minister from 1982.

Although reelected in the 1989 election, his popularity suffered from economic upheaval and allegations of corruption.

After studying law in Spain and Belgium, in 1966 he opened the first labor-law office in his home city of Seville. In 1964 he had joined the PSOE, and he rose rapidly to the position of leader. In 1982 the PSOE won a sweeping electoral victory and González became prime minister. Under his administration left-wing members of the PSOE, disenchanted with González's policies, formed a new party called Social Democracy 1990.

Good Friday in the Christian church, the Friday before Easter, which is observed in memory of the Crucifixion (the death of Jesus on the cross).

Goodman Benny (Benjamin David) 1909–1986. US clarinetist, nicknamed the "King of Swing" for the new jazz idiom he introduced with arranger Fletcher Henderson (1897–1952). In 1934 he founded his own 12-piece band, which combined the expressive improvisatory style of black jazz with disciplined precision ensemble playing. He is associated with such numbers as "Blue Skies" and "Let's Dance." He also recorded with a sextet 1939–41 that included the guitarist Charlie Christian (1916–1942).

When swing lost popularity in the 1950s, Goodman took a series of smaller groups on world tours culminating in a US government-sponsored visit to Moscow in 1962.

Born in Chicago, he studied Classical clarinet with Franz Schoepp of the Chicago Symphony Orchestra before embarking on a successful freelance solo career in 1921, influenced by the New Orleans style. He introduced jazz to New York's Carnegie Hall in 1938.

Goodyear Charles 1800–1860. US inventor who developed rubber coating 1837 and vulcanized rubber 1839, a method of curing raw rubber to make it strong and elastic.

goose aquatic bird of several genera (especially *Anser*) in the family Anatidae, which also includes ducks and swans. Both genders are similar in appearance: they have short, webbed feet, placed nearer the front of the body than in other members of the order Anatidae, and the beak is slightly hooked. They feed entirely on grass and plants.

The graylag goose *Anser anser* is the ancestor of domesticated geese. Other species include the Canada goose *Branta canadensis*, the bean goose *A. fabalis*, the pink-footed goose *A. brachyrhynchus*, and the white-fronted goose *A. albifrons*. The goose builds a nest of grass and twigs on the ground and lays from five to nine eggs, white or cream-colored, according to the species.

Goose Bay settlement at the head of Lake Melville on the Labrador coast of Newfoundland. In World War II it was used as a staging post by US and Canadian troops on their way to Europe. Until 1975 it was used by the US Air Force as a low-level-flying base.

gooseberry several prickly shrubs of the genus *Ribes* in the saxifrage family, native to Eurasia and North America, and closely related to currants in the same genus. The fleshy, red, blackish or green fruits are edible. The pasture gooseberry *R. cyanosbati* is native to North America. The European gooseberry *R. Grossalaria* is cultivated in gardens.

goosefoot any plants of the genus *Chenopodium* in the goosefoot family

Chenopodiaceae, closely related to spinach and beets. The seeds of white goosefoot, *C. album*, were used as food in Europe from Neolithic times, and also from early times in the Americas. White goosefoot grows to 3 ft/ 1 m tall and has lance-or diamond-shaped leaves and packed heads of small inconspicuous flowers. The green part is eaten as a spinach substitute.

gopher burrowing rodent of the genus *Citellus*, family Sciuridae. It is a kind of ground squirrel represented by some 20 species distributed across W North America and Eurasia. Length ranges from 6 in/15 cm to 16 in/90 cm, excluding the furry tail; coloring ranges from plain yellowish to striped and spotted species. The name *pocket gopher* is applied to the eight genera of the North American family Geomyidae.

Gorbachev Mikhail Sergeyevich 1931– . Soviet president, in power 1985–91. He was a member of the Politburo from 1980. As general secretary of the Communist Party (CPSU) 1985–91, and president of the Supreme Soviet 1988–91, he introduced liberal reforms at home (⟡*perestroika* and ⟡*glasnost*), proposed the introduction of multiparty democracy, and attempted to halt the arms race abroad. He became head of state 1989.

He was awarded the Nobel Peace Prize 1990 but his international reputation suffered in the light of harsh state repression of nationalist demonstrations in the Baltic states. Following an abortive coup attempt by hard-liners Aug 1991, international acceptance of independence for the Baltic states, and accelerated moves toward independence in other republics, Gorbachev's power base as Soviet president was greatly weakened and in Dec 1991 he resigned.

Gorbachev, born in the N Caucasus, studied law at Moscow University and joined the CPSU 1952. In 1955–62 he worked for the Komsomol (Communist Youth League) before being appointed regional agriculture secretary. As Stavropol party leader from 1970 he impressed Andropov, and was brought into the CPSU secretariat 1978. Gorbachev was promoted into the Politburo in 1983, when Andropov was general secretary, and took broader charge of the Soviet economy. During the Chernenko administration 1984–85, he was chair of the Foreign Affairs Commission. On Chernenko's death 1985 he was appointed party leader. He initiated wide-ranging reforms and broad economic restructuring, and introduced campaigns against alcoholism, corruption, and inefficiency. In the 1988 presidential election by members of the Soviet parliament, he was the sole candidate. Gorbachev radically changed the style of Soviet leadership, encountering opposition to the pace of change in both conservative and radical camps, but he failed both to realize the depth of hostility this aroused against him in the CPSU and to distance himself from the party. In March 1990 he was elected to a five-year term as executive president with greater powers.

At home his plans for economic reform failed to avert a food crisis in the winter of 1990–91 and his desire to preserve a single, centrally controlled USSR met with resistance from Soviet republics seeking more independence. Early in 1991, Gorbachev shifted to the right in order to placate the conservative wing of the party and appointed some of the hard-liners to positions of power. In late spring, he produced a plan for a new union treaty to satisfy the demands of reformers. This plan alarmed the hard-liners, who, in late summer, temporarily removed him from office. He was saved from this attempted coup mainly by the efforts of Boris ⟡Yeltsin and the ineptness of the plotters. Soon after his reinstatement, Gorbachev was obliged to relinquish his leadership of the party, renounce communism as a state doctrine, suspend all activities of the Communist Party (including its most powerful organs, the Politburo and the Secretariat), and surrender many of his central powers to the states. During the following months he pressed for an agreement on his proposed union treaty in the hope of preventing a distintegration of the Soviet Union, but was unable to maintain control and on Dec 25, 1991 resigned as president, effectively yielding power to Boris Yeltsin.

Gordian knot in Greek mythology, the knot tied by King Gordius of Phrygia that—so an oracle revealed—could be unraveled only by the future conqueror of Asia. According to tradition, Alexander the Great, unable to untie it, cut it with his sword in 334 BC.

Gordimer Nadine 1923– . South African novelist, an opponent of apartheid. Her first novel, *The Lying Days*, appeared in 1953, her other works include *The Conservationist* 1974, the volume of short stories *A Soldier's Embrace* 1980, and *July's People* 1981. She was awarded the Nobel Prize for Literature in 1991.

Gordon Charles (George) 1833–1885. British general sent to Khartoum in the Sudan 1884 to rescue English garrisons that were under attack by the ⟡Mahdi, Mohammed Ahmed; he was himself besieged for ten months by the Mahdi's army. A relief expedition arrived Jan 28, 1885 to find that Khartoum had been captured and Gordon killed two days before.

Gordon served in the ⟡Crimean War and in China 1864, where he earned his nickname "Chinese" Gordon in ending the Taiping Rebellion. In 1874 he was employed by the Khedive of Egypt to open the country and 1877–80 was British governor of the Sudan.

Gore Al (Albert Arnold, Jr) 1948– . US vice-president 1993– under President Bill ⟡Clinton. A Democrat, he served in the House of Representatives 1977–85 and the Senate 1985–93 and became noted for his concern for the environment.

Born in Washington, DC, Gore graduated from Harvard University 1969 and served as a journalist in the army as well as for a newspaper in Nashville, Tennessee 1971–76. His father, Al Gore, Sr, was a prominent senator from Tennessee.

Gorgon in Greek mythology, any of three sisters, Stheno, Euryale, and Medusa, who had wings, claws, enormous teeth, and snakes for hair. Medusa, the only one who was mortal, was killed by ⟡Perseus, but even in death her head was still so frightful that it turned the onlooker to stone.

Gorgonzola town NE of Milan, Italy, famous for cheese.

gorilla largest of the apes, *Gorilla gorilla*, found in the dense forests of West Africa and mountains of central Africa. The male stands about 6 ft/1.8 m, and weighs about 450 lbs/ 200 kg. Females are about half the size. The body is covered with blackish hair, silvered on the back in older males. Gorillas live in family groups; they are vegetarian, highly intelligent, and will attack only in self-defense. They are dwindling in numbers, being shot for food by some local people, or by poachers taking young for zoos, but protective measures are having some effect.

Gorillas construct stoutly built nests in trees for overnight use. The breast-beating movement, once thought to indicate rage, actually signifies only nervous excitement. There are three races of the one species: western lowland, eastern lowland, and mountain gorillas.

Göring Hermann. German spelling of ⟡Goering, Nazi leader.

Gorky Arshile 1904–1948. Armenian-born US painter. He painted Cubist abstracts before developing a more surreal Abstract-Expressionist style, using organic shapes and bold paint strokes.

Among Gorky's major influences were Picasso, Kandinsky, Miró, and Cézanne. His works, such as *The Liver Is the Cock's Comb* 1944 Albright-Knox Art Gallery, Buffalo) are noted for their sense of fantasy. He lived in the US from 1920.

Gorky Maxim. Adopted name of Alexei Peshkov 1868–1936. Russian writer. Born in Nizhni Novgorod (named Gorky 1932–90 in his honor), he was exiled 1906–13 for his revolutionary principles. His works, which include the play *The Lower Depths* 1902 and the memoir *My Childhood* 1913–14, combine realism with optimistic faith in the potential of the industrial proletariat.

Gorky Russian *Gor'kiy* name 1932–90 of ⟡Nizhny Novgorod, city in central Russia.

gorse or *furze* or *whin* Eurasian genus of plants *Ulex*, family Leguminosae, consisting of thorny shrubs with spine-shaped leaves densely clustered along the stems, and bright yellow flowers.

Gorton John Grey 1911– . Australian Liberal politician. He was minister for education and science 1966–68, and prime minister 1968–71.

goshawk or *northern goshawk* woodland hawk *Accipiter gentilis* that is similar in appearance to the peregrine falcon, but with shorter wings and legs. It is used in falconry.

Goshen city in N Indiana, on the Elkhart river, SE of South Bend; seat of Elkhart county. It is situated in an agricultural area and serves as a market town. Industries include steel, rubber, electrical, and building products; population (1990) 23,700.

Gospel (Middle English "good news") in the New Testament generally, the message of Christian salvation; in particular the four written accounts of the life of Jesus by Matthew, Mark, Luke, and John. Although the first three give approximately the same account or synopsis (thus giving rise to the name "Synoptic Gospels"), their differences from John have raised problems for theologians.

The so-called fifth Gospel, or *Gospel of St Thomas* (not connected with the disciple Thomas), is a 2nd-century collection of 114 sayings of Jesus. It was found in a Coptic translation contained in a group of 13 papyrus codices, discovered in Upper Egypt 1945, which may have formed the library of a Gnostic community (see ⟡Gnosticism).

gospel music vocal music developed in the 1920s in the black Baptist churches of the US South from spirituals, which were 18th- and 19th-century hymns joined to the old African pentatonic (five-note) scale. Outstanding among the early gospel singers was Mahalia Jackson (1911–1972), but from the 1930s to the mid-1950s male harmony groups predominated, among them the Dixie Hummingbirds, the Swan Silvertones, and the Five Blind Boys of Mississippi.

Göteborg (German *Gothenburg*) port and industrial (ships, vehicles, chemicals) city (Sweden's second largest) on the W coast of Sweden, on the Göta Canal (built 1832), which links it with Stockholm; population (1990) 433,000.

Goth E Germanic people who settled near the Black Sea around AD 2nd century. There are two branches, the eastern Ostrogoths and the western Visigoths. The *Ostrogoths* were conquered by the Huns 372. They regained their independence 454 and under ▷Theodoric the Great conquered Italy 488–93; they disappeared as a nation after the Byzantine emperor ▷Justinian I reconquered Italy 535–55.

The *Visigoths* migrated to Thrace. Under ▷Alaric they raided Greece and Italy 395–410, sacked Rome, and established a kingdom in S France. Expelled from there by the Franks, they established a Spanish kingdom which lasted until the Moorish conquest of 711.

Gotha town in Thuringia, Germany, former capital of the duchy of Saxe-Coburg-Gotha; population (1981) 57,600. It has a castle and two observatories; pottery, soap, textiles, precision instruments, and aircraft are manufactured here.

Gothic architecture style of architecture that flourished in Europe from the mid-12th century to the end of the 15th century. It is characterized by vertical lines of tall pillars, spires, greater height in interior spaces, the pointed arch, rib vaulting, and the flying buttress.

Gothic architecture originated in Normandy and Burgundy in the 12th century. The term became derisory, perhaps deriving from the 16th-century critic Vasari's attribution of medieval artistic styles to the Goths, who destroyed "Classicism." The style prevailed in W Europe until the 16th century when Classic architecture was revived. The term Gothic was at first used disparagingly of medieval art by Renaissance architects.

In *France*, Gothic architecture may be divided into four periods. *Early Gothic*, 1130–90, saw the introduction of ogival (pointed) vaults, for example Nôtre Dame, Paris, begun 1160. In *lancet Gothic*, 1190–1240, pointed arches were tall and narrow, as in Chartres Cathedral, begun 1194, and Bourges Cathedral, begun 1209. *Radiating Gothic*, 1240–1350, takes its name from the series of chapels that radiate from the cathedral apse, as in Sainte Chapelle, Paris, 1226–30. *Late Gothic* or the Flamboyant style, 1350–1520, is exemplified in St Gervais, Paris.

In *Italy* Gothic had a Classical basis. A notable example of Italian Gothic is Milan cathedral.

In *Germany*, the Gothic style until the end of the 13th century was at first heavily influenced by that of France; for example Cologne Cathedral, the largest in N Europe, was built after the model of Amiens.

In *England* the Gothic style is divided into *Early English* 1200–75, for example Salisbury Cathedral; *Decorated* 1300–75, for example York Minster; and *Perpendicular* 1400–1575, for example Winchester Cathedral.

Gothic art style of painting and sculpture that dominated European art from the late 12th century until the early Renaissance. The great Gothic church façades held hundreds

of sculpted figures and profuse ornamentation, and manuscripts were lavishly decorated. Stained glass replaced mural painting to some extent in N European churches. The *International Gothic* style in painting emerged in the 14th century, characterized by delicate and complex ornamentation and increasing realism.

Gothic novel literary genre established by Horace Walpole's *The Castle of Otranto* 1765 and marked by mystery, violence, and horror; other exponents were the English writers Anne Radcliffe, Matthew "Monk" Lewis, Mary Shelley, the Irish writer Bram Stoker, and Edgar Allan Poe in the US.

Gothic revival the resurgence of interest in Gothic architecture, as displayed in 19th-century Britain and the US. Gothic revival buildings include the Houses of Parliament and St Pancras Station, London; the Town Hall, Vienna; and Princeton University.

The growth of Romanticism led some writers, artists, and antiquaries to embrace a fascination with Gothic forms that emphasized the supposedly bizarre and grotesque aspects of the Middle Ages. During the Victorian period, however, a far better understanding of Gothic forms was achieved, and this resulted in some impressive Neo-Gothic architecture, as well as some desecration of genuine Gothic churches in the name of "restoration" by, for example, Augustus Pugin and George Gilbert Scott.

Gotland Swedish island in the Baltic Sea; area 1,212 sq mi/3,140 sq km; population (1990) 57,100. The capital is Visby. Its products are mainly agricultural (sheep and cattle), and there is tourism. It was an area of dispute between Sweden and Denmark but became part of Sweden 1645.

Götterdämmerung (German "twilight of the gods") in Scandinavian mythology, the end of the world.

Gould Elliott. Adopted name of Elliot Goldstein 1938– . US film actor. A successful child actor, his film debut *The Night They Raided Minsky's* 1968 led rapidly to starring roles in such films as *M.A.S.H.* 1970, *The Long Goodbye* 1972, and *Capricorn One* 1978.

Gould Jay 1836–1892. US financier, born in New York. He is said to have caused the financial panic on "Black Friday," Sept 24, 1869, through his efforts to corner the gold market.

Gould was one of the "Robber Barons" who built the transportation and communications structures of the US while accumulating great wealth. His first major success came when he was made an associate of the Erie Railroad by Cornelius ▷Vanderbilt. Following financial and political scandals, Gould was forced to relinquish control of the Erie Railroad, but he used the large fortune he had amassed to acquire control of western railroads, including the Union Pacific. He also controlled the Western Union Telegraph Company and elevated railroads in New York City.

Gould Stephen Jay 1941– . US paleontologist and author. In 1972 he proposed the theory of punctuated equilibrium, suggesting that the evolution of species did not occur at a steady rate but could suddenly accelerate, with rapid change occurring over a few hundred thousand years. His books include *Ever Since Darwin* 1977, *The Panda's Thumb* 1980, *The Flamingo's Smile* 1985, and *Wonderful Life* 1990.

Gounod Charles François 1818–1893. French composer. His operas include *Sappho* 1851, *Faust* 1859, *Philémon et Baucis* 1860, and *Roméo et Juliette* 1867. He also wrote sacred songs, masses, and an oratorio, *The Redemption* 1882. His music inspired many French composers of the late 19th century.

gourd names applied to various members of the family Cucurbitaceae, including melons, squashes, and pumpkins. In a narrower sense, the name is applied to an inedible, ornamental variety of pumpkin *Cucurbita pepa*.

gout disease, a hereditary form of ▷arthritis, marked by an excess of uric acid crystals in the tissues, causing pain and inflammation in one or more joints (usually of the feet or hands). Acute attacks are treated with ▷anti-inflammatories.

The disease, ten times more common in men, poses a long-term threat to the blood vessels and the kidneys, so ongoing treatment may be needed to minimize the levels of uric acid in the body fluids. It is worsened by drinking alcohol.

government any system whereby political authority is exercised. Modern systems of government distinguish between liberal democracies, totalitarian (one-party) states, and autocracies (authoritarian, relying on force rather than ideology). The Greek philosopher Aristotle was the first to attempt a systematic classification of governments. His main distinctions were between government by one person, by few, and by many (monarchy, oligarchy, and democracy), although the characteristics of each may vary between states and each may degenerate into tyranny (rule by an oppressive elite in the case of oligarchy or by the mob in the case of democracy).

The French philosopher Montesquieu distinguished between constitutional governments—whether monarchies or republics—which operated under various legal and other constraints, and despotism, which was not constrained in this way. Many of the words used (dictatorship, tyranny, totalitarian, democratic) have acquired negative or positive connotations that make it difficult to use them objectively. The term *liberal democracy* was coined to distinguish Western types of democracy from the many other political systems that claimed to be democratic. Its principal characteristics are the existence of more than one political party, open processes of government and political debate, and a separation of powers. *Totalitarian* has been applied to both fascist and communist states and denotes a system where all power is centralized in the state, which in turn is controlled by a single party that derives its legitimacy from an exclusive ideology. *Autocracy* describes a form of government that has emerged in a number of Third World countries, where state power is in the hands either of an individual or of the army; normally ideology is not a central factor, individual freedoms tend to be suppressed where they may constitute a challenge to the authority of the ruling group, and there is a reliance upon force. Other useful distinctions are between *federal* governments (where powers are dispersed among various regions which in certain respects are self-governing) and *unitary* governments (where powers are concentrated in a central authority); and between *presidential* (where the head of state is also the directly elected head of government, not part of the legislature) and *parliamentary* systems (where the government is drawn from an elected legislature that can dismiss it).

governor in engineering, any device that controls the speed of a machine or engine, usually by regulating the intake of fuel or steam.

James ◊Watt invented the steam-engine governor in 1788. It works by means of heavy balls, which rotate on the end of linkages and move in or out because of ◊centrifugal force according to the speed of rotation. The movement of the balls closes or opens the steam valve to the engine. When the engine speed increases too much, the balls fly out, and cause the steam valve to close, so the engine slows down. The opposite happens when the engine speed drops too much.

Gowon Yakubu 1934– . Nigerian politician, head of state 1966–75. Educated at Sandhurst military college in the UK, he became chief of staff, and in the military coup of 1966 seized power. After the Biafran civil war 1967–70, he reunited the country with his policy of "no victor, no vanquished." In 1975 he was overthrown by a military coup.

Goya Francisco José de Goya y Lucientes 1746–1828. Spanish painter and engraver. He painted portraits of four successive kings of Spain, and his etchings include *The Disasters of War*, depicting the French invasion of Spain 1810–14. Among his later works are the "black paintings" (Prado, Madrid), with horrific images such as *Saturn Devouring One of His Sons* c. 1822.

Goya was born in Aragon and was for a time a bullfighter, the subject of some of his etchings. After studying in Italy, he returned to Spain and was employed on a number of paintings for the royal tapestry factory. In 1789 he was court painter to Charles IV.

Goyen Jan van 1596–1656. Dutch landscape painter, active in Leiden, Haarlem, and from 1631 in The Hague. He was a pioneer of the realist style of landscape with Ruisdael, and he sketched from nature and studied clouds and light effects.

Gozzoli Benozzo c. 1421–1497. Florentine painter, a late exponent of the International Gothic style. He painted frescoes 1459 in the chapel of the Palazzo Medici-Riccardi, Florence: the walls are crammed with figures, many of them portraits of the Medici family.

GP in medicine, abbreviation for *general practitioner*.

GPU name (1922–23) for the security service of the Soviet Union; later the ◊KGB.

Graaf Regnier de 1641–1673. Dutch physician and anatomist who discovered the ovarian follicles, which were later named *Graafian follicles*. He named the ovaries and gave exact descriptions of the testicles. He was also the first to isolate and collect the secretions of the pancreas and gall bladder.

Graafian follicle fluid-filled capsule that surrounds and protects the developing egg cell inside the ovary during the ◊menstrual cycle. After the egg cell has been released, the follicle remains and is known as a corpus luteum.

Grable Betty (Elizabeth Ruth) 1916–1973. US actress, singer, and dancer, who starred in *Moon over Miami* 1941, *I Wake Up Screaming* 1941, and *How to Marry a Millionaire* 1953. As a publicity stunt, her legs were insured for a million dollars. Her popularity peaked during World War II when US soldiers voted her their number-one pin-up girl.

Gracchus the brothers *Tiberius Sempronius* 163–133 BC and *Gaius Sempronius* 153–121 BC. Roman agrarian reformers. As ◊tribune (magistrate) 133 BC, Tiberius tried to prevent the ruin of small farmers by making large slave-labor farms illegal but was murdered. Gaius, tribune 123–122 BC, revived his brother's legislation, and introduced other reforms, but was outlawed by the Senate and committed suicide.

Graces in Greek mythology, three goddesses (Aglaia, Euphrosyne, Thalia), daughters of Zeus and Hera, personifications of pleasure, charm, and beauty; the inspirers of the arts and the sciences.

Graf Steffi 1969– . German lawn-tennis player who brought Martina ◊Navratilova's long reign as the world's number-one female player to an end. Graf reached the semifinal of the US Open 1985 at the age of 16, and won five consecutive Grand Slam singles titles 1988–89.

CAREER HIGHLIGHTS

Wimbledon
singles: 1988–89, 1991, 1992
doubles: 1988
US Open
singles: 1988–89
French Open
singles: 1987–88
Australian Open
singles: 1988–90
Olympics
gold: 1988

graffiti (Italian "scratched drawings") inscriptions or drawings carved, scratched, or drawn on public surfaces, such as walls, fences, or public-transport vehicles. *Tagging* is the act of writing an individual logo on surfaces with spray paint or large felt-tip pens.

The term "graffiti" is derived from a traditional technique in Italian art (*sgraffito*) of scratching a design in the thin white plaster on a wall.

grafting in medicine, the operation by which a piece of living tissue is removed from one organism and transplanted into the same or a different organism where it continues growing. In horticulture, it is a technique widely used for propagating plants, especially woody species. A bud or shoot on one plant, termed the *scion*, is inserted into another, the *stock*, so that they continue growing together, the tissues combining at the point of union.

Grafting is usually only successful between species that are closely related and is most commonly practiced on roses and fruit trees. The grafting of non-woody species is more difficult but it is sometimes used to propagate tomatoes and cacti. See also ◊transplant.

Graham Billy (William Franklin) 1918– . US Protestant evangelist, known for the dramatic staging and charismatic eloquence of his preaching. Graham has preached to millions during worldwide crusades and on television, bringing many thousands to a "decision for Christ."

Born in Charlotte, North Carolina, he graduated from Wheaton College (Illinois). His first evangelical crusade was Youth for Christ 1949. From then, under the auspices of the Billy Graham Evangelistic Association 1950, he conducted worldwide tours. Graham wrote *Peace with God* 1953, *World Aflame* 1965, and *The Challenge* 1969.

Graham Martha 1893–1991. US dancer, choreographer, teacher, and director. A leading exponent of modern dance in the US, she developed a distinctive vocabulary of movement, the *Graham Technique*, now taught worldwide. Her pioneering technique, designed to express inner emotion and intention through dance forms, represented the first real alternative to Classical ballet.

Graham founded her own dance school 1927 and started a company with students from the school 1929. She created over 170 works, including *Appalachian Spring* 1944 (score by Aaron Copland), *Clytemnestra* 1958, the first full-length modern dance work, and *Errand into the Maze*.

She danced in most of the pieces she choreographed until her retirement from performance in the 1960s. Graham had a major influence on such choreographers in the contemporary dance movement as Robert ◊Cohan, Glen Tetley, Merce ◊Cunningham, Norman Morrice, Paul Taylor, and Robert North.

Graham Thomas 1805–1869. Scottish chemist who laid the foundations of physical chemistry (the branch of chemistry concerned with changes in energy during a chemical transformation) by his work on the diffusion of gases and liquids. *Graham's Law* 1829 states that the diffusion rate of a gas is inversely proportional to the square root of its density.

His work on ◊colloids (which have larger particles than true solutions) was equally fundamental; he discovered the principle of dialysis, that colloids can be separated from solutions containing smaller molecules by the differing rates at which they pass through a semipermeable membrane (a process he termed "osmosis"). The human kidney uses the principle of dialysis to extract nitrogenous waste.

Grahame Kenneth 1859–1932. Scottish author. The early volumes of sketches of childhood, *The Golden Age* 1895 and *Dream Days* 1898, were followed by his masterpiece *The Wind in the Willows* 1908, an animal fantasy created for his young son, which was dramatized by A A Milne as *Toad of Toad Hall* 1929.

Graham Land mountainous peninsula in Antarctica, formerly a dependency of the Falkland Islands, and from 1962 part of the ◊British Antarctic Territory. It was discovered by John Biscoe in 1832 and until 1934 was thought to be an archipelago.

grain the smallest unit of mass in the three English systems (avoirdupois, troy, and apothecaries' weights) used in the US and UK, equal to 0.0648 g. It was reputedly the weight of a grain of wheat. One pound avoirdupois equals 7,000 grains; one pound troy or apothecaries' weight equals 5,760 grains.

Grainger Percy Aldridge 1882–1961. Australian-born US composer and concert pianist. He is remembered for a number of songs and short instrumental pieces drawing on folk idioms, including *Country Gardens* 1925, and for his settings of folk songs, such as *Molly on the Shore* 1921.

gram metric unit of mass; one-thousandth of a kilogram.

grammar Greek *grammatike tekhne* "art of letters" the principles of the correct use of language, dealing with the rules of structuring words into phrases, clauses, sentences, and paragraphs in an accepted way. Emphasis on the standardizing impact of print has meant that spoken or colloquial language is often perceived as less grammatical than written language, but all forms of a language, standard or otherwise, have their own grammatical systems of differing complexity. People often acquire several overlapping grammatical systems within one language; for example, one formal system for writing and standard communication and one less formal system for everyday and peer-group communication.

Originally "grammar" was an analytical approach to writing, intended to improve the understanding and the skills of scribes, philosophers, and writers. When compared with Latin, English has been widely regarded as having "less" grammar or at least a simpler grammar; it would be truer, however, to say that English and Latin have different grammars, each complex in its own way. In linguistics (the contemporary study of language) grammar, or syntax, refers to the arrangement of the elements in a language for the purposes of acceptable communication in speech, writing, and print.

All forms of a language, standard or otherwise, have their grammars or grammatical systems, which children acquire through use; a child may acquire several overlapping systems within one language (especially a nonstandard form for everyday life and a standard form linked with writing, school, and national life). Not even the most comprehensive grammar book (or grammar) of a language like English, French, Arabic, or Japanese completely covers or fixes the implicit grammatical system that people use in their daily lives. The rules and tendencies of natural grammar operate largely in nonconscious ways but can, for many social and professional purposes, be studied and developed for conscious as well as inherent skills. See also ⬦parts of speech.

Recent theories of the way language functions include ⬦**phrase structure grammar**, ⬦**transformational grammar**, and ⬦**case grammar**.

Grampian Mountains range that separates the Highlands from the Lowlands of Scotland, running NE from Strathclyde. It takes in the S Highland region (which includes **Ben Nevis**, the highest mountain in the British Isles at 4,406 ft/1,340 m), northern Tayside, and the Southern border of Grampian region itself (the Cairngorms, which include **Ben Macdhui** 4,296 ft/1,309 m). The region includes Aviemore, a winter vacation and sports center.

Grampians western end of Australia's eastern highlands, in Victoria; the highest peak is Mount William 3,829 ft/1,167 m.

grampus common name for Risso's dolphin *Grampus griseus*, a slate-gray dolphin found in tropical and temperate seas. These dolphins live in large schools and can reach 13 ft/4 m in length. They have blunt snouts with only a few teeth, and feed on squid and small fish. The name grampus is sometimes also used for the killer ⬦whale.

Gramsci Antonio 1891–1937. Italian Marxist who attempted to unify social theory and political practice. He helped to found the Italian Communist Party 1921 and was elected to parliament 1924, but was imprisoned by the Fascist leader Mussolini from 1926; his *Quaderni di carcere/Prison Notebooks* were published posthumously 1947.

Granada city in the Sierra Nevada in Andalusia, S Spain; population (1986) 281,000.

It produces textiles, soap, and paper. The *Alhambra*, a fortified hilltop palace, was built in the 13th and 14th centuries by the Moorish kings.

history Founded by the Moors in the 8th century, it became the capital of an independent kingdom 1236–1492, when it was the last Moorish stronghold to surrender to the Spaniards. Ferdinand and Isabella, the first sovereigns of a united Spain, are buried in the cathedral (built 1529–1703).

Gran Chaco large lowland plain in N Argentina, W Paraguay, and SE Bolivia; area 251,000 sq mi/650,000 sq km. It consists of swamps, forests (a source of quebracho timber), and grasslands, and there is cattle-raising.

Grand Banks continental shelf in the N Atlantic off SE Newfoundland, where the shallow waters are rich fisheries, especially for cod.

Grand Canal (Chinese *Da Yune*) the world's longest canal. It is 1,000 mi/1,600 km long and runs north from Hangzhou to Tianjin, China; it is 100–200 ft/30–61 m wide, and reaches depths of over 1 mi/1.5 km. The earliest section was completed 486 BC, and the northern section was built AD 1282–92, during the reign of Kublai Khan.

Grand Canyon gorge of multicolored rock strata cut by and containing the Colorado River, N Arizona. It is 217 mi/350 km long, 4–18 mi/6–29 km wide, and reaches depths of over 1.1 mi/1.7 km.

John Wesley Powell and ten companions first traveled down the river through the gorge 1869. It was made a national park 1919. Millions of tourists visit each year.

Grand Design in the early 17th century, a plan attributed by the French minister Sully to Henry IV of France (who was assassinated before he could carry it out) for a great Protestant union against the Holy Roman Empire; the term was also applied to President de Gaulle's vision of France's place in a united Europe.

Grand Forks city in E central North Dakota on the Minnesota border, on the Red River, N of Fargo; seat of Grand Forks County. It serves the surrounding agricultural area; most of its industries, such as food-processing mills and fertilizer plants, are associated with agriculture. The University of North Dakota 1883 is located here; population (1990) 49,400.

Grand Guignol genre of short horror play originally produced at the Grand Guignol theater in Montmartre, Paris (named after the bloodthirsty character Guignol in late 18th-century marionette plays).

Grandi Dino 1895–1988. Italian politician who challenged Mussolini for leadership of the Italian Fascist Party in 1921 and was subsequently largely responsible for Mussolini's downfall in July 1943.

Grand Old Party (GOP) popular name for US ⬦Republican Party.

grand opera type of opera without any spoken dialogue (unlike the *opéra-comique*), as performed at the Paris Opéra 1820s–80s. Using the enormous resources of the state-subsidized opera house, grand operas were extremely long (five acts), and included incidental music and a ballet.

Composers of grand opera include D F E Auber, Giacomo Meyerbeer, and Ludovic Halévy; examples include Verdi's *Don Carlos* 1867 and Meyerbeer's *Les Huguenots* 1836.

Grand Rapids city in W Michigan on the Grand River; population (1990) 189,100. It produces furniture, motor bodies, plumbing fixtures, and electrical goods. A fur-trading post was founded here 1826, and the furniture industry developed in the 1840s.

Gerald Ford, 38th president of the US, lived here.

Grand Remonstrance petition passed by the English Parliament in Nov 1641 that listed all the alleged misdeeds of Charles I and demanded Parliamentary approval for the king's ministers and the reform of the church. Charles refused to accept the Grand Remonstrance and countered by trying to arrest five leading members of the House of Commons (Pym, Hampden, Holles, Hesilrige, and Strode). The worsening of relations between king and Parliament led to the outbreak of the English Civil War in 1642.

grand slam in tennis, the four major tournaments: the Australian Open, the French Open, Wimbledon, and the US Open. In golf, it is also the four major tournaments: the US Open, the British Open, the Masters, and the PGA (Professional Golfers Association). In baseball, a grand slam is a home run with runners on all the bases. A grand slam in bridge is when all 13 tricks are won by one team.

Grand Teton highest point of the spectacular Teton mountain range, NW Wyoming, rising to 13,770 ft/4,197 m. Grand Teton National Park was established 1929.

grand unified theory (GUT) in physics, a sought-for theory that would combine the theory of the strong nuclear force (called ⬦quantum chromodynamics) with the theory of the weak nuclear and electromagnetic forces. The search for the grand unified theory is part of a larger program seeking a ⬦unified field theory, which would combine all the forces of nature (including gravity) within one framework.

Grange Red (Harold Edward) 1903–1991. US football player. Born in Forksville, Pennsylvania, and raised in Illinois, Grange attended the University of Illinois. In both the 1923 and 1924 seasons he was chosen All-American halfback and won the nickname "the Galloping Ghost" for his extraordinary open-field running ability. Leaving college 1925 to join the Chicago Bears professional football team, Grange became one of the first superstars of the newly founded National Football League. He became a charter member of the Football Hall of Fame 1963.

Grange Movement, the in US history, a farmers' protest in the South and Midwest states against economic hardship and exploitation. The National Grange of the Patrons of Husbandry, formed 1867, was a network of local organizations, employing cooperative practices and advocating "granger" laws. The movement petered out in the late 1870s, to be superseded by the ⬦Greenbackers.

Granger (James) Stewart 1913– . British film actor. After several leading roles in British romantic films during World War II, he moved to Hollywood in 1950 and subsequently appeared in such fanciful films as *Scaramouche* 1952, *The Prisoner of Zenda* 1952, and *The Wild Geese* 1978.

granite coarse-grained ⬦igneous rock, typically consisting of the minerals quartz, feldspar, and mica. It may be pink or gray, depending on the composition of the feldspar. Granites are chiefly used as building materials.

Granites often form large intrusions in the core of mountain ranges, and they are usually surrounded by zones of ⟡metamorphic rock (rock that has been altered by heat or pressure). Granite areas have characteristic moorland scenery. In exposed areas the bedrock may be weathered along joints and cracks to produce a tor, consisting of rounded blocks that appear to have been stacked upon one another.

Granite City city in SW Illinois, across the Mississippi river from St Louis, Missouri. An industrial city with its own port on the Chain of Rocks canal, it manufactures steel products, automobile frames, and building materials; population (1990) 32,800.

Grant Cary. Adopted name of Archibald Leach 1904–1986. British-born actor who became a US citizen 1942. His witty, debonair personality made him a screen favorite for more than three decades. He was directed by Alfred ⟡Hitchcock in *Suspicion* 1941, *Notorious* 1946, *To Catch a Thief* 1955, and *North by Northwest* 1959. He received a 1970 Academy Award for general excellence.

His other films include *She Done Him Wrong* 1933, *Bringing Up Baby* 1937, and *The Philadelphia Story* 1940.

Grant Ulysses S(impson) 1822–1885. American Civil War leader and 18th president of the US 1869–77. He was a Union general in the American Civil War and commander in chief from 1864. As a Republican president, he carried through a liberal ⟡Reconstruction policy in the South, reformed the civil service, and ratified the Treaty of Washington with Great Britain 1871. He failed to suppress extensive political corruption within his own party and cabinet, which tarnished the reputation of his second term.

Born Hiram Ulysses Grant in Point Pleasant, Ohio, he graduated from West Point 1843 and had an unsuccessful career in the army 1839–54 and in business. At the outbreak of the Civil War he received a commission on the Mississippi front. His military career nearly ended in failure when Confederate forces surprised him at the Battle of Shiloh 1862, but Abraham ⟡Lincoln's support was unwavering and Grant quickly redeemed himself, showing an aggressive fighting spirit. By his capture of Vicksburg in 1863 he brought the whole Mississippi front under Northern control and slowly wore down the Confederate general Lee's resistance, receiving his surrender at Appomattox 1865. He was elected president 1868 and reelected 1872. His two volume *Memoirs* were very successful and restored his finances.

Granville-Barker Harley 1877–1946. British theater director and author. He was director and manager with J E Vedrenne at the Royal Court Theater, London, 1904–18, producing plays by Shaw, Yeats, Ibsen, Galsworthy, and Masefield.

grape fruit of any vine of the genus *Vitis*, especially *V. vinifera*, of the Vitaceae family. The woody grapevine has small greenish flowers that produce clusters of large, juicy green, red, or black berries. Grapes are eaten as a dessert fruit, the juice is made into wines, and grape seed oil is extracted from the pips. They are also dried as raisins, or sultanas and currants if seedless. Grapes have been cultivated throughout the Old World for thousands of years and were successfully introduced to

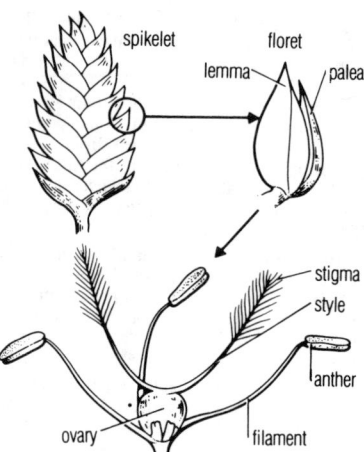

grass *The parts of a grass flower.*

South America and the W coast of North America.

grapefruit round, yellow, juicy, sharp-tasting fruit of the evergreen tree *Citrus paradisi* of the Rutaceae family. The tree grows up to more than 30 ft/10 m and has dark shiny leaves and large white flowers. The large fruits grow in grapelike clusters (hence the name). Grapefruits were first established in the West Indies and subsequently cultivated in Florida by the 1880s; they are now also grown in Israel and South Africa. Some varieties have pink flesh.

graph pictorial representation of numerical data, such as statistical data, or a method of showing the mathematical relationship between two or more variables by drawing a diagram.

There are often two axes or coordinates at right angles intersecting at the origin—the zero point, from which values of the variables (for example, distance and time for a moving object) are assigned along the axes. Pairs of simultaneous values (the distance moved after a particular time) are plotted as points in the area between the axes, and the points then joined by a smooth curve to produce a graph.

graphic notation in music, a sign language referring to unorthodox sound effects, such as electronic sounds, for which Classical music notation is not suitable.

graphics tablet or *bit pad* in computing, an input device in which a stylus or cursor is moved, by hand, over a flat surface. The computer can keep track of the position of the stylus, so enabling the operator to input drawings or diagrams into the computer.

A graphics tablet is often used with a form overlaid for users to mark boxes in positions that relate to specific registers in the computer, although recent developments in handwriting recognition may increase its future versatility.

graphical user interface (GIU) or *WIMP* in computing, a type of user interface in which programs and files appear as ⟡icons, menus drop down from a bar along the top of the screen, and data are displayed in rectangular areas, called window, which the operator can manipulate in various ways. The operator uses a pointing device, typically a ⟡mouse, to make selections and initiate actions.

graphite blackish gray, laminar, crystalline form of ⟡carbon. It is used as a lubricant and as the active component of pencil lead.

The carbon atoms are strongly bonded together in sheets, but the bonds between the sheets are weak so that the sheets are free to slide over one another. Graphite has a very high melting point (6,332°F/3,500°C), and is a good conductor of heat and electricity. In its pure form it is used as a moderator in nuclear reactors.

grass plant of the large family Gramineae of monocotyledons, with about 9,000 species distributed worldwide except in the Arctic regions. The majority are perennial, with long, narrow leaves and jointed, hollow stems; hermaphroditic flowers are borne in spikelets; the fruits are grainlike. Included are bluegrass, wheat, rye, corn, sugarcane, and bamboo.

Grass Günter 1927– . German writer. The grotesque humor and socialist feeling of his novels *Die Blechtrommel/The Tin Drum* 1959 and *Der Butt/The Flounder* 1977 are also characteristic of many of his poems.

Born in Danzig, he studied at the art academies of Düsseldorf and Berlin, worked as a writer and sculptor (first in Paris and later in Berlin), and in 1958 won the coveted "Group 47" prize.

grasshopper insect of the order Orthoptera, usually with strongly developed hind legs, enabling it to leap. The femur of each hind leg in the male usually has a row of protruding joints that produce the characteristic chirping when rubbed against the hard wing veins. Members of the order include ⟡locusts, ⟡crickets, and katydids.

The shorthorned grasshoppers constitute the family Acrididae, and include locusts. All members of the family feed voraciously on vegetation. Eggs are laid in a small hole in the ground, and the unwinged larvae become adult after about six molts.

The American grasshopper *Schistocera americana* is widespread in North America. The longhorned grasshoppers, or katydids, form the family Tettigoniidae, and have a similar life history, but differ from the Acrididae in having long antennae and in producing their chirping by the friction of the wing covers over one another (stridulation).

grass-of-Parnassus or *eastern parnassia* plant (*Parnassia glauca*), unrelated to grasses, found growing in moist grasslands and thickets of North America. It is low-growing, with a rosette of heart-shaped, stalked leaves, and has five-petaled, white flowers with conspicuous green veins.

grass tree Australian plant of the genus *Xanthorrhoea*. The tall, thick stems have a grasslike tuft at the top and are surmounted by a flower spike resembling a spear; this often grows after bushfires and can in some species grow to a height of 10 ft/3 m.

Grateful Dead, the US psychedelic rock group formed 1965. Their shows feature long improvisations and subtle ensemble playing, seldom fully captured in recording; albums include *Live Dead* 1969, *Workingman's Dead* 1970, and *Built to Last* 1989.

Formed at the heart of the San Francisco ⟡hippie scene, the Dead still represent an alternative lifestyle to a core of fans (Deadheads) who follow the constantly touring band around the world. Remaining founder members are Jerry Garcia (1942–), guitar; Phil Lesh (1940–), bass; Bob Weir (1947–), guitar; Bill Kreutzmann (1946–), drums. Out of their vast repertoire of original and nonoriginal material, they are often identified with the song "Truckin'" (from *American Beauty* 1970).

Graubünden (French *Grisons*) Swiss canton, the largest in Switzerland; area 2,743 sq mi/ 7,106 sq km; population (1990) 170,400. The inner valleys are the highest in Europe, and the main sources of the river Rhine rise here. It also includes the resort of Davos and, in the Upper Engadine, St Moritz. The capital is Chur. Romansch is still widely spoken. Graubünden entered the Swiss Confederation 1803.

gravel coarse ◊sediment consisting of pebbles or small fragments of rock, originating in the beds of lakes and streams or on beaches. Gravel is quarried for use in road building, railroad ballast, and for an aggregate in concrete. It is obtained from quarries known as gravel pits, where it is often found mixed with sand or clay. Some gravel deposits also contain metal ores (chiefly tin) or free metals (such as gold and silver).

Some gravel deposits also contain ◊placer deposits of metal ores (chiefly tin) or free metals (such as gold and silver).

Graves Robert (Ranke) 1895–1985. English poet and author. He was severely wounded on the Somme in World War I, and his frank autobiography *Goodbye to All That* 1929 is one of the outstanding war books. Other works include the poems *Over the Brazier* 1916; two historical novels of imperial Rome, *I Claudius* and *Claudius the God*, both 1934; and books on myth—for example, *The White Goddess* 1948.

gravimetry study of the Earth's gravitational field. Small variations in the gravitational field (gravimetric anomalies) can be caused by varying densities of rocks and structure beneath the surface. Such variations are measured by a device called a gravimeter, which consists of a weighted spring that is pulled further downward where the gravity is stronger—at a positive anomaly, also known as the ◊Bouguer anomaly—and the extension of the spring is measured. Gravimetry is used by geologists to map the subsurface features of the Earth's crust, such as underground masses of heavy rock like granite, or light rock like salt.

gravitational force one of the four ◊fundamental forces of nature, the other three being the ◊electromagnetic force, the ◊strong force, and the ◊weak force. The gravitational force is the weakest of the four forces, but it acts over great distances. The particle that is postulated as the carrier of the gravitational force is the ◊graviton.

gravitational lensing bending of light by a gravitational field, predicted by Einstein's general theory of relativity. The effect was first detected 1917 when the light from stars was found to be bent as it passed the totally eclipsed Sun. More remarkable is the splitting of light from distant quasars into two or more images by intervening galaxies. In 1979 the first double image of a quasar produced by gravitational lensing was discovered and a quadruple image of another quasar was later found.

graviton in physics, the ◊gauge boson that is the postulated carrier of gravity.

gravity force of attraction that arises between objects by virtue of their masses. On Earth, gravity is the force of attraction between any object in the Earth's gravitational field and the Earth itself. It is regarded as one of the four ◊fundamental forces of nature, the other three being the ◊electromagnetic force, the ◊strong

nuclear force, and the ◊weak nuclear force. The gravitational force is the weakest of the four forces, but it acts over great distances. The particle that is postulated as the carrier of the gravitational force is the ◊graviton.

According to Newton's law of gravitation, all objects fall to Earth with the same acceleration, regardless of mass. For an object of mass m_1 at a distance r from the center of the Earth (mass m_2), the gravitational force of attraction F equals Gm_1m_2/r^2, where G is the gravitational constant. However, according to Newton's second law of motion, F also equals m_1g, where g is the acceleration due to gravity; therefore $g = Gm_2/r^2$ and is independent of the mass of the object; at the Earth's surface it equals 9.806 meters per second per second.

Einstein's general theory of relativity treats gravitation not as a force but as a curvature of space and time around a body. Relativity predicts the bending of light and the ◊red shift of light in a gravitational field; both have been observed. Another prediction of relativity is **gravitational waves**, which should be produced when massive bodies are violently disturbed. These waves are so weak that they have not yet been detected with certainty, although observations of a ◊pulsar (which emits energy at regular intervals) in orbit around another star have shown that the stars are spiraling together at the rate that would be expected if they were losing energy in the form of gravitational waves.

gravure one of the three main ◊printing methods, in which printing is done from a plate etched with a pattern of recessed cells in which the ink is held. The greater the depth of a cell, the greater the strength of the printed ink. Gravure plates are expensive to make, but the process is economical for high-volume printing and reproduces illustrations well.

gray SI unit (symbol Gy) of absorbed radiation dose. It replaces the rad (1 Gy equals 100 rad), and is defined as the dose absorbed when one kilogram of matter absorbs one joule of ionizing radiation. Different types of radiation cause different amounts of damage for the same absorbed dose; the SI unit of **dose equivalent** is the ◊sievert.

Gray Asa 1810–1888. US botanist who became America's leading botanist and taxonomist, basing his revision of the Linnaean system on fruit form rather than gross morphology. His *Manual of Botany* 1850 remains the standard reference work on flora E of the Rockies. In 1842 he was appointed professor of botany at Harvard and was instrumental in establishing the subject in American university curricula. A friend and supporter of Darwin, Gray was one of the founders of the National Academy of Sciences.

Born in Saquoit, New York, Gray graduated from medical school but chose botany rather than medicine as his career. Gray's major publications include *Elements of Botany* 1836 and the definitive *Flora of North America* 1838, 1843.

Gray Thomas 1716–1771. English poet whose "Elegy Written in a Country Churchyard" 1751 is one of the most quoted poems in English. Other poems include "Ode on a Distant Prospect of Eton College," "The Progress of Poesy," and "The Bard"; these poems are now seen as the precursors of Romanticism.

A close friend of Horace ◊Walpole at Eton, Gray made a continental tour with him 1739–41, an account of which is given in his vivid letters. His first poem, "Ode on a Distant Prospect of Eton College," was published in 1747

and again in 1748 with "Ode on the Spring" in Robert Dodsley's (1703–1764) *A Collection of Poems. By Several Hands.*

grayling freshwater fish *Thymallus arcticus* of the family Salmonidae. It has a long, multirayed dorsal fin and exhibits a coloration shading from silver to purple. It is found in N parts of North America, Europe, and Asia. It was once common in the Great Lakes.

Graz capital of Styria province, and second largest city in Austria; population (1981) 243,400. Industries include engineering, chemicals, iron, and steel. It has a 15th-century cathedral and a university founded 1573. Lippizaner horses are bred near here.

Graziano Rocky (Thomas Rocco Barbella) 1922–1990. US middleweight boxing champion who fought in the 1940s and 1950s. Although he was not noted for his boxing skills or finesse, his colorful, brawling style made him popular. He compiled a record of 67 wins, 10 losses and 6 draws between 1942 and 1952. Three of his bouts, with Tony Zale 1946, 1947, and 1948, were considered classics.

Great Artesian Basin the largest area of artesian water in the world. It underlies much of Queensland, New South Wales, and South Australia, and in prehistoric times formed a sea. It has an area of 676,250 sq mi/ 1,750,000 sq km.

Great Australian Bight broad bay in S Australia, notorious for storms. It was discovered by a Dutch navigator, Captain Thyssen, 1627. The coast was charted by the English explorer Captain Matthew Flinders 1802.

Great Awakening religious revival in the American colonies from the late 1730s to the 1760s, sparked off by George Whitefield (1714–1770), an itinerant English Methodist preacher whose evangelical fervor and eloquence made many converts. A second "great awakening" occurred in the first half of the 19th century, establishing the evangelist tradition in US Protestantism.

Great Barrier Reef chain of coral reefs and islands about 1,250 mi/2,000 km long, off the E coast of Queensland, Australia, at a distance of 10–30 mi/15–45 km. It is believed to be the world's largest living organism and forms an immense natural breakwater, the coral rock forming a structure larger than all human-made structures on Earth combined. The reef is in danger from large numbers of starfish, which are reported to have infested 35% of the reef. Some scientists fear the entire reef will disappear within 50 years.

Annually, a few nights after the full Moon in Nov, 135 species of hard coral release their eggs and sperm for fertilization and the sea turns pink. The phenomenon, one of the wonders of the natural world, was discovered 1983, and is triggered by a mechanism dependent on the Moon, the tides, and water temperatures.

Great Bear popular name for the constellation ◊Ursa Major.

Great Bear Lake lake on the Arctic Circle, in the Northwest Territories; area 12,275 sq mi/ 31,800 sq km.

Great Britain official name for ◊England, ◊Scotland, and ◊Wales, and the adjacent islands (except the Channel Islands and the Isle of Man) from 1603, when the English and Scottish crowns were united under James I of England (James VI of Scotland). With Northern ◊Ireland it forms the ◊United Kingdom.

great circle circle drawn on a sphere such that the diameter of the circle is a diameter of the sphere. On the Earth, all meridians of longitude are half great circles; among the parallels of latitude, only the equator is a great circle.

The shortest route between two points on the Earth's surface is along the arc of a great circle. These are used extensively as air routes although on maps, owing to the distortion brought about by ⊅projection, they do not appear as straight lines.

Great Dane large, short-haired breed of dog, usually fawn in color, standing up to 30 in/76 cm tall, and weighing up to 154 lb/70 kg. It has a long head, a large nose, and small, erect ears. It was used in Europe for hunting boar and stags.

Great Dividing Range E Australian mountain range, extending 2,300 mi/3,700 km N–S from Cape York Peninsula, Queensland, to Victoria. It includes the Carnarvon Range, Queensland, which has many Aboriginal cave paintings, the Blue Mountains in New South Wales, and the Australian Alps.

Great Expectations novel by Charles Dickens, published 1860–61. Philip Pirrip ("Pip"), brought up by his sister and her husband, the blacksmith Joe Gargery, rejects his humble background and pursues wealth, which he believes comes from the elderly, eccentric Miss Havisham. Ultimately, through adversity, he recognizes the value of his origins.

Great Falls city in central Montana, on the Missouri river, NE of Helena; seat of Cascade county. Its main industries are involved with the processing of copper and zinc from nearby mines. The processing of agricultural products and oil refining is also important; population (1990) 55,000. The city is named for nearby waterfalls, first discovered in 1805 by Meriwether Lewis and William Clark.

Great Lakes series of five freshwater lakes along the US-Canada border: Lakes Superior, Michigan, Huron, Erie, and Ontario; total area 94,600 sq mi/245,000 sq km. Interconnecting canals make them navigable by large ships, and they are drained by the ⊅St Lawrence River. The whole forms the St Lawrence Seaway. They are said to contain 20% of the world's surface fresh water.

The principal cargoes are iron ore and grain, both of which originate at Lake Superior ports. Iron ore is carried to other lake ports for transport to steel mills. Grain may be shipped to processing centers such as Buffalo, New York, or sent directly abroad.

Great Leap Forward change in the economic policy of the People's Republic of China introduced by ⊅Mao Zedong under the second five-year plan of 1958–62. The aim was to convert China into an industrially based economy by transferring resources away from agriculture. This coincided with the creation of people's communes. The inefficient and poorly planned allocation of state resources led to the collapse of the strategy by 1960 and a return to more adequate support for agricultural production.

Great Patriotic War (1941–45) war between the USSR and Germany during ⊅World War II.

When Germany invaded the USSR in June 1941, the Soviet troops retreated, carrying out a ⊅scorched earth policy and relocating strategic industries beyond the Ural Mountains.Stalin remained in Moscow and the Soviet forces, inspired to fight on by his patriotic speeches, launched a counter-offensive.

The Allies tried to provide the USSR with vital supplies through Murmansk and Archangel despite German attempts to blockade the ports. In 1942 the Germans failed to take Leningrad and Moscow, and launched an attack toward the river Volga and to capture oil wells at Baku. In Aug 1942 the Germans attacked Stalingrad but it was held by the Russians. The Germans were forced to surrender at Stalingrad in Jan 1943. The Red Army, under the command of Marshal Zhukov, gradually forced the Germans back and by Feb 1945 the Russians had reached the German border. In April 1945 the Russians, who had made tremendous sacrifices (20 million dead and millions more wounded) entered Berlin. In May 1945 the war ended.

Great Plains semiarid region to the E of the Rocky Mountains, stretching as far as the 100th meridian of longitude through Oklahoma, Kansas, Nebraska, and the Dakotas. The plains, which cover one-fifth of the US, extend from Texas in the south over 1,500 mi/2,400 km north to Canada. Ranching and wheat farming have resulted in overuse of water resources to such an extent that available farmland has been reduced by erosion.

Great Power any of the major European powers of the 19th century: Russia, Austria (Austria-Hungary), France, Britain, and Prussia.

Great Red Spot prominent oval feature, 8,500 mi/14,000 km wide and some 20,000 mi/30,000 km long, in the atmosphere of the planet ⊅Jupiter, S of the equator. It was first observed in the 19th century. Space probes show it to be a counterclockwise vortex of cold clouds, colored possibly by phosphorus.

Great Rift Valley longest "split" in the Earth's surface; see ⊅Rift Valley, Great.

Great Sandy Desert desert in N Western Australia; 415,000sq km/160,000 sq mi. It is also the name of an arid region in S Oregon, US.

Great Schism in European history, the period 1378–1417 in which rival popes had seats in Rome and in Avignon; it was ended by the election of Martin V during the Council of Constance 1414–17.

Great Slave Lake lake in the Northwest Territories; area 10,980 sq mi/28,450 sq km. It is the deepest lake (2,020 ft/615 m) in North America.

Great Trek in South African history, the movement of 12,000–14,000 Boer (Dutch) settlers from Cape Colony 1835 and 1845 to escape British rule. They established republics in Natal and the Transvaal. It is seen by many white South Africans as the main event in the founding of the present republic and also as a justification for continuing whites-only rule.

Great Wall of China continuous defensive wall stretching from W Gansu to the Gulf of Liaodong (1,450 mi/2,250 km). It was once even longer. It was built under the Qin dynasty from 214 BC to prevent incursions by the Turkish and Mongol peoples. Some 25 ft/8 m high, it consists of a brick-faced wall of earth and stone, has a series of square watchtowers, and has been carefully restored. It is so large that it can be seen from space.

grebe any of 19 species of water birds belonging to the family Podicipedidae. The great crested grebe *Podiceps cristatus* is the largest of the Old World grebes. It lives in ponds and marshes in Eurasia, Africa, and Australia, feeding on fish. It grows to 20 in/50 cm long and has

a white breast, with chestnut and black feathers on its back and head. The head and neck feathers form a crest, especially prominent during the breeding season.

Greco, El (Doménikos Theotokopoulos) 1541–1614. Spanish painter called "the Greek" because he was born in Crete. He studied in Italy, worked in Rome from about 1570, and by 1577 had settled in Toledo. He painted elegant portraits and intensely emotional religious scenes with increasingly distorted figures and flickering light; for example, *The Burial of Count Orgaz* 1586 (Toledo).

Greece country in SE Europe, comprising the S Balkan peninsula, bounded N by Yugoslavia and Bulgaria, NW by Albania, NE by Turkey, E by the Aegean Sea, S by the Mediterranean Sea, and W by the Ionian Sea.

government The 1975 constitution provides for a parliamentary system of government, with a president who is head of state, a prime minister who is head of government, and a single-chamber parliament. The president, elected by parliament for a five-year term, appoints the prime minister and cabinet. Parliament has 300 members, all elected by universal suffrage for a four-year term, and the prime minister and cabinet are collectively responsible to it. Bills passed by parliament must be ratified by the president, whose veto can be overridden by an absolute majority of the total number of members. In 1986 the constitution was amended, limiting the powers of the president in relation to those of the prime minister.

history For ancient history, see ⊅Greece, ancient. From the 14th century Greece came under Ottoman Turkish rule, and except for the years 1686–1715, when the Peloponnese was occupied by the Venetians, it remained Turkish until the outbreak of the War of Independence 1821. British, French, and Russian intervention 1827, which brought about the destruction of the Turkish fleet at ⊅Navarino, led to the establishment of Greek independence 1829. Prince Otto of Bavaria was placed on the throne 1832; his despotic rule provoked a rebellion 1843, which set up a parliamentary government, and another 1862, when he was deposed and replaced by Prince George of Denmark. Relations with Turkey were embittered by the Greeks' desire to recover Macedonia, Crete, and other Turkish territories with Greek populations. A war 1897 ended in disaster, but the ⊅Balkan Wars 1912–13 won most of the disputed areas for Greece.

In a period of internal conflict from 1914, two monarchs were deposed, and there was a republic 1923–25, when a military coup restored ⊅George II, who in the following year established a dictatorship under Joannis ⊅Metaxas.

monarchy reestablished An Italian invasion 1940 was successfully resisted, but an intensive attack by Germany 1941 overwhelmed the Greeks. During the German occupation of Greece 1941–44, a communist-dominated resistance movement armed and trained a guerrilla army, and after World War II the National Liberation Front, as it was called, wanted to create a socialist state. If the Greek royalist army had not had massive assistance from the US, under the provisions of the ⊅Truman doctrine, this undoubtedly would have happened. A civil war 1946–49 ended when the royalists defeated the communists. The monarchy was reestablished under King Paul, who was succeeded by his son Constantine 1964.

military junta Dissatisfaction with the government and conflicts between the king and his ministers resulted in a coup 1967, replacing the monarchy with a new regime, which, despite its democratic pretensions, was little more than a military dictatorship, with Col George Papadopoulos as its head. All political activity was banned, and opponents of the government were forced out of public life.

republic In 1973 Greece declared itself a republic, and Papadopoulos became president. A civilian cabinet was appointed, but before the year was out another coup brought Lt Gen Phaidon Ghizikis to the presidency, with Adamantios Androutsopoulos as prime minister. The government's failure to prevent the Turkish invasion of ⟡Cyprus led to its downfall, and a former prime minister, Constantine ⟡Karamanlis, was recalled from exile to form a new Government of National Salvation. He immediately ended martial law, press censorship, and the ban on political parties, and in the 1974 general election his New Democracy Party (ND) won a decisive majority in parliament.

A referendum the same year rejected the return of the monarchy, and in 1975 a new constitution for a democratic "Hellenic Republic" was adopted, with Constantine Tsatsos as president. The ND won the 1977 general election with a reduced majority, and in 1980 Karamanlis resigned as prime minister and was elected president.

The following year Greece became a full member of the European Economic Community (EEC), having been an associate since 1962. Meanwhile, the ND was faced with a growing challenge from the Panhellenic Socialist Movement (PASOK), which won an absolute majority in parliament in the 1981 general election. Its leader, Andreas ⟡Papandreou, became Greece's first socialist prime minister.

Greek socialism PASOK had been elected on a radical socialist platform, which included withdrawal from the EEC, the removal of US military bases, and a program of domestic reform. Important social changes, such as lowering the voting age to 18, the legalization of civil marriage and divorce, and an overhaul of the universities and the army, were carried out; but instead of withdrawing from Europe, Papandreou was content to obtain a modification of the terms of entry, and, rather than close US bases, he signed a five-year agreement on military and economic cooperation. In 1983 he also signed a ten-year economic-cooperation agreement with the USSR.

Papandreou defeated Despite introducing austerity measures to deal with rising inflation, PASOK won a comfortable majority in the 1985 elections. Criticism of Papandreou grew 1989 when close aides were implicated in a banking scandal. He lost the general elections 1989 and Tzanis Tzannetakis, an ND backbencher, formed Greece's first all-party government for 15 years. However, this soon broke up and after months of negotiation Xenophon Zolotas (PASOK) put together a government of unity, comprising communists, socialists, conservatives, and nonpolitical figures.

Constantine Mitsotakis of the New Democracy Party (ND) was sworn in as the new premier April 1990 and formed a new all-party government after the ND had failed to win an outright majority in the elections. In June Karamanlis was again elected president. In 1990 an agreement on the siting of US bases in Greece was signed.

Papandreou was cleared of all corruption charges in Jan 1992; he immediately called

Greece
Hellenic Republic (*Elliniki Dimokratia*)

area 50,935 sq mi/131,957 sq km
capital Athens
cities Larisa; ports Piraeus, Thessaloníki, Patras, Iráklion
physical mountainous; a large number of islands, notably Crete, Corfu, and Rhodes
environment acid rain and other airborne pollutants are destroying the Classical buildings and ancient monuments of Athens
features Corinth canal; Mount Olympus; the Acropolis; many Classical archeological sites; the Aegean and Ionian Islands
head of state Constantine Karamanlis from 1990
head of government Constantine Mitsotakis from 1990
political system democratic republic
political parties Panhellenic Socialist Movement (PASOK), democratic socialist; New Democracy Party (ND), center-right; Democratic Renewal (DR); Communist Party; Greek Left Party
exports tobacco, fruit, vegetables, olives, olive oil, textiles, aluminum, iron and steel
currency drachma
population (1990 est) 10,066,000; growth rate 0.3% p.a.
life expectancy men 72, women 76
language Greek
religion Greek Orthodox 97%
literacy men 96%, women 89% (1985)

GDP $40.9 bn (1987); $4,093 per head
chronology
1829 Independence achieved from Turkish rule.
1912–13 Balkan Wars; Greece gained much land.
1941–44 German occupation of Greece.
1946 Civil war between royalists and communists; communists defeated.
1949 Monarchy reestablished with Paul as king.
1964 King Paul succeeded by his son Constantine.
1967 Army coup removed the king; Col George Papadopoulos became prime minister. Martial law imposed, all political activity banned.
1973 Republic proclaimed, with Papadopoulos as president.
1974 Former premier Constantine Karamanlis recalled from exile to lead government. Martial law and ban on political parties lifted; restoration of the monarchy rejected by a referendum.
1975 New constitution adopted, making Greece a democratic republic.
1980 Karamanlis resigned as prime minister and was elected president.
1981 Greece became full member of European Economic Community. Andreas Papandreou elected Greece's first socialist prime minister.
1983 Five-year military and economic cooperation agreement signed with USA; ten-year economic cooperation agreement signed with USSR.
1985 Papandreou reelected.
1988 Relations with Turkey improved. Major cabinet reshuffle after mounting criticism of Papandreou.
1989 Papandreou defeated. Tzannis Tzannetakis became prime minister; his all-party government collapsed. Xenophon Zolotas formed new unity government. Papandreou charged with corruption.
1990 New Democracy Party (ND) won half of parliamentary seats in general election, but no outright majority; Constantine Mitsotakis became premier; formed new all-party government. Karamanlis reelected president.
1992 Papandreou acquitted. Greece opposed recognition of independence of the Yugoslav breakaway republic of Macedonia. Decisive parliamentary vote to ratify Maastricht Treaty.

for a general election but this was refused by the government. In June 1992 Greece attended the Lisbon Summit with other EC nations and gained support for their decision not to recognize the independence declaration of the breakaway republic of Macedonia unless the latter changed its name. In July parliament voted by 286 to 14 to ratify the Maastricht Treaty on greater European union. *See illustration box.*

Greece, ancient the first Greek civilization, known as Mycenaean (*c.* 1600–1200 BC), owed much to the Minoan civilization of Crete and may have been produced by the intermarriage of Greek-speaking invaders with the original inhabitants. From the 14th century BC a new wave of invasions began. The Achaeans overran Greece and Crete, destroying the Minoan and Mycenaean civilizations and penetrating Asia Minor; to this period belongs the siege of Troy (*c.* 1180 BC). The latest of the invaders were the Dorians (*c.* 1100 BC) who settled in the Peloponnese and founded Sparta; that great city-state arose during the obscure period that

followed (1100–800 BC). The mountainous geography of Greece hindered the cities from attaining any national unity, and led the Greeks to take to the sea. During the years 750–550 BC the Greeks not only became great traders, but founded colonies around the coasts of the Mediterranean and the Black Sea, in Asia Minor, Sicily, S Italy, S France, Spain, and N Africa. The main centers of Greek culture in the 6th century BC were the wealthy ⟡Ionian ports of Asia Minor, where Greek philosophy, science, and lyric poetry originated.

Many Greek cities passed from monarchy to the rule of a landowning or merchant oligarchy and from there to democracy. Thus Athens passed through the democratic reforms of Solon (594 BC), the enlightened "tyranny" of Pisistratus (560–527 BC), and the establishment of democracy by Cleisthenes (*c.* 507 BC). Sparta remained unique, a state in which a ruling race, organized on military lines, tyrannized the original population.

After 545 BC the Ionian cities fell under the dominion of the Persian Empire. Aid given them by Athens in an unsuccessful revolt in

499–494 BC provoked Darius of Persia to invade Greece in 490 BC only to be defeated by the Athenians at Marathon and forced to withdraw. Another invasion by the Persian emperor Xerxes, after being delayed by the heroic defense of Thermopylae by 300 Spartans, was defeated at sea off Salamis in 480 BC and on land at Plataea in 479 BC. The Ionian cities were liberated and formed a naval alliance with Athens, the Confederacy of Delos. Pericles, the real ruler of Athens 461–429 BC, attempted to convert this into an Athenian empire and to form a land empire in Greece. Mistrust of his ambitions led to the Peloponnesian War (431–404 BC), which destroyed the political power of Athens. In 5th-century Athens, Greek tragedy, comedy, sculpture, and architecture were at their peak, and Socrates and Plato founded moral philosophy.

After the Peloponnesian War, Sparta became the leading Greek power until it was overthrown by Thebes (378–371 BC). The constant wars between the cities gave Philip II of Macedon (358–336 BC) the opportunity to establish his supremacy over Greece. His son ⟩Alexander the Great overthrew the decadent Persian Empire, conquered Syria and Egypt, and invaded the Punjab. After his death in 323 BC his empire was divided among his generals, but his conquest had nevertheless spread Greek culture to the Middle East.

During the 3rd century BC the cities attempted to maintain their independence against Macedon, Egypt, and Rome by forming federations; for example, the Achaean and Aetolian leagues. Roman intervention began in 212 BC and ended in the annexation of Greece in 146 BC. Under Roman rule Greece remained a cultural center, until the emperor Justinian closed the university of Athens in AD 529.

Greek native to or an inhabitant of ancient or modern Greece or person of Greek descent; also the language and culture. Modern Greek is an Indo-European language, spoken in Greece and by Greek Cypriots; also by people of Greek descent, especially in Canada, the US, and Australia.

Greek architecture the architecture of ancient Greece is the base for virtually all architectural developments in Europe. The Greeks invented the entablature, which allowed roofs to be hipped (inverted V-shape), and perfected the design of arcades with support columns. There were three styles, or orders, of columns: Doric, Ionic, and Corinthian; see also ⟩column and ⟩order.

Of the Greek orders, the **Doric** is the oldest; it is said to have evolved from a former timber prototype. The finest example of a Doric temple is the Parthenon in Athens (447–438 BC). The origin of the **Ionic** is uncertain. The earliest building in which the Ionic capital appears is the temple of Diana in Ephesus (530 BC). The gateway to the Acropolis in Athens (known as the Propylaea) has internal columns of the Ionic order. The most perfect example is the Erechtheum in Athens. The **Corinthian** order belongs to a later period of Greek art. The leading example of the order is the temple of Jupiter (Zeus) Olympus in Athens (174 BC), completed under Roman influence in AD 129. The Mausoleum in Halicarnassus (353 BC) was one of the Seven Wonders of the World.

Greek art sculpture, mosaic, and crafts of ancient Greece (no large-scale painting survives). It is usually divided into three periods: **Archaic** (late 8th century–480 BC), showing Egyptian

influence; **Classical** (480–323 BC), characterized by dignified realism; and **Hellenistic** (323–27 BC), more exuberant or dramatic. Sculptures of human figures dominate all periods, and vase painting was a focus for artistic development for many centuries.

Archaic period Statues of naked standing men (*kouroi*) and draped females (*korai*) show an Egyptian influence in their rigid frontality. By about 500 BC the figure was allowed to relax its weight onto one leg. Subjects were usually depicted smiling.

Classical period Expressions assumed a dignified serenity. Further movement was introduced in new poses, such as in Myron's bronze *Diskobolus/The Discus Thrower* 460–50 BC, and in the rhythmic Parthenon reliefs of riders and horses supervised by Phidias. Polykleitos' sculpture *Doryphoros/The Spear Carrier* 450–440 BC was of such harmony and poise that it set a standard for beautiful proportions. Praxiteles introduced the female nude into the sculptural repertory with the graceful *Aphrodite of Knidos* about 350 BC. It was easier to express movement in bronze, hollow-cast by the lost-wax method, but relatively few bronze sculptures survive, and many are known only through Roman copies in marble.

Hellenistic period Sculptures such as the *Winged Victory of Samothrace* with its dramatic drapery, and the tortured *Laocoön* explored the effects of movement and deeply felt emotion.

vase painting Artists worked as both potters and painters until the 5th century BC, and the works they signed were exported throughout the empire. Made in several standard shapes and sizes, the pots served as functional containers for wine, water, and oil. The first decoration took the form of simple lines and circles, from which the **Geometric style** emerged near Athens in the 10th century BC. It consisted of precisely drawn patterns, such as the key meander. Gradually the bands of decoration multiplied and the human figure, geometrically stylized, was added. About 700 BC the potters of Corinth invented the **Black Figure** technique in which the unglazed red clay was painted in black with mythological scenes and battles in a narrative frieze.

About 530 BC Athenian potters reversed the process and developed the more sophisticated **Red Figure** pottery, which allowed for more detailed and elaborate painting of the figures in red against a black background. This grew increasingly naturalistic, with lively scenes of daily life. The finest examples date from the mid-6th to the mid-5th century BC in Athens. Later painters tried to follow major art trends and represent spatial depth, dissipating the unique quality of their fine linear technique.

crafts The ancient Greeks excelled in carving gems and cameos and in metalwork. They also invented the pictorial mosaic, and from the 5th century BC onwards floors were paved with colored pebbles depicting mythological subjects. Later, specially cut cubes of stone and glass called *tesserae* were used, and Greek artisans working for the Romans reproduced paintings, such as *Alexander at the Battle of Issus* from Pompeii, the originals of which are lost.

Greek language member of the Indo-European language family, which has passed through at least five distinct phases since the 2nd millennium BC: **Ancient Greek** 14th–12th centuries BC; **Archaic Greek**, including Homeric epic language, until 800 BC; **Classical Greek** until 400 BC; **Hellenistic Greek**, the

common language of Greece, Asia Minor, W Asia, and Egypt to the 4th century AD, and **Byzantine Greek**, used until the 15th century and still the ecclesiastical language of the Greek Orthodox Church. **Modern Greek** is principally divided into the general vernacular (**Demotic Greek**) and the language of education and literature (**Katharevousa**).

In its earlier phases Greek was spoken mainly in Greece, the Aegean islands, the west coast of Asia Minor, and in colonies in Sicily, the Italian mainland, S Spain, and S France. Hellenistic Greek was an important language not only in the Middle East but also in the Roman Empire generally, and is the form also known as **New Testament Greek** (in which the Gospels and other books of the New Testament of the Bible were first written). Byzantine Greek was not only an imperial but also an ecclesiastical language, the medium of the Greek Orthodox Church. Modern Greek, in both its forms, is spoken in Greece and in Cyprus, as well as wherever Greeks have settled throughout the world (principally Canada, the US, and Australia). Classical Greek word forms continue to have a great influence in the world's scientific and technical vocabulary, and make up a large part of the technical vocabulary of English.

Greek literature literature of Greece, ancient and modern.

ancient The earliest known works are those of Homer, reputed author of the epic poems the *Iliad* and the *Odyssey*, and Hesiod, whose long poem *Works and Days* deals with agricultural life. The lyric poet Pindar and the historians Herodotus and Thucydides belong to the 6th and 5th centuries BC. The 5th century BC saw the development of Athenian drama through the works of the tragic dramatists Aeschylus, Sophocles, and Euripides, and the comedies of Aristophanes. After the fall of Athens came a period of prose with the historian Xenophon, the idealist philosopher Plato, the orators Isocrates and Demosthenes, and the scientific teacher Aristotle.

After 323 BC Athens lost its political importance, but was still a university town with such teachers as Epicurus, Zeno, and Theophrastus, and the comic dramatist Menander. Meanwhile Alexandria had become the center of Greek culture: at the court of Philadelphus were scientists such as Euclid and the poets Callimachus, Apollonius, and Theocritus. During the 2nd century BC Rome became the new center for Greek literature, and Polybius, a historian, spent most of his life there; in the 1st century BC Rome also sheltered the poets Archias, Antipater of Sidon, Philodemus the Epicurean, and Meleager of Gadara, who compiled the first *Greek Anthology*.

In the 1st century AD Latin writers overshadowed the Greek, but there were still the geographer Strabo, the critic Dionysius of Halicarnassus (active around 10 BC), the Jewish writers Philo Judaeus and Josephus, the New Testament writers, and the biographer Plutarch. A revival came in the 2nd century with the satirical writer Lucian. To the 3rd century belong the historians Cassius Dio and Herodian, the Christian fathers Clement and Origen, and the Neoplatonists. For medieval Greek literature, see ⟩Byzantine literature.

modern After the fall of Constantinople, the Byzantine tradition was perpetuated in the Classical Greek writing of, for example, the 15th-century chronicles of Cyprus, various historical works in the 16th and 17th centuries, and educational and theological works in the 18th century. The 17th and 18th centuries saw much controversy over whether to write in the Greek vernacular (**Demotic**), the Classical language (*Katharevousa*), or the language of the Eastern Orthodox Church. Adamantios Korais (1748–1833), the first great modern writer, produced a compromise language; he was followed by the prose and drama writer and poet Aleksandros Rhangavis ("Rangabe") (1810–92), and many others.

The 10th-century epic of *Digenis Akritas* is usually considered to mark the beginnings of modern Greek vernacular literature, and the Demotic was kept alive in the flourishing Cretan literature of the 16th and 17th centuries, in numerous popular songs, and in the Klephtic ballads of the 18th century. With independence in the 19th century the popular movement became prominent with the Ionian poet Dionysios Solomos (1798–1857), Andreas Kalvos (1796–1869), and others, and later with Iannis Psichari (1854–1929), short-story writer and dramatist, and the prose writer Alexandros Papadiamandis (1851–1911), who influenced many younger writers, for example Konstantinos Hatzopoulos (1868–1921), poet and essayist. After the 1920s, the novel began to emerge with Stratis Myrivilis (1892–1969) and Nikos Kazantzakis (1885–1957), author of *Zorba the Greek* 1946 and also a poet. There were also the Nobel-prize-winning poets George ⟡Seferis and Odysseus ⟡Elytis.

Greek Orthodox Church see ⟡Orthodox Church.

Greeley city in N Colorado, at the point where the Cache de Poudre river flows into the South Platte river, NE of Boulder. A distribution center for the surrounding agricultural area, its main industry is the processing of sugar beets; population (1990) 60,500. It is named for Horace Greeley, one of its founders.

Greeley Horace 1811–1872. US editor, publisher, and politician. He founded the *New York Tribune* 1841 and, as a strong supporter of the Whig party, advocated many reform causes in his newspaper—among them, feminism and abolitionism. He was an advocate of American westward expansion, and is remembered for his advice "Go west, young man." One of the founders of the Republican party 1854, Greeley was the unsuccessful presidential candidate of the breakaway Liberal Republicans 1872.

Born in Amherst, New Hampshire, Greeley was trained as a printer and moved to New York City 1831. He worked on a variety of publications before founding the *New York Tribune*.

Greenaway Kate 1846–1901. English illustrator, known for her drawings of children. In 1877 she first exhibited at the Royal Academy, and began her collaboration with the color-printer Edmund Evans, with whom she produced a number of children's books, including *Mother Goose*.

greenback paper money issued by the US government 1862–65 to help finance the Civil War. It was legal tender but could not be converted into gold.

Greenbacker in US history, a supporter of an alliance of agrarian and industrial organizations, known as the Greenback Labor Party, which campaigned for currency inflation by increasing the paper dollars ("greenbacks") in circulation. In 1880 the party's presidential nominee polled only 300,000 votes;

the movement was later superseded by ⟡Populism.

Green Bay city in NE Wisconsin, where the Little Fox River flows into Green Bay on Lake Michigan; seat of Brown County. It is a port of entry to the US through the St Lawrence Seaway and serves as a distribution center. Industries include paper and food products; population (1990) 96,400. The Green Bay Packers team of the National Football League was organized here 1919.

green belt or **green way** area surrounding a large city, officially designated not to be built on but preserved as open space (for agricultural and recreational use or to be "forever wild").

greenbrier or **catbrier** any of several climbing woody vines of the genus *Smilax* of the lily family, having smooth, shiny green oval leaves and usually black berries. The prickly stems of these plants often form impenetrable thickets.

Greene (Henry) Graham 1904–1991. English writer whose novels of guilt, despair, and penitence are set in a world of urban seediness or political corruption in many parts of the world. They include *Brighton Rock* 1938, *The Power and the Glory* 1940, *The Heart of the Matter* 1948, *The Third Man* 1950, *The Honorary Consul* 1973, and *Monsignor Quixote* 1982.

Greene Nathanael 1742–1786. American military leader. Born in Warwick, Rhode Island, Greene was a member of a Quaker family but showed an exceptional interest in military affairs. As a local militia officer, he was placed in command of the Rhode Island regiments at the outbreak of the Revolutionary War. Greene was later appointed brigadier general in the Continental army and saw action in the siege of Boston, the Battle of Long Island, and Washington's New Jersey campaigns. After service as quartermaster general 1778–80, he commanded the successful American offensive in the South.

greenfinch songbird *Carduelis chloris*, common in Europe and N Africa. The male is green with a yellow breast, and the female is a greenish-brown.

greenfly plant-sucking insect, a type of ⟡aphid.

greenhouse effect in the Earth's atmosphere, the trapping of solar radiation, which, absorbed by the Earth and re-emitted from the surface, is prevented from escaping by various gases in the air. The result is a rise in the Earth's temperature; in a garden greenhouse, the glass walls have the same effect. The main greenhouse gases are carbon dioxide, methane, and ⟡chlorofluorocarbons. Fossil-fuel consumption and forest fires are the main causes of carbon dioxide buildup; methane is a byproduct of agriculture (rice, cattle, sheep). Water vapor is another greenhouse gas. The United Nations Environment Program estimates an increase in average world temperatures of $2.7°F/1.5°C$ with a consequent rise of 7.7 in/20 cm in sea level by 2025.

The concentration of carbon dioxide in the atmosphere is estimated to have risen by 25% since the Industrial Revolution, and 10% since 1950; the rate of increase is now 0.5% a year. Chlorofluorocarbon levels are rising by 5% a year, and nitrous oxide levels by 0.4% a year, resulting in a global warming effect of 0.5% since 1900, and a rise of about $3°F/0.1°C$ a year in the temperature of the world's oceans during the 1980s. Arctic ice was 20–23 ft/6–7 m thick

in 1976 and had reduced to 13–17 ft/4–5 m by 1987. Low-lying areas and entire countries are threatened by flooding, and crops will be affected by the change in climate.

Dubbed the "greenhouse effect" by Swedish scientist Svante Arrhenius, it was first predicted 1827 by French mathematician Joseph Fourier (1768–1830).

Greenland (Greenlandic **Kalaalit Nunaat**) world's largest island, lying between the North Atlantic and Arctic Oceans E of North America
area 840,000 sq mi/2,175,600 sq km
capital Godthaab (Greenlandic *Nuuk*) on the W coast
features the whole of the interior is covered by a vast ice sheet (the remnant of the last glaciation, part of the N Polar icecap); the island has an important role strategically and in civil aviation, and shares military responsibilities with the US; there are lead and cryolite deposits, and offshore oil is being explored
economy fishing and fish-processing
population (1990) 55,500; Inuit (Ammassalik Eskimoan), Danish, and other European
language Greenlandic (Ammassalik Eskimoan)
history Greenland was discovered about 982 by Eric the Red, who founded colonies on the W coast soon after Eskimos from the North American Arctic had made their way to Greenland. Christianity was introduced to the Vikings about 1000. In 1261 the Viking colonies accepted Norwegian sovereignty, but early in the 15th century all communication with Europe ceased, and by the 16th century the colonies had died out, but the Eskimos had moved on to the E coast. It became a Danish colony in the 18th century, and following a referendum 1979 was granted full internal self-government 1981.

Greenland Sea area of the ⟡Arctic Ocean between Spitsbergen and Greenland, and N of the Norwegian Sea.

greenmail payment made by a target company to avoid a takeover; for example, buying back a portion of its own shares from a potential predator (either a person or a company) at an inflated price.

green monkey disease another name for ⟡Marburg disease, a virus originating in Central Africa.

Green Mountain Boys in US history, irregular troops who fought to protect the Vermont part of what was then New Hampshire colony from land claims made by neighboring New York. In the American Revolution they captured ⟡Fort Ticonderoga from the British. Their leader was Ethan Allen (1738–1789), who was later captured by the British. Vermont declared itself an independent republic, refusing to join the Union until 1791. It is popularly known as the Green Mountain State.

green movement collective term for the individuals and organizations involved in efforts to protect the environment. The movement encompasses political parties such as the ⟡Green Party and organizations like ⟡Friends of the Earth and ⟡Greenpeace.

Green Party political party aiming to "preserve the planet and its people," based on the premise that incessant economic growth is unsustainable. The leaderless party structure reflects a general commitment to decentralization. Green parties sprang up in W Europe in the 1970s and in E Europe from 1988. Parties in different countries are linked to one another but unaffiliated with any pressure group. The party had a number of parliamentary seats in 1992: Austria 9, Belgium 13, Finland 8, Italy 20, Luxembourg 2, Republic of Ireland 1, Greece 1, and Germany 2; and 29 members in the European Parliament (Belgium 3, France 8, Italy 7, the Netherlands 2,, Spain 1, and Germany 8).

Greenpeace international environmental pressure group, founded 1971, with a policy of nonviolent direct action backed by scientific research. During a protest against French atmospheric nuclear testing in the S Pacific 1985, its ship *Rainbow Warrior* was sunk by French intelligence agents, killing a crew member.

green revolution in agriculture, a popular term for the change in methods of arable farming in Third World countries. The intent is to provide more and better food for their populations, albeit with a heavy reliance on chemicals and machinery. It was instigated in the 1940s and 1950s, but abandoned by some countries in the 1980s. Much of the food produced is exported as ⬙cash crops, so that local diet does not always improve.

Measures include the increased use of tractors and other machines, artificial fertilizers and pesticides, as well as the breeding of new strains of crop plants (mainly rice, wheat, and corn) and farm animals. Much of the work is coordinated by the Food and Agriculture Organization of the United Nations.

The green revolution was initially successful in SE Asia; India doubled its wheat yield in 15 years, and the rice yield in the Philippines rose by 75%. However, yields have leveled off in many areas and some countries, which cannot afford the dams, fertilizers, and machinery required, have adopted ⬙intermediate technologies.

High-yield varieties of cereal plants require much more nitrogen per acre, more than is available to small farmers in poor countries. The rich farmers therefore enjoy bigger harvests, and the gap between rich and poor in the Third World has grown.

Greensboro city in N central North Carolina, W of Durham; seat of Guilford county. It is noted for its textile, chemical, and tobacco industries. Many schools are located here, including Guilford College 1834 and the University of North Carolina at Greensboro 1891; population (1990) 183,500. The Battle of Guilford Courthouse 1781 was fought nearby.

greenshank grayish shorebird *Tringa nebularia* of the sandpiper group. It has long olive-green legs and a slightly upturned bill. It breeds in N Europe and regularly migrates through the Aleutian Islands.

Greenspan Alan 1926– . US economist who succeeded Paul ⬙Volcker as chair of the ⬙Federal Reserve System 1987 and successfully pumped liquidity into the market to avert a sudden "free fall" into recession after the Wall Street share crash of Oct 1987.

Born in New York and educated at Columbia University, he served as economics adviser and member of a variety of "task forces" under the Republican Presidents Nixon, Ford, and Reagan.

Greenstreet Sydney 1879–1954. British character actor. He made an impressive film debut in *The Maltese Falcon* 1941 and became one of the cinema's best-known villains. His other films include *Casablanca* 1943 and *The Mask of Dimitrios* 1944.

Greenville city in NW South Carolina, on the Reedy River, near the foothills of the Blue Ridge Mountains, SW of Spartanburg; seat of Greenville County. It is known as a major textile manufacturing center. Other industries include lumber and chemicals; population (1990) 44,900.

Greenwich inner borough of Greater London, England; population (1991) 200,800.

Greenwich landmarks include the **Queen's House** 1637, designed by Inigo Jones, the first Palladian-style building in England; the *Royal Naval College*, designed by Christopher Wren 1694; the *Royal Observatory* (founded here 1675). The source of Greenwich Mean Time has been moved, but the Greenwich meridian (0°) remains unchanged. The *Cutty Sark*, one of the great tea clippers, is preserved as a museum of sail.

Greenwich Mean Time (GMT) local time on the zero line of longitude (the *Greenwich meridian*), which passes through the Old Royal Observatory at Greenwich, London. It was replaced 1986 by coordinated universal time (UTC); see ⬙time.

Greenwich Village in New York City, a section of lower Manhattan (from 14th Street south to Houston Street and from Broadway west to the Hudson River), which from the late 19th century became the bohemian and artistic fourth of the city and, despite expensive rentals, remains so.

More generally, its name suggests the spirit of avant-gardism and political radicalism in US culture; it is variously associated with left-wing causes, sexual liberation, experimental art and theater, and new magazines and movements. This attitude caused the adjoining section of the Lower East Side, east of Broadway, now far more outrageous than "the Village," to be called the *East Village*.

Greer Germaine 1939– . Australian feminist who became widely known on the publication of her book *The Female Eunuch* 1970. Later works include *The Obstacle Race* 1979, a study of contemporary women artists, and *Sex and Destiny: The Politics of Human Fertility* 1984. She is also a speaker and activist.

Gregorian chant any of a body of plainsong choral chants associated with Pope Gregory the Great (540–604), which became standard in the Roman Catholic Church.

Gregory Isabella Augusta (born Persse) 1852–1932. Irish playwright, associated with W B Yeats in creating the ⬙Abbey Theatre, Dublin, 1904. Her plays include the comedy *Spreading the News* 1904 and the tragedy *Gaol Gate* 1906. Her journals 1916–30 were published 1946.

Gregory name of 16 popes, including:

Gregory I St, *the Great* c. 540–604. Pope from 590 who asserted Rome's supremacy and exercised almost imperial powers. In 596 he sent St ⬙Augustine to England. He introduced the choral *Gregorian chant* into the liturgy. Feast day March 12.

Gregory VII or *Hildebrand* c. 1023–1085. Chief minister to several popes before his election to the papacy 1073. In 1077 he forced the Holy Roman emperor Henry IV to wait in the snow at Canossa for four days, dressed as a penitent, before receiving pardon. He was driven from Rome and died in exile. His feast day is May 25.

He claimed power to depose kings, denied lay rights to make clerical appointments, and attempted to suppress simony (the buying and selling of church preferments) and to enforce clerical celibacy, making enemies of both rulers and the church.

Gregory XIII 1502–1585. Pope from 1572 who introduced the reformed *Gregorian calendar*, still in use, in which a century year is not a leap year unless it is divisible by 400.

Gregory of Tours, St 538–594. French Christian bishop of Tours from 573, author of a *History of the Franks*. His feast day is Nov 17.

Grenada island country in the Caribbean, the southernmost of the Windward Islands.

government The constitution, which dates from full independence 1974, provides for a system modeled on that of Britain, with a resident governor-general, representing the British monarch, as the formal head of state and a prime minister and cabinet drawn from and collectively responsible to parliament. Parliament consists of two chambers, a 15-member house of representatives, elected by universal suffrage, and a senate of 13, appointed by the governor-general, seven on the advice of the prime minister, three on the advice of the leader of the opposition, and three after wider consultation.

history Prior to the arrival of Christopher ⬙Columbus 1498, Grenada was inhabited by ⬙Carib Indians. The island was eventually colonized by France 1650 and ceded to Britain 1783. Grenada remained a British colony until 1958, when it joined the Federation of the West Indies until its dissolution 1962. Internal self-government was achieved 1967 and full independence within the British ⬙Commonwealth 1974. The early political life of the nation was dominated by two figures: Eric Gairy, a labor-union leader who founded the Grenada United Labor Party (GULP) 1950, and Herbert Blaize, of the Grenada National Party (GNP).

after independence On independence in 1974, Gairy was elected prime minister. He was knighted 1977, but his rule became increasingly autocratic and corrupt, and he was replaced 1979 in a bloodless coup by the leader of the left-wing New Jewel Movement (NJM), Maurice Bishop. Bishop suspended the 1974 constitution, established a People's Revolutionary Government, and announced the formation of a people's consultative assembly to draft a new constitution. He promised a nonaligned foreign policy but became convinced that the US was involved in a plot to destabilize his administration; this was strongly denied.

Grenada's relations with Britain and the US deteriorated while links with Cuba and the USSR grew stronger. In 1983 Bishop tried to improve relations with the US and announced the appointment of a commission to draft a new constitution. His conciliatory attitude was opposed by the more left-wing members of his regime, resulting in a military coup, during which Bishop and three of his colleagues were executed.

US-led invasion A Revolutionary Military Council (RMC), led by General Hudson Austin, took control. In response to the outcry caused by the executions, Austin promised a return to civilian rule as soon as possible, but on Oct 25 about 1,900 US troops, accompanied by 300 from Jamaica and Barbados, invaded the island. It was not clear whether the invasion was in response to a request from the governor-general or on the initiative of the Organization of Eastern Caribbean States. The RMC forces were defeated and Austin and his colleagues arrested.

Grenada

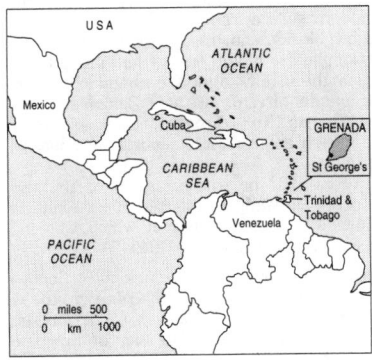

area (including the Grenadines, notably Carriacou) 131 sq mi/340 sq km
capital St George's
cities Grenville, Hillsborough (Carriacou)
physical southernmost of the Windward Islands; mountainous
features Grand-Anse beach; Annandale Falls; the Great Pool volcanic crater
head of state Elizabeth II from 1974 represented by governor-general
head of government Nicholas Braithwaite from 1990
political system emergent democracy
political parties New National Party (NNP), centrist; Grenada United Labor Party (GULP), nationalist, left of center; National Democratic Congress (NDC), centrist
exports cocoa, nutmeg, bananas, mace

currency Eastern Caribbean dollar
population (1990 est) 84,000, 84% of black African descent; growth rate –0.2% p.a.
life expectancy 69
language English (official); some French patois spoken
media two independent weekly newspapers
religion Roman Catholic 60%
literacy 85% (1985)
GDP $139 million (1987); $1,391 per head
chronology
1974 Independence achieved from Britain; Eric Gairy elected prime minister.
1979 Gairy removed in bloodless coup led by Maurice Bishop; constitution suspended and a People's Revolutionary Government established.
1982 Relations with the US and Britain deteriorated as ties with Cuba and the USSR strengthened.
1983 After Bishop's attempt to improve relations with the US, he was overthrown by left-wing opponents. A coup established the Revolutionary Military Council (RMC), and Bishop and three colleagues were executed. The US invaded Grenada, accompanied by troops from other E Caribbean countries; RMC overthrown, 1974 constitution reinstated.
1984 The newly formed NNP won 14 of the 15 seats in the house of representatives and its leader, Herbert Blaize, became prime minister.
1989 Herbert Blaize lost leadership of NNP, remaining as head of government; he died and was succeeded by Ben Jones.
1990 Nicholas Braithwaite of the NDC became prime minister.
1991 Integration into Windward Islands confederation proposed.

new party victory In Nov 1983 the governor-general appointed a nonpolitical interim council, and the 1974 constitution was reinstated. Several political parties emerged from hiding, including Eric Gairy's GULP and Herbert Blaize's GNP. After considerable maneuvering, an informal coalition of center and left-of-center parties resulted in the formation of the New National Party (NNP), led by Blaize. In the 1984 general election the NNP won 14 of the 15 seats in the house of representatives and Blaize became prime minister. The US withdrew most of its forces by the end of 1983 and the remainder by July 1985. In party elections Jan 1989, Blaize lost the leadership of the NNP to the public works minister Keith Mitchell. In Dec 1989 Blaize died and was succeeded by a close colleague, Ben Jones. Elections in 1990 brought Nicholas Braithwaite of the National Democratic Congress to power.

In Sept 1991 representatives of Dominica, St Lucia, St Vincent and the Grenadines, and Grenada proposed that integration with the Windward Islands would benefit the islands politically and economically. *See illustration box.*

grenadier another name for ⟩rat-tail.

Grenadines chain of about 600 small islands in the Caribbean sea, part of the group known as the Windward Islands. They are divided between ⟩St Vincent and ⟩Grenada.

Grendel in the Old English epic poem ⟩Beowulf, the male monster that the hero has to kill.

He is a giant, human in shape, a descendent of Cain, living in a murky pond with his mother, among other strange and vicious sea-beasts.

Grenoble alpine town in Rhône-Alpes region, SE France; population (1982) 159,500, conurbation 392,000. Industries include engineering, nuclear research, hydroelectric power, computers, technology, chemicals, plastics, and gloves. It was the birthplace of the novelist ⟩Stendhal, commemorated by a museum, and the Beaux Arts gallery has a modern collection. There is a 12th–13th-century cathedral, a university 1339, and the Institut Laue-Langevin for nuclear research. The 1968 Winter Olympics were held here.

Grenville George 1712–1770. British Whig politician, prime minister, and chancellor of the Exchequer, whose introduction of the ⟩Stamp Act 1765 to raise revenue from the colonies was one of the causes of the American Revolution. His government was also responsible for prosecuting the radical John ⟩Wilkes.

Grenville William Wyndham, Baron 1759–1834. British Whig politician, foreign secretary from 1791; he resigned along with Prime Minister Pitt the Younger 1801 over George III's refusal to assent to Catholic emancipation. He headed the "All the Talents" coalition of 1806–07 that abolished the slave trade.

Gresham Thomas *c.* 1519–1579. English merchant financier who founded and paid for the Royal Exchange and propounded **Gresham's Law**: "bad money tends to drive out good money from circulation."

Gretzky Wayne 1961– . Canadian ice-hockey player, probably the best in the history of the National Hockey League (NHL). Gretzky played with the Edmonton Oilers 1979–88 and with the Los Angeles Kings from 1988. He took just 11 years to break the NHL scoring record of 1,850 goals (accumulated by Gordie Howe over 26 years) and won the Hart Memorial Trophy as the NHL's most valuable player of the season a record nine times (1980–87, 1989).

Born in Brantford, Ontario, Gretzky played hockey from a very young age. He signed with the Edmonton Oilers 1979 at the age of 18. A prolific goal scorer, he scored a record 215 points in the 1981–82 season. He went on to lead his team to the championship twice (1985, 1988) and in 1984 established the record of scoring or assisting in a score in 51 consecutive games. Traded to the Los Angeles Kings 1988, he continued to rank high in the league in goals and assists during most seasons.

CAREER HIGHLIGHTS

Stanley Cup
1984, 1985, 1987, 1988
Hart Memorial Trophy (NHL's most valuable player)
1980–87, 1989
Ross Trophy (most points in regular season)
1981–90

Grey Charles, 2nd Earl Grey 1764–1845. British Whig politician. He entered Parliament 1786, and in 1806 became First Lord of the Admiralty, and foreign secretary soon afterward. As prime minister 1830–34, he carried the Great Reform Bill that reshaped the parliamentary representative system 1832 and the act abolishing slavery throughout the British Empire 1833.

Grey Henry, 3rd Earl Grey 1802–1894. British politician, son of Charles Grey. He served under his father as undersecretary for the colonies 1830–33, resigning because the cabinet would not back the immediate emancipation of slaves; he was secretary of war 1835–39 and colonial secretary 1846–52.

He granted self-government wherever possible. Yet he advocated transport of convicts to the colonies and opposed Gladstone's Home Rule policy.

Grey Lady Jane 1537–1554. Queen of England for ten days, July 9–19, 1553, the great-granddaughter of Henry VII. She was married 1553 to Lord Guildford Dudley (died 1554), son of the Duke of ⟩Northumberland. Edward VI was persuaded by Northumberland to set aside the claims to the throne of his sisters Mary and Elizabeth. When Edward died on July 6 the same year, Jane reluctantly accepted the crown and was proclaimed queen four days later. Mary, although a Roman Catholic, had the support of the populace, and the Lord Mayor of London announced that she was queen July 19. Grey was executed on Tower Green.

Grey Zane 1875–1939. US author of Westerns, such as *Riders of the Purple Sage* 1912. He wrote more than 80 books and was primarily responsible for the creation of the Western as a literary genre.

greyhound ancient breed of dog, with a long narrow muzzle, slight build, and long legs, renowned for its swiftness. It is up to 2.6 ft/78 cm tall, and can exceed 40 mph/60 kph. Greyhound racing is a popular spectator sport.

greyhound racing spectator sport, invented in the US 1919, that has a number of greyhounds pursuing a mechanical hare around a circular or oval track. It is popular in Great Britain and Australia, attracting much on- and off-course betting.

grid network by which electricity is generated and distributed over a region or country. It contains many power stations and switching centers and allows, for example, high demand in one area to be met by surplus power generated in another. Britain has the world's largest grid system, with over 140 power stations able to supply up to 55,000 megawatts.

The term is also used for any grating system, as in a cattle grid for controlling the movement of livestock across roads, and a conductor in a storage battery or electron gun. In trigonometry, a grid is a network of uniformly spaced vertical and horizontal lines as used to locate points on a map or to construct a graph.

Grieg Edvard Hagerup 1843–1907. Norwegian composer. Much of his music is small-scale, particularly his songs, dances, sonatas, and piano works. Among his orchestral works are the *Piano Concerto* 1869 and the incidental music for Ibsen's *Peer Gynt* 1876.

griffin mythical monster, the supposed guardian of hidden treasure, with the body, tail, and hind legs of a lion, and the head, forelegs, and wings of an eagle.

Griffith D (avid) W (ark) 1875–1948. US film director, an influential figure in the development of cinema as an art. He made hundreds of "one-reelers" 1908–13, in which he pioneered the techniques of masking, fade-out, flashback, crosscut, close-up, and long shot. After much experimentation with photography and new techniques he directed *The Birth of a Nation* 1915, about the aftermath of the Civil War, later criticized as degrading to blacks.

His other films include the epic *Intolerance* 1916, *Broken Blossoms* 1919, *Way Down East* 1920, *Orphans of the Storm* 1921, and *The Struggle* 1931. He was a cofounder of United Artists 1919. With the advent of sound, his silent films lost money, and he lived forgotten in Hollywood until his death.

griffon small breed of dog originating in Belgium; red, black, or black and tan in color and weighing up to 11 lb/5 kg. Griffons are square-bodied and round-headed, and there are rough- and smooth-coated varieties.

griffon vulture Old World vulture *Gyps fulvus* of the family Accipitridae, found in S Europe, W and Central Asia, and parts of Africa. It has a bald head with a neck ruff, and is 3.5 ft/1.1 m long with a wingspan of up to 9 ft/2.7 m.

Grignard François Auguste-Victor 1871–1935. French chemist. In 1900 he discovered a series of organic compounds, the *Grignard reagents*, that found applications as some of the most versatile reagents in organic synthesis. Members of the class contain a hydrocarbon radical, magnesium, and a halogen such as chlorine. He shared the 1912 Nobel Prize for Chemistry.

Grillparzer Franz 1791–1872. Austrian poet and dramatist. His plays include the tragedy *Die Ahnfrau/The Ancestress* 1817, the Classical *Sappho* 1818, and the trilogy *Das goldene Vliess/ The Golden Fleece* 1821.

Born in Vienna, Grillparzer worked for the Austrian government service 1813–56. His historical tragedies *König Ottokars Glück und Ende/King Ottocar, His Rise and Fall* 1825 and *Ein treuer Diener seines Herrn/A True Servant of His Master* 1826 both involved him with the censor. There followed his two greatest dramas, *Des Meeres und der Liebe Wellen/The Waves of Sea and Love* 1831, returning to the Hellenic world, and *Der Traum, ein Leben/A*

Dream Is Life 1834. He wrote a bitter cycle of poems *Tristia ex Ponto* 1835 after an unhappy love affair.

Grimm Jakob Ludwig Karl 1785–1863. German philologist who formulated ◊Grimm's Law and collaborated with his brother Wilhelm Karl (1786–1859) in the *Fairy Tales* 1812–14, based on collected folk tales. Jakob's main work was his *Deutsche Grammatick/German Grammar* 1819, the first historical treatment of the ◊Germanic Languages.

Grimm's law in linguistics, the rule (formulated 1822 by Jacob Grimm) by which certain prehistoric sound changes have occurred in the consonants of Indo-European languages: for example Latin *p* became English and German *f* sound, as in *pater—father, Vater*.

Such correspondences show the kinship between various native English words and those borrowed from the Classical or Romance languages.

Gris Juan 1887–1927. Spanish abstract painter, one of the earliest Cubists. He developed a distinctive geometrical style, often strongly colored. He experimented with paper collage and made designs for Diaghilev's Ballet Russes 1922–23.

Grisons French name for the Swiss canton of ◊Graubünden.

Griswold v Connecticut a US Supreme Court decision 1965 dealing with state bans on the use of birth control. Griswold, the state director of the Planned Parenthood League, was convicted under a Connecticut anticontraceptive law for giving medical advice about birth control to a married couple. The Court overturned the conviction on appeal, ruling that the law was an illegitimate imposition of state police power on marital privacy guaranteed by the 1st, 3rd, 5th, 9th, and 14th Amendments.

Grivas George 1898–1974. Greek Cypriot general who from 1955 led the underground group EOKA's attempts to secure the union (Greek *enosis*) of Cyprus with Greece.

Gromyko Andrei 1909–1989. President of the USSR 1985–88. As ambassador to the US from 1943, he took part in the Tehran, Yalta, and Potsdam conferences; as United Nations representative 1946–49, he exercised the Soviet veto 26 times. He was foreign minister 1957–85. It was Gromyko who formally nominated Mikhail Gorbachev as Communist Party leader 1985.

Groningen most northerly province of the Netherlands
area 907 sq mi/2,350 sq km
population (1991) 554,600
cities capital Groningen; Hoogezand-Sappemeer, Stadskanaal, Veendam, Delfzijl, Winschoten
products natural gas, arable crops, dairy produce, sheep, horses
physical Ems estuary, innermost W Fresian Islands
history under the power of the bishops of Utrecht from 1040, Groningen became a member of the Hanseatic League 1284. Taken by Spain 1580, it was recaptured by Maurice of Nassau 1594.

grooming in biology, the use by an animal of teeth, tongue, feet, or beak to clean fur or feathers. Grooming also helps to spread essential oils for waterproofing. In many social species, notably monkeys and apes, grooming of other individuals is used to reinforce social relationships.

Gropius Walter Adolf 1883–1969. German architect who lived in the US from 1937. He was an early exponent of the international modern style defined by glass curtain walls, cubic blocks, and unsupported corners—for example, the model factory and office building at the 1914 Cologne Werkbund exhibition. A founder-director of the ◊Bauhaus school in Weimar 1919–28, he advocated teamwork in design and artistic standards in industrial production.

From 1937 he was professor of architecture at Harvard. He started the Architects Collaborative, a product of which was the Harvard Graduate Center 1949–50.

grosbeak any of various thick-billed finches of the family Fringillidae. The *pine grosbeak Pinicola enucleator* breeds in Arctic forests. Its plumage is similar to that of the pine ◊crossbill.

gros point embroidery that uses wool to fill netting (see ◊petit point). It is normally used in colorful designs on widely spaced canvas.

gross domestic product (GDP) value of the output of all goods and services produced within a nation's borders, normally given as a total for the year. It thus includes the production of foreign-owned firms within the country, but excludes the income of domestically owned firms located abroad. See also ◊gross national product.

Since output is derived from expenditure on goods and services by firms, consumers, and government net of imports; and income (in the form of wages, salaries, interest, rent, and profits) is derived from the production of goods and services, GDP can be measured either by the sum of total output or expenditure or incomes. However, in practice there is usually a slight discrepancy between the three because of the highly complex calculations involved. GDP fluctuates in relation to the ◊labor cycle and ◊standard of living.

gross national product (GNP) the most commonly used measurement of the wealth of a country.

GNP is defined as the total value of all goods and services produced by firms owned by the country concerned. It is measured as the ◊gross domestic product plus income from abroad, minus income earned during the same period by foreign investors within the country; see also ◊national income.

Grosvenor Gilbert Hovey 1875–1966. US publisher. Born in Constantinople to missionary parents, Grosvenor was educated at Amherst College and named editor of *National Geographic Magazine* 1899. Its financial status was shaky, but Grosvenor soon transformed it to a mass circulation periodical through the use of color photography from 1910.

He also changed the parent body, the National Geographic Society, from a small scientific body to a national institution. As president of the Society 1920–54 and chairman of its directors 1954–66, Grosvenor sponsored scientific expeditions all over the world.

Grosz Georg 1893–1959. German Expressionist painter and illustrator, a founder of the Berlin group of the Dada movement 1918. Grosz excelled in savage satirical drawings criticizing the government and the military establishment. After numerous prosecutions he fled his native Berlin 1932 and became a naturalized American 1938.

Grosz Károly 1930– . Hungarian Communist

politician, prime minister 1987–88. As leader of the ruling Hungarian Socialist Workers' Party (HSWP) 1988–89, he sought to establish a flexible system of "socialist pluralism."

Grotefend George Frederick 1775–1853. German scholar. Although a student of the Classical rather than the oriental languages, he nevertheless solved the riddle of the wedge-like ◊cuneiform script as used in ancient Persia: decipherment of Babylonian cuneiform followed from his work.

Grotius Hugo 1583–1645. Dutch jurist and politician, born in Delft. He became a lawyer, and later received political appointments. In 1618 he was arrested as a republican and sentenced to imprisonment for life. His wife contrived his escape 1620, and he settled in France, where he composed the *De Jure Belli et Pacis/On the Law of War and Peace* 1625, the foundation of international law. He was Swedish ambassador in Paris 1634–45.

ground an electrical connection between an appliance and the ground, which becomes part of the circuit. In the event of a fault in an electrical appliance (for example, involving connection between the live part of the circuit and the outer casing) the current flows to earth, causing no harm to the user.

In most domestic installations, grounding is achieved by a connection to an underground metal water-supply pipe buried in the ground before it enters the premises.

ground water water collected underground in porous rock strata and soils; it emerges at the surface as springs and streams. The groundwater's upper level is called the *water table*. Sandy or other kinds of beds that are filled with groundwater are called *aquifers*. Recent estimates are that usable ground water amounts to more than 90% of all the fresh water on Earth; however, keeping such supplies free of pollutants entering the recharge areas is a critical environmental concern.

Most groundwater near the surface moves slowly through the ground while the water table stays in the same place. The depth of the water table reflects the balance between the rate of infiltration, called recharge, and the rate of discharge at springs or rivers or pumped water wells. The force of gravity makes underground water run "downhill" underground just as it does above the surface. The greater the slope and the permeability, the greater the speed. Velocities vary from 40 in/100 cm per day to 0.2 in/0.5 cm.

Ground-water supplies vary from region to region depending on recharge rates and well use. Some areas such as W Texas and Oklahoma are in danger of depleting their groundwater supplies. In other areas, such as Long Island and New Jersey, overpumping has led to the encroachment of sea water into continental aquifers. Overall, however, the amount of usable fresh water in the ground is enormous.

group in mathematics, a finite or infinite set of elements that can be combined by an operation; formally, a group must satisfy certain conditions. For example, the set of all integers (positive or negative whole numbers) forms a group with regard to addition because: (1) addition is associative, that is, the sum of two or more integers is the same regardless of the order in which the integers are added; (2) adding two integers gives another integer; (3) the set includes an identity element 0, which has no effect on any integer to which it is added (for example, $0 + 3 = 3$); and (4) each integer has an inverse (for instance, 7 has the inverse −7), such that the sum of an integer and its inverse is 0. *Group theory* is the study of the properties of groups.

grouper any of several species of large sea bass, especially the genera *Mycteroperca* and *Epinephelus*, found in warm waters.

grouse fowllike game bird of the subfamily Tetraonidae, in the pheasant family, Phasianidae. The subfamily also includes quail, ptarmigan, and prairie chicken. Grouse are native to North America and N Europe. They are mostly ground-living. During the mating season the males undertake elaborate courtship displays in small individual territories (◊leks).

Among the most familiar are the ruffed grouse *Bonasa umbellus*, common in woods in N and E North America, and the blue grouse *Dendragapus obscurus* of W North America.

Grove City v Bell a US Supreme Court decision 1984 dealing with sexual discrimination in publicly funded schools. Grove City College, a private school in Pennsylvania, refused to comply officially with laws prohibiting sex discrimination. Although as a whole it was not a direct recipient of federal funds, certain programs in the school received federal scholarship money. The government moved to withhold funds from Grove City under the Education Amendments 1972. On appeal, the Court ruled 6–3 that restrictions on sex discrimination could be applied only to programs and not to the school as a whole; federal action was to be taken only on a "program-specific" basis.

growth in biology, the increase in size and weight during the development of an organism. Growth is an increase in biomass (mass of organic material, excluding water) and is associated with cell division.

All organisms grow, although the rate of growth varies over a lifetime. Typically, an organism shows an S-shaped curve, in which growth is at first slow, then fast, then, toward the end of life, nonexistent. Growth may even be negative during the period before death, with decay occurring faster than cellular replacement.

GRP abbreviation for *glass-reinforced plastic*, a plastic material strengthened by glass fibers, usually erroneously known as ◊fiberglass. GRP is a favored material for boat hulls and for the bodies and some structural components of performance automobiles; it is also used in the manufacture of passenger automobiles.

Products are usually molded, mats of fiberglass being sandwiched between layers of a polyester plastic, which sets hard when mixed with a curing agent.

Grünewald (Mathias Gothardt/Neithardt) *c.* 1475–1528. German painter, active in Mainz, Frankfurt, and Halle. He was court painter, architect, and engineer to the archbishop of Mainz 1508–14. His few surviving paintings show an intense involvement with religious subjects.

The *Isenheim altarpiece,* 1515 (Colmar Museum, France), with its horribly tortured figure of Jesus, recalls medieval traditions.

GU abbreviation for *Guam*.

Guadalajara industrial (textiles, glass, soap, pottery) capital of Jalisco state, W Mexico; population (1990) 2,847,000. It is a key communications center. It has a 16th–17th-century cathedral, the Governor's Palace, and an orphanage with murals by the Mexican painter José Orozco.

Guadalcanal largest of the ◊Solomon Islands; area 2,510 sq mi/6,500 sq km; population (1987) 71,000. Gold, copra, and rubber are produced. During World War II it was the scene of a battle that was won by US forces after six months of fighting.

Guadeloupe island group in the Leeward Islands, West Indies, an overseas *département* of France; area 658 sq mi/1,705 sq km; population (1982) 328,400. The main islands are Basse-Terre, on which is the chief town of the same name, and Grande-Terre. Sugar refining and rum distilling are the main industries.

Guam largest of the ◊Mariana Islands in the W Pacific, an unincorporated territory of the US
area 208 sq mi/540 sq km
capital Agaña
cities Apra (port), Tamuning
features major US air and naval base, much used in the Vietnam War; tropical, with much rain
products sweet potatoes, fish; tourism is important
currency US dollar
population (1990) 132,800
language English, Chamorro (basically Malay-Polynesian)
religion 96% Roman Catholic
government popularly elected governor (Ricardo Bordallo from 1985) and single-chamber legislature
recent history ceded by Spain to the US 1898; occupied by Japan 1941–44. Guam achieved full US citizenship and self-government from 1950. A referendum 1982 favored the status of a commonwealth, in association with the US.

guan any of several large, pheasantlike birds of the family Cracidae, living in the forests of South and Central America. They are olive-green or brown.

guanaco hoofed ruminant *Lama guanacoe* of the camel family, found in South America on pampas and mountain plateaus. It grows to 4 ft/1.2 m at the shoulder, with head and body about 5 ft/1.5 m long. It is sandy brown in color, with a blackish face, and has fine wool. It lives in small herds and is the ancestor of the domestic ◊llama and ◊alpaca. It is also related to the other wild member of the camel family, the ◊vicuna.

Guangdong or *Kwantung* province of S China
area 89,320 sq mi/231,400 sq km
capital Guangzhou
features tropical climate; Hainan, Leizhou peninsula, and the foreign enclaves of Hong Kong and Macao in the Pearl river delta
products rice, sugar, tobacco, minerals, fish
population (1990) 62,829,000.

Guangxi or *Kwangsi Chuang* autonomous region in S China
area 85,074 sq mi/220,400 sq km
capital Nanning
products rice, sugar, fruit
population (1990) 42,246,000, including the Zhuang people, allied to the Thai, who form China's largest ethnic minority.

Guantánamo capital of a province of the same name in SE Cuba; population (1989) 200,400; a trading center in a fertile agricultural region producing sugar. Iron, copper, chromium, and manganese are mined nearby. There is a US naval base, for which the Cuban government has refused to accept rent since 1959.

Guanyin in Chinese Buddhism, the goddess of mercy. In Japan she is **Kwannon** or Kannon, an attendant of the Amida Buddha (Amitābha). Her origins were in India as the male bodhisattva Avalokiteśvara.

guarana Brazilian woody climbing plant *Paullinia cupana*, family Sapindaceae. A drink made from its roasted seeds has a high caffeine content, and it is the source of the drug known as zoom in the US. Starch, gum, and several oils are extracted from it for commercial use.

Guaraní member of a South American Indian people who formerly inhabited the area that is now Paraguay, S Brazil, and Bolivia. The Guaraní live mainly in reserves; few retain the traditional ways of hunting in the tropical forest, cultivation, and ritual warfare. About 1 million speak Guaraní, a member of the Tupian language group.

guard cell in plants, a specialized cell on the undersurface of leaves for controlling gas exchange and water loss. Guard cells occur in pairs and are shaped so that a pore, or ⟡stomata, exists between them. They can change shape with the result that the pore disappears. During warm weather, when a plant is in danger of losing excessive water, the guard cells close, cutting down evaporation from the interior of the leaf.

Guardi Francesco 1712–1793. Italian painter. He produced souvenir views of his native Venice that were commercially less successful than Canaletto's but are now considered more atmospheric, with subtler use of reflected light.

Guare John 1938– . US playwright who is particularly known for his screenplay for Louis Malle's *Atlantic City* 1980. His stage plays include *House of Blue Leaves* 1971 and *Six Degrees of Separation* 1990.

Guareschi Giovanni 1909–1968. Italian author of short stories featuring the friendly feud between parish priest Don Camillo and the Communist village mayor.

Guarini Giovanni 1924–1983. Italian architect whose intricate carved Baroque designs were produced without formal architectural training. Guarini was a secular priest of the Theatine Order, and many of his buildings are religious; for example, the Chapel of the Holy Shroud, Turin, 1667–90. His greatest similar work is the undulating Palazzo Carignano, Turin, 1679.

Guarneri family of stringed-instrument makers of Cremona, Italy. Giuseppe "del Gesù" Guarneri (1698–1744) produced the finest models.

Guatemala country in Central America, bounded N and NW by Mexico, E by Belize and the Caribbean Sea, SE by Honduras and El Salvador, and SW by the Pacific Ocean.

Guatemala
Republic of (*República de Guatemala***)**

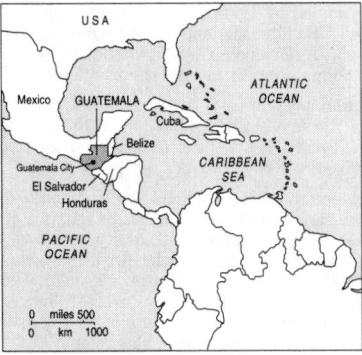

area 42,031 sq mi/108,889 sq km
capital Guatemala City
cities Quezaltenango, Puerto Barrios (naval base)
physical mountainous; narrow coastal plains; limestone tropical plateau in N; frequent earthquakes
environment between 1960 and 1980 nearly 57% of the country's forest was cleared for farming
features Mayan archeological remains, including site at Tikal
head of state and government Jorge Serrano Elías from 1991
political system democratic republic
political parties Guatemalan Christian Democratic Party (PDCG), Christian center-left; Center Party (UCN), centrist; National Democratic Cooperation Party (PDCN), center-right; Revolutionary Party (PR), radical; Movement of National Liberation (MLN), extreme right-wing; Democratic Institutional Party (PID), moderate conservative; Solidarity Action Movement (MAS),

right-wing
exports coffee, bananas, cotton, sugar, beef
currency quetzal
population (1990 est) 9,340,000 (Mayaquiche Indians 54%, mestizos (mixed race) 42%); growth rate 2.8% p.a. (87% of under-fives suffer from malnutrition)
life expectancy men 57, women 61
languages Spanish (official); 40% speak 18 Indian languages
religion Roman Catholic 80%, Protestant 20%
literacy men 63%, women 47% (1985 est)
GDP $7 bn (1987); $834 per head
chronology
1839 Independence achieved from Spain.
1954 Col Carlos Castillo became president in US-backed coup, halting land reform.
1963 Military coup made Col Enrique Peralta president.
1966 Cesar Méndez elected president.
1970 Carlos Araña elected president.
1974 General Kjell Laugerud became president. Widespread political violence precipitated by the discovery of falsified election returns in March.
1978 General Fernando Romeo became president.
1981 Growth of antigovernment guerrilla movement.
1982 General Angel Anibal became president. Army coup installed General Ríos Montt as head of junta and then as president; political violence continued.
1983 Montt removed in coup led by General Mejía Victores, who declared amnesty for the guerrillas.
1985 New constitution adopted; PDCG won congressional elections; Vinicio Cerezo elected president.
1989 Coup attempt against Cerezo foiled. Over 100,000 people killed, and 40,000 reported missing since 1980.
1991 Jorge Serrano Elías of the Solidarity Action Movement elected president. Diplomatic relations with Belize established.

government The 1985 constitution provides for a single-chamber national assembly of 100 deputies, 75 elected directly by universal suffrage and the rest on the basis of proportional representation; they serve a five-year term. The president, also directly elected for a similar term, appoints a cabinet and is assisted by a vice-president, and is not eligible for reelection.

history Formerly part of the ⟡Maya empire, Guatemala became a Spanish colony 1524. Independent from Spain 1821, it then joined Mexico, becoming independent 1823. It was part of the ⟡Central American Federation 1823–39 and was then ruled by a succession of dictators until the presidency of Juan José ⟡Arévalo Bermejo 1944 and his successor, Col Jacobo Arbenz. Their socialist administrations both followed programs of reform, including land appropriation.

era of coups Arbenz's nationalization of the United Fruit Company's plantations 1954 so alarmed the US government that it sponsored a revolution, led by Col Carlos Castillo Armas, who then assumed the presidency. He was assassinated 1963, and the army continued to rule until 1966. There was a brief return to constitutional government until the military returned 1970.

In the 1982 presidential election the government candidate won, but opponents complained that the election had been rigged, and before he could take office there was a coup by a group of young right-wing officers, who installed General Ríos Montt as head of a three-person junta. He soon dissolved the junta, assumed the presidency, and began fighting corruption.

The antigovernment guerrilla movement was growing 1981 and was countered by repressive measures by Montt, so that by 1983 opposition to him was widespread. After several unsuccessful attempts to remove him, a coup led by General Mejía Victores finally succeeded. Mejía Victores declared an amnesty for the guerrillas, the ending of press censorship, and the preparation of a new constitution. After its adoption and elections 1985, the Guatemalan Christian Democratic Party (PDCG) won a majority in the congress as well as the presidency, with Vinicio Cerezo becoming president. In 1989 an attempted coup against Cerezo was put down by the army. By 1989 once more 2% of the population owned over 70% of the land.

deaths and disappearances The army, funded and trained by the US, destroyed some 440 rural villages and killed more than 100,000 civilians 1980–89; 40,000 people disappeared during the same period. From Jan to Nov 1989 almost 2,000 people were killed and 840 disappeared (representing a six-fold increase over the same period in the preceding year).

In presidential elections Jan 1991, Jorge Serrano Elías of the Solidarity Action Movement (MAS), an ally of Montt, received 68% of the vote and his opponent Jorge Carpio Nicolle of the Center Party (UCN) 32%. In Sept 1991 diplomatic relations with Belize were established. *See illustration box.*

Guatemala City capital of Guatemala; population (1983) 1,300,000. It produces textiles, tires, footwear, and cement. It was founded 1776 when its predecessor (Antigua) was destroyed in an earthquake. It was severely damaged by another earthquake 1976.

guava tropical American tree *Psidium guajava* of the myrtle family Myrtaceae; the astringent yellow pear-shaped fruit is used to make guava jelly, or it can be stewed or canned. It has a high vitamin C content.

Guayaquil largest city and chief port of ⬦Ecuador; population (1986) 1,509,100. The economic center of Ecuador, Guayaquil manufactures machinery and consumer goods, processes food, and refines petroleum. It was founded 1537 by the Spanish explorer Francisco de Orellana.

Guderian Heinz 1888–1954. German general in World War II. He created the Panzer (German "armor") divisions that formed the ground spearhead of Hitler's *Blitzkrieg* attack strategy, achieving a significant breakthrough at Sedan in Ardennes, France 1940, and leading the advance to Moscow 1941.

gudgeon any of an Old World genus *Gobio* of freshwater fishes of the carp family, especially *G. gobio* found in Europe and N Asia on the gravel bottoms of streams. It is olive-brown, spotted with black, and up to 8 in/20 cm long, with a distinctive barbel (a sensory fleshy filament) at each side of the mouth.

guelder rose or *snowball tree* cultivated shrub or small tree *Viburnum opulus*, native to Europe and N Africa, with spherical clusters of white flowers and shiny red berries.

It is closely related to high-bush cranberry *V. trilobum* of North America.

Guelph industrial town and agricultural center in SE Ontario, on the Speed River; industries include food processing, electrical goods, and pharmaceuticals; population (1981) 71,250.

Guelph and Ghibelline rival parties in medieval Germany and Italy, which supported the papal party and the Holy Roman emperors respectively.

They originated in the 12th century as partisans of rival German houses, that of Welf (hence Guelph or Guelf) of the dukes of Bavaria, and that of the lords of ⬦Hohenstaufen (whose castle at Waiblingen gave the Ghibellines their name). The Hohenstaufens struggled for the imperial crown after the death of Henry VI in 1197, until the Hohenstaufen dynasty died out 1268. The Guelphs early became associated with the papacy because of their mutual Hohenstaufen enemy. In Italy, the terms were introduced about 1242 in Florence; the names seem to have been grafted on to preexisting papal and imperial factions within the city-republics.

Guercino (Giovanni Francesco Barbieri) 1590–1666. Italian Baroque painter, active chiefly in Rome. In his ceiling painting of *Aurora* 1621–23 (Villa Ludovisi, Rome), the chariot-borne figure of dawn rides across the heavens, and the architectural framework is imitated in the painting, giving the illusion that the ceiling opens into the sky.

Guercino's use of dramatic lighting recalls ⬦Caravaggio, but his brighter colors reflect a contrasting mood. His later works, produced when he had retired from Rome to Bologna, are closer in style to Guido ⬦Reni.

Guérin Camille 1872–1961. French bacteriologist who, with ⬦Calmette, developed the *bacille* Calmette-Guérin (⬦BCG) vaccine for tuberculosis.

Guernica town in the Basque Provinces of Vizcaya, N Spain; population (1981) 18,000. Here the Castilian kings formerly swore to respect the rights of the Basques. It was almost completely destroyed 1937 by German bombers aiding Franco in the Spanish Civil War and

rebuilt 1946. The bombing inspired a painting by Pablo Picasso and a play by Fernando Arrabal.

Guernsey second largest of the ⬦Channel Islands; area 24.3 sq mi/63 sq km; population (1986) 55,500. The capital is St Peter Port. Products include electronics, tomatoes, flowers, and more recently butterflies; from 1975 it has been a major financial center. Guernsey cattle, which are a distinctive pale fawn color and give rich creamy milk, originated here.

Guernsey has belonged to the English crown since 1066, but was occupied by German forces 1940–45.

guerrilla (Spanish "little war") irregular soldier fighting in a small unofficial unit, typically against an established or occupying power, and engaging in sabotage, ambush, and the like, rather than pitched battles against an opposing army. Guerrilla tactics have been used both by resistance armies in wartime (for example, the Vietnam War) and in peacetime by national liberation groups and militant political extremists (for example the ⬦PLO; Tamil Tigers).

The term was first applied to the Spanish and Portuguese resistance to French occupation during the Peninsular War (1808–14). Guerrilla techniques were widely used in World War II—for example, in Greece and the Balkans. Political activists who resort to violence, particularly **urban guerrillas**, tend to be called "freedom fighters" by those who support their cause, "terrorists" by those who oppose it. Efforts by governments to put a stop to their activities have had only sporadic success. The Council of Europe has set up the European Convention on the Suppression of Terrorism, to which many governments are signatories. In the UK the Prevention of Terrorism Act 1984 is aimed particularly at the Irish Republican Army (IRA). The Institute for the Study of Terrorism was founded in London 1986. Violent activities (bombings, kidnappings, hijackings) by such groups as these have proliferated considerably in recent years; in 1984 there were 600 international incidents of politically motivated violence, a 20% increase on the average over the previous five years. Cooperation among the groups (for example in arms supply) has developed, as has state support (such as the US's for the Contras and Libya's for many groups, including the IRA).

Guest Edgar Albert 1881–1959. US journalist and poet. Leaving school at an early age, he worked in various jobs at the *Detroit Free Press* and from 1900 wrote "Breakfast Table Chat," a highly popular daily column of light verse and folksy wisdom, which later was syndicated nationally. Guest's best-selling collections of verse include *A Heap o' Livin'* 1916, *When Day Is Done* 1921, and *Harbor Lights of Home* 1928.

Born in Birmingham, England, Guest came to America 1891 with his parents, settling in Detroit, Michigan. From 1938 to 1942 he was the host of a popular weekly radio program.

Guevara "Che" Ernesto 1928–1967. Latin American revolutionary. He was born in Argentina and trained there as a doctor, but left his homeland 1953 because of his opposition to the right-wing president Perón. In effecting the Cuban revolution of 1959, he was second only to Castro and Castro's brother Raúl. In 1965 he went to the Congo to fight against white mercenaries, and then to Bolivia, where he was killed in an unsuccessful attempt to lead

a peasant rising. He was an orthodox Marxist and renowned for his guerrilla techniques.

GUI in computing, abbreviation for ⬦*graphical user interface*.

Guiana NE part of South America that includes ⬦French Guiana, ⬦Guyana, and ⬦Suriname.

Guido Reni. Italian painter, see ⬦Reni.

Guienne ancient province of SW France which formed the duchy of Aquitaine with Gascony in the 12th century. Its capital was Bordeaux. It became English 1154 and passed to France 1453.

guild or *gild* medieval association, particularly of artisans or merchants, formed for mutual aid and protection and the pursuit of a common purpose, religious or economic. Guilds became politically powerful in Europe but after the 16th century their position was undermined by the growth of capitalism.

Guilds fulfilling charitable or religious functions (for example, the maintenance of schools, roads, or bridges, the assistance of members in misfortune, or the provision of masses for the souls of dead members) flourished in western Europe from the 9th century but were suppressed in Protestant countries at the Reformation.

The earliest form of economic guild, the **guild merchant**, arose during the 11th and 12th centuries; this was an organization of the traders of a town, who had been granted a practical monopoly of its trade by charter. As the merchants often strove to exclude craftworkers from the guild, and to monopolize control of local government, the **craft guilds** came into existence in the 12th and 13th centuries. These, which included journeymen (day workers) and apprentices as well as employers, regulated prices, wages, working conditions, and apprenticeship, prevented unfair practices, and maintained high standards of craft; they also fulfilled many social, religious, and charitable functions. By the 14th century they had taken control of local government, ousting the guild merchant.

Guillaume Charles 1861–1938. Swiss physicist who studied measurement and alloy development. He discovered a nickel–steel alloy, invar, which showed negligible expansion with rising temperatures. He was awarded the Nobel Prize for Physics 1920.

As the son of a clockmaker, Guillaume came early in life to appreciate the value of precision in measurement. He spent most of his life at the International Bureau of Weights and Measures in Sèvres, France, which established the standards for the meter, liter, and kilogram.

guillemot diving seabird of the auk family that breeds in large numbers on rocky N Atlantic and Pacific coasts. The common guillemot *Uria aalge* has a sharp bill and short tail, and sooty-brown and white plumage. The black guillemot *Cepphus grylle* of northern coasts is mostly black, with orange legs when breeding. Guillemots build no nest, but lay one large, almost conical egg.

guillotine beheading device consisting of a metal blade that descends between two posts. It was common in the Middle Ages and was introduced 1791 in an improved design by physician Joseph Ignace Guillotin (1738–1814) in France. It was subsequently used for executions during the French Revolution. It is still in use in some countries.

Guinea
Republic of (*République de Guinée*)

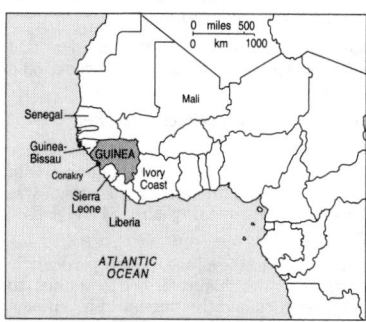

area 94,901 sq mi/245,857 sq km
capital Conakry
cities Labé, Nzérékoré, Kankan
physical flat coastal plain with mountainous interior; sources of rivers Niger, Gambia, and Senegal; forest in SE
environment large amounts of toxic waste from industrialized countries have been dumped in Guinea
features Fouta Djallon, area of sandstone plateaus, cut by deep valleys
head of state and government Lansana Conté from 1984
political system military republic

Guinea country in W Africa, bounded N by Senegal, NE by Mali, SE by the Ivory Coast, S by Liberia and Sierra Leone, W by the Atlantic Ocean, and NW by Guinea-Bissau.
government The 1982 constitution, which provided for an elected national assembly, was suspended 1984 after a military coup. A military committee for national recovery assumed power. The president is head of both state and government and leads an appointed council of ministers. The sole political party, the Democratic Party of Guinea (PDG), was dissolved after the coup, and opposition groups now operate from abroad.
history Formerly part of the Muslim ⬦Mali Empire, which flourished in the region between the 7th and 15th centuries, Guinea's first European visitors were the Portuguese in the mid-15th century, who, together with France and Britain, established the slave trade in the area. In 1849 France proclaimed the Boké region in the east a French protectorate and expanded its territory until by the late 19th century most of W Africa was united under French rule as ⬦French West Africa.
Touré's presidency French Guinea became fully independent 1958, under the name of Guinea, after a referendum rejected a proposal to remain a self-governing colony within the French Community. The first president was Sékou Touré, who made the PDG the only political organization and embarked upon a policy of socialist revolution. There were unsuccessful attempts to overthrow him 1961, 1965, 1967, and 1970, and, suspicious of conspiracies by foreign powers, he put his country into virtual diplomatic isolation. By 1975, however, relations with most of his neighbors had returned to normal.
At first rigidly Marxist, crushing all opposition to his policies, Touré gradually moved toward a mixed economy, with private enterprise becoming legal 1979. His regime was nevertheless authoritarian and harsh. He

political parties none since 1984
exports coffee, rice, palm kernels, alumina, bauxite, diamonds
currency syli or franc
population (1990 est) 7,269,000 (chief peoples are Fulani, Malinke, Susu); growth rate 2.3% p.a.
life expectancy men 39, women 42
languages French (official), African languages
media state-owned, but some criticism of the government tolerated; no daily newspaper
religion Muslim 85%, Christian 10%, local 5%
literacy men 40%, women 17% (1985 est)
GNP $1.9 bn (1987); $369 per head
chronology
1958 Full independence achieved from France; Sékou Touré elected president.
1977 Strong opposition to Touré's rigid Marxist policies forced him to accept return to mixed economy.
1980 Touré returned unopposed for fourth seven-year term.
1984 Touré died. Bloodless coup established a military committee for national recovery, led by Col Lansana Conté.
1985 Attempted coup against Conté while he was out of the country was foiled by loyal troops.
1990 Sent troops to join the multinational force that attempted to stabilize Liberia.
1991 Antigovernment general strike by National Confederation of Guinea Workers (CNTG).

sought closer relations with Western powers, particularly France and the US, and was reelected unopposed 1980, but died 1984.
military rule Before the normal machinery for electing his successor could be put into operation, the army staged a bloodless coup, suspending the constitution and setting up a military committee for national recovery, with Col Lansana Conté at its head. Releasing hundreds of political prisoners and lifting press

restrictions, he also made efforts to restore his country's international standing through a series of overseas visits. He succeeded in persuading some 200,000 Guineans who had fled the country during the Touré regime to return. In 1985 an attempt to overthrow him while he was out of the country was foiled by loyal troops. In 1990 Guinea contributed troops to the multinational force that attempted to stabilize Liberia. The National Confederation of Guinea Workers (CNTG) called a general strike May 1991 in a campaign against the government. *See illustration box.*

Guinea-Bissau country in W Africa, bounded N by Senegal, E and SE by Guinea, and SW by the Atlantic Ocean.
government The 1984 constitution describes the African Party for the Independence of Portuguese Guinea and Cape Verde (PAIGC) as "the leading force in society and in the nation," but was modified 1991 to legalize other parties. Although Cape Verde chose independence, the title of the original party that served the two countries was retained. The constitution provides for a 150-member national people's assembly, all nominees of PAIGC. The assembly elects the president, who is head of both state and government. Policy is determined by PAIGC, and it is there that ultimate political power lies, the president being its secretary-general.
history Guinea-Bissau was first reached by Europeans when the Portuguese arrived 1446 and it became a slave-trading center. Until 1879 it was administered with the Cape Verde Islands, but then became a separate colony under the name of Portuguese Guinea.
Nationalist groups began to form in the 1950s, and PAIGC was established 1956. Portugal refused to grant independence, fighting broke out, and by 1972 PAIGC claimed to control two-thirds of the country. In 1973 the "liberated areas" were declared independent, a national people's assembly was set up, and

Guinea-Bissau
Republic of (*República da Guiné-Bissau*)

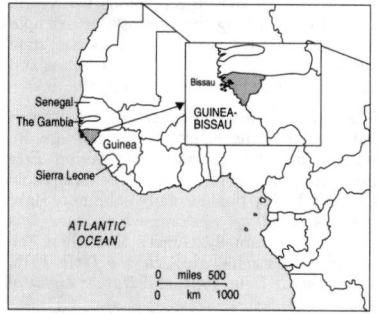

area 13,944 sq mi/36,125 sq km
capital Bissau
cities Mansôa, São Domingos
physical flat coastal plain rising to savanna in E
features the archipelago of Bijagós
head of state and government João Bernardo Vieira from 1980
political system socialist pluralist republic
political party African Party for the Independence of Portuguese Guinea and Cape Verde (PAIGC), nationalist socialist
exports rice, coconuts, peanuts, fish, timber
currency peso

population (1989 est) 929,000; growth rate 2.4% p.a.
life expectancy 42; 1990 infant mortality rate was 14.8%
languages Portuguese (official), Crioulo (Cape Verdean dialect of Portuguese), African languages
religions animism 54%, Muslim 38%, Christian 8%
literacy men 46%, women 17% (1985 est)
GDP $135 million (1987); $146 per head
chronology
1956 PAIGC formed to secure independence from Portugal.
1973 Two-thirds of the country declared independent, with Luiz Cabral as president of a state council.
1974 Independence achieved from Portugal.
1980 Cape Verde decided not to join a unified state. Cabral deposed, and João Vieira became chair of a council of revolution.
1981 PAIGC confirmed as the only legal party, with Vieira as its secretary-general.
1982 Normal relations with Cape Verde restored.
1984 New constitution adopted, making Vieira head of government as well as head of state.
1989 Vieira reelected.
1991 Other parties legalized.
1992 Multiparty electoral commission established.

Luiz Cabral was appointed president of a state council. Some 40,000 Portuguese troops were engaged in trying to put down the uprising and suffered heavy losses, but before a clear outcome was reached a coup in Portugal ended the fighting, and PAIGC negotiated independence with the new government in Lisbon.

after independence In 1974 Portugal formally acknowledged Guinea-Bissau as a sovereign nation. PAIGC began to lay the foundations of a socialist state, intended to include Cape Verde, but in 1980, four days before approval of the constitution, Cape Verde withdrew, feeling that Guinea-Bissau was being given preferential treatment. A coup deposed Cabral, and João Vieira became a chair of a council of revolution.

At its 1981 congress, PAIGC decided to retain its name, despite Cape Verde's withdrawal, and its position as the only party was confirmed, with Vieira as secretary-general. Normal relations between the two countries were restored 1982. In 1984 a new constitution made Vieira head of government as well as head of state. In June 1989 he was reelected for another five-year term. In Jan 1991 PAIGC approved the introduction of "integral multipartyism". *See illustration box.*

Guinea Coast coast of W Africa between Gambia and Cape Lopez.

guinea fowl chickenlike African bird of the family Numididae. The group includes the helmet guinea fowl *Numida meleagris*, which has a horny growth on the head, white-spotted feathers, and fleshy cheek wattles. It is the ancestor of the domestic guinea fowl.

guinea pig species of ⬦cavy, a type of rodent.

Guinevere Welsh *Gwenhwyfar* in British legend, the wife of King ⬦Arthur. Her adulterous love affair with the knight ⬦Lancelot of the Lake led ultimately to Arthur's death.

Guinness Alec 1914– . English actor of stage and screen. His films include *Kind Hearts and Coronets* 1949 (in which he played eight parts), *The Bridge on the River Kwai* 1957 (Academy Award), and *Star Wars* 1977.

Guise Francis, 2nd Duke of Guise 1519–1563. French soldier and politician. He led the French victory over Germany at Metz 1552 and captured Calais from the English 1558. Along with his brother *Charles* (1527–1574), he was powerful in the government of France during the reign of Francis II. He was assassinated attempting to crush the ⬦Huguenots.

Guise Henri, 3rd Duke of Guise 1550–1588. French noble who persecuted the Huguenots and was partly responsible for the Massacre of ⬦St Bartholomew 1572. He was assassinated.

guitar six-stringed, or twelve-stringed, flat-bodied musical instrument, plucked or strummed with the fingers. The *Hawaiian guitar*, laid across the lap, uses a metal bar to produce a distinctive gliding tone; the solid-bodied *electric guitar*, developed in the 1950s, mixes and amplifies vibrations from microphone contacts at different points to produce a range of tone qualities.

Derived from a Moorish original, the guitar spread throughout Europe in medieval times, becoming firmly established in Italy, Spain, and the Spanish American colonies. Its 20th-century revival owes much to Andrés ⬦Segovia, Julian Bream, and John ⬦Williams. The guitar's prominence in popular music can be traced from the traditions of the US mid-West; it played a supporting harmony role in jazz and dance bands during the 1920s and adapted quickly to electric amplification.

Guizhou or *Kweichow* province of S China
area 67,164 sq mi/174,000 sq km
capital Guiyang
products rice, corn, nonferrous minerals
population (1990) 32,392,000.

Guizot François Pierre Guillaume 1787–1874. French politician and historian, professor of modern history at the Sorbonne, Paris 1812–30. He wrote histories of French and European culture and became prime minister 1847. His resistance to all reforms led to the revolution of 1848.

Gujarat or *Gujerat* state of W India
area 75,656 sq mi/196,000 sq km
capital Ahmedabad
features heavily industrialized; includes most of the Rann of Kutch; the Gir Forest (the last home of the wild Asian lion)
products cotton, petrochemicals, oil, gas, rice, textiles
language Gujarati (Gujerati), Hindi
population (1991) 41,174,000.

Gujarati inhabitant of Gujarat on the NW coast of India. The Gujaratis number approximately 30 million and speak their own Indo-European language, Gujarati, which has a long literary tradition. They are predominantly Hindu (90%), with Muslim (8%) and Jain (2%) minorities.

Gujarati language member of the Indo-Iranian branch of the Indo-European language family, spoken in and around the state of Gujarat in W India. It is written in its own script, a variant of the Devanagari script used for Sanskrit and Hindi.

gulag Russian term for the system of prisons and labor camps used to silence dissidents and opponents of the Soviet regime.

In the Stalin era (1920s–1930s), thousands of prisoners died from the harsh conditions of these remote camps.

Gulf Cooperation Council (GCC) Arab organization for promoting peace in the Persian Gulf area, established 1981. Its declared purpose is "to bring about integration, coordination, and cooperation in economic, social, defense, and political affairs among Arab Gulf states." Its members include Bahrain, Kuwait, Oman, Qatar, Saudi Arabia, and the United Arab Emirates; its headquarters are in Riyadh, Saudi Arabia.

Gulfport city in SE Mississippi, on the Gulf of Mexico, W of Biloxi and E of New Orleans, Louisiana; seat of Harrison County and a port of entry to the US; population (1990) 40,700. It is a major shipping point for lumber, cotton, and food products.

Gulf States oil-rich countries sharing the coastline of the ⬦Persian Gulf (Bahrain, Iran, Iraq, Kuwait, Oman, Qatar, Saudi Arabia, and the United Arab Emirates). In the US, the term refers to those states bordering the Gulf of Mexico (Alabama, Florida, Louisiana, Mississippi, and Texas).

Gulf Stream warm ocean ⬦current that flows north from the warm waters of Gulf of Mexico. Part of the current is diverted east across the Atlantic, where it is known as the *North Atlantic Drift*, and warms what would otherwise be a colder climate in the British Isles and NW Europe.

Gulf War war Jan 16–Feb 28, 1991 between Iraq and a coalition of 28 nations led by the US. (It is also another name for the ⬦Iran–Iraq War). The invasion and annexation of Kuwait by Iraq on Aug 2, 1990 provoked a buildup of US troops in Saudi Arabia, eventually totaling over 500,000. The UK subsequently deployed 42,000 troops, France 15,000, Egypt 20,000, and other nations smaller contingents. An air offensive lasting six weeks, in which "smart" weapons came of age, destroyed about one-third of Iraqi equipment and inflicted massive casualties. A 100-hour ground war followed, which effectively destroyed the remnants of the 500,000-strong Iraqi army in or near Kuwait.

A dispute over a shared oil field and the price of oil was one of the main reasons for Iraq's invasion of Kuwait. Resolutions made in Aug 1990 by the United Nations Security Council for immediate withdrawal of Iraqi troops went unheeded, and a trade embargo and blockade were instituted. In Nov the US doubled its troop strength in Saudi Arabia to 400,000, and in Dec 1990 the UN Security Council authorized the use of force if Iraq did not withdraw before Jan 15, 1991. Talks between the US and Iraq failed, as did peace initiatives by the UN and France. By Jan 1991 coalition forces totaled some 725,000. Within 24 hours of the deadline, US and allied forces launched massive air bombardments against Baghdad, hitting strategic targets such as military air bases and communications systems. Saddam Hussein replied by firing missiles at the Israeli cities of Tel Aviv and Haifa (by which tactic he hoped to bring Israel into the war and thus break up the Arab alliance against him), as well as cities in Saudi Arabia; most of these missiles were intercepted.

The ground war started on Feb 24 and the superior range of the US artillery soon devastated the retreating Iraqi forces; by the end of Feb the war was over, Iraq defeated, and Kuwait once more independent, though under a pall of smoke from burning oil wells and facing extensive rebuilding.

Some 100,000 tons of ordnance was dropped by US planes on Iraq and occupied Kuwait, of which precision-guided weapons amounted to 7%; of these, 90% hit their targets whereas only 25% of the conventional bombs did so. British forces dropped 3,000 tons of ordnance, including 6,000 bombs, of which 1,000 were laser-guided. Napalm and fuel-air explosives were also used by coalition forces, but cluster bombs and multiple-launch rockets were predominant. The cost to the US of the war was $61.1 billion, including $43.1 billion contributed by the allies. Estimates of Iraqi casualties are in the range of 80,000–150,000 troops and 100,000–200,000 civilians.

The war created 2–3 million refugees. Severe environmental damage, including ⬦oil spills, and burning oil wells (ignited by retreating Iraqis), affected a large area.

gull seabird of the family Laridae, especially the genus *Larus*. Gulls are usually 10–30 in/25–75 cm long, white with gray or black on the back and wings, and have large beaks.

The common black-headed gull *L. ridibundus*, common on both sides of the Atlantic, is gray and white with (in summer) a dark brown head and a red beak; it breeds in large colonies on wetlands, making a nest of dead rushes and laying, on average, three eggs. The great black-headed gull *L. ichthyaetus* is native to Asia. The herring gull

L. argentatus, common in the northern hemisphere, has white and pearl-gray plumage and a yellow beak. The oceanic great black-backed gull *L. marinus*, found in the Atlantic, is over 75cm/2.5 ft long.

Gulliver's Travels satirical novel by the Irish writer Jonathan ⟡Swift published 1726. The four countries visited by the narrator Gulliver ridicule different aspects of human nature, customs, and politics.

gum in botany, complex polysaccharides (carbohydrates) formed by many plants and trees, particularly by those from dry regions. They form four main groups: plant exudates (gum arabic); marine plant extracts (agar); seed extracts; and fruit and vegetable extracts. Some are made synthetically.

Gums are tasteless and odorless, insoluble in alcohol and ether but generally soluble in water. They are used for adhesives, fabric sizing, in confectionery, medicine, and calico printing.

gum in mammals, the soft tissues surrounding the base of the teeth. Gums are liable to inflammation (gingivitis) or to infection by microbes from food deposits (periodontal disease).

gum arabic substance obtained from certain species of ⟡acacia, with uses in medicine, confectionery, and adhesive manufacture.

gun any kind of firearm or any instrument consisting of a metal tube from which a projectile is discharged; see also ⟡artillery, ⟡machine gun, ⟡pistol, and ⟡small arms.

gun metal type of ⟡bronze, an alloy high in copper (88%), also containing tin and zinc, so-called because it was once used to cast cannons. It is tough, hard-wearing, and resists corrosion.

gunpowder or *black powder* the oldest known ⟡explosive, a mixture of 75% potassium nitrate (saltpeter), 15% charcoal, and 10% sulfur. Sulfur ignites at a low temperature, charcoal burns readily, and the potassium nitrate provides oxygen for the explosion. Although progressively replaced since the late 19th century by high explosives, gunpowder is still widely used for quarry blasting, fuses, and fireworks.

Gunpowder Plot in British history, the Catholic conspiracy to blow up James I and his parliament on Nov 5, 1605. It was discovered through an anonymous letter. Guy ⟡Fawkes was found in the cellar beneath the Palace of Westminster, ready to fire a store of explosives. Several of the conspirators were killed, and Fawkes and seven others were executed.

The event is commemorated annually in England on Nov 5 by fireworks and burning "guys" on bonfires. The searching of the vaults of Parliament before the opening of each new session, however, was not instituted until the "Popish Plot" of 1678.

Guomindang Chinese National People's Party, founded 1894 by ⟡Sun Yat-sen, which overthrew the Manchu Empire 1912. From 1927 the right wing, led by ⟡Chiang Kai-shek, was in conflict with the left, led by Mao Zedong until the Communist victory 1949 (except for the period of the Japanese invasion 1937–45). It survives as the dominant political party of Taiwan, where it is still spelled *Kuomintang*.

Gurdjieff George Ivanovitch 1877–1949. Russian occultist and mystic who influenced the modern human-potential movement. His famous text is *Meetings with Remarkable*

Men (English translation 1963). The mystic Ouspensky was a disciple who expanded his ideas.

After years of wandering in central Asia, in 1912 Gurdjieff founded in Moscow the Institute for the Harmonious Development of Man, based on a system of raising consciousness (involving learning, group movement, manual labor, dance, and a minimum of sleep) known as the Fourth Way. After the 1917 Revolution he established similar schools in parts of Europe.

Gurkha member of a people living in the mountains of Nepal, whose young men have been recruited since 1815 for the British and Indian armies. They are predominantly Tibeto-Mongolians, but their language is Khas, a dialect of a northern Indic language.

guru Hindi *gurū* Hindu or Sikh leader, or religious teacher.

Gush Emunim (Hebrew "bloc of the faithful") Israeli fundamentalist group, founded 1973, which claims divine right to settlement of the West Bank, Gaza Strip, and Golan Heights as part of Israel. The claim is sometimes extended to the Euphrates.

Gustavus or *Gustaf* six kings of Sweden, including:

Gustavus I king of Sweden, better known as ⟡Gustavus Vasa.

Gustavus II king of Sweden, better known as ⟡Gustavus Adolphus.

Gustaf V 1858–1950. King of Sweden from 1907, when he succeeded his father Oscar II. He married Princess Victoria, daughter of the Grand Duke of Baden 1881, thus uniting the reigning Bernadotte dynasty with the former royal house of Vasa.

Gustaf VI 1882–1973. King of Sweden from 1950, when he succeeded his father Gustaf V. He was an archeologist and expert on Chinese art. He was succeeded by his grandson ⟡Carl XVI Gustaf.

Gustavus Adolphus (Gustavus II) 1594–1632. King of Sweden from 1611, when he succeeded his father Charles IX. He waged successful wars with Denmark, Russia, and Poland, and in the ⟡Thirty Years' War became a champion of the Protestant cause. Landing in Germany 1630, he defeated the German general Wallenstein at Lützen, SW of Leipzig Nov 6, 1632, but was killed in the battle. He was known as the "Lion of the North."

Gustavus Vasa (Gustavus I) 1496–1560. King of Sweden from 1523, when he was elected after leading the Swedish revolt against Danish rule. He united and pacified the country and established Lutheranism as the state religion.

gut or *alimentary canal* in the ⟡digestive system, the part of an animal responsible for processing food and preparing it for entry into the blood.

The gut consists of a tube divided into regions capable of performing different functions. The front end (the mouth) is adapted for food capture and for the first stages of digestion. The stomach is a storage area, although digestion of protein by the enzyme pepsin starts here; in many herbivorous mammals this is also the site of cellulose digestion. The small intestine follows the stomach and is specialized for digestion and for absorption. The large intestine, consisting of the colon, cecum, and rectum, has a variety of functions, including cellulose digestion, water absorption, and

storage of feces. The gut has an excellent blood supply, which carries digested food to the liver via the hepatic portal vein, ready for assimilation by the cells.

Gutenberg Johann *c.* 1400–1468. German printer, the inventor of printing from movable metal type, based on the Chinese wood-block-type method (although Laurens Janszoon ⟡Coster has a rival claim).

Gutenberg began work on the process in the 1440s and in 1450 set up a printing business in Mainz with Johann Fust (*c.* 1400–1466) as a backer. By 1455 he had produced the first printed Bible (known as the Gutenberg Bible). Fust seized the press for nonpayment of the loan, but Gutenberg is believed to have gone on to print the Mazarin and Bamberg bibles.

Guthrie Tyrone 1900–1971. British theater director, notable for his experimental approach. Administrator of the ⟡Old Vic and Sadler's Wells theaters 1939–45, he helped found the Ontario (Stratford) Shakespeare Festival 1953 and the Minneapolis theater now named after him.

Guthrie Woody (Woodrow Wilson) 1912–1967. US folk singer and songwriter whose left-wing protest songs, "dustbowl ballads," and "talking blues" influenced, among others, Bob Dylan; they include "Deportees," "Hard Travelin'," and "This Land Is Your Land."

gutta-percha juice of various tropical trees of the sapodilla family (such as the Malaysian *Palaquium gutta*), which can be hardened to form a flexible, rubbery substance used for electrical insulation, dentistry, and golf balls; it has now been largely replaced by synthetics.

guttation secretion of water on to the surface of leaves through specialized pores, or ⟡hydathodes. The process occurs most frequently during conditions of high humidity when the rate of transpiration is low. Drops of water found on grass in early morning are often the result of guttation, rather than dew. Sometimes the water contains minerals in solution, such as calcium, which leaves a white crust on the leaf surface as it dries.

Guyana country in South America, bounded N by the Atlantic Ocean, E by Suriname, S and SW by Brazil, and NW by Venezuela.

government Guyana is a sovereign republic within the British ⟡Commonwealth. The 1980 constitution provides for a single-chamber national assembly of 65 members, 53 elected by universal suffrage and 12 elected by the regions, for a five-year term. The president is the nominee of the party winning most votes in the national assembly elections and serves for the life of the assembly, appointing a cabinet that is collectively responsible to it.

history Inhabited by Arawak, Carib, and Warrau Indians when the first Europeans arrived in the late 1500s, the area now known as Guyana was a Dutch colony 1621–1796, when it was seized by Britain. Ceded to Britain 1814, it was made a British colony 1831 under the name of British Guiana and became part of the Commonwealth until full independence 1966.

The transition from colonial to republican status was gradual and not entirely smooth. In 1953 a constitution providing for free elections to an assembly was introduced, and the left-wing People's Progressive Party (PPP), led by Dr Cheddi Jagan, won the popular vote. Within months, however, the UK government suspended the constitution and put in its own interim administration, claiming that the PPP threatened to become a communist dictatorship.

internal self-government In 1957 a breakaway group from the PPP founded a new party, the People's National Congress (PNC), which was supported mainly by Guyanans of African descent, while PPP followers were mainly of Indian descent. Fresh elections, under a revised constitution, were held 1957, and the PPP won again, with Jagan becoming chief minister. Internal self-government was granted 1961 and, with the PPP again the successful party, Jagan became prime minister. Proportional representation was introduced 1963, and in the 1964 elections (under the new voting procedures) the PPP, although winning most votes, did not have an overall majority, resulting in the formation of a PPP–PNC coalition with PNC leader Forbes Burnham as prime minister.

after independence This coalition took the country through to full independence 1966. The PNC won the 1968 and 1973 elections; in 1970 Guyana became a republic within the Commonwealth. In 1980 a new constitution was adopted, making the president head of both state and government, and as a result of the 1981 elections—which opposition parties claimed were fraudulent—Burnham became executive president. The rest of his administration was marked by economic deterioration (necessitating austerity measures) and cool relations with the Western powers, particularly the US, whose invasion of Grenada he condemned. He died 1985 and was succeeded by Prime Minister Desmond Hoyte.

Guyana
Cooperative Republic of

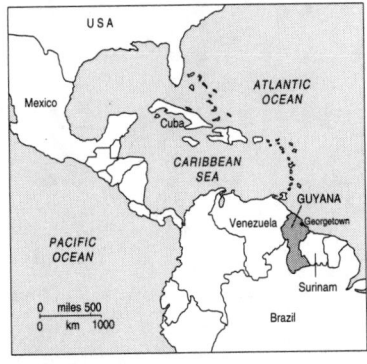

area 82,978 sq mi/214,969 sq km
capital and port Georgetown
cities New Amsterdam, Mabaruma
physical coastal plain rises into rolling highlands with savanna in S; mostly tropical rainforest
features Mount Roraima; Kaietur National Park, including Kaietur Fall on the Potaro (tributary of Essequibo) 821 ft/ 250 m
head of state Desmond Hoyte from 1985
head of government Cheddi Jagan from 1992
political system democratic republic
political parties People's National Congress (PNC), Afro-Guyanan nationalist socialist; People's Progressive Party (PPP), Indian Marxist-Leninist
exports sugar, rice, rum, timber, diamonds, bauxite, shrimps, molasses

return of Jagan In the Aug 1992 general election, the PPP had a decisive win and its veteran leader, Cheddi Jagan, became prime minister. *See illustration box.*

guyot truncated or flat-topped seamount. Such undersea mountains are found throughout the abyssal plains of major ocean basins, and most of them are covered by an appreciable depth of water. They are believed to have started as volcanic cones formed near mid-oceanic ridges, in relatively shallow water, and to have been truncated by wave action as their tops emerged above the surface. They were then transported to deeper waters as the ocean floor moved away on either side of the ridge.

Guzmán Blanco Antonio 1829–1899. Venezuelan dictator and military leader (*caudillo*), who seized power 1870 and remained absolute ruler until 1889. He modernized Caracas to become the political capital; committed resources to education, communications, and agriculture; and encouraged foreign trade.

Gwent county in S Wales
area 533 sq mi/1,380 sq km
cities Cwmbran (administrative headquarters), Abergavenny, Newport, Tredegar
features Wye Valley; Tintern Abbey; Legionary Museum at Caerleon, and Roman amphitheater; Chepstow and Raglan castles
products salmon and trout from the Wye and Usk rivers; iron and steel at Llanwern
population (1991) 432,300
language 2.5% Welsh, English

Gwyn Nell (Eleanor) 1651–1687. English

currency Guyanese dollar
population (1989 est) 846,000 (51% descendants of workers introduced from India to work the sugar plantations after the abolition of slavery, 30% black, 5% Amerindian); growth rate 2% p.a.
life expectancy men 66, women 71
languages English (official), Hindi, Amerindian
media one government-owned daily newspaper; one independent paper published three times a week, on which the government puts pressure by withholding foreign exchange for newsprint; one weekly independent in the same position. There is also legislation that restricts exchange of information between public officials, government, and the press
religions Christian 57%, Hindu 33%, Sunni Muslim 9%
literacy men 97%, women 95% (1985 est)
GNP $359 million (1987); $445 per head
chronology
1831 Became British colony under name of British Guiana.
1953 Assembly elections won by left-wing PPP; Britain suspended constitution and installed interim administration, fearing communist takeover.
1961 Internal self-government granted; Cheddi Jagan became prime minister.
1964 PNC leader Forbes Burnham led PPP-PNC coalition.
1966 Independence achieved from Britain.
1970 Guyana became a republic within the Commonwealth.
1981 Forbes Burnham became first executive president under new constitution.
1985 Burnham died; succeeded by Desmond Hoyte.
1992 PPP had decisive victory in assembly elections; Jagan returned as prime minister.

comedy actress from 1665, formerly an orange-seller at Drury Lane Theater, London. The poet Dryden wrote parts for her, and from 1669 she was the mistress of Charles II.

Gwynedd county in NW Wales
area 1,494 sq mi/3,870 sq km
cities Caernarvon (administrative headquarters), Bangor
products cattle, sheep, gold (at Dolgellau), textiles, electronics, slate
population (1991) 238,600
language 61% Welsh, English
features Snowdonia National Park including Snowdon, the highest mountain in Wales 3,561 ft/1,085 m, and the largest Welsh lake, Llyn Tegid (Bala Lake); Caernarvon Castle.

gymnastics physical exercises, originally for health and training (so-called from the way in which men of ancient Greece trained: *gymnos* "naked"). The *gymnasia* were schools for training competitors for public games. **Men's gymnastics** includes high bar, parallel bars, horse vault, rings, pommel horse, and floor exercises. **Women's gymnastics** includes asymmetrical bars, side horse vault, balance beam, and floor exercises. Also popular are sports acrobatics, performed by gymnasts in pairs, trios, or fours to music, where the emphasis is on dance, balance, and timing, and *rhythmic gymnastics*, choreographed to music and performed by individuals or six-girl teams, with small hand apparatus such as a ribbon, ball, or hoop.

Gymnastics was first revived in 19th-century Germany as an aid to military strength, and was also taken up by educators including ⟡Froebel and ⟡Pestalozzi, becoming a recognized part of the school curriculum. Today it is a popular spectator sport.

gymnosperm (Greek "naked seed") in botany, any plant whose seeds are exposed, as opposed to the structurally more advanced ⟡angiosperms, where they are inside an ovary. The group includes conifers and related plants such as cycads and ginkgos, whose seeds develop in ⟡cones. Fossil gymnosperms have been found in rocks about 350 million years old.

gynecology in medicine, a specialist branch concerned with disorders of the female reproductive system.

gynoecium or *gynaecium* collective term for the female reproductive organs of a flower, consisting of one or more ⟡carpels, either free or fused together.

gypsum common ⟡mineral, composed of hydrous calcium sulfate, $CaSO_4 \cdot 2H_2O$. It ranks 2 on the Mohs' scale of hardness. Gypsum is used for making casts and molds, and for blackboard chalk.

A fine-grained gypsum, called *alabaster*, is used for ornamental work. Burned gypsum is known as *plaster of Paris*, because for a long time it was obtained from the gypsum quarries of the Montmartre district of Paris.

Gypsy English name for a member of the ⟡Romany people.

gyre circular surface rotation of ocean water in each major sea (a type of ⟡current). Gyres are large and permanent, and occupy the N and S halves of the three major oceans. Their movements are dictated by the prevailing winds and the ⟡Coriolis effect. Gyres move clockwise in the northern hemisphere and counterclockwise in the southern hemisphere.

gyroscope mechanical instrument, used as a stabilizing device and consisting, in its simplest form, of a heavy wheel mounted on an axis fixed in a ring that can be rotated about another axis, which is also fixed in a ring capable of rotation about a third axis. Applications of the gyroscope principle include the gyrocompass, the gyropilot for automatic steering, and gyro-directed torpedoes.

The components of the gyroscope are arranged so that the three axes of rotation in any position pass through the wheel's center of gravity. The wheel is thus capable of rotation about three mutually perpendicular axes, and its axis may take up any direction. If the axis of the spinning wheel is displaced, a restoring movement develops, returning it to its initial direction.

H eighth letter of the English alphabet, representing an aspirate in all modern alphabets derived from the Latin except in those languages, especially the Romance languages, where the aspirate is lost. It is used in several diagraphs (conventional two-letter sequences with special values), such as *ch*, *ph*, *sh*, and *th*.

Haakon seven kings of Norway, including:

Haakon I *the Good* c. 915–961. King of Norway from about 935. The son of Harald Hárfagri ("Finehair") (c. 850–930), king of Norway, he was raised in England. He seized the Norwegian throne and tried unsuccessfully to introduce Christianity there. His capital was at Trondheim.

Haakon IV 1204–1263. King of Norway from 1217, the son of Haakon III. Under his rule, Norway flourished both militarily and culturally; he took control of the Faroe Islands, Greenland 1261, and Iceland 1262–64. His court was famed throughout N Europe.

Haakon VII 1872–1957. King of Norway from 1905. Born Prince Charles, the second son of Frederick VIII of Denmark, he was elected king of Norway on separation from Sweden, and in 1906 he took the name Haakon. In World War II he carried on the resistance from Britain during the Nazi occupation of his country. He returned 1945.

Haarlem industrial city and capital of North Holland, the Netherlands, 12 mi/20 km W of Amsterdam; population (1991) 149,500. At Velsea to the north a road-rail tunnel runs under the North Sea Canal, linking North and South Holland. Industries include chemicals, pharmaceuticals, textiles, and printing. Haarlem is renowned for flowering bulbs and has a 15th–16th-century cathedral and a Frans Hals museum.

Habakkuk prophet in, and book of, the Old Testament.

habanera or *havanaise* slow dance in two-four time, originating in Havana, Cuba, which was introduced into Spain during the 19th century. There is a celebrated example of this dance in Bizet's opera *Carmen*.

habeas corpus (Latin "you may have the body") in law, a writ directed to someone who has custody of a person, ordering him or her to bring the person before the court issuing the writ and to justify why the person is detained in custody.

Traditional rights to habeas corpus were embodied in law mainly caused by Lord ◊Shaftesbury, in the English Habeas Corpus Act 1679. The main principles were adopted in the US Constitution.

Haber Fritz 1868–1934. German chemist whose conversion of atmospheric nitrogen to ammonia opened the way for the synthetic fertilizer industry. His study of the combustion of hydrocarbons led to the commercial "cracking" or fractional distillation of natural oil (petroleum) into its components (for example, diesel, gasoline, and paraffin). In electrochemistry, he was the first to demonstrate that oxidation and reduction take place at the electrodes; from this he developed a general electrochemical theory.

In World War I he worked on poison gas and devised gas masks, hence there were protests against his Nobel Prize 1918.

Haber process industrial process in which ammonia is manufactured by direct combination of its elements, nitrogen and hydrogen. The reaction is carried out at 752–932°F/400–500°C and at 200 atmospheric pressure. The two gases, in the proportions of 1:3 by volume, are passed over a ◊catalyst of finely divided iron. Around 10% of the reactants combine, and the unused gases are recycled. The ammonia is separated by either dissolving in water or cooling to liquid ($N_2 + 3H_2 \rightleftharpoons 2NH_3$).

habitat in ecology, the localized ◊environment in which an organism lives. Habitats are often described by the dominant plant type or physical feature, such as a grassland habitat or rocky seashore habitat.

Habsburg European royal family; see ◊Hapsburg.

hacking unauthorized access to a computer, either for fun or for malicious or fraudulent purposes. Hackers generally use microcomputers and telephone lines to obtain access. In computing, the term is used in a wider sense to mean using software for enjoyment or self-education, not necessarily involving unauthorized access. See also computer ◊virus.

Hackman Gene 1931– . US actor. He became a star as "Popeye" Doyle in *The French Connection* 1971 and continued to play major combative roles in such films as *The Conversation* 1974, *The French Connection II* 1975, and *Mississippi Burning* 1988.

haddock marine fish *Melanogrammus aeglefinus* of the cod family found off the N Atlantic coast. It is brown with silvery underparts and black markings above the pectoral fins. It can grow to a length of 3 ft/1 m. Haddock are important food fish; about 100 million lb/45 million kg are taken annually off the New England fishing banks alone.

Hades in Greek mythology, the underworld where spirits went after death, usually depicted as a cavern or pit underneath the Earth, the entrance of which was guarded by the three-headed dog Cerberus. It was presided over by the god Hades or Pluto (Roman Dis). Hades was the brother of Zeus and married ◊Persephone, daughter of Demeter and Zeus.

Tartarus was the section where the wicked were punished, for example, Tantalus.

Hadith collection of the teachings of ◊Mohammed and stories about his life, regarded by Muslims as a guide to living second only to the ◊Koran.

The teachings were at first transmitted orally, but this led to a large number of Hadiths whose origin was in doubt; later, scholars such as Mohammed al-Bukhari (810–870) collected together those believed to be authentic, and these collections form the Hadith accepted by Muslims today.

Hadrian AD 76–138. Roman emperor from 117. Born in Spain, he was adopted by his relative, the emperor Trajan, whom he succeeded. He abandoned Trajan's conquests in Mesopotamia and adopted a defensive policy, which included the building of Hadrian's Wall in Britain.

Hadrian's Wall Roman fortification built AD 122–126 to mark England's northern boundary and abandoned about 383; its ruins run 115 mi/185 km from Wallsend on the river Tyne to Maryport, W Cumbria. In some parts, the wall was covered with a glistening, white coat of mortar. The fort at South Shields, Arbeia, built to defend the eastern end, is being reconstructed.

hadron in physics, a subatomic particle that experiences the strong nuclear force. Each is made up of two or three indivisible particles called quarks. The hadrons are grouped into the ◊baryons (protons, neutrons, and hyperons) and the ◊mesons (particles with masses between those of electrons and protons). Since the 1960s, particle physicists' main interest has been the elucidation of hadron structure.

Hâfiz Shams al-Din Mohammed c. 1326–1390. Persian lyric poet who was born in Shiraz and taught in a Dervish college there. His *Diwan*, a collection of short odes, extols the pleasures of life and satirizes his fellow Dervishes.

hafnium (Latin *Hafnia* "Copenhagen") silvery, metallic element, symbol Hf, atomic number 72, atomic weight 178.49. It occurs in nature in ores of zirconium, the properties of which it resembles. Hafnium absorbs neutrons better than most metals, so it is used in the control rods of nuclear reactors; it is also used for light-bulb filaments.

It was named in 1923 by Dutch physicist Dirk Coster (1889–1950) and Hungarian chemist Georg von Hevesy after the city of Copenhagen, where the element was discovered.

Haganah Zionist military organization in Palestine. It originated under the Turkish rule of the Ottoman Empire before World War I to protect Jewish settlements, and many of its members served in the British forces in both world wars. After World War II it condemned guerrilla activity, opposing the British authorities only passively. It formed the basis of the Israeli army after Israel was established 1948.

Hagerstown city in NW Maryland, on Antietam creek, NW of Baltimore and just S of the Pennsylvania border. Industries include engine and missile parts and furniture; population (1980) 34,132.

Haggadah in Judaism, the part of the Talmudic literature not concerned with religious law (the *Halakah*), but devoted to folklore and legends of heroes.

Haggai minor Old Testament prophet (lived c. 520 BC) who promoted the rebuilding of the Temple in Jerusalem.

Haggard H(enry) Rider 1856–1925. English novelist. He used his experience in the South African colonial service in his romantic adventure tales, including *King Solomon's Mines* 1885 and *She* 1887.

haggis Scottish dish made from a sheep's or calf's heart, liver, and lungs, minced with onion, oatmeal, suet, spices, and salt, mixed with stock, and traditionally boiled in the animal's stomach for several hours.

Hagia Sophia (Greek "holy wisdom") Byzantine building in Istanbul, Turkey, built 532–37 as an Eastern Orthodox cathedral, replacing earlier churches. From 1204 to 1261 it was a Catholic cathedral; 1453–1934 an Islamic mosque; and in 1934 it became a museum.

Hagler Marvin 1954– . US boxer who was the undisputed world middleweight champion from 1980 to 1987. He won 13 of his 15 world title fights, losing only to Sugar Ray Leonard.

Hague, The (Dutch *'s-Gravenhage* or *Den Haag*) capital of South Holland and seat of the Netherlands government, linked by canal with Rotterdam and Amsterdam; population (1991) 444,200. It is also the seat of the United Nations International Court of Justice.

The seaside resort of *Scheveningen* (patronized by Wilhelm II and Winston Churchill), with its Kurhaus, is virtually incorporated.

Hahn Otto 1879–1968. West German physical chemist who discovered nuclear fission (see ⟡nuclear energy). In 1938 with Fritz Strassmann (1902–1980), he discovered that uranium nuclei split when bombarded with neutrons, which led to the development of the atomic bomb. He was awarded the Nobel Prize for Chemistry 1944.

He worked with Ernest Rutherford and William Ramsay, and became director of the Kaiser Wilhelm Institute for Chemistry 1928.

hahnium name proposed by US scientists for the element also known as ⟡unnilpentium (atomic number 105), in honor of German nuclear physicist Otto Hahn. The symbol is Ha.

Haifa port in NE Israel; population (1988) 222,600. Industries include oil refining and chemicals.

Haig Alexander (Meigs) 1924– . US general and Republican politician. He became President Nixon's White House Chief of Staff at the height of the ⟡Watergate scandal, was NATO commander 1974–79, and secretary of state to President Reagan 1981–82.

haiku seventeen-syllable Japanese verse form, usually divided into three lines of five, seven, and five syllables. ⟡Bashō popularized the form in the 17th century. It evolved from the 31-syllable *tanka* form dominant from the 8th century.

hail precipitation in the form of pellets of ice (hailstones). It is caused by the circulation of moisture in strong convection currents, usually within cumulonimbus ⟡clouds.

Water droplets freeze as they are carried upward. As the circulation continues, layers of ice are deposited around the droplets until they become too heavy to be supported by the currents and they fall as a hailstorm.

Haile Selassie Ras (Prince) Tafari ("the Lion of Judah") 1892–1975. Emperor of Ethiopia 1930–74. He pleaded unsuccessfully to the League of Nations against Italian conquest of his country 1935–36, and lived in the UK until his restoration 1941. He was deposed by a military coup 1974 and died in captivity the following year. Followers of the Rastafarian religion (see ⟡Rastafarianism) believe that he was the Messiah, the incarnation of God (Jah).

Hainan island in the South China Sea;

Haiti
Republic of (*République d'Haïti*)

area 10,712 sq mi/27,750 sq km
capital Port-au-Prince
cities Cap-Haïtien, Gonaïves, Les Cayes
physical mainly mountainous and tropical; occupies W third of Hispaniola Island in Caribbean Sea; seriously deforested
features oldest black republic in the world; only French-speaking republic in the Americas; island of La Tortuga off N coast was formerly a pirate lair
interim head of state Joseph Nerette from 1991
head of government Marc Bazin from 1992
political system transitional
political party National Progressive Party (PNP), right-wing military
exports coffee, sugar, sisal, cotton, cocoa, bauxite
currency gourde
population (1990 est) 6,409,000; growth rate 1.7% p.a.; one of highest population densities in the world; about 1.5 million Haitians live outside Haiti (in US and Canada);

about 400,000 live in virtual slavery in the Dominican Republic, where they went or were sent to cut sugar cane
life expectancy men 51, women 54
languages French (official, spoken by literate 10% minority), Creole (spoken by 90% black majority)
religion Christian 95% of which 80% Roman Catholic, voodoo 4%
literacy men 40%, women 35% (1985 est)
GDP $2.2 bn (1987); $414 per head
chronology
1804 Independence achieved from France.
1915 Haiti invaded by US; remained under US control until 1934.
1957 Dr François Duvalier (Papa Doc) elected president.
1964 Duvalier pronounced himself president for life.
1971 Duvalier died, succeeded by his son, Jean-Claude (Baby Doc); thousands murdered during Duvalier era.
1986 Duvalier deposed; replaced by Lt Gen Henri Namphy as head of a governing council.
1988 Feb: Leslie Manigat became president. Namphy staged a military coup in June, but another coup in Sept led by Brig Gen Prosper Avril replaced him with a civilian government under military control.
1989 Coup attempt against Avril foiled; US aid resumed.
1990 Opposition elements expelled; Ertha Pascal-Trouillot acting president.
1991 Jean-Bertrand Aristide elected president but later overthrown in military coup led by Brig Gen Raoul Cedras. Efforts to reinstate Aristide failed. Joseph Nerette became interim head of state.
1992 Economic sanctions imposed since 1991 were eased by the US but increased by the Organization of American States (OAS). Marc Bazin appointed premier.

area 13,124 sq mi/34,000 sq km; population (1990) 6,557,000. The capital is Haikou. In 1987 Hainan was designated a Special Economic Zone; in 1988 it was separated from Guangdong and made a new province. It is China's second largest island.

Hainaut industrial province of SW Belgium; capital Mons; area 1,467 sq mi/3,800 sq km; population (1991) 1,278,800. It produces coal, iron, and steel.

Haiphong industrial port in N Vietnam; population (1989) 456,000. Among its industries are shipbuilding and the making of cement, plastics, phosphates, and textiles.

hair threadlike structure growing from mammalian skin. Each hair grows from a pit-shaped follicle of the outer skin layer (epidermal cells). Hair consists of dead cells impregnated with the protein keratin.

There are about a million hairs on the average person's head. Each grows at the rate of 0.2–0.4 in/5–10 mm per month, lengthening for about three years before being replaced by a new one. A coat of hair helps to insulate mammals by trapping air next to the body. It also aids in camouflage, and its coloring or erection may be used for communication.

hairstreak any of a group of butterflies, belonging to the family Lycaenidae, to which blues and coppers also belong. Hairstreaks live in both temperate and tropical regions. Most

of them are brownish or grayish-blue with hairlike tips at the end of their hind wings.

Haiti country in the Caribbean, occupying the W part of the island of Hispaniola; to the E is the Dominican Republic.
government The 1950 constitution was revised 1957, 1964, 1971, 1983, 1985, and 1987. The 1987 constitution provides for a 27-member senate and 77-member chamber of deputies, all popularly elected, as well as a "dual executive" of a president and prime minister sharing power; but in practice dictatorship has prevailed.
history The island of Hispaniola was once inhabited by ⟡Arawak Indians who had died out by the end of the 16th century owing to conquest, warfare, hard labor, and diseases brought in by the Europeans after the arrival of Christopher Columbus 1492. The island was made a Spanish colony under the name of Santo Domingo, but the western part was colonized by France from the mid-17th century. In 1697 the western third of the island was ceded to France by Spain.
independence achieved The period 1790–1804 was fraught with rebellions against France, tension among blacks, whites, and mulattos, and military intervention by France and Britain. In one such rebellion 1791 the island was taken over by slaves, under ⟡Toussaint L'Ouverture, and slavery was abolished, but it was then reinstated after he was killed

by the French. After independence 1804 the instability continued, with Santo Domingo repossessed by Spain and then by Haiti, and self-proclaimed kings ruling Haiti. In 1844 Haiti and the Dominican Republic became separate states.

Duvalier era Friction between Haitians of African descent and mulattos, and the country's political instability, brought a period of US rule 1915–34. In the 1940s and 1950s there were several coups, the last occurring 1956, which resulted in Dr François Duvalier, a physician, being elected president. After an encouraging start, his administration degenerated into a personal dictatorship, maintained by a private army, the Tontons Macoutes. In 1964 "Papa Doc" Duvalier made himself president for life, with the power to nominate his son as his successor.

On his father's death 1971 Jean-Claude ◊Duvalier came to the presidency at the age of 19 and soon acquired the name of "Baby Doc." Although the young Duvalier repeatedly promised a return to democracy, and his rule was judged to be less despotic than his father's, there was little change. In the 1984 elections about 300 government candidates contested the 59 seats, with no opposition at all. In 1985, political parties were legalized, provided they conformed to strict guidelines, but only one party registered, the National Progressive Party (PNP), which supported Duvalier's policies. He was overthrown and exiled to France 1986.

democratization failed The new military regime led by Lt Gen Henri Namphy offered no protection to the electoral council, and the US government withdrew aid. Elections Nov 1987 were sabotaged by armed gangs of Duvalierists who massacred voters and set fire to polling places and to vehicles delivering ballot papers in the country. Leslie Manigat, with army support, was made president Feb 1988 but four months later was ousted in a coup led by Namphy, who was in turn replaced by Brig Gen Prosper Avril in a coup Sept 1988. Avril installed a largely civilian government, but the army was still in control and a coup attempt April 1989 was quickly put down. Although his regime continued to be criticized by human-rights organizations, the US government resumed food aid Aug 1989. Early in 1990 opposition to Avril grew, but was quickly suppressed. In Aug and Sept 1990 acting president Ertha Pascal-Trouillot defied calls for her resignation, but elections were held in Dec. Jean-Bertrand Aristide, a Catholic priest, won a landslide victory and in Feb 1991, as president, dismissed the entire army high command, with the exception of General Hérard Abraham, who had earlier permitted Haiti's first free elections.

Aristide ousted A military coup, led by Brig Gen Raoul Cedras, overthrew Aristide in Sept 1991. In the following month, the army appointed Joseph Nerette as interim president, with Jean Jacques Honorat as prime minister. There was international condemnation of the coup but efforts to reinstate Aristide failed. Nerette's term of office was extended indefinitely. In early 1992 the US began to modify its 1991 sanctions on Haiti, in an effort to create more jobs there. The Organization of American States (OAS), however, increased its sanctions in May. Marc Bazin replaced Honorat as prime minister in June 1992. *See illustration box.*

Haitink Bernard 1929– . Dutch conductor. He was chief conductor of the Concertgebouw Orchestra, Amsterdam, 1959–86; of the London Philharmonic Orchestra 1967–78; and of the Royal Opera House, Covent Garden, London, from 1983, becoming its music director 1986.

hajj pilgrimage to ◊Mecca that should be undertaken by every Muslim at least once in a lifetime, unless he or she is prevented by financial or health difficulties. A Muslim who has been on hajj may take the additional name Hajji. Many of the pilgrims on hajj also visit Medina, where the prophet Mohammed is buried.

hake any of various marine fishes of the cod family, found in N European, African, and American waters. They have silvery, elongated bodies and attain a length of 3 ft/1 m. They have two dorsal fins and one long anal fin. The silver hake *Merluccius bilinearis* is an important food fish.

Hakluyt Richard 1553–1616. English geographer whose chief work is *The Principal Navigations, Voyages and Discoveries of the English Nation* 1598–1600. He was assisted by Sir Walter Raleigh.

He lectured on cartography at Oxford, became geographical adviser to the East India Company, and was an original member of the Virginia Company.

halal (Arabic "lawful") conforming to the rules laid down by Islam. The term can be applied to all aspects of life, but usually refers to food permissible under Muslim dietary laws, including meat from animals that have been slaughtered in the correct ritual fashion.

Halas George Stanley 1895–1983. US athlete and sports promoter. He devoted himself to professional football from 1921. He was the founder of the Chicago Bears of the National Football League and was an active player until 1929. As coach until retirement 1967, Halas introduced the T-formation and laid special emphasis on the passing offense. He became a charter member of the Football Hall of Fame 1963.

Born in Chicago and educated at the University of Illinois, where he was an exceptional athlete, Halas worked briefly as a railroad engineer and in 1919 briefly played professional baseball for the New York Yankees.

Haldane J(ohn) B(urdon) S(anderson) 1892–1964. English scientist and writer. A geneticist, Haldane was better known as a popular science writer of such books as *The Causes of Evolution* 1933 and *New Paths in Genetics* 1941.

Hale George Ellery 1868–1938. US astronomer who made pioneer studies of the Sun and founded three major observatories. In 1889 he invented the spectroheliograph, a device for photographing the Sun at particular wavelengths. In 1917 he established on Mount Wilson, California, a 100-in/2.5-m reflector, the world's largest telescope until superseded 1948 by the 200-in/5-m reflector on Mount Palomar, which Hale had planned just before he died.

In 1897 he founded the Yerkes Observatory in Wisconsin, with the largest refractor, 40 in/102 cm, ever built at that time.

Hale Nathan 1755–1776. American Revolutionary War hero, hanged by the British as a spy. He crossed British lines disguised as a teacher and told George ◊Washington that he wished "to be useful." He was sent behind enemy lines on Long Island to gather information about the British army. Captured, he was hanged. Reputedly his final words were "I only regret that I have but one life to lose for my country."

Born in Coventry, Connecticut, Hale graduated from Yale 1773 and became a schoolteacher. He fought with the Connecticut militia in the American Revolution.

Halévy Ludovic 1834–1908. French novelist and librettist. He collaborated with Hector Crémieux in the libretto for Offenbach's *Orpheus in the Underworld*; and with Henri Meilhac on librettos for Offenbach's *La Belle Hélène* and *La Vie Parisienne*, as well as for Bizet's *Carmen*.

Haley Bill 1927–1981. US pioneer of rock and roll who was originally a western-swing musician. His songs "Rock Around the Clock" 1954 (recorded with his group the Comets and featured in the 1955 film *Blackboard Jungle*) and "Shake, Rattle and Roll" 1955 became anthems of the early rock-and-roll era.

half-life in physics, the time taken for half the nuclei in a sample of a radioactive isotope to disintegrate. It may vary from millionths of a second to billions of years, even among different isotopes of the same element.

Radioactive substances decay exponentially; thus the time taken for the first 50% of the isotope to decay will be the same as the time taken by the next 25%, and by the 12.5% after that, and so on. For example, carbon-14 takes about 5,730 years for half the material to decay; another 5,730 for half of the remaining half to decay; then 5,730 years for half of that remaining half to decay, and so on. Plutonium-239, one of the most toxic of all radioactive substances, has a half-life of about 24,000 years. In theory, the decay process is never complete and there is always some residual radioactivity. For this reason, the half-life (the time taken for 50% of the isotope to decay) is measured, rather than the total decay time.

halftone process technique used in printing to reproduce the full range of tones in a photograph or other illustration. The intensity of the printed color is varied from full strength to the lightest shades, even if one color of ink is used. The picture to be reproduced is photographed through a screen ruled with a rectangular mesh of fine lines, which breaks up the tones of the original into areas of dots that vary in frequency according to the intensity of the tone. In the darker areas the dots run together; in the lighter areas they have more space between them.

halibut any of several large flatfishes of the genus *Hippoglossus*, in the family Pleuronectidae, found in the Atlantic and Pacific oceans. The largest of the flatfishes, they may grow to 6 ft/2 m and weigh 200–300 lb/90–135 kg. They are very dark mottled brown or green above and pure white beneath. The Atlantic halibut *H. hippoglossus* is caught offshore at depths from 600 ft/180 m to 2,400 ft/730 m.

Halicarnassus ancient city in Asia Minor (now Bodrum in Turkey), where the tomb of Mausolus, built about 350 BC by widowed Queen Artemisia, was one of the Seven Wonders of the World. The Greek historian Herodotus was born there.

halide any compound produced by the combination of a ◊halogen, such as chlorine or iodine, with a less electronegative element (see ◊electronegativity). Halides may be formed by ionic or ◊covalent bonds.

Halifax capital of Nova Scotia, E Canada's main port; population (1986) 296,000. Its industries include oil refining and food processing. There are six military bases in Halifax and it is a major center of oceanography. It was founded by British settlers 1749.

Halifax Charles Montagu, Earl of Halifax 1661–1715. British financier. Appointed commissioner of the Treasury 1692, he raised money for the French war by instituting the National Debt and in 1694 carried out William Paterson's plan for a national bank (the Bank of England) and became chancellor of the Exchequer.

Halifax Edward Frederick Lindley Wood, Earl of Halifax 1881–1959. British Conservative politician, viceroy of India 1926–31. As foreign secretary 1938–40 he was associated with Chamberlain's "appeasement" policy. He received an earldom 1944 for services to the Allied cause while ambassador to the US 1941–46.

halite mineral sodium chloride, NaCl, or common ⬙salt. When pure it is colorless and transparent, but it is often pink, red, or yellow. It is soft and has a low density.

Halite occurs naturally in evaporite deposits that have precipitated on evaporation of bodies of salt water. As rock salt, it forms beds within a sedimentary sequence; it can also migrate upward through surrounding rocks to form salt domes. It crystallizes in the cubic system.

halitosis bad breath. It may be caused by poor oral hygiene; disease of the mouth, throat, nose, or lungs; or disturbance of the digestion.

Hall Charles 1863–1914. US chemist who developed a process for the commercial production of aluminum 1886.

He found that when mixed with cryolite (sodium aluminum fluoride), the melting point of aluminum was lowered and electrolysis became commercially viable. It had previously been as costly as gold. By 1890, Hall was in charge of the Aluminum Company of the US and aluminum utensils began to spread throughout the world.

Hall Peter (Reginald Frederick) 1930– . English theater, opera, and film director. He was director of the Royal Shakespeare Theatre in Stratford-on-Avon 1960–68 and developed the Royal Shakespeare Company 1968–73 until appointed director of the National Theatre 1973–88, succeeding Laurence Olivier. He founded the Peter Hall Company 1988.

Hall's stage productions include *Waiting for Godot* 1955, *The Wars of the Roses* 1963, *The Homecoming* stage 1967 and film 1973, *The Oresteia* 1981, and *Orpheus Descending* 1988. He was appointed artistic director of opera at Glyndebourne 1984, with productions of *Carmen* 1985 and *Albert Herring* 1985–86.

Hall effect production of a voltage across a conductor or semiconductor carrying a current at a right angle to a surrounding magnetic field. It was discovered 1897 by the US physicist Edwin Hall (1855–1938). It is used in the *Hall probe* for measuring the strengths of magnetic fields and in magnetic switches.

Haller Albrecht von 1708–1777. Swiss physician and scientist, founder of ⬙neurology. He studied the muscles and nerves, and concluded that nerves provide the stimulus that triggers muscle contraction. He also showed that it is the nerves, not muscle or skin, that receive sensation.

Halley Edmond 1656–1742. English scientist. In 1682 he observed the comet named after him, predicting that it would return 1759.

Halley's other astronomical achievements include the discovery that stars have their own ⬙proper motion. He was a pioneer geophysicist and meteorologist and worked in many other fields including mathematics. He was a friend of Isaac ⬙Newton, whose *Principia* he financed.

Halley's comet comet that orbits the Sun about every 76 years, named after Edmond Halley who calculated its orbit. It is the brightest and most conspicuous of the periodic comets. Recorded sightings go back over 2,000 years. It travels around the Sun in the opposite direction to the planets. Its orbit is inclined at almost 20° to the main plane of the Solar System and ranges between the orbits of Venus and Neptune. It will next reappear 2061.

The comet was studied by space probes at its last appearance 1986. The European probe *Giotto* showed that the nucleus of Halley's comet is a tiny and irregularly shaped chunk of ice, measuring some 10 mi/15 km long by 5 mi/8 km wide, coated by a layer of very dark material, thought to be composed of carbon-rich compounds. This surface coating has a very low ⬙albedo, reflecting just 4% of the light it receives from the Sun. Although the comet is one of the darkest objects known, it has a glowing head and tail produced by jets of gas from fissures in the outer dust layer. These vents cover 10% of the total surface area and become active only when exposed to the Sun. The force of these jets affects the speed of the comet's travel in its orbit.

hallmark official mark stamped on British gold, silver, and (from 1913) platinum, instituted 1327 (royal charter of London Goldsmiths) in order to prevent fraud. After 1363, personal marks of identification were added. Now tests of metal content are carried out at authorized assay offices in London, Birmingham, Sheffield, and Edinburgh; each assay office has its distinguishing mark, to which is added a maker's mark, date letter, and mark guaranteeing standard.

Halloween evening of Oct 31, immediately preceding the Christian feast of Hallowmas or All Saints' Day. Customs associated with Halloween in the US and UK include children wearing masks or costumes, and "trick or treating"—going from house to house collecting candy, fruit, or money.

Hallstatt archeological site in Upper Austria, SW of Salzburg. The salt workings date from prehistoric times. In 1846 over 3,000 graves were discovered belonging to a 9th–5th century BC Celtic civilization transitional between the Bronze and Iron ages.

hallucinogen any substance that acts on the ⬙central nervous system to produce changes in perception and mood and often hallucinations. Hallucinogens include ⬙LSD, ⬙peyote, and ⬙mescaline. Their effects are unpredictable and they are illegal in most countries.

In some circumstances hallucinogens may produce panic or even suicidal feelings, which can recur without warning several days or months after taking the drug. In rare cases they produce an irreversible psychotic state mimicking schizophrenia. Spiritual or religious experiences are common, hence the ritual use of hallucinogens in some cultures. They work by chemical interference with the normal action of neurotransmitters in the brain.

halogen any of a group of five nonmetallic elements with similar chemical bonding properties: fluorine, chlorine, bromine, iodine, and astatine. They form a linked group in the ⬙periodic table of the elements, descending from fluorine, the most reactive, to astatine, the least reactive. They combine directly with most metals to form salts, such as common salt (NaCl). Each halogen has seven electrons in its valence shell, which accounts for the chemical similarities displayed by the group.

halophyte plant adapted to live where there is a high concentration of salt in the soil, for example, in salt marshes and mud flats.

Halophytes contain a high percentage of salts in their root cells, so that, despite the salt in the soil, water can still be taken up by the process of ⬙osmosis. Some species also have fleshy leaves for storing water, such as the salt marsh *Spartina* and the salt-primrose *Glaux maritima*.

halothane anesthetic agent (a liquid, $CF_3CHBrCl$) that produces a deep level of unconsciousness when inhaled.

Hals Frans c. 1581–1666. Flemish-born painter of lively portraits, such as the *Laughing Cavalier* 1624 (Wallace Collection, London), and large groups of military companies, governors of charities, and others (many examples in the Frans Hals Museum, Haarlem, the Netherlands). In the 1620s he experimented with genre (domestic) scenes.

Halsey William Frederick 1882–1959. US admiral, known as "Bull." He was the commander of the Third Fleet in the S Pacific from 1942 during World War II. The Japanese signed the surrender document ending World War II on his flagship, the battleship *Missouri*.

Halston trade name of Roy Halston Frowick 1932–1990. US fashion designer who showed his first collection 1969 and created a vogue for easy-to-wear clothes that emphasized the body but left it free to move. In 1973 he diversified into loungewear, luggage, and cosmetics.

Hamadán city in NW Iran on the site of the ancient Ecbatana, capital of the Medes; population (1986) 274,300.

Hamburg largest inland port of Europe, in Germany, on the river Elbe; population (1988) 1,571,000. Industries include oil, chemicals, electronics, and cosmetics.

It is capital of the *Land* of Hamburg, and an archbishopric from 834. In alliance with Lübeck, it founded the ⬙Hanseatic League.

Hamburg administrative region (German *Land*) of Germany
area 293 sq mi/760 sq km
capital Hamburg
features comprises the city and surrounding districts; there is a university, established 1919, and the Hamburg Schauspielhaus is one of the republic's leading theaters
products refined oil, chemicals, electrical goods, ships, processed food
population (1990 est) 1,626,000
religion 74% Protestant, 8% Roman Catholic
history in 1510 the emperor Maximilian I made Hamburg a free imperial city, and in 1871 it became a state of the German Empire.

Hameln English form Hamelin town in Lower Saxony, Germany; population (1984) 56,300. Old buildings include the *Rattenhaus* (rat-catcher's house). Hameln is the setting for the Pied Piper legend.

Hamilcar Barca c. 270–228 BC. Carthaginian general, father of ⬙Hannibal. From 247 to

241 BC he harassed the Romans in Italy and then led an expedition to Spain, where he died in battle.

Hamilton capital (since 1815) of Bermuda, on Bermuda Island; population about (1980) 1,617. It was founded 1612.

Hamilton port in Ontario; population (1986) 557,000. Linked with Lake Ontario by the Burlington Canal, it has a hydroelectric plant and steel, heavy machinery, electrical, chemical, and textile industries.

Hamilton industrial and university town on North Island, New Zealand, on Waikato River; population (1989) 104,100. It trades in forestry, horticulture, and dairy-farming products. Waikato University was established here 1964.

Hamilton city in the SW corner of Ohio, on the Great Miami River, NW of Cincinnati; seat of Butler County; population (1990) 61,400. Its industries include livestock processing, metal products, paper, and building materials. The city was built on the site of Fort Hamilton, constructed 1791 by General Arthur St Clair and used as a headquarters by General Anthony Wayne during his campaign in the Northwest Territory 1792–93.

Hamilton Alexander 1757–1804. US politician who influenced the adoption of a constitution with a strong central government and was the first secretary of the Treasury 1789–95. He led the Federalist Party, and incurred the bitter hatred of Aaron ⟡Burr when he voted against Burr and in favor of Thomas Jefferson for the presidency 1801. Challenged to a duel by Burr, Hamilton was wounded and died the next day.

Hamilton, born in the West Indies, served during the American Revolution as captain and was George ⟡Washington's secretary and aide-de-camp 1777–81. After the war he practiced as a lawyer. He was a member of the Constitutional Convention of 1787, and in the *Federalist* influenced public opinion in favor of the ratification of the constitution. He was a strong advocate of the wealthy urban sector of American life and encouraged renewed ties with Britain, remaining distrustful of revolutionary France. As the first secretary of the Treasury, he proved an able controller of the national finances.

Hamilton Edith 1867–1963. German born-US educator and Classical scholar. Among her most important works are *The Greek Way* 1930 and *The Roman Way* 1932. Hamilton is best remembered as a collector and translator of ancient myths. Her anthologies *Mythology* 1942 and *The Great Age of Greek Literature* 1943 were, for many years, standard textbooks.

Born in Dresden and raised in Fort Wayne, Indiana, Hamilton was educated at Bryn Mawr. She was the headmistress of the Bryn Mawr School in Baltimore 1896–1922, later devoting her energies to the study of Greek and Roman civilization.

Hamilton Emma (born Amy Lyon), Lady Hamilton 1765–1815. wife of Sir William Hamilton (1730–1803) from 1791, envoy to the court of Naples, and mistress of Admiral Horatio ⟡Nelson, whom she met in Naples in 1793. After his return from the Nile battle 1798, during the Napoleonic Wars, she became his mistress and their daughter, Horatia, was born 1801. After Nelson's death in battle 1805, Lady Hamilton spent her inheritance and died in poverty in Calais. She had been a great beauty and had posed for the great artists of her youth, especially George ⟡Romney.

Hamito-Semitic language any of a family of languages spoken throughout the world. There are two main branches, the *Hamitic* languages of N Africa and the *Semitic* languages originating in Syria, Mesopotamia, Palestine, and Arabia, but now found from Morocco in the west to the Persian Gulf in the east.

The Hamitic languages include ancient Egyptian, Coptic, and Berber, while the Semitic languages include the largest number of speakers –modern Arabic –as well as Hebrew, Aramaic, and Syriac. The scripts of Arabic and Hebrew are written from right to left.

Hamlet tragedy by William ⟡Shakespeare, first performed 1602. Hamlet, after much hesitation, avenges the murder of his father, the king of Denmark, by the king's brother Claudius, who has married Hamlet's mother. The play ends with the death of all three.

Hamlet's agonized indecision, real or feigned mental disorder, and awareness of role playing have been said to make him the first protagonist in English literature. He is haunted by his father's ghost demanding revenge, is torn between love and loathing for his mother, and becomes responsible for the deaths of his lover Ophelia, her father and brother, and his student companions Rosencrantz and Guildenstern. In the monologue beginning "To be, or not to be" he contemplates suicide.

Hamlin Hannibal 1809–1891. US political leader and vice-president 1861–65. He entered politics as a Democrat and served in the Maine state legislature 1836–41, the US House of Representatives 1843–47, and the US Senate 1848–61 (he was briefly governor of Maine 1857). His opposition to slavery led him to join the Republican Party 1856. Hamlin served as Lincoln's vice-president during his first term 1861–65.

Born in Paris Hill, Maine, Hamlin worked at a succession of jobs before studying law and being admitted to the bar 1833. Returning to the senate as a Radical Republican 1868–80, he later served as US minister to Spain 1881–82.

Hammarskjöld Dag 1905–1961. Swedish secretary-general of the United Nations 1953–61. He opposed Britain over the ⟡Suez Crisis 1956. His attempts to solve the problem of the Congo (now Zaire), where he was killed in a plane crash, were criticized by the USSR. He was awarded the Nobel Peace Prize 1961.

hammer in track and field athletics, a throwing event in which only men compete. The hammer is a spherical weight attached to a chain with a handle. The competitor spins the hammer over his head to gain momentum, within the confines of a circle, and throws it as far as he can. The hammer weighs 16 lb/7.26 kg, and may originally have been a blacksmith's hammer.

Hammer Armand 1898–1990. US entrepreneur, one of the most remarkable business figures of the 20th century. A pioneer in trading with the USSR from 1921, he later acted as a political mediator. He was chair of the US oil company Occidental Petroleum until his death, and was also an expert on art.

Hammer visited the USSR 1921 and acquired the first private concession awarded by the Soviet government: an asbestos mine. He built up fortunes in several business areas, including the import-export business. He was renowned for his dynamism, his championing of East–West relations, and his many philanthropic and cultural activities.

Having received his medical degree from Columbia University, Hammer wanted to use his skills to aid victims of starvation and typhus in the Ural Mountains. While in the USSR, he developed the idea of importing food from the US grain surplus in exchange for luxury goods. Lenin approved, and Hammer established a large import-export business. During the next quarter century, he made a fortune in, among other things, livestock feed and cattle. In 1956, he and his wife each put $50,000 into a struggling oil company, Occidental Petroleum, which became one of America's largest.

Hammerfest fishing port in NW Norway, northernmost town of Europe; population (1991) 6,900.

hammerhead any of several species of shark of the genus *Sphyrna*, found in tropical seas, characterized by having eyes at the ends of flattened extensions of the skull. Hammerheads can grow to 13 ft/4 m.

Hammer (formerly *M C Hammer*) Adopted name of Stanley Kirk Burrell 1963– . US rap vocalist and songwriter. His pop-oriented rap style and exuberant dancing gave him a wide appeal, especially in the video-based market, and his second LP, *Please Hammer Don't Hurt 'Em* 1990, sold 13 million copies in one year.

A born-again Christian who plugs Pepsi-Cola, Hammer is perceived as an all-round family entertainer, the first crossover rapper; his lyrics are intended to be inoffensive and he tours with an elaborate stage show.

Hammerstein Oscar, II 1895–1960. Lyricist and librettist who collaborated with Richard ⟡Rodgers on some of the best-known American musicals, including *Oklahoma* 1943 (Pulitzer Prize), *Carousel* 1945, *South Pacific* 1949 (Pulitzer Prize), *The King and I* 1951, and *The Sound of Music* 1959.

Grandson of opera impresario Oscar Hammerstein, he earned his first successes with *Rose Marie* 1924, music by Rudolf Friml (1879–1972); *Desert Song* 1926, music by Sigmund Romberg (1887–1951); and *Show Boat* 1927, music by Jerome Kern (1885–1945). *Show Boat* represented a major step forward in musical theater in terms of integrated plot and character. After a moderate success at film scoring, he joined Rodgers and launched their 16-year monumentally successful collaboration.

Hammer v Dagenhart US Supreme Court decision 1918 dealing with Congress's power to regulate labor practices in the manufacture of goods for interstate trade. The father of a child who worked in a North Carolina cotton mill sued the mill for an infraction of the Child Labor Law 1916, which prohibited the interstate sale of products of child labor. The Court held that the law was invalid because it regulated local manufacturing under the guise of interstate commerce regulations. ⟡*US* v *Darby Lumber Co* overturned *Hammer*.

Hammett (Samuel) Dashiell 1894–1961. US crime novelist. His works, *The Maltese Falcon* 1930, *The Glass Key* 1931, and the *The Thin Man* 1932, introduced the "hard-boiled" detective character into fiction.

Hammett was a former Pinkerton detective agent. In 1951 he was imprisoned for contempt of court for refusing to testify during the McCarthy era of anticommunist witch hunts. He lived with the playwright Lillian ⟡Hellman for the latter half of his life.

Hammond city in the NW corner of Indiana, on the Calumet River, just S of Chicago, Illinois;

population (1990) 84,200. It is a major transportation center, connecting to Lake Michigan via the Calumet canal. Industries include soap, cereal products, publishing, railroad equipment, and transportation facilities for the city's surrounding steel plants and oil refineries.

Hammond organ electric organ invented in the US by Laurens Hammond 1934 and widely used in gospel music. It was a precursor of the synthesizer.

Hammurabi king of Babylon from *c.* 1792 BC. He united his country and took it to the height of its power, although his consolidation of the legal code listed bloodthirsty punishments.

Hampshire county of S England
area 1,455 sq mi/3,770 sq km
cities Winchester (administrative headquarters), Southampton, Portsmouth, Gosport
features New Forest, area 144 sq mi/373 sq km, a Saxon royal hunting ground
famous people Jane Austen, Charles Dickens, Gilbert White.

Hampton Lionel 1909– . US jazz musician, a top band leader of the 1940s and 1950s. Originally a drummer, Hampton introduced the vibraphone, an electronically vibrated percussion instrument, to jazz music. With the Benny ↻Goodman band from 1936, he fronted his own big band 1941–65 and subsequently led small groups.

Hampton Wade 1818–1902. US politician and Confederate military leader. At the outbreak of the American Civil War, he raised and led a regiment of Confederate volunteers, seeing action at the First Battle of Bull Run. In 1862 Hampton was appointed brigadier general in the cavalry and in 1864 became the commander of the entire Confederate cavalry corps. After the war he returned to South Carolina. He later served as governor 1876–79 and US senator 1879–91.

Born in Charleston, South Carolina, Hampton was educated at Carolina College and later administered his family's plantation.

hamster rodent of the family Cricetidae with a thickset body, short tail, and cheek pouches to carry food. Several genera are found across Asia and in SE Europe. Hamsters are often kept as pets.

Species include the Eurasian black-bellied or common hamster *Cricetus cricetus*, about 10 in/25 cm long, which can be a crop pest and stores up to 200 lb/90 kg of seeds in its burrow. The golden hamster *Mesocricetus auratus* lives in W Asia and SE Europe. All golden hamsters now kept as pets originated from one female and 12 young captured in Syria 1930.

Hamsun Knut 1859–1952. Norwegian novelist whose first novel *Sult/Hunger* 1890 was largely autobiographical. Other works include *Pan* 1894 and *The Growth of the Soil* 1917, which won him a Nobel Prize 1920. His hatred of capitalism made him sympathize with Nazism, and he was fined in 1946 for collaboration.

Han member of the majority ethnic group in China, numbering about 990 million. The Hans speak a wide variety of dialects of the same monosyllabic language, a member of the Sino-Tibetan family. Their religion combines Buddhism, Taoism, Confucianism, and ancestor worship.

Hancock John 1737–1793. US politician and a leader of the American Revolution. As president of the Continental Congress 1775–77, he was the first to sign the Declaration of Independence 1776. Because he signed it in a

large, bold hand (in popular belief, so that it would be big enough for George III to see), his name became a colloquial term for a signature in the US. He coveted command of the Continental Army, deeply resenting the selection of George ↻Washington. He was governor of Massachusetts 1780–85 and 1787–93.

Hand Learned Billings 1872–1961. US jurist. Appointed federal district judge by President Taft 1909, Hand was named to the Second Circuit Court of Appeals by President Coolidge 1924. He became chief judge of that court in 1939. Serving there until 1951, he handed down opinions in landmark copyright, antitrust, and First Amendment cases.

Born in Albany, New York, and educated at Harvard, Hand received his law degree 1896. Although never named to the US Supreme Court, Hand was considered a leading jurist of his day. A collection of his essays, *The Spirit of Liberty*, was published 1952.

Handel Georg Friedrich 1685–1759. German composer who became a British subject 1726. His first opera, *Almira*, was performed in Hamburg 1705. In 1710 he was appointed Kapellmeister to the elector of Hanover (the future George I of England). In 1712 he settled in England, where he established his popularity with such works as the *Water Music* 1717 (written for George I). His great choral works include the *Messiah* 1742 and the later oratorios *Samson* 1743, *Belshazzar* 1745, *Judas Maccabaeus* 1747, and *Jephtha* 1752.

Born in Halle, he abandoned the study of law 1703 to become a violinist at Keiser's Opera House in Hamburg. Visits to Italy (1706–10) inspired a number of operas and oratorios, and in 1711 his opera *Rinaldo* was performed in London. *Saul* and *Israel in Egypt* (both 1739) were unsuccessful, but his masterpiece the *Messiah* was acclaimed on its first performance in Dublin 1742. Other works include the pastoral *Acis and Galatea* 1718 and a set of variations for harpsichord that were later nicknamed "The Harmonious Blacksmith." In 1751 he became totally blind.

Handke Peter 1942– . Austrian novelist and playwright whose first play *Insulting the Audience* 1966 was an example of "antitheater writing." His novels include *Die Hornissen/The Hornets* 1966 and *Die Angst des Tormanns beim Elfmeter/The Goalie's Anxiety at the Penalty Kick* 1970. He wrote and directed the film *Linkshandige Frau/The Left-handed Woman* 1977.

Hangchow alternative transcription of ↻Hangzhou, port in Zhejiang province, China.

hang-gliding technique of unpowered flying using air currents, perfected by US engineer Francis Rogallo in the 1970s. The aeronaut is strapped into a carrier, attached to a sail wing of nylon stretched on an aluminum frame like a paper dart, and jumps into the air from a high place, where updrafts of warm air allow soaring on the "thermals." See ↻gliding.

hanging execution by suspension, usually with a drop of 2–6 ft/0.6–2 m, so that the powerful jerk of the tightened rope breaks the neck. This was once a common form of ↻capital punishment in Europe and is still practiced in some states in the US.

Hangzhou or *Hangchow* port and capital of Zhejiang province, China; population (1989) 1,330,000. It has jute, steel, chemical, tea, and silk industries.

Hangzhou has fine landscaped gardens and

was the capital of China 1127–1278 under the Sung dynasty.

Hanna Mark 1837–1904. US businessman and political leader. As a businessman naturally sympathetic to the Republican Party, he was a supporter of Garfield in 1880 and became McKinley's closest adviser. Named chairman of the Republican National Committee, Hanna engineered McKinley's victories in 1896 and 1900. He served in the US Senate from 1896 until his death.

Born in New Lisbon, Ohio, Hanna attended Case Western Reserve College before joining his father in business. He later became one of Cleveland's civic leaders, founding the Union National Bank and buying the *Cleveland Herald*.

Hannibal 247–182 BC. Carthaginian general from 221 BC, son of Hamilcar Barca. His siege of Saguntum (now Sagunto, near Valencia) precipitated the 2nd ↻Punic War with Rome. Following a campaign in Italy (after crossing the Alps in 218 with 57 elephants), Hannibal was the victor at Trasimene in 217 and Cannae in 216, but he failed to take Rome. In 203 he returned to Carthage to meet a Roman invasion but was defeated at Zama in 202 and exiled in 196 at Rome's insistence.

Hannibal town in Missouri, population (1990) 18,000. Mark Twain lived here as a boy and made it the setting for *The Adventures of Huckleberry Finn*.

Hanoi capital of Vietnam, on the Red River; population (1989) 1,088,900. Central Hanoi has one of the highest population densities in the world: 1,300 people per hectare/3,250 per acre. Industries include textiles, paper, and engineering.

Captured by the French 1873, it was the capital of French Indochina 1887–1946. It was the capital of North Vietnam 1954–76. Hanoi University was founded 1918.

Hanover industrial city, capital of Lower Saxony, Germany; population (1988) 506,000. Industries include machinery, vehicles, electrical goods, rubber, textiles, and oil refining.

From 1386, it was a member of the ↻Hanseatic League, and from 1692 capital of the electorate of Hanover (created a kingdom 1815). ↻George I of England was also Elector of Hanover, and the two countries shared the same monarch until the accession of Victoria 1837. Since Salic Law meant a woman could not rule in Hanover, the throne passed to her uncle, Ernest, Duke of Cumberland. His son was forced by ↻Bismarck to abdicate 1866, and Hanover became a Prussian province. In 1946, Hanover was merged with Brunswick and Oldenburg to form the *Land* of Lower Saxony.

Hanover German royal dynasty that ruled Great Britain and Ireland 1714–1901. Under the Act of ↻Settlement 1701, the succession passed to the ruling family of Hanover, Germany, on the death of Queen Anne. On the death of Queen Victoria, the crown passed to Edward VII of the house of Saxe-Coburg.

Hanseatic League (German *Hanse* "group, society") confederation of N European trading cities from the 12th century to 1669. At its height in the late 14th century the Hanseatic League included over 160 cities and towns, among them Lübeck, Hamburg, Cologne, Breslau, and Kraków. The basis of the league's power was its monopoly of the Baltic trade and its relations with Flanders and England. The decline of the Hanseatic League from the 15th century was caused by the closing and moving of trade routes and the development of nation states.

The earliest association had its headquarters in Visby, Sweden; it included over 30 cities, but was gradually supplanted by that headed by Lübeck. Hamburg and Lübeck established their own trading stations in London in 1266 and 1267 respectively, which coalesced in 1282 with that of Cologne to form the so-called Steelyard. There were three other such stations: Bruges, Bergen, and Novgorod. The last general assembly 1669 marked the end of the league.

Hanukah or *Chanukah* Jewish festival of lights, which lasts eight days in December and celebrates the recapture of the Temple in Jerusalem by Judas Maccabaeus in 164 BC, and the "miracle" of one day's oil lasting for eight days when the Eternal Light was relit.

Hanuman in the Sanskrit epic ⟶*Rāmāyaṇa*, the Hindu monkey god and king of Hindustan (N India). He helped Rama (an incarnation of the god Vishnu) to retrieve his wife Sita, abducted by Ravana of Lanka (now Sri Lanka).

Hanyang former Chinese city, now merged in ⟶Wuhan, in Hubei province.

haploid having a single set of ⟶chromosomes in each cell. Most higher organisms are ⟶diploid—that is, they have two sets—but their gametes (sex cells) are haploid. Some plants, such as mosses, liverworts, and many seaweeds, are haploid, and male honey bees are haploid because they develop from eggs that have not been fertilized. See also ⟶meiosis.

Hapsburg or *Habsburg* European royal family, former imperial house of Austria-Hungary. The name comes from the family castle in Switzerland. The Hapsburgs held the title Holy Roman emperor 1273–91, 1298–1308, 1438–1740, and 1745–1806. They ruled Austria from 1278, under the title emperor 1806–1918.

hara-kiri ritual suicide of the Japanese samurai (military caste) since the 12th century. Today it is illegal. It was carried out to avoid dishonor or to demonstrate sincerity, either voluntarily or on the order of a feudal lord. The correct Japanese term is *seppuku* and, traditionally, the ritual involved cutting open one's stomach with a dagger before one's head was struck off by another samurai's sword.

Harappa ruined city in the Punjab, NW Pakistan, of a prehistoric culture in India, the ⟶Indus Valley civilization, which flourished from 2500 to 1700 BC. It is one of two such great cities known; the other is ⟶Mohenjo Daro.

Harare capital of Zimbabwe, on the Mashonaland plateau, about 5,000 ft/1,525 m above sea level; population (1982) 656,000. It is the center of a rich farming area (tobacco and corn), with metallurgical and food processing industries.

The British occupied the site 1890 and named it Fort Salisbury in honor of Lord Salisbury, then prime minister of the UK. It was capital of the Federation of Rhodesia and Nyasaland 1953–63.

hard disk in computing, a storage device consisting of a rigid metal ⟶disk coated with a magnetic material. Data are read from and written to the disk by means of a unit called a disk drive. The hard disk may be permanently fixed into the drive or in the form of a disk pack that can be removed and exchanged with a different pack. Hard disks vary from large units with

capacities of over 3,000 megabytes, intended for use with mainframe computers, to small units with capacities as low as 20 megabytes, intended for use with microcomputers.

Hardicanute c. 1019–1042. King of England from 1040. Son of Canute, he was king of Denmark from 1028. In England he was considered a harsh ruler.

Hardie (James) Keir 1856–1915. Scottish socialist, member of Parliament 1892–95 and 1900–15. He worked in the mines as a boy and in 1886 became secretary of the Scottish Miners' Federation. In 1888 he was the first Labour candidate to stand for Parliament; he entered Parliament independently as a Labour member 1892 and was a chief founder of the ⟶Independent Labour Party 1893.

Harding Warren G(amaliel) 1865–1923. 29th president of the US 1921–23, a Republican whose administration was known for its corruption. Harding entered the US Senate in 1914. As president he concluded the peace treaties with Germany, Austria, and Hungary, and in the same year called the ⟶Washington Convention. He opposed US membership in the ⟶League of Nations, thus reinforcing the traditional US position of neutrality. There were charges of corruption among members of his cabinet (the ⟶Teapot Dome Scandal), and Harding generally turned a benign eye to the activities of his close associates.

Harding was born in Corsica, Ohio, and graduated from Ohio Central College 1882. Before entering politics, he was a newspaper editor and publisher. He was an Ohio state senator 1898–1904 and lieutenant governor 1904–05. During his presidential administration, the various treaties stemming from the Washington Conference, providing for naval disarmament, and ostensibly stabilizing international relations among the great power signatories, were considered at the time a diplomatic coup for the US and Harding. He died in office shortly after undeniable evidence of corruption in his administration began to surface. He was succeeded by Calvin ⟶Coolidge.

hardness physical property of materials that governs their use. Methods of heat treatment can increase the hardness of metals. A scale of hardness was devised by Friedrich ⟶Mohs in the 1800s, based upon the hardness of certain minerals from soft talc (Mohs hardness 1) to diamond (10), the hardest of all materials.

The *hardness of water* refers to the presence of dissolved minerals in it that prevent soap lathering, particularly compounds of calcium and magnesium. Treatment with a water softener may remove or neutralize them.

Hardouin-Mansart Jules 1646–1708. French architect to Louis XIV from 1675. He designed the lavish Baroque extensions to the palace of Versailles (from 1678) and Grand Trianon. Other works include the Invalides Chapel (1680–91), the Place de Vendôme, and the Place des Victoires, all in Paris.

Hardwar town in Uttar Pradesh, India, on the right bank of the river Ganges; population (1981) 115,513. The name means "door of Hari" (or Vishnu). It is one of the holy places of the Hindu religion and a pilgrimage center. The *Kumbhmela* festival, held every 12th year in honor of the god Siva, attracts about 1 million pilgrims.

hardware the mechanical, electrical, and electronic components of a computer system,

as opposed to the various programs, which constitute ⟶software.

In a microcomputer, hardware might include the circuit boards, the power supply and housing of the processing unit, the VDT (screen), external memory devices such as disk drives, a printer, the keyboard, and so on.

Hardy Oliver 1892–1957. US film comedian, member of the duo ⟶Laurel and Hardy.

Hardy Thomas 1840–1928. English novelist and poet. His novels, set in rural "Wessex" (his native West Country), portray intense human relationships played out in a harshly indifferent natural world. They include *Far From the Madding Crowd* 1874, *The Return of the Native* 1878, *The Mayor of Casterbridge* 1886, *The Woodlanders* 1887, *Tess of the d'Urbervilles* 1891, and *Jude the Obscure* 1895. His poetry includes the *Wessex Poems* 1898, the blank-verse epic of the Napoleonic Wars *The Dynasts* 1904–08, and several volumes of lyrics.

Born in Dorset, Hardy was trained as an architect. His first success was *Far From the Madding Crowd. Tess of the d'Urbervilles*, subtitled "A Pure Woman," outraged public opinion by portraying as its heroine a woman who had been seduced. The even greater outcry that followed *Jude the Obscure* 1895 reinforced Hardy's decision to confine himself to verse.

Hardy–Weinberg equilibrium in population genetics, the theoretical relative frequency of different ⟶alleles within a given population of a species, when the stable endpoint of evolution in an undisturbed environment is reached.

hare mammal of the genus *Lepus* of the family Leporidae (which also includes rabbits) in the order Lagomorpha. Hares are larger than rabbits, with very long, black-tipped ears, long hind legs, and short, upturned tails.

Throughout the long breeding season June–Aug, there are chases and "boxing matches" among males and females; the expression "mad as a March hare" arises from this behavior.

Unlike rabbits, hares do not burrow. Their furred, open-eyed young (leverets) are cared for in a shallow depression rather than a specially prepared nest cavity. Jack rabbits and snowshoe rabbits are actually hares.

harebell perennial plant *Campanula rotundifolia* of the ⟶bellflower family, with bell-shaped blue flowers, found on dry grassland and heaths. It is known in Scotland as the bluebell.

Hare Krishna popular name for a member of the ⟶International Society for Krishna Consciousness, derived from their chant.

harelip congenital facial deformity, a cleft in the upper lip and jaw, which may extend back into the palate (cleft palate). It can be remedied by surgery.

Hare's apparatus in physics, a specific kind of ⟶hydrometer used to compare the relative densities of two liquids, or to find the density of one if the other is known. It was invented by US chemist Robert Hare (1781–1858).

It consists of a vertical E-shaped glass tube, with the long limbs dipping into the two liquids and a tap on the short limb. With the tap open, air is removed from the tops of the tubes and the liquids are pushed up the tubes by atmospheric pressure. When the tap is closed, the heights of the liquids are inversely proportional to their relative densities.

Hargobind 1595–1644. Indian religious leader,

sixth guru (teacher) of Sikhism 1606–44. He encouraged Sikhs to develop military skills in response to growing persecution. At the festival of Diwali, Sikhs celebrate his release from prison.

Hargraves Edward Hammond 1816–1891. Australian prospector, born in England. In 1851 he found gold in the Blue Mountains of New South Wales, thus beginning the first Australian gold rush.

Hargreaves James died 1778. English inventor who co-invented a carding machine for combing wool 1760. About 1764 he invented his "spinning jenny," which enabled a number of threads to be spun simultaneously by one person.

Harijan (Hindi "children of god") member of the Indian ⟡caste of untouchables. The compassionate term was introduced by Mahatma Gandhi during the independence movement.

Harlan John Marshall 1833–1911. US jurist and associate justice of the US Supreme Court 1877–1911. After practicing law and politics in Kentucky, Harlan supported the Union during the Civil War, serving as colonel in the 10th Kentucky Volunteer Infantry and being elected Kentucky attorney general 1863. He was defeated as Republican candidate for governor of Kentucky 1871, 1875. After service on a federal Reconstruction Commission in Louisiana, Harlan was appointed associate justice by President Hayes 1877.

Harlan John Marshall 1899–1971. US jurist and Supreme Court justice. After service in the US attorney's office 1925–27 he joined the staff of the state attorney general 1928–30. Harlan later established a private practice but returned to public life as chief counsel for the New York Crime Commission 1951–53. In 1954 President Eisenhower appointed Harlan to the US Supreme Court. As associate justice, he was a conservative, especially in the areas of free speech and civil and criminal rights.

Born in Chicago and educated at Princeton and Oxford, Harlan studied law at New York University and was admitted to the bar 1925.

Harlem commercial and residential district of Manhattan, New York City. The principal thoroughfare, 125th Street, runs E–W between the Hudson River and the East River. It was a Dutch settlement in 1658; it developed as a black population center from World War I. Harlem's heyday was the 1920s, when it established its reputation as the intellectual, cultural, and entertainment center of black America. Once noted for its music clubs and theaters, it retained the famed Apollo Theater; the Dance Theater and Theater of Harlem are also here.

Harlem Globetrotters US touring basketball team that plays exhibition matches worldwide. Comedy routines as well as their great skills are features of the games. They were founded 1927 by Abraham Saperstein (1903–1966).

Harlem Renaissance movement in US literature in the 1920s that used African-American life and black culture as its subject matter; it was an early manifestation of black pride in the US. The center of the movement was the Harlem section of New York City.

Harlem was the place where aspects of African-American culture, including jazz, flourished from the early 20th century, and attracted a new white audience. The magazine *Crisis*, edited by W E B DuBois (1868–1963), was a forum for the new black consciousness;

writers associated with the movement include Langston Hughes (1902–1967), Zora Neale Hurston (1901–1960), James Weldon Johnson (1871–1938), and Countee Cullen (1903–1946).

Harley Robert, 1st Earl of Oxford 1661–1724. British Tory politician, chief minister to Queen Anne 1711–14, when he negotiated the Treaty of Utrecht 1713. Accused of treason as a ⟡Jacobite after the accession of George I, he was imprisoned 1714–17.

Harlingen city in the SE corner of Texas, S of Corpus Christi and just N of the Mexican border. Connected to the Rio Grande by an intracoastal waterway, it serves as the processing and marketing area for the lower Rio Grande valley. Industries include citrus-fruit processing and cotton products; population (1990) 48,735.

Harlow Jean. Adopted name of Harlean Carpenter 1911–1937. US film actress, the first "platinum blonde" and the wisecracking sex symbol of the 1930s. Her films include *Hell's Angels* 1930, *Red Dust* 1932, *Platinum Blonde* 1932, *Dinner at Eight* 1933, *China Seas* 1935, and *Saratoga* 1937, during the filming of which she died (her part was completed by a double—with rear and long shots).

harmattan in meteorology, a dry and dusty NE wind that blows over W Africa.

harmonica or *mouth organ* pocket-sized reed organ blown directly from the mouth; it was invented by Charles Wheatstone 1829.

The ⟡*glass harmonica* is based on the principle of playing a wine glass with a wet finger.

harmonics in music, a series of partial vibrations that combine to form a musical tone. The number and relative prominence of harmonics produced determines an instrument's tone color (timbre). An oboe is rich in harmonics, the flute has few. Harmonics conform to successive divisions of the sounding air column or string: their pitches are harmonious.

harmonium keyboard reed organ of the 19th century, powered by foot-operated bellows.

Widely adopted in the US as a home and church instrument, in France and Germany the harmonium flourished as a concert solo and orchestral instrument, being written for by Karg-Elert, Schoenberg, and Saint-Saëns.

harmony in music, any simultaneous combination of sounds, as opposed to melody, which is a succession of sounds. Although the term suggests a pleasant or agreeable sound, it is applied to any combination of notes, whether consonant or dissonant. Harmony deals with the formation of chords and their interrelation and logical progression.

The founder of harmonic theory was Jean-Philippe ⟡Rameau. In his *Traité de l'harmonie/Treatise on Harmony* 1722, he established a system of chord classification on which subsequent methods of harmony have been based.

Harold two kings of England:

Harold I died 1040. King of England from 1035. The illegitimate son of Canute, known as *Harefoot*, he claimed the throne 1035 when the legitimate heir Hardicanute was in Denmark. He was elected king 1037.

Harold II *c.* 1020–1066. King of England from Jan 1066. He succeeded his father Earl Godwin 1053 as earl of Wessex. In 1063 William of Normandy (⟡William I) tricked

him into swearing to support his claim to the English throne, and when the Witan (a council of high-ranking religious and secular men) elected Harold to succeed Edward the Confessor, William prepared to invade. Meanwhile, Harold's treacherous brother Tostig (died 1066) joined the king of Norway, Harald III Hardrada (1015–1066), in invading Northumbria. Harold routed and killed them at Stamford Bridge Sept 25. Three days later William landed at Pevensey, Sussex, and Harold was killed at the Battle of Hastings Oct 14, 1066.

harp plucked musical string instrument, with the strings stretched vertically within a wooden frame, normally triangular. The concert harp is now the largest musical instrument to be plucked by hand. It has up to 47 strings, and seven pedals set into the soundbox at the base to alter pitch.

The harp existed in the West as early as the 9th century, and it was common among medieval minstrels. At that time it was quite small, and was normally placed on the knees. It evolved in size because of a need for increased volume following its introduction into the orchestra in the 19th century. The harp has also been used in folk music, as both a solo and accompanying instrument, and is associated with Wales and Ireland.

Harper's Ferry village in W Virginia, where the Potomac and Shenandoah rivers meet. In 1859 antislavery leader John ⟡Brown seized the federal government's arsenal here, an action that helped precipitate the Civil War.

During the war the strategically located settlement was the site of several engagements. In commemoration, Harper's Ferry National Historical Park is here.

harpsichord keyboard musical instrument common in the 16th–18th centuries, until superseded by the piano. The strings are plucked by quills. It was revived in the 20th century for the authentic performance of early music.

Harpy (plural **Harpies**) in early Greek mythology, a wind spirit; in later legend the Harpies have horrific women's faces and the bodies of vultures.

harrier bird of prey of the genus *Circus*, family Accipitridae. Harriers have long wings and legs, short beaks and soft plumage. They are found throughout the world.

The northern harrier or marsh hawk *C. cyaneus* is native to North America.

harrier breed of dog, a small hound originally used for hare-hunting.

Harriman (William) Averell 1891–1986. US diplomat. He was administrator of ⟡lend-lease in World War II and warned of the Soviet Union's aggressive intentions from his post as ambassador to the USSR 1943–46. He became Democratic secretary of commerce 1946–48 in Truman's administration, governor of New York 1955–58, and negotiator of the Nuclear Test Ban Treaty with the USSR 1963. He served the L Johnson administration 1968–69 in the opening rounds of the Vietnam War peace talks at which he was chief negotiator.

Harris southern part of ⟡Lewis with Harris, in the Outer ⟡Hebrides; area 193 sq mi/500 sq km; population (1971) 2,900. It is joined to Lewis by a narrow isthmus. Harris tweeds are produced here.

Harris Arthur Travers 1892–1984. British

marshal of the Royal Air Force in World War II. Known as "Bomber Harris," he was commander in chief of Bomber Command 1942–45.

He was an autocratic and single-minded leader, and was criticized for his policy of civilian-bombing of selected cities in Germany; he authorized the fire-bombing raids on Dresden, in which more than 100,000 died.

Harris Frank 1856–1931. Irish journalist, later in the US, who wrote colorful biographies of Oscar Wilde and George Bernard Shaw, and an autobiography, *My Life and Loves* 1926, originally banned in the US and the UK for its sexual content.

Harris Joel Chandler 1848–1908. US author, born in Georgia. He wrote tales narrated by the former slave "Uncle Remus," based on black folklore, and involving the characters Br'er Rabbit and the Tar Baby.

Harris Louis 1921– . US pollster. He joined the Roper polling organization 1947 and became a partner in that firm 1954. Developing his own research techniques, he founded Louis Harris and Associates 1956. Hired by the 1960 Kennedy presidential campaign, Harris gained a national reputation and later served as a consultant to the CBS television network and as a political columnist.

Born in New Haven, Connecticut, he was educated at the University of North Carolina. After World War II, Harris gained his first experience in testing public opinion in his work for the American Veterans' Committee.

Harris Paul P 1878–1947. US lawyer who founded the first ⟷*Rotary Club* in Chicago 1905.

Harris Richard 1932– . Irish film actor known for playing rebel characters in such films as *This Sporting Life* 1963. His other films include *Camelot* 1967, *A Man Called Horse* 1970, *Robin and Marian* 1976, *Tarzan the Ape Man* 1981, *The Field* 1990, and *Unforgiven* 1992.

He won the 1990 *Evening Standard* Award for best actor in Pirandello's *Henry IV*.

Harris Roy 1898–1979. US composer, born in Oklahoma, who used American folk tunes. Among his works are the 10th symphony 1965 (known as "Abraham Lincoln") and the orchestral *When Johnny Comes Marching Home* 1935.

Harrisburg capital city of Pennsylvania, located in the S central part of the state, on the Susquehanna River; seat of Dauphin County; population (1990) 52,400. Industries include steel, railroad equipment, food processing, printing and publishing, and clothing.

Harrison Benjamin 1833–1901. 23rd president of the US 1889–93, a Republican. He called the first Pan-American Conference, which led to the establishment of the Pan American Union, to improve inter-American cooperation, and develop commercial ties. In 1948 this became the ⟷Organization of American States.

Born in North Bend, Ohio, Harrison graduated from Miami University in Oxford, Ohio, 1852 and practiced law in Indianapolis, Indiana. Active in Republican politics before and after the Civil War, he returned from the war a brigadier general and by 1877 was the Republican leader of Indiana. He served in the US Senate 1881–87 before being nominated as the Republican presidential candidate in the election of 1888.

During his administration, important legislation was enacted 1890: the Sherman Anti-Trust Act; the Sherman Silver Purchase Act, which assured farmers of solvency in the face of falling prices; the McKinley Tariff Act, which protected manufacturers during intense industrialization; and the Dependent Pension Act, which assured disabled Civil War veterans an income.

Harrison Rex (Reginald Carey) 1908–1990. English film and theater actor. He appeared in over 40 films and numerous plays, often portraying sophisticated and somewhat eccentric characters, such as the waspish Professor Higgins in *My Fair Lady* 1964, the musical version of Irish dramatist George Bernard Shaw's play *Pygmalion*. His other films include *Blithe Spirit* 1945, *The Ghost and Mrs Muir* 1947, and *Dr Doolittle* 1967.

Harrison William Henry 1773–1841. 9th president of the US 1841. Elected 1840 as a Whig, he died one month after taking office. His political career was based largely on his reputation as an Indian fighter, and his campaign was constructed to give the impression that he was a man of the people with simple tastes and that the New Yorker, Martin ⟷Van Buren, his opponent, was a "foppish" sophisticate.

Born in Charles City County, Virginia, he joined the army 1791 at the age of 18. He resigned from the army 1798 and served as secretary of the Northwest Territory 1798–1800 and governor of the Indiana Territory 1801–12, where he drove off a minor Indian attack at Tippecanoe Creek, which was reported as a rout. Recalled to the army during the War of 1812, Harrison led his troops in the recapture of Detroit and was victorious at the Battle of the Thames River in Ontario. He served in the US House of Representatives 1816–19 and the Senate 1825–28. Benjamin ⟷Harrison was his grandson.

harrow agricultural implement used to break up the furrows left by the ⟷plow and reduce the soil to a fine consistency or tilth, and to cover the seeds after sowing. The traditional harrow consists of spikes set in a frame; modern harrows use sets of disks.

Hart Gary 1936– . US Democrat politician, senator from Colorado from 1974. In 1980 he contested the Democratic nomination for the presidency, and stepped down from his Senate seat 1986 to run, again unsuccessfully, in the 1988 presidential campaign.

Early in 1987 he withdrew because of a scandal involving an alleged affair with a model; in Dec 1987 he briefly resumed his campaign and once more withdrew.

Hart Moss 1904–1961. US playwright. Born in New York City, Hart had his first play produced in 1922. After working for an independent producer and at Catskill resorts in New York State, he gained Broadway success with *Once in a Lifetime*, written with George S Kaufman 1930. He later collaborated with such major figures as Irving Berlin, Cole Porter, Kurt Weill, and Ira Gershwin. Among Hart's most famous works are *The Man Who Came to Dinner* 1939 and the films *Gentlemen's Agreement* 1947 and *A Star is Born* 1954.

Late in his career he became one of Broadway's most successful directors. His autobiography, *Act One*, appeared 1959.

Harte (Francis) Bret 1839–1902. US writer and humorist of the American West. He founded *The Overland Monthly* 1868, in which he wrote short stories of the pioneer West, such as "The Outcasts of Poker Flat" and "The Luck

of Roaring Camp," and poetry. In 1871, with his popularity at its height, he went East and signed a contract with *The Atlantic Monthly* for $10,000 for 12 stories a year, the most money then offered to a US writer. He entered a creative slump, however, and from 1878 to 1885 served as US consul in Germany and Scotland, where he entertained the literary circles. He then settled permanently in England.

He was born in Albany, New York, and became a California gold miner at 18.

hartebeest large African antelope *Alcelaphus buselaphus* with lyre-shaped horns set close on top of the head in both sexes. It may grow to 5 ft/1.5 m at the rather humped shoulders and up to 6 ft/2 m long. Although they are clumsy-looking runners, hartebeest can reach 40 mph/ 65 kph.

Hartford capital city of Connecticut, located in the N central part of the state, on the Connecticut River, NE of Waterbury. Industries include insurance, firearms, business office equipment, and tools; population (1990) 139,700. The Fundamental Orders of Connecticut, the first constitution that created a democratic government, were signed here 1639.

Hartford Convention in US history, a meeting of ⟷Federalist party delegates from Dec 1814 to Jan 1815 (at the end of the War of ⟷1812) in Hartford, Connecticut. The meeting considered amendments to the US Constitution and the possibility of secession from the union in response to the adverse economic effects of the war on New England. The end of the war forestalled further action.

Hartly Marsden 1877–1943. US avant-garde painter. Born in Lewiston, Maine, he traveled in Europe to study art and was influenced by the Expressionist painters of the time. Hartly returned from Paris and Berlin with an original style that resembled the painting of the *Blaue Reiter* (Blue Rider) school. His paintings range from abstract, brightly colored representations of German soldiers and German military symbols, such as *Military* 1913, to New England landscapes, such as *Log Jam, Penobscot Bay* 1940–41.

hart's-tongue fern *Phyllitis scolopendrium* whose straplike undivided fronds, up to 24 in/ 60 cm long, have prominent brown spore-bearing organs on the undersides. The plant is native to Eurasia and E North America.

Hartz Mountains range running north to south in Tasmania, Australia, with two remarkable peaks: Hartz Mountain (4,113 ft/1,254 m) and Adamsons Peak (4,017 ft/1,224 m).

Harvard University oldest educational institution in the US, founded 1636 at New Towne (later Cambridge), Massachusetts, and named after John Harvard (1607–1638), who bequeathed half his estate and his library to it. Women were first admitted 1969; the women's college of the university is *Radcliffe College*.

harvestman arachnid of the order Opiliones, with very long, thin legs and small bodies. Harvestmen are distinguished from true spiders by the absence of a waist or constriction in the oval body. They are carnivorous and found from the Arctic to the tropics.

harvest mite another name for ⟷chigger.

Harvey Laurence. Adopted name of Lauruska Mischa Skikne 1928–1973. British film actor of Lithuanian descent who worked both in England (*Room at the Top* 1958) and in

Hollywood (*The Alamo* 1960, *The Manchurian Candidate* 1962).

Harvey William 1578–1657. English physician who discovered the circulation of blood. In 1628 he published his book *De Motu Cordis/ On the Motion of the Heart and the Blood in Animals*. He was court physician to James I and Charles I.

After studying at Padua, Italy, under ⍭Fabricius, he set out to question ⍭Galen's account of the action of the heart. Later, Harvey explored the development of chick and deer embryos.

Haryana state of NW India
area 17,061 sq mi/44,200 sq km
capital Chandigarh
features part of the Ganges plain; a center of Hinduism
products sugar, cotton, oilseed, textiles, cement, iron ore
population (1991) 16,317,700
language Hindi.

Hasdrubal Barca Carthaginian general, son of Hamilcar Barca and brother of Hannibal. He remained in command in Spain when Hannibal invaded Italy and, after fighting there against Scipio until 208, marched to Hannibal's relief. He was defeated and killed in the Metaurus valley, NE Italy.

Hašek Jaroslav 1883–1923. Czech writer. His masterpiece is an antiauthoritarian comic satire on military life under Austro-Hungarian rule, *The Good Soldier Schweik* 1923. During World War I he deserted to Russia, and eventually joined the Bolsheviks.

hashish drug made from the resin contained in the female flowering tops of ⍭hemp (or cannabis).

Hasidism or *Chasidism* religious sect of Orthodox Judaism, founded by Ba'al Shem Tov (*c.* 1700–1760), based on study of ⍭kabbala and popular piety. It spread against strong opposition throughout E Europe during the 18th and 19th centuries, led by charismatic leaders, the *zaddikim*. They stressed piety and ecstatic prayer, denouncing the academic approach of Talmudic academies (see ⍭Talmud). A later, more intellectual approach was instituted by the Lubavitch rabbi of Russia, now based in New York City. Hasidic men dress in the black suits and broad-brimmed hats of 18th-century European society, which they conservatively maintain.

Hassam Childe 1859–1935. US Impressionist painter and printmaker. He studied in Paris 1886–89. He became one of the members of *The Ten*, a group of American Impressionists who exhibited together until World War I.

Hassan II 1929– . King of Morocco from 1961. From 1976 he undertook the occupation of Western Sahara when it was ceded by Spain.

The result was a long and damaging guerrilla war against the Polisario fighters. Hassan is a moderate Arab leader, having met with Israeli leaders.

Hastings resort in East Sussex, England; population (1981) 74,803. The chief of the ⍭Cinque Ports, it has ruins of a Norman castle.

Hastings Warren 1732–1818. British colonial administrator. A protégé of Lord Clive, who established British rule in India, Hastings carried out major reforms, and became governor of Bengal 1772 and governor-general of India 1774. Impeached for corruption on his return to England 1785, he was acquitted 1795.

Hastings, Battle of battle Oct 14, 1066 at which William the Conqueror, Duke of Normandy, defeated Harold, King of England. The site is 6 mi/10 km inland from Hastings, at Senlac, Sussex; it is marked by Battle Abbey.

Having defeated an attempt by King Harald Hardrada of Norway at Stamford Bridge, Harold moved south with an army of 9,000 to counter the landing of the duke of Normandy at Pevensey Bay, Kent.

William, having laid a claim to the English throne, dominated the battle with archers supported by cavalry, breaking through ranks of infantry. Both sides suffered heavy losses but the death of Harold allowed William to conquer and become England's king.

Hathor in ancient Egyptian mythology, the sky goddess, identified with ⍭Isis.

Hatshepsut *c.* 1540–*c.* 1481 BC. Queen of Egypt during the 18th dynasty. She was the daughter of Thothmes I, with whom she ruled until the accession to the throne of her husband and half brother Thothmes II. Throughout his reign real power lay with Hatshepsut, and she continued to rule after his death, as regent for her nephew Thothmes III.

Her reign was a peaceful and prosperous time in which Egypt was developing its armies and expanding its territories. The ruins of her magnificent temple at Deir el-Bahri survive.

Hatteras cape on the coast of N Carolina, where the waters of the N Atlantic meet the Gulf Stream, causing great turbulence; it therefore is noted for shipwrecks (more than 700 are said to have occurred here), and is nicknamed "the Graveyard of the Atlantic." Cape Hatteras National Seashore has both natural and historical interest, including a lighthouse and sea life typical of both the temperate and tropical zones.

Haughey Charles 1925– . Irish Fianna Fáil politician of Ulster descent. Dismissed 1970 from Jack Lynch's cabinet for alleged complicity in IRA gun-running, he was afterwards acquitted. He was prime minister 1979–81, March–Nov 1982, and 1986–92, when he was replaced by Albert Reynolds.

Hausa member of an agricultural Muslim people of NW Nigeria, numbering 9 million. The Hausa language belongs to the Chadic subfamily of the Afro-Asiatic language group. It is used as a trade language throughout W Africa.

Haussmann Georges Eugène, Baron Haussmann 1809–1891. French administrator who replanned medieval Paris 1853–70 to achieve the current city plan, with wide boulevards and parks. The cost of his scheme and his authoritarianism caused opposition, and he was made to resign.

haustorium (plural *haustoria*) specialized organ produced by a parasitic plant or fungus that penetrates the cells of its host to absorb nutrients. It may be either an outgrowth of hyphae (see ⍭hypha), as in the case of parasitic fungi, or of the stems of flowering parasitic plants, as in dodders (*Cuscuta*). The suckerlike haustoria of a dodder penetrate the vascular tissue of the host plant without killing the cells.

Haute-Normandie or *Upper Normandy* coastal region of NW France lying between Basse-Normandie and Picardy and bisected by the river Seine; area 4,757 sq mi/12,300 sq km; population (1986) 1,693,000. It comprises the *départements* of Eure and Seine-Maritime; its

capital is Rouen. Major ports include Dieppe and Fécamp. The area has many beech forests.

Havana capital and port of Cuba; population (1989) 2,096,100. Products include cigars and tobacco.

The palace of the Spanish governors and the stronghold of La Fuerza (1583) survive. In 1898 the blowing up of the US battleship *Maine* in the harbor began the ⍭Spanish-American War.

Havel Václav 1936– . Czech playwright and politician, president 1989–92. His plays include *The Garden Party* 1963 and *Largo Desolato* 1985, about a dissident intellectual. Havel became widely known as a human-rights activist. He was imprisoned 1979–83 and again 1989 for support of Charter 77 (see ⍭Czechoslovakia). As president he sought to preserve a united Czechoslovakia. He resigned in recognition of the breakup of the federation 1992.

Haverhill city in NE Massachusetts, on the Merrimac River, N of Boston. Manufactures include paints, chemicals, machine tools, and shoes; population (1990) 51,418.

Havre, Le see ⍭Le Havre, port in France.

Hawaii Pacific state of the US; nickname Aloha State
area 6,485 sq mi/16,800 sq km
capital Honolulu on Oahu
cities Hilo
physical Hawaii consists of a chain of some 20 volcanic islands, of which the chief are: (1) *Hawaii*, noted for Mauna Kea (13,788 ft/ 4,201 m), the world's highest island mountain (site of a UK infrared telescope) and Mauna Loa (13,686 ft/4,170 m), the world's largest active volcanic crater; (2) *Maui*, the second largest of the islands; (3) *Oahu*, the third largest, with the greatest concentration of population and tourist attractions—for example, Waikiki beach and the Pearl Harbor naval base; (4) *Kauai*; and (5) *Molokai*, site of a historic leper colony
products sugar, coffee, pineapples, flowers, women's clothing
population (1990) 1,108,200; 34% European, 25% Japanese, 14% Filipino, 12% Hawaiian, 6% Chinese
language English
religion Christianity; Buddhist minority
famous people Father Joseph Damien, Kamehameha I, Queen Liliuokalani, Sanford Dole
history a Polynesian kingdom from the 6th century until 1893; Hawaii became a republic 1894; ceded itself to the US 1898, and became a US territory 1900. Japan's air attack on Pearl

Hawaii

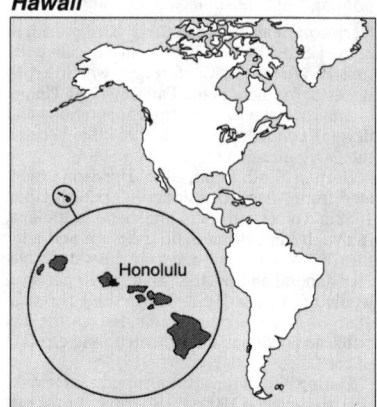

Harbor Dec 7, 1941, crippled the US Pacific fleet and turned the territory into an armed camp, under martial law, for the remainder of the war. Hawaii became a state 1959. Tourism is the chief source of income.

Capt Cook, who called Hawaii the Sandwich Islands, was the first known European visitor 1778. In 1992 a severe tropical storm devastated the island of Kauai.

hawfinch European finch *Coccothraustes coccothraustes* about 7 in/18 cm long. It feeds on berries and seeds, and can crack cherry stones with its large and powerful bill.

hawk any of various small to medium-sized birds of prey of the family Accipitridae, other than eagles, kites, ospreys, and vultures. The name is used especially to describe the genera *Accipiter* and *Buteo*. Hawks have short, rounded wings compared with falcons, and keen eyesight.

hawk person who believes in the use of military action rather than mediation as a means of solving a political dispute. The term first entered the political language of the US during the 1960s, when it was applied metaphorically to those advocating continuation and escalation of the Vietnam War. Those with moderate, or even pacifist, views were known as doves. In general usage today, a hawk is associated with conservative policies.

Hawke Bob (Robert) 1929– . Australian Labor politician, prime minister 1983–91, on the right wing of the party. He was president of the Australian Council of Trade Unions 1970–80. He announced his retirement from politics 1992.

Hawking Stephen 1942– . English physicist who has researched ⟡black holes and gravitational field theory. His books include *A Brief History of Time* 1988, in which he argues that our universe is only one small part of a "super-universe" that has existed forever and that comprises an infinite number of universes like our own.

Professor of gravitational physics at Cambridge from 1977, he discovered that the strong gravitational field around a black hole can radiate particles of matter. Commenting on Einstein's remark, "God does not play dice with the universe," Hawking said: "God not only plays dice, he throws them where they can't be seen."

Hawkins Coleman (Randolph) 1904–1969. US virtuoso tenor saxophonist. He was, until 1934, a soloist in the swing band led by Fletcher Henderson (1898–1952), and was an influential figure in bringing the jazz saxophone to prominence as a solo instrument.

hawk moth or **sphinx moth** any of a family, Sphingidae, of moths with thick bodies and narrow wings. Some 1,000 species are distributed throughout the world, but they are mainly tropical. The large hawk-moth larva usually has a "horn" at the end of its body—for example, the bright-green tomato hornworm *Protoparce quinquemaculata*.

Hawks Howard 1896–1977. US director, writer, and producer of a wide range of classic films, swift-moving and immensely accomplished, including *Scarface* 1932, *Bringing Up Baby* 1938, *The Big Sleep* 1946, and *Gentlemen Prefer Blondes* 1953.

Haworth Norman 1883–1950. English organic chemist who was the first to synthesize a vitamin (ascorbic acid, vitamin C) 1933, for which he shared a Nobel Prize 1937.

hawthorn shrub or tree of the genus *Crataegus* of the rose family Rosaceae. Species are most abundant in E North America, but there are also many in Eurasia. All have alternate, toothed leaves and bear clusters of showy white, pink, or red flowers. Small applelike fruits can be red, orange, blue, or black. Hawthorns are popular as ornamentals.

Hawthorne Nathaniel 1804–1864. US author who wrote about Puritan New England and won fame with *The Scarlet Letter* 1850, a powerful novel set in Boston 200 years earlier. He wrote three other novels (*The House of the Seven Gables* 1851, *The Blithedale Romance* 1852, and *The Marble Faun* 1860), many volumes of short stories, and *Tanglewood Tales* 1853, classic Greek legends retold for children. His short stories, which include "My Kinsman, Major Molineux" and "Young Goodman Brown," helped to establish the short story as an art form.

Born in Salem, Massachusetts, Hawthorne graduated from Bowdoin College and worked as a customs official. He was the US consul 1853–57 in Liverpool, England, and then lived in Italy until 1860. Hawthorne's fiction is marked by its haunting symbolism and its exploration of guilt, sin, and other complex moral and psychological issues. It had a profound effect on writers of his own time, notably his friend Herman Melville, and continues to influence writers.

hay preserved grass used for winter livestock feed. The grass is cut and allowed to dry in the field before being removed for storage in a barn.

The optimum period for cutting is when the grass has just come into flower and contains most feed value. During the natural drying process, the moisture content is reduced from 70–80% down to a safe level of 20%. In normal weather conditions, this takes from two to five days during which time the hay is turned by machine to ensure even drying. Hay is normally baled before removal from the field.

2.47 acres/1 hectare of grass can produce up to 7.3 tons/7.5 tonnes of hay.

Hayden Sterling. Adopted name of John Hamilton 1916–1986. US film actor who played leading Hollywood roles in the 1940s and early 1950s. Although later seen in some impressive character roles, his career as a whole failed to do justice to his talent. His work includes *The Asphalt Jungle* 1950, *Johnny Guitar* 1954, *Dr Strangelove* 1964, and *The Godfather* 1972.

Haydn Franz Joseph 1732–1809. Austrian composer. A teacher of Mozart and Beethoven, he was a major exponent of the Classical sonata form in his numerous chamber and orchestral works (he wrote more than 100 symphonies). He also composed choral music, including the oratorios *The Creation* 1798 and *The Seasons* 1801. He was the first great master of the string quartet.

Born in Lower Austria, he was Kapellmeister 1761–90 to Prince Esterházy. His work also includes operas, church music, and songs, and the "Emperor's Hymn," adopted as the Austrian, and later the German, national anthem.

Hayek Friedrich August von 1899– . Austrian economist. Born in Vienna, he taught at the London School of Economics 1931–50. His *The Road to Serfdom* 1944 was a critical study of socialist trends in Britain. He won the 1974 Nobel Prize for Economics with Gunnar Myrdal.

He was professor of social and moral science at the University of Chicago 1950–62.

Hayes Rutherford Birchard 1822–1893. 19th president of the US 1877–81, a Republican. Born in Ohio, he was a major general on the Union side in the Civil War. During his presidency federal troops (see ⟡Reconstruction) were withdrawn from the Southern states and the Civil Service reformed.

He was noted for his honesty, and his integrity was viewed by many as a way to overcome the aura of corruption that had surrounded the ⟡Grant administration. Under Hayes, the political role of federal employees was curtailed.

hay fever allergic reaction to pollen, causing sneezing, inflammation of the eyes, and asthmatic symptoms. Sufferers experience irritation caused by powerful body chemicals related to ⟡histamine produced at the site of entry. Treatment is by antihistamine drugs.

Hays Office film regulation body in the US 1922–45. Officially known as the Motion Picture Producers and Distributors of America, it was created by the major film companies to improve the industry's image and provide internal regulation, including a strict moral code.

The office was headed by Will H Hays (1879–1954). A Production Code, listing all the subjects forbidden to films, was begun 1930 and lasted until 1966, when it was replaced by a ratings system.

Haywood William Dudley 1869–1928. US labor leader. One of the founders of the Industrial Workers of the World (IWW, "Wobblies") 1905, Haywood was arrested for conspiracy to murder an antiunion politician. His acquittal in 1907 made him a labor hero. Arrested again for sedition during World War I, he spent his later years in exile in the Soviet Union.

Born in Salt Lake City, Utah, and having worked in the mines, Haywood joined the Western Federation of Miners (WFM) 1896. By 1899 he had become a national leader of the WFM and, in his tireless and forceful speaking tours throughout the country, had won the nickname "Big Bill."

Hayworth Rita. Adopted name of Margarita Carmen Cansino 1918–1987. US dancer and film actress who gave vivacious performances in 1940s musicals and steamy, erotic roles in *Gilda* 1946 and *Affair in Trinidad* 1952. She was known as Hollywood's "Goddess" during the height of her career. She was married to Orson Welles 1943–48 and appeared in his films, including *The Lady from Shanghai* 1948. She was perfectly cast in *Pal Joey* 1957 and *Separate Tables* 1958.

Her later appearances were intermittent and she retired in 1972, a victim of Alzheimer's disease.

hazardous substance waste substance, usually generated by industry, which represents a hazard to the environment or to people living or working nearby. Examples include radioactive wastes, acidic resins, arsenic residues, residual hardening salts, lead, mercury, nonferrous sludges, organic solvents, and pesticides. Their economic disposal or recycling is the subject of research.

hazel shrub or tree of the genus *Corylus*, family Corylaceae, including the European common hazel or cob *C. avellana*, of which the filbert is the cultivated variety. North American species include the American hazel *C. americana*.

Hazlitt William 1778–1830. English essayist

and critic whose work is characterized by invective, scathing irony, and a gift for epigram. His critical essays include *Characters of Shakespeare's Plays* 1817–18, *Lectures on the English Poets* 1818–19, *English Comic Writers* 1819, and *Dramatic Literature of the Age of Elizabeth* 1820. Other works are *Table Talk* 1821–22, *The Spirit of the Age* 1825, and *Liber Amoris* 1823.

H-bomb abbreviation for ◊*hydrogen bomb*.

Head Edith 1900–1981. US costume designer for Hollywood films who won eight Academy Awards for her designs, in such films as *The Heiress* 1949, *All About Eve* 1950, and *The Sting* 1973.

headache pain in the head, caused by minor eye strain, stress, neck- or jaw-muscle strain, allergies, or physical illness, such as infectious disease or brain tumor. It is marked by dilation of the cerebral blood vessels and irritation of the brain linings (meninges) and nerves.

health care implementation of the proper regimen to ensure long-lasting good health. Life expectancy is determined by overall efficiency of the body's vital organs and the rate at which these organs deteriorate. Fundamental health-care concerns are:
smoking This is strongly linked to heart disease, stroke, bronchitis, lung cancer, and other serious diseases.
exercise Regular physical exercise improves fitness, slows down the gradual decline in efficiency of the heart and lungs, and so helps to prolong life.
diet A healthy diet contains plenty of vegetable fiber, complex carbohydrates, vitamins, minerals, and enzymes, and polyunsaturated fats (which keep the level of blood cholesterol low), not saturated (animal) fats (which contribute to cholesterol storage in blood vessels).
weight Obesity (defined as generally being 20% or more above the desirable weight for age, sex, build, and height) is associated with many potentially dangerous conditions, such as coronary heart disease, diabetes, and stroke, as well as muscular and joint problems, and breathing difficulties.
alcohol Recommended maximum intake is no more than 21 units of alcohol a week for men, no more than 14 for women. (One glass of beer or wine or a single ounce of liquor is equivalent to one unit.) Doctors recommend at least two alcohol-free days a week. Excessive alcohol intake may lead to dependence and causes liver damage, which suppresses the immune system and may be fatal (see ◊cirrhosis).

health education teaching and counseling on healthy living, including hygiene, nutrition, sex education, and advice on alcohol and drug abuse, smoking, and other threats to health. Health education in most secondary schools is also included within a course of personal and social education, or integrated into subjects such as biology, home economics, or physical education.

health psychology new development within ◊clinical psychology that applies psychological principles to promote physical well-being. For example, people with high blood pressure can learn methods such as relaxation, meditation, and lifestyle changes.

health service government provision of medical care on a national scale.
State and local governments provide some public health services. The US provides care through private physicians and hospitals who

are paid by the federally subsidized schemes **Medicare** and **Medicaid**. The Medicare health-insurance plan provides outpatient care for the elderly and disabled (toward which patients pay a share), and since 1985, fees for Medicare patients to join health-maintenance organizations (HMOs, covering visits to a group of doctors and hospital fees). The Medicaid state plan is paid to the state by the federal government for people unable to afford private care. US private health schemes include Blue Cross (established 1929) and Blue Shield (established 1917), as well as other insurance companies' plans.

Heard Island and McDonald Islands group of islands forming an Australian external territory in the S Indian Ocean, about 2,500 mi/4,000 km SW of Fremantle; area 158 sq mi/410 sq km. They were discovered 1833, annexed by Britain 1910, and transferred to Australia 1947. **Heard Island**, 26 mi/42 km by 12 mi/19 km, is glacier-covered, although the volcanic mountain **Big Ben** (9,000 ft/2,742 m) is still active. A weather station was built 1947. **Shag Island** is 5 mi/8 km to the north and the craggy McDonalds are 26 mi/42 km to the west.

hearing aid any device to improve the hearing of partially deaf people. Hearing aids usually consist of a battery-powered transistorized microphone/amplifier unit and earpiece. Some miniaturized aids are compact enough to fit in the ear or be concealed in the frame of eyeglasses.

Hearn (Patrick) Lafcadio 1850–1904. Greek-born US writer and translator who lived in Japan from 1890 and became a Japanese citizen. His many books on Japanese life and customs introduced the country to many Western readers, for example, *Glimpses of Unfamiliar Japan* 1893 and *In Ghostly Japan* 1904.
A journalist, Hearn was sent to Japan to write an article for a US magazine and never left. His sympathetic understanding of the country and its culture made him accepted and appreciated by the Japanese, and his writings are still widely read. From 1896 he taught English literature at Tokyo University.

hearsay evidence evidence given by a witness based on information passed to that person by others rather than evidence experienced at first hand by the witness. It is usually not admissible as evidence in criminal proceedings.

Hearst William Randolph 1863–1951. US newspaper publisher, celebrated for his introduction of banner headlines, lavish illustration, and the sensationalist approach known as "yellow journalism."
He was also a Hollywood film maker (promoting the career of his long-time mistress Marian Davies) as well as an unsuccessful presidential candidate.
A campaigner in numerous controversies, and a strong isolationist, he was said to be the model for Citizen Kane in the 1941 film of that name by Orson Welles. He collected art treasures, antiques, zoo animals, and castles—one of which, San Simeon (Hearst Castle) in California, is a state museum and zoo.

heart muscular organ that rhythmically contracts to force blood around the body of an animal with a circulatory system. Annelid worms and some other invertebrates have simple hearts consisting of thickened sections of main blood vessels that pulse regularly. An

earthworm has ten such hearts. Vertebrates have one heart. A fish heart has two chambers—the thin-walled **atrium** (once called the auricle) that expands to receive blood, and the thick-walled **ventricle** that pumps it out. Amphibians and most reptiles have two atria and one ventricle; birds and mammals have two atria and two ventricles. The beating of the heart is controlled by the autonomic nervous system and an internal control center or pacemaker, the sinoatrial node.

heart attack sudden onset of gripping central chest pain, often accompanied by sweating and vomiting, caused by death of a portion of the heart muscle following obstruction of a coronary artery by thrombosis (formation of a blood clot). Half of all heart attacks result in death within the first two hours, but in the remainder survival has improved following the widespread use of streptokinase and aspirin to treat heart-attack victims.
After a heart attack, most people remain in hospital for seven to ten days, and may make a gradual return to normal activity over the following months. How soon a patient is able to return to work depends on the physical and mental demands of their job. Despite widespread fears to the contrary, it is safe to return to normal sexual activity within about a month of the attack.

heartbeat the regular contraction and relaxation of the heart, and the accompanying sounds. As blood passes through the heart a double beat is heard. The first is produced by the sudden closure of the valves between the atria and the ventricles. The second, slightly delayed sound, is caused by the closure of the valves found at the entrance to the major arteries leaving the heart. Diseased valves may make unusual sounds, known as heart murmurs.

heartburn burning sensation below the breastbone (sternum). It results from irritation of the lower esophagus (gullet) by excessively acid stomach contents, as sometimes happens during pregnancy and in cases of duodenal ulcer or obesity. It is often due to a weak valve at the entrance to the stomach that allows its contents to well up into the esophagus.

heart disease disorder affecting the heart; for example, ◊ischaemic heart disease, in which the blood supply through the coronary arteries is reduced by ◊atherosclerosis; ◊valvular heart disease, in which a heart valve is damaged; and cardiomyopathy, where the heart muscle itself is diseased.

heart-lung machine apparatus used during heart surgery to take over the functions of the heart and the lungs temporarily. It has a pump to circulate the blood around the body and is able to add oxygen to the blood and remove carbon dioxide from it. A heart-lung machine was first used for open-heart surgery in the US 1953.

Heart of Atlanta Motel Inc v US US Supreme Court decision 1964 dealing with the constitutionality of certain Congressional measures designed to eliminate racial discrimination. The owner of the Heart of Atlanta Motel filed suit in protest of the Civil Rights Act 1964, which prevented him from racially discriminating against his customers. The Court upheld the Civil Rights Act, ruling that since the motel was a business involved in interstate travel, it was subject to federal regulation. This reversed the decision in the ◊Civil Rights Cases

1883 that the government could not proscribe discrimination by private citizens.

Heart of Darkness short novel by Joseph Conrad, published 1902. Marlow, the narrator, tells of his journey by boat into the African interior to meet a company agent, Kurtz, who has adopted local customs and uses barbaric methods to exercise power over the indigenous people.

heat form of internal energy possessed by a substance by virtue of the kinetic energy in the motion of its molecules or atoms. It is measured by ◊temperature. Heat energy is transferred by conduction, convection, and radiation. It always flows from a region of higher temperature (heat intensity) to one of lower temperature. Its effect on a substance may be simply to raise its temperature, or to cause it to expand, melt (if a solid), vaporize (if a liquid), or increase its pressure (if a confined gas).

Quantities of heat are usually measured in units of energy, such as joules (JU) or calories (C). The **specific heat** of a substance is the ratio of the quantity of heat required to raise the temperature of a given mass of the substance through a given range of temperature to the heat required to raise the temperature of an equal mass of water through the same range. It is measured by a ◊calorimeter. **Conduction** is the passing of heat along a medium to neighboring parts with no visible motion accompanying the transfer of heat—for example, when the whole length of a metal rod is heated when one end is held in a fire. **Convection** is the transmission of heat through a fluid (liquid or gas) in currents—for example, when the air in a room is warmed by a fire or radiator. **Radiation** is heat transfer by infrared rays. It can pass through a vacuum, travels at the same speed as light, can be reflected and refracted, and does not affect the medium through which it passes. For example, heat reaches the Earth from the Sun by radiation.

heath in botany, any woody, mostly evergreen shrub of the family Ericaceae, native to Europe, Africa, and North America. Many heaths have bell-shaped pendant flowers. In the Old World the genera *Erica* and *Calluna* are the most common heaths, and include ◊heather.

Included among the heaths are North American blueberries, rhododendrons, mountain laurel, and Labrador tea.

Heath Edward (Richard George) 1916– . British Conservative politician, party leader 1965–75. As prime minister 1970–74 he took the UK into the European Community but was brought down by economic and industrial relations crises at home. He was replaced as party leader by Margaret Thatcher 1975, and became increasingly critical of her policies and her opposition to the UK's full participation in the EC. In 1990 he undertook a mission to Iraq in an attempt to secure the release of British hostages.

heather low-growing evergreen shrub of the heath family, common on sandy or acid soil. The common heather *Calluna vulgaris* is a carpet-forming shrub, growing up to 24 in/60 cm high and bearing pale pink-purple flowers. It is found over much of Europe and has been introduced to North America.

heat pump machine, run by electricity or another power source, that cools the interior of a building by removing heat from interior air and pumping it out or, conversely, heats the inside by extracting energy from the atmosphere or from a hot-water source and pumping it in.

heat shield any heat-protecting coating or system, especially the coating (for example, tiles) used in spacecraft to protect the astronauts and equipment inside from the heat of reentry when returning to Earth. Air friction can generate temperatures of up to 2,700°F/1,500°C on reentry into the atmosphere.

heat storage any means of storing heat for release later. It is usually achieved by using materials that undergo phase changes, for example, Glauber's salt and sodium pyrophosphate, which melts at 158°F/70°C. The latter is used to store off-peak heat in the home: the salt is liquefied by cheap heat during the night and then freezes to give off heat during the day.

Other developments include the use of plastic crystals, which change their structure rather than melting when they are heated. They could be incorporated in curtains or clothing.

heatstroke or **sunstroke** rise in body temperature caused by excessive exposure to heat. Mild heatstroke is experienced as feverish lassitude, sometimes with simple fainting; recovery is prompt following rest and replenishment of salt lost in sweat. Severe heatstroke causes collapse akin to that seen in acute ◊shock, and is potentially lethal without prompt treatment of cooling the body carefully and giving fluids to relieve dehydration.

In severe heatstroke the brain swells resulting in confusion of thought, the body becomes feverish and dehydrated, blood circulation slows, and organs, such as the kidneys, fail to function. Coma may ensue, and possibly cardiac arrest.

heat treatment in industry, the subjection of metals and alloys to controlled heating and cooling after fabrication to relieve internal stresses and improve their physical properties. Methods include ◊annealing and ◊tempering.

heaven in Christianity and some other religions, the abode of God and the destination of the virtuous after death. Theologians now usually describe it as a place or state in which the soul experiences the full reality of God.

Heaviside Oliver 1850–1925. British physicist. In 1902 he predicted the existence of an ionized layer of air in the upper atmosphere, which was known as the Kennelly–Heaviside layer but is now called the ◊E layer of the ◊ionosphere. Deflection from it makes possible the transmission of radio signals around the world, which would otherwise be lost in outer space.

heavy metal in music, a style of rock characterized by loudness, sex-and-violence imagery, and guitar solos. Heavy metal developed out of the hard rock of the late 1960s and early 1970s, was performed by such groups as Led Zeppelin and Deep Purple, and enjoyed a resurgence in the late 1980s. Bands include Van Halen (formed 1974), Def Leppard (formed 1977), and Guns n' Roses (formed 1987).

heavy metal in chemistry, a metallic element of high atomic weight, such as platinum, gold, and lead. Many heavy metals are poisonous and tend to accumulate and persist in living systems—for example, high levels of mercury (from industrial waste and toxic dumping) accumulate in shellfish and fish, which are in turn eaten by humans. Treatment of heavy-metal poisoning is difficult because available drugs are not able to distinguish between the heavy metals that are essential to living cells (zinc, copper) and those that are poisonous.

Various detoxification programs combining nutrition, herbs, fasts, and intestinal irrigation are often successful.

heavy water or **deuterium oxide** D₂O water containing the isotope deuterium instead of hydrogen (molecular weight 20 as opposed to 18 for ordinary water).

Its chemical properties are identical with those of ordinary water, but its physical properties differ slightly. It occurs in ordinary water in the ratio of about one part by mass of deuterium to 5,000 parts by mass of hydrogen, and can be concentrated by electrolysis, the ordinary water being more readily decomposed by this means than the heavy water. It has been used in the nuclear industry.

Hebe in Greek mythology, the goddess of youth, daughter of Zeus and Hera.

Hebei or **Hopei** or **Hupei** province of N China
area 78,242 sq mi/202,700 sq km
capital Shijiazhuang
features includes special municipalities of Beijing and Tianjin
products cereals, textiles, iron, steel
population (1990) 61,082,000.

Hebrew member of the Semitic people who lived in Palestine at the time of the Old Testament and who traced their ancestry to ◊Abraham of Ur, a city of Sumer.

Also the language of the Old Testament and Judaic literature, as well as the official language (since 1948) of the state of Israel, one of the Semitic languages of the Hamito-Semitic (Afro-Asiatic) family. The Hebrew people were widely dispersed during the Roman Empire and learned the languages and cultures of those they lived among in Europe, the Near East, Asia, and (after 1492) the Americas, but continued using liturgical Hebrew in prayer, as well as the ancient Hebrew ◊alphabet to write both sacred works in Hebrew and secular works in ◊Yiddish, a 13th-century High German dialect. In the late 19th century, Hebrew was revived as a modern language, by the European Haskala movement, in both spoken and written forms.

Hebrew Bible the sacred writings of Judaism (some dating from as early as 1200 BC), called by Christians the ◊Old Testament. It includes the Torah (the first five books, ascribed to Moses), historical and prophetic books, and psalms, originally written in Hebrew and later translated into Greek (◊Pentateuch) and other languages.

Hebrew language member of the ◊Hamito-Semitic language family spoken in SW Asia by the ancient Hebrews, sustained for many centuries in the Diaspora as the liturgical language of Judaism, revived by the late-19th-century Haskala movement, and developed in the 20th century as Israeli Hebrew, the national language of the state of Israel. It is the original language of the Old Testament of the Bible.

Such English words as *cherub, chutzpah, Jehovah/Yahweh, kosher, rabbi, sabbath, seraph,* and *shibboleth* are borrowings from Hebrew. The Hebrew alphabet (called the *aleph-beth*) is written from right to left.

Hebrews epistle in the New Testament, probably written to the Hebrew converts to Christianity. It is no longer attributed to Paul, but its authorship is unknown.

Hebrides group of more than 500 islands (fewer than 100 inhabited) off W Scotland; total area 1,120 sq mi/2,900 sq km. The Hebrides were settled by Scandinavians during the 6th to 9th centuries and passed under Norwegian rule from about 890 to 1266.

The **Inner Hebrides** are divided between Highland and Strathclyde regions, and include ▷Skye, ▷Mull, ▷Jura, ▷Islay, ▷Iona, ▷Rum, Raasay, Coll, Tiree, Colonsay, Muck, and uninhabited Staffa. The **Outer Hebrides** form the islands area of the ▷Western Isles administrative area, separated from the Inner Hebrides by the Little Minch. They include ▷Lewis with Harris, North Uist, South Uist, ▷Barra, and ▷St Kilda.

Hebron (Arabic **El Khalil**) town on the West Bank of the Jordan, occupied by Israel 1967; population (1967) 43,000, including 4,000 Jews. It is a front-line position in the confrontation between Israelis and Arabs in the ▷Intifada. Within the mosque is the traditional site of the tombs of Abraham, Isaac, and Jacob.

Hecate in Greek mythology, the goddess of witchcraft and magic, sometimes identified with ▷Artemis and the Moon.

Hecht Ben 1894–1964. US journalist, author, and playwright. A collection of his newspaper feature stories, *1001 Nights in Chicago*, appeared 1922. Hecht's greatest success came in his 1928 collaboration with Charles MacArthur on the popular play *The Front Page*. He then went to Hollywood and wrote many successful screenplays, including *Twentieth Century* 1934 and *Wuthering Heights* 1939, and became known as a script-doctor for others' screenplays. Hecht's autobiography, *Child of the Century*, was published 1954.

Born in New York City and raised in Racine, Wisconsin, Hecht began his writing career as a reporter for the *Chicago Journal* and as a foreign corespondent for the *Chicago Daily News*. Also interested in fiction writing, he published his first novel, *Erik Dorn*, 1921.

hectare metric unit of area equal to 10,000 square meters (2.47 acres), symbol ha.

Hector in Greek mythology, a Trojan prince, son of King Priam and husband of Andromache, who, in the siege of Troy, was the foremost warrior on the Trojan side until he was killed by ▷Achilles.

Hecuba in Greek mythology, the wife of King Priam, and mother of Hector and ▷Paris. She was captured by the Greeks after the fall of Troy.

Hedda Gabler play by Henrik Ibsen, first produced 1891. Trapped in small-town society, Hedda Gabler takes out her spiritual and sexual frustrations on everyone from her ineffectual academic husband to the reformed alcoholic writer Lövborg. When her mean-spirited revenge backfires, she commits suicide.

hedge or **hedgerow** row of closely planted shrubs or low trees, generally acting as a land division and windbreak. Hedges also serve as a source of food and as a refuge for wildlife, and provide a ▷habitat not unlike the understory of a natural forest.

Generally, the older a hedge, the more species are found contained in a given length, roughly one species per century for a 30-yd length. About 309 species of plant occur only in hedgerows. Hedges are part of the landscape in Britain, N France, Ireland, and New England, but many have been destroyed to accommodate altered farming practices and larger machinery.

hedgehog insectivorous mammal of the genus *Erinaceus*, native to Europe, Asia, and Africa. The body, including the tail, is 1 ft/ 30 cm long. It is grayish-brown in color, has a piglike snout, and is covered with sharp spines. When alarmed it can roll itself into a ball. Hedgehogs feed on insects, slugs, and carrion. Long-eared hedgehogs and desert hedgehogs are placed in different genera.

hedonism ethical theory that pleasure or happiness is, or should be, the main goal in life. Hedonist sects in ancient Greece were the ▷Cyrenaics, who held that the pleasure of the moment is the only human good, and the Epicureans (see ▷Epicureanism), who advocated the pursuit of pleasure under the direction of reason. Modern hedonistic philosophies, such as those of the British philosophers Jeremy Bentham and J S Mill, regard the happiness of society, rather than that of the individual, as the aim.

Hefner Hugh Marston 1926– . US publisher, founder of *Playboy* magazine 1953. With its distinctive rabbit logo, monthly "Playmate" centerfolds of nude women, and columns and interviews of opinion, fashion, and personal advice on sex and other topics, *Playboy* helped reshape the social attitudes of the postwar generation. In the early 1960s, the magazine's huge success led to the creation of a national chain of Playboy clubs and resorts.

Hefner, who was born in Chicago and educated at the University of Illinois, also saw *Playboy*'s readership drop steeply in the 1980s, due to the rise of competing men's magazines and feminist protest.

Hegel Georg Wilhelm Friedrich 1770–1831. German philosopher who conceived of consciousness and the external object as forming a unity in which neither factor can exist independently, mind and nature being two abstractions of one indivisible whole. He believed development took place through dialectic: thesis and antithesis (contradiction) and synthesis, the resolution of contradiction. For Hegel, the task of philosophy was to comprehend the rationality of what already exists; leftist followers, including Karl Marx, used Hegel's dialectic to attempt to show the inevitability of radical change and to attack both religion and the social order of the European Industrial Revolution.

He wrote *The Phenomenology of Spirit* 1807, *Encyclopaedia of the Philosophical Sciences* 1817, and *Philosophy of Right* 1821.

He was professor of philosophy at Heidelberg 1817–18 and at Berlin 1818–31. As a rightist, Hegel championed religion, the Prussian state, and the existing order.

hegemony (Greek *hegemonia* "authority") political dominance of one power over others in a group in which all are supposedly equal. The term was first used for the dominance of Athens over the other Greek city-states, later applied to Prussia within Germany, and, in more recent times, to the US and the USSR with regard to the rest of the world.

Hegira the flight of the prophet Mohammed; see ▷Hijrah.

Heidegger Martin 1889–1976. German philosopher. In *Sein und Zeit/Being and Time* 1927 (translated 1962) he used the methods of Edmund ▷Husserl's phenomenology to explore the structures of human existence. His later writings meditated on the fate of a world dominated by science and technology.

He believed that Western philosophy had "forgotten" the fundamental question of the "meaning of Being." Although one of his major concerns was the angst of human existence, he denied that he was an existentialist. His support for Nazism and his unwillingness or inability to defend his position damaged his reputation.

Heidelberg town on the south bank of the river Neckar, 12 mi/19 km SE of Mannheim, in Baden-Württemberg, Germany; population (1988) 136,000. Heidelberg University, the oldest in Germany, was established 1386. The town is overlooked by the ruins of its 13th–17th century castle, 330 ft/100 m above the river.

Heidelberg village near Melbourne, Australia, that gave its name to the **Heidelberg School**—a group of Impressionist artists (including Tom Roberts, Arthur Streeton, and Charles Conder) working in teaching camps in the neighborhood.

Heifetz Jascha 1901–1987. Russian-born US violinist, one of the great virtuosos of the 20th century. He first performed at the age of five, and before he was 17 had played in most European capitals, and in the US, where he settled 1917. His style of playing was calm and objective.

He appeared in several Hollywood movies, played in a trio with Artur ▷Rubinstein and Grigor Piatigorsky (1903–1976), and after returning from the concert stage taught several violinists including Eugene Fodor.

Heike monogatari (Japanese "tales of the Heike") Japanese chronicle, written down in the 14th century but based on oral legend describing events that took place 200 years earlier, recounting the struggle for control of the country between the rival Genji (Minamoto) and Heike (▷Taira) clans. The conflict resulted in the end of the Heian period, and the introduction of the first shogunate (military dictatorship). Many subsequent Japanese dramas are based on material from the chronicle.

Heilongjiang or **Heilungkiang** province of NE China, in ▷Manchuria
area 178,950 sq mi/463,600 sq km
capital Harbin
features China's largest oil field, near Anda
products cereals, gold, coal, copper, zinc, lead, cobalt
population (1990) 35,215,000.

Heilungkiang former name of ▷Heilongjiang, a province of NE China.

Heine Heinrich 1797–1856. German Romantic poet and journalist who wrote *Reisebilder* 1826 and *Buch der Lieder/Book of Songs* 1827. From 1831 he lived mainly in Paris, working as a correspondent for German newspapers. Schubert and Schumann set many of his lyrics to music.

In 1835 he headed a list of writers forbidden to publish in Germany. He contracted a spinal disease 1845 that confined him to his bed from 1848 until his death.

Heinlein Robert A(nson) 1907– . US science-fiction writer, associated with the pulp magazines of the 1940s, who wrote the militaristic novel *Starship Troopers* 1959 and the utopian cult novel *Stranger in a Strange Land* 1961. His work helped to increase the legitimacy of science fiction as a literary genre.

Heinz Henry John 1844–1919. US industrialist. Born in Pittsburgh, Heinz entered his family's brick business but became interested in the possibilities of wholesale food marketing, founding a firm for that purpose 1876. The firm, renamed the H J Heinz Co 1888, specialized in the manufacture of prepared foods and condiments. Heinz popularized the use of ketchup and made famous his company's slogan "57 Varieties."

As president, Heinz oversaw every phase of production, from farming to advertising. Unlike some of his competitors, he was a strong supporter of the 1906 US Pure Food and Drug Act.

Heisenberg Werner Carl 1901–1976. German physicist who developed ◊quantum theory and formulated the ◊uncertainty principle, which concerns matter, radiation, and their reactions, and places absolute limits on the achievable accuracy of measurement. He was awarded a Nobel Prize 1932.

Hejaz former independent kingdom, merged 1932 with Nejd to form ◊Saudi Arabia; population (1970) 2,000,000; the capital is Mecca.

Hel or **Hela** in Norse mythology, the goddess of the underworld.

Helen in Greek mythology, the daughter of Zeus and Leda, and the most beautiful of women. She married Menelaus, King of Sparta, but during his absence, was abducted by Paris, Prince of Troy. This precipitated the Trojan War. Afterwards she returned to Sparta with her husband.

Helena capital of Montana, located in the W central part of the state, near the Big Belt Mountains, S of the Missouri River; population (1990) 24,600. It was settled after gold was discovered 1864. Industries include agricultural products, machine parts, ceramics, paints, sheet metal, and chemicals.

Helena, St c. 248–328. Roman empress, mother of Constantine the Great, and a convert to Christianity. According to legend, she discovered the true cross of Jesus in Jerusalem. Her feast day is Aug 18.

Helicon mountain in central Greece, on which was situated a spring and a sanctuary sacred to the ◊Muses.

helicopter powered aircraft that achieves both lift and propulsion by means of a rotary wing, or rotor, on top of the fuselage. It can take off and land vertically, move in any direction, or remain stationary in the air. It can be powered by piston or jet engine. The ◊autogiro was a precursor.

The rotor of a helicopter has two or more blades of airfoil cross-section like an airplane's wings. Lift and propulsion are achieved by angling the blades as they rotate. Experiments using the concept of helicopter flight date from the early 1900s, with the first successful lift-off and short flight 1907. Igor ◊Sikorsky built the first practical single-rotor craft in the US 1939. A single-rotor helicopter must also have a small tail rotor to counter the torque, or tendency of the body to spin in the opposite direction to the main rotor. Twin-rotor helicopters, like the Boeing Chinook, have their rotors turning in opposite directions to prevent the body from spinning. Helicopters are now widely used in passenger service, rescue missions on land and sea, police pursuits and traffic control, firefighting, and agriculture. In war they carry troops and equipment into difficult terrain, make aerial reconnaissance and attacks, and carry the wounded to aid stations.

Heligoland island in the North Sea, one of the North Frisian Islands; area 0.2 sq mi/ 0.6 sq km. It is administered by the state of Schleswig-Holstein, Germany, having been ceded to Germany by Britain 1890 in exchange for ◊Zanzibar. It was used as a naval base in both world wars.

heliography old method of signaling, used by armies in the late 19th century, which employed sunlight reflected from a mirror to pass messages in ◊Morse code. On a clear day, a heliograph could send over distances in excess of 30 mi/50 km. Also, an early photographic process by which a permanent image was formed on a glass plate.

Heliopolis ancient Egyptian center (the biblical *On*) of the worship of the sun god Ra, NE of Cairo and near the village of Matariah.

Helios in Greek mythology, the sun god and

father of ◊Phaethon, thought to make his daily journey across the sky in a chariot.

heliosphere region of space through which the ◊solar wind flows outward from the Sun. The **heliopause** is the boundary of this region, believed to lie about 100 astronomical units from the Sun, where the flow of the solar wind merges with the interstellar gas.

heliotrope decorative plant of the genus *Heliotropium* of the borage family Boraginaceae, with distinctive spikes of blue, lilac, or white flowers, including the Peruvian or cherry pie heliotrope *H. peruvianum*.

helium (Greek *helios* "Sun") colorless, odorless, gaseous, nonmetallic element, symbol He, atomic number 2, atomic weight 4.0026. It is grouped with the ◊inert gases, is nonreactive, and forms no compounds. It is the second most abundant element (after hydrogen) in the universe, and has the lowest boiling (–452°F/–268.9°C) and melting points (–458°F/–272.2°C) of all the elements. It is present in small quantities in the Earth's atmosphere from gases issuing from radioactive elements (from ◊alpha decay) in the Earth's crust; after hydrogen it is the second lightest element.

Helium is a component of most stars, including the Sun, where the nuclear-fusion process converts hydrogen into helium with the production of heat and light. It is obtained by compression and fractionation of naturally occurring gases. It is used for inflating balloons and as a dilutant for oxygen in deep-sea breathing systems. Liquid helium is used extensively in low-temperature physics (cryogenics).

helix in mathematics, a three-dimensional curve resembling a spring, corkscrew, or screw thread. It is generated by a line that encircles a cylinder or cone at a constant angle.

hell in various religions, a place of posthumous punishment. In Hinduism, Buddhism, and Jainism, hell is a transitory stage in the progress of the soul, but in Christianity and Islam it is eternal (◊purgatory is transitory). Judaism does not postulate such punishment.

In the Bible, the word "hell" is used to translate Hebrew and Greek words all meaning "the place of departed spirits, the abode of the dead." In medieval Christian theology, hell is the place where unrepentant sinners suffer the torments of the damned, but the 20th-century tendency has been to regard hell as a state of damnation (that is, everlasting banishment from the sight of God) rather than a place.

Helle in Greek mythology, the daughter of Athamas, King of Thessaly, and sister of Phryxes. With her brother she ran away from Ino, their cruel stepmother, on a ram with a ◊Golden Fleece. Helle fell into the sea and drowned, thus giving her name to the **Hellespont** ("sea of Helle").

hellebore poisonous European herbaceous plant of the genus *Helleborus* of the buttercup family Ranunculaceae. The stinking hellebore *H. foetidus* has greenish flowers early in the spring.

The white, or false, hellebore *Veratrum viride* of North America is a poisonous member of the lily family Liliaceae.

helleborine temperate Old World orchid of the genera *Epipactis* and *Cephalanthera*, including the marsh helleborine *E. palustris* and the hellebore orchid *E. helleborine* introduced to North America.

rotor rotates horizontally for vertical flight

rotor tilts forward for forward flight

backwards for backward flight

sideways for sideways flight

main rotor

tail rotor

variable pitch of rotor

main rotor control stick controls pitch and tilt of blades

tail rotor control pedals

skid

helicopter *The helicopter is controlled by varying the rotor pitch (the angle of the rotor blade as it moves through the air).*

The rattlesnake orchids (genus *Goodyera*) of North America are sometimes placed in the genus *Epipactis*.

Hellene (Greek *Hellas* "Greece") alternate name for a ◊Greek.

Hellenic period (from *Hellas*, Greek name for Greece) Classical period of ancient Greek civilization, from the first Olympic Games 776 BC until the death of Alexander the Great 323 BC.

Hellenistic period period in Greek civilization from the death of Alexander 323 BC until the accession of the Roman emperor Augustus 27 BC. Alexandria in Egypt was the center of culture and commerce during this period, and Greek culture spread throughout the Mediterranean region.

Heller Joseph 1923– . US novelist. He drew on his experiences in the US air force in World War II to write ◊*Catch-22* 1961, satirizing war and bureaucratic methods. A film based on the book appeared 1970.

After serving in the air force, he entered advertising. His other works include the novels *Something Happened* 1974 and *Good As Gold* 1979, and the plays *We Bombed In New Haven* 1968 and *Clevinger's Trial* 1974.

Hellespont former name of the ◊Dardanelles, the strait that separates Europe from Asia.

Hellman Lillian 1907–1984. US playwright whose work is concerned with contemporary political and social issues. *The Children's Hour* 1934, *The Little Foxes* 1939, and *Toys in the Attic* 1960 are all examples of the "well-made play."

She lived 31 years with the writer Dashiell Hammett, and in her will set up a fund to promote Marxist doctrine. Since her death there has been dispute over the accuracy of her memoirs, for example *Pentimento* 1973.

Helmholtz Hermann Ludwig Ferdinand von 1821–1894. German physiologist, physicist, and inventor of the ophthalmoscope for examining the inside of the eye. He was the first to explain how the cochlea of the inner ear works, and the first to measure the speed of nerve impulses. In physics he formulated the law of conservation of energy, and worked in thermodynamics.

The ophthalmoscope made possible the examination of the inside of the eye. This was a great advance in ophthalmic medicine, as was his ophthalmometer for measuring the curvature of the eye. He also studied magnetism, electricity, and the physiology of hearing.

Helmont Jean Baptiste van 1577–1644. Belgian doctor who was the first to realize that there are gases other than air, and claimed to have coined the word "gas" (from Greek *cháos*).

Helms Richard 1913– . US director of the Central Intelligence Agency 1966–73, when he was dismissed by President Nixon. In 1977 he was convicted of lying before a congressional committee because his oath as chief of intelligence compelled him to keep secrets from the public. He was originally with the Office of Strategic Services, before it developed into the CIA 1947.

Héloïse 1101–1164. Abbess of Paraclete in Champagne, France, correspondent and lover of ◊Abelard. She became deeply interested in intellectual study in her youth and was impressed by the brilliance of Abelard, her teacher, whom she secretly married. After her affair with Abelard, and the birth of a son, Astrolabe, she became a nun 1129, and

with Abelard's assistance, founded a nunnery at Paraclete. Her letters show her strong and pious character and her devotion to Abelard.

helot member of a class of slaves in ancient Sparta who were probably the indigenous inhabitants. Their cruel treatment by the Spartans became proverbial.

Helsingborg (Swedish *Hälsingborg*) port in SW Sweden, linked by ferry with Helsingør across Øre Sound; population (1990) 109,300. Industries include copper smelting, rubber and chemical manufacture, and sugar refining.

Helsingfors Swedish name for ◊Helsinki, capital of Finland.

Helsingør (English *Elsinore*) port in NE Denmark; population (1990) 56,800. It is linked by ferry with Helsingborg across Øre Sound; Shakespeare made it the scene of *Hamlet*.

Helsinki (Swedish *Helsingfors*) capital and port of Finland; population (1990) 492,400, metropolitan area 978,000. Industries include shipbuilding, engineering, and textiles. The homes of the architect Eliel Saarinen and the composer Jean Sibelius outside the town are museums.

Helsinki Conference international meeting 1975 at which 35 countries, including the USSR and the US, attempted to reach agreement on cooperation in security, economics, science, technology, and human rights. This established the ◊Conference on Security and Cooperation in Europe (CSCE).

Helvetia region, corresponding to W Switzerland, occupied by the Celtic Helvetii 1st century BC–5th century AD. In 58 BC Caesar repulsed their invasion of southern Gaul at Bibracte (near Autun) and Helvetia became subject to Rome.

Helvetius Claude Adrien 1715–1771. French philosopher. In *De l'Esprit* 1758 he argued, following David ◊Hume, that self-interest, however disguised, is the mainspring of all human action and that since conceptions of good and evil vary according to period and locality there is no absolute good or evil. He also believed that intellectual differences are only a matter of education.

Helvetius's principle of artificial identity of interests (those manipulated by governments) influenced the utilitarian philosopher Jeremy Bentham. *De l'Esprit* was denounced and burned by the public hangman.

hematite principal ore of iron, consisting mainly of iron(III) oxide, Fe_2O_3. It occurs as ***specular hematite*** (dark, metallic luster), ***kidney ore*** (reddish radiating fibers terminating in smooth, rounded surfaces), and as a red earthy deposit.

hematology branch of medicine concerned with disorders of the blood.

Hemingway Ernest 1898–1961. US writer. War, bullfighting, and fishing are used symbolically in his work to represent honor, dignity, and primitivism—prominent themes in his short stories and novels, which include *A Farewell to Arms* 1929, *For Whom the Bell Tolls* 1940, and *The Old Man and the Sea* 1952. His deceptively simple writing styles attracted many imitators. He received the Nobel Prize for Literature 1954.

He was born in Oak Park, Illinois, and in his youth developed a passion for hunting and adventure. He became a journalist and was wounded while serving on a volunteer ambulance crew in Italy in World War I. His style

was influenced by Gertrude ◊Stein, who also introduced him to bullfighting, a theme in his first novel, *The Sun Also Rises* 1926, and the memoir *Death in the Afternoon* 1932. *A Farewell to Arms* deals with wartime experiences on the Italian front, and *For Whom the Bell Tolls* has a Spanish Civil War setting. He served as war correspondent both in that conflict and in Europe during World War II. After a full life, physical weakness, age, and depression contributed to his suicide.

hemlock plant *Conium maculatum* of the carrot family Umbelliferae, native to Europe, W Asia, and N Africa. Reaching up to 6 ft/2 m high, it bears umbels of small white flowers. The whole plant, especially the root and fruit, is poisonous, causing paralysis of the nervous system. The name hemlock is also applied to members of the genus *Tsuga* of North American and Asiatic conifers of the pine family.

hemoglobin protein that carries oxygen. In vertebrates it occurs in red blood cells, giving them their color. Oxygen attaches to hemoglobin in the lungs or gills where the amount dissolved in the blood is high. This process effectively increases the amount of oxygen that can be carried in the bloodstream. The oxygen is later released in the body tissues where it is at low concentration. Hemoglobin also works in carrying carbon dioxide away from tissues to the lungs or gills.

hemolymph the circulatory fluid of those mollusks and insects that have an "open" circulatory system. Hemolymph contains water, amino acids, sugars, salts, and white cells like those of blood. Circulated by a contractile heart, its main functions are to transport digestive and excretory products around the body. In mollusks, it also transports oxygen and carbon dioxide.

hemolysis destruction of red blood cells. Aged cells are constantly being lyzed (broken down), but increased wastage of red cells is seen in some infections and blood disorders. It may result in ◊jaundice (through the release of too much hemoglobin) and in ◊anemia.

hemophilia any of several inherited diseases in which normal blood clotting is impaired. The sufferer experiences prolonged bleeding from the slightest wound, as well as painful internal bleeding without apparent cause.

Hemophilias are nearly always sex-linked, transmitted through the female line only to male infants; it has afflicted a number of European royal households. Males affected by the most common form are unable to synthesize Factor VIII, a protein involved in the clotting of blood. Treatment is primarily with Factor VIII (now mass-produced from donated blood), but the hemophiliac remains at risk from the slightest incident of bleeding. The disease is a painful one that causes deformities of joints.

hemorrhage loss of blood from the circulatory system. It is "manifest" when the blood can be seen, as when it flows from a wound, and "occult" when the bleeding is internal, as from an ulcer or internal injury.

Rapid, profuse hemorrhage causes ◊shock and may prove fatal if the circulating volume cannot be replaced in time. Slow, sustained bleeding may lead to ◊anemia. Arterial bleeding is potentially more serious than blood lost from a vein. It may be stemmed by pressure above the wound, as by tourniquet.

hemorrhoids distended blood vessels (⬦varicose veins) in the area of the anus, popularly called piles.

hemostasis natural or surgical stoppage of bleeding. In the natural mechanism, the damaged vessel contracts, restricting the flow, and blood ⬦platelets plug the opening, releasing chemicals essential to clotting.

hemp annual plant *Cannabis sativa*, family Cannabaceae. Originally from Asia, it is cultivated in most temperate countries for its fibers, produced in the outer layer of the stem, and used in ropes, twines, and, occasionally, in a type of linen or lace. Marijuana and hashish are obtained from certain varieties of hemp.

The name "hemp" is extended to similar types of fiber: **sisal hemp** and **henequen** obtained from the leaves of *Agave* species native to Yucatán and cultivated in many tropical countries, and **manila hemp** obtained from *Musa textilis*, a plant native to the Philippines and the Moluccas.

Henan or **Honan** province of E central China
area 64,462 sq mi/167,000 sq km
capital Zhengzhou
features river plains of the Huang He (Yellow River); ruins of Xibo, the 16th-century BC capital of the Shang dynasty, were discovered here in the 1980s
products cereals, cotton
population (1990) 85,510,000.

henbane poisonous plant *Hyoscyamus niger* of the nightshade family Solanaceae, found on waste ground throughout most of Europe and W Asia. A branching plant, up to 31 in/80 cm high, it has hairy leaves and a nauseous smell. The yellow flowers are bell-shaped. Henbane is used in medicine as a source of hyoscyamine and scopolamine.

Hench Philip Showalter 1896–1965. US physician who introduced cortisone treatment for rheumatoid arthritis. Hench shared the 1950 Nobel Prize for Medicine with Edward ⬦Kendall and Tadeus ⬦Reichstein.

He noticed that arthritic patients improved greatly during pregnancy or an attack of jaundice and concluded that a ⬦hormone secreted in increased quantity during both these conditions caused the improvement. This turned out to be cortisol, a ⬦steroid converted to cortisone in the liver.

Hendrix Jimi (James Marshall) 1942–1970. US rock guitarist, songwriter, and singer, legendary for his virtuoso experimental technique and flamboyance. *Are You Experienced?* 1967 was his first album. His performance at the 1969 Woodstock festival included a memorable version of "The Star-Spangled Banner" and is recorded in the film *Woodstock*. He greatly expanded the vocabulary of the electric guitar and influenced both rock and jazz musicians.

Hendrix moved to the UK 1966 and formed a trio, the Jimi Hendrix Experience, which produced hit singles with their first recorded songs ("Hey Joe" and "Purple Haze," both 1967), and attracted notice in the US when Hendrix burned his guitar at the 1967 Monterey Pop Festival. The group disbanded early 1969 after three albums; Hendrix continued to record and occasionally perform until his death the following year.

Henie Sonja 1912–1969. Norwegian skater. Champion of her country at 11, she won ten world championships and three Olympic titles. She turned professional 1936 and went on to make numerous films in Hollywood.

CAREER HIGHLIGHTS

Olympic champion
1928, 1932, 1936 (record 3 wins)
World champion
1927–36 (record 10 wins)

Henlein Konrad 1898–1945. Sudeten-German leader of the Sudeten Nazi Party in Czechoslovakia, and closely allied with Hitler's Nazis. He was partly responsible for the destabilization of the Czechoslovak state 1938, which led to the ⬦Munich Agreement and secession of the Sudetenland to Germany.

henna small shrub *Lawsonia inermis* of the loosestrife family Lythraceae, found in Iran, India, Egypt, and N Africa. The leaves and young twigs are ground to a powder, mixed to a paste with hot water, and applied to fingernails and hair, giving an orange-red hue. The color may then be changed to black by applying a preparation of indigo.

Henotikon declaration published by Roman emperor Zeno 482, aimed at reconciling warring theological factions within the early Christian church. It refuted the Council of Chalcedon 451, and reaffirmed the heretical idea that Jesus was one person, not two. The declaration, not accepted by Rome, led to a complete split between Rome and Constantinople 484–519.

Henri Robert. Adopted name of Robert Henry Cozad 1865–1929. US landscape and portrait painter. Although he executed a number of noted works, such as *Himself* and *Herself* 1913, he is best known as a teacher, profoundly influencing such artists as George ⬦Bellows, William ⬦Glackens, Edward ⬦Hopper, Rockwell Kent, and George ⬦Luks.

Born in Cincinnati, Ohio, he was trained at the Pennsylvania Academy of the Fine Arts, after which he studied in Europe before returning to the US.

henry SI unit (symbol H) of ⬦inductance (the reaction of an electric current against the magnetic field that surrounds it). One henry is the inductance of a circuit that produces an opposing voltage of one volt when the current changes at one ampere per second.

It is named after the US physicist Joseph Henry.

Henry Joseph 1797–1878. US physicist, inventor of the electromagnetic motor 1829 and of a telegraphic apparatus. He also discovered the principle of electromagnetic induction, roughly at the same time as Michael ⬦Faraday, and the phenomenon of self-induction. A unit of inductance (henry) is named after him.

Henry Patrick 1736–1799. US politician who in 1775 supported the arming of the Virginia militia against the British by a speech ending, "Give me liberty or give me death!" He was governor of Virginia 1776–79 and 1784–86.

He assisted in the creation of the ⬦Continental Congress of which he was a member. He opposed ratification of the US Constitution, contending that it posed a danger to state sovereignty. His influence, however, helped to ensure the passage of the first ten amendments (see ⬦Bill of Rights).

Henry William 1774–1836. British chemist. In 1803 he formulated **Henry's law**, which states that when a gas is dissolved in a liquid at a given temperature, the mass that dissolves is in direct proportion to the pressure of the gas.

Henry eight kings of England:

Henry I 1068–1135. King of England from 1100. Youngest son of William I, he succeeded his brother William II. He won the support of the Saxons by granting them a charter and marrying a Saxon princess. An able administrator, he established a professional bureaucracy and a system of traveling judges. He was succeeded by Stephen.

Henry II 1133–1189. King of England from 1154, when he succeeded ⬦Stephen. He was the son of ⬦Matilda and Geoffrey of Anjou (1113–1151). He curbed the power of the barons, but his attempt to bring the church courts under control had to be abandoned after the murder of Thomas à ⬦Becket. During his reign the English conquest of Ireland began. He was succeeded by his son Richard I.

He was lord of Scotland, Ireland, and Wales, and count of Anjou, Brittany, Poitou, Normandy, Maine, Gascony, and Aquitaine. He was married to Eleanor of Aquitaine.

Henry III 1207–1272. King of England from 1216, when he succeeded John, but he did not rule until 1227. His financial commitments to the papacy and his foreign favorites led to de ⬦Montfort's revolt 1264. Henry was defeated at Lewes, Sussex, and imprisoned. He was restored to the throne after the royalist victory at Evesham 1265. He was succeeded by his son Edward I.

The royal powers were exercised by a regency until 1232 and by two French nobles, Peter des Roches and Peter des Rivaux, until the barons forced their expulsion 1234, marking the start of Henry's personal rule. While he was in prison, de Montfort ruled in his name. On his release Henry was weak and senile and his eldest son, Edward, took charge of the government.

Henry IV (Bolingbroke) 1367–1413. King of England from 1399, the son of ⬦John of Gaunt. In 1398 he was banished by ⬦Richard II for political activity but returned 1399 to head a revolt and be accepted as king by Parliament. He was succeeded by his son Henry V.

He had difficulty in keeping the support of Parliament and the clergy. To win support he had to conciliate the church by a law for the burning of heretics and to make many concessions to Parliament.

Henry V 1387–1422. King of England from 1413, son of Henry IV. Invading Normandy 1415 (during the Hundred Years' War), he captured Harfleur and defeated the French at ⬦Agincourt. He invaded again 1417–19, capturing Rouen. His military victory forced the French into the Treaty of Troyes 1420, which gave Henry control of the French government. He married ⬦Catherine of Valois 1420 and gained recognition as heir to the French throne by his father-in-law Charles VI, but died before him. He was succeeded by his son Henry VI.

Henry VI 1421–1471. King of England from 1422, son of Henry V. He assumed royal power 1442 and sided with the party opposed to the continuation of the Hundred Years' War with France. After his marriage 1445, he was dominated by his wife, ⬦Margaret of Anjou. The unpopularity of the government, especially after the loss of the English conquests in France, encouraged Richard, Duke of ⬦York, to claim the throne, and though York was killed 1460, his son Edward IV proclaimed himself king 1461 (see Wars of the ⬦Roses). Henry was captured 1465, temporarily restored 1470, but again imprisoned 1471 and then murdered.

Henry VII 1457–1509. King of England from

1485, son of Edmund Tudor, Earl of Richmond (*c.* 1430–1456), and a descendant of ◇John of Gaunt. He spent his early life in Brittany until 1485, when he landed in Britain to lead the rebellion against Richard III which ended with Richard's defeat and death at ◇Bosworth. By his marriage to Elizabeth of York 1486 he united the houses of York and Lancaster. Yorkist revolts continued until 1497, but Henry restored order after the Wars of the ◇Roses by the ◇Star Chamber and achieved independence from Parliament by amassing a private fortune through confiscations. He was succeeded by his son Henry VIII.

Henry VIII 1491–1547. King of England from 1509, when he succeeded his father Henry VII and married Catherine of Aragon, the widow of his brother. During the period 1513–29 Henry pursued an active foreign policy, largely under the guidance of his Lord Chancellor, Cardinal Wolsey who shared Henry's desire to make England a notable nation. Wolsey was replaced by Thomas More 1529 for failing to persuade the pope to grant Henry a divorce. After 1532 Henry broke with papal authority, proclaimed himself head of the church in England, dissolved the monasteries, and divorced Catherine. His subsequent wives were Anne Boleyn, Jane Seymour, Anne of Cleves, Catherine Howard, and Catherine Parr. He was succeeded by his son Edward VI.

Henry demanded his first divorce because his wife had become too old to bear him a (male) heir and he was taken with Anne ◇Boleyn. Thomas ◇Cromwell initiated legislation that made Henry head of the Church of England, allowing him to marry Anne 1533, who later that year gave birth to Elizabeth I. (Jane Seymour was the mother of Edward VI.) Henry's last years were devoted to war with France and Scotland, consequent economic problems, and attempts to hold back the ◇Reformation, which his own interests had unleashed in his nation.

Henri four kings of France:

Henri I 1005–1060. King of France from 1031. He spent much of his reign in conflict with ◇William I the Conqueror, then duke of Normandy.

Henri II 1519–1559. King of France from 1547. He captured the fortresses of Metz and Verdun from the Holy Roman emperor Charles V and Calais from the English. He was killed in a tournament.

In 1526 he was sent with his brother to Spain as a hostage, being returned when there was peace 1530. He married Catherine de' Medici 1533, and from then on was dominated by her, Diane de Poitiers, and Duke Montmorency. Three of his sons, Francis II, Charles IX, and Henri III, became kings of France.

Henri III 1551–1589. King of France from 1574. He fought both the ◇Huguenots (headed by his successor, Henry of Navarre) and the Catholic League (headed by the Duke of Guise). Guise expelled Henry from Paris 1588 but was assassinated. Henry allied with the Huguenots under Henry of Navarre to besiege the city, but was assassinated by a monk.

Henri IV 1553–1610. King of France from 1589. Son of Antoine de Bourbon and Jeanne, Queen of Navarre, he was brought up as a Protestant and from 1576 led the ◇Huguenots. On his accession he settled the religious question by adopting Catholicism while tolerating Protestantism. He restored peace and strong

government to France and brought back prosperity by measures for the promotion of industry and agriculture and the improvement of communications. He was assassinated by a Catholic extremist.

Henry seven Holy Roman emperors:

Henry I *the Fowler* c. 876–936. King of Germany from 919, and duke of Saxony from 912. He secured the frontiers of Saxony, ruled in harmony with its nobles, and extended German influence over the Danes, the Hungarians, and the Slavonic tribes. He was about to claim the imperial crown when he died.

Henry II *the Saint* 973–1024. King of Germany from 1002, Holy Roman emperor from 1014, when he recognized Benedict VIII as pope. He was canonized 1146.

Henry III *the Black* 1017–1056. King of Germany from 1028, Holy Roman emperor from 1039 (crowned 1046). He raised the empire to the height of its power, and extended its authority over Poland, Bohemia, and Hungary.

Henry IV 1050–1106. Holy Roman emperor from 1056, who was involved from 1075 in a struggle with the papacy (see ◇Gregory VII). Excommunicated twice (1076 and 1080), Henry deposed Gregory and set up the antipope Clement III (died 1191) by whom he was crowned Holy Roman emperor 1084.

Henry V 1081–1125. Holy Roman emperor from 1106. He continued the struggle with the church until the settlement of the ◇investiture contest 1122.

Henry VI 1165–1197. Holy Roman emperor from 1190. As part of his plan for making the empire universal, he captured and imprisoned Richard I of England and compelled him to do homage.

Henry VII 1269–1313. Holy Roman emperor from 1308. He attempted unsuccessfully to revive the imperial supremacy in Italy.

Henry of Blois died 1171. Brother of King Stephen of England, he was bishop of Winchester from 1129, and Pope Innocent II's legate to England from 1139. While remaining loyal to Henry II, he tried to effect a compromise between ◇Becket and the king.

Henry the Lion 1129–1195. Duke of Bavaria 1156–80, duke of Saxony 1142–80, and duke of Lüneburg 1180–85. He was granted the Duchy of Bavaria by the Emperor Frederick Barbarossa. He founded Lübeck and Munich. In 1162 he married Matilda, daughter of Henry II of England. His refusal in 1176 to accompany Frederick Barbarossa to Italy led in 1180 to his being deprived of the duchies of Bavaria and Saxony. Henry led several military expeditions to conquer territory in the East.

Henry the Navigator 1394–1460. Portuguese prince, the fourth son of John I. He set up a school for navigators 1419 and under his patronage Portuguese sailors explored and colonized Madeira, the Cape Verde Islands, and the Azores; they sailed down the African coast almost to Sierra Leone.

Henson Jim (James Maury) 1936–1990. US puppeteer who created the television Muppet characters, including Kermit the Frog, Miss Piggy, and Fozzie Bear. The Muppets became popular on the children's educational TV series *Sesame Street*, which first appeared in 1969 and soon became regular viewing in over 80 countries. In 1976 Henson created *The Muppet Show*, which ran for five years and became one

of the world's most widely seen TV programs, reaching 235 million viewers in 100 countries. Three Muppet movies followed. In 1989 the Muppets became part of the ◇Disney empire.

Henze Hans Werner 1926– . German composer whose large and varied output includes orchestral, vocal, and chamber music. He uses traditional symphony and concerto forms, and incorporates a wide range of styles including jazz. Operas include *Das Verratene Meer* (Berlin 1992) based on Yukio Mishima's *The Sailor Who Fell from Grace with the Sea*.

heparin anticoagulant substance produced by cells of the liver, lungs, and intestines. It normally inhibits the clotting of blood by interfering with the production of thrombin, which is necessary for clot formation. Heparin obtained from animals is used medically after surgery to limit the risk of ◇thrombosis, or following pulmonary ◇embolism to ensure that no further clots form.

hepatic of or pertaining to the liver.

hepatitis any inflammatory disease of the liver, usually caused by a virus. Other causes include alcohol, drugs, gallstones, ◇lupus *erythematosus*, and amebic dysentery. Symptoms include weakness, nausea, and jaundice.

The viral disease **hepatitis A** (infectious or viral hepatitis) is spread by contaminated food, often seafood, and via the oro-fecal route. Incubation is about four weeks. Temporary immunity is conferred by injections of normal ◇immunoglobulin (gamma globulin). The virus causing **hepatitis B** (serum hepatitis) was isolated in the 1960s. Contained in all body fluids, it is very easily transmitted. Some people become ◇carriers. Those with the disease may be sick for weeks or months. The illness may be mild, or it may result in death from liver failure. Liver cancer is now recognized as a long-term complication of the disease. A successful vaccine was developed in the late 1970s.

Hepburn Audrey (Audrey Hepburn-Rushton) 1929–1993. British actress of Anglo-Dutch descent who often played innocent, childlike characters. Slender and doe-eyed, she set a different style from the more ample women stars of the 1950s. After playing minor parts in British films in the early 1950s, she became a Hollywood star in such films as *Funny Face* 1957, *My Fair Lady* 1964, *Wait Until Dark* 1968, and *Robin and Marian* 1976.

Hepburn Katharine 1909– . US actress who made feisty self-assurance her trademark. She appeared in such films as *Morning Glory* 1933 (Academy Award), *Little Women* 1933, *Bringing Up Baby* 1938, *The Philadelphia Story* 1940, *Woman of the Year* 1942, *The African Queen* 1951, *Pat and Mike* 1952 (with her frequent partner Spencer Tracy), *Guess Who's Coming to Dinner* 1967 (Academy Award), *Lion in Winter* 1968 (Academy Award), and *On Golden Pond* 1981 (Academy Award). She also had a distinguished stage career.

Hephaestus in Greek mythology, the god of fire and metalcraft (Roman Vulcan), son of Zeus and Hera, husband of Aphrodite. He was lame.

Hepplewhite George died 1786. English furniture maker. He developed a simple, elegant style, working mainly in mahogany or satinwood, adding delicately inlaid or painted decorations of feathers, shells, or ears of wheat. His book of designs, *The Cabinetmaker and Upholsterer's Guide* 1788, was published posthumously.

heptarchy the seven Saxon kingdoms thought to have existed in England before AD 800: Northumbria, Mercia, East Anglia, Essex, Kent, Sussex, and Wessex. The term was coined by 16th-century historians.

heptathlon multi-event athletics discipline for women consisting of seven events over two days: 100 meters hurdles, high jump, shot put, 200 meters (day one); long jump, javelin, 800 meters (day two). Points are awarded for performances in each event in the same way as the ◊decathlon. It replaced the pentathlon (five events) in international competition 1981.

Hera in Greek mythology, a goddess (Roman Juno), sister-consort of Zeus, mother of Hephaestus, Hebe, and Ares; protector of women and marriage.

Heracles in Greek mythology, a hero (Roman Hercules), son of Zeus and Alcmene, famed for strength. While serving Eurystheus, King of Argos, he performed 12 labors, including the cleansing of the Augean stables.

Heraclitus *c.* 544–483 BC. Greek philosopher who believed that the cosmos is in a ceaseless state of flux and motion, fire being the fundamental material that accounts for all change and motion in the world. Nothing in the world ever stays the same, hence the dictum, "one cannot step in the same river twice."

Wisdom came from understanding this eternal dynamic, which unified the diversity of nature, as he wrote in *On Nature*. Heraclitus was born in Ephesus.

Heraclius *c.* 575–641. Byzantine emperor from 610. His reign marked a turning point in the empire's fortunes. Of Armenian descent, he recaptured Armenia 622, and other provinces 622–28 from the Persians, but lost them to the Muslims 629–41.

Heraklion alternate name for *Iráklion*, a Greek port.

heraldry insignia and symbols representing a person, family, or dynasty. Heraldry originated with simple symbols used on banners and shields for recognition in battle. By the 14th century, it had become a complex pictorial language with its own regulatory bodies (courts of chivalry), used by noble families, corporations, cities, and realms. The world's oldest heraldic court is the English College of Arms founded by Henry V; it was incorporated 1484 by Richard III.

Herat capital of Herat province, and the largest city in W Afghanistan, on the north banks of the Hari Rud River; population (1980) 160,000. A principal road junction, it was a great city in ancient and medieval times.

herb any plant (usually a flowering plant) tasting sweet, bitter, aromatic, or pungent, used in cooking, medicine, or perfumery; technically, a herb is any plant in which the aerial parts do not remain above ground at the end of the growing season.

herbaceous plant plant with very little or no wood, dying back at the end of every summer. The herbaceous perennials survive winters as underground storage organs such as bulbs and tubers.

herbarium collection of dried, pressed plants used as an aid to identification of unknown plants and by taxonomists in the ◊classification of plants. The plant specimens are accompanied by information, such as the date and place of collection, by whom collected, details of habitat, flower color, and local names.

Herbaria range from small collections containing plants of a limited region, to the large university and national herbaria (some at ◊botanical gardens) containing millions of specimens from all parts of the world.

Herbert Frank (Patrick) 1920–1986. US science-fiction writer, author of the *Dune* series from 1965 (filmed by David Lynch 1984), large-scale adventure stories containing serious ideas about ecology and religion.

Herbert Victor 1859–1924. Irish-born US conductor and composer. He immigrated to the US in 1886 and played with the New York Metropolitan Opera and Philharmonic Orchestra. In 1893 he was named conductor of the 22nd Regiment Band, also composing light operettas for the New York stage. After serving as conductor of the Pittsburgh Philharmonic 1898–1904, he returned to New York and helped found the American Society of Composers, Authors, and Publishers (ASCAP) 1914.

Born in Dublin and trained as a cellist at the Stuttgart Conservatory, Herbert began his professional musical career in Vienna.

herbicide any chemical used to destroy plants or check their growth; see ◊weedkiller.

herbivore animal that feeds on green plants (or photosynthetic single-celled organisms) or their products, including seeds, fruit, and nectar. The most numerous type of herbivore is thought to be the zooplankton, tiny invertebrates in the surface waters of the oceans that feed on small photosynthetic algae. Herbivores are more numerous than other animals because their food is the most abundant. They form a vital link in the food chain between plants and carnivores.

Herblock popular name of US cartoonist Herbert Lawrence Block 1909– . During the 1950s, he gained a national reputation through his syndicated cartoons. He won Pulitzer prizes 1942 and 1952, published several collections of his work, and took a leading role in the public campaign against the communist witch-hunting tactics of Senator Joseph ◊McCarthy.

He was born in Chicago and joined the staff of the *Chicago Daily News* 1929 as an editorial cartoonist. After serving in the army during World War II, he joined the staff of the *Washington Post* 1946.

herb Robert wild ◊geranium *Geranium robertianum* found throughout Europe and central Asia and naturalized in North America. About 12 in/30 cm high, it bears hairy leaves and small pinkish to purplish flowers.

Herculaneum ancient city of Italy between Naples and Pompeii. Along with Pompeii, it was buried when Vesuvius erupted AD 79. It was excavated from the 18th century onwards.

Hercules Roman form of ◊Heracles.

Hercules in astronomy, the fifth largest constellation, lying in the northern hemisphere. Despite its size it contains no prominent stars. Its most important feature is a ◊globular cluster of stars 22,500 light-years from Earth, one of the best examples in the sky.

Hercules, Pillars of rocks (at Gibraltar and Ceuta) that guard the western entrance to the Mediterranean Sea.

Herder Johann Gottfried von 1744–1803. German poet, critic, and philosopher. Herder's critical writings indicated his intuitive rather than reasoning trend of thought. He collected folk songs of all nations 1778, and in the *Ideen zur Philosophie der Geschichte der Menschheit/ Outlines of a Philosophy of the History of Man* 1784–91 he outlined the stages of human cultural development.

heredity in biology, the transmission of traits from parent to offspring. See also ◊genetics.

Hereford and Worcester county in W central England
area 1,517 sq mi/3,930 sq km
cities Worcester (administrative headquarters), Hereford, Kidderminster, Evesham, Ross-on-Wye, Ledbury
features rivers: Wye, Severn; Malvern Hills (high point Worcester Beacon 1,395 ft/425 m) and Black Mountains; fertile Vale of Evesham.

heresy (Greek *hairesis* "parties" of believers) doctrine opposed to orthodox belief, especially in religion. Those holding ideas considered heretical by the Christian church have included Gnostics, Arians, Pelagians, Montanists, Albigenses, Waldenses, Lollards, and Anabaptists.

Herman Woody (Woodrow) 1913–1987. US bandleader and clarinetist. A child prodigy, he was leader of his own orchestra at 23, and after 1945 formed his famous Thundering Herd band. Soloists in this or later versions of the band included Lester Young and Stan ◊Getz.

hermaphrodite organism that has both male and female sex organs. Hermaphroditism is the norm in species such as earthworms and snails, and is common in flowering plants. Cross-fertilization is the rule among hermaphrodites, with the parents functioning as male and female simultaneously, or as one or the other sex at different stages in their development.

Hermaphroditus in Greek mythology, the son of Hermes and Aphrodite. He was loved by a nymph who prayed for eternal union with him, so that they became one body with dual sexual characteristics, hence the term hermaphrodite.

hermeneutics philosophical tradition concerned with the nature of understanding and interpretation of human behavior and social traditions. From its origins in problems of biblical interpretation, hermeneutics has expanded to cover many fields of inquiry, including aesthetics, literary theory, and science. ◊Dilthey, ◊Heidegger, and Gadamer are influential contributors to this tradition.

Hermes in Greek mythology, a god, son of Zeus and Maia; messenger of the gods; he wore winged sandals, a wide-brimmed hat, and carried a staff around which serpents coiled. Identified with the Roman Mercury and ancient Egyptian Thoth, he protects thieves, travelers, and merchants.

Hermes Trismegistus supposed author of the *Hermetica* (2nd–3rd centuries AD), a body of writings expounding a Hellenistic mystical philosophy in which the Sun is regarded as the visible manifestation of God. In the Renaissance these writings were thought to be by an Egyptian priest contemporary with Moses, and it is possible they contain some Egyptian material.

Hermione in Greek mythology, daughter of ◊Menelaus and ◊Helen, and wife either to ◊Neoptolemos or to ◊Orestes.

hermit religious ascetic living in seclusion, often practicing extremes of mortification (such as the Stylites, early Christians who lived on top of pillars).

The Christian monastic movement developed as a way of organizing into communities the ascetic hermits living in the deserts of ancient Egypt and the Middle East.

hermit crab a kind of ⟩crab.

Hermon (Arabic *Jebel esh-Sheikh*) snow-topped mountain, 9,232 ft/2,814 m high, on the Syria–Lebanon border. According to tradition, Jesus was transfigured here.

Herndon v Lowry US Supreme Court decision 1937 dealing with state restriction of First-Amendment rights in sedition cases. Herndon, a Communist organizer convicted of sedition under a Georgia law, appealed to the US Supreme Court for protection of his right to free speech. The Court reversed Herndon's conviction, ruling that a tendency to incite violent revolt was not sufficient grounds to revoke First-Amendment rights without evidence of a "clear and present danger" to society.

hernia or *rupture* protrusion of part of an internal organ through a weakness in the surrounding muscular wall, usually in the groin or navel. The appearance is that of a rounded soft lump or swelling.

Hero and Leander in Greek mythology, a pair of lovers. Hero was a priestess of Aphrodite at Sestos on the Hellespont, in love with Leander on the opposite shore at Abydos. When he was drowned while swimming across during a storm, she threw herself into the sea.

Herod *the Great* 74–4 BC. King of the Roman province of Judea, S Palestine, from 40 BC. With the aid of Mark Antony, he established his government in Jerusalem 37 BC. He rebuilt the Temple in Jerusalem, but his Hellenizing tendencies made him suspect to orthodox Jewry. His last years were a reign of terror, and in the New Testament Matthew alleges that he ordered the slaughter of all the infants in Bethlehem to ensure the death of Jesus, whom he foresaw as a rival. He was the father of Herod Antipas.

Herod Agrippa I 10 BC–AD 44. Ruler of Palestine from AD 41. His real name was Marcus Julius Agrippa, erroneously called "Herod" in the Bible. Grandson of Herod the Great, he was made tetrarch (governor) of Palestine by the Roman emperor Caligula and king by Emperor Claudius AD 41. He put the apostle James to death and imprisoned the apostle Peter. His son was Herod Agrippa II.

Herod Agrippa II *c.* AD 40–93. King of Chalcis (now S Lebanon), son of Herod Agrippa I. He was appointed by the Roman emperor Claudius about AD 50, and in AD 60 tried the apostle Paul. He helped the Roman emperor Titus take Jerusalem AD 70, then went to Rome, where he died.

Herod Antipas 21 BC–AD 39. Tetrarch (governor) of the Roman province of Galilee, N Palestine, 4 BC–AD 9, son of Herod the Great. He divorced his wife to marry his niece Herodias, who persuaded her daughter Salome to ask for John the Baptist's head when he reproved Herod's action. Jesus was brought before him on Pontius Pilate's discovery that he was a Galilean and hence of Herod's jurisdiction, but Herod returned him without giving any verdict. In AD 38 Herod Antipas went to Rome to try to persuade Emperor Caligula to give him the title of king, but was instead banished.

Herodotus *c.* 484–424 BC. Greek historian.

After four years in Athens, he traveled widely in Egypt, Asia, and eastern Europe, before settling at Thurii in S Italy 443 BC. He wrote a nine-book history of the Greek-Persian struggle that culminated in the defeat of the Persian invasion attempts 490 and 480 BC. Herodotus was the first historian to apply critical evaluation to his material.

heroin or *diamorphine* powerful endogenous ⟩opiate analgesic, an acetyl derivative of ⟩morphine. It is more addictive than morphine but causes less nausea and is one of the most abused drugs in the US. Because of its powerful habit-forming qualities, its manufacture and import are forbidden in the US, even for medical use.

heron large to medium-sized wading bird of the family Ardeidae, which also includes bitterns, egrets, night herons, and boatbills. Herons have sharp bills, broad wings, long legs, and soft plumage. They are found mostly in tropical and subtropical regions, but also in temperate zones.

The great blue heron *Ardea herodias* is native to North America. Gray-blue overall, breeding adults have yellowish bills and ornate plumes on the head, neck, and back. A wader, it feeds mainly on fish and frogs.

Hero of Alexandria Greek mathematician and engineer, probably of the 1st century AD, who invented an automatic fountain and a kind of stationary steam-engine, described in his book *Pneumatica*.

herpes any of several infectious diseases caused by viruses of the herpes group. *Herpes simplex I* is the causative agent of a common inflammation, the cold sore. *Herpes simplex II* is responsible for genital herpes, a highly contagious, sexually transmitted disease characterized by painful blisters in the genital area. It can be transmitted in the birth canal from mother to newborn. *Herpes zoster* causes ⟩shingles; another herpes virus causes chickenpox.

A number of ⟩antivirals treat these infections, which are particularly troublesome in patients whose immune system has been suppressed medically; for example, after a transplant operation.

The Epstein–Barr virus of infectious ⟩mononucleosis also belongs to this group.

Herrick Robert 1591–1674. English poet and cleric, born in Cheapside, London. He published *Hesperides* 1648, a collection of sacred and pastoral poetry admired for its lyric quality, including "Gather ye rosebuds" and "Cherry ripe."

herring any of various marine fishes of the herring family (Clupeidae), but especially the important food fish *Clupea harengus*. A silvered greenish-blue, it swims close to the surface, and may be 10–16 in/25–40 cm long. Herring travel in schools several miles long and wide. They are found in large quantities off the E coast of North America, and the shores of NE Europe. Overfishing and pollution have reduced their numbers.

Herriot Edouard 1872–1957. French Radical socialist politician. An opponent of Poincaré, who as prime minister carried out the French occupation of the Ruhr, Germany, he was briefly prime minister 1924–25, 1926, and 1932. As president of the chamber of deputies 1940, he opposed the policies of the right-wing Vichy government and was arrested and later taken to Germany; he was released 1945 by the Soviets.

Herriot James. Adopted name of James Alfred Wight 1916– . English writer. A practicing veterinary surgeon in Yorkshire from 1940, he wrote of his experiences in a series of books including *If Only They Could Talk* 1970, *All Creatures Great and Small* 1972, and *The Lord God Made Them All* 1981.

Herrmann Bernard 1911–1975. American film composer whose long career began with *Citizen Kane* 1940 and included collaborations with Alfred Hitchcock (*North by Northwest* 1959 and *Psycho* 1960) and François Truffaut (*Fahrenheit 451* 1966). He wrote his best scores for thriller and mystery movies, and was a major influence in the establishment of a distinctively American musical imagery.

Herschel Caroline Lucretia 1750–1848. German-born English astronomer, sister of William ⟩Herschel, and from 1772 his assistant in England. She discovered eight comets and was awarded the Royal Astronomical Society's gold medal for her work on her brother's catalog of star clusters and nebulae.

Herschel John Frederick William 1792–1871. English scientist and astronomer, son of William Herschel. He discovered thousands of close ⟩double stars, clusters, and ⟩nebulae, reported 1847. A friend of the photography pioneer Fox ⟩Talbot, Herschel coined the terms "photography," "negative," and "positive," discovered sodium thiosulfite as a fixer of silver halides, and invented the cyanotype process; his inventions also include astronomical instruments.

He became director of the Cape of Good Hope observatory in South Africa 1834.

Herschel William 1738–1822. German-born English astronomer. He was a skilled telescope maker, and pioneered the study of binary stars and nebulae. He discovered the planet Uranus 1781 and infrared solar rays 1801. He cataloged over 800 double stars, and found over 2,500 nebulae, cataloged by his sister Caroline Herschel; this work was continued by his son John Herschel. By studying the distribution of stars, William established the basic form of our Galaxy, the Milky Way.

Born in Hanover, Germany, he went to England 1757 and became a professional musician and composer while instructing himself in mathematics and astronomy, and constructing his own reflecting telescopes. While searching for ⟩double stars, he found Uranus, and later several of its satellites. This brought him instant fame and, in 1782, the post of private astronomer to George III. He discovered the motion of double stars around one another, and recorded it in his *Motion of the Solar System in Space* 1783. In 1789 he built, at Slough, a 4 ft/1.2 m telescope of 40 ft/12 m focal length (the largest in the world at the time), but he made most use of a more satisfactory 18 in/46 cm instrument.

Hertfordshire county in SE England
area 629 sq mi/1,630 sq km
cities Hertford (administrative headquarters), St Albans, Watford, Hatfield, Hemel Hempstead, Bishop's Stortford, Letchworth (the first garden city, followed by Welwyn 1919 and Stevenage 1947)
features rivers: Lea, Stort, Colne; part of the Chiltern Hills; Hatfield House; Knebworth House (home of Lord Lytton); Brocket Hall (home of Palmerston and Melbourne); home of G B ⟩Shaw at Ayot St Lawrence; Berkhamsted Castle (Norman); Rothamsted agricultural experimental station

products engineering, aircraft, electrical goods, paper and printing; general agricultural goods
population (1991) 951,500
famous people Graham Greene was born at Berkhamsted.

Hertling Count Georg von 1843–1919. German politician who was appointed imperial chancellor Nov 1917. He maintained a degree of support in the Reichstag (parliament) but was powerless to control the military leadership under ▷Ludendorff.

Hertogenbosch see ▷'s-Hertogenbosch, capital of North Brabant, the Netherlands.

hertz SI unit (symbol Hz) of frequency (the number of repetitions of a regular occurrence in one second). Radio waves are often measured in megahertz (MHz), millions of hertz, and the clock rate of a computer is usually measured in megahertz. The unit is named after Heinrich Hertz.

Hertz Heinrich 1857–1894. German physicist who studied electromagnetic waves, showing that their behavior resembles that of light and heat waves.

He confirmed ▷Maxwell's theory of electromagnetic waves. The unit of frequency, the *hertz*, is named after him.

Herzog James Barry Munnik 1866–1942. South African politician, prime minister 1924–39, founder of the Nationalist Party 1913 (the United South African National Party from 1933). He opposed South Africa's entry into both world wars.

Hertzsprung–Russell diagram in astronomy, a graph on which the surface temperatures of stars are plotted against their luminosities. Most stars, including the Sun, fall into a narrow band called the ▷*main sequence*. When a star grows old it moves from the main sequence to the upper right part of the graph, into the area of the giants and supergiants. At the end of its life, as the star shrinks to become a white dwarf, it moves again, to the bottom left area. It is named after the Dane Ejnar Hertzsprung (1873–1967) and the American Henry Norris Russell (1877–1957), who independently devised it in the years 1911–13.

Herzegovina or **Hercegovina** part of ▷Bosnia-Herzegovina (which was formerly, until 1991, a republic of Yugoslavia).

Herzl Theodor 1860–1904. Austrian founder of the *Zionist* movement. He was born in Budapest and became a successful playwright and journalist, mainly in Vienna. The ▷Dreyfus case convinced him that the only solution to the problem of anti-Semitism was the resettlement of the Jews in a state of their own. His book *Jewish State* 1896 launched political ▷Zionism, and he became the first president of the World Zionist Organization 1897.

Herzog Werner 1942– . German maverick film director who often takes his camera to exotic and impractical locations. His highly original and visually splendid films include *Aguirre der Zorn Gottes/Aguirre Wrath of God* 1972, *Nosferatu Phantom der Nacht/Nosferatu Phantom of the Night* 1979, and *Fitzcarraldo* 1982.

Hesiod lived *c.* 700 BC. Greek poet. He is supposed to have lived a little later than Homer, and according to his own account he was born in Boeotia. He is the author of "Works and Days," a poem that tells of the country life, and the *Theogony*, an account of the origin of the world and of the gods.

Hesperides in Greek mythology, the Greek maidens who guarded a tree bearing golden apples in the Islands of the Blessed (also known as the Hesperides).

Hess (Walter Richard) Rudolf 1894–1987. German Nazi leader. Imprisoned with Hitler 1923–25, he became his private secretary, taking down *Mein Kampf* from his dictation. In 1932 he was appointed deputy *Führer* to Hitler. On May 10, 1941 he landed by air in the UK with compromise peace proposals and was held a prisoner of war until 1945, when he was tried at Nuremberg as a war criminal and sentenced to life imprisonment. He died in ▷Spandau prison, Berlin.

He was effectively in charge of the Nazi party organization until his flight 1941. For the last years of his life he was the only prisoner left in Spandau.

Hess Victor 1883–1964. Austrian physicist who emigrated to the US shortly after sharing a Nobel Prize in 1936 for the discovery of cosmic radiation.

He was professor at Fordham University, New York, from 1938.

Hesse Hermann 1877–1962. German writer who became a Swiss citizen 1923. A conscientious objector in World War I and a pacifist opponent of Hitler, he published short stories, poetry, and novels, including *Peter Camenzind* 1904, *Siddhartha* 1922, and *Steppenwolf* 1927. Later works, such as *Das Glasperlenspiel/The Glass Bead Game* 1943, tend toward the mystical. He was awarded the Nobel Prize for Literature 1946.

Hessen administrative region (German *Land*) of Germany
area 8,145 sq mi/21,100 sq km
capital Wiesbaden
cities Frankfurt-am-Main, Kassel, Darmstadt, Offenbach-am-Main
features valleys of the rivers Rhine and Main; Taunus mountains, rich in mineral springs, as at Homburg and Wiesbaden; see also ▷Swabia
products wine, timber, chemicals, automobiles, electrical engineering, optical instruments
population (1988) 5,550,000
religion Protestant 61%, Roman Catholic 33%
history Until 1945, Hessen was divided in two by a strip of Prussian territory, the southern portion consisting of the valleys of the rivers Rhine and the Main, the northern being dominated by the Vogelsberg Mountains (2,442 ft/744 m). Its capital was Darmstadt.

Hestia in Greek mythology, the goddess (Roman Vesta) of the hearth, daughter of ▷Cronus (Roman Saturn) and Rhea.

Heston Charlton. Adopted name of Charles Carter 1924– . US film actor who often starred in biblical and historical epics (as Moses, for example, in *The Ten Commandments* 1956, and in the title role in *Ben-Hur* 1959).

heterophony choral melody singing and playing, found in folk music around the world, in which individual players have some freedom to improvise.

heterosexuality sexual preference for, or attraction mainly to, persons of the opposite sex.

heterosis or *hybrid vigor* improvement in physical capacities that sometimes occurs in the ▷hybrid produced by mating two genetically different parents.

The parents may be of different strains or varieties within a species, or of different species, as in the mule, which is stronger and has a longer life span than either of its parents (donkey and horse). Heterosis is also exploited in hybrid varieties of corn, tomatoes, and other crops.

heterostyly in botany, having ▷styles of different lengths. Certain flowers, such as primroses (*Primula vulgaris*), have different-sized ▷anthers and styles to ensure cross-fertilization (through ▷pollination) by visiting insects.

heterotroph any living organism that obtains its energy from organic substances produced by other organisms. All animals and fungi are heterotrophs, and they include herbivores, carnivores, and saprotrophs (those that feed on dead animal and plant material).

heterozygous in a living organism, having two different ▷alleles for a given trait. In ▷homozygous organisms, by contrast, both chromosomes carry the same allele. In an outbreeding population an individual organism will generally be heterozygous for some genes but homozygous for others.

For example, in humans, alleles for both blue-and brown-pigmented eyes exist, but the "blue" allele is ▷recessive to the dominant "brown" allele. Only individuals with blue eyes are predictably homozygous for this trait; brown-eyed people can be either homozygous or heterozygous.

heuristics in computing, a process by which a program attempts to improve its performance by learning from its own experience.

Hevesy Georg von 1885–1966. Swedish chemist, discoverer of the element hafnium. He was the first to use a radioactive isotope (radioactive form of an element) to follow the steps of a biological process, for which he won the Nobel Prize for Chemistry 1943.

Hewish Antony 1924– . British radio astronomer who was awarded, with Martin ▷Ryle, the Nobel Prize for Physics 1974 for his work on ▷pulsars, rapidly rotating neutron stars that emit pulses of energy.

hexachlorophene $(C_6HCl_3OH)_2CH_2$ white, odorless bactericide, used in minute quantities in soaps and surgical disinfectants.

Trichlorophenol is used in its preparation, and, without precise temperature control, the highly toxic TCDD (tetrachlorodibenzodioxin; see ▷dioxin) may form as a by-product.

hexadecimal number system number system to the base 16, used in computing. In hex (as it is commonly known) the decimal numbers 0–15 are represented by the characters 0, 1, 2, 3, 4, 5, 6, 7, 8, 9, A, B, C, D, E, F. Hexadecimal numbers are easy to convert to the computer's internal ▷binary code and are more compact than binary numbers.

Each place in a number increases in value by a power of 16 going from right to left; for instance, 8F is equal to 15 + (8 × 16) = 143 in decimal.

Heydrich Reinhard 1904–1942. German Nazi, head of the party's security service and Heinrich ▷Himmler's deputy. He was instrumental in organizing the ▷final solution, the policy of genocide used against Jews and others. While deputy "protector" of Bohemia and Moravia from 1941, he was ambushed and killed by three members of the Czechoslovak forces in Britain, who had landed by parachute. Reprisals followed, including several hundred executions and the massacre in ▷Lidice.

Heyerdahl Thor 1914– . Norwegian ethnologist. He sailed on the ancient-Peruvian-style raft ⬦*Kon-Tiki* from Peru to the Tuamotu Archipelago along the Humboldt Current 1947, and in 1969–70 used ancient-Egyptian-style papyrus reed boats to cross the Atlantic. His experimental approach to historical reconstruction is not regarded as having made any important scientific contribution.

His expeditions were intended to establish that ancient civilizations could have traveled the oceans in similar fashion, but his theories are largely discounted by anthropologists, who rely on linguistic, sociological, and archeological information. His voyages are described in *Kon-Tiki*, translated into English 1950, and *The Ra Expeditions*, translated 1971. He also crossed the Persian Gulf 1977, written about in *The Tigris Expedition*, translated 1981.

Hezbollah or *Hizbollah* (Party of God) extremist Muslim organization founded by the Iranian Revolutionary Guards who were sent to Lebanon after the 1979 Iranian revolution. Its aim is to spread the Islamic revolution of Iran among the Shiite population of Lebanon. Hezbollah is believed to be the umbrella movement of the groups that held many of the Western hostages taken since 1984.

Hezekiah in the Old Testament, king of Judah from 719 BC. Against the advice of the prophet Isaiah he rebelled against Assyrian suzerainty in alliance with Egypt, but was defeated by ⬦Sennacherib and had to pay out large amounts in indemnities. He carried out religious reforms.

HF in physics, the abbreviation for *high ⬦frequency*.

HI abbreviation for the state of ⬦*Hawaii*.

Hialeah city in SE Florida, just NW of Miami. Manufactures include clothing, furniture, plastics, and chemicals. Hialeah Park racetrack is a center for horse racing; population (1990) 188,000.

Hiawatha 16th-century North American Indian teacher and Onondaga chieftain. He is said to have welded the Five Nations (later joined by a sixth) of the ⬦Iroquois into the league of the *Long House*, as the confederacy was known in what is now upper New York State. Hiawatha is the hero of Longfellow's epic poem *The Song of Hiawatha*.

hibernation state of ⬦dormancy in which certain animals spend the winter. It is associated with a dramatic reduction in all metabolic processes, including body temperature, breathing, and heart rate. It is a fallacy that animals sleep throughout the winter.

The body temperature of the arctic ground squirrel falls to below 32°F/0°C during hibernation.

hibiscus any plant of the genus *Hibiscus* of the mallow family. Hibiscuses range from large herbaceous plants to trees. Popular as ornamental plants because of their brilliantly colored, red to white, bell-shaped flowers, they include *H. syriacus* and *H. rosa-sinensis* of Asia and the rose mallow *H. palustris* of North America.

Some tropical species provide fruit and timber: *H. tiliaceus* supplies timber and fibrous bark to South Pacific islanders; *H. sabdariffa* is cultivated in the West Indies and elsewhere for its fruit.

hiccup sharp noise caused by a sudden spasm of the ⬦diaphragm with closing of the windpipe, commonly caused by digestive disorder. On rare occasions, hiccups may become continuous, when they are very debilitating; treatment with a muscle relaxant drug may be effective.

Hickok "Wild Bill" (James Butler) 1837–1876. US pioneer and law enforcer, a legendary figure in the West. In the Civil War he was a sharpshooter and scout for the Union army. He then served as marshal in Kansas, killing as many as 27 men. He established his reputation as a gunfighter when he killed a fellow scout, turned traitor. He was a prodigious gambler and was fatally shot from behind while playing poker in Deadwood, South Dakota.

hickory tree of the genus *Carya* of the walnut family, native to North America and Asia. It provides a valuable timber, and all species produce nuts, although some are inedible. The pecan *C. illinoensis* is widely cultivated in the southern US, and the shagbark *C. ovata* in the northern US.

Hickory city in W central North Carolina, in the foothills of the Blue Ridge Mountains, NW of Charlotte. Its main industry is hosiery manufacture. Other products include rope, cotton, and wagons; population (1990) 28,300.

Hidalgo y Costilla Miguel 1753–1811. Catholic priest, known as "the Father of Mexican Independence." A symbol of the opposition to Spain, he rang the church bell Sept 1810 to announce to his parishioners in Dolores that the revolution against the Spanish had begun. He was captured and shot the following year.

hieroglyphic Egyptian writing system of the mid-4th millennium BC–3rd century AD, which combines picture signs with those indicating letters. The direction of writing is normally from right to left, the signs facing the beginning of the line. It was deciphered 1822 by the French Egyptologist J F Champollion (1790–1832) with the aid of the ⬦*Rosetta Stone*, which has the same inscription carved in hieroglyphic, demotic, and Greek.

hi-fi (abbreviation of *high-fidelity*) faithful reproduction of sound from a machine that plays recorded music or speech. A typical hi-fi system includes a turntable for playing vinyl records, a cassette tape deck to play magnetic tape recordings, a tuner to pick up radio broadcasts, an amplifier to serve all the equipment, possibly a compact-disk player, and two or more loudspeakers.

Advances in mechanical equipment and electronics, such as digital recording techniques and compact discs, have made it possible to eliminate many distortions in sound-reproduction processes.

Higgins George V 1939– . US novelist who wrote many detective and underworld novels, often set in Boston, including *The Friends of Eddie Coyle* 1972 and *The Impostors* 1986.

high-definition television (HDTV) ⬦television system offering a significantly greater number of scanning lines, and therefore a clearer picture, than that provided by conventional systems.

higher education in most countries, education beyond the age of 18 leading to a university or college degree or similar qualification.

high jump field event in track and field in which competitors leap over a horizontal crossbar held between rigid uprights at least 12 ft/ 3.66 m apart. The bar is placed at increasingly higher levels. Elimination occurs after three consecutive failures to clear the bar.

Highland Games traditional Scottish outdoor gathering that includes tossing the caber, shot put, running, dancing, and bagpipe playing.

Highland Region administrative region of Scotland
area 10,077 sq mi/26,100 sq km
cities Inverness (administrative headquarters), Thurso, Wick
features comprises almost half the country; Grampian Mountains; Ben Nevis (highest peak in the UK); Loch Ness, Caledonian Canal; Inner Hebrides; the Queen Mother's castle of Mey at Caithness; John O'Groats's House; Dounreay (with Atomic Energy Authority's prototype fast reactor, and a nuclear processing plant)
products oil services, winter sports, timber, livestock, grouse and deer hunting, salmon fishing
population (1991) 209,400

high-level language in computing, a programming language designed to suit the requirements of the programmer; it is independent of the internal machine code of any particular computer. High-level languages are used to solve problems and are often described as *problem-oriented languages*—for example, BASIC was designed to be easily learned by first-time programmers; COBOL is used to write programs solving business problems; and FORTRAN is used for programs solving scientific and mathematical problems. In contrast, low-level languages, such as ⬦assembly languages, closely reflect the machine codes of specific computers, and are therefore described as *machine-oriented languages*.

Unlike low-level languages, high-level languages are relatively easy to learn because the instructions bear a close resemblance to everyday language, and because the programmer does not require a detailed knowledge of the internal workings of the computer.

Each instruction in a high-level language is equivalent to several machine-code instructions. High-level programs are therefore more compact than equivalent low-level programs. However, each high-level instruction must be translated into machine code—by either a ⬦compiler or an ⬦interpreter program—before it can be executed by a computer.

High-level languages are designed to be *portable*—programs written in a high-level language can be run on any computer that has a compiler or interpreter for that particular language.

High Point city in N central North Carolina, SW of Greensboro. The furniture industry is very important to the economy; the Southern Furniture Market is held four times a year. Hosiery is also manufactured; population (1990) 69,500.

high tech (abbreviation for *high technology*) in architecture, buildings that display technical innovation of a high order and celebrate structure and services to create exciting forms and spaces. The Hong Kong and Shanghai Bank, Hong Kong, is a masterpiece of this approach.

highway any road used for automobile traffic open to the public, especially a main road or thoroughfare.

hijacking illegal seizure or taking control of a vehicle and/or its passengers or goods. The term dates from 1923 and originally referred to the robbing of freight trucks. In recent times it (and its derivative, "skyjacking") has been applied to the seizure of aircraft, usually in flight, by an individual or group, often with some political aim. International treaties (Tokyo 1963, The Hague 1970, and Montreal 1971) encourage cooperation against hijackers and make severe penalties compulsory.

Hijrah or *Hegira* the trip from Mecca to Medina of the prophet Mohammed, which took place AD 622 as a result of the persecution of the prophet and his followers. The Muslim calendar dates from this event, and the day of the Hijrah is celebrated as the Muslim New Year.

Hilbert David 1862–1943. German mathematician who founded the formalist school with the publication of *Grundlagen der Geometrie/Foundations of Geometry* 1899, which was based on his idea of postulates. He attempted to put mathematics on a logical foundation through defining it in terms of a number of basic principles, which ◊Gödel later showed to be impossible; nonetheless, his attempt greatly influenced 20th-century mathematicians.

Hildebrand Benedictine monk who became Pope ◊Gregory VII.

Hildegard of Bingen 1098–1179. German scientific writer, abbess of the Benedictine convent of St Disibode, near the Rhine, from 1136. She wrote a mystical treatise, *Liber Scivias* 1141, and an encyclopedia of natural history, *Liber Simplicis Medicinae* 1150–60, giving both Latin and German names for the species described, as well as their medicinal uses; it is the earliest surviving scientific book by a woman.

Hill Joe *c.* 1872–1915. Swedish-born US labor organizer. He immigrated to the US 1901 and, as a member of the Industrial Workers of the World (IWW, "Wobblies"), was a leader of a dockworkers' strike in San Pedro, California. A frequent contributor to the IWW's periodicals *Solidarity* and *Industrial Worker*, Hill is best remembered for his many popular prounion songs. He was arrested and convicted of murder on circumstantial evidence in Salt Lake City, Utah, 1914. Despite calls by President Wilson and the Swedish government for a retrial, Hill was executed 1915, becoming a martyr for the labor movement.

Hill's original name is given variously as Joel Emmanuel Haaglund (or Hagglund) or Joseph Hillstrom.

Hillary Edmund Percival 1919– . New Zealand mountaineer. In 1953, with Nepalese Sherpa mountaineer Tenzing Norgay, he reached the summit of Mount Everest, the first to climb the world's highest peak. As a member of the Commonwealth Transantarctic Expedition 1957–58, he was the first person since Scott to reach the South Pole overland, on Jan 3, 1958.

Hillel 1st century BC Hebrew scholar, lawyer, and teacher; member of the Pharisaic movement (see ◊Pharisee). His work was accepted by later rabbinic Judaism and was noted for its tolerance.

Hilton Conrad Nicholson 1887–1979. US hotel developer. At first successful in banking, Hilton entered the hotel business after World War I. Through the 1930s he steadily expanded his chain of luxury hotels and resorts, reorganizing it as the Hilton Hotel Corporation 1946. Basing his firm's marketing appeal on its recognizable name and high-quality standardized service, Hilton retired 1966. His autobiography, *Be My Guest*, was published 1957.

Born in San Antonio, New Mexico, Hilton attended the New Mexico School of Mines and joined his father in various business ventures after graduation 1909.

Hilton James 1900–1954. English novelist. He settled in Hollywood as one of its most successful scriptwriters, for example, *Mrs Miniver*. His books include *Lost Horizon* 1933, envisaging Shangri-la, a remote district of Tibet where time stands still; *Goodbye, Mr Chips* 1934, a portrait of an old schoolmaster; and *Random Harvest* 1941.

Himachal Pradesh state of NW India
area 21,500 sq mi/55,700 sq km
capital Simla
features mainly agricultural state, one-third forested, with softwood timber industry
products timber, grain, rice, fruit
population (1991) 5,111,000; mainly Hindu
language Pahari
history created as a Union Territory 1948, it became a full state 1971.

Certain hill areas were transferred to Himachal Pradesh from the Punjab 1966.

Himalayas vast mountain system of central Asia, extending from the Indian states of Kashmir in the west to Assam in the east, covering the southern part of Tibet, Nepal, Sikkim, and Bhutan. It is the highest mountain range in the world. The highest peak is *Mount* ◊*Everest*; other major peaks include Kangchenjunga, Makalu, Annapurna, and Nanga Parbat, all over 26,000 ft/8,000 m.

Himes Chester 1909–1984. US novelist. After serving seven years in prison for armed robbery, he published his first novel *If He Hollers Let Him Go* 1945, a depiction of the drudgery and racism in a Californian shipyard.

Himmler Heinrich 1900–1945. German Nazi leader, head of the ◊SS elite corps from 1929, the police and the ◊Gestapo secret police from 1936, and supervisor of the extermination of the Jews in E Europe. During World War II he replaced Goering as Hitler's second-in-command. He was captured May 1945 and committed suicide.

Born in Munich, he joined the Nazi Party in 1925 and became chief of the Bavarian police 1933. His accumulation of offices meant he had command of all German police forces by 1936, which made him one of the most powerful people in Germany. In April 1945 he made a proposal to the Allies that Germany should surrender to the US and Britain but not to the USSR, which was rejected.

Hīnayāna (Sanskrit "lesser vehicle") Mahāyāna Buddhist name for ◊Theravāda Buddhism.

Hindemith Paul 1895–1963. German composer. His Neo-Classical, contrapuntal works include chamber ensemble and orchestral pieces, such as the *Symphonic Metamorphosis on Themes of Carl Maria von Weber* 1944, and the operas *Cardillac* 1926, revised 1952, and *Mathis der Maler/Mathis the Painter* 1938.

A fine viola player, he led the Frankfurt Opera Orchestra at 20, and taught at the Berlin Hochschule for music 1927–33. The modernity of his work, such as the *Philharmonic Concerto* 1932, led to a Nazi ban. In 1939 he went to the US, where he taught at Yale University and in 1951 he became professor of musical theory at Zürich.

Hindenburg Paul Ludwig Hans von Beneckendorf und Hindenburg 1847–1934.

German field marshal and right-wing politician. During World War I he was supreme commander and, with Ludendorff, practically directed Germany's policy until the end of the war. He was president of Germany 1925–33.

Born in Posen of a Prussian Junker (aristocratic landowner) family, he was commissioned 1866, served in the Austro-Prussian and Franco-German wars, and retired 1911. Given the command in East Prussia Aug 1914, he received the credit for the defeat of the Russians at ◊Tannenberg and was promoted to supreme commander and field marshal. Reelected president 1932, he was compelled to invite Hitler to assume the chancellorship Jan 1933.

Hindenburg Line German western line of World War I fortifications built 1916–17.

Hindi language member of the Indo-Iranian branch of the Indo-European language family, the official language of the Republic of India, although resisted as such by the Dravidian-speaking states of the south. Hindi proper is used by some 30% of Indians, in such northern states as Uttar Pradesh and Madhya Pradesh.

Hindi has close historical and cultural links with Sanskrit, the Classical language of Hinduism, and is written (from left to right) in Devanagari script. Bihari, Punjabi, and Rajasthani, the dominant language varieties in the states of Bihar, Punjab, and Rajasthan, are claimed by some to be varieties of Hindi (dialects), by others to be distinct languages.

Hinduism (Hindu *sanatana dharma* "eternal tradition") religion originating in N India about 4,000 years ago, which is superficially and in some of its forms polytheistic, but has a concept of the supreme spirit, ◊Brahman, above the many divine manifestations. These include the triad of chief gods (the Trimurti): Brahma, Vishnu, and Siva (creator, preserver, and destroyer). Central to Hinduism are the beliefs in reincarnation and ◊karma; the oldest scriptures are the *Vedas*. Temple worship is almost universally observed and there are many festivals. There are over 805 million Hindus worldwide. Women are not regarded as the equals of men but should be treated with kindness and respect. Muslim influence in N India led to the veiling of women and the restriction of their movements from about the end of the 12th century.

roots Hindu beliefs originated in the Indus Valley civilization about 4,500 years ago. Much of the tradition that is now associated with Hinduism stems from the ritual and religion of the Aryans who invaded N India about 3,000 years ago.

scriptures The *Veda* collection of hymns, compiled by the Aryans, was followed by the philosophical *Upanishads*, centering on the doctrine of Brahman, and the epics *Rāmāyana* and *Mahābhārata* (which includes the *Bhagavad-Gītā*), all from before the Christian era.

beliefs Hindu belief and ritual can vary greatly even between villages. Some deities achieve widespread popularity such as Krishna, Hanuman, Lakshmi, and Durga; others, more localized and specialized, are referred to particularly in times of sickness or need. Some deities manifest themselves in different incarnations or avatars such as Rama or Krishna, both avatars of the god Vishnu. Underlying this multifaceted worship is the creative strength of Brahman, the Supreme Being. Hindus believe that all living things are part of Brahman: they are sparks of atman or divine life that transmute from one body to another, sometimes descending into the form of a plant or an insect, sometimes the body of a human. This is all according to its karma or past actions which are the cause of its sufferings or joy as it rises and falls in *samsara* (the endless cycle of birth and death). Humans have the opportunity, through knowledge and devotion, to break the karmic chain and achieve final liberation or moksha. The atman is then free to return to Brahman. The creative force of the universe is recognized in the god Brahma. Once he has brought the cosmos into being it is sustained by Vishnu and then annihilated by the god Siva, only to be created once more by Brahma. Vishnu and Siva are, respectively, the forces of light and darkness, preservation and destruction, with Brahma as the balancing force that enables the existence and interaction of life. The cosmos is seen as both real and an illusion (*maya*), since its reality is not lasting; the cosmos is itself personified as the goddess Maya.

practice Hinduism has a complex of rites and ceremonies performed within the framework of the *jati* or caste system under the supervision of the Brahman priests and teachers. In India, caste is traditionally derived from the four classes of early Hindu society: brahmans (priests), kshatriyas (nobles and warriors), vaisyas (traders and cultivators), and sudras (servants). A fifth class, the untouchables, regarded as polluting in its origins, remained (and still largely remains) on the edge of Hindu society. The Indian Constituent Assembly 1947 made discrimination against the Scheduled Castes or Depressed Classes illegal, but strong prejudice continues.

Western influence The International Society for Krishna Consciousness (ISKON), the Western organization of the Hare Krishna movement, was introduced to the West by Swami Prabhupada (1896–1977). Members are expected to lead ascetic lives. It is based on devotion to Krishna which includes study of the *Bhagavad-Gītā*, temple and home ritual, and the chanting of the name Hare (savior) Krishna. Members are expected to avoid meat, eggs, alcohol, tea, coffee, drugs, and gambling. Sexual relationships should be for procreation within the bonds of marriage.

Hindu Kush mountain range in central Asia, length 500 mi/800 km, greatest height Tirich Mir, 25,239 ft/7,690 m, in Pakistan. The narrow **Khyber Pass** (33 mi/53 km long) separates Pakistan from Afghanistan and was used by ◊Zahir and other invaders of India. The present road was built by the British in the Afghan Wars.

Hindustan ("land of the Hindus") the whole of India, but more specifically the plain of the Ganges and Jumna rivers, or that part of India north of the Deccan.

Hindustani member of the Indo-Iranian branch of the Indo-European language family, closely related to Hindi and Urdu and originating in the bazaars of Delhi. It is a ◊lingua franca in many parts of the Republic of India.

Hine Lewis 1874–1940. US sociologist and photographer. His dramatic photographs of child labor conditions in US factories at the beginning of the 20th century led to changes in state and local labor laws.

Trained as a sociologist at the University of Chicago and New York University, Hine began to document social conditions by photographing the immigrants coming into the US at New York's Ellis Island 1904–08, as well as their tenement homes and the places and sweatshops in which they worked. His publication of those photos 1908 is considered the first "photo story." The National Child Labor Committee hired him to travel extensively in the US, photographing child labor conditions 1911–16. In later years, Hine photographed various government projects and construction of the Empire State Building, published 1930 in his *Men at Work*.

Hines Duncan 1880–1959. US travel author and publisher. He published restaurant reviews as *Adventures in Good Eating* 1936 and hotel notes as *Lodging for a Night* 1939. He later founded his own publishing house for cookbooks and entertainment and travel guides. A pioneer travel critic, Hines helped raise the standard of travel accommodation in the US.

He was born in Bowling Green, Kentucky. While working as a traveling salesman, he compiled notes on the many hotels and restaurants he encountered on his trips, which he was encouraged by friends to publish. He later licensed his name to a line of prepackaged cake mixes.

hinge joint in vertebrates, a joint where movement occurs in one plane only. Examples are the elbow and knee, which are controlled by pairs of muscles, the ◊flexors and ◊extensors.

Hinshelwood Cyril Norman 1897–1967. English chemist. He shared the 1956 Nobel Prize for Chemistry with Nikolai Semenov for his work on chemical chain reactions. He also studied the chemistry of bacterial growth.

hip-hop popular music originating in New York in the early 1980s. It uses scratching (a percussive effect obtained by manually rotating a vinyl record) and heavily accented electronic drums behind a ◊rap music vocal. The term "hip-hop" also comprises break dancing and graffiti.

Hipparchus c. 555–514 BC. Greek tyrant. Son of ◊Pisistratus, he was associated with his elder brother Hippias as ruler of Athens 527–514 BC. His affection being spurned by Harmodius, he insulted her sister, and was assassinated by Harmodius and Aristogiton.

Hipparchus c. 190–c. 120 BC. Greek astronomer who invented trigonometry, calculated the lengths of the solar year and the lunar month, discovered the precession of the equinoxes, made a catalog of 800 fixed stars, and advanced Eratosthenes' method of determining the situation of places on the Earth's surface by lines of latitude and longitude.

A native of Nicaea in Bithynia, he lived in Rhodes, and possibly in Alexandria.

hippie member of a youth movement of the late 1960s, also known as *flower power*, which originated in San Francisco, California, and was characterized by nonviolent anarchy, concern for the environment, and rejection of Western materialism. The hippies formed a politically outspoken, antiwar, artistically prolific counterculture in North America and Europe. Their colorful psychedelic style, inspired by drugs such as ◊LSD, emerged in fabric design, graphic art, and music by bands such as Love (1965–71), the ◊Grateful Dead, Jefferson Airplane (1965–74), and ◊Pink Floyd.

Hippocrates c. 460–c. 370 BC. Greek physician, often called the father of medicine. Important Hippocratic ideas include cleanliness (for patients and physicians), moderation in eating and drinking, letting nature take its course, and living where the air is good. He believed that health was the result of the "humors" of the body being in balance; imbalance caused disease. These ideas were later adopted by ◊Galen.

He was born and practiced on the island of Kos and died at Larissa. He is known to have discovered aspirin in willow bark. The *Corpus Hippocraticum*, a group of some 70 works, is attributed to him but was probably not written by him, although the works outline his approach to medicine. They include *Aphorisms* and the *Hippocratic Oath*, which embodies the essence of medical ethics.

Hippolytus in Greek mythology, the son of Theseus. When he rejected the love of his stepmother, Phaedra, she falsely accused him of making advances to her and turned Theseus against him. Killed by Poseidon at Theseus' request, he was restored to life when his innocence was proven.

hippopotamus (Greek "river horse") large herbivorous, even-toed hoofed mammal of the family Hippopotamidae. The common hippopotamus *Hippopotamus amphibius* is found in Africa. It averages over 13 ft/4 m long, 5 ft/1.5 m high, weighs about 5 tons/4,500 kg, and has a brown or slate-gray skin. It is an endangered species.

A social and gregarious animal, the hippopotamus spends the day wallowing in rivers or waterholes, only emerging at night to graze. The pygmy hippopotamus *Choeropsis liberiensis* inhabits W Africa. To the ancient Egyptians, the hippopotamus symbolized both evil and female fertility.

Hirabayashi v US US Supreme Court decision 1943 dealing with wartime legislation restricting the rights of citizens based on national origin. The case was brought in response to special curfews for Japanese-Americans on the US west coast. Hirabayashi charged that this and the forced relocation of Japanese-Americans during World War II was a violation of Fifth-Amendment rights. The Court refused to rule on relocation measures (◊*Korematsu v US* 1944) but upheld Congress's curfew, judging that danger of internal sabotage in the war with Japan warranted this extraordinary measure.

Hirohito 1901–1989. Emperor of Japan from 1926. He succeeded his father Yoshihito. After the defeat of Japan in World War II 1945, he was made constitutional monarch by the US-backed 1946 constitution. He is believed to have played a reluctant role in Prime Minister Hideki Tojo's ((1884-1948) prewar expansion plans. Hirohito ruled postwar occupied Japan with dignity. His era is known as the Showa era. He was succeeded by his son ◊Akihito.

Hirohito was a scholar of botany and zoology and the author of books on marine biology.

Hiroshige Andō 1797–1858. Japanese artist whose landscape prints, often using snow or rain to create atmosphere, include *Tōkaidō gojūsan-tsugi/53 Stations on the Tokaido Highway* 1833. Whistler and van Gogh were among Western painters influenced by him.

Hiroshige was born in Edo (now Tokyo), and his last series was *Meisho Edo Hyakkei/100 Famous Views of Edo* 1856–58, uncompleted before his death. He is thought to have made over 5,000 different prints.

Hiroshima industrial city and port on the S

coast of Honshu, Japan, destroyed by the first wartime use of an atomic bomb Aug 6, 1945. The city has largely been rebuilt since the war; population (1989) 1,057,100.

Toward the end of World War II the city was utterly devastated by the US atomic bomb. More than 4 sq mi/10 sq km was obliterated, with very heavy damage outside that area. Casualties totaled at least 137,000 out of a population of 343,000: 78,150 were found dead; others died later.

Hispanic person of Latin American descent from the Spanish-speaking nations, either native-born or an immigrant.

Hispaniola (Spanish "little Spain") West Indian island, first landing place of Columbus in the New World, Dec 6, 1492; now divided into ◊Haiti and the ◊Dominican Republic.

Hiss Alger 1904– . US diplomat and liberal Democrat, a former State Department official, imprisoned 1950 for perjury. There are doubts about the justice of Hiss's conviction.

Hiss, president of the Carnegie Endowment for International Peace and one of President Roosevelt's advisers at the 1945 ◊Yalta Conference, was accused 1948 by a former Soviet agent, Whittaker Chambers (1901–1961), of having passed information to the USSR during the period 1926–37. He was convicted of perjury for swearing before the House Un-American Activities Committee that he had not spied for the USSR (under the statute of limitations he could not be tried for the original crime). Richard ◊Nixon was a prominent member of the committee, which inspired the subsequent anticommunist witch-hunts of Senator Joseph ◊McCarthy.

histamine inflammatory substance normally released in damaged tissues, which also accounts for many of the symptoms of ◊allergy. Substances that neutralize its activity are known as ◊antihistamines.

It is an amine, $C_5H_9N_3$.

histochemistry study of plant and animal tissue by visual examination, usually with a ◊microscope.

◊Stains are often used to highlight structural characteristics such as the presence of starch or distribution of fats.

histogram in statistics, a graph showing frequency of data, in which the horizontal axis details discrete units or class boundaries, and the vertical axis represents the frequency. Blocks are drawn such that their areas (rather than their height as in a bar chart) are proportional to the frequencies within a class or across several class boundaries. There are no spaces between blocks.

histology in medicine, the laboratory study of cells and tissues.

historical novel fictional prose narrative set in the past. Literature set in the historic rather than the immediate past has always abounded, but in the West Walter Scott began the modern tradition by setting imaginative romances of love, impersonation, and betrayal in a past based on known fact; his use of historical detail, and subsequent imitations of this technique by European writers such as Manzoni, gave rise to the genre.

Some historical novels of the 19th century were overtly nationalistic, but most were merely novels set in the past to heighten melodrama while providing an informative framework; the genre was used by Victor Hugo, Charles Dickens, and James Fenimore Cooper, among many

others. In the 20th century the historical novel also became concerned with exploring psychological states and the question of differences in outlook and mentality in past periods. Examples of this are Robert Graves's novels about the Roman emperor *I, Claudius* and *Claudius the God*, and Margaret Yourcenar's *Memoirs of Hadrian*.

The less serious possibilities of the historical novel were exploited by writers including Kenneth Roberts, James Michener, Jeffery Farnol, Stanley Weyman, and Rafael Sabatini in the early 20th century in the form of the **historical romance**; Dorothy Dunnett and George MacDonald Fraser revived the historical romance with some success in the late 1960s. Subgenres of the historical novel have developed, with their own conventions. Examples include the **Western**, many of which draw on Owen Wister's classic *The Virginian*; and the novels of the South in the period of the Civil War, notably Margaret Mitchell's *Gone With the Wind*. In the late 20th century, generational series of novels about families, often industrialists of the early 19th century, became popular.

history record of the events of human societies. The earliest surviving historical records are the inscriptions denoting the achievements of Egyptian and Babylonian kings. As a literary form in the Western world, historical writing or **historiography** began with the Greek Herodotus in the 4th century BC, who was first to pass beyond the limits of a purely national outlook. Contemporary historians make extensive use of statistics, population figures, and primary records to justify historical arguments.

Herodotus' contemporary Thucydides brought to history not only literary gifts but the interests of a scientific investigator and political philosopher. Later Greek history and Roman history tended toward rhetoric; Sallust preserved the scientific spirit of Thucydides, but Livy and Tacitus, in spite of their insight and literary distinction, tended to subordinate factual accuracy to patriotic or party considerations. Medieval history was dominated by a religious philosophy imposed by the church. English chroniclers of this period are Bede, William of Malmesbury, and Matthew Paris. France produced great chroniclers of contemporary events in Froissart and Comines. The Renaissance revived historical writing and the study of history both by restoring Classical models and by creating the science of textual criticism. A product of the new secular spirit was Machiavelli's *History of Florence* 1520–23. This critical approach continued into the 17th century but the 18th century ◊Enlightenment disposed of the attempt to explain history in theological terms, and an interpretive masterpiece was produced by Edward Gibbon, *The Decline and Fall of the Roman Empire* 1776–88. An attempt to formulate a **historical method** and a philosophy of history, that of the Italian Giovanni Vico, remained almost unknown until the 19th century. Romanticism left its mark on 19th-century historical writing in the tendency to exalt the contribution of the individual "hero," and in the introduction of a more colorful and dramatic style and treatment, variously illustrated in the works of the French historian Jules Michelet (1798–1874), and the British writers Carlyle and Macaulay. During the 20th century the study of history has been revolutionized, partly through the contributions of other disciplines, such as the sciences and anthropology. The deciphering

of the Egyptian and Babylonian inscriptions was of great importance. Researchers and archeologists have traced the development of prehistoric human beings, and have revealed forgotten civilizations such as that of Crete. Anthropological studies of primitive society and religion, which began with James Frazer's *Golden Bough* 1890, have attempted to analyze the bases of later forms of social organization and belief. The changes brought about by the Industrial Revolution and the accompanying perception of economics as a science forced historians to turn their attention to economic questions. Marx's attempt to find in economic development the most significant, although not the only, determining factor in social change, an argument partly paralleled in *History of Civilization in England* 1857 by Henry Thomas Buckle (1821–62), has influenced historians since. History from the point of view of ordinary people is now recognized as an important element in historical study. Associated with this is the collection of spoken records known as **oral history**. A comparative study of civilizations is offered in A J Toynbee's *Study of History* 1934–54, and on a smaller scale by J M Roberts's *History of the World* 1976. Contemporary historians make a distinction between historical evidence or records, historical writing, and historical method or approaches to the study of history. The study of historical method is also known as **historiography**.

history of ideas discipline that studies the history and development of ideas and theories in terms of their origins and influences. The historian of ideas seeks to understand their significance in their original contexts.

Hitchcock Alfred 1899–1980. British film director who became a US citizen in 1955. A master of the suspense thriller, he was noted for his meticulously drawn storyboards that determined his camera angles and for his cameo "walk-ons" in his own films. His *Blackmail* 1929 was the first successful British talking film; *The Thirty-Nine Steps* 1935 and *The Lady Vanishes* 1939 are British suspense classics. He went to Hollywood 1940, where he made *Rebecca* 1940, *Notorious* 1946, *Strangers on a Train* 1951, *Rear Window* 1954, *Vertigo* 1958, *Psycho* 1960, and *The Birds* 1963. He also hosted two US television mystery series, *Alfred Hitchcock Presents* 1955–62 and *The Alfred Hitchcock Hour* 1963–65.

Hitler Adolf 1889–1945. German Nazi dictator, born in Austria. He was *Führer* (leader) of the Nazi Party from 1921 and author of *Mein Kampf/My Struggle* 1925–27. As chancellor of Germany from 1933 and head of state from 1934, he created a dictatorship by playing party and state institutions against each other and continually creating new offices and appointments. His position was not seriously challenged until the "Bomb Plot" July 20, 1944 to assassinate him. In foreign affairs, he reoccupied the Rhineland and formed an alliance with the Italian Fascist Mussolini 1936, annexed Austria 1938, and occupied the Sudetenland under the ◊Munich Agreement. The rest of Czechoslovakia was annexed March 1939. The Hitler–Stalin pact was followed in Sept by the invasion of Poland and the declaration of war by Britain and France (see ◊World War II). He committed suicide as Berlin fell.

Born at Braunau-am-Inn, the son of a customs official, he spent his early years in poverty in Vienna and Munich. After serving as a volunteer in the German army during World War I, he was employed as a spy by the military authorities in Munich and in 1919 joined, in this capacity, the German Workers' Party. By 1921 he had assumed its leadership, renamed it the National Socialist German Workers' Party (Nazi Party for short), and provided it with a program that mixed nationalism with ◊anti-Semitism. Having led an unsuccessful uprising in Munich 1923, he was sentenced to nine months' imprisonment during which he wrote his political testament, *Mein Kampf.* The party did not achieve national importance until the elections of 1930; by 1932, although Field Marshal Hindenburg defeated Hitler in the presidential elections, it formed the largest group in the Reichstag (parliament). As the result of an intrigue directed by Chancellor Franz von Papen, Hitler became chancellor in a Nazi–Nationalist coalition Jan 30, 1933. The opposition was rapidly suppressed, the Nationalists removed from the government, and the Nazis declared the only legal party. In 1934 Hitler succeeded Hindenburg as head of state. Meanwhile, the drive to war began; Germany left the League of Nations, conscription was reintroduced, and in 1936 the Rhineland was reoccupied. Hitler and Mussolini, who were already both involved in Spain, formed an alliance (the Axis) 1936, joined by Japan 1940. Hitler conducted the war in a ruthless but idiosyncratic way, took and ruled most of the neighboring countries with repressive occupation forces, and had millions of Slavs, Jews, Romanies, homosexuals, and political enemies killed in concentration camps and massacres. He narrowly escaped death 1944 from a bomb explosion at a staff meeting, prepared by high-ranking officers. On April 29, 1945, when Berlin was largely in Soviet hands, he married his mistress Eva Braun in his bunker under the chancellery building and on the following day committed suicide with her.

Hitler–Stalin pact nonaggression treaty signed by Germany and the USSR Aug 23, 1939. Under the terms of the treaty both countries agreed to remain neutral and to refrain from acts of aggression against each other if either went to war. Secret clauses allowed for the partition of Poland—Hitler was to acquire western Poland, Stalin the eastern part. On Sept 1, 1939 Hitler invaded Poland. The pact ended when Hitler invaded Russia on June 22, 1941. See also ◊World War II.

Hittite member of a group of people who inhabited Anatolia and N Syria from the 3rd millennium to the 1st millennium BC. The city of Hattusas (now Boğazköy in central Turkey) became the capital of a strong kingdom which overthrew the Babylonian Empire. After a period of eclipse the Hittite New Empire became a great power (about 1400–1200 BC), which successfully waged war with Egypt. The Hittite language is an Indo-European language.

The original Hittites, a people of Armenian/Anatolian type, inhabited a number of city-states in E Anatolia, one of which, Hatti, gained supremacy over the others. An Indo-European people invaded the country about 2000 BC, made themselves the ruling class, and intermarried with the original inhabitants. The Hittites developed advanced military, political, and legal systems. The New Empire concluded a peace treaty with Egypt 1269 BC, but was eventually overthrown by the Sea Peoples. Small Hittite states then arose in N Syria, the most important of which was ◊Carchemish; these were conquered by the Assyrians in the 8th century BC. Carchemish was conquered 717. The Hittites used a cuneiform

script, modeled on the Babylonian, for ordinary purposes, and a hieroglyphic script for inscriptions on monuments. The Hittite royal archives were discovered at Hattusas 1906–07 and deciphered 1915.

HIV abbreviation for **human immuno-deficiency virus**, the infectious agent that causes ◊AIDS.

Hoare–Laval Pact plan for a peaceful settlement to the Italian invasion of Ethiopia in Oct 1935. It was devised by Samuel Hoare (1880–1959), British foreign secretary, and Pierre ◊Laval, French premier, at the request of the ◊League of Nations. Realizing no European country was willing to go to war over Ethiopia, Hoare and Laval proposed official recognition of Italian claims. Public outcry in Britain against the pact's seeming approval of Italian aggression was so great that the pact had to be disowned and Hoare was forced to resign.

hoatzin tropical bird *Opisthocomus hoatzin* found only in the Amazon, resembling a small pheasant in size and appearance. The bill is thick and the facial skin blue. Adults are olive with white markings above and red-brown below.

The young are hatched naked, with claws on their wings, which they use to crawl reptile-fashion about the tree—a possible reminder of their ancestry; these claws later fall off. They fly only reluctantly and prefer to climb among branches using their wings. They cannot grip with their feet.

Hoban James C 1762–1831. Irish-born architect who emigrated to the US. He designed the White House, Washington, DC; he also worked on the Capitol and other public buildings.

Hobart capital and port of Tasmania, Australia; population (1986) 180,000. Products include zinc, textiles, and paper. Founded 1804 as a penal colony, it was named after Lord Hobart, then secretary of state for the colonies.

The University of Tasmania, established 1890, is at Hobart.

Hobbes Thomas 1588–1679. English political philosopher and the first thinker since Aristotle to attempt to develop a comprehensive theory of nature, including human behavior. In *The Leviathan* 1651, he advocates absolutist government as the only means of ensuring order and security; he saw this as deriving from the ◊social contract.

Hobbit, The or *There and Back Again* a fantasy for children by J R R ◊Tolkien, published in the UK 1937. It describes the adventures of Bilbo Baggins, a "hobbit" (small humanoid) in an ancient world, Middle-Earth, populated by dragons, dwarves, elves, and other mythical creatures, including the wizard Gandalf. *The Hobbit,* together with Tolkien's later trilogy *The Lord of the Rings* 1954–55, achieved cult status in the 1960s.

By 1991, 35 million copies had been sold worldwide, more than any other work of fiction.

hobby small falcon *Falco subbuteo* found across Europe and N Asia. It is about 1 ft/30 cm long, with a gray back, streaked front, and chestnut thighs. It is found in open woods and heaths, and feeds on insects and small birds.

Hoboken city and port in NE New Jersey, on the Hudson River; population (1990) 33,397.

Hochhuth Rolf 1931– . Swiss dramatist whose controversial play *Soldaten/Soldiers* 1968 implied that the British politician Churchill was involved in a plot to assassinate the Polish general ◊Sikorski.

Ho Chi Minh adopted name of Nguyen That Tan 1890–1969. North Vietnamese Communist politician, premier and president 1954–69. Having trained in Moscow shortly after the ◊Russian Revolution, he headed the communist Vietminh from 1941 and fought against the French during the Indochina War 1946–54, becoming president and prime minister of the republic at the armistice. Aided by the Communist bloc, he did much to develop industrial potential. He relinquished the premiership 1955, but continued as president. In the years before his death, Ho successfully led his country's fight against US-aided South Vietnam in the Vietnam War 1954–75.

Ho Chi Minh City (until 1976 *Saigon*) chief port and industrial city of S Vietnam; population (1989) 3,169,100. Industries include shipbuilding, textiles, rubber, and food products. Saigon was the capital of the Republic of Vietnam (South Vietnam) from 1954 to 1976, when it was renamed.

Ho Chi Minh Trails North Vietnamese troop and supply routes to South Vietnam via Laos during the Vietnam War 1954–75.

Hockney David 1937– . English painter, printmaker, and designer, resident in California. He exhibited at the Young Contemporaries Show of 1961 and contributed to the Pop art movement. He developed an individual figurative style, as in his portrait *Mr and Mrs Clark and Percy* 1971, Tate Gallery, London, and has prolifically experimented with technique. His views of swimming pools reflect a preoccupation with surface pattern and effects of light. He has also produced drawings, etchings, photo collages, and sets for opera.

Hodgkin Dorothy Crowfoot 1910– . English biochemist who analyzed the structure of penicillin, insulin, and vitamin B_{12}. Hodgkin was the first to use a computer to analyze the molecular structure of complex chemicals, and this enabled her to produce three-dimensional models. She was awarded the Nobel Prize for Chemistry 1964.

Hodgkin's disease rare form of cancer (also known as *lymphoadenoma*), mainly affecting the lymph nodes and spleen. It undermines the immune system, leaving the sufferer susceptible to infection. However, it responds well to radiotherapy, and long-term survival is usual.

Hodza Milan 1878–1944. Czechoslovak politician, prime minister 1936–38. He and President Beneš were forced to agree to the secession of the Sudeten areas of Czechoslovakia to Germany before resigning Sept 22, 1938 (see ◊Munich Agreement).

Hofei alternative transcription of ◊*Hefei*, a city in China.

Hoffa James Riddle "Jimmy" 1913–1975. notorious US labor union leader. A member of the Teamsters' (trucking) Union since 1931, he became its ruthless president 1957. In 1964 he effected the first national contract for the truckers but was also convicted in two trials of fraud and jury tampering. He went to prison 1967 and retained his presidency until 1971, when President Nixon commuted his sentence on condition that he should not engage in union activity until 1980. Hoffa disappeared 1975, however, and is considered to have been murdered.

Hoffman Abbie (Abbot) 1936–1989. US left-wing political activist, founder of the Yippies (Youth International Party), a political offshoot of the ◊hippies. He was a member of the Chicago Seven, a radical group tried for attempting to disrupt the 1968 Democratic Convention.

Hoffman was arrested 52 times and was a fugitive from justice 1973–80. He specialized in imaginative political gestures to gain media attention, for example throwing dollar bills to the floor of the New York Stock Exchange 1967. His books include *Revolution for the Hell of It* 1969. He campaigned against the Vietnam War and, later, for the environment. He committed suicide.

Hoffman Dustin 1937– . US actor, icon of the antiheroic 1960s. He won Academy Awards for his performances in *Kramer vs Kramer* 1979 and *Rain Man* 1988. His other films include *The Graduate* 1967, *Midnight Cowboy* 1969, *Little Big Man* 1970, *All the President's Men* 1976, *Tootsie* 1982, and *Hook* 1991. He appeared on Broadway in the 1984 revival of *Death of a Salesman*, which was also produced for television 1985.

Hoffmann E(rnst) T(heodor) A(madeus) 1776–1822. German composer and writer. He composed the opera *Undine* 1816 and many fairy stories, including *Nussknacker/Nutcracker* 1816. His stories inspired ⇨Offenbach's *Tales of Hoffmann*.

Hoffmann Josef 1870–1956. Austrian architect, one of the founders of the Wiener Werkstätte (a modern design cooperative of early 20th-century Vienna), and a pupil of Otto ⇨Wagner.

Hoffman's voltameter in chemistry, an apparatus for collecting gases produced by the ⇨electrolysis of a liquid.

It consists of a vertical E-shaped glass tube with taps at the upper ends of the outer limbs and a reservoir at the top of the central limb. Platinum electrodes fused into the lower ends of the outer limbs are connected to a source of direct current. At the beginning of an experiment, the outer limbs are completely filled with electrolyte by opening the taps. The taps are then closed and the current switched on. Gases evolved at the electrodes bubble up the outer limbs and collect at the top, where they can be measured.

Hofmann Hans 1880–1966. German-born Abstract Expressionist painter, active in Paris and Munich from 1915 until 1932, when he moved to the US. In addition to bold brushwork (he experimented with dribbling and dripping painting techniques in the 1940s) he used strong expressive colors. In the 1960s he moved toward a hard-edged abstract style.

He opened two art schools, in New York City and Provincetown, Massachusetts, and was influential among New York artists in the 1930s.

Hofstadter Robert 1915–1990. US high-energy physicist who revealed the structure of the atomic nucleus. He demonstrated that the nucleus is composed of a high-energy core and a surrounding area of decreasing density. He shared the 1961 Nobel Prize for Physics with Rudolf Mössbauer.

Educated in New York and Princeton, Hofstadter did his research in California after 1950. He helped to construct a new high-energy accelerator at Stanford University, with which he showed that the proton and the neutron have complex structures and cannot be considered elementary particles. See also ⇨quark.

hog member of the ⇨pig family.

The river hog *Potamochoerus porcus* lives in Africa, south of the Sahara. Reddish or black, up to 4.2 ft/1.3 m long plus tail, and 3 ft/90 cm at the shoulder, this gregarious animal roots for food in many types of habitat. The giant forest hog *Hylochoerus meinerzthageni* lives in thick forests of central Africa and grows up to 6 ft/1.9 m long.

Hogan Ben 1912– . US golfer who won the Masters, the US Open, and the British Open in the same year, 1953. He was a member of four Ryder Cup teams, playing captain in 1947 and 1949.

CAREER HIGHLIGHTS

US Open
1948, 1950, 1951, 1953
US PGA Championship
1946, 1948
Player of the Year: 1948, 1950–51, 1953
US Masters
1951 1953
British Open
1953

Hogan Paul 1940– . Australian TV comic, film actor, and producer. The box-office hit *Crocodile Dundee* (considered the most profitable film in Australian history) 1986 and *Crocodile Dundee II* 1988 (of which he was cowriter, star, and producer) brought him international fame.

Hogarth William 1697–1764. English painter and engraver who produced portraits and moralizing genre scenes, such as the series *A Rake's Progress* 1735. His portraits are remarkably direct and full of character, for example *Heads of Six of Hogarth's Servants* c. 1750–55 (Tate Gallery, London).

Hogarth was born in London and apprenticed to an engraver. He published *A Harlot's Progress*, a series of six engravings, in 1732. Other series followed, including *Marriage à la Mode* 1745, *Industry and Idleness* 1749, and *The Four Stages of Cruelty* 1751. In his book *The Analysis of Beauty* 1753 he proposed a double curved line as a key to successful composition.

hogback geologically formation consisting of a ridge with a short crest and abruptly sloping sides. Hogbacks are the result of differential erosion on steeply dipping rock strata composed of alternating resistant and soft beds. Exposed, almost vertical beds provide the sharp crests.

Hoggar alternate spelling of ⇨*Ahaggar*, a plateau in the Sahara.

Hohenlinden, Battle of in the French ⇨Revolutionary Wars, a defeat of the Austrians by the French Dec 1800. Coming after the defeat at ⇨Marengo, it led the Austrians to make peace at the Treaty of Lunéville 1801.

Hohenlohe-Schillingsfürst Prince Chlodwig von 1819–1901. German imperial chancellor from Oct 1894 until his replacement by Prince von Bülow Oct 1900.

Hohenstaufen German family of princes, several members of which were Holy Roman emperors 1138–1208 and 1214–54. They were the first German emperors to make use of associations with Roman law and tradition to aggrandize their office, and included Conrad III; Frederick I (Barbarossa), the first to use the title Holy Roman emperor (previously the title Roman emperor was used); Henry VI; and Frederick II. The last of the line, Conradin, was executed 1268 with the approval

of Pope Clement IV while attempting to gain his Sicilian inheritance.

Hohenzollern German family, originating in Württemberg, the main branch of which held the titles of ⇨elector of Brandenburg from 1415, king of Prussia from 1701, and German emperor from 1871. The last emperor, Wilhelm II, was dethroned 1918 after the disastrous course of World War I. Another branch of the family were kings of Romania 1881–1947.

Hohhot or *Huhehot* city and capital of Inner Mongolia (Nei Mongol) autonomous region, China; population (1989) 870,000. Industries include textiles, electronics, and dairy products. There are Lamaist monasteries and temples here.

Hokkaido former name (until 1868) *Yezo* or *Ezo* or *Ezochi* northernmost of the four main islands of Japan, separated from Honshu to the south by Tsugaru Strait and from Sakhalin to the north by Soya Strait; area 32,231 sq mi/83,500 sq km; population (1986) 5,678,000, including 16,000 ⇨Ainus. The capital is Sapporo. Natural resources include coal, mercury, manganese, oil and natural gas, timber, and fisheries. Coal mining and agriculture are the main industries.

Snow-covered for half the year, Hokkaido was little developed until the Meiji Restoration 1868 when disbanded samurai were settled here. Intensive exploitation followed World War II, including heavy and chemical industrial plants, development of electric power, and dairy farming. An artificial harbor has been constructed at Tomakomai, and an undersea rail tunnel links Hakodate with Aomori (Honshu) but remains as yet closed to public transport.

Hokusai Katsushika 1760–1849. Japanese artist, the leading printmaker of his time. He published *Fugaku Sanjū-rokkei/36 Views of Mount Fuji* about 1823–29, but he produced outstanding pictures of almost every kind of subject -birds, flowers, courtesans, and scenes from legend and everyday life.

Hokusai was born in Edo (now Tokyo) and studied wood engraving and book illustration. He was interested in Western painting and perspective and introduced landscape as a woodblock-print genre. His *Manga*, a book crammed with inventive sketches, was published in 13 volumes from 1814.

Holbein Hans, *the Elder* c. 1464–1524. German painter, active in Augsburg. His works include altarpieces, such as that of *St Sebastian* 1516 (Alte Pinakothek, Munich). He also painted portraits and designed stained glass.

Holbein Hans, *the Younger* 1497/98–1543. German painter and woodcut artist; the son and pupil of Hans Holbein the Elder. Holbein was born in Augsburg. In 1515 he went to Basel, where he became friendly with Erasmus; he painted three portraits of him in 1523, which were strongly influenced by Quentin Massys. He traveled widely in Europe and was court painter to England's Henry VIII from 1536. He also painted portraits of Thomas More and Thomas Cromwell; a notable woodcut series is *Dance of Death* about 1525. He designed title pages for Luther's New Testament and More's *Utopia*.

Holden William. Adopted name of William Franklin Beedle 1918–1981. US film actor, a star in the late 1940s and 1950s. He played leading roles in *Sunset Boulevard* 1950, *Stalag 17* 1953, *The Wild Bunch* 1969, and *Network* 1976.

holdfast organ found at the base of many sea-weeds, attaching them to the sea bed. It may be a flattened, suckerlike structure, or dissected and fingerlike, growing into rock crevices and firmly anchoring the plant.

holding company company with a controlling stockholding in one or more subsidiaries.

Holiday Billie. Adopted name of Eleanora Gough McKay 1915–1959. US jazz singer, also known as "Lady Day." She made her debut in Harlem clubs and became known for her emotionally charged delivery and idiosyncratic phrasing; she brought a blues feel to performances with swing bands. Songs she made her own include "Stormy Weather," "Strange Fruit" and "I Cover the Waterfront."

Holinshed Ralph *c.* 1520–*c.* 1580. English historian who published two volumes of the *Chronicles of England, Scotland and Ireland* 1578, on which Shakespeare based his history plays.

holism in philosophy, the concept that the whole is greater than the sum of its parts.

holistic medicine umbrella term for an approach that virtually all alternative therapies profess, which considers the overall health and lifestyle profile of a patient, and treats specific ailments not primarily as conditions to be alleviated but rather as symptoms of more fundamental disease.

Holland popular name for the ⬦Netherlands; also two provinces of the Netherlands; see ⬦North Holland and ⬦South Holland.

Holland John Philip 1840–1914. Irish engineer who developed some of the first submarines. He began work in Ireland in the late 1860s and emigrated to the US 1873. His first successful boat was launched 1881 and, after several failures, he built the *Holland* 1893, which was bought by the US Navy two years later.

The first submarine, the *Fenian Ram* 1881, was built with financial support from the Irish Fenian society, who hoped to use it against England. Holland continued after 1895 to build submarines for various navies but died in poverty after his company became embroiled in litigation with backers.

Holland Sidney George 1893–1961. New Zealand politician, leader of the National Party 1940–57 and prime minister 1949–57.

Hollerith Herman 1860–1929. US inventor of a mechanical tabulating machine, the first device for data processing. Hollerith's tabulator was widely publicized after being successfully used in the 1890 census. The firm he established, the Tabulating Machine Company, was later one of the founding companies of ⬦IBM.

After attending the Columbia University School of Mines, Hollerith worked on the 1880 US census and witnessed the huge task of processing so much information. In 1882 he became an instructor at the Massachusetts Institute of Technology, where he developed his machine for counting and collating census data.

holly tree or shrub of the genus *Ilex*, family Aquifoliaceae, generally with glossy, sharp-pointed leaves and red berries. American holly *I. opaca* of the eastern US is used for Christmas decorations. Leaves of the Brazilian holly *I. paraguayensis* are used to make the tea yerba maté.

Holly Buddy. Adopted name of Charles Hardin Holley 1936–1959. US rock-and-roll singer, guitarist, and songwriter, born in Lubbock, Texas.

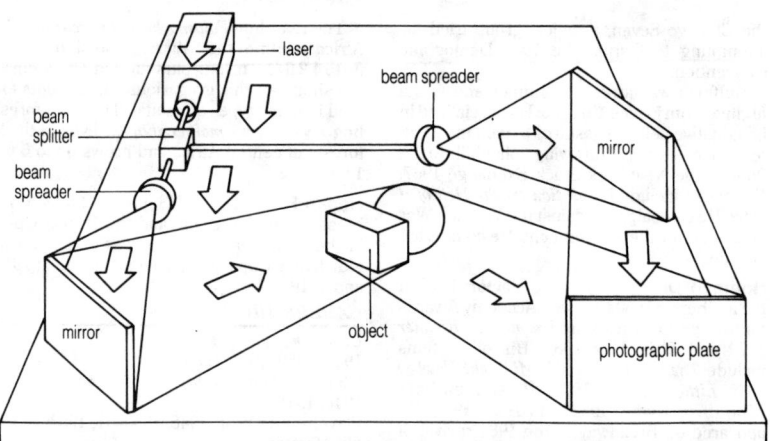

holography *Recording a transmission hologram.*

Holly had a distinctive, hiccuping vocal style and was an early experimenter with recording techniques. Many of his hits with his band, the Crickets, such as "That'll Be the Day" 1957, "Peggy Sue" 1957, and "Maybe Baby" 1958, have become classics. He died in a plane crash.

hollyhock plant of the genus *Althaea* of the mallow family Malvaceae. *A. rosea*, originally a native of Asia, produces spikes of large white, yellow, or red flowers, 10 ft/3 m high when cultivated as a biennial.

Hollywood district in the city of Los Angeles, California; the center of the US film industry from 1911. It is the home of legendary film studios such as 20th Century Fox, MGM, Paramount, Columbia Pictures, United Artists, Disney, and Warner Brothers. Many film stars' homes are situated nearby in Beverly Hills and other communities adjacent to Hollywood.

Although Hollywood lost its commanding position with the decline of the studio system in the late 1950s, the rise of independent producers and the needs of television studios made use of the soundstage and backlot facilities there. MGM Studios has become a major theme park and tourist attraction.

Hollywood city in SE Florida, on the Atlantic Ocean, S of Fort Lauderdale and N of Miami. Its principal industry is tourism; population (1990) 121,700.

Holmes, Sherlock fictitious private detective, created by the English writer Arthur Conan ⬦Doyle in *A Study in Scarlet* 1887 and recurring in novels and stories until 1914. Holmes's ability to make inferences from slight clues always astonishes the narrator, Dr Watson.

The criminal mastermind against whom Holmes repeatedly pits his wits is Professor James Moriarty. Holmes is regularly portrayed at his home, 221b Baker Street, London, where he plays the violin and has bouts of determined action interspersed by lethargy and drug-taking. His characteristic pipe and deerstalker hat were the addition of an illustrator.

Holmes Oliver Wendell 1809–1894. US writer and physician. In 1857 he founded *The Atlantic Monthly* with J R Lowell, in which were published the essays and verse collected in 1858 as *The Autocrat of the Breakfast-Table*, a record of the imaginary conversation of boarding-house guests.

This was followed by *The Professor at the Breakfast-Table* 1860 and other "Breakfast-

Table" collections, and the novel *Elsie Venner* 1861. "The Chambered Nautilus" is among his best-known poems.

Holmes Oliver Wendell 1841–1935. US jurist and Supreme Court justice noted for the elegance of his written opinions. Holmes established a private practice in Boston and gained a reputation as an author and lecturer on legal subjects. Appointed to the Massachusetts Supreme Court 1882 and to the US Supreme Court by President T Roosevelt 1902, Holmes handed down landmark decisions in a number of antitrust, First Amendment, and labor law cases. He retired from the Court 1932.

Son of the writer and physician of the same name, he was born in Boston and educated at Harvard. After service in the US Civil War, he studied law and was admitted to the bar 1867.

holmium (Latin *Holmia* "Stockholm") silvery, metallic element of the ⬦lanthanide series, symbol Ho, atomic number 67, atomic weight 164.93. It occurs in combination with other rare-earth metals and in various minerals such as gadolinite. Its compounds are highly magnetic.

The element was discovered in 1878, spectroscopically, by the Swiss chemists L Soret and Delafontaine, and independently in 1879 by Swedish chemist Per Cleve (1840–1905), who named it after Stockholm, near which it was found.

Holocaust, the the annihilation of an estimated 6 million Jews by the Hitler regime 1933–45 in the numerous extermination and ⬦concentration camps, most notably Auschwitz, Sobibor, Treblinka, and Maidanek in Poland, and Belsen, Buchenwald, and Dachau in Germany. An additional 10 million people died during imprisonment or were exterminated; among them were Ukrainian, Polish, and Russian civilians and prisoners of war, Gypsies, socialists, homosexuals, and others (labeled "defectives"). Victims were variously starved, tortured, experimented on, and worked to death. Millions were executed in gas chambers, shot, or hanged. It was euphemistically termed the ⬦final solution of the Jewish question.

Holocaust museums and memorial sites have been established in Israel and in other countries.

Holocene epoch of geological time that began 10,000 years ago, the second and current epoch of the Quaternary period. The glaciers retreated, the climate became warmer, and humans developed significantly.

holography method of producing three-dimensional (3-D) images by means of ◊laser light. Holography uses a photographic technique (involving the splitting of a laser beam into two beams) to produce a picture, or hologram, that contains 3-D information about the object photographed. Some holograms show meaningless patterns in ordinary light and produce a 3-D image only when laser light is projected through them, but reflection holograms produce images when ordinary light is reflected from them (as found on credit cards).

Although the possibility of holography was suggested as early as 1947, it could not be demonstrated until a pure coherent light source, the laser, became available 1963.

The technique of holography is also applicable to sound, and bats may navigate by ultrasonic holography. Holographic techniques also have applications in storing dental records, detecting stresses and strains in construction and in retail goods, and detecting forged paintings and documents.

Holst Gustav(us Theodore von) 1874–1934. English composer. He wrote operas, including *Savitri* 1916 and *At the Boar's Head* 1925; ballets; choral works, including *Hymns from the Rig Veda* 1911 and *The Hymn of Jesus* 1920; orchestral suites, including *The Planets* 1918; and songs. He was a lifelong friend of Ralph ◊Vaughan Williams, with whom he shared an enthusiasm for English folk music. His musical style, although tonal and drawing on folk song, tends to be severe.

Holt Harold Edward 1908–1967. Australian Liberal politician, prime minister 1966–67. His brief prime ministership was dominated by the Vietnam War, to which he committed increased Australian troops.

Holy Alliance "Christian Union of Charity, Peace, and Love" initiated by Alexander I of Russia 1815 and signed by every crowned head in Europe. The alliance became associated with Russian attempts to preserve autocratic monarchies at any price, and served as an excuse to meddle in the internal affairs of other states.

Ideas of an international army acting in the name of the alliance were rejected by Britain and Austria 1818 and 1820.

Holy Communion another name for the ◊Eucharist, a Christian sacrament.

Holy Grail in medieval Christian legend, the dish or cup used by Jesus at the Last Supper, supposed to have supernatural powers. Together with the spear with which he was wounded at the Crucifixion, it was an object of quest by King Arthur's knights in certain stories incorporated in the Arthurian legend.

According to one story, the blood of Jesus was collected in the Holy Grail by ◊Joseph of Arimathaea at the Crucifixion, and he brought it to Britain where he allegedly built the first church, at Glastonbury. At least three churches in Europe possess vessels claimed to be the Holy Grail.

Holy Island or *Lindisfarne* island in the North Sea, area 4 sq mi/10 sq km, 2 mi/3 km off Northumberland, England, with which it is connected by a causeway. St ◊Aidan founded a monastery here in 635.

Holy Land Christian term for ◊Israel, because of its association with Jesus and the Old Testament.

Holy Roman emperors

emperor	dates of reign
Carolingian kings and emperors	
Charlemagne (Charles the Great)	800–14
Louis I, the Pious	814–40
Lothair I	840–55
Louis II	855–75
Charles II, the Bald	875–77
Charles III, the Fat	881–87
Guido of Spoleto	891–94
Lambert of Spoleto (co-emperor)	892–98
Arnulf (rival)	896–901
Louis III of Provence	901–05
Berengar	905–24
Conrad I of Franconia (rival)	911–18
Saxon kings and emperors	
Henry I, the Fowler	919–36
Otto I, the Great	936–73
Otto II	973–83
Otto III	983–1002
Henry II, the Saint	1014–24
Franconian (Salian) emperors	
Conrad II	1024–39
Henry III, the Black	1039–56
Henry IV	1056–1106
Rudolf of Swabia (rival)	1077–80
Hermann of Luxembourg (rival)	1081–93
Conrad of Franconia (rival)	1093–1101
Henry V	1106–25
Lothair II	1126–37
Hohenstaufen kings and emperors	
Conrad III	1138–52
Frederick I Barbarossa	1152–90
Henry VI	1190–97
Otto IV	1198–1215
Philip of Swabia (rival)	1198–1208
Frederick II	1215–50
Henry Raspe of Thuringia (rival)	1246–47
William of Holland (rival)	1246–47
Conrad IV	1250–54
The Great Interregnum	1254–73
rulers from noble families	
Richard of Cornwall (rival)	1257–72
Alfonso X of Castile (rival)	1257–73
Rudolf I (Hapsburg)	1273–91
Adolph I of Nassau	1292–98
Albert I (Hapsburg)	1298–1303
Henry VII (Luxembourg)	1308–13
Louis IV of Bavaria	1314–47
Frederick of Hapsburg (co-regent)	1314–25
Charles IV (Luxembourg)	1347–78
Wenceslas of Bohemia	1378–1400
Frederick III of Brunswick	1400
Rupert of the Palatinate	1400–10
Sigismund (Luxembourg)	1411–37
Habsburg emperors	
Albert II	1438–39
Frederick III	1440–93
Maximillian I	1493–1519
Charles V	1519–56
Ferdinand II	1556–64
Maximillian II	1564–76
Rudolf II	1576–1612
Mathias	1612–19
Ferdinand III	1619–57
Leopold I	1658–1705
Joseph I	1705–11
Charles VI	1711–40
Charles VII of Bavaria	1742–45
Habsburg-Lorraine emperors	
Francis I of Lorraine	1745–65
Joseph II	1765–90
Leopold II	1790–92
Francis II	1792–1806

Holyoake Keith Jacka 1904–1983. New Zealand National Party politician, prime minister 1957 (for two months) and 1960–72 during which time he was also foreign minister.

holy orders Christian priesthood, as conferred by the laying on of hands by a bishop. It is held by the Roman Catholic, Eastern Orthodox, and Anglican churches to have originated in Jesus' choosing of the apostles.

The Roman Catholic church includes among holy orders bishop, priest, deacon, subdeacon, acolyte, exorcist, reader, and door-keeper, and, outside the priesthood, ◊tertiary.

Holy Roman Empire empire of ◊Charlemagne and his successors, and the German Empire 962–1806, both being regarded as the Christian (hence "holy") revival of the Roman Empire. At its height it comprised much of western and central Europe. See ◊Germany, history and ◊Habsburg.

Holy See the diocese of the ◊pope.

Holy Spirit third person of the Christian ◊Trinity, also known as the Holy Ghost or the Paraclete, usually depicted as a white dove.

Holy Week in the Christian church, the last week of ◊Lent, when Christians commemorate the events that led up to the crucifixion of Jesus. Holy Week begins on Palm Sunday and includes Maundy Thursday, which commemorates the Last Supper.

Home Alec Douglas-Home, Baron Home of the Hirsel 1903– . British Conservative politician. He was foreign secretary 1960–63, and succeeded Harold Macmillan as prime minister 1963. He renounced his peerage (as 14th Earl of Home) to fight (and lose) the general election 1963, and resigned as party leader 1965. He was again foreign secretary 1970–74, when he received a life peerage. The playwright William Douglas-Home was his brother.

Homelands Policy in South Africa, the apartheid policy that set aside ◊Black National States for black Africans.

homeopathy or *homoeopathy* system of medicine based on the principle that symptoms of disease are part of the body's self-healing processes, and on the practice of administering extremely diluted doses of natural substances found to produce in a healthy person the symptoms manifest in the illness being treated. Developed by German physician Samuel Hahnemann (1755–1843), the system is widely practiced today as an alternative to ◊allopathy, and many controlled tests and achieved cures testify its efficacy.

homeostasis maintenance of a constant internal state in an organism, particularly with regard to pH, salt concentration, temperature, and blood sugar levels. Stable conditions are important for the efficient functioning of the ◊enzyme reactions within the cells, which affect the performance of the entire organism.

homeothermy maintenance of a constant body temperature in endothermic (warm-blooded) animals, by the use of chemical body processes to compensate for heat loss or gain when external temperatures change. Such processes include generation of heat by the breakdown of food and the contraction of muscles, and loss of heat by sweating, panting, and other means.

Mammals and birds are homeotherms, whereas invertebrates, fish, amphibians, and reptiles are coldblooded or poikilotherms.

Homeotherms generally have a layer of insulating material to retain heat, such as fur, feathers, or fat (see ◊blubber). Their metabolism functions more efficiently due to homeothermy, enabling them to remain active under most climatic conditions.

Homer lived *c.* 8th century BC. Legendary Greek epic poet. According to tradition, he was a blind minstrel and the author of the ◊*Iliad* and the ◊*Odyssey*, which are probably based on much older stories, passed on orally, concerning war with Troy in the 12th century BC.

Homer Winslow 1836–1910. US painter and lithographer, known for his seascapes, both oils and watercolors, which date from the 1880s and 1890s.

Homer, born in Boston, made his reputation as a realist painter with *Prisoners from the Front* 1866 (Metropolitan Museum of Art, New York), recording miseries of the American Civil War. After a visit to Paris he turned to lighter subjects, studies of country life, which reflect early Impressionist influence.

He stayed in Britain for two years, then settled in Maine, but continued to travel to Canada, the West Indies, and elsewhere.

Home Rule, Irish movement to repeal the Act of ◊Union 1801 that joined Ireland to Britain and to establish an Irish parliament responsible for internal affairs. In 1870 Isaac Butt (1813–1879) formed the Home Rule Association and the movement was led in Parliament from 1880 by Charles ◊Parnell. After 1918 the demand for an independent Irish republic replaced that for home rule.

Gladstone's Home Rule bills 1886 and 1893 were both defeated. A third bill was introduced by the Liberals in 1912, which aroused opposition in Ireland where the Protestant minority in Ulster feared domination by the Catholic majority. Ireland appeared on the brink of civil war but the outbreak of World War I rendered further consideration of Home Rule inopportune. In 1920 the Government of Ireland Act introduced separate parliaments in the North and South.

Homestead Act in US history, an act of Congress 1862 to encourage settlement of land in the west by offering 160-acre/65-hectare plots cheaply or even free to those willing to cultivate and improve the land for a stipulated amount of time. By 1900 about 80 million acres/32 million hectares had been distributed. Homestead lands are available to this day.

homicide in law, the killing of a human being. This may be unlawful, lawful, or excusable, depending on the circumstances. Unlawful homicides include ◊murder, ◊manslaughter, ◊infanticide, and causing death by dangerous driving (vehicular homicide). Lawful homicide occurs where, for example, a police officer is justified in killing a criminal in the course of apprehension. Excusable homicide occurs when a person is killed in self-defense or by accident.

homologous in biology, a term describing an organ or structure possessed by members of different taxonomic groups (for example, species, genera, families, orders) that originally derived from the same structure in a common ancestor. The wing of a bat, the arm of a monkey, and the flipper of a seal are homologous because they all derive from the forelimb of an ancestral mammal.

homologous series any of a number of series of organic chemicals with similar chemical properties in which members differ by a constant molecular weight.

Alkanes (paraffins), alkenes (olefins), and alkynes (acetylenes) form such series in which members differ in mass by 14, 12, and 10 atomic mass units respectively. For example, the alkane homologous series begins with methane (CH_4), ethane (C_2H_6), propane (C_3H_8), butane (C_4H_{10}), and pentane (C_5H_{12}), each member differing from the previous one by a CH_2 group (or 14 atomic mass units).

homonymy aspect of language in which, through historical accident, two or more words may sound and look alike (**homonymy** proper, as in a farmer's *bull* and a papal *bull*), may sound the same but look different (**homophony**, as in *air* and *heir*; *gilt* and *guilt*), or may look the same but sound different (**homography**, as in the *wind* in the trees and roads that *wind*).

Homonyms, homophones, and homographs seldom pose problems of comprehension, because they usually belong in different contexts. Even when brought into the same context for effect ("The *heir* to the throne had an *air* of self-satisfaction"), they are entirely clear. They may, however, be used to make puns (for example, "a papal bull in a china shop").

homophony in music, a melody lead and accompanying harmony, as distinct from **heterophony** and **polyphony** in which different melody lines are combined.

homosexuality sexual preference for, or attraction to, persons of one's own sex; in women it is referred to as ◊lesbianism. Both sexes use the term "gay." Men and women who are attracted to both sexes are referred to as bisexual. The extent to which homosexual behavior is caused by biological or psychological factors is an area of disagreement among experts.

Although some ancient civilizations (notably ancient Greece and Confucian China) accepted homosexuality, other societies have punished homosexual acts. In 12th-century Europe sodomy was punishable by burning and since then homosexuals have suffered varying degrees of prejudice and prosecution. In the latter half of the 20th century discrimination against homosexuals has decreased as a result of pressure from "gay rights" campaigners. However, laws against homosexuality differ from country to country. In the US, for example, many states prohibit homosexual acts while in the EC countries (except the Isle of Man) homosexuality between consenting adults is legal. Male homosexuals fear further discrimination as a result of the discovery of the ◊AIDS virus.

homozygous in a living organism, having two identical ◊alleles for a given trait. Individuals homozygous for a trait always breed true; that is, they produce offspring that resemble them in appearance when bred with a genetically similar individual; inbred varieties or species are homozygous for almost all traits. Recessive alleles (see ◊recessive gene) are only expressed in the homozygous condition. See also ◊heterozygous.

Homs or **Hums** city, capital of Homs district, W Syria, near the Orontes River; population (1981) 355,000. Silk, cereals, and fruit are produced in the area, and industries include silk textiles, oil refining, and jewelry. ◊Zenobia, Queen of Palmyra, was defeated at Homs by the Roman emperor ◊Aurelian 272.

Honan alternate name for ◊*Henan*, a province of China.

Honduras country in Central America, bounded N by the Caribbean Sea, SE by Nicaragua, S by the Pacific Ocean, SW by El Salvador, and W and NW by Guatemala.

government The 1982 constitution, which underwent a major revision 1985, provides for the election of a president, who is head of both state and government, by universal suffrage for a four-year term, and may not serve two terms in succession. A single-chamber national assembly of 134 members is elected in the same way for a similar term.

history Originally part of the ◊Maya civilization, the area was reached by Christopher Columbus 1502, and was colonized by Spain from 1526. Becoming independent from Spain 1821, Honduras was part of the ◊United Provinces of Central America until 1838, when it achieved full independence. From 1939 to 1949 it was a dictatorship under the leader of the National Party (PN).

civilian rule The government changed in a series of military coups, until the return of civilian rule 1980. The army, however, still controlled security and was able to veto cabinet appointments, and although the 1981 general election was won by the Liberal Party of Honduras (PLH) and its leader, Dr Roberto Suazo, became president, power remained in the hands of General Gustavo Alvarez, the commander in chief of the army. In 1982 Alvarez

Alkane	Alcohol	Aldehyde	Ketone	Carboxylic acid	Alkene
CH_4 methane	CH_3OH methanol	HCHO methanal	—	HCOOH methanoic acid	—
CH_3CH_3 ethane	CH_3CH_2OH ethanol	CH_3CHO ethanal	—	CH_3COOH ethanoic acid	CH_2CH_2 ethene
$CH_3CH_2CH_3$ propane	$CH_3CH_2CH_2OH$ propanol	CH_3CH_2CHO propanal	CH_3COCH_3 propanone	CH_3CH_2COOH propanoic acid	CH_2CHCH_3 propene
methane	methanol	methanal	propanone	methanoic acid	ethene

homologous series *The systematic naming of simple straight-chain organic molecules depends on two-part names.*

secured an amendment to the constitution, reducing government control over the armed forces, and was virtually in charge of foreign policy, agreeing 1983 to the establishment of US military bases in the country. The US Central Intelligence Agency was also active in assisting Nicaraguan counterrevolutionary rebels ("Contras") based in Honduras.

tensions with Nicaragua In 1984 Alvarez was ousted by a group of junior officers and the country's close relationship with the US came under review. In the same year divisions arose in the PLH over selection of presidential candidates and in 1985 the electoral law was changed. Suazo was not eligible for the 1985 presidential elections, and although the main PLH candidate was José Azcona. Although the PN nominee won most votes, the revised constitution made Azcona the eventual winner. The presence of Contras on Honduran territory provoked tensions with Nicaragua, which filed a suit against Honduras in the International Court of Justice. The Sandinista government agreed to drop the suit if Contra bases were dismantled and the fighters demobilized, in keeping with the regional peace plan adopted Feb 1989. Thus the presence of the rebels became a distinct political liability for Honduras. In the Nov 1989 presidential election, the PN candidate, Rafael Callejas, was elected; he was inaugurated 1990.

The century-old border dispute with El Salvador, involving 440sq km/170 sq mi, was settled Sept 1992 awarding two-thirds of the territory in question to Honduras. As a result Honduras acquired the region at the delta of the Goascoran River and about four-fifths of two areas along the Negro-Quiagara and the Sazalapa Rivers. *See illustration box.*

Honduras
Republic of (*República de Honduras***)**

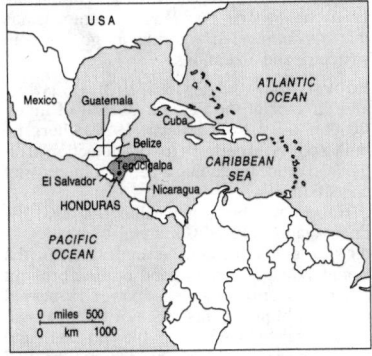

area 43,282 sq mi/112,100 sq km
capital Tegucigalpa
cities San Pedro Sula; ports La Ceiba, Puerto Cortés
physical narrow tropical coastal plain with mountainous interior, Bay Islands
features archeological sites; Mayan ruins at Copán
head of state and government Rafael Leonardo Callejas from 1990
political system democratic republic
political parties Liberal Party of Honduras (PLH), center-left; National Party (PN), right-wing
exports coffee, bananas, meat, sugar, timber (including mahogany, rosewood)
currency lempira

Honecker Erich 1912– . German communist politician, in power 1973–89, elected chair of the council of state (head of state) 1976. He governed in an outwardly austere and efficient manner and, while favoring East–West détente, was a loyal ally of the USSR. In Oct 1989, following a wave of prodemocracy demonstrations, he was replaced as leader of the Socialist Unity Party (SED) and head of state, and in Dec expelled from the Communist Party.

Honecker, the son of a miner, joined the German Communist Party 1929 and was imprisoned for antifascist activity 1935–45. He was elected to the East German parliament (Volkskammer) 1949 and became a member of the SED Politburo during the 1950s. A security specialist, during the 1960s he served as a secretary of the National Defense Council before being appointed first secretary of the SED 1971. After Walter Ulbricht's death 1973, Honecker became leader of East Germany.

In Oct 1989, following large-scale civil disturbances, Honecker was replaced by his protégé Egon Krenz. He was arrested Feb 1990 and charged with high treason, misuse of office, and corruption. In March 1991 he was transferred from a Soviet military hospital to Moscow, but the German government demanded his return to face manslaughter charges in connection with the killing of those illegally crossing the Berlin Wall 1961–89. In July 1992 he was returned to Germany to stand trial.

Honegger Arthur 1892–1955. Swiss composer, one of ◊Les Six. His work was varied in form, for example, the opera *Antigone* 1927, the ballet *Skating Rink* 1922, the oratorio *Le Roi*

population (1989 est) 5,106,000 (90% mestizo (mixed), 10% Indians and Europeans); growth rate 3.1% p.a.
life expectancy men 58, women 62
languages Spanish (official), English, Indian languages
religion Roman Catholic 97%
literacy men 61%, women 58% (1985 est)
GDP $3.5 bn (1987); $758 per head
chronology
1838 Independence achieved from Spain.
1980 After more than a century of mostly military rule, a civilian government was elected, with Dr Roberto Suazo as president; the commander in chief of the army, General Gustavo Alvarez, retained considerable power.
1983 Close involvement with the US in providing naval and air bases and allowing Nicaraguan counterrevolutionaries ("Contras") to operate from Honduras.
1984 Alvarez ousted in coup led by junior officers, resulting in policy review toward US and Nicaragua.
1985 José Azcona elected president after electoral law changed, making Suazo ineligible for presidency.
1989 Government and opposition declared support for Central American peace plan to demobilize Nicaraguan Contras based in Honduras; Contras and their dependents in Honduras in 1989 thought to number about 55,000.
1990 Rafael Callejas (PN) inaugurated as president.
1992 Border dispute with El Salvador dating from 1861 finally resolved.

David/King David 1921, program music (*Pacific 231* 1923), and the *Symphonie liturgique/Liturgical Symphony* 1946.

Hōnen 1133–1212. Japanese Buddhist monk who founded the ◊Pure Land school of Buddhism.

honey sweet syrup produced by honey ◊bees from the nectar of flowers. It is stored in honeycombs and made in excess of their needs as food for the winter. Honey comprises various sugars, mainly levulose and dextrose, with enzymes, coloring matter, acids, and pollen grains. It has antibacterial properties and was widely used in ancient Egypt, Greece, and Rome as a wound salve. It is still popular for sore throats, in hot drinks or in lozenges.

honey-eater or *honey-sucker* small, brightly colored bird of the family Meliphagidae. Honey-eaters have long, curved beaks and long tails, and they use their long tongues to sip nectar from flowers. They are native to Australia.

Honey-eaters from Australasia colonized Hawaii and four species evolved there of which only one, the Kauai oo, survives; thought to be extinct, it was rediscovered 1960.

honey guides in botany, lines or spots on the petals of a flower that indicate to pollinating insects the position of the nectaries (see ◊nectar) within the flower. The orange dot on the lower lip of the butter-and-eggs flower *Linaria vulgaris* is an example. Sometimes the markings reflect only ultraviolet light, which can be seen by many insects although it is not visible to the human eye.

honeysuckle vine or shrub of the genus *Lonicera*, family Caprifoliaceae. The common honeysuckle or woodbine *L. periclymenum* of Europe is a climbing plant with sweet-scented flowers, reddish and yellow-tinted outside and creamy-white inside; it now grows in the northeastern US.

The North American trumpet honeysuckle *L. sempervirens* has unusual vaselike flowers and includes scarlet and yellow varieties.

Hong Kong British crown colony SE of China, in the South China Sea, comprising Hong Kong Island; the Kowloon Peninsula; many other islands, of which the largest is Lantau; and the mainland New Territories. It is due to revert to Chinese control 1997.
area 413 sq mi/1,070 sq km
capital Victoria (Hong Kong City)
cities Kowloon, Tsuen Wan (in the New Territories)
features an enclave of Kwantung province, China, it has one of the world's finest natural harbors; Hong Kong Island is connected with Kowloon by undersea railroad and ferries; a world financial center, its stock market has four exchanges; across the border of the New Territories in China itself is the Shenzhen special economic zone
exports textiles, clothing, electronic goods, clocks, watches, cameras, plastic products; a large proportion of the exports and imports of S China are transshipped here; tourism is important
currency Hong Kong dollar
population (1986) 5,431,000; 57% Hong Kong Chinese, most of the remainder refugees from the mainland
languages English, Chinese
media Hong Kong has the most free press in Asia but its freedoms are not enshrined in law
religion Confucianist, Buddhist, Taoist, with Muslim and Christian minorities

government Hong Kong is a British dependency administered by a crown-appointed governor (Chris Patten from 1992) who presides over an unelected executive council, composed of 4 ex-officio and 11 nominated members, and a legislative council composed of 3 ex-officio members, 29 appointees, and 24 indirectly elected members

history formerly part of China, Hong Kong Island was occupied by Britain 1841, during the first of the ⟡Opium Wars, and ceded by China under the 1842 Treaty of Nanking. The Kowloon Peninsula was acquired under the 1860 Beijing (Peking) Convention and the New Territories secured on a 99-year lease from 1898. The colony, which developed into a major entrepôt for Sino-British trade during the late 19th and early 20th centuries, was occupied by Japan 1941–45. The restored British administration promised, after 1946, to increase self-government. These plans were shelved, however, after the 1949 Communist revolution in China. During the 1950s almost 1 million Chinese (predominantly Cantonese) refugees fled to Hong Kong. Immigration continued during the 1960s and 1970s, raising the colony's population from 1 million in 1946 to 5 million in 1980, leading to the imposition of strict border controls during the 1980s. Since 1975, 160,000 Vietnamese ⟡boat people have fled to Hong Kong; in 1991 some 61,000 remained. The UK government began forced repatriation 1989.

Hong Kong's economy expanded rapidly during the corresponding period and the colony became one of Asia's major commercial, financial, and industrial centers, boasting the world's busiest container port from 1987. As the date (1997) for the termination of the New Territories' lease approached, negotiations on Hong Kong's future were opened between Britain and China 1982. These culminated in a unique agreement, signed in Beijing 1984, in which Britain agreed to transfer full sovereignty of the islands and New Territories to China 1997 in return for Chinese assurance that Hong Kong's social and economic freedom and capitalist lifestyle would be preserved for at least 50 years.

Under this "one country, two systems" agreement, in 1997 Hong Kong would become a special administrative region within China, with its own laws, currency, budget, and tax system, and would retain its free-port status and authority to negotiate separate international trade agreements. In preparation for its withdrawal from the colony, the British government introduced indirect elections to select a portion of the new legislative council 1984, and direct elections for seats on lower-tier local councils 1985. A Sino-British joint liaison group was also established to monitor the functioning of the new agreement, and a 59-member committee (including 25 representatives from Hong Kong) formed in Beijing 1985 to draft a new constitution.

In Dec 1989 the UK government granted British citizenship to 225,000 Hong Kong residents, beginning 1997. In March 1990 the 59-member committee agreed to a "Basic Law" with 18 directly elected members of the legislative council from 1991, rising to 30 in 2003 (out of a total of 60). In Sept 1991, the liberal United Democrats won 16 of the 18 seats in the territory's legislature; they were led by lawyer Martin Lee and teacher Szeto Wah (who had spearheaded Hong Kong's 1989 prodemocracy demonstrations in the wake of the ⟡Tiananmen Square massacre in Beijing). Earlier in the year, the UK and China agreed on the construction of a new airport and seaport, but in 1992 China balked at the high cost of the project. China also objected to Patten's democratic reform, charging that the Basic Law was being violated.

Honiara port and capital of the Solomon Islands, on the NW coast of Guadalcanal island; population (1985) 26,000.

Honolulu (Hawaiian "sheltered bay") capital city and port of Hawaii, on the S coast of Oahu; population (1990) 365,300. It is a vacation resort, noted for its beauty and tropical vegetation, with some industry.

The University of Hawaii's main campus is here, and there is an innovative state capitol building, dating from 1959. Pearl Harbor and Hickam Air Force Base are 7 mi/11 km to the NW. William Brown, a British sea captain, was the first European to see Honolulu, in 1794. It became the Hawaiian royal capital in the 19th century.

Honshu principal island of Japan. It lies between Hokkaido to the NE and Kyushu to the SW; area 89,205 sq mi/231,100 sq km, including 382 smaller islands; population (1986) 97,283,000. A chain of volcanic mountains runs along the island, which is subject to frequent earthquakes. The main cities are Tokyo, Yokohama, Osaka, Kobe, Nagoya, and Hiroshima.

Hooke Robert 1635–1703. English scientist and inventor, originator of ⟡*Hooke's law*, and considered the foremost mechanic of his time. His inventions included a telegraph system, the spirit level, marine barometer, and sea gauge. He coined the term "cell" in biology.

Hooke was born at Freshwater on the Isle of Wight, the son of a priest. He studied elasticity, furthered the sciences of mechanics and microscopy, and helped improve such scientific instruments as watches, microscopes, telescopes, and barometers. He was elected to the Royal Society 1663, and became its curator for the rest of his life. He was professor of geometry at Gresham College, London, and designed several buildings, including the College of Physicians, London.

Hooker Joseph Dalton 1817–1911. English botanist who traveled to the Antarctic and made many botanical discoveries. His works include *Flora Antarctica* 1844–47, *Genera Plantarum* 1862–83, and *Flora of British India* 1875–97.

Hooker Thomas 1586–1647. Colonial American religious leader. In 1633 he immigrated to the Massachusetts Bay Colony, settling in Cambridge. As an opponent of the strong religious leadership of the colony, he led a group of his followers westward to the Connecticut Valley in 1636, founding Hartford. Hooker became the de facto leader of the colony and in 1639 helped to formulate Connecticut's first constitution, the Fundamental Orders.

Born in England and educated as a minister at Cambridge, Hooker served at parishes in England before fleeing to Holland in 1630 because of his Puritan beliefs.

Hooke's law in physics, law stating that the tension in a lightly stretched spring is proportional to its extension from its natural length. It was discovered by Robert Hooke 1676.

hookworm parasitic roundworm (see ⟡worm), of the genus *Necator*, with hooks around the mouth. It lives mainly in tropic and subtropic regions, but also in humid areas in temperate climates. The eggs are hatched in damp soil, and the larvae bore into the host's skin, usually through the soles of the feet. They make their way to the small intestine, where they live by sucking blood. The eggs are expelled with feces, and the cycle starts again. The human hookworm causes anemia, weakness, and abdominal pain. It is common in areas where defecation occurs outdoors.

hoopoe bird *Upupa epops* in the order Coraciiformes, slightly larger than a thrush, with a long, thin bill and a bright, buff-colored crest that expands into a fan shape. The wings are banded with black and white, and the rest of the plumage is black, white, and buff. This bird is the "lapwing" mentioned in the Old Testament.

Hoover Herbert Clark 1874–1964. 31st president of the US 1929–33, a Republican. He was secretary of commerce 1921–28. Hoover lost public confidence after the stock-market crash of 1929, when he opposed direct government aid for the unemployed in the Depression that followed.

As a mining engineer, Hoover traveled widely before World War I. After the war he organized relief work in occupied Europe; a talented administrator, he was subsequently associated with numerous international relief organizations, and became food administrator for the US 1917–19. He defeated the Democratic candidate for the presidency, Al Smith (1873–1944) by a wide margin. The shantytowns or ⟡*Hooverville*s of the homeless that sprang up around large cities were evidence of his failure to cope with the effects of the Depression. He was severely criticized for his adamant opposition to federal relief for the unemployed, even after the funds of states, cities, and charities were exhausted. In 1933 he was succeeded by F D Roosevelt.

Hoover was called upon to administer the European Food Program 1947, and in the late 1950s he headed two Hoover commissions that recommended reforms in government structure and operations.

Hoover J(ohn) Edgar 1895–1972. US lawyer and director of the Federal Bureau of Investigation (FBI) from its start 1924, where he built a powerful network for the detection of organized crime, including a national fingerprint collection.

Hoover was born in Washington, DC. His drive against alleged Communist activities after World War II, and his opposition to the Kennedy administration and others, brought much criticism over abuse of power. He served under eight presidents, none of whom would dismiss him, since he kept files on them and their associates. During his tenure, the FBI (named 1935) grew from a corrupt Bureau of Investigation to a respected and highly professional national police agency, with responsibility for counterespionage within the US as well as counterterrorism. Hoover was accused of waging a personal campaign of harassment against leaders of the civil rights movement, notably Dr Martin Luther ⟡King, Jr. He wrote *Persons in Hiding* 1938, *Masters of Deceit* 1958, and *A Study of Communism* 1962.

Hoover William Henry 1849–1932. US manufacturer who developed the vacuum cleaner. "Hoover" soon became a generic name for vacuum cleaner.

Hoover Dam highest concrete dam in the US, 726 ft/221 m, on the Colorado River at the Arizona–Nevada border. It was begun during the Hoover administration, built 1931–36. Known as Boulder Dam 1933–47, under the Roosevelt administration, its name was restored by President Truman since President Hoover was serving the Truman administration in postwar organization. The dam created Lake Meade, and has a hydroelectric power capacity of 1,300 megawatts.

Hooverville colloquial term for any shantytown built by the unemployed and destitute in the US during the Depression 1929–40, named after US president Herbert ⷧHoover whose policies were blamed for the plight of millions.

Hope Bob. Adopted name of Leslie Towne Hope. 1903– . British-born US comedian, brought to the US in 1907. His earliest success was on Broadway and as a radio star in the 1930s. His film appearances include seven "Road" films made from 1940 with Bing Crosby and Dorothy Lamour. These include *The Road to Singapore* 1940, *The Road to Zanzibar* 1941, *The Road to Morocco* 1942, *The Road to Utopia* 1946, *The Road to Rio* 1946, *The Road to Bali* 1952, and *The Road to Hong Kong* 1953. He made other films, such as *Paleface* 1948, a comic western.

He entertained the troops since World War II. He was a perennial star on radio and television (since 1950) in his own comedy series and specials. He has received several special ⷧAcademy Awards.

Hopei alternative transcription of ⷧ*Hebei*, a province of China.

Hope's apparatus in physics, an apparatus used to demonstrate the temperature at which water has its maximum density. It is named after Thomas Charles Hope (1766–1844).

It consists of a vertical cylindrical vessel fitted with horizontal thermometers through its sides near the top and bottom, and surrounded at the center by a ledge that holds a freezing mixture (ice and salt). When the cylinder is filled with water, this gradually cools, the denser water sinking to the bottom; eventually the upper thermometer records 32°F/0°C (the freezing point of water) and the lower one has a constant reading of 39°F/4°C (the temperature at which water is most dense).

Hopewell North American Indian agricultural culture of the central US, dated about AD 200. The Hopewell built burial mounds up to 40 ft/12 m high and structures such as Serpent Mound in Ohio; see also ⷧMoundbuilder.

Hopi member of a North American Indian people, presently numbering approximately 9,000, who live mainly in pueblos in the SW US, especially NE Arizona. They live in stone and adobe houses, forming small towns on rocky plateaus, farm, and herd sheep. Their language belongs to the Uto-Aztecan family.

Hopkins Anthony 1937– . Welsh actor. Among his stage appearances are *Equus*, *Macbeth*, *Pravda*, and the title role in *King Lear*. His films include *The Lion in Winter* 1968, *A Bridge Too Far* 1977, *The Elephant Man* 1980, *84 Charing Cross Road* 1986, and *The Silence of the Lambs* (Academy Award) 1991.

Hopkins Frederick Gowland 1861–1947. English biochemist whose research into diets revealed the existence of trace substances, now known as vitamins. Hopkins shared the 1929 Nobel Prize for Physiology and Medicine with Christiaan Eijkman, who had arrived at similar conclusions.

Hopkins Gerard Manley 1844–1889. English

poet and Jesuit priest. His work, marked by its religious themes and use of natural imagery, includes "The Wreck of the Deutschland" 1876 and "The Windhover" 1877. His employment of "sprung rhythm" greatly influenced later 20th-century poetry. His poetry was written in secret, and published 30 years after his death by his friend Robert Bridges.

Hopkins Harry Lloyd 1890–1946. US government official. Originally a social worker, in 1935 he became head of the WPA (Works Progress Administration), which was concerned with Depression relief work. After a period as secretary of commerce 1938–40, he was appointed supervisor of the ⷧlend-lease program 1941, and undertook missions to Britain and the USSR during World War II.

Hopkins Mark 1802–1887. US educator and religious leader. In 1830 he was appointed professor of philosophy at Williams College, serving as its president 1836–72. Becoming increasingly involved in religious affairs, Hopkins was ordained a Congregationalist minister 1836 and served as president of the American Board of Commissioners for Foreign Missions 1857–87. He was also known as a popular lecturer and author on religious subjects.

Born in Stockbridge, Massachusetts, Hopkins was educated at Williams College and received an MD degree from Berkshire College 1829.

Hopkinsville city in SW Kentucky, SW of Louisville; population (1990) 29,800. It is a marketplace for tobacco and livestock.

hoplite in ancient Greece, a heavily armed infantry soldier.

Hopper Dennis 1936– . US film actor and director who caused a sensation with the antiestablishment *Easy Rider* 1969, the archetypal "road" film, but whose *The Last Movie* 1971 was poorly received by the critics. He made a comeback in the 1980s. His work as an actor includes *Rebel Without a Cause* 1955, *The American Friend/Der amerikanische Freund* 1977, and *Blue Velvet* 1986.

Hopper Edward 1882–1967. US painter and etcher. His views of New England and New York in the 1930s and 1940s captured the loneliness and superficial glamor of city life, as in *Nighthawks* 1942 (Art Institute, Chicago).

Hopper's teacher Robert ⷧHenri, associated with the ⷧAshcan School, was a formative influence.

Hopper was a realist who never followed avant-garde trends.

Hopper Hedda 1890–1966. US actress and celebrity reporter. From 1915 she appeared in many silent films and after a brief retirement was hired as a radio gossip reporter in 1936. From 1938 Hopper wrote a syndicated newspaper column about the private lives of the Hollywood stars. She carried on a widely publicized feud with rival columnist Louella Parsons.

Born Elda Furry in Hollidaysburg, Pennsylvania, she left home as a teenager to begin a theatrical career. First appearing on the Broadway stage in 1909, she adopted her professional name after marrying actor DeWolf Hopper.

hops female fruit-heads of the hop plant *Humulus lupulus*, family Cannabiaceae; these are dried and used as a tonic and in flavoring beer. In designated areas in Europe, no male

hops may be grown, since seedless hops produced by the unpollinated female plant contain a greater proportion of the alpha acid that gives beer its bitter taste.

Horace 65–8 BC. Roman lyric poet and satirist. He became a leading poet under the patronage of Emperor Augustus. His works include *Satires* 35–30 BC; the four books of *Odes* about 25–24 BC; *Epistles*, a series of verse letters; and a critical work, *Ars poetica*. They are distinguished by their style, wit, and good sense.

Born at Venusia, S Italy, the son of a freedman, Horace fought under Brutus at Philippi, lost his estate, and was reduced to poverty. In about 38 Virgil introduced him to Maecenas, who gave him a farm in the Sabine hills and recommended him to the patronage of Augustus.

horehound any plant of the genus *Marrubium* of the mint family Labiatae. The white horehound *M. vulgare*, found in Europe, N Africa, and W Asia and naturalized in North America, has a thick, hairy stem and clusters of dull white flowers; it has medicinal uses.

horizon the limit to which one can see across the surface of the sea or a level plain, that is, about 3 mi/5 km at 5 ft/1.5 m above sea level, and about 40 mi/65 km at 1,000 ft/300 m.

hormone product of the ⷧendocrine glands, concerned with control of body functions. The main glands are the thyroid, parathyroid, pituitary, adrenal, pancreas, uterus, ovary, and testis. Hormones bring about changes in the functions of various organs according to the body's requirements. The pituitary gland, at the base of the brain, is a center for overall coordination of hormone secretion; the thyroid hormones determine the rate of general body chemistry; the adrenal hormones prepare the organism during stress for "fight or flight"; and the sexual hormones such as estrogen govern reproductive functions.

Many diseases due to hormone deficiency can be relieved with hormone preparations.

hormone-replacement therapy (HRT) use of oral ⷧestrogen and progestogen to help limit the effects of the menopause in women. The treatment was first used in the 1970s.

At the menopause, the ovaries cease to secrete natural estrogen. This results in a number of symptoms, including hot flushes, anxiety, and a change in the pattern of menstrual bleeding. It is also associated with osteoporosis, or a thinning of bone, leading to an increased incidence of fractures, frequently of the hip, in older women. Oral estrogens, taken to replace the decline in natural hormone levels, combined with regular exercise can help to maintain bone strength in women. In order to improve bone density, however, HRT must be taken for five years, during which time the woman will continue to menstruate. Many women do not find this acceptable.

Hormuz or *Ormuz* small island, area 16 sq mi/41 sq km, in the Strait of Hormuz, belonging to Iran. It is strategically important because oil tankers leaving the Persian Gulf for Japan and the West have to pass through the strait to reach the Arabian Sea.

It was occupied by the Portuguese 1515–1622.

horn one of a family of wind instruments, of which the French horn is the most widely used. See ⷧbrass instrument.

Horn Philip de Montmorency, Count of Horn

1518–1568. Flemish politician. He held high offices under the Holy Roman emperor Charles V and his son Philip II. From 1563 he was one of the leaders of the opposition to the rule of Cardinal Granvella (1517–1586) and to the introduction of the Inquisition. In 1567 he was arrested, together with the Resistance leader Egmont, and both were beheaded in Brussels.

hornbeam any tree of the genus *Carpinus* of the birch family Betulaceae. They have oval, serrated leaves and bear pendant clusters of flowers, each with a nutlike seed attached to the base. The trunk is usually twisted, with smooth gray bark.

The American hornbeam *C. caroliniana* is native to the eastern US. The European hornbeam *C. betulus* is sometimes planted as an ornamental.

hornbill bird of the family of Bucerotidae, found in Africa, India, and Malaysia. Omnivorous, it is about 3 ft/1 m long, and has a powerful bill, usually surmounted by a bony growth or casque. During the breeding season, the female walls herself into a hole in a tree, and does not emerge until the young are hatched.

hornblende green or black rock-forming mineral, one of the ◊amphiboles; it is a hydrous silicate of calcium, iron, magnesium, and aluminum. Hornblende is found in both igneous and metamorphic rocks.

hornet kind of ◊wasp.

hornfels ◊metamorphic rock formed by rocks heated by contact with a hot igneous body. It is fine-grained and brittle, without foliation.

Hornfels may contain minerals only formed under conditions of great heat, such as andalusite, Al_2SiO_5, and cordierite, $(Mg,Fe)_2Al_4Si_5O_{18}$. This rock, originating from sedimentary rock strata, is found in contact with large igneous ◊intrusions where it represents the heat-altered equivalent of the surrounding clays. Its hardness makes it suitable for road building and railroad ballast.

Hornsby Rajah (Rogers) 1896–1963. US baseball player. He won the National League batting title six consecutive seasons 1920–25; his .424 batting average 1924 is the highest ever achieved in the National League. In 1925 he was named the Cardinals' player-manager and won the National League's most valuable player award. In that same year, he had become the first player to win baseball's Triple Crown twice. He was traded to the New York Giants 1927 and served variously as player/player-manager for the Boston Braves 1928, the Chicago Cubs 1929–32, the Cardinals 1933, and the St Louis Browns 1933–37. After retiring as a player—with the second-highest lifetime batting average (.358) in history—he became a manager. Hornsby was elected to the Baseball Hall of Fame 1942.

Born in Winters, Texas, Hornsby was signed by the St Louis Cardinals and broke into the major leagues 1915.

hornwort underwater aquatic plant, family Ceratophyllaceae. It has whorls of finely divided leaves and is found in slow-moving water. Hornworts may be up to 7 ft/2 m long.

horoscope in Western astrology, a chart of the position of the Sun, Moon, and planets relative to the ◊zodiac at the moment of birth, used to assess a person's character and forecast future influences.

In casting a horoscope, the astrologer draws a circular diagram divided into 12 sections, or houses, showing the 12 signs of the zodiac around the perimeter and the Sun, Moon, and planets as they were at the subject's time and place of birth. These heavenly bodies are supposed to represent different character traits and influences, and by observing their positions and interrelations the astrologer may gain insight into the subject's personality and foretell the main outlines of his or her career.

Horowitz Vladimir 1904–1989. Russian-born US pianist. He made his debut in the US 1928 with the New York Philharmonic Orchestra. Noted for his commanding virtuoso style, he was a leading interpreter of Liszt, Schumann, and Rachmaninov.

Horowitz toured worldwide until the early 1950s, when nervous disorders forced him to withdraw completely from the stage; he kept recording, however. After a triumphal return at Carnegie Hall 1965, in which it was clear that he had lost none of his ability, he toured briefly in the 1970s and 1980s.

Horowitz married Arturo ◊Toscanini's daughter, Wanda, 1933. In 1986 he made a pilgrimage to his homeland, giving a brilliant performance at the Moscow Conservatory of Music.

horror genre of fiction and film, devoted primarily to scaring the reader or audience, but often also aiming to be cathartic through their exaggeration of the bizarre and grotesque. Dominant figures in the horror tradition are Mary Shelley (*Frankenstein* 1818), Edgar Allan Poe, Bram Stoker, H P Lovecraft and, among contemporary writers, Stephen King and Clive Barker.

Horror is derived from the Gothic novel, which dealt in shock effects, as well as from folk tales and ghost stories throughout the ages. Horror writing tends to use motifs such as vampirism, the eruption of ancient evil, and monstrous transformation, which often derive from folk traditions, as well as more recent concerns such as psychopathology.

horse hoofed, odd-toed, grazing mammal *Equus caballus* of the family Equidae, which also includes zebras and asses. The many breeds of domestic horse of Euro-Asian origin range in color from white to gray, brown, and black. The yellow-brown Mongolian wild horse or Przewalski's horse *E. przewalskii*, named after its Polish "discoverer" about 1880, is the only surviving species of wild horse.

It has become extinct in the wild because of hunting and competition with domestic animals for food; about 800 survive in captivity, and there are plans to reintroduce them to Mongolia.

Breeds include the **Arab**, small and agile; **thoroughbred**, derived from the Arab via English mares, used in horse racing for its speed (the present stock is descended from three Arab horses introduced to Britain in the 18th century); **quarter horse**, used by cowboys for herding; **Lippizaner**, a pure white horse, named after its place of origin in Slovenia; **shire**, the largest draft horse in the world at 17 hands (1 hand = 4 in/10.2 cm), descended from the medieval war horses that carried knights in armor. Ponies combine the qualities of various types of horses with a smaller build (under 14.2 hands, or 58 in/1.47 m). The smallest is the hardy **Shetland**, about 10.5 hands, or 27 in/70 cm high. The **mule**, a hardy pack-animal, is the usually sterile offspring of a female horse and a male ass; the **hinny** is a similarly sterile offspring of a male horse and a female ass, but less useful as a beast of burden.

horsefly any of over 2,500 species of fly, belonging to the family Tabanidae. The females suck blood from horses, cattle, and humans; males live on plants and suck nectar. The larvae are carnivorous.

horsepower imperial unit (abbreviation hp) of power, now replaced by the ◊watt. It was first used by the engineer James ◊Watt, who employed it to compare the power of steam engines with that of horses.

In the UK, one horsepower is equal to 550 foot-pounds per second or 745.7 watts. In the US this figure has been rounded to 746 watts, and in the metric system it is 735.5 watts.

horse racing sport of racing mounted or driven (hitched) horses. Two popular forms in the US are *flat racing*, in which thoroughbred horses are guided over a flat course by a rider called a jockey, and *harness racing*, in which a driver in a two-wheeled cart called a sulky drives a horse in one of two gaits: pacing (both legs on the same side are off the ground at the same time); trotting (diagonal legs are off the ground at the same time).

Flat racing has been popular in the Americas since the early colonial era. Thoroughbreds were introduced to North America from England during the 18th century, and the first thoroughbred course was opened on Long Island 1821. Today, the most famous races in the US for three-year-old horses are the Kentucky Derby, the Preakness, and the Belmont Stakes, collectively known as the Triple Crown. Winning all three races is a major feat. There are race tracks throughout the US, and betting on races is a major attraction for spectators and off-track betters.

Harness racing horses, called standardbreds, usually race on 0.5-mi/0.8-km oval tracks. Harness racing became popular in the early 19th century; the introduction of parimutuel betting and night racing increased its popularity in the mid-20th century. Other types of horse racing include the *steeplechase*, in which horses race around a course that has numerous obstacles over which the horse must jump. These may include fences, barred jumps, hedges, stone walls, and water.

Triple Crown Winners

1919	Sir Barton
1930	Gallant Fox
1935	Omaha
1937	War Admiral
1941	Whirlaway
1943	Count Fleet
1946	Assault
1948	Citation
1973	Secretariat
1977	Seattle Slew
1978	Affirmed

horseradish hardy perennial *Armoracia rusticana*, native to SE Europe but naturalized elsewhere, family Cruciferae. The thick, cream-colored root is strong-tasting and is often made into a condiment.

horseshoe crab marine arthropod of the order Xiphosura, class Merostomata, distantly related to spiders, which lives on the Atlantic coast of North America and the coasts of Asia. The upper side of the body is entirely covered with a rounded shell, and it has a long, spinelike tail. Horseshoe crabs grow up to 2 ft/60 cm long. They crawl along the bottom in coastal waters and lay their eggs in the sand at the high water mark.

horsetail plant of the genus *Equisetum*, related to ferns and club mosses; some species are also called **scouring rush**. There are about 35 living species, bearing their spores on cones at the stem tip. The upright stems are ribbed and often have spaced whorls of branches. Today they are of modest size, but hundreds of millions of years ago giant treelike forms existed.

Horthy Nicholas Horthy de Nagybánya 1868–1957. Hungarian politician and admiral. Leader of the counterrevolutionary White government, he became regent 1920 on the overthrow of the communist Bela Kun regime by Romanian and Czechoslovak intervention. He represented the conservative and military class, and retained power until World War II, trying (although allied to Hitler) to retain independence of action. In 1944 he tried to negotiate a surrender to the USSR but Hungary was taken over by the Nazis and he was deported to Germany. He was released from German captivity the same year by the Western Allies and allowed to go to Portugal, where he died.

horticulture art and science of growing flowers, fruit, and vegetables. Horticulture is practiced in gardens and orchards, along with millions of acres of land devoted to vegetable farming. Some areas, like California, have specialized in horticulture because they have the mild climate and light fertile soil most suited to these crops.

Horus in ancient Egyptian mythology, the hawkheaded sun god, son of Isis and Osiris, of whom the pharaohs were declared to be the incarnation.

Hosea 8th century BC. Prophet in the Old Testament. His prophecy draws parallels between his own marriage and the relationship between God and Israel.

Hoskins Bob 1942– . British character actor who progressed to fame from a series of supporting roles. Films include *The Long Good Friday* 1980, *The Cotton Club* 1984, *Mona Lisa* 1985, *A Prayer for the Dying* 1987, and *Who Framed Roger Rabbit?* 1988.

hospice residential facility specializing in palliative care for terminally ill patients and their relatives.

hospital facility for the care of the sick, injured, and incapacitated.

In ancient times, temples of deities such as ♢Aesculapius offered facilities for treatment and by the 4th century, the Christian church had founded hospitals for lepers, cripples, the blind, the sick, and the poor. The oldest surviving hospital in Europe is the 7th-century Hôtel Dieu, Paris; in Britain, the most ancient are St Bartholomew's 1123 and St Thomas's 1200; and in the Americas the Hospital of Jesus of Nazareth, Mexico, 1524. Medical knowledge advanced during the Renaissance, and hospitals became increasingly secularized after the Reformation. In the 19th century, further progress was made in hospital design, administration, and staffing (Florence ♢Nightingale played a significant role in this). In the 20th century there has been an increasing trend toward specialization and the inclusion of maternity wards. Modern hospitals have abandoned the single-room Nightingale design for wards in favor of four- or six-bedded rooms, where patients have more privacy.

Hospitaller member of the Order of ♢St John.

host organism that is parasitized by another. In ♢commensalism, the partner that does not benefit may also be called the host.

hostage person taken prisoner as a means of exerting pressure on a third party, usually with threats of death or injury.

In 1979, 63 staff members of the US embassy in Tehran were taken by the Iranians. Following the Iraqi invasion of Kuwait Aug 1990, about 9,000 Westerners were held in Kuwait and Iraq; they were gradually released later that year. The Sept–Nov 1991 UN negotiations between Iran and Israel led to UN-mediated exchanges and the eventual release of several hostages. In Sept 1991, Israel freed 51 Lebanese and Palestinian guerrillas from prison after receiving confirmation of the deaths of two Israeli soldiers missing in action since 1986; in Oct, a further 15 Lebanese detainees were set free. Sept–Nov 1991 saw the release of the longest-held British hostages in Lebanon, Terry ♢Waite and John McCarthy (captured Jan 20, 1987 and April 17, 1986 respectively); other hostages released included Jackie Mann (captured May 12, 1989) and Jesse Turner (captured Jan 24, 1987).

hot spot in geology, a hypothetical region of high thermal activity in the Earth's ♢mantle. It is believed to be the origin of many chains of ocean islands, such as Polynesia and the Galápagos.

A volcano forms on the ocean crust immediately above the hot spot, is carried away by ♢plate tectonic movement, and becomes extinct. A new volcano forms beside it, above the hot spot. The result is an active volcano and a chain of increasingly old and eroded volcanic stumps stretching away along the line of plate movement.

Hottentot ("stammerer") South African term for a variety of different African peoples; it is nonscientific and considered derogatory by many. The name ♢Khoikhoi is preferred.

Houdini Harry. Adopted name of Erich Weiss 1874–1926. US escapologist and conjurer. He was renowned for his escapes from ropes and handcuffs, from trunks under water, from straitjackets and prison cells.

He also campaigned against fraudulent mindreaders and mediums.

Houma city in S Louisiana, on the gulf intracoastal waterway, SW of New Orleans; population (1990) 30,500. The seat of Terrebonne parish, it is a supply center for offshore oil rigs in the Gulf of Mexico. Industries include shellfish processing and sugar refining.

Hounsfield Godfrey (Newbold) 1919– . British engineer, a pioneer of ♢tomography, the application of computer techniques to X-raying the human body. He shared the Nobel Prize for Physiology and Medicine 1979 with the US physicist Allan Cormack (1924–).

Houphouët-Boigny Félix 1905– . Ivory Coast right-wing politician. He held posts in French ministries, and became president of the Republic of the Ivory Coast on independence 1960, maintaining close links with France, which helped to boost an already thriving economy and encourage political stability. Pro-Western and opposed to communist intervention in Africa, Houphouët-Boigny has been strongly criticized for maintaining diplomatic relations with South Africa. He was reelected for a seventh term 1990 in multiparty elections, amid allegations of ballot rigging and political pressure.

hour period of time comprising 60 minutes; 24 hours make one calendar day.

Hours, Book of in medieval Europe, a collection of liturgical prayers for the use of the faithful.

Books of Hours contained short prayers and illustrations, with each prayer suitable for a different hour of the day, in honor of the Virgin Mary. The enormous demand for Books of Hours was a stimulus for the development of Gothic illumination. A celebrated example is the *Très Riches Heures du Duc de Berry*, illustrated in the early 15th century by the ♢Limbourg brothers.

House Edward Mandell 1858–1938. US politician and diplomat. As personal adviser to a succession of Texas governors 1892–1904, he was awarded the honorary title of colonel. "Colonel" House was instrumental in obtaining the presidential nomination for Woodrow Wilson 1912 and later served as Wilson's closest adviser. During World War I, House served as US liaison with Great Britain and was an important behind-the-scenes participant in the 1919 Versailles Peace Conference.

Born in Houston, Texas, House attended Cornell University and, after working for many years on his family's holdings, became active in state Democratic politics.

housefly fly of the genus *Musca*, found in and around dwellings, especially *M. domestica*, a common worldwide species. Houseflies are gray, and have mouthparts adapted for drinking liquids and sucking moisture from food and manure.

Houseman John 1902–1988. US theater, film, and television producer and actor, born in Romania. He co-founded the Mercury Theater with Orson Welles, and collaborated with Welles and Nicholas Ray as directors. He won an Academy Award for his acting debut in *The Paper Chase* 1973, and recreated his role in the subsequent TV series.

house music dance music of the 1980s originating in the inner-city clubs of Chicago, combining funk with European high-tech pop, and using dub, digital sampling, and crossfading. *Acid house* has minimal vocals and melody, instead surrounding the mechanically emphasized 4/4 beat with stripped-down synthesizer riffs and a wandering bass line. Other variants include *hip house*, with rap elements, and *acid jazz*.

House of Commons lower chamber of the UK ♢Parliament.

House of Lords upper chamber of the UK ♢Parliament.

Its members are unelected and comprise the *temporal peers*: all hereditary peers of England created to 1707, all hereditary peers of Great Britain created 1707–1800, and all hereditary peers of the UK from 1801 onward; all hereditary Scottish peers (under the Peerage Act 1963); all peeresses in their own right (under the same act); all life peers (both the law lords and those created under the Life Peerages Act 1958); and the *spiritual peers*: the two archbishops and 24 of the bishops (London, Durham, and Winchester by right, and the rest by seniority). Since the Parliament Act 1911 the powers of the Lords have been restricted in that they may delay a bill passed by the Commons but not reject it. The Lords are presided over by the Lord Chancellor.

House of Representatives, US lower chamber of the Congress. Revenue bills and impeachment charges must originate in the House, which also elects the president (as it did in 1800 and 1824) if there is no majority in the electoral college. Once bills are passed in the House, they are sent to the Senate for consideration.

The House started with fewer than 70 members, but grew as new states joined the Union and the US population increased. Since 1910 the number of members has been fixed at 435. States are represented in proportion to their population. In order to serve in the House a person must be 25 years of age, a resident of the state represented, and a US citizen. The term of office is two years. The Speaker of the House is the majority party's leader. In the late 20th century the Democrats controlled the House almost all of the time.

House Un-American Activities Committee (HUAC) Congressional committee, established 1938, noted for its public investigating into alleged subversion, particularly of communists. First headed by Martin Dies, it achieved its greatest notoriety during the 1950s through its hearings on communism in the movie industry. It was later renamed the House Internal Security Committee.

Housman A(lfred) E(dward) 1859–1936. English poet and Classical scholar. His *A Shropshire Lad* 1896, a series of deceptively simple, nostalgic, balladlike poems, was popular during World War I. This was followed by *Last Poems* 1922 and *More Poems* 1936.

Houston port in Texas; population (1990) 1,630,600; linked by canal to the Gulf of Mexico. It is a major center of the petroleum industry and of finance and commerce. It is also one of the busiest US ports.

Industrial products include refined petroleum, oil-field equipment, and petrochemicals, chief of which are synthetic rubber, plastics, insecticides, and fertilizers. Other products include iron and steel, electrical and electronic

machinery, paper products, and milled rice. The Lyndon B Johnson Space Center, the University of Houston, and Rice University are here, as is the Astrodome, the world's first all-purpose, air-conditioned domed stadium. The Texas Medical Center is one of the world's finest, and there are major museums and performing-arts groups. Houston was first settled 1826. Its modern growth dates from the discovery of oil nearby 1901 and the completion of the Houston Ship Channel 1914.

Houston Sam 1793–1863. US general who won independence for Texas from Mexico 1836 and was president of the Republic of Texas 1836–45. Houston, Texas, is named after him.

Houston was governor of the state of Tennessee and later US senator from and governor of the state of Texas. He took Indian citizenship when he married a Cherokee.

hovercraft vehicle that rides on a cushion of high-pressure air, free from all contact with the surface beneath, invented by British engineer Christopher Cockerell 1959. Hovercraft need a smooth terrain when operating overland and are best adapted to use on waterways. They are useful in places where harbors have not been established.

Large hovercraft (SR-N4) operate a swift car-ferry service across the English Channel, taking only about 35 minutes between Dover and Calais. They are fitted with a flexible "skirt" that helps maintain the air cushion.

Howard Catherine *c.* 1520–1542. Queen consort of ◊Henry VIII of England from 1540. In 1541 the archbishop of Canterbury, Thomas Cranmer, accused her of being unchaste before marriage to Henry and she was beheaded 1542 after Cranmer made further charges of adultery.

Howard Charles, 2nd Baron Howard of Effingham and 1st Earl of Nottingham 1536–1624. English admiral, a cousin of Queen Elizabeth I. He commanded the fleet against

the Spanish Armada while Lord High Admiral 1585–1618.

Howard Leslie. Adopted name of Leslie Stainer 1893–1943. English actor whose films include *The Scarlet Pimpernel* 1935, *The Petrified Forest* 1936, *Pygmalion* 1938, and *Gone With the Wind* 1939.

He was killed during a secret wartime mission when the plane he was traveling in was shot down by the Germans, allegedly because Winston Churchill was thought to be aboard.

Howard Trevor (Wallace) 1916–1989. English actor whose films include *Brief Encounter* 1945, *Sons and Lovers* 1960, *Mutiny on the Bounty* 1962, *Ryan's Daughter* 1970, and *Conduct Unbecoming* 1975.

Howe Elias 1819–1867. US inventor, in 1846, of a ◊sewing machine using two threads, thus producing a lock stitch.

Born in Spencer, Massachusetts, Howe worked on several types of sewing machines before arriving at his invention that he marketed successfully in England. Eventually he manufactured the machine in Bridgeport, Connecticut, and marketed it successfully in the US.

Howe James Wong. Adopted name of Wong Tung Jim 1899–1976. Chinese-born director of film photography, who lived in the US from childhood. One of Hollywood's best camera operators, he is credited with introducing the use of hand-held cameras and deep focus. His work ranges from *The Alaskan* 1924 to *Funny Lady* 1975.

Howe Julia Ward 1819–1910. US feminist and abolitionist who in 1862 wrote the poem "The Battle Hymn of the Republic"; sung to the tune of "John Brown's Body," it became associated with the Union side during the Civil War.

Born in New York City, she was an editor of *Commonwealth*, a Boston newspaper on which she worked with her husband, Samuel Gridley Howe. The couple was also active in the abolition movement. She wrote a biography 1883 of Margaret Fuller, a prominent literary figure and a member of Ralph Waldo Emerson's Transcendentalists.

Howe Richard Earl 1726–1799. British admiral. He cooperated with his brother William against the colonists during the American Revolution and in the French Revolutionary Wars commanded the Channel fleets 1792–96.

Howe Samuel Gridley 1801–1876. US educational reformer. Howe became director of a school for the blind in Boston 1831, developing innovative educational techniques that were widely emulated. A close associate of Horace Mann and Dorothea Dix, Howe also campaigned for expanded public education and better mental health facilities. He served as chairman of the Massachusetts Board of State Charities 1865–74.

Born in Boston, Howe was educated at Brown University and received an MD degree from Harvard 1824. A Philhellene, he spent seven years in Greece during its War of Independence.

Howe William, 5th Viscount Howe 1729–1814. British general. During the Revolutionary War he won the Battle of Bunker Hill 1775, and as commander in chief in America 1776–78 captured New York and defeated Washington at Brandywine and Germantown. He resigned in protest at lack of home government support.

Howells William Dean 1837–1920. US novelist and editor. The "dean" of US letters

rudders
tailfins
pushing propellers
control cabin / flight deck
passenger windows
flexible skirt

three kinds of hovercraft

loading ramp

air — fan — open plenum
air — fan — peripheral jet
air — fan — flexible skirt

hovercraft *There are several alternative ways of containing the cushion of air beneath the hull of a hovercraft.*

in the post-Civil War era, and editor of *The Atlantic Monthly*, he championed the realist movement in fiction and encouraged many younger authors. He wrote 35 novels, 35 plays, and many books of poetry, essays, and commentary.

His novels, filled with vivid social detail, include *A Modern Instance* 1882 and *The Rise of Silas Lapham* 1885, about the social fall and moral rise of a New England paint manufacturer, a central fable of the "Gilded Age."

howitzer cannon, in use since the 16th century, with a particularly steep angle of fire. It was much developed in World War I for demolishing the fortresses of the trench system. The multinational NATO FH70 field howitzer is mobile and fires, under computer control, three 95 lb/43 kg shells at 20 mi/32 km range in 15 seconds.

Hoxha Enver 1908–1985. Albanian Communist politician, the country's leader from 1954. He founded the Albanian Communist Party 1941, and headed the liberation movement 1939–44. He was prime minister 1944–54, combining with foreign affairs 1946–53, and from 1954 was first secretary of the Albanian Party of Labor. In policy he was a Stalinist and independent of both Chinese and Soviet communism.

Hoyle Fred(erick) 1915– . English astronomer and writer. In 1948 he joined with Hermann ⟡Bondi and Thomas Gold (1920–) in developing the ⟡steady-state theory. In 1957, with Geoffrey and Margaret Burbidge (1925– and 1919–) and William ⟡Fowler, he showed that chemical elements heavier than hydrogen and helium are built up by nuclear reactions inside stars. He has suggested that life originates in the gas clouds of space and is delivered to the Earth by passing comets. His science-fiction novels include *The Black Cloud* 1957.

hp abbreviation for ⟡*horsepower*.

HQ abbreviation for *headquarters*.

Hsuan Tung name adopted by Henry ⟡P'u-i on becoming emperor of China 1908.

ht abbreviation for *height*.

Hua Guofeng or *Hua Kuofeng* 1920– . Chinese politician, leader of the Chinese Communist Party (CCP) 1976–81, premier 1976–80. He dominated Chinese politics 1976–77, seeking economic modernization without major structural reform. From 1978 he was gradually eclipsed by Deng Xiaoping. Hua was ousted from the Politburo Sept 1982 but remained a member of the CCP Central Committee.

Huambo town in central Angola; population (1970) 61,885. Founded 1912, it was known as *Nova Lisboa* ("New Lisbon") 1928–78, when it was designated by the Portuguese as the future capital. It is an agricultural center.

Huang He or *Hwang Ho* river in China; length 3,395 mi/5,464 km. It takes its name (meaning "yellow river") from its muddy waters. Formerly known as "China's sorrow" because of disastrous floods, it is now largely controlled through hydroelectric works and flood barriers.

The flood barriers, however, are ceasing to work because the silt is continually raising the river bed.

Huáscar c. 1495–1532. King of the Incas. He shared the throne with his half brother

Atahualpa from 1525, but the latter overthrew and murdered him during the Spanish conquest.

Huascaran extinct volcano in the Andes; the highest mountain in Peru, 22,205 ft/6,768 m.

Hubbard L(afayette) Ron(ald) 1911–1986. US science-fiction writer of the 1930s and 1940s, founder in 1954 of ⟡Scientology.

Hubble Edwin Powell 1889–1953. US astronomer who discovered the existence of other ⟡galaxies outside our own, and classified them according to their shape. His theory that the universe is expanding is now generally accepted.

Born in Marshfield, Missouri, Hubble originally studied law before joining ⟡Yerkes Observatory 1914, subsequently moving to Mount Wilson where in 1923 he discovered ⟡Cepheid variable stars outside our own Galaxy. In 1925 he introduced the classification of galaxies as spirals, barred spirals, and ellipticals. In 1929 he announced *Hubble's law*, which states that the galaxies are moving apart at a rate that increases with their distance.

Hubble's constant in astronomy, a measure of the rate at which the universe is expanding, named after Edwin Hubble. Observations suggest that galaxies are moving apart at a rate of 30–60 mps/50–100 kps for every million ⟡parsecs of distance. This means that the universe, which began at one point according to the ⟡Big Bang theory, is between 10 billion and 20 billion years old (closer to 20).

Hubble's law the law that relates a galaxy's distance from us to its speed of recession as the universe expands, announced in 1929 by Edwin Hubble. He found that galaxies are moving apart at speeds that increase in direct proportion to their distance apart. The rate of expansion is known as Hubble's constant.

Hubble Space Telescope (HST) telescope placed into orbit around the Earth, at an altitude of 380 mi/610 km, by the space shuttle *Discovery* in April 1990. It has a main mirror 94 in/2.4 m wide, which suffers from spherical aberration and so cannot be focused properly. Yet, because it is above the atmosphere, the HST outperforms ground-based telescopes. Computer techniques are being used to improve the images from the telescope until the arrival of a maintenance mission to install corrective optics. The HST carries four scientific instruments. In Aug 1991, power failure caused half the Goddard High Resolution Spectroscope, the instrument least affected by the telescope's faulty mirror, to be shut down.

The HST is the most expensive crewless spacecraft so far made, costing $2.5 billion—five times the original estimate—and launched seven years late. An inquiry found both NASA and the contractors to blame for the manufacturing fault in the mirror, which was not recognized until it was in orbit.

Hubei or *Hupei* province of central China, through which flow the river Chang Jiang and its tributary the Han Shui
area 72,375 sq mi/187,500 sq km
capital Wuhan
features high land in the W, the river Chang breaking through from Sichuan in gorges; elsewhere low-lying, fertile land; many lakes
products beans, cereals, cotton, rice, vegetables, copper, gypsum, iron ore, phosphorous, salt
population (1990) 53,969,000.

hubris overweening pride. In ancient Greek

tragedy, hubris was a defiance of the gods and invariably led to the downfall of the hubristic character.

huckleberry berry-bearing bush of the genus *Gaylussacia*; it is closely related to the genus *Vaccinium*, which includes the ⟡blueberry in the US and bilberry in Britain. Huckleberry bushes have edible dark-blue berries.

Hudson river of the northeastern US; length 300 mi/485 km. It rises in the Adirondack Mountains and flows south, emptying into a bay of the Atlantic Ocean at New York City.

It is navigable by small oceangoing vessels as far upstream as Albany and Troy, about 150 mi/240 km from its mouth. On its west shore are the Catskill Mountains, and near its mouth, the Palisades, a vertical rock face. The New York Barge Canal system links the Hudson to Lake Champlain, Lake Erie, and the St Lawrence River. The Hudson forms the boundary between New Jersey and New York, and the states are linked by bridges and tunnels. The Hudson River valley is known for scenery that inspired a school of landscape painters in the 19th century. First sighted at its mouth by the Italian navigator Giovanni da Verrazano in 1524, the river was explored upstream as far as modern Albany in 1609 by Henry Hudson, for whom it is named.

Hudson Henry c. 1565–c. 1611. English explorer. Under the auspices of the Muscovy Company 1607–08, he made two unsuccessful attempts to find the Northeast Passage to China. In Sept 1609, commissioned by the Dutch East India Company, he reached New York Bay and sailed 150 mi/240 km up the river that now bears his name, establishing Dutch claims to the area. In 1610, he sailed from London in the *Discovery* and entered what is now the Hudson Strait. After an icebound winter, he was turned adrift by a mutinous crew in what is now Hudson Bay.

Hudson had heard reports of two possible channels to the Pacific Ocean across North America. One of these had been described by English soldier and colonist John Smith. Since Hudson's search for the Northeast Passage proved unsuccessful, he chose to pursue Smith's suggestion.

Hudson Rock. Adopted name of Roy Scherer Jr 1925–1985. US film actor, a star from the mid-1950s to the mid-1960s, who appeared in several melodramas directed by Douglas Sirk and in three comedies co-starring Doris Day (including *Pillow Talk* 1959). He went on to have a successful TV career in the 1970s.

Hudson W(illiam) H(enry) 1841–1922. British author, born of US parents in Argentina. He was inspired by recollections of early days in Argentina to write the romances *The Purple Land* 1885 and *Green Mansions* 1904, and his autobiographical *Far Away and Long Ago* 1918. He wrote several books on birds, and on the English countryside, for example, *Nature in Down-Land* 1900 and *A Shepherd's Life* 1910.

Hudson Bay inland sea of NE Canada, linked with the Atlantic Ocean by **Hudson Strait** and with the Arctic Ocean by Foxe Channel; area 476,000 sq mi/1,233,000 sq km. It is named after Henry Hudson, who reached it 1610.

Several rivers empty into the bay, including the Churchill, Nelson, and Severn. It is ice-free and navigable during the summer, when grain is shipped from Churchill, Manitoba. The bay abounds in fish, and whales, dolphins, seals, and walruses also inhabit its waters and coastline. The Hudson Bay area is sparsely settled, chiefly by trappers, Indians, and Eskimos.

Hudson River School group of US landscape painters of the early 19th century, inspired by the dramatic scenery of the Hudson River Valley and the Catskill Mountains in New York State.

The first artist to depict the region was Thomas Cole. The group also included Asher B ⬦Durand, Martin Joseph Heade, and Frederic Edwin ⬦Church.

Their works, often in a romantic vein, elevated landscape painting in importance in the US.

Hudson's Bay Company chartered company founded by Prince ⬦Rupert 1670 to trade in furs with North American Indians. In 1783 the rival North West Company was formed, but in 1851 this became amalgamated with the Hudson's Bay Company. It is still Canada's biggest fur company, but today also sells general merchandise through department stores and has oil and natural gas interests.

Hué town in central Vietnam, formerly capital of Annam, 8 mi/13 km from the China Sea; population (1989) 211,100. The Citadel, within which is the Imperial City enclosing the palace of the former emperor, lies to the west of the Old City on the north bank of the Huong (Perfume) River; the New City is on the south bank. Hué was once an architecturally beautiful cultural and religious center, but large areas were devastated, with many casualties, during the Battle of Hué Jan 31–Feb 24, 1968, when US and South Vietnamese forces retook the city after Vietcong occupation.

Hughes Charles Evans 1862–1948. US Supreme Court justice and public official. Hughes was named to the US Supreme Court by President Taft 1910 but resigned to accept the Republican nomination for president 1916. He lost narrowly to the incumbent Wilson and returned to his law practice. He served as secretary of state under Harding 1921–25. Appointed Supreme Court chief justice by Hoover 1930, Hughes presided over the constitutional tests of New Deal legislation. He retired from the Court 1941.

Born in Glens Falls, New York, Hughes received his law degree from Columbia 1884. After joining the Columbia law faculty 1891–93, he directed a state investigation of public utilities 1905 and served two terms as New York governor 1906–10.

Hughes Howard R 1905–1976. US aviator, aircraft designer, film producer, and entrepreneur. He founded the Hughes Aircraft Company and broke the air speed record in a craft of his own design in 1935, reaching a speed of 352 mph/566 kph. His financial empire was based on his inheritance of the Hughes Tool Co, founded by his father. In the 1920s he formed the Hughes film studio and produced *Hell's Angels* 1930, *Scarface* 1932, and *The Outlaw* 1944 (which he also directed). A billionaire for most of his later years, he invested in Las Vegas real estate, airlines, and motion picture studios but lived like a hermit, protected by his staff.

Hughes Langston 1902–1967. US author. After graduation from Lincoln University, Hughes published a collection of his poems, *The Weary Blues* 1926. As one of the foremost black American literary figures, he became known as "the Poet Laureate of Harlem." In addition

to his poetry he wrote a series of novels, short stories, and essays. His autobiography, *The Big Sea*, was published 1940.

Born in Joplin, Missouri, and raised in Cleveland, Ohio, Hughes had a poem published while still in high school. After briefly attending Columbia University, he traveled widely and continued to write.

Hughes Ted 1930– . English poet, poet laureate from 1984. His work includes *The Hawk in the Rain* 1957, *Lupercal* 1960, *Wodwo* 1967, and *River* 1983, and is characterized by its harsh portrayal of the crueler aspects of nature. In 1956 he married the poet Sylvia Plath.

Hughes William Morris 1864–1952. Australian politician, prime minister 1915–23; originally Labor, he headed a national cabinet. After resigning as prime minister 1923, he held many other cabinet posts 1934–41.

Hugo Victor (Marie) 1802–1885. French poet, novelist, and dramatist. The *Odes et poésies diverses* appeared 1822, and his verse play *Hernani* 1830 established him as the leader of French Romanticism. More volumes of verse followed between his series of dramatic novels, which included *The Hunchback of Notre Dame* 1831 and *Les Misérables* 1862.

Born at Besançon, Hugo was the son of one of Napoleon's generals. Originally a monarchist, his support of republican ideals in the 1840s led to his banishment 1851 for opposing Louis Napoleon's coup d'état. He lived in exile in Guernsey until the fall of the empire 1870, later becoming a senator under the Third Republic. He died a national hero and is buried in the Panthéon, Paris (see ⬦panthéon).

Huguenot French Protestant in the 16th century; the term referred mainly to Calvinists. Severely persecuted under Francis I and Henry II, the Huguenots survived both an attempt to exterminate them (the **Massacre of** ⬦**St Bartholomew** Aug 24, 1572) and the religious wars of the next 30 years. In 1598 Henry IV (himself formerly a Huguenot) granted them toleration under the **Edict of** ⬦**Nantes**. Louis XIV revoked the edict 1685, attempting their forcible conversion, and 400,000 emigrated.

Provoked by Louis XIV they left, taking their industrial skills with them; many settled in North America, where they founded such towns as New Rochelle and New Paltz, New York State. Only in 1802 was the Huguenot church again legalized in France.

Huhehot former name of ⬦**Hohhot**, a city in Inner Mongolia.

Hui member of one of the largest minority ethnic groups in China, numbering about 25 million. Members of the Hui live all over China, but are concentrated in the northern central region. They have been Muslims since the 10th century, for which they have suffered persecution both before and since the Communist revolution.

Hull Cordell 1871–1955. US Democratic politician. As F D Roosevelt's secretary of state 1933–44, he opposed German and Japanese aggression. He was identified with the Good Neighbor Policy of nonintervention in Latin America. In his last months of office he paved the way for a system of collective security, for which he was called "father" of the United Nations. He was awarded the Nobel Peace Prize 1945.

He was born in Tennessee. He was a member of Congress 1907–33.

Hull officially *Kingston upon Hull* city and

port on the north bank of the Humber estuary, where the river Hull flows into it, England; population (1991) 252,200. It is linked with the south bank of the estuary by the Humber Bridge. Industries include fish processing, vegetable oils, flour milling, electrical goods, textiles, paint, pharmaceuticals, chemicals, caravans, and aircraft.

Notable buildings include 13th-century Holy Trinity Church, Guildhall, Ferens Art Gallery 1927, and the university 1954.

Hulme Keri 1947– . New Zealand poet and novelist. She won the Commonwealth ⬦Booker Prize with her first novel *The Bone People* 1985. Other works include the novella *Lost Possessions* 1985, *The Windeater/ Te Kaihau* 1986, a collection of short stories, and *Strands* 1990, a book of poetry.

hum, environmental disturbing sound of frequency about 40 Hz, heard by individuals sensitive to this range, but inaudible to the rest of the population. It may be caused by industrial noise pollution or have a more exotic origin, such as the jet stream, a fast-flowing high-altitude (about 50,000 ft/15,000 m) mass of air.

human body the physical structure of the human being. It develops from the single cell of the fertilized ovum, is born at 40 weeks, and usually reaches sexual maturity between 11 and 18 years of age. The bony framework (skeleton) consists of more than 200 bones, over half of which are in the hands and feet. Bones are held together by joints, some of which allow movement. The circulatory system supplies muscles and organs with blood, which provides oxygen and food and removes carbon dioxide and other waste products. Body functions are controlled by the nervous system and hormones. In the upper part of the trunk is the thorax, which contains the lungs and heart. Below this is the abdomen, containing the digestive system (stomach and intestines); the liver, spleen, and pancreas; the urinary system (kidneys, ureters, and bladder); and, in women, the reproductive organs (ovaries, uterus, and vagina). In men, the prostate gland and seminal vesicles only of the reproductive system are situated in the abdomen, the testes being in the scrotum, which, with the penis, is suspended in front of and below the abdomen. The bladder empties through a small channel (urethra); in the female this opens in the upper end of the vulval cleft, which also contains the opening of the vagina, or birth canal; in the male, the urethra is continued into the penis. In both sexes, the lower bowel terminates in the anus, a ring of strong muscle situated between the buttocks.

skeleton The skull is mounted on the spinal column, or spine, a chain of 24 vertebrae. The ribs, 12 on each side, are articulated to the spinal column behind, and the upper seven meet the breastbone (sternum) in front. The lower end of the spine rests on the pelvic girdle, composed of the triangular sacrum, to which are attached the hipbones (ilia), which are fused in front. Below the sacrum is the tailbone (coccyx). The shoulder blades (scapulae) are held in place behind the upper ribs by muscles, and connected in front to the breastbone by the two collarbones (clavicles). Each shoulder blade carries a cup (glenoid cavity) into which fits the upper end of the armbone (humerus). This articulates below with the two forearm bones (radius and ulna). These are articulated at the wrist (carpals) to the bones of the hand (metacarpals and phalanges). The upper end of each thighbone (femur) fits into a depression (acetabulum) in the hipbone; its lower end is articulated at the knee to the shinbone (tibia) and calf bone (fibula), which are articulated at the ankle (tarsals) to the bones of the foot (metatarsals and phalanges). At a moving joint, the end of each bone is formed of tough, smooth cartilage, lubricated by ⟩synovial fluid. Points of special stress are reinforced by bands of fibrous tissue (ligaments).

Muscles are bundles of fibers wrapped in thin, tough layers of connective tissue (fascia); these are usually prolonged at the ends into strong, white cords (tendons, sinews) or sheets (aponeuroses), which connect the muscles to bones and organs, and by way of which the muscles do their work. Membranes of connective tissue also wrap the organs and line the interior cavities of the body. The thorax has a stout muscular floor, the diaphragm, which expands and contracts the lungs in the act of breathing.

The blood vessels of the *circulatory system*, branching into multitudes of very fine tubes (capillaries), supply all parts of the muscles and organs with blood, which carries oxygen and food necessary for life. The food passes out of the blood to the cells in a clear fluid (lymph); this is returned with waste matter through a system of lymphatic vessels that converge into collecting ducts that drain into large veins in the region of the lower neck. Capillaries join together to form veins which return blood, depleted of oxygen, to the heart.

A finely branching *nervous system* regulates the function of the muscles and organs, and makes their needs known to the controlling centers in the central nervous system, which consists of the brain and spinal cord. The inner spaces of the brain and the cord contain cerebrospinal fluid. The body processes are regulated both by the nervous system and by hormones secreted by the endocrine glands. Cavities of the body that open onto the surface are coated with mucous membranes, which secrete a lubricating fluid (mucus).

The exterior surface of the body is coated with *skin*. Within the skin are the sebaceous glands, which secrete sebum, an oily fluid that makes the skin soft and pliable, and the sweat glands, which secrete water and various salts. From the skin grow hairs, chiefly on the head, in the armpits, and around the sexual organs; and nails shielding the tips of the fingers and toes; both hair and nail structures are modifications of skin tissue. The skin also contains ⟩nerves of touch, pain, heat, and cold.

The human *digestive system* is nonspecialized and can break down a wide variety of foodstuffs. Food is mixed with saliva in the mouth by chewing and is swallowed. It enters the stomach, where it is gently churned for some time and mixed with acidic gastric juice. It then passes into the small intestine. In the first part of this, the duodenum, it is broken down further by the juice of the pancreas and duodenal glands, and mixed with bile from the liver, which splits up the fat. The jejunum and ileum continue the work of digestion and absorb most of the nutritive substances from the food. The large intestine completes the process, reabsorbing water into the body, and ejecting the useless residue as feces.

The body, to be healthy, must maintain water and various salts in the right proportions; the process is called *osmoregulation*. The blood is filtered in the two kidneys, which remove excess water, salts, and metabolic wastes. Together these form urine, which has a yellow pigment derived from bile, and passes down through two fine tubes (ureters) into the bladder, a reservoir from which the urine is emptied at intervals (micturition) through the urethra. Heat is constantly generated by the combustion of food in the muscles and glands, and by the activity of nerve cells and fibers. It is dissipated through the skin by conduction and evaporation of sweat, through the lungs in the expired air, and in other excreted substances. Average body temperature is about 100°F/ 38°C (98.4°F/37°C in the mouth).

Human Comedy, The (French *La Comédie humaine*) series of novels by Balzac, published 1842–46, which aimed to depict every aspect of 19th-century French life. Of the 143 planned, 80 were completed. These include studies of human folly and vice, as in *Le Recherche de l'absolu/The Search for the Absolute*, and analyses of professions or ranks, as in *L'Illustre Gaudissart/The Famous Gaudissart* and *Le Curé de village/The Village Parson*.

human–computer interaction exchange of information between a person and a computer, through the medium of a user interface, studied as a branch of ergonomics.

human genome project research scheme, begun 1988, to map the complete nucleotide (see ⟩nucleic acid) sequence of human ⟩DNA. There are approximately 80,000 different ⟩genes in the human genome, and one gene may contain more than 2 million nucleotides. The knowledge gained is expected to help prevent or treat many crippling and lethal diseases, but there are potential ethical problems associated with knowledge of an individual's genetic makeup, and fears that it will lead to genetic engineering.

The Human Genome Organization (HUGO) coordinating the project expects to spend $1 billion over the first five years, making this the largest research project ever undertaken in the life sciences. Work is being carried out in more than 20 centers around the world. By the beginning of 1991, some 2,000 genes had been mapped. Concern that, for example, knowledge of an individual's genes may make that person an unacceptable insurance risk has led to planned legislation on genome privacy in the US, and 3% of HUGO's funds have been set aside for researching and reporting on the ethical implications of the project. Each strand of DNA carries a sequence of chemical building blocks, the nucleotides. There are only four different types, but the number of possible combinations is immense. The different combinations of nucleotides produce different proteins in the cell, and thus determine the structure of the body and its individual variations. To establish the nucleotide sequence, DNA strands are broken into fragments, which are duplicated (by being introduced into cells of yeast or the bacterium *E. coli*) and distributed to the research centers. Genes account for only a small amount of the DNA sequence. Over 90% of DNA appears not to have any function, although it is perfectly replicated each time the cell divides, and handed on to the next generation. Many higher organisms have large amounts of redundant DNA and it may be that this is an advantage, in that there is a pool of DNA available to form new genes if an old one is lost by mutation.

humanism belief in the goodness and high potential of human nature rather than in religious or transcendental values. Humanism culminated as a cultural and literary force in 16th-century Renaissance Europe in line with the period's enthusiasm for Classical literature and art, growing individualism, and the ideal of the all-round male who should be statesman and poet, scholar and warrior. Sir Philip ⟩Sidney is a great exemplar of Renaissance humanism.

human rights civil and political rights of the individual in relation to the state.

Human Rights, Universal Declaration of charter of civil and political rights drawn up by the United Nations 1948. They include the right to life, liberty, education, and equality before the law; to freedom of movement, religion, association, and information; and to a nationality. Under the European Convention of Human Rights 1950, the Council of Europe established the *European Commission of Human Rights* (headquarters in Strasbourg, France), which investigates complaints by states or individuals, and its findings are examined by the *European Court of Human Rights* (established 1959), whose compulsory jurisdiction has been recognized by a number of states, including the UK.

Human Rights Day is Dec 10, commemorating the adoption of the Universal Declaration of Human Rights by the UN General Assembly. The declaration is not legally binding, and the frequent contraventions are monitored by organizations such as ⟩Amnesty International. Human rights were also an issue at the ⟩Helsinki Conference.

Human Rights Watch US nonpartisan pressure group that monitors and publicizes human-rights abuses by governments, especially attacks on those who defend human rights in their own countries. It comprises *Africa Watch*, *Americas Watch*, *Asia Watch*, *Middle East Watch*, and *Helsinki Watch*; the last-named monitors compliance with the 1975 Helsinki accords by the 35 signatory countries.

The first Watch committee was established 1978. By 1990 the organization was sending more than 100 investigative missions to some 60 countries around the world. Human Rights Watch does not accept financial support from governments or government-funded organizations.

human species, origins of evolution of humans from ancestral ⟩primates. The African apes (gorilla and chimpanzee) are shown by anatomical and molecular comparisons to be the closest living relatives of humans. Humans are distinguished from apes by the size of their brain and jaw, their bipedalism, and their elaborate culture. Molecular studies put the date of the split between the human and African ape lines at 5–10 million years ago. There are only fragmentary remains of ape and *hominid* (of the human group) fossils from this period; the oldest known hominids, found in Ethiopia and Tanzania, date from 3.5 to 4 million years ago. These creatures are known as *Australopithecus afarensis*, and they walked upright. They were either direct ancestors or an offshoot of the line that led to modern humans. They may have been the ancestors of *Homo habilis* (considered by some to be a species of *Australopithecus*), who appeared about a million years later, had slightly larger bodies and brains, and were probably the first to use stone tools. *Australopithecus robustus* and *A.*

africanus also lived in Africa at the same time, but these are not generally considered to be our ancestors.

Over 1.5 million years ago, *Homo erectus*, believed by some to be descended from *H. habilis*, appeared in Africa. The *erectus* people had much larger brains, and were probably the first to use fire and the first to move out of Africa. Their remains are found as far afield as China, Java, Spain, Germany, and England. Modern humans, *H. sapiens sapiens*, and the Neanderthals, *H. sapiens neanderthalensis*, are probably descended from *H. erectus*. Analysis of DNA in recent human populations shows that *H. sapiens* originated about 200,000 years ago in Africa. The oldest known fossils of *H. sapiens* also come from Africa, between 150,000 and 100,000 years ago. Separation of human populations occurred later, with separation of Asian, European, and Australian populations between 100,000 and 50,000 years ago. Neanderthals were large-brained and heavily built, probably adapted to the cold conditions of the ice ages. They lived in Europe and the Middle East, and died out about 40,000 years ago, leaving *H. sapiens sapiens* as the only remaining species of the hominid group. The most recent fossil discovery is that of a lower jaw of a fossil ape found in the Otavi Mountains, Namibia. It comes from deposits dated between 10 and 15 million years ago, and it is similar to earlier finds from East Africa and Turkey. This is the first record of a fossil ape from southern Africa and it extends the known range of fossil apes by at least 2,000 mi/3,200 km. It is thought to be close to the initial divergence of the great apes and humans, although genetic studies indicate that the last common ancestor between chimpanzees and humans lived 6 to 8 million years ago.

Humberside county of NE England
area 1,355 sq mi/3,510 sq km
cities Hull (administrative headquarters), Grimsby, Scunthorpe, Goole, Cleethorpes
features Humber Bridge; fertile Holderness peninsula; Isle of Axholme, bounded by rivers Trent, Don, Idle, and Torne, where medieval open-field strip farming is still practiced
products petrochemicals, refined oil, processed fish, cereals, root crops, cattle
population (1991) 845,200
famous people Andrew Marvell, John Wesley, Amy Johnson.

Humbert anglicized form of ♢Umberto, two kings of Italy.

Humboldt Friedrich Heinrich Alexander, Baron von 1769–1859. German botanist and geologist who, with the French botanist Aimé Bonpland (1773–1858), explored the regions of the Orinoco and the Amazon rivers in South America 1800–04, and gathered 60,000 plant specimens. On his return, Humboldt devoted 21 years to writing an account of his travels.

One of the first popularizers of science, he gave a series of lectures later published as *Cosmos* 1845–62, an account of the physical sciences.

Humboldt Current former name of the ♢Peru Current.

Hume David 1711–1776. Scottish philosopher. *A Treatise of Human Nature* 1739–40 is a central text of British empiricism. Hume denies the possibility of going beyond the subjective experiences of "ideas" and "impressions." The effect of this position is to invalidate metaphysics.

chronology: Hundred Years' War

1340	The English were victorious at the naval battle of Sluys.
1346	Battle of Crécy, another English victory.
1347	The English took Calais.
1356	Battle of Poitiers, where Edward the Black Prince defeated the French. King John of France was captured.
late 1350s –early 1360s	France had civil wars, brigandage, and the popular uprising of the ♢Jacquerie.
1360	Treaty of Brétigny-Calais. France accepted English possession of Calais and of a greatly enlarged duchy of Gascony. John was ransomed for £500,000.
1369–1414	The tide turned in favor of the French, and when there was another truce in 1388, only Calais, Bordeaux, and Bayonne were in English hands. A state of half-war continued for many years.
1415	Henry V invaded France and won a victory at Agincourt, followed by conquest of Normandy.
1419	In the Treaty of Toyes, Charles VI of France was forced to disinherit his son, the Dauphin, in favor of Henry V, who was to marry Catherine, Charles's daughter. Most of N France was in English hands.
1422–28	After the death of Henry V his brother Bedford was generally successful.
1429	Joan of Arc raised the siege of Orléans, and the Dauphin was crowned Charles VII at Rheims.
1430–53	Even after Joan's capture and death the French continued their successful counteroffensive, and in 1453 only Calais was left in English hands.

His *History of Great Britain* 1754–62 was popular within his own lifetime but *A Treatise of Human Nature* was indifferently received. He shared many of the beliefs of the British empiricist school (see ♢empiricism), including those of John ♢Locke. **Hume's law** in moral philosophy states that it is never possible to deduce evaluative conclusions from factual premises; this has come to be known as the "is/ought problem."

humerus the upper bone of the forelimb of tetrapods. In humans, the humerus is the bone above the elbow.

humidity the quantity of water vapor in a given volume of the atmosphere (absolute humidity), or the ratio of the amount of water vapor in the atmosphere to the saturation value at the same temperature (relative humidity). At ♢dew point the relative humidity is 100% and the air is said to be saturated. Condensation (the conversion of vapor to liquid) may then occur. Relative humidity is measured by various types of ♢hygrometer.

hummingbird any of various birds of the family Trochilidae, found in the Americas. The name is derived from the sound produced by the rapid vibration of their wings. Hummingbirds are brilliantly colored, and have long, needlelike bills and tongues to obtain nectar from flowers and capture insects. They are the only birds able to fly backward. The Cuban bee hummingbird *Mellisuga helenae*, the world's smallest bird, is 2 in/5.5 cm long, and weighs less than 0.1 oz/2.5 g.

humors, theory of theory prevalent in Classical and medieval times that the human body was composed of four kinds of fluid: phlegm, blood, choler or yellow bile, and melancholy or black bile. Physical and mental characteristics were explained by different proportions of humors in individuals.

Humperdinck Engelbert 1854–1921. German composer. He studied music in Munich and in Italy and assisted Richard ♢Wagner at the Bayreuth Festival Theater. He wrote the musical fairy operas *Hänsel und Gretel* 1893, and *Königskinder/King's Children* 1910.

Humphrey Hubert Horatio 1911–1978. US political leader and vice-president 1965–69. In 1948 he was elected to the US Senate, where

for three terms he distinguished himself as an eloquent and effective promoter of key legislation. An unsuccessful presidential candidate in 1960, he strongly supported the 1964 Civil Rights Act. He served as vice-president under L B Johnson 1965–69 and made another unsuccessful run for the presidency 1968. Briefly professor at the University of Minnesota, Humphrey was reelected to the Senate in 1970 and 1976.

Born in Wallace, South Dakota, Humphrey was trained as a pharmacist. Settling in Minnesota, he became active in Democratic party politics and was elected mayor of Minneapolis 1945.

humus component of ♢soil consisting of decomposed or partly decomposed organic matter, dark in color and usually richer toward the surface. It has a higher carbon content than the original material and a lower nitrogen content, and is an important source of minerals in soil fertility.

Hun member of any of a number of nomad Mongol peoples who were first recorded historically in the 2nd century BC, raiding across the Great Wall into China. They entered Europe about AD 372, settled in the area that is now Hungary, and imposed their supremacy on the Ostrogoths and other Germanic peoples. Under the leadership of Attila they attacked the Byzantine Empire, invaded Gaul, and threatened Rome. After Attila's death in 453 their power was broken by a revolt of their subject peoples. The **White Huns**, or Ephthalites, a kindred people, raided Persia and N India in the 5th and 6th centuries.

Hunan province of S central China
area 81,253 sq mi/210,500 sq km
capital Changsha
features Dongting Lake; farmhouse in Shaoshan village where Mao Zedong was born
products rice, tea, tobacco, cotton; nonferrous minerals
population (1990) 60,660,000.

hundred days, the in European history, the period March 20–June 28, 1815, marking the French emperor Napoleon's escape from imprisonment on Elba to his departure from Paris after losing the battle of Waterloo June 18.

The phrase also describes other periods of new administration. In 1898 Emperor Te Tsung

Hungary
Republic of (*Magyar Köztársaság*)

area 35,910 sq mi/93,032 sq km
capital Budapest
cities Miskolc, Debrecen, Szeged, Pécs
physical Great Hungarian Plain covers E half of country; Bakony Forest, Lake Balaton, and Transdanubian Highlands in the W; rivers Danube, Tisza, and Raba
environment an estimated 35%–40% of the population live in areas with officially "inadmissible" air and water pollution. In Budapest lead levels have reached 30 times the maximum international standards
features more than 500 thermal springs; Hortobágy National Park; Tokay wine area
head of state Árpád Göncz from 1990
head of government József Antall from 1990
political system emergent democratic republic
political parties over 50, including Hungarian Socialist Party (HSP), left of center; Hungarian Democratic Forum (MDF), umbrella prodemocracy grouping; Alliance of Free Democrats (SzDSz), radical free-market opposition group heading coalition with Alliance of Young Democrats, Social Democrats, and Smallholders Party, right-wing
exports machinery, vehicles, iron and steel, chemicals, fruit and vegetables
currency forint
population (1990 est) 10,546,000 (Magyar 92%, Romany 3%, German 2.5%; Hungarian

minority in Romania has caused some friction between the two countries); growth rate 0.2% p.a.
life expectancy men 67, women 74
language Hungarian (or Magyar), one of the few languages of Europe with non-Indo-European origins; it is grouped with Finnish, Estonian, and others in the Finno-Ugric family
religions Roman Catholic 67%, other Christian denominations 25%
literacy men 99.3%, women 98.5% (1980)
GDP $26.1 bn (1987); $2,455 per head
chronology
1918 Independence achieved from Austro-Hungarian empire.
1919 A communist state formed for 133 days.
1920–44 Regency formed under Admiral Horthy, who joined Hitler's attack on the USSR.
1945 Liberated by USSR.
1946 Republic proclaimed; Stalinist regime imposed.
1949 Soviet-style constitution adopted.
1956 Hungarian national uprising; workers' demonstrations in Budapest; democratization reforms by Imre Nagy overturned by Soviet tanks, Kádár installed as party leader.
1968 Economic decentralization reforms.
1983 Competition introduced into elections.
1987 VAT and income tax introduced.
1988 Kádár replaced by Károly Grosz. First free labor union recognized; rival political parties legalized.
1989 May: border with Austria opened. July: new four-person collective leadership of HSWP. Oct: new "transitional constitution" adopted, founded on multiparty democracy and new presidentialist executive. HSWP changed name to Hungarian Socialist Party, with Nyers as new leader. Kádár "retired."
1990 HSP reputation damaged by "Danubegate" bugging scandal. March–April: elections won by right-of-center coalition, headed by Hungarian Democratic Forum (MDF). May: József Antall, leader of the MDF, appointed premier. Aug: Árpád Göncz elected president.
1991 Jan: devaluation of currency. June: legislation approved to compensate owners of land and property expropriated under communist government. Last Soviet troops departed. Dec: Economic Community (EC) association pact signed.
1992 March: EC pact came into effect.

in a form of the Roman alphabet in which *s* corresponds to English *sh*, and *sz* to *s*.

Like the Turks, the Magyars originated in NE Asia; the term "Hungarian" appears to derive from the Turkish *on ogur* ("ten arrows"), describing their ten tribes; this may also be the origin of the English "ogre."

Hungary country in central Europe, bounded N by Czechoslovakia, NE by Ukraine, E by Romania, S by Yugoslavia and Croatia, and W by Austria and Slovenia.

government Under the terms of the "transitional constitution" adopted Oct 1989, Hungary is a unitary state with a one-chamber, 386-member legislature, the national assembly (Orszaggyules). Its members are elected for five-year terms under a mixed system of proportional and direct representation: 176 are directly elected (on a potential two-ballot run-off basis) from local constituencies; 152 are from county and metropolitan lists on a proportional basis; and 58 are elected indirectly from party-nominated national "compensation" lists designed to favor smaller parties. Free competition is allowed in these elections. The national assembly elects a president to serve as head of state and chief executive, and a council of ministers (cabinet) headed by a prime minister. Since 1989 opposition parties have been able to register freely and receive partial state funding. A constitutional court has also been appointed to serve as a watchdog.

history Inhabited by Celts and Slavs, the region became a Roman province. After the Roman era it was overrun at the end of the 4th century AD by Germanic invaders and by Asians who established a ◊Magyar kingdom in the late 9th century, under a chief named Árpád. St Stephen (997–1038) became Hungary's first king; he established a kingdom 1001 and converted the inhabitants to Christianity. After the Árpádian line died out, Hungary was ruled 1308–86 by English kings Henry II and Richard III, and subsequently by other foreign princes.

Turkish rule From 1396, successive rulers fought to keep out Turkish invaders but were finally defeated at Mohács 1526, and the south and center of the country came under Turkish rule for 150 years, while the east was ruled by semiindependent Hungarian princes. By the end of the 17th century the Turks had been driven out by the ◊Hapsburgs, bringing Hungary under Austrian rule. After 1815 a national renaissance began, under the leadership of Louis ◊Kossuth. The revolution of 1848–49 proclaimed a Hungarian republic and abolished serfdom, but Austria suppressed the revolt with Russian help.

Austro-Hungarian empire In 1867 the ◊Austro-Hungarian empire was established, giving Hungary self-government. During World War I, Hungary fought on the German side and, after the collapse of the Austro-Hungarian empire, became an independent state 1918. For 133 days in 1919, Hungary was a communist republic under Béla ◊Kun, but this was brought to an end by intervention from Romania and Czechoslovakia. During 1920–44, Hungary was ruled by Admiral ◊Horthy, acting as regent for an unnamed king. After 1933, Horthy fell more and more under German influence and joined Hitler in the invasion of the USSR 1941.

communism Hungary was overrun by communist forces 1944–45. Horthy fled, and a provisional government, including the communist agriculture minister Imre ◊Nagy, was

---

of China attempted 100 days of reform (June 11–Sept 16), under the guidance of K'ang Yu-wei. In 1931 Mussolini and G Forzano wrote *The 100 Days*. It is also applied to the reform period in the administration of US president F D Roosevelt from his inauguration on March 4, 1933 when much of the legislation for his New Deal program was initiated. English prime minister Harold Wilson used the phrase in *Purpose and Power* 1966.

hundredweight unit (symbol cwt) of mass, equal to 100 lb (45.36 kg) in the US. In the UK and Canada, it equals 112 lb (50.8 kg), and is sometimes called the long hundredweight.

Hundred Years' War series of conflicts between England and France 1337–1453. Its origins lay with the English kings' possession of Gascony (SW France), which the French kings claimed as their ◊fief, and with trade rivalries over ◊Flanders.

The two kingdoms had a long history of

strife before 1337, and the Hundred Years' War has sometimes been interpreted as merely an intensification of these struggles. It was caused by fears of French intervention in Scotland, which the English were trying to subdue, and by the claim of England's ◊Edward III (through his mother Isabel, daughter of Charles IV) to the crown of France.

Hungarian or **Magyar** member of the majority population of Hungary or a person of Hungarian descent; also, their culture and language. Hungarian minorities are found in Czechoslovakia, Yugoslavia, and Romania, where the Székely of Transylvania regard themselves as ethnically distinct but speak Hungarian, as do the Csángó of Moldavia.

Hungarian language member of the Finno-Ugric language group, spoken principally in Hungary but also in parts of Czechoslovakia, Romania, and Yugoslavia. Hungarian is known as **Magyar** among its speakers. It is written formed, distributing land to the peasants. An elected assembly inaugurated a republic 1946, but it soon fell under Soviet domination, although only 70 communists had been returned out of a total of 409 deputies. Under Communist Party leader Matyas Rákosi (1892–1971), a Stalinist regime was imposed 1946–53, with a Soviet-style constitution being adopted 1949, industry nationalized, land collectivized, and a wave of secret-police terror launched.

Hungarian national uprising Liberalization in the economic sphere was experienced 1953–55 when Imre Nagy, supported by Soviet premier Malenkov, replaced Rákosi as prime minister. Nagy was removed from office 1955, after the fall of Malenkov, but in 1956, in the wake of ⟡Khrushchev's denunciation of Stalin in his "secret speech," pressure for democratization mounted. Rákosi stepped down as Communist Party leader and, following student and worker demonstrations in Budapest, Nagy was recalled as prime minister, and János Kádár appointed general secretary of the renamed Hungarian Socialist Workers' Party (HSWP). Nagy lifted restrictions on the formation of political parties, released the anticommunist primate Cardinal ⟡Mindszenty, and announced plans for Hungary to withdraw from the ⟡Warsaw Pact and become a neutral power. These changes were, however, opposed by Kádár, who set up a countergovernment in E Hungary before returning to Budapest with Soviet tanks to overthrow the Nagy government Nov 4. Some 200,000 fled to the West during the 1956 Hungarian national uprising. After a period of strict repression, Kádár proceeded to introduce pragmatic liberalizing reforms after 1960. Hungary remained, however, a loyal member of the Warsaw Pact and ⟡Comecon.

reform Hungary's relations with Moscow significantly improved during the post-Brezhnev era, with Hungary's "market socialism" experiment influencing Mikhail Gorbachev's ⟡perestroika program. Further reforms introduced 1987–88 included additional price deregulation, the establishment of "enterprise councils," the introduction of value-added tax (VAT), and the creation of a stock market. As elsewhere in Eastern Europe, change came quickly to Hungary from 1988. Kádár, who had become an obstacle to reform, was replaced as general secretary of the ruling HSWP party by Károly ⟡Grosz 1988, and was named to a new post, that of party president. Two radical reformers, Rezso Nyers and Imre Pozsgay, were brought into the Politburo. The Hungarian Democratic Forum was formed Sept 1988 as an umbrella movement for opposition groups, and several dozen other political parties were formed 1989–90.

There then began a period of far-reaching political reform in which the rights to demonstrate freely and to form rival political parties and labor unions were ceded. The official verdict on the 1956 events was revised radically, with Nagy being posthumously rehabilitated and cleared of alleged past crimes by the Supreme Court July 1989. In May 1989 the border with Austria was opened, with adverse effects for East Germany as thousands of East Germans escaped to the West through Hungary. Two months later Grosz was forced to cede power to the more radical reformist troika of Nyers (party president), Pozsgay, and Miklos Nemeth (prime minister since Nov 1988), who joined Grosz in a new four-person ruling presidium.

constitutional changes In Oct 1989 a series of constitutional changes, the result of round-table talks held through the summer, were approved by the national assembly. These included the adoption of a new set of electoral rules, the banning of workplace party cells, and the change of the country's name from "People's Republic" to simply "Republic." Also in Oct the HSWP changed its name to the Hungarian Socialist Party (HSP), and adopted Poszgay as its presidential candidate. Conservatives, including Grosz, refused to play an active role in the new party, which had become essentially a social-democratic party committed to multiparty democracy. Despite these changes, the HSP's standing was seriously damaged in the "Danubegate" scandal of Jan 1990, when it was revealed that the secret police had bugged opposition parties and passed the information obtained to the HSP.

foreign relations In Feb 1990 talks were held with the USSR to discuss the withdrawal of Soviet troops stationed in Hungary. In June 1990 the Hungarian government announced the country's decision no longer to participate in Warsaw Pact military exercises and its intention to withdraw altogether from the Pact. As the Warsaw Pact and Comecon had disbanded by July 1991, the country was able to move toward the West more directly. Hungary joined the Council of Europe in Nov 1990. The last Soviet troops left Hungary, on schedule, June 1991.

privatization As the first step in the privatization program, a stock exchange was opened in Budapest. In Jan 1991 the forint was devalued by 15% in an effort to boost exports. A Compensation Bill for owners of land and property expropriated under the communist regime was approved by the national assembly June 1991. It was hoped that, by clearing up the uncertainty over ownership, the bill would stimulate the privatization program and inward foreign investment. Gross national product fell by 7% in 1991, industrial production fell by one-fifth during the first half of 1991, and by the close of 1991 unemployment rose to more than 7%. However, of all the former communist European states, Hungary experienced the smoothest transition toward a market economy. This was credited to the establishment of self-management and privatization before the downfall of the communist regime in 1989. In Dec 1991 Hungary signed a ten-year association agreement with the European Community (EC) and was awarded trade concessions and a guarantee of economic assistance from the EC. The agreement was effective from March 1992. *See illustration box.*

Hun Sen 1950– . Cambodian political leader, prime minister from 1985. Originally a member of the Khmer Rouge army, he defected in 1977 to join Vietnam-based anti-Khmer Cambodian forces. His leadership has been characterized by the promotion of economic liberalization and a thawing in relations with exiled non-Khmer opposition forces as a prelude to a compromise political settlement. In Oct 1991, following a peace accord ending 13 years of civil war in Cambodia, Hun Sen agreed to rule the country in conjunction with the United Nations Transitional Authority in Cambodia (UNTAC) and representatives of the warring factions until UN-administered elections 1993.

Hunt (James Henry) Leigh 1784–1859. English poet and essayist. The appearance in his Liberal newspaper *The Examiner* of an unfavorable article that he had written about the Prince Regent caused him to be convicted for libel and imprisoned 1813. The friend and later enemy of Byron, he also knew Keats and Shelley.

His verse is little appreciated today, but he influenced the Romantics, and his book on London *The Town* 1848 and his *Autobiography* 1850 survive. The character of Harold Skimpole in Dickens's *Bleak House* was allegedly based on him.

Hunt William Holman 1827–1910. English painter, one of the founders of the ⟡Pre-Raphaelite Brotherhood 1848. Obsessed with realistic detail, he traveled from 1854 onwards to Syria and Palestine to paint biblical subjects. His works include *The Awakening Conscience* 1853 (Tate Gallery, London) and *The Light of the World* 1854 (Keble College, Oxford).

Huntington city in W West Virginia, across the Ohio River from Ohio, NW of Charleston; seat of Cabell County; population (1990) 54,800. It is an important transportation center for coal mined to the south. Other industries include chemicals; metal, wood, and glass products; tobacco; and fruit processing.

Huntington's chorea rare hereditary disease that begins in middle age. It is characterized by involuntary movements and rapid mental degeneration progressing to ⟡dementia. There is no known cure.

Huntsville city in NE Alabama; population (1990) 159,800. Manufactured products include textiles, electrical and electronic goods, metal products, chemicals, machinery, and cosmetics. Just outside the city is the Redstone Arsenal, which includes an army missile center and the George C Marshall Space Flight Center. A branch of the University of Alabama and a space and rocket museum are here. Huntsville was settled 1805. During the Civil War, it was occupied and burned by Union troops.

Hunyadi János Corvinus 1387–1456. Hungarian politician and general. Born in Transylvania, reputedly the son of the emperor ⟡Sigismund, he won battles against the Turks from the 1440s. In 1456 he defeated them at Belgrade, but died shortly afterwards of the plague.

Hunza small state in the Gilgit region, on the NW frontier of Kashmir, under the rule of Pakistan.

Hupei alternative transcription of ⟡Hebei, a province of China.

hurdy-gurdy musical stringed instrument resembling a violin in tone but using a form of keyboard to play a melody and drone strings to provide a continuous harmony. An inbuilt wheel, turned by a handle, acts as a bow.

Hurok Solomon "Sol" 1888–1974. Russian-born US theatrical producer. Hurok immigrated to the US 1906. As a lifelong devotee of music, Hurok began to organize concerts for New York unions and social groups. In 1914 he began to produce musical and theatrical events professionally and over the years arranged US appearances for the most prominent figures in European music and dance.

His Russian contacts proved especially valuable, and in later years he worked with the NBC television network producing television specials. His autobiographical *Impresario* and *S Hurok Presents* appeared 1946 and 1953, respectively.

Huron (French *hure* "rough hair of the head") nickname for a member of a confederation of five Iroquoian North American Indian peoples living near lakes Huron, Erie, and Ontario in the 16th and 17th centuries. They were almost wiped out by the Iroquois. In the 17th century, surviving Hurons formed a group called Wyandot, some of whose descendants now live in Québec and Oklahoma.

Huron second largest of the Great Lakes of North America, on the US–Canadian border; area 23,160 sq mi/60,000 sq km. It includes Georgian Bay, Saginaw Bay, and Manitoulin Island.

It receives Lake Superior's waters through the Sault Ste Marie River, and Lake Michigan's through the Straits of Mackinac. It drains S into Lake Erie through the St Clair River–Lake St Clair–Detroit River system. There are a number of small Michigan and Ontario ports on its shores. Jesuit missionaries established the first European settlement, on Georgian Bay, in 1638.

hurricane revolving storm in tropical regions, called *typhoon* in the N Pacific. It originates between 5° and 20° N or S of the equator, when the surface temperature of the ocean is above 80°F/27°C. A central calm area, called the eye, is surrounded by inwardly spiraling winds (counterclockwise in the northern hemisphere) of up to 200 mph/320 kph. A hurricane is accompanied by lightning and torrential rain, and can cause extensive damage. In meteorology, a hurricane is a wind of force 12 or more on the ⌐Beaufort scale. The most intense hurricane recorded in the Caribbean/Atlantic sector was Hurricane Gilbert in 1988, with sustained winds of 175 mph/280 kph and gusts of over 200 mph/320 kph.

Hurston Zora Neale 1901–1960. US novelist and short-story writer, associated with the ⌐Harlem Renaissance. She collected traditional African-American folk tales in *Mules and Men* 1935; her novels include *Their Eyes Were Watching God* 1937.

Hurt William 1950– . US actor whose films include *Altered States* 1980, *The Big Chill* 1983, *Kiss of the Spider Woman* 1985, and *Broadcast News* 1987.

Husák Gustáv 1913–1991. Leader of the Communist Party of Czechoslovakia (CCP) 1969–87 and president 1975–89. After the 1968 Prague Spring of liberalization, his task was to restore control, purge the CCP, and oversee the implementation of a new, federalist constitution. He was deposed in the popular uprising of Nov–Dec 1989 and expelled from the Communist Party Feb 1990.

Husák, a lawyer, was active in the Resistance movement during World War II, and afterwards in the Slovak Communist Party (SCP), and was imprisoned on political grounds 1951–60. Rehabilitated, he was appointed first secretary of the SCP 1968 and CCP leader 1969–87. As titular state president he pursued a policy of cautious reform. He stepped down as party leader 1987, and was replaced as state president by Vaclav ⌐Havel Dec 1989 following the "gentle revolution."

husky any of several breeds of sled dog used in Arctic regions, growing to 2 ft/70 cm high, and weighing about 50 kg/110 lbs, with pricked ears, thick fur, and a bushy tail. The Siberian husky is the best known.

Huss John (Czech *Jan*) *c.* 1373–1415. Bohemian Christian church reformer, rector of Prague University from 1402, who was excommunicated for attacks on ecclesiastical abuses. He was summoned before the Council of Constance 1414, defended the English reformer John Wycliffe, rejected the pope's authority, and was burned at the stake. His followers were called Hussites.

Hussein ibn Ali *c.* 1854–1931. Leader of the Arab revolt 1916–18 against the Turks. He proclaimed himself king of the Hejaz 1916, accepted the caliphate 1924, but was unable to retain it due to internal fighting. He was deposed 1924 by ibn Saud.

Hussein ibn Talal 1935– . King of Jordan from 1952. Great-grandson of Hussein ibn Ali, he became king following the mental incapacitation of his father, Talal. By 1967 he had lost all his kingdom west of the river Jordan in the ⌐Arab-Israeli Wars, and in 1970 suppressed the ⌐Palestine Liberation Organization acting as a guerrilla force against his rule on the remaining East Bank territories. In recent years, he has become a moderating force in Middle Eastern politics. After Iraq's annexation of Kuwait 1990 he attempted to mediate between the opposing sides, at the risk of damaging his relations with both sides.

Hussein Saddam 1937– . Iraqi politician, in power from 1968, president from 1979, progressively eliminating real or imagined opposition factions as he gained increasing dictatorial control. Ruthless in the pursuit of his objectives, he fought a bitter war against Iran 1980–88, with US economic aid, and dealt harshly with Kurdish rebels seeking independence, using chemical weapons against civilian populations. In 1990 he annexed Kuwait, to universal condemnation, before being driven out by a US-dominated coalition army Feb 1991. Iraq's defeat in the ⌐Gulf War undermined Saddam's position as the country's leader; when the Kurds rebelled again after the end of the war, he sent the remainder of his army to crush them, bringing international charges of genocide against him and causing hundreds of thousands of Kurds to flee their homes in northern Iraq. His continued bombardment of Shiites in southern Iraq caused the UN to impose a "no-fly zone" in the area.

Hussein joined the Arab Ba'ath Socialist Party as a young man and soon became involved in revolutionary activities. In 1959 he was sentenced to death and took refuge in Egypt, but a coup in 1963 made his return possible, although in the following year he was imprisoned for plotting to overthrow the regime he had helped to install. After his release he took a leading part in the 1968 revolution, removing the civilian government and establishing a Revolutionary Command Council (RCC). At first discreetly, and then more openly, Hussein strengthened his position and in 1979 became RCC chair and state president. In 1977 Saddam Hussein al-Tikriti abolished the use of surnames in Iraq to conceal the fact that a large number of people in the government and ruling party all came from his home village of Tikrit and therefore bore the same surname. The 1990 Kuwait annexation followed a long-running border dispute and was prompted by the need for more oil resources after the expensive war against Iran. Saddam, who had enjoyed US support for being the enemy of Iran and had used poison gas against his own people in Kurdistan without any falling-off in trade with the West, suddenly found himself almost universally condemned. Iraqi assets were frozen and in the UN, Arab, communist, and capitalist nations east and west agreed on a trade embargo and aid to refugees, with the US and the UK urging aggressive military action. Fears that Saddam might use chemical or even nuclear weapons were raised as predominantly US troops massed on the Saudi Arabian border. With the passing of the UN deadline of Jan 15, 1991 without any withdrawal from Kuwait, allied forces struck Baghdad in a series of air bombardments to which Saddam replied by firing Scud missiles on the Israeli cities of Tel Aviv and Haifa in an unsuccessful effort to bring Israel into the war and thus break up the Arab alliance with the West; he also failed to rally Arab support for a holy war or "jihad" to eject the Western "infidels."

Husserl Edmund (Gustav Albrecht) 1859–1938. German philosopher, regarded as the founder of ⌐phenomenology, a philosophy concentrating on what is consciously experienced. His main works are *Logical Investigations* 1900, *Phenomenological Philosophy* 1913, and *The Crisis of the European Sciences* 1936.

Hussite follower of John ⌐Huss. Opposed to both German and papal influence in Bohemia, the Hussites waged successful war against the Holy Roman Empire from 1419, but Roman Catholicism was finally reestablished 1620.

Huston John 1906–1987. US film director, screenwriter, and actor. An impulsive and individualistic film maker, he often dealt with the themes of greed, treachery in human relationships, and the loner. His works as a director include *The Maltese Falcon* 1941 (his debut), *The Treasure of the Sierra Madre* 1948 (in which his father Walter Huston starred and for which both won Academy Awards), *The African Queen* 1951, and his last, *The Dead* 1987.

He was the son of the actor Walter Huston and the father of the actress Anjelica Huston. His other films include *Key Largo* 1948, *Moby Dick* 1956, *The Misfits* 1961, *Fat City* 1972, and *Prizzi's Honor* 1984.

Huston Walter 1884–1950. Canadian-born US actor. The father of director John Huston, he was born in Toronto and trained as an engineer. After a succession of engineering jobs, he chose a theatrical career, appearing in a vaudeville musical act. Turning to legitimate acting, he won critical acclaim for his Broadway performance in *Desire Under the Elms* 1924. For the rest of his career, Huston alternated between stage acting and appearances in feature films. In 1948 he won the Academy Award as best supporting actor for his role in *The Treasure of Sierra Madre*, a film written and directed by his son.

Hutchinson Anne Marbury 1591–1643. Colonial American religious leader. Hutchinson was a follower of Puritan leader John Cotton and followed him to Massachusetts Bay Colony 1634 with her husband and children. Noted for her intellect and forceful personality, she developed a following in Boston, preaching a unique theology that emphasized the role of faith. The colony's leaders felt threatened by Hutchinson, and the "Antinomian Controversy" ensued. In 1637 Hutchinson was banished and excommunicated; having found asylum in nearby Rhode Island, she later moved to Long Island, where she and her family were killed by Indians.

Hutchinson was born in England.

Hutterian Brethren Christian sect; see ⌐Mennonite.

Hutton James 1726–1797. Scottish geologist, known as the "founder of geology," who formulated the concept of ⌐uniformitarianism.

In 1785 he developed a theory of the igneous origin of many rocks.

His *Theory of the Earth* 1788 proposed that the Earth was indefinitely old. Uniformitarianism suggests that past events could be explained in terms of processes that work today. For example, the kind of river current that produces a certain settling pattern in a bed of sand today must have been operating many millions of years ago, if that same pattern is visible in ancient sandstones.

Hutu member of the majority ethnic group of both Burundi and Rwanda, numbering around 9,500,000. The Hutu tend to live as peasant farmers, while the ruling minority, the Tutsi, are town dwellers. There is a long history of violent conflict between the two groups. The Hutu language belongs to the Bantu branch of the Niger-Congo family.

Huxley Aldous (Leonard) 1894–1963. English writer of novels, essays, and verse. From the disillusionment and satirical eloquence of *Crome Yellow* 1921, *Antic Hay* 1923, and *Point Counter Point* 1928, Huxley developed toward the Utopianism exemplified by *Island* 1962. The science fiction novel *Brave New World* 1932 shows human beings mass-produced in laboratories and rendered incapable of freedom by indoctrination and drugs. He was the grandson of Thomas Henry Huxley and brother of Julian Huxley.

Huxley's later devotion to mysticism led to his experiments with the hallucinogenic drug mescalin, recorded in *The Doors of Perception* 1954. He also wrote the novel *Eyeless in Gaza* 1936, and two historical studies, *Grey Eminence* 1941 and *The Devils of Loudun* 1952.

Huxley Julian 1887–1975. English biologist, first director general of UNESCO, and a founder of the World Wildlife Fund (now the World Wide Fund for Nature).

Huxley Thomas Henry 1825–1895. English scientist and humanist. Following the publication of Charles Darwin's *On the Origin of Species* 1859, he became known as "Darwin's bulldog," and for many years was a prominent champion of evolution. He is considered the founder of scientific ⟡humanism.

Hu Yaobang 1915–1989. Chinese politician, Communist Party (CCP) chair 1981–87. A protégé of the communist leader Deng Xiaoping, Hu presided over a radical overhaul of the party structure and personnel 1982–86. His death ignited the prodemocracy movement, which was eventually crushed in Tiananmen Square June 1989.

Hu, born into a peasant family in Hunan province, joined the Red Army at the age of 14 and was a political commissar during the 1934–36 Long March. In 1941 he served under Deng and later worked under him in provincial and central government. Hu was purged as a "capitalist roader" during the 1966–69 Cultural Revolution and sent into the countryside for "reeducation." He was rehabilitated 1975 but disgraced again when Deng fell from prominence 1976. In Dec 1978, with Deng established in power, Hu was inducted into the CCP Politburo and became head of the revived secretariat 1980 and CCP chair 1981. He attempted to quicken reaction against Mao. He was dismissed Jan 1987 for his relaxed handling of a wave of student unrest Dec 1986.

Huygens Christiaan 1629–1695. Dutch mathematical physicist and astronomer who proposed the wave theory of light. He developed the pendulum clock, discovered polarization, and observed Saturn's rings.

Huysmans J(oris) K(arl) 1848–1907. French novelist of Dutch ancestry. His novel *Marthe* 1876, the story of a courtesan, was followed by other realistic novels, including *A rebours/ Against Nature* 1884, a novel of self-absorbed aestheticism that symbolized the "decadent" movement.

Hwang Ho alternative transcription of ⟡Huang He, a river in China.

HWM abbreviation for **high water mark**.

hyacinth any bulb-producing plant of the genus *Hyacinthus* of the lily family Liliaceae, native to the E Mediterranean and Africa. The cultivated hyacinth *H. orientalis* has large, scented, cylindrical heads of pink, white, or blue flowers. The ⟡water hyacinth, genus *Eichhornia*, is unrelated, a floating plant from South America.

Hyades V-shaped cluster of stars that forms the face of the bull in the constellation Taurus. It is 150 light-years away and contains over 200 stars, although only about 12 are visible to the naked eye.

hyaline membrane disease former name for ⟡respiratory distress syndrome.

hybrid offspring from a cross between individuals of two different species, or two inbred lines within a species. In most cases, hybrids between species are infertile and unable to reproduce sexually. In plants, however, doubling of the chromosomes (see ⟡polyploid) can restore the fertility of such hybrids.

Hybrids between different genera are extremely rare; an example is the *leylandii* cypress which, like some hybrids, shows exceptional vigor, or ⟡heterosis. In the wild, a "hybrid zone" may occur where the ranges of two related species meet.

hydathode specialized pore, or less commonly, a hair, through which water is secreted by hydrostatic pressure from the interior of a plant leaf onto the surface. Hydathodes are found on many different plants and are usually situated around the leaf margin at vein endings. Each pore is surrounded by two crescent-shaped cells and resembles an open ⟡stoma, but the size of the opening cannot be varied as in a stoma. The process of water secretion through hydathodes is known as ⟡guttation.

Hyde Douglas 1860–1949. Irish scholar and politician. Founder president of the Gaelic League 1893–1915, he was president of Eire 1938–45. He was the first person to write a book in modern Irish and to collect Irish folklore, as well as being the author of the first literary history of Ireland. His works include *Love Songs of Connacht* 1894.

From a Protestant family, he founded the Gaelic League to promote a cultural, rather than political, nationalism.

Hyderabad capital city of the S central Indian state of Andhra Pradesh, on the river Musi; population (1981) 2,528,000. Products include carpets, silks, and metal inlay work. It was formerly the capital of the state of Hyderabad. Buildings include the Jama Masjid mosque and Golconda fort.

Hyderabad city in Sind province, SE Pakistan; population (1981) 795,000. It produces gold, pottery, glass, and furniture. The third largest city of Pakistan, it was founded 1768.

hydra in zoology, any member of the family Hydridae, or freshwater polyps, of the phylum Cnidaria (coelenterates). The body is a double-

hydraulics *The hydraulic jack transmits the pressure on a small piston to a larger one.*

layered tube (with six to ten hollow tentacles around the mouth), 0.5 in/1.25 cm long when extended, but capable of contracting to a small knob. Usually fixed to waterweed, hydras feed on minute animals that are caught and paralyzed by stinging cells on the tentacles.

Hydras reproduce asexually in the summer and sexually in the winter. They have no specialized organs except those of reproduction.

Hydra in astronomy, the largest constellation, winding across more than a fourth of the sky between Cancer and Libra in the southern hemisphere. Hydra is named after the multiheaded monster slain by Heracles. Despite its size, it is not prominent; its brightest star is second-magnitude Alphard.

Hydra in Greek mythology, a huge monster with nine heads. If one were cut off, two would grow in its place. One of the 12 labors of Heracles was to kill it.

hydrangea any flowering shrub of the genus *Hydrangea* of the saxifrage family Hydrangeaceae, native to Japan. Cultivated varieties of *H. macrophylla* normally produce round heads of pink flowers, but these may be blue if certain chemicals, such as alum or iron, are in the soil. The name is from the Greek for "water vessel," after the cuplike seed capsules.

hydraulics field of study concerned with utilizing the properties of water and other liquids, in particular the way they flow and transmit pressure, and with the application of these properties in engineering. It applies the principles of ⟡hydrostatics and hydrodynamics. The oldest type of hydraulic machine is the **hydraulic press**, invented by Joseph Bramah (1748-1814) in England 1795. The hydraulic principle of pressurized liquid increasing mechanical efficiency is commonly used on vehicle braking systems, the forging press, and the hydraulic systems of aircraft and excavators.

A hydraulic press consists of two liquid-connected pistons in cylinders, one of narrow bore, one of large bore. A force applied to the narrow piston applies a certain pressure (force per unit area) to the liquid, which is transmitted to the larger piston. Because the area of this piston is larger, the force exerted on it is larger. Thus the original force has been magnified, although the smaller piston must move a great distance to move the larger piston only a little, hence mechanical efficiency is gained in force but lost in movement.

hydrocarbon any of a class of chemical compounds containing only hydrogen and carbon (for example, the alkanes and alkenes). Hydrocarbons are obtained industrially principally from petroleum and coal tar.

hydrocephalus potentially serious increase in the volume of cerebrospinal fluid (CSF) within the ventricles of the brain. In infants, since their skull plates have not fused, it causes enlargement of the head, and there is a risk of brain damage from CSF pressure on the developing brain.

Hydrocephalus may be due to mechanical obstruction of the outflow of CSF from the ventricles or to faulty reabsorption. Treatment usually involves surgical placement of a shunt system to drain the fluid into the abdominal cavity. In infants, the condition is often seen in association with ◊spina bifida.

hydrochloric acid highly corrosive aqueous solution of hydrogen chloride (HCl, a colorless, corrosive gas). It has many industrial uses, including recovery of zinc from galvanized scrap iron and the production of chlorides and chlorine. It is also produced in the stomachs of animals for the purposes of digestion.

hydrocyanic acid or **prussic acid** solution of hydrogen cyanide gas (HCN) in water. It is a colorless, highly poisonous, volatile liquid, smelling of bitter almonds.

hydrodynamics science of nonviscous liquids (for example water, alcohol, ether) in motion.

hydroelectric power (HEP) electricity generated by moving water. In a typical HEP scheme water stored in a reservoir, often created by damming a river, is piped into water ◊turbines, coupled to electricity generators. In ◊pumped storage plants, water flowing through the turbines is recycled. A ◊tidal power station exploits the rise and fall of the tides. About one-fifth of the world's electricity comes from HEP.

HEP plants have prodigious generating capacities. The Grand Coulee plant in Washington State has a power output of some 10,000 megawatts. The Itaipu power station on the Paraná River (Brazil/Paraguay) has a potential capacity of 12,000 megawatts.

hydrofoil wing that develops lift in the water in much the same way that an airplane wing develops lift in the air. A hydrofoil boat is one whose hull rises out of the water due to the lift, and the boat skims along on the hydrofoils. The first hydrofoil was fitted to a boat 1906. The first commercial hydrofoil went into operation 1956. One of the most advanced hydrofoil boats is the Boeing ◊jetfoil.

hydrogen (Greek *hydro* + *gen* "water generator") colorless, odorless, gaseous, nonmetallic element, symbol H, atomic number 1, atomic weight 1.00797. It is the lightest of all the elements and occurs on Earth chiefly in combination with oxygen as water. Hydrogen is the most abundant element in the universe, where it accounts for 93% of the total number of atoms and 76% of the total mass. It is a component of most stars, including the Sun, whose heat and light are produced through the nuclear-fusion process that converts hydrogen into helium. When subjected to a pressure 500,000 times greater than that of the Earth's atmosphere, hydrogen becomes a solid with metallic properties, as in one of the inner zones of Jupiter. Its common and industrial uses include the hardening of oils and fats by hydrogenation and the creation of high-temperature flames for welding.

Its isotopes ◊deuterium and ◊tritium (half-life 12.5 years) are used in nuclear weapons, and deuterons (deuterium nuclei) are used in synthesizing elements. The element's name refers to the generation of water by the combustion of hydrogen, and was coined in 1787 by French chemist Louis Guyton de Morveau (1737–1816).

hydrogenation addition of hydrogen to an unsaturated organic molecule (one that contains ◊double bonds or triple bonds).

It is widely used in the manufacture of margarine and low-fat spreads by the addition of hydrogen to vegetable oils.

hydrogen bomb bomb that works on the principle of nuclear ◊fusion. Large-scale explosion results from the thermonuclear release of energy when hydrogen nuclei are fused to form helium nuclei. The first hydrogen bomb was exploded at Eniwetok Atoll in the Pacific Ocean by the US 1952.

The constant release of energy through nuclear fusion is the continuing reaction in the Sun and other stars; it can be duplicated by the triggering of tritium (hydrogen isotope of atomic weight 3.0170) by an ordinary atomic bomb.

hydrogen cyanide HCN poisonous gas formed by the reaction of sodium cyanide with dilute sulfuric acid; it is used for fumigation.

The salts formed from it are cyanides—for example sodium cyanide, used in hardening steel and extracting gold and silver from their ores. If dissolved in water, hydrogen cyanide gives hydrocyanic acid.

hydrography study and charting of Earth's surface waters in seas, lakes, and rivers.

hydrology study of the location and movement of inland water, both frozen and liquid, above and below ground. It is applied to major civil engineering projects such as irrigation schemes, dams and hydroelectric power, and in planning water supply.

hydrolysis chemical reaction in which the action of water or its ions breaks down a substance into smaller molecules. Hydrolysis occurs in certain inorganic salts in solution, in nearly all nonmetallic chlorides, in esters, and in other organic substances. It is one of the mechanisms for the breakdown of food by the body, as in the conversion of starch to glucose.

hydrometer in physics, an instrument used to measure the density of liquids compared with that of water, usually expressed in grams per cubic centimeter. It consists of a thin glass tube ending in a sphere that leads into a smaller sphere, the latter being weighted so that the hydrometer floats upright, sinking deeper into less dense liquids than into denser liquids. It is used in brewing.

The hydrometer is based on ◊Archimedes' principle.

hydrophily ◊pollination in which the pollen is carried by water. Hydrophily is very rare but occurs in a few aquatic species. In Canadian pondweed *Elodea* and tape grass *Vallisneria*, the male flowers break off whole and rise to the water surface where they encounter the female flowers, which are borne on long stalks. In eel grasses *Zostera*, which are coastal plants growing totally submerged, the filamentous pollen grains are released into the water and carried by currents to the female flowers where they become wrapped around the stigmas.

hydrophobia another name for the disease ◊rabies.

hydrophone underwater ◊microphone and ancillary equipment capable of picking up waterborne sounds. It was originally developed to detect enemy submarines but is now also used, for example, for listening to the sounds made by whales.

hydrophyte plant adapted to live in water, or in waterlogged soil.

Hydrophytes may have leaves with a very reduced or absent ◊cuticle and no ◊stomata (since there is no need to conserve water), a reduced root and water-conducting system, and less supporting tissue since water buoys plants up. There are often numerous spaces between the cells in their stems and roots to make ◊gas exchange with all parts of the plant body possible. Many have highly divided leaves, which lessens resistance to flowing water; an example is spiked water milfoil *Myriophyllum spicatum*.

hydroplane on a submarine, a moveable horizontal fin angled downward or upward when the vessel is descending or ascending. It is also a highly maneuverable motorboat with its bottom rising in steps to the stern, or a ◊hydrofoil boat that skims over the surface of the water when driven at high speed.

hydroponics cultivation of plants without soil, using specially prepared solutions of mineral salts. Beginning in the 1930s, large crops were grown by hydroponic methods, at first in California but since then in many other parts of the world.

J von Sachs (1832–1897) 1860 and W Knop 1865 developed a system of plant culture in water whereby the relation of mineral salts to plant growth could be determined, but it was not until about 1930 that large crops could be grown. The term was first coined by W F Gericke, a US scientist.

hydrosphere the water component of the Earth, usually encompassing the oceans, seas, rivers, streams, swamps, lakes, groundwater, and atmospheric water vapor.

hydrostatics in physics, the branch of ◊statics dealing with the mechanical problems of liquids in equilibrium, that is, in a static condition. Practical applications include shipbuilding and dam design.

hydrothermal in geology, pertaining to a fluid whose principal component is hot water, or to a mineral deposit believed to be precipitated from such a fluid.

hydrothermal vein a crack in rock filled with minerals precipitated through the action of circulating high-temperature fluids. Igneous activity often gives rise to the circulation of heated fluids that migrate outwards and move through the surrounding rock. When such solutions carry metallic ions, ore-mineral deposition occurs in the new surroundings on cooling.

hydroxide any inorganic chemical compound containing one or more hydroxyl (OH) groups and generally combined with a metal. Hydroxides include sodium hydroxide (caustic soda, NaOH), potassium hydroxide (caustic potash, KOH), and calcium hydroxide (slaked lime, $Ca(OH)_2$).

hydroxypropanoic acid technical name for ◊lactic acid.

hyena any of three species of carnivorous mammals in the family Hyaenidae, living in Africa and Asia. Hyenas have extremely powerful jaws. They are scavengers, although they will also attack and kill live prey.

The species are: the striped hyena *Hyaena hyaena* found from Asia Minor to India; the brown hyena *H. brunnea*, found in S Africa;

hygrometer *The most common hygrometer, or instrument for measuring the humidity of a gas, is the wet and dry bulb hygrometer.*

and the spotted hyena *Crocuta crocuta*, common south of the Sahara. The ◊aardwolf also belongs to the hyena family.

Hygieia in Greek mythology, the goddess of health (Roman **Salus**), daughter of Aesculapius.

hygiene the science of the preservation of health and prevention of disease. It is chiefly concerned with such external conditions as the purity of air and water; bodily cleanliness; cleanliness in the home and workplace; and good nutrition, exercise, and sex habits.

hygrometer in physics, any instrument for measuring the humidity, or water vapor content, of a gas (usually air). A wet and dry bulb hygrometer consists of two vertical thermometers, with one of the bulbs covered in absorbent cloth dipped into water. As the water evaporates, the bulb cools producing a temperature difference between the two thermometers. The amount of evaporation, and hence cooling of the wet bulb, depends on the relative humidity of the air.

Other hygrometers work on the basis of a length of natural fiber, such as hair or a fine strand of gut, changing with variations in humidity. In a dew-point hygrometer, a polished metal mirror gradually cools until a fine mist of water (dew) forms on it. This gives a measure of the ◊dew point, from which the air's relative humidity can be calculated.

hygroscopic able to absorb moisture from the air without becoming wet.

Hyksos ("shepherd kings" or "princes of the desert") nomadic, probably Semitic people who invaded Egypt in the 18th century BC and established their own dynasty in the Nile delta, which lasted until 1580 BC. They introduced bronze metallurgy, the wheel, and the use of the horse-drawn chariot.

Hylton v US US Supreme Court decision 1796 in which the Court, for the first time, reviewed the constitutionality of an act of Congress. The suit was a protest of a carriage tax imposed by Congress in 1794. The plaintiff argued that this tax was unconstitutional because, although it was a direct tax, it was not applied to states proportionally, according to population. The Court upheld the tax, voting 3 to 0 that a carriage tax

was not a direct tax, like a head or land tax, but an impost on a consumer good.

Hymen in Greek mythology, either the son of Apollo and one of the Muses, or of Dionysus and Aphrodite. He was the god of marriage, and in painting he is represented as a youth carrying a bridal torch.

hymn song in praise of a deity. Examples include Ikhnaton's hymn to the Aton in ancient Egypt, the ancient Greek Orphic hymns, Old Testament psalms, extracts from the New Testament (such as the "Ave Maria"), and hymns by the British writers John Bunyan ("Who would true valor see") and Charles Wesley ("Hark the herald angels sing"). ◊Gospel music and carols are forms of Christian hymn singing.

hyoscine or *scopolamine* drug that acts on the autonomic nervous system and is frequently included in ◊premedication to dry up lung secretions and as a postoperative sedative. It is an alkaloid, $C_{17}H_{21}NO_2$, obtained from various plants of the nightshade family (such as ◊belladonna).

hyperactivity condition of excessive activity in young children, combined with inability to concentrate and difficulty in learning. The cause is not known, although some food ◊additives have come under suspicion. Modification of the diet may help, and in the majority of cases there is improvement at puberty.

hyperbola in geometry, a curve formed by cutting a right circular cone with a plane so that the angle between the plane and the base is greater than the angle between the base and the side of the cone. All hyperbolae are bounded by two asymptotes (straight lines which the hyperbola moves closer and closer to but never reaches). A hyperbola is a member of the family of curves known as ◊conic sections.

A hyperbola can also be defined as a path traced by a point that moves such that the ratio of its distance from a fixed point (focus) and a fixed straight line (directrix) is a constant and greater than 1; that is, it has an ◊eccentricity greater than 1.

hyperbole expression used in speech; the Greek name suggests "going over the top." When people use hyperbole, they exaggerate, usually to emphasize a point ("If I've told you once I've told you a thousand times not to do that").

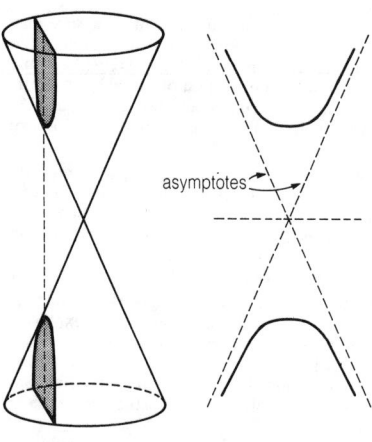

hyperbola *The hyperbola is produced when a cone is cut by a plane.*

hypercharge in physics, a property of certain ◊elementary particles, analogous to electric charge, that accounts for the absence of some expected behavior (such as decay) in terms of the short-range strong nuclear force, which holds atomic nuclei together.

It is a number equal to twice the average charge of the particles concerned, divided by the elementary charge. ◊Protons and ◊neutrons, for example, have a hypercharge of +1, whereas a pion has a hypercharge of 0.

hyperinflation rapid and uncontrolled ◊inflation, or increases in prices, usually associated with political and/or social instability (as in Germany in the 1920s).

hypermarket a very large ◊supermarket.

hyperon in physics, a ◊hadron; any of a group of highly unstable ◊elementary particles that includes all the ◊baryons with a mass greater than the ◊neutron. They are all composed of three quarks. The lambda, xi, sigma, and omega particles are hyperons.

hypertension abnormally high ◊blood pressure due to a variety of causes, leading to excessive contraction of the smooth muscle cells of the walls of the arteries. It increases the risk of kidney disease, stroke, and heart attack.

hypertext system for viewing information (both text and pictures) on a computer screen in such a way that related items of information can easily be reached. For example, the program might display a map of a country; if the user clicks (with a ◊mouse) on a particular city, the program will display some information about that city.

hyperthyroidism or *thyrotoxicosis* overactivity of the thyroid gland due to enlargement or tumor. Symptoms include accelerated heart rate, sweating, anxiety, tremor, and weight loss. Treatment is by drugs or surgery.

hypertrophy abnormal increase in size of a body organ or tissue.

hypha (plural *hyphae*) delicate, usually branching filament, many of which collectively form the mycelium and fruiting bodies of a ◊fungus. Food molecules and other substances are transported along hyphae by the movement of the cytoplasm, known as "cytoplasmic streaming."

Typically hyphae grow by increasing in length from the tips and by the formation of side branches. Hyphae of the higher fungi (the ascomycetes and basidiomycetes) are divided by cross walls or septa at intervals, whereas those of lower fungi (for example, bread mold) are undivided. However, even the higher fungi are not truly cellular, as each septum is pierced by a central pore, through which cytoplasm, and even nuclei, can flow. The hyphal walls contain ◊chitin, a polysaccharide.

Hyphasis Classical name of the river ◊Beas, in India.

hyphen punctuation mark (-) with two functions: to join words, parts of words, syllables, and so on, as an aid to sense; and to mark a word break at the end of a line. Adjectival compounds (see ◊adjective) are hyphenated because they modify the noun jointly rather than separately ("a small-town boy" is a boy from a small town; "a small town boy" is a small boy from a town). The use of hyphens with adverbs is redundant unless an identical adjective exists (*well, late, long*): "late-blooming plant" but "brightly blooming plant."

Phrasal verbs are not hyphenated ("things

turned out well," "it *washed up* on the beach") unless used adjectivally ("a well-*turned-out* crowd," "a *washed-up* athlete"). Nouns formed from phrasal verbs are hyphenated or joined together ("a good *turnout* tonight," "please do the *washing-up*"). In the use of certain prefixes, modern style is moving toward omitting the hyphen (*noncooperation*).

hypnosis artificially induced state of relaxation in which suggestibility is heightened. The subject may carry out orders after being awakened, and may be made insensitive to pain. Hypnosis is sometimes used to treat addictions to tobacco or overeating, or to assist amnesia victims.

hypnotic any substance (such as ⟡barbiturate, ⟡benzodiazepine, alcohol) that depresses brain function, inducing sleep. Prolonged use may lead to physical or psychological addiction.

hypo in photography, a term for sodium thiosulfate, discovered 1819 by John ⟡Herschel, and used as a fixative for photographic images since 1837.

hypocycloid in geometry, a cusped curve traced by a point on the circumference of a circle that rolls around the inside of another larger circle. (Compare ⟡epicycloid.)

hypodermic instrument used for injecting fluids beneath the skin into either muscles or blood vessels. It consists of a small graduated tube with a close-fitting piston and a nozzle onto which a hollow needle can be fitted.

hypogeal term used to describe seed germination in which the ⟡cotyledons remain below ground. It can refer to fruits that develop underground, such as peanuts *Arachis hypogea*.

hypoglycemia condition of abnormally low level of sugar (glucose) in the blood, which starves the brain. It causes weakness, the shakes, and perspiration, sometimes fainting. Untreated victims have suffered paranoia and extreme anxiety. Treatment is by special diet.

Hypoglycemia is rare in combination with other diseases, but in diabetics, low blood sugar occurs when the diabetic has taken too much insulin.

hyponymy in semantics, a relationship in meaning between two words such that one

(for example, *sport*) includes the other (for example, *football*), but not vice versa.

hypotenuse the longest side of a right triangle, opposite the right angle. It is of particular application in Pythagoras' theorem (the square of the hypotenuse equals the sum of the squares of the other two sides), and in trigonometry where the ratios ⟡sine and ⟡cosine are defined as the ratios opposite/hypotenuse and adjacent/hypotenuse respectively.

hypothalamus region of the brain below the ⟡cerebrum which regulates rhythmic activity and physiological stability within the body, including water balance and temperature. It regulates the production of the pituitary gland's hormones and controls that part of the ⟡nervous system regulating the involuntary muscles.

hypothermia condition in which the deep (core) temperature of the body spontaneously drops. If it is not discovered, coma and death ensue. Most at risk are the aged and babies (particularly if premature).

hypothesis in science, an idea concerning an event and its possible explanation. The term is one favored by the followers of the philosopher Karl ⟡Popper, who argue that the merit of a scientific hypothesis lies in its ability to make testable predictions.

hypothyroidism or *myxoedema* deficient functioning of the thyroid gland, causing slowed mental and physical performance, sensitivity to cold, and susceptibility to infection.

This may be due to lack of iodine in the diet or a defect of the thyroid gland, both being productive of ⟡goiter; or to the pituitary gland providing insufficient stimulus to the thyroid gland. Treatment of thyroid deficiency is by the hormone thyroxine (either synthetic or from animal thyroid glands).

hypsometer (Greek *hypsos* "height") instrument for testing the accuracy of a thermometer at the boiling point of water. It was originally used for determining altitude by comparing changes in the boiling point with changes in atmospheric pressure.

The name is also used for any of several instruments for measuring the heights of trees by ⟡triangulation.

hyrax small mammal, forming the order Hyracoidea, that lives among rocks, in deserts, and in forests in Africa, Arabia, and Syria. It is about the size of a rabbit, with a plump body, short legs, short ears, brownish fur, and long, curved front teeth.

There are four toes on the front limbs, and three on the hind, each of which has a tiny hoof. There are nine species. They are related to elephants.

hyssop aromatic herb *Hyssopus officinalis* of the mint family Labiatae, found in Asia, S Europe, and around the Mediterranean. It has blue flowers, oblong leaves, and stems that are woody near the ground but herbaceous above.

hysterectomy surgical removal of all or part of the uterus (womb). The operation is performed to treat fibroids (benign tumors growing in the uterus) or cancer; also to relieve heavy menstrual bleeding. A woman who has had a hysterectomy will no longer menstruate and cannot bear children.

hysteresis phenomenon seen in the elastic and electromagnetic behavior of materials, in which a lag occurs between the application or removal of a force or field and its effect.

If the magnetic field applied to a magnetic material is increased and then decreased back to its original value, the magnetic field inside the material does not return to its original value. The internal field "lags" behind the external field. This behavior results in a loss of energy, called the **hysteresis loss**, when a sample is repeatedly magnetized and demagnetized. Hence the materials used in transformer cores and electromagnets should have a low hysteresis loss.

Similar behavior is seen in some materials when varying electric fields are applied (**electric hysteresis**). **Elastic hysteresis** occurs when a varying force repeatedly deforms an elastic material. The deformation produced does not completely disappear when the force is removed, and this results in energy loss on repeated deformations.

hysteria according to the work of Sigmund ⟡Freud, the conversion of a psychological conflict or anxiety feeling into a physical symptom, such as paralysis, blindness, recurrent cough, vomiting, and general malaise. The term is little used today in diagnosis.

Hz in physics, the symbol for ⟡*hertz*.

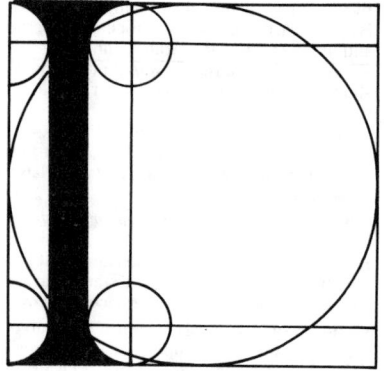

I ninth letter of the English alphabet, deriving, in form, from the sign for one of the several breathings of the Semitic languages. Its vocalic value was first given by the Greeks, who called it *iota* (Ι, ι).

IA abbreviation for the state of ◊*Iowa*.

Iapetus Ocean or *Proto-Atlantic* sea that existed in early ◊Paleozoic times between the continent that was to become Europe and that which was to become North America. The continents moved together in the late Paleozoic, obliterating the ocean. When they moved apart once more, they formed the Atlantic.

Iaşi (German *Jassy*) city in NE Romania; population (1985) 314,000. It has chemical, machinery, electronic, and textile industries. It was the capital of the principality of Moldavia 1568–89.

iatrogenic caused by medical treatment; the term "iatrogenic disease" may be applied to any pathological condition or complication that is caused by the treatment, the facilities, or the staff.

Ibadan city in SW Nigeria and capital of Oyo state; population (1981) 2,100,000. Industries include chemicals, electronics, plastics, and vehicles.

Iban recent replacement term for ◊Dyak.

Ibáñez Vicente Blasco 1867–1928. Spanish novelist and politician, born in Valencia. He was actively involved in revolutionary politics. His novels include *La barraca/The Cabin* 1898, the best of his regional works; *Sangre y arena/Blood and Sand* 1908, the story of a famous bullfighter; and *Los cuatro jinetes del Apocalipsis/The Four Horsemen of the Apocalypse* 1916, a product of the effects of World War I.

Ibarruri Dolores, known as *La Pasionaria* ("the passion flower") 1895–1989. Spanish Basque politician, journalist, and orator; she was first elected to the Cortes in 1936. She helped to establish the Popular Front government and was a Loyalist leader in the Civil War. When Franco came to power in 1939 she left Spain for the USSR, where she was active in the Communist Party. She returned to Spain in 1977 after Franco's death and was reelected to the Cortes (at the age of 81) in the first parliamentary elections since the 1930s.

She joined the Spanish Socialist Party in 1917 and wrote for a workers' newspaper under the adopted name La Pasionaria.

Iberia name given by ancient Greek navigators to the Spanish peninsula, derived from the river Iberus (Ebro). Anthropologists have given the name *"Iberian"* to a Neolithic people, traces of whom are found in the Spanish peninsula, southern France, the Canary Isles, Corsica, and part of North Africa.

Iberville Pierre Le Moyne, Sieur d' 1661–1706. French colonial administrator and explorer. Born in Montreal, Iberville joined the French navy and saw action against the English in the struggle for Canada 1686–97. After the conclusion of the war, he and his brother, the Sieur de Bienville, led an expedition from France to establish a colony at the mouth of the Mississippi River. In 1699–1700 they explored the river and established settlements at the later sites of Biloxi and New Orleans. Iberville ended his military career as commander of French naval forces in the Caribbean.

ibex any of various wild goats found in mountainous areas of Europe, NE Africa, and Central Asia. They grow to 3.5 ft/100 cm, and have brown or gray coats and heavy horns. They are herbivorous and live in small groups.

ibid. abbreviation for *ibidem* (Latin "in the same place"); used in reference citation.

ibis any of various wading birds, about 2 ft/60 cm tall, in the same family, Threskiornidae, as spoonbills. Ibises have long legs and necks, and long, curved beaks. Various species occur in the warmer regions of the world.

The glossy ibis *Plegadis falcinellus* occurs in the SE US and in all continents except South America. The sacred ibis *Threskiornis aethiopica* of ancient Egypt is still found in the Nile basin. The Japanese ibis is in danger of extinction because of loss of its habitat; fewer than 25 birds remain.

Ibiza one of the ◊Balearic Islands, a popular tourist resort; area 230 sq mi/596 sq km; population (1986) 45,000. The capital and port, also called Ibiza, has a cathedral.

IBM (abbreviation for *International Business Machines*) multinational company, the largest manufacturer of computers in the world. The company is a descendant of the Tabulating Machine Company, formed 1896 by Herman ◊Hollerith to exploit his punched-card machines. It adopted its present name 1924. By 1991 it had an annual turnover of $64.8 billion and employed about 345,000 people.

Ibn Battuta 1304–1368. Arab traveler born in Tangiers. In 1325, he went on an extraordinary 75,000 mi/120,675 km journey via Mecca to Egypt, E Africa, India, and China, returning some 30 years later. During this journey he also visited Spain and crossed the Sahara to Timbuktu. The narrative of his travels, *The Adventures of Ibn Battuta*, was written with an assistant, Ibn Juzayy.

Ibn Saud 1880–1953. First king of Saudi Arabia from 1932. His father was the son of the sultan of Nejd, at whose capital, Riyadh, Ibn Saud was born. In 1891 a rival group seized Riyadh, and Ibn Saud went into exile with his father, who resigned his claim to the throne in his son's favor. In 1902 Ibn Saud recaptured Riyadh and recovered the kingdom, and by 1921 he had brought all central Arabia under his rule. In 1924 he invaded the Hejaz, of which he was proclaimed king in 1926.

Nejd and the Hejaz were united 1932 in the kingdom of Saudi Arabia. Ibn Saud introduced programs for modernization with revenue from oil, which was discovered 1936.

Ibn Sina Arabic name of ◊Avicenna, scholar and translator.

Ibo or *Igbo* member of the W African Ibo culture group occupying SE Nigeria and numbering about 18,000,000. Primarily cultivators, they inhabit the richly forested tableland, bounded by the river Niger to the west and the river Cross to the east. They are divided into five main groups, and their languages belong to the Kwa branch of the Niger-Congo family.

Ibrahim Abdullah 1934–1990. South African pianist and composer, formerly known as "Dollar" Brand. He first performed in the US in 1965 and has had a great influence on the fusion of African rhythms with American jazz. His compositions range from songs to large works for orchestra.

Ibsen Henrik (Johan) 1828–1906. Norwegian playwright and poet, whose realistic and often controversial plays revolutionized European theater. Driven into exile 1864–91 by opposition to the satirical *Love's Comedy* 1862, he wrote the verse dramas *Brand* 1866 and *Peer Gynt* 1867, followed by realistic plays dealing with social issues, including *Pillars of Society* 1877, ◊*The Doll's House* 1879, *Ghosts* 1881, *An Enemy of the People* 1882, and ◊*Hedda Gabler* 1891. By the time he returned to Norway, he was recognized as the country's greatest living writer.

His later plays, which are more symbolic, include *The Master Builder* 1892, *Little Eyolf* 1894, *John Gabriel Borkman* 1896, and *When We Dead Awaken* 1899.

Icarus in Greek mythology, the son of ◊Daedalus, who with his father escaped from the labyrinth in Crete by making wings of feathers fastened with wax. Icarus plunged to his death when he flew too near the Sun and the wax melted.

Icarus in astronomy, an ◊Apollo asteroid 1 mi/1.5 km in diameter, discovered 1949. It orbits the Sun every 409 days at a distance of 18–186 million mi/28–300 million km (0.19–2.0 astronomical units). It was the first asteroid known to approach the Sun closer than does the planet Mercury. In 1968 it passed 4 million mi/6 million km from the Earth.

ICBM abbreviation for *intercontinental ballistic missile*; see ◊nuclear warfare.

ice solid formed by water when it freezes. H_2O

ice *The crystal structure of ice in which water molecules are held together by hydrogen bonds.*

It is colorless and its crystals are hexagonal. The water molecules are held together by ▷hydrogen bonds.

The freezing point of ice, used as a standard for measuring temperature, is 0° for the Celsius and Réaumur scales and 32° for the Fahrenheit. Ice expands in the act of freezing (hence burst pipes), becoming less dense than water (0.9175 at 41°F/5°C).

ice form of methamphetamine that is smoked for its stimulating effect; its use has been illegal in the US since 1989. Its effect may be followed by a period of depression and psychosis.

ice age any period of glaciation occurring in the Earth's history, but particularly that in the Pleistocene epoch, immediately preceding historic times. On the North American continent, ▷glaciers reached as far south as the Great Lakes, and an ice sheet spread over N Europe, leaving its remains as far south as Switzerland. There were several glacial advances separated by interglacial stages during which the ice melted and temperatures were higher than today.

Formerly there were thought to have been only three or four glacial advances, but recent research has shown about 20 major incidences. For example, ocean-bed cores record the absence or presence in their various layers of such cold-loving small marine animals as radiolaria, which indicate a fall in ocean temperature at regular intervals. Other ice ages have occurred throughout geological time: there were three in the Precambrian era, one in the Ordovician, and one at the end of the the Carboniferous and beginning of the Permian. The occurrence of an ice age is governed by a combination of factors (the *Milankovitch hypothesis*): (1) the Earth's change of attitude in relation to the Sun, that is, the way it tilts in a 41,000-year cycle and at the same time wobbles on its axis in a 22,000-year cycle, making the time of its closest approach to the Sun come at different seasons; and (2) the 92,000-year cycle of eccentricity in its orbit round the Sun, changing it from an elliptical to a near circular orbit, the severest period of an ice age coinciding with the approach to circularity. There is a possibility that the Pleistocene ice age is not yet over. It may reach another maximum in another 60,000 years.

The theory of ice ages was first proposed in the 19th century by, among others, Swiss civil engineer Ignace Venetz 1821 and Louis Agassiz 1837. The term "ice age" was first used by botanist Karl Schimper in 1837.

major ice ages

name	date (years ago)
Pleistocene	1.7 million–10,000
Permo-Carboniferous	330–250 million
Ordovician	440–430 million
Verangian	615–570 million
Sturtian	820–770 million
Gnejso	940–880 million
Huronian	2,700–1,800 million

Ice Age, Little period of particularly severe winters that gripped N Europe between the 13th and 17th centuries. Contemporary writings and paintings show that Alpine glaciers were much more extensive than at present, and rivers such as the Thames, which do not ice over today, were so frozen that festivals could be held on them.

iceberg floating mass of ice, about 80% of which is submerged, rising sometimes to 300 ft/100 m above sea level. Glaciers that reach the coast become extended into a broad foot; as this enters the sea, masses break off and drift toward temperate latitudes, becoming a danger to shipping.

ice cream rich, creamy, frozen confectionery, made commercially from the early 20th century from various milk products, sugar, and fruit and nut flavorings, usually with additives to improve keeping qualities and ease of serving. Sherbet is a frozen dessert of watered fruit juice, egg white, and sugar, like an ice, but with gelatin and milk added.

ice hockey a game played on ice between two teams of six, developed in Canada from field hockey or bandy. Players, who wear skates and protective clothing, use a curved stick to advance the puck (a rubber disk) and shoot it at the opponents' goal, a netted cage, guarded by the goalie. The other positions are the left and right defensemen and the left wing, center, and right wing. The latter three are offensive players. The team with the most goals scored at the end of the three 20-minute periods wins; an overtime period may be played if a game ends in a tie.

The standard hockey rink is 200 ft/61 m long and 85 ft/26 m wide, with rounded corners and enclosed by a board wall 4 ft/1.3 m high. The goals are on a red line that crosses the rink 10 ft/3 m from each end of the rink. In front of each goal is a rectangular area called the crease, in which the goalie can operate freely, since other players cannot score from that area.

Each period in a game starts with a face-off at the center of the rink (in a face-off the referee drops the puck to the ice, and a player from each team tries with his stick to gain control of the puck). Other players must be at least 10 ft away from the two facing off. Face-offs at center ice (as after a goal) and at other designated spots on the ice are used to restart the game at various times during play.

During a game, substitutions are made frequently, except for the goalie. Substitutions are usually done in groups, such as all three offensive players (the "front line") or both defensemen. Serious rules infractions result in removal from the game to the penalty box for varying amounts of time (usually 2 or 5 min) or, in extreme cases, expulsion from the game.

history ice hockey is believed to have been first introduced in Canada in the 1850s, the first game being played in Kingston, Ontario. The first rules were drawn up at McGill University, Montréal. The governing body is the International Ice Hockey Federation (IIHF) founded 1908.

Canada's first hockey league, the Amateur Hockey Association, was formed 1885. In 1893, Lord Stanley's governor-general gave a cup to be awarded to Canada's champion amateur team. By 1912, there were various professional leagues, and a playoff for the championship was inaugurated. The winner was awarded the Stanley Cup, which has since been the symbol of professional hockey's championship. The National Hockey League (NHL), founded 1917, became the dominant professional league and now consists of two conferences, each with two divisions.

Hockey has been played in the winter Olympic Games since 1920 and enjoys wide popularity in northern and central Europe. A world championship is held each year except during the Olympiad. Top European and North American teams play each other frequently in exhibition games.

Recent Stanley Cup Winners

1983	New York Islanders
1984	Edmonton Oilers
1985	Edmonton Oilers
1986	Montréal Canadiens
1987	Edmonton Oilers
1988	Edmonton Oilers
1989	Calgary Flames
1990	Edmonton Oilers
1991	Pittsburgh Penguins
1992	Pittsburgh Penguins

Içel another name for ▷Mersin, a city in Turkey.

Iceland island country in the N Atlantic Ocean, situated S of the Arctic Circle, between Greenland and Norway.

government The 1944 constitution provides for a president, as head of state, and a legislature, the 63-member Althing, both elected by universal suffrage for a four-year term. Voting is by a system of proportional representation that ensures, as nearly as possible, equality between the proportions of the votes cast and seats won.

Once elected, the Althing divides into an upper house of 21 members and a lower house of 42. The upper-house members are chosen by the Althing itself, and the remainder of 42 automatically constitute the lower house. Members may speak in either house but vote only in the one for which they have been chosen. Legislation must pass through three stages in each house before being submitted to the president for ratification. On some occasions the Althing sits as a single house. The president appoints the prime minister and cabinet on the basis of parliamentary support, and they are collectively responsible to the Althing.

history Iceland was first occupied 874 by Norse settlers, who founded a republic and a parliament 930. In 1000 the inhabitants adopted Christianity and about 1263 submitted to the authority of the king of Norway. In

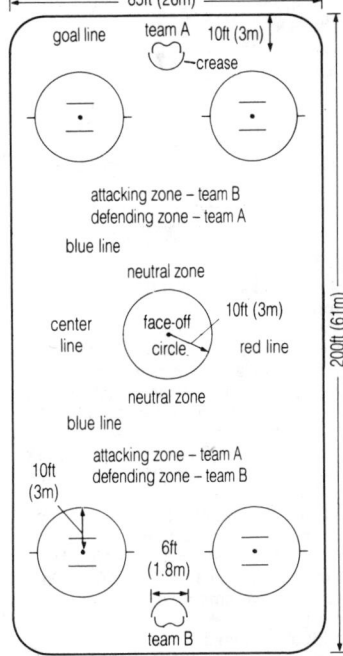

ice hockey

1380 Norway, and with it Iceland, came under Danish rule.

Iceland remained attached to Denmark after Norway became independent 1814. From 1918 it was independent but still recognized the Danish monarch. During World War II Iceland was occupied by British and US forces and voted in a referendum for complete independence 1944. **after independence** In 1949 Iceland joined ⟡NATO and the ⟡Council of Europe, and in 1953 the Nordic Council. Since independence it has been governed by coalitions of the leading parties, sometimes right- and sometimes left-wing groupings, but mostly moderate.

The center and right-of-center parties are the Independents and Social Democrats, while those to the left are the Progressives and the People's Alliance. More recent additions have been the Social Democratic Alliance and the Women's Alliance. **overfishing** Most of Iceland's external problems have been connected with the overfishing of the waters around its coasts. Domestically governments have been faced with the recurring problem of inflation. In 1985 the Althing unanimously declared the country a nuclear-free zone, banning the entry of all nuclear weapons.

The 1987 elections ended control of the Althing by the Independence and Progressive parties, giving more influence to the minor parties, including the Women's Alliance, which doubled its seat tally. In June 1988 Vigdís Finnbogadóttir was reelected president for a third four-year term with 92.7% of the vote. Steingrímur Hermannsson became prime minister. Following a general election April 1991, however, he was replaced by David Oddsson, who led a new center-right coalition of the Independence Party and the Social Democratic Party. In 1992 Iceland announced that it would defy a worldwide ban on whaling in order to resume its own whaling industry. *See illustration box.*

Icelandic language member of the N Germanic branch of the Indo-European language family, spoken only in Iceland and the most conservative in form of the Scandinavian languages. Despite seven centuries of Danish rule, lasting until 1918, Icelandic has remained virtually unchanged since the 12th century.

Since independence in 1918, Icelandic has experienced a revival, as well as governmental protection against such outside linguistic influences as English-language broadcasting. Early Icelandic literature is largely anonymous and seems to have originated in Norse colonies in the British Isles (around 9th–10th centuries). The two Eddas and several Sagas date from this period. Halldor ⟡Laxness, writing about Icelandic life in the style of the Sagas, was awarded a Nobel Prize 1955.

Iceland spar form of ⟡calcite, $CaCO_3$, originally found in Iceland. In its pure form Iceland spar is transparent and exhibits the peculiar phenomenon of producing two images of anything seen through it. It is used in optical instruments. The crystals cleave into perfect rhombohedra.

Iceni ancient people of E England, who revolted against occupying Romans under ⟡Boudicca.

ice-skating see ⟡skating.

I Ching or **Book of Changes** ancient Chinese book of divination based on 64 hexagrams, or patterns of six lines. The lines may be "broken" or "whole" (yin or yang) and are generated by tossing yarrow stalks or coins. The inquirer formulates a question before throwing, and the book gives interpretations of the meaning of the hexagrams.

The *I Ching* is thought to have originated in the 2nd millennium BC, with commentaries added by Confucius and later philosophers. It is proto-Taoist in that it is not used for determining the future but for making the inquirer aware of inherent possibilities and unconscious tendencies.

ichneumon fly any parasitic wasp of the family Ichneumonidae. There are several thousand species in Europe, North America, and other regions. They have slender bodies, and females have unusually long, curved ovipositors (egg-laying instruments) that can pierce several inches of wood. The eggs are laid in the eggs, larvae, or pupae of other insects, usually butterflies or moths.

Ickes Harold LeClair 1874–1952. US public official. A liberal Republican, he was appointed secretary of the interior by F D Roosevelt 1933. Ickes later held other senior posts in the Roosevelt administration, including director of the Public Works Administration (PWA), where he administered New Deal development projects.

Born in Blair County, Pennsylvania, and educated at the University of Chicago, Ickes was admitted to the bar 1907. After resigning from the Truman cabinet 1946, Ickes wrote a newspaper column and published several autobiographical works. *The Secret Diary of Harold L Ickes* appeared 1953.

icon in the Greek or Eastern Orthodox Church, a representation of Jesus, Mary, an angel, or a saint, in painting, low relief, or mosaic. The painted icons were traditionally done on wood. After the 17th century in Russia, a *riza*, or gold and silver covering which leaves only the face and hands visible (and may be adorned with jewels presented by the faithful in thanksgiving), was often added as protection.

Icons were regarded as holy objects, based on the doctrine that God became visible through Christ. Icon painting originated in the Byzantine Empire, but many examples were destroyed by the ⟡iconoclasts in the 8th and 9th centuries. The Byzantine style of painting predominated in the Mediterranean region and in Russia until the 12th century, when Russian, Greek, and other schools developed. Andrei Rublev (c. 1365–1430) was a renowned Russian icon painter.

icon in computing, a small picture on the computer screen, or ⟡VDT, representing an object or function that the user may manipulate or otherwise use. It is a feature of ⟡graphical user interface (GUI) systems. Icons make computers easier to use by allowing the user to point to and click with a ⟡mouse on pictures, rather than type commands.

iconoclast (Greek "image-breaker") literally, a person who attacks religious images, originally in obedience to the injunction of the Second Commandment not to worship "graven images." Under the influence of Islam and Judaism, an iconoclastic movement calling for the destruction of religious images developed in the Byzantine Empire, and was endorsed by the Emperor Leo III in 726. Fierce persecution of those who made and venerated icons followed, until iconoclasm was declared a heresy in the 9th century.

The same name was applied to those opposing the use of images at the Reformation,

Iceland
Republic of (*Lýdöveldidö Ísland*)

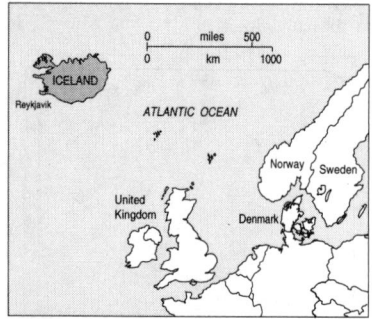

area 39,758 sq mi/103,000 sq km
capital Reykjavík
cities Akureyri, Akranes
physical warmed by the Gulf Stream; glaciers and lava fields cover 75% of the country; active volcanoes (Hekla was once thought the gateway to Hell), geysers, hot springs, and new islands created offshore (Surtsey in 1963); subterranean hot water heats 85% of Iceland's homes
features Thingvellir, where the oldest parliament in the world first met AD 930; shallow lake Mývatn (15 sq mi/38 sq km) in N
head of state Vigdís Finnbogadóttir from 1980
head of government Davíd Oddsson from 1991
political system democratic republic
political parties Independence Party (IP), right of center; Progressive Party (PP), radical socialist; People's Alliance (PA), socialist; Social Democratic Party (SDP), moderate, left of center; Citizens' Party, centrist; Women's Alliance, women- and family-oriented
exports cod and other fish products, aluminum, diatomite
currency krona
population (1990 est) 251,000; growth rate 0.8% p.a.
life expectancy men 74, women 80
language Icelandic, the most archaic Scandinavian language, in which some of the finest sagas were written
religion Evangelical Lutheran 95%
literacy 99.9% (1984)
GDP $3.9 bn (1986); $16,200 per head
chronology
1944 Independence achieved from Denmark.
1949 Joined NATO and Council of Europe.
1953 Joined Nordic Council.
1976 "Cod War" with UK.
1979 Iceland announced 320-km/200-mi exclusive fishing zone.
1983 Steingrímur Hermannsson appointed to lead a coalition government.
1985 Iceland declared itself a nuclear-free zone.
1987 New coalition government formed by Thorsteinn Pálsson after general election.
1988 Vigdís Finnbogadóttir reelected president for a third term; Hermannsson led new coalition.
1991 Davíd Oddsson led new IP–SDP (Independence Party and Social Democratic Party) center-right coalition, becoming prime minister in the general election.
1992 Iceland defied world ban to resume whaling industry.

when there was much destruction in churches. Figuratively, the term is used for a person who attacks established ideals or principles.

iconography in art history, significance attached to symbols that can help to identify subject matter (for example, a saint holding keys usually represents St Peter) and place a work of art in its historical context.

ICU abbreviation for ⟡*intensive care unit*.

id in Freudian psychology, the instinctual element of the human mind, concerned with pleasure, which demands immediate satisfaction. It is regarded as the ⟡unconscious element of the human psyche, and is said to be in conflict with the ⟡ego and the ⟡superego.

id. abbreviation for *idem* (Latin "the same"); used in reference citation.

ID abbreviation for the state of ⟡*Idaho*.

Idaho state of NW US; nickname Gem State
area 83,569 sq mi/216,500 sq km
capital Boise
cities Pocatello, Idaho Falls
features Rocky Mountains; Snake River, which runs through Hell's Canyon (7,647 ft/2,330 m), the deepest in North America, and has the National Reactor Testing Station on the plains of its upper reaches; Sun Valley ski and summer resort; Craters of the Moon National Monument; Nez Percé National Historic Park
products potatoes, wheat, livestock, timber, silver, lead, zinc, antimony
population (1990) 1,006,700
history part of the Louisiana Purchase 1803; explored by Lewis and Clark 1805–06; first permanently settled by Mormons 1860, the same year gold was discovered. Settlement in the 1870s led to a series of battles between US forces and Indian tribes. Idaho became a state in 1890. The timber industry began 1906, and by World War I agriculture was a leading enterprise.

idealism in philosophy, the theory that states that the external world is fundamentally immaterial and a dimension of the mind. Objects in the world exist but, according to this theory, they lack substance.

identikit a set of drawings of different parts of the face used to compose a likeness of a person for identification. It was evolved by Hugh C McDonald (1913–) in the US. It has largely been replaced by photofit, based on photographs, which produces a more realistic likeness.

ideology set of ideas, beliefs, and opinions about the nature of people and society, providing a framework for a theory about how people should live, as well as how society is or should be organized. A nation's ideology is usually reflected in the political system it creates.

Ides in the Roman calendar, the 15th day of March, May, July, and Oct, and the 13th day of all other months (the word originally indicated

Idaho

Boise

HT lead
spark plug lead
ignition coil
condenser
contact breaker
distributor
spark plugs
car key
lead acid battery

— high-tension (20,000 volts)
— earthing
- - - low-tension (12 volts = car battery voltage)

ignition coil *The ignition coil generates a high-tension (voltage) current which flows to the spark plugs through the distributor.*

the full moon); Julius Caesar was assassinated on the Ides of March 44 BC.

idiot savant (French "knowledgeable idiot") person who has a specific mental skill which has developed at the expense of general intelligence. An idiot savant is educationally slow but may be able to calculate the day of the week for any date, or memorize a large quantity of text. Most idiots savants are male.

i.e. abbreviation for *id est* (Latin "that is").

If small French island in the Mediterranean about 2 mi/3 km off Marseille, with a castle, Château d'If, built about 1529. This was used as a state prison and is the scene of the imprisonment of Dante in Dumas's *Count of Monte Cristo*.

Ifugao member of an indigenous people of N Luzon in the Philippines, numbering approximately 70,000. In addition to practicing shifting cultivation on highland slopes, they build elaborate terraced rice fields. Their language belongs to the Austronesian family.

The Ifugao live in scattered hamlets and traditionally recognise a class of nobles, *kadangya*, who are obliged to provide expensive feasts on particular social occasions. Although indigenous beliefs remain, many Ifugao have adopted Christianity. Some Ifugao work as wage laborers outside their highland region.

Ignatius Loyola, St 1491–1556. Spanish noble who founded the ⟡Jesuit order 1540, also called the Society of Jesus.

His deep interest in the religious life began in 1521, when reading the life of Jesus while recuperating from a war wound. He visited the Holy Land in 1523, studied in Spain and Paris, where he took vows with St Francis Xavier, and was ordained 1537. He then moved to Rome and with the approval of Pope Paul III began the Society of Jesus, sending missionaries to Brazil, India, and Japan, and founding Jesuit schools. Feast day July 31.

Ignatius of Antioch, St 1st–2nd century AD.

Christian martyr. Traditionally a disciple of St John, he was bishop of Antioch, and was thrown to the wild beasts in Rome. He wrote seven epistles, important documents of the early Christian church. Feast day Feb 1.

igneous rock rock formed from cooling magma or lava, and solidifying from a molten state. Igneous rocks are classified according to their crystal size, texture, chemical composition, or method of formation. They are largely composed of silica (SiO_2) and they are classified by their silica content into groups: acid (over 66% silica), intermediate (55%–66%), basic (45%–55%), and ultrabasic (under 45%). Igneous rocks that crystallize below the Earth's surface are called plutonic or intrusive, depending on the depth of formation. They have large crystals produced by slow cooling; examples include diabase and granite. Those extruded at the surface are called extrusive or volcanic. Rapid cooling results in small crystals; basalt is an example.

ignition coil ⟡transformer that is an essential part of a gasoline engine's ignition system. It consists of two wire coils wound around an iron core. The primary coil, which is connected to the car battery, has only a few turns. The secondary coil, connected via the ⟡distributor to the ⟡spark plugs, has many turns. The coil takes in a low voltage (usually 12 volts) from the battery and transforms it to a high voltage (about 20,000 volts) to ignite the engine.

When the engine is running, the battery current is periodically interrupted by means of the contact breaker in the distributor. The collapsing current in the primary coil induces a current in the secondary coil, a phenomenon known as ⟡electromagnetic induction. The induced current in the secondary coil is at very high voltage, typically about 15,000–20,000 volts. This passes to the spark plugs to create sparks.

ignition temperature or *fire point* minimum temperature to which a substance must be heated before it will spontaneously burn independently of the source of heat; for example, ethanol has an ignition temperature of 798°F/ 425°C and a ⏦flash point of 54°F/12°C.

Iguaçú Falls or *Iguassú Falls* waterfall in South America, on the border between Brazil and Argentina. The falls lie 12 mi/19 km above the junction of the river Iguaçú with the Paraná. The falls are divided by forested rocky islands and form a spectacular tourist attraction. The water plunges in 275 falls, many of which have separate names. They have a height of 269 ft/ 82 m and a width of about 2.5 mi/4 km.

iguana any lizard, especially the genus *Iguana*, of the family Iguanidae, which includes about 700 species and is chiefly confined to the Americas. The common iguana *I. iguana* of Central and South America is a vegetarian and may reach 6 ft/2 m in length.

iguanodon plant-eating ⏦dinosaur of the order *Ornithiscia*, whose remains are found in deposits of the Lower Cretaceous age, together with the remains of other ornithiscians such as stegosaurus and triceratops. It was 16–32 ft/5– 10 m long and, when standing upright, 13 ft/ 4 m tall. It walked on its hind legs, using its long tail to balance its body.

IJsselmeer lake in the Netherlands, formed 1932 after the Zuider Zee was cut off by a dyke from the North Sea; freshwater since 1944. Area 470 sq mi/1,217 sq km.

ikebana (Japanese "living flower") Japanese art of flower arrangement. It dates from the 6th–7th century when arrangements of flowers were placed as offerings in Buddhist temples, a practice learned from China. In the 15th century, ikebana became a favorite pastime of the nobility. Oldest of the Japanese ikebana schools is Ikenobo at Kyoto (7th century).

Ikhnaton or *Akhenaton* 14th century BC. King of Egypt of the 18th dynasty (*c.* 1379–1362 BC), who may have ruled jointly for a time with his father Amenhotep III. He developed the cult of the Sun, ⏦Aton, rather than the rival cult of ⏦Ammon. Some historians believe that his attention to religious reforms rather than imperial defense led to the loss of most of Egypt's possessions in Asia.

Ikhnaton's favorite wife was Nefertiti, and two of their six daughters were married to his successors Smenkhare and Tutankaton (later known as Tutankhamen).

IL abbreviation for the state of ⏦*Illinois*.

Île-de-France region of N France; area 4,632 sq mi/12,000 sq km; population (1986) 10,251,000. It includes the French capital, Paris, and the towns of Versailles, Sèvres, and St-Cloud and comprises the *départements* of Essonne, Val-de-Marne, Val d'Oise, Ville de Paris, Seine-et-Marne, Hauts-de-Seine, Seine-Saint-Denis, and Yvelines. From here the early French kings extended their authority over the whole country.

ileum part of the small intestine of the ⏦digestive system, between the duodenum and the colon, that absorbs digested food.

Its wall is muscular so that waves of contraction (peristalsis) can mix the food and push it forward. Numerous fingerlike projections, or villi, point inward from the wall, increasing the surface area available for absorption. The ileum has an excellent blood supply, which receives the food molecules passing through the wall and transports them to the liver via the hepatic portal vein.

Iliad Greek epic poem in 24 books, probably written before 700 BC, attributed to ⏦Homer.

Its title is derived from Ilion, the Greek name for Troy. Its subject is the wrath of Achilles, an incident in the 12th century BC during the tenth year of the Trojan War, when Achilles killed Hector to avenge the death of his friend Patroclus. The tragic battle scenes are described in graphic detail.

Iliescu Ion 1930–   . Romanian president from 1990. A former member of the Romanian Communist Party (PCR) and of Nicolae Ceaușescu's government, Iliescu swept into power on Ceaușescu's fall as head of the National Salvation Front.

Iliescu was elected a member of the PCR central committee 1968, becoming its propaganda secretary 1971. Conflict over the launching of a "cultural revolution," and the growth of Ceaușescu's personality cult led to Iliescu's removal from national politics: he was sent to Timișoara as chief of party propaganda. At the outbreak of the "Christmas revolution" 1989, Iliescu was one of the first leaders to emerge, becoming president of the Provisional Council of National Unity Feb 1990. He won an overwhelming victory in the presidential elections in May 1990, despite earlier controversy over his hard line.

Ilium in Classical mythology, an alternate name for the city of ⏦Troy, taken from its founder Ilus.

illegitimacy in law, the status of a child born to a mother who is not legally married; a child may be legitimized by subsequent marriage of the parents. The nationality of the child is usually that of the mother.

Illegitimacy, depending on state laws, affects inheritance rights with repect to a father and may give rise to actions for judicial determination of paternity and subsequent economic responsibility toward the child.

Illich Ivan 1926–   . US radical philosopher and activist, born in Austria. His works, which include *Deschooling Society* 1971, *Towards a History of Need* 1978, and *Gender* 1983, are a critique of contemporary economic development, especially in the Third World.

Illich was born in Vienna and has lived in the US and Latin America. He believes that modern technology and bureaucratic institutions are destroying peasant skills and self-sufficiency and creating a new form of dependency: on experts, professionals, and material goods. True liberation, he believes, can only be achieved by abolishing the institutions on which authority rests, such as schools and hospitals.

Illinois midwest state of the US; nickname Land of Lincoln/Prairie State
area 56,395 sq mi/146,100 sq km
capital Springfield
cities Chicago, Rockford, Peoria, Decatur, Aurora
features Lake Michigan; rivers: Mississippi, Illinois, Ohio, Rock; Cahokia Mounds, the largest group of prehistoric earthworks in the US; the Lincoln Home National Historic Site, Springfield; the University of Chicago; Mormon leader Joseph Smith's home, Nauvoo; the Art Institute and Field Museum, Chicago
products soybeans, cereals, meat and dairy products, machinery, electrical and electronic equipment
population (1990) 11,430,600
famous people Jane Addams, Saul Bellow, Mother Cabrini, Clarence Darrow, Enrico Fermi, Ernest Hemingway, Jesse Jackson, Edgar Lee Masters, Ronald Reagan, Louis Sullivan, Frank Lloyd Wright

Illinois

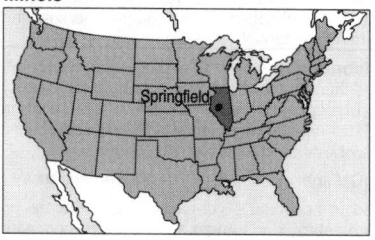

history explored by Marquette and Joliet 1673; settled by the French in the 17th century; ceded to Britain by France 1763; passed to US control 1783; became a state 1818. Much settlement began 1825 following the opening of the Erie Canal. Spurred after the Civil War by the phenomenal growth of Chicago, Illinois became a major agricultural and industrial state, with heavy immigration. Labor unrest was reflected in the Haymarket Riot 1886 and Pullman strike 1894. The importance of heavy industry declined after 1950, but Chicago remained a major transport, trade, and finance center, and the state a leader in farm income; Illinois ranks first in agricultural exports and second in hog production. The enormous Fermi National Accelerator Laboratory is located at Batavia.

illumination the brightness or intensity of light falling on a surface. It depends upon the brightness, distance, and angle of any nearby light sources. The SI unit is the ⏦lux.

Illyria ancient name for the eastern coastal region on the Adriatic, N of the Gulf of Corinth, conquered by Philip of Macedon. It became a Roman province AD 9. The Albanians are the survivors of its ancient peoples.

ilmenite oxide of iron and titanium, iron titanate ($FeTiO_3$); an ore of titanium. The mineral is black, with a metallic luster. It is found in compact masses, grains, and sand.

imaginary number term often used to describe the non-real element of a ⏦complex number. For the complex number ($a + ib$), ib is the imaginary number where $i = \sqrt{-1}$, and b any real number.

Imagism movement in Anglo-American poetry that flourished 1912–14 and affected much US and British poetry and critical thinking thereafter. A central figure was Ezra Pound, who asserted the principles of free verse, complex imagery, and poetic impersonality.

Pound encouraged Hilda Doolittle to sign her verse H D Imagiste and in 1914 edited the *Des Imagistes* anthology. Poets subsequently influenced by this movement include T S Eliot, William Carlos Williams, Wallace Stevens, and Marianne Moore. Imagism established modernism in English-language verse.

imago sexually mature stage of an ⏦insect.

imam (Arabic "leader") in a mosque, the leader of congregational prayer, but generally any notable Islamic leader.

Imbros (Turkish *Imroz*) island in the Aegean Sea; area 108 sq mi/280 sq km; population (1970) 6,786. Occupied by Greece in World War I, it became Turkish under the Treaty of ⏦Lausanne 1923.

IMF abbreviation for ⏦*International Monetary Fund*.

Imhotep *c.* 2800 BC. Egyptian physician and architect, adviser to King Zoser (3rd dynasty). He is thought to have designed the step pyramid at Sakkara, and his tomb (believed to be in the N Sakkara cemetery) became a center of healing. He was deified as the son of ⟩Ptah and was identified with Aesculapius, the Greek god of medicine.

Immaculate Conception in the Roman Catholic Church, the belief that the Virgin Mary was, by a special act of grace, preserved free from ⟩original sin from the moment she was conceived. This article of the Catholic faith was for centuries the subject of heated controversy, opposed by St Thomas Aquinas and other theologians, but generally accepted from about the 16th century. It became a dogma in 1854 under Pope Pius IX.

immigration and emigration movement of people from one country to another. Immigration is movement to a country; emigration is movement from a country. Immigration or emigration on a large scale is often for economic reasons or because of religious, political, or social persecution (which may create ⟩refugees), and often prompts restrictive legislation by individual countries. The US has received immigrants on a larger scale than any other country, more than 50 million during its history.

Immigration and Naturalization Service v Chadha a US Supreme Court decision 1983 dealing with the power of Congress to overrule decisions of the executive branch regarding immigration. Chadha, a foreign student allowed by the Immigration and Naturalization Service (INS) to remain in the country after the expiration of his visa, was deported by the House of Representatives. By the Immigration and Nationality Act, this veto of an INS ruling was within the power of either house of Congress, but Chadha appealed, challenging the constitutionality of the act. The Court ruled to invalidate the provision of the act that allowed a single house to veto INS rulings, judging one-house vetoes to be unconstitutional under any circumstance.

immiscible term describing liquids that will not mix with each other, such as oil and water. When two immiscible liquids are shaken together, a turbid mixture is produced. This normally forms separate layers on being left to stand.

immunity the protection that organisms have against foreign microorganisms, such as bacteria and viruses, and against cancerous cells (see ⟩cancer). The cells that provide this protection are called white blood cells, or leukocytes, and make up the immune system. They include neutrophils and ⟩macrophages, which can engulf invading organisms and other unwanted material, and natural killer cells that destroy cells infected by viruses and cancerous cells. Some of the most important immune cells are the ⟩B cells and ⟩T cells. Immune cells coordinate their activities by means of chemical messengers or ⟩lymphokines, including the antiviral messenger ⟩interferon. The lymph nodes play a major role in organizing the immune response.

Immunity is also provided by a range of physical barriers such as the skin, tear fluid, acid in the stomach, and mucus in the airways. ⟩AIDS is one of many viral diseases in which the immune system is affected.

Immunity has been studied mostly in higher vertebrates, especially rodents, domestic animals, and primates.

immunization conferring immunity to infectious disease by artificial methods. The most widely used technique is ⟩vaccination.

Vaccination against smallpox was developed by Edward ⟩Jenner in 1796. In the late 19th century Louis ⟩Pasteur developed vaccines against cholera, typhoid, typhus, plague, and yellow fever. Immunization is now available against diphtheria, whooping cough, measles, and polio.

immunocompromised lacking a fully effective immune system. The term is most often used in connection with infections such as ⟩AIDS where the virus interferes with the immune response (see ⟩immunity).

Other factors that can impair the immune response are pregnancy, diabetes, old age, malnutrition and extreme stress, making someone susceptible to infections by microorganisms (such as listeria) that do not affect normal, healthy people. Some people are immunodeficient; others could be on ⟩immunosuppressive drugs.

immunodeficient lacking one or more elements of a working immune system. Immune deficiency is the term generally used for patients who are born with such a defect, while those who acquire such a deficiency later in life are referred to as ⟩*immunocompromised* or immunosuppressed.

A serious impairment of the immune system is sometimes known as SCID, or Severe Combined Immune Deficiency. At one time children born with this condition would have died in infancy. They can now be kept alive in a germ-free environment, then treated with a bone-marrow transplant from a relative, to replace the missing immune cells. At present, the success rate for this type of treatment is still fairly low.

immunoglobulin human globulin ⟩protein that can be separated from blood and administered to confer immediate immunity on the recipient. It participates in the immune reaction as the antibody for a specific ⟩antigen (disease-causing agent).

Normal immunoglobulin (gamma globulin) is the fraction of the blood serum that, in general, contains the most antibodies, and is obtained from plasma pooled from about a thousand donors. It is given for short-term (two to three months) protection when a person is at risk, mainly from hepatitis A (infectious hepatitis), or when a pregnant woman, not immunized against ⟩German measles, is exposed to the rubella virus.

Specific immunoglobulins are injected when a susceptible (nonimmunized) person is at risk of infection from a potentially fatal disease, such as hepatitis B (serum hepatitis), rabies, or tetanus. These immunoglobulins are prepared from blood pooled from donors convalescing from the disease.

immunosuppressive any drug that suppresses the body's normal immune responses to infection or foreign tissue. It is used in the treatment of autoimmune disease (see ⟩autoimmunity); as part of chemotherapy for leukemias, lymphomas, and other cancers; and to help prevent rejection following organ transplant.

impala African antelope *Aepyceros melampus* found from Kenya to South Africa in savannas and open woodland. The body is sandy brown. Males have lyre-shaped horns up to 2.5 ft/ 75 cm long. Impala grow up to 5 ft/1.5 m long and 3 ft/90 cm tall. They live in herds and spring high in the air when alarmed.

impeachment judicial procedure by which government officials are accused of wrongdoing and brought to trial before a legislative body. In the US the House of Representatives may impeach offenders to be tried before the Senate, as in the case of President Andrew Johnson 1868. Richard ⟩Nixon to resigned the US presidency 1974 when threatened by impeachment.

impedance the total opposition of a circuit to the passage of alternating electric current. It has the symbol Z. For an ⟩alternating current (AC) it includes the reactance X (caused by electrical ⟩capacitance or ⟩inductance); the impedance can then be found using the equation $Z^2 = R^2 + X^2$.

In acoustics, impedance refers to the ratio of the force per unit area to the volume displaced by the surface across which sound is being transmitted.

imperialism policy of extending the rule or authority of a nation or an empire over foreign nations or of taking and holding foreign colonies. Since the breakup of empires and the granting of independence to most colonies, some refer to the continuing economic domination of these former holdings as ⟩neocolonialism.

impetigo superficial skin infection with either streptococcus or staphylococcus bacteria, characterized by a honey-colored crust on the skin.

It is curable with antibiotics.

implantation in mammals, the process by which the developing ⟩embryo attaches itself to the wall of the mother's uterus and stimulates the development of the ⟩placenta.

In some species, such as seals and bats, implantation is delayed for several months, during which time the embryo does not grow; thus the interval between mating and birth may be a year, although the ⟩gestation period is only seven or eight months.

import product or service that one country purchases from another for domestic consumption, or for processing and reexporting (Hong Kong, for example, is heavily dependent on imports for its export business). Imports may be visible (goods) or invisible (services). If an importing country does not have a counterbalancing value of exports, it may experience balance-of-payments difficulties and accordingly consider restricting imports by some form of protectionism (such as an import tariff or imposing import quotas).

impotence in medicine, a physical inability to perform sexual intercourse (the term is not usually applied to women). Impotent men fail to achieve an erection, and this may be due to illness, the effects of certain drugs, or psychological factors.

General fatigue or lack of interest may also cause impotence. Treatment for ongoing impotence includes counseling, behavioral therapy, and surgical implants.

Impressionism movement in painting that originated in France in the 1860s and dominated European and North American painting in the late 19th century. The Impressionists wanted to depict real life, to paint straight from nature, and to capture the changing effects of light. The term was first used abusively to describe Monet's painting *Impression, Sunrise* 1872 (stolen from the Musée Marmottan, Paris); other Impressionists were Renoir and Sisley, soon joined by Cézanne, Manet, Degas, and others.

The starting point of Impressionism was the *Salon des Refusés*, an exhibition in 1873 of work rejected by the official Salon. This was followed by the Impressionists' own exhibitions

1874–86, where their work aroused fierce opposition. Their styles were diverse, but many experimented with effects of light and movement created with distinct brushstrokes and fragments of color juxtaposed on the canvas rather than mixed on the palette. By the 1880s, the movement's central impulse had dispersed, and a number of new styles emerged, later described as Post-Impressionism.

impressionism in music, a style of composition emphasizing instrumental color and texture. The term was first applied to the music of ◊Debussy.

imprinting in ◊ethology, the process whereby a young animal learns to recognize both specific individuals (for example, its mother) and its own species.

Imprinting is characteristically an automatic response to specific stimuli at a time when the animal is especially sensitive to those stimuli (the **sensitive period**). Thus, goslings learn to recognize their mother by following the first moving object they see after hatching; as a result, they can easily become imprinted on other species, or even inanimate objects, if these happen to move near them at this time. In chicks, imprinting occurs only between 10 and 20 hours after hatching. In mammals, the mother's attachment to her infant may be a form of imprinting made possible by a sensitive period; this period may be as short as the first hour after giving birth.

impromptu in music, a short instrumental piece that suggests spontaneity. Composers of piano impromptus include Schubert and Chopin.

in abbreviation for ◊**inch**, a measure of distance.

IN abbreviation for the state of ◊**Indiana**.

inbreeding in ◊genetics, the mating of closely related individuals. It is considered undesirable because it increases the risk that offspring will inherit copies of rare deleterious ◊recessive alleles (genes) from both parents and so suffer from disabilities.

Inc. abbreviation for **Incorporated**.

Inca member of an ancient Peruvian civilization of Quechua-speaking Indians that began in the Andean highlands about 1200; by the time of the Spanish Conquest in the 1530s, the Inca ruled from Ecuador in the north to Chile in the south.

The Inca empire dominated the Andean region militarily and assimilated many of the conquered peoples, transplanting them into new homelands nearest their capital, Cuzco, until they had been Inca-ized, then resettling them and transporting in the newly conquered to undergo the learning process. They had an agriculturally based theocracy, with priest-rulers at the top of the hierarchy, and with "the Inca," a descendant of the Sun (and his sister-wife), ruling over all. Their extensive road system united the empire of both highland and coastal cities but made them vulnerable to the Spanish, who conquered and enslaved the people in mining and food-producing ventures. Today's Quechua-speaking Indians are descendants of the Inca civilization; many still live in the farming villages of the highlands of Peru.

Incan art art of the Inca people of the Peruvian Andes, South America, of the 11th–16th centuries. The main sites are Cuzco, the old capital, and ◊Machu Picchu, a fortified mountain settlement. Incan artisans produced technically brilliant, highly finished ceramics and textiles, and excellent masonry, consisting of large blocks of stone fitted together with great precision. Animal and human figures are frequent sculptural subjects.

incandescence emission of light from a substance in consequence of its high temperature. The color of the emitted light from liquids or solids depends on their temperature, and for solids generally the higher the temperature the whiter the light. Gases may become incandescent through ◊ionizing radiation, as in the glowing vacuum ◊discharge tube.

The oxides of cerium and thorium are highly incandescent and for this reason are used in gas mantles. The light from an electric filament lamp is due to the incandescence of the filament, rendered white-hot when a current passes through it.

incarnation assumption of living form (plant, animal, human) by a deity, for example the gods of Greece and Rome, Hinduism, and Christianity (Jesus as the second person of the Trinity).

incendiary bomb a bomb containing inflammable matter. Usually dropped by aircraft, incendiary bombs were used in World War I, and were a major weapon in attacks on cities in World War II. To hinder firefighters, delayed-action high-explosive bombs were usually dropped with them. In the Vietnam War, US forces used ◊napalm in incendiary bombs.

incest sexual intercourse between persons thought to be too closely related to marry; the exact relationships that fall under the incest taboo vary widely from society to society. A biological explanation for the incest taboo is based on the necessity to avoid ◊inbreeding.

Within groups in which ritual homosexuality is practiced, for example in New Guinea, an incest taboo applies also to these relations, suggesting that the taboo is as much social as biological in origin.

inch imperial unit of linear measure, a twelfth of a foot, equal to 2.54 centimeters.

It was defined in statute by Edward II of England as the length of three barley grains laid end to end.

Inchon formerly **Chemulpo** chief port of Seoul, South Korea; population (1990) 1,818,300.

It produces steel and textiles.

income tax a direct tax levied on corporate profits and on personal income, mainly wages and salaries, but which may include dividends, interests, rents, royalties, and the value of receipts other than in cash. It is one of the main instruments for achieving a government's income redistribution objectives.

In the US, every citizen (with certain exemptions on the grounds of age or income level) must file an annual report for income-tax consideration. The tax-rates, which are calculated on a percentage basis, and allowances (deductions) are fixed by Congress from year to year. A state income tax is also levied in many states, the amount of tax and allowances varying from state to state; and in a few cases, such as New York City, there is a city income tax as well.

incontinence failure or inability to control evacuation of the bladder or bowel (or both in the case of double incontinence). It may arise as a result of injury, childbirth, disease, or senility.

incubus male demon who in the popular belief of the Middle Ages had sexual intercourse with women in their sleep. Supposedly the women then gave birth to witches and demons. **Succubus** is the female equivalent.

incunabula (Latin "swaddling clothes") the birthplace, or early stages of anything; printed books produced before 1500, when printing was in its infancy.

indemnity in law, an undertaking to compensate another for damage, loss, trouble, or expenses, or the money paid by way of such compensation—for example, under fire insurance agreements.

In some laws, government officials are protected from paying indemnities and as such are "indemnified." Similarly directors of nonprofit corporations may be indemnified or corporations may indemnify their officers and directors by the purchase of insurance.

indenture in law, a ◊deed between two or more people. Historically, an indenture was a contract between a master and an apprentice. The term derives from the practice of writing the agreement twice on paper or parchment and then cutting it with a jagged edge so that both pieces fit together, proving the authenticity of each half.

indentured labor work under a restrictive contract of employment for a fixed period in a foreign country in exchange for payment of passage, accommodation, and food. Indentured labor was the means by which many British people emigrated to North America during the colonial era, and in the 19th–early 20th centuries it was used to recruit Asian workers for employment elsewhere in European colonial empires.

Conditions for indentured workers were usually very poor. Many died during the passage, and during the term of indenture (usually between four and seven years) the worker was not allowed to change employer, although the employer could sell the remaining period of indenture, much as a slave could be sold. Indentured labor was widely used as a source of workers from India for employment on sugar plantations in the Caribbean from 1839, following the abolition of slavery.

Independence city in W Missouri; population (1990) 112,300. Industries include steel, Portland cement, petroleum refining, and flour milling. President Harry S Truman was raised here, and it is the site of the Truman Library and Museum.

Independence Day public holiday in the US, commemorating the adoption of the ◊Declaration of Independence July 4, 1776.

Ties with Britain were severed and the "Fourth of July" has become one of America's most spirited holidays.

Independent Labour Party (ILP) British socialist party, founded in Bradford 1893 by the Scottish member of Parliament Keir Hardie. In 1900 it joined with labour unions and Fabians in founding the Labour Representation Committee, the nucleus of the ◊Labour Party. Many members left the ILP to join the Communist Party 1921, and in 1932 all connections with the Labour Party were severed. After World War II the ILP dwindled, eventually becoming extinct. James Maxton (1885–1946) was its chair 1926–46.

indeterminacy principle alternate name for ◊uncertainty principle.

index in economics, an indicator of a general movement in wages and prices over a specified period.

For example, the consumer price index (CPI) records changes in the ◊cost of living.

India
Republic of (Hindi *Bharat*)

area 1,222,396 sq mi/3,166,829 sq km
capital New Delhi
cities Bangalore, Hyderabad, Ahmedabad, Kanpur, Pune, Nagpur; ports Calcutta, Bombay, Madras
physical Himalaya mountains on N border; plains around rivers Ganges, Indus, Brahmaputra; Deccan peninsula S of the Narmada River forms plateau between Western and Eastern Ghats mountain ranges; desert in W; Andaman and Nicobar Islands, Lakshadweep (Laccadive Islands)
environment the controversial Narmada Valley Project is the world's largest combined hydroelectric irrigation scheme. In addition to displacing a million people, the damming of the holy Narmada River will submerge large areas of forest and farmland and create problems of waterlogging and salinization
features Taj Mahal monument; Golden Temple, Amritsar; archeological sites and cave paintings (Ajanta); world's second most populous country
head of state R Venkataraman from 1987
head of government P V Narasimha Rao from 1991
political system liberal democratic federal republic
political parties All India Congress Committee (I), or Congress (I), cross-caste and cross-religion, left of center; Janata Dal, left of center; Bharatiya Janata Party (BJP), conservative Hindu-chauvinist; Communist Party of India (CPI), pro-Moscow Marxist-Leninist; Communist Party of India–Marxist (CPI–M), West Bengal–based moderate socialist
exports tea (world's largest producer),

coffee, fish, iron and steel, leather, textiles, clothing, polished diamonds
currency rupee
population (1991 est) 844,000,000 (920 women to every 1,000 men); growth rate 2.0% p.a.
life expectancy men 56, women 55
languages Hindi (widely spoken in N India), English, and 14 other official languages: Assamese, Bengali, Gujarati, Kannada, Kashmiri, Malayalam, Marathi, Oriya, Punjabi, Sanskrit, Sindhi, Tamil, Telugu, Urdu
media free press; government-owned broadcasting
religions Hindu 80%, Sunni Muslim 10%, Christian 2.5%, Sikh 2%
literacy men 57%, women 29% (1985 est)
GDP $220.8 bn (1987); $283 per head
chronology
1947 Independence achieved from Britain.
1950 Federal republic proclaimed.
1962 Border skirmishes with China.
1964 Death of Prime Minister Nehru. Border war with Pakistan over Kashmir.
1966 Indira Gandhi became prime minister.
1971 War with Pakistan leading to creation of Bangladesh.
1975–77 State of emergency proclaimed.
1977–79 Janata Party government in power.
1980 Indira Gandhi returned in landslide victory.
1984 Indira Gandhi assassinated; Rajiv Gandhi elected with record majority.
1987 Signing of "Tamil" Colombo peace accord with Sri Lanka; Indian Peacekeeping Force (IPKF) sent there. Public revelation of Bofors corruption scandal.
1988 New opposition party, Janata Dal, established by former finance minister V P Singh. Voting age lowered from 21 to 18.
1989 Congress (I) lost majority in general election, after Gandhi associates implicated in financial misconduct; Janata Dal minority government formed, with V P Singh prime minister.
1990 Central rule imposed in Jammu and Kashmir. V P Singh resigned; new minority Janata Dal government formed by Chandra Shekhar. Interethnic and religious violence in Punjab and elsewhere.
1991 Central rule imposed in Tamil Nadu. Shekhar resigned; elections called for May. May: Rajiv Gandhi assassinated. June: elections resumed, resulting in a Congress (I) minority government led by P V Narasimha Rao. Separatist violence continued.
1992 Congress (I) won control of state assembly and a majority in parliament in Punjab state elections. Split in Janata Dal opposition resulted in creation of National Front coalition party (including part of Janata Dal party).

The ⟩Dow Jones average indicates the general movement of the New York stock exchange.

index (plural *indices*) in mathematics, another term for ⟩exponent, the number that indicates the power to which a term should be raised.

Index Librorum Prohibitorum (Latin "Index of Prohibited Books") the list of books formerly officially forbidden to members of the Roman Catholic church. The process of condemning books and bringing the Index up to date was carried out by a congregation of cardinals, consultors, and examiners from the 16th century until its abolition 1966.

India country in S Asia, bounded N by China, Nepal, and Bhutan; E by Myanmar; NW by Pakistan; and SE, S, and SW by the Indian Ocean. Situated in the NE of India, N of the Bay of Bengal, is Bangladesh.
government India is a federal republic whose 1949 constitution contains elements from the US and British systems of government. It comprises 25 self-governing states, administered by a governor appointed by the federal president, and a council of ministers (headed by a chief minister) drawn from a legislature (legislative assembly) that is popularly elected for a five-year term. Eight of the larger states have a second chamber (legislative council).

The states have primary control over education, health, police, and local government and work in consultation with the center in the economic sphere. In times of crisis, central rule ("president's rule") can be imposed. There are also seven union territories, administered by a lieutenant-governor appointed by the federal president. The central (federal) government has sole responsibility in military and foreign affairs and plays a key role in economic affairs.

The titular, executive head of the federal government is the president, who is elected for five-year terms by an electoral college composed of members from both the federal parliament and the state legislatures. However, real executive power is held by a prime minister and cabinet drawn from the majority party or coalition within the federal parliament.

The two-chamber federal parliament has a 545-member lower house, Lok Sabha (house of the people), which has final authority over financial matters and whose members are directly elected for terms of a maximum of five years from single-member constituencies by universal suffrage, and a 244-member upper house, Rajya Sabha (council of states), whose members are indirectly elected, one-third at a time for six-year terms, by state legislatures on a regional quota basis. (Two seats in the Lok Sabha are reserved for Anglo-Indians, while the president nominates eight representatives of the Rajya Sabha.) Bills to become law must be approved by both chambers of parliament and receive the president's assent.
history For history before 1947, see ⟩India: history. Between 1947 and 1949 India temporarily remained under the supervision of a governor-general appointed by the British monarch until a new constitution was framed and approved. Former princely states (see ⟩India of the Princes; ⟩Kashmir) were integrated, and the old British provinces restructured into new states; in 1950 India was proclaimed a fully independent federal republic.
independent republic During its early years the republic faced the problem of resettling refugees from Pakistan and was involved in border skirmishes over Kashmir. Under the leadership of Prime Minister ⟩Nehru, land reforms, a new socialist economic program (involving protectionism), and an emphasis on heavy industries and government planning, were introduced. Sovereignty of parts of India held by France and Portugal was recovered 1950–61.

In foreign affairs, India remained within the British ⟩Commonwealth, was involved in border clashes with China 1962, and played a leading role in the formation of the ⟩nonaligned movement 1961. In 1964, Nehru died and was succeeded as prime minister by Lal Bahadur ⟩Shastri. There was a second war with Pakistan over Kashmir 1964.
Indira Gandhi's premiership Indira ⟩Gandhi (Nehru's daughter) became prime minister on Shastri's death 1966 and kept broadly to her father's policy program, but drew closer to the USSR with the signing of a 15-year economic and military assistance agreement 1973. In 1971 Indian troops invaded East Pakistan in support of separatist groups. They defeated Pakistan's troops and oversaw the creation of independent ⟩Bangladesh. In 1975, having been found guilty of electoral malpractice during the 1971 election, Indira Gandhi imposed a state of emergency and imprisoned almost 1,000 political opponents.

She was cleared of malpractice by the Supreme Court Nov 1975, but the "emergency" continued for two years, during which period a harsh compulsory birth-control program was introduced.

The state of emergency was lifted March 1977 for elections in which the opposition Janata Party was swept to power, led by Morarji ⟡Desai. The new government was undermined by economic difficulties and internal factional strife. Desai was toppled as prime minister 1979, and a coalition, under Charan Singh, was soon overthrown. In Jan 1980 the Congress (I) Party, led by Indira Gandhi, was returned to power with a landslide victory.

Amritsar massacre The new Gandhi administration was economically successful, but the problems of intercaste violence and regional unrest were such that the Congress (I) Party lost control of a number of states. The greatest unrest was in Punjab, where ⟡Sikh demands (see ⟡Sikhism) for greater religious recognition and for resolution of water and land disputes with neighboring states escalated into calls for the creation of a separate state of "Khalistan." In 1984, troops were sent into the Sikhs' most holy shrine, the Golden Temple at Amritsar, to dislodge the armed Sikh extremist leader Sant Jarnail Singh Bhindranwale, resulting in the deaths of Bhindranwale and hundreds of his supporters. The ensuing Sikh backlash brought troop mutinies, culminating in the assassination of Indira Gandhi by her Sikh bodyguards Oct 1984. In Delhi, retaliating Hindus massacred 3,000 Sikhs before the new prime minister, Rajiv ⟡Gandhi (Indira's elder son), restored order.

In Dec 1984 ⟡Bhopal in central India became the site of a major industrial accident in which more than 2,500 people were killed.

reform In the elections of Dec 1984, Congress (I), benefiting from a wave of public sympathy, gained a record victory. As prime minister, Rajiv Gandhi pledged to modernize and inject greater market efficiency into the Indian economy and to resolve the Punjab, Assam, and Kashmir disputes. Early reforms and the spread of technology, with India launching its first space satellite, augured well. Progress was made toward resolving the ethnic disputes in Assam and the hill areas, with 25 years of rebellion ended in Mizoram, which was made a new state of the Indian Union. However, Gandhi was unable to resolve the Punjab problem, with Sikh-Hindu ethnic conflict continuing, while in N India Hindu-Muslim relations deteriorated. Gandhi's enthusiasm for economic reform also waned from 1986 and his personal reputation was sullied by the uncovering of the "Bofors scandal" by finance minister V P ⟡Singh, involving alleged financial kickbacks received by government-connected organizations from a $1,400-million arms contract with the Swedish Bofors Corporation. In N Sri Lanka, where an Indian Peacekeeping Force (IPKF) had been sent July 1987 as part of an ambitious peace settlement, Indian troops became bogged down in a civil war.

coalition government R Venkataraman was sworn in as president July 1987. Despite bumper harvests 1988–89, Gandhi's popularity continued to fall. V P Singh, who was dismissed from Congress (I) 1987, attacked Gandhi's increasingly dictatorial style and became the recognized leader of the opposition forces, which united under the Janata Dal umbrella Oct 1988. In the general election Nov 1989 a broad anti-Congress electoral pact was forged, embracing the Janata Dal (People's Party),

Bharatiya Janata Party (BJP), both factions of the Communist Party, and the regional-level Telugu Desam. This ensured that Congress (I) failed to secure a working majority. Gandhi resigned from office and V P Singh, widely respected for his incorruptibility, took over at the head of a minority National Front coalition.

separatist violence Singh's main objective was the lowering of racial tensions. However, in Jan 1990 Muslim separatist violence erupted in Kashmir, forcing the imposition of direct rule and leading to a deterioration of relations with Pakistan. Relations were improved with the neighboring states of Bhutan, Nepal (which had been subject to a partial border blockade by India during 1989), and Sri Lanka, with whom a date (March 31, 1990) was agreed for the withdrawal of the IPKF. President's rule was imposed over Jammu and Kashmir July 1990 and over Assam Nov 1990, as a result of the rising tide of separatist violence. Punjab, where interethnic murders climbed to record heights from Nov, was already under president's rule begun 1983.

During the summer and early autumn of 1990 the Janata Dal government of V P Singh was rocked by a series of events, including the prime minister's decision to employ more low-caste workers in government and public-sector jobs, which resulted in protests by high-caste students and a split in the Janata Dal. Chandra Shekhar, a long-time Singh opponent, emerged as the leader of a rebel faction. Hindu militants (the Vishwa Hindu Parishad) announced that on Oct 30, 1990 they would begin to build a "birthplace" temple dedicated to the warrior god Ram on the site of a mosque in the northern city of Ayodhya. This precipitated serious communal tensions, which the government was unable to quell. On Nov 7, after troops had fired on Hindu fanatics who were attempting to storm the Ayodhya mosque, the Singh government was voted out of office.

minority government A new minority government was formed by Chandra Shekhar, who led a tiny Janata Dal socialist faction comprising 56 deputies, and was assured of outside support by the Congress Party of Rajiv Gandhi (who had declined the president's invitation to head a government of his own). Violence continued, with a total of 890 people killed and 4,000 injured in Hindu-Muslim riots and 3,560 people killed in the continuing ethnic strife in Punjab 1990. The higher oil prices due to the crisis in the Persian Gulf badly hit India's economy. At the end of Jan 1991 Shekhar dismissed the opposition-led government of the large southern state of Tamil Nadu, citing the presence of Tamil Tiger rebels from N Sri Lanka. This brought to four the number of states subject to direct rule. In March, Shekhar fell out with his backers, Congress (I), and tendered his resignation, but continued as caretaker premier until elections May 1991.

assassination of Rajiv Gandhi On May 21, 1991, a day after the first round of voting had taken place in the general election, Rajiv Gandhi was assassinated at Sriperumpudur, near Madras, by a bomb strapped to a guerrilla. She was one of the Liberation Tigers of Tamil Eelam (LTTE) who had "targeted" Gandhi ever since he had sent Indian peacekeeping forces into N Sri Lanka 1987. P V Narasimha Rao, an experienced southerner, was unanimously elected Congress (I) party president May 29, 1991.

Congress (I) minority government Gandhi's assassination occurred in the wake of what

had been the most violent election campaign in Indian history, with several hundred dying in election-related violence in N India where Hindu, Muslim, and Sikh communal tensions were acute. Fortunately, there was subsequent calm, with polling being delayed until mid-June 1991 in seats not already contested. In this election, Congress (I), benefiting from a sympathy vote, emerged as the largest single party, capturing, along with its allies, around 240 of the 511 seats contested. The BJP, which had performed particularly strongly before Rajiv Gandhi's assassination, captured 125 seats and 25% of the popular vote, V P Singh's National Front and Left Front (Communist Party) allies captured 125 seats, while the Samajwadi Janata Party of the outgoing premier, Chandra Shekhar, captured only five seats. Congress (I) polled well in central and S India, but was defeated by the BJP in its traditional northern Hindu-belt heartland of Uttar Pradesh, where a BJP state government was subsequently formed. The BJP's rise was the most striking development during this election. A union Congress (I) minority government was established after the election and headed by P V Narasimha Rao, who was named prime minister on June 20. In what some observers termed an "economic revolution," subsidies were slashed, inward foreign investment encouraged, and industrial licensing scrapped, bringing an end to what had been termed the "permit raj," in a new industrial policy July 1991.

violence continues The president's rule was extended over Jammu and Kashmir in Sept 1991 for a further six months and was imposed in Meghalaya in Oct 1991. In Punjab, where killings averaged 600 a month during 1991, the president's rule would remain in force until state elections in Feb 1992. In Sept 1991 a Places of Worship Bill was passed, prohibiting the conversion of any place of worship that existed at the Independence (1947), thus debarring Hindus from converting mosques into temples. Despite the mosque in Ayodyha being exempted from its terms, the bill was opposed by the Hindu-chauvinist BJP.

economic reform Prime Minister Rao continued to introduce reforms designed to make the economy more market-conscious and open it up to greater investment. In Nov 1991, in compliance with the conditions for a loan from the International Monetary Fund of US$ 2.2 billion, it was agreed that fertilizer subsidies should be cut, with small farmers being exempted, and unprofitable factories closed down.

The position of Rao's minority government was strengthened Jan 1992 when a split occurred in the opposition Janata Dal and a number of its deputies left and sought alliance with Congress (I). In elections held Feb 1992 in strife-torn Punjab, Congress (I) won control of the state assembly and a majority in parliament. However, despite heavy security, turnout was only 28%, with the main Sikh nationalist party opponents of Congress boycotting the contest.

foreign relations Despite the breakup of the USSR, economic and military links with Russia remained close. A thaw in relations with China resulted in Dec 1991 after the visit to India of Li Penh, the first Chinese premier to visit India since the border conflict of 1962. In Jan 1992 full diplomatic relations with Israel were established. *See illustration box.*

Indiana state of the midwest US; nickname Hoosier State
area 36,168 sq mi/93,700 sq km
capital Indianapolis

cities Fort Wayne, Gary, Evansville, South Bend
features Wabash River; Wyandotte Cavern; Indiana Dunes National Lakeshore; Indianapolis Motor Speedway and Museum; George Rogers National Historic Park, Vincennes; Robert Owen's utopian commune, New Harmony; Lincoln Boyhood National Memorial
products corn, pigs, soybeans, limestone, machinery, electrical goods, coal, steel, iron, chemicals
population (1990) 5,544,200
famous people Hoagy Carmichael, Eugene V Debs, Theodore Dreiser, Michael Jackson, Cole Porter, Dan Quayle, Wilbur Wright
history explored for France by La Salle 1679–80; first colonial settlements established 1731–35 by French traders; ceded to Britain by France 1763; passed to US control 1783; became a state 1816. Indiana became an important industrial state in the early 20th century, with steel mills, oil refineries, and factories producing automobiles and auto parts. However, the state remained one-third rural in the mid-1980s, and agriculture retained much of its former importance.

Indianapolis capital and largest city of Indiana, on the White River; population (1990) 731,300. It is an industrial center and venue of the "Indianapolis 500" automobile race.

To end its heavy reliance on recession-prone auto manufacturing, the city has exploited its

India: states and union territories

state	capital	area in sq km
Andhra Pradesh	Hyderabad	276,800
Arunachal Pradesh	Itanagar	83,600
Assam	Dispur	78,400
Bihar	Patna	173,900
Goa	Panaji	3,700
Gujarat	Gandhinagar	196,000
Haryana	Chandigarh	44,200
Himachal Pradesh	Simla	55,700
Jammu and Kashmir	Srinagar	101,300
Karnataka	Bangalore	191,800
Kerala	Trivandrum	38,900
Madhya Pradesh	Bhopal	442,800
Maharashtra	Bombay	307,800
Manipur	Imphal	22,400
Meghalaya	Shillong	22,500
Mizoram	Aizawl	21,100
Nagaland	Kohima	16,500
Orissa	Bhubaneswar	155,800
Punjab	Chandigarh	50,400
Rajasthan	Jaipur	342,200
Sikkim	Gangtok	7,300
Tamil Nadu	Madras	130,100
Tripura	Agartala	10,500
Uttar Pradesh	Lucknow	294,400
West Bengal	Calcutta	87,900
Union territory		
Andaman and Nicobar Islands	Port Blair	8,200
Chandigarh	Chandigarh	114
Dadra and Nagar Haveli	Silvassa	490
Daman and Diu	Daman	110
Delhi	Delhi	1,500
Lakshadweep	Kavaratti	32
Pondicherry	Pondicherry	492

India: history

c. 2500–c. 1600 BC	The earliest Indian civilization evolved in the Indus Valley; two major city-states are known, ▷Harappa and ▷Mohenjo Daro. They exhibit permanent architecture with plumbing, city planning, artisans' quarters, granaries, and evidence of basic Hindu religion. Many other sites developed along the rivers from the Himalayas to the Arabian Sea, some 1,000 mi/1,609 km, forming the largest unitary civilization of the ancient world.
c. 1500	**Aryans**, militant horse-riding nomads, began to invade from the NW. They gradually overran the north and the Deccan plateau, intermarrying with the Dravidians, the majority people of the Indian subcontinent. From their religious beliefs developed Brahmanism (an early stage of ▷Hinduism).
c. 500	▷**Buddhism** and ▷Jainism developed.
321 BC–AD 184	The subcontinent, except the far south, was first unified under the **Mauryan emperors**.
c. 300–500	The north was again united under the **Gupta dynasty**; its rule was ended by the raids of the White Huns, which plunged India into anarchy.
11th–12th centuries	Raids on India were made by Muslim adventurers, Turks, Arabs, and Afghans, and in 1206 the first Muslim dynasty was set up at Delhi.
14th–16th centuries	Islam was established throughout the north and the Deccan, although the south maintained its independence under the Hindu **Vijayanagar dynasty**. In the 16th century Portuguese, Dutch, French, and English traders established trading bases on the coast.
1527–1858	The **Mogul emperors** included Babur (▷Zahir ud-din Mohammed) and his grandson Akbar. After 1707 the Mogul Empire fell into decline.
1756–63	During the Seven Years' War the ▷British East India Company overcame their French rivals and made themselves rulers of Bengal and the Carnatic.
1857–58	The ▷Sepoy Rebellion ended the rule of the British East India Company, which was established all over India, and rule was transferred to the British government.
1885	The India National Congress was founded (see Congress Party) as a focus for nationalism.
1915–47	Resistance to UK rule was organized under the leadership of Mohandas ▷Gandhi.
1947	British India was divided into the independent dominions of India (predominantly Hindu) and Pakistan (predominantly Muslim). For subsequent history, see ▷India.

central location to become a warehouse, distribution, and convention center. Educational facilities include the Indiana University Medical Center, and there is a 60,000-seat domed stadium. Indianapolis was settled 1820. In 1967 surrounding Marion County was annexed to the city.

Indianapolis Raceway US motor-sport circuit, built 1910 following the success of Brooklands in the UK. The Indianapolis 500 is staged here at the end of May each year as part of the Memorial Day weekend.

The circuit is 2.5 mi/4 km long and is rectangular with the four corners joined at slightly banked corners. The original circuit was made out of bricks, hence its nickname the "Brickyard."

Indian art the painting, sculpture, and architecture of India. Indian art dates back to the ancient Indus Valley civilization of about 3000 BC (see ▷Harappa and ▷Mohenjo Daro). Sophisticated artistic styles emerged from the 1st century AD. Buddhist art includes sculptures and murals. Hindu artists created sculptural schemes in caves and huge temple complexes; the Hindu style is lively, with voluptuous nude figures. The Islamic Mogul Empire of the 16th–17th centuries created an exquisite style of miniature painting, inspired by Persian examples.

Buddhist art In NW India the Gandhara kingdom produced the first known images of the Buddha in a monumental soft and rounded style that was exported, with the Buddhist religion, to China, Korea, and Japan. The Gupta kingdom, which emerged around the 4th century AD in the Ganges plain, continued to develop Buddhist art. Its sites include Sarnath and the caves of Ajanta, which have extensive remains of murals of the 5th and 6th centuries as well as sculpture.

Hindu art Hinduism advanced further in central and S India. Influenced by Buddhist art, Hindu artists created brilliant sculptural schemes in rock-cut caves at Mamallapuram, and huge temple complexes: for example, in Orissa, Konarak, and Khajuraho. The caves at Ellora are known for their ensemble of religious art (Buddhist, Hindu, and Jain) dating from the 6th and 7th centuries.

Mogul art dates from the Muslim invasion of NW India in the Middle Ages. The invaders destroyed Buddhist and Hindu temple art and introduced their own styles (see ▷Islamic art). An early example of their work is the Q'utb mosque of about 1200 in Delhi. By the 16th century the Moguls had established an extensive empire. Court artists excelled in miniature painting, particularly in the reigns of Jehangir and Shah Jahan (c. 1566–1658). Their subjects ranged from portraiture and histories to birds, animals, and flowers.

Indiana

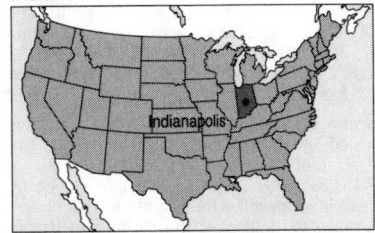

Indianapolis

Indian languages traditionally, the languages of the subcontinent of India; since 1947, the languages of the Republic of India. These number some 200, depending on whether a variety is classified as a language or a dialect. They fall into five main groups, the two most widespread of which are the Indo-European languages (mainly in the north) and the Dravidian languages (mainly in the south).

The Indo-European languages include two Classical languages, Sanskrit and Pali, and such modern languages as Bengali, Hindi, Gujarati, Marathi, Oriya, Punjabi, and Urdu. The Dravidian languages include Kannada, Malayalam, Tamil, and Telugu. A wide range of scripts is used, including Devanagari for Hindi, Arabic for Urdu, and distinct scripts for the various Dravidian languages. The Sino-Tibetan group of languages is used widely in Assam and along the Himalayas.

Indian literature for the literature of ancient India see ▷Sanskrit, ▷Veda, ▷Pali, and ▷Prakrit. In the 19th century Bengali emerged as a literary language, for example in the work of philologist Ram Mohan Roy, founder of Brahma Samaj, who paved the way for such writers as Bankim Chandra Chatterji and Romesh Chunder Dutt (1848–1909). Rabindranath Tagore's Nobel Prize 1913 confirmed the reputation of Bengali in world literature.

Subsequent writers include the poets Buddhadeva Bose (1908–) and Amiya Chakravarty. Other literary languages are Urdu (used by the novelist Prem Chand and poet-philosopher Iqbāl) and Gujarati (used by the poet Nanalal Devi and in the writings of Gandhi). The long association with Britain established English as a literary language, and writers in English—whose work is nonetheless wholly Indian in character—include the novelist Dhan Gopal Mukerji (1879–1949), the poet Sarojini Naidu (1879–1949), Sri Aurobindo (1872–1950), Dom Moraes (1938–), and Nehru. Tagore did little creative writing in English, but translated many of his own works. V S Naipaul is among overseas writers of Indian descent.

Indian music rich and diverse musical culture related to that of the Middle East. A characteristic Classical ensemble consists of two to four players representing solo melody (sitar, vina), drone accompaniment (tamboura), and rhythm (tabla). Players improvise to combinations of established modes (ragas) and rhythms (talas), associated with specific emotions, ritual functions, and times of day. Sitar improvisations are intensely incantatory in style and develop continuously, often for more than an hour. A close rapport exists among players and with audiences. Popular music makes use of larger orchestras including violins and reed organ, both introduced from Europe during the 18th and 19th centuries.

Indian Mutiny see ▷Sepoy Rebellion.

Indian Ocean ocean between Africa and Australia, with India to the N, and the S boundary being an arbitrary line from Cape Agulhas to S Tasmania; area 28,371,000 sq mi/73,500,000 sq km; average depth 12,708 ft/3,872 m. The greatest depth is the Java Trench 25,353 ft/7,725 m.

India of the Princes the 562 Indian states ruled by princes during the period of British control. They occupied an area of 715,964 sq mi/1,854,347 sq km (45% of the total area of pre-partition India) and had a population of over 93 million. At the partition of British

India in 1947 the princes were given independence by the British government but were advised to adhere to either India or Pakistan. Between 1947 and 1950 all except ▷Kashmir were incorporated in either country.

indicator species plant or animal whose presence or absence in an area indicates certain environmental conditions, such as soil type, high levels of pollution, or, in rivers, low levels of dissolved oxygen. Many plants show a preference for either alkaline or acid soil conditions, while certain trees require aluminum, and are found only in soils where it is present. Some lichens are sensitive to sulfur dioxide in the air, and absence of these species indicates atmospheric pollution.

indigenous the people, animals, and plants that are native to a region. Examples of indigenous peoples include Africans, Australian Aborigines, the Pacific Islanders, and American Indians. A World Council of Indigenous Peoples is based in Canada.

indigestion any pain or discomfort in the stomach or abdomen due to problems in the ▷digestive system.

indigo violet-blue vegetable dye obtained from plants of the genus *Indigofera*, family Leguminosae, but now replaced by a synthetic product. It was once a major export crop of India.

indium (Latin *indicum* "indigo") soft, ductile, silver-white, metallic element, symbol In, atomic number 49, atomic weight 114.82. It occurs in nature in some zinc ores, is resistant to abrasion, and is used as a coating on metal parts. It was discovered 1863 by German metallurgists Ferdinand Reich (1799–1882) and Hieronymus Richter (1824–1898), who named it after the two indigo lines of its spectrum.

Indo-Aryan languages another name for the ▷Indo-European languages.

Indochina French former collective name for ▷Cambodia, ▷Laos, and ▷Vietnam, which became independent after World War II.

Indochina War successful war of independence 1946–54 between the nationalist forces of what was to become Vietnam and France, the occupying colonial power.

In 1945 Vietnamese nationalist communist leader Ho Chi Minh proclaimed an independent Vietnamese republic, which soon began an armed struggle against French forces. France in turn set up a noncommunist state four years later. In 1954, after the siege of ▷Dien Bien Phu, a cease-fire was agreed between France and China that resulted in the establishment of two separate states, North and South Vietnam, divided by the 17th parallel.

Attempts at reunification of the country led subsequently to the ▷Vietnam War.

Indo-European languages family of languages that includes some of the world's major Classical languages (Sanskrit and Pali in India, Zend Avestan in Iran, Greek and Latin in Europe), as well as several of the most widely spoken languages (English worldwide; Spanish in Iberia, Latin America, and elsewhere; and the Hindi group of languages in N India). Indo-European languages were once located only along a geographical band from India through Iran into NW Asia, E Europe, the northern Mediterranean lands, N and W Europe and the British Isles.

When first discussed and described in the 19th century, this family was known as the Aryan and then the Indo-Germanic language

family. Because of unwelcome associations with the Nazi idea of "Aryan" racial purity and superiority, both titles have been abandoned by scholars in favor of the neutral "Indo-European."

In general terms, many Indo-European languages (such as English, French, and Hindi) have tended to evolve from the highly inflected to a more open or analytic grammatical style that does not greatly depend on complex grammatical endings to nouns, verbs, and adjectives. Eastern Indo-European languages are often called the *satem* group (Zend "a hundred") while western Indo-European languages are the *centum* group (Latin "a hundred"); this illustrates a split that occurred over 3,000 years ago, between those that had an *s*-sound in certain words and those that had a *k*-sound. Scholars have reconstructed a Proto-Indo-European ancestral language by comparing the sound systems and historical changes within the family, but continue to dispute the original homeland of this ancient form, some arguing for N Europe, others for Russia N of the Black Sea.

Indo-Germanic languages former name for the ▷Indo-European languages.

Indonesia country in SE Asia, made up of over 13,000 islands situated on or near the equator, between the Indian and Pacific oceans.

government Under the 1945 constitution, amended 1950 and 1969, the supreme political body in Indonesia is, in theory, the 1,000-member people's consultative council (Majelis Permusyawaratan Rakyat). This comprises the 500 members of the legislature (house of representatives) as well as 500 appointed representatives from regional assemblies and functional groups (including 200 from the armed forces). It sits at least once every five years to elect an executive president and vice-president, and determines the constitution.

The house of representatives, Dewan Perwakilan Rakyat, functions as a single-chamber legislature, comprising 400 directly elected members and 100 presidential appointees (of whom three-quarters represent the armed forces). It meets at least once a year, with elections every five years. At the head of the executive, and the most powerful political figure in Indonesia, is the president, elected by the people's consultative council for five-year terms. The president works with an appointed cabinet, exercises the right of veto over house of representatives' bills, and appoints governors to supervise local government in each of Indonesia's 27 provinces.

history Between 3000 and 500 BC, immigrants from S China displaced the original Melanesian population of Indonesia. Between AD 700 and 1450, two Hindu empires developed, to be superseded by Islam from the 13th century. During the 16th century English and Portuguese traders were active in Indonesia, but in 1595 Holland took over trade in the area. In the 17th century the Dutch had still only managed to establish trading centers, while extensive Indonesian kingdoms dominated the region, but by the 18th–19th centuries Dutch control was complete and the islands were proclaimed a Dutch colony 1816.

rise of nationalism A nationalist movement developed during the 1920s under the procommunist Indonesian Nationalist Party (PNI), headed by Achmed ▷Sukarno. This was suppressed by the Dutch, but in 1942, after Japan's occupation of the islands, the PNI was

Indonesia
Republic of (*Republik Indonesia*)

area 740,905 sq mi/1,919,443 sq km
capital Jakarta
cities Bandung; ports Surabaya, Semarang, Tandjungpriok
physical comprises 13,677 tropical islands, of the Greater Sunda group (including Java and Madura, part of Borneo (Kalimantan), Sumatra, Sulawesi and Belitung), and the Lesser Sundas/Nusa Tenggara (including Bali, Lombok, Sumbawa, Sumba, Flores, and Timor), as well as Malaku/Moluccas and part of New Guinea (Irian Jaya)
environment comparison of primary forest and 30-year-old secondary forest has shown that logging in Kalimantan has led to a 20% decline in tree species
head of state and government T N J Suharto from 1967
political system authoritarian nationalist republic
political parties Golkar, ruling military-bureaucrat, farmers' party; United Development Party (PPP), moderate Islamic; Indonesian Democratic Party (PDI), nationalist Christian
exports coffee, rubber, timber, palm oil, coconuts, tin, tea, tobacco, oil, liquid natural gas
currency rupiah

population (1989 est) 187,726,000 (including 300 ethnic groups); growth rate 2% p.a.; Indonesia has the world's largest Muslim population; Java is one of the world's most densely populated areas
life expectancy men 52, women 55
language Indonesian (official), closely allied to Malay; Javanese is the most widely spoken local dialect
religions Muslim 88%, Christian 10%, Buddhist and Hindu 2%
literacy men 83%, women 65% (1985 est)
GDP $69.7 bn (1987); $409 per head
chronology
17th century Dutch colonial rule established.
1942 Occupied by Japan; nationalist government established.
1945 Japanese surrender; nationalists declared independence under Sukarno.
1949 Formal transfer of Dutch sovereignty.
1950 Unitary constitution established.
1963 Western New Guinea (Irian Jaya) ceded by the Netherlands.
1965–66 Attempted communist coup; General Suharto imposed emergency administration, carried out massacre of hundreds of thousands.
1967 Sukarno replaced as president by Suharto.
1975 Guerrillas seeking independence for S Moluccas seized train and Indonesian consulate in the Netherlands, held Western hostages.
1976 Forced annexation of former Portuguese colony of East Timor.
1986 Institution of "transmigration program" to settle large numbers of Javanese on sparsely populated outer islands, particularly Irian Jaya.
1988 Partial easing of travel restrictions to East Timor. Suharto reelected for fifth term.
1989 Foreign debt reaches $50 billion; Western creditors offer aid on condition that concessions are made to foreign companies and that austerity measures are introduced.
1991 Democracy forums launched to promote political dialogue. Massacre in East Timor.
1992 The ruling Golkar party won the assembly elections.

installed in power as an anti-Western puppet government. When Japan surrendered to the Allies 1945, President Sukarno proclaimed Indonesia's independence. The Dutch challenged this by launching military expeditions before agreeing to transfer sovereignty 1949.
republic The new republic was planned as a federation of 16 constituent regions but was made unitary 1950. This led to dominance by Java (which has two-thirds of Indonesia's population), provoking revolts in Sumatra and the predominantly Christian South Moluccas. The paramount political figure in the new republic was President Sukarno, who ruled in an authoritarian manner and pursued an ambitious and expansionist foreign policy. He effected the transfer of Dutch New Guinea (Irian Jaya) to Indonesia 1963.
army massacre With the economy deteriorating, in 1965 an attempted coup against Sukarno by groups allegedly connected with the Indonesian Communist Party was firmly put down by army Chief of Staff General ◊Suharto, who then assumed power as emergency ruler 1966.

Suharto coordinated the massacre by the army of between 200,000 and 700,000 people in 1965; it was later revealed that US intelligence was directly linked to this massacre,

having provided the Indonesian military with lists of around 5,000 alleged members of the Indonesian Communist Party.
"New Order" Suharto formally replaced Sukarno as president 1967. He proceeded to institute what was termed a "New Order." This involved the concentration of political power in the hands of a coterie of army and security-force officers, the propagation of Pancasila, which stressed unity and social justice, the pursuit of a liberal economic program, and the fierce suppression of communist activity.

Rising oil exports brought significant industrial and agricultural growth to Indonesia during the 1970s, and self-sufficiency in rice production was attained by the 1980s. In addition, its borders were extended by the forcible annexation of the former Portuguese colony of ◊East Timor 1976. Suharto's authoritarian approach met with opposition from left-wing groups, from radical Muslims, and from separatist groups in outlying islands (most especially in Irian Jaya) and the S Moluccas.
resettlement of Javanese In Irian Jaya, following the suppression of a rebellion organized by the Free Papua Movement (OPM), a "transmigration" program was instituted by the Suharto government 1986, with the aim of resettling 65 million Javanese there and on

other sparsely populated "outer islands" by 2006. This encountered strong opposition from native Melanesians, prompting the emigration of more than 10,000 refugees to neighboring Papua New Guinea. Although travel restrictions were partly eased in East Timor 1988, the United Nations refused to recognize Indonesia's sovereignty over the area; an estimated 200,000 were killed or died of starvation in the years since the territory was closed to the outside world.
prodemocracy forums In April 1991, a 45-member Democracy Forum was launched by leading members of the country's religious and cultural intelligentsia, including Abdurrahman Wahid, leader of the Nahdatul Ulama, the country's largest Muslim association. In Aug 1991 a Forum for the Purification of People's Sovereignty (FPPS) was established by General Hartono Resko Dharsono, the country's most prominent dissident, released from prison Sept 1990. The formation of these groups is seen as an attempt to ventilate ideas about freedom in politics in what remains an authoritarian state.
foreign relations Indonesia has long pursued a nonaligned foreign policy, and is a member of ◊ASEAN. Under General Suharto, its relations with the West improved.
massacre in East Timor On Nov 12, 1991 soldiers opened fire in Dili, capital of East Timor, at the funeral of a student killed by the police during anti-Indonesian demonstrations two weeks earlier. Up to 180 were massacred and a further 300–400 arrested, with up to 60 executed on Nov 15, 1991. The Netherlands, the former colonial power, announced its suspension of foreign aid to Indonesia in response.

In the June 1992 assembly elections, the ruling Golkar party was returned with a reduced majority. *See illustration box.*

Indra Hindu god of the sky, shown as a four-armed man on a white elephant, carrying a thunderbolt. The intoxicating drink ◊soma is associated with him.

indri largest living lemur *Indri indri* of Madagascar. Black and white, almost tailless, it has long arms and legs. It grows to 2.3 ft/70 cm long. It is diurnal and arboreal. Its howl is doglike or human in tone. Like all lemurs, its survival is threatened by the widespread deforestation of Madagascar.

inductance in physics, a measure of the capability of an electronic circuit or circuit component to form a magnetic field or store magnetic energy when carrying a current. Its symbol is L, and its unit of measure is the ◊henry.

The magnetic field produced induces voltages in the same circuit or a nearby circuit.

induction in philosophy, the process of observing particular instances of things in order to derive general statements and laws of nature. It is the opposite of ◊deduction, which moves from general statements and principles to the particular.

Induction was criticized by the Scottish philosopher David ◊Hume because it relied upon belief rather than valid reasoning. In the philosophy of science, the "problem of induction" is a crucial area of debate: however much evidence there is for a proposition, there is the possibility of a future counterinstance that will invalidate the explanation. Therefore, it is argued, no scientific statement can be said to be true.

induction in obstetrics, deliberate intervention to initiate labor before it starts naturally; then it usually proceeds normally. Induction involves rupture of the fetal membranes (amniotomy) and the use of the hormone oxytocin to stimulate contractions of the womb. In biology, induction is a term used for various processes, including the production of an ⟩enzyme in response to a particular chemical in the cell, and the ⟩differentiation of cells in an ⟩embryo in response to the presence of neighboring tissues.

In obstetrics, induction is recommended as a medical necessity where there is risk to the mother or baby in waiting for labor to begin of its own accord.

induction coil type of electrical transformer, similar to an ⟩ignition coil, that produces an intermittent high-voltage alternating current from a low-voltage direct current supply.

It has a primary coil consisting of a few turns of thick wire wound around an iron core and passing a low voltage (usually from a battery). Wound on top of this is a secondary coil made up of many turns of thin wire. An iron armature and make-and-break mechanism (similar to that in an ⟩electric bell) repeatedly interrupts the current to the primary coil, producing a high, rapidly alternating current in the secondary circuit.

inductor device included in an electrical circuit because of its inductance.

indulgence in the Roman Catholic church, the total or partial remission of temporal punishment for sins which remain to be expiated after penitence and confession have secured exemption from eternal punishment. The doctrine of indulgence began as the commutation of church penances in exchange for suitable works of charity or money gifts to the church, and became a great source of church revenue. This trade in indulgences roused Luther in 1517 to initiate the Reformation. The Council of Trent 1563 recommended moderate retention of indulgences, and they continue, notably in "Holy Years."

Indus river in Asia, rising in Tibet and flowing 1,975 mi/3,180 km to the Arabian Sea. In 1960 the use of its waters, including those of its five tributaries, was divided between India (rivers Ravi, Beas, Sutlej) and Pakistan (rivers Indus, Jhelum, Chenab).

industrialization policy usually associated with modernization of developing countries where the process normally starts with the manufacture of simple goods that can replace imports. It is essential for economic development and largely responsible for the growth of cities.

industrial law or **labor law** the body of law relating to relationships between employers (and their representatives), employees (and their representatives), and government.

industrial relations relationship between employers and employees, and their dealings with each other. In most industries, wages and conditions are determined by **free collective bargaining** between employers and ⟩trade unions. Some European and American countries have **worker participation** through profit-sharing and industrial democracy. Another solution is **co-ownership**, in which a company is entirely owned by its employees. The aim of good industrial relations is to achieve a motivated, capable work force that sees its work as creative and fulfilling.

Another approach to industrial relations is that of the Japanese and Israelis, who encourage in their workers a feeling of belonging amounting almost to family membership.

When agreement cannot be reached by collective bargaining, outside arbitration is often sought. In the US, there is a highly developed system for private, third-party arbitration. Unions have long sought such provisions, but employers resisted, agreeing generally only in return for "no-strike" clauses in contracts. Working conditions, unfair treatment, and specific complaints are usually handled through the union *grievance system*, which requires written complaints from workers. New issues are becoming important in the US workplace, such as provision of day care, parental leave, and flexible working hours.

Industrial Revolution the sudden acceleration of technical and economic development that began in Britain in the second half of the 18th century. The traditional agrarian economy was replaced by one dominated by machinery and manufacturing, made possible through technical advances such as the steam engine. This transferred the balance of political power from the landowner to the industrial capitalist and created an urban working class. From 1830 to the early 20th century, the Industrial Revolution spread throughout Europe and the US and to Japan and the various colonial empires.

industrial sector any of the different groups into which industries may be divided: primary, secondary, tertiary, and quaternary. **Primary** industries extract or use raw materials; for example, mining and agriculture. **Secondary** industries are manufacturing industries, where raw materials are processed or components are assembled. **Tertiary** industries supply services such as retailing. The **quaternary** sector of industry is concerned with the professions and those services that require a high level of skill, expertise, and specialization. It includes education, research and development, administration, and financial services such as accounting.

Industrial Workers of the World (IWW) labor movement founded in Chicago 1905, and in Australia 1907, the members of which were popularly known as the **Wobblies**. The IWW was dedicated to the overthrow of capitalism and the creation of a single union for workers, but divided on tactics.

At its peak, (1912–15), the organization claimed to have 100,000 members, mainly in western mining and lumber areas, and in the textile mills of New England. Demonstrations were violently suppressed by the authorities. It gradually declined in popularity after 1917. See also ⟩syndicalism.

industry the extraction and conversion of raw materials, the manufacture of goods, and the provision of services. Industry can be either low technology, unspecialized, and labor-intensive, as in Third World countries, or highly automated, mechanized, and specialized, using advanced technology, as in the industrialized countries. Major trends in industrial activity 1960–90 were the growth of electronic, robotic, and microelectronic technologies, the expansion of the offshore oil industry, and the prominence of Japan and other Pacific-region countries in manufacturing and distributing electronics, computers, and motor vehicles.

Indus Valley civilization one of the four earliest ancient civilizations of the Old World

(the other three being the ⟩Sumerian civilization 3500 BC; ⟩Egypt 3000 BC; and ⟩China 2200 BC), developing in the NW of the Indian subcontinent about 2500 BC.

⟩Mohenjo-Daro and ⟩Harappa were the two main city complexes, but many more existed along the Indus valley, now in Pakistan. Remains include grid-planned streets with municipal drainage, public and private buildings, baths, temples, a standardized system of weights and measures—all of which testify to centralized political control. Evidence exists for trade with Sumer and Akkad. The ⟩Aryan invasion of about 1500 BC probably led to its downfall.

inert gas or **noble gas** any of a group of six elements (helium, neon, argon, krypton, xenon, and radon), so named because they were originally thought not to enter into any chemical reactions. This is now known to be incorrect: in 1962, xenon was made to combine with fluorine, and since then, compounds of argon, krypton, and radon with fluorine and/or oxygen have been described.

The extreme unreactivity of the inert gases is due to the stability of their electronic structure. All their electron shells (⟩energy levels) are filled and, with the exception of helium, all have eight electrons in their outer, or valency, shell (see ⟩atom, electronic structure).

inertia in physics, the tendency of an object to remain in a state of rest or uniform motion until an external force is applied, as stated by Isaac Newton's first law of motion (see ⟩Newton's laws of motion).

INF abbreviation for **intermediate nuclear forces**, as in the ⟩Intermediate Nuclear Forces Treaty.

infant a child below full legal age; see ⟩minor.

infanticide in law, the killing of a child under 12 months old by its mother. More generally, any killing of a newborn child, usually as a method of population control and most frequently of girls (especially in India and China), although boys are killed in countries where bride prices are high.

infantile paralysis former term for poliomyelitis. See ⟩poliomyelitis.

infant mortality rate measure of the number of infants dying under one year of age, usually expressed as the number of deaths per 1,000 live births. Improved sanitation, nutrition, and medical care have considerably lowered figures throughout much of the world; for example in the 18th century in the US and UK infant mortality was about 500 per thousand, compared with under 10 per thousand in 1989. In much of the Third World, however, the infant mortality rate remains high.

infarct or **infarction** death and scarring of a portion of the tissue in an organ, as a result of congestion or blockage of a vessel serving it. Myocardial infarction is the technical term for a heart attack.

infection invasion of the body by disease-causing organisms (pathogens, or germs) that become established, multiply, and produce symptoms. Bacteria and viruses cause most diseases, but there are other microorganisms, protozoans, and other parasites.

Most pathogens enter and leave the body through the digestive or respiratory tracts. Polio, dysentery, and typhoid are examples of diseases contracted by ingestion of contaminated foods or fluids. Organisms present in the saliva or nasal mucus are spread by airborne or droplet infection; fine droplets or dried particles are inhaled by others when the affected individual talks, coughs, or sneezes. Diseases such as measles, mumps, and tuberculosis are passed on in this way. The common cold is passed from hand to hand, which then touches the eye or nose. A less common route of entry is through the skin, either by contamination of an open wound (as in tetanus) or by penetration of the intact skin surface, as in a bite from a malaria-carrying mosquito. Relatively few diseases are transmissible by skin-to-skin contact. Glandular fever and herpes simplex (cold sore) may be passed on by kissing, and the group now officially bracketed as sexually transmitted diseases (⟡STDs) are mostly spread by intimate contact.

inferiority complex in psychology, a ⟡complex described by Alfred ⟡Adler based on physical inferiority; the term has been popularly used to describe general feelings of inferiority and the overcompensation that often ensues.

inferior planet a planet (Mercury or Venus) whose orbit lies between that of the Earth and the Sun.

inferno in astrophysics, a unit for describing the temperature inside a star. One inferno is 1 billion K, or approximately 1 billion °C.

infinite series in mathematics, a series of numbers consisting of a denumerably infinite sequence of terms. The sequence n, n^2, n^3, ... gives the series $n + n^2 + n^3 + ...$. For example, $1 + 2 + 3 + ...$ is a divergent infinite arithmetic series, and $8 + 4 + 2 + 1 + 1/2 + ...$ is a convergent infinite geometric series that has a sum to infinity of 16.

infinity mathematical quantity that is larger than any fixed assignable quantity; symbol ∞. By convention, the result of dividing any number by zero is regarded as infinity.

inflammation defensive reaction of the body tissues to disease or damage, including redness, swelling, and heat. Denoted by the suffix *-itis* (as in appendicitis), it may be acute or chronic, and may be accompanied by the formation of pus. This is an essential part of the healing process.

Inflammation occurs when damaged cells release a substance (⟡histamine) that causes blood vessels to widen and leak into the surrounding tissues. This phenomenon accounts for the redness, swelling, and heat. Pain is due partly to the pressure of swelling and also to irritation of nerve endings. Defensive white blood cells congregate within an area of inflammation to engulf and remove foreign matter and dead tissue.

inflation in economics, a rise in the general level of prices. The many causes include *cost-push inflation* that occurred 1974 as a result of the world price increase in oil, thus increasing production costs. *Demand-pull inflation* results when overall demand exceeds supply. Suppressed inflation occurs in controlled economies and is reflected in rationing, shortages, and black market prices. Deflation, a fall in the general level of prices, is the reverse of inflation.

inflation accounting method of accounting that allows for the changing purchasing power of money due to inflation.

inflection or *inflexion* in grammatical analysis, an ending or other element in a word that indicates its grammatical function (whether plural or singular, masculine or feminine, subject or object, and so on).

In a highly inflected language like Latin, nouns, verbs, and adjectives have many inflectional endings (for example, in the word *amabunt* the base *am* means "love" and the complex *abunt* indicates the kind of verb, the future tense, indicative mood, active voice, third person, and plurality). English has few inflections: for example, the *s* for plural forms (as in *the books*) and for the third person singular of verbs (as in *He runs*).

inflorescence flower-bearing branch, or system of branches, in plants. Inflorescences can be divided into two main types: *cymose* and *racemose*. In a cymose inflorescence, the terminal growing point produces a single flower and subsequent flowers arise on lower lateral branches, as in forget-me-not *Myosotis* and chickweed *Stellaria*; the oldest flowers are found at the apex. A racemose inflorescence consists of a main axis, bearing flowers along its length, with an active growing region at the apex, as in hyacinth and lupin; the oldest flowers are found near the base or, in cases where the inflorescence has become flattened, toward the outside.

An inflorescence is usually separated from the leaves by a stalk or peduncle and comprises two, three, or more individual flowers. The stalk of each individual flower is called a pedicel.

Types of racemose inflorescence include the *raceme* as seen in lupins, a spike which is similar but has stalkless flowers, for example, plantain *Plantago*; and a *corymb*, which is rounded or flat-topped, as in candytuft *Iberis amara*. A *panicle* is a branched inflorescence comprising a number of racemes, as seen in many grasses, for example, oats *Avena*.

An *umbel*, as in members of the carrot family (Umbelliferae), is a special type of racemose inflorescence with all the flower stalks arising from the same point on the main stem. Other types of racemose inflorescence include the ⟡catkin, ⟡spadix, and ⟡capitulum.

influenza any of various virus infections primarily affecting the air passages, accompanied by ⟡systemic effects such as fever, chills, headache, joint and muscle pains, and lassitude. Treatment is with bed rest and analgesic drugs such as aspirin and paracetamol.

Depending on the virus strain, influenza varies in virulence and duration, and there is always the risk of secondary (bacterial) infection of the lungs (pneumonia). Vaccines are effective against known strains but will not give protection against newly evolving viruses. The 1918–19 influenza pandemic (see ⟡epidemic) killed about 20 million people worldwide.

information technology collective term for the various technologies involved in processing and transmitting information. They include computing, telecommunications, and microelectronics.

infrared absorption spectrometry technique used to determine the mineral or chemical composition of artifacts and organic substances, particularly amber. A sample is bombarded by infrared radiation, which causes the atoms in it to vibrate at frequencies characteristic of the substance present, and absorb energy at those frequencies from the infrared spectrum, thus forming the basis for identification. The method is useful for detecting ambers from different sources.

infrared astronomy study of infrared radiation produced by relatively cool gas and dust in space, as in the areas around forming stars. In

1983, the Infra-Red Astronomy Satellite (IRAS) surveyed the entire sky at infrared wavelengths. It found five new comets, thousands of galaxies undergoing bursts of star formation, and the possibility of planetary systems forming around several dozen stars.

infrared radiation invisible electromagnetic radiation of wavelength between about 0.75 micrometers and 1 millimeter—that is, between the limit of the red end of the visible spectrum and the shortest microwaves. All bodies above the ⟡absolute zero of temperature absorb and radiate infrared radiation. Infrared radiation is used in medical photography and treatment, and in industry, astronomy, and criminology.

Infrared absorption spectra are used in chemical analysis, particularly for organic compounds. Objects that radiate infrared radiation can be photographed or made visible in the dark, or through mist or fog, on specially sensitized emulsions. This is important for military purposes and in detecting people buried under rubble. The strong absorption by many substances of infrared radiation is a useful method of applying heat, as in baking and toasting.

infrastructure relatively permanent facilities that service an industrial economy. Infrastructure usually includes roads, railroads, other communication networks, energy and water supply, and education and training facilities. Some definitions also include sociocultural installations such as health-care and leisure facilities.

ingestion process of taking food into the mouth. The method of food capture varies but may involve biting, sucking, or filtering. Many single-celled organisms have a region of their cell wall that acts as a mouth. In these cases surrounding tiny hairs (cilia) sweep food particles together, ready for ingestion.

Ingres Jean Auguste Dominique 1780–1867. French painter, a student of David and leading exponent of the Neo-Classical style. He studied and worked in Rome about 1807–20, where he began the *Odalisque* series of sensuous female nudes, then went to Florence, and returned to France 1824. His portraits painted in the 1840s–50s are meticulously detailed and highly polished.

Ingres's style developed in opposition to the Romanticism of Delacroix. Early works include portraits of Napoleon. Later he painted huge ceilings for the Louvre and for Autun Cathedral. His portraits include *Madame Moitessier* 1856 (National Gallery, London).

inhibition, neural in biology, the process in which activity in one ⟡nerve cell suppresses activity in another. Neural inhibition in networks of nerve cells leading from sensory organs, or to muscles, plays an important role in allowing an animal to make fine sensory discriminations and to exercise fine control over movements.

initiative, referendum, and recall processes used by voters to affect directly law making and the removal of elected representatives. An initiative petition is for the origination of a law or constitutional amendment, which is then either voted on in special or general election or acted on by the legislature. Referendum is a final approval vote on a law or policy. Recall is a petition method to remove an elected representative, by special election, before the term of office expires.

injunction court order that forbids a person from doing something, or orders him or her to take certain action. Breach of an injunction is ⟡contempt of court.

ink colored liquid used for writing, drawing, and printing. Traditional ink (blue, but later a permanent black) was produced from gallic acid and tannic acid, but inks are now based on synthetic dyes.

Inkatha (from the grass coil worn by Zulu women for carrying head loads; its many strands give it strength) South African political organization formed 1975 by Chief Gatsha ▷Buthelezi, leader of 6 million Zulus, the country's biggest ethnic group. Inkatha's avowed aim is to create a nonracial democratic political situation. Inkatha has tried to work with the white regime and, as a result, Buthelezi has been widely regarded as a collaborator. Fighting between Inkatha and African National Congress members cost more than 1,000 lives in the first five months of 1990. In 1991, revelations that Inkatha had received covert financial aid from the South African government during 1989–90 increased the ANC's distrust of its motives.

Inkerman, Battle of battle of the Crimean War, fought on Nov 5, 1854, during which an attack by the Russians on Inkerman Ridge, occupied by the British army besieging Sevastopol, was repulsed.

Inland Sea (Japanese *Seto Naikai*) arm of the Pacific Ocean, 240 mi/390 km long, almost enclosed by the Japanese islands of Honshu, Kyushu, and Shikoku. It has about 300 small islands.

Inness George 1825–1894. US landscape painter influenced by the ▷Hudson River school. His early works, such as *The Delaware Valley* 1865 (Metropolitan Museum of Art, New York), are on a grand scale and show a concern for natural effects of light. Later he moved toward Impressionism.

Innocent thirteen popes including:

Innocent III 1161–1216. Pope from 1198 who asserted papal power over secular princes, in particular over the succession of Holy Roman Emperors. He also made King ▷John of England his vassal, compelling him to accept Stephen ▷Langton as archbishop of Canterbury. He promoted the fourth Crusade and crusades against the non-Christian Livonians and Letts, and the Albigensian heretics of S France.

Innsbruck capital of Tirol state, W Austria; population (1981) 117,000. It is a tourist and winter sports center and a route junction for the Brenner Pass. The 1964 and 1976 Winter Olympics were held here.

inoculation injection into the body of dead or weakened disease-carrying organisms or their toxins (▷vaccine) to produce immunity by inducing a mild form of a disease.

inorganic chemistry branch of chemistry dealing with the chemical properties of the elements and their compounds, excluding the more complex covalent compounds of carbon, which are considered in ▷organic chemistry.

The origins of inorganic chemistry lay in observing the characteristics and experimenting with the uses of the substances (compounds and elements) that could be extracted from mineral ores. These could be classified according to their chemical properties: elements could be classified as metals or nonmetals; compounds as acids or bases, oxidizing or reducing agents, ionic compounds (such as salts), or covalent compounds (such as gases). The arrangement of elements into groups possessing similar properties led to Mendeleyev's ▷periodic table of the elements, which prompted chemists to predict the properties of undiscovered elements that might occupy gaps in the table. This, in turn, led to the discovery of new elements, including a number of highly radioactive elements that do not occur naturally.

input device device for entering information into a computer. Input devices include keyboards, joysticks, mice, light pens, touch-sensitive screens, graphics tablets, speech-recognition devices, and vision systems. Compare ▷output device.

Input devices that are used commercially—for example, by banks, postal services, and supermarkets—must be able to read and capture large volumes of data very rapidly. Such devices include document readers for magnetic-ink character recognition (MICR), optical character recognition (OCR), and optical mark recognition (OMR); mark-sense readers; bar-code scanners; magnetic-strip readers; and point-of-sale (POS) terminals. Punched-card and paper-tape readers were used in earlier commercial applications but are now obsolete.

inquest inquiry held by a coroner into an unexplained death. At an inquest, a coroner is assisted by a jury of between 7 and 11 people. Evidence is on oath, and medical and other witnesses may be summoned.

Inquisition tribunal of the Roman Catholic Church established 1233 to suppress heresy (dissenting views), originally by excommunication. Sentence was pronounced during a religious ceremony, the ▷auto-da-fé. The Inquisition operated in France, Italy, Spain, and the Holy Roman Empire, and was especially active following the ▷Reformation; it was later extended to the Americas. Its trials were conducted in secret, under torture, and penalties ranged from fines, through flogging and imprisonment, to death by burning.

During the course of the Spanish Inquisition, until its abolition 1834, some 60,000 cases were tried. The Roman Inquisition was established 1542 to combat the growth of Protestantism. The Inquisition or Holy Office (renamed Sacred Congregation for the Doctrine of the Faith 1965) still deals with ecclesiastical discipline.

In re Debs a US Supreme Court decision 1895 dealing with the right of the federal government to suppress labor movements. Eugene Debs, a well-known labor leader, was imprisoned for refusing to comply with a federal injunction against a boycott. Debs had helped organize the boycott of all Pullman carriers in support of the Pullman strike against pay cuts. The government arrested him under the Sherman Antitrust Act. Debs's lawyers petitioned for a writ of habeas corpus, arguing that the matter was outside of federal jurisdiction. The Court denied the writ, ruling that the government's actions were legal under its right to regulate interstate commerce and mail transportation.

In re Gault a US Supreme Court decision 1967 that established the right of minors to due process under the 14th Amendment. The parents of Gerald Gault, a 15-year-old sentenced to reform school by the Arizona juvenile court, filed for a writ of habeas corpus on the grounds that their son's detention after only a summary hearing violated his rights to counsel, notice of hearings, and cross examination and his protection against self-incrimination. The Supreme Court found that the juvenile court was in violation of the 14th Amendment, setting a clear precedent that minors were to be guaranteed due process of law.

insanity popular and legal term for mental disorder. In medicine the corresponding term is ▷psychosis.

insect any member of the class Insecta among the ▷arthropods or jointed-legged animals. An insect's body is divided into head, thorax, and abdomen. The head bears a pair of feelers or antennae, and attached to the thorax are three pairs of legs and usually two pairs of wings. The scientific study of insects is termed entomology. More than 1 million species are known, and several thousand new ones are discovered every year. Insects vary in size from 0.007 in/0.02 cm to 13.5 in/35 cm in length.

anatomy The skeleton is external and is composed of chitin. It is membranous at the joints, but elsewhere is hard. The head is the feeding and sensory center. It bears the antennae, eyes, and mouthparts. By means of the antennae, the insect detects odors and experiences the sense of touch. The eyes include compound eyes and simple eyes (ocelli). Compound eyes are formed of a large number of individual facets or lenses; there are about 4,000 lenses to each compound eye in the housefly. The mouthparts include a labrum, or upper lip; a pair of principal jaws, or mandibles; a pair of accessory jaws, or maxillae; and a labium, or lower lip. These mouthparts are modified in the various insect groups, depending on the diet. The thorax is the locomotory center, and is made up of three segments: the pro-, meso-, and metathorax. Each bears a pair of legs, and, in flying insecs, the second and third of these segments also each bear a pair of wings.

Wings are composed of an upper and a lower membrane, and between these two layers they are strengthened by a framework of chitinous tubes known as veins. The abdomen is the metabolic and reproductive center, where digestion, excretion, and the sexual functions take place. In the female, there is very commonly an egg-laying instrument, or ovipositor, and many insects have a pair of tail feelers, or cerci. Most insects breathe by means of fine airtubes called tracheae, which open to the exterior by a pair of breathing pores, or spiracles. Reproduction is by diverse means. In most insects, mating occurs once only, and death soon follows.

growth and metamorphosis When ready to hatch from the egg, the young insect forces its way through the chorion, or eggshell, and growth takes place in cycles that are interrupted by successive molts. After molting, the new cuticle is soft and pliable, and is able to adapt itself to increase in size and change of form.

Most of the lower orders of insects pass through a direct or incomplete metamorphosis. The young closely resemble the parents and are known as nymphs.

The higher groups of insects undergo indirect or complete metamorphosis. They hatch at an earlier stage of growth than nymphs and are termed larvae. The life of the insect is interrupted by a resting pupal stage when no food is taken. During this stage, the larval organs and tissues are transformed into those of the imago, or adult. Before pupating, the insect protects itself by selecting a suitable hiding place, or making a cocoon of some material which will merge in with its surroundings. When an insect is about to emerge from the pupa, or protective sheath, it undergoes its final molt, which consists of shedding the pupal cuticle. Many insects are seen as **pests**. They may be controlled by chemical insecticides (these may also kill useful insects), by importation of natural predators (that may themselves become pests), or, more recently, by the use of artificially reared sterile insects, either the males only, or in "population flushing" both sexes, so sharply reducing succeeding generations.

The **classification** of insects is largely based upon characters of the mouthparts, wings, and metamorphosis. Insects are divided into two subclasses (one with two divisions) and 29 orders.

insecticide any chemical pesticide used to kill insects. Among the most effective insecticides are synthetic organic chemicals such as ⟡DDT and dieldrin, which are chlorinated hydrocarbons. These chemicals, however, have proved persistent in the environment and are also poisonous to all animal life, including humans, and are consequently banned in many countries. Other synthetic insecticides include organic phosphorus compounds such as malathion. Insecticides prepared from plants, such as derris and pyrethrum, are safer to use but need to be applied frequently and carefully.

insectivore any animal whose diet is made up largely or exclusively of insects. In particular, the name is applied to mammals of the order Insectivora, which includes the shrews, hedgehogs, moles, and tenrecs.

insectivorous plant plant that can capture and digest live prey (normally insects), to obtain nitrogen compounds that are lacking in its usual marshy habitat. Some are passive traps, for example, the pitcher plants *Nepenthes* and *Sarracenia*. One pitcher-plant species has container-traps holding 3.5 pt/1.6 l of the liquid that "digests" its food, mostly insects but occasionally even rodents. Others, for example, sundews *Drosera*, butterworts *Pinguicula* and Venus's-flytrap *Dionaea muscipula*, have an active trapping mechanism; see ⟡leaf.

inselberg (German "island mountain") prominent steep-sided hill of resistant solid rock, such as granite, rising out of a plain, usually in a tropical area. Its rounded appearance is caused by so-called onion-skin ⟡weathering, in which the surface is eroded in successive layers.

The Sugar Loaf in Rio de Janeiro harbor in Brazil, and Ayers Rock in Northern Territory, Australia, are famous examples.

insemination, artificial see ⟡artificial insemination.

insider trading illegal use of privileged information in dealing on the stock exchanges—for example, when a company takeover bid is imminent. Insider trading is in theory detected by the Securities and Exchange Commission (SEC), and in 1988 the commission was authorized to offer bounties of up to 10% of the civil penalties to those who turned in inside traders. As one New York investment firm pleaded guilty to insider trading and paid more than $500 million in penalties, other stock markets, notably the French Bourse, suffered major inside-trading scandals.

instinct in ⟡ethology, behavior found in all equivalent members of a given species (for example, all the males, or all the females with young) that is presumed to be genetically determined.

Examples include a male robin's tendency to attack other male robins intruding on its territory and the tendency of many female mammals to care for their offspring. Instincts differ from ⟡reflexes in that they involve very much more complex actions, and learning often plays an important part in their development.

Institute for Advanced Study department of Princeton University in New Jersey, established 1933 to encourage gifted scientists to further their research uninterrupted by teaching duties or an imposed research scheme. Its first professor was Albert Einstein.

instrument landing system landing aid for aircraft that uses radio beacons on the ground and instruments on the flight deck. One beacon (localizer) sends out a vertical radio beam along the center line of the runway. Another beacon (glide slope) transmits a beam in the plane at right angles to the localizer beam at the ideal approach-path angle. The pilot can tell from the instruments how to maneuver to attain the correct approach path.

insulator any poor ⟡conductor of heat, sound, or electricity. Most substances lacking free (mobile) ⟡electrons, such as nonmetals, are electrical or thermal insulators.

Usually, devices of glass or porcelain, called insulators, are used for insulating and supporting overhead wires.

insulin protein ⟡hormone, produced by specialized cells in the islets of Langerhans in the pancreas, that regulates the metabolism (rate of activity) of glucose, fats, and proteins. Insulin was discovered by Canadian physician Frederick ⟡Banting, who pioneered its use in treating ⟡diabetes.

Normally, insulin is secreted in response to rising blood sugar levels (after a meal, for example), stimulating the body's cells to store the excess. Failure of this regulatory mechanism in diabetes mellitus requires treatment with insulin injections or capsules taken by mouth. Types vary from pig and beef insulins to synthetic and bioengineered ones. They may be combined with other substances to make them longer- or shorter-acting. Implanted, battery-powered insulin pumps deliver the hormone at a preset rate, to eliminate the unnatural rises and falls that result from conventional, subcutaneous (under the skin) delivery. Human insulin has now been produced from bacteria by ⟡genetic engineering techniques, but may increase the chance of sudden, unpredictable hypoglycemia, or low blood sugar. In 1990 the Medical College of Ohio developed gelatine capsules and an aspirinlike drug which helps the insulin pass into the bloodstream.

insect classification

class Insecta subclass	order	number of species	common names
Apterygota (wingless insects)			
	Thysanura	350	three-pronged bristletails, silverfish
	Diplura	400	two-pronged bristletails, campodeids, japygids
	Protura	50	minute insects living in soil
	Collembola	1500	springtails
Pterygota (winged insects or forms secondarily wingless)			
Divisions			
Exopterygota (young resemble adults but have externally developing wings)	Ephemeroptera	1,000	mayflies
	Odonata	5,000	dragonflies, damselflies
	Plecoptera	3,000	stoneflies
	Grylloblattodea	12	wingless soil-living insects of North America
	Orthoptera	20,000	crickets, grasshoppers, locusts, mantids, roaches
	Phasmida	2,000	stick insects, leaf insects
	Dermaptera	1,000	earwigs
	Embioptera	150	web-spinners
	Dictyoptera	5,000	cockroaches, praying mantises
	Isoptera	2,000	termites
	Zoraptera	16	tiny insects living in decaying plants
	Psocoptera	1,600	booklice, barklice, psocids
	Mallophaga	2,500	biting lice, mainly parasitic on birds
	Anoplura	250	sucking lice, mainly parasitic on mammals
	Hemiptera	55,000	true bugs, including aphids, shield-and bedbugs, froghoppers, pond skaters, water boatmen
	Thysanoptera	5,000	thrips
Endopterygota (young unlike adults, undergo sudden metamorphosis)	Neuroptera	4,500	lacewings, alder flies, snake flies, ant lions
	Mecoptera	300	scorpion flies
	Lepidoptera	165,000	butterflies, moths
	Trichoptera	3,000	caddis flies
	Diptera	70,000	true flies, including bluebottles, mosquitoes, leatherjackets, midges
	Siphonaptera	1,400	fleas
	Hymenoptera	100,000	bees, wasps, ants, sawflies
	Coleoptera	350,000	beetles, including weevils, ladybirds, glow-worms, woodworms, chafers

insurance contract guaranteeing compensation to the payer of periodic premiums against loss (under stipulated conditions) by fire, death, accident, and the like. Various consumer policies also insure legal or health services, paying bills or portions thereof, within the contracted conditions. Insurance is a major component of business activity, covering potential loss of property, inventory, or goods in transit.

integer any whole number. Integers may be positive or negative; 0 is an integer, and is often considered positive. Formally, integers are members of the set $Z = \{ \ldots -3, -2, -1, 0, 1, 2, 3, \ldots \}$. Fractions, such as 1½ and 0.35, are known as nonintegral numbers ers ("not integers").

integral calculus branch of mathematics using the process of ⊅integration. It is concerned with finding volumes and areas and summing infinitesimally small quantities.

integrated circuit (IC), popularly called **silicon chip**, a miniaturized electronic circuit produced on a single crystal, or chip, of a semiconducting material—usually silicon. It may contain many thousands of components and yet measure only 5 mm square and 1 mm thick. The IC is encapsulated within a plastic or ceramic case, and linked via gold wires to metal pins with which it is connected to a ⊅printed circuit board and the other components that make up such electronic devices as computers and calculators.

Integrated Services Digital Network (ISDN) internationally developed telecommunications system for sending signals in ⊅digital format along optical fibers and coaxial cable. It involves converting the "local loop"—the link between the user's telephone (or private automatic branch exchange) and the digital telephone exchange—from an ⊅analog system into a digital system, thereby greatly increasing the amount of information that can be carried. The first large-scale use of ISDN began in Japan 1988.

ISDN has advantages in higher voice quality, better-quality faxes, and the possibility of data transfer between computers six times faster than current modems. With ISDN's **Basic Rate Access**, a multiplexer divides one voice telephone line into three channels: two B bands and a D band. Each B band offers 64 kilobits per second and can carry one voice conversation or 50 simultaneous data calls at 1,200 bits per second. The D band is a data-signaling channel operating at 16 kilobits per second. With **Primary Rate Access**, ISDN provides 30 B channels.

integration in mathematics, a method in ⊅calculus of evaluating definite or indefinite integrals. An example of a definite integral can be thought of as finding the area under a curve (as represented by an algebraic expression or function) between particular values of the function's variable. In practice, integral calculus provides scientists with a powerful tool for doing calculations that involve a continually varying quantity (such as determining the position at any given instant of a space rocket that is accelerating away from Earth). Its basic principles were discovered in the late 1660s independently by the German philosopher ⊅Leibniz and the British scientist ⊅Newton.

intelligence in psychology, a general concept that summarizes the abilities of an individual in reasoning and problem solving, particularly in novel situations. These consist of a wide range of verbal and nonverbal skills and therefore some psychologists dispute a unitary concept of intelligence. See ⊅intelligence test.

intelligence in military and political affairs, information, often secretly or illegally obtained, about other countries. **Counterintelligence** is information on the activities of hostile agents. Much intelligence is gained by technical means, such as satellites and the electronic interception of data.

The Central Intelligence Agency is responsible for gathering foreign intelligence and for coordinating the reports of the several independent intelligence agencies. These include military intelligence branches within each armed service; the National Security Agency, responsible for technical intelligence gathering; and intelligence officers within the State Department and other executive agencies. Domestic intelligence is the responsibility of the ⊅Federal Bureau of Investigation. Double agents are motivated by money, ideology, or dissatisfaction to provide information to the ostensible enemy, often doing great damage. Moles are double agents who betray their own security services. Sleepers are agents who assume a normal life in the target country, often inactive for years until needed.

intelligence test test that attempts to measure innate intellectual ability, rather than acquired ability.

It is now generally believed that a child's ability in an intelligence test can be affected by his or her environment, cultural background, and teaching. There is skepticism about the accuracy of intelligence tests, but they are still widely used as a diagnostic tool when children display learning difficulties. "Sight and sound" intelligence tests, developed by Christopher Brand in 1981, avoid cultural bias and the pitfalls of improvement by practice. Subjects are shown a series of lines being flashed on a screen at increasing speed, and are asked to identify in each case the shorter of a pair; and when two notes are relayed over headphones, they are asked to identify which is the higher. There is a close correlation between these results and other intelligence test scores.

The French psychologist Alfred Binet (1857–1911) devised the first intelligence test in 1905. The concept of intelligence quotient (IQ) was adopted by US psychologist Lewis Terman in 1915. The IQ is calculated according to the formula: $IQ = MA/CA \times 100$ in which MA is "mental age" (the age at which an average child is able to perform given tasks) and CA is "chronological age," hence an average person has an IQ of 100 ± 10. Intelligence tests were first used on a large scale in the US in 1917 during World War I for two million drafted men, and their subsequent widespread use for education and employment decisions has provoked protests from minority groups who contend the tests are culturally biased and discriminatory.

Intelsat International Telecommunications Satellite Organization, established 1964 to operate a worldwide system of communications satellites. More than 100 countries are members of Intelsat, with headquarters in Washington, DC. Intelsat satellites are stationed in geostationary orbit (maintaining their positions relative to the Earth) over the Atlantic, Pacific, and Indian Oceans. The first Intelsat satellite was *Early Bird*, launched 1965.

intendant official appointed by the French crown under Louis XIV to administer a territorial *département*. Their powers were extensive but counteracted to some extent by other local officials. The term was also used for certain administrators in Spain, Portugal, and Latin America.

intensity in physics, the power (or energy per second) per unit area carried by a form of radiation or wave motion. It is an indication of the concentration of energy present and, if measured at varying distances from the source, of the effect of distance on this. For example, the intensity of light is a measure of its brightness, and may be shown to diminish with distance from its source in accordance with the ⊅inverse square law (its intensity is inversely proportional to the square of the distance).

interactive video (IV) computer-mediated system that enables the user to interact with and control information (including text, recorded speech, or moving images) stored on video disc. IV is most commonly used for training purposes, using analog video discs, but has wider applications with digital video systems such as CD-I (Compact Disc Interactive, from Philips and Sony) and DVI (Digital Video Interactive, from Intel).

Inter-American Development Bank (IADB) bank founded 1959, at the instigation of the Organization of American States, to finance economic and social development, particularly in the less wealthy regions of the Americas. Its membership includes the states of Central and Southern America, the Caribbean, and the US, as well as Austria, Belgium, Denmark, Finland, France, Germany, Israel, Italy, Japan, the Netherlands, Spain, Sweden, Switzerland, and the UK. Its headquarters are in Washington, DC.

interdict ecclesiastical punishment that excludes an individual, community, or realm from participation in spiritual activities except for communion. It was usually employed against heretics or realms whose ruler was an excommunicant.

interest in finance, a sum of money paid by a borrower to a lender in return for the loan, usually expressed as a percentage per annum. **Simple interest** is interest calculated as a straight percentage of the amount loaned or invested. In **compound interest**, the interest earned over a period of time (for example, per annum) is added to the investment, so that at the end of the next period interest is paid on that total.

A sum of $100 invested at 10% per annum simple interest for five years earns $10 a year, giving a total of $50 interest (and at the end of the period the investor receives a total of $150). The same sum of $100 invested for five years at 10% compound interest earns a total of $61.05 interest (with $161.05 returned at the end of the period). The difference arises from adding the previous period's interest to the capital before calculating the next payment.

interface in computing, the point of contact between two programs or pieces of equipment. The term is most often used for the physical connection between the computer and a ⊅peripheral device, which is used to compensate for differences in such operating characteristics as speed, data coding, voltage, and power consumption. For example, a **printer interface** is the cabling and circuitry used to transfer data from a computer to a printer, and to compensate for differences in speed and coding.

interference in physics, the phenomenon of two or more wave motions interacting and combining to produce a resultant wave of larger or smaller amplitude (depending on whether the combining waves are in or out of ⬦phase with each other).

Interference of white light (multiwavelength) results in spectral colored fringes; for example, the iridescent colors of oil films seen on water or soap bubbles (demonstrated by ⬦Newton's rings). Interference of sound waves of similar frequency produces the phenomenon of beats, often used by musicians when tuning an instrument. With monochromatic light (of a single wavelength), interference produces patterns of light and dark bands. This is the basis of ⬦holography, for example. Interferometry can also be applied to radio waves, and is a powerful tool in modern astronomy.

interferometer in physics, a device that splits a beam of light into two parts, the parts being recombined after traveling different paths to form an interference pattern of light and dark bands. Interferometers are used in many branches of science and industry where accurate measurements of distances and angles are needed.

In the Michelson interferometer, a light beam is split into two by a semisilvered mirror. The two beams are then reflected off fully silvered mirrors and recombined. The pattern of dark and light bands is sensitive to small alterations in the placing of the mirrors, so the interferometer can detect changes in their position to within one ten-millionth of a meter. Using lasers, compact devices of this kind can be built to measure distances, for example to check the accuracy of machine tools.

In radio astronomy, interferometers consist of separate radio telescopes, each observing the same distant object, such as a galaxy, in the sky. The signal received by each telescope is fed into a computer. Because the telescopes are in different places, the distance traveled by the signal to reach each differs and the overall signal is akin to the interference pattern in the Michelson interferometer. Computer analysis of the overall signal can build up a detailed picture of the source of the radio waves.

In space technology, interferometers are used in radio and radar systems. These include space-vehicle guidance systems, in which the position of the spacecraft is determined by combining the signals received by two precisely spaced antennae mounted on it.

interferon naturally occurring cellular protein that makes up part of the body's defenses against viral disease. Three types (alpha, beta, and gamma) are produced by infected cells and enter the bloodstream and uninfected cells, making them immune to virus attack.

Interferon was discovered 1957 by Scottish virologist Alick Isaacs. At present, only alpha interferon has any proven therapeutic value, and may be used to treat a rare type of ⬦leukemia.

interior decoration design, decoration, and furnishing of the inside of a building. In recent times the trend has been toward a less ornate and more functional style, fostered by the interaction of architects and designers working in teams, whether to remodel existing interiors, for example Misha Black and Hugh Casson, or in new buildings, for example Gio Ponti's Pirelli building (Milan), Oscar ⬦Niemeyer's capital city of Brasília, and the many works of ⬦Le Corbusier, Eero ⬦Saarinen, and

intermediate technology *The simple windmill is an example of intermediate technology if it utilizes local materials and traditional design.*

Skidmore, Owings, and Merrill. International-style furniture—light, geometric, simple, and functional—was designed, often by architects, to complement modern architecture.

Intermediate Nuclear Forces Treaty agreement signed Dec 8, 1987 between the US and the USSR to eliminate all ground-based nuclear missiles in Europe that were capable of hitting only European targets (including European Russia). It reduced the countries' nuclear arsenals by some 2,000 (4% of the total). The treaty included provisions for each country to inspect the other's bases.

intermediate technology application of mechanics, electrical engineering, and other technologies, based on inventions and designs developed in scientifically sophisticated cultures, but utilizing materials, assembly, and maintenance methods found in technologically less advanced regions (known as the ⬦Third World).

Intermediate technologies aim to allow developing countries to benefit from new techniques and inventions of the "First World," without the burdens of costly maintenance and supply of fuels and spare parts that in the Third World would represent an enormous and probably uneconomic overhead.

intermediate vector boson alternate name for **weakon**, the elementary particle responsible for carrying the weak nuclear force.

intermezzo in music, a short orchestral interlude often used between the acts of an opera to denote the passage of time; by extension, a short piece for an instrument to be played between other more substantial works.

intermolecular force or **van der Waals' force** force of attraction between molecules. Intermolecular forces are relatively weak; hence simple molecular compounds are gases, liquids, or low-melting-point solids.

internal-combustion engine heat engine in which fuel is burned inside the engine, contrasting with an external combustion engine (such as the steam engine) in which fuel is burned in a separate unit. The diesel and ⬦gasoline engine are both internal-combustion engines. Gas turbines and jet and rocket engines are sometimes also considered to be internal-combustion engines because they burn their fuel inside their combustion chambers.

International, the coordinating body established by labor and socialist organizations, including:
First International or *International Working Men's Association* 1864–72, formed in London under Karl ⬦Marx.
Second International 1889–1940, founded in Paris.
Third (Socialist) International or *Comintern* 1919–43, formed in Moscow by the Soviet leader Lenin, advocating from 1933 a popular front (communist, socialist, liberal) against the German dictator Hitler.
Fourth International or *Trotskyist International* 1936, somewhat indeterminate, anti-Stalinist.
Revived Socialist International 1951, formed in Frankfurt, Germany, a largely anticommunist association of social democrats.

International Atomic Energy Agency (IAEA) agency of the United Nations established 1957 to advise and assist member countries in the development and application of nuclear power, and to guard against its misuse. It has its headquarters in Vienna, and is responsible for research centers in Austria and Monaco, and the International Center for Theoretical Physics, Trieste, Italy, established 1964.

International Bank for Reconstruction and Development official name of the ⬦World Bank.

international biological standards drugs (such as penicillin and insulin) of which the activity for a specific mass (called the international unit, or IU) is prepared and stored under specific conditions, serves as a standard for measuring doses. For penicillin, one IU is the activity of 0.0006 mg of the sodium salt of penicillin, so a dose of a million units would be 0.6 g.

International Court of Justice main judicial organ of the ⬦United Nations, in The Hague, the Netherlands. It hears international law disputes as well as playing an advisory role to UN organs. It was set up by the UN charter 1945 and superseded the World Court. There are 15 judges, each from a different member state.

International Date Line (IDL) imaginary line that approximately follows the 180° line of longitude. The date is put forward a day when crossing the line going west, and back a day when going east. The IDL was chosen at the International Meridian Conference 1884.

International Development Association (IDA) agency of the United Nations, established 1960 and affiliated to the ⬦World Bank.

Internationale international revolutionary socialist anthem; composed 1870 and first sung

1888. The words by Eugène Pottier (1816–1887) were written shortly after Napoleon III's surrender to Prussia; the music is by Pierre Degeyter. It was the Soviet national anthem 1917–44.

International Finance Corporation agency of the ▷United Nations affiliated to the ▷World Bank. It was set up 1956 to facilitate loans for private investment to developing countries.

International Fund for Agricultural Development agency of the ▷United Nations, established 1977, to provide funds for benefiting the poor in developing countries.

International Gothic late Gothic style of painting prevalent in Europe in the 14th and 15th centuries. It is characterized by increased stylization and strong decorative qualities. Exponents include Antonio ▷Pisanello and the Franco-Flemish ▷Limbourg brothers.

International Labor Organization (ILO) agency of the United Nations, established 1919, which formulates standards for labor and social conditions. Its headquarters are in Geneva. It was awarded the Nobel Peace Prize 1969.

international law body of rules generally accepted as governing the relations between countries, pioneered by Hugo ▷Grotius, especially in matters of human rights, territory, and war.

Neither the League of Nations nor the United Nations proved able to enforce international law, successes being achieved only when the law coincided with the aims of a predominant major power—for example, in the ▷Korean War. The scope of the law is now extended to space—for example, the 1967 treaty that (among other things) banned nuclear weapons from space.

International Maritime Organization agency of the ▷United Nations concerned with world shipping. Established in 1958; headquarters in London, England.

International Monetary Fund (IMF) specialized agency of the ▷United Nations, headquarters Washington, DC, established under the 1944 ▷Bretton Woods agreement and operational since 1947. It seeks to promote international monetary cooperation and the growth of world trade, and to smooth multilateral payment arrangements among member states. IMF standby loans are available to members in balance-of-payments difficulties (the amount being governed by the member's quota), usually on the basis of acceptance of instruction on stipulated corrective measures.

The Fund also operates other drawing facilities, including several designed to provide preferential credit to developing countries with liquidity problems. Having previously operated in US dollars linked to gold, since 1972 the IMF has used the ▷special drawing right (SDR) as its standard unit of account, valued in terms of a weighted "basket" of major currencies. Since the 1971 Smithsonian agreement permitting wider fluctuations from specified currency parities, IMF rules have been progressively adapted to the increasing prevalence of fully floating exchange rates.

International Settlements, Bank for (BIS) See ▷Bank for International Settlements.

International Society for Krishna Consciousness (ISKCON) or Gaudiya Vaisnavism Hindu sect based on the demonstration of intense love for Krishna (an incarnation of the god Vishnu), especially by

chanting the mantra "Hare Krishna." Members wear distinctive yellow robes, and men often have their heads partly shaven. Their holy books are the Hindu scriptures and particularly the *Bhagavad-Gītā*, which they study daily.

The sect was introduced to the West by Swami Prabhupada (1896–1977). Members believe that by chanting the mantra and meditating on it they may achieve enlightenment and so remove themselves from the cycle of reincarnation. They are expected to live ascetic lives, avoiding meat, eggs, alcohol, tea, coffee, and other drugs, and gambling; sexual relationships should only take place within marriage and solely for procreation.

International Standards Organization international organization founded 1947 to standardize technical terms, specifications, units, and so on. Its headquarters are in Geneva.

International Telecommunication Union body belonging to the Economic and Social Council of the ▷United Nations. It aims to extend international cooperation by improving telecommunications of all kinds.

International Union for Conservation of Nature organization established by the ▷United Nations to promote the conservation of wildlife and habitats as part of the national policies of member states.

It has formulated guidelines and established research programs (for example, International Biological Program, IBP) and set up advisory bodies (such as Survival Commissions, SSC). In 1980, it launched the *World Conservation Strategy* to highlight particular problems, designating a small number of areas as *World Heritage Sites* to ensure their survival as unspoiled habitats (for example, Yosemite National Park in the US, and the Simen Mountains in Ethiopia).

internment detention of suspected criminals without trial. Foreign citizens are often interned during times of war or civil unrest.

interplanetary matter gas and dust thinly spread through the Solar System. The gas flows outwards from the Sun as the ▷solar wind. Fine dust lies in the plane of the Solar System, scattering sunlight to cause the ▷zodiacal light. Swarms of dust shed by comets enter the Earth's atmosphere to cause ▷meteor showers.

Interpol (abbreviation for *International Criminal Police Organization*) agency founded following the Second International Judicial Police Conference 1923 with its headquarters in Vienna, and reconstituted after World War II with its headquarters in Paris. It has an international criminal register, fingerprint file, and methods index.

interpreter computer program that translates and executes a program written in a high-level language. Unlike a ▷compiler, which produces a complete machine-code translation of the high-level program in one operation, an interpreter translates the source program, instruction by instruction, each time that program is run.

Because each instruction must be translated each time the source program is run, interpreted programs run far more slowly than do compiled programs. However, unlike compiled programs, they can be executed immediately without waiting for an intermediate compilation stage.

intersex individual that is intermediate between a normal male and a normal female in

its appearance (for example, a genetic male that lacks external genitalia and so resembles a female).

Intersexes are usually the result of an abnormal hormone balance during development (especially during ▷gestation) or of a failure of the ▷genes controlling sex determination. The term ▷hermaphrodite is sometimes erroneously used for intersexes.

Interstate Commerce Act in US history, an act of Congress 1887 responding to public concern regarding profiteering and malpractice by railroad companies. It required all charges to be reasonable and fair, and established the Interstate Commerce Commission to investigate railroad management. The act proved difficult to enforce.

interstellar molecules over 50 different types of molecule existing in gas clouds in our Galaxy. Most have been detected by their radio emissions, but some have been found by the absorption lines they produce in the spectra of starlight. The most complex molecules, many of them based on ▷carbon, are found in the dense clouds where stars are forming. They may be significant for the origin of life elsewhere in space.

intestacy absence of a will at a person's death. In law, special legal rules apply on intestacy for appointing administrators to deal with the deceased person's affairs, and for disposing of the deceased person's property in accordance with statutory provisions.

By the rules of hotchpot, lifetime gifts made to a person entitled to benefit under intestacy may be taken into account when the estate comes to be distributed.

intestine in vertebrates, the digestive tract from the stomach outlet to the anus. The human *small intestine* is 20 ft/6 m long, 1.5 in/4 cm in diameter, and consists of the duodenum, jejunum, and ileum; the *large intestine* is 5 ft/1.5 m long, 2.5 in/6 cm in diameter, and includes the cecum, colon, and rectum. Both are muscular tubes comprising an inner lining that secretes alkaline digestive juice, a submucous coat containing fine blood vessels and nerves, a muscular coat, and a serous coat covering all, supported by a strong peritoneum, which carries the blood and lymph vessels, and the nerves. The contents are passed along slowly by ▷peristalsis (waves of involuntary muscular action). The term intestine is also applied to the lower digestive tract of invertebrates.

Intifada (Arabic "resurgence" or "throwing off") Palestinian uprising; also the title of the involved *Liberation Army of Palestine*, a loosely organized group of adult and teenage Palestinians active since 1987 in attacks on armed Israeli troops in Israeli-occupied territories claimed by Palestinians. Their campaign for self-determination includes stone-throwing and gasoline bombing.

The uprising began Dec 1987 in Gaza. Rumors that a fatal traffic collision had been caused by Israeli security service agents in retaliation for the stabbing of an Israeli the previous week led to demonstrations by teenagers armed with slingshots. It subsequently spread, despite attempts at repression. Many Palestinian private homes have been dynamited by military order, under a still-valid British emergency regulation promulgated 1946 to put down Jewish guerrillas.

intrauterine device IUD or coil, a contraceptive device that is inserted into the womb (uterus). It is a tiny plastic object, sometimes containing copper. By causing a mild inflammation of the lining of the uterus it prevents fertilized eggs from becoming implanted.

IUDs are not usually given to women who have not had children. They are generally very reliable, as long as they stay in place, with a success rate of about 98%. Some women experience heavier and more painful periods, and there is a very small risk of a pelvic infection leading to infertility.

intravenous method of delivery of a substance directly into a vein.

intrusion mass of ⋄igneous rock that has formed by "injection" of molten rock, or magma, into existing cracks beneath the surface of the Earth, as distinct from a volcanic rock mass which has erupted from the surface. Intrusion features include vertical cylindrical structures such as stocks and necks, sheet structures such as dykes that cut across the strata and sills that push between them, and laccoliths, which are blisters that push up the overlying rock.

intuition rapid, unconscious thought process. In philosophy, intuition is that knowledge of a concept which does not derive directly from the senses. Thus, we may be said to have an intuitive idea of God, beauty, or justice. The concept of intuition is similar to Bertrand ⋄Russell's theory of knowledge by acquaintance. In both cases, it is contrasted with empirical knowledge (see ⋄empiricism).

intuitionism in mathematics, the theory that propositions can be built up only from intuitive concepts that we all recognize easily, such as unity or plurality. The concept of ⋄infinity, of which we have no intuitive experience, is thus not allowed.

Inuit people inhabiting the Arctic coasts of North America, the E islands of the Canadian Arctic, and the ice-free coasts of Greenland. Inuktitut, their language, has about 60,000 speakers; it belongs to the Eskimo-Aleut group. The Inuit object to the name Eskimos ("eaters of raw meat") given them by the Algonquin Indians.

In 1989 the Canadian government made over to the 17,000 Inuit of the E Arctic an area about half the size of France, including rights to hunt, fish, and levy royalties from the exploitation of mineral resources. A cash payment was also agreed in compensation for the Inuit's renunciation of other areas where they formerly lived.

Invar trademark for an alloy of iron containing 36% nickel, which expands or contracts very little when the temperature changes. It is used to make precision instruments (such as pendulums and tuning forks) whose dimensions must not alter.

Inverness town in Highland region, Scotland, lying in a sheltered site at the mouth of the river Ness; population (1985) 58,000. It is a tourist center with tweed, tanning, engineering, and distilling industries.

inverse square law in physics, the statement that the magnitude of an effect (usually a force) at a point is inversely proportional to the square of the distance between that point and the point location of its cause.

Light, sound, electrostatic force (Coulomb's law), gravitational force (Newton's law) and magnetic force (see ⋄magnetism) all obey the inverse square law.

invertebrate an animal without a backbone. The invertebrates form all of the major divisions of the animal kingdom called phyla, with the exception of vertebrates. Invertebrates include the sponges, coelenterates, flatworms, nematodes, annelids, arthropods, mollusks, and echinoderms. Primitive aquatic chordates such as sea squirts and lancelets, which only have notochords and do not possess a vertebral column of cartilage or bone, are sometimes called invertebrate chordates, but this is misleading, since the notochord is the precursor of the backbone in advanced chordates.

investiture contest conflict between the papacy and the Holy Roman Empire 1075–1122, which centered on the right of lay rulers to appoint prelates (investiture).

It began with the decree of 1075 in which Pope Gregory VII (1021–1085) forbade lay investiture and with Henry IV's excommunication the following year after he refused to accept the ruling. There was a lull in the conflict after Henry's death 1106, but in 1111, Henry V captured Paschal II (c. 1050–1118), and forced him to concede that only lay rulers could endow prelates with their temporalities (lands and other possessions). When this was overturned by the Lateran Council of 1112, the church split between pro-papal and pro-imperial factions, and fighting broke out in Germany and Italy. Settlement was reached 1122 at the Diet of Worms, when it was agreed that lay rulers could not appoint prelates but could continue to invest them with their temporalities.

investment in economics, the purchase of any asset with the potential to yield future financial benefit to the purchaser (such as a house, a work of art, stocks and shares, or even a private education).

Invisible Man 1952 novel by US writer Ralph Ellison about an unnamed hero who discovers that because of his blackness he lacks all social identity in postwar US society.

in vitro fertilization (IVF) ("fertilization in glass") allowing eggs and sperm to unite in a laboratory to form embryos. The embryos produced may then either be implanted into the womb of the otherwise infertile mother (an extension of artificial ⋄insemination), or used for research. The first baby to be produced by this method was born 1978 in the UK. In cases where the fallopian tubes are blocked, fertilization may be carried out by *intra-vaginal culture*, in which egg and sperm are incubated (in a plastic tube) in the mother's vagina, then transferred surgically into the uterus.

Recent extensions of the in vitro technique have included the birth of a baby from a frozen embryo (Australia 1984) and from a frozen egg (Australia 1986). British doctors were pioneers in the field. The technique is now common in the US. As yet the success rate is relatively low; only 15%–20% of in vitro fertilizations result in babies.

involute (Latin "rolled in") ⋄spiral that can be thought of as being traced by a point at the end of a taut nonelastic thread being wound onto or unwound from a spool.

Io in Greek mythology, a princess loved by ⋄Zeus, who transformed her into a heifer to hide her from the jealousy of ⋄Hera.

Io in astronomy, the third largest moon of the planet Jupiter, 2,260 mi/3,630 km in diameter, orbiting in 1.77 days at a distance of 262,000 mi/422,000 km. It is the most volcanically active body in the Solar System, covered by hundreds of vents that erupt not lava but sulfur, giving Io an orange-colored surface.

iodine (Greek *iodes* "violet") grayish-black nonmetallic element, symbol I, atomic number 53, atomic weight 126.9044. It is a member of the ⋄halogen group. Its crystals give off, when heated, a violet vapor with an irritating odor resembling that of chlorine. It only occurs in combination with other elements. Its salts are known as iodides, which are found in sea water. As a mineral nutrient it is vital to the proper functioning of the thyroid gland, where it occurs in trace amounts as part of the hormone thyroxine. Iodine is used in photography, in medicine as an antiseptic, and in making dyes.

Its radioactive isotope [131]I (half-life of eight days) is a dangerous fission product from nuclear explosions and from the nuclear reactors in power plants, since, if ingested, it can be taken up by the thyroid and damage it. It was discovered 1811 by French chemist B Courtois (1777–1838).

ion atom, or group of atoms, which is either positively charged (⋄cation) or negatively charged (⋄anion), as a result of the loss or gain of electrons during chemical reactions or exposure to certain forms of radiation.

Ion in Greek mythology, son of Apollo, ancestor of the Ionian or eastern Greeks, and subject of a play by ⋄Euripides.

Iona island in the Inner Hebrides; area 2,100 acres/850 hectares. A center of early Christianity, it is the site of a monastery founded 563 by

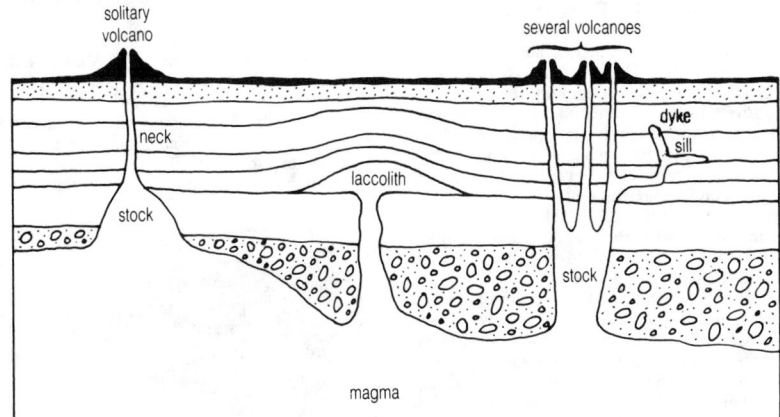

intrusion *Igneous intrusions can be a variety of shapes and sizes.*

St ⟡Columba. It later became a burial ground for Irish, Scottish, and Norwegian kings. It has a 13th-century abbey.

ion engine rocket engine that uses ⟡ions (charged particles) rather than hot gas for propulsion. Ion engines have been successfully tested in space, where they will eventually be used for gradual rather than sudden velocity changes. In an ion engine, atoms of mercury, for example, are ionized (given an electric charge by an electric field) and then accelerated at high speed by a more powerful electric field.

Ionesco Eugène 1912– . Romanian-born French dramatist, a leading exponent of the Theater of the ⟡Absurd. Most of his plays are in one act and concern the futility of language as a means of communication. These include *La Cantatrice chauve/The Bald Prima Donna* 1950 and *La Leçon/The Lesson* 1951. Later full-length plays include *Rhinocéros* 1958 and *Le Roi se meurt/Exit the King* 1961.

He has also written memoirs and a novel, *Le Solitaire/The Hermit* 1973.

ion exchange process whereby an ion in one compound is replaced by a different ion, of the same charge, from another compound.

Ion exchange is the basis of a type of ⟡chromatography in which the components of a mixture of ions in solution are separated according to the ease with which they will replace the ions on the polymer matrix through which they flow. Ion-exchange resins are used to soften water by exchanging the dissolved ions responsible for the water's hardness with others that do not have this effect. The exchange of positively charged ions is called cation exchange; that of negatively charged ions is called anion exchange.

Ionia in Classical times the W coast of Asia Minor, settled about 1000 BC by the Ionians; it included the cities of Ephesus, Miletus, and later Smyrna.

Ionian member of a Hellenic people from beyond the Black Sea who crossed the Balkans around 1980 BC and invaded Asia Minor. Driven back by the ⟡Hittites, they settled all over mainland Greece, later being supplanted by the Achaeans.

Ionian Islands (Greek *Ionioi Nisoi*) island group off the W coast of Greece; area 332 sq mi/860 sq km. A British protectorate from 1815 until their cession to Greece 1864, they include **Cephalonia** (Greek *Kefallínia*); **Corfu** (*Kérkyra*), a Venetian possession 1386–1797; **Cythera** (*Kíthira*); **Ithaca** (*Itháki*), the traditional home of ⟡Odysseus; **Leukas** (*Levkás*); **Paxos** (*Paxoí*); and **Zante** (*Zákynthos*).

Ionian Sea part of the Mediterranean that lies between Italy and Greece, to the S of the Adriatic, and containing the Ionian Islands.

Ionic in Classical architecture, one of the five types of column; see ⟡order.

ionic bond or *electrovalent bond* bond produced when atoms of one element donate electrons to another element that accepts the electrons, forming positively and negatively charged ⟡ions respectively. The electrostatic attraction between the oppositely charged ions constitutes the bond. Sodium chloride (Na^+Cl^-) is a typical ionic compound.

Each ion has the electronic structure of an inert gas (see ⟡noble gas structure). The maximum number of electrons that can be gained is usually two.

ionic compound substance composed of oppositely charged ions. All salts, most bases, and some acids are examples of ionic compounds. They possess the following general properties: they are crystalline solids with a high melting point; are soluble in water and insoluble in organic solvents; and always conduct electricity when molten or in aqueous solution. A typical ionic compound is sodium chloride (Na^+Cl^-).

ionization chamber any device for measuring ionizing radiation. The radiation ionizes the gas in the chamber and the ions formed are collected and measured as an electric charge. Ionization chambers are used for determining the intensity of X-rays or the disintegration rate of radioactive materials.

ionization therapy enhancement of the atmosphere of an environment by instrumentally boosting the negative ion content of the air.

Fumes, dust, cigarette smoke, and central heating cause negative ion deficiency, which particularly affects sufferers from respiratory disorders such as bronchitis, asthma, and sinusitis. Symptoms are alleviated by the use of ionizers in the home or workplace. In severe cases, ionization therapy is used as an adjunct to conventional treatment.

ionizing radiation radiation that knocks electrons from atoms during its passage, thereby leaving ions in its path. Alpha and beta particles are far more ionizing in their effect than are neutrons or gamma radiation.

ionosphere ionized layer of Earth's outer ⟡atmosphere (38–620 mi/60–1,000 km) that contains sufficient free electrons to modify the way in which radio waves are propagated, for instance by reflecting them back to Earth. The ionosphere is thought to be produced by absorption of the Sun's ultraviolet radiation.

ion plating method of applying corrosion-resistant metal coatings. The article is placed in argon gas, together with some coating metal, which vaporizes on heating and becomes ionized (acquires charged atoms) as it diffuses through the gas to form the coating. It has important applications in the aerospace industry.

IOU short for "I owe you"; written acknowledgment of debt, signed by the debtor; see also ⟡bill of exchange.

Iowa state of the midwest US; nickname Hawkeye State
area 56,279 sq mi/145,800 sq km
capital Des Moines
cities Cedar Rapids, Davenport, Sioux City
features Grant Wood Gallery, Davenport; Herbert Hoover birthplace, library, and museum near West Branch; "Little Switzerland" region in the NE, overlooking the Mississippi River; Effigy Mounds National Monument, near Marquette, a prehistoric Indian burial site
products cereals, soybeans, pigs and cattle, chemicals, farm machinery, electrical goods, hardwood lumber, minerals
population (1990) 2,776,800
famous people "Bix" Beiderbecke, "Buffalo Bill" Cody, Herbert Hoover, Glenn Miller, Lillian Russell, Grant Wood
history Sauk and Fox Indians were forced to cede their lands 1832 in what is now E Iowa. Blessed with rich topsoil, Iowa quickly attracted settlers, and it became a state 1846. The economy remains based on agriculture; the state usually leads all others in the production of corn, soybeans, and hogs.

Iowa City city in E Iowa, on the Iowa River, S

of Cedar Rapids, seat of Johnson County. It is a distribution center for the area's agricultural products. Other industries include printed matter and building materials. The University of Iowa 1847 is here; population (1990) 59,700.

ipecacuanha or *ipecac* South American plant *Psychotria ipecacuanha* of the madder family Rubiaceae, the dried roots of which are used as an emetic and in treating amebic dysentery.

Iphigenia in Greek mythology, a daughter of Agamemnon and Clytemnestra.

IQ (abbreviation for *intelligence quotient*) the ratio between a subject's "mental" and chronological ages, multiplied by 100. A score of 100±10 in an ⟡intelligence test is considered average.

Iqbāl Mohammed 1875–1938. Islamic poet and thinker. His literary works, in Urdu and Persian, were mostly verse in the Classical style, suitable for public recitation. He sought through his writings to arouse Muslims to take their place in the modern world.

His most celebrated work, the Persian *Asrā-e khūdī/Secrets of the Self* 1915, put forward a theory of the self that was opposite to the traditional abnegation found in Islam. He was an influence on the movement that led to the creation of Pakistan.

ir in physics, abbreviation for *infrared*.

IRA abbreviation for ⟡*Irish Republican Army*.

Iran country in SW Asia, bounded N by Armenia, Azerbaijan, the Caspian Sea, and Turkmenistan; E by Afghanistan and Pakistan; S and SW by the Gulf of Oman and the Persian Gulf; W by Iraq; and NW by Turkey.

government The constitution, which came into effect on the overthrow of the shah in 1979, provides for a president elected by universal suffrage and a single-chamber legislature, the Majlis (Islamic Consultative Assembly), consisting of 270 members, similarly elected. The president and the assembly serve a four-year term. All legislation passed by the assembly must be sent to the council for the protection of the constitution, consisting of six religious and six secular lawyers, to ensure that it complies with Islamic precepts. The president is the executive head of government but, like the assembly, ultimately subject to the will of the religious leader. Although a number of political parties exist, Iran is fundamentally a one-party state, the Islamic Republican Party having been founded 1978 to bring about the Islamic revolution.

history The name Iran is derived from the Aryan tribes, including the Medes and Persians, who overran Persia (see ⟡Persia, ancient) from 1600 BC. ⟡Cyrus the Great, who seized the Median throne 550, formed an empire including Babylonia, Syria, and Asia Minor, to which Egypt, Thrace, and Macedonia were later added. It was conquered

Iowa

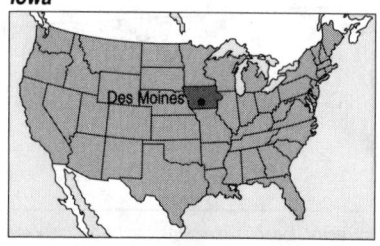

by Alexander the Great 334–328, then passed to his general Seleucus (c. 358–280) and his descendants, until overrun in the 3rd century BC by the Parthians. The Parthian dynasty was overthrown AD 226 by Ardashir, founder of the ◊Sassanian Empire.

During 633–41 Persia was conquered for Islam by the Arabs and then in 1037–55 came under the Turks of the ◊Seljuk Empire. Their empire broke up in the 12th century and was conquered in the 13th by the ◊Mongols. After 1334 Persia was again divided until its conquest by ◊Tamerlane in the 1380s. A period of violent disorder in the later 15th century was ended by the accession of the Safavi dynasty, who ruled 1499–1736 but were deposed by the great warrior Nadir Shah (ruled 1736–47), whose death was followed by instability until the accession of the Qajar dynasty (1794–1925).

During the 18th century Persia was threatened by Russian expansion, culminating in the loss of Georgia 1801 and a large part of Armenia 1828. Persian claims on Herat, Afghanistan, led to war with Britain 1856–57. Revolutions 1905 and 1909 resulted in the establishment of a parliamentary regime. During World War I the country was occupied by British and Russian forces. An officer, Col Reza Khan, was made minister of war following a coup 1921, and was crowned shah 1925; this allowed him to carry out a massive program of modernization.

after World War II During World War II, Iran, as it had become known, was occupied by British, US, and Soviet troops until 1946. Anti-British and anti-American feeling grew, and in 1951 the newly elected prime minister, Dr Mohammed Mossadegh, obtained legislative approval for the nationalization of Iran's largely foreign-owned petroleum industry. With US connivance, he was deposed in a 1953 coup, and the dispute over nationalization was settled the following year when oil-drilling concessions were granted to a consortium of eight companies. The shah took complete control of the government, and Iran enjoyed a period of political stability and economic growth 1965–77, based on oil revenue.

Iranian revolution By 1975 the shah had introduced a one-party system, based on the Rastakhis (Iran National Resurgence Party), but opposition to his regime was growing. The most effective opposition came from the religious leader Ayatollah Khomeini, who campaigned from exile in France. He demanded a return to the principles of Islam, and pressure on the shah became so great that in 1979 he left the country, leaving the way open for Khomeini's return. He appointed a provisional government, but power was placed essentially in the hands of the 15-member Islamic Revolutionary Council, controlled by Khomeini.

Islamic republic Iran was declared an Islamic republic, and a new constitution, based on Islamic principles, was adopted. Relations with the US were badly affected when a group of Iranian students took 63 Americans hostage at the US embassy in Tehran, demanding that the shah return to face trial. Even the shah's death, in Egypt 1980, did little to resolve the crisis, which ended when all the hostages were released Jan 1981.

Iran–Iraq War In its early years several rifts developed within the new Islamic government. Externally, the war with Iraq, which broke out 1980 after a border dispute, continued with considerable loss of life on both sides. Meanwhile, Islamic law was becoming stricter, with amputation as the penalty for theft and flogging for minor sexual offenses. By 1985 the failure to end the ◊Iran–Iraq War and the harshness of the Islamic codes were increasing opposition to Khomeini's regime but his position remained secure. The intervention of the US Navy to conduct convoys through the Gulf 1987–88 resulted in confrontations that proved costly for Iranian forces. Iraq gained the initiative on the battlefield, aided by its use of chemical weapons. By 1987 both sides in the war had increased the scale of their operations, each apparently believing that outright victory was possible. In Aug 1988, under heavy domestic and international pressure, Iran accepted the provisions for a United Nations–sponsored cease-fire. Full diplomatic relations with the UK were restored Dec 1988, but the issuing of a death threat to the author Salman ◊Rushdie caused a severance March 1989.

rebuilding the economy Khomeini's death in June 1989 provoked a power struggle between hard-line revolutionaries and so-called pragmatists who recognized a need for trade and cooperation with the West. Revelations in 1989 that Iran had negotiated secret oil sales to Israel reflected Iran's need for hard currency to rebuild its economy as well as a desire to counter Iraq. Struggle for succession began, ending with the confirmation of the former speaker of the Majlis, Hoshemi Rafsanjani, as president with increased powers. Despite his reputation for moderation and pragmatism, Iran's relations with the West were slow to improve. In Aug 1990 Iran accepted Iraq's generous peace terms, which virtually gave back everything it had claimed at the start of the Iran–Iraq War. During the Kurdish refugee crisis that followed the Gulf War, Iran took in nearly 1 million Kurds; it accused the US and relief agencies of neglecting the Kurds. Iran also condemned the Middle East peace conference held in Spain Nov 1991.

In May 1992 elections supporters of Rafsanjani claimed a majority win, constituting a major setback for Iran's Islamic militants. *See illustration box.*

Irangate US political scandal 1987 involving senior members of the Reagan administration (called this to echo the Nixon administration's ◊Watergate). Congressional hearings 1986–87 revealed that the US government had secretly sold weapons to Iran in 1985 and traded them for hostages held in Lebanon by pro-Iranian militias, and used the profits to supply right-wing Contra guerrillas in Nicaragua with arms. The attempt to get around the law (Boland amendment) specifically prohibiting military assistance to the Contras also broke other laws in the process.

Arms, including Hawk missiles, were sold to Iran via Israel (at a time when the US was publicly calling for a worldwide ban on sending arms to Iran), violating the law prohibiting the

Iran
Islamic Republic of (*Jomhori-e-Islami-e-Irân*; until 1935 **Persia**)

area 636,128 sq mi/1,648,000 sq km
capital Tehran
cities Isfahan, Mashhad, Tabriz, Shiraz, Ahvaz; chief port Abadan
physical plateau surrounded by mountains, including Elburz and Zagros; Lake Rezayeh; Dasht-Ekavir Desert; occupies islands of Abu Musa, Greater Tunb and Lesser Tunb in the Gulf
features ruins of Persepolis; Mount Demavend 18,603 ft/5,670 m
Leader of the Islamic Revolution Seyed Ali Khamenei from 1989
head of government Ali Akbar Hoshemi Rafsanjani from 1989
political system authoritarian Islamic republic
political party Islamic Republican Party (IRP), fundamentalist Islamic
exports carpets, cotton textiles, metalwork, leather goods, oil, petrochemicals, fruit
currency rial
population (1989 est) 51,005,000 (including minorities in Azerbaijan, Baluchistan, Khuzestan/Arabistan, and Kurdistan); growth rate 3.2% p.a.
life expectancy men 57, women 57
languages Farsi (official), Kurdish, Turkish, Arabic, English, French
religion Shiite Muslim (official) 92%, Sunni Muslim 5%, Zoroastrian 2%, Jewish, Baha'i, and Christian 1%
literacy men 62%, women 39% (1985 est)
GDP $86.4 bn (1987); $1,756 per head
chronology
1946 British, US, and Soviet forces left Iran.
1951 Oilfields nationalized by Prime Minister Mohammed Mossadegh.
1953 Mossadegh deposed and the US-backed shah took full control of the government.
1975 The shah introduced single-party system.
1978 Opposition to the shah organized from France by Ayatollah Khomeini.
1979 Shah left the country; Khomeini returned to create Islamic state. Revolutionaries seized US hostages at embassy in Tehran; US economic boycott.
1980 Start of Iran–Iraq War.
1981 US hostages released.
1984 Egyptian peace proposals rejected.
1985 Fighting intensified in Iran–Iraq War.
1988 Cease-fire; talks with Iraq began.
1989 Khomeini called for the death of British writer Salman Rushdie. June: Khomeini died; Ali Khamenei elected interim Leader of the Revolution; speaker of Iranian parliament Hoshemi Rafsanjani elected president. Secret oil deal with Israel revealed.
1990 Generous peace terms with Iraq accepted. Normal relations with UK restored.
1991 Imprisoned British business executive released. Nearly one million Kurds arrived in Iran from Iraq, fleeing persecution by Saddam Hussein after the Gulf War.
1992 Pro-Rafsanjani moderates won assembly elections.

sale of US weapons for resale to a third country listed as a "terrorist nation," as well as the law requiring sales above $14 million to be reported to Congress. The negotiator in the field was Lt Col Oliver North, a military aide to the National Security Council, reporting in the White House to the national-security adviser (first Robert McFarlane, then John Poindexter). North and his associates were also channeling donations to the Contras from individuals and from other countries, including $2 million from Taiwan, $10 million from the sultan of Brunei, and $32 million from Saudi Arabia.

The Congressional Joint Investigative Committee reported, in Nov 1987, that the president bore "ultimate responsibility" for allowing a "cabal of zealots" to seize control of the administration's policy, but found no firm evidence that President Reagan had actually been aware of the Contra diversion. Reagan persistently claimed to have no recall of events, and some evidence was withheld on grounds of "national security." North was tried and convicted in May 1989 on charges of obstructing Congress and unlawfully destroying government documents. Poindexter was found guilty on all counts in 1990.

Iranian language the main language of Iran, more commonly known as ⟡Persian or Farsi.

Iran–Iraq War or *Gulf War* war between Iran and Iraq 1980–88, claimed by the former to have begun with the Iraqi offensive Sept 21, 1980, and by the latter with the Iranian shelling of border posts Sept 4, 1980. Occasioned by a boundary dispute over the ⟡Shatt-al-Arab waterway, it fundamentally arose because of Saddam Hussein's fear of a weakening of his absolute power base in Iraq by Iran's encouragement of the Shiite majority in Iraq to rise against the Sunni government. An estimated 1 million people died in the war.

The war's course was marked by offensive and counter-offensive, interspersed with extended periods of stalemate. Chemical weapons were used, cities and the important oil installations of the area were the target for bombing raids and rocket attacks, and international shipping came under fire in the Persian Gulf (including in 1987 the US frigate *Stark*, which was attacked by the Iraqi airforce). Among Arab states, Iran was supported by Libya and Syria, the remainder supporting Iraq. Iran also benefited from secret US arms shipments, the disclosure of which in 1986 led to considerable scandal in the US, ⟡Irangate. The intervention of the US 1987, ostensibly to keep the sea lanes open, but seen by Iran as support for Iraq, heightened, rather than reduced, tension in the Gulf, and United Nations attempts to obtain a cease-fire failed. The war ended in Aug 1988 after cease-fire talks in Geneva.

Iraq country in SW Asia, bounded N by Turkey, E by Iran, SE by the Persian Gulf and Kuwait, S by Saudi Arabia, and W by Jordan and Syria.
government The 1970 constitution, amended 1973, 1974, and 1980, provides for a president who is head of state, prime minister, and chair of a Revolutionary Command Council (RCC). Day-to-day administration is under the control of a council of ministers over which the president also presides. The president is also regional secretary of the Arab Ba'ath Socialist Party which, although not the only political party in Iraq, so dominates the country's institutions as to make it virtually a one-party state. There is a 250-member national assembly.
history The area now occupied by Iraq was formerly ancient ⟡Mesopotamia and was

the center of the Sumerian, Babylonian, and Assyrian civilizations 6000 BC–AD 100. It was conquered 114 by the Romans and was ruled 266–632 by the native Sassanids before being invaded 633 by the Arabs. In 1065 the country was taken over by the Turks and was invaded by the Mongols 1258; Baghdad was destroyed 1401 by ⟡Tamerlane. Annexed by Suleiman the Magnificent 1533, Iraq became part of the Turkish Ottoman Empire 1638, as the separate *vilayets* (regions) of Basra, Baghdad, and Mosul.

independent kingdom Occupied by Britain in World War I, Iraq was placed under British administration by the League of Nations 1920. In 1932 Iraq became a fully independent kingdom, but until World War II Iraq's increasing formal autonomy masked a continued political and military control by Britain. In 1933 the reigning king, Faisal I, died and was succeeded by his son Ghazi; the leading figure behind the throne was the strongly pro-Western general Nuri-el-Said, who was prime minister 1930–58. In 1939 King Ghazi was killed in an accident, and Faisal II became king at the age of three, his uncle Prince Abdul Ilah acting as regent until 1953 when the king assumed full powers.

In 1955 Iraq signed the ⟡Baghdad Pact, a regional collective security agreement, with the

USSR seen as the main potential threat, and in 1958 joined Jordan in an Arab Federation, with King Faisal as head of state. In July of that year, a revolution overthrew the monarchy, and King Faisal, Prince Abdul Ilah, and General Nuri were all killed.

republic The constitution was suspended, and Iraq was declared a republic, with Brig Abdul Karim Kassem as head of a left-wing military regime. He withdrew from the Baghdad Pact 1959 and was killed 1963 in a coup led by Col Salem Aref, who established a new government, ended martial law, and within two years had introduced a civilian administration. He died in an airplane crash 1966, and his brother, who succeeded him, was ousted 1968 and replaced by Maj Gen Ahmed Hassan al-Bakr. He concentrated power in the hands of a Revolutionary Command Council (RCC) and made himself head of state, head of government, and chair of the RCC.

In 1979 Saddam Hussein, who for several years had been the real power in Iraq, replaced al-Bakr as RCC chair and state president. In 1980 he introduced a National Charter, reaffirming a policy close to the ⟡nonaligned movement and a constitution that provided for an elected national assembly. The first elections took place that year.

Iraq
Republic of (*al Jumhouriya al 'Iraqia* **)**

area 167,881 sq mi/434,924 sq km
capital Baghdad
cities Mosul and port of Basra
physical mountains in N, desert in W; wide valley of rivers Tigris and Euphrates NW–SE
environment a chemical-weapons plant covering an area of 25 sq mi/65 sq km, situated 80 km/50 mi NW of Baghdad, has been described by the UN as the largest toxic waste dump in the world
features reed architecture of the marsh Arabs; ancient sites of Eridu, Babylon, Nineveh, Ur, Ctesiphon
head of state and government Saddam Hussein al-Tikriti from 1979
political system one-party socialist republic
political party Arab Ba'ath Socialist Party, nationalist socialist
exports oil (prior to UN sanctions), wool, dates (80% of world supply)
currency Iraqi dinar
population (1989 est) 17,610,000 (Arabs 77%, Kurds 19%, Turks 2%); growth rate 3.6% p.a.
life expectancy men 62, women 63
languages Arabic (official); Kurdish, Assyrian, Armenian
religions Shiite Muslim 60%, Sunni Muslim

37%, Christian 3%
literacy men 68%, women 32% (1980 est)
GDP $42.3 bn (1987); $3,000 per head
chronology
1920 Iraq became a British League of Nations protectorate.
1921 Hashemite dynasty established, with Faisal I installed by Britain as king.
1932 Independence achieved from British protectorate status.
1958 Monarchy overthrown; Iraq became a republic.
1963 Joint Ba'athist-military coup headed by Col Salem Aref.
1968 Military coup put Maj Gen al-Bakr in power.
1979 Al-Bakr replaced by Saddam Hussein.
1980 War between Iraq and Iran broke out.
1985 Fighting intensified.
1988 Cease-fire; talks began with Iran. Iraq used chemical weapons against Kurdish rebels seeking greater autonomy.
1989 Unsuccessful coup against President Hussein; Iraq launched ballistic missile in successful test.
1990 Peace treaty favoring Iran agreed. Aug: Iraq invaded and annexed Kuwait, precipitating another Gulf crisis. US forces massed in Saudi Arabia at request of King Fahd. United Nations resolutions ordered Iraqi withdrawal from Kuwait and imposed total trade ban on Iraq; UN resolution sanctioning force approved. All foreign hostages released.
1991 Jan 16: US-led forces began aerial assault on Iraq; Iraq's infrastructure destroyed by bombing. Feb 23–28: land-sea-air offensive to free Kuwait successful. Uprisings of Kurds and Shiites brutally suppressed by surviving Iraqi troops. Talks between Kurdish leaders and Saddam Hussein about Kurdish autonomy. Allied troops withdrew after establishing "safe havens" for Kurds in the north, leaving a rapid-reaction force near the Turkish border. Allies threatened to bomb strategic targets in Iraq if full information about nuclear facilities denied to UN.
1992 UN imposed a "no-fly zone" over S Iraq to protect Shiites.

Iran–Iraq War Iraq had, since 1970, enjoyed a fluctuating relationship with Syria, sometimes distant and sometimes close enough to contemplate a complete political and economic union. By 1980, however, the atmosphere was cool. Relations between Iraq and Iran had been tense for some years, with disagreement over their shared border, which runs down the Shatt-al-Arab waterway. The 1979 Iranian revolution made Iraq more suspicious of Iran's intentions, and in 1980 a full-scale war broke out. Despite Iraq's inferior military strength, Iran gained little territory, and by 1986 it seemed as if a stalemate might have been reached. The fighting intensified again in early 1987, by which time hundreds of thousands of lives had been lost on both sides and incalculable damage to industry and property sustained. Following Iranian acceptance of United Nations cease-fire provisions, the war came to an end 1988. Peace talks made little progress on fundamental issues of territory or prisoner-of-war repatriation. Hussein took advantage of the end of hostilities to turn his combat-hardened army against Kurdish separatists, many of whom had sided with Iran. After the war's end, Iraq moved to support Christian forces in Lebanon against Syrian- and Iranian-backed Muslims. The Iraqis also launched a ballistic missile on a successful test, causing concern about Iraq's suspected nuclear-weapons development. In 1989 an unsuccessful coup attempt against President Hussein was reported.

Gulf War In 1990 Hussein reopened a long-standing territorial dispute with neighboring Kuwait while seeking to assume leadership of the Arab world. Following increasing diplomatic pressure, on Aug 2 Iraqi troops invaded and annexed Kuwait, installing a puppet government and declaring it part of Iraq. As Iraqi troops massed on his borders, King Fahd of Saudi Arabia requested help from the US and the UK, and a rapid buildup of US ground and air power and British aircraft began. Meanwhile the UN Security Council condemned the invasion, demanded Iraq's withdrawal, and imposed comprehensive sanctions including an embargo. These were to be enforced by a multinational naval force led by the US. To make its substantial presence in Saudi Arabia seem more legitimate, the US sought contributions from other UN members but with only limited success. Unsuccessful attempts to find a peaceful solution to the dispute were made by Egypt, Jordan, France, the US, the UK, and the UN.

To ensure the safety of his border, President Hussein hastily concluded a permanent peace treaty with Iran, under which he conceded virtually everything for which he had fought the Iran–Iraq War and both countries agreed to release all prisoners of war.

Refusing to withdraw from Kuwait, President Hussein sought to prevent a military strike against him by compelling thousands of non-Iraqi adult males, mainly British and American, living in Iraq to remain there, moving some to unknown strategic locations. Meanwhile, a mass exodus of foreign workers who were allowed to leave created enormous refugee problems in neighboring Jordan.

In Dec 1990 the UN Security Council set a Jan 15, 1991 deadline for Iraq's withdrawal from Kuwait, after which force could be used. Soon afterwards US president Bush offered talks with Iraq and proposed a UN-sponsored international conference to discuss the Middle East's problems. Saddam Hussein then announced that all foreign hostages in Kuwait

and Iraq would be allowed to return home. Nevertheless, Iraqi troops were not removed from Kuwait by the deadline and on Jan 16 the US-led Allied forces began the aerial bombardment of Baghdad as the first phase of operation Desert Storm, the military campaign to liberate Kuwait; the Iraqi military response during the air campaign was largely limited to the firing of Scud missiles into Israel and Saudi Arabia. A last-minute peace initiative by the USSR to avoid a land battle failed, and on Feb 23 the Allied land offensive began, with thousands of Iraqi troops immediately surrendering without a fight to the advancing Allied armies. On Feb 28, 1991, after 100 hours of ground fighting, the Iraqi forces capitulated and agreed to a cease-fire. The total number of Iraqis killed in the war was estimated at around 200,000. By March, Iraq had conceded to peace negotiations.

Various factions in Iraq began uprisings against the government after the withdrawal of the US and allied forces from northern Iraq in July 1991; these were soon quelled by government forces, leading to an immense refugee problem as Kurds in the north and Shiites in the south fled from their homes in fear of reprisals. An autonomy agreement offered to the Kurds was rejected in June and subsequent negotiations saw little progress. In Nov 1991 talks were resumed but Iraqi harassment of Kurds continued. After the initial compromise agreement on UN inspection of suspected arms-production sites in July 1991, Saddam Hussein continued to violate the terms of the cease-fire agreement, rejecting UN resolutions on weapons and human rights, and carrying out further obstruction of UN arms inspections. A coup attempt by Iraq's Republican Guard against Saddam Hussein July 1992 was thwarted by officers loyal to him. The conspiracy allegedly received backing from the US and Jordan although the US did not confirm the reports and Jordan denied any role in the plot. In Aug 1992 the UN Security Council imposed a "no-fly zone" over S Iraq to protect the Shiite community. *See illustration box.*

IRAS acronym for ***Infrared Astronomy Satellite***, a joint US-UK-Dutch satellite launched 1983 to survey the sky at infrared wavelengths, studying areas of star formation, distant galaxies, possible embryo planetary systems around other stars, and discovering five new comets in our own Solar System.

Ireland one of the British Isles, lying to the west of Great Britain, from which it is separated by the Irish Sea. It comprises the provinces of Ulster, Leinster, Munster, and Connacht, and is divided into the Republic of Ireland (which occupies the south, center, and northwest of the island) and Northern Ireland (which occupies the northeast corner and forms part of the United Kingdom).

The center of Ireland is a lowland, about 200–400 ft/60–120 m above sea level; hills are mainly around the coasts, although there are a few peaks over 3,000 ft/1,000 m high, the highest being Carrantuohill ("the inverted reaping hook"), 3,415 ft/1,040 m, in Macgillicuddy's Reeks, County Kerry. The entire western coastline is an intricate alternation of bays and estuaries. Several of the rivers flow in sluggish courses through the central lowland and then cut through fjordlike valleys to the sea. The ◊Shannon in particular falls 100 ft/30 m in its last 16 mi/26 km above Limerick, and is used to produce hydroelectric power.

The lowland bogs that cover parts of central Ireland are intermingled with fertile limestone

country where dairy farming is the chief occupation. The bogs are an important source of fuel in the form of ◊peat, Ireland being poorly supplied with coal.

The climate is mild, moist, and changeable. The annual rainfall on the lowlands varies from 30 in/76 cm in the east to 80 in/203 cm in some western districts, but much higher falls are recorded in the hills.

Ireland: history in prehistoric times Ireland underwent a number of invasions from Europe, the most important of which was that of the Gaels in the 3rd century BC. Gaelic Ireland was divided into kingdoms, nominally subject to an *Ardri* or High King; the chiefs were elected under the tribal or Brehon law, and were usually at war with one another. Christianity was introduced by St ◊Patrick about 432, and during the 5th and 6th centuries Ireland became the home of a civilization which sent out missionaries to Britain and Europe. From about 800 the Danes began to raid Ireland, and later founded Dublin and other coastal towns, until they were defeated by Brian Boru (king from 976) at Clontarf 1014. Anglo-Norman adventurers invaded Ireland 1167, but by the

Ireland: counties

county	administrative headquarters	area sq km
Ulster province		
Antrim	Belfast	2,830
Armagh	Armagh	1,250
Down	Downpatrick	2,470
Fermanagh	Enniskillen	1,680
Londonderry	Derry	2,070
Tyrone	Omagh	3,160
		———
	NORTHERN IRELAND	13,46
Cavan	Cavan	1,890
Donegal	Lifford	4,830
Monaghan	Monaghan	1,290
Munster province		
Clare	Ennis	3,190
Cork	Cork	7,460
Kerry	Tralee	4,700
Limerick	Limerick	2,690
Tipperary (N)	Nenagh	2,000
Tipperary (S)	Clonmel	2,260
Waterford	Waterford	1,840
Leinster province		
Carlow	Carlow	900
Dublin	Dublin	920
Kildare	Naas	1,690
Kilkenny	Kilkenny	2,060
Laois	Port Laoise	1,720
Longford	Longford	1,040
Louth	Dundalk	820
Meath	Trim	2,340
Offaly	Tullamore	2,000
Westmeath	Mullingar	1,760
Wexford	Wexford	2,350
Wicklow	Wicklow	2,030
Connacht province		
Galway	Galway	5,940
Leitrim	Carrick-on-Shannon	1,530
Mayo	Castlebar	5,400
Roscommon	Roscommon	2,460
Sligo	Sligo	1,800
		———
	REPUBLIC OF IRELAND	68,91

end of the medieval period English rule was still confined to the Pale, the territory around Dublin. The Tudors adopted a policy of conquest, confiscation of Irish land, and plantation by English settlers, and further imposed the ⟡Reformation and English law on Ireland. The most important of the plantations was that of Ulster, carried out under James I 1610. In 1641 the Irish took advantage of the developing struggle in England between king and Parliament to begin a revolt which was crushed by Oliver ⟡Cromwell 1649, the estates of all "rebels" being confiscated. Another revolt 1689–91 was also defeated, and the Roman Catholic majority held down by penal laws. In 1739–41 a famine killed one-third of the population of 1.5 million.

The subordination of the Irish parliament to that of England, and of Irish economic interests to English, led to the rise of a Protestant patriot party, which in 1782 forced the British government to remove many commercial restrictions and grant the Irish parliament its independence. This did not satisfy the population, who in 1798, influenced by French revolutionary ideas, rose in rebellion, but were again defeated; and in 1800 William ⟡Pitt induced the Irish parliament to vote itself out of existence by the Act of ⟡Union, effective Jan 1, 1801, which brought Ireland under the aegis of the British crown. During another famine 1845–46, 1.5 million people emigrated, mostly to the US.

By the 1880s there was a strong movement for home rule for Ireland; Gladstone supported it but was defeated by the British Parliament. By 1914, home rule was conceded but World War I delayed implementation.

The **Easter Rising** took place April 1916, when nationalists seized the Dublin general post office and proclaimed a republic. After a week of fighting, the revolt was suppressed by the British army and most of its leaders executed. From 1918 to 1921 there was guerrilla warfare against the British army, especially by the Irish Republican Army (⟡IRA), formed by Michael Collins 1919. This led to a split in the rebel forces, but in 1921 the Anglo-Irish Treaty resulted in partition and the creation of Irish Free State in S Ireland. For history since that date, see ⟡Ireland, Republic of; ⟡Ireland, Northern.

Ireland, Northern constituent part of the UK
area 5,196 sq mi/13,460 sq km
capital Belfast
cities Londonderry, Enniskillen, Omagh, Newry, Armagh, Coleraine
features Mourne mountains, Belfast Lough and Lough Neagh; Giant's Causeway; comprises the six counties (Antrim, Armagh, Down, Fermanagh, Londonderry, and Tyrone) that form part of Ireland's northernmost province of Ulster
exports engineering, especially shipbuilding, textile machinery, aircraft components; linen and synthetic textiles; processed foods, especially dairy and poultry products—all affected by depression and political unrest
currency pound sterling
population (1986) 1,567,000
language English
religion Protestant 54%, Roman Catholic 31%
famous people Montgomery, Alanbrooke
government direct rule from the UK since 1972. Northern Ireland is entitled to send 12 members to the Westminster Parliament.
history for history pre-1921, see ⟡Ireland, history. The creation of Northern Ireland dates from 1921 when the mainly Protestant counties

of Ulster withdrew from the newly established Irish Free State. Spasmodic outbreaks of violence by the ⟡IRA continued, but only in 1968–69 were there serious disturbances arising from Protestant political dominance and discrimination against the Roman Catholic minority in employment and housing. British troops were sent to restore peace and protect Catholics, but disturbances continued and in 1972 the parliament at Stormont was prorogued and superseded by direct rule from Westminster. Under the ⟡Anglo-Irish Agreement 1985, the Republic of Ireland was given a consultative role (via an Anglo-Irish conference) in the government of Northern Ireland, but agreed that there should be no change in its status except by majority consent. The agreement was approved by Parliament, but all 12 Ulster members gave up their seats, so that by-elections could be fought as a form of "referendum" on the views of the province itself. A similar boycotting of the Northern Ireland Assembly led to its dissolution 1986 by the UK government. Job discrimination was outlawed under the Fair Employment Act 1975, but in 1987 Catholics were two and a half times more likely to be unemployed than their Protestant counterparts—a differential that had not improved since 1971. Between 1969 and 1993 violence had claimed nearly 3,000 lives in Northern Ireland.

The question of Northern Ireland's political future was debated in talks held in Belfast April–Sept 1991. The talks represented the first direct negotiations between the political parties for 16 years. No significant progress was made. At the end of 1991 there were 11,000 regular soldiers and 6,000 Ulster Defense Regiment members in Northern Ireland.

Ireland, Republic of country occupying the main part of the island of Ireland, NW Europe. It is bounded E by the Irish Sea, S and W by the Atlantic Ocean, and NE by Northern Ireland.
government The 1937 constitution provides for a president, elected by universal suffrage for a seven-year term, and a two-chamber national parliament, consisting of a senate, Seanad Éireann, and a house of representatives, Dáil Éireann, serving a five-year term. The senate has 60 members, 11 nominated by the prime minister (Taoiseach) and 49 elected by panels representative of most aspects of Irish life. The Dáil consists of 166 members elected by universal suffrage through a system of proportional representation. The president appoints a prime minister who is nominated by the Dáil, which is subject to dissolution by the president when the government has ceased to retain the support of a majority in the Dáil.
history For history pre-1921, see ⟡Ireland: history. In 1921 a treaty gave Southern Ireland dominion status within the British ⟡Commonwealth, while six out of the nine counties of Ulster remained part of the UK, with limited self-government. The Irish Free State, as Southern Ireland was formally called 1921, was accepted by IRA leader Michael Collins but not by many of his colleagues, who shifted their allegiance to the Fianna Fáil party leader Éamon

Ireland 1801–1916: chronology

1800	Act of Union established United Kingdom of Great Britain and Ireland.
1823	Catholic Association founded by Daniel O'Connell to campaign for Catholic political rights.
1828	O'Connell elected for County Clare; forces granting of rights for Catholics to sit in Parliament.
1829	Catholic Emancipation Act.
1838	Tithe Act (abolishing payment) removed a major source of discontent.
1840	Franchise in Ireland reformed. "Young Ireland" formed.
1845–50	Potato famine resulted in widespread death and emigration. Population reduced by 20%.
1850	Irish Franchise Act extended voters from 61,000 to 165,000.
1858	Fenian Brotherhood formed.
1867	Fenian insurrection failed.
1869	Church of Ireland disestablished.
1870	Land Act provided greater security for tenants but failed to halt agrarian disorders. Protestant Isaac Butt formed Home Government Association (Home Rule League).
1874	Home Rule League won 59 Parliamentary seats and adopted a policy of obstruction.
1880	Charles Stuart Parnell became leader of Home Rulers, dominated by Catholic groups. "Boycotts" against landlords unwilling to agree to fair rents.
1881	Land Act greeted with hostility. Parnell imprisoned. "No Rent" movement began.
1882	"Kilmainham Treaty" between government and Parnell agreed conciliation. Chief Secretary Cavendish and Under Secretary Burke murdered in Phoenix Park, Dublin.
1885	Franchise Reform gave Home Rulers 85 seats in new parliament and balance between Liberals and Tories. Home Rule Bill rejected.
1886	Home Rule Bill rejected again.
1890	Parnell cited in divorce case, which split Home Rule movement.
1893	Second Home Rule Bill defeated in House of Lords; Gaelic League founded.
1900	Irish Nationalists reunited under Redmond. 82 MPs elected.
1902	Sinn Féin founded by Arthur Griffith.
1906	Bill for devolution of power to Ireland rejected by Nationalists.
1910	Sir Edward Carson led Unionist opposition to Home Rule.
1912	Home Rule Bill for whole of Ireland introduced. (Protestant) Ulster Volunteers formed to resist.
1913	Home Rule Bill defeated in House of Lords but overridden. (Catholic) Irish Volunteers founded in the South.
1914	Nationalists persuaded to exclude Ulster from Bill for six years but Carson rejected it. Curragh "mutiny" cast doubt on reliability of British troops against Protestants. Extensive gun-running by both sides. World War I deferred implementation.
1916	Easter Rising by members of Irish Republican Brotherhood. Suppressed by troops and leaders executed.

Ireland, Republic of
(Eire)

area 27,146 sq mi/70,282 sq km
capital Dublin
cities ports Cork, Dun Laoghaire, Limerick, Waterford
physical central plateau surrounded by hills; rivers Shannon, Liffey, Boyne
features Bog of Allen, source of domestic and national power; Macgillicuddy's Reeks, Wicklow Mountains; Lough Corrib, lakes of Killarney; Galway Bay and Aran Islands
head of state Mary Robinson from 1990
head of government Albert Reynolds from 1992
political system democratic republic
political parties Fianna Fáil (Soldiers of Destiny), moderate center-right; Fine Gael (Irish Tribe), moderate center-left; Labour Party, moderate, left of center; Progressive Democrats, radical free-enterprise
exports livestock, dairy products, Irish whiskey, microelectronic components and assemblies, mining and engineering products, chemicals, clothing; tourism is important
currency punt

population (1989 est) 3,734,000; growth rate 0.1% p.a.
life expectancy men 70, women 76
languages Irish Gaelic and English (both official)
religion Roman Catholic 94%
literacy 99% (1984)
GDP $21.9 (1987); $6,184 per head
chronology
1916 Easter Rising: nationalists against British rule seized the Dublin general post office and proclaimed a republic; the revolt was suppressed by the British army and most of the leaders were executed.
1918–21 Guerrilla warfare against British army led to split in rebel forces.
1921 Anglo-Irish Treaty resulted in creation of the Irish Free State (Southern Ireland).
1937 Independence achieved from Britain.
1949 Eire left the Commonwealth and became the Republic of Ireland.
1973 Fianna Fáil defeated after 40 years in office; Liam Cosgrave formed a coalition government.
1977 Fianna Fáil returned to power, with Jack Lynch as prime minister.
1979 Lynch resigned, succeeded by Charles Haughey.
1981 Garret FitzGerald formed a coalition.
1983 New Ireland Forum formed, but rejected by the British government.
1985 Anglo-Irish Agreement signed.
1986 Protests by Ulster Unionists against the agreement.
1987 General election won by Charles Haughey.
1988 Relations with UK at low ebb because of disagreement over extradition decisions.
1989 Haughey failed to win majority in general election. Progressive Democrats given cabinet positions in coalition government.
1990 Mary Robinson elected president; John Bruton became Fine Gael leader.
1992 Jan: Haughey resigned after losing parliamentary majority. Feb: Albert Reynolds became Fianna Fáil leader and prime minister. June: National referendum approved ratification of Maastricht Treaty.

◊de Valera; the latter eventually acknowledged the partition 1937 when a new constitution established the country as a sovereign state under the name of Eire.
after independence The IRA continued its fight for an independent, unified Ireland through a campaign of violence, mainly in Northern Ireland but also on the British mainland and, to a lesser extent, in the Irish republic. Eire remained part of the Commonwealth until 1949, when it left, declaring itself the Republic of Ireland, while Northern Ireland remained a constituent part of the UK. In 1973 Fianna Fáil, having held office for over 40 years, was defeated, and Liam Cosgrave formed a coalition of the Fine Gael and Labour parties.

In 1977 Fianna Fáil returned to power, with Jack Lynch as prime minister. In 1979 IRA violence intensified with the killing of Earl Mountbatten in Ireland and 18 British soldiers in Northern Ireland later the same year, and was succeeded by Charles Haughey. His aim was a united Ireland, with considerable independence for the six northern counties. After the 1981 election Garret Fitzgerald, leader of Fine Gael, formed another coalition with Labor but was defeated the following year on budget proposals and resigned. Haughey returned to office with a minority

government, but he, too, had to resign later that year, resulting in the return of FitzGerald.
Anglo-Irish Agreement In 1983 all the main Irish and Northern Irish political parties initiated the New Ireland Forum as a vehicle for discussion. Its report was rejected by Margaret Thatcher's Conservative government in the UK, but discussions between London and Dublin resulted in the signing of the Anglo-Irish Agreement 1985, providing for regular consultation and exchange of information on political, legal, security, and cross-border matters. The agreement also said that the status of Northern Ireland would not be changed without the consent of a majority of the people. The agreement was criticized by the Unionist parties of Northern Ireland, who asked that it be rescinded. FitzGerald's coalition ended 1986, and the Feb 1987 election again returned Fianna Fáil and Charles Haughey.
relations with UK In 1988 relations between the Republic of Ireland and the UK were at a low ebb because of disagreements over extradition decisions. In 1989 Haughey failed to win a majority in the election and entered into a coalition with the Progressive Democrats (a breakaway party from Fianna Fáil), putting two of their members into the cabinet. In Nov 1990, after being dismissed as deputy prime

minister, Brian Lenihan was defeated in the presidential election by the left-wing-backed Mary Robinson. In the same month Alan Dukes resigned the leadership of Fine Gael, to be replaced by the right-winger John Bruton.
Haughey resigns The Progressive Democrat leader Desmond O'Malley withdrew from the coalition after allegations Jan 1992 against Haughey of illegal telephone-tapping. As a result, Haughey lost his parliamentary majority and resigned as Fianna Fáil leader and prime minister. He was succeeded Feb 1992 by Albert Reynolds. Reynolds immediately reconstructed the cabinet, with David Andrews as foreign minister and Bertie Ahern as finance minister. In a national referendum June 1992, Ireland showed its approval of the Maastricht Treaty on European union when 69% voted in favor in a turnout of 57%. Campaigning hard for the treaty, Reynolds said that it was essential for Ireland's economy to maintain close links with the European Community. Fianna Fáil slipped in inconclusive November elections, in which voters approved a more liberal approach to abortion. *See illustration box.*

Irene in Greek mythology, goddess of peace (Roman *Pax*). She was sometimes regarded as one of the Horae, who presided over the seasons and the order of nature, and were the daughters of Zeus and Themis.

Irene, St c. 752–c. 803. Byzantine emperor 797–802. The wife of Leo IV (750–80), she became regent for their son Constantine (771–805) on Leo's death. In 797 she deposed her son, had his eyes put out, and assumed the full title of *basileus* ("emperor"), ruling in her own right until deposed and exiled to Lesvos by a revolt in 802. She was made a saint by the Greek Orthodox church for her attacks on iconoclasts.

Ireton Henry 1611–1651. English Civil War general. He joined the parliamentary forces and fought at Edgehill 1642, Gainsborough 1643, and ◊Naseby 1645. After the Battle of Naseby, Ireton, who was opposed to both the extreme republicans and ◊Levelers, strove for a compromise with Charles I, but then played a leading role in his trial and execution. He married his leader Cromwell's daughter in 1646. Lord Deputy in Ireland from 1650, he died after the capture of Limerick.

Irgun short for *Irgun Zvai Leumi* (National Military Society), a Jewish guerrilla group active against the British administration in Palestine 1946–48. Their bombing of the King David Hotel in Jerusalem July 22, 1946 resulted in 91 fatalities.

Irian Jaya the western portion of the island of New Guinea, part of Indonesia
area 162,000 sq mi/420,000 sq km
capital Jayapura
population (1989) 1,555,700
history part of the Dutch East Indies 1828 as Western New Guinea; retained by the Netherlands after Indonesian independence 1949 but ceded to Indonesia 1963 by the United Nations and remained part of Indonesia by an "Act of Free Choice" 1969. In the 1980s 700,000 acres/283,500 hectares were given over to Indonesia's controversial transmigration program for the resettlement of farming families from overcrowded Java, causing destruction of rainforests and displacing indigenous people. In 1989 Indonesia began construction of a space launching pad on the island of Biak, near the equator where the Earth's atmosphere is least thick.

iridium (Latin *iridis* "rainbow") hard, brittle, silver-white, metallic element, symbol Ir, atomic number 77, atomic weight 192.2. It is twice as heavy as lead and is resistant to tarnish and corrosion. It is one of the so-called platinum group of metals; it occurs in platinum ores and as a free metal (⊳native metal) with osmium in osmiridium, a natural alloy that includes platinum, ruthenium, and rhodium.

It is alloyed with platinum for jewelry and used for watch bearings and in scientific instruments. It was named in 1804 by English chemist Smithson Tennant (1761–1815) for its iridescence in solution.

iris in anatomy, the colored muscular diaphragm that controls the size of the pupil in the vertebrate eye. It contains radial muscle that increases the pupil diameter and circular muscle that constricts the pupil diameter. Both types of muscle respond involuntarily to light intensity.

iris in botany, perennial northern temperate flowering plants of the genus *Iris*, family Iridaceae. The leaves are usually sword-shaped; the purple, white, or yellow flowers have three upright inner petals and three outward- and downward-curving sepals. The wild yellow iris is called ⊳flag.

Irish person of Irish culture from Ireland or person of Irish descent. The Irish mainly speak English, though there are approximately 30,000–100,000 speakers of Irish Gaelic, a Celtic language belonging to the Indo-European family.

Celtic tribes, the ancestors of the Irish, migrated to Ireland about 300 BC. Later known as Gaels (Irishmen), they settled on the Isle of Man and SW Scotland, and established colonies in W Wales, Devon, and Cornwall.

Irish Gaelic first official language of the Irish Republic, but much less widely used than the second official language, English. See ⊳Gaelic language.

Irish language common name for the Irish ⊳Gaelic language. At one time, especially in the form "Erse," also a name for the Gaelic of Scotland.

Irish literature early Irish literature, in Gaelic, consists of the sagas, which are mainly in prose, and a considerable body of verse. The chief cycles are that of Ulster, which deals with the mythological ⊳Conchobar and his followers, and the Ossianic (see ⊳Ossian), which has influenced European literature through Scottish writer James MacPherson's (1736-1796) version.

Early Irish poetry has a unique lyric quality and consists mainly of religious verse and nature poetry, for example, St Patrick's hymn and Ultán's hymn to St Brigit. Much pseudo-historical verse is also extant, ascribed to such poets as Mael Mura (9th century), Mac Liac (10th century), and Flann Mainistrech (11th century). Religious literature in prose includes sermons, saints' lives (for example, those in the *Book of Lismore* and in the writings of Michael O'Clery), and visions. History is represented by annals and by isolated texts like the *Cogad Gaedel re Gallaib*, an account of the Viking invasions by an eye-witness. The "official" or "court" verse of the 13th to 17th centuries was produced by a succession of professional poets, notably Tadhg Dall O' Huiginn (died *c.* 1617), Donnchadh Mór O'Dálaigh (died 1244), and Geoffrey Keating (died 1646), who wrote in both verse and prose.

The bardic schools ceased to exist by the end of the 17th century. Meter became accentual, rather than syllabic. The greatest exponents of the new school were Egan O'Rahilly (early 18th century) and the religious poet Tadhg Gaelach O'Súilleabháin.

The late 19th century onwards saw a resurgence of Irish literature written in English. Oscar ⊳Wilde, G B ⊳Shaw, and James ⊳Joyce represent those who chose to live outside Ireland. More culturally nationalistic were the writers including W B ⊳Yeats who supported the Gaelic League (aiming to revivify the Irish language) and founded the Abbey Theater Company in Dublin: this provided a milieu for the realism and fantasy of J M ⊳Synge and the intensity and compassion of Sean ⊳O'Casey.

Since World War II, Ireland has produced the Nobel Prize-winning playwright Samuel ⊳Beckett, novelists of the caliber of Brian Moore and Edna O'Brien, and poet Seamus Heaney (1939–   ).

Irish nationalism see ⊳Ireland: history and ⊳Ireland, Northern.

Irish Republican Army (IRA) militant Irish nationalist organization whose aim is to create a united Irish socialist republic including Ulster. The paramilitary wing of ⊳Sinn Féin, it was founded 1919 by Michael ⊳Collins and fought a successful war against Britain 1919–21. It came to the fore again 1939 with a bombing campaign in Britain, having been declared illegal in 1936. Its activities intensified from 1968 onwards, as the civil-rights disorders ("the Troubles") in Northern Ireland developed. In 1970 a group in the north broke away to become the **Provisional IRA**; its objective is the expulsion of the British from Northern Ireland.

The IRA is committed to the use of force in trying to achieve its objectives, and it regularly carries out bombings and shootings. In 1979 it murdered Louis ⊳Mountbatten, and its bomb attacks in Britain have included an attempt to kill members of the UK cabinet during the Conservative Party conference in Brighton, Sussex, 1984. Several attacks have been carried out against British military personnel serving outside the UK, especially in Germany.

Irkutsk city in S Siberian Russia; population (1987) 609,000. It produces coal, iron, steel, and machine tools. Founded 1652, it began to grow after the Trans-Siberian railroad reached it 1898.

iron (Germanic *eis* "strong") a hard, malleable and ductile, silver-gray metallic element, symbol Fe (from Latin *ferrum*), atomic number 26, atomic weight 55.847. It is the fourth most abundant element (the second most abundant metal after aluminum) in the Earth's crust. The central core of the Earth, the radius of which is believed to be 2,200 miles, is held to consist principally of iron with some nickel. When the amounts in the crust and core are combined, iron is probably the most abundant constituent element of the planet.

Although it almost always occurs in ores or as compounds, it sometimes occurs as a free metal (⊳native metal), occasionally as fragments of iron or iron-nickel meteorites. Iron is the most common and most useful of all metals; it is strongly magnetic and is noted for becoming oxydized (rusted) in moist air. Iron is an essential component of hemoglobin, the molecule in the red blood cells, where it serves to transport oxygen to all parts of the body. Iron is the basis for steel, an alloy with carbon and other elements. Iron has been worked into

tools by early peoples in both the Old World and the New and its use has persisted since the ⊳Iron Age of prehistory.

Iron Age developmental stage of human technology when weapons and tools were made from iron. Iron was produced in Thailand by about 1600 BC but was considered inferior in strength to bronze until about 1000 when metallurgical techniques improved and the alloy steel was produced by adding carbon during the smelting process.

Iron Age cultures include **Hallstat** (named after a site in Austria), **La Téne** (from a site in Switzerland), and **Marnian** (from the Marne region, France).

ironbark any species of ⊳eucalyptus tree with hard, tough bark.

ironclad wooden warship covered with armor plate. The first to be constructed was the French *Gloire* 1858, but the first to be launched was the British HMS *Warrior* 1859. The first battle between ironclads took place during the American Civil War, when the Union *Monitor* fought the Confederate *Virginia* (formerly the *Merrimack*) March 9, 1862. The design was replaced by battleships of all-metal construction in the 1890s.

The US Navy's Great White Fleet was especially well known.

Iron Cross medal awarded for valor in the German armed forces. Instituted in Prussia 1813, it consists of a Maltese cross of iron, edged with silver.

Iron Curtain in Europe after World War II, the symbolic boundary of the ⊳Cold War between capitalist West and communist East. The term was popularized by the UK prime minister Winston Churchill from 1945.

An English traveler to Bolshevik Russia, Mrs Snowden, used the term with reference to the Soviet border in 1920. The Nazi minister Goebbels used it a few months before Churchill in 1945 to describe the divide between Soviet-dominated and other nations that would follow German capitulation.

Iron Gate (Romanian *Porţile de Fier*) narrow gorge, interrupted by rapids, in Romania. A hydroelectric scheme undertaken 1964–70 by Romania and Yugoslavia transformed this section of the river Danube into a 90 mi/ 145 km long lake and eliminated the rapids as a navigation hazard. Before flooding, in 1965, an archeological survey revealed Europe's oldest urban settlement, Lepenski Vir.

Iron Guard profascist group controlling Romania in the 1930s. To counter its influence, King Carol II established a dictatorship 1938 but the Iron Guard forced him to abdicate 1940.

iron ore any mineral from which iron is extracted. The chief iron ores are ⊳*magnetite*, a black oxide; ⊳*hematite*, or kidney ore, a reddish oxide; ⊳*limonite*, brown, impure oxyhydroxides of iron; and *siderite*, a brownish carbonate.

Iron ores are found in a number of different forms, including distinct layers in igneous intrusions, as components of contact metamorphic rocks, and as sedimentary beds. Much of the world's iron is extracted in Russia, Kazakhstan, and the Ukraine. Other important producers are the US, Australia, France, Brazil, and Canada; over 40 countries produce significant quantities of ore.

iron pyrites or **pyrite** FeS_2 common iron ore. Brassy yellow, and occurring in cubic crystals, it is often called "fool's gold," since only those who have never seen gold would mistake it.

irony literary technique that achieves the effect of "saying one thing and meaning another," through the use of humor or mild sarcasm. It can be traced through all periods of literature, from Classical Greek and Roman epics and dramas to the good-humored and subtle irony of ⍦Chaucer to the 20th-century writer's method for dealing with nihilism and despair, as in Samuel Beckett's *Waiting for Godot.*

The Greek philosopher Plato used irony in his dialogues, in which Socrates elicits truth through a pretence of naivety. Sophocles' use of dramatic irony also has a high seriousness, as in *Oedipus Rex*, where Oedipus prays for the discovery and punishment of the city's polluter, little knowing that it is himself. Eighteenth-century skepticism provided a natural environment for irony, with ⍦Swift using the device as a powerful weapon in *Gulliver's Travels* and elsewhere.

Iroquois member of a confederation of NE North American Indians, the Six Nations (Cayuga, Mohawk, Oneida, Onondaga, and Seneca, with the Tuscarora after 1723), traditionally formed by Hiawatha (actually a priestly title) 1570.

The Iroquois lived in upstate New York, and their descendants live in New York, Ontario, Québec, and Oklahoma, on reservations and among the general public. The Mohawk steelworkers are famous for constructing the girders of skyscrapers such as the Empire State Building.

irradiation in technology, subjecting anything to radiation, including cancer tumors. See also ⍦food irradiation.

In optics, the term refers to the apparent enlargement of a brightly lit object when seen against a dark background.

irrationalism feature of many philosophies rather than a philosophical movement. Irrationalists deny that the world can be comprehended by conceptual thought, and often see the human mind as determined by unconscious forces.

irrational number a number that cannot be expressed as an exact ⍦fraction. Irrational numbers include some square roots (for example, $\sqrt{2}$, $\sqrt{3}$, and $\sqrt{5}$ are irrational) and numbers such as π (the ratio of the circumference of a circle to its diameter, which is approximately equal to 3.14159) and e (the base of ⍦natural logarithms, approximately 2.71828).

Irrawaddy (Myanmar *Ayeryarwady*) chief river of Myanmar (Burma), flowing roughly N to S for 1,300 mi/2,090 km across the center of the country into the Bay of Bengal. Its sources are the Mali and N'mai rivers; its chief tributaries are the Chindwin and Shweli.

irrigation artificial water supply for dry agricultural areas by means of dams and channels. Drawbacks are that it tends to concentrate salts, ultimately causing infertility, and that rich river silt is retained at dams, to the impoverishment of the land and fisheries below them.

Irrigation has been practiced for thousands of years, in Eurasia as well as the Americas. An example is the channeling of the annual Nile flood in Egypt, which has been done from earliest times to its present control by the Aswan High Dam.

Irving Washington 1783–1859. US essayist and short-story writer. He published a mock-heroic *History of New York* in 1809, supposedly written by the Dutchman "Diedrich Knickerbocker." In 1815 he went to England where he published *The Sketch Book of Geoffrey Crayon, Gent.* 1820, which contained such stories as "Rip van Winkle" and "The Legend of Sleepy Hollow."

His other works include *The Alhambra* 1832, sketches about Spanish subjects, and *Tour of the Prairies* 1835, about the American West. His essays and tales remain popular.

Isaac in the Old Testament, Hebrew patriarch, son of ⍦Abraham and Sarah, and father of Esau and Jacob.

Isabella two Spanish queens:

Isabella I *the Catholic* 1451–1504. Queen of Castile from 1474, after the death of her brother Henry IV. By her marriage with Ferdinand of Aragon 1469, the crowns of two of the Christian states in the Moorish-held Spanish peninsula were united. In her reign, during 1492, the Moors were driven out of Spain. She introduced the ⍦Inquisition into Castile, expelled the Jews, and gave financial encouragement to ⍦Columbus. Her youngest daughter was Catherine of Aragon, first wife of Henry VIII of England.

Isabella II 1830–1904. Queen of Spain from 1833, when she succeeded her father Ferdinand VII (1784–1833). The Salic Law banning a female sovereign had been repealed by the Cortes (parliament), but her succession was disputed by her uncle Don Carlos de Bourbon (1788–1855). After seven years of civil war, the ⍦Carlists were defeated. She abdicated in favor of her son Alfonso XII in 1868.

Isabella of France 1292–1358. Daughter of King Philip IV of France, wife of King Edward II of England; she intrigued with her lover, Roger Mortimer, to have the king deposed and murdered.

Isaiah 8th century BC. In the Old Testament, the first major Hebrew prophet. The son of Amos, he was probably of high rank, and lived largely in Jerusalem.

He was influential in the court of ancient Judah until the Assyrian invasion of 701 BC.

Isaurian 8th-century Byzantine imperial dynasty, originating in Asia Minor.

Members of the family had been employed as military leaders by the Byzantines, and they gained great influence and prestige as a result. Leo III acceded in 717 as the first Isaurian emperor, and was followed by Constantine V (718–75), Leo IV (750–80), and Leo's widow Irene, who acted as regent for their son before deposing him 797 and assuming the title of emperor herself. She was deposed 802. The Isaurian rulers maintained the integrity of the empire's borders. With the exception of Irene, they attempted to suppress the use of religious icons.

ISBN (abbreviation for *International Standard Book Number*) code number used for ordering or classifying book titles.

The final digit in each ISBN number is a check digit, which can be used by a computer program to validate the number each time it is input.

ischemia reduction of blood supply to any part of the body.

Ischia volcanic island about 16 mi/26 km SW of Naples, Italy, in the Tyrrhenian Sea; population (1985) 26,000. It has mineral springs (known to the Romans) and beautiful scenery, and is a vacation resort.

Ise city SE of Kyoto, on Honshu, Japan. It is the site of the most sacred Shinto shrine, dedicated to the sun-goddess Amaterasu, rebuilt every 20 years in the form of a perfect thatched house of the 7th century BC and containing the octagonal mirror of the goddess.

Isfahan or *Eṣfahān* industrial (steel, textiles, carpets) city in central Iran; population (1986) 1,001,000. It was the ancient capital (1598–1722) of ⍦Abbas I, and its features include the Great Square, Grand Mosque, and Hall of Forty Pillars.

Isherwood Christopher (William Bradshaw) 1904–1986. English novelist. He lived in Germany 1929–33 just before Hitler's rise to power, a period that inspired *Mr Norris Changes Trains* 1935 and *Goodbye to Berlin* 1939, creating the character of Sally Bowles (the basis of the musical *Cabaret* 1968). Returning to England, he collaborated with W H ⍦Auden in three verse plays.

Ishiguro Kazuo 1954– . Japanese-born British novelist. His novel *An Artist of the Floating World* won the 1986 Whitbread Prize, and *The Remains of the Day* won the 1989 Booker Prize. His work is characterized by a sensitive style and subtle structure.

Ishiguro's first novel, *A Pale View of Hills*, takes place mainly in his native Nagasaki, dealing obliquely with the aftermath of the atomic bomb. *An Artist of the Floating World* is set entirely in Japan but thematically linked to *The Remains of the Day*, which is about an English butler coming to realize the extent of his self-sacrifice and self-deception. All three have in common a melancholy reassessment of the past.

Ishmael in the Old Testament, son of ⍦Abraham and his wife Sarah's Egyptian maid Hagar; traditional ancestor of Mohammed and the Arab people. He and his mother were driven away by Sarah's jealousy. Muslims believe that it was Ishmael, not Isaac, whom God commanded Abraham to sacrifice, and that Ishmael helped Abraham build the ⍦Kaaba in Mecca.

Ishtar goddess of love and war, worshiped by the Babylonians and Assyrians, and personified as the legendary queen Semiramis.

Isidore of Seville c. 560–636. Writer and missionary. His *Ethymologiae* was the model for later medieval encyclopedias and helped to preserve Classical thought during the Middle Ages; his *Chronica Maiora* remains an important source for the history of Visigothic Spain. As bishop of Seville from 600, he strengthened the church in Spain and converted many Jews and Aryan Visigoths.

isinglass pure form of gelatin obtained from the internal membranes of the swim bladder of various fishes, particularly the sturgeon. Isinglass is used in the clarification of wines and beer, and in cooking.

Isis the principal goddess of ancient Egypt. She was the daughter of Geb and Nut (Earth and Sky), and as the sister-wife of Osiris searched for his body after his death at the hands of his brother, Set. Her son Horus then defeated and captured Set but cut off his mother's head because she would not allow Set to be killed. She was later identified with ⍦Hathor. The cult of Isis ultimately spread to Greece and Rome.

Islam (Arabic "submission," that is, to the will of Allah) religion founded in the Arabian peninsula in the early 7th century AD. It emphasizes the oneness of God, his omnipotence, beneficence, and inscrutability. The sacred book is the **Koran** of the prophet ◊Mohammed, the Prophet or Messenger of Allah. There are two main Muslim sects: ◊**Sunni** and ◊**Shiite**. Other schools include **Sufism**, a mystical movement originating in the 8th century.

beliefs The fundamental beliefs of Islam are contained in the Adhan: "I bear witness that there is no God but Allah and Mohammed is the Prophet of Allah." Creation, Fall of Adam, angels and ◊jinns, heaven and hell, Day of Judgment, God's predestination of good and evil, and the succession of scriptures revealed to the prophets, including Moses and Jesus, but of which the perfect, final form is the **Koran** or **Quran**, divided into 114 **suras** or chapters, said to have been divinely revealed to Mohammed; the original is said to be preserved beside the throne of Allah in heaven.

Islamic law Islam embodies a secular law (the **Shari'a** or "Highway"), which is clarified for Shiites by reference to their own version of the **sunna**, "practice" of the Prophet as transmitted by his companions and embodied in the Hadith; the Sunni sect also take into account **ijma'**, the endorsement by universal consent of practices and beliefs among the faithful. For the Sufi, the **Shari'a** is the starting point on the "Sufi Path" to self-enlightenment. A **mufti** is a legal expert who guides the courts in their interpretation. (In Turkey until the establishment of the republic 1924 the mufti had supreme spiritual authority.)

organization There is no organized church or priesthood, although Mohammed's descendants (the Hashim family) and popularly recognized holy men, mullahs, and ayatollahs are accorded respect.

observances The Shari'a includes the observances known as the "Five Pillars of the Faith" which are binding to all adult male believers. The observances include: *shahada* or profession of the faith; *salat* or worship five times a day facing the holy city of ◊Mecca (the call to prayer is given by a muezzin, usually from the minaret or tower of a mosque); *zakat* or obligatory almsgiving; *saum* or fasting sunrise to sunset through Ramadan (ninth month of the year, which varies with the calendar); and the *hajj* or pilgrimage to Mecca at least once in a lifetime.

history Islam began as a militant and missionary religion, and between 711 and 1492 spread east into India, west over N Africa, then north across Gibraltar into the Iberian peninsula. During the Middle Ages, Islamic scholars preserved ancient Greco-Roman learning, while the Dark Ages prevailed in Christian Europe. Islam was seen as an enemy of Christianity by European countries during the Crusades, and Christian states united against a Muslim nation as late as the Battle of Lepanto 1571. Driven from Europe, Islam remained established in N Africa and the Middle East. Islam is a major force in the Arab world and is a focus for nationalism among the peoples of the ◊Central Asian Republics. It is also a significant factor in Pakistan, Indonesia, Malaysia, and parts of Africa.

Islamabad capital of Pakistan from 1967, in the Potwar district, at the foot of the Margala Hills and immediately NW o ◊Rawalpindi; population (1981) 201,000. The city was designed by Constantinos Doxiadis in the 1960s. The Federal Capital Territory of Islamabad has an area of 350 sq mi/907 sq km and a population (1985) of 379,000.

Islamic art art and design of Muslim nations and territories. Because the Koran forbids figurative representation in art, Islamic artistry was channeled into calligraphy and ornament. Despite this, there was naturalistic Persian painting, which inspired painters in the Mogul and Ottoman empires. Ceramic tiles decorated mosques and palaces from Spain (Alhambra, Granada) to S Russia and Mogul India (Taj Mahal, Agra). Wood, stone, and stucco sculpture ornamented buildings. Islamic artists produced intricate metalwork and, in Persia in the 16th–17th centuries, woven textiles and carpets.

Islamic art is found from NW Africa and much of Spain to NW India and Anatolia. Interlacing patterns based on geometry and stylized plant motifs (including the swirling arabesque) swarm over surfaces.

calligraphy From about the 8th century the Arabic script was increasingly elaborate. The cursive script with extended flourishes (Nashki script) was widely adopted, and calligraphy was used to ornament textiles, metalwork, tiles, and pottery.

miniature painting This flourished in Persia, in cities such as Isfahan, Heratt, and Shiraz during the Safavid period 1502–1736 and after 1526 under the Mogul Empire in India.

carpets The royal Persian carpet factories produced huge and luxurious compositions featuring human and animal figures as well as calligraphic, geometrical, and floral motifs.

Islamic Conference Organization (ICO) association of 44 states in the Middle East, Africa, and Asia, established 1971 to promote Islamic solidarity between member countries, and to consolidate economic, social, cultural, and scientific cooperation. Headquarters in Niger.

The ICO also aims to "support international peace and security; to coordinate efforts to safeguard the holy places; to support Palestinians in their efforts to liberate their lands; and to strengthen the struggle of all Muslim people to safeguard their dignity and independence." Mozambique and Nigeria have observer status.

major islands

name and location	sq km	sq mi
Greenland (North Atlantic)	2,175,600	840,000
New Guinea (SW Pacific)	800,000	309,000
Borneo (SW Pacific)	744,100	287,300
Madagascar (Indian Ocean)	587,000	227,000
Baffin (Canadian Arctic)	507,258	195,928
Sumatra (Indian Ocean)	473,600	182,860
Honshu (NW Pacific)	230,966	89,176
Great Britain (N Atlantic)	229,978	88,795
Victoria (Canadian Arctic)	217,206	83,896
Ellesmere (Canadian Arctic)	196,160	75,767
Sulawesi (Indian Ocean)	189,216	73,057
South Island, New Zealand (SW Pacific)	149,883	57,870
Java (Indian Ocean)	126,602	48,900
North Island, New Zealand (SW Pacific)	114,669	44,274
Cuba (Caribbean Sea)	110,800	44,800
Newfoundland (NW Atlantic)	108,860	42,030
Luzon (W Pacific)	104,688	40,420
Iceland (N Atlantic)	103,000	39,800
Mindanao (W Pacific)	94,630	36,537
Ireland—N and the Republic (N Atlantic)	84,400	32,600
Hokkaido (NW Pacific)	83,515	32,245
Sakhalin (NW Pacific)	76,400	29,500
Hispaniola—Dominican Republic and Haiti (Caribbean Sea)	76,000	29,300
Banks (Canadian Arctic)	70,000	27,038
Tasmania (SW Pacific)	67,800	26,200
Sri Lanka (Indian Ocean)	64,600	24,900
Devon (Canadian Arctic)	55,247	21,331

island area of land surrounded entirely by water. Australia is classed as a continent rather than an island, because of its size.

Islands can be formed in many ways. **Continental islands** were once part of the mainland, but became isolated (by tectonic movement, erosion, or a rise in sea level, for example). **Volcanic islands**, such as Japan, were formed by the explosion of underwater volcanoes. **Coral islands** consist mainly of ◊coral, built up over many years. An **atoll** is a circular coral reef surrounding a lagoon; atolls were formed when a coral reef grew up around a volcanic island that subsequently sank or was submerged by a rise in sea level. **Barrier islands** are found by the shore in shallow water, and are formed by the deposition of sediment eroded from the shoreline.

island arc curved chain of islands produced by volcanic activity caused by rising magma behind the ocean trench formed by one tectonic plate sliding beneath another. In such areas (called subductive zones) the lithosphere of the descending plate does so along a curved path, because of the spherical shape of the Earth. Lithosphere depressed into the less rigid asthenosphere of the mantle tends to bend downward along a curved line much in the way a circular dent forms in a ping-pong ball when pressed with the thumb.

Such island arcs are often later incorporated into continental margins during mountain-building episodes. Island arcs are common in the Pacific where they ring the ocean on both sides; the Aleutian Islands of Alaska are an example.

Islay southernmost island of the Inner Hebrides, Scotland, in Strathclyde region, separated from Jura by the Sound of Islay; area 235 sq mi/610 sq km; population (1981) 3,800. The principal towns are Bowmore and Port Ellen. It produces malt whiskey, and its wildlife includes eagles and rare wintering geese.

Isles of the Blessed an alternative title for ◊Elysium in Greek mythology.

islets of Langerhans groups of cells within the pancreas responsible for the secretion of the hormone insulin. They are sensitive to the blood sugar, producing more hormone when glucose levels rise.

Ismail 1830–1895. Khedive (governor) of Egypt 1866–79. A grandson of Mehemet Ali, he became viceroy of Egypt in 1863 and in 1866 received the title of khedive from the Ottoman sultan. He amassed huge foreign debts and in 1875 Britain, at Prime Minister Disraeli's suggestion, bought the khedive's Suez Canal shares for nearly"million, establishing Anglo-French control of Egypt's finances. In 1879 the UK and France persuaded the sultan to appoint Tewfik, his son, khedive in his place.

Ismail I 1486–1524. Shah of Persia from 1501, founder of the **Safavi dynasty**, who established the first national government since the Arab conquest and Shiite Islam as the national religion.

Isma'ili member of an Islamic group, the second largest ♢Shiite community in Islam (after the ♢Twelver Shi'is). Isma'ilis comprise several smaller groups, the most important of which are the Nizari Isma'ilis, from 1094; the Da'udi Isma'ilis; the Musta'li Isma'ilis; and the Sulaymani Isma'ilis.

ISO in photography, a numbering system for rating the speed of films, devised by the International Standards Organization.

isobar line drawn on maps and weather charts linking all places with the same atmospheric pressure (usually measured in millibars). When used in weather forecasting, the distance between the isobars is an indication of the barometric gradient.

Where the isobars are close together, cyclonic weather is indicated, bringing strong winds and a depression, and where far apart anticyclonic, bringing calmer, settled conditions.

Isocrates 436–338 BC. Athenian orator, a pupil of the philosopher Socrates. He was a professional speechwriter and teacher of rhetoric.

isolation in medicine, the segregation of patients to prevent the spread of infection. Today, isolation is most often required for patients who are at unusual risk, mainly those whose immune systems have been undermined by disease or suppressed by antirejection or ♢cytotoxic drugs. Strict isolation is also practiced to prevent infection due to antibiotic-resistant microbes (see ♢nosocomial infection).

isolationism in politics, concentration on internal rather than foreign affairs; a foreign policy having no interest in international affairs that do not affect the country's own interests.

In the US, isolationism is as old as George Washington, who warned against "entangling alliances." Today it is usually associated with the Republican Party, especially politicians of the Midwest (for example, the Neutrality Acts 1935–39). Intervention by the US in both World Wars was initially resisted. In the 1960s some Republicans demanded the removal of the United Nations from American soil.

There has been resistance to use of official US military forces without clearly defined objectives in pursuit of an important national interest. This so-called Vietnam Syndrome was largely dissipated during the presidencies of Ronald Reagan and George Bush,

butane CH₃(CH₂)₂CH₃

methyl propane CH₃CH(CH₃)CH₃

● carbon atom   ○ hydrogen atom
—— covalent bond

isomer The chemicals butane and methyl propane are isomers.

who reasserted international involvements and military action.

Isolde or **Iseult** in Celtic legend, the wife of King Mark of Cornwall who was brought from Ireland by his nephew ♢Tristan. She and Tristan accidentally drank the aphrodisiac given to her by her mother for her marriage, were separated, and finally died together.

isomer chemical compound having the same molecular composition and mass as another, but with different physical or chemical properties owing to the different structural arrangement of its constituent atoms. For example, the organic compounds butane ($CH_3(CH_2)_2CH_3$) and methyl propane ($CH_3CH(CH_3)CH_3$) are isomers, each possessing four carbon atoms and ten hydrogen atoms but differing in the way that these are arranged with respect to each other.

Structural isomers have obviously different constructions, but **geometrical** and **optical isomers** must be drawn or modeled in order to appreciate the difference in their three-dimensional arrangement. Geometrical isomers have a plane of symmetry and arise because of the restricted rotation of atoms around a bond; optical isomers are mirror images of each other. For instance, 1,1-dichloroethene ($CH_2{=}CCl_2$) and 1,2-dichloroethene ($CHCl{=}CHCl$) are structural isomers, but there are two possible geometric isomers of the latter (depending on whether the chlorine atoms are on the same side or on opposite sides of the plane of the carbon-carbon double bond).

isometrics system of muscular exercises without apparatus—for example, by contracting particular sets of muscles. These exercises, some of which can be performed without visible movement, have been recommended to sedentary workers as a way of getting fit, but can be damaging when practiced by the unskilled.

isomorphism the existence of substances of different chemical composition but with similar crystalline form.

isorhythm in music, a form in which a given rhythm constantly repeats, although the

notes may change. Used in European medieval music, and still practiced in Classical Indian music.

isostasy the theoretical balance in buoyancy of all parts of the Earth's ♢crust, as though they were floating on a denser layer beneath. High mountains, for example, have very deep roots, just as an iceberg floats with most of its mass submerged.

Similarly, during an ♢ice age the weight of the ice sheet pushes that continent into the earth's mantle; once the ice has melted, the continent rises again. This accounts for shoreline features being found some way inland in regions that were heavily glaciated during the Pleistocene period.

isotherm line on a map linking all places having the same temperature at a given time.

isotope one of two or more atoms that have the same atomic number (same number of protons), but which contain a different number of neutrons, thus differing in their atomic masses. They may be stable or radioactive, naturally occurring or synthesized. The term was coined by English chemist Frederick Soddy, pioneer researcher in atomic disintegration.

Isozaki Arata 1931– . Japanese architect. One of Kenzo ♢Tange's team 1954–63, his Post-Modernist works include Ochanomizu Square, Tokyo (retaining the existing facades), and buildings for the 1992 Barcelona Olympics.

Israel ancient kingdom of N ♢Palestine, formed after the death of Solomon by Jewish peoples seceding from the rule of his son Rehoboam and electing Jeroboam in his place.

Israel country in SW Asia, bounded N by Lebanon, E by Syria and Jordan, S by the Gulf of Aqaba, and W by Egypt and the Mediterranean Sea.

government Israel has no written constitution. In 1950 the single-chamber legislature, the Knesset, voted to adopt a state constitution by evolution over an unspecified period of time. As in the UK, certain laws are considered to have particular constitutional significance and could, at some time, be codified into a single written document.

Supreme authority rests with the Knesset, whose 120 members are elected by universal suffrage, through a system of proportional representation, for a four-year term. It is subject to dissolution within that period. The president is constitutional head of state and is elected by the Knesset for a five-year term. The prime minister and cabinet are mostly drawn from, and collectively responsible to, the Knesset, but occasionally a cabinet member may be chosen from outside.

history The Zionist movement, calling for an independent community for Jews in their historic homeland of Palestine, began in the 19th century, and in 1917 Britain declared its support for the idea. In 1920 the League of Nations placed Palestine under British administration, and the British government was immediately faced with the rival claims of Jews who wished to settle there and the indigenous Arabs who opposed them. In 1937 Britain proposed separate Arab and Jewish communities; this was accepted by the Jews but not by the Arabs, and fighting broke out between them. In Europe, the Nazi Holocaust killed about 6 million Jews, and hundreds of thousands tried to get to Palestine before, during, and after World War II 1939–45. Many survivors could no longer live in Europe.

Israel
State of (*Medinat Israel*)

area 8,029 sq mi/20,800 sq km (as at 1949 armistice)

capital Jerusalem (not recognized by the United Nations)

cities ports Tel Aviv/Jaffa, Haifa, Acre, Eilat; Bat-Yam, Holon, Ramat Gan, Petach Tikva, Beersheba

physical coastal plain of Sharon between Haifa and Tel Aviv noted since ancient times for fertility; central mountains of Galilee, Samaria, and Judea; Dead Sea, Lake Tiberias, and river Jordan Rift Valley along the E are below sea level; Negev Desert in the S; Israel occupies Golan Heights, West Bank, and Gaza

features historic sites: Jerusalem, Bethlehem, Nazareth, Masada, Megiddo, Jericho; caves of the Dead Sea scrolls

head of state Chaim Herzog from 1983

head of government Yitzhak Rabin from 1992

political system democratic republic

political parties Israel Labor Party, moderate, left of center; Consolidation Party (Likud), right of center **exports** citrus and other fruit, avocados, chinese leaves, fertilizers, diamonds, plastics, petrochemicals, textiles, electronics (military, medical, scientific, industrial), electro-optics, precision instruments, aircraft and missiles

currency shekel

population (1991 est) 4,477,000 (including 750,000 Arab Israeli citizens); under the Law of Return 1950, "every Jew shall be entitled to come to Israel as an immigrant"; those from the East and E Europe are Ashkenazim, and from Mediterranean Europe (Spain, Portugal, Italy, France, Greece) and Arab N Africa are Sephardim (over 50% of the population is now of Sephardic descent). Between Jan 1990 and April 1991, 250,000 Soviet Jews emigrated to Israel. An Israeli-born Jew is a Sabra. About 500,000 Israeli Jews are resident in the US. Growth rate 1.8% p.a.

life expectancy men 73, women 76

languages Hebrew and Arabic (official); English, Yiddish, European and W Asian languages

religions Israel is a secular state, but the predominant faith is Judaism 83%; also Sunni Muslim, Christian, and Druse

literacy Jewish 88%, Arab 70%

GDP $35 bn (1987); $8,011 per head

chronology

1948 Independent State of Israel proclaimed with Ben-Gurion as prime minister; attacked by Arab nations, Israel won the War of Independence. Many displaced Arabs settled in refugee camps in the Gaza Strip and West Bank.

1952 Col Gamal Nasser of Egypt stepped up blockade of Israeli ports and support of Arab guerrillas in Gaza.

1956 Israel invaded Gaza and Sinai.

1959 Egypt renewed blockade of Israeli trade through Suez Canal.

1963 Ben-Gurion resigned, succeeded by Levi Eshkol.

1964 Palestine Liberation Organization (PLO) founded with the aim of overthrowing the state of Israel.

1967 Israel victorious in the Six-Day War. Gaza, West Bank, E Jerusalem, Sinai, and Golan Heights captured.

1968 Israel Labor Party formed, led by Golda Meir.

1969 Golda Meir became prime minister.

1973–74 Yom Kippur War: Israel attacked by Egypt and Syria. Golda Meir succeeded by Yitzhak Rabin.

1975 Suez Canal reopened.

1977 Menachem Begin elected prime minister. Egyptian president addressed the Knesset.

1978 Camp David talks.

1979 Egyptian-Israeli agreement signed. Israel agreed to withdraw from Sinai.

1980 Jerusalem declared capital of Israel.

1981 Golan Heights formally annexed.

1982 Israel pursued PLO fighters in Lebanon.

1983 Agreement reached for withdrawal from Lebanon.

1985 Israeli prime minister Shimon Peres had secret talks with King Hussein of Jordan.

1986 Yitzhak Shamir took over from Peres under power-sharing agreement.

1988 Criticism of Israel's handling of Palestinian uprising in occupied territories; PLO acknowledged Israel's right to exist.

1989 New Likud–Labor coalition government formed under Shamir. Limited progress achieved on proposals for negotiations leading to elections in occupied territories.

1990 Coalition collapsed due to differences over peace process; international condemnation of Temple Mount killings. New Shamir right-wing coalition formed.

1991 Shamir gave cautious response to Middle East peace proposals. Some Palestinian prisoners released. Peace talks began in Barcelona.

1992 Jan: Shamir lost majority in Knesset when fundamentalists withdrew from coalition. June: Labor Party, led by Yitzhak Rabin, won elections; coalition formed under Rabin. Aug: US-Israeli loan agreement signed.

the ⭗Palestine Liberation Organization (PLO), aiming to overthrow Israel.

Arab-Israeli wars During the 1960s there was considerable tension between Israel and Egypt, which, under President ⭗Nasser, had become a leader in the Arab world. His nationalization of the ⭗Suez Canal 1956 provided an opportunity for Israel, with Britain and France, to attack Egypt and occupy the Sinai Peninsula and the Gaza Strip, a part of Palestine that Egypt had controlled since 1949. Israel was forced by UN and US pressure to withdraw 1957. Ten years later, in the Six-Day War, Israel gained the whole of Jerusalem, the West Bank area of Jordan, the Sinai peninsula in Egypt, and the Golan Heights in Syria. All were placed under Israeli law, although the Sinai was returned to Egypt under the terms of the ⭗Camp David Agreements. Ben-Gurion resigned 1963 and was succeeded by Levi Eshkol, leading a coalition government; in 1968 three of the coalition parties combined to form the Israel Labor Party. In 1969 Golda Meir became Labor Party prime minister. In Oct 1973, toward the end of her administration, the Yom Kippur War broke out on the holiest day of the Jewish year. Israel was attacked by Egypt and Syria, and after nearly three weeks of fighting, with heavy losses, a cease-fire was agreed. Golda Meir resigned 1974 and was succeeded by General Yitzhak Rabin, heading a Labor-led coalition.

Camp David Agreements In the 1977 elections the Consolidation Party (Likud) bloc, led by Menachem ⭗Begin, won an unexpected victory, and Begin became prime minister. Within five months relations between Egypt and Israel changed dramatically, mainly owing to initiatives by President ⭗Sadat of Egypt, encouraged by US president Jimmy ⭗Carter. Setting a historical precedent for an Arab leader, Sadat visited Israel to address the Knesset 1977, and the following year the Egyptian and Israeli leaders met at Camp David, in the US, to sign agreements for peace in the Middle East. A treaty was signed 1979, and in 1980 Egypt and Israel exchanged ambassadors, to the dismay of most of the Arab world.

Israeli forces enter Lebanon Israel withdrew from Sinai by 1982 but continued to occupy the Golan Heights. In the same year Israel, without consulting Egypt, entered Lebanon and surrounded W Beirut, in pursuit of 6,000 PLO fighters who were trapped there. A split between Egypt and Israel was avoided by the efforts of the US special negotiator Philip Habib, who secured the evacuation from Beirut to other Arab countries of PLO fighters Aug 1982.

Israel's alleged complicity in permitting Christian Lebanese militias to carry out massacres in two Palestinian refugee camps increased Arab hostility. Talks between Israel and Lebanon, between Dec 1982 and May 1983, resulted in an agreement, drawn up by US secretary of state George Shultz, calling for the withdrawal of all foreign forces from Lebanon within three months. Syria refused to acknowledge the agreement, and left some 30,000 troops, with about 7,000 PLO members, in the northeast; Israel retaliated by refusing to withdraw its forces from the south.

economic problems During this time Begin faced growing domestic problems, including rapidly rising inflation and opposition to his foreign policies. In 1983 he resigned, and Yitzhak Shamir formed a shaky coalition. Elections July 1984 proved inconclusive, with the Labor Alignment, led by Shimon Peres, winning 44 seats in the Knesset, and Likud, led by Shamir, 41. Neither leader was able to form a viable coalition,

creation of Israel In 1947 the British plan for partition was supported by the United Nations, and when Britain ended its Palestinian mandate 1948, an independent State of Israel was proclaimed, with David ⭗Ben-Gurion as prime minister. Neighboring Arab states sent forces to crush Israel but failed, and when a cease-fire agreement was reached 1949, Israel controlled more land than had been originally allocated to it. The non-Jewish-occupied remainder of Palestine, known as the West Bank, was occupied by Jordan. The creation of Israel encouraged Jewish immigration on a large scale, about 2 million having arrived from all over the world by 1962. Hundreds of thousands of Arab residents fled from Israel to neighboring countries, such as Jordan and Lebanon. In 1964 a number of Palestinian Arabs in exile founded but it was eventually agreed that a government of national unity would be formed, with Peres as prime minister for the first 25 months, until Oct 1986, and Shamir as his deputy, and then a reversal of the positions.

Israeli forces withdraw Meanwhile the problems in Lebanon continued. In 1984, under pressure from Syria, President Gemayel of Lebanon abrogated the 1983 treaty with Israel, but the government of national unity in Tel Aviv continued to plan the withdrawal of its forces, although it might lead to outright civil war in S Lebanon. Guerrilla groups of the Shiite community of S Lebanon took advantage of the situation by attacking the departing Israeli troops. Israel retaliated by attacking Shiite villages. Most of the withdrawal was complete by June 1985. Prime Minister Peres met King Hussein of Jordan secretly in the south of France 1985, and later, in a speech to the UN, Peres said he would not rule out the possibility of an international conference on the Middle East. PLO leader Yassir ◊Arafat also had talks with Hussein and later, in Cairo, renounced PLO guerrilla activity outside Israeli-occupied territory. Domestically, the government of national unity was having some success with its economic policies, inflation falling in 1986 to manageable levels.

political crisis The Nov 1988 general election resulted in a hung parliament; after lengthy negotiations, Shamir formed another coalition with Peres and the Labor Party. Shamir's harsh handling of Palestinian protests, and differences over dealings with the PLO, broke the partnership March 1990 when the coalition fell after a vote of no confidence. After a three-month political crisis, Shamir succeeded in forming a new coalition government which included members of Likud and far-right nationalist and religious parties.

proposals for occupied territories Egyptian president Hosni ◊Mubarak proposed a ten-point program for elections in the occupied territories leading toward an unspecified form of autonomous self-rule. Labor quickly agreed to the provisions, and the US approved the plan. In 1989 Likud accepted some of the provisions but remained opposed to any PLO role in the negotiations. In Oct 1990 the killing of at least 19 Palestinians by Israeli police on Jerusalem's Temple Mount drew widespread international condemnation.

In Jan 1991 the Gulf War erupted with UN-coalition air raids against Iraq. In retaliation, Scud missiles were launched against Israel and Israel's nonretaliation was widely praised. In Aug 1991 Shamir agreed to an amended Middle East peace plan, and in Sept released a number of Palestinian prisoners as part of a hostage exchange.

Shamir loses majority The extreme fundamentalists in Shamir's coalition withdrew their support Jan 1992 because of their dissatisfaction with Israel's participation in the Middle East peace talks. This left Shamir with the prospect of a general election to try to restore his majority in the Knesset. In Feb 1992 Yitzhak Rabin replaced Shimon Peres as leader of the Israel Labor Party. In the national elections held June 1992 the Labor party defeated Likud, and a month later Rabin was confirmed as the country's new prime minister. His coalition party was the first Labor-dominated government since Likud had taken power in 1977. In Aug 1992 US-Israeli relations improved when US President Bush and Rabin agreed on a loan pact to aid Israel's absorption of several hundreds of thousands of Soviet Jewish emigrés. The

move solved an issue considered to be a major obstacle in the Middle East peace talks. *See illustration box.*

Israels Jozef 1824–1911. Dutch painter. In 1870 he settled in The Hague and became a leader of the **Hague school** of landscape painters, who shared some of their ideals with the ◊Barbizon school in France. His somber and sentimental scenes of peasant life recall the work of ◊Millet.

Istanbul city and chief seaport of Turkey; population (1990) 6,620,200. It produces textiles, tobacco, cement, glass, and leather. Founded as **Byzantium** about 660 BC, it was renamed **Constantinople** AD 330 and was the capital of the ◊Byzantine Empire until captured by the Turks 1453. As **Istamboul** it was capital of the Ottoman Empire until 1922.

Its *features* include the harbor of the Golden Horn; Hagia Sophia (Emperor Justinian's church of the Holy Wisdom, 537, now a mosque); Sultan Ahmet Mosque, known as the Blue Mosque, from its tiles; Topkapi Palace of the Sultans (with a harem of 400 rooms), now a museum. The Selimye Barracks in the suburb of **Usküdar** (Scutari) was used as a hospital in the Crimean War; the rooms used by Florence Nightingale, with her personal possessions, are preserved as a museum.

isthmus narrow strip of land joining two larger land masses. The Isthmus of Panama joins North and South America.

Itagaki Taisuke 1837–1919. Japanese military and political leader, the founder of Japan's first political party, the (Liberal) Jiyuto 1875–81. Involved in the overthrow of the Tokugawa shogunate and the Meiji restoration 1866–68 (see ◊Mutsuhito), Itagaki became a champion of democratic principles while continuing to serve in the government for short periods.

Itaipu the world's largest dam, situated on the Paraná River, SW Brazil. A joint Brazilian-Paraguayan venture, it started in 1973; it supplies hydroelectricity to a wide area.

Italian native to or an inhabitant of Italy and their descendants, culture, and language. The language belongs to the Romance group of Indo-European languages.

Italian is spoken in S Switzerland and in areas of Italian settlement in the US, Argentina, the UK, and Australia.

Italian architecture architecture of the Italian peninsula after the fall of the Roman Empire. In the earliest styles—Byzantine, Romanesque, and Gothic—the surviving buildings are mostly churches. From the Renaissance and Baroque periods there are also palaces, town halls, and so on.

Byzantine (5th–11th centuries) Italy is rich in examples of this style of architecture, which is a mixture of oriental and Classical elements; examples are the monuments of Justinian in Ravenna and the basilica of S Marco, Venice, about 1063.

Romanesque (10th–13th centuries) In N Italy buildings in this style are often striped in dark and light marble, for example the baptistery, cathedral, and Leaning Tower of Pisa; Sicily has Romanesque churches.

Gothic (13th–15th centuries) Italian Gothic differs a great deal from that of N Europe. Façades were elaborately decorated: mosaics and colored marble were used, and sculpture placed around windows and doors. The enormous cathedral of Milan, 15th century, was built in the N European style.

Renaissance (15th–16th centuries) The style was developed by the Florentine Brunelleschi

and his contemporaries, inspired by Classical models. The sculptor Michelangelo is associated with the basilica of St Peter's, Rome. In Venice the villas of Palladio continued the purity of the High Renaissance.

Baroque (17th century) The Baroque style flourished with the oval spaces of Bernini (for example, the church of S. Andrea al Quirinale, Rome) and Boronini, and the fantasies of Guarini in Turin (such as the church of S. Lorenzo).

Neo-Classicism (18th–19th centuries) In the 18th century Italian architecture was less significant, and a dry Classical revival prevailed. In the 19th century Neo-Classicism was the norm, as in much of Europe.

20th century The Futurist visions of Sant'Elia opened the century. Between World Wars I and II pure Modernism was explored (under the influence of Fascism), together with a stripped Classicism. Nervi's work showed the expressive potential of structural concrete. Rationalism and a related concern with the study of the traditional types of European cities have exerted great influence, led by the work and writings of Aldo Rossi.

Italian art painting and sculpture of Italy from the early Middle Ages to the present. Schools of painting arose in many of the city-states, including Florence and Siena and, by the 15th century, Venice. Florence was a major center of the Renaissance, along with Venice, and Rome was the focus of the High Renaissance and Baroque styles.

13th century (Italian *Duecento*) the painter Cimabue was said by the poet Dante to be the greatest painter of his day. Already there was a strong tradition of fresco painting and monumental painted altarpieces, often reflecting Byzantine art. A type of Gothic Classicism was developed by the sculptors Nicola and Giovanni Pisano.

14th century (*Trecento*) the Florentine painter Giotto broke with prevailing styles. Sienese painting remained decoratively stylized but became less somber, as exemplified by the work of Simone Martini and the Lorenzetti brothers.

Renaissance (15th and 16th centuries) the style was seen as a "rebirth" of the Classical spirit. The earliest artists of the Renaissance were based in Florence. The sculptor Ghiberti worked on the baptistery there; Donatello set new standards in naturalistic and Classically inspired sculpture. Masaccio and Uccello made advances in employing scientific perspective in painting. In the middle and later part of the century dozens of sculptors and painters were at work in Florence: Verrocchio, Pollaiuolo, Botticelli, Fra Angelico, Fra Filippo Lippi, and Filippino Lippi, among others.

In Venice the Bellini family of painters influenced their successors Giorgione and Titian. Tintoretto was Titian's most notable pupil. The High Renaissance was dominated by the many-sided genius of Leonardo da Vinci, the forceful sculptures and frescoes of Michelangelo, and the harmonious paintings of Raphael.

Baroque (17th century) this dramatic style was developed by, among others, the sculptor and architect Bernini, and in painting by Caravaggio, who made effective use of light and shade to create high drama.

Neo-Classicism (18th and early 19th centuries) the style was inspired by the rediscovery of Classical Roman works. The sculptor Canova was an exponent. Piranesi produced engravings.

20th century The Futurist movement, founded 1910, tried to portray phenomena such as speed and electricity in their paintings and sculptures. The first dreamlike Metaphysical paintings of de Chirico date from the same period. Modigliani soon moved to Paris; his paintings are characterized by elongated figures. The sculptures of Marino Marini (1901–1980) and Giacometti created new styles in bronze.

Italian language member of the Romance branch of the Indo-European language family, the most direct descendant of Latin. Broadcasting and films have standardized the Italian national tongue, but most Italians speak a regional dialect as well as standard Italian. The Italian language is also spoken in Switzerland and by people of Italian descent especially in the US, Australia, the UK, and Argentina.

The standard language originates in the Tuscan dialect of the Middle Ages, particularly as used for literary purposes by ⟂Dante Alighieri. Its development parallels the integration of the Italian peninsula and the plains south of the Alps into a cultural and national unity. With a strong infusion of Latin for religious, academic, and educational purposes, written standard Italian has tended to be highly formal and divorced from the many regional dialects, which are often mutually unintelligible. Italian has provided English with much of the vocabulary of music, such as *adagio, arpeggio, cello, crescendo, and pianoforte*; Italian cuisine (*lasagne, macaroni, pasta, pizza, ravioli, spaghetti, tagliatelle*); and an assortment of social comment (*extravaganza, graffiti, imbroglio, mafia, seraglio*).

Italian literature originated in the 13th century with the Sicilian school, which imitated Provençal poetry. The works of St Francis of Assisi and Jacopone da Todi reflect the religious faith of that time. Guido Guinicelli (1230–*c*. 1275) and Guido Cavalcanti (c. 1250–1300) developed the spiritual conception of love and influenced Dante Alighieri, whose *Divina commedia/Divine Comedy* 1307–21 is generally recognized as the greatest work of Italian literature. Petrarch was a humanist and a poet, celebrated for his sonnets, while Boccaccio is principally known for his tales.

The *Divina commedia* marked the beginning of the Renaissance. Boiardo dealt with the Carolingian epics in his *Orlando Innamorato/ Roland in Love* 1480–94, which was completed and transformed by Lodovico Ariosto as *Orlando furioso/The Frenzy of Roland* 1516. Their contemporaries Niccolò Machiavelli and Francesco Guicciardini (1483–1540) are historians of note. Torquato Tasso wrote his epic *Gerusalemme liberata/The Liberation of Jerusalem* 1575 in the spirit of the Counter-Reformation.

The 17th century was characterized by the exaggeration of the poets Giovanni Battista Marini (1569–1625) and Gabriello Chiabrera (1552–1638). In 1690 the "Academy of Arcadia" was formed, including among its members Innocenzo Frugoni (1692–1768) and Metastasio. Other writers include Salvator Rosa, the satirist.

During the 18th century Giuseppe Parini (1729–1799) ridiculed the abuses of his day, while Vittorio Alfieri attacked tyranny in his dramas. Carlo Goldoni wrote comedies, and Ugo Foscolo (1778–1827) is chiefly remembered for his patriotic verse. Giacomo Leopardi is not only the greatest lyrical poet since Dante but also a master of Italian

prose. The Romantic Alessandro Manzoni is best known as a novelist, and influenced among others the novelist Antonio Fogazzaro. A later outstanding literary figure, Giosuè Carducci, was followed by the verbose Gabriele d'Annunzio, writing of sensuality and violence, and Benedetto Croce, historian and philosopher, who between them dominated Italian literature at the turn of the century.

Twentieth-century writers include the realist novelists Giovanni Verga and Grazia Deledda, winner of the Nobel Prize 1926, the dramatist Luigi Pirandello, and the novelists Ignazio Silone and Italo Svevo. Poets of the period include Dino Campana and Giuseppe Ungaretti; and among the modern school are Nobel Prize-winners Eugenio Montale and Salvatore Quasimodo. Novelists of the post-Fascist period include Alberto Moravia, Carlo Levi, Cesare Pavese (1908–50), Vasco Pratolini (1913–), Elsa Morante (1916–), Natalia Ginsburg (1916–), Giuseppe Tomasi, Prince of Lampedusa, and the writers Italo Calvino, Leonardo Sciascia, and Primo Levi.

Italian Somaliland former Italian trust territory on the Somali coast of Africa extending

Italy
Republic of (*Repubblica Italiana*)

area 116,332 sq mi/301,300 sq km
capital Rome
cities Milan, Turin; ports Naples, Genoa, Palermo, Bari, Catania, Trieste
physical mountainous (Maritime Alps, Dolomites, Apennines) with narrow coastal lowlands; rivers Po, Adige, Arno, Tiber, Rubicon; islands of Sicily, Sardinia, Elba, Capri, Ischia, Lipari, Pantelleria; lakes Como, Maggiore, Garda
environment Milan has the highest recorded level of sulfur dioxide pollution of any city in the world. The Po River, with pollution ten times higher than officially recommended levels, is estimated to discharge around 250 tons of arsenic into the sea each year
features continental Europe's only active volcanoes: Vesuvius, Etna, Stromboli; historic towns include Venice, Florence, Siena, Rome; Greek, Roman, Etruscan archeological sites
political parties Christian Democratic Party (DC), Christian, centrist; Democratic Party of the Left (PDS), pro-European socialist; Italian Socialist Party (PSI), moderate socialist; Italian Social Movement–National Right (MSI–DN), neofascist; Italian Republican Party (PRI), social democratic, left of center; Italian Social Democratic Party (PSDI), moderate, left of center; Liberals (PLI), right

to 194,999 sq mi/502,300 sq km. Established 1892, it was extended 1925 with the acquisition of Jubaland from Kenya; administered from Mogadishu; under British rule 1941–50. Thereafter it reverted to Italian authority before uniting with British Somaliland in 1960 to form the independent state of Somalia.

italic style of printing in which the letters slope to the right *like this*, introduced by the printer Aldus Manutius of Venice in 1501. It is usually used side by side with the erect Roman type to distinguish titles of books, films, and so on, and for purposes of emphasis and (mainly in the US) citation. The term "italic" is also used for the handwriting style developed for popular use in 1522 by Vatican chancery scribe Ludovico degli Arrighi, which became the basis for modern italic script.

Italy country in S Europe, bounded N by Switzerland and Austria, E by Slovenia, Croatia, and the Adriatic Sea, S by the Ionian and Mediterranean seas, and W by the Tyrrhenian and Ligurian seas and France. It includes the Mediterranean islands of Sardinia and Sicily.
government The 1948 constitution provides for a two-chamber parliament consisting of a

of center
exports wine (world's largest producer), fruit, vegetables, textiles (Europe's largest silk producer), clothing, leather goods, motor vehicles, electrical goods, chemicals, marble (Carrara), sulfur, mercury, iron, steel
head of state Oscar Luigi Scalfaro from 1992
head of government Giuliano Amato from 1992
political system democratic republic
currency lira
population (1990 est) 57,657,000; growth rate 0.1% p.a.
life expectancy men 73, women 80 (1989)
language Italian; German, French, Slovene, and Albanian minorities
religion Roman Catholic 100% (state religion)
literacy 97% (1989)
GDP $748 bn; $13,052 per head (1988)
chronology
1946 Monarchy replaced by a republic.
1948 New constitution adopted.
1954 Trieste returned to Italy.
1976 Communists proposed establishment of broad-based, left–right government, the "historic compromise;" rejected by Christian Democrats.
1978 Christian Democrat Aldo Moro, architect of the historic compromise, kidnapped and murdered by Red Brigade guerrillas.
1983 Bettino Craxi, a Socialist, became leader of broad coalition government.
1987 Craxi resigned; succeeding coalition fell within months.
1988 Christian Democrats' leader Ciriaco de Mita established a five-party coalition including the Socialists.
1989 De Mita resigned after disagreements within his coalition government; succeeded by Giulio Andreotti. De Mita lost leadership of Christian Democrats; Communists formed "shadow government."
1991 Referendum approved electoral reform.
1992 April: ruling coalition lost its majority in general election; President Cossiga resigned, replaced by Oscar Luigi Scalfaro in May. Giuliano Amato, deputy leader of PDS, accepted premiership. Sept: lira devalued and Italy withdrew from the Exchange Rate Mechanism (ERM).

senate and a 630-member chamber of deputies. Both are elected for a five-year term by universal suffrage, through a system of proportional representation, and have equal powers. The senate's 315 elected members are regionally representative, and there are also seven life senators. The president is constitutional head of state and is elected for a seven-year term by an electoral college consisting of both houses of parliament and 58 regional representatives. The president appoints the prime minister and cabinet (council of ministers), and they are collectively responsible to parliament. Although Italy is not a federal state, each of its 20 regions enjoys a high degree of autonomy, with a regional council elected for a five-year term by universal suffrage.

history The varying peoples inhabiting Italy—Etruscans in Tuscany, Latins and Sabines in middle Italy, Greek colonies in the south and Sicily, and Gauls in the north—were united under Roman rule during the 4th–3rd centuries BC. With the decline of the Roman Empire, and its final extinction AD 476, Italy became exposed to barbarian attacks and passed in turn under the rule of the Ostrogoths and the Lombards. The 8th century witnessed the rise of the papacy as a territorial power, the annexation of the Lombard kingdom by Charlemagne, and his coronation as emperor of the West in 800. From then until 1250 the main issue in Italian history is the relations, at first friendly and later hostile, between the papacy and the Holy Roman Empire. During this struggle the Italian cities seized the opportunity to convert themselves into self-governing republics.

wars and divisions By 1300 five major powers existed in Italy: the city-republics of Milan, Florence, and Venice; the papal states; and the kingdom of Naples. Their mutual rivalries and constant wars laid Italy open 1494–1559 to invasions from France and Spain; as a result Naples and Milan passed under Spanish rule. After 1700 Austria secured Milan and replaced Spain as the dominating power, while Naples passed to a Spanish Bourbon dynasty and Sardinia to the dukes of Savoy. The period of French rule 1796–1814 temporarily unified Italy and introduced the principles of the French Revolution,

Italy: regions

region	capital	area in sq km
Abruzzi	Aquila	10,800
Basilicata	Potenza	10,000
Calabria	Catanzaro	15,100
Campania	Naples	13,600
Emilia-Romagna	Bologna	22,100
Friuli-Venezia Giulia*	Udine	7,800
Lazio	Rome	17,200
Liguria	Genoa	5,400
Lombardy	Milan	23,900
Marche	Ancona	9,700
Molise	Campobasso	4,400
Piedmont	Turin	25,400
Puglia	Bari	19,300
Sardinia*	Cagliari	24,100
Sicily*	Palermo	25,700
Trentino-Alto Adige*	Trento**	13,600
Tuscany	Florence	23,000
Umbria	Perugia	8,500
Valle d'Aosta*	Aosta	3,300
Veneto	Venice	18,400
		301,300

* special autonomous regions
** also Bolzano-Bozen

but after Napoleon's fall Italy was again divided between Austria, the pope, the kingdoms of Sardinia and Naples, and four smaller duchies. Nationalist and democratic ideals nevertheless remained alive and inspired attempts at revolution 1820, 1831, and 1848–49. After this last failure, the Sardinian monarchy assumed the leadership of the national movement.

unification of Italy With the help of Napoleon III, the Austrians were expelled from Lombardy 1859; the duchies joined the Italian kingdom; ◊Garibaldi overthrew the Neapolitan monarchy; and Victor Emmanuel II of Sardinia was proclaimed king of Italy at Turin 1861. Venice and part of Venetia were secured by another war with Austria 1866; in 1870 Italian forces occupied Rome, thus completing the unification of Italy, and the pope ceased to be a temporal ruler until 1929 (see ◊Vatican City State). In 1878 Victor Emmanuel II died and was succeeded by Humbert (Umberto) I, his son, who was assassinated 1900.

colonial empire The formation of a colonial empire began 1869 with the purchase of land on the Bay of Assab, on the Red Sea, from the local sultan. In the next 20 years the Italians occupied all ◊Eritrea, which was made a colony 1889. An attempt to seize Ethiopia was decisively defeated at Adowa 1896. War with Turkey 1911–12 gave Italy Tripoli and Cyrenaica. Italy's intervention on the Allied side in World War I secured it Trieste, the Trentino, and S Tirol.

Fascist era The postwar period was marked by intense political and industrial unrest, culminating 1922 in the establishment of ◊Mussolini's Fascist dictatorship. The regime embraced a policy of aggression with the conquest of Ethiopia 1935–36 and Albania 1939, and Italy entered World War II in 1940 as an ally of Germany. Defeat in Africa 1941–43 and the Allied conquest of Sicily 1943 resulted in Mussolini's downfall; the new government declared war on Germany, and until 1945 Italy was a battlefield of German occupying forces, the Italian underground (partisans), and the advancing Allies.

republic In 1946 Victor Emmanuel III, who had been king since 1900, abdicated in favor of his son Humbert (Umberto) II. The monarchy was abolished after a referendum 1946, and the country became a republic, adopting a new constitution 1948. Between 1946 and 1986 there were nine parliaments and 45 administrations. The Christian Democratic Party was dominant until 1963 and after this participated in most coalition governments. In 1976 the Communists became a significant force, winning over a third of the votes for the chamber of deputies and pressing for what they called the "historic compromise," a broad-based government with representatives from the Christian Democratic, Socialist, and Communist parties, which would, in effect, be an alliance between Communism and Roman Catholicism. The Christian Democrats rejected this. Apart from a brief period 1977–78, the other parties excluded the Communists from power-sharing, forcing them to join the opposition.

coalition governments In 1980 the Socialists returned to share power with the Christian Democrats and Republicans and participated in a number of subsequent coalitions. In 1983, the leader of the Socialist Party, Bettino Craxi, became the republic's first Socialist prime minister, leading a coalition of Christian Democrats, Socialists, Republicans, Social Democrats, and Liberals. Under Craxi's government, which lasted until 1987, the

state of the economy improved, although the north–south divide in productivity and prosperity persists, despite attempts to increase investment in the south. Various short-lived coalition governments followed; in 1989, the veteran Giulio Andreotti put together a new coalition of Christian Democrats, Socialists, and minor parties. In 1990 the Communist Party abandoned Marxism-Leninism and adopted the name Democratic Party of the Left (Partito Democratico della Sinistra). Its leader, Achille Occhetto, was elected secretary-general of the renamed party. A referendum held June 1991 overwhelmingly approved reform of the voting procedure in an attempt to eliminate electoral corruption and to reduce the political influence of the Mafia. In Feb 1992 President Cossiga dissolved parliament two months ahead of schedule and set a general election date of April 6. The election resulted in the ruling coalition losing its majority and the need for the Christian Democrats to forge a new alliance. President Cossiga carried out his threat to resign if a new coalition was not formed within a reasonable time. The election of Oscar Luigi Scalfaro as president in May 1992 was followed in June by the swearing in of Giuliano Amato, leader of the Democratic Party of the Left (PDS), as the new premier. The reshuffled cabinet reflected Amato's intent on reform. In Sept 1992, after unprecedented currency speculation, the government devalued the lira and suspended its membership in the Exchange Rate Mechanism.

foreign relations In foreign affairs Italy has demonstrated its commitment to the European Community (EC) (founder member), NATO, and the United Nations (UN), and in 1983 played an important part in the multinational peacekeeping force in Beirut. Refugees from Albania 1991 strained some towns' resources. *See illustration box.*

itch irritation of nerve endings in skin or mucous membrane that provokes the desire to scratch; also a popular name for the parasitic disorder ◊scabies.

iteration in computing, a method of solving a problem by performing the same steps repeatedly until a certain condition is satisfied. For example, in one method of ◊sorting, adjacent items are repeatedly exchanged until the data are in the required sequence.

iteroparity in biology, the repeated production of offspring at intervals throughout the life cycle. It is usually contrasted with ◊semelparity, where each individual reproduces only once during its life. Most vertebrates are iteroparous.

Ithaca (Greek *Itháki*) Greek island in the Ionian Sea, area 36 sq mi/93 sq km. Important in pre-Classical Greece, Ithaca was (in Homer's poem) the birthplace of ◊Odysseus, though this is sometimes identified with the island of Levkas.

Itō Hirobumi, Prince 1841–1909. Japanese politician, prime minister 1887, 1892–96, 1898, 1900–01. He was a key figure in the modernization of Japan and was involved in the Meiji restoration under ◊Mutsuhito 1866–68 and in government missions to the US and Europe in the 1870s. As minister for home affairs, he helped draft the Meiji constitution of 1889.

Itō was a samurai from Chōshū, a feudal domain that rebelled against the shogunate in the 1850s–60s. In 1863 he became one of the first Japanese to study in England, and in 1871–73 he was a member of a diplomatic mission to Europe and the US. Given responsibility for drafting the constitution, he went abroad again 1882–83 to study European models. He was appointed a government adviser 1885 and went on to become prime minister many times. While resident-general in Korea, he was assassinated by Korean nationalists, which led to Japan's annexation of that country. Politically Itō was a moderate, favoring negotiation and compromise.

Iturbide Agustín de 1783–1824. Mexican military leader (*caudillo*) who led the conservative faction in the nation's struggle for independence from Spain. In 1822 he crowned himself Emperor Agustín I. His extravagance and failure to restore order led all other parties to turn against him, and he reigned for less than a year (see ◊Mexican Empire).

IUCN (abbreviation for **International Union for the Conservation of Nature**) organization established by the United Nations to promote the conservation of wildlife and habitats as part of the national policies of member states.

It has formulated guidelines and established research programs (for example, International Biological Program, IBP) and set up advisory bodies (such as Survival Services Commissions, SSC).

In 1980, it launched the **World Conservation Strategy** to highlight particular problems, designating a small number of areas as **World Heritage Sites** to ensure their survival as unspoiled habitats (for example, Yosemite National Park in California, and the Simen Mountains in Ethiopia).

Ivan six rulers of Russia, including:

Ivan III the Great 1440–1505. Grand duke of Muscovy from 1462, who revolted against Tatar overlordship by refusing tribute to Grand Khan Ahmed 1480. He claimed the title of tsar, and used the double-headed eagle as the Russian state emblem.

Ivan IV the Terrible 1530–1584. Grand duke of Muscovy from 1533; he assumed power 1544 and was crowned as first tsar of Russia 1547. He conquered Kazan 1552, Astrakhan 1556, and Siberia 1581. He reformed the legal code and local administration 1555 and established trade relations with England. In his last years he alternated between debauchery and religious austerities, executing thousands and, in rage, his own son.

Ivan attempted to centralize his rule in Muscovy. He campaigned against the Tatars of Kazan, Astrakhan, and elsewhere, but his policy of forming Russia into an empire led to the fruitless 24-year Livonian war. His regime was marked by brutality, evidenced by the destruction (sacking) of Novgorod.

Ives Charles (Edward) 1874–1954. US composer who experimented with ◊atonality, quarter tones, clashing time signatures, and quotations from popular music of the time. He wrote five symphonies, including *Holidays Symphony* 1904–13, chamber music, including the *Concord Sonata*, and the orchestral *Three Places in New England* 1903–14 and *The Unanswered Question* 1908.

Ives Frederic Eugene 1856–1937. US inventor who developed the ◊halftone process of printing photographs in 1878. The process uses a screen to break up light and dark areas into dots. By 1886 he had evolved the halftone process now generally in use. Among his many other inventions was a three-color printing process (similar to the ◊four-color process).

Iviza alternate spelling of ◊Ibiza, one of the ◊Balearic Islands.

ivory the hard white substance of which the teeth and tusks of certain mammals are composed. Most valuable are elephants' tusks, which are of unusual hardness and density. Ivory is used in carving and other decorative work, and is so valuable that poachers continue to destroy the remaining wild elephant herds in Africa to obtain it illegally.

Poaching for ivory has led to the decline of the African elephant population from 2 million to approximately 600,000, with the species virtually extinct in some countries. Trade in ivory was halted by Kenya 1989, but Zimbabwe continued its policy of controlled culling to enable the elephant population to thrive and to release ivory for export. China and Hong Kong have refused to obey an international ban on ivory trading. *Vegetable ivory* is used for buttons, toys, and cheap ivory goods. It consists of the hard albumen of the seeds of a tropical palm *Phytelephas macrocarpa*, and is imported from Colombia.

Ivory Coast (French *Côte d'Ivoire*) country in W Africa, bounded N by Mali and Burkina Faso, E by Ghana, S by the Gulf of Guinea, and W by Liberia and Guinea.

government The 1960 constitution, amended 1971, 1975, 1980, and 1985, provides for a president who is head of both state and government, elected by universal suffrage for a five-year term, and a single-chamber national assembly of 175 members, also popularly elected and serving a five-year term. The president chooses and heads a council of ministers. The only political party is the Democratic Party of the Ivory Coast (PDCI), and its chair is the state president.

history The area now known as the Ivory Coast/Côte d'Ivoire was once made up of several indigenous kingdoms. From the 16th century the Portuguese, French, and British established trading centers along the coast, dealing in slaves and ivory. During the 19th century France acquired the region by means of treaties with local leaders, eventually incorporating it into ◊French West Africa 1904.

It was given self-government within the French Community 1958 and full independence 1960, when a new constitution was adopted. Félix ◊Houphouët-Boigny is the country's first and only president. He has maintained close links with France since independence, and this support, combined with a good economic growth rate, has given his country a high degree of political stability. He was criticized by some other African leaders for maintaining links with South Africa but defended this policy by arguing that a dialogue between blacks and whites is essential. He has denounced communist intervention in African affairs and has traveled extensively to improve relations with Western powers.

In the Oct and Nov 1990 multiparty elections Houphouët-Boigny and the PDCI were reelected amid widespread criticisms of ballot rigging and political pressure. *See illustration box.*

ivy any tree or shrub of the genus *Hedera* of the ginseng family Araliaceae. English or European ivy *H. helix* has shiny, evergreen, triangular or oval-shaped leaves, and clusters of small, yellowish-green flowers, followed by black berries. It climbs by means of rootlike suckers put out from its stem, and is injurious to trees.

Ground ivy *Glechoma hederacea* is a small, originally European creeping plant of the mint family Labiatae; the North American poison ivy *Rhus radicans* belongs to the cashew family Anacardiaceae.

Ivy League eight long-established colleges and universities in the US with prestigious academic and social reputations: Brown, Columbia, Cornell, Dartmouth, Harvard, Pennsylvania, Princeton, and Yale. The members of the Ivy League compete in intercollegiate athletics.

Iwo Jima largest of the Japanese Volcano Islands in the W Pacific Ocean, 760 mi/1,222 km S of Tokyo; area 8 sq mi/21 sq km. Annexed by Japan 1891, it was captured by the US 1945 after fierce fighting. It was returned to Japan 1968.

Ivory Coast
Republic of (*République de la Côte d'Ivoire***)**

area 124,471 sq mi/322,463 sq km
capital Yamoussoukro
cities Bouaké, Daloa, Man; ports Abidjan, San-Pédro
physical tropical rainforest (diminishing as exploited) in S; savanna and low mountains in N
environment an estimated 85% of the country's forest has been destroyed by humans
features Vridi canal, Kossou dam, Monts du Toura

head of state and government Félix Houphouët-Boigny from 1960
political system emergent democratic republic
political party Democratic Party of the Ivory Coast (PDCI), nationalist, free-enterprise
exports coffee, cocoa, timber, petroleum products
currency franc CFA
population (1990 est) 12,070,000; growth rate 3.3% p.a.
life expectancy men 52, women 55 (1989)
languages French (official), over 60 native dialects
media the government has full control of the media
religions animist 65%, Muslim 24%, Christian 11%
literacy 35% (1988)
GDP $7.6 bn (1987); $687 per head
chronology
1904 Became part of French West Africa.
1958 Achieved internal self-government.
1960 Independence achieved from France, with Félix Houphouët-Boigny as president of a one-party state.
1985 Houphouët-Boigny reelected, unopposed.
1986 Name changed officially from Ivory Coast to Côte d'Ivoire.
1990 Houphouët-Boigny and PDCI reelected.

Iwo Jima, Battle of intense fighting between Japanese and US forces Feb 19–March 17, 1945 during World War II. In Feb 1945, US marines landed on the island of Iwo Jima, a Japanese air base, intending to use it to prepare for a planned final assault on mainland Japan. The Japanese defenses were so strong that 5,000 US marines were killed before the island was captured from the Japanese.

IWW abbreviation for ⇨*Industrial Workers of the World*.

Izhevsk industrial city in central Russia, capital of Udmurt Autonomous Republic; population (1987) 631,000. Industries include steel, agricultural machinery, machine tools, and armaments. It was founded 1760.

Izmir formerly *Smyrna* port and naval base in Turkey; population (1990) 1,757,400. Products include steel, electronics, and plastics. The largest annual trade fair in the Middle East is held here. It is the headquarters of ⇨North Atlantic Treaty Organization SE Command.

history Originally Greek (founded about 1000 BC), it was of considerable importance in ancient times, vying with Ephesus and Pergamum as the first city of Asia. It was destroyed by ⇨Tamerlane in 1402 and became Turkish in 1424. It was developed in the 16th century as an international trading center, much of its trade gained at the expense of Venice. It was occupied by the Greeks in 1919 but retaken by the Turks in 1922; in the same year it was largely destroyed by fire.

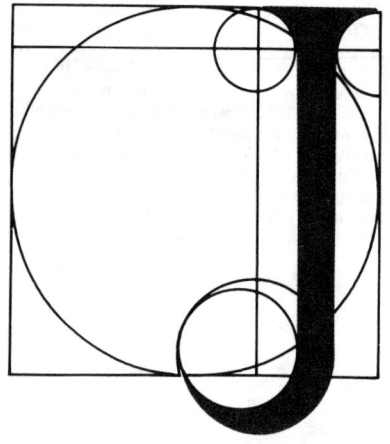

J tenth letter of the English alphabet. The English value of *j* is that of a compound consonant, d followed by the sound *zh* (as in pleasure, pronounced ple*zh*'ur).

J in physics, the symbol for *joule*, the SI unit of energy.

jabiru stork *Jabiru mycteria* found in Central and South America. It is 5 ft/1.5 m high with white plumage. The head is black and red.

jaborandi plant *Pilocarpus microphyllus* of the rue family Rutaceae, native to South America. It is the source of *pilocarpine*, used to contract the pupil of the eye.

jacamar insect-eating bird of the family Galbulidae, in the same order as woodpeckers. Jacamars are found in Central and South America. It has a long, sharp-pointed bill, long tail, and paired toes. The plumage is brilliantly colored. The largest species grows up to 12 in/30 cm.

jacana one of seven species of wading birds, family Jacanidae, with very long toes and claws enabling it to walk on the flat leaves of river plants, hence the name "lily trotter." Jacanas are found in Mexico, Central America, South America, S Asia, and Australia. The female pheasant-tailed jacana *Hydrophasianus chirurgus* of Asia has a "harem" of two to four males.

jacaranda any tropical American tree of the genus *Jacaranda* of the bignonia family Bignoniaceae, with fragrant wood and showy blue or violet flowers, commonly cultivated in the southern US.

jacinth or *hyacinth* red or yellowish-red gem, a variety of ⟡zircon.

jack tool or machine for lifting, hoisting, or moving heavy weights, such as motor vehicles. A *screw jack* uses the principle of the screw to magnify an applied effort; in an automobile jack, for example, turning the handle many times causes the lifting screw to rise slightly, and the effort is magnified to lift heavy weights. A *hydraulic jack* uses a succession of piston strokes to increase pressure in a liquid and force up a lifting ram.

jackal any of several wild dogs of the genus *Canis*, found in S Asia, S Europe, and N Africa. Jackals can grow to 2.7 ft/80 cm long, and have grayish-brown fur and a bushy tail.

The golden jackal *C. aureus* of S Asia, S Europe, and N Africa is 1.5 ft/45 cm high and 2 ft/60 cm long. It is grayish-yellow, darker on the back. Nocturnal, it preys on smaller mammals and poultry, although packs will attack larger animals. It will also scavenge. The side-striped jackal *C. adustus* is found over much of Africa; the black-backed jackal *C. mesomelas* occurs only in the S of Africa.

jackdaw Eurasian bird *Corvus monedula* of the crow family. It is mainly black, but grayish on sides and back of head, and about 1.1 ft/33 cm long. It nests in tree holes or on buildings.

Jackson city in S Michigan, on the Grand River, S of Lansing; seat of Jackson County; population (1990) 37,400. Its industries include motor-vehicle and aircraft parts, tools, plastics, and air-conditioning equipment. The Republican Party was formed here 1854.

Jackson largest city and capital of Mississippi, on the Pearl River; population (1990) 203,000. It produces furniture, cottonseed oil, and iron and steel castings, and owes its prosperity to the discovery of gas fields to the south in the 1930s. Named after Andrew Jackson, later president, it dates from 1821 and was virtually destroyed by Union troops 1863, during the American Civil War.

Educational institutions include Jackson State University, Millsaps College, and the University of Mississippi Medical Center.

Jackson Alexander Young 1882–1974. Canadian landscape painter, a leading member of the *Group of Seven*, who aimed to create a specifically Canadian school of landscape art.

Jackson Andrew 1767–1845. 7th president of the US 1829–37, a Democrat. A major general in the War of 1812, he defeated a British force at New Orleans in 1815 (after the official end of the war in 1814) and was involved in the war that led to the purchase of Florida in 1819. The political organization he built as president, with Martin Van Buren, was the basis for the modern ⟡Democratic Party.

Jackson was born in South Carolina and spent his early life in poverty. After an unsuccessful attempt in 1824, he was elected president in 1828. This was the first election in which electors were chosen directly by voters rather than state legislators. He demanded and received absolute loyalty from his cabinet members and made wide use of his executive powers. In 1832 he vetoed the renewal of the US bank charter and was reelected, whereupon he continued his struggle against the power of finance.

Jackson Glenda 1936– . English actress and politician. She has made many stage appearances, including *Marat/Sade* 1966, and her films include the Oscar-winning *Women in Love* 1969, *Sunday Bloody Sunday* 1971, and *A Touch of Class* 1973. On television she played Queen Elizabeth I in *Elizabeth R* 1971. In 1992 she was elected to Parliament as a Labour Party member.

Jackson Howell Edmunds 1832–1895. US jurist. Born in Paris, Tennessee, Jackson received his law degree from Cumberland University 1856. During the US Civil War, he served as an official in Tennessee's Confederate government. He returned to private practice after the war, was elected to the state legislature 1880, and immediately thereafter was chosen for the US Senate. He was named federal district judge 1886 by Grover Cleveland and chief judge of the circuit court of appeals

1891 by Benjamin Harrison. In 1893 Jackson was appointed to the US Supreme Court by Harrison, but illness prevented him from carrying out his duties.

Jackson Jesse 1941– . US Democrat politician, a cleric and campaigner for minority rights. He contested his party's 1984 and 1988 presidential nominations in an effort to increase voter registration and to put black issues on the national agenda. He is an eloquent public speaker.

Born in North Carolina and educated in Chicago, Jackson emerged as a powerful Baptist preacher and black activist politician, working first with the civil-rights leader Martin Luther King, Jr, then on building the political machine that gave Chicago a black mayor 1983.

Jackson sought to construct what he called a *rainbow coalition* of ethnic-minority and socially deprived groups. He took the lead in successfully campaigning for US disinvestment in South Africa 1986.

Jackson Mahalia 1911–1972. US gospel singer. She made her first recording in 1934, and her version of the gospel song "Move on Up a Little Higher" was a commercial success 1945. Jackson became a well-known radio and television performer in the 1950s and was invited to sing at the presidential inauguration of John F Kennedy.

Born in New Orleans and brought up in a religious home, Jackson began singing religious music in the choir of her local church. In 1927 she left home for Chicago and became a member of the Greater Salem Baptist Church choir, where she distinguished herself as an outstanding soloist.

Jackson Michael 1958– . US rock singer and songwriter whose videos and live performances are meticulously choreographed. His first solo hit was "Got to Be There" 1971; his worldwide popularity peaked with the albums *Thriller* 1982 and *Bad* 1987. The follow-up was *Dangerous* 1991.

He turned professional in 1969 as the youngest member of *the Jackson Five*, who had several hits on Motown Records, beginning with their first single, "I Want You Back." The group left Motown in 1975 and changed its name to *the Jacksons*. Michael was the lead singer, but soon surpassed his brothers in popularity as a solo performer. From *Off the Wall* 1979 to *Bad*, his albums were produced by Quincy Jones (1933–). *Thriller* sold 41 million copies, a world record, and yielded an unprecedented number of hit singles, among them "Billie Jean" 1983.

Jackson Stonewall (Thomas Jonathan) 1824–1863. US Confederate general in the American Civil War. He acquired his nickname and his reputation at the Battle of Bull Run, from the firmness with which his brigade resisted the Northern attack. In 1862 he organized the Shenandoah Valley campaign and assisted Robert E ⟡Lee's invasion of Maryland. He helped to defeat General Joseph E Hooker's Union army at the battle of Chancellorsville, Virginia, but was fatally wounded by one of his own soldiers in the confusion of battle.

A West Point graduate, after serving in the Mexican War 1846–48, he became professor of military tactics at the Virginia military institute.

Jacksonian Democracy in US history, the populist, egalitarian spirit pervading the presidencies of Andrew Jackson and Martin Van Buren 1829–1841, which encouraged greater participation in the democratic process. Recent studies have questioned the professed commitment to popular control, emphasizing Jackson's alleged cult of personality.

Jacksonville port, resort, and commercial center in Florida; population (1990) 635,200. The port has naval installations and ship-repair yards. To the north the Cross-Florida Barge Canal links the Atlantic with the Gulf of Mexico. Manufactured goods include wood and paper products, chemicals, and processed food.

Among the educational institutions are Jacksonville University and the University of North Florida. French Huguenots built a short-lived settlement 1564, but the site of the present city was not settled until 1816. Much of the city was destroyed by Union troops in the American Civil War 1861–65, and there was a destructive fire in 1901. The city absorbed most of Duval County 1968, greatly increasing its area and population.

Jack the Ripper popular name for the unidentified mutilator and murderer of at least five women prostitutes in the Whitechapel area of London in 1888.

Several suspects have been suggested in extensive studies of the case, including members of the royal household.

Jacob in the Old Testament, Hebrew patriarch, son of Isaac and Rebecca, who obtained the rights of seniority from his twin brother Esau by trickery. He married his cousins Leah and Rachel, serving their father Laban seven years for each, and at the time of famine in Canaan joined his son Joseph in Egypt. His 12 sons were the traditional ancestors of the 12 tribes of Israel.

Jacob François 1920– . French biochemist who, with Jacques Monod, pioneered research into molecular genetics and showed how the production of proteins from ◊DNA is controlled. He shared the Nobel Prize for Medicine in 1965.

Jacobin member of an extremist republican club of the French Revolution founded at Versailles 1789, which later used a former Jacobin (Dominican) friary as its headquarters in Paris. Helped by ◊Danton's speeches, they proclaimed the French republic, had the king executed, and overthrew the moderate ◊Girondins 1792–93. Through the Committee of Public Safety, they began the Reign of Terror, led by ◊Robespierre. After his execution 1794, the club was abandoned and the name "Jacobin" passed into general use for any left-wing extremist.

Jacobite in Britain, a supporter of the royal house of Stuart after the deposition of James II in 1688. They include the Scottish Highlanders, who rose unsuccessfully under Viscount Claverhouse (1649–1689) in 1689; and those who rose in Scotland and N England under the leadership of ◊James Edward Stuart, the Old Pretender, in 1715, and followed his son ◊Charles Edward Stuart in an invasion of England that reached Derby in 1745–46. After the defeat at ◊Culloden, Jacobitism disappeared as a political force.

Jacquard Joseph Marie 1752–1834. French textile manufacturer who invented a punched-card system for programming designs on a carpet-making loom. In 1804 he constructed looms that used a series of punched cards to control the pattern of longitudinal warp threads depressed before each sideways passage of the

shuttle. On later machines the punched cards were joined to form an endless loop that represented the "program" for the repeating pattern of a carpet.

Jacquerie French peasant uprising 1358, caused by the ravages of the English army and French nobility during the Hundred Years' War, which reduced the rural population to destitution. The word derives from the nickname for French peasants, Jacques Bonhomme.

jade semiprecious stone consisting of either jadeite, $NaAlSi_2O_6$ (a pyroxene), or nephrite, $Ca_2(Mg,Fe)_5Si_8O_{22}(OH,F)_2$ (an amphibole), ranging from colorless through shades of green to black according to the iron content. Jade ranks 5.5–6.5 on the Mohs' scale of hardness.

The early Chinese civilization discovered jade, bringing it from E Turkestan, and carried the art of jade-carving to its peak. The Olmecs, Aztecs, Maya, and the Maoris have also used jade for ornaments, ceremony, and utensils.

Jade Emperor in Chinese religion, the supreme god, Yu Huang, of pantheistic Taoism, who watches over human actions and is the ruler of life and death.

Jaffa (biblical name *Joppa*) port in W Israel, part of ◊Tel Aviv from 1950.

It was captured during the ◊Crusades in the 12th century, by the French emperor Napoleon in 1799, and by the British field marshal Allenby 1917.

Jaffna capital of Jaffna district, Northern Province, Sri Lanka; population (1990) 129,000. It was the focal point of Hindu Tamil nationalism and the scene of recurring riots during the 1980s.

Jagan Cheddi (Berrat) 1918– . Guyanese left-wing politician. Educated in British Guyana and the US, he led the People's Progressive Party (PPA) from 1950, and was the first prime minister of British Guyana 1961–64. As candidate for president 1992, he opposed privatization as leading to "recolonization." In Aug elections the PPA won a decisive victory, and Jagan as veteran leader replaced Desmond Hoyte.

jaguar largest species of ◊cat *Panthera onca* in the Americas, formerly ranging from the SW US to S South America, but now extinct in most of North America. It can grow up to 8 ft/2.5 m long including the tail. The background color of the fur varies from creamy white to brown or black, and is covered with black spots. The jaguar is usually solitary.

jaguarundi wild cat *Felis yaguoaroundi* found in forests in Central and South America. Up to 3.5 ft/1.1 m long, it is very slim with rather short legs and short rounded ears. It is uniformly colored dark brown or chestnut. A good climber, it feeds on birds and small mammals and, unusually for a cat, has been reported to eat fruit.

Jahangir "Conqueror of the World." Adopted name of Salim 1569–1627. Mogul emperor of India 1605–27, succeeding his father ◊Akbar the Great. He designed the Shalimar Gardens in Kashmir and buildings and gardens in Lahore.

Jahweh another spelling of ◊Jehovah, the Lord (meaning God) in the Hebrew Bible, used by some writers instead of *Adonai* (Lord) or *Hashem* (the Name)— all names used to avoid the representation of God in any form.

jai alai or *pelota* very fast ball game of Basque derivation, popular in Latin American countries

and in the US where it is a betting sport. It is played by two, four, or six players, in a walled court, or *cancha*, and somewhat resembles squash, but each player uses a long, curved, wickerwork basket, or *cesta*, strapped to the hand, to hurl the ball, or pelota (about the size of a baseball), against the walls.

Jainism (Hindi *jaina* "person who overcomes") ancient Indian religion, sometimes regarded as an offshoot of Hinduism. Jains emphasize the importance of not injuring living beings, and their code of ethics is based on sympathy and compassion for all forms of life. They also believe in ◊karma but not in any deity. It is a monastic, ascetic religion. There are two main sects: the Digambaras and the Swetambaras. Jainism practises the most extreme form of nonviolence (*ahimsā*) of all Indian sects, and influenced the philosophy of Mahatma Gandhi. Jains number approximately 6 million; there are Jain communities throughout the world but the majority live in India.

Jainism's sacred books record the teachings of Mahavira (*c.* 540–468 BC), the last in a line of 24 great masters called Tirthankaras (or *jainas*). Mahavira was born in Vessali (now Bihar), E India. He became an ascetic at the age of 30, achieved enlightenment at 42, and preached for 30 years.

During the 3rd century BC two divisions arose regarding the extent of austerities. The Digambaras ("sky-clad") believe that enlightenment can only occur when all possessions have been given up, including clothes, and that it can only be achieved when a soul is born into a human male body. Monks of this sect go naked on the final stages of their spiritual path. The Swetambaras ("white-clad") believe that both human sexes can achieve enlightenment and that nakedness is not a prerequisite.

Jaipur capital of Rajasthan, India; population (1981) 1,005,000. Formerly the capital of the state of Jaipur, which was merged with Rajasthan in 1949. Products include textiles and metal products.

Features include the Jantar Mantar observatory, built by Maharajah Jai Singh II in 1728; it contains the world's largest sundial. The five-story, pink sandstone Hawa Mahal or Palace of the Winds 1799 is a notable landmark. The city is also noted for its blue pottery.

Jakarta or *Djakarta* (former name until 1949 *Batavia*) capital of Indonesia on the NW coast of Java; population (1980) 6,504,000. Industries include textiles, chemicals, and plastics; a canal links it with its port of Tanjung Priok where rubber, oil, tin, coffee, tea, and palm oil are among its exports; also a tourist center. Jakarta was founded by Dutch traders in 1619.

Jalalabad capital of Nangarhar province, E Afghanistan, on the road from Kabul to Peshawar in Pakistan. The city was besieged by mujaheddin rebels in 1989 after the withdrawal of Soviet troops from Afghanistan.

Jamaica island in the Caribbean Sea, S of Cuba and W of Haiti.

government The 1962 constitution follows closely the unwritten British model, with a resident constitutional head of state, the governor-general, representing the British monarch and appointing a prime minister and cabinet, collectively responsible to the legislature. This consists of two chambers, an appointed 21-member senate and a 60-member elected house of representatives. Normally, 13 of the senators are appointed on the advice of the prime minister and 8 on the advice of the leader of the opposition. Members of the house are elected by universal suffrage for a five-year term, but it is subject to dissolution within that period.

history Before the arrival of Christopher ▷Columbus 1494, the island was inhabited by ▷Arawak Indians. From 1509 to 1655 it was a Spanish colony, and after this was in British hands until 1959, when it was granted internal self-government, achieving full independence within the ▷Commonwealth 1962.

The two leading political figures in the early days of independence were Alexander Bustamante, leader of the Jamaica Labor Party (JLP), and Norman Manley, leader of the People's National Party (PNP). The JLP won the 1962 and 1967 elections, led by Bustamante's successor, Hugh Shearer, but the PNP, under Norman Manley's son Michael, was successful 1972. He advocated social reform and economic independence from the industrialized world. Despite high unemployment, Manley was returned to power 1976 with an increased majority, but by 1980 the economy had deteriorated, and, rejecting the conditions attached to a loan from the International Monetary Fund, Manley sought support for his policies of economic self-reliance.

The 1980 general election campaign was extremely violent, despite calls by Manley and the leader of the JLP, Edward Seaga, for moderation. The outcome was a decisive victory for the JLP, with 51 of the 60 seats in the house of representatives. Seaga thus received a mandate for a return to a renewal of links with the US and an emphasis on free enterprise. He severed diplomatic links with Cuba 1981. In 1983 Seaga called an early, snap election, with the opposition claiming they had been given insufficient time to nominate their candidates. The JLP won all 60 seats. There were violent demonstrations when the new parliament was inaugurated, and the PNP said it would continue its opposition outside the parliamentary arena. In 1989 Manley and the PNP were elected. The new prime minister pledged to pursue moderate economic policies and improve relations with the US. In March 1992 Manley resigned the premiership on the grounds of ill health. P J Patterson, the former finance minister, was chosen by the PNP as Manley's successor. *See illustration box.*

James Henry 1843–1916. US novelist, who lived in Europe from 1875 and became a naturalized British subject 1915. His novels deal with the impact of sophisticated European culture on the innocent American. They include *The Portrait of a Lady* 1881, *Washington Square* 1881, *The Bostonians* 1886, *The Ambassadors* 1903, and *The Golden Bowl* 1904. He also wrote more than a hundred shorter works of fiction, notably the supernatural tale *The Turn of the Screw* 1898.

He is assessed, both in the US and Europe, as one of the most significant and influential American writers. His career spanned more than half a century. Other major works include *Roderick Hudson* 1876, *The American* 1877, *The Tragic Muse* 1890, *The Spoils of Poynton* 1897, *The Awkward Age* 1899, *The Wings of the Dove* 1902. His mastery of the novel set the standard for many 20th-century writers.

James Jesse 1847–1882. US bank and train robber, born in Missouri and a leader, with his brother Frank (1843–1915), of the Quantrill raiders, a Confederate guerrilla band in the Civil War. Frank later led his own gang. Jesse was killed by Bob Ford, an accomplice; Frank remained unconvicted and became a farmer.

James P(hyllis) D(orothy) 1920– . British detective novelist, creator of the characters Superintendent Adam Dalgliesh and private investigator Cordelia Gray. She was a tax official, hospital administrator, and civil servant before turning to writing. Her books include *Death of an Expert Witness* 1977, *The Skull Beneath the Skin* 1982, and *A Taste for Death* 1986. She was made a baroness in 1991.

James William 1842–1910. US psychologist and philosopher, brother of the novelist Henry James. He turned from medicine to psychology and taught at Harvard 1872–1907. His books include *Principles of Psychology* 1890, *The Will to Believe* 1897, and *Varieties of Religious Experience* 1902, one of the most important works on the psychology of religion.

James I the Conqueror 1208–1276. King of Aragon from 1213, when he succeeded his father. He conquered the Balearic Islands and took Valencia from the ▷Moors, dividing it with Alfonso X of Castile by a treaty of 1244. Both these exploits are recorded in his autobiography *Libre dels feyts/Chronicle*. He largely established Aragon as the dominant power in the Mediterranean.

James two kings of Britain:

James I 1566–1625. King of England from 1603 and Scotland (as *James VI*) from 1567. The son of Mary Queen of Scots and Lord Darnley, he succeeded on his mother's abdication from the Scottish throne, assumed power 1583, established a strong centralized authority, and in 1589 married Anne of Denmark (1574–1619). As successor to Elizabeth I in England, he alienated the Puritans by his High Church views and Parliament by his assertion of ▷divine right, and was generally unpopular because of his favorites, such as ▷Buckingham, and his schemes for an alliance with Spain. He was succeeded by his son Charles I.

James II 1633–1701. King of England and Scotland (as *James VII*) from 1685, second son of Charles I. He succeeded Charles II. James married Anne Hyde 1659 (1637–1671), mother of Mary II and Anne) and ▷Mary of Modena 1673 (mother of James Edward Stuart). He became a Catholic 1671, which led first to attempts to exclude him from the succession, then to the rebellions of ▷Monmouth and ▷Argyll, and finally to the Whig and Tory leaders' invitation to William of Orange to take the throne in 1688. James fled to France, then led an uprising in Ireland 1689, but after defeat at the Battle of the ▷Boyne 1690 remained in exile in France.

James seven kings of Scotland:

James I 1394–1437. King of Scotland 1406–37, who assumed power 1424. He was a cultured and strong monarch whose improvements in the administration of justice brought him popularity among the common people. He was assassinated by a group of conspirators led by the Earl of Atholl.

James II 1430–1460. King of Scotland from 1437, who assumed power 1449. The only surviving son of James I, he was supported by most of the nobles and parliament. He sympathized with the Lancastrians during the Wars of the ▷Roses, and attacked English possessions in S Scotland. He was killed while besieging Roxburgh Castle.

James III 1451–1488. King of Scotland from 1460, who assumed power 1469. His reign was marked by rebellions by the nobles, including his brother Alexander, Duke of Albany. He was murdered during a rebellion supported by his son, who then ascended the throne as James IV.

Jamaica

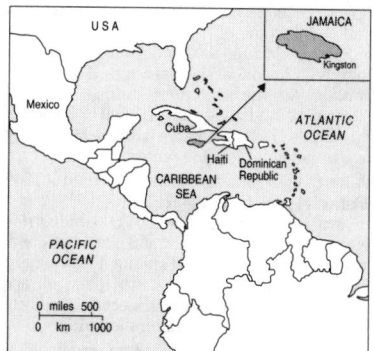

area 4,230 sq mi/10,957 sq km
capital Kingston
cities Montego Bay, Spanish Town, St Andrew
physical mountainous tropical island
features Blue Mountains (so called because of the haze over them) renowned for their coffee; partly undersea ruins of pirate city of Port Royal, destroyed by an earthquake 1692
head of state Elizabeth II from 1962 represented by governor-general (Howard Cooke from 1991)
head of government P J Patterson from 1992
political system constitutional monarchy
political parties Jamaica Labor Party (JLP), moderate, centrist; People's National Party (PNP), left of center
exports sugar, bananas, bauxite, rum, cocoa, coconuts, liqueurs, cigars, citrus
currency Jamaican dollar
population (1990 est) 2,513,000 (African 76%, mixed 15%, Chinese, Caucasian, East Indian); growth rate 2.2% p.a.
life expectancy men 75, women 78 (1989)
languages English, Jamaican Creole
media one daily newspaper 1834–1988 (except 1973–82), privately owned; sensational evening and weekly papers
religions Protestant 70%, Rastafarian
literacy 82% (1988)
GDP $2.9 bn; $1,187 per head (1989)
chronology
1494 Columbus reached Jamaica.
1509–1655 Occupied by Spanish.
1655 Captured by British.
1944 Internal self-government introduced.
1962 Independence achieved from Britain, with Alexander Bustamante of the JLP as prime minister.
1967 JLP reelected under Hugh Shearer.
1972 Michael Manley of the PNP became prime minister.
1980 JLP elected, with Edward Seaga as prime minister.
1983 JLP reelected, winning all 60 seats.
1988 Island badly damaged by Hurricane Gilbert.
1989 PNP won a decisive victory with Michael Manley returning as prime minister.
1992 Manley resigned, succeeded by P J Patterson.

James IV 1473–1513. King of Scotland from 1488, who married Margaret (1489–1541, daughter of Henry VII) in 1503. He came to the throne after his followers murdered his father, James III, at Sauchieburn. His reign was internally peaceful, but he allied himself with France against England, invaded 1513 and was defeated and killed at the Battle of ▷Flodden. James IV was a patron of poets and architects as well as a military leader.

James V 1512–1542. King of Scotland from 1513, who assumed power 1528. During the long period of his minority, he was caught in a struggle between pro-French and pro-English factions. When he assumed power, he allied himself with France and upheld Catholicism against the Protestants. Following an attack on Scottish territory by Henry VIII's forces, he was defeated near the border at Solway Moss 1542.

James VI King of Scotland. See ▷James I of England.

James VII King of Scotland. See ▷James II of England.

James Edward Stuart 1688–1766. British prince, known as the **Old Pretender** (for the ▷Jacobites, he was James III). Son of James II, he was born at St James's Palace and after the revolution of 1688 was taken to France. He landed in Scotland in 1715 to head a Jacobite rebellion but withdrew through lack of support. In his later years he settled in Rome.

James-Lange theory in psychology, a theory that sensory impressions resulting from exposure to an emotional situation are caused by physiological reactions. In this way emotions of pleasure, fear, or amusement may be seen as the result of changes of bodily activity; fear is the sensation of sweating and trembling rather than the emotional reaction to a terrifying situation.

Jameson Leander Starr 1853–1917. British colonial administrator. In South Africa, early in 1896, he led the **Jameson Raid** from Mafeking into Transvaal to support the non-Boer colonists there, in an attempt to overthrow the government (for which he served some months in prison). Returning to South Africa, he succeeded Cecil ▷Rhodes as leader of the Progressive Party of Cape Colony, where he was prime minister 1904–08.

James, St several Christian saints, incuding:

James, St the Great died AD 44. A New Testament apostle, originally a Galilean fisher, he was the son of Zebedee and brother of the apostle John. He was put to death by ▷Herod Agrippa. James is the patron saint of Spain. Feast day July 25.

James, St the Just 1st century AD. The New Testament brother of Jesus, to whom Jesus appeared after the Resurrection. Leader of the Christian church in Jerusalem, he was the author of the biblical Epistle of James.

James, St the Little 1st century AD. In the New Testament, a disciple of Christ, son of Alphaeus. Feast day May 3.

Jamestown first permanent British settlement in North America, established by Captain John Smith 1607. It was capital of Virginia 1624–99.

In the nearby Jamestown Festival Park there is a replica of the original Fort James, and models of the ships (*Discovery*, *Godspeed*, and *Constant*) that carried the 105 pioneers.

The colony initiated the first representative government in North America; it also brought the first slaves and built the first Anglican church there. Subject to a high mortality rate, the population remained small, and the settlement burned 1608. It was about to be abandoned when Lord De La Warr arrived with new supplies.

Jammu and Kashmir state of N India
area 39,102 sq mi/101,300 sq km
capital Jammu (winter); Srinagar (summer)
cities Leh
products timber, grain, rice, fruit, silk, carpets
population (1991) 7,718,700 (Indian-occupied territory)
history part of the Mogul Empire from 1586, Jammu came under the control of Gulab Singh 1820. In 1947 Jammu was attacked by Pakistan and chose to become part of the new state of India. Dispute over the area (see ▷Kashmir) caused further hostilities 1971 between India and Pakistan (ended by the Simla agreement 1972). Since then, separatist agitation has developed, complicating the territorial dispute between India and Pakistan.

Janáček Leoš 1854–1928. Czech composer. He became director of the Conservatoire at Brno in 1919 and professor at the Prague Conservatoire in 1920. His music, highly original and influenced by Moravian folk music, includes arrangements of folk songs, operas (*Jenůfa* 1904, *The Cunning Little Vixen* 1924), and the choral *Glagolitic Mass* 1926.

Janata alliance of political parties in India formed 1971 to oppose Indira Gandhi's Congress Party. Victory in the election brought Morarji Desai to power as prime minister but he was unable to control the various groups within the alliance and resigned 1979. His successors fared little better, and the elections of 1980 overwhelmingly returned Indira Gandhi to office.

Janata Dal (People's Party) Indian center-left coalition, formed Oct 1988 under the leadership of V P ▷Singh and comprising the Janata, Lok Dal (B), Congress (S), and Jan Morcha parties. In a loose alliance with the Hindu fundamentalist Bharatiya Janata Party and the Communist Party of India, the Janata Dal was victorious in the Nov 1989 general election, taking power out of the hands of the Congress (I) Party for the first time since 1947. Following internal splits, its minority government fell in Nov 1990.

Jane Eyre novel by Charlotte Brontë, published 1847. Jane, an orphan, is engaged as governess to Mr Rochester's ward Adèle. Rochester and Jane fall in love, but their wedding is prevented by the revelation that Rochester already has a wife. Jane flees, but later returns to find the house destroyed by fire and Rochester blinded in a vain attempt to save his wife. Jane and Rochester marry.

Janesville city in S Wisconsin, on the Rock River, SE of Madison; seat of Rock County; population (1990) 52,100. Industries include automobiles and car parts, building materials, and electronic equipment. It is a processing and marketing center for the area's agricultural products.

janissary (Turkish *yeniçeri* "new force") bodyguard of the Ottoman sultan, the Turkish standing army 1330–1826. Until the 16th century janissaries were Christian boys forcibly converted to Islam; after this time they were allowed to marry and recruit their own children. The bodyguard ceased to exist when it revolted against the decision of the sultan in 1826 to raise a regular force.

Jan Mayen Norwegian volcanic island in the Arctic, between Greenland and Norway; area 147 sq mi/380 sq km. It is named after a Dutchman who visited it in about 1610, and was annexed by Norway 1929.

Jannequin Clément *c.* 1472–*c.* 1560. French composer. He studied with Josquin ▷Desprez and is remembered for choral works that incorporate images from real life, such as birdsong and the cries of street vendors.

Jansen Cornelius 1585–1638. Dutch Roman Catholic theologian, founder of ▷*Jansenism* with his book *Augustinus* 1640.

Jansenism Christian teaching of Cornelius Jansen, which divided the Roman Catholic Church in France in the mid-17th century. Emphasizing the more predestinatory approach of Augustine's teaching, as opposed to that of the Jesuits, Jansenism was supported by the philosopher Pascal and Antoine Arnauld (a theologian linked with the abbey of ▷Port Royal). Jansenists were excommunicated 1719.

In 1713 a Jansenist work by Pasquier Quesnel (1634–1719), the leader of the Jansenist party, was condemned by Pope Clement XI as heretical, and after Quesnel's death Jansenism disappeared as an organized movement in France. It survived in the Netherlands, where in 1723 a regular Jansenist church was established under the bishop of Utrecht.

jansky unit of radiation received from outer space, used in radio astronomy. It is equal to 10^{-26} watts per square meter per hertz, and is named after US engineer Karl Jansky.

Jansky Karl Guthe 1905–1950. US radio engineer who discovered that the Milky Way galaxy emanates radio waves; he did not follow up his discovery, but it marked the birth of radioastronomy.

Jansky was born in Norman, Oklahoma. In 1928 he joined the Bell Telephone Laboratories, New Jersey, where he investigated causes of static that created interference on radio-telephone calls.

Januarius, St or *San Gennaro* died *c.* 305. Patron saint of Naples, Italy. Traditionally, he suffered martyrdom under the Roman emperor Diocletian. Two phials of his blood preserved in the cathedral at Naples are alleged by the faithful to liquefy miraculously at regular intervals. Feast day Sept 19.

Janus in Roman mythology, god of doorways and passageways, the patron of the beginning of the day, month, and year, after whom January is named; he is represented as having two faces, one looking forward and one back.

Japan country in NE Asia, occupying a group of islands of which the four main ones are Hokkaido, Honshu, Kyushu, and Shikoku. Japan is situated between the Sea of Japan (to the W) and the N Pacific (to the E), E of North and South Korea.

government Japan's 1946 constitution was framed by the occupying Allied forces with the intention of creating a consensual, parliamentary form of government and avoiding an overconcentration of executive authority. The emperor, whose functions are purely ceremonial, is head of state. The Japanese parliament is a two-chamber body composed of a 252-member house of councillors and a 512-member house of representatives. The former chamber comprises 152 representatives elected from 47 prefectural constituencies by the "limited-vote" system and 100 elected nationally by proportional representation. Each member serves a six-year term, the chamber

Japan
(*Nippon*)

area 145,822 sq mi/377,535 sq km
capital Tokyo
cities Fukuoka, Kitakyushu, Kyoto, Sapporo; ports Osaka, Nagoya, Yokohama, Kobe, Kawasaki
physical mountainous, volcanic; comprises over 1,000 islands, the largest of which are Hokkaido, Honshu, Kyushu, and Shikoku
features Mount Fuji, Mount Aso (volcanic), Japan Alps, Inland Sea archipelago
head of state (figurehead) Emperor Akihito from 1989
head of government Kiichi Miyazawa from 1991
political system liberal democracy
political parties Liberal Democratic Party (LDP), right of center; Social Democratic Party of Japan (SDJP), former Socialist Party, left of center but moving toward center; Komeito (Clean Government Party), Buddhist, centrist; Democratic Socialist Party, centrist; Japanese Communist Party (JCP), socialist
exports televisions, cassette and video recorders, radios, cameras, computers, robots, other electronic and electrical equipment, motor vehicles, ships, iron, steel, chemicals, textiles
currency yen
population (1990 est) 123,778,000; growth rate 0.5% p.a.
life expectancy men 76, women 82 (1989)
language Japanese

religions Shinto, Buddhist (often combined), Christian; 30% claim a personal religious faith
literacy 99% (1989)
GDP $2.4 trillion; $19,464 per head (1989)
chronology
1867 End of shogun rule; executive power passed to emperor. Start of modernization of Japan.
1894–95 War with China; Formosa (Taiwan) and S Manchuria gained.
1902 Formed alliance with Britain.
1904–05 War with Russia; Russia ceded southern half of Sakhalin.
1910 Japan annexed Korea.
1914 Joined Allies in World War I.
1918 Received German Pacific islands as mandates.
1931–32 War with China; renewed 1937.
1941 Japan attacked US fleet at Pearl Harbor Dec 7.
1945 World War II ended with Japanese surrender. Allied control commission took power. Formosa and Manchuria returned to China.
1946 Framing of "peace constitution." Emperor Hirohito became figurehead ruler.
1952 Full sovereignty regained.
1958 Joined United Nations.
1968 Bonin and Volcano Islands regained.
1972 Ryukyu Islands regained.
1974 Prime Minister Tanaka resigned over Lockheed bribes scandal.
1982 Yasuhiro Nakasone elected prime minister.
1985 Yen revalued.
1987 Noboru Takeshita chosen to succeed Nakasone.
1988 Recruit scandal cast shadow over government and opposition parties.
1989 Emperor Hirohito died; succeeded by his son Akihito. Many cabinet ministers implicated in Recruit scandal and Takeshita resigned; succeeded by Sosuke Uno. Aug: Uno resigned after sex scandal; succeeded by Toshiki Kaifu.
1990 Feb: new house of councillors' elections won by LDP. Public-works budget increased by 50% to encourage imports.
1991 Japan contributed billions of dollars to the Gulf War and its aftermath. Kaifu succeeded by Kiichi Miyazawa.
1992 Over 100 politicians implicated in new financial scandal. Emperor Akihito made first Japanese imperial visit to China.

Mongol invasions from Korea were repulsed. For the next three centuries the country remained riven by factions, until order was restored 1570–1615 by three great rulers, Oda Nobunaga (1534–1582), Toyotomi Hideyoshi (1537–1598), and ◊Tokugawa Ieyasu; at the battle of Sekigahara 1600 Ieyasu defeated his rivals and established the Tokugawa shogunate (1603–1867).

arrival and expulsion of Europeans Contact with Europe began 1542 when Portuguese traders arrived; they were followed by Spanish and in 1609 by Dutch sailors. Christianity was introduced by Francis ◊Xavier 1549. The fear that Roman Catholic propaganda was intended as a preparation for Spanish conquest led to the expulsion of the Spanish 1624 and the Portuguese 1639 and to the almost total extermination of Christianity by persecution; only the Dutch were allowed to trade with Japan, under irksome restrictions, while Japanese subjects were forbidden to leave the country. Firearms, which the highly skilled Japanese swordsmiths had begun to make in imitation of guns introduced by the Europeans, fell largely into oblivion during this period. Arts, crafts, and theater flourished.

opening of trade relations This isolation continued until 1853, when the US insisted on opening trade relations; during the next few years this example was followed by various European powers. Consequently the isolationist party compelled the shogun to abdicate 1867, and executive power was vested with the emperor, to suit European custom. During the next 30 years the privileges and duties of the feudal nobility were abolished, a uniform code of law was introduced, the educational system revised, and a constitution on the imperial German model was established 1889. The army was modernized and a powerful navy founded. Industry developed steadily, and a considerable export trade was built up.

Japanese expansionism In 1894 a war with China secured Japanese control of Formosa (Taiwan) and S Manchuria, as well as Korea, which was formally annexed 1910. A victory over Russia 1904–05 gave Japan the southern half of Sakhalin and compelled the Russians to evacuate Manchuria. Japan formed an alliance with Britain 1902 and joined the Allies in World War I. At the peace settlement it received the German islands in the N Pacific as mandates. The 1920s saw an advance toward democracy and party government, but after 1932 the government assumed a semiFascist form.

World War II As a result of successful aggression against China 1931–32, a Japanese puppet monarchy under P'u-i, the last emperor of China, was established in Manchuria (see ◊Manchukuo); war with China was renewed 1937 and continued in Asia until Japan entered World War II with its attack on the US territory of Pearl Harbor Dec 7, 1941. Japan at first won a succession of victories in the Philippines, the Malay Peninsula, Burma (now Myanmar), and the Netherlands Indies. US, Australian, and New Zealand troops retook many of the Pacific islands in battles that resulted in heavy casualties; US, French, and UK troops reclaimed much of SE Asia. Japan was compelled to surrender Aug 15, 1945, after the detonation of atomic bombs by the US at ◊Hiroshima and ◊Nagasaki. An Allied control commission took charge, and Japan was placed under military occupation by Allied (chiefly US) troops under General Douglas ◊MacArthur until 1952, when the Japanese Peace Treaty came into force and full sovereignty was regained.

---

being elected half at a time every three years. Representatives to the lower house are elected by universal suffrage for four-year terms in multimember constituencies. The house of representatives is the most powerful chamber, able to override (if a two-thirds majority is gained) vetoes on bills imposed by the house of councillors, and enjoying paramountcy on financial questions. Legislative business is effected through a system of standing committees. Executive administration is entrusted to a prime minister, chosen by parliament, who selects a cabinet that is collectively responsible to parliament.

history Evidence of early human occupation on the Japanese islands exists in the form of 30,000-year-old tools, but the Japanese nation probably arose from the fusion of two peoples, one from the Malay Peninsula or Polynesia, the other from Asia, who conquered the original inhabitants, the ◊Ainu, and forced them into the northernmost islands. Japanese history remains legendary until the leadership of the first

emperor Jimmu was recorded about 660 BC. From 300 BC, agriculture (rice-growing) was introduced, together with bronze, iron, and textile production. During the 4th century AD, the Yamato dynasty unified warring classes in central Honshu and built huge tombs (the largest being nearly 1,640 ft/500 m). Gradually a feudal society was established. By the 5th century AD, the art of writing had been introduced from Korea. After the introduction of Buddhism, also from Korea, in the 6th century, Chinese culture became generally accepted, but although attempts were made in the 7th century to diminish the power of the nobles and set up a strong centralized monarchy on the Chinese model, real power remained in the hands of the great feudal families until recent times.

shogunates A group of warrior families organized local affairs, and the 12th century saw the creation of a military government (shogunate)—a form that persisted until 1867. During the Kamakura shogunate (1192–1333),

After Japan's defeat, Korea was made independent; Manchuria and Formosa (Taiwan) were returned to China; and the islands mandated to Japan after World War I were placed by the United Nations under US trusteeship. Japan regained the ⟡Ryukyu Islands 1972 and the ⟡Bonin and Volcano islands 1968 from the US, and continues to agitate for the return from Russia of the Northern Territories (the islands of the Shikotan and Habomai group) and the southernmost ⟡Kuril Islands (Kunashiri and Etorofu).

democratization and reconstruction During Allied rule, Aug 1945–April 1952, a major "democratization campaign" was launched, involving radical land, social, and educational reform and the framing of a new "Peace Constitution" 1946 in which Emperor Hirohito renounced his claims to divinity and became a powerless figurehead ruler and the nation committed itself to a pacific foreign policy. Japan concentrated during the early postwar years on economic reconstruction, tending toward neutralism in foreign affairs under the protection provided by the 1951 Security Pact.

Postwar politics in Japan were dominated by the Liberal Democratic Party (LDP), formed 1955 from the merger of existing conservative parties and providing a regular succession of prime ministers. Real decision-making, however, centered around a broader, consensual grouping of politicians, senior civil servants, and directors of the major *zaibatsu* (finance and industrial houses). Through a paternalist, guided approach to economic development, epitomized by the operations of the Ministry for International Trade and Industry (MITI), the Japanese economy expanded dramatically during the 1950s and 1960s, with gross national product (GNP) increasing by 10% per year.

During this period, Japan was rehabilitated within the international community, entering the UN 1958 and establishing diplomatic relations with Western nations and, following the lead taken by the Nixon presidency, with Communist China 1972. Japan's internal politics were rocked 1960 and 1968–69 by violent attacks by the anarchic Red Army guerrilla organization protesting against US domination and in 1974 by the resignation of Prime Minister Kakuei Tanaka after a bribery scandal involving the US Lockheed Corporation. This scandal tarnished the image of the LDP and led to the loss of its majority in the house of representatives 1976 and the formation of the New Liberal Club as a breakaway grouping. The LDP remained in power, however, as the largest single party in parliament.

economic impact abroad Japanese economic growth was maintained during the 1970s, though at a reduced annual rate of 4.5%, and the country made a major impact in the markets of North America and Europe as an exporter of electronics, machinery, and motor vehicles. This created resentment overseas as economic recession began to grip Europe and the US during the later 1970s, and led to calls for Japan to open up its internal market to foreign exporters and to assume a greater share of the defense burden for the Asia–Pacific region. Prime ministers Miki, Fukuda, Ohira, and Suzuki resisted these pressures, and in 1976 the Japanese government placed a rigid limit of 1% of GNP on military spending.

liberalization A review of policy was instituted by Prime Minister Yasuhiro ⟡Nakasone, who assumed power 1982. He favored a strengthening of Japan's military capability, a reevaluation of attitudes toward the country's

past, and the introduction of a more liberal, open-market economic strategy at home. The yen was revalued 1985. His policy departures were controversial and only partly implemented. However, he gained a landslide victory in the 1986 elections, and became the first prime minister since Satō (1964–72) to be reelected by the LDP for more than one term. During 1987 his plans for tax reform, including the introduction of a 5% value-added tax (VAT), were overturned by the Diet (parliament). Despite this defeat Nakasone remained popular and was able, after factional deadlock within the LDP, to select Noboru ⟡Takeshita as his successor. It was also Nakasone who went to Iraq in Nov 1990 and obtained the release of 77 hostages.

political scandals Takeshita continued Nakasone's domestic and foreign policies, introducing a 3% sales tax 1988 and lowering income-tax levels to boost domestic consumption. The new sales tax was electorally unpopular, and the government's standing during 1988–89 was further undermined by revelations of insider share-dealing in the ⟡Recruit scandal), in which more than 40 senior LDP and opposition figures, including Takeshita, Nakasone, the deputy prime minister, and the finance and justice ministers, were implicated. The last three were forced to resign, as, eventually, was Takeshita June 1989. This marked an inauspicious start to the new *Heisei* ("achievement of universal peace") era proclaimed on the death Jan 1989 of Hirohito (Shōwa) and the accession of his son Akihito as emperor.

The new prime minister, Sosuke Uno, the former foreign minister, was soon dogged by a sex scandal. His standing was further undermined by the LDP's unprecedented loss of its majority in the house of councillors in elections July 1989, and after only 53 days in office he resigned Aug 1989. He was replaced by Toshiki Kaifu, a former education minister and member of the LDP's small scandal-free Komoto faction. Kaifu formed a new cabinet whose members were comparatively young and which, in an attempt to counter the growing appeal to women of the Japanese Socialist Party (JSP), led by Ms Takako Doi, included two women. Elections in Feb 1990 were won by the LDP, but with large gains for the JSP.

support for Gulf Allies When another insider-trading scandal emerged in the autumn of 1990, it was overshadowed by the crisis in the Persian Gulf, caused by Iraq's annexation of Kuwait. Although Japan is constitutionally debarred from sending troops abroad, the Diet's refusal to pass a bill authorizing the sending of unarmed, noncombatant military personnel damaged Kaifu's standing. However, Japan pledged $13 billion to support the US-led anti-Iraq coalition in the Gulf War. After the war, in 1991, Japan contributed over $2.6 million toward the environmental cleanup, sent teams of experts to help repair desalination plants and remove oil spills, and donated $110 million for the relief of the Kurds and other displaced people.

Kurils In April 1991 Kaifu's government was weakened when a visit by President Gorbachev ended in failure to resolve the conflict over the Kuril Islands, the remaining obstacle to a peace agreement between the USSR and Japan. Russian president Yeltsin's last-minute cancellation of a visit in Sept 1992 was believed to relate to the same issue.

socialists move toward center In June 1991 Takako Doi, leader of the renamed opposition

Social Democratic Party of Japan (SDJP), resigned to take responsibility for her party's crushing defeat in the April 1991 local elections. She was replaced as chair in July by Makoto Tanabe, who sought to continue the process of moving the SDJP towards the centre that Takako Doi had instituted.

Miyazawa's troubled government In Nov 1991 Kaifu was succeeded as LDP leader, and hence prime minister, by Kiichi Miyazawa, whose government included a large number of "rehabilitated" members tainted by the Lockheed and Recruit scandals. In Dec 1991 the Miyazawa government was rocked by LDP by-election reversals, a succession of damaging bribery and corruption scandals that came to light during 1992, and by opposition attempts to secure clarification from Miyazawa of his role in the Recruit affair. The most serious of the new scandals centerd on the Tokyo Sagawa Kyubin company and its enormous political donations and links with organized crime. More than 100 politicians, a seventh of the Diet membership, were implicated, and in Oct it forced the resignation from the Diet of Shin Kanemaru (1914–   ), the LDP's deputy chair and most influential figure. A precipitous fall in the stock market in summer 1992 was stopped short in Sept by an economic rescue package. In Oct, Emperor Akihito made the first visit by a Japanese emperor to China. *See illustration box.*

Japan Current or **Kuroshio** warm ocean ⟡current flowing from Japan to North America.

Japanese inhabitant of Japan; a person of Japanese culture or descent. Japan is an unusually homogeneous society, which has always been adept at assimilating influences from other cultures but has not readily received immigrants; discrimination against foreigners is legal in Japan. The ⟡Japanese language is the only one spoken, though English is considered fashionable and is much used in advertising. Religion is syncretic and it is common for Japanese to take part in both Buddhist and Shinto rituals while professing belief in neither.

Although Japan has a highly distinctive culture, Korean and Chinese influences were absorbed during the early centuries AD. In addition to the art of writing, from the Chinese the Japanese learned skills in the arts, public finance, administration, and animal husbandry. Confucian philosophy and Buddhism were also introduced from China, and after some initial opposition, Buddhism intertwined with Shinto, the indigenous religion. Chinese influence in Japan waned during the decline of the Tang Dynasty (AD 618–907).

The 12th century saw the rise of the code of warriors. Making up approximately 8% of the population, the ⟡samurai had the right to wear two swords, and were the retainers of the daimyos, the hereditary feudal nobles. Merchants, although often wealthier than the samurai, belonged to a lower social order. Some highly skilled craftworkers were allowed to bear family names, a privilege usually reserved for the highest social tier. The lowest social group comprised the *burakumin* or eta, responsible for slaughtering animals and engaged in such trades as tanning leather and shoemaking.

During the late 19th century the feudal society was abolished, compulsory education extended to all, and Japan began to develop its Westernized industrial base. The initially US-financed, rapid economic expansion of the second half of the 20th century has caused the decline of the extended family, in which three or more generations lived under the same roof. Today, large corporations provide a way of life for many Japanese, although this appears to be less the case with the younger generation. The descendants of Japanese migrants are found in Hawaii and North and South America, and Japanese business communities now exist in the cities of most industrial nations.

Japanese art the painting, sculpture, and design of Japan. Early Japanese art was influenced by China. Painting later developed a distinct Japanese character, bolder and more angular, with the spread of Zen Buddhism in the 12th century. Ink painting and calligraphy flourished, followed by book illustration and decorative screens. Japanese prints developed in the 17th century, with multicolor prints invented around 1765. Buddhist sculpture proliferated from 580, and Japanese sculptors excelled at portraits. Japanese pottery stresses simplicity.

Jōmon period (10,000–300 BC) was characterized by cord-marked pottery.

Yayoi period (300 BC–AD 300) elegant pottery with geometric designs and *dōtaku*, bronze bells decorated with engravings.

Kofun period (300–552) burial mounds held *haniwa*, clay figures, some of which show Chinese influence.

Asuka period (552–646) Buddhist art, introduced from Korea 552, flourished in sculpture, metalwork, and embroidered silk banners. Painters' guilds were formed.

Nara period (646–794) religious and portrait sculptures were made of bronze, clay, or dry lacquer. A few painted scrolls, screens, and murals survive. Textiles were decorated with batik, tie-dye, stencils, embroidery, and brocade.

Heian period (794–1185) Buddhist statues became formalized and were usually made of wood. Shinto images emerged. A native style of secular painting (*Yamato-e*) developed, especially in scroll painting, with a strong emphasis on surface design. Lacquerware was also decoratively stylized.

Kamakura period (1185–1392) sculpture and painting became vigorously realistic. Portraits were important, as were landscapes and religious, narrative, and humorous picture scrolls.

Ashikaga or *Muromachi* period (1392–1568) the rapid ink sketch in line and wash introduced by Zen priests from China became popular. Pottery gained in importance from the spread of the tea ceremony. Masks and costumes were made for Nō theater.

Momoyama period (1568–1615) artists produced beautiful screens to decorate palaces and castles. The arrival of Korean potters inspired new styles.

Tokugawa or *Edo* period (1615–1867) the print (*ukiyo-e*) originated in genre paintings of 16th- and 17th-century kabuki actors and teahouse women. It developed into the woodcut and after 1740 the true color print, while its range of subject matter expanded. *Ukiyo-e* artists include Utamaro and Hokusai. Lacquer and textiles became more sumptuous. Tiny *netsuke* figures were mostly carved from ivory or wood.

Meiji period (1868–1912) painting was influenced by styles of Western art, for example Impressionism.

Shōwa period (1926–89) attempts were made to revive the traditional Japanese painting style and to combine traditional and foreign styles.

Japanese language language of E Asia, spoken almost exclusively in the islands of Japan. Traditionally isolated, but possibly related to Korean, Japanese was influenced by Mandarin Chinese especially in the 6th–9th centuries and is written in Chinese-derived ideograms supplemented by two syllabic systems.

Japanese has a well-defined structure of syllables; words end with a vowel or *n* (*futon, jūdō, ninja, kimono, shōgun, sumō, tōfu*). The distinction between long and short vowels affects meaning (long ones are usually, as in this volume, indicated by a macron, or line over the letter).

Japanese is written in a triple system: its *kanji* ideograms are close to their Chinese originals; *hiragana* is a syllabary for the general language; and *katakana* is a syllabary for foreign names and borrowings. In print, the three systems blend on the page much as when italic type is used together with roman.

English words belong in *gairaigo*, the foreign vocabulary expressed in the syllable signs of *katakana* (*fairu* "file," *ereganto* "elegant"), and are often shortened in the process (*fainda* "viewfinder," *wapuro* "word-processor").

Japanese literature earliest surviving works include the 8th-century *Man'yōshū/Collection of a Myriad Leaves*, with poems by Hitomaro and Akahito (the principal form being the *tanka*, a five-line stanza of 5, 7, 5, 7, 7 syllables), and the prose *Kojiki/Record of Ancient Matters*. The late 10th and early 11th centuries produced such writers as Sei Shōnagon and Murasaki Shikibu. During the 14th century the Nō drama developed from ceremonial religious dances, combined with monologues and dialogues.

The 17th century brought such scholars of Chinese studies as Fujiwara Seika (1561–1619) and Arai Hakuseki (1657–1725). This period also saw the beginnings of *kabuki*, the popular drama of Japan, of which Chikamatsu Monzaemon (1653–1724) is the chief exponent; of *haiku* (the stanza of three lines of 5, 7, and 5 syllables), popularized by Bashō; and of the modern novel, as represented by Ihara Saikaku (1642–1693). Among those reacting against Chinese influence was the poet and historian Motoori Norinaga (1730–1801). The late 19th and early 20th centuries saw the replacement of the obsolete Tokugawa style as a literary medium with the modern colloquial language; the influence of Western and Russian literature, producing writers such as the Realist Tsubouchi Shōyo (1859–1935), followed by the Naturalist and "Idealistic" novelists, whose romantic preoccupation with self-expression gave rise to the still popular "I-novels" of, for example, Dazai Osamu (1909–1948).

A reaction against the autobiographical school came from Natsume Sōseki (1867–1916), Nagai Kafū (1879–1959), and Junichirō Tanizaki (1886–1965), who found inspiration in past traditions or in self-sublimation; later novelists include Yasunari Kawabata (1899–1972) and Yukio Mishima (1925–1970). Shimazaki Tōson (1872–1943) introduced Western-style poetic trends, including Symbolism, but the traditional forms of *haiku* and *tanka* are still widely used. Western-style modern drama, inspired by Ibsen and Strindberg, has been growing since the turn of the century (as seen in the work of Shingeki, for example).

Japan, Sea of sea separating Japan from the mainland of Asia.

Jaques-Dalcroze Emile 1865–1950. Swiss composer and teacher. He is remembered for his system of physical training by rhythmical movement to music (◊eurhythmics), and founded the Institut Jaques-Dalcroze in Geneva, in 1915.

jargon language usage that is complex and hard to understand, usually because it is highly technical or occupational, used in the wrong contexts, or designed to impress or confuse ("technical jargon"; "writing in pseudoscientific jargon"; "using a meaningless and barbarous jargon").

Jargon is often also known as *gobbledygook/gobbledegook* and is subcategorized as, for example, *bureaucratese* and *officialese* (the usage of bureaucrats and officials), *journalese* (the languages of newspapers), and *medicalese* (the often impenetrable usage of doctors), and so on. In writing, jargon may be highly formal, whereas in speech it often contains ◊slang expressions.

Jarrett Keith 1945– . US jazz pianist and composer, an eccentric innovator who performs both alone and with small groups. Jarrett was a member of the rock-influenced Charles Lloyd Quartet 1966–67, and played with Miles Davis 1970–71. *The Köln Concert* 1975 is a characteristic solo live recording.

Jaruzelski Wojciech 1923– . Polish general, communist leader from 1981, president 1985–90. He imposed martial law for the first year of his rule, suppressed the opposition, and banned labor-union activity, but later released many political prisoners. In 1989, elections in favor of the free labor union Solidarity forced Jaruzelski to speed up democratic reforms, overseeing a transition to a new form of "socialist pluralist" democracy and stepping down as president 1990.

Jaruzelski, who served with the Soviet army 1939–43, was defense minister 1968–83 and entered the Politburo 1971. At the height of the crisis of 1980–81 he assumed power as prime minister and PUWP first secretary; in 1985 he resigned as prime minister to become president, but remained the dominant political figure in Poland. His attempts to solve Poland's economic problems were unsuccessful. He apologized for the "pain and injustice" suffered by Poles during his term as head of state in his farewell speech of Dec 1990.

Jarvik 7 the first successful artificial heart intended for permanent implantation in a human being. Made from polyurethane plastic and aluminum, it is powered by compressed air. Barney Clark became the first person to receive a Jarvik 7, in Salt Lake City, Utah, in Dec 1982; it kept him alive for 112 days.

The US Food and Drug Administration subsequently withdrew approval for artificial heart transplants because of evidence of adverse reactions.

jasmine any subtropical plant of the genus *Jasminum* of the olive family Oleaceae, with fragrant white or yellow flowers, and yielding jasmine oil, used in perfumes. The common jasmine *J. officinale* has pure white flowers; the Chinese winter jasmine *J. nudiflorum* has bright yellow flowers that appear before the leaves.

Jason in Greek mythology, leader of the Argonauts who sailed in the *Argo* to Colchis in search of the ◊Golden Fleece.

jasper hard, compact variety of ◊chalcedony SiO_2, usually colored red, brown, or yellow. Jasper can be used as a gem.

Jaspers Karl 1883–1969. German philosopher whose works include *General Psychopathology* 1913 and *Philosophy* 1932. He studied medicine and psychology, and in 1921 became professor of philosophy at Heidelberg.

Jat member of an ethnic group living in Pakistan and N India, and numbering about 11 million; they are the largest group in N India. The Jat are predominantly farmers. They speak Punjabi, a language belonging to the Iranian branch of the Indo-European family. They are thought to be related to the Romany people.

Jataka collections of Buddhist legends compiled at various dates in several countries; the oldest and most complete has 547 stories. They were collected before AD 400.

They give an account of previous incarnations of the Buddha, and the verse sections of the text form part of the Buddhist canon. The Jataka stories were one of the sources of inspiration for the fables of Aesop.

jaundice yellow discoloration of the skin and whites of the eyes caused by an excess of bile pigment in the bloodstream. Mild jaundice is common in newborns, but a serious form occurs in rhesus disease (see ◊rhesus factor).

Bile pigment is normally produced by the liver from the breakdown of red blood cells, then excreted into the intestines. A buildup in the blood is due to abnormal destruction of red cells (as in some cases of ◊anemia), impaired liver function (as in ◊hepatitis), or blockage in the excretory channels (as in gallstones or ◊cirrhosis). The jaundice gradually recedes following treatment of the underlying cause.

Java or *Jawa* the most important island of Indonesia, situated between Sumatra and Bali
area (with the island of Madura) 51,000 sq mi/ 132,000 sq km
capital Jakarta (also capital of Indonesia)
cities ports include Surabaya and Semarang
physical about half the island is under cultivation, the rest being thickly forested. Mountains and sea breezes keep temperatures down, but humidity is high, with heavy rainfall from Dec to March
features a chain of mountains, some of which are volcanic, runs along the center, rising to 9,000 ft/2,750 m. The highest mountain, Semeru (12,060 ft/3,676 m) is in the east
products rice, coffee, cocoa, tea, sugar, rubber, quinine, teak, petroleum
population (with Madura; 1989) 107,513,800, including people of Javanese, Sundanese, and Madurese origin, with differing languages
religion predominantly Muslim
history Fossilized early human remains (*Homo erectus*) were discovered 1891–92. In central Java there are ruins of magnificent Buddhist monuments and of the Sivaite temple in Prambanan. The island's last Hindu kingdom, Majapahit, was destroyed about 1520 and followed by a number of short-lived Javanese kingdoms. The Dutch East India company founded a factory in 1610. Britain took over during the Napoleonic period, 1811–16, and Java then reverted to Dutch control. Occupied by Japan 1942–45, Java then became part of the republic of ◊Indonesia.

Javanese member of the largest ethnic group in the Republic of Indonesia. There are more than 50 million speakers of Javanese, which belongs to the western branch of the Austronesian family. Although the Javanese have a Hindu-Buddhist heritage, they are today predominantly Muslim, practicing a branch of

Islam known as *Islam Jawa*, which contains many Sufi features.

The Javanese are known for their performing arts, especially their shadow theater and gamelan orchestras, their high-quality metalwork, and batik resist-dyed cloth.

In pre-independence Indonesia, Javanese society was divided into hierarchical classes ruled by sultans, and differences in status were reflected by strict codes of dress. Arts and crafts flourished at the court.

Although the majority of Javanese depend on the cultivation of rice in irrigated fields, there are many large urban centers with developing industries. To relieve the pressure on the land, farmers have been moved under Indonesia's controversial transmigration scheme to less populated islands such as Sulawesi (Celebes) and Irian Jaya (W New Guinea).

javelin spear used in track and field events. The men's javelin is about 8.5 ft/260 cm long, weighing 28 oz/800 g; the women's 7.5 ft/ 230 cm long, weighing 21 oz/600 g. It is thrown from a scratch line at the end of a run-up. The center of gravity on the men's javelin was altered 1986 to reduce the vast distances (100 yd/90 m) that were being thrown.

jaw one of two bony structures that form the framework of the mouth in all vertebrates except lampreys and hagfishes (the agnathous or jawless vertebrates). They consist of the upper jawbone (maxilla), which is fused to the skull, and the lower jawbone (mandible), which is hinged at each side to the bones of the temple by ◊ligaments.

jay any of several birds of the crow family Corvidae, generally brightly colored and native to Eurasia and the Americas. In the Eurasian common jay *Garrulus glandarius*, the body is fawn with patches of white, blue, and black on the wings and tail.

The blue jay *Cyanocitta cristata*, of the east and central US, has a crest and is very noisy and bold.

Jay John 1745–1829. US diplomat and jurist, a member of the Continental Congress. With Benjamin Franklin and John Adams, he negotiated the Peace of Paris 1783, which concluded the Revolutionary War. President Washington named him first chief justice of the US in 1789. He negotiated Jay's Treaty with England 1795 (which averted another war), then left the Supreme Court to serve as governor of New York 1795–1801.

Jay, born in New York City, was admitted to the bar 1768. He was a member of the Continental Congress 1774–76 and became the first chief justice of New York 1778. He served as president of the Continental Congress 1779 and US minister to Spain 1779–82. Jay later served as foreign secretary for the Continental Congress 1783–89. A strong supporter of the federal constitution, he collaborated with Alexander Hamilton and James Madison on the *Federalist Papers* 1787–88, which helped sway opinion in favor of its ratification.

Jayawardene Junius Richard 1906– . Sri Lankan politician. Leader of the United Nationalist Party from 1973, he became prime minister 1977 and the country's first president 1978–88.

jazz polyphonic, syncopated music characterized by solo virtuosic improvisation, which developed in the US at the turn of the 20th century. Initially music for dancing, often with a vocalist, it had its roots in black American

and other popular music. As jazz grew increasingly complex and experimental, various distinct forms evolved. Seminal musicians include Louis Armstrong, Charlie Parker, and John Coltrane.

chronology
1880–1900 Originated chiefly in New Orleans from ragtime. *1920s* During Prohibition, the center of jazz moved to Chicago (Louis Armstrong, Bix Beiderbecke) and St Louis. By the end of the decade the focus had shifted to New York City (Art Tatum, Fletcher Henderson), to radio and recordings.
1930s The *swing* bands used call-and-response arrangements with improvised solos of voice and instruments (Paul Whiteman, Benny Goodman).
1940s Swing grew into the *big-band* era with jazz composed as well as arranged (Glenn Miller, Duke Ellington); rise of *West Coast* jazz (Stan Kenton) and rhythmically complex, highly improvised *bebop* (Charlie Parker, Dizzy Gillespie, Thelonius Monk). *1950s* Jazz had ceased to be dance music; *cool jazz* (Stan Getz, Miles Davis, Lionel Hampton, Modern Jazz Quartet) developed in reaction to the insistent, "hot" bebop and *hard bop*.
1960s Free-form or *free jazz* (Ornette Coleman, John Coltrane).
1970s Jazz rock (US group Weather Report, formed 1970; British guitarist John McLaughlin, 1942–); jazz funk (US saxophonist Grover Washington Jr, 1943–); more eclectic free jazz (US pianist Keith Jarrett, 1945–).
1980s Resurgence of tradition (US trumpeter Wynton Marsalis, 1962– ; British saxophonist Courtney Pine, 1965–) and avant-garde (US chamber-music Cronus Quartet, formed 1978; anarchic British group Loose Tubes, 1983–89).

Jazz Age the hectic and exciting 1920s in the US, when "hot jazz" became fashionable as part of the general rage for spontaneity and social freedom. The phrase is attributed to the novelist F Scott Fitzgerald.

jazz dance dance based on African techniques and rhythms, developed by black Americans around 1917. It entered mainstream dance in the 1920s, mainly in show business, and from the 1960s the teachers and choreographers Matt Mattox and Luigi expanded its vocabulary. Contemporary choreographers as diverse as Jerome ◊Robbins and Alvin Ailey used it in their work.

J-curve in economics, a graphic illustration of the likely effect of a currency devaluation on the balance of payments. Initially, there will be a deterioration as import prices increase and export prices decline, followed by a decline in import volume and upsurge of export volume.

jeans denim trousers, traditionally blue, originally cut from jean cloth ("jene fustian"), a heavy canvas made in Genoa, Italy. Levi Strauss (1830–1902), a Bavarian immigrant to the US, made sturdy trousers for goldminers in San Francisco out of jean material intended for wagon covers. Hence they became known as "Levis." Later a French fabric, *serge de Nîmes* (corrupted to "denim"), was used.

Jeans James Hopwood 1877–1946. British mathematician and scientist. In physics he worked on the kinetic theory of gases, and on forms of energy radiation; in astronomy, his work focused on giant and dwarf stars, the nature of spiral nebulae, and the origin of the cosmos. He did much to popularize astronomy.

Jedda alternate spelling for the Saudi Arabian port ◊Jiddah.

Jeffers (John) Robinson 1887–1962. US poet. He wrote free verse and demonstrated an antagonism to human society. His collected volumes include *Tamar and Other Poems* 1924, *The Double Axe* 1948, and *Hungerfield and Other Poems* 1954.

Jefferson Thomas 1743–1826. 3rd president of the US 1801–09, founder of the Democratic Republican Party. He published *A Summary View of the Rights of America* 1774 and as a member of the Continental Congresses of 1775–76 was largely responsible for the drafting of the ◊Declaration of Independence. He was governor of Virginia 1779–81, ambassador to Paris 1785–89, secretary of state 1789–93, and vice-president 1797–1801.

Jefferson was born in Virginia into a wealthy family. His interests included music, painting, architecture, and the natural sciences; he was very much a product of the 18th-century Enlightenment. His political philosophy of "agrarian democracy" placed responsibility for upholding a virtuous American republic mainly upon a citizenry of independent yeoman farmers. Ironically, his two terms as president saw the adoption of some of the ideas of his political opponents, the ◊Federalists.

He was supportive of the French Revolution and spent four years in France while dispatching advice through his ally James ◊Madison on the proposals for a Constitutional Convention. Upon his return to the political scene, he carried on his battle with Alexander ◊Hamilton, who held views of America directly opposed to his own agrarian, democratic inclinations.

Jefferson City capital of Missouri, located in the central part of the state, W of St Louis, on the Mississippi River; population (1990) 35,500. Industries include agricultural products, shoes, electrical appliances, and cosmetics.

Jeffreys Alec John 1950– . British geneticist who discovered the DNA probes necessary for accurate ◊genetic fingerprinting so that a murderer or rapist could be identified by, for example, traces of blood, tissue, or semen.

Jehol former name for the city of Chengale in NE Hebei province, N China.

Jehosophat 4th king of Judah *c.* 873–849 BC; he allied himself with Ahab, king of Israel, in the war against Syria.

Jehovah also *Jahweh* in the Old Testament the name of God, revealed to Moses; in Hebrew texts of the Old Testament the name was represented by the letters YHVH (without the vowels "a o a") as it was regarded as too sacred to be pronounced.

The terms *Adonai* ("Lord") and *Hashem* ("the Name") were also used in order to avoid directly mentioning God.

Jehovah's Witness member of a religious organization originating in the US 1872 under Charles Taze Russell (1852–1916). Jehovah's Witnesses attach great importance to Christ's second coming, which Russell predicted would occur 1914, and which Witnesses still believe is imminent. All Witnesses are expected to take part in house-to-house preaching; there are no clergy.

Witnesses believe that after the second coming the ensuing Armageddon and Last Judgment, which entail the destruction of all except the faithful, are to give way to the Theocratic Kingdom. Earth will continue to exist as the home of humanity, apart from 144,000 chosen believers who will reign with Christ in heaven. Witnesses believe that they should not become involved in the affairs of this world, and their tenets, involving rejection of obligations such as military service, have often brought them into conflict with authority. Because of a biblical injunction against eating blood, they will not give or receive blood transfusions. Adults are baptized by total immersion.

The Watch Tower Bible and Tract Society and the Watch Tower Students' Association form part of the movement, which numbered about 1 million members in the 1980s.

Jehu king of Israel *c.* 842–815 BC. He led a successful rebellion against the family of ◊Ahab and was responsible for the death of Jezebel.

Jekyll and Hyde two conflicting sides of a personality, as in the novel by the Scottish writer R L Stevenson, *The Strange Case of Dr Jekyll and Mr Hyde* 1886, where the good Jekyll by means of a potion periodically transforms himself into the evil Hyde.

jellyfish marine invertebrate of the phylum Cnidaria (coelenterates) with an umbrella-shaped body composed of a semitransparent gelatinous substance, with a fringe of stinging tentacles. Most adult jellyfishes move freely, but during parts of their life cycle many are polyplike and attached. They feed on small animals that are paralyzed by stinging cells in the jellyfishes' tentacles.

Jena town SE of Weimar, in the state of Thuringia, Germany, population (1990) 110,000. Industries include the Zeiss firm of optical-instrument makers, founded 1846. Here in 1806 Napoleon defeated the Prussians, and Schiller and Hegel taught at the university, which dates from 1558.

Jencks Charles 1939– . US architectural theorist and furniture designer. He coined the term "Postmodern architecture" and wrote *The Language of Post-Modern Architecture* 1984.

Jenkins's Ear, War of war 1739 between Britain and Spain, arising from Britain's illicit trade in Spanish America; it merged into the War of the ◊Austrian Succession 1740–48. The name derives from the claim of Robert Jenkins, a merchant captain, that his ear had been cut off by Spanish coastguards near Jamaica. The incident was seized on by opponents of Robert ◊Walpole who wanted to embarrass his government's antiwar policy and force war with Spain.

Jenner Edward 1749–1823. English physician who pioneered vaccination. In Jenner's day, smallpox was a major killer. His discovery 1796 that inoculation with cowpox gives immunity to smallpox was a great medical breakthrough. He coined the word "vaccination" from the Latin word for cowpox, *vaccina*.

jerboa small, nocturnal, leaping rodent belonging to the family Dipodidae. There are about 25 species of jerboa, native to N Africa and SW Asia.

Typical is the common N African jerboa *Jaculus orientalis* with a body about 6 in/15 cm long and a 10 in/25 cm tail with a tuft at the tip. At speed it moves in a series of long jumps with its forefeet held close to its body.

Jeremiah 7th–6th century BC. Old Testament Hebrew prophet, whose ministry continued 626–586 BC. He was imprisoned during ◊Nebuchadnezzar's siege of Jerusalem on suspicion of intending to desert to the enemy. On the city's fall, he retired to Egypt.

Jericho Israeli-administered town in Jordan, north of the Dead Sea. It was settled by 8000 BC, and by 6000 BC had become a walled city with 2,000 inhabitants. In the Old Testament it was the first Canaanite stronghold captured by the Israelites, and its walls, according to the Book of ◊Joshua, fell to the blast of Joshua's trumpets. Successive archeological excavations since 1907 show that the walls of the city were destroyed many times.

Jeroboam 10th century BC. First king of Israel *c.* 922–901 BC after it split away from the kingdom of Judah.

Jerome, St *c.* 340–420. One of the early Christian leaders and scholars known as the Fathers of the Church. His Latin versions of the Old and New Testaments form the basis of the Roman Catholic Vulgate. He is usually depicted with a lion. Feast day Sept 30.

Jersey largest of the ◊Channel Islands; capital St Helier; area 45 sq mi/117 sq km; population (1986) 80,000. It is governed by a lieutenant-governor representing the English crown and an assembly. Jersey cattle were originally bred here. Jersey gave its name to a woolen garment.

The island was occupied 1940–45 by German forces. Jersey zoo (founded 1959 by Gerald Durrell) is engaged in breeding some of the world's endangered species.

Jersey City city of NE New Jersey; population (1990) 228,500. It faces Manhattan Island, to which it is connected by tunnels. A former port, it is now an industrial center.

Jerusalem ancient city of Palestine, divided 1948 between Jordan and the new republic of Israel; area (pre-1967) 14.5 sq mi/37.5 sq km, (post-1967) 42 sq mi/108 sq km, including areas of the West Bank; population (1989) 500,000, about 350,000 Israelis and 150,000 Palestinians. In 1950 the western New City was proclaimed as the Israeli capital, and, having captured from Jordan the eastern Old City 1967, Israel affirmed 1980 that the united city was the country's capital; the United Nations does not recognize the claim.

features Seven gates into the Old City through the walls built by Selim I (1467–1520); buildings: the Church of the Holy Sepulchre (built by Emperor Constantine 335) and the mosque of the Dome of the Rock. The latter stands on the site of the ◊Temple built by King Solomon in the 10th century BC, and the Western ("wailing") Wall, held sacred by Jews, is part of the walled platform on which the Temple once stood. The Hebrew University of Jerusalem opened 1925.

religions Christianity, Judaism, and Muslim, with Roman Catholic, Anglican, Eastern Orthodox, and Coptic bishoprics. In 1967 Israel guaranteed freedom of access of all faiths to their holy places.

history
1400 BC Jerusalem was ruled by a king subject to Egypt.
c. 1000 BC David made it the capital of a united Jewish kingdom.
586 BC The city was destroyed by Nebuchadnezzar, king of Babylonia, who deported its inhabitants.
539–529 BC Under Cyrus the Great of Persia the exiled Jews were allowed to return to Jerusalem and a new settlement was made.

c. 445 BC The city walls were rebuilt.
333 BC Conquered by Alexander the Great.
63 BC Conquered by the Roman general Pompey.
AD 29 or 30 Under the Roman governor Pontius Pilate, Jesus was executed here.
70 A Jewish revolt led to the complete destruction of the city by the Roman emperor Titus.
135 On its site the emperor Hadrian founded the Roman city of Aelia Capitolina.
615 The city was pillaged by the Persian Chosroës II while under Byzantine rule.
637 It was first conquered by Islam.
1099 Jerusalem captured by the Crusaders and became the Kingdom of Jerusalem under Godfrey of Bouillon.
1187 Recaptured by Saladin, sultan of Egypt.
1516 Became part of the Ottoman Empire.
1917 Britain occupied Palestine.
1922–1948 Jerusalem was the capital of the British mandate.

Jerusalem artichoke a variety of ▷artichoke.

Jesuit member of the largest and most influential Roman Catholic religious order (also known as the *Society of Jesus*) founded by Ignatius ▷Loyola 1534, with the aims of protecting Catholicism against the Reformation and carrying out missionary work. During the 16th and 17th centuries Jesuits were missionaries in Japan, China, Paraguay, and among the North American Indians. The order had (1991) about 29,000 members (15,000 priests plus students and lay members), and their schools and universities are renowned.

history The Society of Jesus received papal approval 1540. Its main objects were defined as educational work, the suppression of heresy, and missionary work among nonbelievers (its members were not confined to monasteries). Loyola infused into the order a spirit of military discipline, with long and arduous training. Their political influence resulted in their expulsion during 1759–68 from Portugal, France, and Spain, and suppression by Pope Clement XIV 1773. The order was revived by Pius VII 1814, but has since been expelled from many of the countries of Europe and the Americas, and John Paul II criticized the Jesuits 1981 for supporting revolution in South America.

Their head (general) is known as the "Black Pope" from the color of his cassock; the general from 1983 was Pieter-Hans Kolvenbach.

Jesus *c.* 4 BC–AD 29 or 30. Hebrew preacher on whose teachings Christianity was founded. According to the accounts of his life in the four Gospels, he was born in Bethlehem, Palestine, son of God and the Virgin Mary, and brought up by Mary and her husband Joseph as a carpenter in Nazareth. After adult baptism, he gathered 12 disciples, but his preaching antagonized the Roman authorities and he was executed by crucifixion. Three days later there came reports of his resurrection and, later, his ascension to heaven.

Through his legal father Joseph, Jesus belonged to the tribe of Judah and the family of David, the second king of Israel, a heritage needed by the Messiah for whom the Hebrew people were waiting. In AD 26/27 his cousin John the Baptist proclaimed the coming of the promised Messiah and baptized Jesus, who then made two missionary journeys through the district of Galilee. His teaching, summarized in the Sermon on the Mount, aroused both religious opposition from the ▷Pharisees

jet propulsion *Two forms of jet engine.*

and secular opposition from the party supporting the Roman governor, ▷Herod Antipas. When Jesus returned to Jerusalem (probably in AD 29), a week before the Passover festival, he was greeted by the people as the Messiah, and the Hebrew authorities (aided by the apostle Judas) had him arrested and condemned to death, after a hurried trial by the Sanhedrin (supreme Jewish court). The Roman procurator, Pontius Pilate, confirmed the sentence, stressing the threat posed to imperial authority by Jesus' teaching.

jet hard, black variety of lignite, a type of coal. It is cut and polished for use in jewelry and ornaments. Articles made of jet have been found in Bronze Age tombs.

jeté (French "thrown") in dance, a jump from one foot to the other. A *grand jeté* is a big jump in which the dancer pushes off on one foot, holds a brief pose in midair, and lands lightly on the other foot.

jetfoil advanced type of ▷hydrofoil boat built by Boeing, propelled by water jets. It features horizontal, fully submerged hydrofoils fore and aft and has a sophisticated computerized control system to maintain its stability in all waters.

Jetfoils have been in service worldwide since 1975. A jetfoil service operates across the English Channel between Dover and Ostend, Belgium, with a passage time of about 1.5 hours. Cruising speed of the jetfoil is about 50 mph/80 kph.

jet lag the effect of a sudden switch of time zones in air travel, resulting in tiredness and feeling "out of step" with day and night. In 1989 it was suggested that use of the hormone melatonin helped to lessen the effect of jet lag by resetting the body clock. See also ▷circadian rhythm.

jet propulsion method of propulsion in which an object is propelled in one direction by a

jet, or stream of gases, moving in the other. This follows from Isaac ▷Newton's third law of motion: "To every action, there is an equal and opposite reaction." The most widespread application of the jet principle is in the jet engine, the most common kind of aircraft engine.

Jet Propulsion Laboratory NASA installation at Pasadena, California, operated by the California Institute of Technology. It is the command center for NASA's deep-space probes such as the ▷Voyager, ▷Magellan, and ▷Galileo missions, with which it communicates via the Deep Space Network of radio telescopes at Goldstone, California; Madrid, Spain; and Canberra, Australia.

jetsam goods deliberately sunk in the sea to lighten a vessel in a storm, or wreck. See ▷flotsam, jetsam, and lagan.

jet stream narrow band of very fast wind (velocities of over 95 mph/150 kph) found at altitudes of 6–10 mi/10–16 km in the upper troposphere or lower stratosphere. Jet streams usually occur about the latitudes of the Westerlies (35°–60°).

Jew follower of ▷Judaism, the Jewish religion. The term is also used to refer to those who claim descent from the ancient Hebrews, a Semitic people of the Middle East. Today, some may recognize their ethnic heritage but not practice the religious or cultural traditions. The term came into use in medieval Europe, based on the Latin name for Judeans, the people of Judah. Prejudice against Jews is termed ▷anti-Semitism.

jewelweed or *touch-me-not* any of various North American annual herbaceous plants of the genus *Impatiens* of the balsam family, usually growing in wet soil and having yellowish-orange, sometimes spotted flowers with short spurs. Their mature seed pods burst at the slightest touch.

Jewish Agency administrative body created

by the British mandate power in Palestine 1929 to oversee the Jewish population and immigration. In 1948 it took over as the government of an independent Israel.

Jewish-American writing US writing in English shaped by the Jewish experience. It was produced by the children of Eastern European immigrants who came to the US at the end of the 19th century, and by the 1940s second- and third-generation Jewish-American writers had become central to US literary and intellectual life. Nobel Prize-winning authors include Saul Bellow 1976 and Isaac Bashevis Singer 1978.

The first significant Jewish-American novel was Abraham Cahan's *The Rise of David Levinsky* 1917. During the 1920s many writers, including Ludwig Lewisohn and Mary Antin, signaled the Jewish presence in US culture. In the 1930s Mike Gold's *Jews Without Money* and Henry Roth's *Call It Sleep* showed in fiction the immigrant Jewish struggle to adapt to the US experience. Novelists such as Bernard Malamud, Philip Roth, and Norman Mailer, poets such as Karl Shapiro, Delmore Schwartz (1913–1966), and Muriel Rukeyser (1913–1980), playwrights and screenwriters such as Arthur Miller, S N Behrman, Neil Simon, and Woody Allen, and critics such as Lionel Trilling (1905–1975) and Irving Howe made the Jewish experience known as a genre of American letters. In the 1950s the Jewish-American novel, shaped by awareness of the Holocaust, expressed themes of human responsibility. Many subsequent writers, including Stanley Elkin, Joseph Heller, Chaim Potok, Denise Levertov, Grace Paley, and Cynthia Ozick, have extended the tradition.

Jewish Autonomous Region part of the Khabarovsk Territory, E Siberian Russia, on the river Amur; capital Birobidzhan; area 13,900 sq mi/36,000 sq km; population (1986) 211,000. Industries include textiles, leather, metallurgy, light engineering, agriculture, and timber. It was established as a Jewish National District 1928 and became an Autonomous Region 1934 but became only nominally Jewish after the Stalinist purges 1936–47 and 1948–49.

Jew's harp musical instrument consisting of a two-pronged metal frame inserted between the teeth, and a springlike tongue plucked with the finger. The resulting drone excites resonances in the mouth that can be varied in pitch to produce a melody.

Jezebel in the Old Testament, daughter of the king of Sidon. She married King Ahab of Israel, and was brought into conflict with the prophet Elijah by her introduction of the worship of Baal.

Jiang Zemin 1926– . Chinese political leader. The son-in-law of ▷Li Xiannian, he joined the Chinese Communist Party's politburo in 1967 after serving in the Moscow embassy and as mayor of Shanghai. He succeeded ▷Zhao Ziyang as party leader after the Tiananmen Square massacre of 1989. A cautious proponent of economic reform coupled with unswerving adherence to the party's "political line," he subsequently replaced ▷Deng Xiaoping as head of the influential central military commission.

Jiang Jie Shi alternate transcription of ▷Chiang Kai-shek.

Jiang Qing or *Chiang Ching* 1914–1991. Chinese communist politician, third wife of the party leader Mao Zedong. In 1960 she became minister for culture, and played a key role in

the 1966–69 Cultural Revolution as the leading member of the Shanghai-based Gang of Four, who attempted to seize power 1976. Jiang was imprisoned 1981.

Jiang was a Shanghai actress when in 1937 she met Mao Zedong at the communist headquarters in Yan'an; she became his wife 1939. She emerged as a radical, egalitarian Maoist. Her influence waned during the early 1970s and her relationship with Mao became embittered. On Mao's death Sept 1976, the ▷Gang of Four, with Jiang as a leading figure, sought to seize power by organizing military coups in Shanghai and Beijing. They were arrested for treason by Mao's successor Hua Guofeng and tried 1980–81. The Gang were blamed for the excesses of the Cultural Revolution, but Jiang asserted during her trial that she had only followed Mao's orders as an obedient wife. This was rejected, and Jiang received a death sentence Jan 1981, which was subsequently commuted to life imprisonment.

Jiangsu or *Kiangsu* province on the coast of E China
area 39,449 sq mi/102,200 sq km
capital Nanjing
features the swampy mouth of the river Chang Jiang; the special municipality of Shanghai
products cereals, rice, tea, cotton, soybeans, fish, silk, ceramics, textiles, coal, iron, copper, cement
population (1990) 67,057,000
history Jiangsu was originally part of the Wu kingdom, and Wu is still a traditional local name for the province. Jiangsu's capture by Japan in 1937 was an important step in that country's attempt to conquer China.

Jiangxi or *Kiangsi* province of SE China
area 63,613 sq mi/164,800 sq km
capital Nanchang
products rice, tea, cotton, tobacco, porcelain, coal, tungsten, uranium
population (1990) 37,710,000
history the province was Mao Zedong's original base in the first phase of the Communist struggle against the Nationalists.

Jiddah or *Jedda* port in Hejaz, Saudi Arabia, on the E shore of the Red Sea; population (1986) 1,000,000. Industries include cement, steel, and oil refining. Pilgrims pass through here on their way to Mecca.

jihad (Arabic "conflict") holy war undertaken by Muslims against nonbelievers. In the *Mecca Declaration* 1981, the Islamic powers pledged a jihad against Israel, though not necessarily military attack.

Jilin or *Kirin* province of NE China in central ▷Manchuria
area 72,182 sq mi/187,000 sq km
capital Changchun
population (1990) 24,659,000

Jim Crow the systematic practice of segregating black Americans, which was common in the South until the 1960s. *Jim Crow laws* are laws designed to deny civil rights to blacks or to enforce the policy of segregation, which existed until Supreme Court decisions and civil-rights legislation of the 1950s and 1960s (Civil Rights Act 1964, Voting Rights Act 1965) denied their legality. See also ▷black.

Jim Crow was originally a derogatory term white Americans used for a black person.

Jiménez Juan Ramón 1881–1958. Spanish lyric poet. Born in Andalusia, he left Spain during the civil war to live in exile in Puerto Rico. Nobel Prize 1956.

jingoism blinkered, warmongering patriotism. The term originated in 1878, when the British prime minister Disraeli developed a pro-Turkish policy, which nearly involved the UK in war with Russia. His supporters' war song included the line "We don't want to fight, but by jingo if we do ... "

jinn in Muslim mythology, a spirit able to assume human or animal shape.

Jinnah Mohammed Ali 1876–1948. Indian politician, Pakistan's first governor-general from 1947. In 1916 and for the period 1934–48, he was president of the Muslim League, a political organization founded 1906 under the leadership of the Aga Khan, and by 1940 was advocating the need for a separate state of Pakistan; at the 1946 conferences in London he insisted on the partition of British India into Hindu and Muslim states.

Jinsha Jiang river that rises in SW China and forms the ▷Chang Jiang (Yangtze) at Yibin.

Jivaro member of a South American Indian people of the tropical forests of SE Ecuador and NE Peru. They live by farming, hunting, fishing, and weaving; the Jivaro language belongs to the Andean-Equatorial family. They were formerly notorious for preserving the hair and shrunken skin of the heads of their enemies as battle trophies.

jive energetic American dance that evolved from the jitterbug, popular in the 1940s and 1950s; a forerunner of rock and roll.

Joachim of Fiore *c.* 1132–1202. Italian mystic, born in Calabria. In his mystical writings he interpreted history as a sequence of three ages, that of the Father, Son, and Holy Spirit, the last of which, the age of perfect spirituality, was to begin in 1260. His messianic views were taken up enthusiastically by many followers.

Joannitius Hunayn ibn Ishaq al Ibadi 809–873. Arabic translator, a Nestorian Christian, who translated Greek learning—including Ptolemy, Euclid, Plato, and Aristotle—into Arabic or Syrian for the Abbasid court in Baghdad.

Joan of Arc, St 1412–1431. French military leader. In 1429 at Chinon, NW France, she persuaded Charles VII that she had a divine mission to expel the occupying English from N France (see ▷Hundred Years' War) and secure his coronation. She raised the siege of Orléans, defeated the English at Patay, north of Orléans, and Charles was crowned in Reims. However, she failed to take Paris and was captured May 1430 by the Burgundians, who sold her to the English. She was found guilty of witchcraft and heresy by a tribunal of French ecclesiastics who supported the English. She was burned to death at the stake in Rouen May 30, 1431. In 1920 she was canonized.

Job *c.* 5th century BC. In the Old Testament, Hebrew leader who in the *Book of Job* questioned God's infliction of suffering on the righteous while enduring great sufferings himself.

Although Job comes to no final conclusion, his book is one of the first attempts to explain the problem of human suffering in a world believed to be created and governed by a God who is all-powerful and all-good.

Jocasta in Greek mythology, wife of Laius, sister of ▷Creon, and mother and wife of ▷Oedipus, by whom she was mother to ▷Antigone, ▷Eteocles, ▷Polynices, and Ismene. She married Oedipus in ignorance, as his reward for killing the ◊Sphinx. She committed suicide on discovering his identity (◊Sophocles) or after the death of her sons (◊Euripides, and Statius).

Jodl Alfred 1892–1946. German general. In World War II he drew up the Nazi government's plan for the attack on Yugoslavia, Greece, and the USSR. In Jan 1945 he became Chief of Staff and headed the delegation that signed Germany's surrender in Reims May 7, 1945. He was tried for war crimes in Nuremberg 1945–46 and hanged.

Jodrell Bank site in Cheshire, England, of the Nuffield Radio Astronomy Laboratories of the University of Manchester. Its largest instrument is the 250 ft/76 m radio dish (the Lovell Telescope), completed 1957 and modified 1970. A 125 × 82 ft/38 × 25 m elliptical radio dish was introduced 1964, capable of working at shorter wavelengths.

These radio telescopes are used in conjunction with six smaller dishes up to 143 mi/230 km apart in an array called MERLIN (**m**ulti-**e**lement **r**adio-**l**inked **i**nterferometer **n**etwork) to produce detailed maps of radio sources.

Joel prophet of Judah in the Old Testament, who predicts punishments for Judah's sins, to be followed by a restoration of God's grace and the nation's triumph over its enemies.

Joffre Joseph Jacques Césaire 1852–1931. Marshal of France during World War I. He was chief of general staff 1911. The German invasion of Belgium 1914 took him by surprise, but his stand at the Battle of the ◊Marne resulted in his appointment as supreme commander of all the French armies 1915. His failure to make adequate preparations at Verdun 1916 and the military disasters on the ◊Somme led to his replacement by Nivelle in Dec 1916.

Jogjakarta alternate spelling of ◊Yogyakarta, a city in Indonesia.

Johannesburg largest city of South Africa, situated on the Witwatersrand River in Transvaal; population (1985) 1,609,000. It is the center of a large gold-mining industry; other industries include engineering works, meat-chilling plants, and clothing factories.

Notable buildings include the law courts, Escom House (Electricity Supply Commission), the South African Railways Administration Building, the City Hall, Chamber of Mines and Stock Exchange, the Witwatersrand (1921) and Rand Afrikaans (1966) universities, and the Union Observatory. Johannesburg was founded after the discovery of gold 1886 and was probably named after Jan (Johannes) Meyer, the first mining commissioner.

John Augustus (Edwin) 1878–1961. British painter of landscapes and portraits, including *The Smiling Woman* 1910 (Tate Gallery, London) of his second wife, Dorelia.

John Elton. Adopted name of Reginald Kenneth Dwight 1947– . English pop singer, pianist, and composer, noted for his melodies and elaborate costumes and glasses. His best-known LP, *Goodbye Yellow Brick Road* 1973, includes the hit "Bennie and the Jets." His output is prolific and his hits continued intermittently into the 1990s.

From his second album, *Elton John* 1970, to *Blue Moves* 1976 he enjoyed his greatest popularity, especially in the US, and worked exclusively with the lyricist Bernie Taupin.

John *Lackland* 1167–1216. King of England

from 1199 and acting king from 1189 during his brother Richard I's (the Lion-Hearted) absence on the third Crusade. He lost Normandy and almost all the other English possessions in France to Philip II of France by 1205. His repressive policies and excessive taxation brought him into conflict with his barons, and he was forced to seal the ◊Magna Carta 1215. Later repudiation of it led to the first Barons' War 1215–17, during which he died.

John two kings of France, including:

John II 1319–1364. King of France from 1350. He was defeated and captured by the Black Prince at Poitiers 1356 and imprisoned in England. Released 1360, he failed to raise the money for his ransom and returned to England 1364, where he died.

John name of 23 popes, including:

John XXII 1249–1334. Pope 1316–34. He spent his papacy in Avignon, France, engaged in a long conflict with the Holy Roman emperor, Louis of Bavaria, and the Spiritual Franciscans, a monastic order who preached the absolute poverty of the clergy.

John XXIII Angelo Giuseppe Roncalli 1881–1963. Pope from 1958. He improved relations with the USSR in line with his encyclical *Pacem in Terris/Peace on Earth* 1963, established Roman Catholic hierarchies in newly emergent states, and summoned the Second Vatican Council, which reformed church liturgy and backed the ecumenical movement.

"John XXIII" Baldassare Costa died 1419. Antipope 1410–15. In an attempt to end the ◊Great Schism he was elected pope by a council of cardinals in Bologna, but was deposed by the Council of Constance 1415, together with the popes of Avignon and Rome. His papacy is not recognized by the church.

John three kings of Poland, including:

John III Sobieski 1624–1696. King of Poland from 1674. He became commander in chief of the army 1668 after victories over the Cossacks and Tatars. A victory over the Turks 1673 helped to get him elected to the Polish throne, and he saved Vienna from the besieging Turks 1683.

John six kings of Portugal, including:

John I 1357–1433. King of Portugal from 1385. An illegitimate son of Pedro I, he was elected by the Cortes (parliament). His claim was supported by an English army against the rival king of Castile, thus establishing the Anglo-Portuguese Alliance 1386. He married Philippa of Lancaster, daughter of ◊John of Gaunt.

John IV 1603–1656. King of Portugal from 1640. Originally duke of Braganza, he was elected king when the Portuguese rebelled against Spanish rule. His reign was marked by a long war against Spain, which did not end until 1668.

John VI 1769–1826. King of Portugal and regent for his insane mother *Maria I* from 1799 until her death 1816. He fled to Brazil when the French invaded Portugal 1807 and did not return until 1822. On his return Brazil declared its independence, with John's elder son Pedro as emperor.

John Bull imaginary figure who is a personification of England, similar to the American Uncle Sam. He is represented in cartoons and caricatures as a prosperous farmer of the 18th century.

The name was popularized by Dr John Arbuthnot (1667–1735), a Scottish writer and physician, who wrote his *History of John Bull* 1712, advocating the Tory policy of peace with France.

John Chrysostom, St 345–407. Christian scholar, hermit, preacher, and Eastern Orthodox bishop of Constantinople 398–404. He was born in Antioch (now Antakya, Turkey). Feast day Sept 13.

John of Austria Don 1545–1578. Spanish soldier, the illegitimate son of the Holy Roman emperor Charles V. He defeated the Turks at the Battle of ◊Lepanto 1571.

John captured Tunis 1573 but quickly lost it. He was appointed governor-general of the Netherlands 1576 but discovered that real power lay in the hands of William of Orange. John withdrew 1577 and then attacked and defeated the patriot army at Gemblours Jan 31, 1578 with the support of reinforcements from Philip II of Spain. Lack of money stopped him from going any farther. He died of fever.

John of Damascus, St c. 676–c. 754. Eastern Orthodox theologian and hymn writer, a defender of image worship against the iconoclasts (image-breakers). Contained in his *The Fountain of Knowledge* is *An Accurate Exposition of the Orthodox Faith*, an important chronicle of theology from the 4th to 7th centuries. He was born in Damascus, Syria. Feast day Dec 4.

John of Gaunt 1340–1399. English politician, born in Ghent, fourth son of Edward III, Duke of Lancaster from 1362. He distinguished himself during the Hundred Years' War. During Edward's last years, and the years before Richard II attained the age of majority, he acted as head of government, and Parliament protested against his corrupt rule.

John of the Cross, St 1542–1591. Spanish Roman Catholic Carmelite friar from 1564, who was imprisoned several times for attempting to impose the reforms laid down by St Teresa. His verse describes spiritual ecstasy. Feast day Nov 24.

He was beatified 1674 and canonized 1726.

John o' Groats village in NE Highland region, Scotland, about 2 mi/3 km west of Duncansby Head, proverbially Britain's northernmost point. It is named after the Dutchman John de Groot, who built a house there in the 16th century.

John Paul two popes:

John Paul I Albino Luciani 1912–1978. Pope Aug 26–Sept 28, 1978. His name was chosen as the combination of his two immediate predecessors.

John Paul II Karol Wojtyla 1920– . Pope from 1978, the first non-Italian to be elected pope since 1522. He was born near Kraków, Poland. He has upheld the tradition of papal infallibility, condemned artificial contraception, women priests, married priests, and modern dress for monks and nuns—views that have aroused criticism from liberalizing elements in the church.

In 1939, at the beginning of World War II, Wojtyla was conscripted for forced labor by the Germans, working in quarries and a chemical factory, but from 1942 studied for the priesthood illegally in Kraków. After the war he taught ethics and theology at the universities of Lublin and Kraków, becoming archbishop of Kraków 1964. In 1967 he was made a cardinal.

He was shot and wounded by a Turk in an attempt on his life 1981. Although he has warned against the involvement of priests in political activity, he opposed the Gulf War 1991 and has condemned arms manufacturers as sinful.

Johns Jasper 1930– . US painter and printmaker who rejected the abstract in favor of such simple subjects as flags, maps, and numbers. He uses pigments mixed with wax (encaustic) to create a rich surface with unexpected delicacies of color. He has also created collages and lithographs.

Born in Augusta, Georgia, he moved to New York City in 1952. In the 1960s his works became more abstract before veering toward abstract expressionism in the mid-1970s. He was influenced by Marcel ⟩Duchamp.

John, St 1st century AD. New Testament apostle. Traditionally, he wrote the fourth Gospel and the Johannine Epistles (when he was bishop of Ephesus), and the Book of Revelation (while exiled to the Greek island of Patmos). His emblem is an eagle; his feast day Dec 27.

St John is identified with the unnamed "disciple whom Jesus loved." Son of Zebedee, born in Judea, he and his brother James were Galilean fishermen. Jesus entrusted his mother to John at the Crucifixion, where John is often shown dressed in red, with curly hair. Another of his symbols is a chalice with a little snake in it.

Johnson Alvin Saunders 1874–1971. US social scientist and educator. After teaching at several universities, he helped found and became editor of the *New Republic* 1917. Joining with some of America's greatest scholars, Johnson was one of the founders of the New School for Social Research in New York City, serving as its director 1923–45. Johnson's memoir, *Progress: An Autobiography*, was published 1952.

Born near Homer, Nebraska, Johnson was educated at the University of Nebraska, saw service in the Spanish-American War, and received a PhD in economics from Columbia 1902.

Johnson Andrew 1808–1875. 17th president of the US 1865–69, a Democrat. He was a congressman from Tennessee 1843–53, governor of Tennessee 1853–57, senator 1857–62, and vice-president 1865. He succeeded to the presidency on Lincoln's assassination (April 15, 1865). His conciliatory policy to the defeated South after the Civil War involved him in a feud with the Radical Republicans, culminating in his impeachment 1868 before the Senate, which failed to convict him by one vote.

Jackson was born in Raleigh, North Carolina. Among his achievements was the purchase of Alaska from Russia 1867. When he tried to dismiss Edwin Stanton, a cabinet secretary, his political opponents seized on the opportunity to charge him with "high crimes and misdemeanors" and attempted to remove him from office; it was this battle that ended in his impeachment. Jackson's tenure as president was characterized by his frustration and political stalemate. He presided over the reentry of the Southern states into the Union. He was returned to the Senate from Tennessee 1875, but died shortly afterward.

Johnson Earvin ("Magic") 1959– . US basketball player. He played for the Los Angeles Lakers 1979–91, a team that won the National Basketball Association (NBA) championship 1980, 1982, 1985, 1987, and 1988. He was named most valuable player 1980, 1982, and 1987. He played in the 1992 All-Star game and in the victorious 1992 US Olympic basketball team in Barcelona, Spain.

Born in Lansing, Michigan, Johnson played for Michigan State University 1977–79, leading them to the National Collegiate Athletic Association (NCAA) championship 1979. In 1991, he announced that he had contracted the HIV virus and would retire from basketball to devote his time to AIDS awareness and prevention programs. In the fall of 1992, Johnson announced that he would rejoin the Lakers but retired before the season began.

Johnson Eastman 1824–1906. US painter born in Germany, trained in Düsseldorf, The Hague, and Paris. Painting in the open air, he developed a fresh and luminous landscape style.

Johnson had his first success with a nostalgic naturalist scene, *Old Kentucky Home* 1859 (New York Historical Society).

Johnson Hiram Warren 1866–1945. US politician. He was the "Bull Moose" party candidate for vice-president in Theodore Roosevelt's unsuccessful bid to regain the presidency 1912. Elected to the US Senate 1917, Johnson served there until his death. He was an unyielding isolationist, opposing US involvement in the European war and, when World War I was over, membership in the League of Nations and World Court.

Born in Sacramento, California, Johnson attended the University of California and was admitted to the bar 1888. Moving in 1902 to San Francisco, where he established a law practice, Johnson entered politics and served as governor of California 1911–17.

Johnson Jack 1878–1968. US heavyweight boxer. He overcame severe racial prejudice to become the first black heavyweight champion of the world 1908 when he traveled to Australia to challenge Tommy Burns. The US authorities wanted Johnson "dethroned" because of his color but could not find suitable challengers until 1915, when he lost the title in a dubious fight decision to the giant Jess Willard.

CAREER HIGHLIGHTS

fights: 107
wins: 86
draws: 11
defeats: 10

Johnson James Weldon 1871–1938. US writer, lawyer, diplomat, and social critic. He was a strong supporter of Theodore Roosevelt and served him and Taft as US consul in Venezuela and Nicaragua 1906–12. He was editor of *New York Age* 1912–22 and was active in the National Association for the Advancement of Colored People (NAACP). As poet and anthropologist, he became one of the chief figures of the Harlem Renaissance of the 1920s. His autobiography, *Along This Way*, was published 1933.

Born in Jacksonville, Florida, and educated at Atlanta University, Johnson became, in 1897, the first black American admitted to the Florida bar.

Johnson Lyndon Baines 1908–1973. 36th president of the US 1963–69, a Democrat. He was elected to Congress 1937–49 and the Senate 1949–60. Born in Texas, he brought critical Southern support as J F Kennedy's vice-presidential running mate 1960, and became president on Kennedy's assassination. After the ⟩Tonkin Gulf Incident, which escalated US involvement in the ⟩Vietnam War, support won by Johnson's Great Society legislation (civil rights, education, alleviation of poverty) dissipated, and he declined to run for reelection 1968.

Following Kennedy's assassination, Johnson pushed many pieces of civil rights legislation through Congress. His foreign policy met with considerably less success, however.

Johnson Philip (Cortelyou) 1906– . US architect who coined the term "international style." Originally designing in the style of ⟩Mies van der Rohe, he later became an exponent of ⟩Postmodernism. He designed the giant AT&T building in New York 1978, a pink skyscraper with a Chippendale-style cabinet top.

He was director of architecture and design at the Museum of Modern Art, New York 1932–54, where he built the annex and sculpture court.

Johnson Samuel, known as "Dr Johnson," 1709–1784. English lexicographer, author, and critic, also a brilliant conversationalist and the dominant figure in 18th-century London literary society. His *Dictionary*, published 1755, remained authoritative for over a century, and is still remarkable for the vigor of its definitions. In 1764 he founded the Literary Club, whose members included the painter Joshua Reynolds, the political philosopher Edmund Burke, the playwright Oliver Goldsmith, the actor David Garrick, and James ⟩Boswell, Johnson's biographer.

Born in Lichfield, Staffordshire, Johnson became first an usher and then a literary hack. In 1735 he married Elizabeth Porter and opened a private school. When this proved unsuccessful he went to London with his pupil David Garrick, becoming a regular contributor to the *Gentleman's Magazine* and publishing the poem *London* 1738. Other works include the satire imitating Juvenal, *Vanity of Human Wishes* 1749, the philosophical romance *Rasselas* 1759, an edition of Shakespeare 1765, and the classic *Lives of the Most Eminent English Poets* 1779–81. His first meeting with Boswell was 1763. A visit with Boswell to Scotland and the Hebrides 1773 was recorded in *Journey to the Western Isles of Scotland* 1775. He was buried in Westminster Abbey and his house, in Gough Square, London, is preserved as a museum; his wit and humanity are documented in Boswell's classic biography *Life of Samuel Johnson* 1791.

Johnson City city in NE Tennessee, just below the Virginia border, in the Appalachian Mountains NE of Knoxville; population (1990) 49,400. Industries include tobacco, furniture, building materials, metals, textiles, and food processing.

Johnson Space Center NASA installation at Houston, Texas, home of mission control for crewed space missions. It is the main center for the selection and training of astronauts.

Johnston Joseph Eggleston 1807–1891. US military leader. At the outbreak of the US Civil War, he was quartermaster general of the US Army. Joining the Confederacy, Johnston was given commands in Virginia. In late 1862 he was sent west and in 1863 commanded the Army of Tennessee. After the war, Johnston returned to private life, later serving in the US House of Representatives 1879–81 and as federal railroad commissioner 1887–91.

Born near Farmville, Virginia, Johnston graduated from West Point 1829 and saw action in the Seminole War. As a military engineer, he served with distinction during the Mexican War.

Johnstown city in SW Pennsylvania, on the

Conemaugh River, E of Pittsburgh; population (1990) 28,100. Industries include steel, coal and coal by-products, chemicals, building materials, and clothing. Johnstown was the victim of disastrous floods 1889.

John the Baptist, St *c.* 12 BC–*c.* AD 27. In the New Testament, an itinerant preacher. After preparation in the wilderness, he proclaimed the coming of the Messiah and baptized Jesus in the river Jordan. He was later executed by ⬦Herod Antipas at the request of Salome, who demanded that his head be brought to her on a platter.

John was the son of Zacharias and Elizabeth (a cousin of Jesus' mother), and born in Nazareth, Galilee. He and Jesus are often shown together as children.

Johor state in S Peninsular Malaysia; capital Johor Baharu; area 7,334 sq mi/19,000 sq km; population (1990) 2,106,500. The southernmost point of mainland Asia, it is joined to Singapore by a causeway. It is mainly forested, with swamps. There is bauxite and iron.

joint in any animal with a skeleton, a point of movement or articulation. In vertebrates, it is the point where two bones meet. Some joints allow no motion (the sutures of the skull), others allow a very small motion (the sacroiliac joints in the lower back), but most allow a relatively free motion. Of these, some allow a gliding motion (one vertebra of the spine on another), some have a hinge action (elbow and knee), and others allow motion in all directions (hip and shoulder joints), by means of a ball-and-

hinge joint (knee)

femur
ligament
patella (knee-cap)
synovial fluid
ligament
cartilage
tibia
fibula

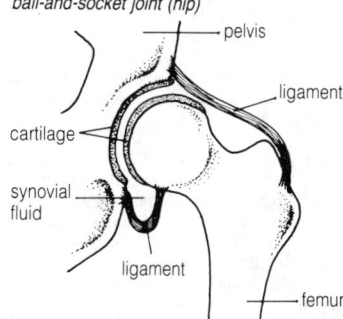

ball-and-socket joint (hip)

pelvis
ligament
cartilage
synovial fluid
ligament
femur

joint *The knee joint is the largest and most complex in the human body.*

socket arrangement. The ends of the bones at a moving joint are covered with cartilage for greater elasticity and smoothness, and enclosed in an envelope (capsule) of tough white fibrous tissue lined with a membrane which secretes a lubricating and cushioning ⬦synovial fluid. The joint is further strengthened by ligaments.

In invertebrates with an ⬦exoskeleton, the joints are places where the exoskeleton is replaced by a more flexible outer covering, the arthrodial membrane, which allows the limb (or other body part) to bend at that point.

joint venture in business, an undertaking in which an individual or legal entity of one country forms a company with those of another country, with risks being shared.

Joliet city in NE Illinois, on the Des Plaines River, SW of Chicago; seat of Will County; population (1990) 76,800. It is a center for barge traffic. Industries include building materials, chemicals, oil refining, heavy construction machinery, and paper. The city is named after the explorer Louis Joliet.

Joliet (or *Jolliet*) Louis 1645–1700. French Canadian explorer. Born in Québec, Joliet was sent by the governor of Canada to undertake an extensive exploration of the Great Lakes 1669. Later, in response to reports that the Mississippi River flowed into the Pacific (and might thereby serve as a trade route to Asia), he and the Jesuit missionary Jacques Marquette were sent to explore the river. Joliet charted the Mississippi down to its junction with the Arkansas River and returned to Canada by way of the Illinois territory. He later explored Labrador and the Hudson Bay.

The city of Joliet, Illinois, is named in his honor.

Joliot-Curie Irène (born Curie) 1897–1956 and Frédéric (born Joliot) 1900–1958. French physicists who made the discovery of artificial radioactivity, for which they were jointly awarded the 1935 Nobel Prize for Chemistry.

Irène was the daughter of Marie and Pierre ⬦Curie and began work at her mother's Radium Institute in 1921. In 1926 she married Frédéric, a pupil of her mother's, and they began a long and fruitful collaboration. In 1934 they found that certain elements exposed to radiation themselves become radioactive.

Jolson Al. Adopted name of Asa Yoelson 1886–1950. Russian-born US singer and entertainer. Popular in Broadway theater and vaudeville, he was chosen to star in the first talking picture, *The Jazz Singer* 1927.

Jolson, who got his start in vaudeville, was also a popular recording star.

Jonah 7th century BC. Hebrew prophet whose name is given to a book in the Old Testament. According to this, he fled by ship to evade his mission to prophesy the destruction of Nineveh. The crew threw him overboard in a storm, as a bringer of ill fortune, and he spent three days and nights in the belly of a whale before coming to land.

Jonathan Chief (Joseph) Leabua 1914–1987. Lesotho politician. A leader in the drive for independence, Jonathan became prime minister of Lesotho in 1965. His rule was ended by a coup in 1986.

Jones Bobby (Robert Tyre) 1902–1971. US golfer. He was the game's greatest amateur player, who never turned professional but won 13 major amateur and professional tournaments, including the Grand Slam of the

amateur and professional opens of both the US and Britain 1930.

Born in Atlanta, Georgia, Jones finished playing competitive golf 1930 and concentrated on his law practice. He maintained his contacts with the sport and was largely responsible for inaugurating the US Masters.

CAREER HIGHLIGHTS

British Open
1926–27, 1930
US Open
1923, 1926, 1929–30
British Amateur
1930
US Amateur
1924–25, 1927–28, 1930
US Walker Cup (team)
1922, 1924, 1926, 1928*, 1930*
* indicates playing captain

Jones Inigo 1573–*c.* 1652. English Classical architect. Born in London, he studied in Italy and was influenced by the works of Palladio. He was employed by James I to design scenery for Ben Jonson's masques. He designed the Queen's House, Greenwich, 1616–35 and his English Renaissance masterpiece, the Banquet House in Whitehall, London, 1619–22.

Jones John Luther "Casey" 1864–1900. US railroad engineer and folk hero. Born in Cayce, Kentucky, Jones gained his nickname from the name of his hometown. Hired by the railroad 1880, he became an engineer for the Illinois Central Railroad 1890. His death at the throttle of a locomotive became the subject of popular legend. Having volunteered for an overnight run on the "Cannonball Express" in April 1900, Jones collided with a stalled freight train. Ordering his fireman to jump to safety, he rode the "Cannonball" to his death. The folk song "Casey Jones," written by Wallace Sanders, is an account of the event.

Jonestown commune of the *People's Temple Sect*, NW of Georgetown, Guyana, established 1974 by the American Jim Jones (1933–1978), who originally founded the sect among San Francisco's black community. After a visiting US congressman was shot dead, Jones enforced mass suicide on his followers by instructing them to drink cyanide; 914 died, including over 240 children.

jonquil species of small daffodil *Narcissus jonquilla*, family Amaryllidaceae, with yellow flowers. Native to Spain and Portugal, it is cultivated elsewhere.

Jonson Ben(jamin) 1572–1637. English dramatist, poet, and critic. *Every Man in his Humour* 1598 established the English "comedy of humors," in which each character embodies a "humor," or vice, such as greed, lust, or avarice. This was followed by *Cynthia's Revels* 1600 and *Poetaster* 1601. His first extant tragedy is *Sejanus* 1603, with Burbage and Shakespeare as members of the original cast. The plays of his middle years include *Volpone, or The Fox* 1606, *The Alchemist* 1610, and *Bartholomew Fair* 1614.

Joplin city in SW Missouri, W of Springfield; population (1990) 41,000. Industries include zinc and lead smelting, leather goods, and furniture.

Joplin Janis 1943–1970. US blues and rock singer, born in Texas. She was lead singer with the San Francisco group Big Brother and the Holding Company 1966–68. Her biggest hit, Kris Kristofferson's "Me and Bobby

McGee," was released on the posthumous *Pearl* LP 1971.

She died of a drug overdose.

Joplin Scott 1868–1917. US ◊ragtime pianist and composer, active in Chicago. His "Maple Leaf Rag" 1899 was the first instrumental sheet music to sell a million copies, and "The Entertainer," as the theme tune of the film *The Sting* 1973, revived his popularity. He was an influence on Jelly Roll Morton and other early jazz musicians.

Joppa ancient name of ◊Jaffa, a port in W Israel.

Jordaens Jacob 1593–1678. Flemish painter, born in Antwerp. His style follows Rubens, whom he assisted in various commissions. Much of his work is exuberant and on a large scale, including scenes of peasant life, altarpieces, portraits, and mythological subjects.

Jordan river rising on Mount Hermon, Syria, at 1,800 ft/550 m above sea level and flowing south for about 200 mi/320 km via the Sea of Galilee to the Dead Sea, 1,290 ft/390 m below sea level. It occupies the northern part of the Great Rift Valley; its upper course forms the boundary of Israel with Syria and the kingdom of Jordan; its lower course runs through Jordan; the West Bank has been occupied by Israel since 1967.

Jordan country in SW Asia, bounded N by Syria, NE by Iraq, E, SE and S by Saudi Arabia, S by the Gulf of Aqaba, and W by Israel.

Jordan
Hashemite Kingdom of (*Al Mamlaka al Urduniya al Hashemiyah***)**

area 34,434 sq mi/89,206 sq km (West Bank 2,269 sq mi/5,879 sq km)
capital Amman
cities Zarqa, Irbid, Aqaba (the only port)
physical desert plateau in E; rift valley separates E and W banks of the river Jordan
features lowest point on Earth below sea level in the Dead Sea (−1,299 ft/−396 m); archeological sites at Jerash and Petra
head of state King Hussein ibn Talai from 1952
head of government Mudar Badran from 1989
political system constitutional monarchy
political parties none
exports potash, phosphates, citrus, vegetables
currency Jordanian dinar
population (1990 est) 3,065,000 (including Palestinian refugees); West Bank (1988) 866,000; growth rate 3.6% p.a.
life expectancy men 67, women 71
languages Arabic (official), English
religions Sunni Muslim 92%, Christian 8%
literacy 71% (1988)

government The king is effectively head of both state and government. The 1952 constitution, amended 1974, 1976, and 1984, provides for a two-chamber national assembly comprising a senate (house of notables) of 30, appointed by the king for an eight-year term, and a 142-member house of representatives (house of deputies), elected by universal suffrage for a four-year term. The house is subject to dissolution within that period. In each chamber there is equal representation for the east and west (occupied) banks of the river Jordan. Three of Jordan's eight administrative provinces have been occupied by Israel since 1967.

The king governs with the help of a council of ministers whom he appoints and who are responsible to the assembly.

history The area forming the kingdom of Jordan was occupied by the independent Nabataeans from the 4th century BC and perhaps earlier, until AD 106 when it became part of the Roman province of Arabia. It was included in the Crusaders' kingdom of Jerusalem 1099–1187. Palestine (partly in the West Bank of present-day Jordan) and Transjordan (the present-day East Bank) were part of the Turkish Ottoman Empire until its dissolution after World War I. Both were then placed under British administration by the League of Nations.

end of British mandates Transjordan acquired greater control of its own affairs than Palestine and separated from it 1923, achieving

GDP $4.3 bn (1987); $1,127 per head (1988)
chronology
1946 Independence achieved from Britain as Transjordan.
1949 New state of Jordan declared.
1950 Jordan annexed West Bank.
1953 Hussein ibn Talai officially became king of Jordan.
1958 Jordan and Iraq formed Arab Federation that ended when the Iraqi monarchy was deposed.
1967 Israel captured and occupied West Bank. Martial law imposed.
1976 Lower house dissolved, political parties banned, elections postponed until further notice.
1982 Hussein tried to mediate in Arab-Israeli conflict.
1984 Women voted for the first time.
1985 Hussein and Yassir Arafat put forward framework for Middle East peace settlement. Secret meeting between Hussein and Israeli prime minister.
1988 Hussein announced decision to cease administering the West Bank as part of Jordan, passing responsibility to Palestine Liberation Organization, and the suspension of parliament.
1989 Prime Minister Zaid al-Rifai resigned; Hussein promised new parliamentary elections following criticism of economic policies. Riots over price increases up to 50% following fall in oil revenues. First parliamentary elections for 22 years; Muslim Brotherhood won 25 of 80 seats but exiled from government; martial law lifted.
1990 Hussein unsuccessfully tried to mediate after Iraq's invasion of Kuwait. Massive refugee problems as thousands fled to Jordan from Kuwait and Iraq.
1991 24 years of martial law ended; ban on political parties lifted.
1992 Political parties allowed to register.

full independence when the British mandate expired 1946. The mandate for Palestine ran out 1948, whereupon Jewish leaders claimed parts of it for a new state of Israel. Israel was attacked by Arab nations and fought until a cease-fire was agreed 1949. By then Transjordan forces had occupied part of Palestine to add to what they called the new state of Jordan. The following year they annexed the West Bank. In 1952 Hussein ibn Talai came to the Jordanian throne at the age of 17 upon the mental incapacity of his father; he was officially made king 1953. In 1958 Jordan and Iraq formed an Arab Federation, which ended five months later when the Iraqi monarchy was overthrown. In 1967, following the Six-Day War (see ◊Arab-Israeli Wars), Israelis captured the West Bank and have remained in occupation since then.

search for peace King Hussein has survived many upheavals in his own country and neighboring states, including attempts on his life, and has kept control of Jordan's affairs as well as playing a central role in Middle East affairs. Political parties were banned 1963, partially restored 1971, then banned again 1976. Relations with his neighbors have fluctuated, but he has generally been a moderating influence. After Israel's invasion of Lebanon 1982, Hussein played a key role in attempts to bring peace to the area, establishing a relationship with ◊Palestine Liberation Organization (PLO) leader Yassir ◊Arafat. By 1984 the Arab world was split into two camps, with the moderates represented by Jordan, Egypt, and Arafat's PLO, and the militant radicals by Syria, Libya, and the rebel wing of the PLO. In 1985 Hussein and Arafat put together a framework for a Middle East peace settlement. It would involve bringing together all interested parties, but Israel objected to the PLO being represented. Further progress was hampered by the PLO's alleged complicity in a number of guerrilla operations in that year. Hussein tried to revive the search for peace by secretly meeting the Israeli prime minister in France and persuading Yassir Arafat to renounce publicly PLO violence in territories not occupied by Israel.

greater democratization In response to mounting unrest within Jordan 1989, Hussein promised greater democratization and in Nov elections to an 80-member parliament were held. Soon afterwards the veteran politician Mudar Badran was made prime minister; he announced the lifting of martial law Dec 1989 (imposed since 1967).

Following the Iraqi invasion and annexation of Kuwait Aug 1990, under popular pressure from his own country, Hussein unsuccessfully attempted to act as a mediator. Meanwhile the United Nations trade embargo on Iraq and the exodus of thousands of refugees into Jordan strained Jordan's resources. Jordan attended the historic Middle East peace conference in Spain in Nov 1991. In July 1992 a draft law to legalize political parties was published. *See illustration box.*

Jordan Michael 1963– . US basketball player. Playing for the Chicago Bulls 1984– , he led them to NBA championship 1991 and 1992. As a rookie he led the National Basketball Association (NBA) in points scored (2,313). During the 1986–87 season he scored 3,000 points, the second player in NBA history to do so.

Born in Brooklyn, New York, and raised in Wilmington, North Carolina, Jordan attended the University of North Carolina where he was a key player for his team when they won the 1982 National Collegiate Athletic Association (NCAA) championship. He also played on the victorious 1984 and 1992 US Olympic basketball teams. "Air Jordan" sneakers were popular in the later 1980s and early 1990s.

Jörgensen Jörgen 1779–1845. Danish sailor who in 1809 seized control of Iceland, announcing it was under the protection of Britain. His brief reign of corruption ended later the same year when he was captured by a British naval ship. After long imprisonment, in about 1823 he was transported to Van Diemen's Land (Tasmania), where he was pardoned. He wrote a dictionary of Australian Aboriginal dialect.

Joseph in the New Testament, the husband of the Virgin Mary, a descendant of King David of the Tribe of Judah, and a carpenter by trade. Although Jesus was not the son of Joseph, Joseph was his legal father. According to Roman Catholic tradition, he had a family by a previous wife, and was an elderly man when he married Mary.

Joseph in the Old Testament, the 11th and favorite son of ◊Jacob, sold into Egypt by his jealous half brothers. After he had risen to power there, they and his father joined him to escape from famine in Canaan.

Joseph Chief c. 1840–1904. American Indian leader of the Nez Percé people. Born in the Wallowa Valley of Oregon, Joseph was the son of a Nez Percé leader who resisted territorial encroachment by the US government. At his father's death in 1873, Joseph assumed the title of chief. Although he advocated passive resistance, initially agreeing to leave tribal lands 1877, Joseph later led his people in armed resistance to General Oliver Howard. After a defeat in Idaho, Joseph ordered a mass retreat to Canada, but the Nez Percé were soon caught by General Nelson Miles. Sent at first to the Indian Territory in Oklahoma, they were transferred to the Colville Reservation in Washington 1885.

Joseph two Holy Roman emperors:

Joseph I 1678–1711. Holy Roman emperor from 1705 and king of Austria, of the house of Hapsburg. He spent most of his reign involved in fighting the War of the ◊Spanish Succession.

Joseph II 1741–1790. Holy Roman emperor from 1765, son of Francis I (1708–1765). The reforms he carried out after the death of his mother, ◊Maria Theresa, in 1780, provoked revolts from those who lost privileges.

Josephine Marie Josèphe Rose Tascher de la Pagerie 1763–1814. As wife of ◊Napoleon Bonaparte, she was empress of France 1796–1809. Born on Martinique, she married in 1779 Alexandre de ◊Beauharnais, who played a part in the French Revolution, and in 1796 Napoleon, who divorced her in 1809 because she had not produced children.

Joseph of Arimathaea, St 1st century AD. In the New Testament, a wealthy Hebrew, member of the Sanhedrin (supreme court), and secret supporter of Jesus. On the evening of the Crucifixion he asked the Roman procurator Pilate for Jesus' body and buried it in his own tomb. Feast day March 17.

Josephson Brian 1940– . British physicist, a leading authority on superconductivity. In 1973 he shared a Nobel Prize for his theoretical predictions of the properties of a supercurrent through a tunnel barrier (the Josephson effect), which led to the development of the Josephson junction.

Josephson junction device used in "superchips" (large and complex integrated circuits) to speed the passage of signals by a phenomenon called "electron tunneling." Although these superchips respond a thousand times faster than the ◊silicon chip, they have the disadvantage that the components of the Josephson junctions operate only at temperatures close to ◊absolute zero. They are named after Brian Josephson.

Josephus Flavius AD 37–c. 100. Jewish historian and general, born in Jerusalem. He became a Pharisee and commanded the Jewish forces in Galilee in their revolt against Rome from AD 66 (which ended with the mass suicide at Masada). When captured, he gained the favor of the Roman emperor Vespasian and settled in Rome as a citizen. He wrote *Antiquities of the Jews*, an early history to AD 66; *The Jewish War*, and an autobiography.

Joshua 13th century BC. In the Old Testament, successor of Moses, who led the Jews in their return to and conquest of the land of Canaan. The city of Jericho was the first to fall—according to the Book of Joshua, the walls crumbled to the blast of his trumpets.

Josiah c. 647–609 BC. King of Judah. Grandson of Manasseh and son of Amon, he succeeded to the throne at the age of eight. The discovery of a Book of Instruction (probably Deuteronomy, a book of the Old Testament) during repairs of the Temple in 621 BC stimulated thorough reform, which included the removal of all sanctuaries except that of Jerusalem. He was killed in a clash at ◊Megiddo with Pharaoh-nechoh, king of Egypt.

Josquin Desprez or **des Prés** 1440–1521. Franco-Flemish composer. His music combines a technical mastery with the feeling for words that became a hallmark of Renaissance vocal music. His works, which include 18 masses, over 100 motets, and secular vocal works, are characterized by their vitality and depth of feeling.

jota traditional northern Spanish dance in lively triple time for one or more couples who play the castanets, accompanied by guitar and singing. There is a *jota* in de ◊Falla's *The Three-Cornered Hat*.

Joubert Petrus Jacobus 1831–1900. Boer general in South Africa. He opposed British annexation of the Transvaal 1877, proclaimed its independence 1880, led the Boer forces in the First ◊South African War against the British 1880–81, defeated ◊Jameson 1896, and fought in the Boer War.

joule SI unit (symbol J) of work and energy, replacing the ◊calorie (one joule equals 4.2 calories).

It is defined as the work done (energy transferred) by a force of one newton acting over one meter and equal to 10^7 ergs. It can also be expressed as the work done in one second by a current of one ampere at a potential difference of one volt. One ◊watt is equal to one joule per second.

Joule James Prescott 1818–1889. English physicist whose work on the relations between electrical, mechanical, and chemical effects led to the discovery of the first law of ◊thermodynamics.

Joule was born in Salford, Lancashire, into a wealthy brewery-owning family. He was educated mainly by private tutors, including the scientist John ◊Dalton, and dedicated his life to precise scientific research. Until neighbors protested, he kept a steam engine in his house in Manchester. He determined the mechanical equivalent of heat (Joule's equivalent), and the SI unit of energy, the ◊joule, is named after him.

Joule–Kelvin effect in physics, the fall in temperature of a gas as it expands adiabatically (without loss or gain of heat to the system) through a narrow jet. It can be felt when, for example, compressed air escapes through the valve of an inflated bicycle tire. Only hydrogen does not exhibit the effect. It is the basic principle of most refrigerators.

journalism the profession of reporting, photographing, or editing news events for the mass media—◊newspapers, magazines, radio, television, documentary films, and newsreels—and for news agencies.

Professional bodies include the Newspaper Guild in the US and the NUJ (National Union of Journalists) in the UK. Standards are set by awards, such as those founded by J ◊Pulitzer.

Jovian 331–364. Roman emperor from 363. Captain of the imperial bodyguard, he was chosen as emperor by the troops after ◊Julian's death in battle with the Persians. He concluded an unpopular peace and restored Christianity as the state religion.

Joyce James (Augustine Aloysius) 1882–1941. Irish writer, born in Dublin, who revolutionized the form of the English novel with his "stream of consciousness" technique. His works include *Dubliners* 1914 (short stories), *Portrait of the Artist as a Young Man* 1916, *Ulysses* 1922, and *Finnegans Wake* 1939.

Ulysses, which records the events of a single Dublin day, experiments with language and combines direct narrative with the unspoken and unconscious reactions of the characters. Banned at first for obscenity in the US and the UK, it enjoyed great impact. It was first published in Paris, where Joyce settled after World War I. *Finnegans Wake* continued Joyce's experiments with language, attempting a synthesis of all existence.

joystick in computing, an input device that signals to a computer the direction and extent of displacement of a hand-held lever. It is similar to the joystick used to control the flight of an aircraft.

Joysticks are sometimes used to control the movement of a cursor (marker) across a display screen, but are much more frequently used to provide fast and direct input for moving the characters and symbols that feature in computer games. Unlike a ◊mouse, which can move a pointer in any direction, simple games joysticks are often only capable of moving an object in one of eight different directions.

JP abbreviation for ◊*justice of the peace*.

Juan Carlos 1938– . King of Spain. The son of Don Juan, pretender to the Spanish throne, he married Princess Sofia in 1962, eldest daughter of King Paul of Greece. In 1969 he was nominated by ◊Franco to succeed on the restoration of the monarchy intended to follow Franco's death; his father was excluded because of his known liberal views. Juan Carlos became king in 1975.

Juan Fernández Islands three small volcanic Pacific islands belonging to Chile; almost uninhabited. The largest is Más-a-Tierra (also sometimes called Juan Fernández Island), where Alexander Selkirk was marooned 1704–

09. The islands were named after the Spanish navigator who reached them in 1563.

Juárez Benito 1806–1872. Mexican politician, president 1861–65 and 1867–72. In 1861 he suspended repayments of Mexico's foreign debts, which prompted a joint French, British, and Spanish expedition to exert pressure. French forces invaded and created an empire for ◊Maximilian, brother of the Austrian emperor. After their withdrawal in 1867, Maximilian was executed, and Juárez returned to the presidency.

He won popularity for nationalizing church property in his first year in office. He was the first Indian (non-Spanish) president of Mexico.

Juba capital of Southern Region, Sudan Republic; situated on the left bank of the White Nile, at the head of navigation above Khartoum, 750 mi/1,200 km to the north; population (1973) 56,700.

Judah or **Judaea** or **Judea** district of S Palestine. After the death of King Solomon 937 BC, Judah adhered to his son Rehoboam and the Davidic line, whereas the rest of Israel elected Jeroboam as ruler of the northern kingdom. In New Testament times, Judah was the Roman province of Judea, and in current Israeli usage it refers to the southern area of the West Bank.

Judah Ha-Nasi "the Prince" c. AD 135–c. 220. Jewish scholar who with a number of colleagues edited the collection of writings known as the *Mishna*, which formed the basis of the ◊*Talmud*, in the 2nd century AD.

Judaism the religion of the ancient Hebrews and their descendants the Jews, based, according to the Old Testament, on a covenant between God and Abraham about 2000 BC, and the renewal of the covenant with Moses about 1200 BC. It rests on the concept of one eternal invisible God, whose will is revealed in the *Torah* and who has a special relationship with the Jewish people. The Torah comprises the first five books of the Bible (the Pentateuch), which contains the history, laws, and guide to life for correct behavior. Besides those living in Israel, there are large Jewish populations today in the US, the former USSR (mostly Russia, Ukraine, Belarus, and Moldova), the UK and Commonwealth nations, and in Jewish communities throughout the world. There are approximately 18 million Jews, with about 9 million in the Americas, 5 million in Europe, and 4 million in Asia, Africa, and the Pacific.

scriptures The *Talmud* combines the *Mishna*, rabbinical commentary on the law handed down orally from AD 70 and put in writing about 200, and the *Gemara*, legal discussions in the schools of Palestine and Babylon from the 3rd and 4th centuries. The *Haggadah* is a part of the *Talmud* dealing with stories of heroes. The *Midrash* is a collection of commentaries on the scriptures written 400–1200, mainly in Palestine. Along with the *Torah* they are regarded as authoritative sources of Jewish ritual, worship, and practice.

observances The synagogue (in US non-Orthodox usage temple) is the local building for congregational worship (originally simply the place where the Torah was read and expounded); its characteristic feature is the Ark, the enclosure where the Torah scrolls are kept. Rabbis are ordained teachers schooled in the Jewish law and ritual who act as spiritual leaders and pastors of their communities; some devote themselves to study. Religious practices include: circumcision, daily services

Judaism

c. 2000 BC	Led by Abraham, the ancient Hebrews emigrated from Mesopotamia to Canaan.
18th century–1580	Some settled on the borders of Egypt and were put to forced labor.
13th century	They were rescued by Moses, who aimed at their establishment in Palestine. Moses received the Ten Commandments from God and brought them to the people. The main invasion of Canaan was led by Joshua about 1274.
12th–11th centuries	During the period of Judges, ascendancy was established over the Canaanites.
c. 1000	Complete conquest of Palestine and the union of all Judea was achieved under David, and Jerusalem became the capital.
10th century	Solomon succeeded David and enjoyed a reputation for great wealth and wisdom; but his lack of a constructive policy led, after his death, to the secession of the north of Judea (Israel) under Jeroboam, with only the tribe of Judah remaining under the house of David as the southern kingdom of Judah.
9th–8th centuries	Assyria became the dominant power in the Middle East. Israel purchased safety by tribute, but the basis of the society was corrupt, and prophets such as Amos, Isaiah, and Micah predicted destruction. At the hands of Tiglathpileser and his successor Shalmaneser IV, the northern kingdom (Israel) was made into Assyrian provinces after the fall of Samaria 721, although the southern kingdom of Judah was spared as an ally.
586–458	Nebuchadnezzar took Jerusalem and carried off the major part of the population to Babylon. Judaism was retained during exile, and was reconstituted by Ezra on the return to Jerusalem.
520	The Temple, originally built by Solomon, was restored.
c. 444	Ezra promulgated the legal code that was to govern the future of the Jewish people.
4th–3rd centuries	After the conquest of the Persian Empire by Alexander the Great, the Syrian Seleucid rulers and the Egyptian Ptolemaic dynasty struggled for Palestine, which came under the government of Egypt, although with a large measure of freedom.
2nd century	With the advance of Syrian power, Antiochus IV attempted intervention in the internal quarrels of the Hebrews, even desecrating the Temple, and a revolt broke out 165 led by the Maccabee family.
63	Judea's near-independence ended when internal dissension caused the Roman general Pompey to intervene, and Roman suzerainty was established.
1st century AD	A revolt led to the destruction of the Temple 66–70 by the Roman emperor Titus. Judean national sentiment was encouraged by the work of Rabbi Johanan ben Zakkai (c. 20–90), and following him the president of the Sanhedrin (supreme court) was recognized as the patriarch of Palestinian Jewry.
2nd–3rd centuries	Greatest of the Sanhedrin presidents was Rabbi Judah (c. 135–220), who codified the traditional law in the *Mishna*. The Palestinian *Talmud* (c. 375) added the *Gemara* to the *Mishna*.
4th–5th centuries	The intellectual leadership of Judaism passed to the descendants of the 6th-century exiles in Babylonia, who compiled the Babylonian *Talmud*.
8th–13th centuries	Judaism enjoyed a golden era, producing the philosopher Saadiah, the poet Jehudah Ha-levi (c. 1075–1141), the codifier Moses Maimonides, and others.
14th–17th centuries	Where Christianity became the dominant or state religion, the Jews were increasingly segregated from mainstream life and trade by the Inquisition, anti-Semitic legislation, or by expulsion. The Protestant and Islamic states, and their colonies, allowed for refuge. Persecution led to messianic hopes strengthened by the 16th century revival of Kabbalism, culminating in the messianic movement of Shabbatai Sevi in the 17th century.
18th–19th centuries	Outbreaks of persecution increased with the rise of European nationalism. Reform Judaism, a rejection of religious orthodoxy and an attempt to interpret it for modern times, began in Germany 1810 and soon was established in England and the US. In the late 19th century, large numbers of Jews fleeing persecution (◊pogrom) in Russia and E Europe emigrated to the US, leading to the development of large Orthodox, Conservative, and Reform communities there. Many became Americanized and lost interest in religion.
20th century	Zionism (founded 1896) is a movement dedicated to achieving a secure homeland where the Jewish people would be free from persecution; this led to the establishment of the state of Israel 1948. Liberal Judaism (more radical than Reform) developed in the US. In 1911 the first synagogue in the UK was founded. The Nazi German regime 1933–45 exterminated 6 million European Jews. Hundreds of thousands of survivors went to Palestine to form the nucleus of the new state of Israel, to the US, and to other nations. Although most Israeli and American Jews were not affiliated with synagogues after the 1950s, they continued to affirm their Jewish heritage. Both Orthodox and Hasidic Judaism, however, flourished in their new homes and grew rapidly in the 1970s and 1980s.

in Hebrew, observance of the Sabbath (sunset on Friday to sunset Saturday) as a day of rest, and, among Orthodox Jews, strict dietary laws (see ⃝kosher). High holy days include *Rosh Hashanah* marking the Jewish New Year (first new moon after the autumn equinox) and, a week later, the religious fast *Yom Kippur* (Day of Atonement). Other holidays are celebrated throughout the year to commemorate various events of Biblical history.

divisions In the late Middle Ages, when Europe and W Asia were divided into Christian and Islamic countries, the Jewish people also found itself divided into two main groups. Jews in central and eastern Europe, namely in Germany and Poland, were called *Ashkenazi*.

Sephardic Jews can trace their tradition back to the Mediterranean countries, particularly Spain and Portugal under Muslim rule. When they were expelled in 1492 they settled in North Africa, the Levant, the Far East, and northern Europe. The two traditions differ in a number of ritual and cultural ways but their theology and basic Jewish practice is the same. The Hasidic sects of eastern Europe and some North African and Oriental countries also differ from other groups in their rites but they, too, maintain the concept of divine authority.

In the 19th and early 20th centuries there was a move by some Jewish groups away from traditional or orthodox observances. This trend gave rise to a number of groups within Judaism. **Orthodox Jews**, who form the majority, assert the supreme authority of the Torah, adhere to all the traditions of Judaism, including the strict dietary laws (see ⃝kosher) and the segregation of women in the synagogue. *Reform Judaism* rejects the idea that Jews are the chosen people, has a liberal interpretation of the dietary laws, and takes a critical attitude toward the Torah. *Conservative Judaism* is a compromise between Orthodox and Reform in its acceptance of the traditional law, making some allowances for modern conditions, although its services and ceremonies are closer to Orthodox than to Reform. *Liberal Judaism*, or *Reconstructionism*, goes further than Reform in attempting to adapt Judaism to the needs of the modern world and to interpret the Torah in the light of current scholarship. In all the groups except Orthodox, women are not segregated in the synagogue, and there are female rabbis in Reform, Liberal and Conservative Judaism. In the 20th century many people who call themselves Jews prefer to identify Judaism with a historical and cultural tradition rather than with strict religious observance, and a contemporary debate (complicated by the history of non-Jewish attitudes toward Jews) centers on the question of how to define a Jew. As in other religions, fundamentalist movements have emerged, for example, Gush Emunim.

Judas Iscariot 1st century AD. In the New Testament, the disciple who betrayed Jesus Christ. Judas was the treasurer of the group. At the last Passover supper, he arranged, for 30 pieces of silver, to point out Jesus to the chief priests so that they could arrest him. Afterwards Judas was overcome with remorse and committed suicide.

Jude, St 1st century AD. Supposed half brother of Jesus and writer of the Epistle of Jude in the New Testament; patron saint of lost causes. Feast day Oct 28.

judge person invested with power to hear and determine legal disputes.

In the US, the federal judiciary is chosen by executive appointments. It consists of Supreme Court justices, judges of the US district courts, magistrates, and administrative law judges. Similar offices exist at the state level with judges elected or appointed. There are also county and municipal judges elected to office.

Judges book of the Old Testament, describing the history of the Israelites from the death of Joshua to the reign of Saul, under the command of several leaders known as Judges (who deliver the people from repeated oppression).

judicial review in the US, the power of a court to decide whether legislative acts or executive actions are constitutional. The ultimate authority for judicial review is the Supreme Court, which established its right to review executive and legislative actions in the ⃝Marbury v Madison decision.

judicial separation action in a court by either husband or wife, in which it is not necessary to prove an irreconcilable breakdown of a marriage, but in which the grounds are otherwise the same as for divorce. It does not end a marriage, but a declaration may be obtained that the complainant need no longer cohabit with the defendant. The court can make similar orders to a divorce court in relation to custody and support of children and maintenance.

judiciary in constitutional terms, the system of courts and body of judges in a country. The independence of the judiciary from other branches of the central authority is generally considered to be an essential feature of a democratic political system. This independence is often written into a nation's constitution and protected from abuse by politicians.

Judith in Biblical legend, a Jewish widow, the heroine of Bethulia, who saved her community from a Babylonian siege by killing the enemy general Holofernes. The Book of Judith is part of the Apocrypha, a section of the Old Testament.

Judith approached Holofernes on the pretext of betraying the besieged Jews. Charming him with her beauty and wit, she made him drunk and cut his head off. By showing it to her compatriots, she incited them to attack and rout the army of ⃝Nebuchadnezzar.

Judith of Bavaria 800–843. Empress of the French. The wife of Louis the Pious (⃝Louis I of France) from 819, she exercised power over her husband to the benefit of their son Charles the Bold.

judo (Japanese *jū do*, "gentle way") form of wrestling of Japanese origin. The two combatants wear loose-fitting, belted jackets and trousers to facilitate holds, and falls are broken by a square mat; when one has established a painful hold that the other cannot break, the latter signifies surrender by slapping the ground with a free hand. Degrees of proficiency are indicated by the color of the belt: for novices, white; after examination, brown (three degrees); and finally, black (nine degrees).

Judo is a synthesis of methods from the many forms of jujitsu, the traditional Japanese skill of self-defense and offense without weapons, which was originally practiced as a secret art by the feudal samurai. Today, judo has been adopted throughout the world in the armed forces, the police, and in many schools. It became an Olympic sport 1964. The world championship was first held 1956 for men, 1980 for women; it is now contested biennially.

Judson Edward Zane Carroll 1823–1886. US author, better known by his adopted name "Ned Buntline." Specializing in short adventure stories, he developed a stereotyped frontier hero in the pages of his own periodicals *Ned Buntline's Magazine* and *Buntline's Own*. In his dime novels in the 1870s, he immortalized Buffalo Bill Cody.

Judson was born in Stamford, New York, served in the US Navy, and became an editor and writer in Cincinnati. Moving to New York, he established *Buntline's Own* and continued in the same literary vein. A violent racist, Judson was one of the founders of the antiforeign "Know-Nothing" party in the 1850s.

Juggernaut or *Jagannath* a name for Vishnu, the Hindu god, meaning "Lord of the World." His temple is in Puri, Orissa, India. A statue of the god, dating from about 318, is annually carried in procession on a large vehicle (hence the word "juggernaut"). Devotees formerly threw themselves beneath its wheels.

jugular vein one of two veins in the necks of vertebrates; they return blood from the head to the superior (or anterior) vena cava and thence to the heart.

Jugurtha died 104 BC. King of Numidia, N Africa, who, after a long resistance, was betrayed to the Romans in 107 BC, and put to death.

jujitsu or *jujutsu* traditional Japanese form of self-defense; the modern form is ⃝judo.

jujube tree of the genus *Zizyphus* of the buckthorn family Thamnaceae, with berrylike fruits.

The common jujube *Z. jujuba* of Asia, Africa, and Australia, cultivated in S Europe and California, has fruit the size of small plums, known as Chinese dates when preserved in syrup.

Julian *the Apostate* c. 331–363. Roman emperor. Born in Constantinople, the nephew of Constantine the Great, he was brought up as a Christian but early in life became a convert to paganism. Sent by Constantius to govern Gaul in 355, he was proclaimed emperor by his troops in 360, and in 361 was marching on Constantinople when Constantius' death allowed a peaceful succession. He revived pagan worship and refused to persecute heretics. He was killed in battle against the Persians.

Juliana 1909– . Queen of the Netherlands 1948–80. The daughter of Queen Wilhelmina (1880–1962), she married Prince Bernhard of Lippe-Biesterfeld in 1937. She abdicated 1980 and was succeeded by her daughter ⃝Beatrix.

Julius II 1443–1513. Pope 1503–13. A politician who wanted to make the Papal States the leading power in Italy, he formed international alliances first against Venice and then against France. He began the building of St Peter's Church in Rome 1506 and was the patron of the artists Michelangelo and Raphael.

July Revolution revolution 27–29 July, 1830 in France that overthrew the restored Bourbon monarchy of Charles X and substituted the constitutional monarchy of Louis Philippe, whose rule (1830–48) is sometimes referred to as the July Monarchy.

jumbo jet popular name for a generation of huge wide-bodied airliners including the *Boeing 747*, which is 232 ft/71 m long, has a wingspan of 196 ft/60 m, a maximum takeoff weight of nearly 400 tons, and can carry more than 400 passengers.

Jumna or *Yamuna* river in India, 860 mi/

1,385 km in length, rising in the Himalayas, in Uttar Pradesh, and joining the river Ganges near Allahabad, where it forms a sacred bathing place. Agra and Delhi are also on its course.

jumping hare or *springhare* either of two African species of long-eared rodents of the only genus (*Pedetes*) in the family Pedetidae. The springhare *P. capensis* is about 16 in/40 cm long and resembles a small kangaroo with a bushy tail. It inhabits dry sandy country in E central Africa.

Juneau ice-free port and state capital of Alaska, on Gastineau Channel in the S Alaska panhandle; population (1980) 19,528. Juneau is the commercial and distribution center for the fur-trading and mining of the Panhandle region; also important are salmon fishing, fish processing, and lumbering.

A campus of the University of Alaska is here. Settled in 1880 by gold prospectors, Juneau was named the capital in 1900. In 1970 its boundaries were extended to cover 2,406 sq mi/6,232 sq km.

juneberry or *serviceberry* any tree or shrub of the genus *Amelanchier* of the rose family, having simple leaves, showy white flowers, and purple-black fruits. The Allegheny serviceberry *Amelanchier lavis*, native to the NE US, grows to a height of 40 ft/12 m and has edible fruit. Several species are grown as ornamentals.

Jung Carl Gustav 1875–1961. Swiss psychiatrist who collaborated with Sigmund ◊Freud until their disagreement in 1912 over the importance of sexuality in causing psychological problems. Jung studied religion and dream symbolism, saw the unconscious as a source of spiritual insight, and distinguished between introversion and extroversion. His books include *Modern Man in Search of a Soul* 1933.

Jungfrau (German "maiden") mountain in the Bernese Oberland, Switzerland; 13,669 ft/4,166 m high. A railroad ascends to the plateau of the Jungfraujoch, 11,340 ft/3,456 m, where there is a winter-sports center.

jungle popular name for ◊rainforest.

juniper aromatic evergreen tree or shrub of the genus *Juniperus* of the cypress family Cupressaceae, found throughout temperate regions. Its berries are used to flavor gin. Some junipers are erroneously called ◊cedars.

junk bond derogatory term for a security officially rated as "below investment grade." It is issued in order to raise capital quickly, typically to finance a takeover to be paid for by the sale of assets once the company is acquired. Junk bonds have a high yield, but are a high-risk investment.

In the US securities market, junk bonds probably diminish since they must now pay an average of more than 5% more than the prevailing treasury bond rate in order to attract investors. Studies suggest that more than 35% of junk-bond issues may default.

Junker member of the landed aristocracy in Prussia; favored by Frederick the Great and ◊Bismarck, they controlled land, industry, trade, and the army, and exhibited privilege and arrogance. From the 15th century until the 1930s they were the source of most of the Prussian civil service and officer corps.

Junkers Hugo 1859–1935. German airplane designer. In 1919 he founded in Dessau the aircraft works named after him. Junkers planes, including dive bombers, night fighters, and

troop carriers, were used by the Germans in World War II.

Juno principal goddess in Roman mythology (identified with the Greek Hera). The wife of Jupiter, the queen of heaven, she was concerned with all aspects of women's lives.

Jupiter or *Jove* in mythology, chief god of the Romans, identified with the Greek ◊Zeus. He was god of the sky, associated with lightning and thunderbolts; protector in battle; and bestower of victory. The son of Saturn, he married his sister Juno, and reigned on Mount Olympus as lord of heaven.

Jupiter the fifth planet from the Sun, and the largest in the Solar System (equatorial diameter 88,700 mi/142,800 km), with a mass more than twice that of all the other planets combined, 318 times that of the Earth's. It takes 11.86 years to orbit the Sun, at an average distance of 484 million mi/778 million km, and has at least 16 moons. It is largely composed of hydrogen and helium, liquefied by pressure in its interior, and probably with a rocky core larger than the Earth. Its main feature is the Great Red Spot, a cloud of rising gases, revolving counterclockwise, 8,500 mi/14,000 km wide and some 20,000 mi/30,000 km long.

Its visible surface consists of clouds of white ammonia crystals, drawn out into belts by the planet's high speed of rotation (9 hr 51 min at the equator, the fastest of any planet). Darker orange and brown clouds at lower levels may contain sulfur, as well as simple organic compounds. Further down still, temperatures are warm, a result of heat left over from Jupiter's formation, and it is this heat that drives the turbulent weather patterns of the planet. The Great Red Spot was first observed 1664. Its top is higher than the surrounding clouds; its color is thought to be due to red phosphorus. Jupiter's strong magnetic field gives rise to a large surrounding magnetic "shell," or magnetosphere, from which bursts of radio waves are detected. The Southern Equatorial Belt in which the Great Red Spot occurs is subject to unexplained fluctuation. In 1989 it sustained a dramatic and sudden fading. The four largest moons, Io, Europa, Ganymede, and Callisto, are the *Galilean satellites*, discovered in 1610 by Galileo (Ganymede is the largest moon in the Solar System). Three small moons were discovered in 1979 by the Voyager space probes, as was a faint ring of dust around Jupiter's equator, 34,000 mi/55,000 km above the cloud tops.

Jura island of the Inner Hebrides; area 147 sq mi/380 sq km; population (with Colonsay, 1971) 343. It is separated from Scotland by the Sound of Jura. The whirlpool Corryvreckan (Gaelic "Brecan's cauldron") is off the north coast.

Jura mountains series of parallel mountain ranges running SW–NE along the French-Swiss frontier between the rivers Rhône and Rhine, a distance of 156 mi/250 km. The highest peak is *Crête de la Neige*, 5,650 ft/1,723 m.

The mountains give their name to a *département* of France, and in 1979 a Jura canton was established in Switzerland, formed from the French-speaking areas of Berne.

Jurassic period of geological time 213–144 million years ago; the middle period of the Mesozoic era. Climates worldwide were equable, creating forests of conifers and ferns, dinosaurs were abundant, birds evolved, and limestones and iron ores were deposited.

The name comes from the Jura mountains in France and Switzerland, where the rocks formed during this period were first studied.

In North America, the Nevadan ◊orogeny marked the beginning of the Sierra Nevadas and other mountains.

Jurgens Curt (Curd Jürgens) 1912–1982. German film and stage actor who was well established in his native country before moving into French and then Hollywood films in the 1960s. His films include *Operette/Operetta* 1940, *Et Dieu créa la Femme/And God Created Woman* 1956, *Lord Jim* 1965, and *The Spy Who Loved Me* 1977.

jurisprudence the science of law in the abstract—that is, not the study of any particular laws or legal system, but of the principles upon which legal systems are founded.

jury body of lay people (usually 12, sometimes 6) sworn to decide the facts of a case and reach a verdict in a court of law. Juries, used mainly in English-speaking countries, are implemented primarily in criminal cases, but also sometimes in civil cases. The members of the jury are carefully selected by both prosecution and defense attorneys.

The British jury derived from Germanic custom. It was introduced into England by the Normans. Originally it was a body of neighbors who gave their opinion on the basis of being familiar with the protagonists and background of a case. Eventually it developed into an impartial panel, giving a verdict based solely on evidence heard in court. The jury's duty is to decide the facts of a case: the judge directs them on matters of law.

The basic principles of the British system have been adopted in the US, most Commonwealth countries, and some European countries (for example, France). Grand juries are still used in the US at both state and federal levels to decide whether there is a case to be referred for trial.

justice of the peace in some states, a public officer (magistrate), usually elected, with limited jurisdiction over a small district or part of a county. This includes the authority to try minor criminal cases, administer oaths, and officiate at marriages.

justiciar the chief justice minister of Norman and early Angevin kings, second in power only to the king. By 1265, the government had been divided into various departments, such as the Exchequer and Chancery, which meant that it was no longer desirable to have one official in charge of all.

Justinian I 483–565. Byzantine emperor from 527. He recovered N Africa from the Vandals, SE Spain from the Visigoths, and Italy from the Ostrogoths, largely owing to his great general Belisarius. He ordered the codification of Roman law, which has influenced European jurisprudence.

Justinian, born in Illyria, was associated with his uncle, Justin I, in the government from 518. He married the actress Theodora, and succeeded Justin in 527. Much of his reign was taken up with an indecisive struggle with the Persians. He built the church of Sta Sophia in Constantinople, and closed the university in Athens in 529.

Justin, St c. 100–c. 163. One of the early Christian leaders and writers known as the Fathers of the Church. Born in Palestine of a Greek family, he was converted to Christianity and wrote two *Apologies* in its defense. He spent the rest of his life as an itinerant missionary, and was martyred in Rome. Feast day June 1.

Jute member of a Germanic people who originated in Jutland but later settled in Frankish territory. They occupied Kent, SE England, about 450, according to tradition under Hengist and Horsa, and conquered the Isle of Wight and the opposite coast of Hampshire in the early 6th century.

jute fiber obtained from two plants of the genus *Corchorus* of the linden family: *C. capsularis* and *C. olitorius*. Jute is used for sacks and sacking, upholstery, webbing, twine, and stage canvas.

In the fabrication of bulk packaging and tufted carpet backing, it is now often replaced by synthetic polypropylene. The world's largest producer of jute is Bangladesh.

Jutland (Danish *Jylland*) peninsula of N Europe; area 11,400 sq mi/29,500 sq km. It is separated from Norway by the Skagerrak and from Sweden by the Kattegat, with the North Sea to the west. The larger northern part belongs to Denmark; the southern part to Germany.

Jutland, Battle of naval battle of World War I, fought between England and Germany on May 31, 1916, off the W coast of Jutland. Its outcome was indecisive, but the German fleet remained in port for the rest of the war.

Juvenal *c.* AD 60–140. Roman satirist and poet. His genius for satire brought him to the unfavorable notice of the emperor Domitian. Juvenal's 16 extant satires give an explicit and sometimes brutal picture of the decadent Roman society of his time.

juvenile delinquency offenses against the law that are committed by young people.

The American judicial system provides special status and treatment for juvenile offenders. Their identities are protected and their records barred from public view. Judicial proceedings are less formal than those of criminal courts. Incarceration may not extend beyond a defendant's majority. Sentencing is tailored to the developmental needs of defendants and may consist of probation, counseling, community service, supervision, or placement in homes for youthful offenders.

Jylland Danish name for the mainland of Denmark, the northern section of the Jutland peninsula. The chief towns are Aalborg, Aarhus, Esbjerg, Fredericia, Horsens, Kolding, Randers, and Vejle.

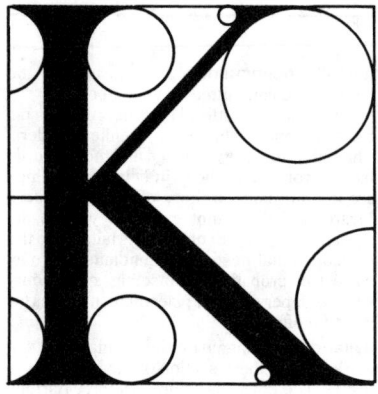

K 11th letter of the English alphabet, derived from the Greek *kappa* (K, κ) and representing the voiceless velar stop. In English, it is silent before *n* at the beginning of a word (for example, in *knee*), a change accomplished, probably, in the 17th century.

K symbol for *kelvin*, a scale of temperature.

K2 or *Chogori* second highest mountain above sea level, 28,261 ft/8,611 m, in the Karakoram range, Kashmir, N India. It was first climbed 1954 by an Italian expedition.

The peak was designated "K2" by Lt-Col Henry Godwin-Austen in his surveying log since it was the second peak in the Karakorams to be surveyed and mapped. It was later unofficially called Mount Godwin-Austen in his honor, although this alternative name has largely gone out of use.

Kaaba (Arabic "chamber") in Mecca, Saudi Arabia, the oblong building in the quadrangle of the Great Mosque, into the NE corner of which is built the Black Stone declared by the prophet Mohammed to have been given to Abraham by the archangel Gabriel, and revered by Muslims.

Kabardino-Balkar autonomous republic of Russia, in the N Caucasus mountains; capital Nalchik; area 4,825 sq mi/12,500 sq km; population (1989) 760,000. Under Russian control from 1557, it was annexed 1827; it was an autonomous republic of the USSR 1936–91.

kabbala or *cabbala* (Hebrew "tradition") ancient esoteric Jewish mystical tradition of philosophy containing strong elements of pantheism yet akin to Neoplatonism. Kabbalistic writing reached its peak between the 13th and 16th centuries. It is largely rejected by current Judaic thought as medieval superstition, but is basic to ◊Hasidism.

Among its earliest documents are the *Sefir Jezirah/The Book of Creation*, attributed to Rabbi Akiba (died 120). The *Zohar/Book of Light* was written in Aramaic in about the 13th century.

Kabinda part of Angola. See ◊Cabinda.

kabuki (Japanese "music, dance, skill") drama originating in late 16th-century Japan, drawing on ◊Nō, puppet plays, and folk dance. Its colorful, lively spectacle became popular in the 17th and 18th centuries. Many kabuki actors specialize in particular types of character, female impersonators (*onnagata*) being the biggest stars.

Kabuki was first popularized in Kyoto 1603 by the dancer Izumo Okuni who gave performances with a chiefly female troupe; from 1629 only men were allowed to act, in the interests of propriety. Unlike Nō actors, kabuki actors do not wear masks. The art was modernized and its following revived in the 1980s by Ennosuke III (1940–).

Kabul capital of Afghanistan, 6,900 ft/2,100 m above sea level, on the river Kabul; population (1984) 1,179,300. Products include textiles, plastics, leather, and glass. It commands the strategic routes to Pakistan via the ◊Khyber Pass.

Kabyle member of a group of Berber peoples of Algeria and Tunisia. As ◊Zouave they served in the colonial French forces, although many were notable in the fight for Algerian independence. Their language belongs to the Afro-Asiatic family.

Kádár János 1912–1989. Hungarian Communist leader, in power 1956–88, after suppressing the national uprising. As Hungarian Socialist Workers' Party (HSWP) leader and prime minister 1956–58 and 1961–65, Kádár introduced a series of market-socialist economic reforms, while retaining cordial political relations with the USSR.

He was ousted as party general secretary May 1988 and forced into retirement May 1989.

kaffir (Arabic *kāfir* "infidel") South African English term, usually regarded as offensive, for a black person. It was formerly the designation of various Bantu-speaking peoples, including the Xhosa and Pondo of Cape Province, living in much of SE Africa. The term is also used in some countries for an unbeliever; for example, in Pakistan to refer to a Christian.

Kafka Franz 1883–1924. Czech novelist, born in Prague, who wrote in German. His three unfinished allegorical novels *Der Prozess/ The Trial* 1925, *Der Schloss/The Castle* 1926, and *Amerika/America* 1927 were posthumously published despite his instructions that they should be destroyed. His short stories include "Die Verwandlung/The Metamorphosis" 1915, in which a man turns into a huge insect. His vision of lonely individuals trapped in bureaucratic or legal labyrinths can be seen as a powerful metaphor for modern experience.

kagu crested bird *Rhynochetos jubatus*, the only member of its family that is placed in the crane order (Gruiformes). It is found in New Caledonia in the S Pacific. About 1.6 ft/50 cm long, it is virtually flightless and nests on the ground. The introduction of cats and dogs has endangered its survival.

Kahn Louis 1901–1974. US architect, born in Estonia. A follower of Mies van de Rohe, he developed a classically romantic style, in which functional "servant" areas, such as stairwells and air ducts, featured prominently, often as towerlike structures surrounding the main living and working, or "served," areas. His projects are characterized by an imaginative use of concrete and brick and include the Salk Institute for Biological Studies, La Jolla, California, and the British Art Center at Yale University.

Kahn taught at the Yale School of Architecture from 1947 and also designed the Yale Art Gallery 1954, as well as the Richards Medical Research Building, University of Pennsylvania.

Kaieteur waterfall on the river Potaro, a tributary of the Essequibo, Guyana. At 822 ft/250 m, it is five times as high as Niagara Falls.

Kaifeng former capital of China, 907–1127, and of Honan province; population (1984) 619,200. It has lost its importance because of the silting-up of the nearby Huang He river.

Kaifu Toshiki 1932– . Japanese conservative politician, prime minister 1989–91. A protégé of former premier Takeo Miki, he was selected as a compromise choice as Liberal Democratic Party (LDP) president and prime minister Aug 1989, following the resignation of Sosuke Uno. Kaifu resigned Nov 1991, having lost the support of important factional leaders in the LDP, and was replaced by Kiichi Miyazawa.

Kaifu entered politics 1961, was deputy chief secretary 1974–76 in the Miki cabinet, and was education minister under Nakasone. He is a member of the minor Komoto faction. In 1987 he received what he claimed were legitimate political donations amounting to about $75,000 from a company later accused of bribing a number of LDP politicians (see ◊Recruit scandal). His popularity as prime minister was dented by the unconstitutional proposal, defeated in the Diet, to contribute Japanese forces to the UN coalition army in the Persian Gulf area after Iraq's annexation of Kuwait 1990. His lack of power led to his replacement as prime minister 1991.

Kaikouras double range of mountains in the NE of South Island, New Zealand, separated by the Clarence river, and reaching 9,465 ft/ 2,885 m.

Kairos in Greek mythology, the personification of Opportunity. He is portrayed in Greek art as bald at the back, but with long hair at the front.

Kairouan Muslim holy city in Tunisia, N Africa, S of Tunis; population (1984) 72,200. It is a center of carpet production. The city, said to have been founded AD 617, ranks after Mecca and Medina as a place of pilgrimage.

Kaiser title formerly used by the Holy Roman emperors, Austrian emperors 1806–1918, and German emperors 1871–1918. The word, like the Russian "tsar," is derived from the Latin *Caesar*.

Kaiser Georg 1878–1945. German playwright, the principal exponent of German ◊Expressionism. His large output includes *Die Bürger von Calais/The Burghers of Calais* 1914 and *Gas* 1918–20.

Kaiser Henry J 1882–1967. US industrialist. He developed steel and motor industries, and his shipbuilding firms became known for the mass production of vessels, including the "Liberty ships"—cheap, quickly produced transport ships—built for the UK in World War II.

kakapo nocturnal, flightless parrot *Strigops habroptilus* that lives in burrows in New Zealand. It is green, yellow, and brown and weighs up to 7.5 lb/3.5 kg. When in danger, its main defense is to keep quite still. Because of the introduction of predators such as dogs, cats, rats, and ferrets, it is in danger of extinction, there being only about 40 birds left.

Kalahari Desert semidesert area forming most of Botswana and extending into Namibia, Zimbabwe, and South Africa; area about 347,400 sq mi/900,000 sq km. The only permanent river, the Okavango, flows into a delta in the NW forming marshes rich in wildlife. Its inhabitants are the nomadic Kung.

Kalamazoo (American Indian "boiling pot") city in SW Michigan, on the Kalamazoo River, SW of Lansing; seat of Kalamazoo County. Its industries include the processing of the area's agricultural products, automobile and transportation machinery parts, chemicals, and metal and paper products; population (1990) 80,300. Kalamazoo is an Indian word for "boiling pot."

kale type of ⟡cabbage.

kaleidoscope optical toy invented by the British physicist David Brewster 1816. It usually consists of a pair of long mirrors at an angle to each other, and arranged inside a triangular tube containing pieces of colored glass, paper, or plastic. An axially symmetrical (hexagonal) pattern is seen by looking along the tube, which can be varied infinitely by rotating or shaking the tube.

Kalevala Finnish national epic poem compiled from legends and ballads by Elias Lönnrot 1835; its hero is Väinämöinen, god of music and poetry.

Kalf Willem 1619–1693. Dutch painter, active in Amsterdam from 1653. He specialized in still lifes set off against a dark background. These feature arrangements of glassware, polished metalwork, decorated porcelain, and fine carpets, with the occasional half-peeled lemon (a Dutch still-life motif).

Kalgan city in NE China, now known as ⟡Zhangjiakou.

Kali in Hindu mythology, the goddess of destruction and death. She is the wife of ⟡Siva.

Kālidāsa lived 5th century AD. Indian epic poet and dramatist. His works, in Sanskrit, include the classic drama *Sakuntala*, the love story of King Dushyanta and the nymph Sakuntala.

Kalimantan province of the republic of Indonesia occupying part of the island of Borneo
area 210,000 sq mi/543,900 sq km
cities Banjermasin and Balikpapan
physical mostly low-lying, with mountains in the north
products petroleum, rubber, coffee, copra, pepper, timber
population (1989 est) 8,677,500.

Kalinin Mikhail Ivanovich 1875–1946. Soviet politician, founder of the newspaper *Pravda*. He was prominent in the 1917 October Revolution, and in 1919 became head of state (president of the Central Executive Committee of the Soviet government until 1937, then president of the Presidium of the Supreme Soviet until 1946).

Kaliningrad formerly *Königsberg* Baltic naval base in W Russia; population (1987) 394,000. Industries include engineering and paper. It was the capital of East Prussia until the latter was divided between the USSR and Poland 1945 under the Potsdam Agreement, when it was renamed in honor of President Kalinin.

Kali-Yuga in Hinduism, the last of the four *yugas* (ages) that make up one cycle of creation. The Kali-Yuga, in which Hindus believe we are now living, is characterized by wickedness and disaster, and leads up to the destruction of this world in preparation for a new creation and a new cycle of yugas.

Kalki in Hinduism, the last avatar (manifestation) of Vishnu, who will appear at the end of the Kali-Yuga, or final age of the world, to destroy it in readiness for a new creation.

Kalmyk or *Kalmuck* autonomous republic in central Russia, on the Caspian Sea; area 29,300 sq mi/75,900 sq km; population (1989) 322,000; capital Elista. Industry is mainly agricultural. It was settled by migrants from China in the 17th century. The autonomous Soviet republic was abolished 1943–57 because of alleged collaboration of the people with the Germans during the siege of Stalingrad, but restored 1958.

Kaltenbrunner Ernst 1901–1946. Austrian Nazi leader. After the annexation of Austria 1938 he joined police chief Himmler's staff, and as head of the Security Police (SD) from 1943 was responsible for the murder of millions of Jews (see the ⟡Holocaust) and Allied soldiers in World War II. After the war, he was tried at Nuremberg for war crimes and hanged.

Kamakura city on Honshu island, Japan, near Tokyo; population 175,000. It was the seat of the first shogunate 1192–1333, which established the rule of the samurai class, and the Hachimangu Shrine is dedicated to the gods of war; the 13th-century statue of Buddha (Daibutsu) is 43 ft/13 m high. From the 19th century, artists and writers (for example, the novelist Kawabata) settled here.

Kamara'n island in the Red Sea, formerly belonging to South Yemen, and occupied by North Yemen 1972. It was included in the territory of the Yemen Republic formed in 1990; area 70 sq mi/180 sq km.

Kamchatka mountainous peninsula separating the Bering Sea and Sea of Okhotsk, forming (together with the Chukchi and Koryak national districts) a region of E Siberian Russia. Its capital, Petropavlovsk, is the only town; agriculture is possible only in the south. Most of the inhabitants are fishers and hunters.

Kamenev Lev Borisovich 1883–1936. Russian leader of the Bolshevik movement after 1917 who, with Stalin and Zinoviev, formed a ruling triumvirate in the USSR after Lenin's death 1924. His alignment with the Trotskyists led to his dismissal from office and from the Communist Party by Stalin 1926. Arrested 1934 after Kirov's assassination, Kamenev was secretly tried and sentenced, then retried, condemned, and shot 1936 for plotting to murder Stalin.

kamikaze (Japanese "wind of the gods") pilots of the Japanese air force in World War II who deliberately crash-dived their planes, loaded with bombs, usually onto ships of the US Navy.

Kampala capital of Uganda; population (1983) 455,000. It is linked by rail with Mombasa. Products include tea, coffee, textiles, fruit, and vegetables.

Kampuchea former name (1975–89) of ⟡Cambodia.

Kanaka (Hawaiian "person") Pacific islander, formerly one kidnapped and taken to Australia or elsewhere in the Pacific as a laborer; an indigenous Hawaiian.

Kananga chief city of Kasai Occidental region, W central Zaire, on the Lulua River; population (1984) 291,000. It was known as *Luluabourg* until 1966.

Kandahar city in Afghanistan, 280 mi/450 km SW of Kabul, capital of Kandahar province and a trading center, with wool and cotton factories; population (1984) 203,200. It is surrounded by a mud wall 25 ft/8 m high. When Afghanistan became independent 1747, Kandahar was its first capital.

Kandinsky Wassily 1866–1944. Russian painter, a pioneer of abstract art. Born in Moscow, he traveled widely, settling in Munich 1896. Around 1910 he produced the first known examples of purely abstract work in 20th-century art. He was an originator of the ⟡*Blaue Reiter* movement 1911–12. From 1921 he taught at the ⟡Bauhaus school of design. He moved to Paris 1933, becoming a French citizen 1939.

Kandinsky originally experimented with Post-Impressionist styles and Fauvism. His highly colored style had few imitators, but his theories on composition, published in *Concerning the Spiritual in Art* 1912, were taken up by the early abstract movement.

Kandy city in central Sri Lanka, former capital of the kingdom of Kandy 1480–1815; population (1990) 104,000. Products include tea. One of the most sacred Buddhist shrines is situated in Kandy.

kangaroo any marsupial of the family Macropodidae found in Australia, Tasmania, and New Guinea. Kangaroos are plant-eaters and most live in groups. They are adapted to hopping, the vast majority of species having very large back legs and feet compared with the small forelimbs. The larger types can jump 30 ft/9 m at a single bound. Most are nocturnal. Species vary from small rat kangaroos, only 1 ft/30 cm long, through the medium-sized wallabies, to the large red and great gray kangaroos, which are the largest living marsupials. These may be 5.9 ft/1.8 m long with 3.5 ft/1.1 m tails.

In New Guinea and N Queensland, tree kangaroos (genus *Dendrolagus*) occur. These have comparatively short hind limbs. The great gray kangaroo *Macropus giganteus* produces a single young ("joey") about 1 in/2 cm long after a very short gestation, usually in early summer. At birth the young kangaroo is too young even to suck. It remains in its mother's pouch, attached to a nipple which squirts milk into its mouth at intervals. It stays in the pouch, with excursions as it matures, for about 280 days.

kangaroo paw bulbous plant *Anigozanthos manglesii*, family Hameodoraceae, with a row of small white flowers emerging from velvety green tubes with red bases. It is the floral emblem of Western Australia.

Ka Ngwane black homeland in Natal province, South Africa; achieved self-governing status 1971; population (1985) 392,800.

Kankakee city in NE Illinois, on the Kankakee River, S of Chicago; seat of Kankakee County. It is a distribution center for corn. Industries also include building materials, furniture, pharmaceuticals, and farm machinery; population (1990) 27,600.

Kano capital of Kano state in N Nigeria, trade center of an irrigated area; population (1983) 487,100. Products include bicycles, glass, furniture, textiles, and chemicals. Founded about 1000 BC, Kano is a walled city, with New Kano extending beyond the walls.

Kansas state in central US; nickname Sunflower State
area 82,296 sq mi/213,200 sq km
capital Topeka
cities Kansas City, Wichita, Overland Park
features Dodge City, once "cowboy capital of the world"; Eisenhower Center, Abilene; Fort Larned and Fort Scott; Pony Express station, Hanover; Wichita Cowtown, a frontier-era reproduction

products wheat, cattle, coal, petroleum, natural gas, aircraft, minerals
population (1990) 2,477,600
famous people Amelia Earhart; Dwight D Eisenhower; William Inge; Buster Keaton; Carry Nation; Charlie Parker
history explored by Francisco de Coronado for Spain 1541 and La Salle for France 1682; ceded to the US 1803 as part of the Louisiana Purchase.

The first permanent settlements were forts Leavenworth 1827, Scott 1842, and Riley 1853, outposts to protect the Santa Fe and Oregon trails. In the 1850s it was the scene of bloody warfare between pro-and antislavery settlers. It became a state 1861. By 1872 two railroads had crossed Kansas, and such towns as Dodge City and Abilene filled with cowboys driving cattle from Texas. Hardy winter wheat was brought to the state by Russian Mennonites. Kansas was hard hit by the Great Depression and dust-bowl soil erosion of the 1930s, but aircraft, oil, and gas industries provided the basis for economic recovery and expansion.

Kansas City city in Kansas, at the confluence of the Kansas and Missouri rivers, adjacent to Kansas City, Missouri; population (1990) 149,800. Food processing, electronics, and automobile-assembly plants are here, as well as the University of Kansas Medical Center. It was laid out in 1857 as Wyandotte and expanded in 1886.

Kansas City city in Missouri, at the confluence of the Kansas and Missouri rivers, adjacent to Kansas City, Kansas; population (1990) 435,100. Industries include steel and electronics manufactures, motor-vehicle assembly, and oil refining, and it is the financial, marketing, and distribution center of the region. The University of Missouri-Kansas City and the Kansas City Art Institute are among the schools here. The site was settled as a trading post by French fur trappers in 1821. It was dominated by boss Tom Pendergast (Democrat) in the 1920s and 1930s, and under his "protection" jazz musicians such as Lester Young, Count Basie, and Charlie Parker performed. Crown Center, a gigantic office, condominium, and shopping complex was completed in the 1970s.

Kansu alternate spelling for the Chinese province ⯈Gansu.

Kant Immanuel 1724–1804. German philosopher who believed that knowledge is not merely an aggregate of sense impressions but is dependent on the conceptual apparatus of the human understanding, which is itself not derived from experience. In ethics, Kant argued that right action cannot be based on feelings or inclinations but conforms to a law given by reason, the *categorical imperative*.

Born in Königsberg (in what was then East Prussia), he attended the university there, and was appointed professor of logic and metaphysics 1770. His first book, *Gedanken von*

Kansas

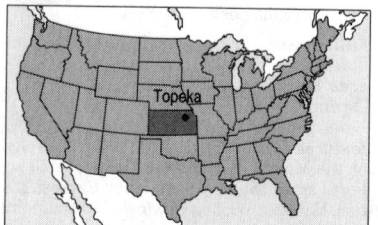

der wahren Schätzung der lebendigen Kräfte/Thoughts on the True Estimates of Living Forces, appeared in 1747 and the *Theorie des Himmels/Theory of the Heavens* in 1755. In the latter he combined physics and theology in an argument for the existence of God. In *Kritik der reinen Vernunft/Critique of Pure Reason* 1781, he argued that God's existence could not be proved theoretically. Other works include *Prolegomena* 1783, *Metaphysik der Sitten/Metaphysic of Ethics* 1785, *Metaphysische Anfangsgründe der Naturwissenschaft/Metaphysic of Nature* 1786, *Kritik der praktischen Vernunft/Critique of Practical Reason* 1788, and *Kritik der Urteilskraft/Critique of Judgement* 1790. In 1797 ill health led to his retirement.

Kanto flat, densely populated region of E Honshu island, Japan; population (1988) 37,867,000; area 12,505 sq mi/32,377 sq km. The chief city is Tokyo.

Kanton and Enderbury two atolls in the Phoenix group, which forms part of the Republic of ⯈Kiribati. They were a UK–US condominium (joint rule) 1939–80. There are US aviation, radar, and tracking stations here.

Kantorovich Leonid 1912–1986. Soviet mathematical economist whose theory that decentralization of decisions in a planned economy could only be made with a rational price system earned him a share (with Tjalling C Koopmans) of the 1975 Nobel Prize for Economics.

KANU (acronym for **Kenya African National Union**) political party founded 1944 and led by Jomo ⯈Kenyatta from 1947, when it was the Kenya African Union; it became KANU on independence. The party formed Kenyatta's political power base in 1963 when he became prime minister; in 1964 he became the first president of Kenya.

kaolinite or **kaolin** ⯈clay mineral, hydrous aluminum silicate, $Al_2Si_2O_5(OH)_4$, formed mainly by the chemical weathering of ⯈feldspar. It is important in the manufacture of porcelain and other ceramics, paper, rubber, paint, textiles, and medicines. It is mined in France, the UK, Germany, China, and the US.

Kapitza Peter 1894–1984. Soviet physicist who in 1978 shared a Nobel Prize for his work on magnetism and low-temperature physics. He was assistant director of magnetic research at the Cavendish Laboratory, Cambridge, England, 1924–32, before returning to the USSR to work at the Russian Academy of Science.

Kaplan Viktor 1876–1934. Austrian engineer who invented a water turbine with adjustable rotor blades. In the machine, patented 1920, the rotor was on a vertical shaft and could be adjusted to suit any rate of flow of water.

Horizontal Kaplan turbines are used at the installation on the estuary of the river Rance in France, the world's first tidal power station.

kapok silky hairs that surround the seeds of certain trees, particularly the **kapok tree** *Bombax ceiba* of India and Malaysia, and the **silk-cotton tree** *Ceiba pentandra*, a native of tropical America. Kapok is used for stuffing cushions and mattresses and for sound insulation; oil obtained from the seeds is used in food and soap preparation.

Kara Bogaz Gol shallow gulf of the Caspian Sea, Turkmenistan; area 8,000 sq mi/20,000 sq km. Rich deposits of sodium chloride, sulfates, and other salts have formed by evaporation.

Karachi largest city and chief seaport of Pakistan, and capital of Sind province, NW of the Indus delta; population (1981) 5,208,000. Industries include engineering, chemicals, plastics, and textiles. It was the capital of Pakistan 1947–59.

Karaite member of an 8th-century sect of Judaism which denied the authority of rabbinic tradition, recognizing only the authority of the scriptures.

Karajan Herbert von 1908–1989. Austrian conductor. He was the principal conductor of the Berlin Philharmonic Orchestra 1955–89 and artistic director of the Vienna State Opera 1956–64. He was also the artistic director of the Salzburg Festival from 1956 to 1960. He was associated with the Classical and Romantic repertoire—Beethoven, Brahms, Mahler, and Richard Strauss.

Kara-Kalpak autonomous republic of Uzbekistan
area 61,000 sq mi/158,000 sq km
capital Nukus
cities Munyak
products cotton, rice, wheat, fish
population (1989) 1,214,000
history named after the Kara-Kalpak ("black hood") people who live south of the Sea of Aral and were conquered by Russia 1867. An autonomous Kara-Kalpak region was formed 1926 within Kazakhstan, transferred to the Soviet republic 1930, made a republic 1932, and attached to Uzbekistan 1936.

Karakoram mountain range in central Asia, divided among China, Pakistan, and India. Peaks include K2, Masharbrum, Gasharbrum, and Mustagh Tower. **Ladakh** subsidiary range is in NE Kashmir on the Tibetan border.

Karakoram highway road constructed by China and Pakistan and completed 1978; runs 500 mi/800 km from Havelian (NW of Rawalpindi), via Gilgit in Kashmir and the Khunjerab Pass (16,000 ft/4,800 m) to Kashi in China.

Karakorum ruined capital of Mongol ruler ⯈Genghis Khan, SW of Ulaanbaatar in Mongolia.

Kara-Kum sandy desert occupying most of ⯈Turkmenistan; area about 120,000 sq mi/310,800 sq km. It is crossed by the Caspian railroad.

karaoke (Japanese "empty orchestra") amateur singing in public to prerecorded backing tapes. Karaoke originated in Japan and spread to other parts of the world in the 1980s. Karaoke machines are jukeboxes of backing tracks to well-known popular songs, usually with a microphone attached and lyrics displayed on a video screen.

In Japan, where karaoke machines have been installed not only in bars but also in taxis, karaoke had become a major industry by the early 1990s. Karaoke machines can hold up to 4,000 songs with on-screen lyrics.

Kara Sea (Russian *Kavaskoye More*) part of the Arctic Ocean off the N coast of Russia, bounded to the NW by the island of Novaya Zemlya and to the NE by Severnaya Zemlya. Novy Port on the Gulf of Ob is the chief port, and the Yenisei also flows into it.

karat or **carat** the unit of purity in gold in the US. Pure gold is 24-karat; 22-karat (the purest used in jewelry) is 22 parts gold and two parts alloy (to give greater strength).

karate (Japanese "empty hand") one of the

⟲martial arts. Karate is a type of unarmed combat derived from kempo, a form of the Chinese Shaolin boxing. It became popular in the West in the 1930s.

Karbala alternate spelling for ⟲Kerbela, holy city in Iraq.

Karelia autonomous republic of NW Russia
area 66,550 sq mi/172,400 sq km
capital Petrozavodsk
town Vyborg
physical mainly forested
features Lake Ladoga
products fishing, timber, chemicals, coal
population (1989) 792,000
history Karelia was annexed to Russia by Peter the Great 1721 as part of the grand duchy of Finland. In 1917 part of Karelia was retained by Finland when it gained its independence from Russia. The remainder became an autonomous region 1920 and an autonomous republic 1923 of the USSR. Following the wars of 1939–40 and 1941–44, Finland ceded 18,000 sq mi/46,000 sq km of Karelia to the USSR. Part of this territory was incorporated in the Russian Soviet Republic and part in the Karelian autonomous republic. A movement for the reunification of Russian and Finnish Karelia emerged in the late 1980s.

Karelian bear dog medium-sized dog, about 2 ft/60 cm high, used to protect Russian settlements from bears. Rather like a husky, the dog is a "national treasure." It was not exported until 1989 when some were sent to Yellowstone Park, to keep bears away from tourists.

Karelian Isthmus strip of land between Lake Ladoga and the Gulf of Finland, Russia, with St Petersburg at the south extremity and Vyborg at the northern. Finland ceded it to the USSR 1940–41 and from 1947.

Karen member of a group of SE Asian peoples, numbering 1.9 million. They live in E Myanmar (formerly Burma), Thailand, and the Irrawaddy delta. Their language belongs to the Thai division of the Sino-Tibetan family. In 1984 the Burmese government began a large-scale military campaign against the Karen National Liberation Army (KNLA), the armed wing of the Karen National Union (KNU).

Kariba dam concrete dam on the Zambia–Zimbabwe border, about 240 mi/386 km downstream from the Victoria Falls, constructed 1955–60 to supply power to both countries. The dam crosses Kariba Gorge, and the reservoir, Lake Kariba, has important fisheries.

Karloff Boris. Adopted name of William Henry Pratt 1887–1969. English-born US actor best known for his work in the US. He achieved Hollywood stardom with his role as the monster in the film *Frankenstein* 1931. Several popular sequels followed as well as starring appearances in other horror films including *Scarface* 1932, *The Lost Patrol* 1934, and *The Body Snatcher* 1945.

In 1941 Karloff gained acclaim on Broadway in *Arsenic and Old Lace*. He continued in television and films until *Targets* 1967, where he appeared as himself.

Born William Henry Pratt in London, he immigrated to Canada around 1911 in search of a theatrical career. Joining a touring stage company and frequently given the role of the play's villain, he adopted the sinister-sounding name Boris Karloff for professional use.

karma (Sanskrit "fate") in Hinduism, the sum of a human being's actions, carried forward from one life to the next, resulting in an improved or worsened fate. Buddhism has a similar belief, except that no permanent personality is envisaged, the karma relating only to the physical and mental elements carried on from birth to birth, until the power holding them together disperses in the attainment of nirvana.

Karmal Babrak 1929– . Afghani communist politician, president 1979–86. In 1965 he formed what became the banned People's Democratic Party of Afghanistan (PDPA) 1977. As president, with Soviet backing, he sought to broaden the appeal of the PDPA but encountered wide resistance from the ⟲Mujaheddin Muslim guerrillas.

Karmal was imprisoned for antigovernment activity in the early 1950s. He was a member of the government 1957–62 and of the national assembly 1965–72. In Dec 1979 he returned from brief exile in E Europe with Soviet support to overthrow President Hafizullah Amin and was installed as the new head of state. Karmal was persuaded to step down as president and PDPA leader May 1986 as the USSR began to search for a compromise settlement with opposition groupings and to withdraw troops. In July 1991, he returned to Afghanistan from exile in Moscow.

Karnak village of modern Egypt, on the E bank of the Nile, that gives its name to the temple of Ammon (constructed by Seti I and Ramses I) around which the major part of the ancient city of ⟲Thebes was built. An avenue of rams leads to ⟲Luxor.

Karnataka formerly (until 1973) *Mysore* state in SW India
area 74,035 sq mi/191,800 sq km
capital Bangalore
products mainly agricultural; minerals include manganese, chromite, and India's only sources of gold and silver
population (1991) 44,817,400
language Kannada
famous people Hyder Ali, Tippu Sultan.

Kärnten German name for ⟲Carinthia, province of Austria.

Karpov Anatoly 1951– . Russian chess player. He succeeded Bobby Fischer of the US as world champion 1975, and held the title until losing to Gary Kasparov 1985.

karri giant ⟲eucalyptus tree *Eucalyptus diversifolia*, found in the extreme SW of Australia. It may reach over 400 ft/120 m. Its exceptionally strong timber is used for girders.

Karroo two areas of semidesert in Cape Province, South Africa, divided into the **Great Karroo** and **Little Karroo** by the Swartberg mountains. The two Karroos together have an area of about 100,000 sq mi/260,000 sq km.

karst landscape characterized by remarkable surface and underground forms, created as a result of the action of water on permeable limestone. The feature takes its name from the Karst region on the Adriatic coast in Slovenia and Croatia, but the name is applied to landscapes throughout the world, the most dramatic of which is found near the city of Guilin in the Guangxi province of China.

Limestone is soluble in the weak acid of rainwater. Erosion takes place most swiftly along cracks and joints in the limestone and these open up into gullies called grikes. The rounded blocks left upstanding between them are called clints.

karyotype in biology, the set of ⟲chromosomes characteristic of a given species. It is described as the number, shape, and size of the chromosomes in a single cell of an organism. In humans for example, the karyotype consists of 46 chromosomes, in mice 40, crayfish 200, and in fruit flies 8.

The diagrammatic representation of a complete chromosome set is called a *karyogram*.

Kashmir former part of Jammu state in the north of British India with a largely Muslim population, ruled by a Hindu maharajah, who joined it to the republic of India 1947. There was fighting between pro-India and pro-Pakistan factions, the former being the Hindu ruling class and the latter the Muslim majority, and open war between the two countries 1965–66 and 1971. It is today divided between the Pakistani area of Kashmir and the Indian state of ⟲Jammu and Kashmir.

Kashmir had been under the sway of Hindu India for many centuries when Muslim rule was established by the 14th century. Mogul rule began in the 16th century but was brought to a halt by the Afghan invasion of 1753. This was followed by a period of Sikh overlordship.

Kashmir Pakistan-occupied area, 30,445 sq mi/78,900 sq km, in the northwest of the former state of Kashmir, now ⟲Jammu and Kashmir. Azad ("free") Kashmir in the west has its own legislative assembly based in Muzaffarabad while Gilgit and Baltistan regions to the north and east are governed directly by Pakistan. The ⟲Northern Areas are claimed by India and Pakistan
population 1,500,000
cities Gilgit, Skardu
features W Himalayan peak Nanga Parbat 26,660 ft/8,126 m, Karakoram Pass, Indus River, Baltoro Glacier.

Kashmiri inhabitant of or native to the state of Jammu and Kashmir, a disputed territory divided between India and Pakistan. There

sex chromosomes { X Y

kangaroo (12 chromosomes)

hawkweed (8 chromosomes)

human (46 chromosomes)

karyotype *The characteristics, or karyotype, of the chromosomes vary according to species.*

are approximately 6 million Kashmiris, 4 million of whom live on the Indian side of the cease-fire line.

Kasparov Gary 1963– . Russian chess player. When he beat his compatriot Anatoly Karpov to win the world title 1985, he was the youngest ever champion at 22 years 210 days.

Kassem Abdul Karim 1914–1963. Iraqi politician, prime minister from 1958; he adopted a pro-Soviet policy. Kassem pardoned the leaders of the pro-Egyptian party who tried to assassinate him 1959. He was executed after the 1963 coup.

Katanga former name of the ⍰Shaba region in Zaire.

Kathiawar peninsula on the W coast of India. Formerly occupied by a number of princely states, all Kathiawar (23,445 sq mi/60,723 sq km) had been included in Bombay state by 1956 but was transferred to Gujarat 1960. Mahatma Gandhi was born in Kathiawar at Porbandar.

Katmai active volcano in Alaska, 6,715 ft/2,046 m. Its major eruption in 1912 created the "Valley of Ten Thousand Smokes."

The lake-filled crater formed from the eruption is lined with glaciers. Katmai National Park, area 6,922 sq mi/17,928 sq km, was designated in 1980.

Katmandu or *Kathmandu* capital of Nepal; population (1981) 235,000. Founded in the 8th century on an ancient pilgrim and trade route from India to Tibet and China, it has a royal palace, Buddhist temples, and monasteries.

Katō Kiyomasa 1562–1611. Japanese warrior and politician who was instrumental in the unification of Japan and the banning of Christianity in the country. He led the invasion of Korea 1592, and helped Toyotomi Hideyoshi (1536–1598) and ⍰Tokugawa Ieyasu in their efforts to unify Japan.

Katō Taka-akira 1860–1926. Japanese politician, prime minister 1924–26. After a long political career with several terms as foreign minister, Katō led probably the most democratic and liberal regime of the Japanese Empire.

Katsura Tarō 1847–1913. Prince of Japan, army officer, politician, and prime minister (1901–06, 1908–11, 1912–13). He was responsible for the Anglo-Japanese treaty of 1902, the successful prosecution of the Russo-Japanese war 1904–05, and the annexation of Korea 1910.

Having assisted in the Meiji restoration (see ⍰Mutsuhito) 1866–68, Katsura became increasingly involved in politics. His support for rearmament, distaste for political parties, and oligarchic rule created unrest; his third ministry Dec 1912–Jan 1913 lasted only seven weeks.

Katyn Forest forest near Smolensk, SW of Moscow, Russia, where 4,500 Polish officer prisoners of war (captured in the German-Soviet partition of Poland 1940) were shot; 10,000 others were killed elsewhere. In 1989 the USSR accepted responsibility for the massacre.

Katz Bernard 1911– . British biophysicist. He shared the 1970 Nobel Prize for Medicine with Ulf von Euler (1905–1983) and Julius Axelrod for work on the biochemistry of the transmission and control of signals in the nervous system, vital in the search for remedies for nervous and mental disorders.

Kaufman George S(imon) 1889–1961. US playwright. Author (often in collaboration with others) of many Broadway hits, including *Of Thee I Sing* 1932, a Pulitzer Prize-winning satire on US politics; *You Can't Take It with You* 1936; *The Man Who Came to Dinner* 1939; and *The Solid Gold Cadillac* 1952. Many of his plays became classic Hollywood films.

Kaunas (formerly until 1917 *Kovno*) industrial river port (textiles, chemicals, agricultural machinery) in Lithuania, on the Niemen River; population (1987) 417,000. It was the capital of Lithuania 1910–40.

Kaunda Kenneth (David) 1924– . Zambian politician, president 1964–91. Imprisoned in 1958–60 as founder of the Zambia African National Congress, he became in 1964 the first prime minister of Northern Rhodesia, then the first president of independent Zambia. In 1973 he introduced one-party rule. He supported the nationalist movement in Southern Rhodesia, now Zimbabwe, and survived a coup attempt 1980 thought to have been promoted by South Africa. He was elected chair of the Organization of African Unity 1987. In 1990 he was faced with wide antigovernment demonstrations, leading to the acceptance of a multiparty political system. He lost the first multiparty election, in Nov 1991, to Frederick Chiluba.

kauri pine New Zealand timber conifer *Agathis australis*, family Araucariaceae. Its fossilized gum deposits are valued in varnishes; the wood is used for carving and handicrafts.

kava narcotic, intoxicating beverage prepared from the roots or leaves of a variety of pepper plant, *Piper methysticum*, found in the South Pacific islands.

Kawabata Yasunari 1899–1972. Japanese novelist, translator of Lady ⍰Murasaki, and author of *Snow Country* 1947 and *A Thousand Cranes* 1952. His novels are characterized by melancholy and loneliness. He was the first Japanese to win the Nobel Prize for Literature, in 1968.

Kawasaki industrial city (iron, steel, shipbuilding, chemicals, textiles) on Honshu island, Japan; population (1989) 1,128,000.

Kay John 1704–c. 1764. British inventor who developed the flying shuttle, a machine to speed up the work of hand-loom weaving. In 1733 he patented his invention but was ruined by the litigation necessary for its defense.

Kayah State division of Myanmar (formerly Burma), area 4,600 sq mi/11,900 sq km, formed 1954 from the Karenni states (Kantarrawaddy, Bawlake, and Kyebogyi) and inhabited mainly by the ⍰Karen people. Kayah State has a measure of autonomy.

kayak long, narrow, sealskin-covered boat with a small opening in the middle for the paddler, used by Inuit fishers and sealers, and now adapted for recreational use.

Kaye Danny. Adopted name of David Daniel Kaminski 1913–1987. US actor, comedian, and singer. He appeared in many films, including *Wonder Man* 1944, *The Secret Life of Walter Mitty* 1946, and *Hans Christian Andersen* 1952.

He achieved success on Broadway in *Lady in the Dark* 1940 and *Let's Face It* 1941. He also starred on television, had his own show 1963–67, toured for UNICEF, and guest-conducted major symphony orchestras in later years.

kayser unit of wave number (number of waves in a unit length), used in spectroscopy. It is expressed as waves per centimeter, and is the reciprocal of the wavelength. A wavelength of 0.1 cm has a wave number of 10 kaysers.

Kayseri (ancient name *Caesarea Mazaca*) capital of Kayseri province, central Turkey; population (1990) 421,400. It produces textiles, carpets, and tiles. In Roman times it was capital of the province of Cappadocia.

Kazakh or *Kazak* member of a pastoral Kyrgyz people of Kazakhstan. Kazakhs also live in China (Xinjiang, Gansu, and Qinghai), Mongolia, and Afghanistan. There are 5–7 million speakers of Kazakh, a Turkic language belonging to the Altaic family. They are predominantly Sunni Muslim, although pre-Islamic customs have survived.

Kazakhs herd horses and make use of camels; they also keep cattle. Traditionally the Kazakhs lived in tents and embarked on seasonal migrations in search of fresh pastures. Collectivized herds were established in the 1920s and 1930s.

Kazakhstan country in central Asia, bounded N by Russia, W by the Caspian Sea, E by China, and S by Turkmenistan, Uzbekistan, and Kyrgyzstan.

government There is a 510-member legislature, the supreme soviet, to which deputies are elected by a majority system, and a second-ballot runoff race in contests in which there is no clear first round majority. The state president, chosen by parliament, works with a cabinet whose head is effectively prime minister.

history Ruled by the Mongols from the 13th century, the region came under Russian control in the 18th century. Inhabited by the traditionally nomadic but now largely sedentary Kazakh people, it joined the USSR as an autonomous republic in 1920 and became a full union republic in 1936. It was the site of Soviet leader Nikita Khrushchev's ambitious "Virgin Lands" agricultural extension program during the 1950s, which not only led to harvest failures during the early 1960s, but also to a large influx of Russian settlers, turning the Kazakhs into a minority in their own republic. There were violent nationalist riots in the capital in Dec 1986 when the long-serving Kazakh Communist Party (KCP) leader Dinmukhamed Kunayed was effectively sacked by the Soviet leader Mikhail Gorbachev and replaced by an ethnic Russian.

reform under Nazarbayev In June 1989 Nursultan Nazarbayev, a "reform communist" in favor of nationalism, assumed leadership of the KCP and in Feb 1990 became the republic's president. He embarked on a pragmatic program of cultural and market-centerd economic reform, involving the privatization of the services and housing sectors. During the spring of 1991 President Nazarbayev pressed for the signing of a new USSR Union Treaty and opposed the Aug 1991 coup attempt against Gorbachev in Moscow, describing it as "illegal and unconstitutional." Soon after the coup was thwarted, the KCP was abolished. However, Nazarbayev played a key role in ensuring that the "uncontrolled disintegration" of the USSR was averted.

independence recognized Kazakhstan joined the new ⍰Commonwealth of Independent States, formed in Dec 1991, and the republic's independence was recognized by the US. In Jan 1992 Kazakhstan was admitted into the ⍰Conference on Security and Cooperation in Europe (CSCE) and in March into the United Nations (UN). Kazakhstan inherited substantial nuclear forces from the USSR,

Kazakhstan
Republic of

area 1,049,150 sq mi/2,717,300 sq km
capital Alma-Ata
cities Karaganda, Semipalatinsk, Petropavlovsk
physical Caspian and Aral seas, Lake Balkhash; Steppe region
features Baikonur Cosmodrome (space launch site at Tyuratam, near Baikonur)
head of state Nursultan Nazarbayev from 1990
head of government Sergey Tereshchenko from 1991
political system emergent democracy
political parties Independent Socialist Party of Kazakhstan (SPK)
products grain, copper, lead, zinc, manganese, coal, oil
population (1990) 16,700,000 (40% Kazakh, 38% Russian, 6% Germans, 5% Ukrainians)
language Russian; Kazakh, related to Turkish
religion Sunni Muslim
chronology
1920 Autonomous republic in USSR.
1936 Joined the USSR and became a full union republic.
1950s Site of Nikita Khrushchev's ambitious "Virgin Lands" agricultural extension program.
1960s A large influx of Russian settlers turned the Kazakhs into a minority in their own republic.
1986 Riots in Alma-Alta after Gorbachev ousted local communist leader.
1989 June: Nazarbayev became leader of the Kazakh Communist Party (KCP) and instituted economic and cultural reform programs.
1990 Feb: Nazarbayev became head of state.
1991 March: support pledged for continued union with USSR; Aug: Nazarbayev condemned attempted anti-Gorbachev coup; CP abolished and replaced by Independent Socialist Party of Kazakhstan (SPK). Dec: joined new Commonwealth of Independent States (CIS); independence recognized by US.
1992 Jan: admitted into Conference on Security and Cooperation in Europe (CSCE). March: became a member of the United Nations (UN). May: trade agreement with US.

and the Nazarbayev administration pledged to remove these to become nuclear-free. A trade agreement was signed with the US May 1992.

Kazan capital of Tatarstan, central Russia, on the river Volga; population (1989) 1,094,000. It is a transport, commercial, and industrial center (engineering, oil refining, petrochemicals, textiles, large fur trade). Formerly capital of a Tatar khanate, Kazan was captured by Ivan IV "the Terrible" 1552.

The "Black Virgin of Kazan," an icon so called because blackened with age, was removed to Moscow (1612–1917), where the great Kazan Cathedral was built to house it 1631; it is now in the US. Among miracles attributed to its presence were the defeat of Poland 1612 and of Napoleon at Moscow 1812.

Kazan Elia 1909–   . US stage and film director, a founder of the ▷Actors Studio 1947. Plays he directed include *The Skin of Our Teeth* 1942, *A Streetcar Named Desire* 1947, and *Cat on a Hot Tin Roof* 1955; films include *Gentlemen's Agreement* 1948, *East of Eden* 1954, and *The Visitors* 1972.

Kazantzakis Nikos 1885–1957. Greek writer whose works include the poem *I Odysseia/ The Odyssey* 1938 (which continues Homer's *Odyssey*), and the novels *Zorba the Greek* 1946, *The Greek Passion*, and *The Last Temptation of Christ*, both 1951.

kazoo simple wind instrument adding a buzzing quality to the singing voice on the principle of "comb and paper" music.

kcal symbol for *kilocalorie* (see ▷calorie).

kea hawklike greenish parrot *Nestor notabilis* found in New Zealand which eats insects, fruits, and sheep offal. The Maori name imitates its cry.

Kean Edmund 1787–1833. British tragic actor, noted for his portrayal of villainy in the Shakespearean roles of Shylock, Richard III, and Iago.

Kearny Philip 1814–1862. US military leader. In 1859 Kearny served in the army of Napoleon III in Italy and received the French Croix de Guerre for his actions.

With the outbreak of the US Civil War, Kearny returned to the US, was named brigadier general of the New Jersey militia, and was killed in action near Chantilly, Virginia. He was the nephew of Stephen W ▷Kearny.

Born in New York, Kearny received a law degree from Columbia 1833. Choosing a career in the military, he obtained a commission in the US Dragoons 1837. He was trained in cavalry techniques in France and saw action in the Mexican War, where he lost an arm.

Kearny Stephen Watts 1794–1848. US military leader. Born in Newark, New Jersey, Kearny attended Columbia University and saw action in the War of 1812. Later serving on the frontier, he was promoted to the rank of brigadier general and given command of the Army of the West 1846. During the Mexican War he was the military governor of New Mexico and joined in the conquest of California 1847. After a dispute with John C Fremont over the priority of conquest, Kearny was named military governor.

In 1848 he served as governor-general of occupied Veracruz and Mexico City. He died of a tropical fever acquired there.

Keating Paul 1954–   . Australian politician, Labor Party (ALP) leader and prime minister from 1991. He was treasurer and deputy leader of the ALP 1983–91.

Keating was active in ALP politics from the

age of 15. He held several posts in Labor's shadow ministry 1976–83. As finance minister 1983–91 under Bob Hawke, Keating was unpopular with the public for his harsh economic policies. He successfully challenged Hawke for the ALP party leadership Dec 1991.

Keaton Buster (Joseph Frank) 1896–1966. US comedian, actor, and film director. After being a star in vaudeville, he took up a career in "Fatty" Arbuckle comedies, and became one of the great comedians of the silent film era, with an inimitable deadpan expression (the "Great Stone Face") masking a sophisticated acting ability. His films include *One Week* 1920, *The Navigator* 1924, *The General* 1927, and *The Cameraman* 1928.

He rivaled Charlie Chaplin in popularity until studio problems ended his creative career. He then made only shorts and guest appearances, as in Chaplin's *Limelight* 1952 and *A Funny Thing Happened on the Way to the Forum* 1966.

Keats John 1795–1821. English Romantic poet who produced work of the highest quality and promise before dying at the age of 25. *Poems* 1817, *Endymion* 1818, the great odes (particularly "Ode to a Nightingale" and "Ode on a Grecian Urn" 1819), and the narratives "Lamia," "Isabella," and "The Eve of St Agnes" 1820, show his lyrical richness and talent for drawing on both Classical mythology and medieval lore.

Born in London, Keats studied at Guy's Hospital 1815–17, but then abandoned medicine for poetry. *Endymion* was harshly reviewed by the Tory *Blackwood's Magazine* and *Quarterly Review*, largely because of Keats's friendship with the radical writer Leigh Hunt (1800–1865). In 1819 he fell in love with Fanny Brawne (1802–1865). Suffering from tuberculosis, he sailed to Italy 1820 in an attempt to regain his health, but died in Rome. Valuable insight into Keats's poetic development is provided by his *Letters*, published 1848.

Keble John 1792–1866. Anglican priest and religious poet. His sermon on the decline of religious faith in Britain, preached 1833, heralded the start of the ▷Oxford Movement, a Catholic revival in the Church of England. Keble College, Oxford, was founded 1870 in his memory.

Kedah state in NW Peninsular Malaysia; capital Alor Setar; area 3,628 sq mi/9,400 sq km; population (1990) 1,412,800. Products include rice, rubber, tapioca, tin, and tungsten. Kedah was transferred by Thailand to Britain 1909, and was one of the Unfederated Malay States until 1948.

Keeling Islands another name for the ▷Cocos Islands, an Australian territory.

keep or *dungeon* or *donjon* the main tower of a castle, containing enough accommodation to serve as living quarters under siege conditions.

Keewatin eastern district of Northwest Territories, Canada, including the islands in Hudson and James bays
area 228,160 sq mi/590,935 sq km
cities (trading posts) Chesterfield Inlet, Eskimo Point, and Coral Harbor (site of an air base set up during World War II)
physical upland plateau in the north, the south low and level, covering the greater part of the Arctic prairies of Canada; numerous lakes
products furs (trapping is main occupation)
history Keewatin District formed 1876, under the administration of Manitoba; it was transferred to Northwest Territories 1905, and in

1912 lost land S of 60° N to Manitoba and Ontario.

Kefallinia (English *Cephalonia*) largest of the Ionian Islands off the west coast of Greece; area 360 sq mi/935 sq km; population (1981) 31,300. It was devastated by an earthquake 1953 that destroyed the capital Argostolion.

Kefauver (Carey) Estes 1903–1963. US Democratic politician. Having established a private law practice in Chattanooga, Tennessee, he was elected to the US House of Representatives 1939, serving there until his election to the US Senate 1948. As chairman of the Senate Judiciary Committee, Kefauver held widely publicized, televised hearings on organized crime 1950–51. An unsuccessful candidate for the Democratic presidential nomination 1952 and 1956, he served in the Senate until his death.

Born near Madisonville, Tennessee, Kefauver was educated at the University of Tennessee and received a law degree from Yale 1927.

Keflavik fishing port in Iceland, 22 mi/35 km SW of Reykjavik; population (1986) 7,500. Its international airport was built during World War II by US forces (who called it Meeks Field). Keflavik became a NATO base in 1951.

Keillor Garrison 1942– . US writer and humorist. His hometown Anoka, Minnesota, in the American Midwest, inspired his stories about Lake Wobegon, including *Lake Wobegon Days* 1985 and *Leaving Home* 1987, which often started as radio monologues about "the town that time forgot, that the decades cannot improve."

He first achieved prominence on National Public Radio's "Prairie Home Companion."

Keitel Wilhelm 1882–1946. German field marshal in World War II, chief of the supreme command from 1938 and Hitler's chief military adviser. He signed Germany's unconditional surrender in Berlin May 8, 1945. Tried at Nuremberg for war crimes, he was hanged.

Kekulé von Stradonitz Friedrich August 1829–1896. German chemist whose theory 1858 of molecular structure revolutionized organic chemistry. He proposed two resonant forms of the ◊benzene ring.

Kelantan state in NE Peninsular Malaysia; capital Kota Baharu; area 5,751 sq mi/14,900 sq km; population (1990) 1,220,100. It produces rice, rubber, copra, tin, manganese, and gold. Kelantan was transferred by Siam to Britain 1909 and until 1948 was one of the Unfederated Malay States.

Keller Helen Adams 1880–1968. US author and campaigner for the blind. She became blind and deaf after an illness when she was only 19 months old, but the teaching of Anne Sullivan, her lifelong companion, enabled her to learn the names of objects and eventually to speak. Keller graduated with honors from Radcliffe College in 1904; published several books, including *The Story of My Life* 1902; and toured the world, lecturing to raise money for the blind. She was born in Alabama.

Kellogg Frank Billings 1856–1937. US political leader and diplomat. Born in Potsdam, New York, Kellogg studied law in Minnesota and was admitted to the bar 1877. After service as a prosecutor of federal antitrust cases, he was elected to the US Senate 1916. Kellogg was named US ambassador to Great Britain by President Harding 1922 and secretary of

state 1925. His greatest achievement was the formulation of the international antiwar resolution, the Kellogg–Briand Pact, for which he was awarded the Nobel Peace Prize 1929. Kellogg later served as judge on the World Court 1930–35.

Kellogg–Briand Pact agreement negotiated 1927 between the US and France to renounce war and seek settlement of disputes by peaceful means. It took its name from the US secretary of state Frank B Kellogg (1856–1937) and the French foreign minister Aristide Briand. Most other nations subsequently signed. Some successes were achieved in settling South American disputes, but the pact made no provision for measures against aggressors and became ineffective in the 1930s, with Japan in Manchuria, Italy in Ethiopia, and Hitler in central Europe.

Kells, Book of 8th-century illuminated manuscript of the Gospels produced at the monastery of Kells in County Meath, Ireland. It is now in Trinity College library, Dublin.

Kelly Emmett 1898–1979. US clown and circus performer. Drifting from circus to circus, Kelly finally unveiled his "Weary Willie" clown character while with the Hagenbeck-Wallace circus 1931. Gaining widespread popularity, he joined the Ringling Brothers and Barnum and Bailey Circus 1942 and made "Weary Willie" one of the most famous clowns in the world. Kelly later became a familiar film and television personality.

Born in Sedan, Kansas, Kelly had early aspirations to be a cartoonist and moved to Kansas City 1917. There he created the hobo character "Weary Willie" that was later to become the inspiration for his circus persona.

Kelly Gene (Eugene Curran) 1912– . US film actor, dancer, choreographer, and director. He was a major star of the 1940s and 1950s in a series of MGM musicals, including *On the Town* 1949, *An American in Paris* 1951, and *Singin' in the Rain* 1952.

He also acted in nonmusicals, such as *Marjorie Morningstar* 1958 and *Inherit the Wind* 1960.

Kelly Grace (Patricia) 1928–1982. US film actress who retired from acting after marrying Prince Rainier III of Monaco 1956. She starred in *High Noon* 1952, *The Country Girl* 1954, for which she received an Academy Award, and *High Society* 1955. She also starred in three Hitchcock classics—*Dial M for Murder* 1954, *Rear Window* 1954, and *To Catch a Thief* 1955.

After her marriage she devoted herself to the principality, raised three children, and was active in charities until she died in an automobile accident.

Kelly Ned (Edward) 1855–1880. Australian ◊bushranger. The son of an Irish convict, he wounded a police officer in 1878 while resisting the arrest of his brother Daniel for horse-stealing. The two brothers escaped and carried out bank robberies. Kelly wore a distinctive home-made armor. In 1880 he was captured and hanged.

keloid in medicine, overgrowth of fibrous tissue, usually produced at the site of a scar. Black skin produces more keloid than does white skin; it has a puckered appearance caused by clawlike offshoots. Surgical removal is often unsuccessful, because the keloid returns.

kelp collective name for large brown seaweeds, such as those of the Fucaceae and

Laminariaceae families. Kelp is also a term for the powdery ash of burned seaweeds, a source of iodine.

The **brown kelp** *Macrocystis pyrifera*, abundant in Antarctic and sub-Antarctic waters, is one of the fastest-growing organisms known, reaching 320 ft/100 m. It is farmed for the alginate industry, its rapid surface growth allowing cropping several times a year, but it is an alien pest in N Atlantic waters.

Kelvin William Thomson, 1st Baron Kelvin 1824–1907. Irish physicist who introduced the **kelvin scale**, the absolute scale of temperature. His work on the conservation of energy 1851 led to the second law of ◊thermodynamics.

Popularly known for his contributions to telegraphy, he greatly improved transatlantic communications. Maritime endeavors led to a tide gauge and predictor, an improved compass, and simpler methods of fixing a ship's position at sea.

kelvin scale temperature scale used by scientists. It begins at ◊absolute zero (−273.16°C) and increases by the same degree intervals as the Celsius scale; that is, 0°C is the same as 273 K and 100°C is 373 K.

Kemal Atatürk Mustafa. Turkish politician; see ◊Atatürk.

Kemble (John) Philip 1757–1823. English actor and theater manager. He excelled in tragedy, including the Shakespearean roles of Hamlet and Coriolanus. As manager of Drury Lane 1788–1803 and Covent Garden 1803–17 in London, he introduced many innovations in theatrical management, costume, and scenery.

Kempe Rudolf 1910–1976. German conductor. Renowned for the clarity and fidelity of his interpretations of the works of Richard Strauss and ◊Wagner's *Ring* cycle, he conducted Britain's Royal Philharmonic Orchestra 1961–75 and was musical director of the Munich Philharmonic from 1967.

Kempis Thomas à. Medieval German monk and religious writer; see ◊Thomas à Kempis.

Kendall Edward 1886–1972. US biochemist. In 1914 he isolated the hormone thyroxine, the active compound of the thyroid gland. He went on to work on secretions from the adrenal gland, among which he discovered a compound E, which was in fact the steroid cortisone. For this Kendall shared the 1950 Nobel Prize for Medicine with Philip Hench (1896–1965) and Tadeus ◊Reichstein.

kendo (Japanese "the way of the sword") one of the Japanese armed ◊martial arts in which combatants fence with bamboo replicas of samurai swords. Masks and padding are worn for protection. The earliest recorded reference to kendo is from AD 789.

Kendrew John 1917– . British biochemist. Kendrew began, in 1946, the ambitious task of determining the three-dimensional structure of the major muscle protein myoglobin. This was completed in 1959 and won for Kendrew a share of the 1962 Nobel Prize for Chemistry with Max Perutz.

Keneally Thomas (Michael) 1935– . Australian novelist who won the Booker Prize with *Schindler's Ark* 1982, a novel based on the true account of Polish Jews saved from the gas chambers in World War II by a German industrialist. Other works include *Woman of the Inner Sea* 1992.

Keneally has also written *The Chant of

Jimmie Blacksmith 1972, filmed in 1978 and based on the life of the Aboriginal bushranger Jimmy Governor, *Confederates* 1980, *A Family Madness* 1986, *The Playmaker* 1987, and *To Asmara* 1989.

Kennedy Anthony 1936– . US jurist and associate justice of the US Supreme Court 1988– . A conservative, he wrote the majority opinion in *Saffle v Parks* 1990 that a writ of habeas corpus may be obtained only according to the laws in force at the time of a prisoner's conviction and in *Washington v Harper* 1990 that the administration of medication for mentally ill prisoners, without the prisoner's consent, is permissible. He supported the majority opinion in the 1989 case, *Texas v Johnson*, that ruled that the burning of the US flag in protest was protected by the First Amendment.

Born in Sacramento, California, he attended Stanford University (spending his fourth year at the London School of Economics) and the Harvard Law School. Kennedy practiced law in private practice in California 1962–75. He taught constitutional law at McGeorge School of Law of the University of the Pacific 1965–88. He was appointed judge of the US Court of Appeals for the Seventh Circuit 1976. In 1988 President Reagan appointed him to the Supreme Court.

Kennedy Edward (Moore) "Ted" 1932– . US Democratic politician. He aided his brothers John and Robert Kennedy in the presidential campaign of 1960, and entered politics as a senator from Massachusetts 1962. He failed to gain the presidential nomination 1980, largely because of questions about his delay in reporting an automobile crash at Chappaquiddick Island, near Cape Cod, Massachusetts, in 1969, in which his passenger, Mary Jo Kopechne, was drowned.

He is a spokesman for liberal causes including national health and gun control.

Kennedy John F(itzgerald) "Jack" 1917–1963. 35th president of the US 1961–63, a Democrat; the first Roman Catholic and the youngest person to be elected president. In foreign policy he carried through the unsuccessful ◊Bay of Pigs invasion of Cuba, and in 1963 secured the withdrawal of Soviet missiles from the island. His program for reforms at home, called the **New Frontier**, was posthumously executed by Lyndon Johnson. Kennedy was assassinated while on a state visit to Dallas, Texas, on Nov 22, 1963 by Lee Harvey Oswald (1939–1963), who was within a few days shot dead by Jack Ruby (1911–1967).

Son of successful financier Joseph Kennedy, John was born in Brookline, Massachusetts, educated at Harvard, and served in the navy in the Pacific during World War II. In 1946 he was elected to the House of Representatives and in 1952 to the Senate from Massachusetts. In 1953 he married socialite Jacqueline Lee Bouvier (1929–). In 1960 he defeated Richard ◊Nixon for the presidency, partly as a result of televised debates, and brought academics and intellectuals to Washington as advisers. The US involvement in the Vietnam War began during Kennedy's administration.

He created the Peace Corps, volunteers who give various types of health, agricultural, and educational aid overseas, and he proposed the Alliance for Progress for aid to Latin America. In the view of many, style was more important than substance in the Kennedy White House, but he inspired a generation of idealists and created an aura of positive activism. His wit and

charisma combined with political shrewdness to disarm many critics. A number of conspiracy theories have developed around the Kennedy assassination, which was investigated by a special commission headed by Chief Justice Earl ◊Warren. The commission determined that Oswald acted alone. Oswald was a malcontent who had gone to live in the USSR in 1959 and later returned. Ruby was a Dallas nightclub owner.

Kennedy Joseph Patrick 1888–1969. US industrialist and diplomat; ambassador to the UK 1937–40. A self-made millionaire, he ventured into the film industry, then set up the Securities and Exchange Commission (SEC) for F D Roosevelt. He groomed each of his four sons—Joseph Patrick Kennedy Jr (1915–1944), John F ◊Kennedy, Robert ◊Kennedy, and Edward ◊Kennedy—for a career in politics. His eldest son, Joseph, was killed in action with the naval air force in World War II.

Kennedy Robert (Francis) 1925–1968. US Democratic politician and lawyer. He was presidential campaign manager for his brother John F ◊Kennedy 1960, and as attorney general 1961–64 pursued a racket-busting policy and promoted the Civil Rights Act of 1964. He was also a key aide to his brother. When John Kennedy's successor, Lyndon Johnson, preferred Hubert H Humphrey for the 1964 vice-presidential nomination, Kennedy resigned and was elected senator from New York. In 1968 he campaigned for the Democratic Party's presidential nomination, but during a campaign stop in California was assassinated by Sirhan Bissara Sirhan (1944–), a Jordanian.

Kennedy William 1928– . US novelist, author of the *Albany Trilogy* consisting of *Legs* 1976, about the gangster "Legs" Diamond; *Billy Phelan's Greatest Game* 1983, about a pool player; and *Ironweed* 1984, about a baseball player's return to the city of Albany, NY. He also wrote *Quinn's Book* 1988.

Kennedy Space Center ◊NASA launch site on Merritt Island, near Cape Canaveral, Florida, used for Apollo and space-shuttle launches. The first flight to land on the Moon (1969) and *Skylab*, the first orbiting laboratory (1973), were launched here.

The Center is dominated by the Vehicle Assembly Building, 525 ft/160 m tall, used for assembly of ◊Saturn rockets and space shuttles. It is named for Pres John F Kennedy.

Kennelly Arthur Edwin 1861–1939. US engineer who gave his name to the Kennelly–Heaviside layer (now the ◊E layer) of the ◊ionosphere. He verified in 1902 the existence of an ionized layer in the upper atmosphere, predicted by ◊Heaviside.

Kennelly–Heaviside layer former term for the ◊E layer.

Kenneth two kings of Scotland:

Kenneth I *MacAlpin* died 858. King of Scotland from *c.* 844. Traditionally, he is regarded as the founder of the Scottish kingdom (Alba) by virtue of his final defeat of the Picts about 844. He invaded Northumbria six times, and drove the Angles and the Britons over the river Tweed.

Kenneth II died 995. King of Scotland from 971, son of Malcolm I. He invaded Northumbria several times, and his chiefs were in constant conflict with Sigurd the Norwegian over the area of Scotland north of the river

Spey. He is believed to have been murdered by his subjects.

Kennewick city in SE Washington, on the Columbia River, SE of Seattle; population (1990) 42,200. Dams built on the Columbia and Snake rivers provide irrigation for the area's grape, sugar beet, alfalfa, and corn crops.

Kenosha city in the SE corner of Wisconsin, on Lake Michigan, SE of Milwaukee, seat of Kenosha County; population (1980) 77,685. Its industries include food-processing equipment, fertilizers, motor vehicles, textiles and clothing, and food products; Kenosha is an Indian word for "pike" or "pickerel."

Kent county in SE England, nicknamed the "garden of England"
area 1,440 sq mi/3,730 sq km
cities Maidstone (administrative headquarters), Canterbury, Chatham, Rochester, Sheerness, Tunbridge Wells; resorts: Folkestone, Margate, Ramsgate
features traditionally, a "man of Kent" comes from east of the Medway and a "Kentish man" from W Kent; New Ash Green, a new town; Romney Marsh; the Isles of Grain, Sheppey (on which is the resort of Sheerness, formerly a royal dockyard) and Thanet; Weald (agricultural area); rivers: Darent, Medway, Stour; Leeds Castle (converted to a palace by Henry VIII); Hever Castle (where Henry VIII courted Anne Boleyn); Chartwell (Churchill's country home), Knole, Sissinghurst Castle and gardens; the Brogdale Experimental Horticulture Station at Faversham has the world's finest collection of apple and other fruit trees; the former RAF Manston became in Oct 1989 Kent International Airport
products hops, apples, soft fruit, coal, cement, paper
population (1991) 1,485,600
famous people Charles Dickens, Edward Heath, Christopher Marlowe.

Kenton Stan 1912–1979. US exponent of progressive jazz, who broke into West Coast jazz in 1941 with his "wall of brass" sound. He helped introduce Afro-Cuban rhythms to US jazz, and combined jazz and Classical music in compositions such as "Artistry in Rhythm" 1943.

Kentucky state in S central US; nickname Bluegrass State
area 40,414 sq mi/104,700 sq km
capital Frankfort
cities Louisville, Lexington, Owensboro, Covington, Bowling Green
features bluegrass country; horse racing at Louisville (Kentucky Derby); Mammoth Cave National Park (main cave 4 mi/6.5 km long, up to 125 ft/38 m high, where Indian councils were once held); Abraham Lincoln's birthplace at Hodgenville; Fort Knox, US gold-bullion depository
products tobacco, cereals, textiles, coal, whiskey, horses, transport vehicles

Kentucky

population (1990) 3,365,300
famous people Mohammed Ali, Daniel Boone, Louis D Brandeis, Kit Carson, Henry Clay, D W Griffith, Thomas Hunt Morgan, Harland "Colonel" Sanders, Robert Penn Warren
history the first region west of the Alleghenies settled by American pioneers. James Harrod founded Harrodsburg 1774; in 1775 Daniel Boone, who blazed his Wilderness Trail 1767, founded Boonesboro. Originally part of Virginia, Kentucky became a state 1792. Badly divided over the slavery question, the state was racked by guerrilla warfare and partisan feuds during the Civil War.

In 1900, Kentucky ranked first among Southern states in per-capita income, but wealth was divided unevenly, and the Great Depression of the 1930s hit hard; by 1940, Kentucky was last among states in per-capita income. Although it remains one of the poorest states, better roads, education, television, and government programs have relieved the isolation of its rural communities.

Kenya country in E Africa, bounded N by Sudan and Ethiopia, E by Somalia, SE by the Indian Ocean, SW by Tanzania, and W by Uganda.
government The 1963 constitution, amended 1964, 1969, 1982, and 1992 provides for a president, elected by universal suffrage for a five-year term, and a single-chamber national assembly, serving a similar term. The president must be endorsed by at least 25% of voters in at least five of the country's eight provinces. The assembly has 202 members, 188 elected by universal suffrage, 12 nominated by the president, and the attorney general and speaker as members by virtue of their office. From 1969 to 1982 Kenya was effectively a one-party state, and in 1983 it became so legally, the only legitimate party being the Kenya African National Union (KANU), whose leader is the state president.
history Archeological evidence shows that the area now known as Kenya was first inhabited at least 5 million years ago by early humans. African tribal groups inhabited the area when, in the 8th century, the coast was settled by Arabs, and during the 15th–18th centuries the region was under Portuguese rule.
independence Kenya became a British protectorate 1895 and colony 1920–64, when it achieved full independence within the British ⟩Commonwealth. There was near civil war during the 20 years before independence, as nationalist groups carried out a campaign of violence. The Kenya African Union (KAU) was founded 1944, and in 1947 Jomo ⟩Kenyatta, a member of Kenya's largest ethnic group, the Kikuyu, became its president. Three years later a secret society of young Kikuyu militants was formed, called Mau Mau, which had the same aims as KAU but sought to achieve them by violent means. Although Kenyatta dissociated himself from Mau Mau, the British authorities distrusted him and imprisoned him 1953. By 1956 the guerrilla campaign had largely ended, the state of emergency was lifted and Kenyatta was released.

Kenya was granted internal self-government 1963, and Kenyatta, who had become leader of the Kenya African National Union (KANU), became prime minister and then president after full independence 1964. During his presidency the country achieved considerable stability. When he died in 1978 he was succeeded by Vice President Daniel arap Moi, who built on Kenyatta's achievements. The East Africa Community (EAC), which Kenya joined in 1967 with Tanzania and Uganda, collapsed 1977.
one-party state An attempted coup by junior air-force officers 1982 was foiled and resulted in political detentions and press censorship. The air force and Nairobi University were temporarily dissolved. In the same year the national assembly declared Kenya a one-party state. President Moi was reelected 1983. He was reelected unopposed for a third successive presidential term Feb 1988. In June 1989 Moi unexpectedly announced the release of all known political detainees. Kenya led the effort 1989 to ban trading in ivory after poaching of elephants became uncontrollable. The deaths of several US tourists on safari provoked Moi to declare a war against poachers.
calls for political reform In July 1990 there were widespread antigovernment riots while more moderate elements called for a multiparty system. Despite the government's refusal to accept this, former vice-president Oginga Odinga launched Feb 1991 a new opposition group, the National Democratic Party. In Dec 1991, after increasing domestic and international pressure for political reform, President Moi announced the imminent introduction of multiparty politics. The Forum for the Restoration of Democracy (FORD) said Jan 1992 that it would reorganize itself as a full political party. In March 1992 the government announced proposals for constitutional changes. An amendment was passed in Aug that was thought to improve Moi's chances of being reelected. To date, Moi has enjoyed some success in tackling corruption and inefficiency in the public services, but his human-rights record has often been criticized. In Feb 1992 plans to revive the East Africa co-operation pact were announced. *See illustration box.*

Kenya, Mount or **Kirinyaga** extinct volcano from which Kenya takes its name, 17,057 ft/5,199 m; the first European to climb it was Halford Mackinder in 1899.

Kenyatta Jomo. Assumed name of Kamau Ngengi c. 1894–1978. Kenyan nationalist politician, prime minister from 1963, as well as the first president of Kenya from 1964 until his death. He led the Kenya African Union from 1947 (**KANU** from 1963) and was active in liberating Kenya from British rule.

Kepler Johannes 1571–1630. German mathematician and astronomer. He formulated what are now called **Kepler's laws** of planetary motion: (1) the orbit of each planet is an ellipse with the Sun at one of the foci; (2) the radius vector of each planet sweeps out equal areas in equal times; (3) the squares of the periods of the planets are proportional to the cubes of their mean distances from the Sun.

Kenya
Republic of (*Jamhuri ya Kenya*)

area 224,884 sq mi/582,600 sq km
capital Nairobi
cities Kisumu, port Mombasa
physical mountains and highlands in W and center; coastal plain in S; arid interior and tropical coast
environment the elephant faces extinction as a result of poaching
features Great Rift Valley, Mount Kenya, Lake Nakuru (salt lake with world's largest colony of flamingos), Lake Turkana (Rudolf), national parks with wildlife, Malindini Marine Reserve, Olduvai Gorge
head of state and government Daniel arap Moi from 1978
political system authoritarian nationalism
political parties Kenya African National Union (KANU), nationalist, centrist; National Democratic Party (NDP), centrist (launched 1991, not accepted by government)
exports coffee, tea, pineapples, petroleum products
currency Kenya shilling
population (1990 est) 25,393,000 (Kikuyu 21%, Luo 13%, Luhya 14%, Kelenjin 11%; Asian, Arab, European); growth rate 4.2% p.a.
life expectancy men 59, women 63 (1989)
languages Kiswahili (official), English; there are many local dialects
religions Protestant 38%, Roman Catholic 28%, indigenous beliefs 26%, Muslim 6%
literacy 50% (1988)
GDP $6.9 bn (1987); $302 per head (1988)
chronology
1895 British East African protectorate established.
1920 Kenya became a British colony.
1944 African participation in politics began.
1950 Mau Mau campaign began.
1953 Nationalist leader Jomo Kenyatta imprisoned by British authorities.
1956 Mau Mau campaign defeated, Kenyatta released.
1963 Achieved internal self-government, with Kenyatta as prime minister.
1964 Independence achieved from Britain as a republic within the Commonwealth, with Kenyatta as president.
1967 East African Community (EAC) formed with Tanzania and Uganda.
1977 Collapse of EAC.
1978 Death of Kenyatta. Succeeded by Daniel arap Moi.
1982 Attempted coup against Moi foiled.
1983 Moi reelected unopposed.
1984 Over 2,000 people massacred by government forces at Wajir.
1985–86 Thousands of forest villagers evicted and their homes destroyed to make way for cash crops.
1988 Moi reelected. 150,000 evicted from state-owned forests.
1989 Moi announced release of all known political prisoners. Confiscated ivory burned in attempt to stop elephant poaching.
1990 Despite antigovernment riots, Moi refused multiparty politics.
1991 Increasing demands for political reform; Moi promised multiparty politics.
1992 Constitutional amendment passed.

Born in Württemberg, Kepler became assistant to Tycho ◊Brahe 1600, and succeeded him 1601 as imperial mathematician to the emperor Rudolph II. Kepler observed in 1604 a supernova, the first visible since the one discovered by Brahe 1572. His analysis of Brahe's observations of the planets, observations published by Kepler in his *Rudolphine Tables* 1627, led to the discovery of his three laws, the first two of which he published in *Astronomia Nova* 1609 and the third in *Harmonices Mundi* 1619. Kepler lived in turbulent times and was faced with many taxing domestic problems, not least of which was the unsuccessful prosecution in Wittenberg 1618 of his mother for witchcraft.

Kerala state of SW India, formed 1956 from the former princely states of Travancore and Cochin
area 15,015 sq mi/38,900 sq km
capital Trivandrum
features most densely populated, and most literate (60%), state of India; strong religious and caste divisions make it politically unstable
products tea, coffee, rice, oilseed, rubber, textiles, chemicals, electrical goods
population (1991) 29,011,200
language Kannada, Malayalam, Tamil.

keratin fibrous protein found in the ◊skin of vertebrates and also in hair, nails, claws, hooves, feathers, and the outer coating of horns in animals such as cows and sheep.

If pressure is put on some parts of the skin, more keratin is produced, forming thick calluses that protect the layers of skin beneath.

Kerbela or *Karbala* holy city of the Shiite Muslims, 60 mi/96 km SW of Baghdad, Iraq; population (1985) 184,600. Kerbela is built on the site of the battlefield where Husein, son of ◊Ali and Fatima, was killed in 680 while defending his succession to the khalifate; his tomb in the city is visited every year by many pilgrims.

Kerekou Mathieu (Ahmed) 1933– . Benin socialist politician and soldier, president 1980–91. In 1972, when deputy head of the Dahomey army, he led a coup to oust the ruling president

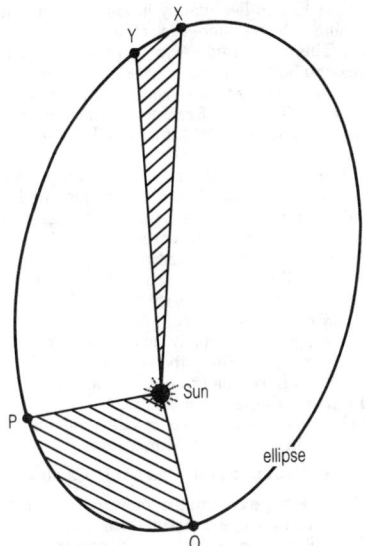

Kepler *Kepler's second law states that the area between X and Y equals the area between P and O if the planet moves from P to O in the same time that it moves from X to Y.*

and establish his own military government. He embarked on a program of "scientific socialism," changing his country's name to Benin to mark this change of direction. In 1987 he resigned from the army and confirmed a civilian administration. He was reelected president 1989, but lost to Nice1phore Soglo in the 1991 presidential elections.

Kerensky Alexandr Feodorovich 1881–1970. Russian revolutionary politician, prime minister of the second provisional government before its collapse Nov 1917, during the ◊Russian Revolution. He was overthrown by the Bolshevik revolution, since he insisted on staying in World War I and mismanaged internal economic affairs. He fled to France 1918 and to the US 1940.

Kerguelen Islands or *Desolation Islands* volcanic archipelago in the Indian Ocean, part of the French Southern and Antarctic Territories; area 2,787 sq mi/7,215 sq km. It was discovered in 1772 by the Breton navigator Yves de Kerguelen and annexed by France in 1949. Uninhabited except for scientists (center for joint study of geomagnetism with Russia), the islands support a unique wild cabbage containing a pungent oil.

Kern Jerome (David) 1885–1945. US composer. Many of Kern's songs have become classics, notably "Smoke Gets in Your Eyes" from his musical *Roberta* 1933. He wrote the operetta *Show Boat* 1927, which includes the song "Ol' Man River."

Based on Edna Ferber's novel, *Show Boat* was the first example of serious musical theater in the US. Kern wrote dozens of hit songs and musicals from 1904 and Hollywood movies from the beginning of the sound era 1927. He worked mainly with lyricist Otto Harbach but also with Ira Gershwin, Oscar Hammerstein II, Dorothy Fields, and Johnny Mercer.

kernel the inner, softer part of a ◊nut, or of a seed within a hard shell.

kerosene thin oil obtained from the distillation of petroleum; a highly refined form is used in jet aircraft fuel. Kerosene is a mixture of hydrocarbons of the ◊paraffin series.

Kerouac Jack 1923–1969. US novelist who named and epitomized the ◊Beat Generation of the 1950s. His books, all autobiographical, include *On the Road* 1957, *Big Sur* 1963, and *Desolation Angel* 1965.

On the Road, written in three weeks in a formless, unpolished style, awoke the nation to the attitudes of a group of young people in pursuit of love, beauty, and new experiences, who were contemptuous of staid American values.

Kerr Deborah 1921– . British actress who often played genteel, ladylike roles. Her performance in British films such as *Major Barbara* 1940 and *Black Narcissus* 1946 led to starring parts in Hollywood such as *Quo Vadis* 1951, *From Here to Eternity* 1953, and *The King and I* 1956. She retired in 1969, but made a comeback with *The Assam Garden* 1985.

Kerry county of Munster province, Republic of Ireland, E of Cork
area 1,814 sq mi/4,700 sq km
county town Tralee
physical western coastline deeply indented; northern part low-lying, but in the south are the highest mountains in Ireland, including Carrantuohill 3,417 ft/1,041 m, the highest peak in Ireland; many rivers and lakes
features Macgillycuddy's Reeks, Lakes of Killarney

products engineering, woolens, shoes, cutlery; tourism is important
population (1991) 121,700.

Kertész André 1894–1986. Hungarian-born US photographer whose spontaneity had a great impact on photojournalism. A master of the 35-mm-format camera, he recorded his immediate environment (Paris, New York) with wit and style.

He lived in Paris 1925–36, where he befriended and photographed many avant-garde artists and writers, and in New York City 1936–86, where he did commercial photography for major American magazines as well as creative photography.

Kesselring Albert 1885–1960. German field marshal in World War II, commander of the Luftwaffe (air force) 1939–40, during the invasions of Poland and the Low Countries and the early stages of the Battle of Britain. He later served under Field Marshal Rommel in N Africa, took command in Italy 1943, and was commander in chief on the western front March 1945. His death sentence for war crimes at the Nuremberg trials 1947 was commuted to life imprisonment, but he was released 1952.

kestrel either of two small species of ◊falcon (genus *Falco*): the Eurasian kestrel *F. tinnunculus*, about 13.5 in/35 cm long, which occasionally visits E North America and the Aleutians; and the American kestrel or sparrowhawk *F. sparverius*, somewhat smaller, of most of North America. Both species are russet, gray, and tan in color, with the male American kestrel having more gray on its wings. They hunt mainly by hovering in mid-air while watching for grasshoppers and small mammals.

ketone member of the group of organic compounds containing the carbonyl group (C=O) bonded to two atoms of carbon (instead of one carbon and one hydrogen as in ◊aldehydes). Ketones are liquids or low-melting-point solids, slightly soluble in water.

An example is propanone (acetone, CH_3COCH_3), used as a solvent.

kettle glacial geologically feature, formed when a block of stagnant ice from a receding glacier becomes isolated and buried in glacial outwash or drift before it finally melts. When the block disappears, it leaves a pit or depression called a kettle, in the drift. These depressions range from 15 ft/5 m to 8 mi/13 km in diameter, and some exceed 100 ft/33 m in depth.

As time passes, water sometimes fills the kettles to form lakes or swamps, features found throughout much of N North America. Lake Ronkonkoma, the largest lake on Long Island, New York, is an example.

Kew Gardens popular name for the Royal Botanic Gardens, Kew, Surrey, England. They were founded 1759 by the mother of King George III as a small garden and passed to the nation by Queen Victoria 1840. By then they had expanded to almost their present size of 368 acres/149 hectares and since 1841 have been open daily to the public. They contain a collection of over 25,000 living plant species and many fine buildings. The gardens are also a center for botanical research.

key in music, the ◊diatonic scale around which a piece of music is written; for example, a passage in the key of C major will mainly use the notes of the C major scale. The term is also used for the lever activated by a keyboard player, such as a piano key.

Key Francis Scott 1779–1843. US lawyer and poet who wrote the song "The Star-Spangled Banner" while Fort McHenry, Baltimore, was besieged by British troops in 1814; since 1931 it has been the national anthem of the US.

Key served as US attorney for the District of Columbia 1833–41.

keyboard in computing, an input device resembling a typewriter keyboard, used to enter instructions and data. There are many variations on the layout and labeling of keys. Extra numeric keys may be added, as may special-purpose function keys, whose effects can be defined by programs in the computer.

Keynes John Maynard, 1st Baron Keynes 1883–1946. English economist, whose *The General Theory of Employment, Interest, and Money* 1936 proposed the prevention of financial crises and unemployment by adjusting demand through government control of credit and currency. He is responsible for that part of economics now known as ⬦*macroeconomics*.

Keynes led the British delegation at the Bretton Woods Conference 1944, which set up the International Monetary Fund. His theories were widely accepted in the aftermath of World War II, and he was one of the most influential economists of the 20th century. His ideas are today often contrasted with those of ⬦monetarism.

Keynesian economics the economic theory of J M Keynes, which argues that a fall in national income, lack of demand for goods, and rising unemployment should be countered by increased government expenditure to stimulate the economy. It is opposed by monetarists (see ⬦monetarism).

Key West town at the tip of the Florida peninsula; population (1980) 24,400. As a tourist resort, it was popularized by the novelist Ernest Hemingway.

In 1967 it became the first US town to take all its fresh water from the sea. It was incorporated 1828 and is the southernmost city in the continental US.

kg symbol for ⬦*kilogram*.

KGB secret police of the USSR, the *Komitet Gosudarstvennoy Bezopasnosti*/Committee of State Security, which was in control of frontier and general security and the forced-labor system. KGB officers held key appointments in all fields of daily life, reporting to administration offices in every major town. The KGB was superseded by the Russian Federal Security Agency on the demise of the Soviet Union 1991.

The KGB had at least 220,000 border guards, with reinforcements of 80,000 volunteer militia members. Many KGB officers were also said to hold diplomatic posts in embassies abroad. Headed by General Vladimir Kryuchkov 1988–91, the KGB coordinated the military crackdown on Azerbaijan in 1990 and on the Baltic states in 1991.

After the attempted anti-Gorbachev coup of 1991, reforms intended to curb the political activities of the KGB were introduced: its leadership was removed and KGB troops were placed under the control of the Defense Ministry; the presidential guard was removed from KGB authority; and government communications were transferred to the aegis of a state committee.

Earlier names for the secret police were *Okhrana* under the tsars; ⬦*Cheka* 1918–23; *GPU* or OGPU (*Obedinyonnoye Gosudarstvnoye Polititcheskoye Upravleniye*/Unified State Political Administration) 1923–34; *NKVD* (*Narodny Komisariat Vnutrennykh Del*/People's Commissariat of Internal Affairs) 1934–46; and *MVD* (Ministry of Internal Affairs) 1946–53. ⬦Smersh was a subsection.

Khabarovsk territory of SE Siberian Russia, bordering the Sea of Okhotsk and drained by the Amur; area 318,501 sq mi/824,600 sq km; population (1985) 1,728,000. The capital is Khabarovsk. Mineral resources include gold, coal, and iron ore.

Khachaturian Aram Il'yich 1903–1978. Armenian composer. His use of folk themes is shown in the ballets *Gayaneh* 1942, which includes the "Saber Dance," and *Spartacus* 1956.

Khaddhafi or *Gaddafi* or *Qaddafi*, Moamer al 1942– . Libyan revolutionary leader. Overthrowing King Idris 1969, he became virtual president of a republic, although he nominally gave up all except an ideological role 1974. He favors territorial expansion in N Africa reaching as far as Zaire, has supported rebels in Chad, and has proposed mergers with a number of countries. His theories, based on those of the Chinese communist leader Mao Zedong, are contained in a *Green Book*.

Khajurāho town in Madhya Pradesh, central India, the former capital of the Candella monarchs. It has 35 sandstone temples—Jain, Buddhist, and Hindu—built in the 10th and 11th centuries. The temples are covered inside and out with erotic sculpture symbolizing mystic union with the deity.

khaki the dust-colored uniform of British and Indian troops in India from about 1850, adopted as camouflage during the South African War 1899–1902, and later standard for military uniforms worldwide.

Khalifa Sudanese leader ⬦Abd Allah.

Khalistan projected independent Sikh state. See ⬦Sikhism.

Khalsa the brotherhood of the Sikhs, created by Guru Gobind Singh at the festival of Baisakhi in 1699. The Khalsa was originally founded as a militant group to defend the Sikh community from persecution.

Khama Seretse 1921–1980. Botswanan politician, prime minister of Bechuanaland 1965, and first president of Botswana from 1966 until his death.

khamsin hot southeasterly wind that blows from the Sahara desert over Egypt and parts of the Middle East from late March to May or June. It is called *sharav* in Israel.

Khan Liaquat Ali 1895–1951. Indian politician, deputy leader of the Muslim League 1941–47, first prime minister of Pakistan from 1947. He was assassinated by objectors to his peace policy with India.

Kharga or *Kharijah* oasis in the Western Desert of Egypt, known to the Romans, and from 1960 headquarters of the New Valley irrigation project. An area twice the size of Italy is watered from natural underground reservoirs.

Kharg Island small island in the Persian Gulf used by Iran as a deep-water oil terminal. Between 1982 and 1988 Kharg Island came under frequent attack during the Iran-Iraq War.

Kharkov capital of the Kharkov region, E Ukraine, 250 mi/400 km E of Kiev; population (1987) 1,587,000. It is a railroad junction and industrial city (engineering, tractors), close to the Donets Basin coalfield and Krivoy Rog iron mines. Kharkov was founded 1654 as a fortress town.

Khartoum capital and trading center of Sudan, at the junction of the Blue and White Nile; population (1983) 476,000, and of Khartoum North, across the Blue Nile, 341,000. ⬦Omdurman is also a suburb of Khartoum, giving the urban area a population of over 1.3 million.

It was founded 1830 by ⬦Mehemet Ali. General ⬦Gordon was killed at Khartoum by the Mahdist rebels 1885. A new city was built after the site was recaptured by British troops under Kitchener 1898.

Khazar member of a people of Turkish origin from the lower Volga basin of Central Asia, who formed a commercial link and a buffer state in the 7th–12th centuries between the Arabs and the Byzantine empire, and later between the Byzantine empire and the Baltic. Their ruler adopted Judaism as the state religion in the 8th century. In the 11th century, Slavonic and nomadic Turks invaded, and by the 13th century the Khazar empire had been absorbed by its neighbors. It has been suggested that the Khazars were the ancestors of some of the Jews living in E European countries and now throughout the world.

khedive title granted by the Turkish sultan to his Egyptian viceroy 1867, retained by succeeding rulers until 1914.

Khe Sanh in the Vietnam War, US Marine outpost near the Laotian border and just south of the demilitarized zone between North and South Vietnam. Garrisoned by 4,000 Marines, it was attacked unsuccessfully by 20,000 North Vietnamese troops Jan 21–April 7, 1968.

Khmer or *Kmer* member of the largest ethnic group in Cambodia, numbering about 7 million. Khmer minorities also live in E Thailand and S Vietnam. The Khmer language belongs to the Mon-Khmer family of Austro-Asiatic languages.

The Kmers live mainly in agricultural and fishing villages under a chief. They practice Theravāda Buddhism and trace descent through both male and female lines. Traditionally, Khmer society was divided into six groups: the royal family, the Brahmans (who officiated at royal festivals), Buddhist monks, officials, commoners, and slaves.

The Khmer empire, an early SE Asian civilization, was founded AD 616 and came under Indian cultural influence as part of the SE Asian kingdom of Funan. The earliest inscriptions in the Khmer language date from the 7th century AD. The Khmer empire reached its zenith in the 9th–13th centuries, with the building of the capital city and temple complex at Angkor. The Khmers were eventually pushed back by the Thais into the territory they occupy today. The anti-French nationalists of Cambodia adopted the name Khmer Republic 1971–75, and the name continues in use by the communist movement called the ⬦Khmer Rouge.

Khmer Republic former name of ⬦Cambodia.

Khmer Rouge communist movement in Cambodia (Kampuchea) formed in the 1960s. Controlling the country 1974–78, it was responsible for mass deportations and executions under the leadership of Pol Pot. Since then it has conducted guerrilla warfare, and in 1991 gained representation in the governing body.

The leader of the Khmer Rouge from 1985 is Khieu Samphan.

The Khmer Rouge formed the largest opposition group to the US-backed regime led by Lon Nol 1970–75. By 1974 they controlled the countryside, and in 1975 captured the capital, Phnom Penh. Initially former prime minister Prince Sihanouk was installed as head of state, but internal disagreements led to the creation of the Pol Pot government 1976. From 1978, when Vietnam invaded the country, the Khmer Rouge conducted a guerrilla campaign against the Vietnamese forces. Pol Pot retired as military leader 1985 and was succeeded by the more moderate Khieu Samphan. After the withdrawal of Vietnamese forces in 1989, the Khmer Rouge continued its warfare against the Vietnamese-backed government, making substantial advances during 1990. A UN-brokered peace treaty Oct 1991 between Cambodia's four warring factions gave the Khmer Rouge its share of representation in the ruling Supreme National Council. The treaty failed to disarm completely the movement's guerrilla army or to win a renunciation of the guerrillas' goal of regaining domination of Cambodia.

Khoikhoi (formerly *Hottentot*) member of a people living in Namibia and the Cape Province of South Africa, and numbering about 30,000. Their language is related to San (spoken by the Kung) and belongs to the Khoisan family. Like the Kung, the Khoikhoi once inhabited a wider area, but were driven into the Kalahari Desert by invading Bantu peoples and Dutch colonists in the 18th century. They live as nomadic hunter-gatherers, in family groups, and have animist beliefs.

Khoisan the smallest group of languages in Africa. It includes fewer than 50 languages, spoken mainly by the people of the Kalahari Desert (including the Khoikhoi and Kung). Two languages from this group are spoken in Tanzania. The Khoisan languages are known for their click consonants (clicking sounds made with the tongue, which function as consonants).

Khomeini Ayatollah Ruhollah 1900–1989. Iranian Shiite Muslim leader, born in Khomein, central Iran. Exiled for opposition to the Shah from 1964, he returned when the Shah left the country 1979, and established a fundamentalist Islamic republic. His rule was marked by a protracted war with Iraq, and suppression of opposition within Iran, executing thousands of opponents.

Khomeini was hostile toward both superpowers, held US embassy hostages 1979–81, and supported terrorist groups.

Khorana Har Gobind 1922–   . Indian-born US biochemist who in 1976 led the team that first synthesized a biologically active gene. In 1968 he shared the Nobel Prize for Medicine for research on the interpretation of the genetic code and its function in protein synthesis.

Khorramshahr former port and oil-refining center in Iran, on the Shatt-al-Arab River and linked by bridge to the island of Abadan. It was completely destroyed in the 1980s by enemy action in the Iran–Iraq war.

Khrushchev Nikita Sergeyevich 1894–1971. Soviet politician, secretary-general of the Communist Party 1953–64, premier 1958–64. He emerged as leader from the power struggle following Stalin's death and was the first official to denounce Stalin, in 1956. His de-Stalinization program gave rise to revolts in Poland and

Hungary 1956. Because of problems with the economy and foreign affairs (a breach with China 1960; conflict with the US in the ⟡Cuban missile crisis 1962), he was ousted by Leonid Brezhnev and Alexei Kosygin.

Born near Kursk, the son of a miner, Khrushchev fought in the post-Revolutionary civil war 1917–20, and in World War II organized the guerrilla defense of his native Ukraine. He denounced Stalinism in a secret session of the party Feb 1956. Many victims of the purges of the 1930s were either released or posthumously rehabilitated, but when Hungary revolted in Oct against Soviet domination, there was immediate Soviet intervention. In 1958 Khrushchev succeeded Bulganin as chair of the council of ministers (prime minister). His policy of competition with capitalism was successful in the space program, which launched the world's first satellite (⟡*Sputnik*). Because of the Cuban crisis and the personal feud with Mao Zedong that led to the Sino-Soviet split, he was compelled to resign 1964, although by 1965 his reputation was to some extent officially restored. In April 1989 his Feb 1956 "secret speech" against Stalin was officially published for the first time.

Khufu *c.* 2600 BC. Egyptian king of Memphis, who built the largest of the pyramids, known to the Greeks as the pyramid of Cheops (the Greek form of Khufu).

Khuzestan province of SW Iran, which includes the chief Iranian oil resources; population (1986) 2,702,533. Towns include Ahvaz (capital) and the ports of Abadan and Khuninshahr. There have been calls for Sunni Muslim autonomy, under the name Arabistan.

Khwārizmī, al- Mohammed ibn-Mūsā *c.* 780–*c.* 850. Persian mathematician from Khwarizm (now Khiva, Uzbekistan), who lived and worked in Baghdad. He wrote a book on algebra, from part of whose title (*al-jabr*) comes the word "algebra," and a book in which he introduced to the West the Hindu-Arabic decimal number system.

The word "algorithm" is a corruption of his name.

He also compiled astronomical tables and was responsible for introducing the concept of zero into Arab mathematics.

Khyber Pass pass 33 mi/53 km long through the mountain range that separates Pakistan from Afghanistan. The Khyber Pass was used by invaders of India. The present road was constructed by the British during the Afghan Wars.

Kiangsi alternate spelling of ⟡Jiangxi, province of China.

Kiangsu alternate spelling of ⟡Jiangsu, province of China.

kibbutz Israeli communal collective settlement with collective ownership of all property and earnings, collective organization of work and decision-making, and communal housing for children. A modified version, the *Moshav Shitufi*, is similar to the ⟡collective farms that were typical of the former USSR. Other Israeli cooperative rural settlements include the *Moshav Ovdim*, which has equal opportunity, and the similar but less strict *Moshav* settlement.

Kidd "Captain" (William) *c.* 1645–1701. Scottish pirate. He spent his youth privateering for the British against the French off the North American coast, and in 1695 was given

a royal commission to suppress piracy in the Indian Ocean. Instead, he joined a group of pirates in Madagascar. On his way to Boston, Massachusetts, he was arrested 1699, taken to England, and hanged.

His execution marked the end of some 200 years of semiofficial condoning of piracy by the British government.

kidnapping the abduction of a person against his or her will. It often involves holding persons for ransom. It may also take place in child-custody disputes or involve psychosexual motives.

kidney in vertebrates, one of a pair of organs responsible for water regulation, excretion of waste products, and maintaining the ionic composition of the blood. The kidneys are situated on the rear wall of the abdomen. Each one consists of a number of long tubules; the outer parts filter the aqueous components of blood, and the inner parts selectively reabsorb vital salts, leaving waste products in the remaining fluid (urine), which is passed through the ureter to the bladder.

The action of the kidneys is vital, although if one is removed, the other enlarges to take over its function. A patient with two defective kidneys may continue near-normal life with the aid of a kidney machine or continuous ambulatory peritoneal ⟡dialysis (CAPD).

Kiefer Anselm 1945–   . German painter. He studied under German sculptor Joseph Beuys (1921-1986), and his works include monumental landscapes on varied surfaces, often with the paint built up into relief with other substances. Much of his highly Expressionist work deals with recent German history.

Kiel Canal formerly *Kaiser Wilhelm Canal* waterway 61 mi/98.7 km long that connects the Baltic with the North Sea. Built by Germany in the years before World War I, the canal allowed the German navy to move from Baltic bases to the open sea without traveling through international waters.

Kierkegaard Søren (Aabye) 1813–1855. Danish philosopher considered to be the founder of ⟡existentialism. Disagreeing with the German dialectical philosopher ⟡Hegel, he argued that no system of thought could explain the unique experience of the individual. He defended Christianity, suggesting that God cannot be known through reason, but only through a "leap of faith." He believed that God and exceptional individuals were above moral laws.

Kierkegaard was born in Copenhagen, where he spent most of his life. The son of a Jewish merchant, he converted to Christianity in 1838, although he became hostile to the established church and his beliefs caused much controversy. He was a prolific author, but his chief works are *Enten-Eller/Either-Or* 1843, *Begrebet Angest/Concept of Dread* 1844, and *Efterskrift/Postscript* 1846, which summed up much of his earlier writings.

Kiev capital of Ukraine, industrial center (chemicals, clothing, leatherwork), on the confluence of the Desna and Dnieper rivers; population (1987) 2,554,000. Kiev was the capital of Russia in the Middle Ages.

history Kiev was founded in the 5th century by ⟡Vikings. The Slav domination of Russia began with the rise of Kiev, the "mother of Russian cities"; Kiev replaced ⟡Novgorod as the capital of Russia 882 and was the original center of the Orthodox Christian faith 988. The city was occupied by Germany 1941, and was the third largest city of the USSR.

features St Sophia cathedral (11th century) and Kiev-Pechersky Monastery (both now museums) survive, as do the remains of the Golden Gate, an arched entrance to the old walled city, built 1037. The gate is surmounted by the small Church of the Annunciation. The Kiev ballet and opera are renowned.

Kigali capital of Rwanda, central Africa; population (1981) 157,000. Products include coffee and minerals.

Kikuyu member of Kenya's dominant ethnic group, numbering about three million. The Kikuyu are primarily cultivators, although many are highly educated and have entered the professions. Their language belongs to the Bantu branch of the Niger-Congo family.

Kildare county of Leinster province, Republic of Ireland, S of Meath
area 652 sq mi/1,690 sq km
county town Naas
physical wet and boggy in the north
features part of the Bog of Allen; the village of Maynooth, with a training college for Roman Catholic priests; the Curragh, a plain that is the site of the national stud and headquarters of Irish horse racing
products oats, barley, potatoes, cattle
population (1991) 122,516.

Kilimanjaro volcano in ⬦Tanzania, the highest mountain in Africa, 19,364 ft/5,900 m.

Kilkenny county of Leinster province, Republic of Ireland, E of Tipperary
area 795 sq mi/2,060 sq km
county town Kilkenny
features river Nore
products agricultural, coal
population (1991) 73,600.

Killarney market town in County Kerry, Republic of Ireland; population (1991) 7,300. A famous beauty spot in Ireland, it has Macgillycuddy's Reeks (a range of mountains) and the Lakes of Killarney to the southwest.

Killeen city in central Texas, S of Fort Worth and N of Austin; population (1990) 63,500. Although some concrete is produced here, the economy relies heavily on the nearby army base, Fort Hood.

killer whale or *orca* toothed whale *Orcinus orca* of the dolphin family, found in all seas of the world. It is black on top, white below, and grows up to 30 ft/9 m long. It is the only whale that has been observed to prey on other whales, as well as on seals and seabirds.

It has been tamed and trained to perform in sea circuses and has proved to be gentle, friendly, intelligent, and hard working, thus prompting use of its alternate name orca in the US.

Killy Jean-Claude 1943– . French skier. He won all three gold medals (slalom, giant slalom, and downhill) at the 1968 Winter Olympics in Grenoble. The first World Cup winner 1967, he retained the title 1968 and also won three world titles.

He was a major force behind France's hosting of the 1992 Winter Olympics.

Kilmer Joyce 1886–1918. US poet. His first collection of poems, *Summer of Love*, was published 1911. Kilmer later gained an international reputation with the title work of *Trees and Other Poems* 1914. At the outbreak of World War I, he joined the 165th Regiment and was killed in action in France.

Born in New Brunswick, New Jersey, Kilmer was educated at Rutgers and Columbia universities. Working briefly as a high school teacher,

he moved to New York and worked in a variety of publishing jobs while pursuing his own literary career.

kiln high-temperature furnace used commercially for drying timber, roasting metal ores, or for making cement, bricks, and pottery. Oil- or gas-fired kilns are used to bake ceramics at up to 3,200°F/1,760°C; electric kilns do not generally reach such high temperatures.

kilobyte (K or KB) in computing, a unit of memory equal to 1,024 ⬦bytes. It is sometimes used, less precisely, to mean 1,000 bytes.

In the metric system, the prefix "kilo-" denotes multiplication by 1,000 (as in kilometer, a unit equal to 1,000 meters). However, computer memory size is based on the ⬦binary number system, and the most convenient binary equivalent of 1,000 is 2^{10}, or 1,024.

kilogram SI unit (symbol kg) of mass equal to 1,000 grams (2.2 lb). It is defined by scientists as a mass equal to that of the international prototype, a platinum-iridium cylinder held at the International Bureau of Weights and Measures at Sèvres, France.

kilometer unit (symbol km) of length equal to 1,000 meters (3,280.89 ft).

kilowatt unit (symbol kW) of power equal to 1,000 watts or about 1.34 horsepower.

kilowatt-hour commercial unit of electrical energy (symbol kWh), defined as the work done by a power of 1,000 watts in one hour. It is used to calculate the cost of electrical energy taken from utility-company supplies.

Kimberley diamond-mining town in Cape Province, South Africa, 95 mi/153 km NW of Bloemfontein; population (1980) 144,923. Its mines have been controlled by de Beers Consolidated Mines since 1887.

kimberlite an igneous rock that is ultrabasic (containing very little silica); a type of alkaline peridotite (see ⬦peridot) containing mica in addition to olivine and other minerals. Kimberlite represents the world's principal source of diamonds.

Kimberlite is found in carrot-shaped pipelike ⬦intrusions called *diatremes*, where mobile material from very deep in the Earth's crust has forced itself upward, expanding in its ascent. The material, brought upward from near the boundary between crust and mantle, often altered and fragmented, includes diamonds. Diatremes are found principally near Kimberley, South Africa, from which the name of the rock is derived, and in the Yakut area of Siberia, Russia.

Kim Il Sung 1912– . North Korean Communist politician and marshal. He became prime minister 1948 and president 1972, retaining the presidency of the Communist Workers' party. He likes to be known as the "Great Leader" and has campaigned constantly for the reunification of Korea. His son *Kim Jong Il* (1942–), known as the "Dear Leader," has been named as his successor.

kimono traditional Japanese costume. Already worn in the Heian period (more than 1,000 years ago), it is still used by women for formal wear and informally by men.

For the finest kimonos a rectangular piece of silk (about 36 ft/11 m x 1.5 ft/0.5 m) is cut into seven pieces for tailoring. The design (which must match perfectly over the seams and for which flowers are the usual motif) is then painted by hand, using various processes, and may be enhanced by embroidery or gilding. The accompanying *obi*, or sash, about 13 ft/4 m

× 4 in/10 cm for men and wider for women, is also embroidered.

Kim Young Sam 1927– . South Korean democratic politician. A member of the National Assembly from 1954 and president of the New Democratic Party (NDP) from 1974, he lost his seat and was later placed under house arrest because of his opposition to President Park Chung Hee. In 1983 he led a prodemocracy hunger strike but in 1987 failed to defeat Roh Tae-Woo in the presidential election. In 1990 he merged the NDP with the ruling party to form the new Democratic Liberal Party (DLP).

kinetic energy the energy of a body resulting from motion. It is contrasted with ⬦potential energy.

kinetics the branch of chemistry that investigates the rates of chemical reactions.

kinetics alternate name for ⬦dynamics. It is distinguished from *kinematics*, which deals with motion without reference to force or mass.

kinetic theory theory describing the physical properties of matter in terms of the behavior—principally movement—of its component atoms or molecules. The temperature of a substance is dependent on the velocity of movement of its constituent particles, increased temperature being accompanied by increased movement. A gas consists of rapidly moving atoms or molecules and, according to kinetic theory, it is their continual impact on the walls of the containing vessel that accounts for the pressure of the gas. The slowing of molecular motion as temperature falls, according to kinetic theory, accounts for the physical properties of liquids and solids, culminating in the concept of no molecular motion at ⬦absolute zero (0K/–273°C). By making various assumptions about the nature of gas molecules, it is possible to derive from the kinetic theory the various gas laws (such as ⬦Avogadro's hypothesis, ⬦Boyle's law, and ⬦Charles's law).

King B B (Riley) 1925– . US blues guitarist, singer, and songwriter, one of the most influential electric-guitar players, who became an international star in the 1960s. His albums include *Blues Is King* 1967, *Lucille Talks Back* 1975, and *Blues 'n' Jazz* 1983.

King Billie Jean (born Moffitt) 1943– . US tennis player. She won a record 20 Wimbledon titles 1961–79 and 39 Grand Slam titles. She won the Wimbledon singles title six times, the US Open singles title four times, the French Open once, and the Australian Open once.

Her first Wimbledon title was the doubles with Karen Hantze 1961, and her last, also doubles, with Martina Navratilova 1979. Her 39 Grand Slam events at singles and doubles are third only to Navratilova and Margaret Court.

CAREER HIGHLIGHTS

Wimbledon
singles: 1966–68, 1972–73, 1975
doubles: 1961–62, 1965, 1967–68, 1970–73, 1979
mixed: 1967, 1971, 1973–74
US Open
singles: 1967, 1971–72, 1974
doubles: 1964, 1967, 1974, 1978, 1980
mixed: 1967, 1971, 1973, 1976
French Open
singles: 1972
doubles: 1972
mixed: 1967, 1970

Australian Open
singles: 1968
mixed: 1968

King Martin Luther Jr 1929–1968. US civil-rights campaigner, black leader, and Baptist minister. He first came to national attention as leader of the ◊Montgomery, Alabama, bus boycott 1955, and was one of the organizers of the massive (200,000 people) march on Washington, DC 1963 to demand racial equality. An advocate of nonviolence, he was awarded the Nobel Peace Prize 1964. He was assassinated in Memphis, Tennessee, by James Earl Ray (1928–).

Born in Atlanta, Georgia, son of a Baptist minister, King founded the ◊Southern Christian Leadership Conference 1957. A brilliant and moving speaker, he was the symbol of, and leading figure in, the campaign for integration and equal rights in the late 1950s and early 1960s. In the mid-1960s his moderate approach was criticized by black militants. He was the target of intensive investigation by the federal authorities, chiefly the FBI under J Edgar ◊Hoover. His personal life was scrutinized and criticized by those opposed to his policies. King's birthday (Jan 15) is observed on the third Monday in Jan as a public holiday in the US.

King Stephen 1946– . US writer of best-selling horror novels with small-town or rural settings. Many of his works have been filmed, including *Carrie* 1974, *The Shining* 1978, and *Christine* 1983.

His recent novels include *It* and *The Tommyknockers* (both 1987), *The Dark Half* 1989 and *Dolores Claiborne* 1992. He has also published three volumes of short stories, several screenplays, and a number of novels under the pseudonym Richard Bachman.

King William Lyon Mackenzie 1874–1950. Canadian Liberal prime minister 1921–26, 1926–30, and 1935–48. He maintained the unity of the English- and French-speaking populations, and was instrumental in establishing equal status for Canada with Britain.

king crab or *Alaskan king crab* large, edible crab *Paralithodescamtschatica*, of the N Pacific. The term "king crab" is sometimes used as another name for the ◊horseshoe crab.

kingdom the primary division in biological ◊classification. At one time, only two kingdoms were recognized: animals and plants. Today most biologists prefer a five-kingdom system, even though it still involves grouping together organisms that are probably unrelated. One widely accepted scheme is as follows: *Kingdom Animalia* (all multicellular animals); *Kingdom Plantae* (all plants, including seaweeds and other algae); *Kingdom Fungi* (all fungi, including the unicellular yeasts, but not slime molds); *Kingdom Protista* or *Protoctista* (protozoa, diatoms, dinoflagellates, slime molds, and various other lower organisms with eukaryotic cells); and *Kingdom Monera* (all prokaryotes—the bacteria and cyanobacteria, or ◊blue-green algae). The first four of these kingdoms make up the eukaryotes.

When only two kingdoms were recognized, any organism with a rigid cell wall was a plant, and so bacteria and fungi were considered plants, despite their many differences. Other organisms, such as the photosynthetic flagellates (euglenoids), were claimed by both kingdoms. The unsatisfactory nature of

the two-kingdom system became evident during the 19th century, and the biologist Ernst Haeckel was among the first to try to reform it. High-power microscopes have revealed more about the structure of cells; it has become clear that there is a fundamental difference between cells without a nucleus (◊prokaryotes) and those with a nucleus (◊eukaryotes). However, these differences are larger than those between animals and higher plants, and are unsuitable for use as kingdoms. At present there is no agreement on how many kingdoms there are in the natural world. Although the five-kingdom system is widely favored, some schemes have as many as 20.

kingfisher heavy-billed bird of the worldwide family Alcedinidae, found near streams, ponds, and coastal areas. Kingfishers plunge-dive for fish and aquatic insects. The nest is usually a burrow in a riverbank.

There are about 90 species, the largest being the Australian ◊kookaburra.

The North American belted kingfisher *Ceryle alcyon* is about 13 in/33 cm long, slate gray and white (the female has a rust-colored band on the belly), and crested in both sexes.

King Lear tragedy by William Shakespeare, first performed 1605–06. Lear, king of Britain, favors his grasping daughters, Goneril and Regan, with shares of his kingdom but refuses his third, honest daughter, Cordelia, a share. Rejected by Goneril and Regan, the old and unbalanced Lear is reunited with Cordelia but dies of grief when she is murdered.

King's Council in medieval England, a court that carried out much of the monarch's daily administration. It was first established in the reign of Edward I, and became the Privy Council 1534–36.

Kingsley Ben (Krishna Banji) 1944– . British film actor who usually plays character parts. He played the title role of *Gandhi* 1982 and appeared in *Betrayal* 1982, *Testimony* 1987, and *Pascali's Island* 1988.

Kingsport city in NE Tennessee, on the Holston River, NE of Knoxville, near the Virginia border. Manufactures include plastics, chemicals, textiles, paper and printing, and cement; population (1990) 36,400. Fort Patrick Henry, built here 1776, protected the Wilderness Road.

Kingston capital and principal port of Jamaica, West Indies, the cultural and commercial center of the island; population (1983) 101,000, metropolitan area 525,000. Founded 1693, Kingston became the capital of Jamaica 1872.

Kingston town in E Ontario, on Lake Ontario; population (1981) 60,313. Industries include shipbuilding yards, engineering works, and grain elevators. It grew from 1782 around the French Fort Frontenac, was captured by the English 1748, and renamed in honor of George III.

Kingston upon Hull official name of ◊Hull, city in Humberside in NE England.

Kingstown capital and principal port of St Vincent and the Grenadines, West Indies, in the SW of the island of St Vincent; population (1989) 29,400.

kinkajou Central and South American carnivore *Potos flavus* of the raccoon family. Yellowish-brown, with a rounded face and slim body, the kinkajou grows to 1.8 ft/55 cm with a 1.6 ft/50 cm tail, and has short legs with sharp

claws. It spends its time in trees and has a prehensile tail. It feeds largely on fruit.

Kinki region of S Honshu island, Japan; population (1988) 22,105,000; area 12,773 sq mi/33,070 sq km. The chief city is Osaka.

Kino Eusebio Francisco *c.* 1644–1711. Italian-born Jesuit missionary. Kino entered the Jesuit order 1665. After teaching at the University of Ingolstadt, he was sent as a missionary to New Spain 1678. Kino arrived in Mexico City 1681 and soon joined a short-lived colony in Baja California. In 1687 he began exploration of Pimería Alta, now modern Sonora, Mexico, and S Arizona. There he established the missions of Tumacacori and San Xavier del Bac near modern Tucson. Kino later explored the Colorado Valley and discovered the massive prehistoric Indian ruins of Casa Grande.

kin selection in biology, the idea that ◊altruism shown to genetic relatives can be worthwhile, because those relatives share some genes with the individual that is behaving altruistically and may continue to reproduce. See ◊inclusive fitness.

Alarm-calling in response to predators is an example of a behavior that may have evolved through kin selection: relatives that are warned of danger can escape and continue to breed, even if the alarm caller is caught.

Kinsey Alfred 1894–1956. US researcher whose studies of male and female sexual behavior 1948–53, based on questionnaires, were the first serious published research on this topic.

The Institute for Sex Research at Indiana University, founded 1947, continues the objective study of human sexual behavior. Many misconceptions, social class differences, and wide variations in practice and expectations have been discovered as a result of Kinsey's work.

Kinshasa formerly *Léopoldville* capital of Zaire on the river Zaïre, 250 mi/400 km inland from Matadi; population (1984) 2,654,000. Industries include chemicals, textiles, engineering, food processing, and furniture. It was founded by the explorer Henry Stanley 1887.

kinship in anthropology, human relationship based on blood or marriage, and sanctified by law and custom. Kinship forms the basis for most human societies and for such social groupings as the family, clan, or tribe.

The social significance of kinship varies from society to society. Most human societies have evolved strict social rules, customs, and taboos regarding kinship and sexual behavior (such as the prohibition of incest), marriage, and inheritance.

Kinski Klaus 1926–1991. German actor of skeletal appearance who featured in Werner Herzog's films *Aguirre Wrath of God* 1972, *Nosferatu* 1978, and *Fitzcarraldo* 1982. His other films include *For a Few Dollars More* 1965, *Dr Zhivago* 1965, and *Venom* 1982. He is the father of the actress Nastassja Kinski (1961–).

Kipling (Joseph) Rudyard 1865–1936. English writer, born in India. *Plain Tales from the Hills* 1888, about Anglo-Indian society, contains the earliest of his masterly short stories. His books for children, including *The Jungle Books* 1894–95, *Just So Stories* 1902, *Puck of Pook's Hill* 1906, and the novel *Kim* 1901, reveal his imaginative identification with the exotic. Poems such as "Danny Deever," "Gunga Din," and "If–" express an empathy with common experience, which contributed to his great popularity, together with a vivid sense of "Englishness" (sometimes denigrated as a kind of jingoist imperialism). His work is increasingly valued for its complex characterization and subtle moral viewpoints. Nobel Prize 1907.

Born in Bombay, Kipling was educated at the United Services College at Westward Ho!, England, which provided the background for *Stalky and Co* 1899. He worked as a journalist in India 1882–89; during these years he wrote *Plain Tales from the Hills*, *Soldiers Three* 1890, *Wee Willie Winkie* 1890, and others. Returning to London he published *The Light that Failed* 1890 and *Barrack-Room Ballads* 1892. He lived largely in the US 1892–96, where he produced the two *Jungle Books* and *Captains Courageous* 1897. Settling in Sussex, SE England, he published *Kim* (set in India), the *Just So Stories*, *Puck of Pook's Hill*, and *Rewards and Fairies* 1910.

Kirchhoff Gustav Robert 1824–1887. German physicist who with ◊Bunsen used the spectroscope to show that all elements, heated to incandescence, have their individual spectra.

Kirchner Ernst Ludwig 1880–1938. German Expressionist artist, a leading member of the group *die* ◊*Brücke* in Dresden from 1905 and in Berlin from 1911. His Dresden work, which includes woodcuts, shows the influence of African art. In Berlin he turned to city scenes and portraits, using lurid colors and bold diagonal paint strokes recalling woodcut technique. He suffered a breakdown during World War I and settled in Switzerland, where he committed suicide.

Kirghiz member of a pastoral people numbering approximately 1.5 million. They inhabit the central Asian region bounded by the Hindu Kush, the Himalayas, and the Tian Shan mountains. The Kirghiz are Sunni Muslims, and their Turkic language belongs to the Altaic family.

The Kirghiz live in Tajikistan, Uzbekistan, Kyrgyzstan, China (Xinjiang), and Afghanistan (Wakhan corridor). The most isolated group, because of its geographical situation and its international border problems, is found in Afghanistan. The highest political authority is traditionally entitled khan. During the winter the Kirghiz live in individual family yurts (tents made of felt). In summer they come together in larger settlements of up to 20 yurts. They herd sheep, goats, and yaks, and use Bactrian camels for transporting their possessions.

Kiribati republic in the W central Pacific Ocean, comprising three groups of coral atolls: the 16 Gilbert Islands, 8 uninhabited Phoenix Islands, 8 of the 11 Line Islands, and the volcanic island of Banaba.

government Kiribati's 1979 constitution provides for a president, the Beretitenti, who is head of both state and government, and is elected by universal suffrage for a four-year term, and a single-chamber legislature, the Maneaba ni Maungatabu. The president may not serve more than three terms. The Maneaba has 39 popularly elected members and one appointed member, representing the island of Banaba, plus the attorney general by virtue of office. It also serves a four-year term. The president governs with the help of a vice-president and cabinet chosen from and responsible to the Maneaba. There are no formal political parties, all candidates for the Maneaba fighting as independents, although government and opposition factions are subsequently formed within the assembly.

history The first Europeans to visit the area were the Spanish 1606. The 16 predominantly Micronesian-peopled Gilbert Islands and 9 predominantly Melanesian-peopled Ellice Islands became a British protectorate 1892, and then the Gilbert and Ellice Islands Colony (GEIC) 1916. The colony was occupied by Japan 1942–43 and was the scene of fierce fighting between Japanese and US forces.

independence In preparation for self-government, a legislative council was set up 1963, and in 1972 a governor took over from the British high commissioner. In 1974 the legislative council was replaced by an elected house of assembly, and in 1975, when the Ellice Islands separated and became Tuvalu, the GEIC was renamed the Gilbert Islands. The islands achieved internal self-government 1977 and full independence within the British ◊Commonwealth 1979, under the name of Kiribati, with Ieremia Tabai as their first president. He was reelected 1982, 1983, and 1987. He was again reelected in the general election of May 1991, but was constitutionally prohibited from serving a further term in office. However, he gave his backing to Vice-President Teatao Teannaki in the contested presidential election July 1991. Tabai was subsequently appointed environment and natural resources minister in Teannaki's ten-member cabinet.

Banaba The once phosphate-rich island of Banaba campaigned for independence or unification with Fiji in the mid-1970s. However, its environment has been ruined by overmining and its people have been forced to resettle on Rabi Island, 2,600 mi/4,160 km away in the Fiji group. *See illustration box.*

Kirin alternate name for ◊Jilin, Chinese province.

Kirk Norman 1923–1974. New Zealand Labor politician, prime minister 1972–74. He entered parliament 1957 and led the Labor Party from 1964. During his office as prime minister he withdrew New Zealand troops from the Vietnam War and attempted to block French nuclear tests in the Pacific.

Kirkland Gelsey 1952– . US ballerina of effortless technique and innate musicality. She joined the New York City Ballet 1968, where George Balanchine staged a new *Firebird* for her 1970 and Jerome Robbins chose her for his *Goldberg Variations* 1971 and other ballets. In 1974 Mikhail Baryshnikov sought her out and she joined the American Ballet Theater, where they danced in partnership, for example in *Giselle*.

Kirkpatrick Jeane 1926– . US politician and professor of political science. She served as US ambassador to the United Nations 1981–85. Originally a Democrat, she often spoke out against Communism and left-wing causes. She joined the Republican Party 1985.

Born in Duncan, Oklahoma, she graduated from Barnard College and Columbia University. She taught at Georgetown University 1967–81 and helped to form the Coalition for a Democratic Majority 1972.

Kirkuk town in NE Iraq; population (1985) 208,000. It is the center of a major oil field. Formerly it was served by several pipelines providing outlets to Lebanon, Syria, and other countries, but closures caused by the Iran–Iraq War left only the pipeline to Turkey operational.

Kirov Sergei Mironovich 1886–1934. Russian Bolshevik leader who joined the party 1904 and played a prominent part in the 1918–20

Kiribati
Republic of

area 277 sq mi/717 sq km
capital and port Bairiki (on Tarawa Atoll)
physical comprises 33 Pacific coral islands: the Kiribati (Gilbert), Rawaki (Phoenix), and Line Islands, Banaba (Ocean Island), and Kiritimati (Christmas Island)
environment the islands are threatened by the possibility of a rise in sea level caused by global warming. A rise of approximately 1 ft/30 cm by the year 2040 will make existing fresh water brackish and undrinkable
features island groups crossed by equator and International Date Line
head of state and government Teatao Teannaki from 1991
political system liberal democracy
political parties National Progressive Party, governing faction; opposition parties: Christian Democratic Party and the Kiribati United Party
exports copra, fish
currency Australian dollar
population (1990 est) 65,600 (Micronesian); growth rate 1.7% p.a.
languages English (official), Gilbertese
religions Roman Catholic 48%, Protestant 45%
literacy 90% (1985)
GDP $26 million (1987); $430 per head (1988)
chronology
1892 Gilbert and Ellice Islands proclaimed a British protectorate.
1937 Phoenix Islands added to colony.
1950s UK tested nuclear weapons on Kiritimati (formerly Christmas Island).
1962 USA tested nuclear weapons on Kiritimati.
1975 Ellice Islands separated to become Tuvalu.
1977 Gilbert Islands granted internal self-government.
1979 Independence achieved from Britain, within the Commonwealth, as the Republic of Kiribati, with Ieremia Tabai as president.
1982 and 1983 Tabai reelected.
1985 Fishing agreement with Soviet state-owned company negotiated, prompting formation of Kiribati's first political party, the opposition Christian Democrats.
1987 Tabai reelected.
1991 Tabai reelected but not allowed under constitution to serve further term; Teatao Teannaki elected president.

civil war. As one of ◊Stalin's closest associates, he became first secretary of the Leningrad Communist Party. His assassination, possibly engineered by Stalin, led to the political trials held during the next four years as part of the ◊purge.

Kirovabad city in Azerbaijan, population (1987) 270,000. Industries include cottons, woolens, and processed foods. The city was known as *Gandzha* until 1804 and again 1918–35, and as *Elizavetpol* 1804–1918.

Kisangani formerly (until 1966) *Stanleyville* town in NE Zaire, on the upper Zaïre River, below Stanley Falls; population (1984) 283,000. It is a communications center.

Kishi Nobusuke 1896–1987. Japanese politician and prime minister 1957–60. A government minister during World War II and imprisoned 1945, he was never put on trial and returned to politics 1953. During his premiership, Japan began a substantial rearmament program and signed a new treaty with the US that gave greater equality in the relationship between the two states.

Kishinev capital of the Republic of Moldova; population (1989) 565,000. Industries include cement, food processing, tobacco, and textiles.

Founded 1436, it became Russian 1812. It was taken by Romania 1918, by the USSR 1940, and by Germany 1941, when it was totally destroyed. The USSR recaptured the site 1944, and rebuilding soon began. Nationalist demonstrations were held in the city during 1989. The republic declared its independence from the Soviet Union Aug 1991.

Kissinger Henry 1923– . German-born US diplomat. After a brilliant academic career at Harvard University, he was appointed national security adviser 1969 by President Nixon, and was secretary of state 1973–77. His missions to the USSR and China improved US relations with both countries, and he took part in negotiating US withdrawal from Vietnam 1973 and in Arab-Israeli peace negotiations 1973–75. Nobel Peace Prize 1973.

Born in Bavaria, Kissinger emigrated to the US 1938. After work in Germany for army counterintelligence, he won a scholarship to Harvard, and subsequently became a government consultant. His secret trips to Beijing and Moscow led to Nixon's visits to both countries and a general détente. In 1973 he shared the Nobel Peace Prize with Le Duc Tho, the North Vietnamese Politburo member, for his part in the Vietnamese peace negotiations, and in 1976 he was involved in the negotiations in Africa arising from the Angola and Rhodesia crises. In 1983, President Reagan appointed him to head a bipartisan commission on Central America. He was widely regarded as the most powerful member of Nixon's administration.

Kiswahili another name for the ◊Swahili language.

Kitakyushu industrial port city (coal, steel, chemicals, cotton thread, plate glass, alcohol) in Japan, on the Hibiki Sea, N Kyushu, formed 1963 by the amalgamation of Moji, Kokura, Tobata, Yawata, and Wakamatsu; population (1989) 1,030,000. A tunnel 1942 links it with Honshu.

Kitasato Shibasaburo 1852–1931. Japanese bacteriologist who discovered the ◊plague bacillus while investigating an outbreak of plague in Hong Kong. Kitasato was the first to grow the tetanus bacillus in pure culture. He and

the German bacteriologist Behring discovered that increasing nonlethal doses of tetanus toxin give immunity to the disease.

He founded the Tokyo Institute for Infectious Diseases 1914, and was a friend and one-time student of Robert ◊Koch.

Kitchener city in SW Ontario; population (1986) 151,000, metropolitan area (with Waterloo) 311,000. Manufacturing includes agricultural machinery and tires. Settled by Germans from Pennsylvania in the 1800s, it was known as Berlin until 1916.

Kitchener Horatio Herbert, Earl Kitchener of Khartoum 1850–1916. British soldier and administrator. He defeated the Sudanese dervishes at Omdurman 1898 and reoccupied Khartoum. In South Africa, he was Chief of Staff 1900–02 during the Boer War, and commanded the forces in India 1902–09. He was appointed war minister on the outbreak of World War I, and drowned when his ship was sunk on the way to Russia.

He was appointed to the Egyptian army 1882 and made commander in chief 1892. He was governor-general of the Sudan 1898–1900. In the Boer War he conducted war by scorched-earth policy and created the earliest ◊concentration camps for civilians.

kite one of about 20 birds of prey in the family Accipitridae, found in all parts of the world.

Kites have long, pointed wings and, usually, a forked tail. North America has five species, including the American swallow-tailed kite *Elanoides forficatus* of the SE US, which catches insects in flight as well as dropping down on snakes and lizards.

Kitimat port near Prince Rupert, British Columbia; population (1981) 4,300. Founded 1955, it has one of the world's largest aluminum smelters, powered by the Kemano hydroelectric scheme.

Kitt Peak National Observatory observatory in the Quinlan Mountains near Tucson, Arizona, operated by AURA (Association of Universities for Research into Astronomy). Its main telescopes are the 4-m/158-in Mayall reflector, opened 1973, and the McMath Solar Telescope, opened 1962, the world's largest of its type. Among numerous other telescopes on the site is a 2.3-m/90-in reflector owned by the Steward Observatory of the University of Arizona.

kiwi flightless bird *Apteryx australis* found only in New Zealand. It has long, hairlike brown plumage and a very long beak with nostrils at the tip. It is nocturnal and insectivorous. The egg is larger in relation to the bird's size (similar to a domestic chicken) than that of any other bird.

All kiwi species have declined since European settlement of New Zealand, and the little spotted kiwi is most at risk. It survives only on one small island reservation, which was stocked with birds from the mainland.

kiwi fruit or *Chinese gooseberry* fruit of a vinelike plant *Actinidithia chinensis*, family Actinidiaceae, commercially grown on a large scale in New Zealand. Kiwi fruits are egg-sized, oval, and of similar flavor to a gooseberry, with a fuzzy brown skin.

Bright-green fuzzless varieties are now available.

Klaipeda formerly *Memel* port in Lithuania, on the Baltic coast at the mouth of the river Dange; population (1987) 201,000. Industries

include shipbuilding and iron foundries. It was founded 1252 as the castle of Memelburg by the Teutonic Knights, joined the ◊Hanseatic League soon after, and has changed hands among Sweden, Russia, and Germany. Lithuania annexed Klaipeda 1923, and after German occupation 1939–45 it was restored to Lithuania.

Klaproth Martin Heinrich 1743–1817. German chemist who first identified the elements uranium, zirconium, cerium, and titanium.

At 16 he was apprenticed to an apothecary; he began research in 1780. The first professor of chemistry at the University of Berlin, he is sometimes called "the father of analytical chemistry."

Klee Paul 1879–1940. Swiss painter. He settled in Munich 1906, joined the ◊Blaue Reiter group 1912, and worked at the Bauhaus school of art and design 1920–31, returning to Switzerland 1933. His style in the 1920s and 1930s was dominated by humorous linear fantasies.

Klee traveled with the painter August Macke to Tunisia 1914, a trip that transformed his sense of color. The Klee Foundation, Berne, has a large collection of his work.

Klein Calvin (Richard) 1942– . US fashion designer whose collections are characterized by the smooth and understated. He set up his own business 1968 specializing in designing coats and suits, and expanded into sportswear in the mid-1970s. His designer jeans became a status symbol during the same period.

Klein Melanie 1882–1960. Austrian child psychoanalyst. She pioneered child psychoanalysis and play studies, and was influenced by Sigmund ◊Freud's theories. She published *The Psychoanalysis of Children* 1960.

Kleist (Bernd) Heinrich (Wilhelm) von 1777–1811. German dramatist whose comedy *Der zerbrochene Krug/The Broken Pitcher* 1808 and drama *Prinz Friedrich von Homburg/The Prince of Homburg* 1811 achieved success only after his suicide.

Kleist entered the Prussian army at the age of 14, remaining for five years. His *Michael Kohlhaus* 1808 describes a righteous schoolmaster led to carry out robbery and murder for political ends.

Klemperer Otto 1885–1973. German conductor who is celebrated for his interpretation of contemporary and Classical music (especially ◊Beethoven and ◊Brahms). He conducted the Los Angeles Orchestra 1933–39 and the Philharmonia Orchestra, London, from 1959.

kleptomania (Greek *kleptes* "thief") behavioral disorder characterized by an overpowering desire to possess articles for which one has no need. In kleptomania, as opposed to ordinary theft, there is no obvious need or use for what is stolen and sometimes the sufferer has no memory of the theft.

Kliegl John H 1869–1959 and Anton T 1872–1927. German-born US brothers who in 1911 invented the brilliant carbon-arc (*klieg*) lights used in television and films. They also created scenic effects for theater and film.

Klimt Gustav 1862–1918. Austrian painter, influenced by Jugendstil ("youth style," a form of Art Nouveau); a founding member of the Vienna Sezession group 1897. His paintings have a jeweled effect similar to mosaics, for example *The Kiss* 1909 (Musée des Beaux-Arts, Strasbourg). His many portraits include *Judith I* 1901 (Österreichische Galerie, Vienna).

Kline Franz 1910–1962. US Abstract Expressionist painter. He created large, graphic compositions in monochrome using angular forms, like magnified calligraphic brushstrokes.

He did not introduce color into his work until the late 1950s.

Klondike former gold-mining area in ⃟Yukon, named after the river valley where gold was found 1896. About 30,000 people moved there during the following 15 years. Silver is still mined there.

km symbol for ⃟*kilometer*.

knapweed any of several weedy plants of the genus *Centaurea*, family Compositae. In the common knapweed *C. nigra*, also known as *hardhead*, the hard bract-covered buds break into purple composite heads. It is native to Europe and has been introduced to North America.

Kneller Godfrey 1646–1723. German-born portrait painter who lived in England from 1674. He was court painter to Charles II, James II, William III, and George I.

Knesset the Israeli parliament, consisting of a single chamber of 120 deputies elected for a period of four years.

Knickerbocker School group of US writers working in New York State in the early 19th century, which included Washington Irving, James Kirke Paulding (1778–1860), and Fitz-Greene Halleck (1790–1867).

knifefish any fish of the genus *Gymnotus* and allied genera of fishes, family Gymnotidae, in which the body is deep at the front, drawn to a narrow or pointed tail at the rear, the main fin being the well-developed long ventral that completes the knifelike shape. The ventral fin is rippled for forward or backward locomotion. Knifefishes produce electrical fields, which they use for navigation.

knighthood, order of fraternity carrying with it the rank of knight, admission to which is granted as a mark of royal favor or as a reward for public services. During the Middle Ages in Europe such fraternities fell into two classes, religious and secular. The first class, including the ⃟*Templars* and the *Knights of* ⃟*St John*, consisted of knights who had taken religious vows and devoted themselves to military service against the Saracens (Arabs) or other non-Christians. The secular orders probably arose from bands of knights engaged in the service of a prince or great noble.

knitting method of making fabric by looping and knotting yarn with two needles. Knitting may have developed from ⃟*crochet*, which uses a single hooked needle, or from *netting*, using a shuttle.

A mechanized process for making stockings was developed in the 16th century, but it was not until the mid-20th century that machine knitting was revolutionized with the introduction of synthetic yarns, colored dyes, and methods of texturing and elasticizing.

Knossos chief city of Minoan Crete (see ⃟Minoan civilization), near present-day Iráklion, 4 mi/6 km SE of Candia. The archeological site excavated by Arthur ⃟Evans 1899–1935, dates from about 2000 BC, and includes the palace throne room and a labyrinth, legendary home of the ⃟Minotaur.

Excavation of the palace of the legendary King Minos showed that the story of Theseus's encounter with the Minotaur in a labyrinth was possibly derived from the ritual "bull-leaping"

slip knot   figure-of-eight   clove hitch

sheet bend   round turn and two half hitches   reef knot

knot *Simple forms of knot have specific applications.*

by young people depicted in the palace frescoes and from the mazelike layout of the palace.

knot wading bird *Calidris canutus* of the sandpiper family. It is about 10 in/25 cm long. In the winter, it is gray above and white below, but in the breeding season, it is brick-red on the head and chest and black on the wings and back. It feeds on insects and mollusks.

Breeding in North American and Eurasian arctic regions, knots travel widely in winter, to be found as far south as South Africa, Australasia, and southern parts of South America.

knot in navigation, unit by which a ship's speed is measured, equivalent to one ⃟nautical mile per hour (one knot equals about 1.15 miles per hour). It is also sometimes used in aviation.

knot intertwinement of parts of one or more ropes, cords, or strings, to bind them together or to other objects. It is constructed so that the strain on the knot will draw it tighter. Bends or hitches are knots used to fasten ropes together or to other objects; when two ropes are joined end to end, they are spliced. The craft of ⃟macramé uses knots to form decorative pieces and fringes.

knotgrass annual plant *Polygonum aviculare* of the dock family. The small lance-shaped leaves have bases that sheathe the slender stems, giving a superficial resemblance to grass. Small pinkish flowers are followed by seeds that are a delicacy for birds. Knotgrass grows worldwide except in the polar regions.

The creeping grass *Paspalum distichum* of North America is sometimes also called knotgrass.

knowledge-based system (KBS) computer program that uses an encoding of human knowledge to help solve problems. It was discovered during research into ⃟artificial intelligence that adding heuristics (rules of thumb) enabled programs to tackle problems that were otherwise difficult to solve by the usual techniques of computer science.

Chess-playing programs have been strengthened by including knowledge of what makes a good position, or of overall strategies, rather than relying solely on the computer's ability to calculate variations.

Knox John c. 1505–1572. Scottish Protestant reformer, founder of the Church of Scotland. He spent several years in exile for his beliefs, including a period in Geneva where he met John ⃟Calvin. He returned to Scotland 1559 to

promote Presbyterianism. His books include *First Blast of the Trumpet Against the Monstrous Regiment of Women* 1558.

Originally a Roman Catholic priest, Knox is thought to have been converted by the reformer George Wishart. When Wishart was burned for heresy, Knox went into hiding, but later preached the reformed doctrines.

Knoxville city in E Tennessee; population (1990) 165,100. It is the center of a mining and agricultural region, and the administrative headquarters of the ⃟Tennessee Valley Authority. The University of Tennessee, founded 1794, is here, and Oak Ridge National Laboratory, one of the world's largest nuclear research facilities, is nearby.

Settlement began 1786, and it was the first state capital (1796–1812; 1817–19). Union troops captured the city 1863, during the Civil War. A world's fair was held here 1982.

koala marsupial *Phascolarctos cinereus* of the family Phalangeridae, found only in E Australia. It feeds almost entirely on eucalyptus shoots. It is about 2 ft/60 cm long, and resembles a bear. The popularity of its grayish fur led to its almost complete extermination by hunters. Under protection since 1936, it has rapidly increased in numbers.

kōan in Zen Buddhism, a superficially nonsensical question or riddle used by a Zen master to help a pupil achieve satori (⃟enlightenment). It is used in the Rinzai school of Zen.

A *kōan* supposedly cannot be understood through the processes of logic; its solution requires attainment of a higher level of insight. An often repeated example is "What is the sound of one hand clapping?"

An answer would be that the word "clapping" by definition involves two hands, and therefore this particular *kōan* is unanswerable.

Kobe deep-water port in S Honshu, Japan; population (1989) 1,438,200. **Port Island**, created 1960–68 from the rock of nearby mountains, area 2 sq mi/5 sq km, is one of the world's largest construction projects.

København Danish name for ⃟Copenhagen, capital of Denmark.

Koblenz city in the Rhineland-Palatinate, Germany, at the junction of the rivers Rhine and Mosel; population (1988) 110,000. The city dates from Roman times. It is a center of communications and the wine trade, with industries (shoes, cigars, paper).

Koch Robert 1843–1910. German bacteriologist. Koch and his assistants devised the techniques to culture bacteria outside the body, and formulated the rules for showing whether or not a bacterium is the cause of a disease. Nobel Prize for Medicine 1905.

His techniques enabled him to identify the bacteria responsible for diseases like anthrax, cholera, and tuberculosis. This was a crucial first step to the later discovery of cures for these diseases. Koch was a great teacher, and many of his pupils, such as ⃝Kitasato, ⃝Ehrlich, and ⃝Behring, became outstanding scientists.

Kodály Zoltán 1882–1967. Hungarian composer. With Béla ⃝Bartók, he recorded and transcribed Magyar folk music, the scales and rhythm of which he incorporated in a deliberately nationalist style. His works include the cantata *Psalmus Hungaricus* 1923, a comic opera *Háry János* 1925–27, and orchestral dances and variations.

Kodiak island off the S coast of Alaska, site of a US naval base; area 3,670 sq mi/9,505 sq km. It is the home of the *Kodiak bear*, the world's largest ⃝bear. The town of Kodiak is one of the largest US fishing ports (mainly salmon).

Koestler Arthur 1905–1983. Hungarian author. Imprisoned by the Nazis in France 1940, he escaped to England. His novel *Darkness at Noon* 1940, regarded as his masterpiece, is a fictional account of the Stalinist purges, and draws on his experiences as a prisoner under sentence of death during the Spanish Civil War. He also wrote extensively about creativity, parapsychology, politics, and culture. He endowed Britain's first chair of parapsychology at Edinburgh, established 1984.

Born in Budapest, and educated as an engineer in Vienna, he became a journalist in Palestine and the USSR. He joined the Communist party in Berlin 1931, but left it 1938 (he recounts his disillusionment with communism in *The God That Failed* 1950). His account of being held by the Nazis is contained in *Scum of the Earth* 1941.

kohl (Arabic) powdered antimony sulfide, used in Asia and the Middle East to darken the area around the eyes. Commonly used eyeliners also contain carbon (bone black, lamp black, carbon black) or black iron oxide.

Kohl Helmut 1930– . German conservative politician, leader of the Christian Democratic Union (CDU) from 1976, West German chancellor (prime minister) 1982–90. He oversaw the reunification of East and West Germany 1989–90 and in 1990 won a resounding victory to become the first chancellor of reunited Germany. His miscalculation of the true costs of reunification and their subsequent effects on the German economy led to a dramatic fall in his popularity.

Kohl studied law and history before entering the chemical industry. Elected to the Rhineland-Palatinate *Land* (state) parliament 1959, he became state premier 1969. After the 1976 Bundestag (federal parliament) elections Kohl led the CDU in opposition. He became federal chancellor 1982, when the Free Democratic Party (FDP) withdrew support from the socialist Schmidt government, and was elected at the head of a new coalition that included the FDP. From 1984 Kohl was implicated in the Flick bribes scandal over the illegal business funding of political parties, but he was cleared of all charges 1986, and was reelected chancellor Jan 1987.

kohlrabi variety of kale *Brassica oleracea*. The leaves of kohlrabi shoot from a globular swelling on the main stem; it is used for food and resembles a turnip.

Kokhba Bar. Adopted name of Simeon bar Koziba. Hebrew leader of the revolt against the Hellenization campaign of Emperor Hadrian 132–35, when Palestine was a province of the Roman Empire. The uprising resulted in the razing of Jerusalem and Kokhba's death in battle.

Kokomo city in N central Indiana, on Wildcat Creek, N of Indianapolis and SW of Fort Wayne; seat of Howard County; population (1990) 45,000. The city's industries produce automobile, radio, and plumbing parts; steel and wire; and electrical machinery. The first automobile to use gasoline was invented and tested here 1893.

Kokoschka Oskar 1886–1980. Austrian Expressionist painter and writer who lived in England from 1938. Initially influenced by the Vienna Sezession painters, he developed a disturbingly expressive portrait style. His writings include several plays.

kola alternate spelling of ⃝cola, a genus of tropical tree.

Kola Peninsula (Russian *Kol'skiy Poluostrov*) peninsula in N Russia, bounded by the White Sea on the south and east and by the Barents Sea on the north; area 50,000 sq mi/129,500 sq km; population 1.3 million (of whom 2,000 Saami). Kola is coterminous with Murmansk region. Apatite and other minerals are exported; heavy pollution from nickel smelting has damaged a large area of forest. There is a heavy concentration of army, naval, and air bases in the Kola Peninsula.

The world's biggest nuclear fleet is stationed in the Kola Peninsula, together with (1990) 22 air bases and 50,000 Soviet troops. The acid (SO_2) emissions from nickel smelting have caused *Waldsterben* (forest die-back) as far away as neighboring Finland. To the NW the low-lying granite plateau adjoins Norway's thinly populated county of Finnmark.

Kolchak Alexander Vasilievich 1875–1920. Russian admiral, commander of the White forces in Siberia after the Russian Revolution. He proclaimed himself Supreme Ruler of Russia 1918, but was later handed over to the Bolsheviks by his own men and shot.

kolkhoz Russian term for a ⃝collective farm, as opposed to a ⃝sovkhoz or state-owned farm.

Kollontai Alexandra 1872–1952. Russian revolutionary, politician, and writer. In 1905 she published *On the Question of the Class Struggle*, and, as commissar for public welfare, was the only female member of the first Bolshevik government. She campaigned for domestic reforms such as acceptance of free love, simplification of divorce laws, and collective child care.

Köln German form of ⃝Cologne, city in Germany.

Komi autonomous republic in N central Russia; area 160,580 sq mi/415,900 sq km; population (1986) 1,200,000. Its capital is Syktyvkar.

Komi member of a Finnish people living mainly in the tundra and coniferous forests of the autonomous republic of Komi in the NW Urals, Russia. They raise livestock, grow timber, and mine coal and oil. Their language, Zyryan, belongs to the Finno-Ugric branch of the Uralic family.

Kommunizma, Pik or *Communism Peak* highest mountain in the ⃝Pamirs, a mountain range in Tajikistan; 24,599 ft/7,495 m. As part of the former USSR, it was known as *Mount Garmo* until 1933 and *Mount Stalin* 1933–62.

Komsomol Russian name for the All-Union Leninist Communist Youth League of the Soviet Union. Founded 1918, it acted as the youth section of the Communist Party.

Kongur Shan mountain peak in China, 25,325 ft/7,719 m high, part of the Pamir range (see ⃝Pamirs). The 1981 expedition that first reached the summit was led by British climber Chris Bonington.

Kong Zi Pinyin form of ⃝Confucius, Chinese philosopher.

Koniev Ivan Stepanovich 1898–1973. Soviet marshal who in World War II liberated Ukraine from the invading German forces 1943 and advanced from the south on Berlin to link up with the British-US forces. He commanded all Warsaw Pact forces 1955–60.

Königsberg German name of ⃝Kaliningrad, port in Russia.

Konoe Fumimaro, Prince 1891–1946. Japanese politician and prime minister 1937–39 and 1940–41. Entering politics in the 1920s, Konoe was active in trying to curb the power of the army in government and preventing an escalation of the war with China. He helped to engineer the fall 1944 of the government of Hideki Tojo (1884-1948) but committed suicide after being suspected of war crimes.

Kon-Tiki legendary creator god of Peru and sun king who ruled the country later occupied by the ⃝Incas and was supposed to have migrated out into the Pacific. The name was used by explorer Thor ⃝Heyerdahl for his raft (made of nine balsawood logs), which he sailed from Peru to the Tuamotu Islands, near Tahiti, on the Humboldt current 1947, in an attempt to show that ancient inhabitants of South America might have reached Polynesia. He sailed from April 28 to Aug 7, 1947, with five companions, over about 5,000 mi/8,000 km. The Tuamotu Archipelago was in fact settled by Austronesian seafarers, and Heyerdahl's theory is largely discounted by anthropologists.

kookaburra or *laughing jackass* largest of the world's ⃝kingfishers *Dacelo novaeguineae*, found in Australia, with an extraordinary laughing call. It feeds on insects and other small creatures. The body and tail measure 18 in/45 cm, the head is grayish with a dark eye stripe, and the back and wings are flecked brown with gray underparts. Its laugh is one of the most familiar sounds of the bush of E Australia.

kora 21-string instrument of W African origin made from gourds, with a harplike sound.

Koran (alternatively transliterated as *Quran*) sacred book of ⃝Islam. Written in the purest Arabic, it contains 114 *suras* (chapters), and is stated to have been divinely revealed to the prophet Mohammed about 616.

Korda Alexander 1893–1956. Hungarian-born British film producer and director, a dominant figure during the 1930s and 1940s. His films include *The Private Life of Henry VIII* 1933, *The Third Man* 1950, and *Richard III* 1956.

Kordofan province of central Sudan, known as the "White Land"; area 56,752 sq mi/146,990 sq km; population (1983) 3,093,300. Although never an independent state, it has a character of its own. It is mainly undulating plain, with acacia scrub producing gum arabic, marketed in the chief town El Obeid. Formerly a rich agricultural region, it has been overtaken by desertification.

Korea peninsula in E Asia, divided into ◊Korea, North, and ◊Korea, South.

Korea: history
2000 BC The foundation of the Korean state traditionally dates back to the *Tangun dynasty*.
1122–4th century The Chinese Kija dynasty.
AD 10th century After centuries of internal war and invasion, Korea was united within its present boundaries.
16th century Japan invaded Korea for the first time, later withdrawing from a country it had devastated.
1905 Japan began to treat Korea as a protectorate.
1910 It was annexed by Japan. Many Japanese colonists settled in Korea, introducing both industrial and agricultural development.
1945 At the end of World War II, the Japanese in Korea surrendered, but the occupying forces at the cease-fire—the USSR north of the ◊38th parallel, and the US south of it—created a lasting division of the country as North and South Korea (see ◊Korea, North, and ◊Korea, South, for history since 1945).

Korean native to or inhabitant of Korea;

Korea, North
Democratic People's Republic of (*Chosun Minchu-chui Inmin Konghwa-guk*)

area 46,528 sq mi/120,538 sq km
capital Pyongyang
cities Chongjin, Nampo, Wonsan
physical wide coastal plain in W rising to mountains cut by deep valleys in interior
environment the building of a hydroelectric dam at Kumgangsan on a tributary of the Han River has been opposed by South Korea as a potential flooding threat to central Korea
features separated from South Korea by a military demarcation line; the richer of the two Koreas in mineral resources (copper, iron ore, graphite, tungsten, zinc, lead, magnesite, gold, phosphor, phosphates)
head of state Kim Il Sung from 1972 (also head of Korean Workers' Party)
head of government Yon Hyong Muk from 1988
political system communism
political parties Korean Workers' Party (KWP), Marxist-Leninist-Kim Il Sungist (leads Democratic Front for the Reunification of the Fatherland, including North Korean Democratic Party and Religious Chungwoo Party)

exports coal, iron, copper, textiles, chemicals
currency won
population (1990 est) 23,059,000; growth rate 2.5% p.a.
life expectancy men 67, women 73 (1989)
language Korean
religions traditionally Buddhist, Confucian, but religious activity curtailed by the state
literacy 99% (1989)
GNP $20 bn; $3,450 per head (1988)
chronology
1910 Korea formally annexed by Japan.
1945 Russian and US troops entered Korea, forced surrender of Japanese, and divided the country in two. Soviet troops occupied North Korea.
1948 Democratic People's Republic of Korea declared.
1950 North Korea invaded South Korea to unite the nation, beginning the Korean War.
1953 Armistice agreed to end Korean War.
1961 Friendship and mutual assistance treaty signed with China.
1972 New constitution, with executive president, adopted. Talks took place with South Korea about possible reunification.
1980 Reunification talks broke down.
1983 Four South Korean cabinet ministers assassinated in Rangoon, Burma (Myanmar), by North Korean army officers.
1985 Increased relations with the USSR.
1989 Increasing evidence shown of nuclear-weapons development.
1990 Diplomatic contacts with South Korea and Japan suggested the beginning of a thaw in North Korea's relations with the rest of the world.
1991 Became a member of the United Nations. Signed nonaggression agreement with South Korea; agreed to ban nuclear weapons.
1992 Signed Nuclear Safeguards Agreement, allowing international inspection of its nuclear facilities. Also signed a pact with South Korea for mutual inspection of nuclear facilities. Passed legislation making foreign investment in the country attractive.

also the language and culture. There are approximately 33 million Koreans in South Korea, 15 million in North Korea, and 3 million elsewhere, principally in Japan, China (Manchuria), Russia, Kazakhstan, Uzbekistan, and the US.

Korean language language of Korea, written from the 5th century AD in Chinese characters until the invention of an alphabet by King Sejong 1443. The linguistic affiliations of Korean are unclear, but it may be distantly related to Japanese.

The alphabet was discouraged as "vulgar letters" (*onmun*) and banned by the colonizing Japanese of the early 20th century. After World War II it was revived and called "top letters" (*hangul*).

Korea, North country in E Asia, bounded NE by Russia, N and NW by China, E by the Sea of Japan, S by South Korea, and W by the Yellow Sea.

government Under the 1972 constitution, which replaced the 1948 Soviet-type constitution, the leading political figure is the president, who is head of the armed forces and executive head of government. The president is appointed for four-year terms by the 687-member supreme people's assembly, which is directly elected by universal suffrage. The

assembly meets for brief sessions once or twice a year, its regular legislative business being carried out by a smaller permanent standing committee (presidium). The president works with and presides over a powerful policy-making and supervisory central people's committee (which is responsible to the assembly for its activities) and an administrative and executive cabinet (administration council).

history For early history, see ◊Korea: history. The Democratic People's Republic of Korea was formed from the zone north of the 38th parallel of latitude, occupied by Soviet troops after Japan's surrender 1945. The USSR installed in power an "Executive Committee of the Korean People," staffed by Soviet-trained Korean communists, before North Korea was declared a People's Republic 1948 under the leadership of the Workers' Party of Korea (KWP), with Kim Il Sung as president. The remaining Soviet forces withdrew 1949.

Korean War In 1950 North Korea, seeking unification of the Korean peninsula, launched a large-scale invasion of South Korea. This began the three-year ◊Korean War which, after intervention by United Nations forces supported by the US (on the side of the South) and by China (on the side of the North), ended in stalemate. The 38th parallel border between North and South was reestablished by the armistice agreement of July 1953, and a UN-patrolled demilitarized buffer zone was created. North Korea has never accepted this agreement and remains committed to reunification.

Despite the establishment 1972 of a North–South coordinating committee to promote peaceful unification relations with the South remained tense and hostile. Border incidents were frequent, and in Oct 1983 four South Korean cabinet ministers were assassinated in Rangoon, Burma (Myanmar), in a bombing incident organized by two North Korean army officers.

economic development Domestically, the years since 1948 have seen economic development in a planned socialist manner. Factories were nationalized and agriculture collectivized in the 1950s, and priority in investment programs has been given to heavy industry and rural mechanization. North Korean economic growth has, however, lagged behind that of its richer and more populous southern neighbor. In foreign affairs, North Korea adopted a neutral stance in the Sino-Soviet dispute, signing a friendship and mutual assistance treaty with China 1961 while at the same time receiving economic and military aid from the USSR. North Korea remained largely immune from the pluralist or market-socialist wave of reform that swept other communist nations 1989–90, making only minor adjustments. Relations with South Korea showed signs of improving.

succession question In the 1980s, North Korean politics became dominated by the succession question, with Kim Il Sung seeking to establish his son, Kim Chong-Il (1941–), as sole heir designate. Kim Chong-Il accompanied Kim Il Sung on diplomatic and factory tours, began to preside over key party and state government meetings, and his portrait was placed on public display across the country. In Jan 1992, Kim Chong-Il replaced his father as supreme commander of the country's armed forces. Elements within the Workers' Party and armed forces appear, however, to oppose Kim's succession aims.

effort to end isolation Recently, North Korea has been anxious to bring to an end its international isolation because of mounting economic shortages. In Sept 1990 Prime Minister Yon Hyong Muk made an unprecedented three-day official visit to South Korea, the highest level official contact since 1948. In Nov–Dec 1990, after four decades of bitter hostility, North Korea had its first formal contact (in Beijing) with the Japanese government. The collapse of communism in the USSR deprived North Korea of considerable military and economic aid and China failed to fill the breach. North Korea was forced to further review its isolationist strategy and began to seek foreign inward investment, especially Japanese aid, promising to establish new free-trade zones. The country was admitted to the United Nations (UN), simultaneously with South Korea, in Sept 1991, and on Dec 13, 1991 a nonaggression pact was signed with South Korea, heralding a move toward formal reconciliation. This provided for the establishment of a military hotline to prevent accidental conflict, the restoration of cross-border communication links, the reunion of divided families, the liberalization of commerce and investment, and the free movement of people and ideas.

In Jan 1992, following an agreement signed with South Korea in Dec banning the production and deployment of nuclear weapons, North Korea also signed the Nuclear Safeguards Agreement, allowing for international inspection of its nuclear facilities. In March it signed a pact with South Korea for mutual inspection of nuclear facilities. In Oct legislation making foreign investment in North Korea attractive was passed. *See illustration box.*

Korean War war 1950–53 between North Korea (supported by China) and South Korea, aided by the United Nations (the troops were mainly US). North Korean forces invaded the South June 25, 1950, and the Security Council of the United Nations, owing to a walk-out by the USSR, voted to oppose them. To begin with the North Koreans held most of the south but US reinforcements arrived Sept 1950 and forced their way through to the North Korean border with China. The Chinese retaliated, pushing them back to the original boundary Oct 1950; truce negotiations began 1951, although the war did not end until 1953.

By Sept 1950 the North Koreans had overrun most of the south, with the UN forces holding a small area, the Pusan perimeter, in the south east. The course of the war changed after the surprise landing of US troops later the same month at Inchon on South Korea's NW coast. The troops, led by General Douglas ◊MacArthur, fought their way through North Korea to the Chinese border in little over a month. On Oct 25, 1950, Chinese troops attacked across the Yalu River, driving the UN forces below the 38th parallel. Truce talks began July 1951, and the war ended two years later, with the restoration of the original boundary on the 38th parallel.

Korea, South country in E Asia, bounded N by North Korea, E by the Sea of Japan, S by the Korea Strait, and W by the Yellow Sea.
government Under the 1987 constitution, executive power is held by the president, who is elected directly by popular vote. The president is restricted to one five-year term of office and governs with a cabinet (state council) headed by a prime minister. Legislative authority resides in the single-chamber, 299-deputy national assembly Kuk Hoe, 224 of whose members are directly elected for four-year terms by universal suffrage in single-

member constituencies, and the remainder of whom are appointed in accordance with a formula designed to reward the largest single assembly party. The assembly has the authority to impeach the president and to override presidential vetoes. There is also a nine-member constitutional court, and guarantees of freedom of speech, press, assembly, and association are written into the constitution.
history For early history, see ◊Korea: history. The Republic of Korea was formed out of the zone south of the 38th parallel of latitude that was occupied by US troops after Japan's surrender 1945. The US military government controlled the country until, following national elections, an independent republic was declared 1948. Dr Syngman ◊Rhee, leader of the right-wing Liberal Party, was the nation's first president in a constitution based on the US model. To begin with, the republic had to cope with a massive influx of refugees fleeing the communist regime in the North; then came the 1950–53 ◊Korean War.

President Syngman Rhee, whose regime had been accused of corruption, resigned 1960 as a result of student-led disorder. A new parliamentary-style constitution gave greater power to the legislature, and the ensuing political instability precipitated a military coup led by General ◊Park Chung-Hee 1961. A presidential system of government was rees-

Korea, South
Republic of Korea (*Daehan Minguk*)

area 38,161 sq mi/98,799 sq km
capital Seoul
cities Taegu, ports Pusan, Inchon
physical southern end of a mountainous peninsula separating the Sea of Japan from the Yellow Sea
features Chomsongdae (world's earliest observatory); giant Popchusa Buddha; granite peaks of Soraksan National Park
head of state Roh Tae Woo from 1988
head of government Chung Won Shik from 1991
political system emergent democracy
political parties Democratic Liberal Party (DLP), right of center; Democratic Party, left of center; Unification National Party (UNP), right of center
exports steel, ships, chemicals, electronics, textiles and clothing, plywood, fish
currency won
population (1990 est) 43,919,000; growth rate 1.4% p.a.
life expectancy men 66, women 73 (1989)
language Korean
media freedom of the press achieved 1987;

tablished, with General Park elected president 1963, and a major program of industrial development began, involving government planning and financial support. This program was remarkably successful, with rapid industrial growth during the 1960s and 1970s as South Korea became a major exporter of light and heavy industrial goods.
opposition to government Opposition to the repressive Park regime mounted during the 1970s. In response, martial law was imposed, and in 1972 a new constitution strengthened the president's powers. A clampdown on political dissent, launched 1975, was partially relaxed for the 1978 elections, but brought protests 1979 as economic conditions briefly deteriorated. President Park was assassinated later that year, and martial law was reimposed. An interim government, led by former prime minister Choi Kyu-Hah, introduced liberalizing reforms, releasing opposition leader Kim Dae Jong 1980. However, as antigovernment demonstrations developed, a new dissident clampdown began, involving the arrest of 30 political leaders, including Kim Dae Jong. After riots in Kim's home city of Kwangju, President Choi resigned 1980 and was replaced by the leader of the army, General Chun Doo Hwan. A new constitution was adopted, and, after Chun Doo Hwan was reelected president 1981, the new Fifth Republic was proclaimed.

large numbers of newspapers with large circulations. It is prohibited to say anything favorable about North Korea
religions traditionally Buddhist, Confucian, and Chondokyo; Christian 28%
literacy 92% (1989)
GNP $171bn (1988); $2,180 per head (1986)
chronology
1910 Korea formally annexed by Japan.
1945 Russian and US troops entered Korea, forced surrender of Japanese, and divided the country in two. US military government took control of South Korea.
1948 Republic proclaimed.
1950–53 War with North Korea.
1960 President Syngman Rhee resigned amid unrest.
1961 Military coup by General Park Chung-Hee. Industrial growth program.
1979 Assassination of President Park.
1980 Military takeover by General Chun Doo Hwan.
1987 Adoption of more democratic constitution after student unrest. Roh Tae Woo elected president.
1988 Former president Chun, accused of corruption, publicly apologized and agreed to hand over his financial assets to the state. Seoul hosted Summer Olympic Games.
1989 Roh reshuffled cabinet, threatened crackdown on protesters.
1990 Two minor opposition parties united with Democratic Justice Party to form ruling Democratic Liberal Party. Diplomatic relations established with the USSR.
1991 Violent mass demonstrations against the government. New opposition grouping, the Democratic Party, formed. Prime Minister Ro Jai Bong replaced by Chung Won Shik. Entered United Nations (UN). Nonaggression and nuclear pacts signed with North Korea.
1992 DLP lost absolute majority in March general election; substantial gains made by Democratic Party and newly formed UNP, led by Chung Ju Wong. Diplomatic relations with China established.

cautious liberalization Under President Chun economic growth resumed, but internal and external criticism of the suppression of civil liberties continued. Cautious liberalization was seen prior to the 1985 assembly elections, with the release of many political prisoners and the return from exile of Kim Dae Jong. The opposition parties emerged in a strengthened position after the 1985 election but they could not agree on a single candidate. They proceeded to launch a campaign for genuine democratization that forced the Chun regime to frame a new, more liberal constitution, which was adopted after a referendum Oct 1987. The ensuing presidential election was won by the ruling party's candidate, Roh Tae Woo, amid opposition charges of fraud. He took over Feb 1988, but in the national assembly elections April 1988 the ruling Democratic Justice Party (DJP) fell short of an overall majority. Only in Feb 1990, when the DJP merged with two minor opposition parties to form the Democratic Liberal Party (DLP), was a stable governing majority secured. The new coalition declared its intention of amending the constitution to replace the presidential executive system with a parliamentary one, led by a powerful prime minister drawn from the majority grouping within the national assembly, moving South Korea's political system closer to Japan's model. In Dec 1990 Kang Young Hoon, who had been prime minister from 1988, was replaced by Ro Jai Bong as part of a broader cabinet reshuffle.

threat of invasion Since 1953 the perceived threat of invasion from the North has been a key factor in South Korean politics, helping to justify stern rule. South Korea has devoted large resources to modernizing its armed forces, which are supported by 36,000 US troops, assuring US intervention in the event of an invasion from the North.

further opposition In July 1990 the 80 members of the Party for Peace and Democracy (PPD), led by Kim Dae Jong, all resigned from the national assembly in protest at what they viewed as government attempts to push through new legislation and demanded the calling of a general election. This followed an outbreak of violence within the assembly itself. The assembly's speaker refused to accept the resignations, but the opposition deputies continued to boycott parliament when it reconvened in Sept. In the same month full diplomatic relations were established with the USSR.

In Dec 1990 the government launched a "purification" campaign designed to improve public morals and reduce materialism. In May 1991 at least 250,000 people demonstrated and six attempted suicide in protests triggered by the beating to death of a student by police. Demands for the resignation of the government and the introduction of economic and political reform were met by the replacement of a home-affairs minister and the prime minister Ro Jai Bong by Chung Won Shik, and emergency powers were given to police and security services.

In June 1991, after the new premier was mobbed by students, the authorities instituted a tougher response to student-led protests. In the same month, the ruling DLP secured a sweeping victory in local elections.

foreign affairs For South Korea the country's economic success and growing world stature was symbolized by Seoul's hosting the 1988 Summer Olympic Games. The country was admitted to the United Nations in Sept 1991.

In the same month, the US announced that all its nuclear weapons in South Korea would be withdrawn and in Nov announced that it planned to reduce its troops in South Korea from 43,000 to 36,000. Despite concerns over North Korea's nuclear aspirations, the prime ministers of the two Koreas met in Seoul on Dec 13, 1991 and signed a nonaggression and confidence-building pact which provided for the restoration of cross-border communications, the reunion of divided families, and the free movement of people and ideas. On Dec 31, 1991 a further pact was signed in Panmunjom in which both states agreed to ban the testing, manufacture, deployment, or possession of nuclear weapons.

1992 general election The country's two-party structure was restored in Sept 1991 when the opposition New Democratic Party, led by Kim Dae Jung, and the small Democratic Party, led by Lee Ki Taek, merged to form the Democratic Party, headed jointly by the two leaders. In Jan 1992 Chung Ju Yong, founder of the giant Hyundai Group, announced that he planned to establish a political party to contest the spring 1992 national assembly elections. The ruling DLP lost its majority in the election held in March; Roh resigned as leader of the DLP in Sept.

In Aug 1992 diplomatic relations with China were established. *See illustration box.*

Korematsu v US a US Supreme Court decision 1944 dealing with congressional measures forcing the relocation of citizens of certain national origins. Korematsu, a Japanese-American, filed suit to challenge a 1942 law excluding Americans of Japanese descent from living on the US W coast. Those Japanese-Americans already living on the coast were removed to inland internment camps. This, Korematsu argued, was a discriminatory violation of Fifth-Amendment rights. Citing the danger of domestic sabotage in the war against Japan, the Court ruled against Korematsu 6–3. The decision to uphold exclusion and relocation laws as legitimate exercises of war powers stood until 1983, when the Korematsu decision was reversed.

Kornberg Arthur 1918– . US biochemist. In 1956, Kornberg discovered the enzyme DNA-polymerase, which enabled molecules of ⬦DNA to be synthesized for the first time. For this work Kornberg shared the 1959 Nobel Prize for Medicine with Severo ⬦Ochoa.

Korngold Erich Wolfgang 1897–1957. Austrian-born composer. He began writing operas while still in his teens and is known for his violin concertos. In 1934 he moved to Hollywood to become a composer for Warner Brothers. His film scores combine a richly orchestrated and romantic style, reflecting the rapid changes of mood characteristic of screen action.

Kornilov Lavr 1870–1918. Russian general, commander in chief of the army, who in Aug 1917 launched an attempted coup, backed by officers, against the revolutionary prime minister, ⬦Kerensky. The coup failed, but brought down the provisional government, thus clearing the way for the Bolsheviks to seize power.

Korolev Sergei Pavlovich 1906–1966. Soviet designer of the first Soviet intercontinental missile, used to launch the first ⬦Sputnik satellite and the first ⬦Vostok spacecraft, also designed by Korolev, in which Yuri Gagarin made the world's first space flight.

Born in Zhitomir, Ukraine, Korolev became

an aircraft designer before turning to rocketry.

Kos or **Cos** fertile Greek island, one of the Dodecanese, in the Aegean Sea; area 111 sq mi/287 sq km. It gives its name to the Cos lettuce.

Kosciusko highest mountain in Australia (7,316 ft/2,229 m), in New South Wales.

The mineralogist Paul Strzelecki, who was born in Prussian Poland, climbed the mountain in 1840. He thought one of the summit tops resembled the grave of the Polish revolutionary hero Tadeusz Kościuszko, and named it after him.

Kościuszko Tadeusz 1746–1817. Polish general and nationalist who served with George Washington in the American Revolution (1776–83). He returned to Poland 1784, fought against the Russian invasion that ended in the partition of Poland, and withdrew to Saxony. He returned 1794 to lead the revolt against the occupation, but was defeated by combined Russian and Prussian forces and imprisoned until 1796.

kosher (Hebrew "appropriate") conforming to religious law with regard to the preparation and consumption of food; in Judaism, conforming to the Mosaic law of the Book of Deuteronomy. For example, only animals that chew the cud and have cloven hooves (cows and sheep, but not pigs) may be eaten. There are rules governing their humane slaughter and preparation (such as complete draining of blood) which also apply to fowl. Only fish with scales and fins may be eaten; shellfish may not. Milk products may not be cooked or eaten with meat or poultry, or until four hours after eating them. Utensils for meat must be kept separate from those for milk as well.

Kosinski Jerzy 1933–1991. Polish-born US author, in the US from 1957. His childhood experiences as a Jew in Poland during World War II are recounted in *The Painted Bird* 1965, a popular success. Later novels include *Being There* 1971, filmed 1979 with Peter Sellers, and *Pinball* 1982.

His other works include *Steps* 1968, which won the National Book Award; and *Passion Play* 1979.

He was born in Lodz, and escaped from Poland through the USSR during World War II. He was then educated as a sociologist at the university in Lodz but eventually went to the US in 1957. He taught himself English, the language in which he wrote.

Kosovo autonomous region (1974–90) in S Serbia, Yugoslavia; capital Priština; area 4,207 sq mi/10,900 sq km; population (1986) 1,900,000, consisting of about 200,000 Serbs and about 1.7 million Albanians. Products include wine, nickel, lead, and zinc. Since it is largely inhabited by Albanians and bordering on Albania, there have been demands for unification with that country, while in the late 1980s Serbians agitated for Kosovo to be merged with the rest of Serbia. A state of emergency was declared Feb 1990 after fighting broke out between ethnic Albanians, police, and the Slavonic minority. The parliament and government were dissolved July 1990 and the Serbian parliament formally annexed Kosovo Sept 1990.

In 1991 the Kosovo assembly, though still technically dissolved, organized a referendum on sovereignty which received 99% support. It elected a provisional government, headed by Bujar Bukoshi, which was recognized by Albania Oct 1991. In May 1992 the Albanian majority held unsanctioned elections, choosing Ibrahim Rugova as president and selecting a 130-member parliament. Serbia regarded the elections as illegal but allowed them to proceed.

Kossuth Lajos 1802–1894. Hungarian nationalist and leader of the revolution of 1848. He proclaimed Hungary's independence of Hapsburg rule, became governor of a Hungarian republic 1849, and, when it was defeated by Austria and Russia, fled first to Turkey and then to exile in Britain and Italy.

Kosygin Alexei Nikolaievich 1904–1980. Soviet politician, prime minister 1964–80. He was elected to the Supreme Soviet 1938, became a member of the Politburo 1946, deputy prime minister 1960, and succeeded Khrushchev as premier (while Brezhnev succeeded him as party secretary). In the late 1960s Kosygin's influence declined.

koto Japanese musical instrument; a long zither of ancient Chinese origin, having 13 silk strings supported by movable bridges. It rests on the floor and the strings are plucked with ivory plectra, producing a brittle sound.

Kourou river and second-largest town of French Guiana, NW of Cayenne, site of the Guiana Space Center of the European Space Agency.

Situated near the equator, it is an ideal site for launches of satellites into ◊geosynchronous orbit.

Koussevitsky Serge 1874–1951. Russian musician and conductor, well known for his work in the US. He was trained at a conservatory in Moscow and became recognized as a virtuoso on the double bass. First appearing as a conductor in Berlin 1908, he established his own orchestra in Moscow in the following year and introduced works of Prokofiev, Rachmaninoff, and Stravinsky. Although named director of the State Symphony after the Bolshevik Revolution, Koussevitsky left the USSR, becoming director of the Boston Symphony Orchestra 1924.

In 1934 he founded the annual Tanglewood summer music festival in W Massachusetts.

Kovalevsky Sonja Vasilevna 1850–1891. Russian mathematician who received a doctorate from Göttingen University 1874 for her dissertation on partial differential equations. She was professor of mathematics at the University of Stockholm from 1884. In 1886 she won the Prix Bordin of the French Academy of Sciences for a paper on the rotation of a rigid body about a point, a problem the 18th-century mathematicians Euler and Lagrange had both failed to solve.

Kowloon peninsula on the Chinese coast forming part of the British crown colony of Hong Kong; the town of Kowloon is a residential area.

The walled city of Kowloon was created 1898, when Britain leased the New Territories from China: China reserved jurisdiction over a disused fort, a site of 6.5 acres/2.6 hectares, and although the UK did not recognize this, some legal anomalies remained (for example, criminals captured in the Walled City were until 1960 deported to China). Although it lacked running water and other amenities, the Walled City became the world's most densely populated area, with 33,000 residents in 1987 and 1,000 industrial and commercial enterprises. The wall was dismantled 1943. Its five hundred buildings of up to 14 floors are less than a meter apart. The Walled City was being cleared in 1991, to be torn down.

kph or **km/h** symbol for **kilometers per hour**.

Krafft-Ebing Baron Richard von 1840–1902. German pioneer psychiatrist and neurologist. He published *Psychopathia Sexualis* 1886.

Educated in Germany, Krafft-Ebing became professor of psychiatry at Strasbourg 1872. His special study was the little-understood relationship between minor paralysis and syphilis, a sexually transmitted disease.

Kragujevac garrison town and former capital (1818–39) of Serbia, Yugoslavia; population (1981) 165,000.

Krajina region on the frontier between Croatia and Bosnia-Herzegovina; the chief town is Knin. Dominated by Serbs, the region proclaimed itself an autonomous Serbian province after Croatia declared its independence from Yugoslavia 1991. Krajina was the scene of intense inter-ethnic fighting during the civil war in Croatia 1991–92 and, following the cease-fire Jan 1992, 10,000 UN troops were deployed here and in E and W Slavonia.

Krakatoa (Indonesian *Krakatau*) volcanic island in Sunda strait, Indonesia, that erupted 1883, causing 36,000 deaths on Java and Sumatra by the tidal waves that followed. The island is now uninhabited.

Kraków or **Cracow** city in Poland, on the river Vistula; population (1990) 750,500. It is an industrial center producing freight cars, paper, chemicals, and tobacco. It was capital of Poland c. 1300–1595.

Founded about 1400, its university, at which the astronomer ◊Copernicus was a student, is one of the oldest in central Europe. There is a 14th-century Gothic cathedral.

Krasnodar territory of SW Russia, in the N Caucasus, adjacent to the Black Sea; area 32,290 sq mi/83,600 sq km; population (1985) 4,992,000. The capital is Krasnodar. In addition to stock rearing and the production of grain, rice, fruit, and tobacco, oil is refined.

Krasnodar formerly **Ekaterinodar** (until 1920) industrial town at the head of navigation of the river Kuban, in SW Russia; population (1987) 623,000. It is linked by pipeline with the Caspian oil fields.

Krasnoyarsk industrial city (locomotives, paper, timber, cement, gold refining, and a large hydroelectric works) in central Siberian Russia; population (1987) 899,000. There is an early-warning and space-tracking radar phased array at nearby Abalakova.

See also ◊Novosibirsk.

Krasnoyarsk territory of Russia in central Siberia stretching north to the Arctic Ocean; area 927,617 sq mi/2,401,600 sq km; population (1985) 3,430,000. The capital is Krasnoyarsk. It is drained by the Yenisei River. Mineral resources include gold, graphite, coal, iron ore, and uranium.

Krebs Hans 1900–1981. German-born British biochemist who discovered the citric acid cycle, also known as the **Krebs cycle**, the final pathway by which food molecules are converted into energy in living tissues. For this work he shared with Fritz Lipmann the 1953 Nobel Prize for Medicine.

Krebs cycle or **citric acid cycle** or **tricarboxylic acid cycle** final part of the chain of biochemical reactions by which organisms break down food using oxygen to release energy (respiration). It takes place within structures called ◊mitochondria in the body's cells, and breaks down food molecules in a series of small steps, producing energy-rich molecules of ◊ATP.

Kreisler Fritz 1875–1962. Austrian violinist and composer, renowned as an interpreter of Brahms and Beethoven. From 1911 he was one of the earliest recording artists of Classical music, including records of his own compositions.

kremlin citadel or fortress of Russian cities. The Moscow kremlin dates from the 12th century, and the name "the Kremlin" was once synonymous with the Soviet government.

Krenek Ernst 1900– . Austrian-born composer. His jazz opera *Jonny spielt auf/Johnny plays up* 1927 received international acclaim.

He moved to the US 1939 and explored the implications of contemporary and Renaissance musical theories in a succession of works and theoretical writings.

krill any of several Antarctic crustaceans of the order Euphausiacea, the most common species being *Euphausia superba*. Shrimplike, it is about 2.5 in/6 cm long, with two antennae, five pairs of legs, seven pairs of light organs along the body, and is colored orange above and green beneath.

Moving in enormous swarms, krill constitute the chief food of the baleen whales, and have been used to produce a protein concentrate for human consumption, and meal for animal feed.

Krishna incarnation of the Hindu god ◊Vishnu. The devotion of the ◊bhakti movement is usually directed toward Krishna; an example of this is the ◊International Society for Krishna Consciousness. Many stories are told of Krishna's mischievous youth, and he is the charioteer of Arjuna in the *Bhagavad-Gītā*.

Krishna Menon Vengalil Krishnan 1897–1974. Indian politician who was a leading light in the Indian nationalist movement. He represented India at the United Nations 1952–62, and was defense minister 1957–62, when he was dismissed by Nehru following China's invasion of N India.

Kristallnacht "night of (broken) glass" 9–Nov 10, 1938 when the Nazi Sturmabteilung (SA) militia in Germany and Austria mounted a concerted attack on Jews, their synagogues, homes, and shops. It followed the assassination of a German embassy official in Paris by a Polish-Jewish youth. Subsequent measures included German legislation against Jews owning businesses or property, and restrictions on their going to school or leaving Germany. It was part of the ◊Holocaust.

More than 200,000 Jewish men were arrested and sent to concentration camps, and 91 Jews were killed during the Kristallnacht. The damage to property is estimated at 25 million marks.

Krivoi Rog (Russian "crooked horn") town in central Ukraine, 80 mi/130 km SW of Dnepropetrovsk; population (1987) 698,000. The surrounding district is rich in iron ore, and there is a metallurgical industry.

Kroeber Alfred Louis 1876–1960. US anthropologist. After establishing a department of anthropology at the University of California at Berkeley, he led archeological expeditions to New Mexico beginning 1915. In 1917 he became president of the American Anthropological Association, a group he helped found.

At Berkeley, Kroeber served as professor 1919–46 and anthropology museum director 1925–46. His extensive research into and analysis of the culture of the California, the Plains, Mexican, and South American Indians dramatically broadened the scope of anthropological studies. His textbook *Anthropology* 1923; 1948 remains a classic and influential work.

Born in Hoboken, New Jersey, Kroeber was the first student of Franz ◊Boas to receive a PhD from Columbia University 1901.

Kronstadt Russian naval base, founded by Peter the Great 1703, on Kotlin island, Gulf of Finland, commanding the sea approach to Leningrad, whose defense under siege 1941–43 was aided by its guns.

Kronstadt uprising revolt in March 1921 by sailors of the Russian Baltic Fleet at their headquarters in Kronstadt, outside Petrograd (now St Petersburg). On the orders of the leading Bolshevik, Leon Trotsky, Red Army troops, dressed in white camouflage, crossed the ice to the naval base and captured it on March 18. The leaders were subsequently shot.

Kropotkin Peter Alexeivich, Prince Kropotkin 1842–1921. Russian anarchist. Imprisoned for revolutionary activities 1874, he escaped to the UK 1876 and later moved to Switzerland. Expelled from Switzerland 1881, he went to France, where he was imprisoned 1883–86. He lived in Britain until 1917, when he returned to Moscow. Among his works are *Memoirs of a Revolutionist* 1899, *Mutual Aid* 1902, and *Modern Science and Anarchism* 1903.

Kropotkin was a noted geologist and geographer. In 1879 he launched an anarchist journal, *Le Révolté*. Unsympathetic to the Bolsheviks, he retired from politics after the Russian Revolution.

Kruger Stephanus Johannes Paulus 1825–1904. President of the Transvaal 1883–1900. He refused to remedy the grievances of the uitlanders (English and other non-Boer white residents) and so precipitated the Second ◊South African War.

Kruger National Park game reserve in NE Transvaal, South Africa, between the Limpopo and Crocodile rivers; it is the largest in the world (about 8,000 sq mi/20,720 sq km). The Sabie Game Reserve was established 1898 by President Kruger, and the park declared 1926.

Kruger telegram message sent by Kaiser Wilhelm II of Germany to President Kruger of the Transvaal Jan 3, 1896 congratulating him on defeating the ◊Jameson raid of 1895. The text of the telegram provoked indignation in Britain and elsewhere, and represented a worsening of Anglo-German relations, in spite of a German government retraction.

Krupp German steelmaking armaments firm, founded 1811 by **Friedrich Krupp** (1787–1826) and developed by **Alfred Krupp** (1812–1887) by pioneering the Bessemer steelmaking process. The company developed the long-distance artillery used in World War I, and supported Hitler's regime in preparation for World War II, after which the head of the firm, **Alfred Krupp** (1907–1967), was imprisoned.

krypton (Greek *kryptos* "hidden") colorless, odorless, gaseous, nonmetallic element, symbol Kr, atomic number 36, atomic weight 83.80. It is grouped with the inert gases and was long believed not to enter into reactions, but it is now known to combine with fluorine under certain conditions; it remains inert to all other reagents. It is present in very small quantities in the air (about 114 parts per million). It is used chiefly in fluorescent lamps, lasers, and gas-filled electronic valves.

Krypton was discovered 1898 in the residue from liquid air by British chemists William Ramsay and Morris Travers; the name refers to their difficulty in isolating it.

Kryukov Fyodor 1870–1920. Russian writer, alleged by Alexander ◊Solzhenitsyn to be the real author of *And Quiet Flows the Don* by Mikhail ◊Sholokhov.

KS abbreviation for the state of ◊*Kansas*.

Kuala Lumpur capital of the Federation of Malaysia; area 93 sq mi/240 sq km; population (1990) 1,237,900. The city developed after 1873 with the expansion of tin and rubber trading; these are now its main industries. Formerly within the state of Selangor, of which it was also the capital, it was created a federal territory 1974.

Kubelik Jan 1880–1940. Czech violinist and composer. He performed in Prague at the age of eight, and became one of the world's greatest virtuosos; he also wrote six violin concertos.

Kubelik Rafael 1914– . Czech conductor and composer, son of violinist Jan Kubelik. His works include symphonies and operas, such as *Veronika* 1947. He was musical director of the Royal Opera House, Covent Garden, London, 1955–58.

Kublai Khan 1216–1294. Mongol emperor of China from 1259. He completed his grandfather ◊Genghis Khan's conquest of N China from 1240, and on his brother Mungo's death 1259 established himself as emperor of China. He moved the capital to Beijing and founded the Yuan dynasty, successfully expanding his empire into Indochina, but was defeated in an attempt to conquer Japan 1281.

Kubrick Stanley 1928– . US-born British film director, producer, and screenwriter. His films include *Paths of Glory* 1957, *Dr Strangelove* 1964, *2001: A Space Odyssey* 1968, *A Clockwork Orange* 1971, and *The Shining* 1979.

More than any of his American contemporaries, Kubrick achieved complete artistic control over his films, which have been eclectic in subject matter and ambitious in both scale and technique. His other films include *Lolita* 1962 and *Full Metal Jacket* 1987.

kudu either of two species of African antelope of the genus *Tragelaphus*. The greater kudu *T. strepsiceros* is fawn-colored with thin white vertical stripes, and stands 4.2 ft/1.3 m at the shoulder, with head and body 8 ft/2.4 m long. Males have long spiral horns. The greater kudu is found in bush country from Angola to Ethiopia. The similar lesser kudu *T. imberbis* lives in E Africa and is 3 ft/1 m at the shoulder.

kudzu Japanese creeper *Pueraria lobata*, family Leguminosae, which helps fix nitrogen (see ◊nitrogen cycle) and can be used as fodder, but became a pest in the southern US when introduced to check soil erosion.

Kuhn Richard 1900–1967. Austrian chemist. Working at Heidelberg University in the 1930s, Kuhn succeeded in determining the structures of vitamins A, B_2, and B_6. He was awarded the 1938 Nobel Prize for Chemistry, but was unable to receive it until after World War II.

Kuhn Thomas S 1922– . US historian and philosopher of science, who showed that social and cultural conditions affect the directions of science. *The Structure of Scientific Revolutions* 1962 argued that even scientific knowledge is relative, dependent on the ◊*paradigm* (theoretical framework) that dominates a scientific field at the time.

Such paradigms (for example, Darwinism and Newtonian theory) are so dominant that they are uncritically accepted as true, until a "scientific revolution" creates a new orthodoxy. Kuhn's ideas have also influenced ideas in the social sciences.

Kuiper Gerard Peter 1905–1973. Dutch-born US astronomer who made extensive studies of the Solar System. His discoveries included the atmosphere of the planet Mars and that of Titan, the largest moon of the planet Saturn.

Kuiper was adviser to many NASA exploratory missions, and pioneered the use of telescopes on high-flying aircraft. The Kuiper Airborne Observatory, one such telescope, is named after him.

Ku Klux Klan US secret society dedicated to white supremacy, founded 1866 in the southern states of the US to oppose ◊Reconstruction after the American ◊Civil War and to deny political rights to the black population.

Members wore hooded white robes to hide their identity, and burned crosses at their night-time meetings. It was publicized in the 1960s for terrorizing civil-rights activists and organizing racist demonstrations.

It was originally headed by former Confederate general Nathan Bedford ◊Forrest and was disbanded in 1869 under pressure from members who opposed violence. Scattered groups continued a campaign of lynching and flogging, prompting anti-Klan laws in 1871. The group reemerged in 1915 as an antiblack, anti-Semitic, anti-Catholic, right-wing group that portrayed itself as fervently patriotic. Today the Klan has evolved into a paramilitary extremist group that has forged loose ties with other white supremacist groups.

Ku Klux Klan Case a US Supreme Court decision (*Ex parte Yarbrough*) 1884 dealing with federal enforcement of the 15th Amendment. Jasper Yarbrough, a Georgia Klansman, was convicted under the Enforcement Act 1870 of harassing a black voter. He appealed to the US Supreme Court on the grounds that the 15th Amendment grants only the right to vote; it does not give Congress the power to protect that right. The Court unanimously upheld the Enforcement Act, ruling that the federal government had legitimate power to protect citizens from racial discrimination in all circumstances surrounding voting in federal elections.

kulak Russian term for a peasant who could afford to hire labor and often acted as village usurer. The kulaks resisted the Soviet government's policy of collectivization, and in 1930 they were "liquidated as a class," with up to 5 million being either killed or deported to Siberia.

Kulturkampf German word for a policy introduced by Chancellor Bismarck in Germany 1873 that isolated the Catholic interest and attempted to reduce its power in order to create a political coalition of liberals and agrarian conservatives. The alienation of such a large section of the German population as the Catholics could not be sustained, and the policy was abandoned after 1876 to be replaced by an antisocialist policy.

Kumasi second largest city in Ghana, W Africa, capital of Ashanti region, with trade in cocoa, rubber, and cattle; population (1984) 376,200.

history From the late 17th century until 1901, when it was absorbed into the British Gold Coast Colony, Kumasi was capital of the Ashanti confederation.

Kumayri formerly (until 1990) *Leninakan*, town in Armenia, 25 m/40 km NW of Yerevan; population (1987) 228,000. Industries include textiles and engineering. It was founded 1837 as a fortress called Alexandropol. The city was virtually destroyed by an earthquake 1926 and again 1988.

kumquat small orange-yellow fruit of any of several evergreen trees of the genus *Fortunella*, family Rutaceae. Native to E Asia, kumquats are cultivated throughout the tropics. The tree grows 8–12 ft/2.4–3.6 m and has dark green shiny leaves and white scented flowers. The fruit is eaten fresh (the skin is edible), preserved, or candied. The oval or Nagami kumquat is the most common variety.

Kun Béla 1885–1938. Hungarian politician who created a Soviet republic in Hungary March 1919, which was overthrown Aug 1919 by a Western blockade and Romanian military actions. The succeeding regime under Admiral Horthy effectively liquidated both socialism and liberalism in Hungary.

Kundera Milan 1929– . Czech writer, born in Brno. His first novel, *The Joke* 1967, brought him into official disfavor in Prague, and, unable to publish further works, he moved to France. Other novels include *The Book of Laughter and Forgetting* 1979 and *The Unbearable Lightness of Being* 1984.

Kung (formerly *Bushman*) member of a small group of hunter-gatherer peoples of the NE Kalahari, southern Africa, still living to some extent nomadically. Their language belongs to the ♢Khoisan family.

kung fu Chinese art of unarmed combat (Mandarin *ch'üan fa*), one of the ♢martial arts. It is practiced in many forms, the most popular being *wing chun*, "beautiful springtime." The basic principle is to use attack as a form of defense.

Kuniyoshi Utagawa 1797–1861. Japanese printmaker. His series *108 Heroes of the Suikoden* depicts heroes of the Chinese classic novel *The Water Margin*. Kuniyoshi's dramatic, innovative style lent itself to warriors and fantasy, but his subjects also include landscapes and cats.

Kunlunshan mountain range on the edge of the great Tibetan plateau, China; 2,500 mi/4,000 km from east to west; highest peak Muztag (23,900 ft/7,282 m).

Kunming formerly *Yunnan* capital of Yunnan province, China, on Lake Dian Chi, about 6,500 ft/2,000 m above sea level; population (1989) 1,500,000. Industries include chemicals, textiles, and copper smelted with nearby hydroelectric power.

Kuomintang original spelling of the Chinese nationalist party, now known (outside Taiwan) as ♢Guomindang.

kurchatovium name proposed by Soviet scientists for the element currently known as ♢unnilquadium (atomic number 104), to honor Soviet nuclear physicist Igor Kurchatov (1903–1960).

Kurd member of the Kurdish culture, living mostly in the Taurus and Sagros mountains of W Iran and N Iraq in the region called Kurdistan. Although divided among more powerful states, the Kurds have nationalist aspirations; there are some 8 million in Turkey (where they suffer from discriminatory legislation), 5 million in Iran, 4 million in Iraq, 500,000 in Syria, and 500,000 in Azerbaijan, Armenia, and Georgia. Several million live elsewhere in Europe. Some 1 million Kurds were made homeless and 25,000 killed as a result of chemical-weapon attacks by Iraq 1984–89, and in 1991 more than 1 million were forced to flee their homes in N Iraq. The Kurdish languages (Kurmanji, Sorani Kurdish, Gurani, and Zaza) are members of the Indo-Iranian branch of the Indo-European family, and the Kurds are a non-Arab, non-Turkic ethnic group. The Kurds are predominantly Sunni Muslims, although there are some Shiites in Iran.

Kurds traditionally owe allegiance to their families, and larger groups are brought together under an agha, or lord. They are predominantly shepherds and farmers, cultivating a wide range of crops and fruit. National dress is still worn in the more mountainous regions and there is a strong tradition of poetry and music. Kurdish professionals are found in many Middle Eastern cities.

Kurdistan or *Kordestan* hilly region in SW Asia near Mount Ararat, where the borders of Iran, Iraq, Syria, Turkey, Armenia, and Azerbaijan meet; area 74,600 sq mi/193,000 sq km; total population around 18 million.

Kuria Muria group of five islands in the Arabian Sea, off the S coast of Oman; area 28 sq mi/72 sq km.

Kuril Islands or *Kuriles* chain of about 50 small islands stretching from the NE of Hokkaido, Japan, to the S of Kamchatka, Russia; area 5,700 sq mi/14,765 sq km; population (1990) 25,000. Some of them are of volcanic origin. Two of the Kurils (Etorofu and Kunashiri) are claimed by Japan and Russia.

The Kurils were discovered 1634 by a Russian navigator and were settled by Russians. Japan seized them 1875 and held them until 1945, when under the Yalta agreement they were returned to the USSR. Japan still claims the southernmost two (Etorofu and Kunashiri) and also the nearby small islands of Habomai and Shikotan (not part of the Kurils). The question of the S Kurils prevents signature of a Japanese-Russian peace treaty.

Kuropatkin Alexei Nikolaievich 1848–1921. Russian general. He distinguished himself as chief of staff during the Russo-Turkish War 1877–78, was commander in chief in Manchuria 1903, and resigned after his defeat at Mukden 1905 in the ♢Russo-Japanese War. During World War I he commanded the armies on the northern front until 1916.

Kurosawa Akira 1929– . Japanese director whose film *Rashōmon* 1950 introduced Western audiences to Japanese cinema. Epics such as *Shichinin no samurai/Seven Samurai* 1954 combine spectacle with intimate human drama.

The nostalgic and visionary *Yume/Dreams* 1990 has autobiographical elements. Kurosawa's films with a contemporary setting include *Drunken Angel* 1948 and *Ikiru/Living* 1952, both using illness as metaphor. *Yōjimbō* 1961, *Kagemusha* 1981, and *Ran* 1985

(loosely based on Shakespeare's *King Lear*) are historical films with an increasingly bleak outlook.

Kuroshio or *Japan Current* warm ocean ♢current flowing from Japan to North America.

Kursk capital city of Kursk region of W Russia; population (1987) 434,000. Industries include chemicals, machinery, alcohol, and tobacco. It dates from the 9th century.

Kūt-al-Imāra or *al Kūt* city in Iraq, on the river Tigris; population (1985) 58,600. It is a grain market and carpet-manufacturing center. In World War I it was under siege by Turkish forces from Dec 1915 to April 1916, when the British garrison surrendered.

Kutch, Rann of salt-marsh area in Gujarat state, India, that forms two shallow lakes (the **Great Rann** and the **Little Rann**) in the wet season and is a salt-covered desert in the dry. It takes its name from the former princely state of Kutch, which it adjoined. An international tribunal 1968 awarded 90% of the Rann of Kutch to India and 10% (about 300 sq mi/800 sq km) to Pakistan, the latter comprising almost all the elevated area above water the year round.

Kutuzov Mikhail Larionovich, Prince of Smolensk 1745–1813. Commander of the Russian forces in the Napoleonic Wars. He commanded an army corps at ♢Austerlitz and the army in its reatreat 1812. After the burning of Moscow that year, he harried the French throughout their retreat and later took command of the united Prussian armies.

Kuwait country in SW Asia, bounded N and NW by Iraq, E by the Persian Gulf, and S and SW by Saudi Arabia.

government The 1962 constitution was partly suspended by the emir 1976 and reinstated 1980. It vests executive power in the hands of the emir, who governs through an appointed prime minister and council of ministers. There is a single-chamber national assembly of 50 members, elected by restricted suffrage for a four-year term. Women do not have the vote. Political parties are not permitted and, despite the appearance of constitutional government, Kuwait is, in effect, a personal monarchy.

history The region was part of the Turkish ♢Ottoman Empire from the 16th century; the ruling family founded the sheikdom of Kuwait 1756. The ruler made a treaty with Britain 1899, enabling it to become a self-governing protectorate until it achieved full independence 1961.

discovery of oil Oil was first discovered 1938, and its large-scale exploitation began after 1945, transforming Kuwait City from a small fishing port into a thriving commercial center. The oil revenues have enabled ambitious public works and education programs to be undertaken. Sheik Abdullah al-Salem al-Sabah took the title of emir 1961 when he assumed full executive power. He died 1965 and was succeeded by his brother, Sheik Sabah al-Salem al-Sabah. He, in turn, died 1977 and was succeeded by Crown Prince Jabir, who appointed Sheik Saad al-Abdullah al-Salem al-Sabah as his heir apparent. In Jan 1990 prodemocracy demonstrations were dispersed by the police.

Kuwait used its considerable wealth not only to improve its infrastructure and social services but also attempting to secure its borders, making, for example, substantial donations to Iraq, which in the past had made territorial claims on it. It has also been a strong supporter of the Arab cause generally.

Iran–Iraq War During the 1980–88 Iran–Iraq War, Kuwait was the target of destabilization efforts by the revolutionary Iranian government. Some Shiites conducted a terrorist bombing campaign as part of an effort to incite the Shiite minority in Kuwait; 17 were arrested 1983 and their freedom was the demand in several hijacking incidents that followed. In 1987 Kuwait sought US protection for its tankers in the wake of attacks on Gulf shipping. Several Kuwaiti tankers were reflagged, and the US Navy conducted convoys through the Gulf. Iranian missiles also struck Kuwaiti installations, provoking fears of an expansion of the conflict. Kuwait released two of the convicted bombers Feb 1989.

Gulf War On Aug 2, 1990 President Saddam Hussein of Iraq reactivated the long-standing territorial dispute and invaded and occupied the country. The emir and most of his family escaped to Saudi Arabia. With more assets outside than in Kuwait, the government in exile was able to provide virtually unlimited financial support to Kuwaitis who had fled and to countries willing to help it regain its territory. On Feb 28, 1991, US-led coalition forces liberated Kuwait. By March 1991 peace negotiations began as part of the effort to restabilize the entire Middle East. In April 1991 the reshuffling of the cabinet provoked criticism from prodemocracy campaigners for leaving power in the hands of the Sabah family.

aftermath of the war About 600 oil wells were sabotaged by the occupying forces; smoke from burning oil created a pall over the whole country. Not until Nov 1991 was Kuwait able to extinguish all the oil-well fires set by the retreating Iraqis. International criticism of a Kuwaiti tribunal which sentenced 21 people to death for alledgedly collaborating with Iraq during the Gulf War resulted in the sentences being reduced to life imprisonment July 1991. Palestinian guest workers who had remained in Kuwait were subjected to reprisals by returning Kuwaitis for alleged collaboration with the Iraqis, and of 350,000 Palestinians in Kuwait before the invasion, only 80,000 remained in 1992. In Oct opposition candidates won a majority of seats in Kuwait's first national-assembly election since 1985. *See illustration box.*

Kuwait City (Arabic *Al Kuwayt*) formerly *Qurein* chief port and capital of the state of Kuwait, on the southern shore of Kuwait Bay; population (1985) 44,300, plus the suburbs of Hawalli, population (1985) 145,100, Jahra, population (1985) 111,200, and as-Salimiya, population (1985) 153,400. Kuwait is a banking and investment center. It was heavily damaged during the Gulf War.

Kuzbas (acronym for *Kuznetsk Basin*) industrial area in Kemerovo region, E Siberian Russia, lying on the Tom River north of the Altai Mountains. Development began in the 1930s. It takes its name from the old town of Kuznetsk.

Kuznets Simon 1901–1985. Russian-born economist who emigrated to the US 1922. He developed theories of national income and economic growth, used to forecast the future, in *Economic Growth of Nations* 1971. He won the Nobel Prize for Economics 1971.

Kuznetsov Anatoli 1930–1979. Russian writer. His novels *Babi Yar* 1966, describing the wartime execution of Jews at Babi Yar, near Kiev, and *The Fire* 1969, about workers in a large metallurgical factory, were seen as anti-Soviet. He lived in Britain from 1969.

kW symbol for ◊*kilowatt*.

Kwakiutl or *Kwa-Gulth* member of a North American Indian people who live on both sides of the northern entrance to the Queen Charlotte Strait in British Columbia. Their language belongs to the Wakashan family. They are one of the northwest-coast tribes famed for their potlatches, status festivals involving a lavish consumption, even destruction, of goods.

Kwa Ndebele black homeland in Transvaal province, South Africa; achieved self-governing status 1981; population (1985) 235,800.

Kwangchow alternative transliteration of Guangzhou, city in China.

Kwangchu or *Kwangju* capital of South Cholla province, SW South Korea; population (1990) 1,144,700. It is at the center of a rice-growing region. A museum in the city houses a large collection of Chinese porcelain dredged up 1976 after lying for over 600 years on the ocean floor.

Kwangsi-Chuang alternative transliteration of ◊Guangxi, region of China.

Kwangtung alternative transliteration of ◊Guangdong, province of China.

Kwannon or *Kannon* in Japanese Buddhism, a female form (known to the West as "goddess of mercy") of the bodhisattva ◊Avalokiteśvara. Kwannon is sometimes depicted with many arms extending compassion.

kwashiorkor severe protein deficiency in children under five years, resulting in retarded growth and a swollen abdomen.

Kwa Zulu black homeland in Natal province, South Africa; population (1985) 3,747,000. It achieved self-governing status 1971.

Kweichow alternative transliteration of ◊Guizhou, province of China.

Kweilin alternative transliteration of Guilin in China.

KY abbreviation for the state of ◊*Kentucky*.

kyanite aluminum silicate, Al_2SiO_5, a pale-blue mineral occurring as blade-shaped crystals. It is an indicator of high-pressure conditions in metamorphic rocks formed from clay sediments. Andalusite, kyanite, and sillimanite are all polymorphs.

Kyd Thomas c. 1557–1595. English dramatist, author in about 1588 of a bloody revenge tragedy, *The Spanish Tragedy*, which anticipated elements present in Shakespeare's *Hamlet*.

Kyoto former capital of Japan 794–1868 (when the capital was changed to Tokyo) on Honshu island, linked by canal with Biwa Lake; population (1989) 1,407,300. Industries include electrical, chemical, and machinery plants; silk weaving; and the manufacture of porcelain, bronze, and lacquerware.

features The city's more than 2,000 temples and shrines include Tō-ji (1380), Kiyomizu-dera (1633), Ryōan-ji with its 15th-century Zen rock and sand garden, Sanjusangendo (1266), and the former Ashikaga shoguns' villas Kinkaku-ji and Ginkaku-ji (the "gold and silver pavilions"). Other features are the Gion teahouse district with traditional geishas, the silk-weavers' district of Nishijin, 17th-century

---

Kuwait
State of (*Dowlat al Kuwait*)

area 6,878 sq mi/17,819 sq km
capital Kuwait (also chief port)
cities Jahra, Ahmadi, Fahaheel
physical hot desert; islands of Failaka, Bubiyan, and Warba at NE corner of Arabian Peninsula
environment during the Gulf War 1990–91, 650 oil wells were set alight and about 300,000 metric tons of oil were released into the waters of the Gulf leading to pollution haze, photochemical smog, acid rain, soil contamination, and water pollution
features there are no rivers and rain is light; the world's largest desalination plants, built in the 1950s
head of state and government Jabir al-Ahmad al-Jabir al-Sabah from 1977
political system absolute monarchy

political parties none
exports oil
currency Kuwaiti dinar
population (1990 est) 2,080,000 (Kuwaitis 40%, Palestinians 30%); growth rate 5.5% p.a.
life expectancy men 72, women 76 (1989)
languages Arabic 78%, Kurdish 10%, Farsi 4%
religion Sunni Muslim 45%, Shiite minority 30%
literacy 71% (1988)
GNP $19.1 bn; $10,410 per head (1988)
chronology
1914 Britain recognized Kuwait as an independent sovereign state.
1961 Full independence achieved from Britain, with Sheik Abdullah al-Salem al-Sabah as emir.
1965 Sheik Abdullah died; succeeded by his brother, Sheik Sabah.
1977 Sheik Sabah died; succeeded by Crown Prince Jabir.
1983 Shiite guerrillas bombed targets in Kuwait; 17 arrested.
1987 Kuwaiti oil tankers reflagged, received US Navy protection; missile attacks by Iran.
1988 Aircraft hijacked by pro-Iranian Shiites demanding release of convicted guerrillas; Kuwait refused.
1990 Prodemocracy demonstrations suppressed. Kuwait annexed by Iraq. Emir set up government in exile in Saudi Arabia.
1991 Feb: Kuwait liberated by US-led coalition forces; extensive damage to property and environment. New government omitted any opposition representatives. Trials of alleged Iraqi collaborators criticized.
1992 Oct: Opposition candidates win majority in national assembly elections.

Kyrgyzstan
Republic of

area 76,641 sq mi/198,500 sq km
capital Bishkek (formerly Frunze)
cities Osh, Przhevalsk, Kyzyl-Kiya, Tormak
physical mountainous, an extension of the Tian Shan range
head of state Askar Akayev from 1990
head of government Tursunbek Chyngyshev from 1991
political system emergent democracy
political party Democratic Kyrgyzstan, nationalist reformist; Asaba (Banner) Party and Free Kyrgyzstan Party, both opposition groupings
products cereals, sugar, cotton, coal, oil, sheep, yaks, horses
population (1990) 4,400,000 (52% Kyrgyz, 22% Russian, 13% Uzbek, 3% Ukrainian, 2% German)
language Kyrgyz, a Turkic language
religion Sunni Muslim
chronology
1917–1924 Part of an independent Turkestan republic.
1924 Became autonomous republic within USSR.
1936 Became full union republic within USSR.
1990 June: ethnic clashes resulted in state of emergency being imposed in Bishkek. Nov: Askar Akayev chosen as state president.
1991 March: Kyrgyz voters endorsed maintenance of Union in USSR referendum. Aug: President Akayev condemned anti-Gorbachev attempted coup in Moscow; Kyrgyz Communist Party, which supported the coup, suspended. Oct: Akayev directly elected president. Dec: joined new Commonwealth of Independent States (CIS) and independence recognized by US.
1992 Jan: admitted into Conference on Security and Cooperation in Europe (CSCE); March: became a member of the United Nations (UN).

sake warehouses in Fushimi, Momoyama castle, and Japan's oldest theater, the Minamiza kabuki theater (early 17th century).

history Like previous Japanese capitals, Kyoto was originally laid out in a grid pattern derived from China. Civil wars, especially that between the Taira and Minamoto clans in the 12th century and the Ōnin war 1467–77, caused great destruction in the capital, and it has been periodically ravaged by fire, most recently in 1864, when almost 80% of the city was laid waste. Although the shogunate was at times based elsewhere, Kyoto remained the seat of the imperial court until the Meiji restoration 1868, and is still a cultural center.

kyphosis exaggerated outward curve of the upper spine, resulting in a lump. It is usually due to spinal disease, arthritis, or bad posture.

Kyprianou Spyros 1932– . Cypriot politician, president 1977–88. Foreign minister 1961–72, he founded the federalist, center-left Democratic Front (DIKO) 1976.

Educated in Cyprus and the UK, he was called to the English Bar 1954. He became secretary to Archbishop Makarios in London 1952 and returned with him to Cyprus 1959. On the death of Makarios 1977 he became acting president and was then elected. He was defeated in the 1988 presidential elections.

Kyrgyzstan or *Kirghizia* country in central Asia, bounded N by Kazakhstan, E by China, W by Uzbekistan, and S by Tajikistan.

government There is a 350-member legislature, the supreme soviet, to which deputies are elected by a majority system, and a second-ballot runoff race in contests in which there is no clear first-round majority. The state president is directly elected for a five-year term, with a limit of two consecutive terms, and works with a cabinet whose head is effectively prime minister.

history Kyrgyzstan is peopled mainly by horse-breeding, mountain-dwelling nomads, the Turkic-speaking descendants of the Mongol invaders who swept across Asia from the 13th century. It was annexed by Russia in 1864. Part of an independent Turkestan republic 1917–24, it then became an autonomous republic within the USSR and, from 1936, a constituent Soviet republic.

anti-Gorbachev coup Long viewed as a bastion of conservatism, the republic overwhelmingly endorsed maintenance of the Union in the March 1991 USSR constitutional referendum and its Communist Party (CP) supported the Aug 1991 coup attempt against President Gorbachev in Moscow. However, Askar Akayev, a "reform communist" who had assumed the republic's presidency in Nov 1990, condemned the coup as unconstitutional. On Aug 28, 1991 he resigned from the Communist Party of the Soviet Union and ordered the suspension of the republic's CP and the nationalization of its property. After the coup was thwarted, Akayev was offered by Gorbachev, but declined to accept, the position of USSR vice-president. He was returned, unchallenged, as Kyrgyzstan's president on Oct 12, 1991 in what was the republic's first ever popular election.

independence and the end of communism Kyrgyzstan joined the ▷Commonwealth of Independent States (CIS) which was formed in Dec 1991. In the same month the US formally acknowledged Kyrgyzstan's independent status and accorded it diplomatic recognition. In Jan 1992 the republic was admitted into the ▷Conference on Security and Cooperation in Europe (CSCE) and in March into the United Nations (UN). It has been described as the "real center of democracy" within former Soviet Central Asia since its former CP is now completely destroyed and discredited. *See illustration box.*

Kyushu southernmost of the main islands of Japan, separated from Shikoku and Honshu by Bungo Channel and Suo Bay, but connected to Honshu by bridge and rail tunnel
area 16,270 sq mi/42,150 sq km, including about 370 small islands
capital Nagasaki
cities Fukuoka, Kumamoto, Kagoshima
physical mountainous, volcanic, with subtropical climate
features the active volcano Aso-take (5,225 ft/1,592 m), with the world's largest crater
products coal, gold, silver, iron, tin, rice, tea, timber
population (1986) 13,295,000.

Kyzyl-Kum desert in Kazakhstan and Uzbekistan, between the Sur-Darya and Amu-Darya rivers; area about 116,000 sq mi/300,000 sq km. It is being reclaimed for cultivation by irrigation and protective tree-planting.

L 12th letter of the English alphabet. The sound represented is one of the most stable in all languages, though in some languages it tends to be lost between a back vowel and a consonant, as in English *half, should*, and so on.

L Roman numeral for 50.

LA abbreviation for the state of ⟡*Louisiana*; *Los Angeles*.

Labanotation comprehensive system of accurate dance notation (*Kinetographie Laban*) devised 1928 by Rudolf von Laban (1879–1958), dancer, choreographer, and dance theorist.

labeled compound or *tagged compound* chemical compound in which a radioactive isotope is substituted for a stable one. The path taken by such a compound through a system can be followed, for example by measuring the radiation emitted.

This powerful and sensitive technique is used in medicine, chemistry, biochemistry, and industry.

labellum lower petal of an orchid flower; it is a different shape from the two lateral petals and gives the orchid its characteristic appearance. The labellum is more elaborate and usually larger than the other petals. It often has distinctive patterning to encourage ⟡pollination by insects; sometimes it is extended backward to form a hollow spur containing nectar.

Labiatae family of 3,000–4,000 species of flowering plants found worldwide. The stems are often quadrangular in sections, with leaves arranged in opposite pairs at right angles to the next pair. The plants are often covered with hairs and glands that emit an aromatic fragrance. Species include basil, marjoram, oregano, peppermint, salvia, and thyme.

Plants of this family have long been used by the food and pharmaceutical industries. They have a natural resistance to insects and in the 1990s were being exploited for the protection of other plants.

Labor Day legal national holiday in honor of workers. In Canada and the US, Labor Day is celebrated on the first Monday in September. In many countries it coincides with ⟡May Day.

Labor, Knights of in US history, a national labor organization founded by Philadelphia

tailor Uriah Stephens in 1869 and committed to cooperative enterprise, equal pay for both sexes, and an eight-hour day. The Knights grew rapidly in the mid-1880s under Terence V Powderly (1849–1924) but gave way to the ⟡American Federation of Labor after 1886.

labor market the market that determines the cost and conditions of the work force. This will depend on the demand of employers, the levels and availability of skills, and social conditions.

Labor Party in Australia, a political party based on socialist principles. It was founded in 1891 and first held office in 1904. It formed governments 1929–31 and 1939–49, but in the intervening periods internal discord provoked splits, and reduced its effectiveness. It returned to power under Gough Whitlam 1972–75, and again under Bob Hawke from 1983.

labor theory of value in Classical economics, the theory that the price (value) of a product directly reflects the amount of labor it involves. According to theory, if the price of a product falls, either the share of labor in that product has declined or that expended in the production of other goods has risen.

⟡Marx adopted and developed the theory but it was not supported by all Classical economists. ⟡Malthus was a dissenter.

labor union organization of employed workers formed to undertake collective bargaining with employers and to try to achieve improved working conditions for its members. Attitudes of government to unions and of unions to management vary greatly from country to country. Probably the most effective labor-union system is that of Sweden, and the most internationally known is the Polish ⟡Solidarity.

history labor unions of a kind existed in the Middle Ages as artisans' guilds, and combinations of wage earners were formed at the time of industrialization in the 18th century; but labor unions did not formally (or legally) come into existence in Britain until the Industrial Revolution in the 19th century. The early history of labor unions is one of illegality and of legislation to prevent their existence. *history, US* the great growth of US labor unionism, apart from the abortive Knights of Labor 1869–86 (see also ⟡American Federation of Labor), came in the post-Depression years. Employers and the US government have historically been more opposed to labor unionism than those in Britain, often using police and armed guards to harass pickets and protect strike breakers, which has led to episodes of violence and bitter confrontation. US legislation includes the Taft–Hartley Act 1947, which among other measures outlaws the closed shop. US unions have the reputation of being open to the acceptance of new techniques, taking a broad view of these as conducive to greater eventual prosperity. In Sweden, for example, conflicts of unions within an industry (demarcation disputes) are largely eliminated, and unions and employers cooperate freely.

labor unionism, international worldwide cooperation between unions. In 1973 a European Trade Union Confederation was established, membership 29 million, and there is an International Labor Organization, established 1919 and affiliated with the United Nations from 1945, which formulates standards for labor and social conditions. Other organizations are the International Confederation of Free Trade Unions (1949), including the American Federation of Labor and Congress of Industrial

Organizations, the UK Trades Union Congress, and the World Federation of Trade Unions (1945).

Labour Party UK political party based on socialist principles, originally formed to represent workers. It was founded in 1900 and first held office in 1924. The first majority Labour government 1945–51 introduced ⟡nationalization and the National Health Service, and expanded ⟡social security. Labour was again in power 1964–70 and 1974–79. The party leader is elected by Labour members of Parliament.

Labrador area of NE Canada, part of the province of Newfoundland, lying between Ungava Bay on the NW, the Atlantic Ocean on the E, and the Strait of Belle Isle on the SE; area 102,699 sq mi/266,060 sq km; population (1986) 28,741. It consists primarily of a gently sloping plateau with an irregular coastline of numerous bays, fjords, inlets, and cliffs (200 ft/60 m to 400 ft/120 m high). Industries include fisheries, timber and pulp, and many minerals. Hydroelectric resources include Churchill Falls on Churchill River, where one of the world's largest underground power houses is situated.

The Canadian Air Force base in Goose Bay is on land claimed by the Innu (or Montagnais-Naskapi) Indian people, who call themselves a sovereign nation (in 1989 they numbered 9,500).

La Bruyère Jean de 1645–1696. French essayist. He was born in Paris, studied law, took a post in the revenue office, and in 1684 entered the service of the French commander the Prince of ⟡Condé. His *Caractères* 1688, satirical portraits of his contemporaries, made him many enemies.

Labuan flat, wooded island off NW Borneo, a Federal Territory of East Malaysia; area 39 sq mi/100 sq km; population (1980) 12,000. Its chief port city is Victoria, population 3,200. Labuan was ceded to Great Britain in 1846, and from 1963 it was included in Sabah, a state of the Federation of Malaysia.

laburnum any flowering tree or shrub of the genus *Laburnum* of the pea family Leguminosae. The seeds are poisonous. *L. anagyroides*, native to the mountainous parts of central Europe, is often grown as an ornamental tree. The flowers, in long drooping clusters, are bright yellow and appear in early spring; some varieties have purple or reddish flowers.

Labyrinth in Greek mythology, the maze designed by the Athenian artisan Daedalus at Knossos in Crete for King Minos as a home for the Minotaur, a monster, half man and half bull. After killing the Minotaur, Theseus, the prince of Athens, was guided out of the Labyrinth by a thread given to him by the king's daughter, Ariadne.

lac resinous incrustation exuded by the female of the lac insect *Laccifer lacca*, which eventually covers the twigs of trees in India and the Far East. The gathered twigs are known as stick lac, and yield a useful crimson dye; shellac, which is used in varnishes, polishes, and leather dressings, is manufactured commercially by melting the separated resin and spreading it into thin layers or flakes.

Laccadive, Minicoy, and Amindivi Islands former name of Indian island group ⟡Lakshadweep.

laccolith intruded mass of igneous rock that forces apart two strata and forms a round lens-shaped mass many times wider than thick. The overlying layers are often pushed upward to form a dome. A classic development of laccoliths is illustrated in the Henry La Sal and Abajo mountains of SE Utah, found on the Colorado plateau.

lace delicate, decorative, openwork textile fabric. Lace is a European craft with centers in Belgium, Italy, France, Germany, and England.

Needlepoint or *point* lace (a development of embroidery) originated in Italy in the late 15th or early 16th centuries. Lace was first made from linen thread and sometimes also with gold, silver, or silk; cotton, wool, and synthetic fibers have been used more recently.

Bobbin or *pillow* ("true") lace is made by twisting threads together in pairs or groups, according to a pattern marked out by pins set in a cushion. It is said to have been invented by Barbara Uttmann (born 1514) of Saxony; elaborate patterns may require over a thousand bobbins.

lacewing insect of the families Hemerobiidae (the brown lacewings) and Chrysopidae (the green lacewings) of the order Neuroptera. Found throughout the world, lacewings are so called because of the intricate veining of their two pairs of semitransparent wings. They have narrow bodies and long thin antennae. The larvae (called aphid lions) are predators, especially on aphids.

The eggs of the golden-eye lacewing *Chrysopa aculata* are laid on the ends of plant stalks.

Lachish ancient city SW of Jerusalem, destroyed 589 BC. Inscribed pottery fragments found there have thrown light on Hebrew manuscripts and the early development of the alphabet.

La Condamine Charles Marie de 1701–1774. French soldier and geographer who was sent by the French Academy of Sciences to Peru 1735–43 to measure the length of an arc of the meridian. On his return journey he traveled the length of the Amazon, writing about the use of the nerve toxin curare, india rubber, and the advantages of inoculation.

lacquer waterproof resinous varnish obtained from Oriental trees *Toxicodendron verniciflua*, and used for decorating furniture and art objects. It can be applied to wood, fabric, leather, or other materials, with or without added colors. The technique of making and carving small lacquerwork objects was developed in China, probably as early as the 4th century BC, and was later adopted in Japan.

La Crosse city in SW Wisconsin, at the confluence of the Black, La Crosse, and Mississippi rivers, NW of Madison; seat of La Crosse County. The processing and marketing center for the area's agricultural products, it also manufactures plastics, rubber products, and electrical machinery; population (1990) 51,000. The city began as a French trading post and grew as a lumber town.

lacrosse Canadian ball game, adopted from the North American Indians, and named after a fancied resemblance of the lacrosse stick (crosse) to a bishop's crosier. Thongs across the curved end of the crosse form a pocket to carry the small rubber ball.

The field is approximately 110 yd/100 m long and a minimum of 60 yd/55 m wide in the men's game, which is played with ten players per side; the women's field is larger, and there are twelve players per side. The goals are just

under 6 ft/2 m square, with loose nets. The world championship were first held in 1967 for men, and in 1969 for women.

lactation secretion of milk from the mammary glands of mammals. In late pregnancy, the cells lining the lobules inside the mammary glands begin extracting substances from the blood to produce milk. The supply of milk starts shortly after birth with the production of colostrum, a clear fluid consisting largely of water, protein, antibodies, and vitamins. The production of milk continues practically as long as the infant continues to suck.

lactic acid or *2-hydroxypropanoic acid* $CH_3CHOHCOOH$ organic acid, a colorless, almost odorless liquid, produced by certain bacteria during fermentation and by active muscle cells when they are exercised hard and are experiencing ◊oxygen debt. It occurs in yogurt, buttermilk, sour cream, poor wine, and certain plant extracts, and is used in food preservation and in the preparation of pharmaceuticals.

lactose white sugar, found in solution in milk; it forms 5% of cow's milk. It is commercially prepared from the whey obtained in cheesemaking. Like table sugar (sucrose), it is a disaccharide, consisting of two basic sugar units (monosaccharides), in this case, glucose and galactose. Unlike sucrose, it is tasteless.

Ladakh subsidiary range of the ◊Karakoram mountains and district of NE Kashmir, India, on the border of Tibet; chief town Leh. After China occupied Tibet in 1951, it made claims on the area.

Ladd Alan 1913–1964. US actor whose first leading role, as the professional killer in *This Gun for Hire* 1942, made him a star. His career declined after the mid-1950s although his last role, in *The Carpetbaggers* 1964, is considered one of his best. His other films include *The Blue Dahlia* 1946 and *Shane* 1953.

Ladin member of an ethnic community (numbering about 16,000) in the Dolomites, S Tyrol, Austria, whose language (Ladin) derives directly from Latin; they may be descended from the Etruscans and other early Italian tribes. They have links with the speakers of ◊Romansch in Switzerland.

Ladoga (Russian *Ladozhskoye*) largest lake on the continent of Europe, in Russia, just NE of St Petersburg; area 7,100 sq mi/18,400 sq km. It receives the waters of several rivers, including the Svir, which drains Lake Onega and runs to the Gulf of Finland by the river Neva.

ladybird or *ladybug* beetle of the family Coccinellidae, generally red or yellow in color, with black spots. There are numerous species which, as larvae and adults, feed on aphids and scale-insect pests.

Laënnec René Théophile Hyacinthe 1781–1826. French physician, inventor of the ◊stethoscope 1814. He introduced the new diagnostic technique of auscultation (evaluating internal organs by listening with a stethoscope) in his book *Traité de l'auscultation médiaté* 1819, which quickly became a medical classic.

Lafarge John 1835–1910. US painter and ecclesiastical designer. He is credited with the revival of stained glass in America and also created woodcuts, watercolors, and murals. Lafarge visited Europe in 1856 and the Far East in 1886. In the 1870s he turned from landscape painting (inspired by the French painter

Jean-Baptiste-Camille ◊Corot) to religious and still-life painting. Decorating the newly built Trinity Church in Boston, Massachusetts, he worked alongside the sculptor Augustus Saint-Gaudens.

Lafayette city in W central Indiana, on the Wabash River, NW of Indianapolis, seat of Tippecanoe County; population (1990) 43,760. A distribution center for the area's agricultural products, its industries also include building materials, chemicals, wire, pharmaceuticals, and automobile parts. Purdue University 1865 is nearby. The Battle of Tippecanoe was fought here 1811.

Lafayette city in S Louisiana, on the Vermilion River, W of New Orleans and SW of Baton Rouge; seat of Lafayette Parish. Its economy centers around the area's oil industry; population (1990) 94,440. Settled by Acadians from Nova Scotia in the late 1700s, Lafayette is in the heart of the area of Louisiana that is associated with French-speaking "Cajuns."

Lafayette Marie Joseph Gilbert de Motier, Marquis de Lafayette 1757–1834. French soldier and politician. He fought against Britain in the American Revolution 1777–79 and 1780–82. During the French Revolution he sat in the National Assembly as a constitutional royalist and in 1789 presented the Declaration of the Rights of Man. After the storming of the ◊Bastille, he was given command of the National Guard. In 1792 he fled the country after attempting to restore the monarchy and was imprisoned by the Austrians until 1797. He supported Napoleon Bonaparte in 1815, sat in the chamber of deputies as a Liberal from 1818, and played a leading part in the revolution of 1830.

He was a popular hero in the US, and the cities of Lafayette in Louisiana and Indiana are named after him, as was the Lafayette Escadrille—American aviators flying for France during World War I, before the US entered 1917.

Lafayette Marie-Madeleine, Comtesse de Lafayette 1634–1693. French author. Her *Mémoires* of the French court are keenly observed, and her *La Princesse de Clèves* 1678 is the first French psychological novel and *roman à clef* ("novel with a key"), in that real-life characters (including the writer François de ◊La Rochefoucauld, who was for many years her lover) are presented under fictitious names.

Lafitte Jean c. 1780–c. 1825. Pirate. Reportedly born in France, Lafitte settled in New Orleans, where he became a smuggler and privateer. Gathering a band of followers around him, he set up headquarters in nearby Barataria Bay. After several years of raiding Spanish shipping in the Gulf of Mexico, he was suspected of complicity with the British and was attacked by American forces soon after the outbreak of the War of 1812. He proved his loyalty to General Andrew Jackson in 1815 by his heroic participation in the Battle of New Orleans. After the war Lafitte established headquarters in Galveston Bay.

La Follette Robert Marion 1855–1925. US political leader. As a US senator 1906–25, La Follette became a leader of the national progressive movement, running for president on the Progressive ticket 1924. His memoirs, *Autobiography, A Personal Narrative of Political Experiences*, appeared in 1913.

Born in Primrose, Wisconsin, La Follette was educated at the state university and was admitted to the bar 1880. Entering politics, he served as district attorney 1880–94 and as a member of the US House of Representatives 1885–91. He was defeated for reelection to Congress 1890 and was elected Wisconsin governor 1900.

La Fontaine Jean de 1621–1695. French poet. He was born at Château-Thierry, and from 1656 lived largely in Paris, the friend of the playwrights Molière and Racine, and the poet Boileau. His works include *Fables* 1668–94 and *Contes* 1665–74, a series of witty and bawdy tales in verse.

Laforgue Jules 1860–1887. French poet who pioneered ◊free verse and who inspired later French and English writers.

lagan legal term for wreckage lying on the ocean floor. See ◊flotsam, jetsam, and lagan.

Lagash Sumerian city N of Shatra, Iraq, under independent and semiindependent rulers from about 3000–2700 BC. Besides objects of high artistic value, it has provided about 30,000 clay tablets giving detailed information on temple administration. Lagash was discovered in 1877 and excavated by Ernest de Sarzec, then French consul in Basra.

lager type of light ◊beer.

Lagerkvist Pär 1891–1974. Swedish author of lyric poetry, dramas (including *The Hangman* 1935), and novels, such as *Barabbas* 1950. He was awarded the 1951 Nobel Prize for Literature.

Lagerlöf Selma 1858–1940. Swedish novelist. Her first work was the romantic historical novel *Gösta Berling's Saga* 1891. The children's fantasy *Nils Holgerssons underbara resa/The Wonderful Voyage of Nils Holgersson* 1906–07 grew from her background as a schoolteacher. She was the first woman to receive a Nobel Prize, in 1909.

lagoon coastal body of shallow salt water, usually with limited access to the sea. The term is normally used to describe the shallow sea area cut off by a ◊coral reef or barrier islands.

Lagos chief port and former capital of Nigeria, located at the western end of an island in a lagoon and linked by bridges with the mainland via Iddo Island; population (1983) 1,097,000. Industries include chemicals, metal products, and fish. One of the most important slaving ports, Lagos was bombarded and occupied by the British 1851, becoming the colony of Lagos 1862. Abuja was established as the new capital 1982.

Lagrange Joseph Louis 1736–1813. French mathematician. His *Mécanique analytique* 1788 applied mathematical analysis, using principles established by Newton, to such problems as the movements of planets when affected by each other's gravitational force. He presided over the commission that introduced the metric system in 1793.

Lagrangian points five locations in space where the centrifugal and gravitational forces of two bodies neutralize each other; a third, less massive body located at any one of these points will be held in equilibrium with respect to the other two. Three of the points, L1–L3, lie on a line joining the two large bodies. The other two points, L4 and L5, which are the most stable, lie on either side of this line. Their existence was predicted in 1772 by Joseph Louis Lagrange.

The *Trojan asteroids* lie at Lagrangian points L4 and L5 in Jupiter's orbit around the Sun. Clouds of dust and debris may lie at the Lagrangian points of the Moon's orbit around the Earth.

La Guardia Fiorello (Henrico) 1882–1947. US Republican politician; congressman 1917, 1919, 1923–33; mayor of New York 1933–45. Elected against the opposition of the powerful Tammany Hall Democratic Party organization, he improved the administration, suppressed racketeering, and organized unemployment relief, slum-clearance schemes, and social services. Although nominally a Republican, he supported the Democratic president F D Roosevelt's ◊New Deal. La Guardia Airport, in New York City, is named after him.

Lahnda language spoken by 15–20 million people in Pakistan and N India. It is closely related to Punjabi and Romany, and belongs to the Indo-Iranian branch of the Indo-European language family.

Lahore capital of the province of Punjab and second city of Pakistan; population (1981) 2,920,000. Industries include engineering, textiles, carpets, and chemicals. It is associated with the Mogul rulers Akbar, Jahangir, and Aurangzeb, whose capital it was in the 16th and 17th centuries.

Lailat ul-Isra Wal Mi'raj Muslim festival that celebrates the prophet Mohammed's ◊Night Journey.

Laing R(onald) D(avid) 1927–1989. Scottish psychoanalyst, originator of the "social theory" of mental illness, for example that schizophrenia is promoted by family pressure for its members to conform to standards alien to themselves. His books include *The Divided Self* 1960 and *The Politics of the Family* 1971.

laissez faire (French "let alone") theory that the state should not intervene in economic affairs, except to break up a monopoly. The phrase originated with the Physiocrats, 18th-century French economists whose maxim was *laissez faire et laissez passer*, (literally, "let go and let pass"—that is, leave the individual alone and let commodities circulate freely). The degree to which intervention should take place is still one of the chief problems of economics. The Scottish economist Adam ◊Smith justified the theory in *The Wealth of Nations*.

Before the 17th century, control by guilds, local authorities, or the state, of wages, prices, employment, and the training of workmen, was taken for granted. As capitalist enterprises developed in the 16th and 17th centuries, entrepreneurs shook off the control of the guilds and local authorities. By the 18th century this process was complete. The reaction against laissez faire began in the mid-19th century and found expression in the factory acts and elsewhere. This reaction was inspired partly by humanitarian protests against the social conditions created by the ◊Industrial Revolution and partly by the wish to counter popular unrest of the 1830s and 1840s by removing some of its causes.

In general the 20th century has seen an increasing degree of state intervention to promote social goals. Environment, safety, and antidiscrimination regulations have been imposed on businesses in some countries, in addition to campaigns to foster corporate responsibility.

A far-reaching program of ◊deregulation was instituted from 1980 by President Reagan as part of an effort to return to a more laissez-faire system.

lake body of still water lying in depressed ground without direct communication with the sea. Lakes are common in formerly glaciated

regions, along the courses of slow rivers, and in low land near the sea. The main classifications are by origin: **glacial lakes**, formed by glacial scouring; **barrier lakes**, formed by landslides and glacial moraines; **crater lakes**, found in volcanoes; and **tectonic lakes**, occurring in natural fissures.

Most lakes are freshwater, such as the Great Lakes in North America, but in hot regions where evaporation is excessive they may contain many salts, the Dead Sea is an example. In the 20th century large artificial lakes have been created in connection with hydroelectric and other works. Some lakes have become polluted as a result of human activity. Sometimes ◊eutrophication (a state of overnourishment) occurs, when agricultural fertilizers leaching into lakes cause an explosion of aquatic life, which then depletes the lake's oxygen supply until it is no longer able to support life.

Lake Veronica. Adopted name of Constance Frances Marie Ockelman 1919–1973. US film actress who was almost as celebrated for her much imitated "peekaboo" hairstyle as for her acting. She co-starred with Alan Ladd in several films during the 1940s, including *This Gun for Hire* and *The Glass Key* both 1942, and *The Blue Dahlia* 1946. She also appeared in *Sullivan's Travels* 1942 and *I Married a Witch* 1942.

Lake Charles city in SW Louisiana, on the Calcasieu River, SW of Baton Rouge, seat of Calcasieu Parish. It is a port of entry on the Gulf of Mexico via a deep-water channel in the Calcasieu River. Most of the city's industries are related to the area's oil and gas resources and major crop, rice; population (1990) 70,580.

Lake District region in Cumbria, England; area 700 sq mi/1,800 sq km. It contains the principal English lakes, which are separated by wild uplands rising to many peaks, including Scafell Pike (3,210 ft/978 m).

The Lake District has associations with the writers Wordsworth, Coleridge, Southey, De Quincey, Ruskin, and Beatrix Potter and was made a national park in 1951.

lake dwelling prehistoric village built on piles driven into the bottom of a lake. Such villages are found throughout Europe, in W Africa, South America, Borneo, and New Guinea.

Lake Havasu City town in Arizona, developed as a tourist resort. Old London Bridge was transported and reconstructed there in 1971.

Lakeland city in W central Florida, NE of Tampa and SW of Orlando, in the lake region and citrus belt; population (1990) 70,576. It serves as a center for the area's citrus products, but its economy depends mainly on its reputation as a winter resort.

Lakshadweep group of 36 coral islands, 10 inhabited, in the Indian Ocean, 200 mi/320 km off the Malabar coast; area 12 sq mi/32 sq km; population (1991) 51,700. The administrative headquarters is on Kavaratti Island. Products include coir, copra, and fish. The religion is Muslim. The first Western visitor was Vasco da Gama in 1499. The islands were British from 1877 until Indian independence and were created a Union Territory of the Republic of India 1956. Formerly known as the Laccadive, Minicoy, and Amindivi Islands, they were renamed Lakshadweep 1973.

Lalique René 1860–1945. French designer and manufacturer of ◊Art Nouveau glass, jewelry, and house interiors. The Lalique factory continues in production at Wingen-sur-Moder, Alsace, under his son Marc and granddaughter Marie-Claude.

major lakes

name and location	sq km	sq mi
Caspian Sea (Azerbaijan/Russia/Kazakhstan/Turkmenistan/Iran)	370,990	143,240
Superior (US/Canada)	82,071	31,700
Victoria (Tanzania/Kenya/Uganda)	69,463	26,820
Aral Sea (Kazakhstan/Uzbekistan)	64,500	24,904
Huron (US/Canada)	59,547	23,000
Michigan (US)	57,735	22,300
Tanganyika (Malawi/Zaire/Zambia/Burundi)	32,880	12,700
Baikal (Russia)	31,456	12,150
Great Bear (Canada)	31,316	12,096
Malawi (Tanzania/Malawi/Mozambique)	28,867	11,150
Great Slave (Canada)	28,560	11,031
Erie (US/Canada)	25,657	9,910
Winnipeg (Canada)	25,380	9,417
Ontario (US/Canada)	19,547	7,550
Balkhash (Kazakhstan)	18,421	7,115
Ladoga (Russia)	17,695	6,835
Chad (Chad/Niger/Nigeria)	16,310	6,300
Maracaibo (Venezuela)	13,507	5,217

Lalo (Victor Antoine) Edouard 1823–1892. French composer. His Spanish ancestry and violin training are evident in the *Symphonie Espagnole* 1873 for violin and orchestra, and *Concerto for cello and orchestra* 1877. He also wrote an opera, *Le Roi d'Ys* 1887.

Lam Wilfredo 1902–1982. Cuban abstract painter. Influenced by Surrealism in the 1930s (he lived in Paris 1937–41), he created a semiabstract style using mysterious and sometimes menacing images and symbols, mainly taken from Caribbean tradition. His *Jungle* series, for example, contains voodoo elements. He visited Haiti and Martinique in the 1940s, Paris 1952, and also made frequent visits to Italy.

Lamaism religion of Tibet and Mongolia, a form of Mahāyāna Buddhism. Buddhism was introduced into Tibet in AD 640, but the real founder of Lamaism was the Indian missionary Padma Sambhava who began his activity about 750. The head of the church is the ⇔Dalai Lama, who is considered an incarnation of the Bodhisattva Avalokiteśvara. On the death of the Dalai Lama great care is taken in finding the infant in whom he has been reincarnated.

In the 15th century Tsongkhapa founded the sect of Geluk-Pa (virtuous), which has remained the most powerful organization in the country. The Dalai Lama, residing at the palace of Potala in Lhasa, exercised both spiritual and temporal authority as head of the Tibetan state until 1959, aided by the ⇔Panchen Lama.

Before Chinese Communist rule, it was estimated that one in four of Tibet's male population was a Lamaist monk, but now their numbers are greatly reduced. Prayer-wheels and prayer-flags, on which were inscribed prayers, were formerly a common sight in the Tibetan countryside; when these were turned by hand or moved by the wind, great spiritual benefit was supposed to accrue.

La Mancha (Arabic *al mansha* "the dry land") former province of Spain now part of the autonomous region of ⇔Castilla-La Mancha. The fictional travels of Cervantes's *Don Quixote de la Mancha* 1605 begin there.

Lamar Lucius Quintus Cincinnatus 1825–1893. US public official and Supreme Court justice. Lamar was a member of the US Senate 1877–85, served as President Cleveland's secretary of the interior 1885–87, and sat on the US Supreme Court 1888–93.

Born in Elbert County, Georgia, and educated at Emory College, Lamar was admitted to the bar 1847. After teaching at the University of Mississippi, he was elected to the US House of Representatives, serving 1857–60. During the American Civil War he served briefly in the Confederate army and was named Confederate envoy to Russia. After the war he returned to the University of Mississippi and sat in the US House of Representatives 1873–77.

Lamarck Jean Baptiste de 1744–1829. French naturalist whose theory of evolution, known as **Lamarckism**, was based on the idea that acquired characteristics (changes acquired in an individual's lifetime) are inherited, and that organisms have an intrinsic urge to evolve into better-adapted forms. His works include *Philosophie Zoologique/Zoological Philosophy* 1809 and *Histoire naturelle des animaux sans vertèbres/Natural History of Invertebrate Animals* 1815–22.

Lamartine Alphonse de 1790–1869. French poet. He wrote romantic poems, including *Méditations poétiques* 1820, followed by *Nouvelles méditations/New Meditations* 1823, and *Harmonies* 1830. His *Histoire des Girondins/History of the Girondins* 1847 helped to inspire the revolution of 1848.

Lamb Charles 1775–1834. English essayist and critic. He collaborated with his sister **Mary Lamb** (1764–1847) on *Tales from Shakespeare* 1807, and his *Specimens of English Dramatic Poets* 1808 helped to revive interest in Elizabethan plays. As "Elia" he contributed essays to the *London Magazine* from 1820 (collected 1823 and 1833).

Born in London, Lamb was educated at Christ's Hospital. He was a contemporary of ⇔Coleridge, with whom he published some poetry in 1796. He was a clerk at India House 1792–1825, when he retired to Enfield. His sister Mary stabbed their mother to death in a fit of insanity in 1796, and Charles cared for her between her periodic returns to an asylum.

Lamb Willis 1913– . US physicist who revised the quantum theory of Paul ⇔Dirac. The hydrogen atom was thought to exist in either of two distinct states carrying equal energies. More sophisticated measurements by Lamb in 1947 demonstrated that the two energy levels were not equal. This discrepancy, since known as the **Lamb shift** won him the 1955 Nobel Prize for Physics.

lambert unit of luminance (the light shining from a surface), equal to one ⇔lumen per square centimeter. In scientific work the ⇔candela per square meter is preferred.

lamina in flowering plants (⇔angiosperms), the blade of the ⇔leaf on either side of the midrib. The lamina is generally thin and flattened, and is usually the primary organ of ⇔photosynthesis. It has a network of veins through which water and nutrients are conducted. More generally, a lamina is any thin, flat plant structure, such as the ⇔thallus of many seaweeds.

lammergeier Old World vulture *Gypaetus barbatus*, also known as the bearded vulture, with a wingspan of 9 ft/2.7 m. It ranges over S Europe, N Africa, and Asia, in wild mountainous areas. It feeds on offal and carrion and drops bones onto rocks to break them and so get at the marrow.

Lampedusa Giuseppe Tomasi di 1896–1957. Italian aristocrat, author of *The Leopard* 1958, a novel set in his native Sicily during the period following its annexation by Garibaldi in 1860. It chronicles the reactions of an aristocratic family to social and political upheavals.

lamprey any of various eel-shaped jawless fishes belonging to the family Petromyzontidae. A lamprey feeds on other fish by fixing itself by its round mouth to its host and boring into the flesh with its toothed tongue. Lampreys breed in fresh water, and the young live as larvae for about five years before migrating to the sea.

Lancashire county in NW England
area 1,173 sq mi/3,040 sq km
cities Preston (administrative headquarters), which forms part of Central Lancashire New Town (together with Fulwood, Bamber Bridge, Leyland, and Chorley); Lancaster, Accrington, Blackburn, Burnley; ports Fleetwood and Heysham; seaside resorts Blackpool, Morecambe, and Southport
features the river Ribble; the Pennines; Forest of Bowland (moors and farming valleys); Pendle Hill
products formerly a world center of cotton manufacture, now replaced with high-technology aerospace and electronics industries
population (1991) 1,365,100.

Lancaster city in Pennsylvania, 70 mi/115 km W of Philadelphia; population (1990) 55,550. It produces textiles and electrical goods. It was capital of the US briefly in 1777, and was the state capital 1799–1812.

Lancaster Burt (Burton Stephen) 1913– . US movie actor, formerly an acrobat. A star from his first film, *The Killers* 1946, he proved himself adept both at action roles and more complex character parts as in such films as *From Here to Eternity* 1953, *The Rose Tattoo* 1955, *Elmer Gantry* 1960, and *The Leopard/Il Gattopardo* 1963.

He was one of the first stars to produce, forming Hecht-Hill-Lancaster. His later films include *The Swimmer* and *Atlantic City*.

Lancaster House Agreement accord reached at a conference held in Sept 1979 at Lancaster House, London, between Britain and representative groups of Rhodesia, including the Rhodesian government under Ian Smith and black nationalist groups. The Agreement enabled a smooth transition to the independent state of Zimbabwe in 1980.

Lancaster, House of English royal house, a branch of the Plantagenets.

It originated in 1267 when Edmund (died 1296), the younger son of Henry III, was granted the earldom of Lancaster. Converted to a duchy for Henry of Grosmont (died 1361), it passed to John of Gaunt in 1362 by his marriage to Blanche, Henry's daughter. John's son, Henry IV, established the royal dynasty of Lancaster in 1399, and he was followed by two more Lancastrian kings, Henry V and Henry VI.

lancelet any one of a variety of marine animals of subphylum cephalocordates (see ⟡chordate), genus *Amphioxus*, about 1 in/ 2.5 cm long. It has no skull, brain, eyes, heart, vertebral column, centralized brain, nor paired limbs, but there is a notochord (a supportive rod) which runs from end to end of the body, a tail, and a number of gill slits. Found in all seas, it burrows in the sand but when disturbed swims freely.

Lancelot of the Lake in British legend, one of King Arthur's knights, the lover of Queen Guinevere. Originally a folk hero, he first appeared in the Arthurian cycle of tales in the 12th century.

Lanchow alternative transcription of ⟡Lanzhou, city in China.

Land (plural *Länder*) federal state of Germany or Austria.

Land Edwin Herbert 1909–1991. US inventor of the Polaroid Land camera 1947, which developed the film in one minute inside the camera and produced an "instant" photograph.

While a student at Harvard, Land became interested in polarized light and invented the sheet polarizer, which imbedded lined-up crystals in a clear plastic sheet. This tremendous advance had implications for camera filters, sunglasses and other optical equipment, and related products. Land set up a laboratory 1932, then established the Polaroid Corporation 1937–80. His research also led to a process for 3-D pictures, "instant" color film, "instant" motion pictures, and a new theory of color perception, the "retinex" theory 1977.

Landau Lev Davidovich 1908–1968. Russian theoretical physicist. He was awarded the 1962 Nobel Prize for Physics for his work on liquid helium.

Landes sandy, low-lying area in SW France, along the Bay of Biscay, about 5,000 sq mi/ 12,950 sq km in extent. Formerly covered with furze and heath, it has in many parts been planted with pine and oak forests. It gives its name to a *département* and extends into the *départements* of Gironde and Lot-et-Garonne. There is a testing range for rockets and missiles at Biscarosse, 45 mi/72 km SW of Bordeaux. There is an oil field in Parentis-en-Born.

Landis Kenesaw Mountain 1866–1944. US judge and baseball commissioner. He was born in Millville, Ohio, and received his law degree 1891. He was appointed federal district judge in Chicago 1905 and presided in important antitrust and labor relations cases. Having served as judge in the fraud trial of the nine members of the infamous "Black Sox" who had conspired to throw the 1919 World Series, Landis was named the first commissioner of major-league baseball 1921. In that position he restored the integrity of the game by establishing strict standards against players' involvement with gamblers.

Land League Irish peasant-rights organization, formed 1879 by Michael ⟡Davitt and Charles ⟡Parnell to fight against tenant evictions. Through its skillful use of the boycott

against anyone who took a farm from which another had been evicted, it forced Gladstone's government to introduce a law in 1881 restricting rents and granting tenants security of tenure.

landlord and tenant in law, the relationship that exists between an owner of land or buildings (the landlord) and a person granted the right to occupy them (the tenant). The landlord grants a lease or tenancy, which may be for a year, a term of years, a week, or any other definite, limited period.

The relationship is known as lessor and lessee, and the lease agreement gives both parties legal rights and obligations.

In the US, there is traditionally a free market in rent prices. Under some circumstances—a wartime housing shortage, for example—the government may impose rent controls. These have been applied at the local level and used in instances, such as in New York City, where the market value of housing would have gone beyond the reach of most wage-earners. Such controls specify allowable increases in rents and may have the unintended effect of reducing available housing stock as landlords sell or withdraw unprofitable units.

Landon Alf(red Mossman) 1887–1987. US public official. After a successful career in business, he entered politics and was elected governor of Kansas 1932. As a popular liberal Republican, Landon ran for president against incumbent F D Roosevelt 1936 but was overwhelmingly defeated. He later accepted a presidential appointment as US delegate to the 1938 Pan-American Conference. After World War II, Landon became a spokesman for the elimination of trade barriers and for international development.

Born in West Middlesex, Pennsylvania, Landon was raised in Kansas and received a law degree from the University of Kansas 1908.

land reform theory that ownership of land should be shared among the workers, the peasants, and the agricultural workers.

Landsbergis Vytautas 1932– . President of Lithuania from 1990. He became active in nationalist politics in the 1980s, founding and eventually chairing the anticommunist Sajudis independence movement 1988.

When Sajudis swept to victory in the republic's elections March 1990, Landsbergis chaired the Supreme Council of Lithuania becoming, in effect, president. He immediately drafted the republic's declaration of independence from the USSR which, after initial Soviet resistance, was recognized Sept 1991.

Landseer Edwin Henry 1802–1873. English painter, sculptor, and engraver of animal studies. Much of his work reflects the Victorian taste for sentimental and moralistic pictures, for example *Dignity and Impudence* 1839 (Tate Gallery, London). The *Monarch of the Glen* (John Dewar and Sons Ltd) 1850, depicting a highland stag, was painted for the House of Lords. His sculptures include the lions at the base of Nelson's Column in Trafalgar Square, London, 1857–67.

Land's End promontory of W Cornwall, 9 mi/ 15 km WSW of Penzance, the westernmost point of England.

An extension of Land's End is a group of dangerous rocks, the Longships, a mile out, marked by a lighthouse.

landslide sudden downward movement of a mass of soil or rocks from a cliff or steep slope.

Landslides happen when a slope becomes unstable, usually because the base has been undercut or because materials within the mass have become wet and slippery.

A *mudflow* happens when soil or loose material is soaked so that it no longer adheres to the slope; it forms a tongue of mud that reaches downhill from a semicircular hollow. A *slump* occurs when the material stays together as a large mass, or several smaller masses, and these may form a tilted steplike structure as they slide. A *landslip* is formed when ⟡beds of rock dipping toward a cliff slide along a lower bed. Earthquakes may precipitate landslides.

Landsteiner Karl 1868–1943. Austrian-born immunologist who discovered the ABO ⟡blood group system 1900–02, and aided in the discovery of the Rhesus blood factors 1940. He also discovered the polio virus.

He was awarded a Nobel Prize in 1930.

Landsteiner worked at the Vienna Pathology Laboratory, and the Rockefeller Institute for Medical Research, New York, where he was involved in the discovery of the MN blood groups in 1927. In 1936 he wrote *The Specificity of Serological Reactions*, which helped establish the science of immunology. He also developed a test for syphilis.

Lanfranc *c.* 1010–1089. Italian archbishop of Canterbury from 1070; he rebuilt the cathedral, replaced English clergy by Normans, enforced clerical celibacy, and separated the ecclesiastical from the secular courts.

His skill in theological controversy did much to secure the church's adoption of the doctrine of transubstantiation. He came over to England with William the Conqueror, whose adviser he was.

Lang Fritz 1890–1976. Austrian film director whose films are characterized by a strong sense of fatalism and alienation. His German films include *Metropolis* 1927, the sensational *M* 1931, in which Peter Lorre starred as a child-killer, and the series of Dr Mabuse films, after which he fled from the Nazis to Hollywood in 1936. His US films include *Fury* 1936, *You Only Live Once* 1937, *Scarlet Street* 1945, *Rancho Notorious* 1952, and *The Big Heat* 1953. He returned to Germany and directed a third picture in the Dr Mabuse series in 1960.

Lange David (Russell) 1942– . New Zealand Labor Party prime minister 1983–89. Lange, a lawyer, was elected to the House of Representatives 1977. Labor had a decisive win in the 1984 general election on a non-nuclear military policy, which Lange immediately put into effect, despite criticism from the US. He introduced a free-market economic policy and was reelected 1987. He resigned Aug 1989 over a disagreement with his finance minister.

Lange Dorothea 1895–1965. US photographer who was hired in 1935 by the federal Farm Security Administration to document the westward migration of farm families from the Dust Bowl of the S central US. Her photographs, characterized by a gritty realism, were widely exhibited and subsequently published as *An American Exodus: A Record of Human Erosion* 1939.

Born in Hoboken, New Jersey, Lange attended a teachers' college before receiving professional training in photography from Clarence White in New York. She established a private studio in San Francisco.

Langevin Paul 1872–1946. French physicist who contributed to the studies of magnetism and X-ray emissions. During World War I he invented an apparatus for locating enemy submarines. The nuclear institute at Grenoble is named after him.

Langley Samuel Pierpoint 1834–1906. US astronomer, scientist, and inventor of the ◊bolometer.

His steam-driven airplane flew for 90 seconds in 1896—the first flight by an engine-equipped aircraft.

From 1887 he was secretary of the Smithsonian Institution in Washington, DC. He founded the Smithsonian Astrophysical Observatory in 1890 and turned to pioneering work in aerodynamics, contributing greatly to the design of early aircraft. He built and tested the first successful (but unmanned) heavier-than-air craft (airplane), which he launched by catapult and which flew over the Potomac River in 1896. The subsequent catapult-launched flights of the ◊Wright brothers at Kitty Hawk owe much to Langley's principles and to the more powerful engines available by the early 1900s, capable of lifting and sustaining piloted craft in flight. The Langley design, now on view at the Smithsonian, was tested in later years by using a model with a modern engine; it flew successfully with a pilot aboard.

Langmuir Irving 1881–1957. US scientist who invented the mercury vapor pump for producing a high vacuum, and the atomic hydrogen welding process; he was also a pioneer of the thermionic valve. In 1932 he was awarded a Nobel Prize for his work on surface chemistry.

Langton Stephen *c.* 1150–1228. English priest who was mainly responsible for drafting the charter of rights, the ◊Magna Carta.

He studied in Paris, where he became chancellor of the university, and in 1206 was created a cardinal. When in 1207 Pope Innocent III secured Langton's election as archbishop of Canterbury, King John refused to recognize him, and he was not allowed to enter England until 1213. He supported the barons in their struggle against John and worked for revisions to both church and state policies.

Langtry Lillie. Adopted name of Emilie Charlotte le Breton 1853–1929. English actress, mistress of the future Edward VII. She was known as the "Jersey Lily" from her birthplace in the Channel Islands and considered to be one of the most beautiful women of her time.

language human communication through speech, writing, or both. Different nationalities or ethnic groups typically have different languages or variations on particular languages; for example, Armenians speaking the Armenian language and the British and Americans speaking distinctive varieties of the English language. One language may have various ◊dialects, which may be seen by those who use them as languages in their own right. The term is also used for systems of communication with languagelike qualities, such as *animal language* (the way animals communicate), *body language* (gestures and expressions used to communicate ideas), *sign language* (gestures for the deaf or for use as a ◊lingua franca, as among American Indians), and *computer languages* (such as BASIC and COBOL).

Natural human language has a neurological basis centered on the left hemisphere of the brain and is expressed through two distinct media in most present-day societies: mouth and ear (the medium of sound, or **phonic**

medium), and hand and eye (the medium of writing, or **graphic medium**). Language appears to develop in all children under normal circumstances, either as a unilingual or multilingual skill, crucially between the ages of one and five, and as a necessary interplay of innate and environmental factors. Any child can learn any language, under the appropriate conditions. When forms of language are as distinct as Dutch and Arabic, it is obvious that they are different languages. When, however, they are mutually intelligible, as are Dutch and Flemish, a categorical distinction is harder to make. Rather than say that Dutch and Flemish are dialects of a common Netherlandic language, as some scholars put it, Dutch and Flemish speakers may, for traditional reasons that include ethnic pride and political distinctness, prefer to talk about two distinct languages. To strengthen the differences among similar languages, groups may emphasize those differences (for example, the historical distancing of Portuguese from Castilian Spanish) or adopt different scripts (Urdu is written in Arabic script, its relative Hindi in Devanagari script). From outside, Italian appears to be a single language; inside Italy, it is a standard variety resting on a base of many very distinct dialects. The terms "language" and "dialect" are not therefore easily defined and distinguished. English is today the most widespread world language, but it has so many varieties (often mutually unintelligible) that scholars now talk about "Englishes" and even "the English languages"—all, however, are united for international purposes by Standard English. When scholars decide that languages are cognate (that is, have a common origin), they group them into a **language family**. Membership of a family is established through a range of correspondences, such as *f* and *p* in certain English and Latin words (as in *father/pater* and *fish/piscis*). By such means, English and Latin are shown to have long ago shared a common "ancestor." Some languages, such as French, Spanish, and Italian, fall easily into family groups, while others, such as Japanese, are not easy to classify, and others still, such as Basque, appear to have no linguistic kin anywhere (and are known as **isolates**). The families into which the languages of the world are grouped include the ◊Indo-European (the largest, with subfamilies or branches from northern India to Ireland), the Hamito-Semitic or Afro-Asiatic (with a Hamitic branch in N Africa and a Semitic branch in W Asia and Africa, and containing Arabic, Hebrew, and Berber), the Finno-Ugric (including Finnish and Hungarian), the Sino-Tibetan (including Chinese and Tibetan), the Malayo-Polynesian or Austronesian (including Malay and Maori), and the Uto-Aztecan (one of many American Indian families, including Ute and Aztec or Nahuatl). Linguists estimate that there may be 4,000–5,000 distinct languages in the world. The number is uncertain because: (1) it is not always easy to establish whether a speech form is a distinct language or a dialect of another language; (2) some parts of the world remain incompletely explored (such as New Guinea); and (3) the rate of **language death** is often unknown (for example, in Amazonia, where many undescribed American Indian languages have died out). It is also difficult to estimate the precise number of speakers of many languages, especially where communities mix elements from several languages elsewhere used separately (as in parts of India). The Indo-European language family is considered to have some 2

billion speakers worldwide, Sino-Tibetan about 1,040 million, Hamito-Semitic some 230 million, and Malayo-Polynesian some 200 million. Chinese (which may or may not be a single language) is spoken by around 1 billion people, English by some 350 million native speakers and at least the same number of non-natives, Spanish by 250 million, Hindi 200 million, Arabic 150 million, Russian 150 million, Portuguese 135 million, Japanese 120 million, German 100 million, French 70 million, Italian 60 million, Korean 60 million, Tamil 55 million, and Vietnamese 50 million.

Languedoc former province of S France, bounded by the river Rhône, the Mediterranean Sea, and the regions of Guienne and Gascony.

Languedoc-Roussillon region of S France, comprising the *départements* of Aude, Gard, Hérault, Lozère, and Pyrénées-Orientales; area 10,576 sq mi/27,400 sq km; population (1986) 2,012,000. Its capital is Montpellier, and products include fruit, vegetables, wine, and cheese.

langur any of various leaf-eating Old World monkeys of several genera, especially the genus *Presbytis*, that lives in trees in S Asia. There are about 20 species. Langurs are related to the colobus monkey of Africa.

lanolin sticky, purified wax obtained from sheep's wool and used in cosmetics, soap, and leather preparation.

Lansing capital of Michigan, at the confluence of the Grand and Red Cedar rivers; population (1990) 127,320. Manufacturing includes motor vehicles, diesel engines, and pumps.

General Motors automobile plants are here, and Michigan State University is the adjoining city of East Lansing. Lansing was settled in the 1840s and has been the state capital since 1847.

lanthanide any of a series of 15 metallic elements (also known as rare earths) with atomic numbers 57 (lanthanum) to 71 (lutetium). One of its members, promethium, is radioactive. All occur in nature. Lanthanides are grouped because of their chemical similarities (they are all bivalent), their properties differing only slightly with atomic number.

Lanthanides were called rare earths originally because they were not widespread and were difficult to identify and separate from their ores by their discoverers. The series is set out in a band in the periodic table of the elements, as are the ◊actinides.

lanthanum (Greek *lanthanein* "to be hidden") soft, silvery, ductile and malleable, metallic element, symbol La, atomic number 57, atomic weight 138.91, the first of the lanthanide series. It is used in making alloys. It was named 1839 by Swedish chemist Carl Mosander (1797–1858).

Lanzhou or *Lanchow* capital of Gansu province, China, on the river Huang He, 120 mi/190 km S of the Great Wall; population (1989) 1,480,000. Industries include oil refining, chemicals, fertilizers, and synthetic rubber.

Laocoon in Classical mythology, a Trojan, brother of Anchises, priest of Apollo and a visionary. He and his sons were killed by serpents when he foresaw disaster for Troy in the ◊Trojan horse left by the Greeks.

The scene of their death is the subject of a Classical marble group, rediscovered in the

Laos
Lao People's Democratic Republic
(*Saathiaranagroat Prachhathippatay Prachhachhon Lao*)

area 91,400 sq mi/236,790 sq km
capital Vientiane
cities Luang Prabang (the former royal capital), Pakse, Savannakhet
physical landlocked state with high mountains in E; Mekong River in W; jungle covers nearly 60% of land
features Plain of Jars, where prehistoric people carved stone jars large enough to hold a person
head of state Kaysone Phomvihane from 1991
head of government General Khamtay Siphandon from 1991
political system communism, one-party state
political party Lao People's Revolutionary Party (only legal party)
exports hydroelectric power from the Mekong is exported to Thailand, timber, teak, coffee, electricity
currency new kip
population (1990 est) 4,024,000 (Lao 48%, Thai 14%, Khmer 25%, Chinese 13%); growth rate 2.2% p.a.
life expectancy men 48, women 51 (1989)
languages Lao (official), French
religions Theravāda Buddhist 85%, animist beliefs among mountain dwellers
literacy 45% (1991)
GNP $500 million (1987); $180 per head (1988)
chronology
1893–1945 Laos was a French protectorate.
1945 Temporarily occupied by Japan.
1946 Retaken by France.
1950 Granted semiautonomy in French Union.
1954 Independence achieved from France.
1960 Right-wing government seized power.
1962 Coalition government established; civil war continued.
1973 Vientiane cease-fire agreement. Withdrawal of US, Thai, and North Vietnamese forces.
1975 Communist-dominated republic proclaimed with Prince Souphanouvong as head of state.
1986 Phoumi Vongvichit became acting president.
1988 Plans announced to withdraw 40% of Vietnamese forces stationed in the country.
1989 First assembly elections since communist takeover.
1991 Constitution approved. Kaysone Phomvihane elected president. General Khamtay Siphandon named as new premier.
1992 Question of US prisoners of war retained in Laos since the end of Vietnam War unresolved.

backed by the royal army, overthrew Souvanna Phouma and set up a pro-Western government headed by Prince Boun Gum. A new Geneva Agreement 1962 established a tripartite (right–left–neutral) government under the leadership of Prince Souvanna Phouma. Fighting continued, however, between the North Vietnamese–backed Pathet Lao and the US-backed neutralists and right wing, until the 1973 Vientiane Agreement established a cease-fire line dividing the country NW to SE, giving the communists two-thirds of the country, but giving the Souvanna Phouma government two-thirds of the population. All foreign forces (North Vietnamese, Thai, and US) were to be withdrawn, and both sides received equal representation in Souvanna Phouma's provisional government 1974.

republic In 1975 the communist Pathet Lao (renamed the Lao People's Front) seized power. King Savang Vatthana (1908–1980), who had succeeded 1959, abdicated, and Laos became a People's Democratic Republic under the presidency of Prince Souphanouvong. Prince Souvanna Phouma remained as an "adviser" to the government, but the real controlling force was now the prime minister and communist party leader, Kaysone Phomvihane.

reform The new administration, which inherited a poor, war-ravaged economy, attempted to reorganize the country along socialist lines, nationalizing businesses and industries and collectivizing agriculture. Faced with a food shortage and the flight of more than 250,000 refugees to Thailand, it modified its approach 1979, introducing production incentives and allowing greater scope for the private sector. Further "liberalization" followed from 1985 under the prompting of the Soviet leader Mikhail Gorbachev, with a new profit-related "socialist business accounting system" being adopted. Phoumi Vongvichit became acting president 1986 due to Souphanouvong's ailing health. National elections were held March 1989. Laos became closely tied to the USSR and Vietnam and attempts were made to improve relations with Thailand and China for economic reasons. In March 1989, multiparty elections were held for the first time since the communists came to power 1975, with the communists retaining political control. In Aug 1989 party-to-party relations were established with China after a ten-year break.

constitution approved At its fifth congress March 1991 the Communist Party leader, Kaysone Phomvihane, called for acceleration of the pace of replacement of agricultural cooperatives by privately owned farms, as part of a deepening of the five-year-old program of economic restructuring. Phomvihane was unanimously elected party president by the congress. A new constitution was endorsed by the supreme people's assembly in Aug 1991. In the same month Phomvihane was elected head of state by the assembly, replacing Phoumi Vongvichit. General Khamtay Siphandon, former vice premier and defense minister, became the new premier.

foreign relations In Nov 1991 the US upgraded its diplomatic representation in Laos to ambassadorial level for the first time since the communists came to power in 1975. Laos remained closely linked to Vietnam. Relations with Thailand, especially commercial links, improved markedly from 1988 when the two countries were involved in a serious border skirmish. The question of American prisoners of war kept in Laos after the Vietnam

Renaissance, and forms an episode in Virgil's *Aeneid*.

Laois or **Laoighis** county in Leinster province, Republic of Ireland
area 664 sq mi/1,720 sq km
county town Port Laoise
physical flat except for the Slieve Bloom Mountains in the northwest
products sugarbeets, dairy products, woolens, agricultural machinery
population (1991) 52,300.

Laon capital of Aisne *département*, Picardie, N France; 75 mi/120 km NE of Paris; population (1982) 29,000. It was the capital of France and a royal residence until the 10th century. It has a 12th-century cathedral.

Laos landlocked country in SE Asia, bounded N by China, E by Vietnam, S by Cambodia, W by Thailand, and NW by Myanmar.
government A constitution was endorsed 1991 providing for an executive president to be elected for a five-year term, and a 79-member supreme people's assembly, with a similar term.

The controlling force and only political party in Laos is the communist party (Lao People's Revolutionary Party), which is dominated by its 11-member political bureau and heads the broader Lao Front for National Reconstruction.
history The original SE Asian tribal groups saw a migration from the 4th–5th centuries of people from China. Laos came under Indian influence and adopted Buddhism during the 7th–11th centuries. As part of the ⬦Khmer empire from the 11th–13th centuries, it experienced much artistic and architectural activity. From the 12th century, the country was invaded by the Lao from Thailand, who established small independent kingdoms and became Buddhists. Laos became an independent kingdom in the 14th century and was first visited by Europeans in the 17th century, becoming a French protectorate 1893–1945. After a brief period of Japanese occupation, France reestablished control 1946 despite opposition from the Chinese-backed Lao Issara (Free Laos) nationalist movement. The country became semiautonomous 1950, when, under the constitutional monarchy of the king of ⬦Luang Prabang, it became an associated state of the French Union.
civil war In 1954, after the Geneva Agreements, Laos gained full independence. Civil war broke out between two factions of former Lao Issara supporters: a moderate, royalist-neutralist group led by Prince Souvanna Phouma, which had supported the 1950 French compromise and was the recognized government for most of the country; and a more extreme communist resistance group, the Pathet Lao ("land of the Lao"), led by ex-Prince Souphanouvong (the half brother of Prince Souvanna) and supported by China and the ⬦Vietminh, which controlled much of N Laos.

A coalition government was established after the 1957 Vientiane Agreement. This soon collapsed, and in 1960 a third, right-wing force emerged when General Phoumi Nosavan,

War remained unresolved when US Senate hearings were conducted in Oct 1992. *See illustration box.*

Laotian member of an Indochinese people who live along the Mekong river system. There are approximately 9 million Laotians in Thailand and 2 million in Laos. The Laotian language is a Thai member of the Sino-Tibetan family.

Lao Zi or Lao Tzu *c.* 604–531 BC. Chinese philosopher, commonly regarded as the founder of ◊Taoism, with its emphasis on the Tao, the inevitable and harmonious way of the universe. Nothing certain is known of his life, and he is variously said to have lived in the 6th or the 4th century BC. The *Tao Tê Ching*, the Taoist scripture, is attributed to him but apparently dates from the 3rd century BC

La Palma see La ◊Palma, one of the Spanish Canary Islands.

laparotomy exploratory surgical procedure involving incision into the abdomen, especially when done at the flanks. The use of laparotomy, as of other exploratory surgery, has decreased sharply with technical advances in scanning and the direct-viewing technique known as ◊endoscopy.

La Paz capital city of Bolivia, in Murillo province, 12,400 ft/3,800 m above sea level; population (1988) 1,049,800. Products include textiles and copper. Founded by the Spanish 1548 as Pueblo Nuevo de Nuestra Senõra de la Paz, it has been the seat of government since 1898.

lapis lazuli rock containing the blue mineral lazurite in a matrix of white calcite with small amounts of other minerals. It occurs in silica-poor igneous rocks and metamorphic limestones found in Afghanistan, Siberia, Iran, and Chile. Lapis lazuli was a valuable pigment of the Middle Ages, also used as a gemstone and in inlaying and ornamental work.

Lapiths in Greek mythology, a people of Thessaly in northern Greece, often represented in Greek art in a battle with their neighbors the ◊centaurs (half man and half horse) at the wedding of their king, Pirithous.

Laplace Pierre Simon, Marquis de Laplace 1749–1827. French astronomer and mathematician. In 1796, he theorized that the Solar System originated from a cloud of gas (the nebular hypothesis). He studied the motion of the Moon and planets, and published a five-volume survey of ◊celestial mechanics, *Traité de méchanique céleste* 1799–1825. Among his mathematical achievements was the development of probability theory.

Lapland region of Europe within the Arctic Circle in Norway, Sweden, Finland, and the Kola Peninsula in NW Russia, without political definition. Its chief resources are chromium, copper, iron, timber, hydroelectric power, and tourism. The indigenous population are the Saami (formerly known as Lapps), a seminomadic herding people. Lapland has low temperatures, with three months' continuous daylight in summer and three months' continuous darkness in winter. There is summer agriculture.

Laptev Sea part of the Arctic Ocean off the north coast of Russia between Taimyr Peninsula and New Siberian Island.

laptop computer portable microcomputer, small enough to be used on the operator's lap. It consists of a single unit, incorporating a keyboard, ◊floppy disk or ◊hard disk drives, and a screen. The screen often forms a lid that folds back in use. It uses a liquid-crystal or gas-plasma display, rather than the bulkier and heavier cathode-ray tubes found in most display terminals. A typical laptop computer measures about 14 in/360 mm × 15 in/380 mm × 4 in/100 mm, and weighs between 6 lb 9 oz/3 kg and 14 lb 2 oz/7 kg.

lapwing Eurasian bird *Vanellus vanellus* of the plover family, also known as the **green plover** and, from its call, as the **peewit**. Bottle-green above and white below, with a long thin crest and rounded wings, it is about 1 ft/30 cm long. It inhabits moorland in Europe and Asia, making a nest scratched out of the ground.

It is an occasional visitor to NE North America.

Laramie town in Wyoming, on the Laramie Plains, a plateau 7,500 ft/2,300 m above sea level, bounded N and E by the Laramie Mountains; population (1990) 26,680. The Laramie River, on which it stands, is linked with the Missouri via the Platte.

It is a commercial and transport center for a ranching and lumber-producing area; its manufactures include cement and wood products. On the overland trail and Pony Express route, Fort Laramie, built 1834, features in western legend. A rail line came through 1868, and Laramie was incorporated 1874.

larceny in the US, and formerly in the UK, theft, the taking of personal property without consent and with the intention of permanently depriving the owner of it.

In some US states, larceny in which the value of the property exceeds a specified amount is grand larceny; larceny involving lesser amounts is petty larceny.

larch any tree of the genus *Larix*, of the family Pinaceae. The common larch *L. decidua* grows to 130 ft/40 m. It is one of the few ◊conifer trees to shed its leaves annually. The small needlelike leaves are replaced every year by new bright-green foliage, which later darkens.

Closely resembling it is the North American tamarack *L. laricina*, and both are timber trees. The golden larch *Pseudolarix amabilis*, a native of China, turns golden in autumn.

Larderello site in the Tuscan hills, NE Italy, where the sulfur springs were used by the Romans for baths and exploited for boric acid in the 18th–19th centuries. Since 1904 they have been used to generate electricity; the water reaches 220°F.

Lardner Ring 1885–1933. US short-story writer. A sports reporter, he based his characters on the people he met professionally. His collected volumes of short stories include *You Know Me, Al* 1916, *Round Up* 1929, and *Ring Lardner's Best Short Stories* 1938, all written in colloquial language.

Laredo city on the Rio Grande, Texas; population (1990) 122,900. It was founded 1755. Industries include oil refining and metal processing. Laredo State University is here. *Nuevo Laredo*, Mexico, on the opposite bank, is a textile center; population (1980) 203,300. It was considered part of Laredo until the international border was established 1848. There is much cross-border trade.

lares and **penates** in Roman mythology, spirits of the farm and of the store cupboard, often identified with the family ancestors, whose shrine was the center of family worship in Roman homes.

Large Electron Positron Collider (LEP) the world's largest particle ◊accelerator, in operation from 1989 at the CERN laboratories near Geneva in Switzerland. It occupies a tunnel 12.5 ft/3.8 m wide and 16.7 mi/27 km long, which is buried 590 ft/180 m underground and forms a ring consisting of eight curved and eight straight sections. In 1989 the LEP was used to measure the mass and lifetime of the Z particle, carrier of the weak nuclear force.

Electrons and positrons enter the ring after passing through the Super Proton Synchrotron accelerator. They travel in opposite directions around the ring, guided by 3,328 bending magnets and kept within tight beams by 1,272 focusing magnets. As they pass through the straight sections, the particles are accelerated by a pulse of radio energy. Once sufficient energy is accumulated, the beams are allowed to collide. Four giant detectors are used to study the resulting shower of particles.

La Rioja region of N Spain; area 1,930 sq mi/5,000 sq km; population (1986) 263,000. It is known for its wine.

Larionov Mikhail Fedorovich 1881–1964. Russian painter, active in Paris from 1919. With his wife Natalia Goncharova, he pioneered a semiabstract style known as Rayonnism in which subjects appear to be deconstructed by rays of light from various sources. Larionov also produced stage sets for Diaghilev's *Ballets Russes* from 1915. In Paris he continued to work as a theatrical designer and book illustrator.

lark songbird of the family Alaudidae, found mainly in the Old World, but also in North America. Larks are brownish-tan in color and usually about 7 in/18 cm long; they nest on the ground in the open. The skylark *Alauda arvensis* sings as it rises almost vertically in the air. It breeds in Britain; it is light-brown, and 7 in/18 cm long.

The skylark has been introduced to Vancouver Island. The North American horned lark *Eremophila alpestris* has black "horns" and only a weak, twittering song.

Larkin Philip 1922–1985. English poet. His perfectionist, pessimistic verse includes *The North Ship* 1945, *The Whitsun Weddings* 1964, and *High Windows* 1974. He edited *The Oxford Book of 20th-Century English Verse* 1973.

larkspur plant of the genus ◊delphinium.

La Rochefoucauld François, duc de La Rochefoucauld 1613–1680. French writer. His *Réflexions, ou sentences et maximes morales/Reflections, or Moral Maxims* 1665 is a collection of brief, epigrammatic, and cynical observations on life and society, with the epigraph "Our virtues are mostly our vices in disguise." He was a lover of Mme de ◊Lafayette.

Born in Paris, he became a soldier, and took part in the ◊Fronde revolts. His later years were divided between the court and literary society.

La Rochelle fishing port in W France; population (1982) 102,000. It is the capital of Charente-Maritime *département*. Industries include shipbuilding, chemicals, and motor vehicles. A Huguenot stronghold, it was taken by Cardinal Richelieu in the siege of 1627–28.

Larousse Pierre 1817–1875. French grammarian and lexicographer. His encyclopedic dictionary, the *Grand dictionnaire universel du XIXème siècle/Great Universal 19th-Century*

Dictionary 1865–76, continues to be published in revised form.

Larsson Carl 1853–1919. Swedish painter, engraver, and illustrator. His watercolors of domestic life, delicately colored and full of detail, were painted for his book *Ett Hem/A Home* 1899.

larva stage between hatching and adulthood in those species in which the young have a different appearance and way of life from the adults. Examples include tadpoles (frogs) and caterpillars (butterflies and moths). Larvae are typical of the invertebrates, some of which (for example, shrimps) have two or more distinct larval stages. Among vertebrates, it is only the amphibians and some fishes that have a larval stage.

The process whereby the larva changes into another stage, such as a pupa (chrysalis) or adult, is known as ⟡metamorphosis.

laryngitis inflammation of the larynx, causing soreness of the throat, a dry cough, and hoarseness. The acute form is due to a virus or other infection, excessive use of the voice, or inhalation of irritating smoke, and may cause the voice to be completely lost. With rest, the inflammation usually subsides in a few days.

larynx in mammals, a cavity at the upper end of the trachea (windpipe), containing the vocal cords. It is stiffened with cartilage and lined with mucous membrane. Amphibians and reptiles have much simpler larynxes, with no vocal cords. Birds have a similar cavity, called the *syrinx*, found lower down the trachea, where it branches to form the bronchi. It is very complex, with well-developed vocal cords.

la Salle René Robert Cavelier, Sieur de la Salle 1643–1687. French explorer. He made an epic voyage through North America, exploring the Mississippi River down to its mouth, and in 1682 founded Louisiana. When he returned with colonists, he failed to find the river mouth again, and was eventually murdered by his mutinous men.

lascar East Indian sailor. The word derives from the Persian *lashkar* ("army"), and lascars were originally a class of sepoy (Indian soldier).

Las Casas Bartolomé de 1474–1566. Spanish missionary, historian, and colonial reformer, known as *the Apostle of the Indies*. He was one of the first Europeans to call for the abolition of Indian slavery in Latin America. He took part in the conquest of Cuba in 1513, but subsequently worked for American Indian freedom in the Spanish colonies. *Apologetica historia de las Indias* (first published 1875–76) is his account of Indian traditions and his witnessing of Spanish oppression of the Indians.

Las Casas sailed to Hispaniola in the West Indies in 1502 and was ordained priest there in 1512. From Cuba he returned to Spain in 1515 to plead for the Indian cause, winning the support of the Holy Roman emperor Charles V. In what is now Venezuela he unsuccessfully attempted to found a settlement of free Indians. In 1530, shortly before the conquest of Peru, he persuaded the Spanish government to forbid slavery there. In 1542 he became bishop of Chiapas in S Mexico. He returned finally to Spain in 1547.

Lascaux cave system in SW France with prehistoric wall paintings. It is richly decorated with realistic and symbolic paintings of buffaloes, horses, and red deer of the Upper Paleolithic period, about 18,000 BC. The caves, near Montignac in the Dordogne, were discovered 1940. Similar paintings are found in ⟡Altamira, Spain. The opening of the Lascaux caves to tourists led to deterioration of the paintings; the caves were closed 1963 and a facsimile opened 1983.

Las Cruces city in S New Mexico, on the Rio Grande, N of the Mexican border; population (1990) 62,120. It is a processing center for the area's crops, such as pecans, cotton, and vegetables. White Sands Missile Range is nearby.

laser (acronym for *light amplification by stimulated emission of radiation*) a device for producing a narrow beam of light, capable of traveling over vast distances without dispersion, and of being focused to give enormous power densities (10^8 watts per cm^2 for high-energy lasers). The laser operates on a principle similar to that of the ⟡maser (a high-frequency microwave amplifier or oscillator). The uses of lasers include communications (a laser beam can carry much more information than can radio waves), cutting, drilling, welding, satellite tracking, medical and biological research, and surgery.

Any substance the majority of whose atoms or molecules can be put into an excited energy state can be used as laser material. Many solid, liquid, and gaseous substances have been used, including synthetic ruby crystal (used for the first extraction of laser light in 1960, and giving a high-power pulsed output) and a helium–neon gas mixture, capable of continuous operation, but at a lower power.

A blue shortwave laser was developed in Japan in 1988. Its expected application is in random access memory (⟡RAM) and ⟡compact disc recording, where its shorter wavelength will allow a greater concentration of digital information to be stored and read. A gallium arsenide chip, produced by IBM in 1989, contains the world's smallest lasers in the form of cylinders of ⟡semiconductor roughly one tenth of the thickness of a human hair; a million lasers can fit on a chip 2.5 in/1 cm square.

Sound wave vibrations from the window glass of a room can be picked up by a reflected laser beam. Lasers are also used as entertainment in theaters, concerts, and light shows.

laser printer computer printer in which the image to be printed is formed by the action of a laser on a light-sensitive drum, then transferred to paper by means of an electrostatic charge. Laser printers are page printers, printing a complete page at a time. The printed image, which can take the form of text or pictures, is made up of tiny dots, or ink particles. The quality of the image generated depends on the fineness of these dots—most laser printers can print up to 300 dots per in/120 dots per cm across the page.

A typical desktop laser printer can print about 4–20 pages per minute. The first low-cost laser printer suitable for office use appeared in 1984.

laser surgery use of intense light sources to cut, coagulate, and vaporize tissue. Less invasive than normal surgery, it destroys diseased tissue gently and allows quicker, more natural healing. It can be used with a flexible endoscope to enable the surgeon to see the diseased area at which the laser needs to be aimed.

Laski Harold 1893–1950. British political theorist. Professor of political science at the London School of Economics from 1926, he taught a modified Marxism and published *A Grammar of Politics* 1925 and *The American Presidency* 1940. He was chairman of the Labour Party 1945–46.

Las Palmas or *Las Palmas de Gran Canaria* tourist resort on the NE coast of Gran Canaria, Canary Islands; population (1991) 347,700. Products include sugar and bananas.

Lassa fever acute disease caused by a virus, first detected in 1969, and spread by a species of rat found only in W Africa. It is characterized by high fever and inflammation of various organs. There is no known cure, the survival rate being less than 50%.

Lassalle Ferdinand 1825–1864. German socialist. He was imprisoned for his part in the ⟡revolution of 1848, during which he met the philosopher Karl ⟡Marx, and in 1863 founded the General Association of German Workers (later the Social-Democratic Party). His publications include *The Working Man's Program* 1862 and *The Open Letter* 1863. He was killed in a duel arising from a love affair.

Las Vegas city in Nevada, known for its night-clubs and gambling casinos; population (1986) 202,000. Founded 1855 in a ranching area, it is the largest city in the state.

Las Vegas entertains millions of visitors and is an important convention center. The University of Nevada-Las Vegas is here, and Nellis Air Force Base, Hoover Dam, and Lake Mead National Recreation Area are nearby. An army base was established here 1864, and the modern community developed with the coming of the railroad 1905. Las Vegas's growth dates from the first casino-hotel 1947, helped by its proximity to S California population centers and the development of air conditioning.

La Tène prehistoric settlement at the east end of Lake Neuchâtel, Switzerland, which has given its name to a culture of the Iron Age. The culture lasted from the 5th century BC to the Roman conquest.

latent heat in physics, the heat absorbed or radiated by a substance as it changes state (for example, from solid to liquid) at constant temperature and pressure.

lateral line system system of sense organs in fishes and larval amphibians (tadpoles) that detects water movement. It usually consists of a row of interconnected pores on either side of the body that divide into a system of canals across the head.

Lateran Treaties series of agreements that marked the reconciliation of the Italian state with the papacy in 1929. They were hailed as a propaganda victory for the Fascist regime. The treaties involved recognition of the sovereignty of the ⟡Vatican City State, the payment of an indemnity for papal possessions lost during unification in 1870, and agreement on the role of the Catholic church within the Italian state in the form of a concordat between Pope Pius XI and the dictator Mussolini.

laterite red residual soil characteristic of tropical rainforests. It is formed by the weathering of basalts, granites, and shales and contains a high percentage of aluminum and iron hydroxides.

latex (Latin "liquid") fluid of some plants (such as the rubber tree and poppy), an emulsion of resins, proteins, and other organic substances. It is used as the basis for making rubber. The name is also applied to a suspension in water of natural or synthetic rubber (or plastic) particles used in rubber goods, paints, and adhesives.

lathe machine tool, used for **turning**. The workpiece to be machined, usually wood or metal, is held and rotated while cutting tools are moved against it. Modern lathes are driven by electric motors, which can drive the spindle carrying the workpiece at various speeds.

latifundium (Latin for "broad" and "farm") in ancient Rome, a large agricultural estate designed to make maximum use of cheap labor, whether free workmen or slaves.

In present-day Italy, Spain, and South America, the term *latifondo* refers to a large agricultural estate worked by low-paid casual or semiservile labor in the interests of absentee landlords.

Latimer Hugh 1490–1555. English Christian church reformer and bishop. After his conversion to Protestantism in 1524 he was imprisoned several times but was protected by Cardinal Wolsey and Henry VIII. After the accession of the Catholic Mary, he was burned for heresy.

Latimer was appointed bishop of Worcester in 1535, but resigned in 1539. Under Edward VI his sermons denouncing social injustice won him great influence, but he was arrested in 1553, once Mary was on the throne, and two years later he was burned at the stake in Oxford.

Latin Indo-European language of ancient Italy. Latin has passed through four influential phases: as the language of (1) republican Rome, (2) the Roman Empire, (3) the Roman Catholic Church, and (4) W European culture, science, philosophy, and law during the Middle Ages and the Renaissance. During the third and fourth phases, much Latin vocabulary entered the English language. It is the parent form of the ◊Romance languages, noted for its highly inflected grammar and conciseness of expression.

The direct influence of Latin in Europe has decreased since Renaissance times but is still considerable, and indirectly both the language and its Classical literature still affect many modern languages and literatures. The insistence of Renaissance scholars upon an exact Classical purity, together with the rise of the European nation-states, contributed to the decline of Latin as an international cultural medium.

Latin vocabulary has entered English in two major waves: as religious vocabulary from Anglo-Saxon times until the Reformation, and as the vocabulary of science, scholarship, and the law from the Middle Ages onward. In the 17th century the makers of English dictionaries deliberately converted Latin words into English, enlarging the already powerful French component of English vocabulary into the language of education and refinement, placing "fraternity" alongside "brotherhood," "comprehend" beside "understand," "feline" beside "catlike," and so on. Many "Latin tags" are in regular use in English: "habeas corpus" ("you may have the body"), "ipse dixit" ("he said it himself"), "non sequitur" ("it does not follow"), and so on. English that consists of many Latin elements is "Latinate" and often has a grandiose and even pompous quality.

Today, with fewer students studying Latin in schools and universities, there is a tendency to make Latin words more conventionally English; for example, "cactuses" rather than "cacti" as the plural of "cactus." This tendency is accompanied by some uncertainty about usage, for example whether words like "data" and "media" are singular or plural. They are technically plural and are so treated by scholars, writers, and editors.

Latin America countries of South and Central America (also including Mexico) in which Spanish, Portuguese, and French are spoken.

Latin American Economic System (*Sistema Económico Latino-Americana* LAES/SELA) international organization for economic, technological, and scientific cooperation in Latin America, aiming to create and promote multinational enterprises in the region and provide markets. Founded in 1975 as the successor to the Latin American Economic Coordination Commission, it has 26 members in Central and South America and parts of the Caribbean, with headquarters in Caracas, Venezuela.

Latin American Integration Association (*Asociación Latino-Americana de Integración* ALADI) organization aiming to create a common market in Latin America; to promote trade it applies tariff reductions preferentially on the basis of the different stages of economic development that individual member countries have reached. Formed in 1980 to replace the Latin American Free Trade Association, it has 11 member countries, all in South America except Mexico. Its headquarters are in Montevideo, Uruguay.

Latin literature only a few hymns and inscriptions survive from the earliest period of Latin literature before the 3rd century BC. Greek influence began with the work of Livius Andronicus (c. 284–204 BC), who translated the *Odyssey* and Greek plays into Latin. Naevius and Ennius both attempted epics on patriotic themes; the former used the native "Saturnian" meter, but the latter introduced the Greek hexameter. Plautus and Terence successfully adapted Greek comedy to the Latin stage. Lucilius (190–103 BC) founded Latin verse satire, while the writings of Cato were the first important works in Latin prose.

In the *De Rerum natura* of Lucretius, and the passionate lyrics of Catullus, Latin verse reached maturity. Cicero set a standard for Latin prose, in his orations, philosophical essays, and letters. To the same period of the Roman republic belong the histories of Caesar. The Augustan age (43 BC–AD 17) is usually regarded as the golden age of Latin literature. There is strong patriotic feeling in the work of the poets Virgil and Horace and the historian Livy, who belonged to the emperor Augustus's court circle. Virgil produced the one great Latin epic, the *Aeneid*, while Horace brought charm and polish to both lyric and satire. Younger poets of the period were Ovid, who dealt with themes of love, and the elegiac poets Tibullus and Propertius.

The silver age of the empire begins with the writers of Nero's reign: the Stoic philosopher Seneca; Lucan, author of the epic *Pharsalia*; the satirist Persius; and, by far the greatest, the realistic novelist Petronius. Around the end of the 1st century and at the beginning of the 2nd came the historian Tacitus and the satirist Juvenal; other writers of the period were the epigrammatist Martial, the scientist Pliny the Elder, the letter-writer Pliny the Younger, the critic Quintilian, the historian Suetonius, and the epic poet Statius.

The 2nd and 3rd centuries produced only one pagan writer of importance, the romancer Apuleius, but there were several able Christian writers, such as Tertullian, Cyprian, Arnobius (died 327), and Lactantius (died 325). In the 4th century there was something of a poetic revival, with Ausonius, Claudian, and the Christian poets Prudentius and St Ambrose. The Classical period ends, and the Middle Ages begin, with St Augustine's *City of God* and St Jerome's translation of the Bible.

Throughout the Middle Ages, Latin remained the language of the church and was normally employed for theology, philosophy, histories, and other learned works. Latin verse, adapted to rhyme and non-Classical meters, was used both for hymns and the secular songs of the wandering scholars. Even after the Reformation, Latin retained its prestige as the international language of scholars and was used as such by the English writers Thomas More, Francis Bacon, John Milton, and many others. Medieval Latin vernacular evolved into the ◊Romance languages including French, Italian, and Spanish.

latitude and longitude angular distances defining position on the globe. *Latitude* (abbreviation lat.) is the angular distance of any point from the ◊equator, measured north or south along the earth's curved surface, equaling the angle between the respective horizontal planes. It is measured in degrees, minutes, and seconds, each minute equaling one nautical mile (1.15 mi/1.85 km) in length. *Longitude* (abbreviation long.) is the angle between the terrestrial meridian through a place, and a standard meridian now taken at Greenwich, England. At the equator one degree of longitude measures approximately 70 mi/113 km.

Point X lies on longitude 60°W

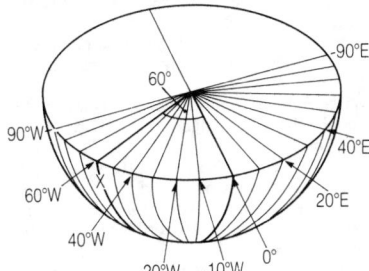

Point X lies on latitude 20°S

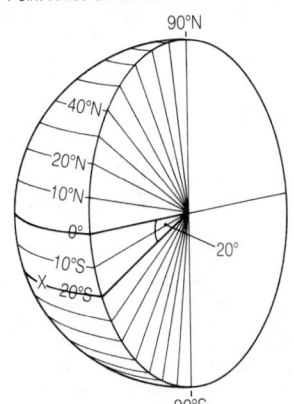

Together longitude 60°W latitude 20°S places point X on a precise position on the globe.

latitude and longitude *Locating a point on a globe using latitude and longitude.*

For map making, latitude is based on the supposition that the Earth is an oblate spheroid. The difference between this (the geographical) and astronomical latitude is the correction necessary for local deviation of plumb line. All determinations of longitude are based on the earth turning through 360° in 24 hours, or the Sun reaching 15° W each hour.

Latium Latin name for ⬦Lazio, a region of W central Italy.

La Tour Georges de 1593–1652. French painter active in Lorraine. He was patronized by the duke of Lorraine and perhaps also by Louis XIII. Many of his pictures are illuminated by a single source of light, with deep contrasts of light and shade. They range from religious paintings to domestic genre scenes.

Latter-day Saint member of the Christian sect the ⬦Mormons.

Latvia country in N Europe, bounded E by Russia, N by Estonia, N and NW by the Baltic Sea, S by Lithuania, and SE by Belarus.
government There is a 210-deputy, popularly elected supreme council (Augstaka Tadone), or parliament, whose members elect a chair (to serve as state president) and a prime minister.
history The Vikings invaded the area now known as Latvia in the 9th century and the Russians attacked in the 10th century. The invasion of the ⬦Teutonic Knights (German crusaders) in the 13th century was resisted in a lengthy struggle, but Latvia eventually came under their control 1230, converted to Christianity, and was governed by them for more than 200 years. By 1562 Poland and Lithuania had taken over most of the country. Sweden conquered the north 1621 and Russia took over control of this area 1710. By 1800 all of Latvia had come under Russian control. The Latvian independence movement began to emerge in the late 1800s and continued to grow in the early 20th century.
struggle for independence Latvia was partly occupied by the Germans during World War I. The USSR reclaimed control 1917 but was overthrown by Germany Feb 1918, when Latvia declared independence. Soviet rule was restored when Germany withdrew Dec 1918, but Soviet rule was again overthrown by British naval and German forces May–Dec 1919, and democratic rule was established. A coup 1934 replaced the established government. In 1939 a secret German-Soviet agreement assigned Latvia to Soviet rule and in 1940 Latvia was incorporated as a constituent republic of the USSR. During World War II Latvia was again occupied by German forces 1941–44, but the USSR regained control 1944.

As in the other Baltic republics, nationalist dissent grew from 1980, influenced by the Polish example and prompted by an influx of Russian workers and officials. A Latvian Popular Front was established Oct 1988 to campaign for independence and in the same month the prewar flag was readopted and official status given to the Latvian language. In the same year Anatolijs Gorbunov was elected president. In Jan 1990 the Latvian Communist Party (LCP) broke its links with Moscow and in May Latvia followed the lead taken by Lithuania when it unilaterally declared independence from the USSR, subject to a transitional period for negotiation. A multiparty system emerged, the 1990 March–April elections resulting in a Popular Front government. In Jan 1991 Soviet paratroopers seized key installations in Riga, killing one civilian, but began to withdraw later that month after international protests.

Latvia
Republic of

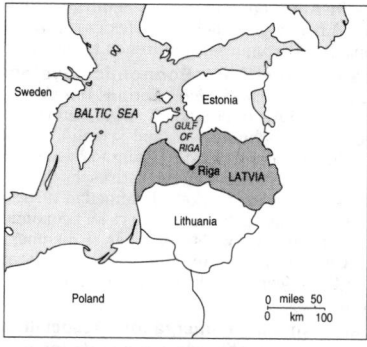

area 24,595 sq mi/63,700 sq km
capital Riga
cities Daugavpils, Liepāja, Jurmala, Jelgava, Ventspils
physical wooded lowland (highest point 1,024 ft/312 m), marshes, lakes; 293 mi/472 km of coastline; mild climate
features Western Dvina River; Riga is largest port on the Baltic after Leningrad
head of state Anatolijs Gorbunov from 1988
head of government Ivars Godmanis from 1990
political system emergent democratic republic
political parties Latvian Popular Front, nationalist; Latvian Social-Democratic Workers' Party
products electronic and communications equipment, electric railroad carriages, motorcycles, consumer durables, timber, paper and woolen goods, meat and dairy products
currency Latvian ruble
population (1990) 2,700,000 (52% Latvian, 34% Russian, 5% Byelorussian, 3% Ukrainian)
language Latvian
religions mostly Lutheran Protestant, with a Roman Catholic minority
chronology
1917 Soviets and Germans contested for control of Latvia.
1918 Feb: Soviet forces overthrown by Germany. Nov: Latvia declared independence. Dec: Soviet rule restored after German withdrawal.
1919 Soviet rule overthrown by British naval and German forces May–Dec; democracy established.
1934 Coup replaced established government.
1939 German-Soviet secret agreement placed Latvia under Russian influence.
1940 Incorporated into USSR as constituent republic.
1941–44 Occupied by Germany.
1944 USSR regained control.
1980 Nationalist dissent began to grow.
1988 Latvian Popular Front established to campaign for independence. Prewar flag readopted; official status given to Latvian language.
1989 Popular Front swept local elections.
1990 Jan: Communist Party's monopoly of power abolished. March–April: Popular Front secured majority in elections. April: Latvian Communist Party (CP) split into pro- independence and pro-Moscow wings. May: unilateral declaration of independence from USSR, subject to transitional period for negotiation.
1991 Jan: Soviet troops briefly seized key installations in Riga. March: overwhelming vote for independence in referendum. Aug: full independence declared at time of anti-Gorbachev coup; CP outlawed. Sept: independence recognized by Soviet government and Western nations; United Nations (UN) membership granted; admitted into Conference on Security and Cooperation in Europe (CSCE).
1992 US reopened its embassy in Latvia. Russia began pullout of ex-Soviet troops, to be completed 1994. July: curbing of rights of noncitizens in Latvia prompted Russia to request minority protection by UN.

A plebiscite in March 1991 voted 73.7% in favor of independence. During the coup attempt against President Gorbachev in USSR, Soviet troops seized the radio and television station in Riga. In response, on Aug 21, 1991, the republic declared its immediate independence (previously it had been in a "period of transition") and outlawed the CP. This declaration was recognized by the Soviet government and Western nations Sept 1991 and the new state was granted membership in the United Nations (UN) and admitted into the ⬦Conference on Security and Cooperation in Europe (CSCE). In Feb 1992 US Vice President Dan Quayle reopened the US embassy, closed since the Baltic takeover 1940. In March Russia agreed to begin a pullout of ex-Soviet troops from Latvia and in August requested money for that pullout, which they said would be completed by 1994. In July Latvia curbed the rights of noncitizens, prompting Russia to ask the UN for the protection of minorities in that country. *See illustration box.*

Latvian language or *Lettish* language of Latvia; with Lithuanian it is one of the two surviving members of the Balto-Slavic branch of the Indo-European language family.

Laud William 1573–1645. English priest; archbishop of Canterbury from 1633. Laud's High Church policy, support for Charles I's unparliamentary rule, censorship of the press, and persecution of the Puritans all aroused bitter opposition, while his strict enforcement of the statutes against enclosures and of laws regulating wages and prices alienated the propertied classes. His attempt to impose the use of the Prayer Book on the Scots precipitated the English ⬦Civil War. Impeached by Parliament 1640, he was imprisoned in the Tower of London, summarily condemned to death, and beheaded.

laudanum alcoholic solution (tincture) of the drug ⬦opium. Used formerly as a narcotic and painkiller, it was available in the 19th century from pharmacists on demand in most of Europe and the US.

Laue Max Theodor Felix von 1879–1960. German physicist who was a pioneer in measuring the wavelength of X-rays by their diffraction through the closely spaced atoms in a crystal. His work led to the powerful technique (⬦X-ray diffraction) now used to elucidate the structure of complex biological materials such as ⬦DNA. He was awarded a Nobel Prize in 1914.

laughing gas popular name for ⬦nitrous oxide, an anesthetic.

laughing jackass another name for the ⬦kookaburra, an Australian kingfisher.

Laughton Charles 1899–1962. English actor who became a US citizen in 1950. Initially a Classical stage actor, he joined the Old Vic 1933. His films were made in Hollywood and include such roles as the king in *The Private Life of Henry VIII* 1933 (Academy Award), Captain Bligh in *Mutiny on the Bounty* 1935, and Quasimodo in *The Hunchback of Notre Dame* 1939. In 1955 he directed *Night of the Hunter* and in 1961 appeared in *Judgment at Nuremberg.*

Laurasia former land mass or supercontinent, formed by the fusion of North America, Greenland, Europe, and Asia. It made up the northern half of ⍿Pangaea, the "world continent" that is thought to have existed between 250 and 200 million years ago. The southern half was ⍿Gondwanaland. Between Laurasia and Gondwanaland was the Tethys Sea. Laurasia broke up with the separation of North America from Europe in the Upper Cretaceous period.

laurel any evergreen tree of the European genus *Laurus*, family Lauraceae, with glossy, aromatic leaves, yellowish flowers, and black berries. The leaves of sweet bay or poet's laurel *L. nobilis* are used in cooking. Several species are cultivated worldwide.

California laurel *Umbellularia californica* of the W US belongs to a different genus in the laurel family.

Laurel and Hardy Stan Laurel (adopted name of Arthur Stanley Jefferson) (1890–1965) and Oliver Hardy (1892–1957). US film comedians who were one of the most successful comedy teams in film history (Stan was slim, Oliver rotund). Their partnership began in 1927, survived the transition from silent films to sound, and resulted in more than 200 short and feature-length films, which were revived as a worldwide cult in the 1970s. Among these are *Pack Up Your Troubles* 1932, *Our Relations* 1936, and *A Chump at Oxford* 1940.

Laurel, a British-born former music-hall comedian, conceived the gags and directed their feature films *Babes in Toyland* 1934, *Way Out West* 1937, and *Swiss Miss* 1938. In 1940 they formed a production company and made films until 1945.

Lauren Ralph 1939– . US fashion designer, producing menswear under the Polo label from 1968, women's wear from 1971, children's wear, and home furnishings from 1983. He also designed costumes for the films *The Great Gatsby* 1973 and *Annie Hall* 1977.

Laurence Margaret 1926–1987. Canadian writer whose novels include *A Jest of God* 1966 and *The Diviners* 1974. She also wrote short stories set in Africa, where she lived for a time.

Laurier Wilfrid 1841–1919. Canadian politician, leader of the Liberal Party 1887–1919 and prime minister 1896–1911. The first French-Canadian to hold the office, he encouraged immigration into Canada from Europe and the US, established a separate Canadian navy, and sent troops to help Britain in the Boer War.

Lausanne resort and capital of Vaud canton, W Switzerland, above the north shore of Lake Geneva; population (1990) 123,200. Industries include chocolate, scientific instruments, and publishing.

Lausanne, Treaty of peace settlement in 1923 between Greece and Turkey after Turkey refused to accept the terms of the Treaty of Sèvres 1920, which would have made peace with the western Allies. It involved the surrender by Greece of Smyrna (now Izmir) to Turkey and the enforced exchange of the Greek population of Smyrna for the Turkish population of Greece.

lava molten material that erupts from a ⍿volcano and cools to form extrusive ⍿igneous rock. A lava high in silica is viscous and sticky and does not flow far, whereas low-silica lava can flow for long distances. Lava differs from its parent ⍿magma in that the fluid "fractionates" on its way to the surface of the Earth; that is, certain heavy or high-temperature minerals settle out and the constituent gases form bubbles and boil away into the atmosphere.

Laval Pierre 1883–1945. French right-wing politician. He was prime minister and foreign secretary 1931–32, and again 1935–36. In World War II he joined Pétain's ⍿Vichy government as vice-premier in June 1940; dismissed in Dec 1940, he was reinstated by Hitler's orders as head of the government and foreign minister in 1942. After the war he was executed.

Laval, born near Vichy, entered the chamber of deputies in 1914 as a socialist, but after World War I moved toward the right. His second period as prime minister was marked by the ⍿Hoare–Laval Pact for concessions to Italy in Abyssinia (now Ethiopia). His part in the deportation of French labor to Germany during World War II made him universally hated. When the Allies invaded, he fled the country but was arrested in Austria, tried for treason, and shot after trying to poison himself.

La Vallière Louise de la Baume le Blance, Duchesse de la Vallière 1644–1710. Mistress of the French king Louis XIV; she gave birth to four children 1661–74. She retired to a convent when superseded in his affections by the Marquise de Montespan.

La Vendée French river; see ⍿Vendée, La.

lavender sweet-smelling herb, genus *Lavandula*, of the mint family Labiatae, native to W Mediterranean countries. The bushy low-growing *L. angustifolia* has long, narrow, erect leaves of a silver-green color. The flowers, borne on a terminal spike, vary in color from lilac to deep purple and are covered with small fragrant oil glands. The oil is extensively used in pharmacy and the manufacture of perfumes.

laver any of several edible red seaweeds, including *Porphyra umbilicalis*. Growing on the shore and below, attached to rocks and stones, laver forms thin, irregularly rounded sheets of tissue up to 8 in/20 cm across. It becomes almost black when dry.

Laver Rod(ney George) 1938– . Australian lawn tennis player. He was one of the greatest left-handed players, and the only player to win the Grand Slam twice (1962 and 1969).

He won four Wimbledon singles titles, the Australian title three times, the US Open twice, and the French Open twice. He turned professional after winning Wimbledon in 1962 but returned when the championships were opened to professionals in 1968.

CAREER HIGHLIGHTS

Wimbledon
singles: 1961–62, 1968–69
doubles: 1971
mixed: 1959–60
US Open
singles: 1962, 1969
French Open
singles: 1962, 1969
doubles: 1961
mixed: 1961
Australian Open
singles: 1960, 1962, 1969
doubles: 1959–61, 1969

Lavoisier Antoine Laurent 1743–1794. French chemist. He proved that combustion needed only a part of the air, which he called oxygen, thereby destroying the theory of phlogiston (an imaginary "fire element" released during combustion). With Pierre de Laplace, the astronomer and mathematician, he showed that water was a compound of oxygen and hydrogen. In this way he established the basic rules of chemical combination.

law body of rules and principles under which justice is administered or order enforced in a state or nation. In western Europe there are two main systems: Roman law and English law. US law is a modified form of English law.

Roman law, first codified in 450 BC and finalized under Justinian AD 528–534, advanced to a system of international law (*jus gentium*), applied in disputes between Romans and foreigners or provincials, or between provincials of different states. Church influence led to the adoption of Roman law throughout western continental Europe, and it was spread to E Europe and parts of Asia by the French *Code Napoléon* in the 19th century. Scotland and Québec (because of their French links) and South Africa (because of its link with Holland) also have it as the basis of their legal systems.

English law derives from Anglo-Saxon customs, which were too entrenched to be broken by the Norman Conquest and still form the basis of the ⍿common law, which by 1250 had been systematized by the royal judges. Unique to English law is the doctrine of *stare decisis* (Latin "to stand by things decided"), which requires that courts abide by former precedents (or decisions) when the same points arise again in litigation. These two concepts are the basis for US law.

law courts bodies that adjudicate in legal disputes. Civil and criminal cases are usually dealt with by separate courts. In many countries there is a hierarchy of courts that provide an appeal system.

Many counties and municipalities also have courts, usually limited to minor offenses. There are also a number of federal and state specialized judicial and quasi-judicial bodies dealing with ⍿administrative law. In the US, the head of the federal judiciary is the Supreme Court, which also hears appeals from the inferior federal courts and from the decisions of the highest state courts. The US Courts of Appeal—organized in circuits—deal with appeals from the US district courts in which civil and criminal cases are heard. State courts deal with civil and criminal cases involving state laws and usually consist of a Supreme Court or appeals court and courts in judicial districts.

Lawrence town in Massachusetts; population (1990) 70,200. Industries include textiles, clothing, paper, and radio equipment. The town was established in 1845 to utilize power from the Merrimack Rapids on a site first settled in 1655.

Lawrence city in NE Kansas, on the Kansas River between Topeka to the W and Kansas City to the E; seat of Douglas County. Its main industries are food processing and chemicals. The University of Kansas 1863 is here; population (1990) 65,600. Lawrence was terrorized by Quantrill's Raiders 1863.

Lawrence D(avid) H(erbert) 1885–1930. English writer whose work expresses his belief in emotion and the sexual impulse as creative and true to human nature. The son of a Nottinghamshire miner, Lawrence studied at University College, Nottingham, and became a teacher. His writing first received attention after the publication of the semi autobiographical *Sons and Lovers*, which includes a portrayal of his mother (died 1911). Other novels include *Sons and Lovers* 1913, *The Rainbow* 1915, *Women in Love* 1921, and *Lady Chatterley's Lover* 1928. Lawrence also wrote short stories (for example "The Woman Who Rode Away") and poetry.

In 1914 he married Frieda von Richthofen, ex-wife of his university professor, with whom he had run away in 1912. Frieda was the model for Ursula Brangwen in *The Rainbow*, which was suppressed for obscenity, and its sequel, *Women in Love*. Lawrence's travels in search of health (he suffered from tuberculosis, from which he eventually died near Nice) prompted books such as *Mornings in Mexico* 1927. *Lady Chatterley's Lover* was banned as obscene in the UK until 1960.

Lawrence Ernest O(rlando) 1901–1958. US physicist. His invention of the cyclotron particle ⟐accelerator pioneered the production of artificial ⟐radioisotopes.

He was professor of physics at the University of California, Berkeley, from 1930 and director from 1936 of the Radiation Laboratory, which he built into a major research center for nuclear physics. He was awarded a Nobel Prize in 1939.

Lawrence Gertrude 1898–1952. English actress who began as a dancer in the 1920s and later took leading roles in musical comedies. Her greatest successes were in the play *Private Lives* 1930–31, written especially for her by Noël Coward, with whom she co-starred, and *The King and I* 1951.

Lawrence T(homas) E(dward), known as *Lawrence of Arabia* 1888–1935. British soldier and writer. Appointed to the military intelligence department in Cairo, Egypt, during World War I, he took part in negotiations for an Arab revolt against the Ottoman Turks, and in 1916 attached himself to the emir Faisal. He became a guerrilla leader of genius, combining raids on Turkish communications with the organization of a joint Arab revolt, described in *The Seven Pillars of Wisdom* 1926.

Lawrence, St Christian martyr. Probably born in Spain, he became a deacon of Rome under Pope Sixtus II and, when summoned to deliver the treasures of the church, displayed the beggars in his charge, for which he was broiled on a gridiron. Feast day Aug 10.

lawrencium synthesized, radioactive, metallic element, the last of the actinide series, symbol Lr, atomic number 103, atomic weight 262. Its only known isotope, Lr-257, has a half-life of 4.3 seconds and was originally synthesized at the University of California at Berkeley 1961 by bombarding californium with boron nuclei. The original symbol, Lw, was officially changed 1963.

The element was named after Ernest Lawrence (1901–1958), the US inventor of the cyclotron.

law, rule of principle that law (as administered by the ordinary courts) is supreme and that all citizens (including members of the government) are equally subject to it and equally entitled to its protection.

Lawton city in SW Oklahoma, on Cache Creek, SW of Oklahoma City, seat of Comanche County. Processing the area's agricultural products is the city's main industry. Fort Sill, an army base, is to the N; population (1980) 80,054.

lawyer a member of the legal profession who provides counsel to clients on matters of civil or criminal law and who represents clients on such matters in negotiations with others, before government agencies, and in civil and criminal courts. An ⟐attorney.

Activities of lawyers include business advice, ⟐conveyancing of property, making ⟐wills and settling estates, ⟐divorce, litigation and criminal prosecution or defense. A lawyer usually obtains a postgraduate Juris Doctor (JD) degree and must pass a bar examination and be admitted to the bar before he or she may practice within a state court's jurisdiction.

laxative substance used to relieve constipation (infrequent bowel movement). Current medical opinion discourages regular or prolonged use. Regular exercise and a diet high in vegetable fiber is believed to be the best means of preventing and treating constipation.

Laxness Halldor 1902– . Icelandic novelist who wrote about Icelandic life in the style of the early sagas. He was awarded a Nobel Prize in 1955.

Lazarus in the New Testament, the brother of Martha, a friend of Jesus, raised by him from the dead. Lazarus is also the name of a beggar in a parable told by Jesus (Luke 16).

Lazarus Emma 1849–1887. US poet, author of the poem on the base of the Statue of Liberty that begins: "Give me your tired, your poor/Your huddled masses yearning to breathe free."

Lazio (Roman *Latium*) region of W central Italy; area 6,639 sq mi/17,200 sq km; capital Rome; population (1990) 5,191,500. Products include olives, wine, chemicals, pharmaceuticals, and textiles. Home of the Latins from the 10th century BC, it was dominated by the Romans from the 4th century BC.

LCD abbreviation for ⟐*liquid-crystal display*.

L-dopa chemical, normally produced by the body, which is converted by an enzyme to dopamine in the brain. It is essential for integrated movement of individual muscle groups.

L-dopa is a left-handed isomer of an amino acid $C_9H_{11}NO_2$. As a treatment, it relieves the rigidity of ⟐Parkinson's disease but may have significant side effects, such as extreme mood changes, hallucinations, and uncontrolled writhing movements. It is often given in combination with other drugs to improve its effectiveness at lower doses.

leaching process by which substances are washed out of the soil. Fertilizers leached out of the soil drain into rivers, lakes, and ponds and cause water pollution. In tropical areas, leaching of the soil after the destruction of forests removes scarce nutrients and leads to a dramatic loss of soil fertility. The leaching of soluble minerals in soils can lead to the formation of distinct soil horizons as different minerals are deposited at successively lower levels.

Leacock Stephen Butler 1869–1944. Canadian humorist whose writings include *Literary Lapses* 1910, *Sunshine Sketches of a Little Town* 1912, and *Frenzied Fiction* 1918.

Born in Hampshire, England, Leacock lived in Canada from 1876 and was head of the department of economics at McGill University, Montreal, 1908–36. He published works on politics and economics, and studies of Mark Twain and Charles Dickens.

lead heavy, soft, malleable, gray, metallic element, symbol Pb (from Latin *plumbum*), atomic number 82, atomic weight 207.19. Usually found as an ore (most often in galena), it occasionally occurs as a free metal (⟐native metal), and is the final stable product of the decay of uranium. Lead is the softest and weakest of the commonly used metals, with a low melting point; it is a poor conductor of electricity and resists acid corrosion. As a cumulative poison, lead enters the body from lead water pipes, lead-based paints, and leaded gasoline. The metal is an effective shield against radiation and is used in batteries, glass, ceramics, and alloys such as pewter and solder.

lead–acid cell type of ⟐battery.

Leadbelly nickname of Huddie ⟐Ledbetter, US musician.

leaded gasoline gasoline containing the lead compound tetraethyllead, $(C_2H_5)_4Pb$, an anti-knock agent. It improves the combustion of gasoline and the performance of an automobile engine. The lead from the exhaust fumes enters the atmosphere, mostly as simple lead compounds.

lead ore any of several minerals from which lead is extracted. The main primary ore is galena or lead sulfite PbS. This is unstable, and on prolonged exposure to the atmosphere it oxidizes into the minerals cerussite $PbCO_3$ and anglesite $PbSO_4$. Lead ores are usually associated with other metals, particularly silver—which can be mined at the same time—and zinc, which can cause problems during smelting.

Most commercial deposits of lead ore are in the form of veins, where hot fluids have leached the ore from cooling igneous masses (see ⟐igneous rock) and deposited it in cracks in the surrounding country rock, and in thermal metamorphic zones (see ⟐metamorphic rock), where the heat of igneous intrusions has altered the minerals of surrounding rocks. Lead is mined in over 40 countries, but half of the world's output comes from the US, Canada, Russia, Kazakhstan, Uzbekistan, and Australia.

leaf lateral outgrowth on the stem of a plant, and in most species the primary organ of ⟐photosynthesis. The chief leaf types are cotyledons (seed leaves), scale leaves (on underground stems), foliage leaves, and bracts (in the axil of which a flower is produced).

Typically leaves are composed of three parts: the sheath or leaf base, the petiole or stalk, and the lamina or blade. The lamina has a network of veins through which water and nutrients are conducted. Structurally the leaf is made up of ⟐mesophyll cells surrounded by the epidermis and usually, in addition, a waxy layer, termed the cuticle, which prevents excessive evaporation of water from the leaf tissues by transpiration. The epidermis is interrupted by small pores, or stomata, through which gas exchange between the plant and the atmosphere occurs.

A simple leaf is undivided, as in the maple or oak. A compound leaf is composed of several leaflets, as in the blackberry, horse chestnut, or ash (the latter being a ⟐pinnate leaf). Leaves that fall in the autumn are termed deciduous, while evergreen leaves are persistent.

leaf-hopper any of numerous species of plant-sucking insects (order Homoptera) of the family Cicadellidae. They feed on the sap of leaves. Each species feeds on a limited range of plants.

leaf insect insect of the order Phasmida, about 4 in/10 cm long, with a green, flattened body, remarkable for closely resembling the foliage on which it lives. It is most common in SE Asia.

Leaf insects are related to walking sticks and ⏵mantises.

League of Nations international organization formed after World War I to solve international disputes by arbitration. Established in Geneva, Switzerland, 1920, the league included representatives from states throughout the world, but was severely weakened by the US decision not to become a member, and had no power to enforce its decisions. It was dissolved 1946. Its subsidiaries included the *International Labour Organization* and the *Permanent Court of International Justice* in The Hague, Netherlands, both now under the auspices of the ⏵United Nations.

The formation of the league was first suggested by President ⏵Wilson in his Fourteen Points as part of the peace settlement for World War I. The US did not become a member since it did not ratify the the the Treaty of ⏵Versailles. Although the league organized conferences, settled minor disputes, and did humanitarian work, it failed to handle the aggression of the 1930s—of Japan against China, Italy in Ethiopia, and Germany against neighboring countries.

Leakey Louis (Seymour Bazett) 1903–1972. British archeologist, born in Kenya. In 1958, with his wife Mary Leakey, he discovered gigantic extinct-animal fossils in the ⏵Olduvai Gorge in Tanzania, as well as many remains of an early human type.

Leakey Mary 1913– . British archeologist. In 1948 she discovered, on Rusinga Island, Lake Victoria, E Africa, the prehistoric ape skull known as *Proconsul*, about 20 million years old; and human remains at Laetolil, to the south, about 3,750,000 years old.

Leakey Richard 1944– . British archeologist. In 1972 he discovered at Lake Turkana, Kenya, an apelike skull, estimated to be about 2.9 million years old; it had some human characteristics and a brain capacity of 800 cu cm. In 1984 his team found an almost complete skeleton of *Homo erectus* some 1.6 million years old. He is the son of Louis and Mary Leakey.

Lean David 1908–1991. British film director. His films, noted for their atmospheric quality, include early work codirected with playwright Noël ⏵Coward. *Brief Encounter* 1946 established Lean as a leading talent. Among his later films are such accomplished epics as *The Bridge on the River Kwai* 1957 (Academy Award), *Lawrence of Arabia* 1962 (Academy Award), and *Dr Zhivago* 1965. The unfavorable reaction to *Ryan's Daughter* 1970 caused him to withdraw from filmmaking for over a decade, but *A Passage to India* 1984 represented a return to form.

Lear Edward 1812–1888. English artist and humorist. His *Book of Nonsense* 1846 popularized the limerick (a five-line humorous verse). He first attracted attention by his paintings of birds, and later turned to landscapes. He traveled to Italy, Greece, Egypt, and India, publishing books on his travels with his own illustrations, and spent most of his later life in Italy.

learning curve graphical representation of the improvement in performance of a person executing a new task.

learning theory in psychology, a theory about how an organism acquires new behaviors. Two main theories are Classical and operant ⏵conditioning.

leasehold in law, land or property held by a tenant (lessee) for a specified period, (unlike freehold, outright ownership) usually at a rent from the landlord (lessor).

least action principle in science, the principle that nature "chooses" the easiest path for moving objects, rays of light, and so on; also known in biology as the *principle of parsimony*.

leather material prepared from the hides and skins of animals, by tanning with vegetable tannins and chromium salts. Leather is a durable and water-resistant material, and is used for bags, shoes, clothing, and upholstery. There are three main stages in the process of converting animal skin into leather: cleaning, tanning, and dressing. Tanning is often a highly polluting process.

The skin, usually cattle hide, is dehydrated after removal to arrest decay. Soaking is necessary before tanning in order to replace the lost water with something that will bind the fibers together. The earliest practice, at least 7,000 years old, was to pound grease into the skin. In about 400 BC the Egyptians began to use vegetable extracts containing tannic acid, a method adopted in medieval Europe. Chemical tanning using mineral salts was introduced in the late 19th century.

Leatherstocking Tales, The five novels by James Fenimore Cooper, describing the ideal US frontiersman, Natty Bumppo, also known as Leatherstocking or the Deerslayer: *The Pioneers* 1823, *The Last of the Mohicans* 1826, *The Prairie* 1827, *The Pathfinder* 1840, and *The Deerslayer* 1841.

The novels follow (though not in order of publication) Natty's life from his youth before the American Revolution to his death after the Louisiana Purchase.

Leaves of Grass collection of poems by US writer Walt Whitman, published anonymously in 1855 and augmented through many editions up to 1892. With its open and "barbaric yawp" meter, the book influenced subsequent US verse.

Leavitt Henrietta Swan 1868–1921. US astronomer who in 1912 discovered the *period–luminosity law* that links the brightness of a ⏵Cepheid variable star to its period of variation. This law allows astronomers to use Cepheid variables as "standard candles" for measuring distances in space.

Lebanon country in W Asia, bounded N and E by Syria, S by Israel, and W by the Mediterranean Sea.

government Under the 1926 constitution, amended 1927, 1929, 1943, 1947, and 1989, legislative power is held by the national assembly, whose 99 members are elected by universal adult suffrage, through a system of proportional representation, in order to give a fair reflection of all the country's religious groups. The assembly serves a four-year term. The president is elected by the assembly for a six-year term and appoints a prime minister and cabinet who are collectively responsible to the assembly. Under the 1943 amended constitution the president is Christian, the prime minister is Sunni Muslim, and the speaker of the national assembly is Shiite Muslim. The

1989 constitution reflects the Muslim majority that has emerged since 1947. The powers of the president have been much diminished, although the post is still reserved for a Maronite Christian.

history The area now known as Lebanon was once occupied by ⏵Phoenicia, an empire that flourished from the 5th century BC to the 1st century AD, when it came under Roman rule. Christianity was introduced during the Roman occupation, and Islam arrived with the Arabs 635. Lebanon was part of the Turkish Ottoman Empire from the 16th century, until administered by France under a League of Nations mandate 1920–41. It was declared independent 1941, became a republic 1943, and achieved full autonomy 1944.

Lebanon has a wide variety of religions, including Christianity and many Islamic sects. For many years these coexisted peacefully, giving Lebanon a stability that enabled it, until the mid-1970s, to be a commercial and financial center. Beirut's thriving business district was largely destroyed 1975–76, and Lebanon's role as an international trader has been greatly diminished.

PLO presence in Lebanon After the establishment of Israel 1948, thousands of Palestinian refugees fled to Lebanon, and the ⏵Palestine Liberation Organization (PLO), founded in Beirut 1964, had its headquarters in Lebanon 1971–82 (it moved to Tunis 1982). The PLO presence in Lebanon has been the main reason for Israeli invasions and much of the subsequent civil strife. Fighting has been largely between left-wing Muslims, led by Kamul Jumblatt of the Progressive Socialist Party, and conservative Christian groups, mainly members of the Phalangist Party. There have also been differences between pro-Iranian traditional Muslims, such as the ⏵Shiites, and Syrian-backed deviationist Muslims, such as the ⏵Druse.

civil war In 1975 the fighting developed into full-scale civil war. A cease-fire was agreed 1976, but fighting began again 1978, when Israeli forces invaded Lebanon in search of PLO guerrillas. The United Nations secured Israel's agreement to a withdrawal and set up an international peacekeeping force, but to little avail. In 1979 Major Saad Haddad, a right-wing Lebanese army officer, with Israeli encouragement, declared an area of about 700 sq mi/1,800 sq km in S Lebanon an "independent free Lebanon," and the following year Christian Phalangist soldiers took over an area N of Beirut. Throughout this turmoil the Lebanese government was virtually powerless. In 1982 Bachir Gemayel (youngest son of Pierre Gemayel, the founder of the Phalangist Party) became president. He was assassinated before he could assume office and his brother Amin took his place. Israeli forces again invaded 1982, driving to Beirut and forcing the expulsion of PLO guerrillas and leaders to Syrian-held areas and to Tunisia.

efforts to end hostilities In 1983, after exhaustive talks between Lebanon and Israel, under US auspices, an agreement declared an end to hostilities and called for the withdrawal of all foreign forces from the country within three months. Syria refused to recognize the agreement and left about 40,000 troops, with about 7,000 PLO fighters, in N Lebanon. Israel responded by refusing to take its forces from the south. Meanwhile, a full-scale war began between Phalangist and Druse soldiers in the Chouf Mountains, ending in a Christian defeat and the creation of a Druse-controlled ministate. The multinational force was drawn gradually but unwillingly into the conflict until it was withdrawn in the spring of 1984. Attempts were made 1985 and 1986 to end the civil war but rifts within Muslim and Christian groups thwarted them. Meanwhile Lebanon, and particularly Beirut, has seen its infrastructure and earlier prosperity virtually destroyed as it continues to be a battlefield for the rival factions.

The civil war in Beirut pitted the E Beirut "administration" of General Michel Aoun, backed by Christian army units and Lebanese militia forces (although 30% of them are Muslim), against the W Beirut "administration"

(Muslim) of Premier Selim al-Hoss, supported by Syrian army and Muslim militia allies, including Walid Jumblatt's Progressive Socialist Party (Druse).

In May 1989 the Arab League secured agreement to a cease-fire between Christians and Muslims and in Sept a peace plan was agreed by all except General Aoun, who dissolved the national assembly. The assembly ignored him and in Nov elected the Maronite-Christian René Muawad as president instead of Aoun, but within days he was killed by an automobile bomb. Elias Hrawi was made his successor and he immediately confirmed the acting prime minister, al-Hoss, in that post. Despite being

replaced as army commander in chief, Aoun continued to defy the constituted government. **Western hostages** In 1990 it was estimated that 18 Westerners, including eight Americans, were being held hostage in Lebanon by pro-Iranian Shiite Muslim groups; many had been held incommunicado for years. In Aug the release of Western ₪hostages began. In Oct government troops, backed by Syria, stormed the presidential palace occupied by General Aoun, who surrendered and took refuge in the French embassy. By Nov the government of Hrawi and al-Hoss had regained control of Beirut and proposals for a new constitution for a Second Republic were being discussed. In Dec Hrawi appointed Umar Karami as prime minister, heading a new government. Following improved relations with Syria and Iran, and strenuous efforts by the UN secretary-general, the remaining Western ₪hostages were progressively released; General Aoun was pardoned by the government and allowed to leave his haven in the French embassy. By 1992 all Western hostages had been released.

Faced with increasing economic problems, Prime Minister Karami resigned May 1992 and was replaced by Rashid al-Solh. By that time the 15 years of civil war had left 144,240 dead, 17,415 missing, and 197,505 injured. The Sept 1992 general election was boycotted by many Christians, resulting in the reelection of the pro-Syrian administration, with Rafik a-Hariri as prime minister.*See illustration box.*

Lebanon
Republic of (*al-Jumhouria al- Lubnaniya*)

area 4,034 sq mi/10,452 sq km
capital and port Beirut
cities ports Tripoli, Tyre, Sidon
physical narrow coastal plain; Bekka valley N–S between Lebanon and Anti-Lebanon mountain ranges
features Mount Hermon; Chouf Mountains; archeological sites at Baalbeck, Byblos, Tyre; until the civil war, the financial center of the Middle East
head of state Elias Hrawi from 1989
head of government Rafik al-Hariri from 1992
political system emergent democratic republic
political parties Phalangist Party, Christian, radical, right-wing; Progressive Socialist Party (PSP), Druse, moderate, socialist; National Liberal Party (NLP), Maronite, center-left; Parliamentary Democratic Front, Sunni Muslim, centrist; Lebanese Communist Party (PCL), nationalist, communist
exports citrus and other fruit, vegetables; industrial products to Arab neighbors
currency Lebanese pound
population (1990 est) 3,340,000 (Lebanese 82%, Palestinian 9%, Armenian 5%); growth rate –0.1% p.a.
life expectancy men 65, women 70 (1989)
languages Arabic, French (both official), Armenian, English
religions Muslim 57% (Shiite 33%, Sunni 24%), Christian (Maronite and Orthodox) 40%, Druse 3%
literacy 75% (1989)
GNP $1.8 bn; $690 per head (1986)
chronology
1920–41 Administered under French mandate.
1944 Independence achieved.
1948–49 Lebanon joined first Arab war against Israel. Palestinian refugees settled

in the south.
1964 Palestine Liberation Organization (PLO) founded in Beirut.
1967 More Palestinian refugees settled in Lebanon.
1971 PLO expelled from Jordan; established headquarters in Lebanon.
1975 Outbreak of civil war between Christians and Muslims.
1976 Cease-fire agreed; Syrian-dominated Arab deterrent force formed to keep the peace but considered by Christians as a occupying force.
1978 Israel invaded S Lebanon in search of PLO fighters. International peacekeeping force established. Fighting broke out again.
1979 Part of S Lebanon declared an "independent free Lebanon."
1982 Bachir Gemayel became president but was assassinated before he could assume office; succeeded by his brother Amin Gemayel. Israel again invaded Lebanon. Palestinians withdrew from Beirut under supervision of international peacekeeping force. PLO moved its headquarters to Tunis.
1983 Agreement reached for the withdrawal of Syrian and Israeli troops but abrogated under Syrian pressure.
1984 Most of international peacekeeping force withdrawn. Muslim militia took control of W Beirut.
1985 Lebanon in chaos; many foreigners taken hostage.
1987 Syrian troops sent into Beirut.
1988 Agreement on a Christian successor to Gemayel failed; he established a military government; Selim al-Hoss set up rival government; threat of partition hung over the country.
1989 Christian leader General Michel Aoun declared "war of liberation" against Syrian occupation; Saudi Arabia and Arab League sponsored talks that resulted in new constitution recognizing Muslim majority; René Muhawad named president, assassinated after 17 days in office; Elias Hrawi named successor; Aoun occupied presidential palace, rejected constitution.
1990 Release of Western hostages began. General Aoun surrendered and legitimate government restored, with Umar Karami as prime minister.
1991 Government extended control to the whole country. Treaty of cooperation with Syria signed. More Western hostages released. General Aoun pardoned.
1992 Karami resigned as prime minister; succeeded by Rashid al-Solh. Remaining Western hostages released. General election boycotted by many Christians; pro-Syrian administration reelected; Rafik al-Hariri became prime minister.

Lebanon city in SE Pennsylvania, NE of Harrisburg, seat of Lebanon County. Industries include iron and steel products, textiles, clothing, and chemicals; population (1990) 24,800.

Lebensraum (German "living space") theory developed by Hitler for the expansion of Germany into E Europe, and in the 1930s used by the Nazis to justify their annexation of neighboring states on the grounds that Germany was overpopulated.

Leblanc Nicolas 1742–1806. French chemist who in 1790 developed a process for making soda ash (sodium carbonate, Na_2CO_3) from common salt (sodium chloride, NaCl).

In the **Leblanc process**, salt was first converted into sodium sulfate by the action of sulfuric acid, which was then roasted with chalk or limestone (calcium carbonate) and coal to produce a mixture of sodium carbonate and sulfide. The carbonate was leached out with water and the solution crystallized. Leblanc devised this method of producing soda ash (for use in making glass, paper, soap, and various other chemicals) to win a prize offered in 1775 by the French Academy of Sciences, but the Revolutionary government granted him only a patent (1791), which they seized along with his factory three years later. A broken man, Leblanc committed suicide.

Lebowa black homeland in Transvaal province, South Africa; it achieved self-governing status 1972; population (1985) 1,836,000.

Lebrun Albert 1871–1950. French politician. He became president of the senate in 1931 and in 1932 was chosen as president of the republic. In 1940 he handed his powers over to Marshal Pétain.

Le Brun Charles 1619–1690. French artist, painter to Louis XIV from 1662. In 1663 he became director of the French Academy and of the Gobelins factory, which produced art, tapestries, and furnishings for the new palace of Versailles. In the 1640s he studied under the painter Poussin in Rome. Returning to Paris in 1646, he worked on large decorative schemes including the *Galerie des glaces* (Hall of Mirrors) at Versailles. He also painted portraits.

Le Carré John. Adopted name of David John Cornwell 1931– . English writer of thrillers. His low-key realistic accounts of complex espionage include *The Spy Who Came in from the Cold* 1963, *Tinker Tailor Soldier Spy* 1974, *Smiley's People* 1980, and *The Russia House* 1989. He was a member of the Foreign Service 1960–64.

Le Chatelier's principle or *Le Chatelier-Braun principle* in science, the principle that if a change in conditions is imposed on a system in equilibrium, the system will react to counteract that change and restore the equilibrium.

First stated in 1884 by French chemist Henri le Chatelier (1850–1936), it has been found to apply widely outside the field of chemistry.

lecithin lipid (fat), containing nitrogen and phosphorus, that forms a vital part of the cell membranes of plant and animal cells. The name is from the Greek *lekithos* "egg yolk," eggs being a major source of lecithin.

Leclanché Georges 1839–1882. French engineer. In 1866 he invented a primary electrical cell, the *Leclanché cell*, which is still the basis of most dry batteries. A Leclanché cell consists of a carbon rod (the ◊anode) inserted into a mixture of powdered carbon and manganese dioxide contained in a porous pot, which sits in a glass jar containing an ◊electrolyte (conducting medium) of ammonium chloride solution, into which a zinc ◊cathode is inserted. The cell produces a continuous current, the carbon mixture acting as a depolarizer; that is, it prevents hydrogen bubbles from forming on the anode and increasing resistance. In a dry battery, the electrolyte is made in the form of a paste with starch.

Leconte de Lisle Charles Marie René 1818–1894. French poet. He was born on the Indian Ocean Island of Réunion, settled in Paris in 1846, and headed the anti-Romantic group Les ◊Parnassiens 1866–76. His work drew inspiration from the ancient world, as in *Poèmes antiques/Antique Poems* 1852, *Poèmes barbares/Barbaric Poems* 1862, and *Poèmes tragiques/Tragic Poems* 1884.

Le Corbusier assumed name of Charles-Édouard Jeanneret 1887–1965. Swiss architect. His functionalist approach to town planning in industrial society was based on the interrelationship between machine forms and the techniques of modern architecture. His concept, *La Ville radieuse*, developed in Marseille, France (1945–50) and Chandigarh, India, placed buildings and open spaces with related functions in a circular formation, with buildings based on standard-sized units mathematically calculated according to the proportions of the human figure (see ◊Fibonacci, ◊golden section).

Le Corbusier was originally a painter and engraver, but turned his attention to the problems of contemporary industrial society. His books *Vers une architecture* 1923 and *Le Modulor* 1948 have had worldwide significance for town planning and building design.

LED abbreviation for ◊*light-emitting diode*.

Leda in Greek mythology, the wife of Tyndareus and mother of Clytemnestra. Zeus, who came to her as a swan, was the father of her other children: Helen of Troy and the twins Castor and Pollux.

Ledbetter Huddie, "Leadbelly" c. 1888–1949. US musician. Better known by his nickname, he was born in Mooringsport, Louisiana, and spent his early years as a farmhand. Drawn to music at an early age, he traveled throughout the South and became well known for his blues guitar playing. In 1934 he was "discovered" by visiting folklorists John and Alan Lomax, who helped him begin a professional concert and recording career. Ledbetter was an important source of inspiration for the urban folk movement of the 1950s. His rendition of "Good Night, Irene" became a folk classic.

Lederberg Joshua 1925– . US geneticist who showed that bacteria can reproduce sexually, combining genetic material so that offspring possess characteristics of both parent organisms.

Lederberg is considered a pioneer of genetic engineering, a science that relies on the possibility of artificially shuffling genes from cell to cell. He realized that bacteriophages, viruses which invade bacteria, can transfer genes from one bacterium to another, a discovery that led to the deliberate insertion by scientists of foreign genes into bacterial cells. In 1958 he shared the Nobel Prize for Medicine with George ◊Beadle and Edward ◊Tatum.

Le Duc Tho 1911–1990. North Vietnamese diplomat who was joint winner (with US Secretary of State Kissinger) of the 1973 Nobel Peace Prize for his part in the negotiations to end the Vietnam War. He indefinitely postponed receiving the award.

Ledyard John 1751–1789. American explorer and adventurer. Born in Groton, Connecticut, Ledyard briefly attended Dartmouth but left school for a life at sea. In 1776, in London, he signed on with Captain Cook for a voyage around the Cape of Good Hope. As a British marine, Ledyard was sent to Long Island during the American Revolution, but, refusing to fight against his own countrymen, he deserted in 1782. Always scheming, he devised a plan for opening the fur trade with China but could not raise the necessary capital. After an ill-fated journey through Siberia, he died in Cairo on his way to find the source of the Niger River.

Led Zeppelin UK rock group 1969–80, founders of the heavy-metal genre. Their overblown style, with long solos, was based on rhythm and blues; songs like "Stairway to Heaven" have become classics.

Lee Bruce. Adopted name of Lee Yuen Kam 1941–1973. US "Chinese Western" film actor, an expert in ◊kung fu, who popularized the oriental martial arts in the West with pictures made in Hong Kong, such as *Fists of Fury* 1972 and *Enter the Dragon* 1973, his last film.

Lee Gyspy Rose 1914–1970. US entertainer. In her teenage years Lee learned the art of the striptease in New York and began performing as an "elegant lady" in burlesque reviews. Unique in her intelligence and friendship with leading literary figures of her time, Lee was herself a published author, writing magazine articles and, after her retirement from stripping, two popular mystery novels, *The G-String Murders* 1941 and *Mother Finds a Body* 1942. Later appearing on Broadway and television, she became a national celebrity. Her autobiography, *Gypsy: A Memoir* 1957, was adapted for stage 1959 and film 1962.

Born Rose Louise Hovick in Seattle, Washington, she began, at about age four, performing song and dance routines with her sister, actress June Havoc.

Lee Henry 1756–1818. American military and political leader. Born in Leesylvania, Virginia, Lee was educated at Princeton and served in the cavalry in the American Revolution. Rising to the rank of major, he won the nickname "Light-Horse Harry" for his lightning attacks. After the war, he entered politics, serving in the Continental Congress 1785–88 and as governor of Virginia 1792–95.

He was a close friend of George Washington and helped suppress the Whiskey Rebellion 1794. Lee was a member of the US House of Representatives 1799–1801 and eventually lost his fortune through bad investments. He was the father of Robert E Lee.

Lee Robert E(dward) 1807–1870. US military leader, Confederate commander in the American ◊Civil War, and military strategist. In 1859 he suppressed John ◊Brown's raid on Harper's Ferry. Lee had freed his own slaves long before the war began, and he was opposed to secession, however his devotion to his native Virginia led him to join the 'Confederacy. At the outbreak of war he became military adviser to Jefferson ◊Davis, president of the Confederacy, and in 1862 commander of the Army of Northern Virginia. Lee actually had been offered command of the Union armies, but he resigned his commission to return to Virginia. During 1862–63 he made several raids into Northern territory but after his defeat at Gettysburg was compelled to take the defensive; he surrendered 1865 at Appomattox.

Lee graduated from West Point and distinguished himself in the Mexican War 1846–48. In 1861 he joined the army of the Confederacy of Southern states; in 1862 he received the command of the Army of Northern Virginia and won the Seven Days' Battle defending Richmond, Virginia, the Confederate capital, against General McClellan's Union forces. In 1863 Lee won victories at Fredericksburg and Chancellorsville, both in Virginia, and in 1864 at Cold Harbor, Virginia, but was besieged in Petersburg, Virginia, June 1864–April 1865. He surrendered to General ◊Grant on April 9, 1865, at Appomattox Courthouse. Following the war he was paroled and served as president of Washington College (now Washington and Lee University). His home had been seized by Union forces and now is part of Arlington National Cemetery.

Lee Spike (Shelton Jackson) 1957– . US film director, actor and writer. His work presents the bitter realities of contemporary African-American life in an aggressive, often controversial manner. His films, in which he sometimes appears, include *She's Gotta Have It* 1986, *Do The Right Thing* 1989, *Jungle Fever* 1991, and *Malcolm X* 1992.

Lee and Yang Lee Tsung Dao (1926–) and Yang Chen Ning (1922–) Chinese physicists who studied how parity operates at the nuclear level. They found no proof for the claim, made by ◊Wigner, that nuclear processes were indistinguishable from their mirror images, and that elementary particles made no distinction between left and right. In 1956 they predicted that parity was not conserved in weak interactions. They shared a Nobel Prize 1957.

leech annelid worm forming the class Hirudinea. Leeches inhabit fresh water, and in tropical countries infest damp forests. As bloodsucking animals they are injurious to people and animals, to whom they attach themselves by means of a strong mouth adapted to sucking.

Formerly, the medicinal leech *Hirudo medicinalis* was used extensively for "bleeding" for a variety of ills. It is still cultivated as the source of the anticoagulant hirudin.

Leeds city in W Yorkshire, England, on the river Aire; population (1991 est) 674,400. Industries include engineering, printing, chemicals, glass, and woolens. Notable buildings include the Town Hall designed by Cuthbert Brodrick, Leeds University 1904, the Art Gallery 1844, Temple Newsam (birthplace of Henry Darnley in 1545, now a museum), and the Cistercian Abbey of Kirkstall 1147. It is a center of communications where road, rail, and canal (to Liverpool and Goole) meet.

Opera North is based here, and the Leeds International Pianoforte Competition is held here every three years.

leek onionlike plant of the genus *Allium* of the lily family Liliaceae. The cultivated leek is a variety of the wild *A. ampeloprasum* of the Mediterranean area and Atlantic islands. The lower leaf parts form the bulb, which is eaten as a vegetable.

Lee Kuan Yew 1923– . Singapore politician, prime minister 1959–90. Lee founded the anticommunist Socialist People's Action Party 1954 and entered the Singapore legislative assembly 1955. He was elected the country's first prime minister 1959, and took Singapore out of the Malaysian federation 1965. He remained in power until his resignation 1990, and was succeeded by Goh Chok Tongo.

Lee Teng-hui 1923– . Taiwanese right-wing politician, vice-president 1984–88, president and Kuomintang (see ⬦Guomindang) party leader from 1988. Lee, the country's first island-born leader, is viewed as a reforming technocrat.

Leeuwenhoek Anton van 1632–1723. Dutch pioneer of microscopic research. He ground his own lenses, some of which magnified up to 200 times. With these he was able to see individual red blood cells, sperm, and bacteria, achievements not repeated for more than a century.

Leeward Islands (1) group of islands, part of the ⬦Society Islands, in ⬦French Polynesia, S Pacific; (2) general term for the northern half of the Lesser ⬦Antilles in the West Indies; (3) former British colony in the West Indies (1871–1956) comprising Antigua, Montserrat, St Christopher/St Kitts—Nevis, Anguilla, and the Virgin Islands.

left-handedness in humans, using the left hand more skillfully and in preference to the right hand for most actions. It occurs in about 9% of the population, predominantly males. It is caused by dominance of the right side of the brain.

left wing in politics, the socialist parties. The term originated in the French National Assembly of 1789, where the nobles sat in the place of honor to the right of the president, and the commons sat to the left. This arrangement has become customary in European parliaments, where the progressives sit on the left and the conservatives on the right. It is also usual to speak of the right, left, and center, when referring to the different elements composing a single party.

legacy in law, a gift of personal property made by a testator in a will and transferred on the testator's death to the legatee. **Specific legacies** are definite named objects; a **general legacy** is a sum of money or item not specially identified; a **residuary legacy** is all the remainder of the deceased's personal estate after debts have been paid and the other legacies have been distributed.

legend (Latin *legere* "to read") a traditional or undocumented story about famous people. The term was originally applied to the books of readings designed for use in Divine Service, and afterwards extended to the stories of saints read in monasteries. A collection of such stories was the 13th-century *Legenda Aurea* by Jacobus de Voragine.

Léger Fernand 1881–1955. French painter, associated with ⬦Cubism. From around 1909 he evolved a characteristic style, composing abstract and semi abstract works with cylindrical forms, reducing the human figure to constructions of pure shape. Mechanical forms are constant themes in his work, including his designs for the Swedish Ballet 1921–22, murals, and the abstract film *Ballet mécanique/ Mechanical Ballet*.

legionnaire's disease pneumonialike disease, so called because it was first identified when it broke out at a convention of the American Legion in Philadelphia in 1976. Legionnaire's disease is caused by the bacterium *Legionella pneumophila*, which breeds in warm water (for example, in the cooling towers of air-conditioning systems). It is spread in minute water droplets, which may be inhaled.

legislature law-making body or bodies in a political system. Some legislatures are unicameral (having one chamber), and some bicameral (with two).

In most democratic countries with bicameral legislatures the "lower," or popular, chamber is the more powerful but there are exceptions, the most notable being in the US, where the upper chamber, the ⬦Senate, is constitutionally more powerful than the lower, the House of Representatives. Most lower or single chambers are popularly elected and upper chambers are filled by appointees or a mixture of appointed and elected members. In the US, both chambers are elected, whereas in the UK, the lower chamber, the ⬦House of Commons, is elected and the upper chamber, the ⬦House of Lords, is filled by hereditary members or appointees.

Legitimist party in France that continued to support the claims of the house of ⬦Bourbon after the revolution of 1830. When the direct line became extinct in 1883, the majority of the party transferred allegiance to the house of Orléans.

Legnano, Battle of defeat of Holy Roman emperor Frederick I Barbarossa by members of the Lombard League in 1176 at Legnano, northwest of Milan. It was a major setback to the emperor's plans for imperial domination over Italy and marked for the first time the power of infantry against feudal cavalry.

Le Guin Ursula K(roeber) 1929– . US writer of science fiction and fantasy. Her novels include *The Left Hand of Darkness* 1969, which questions sex roles; the *Earthsea* trilogy 1968–72; *The Dispossessed* 1974, which compares an anarchist and a capitalist society; *Orsinian Tales* 1976; and *Always Coming Home* 1985.

legume plant of the family Leguminosae, which has a pod containing dry seeds. The family includes peas, beans, lentils, clover, and alfalfa (lucerne). Legumes are important in agriculture because of their specialized roots, which have nodules containing bacteria capable of fixing nitrogen from the air and increasing the fertility of the soil. The edible seeds of legumes are called **pulses**.

Lehár Franz 1870–1948. Hungarian composer. He wrote many operettas, among them *The Merry Widow* 1905, *The Count of Luxembourg* 1909, *Gypsy Love* 1910, and *The Land of Smiles* 1929. He also composed songs, marches, and a violin concerto.

Le Havre industrial port (engineering, chemicals, oil refining) in Normandy, NW France, on the river Seine; population (1982) 255,000. It is the largest port in Europe, and has transatlantic passenger links.

Lehman Herbert Henry 1878–1963. US political leader. In 1932 he became governor of New York, and his subsequent support of F D Roosevelt's policies caused his own administration to be called the "Little New Deal." In 1942 Lehman was appointed director of the federal Office of Foreign Relief and Rehabilitation. He served in the US Senate 1949–57.

Born in New York and educated at Williams College, Lehman joined his family's banking business and served in the army during World War I. Later entering politics, he was an adviser to Al Smith and was elected New York's lieutenant governor 1928.

Leibniz Gottfried Wilhelm 1646–1716. German mathematician and philosopher. Independently of, but concurrently with, the British scientist Isaac Newton he developed the branch of mathematics known as ⬦calculus. In his metaphysical works, such as *The Monadology* 1714, he argued that everything consisted of innumerable units, **monads**, the individual properties of which determined each thing's past, present, and future. Monads, although independent of each other, interacted predictably; this meant that Christian faith and scientific reason need not be in conflict and that "this is the best of all possible worlds." His optimism is satirized in Voltaire's *Candide*.

Leicester Robert Dudley, Earl of Leicester *c.* 1532–1588. English courtier. Son of the Duke of Northumberland, he was created earl of Leicester 1564. Queen Elizabeth I gave him command of the army sent to the Netherlands 1585–87 and of the forces prepared to resist the threat of Spanish invasion of 1588. His lack of military success led to his recall, but he retained Elizabeth's favor until his death.

Leicester's good looks attracted Queen Elizabeth, who made him Master of the Horse 1558 and a privy councillor 1559. But his poor performance in the army ended any chance of marrying the queen. He was a staunch supporter of the Protestant cause.

Leicestershire county in central England
area 984 sq mi/2,550 sq km
cities Leicester (administrative headquarters), Loughborough, Melton Mowbray, Market Harborough
features Rutland district (formerly England's smallest county, with Oakham as its county town); Rutland Water, one of Europe's largest reservoirs; Charnwood Forest; Vale of Belvoir (under which are large coal deposits)
products horses, cattle, sheep, dairy products, coal
population (1991) 860,500
famous people C P Snow, Thomas Babington Macaulay, Titus Oates.

Leiden or *Leyden* city in South Holland province, the Netherlands; population (1991) 111,900. Industries include textiles and cigars. It has been a printing center since 1580, with a university established in 1575. It is linked by canal to Haarlem, Amsterdam, and Rotterdam. The painters Rembrandt and Jan Steen were born here.

Leif Ericsson Norse explorer; see ⏿Ericsson, Leif.

Leigh Vivien. Adopted name of Vivien Mary Hartley 1913–1967. English actress who appeared on the stage in London and New York, and won Academy Awards for her performances as Scarlett O'Hara in *Gone With the Wind* 1939 and as Blanche du Bois in *A Streetcar Named Desire* 1951.

She was born in India. Married to Laurence Olivier 1940–60, she starred with him in the play *Antony and Cleopatra* in 1951. Her films include *Lady Hamilton* 1941, *Anna Karenina* 1948, and *Ship of Fools* 1965.

Leigh-Mallory Trafford 1892–1944. British air chief marshal in World War II. He took part in the Battle of Britain and was Commander in Chief of Allied air forces during the invasion of France.

Leinster SE province of the Republic of Ireland, comprising the counties of Carlow, Dublin, Kildare, Kilkenny, Laois, Longford, Louth, Meath, Offaly, Westmeath, Wexford, and Wicklow; area 7,577 sq mi/19,630 sq km; capital Dublin; population (1991) 1,860,000.

Leipzig city in W Saxony, Germany, 90 mi/ 145 km SW of Berlin; population (1986) 552,000. Products include furs, leather goods, cloth, glass, automobiles, and musical instruments.

leishmaniasis any of several parasitic diseases caused by microscopic protozoans of the genus *Leishmania*, identified by William Leishman (1865–1926), and transmitted by sandflies. Either localized infection or dangerous fever can be a symptom. The diseases are prevalent in NE Africa and S Asia. Kala-azar, characterized by an enlarged spleen and liver, fever, and anemia, is an example.

Leisler Jacob 1640–1691. Public figure in colonial New York. Born in Frankfurt, Germany, Leisler came to New Amsterdam as a mercenary for the Dutch West India Company 1660. He became a successful merchant when the colony passed to English rule and was one of the leaders of a local party that took advantage of the political instability caused by England's Glorious Revolution of 1688. As an officer in the militia, Leisler ousted the royal authorities and assumed command of New York in the name of William and Mary. Deposed in 1691 by troops dispatched from England, Leisler was tried and hanged for treason.

Leitrim county in Connacht province, Republic of Ireland, bounded NW by Donegal Bay
area 591 sq mi/1,530 sq km
county town Carrick-on-Shannon
features rivers: Shannon, Bonet, Drowes, and Duff
products potatoes, cattle, linen, woolens, pottery, coal, iron, lead
population (1991) 25,300.

lek in biology, a closely spaced set of very small ⏿territories each occupied by a single male during the mating season. Leks are found in the mating systems of several ground-dwelling birds (such as grouse) and a few antelopes.

The lek is a traditional site where both males and females congregate during the breeding season. The males display to passing females in the hope of attracting them to mate. Once mated, the females go elsewhere to lay their eggs or to complete gestation.

Lely Peter. Adopted name of Pieter van der Faes 1618–1680. Dutch painter, active in England from 1641, who painted fashionable portraits in Baroque style. His subjects included Charles I, Cromwell, and Charles II. He painted a series of admirals, *Flagmen* (National Maritime Museum, Greenwich), and one of *The Windsor Beauties* (Hampton Court, Richmond), fashionable women of Charles II's court.

Lemaître Georges Edouard 1894–1966. Belgian cosmologist who in 1927 proposed the ⏿Big Bang theory of the origin of the universe. He predicted that the entire universe was expanding, which the US astronomer Edwin ⏿Hubble confirmed. Lemaître suggested that the expansion had been started by an initial explosion, the Big Bang, a theory that is now generally accepted.

Le Mans industrial town in Sarthe *département*, France; population (1982) 150,000, conurbation 191,000. It has a motor-racing circuit where the annual endurance 24-hour race (established 1923) for sports automobiles and their prototypes is held.

lemming small rodent of the family Cricetidae, especially the genus *Lemmus*, comprising four species worldwide in northern latitudes. It is about 5 in/12 cm long, with thick brownish fur, a small head, and a short tail. Periodically, when their population exceeds the available food supply, lemmings undertake mass migrations.

Lemmon Jack (John Uhler III) 1925– . US character actor, often cast as the lead in comedy films, such as *Some Like It Hot* 1959 but equally skilled in serious roles, as in *The China Syndrome* 1979 and *Dad* 1990.

Lemnos (Greek *Límnos*) Greek island in the N of the Aegean Sea
area 184 sq mi/476 sq km
cities Kastron, Mudros
physical of volcanic origin, rising to 1,411 ft/ 430 m
products mulberries and other fruit, tobacco, sheep
population (1981) 15,700.

lemon sour fruit of the small, evergreen, semi-tropical lemon tree *Citrus limon*. It may have originated in NW India, and was introduced into Europe by the Spanish Moors in the 12th or 13th century. It is now grown in Italy, Spain, California, Florida, South Africa, and Australia.

lemon balm perennial herb *Melissa officinalis* of the mint family Labiatae, with lemon-scented leaves. It is widely used in teas, liqueurs, and medicines.

LeMond Greg 1961– . US racing cyclist, the first American to win the Tour de France 1986.

Although his career received a setback in 1987 through injury, he recovered sufficiently to regain his Tour de France title in 1989 by seven seconds, the smallest margin ever. He won it again in 1990. He also won the World Professional Road Race in 1983 and 1989.

lemur prosimian ⏿primate of the family Lemuridae, inhabiting Madagascar and the Comoro Islands. There are about 16 species, ranging from mouse-sized to dog-sized animals. Lemurs are arboreal animals, and some

species are nocturnal. They have long, bushy tails, and feed on fruit, insects, and small animals. Many are threatened with extinction owing to loss of their forest habitat and, in some cases, from hunting.

Lena longest river in Asiatic Russia, 2,730 mi/ 4,400 km, with numerous tributaries. Its source is near Lake Baikal, and it empties into the Arctic Ocean through a delta 240 mi/400 km wide. It is ice-covered for half the year.

Le Nain family of French painters, the brothers Antoine (1588–1648), Louis (1593–1648), and Mathieu (1607–1677). They were born in Laon, settled in Paris, and were among the original members of the French Academy in 1648. Attribution of works among them is uncertain. They chiefly painted somber and dignified scenes of peasant life.

Lenard Philipp Eduard Anton 1862–1947. German physicist who investigated the ⏿photoelectric effect (light causes metals to emit electrons) and cathode rays (the stream of electrodes emitted from the cathode in a vacuum tube). He was awarded a Nobel Prize in 1905.

In later life he became obsessed with the idea of producing a purely "Aryan" physics free from the influence of ⏿Einstein and other Jewish physicists.

Lendl Ivan 1960– . Czech-born American tennis player. He has won eight Grand Slam singles titles, including the US and French titles three times each. He has won more than $15 million in prize money.

CAREER HIGHLIGHTS

US Open 1985–87
French Open 1984, 1986–87
Australian Open 1989–90
Grand Prix Masters 1982–83, 1986–87
Davis Cup 1980 (member of Czechoslavakian team)

lend-lease in US history, an act of Congress passed in March 1941 that gave the president power to order "any defense article for the government of any country whose defense the president deemed vital to the defense of the US." During World War II, the US negotiated many Lend-Lease agreements, notably with Britain and the Soviet Union.

The aim of such agreements was to ignore trade balances among the participating countries during the war effort and to aid the Allied war effort without fanning isolationist sentiments. Lend-lease was officially stopped in Aug 1945, by which time goods and services to the value of $42 billion had been supplied in this way, of which the British Empire had received 65% and the Soviet Union 23%.

Lenin Vladimir Ilyich. Adopted name of Vladimir Ilyich Ulyanov 1870–1924. Russian revolutionary, first leader of the USSR, and communist theoretician. Active in the 1905 Revolution, Lenin had to leave Russia when it failed, settling in Switzerland in 1914. He returned to Russia after the February revolution of 1917 (see ⏿Russian Revolution). He led the Bolshevik revolution in Nov 1917 and became leader of a Soviet government, concluded peace with Germany, and organized a successful resistance to White Russian (pro-tsarist) uprisings and foreign intervention 1918–20. His modification of traditional Marxist doctrine to fit conditions prevailing in Russia became known as *Marxism-Leninism*, the basis of communist ideology.

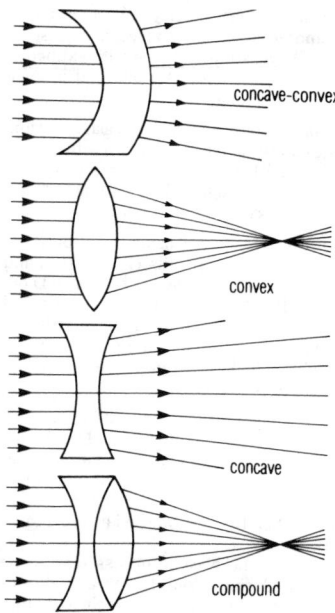

concave-convex

convex

concave

compound

lens *The passage of light through lenses.*

Lenin was born on April 22, 1870 in Simbirsk (now renamed Ulyanovsk), on the river Volga, and became a lawyer in St Petersburg. His brother was executed in 1887 for attempting to assassinate Tsar Alexander III. A Marxist from 1889, Lenin was sent to Siberia for spreading revolutionary propaganda 1895–1900. He then edited the political paper *Iskra* ("The Spark") from abroad, and visited London several times. In *What Is to be Done?* 1902 he advocated that a professional core of Social Democratic Party activists should spearhead the revolution in Russia, a suggestion accepted by the majority (*bolsheviki*) at the London party congress 1903. From Switzerland he attacked socialist support for World War I as aiding an "imperialist" struggle, and wrote *Imperialism* 1917.

After the renewed outbreak of revolution in Feb/March 1917, he returned to Russia in April and called for the transfer of power to the soviets (workers' councils). From the overthrow of the provisional government in Nov 1917 until his death, Lenin effectively controlled the Soviet Union, although an assassination attempt in 1918 injured his health. He founded the Third (Communist) ◊International in 1919. With communism proving inadequate to put the country on its feet, he introduced the private-enterprise ◊New Economic Policy 1921. His embalmed body is in a mausoleum in Red Square, Moscow. In 1898 he married **Nadezhda Konstantinova Krupskaya** (1869–1939), who shared his work and wrote *Memories of Lenin*.

Leninakan former name (to 1990) of Kumayri, town in ◊Armenia.

Leningrad former name (1924–91) of the Russian city ◊St Petersburg.

Lennon John (Ono) 1940–1980. UK rock singer, songwriter, and guitarist, in the US from 1971; a founder member of the ◊Beatles. Both before the band's breakup 1969 and in his solo career, he collaborated intermittently with his wife **Yoko Ono** (1933–). "Give Peace a Chance," a hit 1969, became an anthem of the peace movement. His solo work alternated between the confessional and the political, as on the album *Imagine* 1971. He was shot dead by a fan.

Le Nôtre André 1613–1700. French landscape gardener, creator of the gardens at Versailles and Les Tuileries, Paris.

lens in optics, a piece of a transparent material, such as glass, with two polished surfaces—one concave or convex, and the other plane, concave, or convex—that modifies rays of light. A convex lens brings rays of light together; a concave lens makes the rays diverge. Lenses are essential to glasses, microscopes, telescopes, cameras, and almost all optical instruments.

The image formed by a single lens suffers from several defects or aberrations, notably **spherical aberration** in which a straight line becomes a curved image, and **chromatic aberration** in which an image in white light tends to have colored edges. Aberrations are corrected by the use of compound lenses, which are built up from two or more lenses of different refractive index.

lens, gravitational see ◊gravitational lensing.

Lent in the Christian church, the 40-day period of fasting that precedes Easter, beginning on Ash Wednesday, but omitting Sundays.

lenticel small pore on the stems of woody plants or the trunks of trees. Lenticels are means of gas exchange between the stem interior and the atmosphere. They consist of loosely packed cells with many air spaces in between, and are easily seen on smooth-barked trees such as cherries, where they form horizontal lines on the trunk.

lentil annual Old World plant *Lens culinaris* of the pea family Leguminosae. The plant, which resembles vetch, grows 6–18 in/15–45 cm high and has white, blue, or purplish flowers. The seeds, contained in pods about 0.6 in/1.6 cm long, are widely used as food.

The most common varieties are the grayish French lentil and the red Egyptian lentil.

Lenya Lotte. Adopted name of Karoline Blamauer 1905–1981. Austrian actress and singer. She was married five times, twice to the composer Kurt ◊Weill, first in 1926, with whom she emigrated to the US 1935. She appeared in several of the Brecht–Weill operas, notably *Die Dreigroschenoper/The Threepenny Opera* 1928.

Lenz's law in physics, a law stating that the direction of an electromagnetically induced current (generated by moving a magnet near a wire or a wire in a magnetic field) will oppose the motion producing it. It is named after the German physicist Heinrich Friedrich Lenz (1804–1865), who announced it in 1833.

Leo zodiacal constellation in the northern hemisphere represented as a lion. The Sun passes through Leo from mid-Aug to mid-Sept. Its brightest star is first-magnitude ◊Regulus at the base of a pattern of stars called the Sickle. In astrology, the dates for Leo are between about July 23 and Aug 22 (see ◊precession).

Leo III *the Isaurian* c. 680–740. Byzantine emperor and soldier. He seized the throne in 717, successfully defended Constantinople against the Saracens 717–18, and attempted to suppress the use of images in church worship (see ◊iconoclast).

Leo thirteen popes, including:

Leo I St *the Great* c. 390–461. Pope from 440 who helped to establish the Christian liturgy.

Leo summoned the Chalcedon Council where his Dogmatical Letter was accepted as the voice of St Peter. Acting as ambassador for the emperor Valentinian III (425–455), Leo saved Rome from devastation by the Huns by buying off their king, Attila.

Leo III c. 750–816. Pope from 795. After the withdrawal of the Byzantine emperors, the popes had become the real rulers of Rome. Leo III was forced to flee because of a conspiracy in Rome and took refuge at the court of the Frankish king Charlemagne. He returned to Rome in 799 and crowned Charlemagne emperor on Christmas Day 800, establishing the secular sovereignty of the pope over Rome under the suzerainty of the emperor (who became the Holy Roman emperor).

Leo X Giovanni de' Medici 1475–1521. Pope from 1513. The son of Lorenzo the Magnificent of Florence, he was created a cardinal at 13. He bestowed on Henry VIII of England the title of Defender of the Faith. A patron of the arts, he sponsored the rebuilding of St Peter's Church, Rome. He raised funds for this by selling indulgences (remissions of punishment for sin), a sale that led the religious reformer Martin Luther to rebel against papal authority. Leo X condemned Luther in the bull *Exsurge domine* 1520 and excommunicated him in 1521.

Leo XIII Gioacchino Pecci 1810–1903. Pope from 1878. After a successful career as a papal diplomat, he established good relations between the papacy and European powers, the US, and Japan. He remained intransigent in negotiations with the Italian government over the status of Rome, insisting that he keep control over part of it.

He was the first pope to emphasize the duty of the church in matters of social justice. His encyclical *Rerum novarum* 1891 pointed out the moral duties of employers toward workers.

Leominster city in N central Massachusetts, on the Nashua River, NE of Worcester. Industries include plastics, paper products, clothing, and chemicals; population (1990) 38,140.

León city in W Nicaragua; population (1985) 101,000. Industries include textiles and food processing. Founded in 1524, it was the capital of Nicaragua until 1855.

León city in Castilla-León, Spain; population (1991) 146,300. It was the capital of the kingdom of León from the 10th century until 1230, when it was merged with Castile.

Leonard Elmore (John, Jr) 1925– . US author of westerns and thrillers, marked by vivid dialogue, as in *City Primeval* 1980, *La Brava* 1983, *Stick* 1983, *Glitz* 1985, *Freaky Deaky* 1988, and *Get Shorty* 1990.

Born in New Orleans, Leonard received a PhD in English from the University of Detroit and worked for an advertising agency while he churned out westerns for pulp magazines. His *Hombre* 1961 is considered among the top westerns of all time; it became a motion picture 1967. In the late 1960s Leonard changed genre, writing about city life and crime. His other works include *The Bounty Hunters* 1953, *The Big Bounce* 1969, *The Moonshine War* 1969, *Unknown Man No. 89* 1977, *Split Images* 1982, and *Cat Chaser* 1982. Many of his works were made into motion pictures.

Leonard Sugar Ray 1956– . US boxer. In 1988 he became the first man to have won world titles at five officially recognized weights. In 1976 he was Olympic light-welterweight champion; he won his first professional title in 1979 when he beat Wilfred Benitez for the WBC welterweight title. He later won titles at junior middleweight (WBA version) 1981, middleweight (WBC) 1987, light-heavyweight (WBC) 1988, and super-middleweight (WBC) 1988. In 1989 he drew with Thomas Hearns.

Leonardo da Vinci 1452–1519. Italian painter, sculptor, architect, engineer, and scientist. One of the greatest figures of the Italian Renaissance, he was active in Florence, Milan, and, from 1516, France. As state engineer and court painter to the duke of Milan, he painted the *Last Supper* mural about 1495 (Sta Maria delle Grazie, Milan), and on his return to Florence painted the *Mona Lisa* (Louvre, Paris) about 1503–06. His notebooks and drawings show an immensely inventive and inquiring mind, studying aspects of the natural world from anatomy to aerodynamics.

Leonardo was born at Vinci in Tuscany and studied under ◊Verrocchio in Florence in the 1470s. His earliest dated work is a sketch of the Tuscan countryside 1473 (Uffizi, Florence); his early works include drawings, portraits, and religious scenes, such as the unfinished *Adoration of the Magi* (Uffizi). About 1482 he went to the court of Lodovico Sforza in Milan. In 1500 he returned to Florence (where he was architect and engineer to Cesare Borgia in 1502), and then to Milan in 1506. He went to France in 1516 and died at Château Cloux, near Amboise, on the Loire. Apart from portraits, religious themes, and historical paintings, Leonardo's greatest legacies were his notebooks and drawings. He influenced many of his contemporary artists, including Michelangelo, Raphael, Giorgione, and Bramante. He also revolutionized painting style. Instead of a white background, he used a dark one to allow the overlying color a more three-dimensional existence. He invented "aerial perspective" whereby the misty atmosphere (*sfumato*) blurs and changes the colors of the landscape as it dissolves into the distance. His principle of grouping figures within an imaginary pyramid, linked by their gestures and emotions, became a High Renaissance compositional rule. His two versions of the Madonna and child with St Anne, *Madonna on the Rocks* (Louvre, Paris, and National Gallery, London) exemplify all these ideas. Other chief works include the *Mona Lisa* (wife of Zanoki del Gioconda, hence also known as *La Gioconda*) 1503, Louvre, Paris; and the *Battle of Anghiari* 1504–05, formerly in the Palazzo Vecchio, Florence.

Leoncavallo Ruggiero 1857–1919. Italian operatic composer, born in Naples. He played in restaurants, composing in his spare time, until the success of *Pagliacci* in 1892. His other operas include *La Bohème* 1897 (contemporary with Puccini's version) and *Zaza* 1900.

Leone Sergio 1928–1989. Italian film director, responsible for popularizing "spaghetti" Westerns (Westerns made in Italy and Spain, usually with a US leading actor and a European supporting cast and crew) and making a world star of Clint Eastwood. His films include *Per un pugno di dollari/A Fistful of Dollars* 1964, *C'era una volta il West/Once Upon a Time in the West* 1968, and *C'era una volta il America/Once Upon a Time in America* 1984.

Leonidas died 480 BC. King of Sparta. He was killed while defending the pass of ◊Thermopylae with 300 Spartans, 700 Thespians, and 400 Thebans against a huge Persian army.

leopard or **panther** cat *Panthera pardus*, found in Africa and Asia. The background color of the coat is golden, and the black spots form rosettes, that differ according to the variety; black panthers are simply a color variation and retain the patterning as a "watered-silk" effect. The leopard is 5–8 ft/1.5–2.5 m long, including the tail, which may measure 3 ft/1 m.

The **snow leopard** or **ounce** *P. uncia*, which has irregular rosettes of much larger black spots on a light cream or gray background, is a native of mountains in central Asia. The **clouded leopard** *Neofelis nebulosa* is rather smaller, about 5.8 ft/1.75 m overall, with large blotchy markings rather than rosettes, and is found in SE Asia. There are seven subspecies, of which six are in danger of extinction, including the Amur leopard and the South Arabian leopard. One subspecies, the Zanzibar leopard, may already be extinct.

Leopardi Giacomo, Count Leopardi 1798–1837. Italian romantic poet. The first collection of his uniquely pessimistic poems, *I Versi/ Verses*, appeared in 1824, and was followed by his philosophical *Operette morali/Minor Moral Works* 1827, in prose, and *I Canti/Lyrics* 1831.

Born at Recanati of a noble family, Leopardi wrote many of his finest poems, including his patriotic odes, before he was 21. Throughout his life he was tormented by ill health, by the consciousness of his deformity (he was hunchbacked), by loneliness and a succession of unhappy love affairs, and by his "cosmic pessimism" and failure to find consolation in any philosophy.

Leopold three kings of the Belgians:

Leopold I 1790–1865. King of the Belgians from 1831, having been elected to the throne on the creation of an independent Belgium. Through his marriage, when prince of Saxe-Coburg, to Princess Charlotte Augusta, he was the uncle of Queen Victoria of Great Britain and had considerable influence over her.

Leopold II 1835–1909. King of the Belgians from 1865, son of Leopold I. He financed the US journalist Henry Stanley's explorations in Africa, which resulted in the foundation of the Congo Free State (now Zaire), from which he extracted a huge fortune by ruthless exploitation.

Leopold III 1901–1983. King of the Belgians 1934–51. He surrendered to the German army in World War II 1940. Postwar charges against his conduct led to a regency by his brother Charles and his eventual abdication 1951 in favor of his son Baudouin.

Leopold two Holy Roman emperors:

Leopold I 1640–1705. Holy Roman emperor from 1658, in succession to his father Ferdinand III. He warred against Louis XIV of France and the Ottoman Empire.

Leopold II 1747–1792. Holy Roman emperor in succession to his brother Joseph II. He was the son of Empress Maria Theresa of Austria. His hostility to the French Revolution led to the outbreak of war a few weeks after his death.

Léopoldville former name (until 1966) of ◊Kinshasa, city in Zaire.

Lepanto, Battle of sea battle Oct 7, 1571, fought in the Mediterranean Gulf of Corinth off Lepanto (Italian name of the Greek port of *Naupaktos*), then in Turkish possession, between the Ottoman Empire and forces from Spain, Venice, Genoa, and the Papal States,

jointly commanded by the Spanish soldier Don John of Austria. The combined western fleets overcame Muslim sea power. The Spanish writer Cervantes was wounded in the battle.

Le Pen Jean-Marie 1928– . French extreme right-wing politician. In 1972 he formed the French National Front, supporting immigrant repatriation and capital punishment; the party gained 14% of the national vote in the 1986 election. Le Pen was elected to the European Parliament in 1984.

lepidoptera order of insects, including ◊butterflies and ◊moths, which have overlapping scales on their wings; the order consists of some 165,000 species.

leprosy or **Hansen's disease** chronic, progressive disease caused by a bacterium *Mycobacterium leprae* closely related to that of tuberculosis. The infection attacks the skin and nerves. Once common in many countries, leprosy is now confined almost entirely to the tropics. It is controlled with drugs.

There are two principal manifestations. **Lepromatous leprosy** is a contagious, progressive form distinguished by the appearance of raised blotches and lumps on the skin and thickening of the skin and nerves, with numbness, weakness, paralysis, and ultimately deformity of the affected parts. In **tuberculoid leprosy**, sensation is lost in some areas of the skin; sometimes there is loss of pigmentation and hair. The visible effects of long-standing leprosy (joint damage, paralysis, loss of fingers or toes) are due to nerve damage and injuries of which the sufferer may be unaware. Damage to the nerves remains, and the technique of using the patient's muscle material to encourage nerve regrowth is being explored.

lepton any of a class of light ◊elementary particles that are not affected by the strong nuclear force; they do not interact strongly with other particles or nuclei. The leptons are comprised of the ◊electron, muon, and tau, and their ◊neutrinos (the electron neutrino, muon neutrino, and tau neutrino), plus their six ◊antiparticles.

leptospirosis any of several infectious diseases of domestic animals and humans caused by spirochetes of the genus *Leptospira* found in sewage and natural waters. One such disease in cattle causes abortion; in humans, eyes, liver, and kidneys may be affected; meningitis (inflammation of the membrane surrounding the brain) is another symptom.

Lermontov Mikhail Yurevich 1814–1841. Russian Romantic poet and novelist. In 1837 he was sent into active military service in the Caucasus for writing a revolutionary poem on the death of Pushkin, which criticized court values, and for participating in a duel. Among his works are the psychological novel *A Hero of Our Time* 1840 and a volume of poems *October* 1840.

Lerner Alan Jay 1918–1986. US lyricist, collaborator with Frederick ◊Loewe on musicals including *Brigadoon* 1947, *Paint Your Wagon* 1951, *My Fair Lady* 1956, *Gigi* 1958, and *Camelot* 1960.

lesbianism homosexuality (sexual attraction to one's own sex) between women, so called from the Greek island of Lesbos (now Lesvos), the home of ◊Sappho the poet and her followers to whom the behavior was attributed.

Lesbos alternate spelling of ◊Lesvos, an island in the Aegean Sea.

lesion any change in a body tissue that is a manifestation of disease or injury.

Lesotho landlocked country in southern Africa, an enclave within South Africa.
government Lesotho is an independent monarchy within the British ⟡Commonwealth. Its 1966 constitution was suspended, reinstated, and then suspended again, and all executive and legislative powers are now vested in the hereditary king, assisted by a six-member military council and a council of ministers. The constitution provides for a 99-member, single-chamber elected national assembly.
history The area now known as Lesotho was originally inhabited by the San, or Bushmen. During the 18th–19th centuries they were superseded by the Sotho, who were being driven southward by the Mfecane ("the shaking-up of peoples") caused by the rise of the Zulu nation. Under the name of Basutoland, the Sotho nation was founded by Moshoeshoe I (1790–1870) in 1827, and at his request it became a British protectorate 1868. It achieved internal self-government 1965, with the paramount chief Moshoeshoe II as king, and was given full independence as Lesotho 1966.

The Basotho National Party (BNP), a conservative group favoring limited cooperation with South Africa, held power from independence until 1986. Its leader, Chief Leabua Jonathan, became prime minister 1966 and after 1970, when the king's powers were severely curtailed, the country was effectively under the prime minister's control. From 1975 an organization called the Lesotho Liberation Army (LLA) carried out a number of attacks on BNP members, with alleged South African support. South Africa, while denying complicity, pointed out that Lesotho was allowing the then (until 1990) banned South African nationalist movement, the ⟡African National Congress (ANC), to use it as a base.
relations with South Africa Economically, Lesotho has been dependent on South Africa but it has openly rejected the policy of apartheid. In retaliation, South Africa has tightened its border controls, causing food shortages in Lesotho. It has been alleged that South Africa has encouraged BNP dissenters to form a new party, the Basotho Democratic Alliance (BDA), and plotted with the BDA to overthrow the Lesotho government. Lesotho was also under pressure from South Africa to sign a nonaggression pact between South Africa and Mozambique, but the Lesotho government refused to do so.

In 1986 South Africa imposed a border blockade, cutting off food and fuel supplies to Lesotho, and the government of Chief Jonathan was ousted and replaced in a coup led by General Justin Lekhanya. He announced that all executive and legislative powers would be vested in the king, ruling through a military council chaired by General Lekhanya, and a council of ministers. A week after the coup about 60 ANC members were deported to Zambia, and on the same day the South African blockade was lifted. South Africa denied playing any part in the coup but clearly found the new government more acceptable than the old.

In Nov 1990 the son of the exiled King Moshoeshoe was sworn in as King Letsie III. In 1991 General Lekhanya was ousted in a military coup led by Col Elias Tutsoane Ramaema, and political parties were permitted to operate. Moshoeshoe, the former king, returned from exile in July 1992, but as tribal chief rather than monarch. *See illustration box.*

less developed country (ldc) any country late in developing an industrial base, and dependent on cash crops and unprocessed minerals. The Group of 77 was established in 1964 to pressure industrialized countries into giving greater aid to less developed countries.

The terms "less developed" and "developing" imply that industrial development is desirable or inevitable; many people prefer to use ⟡"Third World".

Lesseps Ferdinand, Vicomte de Lesseps 1805–1894. French engineer, constructor of the ⟡Suez Canal 1859–69; he began the ⟡Panama Canal in 1879, but withdrew after failing to construct it without locks.

Lessing Doris (May) (née Taylor) 1919– . British novelist, born in Iran. Concerned with social and political themes, particularly the place of women in society, her work includes *The Grass is Singing* 1950, the five-novel series *Children of Violence* 1952–69, *The Golden Notebook* 1962, *The Good Terrorist* 1985, and *The Fifth Child* 1988. She has also written an "inner space fiction" series *Canopus in Argus Archives* 1979–83, and under the adopted name "Jane Somers," *The Diary of a Good Neighbour* 1981.

Lessing Gotthold Ephraim 1729–1781. German dramatist and critic. His plays include *Miss Sara Sampson* 1755, *Minna von Barnhelm* 1767, *Emilia Galotti* 1772, and the verse play *Nathan der Weise* 1779. His works of criticism *Laokoon* 1766 and *Hamburgische Dramaturgie* 1767–68 influenced German literature. He also produced many theological and philosophical writings.

Les Six (French "the six") a group of French composers: Georges Auric, Louis Durey (1888–1979), Arthur Honegger, Darius Milhaud, Francis Poulenc, and Germaine Tailleferre (1892–1983). Formed in 1917, the group was dedicated to producing works free from foreign influences and reflecting the contemporary world. It split up in the early 1920s.

Lesvos Greek island in the Aegean Sea, near the coast of Turkey
area 831 sq mi/2,154 sq km
capital Mytilene
products olives, wine, grain
population (1981) 104,620
history ancient name Lesbos; an Aeolian settlement, the home of the poets Alcaeus and Sappho; conquered by the Turks from Genoa 1462; annexed to Greece 1913.

Lethe in Greek mythology, a river of the underworld whose waters, when drunk, brought forgetfulness of the past.

Leto in Greek mythology, a goddess, mother by Zeus of Artemis and Apollo, to whom she gave birth on the Aegean island of Delos, which became their sanctuary.

letter written or printed message, chiefly a personal communication. Letters are valuable as reflections of social conditions and of literary and political life. Legally, ownership of a letter (as a document) passes to the recipient, but the copyright remains with the writer.

Outstanding examples include:
ancient Cicero, Pliny the Younger, and St Paul;
medieval Abelard and Héloïse (12th-century France), the Paston family (15th-century England);

Lesotho
Kingdom of

area 11,717 sq mi/30,355 sq km
capital Maseru
cities Teyateyaneng, Mafeteng, Roma, Quthing
physical mountainous with plateaus, forming part of South Africa's chief watershed
features Lesotho is an enclave within South Africa
political system military-controlled monarchy
head of state King Letsie III from 1990
head of government Col Elias Tutsoane Ramaema from 1991
political parties Basotho National Party (BNP), traditionalist, nationalist; Basutoland Congress Party (BCP); Basotho Democratic Alliance (BDA)
exports wool, mohair, diamonds, cattle, wheat, vegetables
currency maluti
population (1990 est) 1,757,000; growth rate 2.7% p.a. **life expectancy** men 59, women 62 (1989)
languages Sesotho, English (official), Zulu, Xhosa
religions Protestant 42%, Roman Catholic 38%
literacy 59% (1988)
GNP $408 million; $410 per head (1988)
chronology
1868 Basutoland became a British protectorate.
1966 Independence achieved from Britain, within the Commonwealth, as the Kingdom of Lesotho, with Moshoeshoe II as king and Chief Leabua Jonathan as prime minister.
1970 State of emergency declared and constitution suspended.
1973 Progovernment interim assembly established; BNP won majority of seats.
1975 Members of the ruling party attacked by guerrillas backed by South Africa.
1985 Elections canceled because no candidates opposed BNP.
1986 South Africa imposed border blockade, forcing deportation of 60 African National Congress members. General Lekhanya ousted Chief Jonathan in coup. National assembly abolished. Highlands Water Project agreement signed with South Africa. **1990** Moshoeshoe II dethroned by military council; replaced by his son Mohato as King Letsie III.
1991 Lekhanya ousted in military coup led by Col Elias Tutsoane Ramaema. Political parties permitted to operate.
1992 Ex-king Moshoeshoe returned from exile.

16th century Erasmus (the Netherlands), Luther, Melanchthon (Germany), Spenser, Sidney (England);

17th century Donne, Milton, Cromwell, Dorothy Osborne, Wotton (England); Pascal, Mme de Sévigné (France);

18th century Pope, Walpole, Swift, Mary Wortley Montagu, Chesterfield, Cowper, Gray (England); Bossuet, Voltaire, Rousseau (France);

19th century Emerson, J R Lowell (US); Byron, Lamb, Keats, Fitzgerald, Stevenson (England); George Sand, Saint-Beuve, Goncourt brothers (France); Schiller, Goethe (Germany); Gottfried Keller (Switzerland);

20th century T E Lawrence, G B Shaw, Ellen Terry, Katherine Mansfield (England); Rilke (Germany).

letterpress method of printing from raised type, pioneered by Johann ⟡Gutenberg in Europe in the 1450s.

lettuce annual edible plant *Lactuca sativa*, family Compositae, believed to have been derived from the wild species *L. serriola*. There are many varieties, including the cabbage lettuce, with round or loose heads, and the Cos lettuce, with long, upright heads.

Iceberg and Romaine are the two salad varieties grown especially for US supermarkets, but Boston and Redleaf are sometimes shipped to markets.

leucite silicate mineral, KAlSi$_2$O$_6$, occurring frequently in some potassium-rich volcanic rocks. It is dull white to gray, and usually opaque. It is used as a source of potassium for fertilizer.

leucotomy another term for frontal ⟡lobotomy, a brain operation.

leukemia any one of a group of cancers of the blood cells, with widespread involvement of the bone marrow and other blood-forming tissue. The central feature of leukemia is runaway production of white blood cells that are immature or in some way abnormal. These rogue cells, which lack the defensive capacity of healthy white cells, overwhelm the normal ones, leaving the victim vulnerable to infection. Treatment is with radiotherapy and ⟡cytotoxic drugs to suppress replication of abnormal cells, or by bone-marrow transplant.

Abnormal functioning of the bone marrow also suppresses production of red blood cells and blood ⟡platelets, resulting in ⟡anemia and a failure of the blood to clot. Leukemias are classified into acute or chronic, depending on their known rates of progression. They are also grouped according to the type of white cell involved.

leukocyte a white blood cell. Leukocytes are part of the body's defenses and give immunity against disease. There are several different types. Some (⟡phagocytes and ⟡macrophages) engulf invading microorganisms, others kill infected cells, while ⟡lymphocytes produce more specific immune responses. Human blood contains about 11,000 leukocytes to the cubic millimeter—about one to every 500 red cells.

Leukocyte numbers may be reduced (leukopenia) by starvation, pernicious anaemia, and certain infections, such as typhoid and malaria. An increase in the numbers (leukocytosis) is a reaction to normal events such as digestion, exertion, and pregnancy, and to abnormal ones such as loss of blood, cancer, and most infections.

Levant the E Mediterranean region, or more specifically, the coastal regions of Turkey-in-Asia, Syria, Lebanon, and Israel.

Le Vau Louis 1612–1670. French architect who drafted the plan of Versailles, rebuilt the Louvre, and built Les Tuileries in Paris.

levee naturally formed raised bank along the side of a river channel. When a river overflows its banks, the rate of flow in the flooded area is less than that in the channel, and silt is deposited. After the waters have withdrawn the silt is left as a bank that grows with successive floods. Eventually the river, contained by the levee, may be above the surface of the surrounding flood plain. Notable levees are found on the lower reaches of the Mississippi in the US and the Po in Italy.

level or *spirit level* instrument for finding horizontal level, or adjusting a surface to an even level, used in surveying, building construction, and archeology. It has a glass tube of colored liquid, in which a bubble is trapped, mounted in an elongated frame. When the tube is horizontal, the bubble moves to the center.

Levelers democratic party in the English Civil War. The Levelers found wide support among Cromwell's New Model Army and the yeoman farmers, artisans, and small traders, and proved a powerful political force 1647–49. Their program included the establishment of a republic, government by a parliament of one house elected by male suffrage, religious toleration, and sweeping social reforms.

Cromwell's refusal to implement this program led to mutinies by Levelers in the army, which, when suppressed by Cromwell in 1649, ended the movement. They were led by John ⟡Lilburne.

lever simple machine consisting of a rigid rod pivoted at a fixed point called the fulcrum, used for shifting or raising a heavy load or applying force in a similar way. Levers are classified into orders according to where the effort is applied, and the load-moving force developed, in relation to the position of the fulcrum.

A **first-order** lever has the load and the effort on opposite sides of the fulcrum–for example, a see-saw or pair of scissors. A

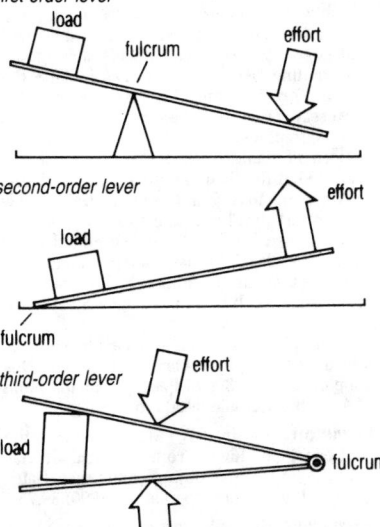

lever Types of lever.

second-order lever has the load and the effort on the same side as the fulcrum, with the load nearer the fulcrum for example a pair of tweezers or tongs. The mechanical advantage of a lever is the ratio of load to effort, equal to the perpendicular distance of the effort's line of action from the fulcrum divided by the distance to the load's line of action. Thus the tweezers, for instance, have a mechanical advantage of less than one.

leveraged buyout in business, the purchase of a controlling proportion of the shares of a company by its own management, financed almost exclusively by borrowing. It is so called because the ratio of a company's long-term debt to its equity (capital assets) is known as its "leverage."

Leverrier Urbain Jean Joseph 1811–1877. French astronomer who predicted the existence and position of the planet Neptune, discovered in 1846.

Lévesque René 1922–1987. French-Canadian politician. In 1968 he founded the Parti Québecois, with the aim of an independent Québec, but a referendum rejected the proposal in 1980. He was premier of Québec 1976–85.

Levi Primo 1919–1987. Italian novelist. He joined the anti-Fascist resistance during World War II, was captured, and sent to the concentration camp at Auschwitz. He wrote of these experiences in *Se questo è un uomo/If This Is a Man* 1947.

leviathan in the Old Testament, a mythical sea monster, identified by later commentators with the whale.

Levi-Montalcini Rita 1909– . Italian neurologist who discovered nerve-growth factor, a substance that controls how many cells make up the adult nervous system. She shared the 1986 Nobel Prize for Medicine with US biochemist Stanley Cohen (1922–).

Levi-Montalcini studied at Turin and worked there until the Fascist anti-Semitic laws forced her to go into hiding. She continued research into the nervous systems of chick embryos. After World War II she moved to the US.

Lévi-Strauss Claude 1908–1990. French anthropologist who sought to find a universal structure governing all societies, as reflected in the way their myths are constructed. His works include *Tristes Tropiques* 1955 and *Mythologiques/Mythologies* 1964–71.

levitation counteraction of gravitational forces on a body. As claimed by medieval mystics, spiritualist mediums, and practitioners of transcendental meditation, it is unproven. In the laboratory it can be produced scientifically; for example, electrostatic force and acoustical waves have been used to suspend water drops for microscopic study. It is also used in technology, for example, in magnetic levitation as in ⟡maglev trains.

Levite in the Old Testament, a member of one of the 12 tribes of Israel, descended from Levi, a son of ⟡Jacob. The Levites performed the lesser services of the Temple; the high priesthood was confined to the descendants of Aaron, the brother of Moses.

Lewes, Battle of battle in 1264 caused by the baronial opposition to the English King Henry III, led by Simon de Montfort, earl of Leicester (1208–65). The king was defeated and captured at the battle.

The barons objected to Henry's patronage of French nobles in the English court, his weak foreign policy, and his support for the papacy against the Holy Roman Empire. In 1258, they forced him to issue the ◊Provisions of Oxford, and when he later refused to implement them, they revolted. They defeated and captured the king at Lewes in Sussex. Their revolt was broken by de Montfort's death and defeat at Evesham in 1265.

Lewis (William) Arthur 1915– . British economist born on St Lucia, West Indies. He specialized in the economic problems of developing countries and created a model relating the terms of trade between less developed and more developed nations to their respective levels of labor productivity in agriculture. He shared the Nobel Prize for Economics with an American, Theodore Schultz, 1979. He wrote many books, including the *Theory of Economic Growth* 1955.

Lewis Carl (Frederick Carleton) 1961– . US track and field athlete who won eight gold medals and one silver in three successive Olympic Games. At the 1984 Olympic Games he equaled the performance of Jesse ◊Owens, winning gold medals in the 100 and 200 meters, 400-meter relay, and long jump.

In the 1988 Olympics, he repeated his golds in the 100 meters and long jump, and won a silver in the 200 meters. Although in the 1992 Olympics he failed to make the US's 100-meter and 200-meter squads, he repeated his success in the long jump and anchored the US's record-breaking 400-meter relay team.

CAREER HIGHLIGHTS

Olympic Games
gold: 100 meters 1984, 1988; 200 meters 1984; 400-meter relay 1984, 1992; long jump 1984, 1988, 1992
silver: 200 meters 1988

Lewis Cecil Day. Irish poet; see ◊Day Lewis.

Lewis C (live) S (taples) 1898–1963. British academic and writer, born in Belfast. His books include the medieval study, *The Allegory of Love* 1936, and the space fiction, *Out of the Silent Planet* 1938. He was a committed Christian and wrote essays in popular theology such as *The Screwtape Letters* 1942 and *Mere Christianity* 1952; the autobiographical *Surprised by Joy* 1955; and a series of books of Christian allegory for children, set in the magic land of Narnia, including *The Lion, the Witch, and the Wardrobe* 1950.

Lewis Jerry. Adopted name of Joseph Levitch 1926– . US comic actor and director. Formerly in partnership with Dean Martin (1946–56), their film debut was in *My Friend Irma* 1949. He was revered as a solo performer by French critics ("Le Roi du Crazy"), but films that he directed such as *The Nutty Professor* 1963 were less well received in the US. He appeared with Robert De Niro in *The King of Comedy* 1982.

Lewis Jerry Lee 1935– . US rock-and-roll and country singer and pianist. His trademark was the "pumping piano" style in hits such as "Whole Lotta Shakin' Going On" and "Great Balls of Fire" 1957; later recordings include "What Made Milwaukee Famous" 1968.

Lewis John L (lewellyn) 1880–1969. US labor leader. Born in Lucas, Iowa, Lewis worked in the coal mines from an early age. He became a regional officer of the United Mine Workers (UMW) and served as its liaison with the American Federation of Labor (AFL) 1911. Elected president of the UMW 1920–60,

he helped found the Congress of Industrial Organizations 1935, the AFL offshoot that unionized workers in mass-production industries. Campaigning for the unionization of workers in heavy industry, he eventually came into conflict with F D Roosevelt. Lewis's militancy led to miners' strikes during and after World War II, and thus to Truman's nationalization of the mines in 1946. His concerns, however, led to the adoption of national mining safety standards.

Lewis Meriwether 1774–1809. US explorer. He was commissioned by president Thomas Jefferson to find a land route to the Pacific with William Clark (1770–1838). They followed the Missouri River to its source, crossed the Rocky Mountains (aided by an Indian woman, Sacajawea) and followed the Columbia River to the Pacific, then returned overland to St Louis 1804–06.

Formerly private secretary to President Jefferson, he was rewarded for his expedition with the governorship of the Louisiana Territory. His death, near Nashville, Tennessee, has been ascribed to suicide, but was more probably murder.

The detailed journals kept of the expedition added to an understanding of the region and facilitated westward expansion.

Lewis (Harry) Sinclair 1885–1951. US novelist. He made a reputation with satirical novels: *Main Street* 1920, depicting American small-town life; *Babbitt* 1922, the story of a real-estate dealer of the Midwest caught in the conventions of his milieu; *Arrowsmith* 1925, a study of the pettiness in medical science; and *Elmer Gantry* 1927, a satiric portrayal of evangelical religion. *Dodsworth*, a gentler novel of a US industrialist, was published 1929. He was the first American to be awarded the Nobel Prize for Literature, in 1930.

Born in Sauk Center, Minnesota, Lewis graduated from Yale University. He stayed for a time at Upton Sinclair's socialist colony in New Jersey, then became a freelance journalist. His other works include *It Can't Happen Here* 1935, *Cass Timberlane* 1945, *Kingsblood Royal* 1947, and *The God-Seeker* 1949.

Lewis (Percy) Wyndham 1886–1957. English writer and artist who pioneered Vorticism, which with its feeling of movement sought to reflect the age of industry. He had a hard and aggressive style in both his writing and his painting. His literary works include the novels *Tarr* 1918 and *The Childermass* 1928, the essay *Time and Western Man* 1927, and autobiographies.

Born off Maine, on his father's yacht, he was educated at the Slade art school and in Paris. On returning to England he pioneered the new spirit of art that his friend the US poet Ezra Pound called Vorticism; he also edited *Blast*, a literary and artistic magazine proclaiming its principles. Of his paintings, his portraits are memorable, such as those of the writers Edith Sitwell and T S Eliot.

Although he has been assessed by some as a leading force of the early 20th century, his support in the 1930s of Fascist principles and of Adolph Hitler alienated most critics.

Lewiston city in SW Maine, across the Androscoggin River from Auburn. It has textile, shoe, and clothing industries. Bates College 1855 is here; population (1990) 39,750.

Lewis with Harris largest island in the Outer Hebrides; area 857 sq mi/2,220 sq km; population (1981) 23,400. Its main town is Stornoway.

It is separated from NW Scotland by the Minch. There are many lakes and peat moors. Harris is famous for its tweeds.

Lexington town in Massachusetts; population (1990) 28,970. Industries include printing and publishing. The Battle of Lexington and Concord, April 19, 1775, opened the American War of Independence.

Lexington or **Lexington–Fayette** town in Kentucky, center of the bluegrass country; population (1990) 225,360. Racehorses are bred in the area, and races and shows are held. There is a tobacco market and the University of Kentucky (1865).

ley area of temporary grassland, sown to produce grazing and hay or silage for a period of one to ten years before being plowed and cropped. Short-term leys are often incorporated in systems of ◊crop rotation.

Leyden alternate form of ◊Leiden, city in the Netherlands.

Leyden Lucas van. See ◊Lucas van Leyden, Dutch painter.

LH abbreviation for ◊*luteinizing hormone*.

Lhasa ("the Forbidden City") capital of the autonomous region of Tibet, China, at 16,400 ft/5,000 m; population (1982) 105,000. Products include handicrafts and light industry. The holy city of ◊Lamaism, Lhasa was closed to Westerners until 1904, when members of a British expedition led by Col Francis E Younghusband visited the city. It was annexed with the rest of Tibet 1950–51 by China, and the spiritual and temporal head of state, the Dalai Lama, fled in 1959 after a popular uprising against Chinese rule. Monasteries have been destroyed and monks killed, and an influx of Chinese settlers has generated resentment. In 1988 and 1989 nationalist demonstrators were shot by Chinese soldiers.

Lhote André 1885–1962. French painter, art teacher, and critic. He opened the Académie Montparnasse 1922 and founded a South American branch of the school in Rio de Janeiro 1952. He also wrote treatises on landscape painting and figure painting. His own paintings are complicated compositions of geometrical forms painted in pure colors, for example *Rugby* (Musée d'Art Moderne, Paris).

liability in accounting, a financial obligation. Liabilities are placed alongside assets on a balance sheet to show the wealth of the individual or company concerned at a given date.

liana woody, perennial climbing plant with very long stems, which grows around trees up to the canopy, where there is more sunlight. Lianas are common in tropical rainforests, where individual stems may grow up to 255 ft/78 m long. They have an unusual stem structure that allows them to retain some flexibility, despite being woody.

Liaoning province of NE China
area 58,300 sq mi/151,000 sq km
capital Shenyang
cities Anshan, Fushun, Liaoyang
features one of China's most heavily industrialized areas
products cereals, coal, iron, salt, oil
population (1990) 39,460,000
history developed by Japan 1905–45, including the *Liaodong Peninsula*, whose ports had been conquered from the Russians.

Libby Willard Frank 1908–1980. US chemist whose development in 1947 of ◊radiocarbon dating as a means of determining the age of organic or fossilized material won him a Nobel Prize in 1960.

liberalism political and social theory that favors representative government, freedom of the press, speech, and worship, the abolition of class privileges, the use of state resources to protect the welfare of the individual, and international ♢free trade. It is historically associated with the Liberal Party in the UK and the Democratic Party in the US.

Liberalism developed during the 17th–19th centuries as the distinctive theory of the industrial and commercial classes in their struggle against the power of the monarchy, the church, and the feudal landowners. Economically it was associated with ♢laissez faire, or nonintervention. In the late 19th and early 20th centuries its ideas were modified by the acceptance of universal suffrage and a certain amount of state intervention in economic affairs, in order to ensure a minimum standard of living and to remove extremes of poverty and wealth. The Classical statement of liberal principles is found in *On Liberty* and other works of the British philosopher J S Mill.

Liberal Party British political party, the successor to the ♢Whig Party, with an ideology of liberalism. In the 19th century, it represented the interests of commerce and industry. Its outstanding leaders were Palmerston, Gladstone, and Lloyd George. From 1914 it declined, and the rise of the Labour Party pushed the Liberals into the middle ground. The Liberals joined forces with the Social Democratic Party (SDP) as the Alliance for the 1983 and 1987 elections. In 1988, a majority of the SDP voted to merge with the Liberals to form the ♢Social and Liberal Democrats.

The term "Liberal," used officially from about 1840 and unofficially from about 1815, marked a shift of support for the party from aristocrats to include also progressive industrialists, backed by supporters of the utilitarian reformer ♢Bentham, Nonconformists (especially in Welsh and Scottish constituencies), and the middle classes. During the Liberals' first period of power 1830–41, they promoted parliamentary and municipal government reform and the abolition of slavery, but their laissez-faire theories led to the harsh Poor Law of 1834. Except for two short periods the Liberals were in power 1846–66, but the only major change was the general adoption of free trade. Liberal pressure forced Peel to repeal the Corn Laws 1846, thereby splitting the Tory party. Extended franchise in 1867 and Gladstone's emergence as leader began a new phase, dominated by the Manchester school with a program of "peace, retrenchment, and reform." Gladstone's 1868–74 government introduced many important reforms, including elementary education and vote by ballot. The party's left, mainly composed of working-class Radicals and led by Charles Bradlaugh (1833-1891), a lawyer's clerk, and Joseph ♢Chamberlain (a wealthy manufacturer), repudiated laissez-faire and inclined toward republicanism, but in 1886 the Liberals were split over the policy of Home Rule for Ireland, and many became Liberal Unionists or joined the Conservatives. Except for 1892–95, the Liberals remained out of power until 1906, when, reinforced by Labour and Irish support, they returned with a huge majority. Old-age pensions, National Insurance, limitation of the powers of the Lords, and the Irish Home Rule Bill followed. Lloyd George's alliance with the Conservatives

Liberia
Republic of

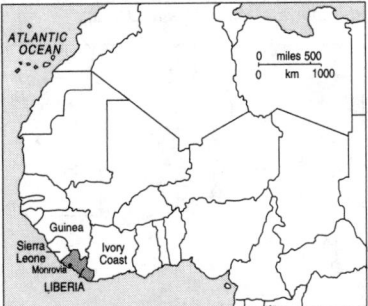

area 42,989 sq mi/111,370 sq km
capital and port Monrovia
cities ports Buchanan, Greenville
physical forested highlands; swampy tropical coast where six rivers enter the sea
features nominally the world's largest merchant marine—minimal registration controls make Liberia's a flag of convenience; the world's largest rubber plantations
head of state and government Amos Sawyer from 1990
political parties National Democratic Party of Liberia (NDLP), nationalist; Liberian Action Party (LAP); Liberian Unity Party (LUP); United People's Party (UPP); Unity Party (UP)
political system emergent democratic republic
exports iron ore, rubber (Africa's largest producer), timber, diamonds, coffee, cocoa, palm oil

currency Liberian dollar
population (1990 est) 2,644,000 (95% indigenous); growth rate 3% p.a.
life expectancy men 53, women 56 (1989)
languages English (official), over 20 Niger-Congo languages
media two daily newspapers, one published under government auspices, the other independent and with the largest circulation (10,000 copies)
religions animist 65%, Muslim 20%, Christian 15% (1985 est)
literacy men 47%, women 23% (1985 est)
GNP $973 million; $410 per head (1987)
chronology
1847 Founded as an independent republic.
1944 William Tubman elected president.
1971 Tubman died; succeeded by William Tolbert.
1980 Tolbert assassinated in coup led by Samuel Doe, who suspended the constitution and ruled through a People's Redemption Council.
1984 New constitution approved. National Democratic Party of Liberia (NDPL) founded by Doe.
1985 NDPL won decisive victory in general election. Unsuccessful coup against Doe.
1990 Rebels under former government minister Charles Taylor controlled nearly entire country by July. Doe killed during a bloody civil war between rival rebel factions. Amos Sawyer became interim head of government.
1991 Amos Sawyer reelected president. Rebel leader Charles Taylor agreed to work with Sawyer. Peace agreement failed but later revived; UN peacekeeping force drafted into republic.
1992 Monrovia under siege by Taylor's rebel forces.

1916–22 divided the Liberal Party between him and his predecessor Asquith, and although reunited in 1923 the Liberals continued to lose votes. They briefly joined the National Government 1931–32. After World War II they were reduced to a handful of members of Parliament. A revival began under the leadership 1956–67 of Jo Grimond and continued under Jeremy Thorpe, who resigned after a period of controversy within the party in 1976. After a caretaker return by Grimond, David Steel became the first party leader in British politics to be elected by party members who were not MPs. In 1977–78 Steel entered into an agreement to support Labour in any vote of confidence in return for consultation on measures undertaken. He resigned in 1988 and was replaced by Paddy Ashdown.

Liberal Party, Australian political party established 1944 by Robert Menzies, after a Labor landslide, and derived from the former United Australia Party. After the voters rejected Labor's extensive nationalization plans, the Liberals were in power 1949–72 and 1975–83 and were led in succession by Harold Holt, John Gorton, William McMahon, Billy Snedden, and Malcolm Fraser.

liberation theology Christian theory of Jesus' primary importance as the "Liberator," personifying the poor and devoted to freeing them from oppression (Matthew 19:21, 25:35, 40). Initiated by the Peruvian priest Gustavo Gutierrez in *The Theology of Liberation* 1969, and enthusiastically (and sometimes violently) adopted in Latin America, it embodies a Marxist interpretation of the class struggle, especially by Third World nations. It has been criticized by some Roman Catholic authorities including Pope John Paul II.

Liberator, the title given to Simón ♢Bolívar, South American revolutionary leader; also a title given to Daniel ♢O'Connell, Irish political leader; and to Bernardo ♢O'Higgins, Chilean revolutionary.

Liberia country in W Africa, bounded N by Guinea, E by the Ivory Coast, S and SW by the Atlantic Ocean, and NW by Sierra Leone.
government The 1984 constitution provides for a two-chamber national assembly consisting of a 26-member senate and a 64-member house of representatives, elected, like the president, by universal suffrage for a six-year term.
history The area now known as Liberia was bought by the American Colonization Society, a philanthropic organization active in the first half of the 19th century. The society's aim was to establish a settlement for liberated black slaves from the southern US. The first settlers arrived 1822, and Liberia was declared an independent republic 1847. The new state suffered from financial difficulties, with bankruptcy 1909 bringing reorganization by US army officers. For almost 160 years the country's leaders were descended from the black American settlers, but the 1980 coup put Africans in power.
military coup William Tubman was president from 1944 until his death 1971 and was succeeded by Vice President William R Tolbert

(1913–1980), who was reelected 1975. In 1980 Tolbert was assassinated in a coup led by Master Sgt Samuel Doe (1952–1990), who suspended the constitution, banned all political parties, and ruled through the People's Redemption Council (PRC). He proceeded to stamp out corruption in the public service, encountering considerable opposition and making enemies who were later to threaten his position.

new constitution A new constitution was approved by the PRC 1983 and by national referendum 1984. Political parties were again permitted, provided they registered with the Special Electoral Commission. In 1984 Doe founded the National Democratic Party of Liberia (NDPL) and announced his intention to stand for the presidency. By 1985 there were 11 political parties, but they complained about the difficulties of the registration process, and only three registered in time for the elections. Doe's party won clear majorities in both chambers, despite alleged election fraud, and he was pronounced president with 51% of the vote. In 1985 there was an unsuccessful attempt to unseat him. Doe alleged complicity by neighboring Sierra Leone and dealt harshly with the coup leaders.

end of Doe regime A gradual movement toward a pluralist political system, with a number of parties registering in opposition to the ruling NDPL, and growing economic problems threatened the stability of the Doe regime. In July 1990 rebel forces under Charles Taylor and a breakaway faction led by Prince Johnson laid siege to Doe in the presidential palace. Doe refused an offer of assistance by the US to leave the country. In Sept Doe was captured and killed by rebel forces. In Nov Amos Sawyer became the head of an interim government and in 1991 he was reelected president. In 1990 a United Nations stabilizing force had been sent to Liberia in an effort to establish peace.

Taylor agreed to work with Sawyer in moves toward peace, and a peace agreement reached Oct 1991, although initially rejected by Raleigh Seekie, leader of the guerrilla group United Liberation Movement of Liberia for Democracy (ULIMO), was finally upheld. However, heavy fighting continued in many areas. In Oct 1992, as fighting increased, Taylor's rebel forces laid siege to Monrovia. *See illustration box.*

liberty in its medieval sense, a franchise, or collection of privileges, granted to an individual or community by the king, and the area over which this franchise extended.

libido in Freudian psychology, the psychic energy, or life force, that is to be found even in a newborn child. The libido develops through a number of phases, identified by Freud as the *oral stage*, when a child tests everything by mouth, the *anal stage*, when the child gets satisfaction from control of its body, and the *genital stage*, when sexual instincts find pleasure in the outward show of love.

Libra faint zodiacal constellation in the southern hemisphere adjoining Scorpius, and represented as the scales of justice. The Sun passes through Libra during Nov. The constellation was once considered to be a part of Scorpius, seen as the scorpion's claws. In astrology, the dates for Libra are between about Sept 23 and Oct 23 (see ♦precession).

library collection of information (usually in the form of books) held for common use. The earliest was at Nineveh in Babylonian times. The first public library was opened in Athens

Libya
Great Socialist People's Libyan Arab Jamahiriya (al-Jamahiriya al-Arabiya al-Libya al-Shabiya al-Ishtirakiya al-Uzma)

area 679,182 sq mi/1,759,540 sq km
capital Tripoli
cities ports Benghazi, Misurata, Tobruk
physical flat to undulating plains with plateaus and depressions stretch S from the Mediterranean coast to an extremely dry desert interior
environment plan to pump water from below the Sahara to the coast risks rapid exhaustion of nonrenewable supply (Great Manmade River Project)
features Gulf of Sirte; rock paintings of about 3000 BC in the Fezzan; Roman city sites include Leptis Magna, Sabratha **political system** one-party socialist state
head of state and government Moamer al-Khaddafi from 1969

political party Arab Socialist Union (ASU), radical, left-wing
exports oil, natural gas
currency Libyan dinar
population (1990 est) 4,280,000 (including 500,000 foreign workers); growth rate 3.1% p.a.
life expectancy men 64, women 69 (1989)
language Arabic
religion Sunni Muslim 97%
literacy 60% (1989)
GNP $20 bn; $5,410 per head (1988)
chronology
1911 Conquered by Italy.
1934 Colony named Libya.
1942 Divided into three provinces: Fezzan (under French control); Cyrenaica, Tripolitania (under British control).
1951 Achieved independence as the United Kingdom of Libya, under King Idris.
1969 King deposed in a coup led by Col Moamer al-Khaddafi. Revolution Command Council set up and the Arab Socialist Union (ASU) proclaimed the only legal party.
1972 Proposed federation of Libya, Syria, and Egypt abandoned.
1980 Proposed merger with Syria abandoned. Libyan troops began fighting in Chad.
1981 Proposed merger with Chad abandoned.
1986 US bombing of Khaddafi's headquarters, following allegations of his complicity in terrorist activities.
1988 Diplomatic relations with Chad restored.
1989 US accused Libya of building a chemical-weapons factory and shot down two Libyan planes; reconciliation with Egypt.
1992 Khaddafi under international pressure to extradite suspected Lockerbie and UTA (Union de Transports Aerians) bombers for trial outside Libya; sanctions imposed.

in 330 BC. All ancient libraries were reference libraries: books could be consulted but not borrowed.

Lending or circulating libraries did not become popular until the 18th century; they became widespread in the 19th century with the rapid development of public libraries. Free public libraries probably began in the 15th century. In the UK, the first documented free public library was established in Manchester in 1852, after the 1850 Public Library Act. The first free, public, tax-supported library in the US was opened in Boston in 1854. Associations of libraries were formed later: the American Library Association was founded in 1876, the Library Association, Great Britain, in 1877.

Books are now usually classified by one of two major systems: Dewey Decimal Classification (now known as Universal Decimal Classification), invented by Melvil Dewey (1851–1931), and the Library of Congress system. Library cataloging systems range from cards to microfiche to computer databases with on-line terminals. These frequently make use of ♦ISBN numbers (International Standard Book Numbers) and, for magazines and journals, ISSN numbers.

major world libraries with date founded

Alexandrian library 284
Vatican Library, Rome 4th century
Bibliothèque nationale, Paris 1520
Bodleian Library, Oxford 1598
British Library, London 1757
Library of Congress, Washington, DC 1800
The New York Public Library, New York City 1895

libretto (Italian "little book") the text of an opera or other dramatic vocal work, or the scenario of a ballet.

Libreville capital of Gabon, on the estuary of the river Gabon; population (1988) 352,000. Products include timber, oil, and minerals. It was founded 1849 as a refuge for slaves freed by the French.

Libya country in N Africa, bounded N by the Mediterranean Sea, E by Egypt, SE by Sudan, S by Chad and Niger, and W by Algeria and Tunisia.

government The 1977 constitution created an Islamic socialist state, and the government is designed to allow the greatest possible popular involvement, through a large congress and smaller secretariats and committees. There is a General People's Congress (GPC) of 1,112 members that elects a secretary-general who was intended to be head of state. The GPC is serviced by a general secretariat, which is Libya's nearest equivalent to a legislature. The executive organ of the state is the General People's Committee, which replaces the structure of ministries that operated before the 1969 revolution. The Arab Socialist Union (ASU) is the only political party, and, despite Libya's elaborately democratic structure, ultimate power rests with the party and its leader.

history The area now known as Libya was inhabited by N African nomads until it came successively under the domination of Phoenicia, Greece, Rome, the Vandals, Byzantium, and Islam, and from the 16th century was part of the Turkish ♦Ottoman Empire.

In 1911 it was conquered by Italy, becoming known as Libya from 1934.

After being the scene of much fighting during World War II, in 1942 it was divided into three provinces: Fezzan, which was placed under French control; Cyrenaica; and Tripolitania, which was placed under British control. In 1951 it achieved independence as the United Kingdom of Libya, Mohammed Idris-as-Sanusi becoming King Idris.

revolution The country enjoyed internal and external stability until a bloodless revolution 1969, led by young nationalist officers, deposed the king and proclaimed a Libyan Arab Republic. Power was vested in a Revolution Command Council (RCC), chaired by Col Moamer al-Khaddhafi, with the Arab Socialist Union (ASU) as the only political party. Khaddhafi soon began proposing schemes for Arab unity, none of which was permanently adopted. In 1972 he planned a federation of Libya, Syria, and Egypt and later that year a merger between Libya and Egypt. In 1980 he proposed a union with Syria and in 1981 with Chad.

Islamic socialism Khaddhafi tried to run the country on socialist Islamic lines, with people's committees pledged to socialism and the teachings of the Koran. The 1977 constitution made him secretary-general of the general secretariat of the GPC, but in 1979 he resigned the post in order to devote more time to "preserving the revolution." His attempts to establish himself as a leader of the Arab world have brought him into conflict with Western powers, particularly the US. The Reagan administration objected to Libya's presence in Chad and its attempts to unseat the French-US-sponsored government of President Habré. The US has linked Khaddhafi to worldwide terrorist activities, despite his denials of complicity, and the killing of a US soldier in a bomb attack in Berlin 1986 by an unidentified guerrilla group prompted a raid by US aircraft, some of them British-based, on Tripoli and Benghazi. Libyan terrorists were also blamed for the bombing of Pan American World Airways Flight 103 over Lockerbie, Scotland, in 1988, killing 270 people and for the 1989 bombing of UTA (Union de Transports Aerians) Flight 772 over Niger.

In Jan 1989 Khaddhafi did not respond to the shooting-down of two of his fighters over the Mediterranean off Libya by the US Navy and has worked at improving external relations, particularly in the Arab world, effecting a reconciliation with Egypt Oct 1989.

International sanctions were imposed against Libya in April 1992 after the country had repeatedly refused to extradite six suspects linked to the Lockerbie and UTA bombings. Foreign air links were severed and Libyan diplomatic staff in several countries were expelled and further sanctions were threatened, including the embargo of the country's oil, if Khaddhafi failed to surrender the suspects for trial outside Libya. *See illustration box.*

license document issued by a government or other recognized authority conveying permission to the holder to do something otherwise prohibited and designed to facilitate accurate records, the maintenance of order, and collection of revenue.

Examples are licenses required for marriage, driving, keeping a gun, and for sale of alcohol. Also permission (in writing or not) granted by a private person or corporation for use of that person's or corporation's property

such as written material, computer software, artistic production, and manufacturing process, product, or likeness.

lichen any organism of the group Lichenes, which consists of a specific fungus and a specific alga existing in a mutually beneficial relationship. Found as colored patches or spongelike masses adhering to trees, rocks, and other substrates, lichens flourish under adverse conditions.

Some lichens have food value, for example, reindeer moss and Iceland moss; others give dyes, such as litmus, or are used in medicine. They are sensitive to atmospheric pollution (see ♢indicator species).

Lichtenstein Roy 1923– . US Pop artist. He uses advertising imagery and comic-strip techniques, often focusing on popular ideals of romance and heroism, as in *Whaam!* 1963 (Tate Gallery, London). He has also produced sculptures in brass, plastic, and enameled metal.

Lichtenstein's reputation was made with an exhibition in New York 1962. His controversial work is a commentary on American culture.

Lick Observatory observatory of the University of California and Mount Hamilton, California. Its main instruments are the 120-in/3.04-m Shane reflector, opened 1959, and a 36-in/91-cm refractor, opened 1988, the second-largest refractor in the world.

Lidice Czechoslovak mining village, replacing one destroyed by the Nazis on June 10, 1942 as a reprisal for the assassination of Reinhard ♢Heydrich. The men were shot, the women sent to concentration camps, and the children taken to Germany. The officer responsible was hanged in 1946.

Lie Trygve (Halvdan) 1896–1968. Norwegian Labor politician and diplomat. He became secretary of the Labor Party in 1926. During the

German occupation of Norway in World War II he was foreign minister in the exiled government 1941–46, when he helped retain the Norwegian fleet for the Allies. He became the first secretary-general of the United Nations 1946–53, but resigned over Soviet opposition to his handling of the Korean War.

Liebig Justus, Baron von 1803–1873. German chemist, a major contributor to agricultural chemistry. He introduced the theory of ♢radicals and discovered chloroform and chloral.

Liebknecht Karl 1871–1919. German socialist, son of Wilhelm Liebknecht. A founder of the German Communist Party, originally known as the Spartacus League (see ♢Spartacist) 1918, he was one of the few socialists who refused to support World War I. He led an unsuccessful revolt with Rosa Luxemburg in Berlin in 1919 and both were murdered by army officers.

Liebknecht Wilhelm 1826–1900. German socialist. A friend of the communist theoretician Karl Marx, with whom he took part in the ♢revolution of 1848, he was imprisoned for opposition to the Franco-Prussian War 1870–71. He was one of the founders of the Social Democratic Party 1875. He was the father of Karl Liebknecht.

Liechtenstein landlocked country in W central Europe, bounded E by Austria and W by Switzerland.

government The 1921 constitution established a hereditary principality with a single-chamber parliament, the Landtag. The prince is formal and constitutional head of state. The Landtag has 25 members, 15 from the Upper Country and 10 from the Lower Country, elected for a four-year term through a system of proportional representation. The Landtag elects five people to form the government for its duration.

Liechtenstein
Principality of (*Fürstentum Liechtenstein***)**

area 62 sq mi/160 sq km
capital Vaduz
cities Balzers, Schaan, Ruggell
physical landlocked Alpine; includes part of Rhine Valley in W
features no airport or railroad station; easy tax laws make it an international haven for foreign companies and banks (some 50,000 companies are registered)
head of state Prince Hans Adam II from 1989
head of government Hans Brunhart from 1978

political system constitutional monarchy
political parties Fatherland Union (VU); Progressive Citizens' Party (FBP)
exports microchips, dental products, small machinery, processed foods, postage stamps
currency Swiss franc
population (1990 est) 30,000 (33% foreign); growth rate 1.4% p.a.
life expectancy men 78, women 83 (1989)
language German (official); an Alemannic dialect is also spoken
religions Roman Catholic 87%, Protestant 8%
literacy 100% (1989)
GNP $450 million (1986)
GDP $1 bn (1987); $32,000 per head
chronology
1342 Became a sovereign state.
1434 Present boundaries established.
1719 Former counties of Schellenberg and Vaduz constituted as the Principality of Liechtenstein.
1921 Adopted Swiss currency.
1923 United with Switzerland in a customs union.
1938 Prince Franz Josef II came to power.
1984 Prince Franz Joseph II handed over power to Crown Prince Hans Adam. Vote extended to women in national elections.
1989 Prince Franz Joseph II died; Hans Adam II succeeded him.
1990 Became a member of the United Nations (UN).
1991 Became seventh member of European Free Trade Association.

history Liechtenstein's history as a sovereign state began 1342; its boundaries have been unchanged since 1434, and it has been known by its present name since 1719. Because of its small population (fewer than 30,000) it has found it convenient to associate itself with larger nations in international matters. For example, since 1923 it formed a customs union with Switzerland, which also 1919–90 represented it abroad. Before this Austria undertook its diplomatic representation.

Liechtenstein is one of the world's richest countries, with an income per head of population greater than that of the US, nearly twice that of the UK, and only slightly less than that of Switzerland. Prince Franz Joseph II came to power 1938, and although he retained the title, he passed the duties of prince to his heir, Hans Adam, 1984. Franz Joseph II died Oct 1989 and Hans Adam II immediately began to press strongly for the country to consider applying for full membership in the United Nations. Despite the growing indications of change, Liechtenstein's political system remains innately conservative. Women did not achieve the right to vote in national elections until 1984 and were debarred from voting in three of the principality's 11 communes until 1986.

Liechtenstein was admitted to the United Nations (UN) in Sept 1990. In May 1991, it became the seventh member of the European Free Trade Association. Previously it had held associate status through its customs union with Switzerland, but had had no vote. *See illustration box.*

lied (German "song," plural lieder) musical setting of a poem, usually for solo voice and piano; referring to Romantic songs of Schubert, Schumann, Brahms, and Hugo Wolf.

lie detector instrument that records graphically certain body activities, such as thoracic and abdominal respiration, blood pressure, pulse rate, and galvanic skin response (changes in electrical resistance of the skin). Marked changes in these activities when a person answers a question may indicate that the person is lying.

liege in the feudal system, the allegiance owed by a vassal to his or her lord (the liege lord).

Liège (German *Luik*) industrial city (weapons, textiles, paper, chemicals), capital of Liège province in Belgium, SE of Brussels, on the river Meuse; population (1991) 194,600. The province of Liège has an area of 1,505 sq mi/3,900 sq km and a population (1991) of 999,600.

lien in law, the right to retain goods owned by another until the owner has satisfied a claim against him by the person in possession of the goods. For example, the goods may have been provided as security for a debt.

life ability to grow, reproduce, and respond to such stimuli as light, heat, and sound. It is thought that life on Earth began about 4 billion years ago. The earliest fossil evidence of life is threadlike chains of cells discovered in 1980 in deposits in NW Australia that have been dated as 3.5 billion years old.

It seems probable that the original atmosphere of Earth consisted of carbon dioxide, nitrogen, and water, and that complex organic molecules, such as ◁amino acids, were created when the then oxygen-(and ozone-)free atmosphere was bombarded by ultraviolet radiation or by lightning. Attempts to replicate these conditions in the laboratory have successfully

life table

shown that amino acids, purine and pyrimidine bases (◁base pairs in DNA), and other vital molecules can be created in this way. It has also been suggested that life could have reached Earth from elsewhere in the universe in the form of complex organic molecules present in meteors or comets, but others argue that this is not really an alternative explanation because these primitive life forms must then have been created elsewhere by much the same process. Once the atmosphere changed to its present composition, life could only be created by living organisms (a process called ◁biogenesis).

Life US weekly magazine of photo journalism, which recorded US and world events pictorially from 1936–72, 1978– . It was founded by Henry Luce, owner of Time Inc., who bought the title of an older magazine. It ceased publication in 1972, although a few "Special Report" issues occasionally appeared after that date. In 1978 the magazine was revived, issued monthly, focusing more on personalities than on current news.

lifeboat small land-based vessel specially built for rescuing swimmers in danger of drowning, or a boat carried aboard a larger ship in case of a need to abandon ship.

life cycle in biology, the sequence of developmental stages through which members of a given species pass. Most vertebrates have a simple life cycle consisting of ◁fertilization of sex cells or ◁gametes, a period of development as an ◁embryo, a period of juvenile growth after hatching or birth, an adulthood including ◁sexual reproduction, and finally death. Invertebrate life cycles are generally more complex and may involve major reconstitution of the individual's appearance (◁metamorphosis) and completely different styles of life. Plants have a special type of life cycle with two distinct phases, known as ◁alternation of generations. Many insects such as cicadas, dragonflies, and mayflies have a long larvae or pupae phase and a short adult phase. Dragonflies live an aquatic life as larvae and an aerial life during the adult phase. In many invertebrates and protozoa there is a sequence of stages in the life cycle, and in parasites different stages often occur in different host organisms.

life insurance an insurance policy that pays money on the death of the holder.

Policies are available in many forms, the most common being term life insurance, in which a policyholder pays equal premiums each year for coverage in the event of death before the end of the contract. The premium rates are higher for the entire term for policyholders

in succeeding age brackets. A whole life policy requires higher annual payments than term life but remains in effect until the death of the holder. The premiums add up and earn dividends so that at the end of a specified number of years the policy pays for itself and an actual cash value exists, against which the policyholder can borrow.

life sciences scientific study of the living world as a whole, a new synthesis of several traditional scientific disciplines including ◁biology, ◁zoology, and ◁botany, and newer, more specialized areas of study such as ◁biophysics and sociobiology (the study of the biological basis of social behavior).

This approach has led to many new ideas and discoveries as well as to an emphasis on ◁ecology, the study of living organisms in their natural environments.

life table way of summarizing the probability that an individual will give birth or die during successive periods of life. From this, the proportion of individuals who survive from birth to any given age (**survivorship**) and the mean number of offspring produced (**net reproductive rate**) can be determined.

Insurance companies use life tables to estimate risks of death in order to set their premiums and governments use them to determine future needs for education and health services.

Liffey river in the eastern Republic of Ireland, flowing from the Wicklow Mountains to Dublin Bay; length 50 mi/80 km.

Ligachev Egor (Kuzmich) 1920– . Soviet politician. He joined the Communist Party 1944, and became a member of the Politburo 1985. He was replaced as the party ideologist in 1988 by Vadim Medvedev.

ligament strong flexible connective tissue, made of the protein collagen, which joins bone to bone at moveable joints. Ligaments prevent bone dislocation (under normal circumstances) but permit joint flexion.

ligature any surgical device (nylon, gut, wire) for tying a blood vessel, limb, or base of a tumor, used to stop the flow of blood or other fluid through it.

Ligeti György (Sándor) 1923– . Hungarian-born Austrian composer who developed a dense, highly chromatic, polyphonic style in which melody and rhythm are sometimes lost in shifting blocks of sound. He achieved international prominence with *Atmosphères* 1961 and *Requiem* 1965, which were used for Stanley Kubrick's film epic *2001: A Space Odyssey* 1968. Other works include an opera *Le Grand Macabre* 1978, and *Poème symphonique* 1962, for 100 metronomes (clockwork time-keeping devices).

light electromagnetic waves in the visible range, having a wavelength from about 400 nanometers in the extreme violet to about 770 nanometers in the extreme red. Light is considered to exhibit particle and wave properties, and the fundamental particle, or quantum, of light is called the photon. The speed of light (and of all electromagnetic radiation) in a vacuum is approximately 186,000 mi/300,000 km per second, and is a universal constant denoted by c.

Newton was the first to discover, 1666, that sunlight is composed of a mixture of light of different colors in certain proportions and that it could be separated into its components by dispersion. Before his time it was supposed that dispersion of light produced color instead of separating already existing colors.

The ancients believed that light traveled at infinite speed; its speed was first measured accurately by Danish astronomer Olaus Roemer 1681.

light bulb incandescent filament lamp, first demonstrated by Joseph Swan in the UK 1878 and Thomas Edison in the US 1879. The present-day light bulb is a thin glass bulb filled with an inert mixture of nitrogen and argon gas. It contains a filament made of fine tungsten wire. When electricity is passed through the wire, it glows white hot, producing light.

light-emitting diode (LED) means of displaying symbols in electronic instruments and devices. An LED is made of ⊳semiconductor material, such as gallium arsenide phosphide, that glows when electricity is passed through it. The first digital watches and calculators had LED displays, but many later models use ⊳liquid-crystal displays.

lighthouse structure carrying a powerful light to warn ships or airplanes that they are approaching a place (usually land) dangerous or important to navigation. The light is magnified and directed out to the horizon or up to the zenith by a series of mirrors or prisms. Increasingly lighthouses are powered by electricity and automated rather than staffed; the more recent models also emit radio signals. Only a minority of the remaining staffed lighthouses still use dissolved acetylene gas as a source of power.

Lights may be either flashing (the dark period exceeding the light) or rotating (the dark period being equal or less); fixed lights are liable to cause confusion. The pattern of lighting is individually varied so that ships or aircraft can identify the lighthouse. Among early lighthouses were the Pharos of Alexandria (about 280 BC) and those built by the Romans at Ostia, Ravenna, Boulogne, and Dover. In England beacons burning in church towers served as lighthouses until the 17th century, and in the earliest lighthouses, such as the Eddystone, first built 1698, open fires or candles were used. Where reefs or sandbanks made erection of a lighthouse impossible, lightships were often installed; increasingly these are being replaced by fixed, small, automated lighthouses. Where it is impossible to install a fixed structure, unattended lightbuoys equipped for up to a year's service may be used. In the UK, these are gradually being converted from acetylene gas in cylinders to solar power. In fog, sound signals are made (horns, sirens, explosives), and in the case of lightbuoys, fog bells and whistles are operated by the movement of the waves. In the US the supervisory authority is the Coast Guard.

lightning high-voltage electrical discharge between two charged rainclouds or between a cloud and the Earth, caused by the buildup of electrical charges. Air in the path of lightning ionizes (becomes conducting), and expands; the accompanying noise is heard as thunder. Currents of 20,000 amperes and temperatures of 54,000°F/30,000°C are common.

light pen in computing, a device resembling an ordinary pen, used to indicate locations on a computer screen. With certain computer-aided design (⊳CAD) programs, the light pen can be used to instruct the computer to change the shape, size, position, and colors of sections of a screen image.

The pen has a photoreceptor at its tip that emits signals when light from the screen passes beneath it. From the timing of this signal and a gridlike representation of the screen in the computer memory, a computer program can calculate the position of the light pen.

light second unit of length, equal to the distance traveled by light in one second. It is equal to 2.997925×10^8 m$/9.835592 \times 10^8$ ft. See ⊳light year.

light watt unit of radiant power (brightness of light). One light watt is the power required to produce a perceived brightness equal to that of light at a wavelength of 550 nanometers and 680 lumens.

light year in astronomy, the distance traveled by a beam of light in a vacuum in one year, approximately 5.88 trillion (million million) mi/9.46 trillion km.

lignin naturally occurring substance produced by plants to strengthen their tissues. It is difficult for ⊳enzymes to attack lignin, so living organisms cannot digest wood, with the exception of a few specialized fungi and bacteria. Lignin is the essential ingredient of all wood and is, therefore, of great commercial importance.

Chemically, lignin is made up of thousands of rings of carbon atoms joined together in a long chain. The way in which they are linked up varies along the chain.

lignite type of ⊳coal that is brown and fibrous, with a relatively low carbon content. In Scandinavia it is burned to generate power.

lignocaine short-term local anesthetic injected into tissues or applied to skin. It is effective for brief, invasive procedures such as dental care or insertion of a cannula (small tube) into a vein. Temporary paralysis to prevent involuntary movement during eye surgery, for example) can be achieved by injection directly into the nerve serving the region.

Rapidly absorbed by mucous membranes (lining tissues), lignocaine may be sprayed into the nose or throat to allow comfortable insertion of a viewing instrument during ⊳endoscopy. Its action makes it a potent antiarrhythmia drug as well: given intravenously during or following a heart attack, it reduces the risk of irregular contractions of the ventricles.

Liguria coastal region of NW Italy, which includes the resorts of the Italian Riviera, lying between the western Alps and the Mediterranean Gulf of Genoa. The region comprises the provinces of Genova, La Spezia, Imperia, and Savona, with a population (1990) of 1,719,200 and an area of 2,093 sq mi/5,418 sq km. Genoa is the chief port city.

Likud alliance of right-wing Israeli political parties that defeated the Labor Party coalition in the May 1977 election and brought Menachem Begin to power. In 1987 Likud became part of an uneasy national coalition with Labor, formed to solve Israel's economic crisis. In 1989 another coalition was formed under Shamir. Likud lost the 1992 general election to Labor.

lilac any flowering Old World shrub of the genus *Syringa* (such as *S. vulgaris*) of the olive family Oleaceae, bearing panicles (clusters) of small, sweetly scented, white or purplish flowers.

Lilburne John 1614–1657. English republican agitator. He was imprisoned 1638–40 for

circulating Puritan pamphlets, fought in the Parliamentary army in the Civil War, and by his advocacy of a democratic republic won the leadership of the Levelers, the democratic party in the English Revolution.

Lilienthal Otto 1848–1896. German aviation pioneer who inspired the US aviators Orville and Wilbur Wright. He made and successfully flew many gliders before he was killed in a glider crash.

Lilith in the Old Testament, an Assyrian female demon of the night. According to Jewish tradition in the ⊳Talmud, she was the wife of Adam before Eve's creation.

Lille (Flemish *Ryssel*) industrial city (textiles, chemicals, engineering, distilling), capital of Nord-Pas-de-Calais, France; population (1982) 174,000, metropolitan area 936,000. The world's first entirely automatic underground system was opened here in 1982.

Lilongwe capital of Malawi since 1975; population (1987) 234,000. Products include tobacco and textiles.

lily plant of the genus *Lilium*, family Liliaceae, of which there are some 80 species, most with showy, trumpet-shaped flowers growing from bulbs. The lily family includes hyacinths, tulips, asparagus, and plants of the onion genus. The term "lily" is also applied to many lilylike plants of allied genera and families.

lily of the valley plant *Convallaria majalis* of the lily family Liliaceae, growing in woods in Europe, N Asia, and North America. The small, pendant, white flowers are strongly scented. The plant is often cultivated.

Lima capital of Peru, an industrial city (textiles, chemicals, glass, cement) with its port at Callao; population (1988) 418,000, metropolitan area 4,605,000. Founded by the conquistador Pizarro 1535, it was rebuilt after destruction by an earthquake in 1746.

Survivals of the colonial period are the university (1551), cathedral (1746), government palace (the rebuilt palace of the viceroys), and the senate house (once the headquarters of the Inquisition).

Lima city in NW Ohio, on the Ottawa River, N of Dayton; seat of Allen County. Industries include motor-vehicle and aircraft parts, heavy machinery, electrical products, and oil processing; population (1990) 45,550.

limbo West Indian dance in which the performer leans backward from the knees to pass under a pole, which is lowered closer to the ground with each attempt. The world record has been unchanged since 1973 at 6⅛ in/15.5 cm, although on roller skates the record is 5¼ in/13.3 cm.

limbo in Christian theology, a region for the souls of those who were not admitted to the divine vision. *Limbus infantum* was a place where unbaptized infants enjoyed inferior blessedness, and *limbus patrum* was where the prophets of the Old Testament dwelt. The word was first used in this sense in the 13th century by St Thomas Aquinas.

Limbourg province of Belgium; capital Hasselt; area 926 sq mi/2,400 sq km; population (1991) 750,400.

Limbourg brothers Franco-Flemish painters, Pol, Herman, and Jan (Hennequin, Janneken), active in the late 14th and early 15th centuries, first in Paris, then at the ducal court of Burgundy. They produced richly detailed manuscript illuminations, including two Books of ⊳Hours.

Patronized by Jean de Berri, duke of Burgundy, from about 1404, they illustrated two Books of Hours that are masterpieces of the International Gothic style, the *Belles Heures* about 1408 (Metropolitan Museum of Art, New York), and *Les très riches Heures du Duc de Berri* about 1413–15 (Musée Condé, Chantilly). Their miniature paintings include a series of scenes representing the months, presenting an almost fairy-tale world of pinnacled castles with lords and ladies, full of detail and brilliant decorative effects. All three brothers were dead by 1416.

Limburg southernmost province of the Netherlands in the plain of the Maas (Meuse); area 838 sq mi/2,170 sq km; population (1991) 1,109,900. Its capital is Maastricht, the oldest city in the Netherlands. The manufacture of chemicals has now replaced coal mining but the coal industry is still remembered at Kerkrade, alleged site of the first European coal mine. The marl soils of S Limburg are used in the manufacture of cement and fertilizer. Mixed arable farming and horticulture are also important.

lime small thorny bush *Citrus aurantifolia* of the rue family Rutaceae, native to India. The white flowers are succeeded by light green or yellow fruits, limes, which resemble lemons but are more globular in shape.

lime or **quicklime** CaO (technical name **calcium oxide**) white powdery substance used in making mortar and cement. It is made commercially by heating calcium carbonate ($CaCO_3$), obtained from limestone or chalk, in a lime kiln. Quicklime readily absorbs water to become calcium hydroxide (CaOH), known as slaked lime, which is used to reduce soil acidity.

Limerick county town of Limerick, Republic of Ireland, the main port of W Ireland, on the Shannon estuary; population (1991) 52,000. It was founded in the 12th century.

Limerick county in the SW Republic of Ireland, in Munster province
area 1,038 sq mi/2,690 sq km
county town Limerick
physical fertile, with hills in the south
products dairy products
population (1991) 161,900.

limestone sedimentary rock composed chiefly of calcium carbonate $CaCO_3$, either derived from the shells of marine organisms or precipitated from solution, mostly in the ocean. Various types of limestone are used as building stone.
◇Marble is metamorphosed limestone. Certain so-called marbles are not in fact marbles but fine-grained fossiliferous limestones that take an attractive polish. Caves commonly occur in limestone. ◇Karst is a type of limestone landscape.

limiting factor any factor affecting the rate of a metabolic reaction. Levels of light or of carbon dioxide are limiting factors in ◇photosynthesis because both are necessary for the production of carbohydrates. In experiments, photosynthesis is observed to slow down and eventually stop as the levels of light decrease.
It is believed that the concentrations of carbon dioxide building up in the atmosphere through the burning of fossil fuels will allow faster plant growth.

limnology study of lakes and other bodies of open fresh water, in terms of their plant and animal biology, and their physical properties.

Limoges city and capital of Limousin, France; population (1982) 172,000. Fine enamels were made here in the medieval period, and it is the center of the modern French porcelain industry. Other industries include textiles, electrical equipment, and metal goods. The city was sacked by the Black Prince, the eldest son of Edward III of England, in 1370.

limonite iron ore, mostly poorly crystalline iron oxyhydroxide, but usually mixed with ◇hematite and other iron oxides. Also known as brown iron ore, it is often found in bog deposits.

Limousin former province and modern region of central France; area 6,544 sq mi/16,900 sq km; population (1986) 736,000. It consists of the *départements* of Corréze, Creuse, and Haute-Vienne. The chief town is Limoges. A thinly populated and largely unfertile region, it is crossed by the mountains of the Massif Central. Fruit and vegetables are produced in the more fertile lowlands. Kaolin is mined.

limpet any of various marine ◇snails belonging to several families and genera, especially *Acmaea* and *Patella*. A limpet has a conical shell and adheres firmly to rocks by its disklike foot. Limpets leave their fixed positions only to graze on seaweeds, always returning to the same spot. They are found in the Atlantic and Pacific.

Limpopo river in SE Africa, rising in the Transvaal and reaching the Indian Ocean in Mozambique; length 1,000 mi/1,600 km.

Lin Biao 1907–1971. Chinese politician and general. He joined the Communists in 1927, became a commander of ◇Mao Zedong's Red Army, and led the Northeast People's Liberation Army in the civil war after 1945. He became defense minister in 1959, and as vice chair of the party in 1969 he was expected to be Mao's successor. But in 1972 the government announced that Lin had been killed in an airplane crash in Mongolia on Sept 17, 1971 while fleeing to the USSR following an abortive coup attempt.

Lincoln industrial city and capital of Nebraska; population (1990) 192,000. Industries include engineering, pharmaceuticals, electronic and electrical equipment, and food processing. Educational institutions include the main campus of the University of Nebraska and Nebraska Wesleyan University. It was known as **Lancaster** until 1867, when it was renamed after Abraham Lincoln and designated the state capital.

Lincoln Abraham 1809–1865. 16th president of the US 1861–65, a Republican. In the American ◇Civil War, his chief concern was the preservation of the Union from which the Confederate (Southern) slave states had seceded on his election. In 1863 he announced the freedom of the slaves with the Emancipation Proclamation. He was reelected in 1864 with victory for the North in sight, but was assassinated at the end of the war.
Lincoln was born in a log cabin in Kentucky. Self-educated, he practiced law from 1837 in Springfield, Illinois. He was a member of the state legislature 1832–42, and was known as Honest Abe. He joined the new Republican Party in 1856, and was elected president in 1860 on a minority vote. His refusal to concede to Confederate demands for the evacuation of the federal garrison at Fort Sumter, Charleston, South Carolina, precipitated the first hostilities of the Civil War. In the Gettysburg Address

1863, he declared the aims of preserving a "nation conceived in liberty, and dedicated to the proposition that all men are created equal." Re-elected with a large majority in 1864 on a National Union ticket, he advocated a reconciliatory policy toward the South "with malice toward none, with charity for all." Five days after General Lee's surrender, Lincoln was shot in a theater audience by an actor and Confederate sympathizer, John Wilkes Booth.

Lincoln Benjamin 1733–1810. American military and political leader. Born in Hingham, Massachusetts, Lincoln served in the legislature and provincial congress prior to the American Revolution. With the outbreak of hostilities, he was named brigadier general in the Continental army and placed in command of troops in New York. After helping to win victory at Saratoga, Lincoln was sent to the South but he had to surrender to the British at Charleston 1780. Lincoln served as secretary of war for the Continental Congress 1781–83, and he led the Massachusetts militia in the suppression of Shays' Rebellion 1787.

Lincolnshire county in E England
area 2,274 sq mi/5,890 sq km
cities Lincoln (administrative headquarters), Skegness
physical Lincoln Wolds; marshy coastline; the Fens in the SE; rivers: Witham, Welland
features 16th-century Burghley House; Belton House, a Restoration mansion
products cattle, sheep, horses, cereals, flower bulbs, oil
population (1991) 573,900
famous people Isaac Newton, Alfred Tennyson, Margaret Thatcher.

Lind Jenny 1820–1887. Swedish soprano of remarkable range, nicknamed the "Swedish nightingale." She toured the US 1850–52 under the management of PT ◇Barnum.

Lindbergh Charles A(ugustus) 1902–1974. US aviator who made the first solo nonstop flight in 33.5 hours across the Atlantic (Roosevelt Field, Long Island, New York, to Le Bourget airport, Paris) 1927 in the *Spirit of St Louis*, a Ryan monoplane designed by him.
Born in Detroit, Michigan, Lindbergh was a barnstorming pilot before attending the US Army School in Texas 1924 and becoming an officer in the Army Air Service Reserve 1925. His son, Charles, Jr (1930–1932), was kidnapped and killed, a crime for which Bruno Hauptmann was convicted and executed. Ensuing legislation against kidnapping was called the Lindbergh Act. Although he admired the Nazi air force and championed US neutrality in the late 1930s, he flew 50 combat missions in the Pacific theater in World War II. He wrote *The Spirit of St Louis* 1953 (Pulitzer Prize).

Lindisfarne site of a monastery off the coast of Northumberland, England; see ◇Holy Island.

Lindsay (Nicholas) Vachel 1879–1931. US poet. He wandered the country, living by reciting his balladlike verse, collected in volumes including *General William Booth Enters into Heaven* 1913, *The Congo* 1914, and *Johnny Appleseed* 1928.

linear accelerator or **linac** see ◇accelerator.

linear equation in mathematics, an equation involving two variables (x, y) of the general form $y = mx + b$, where m is the slope of the line represented by the equation and b is the y-intercept, or the value of y where the line crosses the y-axis in the ◇Cartesian coordinate system. Sets of linear equations can be used to describe the behavior of buildings, bridges, trusses, and other static structures.

linear motor type of electric motor, an induction motor in which the fixed stator and moving armature are straight and parallel to each other (rather than being circular and one inside the other as in an ordinary induction motor). Linear motors are used, for example, to power sliding doors. There is a magnetic force between the stator and armature; this force has been used to support a vehicle, as in the experimental ◊maglev linear motor train.

linear programming in mathematics and economics, a set of techniques for finding the maxima or minima of certain variables governed by linear equations or inequalities. These maxima and minima are used to represent "best" solutions in terms of goals such as maximizing profit or minimizing cost.

Line Islands coral-island group in the Pacific ocean; population (1990) 4,800. Products include coconut and guano. Eight of the islands belong to Kiribati, and two (Palmyra and Jarvis) are administered by the US.

linen yarn spun and the textile woven from the fibers of the stem of the ◊flax plant. Used by the ancient Egyptians, linen was introduced by the Romans to northern Europe, where production became widespread. Religious refugees from the Low Countries in the 16th century helped to establish the linen industry in England, but here and elsewhere it began to decline in competition with cotton in the 18th century.

To get the longest possible fibers, flax is pulled, rather than cut by hand or machine, just as the seed bolls are beginning to set. After preliminary drying, it is steeped in water so that the fiber can be more easily separated from the wood of the stem, then hackled (combed), classified, drawn into continuous fibers, and spun. Bleaching, weaving, and finishing processes vary according to the final product, which can be sailcloth, canvas, sacking, cambric, or lawn. Because of the length of its fiber, linen yarn has twice the strength of cotton, and yet is superior in delicacy, so that it is suitable for lace making. It mixes well with synthetics.

line of force in physics, an imaginary line representing the direction of force at any point in a magnetic or electrical field.

ling any of several deepwater long-bodied fishes of the cod family found in the N Atlantic.

lingam in Hinduism, the phallic emblem of the god ◊Siva, the *yoni* being the female equivalent.

lingua franca (Italian "Frankish tongue") any language that is used as a means of communication by groups who do not themselves normally speak that language; for example, English is a lingua franca used by Japanese doing business in Finland, or by Swedes in Saudi Arabia. The term comes from the mixture of French, Italian, Spanish, Greek, Turkish, and Arabic that was spoken around the Mediterranean from the time of the Crusades until the 18th century.

Many of the world's lingua francas are ◊pidgin or trade languages; for example, Bazaar Hindi (Hindustani), Bazaar Malay, and Neo-Melanesian (also known as Tok Pisin), which became the official language of Papua New Guinea.

linguistics scientific study of language, from its origins (historical linguistics) to

the changing way it is pronounced (phonetics), derivation of words through various languages (etymology), development of meanings (semantics), and the arrangement and modifications of words to convey a message (grammar).

linkage in genetics, the association between two or more genes that tend to be inherited together because they are on the same chromosome. The closer together they are on the chromosome, the less likely they are to be separated by crossing over (one of the processes of ◊recombination) and they are then described as being "tightly linked."

Linnaeus Carolus 1707–1778. Swedish naturalist and physician. His botanical work *Systema naturae* 1735 contained his system for classifying plants into groups depending on shared characteristics (such as the number of stamens in flowers), providing a much-needed framework for identification. He also devised the concise and precise system for naming plants and animals, using one Latin (or Latinized) word to represent the genus and a second to distinguish the species.

For example, in the Latin name of the daisy, *Bellis perennis*, *Bellis* is the name of the genus to which the plant belongs, and *perennis* distinguishes the species from others of the same genus. By tradition the generic name always begins with a capital letter. The author who first described a particular species is often indicated after the name, for example, *Bellis perennis* Linnaeus, showing that the author was Linnaeus.

linnet Old World finch *Acanthis cannabina*. Mainly brown, the males, noted for their song, have a crimson crown and breast in summer.

Linotype trademark for a typesetting machine once universally used for newspaper work, which sets complete lines (slugs) of hot-metal type as operators type the copy at a keyboard. It was invented in the US in 1884 by German-born Ottmar Mergenthaler. It has been replaced by phototypesetting.

Lin Piao alternative transliteration of ◊Lin Biao.

linsang nocturnal, tree-dwelling, carnivorous mammal of the civet family, about 2.5 ft/75 cm long. It is native to Africa and SE Asia.

The African linsang *Poiana richardsoni* is a long, lithe and slender animal about 1.1 ft/33 cm long with a 1.25 ft/38 cm tail. The two species of oriental linsang, genus *Prionodon*, of Asia are slightly bigger.

linseed seeds of the flax plant *Linum usitatissimum*, from which linseed oil is expressed, the residue being used as cattle feed. The oil is used in paint, wood treatments and varnishes, and in the manufacture of linoleum.

lion cat *Panthera leo*, now found only in Africa and NW India. The coat is tawny, the young having darker spot markings that usually disappear in the adult. The male has a heavy mane and a tuft at the end of the tail. Head and body measure about 6 ft/2 m, plus 3 ft/1 m of tail, the lioness being slightly smaller. Lions produce litters of two to six cubs, and often live in prides of several adult males and females with several young.

Capable of short bursts of speed, they skillfully collaborate in stalking herbivorous animals. Old lions whose teeth and strength are failing may resort to eating humans. "Mountain lion" is a name for the ◊puma.

Lipari Islands or *Aeolian Islands* volcanic group of seven islands off NE Sicily, including *Lipari* (on which is the capital of the same name), *Stromboli* (active volcano 3,038 ft/926 m high), and *Vulcano* (also with an active volcano); area 44 sq mi/114 sq km. In Greek mythology, the god Aeolus kept the winds imprisoned in a cave on the Lipari Islands.

Lipchitz Jacques 1891–1973. Lithuanian-born sculptor, active in Paris from 1909; he emigrated to the US in 1941. He was one of the first Cubist sculptors.

The Barnes Foundation, Philadelphia, has many of his early works.

Li Peng 1928– . Chinese communist politician, a member of the Politburo from 1985, and head of government from 1987. During the prodemocracy demonstrations of 1989 he supported the massacre of students by Chinese troops and the subsequent execution of others. He sought improved relations with the USSR prior to its demise, and has favored maintaining firm central and party control over the economy.

Li was born at Chengdu in Sichuan province, the son of the writer Li Shouxun (who took part in the Nanchang rising 1927 and was executed 1930), and was adopted by the communist leader Zhou Enlai. He studied at the communist headquarters of Yanan 1941–47 and trained as a hydroelectric engineer at the Moscow Power Institute from 1948. He was appointed minister of the electric power industry 1981, a vice premier 1983, and prime minister 1987. In 1989 he launched the crackdown on demonstrators in Beijing that led to the massacre in ◊Tiananmen Square.

lipid any of a large number of esters of fatty acids, commonly formed by the reaction of a fatty acid with glycerol (see ◊glycerides). They are soluble in alcohol but not in water. Lipids are the chief constituents of plant and animal waxes, fats, and oils.

Phospholipids are lipids that also contain a phosphate group, usually linked to an organic base; they are major components of biological cell membranes.

Lipmann Fritz 1899–1986. US biochemist. He investigated the means by which the cell acquires energy and highlighted the crucial role played by the energy-rich phosphate molecule, adenosine triphosphate (ATP). For this and further work on metabolism, Lipmann shared the 1953 Nobel Prize for Medicine with Hans Krebs.

Li Po 705–762. Chinese poet. He used traditional literary forms, but his exuberance, the boldness of his imagination, and the intensity of his feeling have won him recognition as perhaps the greatest of all Chinese poets. Although he was mostly concerned with higher themes, he is also remembered for his celebratory verses on drinking.

Lippe river of N Germany flowing into the river Rhine; length 147 mi/230 km; also a former German state, now part of North Rhine–Westphalia.

Lippershey Hans *c.* 1570–1619. Dutch lens maker, credited with inventing the telescope in 1608.

Lippi Filippino 1457–1504. Italian painter of the Florentine school, trained by Botticelli. He produced altarpieces and several fresco cycles, full of detail and drama, elegant and finely drawn. He was the son of Filippo Lippi.

His frescoes, typical of late 15th-century Florentine work, can be found in Sta Maria sopra Minerva, Rome, in Sta Maria Novella, Florence, and elsewhere.

Lippi Fra Filippo 1406–1469. Italian painter whose works include frescoes depicting the lives of St Stephen and St John the Baptist in Prato Cathedral 1452–66. He also painted many altarpieces of Madonnas and groups of saints.

Lippi was born in Florence and patronized by the Medici family. The painter and biographer Giorgio ⟩Vasari gave a colorful account of his life including how, as a monk, he was tried in the 1450s for abducting a nun (the mother of his son Filippino).

Lippizaner pure white horse, named after its place of origin in Lippiza, Slovenia. They are trained at the Spanish Riding School of Vienna.

Lippmann Gabriel 1845–1921. French doctor who invented the direct color process in photography. He was awarded the Nobel Prize for Physics in 1908.

Lippmann Walter 1889–1974. US liberal political commentator. From 1921 Lippmann was the chief editorial writer for the *New York World* and from 1931 wrote the daily column "Today and Tomorrow," which was widely syndicated through the *New York Herald Tribune*. Among his books are *A Preface to Morals* 1929, *The Good Society* 1937, and *The Public Philosophy* 1955.

Born in New York and educated at Harvard, Lippmann was one of the founders of the *New Republic* 1914. After service in army intelligence during World War I, he became an adviser to President Wilson at the Versailles Peace Conference.

liquefied petroleum gas (LPG) liquid form of butane, propane, or pentane, produced by the distillation of petroleum during oil refining. At room temperature these substances are gases, although they can be easily liquefied and stored under pressure in metal containers. They are used for heating and cooking where other fuels are not available: camping stoves and cigarette lighters, for instance, often use liquefied butane as fuel.

liquid state of matter between a ⟩solid and a ⟩gas. A liquid forms a level surface and assumes the shape of its container. Its atoms do not occupy fixed positions as in a crystalline solid, nor do they have freedom of movement as in a gas. Unlike a gas, a liquid is difficult to compress since pressure applied at one point is equally transmitted throughout (Pascal's principle). ⟩Hydraulics makes use of this property.

liquid air air that has been cooled so much that it has liquefied. This happens at temperatures below about –321°F/–196°C. The various constituent gases, including nitrogen, oxygen, argon, and neon, can be separated from liquid air by the technique of ⟩fractionation.

Air is liquefied by the **Linde process**, in which air is alternately compressed, cooled, and expanded, the expansion resulting each time in a considerable reduction in temperature.

liquidation in economics, the termination of a company by converting all its assets into money to pay off its liabilities.

liquid-crystal display (LCD) display of numbers (for example, in a calculator) or pictures (such as on a pocket television screen) produced by molecules of a substance in a semiliquid state with some crystalline properties, so that clusters of molecules align in parallel formations. The display is a blank until the application of an electric field, which "twists" the molecules so that they reflect or transmit light falling on them.

liquidity in economics, the state of possessing sufficient money and/or assets to be able to pay off all liabilities. *Liquid assets* are those such as shares that may be converted quickly into cash, as opposed to property.

Lisbon (Portuguese *Lisboa*) city and capital of Portugal, in the SW of the country, on the tidal lake and estuary formed by the river Tagus; population (1984) 808,000. Industries include steel, textiles, chemicals, pottery, shipbuilding, and fishing. It has been the capital since 1260 and reached its peak of prosperity in the period of Portugal's empire during the 16th century. In 1755 an earthquake killed 60,000 people and destroyed much of the city.

LISP (abbreviation for *list processing*) high-level computer-programming language designed for manipulating lists of data items. It is used primarily in research into ⟩artificial intelligence (AI).

Developed in the 1960s, and until recently common only in university laboratories, LISP is used more in the US than in Europe, where the language ⟩PROLOG is often preferred for AI work.

Lister Joseph, 1st Baron Lister 1827–1912. English surgeon and founder of antiseptic surgery, influenced by Louis ⟩Pasteur's work on bacteria. He introduced dressings soaked

liquid-crystal display *A liquid-crystal display consists of a liquid crystal sandwiched between polarizing filters similar to polaroid sunglasses.*

in carbolic acid and strict rules of hygiene to combat wound sepsis in hospitals.

The number of surgical operations greatly increased following the introduction of anesthetics, and death rates were more than 40%. Under Lister's regime they fell dramatically.

listeriosis disease of animals that may occasionally infect humans, caused by the bacterium *Listeria monocytogenes*. The bacteria multiply at temperatures close to 32°F/0°C, which means they may flourish in precooked frozen meals if the cooking has not been thorough. Listeriosis causes inflammation of the brain and its surrounding membranes, but can be treated with penicillin.

Liszt Franz 1811–1886. Hungarian pianist and composer. An outstanding virtuoso of the piano, he was an established concert artist by the age of 12. His expressive, romantic, and frequently chromatic works include piano music (*Transcendental Studies* 1851), symphonies, piano concertos, and organ music. Much of his music is programmatic; he also originated the symphonic poem. Liszt was taught by his father, then by Carl Czerny (1791–1857). He traveled widely in Europe, producing an opera *Don Sanche* in Paris at the age of 14. As musical director and conductor at Weimar 1848–59, he championed the music of Berlioz and Wagner.

Retiring to Rome, he turned again to his early love of religion, and in 1865 became a secular priest (adopting the title Abbé), but he continued to teach and give concert tours. Many of his compositions are lyrical, often technically difficult, piano works, including the *Liebesträume* and the *Hungarian Rhapsodies*, based on folk music. He also wrote an opera and a symphony; masses and oratorios; songs; and piano arrangements of works by Beethoven, Schubert, and Wagner among others. He died at Bayreuth in Germany.

Litani river rising near Baalbek in the Anti-Lebanon Mountains of E Lebanon. It flows NE–SW through the Beqa'a Valley, then E to the Mediterranean 5 mi/8 km N of Tyre. Israeli forces invaded Lebanon as far as the Litani River 1978.

litany in the Christian church, a form of prayer or supplication led by a priest with set responses by the congregation.

litchi or *lychee* evergreen tree *Litchi chinensis* of the soapberry family Sapindaceae. The delicately flavored ovate fruit is encased in a brownish rough outer skin and has a hard seed. The litchi is native to S China, where it has been cultivated for 2,000 years.

liter metric unit of volume (symbol l), equal since 1964 to one cubic decimeter (61.025 cu in, 1.057 liquid qt, or 0.91 dry qt). It was formerly defined as the volume occupied by one kilogram of pure water at 4°C at standard pressure, but this is slightly larger than one cubic decimeter.

literacy ability to read and write. The level at which functional literacy is set rises as society becomes more complex, and it becomes increasingly difficult for an illiterate person to find work and cope with the other demands of everyday life.

Nearly 1 billion adults in the world, most of them women, are unable to read or write. Africa has the world's highest illiteracy rate: 54% of the adult population. Asia has 666 million illiterates, 75% of the world total. Surveys in the US, the UK, and France in the 1980s found far greater levels of functional illiteracy than official figures suggest, as well as revealing a lack of basic general knowledge, but no standard of measurement has been agreed. For example, in a 1988 survey one in six Britons could not find their country on a map, and in the US 12% of 12-year-olds in 1991 could not find their country on a map; 25 million US adults could not decipher a road sign.

literary criticism establishment of principles governing literary composition, and the assessment and interpretation of literary works. Contemporary criticism offers analyses of literary works from structuralist, semiological, feminist, Marxist, and psychoanalytical perspectives, whereas earlier criticism tended to deal with moral or political ideas, or with a literary work as a formal object independent of its creator.

The earliest systematic literary criticism was the *Poetics* of Aristotle; a later Greek critic was the author of the treatise *On the Sublime*, usually attributed to Longinus. Horace and Quintilian were influential Latin critics. The Italian Renaissance introduced humanist criticism, and the revival of Classical scholarship exalted the authority of Aristotle and Horace. Like literature itself, European criticism then applied Neo-Classical, Romantic, and modern approaches.

literature words set apart in some way from ordinary everyday communication. In the ancient oral traditions, before stories and poems were written down, literature had a mainly public function—mythic and religious. As literary works came to be preserved in writing, and, eventually, printed, their role became more private, serving as a vehicle for the exploration and expression of emotion and the human situation.

In the development of literature, aesthetic criteria have come increasingly to the fore. The English poet and critic Coleridge defined *prose* as words in their best order, and *poetry* as the "best" words in the best order. The distinction between poetry and prose is not always clear-cut, but in practice poetry tends to be metrically formal (making it easier to memorize), whereas prose corresponds more closely to the patterns of ordinary speech. Poetry therefore had an early advantage over prose in the days before printing, which it did not relinquish until comparatively recently. Over the centuries poetry has taken on a wide range of forms, from the lengthy narrative such as the ◊epic, to the lyric, expressing personal emotion in songlike form; from the ◊ballad, and the 14-line ◊sonnet, to the extreme conciseness of the 17-syllable Japanese ◊haiku. Prose came into its own in the West as a vehicle for imaginative literature with the rise of the novel in the 18th century, and ◊fiction has since been divided into various genres such as the historical novel, detective fiction, fantasy, and science fiction. See also the literature of particular countries, under ◊American literature, ◊English literature, ◊French literature, and so on.

lithification another term for ◊diagenesis.

lithium (Greek *lithos* "stone") soft, ductile, silver-white, metallic element, symbol Li, atomic number 3, atomic weight 6.941. It is one of the ◊alkali metals, has a very low density (far less than most woods), and floats on water (specific gravity 0.57); it is the lightest of all metals. Lithium is used to harden alloys, and in batteries; its compounds are used in medicine to treat manic depression.

Lithium was named in 1818 by Swedish chemist Jöns Berzelius, having been discovered the previous year by his student Johan A

Arfwedson (1792–1841). Berzelius named it after "stone" because it is found in most igneous rocks and many mineral springs.

lithography printmaking technique originated in 1798 by Aloys Senefelder, based on the antipathy of grease and water. A drawing is made with greasy crayon on an absorbent stone, which is then wetted. The wet stone repels ink (which is greasy) applied to the surface and the crayon attracts it, so that the drawing can be printed. Lithographic printing is used in book production and has developed this basic principle into complex processes.

lithosphere topmost layer of the Earth's structure, forming the jigsaw of plates that take part in the movements of ◊plate tectonics. The lithosphere comprises the ◊crust and a portion of the upper ◊mantle. It is regarded as being rigid and moves about on the semimolten ◊asthenosphere. The lithosphere is about 47 mi/75 km thick.

Lithuania country in N Europe, bounded N by Latvia, E by Belarus, S by Poland and the Kaliningrad area of Russia, and W by the Baltic Sea.

government There is a 141-deputy, popularly elected supreme council (Auksiansiogi

Taryba), or parliament, whose members elect a chair to serve as state president and a prime minister. The Lithuanian Communist Party is outlawed.

history Lithuania became a single nation at the end of the 12th century. The ◊Teutonic Knights (German crusaders) who attempted to invade in the 13th century were successfully driven back, and Lithuania extended its boundaries in the 14th century to reach almost as far as Moscow and the Black Sea. In 1386 Lithuania was joined with Poland in a mutually beneficial confederation. The two eventually became a single state 1569, and came under the control of the Russian tsar 1795. Revolts 1831 and 1863 failed to win independence for the state, and a more organized movement for the independence of Lithuania emerged in the 1880s. When self-government was demanded 1905, this was refused by the Russians.

struggle for independence During World War I Lithuania was occupied by German troops. After the war, it declared independence but the USSR claimed Lithuania as a Soviet republic 1918. Soviet forces were overthrown by the Germans, Poles, and nationalist Lithuanians 1919, and a democratic republic was established. This was in turn overthrown by a coup 1926 and the new president, Antanas

Lithuania
Republic of

area 25,174 sq mi/65,200 sq km
capital Vilnius
cities Kaunas, Klaipeda, Siauliai, Panevezys
physical central lowlands with gentle hills in W and higher terrain in SE; 25% forested; some 3,000 small lakes, marshes, and complex sandy coastline
features river Nemen; white sand dunes on Kursiu Marios lagoon
head of state Vytautas Landsbergis from 1990
head of government Aleksandras Abisala from 1992
political system emergent democracy
political parties Sajudis (Lithuanian Restructuring Movement), nationalist; Democratic Party, centrist; Humanism and Progress Party, reformist; Social Democratic Party, left of center; Green Party, ecological; Christian Democratic Party, right of center; Democratic Labor Party, "reform communist"
products heavy engineering, electrical goods, shipbuilding, cement, food processing, bacon, dairy products, cereals, potatoes
currency Lithuanian ruble
population (1990) 3,700,000 (Lithuanian 80%, Russian 9%, Polish 7%, Byelorussian 2%)
language Lithuanian
religion predominantly Roman Catholic

chronology
1918 Independence declared following withdrawal of German occupying troops at end of World War I; USSR attempted to regain power.
1919 Soviet forces overthrown by Germans, Poles, and nationalist Lithuanians; democratic republic established.
1920–39 Province and city of Vilnius occupied by Poles.
1926 Coup overthrew established government; Antanas Smetona became president.
1939 Secret German-Soviet agreement brought most of Lithuania under Soviet influence.
1940 Incorporated into USSR as constituent republic.
1941 Lithuania revolted against USSR and established own government. During World War II Germany again occupied the country.
1944 USSR resumed rule.
1944–52 Lithuanian guerrillas fought USSR.
1972 Demonstrations against Soviet government.
1980 Growth in nationalist dissent, influenced by Polish example.
1988 Popular front formed, the Sajudis, to campaign for increased autonomy.
1989 Lithuanian declared the state language; flag of independent interwar republic readopted. Communist Party (CP) split into pro-Moscow and nationalist wings. Communist local monopoly of power abolished.
1990 Feb: nationalist Sajudis won elections. March: Vytautas Landsbergis became president; unilateral declaration of independence resulted in temporary Soviet blockade.
1991 Jan: Albertas Shiminas became prime minister. Soviet paratroopers briefly occupied key buildings in Vilnius. Sept: independence recognized by Soviet government and Western nations; Gediminas Vagnorius elected prime minister; CP outlawed; admitted into United Nations (UN) and Conference on Security and Cooperation in Europe (CSCE).
1992 July: Aleksandras Abisala became prime minister. Nov: Democratic Labor Party, led by Algirdas Brazauskas, won majority vote.

Smetona, assumed increasing authority. In 1939 Germany took control of part of Lithuania, handing it to the USSR later the same year. In 1940 Lithuania was incorporated as a constituent republic of the USSR, designated the Lithuanian Soviet Socialist Republic. In 1941, when German troops had invaded the USSR, Lithuania revolted against Soviet rule and established its own government. The Germans occupied Lithuania 1941–44, after which Soviet rule was restored.

As in the other Baltic republics, there was strong nationalist dissent from 1980, influenced by the Polish example and prompted by the influx of Russian workers and officials. A popular front, the Sajudis (Lithuanian Restructuring Movement), was formed Oct 1988 to campaign for increased autonomy, and in the same month the republic's supreme soviet (state assembly), to the chagrin of Russian immigrants, decreed Lithuanian the state language and readopted the flag of the independent interwar republic. In Dec 1989 the republic's Communist Party split into two, with the majority wing formally breaking away from the Communist Party of the USSR and establishing itself as a social-democratic, Lithuanian-nationalist body. A multiparty system is in place in the republic, Sadjudis-backed pro-separatist candidates having secured a majority in the Feb–March 1990 elections. In March 1990 Lithuania unilaterally declared independence. The USSR responded by imposing an economic blockade, which was lifted July 1990 after the supreme council agreed to suspend the independence declaration.

Criticized by militant nationalists as being too conciliatory toward Moscow, Prime Minister Kazimiera Prunskiene resigned Jan 1991 and went into exile. She was replaced by Albertas Shiminas. Also in Jan, Soviet paratroopers seized political and communications buildings in Vilnius, killing 13 civilians, but began to withdraw the same month. In July four Lithuanian police and two customs officers were killed at a border post with Byelorussia (now Belarus). The OMON black-beret troops of the Soviet Interior Ministry and KGB were suspected.

independence achieved After the failure of the Aug 1991 anti-Gorbachev coup in the USSR, Lithuania's declaration of independence was recognized by the Soviet government and Western nations Sept 1991 and the new state was granted membership in the United Nations (UN) and admitted into the Conference on Security and Cooperation in Europe (CSCE). At the same time, the Communist Party was outlawed, and Gediminas Vagnorius took over as prime minister. In Feb 1992 President Landsbergis demanded the withdrawal of Russian troops from the Baltic enclave of Kaliningrad, formerly Königsberg. The Lithuanian Supreme Council (parliament) chose Aleksandras Abisala as the new prime minister when Vagnorious received a vote of no confidence in July. In Nov elections the Democratic Labor Party, headed by Algirdas Brazauskas, won the majority vote. *See illustration box.*

Lithuanian member of the majority ethnic group living in Lithuania, comprising 80% of the population.

Lithuanian language Indo-European language spoken by the people of Lithuania, which through its geographical isolation has retained many ancient features of the Indo-European language family. It acquired a written form in the 16th century, using the Latin alphabet, and is currently spoken by some 3–4 million people.

litmus dye obtained from various lichens and used in chemistry as an indicator to test the acidic or alkaline nature of aqueous solutions; it turns red in the presence of acid, and blue in the presence of alkali.

Little Bighorn, Battle of the engagement in Montana; Lieutenant Colonel George ▷Custer's defeat by the ▷Sioux Indians, June 25, 1876, under Chiefs ▷Crazy Horse and Sitting Bull, known as Custer's Last Stand. The battle was precipitated by the discovery of gold in the Black Hills and the subsequent violations of the 1868 treaty with the Sioux, which had granted them "sole use" of the area. Custer ignored scouting reports of an overwhelming Indian force and led a column of 265 soldiers into a ravine where thousands of Indian warriors lay in wait. Custer and every one of his command were killed. US reprisals against the Indians followed, abrogating the treaty, ending their rights, and driving them from the area.

Little Dipper another name for the most distinctive part of ▷Ursa Minor, the Little Bear.

The name has also been applied to the stars in the ▷Pleiades open star cluster, the overall shape of the cluster being similar to that of the ▷Big Dipper.

Little Entente series of alliances between Czechoslovakia, Romania, and Yugoslavia 1920–21 for mutual security and the maintenance of existing frontiers. Reinforced by the Treaty of Belgrade 1929, the entente collapsed upon Yugoslav cooperation with Germany 1935–38 and the Anglo-French abandonment of Czechoslovakia in 1938.

Little Red Book, The book written by ▷Mao Zedong, in which he adapted Marxist theory to Chinese conditions.

Little Review, The 1914–29 US literary magazine founded in Chicago by Margaret Anderson. It published many experimental writers including W B Yeats, Ezra Pound, T S Eliot, and William Carlos Williams, and was banned for publishing part of James Joyce's *Ulysses*. The *Little Review* was variously published in New York, Paris, and elsewhere.

Little Richard Adopted name of Richard Penniman 1932– . US rock singer and pianist. He was one of the creators of rock and roll with his wildly uninhibited renditions of "Tutti Frutti" 1956, "Long Tall Sally" 1956, and "Good Golly Miss Molly" 1957. His subsequent career in soul and rhythm and blues was interrupted by periods devoted to gospel music and religion.

Little Rock largest city and capital of Arkansas; population (1990) 175,800. Products include metal goods, oil-field and electronic equipment, chemicals, clothing, and processed food.

Educational institutions include the University of Arkansas at Little Rock. A French trading post was built here 1722, and in 1821 it became the territorial capital. Union forces captured the city 1863, during the Civil War. Federal troops were sent here 1957 to enforce the integration of all-white Central High School.

Little Women novel for children by Louisa M ▷Alcott published in 1868, one of the most popular children's books ever written. It describes the daily life of a New England family in reduced circumstances, and the tensions and harmony between the four teenage daughters, Meg, Jo, Beth, and Amy.

It was followed by a sequel in 1869.

liturgy in the Christian church, any service for public worship; the term was originally limited to the celebration of the ▷Eucharist.

Litvinov Maxim 1876–1951. Soviet politician, commissioner for foreign affairs under Stalin from Jan 1931 until his removal from office in May 1939.

Litvinov believed in cooperation with the West and obtained US recognition of the USSR in 1934. In the League of Nations he advocated action against the ▷Axis (the alliance of Nazi Germany and Fascist Italy); he was therefore dismissed just before the signing of the Hitler–Stalin nonaggression pact 1939. After the German invasion of the USSR, he was ambassador to the US 1941–43.

Liu Shaoqi or *Liu Shao-chi* 1898–1969. Chinese communist politician, in effective control of government 1960–65. A labor organizer, he was a firm proponent of the Soviet style of government based around disciplined one-party control, the use of incentive gradings, and priority for industry over agriculture. This was opposed by Mao Zedong, but began to be implemented by Liu while he was state president 1960–65. Liu was brought down during the ▷Cultural Revolution.

liver large organ of vertebrates, which has many regulatory and storage functions. The human liver is situated in the upper abdomen, and weighs about 4.5 lb/2 kg. It receives the products of digestion, converts glucose to glycogen (a long-chain carbohydrate used for storage), and breaks down fats. It removes excess amino acids from the blood, converting them to urea, which is excreted by the kidneys. The liver also synthesizes vitamins, produces bile and blood-clotting factors, and removes damaged red cells and toxins such as alcohol from the blood.

Liverpool city, seaport, and administrative headquarters of Merseyside, NW England; population (1991 est) 448,300. In the 19th and early 20th centuries it exported the textiles of Lancashire and Yorkshire. Liverpool is the UK's chief Atlantic port with miles of specialized, mechanized quays on the river Mersey.

The Liverpool Institute for the Performing Arts occupies the old Liverpool Institute where former ▷Beatles Paul McCartney and George Harrison went to school. It is planned as an educational center for people involved in graphic design, performance, production, and video.

liverwort plant of the class Hepaticae, of the bryophyte division of nonvascular plants, related to mosses, found growing in damp places.

The main sexual generation consists of a ▷thallus, which may be flat, green, and lobed, like a small leaf, or leafy and mosslike. The spore-bearing generation is smaller, typically parasitic on the thallus, and throws up a capsule from which spores are spread.

Livia Drusilla 58 BC–AD 29. Roman empress, wife of ▷Augustus from 39 BC, she was the mother by her first husband of ▷Tiberius and engaged in intrigue to secure his succession to the imperial crown. She remained politically active to the end of her life.

Livingston Robert R 1746–1813. American public official and diplomat, who, after service in the Continental Congress 1775, helped write the New York Constitution and served as state chancellor 1776–1801. He returned to the Continental Congress 1779 and was named secretary for foreign affairs 1781 and directed negotiations for the Paris Peace Treaty. In 1801 he was named minister to France by Jefferson. With James Monroe, Livingston secured the purchase of the Louisiana Territory 1803.

Born in New York and educated at King's College (now Columbia), Livingston was admitted to the bar 1770.

Livingstone David 1813–1873. Scottish missionary explorer. In 1841 he went to Africa, reached Lake Ngami 1849, followed the Zambezi to its mouth, saw the Victoria Falls 1855, and went to East and Central Africa 1858–64, reaching Lakes Shirwa and Malawi. From 1866, he tried to find the source of the river Nile, and reached Ujiji in Tanganyika in Oct 1871. British explorer Henry Stanley joined Livingstone in Ujiji.

Livingstone not only mapped a great deal of the African continent but also helped to end the Arab slave trade.

Livingstone formerly *Maramba* town in Zambia; population (1988) 98,500. Founded 1905, it was named after explorer David Livingstone, and was capital of N Rhodesia 1907–35. The Victoria Falls are nearby.

Living Theater experimental US theater group, 1947–70, founded by Judith Malina (1926–   ) and Julian Beck (1925–1985), which mounted avant-garde plays by Jack Gelber (1932–   ), John Ashbery (1927–   ), and others. The group production *Paradise Now* 1968 was considered to have expressed the spirit of the sixties. In 1964 the company took up "voluntary exile" in Europe. In 1970 it split into several groups and dispersed.

Livonia former region in Europe on the E coast of the Baltic Sea comprising most of present-day Latvia and Estonia. Conquered and converted to Christianity in the early 13th century by the Livonian Knights, a crusading order, Livonia was independent until 1583, when it was divided between Poland and Sweden. In 1710 it was occupied by Russia, and in 1721 was ceded to Peter the Great, Tsar of Russia.

Livy Titus Livius 59 BC–AD 17. Roman historian, author of a *History of Rome* from the city's foundation to 9 BC, based partly on legend. It was composed of 142 books, of which 35 survive, covering the periods from the arrival of Aeneas in Italy to 293 BC and from 218 to 167 BC.

lizard reptile of the suborder Lacertilia, which together with snakes constitutes the order Squamata. Lizards are generally distinguishable from snakes by having four legs, moveable eyelids, eardrums, and a fleshy tongue, but some lizards are legless and snakelike in appearance. There are over 3,000 species of lizard worldwide.

Like other reptiles, lizards are abundant in the tropics, although some species live as far north as the Arctic circle. There are some 20 families of lizards, including geckos, chameleons, skinks, monitors, agamas, and iguanas. The common or viviparous lizard *Lacerta vivipara*, about 6 in/15 cm long, is found throughout Europe; in the far north, it hibernates through the long winter. Like many other species, it can shed its tail as a defense, later regrowing it. The frilled lizard *Chlamydosaurus kingi* of Australia has an erectile collar to frighten its enemies. There are two poisonous

species of lizard, the Mexican bearded lizard and the gila monster. (For flying lizard see ◊flying dragon.)

Ljubljana (German *Laibach*) capital and industrial city (textiles, chemicals, paper, leather goods) of Slovenia; population (1981) 305,200. It has a nuclear research center and is linked with S Austria by the Karawanken road tunnel under the Alps (1979–83).

llama South American even-toed hoofed mammal *Lama glama* of the camel family, about 4 ft/1.2 m high at the shoulder. Llamas can be white, brown, or dark, sometimes with spots or patches. They are very hardy, and require little food or water. They spit profusely when annoyed.

Llamas are used in Peru as beasts of burden, and also for their wool, milk, and meat. Llamas and alpacas are both domesticated forms of the ◊guanaco.

Llewellyn Richard. Adopted name of Richard Vivian Llewellyn Lloyd 1907–1983. Welsh writer. *How Green Was My Valley* 1939, a novel about a S Wales mining family, was made into a play and a film.

Llewelyn two kings of Wales:

Llewelyn I 1173–1240. King of Wales from 1194 who extended his rule to all Wales not in Norman hands, driving the English from N Wales 1212, and taking Shrewsbury 1215. During the early part of Henry III's reign, he was several times attacked by English armies. He was married to Joanna, illegitimate daughter of King John.

Llewelyn II *c.* 1225–1282. King of Wales from 1246, grandson of Llewelyn I. In 1277 Edward I of England compelled Llewelyn to acknowledge him as overlord and to surrender S Wales. His death while leading a national uprising ended Welsh independence.

Lloyd Harold 1893–1971. US film comedian, noted for his "trademark" of thick horn-rimmed glasses and straw hat, who invented the bumbling cliff-hanger and dangler. He appeared from 1913 in silent and talking films. His silent films include *Grandma's Boy* 1922, *Safety Last* 1923, and *The Freshman* 1925. His first talkie was *Movie Crazy* 1932. He produced films after 1938, including the reissued *Harold Lloyd's World of Comedy* 1962 and *Funny Side of Life* 1964.

Lloyd George David 1863–1945. Welsh Liberal politician, prime minister of Britain 1916–22. A pioneer of social reform, as chancellor of the Exchequer 1908–15 he introduced old-age pensions 1908 and health and unemployment insurance 1911. High unemployment, intervention in the Russian Civil War, and use of the military police force, the ◊Black and Tans, in Ireland eroded his support as prime minister, and the creation of the Irish Free State in 1921 and his pro-Greek policy against the Turks caused the collapse of his coalition government.

Lloyd George was born in Manchester, became a lawyer, and was member of Parliament for Caernarvon Boroughs from 1890. During the Boer War, he was prominent as a pro-Boer. His 1909 budget (with graduated direct taxes and taxing land values) provoked the Lords to reject it, and resulted in the Act of 1911 limiting their powers. He held ministerial posts during World War I until 1916 when there was an open breach between him and Prime Minister ◊Asquith, and he became prime minister of a

coalition government. Securing a unified Allied command, he enabled the Allies to withstand the last German offensive and achieve victory. After World War I he had a major role in the Versailles peace treaty.

In the 1918 elections, he achieved a huge majority over Labour and Asquith's followers. He had become largely distrusted within his own party by 1922, and never regained power.

Lloyd Webber Andrew 1948–   . English composer. His early musicals, with lyrics by Tim Rice, include *Joseph and the Amazing Technicolor Dreamcoat* 1968; *Jesus Christ Superstar* 1970; and *Evita* 1978, based on the life of the Argentine leader Eva Perón. He also wrote *Cats* 1981 and *The Phantom of the Opera* 1986.

Llull Ramon 1232–1316. Catalan scholar and mystic. He began his career at the court of James I of Aragon (1212–1276) in Majorca. He produced treatises on theology, mysticism, and chivalry in Catalan, Latin, and Arabic. His *Ars magna* was a mechanical device, a kind of prototype computer, by which all problems could be solved by manipulating fundamental Aristotelian categories.

He also wrote the prose romance *Blanquerna*, in his native Catalan, the first novel written in a Romance language. In later life he became a Franciscan, and died a martyr at Bugia, Algeria.

loa spirit in ◊voodoo. Loas may be male or female, and include Maman Brigitte, the loa of death and cemeteries, and Aida-Wedo, the rainbow snake. Believers may be under the protection of one particular loa.

loach carplike freshwater fish, family Cobitidae, with a long narrow body, and no teeth in the small, downward-pointing mouth, which is surrounded by barbels. Loaches are native to Asian and European waters.

Lobachevsky Nikolai Ivanovich 1792–1856. Russian mathematician who concurrently with, but independently of, Karl ◊Gauss and the Hungarian János Bolyai (1802–1860), founded non-Euclidean geometry. Lobachevsky published the first account of the subject in 1829, but his work went unrecognized until Georg ◊Riemann's system was published.

lobby individual or pressure group that sets out to influence government action. The lobby is prevalent in the US, where the term originated in the 1830s from the practice of those wishing to influence state policy waiting for elected representatives in the lobby of the Capitol.

lobelia any temperate and tropical plant of the genus *Lobelia* of the bellflower family Lobeliaceae, with white to mauve flowers. Lobelias may grow to shrub size but are mostly small annual plants.

The cardinal lobelia *L. cardinalis* of E North America has large bright red flowers.

Lobengula 1836–1894. King of Matabeleland (now part of Zimbabwe) 1870–93. He was overthrown in 1893 by a military expedition organized by Cecil ◊Rhodes's South African Company.

lobotomy in medicine, the cutting of a lobe. The term usually refers to the operation of **frontal lobotomy** (or *leucotomy*), where the frontal lobes are disconnected from the rest of the brain by cutting the white matter that joins them. This may alleviate the condition of patients with severe depression, anxiety states, or obsessive-compulsive disorders, but it is now rarely performed, and only on patients who have proved resistant to all other forms of treatment. It is irreversible and the degree of personality change is not predictable.

It was pioneered by A E Moniz (1874–1955), who shared the 1949 Nobel Prize for Medicine for his work in brain surgery.

lobster large marine crustacean of the order Decapoda. Lobsters are grouped with freshwater ◇crayfish in the suborder Reptantia ("walking"), although both lobsters and crayfish can also swim, using their fanlike tails. Lobsters have eyes on stalks and long antennae, and are mainly nocturnal. They scavenge and eat dead or dying fish.

True lobsters, family Homaridae, are distinguished by having very large "claws" or pincers on their first pair of legs, and smaller ones on their second and third pairs. Spiny lobsters, family Palinuridae, have no large pincers. They communicate by means of a serrated pad at the base of their antennae, the "sound" being picked up by sensory nerves located on hairlike outgrowths on their fellow lobsters up to 180 ft/60 m away.

Species include the American lobster *Homarus americanus*; and the Norwegian lobster *Nephrops norvegicus*, a small orange species.

local area network (LAN) in computing, a ◇network restricted to a single room or building. Local area networks enable around 500 devices to be connected together.

local government that part of government dealing mainly with matters concerning the inhabitants of a particular area or town, usually financed at least in part by local taxes. In the US and UK, local government has comparatively large powers and responsibilities.

Historically, in European countries such as France, Germany, and the USSR, local government tended to be more centrally controlled than in Britain, although German cities have a tradition of independent action, as exemplified in Berlin, and France from 1969 moved toward regional decentralization. In the US the system shows evidence of the early type of settlement (for example in New England the town is the unit of local government, in the South the county, and in the N central states the combined county and township). A complication is the tendency to delegate power to special authorities in such fields as education. In Australia, although an integrated system similar to the British was planned, the scattered nature of settlement, apart from the major towns, has prevented implementation of any uniform tiered arrangement.

Local Group in astronomy, a cluster of about 30 galaxies that includes our own, the Milky Way. Like other groups of galaxies, the Local Group is held together by the gravitational attraction among its members, and does not expand with the expanding universe. Its two largest galaxies are the Milky Way and the Andromeda galaxy; most of the others are small and faint.

Locarno health resort in the Ticino canton of Switzerland on the N shore of Lago Maggiore, W of Bellinzona; population (1990) 14,200. Formerly in the duchy of Milan, it was captured by the Swiss in 1803.

Locarno, Pact of series of diplomatic documents initialled in Locarno, Switzerland, Oct 16, 1925 and formally signed in London Dec 1, 1925. The pact settled the question of French security, and the signatories—Britain,

France, Belgium, Italy, and Germany—guaranteed Germany's existing frontiers with France and Belgium. Following the signing of the pact, Germany was admitted to the League of Nations.

Lochner Stephan died 1451. German painter, active in Cologne from 1442, a master of the International ◇Gothic style. Most of his work is still in Cologne: for example, the *Virgin in the Rose Garden* (Wallraf-Richartz Museum) and *Adoration of the Magi* (Cologne Cathedral).

Lochner v New York a US Supreme Court decision 1905 dealing with the use of state police power to regulate working conditions. Lochner, an owner of a bakery convicted of violating a New York law that set maximum working hours for bakery workers, filed suit against the state. The US Supreme Court voted narrowly to overrule the New York law, ruling it an excessive use of state police power that violated the 14th-Amendment right to freedom of contract. Dissenting, Justice Holmes criticized the majority ruling for making its decision because of a belief in laissez-faire economics.

Loch Ness see ◇Ness, Loch

lock construction installed in waterways to allow boats or ships to travel from one level to another. The earliest form, the *flash lock*, was first seen in the East in 1st-century-AD China and in the West in 11th-century Holland. By this method barriers temporarily dammed a river and when removed allowed the flash flood to propel the waiting boat through any obstacle. This was followed in 12th-century China and 14th-century Holland by the *pound lock*. In this system the lock has gates at each end. Boats enter through one gate when the levels are the same both outside and inside. Water is then allowed in (or out of) the lock until the

level rises (or falls) to the new level outside the other gate.

Locks are important to shipping where canals link oceans of differing levels, such as the Panama Canal, or where falls or rapids are replaced by these adjustable water "steps."

lock and key devices that provide security, usually fitted to a door of some kind. In 1778 English locksmith Robert Barron made the forerunner of the *mortise lock*, which contains levers that the key must raise to an exact height before the bolt can be moved. The *Yale lock*, a pin-tumbler cylinder design, was invented by US locksmith Linus Yale, Jr, in 1865. More secure locks include *combination locks*, with a dial mechanism that must be turned certain distances backward and forward to open, and *time locks*, which are set to be opened only at specific times.

Locks originated in the Far East over 4,000 years ago. The Romans developed the warded lock, which contains obstacles (wards) that the key must pass to turn.

Locke John 1632–1704. English philosopher. His *Essay concerning Human Understanding* 1690 maintained that experience was the only source of knowledge (empiricism), and that "we can have knowlege no farther than we have ideas" prompted by such experience. *Two Treatises on Government* 1690 helped to form contemporary ideas of liberal democracy.

Locke studied at Oxford, practiced medicine, and in 1667 became secretary to the Earl of Shaftesbury. He consequently fell under suspicion as a Whig and in 1683 fled to Holland, where he lived until the 1688 revolution brought William of Orange to the English throne. In later life he published many works on philosophy, politics, theology, and economics; these include *Letters on Toleration* 1689–92

upper gates open   lower gates shut

upper gates shut   lower gates shut   water let out through sluices

upper gates shut   lower gates open

water let in through sluices to raise level in lock   lower gates shut

lock Travelling downstream, a boat enters the lock with the lower gates closed.

locomotive *In a steam locomotive, a slide valve directs high-pressure steam first to one end of the cylinder and then to the other, driving the piston back and forth.*

and *Some Thoughts concerning Education* 1693. His *Two Treatises on Government* supplied the Classical statement of Whig theory and enjoyed great influence in America and France. It supposed that governments derive their authority from popular consent (regarded as a "contract"), so that a government may be rightly overthrown if it infringes such fundamental rights of the people as religious freedom. He believed that at birth the mind was a blank, and that all ideas came from sense impressions.

lockjaw former name for ◊tetanus, a type of infection.

locomotive engine for hauling railroad trains. In 1804 Richard Trevithick built the first steam engine to run on rails. Locomotive design did not radically improve until George Stephenson built the *Rocket* 1829, which featured a multitube boiler and blastpipe, standard in all following ***steam locomotives***. Today most locomotives are diesel or electric: ***diesel locomotives*** have a powerful diesel engine, and ***electric locomotives*** draw their power from either an overhead cable or a third rail alongside the ordinary track.

In a steam locomotive, fuel (usually coal, sometimes wood) is burned in a furnace. The hot gases and flames produced are drawn through tubes running through a huge water-filled boiler and heat up the water to steam. The steam is then fed to the cylinders, where it forces the pistons back and forth. Movement of the pistons is conveyed to the wheels by cranks and connecting rods. Diesel locomotives have a powerful diesel engine, burning oil. The engine may drive a generator to produce electricity to power electric motors that turn the wheels, or the engine drives the wheels mechanically or through a hydraulic link. A number of ***gas-turbine locomotives*** are in use, in which a turbine spun by hot gases provides the power to drive the wheels.

locus (Latin "place") in mathematics, traditionally the path traced out by a moving point, but now defined as the set of all points on a

curve satisfying given conditions. For example, the locus of a point that moves so that it is always at the same distance from another fixed point is a circle; the locus of a point that is always at the same distance from two fixed points is a straight line that perpendicularly bisects the line joining them.

locus point on a ◊chromosome where a particular ◊gene occurs.

locust swarming grasshopper, with short antennae and auditory organs on the abdomen, in the family Acrididae. As winged adults, flying in swarms, locusts may be carried by the wind hundreds of miles from their breeding grounds; on landing they devour all vegetation. Locusts occur in nearly every continent.

The migratory locust *Locusta migratoria* ranges from Europe to China, and even small swarms may cover several square miles, and weigh thousands of tons. Control by spreading poisoned food among the bands is very effective, but it is cheapest to spray concentrated insecticide solutions from aircraft over the insects or the vegetation on which they feed. They eat the equivalent of their own weight in a day, and, flying at night with the wind, may cover some 300 mi/500 km. The largest known swarm covered 400 sq mi/1,036 sq km, comprising approximately 40 billion insects.

locust tree in botany, any of several trees of the genera *Robinia* and *Gleditsia* of the legume family, with primate compound leaves and many-seeded pods, of E US. The black locust *R. pseudoacacia* and the honeylocust *G. triacanthos* are examples. The name locust tree is also applied to the ◊carob, a small European tree.

lode geological deposit rich in certain minerals, generally consisting of a large vein or set of veins containing ore minerals. A system of veins that can be mined directly forms a lode, for example the mother lode of the California gold rush.

Lodes form because hot liquids and gases from magmas penetrate surrounding rocks, especially when these are limestones; on

cooling, veins of ores formed from the magma then extend from the igneous mass into the local rock.

lodestar or ***loadstar*** a star used in navigation or astronomy, often ◊Polaris, the Pole Star.

Lodge Henry Cabot 1850–1924. US politician, Republican senator from 1893, and chairman of the Senate Foreign Relations Committee after World War I. He supported conservative economic legislation at home but expansionist policies abroad. Nevertheless, he influenced the US to stay out of the ◊League of Nations 1920 as a threat to US sovereignty.

As an advocate of American pursuit of empire, he joined President T ◊Roosevelt in calling for war against Spain 1898. He insisted on modifications to the Treaty of ◊Versailles with its provisions for the League of Nations. President ◊Wilson refused to accede, and the Senate was deadlocked, finally refusing to ratify the treaty.

Lodge Henry Cabot, II 1902–1985. US diplomat. He was Eisenhower's presidential campaign manager and the US representative at the United Nations 1953–60. Ambassador to South Vietnam 1963–64 and 1965–67, he replaced W A Harriman as President Nixon's negotiator in the Vietnam peace talks 1969. He was a grandson of Henry Cabot Lodge.

Born in Nahant, Massachusetts, Lodge served in the US Senate 1937–44, 1947–53.

Łódź industrial town (textiles, machinery, dyes) in central Poland, 75 mi/120 km SW of Warsaw; population (1990) 848,300.

Loeb James 1867–1933. German banker, born in New York, who financed the ***Loeb Classical Library*** of Greek and Latin authors, which gives the original text with a parallel translation.

loess yellow loam, derived from glacial melt-water deposits and accumulated by wind in periglacial regions during the ◊ice ages. Loess usually attains considerable depths, and the soil derived from it is very fertile. There are large deposits in central Europe (Hungary),

China, and North America. It was first described in 1821 in the Rhine area, and takes its name from a village in Alsace.

Loewe Frederick 1901–1988. US composer of musicals. In 1942 he joined forces with the lyricist Alan Jay Lerner (1918–1986), and their joint successes include *Brigadoon* 1947, *Paint Your Wagon* 1951, *My Fair Lady* 1956, *Gigi* 1958, and *Camelot* 1960.

Born in Berlin, the son of an operatic tenor, he studied under Busoni, and in 1924 went with his father to the US.

Loewi Otto 1873–1961. German physiologist whose work on the nervous system established that a chemical substance is responsible for the stimulation of one nerve cell (neuron) by another.

The substance was shown by the physiologist Henry Dale to be acetylcholine, now known to be one of the most vital neurotransmitters. For this work Loewi and Dale were jointly awarded the 1936 Nobel Prize for Medicine.

Lofoten and Vesterålen island group off NW Norway; area 1,750 sq mi/4,530 sq km. Hinnoy, in the Vesterålens, is the largest island of Norway. The surrounding waters are rich in cod and herring. The **Maelström**, a large whirlpool hazardous to ships, which gives its name to similar features elsewhere, occurs in one of the island channels.

log any apparatus for measuring the speed of a ship; also the daily record of events on board a ship or aircraft.

The log originally consisted of a piece of weighted wood attached to a line with knots at equal intervals that was cast from the rear of a ship. The vessel's speed was estimated by timing the passage of the knots with a sandglass (like an egg timer). Today logs use electromagnetism and sonar.

log in mathematics, abbreviation for ⊳*logarithm*.

loganberry hybrid between a ⊳blackberry and a ⊳raspberry with large, tart, dull-red fruit. It was developed by US judge James H Logan in 1881.

logarithm or *log* the ⊳exponent or index of a number to a specified base -usually 10. For example, the logarithm to the base 10 of 1,000 is 3 because $10^3 = 1,000$; the logarithm of 2 is 0.3010 because $2 = 10^{0.3010}$. Before the advent of cheap electronic calculators, multiplication and division could be simplified by being replaced with the addition and subtraction of logarithms.

For any two numbers x and y (where $x = b^a$ and $y = b^c$) $x \times y = b^a \times b^c = b^{a+c}$; hence we would add the logarithms of x and y, and look up this answer in antilogarithm tables. Tables of logarithms and antilogarithms are available that show conversions of numbers into logarithms, and vice versa. For example, to multiply 6,560 by 980, one looks up their logarithms (3.8169 and 2.9912), adds them together (6.8081), then looks up the antilogarithm of this to get the answer (6,428,800). **Natural** or **Napierian** *logarithms* are to the base e, an ⊳irrational number equal to approximately 2.7183.

The principle of logarithms is also the basis of the slide rule. With the general availability of the electronic pocket calculator, the need for logarithms has been reduced. The first log tables (to base e) were published by the Scottish mathematician John Napier in 1614. Base-ten logs were introduced by the Englishman Henry Briggs (1561–1631) and Dutch mathematician Adriaen Vlacq (1600–1667).

logic branch of philosophy that studies valid reasoning and argument. It is also the way in which one thing may be said to follow from, or be a consequence of, another (deductive logic). Logic is generally divided into the traditional formal logic of Aristotle and the symbolic logic derived from Friedrich Frege and Bertrand Russell.

Aristotle's *Organon* is the founding work on logic, and Aristotelian methods, as revived in the medieval church by the French scholar Peter Abelard in the 12th century, were used in the synthesis of ideas aimed at in scholasticism. As befitted the spirit of the Renaissance, the English philosopher Francis Bacon considered many of the general principles used as premises by the scholastics to be groundless; he envisaged that in natural philosophy principles worthy of investigation would emerge by "inductive" logic, which works backward from the accumulated facts to the principle that accounts for them.

logical positivism doctrine that the only meaningful propositions are those that can be verified empirically. Metaphysics, religion, and aesthetics are therefore meaningless.

Logical positivism was characteristic of the Vienna Circle in the 1920s and 1930s, and was influenced by Friedrich Frege, Bertrand Russell, and Ludwig Wittgenstein.

logic gate or *logic circuit* in electronics, one of the basic components used in building ⊳integrated circuits. The five basic types of gate make logical decisions based on the functions NOT, AND, OR, NAND (NOT AND), and NOR (NOT OR). With the exception of the NOT gate, each has two or more inputs.

Information is fed to a gate in the form of binary-coded input signals (logic value 0 stands for "off" or "low-voltage pulse," logic 1 for "on" or "high-voltage"), and each combination of input signals yields a specific output (logic 0 or 1). An *OR* gate will give a logic 1 output if one or more of its inputs receives a logic 1 signal; however, an *AND* gate will yield a logic 1 output only if it receives a logic 1 signal through both its inputs. The output of a *NOT* or *inverter* gate is the opposite of the signal received through its single input, and a *NOR* or *NAND* gate produces an output signal that is the opposite of the signal that would have been produced by an OR or AND gate respectively. The properties of a logic gate, or of a combination of gates, may be defined and presented in the form of a diagram called a **truth table**, which lists the output that will be triggered by each of the possible combinations of input signals. The process has close parallels in computer programming, where it forms the basis of binary logic.

LOGO (Greek *logos* "word") high-level computer programming language designed to teach mathematical concepts. Developed about 1970 at the Massachusetts Institute of Technology, it became popular in schools and with home computer users because of its "turtle graphics" feature. This allows the user to write programs that create line drawings on a computer screen, or drive a small mobile robot (a "turtle" or "buggy") around the floor.

LOGO encourages the use of languages in a logical and structured way, leading to "microworlds," in which problems can be solved by using a few standard solutions.

logos (Greek "word") a term in Greek, Hebrew, and Christian philosophy and theology. It was used by Greek philosophers as the embodiment of "reason" in the universe. Under Greek influence the Jews came to conceive of "wisdom" as an aspect of God's activity. The Jewish philosopher ⊳Philo (1st century AD) attempted to reconcile Platonic, Stoic, and Hebrew philosophy by identifying the logos with the Jewish idea of "wisdom." Several of the New Testament writers took over Philo's conception of the logos, which they identified with Christ and hence with the second person of the Trinity.

Lohengrin son of ⊳Parsifal, hero of a late 13th-century Germanic legend, on which Wagner based his German opera *Lohengrin* 1847. Lohengrin married Princess Elsa, who broke his condition that she never ask his origin, and he returned to the temple of the ⊳Holy Grail.

Loire longest river in France, rising in the Cévennes Mountains, at 4,430 ft/1,350 m and flowing for 650 mi/1,050 km first N then W until it reaches the Bay of Biscay at St Nazaire, passing Nevers, Orléans, Tours, and Nantes. It gives its name to the *départements* of Loire, Haute-Loire, Loire-Atlantique, Indre-et-Loire, Maine-et-Loire, and Saône-et-Loire. There are many chateaux and vineyards along its banks.

Loki in Norse mythology, one of the ⊳Aesir (the principal gods), but the cause of dissension among the gods, and the slayer of ⊳Balder. His children are the Midgard serpent Jörmungander, which girdles the Earth, the wolf Fenris, and Hela, goddess of death.

Lolita novel by Vladimir Nabokov, published 1955. It describes the infatuation of a middle-aged man for a precocious 12-year-old girl, and added the word "nymphet" to the English language.

Lollard follower of the English religious reformer John ⊳Wycliffe in the 14th century. The Lollards condemned the doctrine of the transubstantiation of the bread and wine of the Eucharist, advocated the diversion of ecclesiastical property to charitable uses, and denounced war and capital punishment. They were active from about 1377; after the passing of the statute *De heretico comburendo* ("The Necessity of Burning Heretics") 1401 many Lollards were burned, and in 1414 they raised an unsuccessful revolt in London.

The movement began at Oxford University, where Wycliffe taught, but thereafter included nonacademics, merchants, lesser clergy, and a few members of Richard II's court. Repression began in Henry IV's reign. The 1414 revolt was known as Oldcastle's rebellion, and the Lollards subsequently went underground; much of their policy was advocated by the early Protestants.

Lombard Carole. Adopted name of Jane Alice Peters 1908–1942. US comedy film actress. A warm and witty actress, she starred in some of the best comedies of the 1930s: *Twentieth Century* 1934, *My Man Godfrey* 1936, and *To Be or Not to Be* 1942.

She was married to Clark Gable in 1939.

Lombard or *Langobard* member of a Germanic people who invaded Italy in 568 and occupied Lombardy (named after them) and central Italy. Their capital was Monza. They were conquered by the Frankish ruler Charlemagne in 774.

Lombardi Vince (nt Thomas) 1913–1970. US football coach. He accepted a job as offensive coach with the New York Giants 1954 and remained in professional football for the rest of his career. Lombardi became head coach of the Green Bay Packers 1959 and transformed a losing team into a major power, winning the first two Super Bowls 1967 and 1968. His last coaching position was with the Washington Redskins 1969–70.

Born in Brooklyn, New York, and educated at Fordham University, Lombardi became a successful high-school coach, breaking into the college level as an assistant coach at Fordham 1947–48 and West Point 1949–54.

Lombard league association of N Italian towns and cities (not all of which were in Lombardy) established 1164 to maintain their independence against the Holy Roman emperors' claims of sovereignty. Venice, Padua, Brescia, Milan, and Mantua were among the founders.

Supported by Milan and Pope Alexander III (1105–1181), the league defeated Frederick I Barbarossa at Legnano in N Italy 1179 and effectively resisted Otto IV (1175–1218) and Frederick II, becoming the most powerful champion of the ⟡Guelph cause. Internal rivalries led to its dissolution 1250.

Lombardy (Italian *Lombardia*) region of N Italy, including Lake Como; capital Milan; area 9,225 sq mi/23,900 sq km; population (1990) 8,939,400. It is the country's chief industrial area (chemicals, pharmaceuticals, engineering, textiles).

Lombok (Javanese "chili pepper") island of Indonesia, E of Java, one of the Sunda Islands; area 1,826 sq mi/4,730 sq km; population (1980) 1,957,000. The chief town is Mataram. It has a fertile plain between N and S mountain ranges.

Lomé capital and port of Togo; population (1983) 366,000. It is a center for gold, silver, and marble crafts; industries include steel production and oil refining.

Lomé Convention convention in 1975 that established economic cooperation between the European Community and African, Caribbean, and Pacific countries. It was renewed 1979 and 1985.

lomentum fruit similar to a pod but constricted between the seeds. When ripe, it splits into one-seeded units, as seen, for example, in the fruit of sainfoin *Onobrychis viciifolia* and radish *Raphanus raphanistrum*. It is a type of ⟡schizocarp.

Lomond, Loch largest freshwater Scottish lake, 21 mi/37 km long, area 27 sq mi/70 sq km, divided between Strathclyde and Central regions. It is overlooked by the mountain *Ben Lomond* (3,192 ft/973 m) and is linked to the Clyde estuary.

Lompoc city in SW California, near the Pacific Ocean, W of Santa Barbara. Industries include the processing of oil from the city's oil wells; population (1990) 37,650.

London capital of England and the UK, on the river Thames; area 610 sq mi/1,580 sq km; population (1991) 6,378,600, larger metropolitan area about 9 million. The *City of London*, known as the "square mile," area 677 acres/274 hectares, is the financial and commercial center of the UK. *Greater London* from 1965 comprises the City of London and 32 boroughs. Popular tourist attractions include the Tower of London, St Paul's Cathedral, Buckingham Palace, and Westminster Abbey.

Roman *Londinium* was established soon after the Roman invasion AD 43; in the 2nd century London became a walled city; by the 11th century, it was the main city of England and gradually extended beyond the walls to link with the originally separate Westminster.

Throughout the 19th century London was the largest city in the world (in population).

features The Tower of London, built by William the Conqueror on a Roman site, houses the crown jewels and the royal armories; 15th-century Guildhall; the Monument (a column designed by Wren) marks the site in Pudding Lane where the Great Fire of 1666 began; Mansion House (residence of the lord mayor); Barbican arts and conference center; Central Criminal Court (Old Bailey) and the Inner and Middle Temples; Covent Garden, once a vegetable market, is now a tourist shopping and entertainment area.

architecture London contains buildings in all styles of English architecture since the 11th century. **Norman**: the White Tower, Tower of London; St Bartholomew's, Smithfield; the Temple Church. **Gothic**: Westminster Abbey; Westminster Hall; Lambeth Palace; Southwark Cathedral. **Tudor**: St James's Palace; Staple Inn. **17th century**: Banqueting Hall, Whitehall (Inigo Jones); St Paul's, Kensington Palace; many City churches (Wren). **18th century**: Somerset House (Chambers); St Martin-in-the-Fields; Buckingham Palace. **19th century**: British Museum (Neo-Classical); Houses of Parliament; Law Courts (Neo-Gothic); Westminster Cathedral (Byzantine style). **20th century**: Lloyd's of London.

commerce and industry From Saxon times the Port of London dominated the Thames from Tower Bridge to Tilbury; its activity is now centered outside the metropolitan area, and downstream Tilbury has been extended to cope with container traffic. The prime economic importance of modern London is as a financial center. There are various industries, mainly on the outskirts. There are also recording, broadcasting, television, and film studios; publishing companies; and the works and offices of the national press. Tourism is important. Some of the docks in the East End of London, once the busiest in the world, have been sold to the Docklands Development Corporation, which has built offices, houses, factories, and a railroad. *Canary Wharf* is now the site of the world's largest office development project.

education and entertainment Museums: British, Victoria and Albert, Natural History, Science museums; galleries: National and Tate. London University is the largest in Britain, while the Inns of Court have been the training school for lawyers since the 13th century. London has been the center of English drama since its first theater was built by James Burbage in 1576.

government There has since 1986 been no central authority for Greater London; responsibility is divided between individual boroughs and central government.

The City of London has been governed by a corporation from the 12th century. Its structure and the electoral procedures for its common councillors and aldermen are medievally complex, and it is headed by the lord mayor (who is, broadly speaking, nominated by the former and elected annually by the latter). After being sworn in at the Guildhall, he or she is presented the next day to the lord chief justice at the Royal Courts of Justice in Westminster, and the *Lord Mayor's Show* is a ceremonial procession there in November.

London city in SW Ontario, on the river Thames, 100 mi/160 km SW of Toronto; population (1986) 342,000. The center of a farming district, it has tanneries, breweries, and factories making hosiery, radio and electrical equipment, leather, and shoes. It dates from 1826 and is the seat of the University of Western Ontario.

London Jack (John Griffith) 1876–1916. US novelist, author of the adventure stories *The Call of the Wild* 1903, *The Sea Wolf* 1904, and *White Fang* 1906. By 1906 he was the most widely read writer in the US and had been translated into 68 languages.

Born in San Francisco, London was an adventurer himself, at various times a sailor, a hobo riding freight trains, and a gold prospector in the Klondike. Many of his works, which are uneven in quality, concern the human struggle against extreme natural forces for survival. His many short stories are collected in *The Son of the Wolf* 1900, *The God of His Fathers* 1901, *Children of the Frost* 1902, *Love of Life* 1907, and *Smoke Bellew* 1912. Among his other novels are *The People of the Abyss* 1903, *The Road* 1907, *The Iron Heel* 1907, and *Martin Eden* 1909.

Londonderry former name (until 1984) of the county and city of ⟡Derry in Northern Ireland.

London, Greater the metropolitan area of ⟡London, England, comprising the City of London, which forms a self-governing enclave, and 32 surrounding boroughs; area 610 sq mi/1,580 sq km; population (1991) 6,378,600. Certain powers were exercised over this whole area by the Greater London Council (GLC) until its abolition in 1986.

London, Treaty of secret treaty signed April 26, 1915 between Britain, France, Russia, and Italy. It promised Italy territorial gains (at the expense of Austria-Hungary) on condition that it entered World War I on the side of the Triple Entente (Britain, France, and Russia). Italy's intervention did not achieve the rapid victories expected, and the terms of the treaty (revealed by Russia 1918), angered the US. Britain and France refused to honor the treaty and, in the postwar peace treaties, Italy received far less territory than promised.

London University university originated in 1826 with the founding of University College, to provide higher education free from religious tests. In 1836 a charter set up an examining body with power to grant degrees. London University opened all its degrees to women in 1878, the first British university to do so.

Its complex substructure of smaller colleges had by 1991 been rationalized to 24 colleges, medical schools, and major institutes, plus 19 affiliated centers.

Long Huey 1893–1935. US Democratic politician, nicknamed "the Kingfish," governor of Louisiana 1928–31, US senator from Louisiana 1930–35, legendary as a demagogue. He was popular with poor white voters for his program of social and economic reform, which he called the "Share Our Wealth" program. It represented a significant challenge to F D Roosevelt's ⟡New Deal economic program. Long's scheme called for massive redistribution of wealth through high inheritance taxes and confiscatory taxes on high incomes. His own extravagance, including the state capitol building at Baton Rouge built of bronze and marble, was widely criticized. He was assassinated.

Born in Winnfield, Louisiana, he graduated from Tulane University with a law degree. Although he became a virtual dictator in the state, his slogan was "Every man a king, but no man wears a crown."

Long Beach city in SW California; population (1990) 429,430. A port and industrial city, it also has oil wells and a naval shipyard. Manufactured goods include aircraft, ships, petroleum products, chemicals, fabricated metals, electronic equipment, and processed food. It is also a convention center. Long Beach forms part of Greater Los Angeles and adjoins the San Pedro harbor of Los Angeles.

California State University-Long Beach is here, and the retired ocean liner *Queen Mary* is a tourist attraction. Long Beach was laid out in the 1880s; the port was opened 1909. Oil was discovered 1921, and the aircraft industry dates from World War II.

Longchamp pleasure resort and racecourse in Paris, France, in the Bois de Boulogne. It is on the site of a former nunnery founded in 1260, suppressed in 1790. Many races in France are run at Longchamp including the most prestigous open-age group race in Europe, the *Prix de L'Arc de Triomphe*, which attracts a top-quality field every Oct.

Long Day's Journey into Night play by US writer Eugene O'Neill, the harrowing tragedy of the theatrical Tyrone family, based on the author's own family. Written in 1941 and published posthumously in 1956, it has been repeatedly performed on stage and was made into a film.

Longfellow Henry Wadsworth 1807–1882. US poet, remembered for ballads ("Excelsior," "The Village Blacksmith," "The Wreck of the Hesperus") and the mythic narrative epics *Evangeline* 1847, *The Song of Hiawatha* 1855, and *The Courtship of Miles Standish* 1858.

Born in Portland, Maine, Longfellow graduated from Bowdoin College and taught modern languages there and at Harvard University 1835–54, after which he traveled widely. The most popular US poet of the 19th century, Longfellow was also an adept translator. His other works include six sonnets on Dante, a translation of Dante's *Divine Comedy*, and *Tales of a Wayside Inn* 1863, which includes the popular poem "Paul Revere's Ride."

Longford county of Leinster province, Republic of Ireland
area 401 sq mi/1,040 sq km
county town Longford
features rivers: Camlin, Inny, Shannon (the W boundary); several lakes
population (1991) 30,300.

Long Island island E of Manhattan and SE of Connecticut, separated from the mainland by Long Island Sound and the East River; 120 mi/193 km long by about 30 mi/48km wide; area 1,400 sq mi/3,627 sq km; population (1984) 6,818,480.

The two New York City boroughs of Queens and Brooklyn are the western eighth of the island with a combined population of 4,165,090 (1984). East of them are the counties of Nassau and Suffolk. Along the N shore, facing the sound, are the wealthy Gold Coast communities, such as Great Neck and Oyster Bay. On the S shore, facing the Atlantic, are the popular summer-resort communities of the sandy barrier beaches, Coney Island, the Rockaways, Long Beach, Fire Island, and the Hamptons. The last glaciation of the ▷Ice Age came as far south as Long Island, leaving its rocky moraine to distinguish the cliffed and rolling north shore from the flat and sandy south; the westernmost extent of the moraine is in Jamaica, Queens.

Educational institutions include Adelphi, Hofstra, C W Post, Farmingdale and Stony Brook-SUNY, and various branches of the City University. La Guardia, Kennedy, and MacArthur airports service the region, and several bridges and tunnels connect the island to Manhattan and the Bronx. The island's many public and private facilities include museums, parks, parkways, beaches, marinas, nature preserves, golf, tennis, and country clubs; Jones Beach State Park, Shea Stadium, and Belmont and Aquaduct raceways are here.

The largest employer is Grumman Aircraft, a major military contractor. Vegetable farms, orchards, vineyards, dairies, poultry and horse raising, fishing and shellfishing exist but are losing ground to suburban developments and pollution. Henry Hudson discovered the island 1609, and it was settled by the Dutch from New Amsterdam (in the W) and the English from New England (in the E) from the 1640s.

longitude see ▷latitude and longitude.

long jump field event in which competitors sprint up to and leap from a take-off board into a sandpit measuring 9 meters in length. The take-off board is 1 meter from the landing area. Each competitor usually has six attempts, and the winner is the one with the longest jump.

Long March in Chinese history, the 6,000 mi/10,000 km trek undertaken 1934–35 by ▷Mao Zedong and his Communist forces from SE to NW China, under harassment from the Nationalist army.

Some 100,000 Communists left Jiangxi, Mao's first headquarters, in Oct 1934 and only 8,000 lasted the journey to arrive about a year later in Shanxi, which became their new base. The march cemented Mao Zedong's control of the movement.

The **New Long March** is China's plan to achieve world leadership in science and technology by the year 2000.

Longmont city in N central Colorado, in the Rocky Mountain foothills, S of Fort Collins and NE of Boulder. Industries include business machinery, sugar-beet refining, and recreational vehicles; population (1990) 51,550.

Long Parliament English Parliament 1640–53 and 1659–60, which continued through the Civil War. After the Royalists withdrew in 1642 and the Presbyterian right was excluded in 1648, the remaining ▷Rump ruled England until expelled by Oliver Cromwell in 1653. Reassembled 1659–60, the Long Parliament initiated the negotiations for the restoration of the monarchy.

Longview city in E Texas, E of Dallas; seat of Gregg County. In the heart of the oil fields of E Texas, Longview's industries are mainly oil and natural-gas processing; population (1990) 70,310.

loofah or *luffa* fibrous skeleton of the cylindrical fruit of the dishcloth gourd *Luffa cylindrica*, family Cucurbitaceae, used as a bath sponge.

loom any machine for weaving yarn or thread into cloth. The first looms were used to weave sheep's wool about 5000 BC. A loom is a frame on which a set of lengthwise threads (warp) is strung. A second set of threads (weft), carried in a shuttle, is inserted at right angles over and under the warp.

In most looms the warp threads are separated by a device called a treddle to create a gap, or shed, through which the shuttle can be passed in a straight line. A kind of comb called a reed presses each new line of weave tight against the previous ones. All looms have similar features, but on the power loom, weaving takes place automatically at great speed. Mechanization of weaving began in 1733 when John Kay invented the flying shuttle. In 1785 Edmund Cartwright introduced a steam-powered loom. Among recent developments are shuttleless looms, which work at very high speed, passing the weft through the warp by means of "rapiers," and jets of air or water.

loon any of various birds of the genus *Gavia*, family Gavidae, found in N regions of the N hemisphere. Loons are specialized for swimming and diving. Their legs are set so far back that walking is almost impossible, and they come to land only to nest, but loons are powerful swimmers and good flyers. They have straight bills and long bodies and feed on fish, crustaceans, and some water plants. There are just five species, the largest, the yellow-billed loon *G. adamsii*, being an Arctic species 2.5 ft/75 cm long.

Loos Anita 1888–1981. US writer, author of the humorous fictitious diary *Gentlemen Prefer Blondes* 1925. She became a screenwriter 1912 and worked on more than 60 films, including D W ▷Griffith's *Intolerance* 1916.

loosestrife genus *Lysimachia* of plants of the primrose family (Primulaceae) including swampcandles *L. terrestris* of North America, with yellow and purple-streaked flowers on a spike. The name is also applied to members of the genus *Lythrum* of the loosestrife family, such as the European willow loosestrife *L. salicaria*, now a weed in NE US.

Lope de Vega (Carpio) Felix Spanish poet and dramatist; see ▷Vega, Lope de.

López Carlos Antonio 1790–1862. Paraguayan dictator (in succession to his uncle José Francia) from 1840. He achieved some economic improvement, and he was succeeded by his son Francisco López.

López Francisco Solano 1827–1870. Paraguayan dictator in succession to his father Carlos López. He involved the country in a war with Brazil, Uruguay, and Argentina, during which approximately 80% of the population died.

Lopez Nancy 1957– . US golfer who turned professional in 1977 and in 1979 became the first woman to win $200,000 in a season. She has won the US LPGA title three times and has won more than 35 tour events, and $3 million in prize money.

Lop Nor series of shallow salt lakes with shifting boundaries in the Taklimakan Shamo (desert) in Xinjiang Uyghur, NW China. Marco Polo, the Venetian traveler, visited Lop Nor, then a single lake of considerable extent, about 1273. The area is used for atomic tests.

loquat evergreen tree *Eriobotrya japonica* of the family Rosaceae, native to China and Japan and also known as the *Japan medlar*. The golden pear-shaped fruit has a delicate sweet-sour taste.

Lorain city in N central Ohio, on Lake Erie, NW of Akron and SW of Cleveland. An important Great Lakes port, it has shipbuilding yards and manufactures automobiles and heavy construction equipment; population (1990) 71,240.

Lorca Federico Garcia 1898–1936. Spanish poet and playwright, born in Granada. His plays include *Bodas de sangre/Blood Wedding* 1933 and *La casa de Bernarda Alba/The House* *of Bernarda Alba* 1936. His poems include *Lament*, written for the bullfighter Mejías. Lorca was shot by the Falangists during the Spanish Civil War.

Romancero gitano/Gipsy Ballad-book 1928 shows the influence of the Andalusian songs of the area. In 1929–30 Lorca visited New York, and his experiences are reflected in *Poeta en Nuevo York* 1940. Returning to Spain, he founded a touring theatrical company and began to write plays.

Lord in the UK, prefix used informally as alternative to the full title of a marquess, earl, or viscount; normally also in speaking of a baron, and as a courtesy title before the forename and surname of younger sons of dukes and marquesses.

Lords, House of upper house of the UK ⟡Parliament.

Lord's Prayer in the New Testament, the prayer taught by Jesus to his disciples. It is sometimes called "Our Father" or "Paternoster" from the opening words in English and Latin respectively.

Lord's Supper in the Christian church, another name for the ⟡Eucharist.

Lorelei in Germanic folklore, a river nymph of the Rhine who lures sailors onto the rock where she sits combing her hair. She features in several poems, including "Die Lorelei" by the German Romantic writer Heine. The *Lurlei* rock S of Koblenz is 430 ft/130 m high.

Loren Sophia. Adopted name of Sofia Scicolone 1934– . Italian film actress whose boldly sensual appeal was promoted by her husband, producer Carlo Ponti. Her work includes *Aida* 1953, *The Key* 1958, *La ciociara/Two Women* 1960, *Judith* 1965, and *Firepower* 1979.

Lorentz Hendrik Antoon 1853–1928. Dutch physicist, winner (with his pupil Pieter ⟡Zeeman) of a Nobel Prize in 1902 for his work on the Zeeman effect.

Lorentz spent most of his career trying to develop and improve James ⟡Maxwell's electromagnetic theory. He also attempted to account for the anomalies of the ⟡Michelson–Morley experiment by proposing, independently of George Fitzgerald, that moving bodies contracted in their direction of motion. He took the matter further with his method of transforming space and time coordinates, later known as Lorentz transformations, which prepared the way for Albert Einstein's theory of ⟡relativity.

Lorenz Konrad 1903–1989. Austrian ethologist. Director of the Max Planck Institute for the Physiology of Behavior in Bavaria 1955–73, he wrote the studies of ethology (animal behavior) *King Solomon's Ring* 1952 and *On Aggression* 1966. In 1973 he shared the Nobel Prize for Medicine with Nikolaas Tinbergen and Karl von Frisch.

Lorenz Ludwig Valentine 1829–1891. Danish mathematician and physicist. He developed mathematical formulae to describe phenomena such as the relation between the refraction of light and the density of a pure transparent substance, and the relation between a metal's electrical and thermal conductivity and temperature.

Lorenzetti Ambrogio c. 1319–1347. Italian painter active in Siena and Florence. His allegorical frescoes *Good and Bad Government* 1337–39 (Town Hall, Siena) include a detailed panoramic landscape and a view of the city of Siena that shows an unusual mastery of spatial effects.

Lorenzetti Pietro c. 1306–1345. Italian painter of the Sienese school, active in Assisi. His frescoes in the Franciscan basilica, Assisi, reflect the Florentine painter ⟡Giotto's concern with mass and weight. He was the brother of Ambrogio Lorenzetti.

lorikeet any of various small, brightly colored parrots, found in SE Asia and Australasia.

loris any of various small prosimian primates of the family Lorisidae. Lorises are slow-moving, arboreal, and nocturnal. They have very large eyes; true lorises have no tails. They climb without leaping, gripping branches tightly and moving on or hanging below them.

The slender loris *Loris tardigradus* of S India and Sri Lanka is about 8 in/20 cm long. The tubbier slow loris *Nycticebus coucang* of SE Asia is 1 ft/30 cm. The angwantibo (genus *Arctocebus*), potto (genus *Perodicticus*), and galagos are similar African forms.

Lorrain Claude. French painter; see ⟡Claude Lorrain.

Lorraine region of NE France in the upper reaches of the Meuse and Moselle rivers; bounded to the N by Belgium, Luxembourg, and Germany and to the E by Alsace; area 9,095 sq mi/23,600 sq km; population (1986) 2,313,000. It comprises the *départements* of Meurthe-et-Moselle, Meuse, Moselle, and Vosges, and its capital is Nancy. There are deposits of coal, iron ore, and salt; grain, fruit, and livestock are farmed. In 1871 the region was ceded to Germany as part of Alsace-Lorraine.

Lorraine, Cross of heraldic cross with double crossbars, emblem of the medieval French nationalist Joan of Arc. It was adopted by the ⟡Free French forces in World War II.

Lorre Peter. Adopted name of Lazlo Löwenstein 1904–1964. Hungarian character actor with bulging eyes, high voice, and melancholy mien. He made several films in Germany before moving to Hollywood in 1935. He appeared in *M* 1931, *Mad Love* 1935, *The Maltese Falcon* 1941, *Casablanca* 1942, *Beat the Devil* 1953, and *The Raven* 1963. His last film was *Patsy* 1964.

lory any of various types of Australasian, honey-eating, brilliantly colored ⟡parrot.

Los Alamos town in New Mexico, which has had a center for atomic and space research since 1942. In World War II the first atom (nuclear fission) bomb was designed there (under Robert ⟡Oppenheimer), based on data from other research stations; the ⟡hydrogen bomb was also developed there.

The town has a population of 12,000.

Los Angeles city and port in SW California; population (1990) 3,485,400, the metropolitan area of Los Angeles–Long Beach 14,531,530. Industries include aerospace, electronics, motor vehicles, chemicals, clothing, printing, and food processing.

Features include Hollywood, center of the US film industry since 1911; the Hollywood Bowl concert arena; the Los Angeles Music Center; and the Los Angeles County Museum of Art. Educational institutions include the University of California at Los Angeles and the University of Southern California.

Los Angeles was established as a Spanish settlement 1781, but it was a farming region with orange groves until the early 20th century, when it annexed neighboring communities and acquired distant water supplies, a deepwater port, and the film industry. In the 1920s large petroleum deposits were found in the area. The aircraft industry, with its need for year-round flying weather, developed here soon after and grew rapidly with the advent of World War II. In 1992, racial disturbances resulted in 50 deaths and heavy damage.

Los Angeles Victoria de 1923– . Spanish soprano. She is renowned for her interpretations of Spanish songs and for the roles of Manon and Madame Butterfly in the Italian composer Giacomo Puccini's operas.

Losey Joseph 1909–1984. US film director. Blacklisted as a former communist in the ⟡McCarthy era, he settled in England, where his films included *The Servant* 1963 and *The Go-Between* 1971.

Lost Generation, the disillusioned US literary generation of the 1920s members of which went to live in Paris. The phrase is attributed to the writer Gertrude Stein in Ernest Hemingway's early novel of 1920s Paris, *The Sun Also Rises* 1926.

lost-wax technique method of making sculptures; see ⟡*cire perdue*.

Lot in the Old Testament, Abraham's nephew, who escaped the destruction of Sodom. Lot's wife disobeyed the condition of not looking back at Sodom and was punished by being turned into a pillar of salt.

Lothair 825–869. King of Lotharingia from 855, when he inherited the region from his father, the Holy Roman emperor Lothair I.

Lothair two Holy Roman emperors:

Lothair I 795–855. Holy Roman emperor from 817 in association with his father Louis I. On Louis's death in 840, the empire was divided between Lothair and his brothers; Lothair took N Italy and the valleys of the rivers Rhône and Rhine.

Lothair II c. 1070–1137. Holy Roman emperor from 1133 and German king from 1125. His election as emperor, opposed by the ⟡Hohenstaufen family of princes, was the start of the feud between the ⟡Guelph and Ghibelline factions, who supported the papal party and the Hohenstaufens' claim to the imperial throne respectively.

Lotharingia medieval region W of the Rhine, between the Jura mountains and the North Sea; the northern portion of the lands assigned to Lothair I when the Carolingian empire was divided. It was called after his son King Lothair, and later corrupted to Lorraine; it is now part of Alsace-Lorraine, France.

Lothian region of Scotland
area 695 sq mi/1,800 sq km
cities Edinburgh (administrative headquarters), Livingston
features hills: Lammermuir, Moorfoot, Pentland; Bass Rock in the Firth of Forth, noted for seabirds
products bacon, vegetables, coal, whiskey, engineering, electronics
population (1991) 723,700
famous people Alexander Graham Bell, Arthur Conan Doyle, R L Stevenson.

lottery game of chance in which tickets sold may win a prize.

In the US, the players choose numbers that, if selected in a random drawing, can bring the winner millions of dollars. State-sponsored lotteries are a means of raising revenue, especially for education and other public needs.

Lottery Case popular name for the US Supreme Court decision ⟡Champion v Ames 1903.

Lotto Lorenzo *c.* 1480–1556. Italian painter, born in Venice, active in Bergamo, Treviso, Venice, Ancona, and Rome. His early works were influenced by Giovanni Bellini; his mature style belongs to the High Renaissance. He painted dignified portraits, altarpieces, and frescoes.

lotus any of several different plants, especially the water lily *Nymphaea lotus*, frequent in Egyptian art, and *Nelumbo nucifera*, the pink Asiatic lotus, a sacred symbol in Hinduism and Buddhism, whose flower head floats erect above the water.

Others are those of the genus *Lotus*, family Leguminosae, including the bird's foot trefoil *Lotus corniculatus*; the ⟡jujube shrub *Zizyphus lotus*, known to the ancient Greeks who used its fruit to make a type of bread and also a wine supposed to induce happy oblivion—hence *lotus-eaters*; and the American lotus *Nelumbo lutea*, a pale yellow water lily of southern US.

Lotus 1–2–3 ⟡spreadsheet computer program, produced by Lotus Development Corporation. It first appeared in 1982 and its combination of spreadsheet, graphics display, and data management contributed to the rapid acceptance of the IBM Personal Computer in businesses.

Lotus-Eaters in ⟡Homer's *Odyssey* a mythical people living on the lotus plant, which induced travelers to forget their journey home.

Lotus Sūtra scripture of Mahāyāna Buddhism. It is Buddha Šākyamuni's final teaching, emphasizing that everyone can attain Buddhahood with the help of bodhisattvas. The original is in Sanskrit (*Saddharma-pundarīka Sūtra*) and is thought to date from some time after 100 BC.

loudspeaker electromechanical device that converts electrical signals into sound waves, which are radiated into the air. The most common type of loudspeaker is the *moving-coil speaker*. Electrical signals from, for example, a radio are fed to a coil of fine wire wound around the top of a cone. The coil is surrounded by a magnet. When signals pass through it, the coil becomes an electromagnet, which by moving causes the cone to vibrate, setting up sound waves.

Louis, Prince of Battenberg 1854–1921. German-born British admiral who took British nationality in 1917 and translated his name to Mountbatten.

Mountbatten is also the surname of Prince Philip and the hyphenated version, Mountbatten-Windsor, the surname of his children.

Louis Joe. Assumed name of Joseph Louis Barrow 1914–1981. US boxer, nicknamed "the Brown Bomber." He was world heavyweight champion between 1937 and 1949 and made a record 25 successful defenses (a record for any weight).

Louis was the longest reigning world heavyweight champion at 11 years and 252 days before announcing his retirement in 1949. He made a comeback and lost to Ezzard Charles in a world title fight in 1950.

CAREER HIGHLIGHTS

Professional fights: 66
wins: 63
knockouts: 49
defeats: 3
1st professional fight: July 4, 1934 v. Jack Kracken *(US)*
last professional fight: Oct 26, 1951 v. Rocky Marciano *(US)*

Louis Morris 1912–1962. US abstract painter. From Abstract Expressionism he turned to the color-staining technique developed by Helen ⟡Frankenthaler, using thinned-out acrylic paints poured on rough canvas to create the illusion of vaporous layers of color. The *Veil* paintings of the 1950s are examples.

Louis eighteen kings of France, including:

Louis I *the Pious* 788–840. Holy Roman emperor from 814, when he succeeded his father Charlemagne.

Louis II *the Stammerer* 846–879. King of France from 877, son of Charles II, the Bald. He was dominated by the clergy and nobility, who exacted many concessions from him.

Louis III 863–882. King of N France from 879, while his brother Carloman (866–884) ruled S France. He was the son of Louis II. Louis countered a revolt of the nobility at the beginning of his reign, and his resistance to the Normans made him a hero of epic poems.

Louis IV (d'Outremer) 921–954. King of France from 936. His reign was marked by the rebellion of nobles who refused to recognize his authority. As a result of his liberality they were able to build powerful feudal lordships.

He was raised in England after his father Charles III, the Simple, had been overthrown in 922 by Robert I. After the death of Raoul, Robert's brother-in-law and successor, Louis was chosen by the nobles to be king. He had difficulties with his vassal Hugh the Great, and skirmishes with the Hungarians, who had invaded S France.

Louis V 966–987. King of France from 986, last of the ⟡Carolingian dynasty (descendants of Charlemagne).

Louis VI *the Fat* 1081–1137. King of France from 1108. He led his army against feudal brigands, the English (under Henry I), and the Holy Roman Empire, temporarily consolidating his realm and extending it into Flanders. He was a benefactor to the church, and his advisers included Abbot ⟡Suger.

Louis VII *c.* 1120–1180. King of France from 1137, who led the Second ⟡Crusade.

Louis VIII 1187–1226. King of France from 1223, who was invited to become king of England in place of ⟡John by the English barons, and unsuccessfully invaded England 1215–17.

Louis IX St 1214–1270. King of France from 1226, leader of the 7th and 8th ⟡Crusades. He was defeated in the former by the Muslims, spending four years in captivity. He died in Tunis. He was canonized in 1297.

Louis X *the Stubborn* 1289–1316. King of France who succeeded his father Philip IV in 1314. His reign saw widespread discontent among the nobles, which he countered by granting charters guaranteeing seignorial rights, although some historians claim that by using evasive tactics, he gave up nothing.

Louis XI 1423–1483. King of France from 1461. He broke the power of the nobility (headed by

⟡Charles the Bold) by intrigue and military power.

Louis XII 1462–1515. King of France from 1499. He was duke of Orléans until he succeeded his cousin Charles VIII to the throne. His reign was devoted to Italian wars.

Louis XIII 1601–1643. King of France from 1610 (in succession to his father Henry IV), he assumed royal power in 1617. He was under the political control of Cardinal ⟡Richelieu 1624–42.

Louis XIV *the Sun King* 1638–1715. King of France from 1643, when he succeeded his father Louis XIII; his mother was Anne of Austria. Until 1661 France was ruled by the chief minister, Jules Mazarin, but later Louis took absolute power, summed up in his saying *L'Etat c'est moi* ("I am the state"). Throughout his reign he was engaged in unsuccessful expansionist wars—1667–68, 1672–78, 1688–97, and 1701–13 (the War of the ⟡Spanish Succession)—against various European alliances, always including Britain and the Netherlands. He was a patron of the arts.

In 1660 Louis married the Infanta Maria Theresa of Spain, but he was greatly influenced by his mistresses, including Louise de ⟡La Vallière, Madame de ⟡Montespan, and Madame de ⟡Maintenon.

Louis XV 1710–1774. King of France from 1715, with the Duke of Orléans as regent until 1723. He was the great-grandson of Louis XIV. Indolent and frivolous, Louis left government in the hands of his ministers, the Duke of Bourbon and Cardinal Fleury (1653–1743). On the latter's death he attempted to rule alone but became entirely dominated by his mistresses, Madame de Pompadour and Madame Du Barry. His foreign policy led to French possessions in Canada and India being lost to England.

Louis XVI 1754–1793. King of France from 1774, grandson of Louis XV, and son of Louis the Dauphin. He was dominated by his queen, ⟡Marie Antoinette, and French finances fell into such confusion that in 1789 the ⟡States General (parliament) had to be summoned, and the ⟡French Revolution began. Louis lost his personal popularity in June 1791 when he attempted to flee the country, and in Aug 1792 the Parisians stormed the Tuileries palace and took the royal family prisoner. Deposed in Sept 1792, Louis was tried in Dec, sentenced for treason in Jan 1793, and guillotined.

Louis XVII 1785–1795. Nominal king of France, the son of Louis XVI. During the French Revolution he was imprisoned with his parents in 1792 and probably died in prison.

Louis XVIII 1755–1824. King of France 1814–24, the younger brother of Louis XVI. He assumed the title of king in 1795, having fled into exile in 1791 during the French Revolution, but became king only on the fall of Napoleon I in April 1814. Expelled during Napoleon's brief return (the "hundred days") in 1815, he resumed power after Napoleon's final defeat at Waterloo, pursuing a policy of calculated liberalism until ultra-royalist pressure became dominant after 1820.

Louisiana state in S US; nickname Pelican State

area 52,457 sq mi/135,900 sq km
capital Baton Rouge
cities New Orleans, Shreveport, Lafayette, Lake Charles
features New Orleans French Quarter: jazz, restaurants, Mardi Gras; Cajun country and the Mississippi River delta; Jean Lafitte National

Park and Chalmette National Historical Park; plantation homes near Natchitoches

products rice, cotton, sugar, oil, natural gas, chemicals, sulfur, fish and shellfish, salt, processed foods, petroleum products, timber, paper

population (1990) 4,219,970; including Cajuns, descendants of 18th-century religious exiles from Canada, who speak a French dialect

famous people Louis Armstrong, P G T Beauregard, Huey Long

history explored by the Spanish Piñeda 1519, Cabeza de Vaca 1528, and de Soto 1541 and by the French explorer La Salle 1862, who named it after Louis XIV and claimed it for France. It became Spanish 1762–1800, then French, then passed to the US 1803 under the ⏃Louisiana Purchase; admitted to the Union as a state 1812. The Civil War destroyed the plantation economy. Recovery was slow, but in the 1930s Louisiana became one of the world's major centers of petrochemical manufacturing, based on oil wells in the Gulf of Mexico.

Louisiana Purchase purchase by the US from France 1803 of an area covering about 828,000 sq mi/2,144,000 sq km, including the present-day states of Louisiana, Missouri, Arkansas, Iowa, Nebraska, North Dakota, South Dakota, and Oklahoma.

The purchase, which doubled the size of the US, marked the end of Napoleon's plans for a colonial empire and ensured free navigation on the Mississippi River for the US.

President Thomas ⏃Jefferson, fearing that the French (having just acquired New Orleans from the Spanish) might restrict American access to the Mississippi, offered $10 million for the area to Napoleon, who initially refused. Faced with an impending war with Britain and reverses in his colonial campaigns, the French emperor then offered to sell the entire territory for $15 million. Jefferson's special emissary, James ⏃Monroe, agreed to the purchase, but Jefferson was concerned that he lacked the authority, under the US Constitution, for such an agreement. Although he was eager to seek Congressional assent, Jefferson was forced to act on his own initiative since Napoleon grew impatient, and Secretary of State James ⏃Madison completed the negotiation 1803.

Louis Philippe 1773–1850. King of France 1830–48. Son of Louis Philippe Joseph, Duke of Orléans 1747–93; both were known as **Philippe Egalité** from their support of the 1792 Revolution. Louis Philippe fled into exile 1793–1814, but became king after the 1830 revolution with the backing of the rich bourgeoisie. Corruption discredited his regime, and after his overthrow, he escaped to the UK and died there.

Louisville industrial city and river port on the Ohio River, Kentucky; population (1990) 269,060. Products include electrical goods, agricultural machinery, motor vehicles, tobacco, and whiskey. It is the home of the Kentucky Fair and Exposition Center, and the Kentucky Derby.

The University of Louisville and the Actors Theater of Louisville are here. Louisville was founded 1778.

Lourdes town in SW France, population (1982) 18,000. Its Christian shrine to St ⏃Bernadette has a reputation for miraculous cures.

Lourenço Marques former name of ⏃Maputo, capital of Mozambique.

louse parasitic insect of the order Anoplura, which lives on mammals. It has a flat, segmented body without wings, and a tube attached to the head, used for sucking blood from its host.

Some lice occur on humans including the head louse *Pediculus capitis*, and the body louse *Pediculus corporis*, a typhus carrier. Pediculosis is a skin disease caused by infestation of lice. Most mammals have a species of lice adapted to living on them. Biting lice belong to a different order of insects, Mallophaga, and feed on the skin, feathers, or hair.

Louth smallest county of the Republic of Ireland, in Leinster province; county town Dundalk; area 317 sq mi/820 sq km; population (1991) 90,700.

Louvain (Flemish **Leuven**) industrial town in Brabant province, central Belgium; population (1991) 85,000. Manufacturing includes fertilizers and food processing. Its university dates from 1425 and there is a Science City.

Louvre French art gallery, former palace of the French kings, in Paris. It was converted by Napoleon to an art gallery in 1793 and houses the sculpture *Venus de Milo* and Leonardo da Vinci's painting *Mona Lisa*.

lovebird any small bird of the ⏃parrot family, especially the African genus *Agapornis*.

love-in-a-mist perennial plant of S Europe *Nigella damascena* of the buttercup family Ranunculaceae, with fernlike leaves and delicate blue or white flowers.

Lovelace Richard 1618–1658. English poet. Imprisoned in 1642 for petitioning for the restoration of royal rule, he wrote "To Althea from Prison," and in a second term in jail in 1648 revised his collection *Lucasta* 1649.

Loveland city in N central Colorado, S of Fort Collins. It is a processing and marketing center for the agricultural products of the area. Tourism is important to the economy, and Rocky Mountain National Park is to the west; population (1990) 37,350.

Lovell Bernard 1913– . British radio astronomer, director (until 1981) of ⏃Jodrell Bank Experimental Station (now Nuffield Radio Astronomy Laboratories).

During World War II he worked at the Telecommunications Research Establishment (1939–45), and in 1951 became professor of radio astronomy at the University of Manchester. His books include *Radio Astronomy* 1951 and *The Exploration of Outer Space* 1961.

Loving v Virginia a US Supreme Court decision 1967 dealing with the constitutionality of state antimiscegenation laws. The case was brought by a Virginia couple convicted of violating a state law against interracial marriages. The Court sustained their challenge to the Virginia statute as a violation of the 14th Amendment. According to the 8–1 ruling, states may not prevent marriages solely because of the race of the participants.

Low Juliette Gordon 1860–1927. Founder of the Girl Scouts in the US. Born in Savannah, Georgia, and educated in New York, Low moved temporarily to England, where she became impressed with the scouting organizations founded by Robert Baden-Powell. Returning to the US, she formed a troop of 16 "Girl Guides" in Savannah 1912. Establishing national headquarters in Washington, DC in the following year, she changed the name of the organization to the Girl Scouts of America (GSA).

Low served as president of the GSA 1915–20 and worked tirelessly to establish Girl Scout troops throughout the country.

Low Countries region of Europe that consists of ⏃Belgium and the ⏃Netherlands, and usually includes ⏃Luxembourg.

Lowell city in Massachusetts; population (1990) 103,440. Industries include electronics, plastics, and chemicals. Lowell was a textile center in the 19th century; a substantial part of the old city was designated a national park in 1978 as a birthplace of the US industrial revolution. Wang Laboratories moved its headquarters here 1978.

Lowell Amy (Lawrence) 1874–1925. US poet who began her career by publishing the conventional *A Dome of Many-Colored Glass* 1912 but eventually succeeded Ezra Pound as leader of the Imagists (see ⏃Imagism). Her works, in free verse, include *Sword Blades and Poppy Seed* 1916.

She was a controversial figure who demonstrated her scorn for conventionality by, for example, openly smoking cigars.

Lowell Francis Cabot 1775–1817. US industrialist. Born in Newburyport, Massachusetts, and educated at Harvard, Lowell was a successful merchant. On a trip to England 1810–12, he was impressed with mechanized textile mills and, committing to memory their basic plans, became intent on bringing this technology to the US. With the cutoff of international trade during the War of 1812, Lowell established the Boston Manufacturing Co, a textile mill at Waltham, Massachusetts. After the war he campaigned for tariff protection for the US textile industry. In 1822 the mill town of Lowell, Massachusetts, was established and named for him.

Lowell J(ames) R(ussell) 1819–1891. US poet whose works range from the didactic *The Vision of Sir Launfal* 1848 to such satirical poems as *The Biglow Papers* 1848.

As a critic, he developed a deep awareness of the US literary tradition. He was also a diplomat and served as minister to Spain 1877–80 and England 1880–85.

Born in Cambridge, Massachusetts, Lowell graduated 1840 from Harvard Law School. He taught at Harvard and was editor 1857–61 of *The Atlantic Monthly* and coeditor 1863–72 of *The North American Review*. Among his critical works are essays on great masters, including Shakespeare, Dante, and Coleridge. Lowell was active in the abolitionist movement, publishing more than 50 antislavery articles between 1845 and 1850. Other works include *Leaves from My Italian Journal* 1854.

Lowell Percival 1855–1916. US astronomer who predicted the existence of a "Planet X" beyond Neptune, and started the search that led to the discovery of Pluto in 1930. In 1894 he founded the Lowell Observatory at Flagstaff,

Louisiana

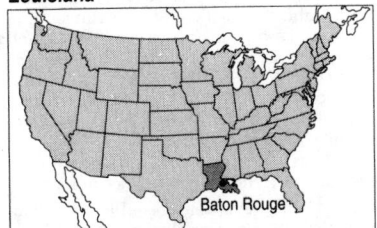

Baton Rouge

Arizona, where he reported seeing "canals" (now known to be optical artifacts) on the surface of Mars.

Lowell Robert (Traill Spence, Jr) 1917–1977. US poet whose work stressed the importance of individualism, especially during times of war. His works include *Lord Weary's Castle* 1946 and *For the Union Dead* 1964.

Much of his poetry is confessional. During World War II he was imprisoned for five months for conscientious objection. Several of his poems, notably "Memories of West Street and Lepke," reflect on this experience. "Skunk Hour," included in *Life Studies* 1959, is another example of his autobiographical poetry.

Other works include *Land of Unlikeness* 1944, *The Mills of the Kaanaughs* 1951, *The Old Glory* 1965, *Near the Ocean* 1967, *Notebook* 1969, *The Dolphin* 1973, and *Day by Day* 1977. In the 1960s he was again a war protestor and also a civil-rights activist.

Lowell Observatory US astronomical observatory founded by Percival Lowell at Flagstaff, Arizona, with a 61-cm/24-in refractor opened in 1896. The observatory now operates other telescopes at a nearby site on Anderson Mesa including the 72-in/1.83-m Perkins reflector of Ohio State and Ohio Wesleyan universities.

Lower Austria (German *Niederösterreich*) largest federal state of Austria; drained by the river Danube; area 7,411 sq mi/19,200 sq km; population (1987) 1,426,000. Its capital is St Pölten. In addition to wine, sugar beets, and grain, there are reserves of oil. Manufactured products include textiles, chemicals, and metal goods.

Lower California English name for ⬦Baja California, Mexico.

Lower Saxony (German *Niedersachsen*) administrative region (German *Land*) of N Germany
area 18,296 sq mi/47,400 sq km
capital Hanover
cities Brunswick, Osnabrück, Oldenburg, Göttingen, Wolfsburg, Salzgitter, Hildesheim
features Lüneburg Heath
products cereals, automobiles, machinery, electrical engineering
population (1988) 7,190,000
religion 75% Protestant, 20% Roman Catholic
history formed 1946 from Hanover, Oldenburg, Brunswick, and Schaumburg-Lippe.

Loy Myrna. Adopted name of Myrna Williams 1905– . US film actress who played Nora Charles in the *Thin Man* series (1934–47) costarring William Powell. Her other films include *The Mask of Fu Manchu* 1932 and *The Rains Came* 1939.

Loyalist member of approximately 30% of the US population remaining loyal to Britain in the ⬦American Revolution. Many Loyalists went to E Ontario after 1783.

Known as Tories, most were crown officials, Anglican clergy, and economically advantaged, although they were represented in every segment of colonial society.

Loyola founder of the Jesuits. See ⬦Ignatius Loyola.

LSD abbreviation for **lysergic acid diethylamide**, a psychedelic drug and a hallucinogen, often producing states resembling those common in psychosis (for example, schizophrenia). It is derived from lysergic acid, originally extracted from poisonous ⬦ergot alkaloids. Its use is illegal.

LSI (abbreviation for **large-scale integration**) the technology that enables whole electrical circuits to be etched into a piece of semiconducting material just a few millimeters square.

By the late 1960s a complete computer processor could be integrated on a single chip, or ⬦integrated circuit, and in 1971 the US electronics company Intel produced the first commercially available ⬦microprocessor. Very large-scale integration (⬦VLSI) results in even smaller chips.

Lualaba another name for the upper reaches of the river ⬦Zaïre in Africa, as it flows north through Zaire from near the Zambia border.

Luanda formerly **Loanda** capital and industrial port (cotton, sugar, tobacco, timber, paper, oil) of Angola; population (1988) 1,200,000. It was founded in 1575 and became a Portuguese colonial administrative center as well as an outlet for slaves transported to Brazil.

Luang Prabang or *Louangphrabang* Buddhist religious center in Laos, on the Mekong at the head of river navigation; population (1984) 44,244. It was the capital of the kingdom of Luang Prabang, incorporated in Laos in 1946, and the royal capital of Laos 1946–75.

Lubbers Rudolph Franz Marie (Ruud) 1939– . Dutch politician, prime minister of the Netherlands from 1982. Leader of the Christian Democratic Appeal (CDA), he is politically right of center. He became minister for economic affairs 1973.

Lubbock city in NW Texas, S of Amarillo; seat of Lubbock County. Industries include heavy farm and construction machinery, cotton, sorghum, and mobile homes; population (1990) 186,200.

Lübeck seaport of Schleswig-Holstein, Germany, on the Baltic Sea, 37 mi/60 km NE of Hamburg; population (1988) 209,000. Founded in 1143, it has five Gothic churches and a cathedral dating from 1173. Once head of the powerful ⬦Hanseatic League, it later lost much of its trade to Hamburg and Bremen, but improved canal and port facilities helped it to retain its position as a center of Baltic trade. Lübeck was a free state of both the empire and the Weimar Republic.

Lubitsch Ernst 1892–1947. German film director known for his stylish comedies, who worked in the US from 1921. His sound films include *Trouble in Paradise* 1932, *Design for Living* 1933, *Ninotchka* 1939, and *To Be or Not to Be* 1942.

Starting as an actor in silent films in Berlin, he turned to writing and directing, including *Die Augen der Mummie Ma*/*The Eyes of the Mummy* 1918 and *Die Austernprinzessin*/*The Oyster Princess* 1919. In the US he directed the silent films *The Marriage Circle* 1924 and *The Student Prince* 1927.

Lublin city in Poland, on the Bystrzyca River, 95 mi/150 km SE of Warsaw; population (1990) 351,400. Industries include textiles, engineering, aircraft, and electrical goods. A trading center from the 10th century, it has an ancient citadel, a 16th-century cathedral, and a university (1918). A council of workers and peasants proclaimed Poland's independence at Lublin in 1918, and a Russian-sponsored committee of national liberation, which proclaimed itself the provincial government of Poland at Lublin on Dec 31, 1944, was recognized by Russia five days later.

Lubovitch Lar 1945– . US modern-dance choreographer and director of the Lar Lubovitch Dance Company, founded 1976. He was the first to use Minimalist music, for which he created a new style of movement in works like *Marimba* 1977 and *North Star* 1978.

lubricant substance used between moving surfaces to reduce friction. Carbon-based (organic) lubricants, commonly called grease and oil, are recovered from petroleum distillation.

Extensive research has been carried out on chemical additives to lubricants, which can reduce corrosive wear, prevent the accumulation of "cold sludge" (often the result of stop-start driving in city traffic jams), keep pace with the higher working temperatures of aviation gas turbines, or provide radiation-resistant greases for nuclear power plants. Silicon-based spray-on lubricants are also used; they tend to attract dust and dirt less than carbon-based ones.

A solid lubricant is graphite, an allotropic form of carbon, either flaked or emulsified (colloidal) in water or oil.

Lubumbashi formerly (until 1986) *Elisabethville* town in Zaire, on the Lualaba River; population (1984) 543,000. It is chief commercial center of the Shaba copper-mining region.

Lucan (Marcus Annaeus Lucanus) AD 39–65. Latin poet, born in Córdoba, Spain, a nephew of the writer Seneca and favorite of Nero until the emperor became jealous of his verse. Lucan then joined a republican conspiracy and committed suicide on its failure. His epic *Pharsalia* deals with the civil wars of the Roman rulers Caesar and Pompey.

Lucas George 1944– . US director and producer whose imagination was fired by the comic books in his father's store. He wrote and directed (in collaboration with Steven Spielberg) *Star Wars* 1977, *The Empire Strikes Back* 1980, and *Return of the Jedi* 1983. His other films include *THX 1138* 1971, *American Graffiti* 1973, *Raiders of the Lost Ark* 1981, *Indiana Jones and the Temple of Doom* 1984, *Willow* 1988, and *Indiana Jones and the Last Crusade* 1989, most of which were box-office hits.

Lucas Robert 1937– . US economist, leader of the University of Chicago school of "new Classical" macroeconomics, which contends that wage and price adjustment is almost instantaneous and that the level of unemployment at any time must be the natural rate (it cannot be reduced by government action except in the short term and at the cost of increasing inflation).

Lucas van Leyden 1494–1533. Dutch painter and engraver, active in Leiden and Antwerp. He was a pioneer of Netherlandish genre scenes, for example *The Chess Players* (Staatliche Museen, Berlin). His woodcuts and engravings were inspired by Albrecht Dürer, whom he met in Antwerp in 1521.

Lucas's work influenced ⬦Rembrandt.

Luce Clare Boothe 1903–1987. US journalist, playwright, and politician. She was managing editor of *Vanity Fair* magazine 1933–34, and wrote several successful plays, including *The Women* 1936 and *Margin for Error* 1940, both of which were made into films. She served as a Republican member of Congress 1943–47 and as ambassador to Italy 1953–57.

She was born in New York and married Time Inc founder Henry Robinson Luce in 1935.

Luce Henry Robinson 1898–1967. US publisher, founder of Time Inc, which publishes the weekly news magazine *Time* 1923, the business magazine *Fortune* 1930, the pictorial magazine *Life* 1936, and the sports magazine *Sports Illustrated* 1954. He married Clare Boothe Luce in 1935.

Born of missionary parents in Tengchow, China, Luce was educated at Yale and Oxford universities. Other publications of Time Inc, include *House and Home*, *Architectural Forum*, and Time-Life Books.

lucerne another name for the plant ⟩alfalfa.

Lucerne (German *Luzern*) capital and tourist center of Lucerne canton, Switzerland, on the river Reuss where it flows out of Lake Lucerne; population (1990) city 59,400, canton 319,500. It developed around the Benedictine monastery, established about 750, and owes its prosperity to its position on the St Gotthard road and railroad.

Lucerne, Lake (German *Luzern*) scenic lake in central Switzerland; area 44 sq mi/ 114 sq km.

Lucian *c.* 125–*c.* 190. Greek writer of satirical dialogues, in which he pours scorn on all religions. He was born at Samosata in Syria and for a time was an advocate at Antioch, but later traveled before settling in Athens about 165. He occupied an official post in Egypt, where he died.

Lucifer (Latin "bearer of light") in Christian theology, another name for the ⟩devil, the leader of the angels who rebelled against God. Lucifer is also another name for the morning star (the planet ⟩Venus).

Lucknow capital and industrial city (engineering, chemicals, textiles, many handicrafts) of the state of Uttar Pradesh, India; population (1981) 1,007,000. During the Indian Mutiny against British rule, it was besieged July 2–Nov 16, 1857.

Lucretia Roman woman, the wife of Collatinus, said to have committed suicide after being raped by Sextus, son of Tarquinius Superbus, the king of Rome. According to tradition, this incident led to the dethronement of Tarquinius and the establishment of the Roman Republic in 509 BC.

Lucretius (Titus Lucretius Carus) *c.* 99–55 BC. Roman poet and ⟩Epicurean philosopher (see ⟩Epicureanism) whose *De Rerum natura/On the Nature of The Universe* envisaged the whole universe as a combination of atoms, and had some concept of evolutionary theory.

According to Lucretius, animals were complex but initially quite fortuitous clusters of atoms, only certain combinations surviving to reproduce.

Lucullus Lucius Licinius 110–56 BC. Roman general and consul. As commander against King Mithridates of Pontus (NE Asia Minor, on the Black Sea) 74–66 he proved to be one of Rome's ablest generals and administrators, until superseded by Pompey. He then retired from politics. His wealth enabled him to live a life of luxury, and Lucullan feasts became legendary.

Lüda or **Hüta** industrial port (engineering, chemicals, textiles, oil refining, shipbuilding, food processing) in Liaoning, China, on Liaodong Peninsula, facing the Yellow Sea; population (1986) 4,500,000. It comprises the naval base of Lüshun (known under 19th-century Russian occupation as Port Arthur) and the commercial port of Dalien (formerly Talien/Dairen).

Both were leased to Russia (which needed an ice-free naval base) in 1898, but were ceded to Japan after the ⟩Russo-Japanese War; Lüshun was under Japanese siege June 1904–Jan 1905. After World War II, Lüshun was occupied by Russian airborne troops (it was returned to China 1955) and Russia was granted shared facilities at Dalien (ended on the deterioration of Sino-Russian relations 1955).

Luddite one of a group of people involved in machine-wrecking riots in N England 1811–16. The organizer of the Luddites was referred to as General Ludd, but may not have existed. Many Luddites were hanged or transported to penal colonies, such as Australia.

The movement, which began in Nottinghamshire and spread to Lancashire, Cheshire, Derbyshire, Leicestershire, and Yorkshire, was primarily a revolt against the unemployment caused by the introduction of machines in the Industrial Revolution.

Ludendorff Erich von 1865–1937. German general, chief of staff to ⟩Hindenburg in World War I, and responsible for the eastern-front victory at the Battle of ⟩Tannenberg in 1914. After Hindenburg's appointment as chief of general staff and Ludendorff's as quartermaster-general in 1916, he was also politically influential. He took part in the Nazi rising in Munich in 1923 and sat in the Reichstag (parliament) as a right-wing Nationalist.

Ludwig Karl Friedrich Wilhelm 1816–1895. German physiologist who invented graphic methods of recording events within the body.

Ludwig demonstrated that the circulation of the blood is purely mechanical in nature and involves no occult vital forces. In the course of this work, he invented the kymograph, a rotating drum on which a stylus charts a continuous record of blood pressure and temperature. This was a forerunner of today's monitoring systems.

Ludwig three kings of Bavaria:

Ludwig I 1786–1868. King of Bavaria 1825–48, succeeding his father Maximilian Joseph I. He made Munich an international cultural center, but his association with the dancer Lola Montez, who dictated his policies for a year, led to his abdication in 1848.

Ludwig II 1845–1886. King of Bavaria from 1864, when he succeeded his father Maximilian II. He supported Austria during the Austro-Prussian War 1866, but brought Bavaria into the Franco-Prussian War as Prussia's ally and in 1871 offered the German crown to the king of Prussia. He was the composer Richard Wagner's patron and built the Bayreuth theater for him. Declared insane 1886, he drowned himself soon after.

Ludwig III 1845–1921. King of Bavaria 1913–18, when he abdicated upon the formation of a republic.

Luening Otto 1900–   . US composer. He studied in Zurich, and privately with the Italian composer Feruccio Busoni. In 1949 he joined the staff at Columbia University, and in 1951 began a series of pioneering compositions for instruments and tape, some in partnership with Vladimir Ussachevsky (1911–   ) (*Incantation* 1952, *Poem in Cycles and Bells* 1954). In 1959 he became co-director, with Milton ⟩Babbitt and Ussachevsky, of the Columbia-Princeton Electronic Music Center.

Luftwaffe German air force. In World War I and, as reorganized by the Nazi leader Hermann Goering in 1933, in World War II. The Luftwaffe also covered antiaircraft defense and the launching of the flying bombs ⟩V1 and V2.

Lugano, Lake lake partly in Italy, between lakes Maggiore and Como, and partly in Switzerland; area 19 sq mi/49 sq km.

Lugansk formerly (1935–58 and 1970–89) *Voroshilovgrad*, industrial city (locomotives, textiles, mining machinery) in Ukraine; population (1987) 509,000.

luge a one- or two-person racing sled, on which riders lie face up. Luges are raced by both men and women in the winter Olympics.

Lugosi Bela. Adopted name of Bela Ferenc Blasko 1882–1956. Hungarian-born US film actor. Acclaimed for his performance in *Dracula* on Broadway 1927, Lugosi began acting in feature films in 1930. His appearance in the film version of *Dracula* 1931 marked the start of Lugosi's long career in horror films—among them, *Murders in the Rue Morgue* 1932, *The Raven* 1935, and *The Wolf Man* 1941.

lugworm any of a genus *Arenicola* of marine annelid worms that grow up to 10 in/25 cm long. They are common burrowers between tidemarks and are useful for their cleansing and powdering of the beach sand, of which they may annually bring to the surface about 2,000 tons per acre/5,000 tonnes per hectare.

Lu Hsün alternative transliteration of Chinese writer ⟩Lu Xun.

Lukács Georg 1885–1971. Hungarian philosopher, one of the founders of "Western" or "Hegelian" Marxism, a philosophy opposed to the Marxism of the official communist movement.

In *History and Class Consciousness* 1923, he argued that the proletariat was the "identical subject-object" of history. Under capitalism, social relations were "reified" (turned into objective things), but the proletariat could grasp the social totality. Lukács himself repudiated the book and spent much of the rest of his life as an orthodox communist. He also made contributions to Marxist aesthetics and literary theory. He believed, as a natural relativist, that the highest art was that which reflected the historical movement of the time: for the 20th century, this meant ⟩Socialist Realism. Lukács joined the Hungarian Communist Party in 1918 and was deputy minister of education during the short-lived Hungarian Soviet Republic, 1919.

Luke, St 1st century AD. Traditionally the compiler of the third Gospel and of the Acts of the Apostles in the New Testament. He is the patron saint of painters; his emblem is a winged ox, and his feast day Oct 18.

Luke is supposed to have been a Greek physician born in Antioch (Antakiyah, Turkey) and to have accompanied Paul after the ascension of Jesus.

Luks George 1867–1933. US painter and graphic artist, a member of the ⟩Ashcan School.

Born in Williamsport, Pennsylvania, he studied at the Pennsylvania Academy of the Fine Arts and worked as an illustrator and cartoonist 1894–96 for various newspapers. Robert ⟩Henri convinced him to take up painting. Luks's painting captured the excitement and color of life in New York City's slums.

Lully Jean-Baptiste. Adopted name of Giovanni Battista Lulli 1632–1687. French composer of

Italian origin who was court composer to Louis XIV. He composed music for the ballet, for Molière's plays, and established French opera with such works as *Alceste* 1674 and *Armide et Renaud* 1686. He was also a ballet dancer.

lumbago pain in the lower region of the back, usually due to strain or faulty posture. If it occurs with ▷sciatica, it may be due to pressure on spinal nerves by a displaced vertebra. Treatment includes rest, application of heat, and skilled manipulation. Surgery may be needed in rare cases.

lumbar puncture or *spinal tap* insertion of a hollow needle between two lumbar (lower back) vertebrae to withdraw a sample of cerebrospinal fluid (CSF) for testing. Normally clear and colorless, the CSF acts as a fluid buffer around the brain and spinal cord. Changes in its quantity, color, or composition may indicate neurological damage or disease.

lumen SI unit (symbol lm) of luminous flux (the amount of light passing through an area per second).

The lumen is defined in terms of the light falling on a unit area at a unit distance from a light source of luminous intensity of one ▷candela. One lumen at a wavelength of 5,550 angstroms equals 0.0014700 watts.

Lumet Sidney 1924– . US film director whose social conscience has sometimes prejudiced his invariably powerful films: *12 Angry Men* 1957, *Fail Safe* 1964, *Serpico* 1973, and *Dog Day Afternoon* 1975.

Lumière Auguste Marie 1862–1954 and Louis Jean 1864–1948. French brothers who pioneered cinematography. In 1895 they patented their cinematograph, a combined camera and projector operating at 16 frames per second, and opened the world's first cinema in Paris to show their films.

The Lumières' first films were short static shots of everyday life such as *La Sorties des Usines Lumière* 1895 about workers leaving a factory and *L'Arroseur Arrosé* 1895, the world's first fiction film. Production was abandoned in 1900.

luminescence emission of light from a body when its atoms are excited by means other than raising its temperature. Short-lived luminescence is called fluorescence; longer-lived luminescence is called phosphorescence.

When exposed to an external source of energy, the outer electrons in atoms of a luminescent substance absorb energy and "jump" to a higher energy level. When these electrons "jump" back to their former level they emit their excess energy as light. Many different exciting mechanisms are possible: visible light or other forms of electromagnetic radiation (ultraviolet rays or X-rays), electron bombardment, chemical reactions, friction, and ▷radioactivity. Certain living organisms produce ▷bioluminescence.

luminism method of painting, associated with the ▷Hudson River School in the 19th century, that emphasized the effects of light on water.

Luminist painters included F H Lane, T Cole, A B Durand, M J Heade, and F E Church. They gave particular attention to the treatment of light in their paintings, stressing precision through technical accuracy.

luminosity or *brightness* in astronomy, the amount of light emitted by a star, measured in ▷magnitudes. The apparent brightness of an object decreases in proportion to the square of its distance from the observer. The luminosity of a star or other body can be expressed in relation to that of the sun.

luminous paint preparation containing a mixture of pigment, oil, and a phosphorescent sulfide, usually calcium or barium. After exposure to light it appears luminous in the dark. The luminous paint used on watch faces contains radium, is radioactive and therefore does not require exposure to light.

Lumumba Patrice 1926–1961. Congolese politician, prime minister of Zaire 1960. Imprisoned by the Belgians, but released in time to attend the conference giving the Congo independence in 1960, he led the National Congolese Movement to victory in the subsequent general election. He was deposed in a coup d'état, and murdered some months later.

Lund city in Malmöhus county, SW Sweden; 10 mi/16 km NE of Malmö; population (1990) 87,700. It has an 11th-century Romanesque cathedral and a university established in 1666. The treaty of Lund was signed in 1676 after Carl XI had defeated the Danes.

lung large cavity of the body, used for ▷gas exchange, or respiration. It is essentially a sheet of thin, moist membrane that is folded so as to occupy less space. Lungs are found in some slugs and snails, particularly those that live on land. Some fishes (lungfish) and most four-limbed vertebrates have a pair of lungs, which occupy the thorax (the upper part of the trunk). Lungs function by bringing inhaled air into close contact with the blood, so that oxygen can pass into the organism and waste carbon dioxide can be passed out; the oxygen is carried by ▷hemoglobin in red blood cells. The lung tissue, consisting of multitudes of air sacs and blood vessels, is very light and spongy.

Air is drawn into the lungs through the trachea and bronchi by the expansion of the ribs and the contraction of the diaphragm. The principal diseases of the lungs are tuberculosis, pneumonia, bronchitis, emphysema, and cancer.

lungfish three genera of fleshy-finned bony fishes of the subclass Dipnoi, found in Africa, South America, and Australia. They have elongated bodies, and grow to about 6 ft/2 m, and in addition to gills have "lungs" with which they can breathe air during periods of drought conditions.

Lungfish are related to the lobefins such as the ▷coelacanth, and were abundant 350 million years ago.

Lunt Alfred 1893–1977. US actor. He went straight from school into the theater, and in 1922 married the actress Lynn Fontanne with whom he subsequently co-starred in more than 30 plays. They formed a sophisticated comedy duo, and the New York Lunt-Fontanne Theater was named after them. Their shows included *Design for Living* by Noël Coward 1933, *There Shall Be No Night* 1940–41, and *The Visit* 1960.

Luo member of the second-largest ethnic group of Kenya, living in the Lake Victoria

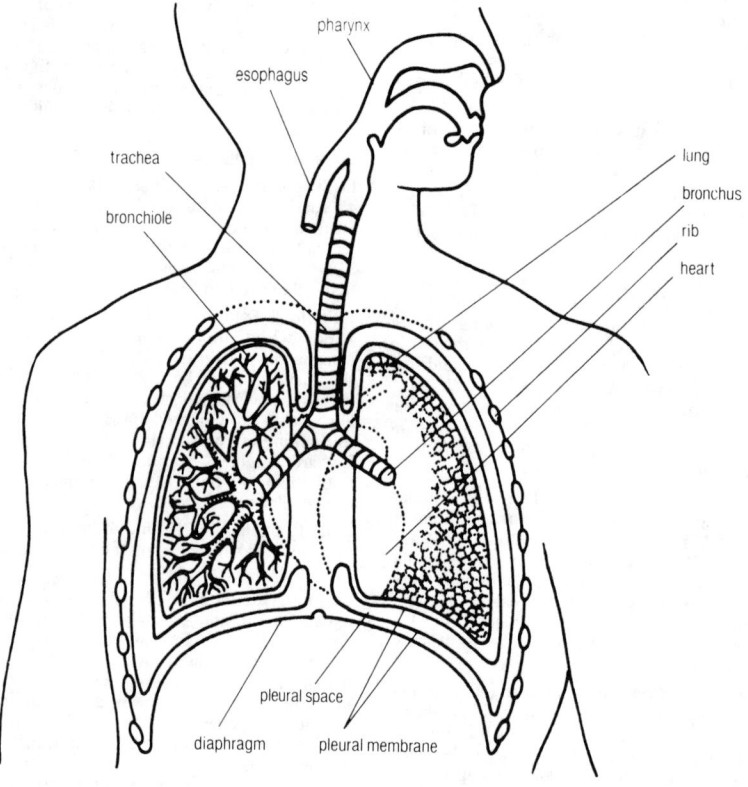

lung *The human lungs contain 300,000 million tiny blood vessels which would stretch for 1,500 mi/2,400 km if laid end to end.*

region and in 1987 numbering some 2,650,000. The Luo traditionally live by farming livestock. The Luo language is of the Nilo-Saharan family.

Luo Guan Zhong or **Luo Kuan-chung** lived 14th-century. Chinese novelist who reworked popular tales into *The Romance of the Three Kingdoms* and *The Water Margin*.

Luoyang or *Loyang* industrial city in Henan province, China, S of the river Huang He; population 1,114,000. Formerly the capital of China, its industries include machinery and tractors.

Lupercalia Roman festival celebrated Feb 15. It took place at the Lupercal, the cave where Romulus and Remus, the twin founders of Rome, were supposedly suckled by a wolf (*lupus*). Lupercalia included feasting, dancing, and sacrificing goats. Priests ran around the city carrying whips made from the hides of the sacrificed goats, a blow from which was believed to cure sterility in women.

lupin any plant of the genus *Lupinus*, of the pea family Leguminosae, including about 300 species. They are native to Mediterranean regions and parts of North and South America. Their spikes of pealike flowers may be white, yellow, blue, or pink. The European lupin *L. albus* is cultivated in some places for cattle fodder and for manure.

lupus in medicine, any of various diseases characterized by lesions of the skin. One form (lupus vulgaris) is caused by the tubercle bacillus (see ◊tuberculosis). The organism produces ulcers that spread and eat away the underlying tissues. Treatment is primarily with standard antituberculous drugs, but ultraviolet light may also be used.

Lupus erythematous (LE) has two forms: *discoid* LE, seen as red, scaly patches on the skin, especially the face; and *disseminated* or *systemic* LE, which may affect connective tissue anywhere in the body, often involving the internal organs. The latter is much more serious. Treatment is with ◊corticosteroids.

Lurie Alison 1926– . US novelist and critic. Her subtly written and satirical novels include *Imaginary Friends* 1967; *The War Between the Tates* 1974; *Foreign Affairs* 1985, a tale of transatlantic relations that won the Pulitzer Prize; and *The Truth About Lorin Jones* 1988.

Luristan or *Lorestan* mountainous province in W Iran; area 11,117 sq mi/28,800 sq km; population (1986) 1,367,000. The capital is Khorramabad. The province is inhabited by Lur tribes who live by their sheep and cattle. Excavation in the area has revealed a culture of the 8th–7th century BC with bronzes decorated with animal forms; its origins are uncertain.

Lusaka capital of Zambia from 1964 (of Northern Rhodesia 1935–64), 230 mi/370 km NE of Livingstone; commercial and agricultural center (flour mills, tobacco factories, vehicle assembly, plastics, printing); population (1988) 870,000.

Lüshun-Dalien see ◊Lüda, port in China.

Lusitania ancient area of the Iberian peninsula, roughly equivalent to Portugal. Conquered by Rome in 139 BC, the province of Lusitania rebelled periodically until it was finally conquered by Pompey 73–72 BC.

Lusitania ocean liner sunk by a German submarine on May 7, 1915 with the loss of 1,200 lives, including some Americans; its destruction helped to bring the US into World War I.

Lü-ta alternative transcription of ◊Lüda, port in China.

lute family of stringed musical instruments of the 14th–18th century, including the mandore, theorbo, and chitarrone. Lutes are pear-shaped and are plucked with the fingers. Members of the lute family were used both as solo instruments and for vocal accompaniment, and were often played in addition to, or instead of, keyboard instruments in larger ensembles and in opera.

luteinizing hormone ◊hormone produced by the pituitary gland. In males, it stimulates the testes to produce androgens (male sex hormones). In females, it works together with follicle-stimulating hormone to initiate production of egg cells by the ovary. If fertilization of the egg cell occurs, it plays a part in maintaining the pregnancy by controlling the levels of the hormones estrogen and progesterone in the body.

lutetium (Latin *Lutetia* "Paris") silver-white, metallic element, the last of the ◊lanthanide series, symbol Lu, atomic number 71, atomic weight 174.97. It is used in the "cracking," or breakdown, of petroleum and in other chemical processes. It was named by its discoverer, French chemist Georges Urbain, (1872–1938) after his native city.

Luther Martin 1483–1546. German Christian church reformer, a founder of Protestantism. While he was a priest at the University of Wittenberg, he wrote an attack on the sale of indulgences (remissions of punishment for sin). The Holy Roman emperor Charles V summoned him to the Diet (meeting of dignitaries of the Holy Roman Empire) of Worms in Germany, in 1521, where he refused to retract his objections. Originally intending reform, his protest led to schism, with the emergence, following the ◊Augsburg Confession 1530 (a statement of the Protestant faith), of a new Protestant church. Luther is regarded as the instigator of the Protestant revolution, and Lutheranism is now the major religion of many N European countries, including Germany, Sweden, and Denmark.

Luther was born in Eisleben, the son of a miner; he studied at the University of Erfurt, spent three years as a monk in the Augustinian convent there, and in 1507 was ordained priest. Shortly afterwards he attracted attention as a teacher and preacher at the University of Wittenberg; and in 1517, after returning from a visit to Rome, he attained nationwide celebrity for his denunciation of the Dominican monk Johann Tetzel (1455–1519), one of those sent out by the Pope to sell indulgences as a means of raising funds for the rebuilding of St Peter's Basilica in Rome.

On Oct 31, 1517, Luther nailed on the church door in Wittenberg a statement of 95 theses concerning indulgences, and the following year he was summoned to Rome to defend his action. His reply was to attack the papal system even more strongly, and in 1520 he publicly burned in Wittenberg the papal bull (edict) that had been launched against him. On his way home from the imperial Diet of Worms he was taken into "protective custody" by the elector of Saxony in the castle of Wartburg. Later he became estranged from the Dutch theologian Erasmus, who had formerly supported him in his attacks on papal authority, and engaged in violent controversies with political and religious opponents. After the Augsburg Confession 1530, Luther gradually retired from the Protestant leadership.

Formerly condemned by communism, Luther had by the 1980s been rehabilitated as a revolutionary socialist hero, and was claimed as patron saint in Germany.

Lutheranism form of Protestant Christianity derived from the life and teaching of Martin Luther; it is sometimes called Evangelical to distinguish it from the other main branch of European Protestantism, the Reformed. The most generally accepted statement of Lutheranism is that of the *Augsburg Confession* 1530 but Luther's Shorter Catechism also carries great weight. It is the largest Protestant body, including some 80 million persons, of whom 40 million are in Germany, 19 million in Scandinavia, 8.5 million in the US and Canada, with most of the remainder in central Europe.

Lutheranism is the principal form of Protestantism in Germany, and is the national faith of Denmark, Norway, Sweden, Finland, and Iceland. The organization may be episcopal (Germany, Sweden) or synodal (the Netherlands and US): the Lutheran World Federation has its headquarters in Geneva. In the US, Lutheranism is particularly strong in the Midwest, where several churches were originally founded by German and Scandinavian immigrants.

The Evangelical Lutherans were formed 1988 from merger of the Lutheran Church of America, the American Lutheran Church and the Association of Evangelical Lutheran Churches. Lutheranism in the US is divided into three main bodies: the Lutheran Church in America, formed 1962 from the United Lutheran Church, Augustana Lutheran Church (Swedish), the Finnish Evangelical Lutheran Church, and the American Evangelical Lutheran Church (Danish); the more conservative Lutheran Church, the Missouri Synod; and the American Lutheran Church (largely Norwegian and centerd in the upper Midwest).

Luthuli or *Lutuli* Albert 1899–1967. South African politician, president of the African National Congress 1952–67. Luthuli, a Zulu tribal chief, preached nonviolence and multiracialism.

Lutosławski Witold 1913– . Polish composer and conductor, born in Warsaw. His early music, dissonant and powerful (*First Symphony* 1947), was criticized by the communist government, so he adopted a more popular style. With the lifting of artistic repression, he quickly adopted avant-garde techniques, including improvisatory and aleatoric forms. He has written chamber, vocal, and orchestral music, including three symphonies; *Livre pour orchestre* 1968 and *Mi-parti* 1976.

Lutyens (Agnes) Elizabeth, 1906–1983. English composer. Her works, using the 12-tone system, are expressive and tightly organized, and include a substantial amount of chamber music, stage, and orchestral works. Her choral and vocal works include a setting of the Austrian philosopher Ludwig ◊Wittgenstein's *Tractatus* and a cantata *The Tears of Night*. She also composed much film and incidental music. Her autobiography *A Goldfish Bowl* was published 1973.

Lützen town in Saxony-Anhalt, Germany, SW of Leipzig, where in 1632 Gustavus Adolphus, king of Sweden, defeated the German commander Wallenstein in the Thirty Years' War; Gustavus was killed in the battle. The French emperor Napoleon Bonaparte overcame the Russians and Prussians here in 1813.

lux SI unit (symbol lx) of illuminance or illumination (the light falling on an object). It is

Luxembourg
Grand Duchy of (*Grand-Duché de Luxembourg*)

area 998 sq mi/2,586 sq km
capital Luxembourg
cities Esch-sur-Alzette, Dudelange
physical on the river Moselle; part of the Ardennes (Oesling) forest in N
features seat of the European Court of Justice, Secretariat of the European Parliament, international banking center; economically linked with Belgium
head of state Grand Duke Jean from 1964
head of government Jacques Santer from 1984
political system liberal democracy
political parties Christian Social Party (PCS), moderate, left of center; Luxembourg Socialist Workers' Party (POSL), moderate, socialist; Democratic Party (PD), center-left; Communist Party of Luxembourg, pro-European left-wing
exports pharmaceuticals, synthetic textiles, steel
currency Luxembourg franc
population (1990 est) 369,000; growth rate 0% p.a.
life expectancy men 71, women 78 (1989)
languages French (official), local Letzeburgesch, German
religion Roman Catholic 97%
literacy 100% (1989)
GNP $4.9 bn; $13,380 per head (1988)
chronology
1354 Became a duchy.
1482 Under Hapsburg control.
1797 Ceded, with Belgium, to France.
1815 Treaty of Vienna created Luxembourg a grand duchy, ruled by the king of the Netherlands.
1830 With Belgium, revolted against Dutch rule.
1890 Link with Netherlands ended with accession of Grand Duke Adolphe of Nassau-Weilburg.
1948 With Belgium and the Netherlands, formed the Benelux customs union.
1960 Benelux became fully effective economic union.
1961 Prince Jean became acting head of state on behalf of his mother, Grand Duchess Charlotte.
1964 Grand Duchess Charlotte abdicated; Prince Jean became grand duke.
1974 Dominance of Christian Social Party challenged by Socialists.
1979 Christian Social Party regained pre-eminence.
1991 Pact agreeing European free-trade area signed in Luxembourg.
1992 Voted in favor of ratification of Maastricht Treaty on European union.

equivalent to one ⟡lumen per square meter or to the illuminance of a surface one meter distant from a point source of one ⟡candela.

Luxembourg capital of Luxembourg; population (1985) 76,000. The 16th-century Grand Ducal Palace, European Court of Justice, and European Parliament secretariat are situated here, but plenary sessions of the parliament are now held only in Strasbourg, in France. Products include steel, chemicals, textiles, and processed food.

Luxembourg landlocked country in W Europe, bounded N and W by Belgium, E by Germany, and S by France.
government Luxembourg is a hereditary and constitutional monarchy. The 1868 constitution, revised 1919 and 1956, provides for a single-chamber legislature, the 60-member chamber of deputies, elected by universal suffrage through a system of proportional representation, for a five-year term. There is also an advisory body, the council of state, whose 21 members are appointed by the grand duke for life. Any of its decisions can be overruled by the chamber of deputies. The grand duke also appoints a prime minister and council of ministers who are collectively responsible to the chamber.
history Formerly part of the Holy Roman Empire, Luxembourg became a duchy 1354. From 1482 it was under ⟡Hapsburg control, and in 1797 was ceded, with Belgium, to France. The 1815 Treaty of Vienna made Luxembourg a grand duchy, ruled by the king of the Netherlands. In 1830 Belgium and Luxembourg revolted against Dutch rule; Belgium achieved independence 1839 and most of Luxembourg became part of it, the rest becoming independent in its own right 1848.
role in Europe Although a small country, Luxembourg occupies an important position in W Europe, being a founding member of many international organizations, including the European Coal and Steel Community, the European Atomic Energy Commission, and the European Economic Community. It formed an economic union with Belgium and the Netherlands 1948 (⟡Benelux), which became fully effective 1960 and was the forerunner of wider European cooperation.

Grand Duchess Charlotte (1896–1985) abdicated 1964 after a reign of 45 years, and was succeeded by her son, Prince Jean. Proportional representation has resulted in a series of coalition governments. The Christian Social Party headed most of these from 1945 to 1974 when its dominance was challenged by the Socialists. It regained pre-eminence 1979, and leads the current administration.

In Oct 1991 the European Community (EC) and the European Free Trade Association (EFTA) reached an agreement at a conference hosted in Luxembourg to establish a Western Europe free-trade area, which would take effect from 1993. The area included the twelve member countries of the EC, including Luxembourg, and the seven members of EFTA.

Luxembourg showed its support for the Maastricht Treaty on European union July 1992 when it voted in favor of ratification.

However, it sought exemption from the treaty's clause requiring that residents from other EC nations be allowed to vote in local elections. About one-third of the duchy's population are foreigners. *See illustration box.*

Luxembourg province of Belgium; capital Arlon; area 1,698 sq mi/4,400 sq km; population (1991) 232,800.

Luxemburg Rosa 1870–1919. Polish-born German communist. She helped found the Polish Social Democratic Party in the 1890s (which later became the Polish Communist Party). She was a leader of the left wing of the German Social Democratic Party from 1898 and collaborator with Karl Liebknecht in founding the communist Spartacus League 1918 (see ⟡Spartacist). She was murdered with him by army officers during the Jan 1919 Berlin workers' revolt.

Luxor (Arabic *al-Uqsur*) small town in Egypt on the E bank of the Nile near the ruins of ⟡Thebes.

Lu Xun Adopted name of Chon Shu-jêu 1881–1936. Chinese short-story writer. His three volumes of satirically realistic stories, *Call to Arms, Wandering,* and *Old Tales Retold*, reveal the influence of the Russian writer Nicolai Gogol.

He is one of the most popular of modern Chinese writers.

Luzern German name of ⟡Lucerne, town in Switzerland.

Luzon largest island of the ⟡Philippines; area 41,750 sq mi/108,130 sq km; capital Quezon City; population (1970) 18,001,270. The chief city is Manila, capital of the Philippines. Products include rice, timber, and minerals. It has US military bases.

In 1991 the volcanic Mt Pinatubo, 55 mi/88 km north of Manila, erupted after lying dormant for 600 years. Volcanic ash covered an area of 1,000 sq mi/2,600 sq km and brought economic catastrophe. The US abandoned Clark Air Base, although Subic Bay naval base, their chief station in the W Pacific, was to be restored, and was leased for a further 10 years.

Lviv (Russian *Lvov*) capital and industrial city of Lviv region, Ukraine; population (1987) 767,000. Industries include textiles, metals, and engineering. The university was founded in 1661. Lviv was formerly a trade center on the Black Sea–Baltic route. Founded in the 13th century by a Galician prince (the name means "city of Leo" or "city of Lev"), it was Polish 1340–1772, Austrian 1772–1919, Polish 1919–39, and annexed by the USSR 1945. It was the site of violent nationalist demonstrations Oct 1989; in 1991, Ukraine became independent.

LW abbreviation for *long wave*, a radio wave with a wavelength of over 3,300 ft/1,000 m; one of the main wavebands into which radio frequency transmissions are divided.

LWM abbreviation for *low water mark*.

Lwów Polish form of ⟡Lviv, city in Ukraine.

lycanthropy in folk belief, transformation of a human being into a wolf; or, in psychology, a delusion involving this belief.

Lyceum ancient Athenian gymnasium and garden, with covered walks, where the philosopher Aristotle taught. It was SE of the city and named after the nearby temple of Apollo Lyceus.

lychee alternate spelling of ⟡litchi, a fruit-bearing tree.

Lycurgus Spartan lawgiver. He is said to have been a member of the royal house of the ancient Greek city-state of Sparta, who, while acting as regent, gave the Spartans their constitution and system of education. Many scholars believe him to be purely mythical.

Lydgate John *c.* 1370–*c.* 1450. English poet. He was a Benedictine monk and later prior. His numerous works were often translations or adaptations, such as *Troy Book* and *Falls of Princes.*

Lydia ancient kingdom in Anatolia (7th–6th centuries BC), with its capital at Sardis. The Lydians were the first Western people to use standard coinage. Their last king, Croesus, was conquered by the Persians in 546 BC.

Lyell Charles 1797–1875. Scottish geologist. In his *Principles of Geology* 1830–33, he opposed the French anatomist Georges Cuvier's theory that the features of the Earth were formed by a series of catastrophes, and expounded the Scottish geologist James Hutton's view, known as ◊uniformitarianism, that past events were brought about by the same processes that occur today—a view that influenced Charles Darwin's theory of evolution.

Lyell trained and practiced as a lawyer, but retired from the law 1827 and devoted himself full time to geology and writing. He implied that the Earth was much older than the 6,000 years of prevalent contemporary theory, and provided the first detailed description of the ◊Tertiary period, dividing it into the Eocene, Miocene, and older and younger Pliocene periods. Although it was only in old age that he accepted that species had changed through evolution, he nevertheless provided Darwin with a geological framework within which evolutionary theories could be placed. Darwin simply applied Lyell's geological method—explaining the past through what is observable in the present—to biology.

lyme disease disease transmitted by tick bites that affects all systems of the body. First described in 1977 following an outbreak in children living around Lyme, Connecticut, it is caused by the microorganism *Borrelia burgdorferi*, isolated by Burgdorfer and Barbor in the US in 1982. Untreated, the disease attacks the nervous system, heart, liver, kidneys, eyes and joints, but responds to the antibiotic tetracycline. The tick that carries the disease, *Ixodes*, lives on deer, while *B. burgdorferi* relies on mice during its life cycle.

lymph fluid found in the lymphatic system of vertebrates.

Lymph is drained from the tissues by lymph capillaries, which empty into larger lymph vessels (lymphatics). These lead to lymph nodes (small, round bodies chiefly situated in the neck, armpit, groin, thorax, and abdomen), which process the ◊lymphocytes produced by the bone marrow, and filter out harmful substances and bacteria. From the lymph nodes, vessels carry the lymph to the thoracic duct and the right lymphatic duct, which lead into the large veins in the neck. Some vertebrates, such as amphibians, have a lymph heart, which pumps lymph through the lymph vessels.

It returns excess, filtered tissue fluid and some protein to the bloodstream. Lymph vessels also transport fat from the digestive tract to the blood. Lymph moves in only one direction; flaplike valves prevent backflow.

lymph nodes small masses of lymphatic tissue in the body that occur at various points along the major lymphatic vessels. Tonsils and adenoids are large lymph nodes. As the lymph passes through them it is filtered, and bacteria and other microorganisms are engulfed by cells known as macrophages.

Lymph nodes are sometimes mistakenly called "lymph glands," and the term "swollen glands" refers to swelling of the lymph nodes caused by infection.

lymphocyte type of white blood cell with a large nucleus, produced in the bone marrow. Most occur in the ◊lymph and blood, and around sites of infection. *B-lymphocytes* or ◊B cells are responsible for producing ◊antibodies. *T-lymphocytes* or ◊T-cells have several roles in the formation of ◊immunity.

lymphogranuloma venerum a sexually transmitted disease caused by the bacterium *Chlamydia trachomatis*, the same organism that causes the eye disease trachoma. The disease is characterized by genital ulcers, inflammation of the urinary tract, and swelling of the lymph nodes in the groin. Chronic pelvic inflammatory disease can result if left untreated.

lymphokines chemical messengers produced by lymphocytes that carry messages between the cells of the immune system (see ◊immunity). Examples include interferon, which initiates defensive reactions to viruses, and the interleukins, which activate specific immune cells.

Lynch "Jack" (John) 1917– . Irish politician, prime minister 1966–73 and 1977–79. A Gaelic footballer and a lawyer, in 1948 he entered the parliament of the republic as a Fianna Fáil member.

Lynchburg city in S central Virginia, on the James River, NE of Roanoke; population (1990) 66,050. Industries include clothing, paper and rubber products, and machine parts.

lynching killing of an alleged offender by an individual or group having no legal authority. In the US it originated in 1780 with creation of a "committee of vigilance" in Virginia; it is named after a member of that committee, Captain William Lynch, to whom is attributed "Lynch's Law." Later examples occurred mostly in the Southern states after the Civil War, and were racially motivated. During 1882–1900 the annual number of lynchings in the US varied between 96 and 231, but today it is an exceptional occurrence.

Similar behavior patterns exist in many societies, especially when access to regular courts is poor.

Lynn industrial city in Massachusetts, on Massachusetts Bay; population (1990) 81,240. Founded as *Saugus* in 1629, it was renamed in 1637 after King's Lynn, England.

Lynn Vera 1917– . British singer, known as the "Forces' Sweetheart" of World War II. She became famous with such songs as "We'll Meet Again," "White Cliffs of Dover," and in 1952 "Auf Wiederseh'n, Sweetheart."

lynx cat *Felis lynx* found in rocky and forested regions of North America and Europe. About 3 ft/1 m in length, it has a short tail and tufted ears, and the long, silky fur is reddish brown or gray with dark spots. The North American bobcat or bay lynx *Felix rufus* looks similar but is smaller. Some zoologists place the lynx, the bobcat, and the ◊caracal in a separate genus, *Lynx.*

Lyon (English *Lyons*) industrial city (textiles, chemicals, machinery, printing) and capital of Rhône *département*, Rhône-Alpes region, and third largest city of France, at the confluence of the rivers Rhône and Saône, 170 mi/275 km NNW of Marseille; population (1982) 418,476, conurbation 1,221,000. Formerly a chief fortress of France, it was the ancient *Lugdunum*, taken by the Romans in 43 BC.

Lyons Joseph Aloysius 1879–1939. Australian politician, founder of the United Australia Party 1931, prime minister 1931–39.

Lyra small but prominent constellation of the northern hemisphere, representing the lyre of Orpheus. Its brightest star is ◊Vega.

Epsilon Lyrae, the "double double," is a system of four gravitationally linked stars. Beta Lyrae is an eclipsing binary. The Ring nebula, M57, is a ◊planetary nebula.

lyre stringed instrument of great antiquity. It consists of a soundbox with two curved arms extended upward to a crosspiece to which four to ten strings are attached. It is played with a plectrum or the fingers. It originated in Asia, and was used in Greece and Egypt.

lyrebird any bird of the order *Passeriformes*, forming the Australian family Menuridae. There are two species, both in the genus *Menura*. The male has a large lyre-shaped tail, brilliantly colored. Lyrebirds nest on the ground, and feed on insects, worms, and snails.

Lysander Spartan general. He brought the Peloponnesian War between Athens and Sparta to a successful conclusion by capturing the Athenian fleet at Aegospotami in 405 BC, and by starving Athens into surrender in the following year. He then aspired to make Sparta supreme in Greece and himself supreme in Sparta; he set up puppet governments in Athens and its former allies, and tried to secure for himself the Spartan kingship, but he was killed in battle with the Thebans.

Lysenko Trofim Denisovich 1898–1976. Soviet biologist who believed in the inheritance of ◊acquired characteristics (changes acquired in an individual's lifetime) and used his position under Joseph Stalin officially to exclude Gregor ◊Mendel's theory of inheritance. He was removed from office after the fall of Khrushchev in 1964.

Lysippus 4th century BC. Greek sculptor. He made a series of portraits of Alexander the Great (Roman copies survive, including examples in the British Museum and the Louvre) and also sculpted the *Apoxyomenos*, an athlete (copy in the Vatican), and a colossal *Hercules* (lost).

lysis in biology, any process that destroys a cell by rupturing its membrane or cell wall (see ◊lysosome).

Lysistrata Greek comedy by Aristophanes, produced 411 BC. The women of Athens, tired of war, refuse to make love with their husbands and occupy the Acropolis to force a peace between the Athenians and the Spartans.

lysosome membrane-enclosed structure, or organelle, inside a ◊cell, principally found in animal cells. Lysosomes contain enzymes that can break down proteins and other biological substances. They play a part in digestion, and in the white blood cells known as phagocytes the lysosome enzymes attack ingested bacteria.

Lytton Edward George Earle Bulwer-Lytton, 1st Baron Lytton of Knebworth 1803–1873. English writer. His novels successfully followed every turn of the public taste of his day and include the Byronic *Pelham* 1828, *The Last Days of Pompeii* 1834, and *Rienzi* 1835. His plays include *Richelieu* 1838.

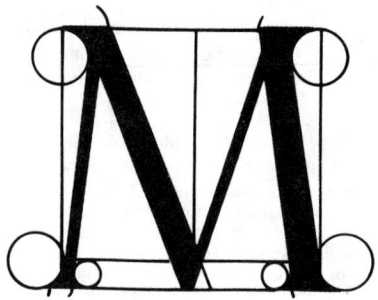

M 13th letter of the English alphabet. It corresponds to the Greek *mu* (M, μ) and the Semitic *mem*, and is almost always sounded as a voiced labial nasal. Finally, or before consonants, it disappears in French, Portuguese, and other languages, leaving a trace in nasalization of the preceding vowel.

M Roman numeral for *1,000*.

MA abbreviation for *Master of Arts*, a degree of education; the state of ⟂*Massachusetts*.

Maas Dutch or Flemish name for the river ⟂Meuse.

Maazel Lorin (Varencove) 1930– . US conductor and violinist. He studied the violin and made his debut as a conductor at the age of nine. He was conductor of the Cleveland Orchestra 1972–82 and the first US director of the Vienna State Opera.

Mabuse Jan. Adopted name of Jan Gossaert *c*. 1478–*c*. 1533. Flemish painter, active chiefly in Antwerp. His common name derives from his birthplace, Maubeuge. His visit to Italy 1508 with Philip of Burgundy started a new vogue in Flanders for Italianate ornament and Classical detail in painting, including sculptural nude figures.

McAdam John Loudon 1756–1836. Scottish engineer, inventor of the macadam road surface. It originally consisted of broken granite bound together with slag or gravel, raised for drainage. Today, it is bound with tar or asphalt.

macadamia edible nut from the tree *Macadamia ternifolia*, family Proteaceae, native to Australia and cultivated in Hawaii, South Africa, Zimbabwe, and Malawi. The nuts are slow-growing; they are harvested when they drop.

McAllen city in S Texas, just north of the Mexican border formed by the Rio Grande, SE of Laredo; population (1990) 84,000. Industries include oil refining and the processing of agricultural products from the Rio Grande valley. It is a US port of entry for Mexicans, and many of the city's inhabitants are Spanish-speaking.

Macao Portuguese possession on the south coast of China, about 40 mi/65 km west of Hong Kong, from which it is separated by the estuary of the Canton River; it consists of a peninsula and the islands of Taipa and Colôane

area 7 sq mi/17 sq km
capital Macao, on the peninsula
features the peninsula is linked to Taipa by a bridge and to Colôane by a causeway, both 1 mi/2 km long
currency pataca
population (1986) 426,000
language Cantonese; Portuguese (official)
religion Buddhist, with 6% Catholic minority.
government Under the constitution ("organic statute") of 1990, Macao enjoys political autonomy. Executive power is held by the governor. The governor works with a cabinet of five appointed secretaries and confers with a 10-member consultative council and a 23-member legislative council, comprising seven government appointees, eight indirectly elected by business associations and eight directly elected by universal suffrage. The legislative council frames internal legislation, but any bills passed by less than a two-thirds majority can be vetoed by the governor. A number of "civic associations" and interest groups function, sending representatives to the legislative council.
history Macao was first established as a Portuguese trading and missionary post in the Far East 1537, and was leased from China 1557. It was annexed 1849 and recognized as a Portuguese colony by the Chinese government in a treaty 1887. The port declined in prosperity during the late 19th and early 20th centuries, as its harbor silted up and international trade was diverted to Hong Kong and the new treaty ports. The colony thus concentrated instead on local "country trade" and became a center for gambling and, later, tourism.

In 1951 Macao became an overseas province of Portugal, sending an elected representative to the Lisbon parliament. After the Portuguese revolution 1974, it became a "special territory" and was granted considerable autonomy under a governor appointed by the Portuguese president.

In 1986 negotiations opened between the Portuguese and the Chinese governments over the question of the return of Macao's sovereignty under "one country, two systems" terms similar to those agreed by China and the UK for ⟂Hong Kong. These negotiations were concluded April 1987 by the signing of the Macao Pact, under which Portugal agreed to hand over sovereignty to the People's Republic Dec 1999, and China agreed in return to guarantee to maintain the port's capitalist economic and social system for at least 50 years.

In May 1990 administrative, economic, and financial autonomy were secured from Portugal; this followed the approval of a new "organic statute" for the territory by both Portugal's parliament and Macao's legislative assembly. In Jan 1991 Macao acceded to GATT (the General Agreement on Tariffs and Trade).

macaque Old World monkey of the genus *Macaca*. Various species of these medium-sized monkeys live in forests from the Far East to N Africa. The ⟂rhesus monkey and the ⟂Barbary ape are part of this group.

Macaques range from long-tailed to tailless types, and have well-developed cheek pouches to carry food.

MacArthur Douglas 1880–1964. US general in World War II, commander of US forces in the Far East and, from March 1942, of the Allied forces in the SW Pacific. After the surrender of Japan he commanded the Allied occupation forces there. During 1950 he commanded the UN forces in Korea, but in April 1951, after

expressing views contrary to US and UN policy, he was relieved of all his commands by President Truman.

Born in Little Rock, Arkansas, the son of an army officer, MacArthur graduated first in his class at West Point 1903, had a distinguished combat record in World War I, and rose to become chief of staff 1930–35. He defended the Philippines against the Japanese 1941–42 and escaped to Australia when his small force was overwhelmed and he was forced to surrender. He vowed at the time, "I shall return." He was responsible for the reconquest of New Guinea 1942–45 and of the Philippines 1944–45, being appointed General of the Army 1944. He retired from the army, but when North Korea crossed the 38th parallel and invaded South Korea 1950, he was asked to command UN forces to support the South's sovereignty. After a surprise landing at Inchon forced the North Koreans to retreat, MacArthur invaded the North until beaten back by Chinese troops. After he was removed from command, he received a hero's welcome on his return to the US.

Macassar another name for ⟂Ujung Pandang, port in the Celebes (Sulawesi), Indonesia.

Macaulay Thomas Babington, Baron Macaulay 1800–1859. English historian, essayist, poet, and politician, secretary of war 1839–41. His *History of England* in five volumes 1849–61 celebrates the Glorious Revolution of 1668 as the crowning achievement of the Whig party.

His works include an essay on Milton 1825 published in the *Edinburgh Review*; a volume of verse, *Lays of Ancient Rome* 1842; and the *History of England* covering the years up to 1702.

macaw any of various large, brilliantly colored, long-tailed tropical American ⟂parrots, especially the genus *Ara*.

Macbeth died 1057. King of Scotland from 1040. The son of Findlaech, hereditary ruler of Moray, he was commander of the forces of Duncan I, King of Scotia, whom he killed in battle 1040. His reign was prosperous until Duncan's son Malcolm III led an invasion and killed him at Lumphanan.

Macbeth tragedy by William Shakespeare, first performed 1605–06. Acting on a prophecy by three witches that he will be king of Scotland, Macbeth, egged on by Lady Macbeth, murders King Duncan and becomes king but is eventually killed by Macduff. The play was based on the 16th-century historian ⟂Holinshed's *Chronicles*.

Maccabee or *Hasmonaean* member of an ancient Hebrew family founded by the priest Mattathias (died 166 BC) who, with his sons, led the struggle for independence against the Syrians in the 2nd century BC. Judas (died 161) reconquered Jerusalem 164 BC, and Simon (died 135) established its independence 142 BC. The revolt of the Maccabees lasted until the capture of Jerusalem by the Romans 63 BC. The story is told in four books of the ⟂Apocrypha.

McCarran Patrick 1876–1954. US Democrat politician. He became senator from Nevada 1932, and as an isolationist strongly opposed ⟂lend-lease during World War II. He sponsored the McCarran–Walter Immigration and Nationality Act of 1952, which severely restricted entry and immigration to the US; the act was amended 1965.

McCarthy Eugene (Joseph) 1916– . US politician. Active in the Democratic-Farmer-Labor party, he was elected to the US House of Representatives 1948 and to the US Senate 1958. An early opponent of the Vietnam War, he ran for president 1968. Although his upset victory in the New Hampshire primary forced incumbent L B Johnson out of the race, McCarthy lost the Democratic nomination to Hubert Humphrey.

Born in Watkins, Minnesota, McCarthy received a master's degree in economics from the University of Minnesota. After another unsuccessful bid for the presidency in 1972, he returned to private life, concentrating on writing and lecturing.

McCarthy Joe (Joseph Raymond) 1908–1957. US right-wing Republican politician. His unsubstantiated claim 1950 that the State Department and US army had been infiltrated by communists started a wave of anticommunist hysteria, wild accusations, and blacklists, which continued until he was discredited 1954. He was censured by the US senate for misconduct.

A lawyer, McCarthy became senator from his native Wisconsin 1946, and in Feb 1950 caused a sensation by claiming to hold a list of about 200 Communist Party members working in the State Department. This was in part inspired by the Alger ◊Hiss case. McCarthy continued a witch-hunting campaign against, among others, members of the ◊Truman administration. When he turned his attention to the army, and it was shown that he and his aides had been falsifying evidence, President ◊Eisenhower renounced him and his tactics. By this time, however, many people in public life and the arts had been unofficially blacklisted as suspected communists or fellow travelers (communist sympathizers). McCarthyism came to represent the practice of using innuendo and unsubstantiated accusations against political adversaries.

McCarthy Mary (Therese) 1912–1989. US novelist and critic. Much of her work looks probingly and scathingly at US society, including the satirical novel *The Groves of Academe* 1952, which describes the early anticommunist "witch hunts" of the era, and *The Group* 1963 (film 1966), her best-known novel, which follows the lives of eight Vassar graduates into their thirties.

Born in Seattle, Washington, McCarthy graduated from Vassar 1933 and was a book reviewer for *The Nation* and *The New Republic*. She also wrote *A Charmed Life* 1955, *Venice Observed* 1956, *The Stones of Florence* 1959, *Vietnam* 1967, *Hanoi* 1968, *Mask of State: Watergate Portraits* 1974, and *Cannibals and Missionaries* 1979. Her short stories are collected in *The Company She Keeps* 1942 and *Cast a Cold Eye* 1950.

McCartney Paul 1942– . UK rock singer, songwriter, and bass guitarist; former member of the ◊Beatles, and leader of the pop group Wings 1971–81. His subsequent solo hits have included collaborations with Michael Jackson and Elvis Costello. Together with composer Carl Davis, McCartney wrote the *Liverpool Oratorio* 1991, his first work of Classical music.

McCauley Mary Ludwig Hays ("Molly Pitcher") 1754–1832. American Revolutionary War heroine, born in Trenton, New Jersey. After working as a domestic servant, she married a local man, John Hays, who joined an artillery company in the 7th Pennsylvania Regiment at the outbreak of the American Revolution. Accompanying her husband to the Battle of Monmouth 1778, she faithfully brought water in a pitcher to the artillerymen during the heat

of the battle, thus gaining her nickname. When her husband became incapacitated, she took over one of the field pieces herself. In recognition of her valor, the Pennsylvania General Assembly awarded her a lifetime annuity.

McClellan George Brinton 1826–1885. American Civil War general, the first general in chief of the Union forces 1861–62. He was dismissed twice by President Lincoln, for various delays in following up and attacking the Confederate army. Early in the Civil War he was replaced by General John Pope, but after the rout at the Second Battle of ◊Bull Run, Lincoln asked McClellan to rebuild and reorganize the Union's Army of the Potomac. He saved Washington, DC, from the threatening Confederate forces but delayed his offense until the opportunity was lost. He was dismissed again at this point, ran unsuccessfully for the presidency against Lincoln on the Democratic ticket 1864, and became governor of New Jersey 1878–81.

McClellan was born in Philadelphia, went to West Point, then served with distinction in the Mexican War. He then worked surveying for the railroads moving west and as a railroad executive until the Civil War.

McClintock Barbara 1902– . US geneticist who worked at the Carnegie Institute, Cold Spring Harbor, New York, in the early days of chromosome mapping, and made some important contributions. She was awarded a Nobel Prize 1983.

McCormick Cyrus Hall 1809–1884. US inventor of the reaping machine 1831, which revolutionized 19th-century agriculture.

MacCready Paul 1925– . US designer of the *Gossamer Condor* aircraft, which made the first controlled flight by human power alone 1977. His *Solar Challenger* flew from Paris to London under solar power, and in 1985 he constructed a powered model of a giant pterosaur, an extinct flying animal.

McCullers Carson (Smith) 1917–1967. US novelist. Most of her writing, including her novels *The Heart is a Lonely Hunter* 1940 and *Reflections in a Golden Eye* 1941, is set in the South, where she was born, and deals with spiritual isolation, containing elements of sometimes macabre violence.

Her novel *A Member of the Wedding* 1946 was made into a successful stage play and film.

Macdonald George 1824–1905. Scottish novelist and children's writer. *David Elginbrod* 1863 and *Robert Falconer* 1868 are characteristic novels but his children's stories, including *At the Back of the North Wind* 1871 and *The Princess and the Goblin* 1872, are today more often read. Mystical imagination pervades all his books and this inspired later writers including G K Chesterton, C S Lewis, and J R R Tolkien.

McDonald (James) Ramsay 1866–1937. British politician, first Labour prime minister Jan–Oct 1924 and 1929–31. Failing to deal with worsening economic conditions, he left the party to form a coalition government 1931, which was increasingly dominated by Conservatives, until he was replaced by Stanley Baldwin 1935.

MacDonald joined the ◊Independent Labour Party 1894, and became first secretary of the new Labour Party 1900. In Parliament he led the party 1906–14 and 1922–31 and was prime minister of the first two Labour governments.

Macdonald John Alexander 1815–1891. Canadian Conservative politician, prime minister 1867–73 and 1878–91. He was born in Glasgow but taken to Ontario as a child. In 1857 he became prime minister of Upper Canada. He took the leading part in the movement for federation, and in 1867 became the first prime minister of Canada. He was defeated 1873 but returned to office 1878 and retained it until his death.

McDonald Observatory observatory of the University of Texas on Mount Locke, Texas. It is the site of a 2.72-m/107-in reflector opened 1969 and a 2.08-m/82-in reflector opened 1939.

Macdonnell Ranges mountain range in central Australia, Northern Territory, with the town of Alice Springs; highest peak Mount Zeil 4,955 ft/1,510 m.

MacDowell Edward Alexander 1860–1908. US Romantic composer, influenced by ◊Liszt. His works include the *Indian Suite* 1896 and piano concertos and sonatas.

Returning to the US after several years in Germany, he played his *Second Piano Concerto in D Minor* 1889, his most successful longer work, in New York City. He was one of the first US composers to receive international acclaim. MacDowell was at his best with short, lyrical piano pieces, such as "To a Wild Rose" from *Woodland Sketches* 1896.

Macedonia ancient region of Greece, forming parts of modern Greece, Bulgaria, and Yugoslavia. Macedonia gained control of Greece after Philip II's victory at Chaeronea 338 BC. His son, ◊Alexander the Great, conquered a vast empire. Macedonia became a Roman province 146 BC.

Macedonia (Greek *Makedhonia*) mountainous region of N Greece, part of the ancient country of Macedonia which was divided between Serbia, Bulgaria, and Greece after the Balkan Wars of 1912–13. Greek Macedonia is bounded to the west and north by Albania and Yugoslavia; area 13,200 sq mi/34,177 sq km; population (1991) 2,263,000. The chief city is Thessaloniki. Fertile valleys produce grain, olives, grapes, tobacco, and livestock. Mount Olympus rises to 9,570 ft/2,918 m on the border with Thessaly.

Macedonia (Serbo-Croatian *Makedonija*) federal republic of Yugoslavia
area 9,920 sq mi/25,700 sq km
capital Skopje
physical mountainous; rivers: Struma, Vardar
population (1981) 2,040,000, 63% Macedonians, 19% Albanians, 4% Turks
language Macedonian, closely allied to Bulgarian and written in Cyrillic
religion Macedonian Orthodox Christian
history the former ancient country of Macedonia was settled by Slavs in the 6th century; conquered by Bulgars in the 7th century, by Byzantium 1014, by Serbia in the 14th century, and by the Ottoman Empire 1355; divided between Serbia, Bulgaria, and Greece after the Balkan Wars of 1912–13. Macedonia was united 1918 in what later became Yugoslavia, but nationalist demands for autonomy persisted. During World War II it was occupied by Bulgaria 1941–44. After increasing tensions between ethnic Macedonians and the Serb-dominated Yugoslav government, the republic declared its independence from Yugoslavia 1992. EC leaders, at Greece's behest, declined in June to recognize the breakaway republic unless it agreed to a name change, on the

grounds that its name implies a territorial claim on the northern Greek province of Macedonia.

Macedonian person of Macedonian culture from Macedonia (Yugoslavia) and the surrounding area, especially Greece, Albania, and Bulgaria. Macedonian, a Slavic language belonging to the Indo-European family, has 1–1.5 million speakers. The Macedonians are predominantly members of the Greek Orthodox Church and write with a Cyrillic script. They are known for their folk arts.

McEnroe John Patrick 1959– . US tennis player whose brash behavior and fiery temper on court dominated the men's game in the early 1980s. He was three times winner of Wimbledon 1981 and 1983–84. He also won three successive US Open titles 1979–81 and again in 1984. A fine doubles player, McEnroe also won ten Grand Slam titles, seven in partnership with Peter Flemming.

McGinley Phyllis 1905–1978. Canadian-born US writer of light verse. She was a contributor to *The New Yorker* magazine and published many collections of social satire. Her works include *One More Manhattan* 1937 and *The Love Letters of Phyllis McGinley* 1954.

McGovern George (Stanley) 1922– . US politician, a Democrat. He was elected to the US House of Representatives 1956, served as an adviser to the Kennedy administration, and was a US senator 1962–80. He campaigned briefly for his party's presidential nomination 1968 and won the nomination 1972, but was soundly defeated by incumbent Richard Nixon.

McGovern was born in Avon, South Dakota. He served as a combat pilot during World War II and received a PhD in history from Northwestern University 1953. McGovern was defeated for reelection to the Senate 1980 and retired to a career of lecturing and writing.

McGraw John Joseph 1873–1934. US baseball manager. Born in Truxton, New York, McGraw began his career 1891 as an infielder with the Baltimore Orioles. He had a successful career with the team (which joined the National League 1892) and became its manager 1899. McGraw became player-manager of the New York Giants 1902 and in this dual capacity led the team to two National League pennants and a World Series championship. After retiring as a player 1906, he managed the Giants to eight more pennants and two world championships. He was elected to the Baseball Hall of Fame 1937.

McGuffey William Holmes 1800–1873. US educator. In 1825 he joined the faculty of Miami University, where he lectured on philosophy and became interested in the issue of public-school reform. McGuffey served as the president of Cincinnati College 1836–39 and Ohio University 1839–45 and as professor at the University of Virginia 1845–73. He is best remembered for his series of reading textbooks, the *Eclectic Readers*, which became standard throughout the US in the 19th century.

Born in Claysville, Pennsylvania, and raised in Ohio, McGuffey attended Washington and Jefferson College.

Mach Ernst 1838–1916. Austrian philosopher and physicist. He was an empiricist, believing that science is a record of facts perceived by the senses, and that acceptance of a scientific law depends solely on its standing the practical test of use; he opposed concepts such as Newton's "absolute motion." He researched airflow, and ⬦Mach numbers are named after him.

Machado de Assis Joaquim Maria 1839–1908. Brazilian writer and poet, regarded as the greatest Brazilian novelist. His skeptical, ironic wit is well displayed in his 30 volumes of novels and short stories, including *Epitaph for a Small Winner* 1880 and *Dom Casmurro* 1900.

Machaut Guillame de 1300–1377. French poet and composer. Born in Champagne, he was in the service of John of Bohemia for 30 years and, later, of King John the Good of France. He gave the forms of the *ballade* and *rondo* a new individuality and ensured their lasting popularity. His *Messe de Nostre Dame* about 1360, written for Reims Cathedral, is an early masterpiece of *ars nova*, "new (musical) art," exploiting unusual rhythmic complexities.

Machel Samora 1933–1986. Mozambique nationalist leader, president 1975–86. Machel was active in the liberation front ⬦Frelimo from its conception 1962, fighting for independence from Portugal. He became Frelimo leader 1966, and Mozambique's first president from independence 1975 until his death in a plane crash near the South African border.

Machiavelli Niccolò 1469–1527. Italian politician and author whose name is synonymous with cunning and cynical statecraft. In his most celebrated political writings, *Il principe/ The Prince* 1513 and *Discorsi/Discourses* 1531, he discussed ways in which rulers can advance the interests of their states (and themselves) through an often amoral and opportunistic manipulation of other people.

Machiavelli was born in Florence and was second chancellor to the republic 1498–1512. On the accession to power of the ⬦Medici 1512, he was arrested and imprisoned on a charge of conspiracy, but in 1513 was released to exile in the country. *The Prince*, based on his observations of Cesare ⬦Borgia, is a guide for the future prince of a unified Italian state (which did not occur until the Risorgimento in the 19th century). In *L'Arte della guerra/The Art of War* 1520 Machiavelli outlined the provision of an army for the prince, and in *Historie fiorentine/History of Florence* he analyzed the historical development of Florence until 1492. Among his later works are the comedies *Clizia* 1515 and *La Mandragola/The Mandrake* 1524.

machine device that allows a small force (the effort) to overcome a larger one (the load). There are three basic machines: the inclined plane (ramp), the lever, and the wheel and axle. All other machines are combinations of these three basic types. Simple machines derived from the inclined plane include the wedge and the screw; the spanner is derived from the lever; the pulley from the wheel.

The two principal features of a machine are its ⬦mechanical advantage, which is the ratio of load to effort, and its ⬦efficiency, which is the work done by the load divided by the work done by the effort; the latter is expressed as a percentage. In a perfect machine, with no friction, the efficiency would be 100%. All practical machines have efficiencies of less than 100%, otherwise perpetual motion would be possible.

machine code in computing, a set of instructions that a computer's central processing unit (CPU) can understand and obey directly, without any translation. Each type of CPU has its own machine code. Because machine-code programs consist entirely of binary digits (bits), most programmers write their programs in an easy-to-use ⬦high-level language. A high-level program must be translated into

machine code -by means of a ⬦compiler or ⬦interpreter program -before it can be executed by a computer.

machine gun rapid-firing automatic gun. The Maxim (named after its inventor, US-born British engineer H S Maxim (1840–1916)) of 1884 was recoil-operated, but some later types have been gas-operated (Bren) or recoil assisted by gas (some versions of the Browning).

The forerunner of the modern machine gun was the Gatling (named after its US inventor R J Gatling 1818–1903), perfected in the US in 1860 and used in the Civil War. It had a number of barrels arranged about a central axis, and the breech containing the reloading, ejection, and firing mechanism was rotated by hand, shots being fired through each barrel in turn.

The **sub-machine-gun**, exploited by Chicago gangsters in the 1920s, was widely used in World War II; for instance, the Thompson, often called the Tommy gun. See ⬦small arms.

machine politics organization of a local political party to ensure its own election by influencing the electorate, and then to retain power through control of key committees and offices. The idea of machine politics was epitomized in the US in the late 19th century, where it was used to control individual cities, most notably Chicago and New York.

machine tool automatic or semiautomatic power-driven machine for cutting and shaping metals. Machine tools have powerful electric motors to force cutting tools into the metal: these are made from hardened steel containing heat-resistant metals such as tungsten and chromium. The use of precision machine tools in ⬦mass-production assembly methods ensures that all duplicate parts produced are virtually identical.

Many machine tools now work under computer control and are employed in factory ⬦automation. The most common machine tool is the ⬦lathe, which shapes shafts and similar objects. A ⬦milling machine cuts metal with a rotary toothed cutting wheel. Other machine tools cut, plane, grind, drill, and polish.

Mach number ratio of the speed of a body to the speed of sound in the undisturbed medium through which the body travels. Mach 1 is reached when a body (such as an aircraft) has a velocity greater than that of sound ("passes the sound barrier"), namely 1,087 ft/331 m per second at sea level. It is named after Austrian physicist Ernst Mach (1838–1916).

Machtpolitik (German) power politics.

Machu Picchu ruined Inca city in Peru, built about AD 1500, NW of Cuzco, discovered 1911 by Hiram Bingham. It stands at the top of cliffs 1,000 ft/300 m high and contains the well-preserved remains of houses and temples.

Macias Nguema former name (until 1979) of ⬦Bioko, an island of Equatorial Guinea in the Bight of Bonny, W Africa.

Macintosh range of microcomputers produced by Apple Computers. The Apple Macintosh, introduced in 1984, was the first popular microcomputer with a ⬦graphical user interface.

The success of the Macintosh prompted other manufacturers and software companies to create their own graphic user interfaces. Most notable of these are **Presentation Manager**, which is part of the IBM OS/2 operating system, and **Windows**, produced for IBM microcomputers by the software company Microsoft.

Macintosh Charles 1766–1843. Scottish manufacturing chemist who invented a waterproof fabric, lined with rubber, that was used for raincoats—hence *mackintosh*. Other waterproofing processes have now largely superseded this method.

Mack Connie. Adopted name of Cornelius McGillicuddy 1862–1956. US baseball manager who led the Philadelphia Athletics ("A's") 1901–51. He began his professional baseball career as a catcher 1883 and became player-manager of the Pittsburgh Pirates 1894. With the establishment of the American League 1901, Mack invested his own money in the A's and became the team's first manager. In his record 50 years with the A's, he led the team to nine American League pennants and five World Series championships. Mack was born in East Brookfield, Massachusetts. He was elected to the Baseball Hall of Fame 1939.

Macke August 1887–1914. German Expressionist painter, a founding member of the ◊Blaue Reiter group in Munich. With Franz ◊Marc he developed a semiabstract style comprising Cubist and Fauve characteristics. He was killed in World War I.

Macke visited Paris 1907. In 1909 he met Marc, and together they went to Paris 1912, where they encountered the abstract style of Robert Delaunay. In 1914 Macke visited Tunis with Paul ◊Klee, and was inspired to paint a series of brightly colored watercolors largely composed of geometrical shapes but still representational.

Mackenzie Alexander c. 1755–1820. British explorer and fur trader. In 1789, he was the first European to see the river, now part of N Canada, named after him. In 1792–93 he crossed the Rocky Mountains to the Pacific coast of what is now British Columbia, making the first known crossing north of Mexico.

He was knighted in 1807.

Mackenzie Compton 1883–1972. Scottish author. He published his first novel *The Passionate Elopement* 1911. Later works were *Carnival* 1912, *Sinister Street* 1913–14 (an autobiographical novel), and the comic *Whisky Galore* 1947. He published his autobiography in ten "octaves" (volumes) 1963–71.

His parents were actors. He was educated at Oxford University.

Mackenzie William Lyon 1795–1861. Canadian politician, born in Scotland. He emigrated to Canada 1820, and led the rebellion of 1837–38, an unsuccessful attempt to limit British rule and establish more democratic institutions in Canada. After its failure he lived in the US until 1849, and in 1851–58 sat in the Canadian legislature as a Radical. He was grandfather of W L Mackenzie King, the Liberal prime minister.

Mackenzie River river in the Northwest Territories, flowing NW from Great Slave Lake to the Arctic Ocean; about 1,120 mi/ 1,800 km long. It is the main channel of the Finlay-Peace-Mackenzie system, 2,635 mi/ 4,241 km long.

It was named after the British explorer Alexander Mackenzie, who saw it 1789.

mackerel any of various fishes of the mackerel family Scombroidia, especially the common mackerel *Scomber Scombrus* found in the N Atlantic and Mediterranean. It weighs about

1.5 lb/0.7 kg, and is blue with irregular black bands down its sides, the latter and the under surface showing a metallic sheen. Like all mackerels, it has a deeply forked tail, and a sleek, streamlined body form.

The largest of the mackerels is the tuna, which weighs up to 1,550 lb/700 kg.

McKinley William 1843–1901. 25th president of the US 1897–1901, a Republican. His term as president was marked by the US's adoption of an imperialist policy, as exemplified by the Spanish-American War 1898 and the annexation of the Philippines. He was first elected to Congress 1876. He was assassinated.

McKinley was born in Niles, Ohio, and became a lawyer. Throughout his political life, he was a trusted friend of business interests, supporting high tariffs for fledgling US industries. He sat in the House of Representatives 1877–83 and 1885–91, and was governor of Ohio 1892–96. As president he presided over a period of prosperity and was drawn into foreign conflicts largely against his will. He annexed the Philippine Islands and implemented the ◊open-door policy with China. He was assassinated in Buffalo, New York, and was succeeded by Theodore Roosevelt.

McKinley, Mount or *Denali* peak in Alaska, the highest in North America, 20,320 ft/ 6,194 m; named after US president William McKinley.

The summit was first reached in 1913 by the Anglo-American explorer Hudson Stuck and three others. Mount McKinley, called Denali, "the high one," by the Indians, rises in the enlarged and renamed (1980) Denali National Park. See ◊Rocky Mountains.

MacLaine Shirley. Adopted name of Shirley MacLean Beatty 1934– . Versatile US actress whose films include Alfred Hitchcock's *The Trouble with Harry* 1955 (her debut), *The Apartment* 1960, and *Terms of Endearment* 1983, for which she won an Academy Award.

MacLaine trained as a dancer and has played in musicals, comedy, and dramatic roles. Her many offscreen interests (politics, writing) have limited her film appearances, which include *Some Came Running* 1958 and *The Turning Point* 1977. She is the sister of Warren Beatty.

Maclean Alistair 1922–1987. Scottish adventure novelist whose first novel, *HMS Ulysses* 1955, was based on wartime experience. It was followed by *The Guns of Navarone* 1957 and other adventure novels. Many of his books were made into films.

Maclean Donald 1913–1983. British spy who worked for the USSR while in the UK civil service. He defected to the USSR 1951 together with Guy ◊Burgess.

Maclean, brought up in a strict Presbyterian family, was educated at Cambridge, where he was recruited by the Soviet ◊KGB. He worked for the UK Foreign Office in Washington 1944 and then Cairo 1948 before returning to London, becoming head of the American Department at the Foreign Office 1950.

McLean John 1785–1861. US Supreme Court justice. Appointed postmaster general by President Monroe 1823, McLean reorganized the post office department, eliminating much corruption and waste. In 1829 he was appointed to the US Supreme Court by President Jackson. During his Court tenure, McLean was an outspoken abolitionist, writing a passionate dissent in the Dred Scott Case 1857.

McLean was born in Morris County, New Jersey, and raised in Ohio; he studied law in Cincinnati and was admitted to the bar 1807. After editing a local newspaper, he served in the US Congress 1813–16 and as a judge on the Ohio Supreme Court 1816–22.

MacLeish Archibald 1892–1982. US poet. He made his name with the long narrative poem "Conquistador" 1932, which describes Cortés's march to the Aztec capital, but his later plays in verse, *Panic* 1935 and *Air Raid* 1938, deal with contemporary problems.

Born in Illinois, he went to France 1923, and during his expatriate years there published his most personal poetry, including "Ars Poetica" 1926. He was assistant secretary of state 1944–45, and helped to draft the constitution of UNESCO. From 1949 to 1962 he was Boylston Professor of Rhetoric at Harvard, and his essays in *Poetry and Opinion* 1950 reflect his feeling that a poet should be "committed," expressing his outlook in his verse.

McLuhan (Herbert) Marshall 1911–1980. Canadian theorist of communication, famed for his views on the effects of technology on modern society. He coined the phrase "the medium is the message," meaning that the form rather than the content of information has become crucial. His works include *The Gutenberg Galaxy* 1962 (in which he coined the phrase "the global village" for the worldwide electronic society then emerging), *Understanding Media* 1964, and *The Medium Is the Massage* (sic) 1967.

MacMahon Marie Edmé Patrice Maurice, Comte de 1808–1893. Marshal of France. Captured at Sedan 1870 during the Franco-Prussian War, he suppressed the ◊Paris Commune after his release, and as president of the republic 1873–79 worked for a royalist restoration until forced to resign.

Macmillan (Maurice) Harold, 1st Earl of Stockton 1894–1986. British Conservative politician, prime minister 1957–63; foreign secretary 1955 and chancellor of the Exchequer 1955–57. In 1963 he attempted to negotiate British entry into the European Economic Community, but was blocked by French president de Gaulle. Much of his career as prime minister was spent defending the retention of a UK nuclear weapon, and was responsible for the purchase of US Polaris missiles 1962.

Macmillan was MP for Stockton 1924–29 and 1931–45, and for Bromley 1945–64. As minister of housing 1951–54 he achieved the construction of 300,000 new houses a year. He became prime minister on the resignation of Anthony ◊Eden after the Suez crisis, and led the Conservative Party to victory in the 1959 elections on the slogan "You've never had it so good" (the phrase was borrowed from a US election campaign). Internationally, his realization of the "wind of change" in Africa advanced the independence of former colonies. Macmillan's nickname Supermac was coined by the cartoonist Vicky.

McMillan Edwin Mattison 1907– . US physicist. In 1940 he discovered neptunium, the first ◊transuranic element, by bombarding uranium with neutrons. He shared a Nobel Prize with Glenn ◊Seaborg 1951 for their discovery of transuranic elements. In 1943 he developed a method of overcoming the limitations of the cyclotron, the first ◊accelerator, for which he shared, 20 years later, an Atoms for Peace award with I Veksler, director of the Soviet Joint Institute for Nuclear Research, who had come to the same discovery independently. McMillan was a professor at the University of California 1946–73.

McMurtry Larry (Jeff) 1936– . US writer. Born in Wichita Falls, Texas, he wrote about the Southwest—in particular, his home state of Texas. Many of his novels were made into films. His works include *Horseman, Pass By* 1961 (film *Hud* 1963), *Leaving Cheyenne* 1963 (film *Lovin' Molly* 1963), *The Last Picture Show* 1966 (film 1971), *Moving On* 1970, *All My Friends Are Going To Be Strangers* 1972, *Terms of Endearment* 1975 (film 1983; Academy Award for Best Picture), *Somebody's Darling* 1978, *Cadillac Jack* 1982, *The Desert Rose* 1983, *Lonesome Dove* 1985 (Pulitzer Prize 1986; TV miniseries 1989), *Texasville* 1987, and *Buffalo Girls* 1990. He also wrote a book of essays, *In a Narrow Grave* 1968.

Macon city in central Georgia, on the Ocmulgee River, NE of Columbus; seat of Bibb County; population (1990) 106,600. An industrial city, Macon produces textiles, building materials, farm machinery, and chemicals; it processes fruits, pecans, and the special kaolin clay that is found nearby.

McPartland Jimmy (James Duigald) 1907–1991. US cornet player, one of the founders of the Chicago school of jazz in the 1920s. He was influenced by Louis Armstrong and Bix Beiderbecke, whom he replaced in a group called the Wolverines 1924. He also recorded with the guitarist Eddie Condon, and from the late 1940s often worked with his wife, the British pianist Marian McPartland (1920–).

McPhee Colin 1900–1964. US composer whose studies of Balinese music 1934–36 produced two works, *Tabuh-tabuhan* for two pianos and orchestra 1936 and *Balinese Ceremonial Music* for two pianos 1940, which influenced John ⏾Cage and later generations of US composers.

McPherson Aimee Semple 1890–1944. Canadian-born US religious leader. As a popular preacher, "Sister Aimee" reached millions through radio broadcasts of her weekly sermons, in which she emphasized the power of faith. Her brief but suspicious 1926 "disappearance" tarnished her reputation; she committed suicide 1944.

Born in Ingersoll, Ontario, she worked as a missionary to China before becoming an itinerant evangelist in the US. Through revival tours, she gained a large following and eventually established the Church of the Four-Square Gospel in Los Angeles 1918.

Macquarie Island outlying Australian territorial possession, a Tasmanian dependency, some 850 mi/1,370 km SE of Hobart; area 65 sq mi/170 sq km; it is uninhabited except for an Australian government research station.

McQueen Steve (Terrence Steven) 1930–1980. US actor, a film star of the 1960s and 1970s, admired for his portrayals of the strong, silent loner, and noted for performing his own stunt work. After television success in the 1950s, he became a film star with *The Magnificent Seven* 1960. His films include *The Great Escape* 1963, *Bullitt* 1968, *Papillon* 1973, and *The Hunter* 1980.

macramé art of making decorative fringes and lacework with knotted threads. The name comes from the Arabic word for "striped cloth," which is often decorated in this way.

macro in computer programming, a new command created by combining a number of existing ones. For example, if a programming language has separate commands for obtaining data from the keyboard and for displaying data on the screen, the programmer might create a macro that performs both these tasks with one command. A *macro key* on the keyboard combines the effects of pressing several individual keys.

macrobiotics dietary system of organically grown foods. It originates in Zen Buddhism, and attempts to balance the principles of ⏾yin and yang, thought to be present in foods in different proportions.

macroeconomics division of economics concerned with the study of whole (aggregate) economies or systems, including such aspects as government income and expenditure, the balance of payments, fiscal policy, investment, inflation, and unemployment. It seeks to understand the influence of all relevant economic factors on each other and thus to quantify and predict aggregate national income.

Modern macroeconomics takes much of its inspiration from the work of Maynard Keynes, whose *General Theory of Employment, Interest, and Money* 1936 proposed that governments could prevent financial crises and unemployment by adjusting demand through control of credit and currency. *Keynesian macroeconomics* thus analyzes aggregate supply and demand and holds that markets do not continuously "clear" (quickly attain equilibrium between supply and demand) and may require intervention if objectives such as full employment are thought desirable. Keynesian macroeconomic formulations were generally accepted well into the postwar era and have been refined and extended by the *neo-Keynesian school*, which contends that in a recession the market will clear only very slowly and that full employment equilibrium may never return without significant demand management (by government). At the same time, however, *neo-classical economics* has experienced a recent resurgence, using tools from ⏾microeconomics to challenge the central Keynesian assumption that resources may be underemployed and that full employment equilibrium requires state intervention. Another important school is *new classical economics*, which seeks to show the futility of Keynesian demand-management policies and stresses instead the importance of *supply-side economics*, believing that the principal factor influencing growth of national output is the efficient allocation and use of labor and capital. A related school is that of the *Chicago monetarists*, led by Milton ⏾Friedman, who have revived the old idea that an increase in money supply leads inevitably to an increase in prices rather than in output; however, whereas the new Classical school contends that wage and price adjustment are almost instantaneous and so the level of employment at any time must be the natural rate, the Chicago monetarists are more gradualist, believing that such adjustment may take some years.

macromolecule in chemistry, a very large molecule, generally a ⏾polymer.

macrophage type of ⏾white blood cell, or leukocyte, found in all vertebrate animals. Macrophages specialize in the removal of bacteria and other microorganisms, or of cell debris after injury. Like phagocytes, they engulf foreign matter, but they are larger than

phagocytes and have a longer life span. They are found throughout the body, but mainly in the lymph and connective tissues, and especially the lungs, where they ingest dust, fibers, and other inhaled particles.

MAD abbreviation for *mutual assured destruction*; the basis of the theory of ⏾deterrence by possession of nuclear weapons.

Madagascar island country in the Indian Ocean, off the coast of E Africa, about 280 mi/400 km from Mozambique.

government The 1975 constitution provides for a single-chamber national people's assembly of 137 members, elected by universal suffrage for a five-year term, and a president elected in the same way for a seven-year term. The president appoints and chairs the Supreme Revolutionary Council (SRC), which acts as "the guardian of the Malagasy Socialist Revolution." A third of its members are nominated by the assembly, and the rest are chosen by the president, who is also secretary-general of the political organization that embraces all the various party factions: the National Front for the Defense of the Malagasy Socialist Revolution (FNDR). Power therefore ultimately lies with the president's party. For day-to-day administration, the president appoints a prime minister and a council of ministers.

history Madagascar was colonized over 2,000 years ago by Africans and Indonesians. They were joined from the 12th century by Muslim traders, and, from 1500, Europeans began to visit the island. Portuguese, Dutch, and English traders having given up, the French established a colony in the mid-17th century but fled after a massacre by local inhabitants. Madagascar was subsequently divided into small kingdoms until the late 18th century when, aided by traders and Christian missionaries, the Merina (the inhabitants of the highland area) united almost all the country under one ruler.

In 1885 the country was made a French protectorate, though French control was not complete until 20 years later.

independence Madagascar remained loyal to ⏾Vichy France during World War II, but it was taken by British forces 1942–43 and then handed over to the Free French. During the postwar period nationalist movements became active, and Madagascar became an autonomous state within the ⏾French Community 1958 and achieved full independence, as a republic, 1960. Its history since independence has been greatly influenced by the competing interests of its two main ethnic groups, the coastal people, or *cotiers*, and the highland Merina.

The first president of the republic was Philibert Tsiranana, leader of the Social Democratic Party (PSD), which identified itself with the *cotiers*. In 1972 the army, representing the Merina, took control of the government and pursued a more nationalistic line than Tsiranana. This caused resentment among the *cotiers* and, with rising unemployment, led to a government crisis 1975 that resulted in the imposition of martial law under a national military directorate and the banning of all political parties. Later that year a new, socialist constitution was approved and Lt-Comdr Didier Ratsiraka, a *cotier*, was elected president of the Democratic Republic of Madagascar. Political parties were permitted again and in 1976 the Front-Line Revolutionary Organization (AREMA) was formed by Ratsiraka as the nucleus of a single party for the state. By 1977 all political

Madagascar
Democratic Republic of (*Repoblika Demokratika n'i Madagaskar***)**

area 226,598 sq mi/587,041 sq km
capital Antananarivo
cities chief port Toamasina, Antseranana, Fianarantsoa, Toliary
physical temperate central highlands; humid valleys and tropical coastal plains; arid in S
environment according to 1990 UN figures, 93% of the forest area has been destroyed and about 100,000 species have been made extinct
features one of the last places to be inhabited, it evolved in isolation with unique animals (such as the lemur, now under threat from deforestation)
head of state Didier Ratsiraka from 1975
head of government Guy Razanamasy from 1991
political system emergent democratic republic
political parties National Front for the Defense of the Malagasy Socialist Revolution (FNDR);

AKFM-Congress and AKFM-Renewal, both left-of-center; Social Democratic Party (PSD), center-left
exports coffee, cloves, vanilla, sugar, chromite, shrimps
currency Malagasy franc
population (1990 est) 11,802,000, mostly of Malayo-Indonesian origin; growth rate 3.2% p.a.
life expectancy men 50, women 53 (1989)
languages Malagasy (official), French, English
religion animist 50%, Christian 40%, Muslim 10%
literacy 53% (1988)
GNP $2.1 bn (1987); $280 per head (1988)
chronology
1885 Became a French protectorate.
1896 Became a French colony.
1960 Independence achieved from France, with Philibert Tsiranana as president.
1972 Army took control of the government.
1975 Martial law imposed under a national military directorate. New Marxist constitution proclaimed the Democratic Republic of Madagascar, with Didier Ratsiraka as president.
1976 Front-Line Revolutionary Organization (AREMA) formed.
1977 National Front for the Defense of the Malagasy Socialist Revolution (FNDR) became the sole legal political organization.
1980 Ratsiraka abandoned Marxist experiment.
1983 Ratsiraka reelected, despite strong opposition from radical socialist National Movement for the Independence of Madagascar (MONIMA) under Monja Jaona.
1989 Ratsiraka reelected for third term after restricting opposition parties.
1990 Political opposition legalized; 36 new parties created.
1991 Antigovernment demonstrations; opposition to Ratsiraka led to general strike. Nov: Ratsiraka formed new unity government.
1992 Constitutional reform approved.

activity was concentrated in FNDR, and all the candidates for the national people's assembly were FNDR nominees.
social and political discontent In 1977 the National Movement for the Independence of Madagascar (MONIMA), a radical socialist party, withdrew from the FNDR and was declared illegal. MONIMA's leader, Monja Jaona, unsuccessfully challenged Ratsiraka for the presidency and, although his party did well in the capital, AREMA won an overwhelming victory in the 1983 elections. Despite this, social and political discontent has continued, particularly among the Merina, who have openly demonstrated their opposition to the government. President Ratsiraka was reelected with a 62% popular vote March 1989, and in May AREMA won 120 of the 137 assembly seats. Calls for a new constitution and democratic reforms were accompanied by strikes and demonstrations June 1991 and a demand for Ratsiraka's resignation.

Opposition forces formed an "alternative government" and in response Ratsiraka declared a state of emergency July 1991. Refusal by the opposition to accept the president's concessions resulted in violence and a declaration of "open war" Aug 1991 by the protesters. Discussions between President Ratsiraka and opposition representatives resulted in the appointment of Guy Razanamasy as prime minister and a widening of the prime minister's

powers. In Oct 1991 Ratsiraka, Razanamasy, and opposition representatives signed an agreement for a new unity government. In Nov 1991 it was announced that President Ratsiraka had formed a new unity government prior to the establishment of a third republic during the next 18 months. In a referendum Aug 1992 a new constitution, providing for multiparty elections, was approved. *See illustration box.*

madder any plant of the genus *Rubia* of the family Rubiaceae, bearing small funnel-shaped flowers, especially the perennial vine *Rubia tinctorum*, the red root of which yields a red dye called alizarin (now made synthetically from coal tar).

Madeira group of islands forming an autonomous region of Portugal off the NW coast of Africa, about 260 mi/420 km N of the Canary Islands. Madeira, the largest, and Porto Santo are the only inhabited islands. The Desertas and Selvagens are uninhabited islets. Their mild climate makes them a year-round resort
area 308 sq mi/796 sq km
capital Funchal, on Madeira
physical Pico Ruivo, on Madeira, is the highest mountain at 6,106 ft/1,861 m
products Madeira (a fortified wine), sugar cane, fruit, fish, handicrafts
population (1986) 269,500
history Portuguese from the 15th century; occupied by Britain 1801 and 1807–14. In 1980

Madeira gained partial autonomy but remains a Portuguese overseas territory.

Maderna Bruno 1920–1973. Italian composer and conductor. He studied with Gian Francesco ◊Malipiero and Hermann ◊Scherchen, and collaborated with Luciano ◊Berio in setting up an electronic studio in Milan. His compositions combine advanced techniques with an elegance of sound, and include a pioneering work for live and prerecorded flute, *Musica su due dimensioni* 1952, numerous concertos, and the aleatoric (involving random choice by the performers) *Aura* for orchestra 1974. *Hyperion* 1965, a "mobile opera," consists of a number of composed events that may be combined in several ways.

Madhya Bharat state of India 1950–56. It was a union of 24 states of which Gwalior and Indore were the most important. In 1956 Madhya Bharat was absorbed in ◊Madhya Pradesh.

Madhya Pradesh state of central India; the largest of the Indian states
area 170,921 sq mi/442,700 sq km
capital Bhopal
cities Indore, Jabalpur, Gwalior, Durg-Bhilainagar, Raipur, Ujjain
products cotton, oilseed, sugar, textiles, engineering, paper, aluminum
population (1991) 66,135,400
language Hindi
history formed 1950 from the former British province of Central Provinces and Berar and the princely states of Makrai and Chattisgarh; lost some SW districts 1956, including ◊Nagpur, and absorbed Bhopal, Madhya Bharat, and Vindhya Pradesh. In 1984 some 2,600 people died in ◊Bhopal from an escape of poisonous gas.

Madison capital of Wisconsin, 120 mi/193 km NW of Chicago, between lakes Mendota and Monona; products include agricultural machinery and medical equipment; population (1990) 191,300.

The main campus of the University of Wisconsin and the US Forest Products Laboratory are here. The city was founded 1836 as the territorial capital and named after James Madison, fourth president of the US.

Madison James 1751–1836. 4th president of the US 1809–17. In 1787 he became a member of the Philadelphia Constitutional Convention and took a leading part in drawing up the US Constitution and the Bill of Rights. He allied himself firmly with Thomas ◊Jefferson against Alexander ◊Hamilton in the struggle between the more democratic views of Jefferson and the aristocratic, upper-class sentiments of Hamilton. As secretary of state in Jefferson's government 1801–09, Madison completed the ◊Louisiana Purchase negotiated by James Monroe. During his period of office the War of 1812 with Britain took place.

Born in Port Conway, Virginia, Madison graduated from the College of New Jersey (now Princeton) 1771. During his presidential administration, the nation was unprepared for the War of 1812, and there were threats of secession by New England states. Madison had long been an articulate champion of the federal structure of government, and as president, as he had done as a member of the Constitutional Convention, he regarded promotion of the Union as his paramount task. Although the War of 1812 ended in stalemate, Madison's fortunes rose with the national expansion that followed.

Madonna Adopted name of Madonna Louise Veronica Ciccone 1958– . US pop singer and actress who presents herself on stage and in videos with an exaggerated sexuality. Her first hit was "Like a Virgin" 1984; others include "Material Girl" 1985 and "Like a Prayer" 1989. Her films include *Desperately Seeking Susan* 1985, *Dick Tracy* 1990, *In Bed with Madonna* 1991, and *A League of Their Own* 1992. Her book *Sex*, a collection of glossy, erotic photographs interspersed with explicit fantasies in the form of short stories, was published 1992, coinciding with the release of the dance album *Erotica*.

Madras industrial port (cotton, cement, chemicals, iron, and steel) and capital of Tamil Nadu, India, on the Bay of Bengal; population (1981) 4,277,000. Fort St George 1639 remains from the East India Company when Madras was the chief port on the east coast. Madras was occupied by the French 1746–48 and shelled by the German ship *Emden* 1914, the only place in India attacked in World War I.

Madras former name of ◊Tamil Nadu, state of India.

Madrid industrial city (leather, chemicals, furniture, tobacco, paper) and capital of Spain and of Madrid province; population (1991) 2,984,600. Built on an elevated plateau in the center of the country, at 2,183 ft/655 m it is the highest capital city in Europe and has excesses of heat and cold. Madrid province has an area of 3,088 sq mi/8,000 sq km and a population of 4,855,000. Madrid began as a Moorish citadel captured by Castile 1083, became important in the times of Charles V and Philip II, and was designated capital 1561.

Features include the Real Academia de Bellas Artes 1752, the Prado Museum 1785, and the royal palace 1764. During the Spanish Civil War, Madrid was besieged by the Nationalists Nov 7, 1936–March 28, 1939.

madrigal form of secular song in four or five parts, usually sung without instrumental accompaniment. It originated in 14th-century Italy. Madrigal composers include Andrea Gabrieli, ◊Monteverdi, Thomas ◊Morley, and Orlando Gibbons.

Madura island in Indonesia, off Surabaya, Java; one of the Sunda Islands.

Madurai city in Tamil Nadu, India; population (1981) 904,000. Founded in the 5th century BC, it is the site of the 16th–17th-century temple of Meenakshi. Industries include textiles (cotton) and brassware manufacturing.

Maeander anglicized form of the ancient Greek name of the river ◊Menderes in Turkey.

maelstrom whirlpool off the Lofoten Islands, Norway, also known as the Moskenesstraumen, which gave its name to whirlpools in general.

maenad in Greek mythology, one of the women participants in the orgiastic rites of ◊Dionysus; maenads were also known as *Bacchae*.

Maeterlinck Maurice, Count Maeterlinck 1862–1949. Belgian poet and dramatist. His plays include *Pelléas et Mélisande* 1892, *L'Oiseau bleu/The Blue Bird* 1908, and *Le Bourgmestre de Stilmonde/The Burgomaster of Stilemonde* 1918. This last celebrates Belgian resistance in World War I, a subject that led to his exile in the US 1940. Nobel Prize 1911.

Mafeking former name of ◊Mafikeng, town in South Africa, incorporated into Bophuthatswana 1980.

Mafia (Italian "swank") secret society reputed to control organized crime such as gambling, loansharking, drug traffic, prostitution, and protection; connected with the ◊Camorra of Naples. It originated in Sicily in the late Middle Ages and now operates chiefly there and in countries to which Italians have emigrated, such as the US and Australia.

It began as a society that avenged wrongs against Sicilian peasants by means of terror and ◊vendetta. In 19th-century Sicily the Mafia was employed by absentee landlords to manage their *latifundia* (landed estates), and through intimidation it soon became the unofficial ruling group. Despite the expropriation and division of the *latifundia* after World War II, the Mafia remains powerful in Sicily. The Italian government has waged periodic campaigns of suppression, notably 1927, when the Fascist leader Mussolini appointed Cesare Mori (1872–?) as prefect of Palermo. Mori's methods were, however, as suspect as those of the people he was arresting, and he was fired 1929. A further campaign was waged 1963–64.

The Mafia grew during ◊Prohibition in the US. Main centers are New York, Las Vegas, Miami, Atlantic City, and Chicago. Organization is in "families," each with its own boss, or *capo*. A code of loyalty and secrecy, combined with intimidation of witnesses, makes it difficult to bring criminal charges against its members. However, Al Capone was sentenced for federal tax evasion and Lucky Luciano was deported. Recent cases of the US government versus the Mafia implicated Sicilian-based operators in the drug traffic that plagues much of the Western world (the "pizza connection"). In 1992 John Gotti, reputedly head of the Gambino "family" of the Mafia, was convicted.

The Mafia, also known in the US as *La Cosa Nostra* ("our affair") or the Mob, features frequently in fiction; for example, in the *Godfather* films from 1972 based on a book by Mario Puzo.

Mafikeng former name (until 1980) *Mafeking* town in Bophuthatswana, South Africa. It was the capital of Bechuanaland, and the British officer Baden-Powell held it under Boer siege Oct 12, 1899–May 17, 1900.

magazine a periodical publication, typically containing articles, essays, reviews, illustrations, and advertising. It is thought that the first magazine was *Le Journal des savants*, published in France 1665. The earliest illustrations were wood engravings; the halftone process was invented 1882 and photogravure was used commercially from 1895. ◊Printing and paper-manufacturing techniques made great progress during the 19th century, making larger print runs possible. Advertising began to appear in magazines around 1800; it was a moderately important factor by 1850 and crucial to most magazines' finances by 1880. Specialty magazines for various interests and hobbies appeared in the 20th century. In the US, subscriptions account for the majority of magazine sales. In Europe, distribution and sales are largely through newsdealers' shops and stands.

history Among the first magazines in the US were Benjamin ◊Franklin's *Poor Richard's Almanac* 1732–57 and the short-lived *The American Magazine* 1741 and *General Magazine* 1741. By the 1800s the magazine industry was flourishing. *North American Review* began 1815. Around the time of the Civil War, such magazines as *Harper's Weekly*, *Harper's Monthly Magazine*, and *The Atlantic Monthly* were

published for the first time. At the beginning of the 1900s *The Nation* and *Illustrated Newspaper* began publication, and soon *The Ladies' Home Journal* and *The Saturday Evening Post* followed. *McClure's*, *Collier's*, and *Cosmopolitan* began as messengers of social reform, attacking government and business policies. The *Reader's Digest* was founded 1921, *Time* 1923, *The New Yorker* 1925, *Fortune* 1930, and *Life* 1936. The 1930s saw the rise of the photojournalism magazine and the introduction of color printing. The US pulp magazines of the 1930s and 1940s, specializing in crime fiction and science fiction, were breeding grounds for writers. The development of cheap offset litho printing made possible the flourishing of the underground press in much of the Western world in the 1960s, although it was limited by unorthodox distribution methods, such as street sales. Prosecutions and economic recession largely killed the underground press; the main survivor in the US is the rock-music magazine *Rolling Stone* 1968.

The *Reader's Digest*, with editions in many different countries and languages, is the world's best-selling magazine. *TV Guide* is the best-selling magazine in the US. The *Ladies' Home Journal*, first published in the late 1800s, led the way for women's magazines in the US. With magazines such as *McCall's*, *Women's Day*, *Ms*, *Good Housekeeping*, *Redbook*, *Vogue*, and *Family Circle*, women's magazines constitute the largest group.

Comic books are usually aimed at children, although in Japan, Latin America, and Europe millions of adults read them. Artistically sophisticated adult comics are produced in the US and several European countries, notably France. They developed from ◊comic strips in newspapers or, like those of Walt ◊Disney, as spinoffs from animated cartoon films. The first superhero, Superman, created 1938 by Jerome Siegel and Joseph Shuster, soon had his own monthly periodical, and others followed; the Marvel Comics group, formed 1961, was selling 50 million copies a year worldwide by the end of the 1960s and found a cult readership among college students for titles such as *Spiderman* and *The Incredible Hulk*.

Magdeburg industrial city (vehicles, paper, textiles, machinery) and capital of Saxony-Anhalt, Germany, on the river Elbe; population (1990) 290,000. A former capital of Saxony, Magdeburg became capital of Saxony-Anhalt on German reunification 1990. In 1938 the city was linked by canal with the Rhine and Ruhr rivers.

Magdeburg was a member of the Hanseatic League, and has a 13th-century Gothic cathedral. Magdeburg county has an area of 4,451 sq mi/11,530 sq km, and a population of 1,250,000.

Magellan Ferdinand 1480–1521. Portuguese navigator. In 1519 he set sail in the *Victoria* from Seville with the intention of reaching the East Indies by a westerly route. He sailed through the **Strait of Magellan** at the tip of South America, crossed an ocean he named the Pacific, and in 1521 reached the Philippines, where he was killed in a battle with the islanders. His companions returned to Seville 1522, completing the voyage under del Cano.

Magellan NASA space probe to ◊Venus, launched May 1989; it went into orbit around Venus Aug 1990 to make a detailed map of the planet by radar. It revealed volcanoes, meteorite craters, and fold mountains on the planet's surface.

Magellanic Clouds in astronomy, the two galaxies nearest to our own galaxy. They are irregularly shaped, and appear as detached parts of the ▷Milky Way, in the southern constellations Dorado and Tucana.

The Large Magellanic Cloud is 169,000 light-years from Earth, and about a third the diameter of our galaxy; the Small Magellanic Cloud, 180,000 light-years away, is about a fifth the diameter of our galaxy. They are named after the navigator Ferdinand Magellan, who first described them.

Magellan, Strait of channel between South America and Tierra del Fuego, named after the navigator Ferdinand ▷Magellan. It is 370 mi/595 km long, and joins the Atlantic and Pacific oceans.

Maggiore, Lago lake partly in Italy, partly in Swiss canton of Ticino, with Locarno on its N shore, 39 mi/63 km long and up to 5.5 mi/9 km wide (area 82 sq mi/212 sq km), with fine scenery.

maggot soft, plump, limbless larva of flies, a typical example being the larva of the blowfly which is deposited as an egg on flesh.

Maghreb name for NW Africa (Arabic "far west," "sunset"). The Maghreb powers—Algeria, Libya, Morocco, Tunisia, and Western Sahara—agreed on economic coordination 1964–65, with Mauritania cooperating from 1970. In 1989 these countries formed an economic union known as the Arab Maghreb Union. Chad and Mali are sometimes included. Compare ▷Mashraq, the Arab countries of the E Mediterranean.

magi priests of the Zoroastrian religion of ancient Persia, noted for their knowledge of astrology. The term is used in the New Testament of the Latin Vulgate Bible where the King James Version gives "wise men." The magi who came to visit the infant Jesus with gifts of gold, frankincense, and myrrh (the Adoration of the Magi) were in later tradition described as "the three kings"—Caspar, Melchior and Balthazar.

magic art of controlling the forces of nature by supernatural means such as charms and ritual. The central ideas are that like produces like (**sympathetic magic**) and that influence carries by contagion or association; for example, by the former principle an enemy could be destroyed through an effigy, by the latter principle through personal items such as hair or nail clippings. See also ▷witchcraft.

It is now generally accepted that most early religious practices and much early art were rooted in beliefs in magical processes. There are similarities between magic and the use of symbolism in religious ritual. Under Christianity existing magical rites were either suppressed (although they survived in modified form in folk custom and superstition) or replaced by those of the church itself. Those still practicing the ancient rites were persecuted as witches.

magic numbers in atomic physics certain numbers of ▷neutrons or ▷protons (2, 8, 20, 28, 50, 82, 126) in the nuclei of elements of outstanding stability, such as lead and helium. Such stability is the result of neutrons and protons being arranged in completed "layers" or "shells."

magic realism in 20th-century literature, a fantastic situation realistically treated, as in the works of many Latin American writers such as Isabel Allende, Jorge Luis ▷Borges, and Gabriel ▷García Márquez.

The technique of magic realism was pioneered in Europe by E T A Hoffman and Hermann Hesse. The term was coined in the 1920s to describe German paintings.

magic square in mathematics, a square array of different numbers in which the rows, columns, and diagonals add up to the same total. A simple example employing the numbers 1 to 9, with a total of 15, is:

$$\begin{array}{ccc} 6 & 7 & 2 \\ 1 & 5 & 9 \\ 8 & 3 & 4 \end{array}$$

Maginot Line French fortification system along the German frontier from Switzerland to Luxembourg built 1929–36 under the direction of the war minister, André Maginot. It consisted of semi underground forts joined by underground passages, and protected by antitank defenses; lighter fortifications continued the line to the sea. In 1940 German forces pierced the Belgian frontier line and outflanked the Maginot Line.

maglev (abbreviation for **magnetic levitation**) high-speed surface transport using the repellent force of superconductive magnets (see ▷superconductivity) to propel and support, for example, a train above a track. Maglev trains have been developed in Japan, where a Tokyo–Osaka line was being planned 1990, and in Germany. A ship launched in Japan 1990 was to be fitted with superconducting thrusters instead of propellers for sea trials 1991.

Technical trials on a maglev train track began in Japan in the 1970s, and a speed of 310 mph/500 kph has been reached, with a cruising altitude of 4 in/10 cm. The train is levitated by electromagnets and forward thrust is provided by linear motors aboard the cars, propelling the train along a reaction plate. A maglev train was being built by a Japanese company for local transport in Las Vegas, 1990. A subway line using maglev carriages began operating in Osaka, Japan, 1990. Maglevs use magnetic forces not to levitate but to propel them forward on rubber wheels, and have a maximum speed of 43 mph/70 kph. They use 30% more electricity than conventional trains but require less space, thus saving money on construction, and there is less wear on the rails and wheels.

Two cylindrical thrusters with electrodes and niobium-titanium superconducting coils, soaked in liquid helium, were to be placed under the Japanese passenger boat *Yamato 1* in 1991. The ship, 100 ft/30 m long, was designed to travel at 8 knots. An electric current passed through the magnetic fields would accelerate the sea water through the thrusters, like air through a jet engine, thus propelling the ship forward.

magma molten rock material beneath the Earth's surface from which ▷igneous rocks are formed. ▷Lava is magma that has reached the surface and solidified, losing some of its components on the way.

Magna Carta (Latin "great charter") in English history, the charter granted by King John 1215, traditionally seen as guaranteeing human rights against the excessive use of royal power. As a reply to the king's demands for excessive feudal dues and attacks on the privileges of the church, Archbishop Langton proposed to the barons the drawing-up of a binding document 1213. John was forced to accept this at Runnymede (now in Surrey) June 15, 1215.

The king's financial demands were caused by a disastrous foreign policy. The charter defined the barons' obligations to the monarch, confirmed the liberties of the English church, and opposed the arbitrary application of justice. Although it did not avert the first Barons' War and was annulled by the pope, it was reissued with changes in 1216, 1217, and 1225. As feudalism declined Magna Carta lost its significance, and under the Tudors was almost forgotten. During the 17th century it was rediscovered and reinterpreted by the Parliamentary party as a democratic document.

Four original copies exist, one each in Salisbury and Lincoln cathedrals and two in the British Library.

magnesia common name for ▷magnesium oxide.

magnesium lightweight, very ductile and malleable, silver-white, metallic element, symbol Mg, atomic number 12, atomic weight 24.305. It is one of the ▷alkaline-earth metals, and the lightest of the commonly used metals. Magnesium silicate, carbonate, and chloride are widely distributed in nature. The metal is used in alloys and flash photography. It is a necessary trace element in the human diet, and green plants cannot grow without it since it is an essential constituent of chlorophyll ($C_{55}H_{72}MgN_4O_5$).

It was named after the ancient Greek city of Magnesia, near where it was first found. It was first recognized as an element by Joseph ▷Black 1755 and discovered in its oxide by Humphry ▷Davy 1808. Pure magnesium was isolated 1828 by Antoine-Alexandre-Brutus Bussy.

magnesium oxide or **magnesia** MgO white powder or colorless crystals, formed when magnesium is burned in air or oxygen; a typical basic oxide. It is used to treat acidity of the stomach, and in some industrial processes; for example, as a lining brick in furnaces, because it is very stable when heated (refractory oxide).

magnet any object that forms a magnetic field (displays ▷magnetism), either permanently or temporarily through induction, causing it to attract materials such as iron, cobalt, nickel, and alloys of these. It always has two ▷magnetic poles, north and south.

magnetic field physical field or region around a permanent magnet, or around a conductor carrying an electric current, in which a force acts on a moving charge or on a magnet placed in the field. The field can be represented by lines of force, which by convention link north and south poles and are parallel to the directions of a small compass needle placed on them. Its magnitude and direction are given by the ▷magnetic flux density, expressed in ▷teslas.

Experiments have confirmed that homing pigeons and some other animals rely on their perception of the Earth's magnetic field for their sense of direction, and by 1979 it was suggested that humans to some extent share this sense.

magnetic flux measurement of the strength of the magnetic field around electric currents and magnets. Its SI unit is the weber; one weber per square meter is equal to one tesla.

The amount of magnetic flux through an area equals the product of the area and the magnetic field strength at a point within that area. It is a measure of the number of magnetic field lines passing through the area.

magnetic pole region on a magnet where its magnetic effects are strongest. Magnets (electromagnets as well as permanent magnets) always have two poles, called north and south. When a magnet is suspended freely, the north pole always points north and the south pole always points south. The north pole of one magnet will be attracted to the south pole of another, but will be repelled by its north pole. Like poles may therefore be said to attract, unlike poles to repel.

Single magnetic poles, called *monopoles*, have never been observed, despite being searched for, although there is no theoretical reason why they could not exist. If monopoles were discovered it would have profound effects on the theory of quantum electrodynamics.

magnetic resonance imaging (MRI) diagnostic scanning system based on the principles of nuclear magnetic resonance. MRI yields finely detailed three-dimensional images of structures within the body without exposing the patient to harmful radiation. The technique is useful for imaging the soft tissues of the body, such as the brain and the spinal cord.

Claimed as the biggest breakthrough in diagnostic imaging since the discovery of X-rays, MRI is a noninvasive technique using the principle that atomic nuclei in a strong magnetic field can be made to give off electromagnetic radiation, the characteristics of which depend on the environment of the nuclei.

magnetic storm in meteorology, a sudden disturbance affecting the Earth's magnetic field, causing anomalies in radio transmissions and magnetic compasses. It is probably caused by ◌sunspot activity.

magnetic tape narrow plastic ribbon coated with an easily magnetizable material on which data can be recorded. It is used in sound recording, audiovisual systems (videotape), and computing. For mass storage on commercial mainframe computers, large reel-to-reel tapes are used, but for the smaller mini- and microcomputers, tape cassettes and cartridges are more usual.

Magnetic tape was first used in *sound recording* 1947, and made overdubbing possible, unlike the direct-to-disk system it replaced. Two-track tape was introduced in the 1950s and four-track in the early 1960s; today, studios use 16-, 24-, or 32-track tape, from which the tracks are mixed down to a stereo master tape.

In computing, magnetic tape was first used to record data and programs in 1951 as part of the UNIVAC 1 system. It was very popular as a storage medium for external memory in the 1950s and 1960s. Since then it has been largely replaced by magnetic ◌disks as a working medium, although tape is still used to make backup copies of important data. Information is recorded on the tape in binary form, with two different strengths of signal representing 1 and 0. It is common for 20,000 ◌bits of information to be recorded on each 0.5 in/1 cm of tape. The tape drives of a mainframe or minicomputer can be capable of reading 16 ft/5 m of tape in a second.

magnetism phenomena associated with ◌magnetic fields. Magnetic fields are produced by moving charged particles: in electromagnets, electrons flow through a coil of wire connected to a battery; in permanent magnets, spinning electrons within the atoms generate the field.

Substances differ in the extent to which they can be magnetized by an external field (susceptibility). Materials that can be strongly magnetized, such as iron, cobalt, and nickel, are said to be *ferromagnetic*; this is due to the formation of areas called ◌domains in which atoms, weakly magnetic because of their spinning electrons, align to form areas of strong magnetism. Magnetic materials lose their magnetism if heated to the ◌Curie temperature. Most other materials are *paramagnetic*, being only weakly pulled toward a strong magnet. This is because their atoms have a low level of magnetism and do not form domains. *Diamagnetic* materials are weakly repelled by a magnet since electrons within their atoms act as electromagnets and oppose the applied magnetic force. *Antiferromagnetic* materials have a very low susceptibility that increases with temperature; a similar phenomenon in materials such as ferrites is called ferrimagnetism.

Apart from its universal application in dynamos, electric motors, and switch gears, magnetism is of considerable importance in advanced technology—for example, in particle ◌accelerators for nuclear research, memory stores for computers, tape recorders, and ◌cryogenics.

magnetite black iron ore, iron oxide (Fe_3O_4). Widely distributed, magnetite is found in nearly all igneous and metamorphic rocks. It is strongly magnetic and some deposits, called *lodestone*, are permanently magnetized. Lodestone has been used as a compass since the first millennium BC.

magneto simple electric generator, often used to provide the electricity for the ignition system of motorcycles and used in early automobiles. It consists of a rotating magnet that sets up an electric current in a coil, providing the spark.

magnetohydrodynamics (MHD) field of science concerned with the behavior of ionized gases or liquid in a magnetic field. Systems have been developed that use MHD to generate electrical power.

magnetosphere volume of space, surrounding a planet, controlled by the planet's magnetic field, and acting as a magnetic "shell." The Earth's magnetosphere extends 40,000 mi/64,000 km toward the Sun, but many times this distance on the side away from the Sun.

The extension away from the Sun is called the *magnetotail*. The outer edge of the magnetosphere is the *magnetopause*. Beyond this is a turbulent region, the *magnetosheath*, where the ◌solar wind is deflected around the magnetosphere. Inside the magnetosphere, atomic particles follow the Earth's lines of magnetic force. The magnetosphere contains the ◌Van Allen radiation belts. Other planets have magnetospheres, notably Jupiter.

magnetron thermionic ◌valve (electron tube) for generating very high-frequency oscillations, used in radar and to produce microwaves in a microwave oven. The flow of electrons from the tube's cathode to one or more anodes is controlled by an applied magnetic field.

magnet school school that specializes in a particular area of the curriculum; for example, science, sport, or the arts. Magnet schools were established in the US from 1954 in some inner cities, with the aim of becoming centers of excellence in their special field.

Critics say that magnet schools attract talented pupils and staff away from equally deserving schools in the surrounding neighborhood.

magnification measure of the enlargement or reduction of an object in an imaging optical system. *Linear magnification* is the ratio of the size (height) of the image to that of the object. *Angular magnification* is the ratio of the angle subtended at the observer's eye by the image to the angle subtended by the object when viewed directly.

magnitude in astronomy, measure of the brightness of a star or other celestial object. The larger the number denoting the magnitude, the fainter the object. Zero or first magnitude indicates some of the brightest stars. Still brighter are those of negative magnitude, such as Sirius, whose magnitude is –1.46. *Apparent magnitude* is the brightness of an object as seen from Earth; *absolute magnitude* is the brightness at a standard distance of 10 parsecs (32.6 light-years).

Each magnitude step is equal to a brightness difference of 2.512 times. Thus a star of magnitude 1 is $(2.512)^5$ or 100 times brighter than a sixth-magnitude star just visible to the naked eye. The apparent magnitude of the Sun is –26.8, its absolute magnitude +4.8.

magnolia tree or shrub of the genus *Magnolia*, family Magnoliaceae, native to North America and E Asia. Magnolias vary in height from 2 ft/60 cm to 150 ft/30 m. The large, fragrant single flowers are white, rose, or purple. The southern magnolia *M. grandiflora* of the US grows up to 24 m/80ft tall and has white flowers 9 in/23 cm across.

magpie any bird of a genus *Pica* in the crow family. It feeds on insects, snails, young birds, and carrion, and is found in Europe, Asia, N Africa, and W North America.

The black-billed magpie *P. pica* of Eurasia and Western N America, about 18 in/45 cm long, has black and white plumage, the long tail having a metallic sheen.

Magritte René 1898–1967. Belgian Surrealist painter whose paintings focus on visual paradoxes and everyday objects taken out of context. Recurring motifs include bowler hats, apples, and windows, for example *Golconda* 1953 where men in bowler hats are falling from the sky to a street below.

Magritte joined the other Surrealists in Paris 1927. Returning to Brussels 1930, he painted murals for public buildings, and throughout his life created variations on themes of mystery treated with apparent literalism.

Magyar member of the largest ethnic group in Hungary, comprising 92% of the population. Magyars are of mixed Ugric and Turkic origin, and they arrived in Hungary toward the end of the 9th century. The Magyar language (see ◌Hungarian) belongs to the Uralic group.

Mahabad Kurdish town in Azerbaijan, W Iran, population (1983) 63,000. Occupied by Russian troops 1941, it formed the center of a short-lived republic (1945–46) before being reoccupied by the Iranians. In the 1980s Mahabad was the focal point of resistance by Iranian Kurds against the Islamic republic.

Mahābhārata (Sanskrit "great poem of the Bharatas") Sanskrit Hindu epic consisting of 18 books and 90,000 stanzas, probably composed in its present form about 300 BC. It forms with the *Rāmāyana* the two great epics of the Hindus. It contains the ◌*Bhagavad-Gītā*, or *Song of the Blessed*, an episode in the sixth book.

The poem, set on the plain of the Upper Ganges, deals with the fortunes of the rival families of the Kauravas and the Pandavas and reveals the ethical values of ancient Indian society and individual responsibility in particular.

Mahādevī (Sanskrit "great goddess") title given to Sakti, the consort of the Hindu god Siva. She is worshiped in many forms, including her more active manifestations as Kali or Durga and her peaceful form as Parvati.

Mahan Alfred Thayer 1840–1914. US naval officer and military historian, author of *The Influence of Sea Power upon History* 1890–92, in which he propounded a global strategy based on the importance of sea power.

Born in Quogue, New York, Mahan graduated from the US Naval Academy 1859. Serving in the blockade of the South during the Civil War, he published a history of the naval operations, *The Gulf and Inland Waters* 1883. In 1885 Mahan was promoted to captain and joined the faculty of the Naval War College. His lectures, published as *The Influence of Sea Power Upon History*, deeply influenced Theodore Roosevelt and Wilhelm II of Germany to expand their respective nations' fleets. Mahan's memoirs were published as *From Sail to Steam* 1907.

Maharashtra state in W central India
area 118,811 sq mi/307,800 sq km
capital Bombay
cities Pune, Nagpur, Ulhasnagar, Sholapur, Nasik, Thana, Kolhapur, Aurangabad, Sangli, Amravati
features cave temples of Ajanta, containing 200 BC–7th century AD Buddhist murals and sculptures; Ellora cave temples 6th–9th century with Buddhist, Hindu, and Jain sculptures
products cotton, rice, groundnuts, sugar, minerals
population (1991) 78,706,700
language Marathi 50%
religion Hindu 80%, Parsee, Jain, and Sikh minorities
history formed 1960 from the southern part of the former Bombay state.

mahatma (Sanskrit "great soul") title conferred on Mohandas K ⟳Gandhi by his followers as the first great national Indian leader.

Mahāyāna (Sanskrit "greater vehicle") one of the two major forms of ⟳Buddhism, common in N Asia (China, Korea, Japan, and Tibet). Veneration of bodhisattvas (those who achieve enlightenment but remain on the human plane in order to help other living beings) is a fundamental belief in Mahāyāna, as is the idea that everyone has within them the seeds of Buddhahood.

A synthesis of Mahāyāna doctrines is found in the *Sūtra of the Golden Light*, stressing that people should obey reason (*prajñā*), which enables them to tell right from wrong; an act of self-sacrifice is the highest triumph of reason. The *Lotus Sūtra* describes the historical Buddha as only one manifestation of the eternal Buddha, the ultimate law (*dharma*) of the cosmos and the omnipresent and compassionate savior.

Mahdi (Arabic "he who is guided aright") in Islam, the title of a coming messiah who will establish a reign of justice on Earth. The title has been assumed by many Muslim leaders, notably the Sudanese sheik Mohammed Ahmed (1848–1885), who headed a revolt 1881 against Egypt and 1885 captured Khartoum.

His great-grandson **Sadiq el Mahdi** (1936–), leader of the Umma party in Sudan, was prime minister 1966–67. He was imprisoned 1969–74 for attempting to overthrow the military regime.

Mahfouz Naguib 1911– . Egyptian novelist and playwright. His novels, which deal with the urban working class, include the semi-autobiographical *Khan al-Kasrain/The Cairo Trilogy* 1956–57. His *Children of Gebelawi* 1959 was banned in Egypt because of its treatment of religious themes. Nobel Prize for Literature 1988.

mah-jong or **mah-jongg** originally an ancient Chinese card game, dating from the Song dynasty 960–1279. It is now usually played by four people with 144 small ivory tiles, divided into six suits.

Mahler Alma (born Schindler) 1879–1964. Austrian pianist and composer. She was the daughter of the artist Anton Schindler and abandoned composing when she married the composer Gustav Mahler 1902. After Mahler's death she lived with the architect Walter Gropius; their daughter Manon's death inspired Berg's Violin Concerto. She later married the writer Franz Werfel.

Mahler Gustav 1860–1911. Austrian composer and conductor whose work displays a synthesis of Romanticism and new uses of chromatic harmonies and musical forms. He composed 14 symphonies, including three unnumbered (as a student), nine massive repertoire symphonies, the titled *Das Lied von der Erde/Song of the Earth* 1909, and the incomplete *Symphony No. 10*. He also wrote song cycles.

Mahler was born in Bohemia (now Czechoslovakia); he studied at the Vienna Conservatoire, and conducted in Prague, Leipzig, Budapest, and Hamburg 1891–97. He was director of the Vienna Court Opera from 1897 and conducted the New York Philharmonic from 1910.

Mahmud two sultans of the Ottoman Empire:

Mahmud I 1696–1754. Ottoman sultan from 1730. After restoring order to the empire in Istanbul 1730, he suppressed the ⟳Janissary rebellion 1731 and waged war against Persia 1731–46. He led successful wars against Austria and Russia, concluded by the Treaty of Belgrade 1739. He was a patron of the arts and also carried out reform of the army.

Mahmud II 1785–1839. Ottoman sultan from 1808 who attempted to westernize the declining empire, carrying out a series of far-reaching reforms in the civil service and army. The pressure for Greek independence after 1821 led to conflict with Britain, France, and Russia, and he was forced to recognize Greek independence 1830.

In 1826 Mahmud destroyed the ⟳Janissaries. Wars against Russia 1807–12 resulted in losses of territory. The Ottoman fleet was destroyed at the Battle of Navarino 1827, and the Ottoman forces suffered defeat in the Russo-Turkish war 1828–29. There was further disorder with the revolt in Egypt of ⟳Mehemet Ali 1831–32, which in turn led to temporary Ottoman-Russian peace. Attempts to control the rebellious provinces failed 1839, resulting in effect in the granting of Egyptian autonomy.

mahogany timber from any of several genera of trees found in the Americas and Africa. Mahogany is a tropical hardwood obtained chiefly by rainforest logging. It has a warm red color and takes a high polish.

True mahogany comes from trees of the genus *Swietenia*, but other types come from the Spanish and Australian cedars, the Indian redwood, and other trees of the mahogany family Meliaceae, native to Africa and the E Indies.

Mahón or **Port Mahon** capital and port of the Spanish island of Minorca; population (1981) 21,900. Probably founded by the Carthaginians, it was in British occupation 1708–56 and 1762–82.

maidenhair any fern of the genus *Adiantum*, especially *A. capillus-veneris*, with hairlike fronds terminating in small kidney-shaped, spore-bearing pinnules. It is widely distributed in the Americas, and is sometimes found in the British Isles.

maidenhair tree another name for ⟳ginkgo, a surviving member of an ancient group of gymnosperms.

Mailer Norman 1923– . US writer and journalist. He gained wide attention with his novel of World War II *The Naked and the Dead* 1948. A commentator on the US social, literary, and political scene, he has run for mayor of New York City.

His other novels include *An American Dream* 1964, *Genius and Lust* 1976, *Ancient Evenings* 1983, *Tough Guys Don't Dance* 1984, and *Harlot's Ghost* 1991. His journalistic work includes *Armies of the Night* 1968 about protest against the Vietnam War, and *The Executioner's Song* 1979 (Pulitzer Prize) about convicted murderer Gary Gilmore. Mailer has also ventured into filmmaking.

Maillol Aristide Joseph Bonaventure 1861–1944. French artist who turned to sculpture in the 1890s. His work is mainly devoted to the female nude. It shows the influence of Classical greek art but tends toward simplified rounded forms.

Maillol was influenced by the ⟳Nabis. A typical example of his work is *Fame* for the Cézanne monument in Aix-en-Provence.

mail merge in computing, a feature offered by some word-processing packages that enables a list of personal details, such as names and addresses, to be combined with a general document outline to produce individualized documents.

For example, a club secretary might create a file containing a mailing list of the names and addresses of the club members. Whenever a letter is to be sent to all club members, a general letter outline is prepared with indications as to where individual names and addresses need to be added. The mail-merge feature then combines the file of names and addresses with the letter outline to produce and print individual letters addressed to each club member.

Maimonides Moses (Moses Ben Maimon) 1135–1204. Jewish rabbi and philosopher, born in Córdoba, Spain. Known as one of the greatest Hebrew scholars, he attempted to reconcile faith and reason.

He left Spain 1160 to escape the persecution of the Jews and settled in Fez, and later in Cairo, where he was personal physician to Sultan Saladin. His codification of Jewish law is known as the *Mishneh Torah/Torah Reviewed* 1180; he also formulated the **Thirteen Principles**, which summarize the basic beliefs of Judaism. His philosophical classic *More nevukhim/The Guide to the Perplexed* 1176–91 helped to introduce Aristotelian thought into medieval philosophy.

Maine

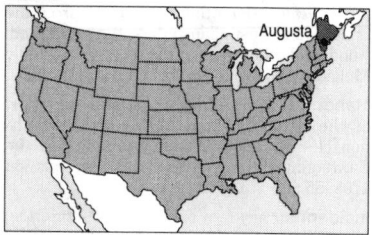

Augusta

Maine northeasternmost state of the US, largest of the New England states; nickname Pine Tree State
area 33,273 sq mi/86,200 sq km
capital Augusta
cities Portland, Lewiston, Bangor
physical Appalachian Mountains; 80% of the state is forested
features Acadia National Park, including Bar Harbor and most of Mount Desert Island; Baxter State Park, including Mount Katahdin; Roosevelt's Campobello International Park; canoeing along the Allagush Wilderness Waterway
products dairy and market garden produce, paper, pulp, timber, footwear, textiles, fish, lobster; tourism is important
population (1990) 1,228,000
famous people Henry Wadsworth Longfellow, Kate Douglas Wiggin, Edward Arlington Robinson, Edna St Vincent Millay
history permanently settled by the British from 1623; absorbed by Massachusetts 1691; became a state 1820.

In colonial days, white-pine masts were built for the Royal Navy at Falmouth (now Portland). Maine produces 98% of the nation's blueberries and has the largest papermaking capacity of any of the 50 states but is generally economically depressed.

mainframe large computer used for commercial data processing and other large-scale operations. Because of the general increase in computing power, the differences between the mainframe, ⟡supercomputer, ⟡minicomputer, and ⟡microcomputer (personal computer) are becoming less marked.

main sequence in astronomy, the part of the ⟡Hertzsprung-Russell diagram that contains most of the stars, including the Sun. It runs diagonally from the top left of the diagram to the lower right. The most massive (and hence brightest) stars are at the top left, with the least massive (coolest) stars at the bottom right.

Main Street classic satirical novel by Sinclair Lewis, published 1920, which made the American small-town Main Street the exemplification of enduring if simplistic social values.

Maintenon Françoise d'Aubigné, Marquise de 1635–1719. Second wife of Louis XIV of France from 1684, and widow of the writer Paul Scarron (1610–1660). She was governess to the children of Mme de Montespan by Louis, and his mistress from 1667. She secretly married the king after the death of Queen Marie Thérèse 1683. Her political influence was considerable and, as a Catholic convert from Protestantism, her religious opinions were zealous.

Mainz (French *Mayence*) capital of Rhineland-Palatinate, Germany, on the Rhine, 23 mi/37 km WSW of Frankfurt-am-Main; population (1988) 189,000. In Roman times it was a fortified camp and became the capital of Germania Superior. Printing was possibly invented here about 1448 by ⟡Gutenberg.

majolica or **maiolica** tin-glazed ⟡earthenware and the richly decorated enamel pottery produced in Italy in the 15th to 18th centuries. The name derives from the Italian form of Majorca, the island from where Moorish lusterware made in Spain was shipped to Italy. During the 19th century the word was used to describe molded earthenware with relief patterns decorated in colored glazes.

Major John 1943– . British Conservative politician, prime minister from Nov 1990. He was foreign secretary 1989 and chancellor of the Exchequer 1989–90. His earlier positive approach to European Community (EC) matters was hindered during 1991 by divisions within the Conservative Party. Despite continuing public dissatisfaction with the poll tax, the National Health Service, and the recession, Major was returned to power in the April 1992 general election. His subsequent handling of a series of political crises called into question his ability to govern the country effectively.

Majorca (Spanish *Mallorca*) largest of the ⟡Balearic Islands, belonging to Spain, in the W Mediterranean
area 1,405 sq mi/3,640 sq km
capital Palma
features the highest mountain is Puig Mayor 4,741 ft/1,445 m
products olives, figs, oranges, wine, brandy, timber, sheep; tourism is the mainstay of the economy
population (1981) 561,215
history captured 797 by the Moors, it became the kingdom of Majorca 1276, and was united with Aragon 1343.

Makarios III 1913–1977. Cypriot politician, Greek Orthodox archbishop 1950–77. A leader of the Resistance organization ⟡EOKA, he was exiled by the British to the Seychelles 1956–57 for supporting armed action to achieve union with Greece (*enosis*). He was president of the republic of Cyprus 1960–77 (briefly deposed by a Greek military coup July–Dec 1974).

Makarova Natalia 1940– . Russian ballerina. She danced with the Kirov Ballet 1959–70, then sought political asylum in the West. Her roles include the title role in *Giselle* and Aurora in *The Sleeping Beauty.*

Makua member of a people living to the north of the Zambezi River in Mozambique. With the Lomwe people, they make up the country's largest ethnic group. The Makua are mainly farmers, living in villages ruled by chiefs. The Makua language belongs to the Niger-Congo family, and has about 5 million speakers.

Malabar Coast coastal area of Karnataka and Kerala states, India, lying between the Arabian Sea and the Western Ghats; about 40 mi/65 km W to E, 450 mi/725 km N to S. A fertile area with heavy rains, it produces food grains, coconuts, rubber, spices; also teak, ebony, and other woods. Lagoons fringe the shore. A district of Tamil Nadu transferred 1956 to Kerala was called Malabar Coast.

Malabo port and capital of Equatorial Guinea, on the island of Bioko; population (1983) 15,253. It was founded in the 1820s by the British as *Port Clarence*. Under Spanish rule it was known as *Santa Isabel* (until 1973).

Malacca or *Melaka* state of W Peninsular Malaysia; capital Malacca; area 656 sq mi/1,700 sq km; products include rubber, tin, and wire; population (1980) 465,000 (about 70% Chinese). The town originated in the 13th century as a fishing village frequented by pirates, and later developed into a trading port. Portuguese from 1511, then Dutch from 1641, it was ceded to Britain 1824, becoming part of the Straits Settlements.

Malacca, Strait of channel between Sumatra and the Malay Peninsula; length 600 mi/965 km; narrows to less than 24 mi/38 km wide. It carries all shipping between the Indian Ocean and the South China Sea.

malachite common ⟡copper ore, basic copper carbonate, $Cu_2CO_3(OH)_2$. It is a source of green pigment and is polished for use in jewelry, ornaments, and art objects.

Málaga industrial seaport (sugar refining, distilling, brewing, olive-oil pressing, shipbuilding) and vacation resort in Andalusia, Spain; capital of Málaga province on the Mediterranean; population (1991) 524,800. Founded by the Phoenicians and taken by the Moors 711, Málaga was capital of the Moorish kingdom of Malaga from the 13th century until captured 1487 by the Catholic monarchs Ferdinand and Isabella.

Malagasy inhabitant of or native to Madagascar. The Malagasy language has about 9 million speakers; it belongs to the Austronesian family.

Despite Madagascar's proximity to Africa, Malagasy contains only a small number of Bantu and Arabic loan words. It seems likely that the earliest settlers came by sea, some 1,500 years ago, from Indonesia. Primarily rice farmers, the Malagasy make use both of irrigated fields and swidden (temporary plot) methods.

Malagasy Republic former name (1958–75) of ⟡Madagascar.

Malamud Bernard 1914–1986. US novelist and short-story writer. He first attracted attention with *The Natural* 1952, making a professional baseball player his hero. Later novels, often dealing with the Jewish immigrant tradition, include *The Assistant* 1957, *The Fixer* 1966, *Dubin's Lives* 1979, and *God's Grace* 1982.

Short story collections include *The Magic Barrel* 1958, *Rembrandt's Hat* 1973, and *The Stories of Bernard Malamud* 1983.

malapropism amusing slip of the tongue, arising from the confusion of similar-sounding words. The term derives from the French *mal à propos* (inappropriate); historically, it is associated with Mrs Malaprop, a character in Sheridan's play *The Rivals* 1775, who was the pineapple (pinnacle) of perfection in such matters.

malaria infectious parasitic disease of the tropics transmitted by mosquitoes, marked by periodic fever and an enlarged spleen. When a female mosquito of the *Anopheles* genus bites a human who has malaria, it takes in with the human blood one of four malaria protozoa of the genus *Plasmodium*. This matures within the insect and is then transferred when the mosquito bites a new victim. Malaria affects some 200 million people a year on a recurring basis.

Inside the human body the parasite settles first in the liver, then multiplies to attack the red blood cells. Within the red blood cells the parasites multiply, eventually causing the cells to rupture and other cells to become infected. The cell rupture tends to be synchronized, occurring every 2–3 days, when the symptoms of malaria become evident. ⟡Quinine was the

Malawi
Republic of (*Malaŵi*)

area 45,560 sq mi/118,000 sq km
capital Lilongwe
cities Blantyre (largest city and commercial center); Mzuzu, Zomba
physical landlocked narrow plateau with rolling plains; mountainous W of Lake Malawi
features one-third is water, including lakes Malawi, Chilara, and Malombe; Great Rift Valley; Nyika, Kasungu, and Lengare national parks; Mulanje Massif; Shire River
head of state and government Hastings Kamusu Banda from 1966 for life
political system one-party republic
political party Malawi Congress Party (MCP), multiracial, right-wing
exports tea, tobacco, cotton, peanuts, sugar
currency kwacha
population (1990 est) 9,080,000 (nearly 1 million refugees from Mozambique); growth rate 3.3% p.a.
life expectancy men 46, women 50 (1989)
languages English, Chichewa (both official)
religions Christian 75%, Muslim 20%
literacy 25% (1989)
GNP $1.2 bn (1987); $160 per head (1988)
chronology
1891 Became the British protectorate Nyasaland.
1964 Independence achieved from Britain, within the Commonwealth, as Malawi.
1966 Became a one-party republic, with Hastings Banda as president.
1971 Banda was made president for life.
1977 Banda released some political detainees and allowed greater freedom of the press.
1986–89 Influx of nearly 1 million refugees from Mozambique.
1992 Calls for multiparty politics. Countrywide industrial riots caused many fatalities. Western aid suspended over human-rights violations.

first drug used against malaria, now replaced by synthetics, such as atabrine to prevent the disease and chloroquine to treat it. Tests on a vaccine were begun 1986 in the US. In Brazil a malaria epidemic broke out among new settlers in the Amazon region, with 287,000 cases 1983 and 500,000 cases 1988.

Malawi country in SE Africa, bounded N and NE by Tanzania; E, S, and W by Mozambique; and W by Zambia.
government The 1966 constitution provides for a president elected for a five-year term but it was amended 1971 to make Hastings ◊Banda president for life. Malawi is a one-party state, all adults being required to be members of the Malawi Congress Party. The single-chamber legislature, the national assembly, has 112 elected members, and the president may appoint any number of additional members. He also appoints a cabinet whose members are directly responsible to him.
history During the 15th–19th centuries the Malawi empire occupied roughly the southern part of the region that makes up present-day Malawi. The difficulty of the terrain and the warfare between the rival Yao and Ngoni groups long prevented penetration of the region by outsiders, though Scottish explorer David ◊Livingstone reached Lake Malawi 1859. In 1891 Britain annexed the country, making it the British protectorate of Nyasaland from 1907. Between 1953 and 1964 it was part of the Federation of Rhodesia and Nyasaland, which comprised the territory that is now Zimbabwe, Zambia, and Malawi.
republic and one-party state Dr Hastings Banda, through the Malawi Congress Party, led a campaign for independence, and in 1963 the federation was dissolved. Nyasaland became independent as Malawi 1964 and two years later became a republic and a one-party state, with Banda as its first president. He has governed his country in a very individual way, tolerating no opposition, and his foreign policies have at times been rather idiosyncratic. He astonished his black African colleagues 1967 by officially recognizing the Republic of South Africa, and in 1971 became the first African head of state to visit that country. In 1976, however, he also recognized the communist government in Angola. Banda's external policies are based on a mixture of national self-interest and practical reality and have enabled Malawi to live in reasonable harmony with its neighbors.
receiving refugees Malawi adopted an "open-door" policy toward refugees fleeing the civil war in neighboring Mozambique; about 70,000 refugees crossed the border Sept 1986. By 1989 the number of refugees had grown to nearly 1 million.
opposition Banda has kept tight control over his government colleagues. In 1977 he released some political detainees and allowed greater press freedom, but human-rights violations and murder of opponents have been reported. There are at least three opposition groups that operate from outside Malawi. During March 1992 the first public calls for multiparty politics were made, and seven high-ranking members of the Roman Catholic church issued a pastoral letter condemning corruption and government censorship and monopoly of the media. In May industrial riots throughout the country resulted in more than 40 deaths. Western nations suspended aid in order to press for greater respect for human rights. *See illustration box.*

Malawi, Lake or *Lake Nyasa* African lake, bordered by Malawi, Tanzania, and Mozambique, formed in a section of the Great ◊Rift Valley. It is about 1,650 ft/500 m above sea level and 350 mi/560 km long, with an area of 14,280 sq mi/37,000 sq km. It is intermittently drained to the south by the river Shiré into the Zambezi.

Malay a member of a large group of peoples comprising the majority population of the Malay Peninsula and Archipelago, also found in S Thailand and coastal Sumatra and Borneo. Their language belongs to the western branch of the Austronesian family.

Malayalam southern Indian language, the official language of the state of Kerala. Malayalam is closely related to Tamil, also a member of the Dravidian language family; it is spoken by about 20 million people. Written records in Malayalam date from the 9th century AD.

Malay language member of the Western or Indonesian branch of the Malayo-Polynesian language family, used in the Malay peninsula and many of the islands of Malaysia and Indonesia. The Malay language can be written in either Arabic or Roman scripts. The dialect of the S Malay peninsula is the basis of both Bahasa Malaysia and Bahasa Indonesia, the official languages of Malaysia and Indonesia. Bazaar Malay is a widespread pidgin variety used for trading and shopping.

Malayo-Polynesian family of languages spoken in Malaysia, better known as the ◊*Austronesian languages*.

Malay Peninsula southern projection of the continent of Asia, lying between the Strait of Malacca, which divides it from Sumatra, and the China Sea. The northern portion is partly in Myanmar (formerly Burma), partly in Thailand; the south forms part of Malaysia. The island of Singapore lies off its southern extremity.

Malaysia country in SE Asia, comprising the Malay Peninsula, bounded N by Thailand, and surrounded E and S by the South China Sea and W by the Strait of Malacca; and the states of Sabah and Sarawak in the northern part of the island of Borneo (S Borneo is part of Indonesia).
government Malaysia is a federation of 13 states: Johore, Kedah, Kelantan, Malacca, Negri Sembilan, Pahang, Penang, Perak, Perlis, Sabah, Sarawak, Selangor, and Trengganu. Each has its own constitution, head of state, and elected assembly, led by a chief minister and cabinet, and legislates on matters outside the federal parliament's sphere. Under the 1957 constitution, a monarch is elected for five-year terms by and from among the hereditary rulers of Johore, Kedah, Kelantan, Negri Sembilan, Pahang, Perak, Perlis, Selangor, and Trengganu. The paramount ruler's powers are similar to those of the British monarch, including discretion in the appointment of a prime minister and in granting a dissolution of parliament. Generally, the monarch acts on the advice of the prime minister and cabinet, who wield effective power.

The two-chamber federal legislature or parliament is composed of a 69-member upper house or Senate, Dewan Negara, comprising 43 members nominated by the head of state and two members elected by each of the 13 state assemblies for six-year terms, and a house of representatives, Dewan Rakyat, whose 180 members are elected for five-year terms from single-member constituencies by universal suffrage. The Senate can only delay bills already approved by the dominant house of representatives, whose majority party or coalition provides the prime minister, who governs with a cabinet selected from parliament.
history The areas that comprise present-day Malaysia were part of the Buddhist Sri Vijaya empire in the 9th–14th centuries. This was

Malaysia

area 127,287 sq mi/329,759 sq km
capital Kuala Lumpur
cities Johor Baharu, Ipoh, Georgetown (Penang), Kuching in Sarawak, Kota Kinabalu in Sabah
physical comprises Peninsular Malaysia (the nine Malay states—Johore, Kedah, Kelantan, Negri Sembilan, Pahang, Perak, Perlis, Selangor, Trengganu—plus Malacca and Penang); and E Malaysia (Sabah and Sarawak); 75% tropical jungle; central mountain range; swamps in E
features Mount Kinabalu (highest peak in SE Asia); Niah caves (Sarawak)
head of state Rajah Azlan Muhibuddin Shah (sultan of Perak) from 1989
head of government Mahathir bin Mohamad from 1981
political system liberal democracy
political parties New United Malays' National Organization (UMNO Baru), Malay-oriented nationalist; Malaysian Chinese Association (MCA), Chinese-oriented conservative; Gerakan Party, Chinese-oriented, left of center; Malaysian Indian Congress (MIC), Indian-oriented; Democratic Action Party (DAP), left of center, multiracial but Chinese-dominated; Pan-Malayan Islamic Party (PAS), Islamic; Semangat '46 (Spirit of 1946), moderate, multiracial
exports pineapples, palm oil, rubber, timber, petroleum (Sarawak), bauxite
currency ringgit
population (1990 est) 17,053,000 (Malaysian 47%, Chinese 32%, Indian 8%, others 13%); growth rate 2% p.a.
life expectancy men 65, women 70 (1989)
languages Malay (official), English, Chinese, Indian, and local languages
religions Muslim (official), Buddhist, Hindu, local beliefs
literacy 80% (1989)
GNP $34.3 bn; $1,870 per head (1988)
chronology
1786 Britain established control.
1826 Became a British colony.
1963 Federation of Malaysia formed, including Malaya, Singapore, Sabah (N Borneo), and Sarawak (NW Borneo).
1965 Secession of Singapore from federation.
1969 Anti-Chinese riots in Kuala Lumpur.
1971 Launch of *bumiputra* ethnic-Malay-oriented economic policy.
1981 Election of Dr Mahathir bin Mohamad as prime minister.
1982 Mahathir bin Mohamad reelected.
1986 Mahathir bin Mohamad reelected.
1987 Arrest of over 100 opposition activists, including DAP leader, as Malay-Chinese relations deteriorated.
1988 Split in ruling UMNO party over Mahathir's leadership style; new UMNO formed.
1989 Semangat '46 set up by former members of UMNO including ex-premier Tunku Abdul Rahman.
1990 Mahathir bin Mohamad reelected.
1991 New economic growth program launched.

overthrown by Majapahit, Java's last Hindu kingdom. After this period of Indian influence came the introduction of Islam, and a powerful Muslim empire developed in the area. Its growth was checked by the Portuguese conquest of Malacca 1511. In 1641 the Dutch ousted the Portuguese, and the area came under British control from 1786, with a brief return to Dutch rule 1818–24. Britain succeeded in unifying its protectorates in Borneo and the Malay Peninsula after World War II, making them a crown colony under the name of the Federation of Malaya 1948.

Federation of Malaysia The Federation of Malaysia was formed 1963 by the union of the 11 states of the Federation of Malaya with the British crown colonies of N Borneo (then renamed Sabah) and Sarawak, and Singapore, which seceded from the federation 1965. Since 1966 the 11 states on the Malay Peninsula have been known as West Malaysia, and Sabah and Sarawak as East Malaysia. The two regions are separated by 400 mi/650 km of the South China Sea. The establishment of the federation was opposed by guerrillas backed by Sukarno of Indonesia 1963–66, and the Philippines disputed the sovereignty of East Malaysia 1968 through their claim on Sabah.

Tunku Abdul ◊Rahman was Malaysia's first prime minister 1963–69, and his multiracial style of government was successful until anti-Chinese riots in Kuala Lumpur 1969 prompted the formation of an emergency administration. These riots followed a fall in support for the United Malays' National Organization (UMNO) in the federal election and were indicative of Malay resentment of the economic success of the Chinese business community. They provoked the resignation of Rahman 1970 and the creation by his successor, Tun Abdul Razak, of a broader governing coalition, including previous opposition parties, in its ranks.

pro-Malay economic policy In addition, a new economic policy was launched 1971, with the aim of raising the percentage of ethnic-Malay-owned businesses from 4% to 30% by 1990 and extending the use of pro-Malay (*bumiputra*) affirmative-action quota systems for university entrance and company employment. During the 1970s Malaysia enjoyed economic growth, but relations with the Chinese community became uneasy later in the decade as a result of the federal government's refusal to welcome Vietnamese refugees. Even more serious has been a revival of fundamentalist Islam in the west and north.

Dr Mahathir bin ◊Mohamad became the new leader of UMNO and prime minister 1981 and pursued a more narrowly Islamic and Malay strategy than his predecessors. He also launched an ambitious industrialization program, seeking to emulate Japan. He was reelected 1982 and 1986 but has encountered opposition from his Malaysian Chinese Association coalition partners, Christian-Muslim conflict in Sabah, and slower economic growth as a result of the fall in world tin, rubber, and palm-oil prices.

new opposition In 1987, in the wake of worsening Malay-Chinese relations, Mahathir ordered the arrest of more than 100 prominent opposition activists, including the Democratic Action Party (DAP)'s leader Lim Kit Siang, and a tightening of press censorship. These moves precipitated a rift in UMNO, with former premier Rahman and former trade and industry minister Razaleigh Hamzah leaving to form a new multiracial party grouping, Semangat '46, in 1989. In 1988 a reconstituted new UMNO had been set up by Mahathir following a high-court ruling that, as a result of irregularities in its 1987 leadership election, the existing UMNO was an "unlawful body." The prime minister also announced some relaxation of the 1971 economic policy that favored ethnic Malays—Malay equity ownership having reached only 18% by 1987—as part of a more consensual "Malay unity" program.

foreign relations Malaysia joined ◊ASEAN 1967 and originally adopted a pro-Western, anticommunist position. During recent years, while close economic links have been developed with Japan and joint ventures encouraged, relations with the communist powers and with Islamic nations also became closer.

In Oct 1990 federal and state elections were held. Prime Minister Mahathir bin Mohamad's ruling coalition captured 127 of the 180 national assembly seats. The expected strong challenge from Mahathir's rival and former colleague Razaleigh failed to materialize: his Semangat '46 party lost 5 of its 12 seats. However, Islamic (PAS) and Chinese (DAP) party allies polled well locally, with the opposition achieving a clean sweep (and control of the state legislature) in Razaleigh's home state of Kelantan.

economic growth policy The pro-Malay economic policy expired Dec 1990 and was replaced by a new program, the "new development policy," which is less discriminatory against non-Malays and aims to achieve a dramatic increase (7% a year) in national income by the year 2000, by which date Malaysia, it is envisaged, will have become a "fully developed state." *See illustration box.*

Malcolm four kings of Scotland, including:

Malcolm III called *Canmore c.* 1031–1093. King of Scotland from 1058, the son of Duncan I (murdered by ◊Macbeth 1040). He fled to England when the throne was usurped by Macbeth, but recovered S Scotland and killed Macbeth in battle 1057. He was killed at Alnwick while invading Northumberland, England.

Malcolm X 1925–1965. US political leader. Born in Omaha, Nebraska, as Malcolm Little, he grew up in foster homes in Michigan, Massachusetts, and New York. Convicted of robbery 1946, he spent seven years in prison, becoming a follower of Black Muslim leader Elijah Mohammed and converting to Islam. In 1952 he officially changed his name to "Malcolm X" to signify his rootlessness in a racist society. Having become an influential national and international leader, Malcolm publicly broke with the Black Muslims 1964 and was assassinated in Harlem 1965. *The Autobiography of Malcolm X* appeared the same year. The film *Malcolm X* by Spike Lee was released 1992.

Maldives
Republic of (*Divehi Jumhuriya*)

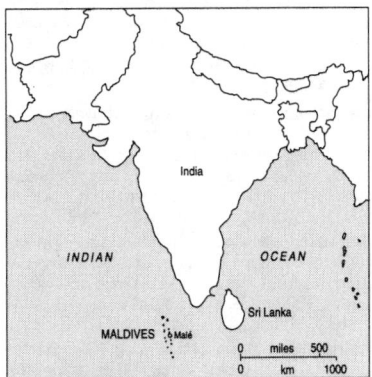

area 115 sq mi/298 sq km
capital Malé
cities Seenu
physical comprises 1,196 coral islands, grouped into 12 clusters of atolls, largely flat, none bigger than 5 sq mi/13 sq km, average elevation 6 ft/1.8 m; 203 are inhabited
environment the threat of rising sea level has been heightened by the frequency of flooding in recent years
features tourism developed since 1972
head of state and government Maumoon Abdul Gayoom from 1978

political system authoritarian nationalism
political parties none; candidates elected on the basis of personal influence and clan loyalties
exports coconuts, copra, bonito (fish related to tuna), garments
currency Rufiya
population (1990 est) 219,000; growth rate 3.7% p.a.
life expectancy men 60, women 63 (1989)
languages Divehi (Sinhalese dialect), English
religion Sunni Muslim
literacy 36% (1989)
GNP $69 million (1987); $410 per head (1988)
chronology
1887 Became a British protectorate.
1953 Long a sultanate, the Maldive Islands became a republic within the Commonwealth.
1954 Sultan restored.
1965 Achieved full independence outside the Commonwealth.
1968 Sultan deposed; republic reinstated with Ibrahim Nasir as president.
1978 Nasir retired; replaced by Maumoon Abdul Gayoom.
1982 Rejoined the Commonwealth.
1983 Gayoom reelected.
1985 Became a founder member of South Asian Association for Regional Cooperation (SAARC).
1988 Gayoom reelected. Coup attempt by mercenaries, thought to have the backing of former president Nasir, was foiled by Indian paratroops.

Maldives group of 1,196 islands in the N Indian Ocean, about 400 mi/640 km SW of Sri Lanka, only 203 of which are inhabited.
government The 1968 constitution provides for a single-chamber citizens' council (Majilis) of 48 members and a president, nominated by the Majilis and elected by referendum. They all serve a five-year term. Forty of the Majilis's members are elected by universal suffrage and eight are appointed by the president, who appoints and leads a cabinet that is responsible to the Majilis. There are no political parties and women are precluded from holding office.
history The islands, under Muslim control from the 12th century, came under Portuguese rule 1518. A dependency of Ceylon 1645–1948, they were under British protection 1887–1965 as the Maldive Islands and became a republic 1953. The sultan was restored 1954, and then, three years after achieving full independence as Maldives 1968, the islands returned to republican status 1968.
independence Maldives became fully independent as a sultanate outside the British ⟡Commonwealth 1965, with Ibrahim Nasir as prime minister. Nasir became president when the sultan was deposed for the second time 1968 and the country became a republic. It rejoined the Commonwealth 1982. Britain had an air-force staging post on the southern island of Gan 1956–75, and its closure meant a substantial loss of income. The president nevertheless refused a Soviet offer 1977 to lease the former base, saying that he did not want it used for military purposes again nor leased to a superpower.

In 1978 Nasir announced that he would not run for reelection, and the Majilis nominated Maumoon Abdul Gayoom, a member of Nasir's cabinet, as his successor. Nasir went to Singapore but was called back to answer charges of misusing government funds. He denied the charges, and attempts to extradite him failed. Despite rumors of a plot to overthrow him, Gayoom was reelected for a further five years 1983. Under Gayoom economic growth accelerated, helped by an expansion in tourism. Overseas, Gayoom broadly adhered to his predecessor's policy of nonalignment, but also began to develop closer links with the Arab nations of the Middle East, and in 1985 rejoined the Commonwealth and was a founder member of the South Asian Association for Regional Cooperation (SAARC) formed 1983 with India, Pakistan, Banlgadesh, Nepal, Sri Lanka, and Bhutan.
coup attempt In Nov 1988, soon after being reelected for a third term, Gayoom was briefly ousted in an attempted coup led by Abdullah Luthufi, an exiled entrepreneur from the atoll of Adu, which favors secession. Luthufi had recruited a force of 200 Tamil mercenaries in Sri Lanka, and was thought to have the backing of former president Nasir. Gayoom was restored to office after the intervention of Indian paratroops; 17 of those captured, including Luthufi, were sentenced to life imprisonment 1989. *See illustration box.*

Malé capital of the Maldives in the Indian Ocean; population (1990) 55,100. It trades in copra, breadfruit, and palm products; it is also a tourist center.

Malebranche Nicolas 1638–1715. French philosopher. His *De la Recherche de la vérité/ Search after Truth* 1674–78 was inspired by René ⟡Descartes; he maintained that exact ideas of external objects are obtainable only through God.

Malenkov Georgi Maximilianovich 1902–1988. Soviet prime minister 1953–55, Stalin's designated successor but abruptly ousted as

Communist Party secretary within two weeks of Stalin's death by ⟡Khrushchev, and forced out as prime minister 1955 by ⟡Bulganin.

Malevich Kasimir 1878–1935. Russian abstract painter. In 1912 he visited Paris and became a Cubist, and 1913 he launched his own abstract movement, ⟡*Suprematism*. Later he returned to figurative themes treated in a semiabstract style.

Malherbe François de 1555–1628. French poet and grammarian, born in Caen. He became court poet about 1605 under Henry IV and Louis XIII. He advocated reform of language and versification, and established the 12-syllable Alexandrine as the standard form of French verse.

Mali landlocked country in NW Africa, bounded to the NE by Algeria, E by Niger, SE by Burkina Faso, S by the Ivory Coast, SW by Senegal and Guinea, and W and N by Mauritania.
government The 1974 constitution, amended 1981 and 1985, provides for a one-party state with a president elected by universal suffrage and an 82-member national assembly elected from a party list for a three-year term. The president serves for six years and may be reelected any number of times.
history From the 7th to the 11th century part of the Ghana Empire (see ⟡Ghana, ancient), then of the Muslim ⟡Mali Empire, which flourished in NW Africa during the 7th–15th centuries, the area now known as Mali came under the rule of the ⟡Songhai Empire during the 15th–16th centuries. In 1591 an invasion by Moroccan forces seeking to take over the W Sudanese gold trade destroyed the Songhai Empire and left the area divided into small kingdoms.

Because of its inland position, the region had little contact with Europeans, who were trading around the coast from the 16th century, and it was not until the 19th century that France, by means of treaties with local rulers, established colonies throughout most of NW Africa. As French Sudan, Mali was part of ⟡French West Africa from 1895. In 1959, with Senegal, it formed the Federation of Mali. In 1960 Senegal left, and Mali became a fully independent republic.
independence Its first president, Modibo Keita, imposed an authoritarian socialist regime, but his economic policies failed, and he was removed in an army coup 1968. The constitution was suspended, political activity was banned, and government was placed in the hands of a Military Committee for National Liberation (CMLN) with Lt Moussa Traoré as president and head of state. In 1969 he became prime minister as well. He promised a return to civilian rule, and in 1974 a new constitution made Mali a one-party state. A new party, the Malian People's Democratic Union (UDPM), was announced 1976. Despite student opposition to a one-party state and army objections to civilian rule, Traoré successfully made the transition so that by 1979 Mali had a constitutional government, while ultimate power lay with the party and the military establishment.
foreign relations In 1983 Mali and Guinea signed an agreement for eventual economic and political integration. In 1985 a border dispute with Burkina Faso resulted in a five-day conflict that was settled by the International Court of Justice.
multiparty system endorsed Violent demonstrations against one-party rule took place Jan

Mali
Republic of (*République du Mali*)

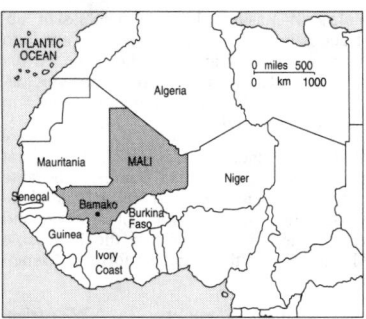

area 478,695 sq mi/1,240,142 sq km
capital Bamako
cities Mopti, Kayes, Ségou, Timbuktu
physical landlocked state with river Niger and savanna in S; part of the Sahara in N; hills in NE; Senegal River and its branches irrigate the SW
environment a rising population coupled with recent droughts has affected marginal agriculture. Once in surplus, Mali has had to import grain every year since 1965
features ancient town of Timbuktu; railroad to Dakar is the only outlet to the sea
head of state and government Alpha Oumar Konare from 1992
political system emergent democratic republic
political parties Alliance for Democracy in Mali (ADEMA), centrist; National Committee for Democratic Initiative (CNID), center-left;

Sudanese Union–African Democratic Rally (US–RDA), Sudanese nationalist
exports cotton, peanuts, livestock, fish
currency franc CFA
population (1990 est) 9,182,000; growth rate 2.9% p.a.
life expectancy men 44, women 47 (1989)
languages French (official), Bambara
religion Sunni Muslim 90%, animist 9%, Christian 1%
literacy 10% (1989)
GNP $1.6 bn (1987); $230 per head (1988)
chronology
1895 Came under French rule.
1959 With Senegal, formed the Federation of Mali.
1960 Became the independent Republic of Mali, with Modibo Keita as president.
1968 Keita replaced in an army coup by Moussa Traoré.
1974 New constitution made Mali a one-party state.
1976 New national party, the Malian People's Democratic Union, announced.
1983 Agreement between Mali and Guinea for eventual political and economic integration signed.
1985 Conflict with Burkina Faso lasted five days; mediated by International Court of Justice.
1991 Demonstrations against one-party rule. Moussa Traoré ousted in a coup led by Lt-Col Amadou Toumani Toure. New multiparty constitution agreed, subject to referendum.
1992 Referendum endorsed new democratic constitution. Alliance for Democracy in Mali (ADEMA) won multiparty elections; Alpha Oumar Konare elected president.

1991. In March 1991 Traoré was ousted in a coup and replaced by Lt-Col Amadou Toumani Toure. A new multiparty constitution was approved by referendum Jan 1992. In presidential elections April 1992 Toure was defeated and replaced by Alpha Oumar Konare. *See illustration box.*

malic acid COOHCH$_2$CH(OH)COOH organic crystalline acid that can be extracted from apples, plums, cherries, grapes, and other fruits, but occurs in all living cells in smaller amounts, being one of the intermediates of the ▷Krebs cycle.

Mali Empire Muslim state in NW Africa during the 7th–15th centuries. Thriving on its trade in gold, it reached its peak in the 14th century under Mansa Musa (reigned 1312–37), when it occupied an area covering present-day Senegal, Gambia, Mali, and S Mauritania. Mali's territory was similar to (though larger than) that of the Ghana Empire (see ▷Ghana, ancient), and gave way in turn to the ▷Songhai Empire.

Malik Yakob Alexandrovich 1906–1980. Soviet diplomat. He was permanent representative at the United Nations 1948–53 and 1968–76, and it was his walkout from the Security Council in Jan 1950 that allowed the authorization of UN intervention in Korea (see ▷Korean War).

Malinovsky Rodion Yakolevich 1898–1967. Russian soldier and politician. In World War II he fought at Stalingrad, commanded in the Ukraine, and led the Soviet advance through the Balkans to capture Budapest 1945. He was minister of defense 1957–67.

Malinowski Bronislaw 1884–1942. Polish-born British anthropologist, one of the

founders of the theory of ▷functionalism in the social sciences. His classic study of the peoples of the Trobriand Islands led him to see customs and practices in terms of their function in creating and maintaining social order.

Malipiero Gian Francesco 1882–1973. Italian composer and editor of ▷Monteverdi and ▷Vivaldi. His own works include operas in a Neo-Classical style, based on Shakespeare's *Julius Caesar* 1934–35 and *Antony and Cleopatra* 1936–37.

mallard common wild duck *Anas platyrhynchos*, found almost worldwide, from which domestic ducks were bred. The male, which can grow to a length of 2 ft/60 cm, usually has a green head and brown breast, while the female is mottled brown. Mallards are omnivorous, dabbling ducks.

Mallarmé Stéphane 1842–1898. French poet who founded the Symbolist school with Paul Verlaine. His belief that poetry should be evocative and suggestive was reflected in *L'Après-midi d'un faune/Afternoon of a Faun* 1876, which inspired the composer Debussy.
    Later works are *Poésies complètes/Complete Poems* 1887, *Vers et prose/Verse and Prose* 1893, and the prose *Divagations/Digressions* 1897.

Malle Louis 1932– . French film director. After a period as assistant to director Robert Bresson, he directed *Les Amants/The Lovers* 1958, audacious for its time in its explicitness. His subsequent films, made in France and the US, include *Zazie dans le métro* 1961, *Viva Maria* 1965, *Pretty Baby* 1978, *Atlantic City* 1980, *Au Revoir les enfants* 1988, and *Milou en mai* 1989.

mallee small trees and shrubs of the genus *Eucalyptus* with many small stems and thick underground roots that retain water. Before irrigation farming began, dense thickets of mallee characterized most of NW Victoria, Australia, known as the mallee region.

Mallorca Spanish form of ▷Majorca, an island in the Mediterranean.

mallow any plant of the family Malvaceae, especially the genus *Malva*, including the North American rose mallow *Hibiscus palustris*, and the European marsh mallow *Althaea officinalis*. Most have showy pink or purple flowers. See also ▷hollyhock, ▷cotton, ▷okra, ▷hibiscus.

Malmö industrial port (shipbuilding, engineering, textiles) in SW Sweden, situated across the Öresund from Copenhagen, Denmark; population (1990) 233,900. Founded in the 12th century, Malmö is Sweden's third largest city.

malnutrition the physical condition resulting from dietary deficiencies. These may be caused by lack of food resources (famine) or by lack of knowledge about ▷nutrition.
    When essential nutrients are missing from the diet, opportunistic infection takes hold in weakened individuals, those with deficiency disease, and may kill before starvation occurs. A high global death rate linked to malnutrition has arisen from famine situations caused by global warming, droughts, and the ▷greenhouse effect as well as by sociopolitical factors, such as alcohol and drug abuse, poverty and war.

Malory Thomas 15th century. English author of the prose romance *Le Morte d'Arthur* about 1470. It is a translation from the French, modified by material from other sources, and it deals with the exploits of King Arthur's knights of the Round Table and the quest for the ▷Holy Grail.
    Malory's identity is uncertain. He is thought to have been the Warwickshire landowner of that name who was member of Parliament for Warwick 1445 and was charged with rape, theft, and attempted murder 1451 and 1452. If that is so, he must have compiled *Morte d'Arthur* during his 20 years in Newgate prison.

Malplaquet, Battle of victory 1709 of the British, Dutch, and Austrian forces over the French forces during the War of the ▷Spanish Succession. The village of Malplaquet is in Nord *département*, France.

malpractice in law, ▷negligence by a professional person, usually a doctor, that may lead to an action for damages by the client. Such legal actions result in doctors having high insurance costs that are reflected in higher fees charged to their patients.

Malraux André 1901–1976. French writer. An active antifascist, he gained international renown for his novel *La Condition humaine/Man's Estate* 1933, set during the Nationalist/Communist Revolution in China in the 1920s. *L'Espoir/Days of Hope* 1937 is set in Civil War Spain, where he was a bomber pilot in the International Brigade. In World War II he supported the Gaullist resistance, and was minister of cultural affairs 1960–69.

malt in brewing, grain (barley, oats, or wheat) artificially germinated and then dried in a kiln. Malts are fermented to make beers or lagers, or fermented and then distilled to produce spirits such as whiskey.

Malta island in the Mediterranean Sea, S of Sicily, E of Tunisia, and N of Libya.
government The 1974 constitution provides for a single-chamber legislature, the 65-member House of Representatives, elected by

Malta
Republic of (*Repubblika Ta'Malta*)

area 124 sq mi/320 sq km
capital and port Valletta
cities Rabat; port of Marsaxlokk
physical includes islands of Gozo 26 sq mi/67 sq km and Comino 1 sq mi/2.5 sq km
features occupies strategic location in central Mediterranean; large commercial dock facilities
head of state Vincent Tabone from 1989
head of government Edward Fenech Adami from 1987
political system liberal democracy
political parties Malta Labour Party (MLP), moderate, left-of-center; Nationalist Party, Christian, centrist, pro-European
exports vegetables, knitwear, handmade lace, plastics, electronic equipment
currency Maltese lira

population (1990 est) 373,000; growth rate 0.7% p.a.
life expectancy men 72, women 77 (1987)
languages Maltese, English
religion Roman Catholic 98%
literacy 90% (1988)
GNP $1.6 bn; $4,750 per head (1988)
chronology
1814 Annexed to Britain by the Treaty of Paris.
1947 Achieved self-government.
1955 Dom Mintoff of the Malta Labour Party (MLP) became prime minister.
1956 Referendum approved MLP's proposal for integration with the UK. Proposal opposed by the Nationalist Party.
1958 MLP rejected the British integration proposal.
1962 Nationalists elected, with Borg Olivier as prime minister.
1964 Independence achieved from Britain, within the Commonwealth. Ten-year defense and economic aid treaty with UK signed.
1971 Mintoff reelected. 1964 treaty declared invalid and negotiations began for leasing the NATO base in Malta.
1972 Seven-year NATO agreement signed.
1974 Became a republic.
1979 British military base closed.
1984 Mintoff retired and was replaced by Mifsud Bonnici as prime minister and MLP leader.
1987 Edward Fenech Adami (Nationalist) elected prime minister.
1989 Vincent Tabone elected president. US–USSR summit held offshore.
1990 Formal application made for EC membership.
1992 Nationalist Party returned to power in general election.

universal suffrage, through a system of proportional representation, for a five-year term. As formal head of state the president is elected by the House for a five-year term and appoints a prime minister and cabinet, drawn from and collectively responsible to the House, which may be dissolved within its five-year term. A 1987 amendment to the constitution made provision for any party winning more than 50% of the votes in a general election to be guaranteed a majority of seats in the House of Representatives, regardless of the number of seats actually won.
history Malta was occupied in turn by Phoenicia, Greece, Carthage, and Rome, and fell to the Arabs 870. In 1090 the Norman count Roger of Sicily conquered Malta, and it remained under Sicilian rule until the 16th century, when the Holy Roman emperor Charles V handed it over to the Knights of ▷St John of Jerusalem 1530. After a Turkish attack 1565 the knights fortified the island and held it until 1798, when they surrendered to Napoleon. After requesting British protection, Malta was annexed by Britain 1814 and became a leading naval base. A vital link in World War II, Malta came under heavy attack and was awarded the British George Cross decoration (the highest British civilian award) 1942 for the country's collective courage.

The island was made self-governing 1947, and in 1955 Dom Mintoff, leader of the Malta Labour Party (MLP), became prime minister. In 1956 the MLP's proposal for integration with the UK was approved by a referendum but opposed by the conservative Nationalist Party, led by Dr Giorgio Borg Olivier. In 1958 Mintoff

rejected the British proposals and resigned, causing a constitutional crisis. By 1961 both parties favored independence, and talks began 1962, with Borg Olivier as prime minister.
independence Malta became a fully independent state within the ▷Commonwealth and under the British crown 1964, having signed a ten-year military and economic aid treaty with the UK. In 1971 Mintoff and the MLP returned to power with a policy of international nonalignment. He declared the 1964 treaty invalid and began to negotiate a new arrangement for leasing the Maltese NATO base and obtaining the maximum economic benefit from it for his country.
republican status agreed A seven-year agreement was signed 1972. Malta became a republic 1974, and in the 1976 general election the MLP was returned with a reduced majority. It again won a narrow majority in the House of Representatives 1981, even though the Nationalists had a bigger share of the popular vote. As a result, Nationalist MPs refused to take their seats for over a year. Relations between the two parties were also damaged by allegations of progovernment bias in the broadcasting service. At the end of 1984 Mintoff announced his retirement, and Dr Mifsud Bonnici succeeded him as MLP leader and prime minister. Three years later, in 1987, the Nationalist Party won the general election and its leader, Edward Fenech Adami, became prime minister. Vincent Tabone was elected president 1989. Malta was the site of the Dec 1989 summit meeting between US president Bush and Soviet president Gorbachev. In Oct 1990 Malta formally applied for European

Community (EC) membership. In the Feb 1992 general election the Nationalist Party, under Prime Minister Adami, was returned for another term. *See illustration box.*

Malta, Knights of another name for members of the military-religious order of the Hospital of ▷St John of Jerusalem.

maltase enzyme found in plants and animals that breaks down the disaccharide maltose into glucose.

Malthus Thomas Robert 1766–1834. English economist and cleric. His *Essay on the Principle of Population* 1798 (revised 1803) argued for population control, since populations increase in geometric ratio and food supply only in arithmetic ratio, and influenced Charles ▷Darwin's thinking on natural selection as the driving force of evolution.

Malthus theory projection of population growth made by Thomas Malthus. He based his theory on the ▷population explosion that was already becoming evident in the 18th century, and argued that the number of people would increase faster than the food supply. Population would eventually reach a resource limit (▷overpopulation). Any further increase would result in a population crash, caused by famine, disease, or war.

Malthus was not optimistic about the outcome and suggested that only "moral restraint" (birth control) could prevent crisis. Recent famines in Ethiopia and other countries, where drought, civil war, and poverty have reduced agricultural output, might suggest that Malthus was correct. In the US, the UK, and many other countries, the agricultural revolution boosted food production, and contraception led to a decline in ▷birth rate; and in some countries ▷population-control policies have been introduced.

maltose $C_{12}H_{22}O_{11}$ a ▷disaccharide sugar in which both monosaccharide units are glucose.
It is produced by the enzymic hydrolysis of starch and is a major constituent of malt, produced in the early stages of beer and whiskey manufacture.

Maluku or *Moluccas* group of Indonesian islands
area 28,764 sq mi/74,500 sq km
capital Ambon, on Amboina
population (1989 est) 1,814,000
history as the Spice Islands, they were formerly part of the Netherlands East Indies, and the S Moluccas attempted secession from the newly created Indonesian republic from 1949; exiles continue agitation in the Netherlands.

Malvern English spa in Hereford and Worcester, on the east side of the *Malvern Hills*, which extend for about 10 mi/16 km and have their high point in Worcester Beacon 1,395 ft/425 m; population (1981) 32,000. The *Malvern Festival* 1929–39, associated with the playwright G B Shaw and the composer Edward Elgar, was revived 1977.

Malvinas Argentine name for the ▷Falkland Islands.

mamba one of two venomous snakes, genus *Dendroaspis*, of the cobra family Elapidae, found in Africa south of the Sahara. Unlike cobras, they are not hooded.
The green mamba *D. angusticeps* is 5 ft/1.5 m long or more and lives in trees, feeding on birds and lizards. The black mamba *D. polylepis* is the largest venomous snake in Africa, occasionally as long as 11 ft/3.4 m, and spends more time on the ground.

mammals: classification

order	typical species
Monotremata	echidna, platypus
Marsupiala	kangaroo, koala, opossum
Insectivora	shrew, hedgehog, mole
Chiroptera	bat
Primates	lemur, monkey, ape, human
Edentata	anteater, armadillo, sloth
Pholidota	pangolin
Dermoptera	flying lemur
Rodentia	rat, mouse, squirrel, porcupine
Lagomorpha	rabbit, hare, pika
Cetacea	whale, dolphin
Carnivora	cat, dog, weasel, bear
Pinnipedia	seal, walrus
Artiodactyla	pig, deer, cattle, camel, giraffe
Perissodactyla	horse, rhinocerous, tapir
Sirenia	dugong, manatee
Tubulidentata	aardvark
Hyracoidea	hyrax
Proboscidea	elephant

Mameluke member of a powerful political class that dominated Egypt from the 13th century until their massacre 1811 by Mehemet Ali.

The Mamelukes were originally descended from freed Turkish slaves. They formed the royal bodyguard in the 13th century, and in 1250 placed one of their own number on the throne. Mameluke sultans ruled Egypt until the Turkish conquest of 1517, and they remained the ruling class until 1811.

Mamet David 1947– . US playwright. His plays, with their vivid, freewheeling language and sense of ordinary US life, include *American Buffalo* 1977, *Sexual Perversity in Chicago* 1978, and *Glengarry Glen Ross* 1984.

mammal any vertebrate that suckles its young and has hair. Mammals maintain a constant body temperature in varied surroundings. Most mammals give birth to live young, but the platypus and echidna lay eggs. There are over 4,000 species, adapted to almost every way of life. The smallest shrew weighs only 0.07 oz/2 g. The largest whale up to 140 tons. Mammals include humans.

mammary gland in female mammals, a milk-producing gland derived from epithelial cells underlying the skin, active only after the production of young. In all but monotremes (egg-laying mammals), the mammary glands terminate in teats which aid infant suckling. The number of glands and their position vary between species. In humans there are two, in cows four, and in pigs between ten and fourteen.

The hatched young of monotremes simply lick milk from a specialized area of skin on the mother's abdomen.

mammography X-ray procedure used to detect breast cancer at an early stage, before the tumors can be seen or felt.

Mammon evil personification of wealth and greed; originally a Syrian god of riches, cited in the New Testament as opposed to the Christian god.

mammoth extinct elephant of genus *Mammuthus*, whose remains are found worldwide. Some were 50% taller than modern elephants.

The woolly mammoth *Elephas primigenius* of northern zones, the size of an Indian elephant, had long fur and large inward-curving tusks. Various species of mammoth were abundant in both the Old World and the New World in Pleistocene times, and were hunted by humans for food.

Mammoth Cave vast limestone cavern in Mammoth Cave National Park 1936, Kentucky. The main cave is 4 mi/6.5 km long, and rises to a height of 125 ft/38 m; it is known for its stalactites and stalagmites. Indian councils were once held here.

Mamoulian Rouben 1898–1987. Armenian stage and film director who lived in the US from 1923. After several years on Broadway he turned to films, making the first sound version of *Dr Jekyll and Mr Hyde* 1932 and *Queen Christina* 1933. His later work includes *The Mark of Zorro* 1940 and *Silk Stockings* 1957.

Man, Isle of island in the Irish Sea, a dependency of the British crown, but not part of the UK
area 220 sq mi/570 sq km
capital Douglas
cities Ramsey, Peel, Castletown
features Snaefell 2,035 ft/620 m; annual TT (Tourist Trophy) motorcycle races, gambling casinos, Britain's first free port, tax haven; tailless Manx cat; tourism, banking, and insurance are important
exports light engineering products
currency the island produces its own coins and notes in UK currency denominations
population (1986) 55,500
language English (Manx, nearer to Scottish than Irish Gaelic, has been almost extinct since the 1970s)
government crown-appointed lieutenant-governor, a legislative council, and the representative House of Keys, which together make up the Court of Tynwald, passing laws subject to the royal assent. Laws passed at Westminster only affect the island if specifically so provided
history Norwegian until 1266, when the island was ceded to Scotland; it came under UK administration 1765.

Man. abbreviation for ▷*Manitoba*, Canadian province.

management process or technique of managing a business. Systems vary according to the type of organization, company, and objectives.

Since the early 1970s, there has been a growing demand for learned management skills, such as those taught in the Harvard Business School, and at the London Business School. By contrast, in Japan, such skills are learned on the job; employees tend to spend their careers with the same company and toward the end of them will acquire management status.

management buyout purchase of control of a company by its management, generally with debt funding, making it a ▷leveraged buyout.

Managua capital and chief industrial city of Nicaragua, on the lake of the same name; population (1985) 682,000. It has twice been destroyed by earthquake and rebuilt, 1931 and 1972; it was also badly damaged during the civil war in the late 1970s.

manakin any bird of the order Passeriformes, family Pipridae, found in South and Central America, about 6 in/15 cm long and often brightly colored. They feed on berries and other small fruits. The males of the genus *Manacus* clear a patch of the forest floor with a small tree as a display perch.

manatee any plant-eating aquatic mammal of the genus *Trichechus* constituting the family Trichechidae in the order Sirenia (sea cows). Manatees occur in marine bays and sluggish rivers, usually in turbid water.

The three species of manatee are the Amazonian manatee, found in the river Amazon, the African manatee, which lives in the rivers and coastal areas of Western Africa, and the West Indian manatee, which lives in the Caribbean Sea and along the east coasts of tropical North and South America. All are in danger of becoming extinct as a result of pollution and because they are hunted for food. Their forelimbs are flippers; their hindlimbs are absent, but they have a short, rounded and flattened tail that is used for propulsion. The marine manatee grows up to about 15 ft/4.5 m long and weighs up to 1,323 lb/600 kg.

Manaus capital of Amazonas, Brazil, on the Rio Negro, near its confluence with the Amazon; population (1991) 996,700. It can be reached by sea-going vessels, although it is 1,000 mi/1,600 km from the Atlantic. Formerly a center of the rubber trade, it developed as a tourist center in the 1970s.

Mancha see ▷La Mancha, former province of Spain.

Manche, La French name for the ▷English Channel. It gives its name to a French *département*.

Manchester city in NW England, on the river Irwell, 31 mi/50 km E of Liverpool. It is a manufacturing (textile machinery, chemicals, rubber, processed foods) and financial center; population (1991) 397,400. It is linked by the Manchester Ship Canal, built 1894, to the river Mersey and the sea.
features Home of the Hallé Orchestra, the Northern College of Music, the Royal Exchange (built 1869, now a theater), a town hall (by English architect Alfred Waterhouse (1830-1905)), and a Cotton Exchange (now a leisure center). The Castlefield Urban Heritage Park includes the Granada television studios, including the set of the soap opera *Coronation Street*, open to visitors, and also the Greater Manchester Museum of Science and Industry.
history Originally a Roman camp, Manchester is mentioned in the Domesday Book, and by the 13th century was already a center for the wool trade. Its damp climate made it ideal for cotton, introduced in the 16th century, and in the 19th century the Manchester area was a world center of manufacture, using cotton imported from North America and India. After 1945 there was a sharp decline, and many disused mills were refurbished to provide alternative industrial uses.

Long a hub of ▷Radical thought, Manchester has always been a cultural and intellectual center; it was the original home of the *Guardian* newspaper (founded as the *Manchester Guardian* 1821). Its pop-music scene flourished in the 1980s.

Manchu last ruling dynasty in China, from 1644 until its overthrow 1912; its last emperor was the infant ▷P'u-i. Originally a nomadic people from Manchuria, they established power through a series of successful invasions from the north, then granted trading rights to the US and Europeans, which eventually brought strife and the ▷Boxer Rebellion.

Manchukuo former Japanese puppet state in Manchuria and Jehol 1932–45.

Manchuria European name for the NE region of China, comprising the provinces of Heilongjiang, Jilin, and Liaoning. It was united with China by the ◊Manchu dynasty 1644, but as the Chinese Empire declined, Japan and Russia were rivals for its control. The Russians were expelled after the ◊Russo-Japanese War 1904–05, and in 1932 Japan consolidated its position by creating a puppet state, *Manchukuo*, which disintegrated on the defeat of Japan in World War II.

Mandaean member of the only surviving Gnostic sect of Christianity (see ◊Gnosticism). The Mandaeans live near the Euphrates, S Iraq, and their sacred book is the *Ginza*. The sect claims descent from John the Baptist, but its incorporation of Christian, Hebrew, and indigenous Persian traditions keeps its origins in dispute.

They are hostile to Jesus as the Christ but revere John the Baptist and see a universe where evil spirits try to keep souls from ascending to God.

Mandalay chief town of the Mandalay division of Myanmar (formerly Burma), on the river Irrawaddy, about 370 mi/495 km N of Yangon (Rangoon); population (1983) 533,000.

Founded by King Mindon Min 1857, it was capital of Burma 1857–85, and has many pagodas, temples, and monasteries.

mandarin variety of the tangerine ◊orange *Citrus reticulata*.

Mandarin (Sanskrit *mantrin* "counselor") standard form of the ◊Chinese language. Historically it derives from the language spoken by *mandarins*, Chinese imperial officials, from the 7th century onwards. It is used by 70% of the population and taught in schools of the People's Republic of China.

mandate in history, a territory whose administration was entrusted to Allied states by the League of Nations under the Treaty of Versailles after World War I. Mandated territories were former German and Turkish possessions (including Iraq, Syria, Lebanon, and Palestine). When the United Nations replaced the League of Nations 1945, mandates that had not achieved independence became known as ◊Trust Territories.

In general, mandate means any official command; in politics also the right (given by the electors) of an elected government to carry out its program of policies.

Mandela Nelson (Rolihlahla) 1918– . South African politician and lawyer, president of the ◊African National Congress (ANC) from 1991. As organizer of the then banned ANC, he was imprisoned 1964. In prison he became a symbol of unity for the worldwide antiapartheid movement. In Feb 1990 he was released, the ban on the ANC having been lifted, and he entered into negotiations with the government about a multiracial future for South Africa. In Sept 1992, Mandela and President de Klerk agreed to hasten the creation of an interim government under which reforms could take place. He was married to the South African civil-rights activist Winnie Mandela 1955–92.

Mandela was born near Umbata, in what is today Transkei, the son of a local chief. In a trial of several ANC leaders, he was acquitted of treason 1961, but was once more arrested 1964 and given a life sentence on charges of sabotage and plotting to overthrow the government. In July 1991 he was elected, unopposed, to the presidency of the ANC.

Mandela Winnie (Nomzamo) 1934– . Civil-rights activist in South Africa and former wife of Nelson Mandela. A leading spokesperson for the African National Congress during her husband's imprisonment 1964–90, she has been jailed for a year and put under house arrest several times. In 1989 she was involved in the abduction of four youths, one of whom, Stompie Seipei, was later murdered. Winnie Mandela was convicted of kidnapping and assault, and given a six-year jail sentence May 1991, with the right to appeal. In April 1992 she and Nelson Mandela separated after 33 years of marriage. In the same year she resigned from her ANC leaderships posts, including her seat on the ANC National Executive Committee Sept 1992.

Mandelbrot Benoit B 1924– . Polish-born US scientist who coined the term *fractal geometry* to describe "self-similar" shape, a motif that repeats indefinitely, each time smaller. The concept is associated with ◊chaos theory.

Mandelshtam Osip Emilevich 1891–1938. Russian poet. Son of a Jewish merchant, he was sent to a concentration camp by the communist authorities in the 1930s, and died there. His posthumously published work, with its classic brevity, established his reputation as one of the greatest 20th-century Russian poets.

His wife Nadezhda's memoirs of her life with her husband, *Hope Against Hope*, were published in the West 1970, but not until 1988 in the USSR.

mandolin musical instrument with four or five pairs of strings, tuned like a violin. It takes its name from its almond-shaped body (Italian *mandorla* "almond").

mandragora or **mandrake** plant of the Old World genus *Mandragora* of almost stemless plants with narcotic properties, of the nightshade family Solanaceae. They have large leaves, pale blue or violet flowers, and globose berries known as devil's apples.

The humanoid shape of the root of *M. officinarum* gave rise to the superstition that it shrieks when pulled from the ground.

mandrake another name for the plant mandragora.

mandrill large W African forest-living baboon *Mandrillus sphinx*, most active on the ground. It has large canine teeth like the drill *M. leucophaeus*, to which it is closely related. The nose is bright red and the cheeks striped with blue. There are red callosities on the buttocks; the fur is brown, apart from a yellow beard.

Manes in ancient Rome, the spirits of the dead, worshiped as divine and sometimes identified with the gods of the underworld (Dis and Proserpine).

Manet Edouard 1832–1883. French painter, active in Paris. Rebelling against the academic tradition, he developed a clear and unaffected Realist style. His subjects were mainly contemporary, such as *Un Bar aux Folies-Bergère/A Bar at the Folies-Bergère* 1882 (Courtauld Art Gallery, London).

Manet, born in Paris, trained under a history painter and was inspired by Goya and Velázquez and also by Courbet. His *Déjeuner sur l'herbe/Picnic on the Grass* 1863 and *Olympia* 1865 (both Musée d'Orsay, Paris) offended conservative tastes in their matter-of-fact treatment of the nude body. He never

exhibited with the Impressionists, although he was associated with them from the 1870s.

mangabey any of the Old World monkeys of the tropical African genus *Cercocebus*. The four species have long tails that can be used for support, although they are not fully prehensile. They feed on shoots, leaves, fruit, and some animal food.

Mangalore industrial port (textiles, timber, food-processing) at the mouth of the Netravati River in Karnataka, S India; population (1981) 306,000.

manganese hard, brittle, gray-white metallic element, symbol Mn, atomic number 25, atomic weight 54.9380. It resembles iron (and rusts), but it is not magnetic and is softer. It is used chiefly in making steel alloys, also alloys with aluminum and copper. It is used in fertilizers, paints, and industrial chemicals. It is a necessary trace element in human nutrition. The name is old, deriving from the French and Italian forms of Latin for *magnesia* (MgO), the white tasteless powder used as an antacid from ancient times.

manganese ore any mineral from which manganese is produced. The main ores are the oxides, such as *pyrolusite*, MnO_2; *hausmannite*, Mn_3O_4; and *manganite*, $MnO(OH)$.

Manganese ores may accumulate in metamorphic rocks or as sedimentary deposits, frequently forming nodules on the sea floor (since the 1970s many schemes have been put forward to harvest deep-sea manganese nodules). The world's main producers are Georgia, Ukraine, South Africa, Brazil, Gabon, and India.

mangelwurzel or **mangold** variety of the common beet *Beta vulgaris* used chiefly as feed for cattle and sheep.

mango evergreen tree *Mangifera indica* of the cashew family Anacardiaceae, native to India but now widely cultivated for its oval fruits in other tropical and subtropical areas, such as the West Indies.

mangrove any of several shrubs and trees, especially of the mangrove family Rhizophoraceae, found in the muddy swamps of tropical coasts and estuaries. By sending down aerial roots from their branches, they rapidly form close-growing mangrove thickets. Their timber is impervious to water and resists marine worms. Mangrove swamps are rich breeding grounds for fish and shellfish. These habitats are being destroyed in many countries.

Manhattan island 12.5 mi/20 km long and 2.5 mi/4 km wide, lying between the Hudson and East rivers and forming a borough of the city of ◊New York. It includes the Wall Street business center and Broadway theaters.

Manhattan Project code name for the development of the ◊atomic bomb in the US in World War II, to which the physicists Enrico Fermi and J Robert Oppenheimer contributed.

manic depression mental disorder characterized by recurring periods of ◊depression which may or may not alternate with periods of inappropriate elation (mania) or overactivity. Sufferers may be genetically predisposed to the condition. Some cases have been improved by taking prescribed doses of ◊lithium.

Manichaeism religion founded by the prophet Mani (Latinized as Manichaeus, c. 216–276).

Despite persecution Manichaeism spread and flourished until about the 10th century. Based on the concept of dualism, it held that the material world is evil, an invasion of the spiritual realm of light by the powers of darkness; particles of divine light imprisoned in evil matter were to be rescued by messengers such as Jesus, and finally by Mani himself.

Mani proclaimed his creed in 241 at the Persian court. Returning from missions to China and India, he was put to death at the instigation of the Zoroastrian priesthood.

manifest destiny in US history, the belief that Americans had a providential mission to extend both their territory and their democratic processes westward across the continent. The phrase was coined by journalist John L O'Sullivan 1845. Reflecting this belief, Texas and California were shortly afterwards annexed by the US. (See ⏱Mexican War).

Manila industrial port (textiles, tobacco, distilling, chemicals, shipbuilding) and capital of the Philippines, on the island of Luzon; population (1990) 1,598,900, metropolitan area (including ⏱Quezon City) 5,926,000.
history Manila was founded by Spain 1571, captured by the US 1898; in 1945 during World War II the old city to the south of the river Pasig was reduced to rubble in fighting between US and Japanese troops. It was replaced as capital by Quezon City 1948–76.

manioc another name for the plant ⏱cassava.

Manipur state of NE India
area 8,646 sq mi/22,400 sq km
capital Imphal
features Loktak Lake; original Indian home of polo
products grain, fruit, vegetables, sugar, textiles, cement
population (1991) 1,826,700
language Hindi
religion Hindu 70%
history administered from the state of Assam until 1947 when it became a Union Territory. It became a state 1972.

Manitoba prairie province of Canada
area 250,900 sq mi/650,000 sq km
capital Winnipeg
features lakes Winnipeg, Winnipegosis, and Manitoba (area 1,814 sq mi/4,700 sq km); 50% forested
exports grain, manufactured foods, beverages, machinery, furs, fish, nickel, zinc, copper, and the world's largest cesium deposits
population (1991) 1,092,600
history trading posts and forts were built here by fur traders in the 18th century. What came to be known as the Red River settlement was first colonized 1811 by dispossessed Scottish Highlanders. The colony became the Canadian

Manitoba

Winnipeg

province of Manitoba 1870 after the Riel Rebellion 1869 ended. The area of the province was extended 1881 and 1912.

Manitoba, Lake lake in Manitoba province, which drains into Lake Winnipeg to the NE through the river Dauphin; area 1,800 sq mi/4,700 sq km.

Manizales city in the Central Cordillera in W Colombia 7,000 ft/2,150 m above sea level, center of a coffee-growing area; population (1985) 328,000. It is linked with Mariquita by the world's longest overhead cable transport system, 45 mi/72 km long.

Manley Michael (Norman) 1924– . Jamaican politician, leader of the socialist People's National Party from 1969, and prime minister 1972–80 and 1989–92. He resigned the premiership because of ill health March 1992 and was succeeded by P J Patterson. Manley left parliament April 1992. His father, *Norman Manley* (1893–1969), was the founder of the People's National Party and prime minister 1959–62.

Mann Anthony. Adopted name of Emil Anton Bundmann 1906–1967. US film director who made a series of violent but intelligent 1950s Westerns starring James Stewart, such as *Winchester '73* 1950. He also directed the epic *El Cid* 1961. His other films include *The Glenn Miller Story* 1954 and *A Dandy in Aspic* 1968.

Mann Heinrich 1871–1950. German novelist who fled to the US 1937 with his brother Thomas Mann. His books include *Im Schlaraffenland/In the Land of Cockaigne* 1901; *Professor Unrat/The Blue Angel* 1904, depicting the sensual downfall of a schoolmaster; a scathing trilogy dealing with the Kaiser's Germany *Das Kaiserreich/The Empire* 1918–25; and two volumes on the career of Henry IV of France 1935–38.

Mann Horace 1796–1859. US political leader and education reformer. He served in the Massachusetts House of Representatives 1827–33 and Massachusetts Senate 1835–37. In 1837, with the passage of a state public-school act, Mann resigned from the legislature to serve as the secretary of the state school board 1837–48. In that position he helped raise the level of funding and instruction for public education.

Born in Franklin, Massachusetts, Mann was educated at Brown University and was admitted to the bar 1823. After serving in the US House of Representatives 1848–53, Mann became president of Antioch College 1853–59.

Mann Thomas 1875–1955. German novelist and critic, concerned with the theme of the artist's relation to society. His first novel was *Buddenbrooks* 1901, which, followed by *Der Zauberberg/The Magic Mountain* 1924, led to a Nobel Prize 1929. Notable among his works of short fiction is *Der Tod in Venedig/Death in Venice* 1913.

Mann worked in an insurance office in Munich and on the staff of the periodical *Simplicissimus*. His opposition to the Nazi regime forced him to leave Germany and in 1940 he became a US citizen. Among his other works are a biblical tetralogy on the theme of Joseph and his brothers 1933–44, *Dr Faustus* 1947, *Die Bekenntnisse des Hochstaplers Felix Krull/Confessions of Felix Krull* 1954, and a number of short stories, including "Tonio Kröger" 1903.

manna sweetish exudation obtained from many trees such as the ash and larch, and used in medicine. The manna of the Bible is thought to have been from the tamarisk tree, or a form of lichen.

Mannerheim Carl Gustav Emil von 1867–1951. Finnish general and politician, leader of the conservative forces in the civil war 1917–18 and regent 1918–19. He commanded the Finnish army 1939–40 and 1941–44, and was president of Finland 1944–46.

After the Russian Revolution 1917, a Red (socialist) militia was formed in Finland with Russian backing, and independence was declared in Dec. The Red forces were opposed by a White (counterrevolutionary) army led by Mannerheim, who in 1918 crushed the socialists with German assistance. In 1944, after leading the defense against Soviet invasion in two wars, he negotiated the peace settlement with the USSR and became president.

Mannerism in painting and architecture, a style characterized by a subtle but conscious breaking of the "rules" of Classical composition—for example, displaying the human body in an off-center, distorted pose, and using harsh, non-blending colors. The term was coined by Giorgio ⏱Vasari and used to describe the 16th-century reaction to the peak of Renaissance classicism as achieved by Raphael, Leonardo da Vinci, and early Michelangelo.

The effect is to unsettle the viewer, who is expected to understand the norms that the Mannerist picture is deliberately violating. Strictly speaking, Mannerism refers to painters and architects in Italy (primarily Rome and Florence) during the years 1520 to 1575 beginning with, and largely derived from, the later works of Michelangelo in painting and architecture, and including the works of the painters Giovanni Rosso and Parmigianino, and the architect Giulio Romano. The term has been extended, however, to cover similar ideas in other arts and in other countries.

Mannheim Karl 1893–1947. Hungarian sociologist who settled in the UK 1933. In *Ideology and Utopia* 1929 he argued that all knowledge, except in mathematics and physics, is ideological, a reflection of class interests and values; that there is therefore no such thing as objective knowledge or absolute truth.

Mannheim distinguished between ruling class ideologies and those of utopian or revolutionary groups, arguing that knowledge is thus created by a continual power struggle between rival groups and ideas. Later works such as *Man and Society* 1940 analyzed contemporary mass society in terms of its fragmentation and susceptibility to extremist ideas and totalitarian governments.

Manoel I 1469–1521. King of Portugal from 1495, when he succeeded his uncle John II (1455–1495). He was known as "the Fortunate," because his reign was distinguished by the discoveries made by Portuguese navigators and the expansion of the Portuguese empire.

manometer instrument for measuring the pressure of liquids (including human blood pressure) or gases. In its basic form, it is a U-tube partly filled with colored liquid; pressure of a gas entering at one side is measured by the level to which the liquid rises at the other.

manor basic economic unit in ⏱feudalism in Europe, established in England under the Norman conquest. It consisted of the lord's house and cultivated land, land rented by free tenants, land held by villagers, common land, woodland, and waste land.

Here and there traces of the system survive in England—the common land may have become an area for public recreation—but the documents sometimes sold at auction and entitling the owner to be called "lord of the manor" seldom have any rights attached to them.

Man Ray adopted name of Emmanuel Rudnitsky 1890–1977. US photographer, painter, and sculptor, active mainly in France; associated with the Dada movement. His pictures often showed Surrealist images like the photograph *Le Violon d'Ingres* 1924.

Man Ray was born in Philadelphia, but lived mostly in Paris from 1921. He began as a painter and took up photography in 1915, the year he met the Dada artist Duchamp in New York. In 1922 he invented the **rayograph**, a black-and-white image obtained without a camera by placing objects on sensitized photographic paper and exposing them to light; he also used the technique of solarization (partly reversing the tones on a photograph). His photographs include portraits of many artists and writers.

Mansart Jules Hardouin. See ◊Hardouin-Mansart, Jules.

Mansfield industrial city (automobile parts, steel and rubber products) in N central Ohio, NE of Columbus, seat of Richland County; population (1990) 50,600.

Mansfield Jayne. Adopted name of Vera Jayne Palmer 1933–1967. US actress who had a short career as a kind of living parody of Marilyn Monroe in films including *The Girl Can't Help It* 1956 and *Will Success Spoil Rock Hunter?* 1957.

manslaughter in English law, the unlawful killing of a human being in circumstances less culpable than ◊murder—for example, when the killer suffers extreme provocation, is in some way mentally ill (diminished responsibility), did not intend to kill but did so accidentally in the course of another crime or by behaving with criminal recklessness, or is the survivor of a genuine suicide pact that involved killing the other person.

Mans, Le see ◊Le Mans.

Manson Patrick 1844–1922. Scottish physician who showed that insects are responsible for the spread of diseases like elephantiasis and malaria.

Manson spent many years in practice in the Far East. On his return to London, he founded the School of Tropical Medicine.

manometer *The manometer indicates gas pressure by the rise of liquid in the tube.*

manta another name for ◊devil ray, a large fish.

Mantegna Andrea *c.* 1431–1506. Italian Renaissance painter and engraver, active chiefly in Padua and Mantua, where some of his frescoes remain. Paintings such as *The Agony in the Garden c.* 1455 (National Gallery, London) reveal a dramatic linear style, mastery of perspective, and strongly Classical architectural detail.

Mantegna was born in Vicenza. Early works include frescoes for the Eremitani Church in Padua painted during the 1440s (badly damaged). From 1460 he worked for Ludovico Gonzaga in Mantua, producing an outstanding fresco series in the Ducal Palace (1470s) and later *The Triumphs of Caesar* (Hampton Court, near London). He was influenced by the sculptor Donatello and in turn influenced the Venetian painter Giovanni Bellini (his brother-in-law) and the German artist Albrecht Dürer.

mantis any insect of the family Mantidae, related to cockroaches. Some species can reach a length of 8 in/20 cm. There are about 2,000 species of mantis, mainly tropical.

Mantises are often called "praying mantises" because of the way they hold their front legs, adapted for grasping prey, when at rest. The eggs are laid in Sept and hatch early in the following summer.

The 4 in/10 cm-long Chinese praying mantis, proficient at garden pest control, is now naturalized in North America.

mantissa in mathematics, the decimal part of a ◊logarithm. For example, the logarithm of 347.6 is 2.5411; in this case, the 0.5411 is the mantissa, and the integral (whole number) part of the logarithm, the 2, is the ◊characteristic.

mantle intermediate zone of the Earth between the crust and the core. It is thought to consist of silicate minerals such as olivine and spinel.

The mantle is separated from the crust by the ◊Mohorovičić discontinuity, and from the core by the Gutenberg discontinuity. The patterns of seismic waves passing through it show that its uppermost as well as its lower layers are solid. However, from 45 mi/72 km to 155 mi/250 km in depth is a zone through which seismic waves pass more slowly (the "low-velocity zone"). The inference is that materials in this zone are close to their melting points and they are partly molten. The low-velocity zone is considered the ◊asthenosphere on which the solid lithosphere rides.

Mantle Mickey (Charles) 1931– . US baseball player. Signed by the New York Yankees, he broke into the major leagues 1951. A powerful switch-hitter (able to bat with either hand), he also excelled as a center-fielder. In 1956 he won baseball's Triple Crown, leading the American League in batting average, home runs, and runs batted in. He retired 1969 after 18 years with the Yankees and seven World Series championships.

Mantle, born in Spavinaw, Oklahoma, was an exceptional high-school athlete in football and basketball as well as baseball.

He enjoyed 12 pennant-winning seasons with the Yankees and was elected to the Baseball Hall of Fame 1974.

mantra in Hindu or Buddhist belief, a word repeatedly intoned to assist concentration and develop spiritual power; for example, *om*, which represents the names of Brahma,

Vishnu, and Siva. Followers of a guru may receive their own individual mantra.

Mantua (Italian *Mantova*) capital of Mantua province, Lombardy, Italy, on an island of a lagoon of the river Mincio, SW of Verona; industry (chemicals, brewing, printing); population (1981) 60,866. The poet Virgil was born near Mantua, which dates from Roman times; it has Gothic palaces and a cathedral founded in the 12th century.

Manu in Hindu mythology, the founder of the human race, who was saved by ◊Brahma from a deluge.

Manuel II 1889–1932. King of Portugal 1908–10. He ascended the throne on the assassination of his father, Carlos I, but was driven out by a revolution 1910, and lived in England.

Manx Gaelic ◊Gaelic language of the Isle of Man.

Maoism form of communism based on the ideas and teachings of the Chinese communist leader ◊Mao Zedong. It involves an adaptation of ◊Marxism to suit conditions in China and apportions a much greater role to agriculture and the peasantry in the building of socialism, thus effectively bypassing the capitalist (industrial) stage envisaged by Marx.

Maori member of the indigenous Polynesian people of New Zealand, who numbered 294,200 in 1986, about 10% of the total population. Their language, Maori, belongs to the eastern branch of the Austronesian family.

In recent years there has been increased Maori consciousness. Only one-third use the Maori language today, but efforts are being made to give it official status and strengthen it after a long period of decline and official indifference. Under the Waitangi Treaty of 1840, the Maoris surrendered their lands to British sovereignty. The Maoris now demand a review of the treaty and claim 70% of the country's land; they have secured a ruling that the fishing grounds of the far north belong solely to local Maori people. The **Maori Unity Movement/Kotahitanga** was founded 1983 by Eva Rickard.

In Maori, New Zealand is *Aotearoa* ("land of the long white cloud") and European settlers are *Pakeha*, a term often used by white New Zealanders when contrasting themselves with the Maori.

Mao Zedong or *Mao Tse-tung* 1893–1976. Chinese political leader and Marxist theoretician. A founder of the Chinese Communist Party (CCP) 1921, Mao soon emerged as its leader. He organized the ◊Long March 1934–36 and the war of liberation 1937–49, following which he established a People's Republic and Communist rule in China; he headed the CCP and government until his death. His influence diminished with the failure of his 1958–60 ◊Great Leap Forward, but he emerged dominant again during the 1966–69 ◊Cultural Revolution. Mao adapted communism to Chinese conditions, as set out in the *Little Red Book*.

Mao, son of a peasant farmer in Hunan province, was once library assistant at Beijing University and a headmaster at Changsha. He became chief of CCP propaganda under the Guomindang (Nationalist) leader Sun Yat-sen (Sun Zhong Shan) until dismissed by Sun's successor Chiang Kai-shek (Jiang Jie Shi). In 1931–34 Mao set up a Communist republic at Jiangxi and, together with Zhu De, marshalled the Red Army and organized the Long March to Shaanxi to evade Nationalist suppressive tactics. CCP head from 1935, Mao secured an alliance with the Nationalist forces 1936–45 aimed at repelling the Japanese invaders. At Yen'an, he built up a people's republic 1936–47 and married his third wife ⟩Jiang Qing 1939. Civil war with the Nationalists was renewed from 1946 until 1949 when Mao defeated them at Nanking and established the People's Republic and Communist party rule under his leadership. During the civil war, he successfully employed mobile, rural-based guerrilla tactics.

Mao served as party head until his death Sept 1976 and as state president until 1959. After the damages of the Cultural Revolution, the Great Helmsman, as he was called, working with his prime minister Zhou Enlai, oversaw a period of reconstruction from 1970 until deteriorating health weakened his political grip in the final years.

Mao's writings and thoughts dominated the functioning of the People's Republic 1949–76. He wrote some 2,300 publications, comprising 3 million words; 740 million copies of his *Quotations* have been printed. He stressed the need for rural rather than urban-based revolutions in Asia, for reducing rural-urban differences, and for perpetual revolution to prevent the emergence of new elites. Mao helped precipitate the Sino-Soviet split 1960 and was a firm advocate of a nonaligned Third World strategy. Since 1978, the leadership of Deng Xiaoping has reinterpreted Maoism, criticized its policy excesses, and commercialized the nation, but many of Mao's ideas remain valued.

map diagrammatic representation of an area—for example, part of the Earth's surface or the distribution of the stars. Modern maps of the Earth are made using satellites in low orbit to take a series of overlapping stereoscopic photographs from which a three-dimensional image can be prepared. The earliest accurate large-scale maps appeared about 1580.

Conventional aerial photography, laser beams, microwaves, and infrared equipment are also used for land surveying. Many different kinds of ⟩map projection (the means by which a three-dimensional body is shown in two dimensions) are used in map-making. Detailed maps requiring constant updating are kept in digital form on computer so that minor revisions can be made without redrafting.

Mapai (Miphlegeth Poale Israel) Israeli Workers' Party or Labor Party, founded 1930. Its leading figure until 1965 was David Ben-Gurion. In 1968, the party allied with two other democratic socialist parties to form the Israeli Labor Party, led initially by Levi Eshkol and later by Golda Meir.

maple deciduous tree of the genus *Acer*, family Aceraceae, with lobed leaves and green flowers, followed by two-winged fruits, or samaras. There are over 200 species, chiefly in northern temperate regions.

About 12 species are native to North America. The North American sugar maple *A. saccharum* is a source of maple syrup. *A. campestre* and *A. pseudoplatanus*, the ⟩sycamore or great maple, are native to Europe. The European plane tree—sometimes erroneously called sycamore—has been introduced worldwide.

Mapplethorpe Robert 1946–1989. US art photographer known for his use of racial and homoerotic imagery in chiefly fine platinum prints. He developed a style of polished elegance in his gallery art works, whose often culturally forbidden subject matter caused controversy.

map projection ways of depicting the spherical surface of the Earth on a flat piece of paper. Traditional projections include the **conic**, **azimuthal**, and **cylindrical**. The most famous cylindrical projection is the ⟩Mercator projection, which dates from 1569. The weakness of these systems is that countries in different latitudes are disproportionately large, and lines of longitude and latitude appear distorted. In 1973 German historian Arno Peters devised the **Peters projection** in which the countries of the world retain their relative areas.

The theory behind traditional map projection is that, if a light were placed at the center of a transparent Earth, the surface features could be thrown as shadows on a piece of paper close to the surface. This paper may be flat and placed on a pole (azimuthal or zenithal), or may be rolled around the equator (cylindrical), or may be in the form of a tall cone resting on the equator (conical). The resulting maps differ from one another, distorting either area or direction, and each is suitable for a particular purpose. For example, projections distorting area the least are used for distribution maps, and those with least distortion of direction are used for navigation charts.

Mapp v Ohio US Supreme Court decision 1961 dealing with the admission into criminal trials of evidence procured through illegal searches and seizures. Mapp, a Cleveland woman, was arrested for the possession of obscene materials discovered by police during an illegal search. Convicted by the state, Mapp appealed to the US Supreme Court, arguing that her Fourth-Amendment rights had been violated. The Court reversed Mapp's conviction, creating the rule that all illegally obtained evidence be excluded from state and federal trials.

Maputo formerly (until 1975) *Lourenço Marques* capital of Mozambique, and Africa's second-largest port, on Delagoa Bay; population (1987) 1,006,800. Linked by rail with Zimbabwe and South Africa, it is a major outlet for minerals, steel, textiles, processed foods, and furniture.

maquis mostly evergreen vegetation common in many Mediterranean countries, consisting of scrub woodland with many low-growing tangled bushes and shrubs, typically including species of broom, gorse, and heather.

Maquis French ⟩resistance movement that fought against the German occupation during World War II.

mara one of two species of rodents, genus *Dolichotis* of the guinea-pig family, occurring in Argentina, with long back limbs and a short tail. They can grow to 2.5 ft/75 cm long and are sometimes known as "Patagonian cavies" or "hares."

marabou stork *Leptoptilos crumeniferus* found in Africa. It is about 4 ft/120 cm tall, has a bald head, and eats snakes, lizards, insects, and carrion. It is largely dark gray and white and has an inflatable throat pouch.

Maracaibo oil-exporting port in Venezuela, on the channel connecting Lake Maracaibo with the Gulf of Venezuela; population (1989) 1,365,308. It is the second largest city in the country.

Maracaibo, Lake lake in NW Venezuela; area 5,400 sq mi/14,000 sq km. Oil was discovered here 1917.

Marat Jean Paul 1743–1793. French Revolutionary leader and journalist. He was elected to the National Convention 1792, where he carried on a long struggle with the right-wing ⟩Girondins, ending in their overthrow May 1793. In July he was murdered by Charlotte ⟩Corday, a member of the Girondins.

Marat was a hero of the Paris revolutionary crowds. He was killed in his bath, where he generally worked, while treating a skin condition.

marathon athletics endurance race over 26 mi/42.195 km. It was first included in the Olympic Games in Athens 1896. The distance varied until it was standardized 1924. More recently, races have been opened to wider participation, including social runners as well as those competing at senior level.

The marathon derives its name from the story of Pheidippides, a Greek soldier who ran the distance of approximately 24 mi/39 km from the battlefield of Marathon to Athens with the news of a Greek victory over the Persians in 490 BC.

The current marathon distance was first used at the 1908 Olympic Games in London when the race was increased by an extra 385 yards so the race would finish in front of the royal box. The best known US marathons are run annually in Boston, New York City, and Los Angeles.

Marathon, Battle of 490 BC. Fought between the Greeks, who were ultimately victorious, and invading Persians on the plain of Marathon, NE of Athens. News of the Persian destruction of the Greek city of Eretria was taken from Athens to Sparta by a courier, Pheidippides, who fell dead on arrival. His feat is commemorated by the **marathon race**.

Marbella port and tourist resort on the Costa del Sol between Málaga and Algeciras in Andalucia, S Spain; population (1991) 80,645. There are three bullrings, a Moorish castle, and the remains of a medieval defensive wall.

marble metamorphosed ⟩limestone that takes and retains a good polish; it is used in building and sculpture. In its pure form it is white and consists almost entirely of calcite $CaCO_3$. Mineral impurities give it various colors and patterns. Carrara, Italy, is known for white marble.

Marburg disease or **green monkey disease** viral disease of central Africa, first occurring in Europe 1967 among research workers in Germany working with African green monkeys. It is characterized by haemorrhage of the mucous membranes, fever, vomiting, and diarrhea; mortality is high.

Marbury v Madison US Supreme Court decision 1803 that affirmed the process of judicial review over Congressional acts. The plaintiff, William Marbury, had been appointed the District of Columbia's justice of the peace by President J Adams shortly before Jefferson replaced Adams in office, but the new secretary of state, James Madison, withheld the letter of appointment. Marbury appealed to the Court to force Madison to produce the letter by issuing a writ of mandamus, a power granted by Congress in the Judiciary Act of 1789. The Court ruled unanimously that Congress did not have the right to expand judiciary powers. Since writs of mandamus were not provided for in the Constitution, the Court was not empowered to issue them. This was the first time the Court nullified an act of Congress on the basis of constitutionality.

Marc Franz 1880–1916. German Expressionist painter, associated with Wassily Kandinsky in founding the ⟡*Blaue Reiter* movement. Animals played an essential part in his view of the world, and bold semiabstracts of red and blue horses are characteristic of his work.

Marceau Marcel 1923– . French mime artist. He is the creator of the clown-harlequin Bip and mime sequences such as "Youth, Maturity, Old Age, and Death."

Marche, Le (English *the Marches*) region of E central Italy consisting of the provinces of Ancona, Ascoli Piceno, Macerata, and Pesaro e Urbino; capital Ancona; area 3,744 sq mi/ 9,700 sq km; population (1990) 1,435,600.

Marches boundary areas of England with Wales, and England with Scotland. In the Middle Ages these troubled frontier regions were held by lords of the Marches, sometimes called *marchiones* and later earls of March. The 1st Earl of March of the Welsh Marches was Roger de Mortimer (*c.* 1286–1330); of the Scottish Marches, Patrick Dunbar (died 1285).

March on Rome, the means by which Fascist leader Benito Mussolini came to power in Italy 1922. A protracted crisis in government and the threat of civil war enabled him to demand the formation of a Fascist government to restore order. On Oct 29, 1922, King Victor Emmanuel III invited Mussolini to come to Rome to take power. The "march" was a propaganda myth: Mussolini traveled overnight by train from Milan to Rome, where he formed a government the following day, Oct 30. Some 25,000 fascist Blackshirts were also transported to the city, where they marched in a ceremonial parade Oct 31.

Marcian 396–457. Eastern Roman emperor 450–457. He was a general who married Pulcheria, sister of Theodosius II, and became emperor at the latter's death. He convened the Council of ⟡Chalcedon (the fourth Ecumenical Council of the Christian Church) 451 and refused to pay tribute to Attila the Hun.

Marciano Rocky (Rocco Francis Marchegiano) 1923–1969. US boxer, world heavyweight champion 1952–56. He retired after 49 professional fights, the only heavyweight champion to retire undefeated.

Born in Brockton, Massachussetts, he was known as the "Brockton Blockbuster." He knocked out 43 of his 49 opponents.

Marciano was killed in a plane crash.

Marconi Guglielmo 1874–1937. Italian electrical engineer and pioneer in the invention and development of radio. In 1895 he achieved radio communication over more than a mile, and in England 1896 he conducted successful experiments that led to the formation of the company that became Marconi's Wireless Telegraph Company Ltd. He shared the Nobel Prize for Physics 1909.

After reading about radio waves, he built a device to convert them into electrical signals. He then tried to transmit and receive radio waves over increasing distances. In 1898 he successfully transmitted signals across the English Channel, and in 1901 established communication with St John's, Newfoundland, from Poldhu in Cornwall, and in 1918 with Australia.

Marco Polo see ⟡Polo, Marco.

Marco Polo bridge incident conflict 1937 between Chinese and Japanese army troops on the border of Japanese-controlled ⟡Manchukuo and China that led to full-scale war

between the two states. It lasted until the Japanese surrender 1945.

Marcos Ferdinand 1917–1989. Filipino rightwing politician, president from 1965 to 1986, when he was forced into exile in Hawaii. He was backed by the US when in power, but in 1988 US authorities indicted him and his wife Imelda Marcos for racketeering, embezzlement, and defrauding US banks; Marcos was too ill to stand trial.

Marcos was convicted while a law student 1939 of murdering a political opponent of his father, but eventually secured his own acquittal. In World War II he was a guerrilla fighter, survived the Japanese prison camps, and became president 1965. His regime became increasingly repressive, with secret pro-Marcos groups terrorizing and executing his opponents. He was overthrown and exiled 1986 by a popular front led by Corazon ⟡Aquino, widow of a murdered opposition leader. A US grand jury investigating Marcos and his wife alleged that they had embezzled over $100 million from the government of the Philippines, received bribes, and defrauded US banks.

Marcos Imelda 1930– . Filipino politician and socialite, wife of Ferdinand Marcos, in exile 1986–91. She was acquitted 1990 of defrauding US banks. Under indictment for misuse of Philippine state funds, she returned to Manila Nov 1991 and was an unsuccessful candidate in the 1992 presidential elections.

After her husband's death 1989, Imelda Marcos stood trial in New York City 1990 in answer to charges of concealing ownership of US property and other goods, purchased with stolen Philippine-government funds. She was acquitted, her lawyer claiming the responsibility had lain solely with her husband.

In 1991, the Philippines' government lifted its ban on Imelda Marcos returning to her homeland in the hope of recouping an estimated $350 million from frozen Marcos accounts in Swiss banks. Simultaneously, they filed 11 charges of tax evasion against her and 18 against her children.

Marcus Aurelius Antoninus AD 121–180. Roman emperor from 161 and Stoic philosopher. Although considered one of the best of the Roman emperors, he persecuted the Christians for political reasons. He wrote the philosophical *Meditations*.

Born in Rome, he was adopted (at the same time as Lucius Aurelius Verus) by his uncle, the emperor Antoninus Pius, whom he succeeded in 161. He conceded an equal share in the rule to Lucius Verus (died 169). Marcus Aurelius spent much of his reign warring against the Germanic tribes and died in Pannonia, where he had gone to drive back the invading Marcomanni.

Marcuse Herbert 1898–1979. US political philosopher, born in Germany. His theories, combining Marxism and Freudianism, greatly influenced the radicalism of the 1960s and 1970s. He preached the overthrow of the existing social order by using the system's very tolerance to ensure its defeat, but he was not an advocate of violent revolution.

A refugee from Hitler's Germany, Marcuse came to the US 1934. He taught philosophy at several universities, including Columbia 1934–40, Brandeis 1954–65, and the University of California at San Diego 1965–79. He wrote several books, including *Eros and Civilization* 1955 and *One-Dimensional Man* 1964.

Mardi Gras (French "fat Tuesday" from the custom of using up all the fat in the household

before the beginning of ⟡Lent) Shrove Tuesday. A festival was traditionally held on this day in Paris, and there are carnivals in many parts of the world, including New Orleans, Louisiana; Italy; and Brazil.

Marduk in Babylonian mythology, the sun god, creator of Earth and humans.

mare (plural *maria*) dark lowland plain on the Moon. The name comes from Latin "sea," because these areas were once wrongly thought to be water.

Marengo, Battle of defeat of the Austrians by the French emperor Napoleon on June 14, 1800, as part of his Italian campaign, near the village of Marengo in Piedmont, Italy.

Margaret (Rose) 1930– . Princess of the UK, younger daughter of George VI and sister of Elizabeth II. In 1960 she married Anthony Armstrong-Jones, later created Lord Snowdon, but they were divorced 1978. Their children are *David, Viscount Linley* (1961–) and *Lady Sarah Armstrong-Jones* (1964–).

Margaret of Anjou 1430–1482. Queen of England from 1445, wife of ⟡Henry VI of England. After the outbreak of the Wars of the ⟡Roses 1455, she acted as the leader of the Lancastrians, but was defeated and captured at the battle of Tewkesbury 1471 by Edward IV.

Her one object had been to secure the succession of her son, Edward (born 1453), who was killed at Tewkesbury. After five years' imprisonment Margaret was allowed in 1476 to return to her native France, where she died in poverty.

Margaret, St 1045–1093. Queen of Scotland, the granddaughter of King Edmund Ironside of England. She went to Scotland after the Norman Conquest, and soon after married Malcolm III. The marriage of her daughter Matilda to Henry I united the Norman and English royal houses.

margarine butter substitute made from animal fats and/or vegetable oils. The French chemist Hippolyte Mège-Mouriès invented margarine 1889. Today, margarines are usually made with vegetable oils, such as soy, corn, or sunflower oil, giving a product low in saturated fats (see ⟡polyunsaturate) and fortified with vitamins A and D.

margay small cat *Felis wiedi* found from southern US to South America in forested areas, where it hunts birds and small mammals. It is about 2 ft/60 cm long with a 1.3 ft/40 cm tail, has a rounded head, and has black spots and blotches on a yellowish-brown coat.

margin in finance, the difference between cost and selling price; also cash or collateral on deposit with a broker or lender to meet legal requirements against loss, as when stocks and other securities have been financed by funds supplied by the lender.

Margin accounts were set at 10% of the selling price before the stock market crash of 1929. Since the establishment of the ⟡Securities and Exchange Commission 1934, margin was set at 50%.

marginal theory in economics, the study of the effect of increasing a factor by one more unit (known as the marginal unit). For example, if a firm's production is increased by one unit, its costs will increase also; the increase in costs is called the marginal cost of production. Marginal theory is a central tool of microeconomics.

margrave German title (equivalent of marquess) for the "counts of the march," who guarded the frontier regions of the Holy Roman Empire from Charlemagne's time. Later the title was used by other territorial princes. Chief among these were the margraves of Austria and of Brandenburg.

Margrethe II 1940– . Queen of Denmark from 1972, when she succeeded her father Frederick IX. In 1967, she married the French diplomat Count Henri de Laborde de Monpezat, who took the title Prince Hendrik. Her heir is Crown Prince Frederick (1968–).

marguerite European plant *Leucanthemum vulgare* of the daisy family Compositae. It is a shrubby perennial and bears white daisylike flowers. Marguerite is also the name of a cultivated variety of ◊chrysanthemum.

Marguerite of Navarre also known as *Margaret d'Angoulême* 1492–1549. Queen of Navarre from 1527, French poet, and author of the *Heptaméron* 1558, a collection of stories in imitation of Boccaccio's *Decameron*. The sister of Francis I of France, she was born in Angoulême. Her second husband 1527 was Henri d'Albret, king of Navarre.

Mari autonomous republic of Russia, E of Nizhni Novgorod and W of the Urals
area 8,900 sq mi/23,200 sq km
capital Yoshkar-Ola
features the Volga flows through the SW; 60% is forested
products timber, paper, grain, flax, potatoes, fruit
population (1989) 750,000; about 43% are ethnic Mari
history the Mari were conquered by Russia 1552. Mari was made an autonomous region 1920, an autonomous republic 1936.

Mariana Islands or *Marianas* archipelago in the NW Pacific E of the Philippines, divided politically into ◊*Guam* (an unincorporated territory of the US) and **Northern Marianas** (a commonwealth of the US with its own internal government, of 16 mountainous islands, extending 350 mi/560 km N from Guam)
area 185 sq mi/480 sq km
capital Garapan on Saipan
government own constitutionally elected government
products sugar, coconuts, coffee
currency US dollar
population (1988) 21,000, mainly Micronesian
languages Chamorro 55%, English
religion mainly Roman Catholic
history sold to Germany by Spain 1899. The islands were mandated by the League of Nations to Japan 1918, and taken by US Marines 1944–45 in World War II. The islands were part of the US Trust Territory of the Pacific 1947–78. Since 1978 they have been a commonwealth of the US.

Mariana Trench lowest region on the Earth's surface; the deepest part of the sea floor. The trench is 1,500 mi/2,400 km long and is situated 200 mi/300 km E of the Mariana Islands, in the NW Pacific Ocean. Its deepest part is the gorge known as the Challenger Deep, which extends 36,210 ft/11,034 m below sea level.

Maria Theresa 1717–1780. Empress of Austria from 1740, when she succeeded her father, the Holy Roman emperor Charles VI; her claim to the throne was challenged and she became embroiled, first in the War of the ◊Austrian Succession 1740–48, then in the ◊Seven Years' War 1756–63; she remained in possession of Austria but lost Silesia. The rest of her reign

was peaceful and, with her son Joseph II, she introduced social reforms.

After 1763 she pursued a consistently peaceful policy, concentrating on internal reforms; although her methods were despotic, she fostered education, codified the laws, and abolished torture. She also expelled the Jesuits. In these measures she was assisted by her son, Joseph II, who became emperor 1765, and succeeded her in the Hapsburg domains.

Marie 1875–1938. Queen of Romania. She was the daughter of the duke of Edinburgh, second son of Queen Victoria, and married Prince Ferdinand of Romania in 1893 (he was king 1922–27). She wrote a number of literary works, notably *Story of My Life* 1934–35. Her son Carol became king of Romania, and her daughters, Elisabeth and Marie, queens of Greece and Yugoslavia respectively.

Marie Antoinette 1755–1793. Queen of France from 1774. She was the daughter of Empress Maria Theresa of Austria, and married ◊Louis XVI of France 1770. Her reputation for extravagance helped provoke the ◊French Revolution of 1789. She was tried for treason Oct 1793 and guillotined.

Marie Antoinette influenced her husband to resist concessions in the early days of the Revolution—for example, ◊Mirabeau's plan for a constitutional settlement. She instigated the disastrous flight to Varennes, which discredited the monarchy, and welcomed foreign intervention against the Revolution, betraying French war strategy to the Austrians 1792.

Marie de' Medici 1573–1642. Queen of France, wife of Henry IV from 1600, and regent (after his murder) for their son Louis XIII. She left the government to her favorites, the Concinis, until Louis XIII seized power and executed them 1617. She was banished, but after she led a revolt 1619, ◊Richelieu effected her reconciliation with her son. When she attempted to oust him again 1630, she was exiled.

Marie Louise 1791–1847. Queen consort of Napoleon I from 1810 (after his divorce from Josephine), mother of Napoleon II. She was the daughter of Francis I of Austria (see Emperor ◊Francis II) and on Napoleon's fall returned with their son to Austria, where she was granted the duchy of Parma 1815.

Marietta industrial town (plastics, metal products, chemicals, and office equipment) in SE Ohio; seat of Washington County; population (1990) 15,000. It lies where the Muskingum River flows into the Ohio River, SE of Columbus, and was the first permanent settlement 1788 in Ohio.

marigold any of several plants of the family Compositae, especially the genus *Tagetes*, including pot marigold *Calendula officinalis* and the tropical American *T. patula*, commonly known as French marigold.

marijuana the dried leaves and flowers of the ◊hemp plant (*Cannabis sativa*), used as a recreational but illegal drug. It is eaten or inhaled and causes euphoria, distortion of time, and heightened sensations of sight and sound.

marimba bass ◊xylophone with wooden rather than metal tubular resonators.

Mariner spacecraft series of US space probes that explored the planets Mercury, Venus, and Mars 1962–75.
Mariner 1 (to Venus) had a failed launch.
Mariner 2 1962 made the first fly-by of Venus,

at 21,000 mi/34,000 km, confirmed the existence of ◊solar wind, and measured Venusian temperature. *Mariner 3* did not achieve its intended trajectory to Mars. *Mariner 4* 1965 passed Mars at a distance of 6,100 mi/9,800 km, and took photographs, revealing a dry, cratered surface. *Mariner 5* 1967 passed Venus at 2,500 mi/4,000 km, and measured Venusian temperature, atmosphere, mass, and diameter. *Mariner 6* and *7* 1969 photographed Mars' equator and southern hemisphere respectively, and also measured temperature, atmospheric pressure and composition, and diameter. *Mariner 8* (to Mars) had a failed launch. *Mariner 9* 1971 mapped the entire Martian surface, and photographed Mars' moons. Its photographs revealed the changing of the polar caps, and the extent of volcanism, canyons, and features, which suggested that there might once have been water on Mars. *Mariner 10* 1974–75 took close-up photographs of Mercury and Venus, and measured temperature, radiation, and magnetic fields.

Mariner 11 and *12* became *Voyager 1* and *2*, which reached Jupiter 1979, Saturn 1980–81, Uranus 1986, Neptune 1989, and continue to the present traveling beyond the Solar System.

marines fighting force that operates both on land and at sea.

The *US Marine Corps* (1775) is constituted as an arm of the US Navy. It is made up of infantry and air support units trained and equipped for amphibious landings under fire.

Marinetti Filippo Tommaso 1876–1944. Italian author who in 1909 published the first manifesto of ◊Futurism, which called for a break with tradition in art, poetry, and the novel, and glorified the machine age.

Marinetti illustrated his theories in *Mafarka le futuriste: Roman africaine/Mafarka the Futurist: African novel* 1909. His best-known work is *Manifesto technico della letteratura futuristica/Technical manifesto of futurist literature* 1912 (translated 1971). He also wrote plays, a volume on theatrical practice 1916, and a volume of poems *Guerra sola igiene del mondo/War the only hygiene of the world* 1915.

He was born in Alexandria.

Marini Marino 1901–1980. Italian sculptor. Inspired by ancient art, he developed a distinctive horse-and-rider theme and a dancers series, reducing the forms to an elemental simplicity. He also produced fine portraits in bronze.

Marion Francis *c.* 1732–1795. American military leader who served in the colonial militia during the Revolutionary War and saw action against the British in the battle for Charleston 1776. After the fall of Charleston 1780, Marion, by then promoted to lieutenant colonel, waged a successful guerrilla war against the British. Establishing his field headquarters in inaccessible areas, he became popularly known as the "Swamp Fox." Marion played a major role in the American victory at Eutaw Springs 1781.

Marion was born in Berkeley County, South Carolina. After the war, he served in the South Carolina Senate.

marionette type of ◊puppet, a jointed figure controlled from above by wires or strings. Intricately crafted marionettes were used in Burma (now Myanmar) and Ceylon (now Sri Lanka) and later at the courts of Italian princes in the 16th–18th centuries.

Mariotte Edme 1620–1684. French physicist and priest known for his recognition in 1676 of ◊Boyle's law about the inverse relationship of volume and pressure in gases, formulated by Irish physicist Robert Boyle 1672. He had earlier, in 1660, discovered the eye's blind spot.

Maritain Jacques 1882–1973. French philosopher. Originally a disciple of Henri ⏵Bergson, as in *La philosophie bergsonienne/Bergsonian Philosophy* 1914, he later became the best-known of the Neo-Thomists, applying the methods of Thomas ⏵Aquinas to contemporary problems, for example *Introduction à la Philosophie/Introduction to Philosophy* 1920.

maritime law that part of the law dealing with the sea: in particular, fishing areas, ships, and navigation. Seas are divided into **internal waters** governed by a state's internal laws (such as harbors, inlets); ⏵**territorial waters** (the area of sea adjoining the coast over which a state claims rights); the **continental shelf** (the seabed and subsoil that the coastal state is entitled to exploit beyond the territorial waters); and the **high seas**, where international law applies.

Marius Gaius 155–86 BC. Roman military commander and politician, born near Arpinum. He was elected consul seven times, the first time in 107 BC. He defeated the Cimbri and the Teutons (Germanic tribes attacking Gaul and Italy) 102–101 BC. Marius tried to deprive Sulla of the command in the east against Mithridates and, as a result, civil war broke out 88 BC. Sulla marched on Rome, and Marius fled to Africa, but later Cinna held Rome for Marius and together they created a reign of terror in Rome.

Marivaux Pierre Carlet de Chamblain de 1688–1763. French novelist and dramatist. His sophisticated comedies include *Le Jeu de l'amour et du hasard/The Game of Love and Chance* 1730 and *Les Fausses confidences/False Confidences* 1737; his novel *La Vie de Marianne/The Life of Marianne* 1731–41 has autobiographical elements. Marivaux gave the word *marivaudage* (oversubtle lovers' conversation) to the French language.

marjoram aromatic herb of the mint family Labiatae. Wild marjoram *Origanum vulgare* is found both in Europe and Asia and has become naturalized in the Americas; the culinary sweet marjoram *O. majorana* is widely cultivated.

Mark Antony Antonius, Marcus 83–30 BC. Roman politician and soldier. He was tribune and later consul under Julius Caesar, serving under him in Gaul. In 44 BC he tried to secure for Caesar the title of king. After Caesar's assassination, he formed the Second Triumvirate with Octavian (⏵Augustus) and Lepidus. In 42 he defeated Brutus and Cassius at Philippi. He took Egypt as his share of the empire and formed a liaison with ⏵Cleopatra. In 40 he returned to Rome to marry Octavia, the sister of Augustus. In 32 the Senate declared war on Cleopatra. Antony was defeated by Augustus at the battle of Actium 31 BC. He returned to Egypt and committed suicide.

market capitalization market value of a company, based on the market price of all its issued securities—a price that would be unlikely to apply, however, if a bid were actually made for control of them.

market forces in economics, the forces of demand (a want backed by the ability to pay) and supply (the willingness and ability to supply).

Some economists argue that resources are allocated most efficiently when producers are able to respond to consumer demand without intervention from "distortions" such as governments and labor unions, and that profits and competition between firms and individuals provide sufficient incentives to produce efficiently (⏵monetarism). Critics of this view suggest that market forces alone may not be efficient because they fail to consider social costs and benefits, and may also fail to provide for the needs of the less well off, since private firms aiming to make a profit respond to the ability to pay.

marketing promoting goods and services to consumers. In the 20th century, marketing has played an increasingly larger role in determining company policy, influencing product development, pricing, methods of distribution, advertising, and promotion techniques. Marketing skills are beginning to appear on the curriculum of some schools and colleges.

Markevich Igor 1912–1983. Russian-born composer and conductor who settled in Paris 1927. He composed the ballet *L'Envol d'Icare/The Flight of Icarus* 1932, and the cantata *Le Paradis Perdu/Paradise Lost* 1933–35 to words by Milton. After World War II he concentrated on conducting.

markhor large wild goat *Capra falconeri*, with spirally twisted horns and long shaggy coat. It is found in the Himalayas.

Markov Andrei 1856–1922. Russian mathematician, formulator of the ⏵Markov chain, an example of a stochastic (random) process.

Markova Alicia. Adopted name of Lilian Alicia Marks 1910– . British ballet dancer. Trained by ⏵Pavlova, she was ballerina with ⏵Diaghilev's company 1925–29, was the first resident ballerina of the Vic-Wells Ballet 1933–35, partnered Anton ⏵Dolin in their own Markova-Dolin Company 1935–37, and danced with the Ballets Russes de Monte Carlo 1938–41 and Ballet Theater, 1941–46. She is associated with the great Classical ballets, such as *Giselle*.

Markov chain in statistics, an ordered sequence of discrete states (random variables) $x_1, x_2, ..., x_i, ..., x_n$ such that the probability of x_i depends only on n and/or the state x_{i-1} which has preceded it. If independent of n, the chain is said to be homogeneous.

Mark, St 1st century AD. In the New Testament, Christian apostle and evangelist whose name is given to the second Gospel. It was probably written AD 65–70, and used by the authors of the first and third Gospels. He is the patron saint of Venice, and his emblem is a winged lion; feast day April 25.

His first name was John, and his mother, Mary, was one of the first Christians in Jerusalem. He was a cousin of Barnabas, and accompanied Barnabas and Paul on their first missionary journey. He was a fellow worker with Paul in Rome, and later became Peter's interpreter after Paul's death. According to tradition he was the founder of the Christian church in Alexandria, and St Jerome says that he died and was buried there.

marl crumbling sedimentary rock, sometimes called **clayey limestone**, including various types of calcareous ⏵clays and fine-grained ⏵limestones. Marls are often laid down in freshwater lakes and are usually soft, earthy, and of a white, gray, or brownish color. They are used in cement-making and as fertilizer.

Marlborough John Churchill, 1st Duke of Marlborough 1650–1722. English soldier, created a duke 1702 by Queen Anne. He was granted the Blenheim mansion in Oxfordshire in recognition of his services, which included defeating the French army outside Vienna in the Battle of Blenheim 1704, during the War of the ⏵Spanish Succession.

Marley Bob (Robert Nesta) 1945–1981. Jamaican reggae singer, a Rastafarian whose songs, many of which were topical and political, popularized reggae worldwide in the 1970s. One of his greatest hit songs is "No Woman No Cry;" his albums include *Natty Dread* 1975 and *Exodus* 1977.

marlin or **spearfish** any of several genera of open-sea fishes known as billfishes, of the family Istiophoridae, order Perciformes. Some 7 ft/2.5 m long, they are found in warmer waters, have elongated snouts, and high-standing dorsal fins. Members of the family include the sailfish *Istiophorus platypterus*, the fastest of all fishes over short distances—reaching speeds of 62 mph/100 kph—and the blue marlin *Makaira nigricans*, highly prized as a "game" fish.

Marlowe Christopher 1564–1593. English poet and dramatist. His work includes the blank-verse plays *Tamburlaine the Great c.* 1587, *The Jew of Malta c.* 1589, *Edward II* and *Dr Faustus*, both *c.* 1592, the poem *Hero and Leander* 1598, and a translation of Ovid's *Amores*.

Marlowe was born in Canterbury and educated at Cambridge University, where he is thought to have become a government agent. His life was turbulent, with a brief imprisonment in connection with a man's death in a brawl (of which he was cleared), and a charge of atheism (following statements by the playwright Thomas ⏵Kyd under torture). He was murdered in a Deptford tavern, allegedly in a dispute over the bill, but it may have been a political killing.

Marmara, Sea of small inland sea separating Turkey in Europe from Turkey in Asia, connected through the Bosporus with the Black Sea, and through the Dardanelles with the Aegean; length 170 mi/275 km, breadth up to 50 mi/80 km.

marmoset small tree-dwelling monkey in the family Callithricidae, found in South and Central America. Most species have characteristic tufted ears, clawlike nails, and a handsome tail, and some only reach a body length of 7 in/18 cm. The tail is not prehensile. Some are known as tamarins.

Best-known is the common marmoset *Callithrix jacchus* of Brazil, often kept there as a pet.

marmot any of several large burrowing rodents of the genus *Marmota*, in the squirrel family Sciuridae. There are about 15 species. They eat plants and some insects. Marmots are found throughout Canada and the US, and from the Alps to the Himalayas. Marmots live in colonies, make burrows (one to each family), and hibernate. In North America they are called **woodchucks** or **groundhogs**.

Marne river in France which rises in the plateau of Langres and joins the Seine at Charenton near Paris; length 928 mi/5,251 km. It gives its name to the *départements* of Marne, Haute Marne, Seine-et-Marne, and Val de Marne; and to two battles of World War I.

Marne, Battles of the in World War I, two unsuccessful German offensives. In the *First Battle* Sept 6–9, 1914, von Moltke's advance was halted by the British Expeditionary Force and the French under Foch; in the *Second*

Battle July 15–Aug 4, 1918, Ludendorff's advance was defeated by British, French, and US troops under the French general Pétain, and German morale crumbled.

Maronite member of a Christian sect deriving from refugee Monothelites (Christian heretics) of the 7th century. They were subsequently united with the Roman Catholic Church and number about 400,000 in Lebanon and Syria, with an equal number scattered in southern Europe and the Americas.

maroon (Spanish *cimarrón* "wild, untamed") in the West Indies and Suriname, a freed or escaped African slave. Maroons were organized and armed by the Spanish in Jamaica in the late 17th century and early 18th century. They harried the British with guerrilla tactics.

Marot Clément 1496–1544. French poet, known for his translation of the *Psalms* 1539–43. His graceful, witty style became a model for later writers of light verse.

Born at Cahors, he accompanied Francis I to Italy 1524 and was taken prisoner at Pavia; he was soon released, and by 1528 was a salaried member of the royal household. Suspected of heresy, he fled to Turin, where he died.

Marquand J(ohn) P(hillips) 1893–1960. US writer. Author of a series of stories featuring the Japanese detective Mr Moto, he later made his reputation with gently satirical novels of Boston society, including *The Late George Apley* 1937 and *H M Pulham, Esq* 1941.

Marquesas Islands (French *Iles Marquises*) island group in ⬦French Polynesia, lying north of the Tuamotu Archipelago; area 490 sq mi/1,270 sq km; population (1988) 7,500. The administrative headquarters is Atuona on Hiva Oa. The islands were annexed by France 1842.

marquess or *marquis* title and rank of a nobleman who in the British peerage ranks below a duke and above an earl. The wife of a marquess is a marchioness.

The first English marquess was created 1385, but the lords of the Scottish and Welsh ⬦Marches were known as *marchiones* before this date.

marquetry inlaying of various woods, bone, or ivory, usually on furniture, to create ornate patterns and pictures. *Parquetry* is the term used for geometrical inlaid patterns. The method is thought to have originated in Germany or Holland.

Marquette Jacques 1637–1675. French Jesuit missionary and explorer. He went to Canada 1666, explored the upper lakes of the St Lawrence River, and in 1673 with Louis Jolliet (1645–1700), set out on a voyage down the Mississippi on which they made the first accurate record of its course.

In 1674 he and two companions camped near the site of present-day Chicago, making them the first Europeans to live there.

Márquez Gabriel García. See ⬦Garcia Márquez, Colombian novelist.

Marquis Don(ald Robert Perry) 1878–1937. US author. He is chiefly known for his humorous writing, including *Old Soak* 1921, which portrays a hard-drinking comic, and *archy and mehitabel* 1927, verse adventures typewritten by a literary cockroach.

Marrakesh historic town in Morocco in the foothills of the Atlas Mountains, about 130 mi/210 km south of Casablanca; population (1982)

549,000. It is a tourist center, and has textile, leather, and food processing industries. Founded 1062, it has a medieval palace and mosques, and was formerly the capital of Morocco.

marram grass coarse perennial grass *Ammophila arenaria*, flourishing on sandy areas. Because of its tough, creeping rootstocks, it is widely used to hold coastal dunes in place.

Marrano (Spanish *marrano* "pig") Spanish or Portuguese Jew who, during the 14th and 15th centuries, converted to Christianity to escape death or persecution at the hands of the ⬦Inquisition. Many continued to adhere secretly to Judaism and carry out Jewish rites. During the Spanish Inquisition thousands were burned at the stake as "heretics."

marriage legally or culturally sanctioned union of one man and one woman (monogamy); one man and two or more women (polygamy); one woman and two or more men (polyandry). The basis of marriage varies considerably in different societies (romantic love in the West; arranged marriages in some other societies), but most marriage ceremonies, contracts, or customs involve a set of rights and duties, such as care and protection, and there is generally an expectation that children will be born of the union to continue the family line, and maintain the family property.

In different cultures and communities there are various conventions and laws that limit the choice of a marriage partner. ***Restrictive factors*** include: age limits, below which no marriage is valid; degrees of consanguinity or other special relationships within which marriage is either forbidden or enjoined; economic factors such as ability to pay a dowry; rank, caste, or religious differences or expectations; medical requirements, such as the blood tests of some US states; the necessity of obtaining parental, family, or community consent; the negotiations of a marriage broker in some cultures, as in Japan or formerly among Jewish communities; color—for example, marriage was illegal until 1985 between "European" and "non-European" people in South Africa, was illegal until 1967 between white and black people in some Southern US states, and was illegal between white and Asian people in some western states.

rights In Western cultures, social trends have led to increased legal equality for some women within marriage: in England married women were not allowed to hold property in their own name until 1882; in California community property laws entail the equal division of all assets between the partners on divorce. Other legal changes have made ⬦divorce easier, notably in the US and increasingly in the UK, so that remarriage is more and more frequent for both sexes within the lifetime of the original partner.

law In most European countries and in the US civil registration of marriage, as well as (or instead of) a religious ceremony, is obligatory. Common-law marriages (that is, cohabitation as man and wife without a legal ceremony) are recognized (for inheritance purposes) in, for example, Scotland and some states of the US. As a step to international agreement on marriage law the United Nations in 1962 adopted a convention on consent to marriage, minimum age for marriage, and registration.

Mars in Roman mythology, the god of war, depicted as a fearless warrior. The month of March is named after him. He is equivalent to the Greek Ares.

Mars fourth planet from the Sun, average distance 141.6 million mi/227.9 million km. It revolves around the Sun in 687 Earth days, and has a rotation period of 24 hr 37 min. It is much smaller than Venus or Earth, with a diameter 4,210 mi/6,780 km, and mass 0.11 that of Earth. Mars is slightly pear-shaped, with a low, level northern hemisphere, which is comparatively uncratered and geologically "young," and a heavily cratered "ancient" southern hemisphere.

The landscape is a dusty, red, eroded lava plain; red atmospheric dust whipped up by winds of up to 125 mph/200 kph accounts for the light pink sky. Mars has white polar caps (water ice and frozen carbon dioxide) that advance and retreat with the seasons. There are four enormous volcanoes near the equator, of which the largest is Olympus Mons 15 mi/24 km high, with a base 375 mi/600 km across, and a crater 40 mi/65 km wide. The atmosphere is 95% carbon dioxide, 3% nitrogen, 1.5% argon, and 0.15% oxygen. Recorded temperatures vary from −148°F/−0100°C to 32°F/0°C. The atmospheric pressure is 7 millibars, equivalent to the pressure 22 mi/35 km above Earth. No proof of life on Mars has been obtained. There are two small satellites: ⬦Phobos and Deimos.

Mars may approach Earth to within 34 million mi/54.7 million km. The first human-made object to orbit another planet was *Mariner 9*. *Viking 1* and *2*, which landed, also provided much information. Studies in 1985 showed that enough water might exist to sustain prolonged missions by space crews. To the east of the four volcanoes lies a high plateau cut by a system of valleys, Valles Marineris, some 2,500 mi/4,000 km long, up to 120 mi/200 km wide and 4 mi/6 km deep; these features are apparently caused by faulting and wind erosion.

Marsala dry or sweet Sicilian dessert wine, with a dark amber color and a caramel flavor. It is fortified with grape juice that has been cooked and reduced to one-third of its original volume.

Marsalis Branford 1960– . US saxophonist. Born in New Orleans, he was taught by his father Ellis Marsalis, and played alto in Art Blakey's Jazz Messengers 1981, alongside brother Wynton Marsalis. He was tenor/soprano lead saxophonist on Wynton's 1982 world tour, and has since recorded with Miles Davis, Tina Turner, and Dizzy Gillespie. His first solo recording was *Scenes in the City* 1983.

Marsalis Wynton 1961– . US trumpet player who has recorded both Classical and jazz music. He was a member of Art Blakey's Jazz Messengers 1980–82 and also played with Miles Davis before forming his own quintet. At one time this included his brother Branford Marsalis on saxophone.

Marseillaise, La French national anthem; the words and music were composed 1792 as a revolutionary song by the army officer Claude Joseph Rouget de Lisle (1760–1836).

Marseille (English *Marseilles*) chief seaport of France, industrial center (chemicals, oil refining, metallurgy, shipbuilding, food processing), and capital of the *département* of Bouches-du-Rhône, on the Golfe du Lion, Mediterranean Sea; population (1982) 1,111,000.

It is surrounded by hills and connected with the river Rhône by a canal, and there are several offshore islands including ⬦If. Its university was founded 1409. In 1991 a grotto was discovered near Marseille, accessible only by an underwater passage. It contains prehistoric wall paintings showing people and animals, which may date from 20,000–12,000 BC; at that time the cave would have been accessible by land as the sea-level was much lower.

history Marseille was founded by mariners of Phocaea in Asia Minor in 600 BC. Under the Romans it was a free city, and then, after suffering successive waves of invaders, became in the 13th century an independent republic, until included in France 1481. Much of the old quarter was destroyed by Germany 1943.

marsh low-lying wetland. Freshwater marshes are common wherever groundwater, surface springs, streams, or run-off causes frequent flooding or more or less permanent shallow water. A marsh is alkaline whereas a ⟡bog is acid. Marshes develop on inorganic silt or clay soils. Rushes are typical marsh plants. Large marshes dominated by papyrus, cattail, and reeds, with standing water throughout the year, are commonly called ⟡swamps. Near the sea, ⟡salt marshes may form.

Marsh Ngaio 1899–1982. New Zealand writer of detective fiction. Her first detective novel *A Man Lay Dead* 1934 introduced her protagonist Chief Inspector Roderick Alleyn.

Marsh Othniel Charles 1831–1899. US paleontologist. He became official paleontologist for the US Geological Survey 1882 and identified many previously unknown fossil species. An early devotee of Darwin's theory of evolution, Marsh wrote *Odontornithes* 1880, *Dinocerata* 1884, and *Dinosaurs of North America* 1896.

Marsh, born in Lockport, New York, was educated at Yale and in Germany. Named to the Yale faculty as the first professor of paleontology in the US, he mounted fossil-hunting expeditions to the West from 1870. He served as president of the American Academy of Sciences 1883–95.

Marshall city in NE Texas, SE of Dallas and across the border from Shreveport, Louisiana; seat of Harrison County; population (1990) 23,700. Industries include food processing, cotton, clothing, building materials, vehicle parts, and chemicals.

Marshall Alfred 1842–1924. English economist, professor of economics at Cambridge University 1885–1908. He was a founder of neo-Classical economics, and stressed the power of supply and demand to generate equilibrium prices in markets, introducing the concept of elasticity of demand relative to price. His *Principles of Economics* 1890 remains perhaps the chief textbook of neo-Classical economics.

Marshall George Catlett 1880–1959. US general and diplomat. He was army Chief of Staff in World War II, secretary of state 1947–49, and secretary of defense Sept 1950–Sept 1951. He initiated the ⟡**Marshall Plan** 1947 and received the Nobel Peace Prize 1953.

Marshall, born in Pennsylvania, was commissioned 1901, served in World War I, and in 1939 became Chief of Staff with the rank of general. Franklin ⟡Roosevelt promoted him to the newly created rank of general of the army. Following Marshall's resignation from the army, President Truman recalled him to serve as a special envoy to China in Nov 1945. He attempted to secure a coalition between the Nationalist and Communist forces against Japan. As defense secretary (a post not normally held by a soldier), he backed Truman's recall of General ⟡MacArthur from Korea.

Marshall John 1755–1835. US jurist and chief justice of the US Supreme Court 1801–35. He

established the independence of the Court, the supremacy of federal over state law, and laid down interpretations of the US constitution in a series of decisions that have since become universally accepted.

Marshall, born in Prince William (now Faquier) County, Virginia, served in the Continental Army on and off until 1780 and then studied law. As a Federalist, he served in the Virginia state legislature and 1797 became a minister to France. He was in the US House of Representatives 1799–1800 and was secretary of state 1800–01. In 1801, President Adams appointed him chief justice.

Marshall's first opinion, rendered in *Marbury* v *Madison* 1801, declared a law unconstitutional and established the principle of judicial review by the Court. He clearly defined the contract clause in the Constitution in the cases *Fletcher* v *Peck* 1810, *Dartmouth College* v *Woodward* 1819, and *Sturges* v *Crowninshield* 1819. The role of the federal government was defined in *McCulloch* v *Maryland* 1819, when Marshall wrote the opinion that when federal and state laws conflict, federal law supersedes that of the states, and in *Gibbons* v *Ogden* 1824, when he wrote that a state could not enact laws that give exclusive rights to its waters.

Marshall presided over the treason trial 1807 of Aaron Burr, in which Burr was found not guilty. Marshall died of injuries sustained in a stagecoach accident.

Marshall Thurgood 1908–1993. US Supreme Court justice from 1967, and civil-rights leader. He appeared frequently before the US Supreme Court in landmark civil rights cases—among them, *Brown* v *Board of Education* 1954. He was named to the US Court of Appeals 1961 and served as US solicitor general 1965–67.

Marshall was born in Baltimore, Maryland, and received a law degree from Howard University 1933. Active in civil rights, he was named director of the National Association for the Advancement of Colored People (NAACP) Legal Defense and Education Fund 1940. In 1967 President Johnson appointed him to the US Supreme Court. The first black associate justice, he remained a strong voice for civil and individual rights until his retirement for health reasons. Clarence ⟡Thomas succeeded to Marshall's seat.

Marshall Islands group of islands, the Radak (13 islands) and Ralik (11 islands) chains in the W Pacific
area 69 sq mi/180 sq km
capital Majuro
features include two atolls used for US atom-bomb tests 1946–63, Eniwetok and Bikini (hence the name given to two-piece swimsuits which supposedly had an explosive impact)—radioactivity will last for 100 years, and the people have made claims for rehabilitation; and Kwajalein atoll (the largest) which has a US intercontinental missile range
products copra, phosphates, fish, tourism
currency US dollar
population (1988) 41,000
language English (official)
religion Christian and local faiths
government internally self-governing
recent history German 1906–19; administered by Japan until 1946, passed to the US as part of the Pacific Islands Trust Territory 1947. They were used for many atomic bomb tests 1946–63, and the islanders are demanding compensation. In 1986 a compact of free association with the US was signed, under

which the islands manage their own internal and external affairs but the US controls military activities in exchange for financial support. In Dec 1990 its membership in the Trust Territory of the Pacific was terminated. It joined the United Nations Sept 1991. The incumbent president Amata Kabua was reelected 1992 for a further four-year term.

Marshall Plan program of US financial aid to Europe, set up at the end of World War II, totaling $13,000 billion 1948–52. Officially known as the European Recovery Program, it was announced by Secretary of State George ⟡Marshall in a speech at Harvard June 1947, but it was in fact the work of a State Department group led by Dean ⟡Acheson. The perceived danger of Communist takeover in postwar Europe was the main reason for the aid effort.

Marshall Space Flight Center NASA installation at Huntsville, Alabama, where the series of ⟡Saturn rockets and the space-shuttle engines were developed. It also manages various payloads for the space shuttle, including the ⟡Spacelab space station.

marsh gas gas consisting mostly of ⟡methane. It is produced in swamps and marshes by the action of bacteria on dead vegetation.

marsh marigold plant *Caltha palustris* of the buttercup family Ranunculaceae, known as the kingcup in the UK and as the cowslip in the US. It grows in moist sheltered spots and has five-sepalled flowers of a brilliant yellow.

Marston Moor, Battle of battle fought in the English Civil War July 2, 1644 on Marston Moor, 7 mi/11 km W of York. The Royalists were conclusively defeated by the Parliamentarians and Scots.

The Royalist forces were commanded by Prince Rupert and the Duke of Newcastle; their opponents by Oliver Cromwell and Lord Leven. Lord Fairfax, on the right of the Parliamentarians, was routed, but Cromwell's cavalry charges were decisive.

marsupial (Greek *marsupion* "little purse") mammal in which the female has a pouch where she carries her young (born tiny and immature) for a considerable time after birth. Marsupials include omnivorous, herbivorous, and carnivorous species, among them the kangaroo, wombat, opossum, phalanger, bandicoot, dasyure, and wallaby.

The marsupial anteater *Myrmecobius* has no pouch.

Martello tower circular tower for coastal defense. Formerly much used in Europe, many were built along the English coast, especially in Sussex and Kent, in 1804, as a defense against the threatened French invasion. The name is derived from a tower on Cape Mortella, Corsica, which was captured by the British with great difficulty 1794, and was taken as a model. They are round towers of solid masonry, sometimes moated, with a flat roof for mounted guns.

marten small bushy-tailed carnivorous mammal of the genus *Martes* in the weasel family Mustelidae. Martens live in North America, Europe, and temperate regions of Asia, and are agile climbers of trees.

The sable *M. zibellina* lives in E Siberia, and provides the most valued fur. The largest marten is the fisher *M. pennanti* of North America, with black fur and reaching 4 ft/125 cm in length.

Martens Wilfried 1936– . Prime minister of Belgium 1979–92, member of the Social

Christian Party. He was president of the Dutch-speaking CVP 1972–79 and, as prime minister, headed several coalition governments in the period 1979–92 when he was replaced by Jean-Luc Dehaene heading a new coalition.

Martha's Vineyard island 20 mi/32 km long off the coast of Cape Cod, Massachusetts; chief town Edgartown. It is the former home of whaling captains, and now a summer resort.

Martial (Marcus Valerius Martialis) AD 41–104. Latin poet and epigrammatist. His poetry, often bawdy, reflects contemporary Roman life. He left over 15 books of miscellaneous verse, mostly elegiac couplets (a hexameter followed by a pentameter).

Born in Bilbilis, Spain, Martial settled in Rome AD 64, and lived by his literary and social gifts. He is renowned for correctness of diction, versification, and form.

martial arts any of several styles of armed and unarmed combat developed in the East from ancient techniques and arts. Common martial arts include ⏵aikido, ⏵judo, ⏵jujitsu, ⏵karate, ⏵kendo, and ⏵kung fu.

martial law replacement of civilian by military authorities in the maintenance of order.

In the US martial law is usually proclaimed by the president or the government of a state in areas of the country where the civil authorities have been rendered unable to act, or to act with safety. The legal position of martial law is neither well defined in the constitution nor laid down in statutes. In effect, when war or rebellion is in progress in an area, the military authorities are recognized as having the powers to maintain order by summary means.

martin any of several species of birds in the swallow family, Hirundinidae.

Only one species, the purple martin *Progne subis*, is native to North America. It is a dark, glossy purplish blue and about 8 in/20 cm long with a notched tail. It winters in South America.

Martin Archer John Porter 1910– . British biochemist who received the 1952 Nobel Prize for Chemistry for work with Richard Synge on paper chromatography in 1944.

Martin John 1789–1854. British Romantic painter of grandiose landscapes and ambitious religious subjects, such as *Belshazzar's Feast* (several versions).

Other examples of his work are *The Great Day of His Wrath* and *The Plains of Heaven* 1851–53 (both Tate Gallery, London). Martin often made mezzotints (types of engraving) from his work.

Martin five popes, including:

Martin V 1368–1431. Pope from 1417. A member of the Roman family of Colonna, he was elected during the Council of Constance, and ended the Great Schism between the rival popes of Rome and Avignon.

Martin du Gard Roger 1881–1958. French novelist who realistically recorded the way of life of the bourgeoisie in the eight-volume *Les Thibault/The World of the Thibaults* 1922–40. Nobel Prize 1937.

Martinet Jean French inspector-general of infantry under Louis XIV whose constant drilling brought the army to a high degree of efficiency—hence the use of his name to mean a strict disciplinarian.

Martinez Maria Montoya 1890–1980. Pueblo Indian potter who revived the traditional silvery black-on-black ware (made without the wheel) at San Ildefonso Pueblo, New Mexico.

Martini Simone *c.* 1284–1344. Italian painter, a master of the Sienese school. He was a pupil of Duccio and continued the graceful linear patterns of Sienese art but introduced a fresh element of naturalism. His patrons included the city of Siena, the king of Naples, and the pope. Two of his frescoes are in the Town Hall in Siena: the *Maestà* about 1315 and the horseback warrior *Guidoriccio da Fogliano* (the attribution of the latter is disputed). From 1333 to 1339 Simone worked at Assisi where he decorated the chapel of St Martin with scenes depicting the life of the saint, regarded by many as his masterpiece.

Martinique French island in the West Indies (Lesser Antilles)
area 417 sq mi/1,079 sq km
capital Fort-de-France
features several active volcanoes; Napoleon's empress Josephine was born in Martinique, and her childhood home is now a museum
products sugar, cocoa, rum, bananas, pineapples
population (1984) 327,000
history Martinique was reached by Spanish navigators 1493, and became a French colony 1635; since 1972 it has been a French overseas region.

Martinmas in the Christian calendar, the feast of St Martin, Nov 11.

On this day fairs were traditionally held, at which farmworkers were hired. In the Middle Ages it was also the day on which cattle were slaughtered and salted for winter consumption.

Martins Peter 1946– . Danish-born US dancer, choreographer, and ballet director, principal dancer with the New York City Ballet (NYCB) from 1965, its joint ballet master (with Anthony Tudor) from 1983, and its director from 1990. He trained with August Bournonville and brought that teacher's influence to the NYCB.

Martins trained at the Royal Danish Ballet School, joining the company 1965, and the same year joined the NYCB as a principal. He created roles in, among others, Robbins's *Goldberg Variations* 1971 and Balanchine's *Violin Concerto* and *Duo Concertant* both 1972, and choreographed, for example, *Calcium Night Light* 1978.

Martin, St 316–400. Bishop of Tours, France, from about 371, and founder of the first monastery in Gaul. He is usually represented as tearing his cloak to share it with a beggar. His feast day is Martinmas, Nov 11.

Martin's Hundred plantation town established in Virginia 1619 and eliminated by an Indian massacre three years later. Its remains, the earliest extensive trace of British colonization in America, were discovered 1970.

Martinů Bohuslav (Jan) 1890–1959. Czech composer who studied in Paris. He settled in New York after the Nazi occupation of Czechoslovakia 1939. The quality of his music varies but at its best it is richly expressive and has great vitality. His works include the operas *Julietta* 1937 and *The Greek Passion* 1959, symphonies, and chamber music.

Martin v Hunter's Lessee a US Supreme Court decision 1816 that established the right of the Supreme Court to overrule certain state court rulings. The Virginia state court refused to return Martin certain property confiscated by state law during the American Revolution, ignoring the treaty with the British that

guaranteed that Loyalists would not be deprived of their properties. When, on appeal, the Supreme Court reversed the decision, the Virginia courts protested that land matters in states were outside of Supreme Court jurisdiction. The Court ruled that, by the Judiciary Act, such matters were within its jurisdiction.

martyr (Greek "witness") one who voluntarily suffers death for refusing to renounce a religious faith. The first recorded Christian martyr was St Stephen, who was killed in Jerusalem shortly after Jesus' alleged ascension to heaven.

Marvell Andrew 1621–1678. English metaphysical poet and satirist. His poems include "To His Coy Mistress" and "Horatian Ode upon Cromwell's Return from Ireland." He was committed to the parliamentary cause, and was member of Parliament for Hull from 1659. He devoted his last years mainly to verse satire and prose works attacking repressive aspects of government.

Marvin Lee 1924–1987. US film actor who began his career playing violent, often psychotic villains and progressed to playing violent, occasionally psychotic heroes. His work includes *The Big Heat* 1953, *The Killers* 1964, and *Cat Ballou* 1965.

Marx Karl (Heinrich) 1818–1883. German philosopher, economist, and social theorist whose account of change through conflict is known as historical, or dialectical, materialism (see ⏵Marxism). His ⏵*Das Kapital/Capital* 1867–95 is the fundamental text of Marxist economics, and his systematic theses on class struggle, history, and the importance of economic factors in politics have exercised an enormous influence on later thinkers and political activists.

Marx was born in Trier, the son of a lawyer, and studied law and philosophy at Bonn and Berlin. During 1842–43, he edited the *Rheinische Zeitung/Rhineland Newspaper* until its suppression. In 1844 he began his life-long collaboration with Friedrich ⏵Engels, with whom he developed the Marxist philosophy, first formulated in their joint works, *Die heilige Familie/The Holy Family* 1844 and *Die deutsche Ideologie/German Ideology* 1846 (which contains the theory demonstrating the material basis of all human activity: "Life is not determined by consciousness, but consciousness by life"), and Marx's *Misère de la philosophie/Poverty of Philosophy* 1847. Both joined the Communist League, a German refugee organization, and in 1847–48 they prepared its program, *The Communist Manifesto*. During the 1848 revolution Marx edited the *Neue Rheinische Zeitung/New Rhineland Newspaper*, until he was expelled from Prussia 1849.

He then settled in London, where he wrote *Die Klassenkämpfe in Frankreich/Class Struggles in France* 1849, *Die Achtzehnte Brumaire des Louis Bonaparte/The 18th Brumaire of Louis Bonaparte* 1852, *Zur Kritik der politischen Ökonomie/Critique of Political Economy* 1859, and his monumental work *Das Kapital/Capital*. In 1864 the International Working Men's Association was formed, whose policy Marx, as a member of the general council, largely controlled. Although he showed extraordinary tact in holding together its diverse elements, it collapsed 1872 due to Marx's disputes with the anarchists, including the Russian ⏵Bakunin. The second and third volumes of *Das Kapital* were edited from his notes by Engels and published posthumously.

Marx's philosophical work owes much to the writings of ♢Hegel, though he rejected Hegel's idealism.

Marx Brothers team of US film comedians: Leonard "Chico" (from the "chicks"—women—he chased) 1887–1961; Adolph, the silent "Harpo" (from the harp he played) 1888–1964; Julius "Groucho" (from his temper) 1890–1977; Milton "Gummo" (from his gumshoes, or galoshes) 1897–1977, who left the team before films; and Herbert "Zeppo" (born at the time of the first zeppelins) 1901–1979, part of the team until 1935. They made a total of 13 zany films 1929–49 including *Animal Crackers* 1930, *Duck Soup* 1933, *A Night at the Opera* 1935, and *Go West* 1940.

They appeared in musical comedy but made their reputation on Broadway in *Cocoanuts* 1926 (later filmed). In Hollywood they made such films as *Monkey Business* 1931 and *A Day at the Races* 1937. After the team disbanded 1948, Groucho, who carried the comedy line, continued to make films and appeared on his own television quiz show, *You Bet Your Life* 1947–62.

Marxism philosophical system, developed by the 19th-century German social theorists ♢Marx and ♢Engels, also known as *dialectical materialism*, under which matter gives rise to mind (materialism) and all is subject to change (from dialectic; see ♢Hegel). As applied to history, it supposes that the succession of feudalism, capitalism, socialism, and finally the classless society is inevitable. The stubborn resistance of any existing system to change necessitates its complete overthrow in the *class struggle*—in the case of capitalism, by the proletariat—rather than gradual modification.

Social and political institutions progressively change their nature as economic developments transform material conditions. The orthodox belief is that each successive form is "higher" than the last; perfect socialism is seen as the ultimate rational system, and it is alleged that the state would then wither away. Marxism has proved one of the most powerful and debated theories in modern history, inspiring both dedicated exponents (Lenin, Trotsky, Stalin, Mao) and bitter opponents. It is the basis of ♢communism.

Mary in the New Testament, the mother of Jesus through divine intervention (see ♢Annunciation), wife of ♢Joseph. The Roman Catholic Church maintains belief in her ♢Immaculate Conception and bodily assumption into heaven, and venerates her as a mediator. Feast day of the Assumption Aug 15.

Traditionally her parents were elderly and named Joachim and Anna. Mary (Hebrew *Miriam*) married Joseph and accompanied him to Bethlehem. Roman Catholic doctrine assumes that the brothers of Jesus were Joseph's sons by an earlier marriage, and that she remained a virgin. Pope Paul VI proclaimed her "Mother of the Church" 1964.

Mary *Queen of Scots* 1542–1587. Queen of Scotland 1542–67. Also known as **Mary Stuart**, she was the daughter of James V. Mary's connection with the English royal line from Henry VII made her a threat to Elizabeth I's hold on the English throne, especially as she represented a champion of the Catholic cause. She was married three times. After her forced abdication she was imprisoned but escaped 1568 to England. Elizabeth I held her prisoner, while the Roman Catholics, who regarded Mary as

rightful queen of England, formed many conspiracies to place her on the throne, and for complicity in one of these she was executed.

Mary's mother was the French Mary of Guise. Born in Linlithgow (now in Lothian region, Scotland), Mary was sent to France, where she married the dauphin, later Francis II. After his death she returned to Scotland 1561, which, during her absence, had turned Protestant. She married her cousin, the Earl of ♢Darnley, 1565, but they soon quarrelled, and Darnley took part in the murder of Mary's secretary, ♢Rizzio. In 1567 Darnley was assassinated as the result of a conspiracy formed by the Earl of ♢Bothwell, possibly with Mary's connivance, and shortly after Bothwell married her. A rebellion followed; defeated at Carberry Hill, Mary abdicated and was imprisoned. She escaped 1568, raised an army, and after its defeat at Langside fled to England, only to be imprisoned again. A plot against Elizabeth I devised by Anthony Babington led to her trial and execution at Fotheringay Castle 1587.

Mary Duchess of Burgundy 1457–1482. Daughter of Charles the Bold. She married Maximilian of Austria 1477, thus bringing the Low Countries into the possession of the Hapsburgs and, ultimately, of Spain.

Mary two queens of England:

Mary I *Bloody Mary* 1516–1558. Queen of England from 1553. She was the eldest daughter of Henry VIII by Catherine of Aragon. When Edward VI died, Mary secured the crown without difficulty in spite of the conspiracy to substitute Lady Jane ♢Grey. In 1554 Mary married Philip II of Spain, and as a devout Roman Catholic obtained the restoration of papal supremacy and sanctioned the persecution of Protestants. She was succeeded by her half sister Elizabeth I.

When Mary died, the Protestant Elizabeth I gained the throne and settled the religious question, for the time, during her long, pivotal reign.

Mary II 1662–1694. Queen of England, Scotland, and Ireland from 1688. She was the Protestant elder daughter of the Catholic ♢James II, and in 1677 was married to her cousin ♢William III of Orange. After the 1688 revolution she accepted the crown jointly with William.

During his absences from England she took charge of the government, and showed courage and resource when invasion seemed possible 1690 and 1692.

Maryland state of E US; nickname Old Line State/Free State

area 12,198 sq mi/31,600 sq km

capital Annapolis

cities Baltimore, Silver Spring, Dundalk, Bethesda

features Chesapeake Bay, an inlet of the Atlantic; horse racing (the Preakness Stakes at Baltimore); yacht racing and the US Naval Academy at Annapolis; historic Fort McHenry; Fort Meade, a government electronic-listening center; Baltimore harbor

products poultry, dairy products, machinery, steel, automobiles and parts, electric and electronic equipment, chemicals, fish and shellfish

population (1990) 4,781,500

famous people Stephen Decatur, Francis Scott Key, Edgar Allan Poe, Frederick Douglass, Harriet Tubman, Upton Sinclair, H L Mencken, Babe Ruth, Billie Holiday

history one of the original Thirteen Colonies, first settled 1634; it became a state 1788.

In 1608 John Smith explored Chesapeake Bay, but the colony of Maryland, awarded by royal grant 1632 to Lord Baltimore for the settlement of English Catholics, dates from 1634. It ratified the federal Constitution 1788. During the British bombardment of Fort McHenry in the War of 1812, Francis Scott Key wrote the poem "The Star-Spangled Banner," which later became the lyrics to the US national anthem. Some Marylanders favored secession during the Civil War, during which the state was largely occupied by Union troops because of its strategic location near Washington, DC and the Confederate armies three times invaded Maryland. In recent times the state has prospered from the growth of the federal government in nearby Washington and the redevelopment of Baltimore, whose port ranks second in handling foreign shipping. Between 1940 and 1980, Maryland's population more than tripled.

Mary Magdalene, St 1st century AD. In the New Testament, the woman whom Jesus cured of possession by evil spirits, was present at the Crucifixion and burial, and was the first to meet the risen Jesus. She is often identified with the woman of St Luke's gospel who anointed Jesus' feet, and her symbol is a jar of ointment; feast day July 22.

Mary of Modena 1658–1718. Queen consort of England and Scotland. She was the daughter of the Duke of Modena, Italy, and married James, Duke of York, later James II, 1673. The birth of their son James Francis Edward Stuart was the signal for the revolution of 1688 that overthrew James II. Mary fled to France.

Masaccio (Tomaso di Giovanni di Simone Guidi) 1401–1428. Florentine painter, a leader of the early Italian Renaissance. His frescoes in Sta Maria del Carmine, Florence, 1425–28, which he painted with Masolino da Panicale (c. 1384–1447), show a decisive break with Gothic conventions. He was the first painter to apply the scientific laws of perspective, newly discovered by the architect Brunelleschi.

Masaccio's frescoes in the Brancacci Chapel of Sta Maria del Carmine include scenes from the life of St Peter (notably *The Tribute Money*) and a moving account of *Adam and Eve's Expulsion from Paradise*. They have a monumental grandeur, without trace of Gothic decorative detail, unlike the work of his colleague and teacher Masolino. Masaccio's figures have solidity and weight and are clearly set in three-dimensional space.

Other works by Masaccio are the *Trinity* c. 1428 (Sta Maria Novella, Florence) and the *Pisa polyptych* (National Gallery, London, Staatliche Museen, Berlin, and Museo di

Maryland

Capodimonte, Naples). Although his career marks a turning point in Italian art, he attracted few imitators (Fra Filippo Lippi's early style followed Masaccio).

Masada rock fortress 1,300 ft/396 m above the western shore of the Dead Sea, Israel. Site of the Hebrews' final stand in their revolt against the Romans (AD 66–72). After withstanding a year-long siege, the Hebrew population of 953 committed mass suicide rather than be conquered and enslaved.

The site was excavated 1963–65, including the palace of Herod, and is now an Israeli national monument.

Masai member of an E African people whose territory is divided between Tanzania and Kenya, and who number about 250,000. They were originally warriors and nomads, breeding humped zebu cattle, but some have adopted a more settled life. Their cooperation is being sought by the Kenyan authorities to help in wildlife conservation. They speak a Nilotic language belonging to the Nilo-Saharan family.

Masaryk Jan (Garrigue) 1886–1948. Czechoslovak politician, son of Tomáš Masaryk. He was foreign minister from 1940, when the Czechoslovak government was exiled in London in World War II. He returned 1945, retaining the post, but as a result of political pressure by the communists committed suicide.

Masaryk Tomáš (Garrigue) 1850–1937. Czechoslovak nationalist politician. He directed the revolutionary movement against the Austrian Empire, founding with Eduard Beneš and Stefanik the Czechoslovak National Council, and in 1918 was elected first president of the newly formed Czechoslovak Republic. Three times reelected, he resigned 1935 in favor of Beneš.

After the communist coup 1948, Masaryk was systematically removed from public memory in order to reverse his semimythological status as the forger of the Czechoslovak nation.

maser (acronym for **microwave amplification by stimulated emission of radiation**) in physics, a high-frequency microwave amplifier or oscillator in which the signal to be amplified is used to stimulate unstable atoms into emitting energy at the same frequency. Atoms or molecules are raised to a higher energy level and then allowed to lose this energy by radiation emitted at a precise frequency. The principle has been extended to other parts of the electromagnetic spectrum as, for example, in the ◊laser.

The two-level ammonia-gas maser was first suggested 1954 by Charles Townes at Columbia University, New York, and independently the same year by Nikolai Basov and Aleksandr Prokhorov in the USSR. The solid-state three-level maser, the most sensitive amplifier known, was envisaged by Nicolaas Bloembergen (1920–) at Harvard 1956. The ammonia maser is used as a frequency standard oscillator (see ◊clock), and the three-level maser as a receiver for satellite communications and radio astronomy.

Maseru capital of Lesotho, southern Africa, on the Caledon River; population (1986) 289,000. Founded 1869, it is a center for trade and diamond processing.

Mashhad or **Meshed** holy city of the Shiites, and industrial center (carpets, textiles, leather goods), in NE Iran; population (1986) 1,464,000. It is the second-largest city in Iran.

Mashraq (Arabic "east") the Arab countries of the E Mediterranean: Egypt, Sudan, Jordan, Syria, and Lebanon. The term is contrasted with ◊Maghreb, comprising the Arab countries of NW Africa.

Masire Quett Ketumile Joni 1925– . President of Botswana from 1980. In 1962, with Seretse ◊Khama, he founded the Botswana Democratic Party (BDP) and in 1965 was made deputy prime minister. After independence 1966, he became vice-president and, on Khama's death 1980, president, continuing a policy of nonalignment.

Maskelyne Nevil 1732–1811. English astronomer who accurately measured the distance from the Earth to the Sun by observing a transit of Venus across the Sun's face 1769. In 1774 he measured the mass of the Earth by noting the deflection of a plumb line near Mount Schiehallion in Scotland.

masochism desire to subject oneself to physical or mental pain, humiliation, or punishment, for erotic pleasure, to alleviate guilt, or out of destructive impulses turned inwards. The term is derived from Leopold von ◊Sacher-Masoch.

Mason James 1909–1984. English actor who portrayed romantic villains in British films of the 1940s. After *Odd Man Out* 1947 he worked in the US, playing intelligent but troubled, vulnerable men, notably in *A Star Is Born* 1954. He returned to Europe 1960, where he made *Lolita* 1962, *Georgy Girl* 1966, and *Cross of Iron* 1977.

Other films include *Five Fingers* 1952 and *North by Northwest* 1959. His final role was *The Shooting Party* 1984.

Mason–Dixon Line in the US, the boundary line between Maryland and Pennsylvania (latitude 39° 43′ 26.3″ N), named after Charles Mason (1730–1787) and Jeremiah Dixon (died 1777), English astronomers and surveyors who surveyed it 1763–67. It was popularly seen as dividing the North from the South.

The two colonies had argued for almost a century and even fought some armed skirmishes over the boundary. In 1760, the two agreed to allow Mason and Dixon to delineate the line.

masque spectacular and essentially aristocratic entertainment with a fantastic or mythological theme in which music, dance, and extravagant costumes and scenic design figured larger than plot. Originating in Italy, it reached its height of popularity at the English court between 1600 and 1640, with the collaboration of Ben ◊Jonson as writer and Inigo ◊Jones as stage designer.

The masque had great influence on the development of ballet and opera, and the elaborate frame in which it was performed developed into the proscenium arch.

mass in physics, the quantity of matter in a body as measured by its inertia. Mass determines the acceleration produced in a body by a given force acting on it, the acceleration being inversely proportional to the mass of the body. The mass also determines the force exerted on a body by ◊gravity on Earth, although this attraction varies slightly from place to place. In the SI system, the base unit of mass is the kilogram.

At a given place, equal masses experience equal gravitational forces, which are known as the weights of the bodies. Masses may, therefore, be compared by comparing the weights of bodies at the same place. The standard unit of mass to which all other masses are compared

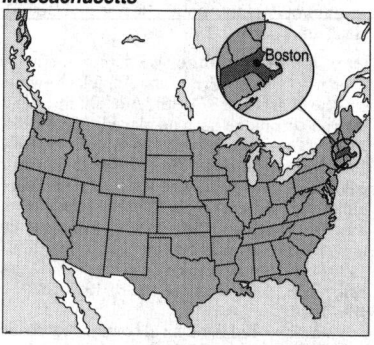

Massachusetts

is a platinum-iridium cylinder of 1 kg, which is kept at the International Bureau of Weights and Measures in Sèvres, France.

Mass in Christianity, the celebration of the ◊Eucharist.

Mass in music, the setting of the invariable parts of the Christian Mass, that is *Kyrie, Gloria, Credo, Sanctus* with *Benedictus*, and *Agnus Dei*. A notable example is Bach's *Mass in B Minor*.

Massachusetts state of US; nickname Bay State/Old Colony State
area 8,299 sq mi/21,500 sq km
capital Boston
cities Worcester, Springfield, New Bedford, Brockton, Cambridge
population (1990) 6,016,400
features Boston landmarks; Harvard University and the Massachusetts Institute of Technology, Cambridge; Cape Cod National Seashore; New Bedford and the islands of Nantucket and Martha's Vineyard, former whaling ports; Berkshire Hills with Tanglewood and other performing-arts centers; the battlefields of Lexington and Concord near Minute Man National Historical Park; Salem, site of witch trials; Plymouth Rock
products electronic, communications, and optical equipment; precision instruments; nonelectrical machinery; fish; cranberries; dairy products
famous people Samuel Adams, Louis Brandeis, Emily Dickinson, Ralph Waldo Emerson, Robert Goddard, Nathaniel Hawthorne, Oliver Wendell Holmes, Winslow Homer, William James, John F Kennedy, Robert Lowell, Paul Revere, Henry Thoreau, Daniel Webster
history one of the original Thirteen Colonies, it was first settled 1620 by the Pilgrims at Plymouth. After the ◊Boston Tea Party 1773, the American Revolution began at Lexington and Concord April 19, 1775, and the British evacuated Boston the following year. Massachusetts became a state 1788.

In the early 19th century the first large-scale factories were built here to turn out textiles. The state also prospered from whaling and shipbuilding. Heavy immigration of Irish, Germans, and Italians greatly modified the Yankee character of Massachusetts by 1900. After World War II, high technology, sophisticated services, and tourism replaced textiles, footwear, and maritime activities as the mainspring of the economy.

massage manipulation of the soft tissue of the body, the muscles, ligaments, and tendons, either to encourage the healing of specific injuries or to produce the general beneficial effects of relaxing muscular tension, stimulating blood circulation, and improving the tone and strength of the skin and muscles.

The benefits of massage were known to the ancient Chinese, Egyptian, and Greek cultures. The techniques most widely practiced today were developed by the Swedish physician Per Henrik Ling (1776–1838).

Massasoit also known as Ousamequin, "Yellow Feather" c. 1590–1661. One of the leaders of the Wampanoag, a people inhabiting the coasts of Massachusetts Bay and Cape Cod. He officially allied himself with the Plymouth Colony 1621 as a political counterbalance against the neighboring Narragansett. In 1638 Massasoit formed an alliance with the founders of the Massachusetts Bay Colony. Upon his death, his son Metacomet, known to the English as "King ⟡Philip," assumed leadership of the Wampanoag.

Massasoit was born in the area of modern Bristol, Rhode Island.

Massawa chief port and naval base of Ethiopia, in Eritrea, on the Red Sea, with salt production and pearl fishing; population (1980) 33,000. It is one of the hottest inhabited spots in the world, the temperature reaching 115°F/46°C in May. Massawa was an Italian possession 1885–1941.

Masséna André 1756–1817. Marshal of France. He served in the French Revolutionary Wars and under the emperor Napoleon was created marshal 1804, duke of Rivoli 1808, and prince of Essling 1809. He was in command in Spain 1810–11 in the Peninsular War and was defeated by British troops under Wellington.

mass–energy equation Albert ⟡Einstein's equation $E = mc^2$, denoting the equivalence of mass and energy, where E is the energy in joules, m is the mass in kilograms, and c is the speed of light, in a vacuum, in meters per second.

Massenet Jules Emile Frédéric 1842–1912. French composer of opera, ballets, oratorios, and orchestral suites.

His many operas include *Hérodiade* 1881, *Manon* 1884, *Le Cid* 1885, and *Thaïs* 1894; among other works is the orchestral suite *Scènes pittoresques* 1874.

Masses, The US left-wing magazine that published many prominent radical writers 1911–17, including John Reed and Max Eastman. It was superseded by *The Liberator* 1918–25 and then by *New Masses*, which advanced the cause of proletarian writing during the Depression years of the 1930s.

Massif Central mountainous plateau region of S central France; area 36,000 sq mi/93,000 sq km, highest peak Puy de Sancy 6,188 ft/1,886 m. It is a source of hydroelectricity.

Massine Léonide 1895–1979. Russian choreographer and dancer with the Ballets Russes. He was a creator of comedy in ballet and also symphonic ballet using concert music.

mass number or **nucleon number** sum (symbol A) of the numbers of protons and neutrons in the nucleus of an atom. It is used along with the ⟡atomic number (the number of protons) in ⟡nuclear notation: in symbols that represent nuclear isotopes, such as $^{14}_{6}C$, the lower number is the atomic number, and the upper number is the mass number.

Masson André 1896–1987. French artist and writer, a leader of Surrealism until 1929. His interest in the unconscious mind led him to experiment with "automatic" drawing—simple pen-and-ink work, and later multitextured accretions of pigment, glue, and sand.

Masson left the Surrealist movement after a quarrel with the writer André Breton. During World War II he moved to the US, then returned to France and painted landscapes.

Massorah collection of philological notes on the Hebrew text of the Old Testament. It was at first an oral tradition, but was committed to writing in the Aramaic language at Tiberias, Palestine, between the 6th and 9th centuries.

mass production manufacture of goods on a large scale, a technique that aims for low unit cost and high output. In factories mass production is achieved by a variety of means, such as division and specialization of labor and ⟡mechanization. These speed up production and allow the manufacture of near-identical, interchangeable parts. Such parts can then be assembled quickly into a finished product on an ⟡assembly line.

Division of labor means that a job is divided into a number of steps, and then groups of workers are employed to carry each step out, specializing and therefore doing the job in a routine way, producing more than if each individually had to carry out all the stages of manufacture. However, the system has been criticized for neglecting the skills of workers and removing their involvement with the end product.

Many of the machines now used in factories are ⟡robots (for example, on car-assembly lines): they work automatically under computer control. Such automation further streamlines production and raises output.

mass spectrograph or **mass spectrometer** in physics, an apparatus for analyzing chemical composition. Positive ions (charged particles) of a substance are separated by an electromagnetic system, designed to focus particles of equal mass to a point where they can be detected. This permits accurate measurement of the relative concentrations of the various ionic masses present, particularly isotopes.

Masters Edgar Lee 1869–1950. US poet. In his book *Spoon River Anthology* 1915, a collection of free-verse epitaphs, the people of a small town tell of their frustrated lives.

He published numerous other volumes of verse, novels, and biographies.

Masters John 1914–1983. British novelist, born in Calcutta, who served in the Indian army 1934–47. He wrote a series of books dealing with the Savage family throughout the period of the Raj—for example, *Nightrunners of Bengal* 1951, *The Deceivers* 1952, and *Bhowani Junction* 1954.

Masterson Bat (William Barclay) 1853–1921. US marshal and sportswriter. In 1878 he succeeded his murdered brother, Edward, as marshal in Dodge City, Kansas, and gunned down his brother's killers. After a brief time in Tombstone, Arizona, where he served with Wyatt Earp 1880, Masterson returned to Kansas. He moved to New York 1902, where he became a sportswriter for the *Morning Telegraph*.

Born in Iroquois County, Illinois, and raised in Kansas, Masterson worked in his early adult years as a buffalo hunter and scout before becoming a deputy marshal in Dodge City 1876.

mastiff breed of powerful dog, usually fawn in color, that was originally bred in Britain for hunting purposes. It has a large head, wide-set eyes, and broad muzzle. It can grow up to 3 ft/90 cm at the shoulder, and weigh 220 lb/100 kg.

mastodon any of an extinct family (Mastodontidae) of mammals of the elephant order (Proboscidea). They differed from elephants and mammoths in the structure of their grinding teeth. There were numerous species, among which the American mastodon *Mastodon americanum*, about 10 ft/3 m high, of the Pleistocene era, is well known. They were hunted by humans for food.

Mastroianni Marcello 1924– . Italian film actor, most popular for his carefully understated roles in such films as Antonioni's *La notte/The Night* 1961. He starred in several films with Sophia Loren, including *Una giornata speciale/A Special Day* 1977, and worked with Fellini in *La dolce vita* 1960, *8 ½* 1963, *Roma* 1971, and *Ginger and Fred* 1986.

Masur Kurt 1928– . German conductor, music director of the New York Philharmonic from 1990. He was conductor of the Dresden Philharmonic Orchestra 1955–58 and 1967–72, before making his London debut 1973 with the New Philharmonia. He was prominent in the political campaigning that took place prior to German unification.

Masurian Lakes lakes in Poland (former East Prussia) which in 1914–15 were the scene of battles in which the Germans defeated the Russians.

Matabeleland western portion of Zimbabwe between the Zambezi and Limpopo rivers, inhabited by the Ndebele people
area 70,118 sq mi/181,605 sq km
cities Bulawayo
features rich plains watered by tributaries of the Zambezi and Limpopo, with mineral resources
language Matabele
famous people Joshua Nkomo
history Matabeleland was granted to the British South Africa Company 1889 and occupied 1893 after attacks on white settlements in Mashonaland; in 1923 it was included in Southern Rhodesia. It is now divided into two administrative regions. Joshua Nkomo was accused of plotting to overthrow the post-independence government of Zimbabwe and then expelled from the cabinet 1981. Zimbabwe African People's Union (ZAPU) supporters, mostly drawn from the Ndebele people, began a loosely organized armed rebellion against the Zimbabwe African National Union (ZANU) government of Robert Mugabe. The insurgency was brought to an end in April 1988, when a unity agreement was reached between ZANU and ZAPU and Nkomo was appointed minister of state in the office of the president.

Matadi chief port of Zaire on the river Zaïre, 70 mi/115 km from its mouth, linked by oil pipelines with Kinshasa; population (1984) 144,700.

Mata Hari Adopted name of Gertrud Margarete Zelle 1876–1917. Dutch courtesan, dancer, and probable spy. In World War I she had affairs with highly placed military and government officials on both sides and told Allied secrets to the Germans. She may have been a double agent, in the pay of both France and Germany. She was shot by the French on espionage charges.

matamata South American freshwater turtle or terrapin *Chelys fimbriata* with a shell up to 15 in/40 cm long.

The head is flattened, with a "snorkel" nose, and the neck has many projections of skin. The movement of these in the water may attract prey, which the matamata catches by opening its mouth suddenly to produce an inrush of water.

match small strip of wood or paper, tipped with combustible material for producing fire. Friction matches containing phosphorus were first made 1816 in France by François Derosne.

A *safety match* is one in which the oxidizing agent and the combustible body are kept apart, the former being incorporated into the striking surface on the side of the box, the latter into the match. Safety matches were patented by a Swede, J E Lundström, 1855. Book matches were invented in the US 1892 by Joshua Pusey.

materialism philosophical theory that there is nothing in existence over and above matter and matter in motion. Such a theory excludes the possibility of deities. It also sees mind as an attribute of the physical, denying idealist theories that see mind as something independent of body; for example, Descartes' theory of "thinking substance."

Like most other philosophical ideas, materialism probably arose among the early Greek thinkers. The Stoics and the Epicureans were materialists, and so were the ancient Buddhists. Among later materialists have been Hobbes, Diderot, d'Holbach, Büchner, and Haeckel; Hume, J S Mill, Huxley, and Spencer showed materialist tendencies.

material product or *social product* system of national accounting used by socialist countries which includes all productive services but usually does not include non-public services and financial activities that would be included in conventional Western national accounts to give gross national product. Gross domestic product (GDP) is a more comprehensive measure of a country's output.

mathematical induction formal method of proof in which the proposition $P(n + 1)$ is proved true on the hypothesis that the proposition $P(n)$ is true. The proposition is then shown to be true for a particular value of n, say k, and therefore by induction the proposition must be true for $n = k + 1, k + 2, k + 3, \ldots$. In many cases $k = 1$, so then the proposition is true for all positive integers.

mathematics science of spatial and numerical relationships. The main divisions of *pure mathematics* include geometry, arithmetic, algebra, calculus, and trigonometry. Mechanics, statistics, numerical analysis, computing, the mathematical theories of astronomy, electricity, optics, thermodynamics, and atomic studies come under the heading of *applied mathematics*.

early history Prehistoric human beings probably learned to count at least up to ten on their fingers. The Chinese, Hindus, Babylonians, and Egyptians all devised methods of counting and measuring that were of practical importance in their everyday lives. The first theoretical mathematician is held to be Thales of Melitus (*c.* 580 BC) who is believed to have proposed the first theorems in plane geometry. His disciple ⇨Pythagoras established geometry as a recognized science among the Greeks. The later school of Alexandrian geometers (4th and 3rd centuries BC) included ⇨Euclid and ⇨Archimedes. Our present decimal numerals are based on a Hindu-Arabic system that reached Europe about AD 100 from Arab mathematicians of the Middle East such as ⇨Khwārizmî.

Europe Western mathematics began to develop from the 15th century. Geometry was revitalized by the invention of coordinate geometry by Descartes 1637; Pascal and Fermat developed probability theory, Napier invented logarithms, and Newton and Leibniz developed calculus. In Russia, Lobachevsky rejected Euclid's parallelism and developed non-Euclidean geometry, a more developed form of which (by Riemann) was later utilized by Einstein in his relativity theory.

the present Higher mathematics has a powerful tool in the high-speed electronic computer, which can create and manipulate mathematical "models" of various systems in science, technology, and commerce. Modern additions to school syllabuses such as sets, group theory, matrices, and graph theory are sometimes referred to as "new" or "modern" mathematics.

Mather Cotton 1663–1728. American theologian and writer. He was a Puritan minister in Boston, and wrote over 400 works of history, science, annals, and theology, including *Magnalia Christi Americana/The Great Works of Christ in America* 1702, a vast compendium of early New England history and experience. Mather appears to have supported the Salem witch-hunts.

Born in Boston, Mather graduated from Harvard with a master's degree 1681 and was ordained a minister 1685. He was a promoter of strict Congregationalism, and a man of great learning. He wrote *Memorable Providences Relating to Witchcraft and Possession* 1689 and told of the witchcraft trials in *Wonders of the Invisible World* 1693.

Mather Increase 1639–1723. Colonial American religious leader. Born in Dorchester, Massachusetts, and educated at Harvard, Mather served as a cleric in England during the Puritan Commonwealth. He returned to Massachusetts 1661, was named teacher of Boston's Second Church 1664, and served as president of Harvard 1685–1701. As a defender of the colonial right to self-government, Mather went to England 1688 to protest revocation of the Massachusetts charter. However, his association with the new governor and his silence during the Salem witch trials of the 1690s lessened his public influence. His eldest son was Cotton ⇨Mather.

Mathewson Christy (Christopher) 1880–1925. US baseball player. Born in Factoryville, Pennsylvania, Mathewson attended Bucknell University. A standout pitcher, he was signed by the New York Giants of the National League 1900. During a 17-year major-league career, Mathewson amassed an impressive record of 373 wins and 188 losses. He retired from play 1916, assuming the job of Cincinnati Reds manager 1916–18. Mathewson was elected to the Baseball Hall of Fame 1936.

Matilda 1102–1167. Claimant to the throne of England. On the death of her father, Henry I, 1135, the barons elected her cousin Stephen to be king. Matilda invaded England 1139, and was crowned by her supporters 1141. Civil war ensued until Stephen was finally recognized as king 1153, with Henry II (Matilda's son) as his successor.

Matilda was recognized during the reign of Henry I as his heir. She married first the Holy Roman emperor Henry V and, after his death, Geoffrey Plantagenet, Count of Anjou (1113–1151).

Matisse Henri 1869–1954. French painter, sculptor, illustrator, and designer; one of the most original creative forces in early 20th-century art. His work concentrates on designs that emphasize curvaceous surface patterns, linear arabesques, and brilliant color. Subjects include odalisques (women of the harem), bathers, and dancers; later works include pure abstracts, as in his collages of colored paper shapes and the designs 1949–51 for the decoration of a chapel for the Dominican convent in Vence, near Nice.

In 1904 Matisse worked with Signac in the south of France in a Neo-Impressionist style. The following year he was the foremost of the Fauve painters exhibiting at the Salon d'Automne, painting with bold brushstrokes, thick paint, and strong colors. He soon abandoned conventional perspective in his continued experiments with color, and in 1910 an exhibition of Islamic art further influenced him toward the decorative. He settled in the south of France 1914. His murals of *The Dance* 1932–33 (Barnes Foundation, Merion, Pennsylvania) are characteristic.

Mato Grosso (Portuguese "dense forest") area of SW Brazil, now forming two states, with their capitals at Cuiaba and Campo Grande. The forests, now depleted, supplied rubber and rare timbers; diamonds and silver are mined.

matriarchy form of social organization in which the mother is recognized as head of the family or group, with descent and kinship traced to the mother, and where women rule or dominate the group's organization. See also ⇨matriliny.

matriliny a form of social organization in which women head the family, and descent and relationship are calculated through the female line. In matrilineal societies, powerful positions are usually held by men but acceded to through female kin.

matrix in mathematics, a square ($n \times n$) or rectangular ($m \times n$) array of elements (numbers or algebraic variables). They are a means of condensing information about mathematical systems and can be used for, among other things, solving ⇨simultaneous linear equations and transformations.

Much early matrix theory was developed by the British mathematician Arthur Cayley, although the term was coined by his contemporary James Sylvester (1814–1897).

matrix in biology, usually refers to the ⇨extracellular matrix.

Matsukata Masayoshi, Prince 1835–1924. Japanese politician, premier 1891–92 and 1896–98. As minister of finance 1881–91 and 1898–1900, he paved the way for the modernization of the Japanese economy.

Matsuoka Yosuke 1880–1946. Japanese politician, foreign minister 1940–41. A fervent nationalist, Matsuoka led Japan out of the League of Nations when it condemned Japan for the seizure of Manchuria. As foreign minister, he allied Japan with Germany and Italy. At the end of World War II, he was arrested as a war criminal but died before his trial.

Matsuyama largest city on Shikoku, Japan; industries (agricultural machinery, textiles, chemicals); population (1989) 437,000. There is a feudal fortress 1634.

Matsys (also *Massys* or *Metsys*) Quentin *c.* 1464–1530. Flemish painter, born in Louvain, active in Antwerp. He painted religious subjects such as the *Lamentation* 1511 (Musées

Royaux, Antwerp) and portraits set against landscapes or realistic interiors.

His works include the *St Anne Altarpiece* 1509 (Musées Royaux, Brussels) and a portrait of *Erasmus* 1517 (Museo Nazionale, Rome).

matter in physics, anything that has mass and can be detected and measured. All matter is made up of ⬦atoms, which in turn are made up of ⬦elementary particles; it exists ordinarily as a solid, liquid, or gas. The history of science and philosophy is largely taken up with accounts of theories of matter, ranging from the hard "atoms" of Democritus to the "waves" of modern quantum theory.

Matterhorn (French **le Cervin**, Italian **il Cervino**) mountain peak in the Alps on the Swiss-Italian border; 14,690 ft/4,478 m.

It was first climbed 1865 by English mountaineer Edward Whymper (1840–1911); four members of his party of seven were killed when a rope broke during their descent.

Matthau Walter. Adopted name of Walter Matuschanskavasky 1922– . US character actor, impressive in both comedy and dramatic roles. He gained film stardom in the 1960s after his stage success in *The Odd Couple* 1965. His many films include *Kotch* 1971, *Charley Varrick* 1973, and *The Sunshine Boys* 1975.

Matthews Stanley 1824–1889. US jurist and associate justice of the US Supreme Court 1881–89. His most important decision, *Hurtado* v *California* 1888, was an important constitutional definition of due process of law.

Born in Cincinnati, Ohio, Matthews graduated from Kenyon College and studied law in Cincinnati. He practiced law in Tennessee and later in Ohio. He served in the Ohio Senate 1855–57 and as a US attorney for the southern district of Ohio 1858–61. After Civil War service, Matthews sat as a judge of the Cincinnati Superior Court and then returned to private practice. He was appointed to the Supreme Court by President Garfield 1881.

Matthew, St 1st century AD. Christian apostle and evangelist, the traditional author of the first Gospel. He is usually identified with Levi, who was a tax collector in the service of Herod Antipas, and was called by Jesus to be a disciple as he sat by the Lake of Galilee receiving customs dues. His emblem is a man with wings; feast day Sept 21.

Matthias Corvinus 1440–1490. King of Hungary from 1458. His aim of uniting Hungary, Austria, and Bohemia involved him in long wars with Holy Roman emperor Frederick III and the kings of Bohemia and Poland, during which he captured Vienna (1485) and made it his capital. His father was János ⬦Hunyadi.

Mature Victor 1915– . US actor, film star of the 1940s and early 1950s. He gave memorable performances in, among others, *My Darling Clementine* 1946, *Kiss of Death* 1947, and *Samson and Delilah* 1949.

Mauchly John William 1907–1980. US physicist and engineer who, in 1946, constructed the first general-purpose computer, the ENIAC, in collaboration with John ⬦Eckert. Their company was bought by Remington Rand 1950, and they built the UNIVAC 1 computer 1951 for the US census.

The idea for ENIAC grew out of work carried out by the two during World War II on ways of automating the calculation of artillery firing tables for the US Army.

Maugham (William) Somerset 1874–1965. English writer. His work includes the novels *Of Human Bondage* 1915, *The Moon and Sixpence* 1919, and *Cakes and Ale* 1930; the short-story collections *The Trembling of a Leaf* 1921 and *Ashenden* 1928; and the plays *Lady Frederick* 1907 and *Our Betters* 1923.

Maugham was born in Paris and studied medicine at St Thomas's, London. During World War I he was a secret agent in Russia; his *Ashenden* spy stories are based on this experience.

Mau Mau Kenyan secret guerrilla movement 1952–60, an offshoot of the Kikuyu Central Association banned in World War II. Its aim was to end British colonial rule. This was achieved 1960 with the granting of Kenyan independence and the election of Jomo Kenyatta as Kenya's first prime minister.

A state of emergency was declared 1952, and by 1956 colonial government forces had killed more than 11,000 Kikuyu. More than 100 Europeans and Asians and 2,000 progovernment Kikuyu were killed by the Mau Mau. The state of emergency was ended 1960, and three years later Kenya achieved independence. Jomo Kenyatta, who was convicted of being the leader of the Mau Mau, became the country's first prime minister.

Mauna Kea astronomical observatory in Hawaii, built on a dormant volcano at 13,784 ft/4,200 m above sea level. Because of its elevation high above clouds, atmospheric moisture, and artificial lighting, Mauna Kea is ideal for infrared astronomy. The first telescope on the site was installed 1970.

Telescopes include the 2.24-m/88-in University of Hawaii reflector 1970. In 1979 three telescopes were erected: the 150 in/3.8 m United Kingdom Infrared Telescope (UKIRT) (also used for optical observations); the 3-m/120-in NASA Infrared Telescope Facility (IRTF); and the 3.6-m/142-in Canada-France-Hawaii Telescope (CFHT), designed for optical and infrared work. The 15-m/50-ft diameter UK/Netherlands James Clerk Maxwell Telescope (JCMT) is the world's largest telescope specifically designed to observe millimeter wave radiation from nebulae, stars, and galaxies. The JCMT is operated via satellite links by astronomers in Europe.

The world's largest optical telescope is the **W M Keck Telescope**. It has a primary mirror 33 ft/10 m across, unique in that it comprises 36 6-ft/2-m hexagonal segments joined together in a giant mosaic, each controlled and adjusted by computer to generate single images of the objects observed. It received its first images in Nov 1990. In May 1991 the W M Keck Foundation donated $74.6 million toward the cost of a twin to the Keck Telescope which will be named Keck II and cost a total of $93.3 million.

The Keck Telescope is built and operated jointly on Mauna Kea by the California Institute of Technology and the University of California.

Mauna Loa active volcano rising to a height of 13,678 ft/4,169 m on the Pacific island of Hawaii; it has numerous craters, including the second-largest active crater in the world.

Maundy Thursday in the Christian church, the Thursday before Easter. The ceremony of washing the feet of pilgrims on that day was instituted in commemoration of Jesus' washing of the apostles' feet and observed from the 4th century to 1754.

Maupassant Guy de 1850–1893. French author who established a reputation with the short story "Boule de Suif/Ball of Fat" 1880 and wrote some 300 short stories in all. His novels include *Une Vie/A Woman's Life* 1883 and *Bel-Ami* 1885. He was encouraged as a writer by Gustave ⬦Flaubert.

Mauriac François 1885–1970. French novelist. His novel *Le Baiser au lépreux/A Kiss for the Leper* 1922 describes the conflict of an unhappy marriage. The irreconcilability of Christian practice and human nature is examined in *Fleuve de feu/River of Fire* 1923, *Le Désert de l'amour/The Desert of Love* 1925, and *Thérèse Desqueyroux* 1927. Nobel Prize for Literature 1952.

Mauritania country in NW Africa, bounded NE by Algeria, E and S by Mali, SW by Senegal, W by the Atlantic Ocean, and NW by Western Sahara.

government The 1961 constitution was suspended 1978 and replaced by a charter that gave executive and legislative power to the Military Committee for National Salvation (CMSN). The chair of the CMSN is also president of the republic, prime minister, and minister of defense. In 1991 the constitution was amended to allow opposition parties to operate.

history Mauritania was the name of the Roman province of NW Africa, after the Mauri, a ⬦Berber people who inhabited it. Berbers occupied the region during the 1st–3rd centuries AD, and it came under the control of the Ghana Empire (see ⬦Ghana, ancient) in the 7th–11th centuries. The Berbers were converted to Islam from the 8th century, and Islamic influence continued to dominate as the area was controlled by the ⬦Almoravids and then the Arabs. French influence began in the 17th century, with the trade in gum arabic, and developed into colonization by the mid-18th century, when France gained control of S Mauritania.

independence In 1920 Mauritania became a French colony as part of ⬦French West Africa. It achieved internal self-government within the French Community 1958 and full independence 1960. Moktar Ould Daddah, leader of the PPM, became president 1961.

Western Sahara conflict In 1975 Spain ceded Western Sahara to Mauritania and Morocco, leaving them to decide how to share it. Without consulting the Saharan people, Mauritania occupied the south, leaving the north to Morocco. A resistance movement developed against this occupation, the Popular Front for Liberation, or the Polisario Front, with Algerian backing, and Mauritania and Morocco found themselves engaged in a guerrilla war, forcing the two former rivals into a mutual defense pact. The conflict weakened Mauritania's economy, and in 1978 President Daddah was deposed in a bloodless coup led by Col Mohamed Khouna Ould Haidalla. Peace with the Polisario was eventually agreed Aug, allowing diplomatic relations with Algeria to be restored.

PPM banned The only political party, the Mauritanian People's Party (PPM), was banned 1978, and some of its exiled supporters now operate from Paris through the Alliance for a Democratic Mauritania (AMI), or from Dakar, in Senegal, through the Organization of Nationalist Mauritanians.

Taya takes over in military coup In Dec 1984, while Col Haidalla was attending a Franco-African summit meeting in Burundi, Col Maaouia Ould Sid Ahmed Taya, a former prime minister, led a bloodless coup to overthrow him. Diplomatic relations with Morocco were broken 1981 and the situation worsened 1984 when Mauritania formally recognized the Polisario regime in Western Sahara. Normal relations were restored 1985. During 1989 there were a number of clashes with Senegalese in border areas resulting in the death of at least 450 people. The presidents of the two countries met to try to resolve their differences. Citizens of each country were forced to return to their native country, with nearly 50,000 people repatriating by June. In 1991 there were calls for the resignation of President Taya, despite the promise of multiparty elections and the amnesty granted to political prisoners.

multiparty system approved Voters approved a new constitution Aug 1991 that increased political freedom, and opposition parties were legalized. Taya formed the Democratic and Social Republican Party (PRDS) as his main political vehicle. The first multiparty elections for the presidency were held Jan 1992 and for the assembly March 1992. Alleging ballot rigging, the opposition parties boycotted the March 1992 elections, allowing the ruling PRDS a clear win. In April 1992 diplomatic relations with Senegal, severed 1989, were restored. *See illustration box.*

Mauritius island country in the Indian Ocean, E of Madagascar.

government Mauritius became a republic 1992 but remained a member of the British ◊Commonwealth. Its 1968 constitution,

Mauritania
Islamic Republic of (*République Islamique de Mauritanie*)

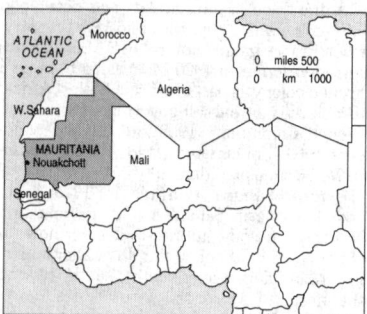

area 397,850 sq mi/1,030,700 sq km
capital Nouakchott
cities port of Nouadhibou, Kaédi, Zouérate
physical valley of river Senegal in S; remainder arid and flat
features part of the Sahara Desert; dusty sirocco wind blows in March
head of state and government Maaouia Ould Sid Ahmed Taya from 1984
political system emergent democratic republic
political parties Democratic and Social Republican Party (PRDS), center-left, militarist; Union of Democratic Forces (UFD), center-left; Rally for Democracy and National Unity (RDUN), centrist; Mauritian Renewal Party (PMR), centrist; Umma, Islamic fundamentalist; Socialist and Democratic Popular Front Union (UDSP), left-of-center
exports iron ore, fish, gypsum
currency ouguiya

amended 1969, provides for a single-chamber legislative assembly of up to 71 members, 62 elected by universal adult suffrage, plus the speaker and up to eight of the most successful nonelected candidates as "additional" members. A president appoints the prime minister and a council of ministers who are collectively responsible to the assembly.

history Uninhabited until the 16th century, the island was colonized on a small scale by the Dutch, who named it Mauricius after Prince Maurice of Nassau. They abandoned it 1710, and in 1715 it was occupied by the French, who imported African slaves to work on their sugar-cane plantations. Mauritius was seized by Britain 1810 and was formally ceded by the Treaty of Paris 1814. The abolition of slavery 1833 brought about the importation of indentured laborers from India, whose descendants now make up about 70% of the island's population. In 1957 Mauritius achieved internal self-government, and full independence within the Commonwealth 1968.

succession of coalition governments Seewoosagur Ramgoolam, leader of the Mauritius Labor Party (MLP), who had led the country since 1959, became its first prime minister. During the 1970s he led a succession of coalition governments, and even in 1976, when the Mauritius Militant Movement (MMM) became the assembly's largest single party, Ramgoolam formed another fragile coalition. Dissatisfaction with the government's economic policies led to Ramgoolam's defeat and the formation in 1982 of an MMM–Mauritius Socialist Party (PSM) coalition government

population (1990 est) 2,038,000 (30% Arab-Berber, 30% black Africans, 30% Haratine —descendants of black slaves, who remained slaves until 1980); growth rate 3% p.a.
life expectancy men 43, women 48 (1989)
languages French (official), Hasaniya Arabic, black African languages
religion Sunni Muslim 99%
literacy 17% (1987)
GNP $843 million; $480 per head (1988)
chronology
1903 Became a French protectorate.
1960 Independence achieved from France, with Moktar Ould Daddah as president.
1975 Western Sahara ceded by Spain. Mauritania occupied the southern area and Morocco the north. Polisario Front formed in Sahara to resist the occupation by Mauritania and Morocco.
1978 Daddah deposed in bloodless coup; replaced by Mohamed Khouna Ould Haidalla. Peace agreed with Polisario Front.
1981 Diplomatic relations with Morocco broken.
1984 Haidalla overthrown by Maaouia Ould Sid Ahmed Taya. Polisario regime formally recognized.
1985 Relations with Morocco restored.
1989 Violent clashes between Mauritanians and Senegalese. Arab-dominated government expelled thousands of Africans into N Senegal; governments had earlier agreed to repatriate each other's citizens (about 250,000).
1991 Amnesty for political prisoners. Multiparty elections promised. Calls for resignation of President Taya.
1992 First multiparty elections won by ruling PRDS. Diplomatic relations with Senegal resumed.

led by Aneerood Jugnauth. Strains developed within the alliance, 12 MMM ministers resigned 1983, and the coalition was dissolved. Jugnauth then founded the Mauritius Socialist Movement (MSM), and the PSM was incorporated in the new party. A general election later that year resulted in an MSM–MLP–Mauritius Social Democratic Party (PMSD) coalition. Jugnauth became prime minister on the understanding that Sir Seewoosagur Ramgoolam would be president if Mauritius became a republic. When the constitutional change failed to get legislative approval, Sir Seewoosagur Ramgoolam was appointed governor-general 1983. He died 1985, and former finance minister Sir Veerasamy Ringadoo replaced him.

On the strength of economic policies that cut inflation and unemployment, Aneerood Jugnauth was reelected 1987. In Aug 1990 an attempt by Jugnauth to make the country a republic was narrowly defeated in the legislative assembly.

Jugnauth coalition re-elected The ruling coalition headed by Jugnauth secured an overwhelming majority in the Sept 1991 general election. In March 1992 the country became a republic but still remained a member of the Commonwealth. Ringadoo became interim president.

foreign policy Mauritius, which has no standing army, has pursued a foreign policy close to that of the ◊nonaligned movement during recent years. *See illustration box.*

Maurois André. Adopted name of Emile Herzog 1885–1967. French novelist and writer whose works include the semi autobiographical *Bernard Quesnay* 1926 and fictionalized biographies, such as *Ariel* 1923, a life of Shelley.

Maury Matthew Fontaine 1806–1873. US naval officer, founder of the US Naval Oceanographic Office. His system of recording oceanographic data is still used today.

Maurya dynasty Indian dynasty c. 321–c. 185 BC, founded by *Chandragupta Maurya* (321–c. 279 BC). Under Emperor ◊Asoka most of India was united for the first time, but after his death in 232 the empire was riven by dynastic disputes.

max. abbreviation for *maximum*.

Maxim Hiram Stevens 1840–1916. US-born British inventor of the first automatic machine gun, in 1884.

Maximilian 1832–1867. Emperor of Mexico 1864–67. He accepted that title when the French emperor Napoleon III's troops occupied the country, but encountered resistance from the deposed president Benito ◊Juárez. In 1866, after the French troops withdrew on the insistence of the US, Maximilian was captured by Mexican republicans and shot.

Maximilian I 1459–1519. Holy Roman emperor from 1493, the son of Emperor Frederick III. He had acquired the Low Countries through his marriage to Mary of Burgundy 1477.

He married his son Philip I (the Handsome) to the heiress to the Spanish throne, and undertook long wars with Italy and Hungary in attempts to extend Hapsburg power. He was the patron of the artist Dürer.

maximum and minimum in ◊coordinate geometry, points at which the slope of a curve representing a ◊function changes from positive to negative (maximum), or from negative to positive (minimum). A tangent to the curve at a maximum or minimum has zero gradient.

maximum and minimum

Maxima and minima can be found by differentiating the function for the curve and setting the differential to zero (the value of the slope at the turning point). For example, differentiating the function for the ◊parabola $y = 2x^2 - 8x$ gives $dy/dx = 4x - 8$. Setting this equal to zero gives $x = 2$, so that $y = -8$ (found by substituting $x = 2$ into the parabola equation). Thus the function has a minimum at the point $(2, -8)$.

maxwell unit (symbol Mx) of magnetic flux (the strength of a ◊magnetic field in an area multiplied by the area). It is now replaced by the SI unit, the ◊weber (one maxwell equals 10^{-8} weber).

Mauritius
Republic of

area 720 sq mi/1,865 sq km; the island of Rodrigues is part of Mauritius; there are several small island dependencies
capital Port Louis
cities Beau Bassin-Rose Hill, Curepipe, Quatre Bornes
physical mountainous, volcanic island surrounded by coral reefs
features unusual wildlife includes flying fox and ostrich; it was the home of the dodo (extinct from about 1680)
interim head of state Veerasamy Ringadoo from 1992
head of government Aneerood Jugnauth from 1982
political system liberal democratic republic
political parties Mauritius Socialist Movement (MSM), moderate socialist-republican; Mauritius Labor Party (MLP), centrist,

Hindu-oriented; Mauritius Social Democratic Party (PMSD), conservative, Francophile; Mauritius Militant Movement (MMM), Marxist-republican; Rodriguais People's Organization (OPR), left-of-center **exports** sugar, knitted goods, tea
currency Mauritius rupee
population (1990 est) 1,141,900, 68% of Indian origin; growth rate 1.5% p.a.
life expectancy men 64, women 71 (1989)
languages English (official), French, Creole, Indian languages
religion Hindu 51%, Christian 30%, Muslim 17%
literacy 94% (1989)
GNP $1.4 bn (1987); $1,810 per head (1988)
chronology
1814 Annexed to Britain by the Treaty of Paris.
1968 Independence achieved from Britain within the Commonwealth, with Seewoosagur Ramgoolam as prime minister.
1982 Aneerood Jugnauth became prime minister.
1983 Jugnauth formed a new party, the Mauritius Socialist Movement. Ramgoolam appointed governor-general. Jugnauth formed a new coalition government.
1985 Ramgoolam died, succeeded by Veersamy Ringadoo.
1987 Jugnauth's coalition reelected.
1990 Attempt to create a republic failed.
1991 Jugnauth's ruling MSM–MMM–OPR coalition won general election; pledge to secure republican status by 1992.
1992 Mauritius became a republic while remaining a member of the Commonwealth. Ringadoo became interim president.

The maxwell is a very small unit, representing a single line of magnetic flux. It is equal to the flux through one square centimeter normal to a magnetic field with an intensity of one gauss.

Maxwell (Ian) Robert (born Jan Ludvik Hoch) 1923–1991. Czech-born British publishing and newspaper proprietor who owned several UK national newspapers, including the *Daily Mirror*, the Macmillan Publishing Company, and the New York *Daily News*. At the time of his death the Maxwell domain carried debts of some $3.9 billion.

Maxwell James Clerk 1831–1879. Scottish physicist. His main achievement was in the understanding of ◊electromagnetic waves: Maxwell's equations bring together electricity, magnetism, and light in one set of relations. He contributed to every branch of physical science—studying gases, optics, and the sensation of color. His theoretical work in magnetism prepared the way for wireless telegraphy and telephony.

His principal works include *Perception of Colour* 1860, *Theory of Heat* 1871, *Electricity and Magnetism* 1873, and *Matter and Motion* 1876. Although thought of as a theoretical physicist, he was an able experimenter; he was ranked by Einstein as second only to Isaac Newton.

Maxwell–Boltzmann distribution in physics, a statistical equation describing the distribution of velocities among the molecules of a gas. It is named after James Maxwell and Ludwig Boltzmann, who derived the equation, independently of each other, in the 1860s.

One form of the distribution is $n = Ne(-E/RT)$, where N is the total number of molecules, n is the number of molecules with energy in excess of E, T is the absolute temperature (temperature in kelvin), R is the ◊gas constant, and e is the exponential constant.

maya (Sanskrit "illusion") in Hindu philosophy, mainly in the *Vedānta*, the cosmos which Isvara, the personal expression of Brahman, or the ◊atman, has called into being. This is real, yet also an illusion, since its reality is not everlasting.

Maya member of a group of Central American Indians who lived in agricultural villages in and around the Yucatán Peninsula and Guatemalan highlands from at least 3000 BC, and who developed a civilization of city-states that flourished from about AD 300 until about 900, when Toltecs from the Valley of Mexico moved south into the area, building new ceremonial centers of their own and dominating the local people. Nevertheless, Mayan sovereignty was maintained, for the most part, until late in the Spanish Conquest 1560s in some areas. The Maya had been ruled by a theocracy supported by taxation and tribute; they traded with their neighbors to the north and south; developed advanced mathematics, astronomy, art, and architecture; a glyph system of writing on stone, ceramics, and in book form; and they celebrated a complex religion with a calendar, many deities, and ceremonies that included a form of ball game and human sacrifice. Today they are Roman Catholic, live in farming and fishing villages, as well as the cities of Yucatán, Guatemala, Belize, and W Honduras. Many still speak Maya, a member of the Totonac-Mayan language family, as well as Spanish.

Mayagüez port in W Puerto Rico with needlework industry and a US agricultural experimental station; population (1986 est) 98,900.

Mayan art art of the Central American civilization of the Maya, between about AD 300 and 900. Mayan figures have distinctive squat proportions and squared-off composition. Large, steeply inclined pyramids were built, such as those at ◊Chichen Itzá, decorated with sculpture and inscription.

Bonampak, Copan, Tikal, and Palenque were other sites of Mayan worship. In sculpture, human heads and giant reclining figures of Mayan deities are frequent motifs. A few intricately painted manuscripts survive (in the Museo de América, Madrid, Spain, for example).

May Day first day of May. In many countries it is a national holiday in honor of labor; see also ◊Labor Day.

Traditionally the first day of summer, in parts of England it is still celebrated as a pre-Christian magical rite; for example, the dance around the maypole (an ancient fertility symbol).

Mayence French name for the German city of ◊Mainz.

Mayenne *département* of W France in Pays-de-Loire region
area 2,033 sq mi/5,212 sq km
capital Laval
features river Mayenne
products iron, slate; paper
population (1982) 271,184.

Mayer Julius Robert von 1814–1878. German physicist who in 1842 anticipated James ◊Joule in deriving the mechanical equivalent of heat, and Hermann von ◊Helmholtz in the principle of conservation of energy.

Mayer Louis B(urt). Adopted name of Eliezer Mayer 1885–1957. Russian-born US film producer. Attracted to the entertainment industry, he became a successful theater-owner in New England and in 1914 began to buy the distribution rights to feature films. Mayer was soon involved in film production, moving to Los Angeles 1918 and becoming one of the founders of Metro-Goldwyn-Mayer (MGM) studios 1924. In charge of production, Mayer instituted the Hollywood "star" system. He retired from MGM 1951.

Mayerling site near Vienna of the hunting lodge of Crown Prince ◊Rudolph of Austria, where he and his mistress were found shot dead in 1889.

Mayfair district of Westminster in London, England, vaguely defined as lying between Piccadilly and Oxford Street, and including Park Lane; formerly a fashionable residential district, but increasingly taken up by offices.

Mayflower the ship in which the ◊Pilgrims sailed 1620 from Plymouth, England, to found Plymouth plantation and Plymouth colony in present-day Massachusetts.

The *Mayflower* was one of two ships scheduled for departure in 1620. The second ship, the *Speedwell*, was deemed unseaworthy, so 102 people were crowded into the 90-foot *Mayflower*, which was bound for Virginia. Tension between Pilgrim and non-Pilgrim passengers threatened to erupt into a mutiny. Blown off course, the ship reached Cape Cod, Massachusetts, in December. The ◊Mayflower Compact was drafted to establish self-rule for the Plymouth colony and to protect the rights of all the settlers.

mayfly any insect of the order Ephemerida (Greek *ephemeros* "lasting for a day," an allusion to the very brief life of the adult). The larval stage, which can last a year or more, is passed in water, the adult form developing gradually from the nymph through successive molts. The adult has transparent, net-veined wings.

Mayo county in Connacht province, Republic of Ireland

area 2,084 sq mi/5,400 sq km

cities Castlebar (administrative town)

features Lough Conn; wild Atlantic coast scenery; Achill Island; the village of Knock, where two women claimed a vision of the Virgin with two saints 1879, now a site of pilgrimage; Croagh Patrick 2,510 ft/765 m, the mountain where St Patrick spent the 40 days of Lent in 441; pilgrims climb the mountain on the last Sunday of July each year

products sheep and cattle farming; fishing

population (1991) 110,700.

Mayo William James 1861–1939. US surgeon, founder, with his brother Charles Horace Mayo (1865–1939), of the **Mayo Clinic** for medical treatment 1889 in Rochester, Minnesota.

mayor title of head of local administration for a town or city. Powers vary widely, although generally mayors oversee financial issues, public education, public safety, planning and zoning, taxation, and other aspects of municipal government.

Mayor of the Palace administrator of the royal court of the ◊Merovingian dynasty from 439 to 751. After the death of Dagobert I (605–639) and the subsequent decline of the Merovingian kings, holders of this office became, in effect, rulers of the kingdom and established a hereditary succession until 751, when the Carolingian line began with ◊Pepin the Short.

Mayotte or *Mahore* island group of the ◊Comoros, off the E coast of Africa, a *collectivité territoriale* of France by its own wish. The two main islands are Grande Terre and Petite Terre

area 144 sq mi/374 sq km

capital Dzaoudzi

products coffee, copra, vanilla, fishing

languages French, Swahili

population (1987) 73,000

history a French colony 1843–1914, and later, with the Comoros, an overseas territory of France. In 1974, Mayotte voted to remain a French dependency.

Mays Willie (Howard Jr) 1931– . US baseball player, born in Westfield, Alabama, who played for 22 years with the New York (later San Francisco) Giants (1951–72) and the New York Mets (1973). He hit 660 career home runs, third best in baseball history, and was also an outstanding fielder and runner. He was elected to the Baseball Hall of Fame 1979.

mayweed any of several species of the daisy family Compositae native to Europe and Asia, and naturalized elsewhere, including the European dog fennel or stinking daisy *Anthemis cotula*, naturalized in North America, and Eurasian pineapple mayweed *Matricaria matricarioides*. All have finely divided leaves.

Mazarin Jules 1602–1661. French politician who succeeded Richelieu as chief minister of France 1642. His attack on the power of the nobility led to the ◊Fronde and his temporary exile, but his diplomacy achieved a successful conclusion to the Thirty Years' War, and, in alliance with Oliver Cromwell during the British protectorate, he gained victory over Spain.

Mazowiecki Tadeusz 1927– . Polish politician, founder member of ◊Solidarity, and Poland's first postwar noncommunist prime minister 1989–90. Forced to introduce unpopular economic reforms, he was knocked out in the first round of the Nov 1990 presidential elections, resigning in favor of his former colleague Lech ◊Wałęsa.

mazurka lively national dance of Poland from the 16th century. In triple time, it is characterized by foot-stamping and heel-clicking, together with a turning movement.

Mazzini Giuseppe 1805–1872. Italian nationalist. He was a member of the revolutionary society, the ◊Carbonari, and founded in exile the nationalist movement Giovane Italia (Young Italy) 1832. Returning to Italy on the outbreak of the 1848 revolution, he headed a republican government established in Rome, but was forced into exile again on its overthrow 1849. He acted as a focus for the movement for Italian unity (see ◊Risorgimento).

Mazzini, born in Genoa, studied law. For his subversive activity with the Carbonari he was imprisoned 1830, then went to France, founding in Marseille the Young Italy movement, followed by an international revolutionary organization, Young Europe, 1834. For many years he lived in exile in France, Switzerland, and the UK, and was condemned to death in his absence by the Sardinian government, but returned to Italy for the ◊revolution of 1848. He conducted the defense of Rome against French forces and, when it failed, he refused to join in the capitulation and returned to London, where he continued to agitate until his death in Geneva, Switzerland.

Mbabane capital (since 1902) of Swaziland, 100 mi/160 km west of Maputo, in the Dalgeni Hills; population (1986) 38,000. Mining and tourism are important.

Mboya Tom 1930–1969. Kenyan politician, a founder of the Kenya African National Union (◊KANU), and minister of economic affairs from 1964 until his assassination.

McMurtry Larry (Jeff) 1936– . US writer. Born in Wichita, Falls, Texas, he wrote about the Southwest—in particular, his home state of Texas. Many of his novels were made into films. His works include *Horseman, Pass By* 1961 (film *Hud* 1963), *Leaving Cheyenne* 1963 (film *Lovin' Molly* 1963), *The Last Picture Show* 1966 (film 1971), *Moving On* 1970, *All My Friends Are Going To Be Strangers* 1972, *Terms of Endearment* 1975 (film 1983; Academy Award for Best Picture), *Somebody's Darling* 1978, *Cadillac Jack* 1982, *The Desert Rose* 1983, *Lonesome Dove* 1985 (Pulitzer Prize 1986; TV miniseries 1989), *Texasville* 1987, and *Buffalo Girls* 1990. He also wrote a book of essays, *In a Narrow Grave* 1968.

MD abbreviation for *Doctor of Medicine*.

MD abbreviation for the state of ◊*Maryland*.

MDMA (3,4-methylenedio-xymethamphetamine) psychedelic drug, also known as ◊ecstasy.

ME abbreviation for *Middle English*, the period of the English language from 1050 to 1550.

ME abbreviation for the state of ◊*Maine*.

ME abbreviation for *myalgic encephalitis*, a debilitating condition also known as ◊*chronic fatigue syndrome*.

mead alcoholic drink made from honey and water fermented with yeast, often with added spices. It was known in ancient times and was drunk by the Greeks, Britons, and Norse.

Mead George Herbert 1863–1931. US philosopher and social psychologist who helped to found the philosophy of pragmatism.

He taught at the University of Chicago during its prominence as a center of social scientific development in the early 20th century, and is regarded as the founder of ◊symbolic interactionism. His work on group interaction had a major influence on sociology, stimulating the development of role theory, ◊phenomenology, and ethnomethodology (the study of social order and routines in people's lives).

Mead Margaret 1901–1978. US anthropologist who popularized cultural relativity and challenged the conventions of Western society with *Coming of Age in Samoa* 1928 and subsequent works. Her fieldwork has later been criticized. She was a popular speaker on civil liberties, ecological sanity, feminism, and population control.

Mead studied at Barnard College 1923 and Columbia University 1929 under Franz ◊Boas. *Coming of Age in Samoa* was a study of differences in temperament between males and females in Samoan and Western societies caused by child-rearing practices. She expanded on this same subject in *Growing Up in New Guinea* 1930 and *Sex and Temperament in Three Primitive Societies* 1935. She also wrote *And Keep Your Powder Dry* 1942, about the US national character, and *Soviet Attitudes Toward Authority* 1951. Her autobiographical works include *Blackberry Winter: My Earlier Years* 1972 and *Letters from the Field, 1925–1975* 1977. She wrote columns for magazines and scholarly papers for journals, appeared on television talk shows, was curator of Pacific Ethnology at the American Museum of Natural History from 1926, and was adjunct professor of anthropology at Columbia University from 1954.

Meade George Gordon 1815–1872. US military leader. At the outbreak of the American Civil War, he was placed in command of Pennsylvania volunteers and participated in the Peninsular Campaign, Bull Run, and Antietam. He led the Army of the Potomac 1863 and the Union forces at Gettysburg. After the war, Meade served as military governor of Georgia, Alabama, and Florida 1868–69.

Born in Cadiz, Spain, Meade graduated from West Point 1835. After working on private railroad and surveying projects 1836–42, he returned to the army, serving in the Mexican War.

Meade James Edward 1907– . British Keynesian economist. He shared a Nobel Prize in 1977 for his work on trade and capital movements, and published a four-volume *Principles of Political Economy* 1965–76.

mean in mathematics, a measure of the average of a number of terms or quantities. The simple *arithmetic mean* is the average value of the quantities, that is, the sum of the quantities divided by their number. The *weighted mean* takes into account the frequency of the terms that are summed; it is calculated by multiplying each term by the number of times it occurs, summing the results and dividing this total by the total number of occurrences. The *geometric mean* of n quantities is the nth root of their product. In statistics, it is a measure of central tendency of a set of data.

meander loop-shaped curve in a river flowing across flat country. As a river flows, any curve in its course is accentuated by the current. The current is fastest on the outside of the curve where it cuts into the bank; on the curve's inside the current is slow and deposits any transported material. In this way the river changes its course across the flood plain.

A loop in a river's flow may become so accentuated that it becomes cut off from the normal course and forms an ◊oxbow lake. The word comes from the river ◊Menderes in Turkey.

mean deviation in statistics, a measure of the spread of a population from the ◊mean.

Thus, if there are n observations with a mean of m, the mean deviation is the sum of the ◊absolute values of the differences of the observation values from m, divided by n.

mean free path in physics, the average distance traveled by a particle, atom, or molecule between successive collisions. It is of importance in the ◊kinetic theory of gases.

measles acute virus disease (rubeola), spread by airborne infection. Symptoms are fever, severe catarrh, small spots inside the mouth, and a raised, blotchy red rash appearing for about a week after two weeks' incubation. Prevention is by vaccination.

In industrialized countries it is not usually a serious disease, though serious complications may develop. Third World children suffer a high mortality, as did the North and South American Indians, who died by the thousands in the 17th, 18th, and 19th centuries.

meat flesh of animals taken as food, in Western countries chiefly from domesticated herds of cattle, sheep, pigs, and poultry. Major exporters include Argentina, Australia, New Zealand, the US, and Denmark (chiefly bacon). The practice of cooking meat is at least 600,000 years old. More than 40% of the world's grain is now fed to animals.

Animals have been hunted for meat since the beginnings of human society. The domestication of animals for meat began during the ◊Neolithic era in the Middle East about 10,000 BC.

Meat is wasteful in production (the same area of grazing land would produce far greater food value in cereal crops). The consumption of meat in 1989 was 244 lb/111 kg per person in the US, 150 lb/68 kg in the UK, 66 lb/30 kg in Japan, 13 lb/6 kg in Nigeria, and 2.2 lb/1 kg in India. Research suggests that, in a healthy diet, consumption of meat (especially with a high fat content) should not exceed the Japanese level.

Meat substitutes are textured vegetable protein (TVP), usually soy-based and extruded in fibers in the same way as plastics.

Grazing lands take up more than 1.4 billion acres/3,000 million hectares and produce about 140 million tons of meat per year.

Meath county in the province of Leinster, Republic of Ireland
area 903 sq mi/2,340 sq km
county town Trim
features Tara Hill, 509 ft/155 m high, was the site of a palace and coronation place of many kings of Ireland (abandoned in the 6th century) and St Patrick preached here
products sheep, cattle
population (1991) 105,600.

Mecca (Arabic *Makkah*) city in Saudi Arabia and, as birthplace of Mohammed, the holiest city of the Islamic world; population (1974) 367,000. In the center of Mecca is the Great Mosque, in the courtyard of which is the ◊Kaaba.

It also contains the well Zam-Zam, associated by tradition with the biblical characters Hagar and Ishmael. Most pilgrims come via the port of ◊Jiddah.

mechanical advantage the amount by which a machine can magnify a force. It is the load (the weight lifted or moved by the machine) divided by the effort (the force used by the operator).

mechanical equivalent of heat in physics, a constant factor relating the calorie (the unit of heat) to the joule (the unit of mechanical energy), equal to 4.1868 joules per calorie. It is redundant in the SI system of units, which measures heat and all forms of energy in joules (so that the mechanical equivalent of heat is 1).

mechanics branch of physics dealing with the motions of bodies and the forces causing these motions, and also with the forces acting on bodies in ◊equilibrium. It is usually divided into ◊dynamics and ◊statics.

Quantum mechanics is the system based on the ◊quantum theory that has superseded Newtonian mechanics in the interpretation of physical phenomena on the atomic scale.

mechanization the use of machines in place of manual labor or the use of animals. Until the 1700s there were few machines available to help people in the home, on the land, or in industry. There were no factories, only cottage industries, in which people carried out work, such as weaving, in their own homes for other people. The 1700s saw a long series of inventions, initially in the textile industry, that ushered in a machine age and brought about the ◊Industrial Revolution.

Among the first inventions in the textile industry were those made by John ◊Kay (flying shuttle, 1773), James ◊Hargreaves (spinning jenny, 1764), and Richard ◊Arkwright (water frame, 1769). Arkwright pioneered the mechanized factory system by installing many of his ◊spinning machines in one building and employing people to work them.

mechanized infantry combat vehicle (MICV) tracked military vehicle designed to fight as part of an armored battle group; that is, with tanks. It is armed with a quick-firing cannon and one or more machine guns. MICVs have replaced armored personnel carriers.

The US Army's MICV is the Bradley and the British Army's equivalent is the Warrior.

Mechnikov Ilya 1845–1916. Russian scientist who discovered the function of white blood cells and ◊phagocytes. After leaving Russia and joining ◊Pasteur in Paris, he described how these "scavenger cells" can attack the body itself (autoimmune disease). He shared the Nobel Prize for Medicine 1908 with Paul ◊Ehrlich.

Mecklenburg–West Pomerania (German *Mecklenburg-Vorpommern*) administrative *Land* (state) of Germany
area 8,840 sq mi/22,887 sq km
capital Schwerin
cities Rostock, Wismar, Stralsund, Neubrandenburg
products fish, ships, diesel engines, electronics, plastics, chalk
population (1990) 2,100,000
history the state was formerly the two grand duchies of Mecklenburg-Schwerin and Mecklenburg-Strelitz, which became free states of the Weimar Republic 1918–34, and were joined 1946 with part of Pomerania to form a region of East Germany. In 1952 it was split into the districts of Rostock, Schwerin, and Neubrandenburg. Following German reunification 1990, the districts were abolished and Mecklenburg–West Pomerania was reconstructed as one of the five new states of the Federal Republic.

Medal of Honor in the US, the highest award for valor. It was established by Congress, originally for the navy (1861) and army (1862). Of differing design, both are bronze stars with the goddess Minerva encircled in their centers. Members of the Marine Corps receive the navy version. The air-force version has Liberty in its center.

medals and decorations coinlike metal pieces, struck or cast to commemorate historic events; to mark distinguished service, whether civil or military (in the latter case in connection with a particular battle, or for individual feats of courage, or for service over the period of a campaign); or as a badge of membership in an order of knighthood, society, or other special group.

Armada medal issued by Elizabeth I following the defeat of the Armada; the first English commemorative medal

George Cross 1940 highest British civilian award for bravery, the medallion in the center of the cross depicting St George and the Dragon

Iron Cross German, see under ◊knighthood

Légion d'honneur French, see under ◊knighthood

Medal of Honor highest award given in the US military for gallantry in action; first given during Civil War (1861–65)

Medal for Merit US civilian, 1942; recognizes exceptional conduct in the performance of outstanding service

Ordre National du Mérite French, civil and military, 1963, replacing earlier merit awards

Order of Merit British, see ⬦Merit, Order of, and ⬦knighthood

Order of the Purple Heart US military, established by Washington 1782, when it was of purple cloth (now made of bronze and enamel); revived by Hoover 1932, when it was issued to those wounded in action from World War I onwards

Pour le Mérite German, instituted by Frederick the Great, military in 1740, and since 1842 for science and art

Presidential Medal of Freedom USA, highest peacetime civilian award since 1963

Gold Star Medal former Soviet Union, civilian and military

Victoria Cross British military, 1856

Waterloo Medal British, established 1816; until the 19th century medals were awarded only to officers; this was the first to be issued to all ranks.

Medan seaport and economic center of the island of Sumatra, Indonesia; population (1980) 1,379,000. It trades in rubber, tobacco, and palm oil.

Medawar Peter (Brian) 1915–1987. Brazilian-born British immunologist who, with Australian physician Macfarlane Burnet (1899–1985), discovered that the body's resistance to grafted tissue is undeveloped in the newborn child, and studied the way it is acquired.

Medawar's work has been vital in understanding the phenomenon of tissue rejection following ⬦transplantation. He shared the 1960 Nobel Prize for Medicine with Burnet (1899–1985), an Australian who also worked on acquired immunological tolerance.

Mede member of a people of NW Iran who in the 9th century BC were tributaries to Assyria, with their capital at Ecbatana (now Hamadán), in the ancient SW Asian country of Media. Allying themselves with Babylon, they destroyed the Assyrian capital of ⬦Nineveh 612 BC, and extended their conquests into central Anatolia. In 550 BC they were overthrown by the Persians, with whom they rapidly merged.

Medea in Greek mythology, the sorceress daughter of the king of Colchis. When ⬦Jason reached the court, she fell in love with him, helped him acquire the Golden Fleece, and they fled together. When Jason married Creusa, Medea killed his bride with the gift of a poisoned garment, and then killed her own two children by Jason.

Medea Greek tragedy by Euripides, produced 431 BC. It deals with the later part of the legend of Medea: her murder of Jason's bride and of her own children.

Medellín industrial town (textiles, chemicals, engineering, coffee) in the Central Cordillera, Colombia, 5,048 ft/1,538 m above sea level; population (1985) 2,069,000. It is the second city of Colombia, and its drug capital, with 7,000 violent deaths in 1990.

There is a museum dedicated to local artist Fernando Botero.

Medford city in SW Oregon, S of Eugene; seat of Jackson County; population (1990) 47,000. It is a summer resort, and tourism is important to the economy. Other industries include processing of the area's agricultural crops and dairy products.

Western medicine: chronology

c. 400 BC	Hippocrates recognized that disease had natural causes.
c. AD 200	Galen consolidated the work of the Alexandrian doctors.
1543	Andreas Vesalius gave the first accurate account of the human body.
1628	William Harvey discovered the circulation of the blood.
1768	John Hunter began the foundation of experimental and surgical pathology.
1785	Digitalis was used to treat heart disease; the active ingredient was isolated 1904.
1798	Edward Jenner published his work on vaccination.
1877	Patrick Manson studied animal carriers of infectious diseases.
1882	Robert Koch isolated the bacillus responsible for tuberculosis.
1884	Edwin Klebs isolated the diphtheria bacillus.
1885	Louis Pasteur produced a vaccine against rabies.
1890	Joseph Lister demonstrated antiseptic surgery.
1895	Wilhelm Röntgen discovered X-rays.
1897	Martinus Beijerinck discovered viruses.
1899	Felix Hoffman developed aspirin; Sigmund Freud founded psychiatry.
1900	Karl Landsteiner identified the first three blood groups, later designated A, B, and O.
1910	Paul Ehrlich developed the first specific antibacterial agent, Salvarsan, a cure for syphilis.
1922	Insulin was first used to treat diabetes.
1928	Alexander Fleming discovered penicillin.
1932	Gerhard Domagk discovered the first antibacterial sulfonamide drug, Prontosil.
1937	Electro-convulsive therapy (ECT) was developed.
1940s	Lithium treatment for manic-depressive illness was developed.
1950	Proof of a link between cigarette smoking and lung cancer was established.
1950s	Antidepressant drugs and beta-blockers for heart disease were developed. Manipulation of the molecules of synthetic chemicals became the main source of new drugs. Peter Medawar studied the body's tolerance of transplanted organs and skin grafts.
1953	Jonas Salk developed a vaccine against polio. Francis Crick and James Watson announced the structure of DNA.
1960s	A new generation of minor tranquilizers called benzodiazepines was developed.
1967	Christian Barnard performed the first human heart-transplant operation.
1971	Viroids, disease-causing organisms even smaller than viruses, were isolated outside the living body.
1972	The CAT scan, pioneered by Godfrey Hounsfield, was first used to image the human brain.
1978	World's first "test-tube baby" was born in the UK.
1980s	AIDS (acquired immune-deficiency syndrome) was first recognized in the US. Barbara McClintock's discovery of the transposable gene was recognized.
1980	The World Health Organization reported the eradication of smallpox.
1983	The virus responsible for AIDS, now known as human immunodeficiency virus (HIV), was identified by Luc Montagnier at the Institut Pasteur, Paris; Robert Gallo at the National Cancer Institute, Maryland discovered the virus independently 1984.
1984	The first vaccine against leprosy was developed.
1987	The world's longest-surviving heart-transplant patient died in France, 18 years after his operation.
1989	Grafts of fetal brain tissue were first used to treat Parkinson's disease.
1991	First successful use of gene therapy (to treat severe combined immune deficiency) was reported in the US.

median in mathematics and statistics, the middle number of an ordered group of numbers. If there is no middle number (because there is an even number of terms), the median is the ⬦mean (average) of the two middle numbers. For example, the median of the group 2, 3, 7, 11, 12 is 7; that of 3, 4, 7, 9, 11, 13 is 8 (the average of 7 and 9).

mediation technical term in ⬦Hegel's philosophy, and in Marxist philosophy influenced by Hegel, describing the way in which an entity is defined through its relations to other entities.

Medici noble family of Florence, the city's rulers from 1434 until they died out 1737. Family members included ⬦Catherine de' Medici, Pope ⬦Leo X, Pope ⬦Clement VII, ⬦Marie de' Medici.

Medici Cosimo de' 1389–1464. Italian politician and banker. Regarded as the model for Machiavelli's *The Prince*, he dominated the government of Florence from 1434 and was a patron of the arts. He was succeeded by his inept son *Piero de' Medici* (1416–1469).

Medici Cosimo de' 1519–1574. Italian politician, ruler of Florence; duke of Florence from 1537 and 1st grand duke of Tuscany from 1569.

Medici Ferdinand de' 1549–1609. Italian politician, grand duke of Tuscany from 1587.

Medici Giovanni de' 1360–1429. Italian entrepreneur and banker, with political influence in Florence as a supporter of the popular party. He was the father of Cosimo de' Medici.

Medici Lorenzo de,' *the Magnificent* 1449–1492. Italian politician, ruler of Florence from 1469. He was also a poet and a generous patron of the arts.

medicine science of preventing, diagnosing, alleviating, or curing disease, both physical and mental; also any substance used in the treatment of disease. The basis of medicine is anatomy (the structure and form of the body) and physiology (the study of the body's functions).

In the West, medicine increasingly relies on new drugs and sophisticated surgical techniques, while diagnosis of disease is more and more by noninvasive procedures. The time and cost of Western-type medical training makes it inaccessible to many parts of the Third World; where health care of this kind is provided it is often by auxiliary medical helpers trained in hygiene and the administration of a limited number of standard drugs for the prevalent diseases of a particular region.

medicine, alternative forms of medical treatment that do not use synthetic drugs or surgery in response to the symptoms of a disease, but aim to treat the patient as a whole (⟩holism). The emphasis is on maintaining health (with diet and exercise) and on dealing with the underlying causes rather than just the symptoms of illness. It may involve the use of herbal remedies and techniques like ⟩acupuncture, ⟩homeopathy, and ⟩chiropractic. Some alternative treatments are increasingly accepted by orthodox medicine, but the absence of enforceable standards in some fields has led to the proliferation of eccentric or untrained practitioners.

medieval art painting and sculpture of the Middle Ages in Europe and parts of the Middle East, dating roughly from the 4th century to the emergence of the Renaissance in Italy in the 1400s. This includes early Christian, Byzantine, Celtic, Anglo-Saxon, and Carolingian art. The Romanesque style was the first truly international style of medieval times, superseded by Gothic in the late 12th century. Religious sculpture, frescoes, and manuscript illumination proliferated; panel painting came only toward the end of the period.

early Christian art (3rd–5th centuries AD) when Christianity was made one of the official religions of the Roman state, churches were built and artistic traditions adapted to the portrayal of the new Christian saints and symbols. Roman burial chests (*sarcophagi*) were adopted by the Christians and their imagery of pagan myths gradually changed into biblical themes.

Byzantine style (4th century–1453) developed in the eastern empire, centered on Constantinople. The use of mosaic associated with Byzantine art also appears in church decoration in the West: for example, in Ravenna. Churches there, built in the 5th and 6th centuries, present powerful religious images on walls and vaults in brilliant, glittering color. Byzantine art soon froze into religious stereotypes and iconlike figures. The Byzantine style continued in icon painting, a strong theme in the art of Greece and Russia.

early medieval art (4th–10th centuries) S Europe was overrun by people from the north, and their art consisted mainly of portable objects, articles for personal use or adornment. They excelled in metalwork and jewelry, often in gold with garnet or enamel inlays, ornamented with highly stylized, animal-based interlace patterns. This type of ornament was translated into manuscript illumination produced in Christian monasteries, such as the decorated pages of the Northumbrian *Lindisfarne Gospels* (British Museum, London) 7th century or the Celtic 8th-century *Book of Kells* (Trinity College, Dublin, Ireland).

Carolingian art (late 8th–early 9th centuries) manuscript painting flourished in Charlemagne's empire, drawing its inspiration from the late Classical artistic traditions of the early Christian and Byzantine styles. Several monasteries produced richly illustrated prayer books and biblical texts.

Romanesque or *Norman art* (10th–12th centuries) is chiefly evident in church sculpture, on capitals and portals, and in manuscript illumination. Romanesque art combined naturalistic elements with the fantastic, poetical, and pattern-loving Celtic and Germanic tradition. Imaginary beasts and medieval warriors mingle with biblical themes. Fine examples remain throughout Europe, from N Spain and Italy to France, the Germanic lands of the Holy Roman Empire, and England. The Romanesque style arrived in Scandinavia in the late 11th century.

Gothic art (late 12th–15th centuries) as large cathedrals were built in Europe, sculptural decoration became more monumental and stained glass filled the tall windows; as in Chartres Cathedral, France. Figures were also carved in wood. Court patronage produced exquisite small ivories, goldsmith's work, devotional books illustrated with miniatures, and tapestries depicting romantic tales. Panel painting, initially on a gold background, evolved in N Europe into the more realistic International Gothic style. In Italy fresco painting made great advances; a seminal figure in this development was the artist Giotto, whose cycle of the lives of Mary and Jesus in the Arena Chapel, Padua (completed 1306), is seen as proto-Renaissance.

Medina (Arabic *Madinah*) Saudi Arabian city, about 220 mi/355 km N of Mecca; population (1974) 198,000. It is the second holiest city in the Islamic world, and is believed to contain the tomb of Mohammed. It produces grain and fruit.

It also contains the tombs of the caliphs or Muslim leaders Abu Bakr, Omar, and Fatima, Mohammed's daughter.

meditation act of spiritual contemplation, practiced by members of many religions or as a secular exercise. It is a central practice in Buddhism. The Sanskrit term is *dhyāna*. See also ⟩transcendental meditation (TM).

Mediterranean climate climate characterized by hot dry summers and warm wet winters. Mediterranean zones are situated in either hemisphere on the western side of continents, between latitudes of 30° and 60°.

During the winter rain is brought by the ⟩Westerlies; in summer Mediterranean zones are under the influence of the ⟩trade winds. The regions bordering the Mediterranean Sea, California, central Chile, the Cape of Good Hope, and parts of S Australia have such climates.

Mediterranean Sea inland sea separating Europe from N Africa, with Asia to the east; extreme length 2,300 mi/3,700 km; area 1,145,000 sq mi/2,966,000 sq km. It is linked to the Atlantic (at the Strait of Gibraltar), Red Sea, and Indian Ocean (by the Suez Canal), Black Sea (at the Dardanelles and Sea of Marmara). The main subdivisions are the Adriatic, Aegean, Ionian, and Tyrrhenian seas. It is highly polluted.

The Mediterranean is almost tideless, and is saltier and warmer than the Atlantic; shallows from Sicily to Cape Bon (Africa) divide it into an east and a west basin. Dense salt water forms a permanent deep current out into the Atlantic.

The Mediterranean is severely endangered by human and industrial waste pollution; 100 million people live along the coast, 85% of sewage near the coast is discharged directly into the water, and it is regularly crossed by oil tankers. The Barcelona Convention 1976 to clean up the Mediterranean was signed by 17 countries and led to a ban on dumping of mercury, cadmium, persistent plastics, DDT, crude oil, and hydrocarbons.

medlar small shrub or tree *Mespilus germanica* of the rose family Rosaceae. Native to SE Europe, it is widely cultivated for its fruit, resembling a small brown-green pear or quince. These are palatable when decay has set in.

Médoc French district bordering the Gironde in Aquitaine region, N of Bordeaux. It is famed for its wines, Margaux and St Julien being two of the most popular varieties. Lesparre and Pauillac are the chief towns.

medulla central part of an organ. In the mammalian kidney, the medulla lies beneath the outer cortex and is responsible for the reabsorption of water from the filtrate. In plants, it is a region of packing tissue in the center of the stem. In the vertebrate brain, the medulla is the posterior region responsible for the coordination of basic activities, such as breathing and temperature control.

medusa jellyfish stage in the life cycle of coelenterates (order Cnidaria).

Medusa in Greek mythology, a mortal woman who was transformed into a ⟩Gorgon. Medusa was slain by Perseus; the winged horse ⟩Pegasus was supposed to have sprung from her blood.

meerschaum aggregate of minerals, usually the soft white mineral *sepiolite*, hydrous magnesium silicate. It floats on water and is used for making pipe bowls.

megabyte (Mb) in computing, a unit of memory equal to 1,024 ⟩kilobytes. It is sometimes used, less precisely, to mean 1 million bytes.

megalith prehistoric stone monument of the late Neolithic or early Bronze Age. Megaliths include single, large uprights (menhirs); rows; circles, generally with a central "altar stone" (for example Stonehenge); and the remains of burial chambers with the covering earth removed, looking like a hut (dolmens).

megamouth deep-sea shark *Megachasma pelagios*, which feeds on plankton. It was first discovered 1976. It has a bulbous head with protruding jaws and blubbery lips, is 15 ft/4.5 m long, and weighs 1,650 lb/750 kg.

megapode large (up to 2.3 ft/70 cm long) chickenlike bird of the family Megapodiidae, found mainly in Australia, but also in SE Asia. Megapodes lay their eggs in a pile of rotting vegetation 13 ft/4 m across, and the warmth from this provides the heat for incubation. The male bird feels the mound with his tongue and adds or takes away vegetation to provide the correct temperature.

megatherium genus of extinct giant ground sloth of North and South America. Various species lived from about 7 million years ago until geologically recent times. They were plant-eaters, and some grew to 20 ft/6 m long.

megaton one million (10⁶) tons. Used with reference to the explosive power of a nuclear weapon, it is equivalent to the explosive force of one million tons of trinitrotoluene (TNT).

megavitamin therapy the administration of large doses of vitamins to combat conditions considered wholly or in part due to their deficiency.

Developed by US chemist Linus Pauling in the 1960s, and alternatively known as "orthomolecular psychiatry," the treatment has proved effective with addicts, schizophrenics, alcoholics, and depressives.

Meghalaya state of NE India
area 8,685 sq mi/22,500 sq km
capital Shillong
features mainly agricultural and comprises tribal hill districts
products potatoes, cotton, jute, fruit
minerals coal, limestone, white clay, corundum, sillimanite
population (1991) 1,760,600, mainly Khasi, Jaintia, and Garo
religion Hindu 70%
languages various.

Megiddo site of a fortress town in N Israel, where Thothmes III defeated the Canaanites about 1469 BC; the Old Testament figure Josiah was killed in battle about 609 BC; and in World War I the British field marshal Allenby broke the Turkish front 1918. It is identified with ⌂Armageddon.

Mehemet Ali 1769–1849. Pasha (governor) of Egypt from 1805, and founder of the dynasty that ruled until 1953. An Albanian in the Ottoman service, he had originally been sent to Egypt to fight the French. As pasha, he established a European-style army and navy, fought his Turkish overlord 1831 and 1839, and conquered Sudan.

Mehta Zubin 1936– . Indian conductor who became music director of the New York Philharmonic 1978. He is known for his flamboyant style of conducting and his interpretations of the Romantic composers.

His father, Mehli Mehta, helped found the Bombay Symphony and exposed his son to Western music from an early age. Zubin Mehta's fame spread rapidly when he toured with the Royal Liverpool Philharmonic, the first orchestra that he conducted. He was appointed music director of the Montreal Symphony 1961–67 and of the Los Angeles Philharmonic 1962–78, thus becoming the first person to direct two North American symphony orchestras simultaneously.

Meier Richard 1934– . US architect whose white designs spring from the poetic modernism of the ⌂Le Corbusier villas of the 1920s. His abstract style is at its most mature in the Museum für Kunsthandwerk (Museum of Arts and Crafts), Frankfurt, Germany, which was completed 1984.

Earlier schemes are the Bronx Developmental Center, New York (1970–76), and the Athenaeum–New Harmony, Indiana (1974). He is the architect for the Getty Museum, Los Angeles.

Meiji Mutsuhito 1852–1912. Emperor of Japan from 1867, when he took the title *meiji tennō* ("enlightened sovereign"). During his reign (known as the Meiji era) Japan became a world industrial and naval power. He abolished the feudal system and discrimination against the lowest caste, established state schools, and introduced conscription, the Western calendar, and other measures in an attempt to modernize Japan, including a constitution 1889.

The son of Emperor Komei, he took the personal name Mutsuhito when he became crown prince 1860.

Meiji era in Japanese history, the reign of Emperor ⌂Meiji 1867–1912.

Meinhof Ulrike 1934–1976. West German urban guerrilla, member of the ⌂*Baader–Meinhof gang* in the 1970s.

A left-wing journalist, Meinhof was converted to the use of violence to achieve political change by the imprisoned Andreas Baader.

She helped free Baader and they became joint leaders of the urban guerrilla organization the Red Army Faction. As the faction's chief ideologist, Meinhof was arrested in 1972 and, in 1974, sentenced to eight years' imprisonment. She committed suicide in 1976 in the Stammheim high-security prison.

Mein Kampf (German "my struggle") book dictated by Adolf ⌂Hitler to Rudolf Hess 1923–24 during Hitler's jail sentence for his part in the abortive 1923 Munich beer-hall putsch. Part autobiography, part political philosophy, the book presents Hitler's ideas of German expansion, anticommunism, and anti-Semitism. It was published in two volumes, 1925 and 1927.

meiosis in biology, a process of cell division in which the number of ⌂chromosomes in the

nuclear membrane
cytoplasm
pair of chromosomes
centrioles
Parent cell with 4 chromosomes
chromosomes pair up
centrioles migrate to opposite ends of the cell
chromatids cross over
chromatids (2 strands of a chromosome) become visible
chromatids altered where crossing over took place
nuclear spindles form
whole chromosomes separated
chromosomes group but no new nuclear membrane forms
2 new spindles form
chromatids separate
nuclear membrane
4 nuclear membranes form
4 daughter cells with 2 chromosomes each. None of the new chromosomes are exactly like the original chromosomes

meiosis *Meiosis is a type of cell division that produces gametes (sex cells, sperm and egg).*

cell is halved. It only occurs in eukaryotic cells (see ⌂eukaryote) and is part of a life cycle that involves sexual reproduction because it allows the genes of two parents to be combined without the total number of chromosomes increasing.

In sexually reproducing ⌂diploid animals (having two sets of chromosomes per cell), meiosis occurs during formation of the ⌂gametes (sex cells, sperm and egg), so that the gametes are ⌂haploid (having only one set of chromosomes). When the gametes unite during ⌂fertilization, the diploid condition is restored. In plants, meiosis occurs just before spore formation. Thus the spores are haploid and in lower plants such as mosses they develop into a haploid plant called a gametophyte which produces the gametes (see ⌂alternation of generations). See also ⌂mitosis.

Meir Golda 1898–1978. Israeli Labor (*Mapai*) politician. Born in Russia, she emigrated to the US 1906, and in 1921 went to Palestine. She was foreign minister 1956–66 and prime minister 1969–74. Criticism of the Israelis' lack of preparation for the 1973 Arab-Israeli War led to election losses for Labor and, unable to form a government, she resigned.

Meissen city in the state of Saxony, Germany, on the river Elbe; known for Meissen or Dresden porcelain from 1710; population (1983) 38,908. The porcelain factory, formerly owned by the king of Saxony, remained in public hands in 1990 when the newly formed Saxony government took over the capital of the firm.

Meistersinger (German "master singer") one of a group of German lyric poets, singers, and musicians of the 14th–16th centuries, who formed guilds for the revival of minstrelsy. Hans ⌂Sachs was a Meistersinger, and Richard Wagner's opera, *Die Meistersinger von Nürnberg* 1868, depicts the tradition.

Meitner Lise 1878–1968. Austrian physicist who worked with Otto ⌂Hahn and was the first to realize that they had inadvertently achieved the fission of uranium. Driven from Nazi Germany because of her Jewish origin, she later worked in Sweden, where she published the results of their work. She refused to work on the atomic bomb.

Meknès (Spanish *Mequinez*) city in N Morocco, known for wine and carpet-making; population (1981) 487,000. One of Morocco's four imperial cities, it was the capital until 1728, and is the site of the tomb of Sultan Moulay Ismail.

Mekong river rising as the Za Qu in Tibet and flowing to the South China Sea, through a vast delta (about 77,000 sq mi/200,000 sq km); length 2,750 mi/4,425 km. It is being developed for irrigation and hydroelectricity by Cambodia, Laos, Thailand, and Vietnam.

melaleuca tree or *paperbark* tropical tree *Melaleuca leucadendron*, family Myrtaceae. The leaves produce *cajuput oil*, which has medicinal uses.

In favorable conditions, such as in the Florida Everglades, the tree reproduces rapidly. Attempts are being made to extirpate it because in a forest fire its crown becomes a ball of flame, accelerating the spread of the blaze in all directions.

melamine $C_3N_6H_6$ thermosetting ⌂polymer based on urea–formaldehyde. It is extremely resistant to heat and is also scratch-resistant. Its uses include synthetic resins.

Melanchthon Philip. Assumed name of Philip Schwarzerd 1497–1560. German theologian who helped Luther prepare a German translation of the New Testament. In 1521 he issued the first systematic formulation of Protestant theology, reiterated in the *Confession of ▷Augsburg* 1530.

Melanesia islands in the SW Pacific between Micronesia to the north and Polynesia to the east, embracing all the islands from the New Britain archipelago to Fiji.

Melanesian indigenous inhabitant of Melanesia; a member of any of the Pacific peoples of Melanesia. The Melanesian languages belong to the Austronesian family.

Melanesian languages see ▷Malayo-Polynesian languages.

Melanesian pidgin English or *Tok Pisin* or *Neo-Melanesian* a form of pidgin English; see ▷pidgin language.

melanism black coloration of animal bodies caused by large amounts of the pigment melanin. Melanin is of significance in insects, because melanic ones warm more rapidly in sunshine than do pale ones, and can be more active in cool weather. A fall in temperature may stimulate such insects to produce more melanin. In industrial areas, dark insects and pigeons match sooty backgrounds and escape predation, but they are at a disadvantage in rural areas where they do not match their backgrounds. This is known as *industrial melanism*.

melanoma mole or growth containing the dark pigment melanin. Malignant melanoma is a type of skin cancer developing in association with a pre-existing mole. Unlike other skin cancers, it is associated with brief but excessive exposure to sunlight.

Once rare, this disease is now frequent, owing to the increasing popularity of vacations in the sun. Most at risk are those with fair hair and light skin, and those who have had a severe sunburn in childhood.

Melba Nellie, adopted name of Helen Porter Mitchell 1861–1931. Australian soprano. One of her finest roles was Donizetti's *Lucia*. *Peach melba* (half a peach plus vanilla ice cream and melba sauce, made from sweetened, fresh raspberries) and *melba toast* (crisp, thin toast) are named after her.

Melbourne capital of Victoria, Australia, near the mouth of the river Yarra; population (1990) 3,080,000. Industries include engineering, shipbuilding, electronics, chemicals, food processing, clothing, and textiles.

Founded 1835, it was named after Lord Melbourne 1837, grew in the wake of the gold rushes, and was the seat of the Commonwealth government 1901–27. It is the country's second-largest city, with three universities, and was the site of the 1956 Olympics.

Melbourne industrial city (food processing and electronic and aviation equipment) on the E coast of Florida, on the Indian River, SE of Orlando; population (1990) 59,600. Tourism is also important to the economy.

Melbourne William Lamb, 2nd Viscount 1779–1848. British Whig politician. Home secretary 1830–34, he was briefly prime minister in 1834 and again 1835–41. Accused in 1836 of seducing Caroline ▷Norton, he lost the favor of William IV.

Melchite or *Melkite* member of a Christian church in Syria, Egypt, Lebanon, and Israel. The Melchite Church was founded in Syria in the 6th–7th centuries and is now part of the Eastern Orthodox Church.

The Melchites accepted Byzantine rule at the council of Chalcedon 451 (unlike the ▷Maronites). In 1754 some Melchites broke away to form a ▷Uniate Church with Rome.

Méliès Georges 1861–1938. French film pioneer. From 1896 to 1912 he made over 1,000 films, mostly fantasies (*Le Voyage dans la Lune/A Trip to the Moon* 1902). He developed trick effects, slow motion, double exposure, and dissolves, and in 1897 built Europe's first film studio at Montreuil.

Melilla port and military base on the NE coast of Morocco; area 5 sq mi/14 sq km; population (1986) 56,000. It was captured by Spain 1496 and is still under Spanish rule. Also administered from Melilla are three other Spanish possessions: Peña ("rock") de Velez de la Gomera, Peña d'Alhucemas, and the Chaffarine Islands.

melitin (Greek "bee") extract of honey-bee poison used as a powerful antibiotic.

Mellon Andrew William 1855–1937. US financier who donated his art collection to found the National Gallery of Art, Washington, DC, in 1937. His son, *Paul Mellon* (1907–) was its president 1963–79. He funded Yale University's Center for British Art, New Haven, Connecticut, and donated major works of art to both collections.

Born in Pittsburgh, Mellon attended Western University of Pennsylvania and entered the family banking firm. Through farsighted investments and loans to the expanding steel and oil industries of Pennsylvania, Mellon became one of the wealthiest men in America. He founded the Mellon National Bank 1902. He was appointed secretary of the treasury by President Harding 1921 and held the post until 1932, under presidents Coolidge and Hoover.

melodrama play or film with romantic and sensational plot elements, often unsubtly acted. Originally it meant a play accompanied by music. The early melodramas used extravagant theatrical effects to heighten violent emotions and actions artificially. By the end of the 19th century, melodrama had become a popular genre of stage play.

melody in music, a distinctive sequence of notes. A melody may be a tune in its own right, or it may form a theme running through a longer piece of music.

melon any of several large, juicy (95% water), thick-skinned fruits of trailing plants of the gourd family Cucurbitaceae. The muskmelon *Cucumis melo* and the large red watermelon *Citrullus vulgaris* are two of the many edible varieties.

Thought to have originated in Asia, the melon became naturalized in the Nile Valley and was introduced to Europe at the end of the 15th century.

Melos (modern Greek *Mílos*) Greek island in the Aegean, one of the Cyclades; area 60 sq mi/155 sq km. The sculpture of *Venus de Milo* was discovered here 1820 (now in the Louvre). The capital is Plaka.

meltdown the melting of the core of a nuclear reactor, due to overheating. To prevent such accidents all reactors have equipment intended to flood the core with water in an emergency. The reactor is housed in a strong containment vessel, designed to prevent radiation escaping into the atmosphere. The result of a meltdown is an area radioactively contaminated for 25,000 years or more.

At Three Mile Island, Pennsylvania, in March 1979, a partial meltdown occurred caused by a combination of equipment failure and operator error, and some radiation was released into the air. In April 1986, a reactor at ▷Chernobyl, near Kiev, Ukraine, exploded, causing a partial meltdown of the core. Radioactive ▷fallout was detected as far away as Canada and Japan.

melting point temperature at which a substance melts, or changes from a solid to liquid form. A pure substance under standard conditions of pressure (usually one atmosphere) has a definite melting point. If heat is supplied to a solid at its melting point, the temperature does not change until the melting process is complete. The melting point of ice is 0°C or 32°F.

Melville Herman 1819–1891. US writer whose ▷*Moby-Dick* 1851 was inspired by his whaling experiences in the South Seas. These experiences were also the basis for earlier fiction, such as *Typee* 1846 and *Omoo* 1847. *Billy Budd* was completed just before his death and published 1924. Although most of his works were unappreciated during his lifetime, today he is one of the most highly regarded of US authors.

Melville was born in Albany, New York. His family was left destitute when his father became bankrupt and died when Melville was 12. He went to sea as a cabin boy in 1839. His love for the sea was inspired by this and later voyages. He published several volumes of verse, as well as short stories (*The Piazza Tales* 1856). Melville worked in the New York customs office 1866–85, writing no prose from 1857 until *Billy Budd*. A friend of Nathaniel Hawthorne, he explored the dark, troubled side of American experience in novels of unusual form and great philosophical power.

He died in obscurity. *Moby-Dick* was filmed by John Huston in 1956. *Billy Budd* was the basis of an opera by Benjamin Britten 1951, which was made into a film 1962.

membrane in living things, a continuous layer, made up principally of fat molecules, that encloses a ▷cell or ▷organelles within a cell. Certain small molecules can pass through the cell membrane, but most must enter or leave the cell via channels in the membrane made up of special proteins. The ▷Golgi apparatus within the cell is thought to produce certain membranes.

In cell organelles, enzymes may be attached to the membrane at specific positions, often alongside other enzymes involved in the same process, like workers at a conveyor belt. Thus membranes help to make cellular processes more efficient.

Memel German name for ▷Klaipeda, port in Lithuania.

Memling (or *Memlinc*) Hans c. 1430–1494. Flemish painter, born near Frankfurt-am-Main, Germany, but active in Bruges. He painted religious subjects and portraits. Some of his works are in the Hospital of St John, Bruges, including the *Adoration of the Magi* 1479.

Memling is said to have been a pupil of van der Weyden, but his style is calmer and softer. His portraits include *Tommaso Portinari and His Wife* (Metropolitan Museum of Art, New York), and he decorated the *Shrine of St Ursula* 1489 (Hospital of St John, Bruges).

Memorial Day in the US, a day of remembrance (formerly Decoration Day) instituted 1868 for those killed in the US Civil War. Since World War I it has been observed as a national holiday on the last Monday in May, traditionally falling on May 30, in remembrance of all Americans killed in war.

memory in computing, the part of a system used to store data and programs either permanently or temporarily. There are two main types: immediate access memory and backing storage. Memory capacity is measured in ▷bytes or, more conveniently, in kilobytes (units of 1,024 bytes) or megabytes (units of 1,024 kilobytes).

Immediate access memory, or *internal memory*, describes the memory locations that can be addressed directly and individually by the central processing unit. It is either read-only (stored in ROM, PROM, and EPROM chips) or read/write (stored in RAM chips). Read-only memory stores information that must be constantly available or accessed very quickly, and is unlikely to be changed. It is nonvolatile—that is, it is not lost when the computer is switched off. Read/write memory is volatile—it stores programs and data only while the computer is switched on.

Backing storage, or *external memory*, is nonvolatile memory, located outside the central processing unit, used to store programs and data that are not in current use. Backing storage is provided by such devices as magnetic ▷disks (floppy and hard disks), ▷magnetic tape (tape streamers and cassettes), optical disks (such as ▷CD-ROM), and ▷bubble memory. By rapidly switching blocks of information between the backing storage and the immediate-access memory, the limited size of the immediate-access memory may be increased artificially. When this technique is used to give the appearance of a larger internal memory than physically exists, the additional capacity is referred to as ▷virtual memory.

memory ability to store and recall observations and sensations. Memory does not seem to be based in any particular part of the brain; it may depend on changes to the pathways followed by nerve impulses as they move through the brain. Memory can be improved by regular use as the connections between ▷nerve cells (neurons) become "well-worn paths" in the brain. Events stored in *short-term memory* are forgotten quickly, whereas those in *long-term memory* can last for many years, enabling recall of information and recognition of people and places over long periods of time. Research is just beginning to uncover the biochemical and electrical bases of the human memory.

Memphis ruined city beside the Nile, 12 mi/19 km S of Cairo, Egypt. Once the center of the worship of Ptah, it was the earliest capital of a united Egypt under King Menes about 3200 BC, but was superseded by Thebes under the new empire 1570 BC.

Memphis was later used as a stone quarry, but the "cemetery city" of Sakkara survives, with the step pyramid built for King Zoser by ▷Imhotep, probably the world's oldest stone building.

Memphis industrial port city (pharmaceuticals, food processing, cotton, timber, tobacco) on the Mississippi River, in Tennessee; population (1990) 610,300. Its musical history includes Beale Street, home of the blues composer W C Handy, and Graceland, the home of Elvis Presley. The French built a fort here 1739, but Memphis was not founded until 1819.

Memphis's recording studios and record companies (Sun 1953–68, Stax 1960–75) made it a focus of the music industry. During the Civil War the city was captured 1862 by Union forces after a river battle. Martin Luther King, Jr, was assassinated here April 4, 1968.

A 1980s industry of handmade ultramodern furniture is called Memphis style and copied by Italian and French firms.

Menam another name for the river ▷Chao Phraya, Thailand.

Menander c. 342–291 BC. Greek comic dramatist, born in Athens. His work was virtually unknown until the discovery 1905 of substantial fragments of four of his plays in Eygptian papyri (many had been used as papier-mâché for Egyptian mummy cases). In 1957 the only complete Menander play, *Dyscholos/The Bad-Tempered Man*, was found.

Mencius Latinized name of Mengzi c. 372–289 BC. Chinese philosopher and moralist, in the tradition of Confucius. Mencius considered human nature innately good, although this goodness required cultivation, and based his conception of morality on this conviction.

Born in Shantung (Shandong) province, he was founder of a Confucian school. After 20 years' unsuccessful search for a ruler to put into practice his enlightened political program, based on people's innate goodness, he retired. His teachings are preserved as the *Book of Mengzi*.

Mencken H(enry) L(ouis) 1880–1956. US essayist and critic, known as "the sage of Baltimore." His unconventionally phrased, satiric contributions to the periodicals *The Smart Set* and *American Mercury* (both of which he edited) aroused controversy.

His critical reviews and essays were gathered in *Prejudices* 1919–27, comprising six volumes. He did not restrict himself to literary criticism, but took nearly every US institution to task in his writings. His book, *The American Language* 1918, is often revised.

Mende member of a W African people living in the rainforests of central east Sierra Leone and W Liberia. They number approximately 1 million. The Mende are farmers as well as hunter-gatherers, and each of their villages is led by a chief and a group of elders. The Mende language belongs to the Niger-Congo family.

Mendel Gregor Johann 1822–1884. Austrian biologist, founder of ▷genetics. His experiments with successive generations of peas gave the basis for his theory of particulate inheritance rather than blending, involving dominant and recessive characters; see ▷Mendelism. His results, published 1865–69, remained unrecognized until the early 20th century.

Mendel was abbot of the Augustinian abbey at Brünn (now Brno, Czechoslovakia) from 1868.

mendelevium synthesized, radioactive metallic element of the ▷actinide series, symbol Md, atomic number 101, atomic weight 258. It was first produced by bombardment of Es-253 with helium nuclei. Its longest-lived isotope, Md-258, has a half-life of about two months. The element is chemically similar to thulium. It was named by the US physicists at the University of California at Berkeley who first synthesized it 1955 after the Russian chemist Mendeleyev, who in 1869 devised the basis for the periodic table of the elements.

Mendeleyev Dmitri Ivanovich 1834–1907. Russian chemist who framed the periodic law in chemistry 1869, which states that the chemical properties of the elements depend on their atomic weights. This law is the basis of the ▷periodic table of the elements, in which the elements are arranged by atomic number and organized by their related groups.

For this work, Mendeleyev and Lothar ▷Meyer (who presented a similar but independent classification of the elements) received the Davy medal in 1882. From his table Mendeleyev predicted the properties of elements then unknown (gallium, scandium, and germanium).

Mendelism in genetics, the theory of inheritance originally outlined by Gregor Mendel. He suggested that, in sexually reproducing species, all characteristics are inherited through indivisible "factors" (now identified with ▷genes) contributed by each parent to its offspring.

Mendelssohn (-Bartholdy) (Jakob Ludwig) Felix 1809–1847. German composer, also a pianist and conductor. As a child he composed and performed with his own orchestra and as an adult was helpful to ▷Schumann's career. Among his best-known works are *A Midsummer Night's Dream* 1827; the *Fingal's Cave* overture 1832; and five symphonies, which include the Reformation 1830, the Italian 1833, and the Scottish 1842. He was instrumental in promoting the revival of interest in J S Bach's music.

Mendelssohn wrote chamber music; two violin concertos, including the renowned E minor 1844; operas, including *Son and Strangers* 1829; piano works; choral works; and songs.

Menderes (Turkish *Büyük Menderes*) river in European Turkey, about 250 mi/400 km long, rising near Afyonkarahisar and flowing along a winding course into the Aegean Sea. The word "meander" is derived from the ancient Greek name for the river.

Mendes Chico (Filho Francisco) 1944–1988. Brazilian environmentalist and labor leader. Opposed to the destruction of Brazil's rainforests, he organized itinerant rubber tappers into the Workers' Party (PT) and was assassinated by Darci Alves, a cattle rancher's son. Of 488 similar murders in land conflicts in Brazil 1985–89, his was the first to come to trial.

Mendès-France Pierre 1907–1982. French prime minister and foreign minister 1954–55. He extricated France from the war in Indochina, and prepared the way for Tunisian independence.

mendicant order religious order dependent on alms. In the Roman Catholic Church there are four orders of mendicant friars: Franciscans, Dominicans, Carmelites, and Augustinians. Hinduism has similar orders.

Mendoza capital of the Argentine province of the same name; population (1991) 121,700. Founded 1561, it developed because of its position on the Trans-Andean railroad; it lies at the center of a wine-producing area.

Mendoza Antonio de c. 1490–1552. First Spanish viceroy of New Spain (Mexico) 1535–51. He attempted to develop agriculture and mining and supported the church in its attempts to convert the Indians. The system he established lasted until the 19th century. He was subsequently viceroy of Peru 1551–52.

Menelaus in Greek mythology, king of Sparta, son of Atreus, brother of Agamemnon, and

meniscus *The curved shape, or meniscus, of a liquid surface is caused by the attraction or repulsion between liquid and container molecules.*

husband of Helen. With his brother he was joint leader of the Greek expedition against ▷Troy.

Menelik II 1844–1913. Negus (emperor) of Abyssinia (now Ethiopia) from 1889. He defeated the Italians 1896 at ▷Aduwa and thereby retained the independence of his country.

Menem Carlos (Saul) 1935– . Argentine politician, president from 1989; leader of the Peronist (Justicialist Party) movement. As president, he introduced sweeping privatization and public spending cuts, released hundreds of political prisoners jailed under the Alfonsin regime, and sent two warships to the Gulf to assist the US against Iraq in the 1992 Gulf War (the only Latin American country to offer support to the US). He also improved relations with the UK.

Menéndez de Avilés Pedro 1519–1574. Spanish colonial administrator. Born in Avilés, Spain, he saw service in the navy of Charles V and was named to the vital post of captain general of the Indies fleet 1554. With the accession of Philip II, Menéndez was granted the right to establish a colony in Florida to counter French presence there. In 1565 he founded St Augustine, repulsed a French attack, and eventually destroyed their outpost at Fort Caroline. Although his later attempts to establish colonies in the Chesapeake region were unsuccessful, Menéndez established a firm Spanish claim on the Florida peninsula.

Menes c. 3200 BC. Traditionally, the first king of the first dynasty of ancient Egypt. He is said to have founded Memphis and organized worship of the gods.

Mengistu Haile Mariam 1937– . Ethiopian soldier and socialist politician, head of state 1977–91 (president 1987–91). He seized power in a coup and was confronted with severe problems of drought and secessionist uprisings, but survived with help from the USSR and the West until his violent overthrow.

Mengs Anton Raffael 1728–1779. German Neo-Classical painter, born in Bohemia. He was court painter in Dresden 1745 and in Madrid 1761; he then worked alternately in Rome and Spain. The ceiling painting *Parnassus* 1761 (Villa Albani, Rome) is an example of his work.

menhir (Breton "long stone") prehistoric standing stone; see ▷megalith.

Ménière's disease or *Ménière's syndrome* recurring condition of the inner ear affecting mechanisms of both hearing and balance. It usually develops in the middle or later years. Symptoms, which include ringing in the ears, nausea, vertigo, and loss of balance, may be relieved by drugs.

meningitis inflammation of the meninges (membranes) surrounding the brain, caused by bacterial or viral infection. Bacterial meningitis, though treatable by antibiotics, is the more serious threat. Diagnosis is by ▷lumbar puncture.

The severity of the disease varies from mild to rapidly lethal, and symptoms include fever, headache, nausea, neck stiffness, delirium, and (rarely) convulsions. Many common viruses can cause the occasional case of meningitis, although not usually in its more severe form. The treatment for viral meningitis is rest.

meniscus in physics, the curved shape of the surface of a liquid in a thin tube, caused by the cohesive effects of ▷surface tension (capillary action). When the walls of the container are made wet by the liquid, the meniscus is concave, but with highly viscous liquids (such as mercury) the meniscus is convex. Meniscus is also the name of a concavo-convex or convexo-concave ▷lens.

Menninger Karl Augustus 1893–1990. US psychiatrist. With his father, prominent psychiatrist Charles Menninger, he founded the Menninger Clinic in Topeka 1920. With his brother William, also a psychiatrist, he established the Menninger Foundation for clinical research and public education 1941. Menninger was instrumental in reforming public mental-health facilities.

Born in Topeka, Kansas, and educated at the University of Kansas, Menninger received his MD degree from Harvard 1917. Among his influential books were *The Human Mind* 1930, *Man Against Himself*, and *The Vital Balance* 1963.

Mennonite member of a Protestant Christian sect, originating as part of the ▷Anabaptist movement in Zürich, Switzerland, 1523. Members refuse to hold civil office or do military service, and reject infant baptism. They were named Mennonites after Menno Simons (1496–1559), leader of a group in Holland. Persecution drove other groups to Russia and North America.

Some Swiss and German Mennonites settled in Germantown, Pennsylvania, in 1683. From there they eventually spread to the Midwest and Canada. Additional groups went to the Great Plains and to the prairie provinces of Canada after Russia began military conscription in the 1880s. Of the 600,000 Mennonites in the world, some 250,000 are in the US.

menopause in women, the cessation of reproductive ability, characterized by menstruation (see ▷menstrual cycle) becoming irregular and eventually ceasing. The onset is at about the age of 50, but varies greatly. Menopause is usually uneventful, but some women suffer from complications such as flushing, excessive bleeding, and nervous disorders. Since the 1950s, ▷hormone replacement therapy (HRT), using ▷estrogen alone or with ▷progesterone, has been developed to counteract such effects.

Long-term use of HRT was previously associated with an increased risk of cancer of the uterus, and of clot formation in the blood vessels, but newer formulations using natural estrogens are not associated with these risks. Without HRT there is increased risk of ▷osteoporosis (thinning of the bones) leading to broken bones, which may be indirectly fatal, particularly in the elderly.

The menopause is also known as the "change of life."

Menorca Spanish form of ▷Minorca, one of the Balearic Islands.

Menotti Gian Carlo 1911– . Italian-born US composer. He was colibrettist with Samuel ▷Barber for the latter's *Vanessa* and *A Hand of Bridge*, and wrote both music and libretti for operas, including *The Medium* 1946, *The Telephone* 1947, *The Consul* 1950, *Amahl and the Night Visitors* 1951 (the first opera to be written for television), and *The Saint of Bleecker Street* 1954. He has also written orchestral and chamber music.

Menshevik (Russian *menshinstvo* "minority") member of the minority of the Russian Social Democratic Party, who split from the ▷Bolsheviks 1903. The Mensheviks believed in a large, loosely organized party and that, before socialist revolution could occur in Russia, capitalist society had to develop further. During the Russian Revolution they had limited power and set up a government in Georgia, but were suppressed 1922.

menstrual cycle cycle that occurs in female mammals of reproductive age, in which the body is prepared for pregnancy. At the beginning of the cycle, a Graafian (egg) follicle develops in the ovary, and the inner wall of the uterus forms a soft spongy lining. The egg is released from the ovary, and the lining of the uterus becomes vascularized (filled with blood vessels). If fertilization does not occur, the corpus luteum (remains of the Graafian follicle) degenerates, and the uterine lining breaks down, and is shed. This is what causes the loss of blood that marks menstruation. The cycle then begins again. Human menstruation takes place from puberty to menopause, occurring about every 28 days.

The cycle is controlled by a number of ▷hormones, including ▷estrogen and ▷progesterone. If fertilization occurs, the corpus luteum persists and goes on producing progesterone.

mental handicap impairment of intelligence. It can be very mild, but in more severe cases, it is associated with social problems and difficulties in living independently. A person may be born with a mental handicap (for example, ▷Down's syndrome) or may acquire it through brain damage. There are between 90 and 130 million people in the world suffering such disabilities.

mental illness abnormal working of the mind. Since normal working cannot easily be defined, the borderline between mild mental illness and normality is a matter of opinion (not to be confused with normative behavior; see ▷norm). Mild forms are known as *neuroses*, affecting the emotions, whereas more severe forms, *psychoses*, distort conscious reasoning.

menthol pungent, waxy, crystalline alcohol $C_{10}H_{19}OH$, derived from oil of peppermint and used in medicines and cosmetics.

Mentor in Homer's ▷*Odyssey*, an old man, adviser to ▷Telemachus in the absence of his father Odysseus. His form is often taken by the goddess Athene.

menu in computing, a list of options, displayed on screen, from which the user may make a choice—for example, the choice of services offered to the customer by a bank cash dispenser: withdrawal, deposit, balance, or statement. Menus are used extensively in ▷graphical user interface (GUI) systems, where the menu options are often selected using a pointing device called a ▷mouse.

Menuhin Yehudi 1916– . US-born violinist and conductor. A child prodigy, he achieved great depth of interpretation, and was often accompanied on the piano by his sister *Hephzibah* (1921–1981). He conducted his own chamber orchestra and founded schools in Surrey, England, and Gstaad, Switzerland, for training young musicians.

Menzies Robert Gordon 1894–1978. Australian politician, leader of the United Australia (now Liberal) Party and prime minister 1939–41 and 1949–66.

Mephistopheles or *Mephisto* another name for the ⍐devil, or an agent of the devil, associated with the ⍐Faust legend.

Mequinez Spanish name for ⍐Meknés, a town in Morocco.

Mercalli scale scale used to measure the intensity of an ⍐earthquake. It differs from the ⍐Richter scale, which measures **magnitude**. It is named after the Italian seismologist Giuseppe Mercalli (1850–1914).

Intensity is a subjective value, based on observed phenomena, and varies from place to place with the same earthquake.

mercantilism economic theory, held in the 16th–18th centuries, that a nation's wealth (in the form of bullion or treasure) was the key to its prosperity. To this end, foreign trade should be regulated to create a surplus of exports over imports, and the state should intervene where necessary (for example, subsidizing exports and taxing imports). The bullion theory of wealth was demolished by Adam ⍐Smith in Book IV of *The Wealth of Nations* 1776.

Mercator Gerardus 1512–1594. Latinized form of the name of the Flemish map-maker Gerhard Kremer. He devised the first modern atlas, showing *Mercator's projection* in which the parallels and meridians on maps are drawn uniformly at 90°. It is often used for navigational charts, because compass courses can be drawn as straight lines, but the true area of countries is increasingly distorted the further north or south they are from the equator. For other types, see ⍐map projection.

Mercedes-Benz German car-manufacturing company created by a merger of the Daimler and Benz factories 1926. The first automobiles to carry the Mercedes name were those built by Gottlieb ⍐Daimler 1901.

In the 1930s, Mercedes-Benz dominated Grand Prix races. The W196, which made its debut 1954, was one of the finest racing automobiles of the postwar era. Following a disaster at Le Mans 1955, when 80 spectators lost their lives after an accident involving a Mercedes, the company withdrew from motor sport until 1989.

mercenary soldier hired by the army of another country or by a private army. Mercenary military service originated in the 14th century, when cash payment on a regular basis was the only means of guaranteeing soldiers' loyalty. In the 20th century mercenaries have been common in wars and guerrilla activity in Asia, Africa, and Latin America.

Most famous of the mercenary armies was the *Great Company* of the 14th century, which was in effect a glorified protection racket, comprising some 10,000 knights of all nationalities and employing *condottieri*, or contractors, to serve the highest bidder. By the end of the 14th century, condottieri and *freelances* were an institutionalized aspect of warfare. In the 18th century, Swiss cantons and some German states regularly provided the

French with troops for mercenary service as a means of raising money; they were regarded as the best forces in the French army. Britain employed 20,000 German mercenaries to make up its numbers during the Seven Years' War 1756–63 and used Hessian forces during the American Revolution 1775–83.

Article 47 of the 1977 Additional Protocols to the Geneva Convention stipulates that "a mercenary shall not have the right to be a combatant or a prisoner of war" but leaves a party to the Protocols the freedom to grant such status if so wished.

Merchant Ismail 1936– . Indian film producer, known for his stylish collaborations with James Ivory on films including *Shakespeare Wallah* 1965, *The Europeans* 1979, *Heat and Dust* 1983, *A Room with a View* 1985, *Maurice* 1987, and *Howard's End* 1992.

merchant bank financial institution that specializes in the provision of corporate finance and financial and advisory services for business. Originally developed in the UK during the 19th century, merchant banks now offer many of the services provided by the commercial banks.

Merchant banks developed from merchant houses trading in various parts of the world. As such houses became known, they found that a remunerative way to finance trade was to accept bills of exchange from lesser-known traders.

merchant navy the passenger and cargo ships of a country. Most are owned by private companies. To avoid strict regulations on safety, union rules on crew wages, and so on, many ships are today registered under "flags of convenience," that is, flags of countries that do not have such rules.

During wartime, merchant shipping may be drafted by the national government for military purposes.

Merchant of Venice, The comedy by William Shakespeare, first performed 1596–97. Antonio, a rich merchant, borrows money from Shylock, a Jewish moneylender, promising a pound of flesh if the sum is not repaid; when Shylock presses his claim, the heroine, Portia, disguised as a lawyer, saves Antonio's life.

Merchants Adventurers English trading company founded 1407, which controlled the export of cloth to continental Europe. It comprised guilds and traders in many N European ports. In direct opposition to the Hanseatic League, it came to control 75% of English overseas trade by 1550. In 1689 it lost its charter for furthering the traders' own interests at the expense of the English economy. The company was finally dissolved 1806.

Mercia Anglo-Saxon kingdom that emerged in the 6th century. By the late 8th century it dominated all England south of the Humber, but from about 825 came under the power of ⍐Wessex. Mercia eventually came to denote an area bounded by the Welsh border, the river Humber, East Anglia, and the river Thames.

Merckx Eddie 1945– . Belgian cyclist known as "the Cannibal." He won the Tour de France a joint record five times 1969–74.

mercury or *quicksilver* heavy, silver-gray, metallic element, symbol Hg (from Latin *hydrargyrum*), atomic number 80, atomic weight 200.59. It is a dense, mobile liquid with a low melting point (–37.96°F/–38.87°C). Its chief source is the mineral cinnabar, HgS, but it sometimes occurs in nature as a free metal.

Its alloys with other metals are called amalgams (a silver-mercury amalgam is used in dentistry for filling cavities in teeth). Industrial uses include drugs and chemicals, mercury-vapor lamps, arc rectifiers, power-control switches, barometers, and thermometers.

Mercury is a cumulative poison that can contaminate the food chain, and cause intestinal disturbance, kidney and brain damage, and birth defects in humans. The discharge into the sea by industry of organic mercury compounds such as dimethylmercury is the chief cause of mercury poisoning in the latter half of the 20th century. Between 1953 and 1975, 684 people in the Japanese fishing village of Minamata were poisoned (115 fatally) by organic mercury wastes that had been dumped into the bay and had accumulated in the bodies of fish and shellfish.

The element was known to the ancient Chinese and Hindus, and is found in Egyptian tombs of about 1500 BC. It was named by the alchemists after the fast-moving god, for its fluidity.

Mercury in astronomy, the closest planet to the Sun, at an average distance of 36 million mi/58 million km. Its diameter is 3,030 mi/ 4,880 km, its mass 0.056 that of Earth. Mercury orbits the Sun every 88 days, and spins on its axis every 59 days. On its sunward side the surface temperature reaches over 752°F/ 400°C, but on the "night" side it falls to –274°F/ –170°C. Mercury has an atmosphere with minute traces of argon and helium. In 1974 the US space probe *Mariner 10* discovered that its surface is cratered by meteorite impacts. Mercury has no moons.

Its largest known feature is the Caloris Basin, 870 mi/1,400 km wide. There are also cliffs hundreds of miles long and up to 2.5 mi/ 4 km high, thought to have been formed by the cooling of the planet billions of years ago. Inside is an iron core three-quarters of the planet's diameter, which produces a magnetic field 1% the strength of the Earth's.

Mercury Roman god, identified with the Greek Hermes, and like him represented with winged sandals and a winged staff entwined with snakes. He was the messenger of the gods.

mercury fulminate highly explosive compound used in detonators and percussion caps. It is a gray, sandy powder and extremely poisonous.

Mercury project US project to put a human in space in the one-seat Mercury spacecraft 1961–63.

The first two Mercury flights, on Redstone rockets, were short flights to the edge of space and back. The orbital flights, beginning with the third in the series (made by John ⍐Glenn), were launched by Atlas rockets.

Meredith George 1828–1909. English novelist and poet. He published the first realistic psychological novel *The Ordeal of Richard Feverel* 1859. Later works include *Evan Harrington* 1861, *The Egoist* 1879, *Diana of the Crossways* 1885, and *The Amazing Marriage* 1895. His verse includes *Modern Love* 1862 and *Poems and Lyrics of the Joy of Earth* 1883.

merengue Latin American dance music with a lively 2/4 beat. Accordion and saxophone are prominent instruments, with ethnic percussion. It originated in the Dominican Republic and became popular in New York in the 1980s.

merganser any of several diving ducks of the genus *Mergus* with long, serrated bills for catching fish, including the common merganser or goosander *M. merganser* and the red-breasted merganser *M. serrator*. Most have crested heads. They are widely distributed in the northern hemisphere.

Mergenthaler Ottmar 1854–1899. German-born American who invented a typesetting method. He went to the US in 1872 and developed the first linotype machine (for casting hot-metal type in complete lines) 1876–86.

merger the linking of two or more companies, either by creating a new organization by consolidating the original companies or by absorption by one company of the others. Unlike a takeover, which is not always a voluntary fusion of the parties, a merger is the result of an agreement.

Mérida capital of Yucatán state, Mexico, a center of the sisal industry; population (1986) 580,000. It was founded 1542, and has a cathedral 1598. Its port on the Gulf of Mexico is Progreso.

Meriden industrial city (plastics, silver, and electronics) in S central Connecticut, E of Waterbury; population (1990) 59,500.

meridian half a ⟡great circle drawn on the Earth's surface passing through both poles and thus through all places with the same longitude. Terrestrial longitudes are usually measured from the Greenwich Meridian.

An astronomical meridian is a great circle passing through the celestial pole and the zenith (the point immediately overhead).

Mérimée Prosper 1803–1870. French author. Among his works are the short novels *Colomba* 1841, *Carmen* 1846, and the *Lettres à une inconnue/Letters to an Unknown Girl* 1873.

Born in Paris, he entered the public service and under Napoleon III was employed on unofficial diplomatic missions.

merino breed of sheep. Its close-set, silky wool is highly valued. The merino, originally from Spain, is now found all over the world, and is the breed on which the Australian wool industry is built.

meristem region of plant tissue containing cells that are actively dividing to produce new tissues (or have the potential to do so). Meristems found in the tip of roots and stems, the apical meristems, are responsible for the growth in length of these organs.

The ⟡cambium is a lateral meristem that is responsible for increase in girth in perennial plants. Some plants also have intercalary meristems, as in the stems of grasses, for example. These are responsible for their continued growth after cutting or grazing has removed the apical meristems of the shoots.

Meristem culture involves growing meristems taken from shoots on a nutrient-containing medium, and using them to grow new plants. It is used to propagate infertile plants or hybrids that do not breed true from seed and to generate virus-free stock, since viruses rarely infect apical meristems.

meritocracy system (of, for example, education or government) in which selection is by performance (in education, by competitive examinations), which therefore favors intelligence and ability rather than social position or wealth.

The Chinese Mandarin system was based on the testing of scholars to work for the emperor; they rose through the ranks, as do civil service employees.

Merleau-Ponty Maurice 1908–1961. French philosopher, one of the most significant contributors to ⟡phenomenology after Edmund ⟡Husserl. He attempted to move beyond the notion of a pure experiencing consciousness, arguing in *The Phenomenology of Perception* 1945 that perception is intertwined with bodily awareness and with language. In his posthumously published work *The Visible and the Invisible* 1964, he argued that our experience is inherently ambiguous and elusive and that the traditional concepts of philosophy are therefore inadequate to grasp it.

merlin small ⟡falcon *Falco columbarius* of Eurasia and North America, where it is also called *pigeon hawk*. The male, 10 in/26 cm long, has a gray-blue back and reddish brown barred front; the female, 13 in/32 cm long, is brown with streaks.

Merlin legendary magician and counselor to King ⟡Arthur. Welsh bardic literature has a cycle of poems attributed to him, and he may have been a real person.

mermaid mythical sea creature (the male is a *merman*), having a human head and torso and a fish's tail. The dugong and seal are among suggested origins for the idea.

Meroe ancient city in Sudan, on the Nile near Khartoum, capital of Nubia from about 600 BC to AD 350. Tombs and inscriptions have been excavated, and iron-smelting slag heaps have been found.

Merovingian dynasty Frankish dynasty, named after its founder, *Merovech* (5th century AD). His descendants ruled France from the time of Clovis (481–511) to 751.

Mersey river in NW England; length 70 mi/112 km. Formed by the confluence of the Goyt and Etherow rivers, it flows west to join the Irish Sea at Liverpool Bay. It is linked to the Manchester Ship Canal. It is polluted by industrial waste, sewage, and chemicals.

Mersey beat pop music of the mid-1960s that originated in the northwest of England. It was also known as the Liverpool sound or ⟡beat music in the UK. It was almost exclusively performed by all-male groups, of whom the most popular was the Beatles.

mesa (Spanish "table") flat-topped steep-sided plateau, consisting of horizontal weak layers of rock topped by a resistant formation; in particular, those found in the desert areas of the US and Mexico. A small mesa is called a butte.

Mesa Verde (Spanish "green table") wooded clifftop in Colorado, with Pueblo dwellings, called the Cliff Palace, built into its side. Dating from about 1000 BC, with 200 rooms and 23 circular ceremonial chambers (kivas), it had an estimated population of about 400 people and was probably a regional center.

mescaline psychedelic drug derived from a small, spineless cactus *Lophophora williamsii* of N Mexico and the SW US, known as ⟡peyote. The tops (called mescal buttons), which scarcely appear above ground, are dried and chewed, or added to alcoholic drinks. Mescaline is a crystalline alkaloid $C_{11}H_{17}NO_3$. It is used by some North American Indians in religious rites.

Meshed variant spelling of ⟡Mashhad, a town in Iran.

Mesmer Friedrich Anton 1734–1815. Austrian physician, an early experimenter in ⟡hypnosis, which was formerly (and popularly) called *mesmerism* after him.

He claimed to reduce people to trance state by consciously exerted "animal magnetism," their willpower being entirely subordinated to his. Expelled by the police from Vienna, he created a sensation in Paris in 1778, but was denounced as a charlatan in 1785.

mesmerism former term for ⟡hypnosis, after Friedrich Mesmer.

Mesolithic the Middle Stone Age developmental stage of human technology and of ⟡prehistory.

meson in physics, an unstable subatomic particle made up of two indivisible elementary particles called quarks. It has a mass intermediate between that of the electron and that of the proton, is found in cosmic radiation, and is emitted by nuclei under bombardment by very high-energy particles.

The mesons form a subclass of the hadrons and include the kaons and pions. Their existence was predicted in 1935 by Japanese physicist Hideki Yukawa.

mesophyll the tissue between the upper and lower epidermis of a leaf blade (⟡lamina), consisting of parenchymalike cells containing numerous ⟡chloroplasts.

In many plants, mesophyll is divided into two distinct layers. The *palisade mesophyll* is usually just below the upper epidermis and is composed of regular layers of elongated cells. Lying below them is the *spongy mesophyll*, composed of loosely arranged cells of irregular shape. This layer contains fewer chloroplasts and has many intercellular spaces for the diffusion of gases (required for ⟡respiration and ⟡photosynthesis), linked to the outside by means of ⟡stomata.

Mesopotamia the land between the Tigris and Euphrates rivers, now part of Iraq. Here the civilizations of Sumer and Babylon flourished. Sumer (3500 BC) may have been the earliest civilization.

mesosphere layer in the Earth's ⟡atmosphere above the stratosphere and below the thermosphere. It lies between about 31 mi/50 km and 50 mi/80 km above the ground.

Mesozoic era of geological time 245–65 million years ago, consisting of the Triassic, Jurassic, and Cretaceous periods. At the beginning of the era, the continents were joined together as Pangaea; dinosaurs and other giant reptiles dominated the sea and air; and ferns, horsetails, and cycads thrived in a warm climate worldwide. By the end of the Mesozoic era, the continents had begun to assume their present positions, flowering plants were dominant, and many of the large reptiles and marine fauna were becoming extinct.

Messalina Valeria *c.* AD 22–48. Third wife of the Roman emperor ⟡Claudius, whom she dominated. She was notorious for her immorality, forcing a noble to marry her AD 48, although still married to Claudius, who then had her executed.

Messerschmitt Willy 1898–1978. German airplane designer whose Me-109 was a standard Luftwaffe fighter in World War II, and whose Me-262 (1942) was the first mass-produced jet fighter.

Messiaen Olivier 1908–1992. French composer and organist. His music is mystical in character, vividly colored, and incorporates transcriptions of birdsong. Among his works are the *Quartet for the End of Time* 1941, the large-scale *Turangalîla Symphony* 1949, and solo organ and piano pieces.

His theories of melody, harmony, and rhythm, drawing on medieval and oriental music, have inspired contemporary composers such as ◇Boulez and ◇Stockhausen.

Messiah (from Hebrew *māshîach* "anointed") in Judaism and Christianity, the savior or deliverer. Jews from the time of the Old Testament exile in Babylon have looked forward to the coming of the Messiah. Christians believe that the Messiah came in the person of ◇Jesus, and hence called him the Christ.

Messier Charles 1730–1817. French astronomer who discovered 15 comets and in 1781 published a list of 103 star clusters and nebulae. Objects on this list are given M (for Messier) numbers, which astronomers still use today, such as M1 (the Crab nebula) and M31 (the Andromeda galaxy).

Messina city and port in NE Sicily; population (1988) 271,000. It produces soap, olive oil, wine, and pasta. Originally an ancient Greek settlement (Zancle), it was taken first by Carthage and then by Rome. It was rebuilt after an earthquake 1908.

Messina, Strait of channel in the central Mediterranean separating Sicily from mainland Italy; in Greek legend a monster (Charybdis), who devoured ships, lived in the whirlpool on the Sicilian side, and another (Scylla), who devoured sailors, in the rock on the Italian side. The Classical hero Odysseus passed safely between them.

Meštrović Ivan 1883–1962. Yugoslav sculptor, a US citizen from 1954. His works include portrait busts of the sculptor Rodin (with whom he is often compared), President Hoover, Pope Pius XI, and many public monuments.

metabolism the chemical processes of living organisms: a constant alternation of building up (**anabolism**) and breaking down (**catabolism**). For example, green plants build up complex organic substances from water, carbon dioxide, and mineral salts (photosynthesis); by digestion animals partially break down complex organic substances, ingested as food, and subsequently resynthesize them in their own bodies.

Metacomet Wampanoag leader better known as King ◇Philip.

metal any of a class of chemical elements with certain chemical characteristics (◇metallic character) and physical properties: they are good conductors of heat and electricity; opaque but reflect light well; malleable, which enables them to be coldworked and rolled into sheets; and ductile, which permits them to be drawn into thin wires.

Metallic elements compose about 75% of the 109 elements shown in the ◇periodic table of the elements. They form alloys with each other, ◇bases with the hydroxyl radical (OH), and replace the hydrogen in an ◇acid to form a salt. The majority are found in nature in the combined form only, as compounds or mineral ores; about 16 of them also occur in the elemental form, as ◇native metals. Their chemical properties are largely determined by the extent to which their atoms can lose one or more electrons and form positive ions (cations). They have been put to many uses, both structural and decorative, since prehistoric times, and the Copper Age, Bronze Age, and Iron Age are named for the metal that formed the technological base for that stage of human evolution.

metal detector electronic device for detecting metal, usually below ground, developed from the wartime mine detector. In the head of the metal detector is a coil, which is part of an electronic circuit. The presence of metal causes the frequency of the signal in the circuit to change, setting up an audible note in the headphones worn by the user.

They are used to survey areas for buried metallic objects, occasionally by archeologists. However, their indiscriminate use by treasure hunters has led to their being banned on recognized archeological sites in some countries.

metal fatigue condition in which metals fail or fracture under relatively light loads, when these loads are applied repeatedly. Structures that are subject to flexing, such as the airframes of aircraft, are prone to metal fatigue.

metallic bond the force of attraction operating in a metal that holds the atoms together. In the metal the ◇valency electrons are able to move within the crystal and these electrons are said to be delocalized (see ◇electrons, delocalized). Their movement creates short-lived, positively charged ions. The electrostatic attraction between the delocalized electrons and the ceaselessly forming ions constitutes the metallic bond.

metallic character chemical properties associated with those elements classed as metals. These properties, which arise from the element's ability to lose electrons, are: the displacement of hydrogen from dilute acids; the formation of ◇basic oxides; the formation of ionic chlorides; and their reducing reaction, as in the ◇thermite process.

In the periodic table of the elements, metallic character increases down any group and across a period from right to left.

metalloid or **semimetal** any chemical element having some of but not all the properties of metals; metalloids are thus usually electrically semiconducting. They comprise the elements germanium, arsenic, antimony, and tellurium.

metallurgy the science and technology of producing metals, which includes extraction, alloying, and hardening. Extractive, or **process, metallurgy** is concerned with the extraction of metals from their ◇ores and refining and adapting them for use. **Physical metallurgy** is concerned with their properties and application. **Metallography** establishes the microscopic structures that contribute to hardness, ductility, and strength.

Metals can be extracted from their ores in three main ways: **dry processes**, such as smelting, volatilization, or amalgamation (treatment with mercury); **wet processes**, involving chemical reactions; and **electrolytic processes**, which work on the principle of ◇electrolysis.

The foundations of metallurgical science were laid about 3500 BC in Egypt, Mesopotamia, China, and India, where the art of ◇smelting metals from ores was discovered, starting with the natural alloy bronze. Later, gold, silver, copper, lead, and tin were worked in various ways, although they had been coldhammered as native metals for thousands of years. The smelting of iron was discovered about 1500 BC. The Romans hardened and tempered iron into steel, using ◇heat treatment. From then until about AD 1400, advances in metallurgy came into Europe by way of Arabian chemists. Cast iron began to be made in the

14th century in a crude blast furnace. The demands of the Industrial Revolution led to an enormous increase in ◇wrought iron production. The invention by Henry Bessemer of the ◇Bessemer process in 1856 made cheap steel available for the first time, leading to its present widespread use and the industrial development of many specialized steel alloys.

metamorphic rock rock altered in structure and composition by pressure, heat, or chemically active fluids after original formation. (If heat is sufficient to melt the original rock, technically it becomes an igneous rock upon cooling.)

The mineral assemblage present in a metamorphic rock depends on the composition of the starting material (which may be sedimentary or igneous) and the temperature and pressure conditions to which it is subjected. For example, a clay rich in sediment might become a slate when metamorphosed at low temperature and pressure, a mica-schist at a higher temperature and pressure, or a gneiss if temperature and pressure are very high.

Thermal metamorphism involves mainly heat changes as in rocks adjacent to an igneous body; *dynamic metamorphism* occurs with changes in stress as in a fault. *Regional metamorphism* involves both heat and pressure and is associated with rock deformation taking place at convergent plate boundaries (see ◇plate tectonics). Most metamorphism involves little change in bulk chemistry except for loss or gain of water and other volatiles; chemical changes may, however, occur owing to the action of fluids. Very high-grade metamorphism can cause a rock to melt, and some granites appear to have been formed in this way.

metamorphism geological term referring to the changes in rocks of the Earth's crust caused by increasing pressure and temperature. The resulting rocks are metamorphic rocks. All metamorphic changes take place in solid rocks. If the rocks melt and then harden, they become ◇igneous rocks.

metamorphosis period during the life cycle of many invertebrates, most amphibians, and some fish, during which the individual's body changes from one form to another through a major reconstitution of its tissues. For example, adult frogs are produced by metamorphosis from tadpoles, and butterflies are produced from caterpillars following metamorphosis within a pupa.

In Classical thought and literature, metamorphosis is the transformation of a living being into another shape, either living or inanimate (for example ◇Niobe). The Roman poet ◇Ovid wrote about this theme.

metaphor (Greek "transfer") figure of speech using an analogy or close comparison between two things that are not normally treated as if they had anything in common. Metaphor is a common means of extending the uses and references of words. See also ◇simile.

If we call people cabbages or foxes, we are indicating that in our opinion they share certain qualities with those vegetables or animals: an inert quality in the case of cabbages, a cunning quality in the case of foxes, which may lead on to calling people "foxy" and saying "He really foxed them that time," meaning that he tricked them. If a scientist is doing research in the *field* of nuclear physics, the word "field" results from comparison between scientists and farmers (who literally work in fields). Such usages are metaphorical.

metaphysical poet member of a group of 17th-century English poets whose work is characterized by conciseness; ingenious, often highly intricate wordplay; and striking imagery. Among the exponents of this genre are John ⟡Donne and George ⟡Herbert.

metaphysics branch of philosophy that deals with first principles, in particular "being" (ontology) and "knowing" (⟡epistemology), and that is concerned with the ultimate nature of reality. It has been maintained that no certain knowledge of metaphysical questions is possible.

Epistemology, or the study of how we know, lies at the threshold of the subject. Metaphysics is concerned with the nature and origin of existence and of mind, the interaction between them, the meaning of time and space, causation, determinism and free will, personality and the self, arguments for belief in God, and human immortality. The foundations of metaphysics were laid by ⟡Plato and ⟡Aristotle. St Thomas ⟡Aquinas, basing himself on Aristotle, produced a metaphysical structure that is accepted by the Catholic church. The subject has been advanced by Descartes, Spinoza, Leibniz, Berkeley, Hume, Locke, Kant, Hegel, Schopenhauer, and Marx; and in the 20th century by Bergson, Bradley, Croce, McTaggart, Whitehead, and Wittgenstein.

Metaxas Ioannis 1870–1941. Greek general and politician, born in Ithaca. He restored ⟡George II (1890–1947) as king of Greece, under whom he established a dictatorship as prime minister from 1936, and introduced several necessary economic and military reforms. He led resistance to the Italian invasion of Greece in 1941, refusing to abandon Greece's neutral position.

metazoa another name for animals. It reflects an earlier system of classification, in which there were two main divisions within the animal kingdom, the multicellular animals, or metazoa, and the single-celled "animals" or protozoa. The ⟡protozoa are no longer included in the animal kingdom, so only the metazoa remain.

metempsychosis another name for ⟡reincarnation.

meteor flash of light in the sky, popularly known as a *shooting* or *falling star*, caused by a particle of dust, a *meteoroid*, entering the atmosphere at speeds up to 45 mps/70 kps and burning up by friction at a height of around 60 mi/100 km. On any clear night, several *sporadic meteors* can be seen each hour.

Several times each year the Earth encounters swarms of dust shed by comets, which give rise to a *meteor shower*. This appears to radiate from one particular point in the sky, after which the shower is named; the Perseid meteor shower in Aug appears in the constellation Perseus. A brilliant meteor is termed a *fireball*. Most meteoroids are smaller than grains of sand. The Earth sweeps up an estimated 16,000 tons of meteoric material every year.

meteor-burst communications technique for sending messages by bouncing radio waves off the fiery tails of ⟡meteors. High-speed computer-controlled equipment is used to sense the presence of a meteor and to broadcast a signal during the short time that the meteor races across the sky.

The system, first suggested in the late 1920s, remained impracticable until data-compression techniques were developed, enabling messages to be sent in automatic high-speed bursts each time a meteor trail appeared. There are usually enough meteor trails in the sky at any time to permit continuous transmission of a message. The technique offers a communications link that is difficult to jam, undisturbed by storms on the Sun, and would not be affected by nuclear war.

meteorite piece of rock or metal from space that reaches the surface of the Earth, Moon, or other body. Most meteorites are thought to be fragments from asteroids, although some may be pieces from the heads of comets. Most are stony, although some are made of iron and a few have a mixed rock-iron composition. Meteorites provide evidence for the nature of the Solar System and may be similar to the Earth's core and mantle, neither of which can be observed directly.

Thousands of meteorites hit the Earth each year, but most fall in the sea or in remote areas and are never recovered. The largest known meteorite is one composed of iron, weighing 66 tons, which lies where it fell in prehistoric times at Grootfontein, Namibia. Meteorites are slowed down by the Earth's atmosphere, but if they are moving fast enough they can form a ⟡crater on impact. Meteor Crater in Arizona, about 4,000 ft/1,200 m in diameter and 650 ft/200 m deep, is the site of a meteorite impact about 50,000 years ago.

meteoroid chunk of rock in interplanetary space. There is no official distinction between meteoroids and asteroids, except that the term asteroid is generally reserved for objects larger than 1 mi/1.6 km in diameter, whereas meteoroids can range anywhere from pebble-size up.

Meteoroids are believed to result from the fragmentation of asteroids after collisions. Some meteoroids strike the Earth's atmosphere, and their fiery trails are called meteors. If they fall to Earth, they are named meteorites.

meteorology scientific observation and study of the ⟡atmosphere, so that weather can be accurately forecast. Data from meteorological stations and weather satellites are collated by computer at central agencies, and forecast and ⟡weather maps based on current readings are issued at regular intervals. Modern analysis can give useful forecasts for up to six days ahead.

At meteorological stations readings are taken of the factors determining weather conditions: atmospheric pressure, temperature, humidity, wind (using the ⟡Beaufort scale), cloud cover (measuring both type of cloud and coverage), and precipitation such as rain, snow, and hail (measured at 12-hour intervals). Satellites are used either to relay information transmitted from the Earth-based stations, or to send pictures of cloud development, indicating wind patterns, and snow and ice cover.

meter any instrument used for measurement. The term is often compounded with a prefix to denote a specific type of meter: for example, ammeter, voltmeter, flowmeter, or pedometer.

meter SI unit (symbol m) of length, equivalent to 1.093 yards or 39.37 inches. It is defined by scientists as the length of the path traveled by light in a vacuum during a time interval of 1/299,792,458 of a second.

methanal (common name *formaldehyde*) HCHO gas at ordinary temperatures, condensing to a liquid at −5.8°F/−21°C. It has a powerful, penetrating smell. Dissolved in water, it is used as a biological preservative. It is used in the manufacture of plastics, dyes, foam (for example urea-formaldehyde foam, used in insulation), and in medicine.

methane CH_4 the simplest hydrocarbon of the paraffin series. Colorless, odorless, and lighter than air, it burns with a bluish flame and explodes when mixed with air or oxygen. It is the chief constituent of natural gas and also occurs in the explosive firedamp of coal mines. Methane emitted by rotting vegetation forms marsh gas, which may ignite by spontaneous combustion to produce the pale flame seen over marshland and known as will-o'-the-wisp.

Methane causes about 38% of the warming of the globe through the ⟡greenhouse effect; the amount of methane in the air is predicted to double over the next 60 years. An estimated 15% of all methane gas into the atmosphere is produced by cows and other cud-chewing animals.

methanogenic bacteria one of a group of primitive bacteria (⟡archaebacteria). They give off methane gas as a by-product of their metabolism, and are common in sewage treatment plants and hot springs, where the temperature is high and oxygen is absent.

methanol (common name *methyl alcohol*) CH_3OH the simplest of the alcohols. It can be made by the dry distillation of wood (hence it is also known as wood alcohol), but is usually made from coal or natural gas. When pure, it is a colorless, flammable liquid with a pleasant odor, and is highly poisonous.

Methanol is used to produce formaldehyde (from which resins and plastics can be made), methyl-ter-butyl ether (MTB, a replacement for lead as an octane-booster in gasoline), vinyl acetate (largely used in paint manufacture), and gasoline.

Method US adaptation of ⟡Stanislavsky's teachings on acting and direction, in which importance is attached to the psychological building of a role rather than the technical side of its presentation. Emphasis is placed on improvisation, aiming for a spontaneous and realistic style of acting. One of the principal exponents of the Method was the US actor and director Lee Strasberg, who taught at the ⟡Actors Studio in New York.

Methodism evangelical Protestant Christian movement that was founded by John ⟡Wesley 1739 within the Church of England, but became a separate body 1795. The Methodist Episcopal Church was founded in the US 1784. There are over 50 million Methodists worldwide.

The itinerant, open-air preaching of John and Charles Wesley and George Whitefield drew immense crowds and led to a revival of faith among members of the English working and agricultural classes who were alienated from the formalism and conservatism of the Church of England. The Methodist emphasis on emotion and the conversion experience proved equally popular in America, where the Wesleys went to preach in 1735. As the movement grew there during the Great Awakening, Wesley encouraged the formation of an independent American Methodist Church. Methodist doctrines are contained in Wesley's sermons and *Notes on the New Testament*. There are now more than 20 separate Methodist groups in the US. The largest, the Methodist Church, was formed through the merger of various Methodist groups in 1938 and 1968.

Methodius, St c. 825–884. Greek Christian bishop, who with his brother Cyril (see ⟡Cyril and Methodius, Sts) translated much of the Bible into Slavonic. Feast day Feb 14.

Methuselah in the Old Testament, Hebrew patriarch who lived before the Flood; his life span of 969 years makes him a byword for longevity.

methyl alcohol common name for ⬦methanol.

methylated spirit alcohol that has been rendered undrinkable, and is used for industrial purposes, as a fuel for spirit burners or a solvent.

It is nevertheless drunk by some individuals, resulting eventually in death. One of the poisonous substances in it is ⬦methanol, or methyl alcohol, and this gives it its name. (The "alcohol" of alcoholic drinks is ethanol.)

methyl benzene alternate name for ⬦toluene.

methyl orange $C_{14}H_{14}N_3NaO_3S$ orange-yellow powder used as an acid–base indicator in chemical tests, and as a stain in the preparation of slides of biological material. Its color changes with pH; below pH 3.1 it is red, above pH 4.4 it is yellow.

metonymy (Greek "transferred title") figure of speech that works by association, naming something closely connected with what is meant; for example, calling the theatrical profession "the stage," horse racing "the turf," or journalists "the press." See also ⬦synecdoche.

metric system system of weights and measures developed in France in the 18th century and recognized by other countries in the 19th century. In 1960 an international conference on weights and measures recommended the universal adoption of a revised International System (Système International d'Unités, or SI), with seven prescribed "base units": the meter (m) for length, kilogram (kg) for mass, second (s) for time, ampere (A) for electric current, kelvin (K) for thermodynamic temperature, candela (cd) for luminous intensity, and mole (mol) for quantity of matter.

Two supplementary units are included in the SI system—the radian (rad) and steradian (sr)—used to measure plane and solid angles. In addition, there are recognized derived units that can be expressed as simple products or divisions of powers of the basic units, with no other integers appearing in the expression; for example, the watt.

Some non-SI units, well established and internationally recognized, remain in use in conjunction with SI: minute, hour, and day in measuring time; multiples or submultiples of base or derived units which have long-established names, such as tonne for mass, the liter for volume; and specialist measures such as the metric carat for gemstones.

Prefixes used with metric units are tera (T) million million times; giga (G) billion (thousand million) times; mega (M) million times; kilo (k) thousand times; hecto (h) hundred times; deka (da) ten times; deci (d) tenth part; centi (c) hundredth part; milli (m) thousandth part; micro (μ) millionth part; nano (n) billionth part; pico (p trillionth part; femto (f) quadrillionth part; atto (a) quintillionth part.

The metric system was made legal for most purposes in the US in the 19th century. A Metric Act was passed in the US in 1975 to promote the use, without compulsion, of the metric system.

metric ton or tonne unit of mass (symbol t or T) equal to 2,205 lb/1,000 kg.

metronome clockwork device, invented by Johann Maelzel 1814, using a sliding weight to regulate the speed of a pendulum to assist in keeping time, particularly in music.

metropolitan (Greek "mother-state, capital") in the Christian church generally, a bishop who has rule over other bishops (termed **suffragans**). In the Eastern Orthodox Church, a metropolitan has a rank between an archbishop and a ⬦patriarch.

Metropolitan Opera Company foremost opera company in the US, founded 1883 in New York City. The Metropolitan Opera House (opened 1883) was demolished 1966, and the company moved to the new Metropolitan Opera House at Lincoln Center.

The first production of the Metropolitan Opera House Co, Ltd, was Gounod's *Faust*. Highlights of its history include: the "Golden Age" 1898–1903, when artists from all over the world appeared at the "Met"; the 1903 New York debut of Enrico ⬦Caruso; the 1955 appearance of Marian ⬦Anderson, the first black to sing in a lead role there, in Verdi's *Un Ballo in Maschera*; and the first live telecast of a Metropolitan Opera production, Puccini's *La Bohème*, featuring Renata Scotto and Luciano Pavarotti, 1977.

Metternich Klemens (Wenzel Lothar), Prince von Metternich 1773–1859. Austrian politician, the leading figure in European diplomacy after the fall of Napoleon. As foreign minister 1809–48 (as well as chancellor from 1821), he tried to maintain the balance of power in Europe, supporting monarchy and repressing liberalism.

At the Congress of Vienna 1815, Metternich advocated cooperation by the great powers to suppress democratic movements. The ⬦revolution of 1848 forced him to flee to the UK; he returned 1851 as a power behind the scenes.

Metz industrial city (shoes, metal goods, tobacco) in Lorraine region, NE France, on the Moselle River; population (1982) 186,000. Part of the Holy Roman Empire 870–1552, it became one of the great frontier fortresses of France, and was in German hands 1871–1918.

Meuse (Dutch **Maas**) river flowing through France, Belgium, and the Netherlands; length 560 mi/900 km. It was a line of battle in both world wars.

Mexicali city in NW Mexico; population (1984) 500,000. It produces soap and cottonseed oil. The availability of cheap labor attracts many US companies (Hughes Aerospace, Rockwell International, and others).

Mexican Empire short-lived empire 1822–23 following the liberation of Mexico from Spain. The empire lasted only eight months, under the revolutionary leader Agustin de ⬦Iturbide.

When the French emperor Napoleon I put his brother Joseph on the Spanish throne in 1808, links between Spain and its colonies weakened and an independence movement grew in Mexico. There were several unsuccessful uprisings until, in 1821, General Agustin de Iturbide published a plan promising independence, protection for the church, and the establishment of a monarchy. As no European came forward, he proclaimed himself emperor 1822. Forced to abdicate, he went into exile; on his return to Mexico he was shot by republican leaders Guadalupe Victoria and Santa Anna. Victoria became the first president of Mexico.

Mexican War war between the US and Mexico 1846–48, begun in territory disputed between Texas (annexed by the US 1845 but claimed by Mexico) and Mexico. It began when General Zachary Taylor invaded New Mexico after efforts to purchase what are now California and New Mexico failed. Mexico City was taken 1847, and under the Treaty of Guadaloupe Hidalgo that ended the war, the US acquired New Mexico and California, as well as clear title to Texas in exchange for $15 million.

Tensions were high between the US and Mexico as a result of continuing border disputes and the annexation of Texas. President James ⬦Polk determined to pursue his notion of ⬦manifest destiny for the US and dispatched Taylor to add the disputed territories, by force if necessary. After repeated defeats and invasion of its home territory, a Mexican government was formed that was willing to negotiate a settlement. Presidential envoy Nicholas Trist was ordered home, but he ignored his orders and negotiated the pact ceding vast Mexican territories to the US. Polk was enraged but had little choice but to submit the exceptionally favorable treaty to the Senate, which ratified it.

Mexico country in Central America, bounded N by the US, E by the Gulf of Mexico, SE by Belize and Guatemala, and SW and W by the Pacific Ocean.

government Mexico is a federal republic of 31 states and a federal district, based in Mexico City. The constitution dates from 1917. Legislative power rests with a two-chamber national congress of senate, chamber of deputies, and directly elected president, all serving a six-year term. The president chooses the cabinet. The senate has 64 members, each state and the federal district being represented by two senators. The chamber has 400 members: 300 representing single-member constituencies and 100 elected by proportional representation so as to give due weight to minority parties. Members of congress are elected by universal suffrage. Each state has an elected governor and chamber of deputies, elected for a six-year term.

history Mexico was the region of the New World where many civilizations developed, including the Olmec, Maya, Toltec, Mixtec, Zapotec, and the Aztec, who settled on the central plateau and whose last king, Montezuma II, was killed 1520 during the Spanish conquest. The indigenous population was reduced from 21 million in 1519 to 1 million by 1607, with many deaths from Old World diseases to which they had no resistance.

In 1535 Mexico became the viceroyalty of New Spain. Spanish culture and Catholicism were established, and the country's natural resources were exploited. Colonial rule became increasingly oppressive; the struggle for independence began 1810, and Spanish rule was ended 1821. The ⬦Mexican Empire followed 1822–23.

Mexican War Mexico's early history as an independent nation was marked by civil and foreign wars and was dominated until 1855 by the dictator Antonio López de ⬦Santa Anna. The US annexation of Texas 1835 brought about the ⬦Mexican War 1846–48, in the course of which Mexico suffered further losses, including New Mexico and California. Santa Anna was overthrown 1855 by Benito Juárez, whose liberal reforms included many anticlerical measures.

Hapsburg rule In 1861, enticed by the offer of 30% of the proceeds, France planned to intervene in the recovery of 79 million francs owed to a Swiss banker by former Mexican

Mexico
United States of (*Estados Unidos Mexicanos*)

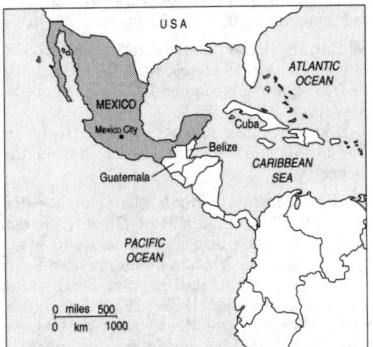

area 756,198 sq mi/1,958,201 sq km
capital Mexico City
cities Guadalajara, Monterrey; port Veracruz
physical partly arid central highlands; Sierra Madre mountain ranges E and W; tropical coastal plains
environment during the 1980s, smog levels in Mexico City exceeded World Health Organization standards on more than 300 days of the year. Air is polluted by 130,000 factories and 2.5 million vehicles
features Rio Grande; 2,000 mi/3,218 km frontier with US; resorts Acapulco, Cancun, Mexicali, Tijuana; Baja California, Yucatán peninsula; volcanoes, including Popocatepetl; pre-Columbian archeological sites
head of state and government Carlos Salinas de Gortari from 1988

political system federal democratic republic
political parties Institutional Revolutionary Party (PRI), moderate, left-wing; National Action Party (PAN), moderate Christian socialist
exports silver, gold, lead, uranium, oil, natural gas, handicrafts, fish, shellfish, fruits and vegetables, cotton, machinery
currency peso
population (1990 est) 88,335,000 (60% mixed descent, 30% Indian, 10% Spanish descent); 50% under 20 years of age; growth rate 2.6% p.a.
life expectancy men 67, women 73
languages Spanish (official) 92%, Nahuatl, Maya, Mixtec
religion Roman Catholic 97%
literacy men 92%, women 88% (1989)
GNP $126 bn (1987); $2,082 per head
chronology
1821 Independence achieved from Spain.
1846–48 Mexico at war with US; loss of territory.
1848 Maya Indian revolt suppressed.
1864–67 Maximilian of Austria was emperor of Mexico.
1917 New constitution introduced, designed to establish permanent democracy.
1983–84 Financial crisis.
1985 Institutional Revolutionary Party (PRI) returned to power. Earthquake in Mexico City.
1986 IMF loan agreement signed to keep the country solvent until at least 1988.
1988 PRI candidate Carlos Salinas Gotari elected president. Debt reduction accords negotiated with US.
1991 PRI won general election. President Salinas promised constitutional reforms.
1992 Public outrage following Guadalajara gas-explosion disaster.

of the ⟡Contadora Group, has argued for the withdrawal of all foreign advisers from the region. *See illustration box.*

Mexico City (Spanish *Ciudad de México*) capital, industrial (iron, steel, chemicals, textiles), and cultural center of Mexico, 7,400 ft/2,255 m above sea level on the southern edge of the central plateau; population (1986) 18,748,000. It is thought to be one of the world's most polluted cities because of its position in a volcanic basin 7,400 ft/2,000 m above sea level. Pollutants gather in the basin causing a smog cloud.

Notable buildings include the 16th-century cathedral, the national palace, national library, Palace of Justice, and national university; the Ministry of Education has murals 1923–27 by Diego Rivera.

The city dates from about 1325, when the Aztec capital Tenochtitlán was founded on an island in Lake Texcoco. This city was leveled 1521 by the Spaniards, who in 1522 founded a new city on the site. It was the location of the 1968 Summer Olympics. In 1984, the explosion of a liquefied gas tank caused the deaths of over 450 people, and in 1985, over 2,000 were killed by an earthquake.

Meyerbeer Giacomo. Adopted name of Jakob Liebmann Beer 1791–1864. German composer of spectacular operas, including *Robert le Diable* 1831 and *Les Huguenots* 1836. From 1826 he lived mainly in Paris, returning to Berlin after 1842 as musical director of the Royal Opera.

mezuza in Judaism, a small box containing a parchment scroll inscribed with a prayer, the Shema from Deuteronomy 6:4–9; 11:13–21, which is found on the doorpost of every home and every room in a Jewish house, except the bathroom.

mezzanine (Italian *mezzano* "middle") architectural term for a story with a lower ceiling placed between two main stories, usually between the ground and first floors of a building.

mezzotint print produced by a method of etching in density of tone rather than line, popular in the 18th and 19th centuries. A copper or steel plate is worked with a tool that raises a burr (rough edge), which will hold ink. The burr is then scraped away to produce a range of lighter tones.

Mfecane in African history, a series of disturbances in the early 19th century among communities in what is today the eastern part of South Africa. They arose when chief ⟡Shaka conquered the Nguni peoples between the Tugela and Pongola rivers, then created by conquest a centralized, militaristic Zulu kingdom from several communities, resulting in large-scale displacement of people.

mg symbol for *milligram*.

mi symbol for ⟡*mile*.

MI abbreviation for the state of ⟡*Michigan*.

Miami industrial city (food processing, transportation and electronic equipment, clothing, and machinery) and port in Florida; population (1990) 358,500. It is the hub of finance, trade, and air transport for the US, Latin America, and the Caribbean. There has been an influx of immigrants from Cuba, Haiti, Mexico, and South America since 1959.

The first permanent non-Indian settlement dates from the 1870s. In 1896 a railroad was extended to Miami, and the city was subsequently promoted as a tourist resort for its

president Miramon, who was overthrown and exiled by Juárez 1860. Seeking to regain power, in 1862 Miramon appealed to Empress Eugénie, consort of Napoleon III, saying that steps must be taken against Juárez and his anti-Christian policies. Eugénie proposed ⟡Maximilian, the brother of Emperor Franz-Joseph of Austria. Napoleon agreed, since the plan suited his colonial ambitions, and in 1864 Maximilian accepted the crown offered him by conservative opponents of Juárez. Juárez and his supporters continued to fight against this new branch of the Hapsburg empire, and in 1867 the monarchy collapsed and Maximilian was executed.

gradual reform There followed a capitalist dictatorship under General Porfirio Diaz, who gave the country stability but whose handling of the economy made him unpopular. He was overthrown 1910 by Madero, who reestablished a liberal regime but was himself assassinated 1913. The 1910 revolution brought changes in land ownership, labor legislations, and reduction in the powers of the Roman Catholic Church. After a brief period of civil war 1920, Mexico experienced gradual agricultural, political, and social reforms. In 1938 all foreign-owned oil wells were nationalized; compensation was not agreed until 1941. The years after Diaz were marked by political and military strife with the US, culminating in the unsuccessful US expedition 1916–17 to kill the revolutionary Francisco "Pancho" Villa (1877–1923).

PRI domination The broadly based Institutional Revolutionary Party (PRI) has dominated Mexican politics since the 1920s,

pursuing moderate, left-of-center policies. Its popularity has been damaged in recent years by the country's poor economic performance and rising international debts. However, despite criticisms from vested-interest groups such as the labor unions and the church, the PRI scored a clear win in the 1985 elections. The government's problems grew worse later that year when an earthquake in Mexico City caused thousands of deaths and made hundreds of thousands homeless.

PRI under challenge The PRI faced its strongest challenge to date in the 1988 elections. Despite claims of fraud during the elections, the PRI candidate, Carlos Salinas de Gortari, was declared president by the electoral college. He subsequently led campaigns against corrupt labor unions and drug traffickers. President Salinas also worked closely with the Bush administration to negotiate debt reductions. In 1991, amid claims of ballot rigging, the PRI decisively won the general elections. In Nov 1991, President Salinas promised widespread constitutional reforms that would affect education, agriculture, and the church. In 1992 public outrage followed a gas sewerline explosion in Mexico's second largest city, Guadalajara, in April, in which 194 died and 1,400 were injured. In July 1992 state-governor elections, the PRI suffered its second defeat in 63 years in Chihuahua state, losing to a PAN candidate.

foreign policy Mexico's foreign policy has been influenced by its proximity to the US. At times the Mexican government has criticized US policy in Central America, and as a member, with Colombia, Panama, and Venezuela, beaches. It is also a center for oceanographic research. The Florida land boom of the 1920s led to rapid development. By the 1980s large amounts of illegal drugs were said to come to the US through Miami. Destructive riots in 1980 and 1982 followed charges of police misconduct.

mica group of silicate minerals that split easily into thin flakes along lines of weakness in their crystal structure (perfect basal cleavage). They are glossy, have a pearly luster, and are found in many igneous and metamorphic rocks. Their good thermal and electrical insulation qualities make them valuable in industry.

Their chemical composition is complicated, but they are silicates with silicon-oxygen tetrahedra arranged in continuous sheets, with weak bonding betwen the layers, resulting in perfect cleavage. A common example of mica is muscovite (white mica), $KAl_2Si_3Al_{10}(OH)_4$.

Micah 8th century BC. In the Old Testament, a Hebrew prophet whose writings denounced the oppressive ruling class of Judah and demanded justice.

Michael in the Old Testament, an archangel, referred to as the guardian angel of Israel. In the New Testament Book of Revelation he leads the hosts of heaven to battle against Satan. In paintings, he is depicted with a flaming sword and sometimes a pair of scales. Feast day Sept 29 (Michaelmas).

Michael Mikhail Fyodorovich Romanov 1596–1645. Tsar of Russia from 1613. He was elected tsar by a national assembly, at a time of chaos and foreign invasion, and was the first of the Romanov dynasty, which ruled until 1917.

Michael 1921– . King of Romania 1927–30 and 1940–47. The son of Carol II, he succeeded his grandfather as king 1927 but was displaced when his father returned from exile 1930. In 1940 he was proclaimed king again on his father's abdication, overthrew 1944 the fascist dictatorship of Ion Antonescu (1882–1946), and enabled Romania to share in the victory of the Allies at the end of World War II. He abdicated and left Romania 1947.

On Dec 25, 1990 King Michael, with his wife Anne and daughter Sophia, attempted to return to Romania, but he was expelled early the following day.

Michelangelo Buonarroti 1475–1564. Italian sculptor, painter, architect, and poet, active in his native Florence and in Rome. His giant talent dominated the High Renaissance. The marble *David* 1501–04 (Accademia, Florence) set a new standard in nude sculpture. His massive figure style was translated into fresco in the Sistine Chapel 1508–12 and 1536–41 (Vatican). Other works in Rome include the dome of St Peter's basilica.

Born near Florence, he was a student of Ghirlandaio and trained under the patronage of Lorenzo de' Medici. His patrons later included several popes and Medici princes. In 1496 he completed the *Pietà* (St Peter's, Rome), a technically brilliant piece that established his reputation. Also in Rome he began the great tomb of Pope Julius II: *The Slaves* (Louvre, Paris) and *Moses* (S Pietro in Vincoli, Rome) were sculpted for this unfinished project. His grandiose scheme for the Sistine Chapel tells, on the ceiling, the Old Testament story from Genesis to the Deluge, and on the altar wall he later added a vast *Last Judgement*.

From 1516 to 1534 he was again in Florence, where his chief work was the design of the

Michigan

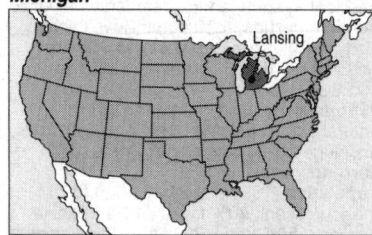

Medici sepulchral chapel in S Lorenzo. Back in Rome he became chief architect of St Peter's in 1547. His friendship with Vittoria Colonna (1492–1547), a noblewoman, inspired many of his sonnets and madrigals.

Michels Robert 1876–1936. German social and political theorist. Originally a radical, he became a critic of socialism and Marxism, and in his last years supported Hitler and Mussolini. In *Political Parties* 1911 he propounded the *Iron Law of Oligarchy*, arguing that in any organization or society, even a democracy, there is a tendency toward rule by the few in the interests of the few, and that ideologies such as socialism and communism were merely propaganda to control the masses. He believed that the rise of totalitarian governments—both fascist and communist—in the 1930s confirmed his analysis and proved that the masses were incapable of asserting their own interests.

Michelson Albert Abraham 1852–1931. German-born US physicist. In conjunction with Edward Morley, he performed in 1887 the *Michelson–Morley experiment* to detect the motion of the Earth through the postulated ether (a medium believed to be necessary for the propagation of light). The failure of the experiment indicated the nonexistence of the ether, and led ⊅Einstein to his theory of ⊅relativity. Michelson was the first American to be awarded a Nobel Prize, in 1907.

He invented the *Michelson interferometer* and made precise measurement of the speed of light. From 1892 he was professor of physics at the University of Chicago.

Michigan state in north central US; nickname Wolverine State/Great Lake State
area 58,518 sq mi/151,600 sq km
capital Lansing
cities Detroit, Grand Rapids, Flint
features Great Lakes: Superior, Michigan, Huron, Erie; Porcupine Mountains; Muskegon, Grand, St Joseph, and Kalamazoo rivers; over 50% forested; Isle Royale National Park; Pictured Rocks and Sleeping Bear national seashores; Henry Ford Museum and Greenfield Village, Dearborn
products motor vehicles and equipment; nonelectrical machinery; iron and steel; chemicals; pharmaceuticals; dairy products
population (1990) 9,295,300
famous people Edna Ferber, Gerald Ford, Henry Ford, Jimmy Hoffa, Iggy Pop, Diana Ross
history temporary posts established in early 17th century by French explorers Brulé, Marquette, Joliet, and La Salle; first settled 1668 at Sault Sainte Marie; present-day Detroit settled 1701; passed to the British 1763 and to the US 1796; statehood 1837.

Henry Ford's establishment of the moving assembly line in 1913–14 made Detroit the motor-vehicle-production capital of the world. Since then the state's fortunes have been

closely tied to the fortunes of the motor industry, prospering in the 1920s, 1940s, and 1950s, but badly hurt by the Great Depression of the 1930s and competition from Japanese manufacturers since the 1970s.

Michigan, Lake lake in north central US, one of the Great Lakes; area 22,390 sq mi/58,000 sq km. Chicago and Milwaukee are its main ports.

Lake Michigan is joined to Lake Huron by the Straits of Mackinac. Green Bay is the largest inlet.

Mickey Mouse cartoon character created 1928 by US animator Walt Disney, characterized by black disc-shaped ears and white gloves. He made his film debut in *Plane Crazy* and starred in the first synchronized sound cartoon, *Steamboat Willie* 1928. The comic book *Mickey Mouse Weekly* started 1936 and ran 920 issues. Mickey Mouse also appeared in the feature-length animated films *Fantasia* 1940, *Fun and Fancy Free* 1947, and *The Simple Things* 1953.

Mickiewicz Adam 1798–1855. Polish revolutionary poet, whose *Pan Tadeusz* 1832–34 is Poland's national epic. He died in Constantinople while raising a Polish corps to fight against Russia in the Crimean War.

micro- prefix (symbol μ) denoting a one-millionth part. For example, a micrometer (μm), or micron, is one-millionth of a meter.

microbe another name for ⊅microorganism.

microbiological warfare use of harmful microorganisms as a weapon. See ⊅biological warfare.

microbiology the study of organisms that can only be seen under the microscope, mostly viruses and single-celled organisms such as bacteria, protozoa, and yeasts. The practical applications of microbiology are in medicine (since many microorganisms cause disease); in brewing, baking, and other food and beverage processes, where the microorganisms carry out fermentation; and in genetic engineering, which is creating increasing interest in the field of microbiology.

microchip popular name for the silicon chip, or ⊅integrated circuit.

microcomputer or *micro* or *personal computer* small desktop or portable computer, typically designed to be used by one person at a time, although individual computers can be linked in a network so that users can share data and programs. Its central processing unit is a ⊅microprocessor, contained on a single integrated circuit.

Microcomputers are the smallest of the four classes of computer (the others are ⊅supercomputer, ⊅mainframe, and ⊅minicomputer). Since the appearance in 1975 of the first commercially available microcomputer, the Altair 8800, micros have become widely accepted in commerce, industry, and education.

microeconomics the division of economics concerned with the study of individual decision-making units within an economy: a consumer, firm, or industry. Unlike macroeconomics, it looks at how individual markets work and how individual producers and consumers make their choices and with what consequences. This is done by analyzing how relevant prices of goods are determined and the quantities that will be bought and sold.

For simplicity, microeconomics begins by analyzing a market in which there is *perfect*

anvil spindle sleeve thimble ratchet

vernier scale

frame

micrometer *A micrometer gauge measures small lengths with great accuracy.*

competition, a theoretical state that exists only when no individual producer or consumer can influence the market price. In the real world, there is always imperfect competition for various reasons (monopoly practices, barriers to trade, and so on), and microeconomics examines what effect these have on wages and prices.

Underlying these and other concerns of microeconomics is the concept of *optimality*, first advanced by Vilfredo ⌔Pareto in the 19th century. Pareto's perception of the most efficient state of an economy, when there is no scope to reallocate resources without making someone worse off, has been of great influence.

microfiche sheet of film on which printed text is photographically reduced. See ⌔microform.

microform generic name for media on which text or images are photographically reduced. The main examples are **microfilm** (similar to the film in an ordinary camera) and **microfiche** (flat sheets of film, generally 4 in/105 mm × 6 in/148 mm, holding the equivalent of 420 A4 sheets). Microform has the advantage of low reproduction and storage costs, but it requires special devices for reading the text. It is widely used for archiving and for storing large volumes of text, such as library catalogs.

micrometer instrument for measuring minute lengths or angles with great accuracy; different types of micrometer are used in astronomical and engineering work.

The type of micrometer used in astronomy consists of two fine wires, one fixed and the other movable, placed in the focal plane of a telescope; the movable wire is fixed on a sliding plate and can be positioned parallel to the other until the object appears between the wires. The movement is then indicated by a scale on the adjusting screw.

The **micrometer caliper**, of great value in engineering, has its adjustment effected by an extremely accurate fine-pitch screw (⌔vernier).

micrometer or micron one-millionth of a meter.

microminiaturization reduction in size and weight of electronic components. The first size reduction in electronics was brought about by the introduction of the ⌔transistor. Further reductions were achieved with ⌔integrated circuits and the ⌔silicon chip.

Micronesia islands in the Pacific Ocean lying N of ⌔Melanesia, including the Federated States of Micronesia, Belau, Kiribati, the Mariana and Marshall Islands, Nauru, and Tuvalu.

Micronesia, Federated States of island group in the W Pacific comprising four constituent states—Kosrae, Ponape, Chuuk

(formerly Truk), and Yap; capital Kolonia, on Pohnpei; area 270 sq mi/700 sq km; population (1988) 86,000. Federal authority resides with an executive president. Its people are Micronesian and Polynesian, and the main languages are Kosrean, Ponapean, Trukese, and Yapese, although the official language is English. Purchased by Germany from Spain 1898, the islands were occupied 1914 by Japan. They were captured by the US in World War II, and were part of the US Trust Territory of the Pacific 1947–90. Micronesia became internally self-governing from 1979, and in free association with the US from 1986. Although independent from 1990 the US controls its defense and foreign relations. Micronesia became a member of the United Nations 1991.

Micronesian member of any of the indigenous Australoid and Polynesian peoples of Micronesia, including Pacific islands N of the equator, such as the Caroline, Marshall, Mariana, and Gilbert islands. Their languages belong to the Austronesian family.

microorganism or **microbe** living organism invisible to the naked eye but visible under a microscope. Microorganisms include viruses and single-celled organisms such as bacteria, protozoa, yeasts, and some algae. The term has no taxonomic significance in biology. The study of microorganisms is known as microbiology.

microphone primary component in a sound-reproducing system, whereby the mechanical energy of sound waves is converted into electrical signals by means of a ⌔transducer. One of the simplest is the telephone receiver mouthpiece, invented by Alexander Graham Bell in 1876; other types of microphone are used with broadcasting and sound-film apparatus.

Telephones have a **carbon microphone**, which reproduces only a narrow range of frequencies. For live music, a **moving-coil microphone** is often used. In it, a diaphragm that vibrates with sound waves moves a coil through a magnetic field, thus generating an electric current. The **ribbon microphone** combines the diaphragm and coil. The **condenser microphone** is most commonly used in recording and works by a ⌔capacitor.

microprocessor complete computer ⌔central processing unit contained on a single ⌔integrated circuit, or chip. The appearance of the first microprocessors in 1971 heralded the introduction of the microcomputer. The microprocessor has led to a dramatic fall in the size and cost of computers, and ⌔dedicated computers can now be found in washing machines, automobiles, and so on.

microscope instrument for magnification with high resolution for detail. Optical and

electron microscopes are the ones chiefly in use; other types include acoustic and X-ray. In 1988 a scanning tunneling microscope was used to photograph a single protein molecule for the first time. Laser microscopy is under development.

The **optical microscope** usually has two sets of glass lenses and an eyepiece. It was invented 1609 in the Netherlands by Zacharias Janssen (1580–*c.* 1638). **Fluorescence microscopy** makes use of fluorescent dyes to illuminate samples, or to highlight the presence of particular substances within a sample.

The **electron microscope**, developed from 1932, passes a beam of electrons, instead of a beam of light, through a specimen. Since electrons are not visible, the eyepiece is replaced with a fluorescent screen or photographic plate; far higher magnification and resolution are possible than with the optical microscope.

The **scanning electron microscope** (SEM), developed in the mid-1960s, moves a fine beam of electrons over the surface of a specimen, the reflected electrons being collected to form the image. The specimen has to be in a vacuum chamber.

The **acoustic microscope** passes an ultrasonic (ultrahigh-frequency sound) wave through the specimen, the transmitted sound being used to form an image on a computer screen.

The **scanned-probe microscope**, developed in the late 1980s, runs a probe, with a tip so fine that it may consist only of a single atom, across the surface of the specimen, which requires no special preparation. In the **scanning tunnelling microscope**, an electric current that flows through the probe is used to construct an image of the specimen. In the **atomic force microscope**, the force felt by the probe is measured and used to form the image. These instruments can magnify a million times and give images of single atoms.

microsurgery surgical operation—rejoining a severed limb, for example—performed with the aid of a binocular microscope. Sewing of

eyepiece
lens

light paths

coarse focusing adjustment

fine focusing adjustment

barrel

alternative objective lenses

objective lens

slide

moves slide

stage light source

condenser

stage

mirror   stand   condenser focus adjuster

microscope

Mid-Atlantic Ridge *The Mid-Atlantic Ridge is the boundary between the crustal plates that form America, and Europe and Africa.*

the nerves and blood vessels is done with a nylon thread so fine that it is only just visible to the naked eye. Restoration of movement and sensation in such cases may be comparatively limited.

microtubules tiny tubes found in almost all cells with a nucleus. They help to define the shape of a cell by forming scaffolding for cilia and form fibers of mitotic spindle.

microwave ◊electromagnetic wave with a wavelength in the range 0.3 to 0.1 in/30 cm to 12 in, or 300–300,000 megahertz (between radio waves and ◊infrared radiation). They are used in radar, as carrier waves in radio broadcasting, and in microwave heating and cooking.

microwave heating heating by means of microwaves. Microwave ovens use this form of heating for the rapid cooking or reheating of foods, where heat is generated throughout the food simultaneously. If food is not heated completely, there is a danger of bacterial growth that may lead to food poisoning. Industrially, microwave heating is used for destroying insects in grain and enzymes in processed food, pasteurizing and sterilizing liquids, and drying timber and paper.

MICV abbreviation for ◊*mechanized infantry combat vehicle.*

Midas in Greek legend, a king of Phrygia who was granted the gift of converting all he touched to gold, and who, for preferring the music of Pan to that of Apollo, was given ass's ears by the latter.

MIDAS acronym for *Missile Defense Alarm System*.

Mid-Atlantic Ridge ◊ocean ridge, formed by the movement of plates described by ◊plate tectonics, that runs along the center of the Atlantic Ocean, parallel to its edges, for some 8,800 mi/14,000 km—almost from the Arctic to the Antarctic.

The Mid-Atlantic Ridge is central because the ocean crust beneath the Atlantic Ocean has continually grown outwards from the ridge at a steady rate during the past 200 million years. Iceland straddles the ridge and was formed by volcanic outpourings.

Middle Ages period of European history between the fall of the Roman Empire in the 5th century and the Renaissance in the 15th. Among the period's distinctive features were the unity of W Europe within the Roman Catholic Church, the feudal organization of political, social, and economic relations, and the use of art for largely religious purposes.

It can be divided into three subperiods:

The *early Middle Ages*, 5th–11th centuries, when Europe was settled by pagan Germanic tribes who adopted the vestiges of Roman institutions and traditions, were converted to Christianity by the church (which had preserved Latin culture after the fall of Rome), and who then founded feudal kingdoms;

The *high Middle Ages*, 12th–13th centuries, which saw the consolidation of feudal states, the expansion of European influence during the ◊Crusades, the flowering of ◊scholasticism and monasteries, and the growth of population and trade;

The *later Middle Ages*, 14th–15th centuries, when Europe was devastated by the ◊Black Death and incessant warfare, ◊feudalism was transformed under the influence of incipient nation-states and new modes of social and economic organization, and the first voyages of discovery were made.

middle C white note at the center of the piano keyboard, indicating the division between left- and right-hand regions and between the treble and bass staves of printed music.

Middle East indeterminate area now usually taken to include the Balkan States, Egypt, and SW Asia. Until the 1940s, this area was generally called the Near East, and the term Middle East referred to the area from Iran to Burma (the latter is now Myanmar).

Middle English the period of the ◊English language from about 1050 to 1550.

Middle Kingdom period of Egyptian history extending from the late 11th to the 13th dynasty (roughly 2040–1670 BC); Chinese term for China and its empire until 1912, describing its central position in the Far East.

Middle Range or *Middleback Range* mountain range in the NE of Eyre Peninsula, South Australia, about 40 mi/65 km long, parallel with the west coast of Spencer Gulf. Iron deposits are mined at Iron Baron, Iron Knob, and Iron Monarch.

Middlesbrough industrial port city on the Tees, Cleveland, England, commercial and cultural center of the urban area formed by Stockton-on-Tees, Redcar, Billingham, Thornaby, and Eston; population (1991) 141,100. Formerly a center of heavy industry, it diversified its products in the 1960s. It is the birthplace of the navigator Captain James Cook.

Middlesex former English county, absorbed by Greater London in 1965. It was settled in

the 6th century by Saxons, and its name comes from its position between the kingdoms of the East and West Saxons. Contained within the Thames basin, it provided good agricultural land before it was built over.

The name is still used, as in Middlesex County Cricket Club.

Middleton Thomas *c.* 1570–1627. English dramatist. He produced numerous romantic plays, tragedies, and realistic comedies, both alone and in collaboration, including *A Fair Quarrel* and *The Changeling* 1622 with Rowley; *The Roaring Girl* with Dekker; and *Women Beware Women* 1621.

Middletown city in S central Connecticut, on the Connecticut River, S of Hartford; population (1990) 42,800. Industries include insurance, banking, vehicle parts, electronics, hardware, and paper products. Wesleyan University is here.

Middletown industrial city (steel, paper products, and aircraft parts) in SW Ohio, on the Miami River, N of Cincinnati; population (1990) 46,000.

Middle Way the path to enlightenment, taught by Buddha, which avoids the extremes of indulgence and asceticism.

midge common name for many insects resembling ◊gnats, generally divided into biting midges (family Ceratopogonidae) that suck blood, and non-biting midges (family Chironomidae).

The larvae of some midges are the "bloodworms" of stagnant water.

Mid Glamorgan (Welsh *Morgannwg Ganol*) county in S Wales
area 394 sq mi/1,020 sq km
cities administrative headquarters Cardiff; resort Porthcawl; Aberdare, Merthyr Tydfil, Bridgend, Pontypridd
features Caerphilly Castle, with its water defenses
products the north was formerly a leading coal (Rhondda) and iron and steel area; Royal Mint at Llantrisant; agriculture in the south; Caerphilly mild cheese
population (1991) 536,500
language 8% Welsh, English
famous people Geraint Evans.

MIDI acronym for *musical instrument digital interface*, a manufacturer's standard allowing different pieces of digital music equipment used in composing and recording to be freely connected.

The information-sending device (any electronic instrument) is called a controller, and the reading device (such as a computer) the sequencer. Pitch, dynamics, decay rate, and stereo position can all be transmitted via the interface.

Midi-Pyrénées region of SW France, comprising the *départements* of Ariège, Aveyron, Haute-Garonne, Gers, Lot, Haute-Pyrénées, Tarn, and Tarn-et-Garonne
area 17,486 sq mi/45,300 sq km
population (1986) 2,355,000
cities capital Toulouse; Montauban, Cahors, Rodez, and Lourdes
products fruit, wine, livestock
features several spa towns, winter resorts, and prehistoric caves
history occupied by the Basques since prehistoric times, this region once formed part of the prehistoric province of Gascony that was taken by the English 1154, recaptured by the

French 1453, inherited by Henry of Navarre, and reunited with France 1607.

Midland industrial city (chemicals and concrete) in central Michigan, on the Tittabawassee River, NW of Saginaw; oil and gas wells are here; population (1990) 38,100.

Midland city in W Texas, halfway between Fort Worth and El Paso; population (1990) 89,400. The city's economy depends on the oil companies located here after the discovery of oil 1923.

Midlands area of England corresponding roughly to the Anglo-Saxon kingdom of ◊Mercia. The *E Midlands* comprises Derbyshire, Leicestershire, Northamptonshire, and Nottinghamshire. The *W Midlands* covers the former metropolitan county of West Midlands created from parts of Staffordshire, Warwickshire, and Worcestershire; and (often included) the *S Midlands* comprises Bedfordshire, Buckinghamshire, and Oxfordshire.

In World War II, the E Midlands was worked for oil, and substantial finds were made in the 1980s; the oilbearing E Midlands Shelf extends into Yorkshire and Lincolnshire.

midnight sun the constant appearance of the Sun (within the Arctic and Antarctic circles) above the ◊horizon during the summer.

Midrash (Hebrew "inquiry") medieval Hebrew commentaries on the Bible, in the form of sermons, in which allegory and legendary illustration are used. They were compiled mainly in Palestine between AD 400 and 1200.

midshipman trainee naval officer.

In the US, a midshipman is a student in training for the rank of ensign, in particular one at the US Naval Academy at Annapolis. In the British navy, a midshipman is a junior naval officer ranking just below sublieutenant.

midsummer the time of the summer solstice (when the Sun is farthest north of the celestial equator), about June 21. Midsummer Day, June 24, is the Christian festival of St John the Baptist.

Midsummer Night's Dream, A comedy by William Shakespeare, first performed 1595–96. Hermia, Lysander, Demetrius, and Helena in their various romantic endeavors are subjected to the playful manipulations of the fairies Puck and Oberon in a wood near Athens. Titania, queen of the fairies, is similarly bewitched and falls in love with Bottom, a stupid weaver, whose head has been replaced with that of an ass.

Midway Islands two islands in the Pacific, 1,120 mi/1,800 km NW of Honolulu; area 2 sq mi/5 sq km; population (1980) 500. They were annexed by the US 1867, and are now administered by the US Navy. The naval *Battle of Midway* June 3–6, 1942, between the US and Japan, was a turning point in the Pacific in World War II; the US victory marked the end of Japanese expansion in the Pacific.

Midwest or *Middle West* large area of the N central US. It is loosely defined, but is generally taken to comprise the states of Illinois, Iowa, Wisconsin, Minnesota, Nebraska, Kansas, Missouri, North Dakota, and South Dakota and the portions of Montana, Wyoming, and Colorado that lie east of the Rocky Mountains. Ohio, Michigan, and Indiana are often variously included, as well. Traditionally its economy is divided between agriculture and heavy industry. The main urban Midwest center is Chicago.

The majority of Midwesterners tend to be conservative socially and politically and less interested in international affairs than the general public in other parts of the country, but liberal and socialistic ideals have a long tradition in the states that championed the Populist and Granger movements of the 19th century. The region is generally flat and well-watered, with good transportation links.

In its broadest sense, the Midwest has an area of 986,800 sq mi/2,556,000 sq km and a population of about 61.5 million—roughly one-fourth of the national total.

midwifery assistance of women in childbirth. Traditionally, it was undertaken by experienced specialists; in modern medical training it is a nursing specialty for practitioners called midwives.

The English physician William Harvey's 1653 work on generation contained an influential chapter on labor. Dr Peter Chamberlen II (1560–1631) made an important contribution to midwifery, particularly with his development of the first midwifery forceps.

Mies van der Rohe Ludwig 1886–1969. German architect who practiced in the US from 1937. He succeeded Walter ◊Gropius as director of the ◊Bauhaus 1929–33. He designed the bronze-and-glass Seagram building in New York City 1956–59 and numerous apartment buildings.

He became professor at the Illinois Technical Institute 1938–58, for which he designed new buildings on characteristically functional lines from 1941. He also designed the National Gallery, Berlin 1963–68.

Mifune Toshiro 1920– . Japanese actor who appeared in many films directed by Akira ◊Kurosawa, including *Rashomon* 1950, *Shichinin no samurai/Seven Samurai* 1954, and *Throne of Blood* 1957. He has also appeared in European and American films: *Grand Prix* 1966, *Hell in the Pacific* 1969.

mignonette sweet-scented plant *Reseda odorata*, native to N Africa, bearing yellowish-green flowers in racemes (along the main stem), with abundant foliage; it is widely cultivated.

migraine acute, sometimes incapacitating headache (generally only on one side), accompanied by nausea, that recurs, often with advance symptoms such as flashing lights. No cure has been discovered, but ◊ergotamine normally relieves the symptoms. Some sufferers learn to avoid certain foods, such as chocolate, which suggests an allergic factor.

In 1990 Hammersmith Hospital in London, England, reported successful treatment with goggles that depress beta waves in the brain (associated with stress) and stimulate alpha waves (whose effect is calming).

migrant labor people who move from place to place to work or harvest seasonal crops. Economic or political pressures often cause people to leave their homelands to earn wages in this way, but some families live this way for several generations. Since the Great Depression of the 1930s, many families lost land and homes and took to the road. Since the 1960s, unions for migrant farm workers have been formed, principally by Cesar ◊Chavez.

The world's pool of legal and illegal immigrants has been exploited by business and has become an important economic and social factor. Migrants from the Caribbean and Central and South America enter this job market in

the US and Canada just as South Europeans and Middle Easterners provide such labor in industrialized northern European countries. Some go home after each seasonal round, while others try to stay and become citizens if possible.

migration the movement, either seasonal or as part of a single life cycle, of certain animals, chiefly birds and fish, to distant breeding or feeding grounds.

The precise methods by which animals navigate and know where to go are still obscure. Birds have much sharper eyesight and better visual memory of ground clues than humans, but in long-distance flights appear to navigate by the Sun and stars, possibly in combination with a "reading" of the Earth's magnetic field through an inbuilt "magnetic compass," which is a tiny mass of tissue between the eye and brain in birds. Similar cells occur in "homing" honeybees and in certain bacteria that use it to determine which way is "down." Most striking, however, is the migration of young birds that have never flown a route before and are unaccompanied by adults. It is postulated that they may inherit as part of their genetic code an overall "sky chart" of their journey that is triggered into use when they become aware of how the local sky pattern, above the place in which they hatch, fits into it. Similar theories have been advanced in the case of fish, such as eels and salmon, with whom vision obviously plays a lesser role, but for whom currents and changes in the composition and temperature of the sea in particular locations may play a part—for example, in enabling salmon to return to the precise river in which they were spawned. Migration also occurs with land animals; for example, lemmings and antelope.

Related to migration is the homing ability of pigeons, bees, and other creatures.

Mihailović Draza 1893–1946. Yugoslav soldier, leader of the guerrilla ◊Chetniks of World War II against the German occupation. His feud with Tito's communists led to the withdrawal of Allied support and that of his own exiled government from 1943. He turned for help to the Italians and Germans, and was eventually shot for treason.

mikado (Japanese "honorable palace gate") title until 1867 of the Japanese emperor, when it was replaced by the term *tennō* ("heavenly sovereign").

Milan (Italian *Milano*) industrial city (aircraft, automobiles, locomotives, textiles), financial and cultural center, capital of Lombardy, Italy; population (1988) 1,479,000.

features The Gothic cathedral, built about 1450, crowned with pinnacles, can hold 40,000 worshipers; the Brera art gallery; the convent with Leonardo da Vinci's *Last Supper* 1495–97; La Scala opera house (Italian *Teatro alla Scala*) 1778; an annual trade fair.

history Settled by the Gauls in the 5th century BC, it was conquered by the Roman consul Marcellus 222 BC to become the Roman city of *Mediolanum*. Under Diocletian, in AD 286 Milan was capital of the Western empire. Destroyed by Attila the Hun 452, and again by the Goths 539, the city regained its power through the political importance of its bishops. It became an autonomous commune 1045; then followed a long struggle for supremacy in Lombardy.

The city was taken by ◊Frederick I (Barbarossa) 1162; only in 1176 were his forces finally defeated, at the battle of Legnano.

Milanese forces were again defeated by the emperor at the battle of Cortenuova 1237. In the Guelph-Ghibelline struggle the Visconti family emerged at the head of the Ghibelline faction; they gained power 1277, establishing a dynasty which lasted until 1450 when Francesco Sforza seized control and became duke. The Sforza court marked the high point of Milan as a cultural and artistic center. Control of the city passed to Louis XII of France 1499, and in 1540 it was annexed by Spain, beginning a long decline. The city was ceded to Austria by the Treaty of ⇨Utrecht 1714, and in the 18th century began a period of intellectual enlightenment. Milan was in 1796 taken by Napoleon, who made it the capital of the Cisalpine Republic 1799, and in 1805 capital of the kingdom of Italy until 1814, when it reverted to the Austrians. In 1848, Milan rebelled unsuccessfully (the *Cinque Giornate*/Five Days), and in 1859 was joined to Piedmont.

Milankovitch hypothesis the combination of factors governing the occurrence of ⇨ice ages proposed in 1930 by the Yugoslav geophysicist M Milankovitch (1879–1958).

mildew any fungus that appears as a destructive growth on plants, paper, leather, or wood when exposed to damp; such fungi usually form a thin white coating.

mile imperial unit of linear measure. A statute mile is equal to 1,760 yards (1.60934 km), and an international nautical mile is equal to 2,026 yards (1,852 m).

Miletus ancient Greek city in SW Asia Minor, with a port that eventually silted up. It was famous for its woolen goods, and traded with the whole Mediterranean coast.

milfoil another name for the herb ⇨yarrow. Water milfoils, plants of the genus *Miriophyllum*, are unrelated; they have whorls of fine leaves and grow underwater.

Milford industrial city (fabricated metal, writing pens, and electronics) in SW Connecticut, situated by the Housatonic River and Long Island Sound, W of New Haven; population (1990) 49,900.

Milhaud Darius 1892–1974. French composer, a member of the group of composers known as Les Six (see ⇨Six, Les). Among his works are the operas *Christophe Colombe* 1928 and *Bolívar* 1943, and the jazz ballet *La Création du monde* 1923. He lived in both France and the US.

He collaborated on ballets with Paul ⇨Claudel. In 1940 he went to the US as professor of music at Mills College, California, and became professor of composition at the National Conservatoire in Paris 1947. Much of his later work—which includes chamber, orchestral, and choral music—is polytonal.

miliaria itchy blisters formed in the skin condition ⇨prickly heat.

military-industrial complex conjunction of the military establishment and the arms industry, both inflated by Cold War demands. The phrase was first used by US president and former general Dwight D Eisenhower in 1961 to warn Americans of the potential misplacement of power.

military law articles or regulations that apply to members of the armed forces.

milk secretion of the ⇨mammary glands of female mammals, with which they suckle their young (during ⇨lactation). Over 85% is water,

the remainder comprising protein, fat, lactose (a sugar), calcium, phosphorus, iron, and vitamins. The milk of cows, goats, and sheep is often consumed by humans, but only Western societies drink milk after infancy; for people in most of the world, milk causes flatulence and diarrhea.

milking machine machine that uses suction to milk cows. The first milking machine was invented in the US by L O Colvin in 1860. Later it was improved so that the suction was regularly released by a pulsating device, since it was found that continuous suction is harmful to cows.

Milky Way faint band of light crossing the night sky, consisting of stars in the plane of our Galaxy. The name Milky Way is often used for the Galaxy itself. It is a spiral ⇨galaxy, about 100,000 light-years in diameter, containing at least 100 billion stars. The Sun is in one of its spiral arms, about 25,000 light-years from the center.

The densest parts of the Milky Way, toward the Galaxy's center, lie in the constellation Sagittarius. In places, the Milky Way is interrupted by lanes of dark dust that obscure light from the stars beyond, such as the Coalsack nebula in Crux (the Southern Cross).

Mill James 1773–1836. Scottish philosopher and political thinker who developed the theory of ⇨utilitarianism. He is remembered for his political articles, and for the rigorous education he gave his son John Stuart Mill.

Born near Montrose, Mill moved to London 1802. Associated for most of his working life with the East India Company, he wrote a vast *History of British India* 1817–18. He was one of the founders of University College, London, together with his friend and fellow utilitarian Jeremy Bentham.

Mill John Stuart 1806–1873. English philosopher and economist who wrote *On Liberty* 1859, the classic philosophical defense of liberalism, and *Utilitarianism* 1863, a version of the "greatest happiness for the greatest number" principle in ethics. His progressive views inspired *On the Subjection of Women* 1869.

He was born in London, the son of James Mill. In 1822 he entered the East India Company, where he remained until retiring in 1858. In 1826, as described in his *Autobiography* 1873, he passed through a mental crisis; he found his father's bleakly intellectual Utilitarianism emotionally unsatisfying and abandoned it for a more human philosophy influenced by Coleridge. In *Utilitarianism*, he states that actions are right if they bring about happiness and wrong if they bring about the reverse of happiness. *On Liberty* moved away from the utilitarian notion that individual liberty was necessary for economic and governmental efficiency and advanced the Classical defense of individual freedom as a value in itself and the mark of a mature society; this change can be traced in the later editions of *Principles of Political Economy* 1848. He sat in Parliament as a Radical 1865–68 and introduced a motion for women's suffrage. His philosophical and political writings include *A System of Logic* 1843 and *Considerations on Representative Government* 1861.

Millais John Everett 1829–1896. British painter, a founder member of the ⇨**Pre-Raphaelite Brotherhood** (PRB) in 1848. By the late 1850s he had dropped out of the PRB, and his style became more fluent and less detailed.

One of his PRB works, *Christ in the House of His Parents* 1850 (Tate Gallery, London),

caused an outcry on its first showing, since its realistic detail was considered unfitting to the sacred subject.

Millay Edna St Vincent 1892–1950. US poet who wrote romantic, emotional verse, including *Renascence and Other Poems* 1917 and *The Harp-Weaver and Other Poems* 1923 (Pulitzer Prize 1924).

She was a favorite of the free-spirited youth of the 1920s.

Born in Rockland, Maine, she moved to New York City's Greenwich Village and became a voice for political and social causes through such works as *A Few Figs from Thistles* 1920 and *Second April* 1921. Her other works include the sonnet sequence *Fatal Interview* 1931, *Make Bright the Arrows*, and several verse plays.

millennium period of 1,000 years. Some quasi-Christian sects, such as Jehovah's Witnesses, believe that Jesus will return to govern the Earth in person at the next millennium, the 6001st year after the creation (as located by Archbishop Usher at 4004 BC).

This belief, *millenarianism*, also called chiliasm (from the Greek for 1,000), was widespread in the early days of Christianity. As hopes were disappointed, belief in the imminence of the second coming tended to fade, but millenarian views have been expressed at periods of great religious excitement, such as the Reformation.

Miller Arthur 1915– . US playwright. His plays deal with family relationships and contemporary American values, and include *Death of a Salesman* 1949 and *The Crucible* 1953, based on the Salem witch trials and reflecting the Communist witch-hunts of Senator Joe ⇨McCarthy. He was married 1956–61 to the film star Marilyn Monroe, for whom he wrote the film *The Misfits* 1960.

Among other plays are *All My Sons* 1947, *A View from the Bridge* 1955, and *After the Fall* 1964, based on his relationship with Monroe. He also wrote the television film *Playing for Time* 1980.

Miller Glenn 1904–1944. US trombonist and, as bandleader, exponent of the big-band swing sound from 1938. He composed his signature tune "Moonlight Serenade" (a hit 1939). Miller became leader of the US Army Air Force Band in Europe 1942, made broadcasts to troops throughout the world during World War II, and disappeared without a trace on a flight between England and France.

Miller Henry 1891–1980. US writer. From 1930 to 1940 he lived a bohemian life in Paris, where he wrote his novels *Tropic of Cancer* 1934 and *Tropic of Capricorn* 1938. They were so outspoken and sexually frank that they were banned in the US and England until the 1960s.

Born in New York City, Miller settled in Big Sur, California, in the 1940s and wrote the autobiographical *Rosy Crucifixion* trilogy, consisting of *Sexus* 1949, *Plexus* 1949, and *Nexus* 1957 (published as a whole in the US 1965). His bohemian image made him a favorite of the ⇨Beat Generation. Other works include *The Colossus of Maroussi* 1941, *The Air-Conditioned Nightmare* 1945, and *Letters to Anaïs Nin* 1965.

Miller Stanley 1930– . US chemist. In the early 1950s, under laboratory conditions, he tried to imitate the original conditions of the Earth's atmosphere (a mixture of methane, ammonia, and hydrogen), added an electrical discharge, and waited. After a few days he found that amino acids, the ingredients of protein, had been formed.

Miller William 1782–1849. US religious leader. Born in Pittsfield, Massachusetts, and raised in New York, Miller later settled in Vermont. Convinced that the Second Coming of Jesus was imminent, he began to preach about the millennium. Ordained as a Baptist minister 1833, Miller lectured and preached about the Second Advent, which he predicted would occur 1844. As the time neared, many of Miller's followers sold their property in expectation of the end of the world. Although Miller's movement disbanded soon after, his teachings paved the way for later Adventist sects.

millet any of several grasses, family Gramineae, of which the grains are used as a cereal food and the stems as fodder.

Species include *Panicum miliaceum*, extensively cultivated in the warmer parts of Europe, and *Sorghum bicolor*, also known as ◊durra.

Millet Jean François 1814–1875. French artist, a leading member of the ◊Barbizon school, who painted scenes of peasant life and landscapes. *The Angelus* 1859 (Musée d'Orsay, Paris) was widely reproduced in his day.

Millett Kate 1934– . US radical feminist lecturer, writer, and sculptor whose book *Sexual Politics* 1970 was a landmark in feminist thinking. She was a founding member of the **National Organization of Women** (NOW). Later books include *Flying* 1974, *The Prostitution Papers* 1976, *Sita* 1977, and *The Loony Bin Trip* 1991, describing a period of manic depression and drug therapy.

millibar unit of pressure, equal to one-thousandth of a ◊bar.

Millikan Robert Andrews 1868–1953. US physicist, awarded a Nobel Prize 1923 for his determination of the ◊electric charge on an electron 1913.

His experiment, which took five years to perfect, involved observing oil droplets, charged by external radiation, falling under gravity between two horizontal metal plates connected to a high-voltage supply. By varying the voltage, he was able to make the electrostatic field between the plates balance the gravitational field so that some droplets became stationary and floated. If a droplet of weight W is held stationary between plates separated by a distance d and carrying a potential difference V, the charge, e, on the drop is equal to Wd/V.

milliliter one-thousandth of a liter (ml), equivalent to 1 cu cm (cc) or 0.0338 fluid ounce.

millimeter of mercury unit of pressure, used in barometers for measuring atmospheric pressure, defined as the pressure exerted by a column of mercury one millimeter high, at standard gravity and at a temperature of 32°F/0°C.

milling metal machining method that uses a rotating toothed cutting wheel to shape a surface. The term also applies to grinding grain, cacao, coffee, pepper, and other spices.

millipede any arthropod of the class Diplopoda. It has a segmented body, each segment usually bearing two pairs of legs, and the distinct head bears a pair of short clubbed antennae. Most millipedes are no more than 1 in/2.5 cm long; a few in the tropics are 12 in/30 cm.

Millipedes live in damp, dark places, feeding mainly on rotting vegetation. Some species injure crops by feeding on tender roots, and some produce a poisonous secretion in defense. Certain orders have silk glands.

Mills C Wright 1916–1962. US sociologist whose concern for humanity, ethical values, and individual freedom led him to criticize the US establishment.

Originally in the liberal tradition, Mills later adopted Weberian and even Marxist ideas. He aroused considerable popular interest in sociology with such works as *White Collar* 1951; *The Power Elite* 1956, depicting the US as ruled by businessmen, military experts, and politicians; and *Listen, Yankee* 1960.

Mills John 1908– . English actor who appeared in films such as *In Which We Serve* 1942, *The Rocking Horse Winner* 1949, *The Wrong Box* 1966, and *Oh! What a Lovely War* 1969. He received an Academy Award for *Ryan's Daughter* 1971. He is the father of the actresses Hayley Mills and Juliet Mills.

Mills Brothers US vocal group who specialized in close-harmony vocal imitations of instruments, comprising Herbert Mills (1912–), Harry Mills (1913–1982), John Mills (1889–1935), and Donald Mills (1915–). Formed 1922, the group first broadcast on radio in 1925, and continued to perform until the 1950s. Their 70 hits include "Lazy River" 1948 and "You Always Hurt the One You Love" 1944.

Millville city in SW New Jersey, on the Maurice River, SE of Philadelphia; products include vegetables, poultry, and glass; population (1990) 26,000.

Milne A(lan) A(lexander) 1882–1956. English writer. His books for children were based on the teddy bear and other toys of his son Christopher Robin (*Winnie-the-Pooh* 1926 and *The House at Pooh Corner* 1928). He also wrote children's verse (*When We Were Very Young* 1924 and *Now We Are Six* 1927) and plays, including an adaptation of Kenneth Grahame's *The Wind in the Willows* as *Toad of Toad Hall* 1929.

Milosevic Slobodan 1941– . Serbian communist politician, party chief and president of Serbia from 1986; reelected Dec 1990 in multiparty elections. Milosevic wielded considerable influence over the Serb-dominated Yugoslav federal army during the 1991–92 civil war and continued to back Serbian militia in ◊Bosnia-Herzegovina 1992, although publicly disclaiming any intention to "carve up" the newly independent republic.

Miłosz Czesław 1911– . Polish writer, born in Lithuania. He became a diplomat before defecting and becoming a US citizen. His poetry in English translation, Classical in style, includes *Selected Poems* 1973 and *Bells in Winter* 1978.

His collection of essays *The Captive Mind* 1953 concerns the impact of communism on Polish intellectuals. Among his novels are *The Seizure of Power* 1955, *The Issa Valley* 1981, and *The Land of Ulro* 1984. Nobel Prize for Literature 1980.

Milstein César 1927– . Argentine-born British molecular biologist who developed monoclonal antibodies, giving immunity against specific diseases. He shared the Nobel Prize for Medicine 1984.

Milstein and his colleagues, while working at Britain's Cambridge University, devised a means of accessing the immune system for purposes of research, diagnosis, and treatment. They developed monoclonal antibodies (MABs), cloned cells that, when introduced into the body, can be targeted to seek out sites of disease. The full potential of this breakthrough is still being investigated. However, MABs, which can be duplicated in limitless quantities, are already in use to combat disease. Milstein shared the Nobel Prize 1984 for Medicine with two colleagues, Georges Köhler and Niels Jerne.

Milton John 1608–1674. English poet whose epic ◊*Paradise Lost* 1667 is one of the landmarks of English literature. Early poems including *Comus* (a masque performed 1634) and *Lycidas* (an elegy 1638) showed Milton's superlative lyric gift. Latin secretary to Oliver Cromwell during the Commonwealth period, he also wrote many pamphlets and prose works, including *Areopagitica* 1644, which opposed press censorship.

Born in London and educated at Christ's College, Cambridge, Milton was a scholarly poet, ambitious to match the Classical epics, and with strong theological views. Of polemical temperament, he published prose works on republicanism and church government. His middle years were devoted to the Puritan cause and pamphleteering, including one on divorce (*The Doctrine and Discipline of Divorce* 1643, which was based on his own experience of marital unhappiness) and another (*Areopagitica*) advocating freedom of the press. From 1649 he was (Latin) secretary to the Council of State. His assistants (as his sight failed) included Andrew ◊Marvell. He married Mary Powell 1643, and their three daughters were later his somewhat unwilling scribes. After Mary's death 1652, the year of his total blindness, he married twice more, his second wife Catherine Woodcock dying in childbirth, while Elizabeth Minshull survived him for over half a century.

Paradise Lost 1667 and the less successful sequel *Paradise Regained* 1671 were written when he was blind and in some political danger (after the restoration of Charles II), as was *Samson Agonistes* 1671, a powerful if untheatrical play.

He is buried in St Giles's, Cripplegate, London.

Milton Keynes industrial new town (engineering, electronics) in Buckinghamshire, England; population (1983) 146,000. It was developed 1967 around the old village of the same name, following a grid design by Richard Llewelyn-Davies; it is the headquarters of the Open University.

Milwaukee industrial port (meatpacking, brewing, engineering, machinery, electronic and electrical equipment, chemicals) in Wisconsin, on Lake Michigan; population (1990) 628,100. The site was settled 1818 and drew a large influx of German immigrants, beginning in the 1840s.

Educational institutions include Marquette University.

mime type of acting in which gestures, movements, and facial expressions replace speech. It has developed as a form of theater, particularly in France, where Marcel ◊Marceau and Jean Louis ◊Barrault have continued the traditions established in the 19th century by Deburau and the practices of the ◊commedia dell'arte in Italy. In ancient Greece, mime was a crude, realistic comedy with dialogue and exaggerated gesture.

mimicry imitation of one species (or group of species) by another. The most common form is **Batesian mimicry** (named after H W �Bates), where the mimic resembles a model that is poisonous or unpleasant to eat, and has aposematic, or warning, coloration; the mimic thus benefits from the fact that predators have learned to avoid the model. Hoverflies that resemble bees or wasps are an example. Appearance is usually the basis for mimicry, but calls, songs, scents, and other signals can also be mimicked.

In **Mullerian mimicry**, two or more equally poisonous or distasteful species have a similar color pattern, thereby reinforcing the warning each gives to predators. In some cases, mimicry is not for protection, but allows the mimic to prey on, or parasitize, the model.

mimosa tree, shrub, or herb of the genus *Mimosa* of the family Mimosaceae, found in tropical and subtropical regions. All bear small, fluffy, golden, ball-like flowers.

Certain species, such as the sensitive plant of Brazil *M. pudica*, shrink momentarily on being touched.

min. abbreviation for **minute** (time); **minimum**.

Minamoto or **Genji** in Japanese history, an ancient Japanese clan, the members of which were the first ruling shoguns 1192–1219. Their government was based in Kamakura, near present-day Tokyo. After the death of the first shogun, Minamoto Yoritomo (1147–1199), the real power was exercised by the regent for the shogun; throughout the Kamakura period (1192–1333), the regents were of the Hōjō family.

The Minamoto claimed descent from a 9th-century emperor. Minamoto Yoriyoshi (988–1075) was a warlord who built up a power base in the Kanto region when appointed by the court to put down a rebellion there. During the 11th and 12th centuries the Minamoto and the �Taira were rivals for power at the court and in the country. The Minamoto emerged victorious in 1185 and Yoritomo received the patent of shogun 1192. Zen teaching and Buddhist sculpture flourished during their shogunate.

Minangkabau member of an Indonesian people of W Sumatra. In addition to approximately 3 million Minangkabau in W Sumatra, there are sizeable communities in the major Indonesian cities. The Minangkabau language belongs to the Austronesian family.

minaret slender turret or tower attached to a Muslim mosque or to buildings designed in that style. It has one or more balconies, from which the *muezzin* calls the people to prayer five times a day. (See also �Islamic architecture.)

Minas Gerais state in SE Brazil; center of the country's iron ore, coal, diamond and gold mining industries; area 226,710 sq mi/ 587,172 sq km; population (1991) 16,956,900; capital Belo Horizonte.

mind in philosophy, the presumed mental or physical being or faculty that enables a person to think, will, and feel; the seat of the intelligence and of memory; sometimes only the cognitive or intellectual powers, as distinguished from the will and the emotions.

Mind may be seen as synonymous with the merely random chemical reactions within the brain, or as a function of the brain as a whole, or (more traditionally) as existing independently of the physical brain, through which it

expresses itself, or even as the only reality, matter being considered the creation of intelligence. The relation of mind to matter may be variously regarded. Traditionally, materialism identifies mental and physical phenomena equally in terms of matter and motion. Dualism holds that mind and matter exist independently side by side. Idealism maintains that mind is the ultimate reality and that matter does not exist apart from it.

Mindanao the second-largest island of the Philippines
area 36,526 sq mi/94,627 sq km
cities Davao, Zamboanga
physical mountainous rainforest
features in 1971, an isolated people, the Tasaday, were reputedly first seen by others (this may be a hoax). The active volcano Apo reaches 9,600 ft/2,954 m, and Mindanao is subject to severe earthquakes. There is a Muslim guerrilla resistance movement
products pineapples, coffee, rice, coconut, rubber, hemp, timber, nickel, gold, steel, chemicals, fertilizer
population (1980) 10,905,250.

Mindoro island of the Philippine Republic, S of Luzon
area 3,995 sq mi/10,347 sq km
cities Calapan
features Mount Halcon 8,500 ft/2,590 m
population (1980) 500,000.

Mindszenty József 1892–1975. Roman Catholic primate of Hungary. He was imprisoned by the communist government 1949, but escaped 1956 to take refuge in the US legation. The pope persuaded him to go into exile in Austria 1971, and he was "retired" when Hungary's relations with the Vatican improved 1974. His remains were returned to Hungary from Austria and reinterred at Esztergom 1991.

mine explosive charge on land or sea, or in the atmosphere, designed to be detonated by contact, vibration (for example, from an enemy engine), magnetic influence, or a timing device. Countermeasures include metal detectors (useless for plastic types), specially equipped helicopters, and (at sea) �minesweepers.

mineral naturally formed inorganic substance with a particular chemical composition and an ordered internal structure. Either in their perfect crystalline form or otherwise, minerals are the constituents of �rocks. In more general usage, a mineral is any substance economically valuable for mining (including coal and oil, despite their organic origins).

Ice is also a mineral, the crystalline form of water, H_2O.

mineral dressing preparing a mineral ore for processing. Ore is seldom ready to be processed when it is mined; it often contains unwanted rock and dirt. Therefore it is usually crushed into uniform size and then separated from the dirt, or gangue. This may be done magnetically (some iron ores), by washing (gold), by treatment with chemicals (copper ores), or by flotation.

mineralogy study of minerals. The classification of minerals is based chiefly on their chemical composition and the kind of chemical bonding that holds these atoms together. The mineralogist also studies their crystallographic and physical characters, occurrence, and mode of formation.

The systematic study of minerals began in the 18th century, with the division of minerals

into four classes: earths, metals, salts, and bituminous substances, distinguished by their reactions to heat and water.

mineral oil oil obtained from mineral sources, for example coal or petroleum, as distinct from oil obtained from vegetable or animal sources.

mineral salt in nutrition, a simple inorganic chemical that is required by living organisms. Plants usually obtain their mineral salts from the soil, while animals get theirs from their food. Important mineral salts include iron salts (needed by both plants and animals), magnesium salts (needed mainly by plants, to make chlorophyll), and calcium salts (needed by animals to make bone or shell). A �trace element is required only in tiny amounts.

mineral water water with mineral constituents gathered from the rocks with which it comes in contact, and classified by these into earthy, brine, and oil mineral waters; also water with artificially added minerals and, sometimes, carbon dioxide.

Many people believe that mineral waters have curative powers, the types of these medicinal waters being alkaline (Vichy), bitter (Seidlitz), chalybeate (iron: Tunbridge Wells) salt (Droitwich), earthy (Bath), sulfurous (Saratoga Springs), and special varieties, such as barium (Harrogate). The most widely sold mineral water is Perrier, from the French village of Vergèze in W Provence. In 1990 minute traces of benzene, a cancer-causing chemical, were found in samples of Perrier, and 160 million bottles were recalled. Production was resumed once charcoal filters at the bottling plant had been replaced. Evian water comes from Haute-Savoie *département*, France, and Malvern water from Hereford and Worcester, England.

Minerva in Roman mythology, the goddess of intelligence, and of the handicrafts and arts, counterpart of the Greek ⟩Athena. From the earliest days of ancient Rome, there was a temple to her on the Capitoline Hill, near the Temple of Jupiter.

minesweeper small naval vessel for locating and destroying mines at sea. A typical minesweeper weighs about 725 tons, and is built of reinforced plastic (immune to magnetic and acoustic mines). Remote-controlled miniature submarines may be used to lay charges next to the mines and destroy them.

Mingus Charles 1922–1979. US jazz bassist and composer. He played with Louis Armstrong, Duke Ellington, and Charlie Parker. His experimentation with atonality and dissonant effects opened the way for the new style of free collective jazz improvisation of the 1960s.

Based on the West Coast until 1951, Mingus took part in the development of cool jazz. Subsequently based in New York, he worked with a number of important musicians and expanded the scope of the bass as a lead instrument. Recordings include *Pithecanthropus Erectus* 1956 and *Mingus at Monterey* 1964.

miniature painting (Latin *miniare* "to paint with minium" (a red color)) painting on a very small scale, notably early manuscript paintings, and later miniature portraits, sometimes set in jeweled cases. The art of manuscript painting was developed in Classical times in the West and revived in the Middle Ages. Several Islamic countries, for example Persia and India, developed strong traditions of manuscript art. Miniature portrait painting enjoyed a vogue in France and England in the 16th–19th centuries.

Jean Clouet and Holbein the Younger both practiced the art for royal patrons. Later in the 16th century Nicholas Hilliard painted miniatures exclusively and set out the rules of this portrait style in his treatise *The Art of Limning*.

minicomputer multiuser computer with a size and processing power between those of a ⊅mainframe and a ⊅microcomputer.

Minicomputers are often used in medium-sized businesses and in university departments handling ⊅database or other commercial programs and running scientific or graphical applications requiring a great deal of numerical computation.

Minimalism movement beginning in the late 1960s in abstract art and music toward a severely simplified composition. In *painting*, it emphasized geometrical and elemental shapes. In *sculpture*, Carl André focused on industrial materials. In *music*, large-scale statements are based on layers of imperceptibly shifting repetitive patterns; its major exponents are Steve ⊅Reich and Philip ⊅Glass.

The idea of hypnotic repetition is a feature of US music from the Balinese transcriptions of Colin ⊅McPhee and the rhythmic experiments of ⊅Nancarrow to the tape music of Terry Riley (1935–) in about 1964.

mining extraction of minerals from under the land or sea for industrial or domestic uses. Exhaustion of traditionally accessible resources has led to development of new mining techniques; for example, extraction of oil from offshore deposits and from land shale reserves. Technology is also under development for the exploitation of minerals from entirely new sources such as mud deposits and mineral nodules from the sea bed.

Mud deposits are laid down by hot springs (about 660°F/350°C): sea water penetrates beneath the ocean floor and carries copper, silver, and zinc with it on its return. Such springs occur along the midocean ridges of the Atlantic and Pacific and in the geological rift between Africa and Arabia under the Red Sea.

Mineral nodules form on the ocean bed and contain manganese, cobalt, copper, molybdenum, and nickel; they stand out on the surface, and "grow" by only a few millimeters every 100,000 years.

mink two species of carnivores of the weasel family, genus *Mustela*, usually found in or near water. They have rich, brown fur, and are up to 1.6 ft/50 cm long with bushy tails 8 in/20 cm long. They live in Eurasia (*Mustela lutreola*) and North America (*M. vison*).

They produce an annual litter of six in their riverbank burrows. The demand for their fur led to the establishment from the 1930s of mink ranches for breeding of the animals in a wide range of fur colors.

Minneapolis city in Minnesota, forming with St Paul the Twin Cities area; population (1990) 368,400, metropolitan area 2,464,100. It is at the head of navigation of the Mississippi River. Industries include food processing and the manufacture of machinery, electrical and electronic equipment, precision instruments, transport machinery, and metal and paper products.

The powerful Cray computers are built here, used for long-range weather forecasting, spacecraft design, and code-breaking. Shopping areas of the city center are glass-covered against the difficult climate; there is

an arts institute, a symphony orchestra, the University of Minnesota, and Tyrone ⊅Guthrie theater. Minneapolis was incorporated as a village 1855.

Minnelli Liza 1946– . US actress and singer, daughter of Judy ⊅Garland and the director Vincente Minnelli. She achieved stardom in the Broadway musical *Flora, the Red Menace* 1965 and in the film *Cabaret* 1972. Her subsequent films include *New York, New York* 1977 and *Arthur* 1981.

Minnelli Vincente 1910–1986. US film director who specialized in musicals and occasional melodramas. His best films, such as *Meet Me in St Louis* 1944 and *The Band Wagon* 1953, display a powerful visual flair.

Minnesinger any of a group of German lyric poets of the 12th and 13th centuries who, in their songs, dealt mainly with the theme of courtly love without revealing the identity of the object of their affections. Minnesingers included Dietmar von Aist, Friedrich von Hausen, Heinrich von Morungen, Reinmar, and Walther von der Vogelweide.

Minnesota state in N midwest US; nickname Gopher State/North Star State
area 84,418 sq mi/218,700 sq km
capital St Paul
cities Minneapolis, Duluth, Bloomington, Rochester
features sources of the Mississippi River and the Red River of the North; Voyageurs National Park near the Canadian border; Minnehaha Falls at Minneapolis; Mayo Clinic at Rochester; more than 15,000 lakes
products cereals, soybeans, livestock, meat and dairy products, iron ore (about two-thirds of US output), nonelectrical machinery, electronic equipment
population (1990) 4,375,100
famous people F Scott Fitzgerald, Hubert H Humphrey, Sinclair Lewis, Charles and William Mayo
history first European exploration, by French fur traders, in the 17th century; region claimed for France by Daniel Greysolon, Sieur Duluth, 1679; part east of Mississippi River ceded to Britain 1763 and to the US 1783; part west of Mississippi passed to the US under the Louisiana Purchase 1803; became a territory 1849; statehood 1858.

With the coming of the railroad in 1867, Minneapolis became the major US flour-milling center. Iron ore was discovered in the Mesabi, Cuyuna, and Vermilion ranges in the 1880s, and Duluth became a major Great Lakes port. In 1848 the value of manufactured products exceeded farm cash receipts for the first time as the state became increasingly urbanized and industrial.

minnow various small freshwater fishes of the carp family (Cyprinidae), found in streams and ponds worldwide. Most species are small and dully colored, but some are brightly colored. They feed on larvae and insects.

Minnesota

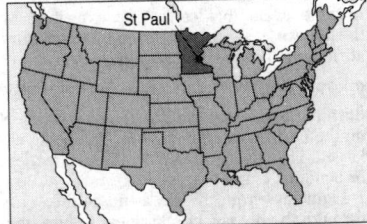

Red-bellied daces, genus *Chrosomus*, and cut-lipped minnows, genus *Exoglossum* are North American representatives.

Minoan civilization Bronze Age civilization on the Aegean island of Crete. The name is derived from Minos, the legendary king of Crete, reputed to be the son of the god Zeus. The civilization is divided into three main periods: early Minoan, about 3000–2200 BC; middle Minoan, about 2200–1580 BC; and late Minoan, about 1580–1100 BC. Known from the Minoan civilization are the palaces of Knossos, Phaistos, and Mallia; sophisticated metalwork; and linear scripts. The Minoan language was deciphered by Michael ⊅Ventris. The civilization was suddenly destroyed by earthquake or war.

No paleolithic remains have yet been found in Crete, but in the Neolithic Age some centuries before 3000 BC the island was inhabited by people coming probably from SW Asia Minor, and akin to the early Bronze Age inhabitants of the Greek mainland. With the opening of the Bronze Age, about 3000 BC, the Minoan culture proper began. Each period was marked by cultural advances in copper and bronze weapons, pottery of increasingly intricate design, frescoes, and the construction of palaces and fine houses. About 1400 BC, in the late Minoan period, the civilization was suddenly destroyed by earthquake or war. A partial revival continued until about 1100.

In religion the Minoans seem to have worshiped principally a great mother goddess with whom was associated a young male god. The tales of Greek mythology about Rhea, the mother of Zeus, and the birth of Zeus himself in a Cretan cave seem to be based on Minoan religion.

minor legal term for those under the age of majority, which varies from country to country but is usually between 18 and 21. In the US (from 1971 for voting, and in some states for nearly all other purposes) and certain European countries (in Britain since 1970) the age of majority is 18.

Most civic and legal rights and duties only accrue at the age of majority: for example, the rights to vote, to make a will, and (usually) to make a fully binding contract, and the duty to act as a juror.

Minorca (Spanish *Menorca*) second largest of the ⊅Balearic Islands in the Mediterranean
area 266 sq mi/689 sq km
cities Mahon, Ciudadela
products copper, lead, iron; tourism is important
population (1985) 55,500.

minor planet another name for an ⊅asteroid.

Minos in Greek mythology, a king of Crete (son of ⊅Zeus and ⊅Europa).

Minotaur in Greek mythology, a monster, half man and half bull, offspring of Pasiphaë, wife of King Minos of Crete, and a bull. It lived in the Labyrinth at Knossos, and its victims were seven girls and seven youths, sent in annual tribute by Athens, until ⊅Theseus killed it, with the aid of Ariadne, the daughter of Minos.

Minsk or *Mensk* industrial city (machinery, textiles, leather; a center of the Russian computer industry) and capital of Belarus; population (1987) 1,543,000.

Minsk dates from the 11th century and has in turn been held by Lithuania, Poland, Sweden, and Russia. The city was devastated by Napoleon 1812 and heavily damaged by German forces 1944. Mass graves from between

1937 and 1941 of more than 30,000 victims of Joseph Stalin's terror were discovered in a forest outside Minsk 1989.

mint in botany, any aromatic plant, genus *Mentha*, of the family Labiatae, widely distributed in temperate regions. The plants have square stems, creeping rootstocks, and flowers, usually pink or purplish, that grow in a terminal spike. Mints include garden mint *M. spicata* and peppermint *M. piperita*.

mint in economics, a place where coins are stamped from metal under government authority.

In the US the official mint is the Bureau of the Mint, a division of the Treasury Department. The official Mint of the United States was established by the Coining Act 1792 in Philadelphia. The US Mint has general supervision of the four current coinage mints—in Denver, West Point, San Francisco, and Philadelphia—all of which are assay offices and bullion depositories. It directs the coinage of money, the manufacture of medals, and the custody of bullion.

Mintoff Dom(inic) 1916–   . Labour prime minister of Malta 1971–84. He negotiated the removal of British and other foreign military bases 1971–79 and made treaties with Libya.

Minton Thomas 1765–1836. English potter. He first worked under the potter Josiah Spode, but in 1789 established himself at Stoke-on-Trent as an engraver of designs (he originated the "willow pattern") and in the 1790s founded a pottery there, producing high-quality bone china, including tableware.

minuet European courtly dance of the 17th century, later used with the trio as the third movement in a Classical symphony.

Minuit Peter *c.* 1580–1638. Dutch colonial administrator, born in Prussia. He took part in the colonization activities of the Dutch West India Company and established the settlement of New Amsterdam on Manhattan Island 1626. Appointed director general of the colony, he conducted purchase negotiations with the local Indians and supervised the construction of Fort Amsterdam. Minuit was relieved of his post 1631 owing to a personal conflict with the Dutch Reformed Church, and he later participated in a Swedish colonization effort, founding Fort Christina at the modern site of Wilmington, Delaware, 1638. He was lost in a hurricane in the West Indies.

minute unit of time consisting of 60 seconds; also a unit of angle equal to one sixtieth of a degree.

Minuteman in weaponry, a US three-stage intercontinental ballistic missile (ICBM) with a range of about 5,000 mi/8,000 km. In US history the term was applied to members of the citizens' militia in the 1770s. These volunteer soldiers had pledged to be available for battle at a "minute's notice" during the ⟡American Revolution.

Miocene ("middle recent") fourth epoch of the Tertiary period of geological time, 25–5 million years ago. At this time grasslands spread over the interior of continents, and hoofed mammals rapidly evolved.

mips (acronym for **m**illion **i**nstructions **p**er **s**econd) in computing, a measure of the speed of a processor. It does not equal the computer power in all cases.

The original IBM personal computer had a speed of one-quarter mips.

Miquelon Islands small group of islands off the S coast of Newfoundland which with St Pierre form a French overseas *département*. See ⟡St Pierre and Miquelon
area 83 sq mi/216 sq km
products cod; silver fox and mink are bred
population (with St Pierre, 1982) 6,045.

mir (Russian "peace" or "world") in Russia before the 1917 Revolution, a self-governing village community in which the peasants distributed land and collected taxes.

Mir (Russian "peace" or "world") Soviet space station, the core of which was launched Feb 20, 1986. *Mir* is intended to be a permanently occupied space station.

Mir weighs almost 23 tons, is approximately 44 ft/13.5 m long, and has a maximum diameter of 13.6 ft/4.15 m. It carries a number of improvements over the earlier ⟡Salyut series of space stations, including six docking ports; four of these can have scientific and technical modules attached to them. The first of these was the *Kvant* (quantum) *Astrophysics Module*, launched 1987. This had two main sections: a main experimental module and a service module, which would be separated in orbit. The experimental module was 19 ft/5.8 m long and had a maximum diameter matching that of *Mir*. When attached to the *Mir* core, *Kvant* added a further 1,413 cu ft/40 cu m of workspace to that already there. Among the equipment carried by *Kvant* were several X-ray telescopes and an ultraviolet telescope.

Mira or **Omicron Ceti** brightest long-period pulsating ⟡variable star, located in the constellation ⟡Cetus. Mira was the first star discovered to vary periodically in brightness.

In 1596 Dutch astronomer David Fabricus noticed Mira as a third-magnitude object. Because it did not appear on any of the star charts available at the time, he mistook it for a ⟡nova. The German astronomer Johann Bayer included it on his star atlas 1603 and designated it Omicron Ceti. The star vanished from view again, only to reappear within a year. Continued observation revealed a periodic variation between third or fourth magnitude and ninth magnitude over an average period of 331 days. Mira can sometimes reach second magnitude and once, in 1779, it almost attained first magnitude.

Mirabeau Honoré Gabriel Riqueti, Comte de 1749–1791. French politician, leader of the National Assembly in the French Revolution. He wanted to establish a parliamentary monarchy on the English model. From May 1790 he secretly acted as political adviser to the king.

Mirabeau was from a noble Provençal family. Before the French Revolution he had a stormy career, was three times imprisoned, and spent several years in exile. In 1789 he was elected to the States General. His eloquence won him the leadership of the National Assembly; nevertheless, he was out of sympathy with the majority of the deputies, whom he regarded as mere theoreticians.

miracle event that cannot be explained by the known laws of nature and is therefore attributed to divine intervention.

miracle play another name for ⟡mystery play.

mirage illusion seen in hot climates of water on the horizon, or of distant objects being enlarged. The effect is caused by the ⟡refraction, or bending, of light.

Light rays from the sky bend as they pass through the hot layers of air near the ground, so that they appear to come from the horizon. Because the light is from a blue sky, the horizon appears blue and watery. If, during the night, cold air collects near the ground, light can be bent in the opposite direction, so that objects below the horizon appear to float above it. In the same way, objects such as trees or rocks near the horizon can appear enlarged.

Miranda Carmen. Adopted name of Maria de Carmo Miranda da Cunha 1909–1955. Portuguese dancer and singer who lived in Brazil from childhood. Her Hollywood musicals include *Down Argentine Way* 1940 and *The Gang's All Here* 1943. Her hallmarks were extravagant costumes and headgear adorned with tropical fruits, a staccato singing voice, and fiery temperament.

Successful in Brazilian films, she went to Hollywood 1939 via Broadway and appeared in over a dozen musicals.

Miranda v Arizona US Supreme Court decision 1966 dealing with the admission into a trial of evidence obtained from suspects who are unaware of their rights. The petitioner, Ernesto Miranda, was convicted of kidnapping and rape after confessing to police interrogators. Miranda appealed the conviction, arguing that due process had been violated because he had not been informed of his rights before his confession. The Court voted 5 to 4 to overturn Miranda's conviction. The ruling mandated that in order for testimony to be admissible in criminal trials, suspects must have been informed (1) of the right to remain silent, (2) that anything they do or say will be used against them in court, (3) of the right to an attorney, and (4) of the right to a court-appointed attorney if unable to afford one.

Mirandola Italian 15th-century philosopher. See ⟡Pico della Mirandola.

Miró Joan 1893–1983. Spanish Surrealist painter, born in Barcelona. In the mid-1920s he developed a distinctive abstract style with ameba shapes, some linear, some highly colored, generally floating on a plain background.

During the 1930s his style became more somber and after World War II he produced larger abstracts. He experimented with sculpture and printmaking and produced ceramic murals (including two in the UNESCO building, Paris, 1958). He also designed stained glass and sets for the ballet director Sergei Diaghilev.

mirror any polished surface that reflects light; often made from "silvered" glass (in practice, a mercury-alloy coating of glass). A plane (flat) mirror produces a same-size, erect "virtual" image located behind the mirror at the same distance from it as the object is in front of it. A spherical concave mirror produces a reduced, inverted real image in front or an enlarged, erect virtual image behind it (as in a shaving mirror), depending on how close the object is to the mirror. A spherical convex mirror produces a reduced, erect virtual image behind it (as in a car's rear-view mirror).

In a plane mirror the light rays appear to come from behind the mirror but do not actually do so. The inverted real image from a spherical concave mirror is an image in which the rays of light pass through it. The ⟡focal length *f* of a spherical mirror is half the radius of curvature; it is related to the image distance *v* and object distance *u* by the equation $1/v + 1/u = 1/f$.

MIRV abbreviation for *multiple independently targeted re-entry vehicle*, used in �ŷnuclear warfare.

miscarriage spontaneous expulsion of a fetus from the womb before it is capable of independent survival. Often, miscarriages are due to an abnormality in the developing fetus.

misdemeanor in US law, an offense less serious than a ⟩felony. A misdemeanor is an offense punishable by a relatively insevere penalty, such as a fine or short term in prison or a term of community service, while a felony carries more severe penalties, such as a term of imprisonment of a year or more up to the death penalty.

Mishawaka industrial city (plastics, rubber, missiles, and vehicle and aircraft parts) in N central Indiana, east of South Bend; population (1990) 42,600.

Mishima Yukio 1925–1970. Japanese novelist whose work often deals with sexual desire and perversion, as in *Confessions of a Mask* 1949 and *The Temple of the Golden Pavilion* 1956. He committed hara-kiri (ritual suicide) as a protest against what he saw as the corruption of the nation and the loss of the samurai warrior tradition.

Mishna or **Mishnah** collection of commentaries on written Hebrew law, consisting of discussions between rabbis, handed down orally from their inception in AD 70 until around 200, when, with the Gemara (the main body of rabbinical debate on interpretations of the Mishna) it was committed to writing to form the Talmud.

Miskito member of an American Indian people of Central America, living mainly in the area that is now Nicaragua.

Misr Egyptian name for ⟩Egypt and for ⟩Cairo.

missal in the Roman Catholic Church, a service book containing the complete office of Mass for the entire year. A simplified missal in the vernacular was introduced 1969 (obligatory from 1971): the first major reform since 1570.

missile rocket-propelled weapon, which may be nuclear-armed (see ⟩nuclear warfare). Modern missiles are often classified as surface-to-surface missiles (SSM), air-to-air missiles (AAM), surface-to-air missiles (SAM), or air-to-surface missiles (ASM). A *cruise missile* is in effect a pilotless, computer-guided aircraft; it can be sea-launched from submarines or surface ships, or launched from the air or the ground.

Rocket-propelled weapons were first used by the Chinese about AD 1100, and were encountered in the 18th century by the British forces. The rocket missile was then re-invented by Sir William ⟩Congreve in England around 1805, and remained in use with various armies in the 19th century. The first wartime use of a long-range missile was against England in World War II, by the jet-powered German ⟩V1 (*Vergeltungswaffe*, "revenge weapon" or Flying Bomb), a monoplane (wingspan about 18 ft/6 m, length 26 ft/8.5 m); the first rocket-propelled missile with a preset guidance system was the German V2, also launched by Germany against Britain in World War II.

Modern missiles are also classified as strategic or tactical: strategic missiles are the large, long-range **intercontinental ballistic missiles** (ICBMs, capable of reaching targets over 3,400 mi/5,500 km), and tactical missiles are the short-range weapons intended for use in limited warfare (with a range under 680 mi/1,100 km).

Not all missiles are large. There are many missiles that are small enough to be carried by one person. The Stinger, for example, is an antiaircraft missile fired by a single soldier from a shoulder-held tube. Most fighter aircraft are equipped with missiles to use against enemy aircraft or against ground targets. Other small missiles are launched from a type of truck, called a MLRS (multiple-launch rocket system), that can move around a battlefield. Ship-to-ship missiles like the Exocet have proved very effective in naval battles.

The vast majority of missiles have systems that guide them to their target. The guidance system may consist of radar and computers, either in the missile or on the ground. These devices track the missile and determine the correct direction and distance required for it to hit its target. In the radio-guidance system, the computer is on the ground, and guidance signals are radio-transmitted to the missile. In the inertial guidance system, the computer is on board the missile. Some small missiles have heat-seeking devices fitted to their noses to seek out the engines of enemy aircraft, or are guided by laser light reflected from the target. Others (called TOW missiles) are guided by signals sent along wires that trail behind the missile in flight.

Outside the industrialized countries, 22 states had active ballistic-missile programs by 1989, and 17 had deployed these weapons: Afghanistan, Argentina, Brazil, Cuba, Egypt, India, Iran, Iraq, Israel, North Korea, South Korea, Libya, Pakistan, Saudi Arabia, South Africa, Syria, and Taiwan. Non-nuclear short-range missiles were used during the Iran–Iraq War 1980–88 against Iraqi cities.

Battlefield missiles used in the 1991 Gulf War include antitank missiles and short-range attack missiles. NATO announced in 1990 that it was phasing out ground-launched nuclear battlefield missiles, and these are being replaced by types of tactical air-to-surface missile (TASM), also with nuclear warheads.

In the Falklands conflict 1982, small, conventionally armed sea-skimming missiles were used (the French Exocet) against British ships by the Argentine forces, and similar small missiles have been used against aircraft and ships elsewhere.

Mission city in S Texas, near the Rio Grande, W of McAllen; population (1990) 28,700. The economy is based on processing the area's citrus fruits and vegetables, and on nearby oil wells.

mission organized attempt to spread a religion. Throughout history, Christianity has been the most aggressive missionary religion; its activities during the colonization of what are now Third World nations was in some instances excessive, and it has frequently been criticized for obliterating both the beliefs and the people of some indigenous societies, as during the Spanish Conquest. During the 20th century, sects such as the Mormons and Jehovah's Witnesses proselytize regularly and systematically. Islam also has a history of militant missionizing, but in the 20th century has found ready converts in the Black Muslim movement of the US. Buddhism was spread both historically and recently by the teaching spirit of the wandering Buddha and his followers.

Mississippi

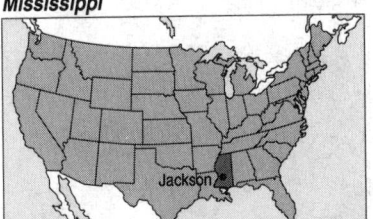

Jackson

In developmental terms, the transition from tribal religions to the Great World Religions can be traced to the missionary movement that emerged in the ancient Near East even before the beginning of the Christian era.

Mississippi river in the US, the main arm of the great river system draining the US between the Appalachian and the Rocky mountains. The length of the Mississippi is 2,350 mi/3,780 km; with its tributary the Missouri 3,740 mi/6,020 km.

The Mississippi rises in the lake region of N Minnesota, with St Anthony Falls at Minneapolis. Below the tributaries Minnesota, Wisconsin, Des Moines, and Illinois, the confluence of the Missouri and Mississippi occurs at St Louis. Turning at the Ohio junction, it passes Memphis, and takes in the St Francis, Arkansas, Yazoo, and Red tributaries before reaching its delta on the Gulf of Mexico beyond New Orleans.

In spring, warm air from the Gulf of Mexico collides with cold fronts from the north to create tornadoes along the Red River, a western tributary. The Spanish explorer Hernando de Soto reached a point on the Mississippi near present-day Memphis 1541. The Sieur de La Salle, a French explorer, reached the river's mouth 1682 after descending from the Great Lakes. Before the coming of the railroad, river commerce was of greater importance, and the securing of the Mississippi 1861–63, in the American Civil War, was a vital objective of the Union forces.

Levees extend over more than 1,600 mi/2,575 km of its course because of the potentially dangerous spring flooding. St Louis is the chief central port on its banks. Waterborne commerce consists mainly of bulk commodities such as petroleum and petroleum products, grain, and iron ore. Passenger traffic was important during the 19th century, today excursion boats, especially paddle-wheel craft, provide day trips or longer cruises.

Mississippi state in SE US; nickname Magnolia State/Bayou State
area 47,710 sq mi/123,600 sq km
capital Jackson
cities Biloxi, Meridian, Hattiesburg
features rivers: Mississippi, Pearl, Big Black; Vicksburg National Military Park (Civil War site); Gulf Islands National Seashore; mansions and plantations, many in the Natchez area
products cotton, rice, soybeans, chickens, fish and shellfish, lumber and wood products, petroleum and natural gas, transportation equipment, chemicals
population (1990) 2,573,200
famous people Jefferson Davis, William Faulkner, Elvis Presley, Leontyne Price, Eudora Welty, Tennessee Williams, Richard Wright
history first explored by Hernando de Soto for Spain 1540; settled by the French 1699,

Missouri

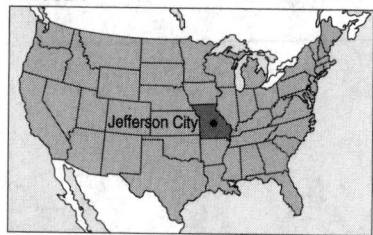

the English 1763; ceded to US 1798; statehood achieved 1817.

After secession from the Union during the Civil War, Mississippi was the scene of heavy fighting that left it devastated. Tenant farming replaced plantations, and only in the mid-1960s did manufacturing pass farming as a source of jobs. The legal segregation of blacks was dismantled during this period. Mississippi remains the poorest of the states in many respects, including personal income per head of population.

Mississippian US term for the lower ◇Carboniferous period of geological time, named after the state of Mississippi.

Missouri state in central US; nickname Show Me State/Bullion State
area 69,712 sq mi/180,600 sq km
capital Jefferson City
cities St Louis, Kansas City, Springfield, Independence
features rivers: Mississippi, Missouri; Pony Express Museum at St Joseph; birthplace of Jesse James; Mark Twain and Ozark state parks; Harry S Truman Library at Independence
products meat and other processed food, aerospace and transport equipment, lead, zinc
population (1990) 5,117,100
famous people George Washington Carver, T S Eliot, Jesse James, Joseph Pulitzer, Harry S Truman, Mark Twain
history explored by de Soto 1541; acquired by the US under the Louisiana Purchase 1803; achieved statehood 1821, following the Missouri Compromise of 1820.

Strong sympathy for both sides existed, but the state remained Union during the Civil War; many battles and skirmishes fostered a general lawlessness that continued in the postwar exploits of such bandits as Jesse and Frank James. While St Louis was eclipsed by Chicago as the commercial center of the Midwest, Kansas City benefited from the growth of the railroads. Increasingly urbanized and industrialized in the 20th century, Missouri is second to Michigan in producing automobiles and ranks high in aerospace production.

Missouri major river in the central US, a tributary of the Mississippi, which it joins N of St Louis; length 2,683 mi/4,320 km.

It is formed by the confluence of the Jefferson, Gallatin, and Madison rivers in SW Montana and flows SE through the states of Montana, North Dakota, and South Dakota to Sioux City, Iowa, where it turns S and forms the borders between Iowa and Nebraska and between Kansas and Missouri. Kansas City, Missouri, is the largest city on its banks. Since 1944 the muddy, turbulent river has been tamed by a series of locks and dams for irrigation and flood control.

Missouri Compromise in US history, the solution by Congress (1820–21) of a sectional crisis caused by the 1819 request from Missouri for admission to the union as a slave state, despite its proximity to existing nonslave states. The compromise was the simultaneous admission of Maine as a nonslave state to keep the same ratio.

mistletoe any of several parasitic evergreen shrubs of the genera *Viscum* and *Phoradendron* of the family Loranthaceae, especially American mistletoe *P. flavescens*, parasitic on broadleaved trees, and European mistletoe *V. album*. They grow on trees as branched bushes, with translucent white berries, and are used as Christmas decorations. See ◇Druidism. The seeds of the European mistletoe are dispersed by birds, but the dwarf mistletoe *Arceuthobium pusillum* of North America shoots its seeds at 60 mph/100 kph as far as 16 yd/15 m. Mistletoes lose water more than ten times as fast as other plants to draw nutrients to them.

mistral cold, dry, northerly wind that occasionally blows during the winter on the Mediterranean coast of France. It has been known to reach a velocity of 90 mph/145 kph.

Mistral Gabriela. Adopted name of Lucila Godoy de Alcayaga 1889–1957. Chilean poet who wrote *Sonnets of Death* 1915. She was awarded the Nobel Prize for Literature 1945.

She was consul of Chile in Spain, and represented her country at the League of Nations and the United Nations.

Mitchell Arthur 1934–1990. US dancer, director of the Dance Theater of Harlem, which he founded with Karel Shook (1920–) in 1968. Mitchell was a principal dancer with the New York City Ballet 1956–68, creating many roles in Balanchine's ballets.

Mitchell Margaret 1900–1949. US novelist, born in Atlanta, Georgia, which is the setting for her one book, the bestseller *Gone With the Wind* 1936, a story of the US Civil War. It was filmed starring Vivien Leigh and Clark Gable in 1939.

Mitchell Peter 1920–1992. British chemist. He received a Nobel Prize in 1978 for work on the conservation of energy by plants during respiration and photosynthesis.

Mitchum Robert 1917– . US film actor, a star for more than 30 years as the big, strong, relaxed modern hero. His films include *Out of the Past* 1947, *The Night of the Hunter* 1955, and *The Friends of Eddie Coyle* 1973.

mite minute ◇arachnid of the subclass Acari.

Some mites are free-living scavengers or predators. Some are parasitic, such as the itch mite *Sarcoptes scabiei*, which burrows in human skin, and the red mite *Dermanyssus gallinae*, which sucks blood from poultry and other birds. Others parasitize plants.

miter in the Christian church, the headdress worn by bishops, cardinals, and mitered abbots at solemn services. There are miters of many different shapes, but in the Western church they usually take the form of a tall cleft cap. The miter worn by the pope is called a tiara.

Mitford sisters the six daughters of British aristocrat Lord Redesdale, including:
Nancy (1904–1973), author of the semi autobiographical *The Pursuit of Love* 1945 and *Love in a Cold Climate* 1949, and editor and part author of *Noblesse Oblige* 1956 elucidating "U" (upper-class) and "non-U" behavior;
Diana (1910–), who married Oswald ◇Mosley;
Unity (1914–1948), who became an admirer of Hitler;

Jessica (1917–), author of the autobiographical *Hons and Rebels* 1960 and *The American Way of Death* 1963.

Mithras in Persian mythology, the god of light. Mithras represented the power of goodness, and promised his followers compensation for present evil after death. He was said to have captured and killed the sacred bull, from whose blood all life sprang. Mithraism was introduced into the Roman Empire 68 BC. By about AD 250, it rivaled Christianity in strength.

A bath in the blood of a sacrificed bull formed part of the initiation ceremony of the Mithraic

mitosis *The stages of mitosis, the process of cell division that takes place when a plant or animal cell divides for growth or repair.*

cult, which spread rapidly, gaining converts especially among soldiers. In 1954 remains of a Roman temple dedicated to Mithras were discovered in the City of London.

Mithridates VI Eupator known as **the Great** 132–63 BC. King of Pontus (NE Asia Minor, on the Black Sea) from 120 BC. He massacred 80,000 Romans in overrunning the rest of Asia Minor and went on to invade Greece. He was defeated by ⊳Sulla in the First Mithridatic War 88–84; by ⊳Lucullus in the Second 83–81; and by ⊳Pompey in the Third 74–64. He was killed by a soldier at his own order rather than surrender.

Mitilíni modern Greek name of ⊳Mytilene, town on the island of Lesvos.

mitochondria (singular **mitochondrion**) membrane-enclosed organelles within eukaryotic cells (see ⊳eukaryote), containing enzymes responsible for energy production during ⊳aerobic respiration. These rodlike or spherical bodies are thought to be derived from free-living bacteria that, at a very early stage in the history of life, invaded larger cells and took up a symbiotic way of life inside. Each still contains its own small loop of DNA, and new mitochondria arise by division of existing ones.

mitosis in biology, the process of cell division. The genetic material of eukaryotic cells (see ⊳eukaryote) is carried on a number of ⊳chromosomes. To control their movements during cell division so that both new cells get a full complement, a system of protein tubules, known as the spindle, organizes the chromosomes into position in the middle of the cell before they replicate. The spindle then controls the movement of chromosomes as the cell goes through the stages of division: **interphase, prophase, metaphase, anaphase**, and **telophase**. See also ⊳meiosis.

Mitre Bartólomé 1821–1906. Argentine president 1862–68. In 1852 he helped overthrow the dictatorial regime of Juan Manuel de Rosas, and in 1861 helped unify Argentina. Mitre encouraged immigration and favored growing commercial links with Europe. He is seen as a symbol of national unity.

Mitsotakis Constantine 1918– . Greek politician, leader of the conservative New Democracy Party from 1984, prime minister from April 1990. Minister for economic coordination 1965 (a post he held again 1978–80), he was arrested by the military junta 1967, but escaped from house arrest and lived in exile until 1974. In 1980–81 he was foreign minister.

Mitterrand François 1916– . French socialist politician, president from 1981. He held ministerial posts in 11 governments 1947–58, and founded the French Socialist Party (PS) 1971. In 1985 he introduced proportional representation, allegedly to weaken the growing opposition from left and right. Since 1982 his administrations have combined economic orthodoxy with social reform.

Mitterrand studied law and politics in Paris. During World War II he was prominent in the Resistance. He entered the National Assembly as a center-left deputy for Nièvre. Opposed to General de Gaulle's creation of the Fifth Republic 1958, he formed the center-left anti-Gaullist Federation of the Left in the 1960s. In 1971 he became leader of the new PS. An electoral union with the Communist Party 1972–77 established the PS as the most popular party in France.

Mitterrand was elected president 1981. His program of reform was hampered by deteriorating economic conditions after 1983. When the socialists lost their majority March 1986, he was compelled to work with a right-wing prime minister, Jacques Chirac, and grew in popularity. He defeated Chirac to secure a second term in the presidential election May 1988.

Mitylene alternate spelling of ⊳Mytilene, Greek city on the island of Lesvos.

Mix Tom (Thomas) 1880–1940. US actor who was the most colorful cowboy star of silent films. At their best, his films, such as *The Range Riders* 1910 and *King Cowboy* 1928, were fast-moving and full of impressive stunts.

His talkies include *Destry Rides Again* 1932 and *The Miracle Rider* 1935, a serial. After his death in an auto accident, his character lived on into the 1940s in a radio serial.

mixture in chemistry, a substance containing two or more compounds that still retain their separate physical and chemical properties. There is no chemical bonding between them and they can be separated from each other by physical means (compare ⊳compound).

Miyamoto Musashi *c.* 1584–1645. Japanese samurai, author of a manual on military strategy and sword fighting, *Gorinsho/The Book of Five Rings* 1645, which in English translation 1974 became popular in the US as a guide to business success.

In Japan, Miyamoto Musashi is popular as the hero of a long historical novel that glamorizes his martial-arts exploits and has been the basis for a series of films and comic books. The historical Miyamoto was a painter as well as a fencer, and spent his life traveling Japan in search of Zen enlightenment.

Mizoguchi Kenji 1898–1956. Japanese film director whose *Ugetsu Monogatari* 1953 confirmed his international reputation. Notable for his sensitive depiction of female psychology, he also directed *Blood and Soul* 1923, *The Poppies* 1935, *Sansho daiyu/Sansho the Bailiff* 1954, and *Street of Shame* 1956.

Mizoram state of NE India
area 8,145 sq mi/21,100 sq km
capital Aizawl
products rice, hand-loom weaving
population (1991) 686,200
religion 84% Christian
history made a Union Territory 1972 from the Mizo Hills District of Assam. Rebels carried on a guerrilla war 1966–76, but 1976 acknowledged Mizoram as an integral part of India. It became a state 1986.

ml symbol for **milliliter**.

Mladenov Petar 1936– . Bulgarian Communist politician, secretary-general of the Bulgarian Communist Party from Nov 1989, after the resignation of ⊳Zhivkov, until Feb 1990. He was elected state president in April 1990 but replaced four months later.

mm symbol for **millimeter**.

Mmabatho or **Sun City** capital of Bophuthatswana, South Africa; population (1985) 28,000. It is a casino resort frequented by many white South Africans.

mmHg symbol for ⊳**millimeter of mercury**.

MN abbreviation for the state of ⊳**Minnesota**.

MO abbreviation for the state of ⊳**Missouri**.

moa extinct flightless kiwilike bird, order Dinornithoformes, 19 species of which lived in

New Zealand. They varied from 2 to 12 ft/0.5 to 3.5 m, with strong limbs, a long neck, and no wings. The last moa was killed in the 1800s.

The Maoris used them as food, and with the use of European firearms killed them in excessive numbers.

Moab ancient country in Jordan east of the southern part of the river Jordan and the Dead Sea. The inhabitants were closely akin to the Hebrews in culture, language, and religion, but were often at war with them, as recorded in the Old Testament. Moab eventually fell to Arab invaders. The **Moabite Stone**, discovered 1868 at Dhiban, dates from the 9th century BC and records the rising of Mesha, king of Moab, against Israel.

Mobile industrial city (meatpacking, paper, cement, clothing, chemicals) and only seaport in Alabama; population (1990) 196,300. Founded 1702 by the French a little to the north of the present city, Mobile was capital of the French colony of Louisiana until 1763. It was then British until 1780, and Spanish to 1813.

Möbius August Ferdinand 1790–1868. German mathematician, discoverer of the Möbius strip and considered one of the founders of ⊳topology.

Möbius strip structure made by giving a half twist to a flat strip of paper and joining the ends together. It has certain remarkable properties, arising from the fact that it has only one edge and one side. If cut down the center of the strip, instead of two new strips of paper, only one long strip is produced. It was invented by the German mathematician August Möbius.

Mobutu Sese Seko Kuku Ngbeandu Wa Za Banga 1930– . Zairean president from 1965. He assumed the presidency in a coup, and created a unitary state under a centralized government. The harshness of some of his policies and charges of corruption have attracted widespread international criticism. In 1991 opposition leaders forced Mobutu to agree formally to give up some of his powers.

Mobutu Sese Seko Lake lake on the border of Uganda and Zaire in the Great ⊳Rift Valley; area 1,650 sq mi/4,275 sq km. The first European to see it was the British explorer Samuel Baker, who named it Lake Albert after the Prince Consort. It was renamed 1973 by Zaire's president Mobutu after himself.

Moby-Dick or **The Whale** US novel by Herman Melville, published 1851. Its story of the conflict between the monomaniac Captain Ahab and the great white whale explores the mystery and the destructiveness of both man and nature's power.

Moche or **Mochica** pre-Inca civilization on the coast of Peru AD 100–800. Remains include cities, massive platform tombs (*adobe*), and pottery that details daily and ceremonial life.

In 1988 the burial of one of their warrior-priest rulers was discovered. He was nicknamed the "Great Lord of Sipan" after the village near the site of his pyramid tomb (*huaca*). It contained a priceless treasure hoard, including a gold mask and ear pendants.

mockingbird North American songbird *Mimus polyglottos* of the mimic thrush family Mimidae, found in the US and Mexico. About 10 in/25 cm long, it is brownish gray, with white markings on the black wings and tail. It is remarkable for its ability to mimic the songs of other species.

mock orange or **syringa** deciduous shrub of the genus *Philadelphus*, family

Philadelphaceae, including *P. coronarius*, which has white, strongly scented flowers, resembling those of the orange.

The common mock orange *P. inodorus* is native to the S US.

mode in mathematics, the element that appears most frequently in a given group. For example, the mode of the group 0, 0, 9, 9, 9, 12, 87, 87 is 9. (Not all groups have modes.)

Model Parliament English parliament set up 1295 by Edward I; it was the first to include representatives from outside the clergy and aristocracy, and was established because Edward needed the support of the whole country against his opponents: Wales, France, and Scotland. His sole aim was to raise money for military purposes, and the parliament did not pass any legislation.

modem (acronym for *modulator/demodulator*, also called an *acoustic coupler*) device for transmitting computer data over telephone lines. Such a device is necessary because the ◊digital signals produced by computers cannot, at present, be transmitted directly over the telephone network, which uses ◊analog signals. The modem converts the digital signals to analog, and back again. Modems are used for linking remote terminals to central computers and enable computers to communicate with each other anywhere in the world.

Modena city in Emilia, Italy, capital of the province of Modena, 23 mi/37 km NW of Bologna; population (1988) 177,000. It has a 12th-century cathedral, a 17th-century ducal palace, and a university 1683, known for its medical and legal faculties.

moderator in a nuclear reactor, a material such as graphite or heavy water used to reduce the speed of high-energy neutrons. Neutrons produced by nuclear fission are fast-moving and must be slowed to initiate further fission so that nuclear energy continues to be released at a controlled rate.

Slow neutrons are much more likely to cause ◊fission in a uranium-235 nucleus than to be captured in a U-238 (nonfissile uranium) nucleus. By using a moderator, a reactor can thus be made to work with fuel containing only a small proportion of U-235.

modern dance 20th-century dance idiom that evolved in opposition to traditional ballet by those seeking a freer and more immediate means of dance expression. Leading exponents include Martha ◊Graham and Merce ◊Cunningham in the US, Isadora ◊Duncan and Loie Fuller in Europe.

Modern dance was pioneered by US women seeking individual freedom but it is from Ruth St Denis and Ted Shawn's Denishawn School in Los Angeles 1915, that the first generation of modern dance—Martha Graham, Doris Humphrey, and Charles Weidman—emerged.

In the UK, the London Contemporary Dance Theatre and school was set up 1967 by Graham's pupil, Robert Cohan. It is the only European institute authorized to teach Graham Technique.

In Germany, the originators of a modernist movement known as Central European dance were Jacques Dalcroze and Rudolph Laban. The leading exponents, Mary Wigman, Harald Kreutzberg, and Kurt Joss, had some influence on modern dance through their visits to the US and through Hanya Holm, a former Wigman dancer who settled and taught in New York, and with whom Alwyn Nikolais was originally associated.

Modernism in Protestantism, liberal thought which emerged early in the 20th century and attempted to reconsider Christian beliefs in the light of modern scientific theories and historical methods, without abandoning the essential doctrines. It was against modernism that the Fundamentalist movement defined itself. The term was originally used for liberal tendencies in the Roman Catholic Church. Modernism was condemned by Pope Pius X in 1907.

Modernism in the arts, a general term used to describe the 20th century's conscious attempt to break with the artistic traditions of the 19th century; it is based on a concern with form and the exploration of technique as opposed to content and narrative.

In the visual arts, direct representationalism gave way to abstraction (see ◊abstract art); in literature, writers experimented with alternatives to orthodox sequential storytelling, such as ◊stream of consciousness; in music, the traditional concept of key was challenged by ◊atonality; and in architecture, Functionalism ousted decorativeness as a central objective. Critics of Modernism have found in it an austerity that is seen as dehumanizing. Modernism as a movement was followed by ◊Postmodernism.

Modern Jazz Quartet US jazz group specializing in group improvisation, formed 1952 (disbanded 1974 and re-formed 1981). Noted for elegance and mastery of form, the quartet has sometimes been criticized for being too "Classical."

Modesto city in central California, on the Tuolumne River, SE of San Francisco, on the fringes of the San Joaquin Valley; population (1990) 164,700. It is an agricultural center for wine, apricots, melons, beans, peaches, and livestock.

Modigliani Amedeo 1884–1920. Italian artist, active in Paris from 1906. He painted and sculpted graceful nudes and portrait studies. His paintings—for example, the portrait of *Jeanne Hebuterne* 1919 (Guggenheim Museum, New York)—have a distinctive elongated, linear style.

Modigliani was born in Livorno. He was encouraged to sculpt by Constantin Brancusi, and his series of strictly simplified heads reflects a shared interest in archaic sculptural styles. He led a dissolute life and died of the combined effects of alcoholism, drug addiction, and tuberculosis.

modulation in radio transmission, the intermittent change of frequency, or amplitude, of a radio carrier wave, in accordance with the audio characteristics of the speaking voice, music, or other signal being transmitted. See ◊pulse-code modulation, ◊AM (amplitude modulation), and ◊FM (frequency modulation).

module in construction, a standard or unit that governs the form of the rest. For example, Japanese room sizes are traditionally governed by multiples of standard tatami floor mats; today prefabricated buildings are mass-produced in a similar way. The components of a spacecraft are designed in coordination; for example, for the Apollo Moon landings the craft comprised a command module (for working, eating, sleeping), service module (electricity generators, oxygen supplies, maneuvering rocket), and lunar module (to land and return the astronauts).

modulus in mathematics, a number that divides exactly into the difference between two

given numbers. Also, the multiplication factor used to convert a logarithm of one base to a logarithm of another base. Also, another name for ◊absolute value.

Mogadishu or **Mugdisho** capital and chief port of Somalia; population (1988) 1,000,000. It is a center for oil refining, food processing, and uranium mining. During the struggle to overthrow President Barre and the ensuing civil war 1991–92, much of the city was devastated and many thousands killed. In April 1992 the UN Security Council voted to send military observers to monitor a cease-fire in the city.

It has mosques dating from the 13th century, and a cathedral built 1925–28.

Mogul emperors N Indian dynasty 1526–1857, established by ◊Zahir ("Babur"). Muslim descendants of Tamerlane, the 14th-century Mongol leader, the Mogul emperors ruled until the last one was dethroned and exiled by the British 1857; they included ◊Akbar, ◊Aurangzeb, and ◊Shah Jahan.

Mohács, Battle of Austro-Hungarian defeat of the Turks 1687, which effectively marked the end of Turkish expansion into Europe. Named after the river port of that name on the Danube in Hungary, which is also the site of a Turkish victory 1526.

mohair (Arabic *mukhayyar* "goat") yarn made from the long, lustrous hair of the ◊Angora goat or rabbit, loosely woven with cotton, silk, or wool to produce a fuzzy texture. It became popular for jackets, coats, and sweaters in the 1950s. Commercial mohair is now obtained from cross-bred animals, pure-bred supplies being insufficient to satisfy demand.

Mohamad Mahathir bin 1925– . Prime minister of Malaysia from 1981 and leader of the United Malays' National Organization (UMNO). His "look east" economic policy emulates Japanese industrialization.

Mahathir bin Mohamad was elected to the House of Representatives 1964 and gained the support of the dominant UMNO's radical youth wing as an advocate of economic help to *bumiputras* (ethnic Malays) and as a proponent of a more Islamic social policy. Mahathir held a number of ministerial posts from 1974 before being appointed prime minister and UMNO leader 1981. He was reelected 1986, but has alienated sections of UMNO by his authoritarian leadership.

Mohammed or **Muhammed**, **Mahomet** c. 570–632. Founder of Islam, born in Mecca on the Arabian peninsula. In about 616 he claimed to be a prophet and that the *Koran* was revealed to him by God (it was later written down by his followers). He fled from persecution to the town now known as Medina in 622: the flight, Hegira, marks the beginning of the Islamic era.

Originally a shepherd and caravan conductor, he found leisure for meditation by his marriage with a wealthy widow in 595, and received his first revelation in 610. After some years of secret teaching, he openly declared himself the prophet of God, and, as the number of his followers increased, he was forced to flee to Medina. After the battle of Badr in 623, he was continuously victorious, entering Mecca as the recognized prophet of Arabia 630. The succession was troubled.

Mohammedanism misnomer for ◊Islam, the religion founded by Mohammed.

Mohave Desert arid region in S California, part of the Great Basin; area 15,000 sq mi/ 38,500 sq km.

The US military has appropriated thousands of acres for bombing ranges and test stations, including Edwards Air Force Base, landing base for space shuttles.

Mohawk member of a North American Indian people, part of the ◊Iroquois confederation, who lived in the Mohawk Valley, New York, and now live on reservations in Ontario, Québec, and New York State, as well as among the general population. Their language belongs to the Macro-Siouan group. In 1990 Mohawks south of Montréal mounted a blockade in a dispute over land with the government of Québec province.

Mohenjo Daro ("mound of the dead") site of a city about 2500–1600 BC on the lower Indus River, Pakistan, where excavations from the 1920s have revealed the ◊Indus Valley civilization. The most striking artistic remains are soapstone seals of elephants and snakes. ◊Harappa in India was built by the same civilization.

Mohican and Mohegan or *Mahican* two closely related North American Indian peoples, speaking an Algonquian language, who formerly occupied the Hudson Valley and parts of Connecticut, respectively. The novelist James Fenimore ◊Cooper confused the two peoples in his fictional account *The Last of the Mohicans* 1826.

Mohole US project for drilling a hole through the Earth's crust, so named after the ◊Mohorovičić discontinuity that marks the transition from crust to mantle. Initial tests were made in the Pacific 1961, but the project was subsequently abandoned.

The cores that were brought up illuminated the geological history of the Earth and aided the development of geophysics.

Moholy-Nagy Laszlo 1895–1946. US photographer, born in Hungary. He lived in Germany 1923–29, where he was a member of the Bauhaus school, and fled from the Nazis 1935. Through the publication of his illuminating theories and practical experiments, he had great influence on 20th-century photography and design.

Mohorovicic discontinuity also *Moho* or *M-discontinuity* boundary that separates the Earth's crust and mantle, marked by a rapid increase in the speed of earthquake waves. It follows the variations in the thickness of the crust and is found approximately 20 mi/32 km below the continents and about 6 mi/10 km below the oceans. It is named after the Yugoslav geophysicist Andrija Mohorovičić (1857–1936) who suspected its presence after analyzing seismic waves from the Kulpa Valley earthquake 1909.

Mohs' scale scale of hardness for minerals (in ascending order): 1 talc; 2 gypsum; 3 calcite; 4 fluorite; 5 apatite; 6 orthoclase; 7 quartz; 8 topaz; 9 corundum; 10 diamond.

The scale is useful in mineral identification because any mineral will scratch any other mineral lower on the scale than itself, and similarly it will be scratched by any other mineral higher on the scale.

Moi Daniel arap 1924– . Kenyan politician, president from 1978. Leader of Kenya African National Union (KANU), he became minister of home affairs 1964, vice-president 1967, and succeeded Jomo Kenyatta as president. He enjoys the support of Western governments but has been widely criticized for Kenya's poor human-rights record. From 1988 his rule became increasingly authoritarian and in 1991, in the face of widespread criticism, he promised an eventual introduction of multiparty politics.

Moissan Henri 1852–1907. French chemist. For his preparation of pure fluorine 1886, Moissan was awarded the 1906 Nobel Prize for Chemistry. He also attempted to create artificial diamonds by rapidly cooling carbon heated to high temperatures. His claims of success were treated with suspicion.

moksha (Sanskrit "liberation") in Hinduism, liberation from the cycle of reincarnation and from the illusion of ◊maya. In Buddhism, ◊enlightenment.

molar one of the large teeth found toward the back of the mammalian mouth. The structure of the jaw, and the relation of the muscles, allows a massive force to be applied to molars. In herbivores the molars are flat with sharp ridges of enamel and are used for grinding, an adaptation to a diet of tough plant material. Carnivores have sharp powerful molars called carnassials, which are adapted for cutting meat.

molar volume volume occupied by one ◊mole (the molecular mass in grams) of any gas at standard temperature and pressure, equal to 2.24136×10^{-2} m^3.

molasses thick, usually dark, syrup obtained during the refining of sugar (either cane or beet) or made from varieties of sorghum. Fermented sugar-cane molasses produces rum; fermented beet-sugar molasses yields ethyl alcohol.

Unsulfured raw molasses, called blackstrap, is a nutritious food, containing in 1 tablespoon 585 mg of potassium.

mold mainly saprophytic ◊fungi living on foodstuffs and other organic matter, a few being parasitic on plants, animals, or each other. Many are of medical or industrial importance; for example, penicillin.

Moldavia former principality in E Europe, on the river Danube, occupying an area divided today between Moldova (formerly a Soviet republic) and Romania. It was independent between the 14th and 16th centuries, when it became part of the Ottoman Empire. In 1861 Moldavia was united with its neighboring principality Wallachia as Romania. In 1940 the eastern part, ◊Bessarabia, became part of the USSR, whereas the western part remained in Romania.

Moldavian member of the majority ethnic group living in Moldova, comprising almost two-thirds of the population; also, an inhabitant of the Romanian province of Moldavia. The Moldavian language is a dialect of Romanian, and belongs to the Romance group of the Indo-European family.

molding the use of a pattern, hollow form, or matrix to give a specific shape to something in a plastic or molten state. Molds are commonly used for shaping plastics, clays, and glass. In injection molding, molten plastic, for example, is injected into a water-cooled mold and takes the shape of the mold when it solidifies. In blow molding, air is blown into a blob of molten plastic inside a hollow mold. In compression molding, synthetic resin powder is simultaneously heated and pressed into a mold. When metals are used, the process is called ◊casting.

Moldova or *Moldavia* country in E central Europe, bounded N, S, and E by Ukraine, and W by Romania.

government There is a 380-member legislature, the Moldova Parliament, to which deputies are elected by the majority system, and a second ballot "run-off" race in contests in which there is no clear first round majority. The executive state president is directly elected.

history Formerly a principality in Eastern Europe, occupying an area divided today between the republic of Moldova and modern Romania, the region was independent from the 14th to the 16th century, when it became part of the Ottoman Empire. Its eastern part, Bessarabia, was ruled by Russia 1912–18, but then transferred to Romania. Romania was forced to cede Bessarabia June 1940 and it was joined with part of the Soviet-controlled Autonomous Moldavian Republic to form the Moldavian Socialist Republic Aug 1940.

nationalist revival Before and after World War II the republic was brutally "sovietized." Agriculture was collectivized, private enterprises were taken over by the state, and Russians and Ukrainians settled in the republic. The republic witnessed significant urban and industrial growth from the 1950s. ◊Glasnost brought a resurgence of Moldavian nationalism from the late 1980s, and there was pressure for language reform and calls for reversion from the Cyrillic to the Latin alphabet. In 1988 a Moldavian Movement in Support of ◊Perestroika was formed and a year later, in May 1989, the Moldavian Popular Front (MPF) was established. In Aug 1989 the MPF persuaded the republic's government, led since July 1989 by the sympathetic communist president Mircea Snegur, to make Romanian the state language and reinstate the Latin script. This provoked demonstrations and strikes by the republic's Russian speakers and led the Turkish-speaking Gagauz minority, concentrated in the southwest, to campaign for autonomy. In Nov 1989, after MPF radicals had staged a gasoline bomb assault on the Interior Ministry headquarters in Chisinau, the Moldavian Communist Party's (MCP) conservative leader, Semyon Grossu, was dismissed and replaced by the more conciliatory Pyotr Luchinsky. In the wake of the Chisinau riots, with inter-ethnic strife worsening, a temporary state of emergency was imposed and a ban placed on public meetings. This restricted campaigning for the Feb 1990 supreme soviet elections, in which, nevertheless, the MPF polled strongly. After this election the movement toward independence gathered momentum, and a "sovereignty" declaration was made June 1990, followed by the creation of a republican guard Nov 1990.

independence recognized In March 1991 the republic boycotted the USSR referendum on preservation of the Union on the grounds that it might worsen inter-ethnic tensions. During the Aug 1991 anti-Gorbachev attempted coup in Moscow, which was denounced by President Snegur but supported by the Dnestr and Gagauz regions, there were large prodemocracy demonstrations in Chisinau. After the coup, MCP activity was banned in workplaces and on Aug 27, 1991 the republic formally declared its independence. Immediate recognition was accorded by Romania. However, the predominantly Russian Dnestr region in the east, centerd around Tiraspol and with a population of 700,000, declared its independence from Moldova Sept 2, 1991 and adopted a separate constitution. The declaration was rejected by Moldova. The republic joined the ◊Commonwealth of Independent

Moldova
Republic of

area 13,012 sq mi/33,700 sq km
capital Chisinau (Kishinev)
cities Tiraspol, Beltsy, Bendery
physical hilly land lying largely between the rivers Prut and Dnestr; northern Moldova comprises the level plain of the Beltsy Steppe and uplands; the climate is warm and moderately continental
features Black Earth region
head of state Mircea Snegur from 1989
head of government Andrei Sangheli from 1992
political system emergent democracy
political parties Moldavian Popular Front (MRF), Romanian nationalist; Gagauz-Khalky People's Movement (GKPM), Gagauz separatist
products wine, tobacco, canned goods
population (1990) 4,400,000 (Moldavian 64%, Ukrainian 14%, Russian 13%, Gagauzi 4%, Bulgarian 2%)
language Moldavian, allied to Romanian
religion Russian Orthodox
chronology
1940 Bessarabia in the E became part of the Soviet Union whereas the W part remained in Romania.
1941 Bessarabia taken over by Romania-Germany.
1944 Red army reconquered Bessarabia.
1946–47 Widespread famine.
1988 A popular front, the Democratic Movement for Perestroika, campaigned for accelerated political reform.
1989 Jan–Feb: nationalist demonstrations in Chisinau. May: Moldavian Popular Front established. July: Snegur became head of state. Aug: Moldavian language granted official status triggering clashes between ethnic Russians and Moldavians. Nov: Gagauz-Khalky People's Movement formed to campaign for Gagauz autonomy.
1990 Feb: Popular Front polled strongly in supreme soviet elections. June: economic and political sovereignty declared; renamed Republic of Moldova. Oct: Gagauz held unauthorized elections to independent parliament; state of emergency declared after inter-ethnic clashes.
1991 March: Moldavia boycotted the USSR's constitutional referendum. Aug: independence declared after abortive anti-Gorbachev coup; Communist Party (CP) outlawed. Sept: Dnestr region declared independence from Moldova. Dec: Moldova joined new Commonwealth of Independent States (CIS).
1992 Jan: admitted into the Conference on Security and Cooperation in Europe (CSCE). Possible union with Romania discussed. March: state of emergency imposed; admitted into United Nations (UN); diplomatic recognition granted by USA. May: further meeting on unification with Romania; Dnestr-region fighting intensified. July: Andrei Sangheli became premier; Moldova agreed to outside peacekeeping force. Aug: talks between Moldova and Russia began; Russian peacekeeping force reportedly deployed.

States (CIS) Dec 1991. Also in Dec 1991 Snegur was directly elected president; he was unopposed after two challengers withdrew. In the same month, the Dnestr and Gagauz regions held separate presidential elections and plebiscites on independence from Moldova which received overwhelming support. In Jan 1992 Moldova was admitted into the ⟡Conference on Security and Cooperation in Europe (CSCE). United Nations (UN) membership and US diplomatic recognition was granted March 1992.

union with Romania Following pro-unification border rallies, the Moldovan and Romanian presidents met Jan and May 1992 to discuss the possibility of union. President Snegur favored a gradual approach toward unification with Romania.

Dnestr-region violence escalated In March 1992 a state of emergency was declared following upsurge of fighting in Dnestr region between Moldovan security forces and ethnic Russians and Ukrainians, fearful of the proposed merger with Romania. Between May and July hundreds died in the fighting, with Russian troops present in the republic accused of assisting the Slav separatists. In July President Snegur agreed to deployment of an outside peacekeeping force, and in Aug talks began between Moldova and Russia on implementing an agreement to preserve peace in the Dnestr region and to improve economic ties between the two countries. By mid-August a Russian peacekeeping force was reportedly deployed in the troubled region.

mole burrowing insectivore of the family Talpidae. Moles grow to 7 in/18 cm, and have acute senses of hearing, smell, and touch, but poor vision. They have shovellike, clawed front feet for burrowing, and eat insects, grubs, and worms.

Some members of the family are aquatic, such as the Russian desman *Desmana moschata* and the North American star-nosed mole *Condylura cristata*.

The eastern American mole *Scalopus aquaticus*, about 6 in/15 cm long, has blackish to coppery soft, dense fur and a long snout. Its eyes and ears are not visible externally. It excavates tunnels just under the surface, leaving raised ridges, in search of earthworms and insect larvae.

mole SI unit (symbol mol) of the amount of a substance. One mole of an element that exists as single atoms weighs as many grams as its ⟡atomic number (so one mole of carbon weighs 12 g), and it contains 6.022045×10^{23} atoms, which is ⟡Avogadro's number.

One mole of a substance is defined as the amount of that substance that contains as many elementary entities (atoms, molecules, and so on) as there are atoms in 12 g of the ⟡isotope carbon-12.

mole in construction, a mechanical device for boring horizontal holes underground without the need for digging trenches. It is used for laying pipes and cables.

mole person working subversively within an organization. The term has come to be used broadly for someone who gives out ("leaks") secret information in the public interest; it originally meant a person who spends several years working for a government department or a company with the intention of passing secrets to an enemy or a rival.

molecular biology study of the molecular basis of life, including the biochemistry of molecules such as DNA, RNA, and proteins, and the molecular structure and function of the various parts of living cells.

molecular clock use of rates of ⟡mutation in genetic material to calculate the length of time elapsed since two related species diverged from each other during evolution. The method can be based on comparisons of the DNA or of widely occurring proteins, such as haemoglobin.

Since mutations are thought to occur at a constant rate, the length of time that must have elapsed in order to produce the difference between two species can be estimated. This information can be compared with the evidence obtained from paleontology to reconstruct evolutionary events.

molecule smallest unit of an ⟡element or ⟡compound that can exist and still retain the characteristics of the element or compound. A molecule of an element consists of one or more like ⟡atoms; a molecule of a compound consists of two or more different atoms bonded together. They vary in size and complexity from the hydrogen molecule (H_2) to the large ⟡macromolecules of proteins. They are held together by ionic bonds, in which the atoms gain or lose electrons to form ⟡ions, or covalent bonds, where electrons from each atom are shared in a new molecular orbital.

The symbolic representation of a molecule is known as its formula. The presence of more than one atom is denoted by a subscript figure—for example, one molecule of the compound water, having two atoms of hydrogen and one atom of oxygen, is shown as H_2O.

Molière Adopted name of Jean Baptiste Poquelin 1622–1673. French satirical playwright from whose work modern French comedy developed. One of the founders of the Illustre Théâtre 1643, he was later its leading actor. In 1655 he wrote his first play, *L'Etourdi*, followed by *Les Précieuses Ridicules* 1659. His satires include *L'Ecole des femmes* 1662, *Le Misanthrope* 1666, *Le Bourgeois Gentilhomme* 1670, and *Le Malade imaginaire* 1673. Other satiric plays include *Tartuffe* 1664 (banned until 1697 for attacking the hypocrisy of the clergy), *Le Médecin malgré lui* 1666, and *Les Femmes savantes* 1672.

Molière's comedies, based on the exposure of hypocrisy and cant, made him vulnerable to many attacks (from which he was protected by Louis XIV) and marked a new departure in the French theater away from reliance on Classical Greek themes.

Moline industrial city (farm implements, furniture, and metal products) in NW Illinois, on the Mississippi River, W of Chicago; population (1990) 43,200.

mollusks: classification

phylum	*Mollusca*
class *Monoplacophora*	primitive marine forms, including Neopilina (2 species)
class *Amphineura*	(1,150 species)
1 Aplacophora	wormlike marine forms
2 Polyplacophora	chitons, coat-of-mail shells
class *Gastropoda*	snaillike mollusks, with single or no shell (9,000 species)
1 Prosobranchia	limpets, winkles, whelks
2 Opisthobranchia	seaslugs
3 Pulmonata	land and freshwater snails, slugs
class *Scaphopoda*	tusk shells, marine burrowers (350 species)
class *Bivalvia*	mollusks with a double (two-valved) shell (15,000 species): mussels, oysters, clams, cockles, scallops, tellins, razor shells, shipworms
class *Cephalopoda*	mollusks with shell generally reduced, arms to capture prey, and beaklike mouth; body bilaterally symmetrical and nervous system well developed (750 species): squids, cuttlefish, octopuses, pearly nautilus, argonaut

Molinos Miguel de 1640–1697. Spanish mystic and Roman Catholic priest. He settled in Rome and wrote several devotional works in Italian, including the *Guida spirituale/Spiritual Guide* 1675, which aroused the hostility of the Jesuits. In 1687 he was sentenced to life imprisonment. His doctrine is known as ▷quietism.

Molise mainly agricultural region of S central Italy, comprising the provinces of Campobasso and Isernia; area 1,698 sq mi/4,400 sq km; population (1990) 336,500. Its capital is Campobasso.

mollusk any invertebrate of the phylum Mollusca with a body divided into three parts, a head, a foot, and a visceral mass. The majority of mollusks are marine animals, but some inhabit fresh water, and a few are terrestrial. They include bivalves, mussels, octopuses, oysters, snails, slugs, and squids. The body is soft, limbless, and coldblooded. There is no internal skeleton, but many species have a hard shell covering the body.

Mollusks vary in diet, the carnivorous species feeding chiefly upon other members of the phylum. Some are vegetarian. Reproduction is by means of eggs and is sexual; many species are hermaphrodite. The shells of mollusks take a variety of forms: univalve (snail), bivalve (clam), chambered (nautilus), and many other variations. In some cases (for example cuttlefish and squid), the shell is internal. Every mollusk has a fold of skin, the mantle, which covers the whole body or the back only, and secretes the calcareous substance forming the shell. The lower ventral surface forms the locomotory organ, or foot.

Molly Maguires, the in US history, a secret Irish coalminers' organization in the 1870s that staged strikes and used violence against coal-company officials and property in the anthracite fields of Pennsylvania, prefiguring a long period of turbulence in industrial relations. The movement was infiltrated by ▷Pinkerton agents (detectives), and 1876 trials led to convictions and executions.

Molnár Ferenc 1878–1952. Hungarian novelist and playwright. His play *Liliom* 1909 is a study of a circus barker (a person who calls out to attract the attention of members of the public), adapted as the musical *Carousel.*

Moloch or *Molech* in the Old Testament, a Phoenician deity worshiped in Jerusalem in the 7th century BC, to whom live children were sacrificed by fire.

Molokai mountainous island of Hawaii, SE of Oahu.

area 259 sq mi/673 sq km
features Kamakou 4,960 ft/1,512 m is the highest peak
population (1980) 6,049
history the island was the site of a leper colony organized 1873–89 by Belgian missionary Joseph De Veuster (Father ▷Damien).

Molotov former name (1940–62) for the port of ▷Perm in Russia.

Molotov Vyacheslav Mikhailovich. Assumed name of V M Skriabin 1890–1986. Soviet communist politician. He was chair of the Council of People's Commissars (prime minister) 1930–41 and foreign minister 1939–49 and 1953–56. He negotiated the 1939 nonaggression treaty with Germany (the ▷Hitler–Stalin pact), and, after the German invasion 1941, the Soviet partnership with the Allies. His postwar stance prolonged the Cold War and in 1957 he was expelled from the government for Stalinist activities.

Molotov cocktail or *gasoline bomb* homemade weapon consisting of a bottle filled with gasoline, plugged with a rag as a wick, ignited, and thrown as a grenade. Resistance groups during World War II named them after the Soviet foreign minister Molotov.

molting the periodic shedding of the hair or fur of mammals, feathers of birds, or skin of reptiles. In mammals and birds, molting is usually seasonal and is triggered by changes of day length.

The term is also often applied to the shedding of the ▷exoskeleton of arthropods, but this is more correctly called ▷ecdysis.

Moltke Helmuth Carl Bernhard, Count von 1800–1891. Prussian general. He became chief of the general staff 1857, and was responsible for the Prussian strategy in the wars with Denmark 1863–64, Austria 1866, and France 1870–71.

Moltke Helmuth Johannes Ludwig von 1848–1916. German general (nephew of Count von Moltke, the Prussian general), chief of the German general staff 1906–14. His use of General Alfred von Schlieffen's (1833–1913) plan for a rapid victory on two fronts failed and he was relieved of command after the defeat at the Marne.

Moluccas another name for ▷Maluku, Indonesia.

molybdenite molybdenum sulfide, MoS_2, the chief ore mineral of molybdenum. It possesses a hexagonal crystal structure similar to graphite, has a blue metallic luster, and is very soft (1–1.5 on Mohs' scale).

The largest source of molybdenite is a deposit in Colorado.

molybdenum (Greek *malybdos* "lead") heavy, hard, lustrous, silver-white, metallic element, symbol Mo, atomic number 42, atomic weight 95.94. The chief ore is the mineral molybdenite. The element is highly resistant to heat and conducts electricity easily. It is used in alloys, often to harden steels. It is a necessary trace element in human nutrition. It was named 1781 by Swedish chemist Karl Scheele, after its isolation by P J Hjelm (1746–1813), for its resemblance to lead ore.

Mombasa industrial port (oil refining, cement) in Kenya (serving also Uganda and Tanzania), built on Mombasa Island and adjacent mainland; population (1984) 481,000. It was founded by Arab traders in the 11th century and was an important center for ivory and slave trading until the 16th century.

moment of a force in physics, measure of the turning effect, or torque, produced by a force acting on a body. It is equal to the product of the force and the perpendicular distance from its line of action to the point, or pivot, about which the body will turn. Its unit is the newton meter.

moment of inertia in physics, the sum of all the point masses of a rotating object multiplied by the squares of their respective distances from the axis of rotation. It is analogous to the ▷mass of a stationary object or one moving in a straight line.

In linear dynamics, Newton's second law of motion states that the force F on a moving object equals the products of its mass m and acceleration a ($F = ma$); the analogous equation in rotational dynamics is $T = I\alpha$, where T is the torque (the turning effect of a force) that causes an angular acceleration α and I is the moment of inertia. For a given object, I depends on its shape and the position of its axis of rotation.

momentum in physics, the product of the mass of a body and its linear velocity. The **angular momentum** of a body in rotational motion is the product of its moment of inertia and its angular velocity. The momentum of a body does not change unless it is acted on by an external force; angular momentum does not change unless it is acted upon by a turning force, or torque.

The law of conservation of momentum is one of the fundamental concepts of Classical physics. It states that the total momentum of all bodies in a closed system is constant and unaffected by processes occurring within the system. Angular momentum is similarly conserved in a closed system.

Momoh Joseph Saidu 1937– . Sierra Leone soldier and politician, president 1985–92. An army officer who became commander 1983, with the rank of major general, he succeeded Siaka Stevens as president when he retired; Momoh was endorsed by Sierra Leone's one political party, the All-People's Congress. He dissociated himself from the policies of his predecessor, pledging to fight corruption and improve the economy. In April 1992 he fled to neighboring Guinea after a military takeover.

Momoyama in Japanese history, the period 1568–1616 or 1573–1603. During this time three great generals, Oda Nobunaga (1534–1582), Toyotomi Hideyoshi (1537–1598), and ▷Tokugawa Ieyasu, successively held power; Ieyasu established the Tokugawa shogunate. Portuguese missionaries and traders were an

Monaco
Principality of

area 0.75 sq mi/1.95 sq km
capital Monaco-Ville
cities Monte Carlo, La Condamine; heliport Fontvieille
physical steep and rugged; surrounded landwards by French territory; being expanded by filling in the sea
features aquarium and oceanographic center; Monte Carlo film festival, motor races, and casinos; world's second smallest state
head of state Prince Rainier III from 1949
head of government Jean Ausseil from 1986
political system constitutional monarchy under French protectorate
political parties National and Democratic Union (UND); Democratic Union Movement; Monaco Action; Monégasque Socialist Party
exports some light industry; economy dependent on tourism and gambling
currency French franc
population (1989) 29,000; growth rate −0.5% p.a.
languages French (official), English, Italian
religion Roman Catholic 95%
literacy 99% (1985)
chronology
1861 Became an independent state under French protection.
1918 France given a veto over succession to the throne.
1949 Prince Rainier III ascended the throne.
1956 Prince Rainier married US actress Grace Kelly.
1958 Birth of male heir, Prince Albert.
1959 Constitution of 1911 suspended.
1962 New constitution adopted.

influence at this time, and ▷Japanese art, architecture (castles), and the tea ceremony flourished. The period is named after a castle built by Hideyoshi in Fushimi, central Honshu.

Monaco small sovereign state forming an enclave in S France, with the Mediterranean Sea to the south.

government Under the 1911 constitution, modified 1917 and largely rewritten 1962, Monaco is a hereditary principality, but an earlier concept of endowing the prince with a divine right to rule has been deleted. Legislative power is shared between the prince and a single-chamber national council, with 18 members elected by universal suffrage for a five-year term. Executive power is formally vested in the prince but in practice is exercised by a four-member council of government.

France is closely involved in the government of Monaco, providing a civil servant, of the prince's choosing, to head its council of government. Agreements between France and Monaco state that Monaco will be incorporated into France if the reigning prince dies without a male heir.

history Formerly part of the Roman Empire, Monaco became a Genoese possession in the 12th century and has been ruled since 1297 by the Grimaldi family. It was a Spanish protectorate 1542–1641, then came under French protection and during the French revolution was annexed by France. The ruling family was imprisoned (one was guillotined) but regained power after the 1814 Treaty of Paris. In 1815 Monaco became a protectorate of Sardinia but reverted to French protection 1861. In 1940 it was occupied by Italy and in 1943 by Germany but was liberated 1945. Prince Rainier III came to the throne 1949 and a male heir, Prince Albert, was born 1958. *See illustration box.*

monad philosophical term deriving from the work of Gottfried Leibniz, suggesting a soul or metaphysical unit that has a self-contained life. The monads are independent of each other but coordinated by a "preestablished harmony."

Monadnock mountain in New Hampshire, 3,186 ft/1,063 m high. The term "monadnock" is also used to mean any isolated hill or mountain.

Monaghan (Irish *Mhuineachain*) county of the NE Republic of Ireland, province of Ulster; area 498 sq mi/1,290 sq km; products include cereals, linen, potatoes, and cattle; population (1991) 51,300. The county town is Monaghan. The county is low and rolling, and includes the rivers Finn and Blackwater.

Monarchianism form of belief in the Christian Trinity that emphasizes the undifferentiated unity of God. It was common in the early 3rd century.

monasticism devotion to religious life under vows of poverty, chastity, and obedience, known to Judaism (for example ▷Essenes), Buddhism, and other religions, before Christianity. In Islam, the Sufis formed monastic orders from the 12th century.

history, Christian
3rd century The institution of monasticism is ascribed to St Anthony in Egypt, but the inauguration of communal life is attributed to his disciple St Pachomius. Possibly communities for women (nuns, from Latin *nonna* "elderly woman") preceded those for men, and most male orders have their female counterpart.
6th century Full adaptation to conditions in W Europe was made by St Benedict, his "rule" being adopted.
10th century In 910 the founding of Cluny began the system of orders whereby each monastery was subordinated to a central institution.
11th century During the Middle Ages other forms of monasticism were established, including the hermitlike Carthusians 1084 and the Augustinian Canons, who were clerics organized under a monastic system.
12th century The military Knights Templar and Knights Hospitallers of St John were formed.
13th century The four mendicant orders of friars—Franciscans, Dominicans, Carmelites, and Augustinians—were established, and monasticism reached the height of its influence.

16th century Already weakened by the wars, plagues, and schisms of the 14th and 15th centuries, monasticism was severely affected by the Reformation. A revival came with the foundation of orders dedicated to particular missions, such as the great weapon of the Counter-Reformation, the Society of Jesus (Jesuits) 1540.
17th century The Trappist Cistercians were founded at La Trappe.
18th century The French Revolution exercised a repressive influence.
20th century Since the Vatican II Council, the trend in many orders is toward modern dress and involvement outside the monastery, despite disapproval by Pope John Paul II.

monazite mineral, $(Ce,La,Y,Th)PO_4$, yellow to red, valued as a source of ▷lanthanides or rare earths, including cerium and europium; generally found in placer deposit (alluvial) sands.

Mönchengladbach industrial city in North Rhine–Westphalia, Germany, on the river Niers near Düsseldorf; industries include textiles, machinery, paper; population (1988) 255,000. It is the NATO headquarters for N Europe.

Mondale Walter "Fritz" 1928– . US Democrat politician, unsuccessful presidential candidate 1984. He was a senator 1964–76 from his home state of Minnesota, and vice-president to Jimmy Carter 1977–81. After losing the 1984 presidential election to Ronald Reagan, Mondale retired from national politics to resume his law practice.

Monday second day of the week, following Sunday. The name derives from its having been considered sacred to the Moon (Old English *Mōnandaeg* and Latin *Lunae dies*).

Mondrian Piet (Pieter Mondriaan) 1872–1944. Dutch painter, a pioneer of abstract art. He lived in Paris 1919–38, then in London, and from 1940 in New York. He was a founder member of the de ▷Stijl movement and chief exponent of Neo-Plasticism, a rigorous abstract style based on the use of simple geometric forms and pure colors. He typically painted parallel horizontal black lines which intersected vertical ones, creating square and rectangular blocks within the framework, some of which he filled with primary colors, mid-gray, or black, others being left white.

In Paris from 1911 Mondrian was inspired by Cubism. He returned to the Netherlands during World War I, where he used a series of still lifes and landscapes to refine his ideas, ultimately developing a pure abstract style. His aesthetic theories were published in the journal *De Stijl* from 1917, in *Neoplasticism* 1920, and in the essay "Plastic Art and Pure Plastic Art" 1937. From the New York period his *Broadway Boogie-Woogie* 1942–43 (Museum of Modern Art, New York) reflects a late preoccupation with jazz rhythms.

Monet Claude 1840–1926. French painter, a pioneer of Impressionism and a lifelong exponent of its ideals; his painting *Impression, Sunrise* 1872 gave the movement its name. In the 1870s he began painting the same subjects at different times of day to explore the effects of light on color and form; the *Haystacks* and *Rouen Cathedral* series followed in the 1890s, and from 1899 he painted a series of *Water Lilies* in the garden of his house at Giverny, Normandy (now a museum).

Monet was born in Paris. In Le Havre in the 1850s he was encouraged to paint by Boudin, and met Jongkind, whose light and airy seascapes made a lasting impact. From 1862 in Paris he shared a studio with Renoir, Sisley, and others, and they showed their work together at the First Impressionist Exhibition 1874.

Monet's work from the 1860s onwards concentrates on the evanescent effects of light and color, and from the late 1860s he painted in the classic Impressionist manner, juxtaposing brushstrokes of color to create an effect of dappled, glowing light. His first series showed the Gare St Lazare in Paris with its puffing steam engines. Views of the water garden in Giverny gradually developed into large, increasingly abstract color compositions. Between 1900 and 1909 he produced a series of water-lily mural panels for the French state (the Orangerie, Paris).

monetarism economic policy, advocated by the economist Milton Friedman and the Chicago school of economists, that proposes control of a country's money supply to keep it in step with the country's ability to produce goods, with the aim of curbing inflation. Cutting government spending is advocated, and the long-term aim is to return as much of the economy as possible to the private sector, allegedly in the interests of efficiency.

Central banks (in the US, the Federal Reserve Bank) use the ◊discount rate and other tools to restrict or expand the supply of money to the economy. Unemployment may result from some efforts to withdraw government "safety nets," but monetarists claim it is less than eventually occurs if the methods of ◊Keynesian economics are adopted. Monetarist policies were widely adopted in the 1980s in response to the inflation problems caused by spiraling oil prices in 1979. See also ◊deregulation, ◊privatization.

monetary policy economic policy aimed at controlling the amount of money in circulation, usually through controlling the level of lending or credit. Increasing interest rates is an example of a contractionary monetary policy, which aims to reduce inflation by reducing the rate of growth of spending in the economy.

money any common medium of exchange acceptable in payment for goods or services or for the settlement of debts; legal tender. Money is usually coinage (invented by the Chinese in the second millennium BC) and paper notes (used by the Chinese from about AD 800). Developments such as the check and credit card fulfill many of the traditional functions of money.

money supply the quantity of money present in an economy at a given moment. Monetarists hold that a rapid increase in money supply inevitably provokes an increase in the rate of inflation.

The money-supply classification M-1 consists of currency and demand deposits. Since the ◊Federal Reserve System holds some currency, only circulating currency is included in M-1. Bank deposits, payable on demand, constitute as much as three-fourths of the money supply. Some economists consider near-money, such as time deposits or liquid assets, as part of M-1. The government can expand or restrict M-1 through ◊monetary policy.

Mongol member of any of the various Mongol (or Mongolian) ethnic groups of Central Asia. Mongols live in Mongolia, Russia, Inner Mongolia (China), Tibet, and Nepal. The Mongol language belongs to the Altaic family; some groups of Mongol descent speak languages in the Sino-Tibetan family, however.

Mongolia
State of (Outer Mongolia until 1924; **People's Republic of Mongolia** until 1991)

area 604,480 sq mi/1,565,000 sq km
capital Ulaanbaatar
cities Darhan, Choybalsan
physical high plateau with desert and steppe (grasslands)
features Altai Mountains in SW; salt lakes; part of Gobi Desert in SE
head of state Punsalmaagiyn Ochirbat from 1990
head of government Puntsagiyn Jasray from 1992
political system emergent democracy
political parties Mongolian People's Revolutionary Party (MPRP), reform-communist; Mongolian Democratic Party (MDP), main opposition party; Mongolian Democratic Union

exports meat and hides, minerals, wool, livestock, grain, cement, timber
currency tugrik
population (1990 est) 2,185,000; growth rate 2.8% p.a.
life expectancy men 63, women 67 (1989)
languages Khalkha Mongolian (official), Chinese, Russian, and Turkic languages
religion officially none (Tibetan Buddhist Lamaism suppressed 1930s)
literacy 89% (1985)
GNP $3.6 bn; $1,820 per head (1986)
chronology
1911 Outer Mongolia gained autonomy from China.
1915 Chinese sovereignty reasserted.
1921 Chinese rule overthrown with Soviet help.
1924 People's Republic proclaimed.
1946 China recognized Mongolia's independence.
1966 20-year friendship, cooperation, and mutual-assistance pact signed with USSR. Relations with China deteriorated.
1984 Yumjaagiyn Tsedenbal, effective leader, deposed and replaced by Jambyn Batmonh.
1987 Soviet troops reduced; Mongolia's external contacts broadened.
1989 Further Soviet troop reductions.
1990 Democratization campaign launched by Mongolian Democratic Union. Ochirbat's MPRP elected in free multiparty elections. Mongolian script readopted.
1991 Massive privatization program launched as part of move toward a market economy. The word "Republic" dropped from country's name.
1992 Jan: New constitution introduced. Economic situation worsened. Prime minister Dashiyn Byambasuren's resignation refused. July: Puntsagiyn Jasray appointed new prime minister.

The Mongols are primarily pastoral nomads, herding sheep, horses, cattle, and camels. Traditionally the Mongols moved with their animals in summer to the higher pastures, returning in winter to the lower steppes. The government of Mongolia now encourages more sedentary forms of pastoralism, and winter quarters are often more permanent. About 60% of the Mongolian population live in felt-covered domed tents known as gers. Many Mongols are Buddhist, although the Mongolian government has been communist since 1924. During the 13th century AD, under Genghis Khan, the Mongols conquered central Asia and attacked E Europe. Kublai Khan, the grandson of Genghis Khan, was the first emperor of the Yuan dynasty (1279–1368) in China.

Mongol Empire empire established by Genghis Khan, who extended his domains from Russia to N China and became khan of the Mongol tribes 1206. His grandson Kublai Khan conquered China and used foreigners such as Marco Polo as well as subjects to administer his empire. The Mongols lost China 1367 and suffered defeats in the West 1380; the empire broke up soon afterwards.

Mongolia country in E Central Asia, bounded N by Russia and S by China.
government Under the 1992 constitution, the parliament, the 430-member People's Great Hural (assembly), is elected for a six-year term. Political parties within the Great Hural nominate candidates for the presidency, to be elected to four-year terms. Presidential vetoes of legislation may be overturned by a majority vote in the Great Hural.

history Inhabited by nomads from N Asia, the area was united under Genghis Khan 1206 and by the end of the 13th century was part of the Mongol empire that stretched across Asia. From 1689 it was part of China.

After the revolution of 1911–12 Mongolia became autonomous under the Lamaist religious ruler Jebsten Damba Khutukhtu. From 1915 it increasingly fell under Chinese influence and not until 1921, with the support of the USSR, were Mongolian nationalists able to cast off the Chinese yoke.

"Sovietization" In 1924 it adopted the Soviet system of government and, after proclaiming itself a people's republic, launched a program of "defeudalization," involving the destruction of Lamaism. In 1931, when two provinces revolted against the Communist Party, religious buildings were destroyed and mass executions carried out on the orders of the Soviet dictator Stalin. An armed uprising by antigovernment forces 1932 was suppressed with Soviet assistance. China recognized its independence 1946, but relations deteriorated as Mongolia took the Soviet side in the Sino-Soviet dispute. In 1966 Mongolia signed a 20-year friendship, cooperation and mutual-assistance pact with the USSR, and some 60,000 Soviet troops based in the country caused China to see it as a Russian colony.

economic change Isolated from the outside world during the 1970s, under the leadership of Yumjaagiyn Tsedenbal (1916–1991)—the nation's dominant figure from 1958—Mongolia underwent great economic change as urban industries developed and settled agriculture on the collective system spread, with new areas being brought under cultivation. Tsedenbal was deposed 1984.

foreign contact and influence After the accession to power in the USSR of Mikhail Gorbachev, Mongolia was encouraged to broaden its outside contacts. Cultural exchanges with China increased, diplomatic relations were established with the US, and between 1987 and 1990 the number of Soviet troops stationed in the country was reduced from 80,000 to 15,000. Influenced by events in Eastern Europe, an opposition grouping, the Mongolian Democratic Union, was illegally formed Dec 1989 and during 1990 it spearheaded a campaign demanding greater democratization.

multiparty system introduced Free multiparty national elections and local municipal and people's hurals were held July 1990. The MPRP secured 83% of the seats of the central parliament and 62% of the seats in the Little Hural. The principal opposition body, the Democratic Party (MDP), led by Erdenijn Bat-Uul, captured only 5% of the seats. In Sept 1990 the new assembly elected the MPRP's Punsalmaagiyn Ochirbat as president and Dashiyn Byambasuren as prime minister. In March 1991 Budragchaa Dashyondon was elected head of the MPRP to replace the allegedly too conservative Gombojavyn Ochirbat. In the wake of the anticommunist repercussions of the failed Aug 1991 anti-Gorbachev coup in the USSR, President Punsalmaagiyn Ochirbat resigned from the MPRP. In Aug 1991 twelve former members of the ruling MPRP were charged with corruption during their terms in office.

The government embarked on an ambitious but, in the short term, painful program to achieve the transition from central planning to a market economy by 1994. Prices were freed, the currency was massively devalued, a new banking system and stock exchange were established, privatizations began, and the country joined the International Monetary Fund and Asian Development Bank.

In June 1991, the word "Republic" was dropped from the name and in Oct 1991 a law was passed providing for the private ownership of land. In Jan 1992 a new constitution came into force. Faced with a rapidly deteriorating economic situation, premier Byambasuren attempted to resign Jan, but his request was rejected. In June parliamentary elections the MPRP won a resounding victory, advocating and in July free-market economist Puntsagiyn Jasray was elected prime minister by an overwhelming majority. *See illustration box.*

Mongolia, Inner (Chinese *Nei Mongol*) autonomous region of NE China from 1947
area 173,700 sq mi/450,000 sq km
capital Hohhot
features strategic frontier area with Russia; known for Mongol herders, now becoming settled farmers
physical grassland and desert
products cereals under irrigation; coal; reserves of rare earth oxides europium, and yttrium at Bayan Obo
population (1990) 21,457,000.

mongolism former name (now considered offensive) for ◊Down's syndrome.

Mongoloid referring to one of the three major varieties (see ◊races) of humans, *Homo*

sapiens sapiens, including the indigenous peoples of Asia, the Indians of the Americas, Polynesians, and the Eskimos and Aleuts. General physical traits include dark eyes with epicanthic folds; straight to wavy dark hair; little beard or body hair; fair to tawny skin; low to medium-bridged noses; thin to medium lips. See also ◊Caucasoid, ◊Negroid.

mongoose any of various carnivorous mammals of the family Viverridae, especially the genus *Herpestes*. The Indian mongoose *H. mungo* is grayish in color and about 1.5 ft/50 cm long, with a long tail. It may be tamed and is often kept for its ability to kill snakes. The white-tailed mongoose *Ichneumia albicauda* of central Africa has a distinctive gray or white bushy tail.

monism in philosophy, the theory that reality is made up of only one substance. This view is usually contrasted with ◊dualism, which divides reality into two substances, matter and mind. The Dutch philosopher Baruch Spinoza saw the one substance as God or Nature. Monism is also sometimes used as a description of a political system in which only one party is permitted to operate.

monitor any of various lizards of the family Varanidae, found in Africa, S Asia, and Australasia. Monitors are generally large and carnivorous, with well-developed legs and claws and a long powerful tail that can be swung in defense.

Monitors include the Komodo dragon, the largest of all lizards, and also the slimmer Salvador's monitor *Varanus salvadorii*, which may reach 8 ft/2.5 m. Several other monitors, such as the lace monitor *Varanus varius*, the perentie *Varanus giganteus* of Australia, and the Nile monitor *Varanus niloticus* of Africa, are up to 6 ft/2 m long.

monk man belonging to a religious order under the vows of poverty, chastity, and obedience, and living under a particular rule; see ◊monasticism.

Monk Thelonious (Sphere) 1917–1982. US jazz pianist and composer who took part in the development of ◊bebop. He had a highly idiosyncratic style, but numbers such as "Round Midnight" and "Blue Monk" have become standards.

Monk worked in Harlem, New York, during the Depression, and became popular in the 1950s.

monkey any of the various smaller, mainly tree-dwelling anthropoid primates, excluding humans and the ◊apes. The 125 species live in Africa, Asia, and tropical Central and South America. Monkeys eat mainly leaves and fruit, and also small animals. Several species are endangered due to loss of forest habitat, for example the woolly spider monkey and black saki of the Amazonian forest.

Old World monkeys, family Cercopithecidae, of tropical Africa and Asia are distinguished by their close-set nostrils and differentiated thumbs, some also having cheek pouches and rumps with bare patches (callosities) of hardened skin. They include ◊baboons, ◊langurs, ◊macaques, and guenons.

New World monkeys of Central and South America are characterized by wide-set nostrils, and some have highly sensitive prehensile tails. They include two families:
(1) the family Cebidae, which includes the larger species saki, ◊capuchin, squirrel, howler, and spider monkeys;

(2) the family Callithricidae, which includes the small ◊marmosets and tamarins.

monkey puzzle or **Chilean pine** coniferous evergreen tree *Araucaria araucana* (see ◊araucaria), native to Chile; it has whorled branches covered in prickly leaves of a leathery texture.

Monmouth James Scott, Duke of Monmouth 1649–1685. Claimant to the English crown, the illegitimate son of Charles II and Lucy Walter. After James II's accession 1685, Monmouth landed in England at Lyme Regis, Dorset, claimed the crown, and raised a rebellion, which was crushed at Sedgemoor in Somerset. He was executed with 320 of his accomplices.

When ◊James II converted to Catholicism, the Whig opposition attempted unsuccessfully to secure Monmouth the succession to the crown by the Exclusion Bill, and having become implicated in a Whig conspiracy, the ◊Rye House Plot 1683, he fled to Holland.

Monnet Jean 1888–1979. French economist. The originator of Winston Churchill's offer of union between the UK and France 1940, he devised and took charge of the French modernization program under Charles de Gaulle 1945. In 1950 he produced the "Shuman Plan" initiating the coordination of European coal and steel production in the European Coal and Steel Community (ECSC), which developed into the Common Market (EC).

monocarpic or **hapaxanthic** describing plants that flower and produce fruit only once during their lifecycle, after which they die. Most ◊annual plants and ◊biennial plants are monocarpic, but there are also a small number of monocarpic ◊perennial plants that flower just once, sometimes after as long as 90 years, dying shortly afterwards, for example, century plant *Agave* and some species of bamboo *Bambusa*. The general biological term related to organisms that reproduce only once during their lifetime is ◊semelparity.

monoclonal antibody (MAB) antibody produced by fusing an antibody-producing lymphocyte with a cancerous myeloma (bone-marrow) cell. The resulting fused cell, called a hybridoma, is immortal and can be used to produce large quantities of a single, specific antibody. By choosing antibodies that are directed against antigens found on cancer cells, and combining them with cytotoxic drugs, it is hoped to make so-called magic bullets that will be able to pick out and kill cancers.

It is the antigens on the outer cell walls of germs entering the body that provoke the production of antibodies as a first line of defense against disease. Antibodies "recognize" these foreign antigens, and, in locking on to them, cause the release of chemical signals in the bloodstream to alert the immune system for further action. MABs are copies of these natural antibodies, with the same ability to recognize specific antigens. Introduced into the body, they can be targeted at disease sites.

The full potential of these biological missiles, developed by César ◊Milstein and others at Cambridge University, England, 1975, is still under investigation. However, they are already in use in blood-grouping, in pinpointing viruses and other sources of disease, in tracing cancer sites, and in developing vaccines.

monocotyledon angiosperm (flowering plant) having an embryo with a single cotyledon, or seed leaf (as opposed to ◊dicotyledons, which have two). Monocotyledons usually have narrow leaves with parallel veins and smooth edges, and hollow or soft stems. Their flower parts are arranged in threes. Most are small plants such as orchids, grasses, and lilies, but some are trees such as palms.

monoculture farming system where only one crop is grown. In Third World countries this is often a ♢cash crop, grown on ♢plantations. Cereal crops in the industrialized world are also frequently grown on a monoculture basis; for example, wheat in the Canadian prairies.

Monoculture allows the farmer to tailor production methods to the requirements of one crop, but it is a high-risk strategy since the crop may fail (because of pests, disease, or bad weather) and world prices for the crop may fall. Monoculture without ♢crop rotation is likely to result in reduced soil quality despite the addition of artificial fertilizers, and it contributes to ♢soil erosion.

Monod Jacques 1910–1976. French biochemist who shared the 1965 Nobel Prize for Medicine (with two colleagues) for research in genetics and microbiology.

monody in music, declamation by accompanied solo voice, used at the turn of the 16th and 17th centuries.

monoecious having separate male and female flowers on the same plant. Maize (*Zea mays*), for example, has a tassel of male flowers at the top of the stalk and a group of female flowers (on the ear, or cob) lower down. Monoecism is a way of avoiding self-fertilization. ♢Dioecious plants have male and female flowers on separate plants.

monogamy practice of having only one husband or wife at a time in ♢marriage.

monohybrid inheritance pattern of inheritance seen in simple ♢genetics experiments, where the two animals (or two plants) being crossed are genetically identical except for one gene.

This gene may code for some obvious external features such as seed color, with one parent having green seeds and the other having yellow seeds. The offspring are monohybrids, that is, hybrids for one gene only, having received one copy of the gene from each parent. Known as the F1 generation, they are all identical, and usually resemble one parent, whose version of the gene (the dominant ♢allele) masks the effect of the other version (the recessive allele). Although the characteristic coded for by the recessive allele (for example, green seeds) completely disappears in this generation, it can reappear in offspring of the next generation if they have two recessive alleles. On average, this will occur in one out of four offspring from a cross between two of the monohybrids. The next generation (called F2) show a 3:1 ratio for the characteristic in question, 75% being like the original parent with the recessive allele. Gregor ♢Mendel first carried out experiments of this type (crossing varieties of artificially bred plants, such as peas) and they revealed the principles of genetics. The same basic mechanism underlies all inheritance, but in most plants and animals there are so many genetic differences interacting to produce the external appearance (phenotype) that such simple, clear-cut patterns of inheritance are not evident.

mononucleosis viral disease (also called "kissing disease," since it may be passed by body fluids, including saliva) characterized at onset by fever and painfully swollen lymph nodes (in the neck); there may also be digestive upset, sore throat, and skin rashes. Lassitude persists for months and even years, and recovery is often very slow. It is caused by the Epstein-Barr virus. A serious to fatal complication may be hepatitis.

Monophysite (Greek "one-nature") member of a group of Christian heretics of the 5th–7th centuries who taught that Jesus had one nature, in opposition to the orthodox doctrine (laid down at the Council of Chalcedon 451) that he had two natures, the human and the divine. Monophysitism developed as a reaction to ♢Nestorianism and led to the formal secession of the Coptic and Armenian churches from the rest of the Christian church. Monophysites survive today in Armenia, Syria, and Egypt.

monopoly in economics, the domination of a market for a particular product or service by a single company, which therefore has no competition and can keep prices high. In practice, a company can be said to have a monopoly when it controls a significant proportion of the market (technically an ♢oligopoly).

In the US, antitrust legislation has been used vigorously to break up and/or prevent the growth of monopolies. Even some closely regulated monopolies, such as the American Telegraph & Telephone Company, have been broken up to ensure competition. A monopsony is a situation in which there is only one buyer; for example, most governments are the only legal purchasers of military equipment inside their countries.

monorail railroad that runs on a single rail; the cars can be balanced on it or suspended from it. It was invented 1882 to carry light loads, and when run by electricity was called a *telpher*.

The Wuppertal Schwebebahn, which has been running in Germany since 1901, is a suspension monorail, where the passenger cars hang from an arm fixed to a trolley that runs along the rail. Today most monorails are of the straddle type, where the passenger cars run on top of the rail. They are used to transport passengers between terminals at some airports; Japan has a monorail (1964) running from the city center to Hameda airport.

monosaccharide or *simple sugar* ♢carbohydrate that cannot be hydrolyzed (split) into smaller carbohydrate units. Examples are glucose and fructose, both of which have the molecular formula $C_6H_{12}O_6$.

monosodium glutamate (MSG) $NaC_5H_8NO_4$ a white, crystalline powder, the sodium salt of glutamic acid (an ♢amino acid found in proteins that plays a role in the metabolism of plants and animals). It is used to enhance the flavor of many packaged and "fast foods," and in Chinese cooking. Ill effects may arise from its overconsumption, and some people are very sensitive to it, even in small amounts. It is commercially derived from vegetable protein.

monotheism belief or doctrine that there is only one God; the opposite of polytheism.

It is the unifying theme of the Old Testament.

Monothelite member of a group of Christian heretics of the 7th century who sought to reconcile the orthodox and ♢Monophysite theologies by maintaining that, while Christ possessed two natures, he had only one will. Monothelitism was condemned as a heresy by the Third Council of Constantinople 680.

monotreme any member of the order Monotremata, the only living egg-laying mammals, found in Australasia. They include the echidnas and the platypus.

Monroe city in NE Louisiana, on the Ouachita River, E of Shreveport; industries include furniture, chemicals, paper, natural gas, and soybeans; population (1990) 54,900.

Monroe James 1758–1831. 5th president of the US 1817–25, a Democratic Republican. He served in the American Revolution, was minister to France 1794–96, and in 1803 negotiated the ♢Louisiana Purchase. He was secretary of state 1811–17. His name is associated with the ♢Monroe Doctrine.

Monroe was born in Westmoreland County, Virginia. He attended the College of William and Mary and studied law under his lifelong friend Thomas ♢Jefferson. Monroe served in the Virginia legislature 1782, in the US Senate 1790–94, and as governor of Virginia 1799–1802. During the Constitutional Convention he opposed ratification, fearing a central government with excessive power. As president, he presided over the so-called Era of Good Feeling, a period of domestic tranquility. He took no firm stand on the question of slavery, making his mark in foreign policy.

Monroe Marilyn. Adopted name of Norma Jean Mortenson or Baker 1926–1962. US film actress, the voluptuous blonde sex symbol of the 1950s, who made adroit comedies such as *Gentlemen Prefer Blondes* 1953, *How to Marry a Millionaire* 1953, *The Seven Year Itch* 1955, *Bus Stop* 1956, and *Some Like It Hot* 1959. Her second husband was baseball star Joe di Maggio, and her third was playwright Arthur ♢Miller, who wrote *The Misfits* 1961 for her, a serious film that became her last. She committed suicide, taking an overdose of sleeping pills.

Monroe Doctrine declaration by US president James Monroe 1823 that any further European colonial ambitions in the western hemisphere would be threats to US peace and security, made in response to proposed European intervention against newly independent former Spanish colonies in South America. In return the US would not interfere in European affairs. The doctrine, subsequently broadened, has been a recurrent theme in US foreign policy, although it has no basis in US or international law.

At the time of the declaration, the US was militarily incapable of enforcing its sweeping proclamations. The impetus for and the power behind the doctrine came from the British, whose commercial interests were at risk in the event of a Franco-Spanish reassertion of colonial influence. President Theodore ♢Roosevelt drew on the doctrine to proclaim a US right to intervene in the internal affairs of Latin American states.

Monrovia capital and port of Liberia; population (1985) 500,000. Industries include rubber, cement, and gasoline processing.

It was founded 1821 for slaves repatriated from the US. Originally called *Christopolis*, it was renamed after US president James Monroe.

Mons (Flemish *Bergen*) industrial city (coal-mining, textiles, sugar) and capital of the province of Hainaut, Belgium; population (1991) 91,700. The military headquarters of NATO is at nearby Chièvres-Casteau.

Monsarrat Nicholas 1910–1979. English novelist who served with the navy in the Battle of

Montana

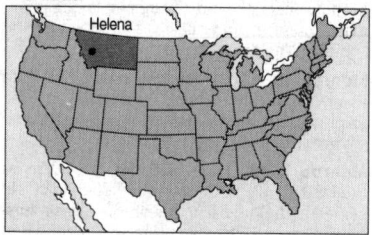

Helena

the ⬡Atlantic Ocean, the subject of his book *The Cruel Sea* 1951.

monsoon wind system that dominates the climate of a wide region, with seasonal reversals of direction; in particular, the wind in S Asia that blows toward the sea in winter and toward the land in summer, bringing heavy rain. The monsoon may cause destructive flooding all over India and SE Asia from April to Sept. Thousands of people are rendered homeless each year. The Guinea monsoon is a southwesterly wind that blows in W Africa from April to Sept, throughout the rainy season.

monstera or *Swiss cheese plant* evergreen climbing plant, genus *Monstera*, of the arum family Araceae, native to tropical America. *M. deliciosa* is cultivated as a house plant. Areas between the veins of the leaves dry up, creating deep marginal notches and ultimately holes.

Montagnard member of a group in the legislative assembly and National Convention convened after the ⬡French Revolution. They supported the more extreme aims of the revolution, and were destroyed as a political force after the fall of Robespierre 1794.

Montagu Ashley 1905– . British-born US anthropologist. A strong critic of theories of racial determinism, Montagu became a forceful defender of human rights, as evidenced in writings such as *Man's Most Dangerous Myth: The Fallacy of Race* 1942. In 1950 he helped draft the definitive UNESCO "Statement on Race." He became well known for popularizing social issues, such as "psychoclerosis," the so-called hardening of the psyche, in *Growing Young* 1981.

Montaigne Michel Eyquem de 1533–1592. French writer, regarded as the creator of the essay form. In 1580 he published the first two volumes of his *Essais*; the third volume appeared in 1588. Montaigne deals with all aspects of life from an urbanely skeptical viewpoint. Through the translation by John Florio in 1603, he influenced Shakespeare and other English writers.

He was born at the Château de Montaigne near Bordeaux, studied law, and in 1554 became a counselor of the Bordeaux *parlement*. Little is known of his earlier life, except that he regularly visited Paris and the court of Francis II. In 1571 he retired to his estates, relinquishing his magistracy. He toured Germany, Switzerland, and Italy 1580–81, returning upon his election as mayor of Bordeaux, a post he held until 1585.

Montale Eugenio 1896–1981. Italian poet and writer. His pessimistic poetry, for which he was awarded a Nobel Prize in 1975, includes *Ossi di seppia/Cuttlefish bones* 1925 and *Le Occasioni/Occasions* 1939. In 1989 it was revealed that much of his literary journalism, such as his regular column in the *Corriere della Sera* newspaper, was in fact written by an American, Henry Frost.

Montana state of the W US, on the Canadian border; nickname Treasure State
area 147,143 sq mi/318,100 sq km
capital Helena
cities Billings, Great Falls, Butte
physical mountainous forests in the west, rolling grasslands in the east
features rivers: Missouri, Yellowstone, Little Bighorn; Glacier National Park on the Continental Divide and Yellowstone National Park; Museum of the Plains Indian; Custer Battlefield National Monument; hunting and ski resorts
products wheat (under irrigation), cattle, coal, copper, oil, natural gas, lumber, wood products
population (1990) 799,100
famous people Gary Cooper, Myrna Loy
history explored for France by Verendrye early 1740s; passed to the US 1803 in the Louisiana Purchase; first settled 1809; W Montana obtained from Britain in the Oregon Treaty 1846; influx of gold-seeking immigrants mid-19th century; fierce Indian wars 1867–77, which included "Custer's Last Stand" at the Little Bighorn with the Sioux; achieved statehood 1889.

Energy production, in the form of oil, natural gas, and strip-mined coal, has replaced precious metals and copper in mineral exploitation. The plains area still produces grain crops, sheep, and cattle.

Montana Joe 1956– . US football player who has appeared in four winning Super Bowls as quarterback for the San Francisco 49ers 1982, 1985, 1989, and 1990, winning the Most Valuable Player award in 1982, 1985, and 1990. He threw a record five touchdown passes in the 1990 Super Bowl.

He graduated from Notre Dame University, where he led his team to the national college championship 1978. He was the leading passer in the National Football Conference 1981, 1984, and 1985. He recovered from a serious back injury in 1986 to become the leading passer in the National Football League 1987, setting league records for touchdowns thrown (31) and consecutive completions (22). In the 1989 Super Bowl, he set a record for passing yardage and the most passes without an interception (33).

Montand Yves 1921–1991. French actor and singer who achieved fame in the thriller *Le Salaire de la peur/The Wages of Fear* 1953 and continued to be popular in French and American films, including *Let's Make Love* 1960 (with Marilyn Monroe), *Le Sauvage/The Savage* 1976, *Jean de Florette* 1986, and *Manon des sources* 1986.

Montanism movement within the early Christian church that strove to return to the purity of primitive Christianity. It originated in Phrygia in about 156 with the teaching of a prophet named Montanus, and spread to Anatolia, Rome, Carthage, and Gaul. The theologian ⬡Tertullian was a Montanist.

Mont Blanc (Italian *Monte Bianco*) highest mountain in the ⬡Alps, between France and Italy; height 15,772 ft/4,807 m. It was first climbed 1786.

montbretia European plant *Tritonia crocosmiflora* of the iris family Iridaceae, native to South Africa, with orange or reddish flowers on long stems.

Montcalm Louis-Joseph de Montcalm-Gozon, Marquis de 1712–1759. French general, appointed military commander in Canada 1756.

He won a succession of victories over the British during the French and Indian War, but was defeated in 1759 by James ⬡Wolfe at Québec, where both he and Wolfe were killed; this battle marked the end of French rule in Canada.

Monte Bello Islands group of uninhabited islands in the Indian Ocean, off Western Australia, used by the UK for nuclear-weapons testing 1952; the largest of the group is Barrow Island.

Monte Carlo town and luxury resort in ⬡Monaco, known for its casino (opened 1861) and the Monte Carlo car rally and Monaco Grand Prix; population (1982) 12,000.

Montego Bay port and resort on the NW coast of Jamaica; population (1982) 70,200.

Montenegrin Slavic inhabitant of Montenegro (Yugoslavia) whose culture has much in common with the Serbs.

Montenegro (Serbo-Croatian *Crna Gora*) constituent republic of Yugoslavia
area 5,327 sq mi/13,800 sq km
capital Titograd
town Cetinje
features smallest of the republics; Skadarsko Jezero (Lake Scutari) shared with Albania
physical mountainous
population (1986) 620,000, including 400,000 Montenegrins, 80,000 Muslims, and 40,000 Albanians
language Serbian variant of Serbo-Croat
religion Serbian Orthodox
famous people Milovan Djilas
history part of ⬡Serbia from the late 12th century, it became independent (under Venetian protection) after Serbia was defeated by the Turks 1389. It was forced to accept Turkish suzerainty in the late 15th century, but was never completely subdued by Turkey. It was ruled by bishop princes until 1851, when a monarchy was founded, and became a sovereign principality under the Treaty of Berlin 1878. The monarch used the title of king from 1910 with Nicholas I (1841–1921). Montenegro participated in the Balkan Wars 1912 and 1913. It was overrun by Austria in World War I, and in 1918 voted after the deposition of King Nicholas to become part of Serbia. In 1946 Montenegro became a republic of Yugoslavia. In a referendum March 1992 Montengrins voted to remain part of the Yugoslav federation; the referendum was boycotted by Montenegro's Muslim and Albanian communities.

In Jan 1989 the entire Communist Party leadership resigned after mass protests which secured the replacement of the party and state leaderships. The republic held multiparty elections for the first time in Dec 1990; the League of Communists of Montenegro remained in power. A staunch ally of Serbia, Montenegro sided with Serbia in the 1991 conflict with Slovenia and Croatia and approved a Serbian plan which called for a new, overwhelmingly Serb, Yugoslav federation Aug 1991. Montenegro is the poorest of the Yugoslav republics and had 25% unemployment 1990.

Monterey fishing port on Monterey Bay in California, once the state capital; population (1990) 32,000. It is the setting for John Steinbeck's novels *Cannery Row* 1945 and *Tortilla Flat* 1935, dealing with migrant fruit workers.

Monterrey industrial city (iron, steel, textiles, chemicals, food processing) in NE Mexico; population (1986) 2,335,000. It was founded 1597.

Montespan Françoise-Athénaïs de Rochechouart, Marquise de Montespan 1641–1707. Mistress of Louis XIV of France from 1667. They had seven children, for whom she engaged as governess the future Madame de ◊Maintenon, who later supplanted her. She retired to a convent in 1691.

Montesquieu Charles Louis de Secondat, baron de la Brède 1689–1755. French philosophical historian, author of the *Lettres persanes/Persian Letters* 1721. *De l'Esprit des lois/The Spirit of the Laws* 1748, a 31-volume philosophical disquisition on politics and sociology as well as legal matters, advocated the separation of powers within government, a doctrine that became the basis of liberal constitutions.

Born near Bordeaux, Montesquieu became adviser to the Bordeaux parliament 1714. After the success of *Lettres persanes*, he adopted a literary career, writing *Considérations sur les causes de la grandeur des Romains et de leur décadence/Considerations on the Greatness and Decadence of the Romans* 1734.

Montessori Maria 1870–1952. Italian educator. From her experience with mentally handicapped children, she developed the *Montessori method*, an educational system for all children based on an informal approach, incorporating instructive play and allowing children to develop at their own pace.

Monteux Pierre 1875–1964. French conductor. Ravel's *Daphnis and Chloe* and Stravinsky's *Rite of Spring* were first performed under his direction. He conducted Sergei ◊Diaghilev's Ballets Russes 1911–14 and 1917, and the San Francisco Symphony Orchestra 1935–52.

Monteverdi Claudio (Giovanni Antonio) 1567–1643. Italian composer. He contributed to the development of the opera with *Orfeo* 1607 and *The Coronation of Poppea* 1642. He also wrote madrigals, ◊motets, and sacred music, notably the *Vespers* 1610.

Montevideo capital and chief port (grain, meat products, hides) of Uruguay, on the Río de la Plata; population (1985) 1,250,000. It was founded 1726.

Montez Lola. Adopted name of Maria Gilbert 1818–1861. Irish actress and dancer. She appeared on the stage as a Spanish dancer, and in 1847 became the mistress of King Ludwig I of Bavaria, whose policy she dictated for a year. Her liberal sympathies led to her banishment through Jesuit influence in 1848. She died in poverty in the US.

Montezuma II 1466–1520. Aztec emperor 1502–20. When the Spanish conquistador Cortés invaded Mexico, Montezuma was imprisoned and killed during the Aztec attack on Cortés's force as it tried to leave Tenochtitlán, the Aztec capital city.

Montfort Simon de Montfort, Earl of Leicester *c.* 1208–1265. English politician and soldier. From 1258 he led the baronial opposition to Henry III's misrule during the second ◊Barons' War and in 1264 defeated and captured the king at Lewes, Sussex. In 1265, as head of government, he summoned the first parliament in which the towns were represented; he was killed at the Battle of Evesham during the last of the Barons' Wars.

Montgolfier Joseph Michel 1740–1810 and Etienne Jacques 1745–1799. French brothers whose hot-air balloon was used for the first successful human flight Nov 21, 1783.

They were papermakers of Annonay, near Lyon, where on June 5, 1783 they first sent up a balloon filled with hot air. After further experiments with wood-fueled paper balloons, they went aloft themselves for 20 minutes above Paris. The Montgolfier experiments greatly stimulated scientific interest in aviation.

Montgomery state capital of Alabama; population (1990) 187,100. The *Montgomery Bus Boycott* 1955 began here when a black passenger, Rosa Parks, refused to give up her seat to a white. Led by Martin Luther ◊King, Jr, the boycott was a landmark in the civil-rights campaign.

Two settlements on the site of the present-day city were consolidated 1819. Montgomery was the capital of the Confederacy in the first months of the American Civil War.

Montgomery Bernard Law, 1st Viscount Montgomery of Alamein 1887–1976. British field marshal. In World War II he commanded the 8th Army in N Africa in the Second Battle of El ◊Alamein 1942. As commander of British troops in N Europe from 1944, he received the German surrender 1945.

At the start of World War II he commanded part of the British Expeditionary Force in France 1939–40 and took part in the evacuation from Dunkirk. In Aug 1942 he took command of the 8th Army, then barring the German advance on Cairo; the victory of El ◊Alamein in Oct turned the tide in N Africa and was followed by the expulsion of Field Marshal Rommel from Egypt and rapid Allied advance into Tunisia. In Feb 1943 Montgomery's forces came under US general Eisenhower's command, and they took part in the conquest of Tunisia and Sicily and the invasion of Italy. Montgomery was promoted to field marshal in 1944. In 1948 he became permanent military chair of the Commanders-in-Chief Committee for W European defense, and 1951–58 was deputy Supreme Commander Europe. Created 1st Viscount Montgomery of Alamein 1946.

Montgomery Robert (Henry) 1904–1981. US film actor of the 1930s and 1940s. He directed some of his later films, such as *Lady in the Lake* 1947, before turning to television and Republican politics. His other films include *Night Must Fall* 1937 and *Mr and Mrs Smith* 1941.

month unit of time based on the motion of the Moon around the Earth. The time from one new or full Moon to the next (the **synodic** or **lunar month**) is 29.53 days. The time for the Moon to complete one orbit around the Earth relative to the stars (the **sidereal month**) is 27.32 days. The **solar month** equals 30.44 days, and is exactly one-twelfth of the solar or tropical year, the time taken for the Earth to orbit the Sun. The **calendar month** is a human invention, devised to fit the calendar year.

Montherlant Henri Millon de 1896–1972. French author. He was a Nazi sympathizer. His novels, which are marked by an obsession with the physical, include *Aux Fontaines du désir/To the Fountains of Desire* 1927 and *Pitié pour les femmes/Pity for Women* 1936. His most critically acclaimed work is *Le Chaos et la nuit/Chaos and Night* 1963.

Montmartre district of Paris, France, dominated by the basilica of Sacré Coeur 1875. It is situated in the N of the city on a 400 ft/120 m high hill.

Montparnasse district of Paris, France, frequented by artists and writers. The Pasteur Institute is also here.

Montpelier capital of Vermont, in the Green Mountains in the central part of the state, on the Winooski River; industries include granite, insurance, and tourism; population (1990) 8,200.

Montréal inland port, industrial city (aircraft, chemicals, oil and petrochemicals, flour, sugar, brewing, meat packing) of Québec, on Montreal island at the junction of the Ottawa and St Lawrence rivers; population (1986) 2,921,000.

features Mont Réal (Mount Royal, 753 ft/230 m) overlooks the city; an artificial island in the St Lawrence (site of the international exhibition 1967); three universities; except for Paris, the world's largest French-speaking city

history Jacques ◊Cartier reached the site 1535, Samuel de ◊Champlain established a trading post 1611, and the original Ville Marie (later renamed Montréal) was founded 1642 by Paul de Chomédy, Sieur de Maisonneuve (1612–1676). It was the last town surrendered by France to Britain 1760. Nevertheless, when troops of the rebel Continental Congress occupied the city 1775–76, the citizens refused to be persuaded (even by a visit from Benjamin Franklin) to join the future US in its revolt against Britain.

Montreux winter resort in W Switzerland on Lake Geneva; population (1990) 19,900. It is the site of the island rock fortress of Chillon, where François Bonivard (commemorated by the poet Byron), prior of the Abbey of St Victor, was imprisoned 1530–36 for his opposition to the duke of Savoy. At the annual television festival (first held 1961), the premier award is the *Golden Rose of Montreux*.

Montreux, Convention of international agreement 1936 allowing Turkey to remilitarize the Dardenelles.

Mont St Michel islet in NW France converted to a peninsula by an artificial causeway; it has a Benedictine monastery, founded 708.

Montserrat volcanic island in the West Indies, one of the Leeward group, a British crown colony; capital Plymouth; area 42 sq mi/110 sq km; population (1985) 12,000. Practically all buildings were destroyed by hurricane Hugo Sept 1989.

Montserrat produces cotton, cotton-seed, coconuts, citrus and other fruits, and vegetables. Its first European visitor was Christopher ◊Columbus 1493, who named it after the mountain in Spain. It was first colonized by English and Irish settlers who moved from St Christopher 1632. The island became a British crown colony 1871.

Monza town in N Italy, known for its motor-racing circuit; population (1988) 123,000. Once the capital of the ◊Lombards, it preserves the Iron Crown of Lombardy in the 13th-century cathedral. Umberto I was assassinated here.

Moody Dwight Lyman 1837–1899. US evangelist. During the American Civil War, Moody worked with the Young Men's Christian Association (YMCA), providing medical and moral support to the troops. In the 1870s he became a popular evangelist, touring in company with organist Ira D Sankey. In Northfield, Massachusetts, Moody founded the Northfield Seminary (now School) for girls 1879 and the Mount Hermon School for boys 1881.

Born in East Northfield, Massachusetts, Moody moved to Boston as a young man and joined the Congregational Church 1856. Later settling in Chicago, he established a church school and devoted himself to preaching among the poor. In 1889 he founded the Chicago (later Moody) Bible Institute.

Moody Helen Wills married name of US tennis player Helen Newington ⟡Wills.

moon in astronomy, any natural ⟡satellite that orbits a planet. Mercury and Venus are the only planets in the Solar System that do not have moons.

Moon natural satellite of Earth, 2,160 mi/3,476 km in diameter, with a mass 0.012 (approximately one-eightieth) that of Earth. Its surface gravity is only 0.16 (one-sixth) that of Earth. Its average distance from Earth is 238,857 mi/384,404 km, and it orbits in a west-to-east direction every 27.32 days (the *sidereal month*). It spins on its axis with one side permanently turned toward Earth. The Moon has no atmosphere or water.

The Moon is illuminated by sunlight, and goes through a cycle of phases of shadow, waxing from *new* (dark) via *first quarter* (half Moon) to *full*, and waning back again to new every 29.53 days (the *synodic month*, also known as a *lunation*). On its sunlit side, temperatures reach 230°F/110°C, but during the two-week lunar night the surface temperature drops to –274°F/–170°C.

The origin of the Moon is still open to debate. Scientists suggest the following theories: that it split from the Earth; that it was a separate body captured by Earth's gravity; that it formed in orbit around Earth; or that it was formed from debris thrown off when a body the size of Mars struck Earth. Future exploration of the Moon may detect water permafrost, which could be located at the permanently shadowed lunar poles.

Much of our information about the Moon has been derived from photographs and measurements taken by US and Soviet Moon probes; from geological samples brought back by US Apollo astronauts and by Soviet Luna probes; and from experiments set up by the US astronauts 1969–72. The Moon's composition is rocky, with a surface heavily scarred by ⟡meteorite impacts that have formed craters up to 150 mi/240 km across. Rocks brought back by astronauts show the Moon is 4.6 billion years old, the same age as Earth. It differs from Earth in that most of the Moon's surface features were formed within the first billion years of its history when it was hit repeatedly by meteorites. The youngest craters are surrounded by bright rays of ejected rock. The largest scars have been filled by dark lava to produce the lowland plains called seas, or *maria* (plural of ⟡mare). These dark patches form the so-called "man-in-the-Moon" pattern.

Moon Sun Myung 1920–   . Korean industrialist and founder of the ⟡Unification Church (*Moonies*) 1954. From 1973 he launched a major mission in the US and elsewhere. The church has been criticized for its manipulative methods of recruiting and keeping members. He was convicted of tax fraud in the US 1982.

Moon has allegedly been associated with extreme right-wing organizations, arms manufacture, and the Korean Central Intelligence Agency.

Moonie popular name for a follower of the ⟡Unification Church, a religious sect founded by Sun Myung Moon.

Moon probe crewless spacecraft used to investigate the Moon. Early probes flew past the Moon or crash-landed on it, but later ones achieved soft landings or went into orbit. Soviet probes included the Luna/Lunik series. US probes (Ranger, Surveyor, Lunar Orbiter) prepared the way for the Apollo crewed flights.

The first space probe to hit the Moon was the Soviet *Lunik 2*, on Sept 13, 1959 (*Lunik 1* had missed the Moon eight months earlier). In Oct 1959, *Lunik 3* sent back the first photographs of the Moon's far side. *Lunik 9* was the first probe to soft-land on the Moon, on Feb 3, 1966, transmitting photographs of the surface to Earth. *Lunik 16* was the first probe to return automatically to Earth carrying Moon samples, in Sept 1970, although by then Moon rocks had already been brought back by US ⟡Apollo astronauts who had landed on the Moon on July 20, 1969 and in Nov 1969. *Lunik 17* landed in Nov 1970 carrying a lunar rover, Lunokhod, which was driven over the Moon's surface by remote control from Earth.

The first successful US Moon probe was *Ranger 7*, which took close-up photographs before it hit the Moon on July 31, 1964. *Surveyor 1*, on June 2, 1966, was the first US probe to soft-land on the lunar surface. It took photographs, and later Surveyors analyzed the surface rocks. Between 1966 and 1967 a series of five Lunar Orbiters photographed the entire Moon in detail, in preparation for the Apollo landings, when Neil Armstrong and Edwin Aldrin became the first men to walk on the Moon.

moonstone translucent, pearly variety of potassium sodium ⟡feldspar, found in Sri Lanka and Myanmar, and distinguished by a blue, silvery, or red opalescent tint. It is valued as a gem.

Moor any of the NW African Muslims, of mixed Arab and Berber origin, who conquered Spain and ruled its southern part from 711 to 1492. The name (English form of Latin *Maurus*) was originally applied to an inhabitant of the Roman province of Mauritania, in NW Africa.

Moore Charles 1925–   . US architect with an eclectic approach to design. He was an early exponent of Postmodernism in, for example, his students' housing for Kresge College, University of California at Santa Cruz, 1973–74, and the Piazza d'Italia in New Orleans, 1975–78, which is one of the key monuments of Post-Modernism.

Sea Ranch, California 1964–65, one of his earliest projects, is in the vernacular timber tradition. At Kresge College he created a stage set of streets and fora. The Piazza d'Italia was built for the local Italian community and has a fountain in the shape of Italy.

Moore Dudley 1935–   . English actor, comedian, and musician, formerly teamed with comedian Peter Cook. Moore became a Hollywood star after appearing in "*10*" 1979. His other films, mostly comedies, include *Bedazzled* 1968, *Arthur* 1981, and *Santa Claus* 1985.

He has played Classical piano concerts, including Carnegie Hall.

Moore G(eorge) E(dward) 1873–1958. British philosopher. Educated at Trinity College, Cambridge University, he was professor of philosophy at the university 1925–39, and edited the journal *Mind*, to which he contributed 1921–47. His books include *Principia Ethica* 1903, in which he attempted to analyze the moral question "What is good?," and *Some Main Problems of Philosophy* 1953, but his chief influence was as a teacher.

Moore Henry 1898–1986. British sculptor. His subjects include the reclining nude, mother and child groups, the warrior, and interlocking abstract forms. Many of his post-1945 works are in bronze or marble, including monumental semiabstracts such as *Reclining Figure* 1957–58 (outside the UNESCO building, Paris), and often designed to be placed in landscape settings.

Moore claimed to have learned much from archaic South and Central American sculpture, and this is reflected in his work from the 1920s. By the early 1930s most of his main themes had emerged, and the Surrealists' preoccupation with organic forms in abstract works proved a strong influence; Moore's hollowed wooden shapes strung with wires date from the late 1930s. Abstract work suggesting organic structures recurs after World War II, for example in the interwoven bonelike forms of the *Hill Arches* and the bronze *Sheep Pieces* 1970s, set in fields by his studio in Hertfordshire.

Moore Marianne 1887–1972. US poet. She edited the literary magazine *The Dial* 1925–29, and published several volumes of witty and intellectual verse, including *Observations* 1924, *What are Years* 1941, and *A Marianne Moore Reader* 1961. She also published translations and essays. Her work is noted for its observation of detail. T S Eliot was an admirer of her poetry.

Moore Roger 1928–   . English actor who starred in the television series *The Saint* 1962–70, and assumed the film role of James Bond in 1973 in *Live and Let Die*.

His films include *Diane* 1955, *Gold* 1974, *The Wild Geese* 1978, and *Octopussy* 1983.

Moorhead city in W Minnesota, on the Red River, opposite Fargo, North Dakota; population (1990) 32,300. It is a center for an agricultural region that produces sugar beets, potatoes, grain, and dairy products.

moorhen marsh bird *Gallinula chloropus* of the rail family, common in water of swamps, lakes, and ponds in Eurasia, Africa, and North and South America. It is about 13 in/33 cm long, and mainly brown and gray, but with a red bill and forehead, and a vivid white underside to the tail. The big feet are not webbed or lobed, but the moorhen can swim well.

moose large ⟡deer *Alces alces* inhabiting N Asia and N Europe, where it is known as the elk. It is brown in color, stands about 6 ft/2 m at the shoulders, and has very large palmate antlers, a fleshy muzzle, a short neck, and long legs. It feeds on leaves and shoots.

Moose Jaw town in S Saskatchewan, with grain elevators, extensive stockyards, petroleum refineries; population (1985) 35,500.

moot legal and administrative assembly found in nearly every community in medieval England.

moraine rocky debris or ⟡till carried along and deposited by a ⟡glacier. Material eroded from the side of a glaciated valley and carried along the glacier's edge is called lateral moraine; that worn from the valley floor and carried along the base of the glacier is called ground moraine. Rubble dropped at the foot of a melting glacier is called terminal moraine.

When two glaciers converge their lateral moraines unite to form a medial moraine. Debris that has fallen down crevasses and become embedded in the ice is termed englacial moraine; when this is exposed at the surface due to partial melting it becomes ablation moraine.

morality play didactic medieval European verse drama, in part a development of the

⟁mystery play (or miracle play), in which human characters are replaced by personified virtues and vices, the limited humorous elements being provided by the Devil. Morality plays, such as *Everyman*, flourished in the 15th century. They exerted an influence on the development of Elizabethan drama and comedy.

Moravia (Czech *Morava*) district of central Europe, from 1960 two regions of Czechoslovakia:
South Moravia (Czech *Jihomoravský*)
area 5,802 sq mi/15,030 sq km
capital Brno
population (1991) 2,048,900.
North Moravia (Czech *Severomoravský*)
area 4,273 sq mi/11,070 sq km
capital Ostrava
population (1991) 1,961,500.
features (N and S) river Morava; 25% forested
products corn, grapes, wine in the south; wheat, barley, rye, flax, sugar beet in the north; coal and iron
history part of the Avar territory since the 6th century; conquered by Charlemagne's Holy Roman Empire. In 874 the kingdom of Great Moravia was founded by the Slavic prince Sviatopluk, who ruled until 894. It was conquered by the Magyars 906, and became a fief of Bohemia 1029. It was passed to the Hapsburgs 1526, and became an Austrian crown land 1849. It was incorporated in the new republic of Czechoslovakia 1918, forming a province until 1949.

Moravia Alberto. Adopted name of Alberto Pincherle 1907–1991. Italian novelist. His first successful novel was *Gli indifferenti/The Time of Indifference* 1929, but its criticism of Mussolini's regime led to the government censoring his work until after World War II. Later books include *La romana/Woman of Rome* 1947, *La ciociara/Two Women* 1957, and *La noia/The Empty Canvas* 1961, a study of an artist's obsession with his model.

Moravian member of a Christian Protestant sect, the *Moravian Brethren*. An episcopal church that grew out of the earlier Bohemian Brethren, it was established by the Lutheran Count Zinzendorf in Saxony 1722.

Persecution of the Bohemian Brethren began 1620, and they were held together mainly by the leadership of their bishop, Comenius. Driven out of Bohemia in 1722, they spread into Germany, England, and North America. In 1732 missionary work began.

It is an unworldly practice, in doctrine close to Lutheranism, with a simplified church hierarchy and liturgy. There are about 63,000 Moravians in the US.

Morazán Francisco 1792–1842. Central American politician, born in Honduras. He was elected president of the United Provinces of Central America in 1830. In the face of secessions he attempted to hold the union together by force but was driven out by the Guatemalan dictator Rafael Carrera. Morazán was eventually captured and executed in 1842.

Mordred in Arthurian legend, nephew and final opponent of King ⟁Arthur. What may be an early version of his name (Medraut) appears with Arthur in annals from the 10th century, listed under the year AD 537.

Mordvin Finnish people inhabiting the middle Volga Valley in W Asia. They are known to have lived in the region since the 1st century AD. There are 1 million speakers of Mordvin

scattered throughout W Russia, about one-third of whom live in the Mordvinian republic. Mordvin is a Finno-Ugric language belonging to the Uralic family.

Mordvinia or *Mordovia* autonomous republic of central Russia
area 10,100 sq mi/26,200 sq km
capital Saransk
features river Sura on the east; forested in the west
products sugar beet, grains, potatoes; sheep and dairy farming; timber, furniture, and textiles
population (1986) 964,000
language Russian, Mordvin
history Mordvinia was conquered by Russia during the 13th century. It was made an autonomous region 1930, and an Autonomous Soviet Socialist Republic 1934. It remained an autonomous republic of Russia after the dissolution of the Soviet Union 1991.

More (St) Thomas 1478–1535. English politician and author. From 1509 he was favored by ⟁Henry VIII and employed on foreign embassies. He was a member of the privy council from 1518 and Lord Chancellor from 1529 but resigned over Henry's break with the pope. For refusing to accept the king as head of the church, he was executed. The title of his political book *Utopia* 1516 has come to mean any supposedly perfect society.

Before his execution More was imprisoned in the Tower of London for a year. He was canonized in 1935.

Moreau Gustave 1826–1898. French Symbolist painter. His works are atmospheric: biblical, mythological, and literary scenes, richly colored and detailed; for example, *Salome Dancing Before Herod* 1876.

In the 1890s Moreau taught at the Ecole des Beaux-Arts in Paris, where his pupils included Matisse and Rouault. Much of his work is in the Musée Moreau, Paris.

Moreau Jean Victor Marie 1763–1813. French general in the Revolutionary Wars who won a brilliant victory over the Austrians at ⟁Hohenlinden 1800; as a republican he intrigued against Napoleon and, when banished, joined the Allies and was killed at the Battle of Dresden.

Moreau Jeanne 1928– . French actress who has appeared in international films, often in passionate, intelligent roles. Her work includes *Les Amants/The Lovers* 1958, *Jules et Jim/Jules and Jim* 1961, *Chimes at Midnight* 1966, and *Querelle* 1982.

morel any edible mushroom of the genus *Morchella*. The common morel *M. esculenta* grows in Europe and North America. The yellowish-brown cap is pitted like a sponge and about 1 in/2.5 cm long. It is used for seasoning gravies, soups, and sauces and is second only to the truffle as the world's most sought-after mushroom.

mores (Latin) the customs and manners of a society.

Morgagni Giovanni Battista 1682–1771. Italian anatomist. As professor of anatomy at Padua, Morgagni carried out more than 400 autopsies, and developed the view that disease was not an imbalance of the body's humors but a result of alterations in the organs. His work *On the Seats and Causes of Diseases as Investigated by Anatomy* 1761 formed the basis of ⟁pathology.

Morgan Henry *c.* 1635–1688. Welsh buccaneer in the Caribbean. He made war against

Spain, capturing and sacking Panama 1671. In 1674 he was knighted and appointed lieutenant governor of Jamaica.

Morgan J(ohn) P(ierpont) 1837–1913. US financier and investment banker whose company (sometimes criticized as "the money trust") became the most influential private banking house after the Civil War, being instrumental in the formation of many trusts to stifle competition. He set up the US Steel Corporation 1901 and International Harvester 1902.

They were powerful enough to bail out the Federal Reserve System 1895 and stabilized the economy after the crisis of 1907 when, in response to increasingly large US trust companies acting as banks under inadequate regulation, the Knickerbocker Trust Co. closed its doors to prevent a run on the firm Oct 22, 1907. Bailed out by Morgan and others, the panic was limited and its effects were not widespread.

Morgan Lewis Henry 1818–1881. US anthropologist who pioneered the study of NE American Indian culture and was adopted by the Iroquois.

Morgan Thomas Hunt 1866–1945. US geneticist, awarded the 1933 Nobel Prize for Medicine for his pioneering studies in Classical genetics. He was the first to work on the fruit fly *Drosophila*, which has since become a major subject of genetic studies. He helped establish that the genes were located on the chromosomes, discovered sex chromosomes, and invented the techniques of genetic mapping.

Morgan le Fay in the romance and legend of the English king ⟁Arthur, an enchantress and healer, ruler of ⟁Avalon and sister of the king, whom she tended after his final battle. In some versions of the legend she is responsible for the suspicions held by the king of his wife ⟁Guinevere.

Morgenthau Plan proposals for Germany after World War II, originated by Henry Morgenthau Jr (1891–1967), US secretary of the treasury, calling for the elimination of war industries in the Ruhr and Saar basins and the conversion of Germany "into a country primarily agricultural and pastoral in character." The plan had already been dropped by the time the Allied leaders Churchill, Roosevelt, and Stalin met at Yalta Feb 1945.

Morisco one of the Spanish Muslims and their descendants who accepted Christian baptism. They were all expelled from Spain in 1609.

Morley Edward 1838–1923. US physicist who collaborated with Albert ⟁Michelson on the *Michelson–Morley experiment* 1887. In 1895 he established precise and accurate measurements of the densities of oxygen and hydrogen.

Morley Malcolm 1931– . British painter, active in New York from 1964. He coined the term *Superrealism* for his work in the 1960s.

Morley Robert 1908–1992. English actor and playwright, active in both Britain and the US. His film work has been mainly character roles, in such movies as *Marie Antoinette* 1938, *The African Queen* 1952, and *Oscar Wilde* 1960.

Morley Thomas 1557–1602. English composer. A student of William ⟁Byrd, he became organist at St Paul's Cathedral, London, and obtained a monopoly on music printing. A composer of the English madrigal school, he also wrote sacred music, songs for Shakespeare's plays, and a musical textbook.

Mormon or **Latter-day Saint** member of a Christian sect, the Church of Jesus Christ of Latter-day Saints, founded at Fayette, New York, 1830 by Joseph ◊Smith. According to Smith, Mormon was an ancient prophet in North America; his *Book of Mormon* is accepted by Mormons as part of the Christian scriptures. Smith said he found the book, inscribed on golden tablets, with the help of the angel Moroni in 1827, and that he translated it from "reformed Egyptian" by using special glasses. Originally persecuted, the Mormons migrated West under Brigham ◊Young's leadership and prospered. Today the worldwide membership in the Mormon church is about 6 million.

The *Book of Mormon* describes American Indians as descendants of ancient Hebrews who came to North America across the Pacific. Christ is said to have appeared to them after his ascension to establish his church in the New World. The Mormon church claims to be a reestablishment of this pure, original Christianity by divine intervention. The church grew rapidly, especially in the Midwest, but its controversial doctrines and rumors that Smith had taken several wives (as allowed in the Old Testament) provoked persecution, and Smith was killed in Illinois. Further settlements were rapidly established despite opposition, and in 1847 Brigham Young led a westward migration of most of the church's members to the Valley of the Great Salt Lake in what is now Utah. The Mormons under Young openly practiced polygamy, but the church repudiated the practice in 1890, following Congressional pressure related to the proposed admission of Utah as a state. Mormons hold several doctrines not held by other Christians, including the belief that God has a physical body and that human beings may become gods, just as God was once a man. They advocate a strict sexual morality, large families, and respect for authority. They forbid the consumption of alcohol, coffee, tea, and tobacco.

morning glory any twining or creeping plant of the genus *Ipomoea*, especially *I. purpurea*, family Convolvulaceae, native to tropical America, with dazzling blue flowers. Small quantities of substances similar to the hallucinogenic drug ◊LSD are found in the seeds of some species.

Big-root morning glory *I. pandurata* is native to the E US.

Moro Aldo 1916–1978. Italian Christian Democrat politician. Prime minister 1963–68 and 1974–76, he was expected to become Italy's president, but he was kidnapped and shot by Red Brigade urban guerrillas.

Moroccan Crises two periods of international tension 1905 and 1911 following German objections to French expansion in Morocco. Their wider purpose was to break up the Anglo-French entente 1904, but both crises served to reinforce the entente and isolate Germany.

Morocco country in NW Africa, bounded N and NW by the Mediterranean Sea, E and SE by Algeria, and S by Western Sahara.

government Morocco is an unusual constitutional monarchy in that the king, as well as being the formal head of state, presides over his appointed cabinet and has powers, under the 1972 constitution, to dismiss the prime minister and other ministers, as well as to dissolve the legislature. This consists of a 306-member chamber of representatives, serving a six-year term; 206 are directly elected by universal suffrage, and 100 are chosen by an electoral college of local councillors and employers' and employees' representatives.

history Originally occupied by ◊Berber tribes, the coastal regions of the area now known as Morocco were under Phoenician rule during the 10th–3rd centuries BC, and became a Roman colony in the 1st century AD. It was invaded in the 5th century by the ◊Vandals, in the 6th century by the Visigoths, and in the 7th century began to be conquered by the Arabs. From the 11th century the region was united under the ◊Almoravids, who ruled a Muslim empire that included Spain, Morocco, and Algeria. They were followed by the ◊Almohads, another Muslim dynasty, whose empire included Libya and Tunisia.

In the 15th century Portugal occupied the Moroccan port of Ceuta but was defeated 1578. Further European influence began in the 19th century and was more lasting, with Morocco being divided 1912 into French and Spanish protectorates. It became fully independent as the Sultanate of Morocco 1956 under Mohammed V (sultan since 1927). The former Spanish protectorate joined the new state, with Tangier, which had previously been an international zone. The sultan was restyled king of Morocco 1957. After his death 1961 he was succeeded by King Hassan II, who has survived several attempted coups and assassinations. Between 1960 and 1972 several constitutions were formulated in an attempt to balance personal royal rule with demands for greater democracy.

Western Sahara dispute Hassan's reign has been dominated by the dispute over ◊Western Sahara, a former Spanish colony seen as historically Moroccan. In 1975 Spain ceded it to Morocco and Mauritania, leaving them to divide it. The inhabitants, who had not been consulted, reacted violently through an independence movement, the Polisario Front. Less than a year later, Morocco and Mauritania were involved in a guerrilla war.

With Algerian support, Polisario set up a government in exile in Algiers, the Sahrawi Arab Democratic Republic (SADR). This prompted Hassan to sever diplomatic relations with Algeria 1976. In 1979 Mauritania agreed a peace treaty with Polisario, and Morocco annexed the part of Western Sahara that Mauritania had vacated. Polisario reacted by intensifying its operations.

In 1983 the Organization of African Unity (OAU) proposed a cease-fire, direct negotiations between Morocco and Polisario, and a referendum in Western Sahara. Morocco agreed but refused to deal directly with Polisario.

Although the war was costly, it allowed Hassan to capitalize on the patriotism it generated in his country. In 1984 he unexpectedly signed an agreement with Col Khaddhafi of Libya, who had been helping Polisario, for

---

Morocco
Kingdom of (*al-Mamlaka al-Maghrebia*)

area 177,070 sq mi/458,730 sq km (excluding Western Sahara)
capital Rabat
cities Marrakesh, Fez, Meknès; ports Casablanca, Tangier, Agadir
physical mountain ranges NE–SW; fertile coastal plains in W
features Atlas Mountains; the towns Ceuta (from 1580) and Melilla (from 1492) are held by Spain; tunnel crossing the Strait of Gibraltar to Spain proposed 1985
head of state Hassan II from 1961
head of government Mohamed Lamrani from 1992
political system constitutional monarchy
political parties Constitutional Union (UC), right-wing; National Rally of Independents (RNI), royalist; Popular Movement (MP), moderate socialist; Istiqlal, nationalist, right-of-center; Socialist Union of Popular Forces (USFP), progressive socialist; National Democratic Party (PND), moderate, nationalist

exports dates, figs, cork, wood pulp, canned fish, phosphates
currency dirham (DH)
population (1990 est) 26,249,000; growth rate 2.5% p.a.
life expectancy men 62, women 65 (1989)
languages Arabic (official) 75%, Berber 25%, French, Spanish
religion Sunni Muslim 99%
literacy men 45%, women 22% (1985 est)
GNP $18.7 bn; $750 per head (1988)
chronology
1912 Morocco divided into French and Spanish protectorates.
1956 Independence achieved as the Sultanate of Morocco.
1957 Sultan restyled king of Morocco.
1961 Hassan II came to the throne.
1969 Former Spanish province of Ifni returned to Morocco.
1972 Major revision of the constitution.
1975 Western Sahara ceded by Spain to Morocco and Mauritania.
1976 Guerrilla war in Western Sahara with the Polisario Front. Sahrawi Arab Democratic Republic (SADR) established in Algiers. Diplomatic relations between Morocco and Algeria broken.
1979 Mauritania signed a peace treaty with Polisario.
1983 Peace formula for Western Sahara proposed by the Organization of African Unity (OAU); Morocco agreed but refused to deal directly with Polisario.
1984 Hassan signed an agreement for cooperation and mutual defense with Libya.
1987 Cease-fire agreed with Polisario, but fighting continued.
1988 Diplomatic relations with Algeria restored.
1989 Diplomatic relations with Syria restored.
1992 Mohamed Lamrani appointed prime minister; new constitution approved in national referendum.

economic and political cooperation and mutual defense. Meanwhile, Morocco was becoming more isolated as the SADR gained wider recognition. Towards the end of 1987 the Polisario guerrillas agreed a cease-fire and in Aug 1988 a United Nations peace plan was accepted by both sides, calling for a referendum to permit the area's inhabitants to choose independence or incorporation into Morocco. Full diplomatic relations with Algeria were restored May 1988, and with Syria Jan 1989.

In 1990–91 Morocco officially opposed Iraq's invasion of Kuwait, although there was much popular support for Iraq. Domestically, the surge in Islamic fundamentalism concerned the government. In Aug 1992 King Hassan appointed the veteran politician Mohamed Lamrani to head a government of independents. In Sept a new constitution was approved by national referendum. *See illustration box.*

Moroni capital of the Comoros Republic, on Njazidja (Grand Comore); population (1980) 20,000. It has a small natural harbor from which coffee, cacao, and vanilla are exported.

Morpheus in Greek and Roman mythology, the god of dreams, son of Hypnos or Somnus, god of sleep.

morphine narcotic alkaloid $C_{17}H_{19}NO_3$ derived from ◊opium and prescribed only to alleviate severe pain. Its use produces serious side effects, including nausea, constipation, tolerance, and addiction, but it is highly valued for the relief of the terminally ill.

morphogen in medicine, one of a class of substances believed to be present in the growing embryo, controlling its growth pattern. It is thought that variations in the concentration of morphogens in different parts of the embryo cause them to grow at different rates.

morphology in biology, the study of the physical structure and form of organisms, in particular their soft tissues.

Morris Robert 1734–1806. American merchant and political leader; signer of the Declaration of Independence. He became a cautious supporter of American independence, serving in the Continental Congress 1775–78 and signing the Declaration of Independence 1776. In 1781 he was appointed superintendent of finance by the Continental Congress and dealt with the pressing economic problems of the new nation. After attending the Constitutional Convention 1787, he served as one of Pennsylvania's first US senators 1789–95. Poor investments and bankruptcy plagued him in later years.

Born in Liverpool, England, Morris immigrated to America 1747, joining a merchant firm in Philadelphia.

Morris William 1834–1896. English designer, a founder of the ◊Arts and Crafts movement, socialist, and writer who shared the Pre-Raphaelite painters' fascination with medieval settings. In 1861 he cofounded a firm that designed and produced furniture, carpets, and a wide range of decorative wallpapers, many of which are still produced today. His Kelmscott Press, set up 1890 to print beautifully designed books, influenced printing and book design. The prose romances *A Dream of John Ball* 1888 and *News from Nowhere* 1891 reflect his socialist ideology. He also lectured on socialism.

Morris abandoned his first profession, architecture, to study painting, but had a considerable influence on such architects as William Lethaby and Philip ◊Webb. As a

founder of the Arts and Crafts movement, Morris did much to raise British craft standards. His first book of verse was *The Defence of Guenevere* 1858.

morris dance English folk dance. In early times it was usually performed by six men, one of whom wore girl's clothing while another portrayed a horse. The others wore costumes decorated with bells. Morris dancing probably originated in pre-Christian ritual dances and is still popular in the US and UK.

Morrison Toni 1931– . US novelist whose fiction records black life in the South. Her works include *Song of Solomon* 1978, *Tar Baby* 1981, *Beloved* 1987, based on a true story about infanticide in Kentucky, which won the Pulitzer Prize 1988, and *Jazz* 1992.

Morse Samuel (Finley Breese) 1791–1872. US inventor. In 1835 he produced the first adequate electric telegraph (see ◊telegraphy), and in 1843 was granted $30,000 by Congress for an experimental line between Washington, DC and Baltimore. With his assistant Alexander Bain (1810–1877) he invented the Morse code.

Born in Charlestown, Massachusetts, Morse graduated from Yale 1810 and studied art in England. He served as the first president of the National Academy of Design 1826–45, which he helped to found, and taught at New York University from 1832. The first message 1844 transmitted between Washington and Baltimore was "What hath God wrought!"

Morse code international code for transmitting messages by wire or radio using signals of short (dots) and long (dashes) duration, originated by Samuel Morse for use on his invention, the telegraph (see ◊telegraphy).

The letters SOS (3 short, 3 long, 3 short) form the international distress signal, being distinctive and easily transmitted (popularly but erroneously *save our souls*). By radio telephone the distress call is "Mayday," for similar reasons (popularly alleged to derive from French *m'aidez*, help me).

mortar method of projecting a bomb via a high trajectory at a target up to 3–4 mi/6–7 km away. A mortar bomb is stabilized in flight by means of tail fins. The high trajectory results in a high angle of attack and makes mortars more suitable than artillery for use in built-up areas or mountains; mortars are not as accurate, however. Artillery also differs in firing a projectile through a rifled barrel, thus creating greater muzzle velocity.

Morte D'Arthur, Le series of episodes from the legendary life of King Arthur by Thomas

A	B	C	D	E	F
·–	–···	–·–·	–··	·	··–·
G	H	I	J	K	L
––·	····	··	·–––	–·–	·–··
M	N	O	P	Q	R
––	–·	–––	·––·	––·–	·–·
S	T	U	V	W	X
···	–	··–	···–	·––	–··–
		Y	Z		
		–·––	––··		
1	2	3	4	5	
·––––	··–––	···––	····–	·····	
6	7	8	9	0	
–····	––···	–––··	––––·	–––––	

Morse code

◊Malory, completed 1470, regarded as the first great prose work in English literature. Only the last of the eight books composing the series is titled *Le Morte D'Arthur*.

mortgage the pledging of real property—usually a building—as security for repayment of a loan. The loan and contracted interest is repaid over a contracted period of years, at which time ownership of the property reverts to the titleholder.

Mortimer John 1923– . English lawyer and writer. His works include the plays *The Dock Brief* 1958 and *A Voyage Round My Father* 1970, the novel *Paradise Postponed* 1985, and the television series *Rumpole of the Bailey*, from 1978, centered on a fictional lawyer.

Mortimer Roger de, 8th Baron of Wigmore and 1st Earl of March *c.* 1287–1330. English politician and adventurer. He opposed Edward II and with Edward's queen, Isabella, led a rebellion against him 1326, bringing about his abdication. From 1327 Mortimer ruled England as the queen's lover, until Edward III had him executed.

mortmain lands held by a corporate body, such as the church, in perpetual or inalienable tenure.

In the Middle Ages, alienation in mortmain, usually to a church in return for a chantry foundation, deprived the feudal lord of his future incidents (payments due to him when the land changed ownership) and rights of wardship, and so attempts were often made to regulate the practice.

Morton Jelly Roll. Adopted name of Ferdinand Joseph La Menthe 1885–1941. US New Orleans-style jazz pianist, singer, and composer. Influenced by Scott Joplin, he was a pioneer in the development of jazz from ragtime to swing by improvising and imposing his own personality on the music. His 1920s band was called the Red Hot Peppers.

Morton William Thomas Green 1819–1868. US dentist who in 1846, with C Thomas Jackson (1805–1880), a chemist and physician, introduced ◊ether as an anesthetic. They patented the process and successfully publicized it.

mosaic design or picture, usually for a floor or wall, produced by inlaying small pieces of marble, glass, or other materials. Mosaic was commonly used by the Romans for their baths and villas (for example Hadrian's Villa at Tivoli) and by the Byzantines, especially for church decoration.

The art was revived by the Italians during the 13th century, when it was used chiefly for the decoration of churches (for example San Vitale, ◊Ravenna).

Moscow (Russian *Moskva*) industrial city, capital of Russia and of the Moskva region, and formerly (1922–91) of the USSR, on the Moskva River 400 mi/640 km SE of St Petersburg; population (1987) 8,815,000. Its industries include machinery, electrical equipment, textiles, chemicals, and many food products.

features The 12th-century Kremlin (Citadel), at the center of the city, is a walled enclosure containing a number of historic buildings, including three cathedrals, one of them the burial place of the tsars; the Ivan Veliki tower 300 ft/90 m, a famine-relief work commissioned by Boris Godunov 1600; various palaces, including the former imperial palace; museums; and the Tsar Kolokol, the world's largest bell (200 tons) 1735. The walls of the Kremlin are crowned by 18 towers and have five gates. Red Square, used for political demonstrations and processions, contains St Basil's Cathedral, the state department store GUM, and Lenin's tomb. The headquarters of the ▷KGB, with Lubyanka Prison behind it, is in Dzerzhinsky Square; the underground railroad was opened 1935. Institutions include Moscow University 1755 and People's Friendship University (for foreign students) 1953; the Academy of Sciences, which moved from Leningrad (now St Petersburg) in 1934; Tretyakov Gallery of Russian Art 1856; Moscow State Circus. Moscow is the seat of the patriarch of the Russian Orthodox Church. On the city outskirts is Star City (Zvezdnoy Gorodok), the space center.

Moscow is the largest industrial center of the Commonwealth of Independent States, linked with Stavropol by oil pipeline 300 mi/480 km, built 1957.

history Moscow, founded as the city-state of *Muscovy* 1127, was destroyed by the Mongols during the 13th century, but rebuilt 1294 by Prince Daniel (died 1303) as the capital of his principality. During the 14th century, it was under the rule of ▷Alexander Nevski, Ivan I (1304–1341), and Dmitri Donskai (1350–1389), and became the foremost political power in Russia, and its religious capital. It was burned in 1571 by the khan of the Crimea, and ravaged by fire in 1739, 1748, and 1753; in 1812 it was burned by its own citizens to save it from Napoleon's troops, or perhaps by accident. It became capital of the Russian Soviet Federated Social Republic (RSFSR) 1918, and of the Union of Soviet Socialist Republics (USSR) 1922. In World War II Hitler's troops were within 20 mi/30 km of Moscow on the northwest by Nov 1941, but the stubborn Russian defense and severe winter weather forced their withdrawal in Dec.

Moseley Henry Gwyn-Jeffreys 1887–1915. English physicist who from 1913 to 1914 devised the series of atomic numbers (reflecting the charges of the nuclei of different elements) that led to the revision of the Mendeleyev's ▷periodic table of the elements.

Moseley was a student of Ernest ▷Rutherford, and devoted his career to research on the structure of the atom. He concluded that the atomic number is equal to the charge on the nucleus; therefore his periodic table was arranged by atomic number (instead of atomic mass, as presented by Mendeleyev). When the elements are so arranged, problems appearing in the Mendeleyev version are resolved. Moseley was killed during the Gallipoli campaign of World War I.

Moselle or *Mosel* river in W Europe some 320 mi/515 km long; it rises in the Vosges, France, and is canalized from Thionville to its confluence with the ▷Rhine at Koblenz in Germany. It gives its name to the *départements* of Moselle and Meurthe-et-Moselle in France.

Moses c. 13th century BC. Hebrew lawgiver and judge who led the Hebrews out of slavery in Egypt (Exodus) and, after wandering 40 years in the desert, brought them to the border (E of the Jordan) of the promised land of Canaan. On Mount Sinai he claimed to have received from Jehovah the **Ten Commandments** engraved on tablets of stone. The first five books of the Old Testament—in Judaism, the ▷Torah—are called the *Five Books of Moses*.

According to the Torah, the infant Moses was hidden among the bulrushes on the banks of the Nile when the pharaoh commanded that all newborn male Hebrew children should be destroyed. He was found by a daughter of pharaoh, who reared him. His brother ▷Aaron helped him lead and he and his descendants are the high priests of Judaism. Moses died at the age of 120, being allowed only a view of the promised land (from Mt Pisgah).

Moses "Grandma" (born Anna Mary Robertson) 1860–1961. US painter. She was self-taught, and began full-time painting in about 1927, after many years as a farmer's wife. She painted naive and colorful scenes from rural American life.

Moses Ed(win Corley) 1955– . US track athlete and 400 meters hurdler. Between 1977 and 1987 he ran 122 races without defeat.

He first broke the world record in 1976, and set a time of 47.02 seconds in 1983. He was twice Olympic champion and twice world champion.

CAREER HIGHLIGHTS

Olympic champion
400 meters hurdles: 1976, 1984
world champion
400 meters hurdles: 1983, 1987

Moses Robert 1888–1981. US public official and urban planner. Although never elected to public office, he had tremendous power for more than 40 years and was known as a power broker. As parks commissioner for New York State 1924–64 and New York City 1934–60, he oversaw the development of bridges, highways, and public facilities. Moses was the unsuccessful Republican candidate for New York governor 1934.

Born in New Haven, Connecticut, and educated at Yale and Oxford universities, Moses received his PhD from Columbia University 1914. He was hired by the New York City municipal government, later headed a state redevelopment program, and served as New York secretary of state 1927–28. Moses served as chair of the Triborough Bridge and Tunnel Authority 1946–68, chair of the New York State Power Authority 1954–63, and president of the 1964–65 New York World's Fair.

Moskva Russian name for ▷Moscow, the capital of Russia.

Moslem alternate spelling of *Muslim*, a follower of ▷Islam.

Mosley Oswald (Ernald) 1896–1980. British politician, founder of the British Union of Fascists (BUF). He was a member of Parliament 1918–31, then led the BUF until his internment 1940–43 during World War II. In 1946 Mosley was denounced when it became known that Italy had funded his prewar efforts to establish ▷fascism in Britain, but in 1948 he resumed fascist propaganda with his Union Movement, the revived BUF.

mosque (Arabic *mesjid*) in Islam, a place of worship. Chief features are: the dome; the minaret, a balconied turret from which the faithful are called to prayer; the *mihrab*, or prayer niche, in one of the interior walls, showing the direction of the holy city of Mecca; and an open court surrounded by porticoes.

The earliest mosques were based on the plan of Christian basilicas, although different influences contributed toward their architectural development. Mosques vary a great deal in style in various parts of the world.

mosquito any fly of the family Culicidae. The female mosquito has needlelike mouthparts, and sucks blood before laying eggs. Males feed on plant juices. Some mosquitoes carry diseases such as ▷malaria.

Human odor in general is attractive to mosquitos, also lactic acid in sweat and heat at close range. Peoples' varying reactions to mosquito bites depend on the general allergic reaction and not on the degree of the bite; the allergic reaction is caused by the saliva injected from the mosquito's salivary glands to prevent coagulation of the host's blood. Natural mosquito repellents include lavender oil, citronella (from lemon grass), thyme, and eucalyptus oils.

Mosquito Coast Caribbean coast of Honduras and Nicaragua, characterized by swamp, lagoons, and tropical rainforest. The territory is inhabited by Miskito Indians, Garifunas, and Zambos, many of whom speak English. Between 1823 and 1860 Britain maintained a protectorate over the Mosquito Coast which was ruled by a succession of "Mosquito Kings."

The area was designated a biosphere reserve by the United Nations in 1992, but the government sold the rights to exploit it (energy, road-building) to a US packaging giant (the Stone Container Corporation). The project threatens local people, whose numbers are diminishing.

moss small nonflowering plant of the class Musci (10,000 species), forming with the ▷liverworts and the ▷hornworts the order Bryophyta. The stem of each plant bears ▷rhizoids that anchor it; there are no true roots. Leaves spirally arranged on its lower portion have sexual organs at their tips. Most mosses flourish best in damp conditions where other vegetation is thin. The peat or bog moss *Sphagnum* was formerly used for surgical dressings.

Moss gardens are popular in Japan; there is one at the Moss Temple, near Kyoto.

Mossadegh Mohammed 1880–1967. Iranian prime minister 1951–53. A dispute arose with the Anglo-Iranian Oil Company when he called for the nationalization of Iran's oil production, and when he failed in his attempt to overthrow the shah he was arrested by loyalist forces with support from the US. From 1956 he was under house arrest.

Mössbauer Rudolf 1929– . German physicist who discovered in 1958 that in certain conditions a nucleus can be stimulated to emit very sharply defined beams of gamma rays. This became known as the *Mössbauer effect*. Such a beam was used in 1960 to provide the first laboratory test of ▷Einstein's general theory of relativity. For his work on gamma rays Mössbauer shared the 1961 Nobel Prize for Physics with Robert ▷Hofstadter.

Mossi member of the majority ethnic group living in Burkina Faso. Their social structure, based on a monarchy and aristocracy, was established in the 11th century. The Mossi have been prominent traders, using cowrie shells as currency. There are about 4 million speakers of Mossi, a language belonging to the Gur branch of the Niger-Congo family.

Mostel Zero (Samuel Joel) 1915–1977. US comedian and actor, mainly in the theater. His films include *Panic in the Streets* 1950, *A Funny Thing Happened on the Way to the Forum* 1966, *The Producers* 1967, and *The Front* 1976.

motet sacred, polyphonic music for unaccompanied voices in a form that originated in 13th-century Europe.

moth any of the various families of mainly night-flying insects of the order Lepidoptera, which also includes the butterflies. Their wings are covered with microscopic scales. The mouthparts are formed into a sucking proboscis, but certain moths have no functional mouthparts, and rely upon stores of fat and other reserves built up during the caterpillar stage. At least 100,000 different species of moth are known.

Moths feed chiefly on the nectar of flowers, and other fluid matter; some, like the ▷hawk moths, frequent flowers and feed while hovering. The females of some species (such as bagworm moths) have wings either absent or reduced to minute flaps. Moths vary greatly in size. In many cases the males are smaller and more brightly colored than the females. The minute Nepticulidae sometimes have a wingspread less than 0.1 in/3 mm, while the giant Noctuid or owlet moth *Erebus agrippina* measures about 11 in/280 mm across.

The larvae (caterpillars) have a well-developed head and three thoracic and ten abdominal segments. Each thoracic segment bears a pair of short legs, ending in single claws; a pair of suckerlike abdominal feet is present on segments three to six and ten of the hind-body. In the family Geometridae the caterpillars bear the abdominal feet only on segments six and ten of the hind body. They move by a characteristic looping gait and are known as "loopers,""inchworms," or geometers. Projecting from the middle of the lower lip of a caterpillar is a minute tube or spinneret, through which silk is emitted to make a cocoon within which the change to the pupa or chrysalis occurs. Silk glands are especially large in the ▷silkworm moth. Many caterpillars, including the geometers, which are sought by birds, are protected by their resemblance in both form and coloration to their immediate surroundings. Others, which are distasteful to such enemies, are brightly colored or densely hairy.

The feeding caterpillars of many moths cause damage: the codling moth, for example, attacks fruit trees; and several species of clothes moth eat natural fibers.

The corn earworm moth infests corn. The largest North American moths are the cecropia moth and polyphemus moth with wingspreads up to 5.5 in/14 cm.

mother-of-pearl or *nacre* the smooth lustrous lining in the shells of certain mollusks —for example pearl oysters, abalones, and mussels. When this layer is especially heavy it is used commercially for jewelry and decorations. Mother-of-pearl consists of calcium carbonate. See ▷pearl.

Mother's Day day set apart in the US, UK, and many European countries for honoring mothers. It is thought to have originated in Grafton, West Virginia, in 1908 when Anna Jarvis observed the anniversary of her mother's death.

In the US, Australia, and Canada Mother's Day is observed on the second Sunday in May; in the UK it is known as Mothering Sunday and observed on the fourth Sunday of Lent.

Motherwell Robert 1915–1991. US painter associated with the New York school of ▷action painting. Borrowing from Picasso, Matisse, and the Surrealists, Motherwell's style of Abstract Expressionism retained some suggestion of the figurative. His works include the "Elegies to the Spanish Republic" 1949–76, a series of over 100 paintings devoted to the Spanish Revolution.

Born in Aberdeen, Washington, Motherwell studied art in California and at Harvard and Columbia universities.

motion picture or *moving picture* see ▷cinema.

motion sickness nausea and vomiting caused by the motion of automobiles, boats, or aircraft. Constant vibration and movement sometimes stimulates changes in the fluid of the semicircular canals (responsible for balance) of the inner ear, to which the individual fails to adapt, and to which are added visual and psychological factors.

Space sickness is a special case where normal body movements result in unexpected and unfamiliar signals to the brain, due to the unique environment of weightlessness. Astronauts achieve some control over symptoms by wedging themselves in their bunks.

motor anything that produces or imparts motion; a machine that provides mechanical power, particularly an ▷electric motor. Machines that burn fuel (gasoline, diesel) are usually called engines, but the internal-combustion engine that propels vehicles has long been called a motor, hence "motoring" and "motorcar" were used as early automotive terms. Actually the motor is a part of the ▷automobile engine.

motorboat small, waterborne craft for pleasure cruising or racing, powered by a gasoline, diesel, or gas-turbine engine. A boat not equipped as a motorboat may be converted by a detachable outboard motor. For increased speed, such as in racing, motorboat hulls are designed to skim the water (aquaplane) and reduce frictional resistance. Plastics, steel, and light alloys are now used in construction as well as the traditional wood.

In recent designs, drag is further reduced with hydrofins and ▷hydrofoils, which enable the hull to rise clear of the water at normal speeds. Notable events in motorboat or "powerboat" racing include the American Gold Cup 1947 (over a 90 mi/145 km course) and the Round-Britain race 1969.

motorcycle or *motorbike* two-wheeled vehicle propelled by a ▷gasoline engine. The motorbike is the lightweight version, with less power than the motorcycle, which may be equipped with a sidecar. The first successful motorized bicycle was built in France 1901, and British and US manufacturers first produced motorbikes 1903.

In 1868 Ernest and Pierre Michaux in France experimented with a steam-powered bicycle, but the steam power unit was too heavy and cumbersome. Gottlieb ▷Daimler, a German engineer, created the first motorcycle when he installed his lightweight gasoline engine in a bicycle frame 1885. Daimler soon lost interest in two wheels in favor of four and went on to pioneer the ▷automobile.

The first really successful two-wheel design was devised by Michael and Eugene Werner in France 1901. They adopted the classic motorcycle layout with the engine low down between the wheels. Harley Davidson in the US and Triumph in the UK began manufacture 1903. Road races like the Isle of Man TT (Tourist Trophy), established 1907, helped improve motorcycle design and it soon evolved into more or less its present form. Until the 1970s British manufacturers predominated but today Japanese motorcycles, such as Honda, Kawasaki, Suzuki, and Yamaha, dominate the world market. They make a wide variety of machines, from mopeds (lightweights with pedal

assistance) to streamlined superbikes capable of speeds up to 160 mph/250 kph. There is still a smaller but thriving Italian motorcycle industry, making more specialist bikes. Laverda, Moto Guzzi, and Ducati continue to manufacture in Italy.

The lightweight bikes are generally powered by a two-stroke gasoline engine (see ▷two-stroke cycle), while bikes with an engine capacity of 250 cc or more are generally four-strokes (see ▷four-stroke cycle). However, many special-use larger bikes (such as those developed for off-road riding and racing) are two-stroke. Most motorcycles are air-cooled—their engines are surrounded by metal fins to offer a large surface area—although some have a water-cooling system similar to that of an automobile. Most small bikes have single-cylinder engines, but larger machines can have as many as six. The single-cylinder engine was economical and was popular in British manufacture, then the Japanese developed multiple-cylinder models, but there has recently been some return to single-cylinder engines. A revived British Norton racing motorcycle uses a Wankel (rotary) engine. In the majority of bikes a chain carries the drive from the engine to the rear wheel, though some machines are now fitted with shaft drive.

motorcycle racing speed contests on motorcycles. It has many different forms: *road racing* over open roads; *circuit racing* over purpose-built tracks; *speedway* over oval-shaped dirt tracks; *motocross* over natural terrain, incorporating hill climbs; and *trials*, also over natural terrain, but with the addition of artificial hazards.

For finely tuned production machines, there exists a season-long world championship Grand Prix series with various categories for machines with engine sizes 125 cc–500 cc. Major events are the world championship, which has been in existence since 1949 (the blue riband event is the 500 cc class), and the Isle of Man Tourist Trophy, the principal race of which is the Senior TT.

motor effect tendency of a wire carrying an electric current in a magnetic field to move. The direction of the movement is given by the left-hand rule (see ▷Fleming's rules). This effect is used in the ▷electric motor. It also explains why streams of electrons produced, for instance, in a television tube can be directed by electromagnets.

motor nerve in anatomy, any nerve that transmits impulses from the central nervous system to muscles or body organs. Motor nerves cause voluntary and involuntary muscle contractions, and stimulate glands to secrete hormones.

motor neuron disease incurable wasting disease in which the nerve cells (neurons) controlling muscle action gradually die, causing progressive weakness and paralysis. It results from infection in childhood with the ▷poliomyelitis virus; this is now largely eradicated, and it is thought that motor neuron disease will disappear by 2010.

Motown first black-owned US record company, founded in Detroit (Mo[tor] Town) 1959 by Berry Gordy, Jr (1929–). Its distinctive, upbeat sound (exemplified by the Four Tops and the ▷Supremes) was a major element in 1960s pop music.

The Motown sound was created by in-house producers and songwriters such as Smokey Robinson and the team of Holland–Dozier–Holland; performers included Stevie Wonder, Marvin Gaye, and the Temptations. Its influence faded after the company's move to Los Angeles 1971, but it still served as a breeding ground for such singers as Lionel Richie (1950–) and Michael Jackson. Gordy sold Motown to the larger MCA company in 1988.

Mott Nevill Francis 1905– . English physicist who researched the electronic properties of metals, semiconductors, and noncrystalline materials. He shared the Nobel Prize for Physics 1977 with US physicists Philip Anderson (1923–) and John Van Vleck (1899–1980).

mouflon sheep *Ovis ammon* found wild in Cyprus, Corsica, and Sardinia. It has woolly underfur in winter, but this is covered by heavy guard hairs. The coat is brown with white belly and rump. Males have strong, curving horns. The mouflon lives in mountain areas.

Moundbuilder member of any of the various North American Indian peoples of the Midwest and the South who built earth mounds, from about 300 BC. The mounds were linear and pictographic in form for tombs, such as the Great Serpent Mound in Ohio, and truncated pyramids and cones for the platforms of chiefs' houses and temples. The ⟡Hopewell and ⟡Natchez were Moundbuilders.

The Moundbuilders carried out group labor projects under the rule of an elite. An important site is Monk's Mound in Mississippi. They were in decline by the time of the Spanish invasion, but traces of their culture live on in the folklore of the Choctaw and ⟡Cherokee Indians.

mountain natural upward projection of the Earth's surface, higher and steeper than a hill. The process of mountain building (orogeny) consists of volcanism, folding, faulting, and thrusting, resulting from the collision and welding together of two tectonic plates.

mountain ash or *rowan* flowering tree of the genus *Sorbus*, family Rosaceae. It has pinnate leaves and large clusters of whitish flowers, followed by scarlet berries. The American mountain ash *S. americana* grows to 30 ft/9 m and is native to NE US. The European mountain ash or rowan tree *S. aucaparia* is planted widely as an ornamental.

mountain biking recreational sport that enjoyed increasing popularity in the 1990s. Mountain bikes first appeared on the mass market in the US in 1981, in the UK in 1984, and have been used in all aspects of cycling. However, it is also a competition sport, and the first world championship was held in France in 1987. The second world championship was held 1990 in Mexico. National mountain-bike championships have been held in the US since 1983 and in the UK since 1984. Mountain bikes have 10–15 gears, a toughened frame, and wider treads on the tires than ordinary bicycles.

mountaineering art and practice of mountain climbing. For major peaks of the Himalayas it was formerly thought necessary to have elaborate support from Sherpas (local people), fixed ropes, and oxygen at high altitudes (*siege-style* climbing). In the 1980s the *Alpine style* was introduced. This dispenses with these aids, and relies on human ability to adapt, Sherpa-style, to high altitude.

In 1854 *Wetterhorn*, Switzerland, was climbed by Alfred Wills, thereby founding the sport; 1865 *Matterhorn*, Switzerland–Italy, by Edward ⟡Whymper; 1897 *Aconcagua*, Argentina, by Zurbriggen; 1938 *Eiger* (north face), Switzerland, by Heinrich Harrer; 1953

Everest, Nepal–Tibet, by Edmund ⟡Hillary and Norgay ⟡Tenzing; 1981 *Kongur*, China, by British mountaineer Chris Bonington (1934–).

mountain lion another name for ⟡puma.

Mountbatten Louis, 1st Earl Mountbatten of Burma 1900–1979. British admiral and administrator. In World War II he became chief of combined operations 1942 and commander in chief in SE Asia 1943. As last viceroy of India 1947 and first governor-general of India until 1948, he oversaw that country's transition to independence. He was killed by an Irish Republican Army bomb aboard his yacht in the Republic of Ireland.

He was a favorite relative of the royal family and counselor to Prince Charles.

Mounties popular name for the *Royal Canadian Mounted Police*, known for their uniform of red jacket and broad-brimmed hat. Their Security Service, established 1950, was disbanded 1981 and replaced by the independent Canadian Security Intelligence Service.

Mount Vernon village in Virginia, on the Potomac River, where George Washington lived 1752–99 and was buried on the family estate, now a national monument.

Mount Wilson site near Los Angeles, California, of the 2.5-m/100-in Hooker telescope, opened 1917, with which Edwin Hubble discovered the expansion of the universe. It was closed in 1985 when the Carnegie Institution withdrew its support. Two solar telescopes in towers 60 ft/18.3 m and 150 ft/45.7 m tall, and a 60-in/1.5-m reflector, opened 1908, still operate there.

Mourning Becomes Electra 1931 trilogy of plays by Eugene O'Neill that retells the Orestes legend (see ⟡Agamemnon), setting it in the world of 19th-century New England. The three are considered among the greatest of modern US plays.

mouse in computing, an input device used to control a pointer on a computer screen. It is a feature of ⟡graphical user interface (GUI) systems. The mouse is about the size of a pack of playing cards, is connected to the computer by a wire, and incorporates one or more buttons that can be pressed. Moving the mouse across a flat surface causes a corresponding movement of the pointer. In this way, the operator can manipulate objects on the screen and make menu selections.

The mouse was invented 1963 at the Stanford Research Institute, by Douglas Engelbart, and developed by the Xerox Corporation in the 1970s. The first was made of wood; the Microsoft mouse was introduced 1983, and the Macintosh mouse 1984. Mice work either mechanically (with electrical contacts to sense the movement in two planes of a ball on a level surface), or optically (photoelectric cells detecting movement by recording light reflected from a grid on which the mouse is moved).

mouse in zoology, one of a number of small rodents with small ears and a long, thin tail, belonging largely to the Old World family Muridae. The house mouse *Mus musculus* is distributed worldwide. It is 3 in/75 mm long, with a naked tail of equal length, and has a gray-brown body.

Native New World mice all belong to the family Cricetidae that is represented worldwide. American cricitids, sometimes called mice, include ⟡voles and deer mice. *Jumping*

mice, family Zapodidae, with enlarged back legs, live across the northern hemisphere.

mousebird bird of the order Coliiformes, including a single family (Coliidae) of small crested species peculiar to Africa. They have hairlike feathers, long tails, and mouselike agility. The largest is the blue-naped mousebird *Colius macrourus*, about 14 in/35 cm long.

mouse-hare another name for ⟡pika.

Moustier, Le cave in the Dordogne, SW France, with prehistoric remains, giving the name *Mousterian* to the flint-tool culture of Neanderthal peoples; the earliest ritual burials are linked with Mousterian settlements (150,000 years ago).

mouth cavity forming the entrance to the digestive tract. In land vertebrates, air from the nostrils enters the mouth cavity to pass down the trachea. The mouth in mammals is enclosed by the jaws, cheeks, and palate.

movie camera or *motion picture camera* camera that takes a rapid sequence of still photographs—24 frames (pictures) each second. When the pictures are projected one after the other at the same speed onto a screen, they appear to show movement, because our eyes hold onto the image of one picture before the next one appears.

The movie camera differs from an ordinary still camera in having a motor that winds on the film continuously, but the film is held still by a claw mechanism while each frame is exposed. When the film is moved between frames, a semicircular disk slides between the lens and the film and prevents exposure.

Mozambique country in SE Africa, bounded N by Zambia, Malawi, and Tanzania; E and S by the Indian Ocean; SW by South Africa and Swaziland; and W by Zimbabwe.
government The 1975 constitution, revised 1978, provides for a one-party socialist state, based on the National Front for the Liberation of Mozambique (Frelimo). The president heads its political bureau and central committee secretariat. There is a 250-member people's assembly, comprising 130 members of Frelimo's central committee plus 120 others from central and provincial governments, the armed forces, and citizens' representatives. The assembly is convened by the president and meets twice a year. Its functions are performed in its absence by a 15-member inner group, called the permanent commission, also convened and presided over by the president.
history Mozambique's indigenous peoples are of Bantu origin. By the 10th century the Arabs had established themselves on the coast. The first European to reach Mozambique was Vasco da ⟡Gama 1498, and the country became a Portuguese colony 1505. Portugal exploited Mozambique's resources of gold and ivory and used it as a source of slave labor, both locally and overseas. By 1820 the slave trade accounted for 85% of all exports. The trade continued as late as 1912, and 2 million people were shipped to the sugar plantations of Brazil and Cuba; others to neighboring colonies. In 1891 Portugal leased half the country to two British companies who seized African lands and employed forced labor. In 1895 the last indigenous resistance leader was crushed. From 1926 to 1968 the Portuguese were encouraged to emigrate to Mozambique, where they were given land and use of forced labor. Mozambicans were forbidden by law to trade or run their own business.

Mozambique
People's Republic of (*República Popular de Moçambique*)

area 308,561 sq mi/799,380 sq km
capital (and chief port) Maputo
cities Beira, Nampula
physical mostly flat tropical lowland; mountains in W
features rivers Zambezi, Limpopo; "Beira Corridor" rail, road, and pipeline link with Zimbabwe
head of state and government Joaquim Alberto Chissano from 1986
political system emergent democratic republic
political parties National Front for the Liberation of Mozambique (Frelimo), Marxist-Leninist; Renamo, or Mozambique National Resistance (MNR), former rebel movement
exports prawns, cashews, sugar, cotton, tea, petroleum products, copra

currency metical (replaced escudo 1980)
population (1990 est) 14,718,000 (mainly indigenous Bantu peoples; Portuguese 50,000); growth rate 2.8% p.a.; nearly 1 million refugees in Malawi
life expectancy men 45, women 48 (1989)
languages Portuguese (official), 16 African languages
religion animist 60%, Roman Catholic 18%, Muslim 16%
literacy men 55%, women 22% (1985 est)
GDP $4.7 bn; $319 per head (1987)
chronology
1505 Mozambique became a Portuguese colony.
1962 Frelimo (liberation front) established.
1975 Independence achieved from Portugal as a socialist republic, with Samora Machel as president and Frelimo as the sole legal party.
1977 Renamo resistance group formed.
1983 Re-establishment of good relations with Western powers.
1984 Nkomati accord of nonaggression signed with South Africa.
1986 Machel killed in airplane crash; succeeded by Joaquim Chissano.
1988 Tanzania announced withdrawal of its troops. South Africa provided training for Mozambican forces.
1989 Frelimo offered to abandon Marxist-Leninism; Chissano reelected. Renamo continued attacks on government facilities and civilians.
1990 One-party rule officially ended. Partial cease-fire agreed.
1991 Peace talks resumed in Rome, delaying democratic process. Attempted antigovernment coup thwarted.
1992 Aug: peace accord agreed upon, but fighting continued. Oct: peace accord signed, but awaited ratification by government.

Frelimo Guerrilla groups opposed Portuguese rule from the early 1960s, the various left-wing factions combining to form Frelimo. Its leader, Samora Machel, demanded complete independence, and in 1974 internal self-government was achieved, with Joaquim Chissano, a member of Frelimo's central committee, as prime minister.
problems following independence Becoming president of an independent Mozambique 1975, Machel was faced with the emigration of hundreds of thousands of Portuguese settlers, leaving no trained replacements in key economic positions. Two activities had been the mainstay of Mozambique's economy: transit traffic from South Africa and ⊅Rhodesia and the export of labor to South African mines. Although Machel supported the African National Congress (ANC) in South Africa and the Patriotic Front in Rhodesia, he knew he must coexist and trade with his two white-governed neighbors. He put heavy pressure on the Patriotic Front for a settlement of the guerrilla war, and this eventually bore fruit in the 1979 ⊅Lancaster House Agreement and the election victory in Zimbabwe of Robert Mugabe, a reliable friend of Mozambique, as leader of the newly independent Zimbabwe.
From 1980 Mozambique was faced with widespread drought, which affected most of southern Africa, and attacks by mercenaries under the banner of the Mozambique National Resistance (MNR), also known as Renamo, who were covertly but strongly backed by South Africa. The attacks concentrated on

Mozambique's transport system. MNR forces killed an estimated 100,000 Mozambicans 1982–87; 25% of the population were forced to become refugees. 100,000 people died in the famine between 1983 and 1984.
foreign relations Machel, showing considerable diplomatic skill, had by 1983 repaired relations with the US, undertaken a successful European tour, and established himself as a respected African leader. In 1984 he signed the Nkomati accord, under which South Africa agreed to deny facilities to the MNR, and Mozambique in return agreed not to provide bases for the banned ANC. Machel took steps to honor his side of the bargain but was doubtful about South Africa's good faith. In Oct 1986 he died in an airplane crash near the South African border. Despite the suspicious circumstances, two inquiries pronounced his death an accident.
The following month Frelimo's central committee elected former prime minister Joaquim Chissano as Machel's successor. Chissano immediately pledged to carry on the policies of his predecessor. He strengthened the ties forged by Machel with Zimbabwe and Britain and in 1987 took the unprecedented step of requesting permission to attend the British ⊅Commonwealth heads-of-government summit that year.
Mozambique's economic problems were aggravated 1987 by food shortages, after another year of drought. The MNR also continued to attack government facilities and kill civilians, by some estimates as many as 100,000. In May

1988, South Africa announced that it would provide training and nonlethal material to Mozambican forces to enable them to defend the Cabora Bassa dam from MNR attack. In 1988 President Chissano met South African state president Botha and later that year, as tension was reduced, Tanzanian troops were withdrawn from the country. In July 1989, at its annual conference, Frelimo offered to abandon Marxism-Leninism to achieve a national consensus and Chissano was reelected president and party leader.
peace pact signed In Aug 1990 one-party rule was formally ended and in Dec a partial cease-fire was agreed. In 1991 peace talks were held in Rome, and an attempted coup against the government was thwarted. In Aug 1992 a peace accord was agreed, but fighting by right-wing rebels continued; the accord was signed Oct by the opposing factions, but awaited ratification by the Mozambican government.*See illustration box.*

Mozart Wolfgang Amadeus 1756–1791. Austrian composer and performer who showed astonishing precocity as a child and was an adult virtuoso. He was trained by his father, *Leopold Mozart* (1719–1787). From an early age he composed prolifically, his works including 27 piano concertos, 23 string quartets, 35 violin sonatas, and more than 50 symphonies including the E flat K543, G minor K550, and C major K551 ("Jupiter") symphonies, all composed 1788. His operas include *Idomeneo* 1781, *Le Nozze di Figaro/The Marriage of Figaro* 1786, *Don Giovanni* 1787, *Così fan tutte/Thus Do All Women* 1790, and *Die Zauberflöte/The Magic Flute* 1791. Strongly influenced by ⊅Haydn, Mozart's music marks the height of the Classical age in its purity of melody and form.
Mozart's career began when, with his sister, Maria Anna, he was taken on a number of tours 1762–79, visiting Vienna, the Rhineland, Holland, Paris, London, and Italy. Mozart not only gave public recitals, but had already begun to compose. In 1772 he was appointed master of the archbishop of Salzburg's court band. He found the post uncongenial, since he was treated as a servant, and in 1781 he was suddenly dismissed. From then on he lived mostly in Vienna, and married Constanze Weber in 1782. He supported himself as a pianist, composer, and teacher, but his lack of business acumen often resulted in financial difficulties. His *Requiem*, unfinished at his death, was completed by a pupil. Mozart had been in failing health, and died impoverished. His works were cataloged chronologically by the musicologist Ludwig von Köchel (1800–1877) in 1862. The K-number system of identifying Mozart's works, which is still used, is based on this catalog.

MP abbreviation for *member of Parliament*.

mpg abbreviation for *miles per gallon*.

mph abbreviation for *miles per hour*.

MPLA (abbreviation for *Movimento Popular de Libertaçaõ de Angola*/Popular Movement for the Liberation of Angola) socialist organization founded in the early 1950s that sought to free Angola from Portuguese rule 1961–75 before being involved in the civil war against its former allies ⊅UNITA and ⊅FNLA 1975–76. The MPLA took control of the country, but UNITA guerrilla activity continues, supported by South Africa.

Mr abbreviation for *mister*; title used before a name to show that the person is male.

Mr was originally the abbreviation for "master," and "mister" is a corrupted pronunciation of the abbreviation.

Mrs title used before a name to show that the person is married and female; partly superseded by Ms, which does not indicate marital status. Pronounced "missus," Mrs was originally an abbreviation for *mistress*.

Ms title used before a woman's name; pronounced "miz." Unlike Miss or Mrs, it can be used by married or unmarried women, and was introduced by the women's movement in the 1970s to parallel Mr, which also does not distinguish marital status.

MS abbreviation for the state of ⟨⟩*Mississippi*.

MSc in education, abbreviation for *Master of Science* degree. The US abbreviation is *M.S.*

MS-DOS (abbreviation for *Microsoft Disk Operating System*) computer ⟨⟩operating system produced by Microsoft Corporation, widely used on ⟨⟩microcomputers with 16-bit microprocessors. A version called PC-DOS is sold by IBM specifically for their range of personal computers. MS-DOS and PC-DOS are usually referred to as DOS. MS-DOS first appeared in the early 1980s, and was based on an earlier system for computers with 8-bit microprocessors, CP/M.

MS(S) abbreviation for *manuscript(s)*.

MT abbreviation for the state of ⟨⟩*Montana*.

Mubarak Hosni 1928– . Egyptian politician, president from 1981. Vice president to Anwar Sadat from 1975, Mubarak succeeded him on his assassination. He has continued to pursue Sadat's moderate policies, and has significantly increased the freedom of the press and of political association, while trying to repress the growing Islamic fundamentalist movement.

Mubarak commanded the air force 1972–75 and was responsible for the initial victories in the Egyptian campaign of 1973 against Israel. He led Egypt's opposition to Iraq's 1990 invasion of Kuwait and had an instrumental role in arranging the Middle East peace conference in Nov 1991.

Muckrakers, the movement of US writers and journalists about 1880–1914 who aimed to expose political, commercial, and corporate corruption, and record frankly the age of industrialism, urban poverty, and conspicuous consumption. Novelists included Frank Norris, Theodore Dreiser, Jack London, and Upton Sinclair.

Major figures of the earlier period include Rebecca Harding Davis, Henry George (*Progress and Poverty* 1879), and Henry Demarest Lloyd (1847–1903). Later, with the growth of journals like *McClure's Magazine*, the movement included Lincoln Steffens (1866–1936) (*The Shame of the Cities* 1904), Ida M Tarbell, and Thorstein Veblen (*The Theory of the Leisure Class* 1904).

Also associated with the Progressive movement in politics, it gave to both US literature and journalism a critical role it was to maintain.

mucous membrane thin skin lining all animal body cavities and canals that come into contact with the air (for example, eyelids, breathing and digestive passages, genital tract). It secretes mucus, a moistening, lubricating, and protective fluid.

mucus lubricating and protective fluid, secreted by mucous membranes in many different parts of the body. In the gut, mucus smooths the passage of food and keeps potentially damaging digestive enzymes away from the gut lining. In the lungs, it traps airborne particles so that they can be expelled.

mudnester any of an Australian group of birds that make their nests from mud, including the apostle bird *Struthidea cinerea* (so called from its appearance in little flocks of about 12), the white-winged chough *Corcorax melanorhamphos*, and the magpie lark *Grallina cyanoleuca*.

mudpuppy brownish salamander of the genus *Necturus* in the family Proteidae. There are five species, living in fresh water in North America. They all breathe in water using external gills. *Necturus maculatus* is about 8 in/ 20 cm long. Mudpuppies eat fish, snails, and other invertebrates.

mudskipper fish of the goby family, genus *Periophthalmus*, found in brackish water and shores in the tropics, except for the Americas. It can walk or climb over mudflats, using its strong pectoral fins as legs, and has eyes set close together on top of the head. It grows up to 12 in/30 cm long.

mudstone fine-grained sedimentary rock made up of clay-to silt-sized particles (up to 0.0025 in/0.0625 mm).

muezzin (Arabic) a person whose job is to perform the call to prayer five times a day from the minaret of a Muslim mosque.

muffler device in the exhaust system of automobiles and motorbikes. Gases leave the engine at supersonic speeds. The exhaust system and muffler are designed to slow them down, thereby silencing them.

Some mufflers use baffle plates (plates with holes, which disrupt the airflow): others use perforated tubes and an expansion box (a large chamber that slows down airflow).

Mugabe Robert (Gabriel) 1925– . Zimbabwean politician, prime minister from 1980 and president from 1987. He was in detention in Rhodesia for nationalist activities 1964–74, then carried on guerrilla warfare from Mozambique. As leader of ⟨⟩ZANU he was in an uneasy alliance with Joshua ⟨⟩Nkomo of ZAPU (Zimbabwe African People's Union) from 1976. The two parties merged 1987.

His failure to anticipate and respond to the 1991–92 drought in southern Africa adversely affected his popularity.

mugwump (from an Indian word meaning "chief") in US political history, a colloquial name for the Republicans who voted in the 1884 presidential election for Grover Cleveland, the Democratic candidate, rather than for their Republican nominee, James G Blaine (1830–1893). Blaine was accused of financial improprieties, and the reform-minded mugwumps were partly responsible for his defeat. The term has come to mean a politician who remains neutral on divisive issues.

Muir John 1838–1914. Scottish-born US conservationist. Beginning in 1880, he headed a campaign that led to the establishment of Yosemite National Park. He was named adviser to the National Forestry Commission 1896 and continued to campaign for the preservation of wilderness areas for the rest of his life.

Muir came to the US with his family 1849. After attending the University of Wisconsin, he traveled widely and compiled detailed nature journals of his trips. He moved to California 1868 and later explored Glacier Bay in Alaska and mounted other expeditions to Australia and South America.

Mujaheddin (Arabic *mujahid* "fighters," from *jihad* "holy war") Islamic fundamentalist guerrillas of contemporary Afghanistan and Iran.

Mukden former name of ⟨⟩Shenyang, city in China.

Mukden, Battle of taking of Mukden (now Shenyang), NE China, from Russian occupation by the Japanese 1905, during the ⟨⟩Russo-Japanese War. Mukden was later the scene of a surprise attack Sept 18, 1931 by the Japanese on the Chinese garrison, which marked the beginning of their invasion of China.

mulberry any tree of the genus *Morus*, family Moraceae, consisting of a dozen species, including the black mulberry *M. nigra*. It is native to W Asia and has heart-shaped, toothed leaves, and spikes of whitish flowers. It is widely cultivated for its fruit, which, made up of a cluster of small drupes, resembles a raspberry. The leaves of the Asiatic white mulberry *M. alba* are those used in feeding silkworms.

The red mulberry *M. rubra* of the E US also has large edible multiple fruit.

Muldoon Robert David 1921–1992. New Zealand National Party politician, prime minister 1975–84, during which time he pursued austere economic policies such as a wage-and-price policy to control inflation.

mule hybrid animal, usually the offspring of a male ass and a female horse.

Mulhouse (German *Mülhausen*) industrial city (textiles, engineering, electrical goods) in Haut-Rhin *département*, Alsace, E France; population (1982) 221,000.

Mull second largest island of the Inner Hebrides, Strathclyde, Scotland; area 367 sq mi/950 sq km; population (1981) 2,600. It is mountainous, and is separated from the mainland by the Sound of Mull. There is only one town, Tobermory. The economy is based on fishing, forestry, tourism, and some livestock.

mullah (Arabic "master") a teacher, scholar, or religious leader of Islam. It is also a title of respect given to various other dignitaries who perform duties connected with the sacred law.

mullein any plant of the genus *Verbascum*, family Scrophulariaceae. The great mullein *Verbascum thapsus* has lance-shaped leaves 12 in/30 cm or more in length, covered in woolly down, and a large spike of yellow flowers. It is found in Europe and Asia and is naturalized in North America.

Muller Hermann Joseph 1890–1967. US geneticist who discovered the effect of radiation on genes by his work on fruit flies. He was awarded the Nobel Prize for Medicine 1946.

Müller Johannes Peter 1801–1858. German comparative anatomist whose studies of nerves and sense organs opened a new chapter in physiology by demonstrating the physical nature of sensory perception. His name is associated with a number of discoveries, including the *Müllerian ducts* in the mammalian fetus and the lymph heart in frogs.

Müller Paul 1899–1965. Swiss chemist awarded a Nobel Prize in 1948 for his discovery 1939 of the first synthetic contact insecticide, DDT.

Muller v Oregon a US Supreme Court decision 1908 dealing with the constitutionality of state laws regulating working conditions for women. Muller, an Oregon laundry owner, was convicted for requiring his female employees to work longer than 10 hours a day, exceeding the legal maximum for women according to state law. He appealed the conviction on the grounds that the state law violated the 14th-Amendment right to freedom of contracts. The Court upheld the conviction, ruling that the law legitimately promoted public health; since women were at greater risk in the workplace, they warranted state protection.

mullet blunt-nosed warm-water fish of the family Muglidae, found in the Atlantic and Pacific. The striped mullet *Mugil cephalus*, about 2 ft/60 cm long, is commonly netted and smoked. The name mullet is sometimes used for goatfishes, tropical reef fishes of the family Mullidae.

Mulliken Robert Sanderson 1896–1986. US chemist and physicist who received the 1966 Nobel Prize for Chemistry for his development of the molecular orbital theory.

He was professor at the University of Chicago 1931–61.

Mulroney Brian 1939– . Canadian politician. A former businessman, he replaced Joe Clark as Progressive Conservative Party leader 1983 and achieved a landslide in the 1984 election to become prime minister. He won the 1988 election on a platform of free trade with the US, and by the end of 1988 the Canada–US trade agreement was approved. Opposition within Canada to the Meech Lake agreement, a prerequisite to signing the 1982 Constitution, continued to plague Mulroney in his second term.

A compromise reached to persuade Quebec to sign the constitution, the Meech Lake agreement 1987 acknowledged Quebec's separateness and offered more powers and federal funding to all provinces. Not all provinces would agree to the compromise, however, and it collapsed in 1990, contributing to the decline in Mulroney's popularity with the electorate.

Multan industrial city (textiles, precision instruments, chemicals, pottery, jewelry) in Punjab province, central Pakistan, 190 mi/205 km SW of Lahore; population (1981) 732,000. It trades in grain, fruit, cotton, and wool. It is on a site inhabited since the time of Alexander the Great.

multilateralism trade among more than two countries without discrimination over origin or destination and regardless of whether a large trade gap is involved.

Unlike ⟨⟩bilateralism, multilateralism does not require the trade flow between countries to be of the same value.

multimedia computer system that combines audio and video components to create an interactive application that uses text, sound, and graphics (still, animated, and video sequences). For example, a multimedia database of musical instruments may allow a user not only to search and retrieve text about a particular instrument but also to see pictures of it and hear it play a piece of music.

Multimedia systems are still at an early stage of development. ⟨⟩CD-ROM is frequently used as a back-up storage for such systems because of its high storage capacity.

In training applications based on multimedia, the student's responses to questions displayed using pictures, text, and sound are monitored by the computer and the student's route through the training material is adjusted accordingly.

multinational corporation company or enterprise operating in several countries, usually defined as one that has 25% or more of its output capacity located outside its country of origin.

multiple birth in humans, the production of more than two babies from one pregnancy. Multiple births can be caused by more than two eggs being produced and fertilized (often as the result of hormone therapy to assist pregnancy), or by a single fertilized egg dividing more than once before implantation.

multiple independently targeted re-entry vehicle (MIRV) nuclear-warhead-carrying part of a ballistic ⟨⟩missile that splits off in midair from the main body. Since each is individually steered and controlled, MIRVs can attack separate targets over a wide area.

The US, former Soviet, UK, and French nuclear missiles are all equipped with MIRVs.

Multiple Mirror Telescope unique telescope on Mount Hopkins, Arizona, opened 1979, consisting of six 72-in/1.83-m mirrors mounted in a hexagon, the light-collecting area of which equals that of a single mirror of 176 in/4.5 m diameter. It is planned to replace the six mirrors with a single mirror 256 in/6.5 m wide.

multiple sclerosis (MS) incurable chronic disease of the central nervous system, occurring in young or middle adulthood. It is characterized by degeneration of the myelin sheath that surrounds nerves in the brain and spinal cord. It is also known as disseminated sclerosis. Its cause is unknown.

Depending on where the demyelination occurs—which nerves are affected—the symptoms of MS can mimic almost any neurological disorder. Typically seen are unsteadiness, ataxia (loss of muscular coordination), weakness, speech difficulties, and rapid involuntary movements of the eyes. The course of the disease is episodic, with frequent intervals of remission (apparent abatement of symptoms).

multiplier in economics, the theoretical concept, formulated by John Maynard Keynes, of the effect on national income or employment by an adjustment in overall demand. For example, investment by a company in a new plant will stimulate new income and expenditure, which will in turn generate new investment, and so on, so that the actual increase in national income may be several times greater than the original investment.

multistage rocket rocket launch vehicle made up of several rocket stages (often three) joined end to end. The bottom stage fires first, boosting the vehicle to high speed, then it falls away. The next stage fires, thrusting the now lighter vehicle even faster. The remaining stages fire and fall away in turn, boosting the vehicle's payload (cargo) to an orbital speed that can reach 17,500 mph/28,000 kph.

multitasking or *multiprogramming* in computing, a system in which one processor appears to run several different programs (or different parts of the same program) at the same time. All the programs are held in memory together and each is allowed to run for a certain period.

For example, one program may run while other programs are waiting for a ⟨⟩peripheral device to work or for input from an operator.

The ability to multitask depends on the ⟨⟩operating system rather than the type of computer. Unix is one of the commonest.

multiuser system or *multiaccess system* in computing, an operating system that enables several users to access the same computer apparently at the same time. Each user has a terminal, which may be local (connected directly to the computer) or remote (connected to the computer via a modem and a telephone line). Multiaccess is usually achieved by *timesharing*: the computer switches very rapidly between terminals and programs so that each user has sole use of the computer for only a fraction of a second but can work as if she or he had continuous access.

Mumford Lewis 1895–1990. US urban planner and social critic, concerned with the adverse effect of technology on contemporary society.

He was also concerned about the dehumanization of the individual as a response to a deadening environment. His writings show faith in human capacity to renew the world, however. He is noted for *The Culture of Cities* 1938 and *The City in History* 1961.

mummers' play or *St George play* British folk drama enacted in dumb show by a masked cast, performed on Christmas Day to celebrate the death of the old year and its rebirth as the new year. The plot usually consists of a duel between St George and an infidel knight, in which one of them is killed but later revived by a doctor. Mummers' plays are still performed in some parts of Britain.

mummy any dead body, human or animal, that has been naturally or artificially preserved. Natural mummification can occur through freezing (for example, mammoths in glacial ice from 25,000 years ago), drying, or preservation in bogs or oil seeps. Artificial mummification may be achieved by embalming (for example, the mummies of ancient Egypt) or by freeze-drying (see ⟨⟩cryonics).

mumps virus infection marked by fever and swelling of the parotid salivary glands (such as those under the ears). It is usually minor in children, although meningitis is a possible complication. In adults the symptoms are severe and it may cause sterility in adult men.

Mumps is the most common form of ⟨⟩meningitis in children, but it follows a much milder course than bacterial meningitis, and a complete recovery is usual. Rarely, mumps meningitis may lead to deafness. An effective vaccine against mumps, measles, and rubella (MMR vaccine) is now offered to children aged 18 months.

Munch Edvard 1863–1944. Norwegian painter and printmaker. He studied in Paris and Berlin, and his major works date from the period 1892–1908, when he lived mainly in Germany. His paintings often focus on neurotic emotional states. The *Frieze of Life* 1890s, a sequence of highly charged, symbolic paintings, includes some of his most characteristic images, such as *Skriket/The Scream* 1893. He later reused these in etchings, lithographs, and woodcuts.

Munch was influenced by van Gogh and Gauguin but soon developed his own expressive style, reducing his compositions to broad areas of color with sinuous contours emphasized by heavy brushstrokes, distorting faces and figures. His first show in Berlin 1892 made a great impact on young German artists. In 1908 he suffered a nervous breakdown and returned to Norway. Later works include a series of murals 1910–15 in the assembly halls of Oslo University.

Münchhausen Karl Friedrich, Freiherr (Baron) von 1720–1797. German soldier, born in Hanover. He served with the Russian army against the Turks, and after his retirement in 1760 told exaggerated stories of his adventures. This idiosyncrasy was utilized by the German writer Rudolph Erich Raspe (1737–1794) in his extravagantly fictitious *Adventures of Baron Munchausen* 1785, which he wrote in English while living in London.

Münchhausen's syndrome emotional disorder in which a patient feigns or invents symptoms to secure medical treatment. In some cases the patient will secretly ingest substances to produce real symptoms. It was named after the exaggerated tales of Baron Münchhausen.

Muncie city in E central Indiana, NE of Indianapolis; industries include vehicle parts, livestock, dairy products, steel forgings, and wire; population (1990) 71,000. It was the subject of Robert and Helen Lynd's *Middletown*, a sociological study of a midwestern city.

Munda member of any one of several groups living in NE and central India, numbering about 5 million (1983). Their most widely spoken languages are Santali and Mundari, languages of the Munda group, an isolated branch of the Austro-Asiatic family. The Mundas were formerly nomadic hunter-gatherers, but now practice shifting cultivation. They are Hindus, but retain animist beliefs.

Munich (German *München*) industrial city (brewing, printing, precision instruments, machinery, electrical goods, textiles), capital of Bavaria, Germany, on the river Isar; population (1986) 1,269,400.
features Munich owes many of its buildings and art treasures to the kings ◊Ludwig I and Maximilian II of Bavaria. The cathedral is late 15th century. The Alte Pinakothek contains paintings by old masters, and the Neue Pinakothek, modern paintings; there is the Bavarian National Museum, the Bavarian State Library, and the Deutsches Museum (science and technology). The university, founded at Ingolstadt 1472, was transferred to Munich 1826; to the NE at Garching there is a nuclear research center.
history Dating from the 12th century, Munich became the residence of the dukes of Wittelsbach in the 13th century, and the capital of independent Bavaria. It was the scene of the November revolution of 1918, the "Soviet" republic of 1919, and the Hitler putsch of 1923. It became the center of the Nazi movement, and the Munich Agreement of 1938 was signed there. When the 1972 Summer Olympics were held in Munich, a number of Israeli athletes were killed by guerrillas.

Munich Agreement pact signed on Sept 29, 1938 by the leaders of the UK (Neville ◊Chamberlain), France (Edouard ◊Daladier), Germany (Hitler), and Italy (Mussolini), under which Czechoslovakia was compelled to surrender its Sudeten-German districts (the **Sudetenland**) to Germany. Chamberlain claimed it would guarantee "peace in our time," but it did not prevent Hitler from seizing the rest of Czechoslovakia in March 1939.

Most districts were not given the option of a plebiscite under the agreement. After World War II the Sudetenland was returned to Czechoslovakia, and over 2 million German-speaking people were expelled from the country.

Munn v Illinois a US Supreme Court decision (one of the "Granger Cases") 1877 dealing with state regulation of industry. The owners of Illinois grain elevators filed suit against the state legislature over an 1873 law, which established maximum legal rates for grain storage. The petitioners claimed that this populist legislation interfered with federal regulation of interstate commerce and violated the due process clause. The Court voted 7 to 2 to uphold the Illinois law, ruling that it was a legitimate use of state police power in the public interest.

Munro Alice 1931– . Canadian author, known for her insightful short stories. Collections of her work include *Dance of the Happy Shades* 1968 and *The Progress of Love* 1987. She has written only one novel, *Lives of Girls and Women* 1971.

Munro H(ugh) H(ector) English author who wrote under the adopted name ◊Saki.

Munster southern province of the Republic of Ireland, comprising the counties of Clare, Cork, Kerry, Limerick, North and South Tipperary, and Waterford; area 9,318 sq mi/24,140 sq km; population (1991) 1,008,400.
It was a kingdom until the 12th century, and was settled in plantations by the English from 1586.

Münster industrial city (wire, cement, iron, brewing, and distilling) in North Rhine–Westphalia, NW Germany, formerly the capital of Westphalia; population (1988) 268,000. The Treaty of Westphalia was signed simultaneously here and at Osnabrück 1648, ending the Thirty Years' War.
Its university was founded 1773. Badly damaged in World War II, its ancient buildings, including the 15th-century cathedral and town hall, have been restored or rebuilt.

muntjac small deer, genus *Muntiacus*, found in SE Asia. There are about six species. Males have short spiked antlers and two sharp canine teeth forming tusks. They are sometimes called "barking deer" because of their voices.
Muntjac live mostly in dense vegetation and do not form herds.

Murakami Haruki 1949– . Japanese novelist and translator, one of Japan's best-selling writers, influenced by 20th-century US writers and popular culture. His dreamy, gently surrealist novels include *A Wild Sheep Chase* 1982 and *Norwegian Wood* 1987.

mural painting (Latin *murus* "wall") decoration of walls, vaults, and ceilings by means of ◊fresco, oil, ◊tempera, or ◊encaustic painting methods. Mural painters include Cimabue, Giotto, Masaccio, Ghirlandaio, and, in the 20th century, Diego Rivera.

Murasaki Shikibu *c.* 978–*c.* 1015. Japanese writer, a lady at the court. Her masterpiece of fiction, *The Tale of Genji*, is one of the classic works of Japanese literature, and may be the world's first novel.
She was a member of the Fujiwara clan, but her own name is not known; scholars have given her the name Murasaki after a character in the book. It deals with upper-class life in Heian Japan, centering on the affairs of Prince Genji. A portion of her diary and a number of poems also survive.

Murat Joachim 1767–1815. King of Naples 1808–1815. An officer in the French army, he

was made king by Napoleon, but deserted him in 1813 in the vain hope that Austria and Great Britain would recognize him. In 1815 he attempted unsuccessfully to make himself king of all Italy, but when he landed in Calabria in an attempt to gain the throne he was captured and shot.

Murcia autonomous region of SE Spain; area 4,362 sq mi/11,300 sq km; population (1986) 1,014,000. It includes the cities Murcia and Cartagena, and produces esparto grass, lead, zinc, iron, and fruit.

murder unlawful killing of one person by another. In the US, first-degree murder requires proof of premeditation; second-degree murder falls between first-degree murder and ◊manslaughter.
If the killer can show provocation by the victim (action or words that would make a reasonable person lose self-control) or diminished responsibility (an abnormal state of mind caused by illness, injury, or mental subnormality), the charge may be reduced to a less serious one. See also ◊assassination and ◊homicide.

"Murders in the Rue Morgue, The" 1841 tale by the US writer Edgar Allan Poe, acknowledged as the first detective story. Poe's detective Auguste Dupin points to the clues leading to the solution of the macabre mystery in what Poe called a "tale of ratiocination."

Murdoch (Keith) Rupert 1931– . Australian-born US media magnate with worldwide interests. His UK newspapers, generally rightwing, include the *Sun*, the *News of the World*, and *The Times*; in the US, he has a 50% share of 20th Century Fox, six Metromedia TV stations, and newspaper and magazine publishing companies. He purchased a 50% stake in a Hungarian tabloid, *Reform*, from 1989.
He became a US citizen in 1985.

Murdoch Iris 1919– . English novelist, born in Dublin. Her novels combine philosophical speculation with often outrageous situations and tangled human relationships. They include *The Sandcastle* 1957, *The Sea, The Sea* 1978, and *The Message to the Planet* 1989.

Murillo Bartolomé Esteban *c.* 1617–1682. Spanish painter, active mainly in Seville. He painted sentimental pictures of the Immaculate Conception; he also specialized in studies of street urchins.
Murillo was born in Seville. Visiting Madrid in the 1640s, he was befriended by the court painter Velázquez. After his return to Seville he received many religious commissions. He founded the academy of painting in Seville 1660 with the help of Herrera the Younger.

Murmansk seaport in NW Russia, on the Barents Sea; population (1987) 432,000. It is the largest city in the Arctic, Russia's most important fishing port, and the base of naval units and the icebreakers that keep the Northeast Passage open.
It is the center of Russian Lapland and the only port on the Russian Arctic coast that is in use all year round. The Festival of the North in March marks the end of the two-month Arctic night.
After the entry of the USSR into World War II in 1941, supplies from the UK and later from the US were unloaded there.

Murnau F W. Adopted name of Friedrich Wilhelm Plumpe 1889–1931. German silent-film director, known for his expressive images and "subjective" use of a moving camera in *Der letzte Mamm/The Last Laugh* 1924. Other films include *Nosferatu* 1922 (a version of the Dracula story), *Sunrise* 1927, and *Tabu* 1931.

Muromachi in Japanese history, the period 1392–1568, comprising the greater part of the rule of the ⇨Ashikaga shoguns; it is named after the area of Kyoto where their headquarters were sited.

Murphy Audie 1924–1971. US actor and war hero who starred mainly in low-budget Westerns. His work includes *The Red Badge of Courage* 1951, *The Quiet American* 1958, and *The Unforgiven* 1960.

He was the most decorated soldier of World War II, and was promoted by Hollywood as such, in the film story of his war years *To Hell and Back* 1955, in which he starred.

Murphy Eddie 1961– . US film actor and comedian. His first film, *48 Hours* 1982, introduced the street-wise, cocksure character that has become his specialty. Its great success, and that of his next two films, *Trading Places* 1983 and *Beverly Hills Cop* 1984, made him one of the biggest box-office draws of the 1980s.

Murphy began his career at 15 as a stand-up comedian before becoming a regular on the US television show *Saturday Night Live*. Other films include *Beverley Hills II* 1987, his filmed live show *Eddie Murphy Raw* 1987, *Coming to America* 1988, which he co-wrote, *Harlem Nights* 1989, which he produced and directed, and *Boomerang* 1992.

Murray principal river of Australia, 1,600 mi/2,575 km long. It rises in the Australian Alps near Mount Kosciusko and flows west, forming the boundary between New South Wales and Victoria, and reaches the sea at Encounter Bay, South Australia. With its main tributary, the Darling, it is 2,330 mi/3,750 km long.

Its other tributaries include the Lachlan and the Murrumbidgee. The Dartmouth Dam (1979) in the Great Dividing Range supplies hydroelectric power and has drought-proofed the Murray River system, but irrigation (for grapes, citrus and stone fruits) and navigation schemes have led to soil salinization.

Murray James Augustus Henry 1837–1915. Scottish philologist. He was the first editor of the *Oxford English Dictionary* (originally the *New English Dictionary*) from 1878 until his death; the first volume was published 1884.

Murray Joseph E 1919– . US surgeon whose work in the field of controlling rejection of organ transplants earned him a shared Nobel Prize for Medicine 1990.

Murrow Edward R(oscoe) 1908–1965. US broadcast journalist. Hired by the Columbia Broadcasting System (CBS) 1935 to plan its educational programs, Murrow was named director of its European Bureau 1937. From London he covered the events of World War II. Murrow hosted the popular radio show "Hear It Now" 1948–51 and television shows "See It Now" 1951–58, "Person to Person" 1953–58, and "Small World" 1958–60. After leaving CBS, he served as director of the US Information Agency 1961–64.

Born in Greensboro, North Carolina, Murrow attended Washington State College and joined the staff of the Institute of International Education 1932.

Murrumbidgee river of New South Wales, Australia; length 1,050 mi/1,690 km. It rises in the Australian Alps, flows north to the Burrinjuck reservoir, and then west to meet the river ⇨Murray.

Musashi Miyamoto see ⇨Miyamoto Musashi, Japanese samurai.

Muscat or *Masqat* capital of Oman, E Arabia, adjoining the port of Matrah, which has a deep-water harbor; combined population (1982) 80,000. It produces natural gas and chemicals.

Muscat and Oman former name of ⇨Oman, country in the Middle East.

muscle contractile animal tissue that produces locomotion and maintains the movement of body substances. Muscle is made of long cells that can contract to between one-half and one-third of their relaxed length.

Striped muscles are activated by ⇨motor nerves under voluntary control; their ends are usually attached via tendons to bones. *Involuntary* or *smooth* muscles are controlled by motor nerves of the ⇨autonomic nervous system, and are located in the gut, blood vessels, iris, and various ducts. *Cardiac* muscle occurs only in the heart, and is also controlled by the autonomic nervous system.

An artificial muscle fiber was developed in the US 1990. Besides replacing muscle fiber, it can be used for substitute ligaments and blood vessels and to prevent tissues sticking together after surgery.

muscovite white mica, $KAl_2(Si_3AlO_{10}(OH,F)_2$, a common silicate mineral. It is colorless to silvery white with shiny surfaces, and like all micas it splits into thin flakes along its one perfect cleavage. Muscovite is a metamorphic mineral occurring mainly in schists; it is also found in some granites, and appears as shiny flakes on bedding planes of some sandstones.

muscular dystrophy any of a group of inherited chronic muscle disorders marked by weakening and wasting of muscle. Muscle fibers degenerate, to be replaced by fatty tissue, although the nerve supply remains unimpaired. Death occurs in early adult life.

The commonest form, Duchenne muscular dystrophy, strikes boys, usually before the age of four. The child develops a waddling gait and an inward curvature (lordosis) of the lumbar spine. The muscles affected by dystrophy and the rate of progress vary. There is no cure, but physical treatments can minimize disability.

Muses in Greek mythology, the nine daughters of Zeus and Mnemosyne (goddess of memory) and inspirers of creative arts: Calliope, epic poetry; Clio, history; Erato, love poetry; Euterpe, lyric poetry; Melpomene, tragedy; Polyhymnia, hymns; Terpsichore, dance; Thalia, comedy; and Urania, astronomy.

Museveni Yoweri Kaguta 1945– . Ugandan general and politician, president from 1986. He led the opposition to Idi Amin's regime 1971–78 and was minister of defense 1979–80 but, unhappy with Milton Obote's autocratic leadership, formed the National Resistance Army (NRA). When Obote was ousted in a coup in 1985, Museveni entered into a brief power-sharing agreement with his successor, Tito Okello, before taking over as president. Museveni leads a broad-based coalition government.

Musgrave Ranges Australian mountain ranges on the border between South Australia and the Northern Territory; the highest peak is Mount Woodruffe 5,000 ft/1,525 m. The area is an Aboriginal reserve.

mushroom fruiting body of certain fungi, consisting of an upright stem and a spore-producing cap with radiating gills on the undersurface. There are many edible species belonging to the genus *Agaricus*. See also ⇨fungus and ⇨toadstool.

Musial Stan(ley Frank). Nicknamed "Stan the Man." 1920– . US baseball player. Born in

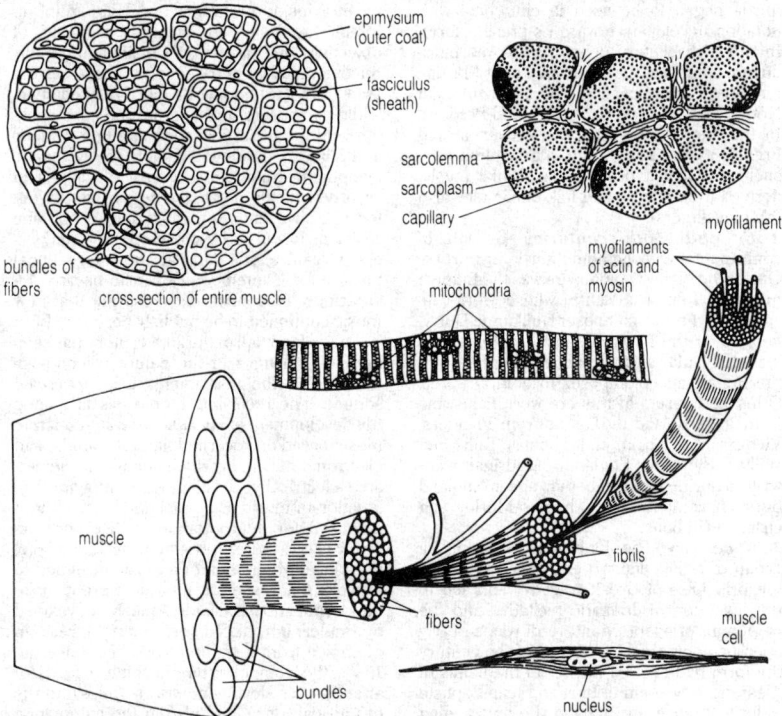

muscle *The movements of the arm depend on two muscles, the biceps and the triceps.*

Donora, Pennsylvania, Musial was an outstanding high-school athlete and was signed by the St Louis Cardinals 1938. As a Cardinal outfielder and first baseman from 1941, Musial played 22 years, during which he led the National League 6 times in hits, 8 times in doubles, 5 times in triples, and 7 times in batting average. He played his last season 1963 and was hired by the Cardinals as an executive. Musial was elected to the Baseball Hall of Fame 1969.

music art of combining sounds into a coherent perceptual experience, typically in accordance with fixed patterns and for an aesthetic purpose. Music is generally categorized as Classical, ⬦jazz, ⬦pop music, ⬦country and western, and ⬦jazz.

The Greek word *mousikē* covered all the arts presided over by the Muses. The various civilizations of the ancient and modern world developed their own musical systems. Eastern music recognizes subtler distinctions of pitch than does Western music and also differs from Western music in that the absence, until recently, of written notation ruled out the composition of major developed works; it fostered melodic and rhythmic patterns, freely interpreted (as in the Indian *raga*) by virtuosos.

Western classical music

Middle Ages The documented history of Western music since Classical times begins with the liturgical music of the medieval Catholic church, derived from Greek and Hebrew antecedents. The four scales, or modes, to which the words of the liturgy were chanted were traditionally first set in order by St Ambrose in AD 384. St Gregory the Great added four more to the original Ambrosian modes, and this system forms the basis of Gregorian ⬦plainsong, still used in the Roman Catholic Church. The organ was introduced in the 8th century, and in the 9th century harmonized music began to be used in churches, with notation developing toward its present form. In the 11th century counterpoint was introduced, notably at the monastery of St Martial, Limoges, France, and in the late 12th century at Nôtre Dame in Paris (by Léonin and Perotin). In the late Middle Ages the Provençal and French ⬦troubadours and court composers, such as Machaut, developed a secular music, derived from church and folk music (see also ⬦Minnesingers).

15th and 16th centuries Growth of contrapuntal or polyphonic music in Europe. One of the earliest composers was the English musician John Dunstable, whose works inspired the French composer Guillaume Dufay, founder of the Flemish school; its members included Dufay's pupil Joannes Okeghem and the Renaissance composer Josquin Desprez. Other composers of this era were Palestrina from Italy, Roland de Lassus from Flanders, Victoria from Spain, and Thomas Tallis and William Byrd from England. ⬦Madrigals were written during the Elizabethan age in England by such composers as Thomas Morley and Orlando Gibbons.

17th-century The Florentine Academy, a group of artists and writers, aimed to revive the principles of Greek tragedy. This led to the invention of dramatic recitative and the beginning of opera. Monteverdi was an early operatic composer; by the end of the century the form had evolved further in the hands of Alessandro Scarlatti in Italy and Jean-Baptiste Lully in France. In England the outstanding composer of the period was Purcell.

18th century The early part of the century was dominated by J S Bach and Handel. Bach was a master of harmony and counterpoint. Handel is renowned for his dramatic oratorios. Bach's sons C P E Bach and J C Bach reacted against contrapuntal forms and developed sonata form, the basis of the Classical sonata, quartet, and symphony. In these types of composition, mastery of style was achieved by the Viennese composers Haydn and Mozart. With Beethoven, music assumed new dynamic and expressive functions.

19th century Romantic music, represented in its early stages by Weber, Schubert, Schumann, Mendelssohn, and Chopin, tended to be subjectively emotional. Orchestral color was increasingly exploited—most notably by Berlioz—and harmony became more chromatic. Nationalism became prominent at this time, as evidenced by the intense Polish nationalism of Chopin; the exploitation of Hungarian music by Liszt; the Russians Rimsky-Korsakov, Borodin, Mussorgsky, and, less typically, Tchaikovsky; the works of the Czechs Dvořák and Smetana; and the Norwegian Grieg. Revolutionary changes were brought about by Wagner in the field of opera, although traditional Italian lyricism continued in the work of Rossini, Verdi, and Puccini. Wagner's contemporary Brahms stood for Classical discipline of form combined with Romantic feeling. The Belgian César Franck, with a newly chromatic idiom, also renewed the tradition of polyphonic writing.

20th century Around 1900 a reaction against Romanticism became apparent in the impressionism of Debussy and Ravel, and the exotic chromaticism of Stravinsky and Scriabin. In Austria and Germany, the tradition of Bruckner, Mahler, and Richard Strauss faced a disturbing new world of atonal expressionism in Schoenberg, Berg, and Webern. After World War I Neo-Classicism, represented by Stravinsky, Prokofiev, and Hindemith, attempted to restore 18th-century principles of objectivity and order while maintaining a distinctively 20th-century tone. In Paris *Les Six* (see ⬦*Six, Les*) adopted a more relaxed style, while composers further from the cosmopolitan centers of Europe, such as Elgar, Delius, and Sibelius, continued loyal to the Romantic symphonic tradition. The rise of radio and recorded media created a new mass market for Classical and Romantic music, but one resistant to music by contemporary composers. Organizations such as the International Society for Contemporary Music became increasingly responsible for ensuring that new music continued to be publicly performed.

The second half of the 20th century has seen dramatic changes in the nature of composition and in the instruments used to create sounds. The recording studio has facilitated the development of *musique concrète*/concrete music based on recorded natural sounds, and electronic music, in which sounds are generated electrically, developments implying the creation of music as a finished object without the need for interpretation by live performers. Chance music, promoted by John Cage, introduced the notion of a music designed to provoke unforeseen results and thereby make new connections; aleatoric music, developed by Boulez, introduced performers to freedom of choice from a range of options. Since the 1960s the computer has become a focus of attention for developments in the synthesis of musical tones, and also in the automation of compositional techniques, most notably at

Stanford University and MIT in the US, and at IRCAM in Paris.

musical 20th-century form of dramatic musical performance, combining elements of song, dance, and the spoken word, often characterized by lavish staging and large casts. It developed from the operettas and musical comedies of the 19th century.

The **operetta** is a light-hearted entertainment with extensive musical content: Jaques Offenbach, Johann Strauss, Franz Lehár, and Gilbert and Sullivan all composed operettas. The **musical comedy** is an anglicization of the French *opéra bouffe*, of which the first was *A Gaiety Girl* 1893, mounted by George Edwardes (1852–1915) at the Gaiety Theater, London. Typical musical comedies of the 1920s were *Rose Marie* 1924 by Rudolf Friml (1879–1972); *The Student Prince* 1924 and *The Desert Song* 1926, both by Sigmund Romberg (1887–1951); and *No, No, Nanette* 1925 by Vincent Youmans (1898–1946). The 1930s and 1940s were an era of sophisticated musical comedies with many filmed examples and a strong US presence (Irving Berlin, Jerome Kern, Cole Porter, and George Gershwin). In England Noël Coward and Ivor Novello also wrote musicals.

In 1943 Rodgers and Hammerstein's *Oklahoma!* introduced an integration of plot and music, which was developed in Lerner and Loewe's *My Fair Lady* 1956 and Leonard Bernstein's *West Side Story* 1957. Sandy Wilson's *The Boy Friend* 1953 revived the British musical and was followed by hits such as Lionel Bart's *Oliver!* 1960. Musicals began to branch into religious and political themes with *Oh What a Lovely War!* 1963, produced by Joan Littlewood and Charles Chiltern, and the Andrew Lloyd Webber musicals *Jesus Christ Superstar* 1970 and *Evita* 1978. Another category of musical, substituting a theme for conventional plotting, includes Stephen Sondheim's *Company* 1970, Hamlisch and Kleban's *A Chorus Line* 1975, and Lloyd Webber's *Cats* 1981, using verses by T S Eliot. In the 1980s 19th-century melodrama was popular, for example *Phantom of the Opera* 1986 and *Les Misérables* 1987.

music hall British light theatrical entertainment, in which singers, dancers, comedians, and acrobats perform in "turns." The music hall's heyday was at the beginning of the 20th century, with such artistes as Marie Lloyd, Harry Lauder, and George Formby. The US equivalent is ⬦vaudeville.

music theater staged performance of vocal music that deliberately sets out to get away from the grandiose style and scale of traditional opera.

Its origins can be traced to the 1920s and 1930s, to plays with music like Kurt Weill's *Mahagonny-Songspiel*, but it came into its own as a movement in the 1960s. It includes not just contemporary opera (such as Alexander Goehr's *Naboth's Vineyard* 1968) but also works like Peter Maxwell Davies's *Eight Songs for a Mad King* 1969.

musk in botany, perennial plant *Mimulus moschatus* of the family Scrophulariaceae; its small oblong leaves exude the musky scent from which it takes its name; it is also called **monkey flower**. Also any of several plants with a musky odor, including the musk mallow *Malva moschata* and the musk rose *Rosa moschata*.

musk deer small deer *Moschus moschiferus* native to mountains of central Asia. A solitary

Western music: chronology

AD 590	St Gregory the Great was elected pope. His enlightened leadership inspired church music to new heights, initiating Gregorian chant.
1026	The Italian monk Guido d'Arezzo completed his treatise *Micrologus*. He founded modern notation and tonic sol-fa.
1207	Walther von der Vogelweide, Tannhauser, and Wolfram von Eschenbach competed in a song contest at Wartburg Castle, as the age of the Minnesingers or German poet-musicians approached its height.
1240	The earliest known canon, *Sumer is Icumen In*, was composed around this year.
1320	*Ars nova*, a tract by Philippe de Vitry, gave its name to a new, more graceful era in music.
1364	Music's first large-scale masterpiece, the *Notre Dame Mass* of Guillaume de Machaut, was performed in Rheims at the coronation of Charles V of France.
1473	The earliest known printed music, the *Collectorium super Magnificat* by Johannes Gerson, was published in Esslingen, near Stuttgart.
1564	The violin was designed and manufactured by Andrea Amati in Cremona.
1575	Thomas Tallis and William Byrd jointly published their *Cantiones sacrae*, a collection of 34 motets.
1597	The first opera, *La Dafne* by Jacopo Peri, was staged privately at the Corsi Palazzo in Florence.
1610	Monteverdi's *Vespers* was published in Venice.
1637	The world's first opera house opened in Venice.
1644	Antonio Stradivarius was born. More than 600 of his violins, made in Cremona, survived into the 20th century.
1709	Bartolemmeo Cristofori built the first piano in Florence.
1721	Bach completed his six *Brandenburg Concertos*.
1722	Jean-Philippe Rameau's book *Traité de l'harmonie* founded modern harmonic theory.
1725	Vivaldi's *The Four Seasons* was published in Amsterdam.
1742	Handel's *Messiah* received its world premiere in Dublin.
1761	Haydn took up service as vice kapellmeister with the aristocratic Esterházy family, to whom he was connected until his death 1809.
1788	Mozart completed his last three symphonies, numbers 39–41, in six weeks.
1795	The composer and inventor Thomas Wright introduced metronome markings.
1805	Beethoven's *Eroica Symphony* vastly expanded the horizons of orchestral music.
1815	Schubert's output for this year included two symphonies, two masses, 20 waltzes, and 145 songs.
1821	Weber's *Der Freischutz* introduced heroic German Romanticism to opera.
1828	The limits of instrumental virtuosity were redefined by violinist Paganini's Vienna debut.
1830	Berlioz's dazzlingly avant-garde and programmatic *Symphonie fantastique* startled Paris concertgoers.
1831	Grand opera was inaugurated with *Robert elle diable* by Giacomo Meyerbeer.
1854	In Weimar, Liszt conducted the premieres of his first symphonic poems.
1855	Like most orchestras around this date, the New York Philharmonic for the first time sat down while playing (cellists were already seated).
1865	Wagner's opera *Tristan and Isolde* scaled new heights of expressiveness using unprecedented chromaticism. Schubert's *Unfinished Symphony* (1822) was premiered in Vienna.
1875	The first of a series of collaborations between Arthur Sullivan and the librettist W S Gilbert, *Trial by Jury*, was given its premiere.
1876	Wagner's *The Ring of the Nibelung* was produced in Bayreuth. Brahms's *First Symphony* was performed in Karlsruhe.
1877	Edison invented the cylindrical tin-foil phonograph, but few showed interest.
1883	The Metropolitan Opera House opened in New York with a production of Gounod's *Faust*.
1885	Liszt composed *Bagatelle without Tonality* (his *Faust Symphony* of 1857 opened with a 12-note row).
1894	Debussy's *Prélude à l'après-midi d'un faune* anticipated 20th-century composition with its use of the whole-tone scale.
1899	Scott Joplin's "Maple Leaf Rag" was published in Sedalia, Missouri.
1902	Caruso recorded ten arias in a hotel room in Milan, the success of which established the popularity of the phonograph. By the time of his death 1921 he had earned $2 million from sales of his recordings.
1911	Irving Berlin had his first big success as a songwriter with "Alexander's Ragtime Band."
1912	Schoenberg's atonal *Pierrot Lunaire*, for reciter and chamber ensemble, foreshadowed many similar small-scale quasi-theatrical works.
1913	Stravinsky's ballet *The Rite of Spring* precipitated a riot at its premiere in Paris.
1925	Louis Armstrong made his first records with the Hot Five. Duke Ellington's Washingtonians also started recording.
1927	Jerome Kern's *Showboat*, with libretto by Oscar Hammerstein II, laid the foundations of the US musical.
1937	Arturo Toscanini, one of the greatest conductors in the history of music, began his 17-year association with the NBC Symphony Orchestra.
1938	Prokofiev's score for Eisenstein's *Alexander Nevsky* raised film music to new levels. Big-band music became popular.
1940	Walt Disney's *Fantasia* introduced Classical music, conducted by Leopold Stokowski, to a worldwide audience of filmgoers.
1942	In Chicago, John Cage conducted the premiere of his *Imaginary Landscape no 3*, scored for marimbula, gongs, tin cans, buzzers, plucked coil, electric oscillator, and generator.
1945	Bebop jazz was initiated. The jazz greats Charlie Parker and Dizzy Gillespie first recorded together.
1954	Stockhausen's *Electronic Studies* for magnetic tape were broadcast in Cologne. Edgard Varèse's *Déserts*, the first work to combine instruments and prerecorded magnetic tape, was performed in Paris. Elvis Presley made his first rock-and-roll recordings.
1957	Leonard Bernstein's *West Side Story* was premiered in New York. A computer, programed at the University of Illinois by Lejaren Hiller and Leonard Isaacson, composed the *Illiac Suite* for string quartet.
1965	Robert Moog invented a synthesizer that considerably widened the scope of electronic music. The film soundtrack of *The Sound of Music*, with music by Rodgers and lyrics by Hammerstein, was released, and stayed in the sales charts for the next two years. Bob Dylan used electric instrumentation on *Highway 61 Revisited*.
1967	The Beatles' album *Sgt Pepper's Lonely Hearts Club Band*, which took over 500 hours to record, was released. The first Velvet Underground album was released. Psychedelic rock spread from San Francisco, and hard rock developed in the US and the UK.
1972	Bob Marley's LP *Catch a Fire* began popularization of reggae beyond Jamaica.
1976	Philip Glass's opera *Einstein on the Beach*, using the repetitive techniques of minimalism, was given its first performance in Paris. Punk rock arrived with the Sex Pistols' "Anarchy in the UK."
1977	The Institute for Research and Coordination of Acoustics and Music (IRCAM) was founded in Paris under the direction of Boulez, for visiting composers to make use of advanced electronic equipment.
1981	MTV (Music Television) started broadcasting nonstop pop videos on cable in the US, growing into a worldwide network in the following decade.
1983	Messiaen's only opera, *Saint François d'Assise*, was given its first performance in Paris. Lutosławski's Third Symphony was premiered to worldwide acclaim by the Chicago Symphony Orchestra under Georg Solti. Compact disks were launched in the West.
1986	Paul Simon's *Graceland* album drew on and popularized world music.
1990	Many record chain stores ceased to stock seven-inch singles, accelerating the decline of vinyl records' share of the market.
1991	US rap group NWA declared not obscene by a UK court. Various attempts, especially in the US, to limit freedom of speech in popular music were generally unsuccessful.
1992	DCC (Digital Compact Cassettes) and MiniDisc (MD), two new audio formats, were launched by Philips and Sony, respectively.

animal, it is about 20 in/50 cm high, sure-footed, and has large ears and no antlers. Males have tusklike upper canine teeth. It is hunted and farmed for the musk secreted by an abdominal gland, which is used as medicine or perfume.

Muskegon city in W Michigan, on the Muskegon River where it enters into Lake Michigan, NW of Grand Rapids; industries include heavy machinery, metal products, vehicle parts, and sporting goods; population (1990) 40,300.

musk ox ruminant *Ovibos moschatus* of the family Bovidae, native to the Arctic regions of North America. It displays characteristics of sheep and oxen, is about the size of a small domestic cow, and has long brown hair. At certain seasons it exhales a musky odor.

Its underwool (*qiviut*) is almost as fine as vicuna, and musk-ox farms have been established in Alaska, Québec, and Norway.

muskrat rodent *Ondatra zibethicus* of the family Cricetidae, about 30 cm/12in long, living along streams, rivers, and lakes in North America. It has webbed hind feet, a side-to-side flattened tail, and shiny, light-brown fur. It builds up a store of food, plastering it over with mud, for winter consumption. It is hunted for its fur.

Muslim or *Moslem*, a follower of ⟡Islam.

Muslim Brotherhood movement founded by members of the Sunni branch of Islam in Egypt in 1928. It aims at the establishment of a theocratic Islamic state and is headed by a "supreme guide." It is also active in Jordan, Sudan, and Syria.

mussel one of a number of bivalve mollusks, some of them edible, such as *Mytilus edulis*, found in clusters attached to rocks around the N Atlantic and American coasts. It has a blue-black shell.

Freshwater pearl mussels, such as *Unio margaritiferus*, are found in some North American and European rivers. *Margaritifera margaritifera* became a protected species in 1991 having suffered from pollution and from amateur fishers who, unlike professionals, are not able to extract the pearl without killing the mussel itself. The green-lipped mussel, found only off New Zealand, produces an extract that is used in the treatment of arthritis.

Musset Alfred de 1810–1857. French poet and playwright. He achieved success with the volume of poems *Contes d'Espagne et d'Italie/Stories of Spain and Italy* 1829. His *Confession d'un enfant du siècle/Confessions of a Child of the Century* 1835 recounts his broken relationship with George Sand.

Mussolini Benito 1883–1945. Italian dictator 1925–43. As founder of the Fascist Movement (see ⟡fascism) 1919 and prime minister from 1922, he became known as *Il Duce* ("the leader"). He invaded Ethiopia 1935–36, intervened in the Spanish Civil War 1936–39 in support of Franco, and conquered Albania 1939. In June 1940 Italy entered World War II supporting Hitler. Forced by military and domestic setbacks to resign 1943, Mussolini established a breakaway government in N Italy 1944–45, but was killed trying to flee the country.

Mussolini was born in the Romagna, the son of a blacksmith, and worked in early life as a teacher and journalist. He became active in the socialist movement, from which he was expelled 1914 for advocating Italian intervention in World War I. In 1919 he founded the Fascist Movement, whose program combined violent nationalism with demagogic republican and anticapitalist slogans, and launched a campaign of terrorism against the socialists. This movement was backed by many landowners and industrialists and by the heads of the army and police, and in Oct 1922 Mussolini was in power as prime minister at the head of a coalition government. In 1925 he assumed dictatorial powers, and in 1926 all opposition parties were banned. During the years that followed, the political, legal, and education systems were remodeled on Fascist lines.

Mussolini's Blackshirt followers were the forerunners of Hitler's Brownshirts, and his career of conquest drew him into close cooperation with Nazi Germany. Italy and Germany formed the ⟡Axis alliance 1936. During World War II, Italian defeats in N Africa and Greece, the Allied invasion of Sicily, and discontent at home destroyed Mussolini's prestige, and in July 1943 he was compelled to resign by his own Fascist Grand Council. He was released from prison by German parachutists in Sept 1943 and set up a "Republican Fascist" government in N Italy. In April 1945 he and his mistress, Clara Petacci, were captured by partisans at Lake Como while heading for the Swiss border, and shot. Their bodies were taken to Milan and hung upside down in a public square.

Mussorgsky Modest Petrovich 1839–1881. Russian composer who was largely self-taught. His opera *Boris Godunov* was completed in 1869, although not produced in St Petersburg until 1874. Some of his works were "revised" by ⟡Rimsky-Korsakov, and only recently has their harsh original beauty been recognized.

Mussorgsky, born in Karevo, resigned his commission in the army in 1858 to concentrate on music while working as a government clerk. A member of the group of nationalist composers, the Five, he was influenced by both folk music and literature. Among his other works are the incomplete operas *Khovanshchina* and *Sorochintsy Fair*, the orchestral *A Night on Bald Mountain* 1867, the suite for piano *Pictures at an Exhibition* 1874, and many songs. Mussorgsky died in poverty, from alcoholism.

Mustafa Kemal Turkish leader who assumed the name of ⟡Atatürk.

mustard any of several annual plants of the family Cruciferae, with sweet-smelling yellow flowers. Brown and white mustard are cultivated as a condiment in Europe and North America. The seeds of brown mustard *Brassica juncea* and white mustard *Sinapis alba* are used in the preparation of table mustard.

Brown mustard replaced black mustard *Brassica nigra* in commercial mustard products during the 1950s with the introduction of mechanized harvesting. *B. nigra* is unsuitable for mechanized harvesting since its pods are dehiscent (that is, they split open to release their seeds), whereas *B. juncea* is indehiscent.

Table mustard is most often used as an accompaniment to meat, although it can also be used in sauces and dressings, and with fish. **English mustard** is made from finely milled brown and white mustard seed to which turmeric is added as a colorant. French **Dijon mustard** contains brown mustard seed, verjuice (the juice of unripe grapes), oil, and white wine. Other varieties are made with vinegar, and may be flavored with herbs or garlic.

The seedlings of white mustard are used in salads. White mustard is also sometimes grown by farmers and plowed back to enrich the soil. Brown mustard is grown on a large scale as an oil-seed crop throughout India, China, and southern Russia.

Mustique island in the Caribbean. See under ⟡St Vincent and the Grenadines.

mutagen any substance that makes ⟡mutation of genes more likely. A mutagen is likely to also act as a ⟡carcinogen.

mutation in biology, a change in the genes produced by a change in the ⟡DNA that makes up the hereditary material of all living organisms. Mutations, the raw material of evolution, result from mistakes during replication (copying) of DNA molecules. Only a few improve the organism's performance and are therefore favored by ⟡natural selection. Mutation rates are increased by certain chemicals and by radiation.

Common mutations include the omission or insertion of a base (one of the chemical subunits of DNA); these are known as **point mutations**. Larger-scale mutations include removal of a whole segment of DNA or its inversion within the DNA strand. Not all mutations affect the organism, because there is a certain amount of redundancy in the genetic information. If a mutation is "translated" from DNA into the protein that makes up the organism's structure, it may be in a nonfunctional part of the protein and thus have no detectable effect. This is known as a **neutral mutation**, and is of importance in ⟡molecular clock studies because such mutations tend to accumulate gradually as time passes. Some mutations do affect genes that control protein production or functional parts of protein, and most of these are lethal to the organism.

mute in music, any device used to dampen the vibration of an instrument and so affect the tone. Brass instruments use plugs of metal or cardboard inserted in the bell, while orchestral strings apply a form of clamp to the bridge.

A cloth applied to the skin of a kettledrum, or inserted into the bell of a saxophone or clarinet, has a similar effect.

Muti Riccardo 1941– . Italian conductor of the Philharmonia Orchestra, London, 1973–82, the Philadelphia Orchestra from 1981, and artistic director of La Scala, Milan, from 1986. He is known as a purist, devoted to carrying out a composer's intentions to the last detail.

mutiny organized act of disobedience or defiance by two or more members of the armed services. In naval and military law, mutiny has always been regarded as one of the most serious of crimes, punishable in wartime by death.

mutton bird any of various shearwaters and petrels that breed in burrows on Australasian islands. The young are very fat, and are killed for food and oil.

mutual fund a company that invests its clients' funds in other companies, equities, or securities. The owner of stock in the investment company holds a proportional interest in the investment company based on the number of shares in the portfolio holdings of the company. In this way a small investor may benefit from professional judgment and a much broader range of investments than might be possible individually.

Mutual funds are generally of two types: open-end investment, companies that issue new stock whenever they sell shares to purchasers, and closed-end investment, companies that issue a fixed number of shares that must be purchased through a stock broker. In open-end funds, the investor is not generally committed to hold the stock for a specified period. Closed-end funds are sometimes sold on a contractual basis requiring a minimum investment and holdings kept for a minimum period.

mutual induction in physics, the production of an electromotive force (emf) or voltage in an electric circuit caused by a changing ⟡magnetic flux in a neighboring circuit. The two circuits are often coils of wire, as in a ⟡transformer, and the size of the induced emf depends largely on the numbers of turns of wire in each of the coils.

mutualism an association between two organisms of different species whereby both profit from the relationship. See also ⟡symbiosis.

Muybridge Eadweard. Adopted name of Edward James Muggeridge 1830–1904. British photographer. He made a series of animal locomotion photographs in the US in the 1870s and proved that, when a horse trots, there are times when all its feet are off the ground. He also explored motion in birds and humans.

Muzorewa Abel (Tendekayi) 1925– . Zimbabwean politician and Methodist bishop. He was president of the African National Council 1971–85 and prime minister of Rhodesia/Zimbabwe 1979–80. He was detained for a year in 1983–84. He is leader of the minority United Africa National Council.

Muzorewa was educated at Methodist colleges in Rhodesia and Nashville, Tennessee.

MVD acronym for the Soviet Ministry of Internal Affairs, name (1946–53) of the Soviet secret police; later the ⟡KGB.

Mwinyi Ali Hassan 1925– . Tanzanian socialist politician, president from 1985, when he succeeded Julius Nyerere. He began a revival of private enterprise and control of state involvement and spending.

myalgic encephalomyelitis see ⟡ME.

Myanmar formerly (until 1989) *Burma* country in SE Asia, bounded NW by India and Bangladesh, NE by China, SE by Laos and Thailand, and SW by the Bay of Bengal.

government Under the 1974 constitution, suspended from Sept 1988, Myanmar is a unitary republic. The highest organ of state power is the 489-member people's assembly (Pyithu Hluttaw), elected by universal suffrage every four years. The people's assembly elects the nation's executive, the 30-member state council, which has a representative from each of Myanmar's 14 states and divisions and is headed by a chair who acts as president. It is the sole legislature and elects a council of ministers, headed by a prime minister, in charge of day-to-day administration.

history The Burmese date their era from AD 638, when they had arrived from the region

where China meets Tibet. By 850 they had organized a state in the center of the plain at Pagan, and in the period 1044–1287 maintained a hegemony over most of the area. In 1287 Kublai Khan's grandson Ye-su Timur occupied the region after destroying the Pagan dynasty. After he withdrew, anarchy supervened. From about 1490 to 1750 the Toungoo dynasty maintained itself, with increasing difficulty; in 1752 Alaungpaya reunited the country and founded Rangoon (now Yangon) as his capital.

Burmese wars In a struggle with Britain 1824–26, Alaungpaya's descendants lost the coastal strip from Chittagong to Cape Negrais. The second Burmese War 1852 resulted in the British annexation of Lower Burma, including Rangoon. Thibaw, the last Burmese king, precipitated the third Burmese War 1885, and the British seized Upper Burma 1886. The country was united as a province of India until 1937, when it was made a crown colony with a degree of self-government.

Burma was occupied 1942–45 by Japan, under a government of anti-British nationalists. The nationalists, led by Aung San and U Nu, later founded the Anti-Fascist People's Freedom League (AFPFL). Burma was liberated 1945 and achieved full independence outside the British ⟡Commonwealth 1948.

republic A parliamentary democracy was established under the Socialist AFPFL led by Prime Minister U Nu. The republic was weakened by civil war between the Karen National Liberation Army (KNLA), communist guerrillas, and ethnic group separatists. Splits within the AFPFL forced the formation of an emergency caretaker government by General Ne Win (1911–) 1958–60, leading to a military coup 1962 and abolition of the parliamentary system. Ne Win became head of a revolutionary council and established a strong one-party state.

In 1974 a new constitution was adopted and the revolutionary council was dissolved. The military leaders became civilian rulers. Ne Win became president and was reelected 1978, before stepping down to be replaced by U San Yu (1918–) 1981.

Burmese socialism The post-1962 government adopted a foreign policy of neutralist isolationism while at home it pursued its unique, self-reliant, Buddhist-influenced "Burmese Way toward Socialism," founded on state ownership in the commercial-industrial sector and strict agricultural price control. Internal opposition by armed separatist groups continued after 1962, causing the economy to deteriorate. The Burmese Communist Party, which received Chinese funding during the 1960s, established control over parts of the north; the Karen National Liberation Army in the southeast; and the Kachin Independence Army in the northeast.

opposition movement In 1975 the non-communist ethnic separatist groups joined together to form the broad National Democratic Front with the aim of creating a federal union. In 1974 and 1976 worsening economic conditions prompted a wave of food riots and in Sept 1987 student demonstrations broke out in Rangoon. Workers' riots followed in the spring of 1988. Initially they were violently suppressed, at the cost of several hundred lives. In the summer of 1988 San Yu and Ne Win, the leader of the ruling party, were forced to resign, as was the newly appointed president, Brig Gen Sein Lwin, after the murder of 3,000 unarmed demonstrators. With government control crumbling, as a widely supported prodemocracy movement swept the nation, the

Myanmar
Union of (*Thammada Myanmar Naingngandaw*) (formerly **Burma**, until 1989)

area 261,228 sq mi/676,577 sq km
capital (and chief port) Yangon (formerly Rangoon)
cities Mandalay, Moulmein, Pegu
physical over half is rainforest; rivers Irrawaddy and Chindwin in central lowlands ringed by mountains in N, W, and E
environment landslides and flooding during the rainy season (June–Sept) are becoming more frequent as a result of deforestation
features ruined cities of Pagan and Mingun
head of state and government Than Shwe from 1992
political system military republic
political parties National Unity Party (NUP), military-socialist ruling party; National League for Democracy (NLD), pluralist opposition grouping
exports rice, rubber, jute, teak, jade, rubies, sapphires

currency kyat
population (1990 est) 41,279,000; growth rate 1.9% p.a. (includes Shan, Karen, Raljome, Chinese, and Indian minorities)
life expectancy men 53, women 56 (1989)
language Burmese
religion Hinayana Buddhist 85%, animist, Christian
literacy 66% (1989)
GNP $9.3 bn (1988); $210 per head (1989)
chronology
1886 United as province of British India.
1937 Became crown colony in the British Commonwealth.
1942–45 Occupied by Japan.
1948 Independence achieved from Britain. Left the Commonwealth.
1962 General Ne Win assumed power in army coup.
1973–74 Adopted presidential-style "civilian" constitution.
1975 Opposition National Democratic Front formed.
1986 Several thousand supporters of opposition leader Suu Kyi arrested.
1988 Government resigned after violent demonstrations. General Saw Maung seized power in military coup Sept; over 1,000 killed.
1989 Martial law declared; thousands arrested including advocates of democracy and human rights. Country renamed Myanmar and capital Yangon.
1990 Breakaway opposition group formed "parallel government" on rebel-held territory.
1991 Martial law and human-rights abuses continued. Military offensives continued. Opposition leader, Aung San Suu Kyi, received Nobel Prize for Peace.
1992 Jan–April: Pogrom against Muslim community in Arakan province, W Myanmar, carried out with army backing. April: Saw Maung replaced by Than Shwe. Several political prisoners liberated. Sept: martial law lifted, but restrictions on political freedom remained.

more reformist Maung Maung took over as president and free multiparty elections were promised "within three months."

military rule However, in Sept 1988 a military coup was staged by General Saw Maung, with the constitution being suspended, martial law imposed, and authority transferred to a 19-member state law and order restoration council. The new regime proceeded to pursue a more liberal economic course. Officially it legalized the formation of political parties, but popular opposition leaders, including ▷Aung San Suu Kyi the daughter of the late Aung San, and U Nu, were barred from running in the elections of May 1990. Behind the scenes, Ne Win remained in control. In June 1989 the country's change of name to Myanmar was recognized by the United Nations (UN).

The May 1990 elections resulted in an overwhelming victory for opposition parties but in practice martial law prevailed. An opposition "parallel government" headed by Dr Sein Win was formed Dec 1990. It was supported by ethnic rebel forces, but denounced by the bulk of the main opposition force, whose leader Suu Kyi was placed under house arrest July 1989. In Oct 1991 she was awarded the Nobel Prize for Peace. The socialist party headed by U Nu, also under house arrest was outlawed in 1991.

military crackdown Serious human rights abuses continued. The ruling junta waged military offensives against Karen ethnic insurgents and moved 75,000 troops into Arakan state, in SW Myanmar, in an attempt to stamp out a Muslim-led pro-independence movement. The latter prompted the flight of 50,000 Rohingya Muslims to Bangladesh during late 1991. The West imposed sanctions against Myanmar. The ▷Association of South East Asian Nations (ASEAN) pursued a more positive policy of "constructive engagement." As many as 60,000 Muslims fled Myanmar following a further military crackdown on Karen rebels Jan–Feb 1992.

martial law ended In April 1992 Saw Maung stepped down on the grounds of ill health, and was succeeded by Than Shwe, the former defense minister. Real power in the junta was said to rest with Khin Nyunt, head of military intelligence, and the former dictator, Ne Win. In the same month, U Nu was released from jail along with several other political prisoners. In Sept 1992 the government ended martial law but the military retained a tight control over political activities. *See illustration box.*

myasthenia gravis in medicine, an uncommon condition characterized by loss of muscle power, especially in the face and neck. The muscles tire rapidly and fail to respond to repeated nervous stimulation. ▷Autoimmunity is the cause.

mycelium interwoven mass of threadlike filaments or ▷hyphae, forming the main body of most fungi. The reproductive structures, or "fruiting bodies," grow from the mycelium.

Mycenae ancient Greek city in the E Peloponnese, which gave its name to the Mycenaean (Bronze Age) civilization. Its peak was 1400–1200 BC, when the Cyclopean walls (using close-fitting stones) were erected. The city ceased to be inhabited after about 1120 BC.

Mycenaean civilization Bronze Age civilization that flourished in Crete, Cyprus, Greece, the Aegean Islands, and W Anatolia about 4000–1000 BC. During this period, magnificent architecture and sophisticated artifacts were produced.

Originating in Crete, it spread into Greece about 1600 BC, where it continued to thrive, with its center at Mycenae, after the decline of Crete in about 1400. It was finally overthrown by the Dorian invasions, about 1100. The system of government was by kings, who also monopolized priestly functions. The Mycenaeans have been identified with the Achaeans of Homer (see ▷Achaea), and were among the besiegers at ▷Troy. They may also have been the marauding sea peoples of Egyptian records. They used a form of Greek deciphered by Michael ▷Ventris. Their palaces were large and luxurious, and contained highly efficient sanitary arrangements. Commercial relations were maintained with Egypt. Pottery, frescoes, and metalwork reached a high artistic level. Evidence of the civilization was brought to light by the excavations of Heinrich ▷Schliemann at Troy, Mycenae, and Tiryns (a stronghold on the plain of Argolis) from 1870 onwards, and of Arthur ▷Evans in Crete from 1899.

mycorrhiza mutually beneficial (mutualistic) association occurring between plant roots and a soil fungus. Mycorrhizal roots take up nutrients more efficiently than non-mycorrhizal roots, and the fungus benefits by obtaining carbohydrates from the tree.

An **ectotrophic mycorrhiza** occurs on many tree species, which usually grow much better, most noticeably in the seeding stage, as a result. Typically the roots become repeatedly branched and corallike, penetrated by hyphae of a surrounding fungal ▷mycelium. In an **endotrophic mycorrhiza**, the growth of the fungus is mainly inside the root, as in orchids. Such plants do not usually grow properly, and may not even germinate, unless the appropriate fungus is present.

myelin sheath insulating layer that surrounds nerve cells in vertebrate animals. It acts to speed up the passage of nerve impulses. Myelin is made up of fats and proteins and is formed from up to a hundred layers, laid down by special cells, the *Schwann cells*.

My Lai massacre killing of 109 civilians in My Lai, a village in South Vietnam, by US troops in March 1968. An investigation in 1969 was followed by the conviction of Lt William Calley, commander of the platoon.

Sentenced to life imprisonment 1971, Calley was later released on parole. His superior officer was acquitted but the trial revealed a US Army policy of punitive tactics against civilians. News of the massacre contributed to domestic pressure for the US to end its involvement in Vietnam.

The incident also focused attention on the emotional pressures faced by US forces in Vietnam. Often unable to identify the enemy, soldiers adopted a policy of firing quickly.

mynah any of various tropical starlings, family Sturnidae, of SE Asia. The glossy blackhill mynah *Gracula religiosa* of India is a realistic mimic of sounds and human speech.

myoglobin globular protein, closely related to ▷hemoglobin and located in vertebrate muscle. Oxygen binds to myoglobin and is released only when the haemoglobin can no longer supply adequate oxygen to muscle cells.

myopia or *short-sightedness* defect of the eye in which a person can see clearly only those objects that are close up. It is caused either by the eyeball being too long or by the cornea and lens system of the eye being too powerful, both

of which cause the images of distant objects to be formed in front of the retina instead of on it. Nearby objects are sharply perceived. Myopia can be corrected by suitable eyeglasses or contact lenses.

myopia, low-luminance poor night vision. About 20% of people have poor vision in twilight and nearly 50% in the dark. Low-luminance myopia does not show up in normal optical tests, but in 1989 a method was developed of measuring the degree of blurring by projecting images on a screen using a weak laser beam.

Myrdal Gunnar 1898–1987. Swedish economist, author of many works on development economics. He shared a Nobel Prize in 1974 with F A Hayek.

myrmecophyte plant that lives in association with a colony of ants and possesses specialized organs in which the ants live. For example, *Myrmecodia*, an epiphytic plant from Malaysia, develops root tubers containing a network of cavities inhabited by ants.

Several species of *Acacia* from tropical America have specialized hollow thorns for the same purpose. This is probably a mutualistic (mutually beneficial) relationship, with the ants helping to protect the plant from other insect pests and in return receiving shelter.

Myron c. 500–440 BC. Greek sculptor. His *Discobolus/Discus-Thrower* and *Athene and Marsyas*, much admired in his time, are known through Roman copies. They confirm his ancient reputation for brilliant composition and naturalism.

myrrh gum resin produced by small trees of the genus *Commiphora* of the bursera family, especially *C. myrrha*, found in Ethiopia and Arabia. In ancient times it was used for incense and perfume and in embalming.

myrtle evergreen shrub of the Old World genus *Myrtus*, family Myrtaceae. The commonly cultivated Mediterranean myrtle *M. communis* has oval opposite leaves and white flowers followed by purple berries, all of which are fragrant.

The Oregon myrtle or California laurel *Umbellularia california* belongs to the ▷laurel family. The wax myrtles (genus *Myrica*) of the US bear wax-covered nuts collected for candle making.

mystery play or *miracle play* medieval religious drama based on stories from the Bible. Mystery plays were performed around the time of church festivals, reaching their height in Europe during the 15th and 16th centuries. A whole cycle running from the Creation to the Last Judgment was performed in separate scenes on mobile wagons by various town guilds.

mystery religion any of various cults of the ancient world, open only to the initiated; for example, the cults of Demeter (see ▷Eleusinian Mysteries), Dionysus, Cybele, Isis, and Mithras. Underlying some of them is a fertility ritual, in which a deity undergoes death and resurrection and the initiates feed on the flesh and blood to attain communion with the divine and ensure their own life beyond the grave. The influence of mystery religions on early Christianity was considerable.

mysticism religious belief or spiritual experience based on direct, intuitive communion with the divine. It does not always involve an orthodox deity, though it is found in all the major religions—for example, kabbalism in Judaism, Sufism in Islam, and the bhakti movement in Hinduism. The mystical experience is often rooted in ascetism and can involve visions, trances, and ecstasies; many religious traditions prescribe meditative and contemplative techniques for achieving mystical experience. Official churches fluctuate between acceptance of mysticism as a form of special grace, and suspicion of it as a dangerous deviation, verging on the heretical.

3rd century Mysticism was first introduced to W Europe through Neoplatonism, which was largely affected by Oriental schools of thought, and in its turn influenced the rise of Christian mysticism.

8th century Beginning of Sufism, an Islamic mystical movement.

11th–12th century Ramanuja, a Tamil Brahmin, taught that the way of devotion (*bhakti*) in Hinduism was superior to the way of knowledge.

13th century A kabbalistic movement in Judaism arose in S France and Spain.

14th–16th centuries Among the Christian mystics of this era, when feudalism was breaking down, were Thomas à Kempis, Jacob Boehme, and Meister Eckhart in Germany, and Julian of Norwich and the author of *The Cloud of Unknowing* in England. The Counter-Reformation produced Catholic mystics such as St Teresa and St John of the Cross.

17th century Quietism spread from Spain to France, while the Quakers (Friends) originated in England.

18th century Two great English mystics: William Law and William Blake.

19th century The scientific study of mysticism was begun by the American William James and others.

20th century A renewed interest in mysticism in the US and the UK was expressed in, for example, the works of the poet W B Yeats, the novelist Aldous Huxley (often drawing on Eastern religions and psychedelic experiences), and the Catholic monk and writer Thomas Merton.

From the 1960s an interest in Zen Buddhism, Tantric Buddhism, Taoism, and other mystical Asian religions became widespread.

mythology study and interpretation of the stories symbolically underlying a given culture and of how they relate to similar stories told in other cultures. These stories describe gods and other supernatural beings, with whom humans may have relationships, and are intended to explain the workings of the universe and human history.

Ancient mythologies, with the names of the chief god of each, include those of Egypt (Osiris), Greece (Zeus), Rome (Jupiter), India (Brahma), and the Teutonic peoples (Odin or Woden).

Mytilene (modern Greek *Mitilíni*) port, capital of the Greek island of Lesvos (to which the name Mytilene is sometimes applied) and a center of sponge fishing; population (1981) 24,000.

myxedema thyroid-deficiency disease developing in adult life, most commonly in middle-aged women. The symptoms are loss of energy and appetite, inability to keep warm, mental dullness, and dry, puffy skin. It is completely reversed by giving the thyroid hormone known as thyroxine.

myxomatosis contagious, usually fatal, virus infection of rabbits which causes much suffering. It has been deliberately introduced in the UK and Australia since the 1950s to reduce the rabbit population.

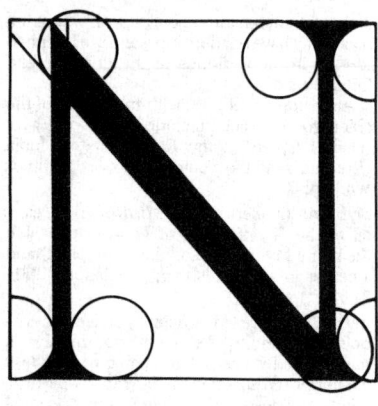

N 14th letter of the English alphabet, from the Greek *nu* (N, ν). N when spoken represents an alveolar nasal sound. In several Romance languages it disappears in many cases, with nasalization of the preceding vowel.

N abbreviation for *north*, ◊*newton*, and the chemical symbol for *nitrogen*.

n. abbreviation for ◊*noun*, *neuter*, and, in mathematics, an *indefinite number*.

NAACP abbreviation for ◊*National Association for the Advancement of Colored People*, a US civil rights organization.

Nabis, les (Hebrew "prophets") group of French artists, active in the 1890s in Paris, united in their admiration of Paul Gauguin—the mystic content of his work, the surface pattern and intense color. In practice their work was decorative. Pierre ◊Bonnard and Edouard ◊Vuillard were members.

Nablus market town on the West Bank of the River Jordan, N of Jerusalem; the largest Palestinian town, after E Jerusalem, in Israeli occupation; population (1971) 64,000. Formerly Shechem, it was the ancient capital of Samaria, and a few ◊Samaritans remain. The British field marshal Allenby's defeat of the Turks here 1918 completed the conquest of Palestine.

Nabokov Vladimir 1899–1977. US writer who left his native Russia 1917 and began writing in English in the 1940s. His most widely known book is *Lolita* 1955, the story of the middle-aged Humbert Humbert's infatuation with a precocious girl of 12. His other books include *Laughter in the Dark* 1938, *The Real Life of Sebastian Knight* 1945, *Pnin* 1957, and his memoirs *Speak, Memory* 1947.

Born in St Petersburg, Nabokov settled in the US 1940, and became a US citizen 1945. He was professor of Russian literature at Cornell University 1948–59, producing a translation and commentary on Pushkin's *Eugene Onegin* 1963. He was also a lepidopterist (a collector of butterflies and moths), a theme used in his book *Pale Fire* 1962.

Nadar adopted name of Gaspard-Félix Tournachon 1820–1910. French portrait photographer and caricaturist. He took the first aerial photographs (from a balloon 1858) and was the first to take flash photographs (using magnesium bulbs).

Nader Ralph 1934– . US lawyer and consumer advocate. Called the "scourge of corporate morality," he led many major consumer campaigns. His book *Unsafe at Any Speed* 1965 led to US car-safety legislation.

The Traffic Safety Act 1966 gave the federal government the right to establish safety standards for automobiles sold in the US.

Born in Winsted, Connecticut, he graduated from Princeton and Harvard universities and practiced law in Connecticut and Washington, DC. He investigated the lack of safety of color televisions, nuclear plants, and X-rays, as well as the procedures used by food and drug companies, overall job safety standards, and environmental pollution. The people who worked with and for him became known as "Nader's Raiders." Nader also cowrote *Who's Poisoning America: Corporate Polluters and Their Victims in the Chemical Age* 1981 and *The Big Boys: Styles of Corporate Power* 1986.

nadir the point on the celestial sphere vertically below the observer and hence diametrically opposite the **zenith**. The term is used metaphorically to mean the low point of a person's fortunes.

Nadir Shah (Khan) *c.* 1880–1933. King of Afghanistan from 1929. Nadir played a key role in the 1919 Afghan War, but was subsequently forced into exile in France. He returned to Kabul in 1929 to seize the throne and embarked on an ambitious modernization program. This alienated the Muslim clergy and in 1933 he was assassinated by fundamentalists. His successor as king was his son ◊Zahir Shah.

Naga member of any of the various peoples who inhabit the highland region near the Indian–Myanmar (Burma) border; they number approximately 800,000. These peoples do not possess a common name; some of the main groups are Ao, Konyak, Sangtam, Lhota, Sema, Rengma, Chang, and Angami. They live by farming, hunting, and fishing. Their languages belong to the Sino-Tibetan family.

Nagaland state of NE India, bordering Myanmar (Burma) on the E
area 6,456 sq mi/16,721 sq km
capital Kohima
products rice, tea, coffee, paper, sugar
population (1991) 1,215,600
history formerly part of Assam, the area was seized by Britain from Burma (now Myanmar) 1826. The British sent 18 expeditions against the Naga peoples in the north 1832–87. After India attained independence 1947, there was Naga guerrilla activity against the Indian government; the state of Nagaland was established 1963 in response to demands for self-government, but fighting continued sporadically.

Nagasaki industrial port (coal, iron, shipbuilding) on Kyushu island, Japan; population (1989) 442,400. Nagasaki was the only Japanese port open to European trade from the 16th century until 1859. An atomic bomb was dropped on it by the US Aug 9, 1945.

Three days after ◊Hiroshima, the second atomic bomb was dropped here at the end of World War II. Of Nagasaki's population of 212,000, 73,884 were killed and 76,796 injured, not counting the long-term victims of radiation.

Nagorno-Karabakh autonomous region of ◊Azerbaijan
area 1,700 sq mi/4,400 sq km
capital Stepanakert
products cotton, grapes, wheat, silk

population (1987) 180,000 (76% Armenian, 23% Azeri), the Christian Armenians forming an enclave within the predominantly Shiite Muslim Azerbaijan
history an autonomous protectorate after the Russian Revolution 1917, Nagorno-Karabakh was annexed to Azerbaijan 1923 against the wishes of the largely Christian-Armenian population. Since the local council declared its intention to transfer control of the region to Armenia 1989, the enclave has been racked by fighting between Armenian and Azeri troops, both attempting to assert control. By Feb 1992, the conflict had caused the loss of at least 1,000 lives (501 during 1991 alone) and the displacement of some 270,000 people, half of them Armenian and half Azeri.

In 1920, inter-ethnic clashes in the Karabakh town of Shusha resulted in the deaths of 30,000 Armenians and 15,000 Azeris. The conflict, rooted in many centuries of Christian Armenian and Shiite Muslim Azeri enmity, re-erupted 1988 and the region has since been the subject of violent disputes between Azerbaijan and neighboring Armenia. The violence was provoked by the local council's vote to transfer the region's administrative control to Armenia and in response the area was placed under direct rule from Moscow Jan–Nov 1989. The conflict escalated fall 1989, with Azerbaijan first imposing an economic blockade on Armenia, and then descending into civil war and threatening secession from the USSR, which resulted in 20,000 Soviet troops being sent to the republic Jan 1990. A cease-fire, brokered by the presidents of Russia and Kazakhstan and signed by Armenia and Azerbaijan Sept 1991, broke down in Nov when the Azerbaijani parliament voted to annul Nagorno-Karabakh's autonomous status. Following a referendum and elections early Dec 1991, and the withdrawal of Soviet troops, the 81-member parliament of Nagorno-Karabakh declared its independence. This was not recognized by Azerbaijan and conflict within the enclave worsened, with the unofficial National Defense Army, headed by Azeri nationalist Musa Mehmedov, imposing a siege and launching an all-out artillery attack on the capital, Stepanakert, while Armenian troops laid siege to the Azeri-held town of Shusha. In May 1992 Armenian troops overran Shusha and made significant advances in the enclave, only to be repulsed by a surprise Azerbaijani counter-offensive in June which left hundreds of Armenian troops dead. On Aug 15 the ethnic Armenian government resigned.

A CSCE fact-finding mission was sent into the enclave Feb 1992.

Nagoya industrial seaport (cars, textiles, clocks) on Honshu island, Japan; population (1989) 2,101,000. It has a shogun fortress 1610 and a notable Shinto shrine, Atsuta Jingu.

Nagpur industrial city (textiles, metals) in Maharashtra, India; population (1981) 1,298,000.

Nagy Imre 1895–1958. Hungarian politician, prime minister 1953–55 and 1956. He led the Hungarian revolt against Soviet domination in 1956, for which he was executed.

Nagy, an Austro-Hungarian prisoner of war in Siberia during World War I, became a Soviet citizen after the Russian Revolution, and lived in the USSR 1930–44. In 1953, after Stalin's death, he became prime minister, introducing liberal measures such as encouraging the production of consumer goods, but was dismissed 1955 by hard-line Stalinist premier Rákosi. Reappointed Oct 1956 during the Hungarian uprising, he began taking liberalization further than the Soviets wanted; for example, announcing Hungarian withdrawal from the Warsaw Pact. Soviet troops entered Budapest, and Nagy was dismissed Nov 1956. He was captured by the KGB and shot. In 1989 the Hungarian Supreme Court recognized his leadership of a legitimate government and quashed his conviction for treachery.

Nahayan Sheik Sultan bin Zayed al- 1918– . Emir of Abu Dhabi from 1969, when he deposed his brother, Sheik Shakhbut. He was elected president of the supreme council of the United Arab Emirates 1971. In 1991 he was implicated, through his majority ownership, in the international financial scandals associated with the Bank of Commerce and Credit International.

Before 1969 Sheik Nahayan was governor of the eastern province of Abu Dhabi, one of seven ⟩Trucial States in the Persian Gulf and Gulf of Oman, then under British protection. An absolute ruler, he was unanimously reelected emir 1986 by other UAE sheiks, among whom he enjoys considerable popularity.

Nahuatl member of any of a group of Mesoamerican Indian peoples (Mexico and Central America), of which the best-known group were the Aztecs. The Nahuatl are the largest ethnic group in Mexico, and their languages, which belong to the Uto-Aztecan (Aztec-Tanoan) family, are spoken by over a million people today.

Nāhum 7th century BC. In the Old Testament, a Hebrew prophet, possibly born in Galilee, who forecast the destruction of Nineveh, the Assyrian capital, by the Medes in 612 BC.

naiad in Classical mythology, a water nymph. Naiads lived in rivers and streams; ⟩nereids in the sea.

nail in biology, a hard, flat, flexible outgrowth of the digits of primates (humans, monkeys, and apes). Nails are derived from the ⟩claws of ancestral primates.

Naipaul V(idiadhar) S(urajprasad) 1932– . British writer, born in Trinidad of Hindu parents. His novels include *A House for Mr Biswas* 1961, *The Mimic Men* 1967, *A Bend in the River* 1979, and *Finding the Centre* 1984. His brother **Shiva(dhar) Naipaul** (1940–1985) was also a novelist (*Fireflies* 1970) and journalist.

Nairobi capital of Kenya, in the central highlands at 5,450 ft/1,660 m; population (1985) 1,100,000. It has light industry and food processing and is the headquarters of the United Nations Environment Program.

Nairobi was founded 1899. It has the International Louis Leakey Institute for African Prehistory 1977, and the International Primate Research Institute is nearby.

Naismith James 1861–1939. Canadian-born inventor of basketball. While attending the YMCA Training School in Springfield, Massachusetts, 1891, Naismith invented basketball as a game to be played indoors during the winter. He later received an MD degree from the University of Colorado and served on the physical education faculty of the University of Kansas 1898–1937. Among his books is *Basketball, Its Origin and Development*, published posthumously 1941.

Born in Almonte, Ontario, Naismith was educated at McGill University, where he later served as director of physical education.

Najibullah Ahmadzai 1947– . Afghan communist politician, state president 1986–92. A member of the Politburo from 1981, he was leader of the People's Democratic Party of Afghanistan (PDPA) from 1986. Although his government initially survived the withdrawal of Soviet troops Feb 1989, continuing pressure from the mujaheddin forces resulted in his eventual overthrow.

Nakasone Yasuhiro 1917– . Japanese conservative politician, leader of the Liberal Democratic Party (LDP) and prime minister 1982–87. He stepped up military spending and increased Japanese participation in international affairs, with closer ties to the US. He was forced to resign his party post May 1989 as a result of having profited from insider trading in the ⟩Recruit scandal. After serving a two-year period of atonement, he rejoined the LDP April 1991.

Nakhichevan autonomous republic forming part of Azerbaijan, even though it is entirely outside the Azerbaijan boundary, being separated from it by Armenia; area 2,120 sq mi/5,500 sq km; population (1986) 272,000. Taken by Russia in 1828, it was annexed to Azerbaijan in 1924. 85% of the population are Muslim Azeris who maintain strong links with Iran to the south. Nakhichevan has been affected by the Armenia–Azerbaijan conflict; many Azeris have fled to Azerbaijan, and in Jan 1990 frontier posts and border fences with Iran were destroyed. In May 1992 Armenian forces made

advances in the region, but Azerbaijan forces had regained control by Aug. The republic has sought independence from Azerbaijan.

Namaqualand or **Namaland** near-desert area on the SW coast of Africa divided between Namibia and South Africa. *Great Namaqualand* is in Namibia, N of the Orange River, area 150,000 sq mi/388,500 sq km; sparsely populated by the Nama, a Hottentot people. *Little Namaqualand* is in Cape Province, South Africa, S of the Orange River, area 20,000 sq mi/52,000 sq km; copper and diamonds are mined here.

Namath Joe (Joseph William) 1943– . US football player. In 1965 Namath signed with the New York Jets of the newly established American Football League. In 1969 Namath led the Jets to a historic upset victory over the Baltimore Colts in Super Bowl III. After leaving the Jets 1977, Namath joined the Los Angeles Rams; however, knee injuries forced his retirement as a player the following year. He later became a sports broadcaster and actor.

Born in Beaver Falls, Pennsylvania, Namath played quarterback for the University of Alabama, leading his team to victory in the 1965 Orange Bowl.

Namib Desert coastal desert region in Namibia between the Kalahari Desert and the Atlantic Ocean. Its sand dunes are among the tallest in the world, reaching heights of 1,200 ft/370 m.

Namibia
Republic of (formerly **South West Africa**)

area 318,262 sq mi/824,300 sq km
capital Windhoek
cities Swakopmund, Rehoboth, Rundu
physical mainly desert
features Namib and Kalahari deserts; Orange River; Caprivi Strip links Namibia to Zambezi River; includes the enclave of Walvis Bay (area 432 sq mi/1,120 sq km)
head of state Sam Nujoma from 1990
head of government Hage Geingob from 1990
political system democratic republic
political parties South-West Africa People's Organization (SWAPO), socialist Ovambo-oriented; Democratic Turnhalle Alliance (DTA), moderate, multiracial coalition; United Democratic Front (UDF), disaffected ex-SWAPO members; National Christian Action (ACN), white conservative
exports diamonds, uranium, copper, lead, zinc
currency South African rand

population (1990 est) 1,372,000 (85% black African, 6% European)
life expectancy blacks 40, whites 69
languages Afrikaans (spoken by 60% of white population), German, English (all official), several indigenous languages
religion 51% Lutheran, 19% Roman Catholic, 6% Dutch Reformed Church, 6% Anglican
literacy whites 100%, nonwhites 16%
GNP $1.6 bn; $1,300 per head (1988)
chronology
1884 German and British colonies established.
1915 German colony seized by South Africa.
1920 Administered by South Africa, under League of Nations mandate, as British South Africa.
1946 Full incorporation in South Africa refused by United Nations (UN).
1958 South-West Africa People's Organization (SWAPO) set up to seek racial equality and full independence.
1966 South Africa's apartheid laws extended to the country.
1968 Redesignated Namibia by UN.
1978 UN Security Council Resolution 435 for the granting of full sovereignty accepted by South Africa and then rescinded.
1988 Peace talks between South Africa, Angola, and Cuba led to agreement on full independence for Namibia.
1989 Unexpected incursion by SWAPO guerrillas from Angola into Namibia threatened agreed independence. Transitional constitution created by elected representatives; SWAPO dominant party.
1990 Liberal multiparty "independence" constitution adopted; independence achieved. Sam Nujoma elected president.
1991 Agreement on joint administration of Walvis Bay reached with South Africa, pending final settlement of dispute.
1992 Agreement on establishment of Walvis Bay Joint Administrative Body.

Namibia formerly (to 1968) *South West Africa* country in SW Africa, bounded N by Angola and Zambia, E by Botswana and South Africa, and W by the Atlantic Ocean. Walvis Bay, part of South Africa, forms an enclave in Namibia on the Atlantic coast.

government A new constitution was framed by the transitional 72-member constituent assembly elected by proportional representation Nov 1989. Unanimously approved Feb 1990, it entrenches a multiparty system with an independent judiciary and bill of fundamental human rights. Executive authority is wielded by a president who may serve a maximum of two five-year terms.

history Originally inhabited by the Damara people, it was annexed, with the exception of the British/Cape Colony enclave of ◊Walvis Bay, by Germany 1884; it was occupied in World War I by South African forces under Louis Botha, and was mandated to South Africa 1920.

South African rule South Africa did not accept the termination of the mandate by the United Nations 1966, although briefly accepting the principle of ultimate independence 1978 (UN Security Council Resolution 435); in 1968 the UN renamed the territory Namibia. South Africa's apartheid laws were extended to the colony 1966 and in opposition to such racial discrimination Sam Nujoma, an Ovambo, led a political (from 1958) and then (from the mid-1960s) an armed resistance campaign for independence, forming the South-West Africa People's Organization (SWAPO) and the People's Liberation Army of Namibia (PLAN). Following harassment, he was forced into exile 1960, establishing guerrilla bases in Angola and Zambia. Military conflict in Namibia escalated from the mid-1970s as the Pretoria regime attempted to topple the Marxist government in neighboring Angola. In 1985 South Africa installed a puppet regime in Namibia, the Transitional Government of National Unity (TGNU), a multiracial body, but including only one Ovambo minister. It attempted to reform the apartheid system but was internally divided between moderate reformist and conservative wings, and failed to secure UN recognition.

peace settlement In 1988 progress was finally made toward a peace settlement in Namibia as a result of both South Africa and the USSR (via Cuba) tiring of the cost of their proxy military involvement in the civil wars of both the colony and neighboring Angola. In Aug 1988 the South African and Angolan governments agreed an immediate cease-fire, followed by the rapid withdrawal of South African forces from Angola and, during 1989, the phased withdrawal of Cuba's troops from Angola and South Africa's from Namibia. From April 1989, a UN peacekeeping force was stationed in Namibia to oversee the holding of multiparty elections in Nov. These were won by SWAPO, but its 57% share of the seats in the constituent assembly, which had the task of framing a new "independence constitution," fell short of the two-thirds majority required for it to dominate the proceedings. As a consequence, a moderate multiparty constitution was adopted Feb 1990. Sam Nujoma was unanimously elected Namibia's first president by the assembly Feb 16, 1990, and was formally sworn in by the UN secretary-general on independence day, March 21, 1990. Hage Geingob became prime minister. The retention of the commercially important Walvis Bay by South Africa on Namibia's independence caused tension between the two countries. Inconclusive talks

were held in March 1991 over its future possession. However, in Sept 1991 it was announced that South Africa and Namibia had agreed to a joint administration of the enclave; in Aug 1992 it was agreed that a Walvis Bay Joint Administrative Body would be established. *See illustration box on p. 737.*

Namur (Flemish *Naemen*) industrial city (cutlery, porcelain, paper, iron, steel), capital of the province of Namur, in S Belgium, at the confluence of the Sambre and Meuse rivers; population (1991) 103,400. It was a strategic location during both world wars. The province of Namur has an area of 1,428 sq mi/3,700 sq km and a population (1991) of 423,300.

Nanaimo coal-mining center of British Columbia, on the E coast of Vancouver Island; population (1985) 50,500.

Nanak 1469–*c.* 1539. Indian guru and founder of Sikhism, a religion based on the unity of God and the equality of all human beings. He was strongly opposed to caste divisions.

At 50, after many years traveling and teaching, he established a new town: Kartarpur, in the Punjab. Here he met his most trusted follower, Lehna. On his death-bed, Guru Nanak announced Lehna as his successor, and gave him the name Guru Angad.

Nanchang industrial (textiles, glass, porcelain, soap) capital of Jiangxi province, China, about 160 mi/260 km SE of Wuhan; population (1989) 1,330,000.

Nanchang is a road and rail junction. It was originally a walled city built in the 12th century. The first Chinese Communist uprising took place here Aug 1, 1927.

Nancy capital of the *département* of Meurthe-et-Moselle and of the region of Lorraine, France, on the River Meurthe 175 mi/280 km E of Paris; population (1982) 307,000. Nancy dates from the 11th century.

Nanda Devi peak in the Himalayas, Uttar Pradesh, N India; height 25,645 ft/7,817 m. Until Kanchenjunga was absorbed into India, Nanda Devi was the country's highest mountain.

NAND gate a type of ◊logic gate.

Nanjing or *Nanking* capital of Jiangsu province, China, 165 mi/270 km NW of Shanghai; center of industry (engineering, shipbuilding, oil refining), commerce, and communications; population (1989) 2,470,000. The bridge 1968 over the River Chang Jiang is the longest in China at 22,000 ft/6,705 m.

The city dates from the 2nd century BC, perhaps earlier. It received the name Nanjing ("southern capital") under the Ming dynasty (1368–1644) and was the capital of China 1368–1403, 1928–37, and 1946–49.

Nanking alternate name for ◊Nanjing, city in China.

Nanning industrial river port, capital of Guangxi Zhuang autonomous region, China, on the River You Jiang; population (1989) 1,050,000. It was a supply town during the Vietnam War and the Sino-Vietnamese confrontation 1979.

nano- prefix used in ◊SI units of measurement, equivalent to a one-billionth part (10^{-9}). For example, a nanosecond is one-billionth of a second.

nanotechnology the building of devices on a molecular scale. Micromachines, such as

gears smaller in diameter than a human hair, have been made at the AT&T Bell laboratories in New Jersey. Building large molecules with useful shapes has been accomplished by research groups in the US. A robot small enough to travel through the bloodstream and into organs of the body, inspecting or removing diseased tissue, was under development in Japan 1990.

The scanning electron ◊microscope can be used to see and position single atoms and molecules, and to drill holes a nanometer (billionth of a meter) across in a variety of materials. The instrument can be used for ultrafine etching; the entire 28 volumes of the *Encyclopedia Britannica* could be engraved on the head of a pin. A complete electric motor has been built in the US; it is less than 0.1 mm across with a top speed of 600,000 rpm. It is etched out of silicon, using the ordinary methods of chip manufacturers.

The idea of manipulating material on a nanometer scale—atom by atom—was first discussed by Richard ◊Feynman in 1959. Nanotechnology enthusiasts say that it will eventually be possible to build computers on the molecular scale, produce ultrastrong materials, and allow the molecular correction of most diseases, even the repair of aging cells.

Nansen Fridtjof 1861–1930. Norwegian explorer and scientist. In 1893, he sailed to the Arctic in the *Fram*, which was deliberately allowed to drift north with an iceflow. Nansen, accompanied by F Hjalmar Johansen (1867–1923), continued north on foot and reached 86° 14′ N, the highest latitude then attained. After World War I, Nansen became League of Nations high commissioner for refugees. Nobel Peace Prize 1923.

He made his first voyage to Greenland waters in a sealing ship 1882, and in 1888–89 attempted to cross the Greenland icefield. He was professor of zoology and oceanography at the University of Christiania (now Oslo). Norwegian ambassador in London 1906–08.

Nantes industrial port in W France on the river Loire, capital of Pays de la Loire region; industries include oil, sugar refining, textiles, soap, and tobacco; population (1982) 465,000. It has a cathedral 1434–1884 and a castle founded 938. It is the birthplace of the writer Jules Verne.

Nantes, Edict of decree by which Henry IV of France granted religious freedom to the ◊Huguenots 1598. It was revoked 1685 by Louis XIV.

Nantucket island and resort in Massachusetts, S of Cape Cod, 46 sq mi/120 sq km. In the 18–19th centuries, Nantucket was a whaling port; it is now a popular summer resort because of its excellent beaches.

The island was discovered 1602, settled 1659 by Quakers, and became part of Massachusetts 1692.

Napa city in NW California on the Napa river, NE of San Francisco on San Pablo Bay. It is a major trading center for wine; other products include fruits and clothing; population (1990) 61,800.

napalm fuel used in flamethrowers and incendiary bombs. Produced from jellied gasoline, it is a mixture of *na*phthenic and *palm*itic acids. Napalm causes extensive burns because it sticks to the skin even when aflame. It was widely used by the US Army during the Vietnam War.

naphtha the mixtures of hydrocarbons obtained by destructive distillation of petroleum, coal tar, and shale oil. It is raw material for the petrochemical and plastics industries. The term was originally applied to naturally occurring liquid hydrocarbons.

naphthalene $C_{10}H_8$ a solid, white, shiny, aromatic hydrocarbon obtained from coal tar. The smell of moth-balls is due to their napthalene content. It is used in making indigo and certain azo dyes, as a mild disinfectant, and as an insecticide.

Napier John 1550–1617. Scottish mathematician who invented ◊logarithms 1614 and "Napier's bones," an early mechanical calculating device for multiplication and division.

Napier Robert Cornelis, 1st Baron Napier of Magdala 1810–1890. British field marshal. Knighted for his services in relieving Lucknow during the ◊Indian Mutiny, he took part in capturing Peking (Beijing) 1860 during the war against China in 1860. He was commander in chief in India 1870–76 and governor of Gibraltar 1876–82.

Naples (Italian *Napoli*) industrial port (shipbuilding, automobiles, textiles, paper, food processing) and capital of Campania, Italy, on the Tyrrhenian Sea; population (1988) 1,201,000. To the south is the Isle of Capri, and behind the city is Mount Vesuvius, with the ruins of Pompeii at its foot.

Naples is the third largest city of Italy, and as a port second in importance only to Genoa. Buildings include the royal palace, the San Carlo Opera House, the Castel Nuovo 1283, and the university 1224.

The city began as the Greek colony Neapolis in the 6th century BC and was taken over by Romans 326 BC; it became part of the Kingdom of the Two ◊Sicilies 1140 and capital of the Kingdom of Naples 1282.

Naples, Kingdom of the southern part of Italy, alternately independent and united with ◊Sicily in the Kingdom of the Two Sicilies.

Naples was united with Sicily 1140–1282, first under Norman rule 1130–94, then Hohenstaufen 1194–1266, then Angevin from 1268; apart from Sicily, but under continued Angevin rule to 1435; reunited with Sicily 1442–1503, under the house of Aragon to 1501; a Spanish Hapsburg possession 1504–1707 and Austrian 1707–35; under Spanish Bourbon rule 1735–99. The *Neapolitan Republic* was established 1799 after Napoleon had left Italy for Egypt, but fell after five months to the forces of reaction under Cardinal Ruffo, with the British admiral Nelson blockading the city by sea; many prominent citizens were massacred after the capitulation. The Spanish Bourbons were restored 1799, 1802–05, and 1815–60, when Naples joined the Kingdom of Italy.

Napoleon I Bonaparte 1769–1821. Emperor of the French 1804–14 and 1814–15. A general from 1796 in the ◊Revolutionary Wars, in 1799 he overthrew the ruling Directory (see ◊French Revolution) and made himself dictator. From 1803 he conquered most of Europe (the *Napoleonic Wars*) and installed his brothers as puppet kings (see ◊Bonaparte). After the Peninsular War and retreat from Moscow 1812, he was forced to abdicate 1814 and was banished to the island of Elba. In March 1815 he reassumed power but was defeated by British forces at the Battle of ◊Waterloo and exiled to the island of St Helena. His internal administrative reforms and laws are still evident in France.

Napoleon, born in Ajaccio, Corsica, received a commission in the artillery 1785 and first distinguished himself at the siege of ◊Toulon 1793. Having suppressed a royalist uprising in Paris 1795, he was given command against the Austrians in Italy and defeated them at Lodi, Arcole, and Rivoli 1796–97. Egypt, seen as a halfway house to India, was overrun and Syria invaded, but his fleet was destroyed by the British admiral ◊Nelson at the Battle of the Nile. Napoleon returned to France and carried out a coup against the government of the Directory to establish his own dictatorship, nominally as First Consul. The Austrians were again defeated at Marengo 1800 and the coalition against France shattered, a truce being declared 1802. A plebiscite the same year made him consul for life. In 1804 a plebiscite made him emperor.

While retaining and extending the legal and educational reforms of the Jacobins, Napoleon replaced the democratic constitution established by the Revolution with a centralized despotism, and by his ◊concordat with Pius VII conciliated the Catholic church. The *Code Napoléon* remains the basis of French law.

War was renewed by Britain 1803, aided by Austria and Russia from 1805 and Prussia from 1806. Prevented by the British navy from invading Britain, Napoleon drove Austria out of the war by victories at Ulm and Austerlitz 1805, and Prussia by the victory at Jena 1806. Then, after the battles of Eylau and Friedland, he formed an alliance with Russia at Tilsit 1807. Napoleon now forbade entry of British goods to Europe, attempting an economic blockade known as the ◊Continental System, occupied Portugal, and in 1808 placed his brother Joseph on the Spanish throne. Both countries revolted, with British aid, and Austria attempted to reenter the war but was defeated at Wagram. In 1796 Napoleon had married ◊Josephine de Beauharnais, but in 1809, to assert his equality with the Hapsburgs, he divorced her to marry the Austrian emperor's daughter, ◊Marie Louise.

When Russia failed to enforce the Continental System, Napoleon marched on and occupied Moscow, but his army's retreat in the bitter winter of 1812 encouraged Prussia and Austria to declare war again 1813. He was defeated at Leipzig and driven from Germany. Despite his brilliant campaign on French soil, the Allies invaded Paris and compelled him to abdicate April 1814; he was banished to the island of Elba, off the west coast of Italy. In March 1815 he escaped and took power for a hundred days, with the aid of Marshal ◊Ney, but Britain and Prussia led an alliance against him at Waterloo, Belgium, in June. Surrendering to the British, he again abdicated, and was exiled to the island of St Helena, 1,200 mi/1,900 km west of Africa, where he died. His body was brought back 1840 to be interred in the Hôtel des Invalides, Paris.

Napoleon II 1811–1832. Title given by the Bonapartists to the son of Napoleon I and ◊Marie Louise; until 1814 he was known as the king of Rome and after 1818 as the duke of Reichstadt. After his father's abdication 1814 he was taken to the Austrian court, where he spent the rest of his life.

Napoleon III 1808–1873. Emperor of the French 1852–70, known as *Louis-Napoleon*. After two attempted coups (1836 and 1840) he was jailed, then went into exile, returning for the revolution of 1848, when he became president of the Second Republic but soon turned

authoritarian. In 1870 he was maneuvered by the German chancellor Bismarck into war with Prussia (see ◊Franco-Prussian War); he was forced to surrender at Sedan, NE France, and the empire collapsed.

He fled to England.

Napoleonic Wars 1803–15 a series of European wars conducted by Napoleon I following the ◊Revolutionary Wars, aiming for French conquest of Europe.

1803 Britain renewed the war against France, following an appeal from the Maltese against Napoleon's 1798 seizure of the island.

1805 Napoleon's planned invasion of Britain from Boulogne ended with Nelson's victory at ◊Trafalgar. Coalition formed against France by Britain, Austria, Russia, and Sweden. Austria defeated at Ulm; Austria and Russia at ◊Austerlitz.

1806 Prussia joined the coalition and was defeated at Jena; Napoleon instituted an attempted blockade, the *Continental System*, to isolate Britain from Europe.

1807 Russia defeated at Eylau and Friedland and, on making peace with Napoleon under the *Treaty of Tilsit*, changed sides, agreeing to attack Sweden, but was forced to retreat.

1808 Napoleon's invasion of Portugal and strategy of installing his relatives as puppet kings led to the ◊*Peninsular War*.

1809 Revived Austrian opposition to Napoleon was ended by defeat at ◊*Wagram*.

1812 The Continental System finally collapsed on its rejection by Russia, and Napoleon made the fatal decision to invade; he reached *Moscow* but was defeated by the Russian resistance and by the bitter winter as he retreated through a countryside laid waste by the retreating Russians (380,000 French soldiers died).

1813 Britain, Prussia, Russia, Austria, and Sweden formed a new coalition, which defeated Napoleon at the *Battle of the Nations*, Leipzig, Germany. He abdicated and was exiled to Elba.

1814 Louis XVIII became king of France, and the Congress of Vienna met to conclude peace.

1815 Napoleon returned to Paris. On June 16 the British commander Wellington defeated the French marshal Ney at Quatre Bras (in Belgium, SE of Brussels), and Napoleon was finally defeated at *Waterloo*, S of Brussels, June 18.

During the Napoleonic Wars, the annual cost of the British army was between 60% and 90% of total government income. About half of Napoleon's army was made up of foreign mercenaries, mainly Swiss and German.

Nara city in Japan, in the south of Honshu island, the capital of the country 710–84; population (1989) 346,300. It was the birthplace of Japanese art and literature and has ancient wooden temples.

Narasimha Rao P(amulaparti) V(enkata) 1921– . Indian politician, prime minister of India from 1991 and Congress (I) leader. He governed the state of Andhra Pradesh as chief minister 1971–73, and served in the Congress (I) cabinets of Indira and Rajiv Gandhi as minister of external affairs 1980–85 and 1988–90 and of human resources 1985–88. He took over the party leadership after the assassination of Rajiv Gandhi. Elected prime minister the following month, he instituted a reform of the economy.

narcissism in psychology, an exaggeration of normal self-respect and self-involvement which may amount to mental disorder when it precludes relationships with other people.

narcissus any bulbous plant of the genus *Narcissus*, family Amaryllidaceae. Species include the daffodil, jonquil, and narcissus. All have flowers with a cup projecting from the center.

Narcissus in Greek mythology, a beautiful youth who rejected the love of the nymph ▷Echo and was condemned to fall in love with his own reflection in a pool. He pined away and in the place where he died a flower sprang up that was named after him.

narcolepsy rare disorder characterized by bouts of overwhelming sleepiness and loss of muscle power. It is controlled by drugs.

narcotic pain-relieving and sleep-inducing drug. The chief narcotics induce dependency, and include opium, its derivatives and synthetic modifications (such as morphine and heroin); alcohols (such as ethanol); and barbiturates.

Narmada River river that rises in the Maikala range in Madhya Pradesh state, central India, and flows 778 mi/1,245 km WSW to the Gulf of Khambat, an inlet of the Arabian Sea. Forming the traditional boundary between Hindustan and Deccan, the Narmada is a holy river of the Hindus. India's Narmada Valley Project is one of the largest and most controversial river development projects in the world. Between 1990 and 2040 it is planned to build 30 major dams, 135 medium-sized dams, and 3,000 smaller dams in a scheme that will involve moving 1 million of the valley's population of 20 million people.

Narragansett Bay Atlantic inlet, Rhode Island. Running inland for 28 mi/45 km, it encloses a number of islands.

At the head of the bay is Providence, the state capital; at its mouth is the island of Aquidneck with Newport, site of the US Naval War College (1885), the America's Cup yachting races, a jazz festival, the Tennis Hall of Fame, and summer mansions of the wealthy (many open as museums).

Narvik seaport in Nordland county, N Norway, on Ofot Fjord, exporting Swedish iron ore; population (1991) 18,600. To secure this ore supply Germany seized Narvik in April 1940. British, French, Polish, and Norwegian forces recaptured the port but had to abandon it on June 10 to cope with the worsening Allied situation elsewhere in Europe.

narwhal toothed whale *Monodon monoceros*, found only in the Arctic Ocean. It grows to 16 ft/5 m long, has a gray and black body, a small head, and short flippers. The male has a single spirally fluted tusk that may be up to 9 ft/2.7 m long.

NASA (acronym for *National Aeronautics and Space Administration*) US government agency, founded 1958, for spaceflight and aeronautical research. Its headquarters are in Washington, DC and its main installation is at the ▷Kennedy Space Center in Florida. NASA's early planetary and lunar programs included Pioneer spacecraft from 1958, which gathered data for the later crewed missions, the most famous of which took the first people to the Moon in *Apollo 11* on 16–24 July, 1969.

Other installations are located in Virginia (Langley Research Center and Wallops Station); California (Ames Research Center, Flight Research Center, and the Jet Propulsion Laboratory); Ohio (Lewis Research Center); Alabama (George C Marshall Space Flight Center); Maryland (Goddard Space Flight Center), and Texas (Manned Spacecraft Center). The Office of Manned Space Flight is responsible for space missions with crews and for the space-station and space-shuttle programs. The Office of Space Science and Applications deals with the scientific exploration of space. The Office of Advanced Research and Technology plans future flights and research. The Office of Tracking and Data Acquisition provides a network for tracking flights and accumulating data.

The agency was founded 1958 by the National Aeronautics and Space Act.

Naseby, Battle of decisive battle of the English Civil War June 14, 1645, when the Royalists, led by Prince Rupert, were defeated by Oliver Cromwell and General Fairfax. It is named after the nearby village of Naseby, 20 mi/32 km S of Leicester.

Nash (Frederic) Ogden 1902–1971. US poet and wit. He published numerous volumes of humorous, quietly satirical light verse, characterized by unorthodox rhymes and puns. They include *I'm a Stranger Here Myself* 1938, *Versus* 1949, and *Bed Riddance* 1970. Most of his poems first appeared in the *New Yorker*, where he held an editorial post and did much to establish the magazine's tone.

Born in Rye, New York, Nash also wrote children's books and lyrics for such musicals as *A Touch of Venus* 1943.

Nash Walter 1882–1968. New Zealand Labor politician. He was born in England, and emigrated to New Zealand 1909. He held ministerial posts 1935–49, was prime minister 1957–60, and leader of the Labor Party until 1963.

Nashua city in S New Hampshire on the Nashua River where it meets the Merrimack River, just N of the Massachusetts border. Industries include electronics, asbestos, chemicals, and glass products; population (1990) 79,600.

Nashville port on the Cumberland River and capital of Tennessee; population (1990) 488,300. It is a banking and commercial center, and has large printing, music-publishing, and recording industries.

Most of the Bibles in the US are printed here, and it is the hub of the country-music business. It is the home of the Country Music Hall of Fame and Museum and Opryland. Educational institutions include Vanderbilt and Fisk universities. The Southern Baptist Convention is headquartered here.

Nashville dates from 1778, and the Confederate army was defeated here 1864 in the Civil War. In 1963 Nashville merged with surrounding Davidson County.

Nassau capital and port of the Bahamas, on New Providence Island; population (1980) 135,000.

A tourist center, it is known for fine beaches and the resort community of Paradise Island across the harbor. The College of the Bahamas is here. English settlers founded it in the 17th century, and it was a supply base for Confederate blockade runners during the American Civil War.

Nasser Gamal Abdel 1918–1970. Egyptian politician, prime minister 1954–56 and from 1956 president of Egypt (the United Arab Republic 1958–71). In 1952 he was the driving power behind the Neguib coup, which ended the monarchy. His nationalization of the Suez Canal 1956 led to an Anglo-French invasion and the ▷Suez Crisis, and his ambitions for an Egyptian-led union of Arab states led to disquiet in the Middle East (and in the West). Nasser was also an early and influential leader of the nonaligned movement.

Nasser entered the army from Cairo Military Academy, and was wounded in the Palestine War of 1948–49. Initially unpopular after the 1952 coup, he took advantage of demands for change by initiating land reform and depoliticizing the army. His position was secured by an unsuccessful assassination attempt 1954 and his handling of the Suez Crisis 1956.

Nast Thomas 1840–1902. German-born US illustrator and cartoonist. During the American Civil War, Nast served as a staff artist for *Harper's Weekly* and later drew its editorial cartoons. His vivid caricatures helped bring down New York's Boss ▷Tweed and established the donkey and the elephant as the symbols of Democrats and Republicans, respectively.

Nast came to the US with his family in 1846. After attending the National Academy of Design in New York, he worked as an illustrator for several popular New York weeklies, eventually being sent to Europe as a foreign correspondent.

nastic movement plant movement that is caused by an external stimulus, such as light or temperature, but is directionally independent of its source, unlike ▷tropisms. Nastic movements occur as a result of changes in water pressure within specialized cells or differing rates of growth in parts of the plant. Examples include the opening and closing of crocus flowers following an increase or decrease in temperature (**thermonasty**), and the opening and closing of evening-primrose *Oenothera* flowers on exposure to dark and light (▷**photonasty**).

The leaf movements of the Venus flytrap *Dionaea muscipula* following a tactile stimulus, and the rapid collapse of the leaflets of the sensitive plant *Mimosa pudica* are examples of **haptonasty**. Sleep movements, where the leaves or flowers of some plants adopt a different position at night, are described as **nyctinasty**. Other movement types include **hydronasty**, in response to a change in the atmospheric humidity, and **chemonasty**, in response to a chemical stimulus.

nasturtium any plant of the genus *Nasturtium*, family Cruciferae, including watercress *N. officinale*, a perennial aquatic plant of Europe and Asia, grown as a salad crop. It also includes plants of the South American family Tropaeolaceae, including the cultivated species *Tropaeolum majus*, with orange or scarlet flowers, and *T. minus*, which has smaller flowers.

Natal province of South Africa, NE of Cape Province, bounded on the east by the Indian Ocean
area 35,429 sq mi/91,785 sq km
capital Pietermaritzburg
cities Durban
physical slopes from the Drakensberg to a fertile subtropical coastal plain
features Ndumu Game Reserve, Kosi Bay Nature Preserve, Sodwana Bay National Park, Maple Lane Nature Preserve, and St Lucia National Park, which extends from coral reefs of the Indian Ocean N of Umfolozi River (whales, dolphins, turtles, crayfish), over forested sandhills to inland grasslands and swamps of Lake St Lucia, 125 sq mi/324 sq km (reedbuck, buffalo, crocodile, hippopotamus, black rhino, cheetah, pelican, flamingo, stork). It is under threat from titanium mining

products sugar cane, black wattle *Acacia mollissima*, corn, fruit, vegetables, tobacco, coal

population (1985) 2,145,000

history called Natal ("of [Christ's] birth") because Vasco da Gama reached it Christmas Day 1497; part of the British Cape Colony from 1843 until 1856, when it was made into a separate colony. Zululand was annexed to Natal 1897, and the districts of Vrijheid, Utrecht, and part of Wakkerstroom were transferred from the Transvaal to Natal 1903; the colony became a part of the Union of South Africa 1910.

Natchez member of a North American Indian people of the Mississippi area, one of the Moundbuilder group of peoples. They had a highly developed caste system unusual in North America, headed by a ruler priest (the "Great Sun"). Members of the highest caste always married members of the lowest caste. The system lasted until French settlers colonized the area 1731. Only a few Natchez now survive in Oklahoma. Their Muskogean language is extinct.

Natchez city in Mississippi, on the E bluffs above the Mississippi River; population (1990) 19,400. It has many houses of the antebellum period and was important in the heyday of steamboat traffic.

The Natchez Trace National Parkway is a restoration of the frontier road that followed Indian pathways and linked the city to Nashville, Tennessee.

Nation Carrie Amelia Moore 1846–1911. US temperance crusader. Born in Kentucky, she briefly taught school in Missouri. After the death of her alcoholic husband, Dr Charles Gloyd, she began a campaign against the use of alcohol. Moving to Kansas, where she married David Nation, she began to protest the flagrant disregard of that state's prohibition law. Marching into illegal saloons with a hatchet, Nation would lecture the patrons and then perform a "hatchetation" on bottles and bar. As the publisher of the *Smasher's Mail*, she was the most outspoken prohibitionist in the country.

national anthem patriotic song for official occasions. The US national anthem, "The Star-Spangled banner," was written during the war of 1812 by Francis Scott ⋄Key and was adopted officially in 1931. In Britain "God Save the King/Queen" has been accepted as such since 1745, although both music and words are of much earlier origin. The German anthem "Deutschland über Alles/Germany before everything" is sung to music by Haydn. The French national anthem, the ⋄ "Marseillaise," dates from 1792.

National Association for the Advancement of Colored People (NAACP) US civil-rights organization dedicated to ending inequality and segregation for African-Americans through nonviolent protest. Founded 1910, its first aim was to eradicate lynching. The NAACP campaigned to end segregation in state schools; it funded test cases that eventually led to the Supreme Court decision 1954 outlawing school segregation, although it was only through the ⋄civil rights movement of the 1960s that desegregation was achieved. In 1987 the NAACP had about 500,000 members, black and white.

The NAACP was founded by a group of white liberals, including William Walling, Oswald Villard, social worker Jane Addams, philosopher John Dewey, and novelist William Dean Howells. Most of the officials were white, but most of the members were drawn from the ranks of the black bourgeoisie. It merged with the Niagara Movement founded 1905 by W E B DuBois. During World War II its membership increased from 50,000 to 400,000. The organization has been criticized by militants and black separatists for its moderate stance and its commitment to integration. See also **history** under ⋄black.

The NAACP has focused on bringing to court challenges to discriminatory practices, and many famous lawyers—among them Thurgood ⋄Marshall—have argued their case. The ⋄Brown v Board of Education case was a major triumph, forcing the end of overt segregation of public schools. It has also been criticized for depending too heavily on funds from white liberals.

national debt debt incurred by the central government of a country to its own people and institutions and also to overseas creditors. A government can borrow from the public by means of selling interest-bearing bonds, for example, or from abroad. Traditionally, a major cause of incurring national debt was the cost of war but in recent decades governments have borrowed heavily in order to finance development or nationalization, to support an ailing currency, or to avoid raising taxes.

Government budgets are often planned with a deficit that is funded by overseas borrowing. In the 1980s most governments adopted monetary policies designed to limit their borrowing requirements, both to reduce the cost of servicing the debt and because borrowing money tends to cause inflation.

In the US the net government debt as a proportion of gross national product rose steadily in the 1980s from only 19% in 1981 to 31% in 1988, as its borrowing increased to finance a huge influx of imported goods and to support increased defense spending.

National Guard militia force recruited by each state of the US. The volunteer National Guard units are under federal orders in emergencies, and under the control of the governor in peacetime, and are now an integral part of the US Army. The National Guard has been used against demonstrators; in May 1970 at Kent State University, Ohio, they killed four students who were protesting against the bombing of Cambodia by the US.

national income the total income earned, not necessarily received, by all persons in a country over a specified time period. It consists of wages, interest, rent, profits, and the net income of the self-employed. Profits of government enterprises are not included. See ⋄national income and products accounts.

national income and products accounts a detailed description of the volume, composition, and use of a nation's output of goods and services. There are two basic components: the value of all goods and services produced (product side) and the costs incurred and payments received in the course of producing all goods and services (income side). These accounts are basic tools used in analyzing current economic performance and in forecasting future developments. See also ⋄Gross National Product (GNP).

nationalism in music, a 19th-century movement in which composers (such as Smetana and Grieg) included the folk material of their country in their works, projecting the national spirit and its expression.

nationalism in politics, a movement that consciously aims to unify a nation, create a state, or liberate it from foreign or imperialistic rule. Nationalist movements became a potent factor in European politics during the 19th century; since 1900 nationalism has become a strong force in Asia and Africa and in the late 1980s revived strongly in E Europe.

Stimulated by the French Revolution, movements arose in the 19th century in favor of national unification in Germany and Italy and national independence in Ireland, Italy, Belgium, Hungary, Bohemia, Poland, Finland, and the Balkan states. Revival of interest in the national language, history, traditions, and culture has accompanied and influenced most political movements.

In political terms, nationalism can be pursued as an ideology which stresses the superiority of a nation and its inhabitants compared with other nations and peoples. Most countries enjoy, and wish to demonstrate, national pride but—carried to an extreme—nationalism can produce dangerous regimes and political systems (such as that in Nazi Germany in the 1930s).

nationalization policy of bringing a country's essential services and industries under public ownership. It was pursued, for example, by the UK Labour government 1945–51. In recent years the trend toward nationalization has slowed and in many countries (the UK, France, and Japan) reversed (⋄privatization). Assets in the hands of foreign governments or companies may also be nationalized; for example, Iran's oil industry (see ⋄Abadan), the ⋄Suez Canal, and US-owned fruit plantations in Guatemala, all in the 1950s.

National Labor Relations Board v Jones and Laughlin Steel Co a US Supreme Court decision 1937 dealing with federal jurisdiction over intrastate trade. Jones and Laughlin appealed an NLRB order to reinstate several employees fired for union activities. The steel company argued that as an exclusively intrastate trader, it was immune to federal regulatory measures. The Court voted 5 to 4 to uphold the NLRB ruling, judging that since the steel industry was so intrinsically an interstate business the actions of Jones and Laughlin must have affected interstate commerce. The Court ruled that the "stream of commerce" placed local steel companies within federal jurisdiction.

national park land set aside and conserved for public enjoyment. The first was Yellowstone National Park, established 1872. National parks include not only the most scenic places, but also places distinguished for their historic, prehistoric, or scientific interest, or for their superior recreational assets. They range from areas the size of small countries to pockets of just a few acres.

National Party, Australian Australian political party representing the interests of the farmers and people of the smaller towns. It developed from about 1860 as the *National Country Party*, and holds the power balance between Liberals and Labor. It gained strength following the introduction of proportional representation 1918, and has been in coalition with the Liberals since 1949.

national security adviser an appointee of the executive branch, the head of the ⋄National Security Council, which, since the National Security Act 1947, coordinates the defense and foreign policy of the US. The national security adviser appointed 1989 was Lt Gen Brent

Scowcroft, the author of a 1983 weapons report proposing MX missiles.

The office was originally a clerical post but took on greater stature when held by McGeorge Bundy 1961–66, Walt Rostow 1966–69, and Henry ◊Kissinger 1969–75, who exceeded Secretary of State William Rogers in influence with President Nixon. Zbigniew ◊Brzezinski, appointed 1977, struggled with Secretary of State Vance for influence on President Carter. President Reagan's adviser, Admiral John Poindexter, who succeeded Robert McFarlane (1937–) in 1985, was forced to resign 1986 because of his part in the illicit sale of arms to Iran (see ◊Irangate). His successors included Lt Gen Colin Powell (1937–) and Scowcroft.

National Security Agency (NSA) largest and most secret of US intelligence agencies. Established 1952 to intercept foreign communications as well as to safeguard US transmissions, the NSA collects and analyses computer communications, telephone signals, and other electronic data, and gathers intelligence. Known as the Puzzle Palace, its headquarters are at Fort Meade, Maryland (with a major facility at Menwith Hill, England).

The NSA was set up by a classified presidential memorandum and its very existence was not acknowledged until 1962. It operates outside normal channels of government accountability, and its budget (also secret) is thought to exceed several billion dollars. Fort Meade has several Cray supercomputers.

In 1976, NSA's Harvest computer system intercepted 75 million individual messages, of which 1.8 million received further analysis.

National Security Council US federal executive council that was established under the National Security Act of 1947. The membership includes the president, vice-president, and secretaries of state and defense. Their special advisers include the head of the Joint Chiefs of Staff and the director of the Central Intelligence Agency. The national security adviser heads the council's staff.

national security directive in the US, secret decree issued by the president that can establish national policy and commit federal funds without the knowledge of Congress, under the National Security Act 1947. The National Security Council alone decides whether these directives may be made public; most are not. The directives have been criticized as unconstitutional, since they enable the executive branch of government to make laws.

history In 1950 President Truman issued a secret directive for covert operations to foment "unrest and revolt" in the Eastern bloc. J F Kennedy authorized an invasion of Cuba by this means (see ◊Bay of Pigs), and Lyndon Johnson approved military incursions into Laos during the Vietnam War. The US invasion of Grenada and the allocation of $19 million for the CIA to start arming and training Contras in Central America were also authorized by national security directives.

National Socialism official name for the ◊Nazi movement in Germany; see also ◊fascism.

Native American the modern, politically conscious term used by North ◊American Indians, ◊Eskimos, and Aleuts to describe themselves as a group, although each society maintains its autonomy and its own name. See ◊Hopi, ◊Navaho, ◊Cherokee, ◊Sioux.

native companion another name for the ◊brolga, so called because these birds are often seen in pairs.

native element any nongaseous element that occurs naturally, uncombined with any other element(s). Examples of native nonmetals are carbon and sulfur.

native metal or *free metal* any of the metallic elements that occur in nature in the chemically uncombined or elemental form (in addition to any combined form). They include bismuth, cobalt, copper, gold, iridium, iron, lead, mercury, nickel, osmium, palladium, platinum, ruthenium, rhodium, tin, and silver. Some are commonly found in the free state, such as gold; others occur almost exclusively in the combined state, but under unusual conditions do occur as native metals, such as mercury.

nativity Christian festival celebrating a birth: *Christmas* is celebrated Dec 25 from AD 336 in memory of the birth of Jesus in Bethlehem; *Nativity of the Virgin Mary* is celebrated Sept 8 by the Catholic and Eastern Orthodox churches; *Nativity of John the Baptist* is celebrated June 24 by the Catholic, Eastern Orthodox, and Anglican churches.

NATO abbreviation for ◊*North Atlantic Treaty Organization*.

natural in music, a sign cancelling a sharp or flat. A *natural trumpet* or *horn* is an instrument without valves, thus restricted to playing natural harmonics.

Natural Bridge village in Virginia, 115 mi/185 km W of Richmond. The nearby Cedar Creek is straddled by an arch of limestone 215 ft/66 m high and 90 ft/27 m wide.

natural frequency the frequency at which a mechanical system will vibrate freely. A pendulum, for example, always oscillates at the same frequency when set in motion. More complicated systems, such as bridges, also vibrate with a fixed natural frequency. If a varying force with a frequency equal to the natural frequency is applied to such an object the vibrations can become violent, a phenomenon known as ◊resonance.

natural gas mixture of flammable gases found in the Earth's crust (often in association with petroleum), now or e of the world's three main fossil fuels (with coal and oil). Natural gas is a mixture of ◊hydrocarbons, chiefly methane, with ethane, butane, and propane.

Before the gas is piped to storage tanks and on to consumers, butane and propane are removed and liquefied to form "bottled gas." Natural gas is liquefied for transport and storage, and is therefore often used where other fuels are scarce and expensive.

Test flights of the first aircraft powered by liquefied natural gas began 1989. The Soviet-produced craft will save 8.9 tons/9 tonnes of kerosene on a journey of 1,250 mi/2,000 km.

natural logarithm in mathematics, the ◊exponent of a number expressed to base *e*, where *e* represents the ◊irrational number 2.71828... . Natural ◊logarithms are also called Napierian logarithms, after their inventor, the Scottish mathematician John Napier.

natural radioactivity radioactivity generated by those radioactive elements that exist in the Earth's crust. All the elements from polonium (atomic number 84) to uranium (atomic number 92) are radioactive. ◊Radioisotopes of some lighter elements are also found in nature (for example potassium-40).

natural selection the process whereby gene frequencies in a population change through certain individuals producing more descendants than others because they are better able to survive and reproduce in their environment. The accumulated effect of natural selection is to produce ◊adaptations such as the insulating coat of a polar bear or the spadelike forelimbs of a mole. The process is slow, relying firstly on random variation in the genes of an organism being produced by ◊mutation and secondly on the genetic ◊recombination of sexual reproduction. It was recognized by Charles Darwin and Alfred Russel Wallace as the main process driving ◊evolution.

nature the living world, including plants, animals, fungi, and all microorganisms, and naturally formed features of the landscape, such as mountains and rivers.

nature–nurture controversy or *environment–heredity controversy* long-standing dispute among philosophers and psychologists over the relative importance of environment, that is upbringing, experience and learning ("nurture"), and heredity, that is genetic inheritance ("nature"), in determining the makeup of an organism, as related to human personality and intelligence.

One area of contention is the reason for differences between individuals, for example in performing intelligence tests. The environmentalist position assumes that individuals do not differ significantly in their inherited mental abilities and that subsequent differences are due to learning, or to differences in early experiences. Opponents insist that certain differences in the capacities of individuals (and hence their behavior) can be attributed to inherited differences in their genetic makeup.

nature preserve area set aside to protect a habitat and the wildlife that lives within it, with only restricted admission for the public. A nature preserve often provides a sanctuary for rare species, and rare habitats, such as marshlands. The world's largest is Etosha Reserve, Namibia; area 38,415 sq mi/99,520 sq km.

Many state and local preserves have been established in the US since 1970. Some are called greenbelts and some are designated "forever wild," as well as those that are administered for limited or educational access.

Nauru island country in Polynesia, SW Pacific, W of Kiribati.

government The constitution dates from independence 1968. It provides for a single-chamber parliament of 18 members, elected by universal suffrage for a three-year term, and a president who is both head of state and head of government. The president and cabinet are elected by parliament and responsible to it. The size of the country allows an intimate style of government, with the president combining several portfolios in a cabinet of only five. Voting in parliamentary elections is compulsory.

Traditionally, members of parliament have been elected as independents and then grouped themselves into pro- and antigovernment factions. In 1987, however, the Democratic Party of Nauru was formed by the then opposition leader Kennan Adeang.

history The first Europeans, Britons, arrived 1798 and called it Pleasant Island. The German empire seized it 1888. Nauru was placed under Australian administration by the League of Nations 1920, with the UK and New Zealand as cotrustees. Japan occupied and devastated Nauru 1942–45, destroying its mining facilities and deporting two-thirds of its population to Truk Atoll in ⟩Micronesia, 1,000 mi/1,600 km to the northwest. In 1947 Nauru became a United Nations trust territory administered by Australia.

independence Internal self-government was attained 1966, and in 1968, on achieving full independence, Nauru became a "special member" of the British ⟩Commonwealth, with no direct representation at meetings of heads of government. The chief of Nauru, Hammer DeRoburt, was elected president 1968 and reelected until 1983 with one interruption, 1976–78, when Bernard Dowiyogo was president. The Dec 1986 elections resulted in a hung parliament.

In the 1987 elections, DeRoburt secured a narrow majority. This prompted the defeated Kennan Adeang, who had briefly held power 1986, to establish the Democratic Party of Nauru as a formal opposition grouping. In Aug 1989 Adeang secured the casting of DeRoburt on a vote of no confidence and Kensas Aroi became president, with Adeang as finance minister in the new government. According to Australian government sources, Aroi was DeRoburt's "unacknowledged natural son." Four months later Aroi resigned on the grounds of ill health and in the subsequent election was defeated by Bernard Dowiyogo. DeRobert died in Melbourne, Australia, July 1992.

resources Nauru is attempting to sue its former trustees (Australia, New Zealand, and the UK) for removing nearly all the island's phosphate-rich soil 1922–68, leaving it barren. Nauru received $2.5 million for phosphate worth $65 million and had to pay Australia $20 million to keep the remaining soil. Nauru's residual phosphate supplies, which have earned $80 million a year, are due to run out 1995 and an economic diversification program has been launched. *See illustration box.*

nautical mile formerly various units of distance used in navigation; since 1959, an internationally agreed-on standard equaling the average length of one minute of arc on a great circle of the Earth, or 6,076.12 ft/ 1,852 m.

nautilus shelled ⟩cephalopod, genus *Nautilus*, found in the Indian and Pacific oceans. The pearly nautilus *N. pompilius* has a chambered spiral shell about 8 in/20 cm in diameter. Its body occupies the outer chamber. The nautilus has a large number of short, grasping tentacles surrounding a sharp beak.

The living nautiluses are representatives of a group common 450 million years ago. Paper nautilus is another name for the ⟩argonaut, a type of octopus.

Nautilus is also the name of the world's first nuclear-powered submarine, launched by the US 1954; it sailed under the icecap to the North Pole.

Navaho member of a peaceable agricultural North American Indian people related to the ⟩Apache; population about 200,000. They were attacked by Kit ⟩Carson and US troops 1864, and were rounded up and exiled. Their reservation, created 1868, is the largest in the US (25,000 sq mi/65,000 sq km), and is mainly in NE Arizona but extends into NW New Mexico and SE Utah. Many Navaho now herd sheep and earn an income from tourism, making and selling rugs, blankets, and silver and turquoise jewelry. Like the Apache, they speak a Southern Athabaskan language.

Navarino, Battle of decisive naval action Oct 20, 1827 off Pylos in the Greek war of liberation that was won by the combined fleets of the English, French, and Russians under Vice-Admiral Edward Codrington (1770–1851) over the Turkish and Egyptian fleets. Navarino is the Italian and historic name of Pylos Bay, Greece, on the SW coast of the Peloponnese.

Navarre (Spanish *Navarra*) autonomous mountain region of N Spain
area 4,014 sq mi/10,400 sq km
capital Pamplona
features Monte Adi 4,933 ft/1,503 m; rivers: Ebro, Arga
population (1986) 513,000
history part of the medieval kingdom of Navarre. Estella, to the SW, where Don Carlos

was proclaimed king 1833, was a center of agitation by the ⟩Carlists.

Navarre, Kingdom of former kingdom comprising the Spanish province of Navarre and part of what is now the French *département* of Basses-Pyrénées. It resisted the conquest of the ⟩Moors and was independent until it became French 1284 on the marriage of Philip IV to the heiress of Navarre. In 1479 Ferdinand of Aragon annexed Spanish Navarre, with French Navarre going to Catherine of Foix (1483–1512), who kept the royal title. Her grandson became Henry IV of France, and Navarre was absorbed in the French crown lands 1620.

nave in architecture, the central part of a church, between the choir and the entrance.

navel small indentation in the center of the abdomen of mammals, the remains of the site of attachment of the ⟩umbilical cord, which connects the fetus to the ⟩placenta.

navigation the science and technology of finding the position, course, and distance traveled by a ship, plane, or other craft. Traditional methods include the magnetic ⟩compass and ⟩sextant. Today the gyrocompass is usually used, together with highly sophisticated electronic methods, employing beacons of radio signals. Satellite navigation uses satellites that broadcast time and position signals.

The US Global Positioning System, when complete, will feature 18 Navstar satellites that will enable users (including eventually motorists and walkers) to triangulate their position (from any three satellites) to within 50 ft/15 m.

Navigation Acts in British history, a series of acts of Parliament passed from 1381 to protect English shipping from foreign competition and to ensure monopoly trading between Britain and its colonies. The last was repealed 1849 (coastal trade exempt until 1853). The Navigation Acts helped to establish England as a major sea power, although they led to higher prices. They ruined the Dutch merchant fleet in the 17th century, and were one of the causes of the ⟩American Revolution.
1650 "Commonwealth Ordinance" forbade foreign ships to trade in English colonies.
1651 Forbade the importation of goods except in English vessels or in vessels of the country of origin of the goods. This act led to the Anglo-Dutch War 1652–54.
1660 All colonial produce was required to be exported in English vessels.
1663 Colonies were prohibited from receiving goods in foreign (rather than English) vessels.

navigation, biological the ability of animals or insects to navigate. Although many animals navigate by following established routes or known landmarks, many animals can navigate without such aids; for example, birds can fly several thousand miles back to their nest site, over unknown terrain. Such feats may be based on compass information derived from the position of the Sun, Moon, or stars, or on the characteristic patterns of Earth's magnetic field.

Biological navigation refers to the ability to navigate both in long-distance ⟩migrations and over shorter distances when foraging (for example, the honey bee finding its way from the hive to a nectar site and back). Where reliant on known landmarks, birds may home on features that can be seen from very great distances (such as the cloud caps that often form above isolated mid-ocean islands). Even smells

Nauru
Republic of (*Naoero*)

area 8 sq mi/21 sq km
capital (seat of government) Yaren District
physical tropical island country in SW Pacific; plateau encircled by coral cliffs and sandy beaches
features lies just S of equator; one of three phosphate rock islands in the Pacific
head of state and government Bernard Dowiyogo from 1989
political system liberal democracy
political party Democratic Party of Nauru

(DPN), opposition to government
exports phosphates
currency Australian dollar
population (1990 est) 8,100 (mainly Polynesian; Chinese 8%, European 8%); growth rate 1.7% p.a.
languages Nauruan (official), English
religion Protestant 66%, Roman Catholic 33%
literacy 99% (1988)
GNP $160 million (1986); $9,091 per head (1985)
chronology
1888 Annexed by Germany.
1920 Administered by Australia, New Zealand, and UK until independence, except 1942–45, when it was occupied by Japan.
1968 Independence achieved from Australia, New Zealand, and UK with "special member" Commonwealth status. Hammer DeRoburt elected president.
1976 Bernard Dowiyogo elected president.
1978 DeRoburt reelected.
1986 DeRoburt briefly replaced as president by Kennan Adeang.
1987 DeRoburt reelected; Adeang established the Democratic Party of Nauru.
1989 DeRoburt replaced by Kensas Aroi, who was later succeeded by Bernard Dowiyogo.
1992 DeRoburt died in Melbourne, Australia.

can act as a landmark. Aquatic species like salmon are believed to learn the characteristic taste of the river where they hatch and return to it, often many years later. Brain cells in some birds have been found to contain ◊magnetite and may therefore be sensitive to the Earth's magnetic field.

Navratilova Martina 1956– . Czech tennis player who became a naturalized US citizen 1981. The most outstanding woman player of the 1980s, she had 55 Grand Slam victories by 1991, including 18 singles titles. She has won the Wimbledon singles title a record nine times, including six in succession 1982–87.

Navratilova won her first Wimbledon title in 1976 (doubles with Chris Evert). Between 1974 and 1988 she won 52 Grand Slam titles (singles and doubles), second only to Margaret ◊Court. Her first Grand Slam win was mixed doubles at the 1974 French Championship (with Ivan Molina, Colombia).

CAREER HIGHLIGHTS

Wimbledon
singles: 1978–79, 1982–87, 1990
doubles: 1976, 1979, 1981–84, 1986
mixed: 1985
US Open
singles: 1983–84, 1986–87
doubles: 1977–78, 1980, 1983–84, 1986–90
mixed: 1985, 1987
French Open
singles: 1982, 1984
doubles: 1975, 1982, 1984–88
mixed: 1974, 1985
Australian Open
singles: 1981, 1983, 1985
doubles: 1980, 1982–85, 1987–89

navy fleet of ships, usually a nation's ◊warships and the organization to maintain them. The USSR had one of the world's largest merchant fleets and the world's largest fishing, hydrographic, and oceanographic fleets, in which all ships had intelligence-gathering equipment.

5th century BC Naval power was an important factor in the struggle for supremacy in the Mediterranean; for example, the defeat of Persia by Greece at Salamis.

311 BC The first permanent naval organization was established by the Roman Empire with the appointment of navy commissioners to safeguard trade routes from pirates and eliminate the threat of rival sea power.

878 Alfred the Great of England overcame the Danes with a few king's ships, plus ships from the shires and some privileged coastal towns.

12th century Turkish invasions ended Byzantine dominance.

13th century The first French royal fleet was established by Louis IX. His admirals came from Genoa.

1339–1453 During the Hundred Years' War there was a great deal of cross-Channel raiding by England and France.

16th century Spain built a large navy for exploration and conquest in the early part of the century. In England, building on the beginnings made by his father Henry VII, Henry VIII raised a force that included a number of battleships, such as the *Mary Rose*, created the long-enduring administrative machinery of the Admiralty, and, by mounting heavy guns low on a ship's side, revolutionized strategy by the use of the "broadside". Elizabeth I encouraged Drake, Frobisher, Hawkins, Raleigh, and other navigators to enlarge the empire.

1571 The Battle of Lepanto was one of the last to be fought with galleys, or oar-propelled ships.

1588 The defeat of the Spanish Armada began the decline of the sea power of Spain.

17th century There was a substantial development in naval power among the powers of N Europe; for example, in the Netherlands, which then founded an empire in the Americas and the East; France, where a strong fleet was built up by Richelieu and Louis XIV that maintained the links with possessions in India and North America; and England, comparatively briefly under Cromwell. In the late 17th century the British overtook the Dutch as the leading naval power.

1775–83 The US navy grew out of the coastal colonies' need to protect their harbors during the American Revolution, as well as the need to capture British war supplies. In late 1775 Washington prepared five schooners and a sloop, manned with army personnel, and sent them to prey on inbound supply vessels. By the time of the Declaration of Independence 1776 these were augmented by armed brigs and sloops from the various colonies. The hero of the period was John Paul Jones.

1805 Effectively reorganized by Pitt in time for the French Revolutionary Wars, the Royal Navy under Nelson won a victory over the French at Trafalgar, which ensured British naval supremacy for the rest of the 19th century.

19th century The US fleet was successful in actions against pirates off Tripoli 1803–05 and the British navy 1812-14, and rapidly expanded during the Civil War and again for the Spanish-American War 1898.

World War I Britain maintained naval supremacy in the face of German U-boat and surface threats.

1918–41 Between the wars the US fleet was developed to protect US trade routes, with an eye to the renewed German threat in the Atlantic and the danger from Japan in the Pacific.

1950s After World War II the US fleet emerged as the world's most powerful. *1962* The Cuban missile crisis (when the US forced the removal of Soviet missiles from Cuba) demonstrated the USSR's weakness at sea and led to its development under Admiral Sergei Gorshkov.

1980s The Soviet fleets (based in the Arctic, Baltic, Mediterranean, and Pacific) continued their expansion, rivaling the combined NATO fleets. The new pattern of the Soviet navy reflected that of other fleets: over 400 submarines, many with ballistic-missile capability, and over 200 surface combat vessels (mostly of recent date) including helicopter carriers, cruisers, destroyers, and escort vessels. The US maintained aircraft-carrier battle groups and recommissioned World War II battleships to give its fleet superior firepower, as well as smaller support vessels.

1990s With the end of the Cold War, the powerful Soviet navy began to fall apart. The Black Sea fleet was split between Russia and the Ukraine, and the Baltic fleet lost its main ports to the newly independent Baltic states, and the Northern and Far Eastern fleets curtailed their operations for lack of resources. All leading Western nations, including the US, announced plans to reduce in size.

Náxos island of Greece, the largest of the Cyclades, area 175 sq mi/453 sq km. Known since early times for its wine, it was a center for the worship of Bacchus, who, according to Greek mythology, found the deserted Ariadne on its shore and married her.

Nazareth town in Galilee, N Israel, SE of Haifa; population (1981) 64,000. According to the New Testament, it was the boyhood home of Jesus.

Nazarite or *Nazirite* Hebrew under a vow to God to observe certain rules, including not to cut his hair, drink wine, or have contact with dead bodies. Some took the vow for life, others for only a certain period. ◊Samson and ◊Samuel in the Old Testament were Nazarites from birth.

Nazca town S of Lima, Peru, near a plateau that has geometric linear markings interspersed with giant outlines of birds and animals. The markings were made by American Indians, possibly in the 6th century AD, and their function is thought to be ritual rather than astronomical.

Nazism ideology based on racism, nationalism, and the supremacy of the state over the individual. The German Nazi party, the *Nationalsozialistische Deutsche Arbeiterpartei* (National Socialist German Workers' Party), was formed from the German Workers' Party (founded 1919) and led by Adolf ◊Hitler 1921–45.

During the 1930s, many similar parties were created throughout Europe and the US, although only those of Austria, Hungary, and Sudetenland were of major importance. These parties collaborated with the German occupation of Europe 1939–45. After the Nazi atrocities of World War II (see ◊SS, ◊concentration camp, ◊Holocaust), the party was banned in Germany, but today parties with Nazi or neo-Nazi ideologies exist in many countries.

Nazi–Soviet pact see ◊Hitler–Stalin pact.

NB abbreviation for ◊*New Brunswick*; *nota bene* (Latin "note well"), used in references and citations.

NBS abbreviation for *National Bureau of Standards*, the US federal standards organization, on whose technical standards all US weights and measures are based.

NC abbreviation for the state of ◊*North Carolina*.

ND abbreviation for the state of ◊*North Dakota*.

N'djamena capital of Chad, at the confluence of the Chari and Logone rivers, on the Cameroon border; population (1988) 594,000. Founded 1900 by the French at the junction of caravan routes, it was used 1903–12 as a military center against the kingdoms of central Sudan. Its name until 1973 was *Fort Lamy*.

Ndola mining center and chief city of the Copperbelt province of central Zambia; population (1988) 442,700.

NE abbreviation for the state of ◊*Nebraska*, *New England*.

Neagh, Lough lake in Northern Ireland, 15 mi/25 km W of Belfast; area 153 sq mi/396 sq km. It is the largest lake in the British Isles.

Neanderthal hominid of the Mid-Late Paleolithic, named after the Neander Thal (valley) near Düsseldorf, Germany, where a skeleton was found in 1856. *Homo sapiens neanderthalensis* lived from about 100,000 to

Nebraska

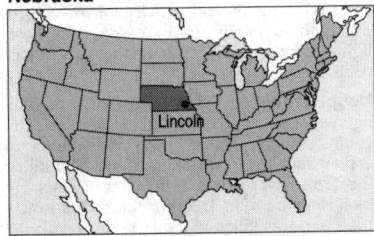

35,000 years ago and was similar in build to present-day people, but slightly smaller, stockier, and heavier-featured with a strong jaw and prominent brow ridges on a sloping forehead.

They lived in Europe, the Near East, and Africa. They looked after their disabled and buried their dead ritualistically. Recent evidence suggests their physical capacity for the sounds of speech. They were replaced throughout Europe by, or possibly interbred with, *Homo sapiens sapiens* (Cro-Magnon Man).

Near East term used until the 1940s to describe the area of the Balkan states, Egypt, and SW Asia, now known as the ▷Middle East.

nearsightedness alternate name for ▷myopia.

Near v Minnesota a US Supreme Court decision 1931 dealing with restrictions on the free press imposed by state libel laws. The Court overruled the actions of Minnesota officials who shut down Near's newspaper because it criticized law enforcement in the state. The Court found the Minnesota statute prohibiting scandalous publications unconstitutional because it allowed the state to suppress material before it was written rather than prosecuting authors of scandalous material after publication.

Nebraska state in central US; nickname Cornhusker State/Blackwater State
area 77,354 sq mi/200,400 sq km
capital Lincoln
cities Omaha, Grand Island, North Platte
population (1990) 1,578,300
features Rocky Mountain foothills; tributaries of the Missouri; Boys' Town for the homeless, near Omaha; the ranch of Buffalo Bill; the only unicameral legislature
products cereals, livestock, processed foods, fertilizers, oil, natural gas
famous people Fred Astaire, William Jennings Bryan, Johnny Carson, Willa Cather, Henry Fonda, Harold Lloyd, Malcom X
history exploited by French fur traders in the early 1700s; ceded to Spain by France 1763; retroceded to France 1801; part of the Louisiana Purchase 1803; explored by Lewis and Clark 1804–06; first settlement at Bellevue 1823; became a territory 1854 and a state 1867 after the Union Pacific began its transcontinental railroad at Omaha 1865. Nebraska's farm economy was weakened in the 1930s by the Great Depression and dust storms, but World War II brought military airfields and war industries. Much of the industry developed since that time is related to agriculture.

Nebuchadnezzar or *Nebuchadrezzar II* king of Babylonia from 60 BC. Shortly before his accession he defeated the Egyptians at Carchemish and brought Palestine and Syria into his empire. Judah revolted, with Egyptian assistance, 596 and 587–586 BC; on both occasions he captured Jerusalem and took many

Hebrews into captivity. He largely rebuilt Babylon and constructed the hanging gardens.

nebula cloud of gas and dust in space. Nebulae are the birthplaces of stars, but some nebulae are produced by gas thrown off from dying stars (see ▷planetary nebula; ▷supernova). Nebulae are classified depending on whether they emit, reflect, or absorb light.

An *emission nebula*, such as the ▷Orion nebula, glows brightly because its gas is energized by stars that have formed within it. In a *reflection nebula*, starlight reflects off grains of dust in the nebula, such as surround the stars of the ▷Pleiades cluster. A *dark nebula* is a dense cloud, composed of molecular hydrogen, which partially or completely absorbs light behind it. Examples include the Coalsack nebula in ▷Crux and the Horsehead nebula in Orion.

neck the structure between the head and the trunk in animals. In the back of the neck are the upper seven vertebrae, and there are many powerful muscles that support and move the head. In front, the neck region contains the pharynx and trachea, and behind these the esophagus. The large arteries (carotid, temporal, maxillary) and veins (jugular) that supply the brain and head are also located in the neck.

Necker Jacques 1732–1804. French politician. As finance minister 1776–81, he attempted reforms, and was dismissed through Queen Marie Antoinette's influence. Recalled 1788, he persuaded Louis XVI to summon the States General (parliament), which earned him the hatred of the court, and in July 1789 he was banished. The outbreak of the French Revolution with the storming of the Bastille forced his reinstatement, but he resigned Sept 1790.

necrosis death or decay of tissue in a particular part of the body, usually due to bacterial poisoning or loss of local blood supply.

nectar sugary liquid secreted by some plants from a nectary, a specialized gland usually situated near the base of the flower. Nectar often accumulates in special pouches or spurs, not always in the same location as the nectary. Nectar attracts insects, birds, bats, and other animals to the flower for ▷pollination and is the raw material used by bees in the production of honey.

nectarine smooth, shiny-skinned variety of ▷peach, usually smaller than other peaches and with firmer flesh. It arose from a natural mutation.

needlefish any bony fish of the marine family Belonidae, with an elongated body and long jaws lined with many sharp teeth.

Neenah city in E Wisconsin, on the Fox River near Lake Winnebago, N of Oshkosh. To its E is Menasha, with which it forms one community. It is a processing and marketing center for the area's agricultural products; population (1990) 23,200.

Nefertiti or *Nofretete* queen of Egypt who ruled *c.* 1372–1350 BC; wife of the pharaoh ▷Ikhnaton.

She disappeared from the records about 12 years after the marriage, and her name was defaced on monuments at some later date. A small gold scarab bearing her name, inscribed within the royal cartouche that marks the name of a pharaoh, was recovered in 1986 from an ancient wreck and confirms that she briefly ruled in her own right.

negative/positive in photography, a reverse image, which when printed is again reversed,

restoring the original scene. It was invented by Fox ▷Talbot about 1834.

Today the most common snapshots and photos are printed positives (on paper) made from film negatives.

Negev desert in S Israel that tapers to the port of Eilat. It is fertile under irrigation, and minerals include oil and copper.

negligence in law, doing some act that a "prudent and reasonable" person would not do, or omitting to do some act that such a person would do. Negligence may arise in respect of a person's duty toward an individual or toward other people in general. Breach of the duty of care that results in reasonably foreseeable damage is a tort.

Contributory negligence is a defense sometimes raised where the defendant to an action for negligence claims that the plaintiff by his own negligence contributed to the cause of the action.

A person's duty toward an individual may cover parenthood, guardianship, trusteeship, or a contractual relationship; a person's duty toward other people may include the duties owed to the community, such as care upon the public highway, and the maintenance of structures in a safe condition.

Negri Sembilan state of S Peninsular Malaysia; area 2,565 sq mi/6,646 sq km; population (1990) 723,800. It is mainly mountainous; products include rice and rubber. The capital is Seremban.

Negrito member of any of several groups living on various islands in SE Asia. The Negritos are long-established inhabitants of the region. They include the cave-dwelling Vedda of Sri Lanka, the Andamanese of the Andaman Islands, and the Semang of Malaysia.

Negroid referring to one of the three major varieties (see ▷races) of humans, *Homo sapiens sapiens*, mainly the indigenous peoples of Subsaharan Africa and some of the nearby islands in the Indian Ocean and the W Pacific. General physical traits include dark eyes, tightly curled dark hair, brown to very dark skin, little beard or body hair, low to medium-bridged wide noses, and wide or everted lips. See ▷Caucasoid, ▷Mongoloid.

Nehemiah Hebrew governor of Judea under Persian rule. He rebuilt Jerusalem's walls 444 BC, and made religious and social reforms.

Nehru Jawaharlal 1889–1964. Indian nationalist politician, prime minister from 1947. Before the partition (the division of British India into India and Pakistan), he led the socialist wing of the Nationalist Congress Party, and was second in influence only to Mohandas ▷Gandhi. He was imprisoned nine times by the British 1921–45 for political activities. As prime minister from the creation of the dominion (later republic) of India in Aug 1947, he originated the idea on which the ▷nonaligned movement (neutrality toward major powers) is based. His daughter was Prime Minister Indira ▷Gandhi.

Nejd region of central Arabia consisting chiefly of desert; area about 800,000 sq mi/2,072,000 sq km. It forms part of the kingdom of Saudi Arabia and is inhabited by Bedouins. The capital is Riyadh.

Nelson Horatio, Viscount Nelson 1758–1805. English admiral. He joined the navy in 1770. In the Revolutionary Wars against France he lost the sight in his right eye 1794 and lost his right arm 1797. He became a national hero, and rear admiral, after the victory off Cape St Vincent,

Portugal. In 1798 he tracked the French fleet to Aboukir Bay and almost entirely destroyed it in the Battle of the Nile. In 1801 he won a decisive victory over Denmark at the Battle of ⊳Copenhagen, and in 1805, after two years of blockading Toulon, another over the Franco-Spanish fleet at the Battle of ⊳Trafalgar, near Gibraltar.

The son of a clergyman, he was almost continuously on active service in the Mediterranean 1793–1800 and lingered at Naples for a year, during which he helped to crush a democratic uprising and fell completely under the influence of Lady ⊳Hamilton. In 1800 he returned to England and soon after separated from his wife, Frances Nisbet. He was promoted to vice admiral 1801 and sent to the Baltic to operate against the Danes, nominally as second-in-command; in fact, it was Nelson who was responsible for the victory of Copenhagen and for negotiating peace with Denmark.

In 1803 he received the Mediterranean command, and for nearly two years blockaded Toulon. On Oct 21, 1805, he defeated the combined French and Spanish fleets off Cape Trafalgar, 20 of the enemy ships being captured, but Nelson himself was mortally wounded.

nematode unsegmented worm of the phylum Aschelminthes. Nematodes are pointed at both ends, with a tough, smooth outer skin. They include many free-living species found in soil and water, including the sea, but a large number are parasites, such as the roundworms and pinworms that live in humans, or the eelworms that attack plant roots. They differ from ⊳flatworms in that they have two openings to the gut (a mouth and an anus).

Nemerov Howard 1920– . US poet, critic, and novelist. He published his poetry collection *Guide to the Ruins* 1950, a short-story collection *A Commodity of Dreams* 1959, and in 1977 his *Collected Poems* won both the National Book Award and the Pulitzer Prize.

Nemesis in Greek mythology, the goddess of retribution, who especially punished hubris (Greek *hybris*), the arrogant defiance of the gods.

nemesis theory theory of animal extinction, suggesting that a sister star to the Sun caused the extinction of groups of animals such as dinosaurs. The theory holds that the movement of this as yet undiscovered star disrupts the ⊳Oort cloud of comets every 26 million years, resulting in the Earth suffering an increased bombardment from comets at these times. The theory was proposed in 1984 to explain the newly discovered layer of iridium—an element found in comets and meteorites—in rocks dating from the end of dinosaur times. However, many paleontologists deny any evidence for a 26-million-year cycle of extinctions.

neo-classical economics school of economic thought based on the work of 19th-century economists, such as Alfred Marshall, using ⊳marginal theory to modify Classical economic theories. Mathematics became extremely important, as did microeconomic theoretical systems. Neo-classicists believed competition to be the regulator of economic activity that would establish equilibrium between output and consumption. Neo-classical economics was largely superseded from the 1930s by the work of Maynard ⊳Keynes.

Neo-Classicism movement in art and architecture in Europe and North America about

1750–1850, a revival of Classical art, which superseded the Rococo style. It was partly inspired by the excavation of the Roman cities of Pompeii and Herculaneum. The architect Piranesi was an early Neo-Classicist; in sculpture Antonio ⊳Canova and in painting Jacques Louis David were exponents.

Others include Thorvaldsen (sculpture), Ingres (painting), and Robert Adam (architecture).

neocolonialism disguised form of ⊳imperialism, by which a country may grant independence to another country but continue to dominate it by control of markets for goods or raw materials.

This system was analyzed in the Ghanaian leader Kwame Nkrumah's book *Neo-Colonialism, the Last Stage of Imperialism* 1965.

neo-Darwinism the modern theory of ⊳evolution, built up since the 1930s by integrating Charles ⊳Darwin's theory of evolution through natural selection with the theory of genetic inheritance founded on the work of Gregor ⊳Mendel.

neodymium yellowish metallic element of the ⊳lanthanide series, symbol Nd, atomic number 60, atomic weight 144.24. Its rose-colored salts are used in coloring glass, and neodymium is used in lasers.

It was named in 1885 by Austrian chemist Carl von Welsbach (1858–1929), who fractionated it away from didymium (originally thought to be an element but actually a mixture of rare-earth metals consisting largely of neodymium, presodymium, and cerium).

Neo-Impressionism movement in French painting in the 1880s, an extension of the Impressionists' technique of placing small strokes of different color side by side. Seurat was the chief exponent; his minute technique became known as "pointillism." Signac and Pissarro practiced the same style for a few years.

Neolithic last period of the ⊳Stone Age, characterized by settled communities based on agriculture and domesticated animals, and identified by sophisticated, finely honed stone tools, and ceramic wares. The earliest Neolithic communities appeared about 9000 BC in the Middle East, followed by Egypt, India, and China. In Europe farming began in about 6500 BC in the Balkans and Aegean, spreading north and east by 1000 BC.

neon (Greek *neon* "new") colorless, odorless, nonmetallic, gaseous element, symbol Ne, atomic number 10, atomic weight 20.183. It is grouped with the ⊳inert gases, is non-reactive, and forms no compounds. It occurs in small quantities in the Earth's atmosphere.

Tubes containing neon are used in electric advertising signs, giving off a fiery red glow; it is also used in lasers. Neon was discovered by Scottish chemist William Ramsay and the Englishman Morris Travers.

neoplasm (Greek "new growth") any lump or tumor, which may be benign or malignant (cancerous).

Neoplatonism school of philosophy that flourished during the declining centuries of the Roman Empire (3rd–6th centuries AD). Neoplatonists argued that the highest stage of philosophy is attained not through reason and experience, but through a mystical ecstasy. Many later philosophers, including Nicholas of Cusa, were influenced by Neoplatonism.

neoprene synthetic rubber, developed in the US 1931 from the polymerization of chloroprene. It is much more resistant to heat, light, oxidation, and petroleum than is ordinary rubber.

Neoptolemos or *Pyrrhus* in Greek mythology, son of Achilles. With ⊳Odysseus he conducted the Trojan hero Philoctetes to ⊳Troy after the death of his father, and killed the Trojan king Priam at the altar of Zeus. He took Hector's wife, Andromache, as his concubine, and was killed in a quarrel at the shrine of Delphi.

Neo-Realism movement in Italian cinema that emerged in the 1940s. It is characterized by its naturalism, social themes, and the visual authenticity achieved through location filming. Exponents include the directors de Sica, Visconti, and Rossellini.

neoteny in biology, the retention of some juvenile characteristics in an animal that seems otherwise mature. An example is provided by the axolotl, a salamander that can reproduce sexually although still in its larval form.

It has been suggested that new species could arise in this way, and that the ⊳human species evolved from its apelike ancestors by neoteny: in human fossil skulls, we see a developmental trend—that facially we resemble a young ape.

NEP abbreviation for the Soviet leader Lenin's ⊳*New Economic Policy*.

Nepal landlocked country in the Himalayan mountain range in Central Asia, bounded N by Tibet (an autonomous region of China), E, S, and W by India.

government Under the constitution of 1990, Nepal is a pluralist, parliamentary democracy headed by a constitutional monarch. It has a two-chamber legislature, comprising a 205-member, directly elected House of Representatives and a 60-member National Council, which consists of 10 appointees of the king, 35 members elected by the lower house, and 15 selected from the country's five development zones. Executive power is vested jointly in the king and a council of ministers which is headed by a prime minister drawn from the House of Representatives' majority party grouping. The constitution explicitly guarantees freedom of expression, press, peaceful assembly, association, and movement.

history From one of a group of small principalities, the Gurkhas emerged to unite Nepal under King Prithivi Narayan Shah 1768. In 1816, after the year-long Anglo-Nepali "Gurkha War," a British resident (government representative) was stationed in Katmandu and the kingdom became a British-dependent buffer state. The country was recognized as fully independent by Britain 1923 although it remained bound by treaty obligations until 1947, the year of India's independence. Between 1846 and 1951 Nepal was ruled by a hereditary prime minister of the Rana family. The Ranas were overthrown in a revolution led by the Nepali congress, and the monarchy, in the person of King Tribhuvan, was restored to power.

first constitution In 1959 King Mahendra Bir Bikram Shah, who had succeeded his father 1955, promulgated the nation's first constitution and held elections. The Nepali Congress Party leader B P Koirala became prime minister and proceeded to clash with the king over policy. King Mahendra thus dissolved parliament Dec 1960 and issued a ban on political parties Jan 1961. In Dec 1962 he introduced a new, monarch-dominated constitution with an indirectly elected national assembly and tiered system of *panchayats* (councils).

amended constitution King Mahendra died 1972. His son Birendra (1945–), faced with mounting agitation for political reform led by B P Koirala, held a referendum on the constitution. As a result, it was amended, and the first elections to the national assembly were held May 1981. They led to the defeat of a third of the progovernment candidates and returned a more independently minded national assembly, which in July 1983 unseated Prime Minister Surya Bahadur Thapa, despite his royal support, and installed in office Lokendra Bahadur Chand. In May 1986 elections to the national assembly returned a majority of members opposed to the partyless *panchayat* system and resulted in the replacement of Prime Minister Chand. In April 1990, following mass prodemocracy demonstrations, during which police shot 150 protesters, King Birendra lifted the ban on opposition parties and abolished the *panchayat* system. An interim government was installed in preparation for the 1991 free, multiparty elections.

foreign affairs In foreign affairs, Nepal has adhered to the policies of the ⟡nonaligned movement, seeking to create a "zone of peace" in S Asia between India and China. In recent years commercial links with China have increased. This has been resented by India who, in March 1989, imposed a partial blockade on Nepal's borders as part of a dispute over the renegotiation of expired transit and trade duties. In June 1990 India agreed to restore the trade and transit concessions.

democratization process In Sept 1990 King Birendra approved a new draft constitution that would transfer political power from the monarchy to an elected government, transforming the state into a constitutional monarchy. In readiness for the 1991 elections, two factions of the Communist Party sank their differences to become the United Nepal Communist Party. Marking the culmination of a 15-month democratization process, on May 12, 1991 the Nepali Congress Party secured a narrow majority of seats in the 205-member house of representatives in the first pluralist general election since 1959. Girija Prasad Koirala, the party's general secretary and brother of former prime minister B P Koirala, was appointed prime minister May 26, 1991. In 1992 communist-led demonstrations in Katmandu and Pátan campaigned for the government's resignation. *See illustration box.*

Nepal
Kingdom of (*Nepal Adhirajya*)

area 56,850 sq mi/147,181 sq km
capital Katmandu
cities Pátan, Moráng, Bhádgáon
physical descends from the Himalayan mountain range in N through foothills to the River Ganges plain in S
environment described as the world's highest rubbish dump, Nepal attracts 270,000 tourists, trekkers, and mountaineers each year. An estimated 1,100 lb of rubbish is left by each expedition trekking or climbing in the Himalayas. Since 1952 the foothills of the Himalayas have been stripped of 40% of their forest cover
features Mount Everest, Mount Kangchenjunga; the only Hindu kingdom in the world; Lumbini, birthplace of the Buddha
head of state King Birendra Bir Bikram Shah Dev from 1972
head of government Girija Prasad Koirala from 1991
political system constitutional monarchy
political parties Nepali Congress Party (NCP), left-of-center; United Nepal Communist Party (UNCP), Marxist-Leninist-Maoist;

United Liberation Torchbearers; Democratic Front, radical republican
exports jute, rice, timber, oilseed
currency Nepalese rupee
population (1990 est) 19,158,000 (mainly known by name of predominant clan, the Gurkhas; the Sherpas are a Buddhist minority of NE Nepal); growth rate 2.3% p.a.
life expectancy men 50, women 49 (1989)
language Nepali (official); 20 dialects spoken
religion Hindu 90%; Buddhist, Muslim, Christian
literacy men 39%, women 12% (1985 est)
GNP $3.1 bn (1988); $160 per head (1986)
chronology
1768 Nepal emerged as unified kingdom.
1815–16 Anglo-Nepali "Gurkha War"; Nepal became a British-dependent buffer state.
1846–1951 Ruled by the Rana family.
1923 Independence achieved from Britain.
1951 Monarchy restored.
1959 Constitution created elected legislature.
1960–61 Parliament dissolved by king; political parties banned.
1980 Constitutional referendum held following popular agitation.
1981 Direct elections held to national assembly.
1983 Overthrow of monarch-supported prime minister.
1986 New assembly elections returned a majority opposed to *panchayat* system of partyless government.
1988 Strict curbs placed on opposition activity; over 100 supporters of banned opposition party arrested; censorship imposed.
1989 Border blockade imposed by India in treaty dispute.
1990 *Panchayat* system collapsed after mass prodemocracy demonstrations; new constitution introduced; elections set for May 1991.
1991 Nepali Congress Party, led by Girija Prasad Koirala, won the general election.
1992 Communists led antigovernment demonstrations in Katmandu and Pátan.

nepenth or **nepenthes** mythical drug that makes people forget cares or worries, used by ⟡Helen of Troy in ⟡Homer's *Odyssey*.

neper unit used in telecommunications to express a ratio of powers and currents. It gives the attenuation of amplitudes as the natural logarithm of the ratio.

nephrectomy surgical removal of a kidney.

nephritis inflammation of the kidneys, caused by bacterial infection or, sometimes, by a body disorder that affects the kidneys, such as streptococcal infection of the throat. The degree of illness varies, and it may be acute or chronic, requiring a range of treatments from antibiotics to ⟡dialysis. Acute nephritis is also known as *Bright's disease*.

nephron microscopic unit in vertebrate kidneys that forms **urine**. A human kidney is composed of over a million nephrons. Each nephron consists of a filter cup surrounding a knot of blood capillaries and a long narrow collecting tubule in close association with yet more capillaries. Waste materials and water pass from the bloodstream into the filter cup, and essential minerals and some water are reabsorbed from the tubule back into the blood. The urine that is left eventually passes out from the body.

Neptune in Roman mythology, god of the sea, the equivalent of the Greek ⟡Poseidon.

Neptune in astronomy, the eighth planet in average distance from the Sun. Neptune orbits the Sun every 164.8 years at an average distance of 2.794 billion mi/4.497 billion km. It is a giant gas (hydrogen, helium, methane) planet, with a diameter of 30,200 mi/48,600 km and a mass 17.2 times that of Earth. Its rotation period is 16 hours 7 minutes. The methane in its atmosphere absorbs red light and gives the planet a blue coloring. It is believed to have a central rocky core covered by a layer of ice. Neptune has eight known moons.

Neptune was located 1846 by the German astronomers J G ⟡Galle and Heinrich d'Arrest (1822–1875) after calculations by the English astronomer J C Adams and the French mathematician Urbain Leverrier had predicted its existence from disturbances in the movement of Uranus. *Voyager 2*, which passed Neptune in Aug 1989, revealed various cloud features, notably an Earth-sized oval storm cloud, the Great Dark Spot, similar to the Great Red Spot on Jupiter.

Neptune has three faint rings and of its eight moons, two (⟡Triton and Nereid) are visible from Earth. Six were discovered by the *Voyager 2* probe in 1989, of which Proteus (diameter 260 mi/415 km) is larger than Nereid (200 mi/ 300 km).

neptunium silvery, radioactive metallic element of the ⟡actinide series, symbol Np, atomic number 93, atomic weight 237.048. It occurs in nature in minute amounts in ⟡pitchblende and other uranium ores, where it is produced from the decay of neutron-bombarded uranium in these ores. The longest-lived isotope, Np-237, has a half-life of 2.2 million years. The element can be produced by bombardment of U-238 with neutrons and is chemically highly reactive.

It was first synthesized in 1940 by US physicists E McMillan (1907–) and P Abelson (1913–), who named it for the planet Neptune (since it comes after uranium as the planet Neptune comes after Uranus). Neptunium was the first ⟡transuranic element to be synthesized.

Nereid in Greek mythology, any of 50 sea goddesses who sometimes mated with mortals. Their father was Nereus, a sea god, and their mother was Doris.

Nergal Babylonian god of the Sun, war, and pestilence, ruler of the underworld, symbolized by a winged lion.

Nernst (Walther) Hermann 1864–1941. German physical chemist. His investigations, for which he won the 1920 Nobel Prize for Chemistry, were concerned with heat changes in chemical reactions. He proposed in 1906 the principle known as the *Nernst heat theorem* or the third law of thermodynamics: the law states that chemical changes at the temperature of ⬦absolute zero involve no change of ⬦entropy (disorder).

Born in Briesen, Prussia, Nernst was professor of chemistry at Göttingen 1905, and Berlin. He suffered under the Nazi regime because two of his daughters married Jews.

Nero AD 37–68. Roman emperor from 54. He is said to have murdered his stepfather ⬦Claudius' son Britannicus, his own mother, his wives Octavia and Poppaea, and many others. After the great fire of Rome 64, he persecuted the Christians, who were suspected of causing it. Military revolt followed 68; the Senate condemned Nero to death, and he committed suicide.

Son of Domitius Ahenobarbus and Agrippina, Nero was adopted by Claudius, and succeeded him as emperor in 54. He was a poet and connoisseur of art, and performed publicly as an actor and a singer.

Neruda Pablo. Adopted name of Neftali Ricardo Reyes y Basualto 1904–1973. Chilean poet and diplomat. His work includes lyrics and the epic poem of the American continent *Canto General* 1950. He was awarded the Nobel Prize for Literature 1971. He served as consul and ambassador to many countries.

After World War II he entered political life in Chile as a communist, and was a senator 1945–48. He went into exile in 1948 but returned in 1952; he later became consul to France 1971–72.

Nerva Marcus Cocceius Nerva AD *c.* 35–98. Roman emperor. He was proclaimed emperor on Domitian's death AD 96, and introduced state loans for farmers, family allowances, and allotments of land to poor citizens.

Nerval Gérard de. Adopted name of Gérard Labrunie 1808–1855. French writer and poet, precursor of French ⬦Symbolism and ⬦Surrealism. His writings include the travelogue *Voyage en Orient* 1851; short stories, including the collection *Les Filles du feu* 1854; poetry; a novel *Aurélia* 1855, containing episodes of visionary psychosis; and drama. He lived a wandering life, and suffered from periodic insanity, finally taking his own life.

nerve strand of nerve cells enclosed in a sheath of connective tissue joining the ⬦central and the ⬦autonomic nervous systems with receptor and effector organs. A single nerve may contain both ⬦motor and sensory nerve cells, but they act independently.

nerve cell or *neuron* elongated cell, part of the ⬦nervous system, that transmits information between different parts of the body. A nerve impulse is a traveling wave of chemical and electrical changes that affects the surface membrane of the nerve fiber. Sequential changes in the permeability of the membrane to positive sodium (Na⁺) ions and potassium (K⁺) ions, produce electrical signals called action potentials. Impulses are received by the cell body and passed, as a pulse of electric charge, along the ⬦axon. At the far end of the axon, the impulse triggers the release of chemical ⬦neurotransmitters across a ⬦synapse (junction), thereby stimulating another nerve cell or the action of an effector organ (for example, a muscle). Nerve impulses travel quickly, in humans as fast as 525 ft/160 m per second along a nerve cell.

Nervi Pier Luigi 1891–1979. Italian architect who used soft steel mesh within concrete to give it flowing form. For example, the Turin exhibition hall 1949, the UNESCO building in Paris 1952, and the cathedral at New Norcia, near Perth, Australia, 1960.

nervous breakdown popular term for a reaction to overwhelming psychological stress. It has no equivalent in medicine: patients said to be suffering from a nervous breakdown may in fact be going through an episode of depression, manic depression, anxiety, or even schizophrenia.

nervous system the system of interconnected ⬦nerve cells of most invertebrates and all vertebrates. It is composed of the ⬦central and ⬦autonomic nervous systems. It may be as simple as the nerve net of coelenterates (for example, jellyfishes) or as complex as the mammalian nervous system, with a central nervous system comprising brain and spinal cord, and a peripheral nervous system connecting up with sensory organs, muscles, and glands.

Ness, Loch lake in Highland region, Scotland, forming part of the Caledonian Canal; 22.5 mi/36 km long, 754 ft/229 m deep. There have been unconfirmed reports of a *Loch Ness monster* since the 15th century.

nerve cell *The anatomy and action of a nerve cell.*

Nestorianism Christian doctrine held by the Syrian ecclesiastic Nestorius (died *c.* 457), patriarch of Constantinople 428–31. He asserted that Jesus had two natures, human and divine. He was banished for maintaining that Mary was the mother of the man Jesus only, and therefore should not be called the Mother of God. His followers survived as the Assyrian church in Syria, Iraq, Iran, and as the Christians of St Thomas in S India.

Netherlands, the country in W Europe on the North Sea, bounded E by Germany and S by Belgium.

government The Netherlands is a hereditary monarchy. Its constitution 1983, based on that of 1814, provides for a two-chamber legislature called the States-General, consisting of a First Chamber of 75 and a Second Chamber of 150. Members of the First Chamber are indirectly elected by representatives of 11 provincial councils for a six-year term, half retiring every three years, and Second Chamber members are elected by universal adult suffrage, through a system of proportional representation, for a four-year term. Legislation is introduced and bills amended in the Second Chamber, while the First has the right to approve or reject.

The monarch appoints a prime minister as head of government, and the prime minister chooses the cabinet. Cabinet members are not permitted to be members of the legislature, but they may attend its meetings and take part in debates, and they are collectively responsible to it. There is also a council of state, the government's oldest advisory body, whose members are intended to represent a broad cross section of the country's life, and include former politicians, scholars, judges, and business people, all appointed for life. The sovereign is its formal president but appoints a vice-president to chair it.

Although not a federal state, the Netherlands gives considerable autonomy to its 11 provinces, each of which has an appointed governor and an elected council.

history The land south of the Rhine, inhabited by ⬦Celts and Germanic peoples, was brought under Roman rule by Julius Caesar as governor of ⬦Gaul 51 BC. The ⬦Franks followed, and their kings subdued the ⬦Frisians and Saxons north of the Rhine in the 7th–8th centuries and imposed Christianity on them. After the empire of ⬦Charlemagne broke up, the local feudal lords, headed by the count of Holland and the bishop of ⬦Utrecht, became practically independent, although they owed nominal allegiance to the German or Holy Roman Empire. Many Dutch towns during the Middle Ages became prosperous trading centers, usually ruled by small groups of merchants. In the 15th century the Netherlands or Low Countries (Holland, Belgium, Flanders) passed to the dukes of Burgundy, and in 1504 to the Spanish Hapsburgs.

war of independence The Dutch aspired to political freedom and Protestantism and rebelled from 1568 against the tyranny of the Catholic Philip II of Spain. William the Silent, Prince of Orange, and his sons Maurice (1567–1625) and Frederick Henry (1584–1647) were the leaders of the revolt and of a confederation established in the north, the United Provinces, that repudiated Spain 1581. The south (now Belgium and Luxembourg) was reconquered by Spain, but not the north, and in 1648 its independence as the Dutch Republic was finally recognized under the Treaty of ⬦Westphalia. A long struggle followed between the Orangist or popular party, which favored centralization under the Prince of Orange as chief magistrate or *stadholder*, and the oligarchical or states' rights party. The latter, headed by Johann de ♢Witt, seized control 1650, but ♢William of Orange (William III of England) recovered the stadholderate with the French invasion 1672.

Batavian Republic Despite the long war of independence, during the early 17th century the Dutch led the world in trade, art, and science, and founded an empire in the East and West Indies. Commercial and colonial rivalries led to naval wars with England 1652–54, 1665–67, and 1672–74. Thereafter until 1713 Dutch history was dominated by a struggle with France under Louis XIV. These wars exhausted the Netherlands, which in the 18th century ceased to be a great power. The French revolutionary army was welcomed 1795 and created the Batávian Republic. In 1806 Napoleon made his brother Louis king of Holland and 1810–13 annexed the country to France. The Congress of ♢Vienna united N and S Netherlands under King William I (son of Prince William V of Orange), but the south broke away 1830 to become independent Belgium.

cooperation with neighbors Under William I (reigned 1814–40), William II (1840–49), William III (1849–90), and Queen Wilhelmina (1890–1948), the Netherlands followed a path of strict neutrality, but its brutal occupation by Germany 1940–45 persuaded it to adopt a policy of cooperation with its neighbors. It became a member of the Western European Union, the North Atlantic Treaty Organization (NATO), the Benelux customs union, the European Coal and Steel Community, the European Atomic Energy Community (Euratom), and the European Economic Community. In 1980 Queen Juliana, who had reigned since 1948, abdicated in favor of her eldest daughter, Beatrix.

The granting of independence to former colonies (Indonesia 1949, with the addition of W New Guinea 1963; Suriname 1975; see also ♢Netherlands Antilles) increased immigration and unemployment. All governments since 1945 have been coalitions, with the parties differing mainly over economic policies. In the Sept 1989 elections, fought largely on environmental issues, Ruud Lubbers's Christian Democrats won the most parliamentary seats. Lubbers formed a coalition government with the leftist Labor Party.

In Dec 1991 Maastricht hosted a meeting of European Community (EC) members who signed the Maastricht Treaty on political and monetary union in Europe. *See illustration box.*

Netherlands Antilles two groups of Caribbean islands, part of the Netherlands with full internal autonomy, comprising ♢Curaçao and Bonaire off the coast of Venezuela (♢Aruba is considered separately), and St Eustatius, Saba, and the southern part of St Maarten in the Leeward Islands, 500 mi/800 km NE

area 308 sq mi/797 sq km
capital Willemstad on Curaçao
products oil from Venezuela refined here; tourism is important
language Dutch (official), Papiamento, English
population (1983) 193,000.

Netherlands East Indies former name of ♢Indonesia (1798–1945).

netsuke toggle of ivory, wood, or other materials, made to secure a purse or tobacco pouch, for men wearing Japanese traditional costume. Made especially in the Edo period in Japan 1601–1867, the miniature sculptures are valued as works of art.

nettle any plant of the genus *Urtica*, family Urticaceae. Stinging hairs on the generally ovate leaves can penetrate the skin, causing inflammation. The common nettle *U. dioica* grows on waste ground in Europe and North America, where it was introduced.

network in computing, a method of connecting computers so that they can share data and ♢peripheral devices, such as printers. The main types are classified by the pattern of the connections—star or ring network, for example—or by the degree of geographical spread allowed; for example, local area networks (LANs) for communication within a room or building, and wide area networks (WANs) for more remote systems.

Among proprietary networking systems is Ethernet, developed in the 1970s (released 1980) at Xerox's Palo Alto Research Center, California, by Rich Seifert, Bob Printis, and Dave Redell.

Netzahualcóyotl Mexican city lying to the S of Lake Texcoco, forming a suburb to the NE of Mexico City; population (1980) 1,341,200.

neuralgia sharp or burning pain originating in a nerve and spreading over its area of distribution. Trigeminal neuralgia, a common form, is a severe pain on one side of the face.

neurasthenia obsolete term for nervous exhaustion, covering mild ♢depression and various symptoms of ♢neurosis. Formerly thought to be a bodily malfunction, it is now generally considered to be mental in origin. Dating from the mid-19th century, the term became widely used to describe the symptoms of soldiers returning from the front in World War I.

neuritis nerve inflammation caused by injury, poisoning, or disease, and accompanied by sensory and motor changes in the area of the affected nerve.

neurofibromatosis rare genetic disorder characterized by multiple soft skin swellings all over the body and by benign tumors of nerve sheaths (neurofibromas). There is no cure.

neuroleptic alternate name for ♢antipsychotic.

neurology the branch of medicine concerned with the study and treatment of the brain, spinal cord, and peripheral nerves.

neuron another name for a ♢nerve cell.

neurosis in psychology, a general term referring to emotional disorders, such as anxiety, depression, and obsessions. The main disturbance tends to be one of mood; contact with

Netherlands
Kingdom of the (*Koninkrijk der Nederlanden*), popularly referred to as **Holland**

area 16,169 sq mi/41,863 sq km
capital Amsterdam
cities The Hague (seat of government), Utrecht, Eindhoven, Maastricht; chief port Rotterdam
physical flat coastal lowland; rivers Rhine, Scheldt, Maas; Frisian Islands
territories Aruba, Netherlands Antilles (Caribbean)
environment the country lies at the mouths of three of Europe's most polluted rivers, the Maas, Rhine, and Scheldt. Dutch farmers contribute to this pollution by using the world's highest quantities of nitrogen-based fertilizer per acre/hectare per year
features polders (reclaimed land) make up over 40% of the land area; dyke (*Afsluitdijk*) 20 mi/32 km long 1932 has turned the former Zuider Zee inlet into the freshwater IJsselmeer; Delta Project series of dams 1986 forms sea defense in Zeeland delta of the Maas, Scheldt, and Rhine
head of state Queen Beatrix Wilhelmina Armgard from 1980
head of government Ruud Lubbers from 1989
political system constitutional monarchy
political parties Christian Democratic Appeal (CDA), Christian, right-of-center; Labor Party (PvdA), moderate, left-of-center; People's Party for Freedom and Democracy (VVD), free enterprise, centrist
exports dairy products, flower bulbs, vegetables, petrochemicals, electronics
currency guilder
population (1990 est) 14,864,000 (including 300,000 of Dutch-Indonesian origin absorbed 1949–64 from former colonial possessions); growth rate 0.4% p.a.
life expectancy men 74, women 81 (1989)
language Dutch
religion Roman Catholic 40%, Protestant 31%
literacy 99% (1989)
GNP $223 bn (1988); $13,065 per head (1987)
chronology
1940–45 Occupied by Germany during World War II.
1947 Joined Benelux customs union.
1948 Queen Juliana succeeded Queen Wilhelmina to the throne.
1949 Became a founding member of North Atlantic Treaty Organization (NATO).
1953 Dykes breached by storm; nearly 2,000 people and tens of thousands of cattle died in flood.
1958 Joined European Economic Community.
1980 Queen Juliana abdicated in favor of her daughter Beatrix.
1981 Opposition to cruise missiles averted their being sited on Dutch soil.
1989 Prime Minister Lubbers resigned; new Lubbers-led coalition elected.
1991 Treaty on political and monetary union signed by European Community (EC) members at Maastricht.

reality is relatively unaffected, in contrast to the effects of ◊psychosis.

neuroticism personality dimension described by Hans Eysenck. People with high neuroticism are worriers, emotional, and moody.

neurotoxin any substance that destroys nerve tissue.

neurotransmitter chemical that diffuses across a ◊synapse, and thus transmits impulses between ◊nerve cells, or between nerve cells and effector organs (for example, muscles). Common neurotransmitters are norepinephrine (which also acts as a hormone) and acetylcholine, the latter being most frequent at junctions between nerve and muscle. Nearly 50 different neurotransmitters have been identified.

Neutra Richard Joseph 1892–1970. Austrian-born architect who became a US citizen 1929. His works, often in impressive landscape settings, include Lovell Health House, Los Angeles (1929), and Mathematics Park, Princeton, New Jersey.

neutrality the legal status of a country that decides not to choose sides in a war. Certain states, notably Switzerland and Austria, have opted for permanent neutrality. Neutrality always has a legal connotation. In peacetime, neutrality toward the big power alliances is called **nonalignment** (see ◊nonaligned movement).

neutralization in chemistry, a process occurring when the excess acid (or excess base) in a substance is reacted with added base (or added acid) so that the resulting substance is neither acidic nor basic.

In theory neutralization involves adding acid or base as required to achieve ◊pH7. When the color of an indicator (a compound that changes its structure and color in response to its environment) is used to test for neutralization, the final pH may differ from pH7 depending upon the indicator used.

neutrino in physics, any of three uncharged ◊elementary particles (and their antiparticles) of the ◊lepton class, having a mass too close to zero to be measured. The most familiar type, the antiparticle of the electron neutrino, is emitted in the beta decay of a nucleus. The other two are the muon neutrino and the tau neutrino.

Supernova 1987A was the first object outside the Solar System to be observed by neutrino emission.

neutron one of the three main subatomic particles, the others being the proton and the electron. The neutron is a composite particle, being made up of three quarks, and therefore belongs to the ◊baryon group of the ◊hadrons. Neutrons have about the same mass as protons but no electric charge, and occur in the nuclei of all atoms except hydrogen. They contribute

Nevada

to the mass of atoms but do not affect their chemistry.

For instance, the ◊isotopes of a single element differ only in the number of neutrons in their nuclei but have identical chemical properties. Outside a nucleus, a free neutron is radioactive, decaying with a half-life of 11.6 minutes into a proton, an electron, and an antineutrino. The neutron was discovered by the British chemist James Chadwick 1932.

neutron beam machine nuclear reactor or accelerator producing a stream of neutrons, which can "see" through metals. It is used in industry to check molecular changes in metal under stress.

neutron bomb small hydrogen bomb for battlefield use that kills by radiation without destroying buildings and other structures. See ◊nuclear warfare.

neutron star very small, "superdense" star composed mostly of ◊neutrons. They are thought to form when massive stars explode as ◊supernovae, during which the protons and electrons of the star's atoms merge, owing to intense gravitational collapse, to make neutrons. A neutron star may have the mass of up to three Suns, compressed into a globe only 12 mi/20 km in diameter.

If its mass is any greater, its gravity will be so strong that it will shrink even further to become a ◊black hole. Being so small, neutron stars can spin very quickly. The rapidly flashing radio stars called ◊pulsars are believed to be neutron stars. The flashing is caused by a rotating beam of radio energy similar in behavior to a lighthouse beam of light.

Nevada state in W US; nickname Silver State/Sagebrush State

area 110,550 sq mi/286,400 sq km

capital Carson City

cities Las Vegas, Reno

population (1990) 1,201,800

physical Mohave desert; lakes: Tahoe, Pyramid, Mead; mountains and plateaus alternating with valleys

features legal gambling and prostitution (in some counties); entertainment at Las Vegas and Reno casinos; Lehman Caves National Monument

products mercury, barite, gold

history explored by Kit Carson and John C Fremont 1843–45; ceded to the US after the Mexican War 1848; first permanent settlement a Mormon trading post 1848. Discovery of silver (the Comstock Lode) 1858 led to rapid population growth and statehood 1864. The building of the Hoover Dam in the 1930s provided the water and power needed for the growth of Las Vegas. In 1931 the state created two industries: divorce (Reno) and gambling (Las Vegas). Oil was discovered 1954, but gold exceeds all other mineral production. Tourism and gambling now generate more than half of the state's income.

nevus any birthmark, mole, or colored spot on the skin, especially the kind called a "port-wine mark." This is a maroon-colored area of the skin, consisting of a mass of small blood vessels.

A nevus of moderate size is harmless, and such marks are usually disguised cosmetically unless they are extremely disfiguring, when they can sometimes be treated by cutting out, by burning with an electric needle, by freezing with carbon dioxide snow, or by argon laser treatment.

new age movement of the late 1980s characterized by an emphasis on the holistic view of body and mind, alternative (or complementary) medicines, personal growth therapies, and a loose mix of theosophy, ecology, oriental mysticism, and a belief in the dawning of an astrological age of peace and harmony.

Drawing on the hippie counterculture of the 1960s, new-age ideas include ◊monism and ◊pantheism, preferring intuition and direct experience to rationality and science. Critics of new-age thinking argue that it is so eclectic that it is incoherent. Nonetheless, new-age principles have inspired many business organizations to decentralize and produce less rigid management hierarchies. The rise of European ◊Green parties provided the new-age philosophy with a practical and political forum for its ideas.

new-age music instrumental or ambient music of the 1980s, often semiacoustic or electronic; less insistent than rock.

Newark largest city (industrial and commercial) of New Jersey; industries include electrical equipment, machinery, chemicals, paints, canned meats; population (1990) 275,200. The city dates from 1666, when a settlement called Milford was made on the site.

Since World War II, Newark has suffered from poverty and urban decay, and there was a major racial disturbance 1967. The airport was upgraded and modernized in the 1970s to serve New York City, and urban renewal projects in the 1980s have kept it a center for business and finance, especially insurance.

New Bedford city in SE Massachusetts, on the Acushnet River near Buzzards Bay, S of Boston; population (1990) 99,900. Industries include electronics, rubber and metal products, and fishing. During the 1800s it was a prosperous whaling town.

New Britain largest island in the ◊Bismarck Archipelago, part of Papua New Guinea; capital Rabaul; population (1985) 253,000.

New Britain city in central Connecticut, SW of Hartford and NE of Waterbury. Long an industrial city, its manufactures include tools, hardware, and household appliances; population (1990) 75,400.

New Brunswick maritime province of E Canada

area 28,332 sq mi/73,400 sq km

capital Fredericton

cities St John, Moncton

features Grand Lake, St John River; Bay of Fundy

products cereals, wood, paper, fish, lead, zinc, copper, oil, natural gas

population (1991) 725,600; 37% French-speaking

history first reached by Europeans (Cartier) 1534; explored by Champlain 1604; remained

New Brunswick

a French colony as part of Nova Scotia until ceded to England 1713. After the American Revolution many United Empire Loyalists settled there, and it became a province of the Dominion of Canada 1867.

New Caledonia island group in the S Pacific, a French overseas territory between Australia and the Fiji Islands
area 7,170 sq mi/18,576 sq km
capital Nouméa
physical fertile, surrounded by a barrier reef
products nickel (the world's third largest producer), chrome, iron
currency CFP franc
population (1983) 145,300, 43% Kanak (Melanesian), 37% European, 8% Wallisian, 5% Vietnamese and Indonesian, 4% Polynesian
language French (official)
religion Roman Catholic 60%, Protestant 30%
history New Caledonia was visited by Captain Cook 1774 and became French 1853. A general strike to gain local control of nickel mines 1974 was defeated. In 1981 the French socialist government promised moves toward independence. The 1985 elections resulted in control of most regions by Kanaks, but not the majority of seats. In 1986 the French conservative government reversed the reforms. The Kanaks boycotted a referendum Sept 1987 and a majority were in favor of remaining a French dependency. In 1989 the leader of the Socialist National Liberation front (the most prominent separatist group), Jean-Marie Tjibaou, was murdered.

Newcastle Thomas Pelham-Holles, Duke of Newcastle 1693–1768. British Whig politician, prime minster 1754–56 and 1757–62. He served as secretary of state for 30 years from 1724, then succeeded his younger brother, Henry Pelham (1696-1754), as prime minister 1754. In 1756 he resigned as a result of setbacks in the Seven Years' War, but returned to office 1757 with ⟁Pitt the Elder (1st Earl of Chatham) taking responsibility for the conduct of the war.

Newcastle-upon-Tyne industrial port (coal, shipbuilding, marine and electrical engineering, chemicals, metals), commercial and cultural center, in Tyne and Wear, NE England, administrative headquarters of Tyne and Wear and Northumberland; population (1991 est) 263,000.
history Chiefly known as a coaling center, Newcastle first began to trade in coal in the 13th century. In 1826 ironworks were established by George ⟁Stephenson, and the first engine used on the Stockton and Darlington railroad was made in Newcastle.

New Deal in US history, the program introduced by President F D ⟁Roosevelt 1933 to counter the ⟁Depression of 1929, including employment on public works, farm loans at low rates, and social reforms such as old-age and unemployment insurance, prevention of child labor, protection of employees against unfair practices by employers, and loans to local authorities for slum clearance. In the first 100 days of Roosevelt's administration, he introduced and pushed through Congress hundreds of programs and economic initiatives. Critics from the right called his approach too socialistic, and the role of the federal government in the nation's economic life was strengthened to include policies that remain today. Some of his programs' provisions were declared unconstitutional by the Supreme Court 1935–36, and full employment was not established until the military-industrial needs of World War II.

The Public Works Administration (PWA) was given $3.3 billion to spend on roads, public buildings, and similar developments (the ⟁Tennessee Valley Authority was a separate project). The Agricultural Adjustment Administration (AAA) raised agricultural prices by restriction of output. In 1935 Harry L ⟁Hopkins was put in charge of a new agency, the Works Progress Administration (WPA), which, in addition to taking over the public works, created something of a cultural revolution with its federal theater, writers,' and arts projects. When the WPA was disbanded in 1943 it had found employment for 8.5 million persons. The New Deal encouraged the growth of labor-union membership, brought previously unregulated areas of the US economy under federal control, and revitalized cultural life and community spirit. Although it did not succeed in restoring full prosperity, it did bring hope and political stability.

New Delhi city in the Union Territory of Delhi, capital of India since 1912; population (1991) 294,100. The city was designed by British architect Edwin Lutyens.

New Democratic Party (NDP) Canadian political party, moderately socialist, formed 1961 by a merger of the Labor Congress and the Cooperative Commonwealth Federation.

There are also provincial and territorial New Democratic Parties, which have formed governments in British Columbia, Saskatchewan, Manitoba, and Yukon.

New Economic Policy (NEP) economic policy of the USSR 1921–29 devised by the Soviet leader Lenin. Rather than requisitioning all agricultural produce above a stated subsistence allowance, the state requisitioned only a fixed proportion of the surplus; the rest could be traded freely by the peasant. The NEP thus reinstated a limited form of free-market trading, although the state retained complete control of major industries.

The NEP was introduced in March 1921 after a series of peasant revolts and the ⟁Kronstadt uprising. Aimed at reestablishing an alliance with the peasantry, it began as an agricultural measure to act as an incentive for peasants to produce more food. The policy was ended in 1928 by Stalin's first Five-Year Plan, which began the collectivization of agriculture.

New England region of NE US, comprising the states of Maine, New Hampshire, Vermont, Massachusetts, Rhode Island, and Connecticut. It is a geographic region rather than a political entity, with an area of 66,672 sq mi/172,681 sq km. Boston is the principal urban center of the region, and Harvard and Yale its major universities.

Originally settled by Pilgrims and Puritans from England, the area is still heavily forested and the economy relies on tourism and services as well as industry.

Its share of US income is larger than its share of population.

Newfoundland breed of dog, said to have originated in Newfoundland. Males can grow to 2.3 ft/70 cm tall, and weigh 145 lb/65 kg; the females are slightly smaller. They have an oily, water-repellent undercoat and are excellent swimmers. Gentle in temperament, their fur is dense, flat, and usually dull black. Newfoundlands that are black and white or brown and white are called *Landseers*.

Newfoundland and Labrador Canadian province on the Atlantic Ocean

area 156,600 sq mi/405,700 sq km
capital St John's
cities Corner Brook, Gander
physical Newfoundland island and ⟁Labrador on the mainland on the other side of the Straits of Belle Isle; rocky
features Grand Banks section of the continental shelf rich in cod; home of the Newfoundland and Labrador dogs
products newsprint, fish products, hydroelectric power, iron, copper, zinc, uranium, offshore oil
population (1991) 571,600
history colonized by Vikings about AD 1000; Newfoundland reached by the English, under the Italian navigator Giovanni ⟁Caboto, 1497. It was the first English colony, established 1583. French settlements made; British sovereignty was not recognized until 1713, although France retained the offshore islands of St Pierre and Miquelon. Internal self-government was achieved 1855. In 1934, as Newfoundland had fallen into financial difficulties, administration was vested in a governor and a special commission. A 1948 referendum favored federation with Canada and the province joined Canada 1949.

New Guinea island in the SW Pacific, N of Australia, comprising Papua New Guinea and the Indonesian province of West Irian (Irian Jaya area); total area about 342,000 sq mi/885,780 sq km. Part of the Dutch East Indies from 1828, West Irian was ceded by the United Nations to Indonesia 1963.
history The western half of New Guinea was annexed by the Dutch 1828. In 1884 the area of Papua on the SE coast was proclaimed a protectorate by the British, and in the same year Germany took possession of the NE quarter of New Guinea. Under Australian control 1914–21, German New Guinea was administered as a British mandate and then united with Papua 1945. Papua and New Guinea jointly gained full independence as Papua New Guinea 1975. The Dutch retained control over the western half of the island (West Irian) after Indonesia gained its independence 1949, but were eventually forced to transfer administrative reponsibility to Indonesia 1963.

Tension between Papua New Guinea and Indonesia has heightened as a result of a growing number of border incidents involving Indonesian troops and Irianese separatist guerrillas. At the same time large numbers of refugees have fled eastward into Papua New Guinea from West Irian. Its tropical rainforest and the 0.5 million hunter-gatherers who inhabit it are under threat from logging companies and resettlement schemes.

New Hampshire state in NE US; nickname Granite State
area 9,264 sq mi/24,000 sq km

Newfoundland

New Hampshire

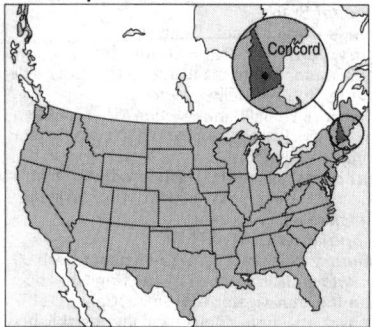

capital Concord
cities Manchester, Nashua
population (1990) 1,109,200
features White Mountains, including Mount Washington, the tallest peak E of the Rockies (with its cog railroad), and Mount Monadnock; the Connecticut River forms boundary with Vermont; earliest presidential-election party primaries every four years; no state income tax or sales tax; ski and tourist resorts
products dairy, poultry, fruits and vegetables; electrical and other machinery; pulp and paper
famous people Mary Baker Eddy, Robert Frost
history settled as a fishing colony near Rye and Dover 1623; separated from Massachusetts colony 1679. As leaders in the Revolutionary cause, its leaders received the honor of being the first to declare independence of Britain on July 4, 1776. It became a state 1788, one of the original 13 states.

In the 19th century, abundant water power allowed textile mills to flourish, but the industry later declined. The state experienced rapid growth after 1970, as people and industry—especially high-technology businesses—moved N from the Boston area into S New Hampshire.

New Haven port town in Connecticut, on Long Island Sound; population (1990) 130,400. **Yale University**, third oldest in the US, was founded here 1701 and named after Elihu Yale (1648–1721), an early benefactor. New Haven was founded in 1683 by English Protestants.

New Hebrides former name (until 1980) of ◊Vanuatu.

Ne Win adopted name of Maung Shu Maung 1911– . Myanmar (Burmese) politician, prime minister 1958–60, ruler from 1962 to 1974, president 1984–81, and chair until 1988 of the ruling Burma Socialist Program Party (BSPP). His domestic "Burmese Way to Socialism" policy program brought the economy into serious decline.

New Jersey state in NE US; nickname Garden State
area 7,797 sq mi/20,200 sq km
capital Trenton
cities Newark, Jersey City, Paterson, Elizabeth
population (1985) 7,562,000
features about 125 mi/200 km of seashore, including legalized gambling in Atlantic City and the Victorian beach resort of Cape May; Delaware Water Gap; Palisades along the W bank of the Hudson River; Princeton University; Morristown National Historic Park; Edison National Historic Site, Menlo Park; Walt Whitman House, Camden; Statue of Liberty National Monument (shared with New York); the Meadowlands stadium

products fruits and vegetables, fish and shellfish, chemicals, pharmaceuticals, soaps and cleansers, transport equipment, petroleum refining
famous people Stephen Crane, Thomas Edison, Thomas Paine, Paul Robeson, Frank Sinatra, Bruce Springsteen, Woodrow Wilson
history colonized in the 17th century by the Dutch (New Netherlands); ceded to England 1664; became a state 1787. It was one of the original 13 states.

Wedged between the growing cities of Philadelphia and New York, New Jersey saw much fighting during the Revolution and became increasingly urban and industrial in the 19th century. In the 20th century, much of the state remains a farming region but also has experienced much air and water pollution as well as the dumping of toxic wastes in landfills. It remains a favored site for development, however, and ranks near the top among states in per-capita income; much urban renewal has occurred in the industrial port cities along the Hudson since the 1970s.

New London port city in SE Connecticut, on Long Island Sound at the mouth of the Thames River; population (1990) 28,500.

It is a naval base and home of the US Coast Guard Academy and the US Submarine Officers School. Industries include submarine production, pharmaceuticals, and chemicals. Tourism is also important to the economy. Connecticut College is here. Settled 1646 as part of the Massachusetts Bay Colony, it served as a privateering base during the American Revolution, a whaling center during the 1800s, and an important base for ships during World War II.

newly industrialized country (NIC) country that has in recent decades experienced a breakthrough into manufacturing and rapid export-led economic growth. The prime examples are Taiwan, Hong Kong, Singapore, and South Korea. Their economic development during the 1970s and 1980s was partly due to a rapid increase of manufactured goods in their exports.

New Madrid seismic fault zone the largest system of geological faults in the eastern US, centered on New Madrid, Missouri. Geologists estimate that there is a 50% chance of a magnitude 6 earthquake in the area by the year 2000. This would cause much damage because the solid continental rocks would transmit the vibrations over a wide area, and buildings in the region have not been designed with earthquakes in mind.

The zone covers a rift in the continental plate running 125 mi/200 km along the

New Jersey

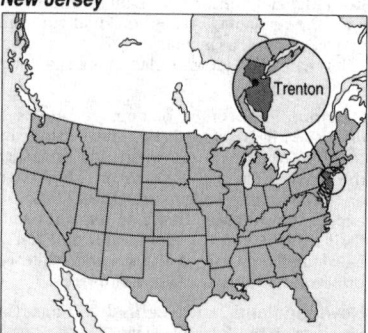

Mississippi River from northern Arkansas to southern Illinois. There are several hundred earthquakes along the fault every year, most of them too small to be felt. A series of very severe earthquakes in 1811–12 created a lake 14 mi/22 km long and were felt as far away as Washington, DC and Canada.

Newman Barnett 1905–1970. US painter, sculptor, and theorist. His paintings are solid-colored canvases with a few sparse vertical stripes. They represent a mystical pursuit of simple or elemental art. His sculptures, such as *Broken Obelisk* 1963–67, consist of geometric shapes on top of each other.

Born in New York City, he was involved in the development of colorfield painting.

Newman John Henry 1801–1890. English Roman Catholic theologian. While still an Anglican, he wrote a series of *Tracts for the Times*, which gave their name to the Tractarian Movement (subsequently called the ◊Oxford Movement) for the revival of Catholicism. He became a Catholic 1845 and was made a cardinal 1879. In 1864 his autobiography, *Apologia pro vita sua*, was published.

Newman, born in London, was ordained in the Church of England in 1824, and in 1827 became vicar of St Mary's, Oxford. There he was influenced by the historian R H Froude and the Anglican priest Keble, and in 1833 published the first of the *Tracts for the Times*. His poem *The Dream of Gerontius* appeared in 1866, and *The Grammar of Assent*, and analysis of the nature of belief, in 1870.

Newman Paul 1925– . US actor and director, Hollywood's leading male star of the 1960s and 1970s. His films include *Somebody Up There Likes Me* 1956, *Cat on a Hot Tin Roof* 1958, *The Hustler* 1961, *Sweet Bird of Youth* 1962, *Hud* 1963, *Cool Hand Luke* 1967, *Butch Cassidy and the Sundance Kid* 1969, *The Sting* 1973, *The Verdict* 1983, *The Color of Money* 1986 (for which he won an Academy Award), and *Mr and Mrs Bridge* 1991.

He directed his wife Joanne Woodward in *Rachel, Rachel* 1968 and other films and was noted as a race-car driver and for his philanthropic activities. The profits from his Newman's Own specialty foods were donated to charity.

New Mexico state in SW US; nickname Land of Enchantment
area 121,590 sq mi/315,000 sq km
capital Santa Fe
cities Albuquerque, Las Cruces, Roswell
population (1990) 1,515,000
physical more than 75% of the area lies over 3,900 ft/1,200 m above sea level; plains, mountains, caverns
features Great Plains; Rocky Mountains; Rio Grande; Carlsbad Caverns, the largest known; Los Alamos atomic and space research center; White Sands Missile Range (also used by space shuttle); Kiowa Ranch, site of D H Lawrence's

New Mexico

stay in the Sangre de Christos mountains; Taos art colony; Santa Fe Opera Company; Navaho and Hopi Indian reservations; White Sands and Gila Cliff Dwellings national monuments

products uranium, potash, copper, oil, natural gas, petroleum and coal products; sheep farming; cotton; pecans; vegetables

famous people Billy the Kid, Kit Carson, Georgia O'Keeffe

history explored by Francisco de Coronado for Spain 1540–42; Spanish settlement 1598 on the Rio Grande; Santa Fe founded 1610; most of New Mexico ceded to the US by Mexico 1848; became a state 1912. The first atomic bomb, a test device, was exploded in the desert near Alamogordo July 16, 1945. Oil and gas development and tourism now contribute greatly to the state economy.

New Model Army army created 1645 by Oliver Cromwell to support the cause of Parliament during the English ⟩Civil War. It was characterized by organization and discipline. Thomas Fairfax was its first commander.

New Orleans city and Mississippi River port in Louisiana; population (1980) 557,500. With an outlet to the Gulf of Mexico, New Orleans has led all US ports in shipping tonnage handled. It is a commercial and manufacturing center, with the chief products refined petroleum and petrochemicals. Educational institutions include Tulane University. In the 18th century New Orleans was the capital of Louisiana Territory. It passed to the US with the ⟩Louisiana Purchase, and by 1852 it was the third-largest US city. It is the traditional birthplace of jazz.

Founded by the French in 1718, it still has a distinctive French Quarter and Mardi Gras celebrations. Dixieland jazz exponents still play at Preservation Hall. The Superdome sports palace is among the world's largest enclosed stadiums and is adaptable to various games and expected audience size.

Newport News industrial city (engineering, shipbuilding) and port of SE Virginia, at the mouth of the River James; population (1990) 170,000. With neighboring Chesapeake, Norfolk, and Portsmouth, it forms the Port of Hampton Roads, one of the chief US ports. It is the site of one of the world's largest shipyards.

The site was settled by the British around 1620. During the Civil War the first battle between ironclad ships (the *Monitor* and the *Merrimac*) 1862 took place off Newport News.

New Rochelle residential suburb of New York on Long Island Sound; population (1990) 67,200.

news agency business handling news stories and photographs that are then sold to newspapers and magazines. International agencies include the Associated Press (AP, 1848), Agence France-Presse (AFP, 1944), United Press International (UPI, 1907), and ⟩Reuters.

Journalists write and edit their material on a VDT (visual display terminal), then press a button to transmit it to the agency headquarters. Stories are coded to arrive at the editor's desk in order of priority (such as flash or urgent) for worldwide distribution to individual newspapers. Third World countries dislike the dominance of the agencies, which they accuse of Western bias, and have attempted to start their own system.

New South Wales state of SE Australia

area 309,418 sq mi/801,600 sq km
capital Sydney
cities Newcastle, Wollongong, Broken Hill
physical Great Dividing Range (including Blue Mountains) and part of the Australian Alps (including Snowy Mountains and Mount Kosciusko); Riverina district, irrigated by the Murray-Darling-Murrumbidgee river system
features a radio telescope at Parkes; Siding Spring Mountain 2,817 ft/859 m NW of Sydney, with telescopes that can observe the central sector of the galaxy. ⟩Canberra forms an enclave within the state, and New South Wales administers the dependency of ⟩Lord Howe Island
products cereals, fruit, sugar, tobacco, wool, meat, hides and skins, gold, silver, copper, tin, zinc, coal; hydroelectric power from the Snowy River
population (1987) 5,570,000; 60% in Sydney
history called New Wales by James ⟩Cook, who landed at Botany Bay 1770 and thought that the coastline resembled that of Wales. It was a convict settlement 1788–1850; opened to free settlement by 1819; achieved self-government 1856; became a state of the Commonwealth of Australia 1901. Since 1973 there has been decentralization to counteract the pull of Sydney, and the New England and Riverina districts have separatist movements.

newspaper a daily or weekly publication in the form of folded sheets containing news, illustrations, timely comments, and advertising. Newsheets became commercial undertakings after the invention of printing and were introduced 1609 in Germany, 1616 in the Netherlands. In 1620, the first newspaper in English appeared in the Netherlands. In England, Addison and Steele published the *Tatler* 1709–11 and the *Spectator* 1711–12. The first newspaper in colonial America was *Publick Occurrences Both Forreign and Domestick*. It was planned as a monthly publication, but it was only published once, in Boston 1690. It was not until 1704 that another paper, the *News-Letter*, also published in Boston, appeared.

history One of the earliest newspapers, the Roman *Acta Diurna*, said to have been started by the emperor Julius Caesar, contained hand-written announcements of marriages, deaths, military appointments, and so on, and was posted in public places. In colonial America, small newspapers were in abundance. By the time of the Revolutionary War, newspapers were used to give opinions from both sides; Thomas Paine's first *Crisis* letters 1776 were published in the *Pennsylvania Journal*. Later, newspapers represented political parties; *The Federalist* essays were first published in the *Independent Journal*, while the *National Gazette* represented Republican views. From 1830, newspapers became more like they are today. News was presented along with human interest stories, crime and court happenings, and other things to attract readership.

Most newspapers are issued daily, but many are weeklies. There are almost 2,000 daily newspapers in the US today. The most well-known and most widely read newspapers are *The New York Times*, the *Los Angeles Times*, and the *Washington Post*. Newspapers such as the *Wall Street Journal* and *Women's Wear Daily* are aimed at special interests and are widely read.

New Style the Gregorian ⟩calendar introduced in 1582 and now used throughout most of the Christian world.

newt small salamander, of the family Salamandridae, found in Eurasia, NW Africa, and North America. The European newts, such as the smooth newt *Triturus vulgaris*, live on land for part of the year but enter a pond or lake to breed in the spring.

The red-spotted newt *Notophthalmus viridescens* of E North America, about 3.5 in/9 cm long, is olive green with red spots when adult. The young, called red efts, are bright orange and are terrestrial.

New Testament the second part of the ⟩Bible, recognized by the Christian church from the 4th century as sacred doctrine. The New Testament includes the Gospels, which tell of the life and teachings of Jesus, the history of the early church, the teachings of St Paul, and mystical writings. It was written in Greek during the 1st and 2nd centuries AD, and the individual sections have been ascribed to various authors by Biblical scholars.

newton SI unit (symbol N) of ⟩force. One newton is the force needed to accelerate an object with mass of one kilogram by one meter per second per second. To accelerate an automobile weighing 2,200 lb/1,000 kg from 0 to 60 mph in 30 seconds would take about 2.5 x 10^5 N.

Newton Isaac 1642–1727. English physicist and mathematician who laid the foundations of physics as a modern discipline. He discovered the law of gravity, created calculus, discovered that white light is composed of many colors, and developed the three standard laws of motion still in use today. During 1665–66, he discovered the binomial theorem, and differential and integral calculus, and also began to investigate the phenomenon of gravitation. In 1685, he expounded his universal law of gravitation. His *Philosophiae naturalis principia mathematica*, usually referred to as *Principia*, was published in 1687, with the aid of Edmund ⟩Halley.

Newton's universal law of gravitation states: "Every particle of matter in the universe attracts every other particle with a force whose direction is that of the joining of the two, and whose magnitude is directly as [proportional to] the product of the masses, and inversely as [proportional to] the square of their distance from each other."

Newtonian physics ⟩physics based on the concepts of Isaac ⟩Newton, before the formulation of quantum theory or relativity theory.

Newton's laws of motion in physics, three laws that form the basis of Newtonian mechanics. (1) Unless acted upon by a net force, a body at rest stays at rest, and a moving body continues moving at the same speed in the same straight line. (2) A net force applied to a body gives it a rate of change of ⟩momentum proportional to the force and in the direction of the force. (3) When a body A exerts a force on a body B, B exerts an equal and opposite force on A; that is, to every action there is an equal and opposite reaction.

Newton's rings in optics, an ⟩interference phenomenon seen (using white light) as concentric rings of spectral colors where light passes through a thin film of transparent medium, such as the wedge of air between a large-radius convex lens and a flat glass plate. With monochromatic light (light of a single wavelength), the rings take the form of alternate light and dark bands. They are caused by interference (interaction) between light rays reflected from the plate and those reflected from the curved surface of the lens.

New Wave in pop music, a style that evolved parallel to punk in the second half of the 1970s. It shared the urban aggressive spirit of punk but was musically and lyrically more sophisticated; examples are the early work of Elvis Costello and Talking Heads.

New Wave (French *nouvelle vague*) French literary movement of the 1950s, a cross-fertilization of the novel, especially the ⟡*nouveau roman* (Marguerite Duras, Alain Robbe-Grillet, Nathalie Sarraute), and film (directors Jean-Luc Godard, Alain Resnais, and François Truffaut).

New World the Americas, so called by the first Europeans who reached them. The term also describes animals and plants of the western hemisphere.

New York largest city in the US, industrial port (printing, publishing, clothing), cultural, financial, and commercial center, in S New York State, at the junction of the Hudson and East rivers and including New York Bay. It comprises the boroughs of the Bronx, Brooklyn, Manhattan, Queens, and Staten Island; population (1990 census) 7,322,500, white 43.2%, black 25.2%, Hispanic 24.4%. New York is also known as the Big Apple.

New York is the nation's corporate, financial, and media center. Real estate is one of its biggest businesses. It remains an important manufacturing center, although a declining one. It is the nation's center for book and magazine publishing and the visual and performing arts. It also ranks first among US cities in wholesale and retail trade. The two major airports are Kennedy International and La Guardia. The Port of New York is the nation's second-busiest harbor, although most active piers and harbors are now in New Jersey and Brooklyn. Tourism, conventions, and educational institutions are also important to the city's economy.

The Statue of Liberty stands on Liberty Island (called Bedloe's Island until 1956) in the inner harbor of New York Bay. Skyscrapers include the twin towers of the World Trade Center (1,350 ft/412 m) and the art deco Empire State Building (1,250 ft/381 m) and Chrysler Building. St Patrick's Cathedral is 19th-century Gothic. Notable art museums include the Frick Collection, the Metropolitan Museum of Art (with a medieval department, the ⟡Cloisters), the Museum of Modern Art, the Guggenheim (designed by Frank Lloyd Wright), the Whitney, and the Morgan Library. Columbia University 1754 is the best known of a number of institutions of higher education. Other features include Central Park, Rockefeller Center, the United Nations complex, Carnegie Hall, Lincoln Center for the Performing Arts, the Broadway theater district, the New York Stock Exchange, Chinatown, Greenwich Village, and South Street Seaport.

The Italian navigator Giovanni da Verrazano (?1485–?1528) reached New York Bay 1524, and Henry Hudson explored it 1609. The Dutch established a settlement on Manhattan 1624, named New Amsterdam, and on Governor's Island in New York Bay; they also settled in Brooklyn, Queens, and Staten Island by the 1640s; all this was captured by the English in 1664 and renamed New York. During the American Revolution, British troops occupied New York 1776–84. After the Revolution, New

York was the capital of the US 1785–89. In the early 19th century, it passed Philadelphia to become the nation's largest city, and for the next 100 years it swelled with immigrants. In 1898 the five boroughs joined together to form the City of Greater New York. In the 1960s New York began declining in population, and its economy suffered because of high taxation (which led businesses to move to tax-free, nearby localities) and the departure of the middle class. In the 1970s a severe municipal financial crisis threatened, but in the 1980s the economy recovered, based on gains in service employment (particularly in financial services), office construction, and the cooperative real-estate market. From the late 1980s, the city's economy was once again threatened.

New York state in NE US; nickname Empire State/Excelsior State
area 49,099 sq mi/127,200 sq km
capital Albany
cities New York, Buffalo, Rochester, Yonkers, Syracuse
population (1990) 17,990,400
physical mountains: Adirondacks, Catskills; lakes: Champlain, Placid, Erie, Ontario; rivers: Mohawk, Hudson, St Lawrence (with Thousand Islands); Niagara Falls; Long Island; New York Bay
features West Point, site of the US Military Academy 1801; National Baseball Hall of Fame, Cooperstown; horse racing at Belmont, Aqueduct, Saratoga Springs; colleges: Colgate, Cornell, Columbia, New York University, CUNY, SUNY, Rensselaer Polytech, Pratt, Juilliard, and Vassar; Washington Irving's home at Philipsburg Manor; Fenimore House (J F ⟡Cooper), Cooperstown; home of F D Roosevelt at Hyde Park, and the Roosevelt Library; home of Theodore Roosevelt, Oyster Bay; Statue of Liberty National Monument; Erie Canal; United Nations headquarters; New York City
products dairy products, apples, clothing, periodical and book printing and publishing, electronic components and accessories, office machines and computers, communications equipment, motor vehicles and equipment, pharmaceuticals, aircraft and parts
famous people Aaron Burr, Grover Cleveland, James Fenimore Cooper, George Gershwin, Alexander Hamilton, Fiorello La Guardia, Washington Irving, Henry James, Herman Melville, Arthur Miller, Nelson Rockefeller, Franklin D Roosevelt, Theodore Roosevelt, Peter Stuyvesant, Walt Whitman
history explored by Giovanni da Verrazano for France 1524; explored by Champlain for France and Hudson for the Netherlands 1609; colonized by the Dutch from 1614; first permanent settlement at Albany (Fort Orange) 1624; Manhattan Island purchased by Peter Minuit 1625; New Amsterdam annexed by the English 1664. The first constitution was adopted 1777, when New York became one of the original thirteen states. The Battle of Saratoga 1777, following which British troops surrendered, is considered the turning point of the American Revolution. By 1810 New York was the most populous of the states, a rank it maintained until the 1960s. The Erie Canal, completed 1825, fostered commerce by providing a link between the Atlantic and the Great Lakes. After the Civil War, New York was transformed from a chiefly agricultural state to an industrial giant. By 1970, however, the state was suffering economic decline, particularly in manufacturing. But it remains an important industrial state,

and in New York City it contains the commercial, financial (Wall Street), and cultural capital of the country.

New Yorker sophisticated US weekly magazine founded 1925 by Harold Ross (1892–1951), which contains entertainment listings, general articles, fiction, poetry, criticism, and cartoons. It has nurtured many writers, including Dorothy Parker, James Thurber, J D Salinger, John Updike, and S J Perelman.

As editor, Ross was succeeded 1952 by William Shawn (1907–), who was replaced 1987 by Robert Gottlieb (1931–). In 1992 British fashion journalist Tina Brown was transferred to the editorship from another Newhouse magazine.

New York Times v Sullivan a US Supreme Court decision 1964 imposing limits on the power of public officials to bring libel suits against people who criticize their actions as public servants. The case was brought by Police Commissioner Sullivan of Montgomery, Alabama, in response to a paid advertisement in the *Times* that accused Sullivan's police force of brutality and repression. The Court ruled that Sullivan's case should not be sustained, finding unanimously that public officials cannot recover damages in libel suits without proof that defamatory falsehoods have been published intentionally and with actual malice.

New Zealand or *Aotearoa* country in the SW Pacific Ocean, SE of Australia, comprising two main islands, North Island and South Island, and other small islands.

government New Zealand is a constitutional monarchy. As in Britain, the constitution is the gradual product of legislation, much of it passed by the British Parliament in London. The governor-general represents the British monarch as formal head of state and appoints the prime minister, who chooses the cabinet. All ministers are drawn from and collectively responsible to the single-chamber legislature, the House of Representatives. This has 97 members, including four ⟡Maoris, elected by universal suffrage from single-member constituencies. It has a maximum life of three years and is subject to dissolution within that period.

history New Zealand was occupied by the Polynesian ⟡Maoris some time before the 14th century. The Dutch explorer Abel ⟡Tasman reached it 1642 but the Maoris would not let him land. The English captain James ⟡Cook explored the coasts 1769, 1773, and 1777. British missionaries began to arrive from 1815. By the Treaty of Waitangi 1840 the Maoris accepted British sovereignty; colonization began, and large-scale sheep farming was developed. The colony achieved self-government 1853. The Maoris resented the loss of their land and rose in revolt 1845–47 and 1860–72, until concessions were made, including representation in parliament. George Grey, governor 1845–53 and 1861–70 and Radical prime minister 1877–

New York

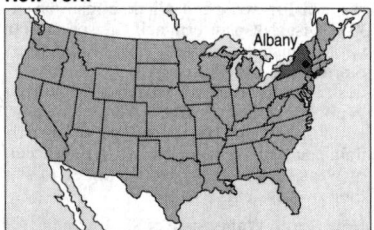

84, was largely responsible for the conciliation of the Maoris and the introduction of male suffrage.

independence The Conservatives held power 1879–90 and were succeeded by a Liberal government that ruled with labor union support; this government introduced women's suffrage 1893 and old-age pensions 1898, and was a pioneer in labor legislation. After 1912 the Reform (formerly Conservative) Party regained power, and the labor unions broke with the Liberals to form the Labor Party. The Reform and Liberal parties united to become the National Party 1931. New Zealand became a dominion in the British Empire 1907 and was granted full independence 1931. New Zealand troops had served in the Boer War in South Africa, and more than 100,000 fought in world wars I and II. Independence was formally accepted by the New Zealand legislature 1947.

political stability The country has a record of political stability, with the centrist National Party holding office from the 1930s until it was replaced by a Labor Party administration, led by Norman Kirk, 1972. During this period New Zealand built up a good social security system. The economy was thriving at the time Kirk took office, but growing inflation was aggravated by the 1973–74 energy crisis that resulted in a balance-of-payments deficit. The Labor government's foreign policy line was influenced by the UK's decision to join the European Economic Community, which was likely to affect New Zealand's future exports. It began a phased withdrawal from some of the country's military commitments in SE Asia and established diplomatic relations with China. Norman Kirk died Aug 1974 and was succeeded by the finance minister, Wallace Rowling. The state of the economy worsened, and in 1975 the National Party, led by Robert ⇨Muldoon, was returned to power. However, the economy failed to revive, and in 1984 Muldoon introduced controversial labor legislation. To renew his mandate, he called an early election but was swept out of office by the Labor Party.

non-nuclear military policy The Labor government elected Aug 1987 (with the same majority as in the previous parliament) had fought the election on a non-nuclear military policy, which its leader Prime Minister David Lange immediately put into effect, forbidding any vessels carrying nuclear weapons or powered by nuclear energy from entering New Zealand's ports. This put a strain on relations with the US, resulting in a suspension of several military-related provisions of the ⇨ANZUS pact. In 1985 the trawler *Rainbow Warrior*, the flagship of the environmentalist pressure group ⇨Greenpeace, which was monitoring nuclear tests in French Polynesia, was mined in Auckland harbor by French secret service agents, killing a Portuguese photographer aboard. The French prime minister eventually admitted responsibility, and New Zealand demanded compensation.

James McLay was leader of the National Party 1984–86, replaced by Jim Bolger. In the 1984 general election Labor won 56 seats in the House, and the National Party, 37. In July 1987 the National Party gave its support to the government in a bipartisan non-nuclear policy, and as a result the US reclassified New Zealand as a "friendly," rather than an "allied" country. In Aug Lange was reelected with a majority of 17. In Aug 1989, Lange resigned, citing health reasons, and was replaced by Geoffrey Palmer. In Sept 1990, faced with a "no confidence" vote, Prime Minister Palmer resigned and was replaced by a former foreign-affairs minister, Mike Moore. In the Oct 1990 general election the ruling Labor Party was defeated and the National Party leader, Jim Bolger, became the new prime minister. In Nov 1991 Robert Muldoon criticized Bolger's right-wing social policies and announced his planned retirement from parliament for early 1992.

In Dec 1991 New Zealand's traditional two-party party political system was challenged by the formation of the Alliance Party, comprising the Democratic Party, the New Labor Party (NLP), the Green Party, and the (mainly Maori) New Zealand Self-Government Party.

In July 1992 the ban imposed on visits by US warships was lifted and in Sept a referendum approved a change in the voting system, to make it semiproportional, with effect from 1996. *See illustration box.*

New Zealand
Dominion of

area 103,777 sq mi/268,680 sq km
capital and port Wellington
cities Hamilton, Palmerston North, Christchurch, Dunedin; port Auckland
physical comprises North Island, South Island, Stewart Island, Chatham Islands, and minor islands; mainly mountainous
overseas territories Tokelau (three atolls transferred 1926 from former Gilbert and Ellice Islands colony); Niue Island (one of the Cook Islands, separately administered from 1903: chief town Alafi); Cook Islands are internally self-governing but share common citizenship with New Zealand; Ross Dependency in Antarctica
features Ruapehu on North Island, 9,180 ft/ 2,797 m, highest of three active volcanoes; geysers and hot springs of the Rotorua district; Lake Taupo (238 sq mi/616 sq km), source of Waikato River; Kaingaroa state forest. On South Island are the Southern Alps and Canterbury Plains
head of state Elizabeth II from 1952 represented by governor-general (Catherine Tizard from 1990)
head of government Jim Bolger from 1990
political system constitutional monarchy
political parties Labor Party, moderate, left-of-center; New Zealand National Party, free enterprise, center-right; Alliance Party, left-of-center, ecologists
exports lamb, beef, wool, leather, dairy products, processed foods, kiwi fruit; seeds and breeding stock; timber, paper, pulp, light aircraft
currency New Zealand dollar
population (1990 est) 3,397,000 (European (mostly British) 87%; Polynesian (mostly Maori) 12%); growth rate 0.9% p.a.
life expectancy men 72, women 78 (1989)
languages English (official), Maori
religion Protestant 50%, Roman Catholic 15%
literacy 99% (1989)
GNP $37 bn; $11,040 per head (1988)
chronology
1840 New Zealand became a British colony.
1907 Created a dominion of the British Empire.
1931 Granted independence from Britain.
1947 Independence within the Commonwealth confirmed by the New Zealand parliament.
1972 National Party government replaced by Labor Party, with Norman Kirk as prime minister.
1974 Kirk died; replaced by Wallace Rowling.
1975 National Party returned, with Robert Muldoon as prime minister.
1984 Labor Party returned under David Lange.
1985 Non-nuclear military policy created disagreements with France and the US.
1987 National Party declared support for the Labor government's non-nuclear policy. Lange reelected. New Zealand officially classified as a "friendly" rather than "allied" country by the US because of its non-nuclear military policy.
1988 Free-trade agreement with Australia signed.
1989 Lange resigned over economic differences with finance minister (he cited health reasons); replaced by Geoffrey Palmer.
1990 Palmer replaced by Mike Moore. Labor Party defeated by National Party in general election; Jim Bolger became prime minister.
1991 Formation of amalgamated Alliance Party set to challenge two-party system.
1992 Ban on visits by US warships lifted. Constitutional change agreed upon.

New Zealand literature prose and poetry of New Zealand. Among interesting pioneer records of the mid- to late 19th century are those of Edward Jerningham Wakefield and F E Maning; and *A First Year in Canterbury Settlement* by Samuel ⇨Butler. Earliest of the popular poets was Thomas Bracken, author of the New Zealand national song, followed by native-born Jessie Mackay and W Pember Reeves, though the latter is better known as the author of the prose account of New Zealand *The Long White Cloud*; and Ursula Bethell (1874–1945).

In the 20th century New Zealand literature gained an international appeal with the short stories of Katherine ⇨Mansfield, produced an exponent of detective fiction in Dame Ngaio ⇨Marsh, and struck a specifically New Zealand note in *Tutira, the Story of a New Zealand Sheep Station* 1926, by W H Guthrie Smith (1861–1940). Poetry of a new quality was written by R A K Mason (1905–1971) in the 1920s, and in the 1930s by a group of which A R D Fairburn (1904–1957), with a witty conversational turn, and Allen Curnow (1911–   ), poet, critic, and anthologist, are the most striking. In fiction the 1930s were remarkable for the short stories of Frank Sargeson (1903–   ) and Roderick Finlayson (1904–   ), and the talent of John Mulgan (1911–1945), who is remembered both for his novel *Man Alone* and for his posthumous factual account of World War II, in which he died, *Report on Experience* 1947. Kendrick Smithyman (1922–   ) struck a metaphysical note in poetry, James K Baxter (1926–

1972) published fluent lyrics, and Janet Frame (1924–   ) has a brooding depth of meaning in such novels as *The Rainbirds* 1968 and *Intensive Care* 1970. In 1985 Keri Hulme (1947–   ) won Britain's Booker Prize for her novel *The Bone People*.

Ney Michael, Duke of Elchingen, Prince of Ney 1769–1815. Marshal of France under ⊳Napoleon I, who commanded the rearguard of the French army during the retreat from Moscow, and for his personal courage was called "the bravest of the brave." When Napoleon returned from Elba, Ney was sent to arrest him, but instead deserted to him and fought at Waterloo. He was subsequently shot for treason.

NF abbreviation for ⊳*Newfoundland*.

NH abbreviation for the state of ⊳*New Hampshire*.

niacin one of the "B group" ⊳vitamins, deficiency of which gives rise to ⊳pellagra.

Niacin is the collective name for compounds that satisfy the dietary need for this function. Nicotinic acid ($C_5H_5N.COOH$) and nicotinamide ($C_5H_5N.CONH_2$) are both used by the body. Common natural sources are yeast, wheat, and meat.

Niagara Falls two waterfalls on the Niagara River, on the Canada–US border, between lakes Erie and Ontario and separated by Goat Island. The *American Falls* are 167 ft/51 m high, 1,080 ft/330 m wide; *Horseshoe Falls*, in Canada, are 160 ft/49 m high, 2,600 ft/790 m across.

On the W bank of the river is *Niagara Falls*, a city in Ontario; population (1981) 71,000; on the E bank is *Niagara Falls*, New York State; population (1990) 61,800. Their economy is based on hydroelectric generating plants, diversified industry, and tourism.

The French explorer Samuel de Champlain may have seen Niagara Falls 1613, and Father Louis Hennepin viewed this natural wonder 1678. The use of hydroelectric power in North America was pioneered here 1881.

Niamey river port and capital of ⊳Niger; population (1983) 399,000. It produces textiles, chemicals, pharmaceuticals, and foodstuffs.

Nibelungenlied *Song of the Nibelungs*, anonymous 12th-century German epic poem, derived from older sources. The composer Richard ⊳Wagner made use of the legends in his *Ring* cycle.

⊳Siegfried, possessor of the Nibelung treasure, marries Kriemhild (sister of Gunther of Worms) and wins Brunhild as a bride for Gunther. However, Gunther's vassal Hagen murders Siegfried, and Kriemhild achieves revenge by marrying Etzel (Attila) of the Huns, at whose court both Hagen and Gunther are killed.

Nicaea ruined city (modern Iznik) in Turkey, capital of the ancient kingdom of Bithynia. It was the site of the Council of Nicaea AD 325 and of another ecumenical council AD 787. Between 1205 and 1261 it was the seat of the Byzantine emperors, and in 1330 it was conquered by Turkish forces.

Nicaea, Council of Christian church council held in Nicaea (now Iznik, Turkey) in 325, called by the Roman emperor Constantine. It condemned ⊳Arianism as heretical and upheld the doctrine of the Trinity in the ⊳Nicene Creed.

Nicaragua country in Central America, between the Pacific Ocean and the Caribbean

Sea, bounded N by Honduras and S by Costa Rica.

government The constitution dates from Jan 1987. The 96-member National Constituent Assembly is elected by universal suffrage through a system of proportional representation, and a president, also popularly elected, serves a six-year term, with the assistance of a vice-president and an appointed cabinet.

history For early history, see ⊳American Indian. The first European to reach Nicaragua was Gil Gonzalez de Avila 1522, who brought it under Spanish rule. It remained Spanish until 1821 and was then briefly united with Mexico. Nicaragua achieved full independence 1838.

In 1912, at the Nicaraguan government's request, the US established military bases in the country. Their presence was opposed by a guerrilla group led by Augusto César Sandino. The US withdrew its forces 1933, but not before it had set up and trained a national guard, commanded by a trusted nominee, General Anastasio Somoza. Sandino was assassinated 1934, reputedly on Somoza's orders, but some of his followers continued their guerrilla activity.

Somoza rule The Somoza family began a near-dictatorial rule that was to last for over 40 years. During this time they developed wide business interests and amassed a huge personal fortune. General Anastasio Somoza was elected president 1936 and stayed in office until his assassination 1956, when he was succeeded by his son Luis. The left-wing Sandinista National Liberation Front (FSLN),

named after the former guerrilla leader, was formed 1962 with the object of overthrowing the Somozas by revolution. Luis Somoza was followed by his brother Anastasio, who headed an even more notorious regime. In 1979, after considerable violence and loss of life, Somoza was ousted; see ⊳Nicaraguan Revolution. The FSLN established a provisional junta of national reconstruction led by Daniel Ortega Saavedra, published a guarantee of civil rights, and appointed a council of state, prior to an elected national assembly and a new constitution.

relations with US Nicaragua's relations with the US deteriorated rapidly with the election of President Reagan. He froze the package of economic assistance arranged by his predecessor, Jimmy ⊳Carter, alleging that the Sandinista government was supporting attempts to overthrow the administration in El Salvador. In March 1982 the Nicaraguan government declared a state of emergency in the wake of attacks on bridges and petroleum installations. The Reagan administration embarked on a policy of destabilizing Nicaragua's government and economy by actively supporting the counterrevolutionary forces (the Contras)—known to have executed prisoners, killed civilians, and engaged in forced conscription—and by covert ⊳Central Intelligence Agency operations, including the mining of Nicaraguan harbors 1984.

In Feb 1985 Reagan denounced Ortega's regime, saying that his objective was to "remove it in the sense of its present structure." In

Nicaragua
Republic of (*República de Nicaragua***)**

area 49,363 sq mi/127,849 sq km
capital Managua
cities León, Granada; chief ports Corinto, Puerto Cabezas, El Bluff
physical narrow Pacific coastal plain separated from broad Atlantic coastal plain by volcanic mountains and lakes Managua and Nicaragua
features largest state of Central America and most thinly populated; Mosquito Coast, Fonseca Bay, Corn Islands
head of state and government Violeta Barrios de Chamorro from 1990
political system emergent democracy
political parties Sandinista National Liberation Front (FSLN), Marxist-Leninist; Democratic Conservative Party (PCD), centrist; National Opposition Union (UNO), loose, US-backed coalition
exports coffee, cotton, sugar, bananas, meat
currency cordoba

population (1990) 3,606,000 (70% mestizo, 15% Spanish descent, 10% Indian or black); growth rate 3.3% p.a.
life expectancy men 61, women 63 (1989)
languages Spanish (official), Indian, English
religion Roman Catholic 95%
literacy 66% (1986)
GNP $2.1 bn; $610 per head (1988)
chronology
1838 Independence achieved from Spain.
1926–1933 Occupied by US marines.
1936 General Anastasio Somoza elected president; start of near-dictatorial rule by Somoza family.
1962 Sandinista National Liberation Front (FSLN) formed to fight Somoza regime.
1979 Somoza government ousted by FSLN.
1982 Subversive activity against the government promoted by the US. State of emergency declared.
1984 The US mined Nicaraguan harbors.
1985 Denunciation of Sandinista government by US president Reagan. FSLN won assembly elections.
1987 Central American peace agreement cosigned by Nicaraguan leaders.
1988 Peace agreement failed. Nicaragua held talks with Contra rebel leaders. Hurricane left 180,000 people homeless.
1989 Demobilization of rebels and release of former Somozan supporters; cease-fire ended.
1990 FSLN defeated by UNO, a US-backed coalition; Violeta Barrios de Chamorro elected president. Antigovernment riots.
1991 First presidential state visit to US for over fifty years.
1992 June: US aid suspended because of concern over role of Sandinista in Nicaraguan government. Sept: around 16,000 made homeless by earthquake.

May 1986 Eden Pastora, a Contra leader, gave up the fight against the Sandinistas and was granted asylum in Costa Rica. The following month the US Congress approved $100 million in overt military aid to the Contras.

Political parties were ostensibly legalized under the terms of a regional peace plan signed by the presidents of El Salvador, Guatemala, Costa Rica, Honduras, and Nicaragua, and peace talks with the Contra rebels had several false starts. In March 1989, 1,900 members of the former National Guard of Anastasia Somoza were released. In June 1989, an electoral council was named in preparation for 1990 elections.

Sandinista government defeated By mid-1989, there were 17 parties cleared to participate in the balloting. Despite international concern about the viability of the promised elections, they were held Feb 1990 and brought a victory by Violeta Barrios de Chamorro of the US-backed National Opposition Union (UNO). The Bush administration spent $9 million on her election campaign. The US lifted its economic embargo in March. By the end of June the Contra rebel army had been disbanded and the government had committed itself to reducing armed forces by 50%. In July violent riots occurred as people protested about land rights, inflation, and unemployment. Eventually a peace agreement was reached.

Chamorro's state visit to the US in April 1991 was the first by a Nicaraguan president in more than 50 years. US President Bush pledged economic support for Nicaragua, whose total international debt was almost $10 billion. US aid was suspended June 1992 due to concern over the extent of Sandinista's influence in Chamorro's government. An earthquake Sept 1992 claimed 116 victims with more than 150 people declared missing and over 16,000 made homeless. In an effort to end the suspension of US aid Chamorro dismissed 12 high-level police officers linked with Sandinista. *See illustration box.*

Nicaragua, Lake lake in Nicaragua, the largest in Central America; area 3,185 sq mi/ 8,250 sq km.

Nicaraguan Revolution the revolt 1978–79 in Nicaragua, led by the socialist *Sandinistas* against the US-supported right-wing dictatorship established by Anastasio ⟡Somoza. His son, President Anastasio (Debayle) Somoza (1925–1980), was forced into exile 1979 and assassinated in Paraguay. The Sandinista National Liberation Front (FSLN) was named after Augusto César Sandino, a guerrilla leader killed by the US-trained National Guard 1934.

Nice city on the French Riviera; population (1982) 449,500. Founded in the 3rd century BC, it repeatedly changed hands between France and the Duchy of Savoy from the 14th to the 19th century. In 1860 it was finally transferred to France.

There is an annual Battle of Flowers, and chocolate and perfume are made. Chapels in the nearby village of Vence have been decorated by Marc Chagall and Henri Matisse, and Nice has a Chagall museum.

Nicene Creed one of the fundamental ⟡creeds of Christianity, promulgated by the Council of ⟡Nicaea 325.

niche in ecology, the "place" occupied by a species in its habitat, including all chemical, physical, and biological components, such as what it eats, the time of day at which the species feeds, temperature, moisture, the parts of the habitat that it uses (for example, trees or open grassland), the way it reproduces, and how it behaves.

It is believed that no two species can occupy exactly the same niche, because they would be in direct competition for the same resources at every stage of their life cycle.

Nichiren 1222–1282. Japanese Buddhist monk, founder of the sect that bears his name. It bases its beliefs on the *Lotus Sūtra*, which Nichiren held to be the only true revelation of the teachings of Buddha, and stresses the need for personal effort to attain enlightenment.

Nicholas two tsars of Russia:

Nicholas I 1796–1855. Tsar of Russia from 1825. His Balkan ambitions led to war with Turkey 1827–29 and the Crimean War 1853–56.

Nicholas II 1868–1918. Tsar of Russia 1894–1917. He was dominated by his wife, Tsarina ⟡Alexandra, who was under the influence of the religious charlatan ⟡Rasputin. His mismanagement of the Russo-Japanese War and of internal affairs led to the revolution of 1905, which he suppressed, although he was forced to grant limited constitutional reforms. He took Russia into World War I in 1914, was forced to abdicate in 1917 after the ⟡Russian Revolution and was executed with his family.

Nicholas of Cusa or *Nicolaus Cusanus* 1401–1464. German philosopher, involved in the transition from scholasticism to the philosophy of modern times. He argued that knowledge is learned ignorance (*docta ignorantia*) since God, the ultimate object of knowledge, is above the opposites by which human reason grasps the objects of nature. He also asserted that the universe is boundless and has no circumference, thus breaking with medieval cosmology.

Nicholas, St also known as *Santa Claus* 4th century AD. In the Christian church, patron saint of Russia, children, merchants, sailors, and pawnbrokers; bishop of Myra (now in Turkey). His legendary gifts of dowries to poor girls led to the custom of giving gifts to children on the eve of his feast day, Dec 6, still retained in some countries, such as the Netherlands; elsewhere the custom has been transferred to Christmas Day. His emblem is three balls.

Nicholson Ben 1894–1982. English abstract artist. After early experiments influenced by Cubism and de Stijl (see ⟡Mondrian), Nicholson developed a style of geometrical reliefs, notably a series of white reliefs (from 1933).

Nicholson Jack 1937– . US film actor who, in the late 1960s, captured the mood of nonconformist, uncertain young Americans in such films as *Easy Rider* 1969 and *Five Easy Pieces* 1970. He subsequently became a mainstream Hollywood star, appearing in *Chinatown* 1974, *One Flew over the Cuckoo's Nest* (Academy Award) 1975, *The Shining* 1979, *Terms of Endearment* (Academy Award) 1983, *Batman* 1989 and *A Few Good Men* 1992.

nickel hard, malleable and ductile, silver-white metallic element, symbol Ni, atomic number 28, atomic weight 58.71. It occurs in igneous rocks and as a free metal (⟡native metal), occasionally occurring in fragments of iron-nickel meteorites. It is a component of the Earth's core, which is held to consist principally of iron with some nickel. It has a high melting point, low electrical and thermal conductivity, and can be magnetized. It does not tarnish and therefore is much used for alloys, electroplating, and for coinage.

It was discovered in 1751 by Swedish mineralogist Axel Cronstedt (1722–1765) and the name given as an abbreviated form of *kopparnickel*, Swedish "false copper," since the ore in which it is found resembles copper but yields none.

nickel ore any mineral ore from which nickel is obtained. The main minerals are arsenides such as chloanthite ($NiAs_2$), and the sulfides millerite (NiS) and pentlandite ($Ni,Fe)_9S_8$, the commonest ore. The chief nickel-producing countries are Canada, Russia, Kazakhstan, Cuba, and Australia.

Nicklaus Jack (William) 1940– . US golfer, nicknamed "the Golden Bear." He won a record 20 major titles, including 18 professional majors between 1962 and 1986.

Nicklaus played for the US Ryder Cup team six times 1969–81 and was nonplaying captain 1983 and 1987 when the event was played over the course he designed at Muirfield Village, Ohio.

He was voted the "Golfer of the Century" 1988.

CAREER HIGHLIGHTS

US Amateur
1959, 1961
US Open
1962, 1967, 1972, 1980
British Open
1966, 1970, 1978
US Masters
1963, 1965–66, 1972, 1975, 1986
US PGA Championship
1963, 1971, 1973, 1975, 1980
US Ryder Cup (team)
1969, 1971, 1973, 1975, 1977

Nicobar Islands group of Indian islands, part of the Union Territory of ⟡Andaman and Nicobar Islands.

Nicolle Charles 1866–1936. French bacteriologist whose discovery in 1909 that typhus is transmitted by the body louse made the armies of World War I introduce delousing as a compulsory part of the military routine. Nobel Prize for Medicine 1928.

Nicosia capital of Cyprus, with leather, textile, and pottery industries; population (1987) 165,000. Nicosia was the residence of Lusignan kings of Cyprus 1192–1475. The Venetians, who took Cyprus 1489, surrounded Nicosia with a high wall, which still exists; the city fell to the Turks 1571. It was again partly taken by the Turks in the invasion 1974.

nicotine $C_{10}H_{14}N_2$ an ⟡alkaloid (nitrogenous compound) obtained from the dried leaves of the tobacco plant *Nicotiana tabacum* and used as an insecticide. A colorless oil, soluble in water, it turns brown on exposure to the air.

Nicotine in its pure form is one of the most powerful poisons known. It is the component of cigarette smoke that causes physical addiction. It is named after a 16th-century French diplomat, Jacques Nicot, who introduced tobacco to France.

Niebuhr Reinhold 1892–1971. US Protestant theologian, a Lutheran minister. His *Moral Man and Immoral Society* 1932 attacked depersonalized modern industrial society but denied the possibility of fulfilling religious and political utopian aspirations, a position that came to be known as Christian Realism. Niebuhr was a pacifist, activist, and socialist but advocated war to stop totalitarianism in the 1940s.

Niebuhr taught for more than 30 years at the Union Theological Seminary in New York City. Originally a strong exponent of Christian socialism, he became increasingly pessimistic about the possibility of achieving it, given humanity's irreducible egoistic pride, which he identified with original sin. He came to believe that liberal democracy must be sustained not because it can bring about human perfection but as a way of avoiding the systematic cruelty that comes with unrestrained power. From 1945 he founded Americans for Democratic Action and became an adviser to the State Department.

nielsbohrium name proposed by Soviet scientists for the element currently known as ▷unnilpentium (atomic number 105), to honor Danish physicist Niels Bohr.

Niemeyer Oscar 1907– . Brazilian architect, joint designer of the United Nations headquarters in New York and of many buildings in Brasília, capital of Brazil.

Niepce Joseph Nicéphore 1765–1833. French pioneer of photography. Niepce invented heliography, a precursor of photography that fixed images onto pewter plates coated with pitch and required eight-hour exposures. He produced the world's first photograph from nature 1826 and later collaborated with ▷Daguerre on the faster daguerreotype process.

The first photograph was a positive image, a view from Niepce's attic bedroom. The image was captured, after an eight-hour exposure, in a camera obscura on a metal plate coated with light-sensitive bitumen. The place has survived and is to be found in the University of Texas.

Nietzsche Friedrich Wilhelm 1844–1900. German philosopher who rejected the accepted absolute moral values and the "slave morality" of Christianity. He argued that "God is dead" and therefore people were free to create their own values. His ideal was the *Übermensch*, or "Superman," who would impose his will on the weak and worthless. Nietzsche claimed that knowledge is never objective but always serves some interest or unconscious purpose.

His insights into the relation between thought and language were a major influence on philosophy. Although claimed as a precursor by Nazism, many of his views are incompatible with totalitarian ideology. He is a profoundly ambivalent thinker whose philosophy can be appropriated for many purposes.

Born in Röcken, Saxony, he attended Bonn and Leipzig universities and was professor of Greek at Basel, Switzerland, 1869–80. He had abandoned theology for philology, and was influenced by the writings of Schopenhauer and the music of Wagner, of whom he became both friend and advocate. Both these attractions passed, however, and ill-health caused his resignation from the university. He spent his later years in northern Italy, in the Engadine, and in southern France. He published *Morgenröte/The Dawn* 1880–81, *Die fröhliche Wissenschaft/The Gay Science* 1881–82, *Also sprach Zarathustra/Thus Spoke Zarathustra* 1883–85, *Jenseits von Gut und Böse/Between Good and Evil* 1885–86, *Zur Genealogie der Moral/Towards a Genealogy of Morals* 1887, and *Ecce Homo* 1888. He suffered a permanent breakdown in 1889 from overwork and loneliness.

Niger third longest river in Africa, 2,600 mi/4,185 km from the highlands bordering Sierra Leone and Guinea NE through Mali, then SE

Niger
Republic of (*République du Niger*)

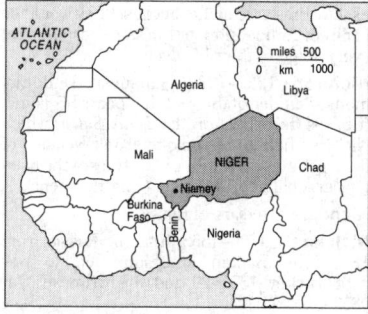

area 457,953 sq mi/1,186,408 sq km
capital Niamey
cities Zinder, Maradi, Tahoua
physical desert plains between hills in N and savanna in S; River Niger in SW, Lake Chad in SE
features part of the Sahara Desert and subject to Sahel droughts
head of state Ali Saibu from 1987
head of government to be elected

political system military republic
political parties banned from 1974
exports peanuts, livestock, gum arabic, uranium
currency franc CFA
population (1990 est) 7,691,000; growth rate 2.8% p.a.
life expectancy men 48, women 50 (1989)
languages French (official), Hausa, Djerma, and other minority languages
religion Sunni Muslim 85%, animist 15%
literacy men 19%, women 9% (1985 est)
GNP $2.2 bn; $310 per head (1987)
chronology
1960 Achieved full independence from France; Hamani Diori elected president.
1974 Diori ousted in army coup led by Seyni Kountché.
1977 Cooperation agreement signed with France.
1987 Kountché died; replaced by Col Ali Saibu.
1989 Ali Saibu elected president without opposition.
1990 Multiparty politics promised.
1991 Saibu stripped of executive powers; transitional government formed.
1992 Transitional government collapsed.

through Niger and Nigeria to an inland delta on the Gulf of Guinea. Its flow has been badly affected by the expansion of the Sahara Desert. It is sluggish and frequently floods its banks. It was explored by Mungo Park 1795–96.

Niger landlocked country in NW Africa, bounded N by Algeria and Libya, E by Chad, S by Nigeria and Benin, and W by Burkina Faso and Mali.
government A new constitution was approved 1983. Niger is ruled by a supreme military council of army officers and a council of ministers appointed by the president, who is head of state as well as head of government and also combines the portfolios of interior and national defense. The National Development Council has 150 elected members.
history Niger was part of ancient and medieval empires in ▷Africa. European explorers arrived in the late 18th century, and Tuareg people invaded the area from the north. France seized it from the Tuaregs 1904 and made it part of ▷French West Africa, although fighting continued until 1922. It became a French overseas territory 1946 and an autonomous republic within the French Community 1958.
independence Niger achieved full independence 1960, and Hamani Diori was elected president. Maintaining close relations with France, Diori seemed to have established one of the most stable regimes in Africa, and the discovery of uranium deposits promised a sound economic future.
military takeover A severe drought 1968–74 resulted in widespread civil disorder, and in April 1974 Diori was ousted by the army led by the Chief of Staff, Lt-Col Seyni Kountché. Having suspended the constitution and established a military government with himself as president, he tried to restore the economy and negotiated a more equal relationship with France through a cooperation agreement 1977. Kountché tried to widen his popular support by liberalizing his regime and releasing political prisoners, including former president Hamani Diori. More civilians were introduced into the government with the prospect of an eventual

return to constitutional rule. When Kountché died 1987, the supreme military council appointed Col Ali Saibu acting president. He was elected without opposition in elections 1989.

In July 1990 the government announced plans for the introduction of a multiparty political system and in Nov these were endorsed by President Saibu who also agreed to hold a constitutional conference attended by representatives of all political views. The conference opened in July 1991 and in Aug Saibu was stripped of his executive powers, although allowed to retain the title of head of state until a new constitution was agreed. A transitional government consisting of a 15-member High Council of the Republic (HCR) was set up, but collapsed March 1992, leaving an unstable political situation. *See illustration box.*

Niger-Congo languages the largest group of languages in Africa. It includes about 1,000 languages and covers a vast area south of the Sahara desert, from the west coast to the east, and down the east coast as far as South Africa. It is divided into groups and subgroups; the most widely spoken Niger-Congo languages are Swahili (spoken on the east coast), the members of the Bantu group (southern Africa), and Yoruba (Nigeria).

Nigeria country in W Africa on the Gulf of Guinea, bounded N by Niger, E by Chad and Cameroon, and W by Benin.
government The constitution is based on one of 1979, amended after military coups 1983 and 1985. The president is head of state, commander in chief of the armed forces, and chair of the 28-member Armed Forces Ruling Council (AFRC), composed of senior officers of the army and police force. The AFRC appoints the National Council of Ministers, which is also headed by the president.

Nigeria is a federal republic of 30 states. Each of the states has a military governor, appointed by the AFRC, who in turn appoints and leads a state executive council. There is also a coordinating federal body called the National Council of States, which includes the president and all the state governors.

Nigeria
Federal Republic of

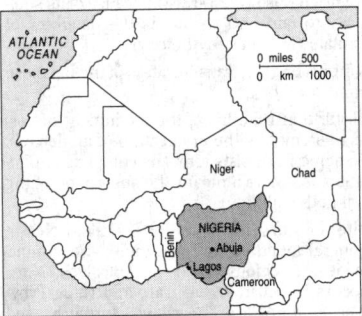

area 356,576 sq mi/923,773 sq km
capital (and chief port) Lagos; Abuja (capital-designate)
cities administrative headquarters Abuja; Ibadan, Ogbomosho, Kano; ports Port Harcourt, Warri, Calabar
physical arid savanna in N; tropical rainforest in S, with mangrove swamps along the coast; River Niger forms wide delta; mountains in SE
environment toxic waste from northern industrialized countries has been dumped in Nigeria
features harmattan (dry wind from the Sahara); rich artistic heritage—for example, Benin bronzes
head of state and government Ibrahim Babangida from 1985
political system military republic pending promised elections
political parties Social Democratic Party (SDP), left of center; National Republican Convention (NRC), right of center
exports petroleum (largest oil resources in Africa), cocoa, peanuts, palm oil (Africa's largest producer), cotton, rubber, tin
currency naira

population (1991) 88,514,500 (Yoruba in W, Ibo in E, and Hausa-Fulani in N); growth rate 3.3% p.a.
life expectancy men 47, women 49 (1989)
languages English (official), Hausa, Ibo, Yoruba
media all radio and television stations and almost 50% of all publishing owned by the federal government or the Nigerian states
religion Sunni Muslim (50%) in N, Christian (40%) in S, local beliefs (10%)
literacy men 54%, women 31% (1985 est)
GNP $78 bn (1987); $790 per head (1984)
chronology
1914 N Nigeria and S Nigeria united to become Britain's largest African colony.
1954 Nigeria became a federation.
1960 Independence achieved from Britain within the Commonwealth.
1963 Became a republic, with Nnamdi Azikiwe as president.
1966 Military coup, followed by a counter-coup led by General Yakubu Gowon. Slaughter of many members of the Ibo tribe in north.
1967 Conflict over oil revenues led to declaration of an independent Ibo state of Biafra and outbreak of civil war.
1970 Surrender of Biafra and end of civil war.
1975 Gowon ousted in military coup; second coup put General Olusegun Obasanjo in power.
1979 Shehu Shagari became civilian president.
1983 Shagari's government overthrown in coup by Maj Gen Mohammedu Buhari.
1985 Buhari replaced in a bloodless coup led by Maj General Ibrahim Babangida.
1989 Two new political parties approved. Babangida promised a return to pluralist politics; date set for 1992.
1991 Nine new states created. Babangida confirmed his commitment to democratic rule for 1992.
1992 Multiparty elections won by Babangida's Social Democratic Party. Primary elections to be introduced.

history Nigeria has been inhabited since at least 700 BC. In the 12th–14th centuries civilizations developed in the Yoruba area and, in the Muslim north, Portuguese and British slave traders raided from the 15th century (see ⟂slavery).

⟂Lagos was supposedly bought from a chief by British traders 1861; in 1886 it became the colony and protectorate of Lagos. The Niger River valley was developed by the National African Company (later the Royal Niger Company), which ceased 1899, and in 1900 two protectorates were set up: N Nigeria and S Nigeria, with Lagos joined to S Nigeria 1906. Britain's largest African colony, Nigeria, was united 1914.
republic Nigeria became a federation 1954 and achieved full independence, as a constitutional monarchy within the British ⟂Commonwealth, 1960. In 1963 it became a republic, based on a federal structure so as to accommodate the many different ethnic groups, which included the Ibo, the Yoruba, the Aro, the Angas, and the Hausa. Nigeria's first president was Dr Nnamdi Azikiwe, an Ibo; he was a banker and proprietor of a newspaper group, and had played a leading part in the movement for independence. His chief rival was Abubakar ⟂Tafawa Balewa, who was prime minister from 1957 until he was assassinated in a military coup 1966. The coup had been led mainly by Ibo junior officers from the

eastern region, which had become richer after the discovery of oil there 1958. The offices of president and prime minister were suspended, and it was announced that the state's federal structure would be abandoned. Before this could be done, the new military government was overturned in a counter-coup by a mostly Christian group from the north, led by Gen Yakubu ⟂Gowon. He reestablished the federal system and appointed a military governor for each region. Soon afterwards tens of thousands of Ibos in the north were killed.
civil war In 1967 a conflict developed between Gowon and the military governor of the eastern region, Col Chukwuemeka Odumegwu-Ojukwu, about the distribution of oil revenues, which resulted in Ojukwu's declaration of an independent Ibo state of ⟂Biafra. Gowon, after failing to pacify the Ibos, ordered federal troops into the eastern region, and a civil war began, lasting until Jan 1970, when Biafra surrendered to the federal forces. It was the first war among black Africans, and it left the economy gravely weakened. Warfare and famine together took an estimated 1 million lives.
bloodless coups In 1975, while he was out of the country, Gowon was replaced in a bloodless coup led by Brig Murtala Mohammad, but he was killed within a month and replaced by General Olusegun Obasanjo. He announced a gradual return to civilian rule, and in 1979 the

leader of the National Party of Nigeria, Shehu Shagari, became president. In Dec 1983, with the economy suffering from falling oil prices, Shagari's civilian government was deposed in another bloodless coup, led by Maj Gen Mohammedu Buhari. In 1985 another peaceful coup replaced Buhari with a new military government, led by Maj Gen Ibrahim Babangida, the army Chief of Staff. At the end of the year an attempted coup by rival officers was thwarted.
Babangida regime President Babangida promised a return to a democratic civilian government 1992, although in an effort to end the corruption that has existed since independence, he banned all persons who have ever held elective office from being candidates for the new civilian government. The ban on political activity was also lifted May 1989, but the government has rejected the applications of former political associations for recognition as political parties, instead creating two official parties, one to the left and one to the right of the political spectrum. An official population policy encouraging mothers to have no more than four children was ratified 1988. Half the population is under 15. In 1990 inflation was running at 51%. Austerity measures, prescribed by the International Monetary Fund in response to economic assistance, created widespread dissatisfaction with the government. The government announced Aug 1991 the creation of nine new states, bringing the total to thirty. In the same month, the total of local government councils increased to 500 with the addition of 47 new ones. The changes were seen as moves toward the decentralization of power. At the same time President Babangida reiterated his commitment to the introduction of civilian rule in 1992. In Dec 1991 the ban prohibiting existing government officials running for office in a new government was lifted. In Aug 1992 it was announced that a system of primary elections, on the US model, was to be introduced to reduce electoral fraud. *See illustration box.*

nightingale songbird of the thrush family with a song of great beauty, heard at night as well as by day. About 6.5 in/16.5 cm long, it is dull brown, lighter below, with a reddishbrown tail. It migrates to Europe and winters in Africa. It feeds on insects and small animals.

Nightingale Florence 1820–1910. English nurse, the founder of nursing as a profession. She took a team of nurses to Scutari (now Üsküdar, Turkey) in 1854 and reduced the ⟂Crimean War hospital death rate from 42% to 2%. In 1856 she founded the Nightingale School and Home for Nurses in London.

nightjar any of about 65 species of night-hunting birds forming the family Caprimulgidae. They have wide, bristly mouths for catching flying insects. Their distinctive calls have earned them such names as whippoor-will and church-will's-widow. Some are called nighthawks.

The whippoorwill of North America *Caprimulgus vociferus* measures about 10 in/25 cm in length, and is mottled gray-brown.

Night Journey or *al-Miraj* (Arabic "the ascent") in Islam, the journey of the prophet Mohammed, guided by the archangel Gabriel, from Mecca to Jerusalem, where he met the earlier prophets, including Adam, Moses, and Jesus; he then ascended to paradise, where he experienced the majesty of Allah, and was also shown hell.

nightshade any of several plants in the family Solanaceae, which includes the black nightshade *Solanum nigrum*, bittersweet or woody nightshade *S. dulcamara*, and deadly nightshade or ◊belladonna.

Nihilist member of a group of Russian revolutionaries in the reign of Alexander II 1855–81. The name, popularized by the writer Turgenev, means "one who approves of nothing" (Latin *nihil*) belonging to the existing order. In 1878 the Nihilists launched a guerrilla campaign leading to the murder of the tsar 1881.

Nijinsky Vaslav 1890–1950. Russian dancer and choreographer. Noted for his powerful but graceful technique, he was a legendary member of ◊Diaghilev's Ballets Russes, for whom he choreographed Debussy's *Prélude à l'Après-midi d'un faune* 1912 and *Jeux* 1913, and Stravinsky's *The Rite of Spring* 1913.

Nijinsky also took lead roles in ballets such as *Petrushka* 1911. He rejected conventional forms of Classical ballet in favor of free expression. His sister was the choreographer *Bronislava Nijinska* (1891–1972).

Nijmegen industrial city (brewery, electrical engineering, leather, tobacco) in E Netherlands, on the River Waal; population (1988) 241,000. The Roman *Noviomagus*, Nijmegen was a free city of the Holy Roman Empire and a member of the Hanseatic League.

Nijmegen, Treaties of peace treaties 1678–79 between France on the one hand and the Netherlands, Spain, and the Holy Roman Empire on the other, ending the Third Dutch War.

Nike in Greek mythology, goddess of victory, represented as "winged," as in the statue from Samothrace in the Louvre, Paris. One of the most beautiful architectural monuments of Athens was the temple of Nike Apteros.

Nile river in Africa, the world's longest, 4,160 mi/6,695 km. The *Blue Nile* rises in Lake Tana, Ethiopia, the *White Nile* at Lake Victoria, and they join at Khartoum, Sudan. It enters the Mediterranean at a vast delta in N Egypt.

Its remotest headstream is the Luvironza, in Burundi. The Nile proper begins on leaving Lake Victoria above ◊Owen Falls. From Lake Victoria it flows over rocky country, and there are many cataracts and rapids, including the Murchison Falls, until it enters Lake Mobutu (Albert). From here it flows across flat country and in places spreads out to form lakes. At Lake No it is joined by the Bahr el Ghazal, and from this point to Khartoum it is called the White Nile. At Khartoum it is joined by the Blue Nile, which rises in the Ethiopian highlands, and 200 mi/320 km below Khartoum it is joined by the Atbara. From Khartoum to ◊Aswan there are six cataracts. The Nile is navigable to the second cataract, a distance of 960 mi/1,545 km. The delta of the Nile is 120 mi/190 km wide. From 1982 Nile water has been piped beneath the Suez Canal to irrigate ◊Sinai. The water level behind the Aswan Dam fell from 558 ft/170 m (1979) to 492 ft/150 m (1988), threatening Egypt's hydroelectric power generation. The 1988 water level was the lowest in a century.

Nile, Battle of the alternate name for the Battle of ◊Aboukir Bay.

nilgai large antelope *Boselaphus tragocamelus* native to India. The bull has short conical horns and is bluish-gray. The female is brown.

Nîmes capital of Gard *département*, Languedoc-Roussillon, S France; population (1982) 132,500. Roman remains include an amphitheater dating from the 2nd century and

the Pont du Gard (aqueduct). The city gives its name to the cloth known as denim (*de Nîmes*); it is the birthplace of the writer Alphonse Daudet.

Nimitz Chester William 1885–1966. US admiral, commander in chief of the US Pacific fleet. He reconquered the Solomon Islands 1942–43, Gilbert Islands 1943, the Marianas and Marshalls 1944, and signed the Japanese surrender 1945 as the US representative.

Nin Anaïs 1903–1977. US novelist and diarist. Her extensive and impressionistic diaries, published 1966–76, reflect her interest in dreams, which along with her psychoanalysis are recurring themes of her gently erotic novels (such as *House of Incest* 1936 and *A Spy in the House of Love* 1954).

Born in Paris, she started out as a model and dancer, but later took up the study of psychoanalysis. She emigrated to the US in 1940, becoming a prominent member of Greenwich Village literary society in New York.

Nineteen Eighty-Four futuristic novel by George Orwell, published 1949, which tells of an individual's battle against, and eventual surrender to, a totalitarian state where Big Brother rules. It is a dystopia (the opposite of utopia) and many of the words and concepts in it have passed into common usage (newspeak, doublethink, thought police).

Nineveh capital of the Assyrian Empire from the 8th century BC until its destruction by the Medes under King Cyaxares in 612 BC, as forecast by the Old Testament prophet Nahum. It was situated on the River Tigris (opposite the present city of Mosul, Iraq) and was adorned with palaces.

Excavations from 1842 onwards by Emile Botta (1802–1870), French consul in Iraq, and the British archeologist Austen Layard (1817–1894) brought to light the ruins of Nineveh (including the library of King Ashurbanipal) under the mounds, or tells, of Kuyunjik and Nebi Yunus.

Ningbo or *Ningpo* port and special economic zone in Zhejiang province, E China; industries (fishing, shipbuilding, high-tech); population (1984) 615,600. Already a center of foreign trade under the Tang dynasty (618–907), it was one of the original treaty ports 1842.

Ningxia or *Ningxia Hui* autonomous region (formerly *Ninghsia-Hui*) of NW China
area 65,620 sq mi/170,000 sq km
capital Yinchuan
physical desert plateau
products cereals and rice under irrigation; coal
population (1990) 4,655,000; including many Muslims and nomadic herders.

Niobe in Greek mythology, the daughter of Tantalus and wife of Amphion, the king of Thebes. She was contemptuous of the goddess Leto for having produced only two children, Apollo and Artemis. She died of grief when her own 12 offspring were killed by them in revenge, and was changed to stone by Zeus.

niobium soft, gray-white, somewhat ductile and malleable, metallic element, symbol Nb, atomic number 41, atomic weight 92.906. It occurs in nature with tantalum, which it resembles in chemical properties. It is used in making stainless steel and other alloys for jet engines and rockets and for making superconductor magnets.

Niobium was discovered in 1801 by English chemist Charles Hatchett (1765–1847), who

named it columbium (symbol Cb), a name that is still used in metallurgy. In 1844 it was renamed after Niobe by German chemist Heinrich Rose (1795–1864) because of its similarity to tantalum (Niobe is the daughter of Tantalus in Greek mythology).

Nippon English transliteration of the Japanese name for ◊Japan.

nirvana in Buddhism, the attainment of perfect serenity by the eradication of all desires. To some Buddhists it means complete annihilation, to others it means the absorption of the self in the infinite.

niter or *saltpeter* potassium nitrate, KNO_3, a mineral found on and just under the ground in desert regions; used in explosives. Niter occurs in Bihar, India, Iran, and Cape Province, South Africa. The salt was formerly used for the manufacture of gunpowder, but the supply of niter for explosives is today largely met by making the salt from nitratine (also called Chile saltpeter, $NaNO_3$). Saltpeter is a ◊preservative and is widely used for curing meats.

Niter formed in limestone caverns, associated with bat guano, was used by the confederacy during the US Civil War.

nitrate any salt of nitric acid, containing the NO_3^- ion. Nitrates of various kinds are used in explosives, in the chemical industry, in curing meat (see ◊niter), and as inorganic fertilizers. They are the most water-soluble salts known.

Nitrates in the soil, whether naturally occurring or from inorganic or organic fertilizers, can be used by plants to make proteins and nucleic acids. Being soluble in water, nitrates are leached out by rain into streams and reservoirs. High levels are now found in drinking water in arable areas. These may be harmful to newborn babies, and it is possible that they contribute to stomach cancer, although the evidence for this is unproven.

nitric acid or *aqua fortis* HNO_3 fuming acid obtained by the oxidation of ammonia or the action of sulfuric acid on potassium nitrate. It is a highly corrosive acid, dissolving most metals, and a strong oxidizing agent. It is used in the nitration and esterification of organic substances, and in the making of sulfuric acid, nitrates, explosives, plastics, and dyes.

nitrification process that takes place in soil when bacteria oxidize ammonia, turning it into nitrates. Nitrates can be absorbed by the roots of plants, so this is a vital stage in the ◊nitrogen cycle.

nitrite salt or ester of nitrous acid, containing the nitrite ion (NO_2^-). Nitrites are used as preservatives (for example, to prevent the growth of botulism spores) and as coloring agents in cured meats such as bacon and sausages.

nitrocellulose series of esters with two to six nitrate (NO_3) groups per molecule, made by the action of concentrated nitric acid on cellulose (for example, cotton waste) in the presence of concentrated sulfuric acid. Those with five or more nitrate groups are explosive (gun cotton), but those with less were once used in lacquers, rayon, and plastics, such as colored and photographic film, until replaced by nonflammable cellulose acetate.

nitrogen (Greek *nitron* "native soda," sodium or potassium nitrate) colorless, odorless, tasteless, gaseous, nonmetallic element, symbol N, atomic number 7, atomic weight 14.0067. It forms almost 80% of the Earth's atmosphere by volume and is a constituent of all plant and animal tissues (in proteins and nucleic acids). Nitrogen is obtained for industrial use by the liquefaction and fractional distillation of air. Its compounds are used in the manufacture of foods, drugs, fertilizers, dyes, and explosives.

Nitrogen has been recognized as a plant nutrient, found in manures and other organic matter, from early times, long before the complex cycle of ♢nitrogen fixation was understood. It was isolated in 1772 by English chemist Daniel Rutherford (1749–1819) and named in 1790 by French chemist Jean Chaptal (1756–1832).

nitrogen cycle the process of nitrogen passing through the ecosystem. Nitrogen, in the form of inorganic compounds (such as nitrates) in the soil, is absorbed by plants and turned into organic compounds (such as proteins) in plant tissue. A proportion of this nitrogen is eaten by ♢herbivores, with some of this in turn being passed on to the carnivores, which feed on the herbivores. The nitrogen is ultimately returned to the soil as excrement and when organisms die and are converted back to inorganic form by ♢decomposers.

Although about 78% of the atmosphere is nitrogen, this cannot be used directly by most organisms. However, certain bacteria and cyanobacteria (see ♢blue-green algae) are capable of nitrogen fixation. Some nitrogen-fixing bacteria live mutually with leguminous plants (peas and beans) or other plants (for example, alder), where they form characteristic nodules on the roots. The presence of such plants increases the nitrate content, and hence the fertility, of the soil.

nitrogen fixation the process by which nitrogen in the atmosphere is converted into nitrogenous compounds by the action of microorganisms, such as cyanobacteria (see ♢blue-green algae) and bacteria, in conjunction with certain ♢legumes. Several chemical processes duplicate nitrogen fixation to produce fertilizers; see nitrogen cycle.

nitrogen oxide any chemical compound that contains only nitrogen and oxygen. All nitrogen oxides are gases. Nitrogen monoxide and nitrogen dioxide contribute to air pollution (see also ♢nitrous oxide).

Nitrogen monoxide (NO) is a colorless gas released when metallic copper reacts with concentrated ♢nitric acid. It is also produced when nitrogen and oxygen combine at high temperature. On contact with air it is oxidized to nitrogen dioxide.

Nitrogen dioxide (nitrogen(IV) oxide, NO_2) is a brown, acidic, pungent gas that is harmful if inhaled and contributes to the formation of ♢acid rain, as it dissolves in water to form nitric acid. It is the most common of the nitrogen oxides and is obtained by heating most nitrate salts (for example ♢lead(II) nitrate, $Pb(NO_3)_2$). If liquefied, it gives a colorless solution (N_2O_4). It has been used in rocket fields.

nitroglycerine $C_3H_5(ONO_2)_3$ flammable, explosive oil produced by the action of nitric and sulfuric acids on glycerol. Although poisonous, it is used in cardiac medicine. It explodes with great violence if heated in a confined space and is used in the preparation of dynamite, cordite, and other high explosives.

nitrous oxide or **dinitrogen oxide** N_2O colorless, nonflammable gas that reduces sensitivity to pain. In higher doses it is an anesthetic. Well tolerated, but less potent than some other anesthetic gases, it is often combined with other drugs to allow lower doses to be used. It may be self-administered; for example, in childbirth. It is popularly known as "laughing gas."

Niue coral island in the S Pacific, W of the Cook Islands; overseas territory of New Zealand
area 100 sq mi/260 sq km
cities port Alofi
products coconuts, passion fruit, honey
population (1989) 2,300
history inhabited by warriors who stopped Captain Cook from landing 1774; British protectorate 1900; annexed by New Zealand 1901; attained self-government in free association with New Zealand (with which there is common citizenship) 1974.

Niven David 1909–1983. Scottish-born US film actor, in Hollywood from the 1930s. His films include *Wuthering Heights* 1939, *Separate Tables* 1958 (Academy Award), *The Guns of Navarone* 1961, and *The Pink Panther* 1964. He published two best-selling volumes of autobiography, *The Moon's a Balloon* 1972 and *Bring on the Empty Horses* 1975.

Nixon Richard (Milhous) 1913– . 37th president of the US 1969–74, a Republican. He attracted attention as a member of the Un-American Activities Committee 1948, and was vice-president to Eisenhower 1953–61. As president he was responsible for US withdrawal from Vietnam, and forged new links with China, but at home his culpability in the cover-up of the ♢Watergate scandal and the existence of a "slush fund" for political machinations during his reelection campaign 1972 led to his resignation 1974 when threatened with ♢impeachment.

Of a Quaker family, Nixon grew up in Whittier, California; he became a lawyer, entered Congress in 1947, and in 1948, as a member of the Un-American Activities Committee, pressed for the investigation of Alger ♢Hiss, accused of being a spy. Nixon was senator for California from 1951 until elected vice-president. He lost the presidential election 1960 to J F Kennedy, partly because televised electoral debates put him at a disadvantage. He did not seek presidential nomination in 1964, but in a "law and order" campaign defeated Vice-President Humphrey 1968 in one of the most closely contested elections in US history.

In 1969 he formulated the Nixon Doctrine abandoning close involvement with Asian countries, but escalated the war in Cambodia by massive bombing. Reelected 1972 in a landslide victory over George McGovern, he resigned 1974, the first US president to do so, under threat of impeachment on three counts: obstruction of the administration of justice in the investigation of Watergate; violation of constitutional rights of citizens, for example attempting to use the Internal Revenue Service, Federal Bureau of Investigation, and Central Intelligence Agency as weapons against political opponents; and failure to produce "papers and things" as ordered by the Judiciary Committee. He was granted a pardon 1974 by President Ford and turned to lecturing and writing.

Nixon Doctrine political principle formulated in 1969 by US president Nixon, which called for the US to supply military aid and arms, but no troops, to Asian nations fighting communist insurgencies. It was issued during opposition to US fighting in Vietnam.

Nizhny Novgorod formerly (1932–90) *Gorky* city in central Russia; population (1987) 1,425,000. Cars, locomotives, and aircraft are manufactured here.

NJ abbreviation for the state of ♢*New Jersey*.

Nkomo Joshua 1917– . Zimbabwean politician, vice-president from 1988. As president of ZAPU (Zimbabwe African People's Union) from 1961, he was a leader of the black nationalist movement against the white Rhodesian regime. He was a member of Robert ♢Mugabe's cabinet 1980–82 and from 1987.

After completing his education in South Africa, Joshua Nkomo became a welfare officer on Rhodesian Railways and later organizing secretary of the Rhodesian African Railway Workers' Union. He entered politics 1950 and rose to become president of ZAPU. He was soon arrested, with other black African politicians, and was in detention during 1963–74. After his release he joined forces with Robert Mugabe as a joint leader of the Patriotic Front 1976, opposing the white-dominated regime of Ian Smith. Nkomo took part in the Lancaster House Conference, which led to Rhodesia's independence as the new state of Zimbabwe, and became a cabinet minister and vice-president.

Nkrumah Kwame 1909–1972. Ghanaian nationalist politician, prime minister of the Gold Coast (Ghana's former name) 1952–57 and of newly independent Ghana 1957–60. He became Ghana's first president 1960 but was overthrown in a coup 1966. His policy of "African socialism" led to links with the communist bloc.

NKVD (Russian "People's Commissariat of Internal Affairs") the Soviet secret police 1934–38, replaced by the ♢KGB. The NKVD was reponsible for Stalin's infamous ♢purges.

NM abbreviation for the state of ♢*New Mexico*.

Nō or **Noh** the Classical, aristocratic Japanese drama, which developed from the 14th to the 16th centuries and is still performed. There is a repertory of some 250 pieces, of which five, one from each of the several classes devoted to different subjects, may be put on in a performance lasting a whole day. Dance, mime, music, and chanting develop the mythical or historical themes. All the actors are men, some of whom wear masks and elaborate costumes; scenery is limited. Nō influenced ♢kabuki drama.

Nō developed from popular rural entertainments and religious performances staged at shrines and temples by traveling companies. The leader of one of these troupes, Kan'ami (1333–1384), and his son and successor Zeami (1363–1443/4) wrote a number of Nō plays and are regarded as the founders of the form. The plots often feature a ghost or demon seeking rest or revenge, but the aesthetics are those of Zen Buddhism. Symbolism and suggestion take precedence over action, and the slow, stylized dance is the strongest element. Flute, drums, and chorus supply the music.

no. or **No.** abbreviation for **number**.

Noah in the Old Testament, the son of Lamech and father of Shem, Ham, and Japheth, who, according to God's instructions, built a ship, the ark, so that he and his family and specimens of all existing animals might survive the ♢Flood. There is also a Babylonian version of the tale, *The Epic of Gilgamesh*.

Nobel Alfred Bernhard 1833–1896. Swedish chemist and engineer. He invented ♢dynamite in 1867 and ballistite, a smokeless gunpowder, in 1889. He amassed a large fortune from the manufacture of explosives and the exploitation of the Baku oil fields in Azerbaijan, near the Caspian Sea. He left this fortune in trust for the endowment of five ♢Nobel Prizes.

nobelium synthesized, radioactive, metallic element of the ⬦actinide series, symbol No, atomic number 102, atomic weight 259. It is synthesized by bombarding curium with carbon nuclei.

It was named in 1957 for the Nobel Institute in Stockholm, Sweden, where it was claimed to have been first synthesized. Later evaluations determined that this was in fact not so, as the successful 1958 synthesis at the University of California at Berkeley produced a different set of data. The name was not, however, challenged.

Nobel Prize annual international prize, first awarded 1901 under the will of Alfred Nobel, Swedish chemist, who invented dynamite. The interest on the Nobel endowment fund is divided annually among the persons who have made the greatest contributions in the fields of physics, chemistry, medicine, literature, and world peace.

The first four are awarded by academic committees based in Sweden, while the peace prize is awarded by a committee of the Norwegian parliament. A sixth prize, for economics, financed by the Swedish National Bank, was first awarded 1969. The prizes have a large cash award and are given to organizations—such as the United Nations peacekeeping forces, which received the Nobel Peace Prize in 1988 – as well as individuals.

nobility the ranks of society who originally enjoyed certain hereditary privileges. Their wealth was mainly derived from land. In many societies until the 20th century, they provided the elite personnel of government and the military.

noble gas alternate name for ⬦inert gas.

noble gas structure the configuration of electrons in noble or ⬦inert gases (helium, neon, argon, krypton, xenon, and radon).

This is characterized by full electron shells around the nucleus of an atom, which render the element stable. Any ion, produced by the gain or loss of electrons, that achieves an electronic configuration similar to one of the inert gases is said to have a noble gas structure.

Noble Savage, the ⬦Enlightenment idea of the virtuous innocence of "savage" peoples, often embodied in the American Indian, and celebrated by the writers J J Rousseau, Chateaubriand (in *Atala* 1801), and James Fenimore Cooper.

nocturne in music, a lyrical, dreamy piece, often for piano, introduced by John Field (1782–1837) and adopted by Frédéric Chopin.

node in physics, a position in a ⬦standing wave pattern at which there is no vibration. Points at which there is maximum vibration are called *antinodes*. Stretched strings, for example, can show nodes when they vibrate.

Guitarists can produce special effects (⬦harmonics) by touching a sounding string lightly to produce a node.

nodule in geology, a lump of mineral or other matter found within rocks or formed on the seabed surface; ⬦mining technology is being developed to exploit them.

Nofretete alternate name for ⬦Nefertiti, queen of Egypt.

noise pollution unwanted and damaging sound. Permanent, incurable loss of hearing can be caused by prolonged exposure to high noise levels (above 85 decibels).

If the noise is in a narrow frequency band, temporary hearing loss can occur even though the level is below 85 decibels or exposure is only for short periods. Lower levels of noise are an irritant, but seem not to increase fatigue or affect efficiency to any great extent.

Noland Kenneth 1924– . US painter, associated with Abstract Expressionism. In the 1950s and early 1960s he painted targets, or concentric circles of color, in a clean, hard-edged style on unprimed canvas. His work centered on geometry, color, and symmetry. His later 1960s paintings experimented with the manipulation of color vision and afterimages, pioneering the field of ⬦Op art.

Nobel Prizewinners: recent winners

Peace

1983	Lech Wałłesa (*Poland*)
1984	Bishop Desmond Tutu (*South Africa*)
1985	International Physicians for the Prevention of Nuclear War
1986	Elie Wiesel (*US*)
1987	President Oscar Arias Sanchez (*Costa Rica*)
1988	The United Nations peacekeeping forces
1989	The Dalai Lama (*Tibet*)
1990	President Mikhail Gorbachev (*USSR*)
1991	Aung San Suu Kyi (*Myanmar*)
1992	Rigoberta Menche (*Guatemala*)

Literature

1983	William Golding (*UK*)
1984	Jaroslav Seifert (*Czechoslovakia*)
1985	Claude Simon (*France*)
1986	Wole Soyinka (*Nigeria*)
1987	Joseph Brodsky (*USSR/US*)
1988	Naguib Mahfouz (*Egypt*)
1989	Camilo José Cela (*Spain*)
1990	Octavio Paz (*Mexico*)
1991	Nadine Gordimer (*South Africa*)
1992	Derek Walcott (*St Lucia*)

Economics

1983	Gérard Debreu (*US*)
1984	Richard Stone (*UK*)
1985	Franco Modigliani (*US*)
1986	James Buchanan (*US*)
1987	Robert Solow (*US*)
1988	Maurice Allais (*France*)
1989	Trygve Haavelmo (*Norway*)
1990	Harry M Markowitz (*US*), Merton H Miller (*US*), and William F Sharpe (*US*)
1991	Ronald H Coase (*US*)
1992	Gary S Becker (*US*)

Chemistry

1983	Henry Taube (*US*)
1984	Bruce Merrifield (*US*)
1985	Herbert A Hauptman (*US*) and Jerome Karle (*US*)
1986	Dudley Herschbach (*US*), Yuan Lee (*US*), and John Polanyi (*Canada*)
1987	Donald Cram (*US*), Jean-Marie Lehn (*France*), and Charles Pedersen (*US*)
1988	Johann Deisenhofer (*West Germany*), Robert Huber (*West Germany*), and Hartmut Michel (*West Germany*)
1989	Sydney Altman (*US*) and Thomas Cech (*US*)
1990	Elias James Corey (*US*)
1991	Richard R Ernst (*Switzerland*)
1992	Rudolph A Marcus (*US*)

Physics

1983	Subrahmanyan Chandrasekhar (*US*) and William A Fowler (*US*)
1984	Carlo Rubbia (*Italy*) and Simon van der Meer (*Netherlands*)
1985	Klaus von Klitzing (*West Germany*)
1986	Ernst Ruska (*West Germany*), Gerd Binnig (*West Germany*), and Heinrich Rohrer (*Switzerland*)
1987	Georg Bednorz (*West Germany*) and Alex Müller (*Switzerland*)
1988	Leon Lederman (*US*), Melvin Schwartz (*US*), and Jack Steinberger (*US*)
1989	Norman Ramsey (*US*), Hans Dehmeit (*US*), and Wolfgang Paul (*West Germany*)
1990	Richard E Taylor (*Canada*), Jerome I Friedman (*US*), and Henry W Kendall (*US*)
1991	Pierre-Gilles de Gennes (*France*)
1992	Georges Charpak (*France*)

Physiology or Medicine

1983	Barbara McClintock (*US*)
1984	Niels Jerne (*Denmark*), Georges Köhler (*West Germany*), and César Milstein (*UK*)
1985	Michael Brown (*US*) and Joseph L Goldstein (*US*)
1986	Stanley Cohen (*US*) and Rita Levi-Montalcini (*Italy*)
1987	Susumu Tonegawa (*Japan*): process by which genes alter to produce a range of different antibodies
1988	James Black (*UK*), Gertrude Elion (*US*), and George Hitchings (*US*)
1989	Michael Bishop (*US*) and Harold Varmus (*US*)
1990	Joseph Murray (*US*) and Donnall Thomas (*US*)
1991	Erwin Neher (*Germany*) and Bert Sakmann (*Germany*)
1992	Edmond Fisher (*US*) and Edwin Krebs (*US*)

Noland was born in Asheville, North Carolina. In *Graded Exposure* 1967, he used large stripes to form a plaid.

Nolde Emil. Adopted name of Emil Hansen 1867–1956. German Expressionist painter. Nolde studied in Paris and Dachau, joined the group of artists known as Die Brücke 1906–07, and visited Polynesia 1913; he then became almost a recluse in NE Germany. Many of his themes were religious.

noli me tangere (Latin "touch me not") in the Bible, the words spoken by Jesus to Mary Magdalene after the Resurrection (John 20:17); in art, the title of many works depicting this scene; in botany, a plant of the genus *Impatiens*.

Nom Chinese-style characters used in writing the Vietnamese language. Nom characters were used from the 13th century for Vietnamese literature, but were replaced in the 19th century by a romanized script known as Quoc Ngu. The greatest Nom writer was the poet Nguyen Du.

nomadic pastoralism farming system where animals (cattle, goats, camels) are taken to different locations in order to find fresh pastures. It is practiced in the developing world; for example, in central Asia and the Sahel region of W Africa. Increasing numbers of cattle may lead to overgrazing of the area and desertification (creation of desert by changes in climate.)

The increasing enclosure of land has reduced the area available for nomadic pastoralism and, as a result, this system of farming is under threat. The movement of farmers in this way contrasts with ▷sedentary agriculture.

nominalism trend in the medieval philosophy of scholasticism. In opposition to the Realists, who maintained that universals have a real existence, the Nominalists taught that they are mere names invented to describe the qualities of real things; that is, classes of things have no independent reality. William of ▷Occam was a leading medieval exponent of nominalism. Dispute over on the issue continued at intervals from the 11th to the 15th centuries.

nominative in the grammar of some inflected languages—such as Latin, Russian, and Sanskrit—the form of a word used to indicate that a noun or pronoun is the subject of a finite verb.

nonaligned movement countries adopting a strategic and political position of neutrality ("nonalignment") toward major powers, specifically the US and former USSR. Although originally used by poorer states, the nonaligned position was later adopted by oil-producing nations. The 1989 summit in Belgrade was attended by 102 member states. With the ending of the Cold War, the movement's survival was in doubt.

The term was originally used by the Indian prime minister Nehru, and was adopted 1961 at an international conference in Belgrade, Yugoslavia, by the country's president Tito, in general opposition to colonialism, neocolonialism, and imperialism, and to the dominance of dangerously conflicting East and West alliances. However, many members were in receipt of aid from either East or West or both, and some went to war with one another (Vietnam–Cambodia, Ethiopia–Somalia).

Nonconformist in religion, originally a member of the Puritan section of the Church of England clergy who, in the Elizabethan age, refused to conform to certain practices, for example the wearing of the surplice and kneeling to receive Holy Communion.

After 1662 the term was confined to members of independent Protestant churches in Great Britain.

nonmetal one of a set of elements (around 20 in total) with certain physical and chemical properties opposite to those of metals. Nonmetals accept electrons (see ▷electronegativity) and are sometimes called electronegative elements.

Nono Luigi 1924–1990. Italian composer. His early vocal compositions have something of the spatial character of ▷Gabrieli, for example *Il Canto Sospeso* 1955–56. After the opera *Intolleranza* 1960 his style moved away from ▷serialism to become increasingly expressionistic. His music is frequently polemical in subject matter, and a number of works incorporate tape-recorded elements.

nonrenewable resource natural resource, such as coal or oil, that takes thousands or millions of years to form naturally and can therefore not be replaced once it is consumed. The main energy sources used by humans are nonrenewable; ▷renewable sources, such as solar, tidal, and geothermal power, have so far been less exploited.

nonsteroidal anti-inflammatory drug full name of ▷NSAID.

nonviolence the principle or practice of abstaining from the use of violence. The Indian nationalist leader Mahatma Gandhi adopted a campaign of passive resistance 1907–14 in response to the attempts by the Transvaal government to discriminate against Indians in South Africa. Later, in India, Gandhi employed nonviolent methods, including the boycotting of British goods and hunger strikes. Martin Luther ▷King led a nonviolent civil-rights movement in the US. He organized a boycott against segregated seating on the buses in Montgomery, Alabama. In June 1963 he led a peaceful demonstration in Washington and in March 1965 led a civil-rights march from Selma to Montgomery.

noradrenaline in the body, a ▷catecholamine that acts directly on specific receptors to stimulate the sympathetic nervous system. Released by nerve stimulation or by drugs, it causes an increase in blood pressure mainly by constricting arterioles (small, thin-walled divisions of arteries) and so raising total peripheral resistance. It is used therapeutically to treat septic shock.

Nordenskjöld Nils Adolf Erik 1832–1901. Swedish explorer. He made voyages to the Arctic with the geologist Torell and in 1878–79 discovered the Northeast Passage. He published the results of his voyages in a series of books, including *Voyage of the Vega round Asia and Europe* 1881.

Nordic ethnic designation for any of the various Germanic peoples, especially those of Scandinavia. The physical type of Caucasoid described under that term is tall, long-headed, blue-eyed, fair of skin and hair. The term is no longer in current scientific use.

Nord-Pas-de-Calais region of N France; area 4,786 sq mi/12,400 sq km; population (1986) 3,923,000. Its capital is Lille, and it consists of the *départements* of Nord and Pas-de-Calais.

Pas-de-Calais is the French term for the Straits of Dover.

Norfolk county on the E coast of England
area 2,069 sq mi/5,360 sq km
cities Norwich (administrative headquarters), King's Lynn; resorts: Great Yarmouth, Cromer, Hunstanton

physical rivers: Ouse, Yare, Bure, Waveney; the Norfolk Broads; Halvergate Marshes wildlife area
features traditional reed thatching; Grime's Graves (Neolithic flint mines); shrine of Our Lady of Walsingham, a medieval and present-day center of pilgrimage; Blickling Hall (Jacobean); residence of Elizabeth II at Sandringham (built 1869–71)
products cereals, turnips, sugar beets, turkeys, geese, offshore natural gas
population (1991) 736,700

Norfolk seaport in SE Virginia, on the Atlantic Ocean at the mouth of the James and Elizabeth rivers; population (1990) 261,200. It is one of the nation's busiest ports, the headquarters of the US Navy's Atlantic fleet, and the home of 22 other Navy commands. Industries include shipbuilding, chemicals, and motor-vehicle assembly.

The Chesapeake Bay Bridge-Tunnel links it to the Delmarva peninsula. Old Dominion University is here. Norfolk was laid out in 1682. It suffered heavy damage during the American Revolution, was captured by Union forces in the Civil War, and grew rapidly during both world wars.

Norfolk Island Pacific island territory of Australia, S of New Caledonia
area 15 sq mi/40 sq km
products citrus fruit, bananas; tourist industry
population (1986) 2,000
history reached by English navigator James Cook 1774: settled 1856 by descendants of the mutineers of the *Bounty* (see ▷Bligh) from ▷Pitcairn Island; Australian territory from 1914: largely self-governing from 1979.

Noriega Manuel (Antonio Morena) 1940– . Panamanian soldier and politician, effective ruler of Panama from 1982, as head of the National Guard, until deposed by the US 1989. An informer for the US Central Intelligence Agency, he was known to be involved in drug trafficking as early as 1972. He enjoyed US support until 1987. In the 1989 US invasion of Panama, he was forcibly taken to the US, tried, and convicted of trafficking in 1992.

Noriega was commissioned in the National Guard 1962, and received US counterintelligence training. He became intelligence chief 1970 and Chief of Staff 1982. He wielded considerable political power behind the scenes, which led to his enlistment by the CIA, and he was seen as an ally against Nicaragua until the ▷Irangate scandal limited US covert action there. In the 1984 and 1989 presidential elections, Noriega claimed a fraudulent victory for his candidate. Bribes accepted by Noriega for tacitly permitting money laundering and the transshipment of cocaine are estimated at $15 million, but after 1985 he cooperated with the US Drug Enforcement Administration. However, relations between Panama and the US deteriorated and in Dec 1989 President Bush ordered an invasion of the country by 24,000 US troops. Noriega was seized and taken to the US for trial. In April 1992 he was given a 40-year prison sentence for drug trafficking and racketeering.

Norilsk world's northernmost industrial city (nickel, cobalt, platinum, selenium, tellurium, gold, silver) in Siberian Russia; population (1987) 181,000. The permafrost is 1,000 ft/300 m deep, and the winter temperature may reach –67°F (–55°C).

It is the most polluted city in Russia, with more than 2.3 million tons of toxins emitted into the air every year, mostly from nickel mining and smelting. Norilsk was founded 1935 by Stalin as the administrative center of the gulag network of prison camps.

norm informal guideline about what is, or is not, considered normal social behavior (as opposed to rules and laws, which are formal guidelines). Such shared values and expectations may be measured by statistical sampling and vary from one society to another and from one situation to another; they range from crucial taboos such as those against incest or cannibalism to trivial customs and traditions, such as the correct way to hold a fork. Norms play a key part in social control and social order.

Normal city in central Illinois, NE of Bloomington. It is a marketing center for the livestock and grains produced in the surrounding area. Illinois State University is here; population (1990) 40,000.

Norman any of the descendants of the Norsemen (to whose chief, Rollo, Normandy was granted by Charles III of France 911) who adopted French language and culture. During the 11th and 12th centuries they conquered England 1066 (under William the Conqueror), Scotland 1072, parts of Wales and Ireland, S Italy, Sicily, and Malta, and took a prominent part in the Crusades.

They introduced feudalism, Latin as the language of government, and Norman French as the language of literature. Church architecture and organization were also influenced by the Normans, although they ceased to exist as a distinct people after the 13th century.

Norman Greg 1955– . Australian golfer, nicknamed "the Great White Shark." After many wins in his home country, he enjoyed success on the European PGA Tour before joining the US Tour. He has won the World Match-Play title three times.

Norman Jessye 1945– . US soprano, born in Augusta, Georgia. She made her operatic debut at the Deutsche Oper, Berlin, 1969. She is acclaimed for her interpretation of *Lieder*, as well as operatic roles, and for her powerful voice.

Normandy two regions of NW France: ◊Haute-Normandie and ◊Basse-Normandie. It was named after the Viking Norsemen (Normans), the people who conquered and settled in the area in the 9th century. As a French duchy it reached its peak under William the Conqueror and was renowned for its centers of learning established by Lanfranc and St Anselm. Normandy was united with England 1100–35. England and France fought over it during the Hundred Years' War, England finally losing it 1449 to Charles VII. In World War II the Normandy beaches were the site of the Allied invasion on D-day, June 6, 1944.

The main towns are Alençon, Bayeux, Caen, Cherbourg, Dieppe, Deauville, Lisieux, Le Havre, and Rouen. Features of Normandy include the painter Monet's restored home and garden at Giverny; Mont St Michel; Château Miromesnil, the birthplace of de Maupassant; Victor Hugo's house at Villequier; and ◊Calvados apple brandy.

Normandy landings alternate name for ◊D-day.

Norman French the form of French used by the Normans in Normandy from the 10th century, and by the Norman ruling class in England after the Conquest 1066. It remained the language of the English court until the 15th century, the official language of the law courts until the 17th century, and is still used in the Channel Islands.

Norn in Scandinavian mythology, any of three goddesses of fate—the goddess of the past (Urd), the goddess of the present (Verdandi), and the goddess of the future (Skuld).

Norris Frank 1870–1902. US novelist. A naturalist writer, he wrote *McTeague* 1899, about a brutish San Francisco dentist and the love of gold. He completed only two parts of his projected trilogy, the *Epic of Wheat*: *The Octopus* 1901, dealing with the struggles between wheat farmers, and *The Pit* 1903, describing the Chicago wheat exchange.

Norse or **Norseman** a member of any of the ancient Scandinavian peoples, also called ◊Vikings when they traded, explored, and raided far afield from their homelands during the 8th–11th centuries, settling in Iceland, Greenland, Russia, the British Isles, and N France. The term is sometimes used to refer specifically to W Scandinavians or just to Norwegians.

North Frederick, 8th Lord North 1732–1792. British Tory politician. He entered Parliament in 1754, became chancellor of the Exchequer in 1767, and was prime minister in a government of Tories and "king's friends" from 1770. His hard line against the American colonies was supported by George III, but in 1782 he was forced to resign by the failure of his policy. In 1783 he returned to office in a coalition with Charles ◊Fox, and after its defeat retired from politics.

North Oliver 1943– . US Marine lieutenant colonel. In 1981 he joined the staff of the National Security Council (NSC), where he supervised the mining of Nicaraguan harbors 1983, an air-force bombing raid on Libya 1986, and an arms-for-hostages deal with Iran 1985, which, when uncovered 1986 (◊Irangate), forced his dismissal and trial.

North was born into a San Antonio, Texas, military family and was a graduate of the US Naval Academy. He led a Marine platoon in the Vietnam War 1968–69.

After Irangate, North was convicted on felony charges of obstructing Congress, mutilating government documents, and taking an illegal gratuity. In Sept 1991, all charges against him were dropped on the grounds that, since his evidence before Congressional committees July 1987 had been widely televised, it was impossible to give him a fair trial.

North America third largest of the continents (when including Central America)
area 9,500,000 sq mi/24,000,000 sq km
largest cities (over 1 million) Mexico City, New York, Chicago, Toronto, Los Angeles, Montreal, Guadalajara, Monterrey, Philadelphia, Houston, Guatemala City, Vancouver, Detroit
population (1990) 395 million; the aboriginal American Indian, Inuit, and Aleut peoples are now a minority within a population predominantly of European immigrant origin. Many Africans were brought in as laborers by the slave trade. Asians were also brought in as laborers, and today immigration from Asia and Latin America is on the increase
physical mountain belts to the E (Appalachians) and W (see ◊Cordilleras), the latter including the Rocky Mountains and the Sierra Madre; coastal plain on the Gulf of Mexico, into which the Mississippi River system drains from the central Great Plains; the St Lawrence River and the Great Lakes form a rough crescent with the Great Bear and Great Slave lakes and Lakes Athabasca and Winnipeg around the exposed rock of the great Canadian/Laurentian Shield, into which Hudson Bay breaks from the N
features wide climatic range, from arctic in Alaska and N Canada (only above freezing June–Sept) to the tropical in Central America, and arid in much of the W US; also, great extremes within the range, due to the vast size of the land mass
products the immensity of the US home market makes it less dependent on imports; the industrial and technological strengths of the US automatically tend to exert a pull on Canada, Mexico, and Central America. The continent is unique in being dominated in this way by a single power, which also exerts great influence over the general world economy
language predominantly English, Spanish, French
religion predominantly Christian
history according to archeological evidence, human settlement in North America began 100,000 to 40,000 years ago, when Mongoloid peoples from Asia migrated, over the Bering land bridge and E of the Brooks range in Alaska into the heart of the continent.

Settlement by these ancestors of the North American Indians then proceeded S and E. These Stone Age people lived by hunting, fishing, and harvesting fruits, nuts, and the seeds of wild plants. By 7000 BC, however, agriculture was known in Mexico and upper Central America, and by 1400 BC, ◊civilization had developed in these areas. Among the pre-Columbian civilizations were those of the Olmecs (1400–400 BC), Maya (1200 BC-1521AD), and Aztecs (1325–1521).

The first-known European settlement in North America was by Vikings in what they called Vinland; a Norse settlement, dating from about 1000, has been found at L'Anse-aux-Meadows, Newfoundland. But permanent settlement came only after Christopher Columbus's voyage to the West Indies in 1492. In 1521 the Spanish, under Hernándo Cortés, destroyed the Aztec empire and imposed their rule on Mexico. The Spanish also colonized Central America and parts of what is now the S US, but most of the present US and Canada was claimed and explored by traders, trappers, and colonizers from the Netherlands, France, and England.

The American Revolution 1775–83 ended in the emergence of the US, stretching from the Atlantic west to the Mississippi River; its area was doubled by the Louisiana Purchase from France in 1803. Mexico and Central America won their independence from Spain in 1821. The US reached its present continental extent by acquiring its Southwest in 1848 and 1851 as a result of war with Mexico, and by purchasing Alaska from Russia in 1867. N of the US, a Canadian confederation, with continuing links to Great Britain, was formed in 1867. Geographically, North America (including the West Indies) now consists of 22 independent nations; several British, Dutch, French, and US island dependencies; and the Danish territory of Greenland.

North American Indian indigenous inhabitant of North America. Many describe themselves as "Native Americans" rather than

"American Indians," the latter term having arisen because Columbus believed he had reached the East Indies. See also ⟡American Indian.

North American Indian religions beliefs and myths of the North American Indians. Common features include a belief that everything in nature is alive and contains powerful forces that can be helpful or harmful to humans. The forces must be treated with respect, and so hunting and other activities require ritual and preparation. Certain people are believed to be in contact with the spirit world (⟡shamans) and to have special powers, but each individual can also seek power and vision through ordeals and fasting.

Northamptonshire county in central England
area 915 sq mi/2,370 sq km
cities Northampton (administrative headquarters), Kettering
features River Nene; Canons Ashby, Tudor house, home of the Drydens for 400 years; churches with broached spires
products cereals, cattle
population (1991) 568,900
famous people John Dryden, Richard III, Robert Browne.

North Atlantic Drift warm ocean ⟡current in the N Atlantic Ocean; an extension of the ⟡Gulf Stream. It flows east across the Atlantic and has a mellowing effect on the climate of NW Europe, particularly the British Isles and Scandinavia.

North Atlantic Treaty agreement signed April 4, 1949 by Belgium, Denmark, France, Iceland, Italy, Luxembourg, the Netherlands, Norway, Portugal, the UK, the US; Greece, Turkey 1952; West Germany 1955; and Spain 1982. They agreed that "an armed attack against one or more of them in Europe or North America shall be considered an attack against them all." The North Atlantic Treaty Organization (NATO) is based on this agreement.

North Atlantic Treaty Organization (NATO) association set up 1949 to provide for the collective defense of the major W European and North American states against the perceived threat from the USSR. Its chief body is the Council of Foreign Ministers (who have representatives in permanent session), and there is an international secretariat in Brussels, Belgium, and also the Military Committee consisting of the Chiefs of Staff. The military headquarters SHAPE (Supreme Headquarters Allied Powers, Europe) is in Chièvres, near Mons, Belgium. After the E European ⟡Warsaw Pact was disbanded 1991, an adjunct to NATO, the *North Atlantic Cooperation Council*, was established, including all the former Soviet republics, with the aim of building greater security in Europe.

Both the Supreme Allied Commanders (Europe and Atlantic) are from the US, but there is also an Allied Commander, Channel (a British admiral). In 1960 a permanent multinational *Allied Mobile Force* (AMF) was established to move immediately to any NATO country under threat of attack; headquarters in Heidelberg, Germany.

France withdrew from the military integration (not the alliance) 1966; Greece withdrew politically but not militarily 1974. In 1980 Turkey was opposed to Greek reentry because of differences over rights in the Aegean Sea. NATO has encountered numerous problems since its inception over such issues as the hegemonial position of the US, the presence in Europe of US nuclear weapons, burden

sharing, and standardization of weapons. In 1990, after a meeting in London, NATO declared that nuclear weapons were "weapons of last resort" rather than "flexible response," and offered to withdraw all nuclear artillery shells from Europe if the USSR did the same. NATO's counterpart was the Warsaw Pact, until the abandonment of its military role 1990. In Oct 1991, it was agreed that NATO's ground-launched and air-delivered nuclear arsenal in Europe would be reduced by 80%. There were also plans for NATO forces to be reduced by up to 30% by the mid-1990s. It was agreed July 1992 that the Conference on Security and Cooperation in Europe (CSCE) would in future authorize all NATO's military responses within Europe.

President Bush's unilateral reductions in US nuclear arms in Oct 1991 resulted in reductions in NATO arms.

North Brabant (Dutch *Noordbrabant*) southern province of the Netherlands, lying between the Maas (Meuse) and Belgium; area 1,907 sq mi/4,940 sq km; population (1991) 2,209,000. The capital is 's Hertogenbosch. Former heathland is now under mixed farming. Towns such as Breda, Tilburg, and Eindhoven are centers of brewing, engineering, microelectronics, and textile manufacture.

North Cape (Norwegian *Nordkapp*) cape in the Norwegian county of Finnmark; the most northerly point of Europe.

North Carolina state in E US; nickname Tar Heel State/Old North State
area 52,650 sq mi/136,400 sq km
capital Raleigh
cities Charlotte, Greensboro, Winston-Salem
population (1990) 6,628,600
features Appalachian Mountains (including Blue Ridge and Great Smoky mountains), site of Fort Raleigh on Roanoke Island, Wright Brothers National Memorial at Kitty Hawk, the Research Triangle established 1956 (Duke University, University of North Carolina, and North Carolina State University) for high-tech industries, Cape Hatteras and Cape Lookout national seashores
products tobacco, corn, soybeans, livestock, poultry, textiles, clothing, cigarettes, furniture, chemicals, machinery
famous people Billy Graham, O Henry, Jesse Jackson, Thomas Wolfe
history after England's Roanoke Island colony was unsuccessful 1585 and 1587, permanent settlement was made 1663; it was one of the original 13 states 1789.

In the Civil War, North Carolina was the last state to join the Confederacy but provided more troops than any other Southern state. After postwar recovery, textiles, tobacco products, and furniture came to dominate the economy. Per-capita income rose from 47% of the national average in 1930 to almost 83%

in 1983. However, many of the state's industries offer predominantly low-skill, low-wage jobs and are, moreover, threatened by foreign competition. Tourism is important to the state's economy, and the mild climate has been attractive to retirement communities.

Walter Raleigh sent out 108 colonists from Plymouth, England, 1585 under his cousin Richard Grenville, who established the first English settlement in the New World on Roanoke Island; Virginia Dare was born there 1587, the first child of English parentage born in America; the survivors were taken home by Drake 1586. Further attempts failed there, since the settlers were found to have disappeared.

North Dakota state in N US; nickname Flickertail State/Sioux State
area 70,677 sq mi/183,100 sq km
capital Bismarck
cities Fargo, Grand Forks, Minot
population (1990) 638,800
features fertile Red River valley, Missouri Plateau; Garrison Dam on the Missouri River; Badlands, so called because the pioneers had great difficulty in crossing them (also site of Theodore Roosevelt's Elkhorn Ranch); International Peace Garden, on Canadian border; 90% of the land is cultivated
products cereals, meat products, farm equipment, oil, coal
famous people Maxwell Anderson, Louis L'Amour
history explored by Verendrye's French Canadian expedition 1738–40; acquired by the US partly in the Louisiana Purchase 1803 and partly by treaty with Britain 1813. The earliest settlement was Pembina 1812, by Scottish and Irish families, and North Dakota became a state 1889, attracting many German and Norwegian settlers.

They and their descendants were hard hit by low prices in the 1920s and 1930s for the state's abundant wheat. Since 1950, North Dakota's oil, natural-gas, and lignite resources have contributed to a more diversified economic base, but it remains the most rural of all the states.

North-East Frontier Agency former name (until 1972) for ⟡Arunachal Pradesh, territory of India.

Northeast Passage sea route from the N Atlantic, around Asia, to the N Pacific, pioneered by Swedish explorer ⟡Nordenskjöld 1878–79 and developed by the USSR in settling N Siberia from 1935. Russia owns offshore islands and claims it as an internal waterway; the US claims that it is international.

Northern Areas districts N of Azad Kashmir, directly administered by Pakistan but not merged with it. India and Azad Kashmir each claim them as part of disputed Kashmir. They include Baltistan, Gilgit, Skardu, and Hunza (an independent principality for 900 years until 1974).

North Carolina

North Dakota

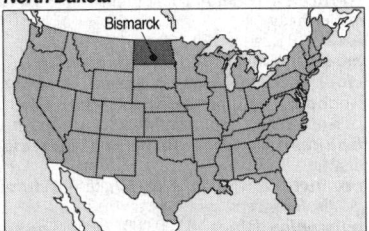

Northern Ireland see �Ireland, Northern.

northern lights common name for the ⟡aurora borealis.

Northern Rhodesia former name (until 1964) of ⟡Zambia.

Northern Securities Co v US a US Supreme Court decision 1904 dealing with the right of the federal government to restrict monopolistic business practices. Two competitors, the Great Northern and the Northern Pacific railroad companies, joined finances to form the Northern Securities holding company. Convicted under the Sherman Antitrust Act 1890, the holding company appealed to the Supreme Court, arguing that the financial merger was not illegal because it was not intended for the restraint of trade. The Court voted 5 to 4 to uphold the conviction, rejuvenating federal authority under the antitrust laws.

Northern Territory territory of Australia
area 519,633 sq mi/1,346,200 sq km
capital Darwin (chief port)
cities Alice Springs
features mainly within the tropics, although with wide range of temperature; very low rainfall, but artesian bores are used; Macdonnell Ranges (Mount Zeil 4,956 ft/1,510 m); ⟡Cocos Islands and ⟡Christmas Island included in the territory 1984; 50,000–60,000-year-old rock paintings of animals, birds, and fish in Kakadu National Park
products beef cattle, prawns, bauxite (Gove), gold and copper (Tennant Creek), uranium (Ranger)
population (1987) 157,000
government there is an administrator and a legislative assembly, and the territory is also represented in the federal parliament
history originally part of New South Wales, it was annexed 1863 to South Australia but from 1911 until 1978 (when self-government was introduced) was under the control of the Commonwealth of Australia government. Mineral discoveries on land occupied by Aborigines led to a royalty agreement 1979.

North Holland (Dutch *Noord-Holland*) low-lying coastal province of the Netherlands occupying the peninsula jutting northward between the North Sea and the IJsselmeer; area 1,031 sq mi/2,670 sq km; population (1991) 2,397,000. Most of it is below sea level, protected from the sea by a series of sand dunes and artificial dykes. The capital is Haarlem; other towns are Amsterdam, Hilversum, Den Helder, and the cheese centers Alkmaar and Edam. Famous for its bulbfields, the province also produces grain and vegetables.

North Korea see ⟡Korea, North.

North Pole the northern point where an imaginary line penetrates the Earth's surface by the axis about which it revolves; see also ⟡Poles and ⟡Arctic.

North Rhine–Westphalia (German *Nordrhein-Westfalen*) administrative *Land* of Germany
area 13,163 sq mi/34,100 sq km
capital Düsseldorf
cities Cologne, Essen, Dortmund, Duisburg, Bochum, Wuppertal, Bielefeld, Bonn, Gelsenkirchen, Münster, Mönchengladbach
features valley of the Rhine; Ruhr industrial district
products iron, steel, coal, lignite, electrical goods, fertilizers, synthetic textiles
population (1988) 16,700,000

religion 53% Roman Catholic, 42% Protestant
history see ⟡Westphalia.

Northrop John 1891–1987. US chemist. In the 1930s he crystallized a number of enzymes, including pepsin and trypsin, showing conclusively that they were proteins. He shared the 1946 Nobel Prize for Chemistry with Wendell ⟡Stanley and James ⟡Sumner.

North Sea sea to the east of Britain and bounded by the coasts of Belgium, the Netherlands, Germany, Denmark, and Norway; area 202,000 sq mi/523,000 sq km; average depth 180 ft/55 m, greatest depth 2,165 ft/660 m. In the northeast it joins the Norwegian Sea, and in the south it meets the Strait of Dover.

It has fisheries, oil, and gas. Despite the 1972 Oslo Treaty, Britain still dumps the largest quantity of sewage sludge in the North Sea; see ⟡sewage disposal. In 1987, Britain dumped more than 4,700 tons of sewage sludge into the North Sea; Britain is also responsible for the highest input of radioactive isotopes, atmospheric nitrogen, and hydrocarbons. In 1991 the North Sea received more than 2 million tons of liquid chemical waste. The effects of pollution are most noted along the E coast of the North Sea.

North–South divide geographical division of the world that theoretically demarcates the rich from the poor. The South includes all of Asia except Japan, Australia, and New Zealand; all of Africa, the Middle East, Central and South America. The North includes Europe, the US, and all republics of the former Soviet Union. Newly industrialized countries such as South Korea and Taiwan could, however, be said to have more in common with the industrialized North than with ⟡Third World countries.

The gulf between rich and poor is widening: in 1880 the average income of a European was twice that of an Indian or Chinese; by 1965 the ratio was 40:1; in 1991 it was 70:1. The richest 20% of the world's people had (1992) 150 times the income of the poorest 20%.

Northumberland county in N England
area 1,942 sq mi/5,030 sq km
cities Newcastle-upon-Tyne (administrative headquarters), Berwick-upon-Tweed, Hexham
features Cheviot Hills; rivers: Tweed, upper Tyne; Northumberland National Park in the west; ⟡Holy Island; the Farne island group; part of Hadrian's Wall and Housestead's Fort; Alnwick and Bamburgh castles; large moorland areas are used for military maneuvers; Longstone Lighthouse from which Grace Darling rowed to the rescue is no longer inhabited, the crew having been replaced by an automatic light; wild white cattle of Chillingham
products sheep
population (1991) 300,600

Northumberland John Dudley, Duke of Northumberland *c.* 1502–1553. English politician, son of the privy councillor Edmund Dudley (beheaded 1510), and chief minister until Edward VI's death 1553. He tried to place his daughter-in-law Lady Jane ⟡Grey on the throne, but was executed on Mary I's accession.

Northumbria Anglo-Saxon kingdom that covered NE England and SE Scotland, comprising the 6th-century kingdoms of Bernicia (Forth–Tees) and Deira (Tees–Humber), united in the 7th century. It accepted the supremacy of Wessex 827 and was conquered by the Danes in the late 9th century.

North-West Frontier Province province of Pakistan; capital Peshawar; area 28,757 sq mi/74,500 sq km; population (1985) 12,287,000. It was a province of British India 1901–47. It includes the strategic Khyber Pass, the site of constant struggle between the British Raj and the ⟡Pathan warriors. In the 1980s it had to accommodate a stream of refugees from neighboring Afghanistan.

Northwest Passage Atlantic–Pacific sea route around the north of Canada. Canada, which owns offshore islands, claims it as an internal waterway; the US insists that it is an international waterway and sent an icebreaker through without permission 1985.

Early explorers included the Englishmen Martin ⟡Frobisher and, later, John Franklin, whose failure to return 1847 led to the organization of 39 expeditions in the next ten years. John Ross reached Lancaster Sound in 1818 but mistook a bank of cloud for a range of mountains and turned back. R McClune explored the passage 1850–53 although he did not cover the whole route by sea. The polar explorer ⟡Amundsen was the first European to sail through 1903–06.

Northwest Territories territory of Canada
area 1,322,552 sq mi/3,426,300 sq km
capital Yellowknife
physical extends to the North Pole, to Hudson's Bay in the east, and in the west to the edge of the Canadian Shield
features Mackenzie River; lakes: Great Slave, Great Bear; Miles Canyon
products oil, natural gas, zinc, lead, gold, tungsten, silver
population (1991) 54,000; over 50% native peoples (Indian, Inuit)
history the area was the northern part of Rupert's Land, bought by the Canadian government from the Hudson's Bay Company 1869. An act of 1952 placed the Northwest Territories under a commissioner acting in Ottawa under the Ministry of Northern Affairs and Natural Resources. In 1990 territorial control of over 135,000 sq mi/350,000 sq km of the Northwest Territories was given to the ⟡Inuit.

North Yorkshire county in NE England
area 3,212 sq mi/8,320 sq km
cities Northallerton (administrative headquarters), York; resorts: Harrogate, Scarborough, Whitby
features England's largest county; including part of the Pennines, the Vale of York, and the Cleveland Hills and North Yorkshire Moors, which form a national park (within which is Fylingdales radar station to give early warning—4 min—of nuclear attack); and Rievaulx Abbey; Yorkshire Dales National Park (including Swaledale, Wensleydale, and Bolton Abbey in Wharfedale); rivers: Derwent, Ouse;

Northwest Territories

Fountains Abbey near Ripon, with Studley Royal Gardens; York Minster; Castle Howard, designed by Vanbrugh, has Britain's largest collection of 18th–20th-century costume
products cereals, wool and meat from sheep, dairy products, coal, electrical goods
population (1991) 698,000
famous people Alcuin, W H Auden, Guy Fawkes.

Norwalk city in SW Connecticut, on the Norwalk River where it flows into Long Island Sound, NE of Stamford; population (1990) 78,300. Industries include electronic equipment, clothing, hardware, and furniture.

Norway country in NW Europe, on the Scandinavian peninsula, bounded E by Sweden, NE by Finland and Russia, S by the North Sea, W by the Atlantic Ocean, and N by the Arctic Ocean.

government Norway's constitution dates from 1814. The hereditary monarch is the formal head of state, and the legislature consists of a single-chamber parliament, the Storting. The monarch appoints a prime minister and state council on the basis of support in the Storting, to which they are all responsible.

The Storting has 157 members, elected for a four-year term by universal suffrage through a system of proportional representation. Once elected, it divides itself into two parts, a fourth of the members being chosen to form an upper house, the Lagting, and the remainder a lower house, the Odelsting. All legislation

must be first introduced in the Odelsting and then passed to the Lagting for approval, amendment, or rejection. Once a bill has had parliamentary approval it must receive the royal assent.

history Norway was originally inhabited by the Saami (Lapps) and other nomads and was gradually invaded by ▷Goths. It was ruled by local chieftains until unified by Harald Fairhair (reigned 872–933) as a feudal country. Norway's ▷Vikings raided and settled in many parts of Europe in the 8th–11th centuries. Christianity was introduced by ▷Olaf II in the 11th century; he was defeated 1030 by rebel chiefs backed by ▷Canute, but his son Magnus I regained the throne 1035. Haakon IV (1217–1263) established the authority of the crown over the nobles and the church and made the monarchy hereditary.

▷Denmark and Norway were united by marriage 1380, and in 1397 Norway, Denmark, and Sweden became united under one sovereign. Sweden broke away 1523, but Norway remained under Danish rule until 1814, when it was ceded to Sweden. Norway rebelled, Sweden invaded, and a compromise was reached whereby Norway kept its own parliament but was united with Sweden under a common monarch.

independence Conflict between the Norwegian parliament and the Swedish crown continued until 1905, when the parliament declared Norway completely independent. This was confirmed by plebiscite, and Prince Carl of

Denmark was elected king as Haakon VII. He ruled for 52 years until his death 1957. He was succeeded by his son ▷Olaf V.

since World War II The experience of German occupation 1940–45 persuaded the Norwegians to abandon their traditional neutral stance and join the North Atlantic Treaty Organization (NATO) 1949, the Nordic Council 1952, and the European Free Trade Association (EFTA) 1960. Norway was accepted into membership in the European Economic Community 1972, but a referendum held that year rejected the proposal and the application was withdrawn. Its exploitation of North Sea oil and gas resources have given it a higher income per head of population than most of its European neighbors, and during the Cold War it succeeded in maintaining good relations with the USSR without damaging its commitments in the West.

Norway has enjoyed stability under a series of coalition governments. In Nov 1988 Prime Minister Gro Harlem Brundtland was awarded the annual Third World Prize for her work on environmental issues but in the Sept 1989 election her party lost seats to the far right and the far left. Following a vote of no confidence, she resigned Oct 1989 and was succeeded by the Conservative Jan P Syze. In Oct 1990 the Syze coalition collapsed and Brundtland returned to power, leading a minority Labor government. Olav V died Jan 1991 and was succeeded by his son, Harald V. In 1992, Norway joined Iceland in defying a worldwide ban on whaling in order to resume its own whaling industry. *See illustration box.*

Norwegian person of Norwegian culture. There are 4–4.5 million speakers of Norwegian (including some in the US), a Germanic language belonging to the Indo-European family. The seafaring culture of the Norwegians can be traced back to the Viking age from about AD 800–1050, when people of Norwegian descent settled Iceland and Greenland, and undertook expeditions to Vinland (coast of Newfoundland).

The Norwegians have a long tradition of woodworking going back to the Vikings and are known for their stave (timber) churches.

Norwegian Sea part of the ▷Arctic Ocean.

Norwich cathedral city in Norfolk, E England; population (1991) 121,000. Industries include shoes, clothing, chemicals, confectionery, engineering, and printing. It has a Norman castle, 15th-century Guildhall, medieval churches, Tudor houses, and a Georgian Assembly House.

The cathedral was founded 1096. The castle has a collection of paintings by the Norwich school. The University of East Anglia 1963 has the Sainsbury Art Center for Visual Arts on its campus. The Sainsbury Laboratory 1987, in association with the John Innes Institute, was founded here to study the molecular causes of disease.

Norwich city in SE Connecticut, at the confluence of the Yantic and Quinebaug rivers that form the Thames River, N of New London; seat of New London County; population (1990) 37,400. Industries include leather, paper, and metal products; electronic equipment; and clothing. In the 1700s it was a shipping and shipbuilding center.

nose in humans, the upper entrance of the respiratory tract; the organ of the sense of smell. The external part is divided down the middle by a septum of ▷cartilage. The nostrils

---

Norway
Kingdom of (*Kongeriket Norge*)

area 149,421 sq mi/387,000 sq km (includes Svalbard and Jan Mayen)
capital Oslo
cities Bergen, Trondheim, Stavanger
physical mountainous with fertile valleys and deeply indented coast; forests cover 25%; extends N of Arctic Circle
territories dependencies in the Arctic (Svalbard and Jan Mayen) and in Antarctica (Bouvet and Peter I Island, and Queen Maud Land)
environment an estimated 80% of the lakes and streams in the southern half of the country have been severely acidified by acid rain
features fjords, including Hardanger and Sogne, longest 115 mi/185 km, deepest 4,086 ft/1,245 m; glaciers in north; midnight sun and northern lights
head of state Harald V from 1991
head of government Gro Harlem Brundtland from 1990
political system constitutional monarchy
political parties Norwegian Labor Party

(DNA), moderate, left-of-center; Conservative Party, progressive, right-of-center; Christian People's Party (KrF), Christian, center-left; Center Party (SP), left-of-center, rural-oriented
exports petrochemicals from North Sea oil and gas, paper, wood pulp, furniture, iron ore and other minerals, high-tech goods, sports goods, fish
currency krone
population (1990 est) 4,214,000; growth rate 0.3% p.a.
life expectancy men 73, women 80 (1989)
languages Norwegian (official); there are Saami (Lapp) and Finnish-speaking minorities
religion Evangelical Lutheran (endowed by state) 94%
literacy 100% (1989)
GNP $89 bn (1988); $13,790 per head (1984)
chronology
1814 Became independent from Denmark; ceded to Sweden.
1905 Links with Sweden ended; full independence achieved.
1940–45 Occupied by Germany.
1949 Joined North Atlantic Treaty Organization (NATO).
1952 Joined Nordic Council.
1957 King Haakon VII succeeded by his son Olaf V.
1960 Joined European Free Trade Association (EFTA).
1972 Accepted into membership in European Economic Community; application withdrawn after a referendum.
1988 Gro Harlem Brundtland awarded Third World Prize.
1989 Jan P Syze became prime minister.
1990 Brundtland returned to power.
1991 King Olaf V died; succeeded by his son Harald V.
1992 Defies whaling ban to resume whaling industry.

contain plates of cartilage that can be moved by muscles and have a growth of stiff hairs at the margin to prevent foreign objects from entering. The whole nasal cavity is lined with a ⬦mucous membrane that warms and moistens the air and ejects dirt. In the upper parts of the cavity the membrane contains 50 million olfactory receptor cells (cells sensitive to smell).

nosebleed bleeding from the nose. Although usually minor and easily controlled, the loss of blood may occasionally be so rapid as to be life-threatening, particularly in small children. Most nosebleeds can be stopped by simply squeezing the nose for a few minutes with the head tilted back, but in exceptional cases transfusion may be required and the nose may need to be packed with ribbon gauze or cauterized.

nosocomial description of any infection acquired in a hospital or other medical facility, whether its effects are seen during the patient's stay or after discharge. Widely prevalent in some hospitals, nosocomial infections threaten patients who are seriously ill or whose immune systems have been suppressed. The threat is compounded by the prevalence of drug-resistant ⬦pathogens endemic to the hospital environment.

Nostradamus Latinized name of Michel de Nôtredame 1503–1566. French physician and astrologer who was consulted by Catherine de' Medici and was physician to Charles IX. His book of prophecies in rhyme, *Centuries* 1555, has had a number of interpretations.

nostril in vertebrates, the opening of the nasal cavity, in which cells sensitive to smell are located. (In fish, these cells detect water-borne chemicals, so they are effectively organs of taste.) In vertebrates with lungs (lungfish and tetrapod vertebrates), the nostrils also take in air. In humans, and most other mammals, the nostrils are located on a ⬦nose.

notation in music, the use of symbols to represent individual sounds (such as the notes of the chromatic scale) so that they can be accurately interpreted and reproduced.

The earliest system was developed by the ancient Sumerians; later the Greeks and Romans devised systems for their music dramas. The system in use today goes back to the Middle Ages, to the Italian monk Guido d'Arezzo 1026.

notation in dance, the recording of dances by symbols. There are several dance notation systems; prominent among them is ⬦Labanotation.

note in music, the written symbol indicating pitch and duration, the sound of which is a tone.

notochord the stiff but flexible rod that lies between the gut and the nerve cord of all embryonic and larval chordates, including the vertebrates. It forms the supporting structure of the adult lancelet, but in vertebrates it is replaced by the vertebral column, or spine.

Nottingham industrial city (engineering, coal-mining, bicycles, textiles, knitwear, pharmaceuticals, tobacco, lace, electronics) and administrative headquarters of Nottinghamshire, England; population (1991) 261,500.

Features include the university 1881, the Playhouse (opened 1963), and the Theater Royal. Nearby are Newstead Abbey, home of Byron, and D H Lawrence's home at Eastwood.

Nottinghamshire county in central England
area 834 sq mi/2,160 sq km
cities Nottingham (administrative headquarters), Mansfield, Worksop

features River Trent; the remaining areas of Sherwood Forest (home of ⬦Robin Hood), formerly a royal hunting ground, are included in the "Dukeries"; Cresswell Crags (remains of prehistoric humans); D H Lawrence commemorative walk from Eastwood (where he lived) to Old Brinsley Colliery
products cereals, cattle, sheep, light engineering, footwear, limestone, ironstone, oil
population (1991) 980,600
famous people William Booth, D H Lawrence, Alan Sillitoe
history In World War II Nottinghamshire produced the only oil out of U-boat reach, and drilling revived in the 1980s.

Nouakchott capital of Mauritania; population (1985) 500,000. Products include salt, cement, and insecticides.

noun grammatical ⬦part of speech that names a person, animal, object, quality, idea, or time. Nouns can refer to objects such as *house*, *tree* (**concrete nouns**); specific persons and places such as John Alden, the *White House* (**proper nouns**); ideas such as *love*, *anger* (**abstract nouns**). In English many simple words are both noun and verb (*jump*, *reign*, *rain*). Adjectives are sometimes used as nouns ("a *local* man," "one of the *locals*").

A common noun does not begin with a capital letter (*child*, *cat*), whereas a proper noun does, because it is the name of a particular person, animal, or place (*Jane*, *Rover*, *Norfolk*). A concrete noun refers to things that can be sensed (*dog*, *box*), whereas an abstract noun relates to generalizations abstracted from life as we observe it (*fear*, *condition*, *truth*). A **countable noun** can have a plural form (*book*: *books*), while an **uncountable noun** or mass noun cannot (*dough*). Many English nouns can be used both countably and uncountably (*wine*: "Have some *wine*; it's one of our best *wines*"). A **collective noun** is singular in form but refers to a group (*flock*, *group*, *committee*), and a **compound noun** is made up of two or more nouns (*teapot*, *baseball team*, *car-factory strike committee*). A **verbal noun** is formed from a verb as a ⬦gerund or otherwise (*build*: *building*; *regulate*: *regulation*).

nouveau roman (French "new novel") experimental literary form produced in the 1950s by French novelists of the ⬦New Wave, including Alain Robbe-Grillet and Nathalie Sarraute. In various ways, these writers seek to eliminate character, plot, and authorial subjectivity in order to present the world as a pure, solid "thing in itself."

Robbe-Grillet's *Le Voyeur* 1955 and Sarraute's *Le Planetarium* 1959 are critically successful examples. Michel Butor, Claude Ollier, and Marguerite Duras also contribute to this form, which is sometimes labeled the "anti-novel" because of its subversion of traditional methods.

nouvelle cuisine (French "new cooking") contemporary French cooking style that avoids traditional rich sauces, emphasizing fresh ingredients and attractive presentation. The phrase was coined in the British magazine *Harpers & Queen* in June 1975.

nova (plural *novae*) faint star that suddenly erupts in brightness by 10,000 times or more. Novae are believed to occur in close ⬦double star systems, where gas from one star flows to a companion ⬦white dwarf. The gas ignites and is thrown off in an explosion at speeds of 930 mps/1,500 kps or more. Unlike a ⬦supernova,

the star is not completely disrupted by the outburst. After a few weeks or months it subsides to its previous state; it may erupt many more times.

The name comes from the Latin "new," although novae are not new stars at all.

Novak Kim (Marilyn Pauline) 1933– . US film actress who starred in such films as *Pal Joey* 1957, *Bell, Book and Candle* 1958, *Vertigo* 1958, *Kiss Me Stupid* 1964, and *The Legend of Lyla Clare* 1968.

Novalis Adopted name of Friedrich Leopold von Hardenberg 1772–1801. Pioneer German Romantic poet who wrote *Hymnen an die Nacht/Hymns to the Night* 1800, prompted by the death of his fiancée Sophie von Kühn. He left two unfinished romances, *Die Lehrlinge zu Sais/The Novices of Sais* and *Heinrich von Ofterdingen*.

Nova Lisboa former name (1928–73) for ⬦Huambo, town in Angola.

Nova Scotia province of E Canada
area 21,423 sq mi/55,500 sq km
capital Halifax (chief port)
cities Dartmouth, Sydney
features Cabot Trail (Cape Breton Island); Alexander Graham Bell Museum; Fortress Louisbourg; Strait of Canso Superport, the largest deepwater harbor on the Atlantic coast of North America
products coal, gypsum, dairy products, poultry, fruit, forest products, fish products (including scallop and lobster)
population (1991) 897,500
history Nova Scotia was visited by the navigator Giovanni ⬦Caboto 1497. A French settlement was established 1604, but expelled 1613 by English colonists from Virginia. The name of the colony was changed from **Acadia** to Nova Scotia 1621. England and France contended for possession of the territory until Nova Scotia (which then included present-day New Brunswick and Prince Edward Island) was ceded to Britain 1713; Cape Breton Island remained French until 1763. Nova Scotia was one of the four original provinces of the Dominion of Canada.

Novaya Zemlya Arctic island group off NE Russia; area 31,394 sq mi/81,279 sq km; population, a few Samoyed. It is rich in birds, seals, and walrus.

novel extended fictional prose narrative, often including some sense of the psychological development of the central characters and of their relationship with a broader world. The European novel is said to have originated in Greece in the 2nd century BC. The modern novel took its name and inspiration from the Italian *novella*, the short tale of varied character which became popular in the late 13th century. As the main form of narrative fiction in the

Nova Scotia

Halifax

20th century, the novel is frequently classified according to genres and subgenres such as the ⟳historical novel, ⟳detective fiction, ⟳fantasy fiction, and ⟳science fiction.

Ancient Greek examples include the *Daphnis and Chloë* of Longus; almost the only surviving Latin work that could be called a novel is the *Golden Ass* of Apuleius (late 2nd century), based on a Greek model. There is a similar, but until the 19th century independent, tradition of prose narrative including psychological development in the Far East, notably in Japan, with for example *The Tale of Genji* by Murasaki Shikibu (978–*c*. 1015).

The works of the Italian writers Boccaccio and Matteo Bandello (1485–1561) were translated into English in such collections as William Painter's *Palace of Pleasure* 1566–67, and inspired the Elizabethan novelists, including John Lyly, Philip Sidney, Thomas Nash, and Thomas Lodge. In Spain, Cervantes's *Don Quixote* 1604 contributed to the development of the novel through its translation into other European languages, but the 17th century was dominated by the French romances of Gauthier de Costes de La Calprenède (1614–1663) and Madelaine de Scudéry (1607–1691), although William Congreve and Aphra Behn continued the English tradition.

In the 18th century the realistic novel was established in England by the work of Defoe, Richardson, Fielding, Sterne, and Smollett. Walpole, and later Mary Shelley, developed the Gothic novel; in the early 19th century Sir Walter Scott developed the historical novel, and Jane Austen wrote "novels of manners." Celebrated novelists of the Victorian age in Britain were Dickens, Thackeray, the Brontës, George Eliot, Trollope, and Stevenson. The 19th century was also a great period for the novel in the US, with Cooper, Melville, Hawthorne, and Twain; in France, with Hugo, Balzac, the two Dumas, George Sand, and Zola; in Germany, with Goethe and Jean Paul; and in Russia, with Gogol, Turgenev, Dostoievsky, and Tolstoy.

From the end of the 19th century the US produced novelists in such schools as realism (Wharton, Crane, Howells, and Cather) and naturalism/social protest (Dreiser, Sinclair, Norris, and London). Before World War II Ferber, Lewis, Buck, Hemingway, Fitzgerald, Steinbeck, Thomas Wolfe, and Faulkner had made names for themselves; many of them continued to enjoy success after the war too.

In Britain the transition period from Victorian times to the 20th century includes Meredith, Butler, Hardy, Henry James, Kipling, Conrad, Wells, and Galsworthy. Slightly later are W Somerset Maugham, E M Forster, James Joyce, D H Lawrence, and Virginia Woolf—the last three being influential in the development of novel technique. Among those who began writing in the 1920s are J B Priestley, Aldous Huxley, Christopher Isherwood, Graham Greene, V S Pritchett, and Evelyn Waugh. The 1930s produced Joyce Cary, Lawrence Durrell, and George Orwell; more recent British writers include Anthony Powell, John Fowles, Kingsley Amis, Anthony Burgess, Iris Murdoch, Doris Lessing, and Salman Rushdie.

After World War II a new generation of US novelists reached maturity, with many of them crossing into poetry and short stories as well. This group includes Mailer, Jones, Heller, Warren, Capote, Hellman, Porter, McCullers, O'Connor, Salinger, Baldwin, Roth, Bellow, Oates, Vonnegut, and Updike.

Twentieth-century European novelists include Lion Feuchtwanger, Thomas Mann, Franz Kafka, Ernst Wiechert, Stefan Zweig, Christa Wolff, Heinrich Böll, and Gunter Grass (Germany); André Gide, Marcel Proust, Jules Romains, François Mauriac, Michel Butor, Nathalie Sarraute, and Alain Robbe-Grillet (French); Gabriele d'Annunzio, Ignazio Silone, Alberto Moravia, Italo Calvino, Primo Levi, and Natalia Ginzburg (Italian); Maxim Gorky, Mikhail Sholokhov, Aleksei Tolstoi, Boris Pasternak, and Alexander Solzhenitsyn (Russian); Arturo Baréa, Pío Baroja and Ramón Pérez de Ayala (Spain). In Latin America contemporary novelists include Mario Vargas Llosa and Gabriel Garcia Márquez. Canadians who have received acclaim include Morley Callaghan, Robertson Davies, Mordecai Richler, and Margaret Atwood.

Noverre Jean-Georges 1727–1810. French choreographer, writer, and ballet reformer. He promoted ⟳*ballet d'action* (with a plot) and simple, free movement, and is often considered the creator of modern Classical ballet. *Les Petits Riens* 1778 was one of his works.

Novgorod industrial (chemicals, engineering, clothing, brewing) city on the Volkhov River, NW Russia; a major trading city in medieval times; population (1987) 228,000.

Novgorod was the original capital of the Russian state, founded at the invitation of the people of the city by the Viking (Varangian) chieftain Rurik 862. The Viking merchants who went there quickly became fully assimilated into the native Slav population. In 912 the capital of the principality moved to Kiev, but this did little to harm Novgorod. It developed a strong municipal government run by the leaders of the craft guilds and, until the 13th century, flourished as a major commercial center (with a monopoly on the Russian fur trade) for trade with Scandinavia, the Byzantine empire, and the Muslim world. (It was known in Russia as "Lord Novgorod the Great" because of its position on the trade route between the Baltic and Black Seas.) It became one of the principal members of the ⟳Hanseatic League, but its economy had already started to decline. This was hastened during the 15th-century rule of the boyars, nobles who had seized power from the guilds 1416. It came under the control of Ivan the Great III 1478 and was sacked by Ivan the Terrible 1570.

Novi Sad industrial and commercial (pottery and cotton) city, capital of the autonomous province of Vojvodina in N Serbia, Yugoslavia, on the River Danube; population (1981) 257,700. Products include leather, textiles, and tobacco.

Novocaine trade name of *procaine*, the first synthetic local anesthetic, invented 1905. It has now been replaced by agents such as ⟳lignocaine. It is as effective as cocaine, formerly used as a painkiller, when injected, but only one-third as toxic and not habit-forming. It is not so effective when used as a surface anesthetic. It is always used with adrenaline.

Novokuznetsk industrial city (steel, aluminum, chemicals) in the Kuzbas, S central Russia; population (1987) 589,000. It was called **Stalinsk** 1932–1961.

Novosibirsk industrial city (engineering, textiles, chemicals, food processing) in W Siberian Russia, on the River Ob; population (1987) 1,423,000. Winter lasts eight months here.

At *Akademgorodok* ("Science City"), population 25,000, advanced research is carried on into Siberia's local problems.

Noyce Robert Norton 1927–1990. US scientist and inventor, with Jack Kilby, of the ⟳integrated circuit (chip), which revolutionized the computer and electronics industries in the 1970s and 1980s. In 1968 he and six colleagues founded Intel Corporation, which became one of the US's leading semiconductor manufacturers.

Noyes John Humphrey 1811–1886. US religious and communal leader. Founding a religious community 1836 in Putney, Vermont, he experimented with alternate forms of marriage, formulating the doctrine of free love in 1837. In 1848 he established an even larger religious society in central New York. This Oneida Community, as it was called, served for 30 years as a forum for Noyes's experiments in "complex marriage." By 1879, internal doubts and tensions had risen to such a degree that Noyes moved to Canada to avoid legal actions against him, and the community, which made silverware and steel traps, ended the social experiment and in 1881 became a joint stock company.

Born in Brattleboro, Vermont, Noyes was educated at Dartmouth and the Andover Seminary. While at Yale Divinity School, he developed ideas about the possibility of overcoming sin, and in 1834, when he announced that he had achieved human perfection, he was promptly expelled from Yale.

NS abbreviation for ⟳*Nova Scotia*.

NSAID abbreviation for *nonsteroidal anti-inflammatory drug*. There are several, and they are effective in the long-term treatment of rheumatoid ⟳arthritis and osteoarthritis, and act to reduce swelling and pain in soft tissues. Bleeding into the digestive tract is a serious side effect: NSAIDs should not be taken by persons with peptic ulcers.

NT abbreviation for ⟳*Northern Territory*, Australia.

Nu U (Thakin) 1907– . Myanmar politician, prime minister of Burma (now Myanmar) for most of the period from 1948 to the military coup of 1962. Exiled from 1966, U Nu returned to the country 1980 and, in 1988, helped found the National League for Democracy opposition movement.

Nuba member of a minority ethnic group living in S Sudan, numbering about 1 million (1991). They speak related dialects of Nubian, which belongs to the Chari-Nile family. Forced Islamization threatens their cultural identity, and thousands were killed in the Sudan civil war.

The Nuba farm terraced fields in the Nuba mountains, to the west of the White Nile. Army massacres, forced "disappearances," and extrajudicial executions took place in the late 1980s and early 1990s, as the Muslim Sudanese of the north attempted to dominate the south, and many Nuba were driven from their homes.

Nubia former African country now divided between Egypt and Sudan; it gives its name to the *Nubian Desert* south of Lake Nasser.

Ancient Egypt, which was briefly ruled by Nubian kings in the 8th–7th centuries BC, knew the north as Wawat and the south as Kush, with the dividing line roughly at Dongola. Egyptian building work in the area included temples at ⟳Abu Simbel, Philae, and a defensive chain of forts that established the lines of development of medieval fortification. Nubia's capital about 600 BC–AD 350 was Meroe, near Khartoum. About AD 250–550 most of Nubia was occupied by the x-group people, of whom little is known; their royal mound tombs (mistaken by earlier investigations for natural mounds created by wind erosion) were excavated in the 1930s and many horses and attendants were found to have been slaughtered to accompany the richly jeweled dead.

nuclear arms verification the process of checking the number and types of nuclear weapons held by a country in accordance with negotiated limits. The chief means are:
reconnaissance satellites that detect submarines or weapon silos, using angled cameras to give three-dimensional pictures of installations, penetrating camouflage by means of scanners, and partially seeing through cloud and darkness by infrared devices;
telemetry, or radio transmission of instrument readings;
interception to get information on performance of weapons under test;
on-site inspection by experts visiting bases, launch sites, storage facilities, and test sites in another country;
radar tracking of missiles in flight;
seismic monitoring of underground tests, in the same way as with earthquakes. This is not accurate and on-site inspection is needed. Tests in the atmosphere, space, or the oceans are forbidden, and the ban is accepted because explosions are not only dangerous to all but immediately detectable.

nuclear energy energy from the inner core or ⭕nucleus of the atom, as opposed to energy released in chemical processes, which is derived from the electrons surrounding the nucleus.
Nuclear fission, as in an atomic bomb, is achieved by allowing a ⭕neutron to strike the nucleus of an atom of fissile material (such as uranium-235 or plutonium-239), which then splits apart to release two or three other neutrons. If the uranium-235 is pure, a ⭕chain reaction is set up when these neutrons in turn strike other nuclei. This happens very quickly, resulting in the tremendous release of energy seen in nuclear weapons. The process is controlled inside the reactor of a nuclear power plant by absorbing excess neutrons in control rods and slowing down their speed.

Nuclear fusion is the release of thermonuclear energy by the conversion of hydrogen nuclei to helium nuclei, a continuing reaction in the Sun and other stars. Nuclear fusion is the principle behind thermonuclear weapons (the ⭕hydrogen bomb). Attempts to harness fusion for commercial power production have so far not succeeded.

nuclear fusion process whereby two atomic nuclei are fused, with the release of a large amount of energy. Very high temperatures and pressures are thought to be required in order for the process to happen. Under these conditions the atoms involved are stripped of all their electrons so that the remaining particles, which together make up ⭕plasma, can come close together at very high speeds and overcome the mutual repulsion of the positive charges on the atomic nuclei. At very close range another nuclear force will come into play, fusing the particles together to form a larger nucleus. As fusion is accompanied by the release of large amounts of energy, the process might one day be harnessed to form the

basis of commercial energy production. Methods of achieving controlled fusion are therefore the subject of research around the world.

Fusion is the process by which the Sun and the other stars produce their energy.

nuclear physics the study of the properties of the nucleus of the ⭕atom, including the structure of nuclei; nuclear forces; the interactions between particles and nuclei; and the study of radioactive decay. The study of elementary particles is ⭕particle physics.

nuclear reactor device for producing ⭕nuclear energy in a controlled manner. There are various types of reactor in use, all using nuclear fission. In a gas-cooled reactor, a circulating gas under pressure (such as carbon dioxide) removes heat from the core of the reactor, which usually contains natural uranium. The efficiency of the fission process is increased by slowing neutrons in the core by using a ⭕moderator such as carbon. The reaction is controlled with neutron-absorbing rods made of boron. An advanced gas-cooled reactor (AGR) generally has enriched uranium as its fuel. A water-cooled reactor, such as the steam-generating heavy water (deuterium oxide) reactor, has water circulating through the hot core. The water is converted to steam, which drives turbo-alternators for generating electricity. The most widely used reactor is the pressurized-water reactor, which contains a sealed system of pressurized water that is heated to form steam in heat exchangers in an external circuit. The ⭕breeder reactor has no moderator and uses fast neutrons to bring about fission; it produces more fuel than it consumes.

nuclear safety the use of nuclear energy has given rise to concern over safety. Anxiety has been heightened by accidents such as those at Windscale (UK), Three Mile Island (US), and Chernobyl (Ukraine). There has also been mounting concern about the production and disposal of nuclear waste, the ⭕radioactive and toxic by-products of the nuclear energy industry. Burial on land or at sea raises problems of safety, environmental pollution, and security. Nuclear waste has an active half-life of thousands of years and no guarantees exist for the safety of the various methods of disposal. Nuclear safety is still a controversial subject since governments will not recognize the haz-

ards of ⭕radiation and ⭕radiation illness. In 1990 a scientific study revealed an increased risk of leukemia in children whose fathers had worked at Sellafield between 1950 and 1985. Sellafield (UK) is the world's greatest discharger of radioactive waste, followed by Hanford, Washington (US).

nuclear warfare war involving the use of nuclear weapons. The worldwide total of nuclear weapons in 1990 was about 50,000, and the number of countries possessing nuclear weapons stood officially at five—USA, USSR, UK, France, and China—although some other nations were thought either to have a usable stockpile of these weapons (Israel) or the ability to produce them quickly (Brazil, India, Pakistan, South Africa). Nuclear-weapons research began in Britain 1940, but was transferred to the US after it entered World War II. The research program, known as the Manhattan Project, was directed by J Robert Oppenheimer.
atom bomb The original weapon relied on use of a chemical explosion to trigger a chain reaction. The first test explosion was at Alamogordo, New Mexico, July 16, 1945; the first use in war was by the US against Japan Aug 6, 1945 over Hiroshima and three days later at Nagasaki.

hydrogen bomb A much more powerful weapon than the atomic bomb, it relies on the release of thermonuclear energy by the condensation of hydrogen nuclei to helium nuclei (as happens in the Sun). The first detonation was at Eniwetok Atoll, Pacific Ocean, 1952 by the US.

neutron bomb or *enhanced radiation weapon* (ERW) A very small hydrogen bomb that has relatively high radiation but relatively low blast, designed to kill (in up to six days) by a brief neutron radiation that leaves buildings and weaponry intact.

nuclear methods of attack now include aircraft bombs, missiles (long- or short-range, surface to surface, air to surface, and surface to air), depth charges, and high-powered landmines ("atomic demolition munitions") to destroy bridges and roads.

nuclear waste the radioactive and toxic by-products of the nuclear-energy and nuclear-weapons industries. Nuclear waste may have an active life of several thousand years. Reactor

nose cone
nuclear warheads
bus
silo
second stage
first stage

When the missiles have been launched into space, the individual warheads separate from the "bus" that carries them, and re-enter the atmosphere independently, each heading for a different target.

ᵗnuclear warfare *The multiple independently targetable reentry vehicle, or MIRV.*

waste is of three types: high-level spent fuel, or the residue when nuclear fuel has been removed from a reactor and reprocessed; intermediate, which may be long-or short-lived; and low-level, but bulky, waste from reactors, which has only short-lived radioactivity. Disposal, by burial on land or at sea, has raised problems of safety, environmental pollution, and security. In absolute terms, nuclear waste cannot be safely relocated or disposed of.

The dumping of nuclear waste at sea officially stopped 1983, when a moratorium was agreed by the members of the London Dumping Convention (a United Nations body that controls disposal of wastes at sea). Covertly, the USSR continued dumping, and deposited thousands of tonnes of nuclear waste and three faulty reactors in the sea 1964–86.

nuclear winter possible long-term effect of a widespread nuclear war. In the wake of the destruction caused by nucle2r blasts and the subsequent radiation, it has been suggested that atmospheric pollution by dust, smoke, soot, and ash could prevent the Sun's rays from penetrating for a period of time sufficient to eradicate most plant life on which other life depends, and create a new Ice Age.

Even after it had settled, ash would still reflect the Sun's rays and delay the planet's return to normal warmth. Insects, grasses, and sea life would have the best prospects of survival, as well as microorganisms. The cold would be intense, and a great increase in snow and ice worldwide would occur.

nucleic acid complex organic acid made up of a long chain of nucleotides. The two types, known as DNA (deoxyribonucleic acid) and RNA (ribonucleic acid), form the basis of heredity. The nucleotides are made up of a sugar (deoxyribose or ribose), a phosphate group, and one of four purine or pyrimidine bases. The order of the bases along the nucleic acid strand contains the genetic code.

nucleolus in biology, a structure found in the nucleus of eukaryotic cells (◊eukaryote). It produces the RNA that makes up the ◊ribosomes, from instructions in the DNA.

nucleon in particle physics, either a ◊proton or a ◊neutron, both particles present in the atomic nucleus. **Nucleon number** is an alternate name for the ◊mass number of an atom.

nucleotide organic compound consisting of a purine (adenine or guanine) or a pyrimidine (thymine, uracil, or cytosine) base linked to a sugar (deoxyribose or ribose) and a phosphate group. ◊DNA and ◊RNA are made up of long chains of nucleotides.

nucleus in physics, the positively charged central part of an ◊atom, which constitutes almost all its mass. Except for hydrogen nuclei, which have only protons, nuclei are composed of both protons and neutrons. Surrounding the nuclei are electrons, which contain a negative charge equal to the protons, thus giving the atom a neutral charge.

The nucleus was discovered by New Zealand physicist Ernest Rutherford in 1911 as a result of experiments in passing alpha particles through very thin gold foil.

A few of the particles were deflected back, and Rutherford deduced that the deflection was due to the positively charged alpha particles being repelled by approaching a small but dense positively charged nucleus.

nucleus in biology, the central, membrane-enclosed part of a ◊eukaryotic cell, containing the chromosomes.

nuclide in physics, one of two or more atoms having the same atomic number (number of protons) and mass number (number of nucleons); compare ◊isotope.

nuisance in law, interference with enjoyment of, or rights over, land. There are two kinds of nuisance. *Private nuisance* affects a particular occupier of land, such as noise from a neighbor; the aggrieved occupier can apply for an ◊injunction and claim ◊damages. *Public nuisance* affects an indefinite number of members of the public, such as obstructing the highway; it is a criminal offense. In this case, individuals can claim damages only if they are affected more than the general public.

Nukua'lofa capital and port of Tonga on Tongatapu; population (1986) 29,000.

Nullarbor Plain (Latin *nullus arbor* "no tree") arid coastal plateau area divided between Western and South Australia; there is a network of caves beneath it. Atom-bomb experiments were carried out in the 1950s at Maralinga, bordering the Great Victoria Desert in the NE.

Numa Pompilius legendary king of Rome c. 716–c. 679 BC, who succeeded Romulus

and was credited with the introduction of religious rites.

numbat or *banded anteater* Australian marsupial anteater *Myrmecobius fasciatus*. It is brown with white stripes on the back and has a long tubular tongue to gather termites and ants. The body is about 10 in/25 cm long, and the tongue can be extended 4 in/10 cm.

number symbol used in counting or measuring. In mathematics, there are various kinds of numbers. The everyday number system is the decimal ("proceeding by tens") system, using the base ten. ◊Real numbers include all rational numbers (integers, or whole numbers, and fractions) and irrational numbers (those not expressible as fractions). ◊Complex numbers include the real and unreal numbers (real-number multiples of the square root of –1). The ◊binary number system, used in computers, has two as its base.

The ordinary numerals, 0, 1, 2, 3, 4, 5, 6, 7, 8, and 9, give a counting system that, in the decimal system, continues 10, 11, 12, 13, and so on. These are whole numbers (positive integers), with fractions represented as, for example, 1/4, 1/2, 3/4, or as decimal fractions (0.25, 0.5, 0.75). They are also rational numbers. Irrational numbers cannot be represented in this way and require symbols, such as $\sqrt{2}$, π, and e. They can be expressed numerically only as the (inexact) approximations 1.414, 3.142 and 2.718 (to three places of decimals) respectively. The symbols π and e are also examples of transcendental numbers, because they (unlike $\sqrt{2}$) cannot be derived by solving a ◊polynomial equation (an equation with one ◊variable quantity) with rational ◊coefficients (multiplying factors). Complex numbers, which include the real numbers as well as unreal numbers, take the general form $a + bi$, where $i = \sqrt{-1}$ (that is, $i^2 = -1$), and a is the real part and bi the unreal part.

history The ancient Egyptians, Greeks, Romans, and Babylonians all evolved number systems, although none had a zero, which was introduced from India by way of Arab mathematicians in about the 6th century AD and allowed a place-value system to be devised on which the decimal system is based. Other number systems have since evolved and have found applications. For example, numbers to base two (binary numbers), using only 0 and 1, are commonly used in digital computers to represent the two-state "on" or "off" pulses of electricity. Binary numbers were first developed by Gottfried Leibniz in the late 17th century.

Numidia ("nomads' land") Roman N African territory, now E ◊Algeria.

numismatics the study of ◊coins, and ◊medals and decorations.

nun (Latin *nonna* "elderly woman") woman belonging to a religious order under the vows of poverty, chastity, and obedience, and living under a particular rule. Christian convents are ruled by a superior (often elected), who is subject to the authority of the bishop of the diocese or sometimes directly to the pope. See ◊monasticism.

It is possible that the institution of Christian communities for nuns preceded the establishment of monasteries. The majority of the male orders have their female counterparts.

nuncio (Italian "messenger") diplomatic representative of the pope, from the 16th century, performing the functions of a papal ambassador.

submarine
trident missile
engine room
nuclear reactor
control room
torpedo bay
warhead

Nuremberg (German *Nürnberg*) industrial city (electrical and other machinery, precision instruments, textiles, toys) in Bavaria, Germany; population (1988) 467,000. From 1933 the Nuremberg rallies were held here, and in 1945 the Nuremberg trials of war criminals.

Created an imperial city 1219, it has an 11th–16th-century fortress and many medieval buildings (restored after destruction of 75% of the city in World War II), including the home of the 16th-century composer Hans ⬦Sachs, where the ⬦Meistersingers met. The artist Dürer was born here.

Nuremberg rallies annual meetings 1933–38 of the German Nazi Party (see ⬦Nazism). They were characterized by extensive torchlight parades, marches in party formations, and mass rallies addressed by Nazi leaders such as Hitler and Goebbels.

Nuremberg trials after World War II, the trials of the 24 chief Nazi war criminals (see ⬦Nazism) Nov 1945–Oct 1946 by an international military tribunal consisting of four judges and four prosecutors: one of each from the US, UK, USSR, and France. An appendix accused the German cabinet, general staff, high command, Nazi leadership corps, ⬦SS, ⬦Sturmabteilung, and ⬦Gestapo of criminal behavior.

The main charges in the indictment were: (1) conspiracy to wage wars of aggression; (2) crimes against peace; (3) war crimes: for example, murder and ill-treatment of civilians and prisoners of war, deportation to slave labor, and killing of hostages; (4) crimes against humanity: for example, mass murder of the Jews and other peoples, and murder and ill-treatment of political opponents.

Of the accused, Krupp was too ill to be tried; Ley (1890–1945) committed suicide during the trial; and ⬦Bormann, who had fled, was sentenced to death in his absence. Fritsche (1899–1953), Schacht (1877–1970), and ⬦Papen were acquitted. The other 18 were found guilty on one or more counts. ⬦Hess, Walther Funk (1890–1960), and ⬦Raeder were sentenced to life imprisonment; Shirach (1907–1974) and Speer (1905–1981) to 20 years; Neurath (1873–1956) to 15 years; and Doenitz (1891–1980) to 10 years. The remaining 11 men, sentenced to death by hanging, were Hans Frank (1900–1946), Wilhelm Frick (1877–1946), ⬦Goering (who committed suicide before he could be executed), ⬦Jodl, ⬦Kaltenbrunner, ⬦Keitel, ⬦Ribbentrop, ⬦Rosenberg, Fritz Sauckel (1894–1946), Arthur Seyss-Inquart (1892–1946), and Julius Streicher (1885–1946). The SS and Gestapo were declared criminal organizations.

Nureyev Rudolf 1938–93. Russian dancer and choreographer. A soloist with the Kirov Ballet, he defected to the West during a visit to Paris in 1961. Mainly associated with the Royal Ballet (London) and as Margot ⬦Fonteyn's principal partner, he was one of the most brilliant dancers of the 1960s and 1970s. Nureyev danced in such roles as Prince Siegfried in *Swan Lake* and Armand in *Marguerite and Armand*, which was created specifically for Fonteyn and Nureyev. He also danced and acted in films and on television and choreographed several ballets.

nursery rhyme children's jingle. Usually limited to a couplet or quatrain with strongly marked rhythm and rhymes, nursery rhymes have often been handed down by oral tradition.

Some of the oldest nursery rhymes are connected with a traditional tune and were sung as accompaniment to ancient ring games, such as "Here we go round the mulberry bush," which was part of the May Day festivities. Others contain fragments of incantations and other rites; still others have a factual basis and commemorated popular figures, such as Jack Sprat and Jack Horner.

nursing care of the sick, the very young, the very old, and the disabled. Organized training originated 1836 in Germany, and was developed in Britain by the work of Florence ⬦Nightingale, who, during the Crimean War, established standards of scientific, humanitarian care in military hospitals. Nurses give day-to-day care and carry out routine medical and surgical procedures under the supervision of a physician.

In ancient times very limited care was associated with some temples, and in Christian times nursing became associated with the religious orders until the Reformation brought it into secular hands in Protestant countries. Many specialties and qualifications now exist in Western countries, standards being maintained by professional bodies and boards.

In the US, although registration (RN) is the responsibility of individual states, an almost uniform standard has been established by the National League for Nursing (1952). There are a variety of degree programs.

Nusa Tenggara or *Lesser Sunda Island* volcanic archipelago in Indonesia, including ⬦Bali, ⬦Lombok, and ⬦Timor; area 28,241 sq mi/73,144 sq km. The islands form two provinces of Indonesia: *Nusu Tenggara Barat*, population (1980) 2,724,500; and *Nusu Tenggara Timur*, population (1980) 2,737,000.

nut any dry, single-seeded fruit that does not split open to release the seed, such as the chestnut. A nut is formed from more than one carpel, but only one seed becomes fully formed, the remainder aborting. The wall of the fruit, the pericarp, becomes hard and woody, forming the outer shell.

Examples of true nuts are the acorn and hazelnut. The term also describes various hard-shelled fruits and seeds, including almonds and walnuts, which are really the stones of ⬦drupes, and brazil nuts and shelled peanuts, which are seeds.

The kernels of most nuts provide a concentrated, nutritious food, containing vitamins, minerals, and enzymes, about 50% fat, and 10–20% protein, although a few, such as chestnuts, are high in carbohydrates and have only a moderate protein content of 5%. Nuts also provide edible and industrial oils. Most nuts are produced by perennial trees and shrubs.

Whereas the majority of nuts are obtained from plantations, considerable quantities of pecans and brazil nuts are still collected from the wild. World production in the mid-1980s was about 4 million tons per year.

nut and bolt common method of fastening pieces of metal or wood together. The nut consists of a small block (usually metal) with a threaded hole in the center for screwing on to a threaded rod or pin (bolt or screw). The method came into use at the turn of the 19th century, following Henry Maudslay's invention of a precision screw-cutting ⬦lathe.

nutation in botany, the spiral movement exhibited by the tips of certain stems during growth; it enables a climbing plant to find a suitable support. Nutation sometimes also occurs in tendrils and flower stalks.

nutation in astronomy, a slight "nodding" of the Earth in space, caused by the varying gravitational pulls of the Sun and Moon. Nutation changes the angle of the Earth's axial tilt (average 23.5°) by about 9 seconds of arc to either side of its mean position, a complete cycle taking just over 18.5 years.

nutcracker either of two jaylike birds of the genus *Nucifraga*, in the crow family (Corvidae).

One, *N. caryocatactes*, is native to Eurasia; the other, Clark's nutcracker *N. columbiana*, 12 in/30 cm long, lives in W North America and has gray and black plumage and a powerful beak.

nuthatch small bird of the family Sittidae, with a short tail and pointed beak. Nuthatches climb head first up, down, and around tree trunks and branches, foraging for insects and their larvae.

The 5.5 in/14 cm long white-breasted nuthatch *Sitta carolinensis* of North America has a black cap, gray wings, and white underparts.

nutmeg kernel of the seed of the evergreen tree *Myristica fragrans*, native to the Moluccas. Both the nutmeg and its secondary covering, known as *mace*, are used as spice in cooking.

nutria or *coypu* South American water rodent *Myocastor coypus*, about 2 ft/60 cm long and weighing up to 20 lb/9 kg. It has a scaly, ratlike tail, webbed hind feet, a blunt, muzzled head, and large, orange incisors. The fur is reddish brown. It feeds on vegetation and lives in burrows in river and lake banks.

Taken to Europe and then to North America to be farmed for their fur, many escaped or were released and became established, often to the detriment of native species.

nutrition the science of food, and its effect on human and animal life, health, and disease. Nutrition is the study of the basic nutrients required to sustain life, their bioavailability in foods and overall diet, and the effects upon them of cooking and storage.

Malnutrition can be caused by underfeeding, an imbalanced diet, and overfeeding. Nutrition is also the study of feeds for farm animals, pets, and wild animals kept in captivity.

Nuuk Greenlandic for ⬦Godthaab, capital of Greenland.

NV abbreviation for the state of ⬦*Nevada*.

NY abbreviation for the state of ⬦*New York*.

nyala antelope *Tragelaphus angasi* found in the thick bush of sothern Africa. About 3 ft/1 m at the shoulder, it is grayish-brown with thin vertical white stripes. Males have horns up to 2.6 ft/80 cm long.

Nyanja member of a central African people living mainly in Malawi, and numbering about 400,000 (1984). The Nyanja are predominantly farmers, living in villages under a hereditary monarchy. They speak a Bantu language belonging to the Niger-Congo family.

Nyasa former name for Lake ⬦Malawi.

Nyasaland former name (until 1964) for ⬦Malawi.

Nyerere Julius (Kambarage) 1922– . Tanzanian socialist politician, president 1964–85. He devoted himself from 1954 to the formation of the Tanganyika African National Union and subsequent campaigning for independence. He became chief minister 1960, was prime minister of Tanganyika 1961–62, president of the newly formed Tanganyika Republic 1962–64, and first president of Tanzania 1964–85.

nylon synthetic long-chain polymer similar in chemical structure to protein. Nylon was the first all-synthesized fiber, made from petroleum, natural gas, air, and water by the Du Pont firm in 1938. It is used in the manufacture of molded articles, textiles, and medical sutures. Nylon fibers are stronger and more elastic than silk and are relatively insensitive to moisture and mildew. Nylon is used for hosiery and woven goods, simulating other materials such as silks and furs; it is also used for carpets.

nymph in Greek mythology, a guardian spirit of nature. *Hamadryads* or *dryads* guarded trees; *naiads*, springs and pools; *oreads*, hills and rocks; and *nereids*, the sea.

nymph in entomology, the immature form of insects that do not have a pupal stage; for example, grasshoppers and dragonflies. Nymphs generally resemble the adult (unlike larvae), but do not have fully formed reproductive organs or wings.

NZ abbreviation for ⇨*New Zealand*.

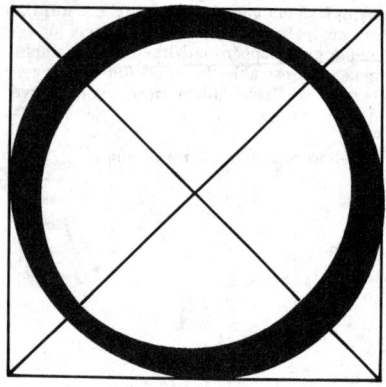

O 15th letter of the English alphabet, whose form was derived from the Semitic alphabet. In modern English it represents a wide range of sounds, from the diphthong Ō (*so*) to the open sounds in *or*, and *on*, and the oo-sound in *wolf*.

Oahu island of Hawaii, in the N Pacific
area 589 sq mi/1,525 sq km
cities Honolulu (state capital)
physical formed by two extinct volcanoes
features Waikiki beach; Pearl Harbor naval base; Diamond Head; punchbowl craters
products sugar, pineapples; tourism is a major industry
history settled by Polynesians from other Pacific islands 300–600 AD. Kamehameha I, ruler 1824–54 of Hawaii, had taken Oahu by 1810. He made Honolulu the capital city of the Hawaiian kingdom.

oak any tree or shrub of the genus *Quercus* of the beech family Fagaceae, with over 300 known species widely distributed in temperate zones. Oaks are valuable for timber, the wood being durable and straight-grained. Their fruits are called acorns.

The 60 species of North American oaks are divided into two groups: white oaks and red oaks. Most white oaks have leaves with rounded lobes, and their acorns are sweet and mature in one season. Red oaks characteristically have spiny, pointed lobes on their leaves, and their bitter acorns take two years to mature. The white oak *Q. alba* of E US and the northern red oak *Q. rubra* are typical examples. The evergreen live oaks (such as *Q. virginiana*) form a subsection in the red oak group.

Oakland industrial port (vehicles, textiles, chemicals, food processing, shipbuilding) in California, on the E coast of San Francisco Bay; population (1990) 372,200. It is linked by bridge (1936) with San Francisco. A major earthquake 1989 buckled the bay bridge and an Oakland freeway section, causing more than 60 deaths.

An army terminal and naval air station are here. The community was laid out 1852 and became a terminus of the first transcontinental railroad 1869.

Oakley Annie (Phoebe Anne Oakley Mozee) 1860–1926. US sharpshooter, member of Buffalo Bill's Wild West Show (see William ⟡Cody).

Even though she was partially paralyzed in a train crash 1901, she continued to astound audiences with her ability virtually until her death. Kaiser Wilhelm of Germany had such faith in her talent that he allowed her to shoot a cigarette from his mouth.

Oak Ridge town in Tennessee, E USA, on the River Clinch, noted for the Oak Ridge National Laboratory 1943, which manufactures plutonium for nuclear weapons; population (1990) 27,300. The community was founded 1942 as part of the Manhattan Project to develop an atomic bomb; by the end of World War II its population was more than 75,000. Ownership of the community passed to the residents in the late 1950s.

Electronic equipment and scientific instruments are also manufactured here. Oak Ridge Associated Universities is a research and educational center.

oarfish any of a family *Regalecidae* of deep-sea bony fishes, found in warm parts of the Atlantic, Pacific, and Indian oceans. Oarfish are large, up to 30 ft/9 m long, elongated, and compressed, with a fin along the back and a manelike crest behind the head. They have a small mouth, no teeth or scales, and large eyes. They are often reported as sea serpents.

oarweed or **tangleweed** any of several large, coarse, brown seaweeds (algae) found on the lower shore and below, especially *Laminaria digitata*. This species has fronds 3–6 ft/1–2 m long, a thick stalk, and a frond divided into flat fingers. In Japan and Korea it is cultivated and harvested commercially.

OAS abbreviation for ⟡*Organization of American States*.

oasis area of land made fertile by the presence of water near the surface in an otherwise arid region. The occurrence of oases affects the distribution of plants, animals, and people in the desert regions of the world.

oat type of grass, genus *Avena*, a cereal food. The plant has long, narrow leaves and a stiff straw stem; the panicles of flowers, and later of grain, hang downward. The cultivated oat *Avena sativa* is produced for human and animal food.

It was an early domesticant (as a weed in the wheatfields) and survived cool temperatures where wheat had trouble growing. It is especially hardy in N Europe.

Oates Joyce Carol 1938– . US writer. Her novels, often containing surrealism and violence, include *A Garden of Earthly Delights* 1967, *Them* 1969, *Unholy Loves* 1979, *A Bloodsmoor Romance* 1982, and *Because It Is Bitter, and Because It Is My Heart* 1990.

Born in Lockport, New York, Oates uses genres that range from romance to mystery to history, but most of her novels have supernatural elements. She also has written many short stories—notably, "Where Are You Going, Where Have You Been?"—poems, reviews, and critical essays. Her other works include *Goddess and Other Women* 1974, *The Assassins* 1975, *Bellefleur* 1980, *Angel of Light* 1981, *Last Days* 1984, *Marya: A Life* 1986, *You Must Remember This* 1987, *The Assignation* 1988, and *American Appetites* 1989.

oath solemn promise to tell the truth or perform some duty, combined with an appeal to a deity or something held sacred. In the US witnesses raise their right hand in taking the oath.

OAU abbreviation for ⟡*Organization of African Unity*.

Oaxaca capital of a state of the same name in the Sierra Madre del Sur mountain range, central Mexico; population (1990) 212,900; former hometown of presidents Benito Juárez and Porfirio Diaz; industries include food processing, textiles, and handicrafts.

Ob river in Asian Russia, flowing 2,100 mi/ 3,380 km from the Altai Mountains through the W Siberian Plain to the Gulf of Ob in the Arctic Ocean. With its main tributary, the **Irtysh**, it is 3,480 mi/5,600 km.

Although frozen for half the year, and subject to flooding, the Ob is a major transportation route. Novosobirsk and Barnaul are the main ports.

obelisk tall, tapering column of stone, much used in ancient Egyptian and Roman architecture. Examples are Cleopatra's Needles 1475 BC, one of which is in London, the other in New York.

Oberammergau village in Bavaria, Germany, 45 mi/72 km SW of Munich; population (1980) 5,000. A Christian ⟡passion play has been performed here every ten years since 1634 (except during the world wars) to commemorate the ending of the Black Death plague.

Oberon in folklore, king of the elves or fairies and, according to the 13th-century French romance *Huon of Bordeaux*, an illegitimate son of Julius Caesar. Shakespeare used the character in *A Midsummer Night's Dream*.

obesity condition of being overweight (generally, 20% or more above the desirable weight for one's sex, build, and height). Obesity increases susceptibility to disease, strains the vital organs, and lessens life expectancy; it is remedied by healthy diet and exercise, unless caused by systemic (glandular) problems.

obi or **obeah** form of witchcraft practiced in the West Indies. It combines elements of Christianity and African religions, such as snake worship.

object-oriented programming (OOP) computer programming based on "objects," in which data are closely linked to the procedures that operate on them. For example, a circle on the screen might be an object: it has data, such as a center point and a radius, as well as procedures for moving it, erasing it, changing its size, and so on.

The technique originated with the Simula and Smalltalk languages in the 1960s and early 1970s, but it has now been incorporated into many general-purpose programming languages.

oboe musical instrument of the ⟡woodwind family. Played vertically, it is a wooden tube with a bell, is double-reeded, and has a yearning, poignant tone. Its range is almost three octaves. Oboe concertos have been composed by Vivaldi, Albinoni, Richard Strauss, and others.

The ⟡cor anglais is similar to the oboe but pitched lower. The **oboe d'amore**, commonly used by Bach and other 18th-century composers, has a narrower bore than the modern instrument.

Obote (Apollo) Milton 1924– . Ugandan politician who led the independence movement from 1961. He became prime minister 1962 and was president 1966–71 and 1980–85, being overthrown by first Idi ⟡Amin and then by Lt Gen Tito Okello.

Obrenovich Serbian dynasty that ruled 1816–42 and 1859–1903. The dynasty engaged in a feud with the rival house of Karageorgevich, which obtained the throne by the murder of the last Obrenovich 1903.

obscenity law law prohibiting the publishing of any material that tends to deprave or corrupt. Publication of any books, films, etc., that, when judged by contemporary standards, are found to have a prurient interest in sex, be patently offensive, and have no serious artistic, scientific, or social value is an offense.

observation in science, the perception of a phenomenon—for example, examining the Moon through a telescope, watching mice to discover their mating habits, or seeing how a plant grows.

Traditionally, observation was seen as entirely separate from theory, free from preconceptions and therefore lending support to the idea of scientific objectivity. However, as the preceding examples show, observations are ordered according to a pre-existing theory; for instance, one cannot observe mating behavior without having decided what mating behavior might look like. In addition many observations actually affect the behavior of the observed (for instance, of mating mice).

observatory site or facility for observing astronomical or meteorological phenomena. The earliest recorded observatory was in Alexandria, N Africa, built by Ptolemy Soter in about 300 BC. The modern observatory dates from the invention of the telescope. Observatories may be ground-based, carried on aircraft, or sent into orbit as satellites, in space stations, and on the space shuttle.

The erection of observatories was revived in W Asia about AD 1000, and extended to Europe. The observatory built on the island of Hven (now Ven) in Denmark 1576 for Tycho ⃝Brahe was elaborate, but survived only to 1597. It was followed by those in Paris 1667, Greenwich (the ⃝Royal Greenwich Observatory) 1675, and Kew, England. Most early observatories were near towns, but with the advent of big telescopes, clear skies with little background light, and hence high, remote sites, became essential.

The most powerful optical telescopes covering the sky are at ⃝Mauna Kea; Mount ⃝Palomar; Kitt Peak, Arizona; La Palma, Canary Islands; Cerro Tololo and La Silla, Chile; Siding Spring, Australia; and Mount Semirodniki in the Caucasus. ⃝Radio astronomy observatories include ⃝Jodrell Bank; the Mullard, Cambridge, England; ⃝Arecibo; Effelsberg, Germany; and ⃝Parkes. The Hubble Space Telescope was launched into orbit April 1990. The Very Large Telescope is under construction by the European Southern Observatory (ESO) in the mountains of N Chile, for completion by 1997.

obsession repetitive unwanted thought or compulsive action that is often recognized by the sufferer as being irrational, but which nevertheless causes distress. It can be associated with the irresistible urge of an individual to carry out a repetitive series of actions.

For example, a person may fear that the gas is not switched off. However irrational the fear, the gas tap will be checked again and again.

obsidian black or dark-colored glassy volcanic rock, chemically similar to ⃝granite, but formed by cooling rapidly on the Earth's surface at low pressure.

The glassy texture is the result of rapid cooling, which inhibits the growth of crystals. Obsidian was valued by the early civilizations of Mexico for making sharp-edged tools and ceremonial sculptures.

obstetrics medical specialty concerned with the management of pregnancy, childbirth, and the immediate postnatal period.

Ocala city in N central Florida, SE of Gainesville; seat of Marion County; population (1990) 42,000. It is a marketing and shipping center for the citrus, poultry, cotton, and tobacco products grown in the surrounding area. Tourism is also vital to the economy.

O'Casey Sean. Adopted name of John Casey 1884–1964. Irish dramatist. His early plays are tragicomedies, blending realism with symbolism and poetic with vernacular speech: *The Shadow of a Gunman* 1922, *Juno and the Paycock* 1925, and *The Plough and the Stars* 1926. Later plays include *Red Roses for Me* 1946 and *The Drums of Father Ned* 1960.

He also wrote the antiwar drama *The Silver Tassie* 1929, *The Star Turns Red* 1940, *Oak Leaves and Lavender* 1947, and a six-volume autobiography.

Occam or *Ockham* William of c. 1300–1349. English philosopher and scholastic logician who revived the fundamentals of nominalism. As a Franciscan monk he defended evangelical poverty against Pope John XXII, becoming known as the Invincible Doctor. He was imprisoned in Avignon, France, on charges of heresy 1328 but escaped to Munich, Germany, where he died. The principle of reducing assumptions to the absolute minimum is known as *Occam's razor*.

occultation in astronomy, the temporary obscuring of a star by a body in the Solar System. Occultations are used to provide information about changes in an orbit, and the structure of objects in space, such as radio sources.

The exact shapes and sizes of planets and asteroids can be found when they occult stars. The rings of Uranus were discovered when that planet occulted a star 1977.

occupational psychology study of human behavior at work. It includes dealing with problems in organizations, advising on management difficulties, and investigating the relationship between humans and machines (as in the design of aircraft controls; see also ⃝ergonomics). Another area is ⃝psychometrics and the use of assessment to assist in selection of personnel.

ocean great mass of salt water. Strictly speaking three oceans exist—the Atlantic, Indian, and Pacific—to which the Arctic is often added. They cover approximately 70% or 140,000,000 sq mi/363,000,000 sq km of the total surface area of the Earth. Water levels recorded in the world's oceans have shown an increase of 4–6 in/10–15 cm over the past 100 years.

depth (average) 12,000 ft/3,660 m, but shallow ledges 600 ft/180 m run out from the continents, beyond which the continental slope reaches down to the ⃝abyssal zone, the largest area, ranging from 6,500–19,500 ft/2,000–6,000 m. Only the deep-sea trenches go deeper, the deepest recorded being 36,201 ft/11,034 m (by the *Vityaz*, USSR) in the Mariana Trench of the W Pacific 1957

features deep trenches (off E and SE Asia, and western South America), volcanic belts (in the W Pacific and E Indian Ocean), and ocean ridges (in the mid-Atlantic, E Pacific, and Indian Ocean)

temperature varies on the surface with latitude (–2°C to +29°C); decreases rapidly to 1,200 ft/370 m, then more slowly to 7,200 ft/2,200 m; and hardly at all beyond that

water contents salinity averages about 3%; minerals commercially extracted include bromine, magnesium, potassium, salt; those potentially recoverable include aluminum, calcium, copper, gold, manganese, silver.

oceanarium large display tank in which aquatic animals and plants live together much as they would in their natural environment. The first oceanarium was created by the explorer and naturalist W Douglas Burden 1938 in Florida.

oceanography study of the oceans, their origin, composition, structure, history, and wildlife (seabirds, fish, plankton, and other organisms). Much oceanography uses computer simulations to plot the possible movements of the waters, and many studies are carried out by remote sensing.

Oceanography involves the study of water movements—currents, waves, and tides—and the chemical and physical properties of the seawater. It deals with the origin and topography of the ocean floor—ocean trenches and ridges formed by ⃝plate tectonics, and continental shelves from the submerged portions of the continents.

The World Ocean Circulation Experiment, a seven-year project begun 1990, involves researchers from 44 countries examining the physics of the ocean and its role in the climate of the Earth. It is based at Southampton University, England.

ocean ridge mountain range on the seabed indicating the presence of a constructive plate margin (where tectonic plates are moving apart and magma rises to the surface; see ⃝plate tectonics). Ocean ridges, such as the ⃝Mid-Atlantic Ridge, consist of many segments offset along ⃝faults, and can rise thousands of meters above the surrounding seabed.

Ocean ridges usually have a ⃝rift valley along their crests, indicating where the flanks are being pulled apart by the growth of the plates of the ⃝lithosphere beneath. The crests are generally free of sediment; increasing depths of sediment are found with increasing distance down the flanks.

ocean trench deep trench in the seabed indicating the presence of a destructive margin (produced by the movements of ⃝plate tectonics). The subduction or dragging downward of one plate of the ⃝lithosphere beneath another means that the ocean floor is pulled down. Ocean trenches are found around the edge of the Pacific Ocean and the NE Indian Ocean; minor ones occur in the Caribbean and near the Falkland Islands.

Ocean trenches represent the deepest parts of the ocean floor, the deepest being the ⃝Mariana Trench which has a depth of 36,201 ft/11,034 m. At depths of below 3.6 mi/6 km there is no light and very high pressure; ocean trenches are inhabited by crustaceans, coelenterates (for example, sea anemones), polychaetes (a type of worm), mollusks, and echinoderms.

Oceanus in Greek mythology, one of the ⃝Titans, the god of a river supposed to encircle the Earth. He was the ancestor of other river gods and the nymphs of the seas and rivers.

ocelot wild cat *Felis pardalis* of the southwestern US, Mexico, and Central and South America, up to 3 ft/1 m long with a 1.5 ft/45 cm tail. It weighs about 40 lb/18 kg and has a pale yellowish coat marked with longitudinal stripes and blotches. Hunted for its fur, it is close to extinction.

Ochoa Severo 1905– . Spanish-born US biochemist. He discovered an enzyme able to assemble units of the nucleic acid ▷RNA in 1955, while working at New York University. For his work toward the synthesis of RNA, Ochoa shared the 1959 Nobel Prize for Medicine with Arthur ▷Kornberg.

Ochs Adolph Simon 1858–1935. US newspaper publisher. In 1896 he gained control of the then-faltering *New York Times* and transformed it into a serious, authoritative publication. Among Ochs's innovations were a yearly index and a weekly book-review section.

Born in Cincinnati, Ohio, and raised in Tennessee, Ochs began his career in the newspaper industry as an office boy for the *Knoxville Chronicle* 1869. Moving to Chattanooga, he worked at various jobs before borrowing funds to purchase the *Chattanooga Times*. Ochs was successful with this paper and in 1891 founded the Southern Associated Press, later moving to take over *The New York Times*.

O'Connell Daniel 1775–1847. Irish politician, called "the Liberator." Although ineligible, as a Roman Catholic, to take his seat, he was elected member of Parliament for County Clare 1828 and so forced the government to grant Catholic emancipation. In Parliament he cooperated with the Whigs in the hope of obtaining concessions until 1841, when he launched his campaign for repeal of the union.

In 1823 he founded the Catholic Association to press Roman Catholic claims.

O'Connor Flannery 1925–1964. US novelist and short-story writer. Her works have a great sense of evil and sin, and often explore the religious sensibility of the Deep South. Her short stories include *A Good Man Is Hard to Find* 1955, *Everything That Rises Must Converge* 1965, *The Habit of Being* 1979, and *Flannery O'Connor: Collected Works* 1988.

Her novels are *Wise Blood* 1952 and *The Violent Bear It Away* 1960. Her work exemplifies the postwar revival of the ▷Gothic novel in Southern US fiction.

O'Connor Sandra Day 1930– . US jurist and the first female associate justice of the US Supreme Court 1981– . Considered a moderate conservative, she dissented in *Texas v Johnson* 1990, a decision that ruled that the legality of burning the US flag in protest was protected by the First Amendment.

Born in El Paso, Texas, O'Connor attended Stanford University and Stanford University Law School. She practiced law in California, in Germany with the US Quartermaster Corps, and in Arizona, where she also became active in the Republican Party. In 1965 she became an assistant Arizona attorney general and in 1969 was appointed to a vacancy in the state senate, to which she was later elected and of which she became majority leader 1972. In 1974 she was elected a county court judge and in 1979 was appointed to the state court of appeals. In 1981 President Reagan appointed her to the US Supreme Court, where she generally espoused a conservative position.

OCR abbreviation for ▷*optical character recognition*.

octal number system number system to the base eight, used in computing. The highest digit that can appear in the octal system is seven. Normal decimal, or base-ten, numbers

may be considered to be written under column headings based on the number ten. For example, the decimal number 567 stands for:

100s	10s	1s
(10^2)	(10^1)	(10^0)
5	6	7

Octal, or base-eight, numbers can be thought of as written under column headings based on the number eight. For example, the octal number 567 stands for:

64s	8s	1s
(8^2)	(8^1)	(8^0)
5	6	7

The octal number 567 is therefore equivalent to the decimal number 375, since $(5 \times 64) + (6 \times 8) + (7 \times 1) = 375$.

The octal number system is sometimes used by computer programmers as an alternative to the ▷hexadecimal number system.

octane rating numerical classification of petroleum fuels indicating their combustion characteristics.

The efficient running of an ▷internal-combustion engine depends on the ignition of a gasoline–air mixture at the correct time during the cycle of the engine. Higher-rated gasoline burns faster than lower-rated fuels. The use of the correct grade must be matched to the engine.

Octans constellation in the southern hemisphere containing the southern celestial pole. The closest naked-eye star to the south celestial pole is fifth-magnitude Sigma Octantis.

It is one of the 14 constellations conceived by the French astronomer La Caille in the 18th century to fill the star-poor regions near the South Pole still undelineated by his time.

octave in music, a distance of eight notes as measured on the white notes of a piano keyboard. It corresponds to the consonance of first and second harmonics.

Octavian original name of ▷Augustus, the first Roman emperor.

octet rule in chemistry, rule stating that elements combine in a way that gives them the electronic structure of the nearest ▷inert gas. All the inert gases except helium have eight electrons in their outermost shell, hence the term octet.

October Revolution second stage of the ▷Russian Revolution 1917, when, on Oct 24 (Nov 6 in the Western calendar), the Red Guards under Trotsky, and on orders from Lenin, seized the Winter Palace and arrested members of the Provisional Government. The following day the Second All-Russian Congress of Soviets handed over power to the Bolsheviks.

Octobrists group of Russian liberal constitutional politicians who accepted the reforming October Manifesto instituted by Tsar Nicholas II after the 1905 revolution and rejected more radical reforms.

octopus any of an order (Octopoda) of ▷cephalopods, genus *Octopus*, having a round or oval body and eight arms with rows of suckers on each. They occur in all temperate and tropical seas, where they feed on crabs and other small animals.

Octopuses can vary their coloration according to their background and can swim using their arms as well as by a type of jet propulsion by means of their funnel. They are as intelligent as some vertebrates and not easily stimulated to aggression. Octopuses are shy creatures that release clouds of ink when frightened.

The common octopus *O. vulgaris* may reach 6 ft/2 m, and the rare, deep-sea giant octopus *O. apollyon* may span more than 32 ft/10 m. There are a few species of Australian blue-ringed octopods, genus *Hapalochlaena*; they can kill a human being in 15 minutes as a result of their venomous bite.

ode lyric poem of complex form, originally chanted to a musical accompaniment. Ancient Greek writers of odes include Sappho, Pindar, Horace, and Catullus; and, among English poets, Spenser, Milton, Dryden, and Keats.

Oder (Polish **Odra**) European river flowing N from Czechoslovakia to the Baltic Sea (the river Neisse is a tributary); length 550 mi/885 km.

Oder–Neisse Line border between Poland and East Germany agreed at the Potsdam Conference 1945 at the end of World War II, named after the two rivers that formed the frontier.

Odessa seaport in Ukraine, on the Black Sea, capital of Odessa region; population (1989) 1,115,000. Products include chemicals, pharmaceuticals, and machinery.

Odessa was founded by Catherine II 1795 near the site of an ancient Greek settlement. Occupied by Germany 1941–44, it suffered severe damage under the Soviet scorched-earth policy and from German destruction.

Odessa city in W Texas, SW of Big Springs; seat of Ector County; population (1990) 89,700. It grew up among the oil fields located here. Industries include petroleum products; it is also a livestock processing and shipping center.

Odets Clifford 1906–1963. US playwright, famous for his play about a taxi drivers' strike, *Waiting for Lefty* 1935. The most renowned of the Depression-era social-protest playwrights, he also wrote such plays as *Awake and Sing* 1935, perhaps his finest, and *Golden Boy* 1937. In the late 1930s he went to Hollywood and became a successful film writer and director, but he continued to write plays, including *The Country Girl* 1950.

Odin chief god of Scandinavian mythology, the **Woden** or **Wotan** of the Germanic peoples. A sky god, he lives in Asgard, at the top of the world-tree, and from the Valkyries (the divine maidens) receives the souls of heroic slain warriors, feasting with them in his great hall, Valhalla. The wife of Odin is Freya, or Frigga, and Thor is their son. Wednesday is named after Odin.

Odoacer 433–493. King of Italy from 476, when he deposed Romulus Augustulus, the last Roman emperor. He was a leader of the barbarian mercenaries employed by Rome. He was overthrown and killed by Theodoric the Great, king of the Ostrogoths.

Odysseus chief character of Homer's *Odyssey*, and mentioned also in the *Iliad* as one of the leaders of the Greek forces at the siege of Troy, a man of courage and ingenuity. He is said to have been the ruler of the island of Ithaca.

Odyssey Greek epic poem in 24 books, probably written before 700 BC, attributed to ▷Homer. It describes the ten-year voyage of Odysseus after the fall of Troy in the 12th century BC and the vengeance he takes on the suitors of his wife, Penelope, on his return. During his wanderings he has many adventures, including encounters with the Cyclops, Circe, Scylla and Charybdis, and the Sirens.

OE abbreviation for **Old English**; see ▷English language.

OECD abbreviation for ⇨*Organization for Economic Cooperation and Development.*

Oedipus in Greek legend, king of Thebes who unwittingly killed his father and married his mother, in fulfillment of a prophecy. When he learned what he had done, he put out his eyes.

Left to die at birth because his father Laius had been warned by an oracle that his son would kill him, Oedipus was saved and brought up by the king of Corinth. Oedipus killed Laius in a quarrel (without recognizing him). Because Oedipus saved Thebes from the Sphinx, he was granted the Theban kingdom and Jocasta (wife of Laius and his own mother) as his wife. After four children had been born, the truth was discovered. Jocasta hanged herself, Oedipus blinded himself, and as an exiled wanderer was guided by his daughter, Antigone.

Oedipus complex in psychology, term coined by Sigmund ⇨Freud for the unconscious antagonism of a son to his father, whom he sees as a rival for his mother's affection. For a girl antagonistic to her mother, as a rival for her father's affection, the term is *Electra complex.*

Freud saw this as a universal part of childhood development, which in most children is resolved during late childhood. Contemporary theory places less importance on the Oedipus/Electra complex than did Freud and his followers.

Oedipus Tyrannus or **Oedipus the King** 409 BC and *Oedipus at Colonus* 401 BC, two Greek tragedies by ⇨Sophocles based on the legend of Oedipus, king of Thebes.

oersted unit (symbol Oe) of ⇨magnetic field strength, now replaced by the SI unit ampere per meter. It is equal to a force of one dyne acting upon a unit magnetic pole in a vacuum. The Earth's magnetic field is about 0.5 oersted; the field near the poles of a small bar magnet is several hundred oersteds; and a powerful ⇨electromagnet can have a field strength of 30,000 oersteds.

Oersted Hans Christian 1777–1851. Danish physicist who founded the science of electromagnetism. In 1820 he discovered the ⇨magnetic field associated with an electric current.

O'Faolain Sean (John Whelan) 1900–1991. Irish novelist, short-story writer, and biographer. His first novel, *A Nest of Simple Folk* 1933, was followed by an edition of translated Gaelic, *The Silver Branch* 1938. His many biographies include *Daniel O'Connell* 1938 and *De Valera* 1939, about the nationalist whom he had fought beside in the Irish Republican Army.

Offa died 796. King of Mercia, England, from 757. He conquered Essex, Kent, Sussex, and Surrey; defeated the Welsh and the West Saxons; and established Mercian supremacy over all England south of the river Humber.

Offaly county of the Republic of Ireland, in the province of Leinster, between Galway on the W and Kildare on the E; area 772 sq mi/2,000 sq km; population (1991) 58,500.

Towns include the county town of Tullamore. Features include the rivers Shannon (along the W boundary), Brosna, Clodagh, and Broughill and the Slieve Bloom mountains in the SE.

Offa's Dyke defensive earthwork along the Welsh border, of which there are remains from the mouth of the River Dee to that of the River Severn. It represents the boundary secured by ⇨Offa's wars with Wales.

The dyke covered a distance of 149 mi/240 km, of which 81 mi/130 km are still standing.

Offenbach Jacques 1819–1880. French composer. He wrote light opera, initially for presentation at the *Bouffes parisiens.* Among his works are *Orphée aux enfers/Orpheus in the Underworld* 1858, *La belle Hélène* 1864, and *Les contes d'Hoffmann/The Tales of Hoffmann* 1881.

offset printing the most common method of ⇨printing, which uses smooth (often rubber) printing plates. It works on the principle of ⇨lithography: that grease and water repel one another.

The printing plate is prepared using a photographic technique, resulting in a type image that attracts greasy printing ink. On the printing press the plate is wrapped around a cylinder and wetted and inked in turn. The ink adheres only to the type area, and this image is then transferred via an intermediate blanket cylinder to the paper.

O'Flaherty Liam 1897–1984. Irish author, best known for his short stories published in volumes such as *Spring Sowing* 1924, *The Tent* 1926, and *Two Lovely Beasts* 1948. His novels, set in County Mayo, include *The Neighbour's Wife* 1923, *The Informer* 1925, and *Land* 1946.

Ogaden desert region in Harar province, SE Ethiopia, that borders on Somalia. It is a desert plateau, rising to 3,280 ft/1,000 m, inhabited mainly by Somali nomads practicing arid farming. The area became one of five new autonomous provinces created in Ethiopia 1987.

A claim to the area was made by Somalia in the 1960s, resulting in guerrilla fighting and major Somali advances during 1977. By 1980 Ethiopia, backed by the USSR and Cuba, was again in virtual control of the area, but armed clashes continued. In 1988 diplomatic relations were restored between Ethiopia and Somalia and troops withdrawn from their shared border. Internal troubles in Somalia 1990 created a large refugee population in E Ogaden.

Ogallala Aquifer the largest source of groundwater in the US, stretching from southern South Dakota to NW Texas. The overexploitation of this water resource has resulted in the loss of over 18% of the irrigated farmland of Oklahoma and Texas in the period 1940–90.

Ogden city in N Utah, on the Weber and Ogden rivers, N of Salt Lake City; population (1990) 63,900. It is a railroad, trading, and military supply center; Hill Air Force Base is nearby. Tourism is also important to the economy.

Oglethorpe James Edward 1696–1785. English soldier and colonizer of Georgia. He served in parliament for 32 years and in 1732 obtained a charter for the colony of Georgia, intended as a refuge for debtors and for European Protestants.

The colony was also intended by the British to act as a buffer against Spanish Florida. The colonists were selected carefully, and every aspect of life was planned and supervised.

Oglethorpe served as Georgia's first colonial governor 1733–34. In 1743, frustrated by settlers' complaints, he returned to England.

OGPU name 1923–34 of the Soviet secret police, later the ⇨KGB.

Ogun state of SW Nigeria; population (1988) 3,397,900; area 6,474 sq mi/16,762 sq km; capital Abeokuta.

OH abbreviation for the state of ⇨*Ohio.*

Ohio

Columbus

O Henry adopted name of US author William Sydney ⇨Porter.

O'Higgins Bernardo 1778–1842. Chilean revolutionary, known as "the Liberator of Chile." He was a leader of the struggle for independence from Spanish rule 1810–17 and head of the first permanent national government 1817–23.

Ohio river in the US, 980 mi/1,580 km long; it is formed by the union of the Allegheny and Monongahela at Pittsburgh, Pennsylvania, and flows SW until it joins the River Mississippi at Cairo, Illinois.

The Ohio carries twice the freight tonnage of the Panama Canal—bulk cargos such as iron ore, oil, chemicals, metals, salt, sand, gravel, and, especially, coal from West Virginia, Indiana, Kentucky, and E Ohio fields. Cincinnati, Ohio, and Louisville, Kentucky, are the chief cities on its banks. Flooding periodically has damaged river communities, most severely in 1937.

Ohio state in N central US; nickname Buckeye State
area 41,341 sq mi/107,100 sq km
capital Columbus
cities Cleveland, Cincinnati, Dayton, Akron, Toledo, Youngstown, Canton
population (1990) 10,847,100
features Ohio River; Lake Erie; Serpent Mound, a 4-ft/1.3-m embankment, 1,330 ft/405 m long and about 18 ft/5 m across (built by ⇨Hopewell Indians about 2nd–1st centuries BC)
products coal, cereals, livestock, dairy foods, machinery, chemicals, steel, motor vehicles, automotive and aircraft parts, rubber products, office equipment, refined petroleum
famous people Sherwood Anderson, Neil Armstrong, Hart Crane, Thomas Edison, James Garfield, John Glenn, Ulysses S Grant, Zane Grey, Warren Harding, Benjamin Harrison, William H Harrison, Rutherford B Hayes, William McKinley, Paul Newman, Jesse Owens, John D Rockefeller, William T Sherman, William H Taft, James Thurber, Orville and Wilbur Wright
history explored for France by René La Salle 1669; ceded to Britain by France 1763; first settled at Marietta (capital of the Northwest Territory) by Europeans 1788; statehood 1803. By 1850 Ohio was the third most populous state. In the Civil War, Ohio gave the Union its greatest generals—U S Grant, W T Sherman, and P Sheridan. In the 1870s J D Rockefeller of Cleveland organized the Standard Oil Company, which soon controlled oil refining and distribution throughout the nation. At the same time, Akron became rubber capital of the world. For a century, Ohio remained a leader in heavy industry, but manufacturing peaked in 1969; agriculture and mining remain important.

Seeking service and high-technology industries, the state needs to overcome an aging infrastructure and urban pollution and decay.

Tourism continues as a valuable revenue producer.

ohm SI unit (symbol Ω) of electrical ⟡resistance (the property of a substance that restricts the flow of electrons through it).

It was originally defined with reference to the resistance of a column of mercury, but is now taken as the resistance between two points when a potential difference of one volt between them produces a current of one ampere.

Ohm Georg Simon 1787–1854. German physicist who studied electricity and discovered the fundamental law that bears his name. The SI unit of electrical resistance is named after him, and the unit of conductance (the reverse of resistance) was formerly called the mho, which is Ohm spelled backward.

ohmic heating method of heating used in the food-processing industry, in which an electric current is passed through foodstuffs to sterilize them before packing. The heating effect is similar to that obtained by microwaves in that electrical energy is transformed into heat throughout the whole volume of the food, not just at the surface.

Ohmic heating is suitable for foods containing chunks of meat or fruit. It is an alternative to in-can sterilization and has been used to produce canned foods such as meat chunks, prawns, baked beans, fruit, and vegetables.

Ohm's law law that states that the current flowing in a metallic conductor maintained at constant temperature is directly proportional to the potential difference (voltage) between its ends. The law was discovered by Georg Ohm 1827.

If a current of I amperes flows between two points in a conductor across which the potential difference is V volts, then V/I is a constant called the ⟡resistance R ohms between those two points. Hence:

$$V/I = R$$

or

$$V = IR$$

Not all conductors obey Ohm's law; those that do are called **ohmic conductors**.

Ohrid, Lake lake on the frontier between Albania and Yugoslavia; area 135 sq mi/ 350 sq km.

oil flammable substance, usually insoluble in water, and composed chiefly of carbon and hydrogen. Oils may be solids (fats and waxes) or liquids. The three main types are: ⟡**essential oils**, obtained from plants; **fixed oils**, obtained from animals and plants; and **mineral oils**, obtained chiefly from the refining of ⟡petroleum.

Essential oils are volatile liquids that have the odor of their plant source and are used in perfumes, flavoring essences, and in aromatherapy. Fixed oils are mixtures of ⟡lipids, of varying consistency, found in both animals (for example, fish oils) and plants (in nuts and seeds); they are used as foods and as lubricants, and in the making of soaps, paints, and varnishes. Mineral oils are composed of a mixture of hydrocarbons, and are used as fuels and lubricants. Eight of the 14 top-earning companies in the US in 1990 (led by Exxon with $7 billion in sales) are in the global petroleum industry.

oil palm African ⟡palm tree *Elaeis guineensis*, the fruit of which yields valuable oils, used as food or processed into margarine, soaps, and livestock feeds.

oil spill leakage of oil from an oceangoing tanker, a pipeline, or other source. Oil spills are frequent and may cause enormous ecological harm. In Feb 1991 Iraqi military forces opened oil pipelines to leak into the Persian Gulf as part of military tactics during the Gulf War; the coalition forces also damaged oil facilities causing leakage. Together the largest-ever oil spill pollutes the Gulf. In March 1989 the *Exxon Valdez* went aground, covering in oil 4,800 sq mi/ 1,850 sq km in Prince William Sound, Alaska, and killing 35,000 sea birds, 10,000 otters, and at least nine whales. The spill left pools of oil up to 3 ft/1 m deep on some beaches.

In Dec 1989 an Iranian tanker leaked 70,000 tons (19 million gallons) off the coast of Morocco. In Jan 1990 a broken Exxon pipeline leaked 567,000 gallons into New York harbor; in June 1990 another 260,000 gallons was spilled in New York harbor and a tanker carrying 38 million gallons caught fire and leaked oil in the Gulf of Mexico, posing a serious threat to local shrimp nurseries and wildlife refuges. In Feb 1990 300,000 gallons leaked from a damaged tanker off Southern California, fouling miles of shoreline.

Oistrakh David Fyodorovich 1908–1974. Soviet violinist, celebrated for performances of both standard and contemporary Russian repertoire. Shostakovich wrote both his violin concertos for him. His son *Igor* (1931–) is equally renowned as a violinist.

He was born in Odessa, S Ukraine.

OK abbreviation for the state of ⟡*Oklahoma*.

okapi ruminant *Okapia johnstoni* of the giraffe family, although with much shorter legs and neck, found in the tropical rainforests of central Africa. Purplish brown with a creamy face and black and white stripes on the legs and hindquarters, it is excellently camouflaged. Okapis have remained virtually unchanged for millions of years.

The okapi was unknown to Europeans until 1901; now only a few hundred are thought to survive.

Okeechobee lake in the N Everglades, Florida; 40 mi/65 km long and 25 mi/40 km wide. It is the largest lake in S US, about 700 sq mi/1,800 sq km.

Okeechobee has no single outlet but flows S through the Everglades.

O'Keeffe Georgia 1887–1986. US painter, based mainly in New York and New Mexico, known chiefly for her large, semiabstract studies of flowers and bones, such as *Black Iris* 1926 (Metropolitan Museum of Art, New York) and the *Pelvis Series* of the 1940s.

Her mature style stressed contours and subtle tonal transitions, which often transformed the subject into a powerful and erotic abstract image. In 1946 she settled in New Mexico, where the desert landscape inspired many of her paintings.

She was married (1924–46) to photographer and art exhibitor Alfred Stieglitz, in whose gallery her work was first shown.

Okefenokee swamp in SE Georgia and NE Florida, rich in alligators, bears, deer, and birds. Much of its 660 sq mi/1,700 sq km forms a natural wildlife refuge. It is drained by the St Marys and Suwannee rivers.

Okhotsk, Sea of arm of the N Pacific between the Kamchatka Peninsula and Sakhalin and bordered southward by the Kuril Islands; area 361,700 sq mi/937,000 sq km. Free of ice only in summer, it is often fogbound.

Okinawa largest of the Japanese ⟡Ryukyu Islands in the W Pacific
area 869 sq mi/2,250 sq km

Oklahoma

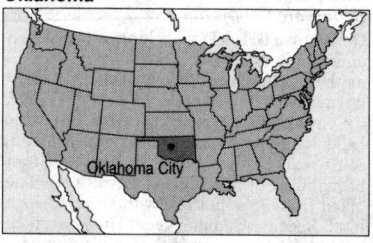

capital Naha
population (1990) 3,145,500
history captured by the US in the **Battle of Okinawa** Apr 1–June 21, 1945, with 47,000 US casualties (12,000 dead) and 60,000 Japanese (only a few hundred survived as prisoners). During the invasion over 150,000 Okinawans, mainly civilians, died; many massacred by Japanese forces. The island was returned to Japan 1972.

Oklahoma state in S central US; nickname Sooner State
area 69,905 sq mi/181,100 sq km
capital Oklahoma City
cities Tulsa, Lawton, Norman, Enid
features Arkansas, Red, and Canadian rivers; Wichita and Ozark mountain ranges; the high plains have Indian reservations (Cherokee, Chickasaw, Choctaw, Creek, and Seminole); American Indian Hall of Fame; Chicasaw National Recreation Area
products cereals, peanuts, cotton, livestock, oil, natural gas, helium, machinery and other metal products
population (1990) 3,145,600
famous people John Berryman, Ralph Ellison, Woody Guthrie, Mickey Mantle, Will Rogers, Jim Thorpe
history explored for Spain by Francisco de Coronado 1541; most acquired by the US from France with the ⟡Louisiana Purchase 1803.

The W Panhandle became US territory when Texas was annexed 1845. It was divided into Indian Territory and Oklahoma Territory 1890, part of which was thrown open to settlers with lotteries and other hurried distribution of land. Together with what remained of Indian Territory, it became a state 1907. Oil was struck 1897, and the state led all others in oil production until 1928. The 1930s brought drought, dust storms, and an exodus of many, especially to California. Economic growth resumed thereafter, particularly in the 1970s, when world oil prices rose.

Oklahoma City industrial city (oil refining, machinery, aircraft, telephone equipment), capital of Oklahoma, on the Canadian River; population (1990) 444,700. On April 22, 1889, a tent city of nearly 10,000 inhabitants was set up overnight as the area was opened to settlement. In 1910 Oklahoma City had 64,000 people and became the state capital.

Oil was discovered in 1928, and derricks are situated even on the state capitol grounds. A General Motors auto plant was established here 1979.

Okuma Shigenobu 1838–1922. Japanese politician and prime minister 1898 and 1914–16. He presided over Japanese pressure for territorial concessions in China, before retiring 1916.

Olaf five kings of Norway, including:

Olaf I Tryggvesson 969–1000. King of Norway from 995. He began the conversion of Norway to Christianity and was killed in a sea battle against the Danes and Swedes.

Olaf II Haraldsson 995–1030. King of Norway from 1015. He offended his subjects by his centralizing policy and zeal for Christianity, and was killed in battle by Norwegian rebel chiefs backed by ◊Canute of Denmark. He was declared the patron saint of Norway 1164.

Olaf V 1903–1991. King of Norway from 1957, when he succeeded his father, Haakon VII.

Olbers Heinrich 1758–1840. German astronomer. A medical doctor, Olbers was a keen amateur astronomer and a founder member of the *Celestial Police*, a group of astronomers who attempted to locate a supposed "missing planet" between Mars and Jupiter.

During his search he discovered two ◊asteroids, Pallas 1802 and Vesta 1807. Also credited to Olbers are a number of comet discoveries, a new method of calculating cometary orbits, and the stating of Olbers' paradox. In 1820 Olbers retired from medicine to devote himself to astronomy.

Olbers' paradox question put forward 1826 by Heinrich Olbers, who asked: If the universe is infinite in extent and filled with stars, why is the sky dark at night? The answer is that the stars do not live infinitely long, so there is not enough starlight to fill the universe. A wrong answer, frequently given, is that the expansion of the universe weakens the starlight.

old age later years of life. The causes of progressive degeneration of bodily and mental processes associated with it are still not precisely known, but every one of the phenomena of ◊aging can occur at almost any age, and the process does not take place throughout the body at an equal rate. *Geriatrics* is the branch of medicine dealing with old age and its diseases.

Normally, aging begins after about 30. The arteries start to lose their elasticity, so that a greater strain is placed on the heart. The resulting gradual impairment of the blood supply is responsible for many of the changes, but between 30 and 60 there is a period of maturity in which aging usually makes little progress. Research into the process of old age (*gerontology*) includes study of dietary factors and the mechanisms behind structural changes in arteries and bones.

Old Catholic one of various breakaway groups from Roman Catholicism—including those in Holland (such as the *Church of Utrecht*, who separated from Rome 1724 after accusations of ◊Jansenism) and groups in Austria, Czechoslovakia, Germany, and Switzerland—who rejected the proclamation of ◊papal infallibility of 1870. Old Catholic clergy are not celibate.

The Old Catholic Church entered full communion with the Church of England 1931. Anglican and Old Catholic bishops have joined in the consecration of new bishops so that their consecration can be traced back to the time of an undivided church.

Oldenburg Claes 1929– . US Pop artist, known for "soft sculptures," gigantic replicas of everyday objects and foods, made of stuffed canvas or vinyl. One characteristic work is *Lipstick* 1969 (Yale University).

Old English general name for the range of dialects spoken by Germanic settlers in England between the 5th and 11th centuries AD, also known as ◊Anglo-Saxon. The literature of the period includes *Beowulf*, an epic in West Saxon dialect.

Other Old English literature includes shorter poems such as *The Wanderer* and *The Seafarer*, prose chronicles, Bible translations, spells, and charms. See also ◊English language.

Oldfield Barney 1878–1946. US race-car driver. Born in Wauseon, Ohio, Oldfield established a reputation as a successful bicycle racer as a youth and came to the attention of Henry Ford, who was seeking a driver for his experimental race car. Oldfield accepted the job 1902 and in the following year set the world land speed record of 60 mph/96.6 kph. In 1910 Oldfield reached a speed in excess of 130 mph/209 kph.

A familiar figure at races across the country, Oldfield retired from competitive driving 1918 and spent the rest of his career as a consultant to various automobile and tire makers.

Old Pretender nickname of ◊James Edward Stuart, the son of James II of England.

Olds Ransom Eli 1864–1950. US automobile manufacturer. Born in Geneva, Ohio, and raised in Michigan, Olds began to experiment with steam-powered prototype automobiles 1886. He produced a gas-powered car 1895 and in the following year founded the Olds Motor Vehicle Company. He reorganized the operation as the Olds Motor Works and began producing his popular Oldsmobiles 1899 in Detroit. Olds pioneered the assembly-line method of auto production that would later be refined by Henry Ford. After selling the Olds Motor Works 1904, Olds established the Reo Motor Car Company, serving as its president 1904–24 and chair of the board 1924–36.

Old Style qualification, often abbreviated to "OS," of dates before the year 1752 in England as quoted in later writings. In that year the ◊calendar in use in England was reformed by the omission of 11 days, in order to bring it into line with the more exact Gregorian system, and the beginning of the year was put back from March 25 to Jan 1.

Old Testament Christian term for the Hebrew ◊Bible, which is the first part of the Christian Bible. It contains 39 (according to Christianity) or 24 (according to Judaism) books, which include the origins of the world, the history of the ancient Hebrews and their covenant with God, prophetical writings, and religious poetry. The first five books (*The five books of Moses*) are traditionally ascribed to Moses and known as the Pentateuch (by Christians) or the Torah (by Jews).

The language of the original text was Hebrew, dating from the 12th–2nd centuries BC. The earliest known manuscripts containing part of the text were found among the ◊Dead Sea Scrolls. The traditional text (translated first into Greek and then other languages) was compiled by rabbinical authorities around the 2nd century AD.

Olduvai Gorge deep cleft in the Serengeti steppe, Tanzania, where Louis and Mary ◊Leakey found prehistoric stone tools in the 1930s. They discovered Pleistocene remains of prehumans and gigantic animals 1958–59. The gorge has given its name to the *Olduvai culture*, a simple stone-tool culture of prehistoric hominids, dating from 2–0.5 million years ago.

The Pleistocene remains include sheep the size of a drafthorse, pigs as big as rhinoceroses, and a gorilla-sized baboon. The skull of an early hominid (1.75 million years old), *Australopithecus boisei* (its massive teeth earned it the nickname "Nutcracker Man") was also found here, as well as remains of *Homo habilis* and primitive types of *Homo erectus*.

Old Vic theater in S London, England, former home of the National Theater (1963–76). It was founded in 1818 as the Coburg. Taken over by Emma Cons 1880 (as the Royal Victoria Hall), it became a popular center for opera and drama, and was affectionately dubbed the Old Vic.

In 1898 Lilian Baylis, niece of Emma Cons, assumed the management, and in 1914 began a celebrated series of Shakespeare productions. Badly damaged in air raids 1940, the Old Vic reopened 1950–81. In 1963 it became the home of the National Theater until the latter moved to its South Bank building in 1976. In 1983 the Old Vic was bought by Ed Mirvish, a Canadian businessman, and was refurbished 1985.

Old World the continents of the eastern hemisphere, so called because they were familiar to Europeans before the Americas. The term is used as an adjective to describe animals and plants that live in the eastern hemisphere.

oleander or *rose bay* evergreen Mediterranean shrub *Nerium oleander* of the dogbane family Apocynaceae, with pink or white flowers and aromatic leaves that secrete the poison oleandrin.

olefin common name for ◊alkene.

Olga, St the wife of Igor, the Scandinavian prince of Kiev. Her baptism around 955 was a decisive step in the Christianization of Russia.

oligarchy rule of the few, in their own interests. It was first identified as a form of government by the Greek philosopher Aristotle. In modern times there have been a number of oligarchies, sometimes posing as democracies; the paramilitary rule of the ◊Duvalier family in Haiti, 1957–86, is an example.

Oligocene third epoch of the Tertiary period of geological time, 38–25 million years ago. The name, from Greek, means "a little recent," referring to the presence of the remains of some modern types of animals existing at that time.

oligopoly in economics, a situation in which a few companies control the major part of a particular market and concert their actions to perpetuate such control. This may include an agreement to fix prices (a ◊cartel).

oligosaccharide ◊carbohydrate comprising a few ◊monosaccharide units linked together. It is a general term used to indicate that a carbohydrate is larger than a simple di -or trisaccharide but not as large as a polysaccharide.

Olivares Count-Duke of (born Gaspar de Guzmán) 1587–1645. Spanish prime minister 1621–43. He overstretched Spain in foreign affairs and unsuccessfully attempted domestic reform. He committed Spain to recapturing the Netherlands and to involvement in the Thirty Years' War 1618–48, and his efforts to centralize power led to revolts in Catalonia and Portugal, which brought about his downfall.

olive evergreen tree *Olea europaea* of the family Oleaceae. Native to Asia but widely cultivated in Mediterranean and subtropical areas, it grows up to 50 ft/15 m high, with twisted branches and opposite, lance-shaped silvery leaves. The white flowers are followed by green oval fruits that ripen a bluish black. They are preserved in brine or oil, dried, or pressed to make olive oil.

The oil, which is a pale, greenish yellow and chiefly composed of glycerides, is widely consumed; it is also used in soaps and ointments, and as a lubricant.

olive branch ancient symbol of peace; in the

Bible (Genesis 9), an olive branch is brought back by the dove to Noah to show that the flood has abated.

olivenite basic copper arsenate, $Cu_2(AsO_4)(OH)$, occurring as a mineral in olive-green prisms.

Olives, Mount of range of hills E of Jerusalem, associated with the Christian religion: a former chapel (now a mosque) marks the traditional site of Jesus' ascension to heaven, with the Garden of Gethsemane at its foot.

Olivier Laurence (Kerr), Baron Olivier 1907–1989. English actor and director. For many years associated with the Old Vic theater, he was director of the National Theater company 1962–73. His stage roles include Henry V, Hamlet, Richard III, and Archie Rice in John Osborne's *The Entertainer*. His acting and direction of filmed versions of Shakespeare's plays received critical acclaim for example, *Henry V* 1944 and *Hamlet* 1948.

Olivier appeared on screen in many films, including *Wuthering Heights* 1939, *Rebecca* 1940, *Sleuth* 1972, *Marathon Man* 1976, and *The Boys from Brazil* 1978. The Olivier Theater (part of the National Theater on the South Bank, London) is named after him.

olivine greenish mineral, magnesium iron silicate, $(Mg,Fe)_2SiO_4$. It is a rock-forming mineral, present in, for example, peridotite, gabbro, and basalt. Olivine is called *peridot* when pale green and transparent, and used in jewelry.

olm cave-dwelling aquatic salamander *Proteus anguinus*, the only European member of the family Proteidae, the other members being the North American mudpuppies. Olms are found in underground caves along the Adriatic seaboard in Italy, Croatia, and Yugoslavia. The adult is permanently larval in form, about 10 in/25 cm long, almost blind, with external gills and under-developed limbs. See ⟩neoteny.

Olmstead v US a US Supreme Court decision 1928 dealing with the legality of telephone wiretapping in criminal investigations. The petitioner, a man convicted of selling alcohol illegally, appealed the case on the grounds that, in violation of the Fourth Amendment, the evidence against him had been obtained through telephone wiretaps. The Court upheld the conviction, ruling 5 to 4 that, since law enforcement officers made no actual entry into Olmstead's house, the surveillance was constitutional.

Olmsted Frederick Law 1822–1903. US landscape designer. Appointed superintendent of New York's Central Park 1857, Olmsted and his partner Calvert Vaux directed its design and construction. After the Civil War, he became a sought-after planner of public parks. In 1893 he designed the grounds of the World's Columbian Exposition; he also planned several garden communities and landscaped urban building complexes.

Born in Hartford, Connecticut, Olmsted became interested in scientific farming and founded a successful nursery business 1844. A keen observer of social and economic conditions, he published his travel journals of the South as *Journeys and Explorations in the Cotton Kingdom* 1861.

Olson Charles 1910–1970. US poet, associated with the Black Mountain school of experimental poets and originator of the theory of "composition by field." His *Maximus Poems* published in volumes 1953–75 were a striking

attempt to extend the American epic poem beyond Ezra Pound's *Cantos* or William Carlos Williams's *Paterson*.

Olympia sanctuary in the W Peloponnese, ancient Greece, with a temple of Zeus, and the stadium (for foot races, boxing, wrestling) and hippodrome (for chariot and horse races), where the original Olympic Games were held.

Olympia capital of Washington, located in the W central part of the state, on the Deschutes river near Puget Sound; population (1990) 30,800. It is a deep-water port; fishing and tourism are important to the economy.

Olympic Games sporting contests originally held in Olympia, ancient Greece, every four years during a sacred truce; records were kept from 776 BC. Women were forbidden to be present, and the male contestants were naked. The ancient Games were abolished AD 394. The present-day Games have been held every four years since 1896. Since 1924 there has been a separate winter Games program. From 1994 the winter and summer Games will be held two years apart.

The first modern Games were held in Athens, Greece. They were revived by Frenchman Pierre de Fredi, Baron de Coubertin (1863–1937), and have been held every four years with the exception of 1916, 1940, and 1944, when the two world wars intervened. Special tenth-anniversary Games were held in Athens 1906. At the first revived Games, 311 competitors represented 13 nations in nine sports. At Seoul, South Korea, in 1988, nearly 10,000 athletes represented nearly 150 nations in 23 sports, plus demonstration sports like tenpin bowling, baseball, and tae kwon do (a form of martial arts). The Olympic flag bears the emblem of five colored rings (red, yellow, blue, black, and green), representing the five continents.

Olympic venues

summer games/winter games
1896 Athens, Greece
1900 Paris, France
1904 St Louis
1908 London, England
1912 Stockholm, Sweden
1920 Antwerp, Belgium
1924 Paris, France/Chamonix, France
1928 Amsterdam, Holland/St Moritz, Switzerland
1932 Los Angeles/Lake Placid, New York
1936 Berlin, Germany/Garmisch-Partenkirchen, Germany
1948 London, England/St Moritz, Switzerland
1952 Helsinki, Finland/Oslo, Norway
1956 Melbourne, Australia*/Cortina d'Ampezzo, Italy
1960 Rome, Italy/Squaw Valley, Colorado
1964 Tokyo, Japan/Innsbruck, Austria
1968 Mexico City, Mexico/Grenoble, France
1972 Munich, West Germany/Sapporo, Japan
1976 Montréal/ Innsbruck, Austria
1980 Moscow, USSR/Lake Placid, New York
1984 Los Angeles/Sarajevo, Yugoslavia
1988 Seoul, South Korea/Calgary
1992 Barcelona, Spain/Albertville, France
1994 Lillehammer, Norway (winter games)
1996 Atlanta, Georgia (summer games)
* Because of quarantine restrictions, equestrian events were held in Stockholm, Sweden.

Olympus (Greek *Olimbos*) several mountains in Greece and elsewhere, one of which is **Mount Olympus** in N Thessaly, Greece, 9,577 ft/2,918 m high. In ancient Greece it was considered the home of the gods.

Om sacred word in Hinduism, used to begin prayers and placed at the beginning and end of books. It is composed of three syllables, symbolic of the Hindu Trimurti, or trinity of gods.

Omaha city in E Nebraska, on the Missouri River; population (1990) 335,800. It is a livestock-market center, with food-processing and meatpacking industries.

Creighton University and the University of Nebraska Medical Center are here. Omaha was laid out in 1854. Its location at the E terminus of the Union Pacific Railroad (1869) spurred economic growth.

Oman country at the SE end of the Arabian peninsula, bounded W by the United Arab Emirates, Saudi Arabia, and Yemen, SE by the Arabian Sea, and NE by the Gulf of Oman.

government Oman has no written constitution, and the sultan has absolute power, ruling by decree. There is no legislature. The sultan takes advice from an appointed cabinet. There is also a consultative assembly of 55 nominated members.

history For early history, see ⟩Arabia. The city of ⟩Muscat has long been a trading post. The country was in Portugal's possession 1508–1658 and was then ruled by Persia until 1744. By the early 19th century, the state of Muscat and Oman was the most powerful in Arabia: it ruled Zanzibar until 1861 and also coastal parts of Persia and Pakistan.

independent sultanate In 1951 it became the independent Sultanate of Muscat and Oman and signed a treaty of friendship with Britain. Said bin Taimur, who had been sultan since 1932, was overthrown by his son, Qaboos bin Said, in a bloodless coup 1970, and the country was renamed the Sultanate of Oman. Qaboos embarked on a more liberal and expansionist policy than his father. The Popular Front for the Liberation of Oman has been fighting to overthrow the sultanate since 1965.

Oman's wealth is based on a few oil fields. Conflicts in nearby countries, such as Yemen, Iran, Iraq, Kuwait, and Afghanistan, have not only emphasized the country's strategic importance but put its own security at risk. The sultan has tried to follow a path close to that of the ⟩nonaligned movement, while maintaining close ties with the US and other NATO countries. In 1991, as part of the Gulf Cooperation Council, Oman troops fought in Operation Desert Storm against Iraqi troops occupying Kuwait. *See illustration box.*

Omar 581–644. Adviser of the prophet Mohammed. In 634 he succeeded Abu Bakr as caliph (civic and religious leader of Islam), and conquered Syria, Palestine, Egypt, and Persia. He was assassinated by a slave. The Mosque of Omar in Jerusalem is attributed to him.

Omar Khayyám c. 1050–1123. Persian astronomer, mathematician, and poet. In the West, he is chiefly known as a poet through Edward ⟩Fitzgerald's version of *The Rubaiyat of Omar Khayyám* 1859.

Khayyám was born in Nishapur. He founded a school of astronomical research and assisted in reforming the calendar. The result of his observations was the *Jalālī* era, begun 1079. He wrote a study of algebra, which was known in Europe as well as in the East.

Omayyad dynasty Arabian dynasty of the Islamic empire who reigned as caliphs (civic and religious leaders of Islam) 661–750, when they were overthrown by Abbasids. A member of the family, Abd Al-Rahma1m, escaped to Spain and in 756 assumed the title of emir of

Oman
Sultanate of (*Saltanat 'Uman***)**

area 105,000 sq mi/272,000 sq km
capital Muscat
cities Salalah, Nizwa
physical mountains to N and S of a high arid plateau; fertile coastal strip
features Jebel Akhdar highlands; Kuria Muria islands; Masirah Island is used in aerial reconnaissance of the Arabian Sea and Indian Ocean; exclave on Musandam Peninsula controlling Strait of Hormuz

head of state and government Qaboos bin Said from 1970
political system absolute monarchy
political parties none
exports oil, dates, silverware, copper
currency rial Omani
population (1990 est) 1,305,000; growth rate 3.0% p.a.
life expectancy men 55, women 58 (1989)
languages Arabic (official), English, Urdu, other Indian dialects
religion Ibadhi Muslim 75%, Sunni Muslim, Shiite Muslim, Hindu
literacy 20% (1989)
GNP $7.5 bn (1987); $5,070 per head (1988)
chronology
1951 The Sultanate of Muscat and Oman achieved full independence from Britain. Treaty of Friendship with Britain signed.
1970 After 38 years' rule, Sultan Said bin Taimur replaced in coup by his son Qaboos bin Said. Name changed to Sultanate of Oman.
1975 Left-wing rebels in south defeated.
1982 Memorandum of Understanding with UK signed, providing for regular consultation on international issues.
1985 Diplomatic ties established with USSR.
1991 Sent troops to Operation Desert Storm, as part of coalition opposing Iraq's occupation of Kuwait.

Córdoba. His dynasty, which took the title of caliph in 929, ruled in Córdoba until the early 11th century.

ombudsman (Swedish "commissioner") official who acts on behalf of the private citizen in investigating complaints against the government. The post is of Scandinavian origin; it was introduced in Sweden 1809, Denmark 1954, and Norway 1962, and spread to other countries from the 1960s.

Hawaii was the first state to appoint an ombudsman 1967.

Omdurman city in Sudan, on the White Nile, a suburb of Khartoum; population (1983) 526,000. It was the residence of the Sudanese sheik known as the Mahdi 1884–98.

Omdurman, Battle of battle on Sept 2, 1898 in which the Sudanese, led by the Khalifa, were defeated by British and Egyptian troops under General Kitchener.

omnivore animal that feeds on both plant and animal material. Omnivores have digestive adaptations intermediate between those of ⬦herbivores and ⬦carnivores, with relatively unspecialized digestive systems and gut microorganisms that can digest a variety of foodstuffs.

On occasion, when regular food supplies are low, most mammals become omnivores.

omphalos in Classical antiquity, a conical navel-stone, thought to mark the center of the world, such as that in the temple of Apollo at ⬦Delphi in Greece.

Omsk industrial city (agricultural and other machinery, food processing, lumber mills, oil refining) in Russia, capital of Omsk region, W Siberia; population (1987) 1,134,000. Its oil refineries are linked with Tuimazy in the Bashkir republic by a 1,000-mi/1,600-km pipeline.

onager wild ass *Equus hemionus* found in W Asia. Onagers are sandy brown, lighter underneath, and about the size of a small horse.

Onassis Aristotle (Socrates) 1906–1975. Turkish-born Greek shipowner. In 1932 he

started what became the largest independent shipping line and during the 1950s he was one of the first to construct supertankers. In 1968 he married Jacqueline Kennedy, widow of US president John F Kennedy.

onchocerciasis or ***river blindness*** disease found in tropical Africa and Central America. It is transmitted by bloodsucking black flies, which infect the victim with parasitic filarial worms (genus *Oncocerca*), producing skin disorders and intense itching; some invade the cornea and may cause blindness.

It is treated with the drug diethylcarbamazine. Newer antiparasitic drugs like mebendazole are effective but too expensive to be practical in the Third World.

oncogene gene carried by a virus that induces a cell to divide abnormally, forming a ⬦tumor. Oncogenes arise from mutations in genes (proto-oncogenes) found in all normal cells. They are usually also found in viruses that are capable of transforming normal cells to tumor cells. Such viruses are able to insert their oncogenes into the host cell's DNA, causing it to divide uncontrollably. More than one oncogene may be necessary to transform a cell in this way.

In 1989 US scientists J Michael Bishop and Harold Varmus were jointly awarded the Nobel Prize for Medicine for their concept of oncogenes, although credit for the discovery was claimed by a French cancer specialist, Dominique Stehelin.

oncology branch of medicine concerned with the diagnosis and treatment of ⬦neoplasms, especially cancer.

ondes Martenot (French "Martenot waves") electronic musical instrument invented by Maurice Martenot (1898–1980), a French musician, teacher, and writer who first demonstrated his invention 1928 at the Paris Opéra. A melody of considerable range and voicelike timbre is produced by sliding a contact along a conductive ribbon, the left hand controlling the tone color.

In addition to inspiring works from Messiaen, Varèse, Jolivet, and others, the instrument has been in regular demand among composers of film and radio incidental music.

Onega, Lake second largest lake in Europe, NE of St Petersburg, partly in Karelia, Russia; area 3,710 sq mi/9,600 sq km. The *Onega Canal*, along its south shore, is part of the Mariinsk system linking St Petersburg with the River Volga.

Oneida town in New York State, named after the Oneida people (a nation of the ⬦Iroquois confederacy). It became known from 1848 for the *Oneida Community*, a religious sect that practiced a form of "complex marriage" until its dissolution 1879.

O'Neill Eugene (Gladstone) 1888–1953. US playwright, widely regarded as the greatest US dramatist. His plays, although tragic, are characterized by a down-to-earth quality and are often experimental in form, influenced by German expressionism, Strindberg, and Freud. They were a radical departure from the romantic and melodramatic American theater entertainments. They include the Pulitzer Prize-winning plays *Beyond the Horizon* 1920 and *Anna Christie* 1921, as well as *The Emperor Jones* 1920, *The Hairy Ape* 1922, *Desire Under the Elms* 1924, *The Iceman Cometh* 1946, and the posthumously produced autobiographical drama *Long Day's Journey into Night* 1956 (written 1940), also a Pulitzer Prize winner. He was awarded the Nobel Prize for Literature 1936.

O'Neill was born in New York City, the son of stage actors James O'Neill and Ella Quinlan. His tumultuous family relationships would later provide much material for his plays. He left Princeton University after a year to learn about life but nearly died from heavy drinking and a suicide attempt while living a derelict's lifestyle. The sailors, prostitutes, and other down-and-out people he met during this period, like the members of his family, people his plays. His other plays include *The Straw* 1921; *All God's Chillun Got Wings* 1924; *The Great God Brown* 1925; *Strange Interlude* 1928, a revolutionary five-hour drama; *Mourning Becomes Electra* 1931, a trilogy based on the story of Orestes from Greek mythology; and *A Moon for the Misbegotten* 1952. Many of his plays were first produced by the Provincetown Players in Provincetown, Massachusetts. It was largely through the work of O'Neill that the American theater became a forum for serious and significant ideas.

one-party state state in which there is a ban, constitutional or unofficial, on the number of political parties permitted to run for election. In some cases there may be no legal alternative parties. For example, in the USSR up until the 1990s members of only one political party ran for election; in other instances a few token members of an opposition party may be tolerated, as in Mexico; or one party may be permanently in power with no elections.

onion bulbous plant *Allium cepa* of the lily family Liliaceae. Cultivated from ancient times, it may have originated in Asia. The edible part is the bulb, containing an acrid volatile oil and having a strong flavor.

The onion is a biennial, the common variety producing a bulb in the first season and seeds in the second.

on-line system in computing, a system that allows the computer to work interactively with its users, responding to each instruction as it

Ontario

Toronto

is given and prompting users for information when necessary. With the falling cost of computer operation, on-line operation has become increasingly attractive commercially.

onomatopoeia (Greek "name-making") expression in speech that copies natural sounds. Thus the word or name "cuckoo" imitates the sound that the cuckoo makes.

Onsager Lars 1903–1976. Norwegian-born US physical chemist. He worked on the application of the laws of thermodynamics to systems not in equilibrium, and received the 1968 Nobel Prize for Chemistry.

Ont. abbreviation for ⟡*Ontario*.

Ontario province of central Canada
area 412,480 sq mi/1,068,600 sq km
capital Toronto
cities Hamilton, Ottawa (federal capital), London, Windsor, Kitchener, St Catharines, Oshawa, Thunder Bay, Sudbury
features Black Creek Pioneer Village; ⟡Niagara Falls; richest, chief manufacturing, most populated, and leading cultural province of English-speaking Canada
products nickel, iron, gold, forest products, motor vehicles, iron, steel, paper, chemicals, copper, uranium
population (1986) 9,114,000
history first explored by the French in the 17th century, it came under British control 1763 (Treaty of Paris). An attempt 1841 to form a merged province with French-speaking Québec failed, and Ontario became a separate province of Canada 1867. Under the protectionist policies of the new federal government, Ontario gradually became industrialized and urban. Since World War II, more than 2 million immigrants, chiefly from Europe, have settled in Ontario.

Ontario, Lake smallest and easternmost of the Great Lakes, on the US–Canadian border; area 7,400 sq mi/19,200 sq km. It is connected to Lake Erie by the Welland Canal and the Niagara River, and drains into the St Lawrence River. Its main port is Toronto.

ontogeny the process of development of a living organism, including the part of development that takes place after hatching or birth. The idea that "ontogeny recapitulates phylogeny" (the development of an organism goes through the same stages as its evolutionary history), proposed by the German scientist Haeckel, has now been greatly modified.

ontology that branch of philosophy concerned with the study of being. In the 20th century, ⟡Heidegger distinguished between an "ontological" inquiry (an inquiry into "Being") and an "ontic" inquiry (an inquiry into a specific kind of entity).

onyx semiprecious variety of chalcedonic

⟡silica (SiO₂) in which the crystals are too fine to be detected under a microscope, a state known as cryptocrystalline. It has straight parallel bands of different colors: milk-white, black, and red.

Sardonyx, an onyx variety, has layers of brown or red carnelian alternating with lighter layers of onyx. It can be carved into cameos.

oolite limestone made up of tiny spherical carbonate particles called *ooliths*. Ooliths have a concentric structure with a diameter up to 0.08 in/2 mm. They were formed by chemical precipitation and accumulation on ancient sea floors.

The surface texture of oolites is rather like that of fish roe. The late Jurassic limestones of the British Isles are mostly oolitic in nature.

Oort Jan Hendrik 1900–1992. Dutch astronomer. In 1927, he calculated the mass and size of our Galaxy, the Milky Way, and the Sun's distance from its center, from the observed movements of stars around the Galaxy's center. In 1950 Oort proposed that comets exist in a vast swarm, now called the *Oort cloud*, at the edge of the Solar System.

In 1944 Oort's student Hendrik van de Hulst (1918–) calculated that hydrogen in space would emit radio waves at 8.3 in/21 cm wavelength, and in the 1950s Oort's team mapped the spiral structure of the Milky Way from the radio waves given out by interstellar hydrogen.

Oort cloud spherical cloud of comets beyond Pluto, extending out to about 100,000 astronomical units (1.5 light-years) from the Sun. The gravitational effect of passing stars and the rest of our Galaxy disturbs comets from the cloud so that they fall in toward the Sun on highly elongated orbits, becoming visible from Earth. As many as 10 trillion comets may reside in the Oort cloud, named after Jan Oort who postulated it 1950.

oosphere another name for the female gamete, or ⟡ovum, of certain plants such as algae.

ooze sediment of fine texture consisting mainly of organic matter found on the ocean floor at depths greater than 6,600 ft/2,000 m. Several kinds of ooze exist, each named after its constituents.

Siliceous ooze is composed of the ⟡silica shells of tiny marine plants (diatoms) and animals (radiolarians). *Calcareous ooze* is formed from the ⟡calcite shells of microscopic animals (foraminifera) and floating algae (coccoliths).

opal form of ⟡silica (SiO₂), often occurring as stalactites and found in many types of rock. The common opal is translucent, milk-white, yellow, red, blue, or green, and lustrous. Precious opal is opalescent, the characteristic play of colors being caused by close-packed silica spheres diffracting light rays within the stone.

Opal is cryptocrystalline; that is, the crystals are too fine to be detected under a microscope. Opals are found in Hungary; New South Wales, Australia (black opals were first discovered there 1905); and Mexico (red fire opals).

Op art movement in modern art, popular in the 1960s. It uses scientifically based optical effects that confuse the spectator's eye. Precisely painted lines or dots are arranged in carefully regulated patterns that create an illusion of surface movement. Exponents include Victor Vasarely and Bridget Riley.

op. cit. abbreviation for *opere citato* (Latin "in the work cited"), used in reference citation.

OPEC acronym for ⟡*Organization ol Petroleum-Exporting Countries*.

open-door policy economic philosophy of equal access by all nations to another nation's markets.

The term was applied Sept 1899 by Secretary of State John Hay to the US policy toward China. Several European powers had carved out spheres of influence in China, and US and British interests were excluded from those areas. Hay called on all nations to preserve and respect China's territorial and administrative independence and integrity. The US reaffirmed its position 1931 and 1937 when Japan attacked China.

open-hearth furnace method of steelmaking, now largely superseded by the ⟡basic-oxygen process. It was developed in England by German-born William and Friedrich Siemens, and improved by Pierre and Emile Martin 1864. In the furnace, which has a wide, saucer-shaped hearth and a low roof, molten pig iron and scrap are packed into the shallow hearth and heated by overhead gas burners using preheated air.

open shop factory or other business employing men and women not belonging to labor unions, as opposed to the ⟡closed shop, which employs labor unionists only.

opera dramatic musical work in which singing takes the place of speech. In opera the music accompanying the action has paramount importance, although dancing and spectacular staging may also play their parts. Opera originated in late 16th-century Florence when the musical declamation, lyrical monologues, and choruses of Classical Greek drama were reproduced in current forms.

One of the earliest opera composers was Jacopo Peri (1561–1633), whose *Euridice* influenced Monteverdi. At first solely a court entertainment, opera soon became popular, and in 1637 the first public opera house was opened in Venice. In the later 17th century the elaborately conventional aria, designed to display the virtuosity of the singer, became predominant, overshadowing the dramatic element. Composers of this type of opera included Cavalli, Cesti, and Alessandro Scarlatti. In France opera was developed by Lully and Rameau, and in England by Purcell, but the Italian style retained its ascendancy, as exemplified by Handel.

Comic opera (*opera buffa*) was developed in Italy by such composers as Pergolesi, while in England *The Beggar's Opera* 1728 by John Gay started the vogue of the *ballad opera*, using popular tunes and spoken dialogue. *Singspiel* was the German equivalent (although its music was newly composed). A lessening of artificiality began with Gluck, who insisted on the preeminence of the dramatic over the purely vocal element. Mozart learned much from Gluck in writing his serious operas, but excelled in Italian *opera buffa*. In works such as *The Magic Flute*, he laid the foundations of a purely German-language opera, using the *Singspiel* as a basis. This line was continued by Beethoven in *Fidelio* and by the work of Weber, who introduced the Romantic style for the first time in opera.

The Italian tradition, which placed the main stress on vocal display and melodic suavity (*bel canto*), continued unbroken into the 19th century in the operas of Rossini, Donizetti, and Bellini. It is in the Romantic operas of Weber and Meyerbeer that the work of Wagner has its roots. Dominating the operatic scene of his time, Wagner attempted to create, in his "music-dramas," a new art form, and completely transformed the 19th-century conception of opera. In Italy, Verdi assimilated, in his mature work, much of the Wagnerian technique, without sacrificing the Italian virtues of vocal clarity and melody. This tradition was continued by Puccini. In French opera in the mid-19th century, represented by such composers as Delibes, Gounod, Saint-Saëns, and Massenet, the drama was subservient to the music. More serious artistic ideals were put into practice by Berlioz in *The Trojans*, but the merits of his work were largely unrecognized in his own time.

Bizet's *Carmen* began a trend toward realism in opera; his lead was followed in Italy by Mascagni, Leoncavallo, and Puccini. Debussy's *Pelléas and Melisande* represented a reaction against the over-emphatic emotionalism of Wagnerian opera. National operatic styles were continued in Russia by Glinka, Rimsky-Korsakov, Mussorgsky, Borodin, and Tchaikovsky, and in Bohemia by Smetana. Several composers of light opera emerged, including Sullivan, Lehár, Offenbach, and Johann Strauss.

In the 20th century the Viennese school produced an outstanding opera in Berg's *Wozzeck*, and the Romanticism of Wagner was revived by Richard Strauss in *Der Rosenkavalier*. Other 20th-century composers of opera include Gershwin, Bernstein, and John Adams in the US; Tippett, Britten, and Harrison Birtwistle in the UK; Henze in Germany; Petrassi in Italy; and the Soviet composers Prokofiev and Shostakovich.

opera buffa (Italian "comic opera") type of humorous opera with characters taken from everyday life. The form began as a musical intermezzo in the 18th century and was then adopted in Italy and France for complete operas. An example is Rossini's *The Barber of Seville*.

opéra comique (French "comic opera") opera that includes text to be spoken, not sung; Bizet's *Carmen* is an example. Of the two Paris opera houses in the 18th and 19th centuries, the *Opéra* (which aimed at setting a grand style) allowed no spoken dialogue, whereas the *Opéra Comique* did.

opera seria (Italian "serious opera") type of opera distinct from *opera buffa*, or humorous opera. Common in the 17th and 18th centuries, it tended to treat Classical subjects in a formal style, with most of the singing being by solo voices. Examples include many of Handel's operas based on mythological subjects.

operating system (OS) in computing, a program that controls the basic operation of a computer. A typical OS controls the ◊peripheral devices, organizes the filing system, provides a means of communicating with the operator, and runs other programs.

Some operating systems were written for specific computers, but some are accepted standards. These include CP/M (by Digital Research), widely used for computers with 8-bit microprocessors; MS-DOS (by Microsoft) for microcomputers with 16-bit microprocessors; and Unix (by Bell Laboratories) for minicomputers.

operetta light form of opera, with music, dance, and spoken dialogue. The story line is romantic and sentimental, often employing farce and parody. Its origins lie in the 19th-century *opéra comique* and is intended to amuse. Examples of operetta are Jacques Offenbach's *Orphée aux enfers/Orpheus in*

the *Underworld* 1858, Johann's Strauss's *Die Fledermaus/The Bat* 1874, and Gilbert and Sullivan's *Pirates of Penzance* 1879 and *The Mikado* 1885.

operon group of genes that are found next to each other on a chromosome, and are turned on and off as an integrated unit. They usually produce enzymes that control different steps in the same biochemical pathway. Operons were discovered 1961 (by the French biochemists F Jacob and J Monod) in bacteria.

They are less common in higher organisms where the control of metabolism is a more complex process.

Ophiuchus large constellation along the celestial equator, known as the serpent bearer because the constellation Serpens is wrapped around it. The Sun passes through Ophiuchus each Dec, but the constellation is not part of the zodiac. Ophiuchus contains ◊Barnard's star.

ophthalmia inflammation of the eyeball or conjunctiva. **Sympathetic ophthalmia** is the diffuse inflammation of the sound eye that is apt to follow septic inflammation of the other.

Ophthalmia neonatorum ("of the newborn") is an acute inflammation of a baby's eyes at birth with the organism of gonorrhea caught from the mother.

ophthalmology medical specialty concerned with diseases of the eye and its surrounding tissues.

opiate, endogenous naturally produced chemical in the body that has effects similar to morphine and other opiate drugs; a type of neurotransmitter. Examples include ◊endorphins and ◊encephalins.

opinion poll attempt to measure public opinion by taking a survey of the views of a representative sample of the electorate; the science of opinion sampling is called *psephology*. Most standard polls take random samples of around a thousand voters which gives results that should be accurate to within three percentage points, 95% of the time. The first accurately sampled opinion poll was carried out by George ◊Gallup during the US presidential election 1936.

Opinion polls have encountered criticism on the grounds that their publication may influence the outcome of an election. Rather than simply predicting how people will vote, poll results may alter voters' intentions—for example, by establishing one party as likely to win and making the voters wish to join the winning side, or by making the lead of one party seem so great that its supporters feel they need not bother to vote.

opium drug extracted from the unripe seeds of the opium poppy *Papaver somniferum* of SW Asia. An addictive narcotic, it contains several alkaloids, including *morphine*, one of the most powerful natural painkillers and addictive narcotics known, and *codeine*, a milder painkiller.

Heroin is a synthetic derivative of morphine and even more powerful as a drug. Opium is still sometimes given as a tincture, dissolved in alcohol and known as *laudanum*. Opium also contains the highly poisonous alkaloid *thebaine*.

Opium Wars two wars, the *First Opium War* 1839–42 and the *Second Opium War* 1856–60, waged by Britain against China to enforce the opening of Chinese ports to trade in opium. Opium from British India paid for Britain's imports from China, such as porcelain, silk, and, above all, tea.

The First Opium War, between Britain and China, resulted in the cession of Hong Kong to Britain and the opening of five treaty ports. Other European states were also subsequently given concessions.

The Second Opium War followed between Britain and France in alliance against China, when there was further Chinese resistance to the opium trade. China was forced to give the European states greater trading privileges, at the expense of its people.

Oporto alternate form of ◊Porto in Portugal.

opossum any of a family (Didelphidae) of marsupials native to North and South America. Most opossums are tree-living, nocturnal animals, with prehensile tails, and hands and feet well adapted for grasping. They range from 4 in/10 cm to 20 in/50 cm in length and are insectivorous, carnivorous, or, more commonly, omnivorous.

The name is also popularly applied to some of the similar-looking phalangers found in Australia.

Most true opossums are confined to Central and South America, but the American opossum *Didelphis marsupialis*, with yellowish-gray fur, has spread its range into North America.

Oppenheimer J(ulius) Robert 1904–1967. US physicist. As director of the Los Alamos Science Laboratory 1943–45, he was in charge of the development of the atomic bomb (the Manhattan Project). When later he realized the dangers of radioactivity, he objected to the development of the hydrogen bomb, and was alleged to be a security risk 1953 by the US Atomic Energy Commission (AEC).

Oppenheimer was the son of a German immigrant. Before World War II he worked with the physicist Ernest Rutherford in Cambridge. In 1963 the AEC, under G T Seaborg, granted him the Fermi award in physics.

opposition in astronomy, the moment at which a body in the Solar System lies opposite the Sun in the sky as seen from the Earth and crosses the ◊meridian at about midnight.

Although the ◊inferior planets cannot come to opposition, it is the best time for observation of the superior planets as they can then be seen all night.

optical aberration see ◊aberration, optical.

optical activity in chemistry, the ability of certain crystals, liquids, and solutions to rotate the plane of ◊polarized light as it passes through them. The phenomenon is related to the three-dimensional arrangement of the atoms making up the molecules concerned. Only substances that lack any form of structural symmetry exhibit optical activity.

optical character recognition (OCR) in computing, a technique for inputting text to a computer by means of a document reader. First, a ◊scanner produces a digital image of the text; then character-recognition software makes use of stored knowledge about the shapes of individual characters to convert the digital image to a set of internal codes that can be stored and processed by computer.

OCR originally required specially designed characters but current devices can recognize most standard typefaces and even handwriting. OCR is used, for example, by gas and electricity companies to input data collected on meter-reading cards.

optical computer computer in which both light and electrical signals are used in the ◊central processing unit. The technology is still not fully developed, but such a computer promises to be faster and less vulnerable to outside electrical interference than one that relies solely on electricity.

optical contouring in medicine, computerized monitoring of a light pattern projected onto a patient to detect discrepancies in movements during breathing.

optical fiber very fine, optically pure glass fiber through which light can be reflected to transmit an image or information from one end to the other. Optical fibers are increasingly being used to replace copper wire in telephone cables, the messages being coded as pulses of light rather than a fluctuating electric current.

Bundles of optical fibers are also used in endoscopes to inspect otherwise inaccessible parts of machines or of the living body (see ▷endoscopy).

optical illusion scene or picture that fools the eye. An example of a natural optical illusion is that the Moon appears bigger when it is on the horizon than when it is high in the sky, owing to the ▷refraction of light rays by the Earth's atmosphere.

optical instrument device that uses one or more ▷lenses or ▷mirrors to produce an image. See ▷eye, ▷microscope, ▷periscope, ▷projector, and ▷telescope.

optic nerve large nerve passing from the eye to the brain, carrying visual information. In mammals, it may contain up to a million nerve fibers, connecting the sensory cells of the retina to the optical centers in the brain. Embryologically, the optic nerve develops as an outgrowth of the brain.

optics branch of physics that deals with the study of light and vision—for example, shadows and mirror images, lenses, microscopes, telescopes, and cameras. For all practical purposes light rays travel in straight lines, although ▷Einstein demonstrated that they may be "bent" by a gravitational field. On striking a surface they are reflected or refracted with some absorption of energy, and the study of this is known as geometrical optics.

option in business, a contract giving the owner the right (as opposed to the obligation, as with futures contracts; see ▷futures trading) to buy or sell a specific quantity of a particular commodity or currency at a future date and at an agreed price, in return for a premium. The buyer or seller can decide not to exercise the option if it would prove disadvantageous.

optoelectronics branch of electronics concerned with the development of devices (based

which is larger
A or B?

are the two inner lines parallel?

optical illusion

on the ▷semiconductor gallium arsenide) that respond not only to the ▷electrons of electronic data transmission, but also to ▷photons.

In 1989, scientists at IBM in the US built a gallium arsenide microprocessor ("chip") containing 8,000 transistors and four photodetectors. The densest optoelectronic chip yet produced, this can detect and process data at a speed of 1 billion bits per second.

opuntia any cactus of the genus *Opuntia* of plants to which the ▷prickly pear belongs. They all have showy flowers and fleshy, jointed stems.

opus (Latin "work") in music, a term, used with a figure, to indicate the numbering of a composer's works, usually in chronological order.

Opus Dei (Latin "God's work") Roman Catholic institution aimed at the dissemination of the ideals of Christian perfection. Founded in Madrid 1928, and still powerful in Spain, it is now international. Its members may be of either sex, and lay or clerical.

OR abbreviation for the state of ▷*Oregon*.

oracle Greek sacred site where answers (also called oracles) were given by a deity to inquirers about future events; these were usually ambivalent, so that the deity was proven right whatever happened.

The earliest was probably at Dodona (in ▷Epirus), where priests interpreted the sounds made by the sacred oaks of ▷Zeus, but the most celebrated was that of Apollo at ▷Delphi.

oral literature stories that are or have been transmitted in spoken form, such as public recitation, rather than through writing or printing. Most preliterate societies have had a tradition of oral literature, including short folk tales, legends, myths, proverbs, and riddles as well as longer narrative works; and most of the ancient epics—such as the Greek *Odyssey* and the Mesopotamian *Gilgamesh*—seem to have been composed and added to over many centuries before they were committed to writing.

Some ancient stories from oral traditions were not written down as literary works until the 19th century, such as the Finnish *Kalevala* (1822); many fairy tales, such as those collected in Germany by the Grimm brothers, also come into this category. Much of this sort of **folk literature** may have been consciously embellished and altered, as happened in 19th-century Europe for nationalistic purposes.

Oran (Arabic **Wahran**) seaport in Algeria; population (1983) 663,500. Products include iron, textiles, footwear, and processed food; the port trades in grain, wool, vegetables, and native esparto grass.

Oran was part of the Ottoman Empire, except when it was under Spanish rule 1509–1708 and 1732–91. It was occupied by France 1831. After the surrender of France to Germany 1940, the French warships in the naval base of Mers-el-Kebir nearby were put out of action by the British navy to prevent them from falling into German hands.

orange any of several evergreen trees of the genus *Citrus*, family Rutaceae, which bear blossom and fruit at the same time. Thought to have originated in SE Asia, orange trees are commercially cultivated in Spain, Israel, the US, Brazil, South Africa, and elsewhere. The sweet orange *C. sinensis* is the one commonly eaten fresh; the Jaffa, blood, and navel orange are varieties of this species.

Tangerines and mandarins belong to a related species *C. reticulata*. The sour orange or Seville *C. aurantium* is the bitter orange used in making marmalade. Oranges yield several essential oils.

Orange river in South Africa, rising on the Mont aux Sources in Lesotho and flowing W to the Atlantic; length 1,300 mi/2,100 km. It runs along the S boundary of the Orange Free State and was named 1779 after William of Orange. Water from the Orange is diverted via the Orange-Fish River Tunnel 1975 to irrigate the semiarid E Cape Province.

Orange town in France, N of Avignon; population (1982) 27,500. It has the remains of a Roman theater and arch. It was a medieval principality from which came the royal house of Orange.

Orange County metropolitan area of S California; area 801 sq mi/2,075 sq km; it adjoins Los Angeles County; population (1980) 1,932,700. Industries include aerospace and electronics. Oranges and strawberries are grown. Disneyland is here, and Santa Ana is the chief town.

Orange Free State province of the Republic of South Africa
area 49,405 sq mi/127,993 sq km
capital Bloemfontein
features plain of the High Veld; Lesotho forms an enclave on the Natal–Cape Province border
products grain, wool, cattle, gold, oil from coal, cement, pharmaceuticals
population (1987) 1,863,000; 82% ethnic Africans
history original settlements from 1810 were complemented by the ▷Great Trek, and the state was recognized by Britain as independent 1854. Following the South African, or Boer, War 1899–1902, it was annexed by Britain until it entered the union as a province 1910.

Orange, House of royal family of the Netherlands. The title is derived from the small principality of Orange in S France, held by the family from the 8th century to 1713. They held considerable possessions in the Netherlands, to which, after 1530, was added the German county of Nassau.

From the time of William, Prince of Orange, the family dominated Dutch history, bearing the title of stadholder (magistrate) for the greater part of the 17th and 18th centuries. The son of Stadholder William V became King William I 1815.

Orangeman member of the Ulster Protestant **Orange Society** established 1795 in opposition to the United Irishmen and the Roman Catholic secret societies. It was a revival of the Orange Institution 1688, formed in support of William (III) of Orange, whose victory over the Catholic James II at the Battle of the Boyne 1690 is commemorated annually by Protestants in parades on July 12.

orangutan ape *Pongo pygmaeus*, found solely in Borneo and Sumatra. Up to 5.5 ft/1.65 m in height, it is covered with long, red-brown hair and mainly lives a solitary, arboreal life, feeding chiefly on fruit. Now an endangered species, it is officially protected because its habitat is being systematically destroyed by ▷deforestation.

Orangutans are slow-moving and have been hunted for food, as well as by animal collectors. They are sometimes considered the most intelligent of the apes. The name means "man of the forest."

Orasul Stalin name 1948–56 of the Romanian town ⟡Brasov.

Oratorian member of the Roman Catholic order of secular priests, called in full **Congregation of the Oratory of St Philip Neri**, formally constituted by Philip Neri 1575 in Rome, and characterized by the degree of freedom allowed to individual communities.

oratorio dramatic, non-scenic musical setting of religious texts, scored for orchestra, chorus, and solo voices. Its origins lie in the *Laudi spirituali* performed by St Philip Neri's Oratory in Rome in the 16th century, followed by the first definitive oratorio in the 17th century by Cavalieri. The form reached perfection in such works as J S Bach's *Christmas Oratorio*, and Handel's *Messiah*.

Other examples of oratorios are Haydn's *The Creation* and *The Seasons*, Mendelssohn's *Elijah*, and Elgar's *The Dream of Gerontius*.

Orbison Roy 1936–1988. US pop singer and songwriter specializing in slow, dramatic ballads, such as "Only the Lonely" 1960 and "Running Scared" 1961. His biggest hit was the jaunty "Oh, Pretty Woman" 1964.

Born in Texas, Orbison began in the mid-1950s as a rockabilly singer on Sun Records. In the 1970s he turned to country material but made a pop comeback 1988 as a member of the Traveling Wilburys with Bob Dylan, George Harrison (ex-Beatle), Tom Petty (1952–), and Jeff Lynne (1947–).

orbit path of one body in space around another, such as the orbit of Earth around the Sun, or the Moon around Earth. When the two bodies are similar in mass, as in a ⟡double star, both bodies move around their common center of mass. The movement of objects in orbit follows Johann ⟡Kepler's laws, which apply to artificial satellites as well as to natural bodies.

As stated by the laws, the orbit of one body around another is an ellipse. The ellipse can be highly elongated, as are comet orbits around the Sun, or it may be almost circular, as are those of some planets. The closest point of a planet's orbit to the Sun is called **perihelion**; the most distant point is **aphelion**. (For a body orbiting the Earth, the closest and furthest points of the orbit are called **perigee** and **apogee**.)

orbital, atomic region around the nucleus of an atom (or, in a molecule, around several nuclei) in which an ⟡electron is most likely to be found. According to ⟡quantum theory, the position of an electron is uncertain; it may be found at any point. However, it is more likely to be found in some places than in others, and it is these that make up the orbital.

An atom or molecule has numerous orbitals, each of which has a fixed size and shape. An orbital is characterized by three numbers, called **quantum numbers**, representing its energy (and hence size), its angular momentum (and hence shape), and its orientation. Each orbital can be occupied by one or (if their spins are aligned in opposite directions) two electrons.

orca another name for ⟡killer whale.

orchestra group of musicians playing together on different instruments. In Western music, an orchestra typically contains various bowed string instruments and sections of wind, brass, and percussion. The size and format may vary according to the needs of composers.

The term was originally used in Greek theater for the semicircular space in front of the stage, and was adopted in 17th-century France to refer first to the space in front of the stage

where musicians sat, and later to the musicians themselves.

The string section is commonly divided into two groups of violins (first and second), violas, cellos, and double basses. The woodwind section became standardized by the end of the 18th century, when it consisted of two each of flutes, oboes, clarinets, and bassoons, to which were later added piccolo, cor anglais, bass clarinet, and double bassoon. At that time, two timpani and two horns were also standard, and two trumpets were occasionally added. During the 19th century, the brass section was gradually expanded to include four horns, three trumpets, three trombones, and tuba. To the percussion section a third timpano was added, and from Turkey came the bass drum, side drum, cymbals, and triangle. One or more harps became common and, to maintain balance, the number of string instruments to a part also increased. Other instruments used in the orchestra include xylophone, ⟡celesta, piano, and organ. The orchestra used to be conducted by means of a violin bow, but by Mendelssohn's time the baton was implemented.

The term may also be applied to non-Western ensembles such as the Indonesian gamelan orchestra, consisting solely of percussion instruments, mainly tuned gongs and bells.

orchid any plant of the family Orchidaceae, which contains at least 15,000 species and 700 genera, distributed throughout the world except in the coldest areas, and most numerous in damp equatorial regions. The flowers are the most evolved of the plant kingdom, have three sepals and three petals and are sometimes solitary, but more usually borne in spikes, racemes, or panicles, either erect or drooping.

Such orchids include the showy orchis *Orchis spectabilis* and rattlesnake orchids (genus *Goodyera*) of North America.

ordeal, trial by in tribal societies and in Europe until the Renaissance, a method of testing guilt of an accused person based on the belief in heaven's protection of the innocent. Examples of such ordeals are walking barefoot over heated iron, dipping the hand into boiling water, and swallowing consecrated bread (causing the guilty to choke).

order in Classical ⟡architecture, the ⟡column (including capital, shaft, and base) and the entablature, considered as an architectural whole. The five orders are Doric, Ionic, Corinthian, Tuscan, and Composite.

The earliest order was the Doric (which had no base), which originated before the 5th century BC, soon followed by the Ionic, which was first found in Asia Minor. The Corinthian (with leaves in the capitals) dates from the end of the 5th century BC, while the Composite appears first on the arch of Titus in Rome AD 82. No Tuscan columns survive from antiquity, although the order was thought to originate in Etruscan times. The five orders were described in detail by the Italian Sebastiano Serlio in his treatise on architecture 1537.

order in biological classification, a group of related ⟡families. For example, the horse, rhinoceros, and tapir families are grouped in the order Perissodactyla, the odd-toed ungulates, because they all have either one or three toes on each foot. The names of orders are not shown in italic (unlike genus and species names) and by convention they have the ending "-formes" in birds and fish: "-a" in mammals, amphibians, reptiles, and other animals;

and "-ales" in fungi and plants. Related orders are grouped together in a ⟡class.

ordinal number in mathematics, one of the series first, second, third, fourth, ... Ordinal numbers relate to order, whereas ⟡cardinal numbers (1, 2, 3, 4, ...) relate to quantity, or count.

ordination religious ceremony by which a person is accepted into the priesthood or monastic life in various religions. Within the Christian church, ordination authorizes a person to administer the sacraments. The Roman Catholic and Eastern Orthodox churches refuse to ordain women; the synod of the Church of England voted in favor of the ordination of women Nov 1992.

ordination of women Many Protestant denominations, such as the Methodists and Baptists, ordain women as ministers.

Ordovician period of geological time 510–439 million years ago; the second period of the ⟡Paleozoic era. Animal life was confined to the sea: reef-building algae and the first jawless fish are characteristic.

The period is named after the Ordovices, an ancient Welsh people, because the system of rocks formed in the Ordovician period was first studied in Wales.

ore body of rock, a vein within it, or a deposit of sediment, worth mining for the economically valuable mineral it contains. The term is usually applied to sources of metals. Occasionally metals are found uncombined (native metals), but more often they occur as compounds such as carbonates, sulfides, or oxides. The ores often contain unwanted impurities that must be removed when the metal is extracted.

Commercially valuable ores include bauxite (aluminum oxide, Al_2O_3) hematite (iron(III) oxide, Fe_2O_3), zinc blende (zinc sulfide, ZnS), and rutile (titanium dioxide, TiO_2).

Hydrothermal ore deposits are formed from fluids such as saline water passing through fissures in the host rock at an elevated temperature. Examples are the "porphyry copper" deposits of Chile and Bolivia, the submarine copper–zinc–iron sulfide deposits recently discovered on the East Pacific Rise, and the limestone lead–zinc deposits that occur in the southern US and in the Pennines of Britain.

Other ores are concentrated by igneous processes, causing the ore metals to become segregated from a magma—for example, the chromite and platinum-metal-rich bands within the Bushveld, South Africa. Erosion and transportation in rivers of material from an existing rock source can lead to further concentration of heavy minerals in a deposit—for example, Malaysian tin deposits.

Weathering of rocks in situ can result in residual metal-rich soils, such as the nickel-bearing laterites of New Caledonia.

Oregon state in NW US, on the Pacific; nickname Beaver State
area 97,079 sq mi/251,500 sq km
capital Salem
cities Portland, Eugene
population (1990) 2,842,300
features fertile Willamette River valley; rivers: Columbia, Snake; Crater Lake, deepest in the US (1,933 ft/589 m); mountains: Coast and Cascades; Oregon Dunes National Recreation Area, on Pacific coast; the Oregon Trail (2,000 mi/3,200 km from Independence, Missouri, to the Columbia River) was the pioneer route across the US 1804–60.
products wheat, livestock, timber, electronics

Oregon

famous people Chief Joseph, Ursula LeGuin, Linus Pauling, John Reed

history coast sighted by Spanish and English sailors 16th–17th centuries; part of coastline charted by James Cook 1778 on his search for the Northwest Passage; claimed for the US 1792 by Robert Gray, whose ship *Columbia* sailed into the river now named for it; explored by Lewis and Clark 1805; Astoria, John Jacob Astor's fur depot, founded at the mouth of the Columbia 1811; boundary between US settlers and the Hudson's Bay Company fixed 1846 by Oregon Treaty. Oregon Territory included Washington until 1853; Oregon achieved statehood 1859.

It remained relatively isolated until the completion of the first transcontinental railroad link 1883. Improved transportation helped make it the nation's leading lumber producer and a major exporter of food products. Development also was aided by hydroelectric projects, many of them undertaken by the federal government.

Orellana Francisco de 1511–1546. Spanish explorer who traveled with Francesco ⬦Pizarro from Guayaquil, on the Pacific coast of South America, to Quito in the Andes. He was the first person known to have navigated the full length of the Amazon from the Napo River to the Atlantic Ocean 1541–43.

Orem city in N central Utah, SE of Salt Lake City; population (1990) 67,500. It was settled by Mormons 1861. Industries include electronics and steel.

Oresteia trilogy of tragic Greek plays by ⬦Aeschylus—*Agamemnon, Choephoroe,* and *The Eumenides*—which won first prize at the festival of Dionysus in 458 BC. They describe the murder of Agamemnon by his wife Clytemnestra and the consequent vengeance of his son Orestes and daughter Electra.

Orestes in Greek legend, the son of ⬦Agamemnon and ⬦Clytemnestra, who killed his mother because she and her lover Aegisthus had murdered his father.

Öresund strait between Sweden and Denmark; in English called the ⬦Sound.

organ musical wind instrument of ancient origin. It produces sound from pipes of various sizes under applied pressure and has keyboard controls. Apart from its continued use in serious compositions and for church music, the organ has been adapted for light entertainment.

One note only is sounded by each pipe, but these are grouped into stops, which are ranks or scales of pipes prepared to "speak" by a knob. These, in turn, form part of a sectional organ, one of the tonal divisions comprising the whole organ. These separate manuals are the great, swell, choir, solo, echo, and pedal organs, controlled by the player's hands and feet. By this grouping and subdivision, extremes of tone and volume are obtained.

The organ developed from the panpipes and hydraulis (water organ), and is mentioned in writings as early as the 3rd century BC. Organs were imported to France from Byzantium in the 8th and 9th centuries, after which their manufacture in Europe began. The superseding of the old drawslides by the key system dates from the 11th–13th centuries, the first chromatic keyboard from 1361. The more recent designs date from 1809 when the composition pedal was introduced.

The electric tone-wheel organ was invented 1934 by the US engineer Laurens Hammond (1895–1973). Other types of electric organ were developed in the 1960s. Electrically controlled organs substitute electrical impulses and relays for some of the air-pressure controls. These, such as the Hammond organs, built during the 1930s for the large cinemas of the period, include many special sound effects as well as color displays. In electronic organs the notes are produced by electronic oscillators and are amplified at will.

organ in biology, part of a living body, such as the liver or brain, that has a distinctive function or set of functions.

organelle discrete and specialized structure in a living cell; organelles include mitochondria, chloroplasts, lysosomes, ribosomes, and the nucleus.

formula	name	atomic bonding
CH_3	Methyl	
CH_2CH_3	Ethyl	
CC	Double bond	
CHO	Aldehyde	
CH_2OH	Alcohol	
CO	Ketone	
$COOH$	Acid	
CH_2NH_2	Amine	
C_6H_6	Benzene ring	

organic chemistry *Common organic-molecule groupings.*

organic chemistry branch of chemistry that deals with carbon compounds. Organic compounds form the chemical basis of life and are more abundant than inorganic compounds. In a typical organic compound, each carbon atom forms bonds covalently with each of its neighboring carbon atoms in a chain or ring, and additionally with other atoms, commonly hydrogen, oxygen, nitrogen, or sulfur.

The basis of organic chemistry is the ability of carbon to form long chains of atoms, branching chains, rings, and other complex structures. Compounds containing only carbon and hydrogen are known as **hydrocarbons**.

organic farming farming without the use of synthetic fertilizers (such as ⬦nitrates and phosphates) or ⬦pesticides (herbicides, insecticides, and fungicides) or other agrochemicals (such as hormones, growth stimulants, or fruit regulators).

In place of artificial fertilizers, compost, manure, seaweed, or other substances derived from living things are used (hence the name "organic"). Growing a crop of a nitrogen-fixing plant such as lucerne, then plowing it back into the soil, also fertilizes the ground. Some organic farmers use naturally occurring chemicals such as nicotine or pyrethrum to kill pests, but control by non-chemical methods is preferred. Those methods include removal by hand, intercropping (planting with companion plants which deter pests), mechanical barriers to infestation, crop rotation, better cultivation methods, and ⬦biological control. Weeds can be controlled by hoeing, mulching (covering with manure, straw, or black plastic), or burning off. Organic farming methods produce food without pesticide residues and greatly reduce pollution of the environment. They are more labor intensive, and therefore more expensive, but use less fossil fuel. Soil structure is greatly improved by organic methods, and recent studies show that a conventional farm can lose four times as much soil through erosion as an organic farm, although the loss may not be immediately obvious.

Organisation de l'Armée Secrète (OAS) guerrilla organization formed 1961 by French settlers devoted to perpetuating their own rule in Algeria (Algérie Française). It collapsed on the imprisonment 1962–68 of its leader, General Raoul Salan.

Organization for Economic Cooperation and Development (OECD) international organization of 24 industrialized countries that provides a forum for discussion and coordination of member states' economic and social policies. Founded 1961, with its headquarters in Paris, the OECD superseded the Organization for European Economic Cooperation, which had been established 1948 to implement the ⬦Marshall Plan.

Organization of African Unity (OAU) association established 1963 to eradicate colonialism and improve economic, cultural, and political cooperation in Africa. Its membership expanded to 51 countries when Namibia joined after independence 1990. The secretary-general is Salim Ahmed Salim of Tanzania. Its headquarters are in Addis Ababa, Ethiopia.

The French-speaking Organisation Commune Africaine et Mauricienne/Joint African and Mauritian Organization (OCAM) works within the framework of the OAU for African solidarity.

Organization of American States (OAS) association founded 1948 by a charter signed by representatives of 30 North, Central, and South American states. It aims to maintain peace and solidarity within the hemisphere, and is also concerned with the social and economic development of Latin America.

The OAS is based on the International Union of American Republics 1890–1910 and Pan-American Union 1910–48, set up to encourage friendly relations between countries of North and South America. Cuba was suspended from membership 1962. Canada held observer status from 1972 and became a full member 1990. Belize and Guyana were admitted 1991, by which time OAS membership had expanded to 35. Its headquarters are in Washington, DC.

Organization of Arab Petroleum Exporting Countries (OAPEC) body established 1968 to safeguard the interests of its members and encourage cooperation in economic activity within the petroleum industry. Its members are Algeria, Bahrain, Egypt, Iraq, Kuwait, Libya, Qatar, Saudi Arabia, Syria, and the United Arab Emirates; headquarters in Kuwait.

Organization of Central American States ODECA (*Organización de Estados Centroamericanos*) international association, first established 1951 and superseded 1962, promoting common economic, political, educational, and military aims in Central America. Its members are Costa Rica, El Salvador, Guatemala, Honduras, and Nicaragua, provision being made for Panama to join at a later date. The permanent headquarters are in Guatemala City.

ODECA comprises executive, legislative, and economic councils and the Central American Court of Justice. The association was responsible for establishing the ⟡Central American Common Market 1960.

Organization of Petroleum-Exporting Countries (OPEC) body established 1960 to coordinate price and supply policies of oil-producing states. Its concerted action in raising prices in the 1970s triggered worldwide recession but also lessened demand so that its influence was reduced by the mid-1980s. OPEC members in 1991 were: Algeria, Ecuador, Gabon, Indonesia, Iran, Iraq, Kuwait, Libya, Nigeria, Qatar, Saudi Arabia, the United Arab Emirates, and Venezuela.

OPEC also aimed to improve the position of Third World states by forcing Western states to open their markets to the resultant products.

The body's importance in the world market was reflected in its ability to implement oil price increases from $3 a barrel 1973 to $30 a barrel 1980. In the 1980s, OPEC's dominant position was undermined by reduced demand for oil in industrialized countries, increased non-OPEC oil supplies, and production of alternative energy. These factors contributed to the dramatic fall in world oil prices to $10 a barrel in July 1986 from $28 at the beginning of the year. OPEC's efforts to stabilize oil prices through mandatory reduced production have been resisted by various members.

organizer in embryology, a part of the embryo that causes changes to occur in another part, through ⟡induction, thus "organizing" development and ⟡differentiation.

organum in music, a form of early medieval harmony in which voices move in parallel.

orienteering sport of cross-country running and route-finding. Competitors set off at one-minute intervals and have to find their way, using map and compass, to various checkpoints (approximately 0.5 mi/0.8 km apart),

where their control cards are marked. World championships have been held since 1966.

origami art of folding paper into forms such as dolls and birds, originating in Japan in the 10th century.

original sin Christian doctrine that Adam's fall rendered humanity innately tainted and unable to achieve salvation except through divine grace.

Orinoco river in N South America, flowing for about 1,500 mi/2,400 km through Venezuela and forming for about 200 mi/320 km the boundary with Colombia; tributaries include the Guaviare, Meta, Apure, Ventuari, Caura, and Caroni. It is navigable by large steamers for 700 mi/1,125 km from its Atlantic delta; rapids obstruct the upper river.

oriole any of two families of brightly colored songbirds. The Old World orioles of Africa and Eurasia belong to the family Oriolidae. New World orioles belong to the family Icteridae.

Icteridae also includes blackbirds, bobolinks, grackles, meadowlarks, cowbirds, and tanagers. The northern oriole *Icterus galbula* of North America has a black head and wings and bright orange underparts.

Orion in astronomy, a very prominent constellation in the equatorial region of the sky, identified with the hunter of Greek mythology.

It contains the bright stars Betelgeuse and Rigel, as well as a distinctive row of three stars that make up Orion's belt. Beneath the belt, marking the sword of Orion, is the Orion nebula; nearby is one of the most distinctive dark nebulae, the Horsehead.

Orion in Greek mythology, a giant of ⟡Boeotia, famed as a hunter.

Orion nebula luminous cloud of gas and dust 1,500 light-years away, in the constellation Orion, from which stars are forming. It is about 15 light-years in diameter, and contains enough gas to make a cluster of thousands of stars.

At the nebula's center is a group of hot young stars, called the **Trapezium**, which make the surrounding gas glow. The nebula is visible to the naked eye as a misty patch below the belt of Orion.

Orissa state of NE India
area 60,139 sq mi/155,800 sq km
capital Bhubaneswar
cities Cuttack, Rourkela
features mainly agricultural; Chilka lake with fisheries and game; temple of Jagannath or Juggernaut at Puri
products rice, wheat, oilseed, sugar, timber, chromite, dolomite, graphite, iron
population (1991) 31,512,000
language Oriya (official)
religion 90% Hindu
history administered by the British 1803–1912 as a subdivision of Bengal, it joined with Bihar to become a province.

In 1936 Orissa became a separate province, and in 1948–49 its area was almost doubled before its designation as a state 1950.

Orizaba Spanish name for ⟡Citlaltépetl, mountain in Mexico.

Orkney Islands island group off the NE coast of Scotland
area 375 sq mi/970 sq km
cities Kirkwall (administrative headquarters), on Mainland (Pomona)
features comprises about 90 islands and islets, low-lying and treeless; mild climate owing to the Gulf Stream; Skara Brae, a well-preserved

Neolithic village on Mainland. Population, long falling, has in recent years risen as the islands' remoteness from the rest of the world attracts new settlers. Scapa Flow, between Mainland and Hoy, was a naval base in both world wars, and the German fleet scuttled itself here June 21, 1919
products fishing and farming, wind power (Burgar Hill has the world's most productive wind-powered generator; a 300 KW wind turbine with blades 197 ft/60 m diameter, capable of producing 20% of the islands' energy needs)
population (1989) 19,400
famous people Edwin Muir, John Rae
history Harald I (Fairhair) of Norway conquered the islands 876; pledged to James III of Scotland 1468 for the dowry of Margaret of Denmark and annexed by Scotland (the dowry unpaid) 1472.

Orkneys, South islands in the British Antarctic Territory; see ⟡South Orkney Islands.

Orlando industrial city in Florida; population (1990) 164,600. It is a winter resort and tourist center, with Walt Disney World and Epcot Center nearby. Electronic and aerospace equipment are manufactured in the city, and citrus-fruit products are processed here. Educational institutions include the University of Central Florida. Orlando was settled 1843.

Orlando Vittorio Emanuele 1860–1952. Italian politician, prime minister 1917–19. He attended the Paris Peace Conference after World War I, but dissatisfaction with his handling of the Adriatic settlement led to his resignation. He initially supported Mussolini but was in retirement 1925–46, when he returned to the assembly and then the senate.

Orléans industrial city of France, on the River Loire; 70 mi/115 km SW of Paris; population (1982) 220,500. It is the capital of Loiret *département*. Industries include engineering and food processing.

Orléans, of pre-Roman origin and formerly the capital of the old province of Orléanais, is associated with Joan of Arc, who liberated it from English rule 1429.

Ormandy Eugene 1899–1985. Hungarian-born US conductor, music director of the Philadelphia Orchestra 1936–80. Originally a violin virtuoso, he championed ⟡Rachmaninov and ⟡Shostakovich.

ormolu (French *or moulu* "ground gold") alloy of copper, zinc, and sometimes tin, used for furniture decoration.

ornithology study of birds. It covers scientific aspects relating to their structure and classification, and their habits, song, flight, and value to agriculture as destroyers of insect pests. Worldwide scientific banding (or the fitting of coded rings to captured specimens) has resulted in accurate information on bird movements and distribution. There is an International Council for Bird Preservation with its headquarters at the Natural History Museum, London.

Interest in birds has led to the formation of societies for their protection, of which the Society for the Protection of Birds 1889 in Britain was the first. The Audubon Society 1905 in the US has similar aims; other countries now have similar societies.

ornithophily ⟡pollination of flowers by birds. Ornithophilous flowers are typically brightly colored, often red or orange. They produce large quantities of thin, watery nectar, and are scentless because most birds do not respond well to smell. They are found mostly in tropical areas, with hummingbirds being important pollinators in North and South America, and the sunbirds in Africa and Asia.

orogeny or *orogenesis* the formation of mountains. It is closely associated with the movements of the rigid plates making up the Earth's crust (described by ⟡plate tectonics). Where two plates collide crustal rocks become folded and lifted to form chains of fold mountains (such as the young fold mountains of the Himalayas).

Oromo a member of a group of E African peoples, especially of S Ethiopia, who speak a Hamito-Semitic (Afro-Asiatic) language.

Orozco José Clemente 1883–1949. Mexican painter who painted murals inspired by the Mexican revolution of 1910, such as the series in the Palace of Government, Guadalajara, 1949.

Orpheus mythical Greek poet and musician. The son of Apollo and a muse, he married Eurydice, who died from the bite of a snake. Orpheus went down to Hades to bring her back and her return to life was granted on condition that he walk ahead of her without looking back. But he did look back and Eurydice was irretrievably lost. In his grief, he offended the Maenad women of Thrace, and was torn to pieces by them.

Orphism ancient Greek mystery cult, of which the Orphic hymns formed a part. Secret rites, accompanied by a harsh lifestyle, were aimed at securing immortality.

Orr Bobby (Robert) 1948– . Canadian ice-hockey player who played for the Boston Bruins 1967–76 and the Chicago Blackhawks 1976–79 of the National Hockey League. He was voted the best defense every year 1967–75, and was Most Valuable Player 1970–72. He was the first defense to score 100 points in a season, and was leading scorer 1970 and 1975.

orris root underground stem of a species of ⟡iris grown in S Europe. Violet-scented, it is used in perfumery and herbal medicine.

Orsini Felice 1819–1858. Italian political activist, a member of the ⟡Carbonari secret revolutionary group, who attempted unsuccessfully to assassinate Napoleon III in Paris Jan 1858. He was subsequently executed, but the Orsini affair awakened Napoleon's interest in Italy and led to a secret alliance with Piedmont at Plombières 1858, directed against Italy.

Ortega Saavedra Daniel 1945– . Nicaraguan socialist politician, head of state 1981–90. He was a member of the Sandinista Liberation Front (FSLN), which overthrew the regime of Anastasio Somoza 1979. US-sponsored ⟡Contra guerrillas opposed his government from 1982.

A participant in underground activities against the Somoza regime from an early age, Ortega was imprisoned and tortured several times. He became a member of the national directorate of the FSLN and fought in the two-year campaign for the ⟡Nicaraguan Revolution. Ortega became a member of the junta of national reconstruction, and its coordinator two years later. The FSLN won the free 1984 elections, but in Feb 1990, Ortega lost the presidency to US-backed Violeta Chamorro.

Ortega y Gasset José 1883–1955. Spanish philosopher and critic. He considered communism and fascism the cause of the downfall of Western civilization. His *Toward a Philosophy of History* 1941 contains philosophical

reflections on the state and an interpretation of the meaning of human history.

orthochromatic photographic film or paper of decreased sensitivity, which can be processed with a red safelight. Using it, blue objects appear lighter and red ones darker because of increased blue sensitivity.

orthodontics branch of ⟡dentistry, mainly dealing with correction of malocclusion (faulty position of teeth).

Orthodox Church or *Eastern Orthodox Church* or *Greek Orthodox Church* federation of self-governing Christian churches mainly found in SE and E Europe and parts of Asia. The center of worship is the Eucharist. There is a married clergy, except for bishops; the Immaculate Conception is not accepted. The highest rank in the church is that of Ecumenical Patriarch, or Bishop of Istanbul. There were approximately 130 million adherents in 1991.

The church's teaching is based on the Bible, and the ⟡Nicene Creed (as modified by the Council of Constantinople 381) is the only confession of faith used. The celebration of the Eucharist has changed little since the 6th century. The ritual is elaborate, and accompanied by singing in which both men and women take part, but no instrumental music is used. Besides the seven sacraments, the prayer book contains many other services for daily life. During the marriage service, the bride and groom are crowned.

Its adherents include Greeks, Russians, Romanians, Serbians, Bulgarians, Georgians, and Albanians. In the last 200 years the Orthodox Church has spread into China, Korea, Japan, and the US, as well as among the people of Siberia and central Asia. Some of the churches were founded by the apostles and their disciples; all conduct services in their own languages and follow their own customs and traditions, but are in full communion with one another. There are many monasteries, including one on Mount Athos in Greece, which has flourished since the 10th century. The senior church of Eastern Christendom is that of Constantinople (Istanbul).

orthopedics branch of medicine concerned with the surgery of bones and joints.

ortolan songbird *Emberiza hortulana* of the bunting family, common in Europe and W Asia, migrating to Africa in the winter. Long considered a delicacy among gourmets, it has become rare and is now a protected species.

Orvieto town in Umbria, Italy, NE of Lake Bolsena, population (1981) 22,800. Built on the site of *Volsinii*, an Etruscan town destroyed by the Romans 280 BC, Orvieto has many Etruscan remains. The name is from Latin *Urbs Vetus* "old town."

Orwell George. Adopted name of Eric Arthur Blair 1903–1950. English author. His books include the satire *Animal Farm* 1945, which included such sayings as "All animals are equal, but some are more equal than others," and the prophetic *Nineteen Eighty-Four* 1949, portraying the dangers of excessive state control over the individual. Other works include *Down and Out in Paris and London* 1933.

Born in India and educated in England, he served for five years in the Burmese police force, an experience reflected in the novel *Burmese Days* 1935. Life as a dishwasher and tramp were related in *Down and Out in Paris and London*, and service for the Republican

cause in the Spanish Civil War in *Homage to Catalonia* 1938. He also wrote numerous essays.

oryx any of the genus *Oryx* of large antelopes native to Africa and Asia. The Arabian oryx *O. leucoryx*, at one time extinct in the wild, has been successfully reintroduced into its natural habitat using stocks bred in captivity.

The scimitar-horned oryx *O. tao* of the Sahara is also rare. Beisaoryx *O. beisa* in E Africa and gemsbok *O. gazella* in the Kalahari are more common. In profile the two long horns appear as one, which may have given rise to the legend of the unicorn.

OS/2 single-user computer ⟡operating system produced jointly by Microsoft Corporation and IBM for use on large microcomputers. Its main features are ⟡multitasking and the ability to access large amounts of internal ⟡memory.

It was announced 1987, and is partly based on an earlier system, ⟡MS-DOS.

Osaka industrial port (iron, steel, shipbuilding, chemicals, textiles) on Honshu island; population (1989) 2,535,000, metropolitan area 8,000,000. It is the oldest city of Japan and was at times the seat of government in the 4th–8th centuries.

Lying on a plain sheltered by hills and opening onto Osaka Bay, Osaka is honeycombed with waterways. It is a tourist center for Kyoto and the Seto Inland Sea and is linked with Tokyo by fast electric train 124 mph/200 kph. An underground shopping and leisure center 1951 has been used as a model for others throughout Japan. It was a mercantile center in the 18th century, and in the 20th century set the pace for Japan's revolution based on light industries.

Osborne John (James) 1929– . English dramatist. He became one of the first ⟡Angry Young Men (antiestablishment writers of the 1950s) of British theater with his debut play, *Look Back in Anger* 1956. Other plays include *The Entertainer* 1957, *Luther* 1960, and *Watch It Come Down* 1976.

Oscar in cinema, popular name for ⟡Academy Award.

Oscar two kings of Sweden and Norway:

Oscar I 1799–1859. King of Sweden and Norway from 1844, when he succeeded his father, Charles XIV. He established freedom of the press, and supported Denmark against Germany 1848.

Oscar II 1829–1907. King of Sweden and Norway 1872–1905, king of Sweden until 1907. He was the younger son of Oscar I, and succeeded his brother Charles XV. He tried hard to prevent the separation of his two kingdoms but relinquished the throne of Norway to Haakon VII 1905.

oscillating universe in astronomy, a theory that states that the gravitational attraction of the mass within the universe will eventually slow down and stop the expansion of the universe. The outward motions of the galaxies will then be reversed, eventually resulting in a "Big Crunch" where all the matter in the universe would be contracted into a small volume of high density. This could undergo a further ⟡Big Bang, thereby creating another expansion phase. The theory suggests that the universe would alternately expand and collapse through alternate Big Bangs and Big Crunches.

oscillator any device producing a desired oscillation (vibration). There are many types of oscillator for different purposes, involving various arrangements of thermionic ⟩valves or components such as ⟩transistors, ⟩inductors, ⟩capacitors, and ⟩resistors.

An oscillator is an essential part of a radio transmitter, generating the high-frequency carrier signal necessary for radio communication. The ⟩frequency is often controlled by the vibrations set up in a crystal (such as quartz).

oscillograph instrument for displaying or recording the values of rapidly changing oscillations, electrical or mechanical.

oscilloscope or *cathode-ray oscilloscope* (CRO) instrument used to measure electrical voltages that vary over time and to display the waveforms of electrical oscillations or signals, by means of the deflection of a beam of ⟩electrons. Readings are displayed graphically on the screen of a ⟩cathode-ray tube.

Oshkosh city in E central Wisconsin, where the Fox River flows into Lake Winnebago, NW of Milwaukee; seat of Winnebago County. Industries include clothing, machinery, lumber, and electronics; population (1990) 55,000.

osier any of several trees and shrubs of the willow genus *Salix*, cultivated for basket making; in particular, *S. viminalis*.

The name is also applied to several North American ⟩dogwoods.

Osiris ancient Egyptian god, the embodiment of goodness, who ruled the underworld after being killed by ⟩Set. The sister-wife of Osiris was ⟩Isis or Hathor, and their son ⟩Horus captured his father's murderer.

Under ⟩Ptolemy I's Greco-Egyptian empire Osiris was developed (as a means of uniting his Greek and Egyptian subjects) into *Serapis* (Osiris+Apis, the latter being the bull god of Memphis who carried the dead to the tomb), elements of the cults of Zeus and Hades being included, which did not please the Egyptians; the greatest temple of Serapis was the Serapeum in Alexandria. The cult of Osiris, and that of Isis, later spread to Rome.

Oslo capital and industrial port (textiles, engineering, timber) of Norway; population (1991) 461,600. The first recorded settlement was made in the 11th century by Harald III, but after a fire 1624, it was entirely replanned by Christian IV and renamed *Christiania* 1624–1924.

The port is built at the head of Oslo fjord, which is kept open in winter by icebreakers. There is a Viking museum, the 13th-century Akershus Castle, a 17th-century cathedral, and the National Gallery, which includes many paintings by Edvard Munch.

Osman I or *Othman I* 1259–1326. Turkish ruler from 1299. He began his career in the service of the Seljuk Turks, but in 1299 he set up a kingdom of his own in Bithynia, NW Asia, and assumed the title of sultan. He conquered a great part of Anatolia, so founding a Turkish empire. His successors were known as "sons of Osman," from which the term ⟩Ottoman Empire is derived.

osmium (Greek *osme* "odor") hard, heavy, bluishwhite, metallic element, symbol Os, atomic number 76, atomic weight 190.2. It is the densest of the elements, and is resistant to tarnish and corrosion. It occurs in platinum ores and as a free metal (see ⟩native metal) with iridium in a natural alloy called osmiridium, containing traces of platinum, ruthenium, and rhodium. Its uses include pen points and light-bulb filaments; like platinum, it is a useful catalyst.

It was discovered in 1803 and named in 1804 by English chemist Smithson Tennant (1761–1815) after the irritating smell of one of its oxides.

osmoregulation process whereby the water content of living organisms is maintained at a constant level. If the water balance is disrupted, the concentration of salts will be too high or too low, and vital functions, such as nerve conduction, will be adversely affected.

In mammals, loss of water by evaporation is counteracted by increased intake and by mechanisms in the kidneys that enhance the rate at which water is resorbed before urine production. Both these responses are mediated by hormones, primarily those of the adrenal cortex (see ⟩adrenal gland).

osmosis movement of solvent (liquid) through a semipermeable membrane separating solutions of different concentrations. The solvent passes from a less concentrated solution to a more concentrated solution until the two concentrations are equal. Applying external pressure to the solution on the more concentrated side arrests osmosis, and is a measure of the osmotic pressure of the solution.

Many cell membranes behave as semipermeable membranes, and osmosis is a vital mechanism in the transport of fluids in living organisms—for example, in the transport of water from the roots up the stems of plants.

Fish have kidney mechanisms to counteract the effects of osmosis fluid transport between their bodies and the surrounding water (outwards in saltwater fish, inwards in freshwater fish).

Osnabrück industrial city in Lower Saxony, Germany; 71 mi/115 km W of Hanover; population (1988) 154,000. Industries include engineering, iron, steel, textiles, clothing, paper, and food processing. Before World War II, Osnabrück contained fine examples of Gothic and Renaissance architecture.

Osnabrück bishopric was founded by Charlemagne 783. The Treaty of Westphalia was signed at Osnabrück and Münster 1648, ending the Thirty Years' War. A type of rough fabric, *osnaburg*, was originally made here.

osprey bird of prey *Pandion haliaetus*, the single member of the family Pandionidae; sometimes erroneously called "fish hawk." To catch fish, it plunges feet first into the water. Dark brown above and a striking white below,

before osmosis

after osmosis

osmosis *The movement of liquid through a semipermeable membrane separating solutions of different concentrations, is essential for life.*

the osprey measures 2 ft/60 cm with a 6 ft/2 m wingspan. Once extinct in Britain, it is now breeding again in Scotland.

Ospreys occur on all continents except Antarctica and have faced extinction in several areas of habitation. Efforts to preserve the species have been successful.

Ossa mountain in Thessaly, Greece; height 6,490 ft/1,978 m. In mythology, two of Poseidon's giant sons were said to have tried to dislodge the gods from Olympus by piling nearby Mount Pelion on top of Ossa to scale the great mountain.

Ossa, Mount the highest peak on the island of Tasmania, Australia; height 5,250 ft/1,617 m.

Ossetia region in the Caucasus, on the border between Russia and Georgia. It is inhabited by the Ossets, who speak the Iranian language Ossetic, and who were conquered by the Russians 1802. Some live in *North Ossetia*, an autonomous republic in southwestern Russia; area 3,088 sq mi/8,000 sq km; population (1989) 634,000; capital Vladikavkaz (formerly Ordzhonikidze). The rest live in *South Ossetia*, an autonomous region of the Georgian republic, population (1989) 99,000; capital Tshkinvali. The region has been the scene of Osset–Georgian interethnic conflict since 1989.

The Ossets demanded that South Ossetia be upgraded to an autonomous republic as a preliminary to reunification with North Ossetia, and in Sept 1990 declared the region independent of the USSR (a claim rejected by President Gorbachev). Separatist moves were violently suppressed by Georgian authorities and states of emergency imposed Dec 1990 in the capital, Tskhinvali, and in the town of Dzhava, following clashes between police and Ossets. During 1991 several hundred lives were claimed in interethnic gun battles. The violence escalated June 1992, when armed South Ossetian nationalists launched a drive to unite the two regions, spreading violence to North Ossetia and heightening tensions between Georgia and Russia. A peace accord reached June 24 had little effect, and from July Georgian and Russian peace-keeping troops were deployed.

Ossian (Celtic *Oisin*) legendary Irish hero, invented by the Scottish writer James ⟩Macpherson. He is sometimes represented as the son of ⟩Finn Mac Cumhaill, about 250, and as having lived to tell the tales of Finn and the Ulster heroes to St Patrick, about 400. The publication 1760 of Macpherson's poems, attributed to Ossian, made Ossian's name familiar throughout Europe.

ossification process whereby bone is formed in vertebrate animals by special cells (*osteoblasts*) that secrete layers of ⟩extracellular matrix on the surface of the existing ⟩cartilage. Conversion to bone occurs through the deposition of calcium phosphate crystals within the matrix.

Ossory ancient kingdom, lasting until 1110, in Leinster, Ireland; the name is preserved in some Church of Ireland and Roman Catholic bishoprics.

Ostend (Flemish *Oostende*) seaport and pleasure resort in W Flanders, Belgium; 67 mi/108 km NW of Brussels; population (1989) 68,400. There are large docks, and the Belgian fishing fleet has its headquarters here. There are ferry links to Dover and Folkestone, England.

osteoarthritis degenerative disease of the joints in later life, sometimes resulting in disabling stiffness and wasting of muscles. Formerly thought to be due to wear and tear, it has been shown to be less common in the physically active. It appears to be linked with crystal deposits (in the form of calcium phosphate) in cartilage.

osteology part of the science of ⬦anatomy, dealing with the structure, function, and development of bones.

osteomalacia softening of the bones, a condition caused by lack of vitamin D in adult life. It results in pain and muscle cramps, bone deformity, and a tendency to spontaneous fracture.

osteomyelitis infection of bone, with spread of pus along the marrow cavity. Now quite rare, it may follow from a compound fracture (where broken bone protrudes through the skin), or from infectious disease elsewhere in the body.

The symptoms are high fever, severe illness, and pain over the limb. If the infection is at the surface of the bone it may quickly form an abscess; if it is deep in the bone marrow it may spread into the circulation and lead to blood poisoning. Most cases can be treated with antibiotics, but sometimes surgery is needed.

osteoporosis disease in which the bone substance becomes porous and brittle. It is common in older people, affecting more women than men. It may be treated with calcium supplements and etidronate.

Osteoporosis may occur in women whose ovaries have been removed, unless hormone-replacement therapy (HRT) is instituted; it may also occur as a side effect of long-term treatment with ⬦corticosteroids. Early menopause in women, childlessness, small body build, lack of exercise, heavy drinking, smoking, and hereditary factors may be contributory factors.

Osteoporosis may also be seen in the bones of a young person whose limb has been immobilized.

Ostia ancient Roman town near the mouth of the Tiber. Founded about 330 BC, it was the port of Rome and had become a major commercial center by the 2nd century AD. It was abandoned in the 9th century. The present-day seaside resort *Ostia Mare* is situated nearby.

Ostpolitik (German "eastern policy") West German chancellor Willy ⬦Brandt's policy of reconciliation with the communist bloc from 1971, pursued to a modified extent by his successors Schmidt and Kohl. The policy attained its goal with the reunification of Germany 1990.

ostracism deliberate exclusion of an individual, or group, from society. It was an ancient Athenian political device to preserve public order. Votes on pieces of broken pot (Greek *ostrakon*) were used to exile unpopular politicians for ten years.

Ostrava industrial city (iron works, furnaces, coal, chemicals) in Czechoslovakia, capital of Severomoravsky region, NE of Brno; population (1991) 327,600.

ostrich large flightless bird *Struthio camelus*, found in Africa. The male may be about 8 ft/ 2.5 m tall and weigh 300 lb/135 kg, and is the largest living bird. It has exceptionally strong legs and feet (two-toed) that enable it to run at high speed, and are also used in defense. It lives in family groups of one cock with several hens.

Ostriches are bred in South Africa and elsewhere for leather and also for their tail feathers.

Ostrogoth member of a branch of the E Germanic people, the ⬦Goths.

Ostwald Wilhelm 1853–1932. German chemist who devised the Ostwald process (the oxidation of ammonia over a platinum catalyst to give nitric acid). His work on catalysts laid the foundations of the petrochemical industry. He won the Nobel Prize for Chemistry 1909.

Oswald, St c. 605–642. King of Northumbria from 634, after killing the Welsh king Cadwallon. He became a Christian convert during exile on the Scottish island of Iona. With the help of St Aidan he furthered the spread of Christianity in N England.

Oswald was defeated and killed by King Penda of Mercia. His feast day is Aug 9.

Oswiecim (German ⬦*Auschwitz*) town in S Poland, site of the World War II extermination and ⬦concentration camp.

OT abbreviation for ⬦*Old Testament*.

Otago peninsula and coastal plain on South Island, New Zealand, constituting a district; area 25,220 sq mi/64,230 sq km; chief cities include Dunedin and Invercargill.

Othello tragedy by William Shakespeare, first performed 1604–05. Othello, a Moorish commander in the Venetian army, is persuaded by Iago that his wife Desdemona is having an affair with his friend Cassio. Othello murders Desdemona; on discovering her innocence, he kills himself.

Othman c. 574–656. Third caliph (leader of the Islamic empire) from 644, a son-in-law of the prophet Mohammed. Under his rule the Arabs became a naval power and extended their rule to N Africa and Cyprus, but Othman's personal weaknesses led to his assassination. He was responsible for the compilation of the authoritative version of the Koran, the sacred book of Islam.

Othman I another name for the Turkish sultan ⬦Osman I.

Otho I 1815–1867. King of Greece 1832–62. As the 17-year-old son of King Ludwig I of Bavaria, he was selected by the European powers as the first king of independent Greece. He was overthrown by a popular revolt.

Otis Elisha Graves 1811–1861. US engineer who developed an elevator that incorporated a safety device, making it acceptable for passenger use in the first skyscrapers. The device, invented 1852, consisted of vertical ratchets on the sides of the elevator shaft into which spring-loaded catches engage and "lock" the elevator into position in the event of cable failure.

otitis inflammation of the ear. *Otitis externa*, occurring in the outer ear canal, is easily treated with antibiotics. Inflamed conditions of the middle ear (*otitis media*) or inner ear (*otitis interna*) are more serious, carrying the risk of deafness and infection of the brain.

O'Toole Peter 1932– . Irish-born English actor who made his name as *Lawrence of Arabia* 1962, and who then starred in such films as *Becket* 1964 and *The Lion in Winter* 1968. Subsequent appearances were few and poorly received by critics until *The Ruling Class* 1972, *The Stuntman* 1978, and *High Spirits* 1988.

otosclerosis overgrowth of bone in the middle ear causing progressive deafness. This inherited condition is gradual in onset, developing usually before middle age. It is twice as common in women as in men.

The middle ear cavity houses the sound-conduction mechanism called the ossicular chain, consisting of three tiny bones (ossicles) that magnify vibrations received at the eardrum for onward transmission to the inner ear. In otosclerosis, extraneous growth of spongy bone immobilizes the chain, preventing the conduction of sound. Surgery is necessary to remove the diseased bone and reconstruct the ossicular chain.

Otranto seaport in Puglia, Italy, on the **Strait of Otranto**; population (1981) 5,000. It has Greek and Roman remains, a ruined castle (the inspiration for Horace Walpole's novel *The Castle of Otranto* 1764), and a cathedral begun 1080. The port is linked by ferry with Corfu.

Ottawa capital of Canada, in E Ontario, on the hills overlooking the Ottawa river and divided by the Rideau Canal into the Upper (western) and Lower (eastern) towns; population (1986) 301,000, metropolitan area (with adjoining Hull, Québec) 819,000. Industries include timber, pulp and paper, engineering, food processing, and publishing. It was founded 1826–32 as Bytown, in honor of John By (1781–1836), whose army engineers were building the Rideau Canal. It was renamed 1854 after the Outaouac Indians.

Features include the National Museum, National Art Gallery, Observatory, Rideau Hall (the governor-general's residence), and the National Arts Center 1969 (with an orchestra and English/French theater). In 1858 it was chosen by Queen Victoria as the country's capital.

otter any of various aquatic carnivores of the weasel family, found on all continents except Australia. Otters have thick, brown fur, short limbs, webbed toes, and long, compressed tails. They are social, playful, and agile.

The genus *Lutra* includes the river otters of North America and Eurasia, about 3.5 ft/1 m long, including the tail. The sea otter *Enhydra lutris* of the N Pacific is the most aquatic. It sometimes lies on its back in the water, resting a stone on its chest, on which it breaks shellfish. The giant otter *Pteronura brasiliensis* of South America reaches 5 ft/1.5 m plus a 2.3 ft/ 70 cm tail.

Otto four Holy Roman emperors, including:

Otto I 912–973. Holy Roman emperor from 936. He restored the power of the empire, asserted his authority over the pope and the nobles, ended the Magyar menace by his victory at the Lechfeld 955, and refounded the East Mark, or Austria, as a barrier against them.

Otto IV c. 1182–1218. Holy Roman emperor, elected 1198. He engaged in controversy with Pope Innocent III, and was defeated by the pope's ally, Philip of France, at Bouvines 1214.

Otto cycle alternate name for the ⬦four-stroke cycle, introduced by the German engineer Nikolaus Otto (1832–1891) in 1876. It improved on existing piston engines by compressing the fuel mixture in the cylinder before it was ignited.

Ottoman Empire Muslim empire of the Turks 1300–1920, the successor of the ⬦Seljuk Empire. It was founded by ⬦Osman I and reached its height with ⬦Suleiman in the 16th century. Its capital was Istanbul (formerly Constantinople).

At its greatest extent the Ottoman Empire's boundaries were Europe as far as Hungary, part of S Russia, Iran, the Palestinian coastline, Egypt, and N Africa. From the 17th century it was in decline. There was an attempted revival and reform under the Young Turk party 1908, but the regime crumbled when Turkey sided with Germany in World War I. The sultanate was abolished by Kema Atatürk 1922; the last sultan was Mohammed VI.

Otway Thomas 1652–1685. English dramatist. His plays include the tragedies *Alcibiades* 1675, *Don Carlos* 1676, *The Orphan* 1680, and *Venice Preserv'd* 1682.

Ouagadougou capital and industrial center of Burkina Faso; population (1985) 442,000. Products include textiles, vegetable oil, and soap.

Oudenaarde town of E Flanders, W Belgium, on the River Scheldt, 18 mi/28 km SSW of Ghent; population (1991) 27,200. It is a center of tapestry-making and carpet-weaving. Oudenaarde was the site of the victory by the British, Dutch, and Austrians over the French 1708 during the War of the Spanish Succession.

Oudh region of N India, now part of Uttar Pradesh. An independent kingdom before it fell under Mogul rule, Oudh regained independence 1732–1856, when it was annexed by Britain. Its capital was Lucknow, center of the ◊Indian Mutiny 1857–58. In 1877 it was joined with Agra, from 1902 as the United Provinces of Agra and Oudh, renamed Uttar Pradesh 1950.

Oughtred William 1575–1660. English mathematician, credited as the inventor of the slide rule 1622. His major work *Clavis mathematicae/The Key to Mathematics* 1631 was a survey of the entire body of mathematical knowledge of his day. It introduced the "×" symbol for multiplication, as well as the abbreviations "sin" for sine and "cos" for cosine.

ounce another name for the snow ◊leopard.

ounce unit of mass, one-sixteenth of a pound ◊avoirdupois, equal to 437.5 grains (28.35 g); also one-twelfth of a pound troy, equal to 480 grains.

The *fluid ounce* is a measure of capacity, in the US equivalent to one-sixteenth of a pint, or eight fluid drams. In the UK and Canada, it equals one-twentieth of a pint.

Ouse (Celtic "water") several British rivers: The *Great Ouse* rises in Northamptonshire and winds its way across 160 mi/250 km to enter the Wash N of King's Lynn. A large sluice across the Great Ouse, near King's Lynn, was built as part of extensive flood-control works 1959. The *Little Ouse* flows for 24 mi/38 km along part of the Norfolk–Suffolk border and is a tributary of the Great Ouse. The Yorkshire *Ouse* is formed by the junction of the Ure and Swale near Boroughbridge and joins the river Trent to form the Humber. The Sussex *Ouse* rises between Horsham and Cuckfield and flows through the South Downs to enter the English Channel at Newhaven.

outback the inland region of Australia. Its main inhabitants are Aborigines, miners (including opal miners), and cattle ranchers. Its harsh beauty has been recorded by such artists as Sidney Nolan.

output device in computing, any device for displaying, in a form intelligible to the user, the results of processing carried out by a computer.

The most common output devices are the VDT (visual display terminal) and the printer.

Ovamboland region of N Namibia stretching along the Namibia–Angola frontier; the scene of conflict between SWAPO guerrillas and South African forces in the 1970s and 1980s.

ovary in female animals, the organ that generates the ◊ovum. In humans, the ovaries are two whitish rounded bodies about 1 in/25 mm

by 1.5 in/35 mm, located in the abdomen near the ends of the ◊Fallopian tubes. Every month, from puberty to the onset of the menopause, an ovum is released from the ovary. This is called ovulation, and forms part of the ◊menstrual cycle. In botany, an ovary is the expanded basal portion of the ◊carpel of flowering plants, containing one or more ◊ovules. It is hollow with a thick wall to protect the ovules. Following fertilization of the ovum, it develops into the fruit wall or pericarp.

The ovaries of female animals secrete the hormones responsible for the secondary sexual characteristics of the female, such as smooth, hairless facial skin and enlarged breasts. An ovary in a half-grown human fetus contains 5 million eggs, and it is possible that infertile women may grow new ovaries as a result of minute cell-transplant operations from such immature eggs.

In botany, the relative position of the ovary to the other floral parts is often a distinguishing character in classification; it may be either inferior or superior, depending on whether the petals and sepals are inserted above or below.

overfishing fishing at rates that exceed the ◊sustained-yield cropping of fish species, resulting in a net population decline. For example, in the North Atlantic, herring has been fished to the verge of extinction and the cod and haddock populations are severely depleted. In the Third World, use of huge factory ships, often by fisheries from industrialized countries, has depleted stocks for local people who cannot obtain protein in any other way. See also ◊fishing and fisheries.

overhead in economics, fixed costs in a business that do not vary in the short term. These might include property rental, heating and lighting, insurance, and administration costs.

Overijssel province of the E central Netherlands
area 1,289 sq mi/3,340 sq km
cities capital Zwolle; Enschede, Hengelo, Deventer
physical it is generally flat and contains the rivers Ijssel and Vecht
products livestock, dairy products, textiles
population (1991) 1,026,300
history ruled by the bishops of Utrecht during the Middle Ages, Overijssel was sold to Charles V of Spain 1527. Joining the revolt against Spanish authority, it became one of the United Provinces of the Netherlands 1579.

Overlord, Operation Allied invasion of Normandy June 6, 1944 (D-day) during World War II.

overpopulation too many people for the resources available in an area (such as food, land, and water). The consequences were first set out in the ◊Malthus theory.

Although there is often a link between overpopulation and population density, high densities will not always result in overpopulation. In many countries, resources are plentiful and the ◊infrastructure and technology are well developed. This means that a large number of people can be supported by a small area of land. In some developing countries, such as Bangladesh, Ethiopia, and Brazil, insufficient food, minerals, and energy, and inequitable income distribution result in poverty and often migration in search of better living conditions. Here even low population densities may amount to overpopulation. Overpopulation may also result from a decrease in resources or an increase in population or a combination of both.

overtone note that has a frequency or pitch that is a multiple of the fundamental frequency, the sounding body's ◊natural frequency. Each sound source produces a unique set of overtones, which gives the source its quality or timbre.

overture piece of instrumental music, usually preceding an opera. There are also overtures to suites and plays, ballets, and "concert" overtures, such as Elgar's *Cockaigne* and John Ireland's descriptive *London Overture*.

The use of an overture in opera began during the 17th century; the "Italian" overture consisting of two quick movements separated by a slow one, and the "French" of a quick movement between two in slower tempo.

Ovid (Publius Ovidius Naso) 43 BC–AD 17. Roman poet whose poetry deals mainly with the themes of love (*Amores* 20 BC, *Ars amatoria/The Art of Love* 1 BC), mythology (*Metamorphoses* AD 2), and exile (*Tristia* AD 9–12).

Born at Sulmo, Ovid studied rhetoric in Rome in preparation for a legal career, but soon turned to literature. In 8 BC he was banished by Emperor Augustus to Tomi, on the Black Sea, where he died. This punishment, supposedly for his immoral *Ars amatoria*, was probably due to some connection with Julia, the profligate daughter of Augustus.

ovipary method of animal reproduction in which eggs are laid by the female and develop outside her body, in contrast to ovovivipary and vivipary. It is the most common form of reproduction.

ovovivipary method of animal reproduction in which fertilized eggs develop within the female (unlike ovipary), and the embryo gains no nutritional substances from the female (unlike vivipary). It occurs in some invertebrates, fishes, and reptiles.

ovulation in female animals, the process of releasing egg cells (ova) from the ◊ovary. In mammals it occurs as part of the ◊menstrual cycle.

ovule structure found in seed plants that develops into a seed after fertilization. It consists of an ◊embryo sac containing the female gamete (◊ovum or egg cell), surrounded by nutritive tissue, the nucellus. Outside this there are one or two coverings that provide protection, developing into the testa, or seed coat, following fertilization.

In ◊angiosperms (flowering plants) the ovule is within an ◊ovary, but in ◊gymnosperms (conifers and their allies) the ovules are borne on the surface of an ovuliferous (ovule-bearing) scale, usually within a ◊cone, and are not enclosed by an ovary.

ovum (plural *ova*) female gamete (sex cell) before fertilization. In animals it is called an egg, and is produced in the ovaries. In plants, where it is also known as an egg cell or oosphere, the ovum is produced in an ovule. The ovum is nonmotile. It must be fertilized by a male gamete before it can develop further, except in cases of ◊parthenogenesis.

Owen Robert 1771–1858. British socialist, born in Wales. In 1800 he became manager of a mill at New Lanark, Scotland, where by improving working and housing conditions and providing schools he created a model community. His ideas stimulated the ◊cooperative movement (the pooling of resources for joint economic benefit).

Owen Wilfred 1893–1918. English poet. His verse, owing much to the encouragement of

Siegfried ▷Sassoon, expresses his hatred of war, for example *Anthem for Doomed Youth*, published 1921.

Owen Falls waterfall in Uganda on the White Nile, 2.5 mi/4 km below the point at which the river leaves Lake Victoria. A dam, built 1949–60, provides hydroelectricity for Uganda and Kenya and helps to control the flood waters.

Owens Jesse (James Cleveland) 1913–1980. US track and field athlete who excelled in the sprints, hurdles, and the long jump. At the 1936 Berlin Olympics he won four gold medals.

The Nazi leader Hitler is said to have stormed out of the stadium at the 1936 Berlin Olympic Games, in disgust at the black man's triumph. Owens held the world long-jump record for 25 years 1935–60. At Ann Arbor, Michigan, on May 25, 1935, he broke six world records in less than an hour.

CAREER HIGHLIGHTS

Olympic Games
gold: 100 meters, 200 meters, 4 × 100 meters relay, long jump: 1936
World Records:
100 meters: 1936
100 yards: 1935, 1936
200 meters: 1935
220 yards: 1935
200 meters hurdles: 1935
220 yards hurdles: 1935
4 × 100 meters relay: 1936 (US National team)
long jump: 1935

Owensboro city in NW Kentucky on the Ohio River, SW of Louisville; seat of Daviess County. Industries include bourbon, electronics, tobacco, and steel; population (1990) 53,500.

owl any bird of the order Strigiformes, found worldwide. They are mainly nocturnal birds of prey, with mobile heads, soundless flight, acute hearing, and forward-facing immobile eyes, surrounded by "facial disks" of rayed feathers. All species lay white eggs, and begin incubation as soon as the first is laid. They regurgitate indigestible remains of their prey in pellets (castings).

Owls comprise two families: typical owls, family Strigidae, of which there are about 120 species; and barn owls, family Tytonidae, of which there are 10 species.

The short-eared owl *Asio flammeus*, of North America, South America, and Eurasia, is a streaked tawny color, about 15 in/38 cm long; it hunts at dawn and dusk and roosts mainly on the ground. The great horned owl *Bubo virginianus*, of North and South America, measures 56 cm/22in, has long ear-tufts, and lives in forests, grasslands, and deserts. The snowy owl *Nyctea scandiaca* lives in the Arctic. The largest of the owls are the eagle owl *B. bubo*, of Eurasia, and the powerful owl *Ninox strenua*, of Australia, both up to 2.25 ft/0.75 m long. The worldwide common barn owl *Tyto alba* is now diminished by pesticides and loss of habitat; in Malaysia, it is used for rat control.

"Owl and the Nightingale" early Middle English poem, written about 1200, which takes the form of an argument between an owl, who may represent wisdom and respectability, and a nightingale, who may symbolize gaiety and ▷courtly love.

ox castrated male of domestic species of cattle, used in Third World countries for plowing and other agricultural purposes. Also the extinct wild ox or ▷aurochs of Europe, and extant wild species such as buffaloes and yaks.

oxalic acid (COOH)$_2$·2H$_2$O white, poisonous solid, soluble in water, alcohol, and ether. Oxalic acid is found in rhubarb, and its salts (oxalates) occur in wood sorrel (genus *Oxalis*, family Oxalidaceae) and other plants. It is used in the leather and textile industries, in dyeing and bleaching, ink manufacture, metal polishes, and for removing rust and ink stains.

oxbow lake curved lake found on the flood plain of a river. Oxbows are caused by the loops of ▷meanders being cut off at times of flood and the river subsequently adopting a shorter course. In the US, the term ▷bayou is often used.

Oxbridge generic term for Oxford and Cambridge, the two oldest universities in the UK.

Oxenstjerna Axel Gustafsson, Count Oxenstjerna 1583–1654. Swedish politician, chancellor from 1612. He pursued Gustavus Adolphus's foreign policy, acted as regent for Queen Christina, and conducted the Thirty Years' War to a successful conclusion.

Oxfam (abbreviation for *Oxford Committee for Famine Relief*) charity working to relieve poverty and famine worldwide. It was established in the UK 1942 by Canon Theodore Richard Milford (1896–1987), initially to assist the starving people of Greece.

Oxford university city and administrative center of Oxfordshire in S central England, at the confluence of the rivers Thames and Cherwell; population (1991) 109,000. Features include Oxford University (1249), the Bodleian Library (1488), the Ashmolean Museum (1683), and Christopher Wren's Sheldonian Theater (1664–68).

Oxford Movement also known as *Tractarian Movement* or *Catholic Revival* movement that attempted to revive Catholic religion in the Church of England. Cardinal Newman dated the movement from ▷Keble's sermon in Oxford 1833. The Oxford Movement by the turn of the century had transformed the Anglican communion, and survives today as Anglo-Catholicism.

Oxfordshire county in S central England
area 1,007 sq mi/2,610 sq km
cities Oxford (administrative headquarters), Abingdon, Banbury, Henley-on-Thames, Witney, Woodstock
features River Thames and tributaries; Cotswolds and Chiltern Hills; Vale of the White Horse (chalk hill figure 374 ft/114 m long); Oxford University; Europe's major fusion project JET (Joint European Trust) at the UK Atomic Energy Authority's fusion laboratories at Culham; Blenheim Palace, Woodstock
products cereals, automobiles, paper, bricks, cement
population (1991) 553,800
famous people William Davenant, Flora Thompson, Winston Churchill.

Oxford University oldest British university, established during the 12th century, the earliest existing college being founded 1249. After suffering from land confiscation during the Reformation, it was reorganized by Elizabeth I 1571. In 1985 there were 9,000 undergraduate and 3,000 postgraduate students.

oxidation in chemistry, the loss of ▷electrons, gain of oxygen, or loss of hydrogen by an atom, ion, or molecule during a chemical reaction.

Oxidation may be brought about by reaction with another compound (oxidizing agent), which simultaneously undergoes reduction, or electrically at the anode (positive electrode) of an electrolytic cell.

oxide compound of oxygen and another element, frequently produced by burning the element or a compound of it in air or oxygen.

Oxides of metals are normally ▷bases and will react with an acid to produce a ▷salt in which the metal forms the cation (positive ion). Some of them will also react with a strong alkali to produce a salt in which the metal is part of a complex anion (negative ion; see ▷amphoteric). Most oxides of nonmetals are acidic (dissolve in water to form an ▷acid). Some oxides display no pronounced acidic or basic properties.

Oxnard city in SW California, NW of Los Angeles; population (1990) 142,200. Industries include paper products, aircraft parts, and oil refining.

oxpecker African bird, of the genus *Buphagus*, of the starling family. It clambers about the bodies of large mammals, feeding on ticks and other parasites. It may help to warn the host of approaching dangers.

Oxus ancient name of ▷Amu Darya, river in Russia.

oxygen (Greek *oxys* "acid" *genes* "forming") colorless, odorless, tasteless, nonmetallic, gaseous element, symbol O, atomic number 8, atomic weight 15.9994. It is the most abundant element in the Earth's crust (almost 50% by mass), forms about 21% by volume of the atmosphere, and is present in combined form in water and many other substances. Life on Earth evolved using oxygen, which is a byproduct of ▷photosynthesis and the basis for ▷respiration in plants and animals.

Oxygen is very reactive and combines with all other elements except the ▷inert gases and fluorine. It is present in carbon dioxide, silicon dioxide (quartz), iron ore, calcium carbonate (limestone). In nature it exists as a molecule composed of two atoms (O$_2$); single atoms of oxygen are very short-lived owing to their reactivity. They can be produced in electric sparks and by the Sun's ultraviolet radiation in space, where they rapidly combine with molecular oxygen to form ozone (an allotrope of oxygen).

Oxygen is obtained for industrial use by the fractional distillation of liquid air, by the electrolysis of water, or by heating manganese(IV) oxide with potassium chlorate. It is essential for combustion, and is used with ethyne (acetylene) in high-temperature oxyacetylene welding and cutting torches.

The element was first identified by English chemist Joseph Priestley 1774 and independently in the same year by Swedish chemist Karl Scheele. It was named by French chemist Antoine Lavoisier 1777.

oxygen debt physiological state produced by vigorous exercise, in which the lungs cannot supply all the oxygen that the muscles need.

Oxygen is required for the release of energy from food molecules (aerobic ▷respiration). Instead of breaking food molecules down fully, muscle cells switch to a form of partial breakdown that does not require oxygen (anaerobic respiration) so that they can continue to generate energy. This partial breakdown produces ▷lactic acid, which results in a sensation of fatigue when it reaches certain levels in the muscles and the blood. Once the vigorous muscle movements cease, the body breaks down the lactic acid, using up extra oxygen to do so. Panting after exercise is an automatic reaction to "pay off" the oxygen debt.

oxyhemoglobin the oxygenated form of

hemoglobin, the pigment found in the red blood cells. All vertebrates, and some invertebrates, use hemoglobin for oxygen transport because the two substances can combine reversibly. In mammals oxyhemoglobin forms in the lungs and is transported to the rest of the body, where the oxygen is released. The deoxygenated blood is then returned to the lungs. Hemoglobin will combine also with carbon monoxide, to form carboxyhemoglobin, but in this case the reaction is irreversible. Asphyxiation can result when oxyhemoglobin cannot form in sufficient quantities.

oxytocin hormone that stimulates the uterus in late pregnancy to initiate and sustain labor. After birth, it stimulates the uterine muscles to contract, reducing bleeding at the site where the placenta was attached.

Intravenous injections of oxytocin may be given to induce labor, improve contractions, or control haemorrhage after birth. It is also secreted during lactation. Oxytocin sprayed in the nose a few minutes before nursing improves milk production. It is secreted by the pituitary gland.

oyster bivalve ◊mollusk constituting the Ostreidae, or true oyster, family, having the upper valve flat, the lower concave, hinged by an elastic ligament. The mantle, lying against the shell, protects the inner body, which includes respiratory, digestive, and reproductive organs. Oysters commonly change their sex annually or more frequently; females may discharge up to a million eggs during a spawning period.

Among the species commercially exploited for food are the North American eastern oyster *Crassostrea virginica* of the Atlantic coast and the European oyster *Ostrea edulis*. The former is oviparous (eggs are discharged straight into the water) and the latter is larviparous (eggs

and larvae remain in the mantle cavity for a period before release). Oyster farming is increasingly practiced, the beds being specially cleansed for the easy setting of the free-swimming larvae (known as "spats"), and the oysters later properly spaced for growth and fattened.

Valuable ◊pearls are not obtained from members of the true oyster family; they occur in pearl oysters (family Pteriidae). There are also tree oysters (family Isognomonidae) and thorny oysters (family Spondylidae).

oyster catcher chunky shorebird of the family Haematopodidae, with a laterally flattened, heavy bill that can pry open mollusk shells.

The black and white American oyster catcher *Haematopus palliatus* is found on the Atlantic and S Pacific coasts.

oz abbreviation for ◊*ounce*.

Ozal Turgut 1927– . Turkish Islamic right-wing politician, prime minister 1983–89, president from 1989. He has been responsible for improving his country's relations with Greece, but his prime objective has been to strengthen Turkey's alliance with the US.

Ozal first entered government service, then worked for the World Bank 1971–79. In 1980 he was deputy to Prime Minister Bulent Ulusu under the military regime of Kenan Evren, and, when political pluralism returned 1983, he founded the Islamic, right-of-center Motherland Party (ANAP) and led it to victory in the elections of that year. In the 1987 general election he retained his majority and Nov 1989 replaced Evren as Turkey's first civilian president for 30 years.

Ozalid process trademarked copying process used to produce positive prints from drawn or printed materials or film, such as printing proofs from film images. The film is placed

on top of chemically treated paper and then exposed to ultraviolet light. The image is developed dry using ammonia vapor.

Ozark Mountains area in the US (shared by Arkansas, Illinois, Kansas, Mississippi, Oklahoma) of ridges, valleys, and streams; highest point only 2,300 ft/700 m; area 50,000 sq mi/130,000 sq km. This heavily forested region between the Missouri and Arkansas rivers has agriculture and lead and zinc mines.

ozone O_3 highly reactive pale-blue gas with a penetrating odor. Ozone is an allotrope of oxygen (see ◊allotropy), made up of three atoms of oxygen. It is formed when the molecule of the stable form of oxygen (O_2) is split by ultraviolet radiation or electrical discharge. It forms a layer in the upper atmosphere, which protects life on Earth from ultraviolet rays, a cause of skin cancer. At lower atmospheric levels it is an air pollutant and contributes to the ◊greenhouse effect.

At ground level, ozone can cause asthma attacks, stunted growth in plants, and corrosion of certain materials. It is produced by the action of sunlight on car exhaust fumes, and is a major air pollutant in hot summers. Ozone is a powerful oxidizing agent and is used industrially in bleaching and air-conditioning.

ozone depleter any chemical that destroys the ozone in the stratosphere. Most ozone depleters are chemically stable compounds containing chlorine or bromine, which remain unchanged for long enough to drift up to the upper atmosphere. The best known are ◊chlorofluorocarbons (CFCs), but many other ozone depleters are known, including halons, used in some fire extinguishers; methyl chloroform and carbon tetrachloride, both solvents; some CFC substitutes; and the pesticide methyl bromide

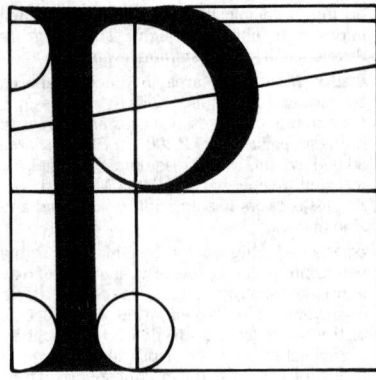

P 16th letter of the English alphabet. In Semitic languages, in Greek, and in Latin *p* had much the same sound as it normally has today in English when final, or when following *s* at the beginning of a word, the sound of an unvoiced labial stop. In other positions in English, and especially when initial, *p* is aspirated.

p in music, abbreviation for ***piano*** (Italian "softly").

p(p). abbreviation for ***page(s)***.

PA abbreviation for the state of ◊***Pennsylvania***.

Pabst G(eorg) W(ilhelm) 1885–1967. German film director whose films include *Die Büchse der Pandora/Pandora's Box* 1928, *Das Tagebuch einer Verlorenen/The Diary of a Lost Girl* 1929, both starring Louise ◊Brooks, the striking antiwar story *Westfront 1918* 1930, and *Die Dreigroschenoper/The Threepenny Opera* 1931.

paca large, tailless, nocturnal, burrowing ◊rodent of the genus *Cuniculus*, in the family Dasyproctidae, which also includes the agoutis. The paca, about 2 ft/60 cm long, is native to Central and South America.

Pacaraima, Sierra mountain range along the Brazil–Venezuela frontier, extending into Guyana; length 385 mi/620 km; highest point **Mount Roraima**, a plateau about 20 sq mi/ 50 sq km, 9,222 ft/2,810 m above sea level, surrounded by 1,000-ft/300-m cliffs, at the conjunction of the three countries. Formed 300 million years ago, it has unique fauna and flora, because of its isolation, consisting only of grasses, bushes, flowers, insects, and small amphibians.

pacemaker medical device implanted in a patient whose heart beats irregularly. It delivers minute electric shocks to stimulate the heart muscles at regular intervals and restores normal heartbeat. The latest pacemakers are powered by radioactive isotopes for long life and weigh no more than 0.5 oz/15 g. They are implanted under the skin.

Pacific Islands former (1947–1990) UN Trust Territory in the W Pacific captured from Japan during World War II. The territory comprised over 2,000 islands and atolls and was assigned to the US 1947. The islands were divided into four governmental units: the Northern Marianas (except Guam) which became a self-governing commonwealth in union with the US 1975; the ◊Marshall Islands, the Federated States of ◊Micronesia, and the Republic of ◊Belau (formerly Palau) became self-governing 1979–80, signing agreements of free association with the US 1982. In Dec 1990 the United Nations Security Council voted to dissolve its trusteeship over the islands with the exception of Belau.

Pacific Ocean world's largest ocean, extending from Antarctica to the Bering Strait; area 64,170,000 sq mi/166,242,500 sq km; average depth 13,749 ft/4,188 m; greatest depth of any ocean 36,210 ft/11,034 m in the ◊Mariana Trench.

Pacific Security Treaty military alliance agreement between Australia, New Zealand, and the US, signed 1951 (see ◊ANZUS). Military cooperation between the US and New Zealand has been restricted by the latter's policy of banning ships that might be carrying nuclear weapons or nuclear power sources.

Pacific War war 1879–83 fought by an alliance of Bolivia and Peru against Chile. Chile seized Antofagasta and the coast between the mouths of the rivers Loa and Paposo, rendering Bolivia landlocked, and also annexed the southern Peruvian coastline from Arica to the mouth of the Loa, including the nitrate fields of the Atacama Desert.

Bolivia has since tried to regain Pacific access, either by a corridor across its former Antofagasta province or by a twin port with Arica at the end of the rail link from La Paz. Brazil supports the Bolivian claims, which would facilitate its own transcontinental traffic.

pacifism belief that violence, even in self-defense, is unjustifiable under any conditions and that arbitration is preferable to war as a means of solving disputes. In the East, pacifism has roots in Buddhism, and nonviolent action was used by Mahatma ◊Gandhi in the struggle for Indian independence.

Pacino Al(berto) 1940– . US film actor who played powerful, introverted but violent roles in films such as *The Godfather* 1972, *Serpico* 1973, and *Scarface* 1983. *Dick Tracy* 1990 added comedy to his range of acting styles, and *The Godfather Part III* added subdued style to his virtuoso performances. In *Scent of a Woman* 1992, he played a retired blind army officer.

pact of steel military alliance between Nazi Germany and Fascist Italy, instituted 1939.

Paderewski Ignacy Jan 1860–1941. Polish pianist, composer, and politician. After his debut in Vienna 1887 he became celebrated in Europe and the US as an interpreter of the piano music of Chopin. During World War I he helped organize the Polish army in France; in 1919 he became prime minister of the newly independent Poland, which he represented at the Peace Conference, but continuing opposition forced him to resign the same year. He resumed a musical career 1922, was made president of the Polish National Council in Paris 1940, and died in New York.

Padua (Italian **Padova**) city in N Italy, 28 mi/45 km W of Venice; population (1988) 224,000. The astronomer Galileo taught at the university, founded 1222.

The 13th-century Palazzo della Ragione, the basilica of S Antonio, and the botanical garden laid out in 1545 are notable. Padua is the birthplace of the Roman historian Livy and the painter Andrea Mantegna.

Paestum ancient Greek city, near Salerno in S Italy. It was founded about 600 BC as the Greek colony Posidonia, and a number of Doric temples remain.

Pagalu former name (1973–79) of ◊Annobón, an island in Equatorial Guinea.

Pagan archeological site in Myanmar with the ruins of the former capital (founded 847, taken by Kublai Khan 1287). These include Buddhist pagodas, shrines, and temples with wall paintings of the great period of Burmese art (11th–13th centuries).

Paganini Niccolò 1782–1840. Italian violinist and composer, a virtuoso soloist from the age of nine. He invented all the virtuoso techniques that have since been included in violin composition. His works for the violin ingeniously exploit the potential of the instrument. His raffish appearance, wild amours, and virtuosity (especially on a single string) fostered a rumor of his being in league with the devil.

Page Frederick Handley 1885–1962. British aircraft engineer, founder 1909 of one of the earliest aircraft-manufacturing companies and designer of long-range civil airplanes and multi-engined bombers in both world wars; for example, the Halifax, flown in World War II.

pageant originally the wagon on which medieval ◊mystery plays were performed. The term was later applied to the street procession of songs, dances, and historical tableaux that became fashionable during the 1920s.

paging method of increasing a computer's apparent memory capacity. See ◊virtual memory.

Pagnol Marcel 1895–1974. French film director, producer, author, and playwright whose work includes *Fanny* 1932 and *Manon des sources* 1952. His autobiographical *La Gloire de mon père/My Father's Glory* 1957 was filmed 1991. He regarded the cinema as recorded theater; thus his films, although strong on character and background, fail to exploit the medium fully as an independent art form.

Pago Pago chief port of American Samoa on the island of Tutuila; population (1980) 3,060. Formerly a naval coaling station, it was acquired by the US under a commercial treaty with the local king 1872.

Pahang state of E Peninsular Malaysia; capital Kuantan; area 13,886 sq mi/36,000 sq km; population (1980) 799,000. It is mountainous and forested and produces rubber, tin, gold, and timber. There is a port at Tanjung Gelang. Pahang is ruled by a sultan.

Pahlavi dynasty Iranian dynasty founded by Reza Khan (1877–1944), an army officer who seized control of the government 1921 and was proclaimed shah 1925. During World War II, Britain and the USSR were nervous about his German sympathies and occupied Iran 1941–46. They compelled him to abdicate 1941 in favor of his son Mohammed Reza Shah Pahlavi, who took office in 1956, with US support, and was deposed in the Islamic revolution of 1979.

Pahsien alternative transliteration for ◊***Chongqing***, port in SW China.

Paige Satchel (Leroy Robert) 1906–1982. US baseball player. As a pitcher, Paige established a near-legendary record, leading the Kansas City Monarchs of the Negro National League to the championship 1942. In 1948, with the end of racial segregation in the major leagues, Paige joined the Cleveland Indians. He later played with the St Louis Browns 1951–53 and was elected to the Baseball Hall of Fame 1971.

Born in Mobile, Alabama, Paige began playing professional baseball in the Negro leagues in the 1920s and traveled extensively throughout the US and Latin America.

pain sense that gives an awareness of harmful effects on or in the body. It may be triggered by stimuli such as trauma, inflammation, and heat. Pain is transmitted by specialized nerves and also has psychological components controlled by higher centers in the brain.

A pain message to the brain travels along the sensory nerves as electrical impulses. When these reach the gap between one nerve and another, biochemistry governs whether this gap is bridged and may also either increase or decrease the attention the message receives or modify its intensity in either direction. The main type of pain transmitter is known simply as "substance P," a neuropeptide concentrated in a certain area of the spinal cord. Substance P has been found in fish, and there is also evidence that the same substances that cause pain in humans (for example, bee venom) cause a similar reaction in insects and arachnids (for instance, spiders).

Since the sensation of pain is transmitted by separate nerves from that of fine touch, it is possible in diseases such as syringomyelia to have no sense of pain in a limb, yet maintain a normal sense of touch. Such a desensitized limb is at great risk of infection from unnoticed cuts and abrasions.

Paine Thomas 1737–1809. English left-wing political writer, active in the American and French revolutions. His pamphlet *Common Sense* 1776 ignited passions in the American Revolution; others include *The Rights of Man* 1791 and *The Age of Reason* 1793. He advocated republicanism, deism, the abolition of slavery, and the emancipation of women.

Paine, born in Thetford, Norfolk, was a friend of US scientist and politician Benjamin Franklin and went to America 1774, where he published several republican pamphlets and fought for the colonists in the revolution. In 1787 he returned to Britain. *The Rights of Man* is an answer to the conservative theorist Burke's *Reflections on the Revolution in France*. In 1792, Paine was indicted for treason and escaped to France, to represent Calais in the National Convention. Narrowly escaping the guillotine, he regained his seat after the fall of Robespierre. Paine returned to the US 1802 and died in New York.

painkiller agent for relieving pain. Types of painkiller include ◊aspirin and aspirin substitutes, ◊morphine, ◊codeine, paracetamol, and synthetic versions of the natural inhibitors, the encephalins and endorphins, which avoid the side effects of the others.

Topical nerve irritants are also used in salves, such as camphor and eucalyptus; they cause the nerve endings to react to them, bringing increased blood flow to the areas and alleviating localized and joint pain.

paint any of various materials used to give a protective and decorative finish to surfaces or for making pictures. A paint consists of a pigment suspended in a vehicle, or binder, usually with added solvents. It is the vehicle that dries and hardens to form an adhesive film of paint. Among the most common kinds are cellulose

paints (or lacquers), oil-based paints, emulsion paints, and special types such as enamels and primers.

Lacquers consist of a synthetic resin (such as an acrylic resin or cellulose acetate) dissolved in a volatile organic solvent, which evaporates rapidly to give a very quick-drying paint. A typical *oil-based paint* has a vehicle of a natural drying oil (such as linseed oil), containing a prime pigment of iron, lead, titanium, or zinc oxide, to which colored pigments may be added. The finish—gloss, semimatte, or matte—depends on the amount of inert pigment (such as clay or silicates). Oil-based paints can be thinned, and brushes cleaned, in a solvent such as turpentine or white spirit (a petroleum product). **Emulsion paints**, sometimes called latex paints, consist of pigments dispersed in a water-based emulsion of a polymer (such as polyvinyl chloride [PVC] or acrylic resin). They can be thinned with water, which can also be used to wash the paint out of brushes and rollers. **Enamels** have little pigment, and they dry to an extremely hard, high-gloss film. **Primers** for the first coat on wood or metal, on the other hand, have a high pigment content (as do undercoat paints). Aluminum or bronze powder may be used for priming or finishing objects made of metal.

painting application of color, pigment, or paint to a surface. The chief methods of painting are **tempera** emulsion painting, with a gelatinous (for example, egg yolk) rather than oil base; known in ancient Egypt; **fresco** watercolor painting on plaster walls; the palace of Knossos, Crete, contains examples from about 2,000 BC; **ink** developed in China from calligraphy in the Sung period and highly popular in Japan from the 15th century; **oil** ground pigments in linseed, walnut, or other oil; spread from N to S Europe in the 15th century; **watercolor** pigments combined with gum arabic and glycerol, which are diluted with water; the method was developed in the 15th–17th centuries from wash drawings; **acrylic** synthetic pigments developed after World War II; the colors are very hard and brilliant.

For the history of painting see ◊ancient art; ◊medieval art; ◊Chinese art, and so on. Individual painters and art movements are listed alphabetically.

Pakistan country in S Asia, stretching from the Himalayas to the Arabian Sea, bounded W by Iran, NW by Afghanistan, NE by China, and E by India.

government The 1973 constitution, suspended 1977, was restored in part and amended 1985 to make the president the dominant political figure. Primary power resides with the central government, headed by an executive president who is elected for five-year terms by a joint sitting of the federal legislature. Day-to-day administration is performed by a prime minister (drawn from the national assembly) and cabinet appointed by the president. After the death of General Zia 1988 and the election of Benazir Bhutto, power shifted from the president to the prime minister in what has become a dual administration.

Pakistan is a federal republic comprising four provinces: Sind, Punjab, North-West Frontier Province, and Baluchistan, administered by appointed governors and local governments drawn from elected provincial assemblies; ◊Tribal Areas, which are administered by the central government; and the Federal Capital Territory of Islamabad. The

federal legislature, Majlis i-Shura, comprises two chambers: a lower house (national assembly) composed of 168 members directly elected for five-year terms by universal suffrage, and 20 women and 10 minority group appointees; and an upper chamber (Senate) composed of 87 members elected, a third at a time, for six-year terms by provincial assemblies and Tribal Areas following a quota system. The National Assembly has sole jurisdiction over financial affairs.

history For history before 1947, see ◊Indus Valley Civilization and ◊India. The name "Pakistan" for a Muslim division of British India was put forward 1930 by Choudhary Rahmat Ali (1897–1951) from names of the Muslim parts of the subcontinent: *P*unjab, the *A*fghan NW Frontier, *K*ashmir, *S*ind, and Ba-luch*istan*. *Pak* means "pure" in Urdu and *stan* means "land." Fear of domination by the Hindu majority in India led in 1940 to a serious demand for a separate Muslim state, which delayed India's independence for some years. In 1947 British India was divided into two dominions, India and Pakistan.

republic After the death of its leader ◊Jinnah 1948, Pakistan remained a dominion with the British monarch as head of state until a republic was declared 1956. Its new constitution was abrogated 1958, and military rule was imposed through a coup by General Mohammed Ayub Khan. The country experienced rapid economic growth during the 1960s, but regional tension mounted between demographically dominant East Pakistan and West Pakistan, where political and military power was concentrated. After serious strikes and riots 1969, General Ayub Khan stepped down and was replaced by General Agha Mohammed Yahya Khan.

civil war Pakistan's first elections with universal suffrage were held 1970 to elect an assembly to frame a new constitution. Sheik Mujib ur-Rahman's Awami League, which proposed autonomy, gained a majority of seats in East Pakistan, and the Pakistan People's Party (or PPP) in West Pakistan. East Pakistan declared its independence from the West 1971, precipitating a civil war. India intervened on East Pakistan's side, and the independent republic of ◊Bangladesh emerged.

parliamentary government General Yahya Khan resigned, passing power in (W) Pakistan to the People's Party leader Zulfiqar Ali ◊Bhutto, who introduced a new federal parliamentary constitution 1973 and a socialist economic program of land reform and nationalization. From the mid-1970s the Sind-based Bhutto faced deteriorating economic conditions and growing regional opposition, particularly from Baluchistan and from ◊Pathans campaigning for an independent Pakhtoonistan.

martial law Bhutto won a majority in the 1977 assembly elections but was accused of ballot rigging by the Pakistan National Alliance opposition. Riots ensued, and after four months of unrest, the Punjabi Muslim army Chief of Staff, General ◊Zia ul-Haq, seized power in a bloodless coup 1977. Martial law was imposed; Bhutto was imprisoned for alleged murder and hanged 1979.

Islamization program Between 1979 and 1981 General Zia imposed severe restrictions on political activity. He introduced a broad Islamization program aimed at deepening his support base and appeasing Islamic fundamentalists. This was opposed by middle-class professionals and by the Shiite minority. In

1981, nine banned opposition parties, including the People's Party of Pakistan, formed the Movement for the Restoration of Democracy alliance to campaign for a return to parliamentary government. The military government responded by arresting several hundred opposition politicians. A renewed democracy campaign 1983 resulted in considerable anti-government violence in Sind province. From 1982, however, General Zia slowly began enlarging the civilian element in his government and, in 1984, he held a successful referendum on the Islamization process, which was taken to legitimize his continuing as president for a further five-year term. In 1985, direct elections were held to the national and provincial assemblies, but on a nonparty basis. A new civilian cabinet was formed and an amended constitution adopted.

civilian government In 1985, martial law and the ban on political parties were lifted, military courts were abolished, and military administrators stepped down in favor of civilians. A government was formed by the Pagaro faction of the Pakistan Muslim League (PML) led by Mohammad Khan Junejo, which was subservient to General Zia. Benazir �ϿBhutto, the daughter of Zulfiqar Ali Bhutto and leader of the PPP, returned 1986 from self-exile

in London to launch a popular campaign for immediate open elections. Riots erupted in Lahore, Karachi, and rural Sind, where troops were sent in, and PPP leaders were arrested.

Islamic law In 1988, concerned with the deteriorating state of the economy and anxious to accelerate the Islamization process, President Zia dismissed the Junejo government and dissolved the National Assembly and provincial legislatures, promising fresh elections within 90 days. Ruling by ordinance, Zia decreed that the *Shari'a*, the Islamic legal code, would immediately become the country's supreme law. A month later the president was killed, along with senior army officers, in a military airplane crash near Bahawalpur. Sabotage was suspected. Ghulam Ishaq Khan, the Senate's elderly chair, succeeded as president, but in the free multiparty elections, the PPP, which had moved toward the center in its policy stance, emerged as the largest single party, with 45% of the National Assembly's elective seats.

Benazir Bhutto's government After forging a coalition with the Mohajir National Movement (MQM), Benazir Bhutto was sworn in as prime minister Nov 1988, and Ghulam Ishaq Khan was elected as president. The new Bhutto administration pledged itself to a

free-market economic program, support of the Afghan mujaheddin, and to leave untouched the military budget. In Oct 1989 the MQM withdrew from the ruling coalition and allied itself with the opposition Islamic Democratic Alliance (IDA). The Bhutto government narrowly survived a vote of no confidence a month later.

Sharif's government Benazir Bhutto's government was dismissed from office by president Ghulam Ishaq Khan Aug 1990 on accusations of incompetence, corruption, and abuse of power. The National Assemblies were also dissolved. In Oct 1990 the opposition was swept to victory and Nawaz Sharif, Bhutto's former chief minister of Punjab province, was sworn in as prime minister. Sharif had headed the IDA, which incorporated the PML (led by former premier Mohammad Khan Junejo). The IDA captured 105 of the 207 parliamentary seats contested to the 45 of Bhutto's PPP. It also secured control of three of the four provincial assemblies, Bhutto's Sind stronghold being the exception. Sharif promised to pursue a free-market economic program and was supported by the military, state bureaucracy, and mullahs.

The US suspended military aid to Pakistan Oct 1990 after learning that the latter was seeking to develop nuclear weapons. (Benazir Bhutto admitted Sept 1991 that Pakistan did have the ability to build a nuclear weapon rapidly in response to a possible threat from India.)

Islamic law enforced In May 1991 a *Shari'a* bill, enforcing Islamic law and designed to create an "Islamic welfare state" was enacted. The opposition PPP, though welcoming parts of the social reform program, unsuccessfully voted against the bill. However, most objective observers saw the bill as a skillfully pragmatic, nonfundamentalist measure. Nawaz Sharif also enthusiastically set about launching a privatization and deregulation program. However, these reforms were soon upset by labor unrest and a rash of bomb attacks, kidnappings, murders, and bank robberies during the summer months of 1991 and by the uncovering of a financial scandal involving Nawaz Sharif's family and members of the government.

foreign affairs In foreign affairs, Pakistan's relations with India have been strained since independence, with border wars over Kashmir 1965 and East Pakistan 1971. It left the Commonwealth 1972, when the new state of Bangladesh was accepted, but rejoined 1989. As a result of shared hostility to India, Pakistan has been allied with China since the 1950s; during the 1970s it developed close relations with the US, providing support for the US-backed Afghan rebels, while at the same time joining the Ͻnonaligned movement 1979 and drawing closer to the Islamic states of the Middle East and Africa. During the Gulf crisis and war against Iraq of 1990–91, Pakistan sent 11,000 troops to Saudi Arabia to guard Islamic shrines, but there was considerable anti-Americanism within the country and popular support for Saddam Hussein. In 1992 Pakistan was elected to the UN Security Council for the period 1993–95. *See illustration box.*

Pakistan
Islamic Republic of

area 307,295 sq mi/796,100 sq km; one-third of Kashmir under Pakistani control
capital Islamabad
cities Karachi, Lahore, Rawalpindi, Peshawar
physical fertile Indus plain in E; Baluchistan plateau in W, mountains in N and NW
environment about 68% of irrigated land is waterlogged or suffering from salinization
features the "five rivers" (Indus, Jhelum, Chenab, Ravi, and Sutlej) feed the world's largest irrigation system; Tarbela (world's largest earthfill dam); K2 mountain; Khyber Pass; sites of the Indus Valley civilization
head of state Ghulam Ishaq Khan from 1988
head of government Nawaz Sharif from 1990
political system emergent democracy
political parties Pakistan People's Party (PPP), moderate, Islamic, socialist; Islamic Democratic Alliance (IDA), including the Pakistan Muslim League (PML), Islamic conservative; Mohajir National Movement (MQM), Sind-based *mohajir* (Muslims previously living in India) settlers
exports cotton textiles, rice, leather, carpets
currency Pakistan rupee
population (1990 est) 113,163,000 (66%

Punjabi, 13% Sindhi); growth rate 3.1% p.a.
life expectancy men 54, women 55 (1989)
languages Urdu and English (official); Punjabi, Sindhi, Pashto, Baluchi, other local dialects
religion Sunni Muslim 75%, Shiite Muslim 20%, Hindu 4%
literacy men 40%, women 19% (1985 est)
GDP $39 bn (1988); $360 per head (1984)
chronology
1947 Independence achieved from Britain, Pakistan formed following partition of British India.
1956 Proclaimed a republic.
1958 Military rule imposed by General Ayub Khan.
1969 Power transferred to General Yahya Khan.
1971 Secession of East Pakistan (Bangladesh). After civil war, power transferred to Zulfiqar Ali Bhutto.
1977 Bhutto overthrown in military coup by General Zia ul-Haq; martial law imposed.
1979 Bhutto executed.
1981 Opposition Movement for the Restoration of Democracy formed. Islamization process pushed forward.
1985 Nonparty elections held, amended constitution adopted, martial law and ban on political parties lifted.
1986 Agitation for free elections launched by Benazir Bhutto.
1988 Zia introduced Islamic legal code, the *Shari'a*. He was killed in a military plane crash in Aug. Benazir Bhutto elected prime minister Nov.
1989 Pakistan rejoined the British Commonwealth.
1990 Army mobilized in support of Muslim separatists in Indian Kashmir. Bhutto dismissed on charges of incompetence and corruption. Islamic Democratic Alliance (IDA), led by Nawaz Sharif, won Oct general election.
1991 *Shari'a* (Islamic legal code) bill enacted; privatization and economic deregulation program launched.
1992 Pakistan elected to United Nations (UN) Security Council 1993–95.

Pakula Alan J 1928– . US film director, formerly a producer, whose compelling films include *Klute* 1971, *The Parallax View* 1974, and *All the President's Men* 1976. His later work includes *Sophie's Choice* 1982 and *Presumed Innocent* 1990.

In his role as producer he was involved with *Fear Strikes Out* 1957, *To Kill A Mockingbird*

1962 and *The Stalking Moon* 1969, all directed by Robert Mulligan (1925–).

Palamas Kostes 1859–1943. Greek poet. He enriched the Greek vernacular by his use of it as a literary language, particularly in his poetry, such as in *Songs of My Fatherland* 1886 and *The Flute of the King* 1910, which expresses his vivid awareness of Greek history.

Palance Jack. Adopted name of Walter Jack Palahnuik 1920– . US film actor, often cast as a brooding villain: his films include *Shane* 1953, *Contempt* 1963, and *Batman* 1989. In 1992 he received an Academy Award as best supporting actor in *City Slickers* 1991.

palate in mammals, the ceiling of the mouth. The bony front part is the hard palate, the muscular rear part the soft palate. Incomplete fusion of the two lateral halves of the palate causes interference with speech.

Technically, the mammalian palate is a secondary structure and parallel to the original mouth roof of fishes, amphibians, reptiles, and birds.

Palatinate (called the *Pfalz* in Germany) historic division of Germany, dating from before the 8th century. It was ruled by a *count palatine* (a count with royal prerogatives) and varied in size.

When the Palatinate was attached to Bavaria 1815 it consisted of two separate parts: Rhenish (or Lower) Palatinate on the Rhine (capital Heidelberg), and Upper Palatinate (capital Amberg on the Vils) 130 mi/210 km to the E. In 1946 Rhenish Palatinate became an administrative division of the *Land* (German region) of Rhineland-Palatinate with its capital at Neustadt; Upper Palatinate remained an administrative division of Bavaria with its capital at Regensburg.

Palau former name (until 1981) of the Republic of ⇨Belau.

Paleocene (Greek "old" + "recent") first epoch of the Tertiary period of geological time, 65–55 million years ago. Many types of mammals spread rapidly after the disappearance of the great reptiles of the Mesozoic.

Paleolithic earliest stage of human technology and development of the Stone Age; see ⇨prehistory.

paleomagnetism science of the reconstruction of the Earth's ancient magnetic field and the former positions of the continents, from the evidence of what is called remanent magnetization in ancient rocks. Remanent magnetization is the record of magnetization acquired by igneous rocks as they cool past the point where they can be influenced by any later magnetization through the presence of the Earth's magnetic field. This permanent record of the direction of the Earth's magnetic field at the time of formation permits geologists to reconstruct the intervals at which the Earth's magnetic field has changed direction, or become reversed. Paleomagnetism shows that such events occur with some regularity—the magnetic north pole becoming the magnetic south pole, and vice versa at approximate half-million-year intervals, with shorter reversal periods in between the major spans.

Starting in the 1960s, this known pattern of magnetic reversals was used to demonstrate seafloor spreading or the formation of new ocean crust on either side of midoceanic ridges. As new material hardened on either side of a ridge, it would retain the imprint of the magnetic field, furnishing datable proof that material was spreading steadily outward. Paleomagnetism is also used to demonstrate continental drift, of the movement of continents on tectonic plates, through time, by determining the direction of the magnetic field of dated rocks from different continents.

paleontology in geology, the study of ancient life that encompasses the structure of ancient organisms and their environment, evolution, and ecology, as revealed by their ⇨fossils.

The practical aspects of paleontology are based on using the presence of different fossils to date particular rock strata and to identify rocks that were laid down under particular conditions, for instance giving rise to the formation of oil. The term paleontology was first used in 1834, during the period when the first ⇨dinosaur remains were discovered.

Paleozoic era of geological time 590–248 million years ago. It comprises the Cambrian, Ordovician, Silurian, Devonian, Carboniferous, and Permian periods. The Cambrian, Ordovician, and Silurian constitute the Lower Paleozoic; the Devonian, Carboniferous, and Permian make up the Upper Paleozoic. The era includes the evolution of hard-shelled multicellular life forms in the sea; the invasion of land by plants and animals; and the evolution of fish, amphibians, and early reptiles. The earliest identifiable fossils date from this era. The climate was mostly warm with short ice ages. The continents were very different from the present ones but, toward the end of the era, all were joined together as a single world continent called ⇨Pangaea.

Palermo capital and seaport of Sicily; population (1988) 729,000. Industries include shipbuilding, steel, glass, and chemicals. It was founded by the Phoenicians in the 8th century BC.

Palestine (Arabic *Falastin* "Philistines") (also called the *Holy Land* because of its links with Judaism, Christianity, and Islam) area between the Mediterranean and the river Jordan, with Lebanon to the N and Sinai to the S. The homeland of the ancient Hebrews, it was from ancient to modern times dominated in turn by Egypt, Assyria, Babylonia, Persia, Macedonia, the Ptolemies, the Seleucids, and the Roman, Byzantine, and Ottoman empires. Captured by the British in World War I, it became a British mandate (1923–48), and Jewish immigration increased dramatically. Since 1948, when Israel was established, it has been part of that country. The majority of the inhabitants are Jews. The Palestinian Arabs are widely distributed (about 1 million in the West Bank, E Jerusalem, and the Gaza Strip; 1.2 million in Jordan; 750,000 in Israel; 300,000 in Lebanon; and 100,000 in the US).

Palestine Liberation Organization (PLO) Arab organization founded 1964 to bring about an independent state of Palestine. It consists of several distinct groupings, the chief of which is al-⇨Fatah, led by Yassir ⇨Arafat, the president of the PLO from 1969. The PLO has pursued diplomatic initiatives, but also operates as a guerrilla movement.

Beirut, Lebanon, became PLO headquarters 1970–71 after its defeat in the Jordanian civil war. In 1974 the PLO became the first nongovernmental delegation to be admitted to a session of the UN General Assembly. When Israel invaded Lebanon 1982 the PLO had to abandon its headquarters there; it moved on to Tunis, Tunisia, and in 1986 to Baghdad, Iraq. PLO members who remained in Lebanon after the expulsion were later drawn into the internal conflict (see ⇨Arab-Israeli Wars). In 1986 Jordan suspended "political coordination" with the PLO and expelled Arafat's deputy, dealing instead directly with Palestinians in Israeli-

Palestine: history

AD 636	Conquest by the Muslim Arabs, which made it a target for the ⇨Crusades (see also ⇨Jerusalem).
1516	Conquest by the *Ottoman* Turks.
1880–1914	As a result of pogroms in Russia and Poland, Jewish immigration increased.
1897	At the first Zionist Congress, Jews called for a permanent homeland in Palestine.
1909	Tel Aviv, the first all-Jewish town in Palestine, was founded.
1917–18	Turks driven out by General ⇨Allenby in World War I.
1922	Britain received Palestine as a League of Nations mandate (incorporating the ⇨Balfour Declaration) to administer both historic Palestine and lands across the river Jordan that were recognized 1923 as the Hashemite Kingdom of Jordan.
1929 and 1936–38	Arab revolts fueled by Jewish immigration (300,000 during 1920–39).
1937	Pan-Arab Congress.
1939	British White Paper for Palestine restricted Jewish immigration to 15,000 per year.
1939–45	Both Arab and Jewish Palestinians served in the Allied forces in World War II.
1947	Following Jewish guerrilla activities, prompted by restriction of Jewish immigration, Britain put the question before the United Nations, which voted for partition.
1948	May 15 (eight hours before Britain's renunciation of the mandate was due) a Jewish state of ⇨Israel was proclaimed. A series of ⇨Arab–Israeli Wars resulted in the displacement of large numbers of Palestinian Arabs.
1964	The ⇨Palestine Liberation Organization (PLO) was formed and a guerrilla war was waged against the Jewish state.
1974	The PLO became the first nongovernmental delegation to be admitted to a plenary session of the United Nations General Assembly.
1987	Palestinian uprising (⇨*Intifada*) began in occupied territories.
1988	PLO leader Yassir ⇨Arafat renounced terrorism; US agreed to meetings.
1989	Israeli prime minister Yitzhak Shamir proposed Palestinian elections in the West Bank/Gaza Strip.
1991	Gulf War against Iraq's annexation of Kuwait caused diplomatic reconsideration of a Palestinian state in an effort to stabilize the Middle East. A peace conference in Spain in Nov included Israel and Arab states.
1992	Direct negotiations between Israelis and Palestinians.

occupied territories. In 1988, the Palestine National Council voted to create a state of Palestine, but at the same time endorsed United Nations resolution 242, recognizing Israel's right to exist.

Discussions with the US government began for the first time when Arafat renounced terrorism as a policy.

Palestine Wars another name for the ⇨Arab-Israeli Wars.

Paley Grace 1922– . US short-story writer and critic. Her stories express Jewish and feminist experience with bitter humor, as in *The Little Disturbances of Man* 1960 and *Later the Same Day* 1985.

Pali ancient Indo-European language of N India, related to Sanskrit, and a Classical language of Buddhism.

Palikur member of a South American Indian people living in N Brazil and numbering about 1 million (1980). Formerly a warlike people, they occupied a vast area between the Amazon and Orinoco rivers.

Palladio Andrea 1518–1580. Italian Renaissance architect noted for his harmonious and balanced Classical structures. He designed numerous country houses in and around Vicenza, Italy, making use of Roman Classical forms, symmetry, and proportion. The Villa Malcontenta and the Villa Rotonda are examples of houses designed from 1540 for patrician families of the Venetian Republic. He also designed churches in Venice and published his studies of Classical form in several illustrated books.

His ideas were revived in England in the early 17th century by Inigo Jones and in the 18th century by Lord Burlington and later by architects in Italy, Holland, Germany, Russia, and the US, where his ideas were introduced by Thomas Jefferson and had wide influence on Federal-period architecture.

palladium in Greek mythology, an image of the goddess of war and wisdom, Pallas Athena, a gift from Zeus to the city of Troy. According to legend, the city could not be captured while the image remained there. It was stolen by the Greek leaders Odysseus and Diomedes and was later alleged to have been taken to Rome by the Trojan prince Aeneas.

palladium lightweight, ductile and malleable, silver-white, metallic element, symbol Pd, atomic number 46, atomic weight 106.4.

It is one of the so-called platinum group of metals, and is resistant to tarnish and corrosion. It often occurs in nature as a free metal (see ⇨native metal) in a natural alloy with platinum. Palladium is used as a catalyst, in alloys of gold (to make white gold) and silver, in electroplating, and in dentistry.

It was discovered 1803 by British physicist William Wollaston (1766–1828), and named after the then recently discovered asteroid Pallas (found 1802).

palliative in medicine, any treatment given to relieve symptoms rather than to cure the underlying cause. In conditions that will resolve of their own accord (for instance, the common cold) or that are incurable, the entire treatment may be palliative.

palm plant of the family Palmae, characterized by a single tall stem bearing a thick cluster of large palmate or pinnate leaves at the top. The majority of the numerous species are tropical or subtropical. Some, such as the coconut, date, sago, and oil palms, are important economically.

Several palms are native to Florida.

Palma, La one of the Canary Islands, Spain
area 282 sq mi/730 sq km
capital Santa Cruz de la Palma
features forested
products wine, fruit, honey, silk; tourism is important
population (1981) 77,000.

Palma (Spanish *Palma de Mallorca*) industrial port (textiles, cement, paper, pottery), resort, and capital of the Balearic Islands, Spain, on Majorca; population (1991) 308,600. Palma was founded 276 BC as a Roman colony. It has a Gothic cathedral begun 1229.

Palmas, Las port in the Canary Islands; see ⇨Las Palmas.

Palm Beach luxurious winter resort in Florida, on an island between Lake Worth and the Atlantic; population (1990) 9,800.

Henry Flagler first developed the community as a resort in the 1890s, when he built the Royal Poinciana Hotel. It now has mansions, clubs, and large estates as well as resort hotels.

Palme (Sven) Olof 1927–1986. Swedish social-democratic politician, prime minister 1969–76 and 1982–86. As prime minister he carried out constitutional reforms, turning the Riksdag into a single-chamber parliament and stripping the monarch of power, and was widely respected for his support of Third World Countries. He was assassinated Feb 1986.

Palme, educated in Sweden and the US, joined the SAP 1949 and became secretary to the prime minister 1954. He led the SAP youth movement 1955–61. In 1963 he entered government and held several posts before becoming leader of the Social Democratic Labor Party (SAP) 1969. Palme was shot by an unknown assassin in the center of Stockholm while walking home with his wife after an evening visit to a cinema.

Palmer A(lexander) Mitchell 1872–1936. US public official. After establishing a private legal practice in Stroudsburg, Pennsylvania, he became active in state Democratic politics and sat in the US House of Representatives 1909–15. Owing to his Quaker beliefs, Palmer declined an appointment as secretary of war by President Wilson, serving instead as custodian of alien property during World War I. As US attorney general 1919–21, he led the controversial "Palmer Raids" against alleged political radicals.

Born in Moosehead, Pennsylvania, Palmer was educated at Swarthmore College and was admitted to the bar 1893.

Palmer Arnold (Daniel) 1929– . US golfer who helped to popularize the professional sport in the US in the 1950s and 1960s. He won the Masters 1958, 1960, 1962, and 1964; the US Open 1960; and the British Open 1961 and 1962.

Born in Pennsylvania, he won the US amateur title 1954, and went on to win all the world major professional trophies except the US PGA Championship. In the 1980s he enjoyed a successful career on the US Seniors Tour.

CAREER HIGHLIGHTS

US Open: 1960
British Open: 1961–62
Masters: 1958, 1960, 1962, 1964
World Match-Play: 1964, 1967
US Ryder Cup: 1961, 1963*, 1965, 1967, 1971, 1973, 1975**
* playing captain; ** nonplaying captain

Palmer Geoffrey Winston Russell 1942– . New Zealand Labor politician, prime minister 1989–90, deputy prime minister and attorney-general 1984–89.

A graduate of Victoria University, Wellington, Palmer was a law lecturer in the US and New Zealand before entering politics, becoming Labor member for Christchurch in the House of Representatives 1979. He succeeded David ⇨Lange on Lange's resignation as prime minister but resigned himself the following year.

Palmerston Henry John Temple, 3rd Viscount 1781–1865. British politician. Initially a Tory, in Parliament from 1807, he was secretary-at-war 1809–28. He broke with the Tories 1830 and sat in the Whig cabinets of 1830–34, 1835–41, and 1846–51 as foreign secretary. He was prime minister 1855–58 (when he rectified Aberdeen's mismanagement of the Crimean War, suppressed the Indian (Sepoy) Mutiny, and carried through the Second Opium War) and 1859–65 (when he almost involved Britain in the American Civil War on the side of the South).

He was responsible for the warship ⇨*Alabama* going to the Confederate side in the American Civil War.

Palm Springs resort and spa in S California, about 100 mi/160 km E of Los Angeles; population (1990) 40,200.

Palm Sunday in the Christian calendar, the Sunday before Easter and first day of Holy Week, commemorating Jesus' entry into Jerusalem, when the crowd strewed palm leaves in his path.

Palmyra ancient city and oasis in the desert of Syria, about 150 mi/240 km NE of Damascus. Palmyra, the biblical *Tadmor*, was flourishing by about 300 BC. It was destroyed AD 272 after Queen Zenobia had led a revolt against the Romans. Extensive temple ruins exist, and on the site is a village called Tadmor.

Palmyra coral atoll 1,000 mi/1,600 km SW of Hawaii, in the Line Islands, S Pacific, purchased by the US from a Hawaiian family 1979 for the storage of highly radioactive nuclear waste from 1986.

Palo Alto city in California, situated SE of San Francisco at the center of the high-tech region known as "Silicon Valley;" population (1990) 55,900. It is the site of Stanford University.

Palomar, Mount astronomical observatory, 50 mi/80 km NE of San Diego, California. It has a 200-in/5-m diameter reflector called the Hale. Completed 1948, it was the world's premier observatory during the 1950s.

Pamirs central Asian plateau mainly in Tajikistan, but extending into China and Afghanistan, traversed by mountain ranges. Its highest peak is Kommunizma Pik (Communism Peak 24,600 ft/7,495 m) in the Akademiya Nauk range.

Pampas flat, treeless, Argentine plains, lying between the Andes and the Atlantic and rising gradually from the coast to the lower slopes of the mountains. The E Pampas contain large cattle ranches and the flax- and grain-growing area of Argentina; the W Pampas are arid and unproductive.

pampas grass any grass of the genus *Cortaderia*, native to South America, especially *C. argentea*, which is grown in gardens and has tall leaves and large panicles of white flowers.

Pamplona industrial city (wine, leather, shoes, textiles) in Navarre, N Spain, on

Panama
Republic of (*República de Panamá*)

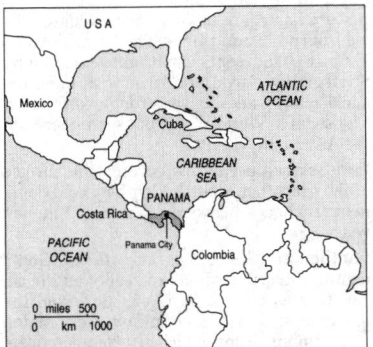

area 29,768 sq mi/77,100 sq km
capital Panamá (Panama City)
cities Cristóbal, Balboa, Colón, David
physical coastal plains and mountainous interior; tropical rainforest in E and NW; Pearl Islands in Gulf of Panama
features Panama Canal; Barro Colorado Island in Gatún Lake (reservoir supplying the canal), a tropical forest reserve since 1923; Smithsonian Tropical Research Institute
head of state and government Guillermo Endara from 1989
political system emergent democratic republic
political parties Democratic Revolutionary Party (PRD), right-wing; Labor Party (PALA), right-of-center; Panamanian Republican Party (PPR), right-wing; Nationalist Liberal Republican Movement (MOLIRENA), left-of-center; Authentic Panamanian Party (PPA), centrist; Christian Democratic Party (PDC), center-left
exports bananas, petroleum products, copper, shrimps, sugar

currency balboa
population (1990 est) 2,423,000 (70% mestizo (mixed race), 14% W Indian, 10% European descent, 6% Indian (Cuna, Choco, Guayami)); growth rate 2.2% p.a.
life expectancy men 71, women 75 (1989)
languages Spanish (official), English
religion Roman Catholic 93%, Protestant 6%
literacy 87% (1989)
GNP $4.2 bn (1988); $1,970 per head (1984)
chronology
1821 Achieved independence from Spain; joined Gran Colombia.
1903 Full independence achieved on separation from Colombia.
1974 Agreement to negotiate full transfer of the Panama Canal from the US to Panama.
1977 USA–Panama treaties transferred the canal to Panama, effective 1999, with the US guaranteeing its protection and an annual payment.
1984 Nicolás Ardito Barletta elected president.
1985 Barletta resigned; replaced by Eric Arturo del Valle.
1987 General Noriega resisted calls for his removal, despite suspension of US military and economic aid.
1988 Del Valle replaced by Manuel Solis Palma. Noriega, charged with drug smuggling by the US, declared a state of emergency.
1989 Opposition won election; Noriega declared results invalid; Francisco Rodríguez sworn in as president; coup attempt against Noriega failed; Noriega declared head of government by assembly; "state of war" with the US announced; US invasion deposed Noriega; Guillermo Endara installed as president; Noriega sought asylum in Vatican embassy; later surrendered and taken to US for trial.
1991 Attempted antigovernment coup foiled. Army abolished.
1992 Noriega found guilty of drug offenses. Constitutional reform referendum voted down overwhelmingly.

as the Canal Zone, in perpetuity. Panama was guaranteed US protection and an annuity. In 1939 Panama's protectorate status was ended by mutual agreement, and in 1977 two treaties were signed by Panama's president (1968–78), General Omar Torrijos Herrera, and US president Carter. One transferred ownership of the canal to Panama effective 1999 and the other guaranteed its subsequent neutrality, with the conditions that only Panamanian forces would be stationed in the zone, and that the US would have the right to use force to keep the canal open if it became obstructed.

deterioration of economy The 1980s saw a deterioration in the state of Panama's economy, with opposition to the austerity measures that the government introduced to try to halt the decline. Unade won 40 seats in the 1984 general election; ADO won 27 seats. After a very close result, Dr Nicolás Ardito Barletta, the Democratic Revolutionary Party (PRD) candidate, was declared president, but in 1985 he resigned, amid speculation that he had been forced to do so by the commander of the National Guard. Relations between Panama and the US deteriorated with the departure of President Barletta, and the Reagan administration cut and later suspended its financial aid.

Barletta was succeeded by Eric Arturo del Valle, but the country was, from 1983, effectively ruled by the army commander in chief, General Manuel Noriega. Although the 1977 Torrijos–Carter Canal Treaties specified that US forces in Panama were present purely to defend the canal, Noriega cooperated in allowing the US to use Panama as an intelligence, training, resupply, and weapons base for the Reagan administration's campaigns in Nicaragua and El Salvador.

accusations against Noriega In 1987 Noriega was accused of corruption, election rigging, involvement in the cocaine trade, and the murder of a political opponent. Noriega's forces were allegedly responsible for up to a dozen political killings between 1983 and 1989. Political parties, labor and student unions, and business groups united as the National Civic Crusade to campaign for his removal; demonstrations were suppressed by riot police. In July 1987 Noriega successfully resisted calls for his removal, despite the suspension of US military and economic aid. He declared the May 1989 assembly elections invalid and in Sept Francisco Rodríguez, with army backing, was made president. In the following month an attempted coup against Noriega was put down.

US invasion In Dec 1989, after mounting harassment of Americans in the Canal Zone, US president Bush ordered troops to invade the country with the declared object of arresting Noriega and bringing him to trial. Several hundred people were killed and more were made homeless in the US invasion. The US and Panamanian forces raided newspaper offices and rounded up hundreds of dissidents, many of whom were imprisoned without charge. Noriega sought refuge in the Vatican embassy but eventually surrendered and was taken to the US, where he was convicted 1992 of charges relating to drug trafficking. Guillermo Endara became president and worked to balance Panama's aims against pressures from the US, its most important partner, in such areas as banking. In Oct 1991 an attempted antigovernment coup by former officers loyal to Noriega was thwarted. In Dec 1991 the army was formally abolished. A referendum Nov 1992 voted overwhelmingly against constitutional reform. *See illustration box.*

---

the Arga River; population (1986) 184,000. A pre-Roman town, it was rebuilt by Pompey 68 BC, captured by the Visigoths 476, sacked by Charlemagne 778, became the capital of Navarre, and was taken by the Duke of Wellington in the Peninsular War 1813. An annual running of bulls takes place in the streets in July.

Pan in Greek mythology, the god (Roman *Sylvanus*) of flocks and herds, shown as a man with the horns, ears, and hoofed legs of a goat, and playing a shepherd's panpipe (or syrinx).

panacea any supposed remedy for all known disease; a cure-all.

Pan-Africanist Congress (PAC) militant black South African nationalist group, which broke away from the African National Congress (ANC) 1959. More radical than the ANC, the Pan-Africanist Congress has a black-only policy for Africa. PAC was outlawed from 1960 to 1990. Its military wing is called Poqo ("we alone").

Panama country in Central America, on a narrow isthmus between the Caribbean and the Pacific Ocean, bounded W by Costa Rica and E by Colombia.
government The constitution was revised 1983, when a new, single-chamber legislative assembly of 67 members, elected by universal suffrage for a five-year term, was created. The

president, elected in the same way for a similar period of office, is assisted by two elected vice-presidents and an appointed cabinet. There are a large number of political organizations, the most significant being represented in the assembly by two coalitions, the center-right National Democratic Union (Unade) and the center-left Democratic Opposition Alliance (ADO). Panama is divided into nine provinces, each with its own governor, appointed by the president. There are also three Indian reservations, which enjoy a high degree of self-government.
history For early history, see ◊American Indian. Panama was visited by Christopher ◊Columbus 1502. Vasco Núñez de ◊Balboa found the Pacific from the Darien isthmus 1513. Spanish settlements were sacked by Francis ◊Drake 1572–95 and Henry ◊Morgan 1668–71; Morgan destroyed the old city of Panama, which dated from 1519. Remains of Fort St Andrews, built by Scottish settlers 1698–1701, were discovered 1976. Panama remained part of the viceroyalties of Peru and New Granada until 1821, when it gained independence from Spain; it joined Gran Colombia 1822.
independence Panama achieved full independence 1903 with US support. At the same time the US bought the rights to build the Panama Canal and was given control of a strip of territory 10 mi/16 km wide, known

Panama Canal canal across the Panama isthmus in Central America, connecting the Pacific and Atlantic oceans; length 50 mi/80 km, with 12 locks. Built by the US 1904–14 after an unsuccessful attempt by the French, it was formally opened 1920. The *Panama Canal Zone* was acquired "in perpetuity" by the US 1903, comprising land extending about 3 mi/5 km on either side of the canal. The zone passed to Panama 1979, and control of the canal itself was ceded to Panama by the US in Jan 1990 under the terms of the Panama Canal Treaty 1977. The Canal Zone has several US military bases.

Panama City capital of the Republic of Panama, near the Pacific end of the Panama Canal; population (1990) 584,800. Products include chemicals, plastics, and clothing. An earlier Panama, to the NE, founded 1519, was destroyed 1671, and the city was founded on the present site 1673.

Pan-American Highway road linking the US with Central and South America; length 15,700 mi/25,300 km. Starting from the US–Canadian frontier (where it links with the Alaska Highway), it runs through San Francisco, Los Angeles, and Mexico City to Panama City, then down the west side of South America to Valparaíso, Chile, where it crosses the Andes and goes to Buenos Aires, Argentina. The road was first planned 1923.

Pan-American Union former name (1910–48) of the ▷Organization of American States.

Panay one of the Philippine islands, lying between Mindoro and Negros
area 4,446 sq mi/11,515 sq km
capital Iloilo
features mountainous, 7,265 ft/2,215 m in Madiaás
products rice, sugar, pineapples, bananas, copra, copper
history seized by Spain 1569; occupied by Japan 1942–45.

Panchen Lama 10th incarnation 1935–1989. Tibetan spiritual leader, second in importance to the ▷Dalai Lama. A protégé of the Chinese since childhood, the present Panchen Lama is not universally recognized. When the Dalai Lama left Tibet 1959, the Panchen Lama was deputed by the Chinese to take over, but was stripped of power 1964 for refusing to denounce the Dalai Lama. He did not appear again in public until 1978.

panchromatic in photography, a term describing highly sensitive black-and-white film made to render all visible spectral colors in correct gray tones. Panchromatic film is always developed in total darkness.

pancreas in vertebrates, an accessory gland of the digestive system located close to the duodenum. When stimulated by the hormone secretin, it secretes enzymes into the duodenum that digest starches, proteins, and fats. In humans, it is about 7 in/18 cm long, and lies behind and below the stomach. It contains groups of cells called the *islets of Langerhans*, which secrete the hormones insulin and glucagon that regulate the blood sugar level.

panda one of two carnivores of different families, native to NW China and Tibet. The *giant panda Ailuropoda melanoleuca* has black-and-white fur with black eye patches, and feeds mainly on bamboo shoots. It can grow up to 4.5 ft/1.5 m long, and weigh up to 300 lb/140 kg. It is an endangered species. The *lesser,*

or red, panda Ailurus fulgens, of the raccoon family, is about 1.5 ft/50 cm long, and is black and chestnut, with a long tail.

Destruction of the giant pandas' natural habitats threatens to make them extinct in the wild, and they are the focus of conservation efforts. There is dispute about whether they should be included in the bear family or the raccoon family, or classified as a family of their own.

Pandora in Greek mythology, the first mortal woman. Zeus sent her to Earth with a box of evils (to counteract the blessings brought to mortals by ▷Prometheus' gift of fire); she opened the box, and the evils all flew out. Only hope was left inside as a consolation.

Pangaea or *Pangea* world continent, named by Alfred ▷Wegener, that existed between 250 and 200 million years ago, made up of all the continental masses. It may be regarded as a combination of ▷Laurasia in the north and ▷Gondwanaland in the south, the rest of Earth being covered by the ▷Panthalassa ocean.

Pan-Germanism movement that developed during the 19th century to encourage unity between German- and Dutch-speaking peoples in Austria, the Netherlands, Flanders, Luxembourg, and Switzerland. Encouraged by the unification of Germany after 1871, the movement had an increasingly high profile in the period up to 1914.

Pan-Germanism also had an impact in Belgium (Flemish separatism) and in Poland during World War I. Despite the defeat of Germany in 1919, its ideas were revived under Hitler's plans to expand through Europe.

pangolin or *scaly anteater* any toothless mammal of the order Pholidota. There is only one genus (*Manis*), with seven species found in tropical Africa and SE Asia. They are long-tailed and covered with large, overlapping scales. The elongated skull contains a long, extensible tongue. Pangolins measure up to 3 ft/1 m in length; some are arboreal and others are terrestrial. All live on ants and termites.

Panipat town in Punjab, India; scene of three decisive battles: 1526, when Babur (1483–1530), great-grandson of Tamerlane, defeated the emperor of Delhi and founded the Mogul empire; 1556, won by his descendant ▷Akbar; 1761, when the ▷Marathas were defeated by ▷Ahmad Shah Durrani of Afghanistan.

Pankhurst Emmeline (born Goulden) 1858–1928. English suffragist. Founder of the Women's Social and Political Union 1903, she launched the militant suffragist campaign 1905. In 1926 she joined the Conservative Party and was a prospective Parliamentary candidate.

pansy cultivated violet derived from the European wild pansy *Viola tricolor*, and including many different varieties and strains. The flowers are usually purple, yellow, cream, or a mixture, and there are many highly developed varieties bred for size, color, or special markings. Several of the 400 different species are scented.

Pantanal large area of swampland in the Mato Grosso of SW Brazil, occupying 84,975 sq mi/220,000 sq km in the upper reaches of the Paraguay River; one of the world's great wildlife refuges of which 530 sq mi/1,370 sq km were designated a national park in 1981.

Pantelleria volcanic island in the Mediterranean, 62 mi/100 km SW of Sicily and part of that region of Italy

area 45 sq mi/115 sq km
town Pantelleria
products sheep, fruit, olives, capers
population (1981) 7,800
history Pantelleria has drystone dwellings dating from prehistoric times. The Romans called it *Cossyra* and sent people into exile there. Strategically placed, the island has been the site of many battles. It was strongly fortified by Mussolini in World War II but surrendered to the Allies June 11, 1943.

Panthalassa ocean that covered the surface of the Earth not occupied by the world continent ▷Pangaea between 250 and 200 million years ago.

pantheism (Greek *pan* "all;" *theos* "God") doctrine that regards all of reality as divine, and God as present in all of nature and the universe. It is expressed in Egyptian religion and Brahmanism; stoicism, Neoplatonism, Judaism, Christianity, and Islam can be interpreted in pantheistic terms. Pantheistic philosophers include Bruno, Spinoza, Fichte, Schelling, and Hegel.

pantheon originally a temple for worshiping all the gods, such as that in ancient Rome, rebuilt by the emperor Hadrian and still used as a church. In more recent times, the name has been used for a building where famous people are buried (as in the Panthéon, Paris).

panther another name for the ▷leopard.

pantothenic acid $C_9H_{17}NO_5$ one of the water-soluble B ▷vitamins, occurring widely throughout a normal diet. There is no specific deficiency disease associated with pantothenic acid but it is known to be involved in the breakdown of fats and carbohydrates.

panzer German mechanized divisions and regiments in World War II, used in connection with armored vehicles, mainly tanks.

papacy the office of the ▷pope or bishop of Rome, as head of the Roman Catholic Church.

papal infallibility doctrine formulated by the Roman Catholic Vatican Council 1870, which stated that the pope, when speaking officially on certain doctrinal or moral matters, was protected from error by God, and therefore such rulings could not be challenged.

Papal States area of central Italy in which the pope was temporal ruler from 756 until the unification of Italy 1870.

Papandreou Andreas 1919– . Greek socialist politician, founder of the Pan-Hellenic Socialist Movement (PASOK), and prime minister 1981–89, when he became implicated in the alleged embezzlement and diversion of funds to the Greek government of $200 million from the Bank of Crete, headed by George Koskotas, and as a result lost the election. In Jan 1992 a trial cleared Papandreou of all corruption charges.

Son of a former prime minister, he studied law in Athens and at Harvard. He was director of the Center for Economic Research in Athens 1961–64, and economic adviser to the Bank of Greece. He was imprisoned April–Dec 1967 for his political activities, after which he founded PASOK. After another spell in overseas universities, he returned to Greece 1974. He was leader of the opposition 1977–81, and became Greece's first socialist prime minister. He was reelected 1985, but defeated 1989 after damage to his party and himself from the Koskotas affair.

papaya tropical tree *Carica papaya* of the family Caricaceae, native from Florida to South

America. Varieties are grown throughout the tropics. The edible fruits resemble a melon, with orange-colored flesh and numerous blackish seeds in the central cavity; they may weigh up to 20 lb/9 kg.

The fruit juice and the tree sap contain papain, an enzyme used to tenderize meat and aid digestion.

Papeete capital and port of French Polynesia on the NW coast of Tahiti; population (1983) 79,000. Products include vanilla, copra, and mother-of-pearl.

Papen Franz von 1879–1969. German right-wing politician. As chancellor 1932, he negotiated the Nazi–Conservative alliance that made Hitler chancellor 1933. He was envoy to Austria 1934–38 and ambassador to Turkey 1939–44. Although acquitted at the ⇨Nuremberg trials, he was imprisoned by a German denazification court for three years.

paper thin, flexible material made in sheets from vegetable fibers (such as wood pulp) or rags and used for writing, drawing, printing, packaging, and various household needs. The name comes from papyrus, a form of writing material made from water reed, used in ancient Egypt. The invention of true paper, originally made of pulped fishing nets and rags, is credited to Tsai Lun, Chinese minister of agriculture, AD 105.

Paper came to the West with Arabs who had learned the secret from Chinese prisoners of war in Samarkand in 768. It spread to Moorish Spain and to Byzantium in the 11th century, then to the rest of Europe. All early paper was handmade within frames.

With the spread of literacy there was a great increase in the demand for paper. Production by hand of single sheets could not keep pace with this demand, which led to the invention, by Louis Robert (1761–1828) in 1799, of a machine to produce a continuous reel of paper. The process was developed and patented in 1801 by François Didot, Robert's employer. Today most paper is made from ⇨wood pulp on a Foudrinier machine, then cut to size. Paper products absorb 35% of the world's annual commercial wood harvest; recycling avoids some of the enormous waste of trees, and most papermakers plant and replant their own forests of fast-growing stock.

Paphos resort town on the SW coast of Cyprus; population (1985) 23,200. It was the capital of Cyprus in Roman times and the legendary birthplace of the goddess Aphrodite, who rose out of the sea. Archeological remains include the 2,300-year-old underground "Tombs of the Kings," the Roman villa of Dionysus, and a 7th-century Byzantine castle.

papier mâché craft technique that involves building up layer upon layer of pasted paper, which is then baked or left to harden. Used for trays, decorative objects, and even furniture, it is often painted, lacquered, or decorated with mother-of-pearl.

Papineau Louis Joseph 1786–1871. Canadian politician. He led a mission to England to protest against the planned union of Lower Canada (Québec) and Upper Canada (Ontario), and demanded economic reform and an elected provincial legislature. In 1835 he gained the cooperation of William Lyon ⇨Mackenzie in Upper Canada, and in 1837 organized an unsuccessful rebellion of the French against British rule in Lower Canada. He fled the country, but returned 1847 to sit in the United Canadian legislature until 1854.

Papp Joseph 1921–1991. US theater director, and founder of the New York Shakespeare Festival 1954 held in an open-air theater in the city's Central Park. He also founded the New York Public Theater 1967, an off-Broadway forum for new talent, which staged the first productions of the musicals *Hair* 1967 and *A Chorus Line*.

Productions directed by Papp include *The Merchant of Venice* and a musical version of *The Two Gentlemen of Verona* (Tony award 1972). Many of Papp's productions achieved great success when transferred to Broadway.

pappus (plural *pappi*) in botany, a modified ⇨calyx comprising a ring of fine, silky hairs, or sometimes scales or small teeth, that persists after fertilization. Pappi are found in members of the daisy family (Compositae) such as the dandelions *Taraxacum*, where they form a parachutelike structure that aids dispersal of the fruit.

Pap test or *Pap smear* common name for ⇨cervical smear.

Papua original name of the island of New Guinea, but latterly its SE section, now part of ⇨Papua New Guinea.

Papuan native to or inhabitant of Papua New Guinea; a speaker of a Papuan language, used mainly on the island of New Guinea, although some 500 are used in New Britain, the Solomon Islands, and the islands of the SW Pacific. The Papuan languages belong to the Indo-Pacific family.

Papuan is a more geographic than linguistic term, since the languages are so varied that it is doubtful that they belong to the same family. Two of the best known languages in Irian Jaya are Marind and Nimborau. In Papua New Guinea, Enga, Kate, Kiwai, and Orokoto are spoken, while Baining is used in New Britain.

Papua New Guinea country in the SW Pacific, comprising the eastern part of the island of New Guinea, the Bismarck Archipelago, and part of the Solomon Islands.

government The British monarch is the formal head of state, represented by a resident governor-general. The governor-general appoints the prime minister and cabinet, who are drawn from and responsible to the parliament.

The constitution from 1975 provides for a single-chamber legislature, the National Parliament, consisting of 109 members elected by universal suffrage for a five-year term, 89 representing local single-member constituencies and 20 provincial constituencies. Although Papua New Guinea is not a federal state, it has 20 provincial governments with a fair degree of autonomy. The 12 political parties include the Papua New Guinea Party (Pangu Pati: PP), People's Democratic Movement (PDM), National Party (NP), Melanesian Alliance (MA), and People's Progress Party (PPP).

history New Guinea has been inhabited for at least 50,000 years, probably by people arriving from the E Indonesian islands. Agricultural economy dates back some 6,000 years. In the Western Highlands, a permanent system with

Papua New Guinea

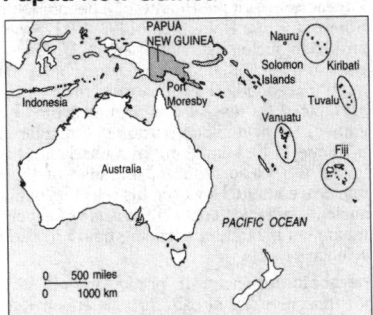

area 178,656 sq mi/462,840 sq km
capital Port Moresby (on E New Guinea)
cities Lae, Rabaul, Madang
physical mountainous; includes tropical islands of New Ireland, New Britain, and Bougainville; Admiralty Islands, D'Entrecasteaux Islands, and Louisiade Archipelago
features one of world's largest swamps on SW coast; world's largest butterfly, orchids; Sepik River
head of state Elizabeth II, represented by governor-general
head of government Paias Wingti from 1992
political system liberal democracy
political parties Papua New Guinea Party (Pangu Pati: PP), urban-and coastal-oriented nationalist; People's Democratic Movement (PDM), 1985 breakaway from the PP; National Party (NP), highlands-based; Melanesian Alliance (MA), Bougainville-based autonomy; People's Progress Party (PPP), conservative
exports copra, coconut oil, palm oil, tea, copper, gold, coffee

currency kina
population (1989 est) 3,613,000 (Papuans, Melanesians, Negritos, various minorities); growth rate 2.6% p.a.
life expectancy men 53, women 54 (1987)
languages English (official); pidgin English, 715 local languages
religion Protestant 63%, Roman Catholic 31%, local faiths
literacy men 55%, women 36% (1985 est)
GNP $2.5 bn; $730 per head (1987)
chronology
1883 Annexed by Queensland; became the Australian Territory of Papua.
1884 NE New Guinea annexed by Germany; SE claimed by Britain.
1914 NE New Guinea occupied by Australia.
1921–42 Held as a League of Nations mandate.
1942–45 Occupied by Japan.
1975 Independence achieved from Australia, within the Commonwealth, with Michael Somare as prime minister.
1980 Julius Chan became prime minister.
1982 Somare returned to power.
1985 Somare challenged by deputy prime minister, Paias Wingti, who later formed a five-party coalition government.
1988 Wingti defeated on no-confidence vote and replaced by Rabbie Namaliu, who established a six-party coalition government.
1989 State of emergency imposed on Bougainville in response to separatist violence.
1991 Peace accord signed with Bougainville secessionists. Economic boom as gold production doubled. Wiwa Korowi elected as new governor-general. Deputy prime minister, Ted Diro, resigned, having been found guilty of corruption.
1992 April: killings by outlawed Bougainville secessionists reported. July: Wingti elected premier.

drainage and garden tools was established 2,500 years ago. The sweet potato, introduced 1,200 years, ago became the staple crop of the highlands, the yam and taro being grown in lowland areas. The first European to reach New Guinea was probably the Portuguese explorer Jorge de Menezes in about 1526, who named it "Ilhas dos Papuas." It was visited by several Dutch traders in the 17th century, and by the Englishman William Dampier 1700, who named the island of New Britain. French explorer Louis Antoine de Bougainville was in the area 1768. The Dutch East India Company took control of the western half of the island, and in 1828 it became part of the Dutch East Indies. In 1884 the southeast was claimed by Britain, the northeast by Germany. The British part, Papua, was transferred to Australia 1905. The German part was transferred after World War I, when Australia was granted a League of Nations mandate and then a trusteeship over the area.

independence Freed from Japanese occupation 1945, the two territories were jointly administered by Australia and, after achieving internal self-government as Papua New Guinea, became fully independent within the Commonwealth 1975. The first prime minister after independence was Michael Somare, leader of the PP. Despite allegations of incompetence, he held office until 1980, when Julius Chan, leader of the PPP, succeeded him. Somare returned to power 1982, but in 1985 he lost a no-confidence motion in parliament and was replaced by Paias Wingti, leader of the breakaway PDM, with former prime minister Chan as his deputy. In 1987 Prime Minister Wingti returned to power with a slender majority of three votes. He announced a more independent foreign policy of good relations with the USSR, Japan, and China.

six-party coalition In 1988, following shifts in coalition alliances, Wingti lost a no-confidence vote and was replaced as prime minister by the former foreign minister and PP's new leader, Rabbie Namaliu. Somare became foreign minister in the new six-party coalition government. Faced with deteriorating internal law and order—soldiers rioting in Port Moresby in Feb 1989 over inadequate pay increases—the government imposed a state of emergency on ◊Bougainville island from June 1989 because of the growing strength there of the guerrilla separatist movement, which had forced the closure a month earlier of the island's Panguna copper and gold mine, which provided 40% of the country's export revenue. The government withdrew its troops from the island March 1990. In May 1990 the secessionist Bougainville Revolutionary Army (BRA) issued a unilateral declaration of independence, to which the government responded by imposing a blockade. An interim peace accord—the "Endeavour Accord"—Aug 1990 was followed by a peace accord signed Jan 1991, and intended to be permanent.

In Oct 1991 the governor-general Vincent Serei Eri was removed after his refusal to dismiss deputy prime minister Ted Diro who was found guilty of corruption in Oct. On Nov 11, 1991 Wiwa Korowi was elected to replace Eri. In April 1992 an outlawed Bougainville separatist group were responsible for the deaths of a peace negotiator and six others, damaging chances of a negotiated peace settlement. In July Wingti was elected premier for a second term.

economic slump After a slump during 1989–90 caused by the closure of the Bougainville

mine and falling world prices for its coffee and cocoa exports, Papua New Guinea has enjoyed an economic boom, with gold production doubling 1990–92 as a result of the discovery of huge new deposits. *See illustration box.*

papyrus type of paper made by the ancient Egyptians from the stem of the papyrus or paper reed *Cyperus papyrus*, family Cyperaceae. ◊Belém.

parabola in mathematics, a curve formed by cutting a right circular cone with a plane parallel to the sloping side of the cone. A parabola is one of the family of curves known as ◊conic sections. The graph of $y = x^2$ is a parabola.

It can also be defined as a path traced out by a point that moves in such a way that the distance from a fixed point (focus) is equal to its distance from a fixed straight line (directrix); it thus has an ◊eccentricity of 1.

The trajectories of missiles within the Earth's gravitational field approximate closely to parabolas (ignoring the effect of air resistance). The corresponding solid figure, the paraboloid, is formed by rotating a parabola about its axis. It is a common shape for headlight reflectors, dish-shaped microwave and radar aerials, and radiotelescopes, since a source of radiation placed at the focus of a paraboloidal reflector is propagated as a parallel beam.

Paracels (Chinese **Xisha**; Vietnamese **Hoang Sa**) group of about 130 small islands in the S China Sea. Situated in an oil-bearing area, they were occupied by China following a skirmish with Vietnam 1974.

Paracelsus Adopted name of Theophrastus Bombastus von Hohenheim 1493–1541. Swiss physician, alchemist, and scientist. He developed the idea that minerals and chemicals might have medical uses (iatrochemistry). He introduced the use of ◊laudanum (which he named) for pain-killing purposes. Considered by some to be something of a charlatan, his books were also criticized because of their mystical content. However, his rejection of the ancients and insistence on the value of experimentation make him a leading figure in early science.

paracetamol analgesic, particularly effective for musculoskeletal pain. It is as effective as aspirin in reducing fever, and less irritating to the stomach, but has little antiinflammatory action (as for joint pain). An overdose can cause severe, often irreversible or even fatal, liver and kidney damage.

Technically, it is acetaminophenol, a white crystalline powder $CH_3CONHC_6H_4OH$. It is sold under numerous trademarks (for example, Tylenol).

parachute any canopied fabric device strapped to a person or a package, used to slow down descent from a high altitude, or returning spent missiles or parts to a safe speed for landing, or sometimes to aid (through braking) the landing of a plane or missile. Modern designs enable the parachutist to exercise considerable control of direction, as in ◊skydiving.

Leonardo da Vinci sketched a parachute design, but the first descent, from a balloon at a height of 2,200 ft/670 m over Paris, was not made until 1797 by André-Jacques Garnerin (1769–1823). The first descent from an aircraft was made by Capt Albert Berry 1912 from a height of 1,500 ft/457 m over Missouri.

A parachute is typically folded into a pack from which it is released by a rip cord or oth-

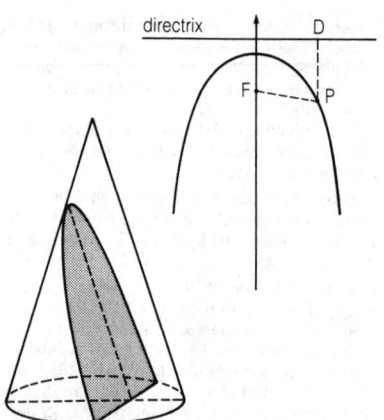

parabola *The parabola is a curve produced when a cone is cut by a plane.*

er device. It originally consisted of some two dozen panels of silk (later nylon) in a circular canopy with shroud lines to a harness. Modern parachutes are variously shaped, often small and rectangular.

In *parascending* the parachuting procedure is reversed, the canopy (parafoil) to which the person is attached being towed behind a vehicle to achieve an ascent.

paradigm all those factors, both scientific and sociological, that influence the research of the scientist. The term, first used by the US historian of science T S ◊Kuhn, has subsequently spread to social studies and politics.

paradise (Persian "pleasure garden") in various religions, a place or state of happiness. Examples are the Garden of ◊Eden and the Messianic kingdom; the Islamic paradise of the Koran is a place of sensual pleasure.

Paradise Lost epic poem in 12 books, by John Milton, first published 1667. The poem describes the Fall of Man and the battle between God and Satan, as enacted through the story of Adam and Eve in the Garden of Eden. A sequel, *Paradise Regained*, was published 1671 and relates the temptation of Christ in the wilderness.

paraffin common name for ◊alkane, any member of the series of hydrocarbons with the general formula C_nH_{2n+2}. The lower members are gases, such as methane (marsh or natural gas). The middle ones (mainly liquid) form the basis of gasoline, kerosene, and lubricating oils, while the higher ones (paraffin waxes) are used in ointment and cosmetic bases.

Paraguay landlocked country in South America, bounded NE by Brazil, S by Argentina, and NW by Bolivia.

government The 1967 constitution provides for a president and a two-chamber legislature, the National Congress, consisting of the Senate and Chamber of Deputies, all elected by universal suffrage for a five-year term. The president appoints and leads the cabinet, which is called the Council of Ministers.

The Senate has 30 members and the Chamber 60, and the party winning the largest number of votes in the congressional elections is allocated two-thirds of the seats in each chamber. A law passed 1981 prescribes that a political party must have a minimum of 10,000 members and must contest at least a third of the constituencies before it can operate.

history For early history, see ◊American Indian. The Guarani Indians had a settled agricultural civilization before the arrival of Europeans: Sebastian ▷Cabot 1526–30, followed by Spanish colonists, who founded the city of Asunción 1537. From about 1600 until 1767, when they were expelled, Jesuit missionaries administered much of the country. It became a province subordinate to the Spanish viceroyalty of Peru, then from 1776 part of the viceroyalty of Buenos Aires.

independence In 1811 Paraguay declared its independence. The first president was J G R Francia (ruled 1816–40), a despot; he was followed by his nephew C A López and in 1862 by his son F S López, who involved Paraguay in a war with Brazil, Argentina, and Uruguay. Paraguay was invaded and López killed at Aquidabán 1870. When the war was finally over, the population consisted mainly of women and children. Recovery was slow, with many revolutions. Continuing disputes with Bolivia over the frontier in the torrid Chaco zone of the north flared up into war 1932–35; arbitration by the US and five South American republics reached a peace settlement 1938.

military governments Since 1940 Paraguay has been mostly under the control of military governments led by strong, autocratic leaders. General Morínigo was president 1940–48 and General Alfredo Stroessner 1954–89. During the US presidency of Jimmy ▷Carter the Stroessner regime came under strong criticism for its violation of human rights, and this resulted in a tempering of the general's iron rule. Stroessner maintained his supremacy by ensuring that the armed forces and business community shared in the spoils of office and by preventing opposition groups from coalescing into a credible challenge. In the 1983 Congress elections the National Republican Party (Colorado Party), led by the president, with the largest number of votes, automatically secured 20 Senate and 40 Chamber seats. The Radical Liberal Party was placed second, with six Senate and 13 Chamber seats.

Stroessner sought and won an eighth consecutive term only to be ousted, in Feb 1989, by General Andrés Rodríguez who, in May 1989, was elected president. The Colorado Party was also successful in the congressional elections. During 1989–90, Rodríguez made progress on economic growth and political democracy. In Dec 1991 the Colorado Party won 58% of the vote for an assembly to write a new constitution. *See illustration box.*

parakeet any of various small ▷parrots.

parallax the change in the apparent position of an object against its background when viewed from two different positions. In astronomy, nearby stars show a shift owing to parallax when viewed from different positions on the Earth's orbit around the Sun. A star's parallax is used to deduce its distance.

Nearer bodies such as the Moon, Sun, and planets also show a parallax caused by the motion of the Earth. *Diurnal parallax* is caused by the Earth's rotation.

parallel circuit electrical circuit in which the components are connected side by side. The current flowing in the circuit is shared by the components.

parallel lines and parallel planes in mathematics, straight lines or planes that always remain a constant distance from one another no matter how far they are extended. This is a principle of Euclidean geometry. Some non-Euclidean geometries, such as elliptical and hyperbolic geometry, however, reject Euclid's parallel axiom.

parallelogram in mathematics, a quadrilateral (four-sided plane figure) with opposite pairs of

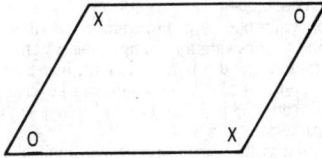

parallax *The parallax of a star, the apparent change of its position during the year, can be used to find its distance from the earth.*

sides equal in length and parallel, and opposite angles equal. The diagonals of a parallelogram bisect each other. Its area is the product of the length of one side and the perpendicular distance between this and the opposite side. In the special case when all four sides are equal in length, the parallelogram is known as a rhombus, and when the internal angles are right angles, it is a rectangle or square.

parallelogram of forces in physics and applied mathematics, a method of calculating the resultant (combined effect) of two different forces acting together on an object. Because a force has both magnitude and direction it is a ▷vector quantity and can be represented by a straight line. A second force acting at the same

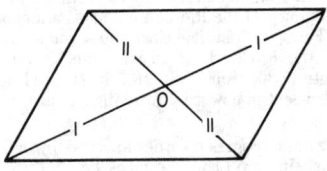

(i) opposite sides & angles are equal

(ii) diagonals bisect each other at 0.

(iii) area of a parallelogram is ah or bH

parallelogram *Some properties of a parallelogram.*

Paraguay
Republic of (*República del Paraguay*)

area 157,006 sq mi/406,752 sq km
capital Asunción
cities Puerto Presidente Stroessner, Pedro Juan Caballero; port Concepción
physical low marshy plain and marshlands; divided by Paraguay River; Paraná River forms SE boundary
features Itaipú dam on border with Brazil; Gran Chaco plain with huge swamps
head of state and government General Andrés Rodríguez from 1989

political system emergent democratic republic
political parties National Republican Association (Colorado Party), right-of-center; Liberal Party (PL), right-of-center; Radical Liberal Party (PLR), centrist
exports cotton, soybeans, timber, vegetable oil, maté
currency guaraní
population (1990 est) 4,660,000 (95% mixed Guarani Indian–Spanish descent); growth rate 3.0% p.a.
life expectancy men 67, women 72 (1989)
languages Spanish 6% (official), Guarani 90%
religion Roman Catholic 97%
literacy men 91%, women 85% (1985 est)
GNP $7.4 bn; $1,000 per head (1987)
chronology
1811 Independence achieved from Spain.
1865–70 War with Argentina, Brazil, and Uruguay; much territory lost.
1932–35 Territory won from Bolivia during the Chaco War.
1940–48 Presidency of General Higinio Morínigo.
1948–54 Political instability; six different presidents.
1954 General Alfredo Stroessner seized power.
1989 Stroessner ousted in coup led by General Andrés Rodríguez. Rodríguez elected president; Colorado Party won the congressional elections.
1991 Colorado Party successful in assembly elections.

point in a different direction can be represented by another line drawn at an angle to the first. By completing the parallelogram (of which the two lines are sides) a diagonal may be drawn from the original angle to the opposite corner to represent the resultant force vector.

parallel processing emerging computer technology that allows more than one computation at the same time. Although in the 1980s this technology enabled only a small number of computer processor units to work in parallel, in theory thousands or millions of processors could be used at the same time.

Parallel processing, which involves breaking down computations into small parts and performing thousands of them simultaneously, rather than in a linear sequence, offers the prospect of a vast improvement in working speed for certain repetitive applications.

paralysis loss of voluntary movement due to failure of nerve impulses to reach the muscles involved. It may result from almost any disorder of the nervous system, including brain or spinal-cord injury, poliomyelitis, stroke, and progressive conditions such as a tumor or multiple sclerosis. Paralysis may also involve loss of sensation due to sensory-nerve disturbance.

Paramaribo port and capital of Suriname, South America, 15 mi/24 km from the sea on the river Surinamee; population (1980) 193,000. Products include coffee, fruit, timber, and bauxite. It was founded by the French on an Indian village 1540, made capital of British Suriname 1650, and placed under Dutch rule 1816–1975.

parameter variable factor or characteristic. For example, length is one parameter of a rectangle; its height is another. In computing, it is frequently useful to describe a program or object with a set of variable parameters rather than fixed values.

For example, if a programmer writes a routine for drawing a rectangle using general parameters for the length, height, line thickness, and so on, any rectangle can be drawn by this routine by giving different values to the parameters.

Similarly, in a word-processing application that stores parameters for font, page layout, type of justification, and so on, these can be changed by the user.

Paraná river in South America, formed by the confluence of the Río Grande and Paranaiba; the Paraguay joins it at Corrientes, and it flows into the Rio de la Plata with the Uruguay; length 2,800 mi/4,500 km. It is used for hydroelectric power by Argentina, Brazil, and Paraguay.

paranoia mental disorder marked by delusions (in psychiatry, a false belief that is unshakeably held) of grandeur or persecution. In popular usage, paranoia means baseless or exaggerated fear and suspicion.

paraplegia paralysis of the lower limbs, involving loss of both movement and sensation; it is usually due to spinal injury.

parapsychology (Greek *para* "beyond") study of phenomena that are not within range of, or explicable by established science—for example, extra-sensory perception. The faculty allegedly responsible for such phenomena, and common to humans and other animals, is known as *psi*.

Parapsychological phenomena include: *mediumship*, supposed contact with the spirits of the dead, usually via an intermediate

"guide" in the other world; *precognition*, foreknowledge of events, as in "second sight;" *telekinesis*, movement of objects from one position to another by human mental concentration; and *telepathy*, a term coined by English essayist W H Myers (1843–1901) for "communication of impressions of any kind from one mind to another, independently of the recognized channels of sense." Most scientists are skeptical, but a chair of parapsychology was established 1984 at Edinburgh University, endowed by the Hungarian author Arthur Koestler.

paraquat $CH_3(C_5H_4N)_2CH_3 \cdot 2CH_3SO_4$ (technical name *1,1-dimethyl-4,4-dipyridylium*) nonselective herbicide (weedkiller). Although quickly degraded by soil microorganisms, it is deadly to human beings if ingested.

parasite organism that lives on or in another organism (called the "host"), and depends on it for nutrition, often at the expense of the host's welfare. Parasites that live inside the host, such as liver flukes and tapeworms, are called *endoparasites*; those that live on the outside, such as fleas and lice, are called *ectoparasites*.

parathyroid one of a pair of small ▷endocrine glands. Most tetrapod vertebrates, including humans, possess two such pairs, located behind the ▷thyroid gland. They secrete parathyroid hormone, which regulates the amount of calcium in the blood.

paratyphoid fever infective fever of the intestinal tract, similar to typhoid but milder and less dangerous. It is caused by bacteria of the genus *Salmonella* and is treated with antibiotics.

Paré Ambroise 1509–1590. French surgeon who introduced modern principles to the treatment of wounds. As a military surgeon, Paré developed new ways of treating wounds and amputations, which greatly reduced the death rate among the wounded. He abandoned the practice of cauterization (sealing with heat), using balms and soothing lotions instead, and used ligatures to tie off blood vessels.

parenchyma plant tissue composed of loosely packed, more or less spherical cells, with thin cellulose walls. Although parenchyma often has no specialized function, it is usually present in large amounts, forming a packing or ground tissue. It usually has many intercellular spaces.

parental care in biology, the time and energy spent by a parent in order to rear its offspring to maturity. Among animals, it ranges from the simple provision of a food supply for the hatching young at the time the eggs are laid (for example, many wasps) to feeding and protection of the young after hatching or birth, as in birds and mammals. In the more social species, parental care may include the teaching of skills—for example, female cats teach their kittens to hunt.

parent–teacher association (PTA) group attached to a school consisting of parents and teachers who support the school by fund raising and other activities. Throughout the US, PTAs are active as political pressure groups and as a way to involve parents in the public education process.

Pareto Vilfredo 1848–1923. Italian economist and political philosopher. A vigorous opponent of socialism and liberalism, he justified inequality of income on the grounds of his empirical observation (*Pareto's law*) that income distribution remained constant whatever efforts were made to change it.

Pareto was born in Paris. He produced the first account of society as a self-regulating and interdependent system that operates independently of human attempts at voluntary control. A founder of welfare economics, he put forward a concept of "optimality," which contends that optimum conditions exist in an economic system if no one can be made better off without at least one other person becoming worse off.

Paris port and capital of France, on the River Seine; *département* in the Ile de France region; area 40.5 sq mi/105 sq km; population (1990) 2,175,200. Products include metal, leather, and luxury goods and chemicals, glass, and tobacco.

features the River Seine is spanned by 32 bridges; the oldest is the Pont Neuf 1578. Churches include Notre Dame cathedral built 1163–1250; the Invalides, housing the tomb of Napoleon; the Gothic Sainte-Chapelle; and the 19th-century basilica of Sacré-Coeur, 410 ft/125 m high. Notable buildings include the Palais de Justice, the Hôtel de Ville, the Luxembourg Palace and Gardens. The former palace of the Louvre is one of the world's major art galleries; the Musée de Orsay 1986 has Impressionist and other paintings from the period 1848–1914; the Pompidou Center (Beaubourg) 1977 exhibits modern art. Other landmarks are the Tuileries gardens, the Place de la Concorde, the Eiffel Tower, and the Champs-Elysées avenue leading to the Arc de Triomphe. Central Paris was replanned in the 19th century by Baron Haussmann. To the west is the Bois de Boulogne; Montmartre is in the north of the city; the university, founded about 1150, is on the Left Bank.

history Paris, the Roman *Lutetia*, capital of the Parisii, a Gaulish people, was occupied by Julius Caesar 53 BC. The Merovingian king Clovis made Paris the capital in about AD 508, and the city became important under the Capetian kings 987–1328. Paris was occupied by the English 1420–36, and was besieged by Henry IV 1590–94. The Bourbon kings did much to beautify the city. Napoleon I added new boulevards, bridges, and triumphal arches, as did Napoleon III. Paris was the center of the revolutions of 1789–94, 1830, and 1848. It was besieged by Prussia 1870–71, and by government troops during the Commune period (local socialist government) from March to May 1871. During World War I it suffered from air raids and bombardment, and in World War II it was occupied by German troops June 1940–Aug 1944.

Paris in Greek legend, a prince of Troy whose abduction of Helen, wife of King Menelaus of Sparta, caused the Trojan War.

Paris Commune two periods of government in France:

The Paris municipal government 1789–94 was established after the storming of the ▷Bastille and remained powerful in the French Revolution until the fall of Robespierre 1794.

The provisional national government March 18–May 1871 was formed while Paris was besieged by the Germans during the Franco-Prussian War. It consisted of socialists and left-wing republicans, and is often considered the first socialist government in history. Elected after the right-wing National Assembly at Versailles tried to disarm the National Guard, it fell when the Versailles troops captured Paris and massacred 20,000–30,000 people May 21–28.

parish in the US, the ecclesiastical unit committed to one minister or priest. In Britain, a subdivision of a county often coinciding with an original territorial subdivision in Christian church administration, served by a parish church.

The origins of the parish lay in early medieval Italian cities, and by the 12th century most of Christian Europe was divided into parishes. The parish has frequently been the center of community life, especially in rural areas.

Paris, Treaty of any of various peace treaties signed in Paris, including: *1763* ending the ◊Seven Years' War; *1783* recognizing American independence; *1814* and *1815* following the abdication and final defeat of ◊Napoleon I; *1856* ending the ◊Crimean War; *1898* ending the ◊Spanish-American War; *1919–20* the conference preparing the Treaty of ◊Versailles at the end of World War I was held in Paris; *1946* after World War II, the peace treaties between the ◊Allies and Italy, Romania, Hungary, Bulgaria, and Finland; *1951* treaty signed by France, West Germany, Italy, Belgium, Netherlands and Luxembourg, embodying the Schuman Plan to set up a single coal and steel authority; *1973* ending US participation in the ◊Vietnam War.

parity in economics, equality of price, rate of exchange, wages, and buying power. Parity ratios may be used in the setting of wages to establish similar status to different work groups. Parity in international exchange rates means that those on a par with each other share similar buying power. In the US, agricultural output prices are regulated by a parity system.

parity of a number, the state of being either even or odd. In computing, the term refers to the number of 1s, in the binary codes used to represent data. A binary representation has **even parity** if it contains an even number of 1s and **odd parity** if it contains an odd number of 1s.

For example, the binary code 1000001, commonly used to represent the character "A," has even parity because it contains two 1s, and the binary code 1000011, commonly used to represent the character "C," has odd parity because it contains three 1s. A **parity bit** is sometimes added to each binary representation to adjust its parity and enable a validation check to be carried out each time data are transferred from one part of the computer to another. The parity bit is added as either a 1 or a 0 so that, after it has been added, every binary representation has the same parity. So, for example, the codes 1000001 and 1000011 could have parity bits added and become *0*1000001 and *1*1000011, both with even parity. If any bit in these codes should be altered in the course of processing the parity would change and the error would be quickly detected.

Park Mungo 1771–1806. Scottish explorer who traced the course of the Niger River 1795–97. He disappeared and probably drowned during a second African expedition 1805–06. He published *Travels in the Interior of Africa* 1799.

Park spent eighteen months in the Niger Basin while tracing the river. Even though he did not achieve his goal of reaching Timbuktu, he proved that it was feasible to travel through the interior of Africa.

Park Chung Hee 1917–1979. President of South Korea 1963–79. Under his rule South Korea had one of the world's fastest-growing economies, but recession and his increasing authoritarianism led to his assassination 1979.

Parker Bonnie 1911–1943. US criminal; see ◊Bonnie and Clyde.

Parker Charlie (Charles Christopher "Bird," "Yardbird") 1920–1955. US alto saxophonist and jazz composer, associated with the trumpeter Dizzy Gillespie in developing the ◊bebop style. His mastery of improvisation inspired performers on all jazz instruments.

Parker's most important recordings were made in the 1940s, many with a group that included Miles Davis on trumpet. He was also very influential as a live performer.

Parker Dorothy (born Rothschild) 1893–1967. US writer and wit, a leading member of the Algonquin Round Table. She reviewed for the magazines *Vanity Fair* and *The New Yorker*, and wrote wittily ironic verses, collected in several volumes including *Not So Deep As a Well* 1940, and short stories.

She also wrote screenplays in Hollywood, having moved there from New York City along with other members of her circle.

Parkersburg city in NW West Virginia, where the Little Kanawha River flows into the Ohio River, north of Charleston. Industries include chemicals, glassware, paper, and plastics; population (1990) 33,900.

Parkinson Cyril Northcote 1909– . English writer and historian, celebrated for his study of public and business administration, *Parkinson's Law* 1958, which included the dictum: "Work expands to fill the time available for its completion."

Parkinson James 1755–1824. British neurologist who first described Parkinson's disease.

Parkinson's disease or *parkinsonism* or *paraboxlysis agitans* degenerative disease of the brain characterized by a progressive loss of mobility, muscular rigidity, tremor, and speech difficulties. The condition is mainly seen in people over the age of 50.

Parkinson's disease destroys a group of cells called the *substantia nigra* ("black substance") in the upper part of the ◊brainstem. These cells are concerned with the production of a neurotransmitter known as dopamine, which is essential to the control of voluntary movement. The almost total loss of these cells, and of their chemical product, produces the disabling effects.

The introduction of the drug ◊L-dopa in the 1960s seemed at first the answer to Parkinson's disease. However, it became evident that long-term use brings considerable problems. At best, it postpones the terminal phase of the disease. Brain grafts with dopamine-producing cells were pioneered in the early 1980s, and attempts to graft Parkinson's patients with fetal brain tissue have been made. In 1989 a large US study showed that the drug deprenyl may slow the rate at which disability progresses in patients with early Parkinson's disease.

Parkman Francis 1823–1893. US historian and traveler who chronicled the European exploration and conquest of North America in such books as *The California and Oregon Trail* 1849 and *La Salle and the Discovery of the Great West* 1879.

Parkman viewed the defeat by England of the French at Québec 1759 (described in his *Montcalm and Wolfe* 1884) as the turning point of North American history, insofar as it swung the balance of power in North America toward the British colonies, which would form the United States of America.

parliament (French "speaking") legislative body of a country. The world's oldest parliament is the Icelandic Althing which dates

from about 930. The UK Parliament is usually dated from 1265. The legislature of the US is called ◊Congress and comprises the ◊House of Representatives and the ◊Senate.

In the UK, Parliament is the supreme legislature, comprising the ◊*House of Commons* and the ◊*House of Lords*. The origins of Parliament are in the 13th century, but its powers were not established until the late 17th century. The powers of the Lords were curtailed 1911, and the duration of parliaments was fixed at five years, but any parliament may extend its own life, as happened during both world wars. The UK Parliament meets in the Palace of Westminster, London.

Parliament, Houses of building where the UK legislative assembly meets. The present Houses of Parliament in London, designed in Gothic Revival style by the architects Charles Barry and A W Pugin, were built 1840–60, the previous building having burned down 1834. It incorporates portions of the medieval Palace of Westminster.

The Commons debating chamber was destroyed by incendiary bombs 1941: the rebuilt chamber (opened 1950) is the work of architect G G Scott and preserves its former character.

Parma city in Emilia-Romagna, N Italy; industries include food processing, textiles, and engineering; population (1988) 175,000. Founded by the Etruscans, it was the capital of the duchy of Parma 1545–1860. It has given its name to Parmesan cheese.

Parmenides c. 510–450 BC. Greek pre-Socratic philosopher, head of the Eleatic school (so called after Elea in S Italy). Against Heraclitus' doctrine of Becoming, Parmenides advanced the view that nonexistence was impossible, that everything was permanently in a state of being. Despite evidence of the senses to the contrary, motion and change are illusory—in fact, logically impossible—because their existence would imply a contradiction. Parmenides saw speculation and reason as more important than the evidence of the senses.

Parmigianino Francesco 1503–1540. Italian painter and etcher, active in Parma and elsewhere. He painted religious subjects and portraits in a Mannerist style, with elongated figures, for example *Madonna of the Long Neck* c. 1535 (Uffizi, Florence).

Parnassiens, Les school of French poets including Leconte de Lisle, Mallarmé, and Verlaine, which flourished 1866–76. Named after the review *Parnasse Contemporain*, it advocated "art for art's sake" in opposition to the ideas of the Romantics.

Parnassus mountain in central Greece, height 8,064 ft/2,457 m, revered by the ancient Greeks as the abode of Apollo and the Muses. The sacred site of Delphi lies on its southern flank.

Parnell Charles Stewart 1846–1891. Irish nationalist politician. He supported a policy of obstruction and violence to attain ◊Home Rule, and became the president of the Nationalist Party 1877. In 1879 he approved the ◊Land League, and his attitude led to his imprisonment 1881. His career was ruined 1890 when he was cited as corespondent in a divorce case.

Parnell, born in County Wicklow, was elected member of Parliament for Meath 1875. He welcomed Gladstone's Home Rule Bill, and continued his agitation after its defeat 1886. In 1887 his reputation suffered from an unfounded accusation by *The Times* of complicity in the murder of Lord Frederick ⊅Cavendish, chief secretary to the Lord-lieutenant of Ireland. Three years later came the adultery scandal, and for fear of losing the support of Gladstone, Parnell's party deposed him. He died suddenly of rheumatic fever at the age of 45.

parody in literature and the other arts, a work that imitates the style of another work, usually with mocking or comic intent; it is related to ⊅satire.

Parr Catherine 1512–1548. Sixth wife of Henry VIII of England. She had already lost two husbands when in 1543 she married Henry VIII. She survived him, and in 1547 married Lord Seymour of Sudeley (1508–1549).

parrot any bird of the order Psittaciformes, abundant in the tropics, especially in Australia and South America. They are mainly vegetarian, and range in size from the 3.5 in/8.5 cm pygmy parrot to the 40 in/100 cm Amazon parrot. The smaller species are commonly referred to as parakeets. The plumage is often very colorful, and the call is usually a harsh screech. Several species are endangered.

Parrots all have hooked bills and feet adapted for tree climbing. One of the rarest is the imperial parrot, found only in Dominica in the Caribbean, which is threatened by deforestation. The talent for imitating human speech is marked in the gray parrot *Psittacus erithacus* of Africa. In 1986, 600,000 parrots were caught and sold.

Parry William Edward 1790–1855. English admiral and Arctic explorer. He made detailed charts during explorations of the Northwest Passage (the sea route between the Atlantic and Pacific oceans) 1819–20, 1821–23, and 1824–25.

He made an attempt to reach the North Pole 1827. The Parry Islands, Northwest Territories, are named after him.

parsec in astronomy, a unit (symbol pc) used for distances to stars and galaxies. One parsec is equal to 3.2616 ⊅light years, 2.063 × 10⁵ ⊅astronomical units, and 3.086 x 10¹³ km.

It is the distance at which a star would have a ⊅parallax (apparent shift in position) of one second of arc when viewed from two points the same distance apart as the Earth's distance from the Sun; or the distance at which one astronomical unit subtends an angle of one second of arc.

Parsee or **Parsi** follower of the religion ⊅Zoroastrianism. The Parsees fled from Persia after its conquest by the Arabs, and settled in India in the 8th century AD. About 100,000 Parsees now live mainly in Bombay State.

Parsifal in Germanic legend, one of the knights who sought the Holy Grail; the father of ⊅Lohengrin.

parsley biennial herb *Petroselinum crispum* of the carrot family, Umbelliferae, cultivated for flavoring and its nutrient properties, being rich in vitamin C and minerals. Up to 1.5 ft/45 cm high, it has pinnate, aromatic leaves and yellow umbelliferous flowers.

parsnip temperate Eurasian biennial *Pastinaca sativa* of the carrot family Umbelliferae, with a fleshy edible root.

Parsons Talcott 1902–1979. US sociologist who attempted to integrate all the social sciences into a science of human action. He was professor of sociology at Harvard University from 1931 until his death, and author of over 150 books and articles. His theory of structural functionalism dominated US sociology from the 1940s to the 1960s, and as an attempt to explain social order and individual behavior, it was a major step in establishing sociology as an academic and scientific discipline.

part. in grammar, abbreviation for ⊅*participle*.

parthenocarpy in botany, the formation of fruits without seeds. This phenomenon, of no obvious benefit to the plant, occurs naturally in some plants, such as bananas. It can also be induced in some fruit crops, either by breeding or by applying certain plant hormones.

parthenogenesis development of an ovum (egg) without any genetic contribution from a male. Parthenogenesis is the normal means of reproduction in a few plants (for example, dandelions) and animals (for example, certain fish). Some sexually reproducing species, such as aphids, show parthenogenesis at some stage in their life cycle.

In most cases, there is no sperm contribution of any kind, but in some the stimulus of being penetrated by a sperm is needed by the egg to start dividing, although the male's chromosomes are not combined with those of the female. Parthenogenesis can be artificially induced in many animals (such as sea urchins and rabbits) by cooling, pricking, or applying acid to an egg.

Parthenon temple of Athena Parthenos ("the Virgin") on the Acropolis at Athens; built 447–438 BC by Callicrates and Ictinus under the supervision of the sculptor Phidias, and the most perfect example of Doric architecture. In turn a Christian church and a Turkish mosque, it was then used as a gunpowder store, and reduced to ruins when the Venetians bombarded the Acropolis 1687. The ⊅Elgin marbles were removed from the Parthenon in the early 19th century and are now in the British Museum, London.

Parthia ancient country in W Asia in what is now NE Iran, capital Ctesiphon. Originating about 248 BC, it reached the peak of its power under Mithridates I in the 2nd century BC, and was annexed to Persia under the Sassanids AD 226. Parthian horsemen feigned retreat and shot their arrows unexpectedly backward, hence the use of "Parthian shot," to mean a remark delivered in parting.

participle in grammar, a form of the verb, in English either a **present participle** ending in -*ing* (for example, "work*ing*" in "They were work*ing*," "work*ing* men," and "a hard-work*ing* team") or a **past participle** ending in -*ed* in regular verbs (for example, "train*ed*" in "They have been train*ed* well," "*trained* soldiers," and "a well-*trained* team").

particle physics the study of the properties of ⊅elementary particles and of fundamental interactions (see ⊅fundamental forces).

Pioneering research took place at the Cavendish laboratory, Cambridge, England. In 1895 Joseph Thomson discovered that all atoms contain identical, negatively charged particles called electrons that could easily be freed. By 1913 Ernest Rutherford had shown that electrons surround a very small, positively-charged nucleus, (which in the case of a hydrogen atom consists of a single positively charged particle, a proton, identified by James Chadwick 1932). The nuclei of all the other elements are made up of protons and uncharged particles called neutrons.

1932 also saw the discovery of a particle (predicted in 1928 by Paul Dirac), with the mass of an electron, but an equal and opposite charge, called the positron. This was the first example of an antiparticle; it is now known that almost all particles have corresponding antiparticles. In 1933 Wolfgang ⊅Pauli argued that a hitherto unsuspected particle must accompany electrons in beta-ray emission—the so-called electron-neutrino.

particles and fundamental forces By the mid-1930s, four fundamental kinds of ⊅force had been identified: (1) The electromagnetic force acts between all particles with electric charge, and was thought to be related to the exchange between the particles of photons, packets of electromagnetic radiation. (2) In 1935 the Japanese physicist Hideki Yukawa suggested that the strong force (holding protons and neutrons together in the nucleus) was caused by the exchange of particles with a mass of about a tenth that of a proton; these particles, called pions (originally pi-mesons), were found by British physicist Cecil Powell in 1946. (3) Theoretical work on the weak nuclear force began with Enrico ⊅Fermi in the 1930s. The existence of the particles that carry the weak force, the W and Z particles (weakons), was confirmed in 1983 at ⊅CERN. (4) The fourth fundamental force, gravitation, is experienced by all matter, the postulated carrier of this force being the graviton.

leptons, hadrons, and quarks The electron, three types of neutrinos, and the positive and negative muons are the leptons—particles with half-integral spin that "feel" the weak, but not the strong, force. The muon (found by US physicist Carl Anderson in cosmic radiation in 1937) produces the muon neutrino when it decays. The tauon, a surprise discovery of the 1970s, produces the tauon neutrino when it decays.

Hadrons (particles that "feel" the strong force) started to turn up in bewildering profusion in experiments in the 1950s and 1960s. They are classified into ⊅mesons, with whole-number or zero spins, and baryons (which include protons and neutrons), with half-integral spins. It was shown in the early 1960s that if hadrons of the same spin are represented as points on suitable charts, simple patterns are formed. This symmetry enabled a hitherto unknown particle, the omega-minus, to be predicted from a gap in one of the patterns; it then turned up in experiments. In 1964, Murray Gell-Mann suggested that all hadrons were composed of just three types or "flavors" of a new particle with half-integral spin and a charge of magnitude either 1/3 or 2/3 that of an electron; Gell-Mann christened the particle ⊅"quark." Mesons are quark-antiquark pairs (spins either add to one or cancel to zero), and baryons are quark triplets. To account for new mesons, such as the psi, the number of quark flavors was discovered to be six by 1985 (up, down, top, bottom, strange, and charm).

particle, subatomic see ⊅subatomic particle.

partisan member of an armed group that operates behind enemy lines or in occupied territories during wars. The name "partisans" was first given to armed bands of Russians who operated against Napoleon's army in Russia during 1812, but has since been used to describe Russian, Yugoslav, Italian, Greek, and Polish Resistance groups against the Germans during World War II.

Partisan Review US intellectual and literary magazine, founded 1934 to express Marxist principles. In the later 1930s it departed from the orthodox line, and committed itself to Modernist literature. During the 1950s the magazine published many of the major writers and critics of the time, including Saul Bellow, Mary McCarthy, and Lionel Trilling.

partnership two or more persons carrying on a common business for shared profit. The business can be of any kind—for instance, lawyers, shop owners, or window cleaners. A partnership differs from a corporation in that the individuals remain separate in identity and are not protected by limited liability, so that each partner is personally responsible for any debts of the partnership.

In a limited partnership, a general partner or partners with a limited liability manage the enterprise, while limited partners have no management rights and their liability is limited to their investment.

part of speech grammatical function of a word, described in the grammatical tradition of the Western world, based on Greek and Latin. The four major parts of speech are the noun, verb, adjective, and adverb; the minor parts of speech vary according to schools of grammatical theory, but include the article, conjunction, preposition, and pronoun.

In languages like Greek and Latin, the part of speech of a word tends to be invariable (usually marked by an ending, or ⟩inflection); in English, it is much harder to recognize the function of a word simply by its form. Some English words may have only one function (for example, *and* as a conjunction). Others may have several functions (for example, *fancy*, which is a noun in the phrase "flights of *fancy*," a verb in "*Fancy* that!" and an adjective in "a *fancy* hat").

Parton Dolly 1946– . US country and western singer and songwriter whose combination of cartoonlike sex-symbol looks and intelligent, assertive lyrics made her popular beyond the genre, with hits like "Jolene" 1974, but deliberate crossover attempts were less successful. She has also appeared in films, beginning with *9 to 5* 1980, and established a theme park Dollywood in Tennessee 1986.

partridge any of various medium-sized ground-dwelling fowl of the family Phasianidae, which also includes pheasants, quail, and chickens.

Partridges are Old World birds, some of which have become naturalized in North America, especially the European gray partridge *Perdix perdix*, with mottled brown back, gray speckled breast, and patches of chestnut on the sides.

Partridge Eric 1894–1979. New Zealand lexicographer. He studied at Oxford University and settled in England to write a number of dictionaries, including *A Dictionary of Slang and Unconventional English* 1934 and 1970, and *Dictionary of the Underworld, British and American* 1950.

Parvati in Hindu mythology, the consort of Siva in one of her gentler manifestations, and the mother of Ganesa, the god of prophecy; she is said to be the daughter of the Himalayas.

Pasadena city in SW California, part of Greater ⟩Los Angeles; population (1990) 131,600. Manufactures include electronic equipment and precision instruments.

The California Institute of Technology and the Jet Propulsion Laboratory (administered jointly by the institute and the federal government) are here. Each New Year's Day,

Pascal *In Pascal's triangle, each number is the sum of the numbers above it—for example, 2 is the sum of 1 and 1, and 6 is the sum of 3 and 3.*

Pasadena is host to the Tournament of Roses parade and a major college football game at the Rose Bowl. Farmers from Indiana founded a settlement here 1874.

Pascagoula city in SE Mississippi, at the mouth of the Pascagoula River, E of Biloxi. Industries include fishing, shipbuilding, paper, petroleum, and chemicals; population (1990) 25,900. A French fort 1718, it was at other times owned by Britain, Spain, and the free state of West Florida.

PASCAL (French acronym for *program appliqué à la selection et la compilation automatique de la littérature*) a high-level computer-programming language. Designed by Niklaus Wirth (1934–) in the 1960s as an aid to teaching programming, it is still widely used as such in universities, but is also recognized as a good general-purpose programming language. It was named after 17th-century French mathematician Blaise Pascal.

pascal SI unit (symbol Pa) of pressure, equal to one newton per square meter. It replaces ⟩bars and millibars (10^5 Pa equals one bar). It is named after the French scientist Blaise Pascal.

Pascal Blaise 1623–1662. French philosopher and mathematician. He contributed to the development of hydraulics, the ⟩calculus, and the mathematical theory of ⟩probability.

In mathematics, Pascal is known for his work on conic sections and, with Pierre de Fermat, on the probability theory. In physics, Pascal's chief work concerned fluid pressure and hydraulics. *Pascal's principle* states that the pressure everywhere in a fluid is the same, so that pressure applied at one point is transmitted equally to all parts of the container. This is the principle of the hydraulic press and jack.

Pascal's triangle is a triangular array of numbers in which each number is the sum of the pair of numbers above it. Plotted at equal distances along a horizontal axis, the numbers in the rows give the binomial probability distribution with equal probability of success and failure, such as when tossing fair coins.

In 1654 Pascal went into the Jansenist monastery of Port Royal and defended a prominent Jansenist, Antoine Arnauld (1612–1694), against the Jesuits in his *Lettres Provinciales* 1656. His *Pensées* 1670 was part of an unfinished defense of the Christian religion.

Pasco city in SE Washington, on the Columbia River, seat of Franklin county; population (1990) 20,300.

Pas-de-Calais French name for the Strait of Dover and of the French *département* bordering it, of which Arras is the capital and Calais the chief port. See also ⟩Nord-Pas-de-Calais.

pas de deux dance for two performers. A *grand pas de deux* is danced by the prima ballerina and the premier danseur.

Pashto language or *Pushto* or *Pushtu* Indo-European language, the official language of Afghanistan, also spoken in N Pakistan.

Pasiphae in Greek mythology, wife of King Minos of Crete and mother of ⟩Phaedra and of the Minotaur, the monstrous offspring of her sexual union with a bull sent from the sea by the god Poseidon.

Pasolini Pier Paolo 1922–1975. Italian director, poet, and novelist. His early work is colored by his experience of life in the poor districts of Rome, where he lived from 1950. From his Marxist viewpoint, he illustrates the decadence and inequality of society, set in a world ravaged by violence and sexuality. Among his films are *Il vangelo secondo Mateo/The Gospel According to St Matthew* 1964, *The Decameron* 1970, *I racconti de Canterbury/The Canterbury Tales* 1972, and the notorious *Salò/Salo—The 120 Days of Sodom* 1975, which included explicit scenes of sexual perversion.

Pasolini's writings (making much use of first Friulan and later Roman dialect) include the novels *Ragazzi di vita/The Ragazzi* 1955 and *Una vita violenta/A Violent Life* 1959, filmed with success as *Accattone!* 1961. He was murdered by a 17-year-old youth.

pasqueflower plant *Anemone patens* of the buttercup family, native to the central US. It has a hairy stalk and hairy leaves near the base. The showy lavender-blue flowers are 2 in/5 cm across.

Passaic city in NW New Jersey, on the Passaic River, N of Jersey City. Manufactures include television cables, chemicals, plastics, pharmaceuticals, and clothing; population (1990) 58,000.

Passau town in SE Bavaria, Germany, at the junction of the rivers Inn and Ilz with the Danube. The Treaty of Passau 1552 between Maurice, Elector of Saxony, and the future emperor Ferdinand I allowed the Lutherans full religious liberty and prepared the way for the Peace of Augsburg: see ⟩Reformation.

Passchendaele village in W Flanders, Belgium, near Ypres. The Passchendaele ridge before Ypres was the object of a costly and unsuccessful British offensive in World War I, between July and Nov 1917; British casualties numbered nearly 400,000.

passion flower climbing plant of the tropical American genus *Passiflora*, family Passifloraceae. It bears distinctive flower heads comprising a saucer-shaped petal base, a fringelike corona, and a central stalk bearing the stamens and ovary. Some species produce edible fruit.

passion play play representing the death and resurrection of a god, such as Osiris, Dionysus, or Jesus; it has its origins in medieval ⟩mystery plays. Traditionally, a passion play takes place every ten years at ⟩Oberammergau, Germany.

pass laws South African laws that required the black population to carry passbooks (identity documents) at all times and severely restricted freedom of movement. The laws, a major cause of discontent, formed a central part of the policies of ⟩apartheid. They were repealed 1986.

Passover also called *Pesach* in Judaism, an eight-day spring festival which commemorates the exodus of the Israelites from Egypt and the passing over by the Angel of Death of the Jewish houses, so that only the Egyptian firstborn sons were killed, redressing Pharaoh's mudering of all Jewish male infants.

milk out to bottle fillers

cooler

regenerator

control panel

flow diversion valve

heater

holder

milk pump

balance tank

cold milk from storage tank

pasteurization *In a pasteurization machine, milk is heated to a high temperature for about 15 seconds to kill disease-causing bacteria.*

The Last Supper was a Passover seder.

passport document issued by a national government authorizing the bearer to go abroad and guaranteeing the bearer the state's protection. Some countries require an intending visitor to obtain a special endorsement or visa.

Passy Frédéric 1822–1912. French economist who shared the first Nobel Peace Prize 1901 with Jean-Henri Dunant. He founded the International League for Permanent Peace 1867, and was cofounder, with the English politician William Cremer (1828–1908), of the Inter-Parliamentary Conferences on Peace and on Arbitration 1889.

pasta food made from a dough of durum-wheat flour or semolina, water, and, sometimes egg, and cooked in boiling water. It is usually served with a sauce. Pasta is available either fresh or dried, and comes in a wide variety of shapes. It may be creamy yellow or colored green with spinach or red with tomato. Pasta has been used in Italian cooking since the Middle Ages, but is now popular in many other countries.

Italian pasta shapes include narrow strands (spaghetti, vermicelli), flat sheets or ribbons (lasagne, tagliatelle, fettucine), shell-shaped (*conchiglie*, *lumache*), butterfly-shaped (*farfalle*), tubular (cannelloni, macaroni, *penne*), and twisted (*fusilli*). Some varieties are sold ready stuffed with a meat, cheese, herb, or vegetable filling (ravioli, agnolotti, tortellini). Some types of Far Eastern pasta are made from buckwheat.

Pasternak Boris Leonidovich 1890–1960. Russian poet and novelist. His novel ◊*Dr Zhivago* 1957 was banned in the USSR as a "hostile act," and was awarded a Nobel Prize (which Pasternak declined). *Dr Zhivago* has since been unbanned and Pasternak has been posthumously rehabilitated.

Born in Moscow, he remained in Russia when his father, the artist Leonid Pasternak (1862–1945), emigrated. His volumes of lyric poems include *A Twin Cloud* 1914 and *On Early Trains* 1943, and he translated Shakespeare's tragedies into Russian.

Pasteur Louis 1822–1895. French chemist and microbiologist who discovered that fermentation is caused by microorganisms. He also developed a vaccine for ◊rabies, which led to the foundation of the Institut Pasteur in Paris 1888.

Pasteur saved the French silkworm industry by identifying two microbial diseases that were decimating the worms. He discovered the pathogens responsible for ◊anthrax and chicken cholera, and developed vaccines for these diseases. He inspired his pupil Joseph ◊Lister's work in antiseptic surgery. *Pasteurization* to make dairy products free from the tuberculosis bacteria is based on his discoveries. See also ◊food technology.

pasteurization treatment of food to reduce the number of microorganisms it contains and so protect consumers from disease. Harmful bacteria are killed and the development of others is delayed. For milk, the method involves heating it to 161°F/72°C for 15 seconds followed by rapid cooling to 50°F/10°C or lower. The process also kills beneficial bacteria and reduces the nutritive property of milk.

The experiments of Louis Pasteur on wine and beer in the 1850s and 1860s showed how heat treatment slowed the multiplication of bacteria and thereby the process of souring. Pasteurization of milk made headway in the dairy industries of Scandinavia and the US before 1900 because of the realization that it also killed off bacteria associated with the diseases of tuberculosis, typhoid, diphtheria, and dysentery.

pastry baked dough made from flour, fat, water, and salt. It makes a useful base or container for soft, moist fillings, and is widely used for tarts, pies, quiches, and pasties. Richer pastries may include eggs, yeast, or sugar, or may use ground nuts instead of flour. Types include short pastry, flaky pastry, suet crust, filo, and choux. *Puff pastry* is made with a higher proportion of fat. Its preparation involves repeated folding, which, with the fat, makes it flaky.

Patagonia geographic area of South America, south of latitude 40° S, with sheep farming, and coal and oil resources. Sighted by Ferdinand Magellan 1520, it was claimed by both Argentina and Chile until divided between them 1881.

patchouli soft-wooded E Indian shrub *Pogostemon heyneanus* of the mint family Labiateae, source of the perfume patchouli.

Patel Vallabhbhai Jhaverbhai 1875–1950. Indian political leader. A fervent follower of Mahatma Gandhi and a leader of the Indian National Congress, he held a number of positions in Pandit Jawaharlal Nehru's first government after independence.

patella or *knee cap* a flat bone embedded in the knee tendon of birds and mammals, which protects the joint from injury.

patent or *letters patent* documents conferring the exclusive right to make, use, and sell an invention for a limited period. Ideas are not eligible; neither is anything not new.

In the US, the period of patent is 17 years. In 1987 the US began issuing patents for new animal forms (new types of livestock and assorted organisms) being created by DNA research, recombinant DNA, and other forms of genetic tampering.

Paterson William 1745–1806. Irish-born US Supreme Court justice and political leader. He was a member of the Constitutional Convention 1787 and was elected one of New Jersey's first US senators 1789. After serving as New Jersey governor 1790–93, Paterson was appointed to the US Supreme Court by President Washington, where he served as associate justice 1793–1806. He was noted for his vigorous prosecution of cases under the Sedition Act of 1798.

Paterson immigrated to America with his family 1747 and graduated from Princeton 1763. Admitted to the bar 1769, he served as a member of the provincial congress 1775–76 and as New Jersey attorney general 1776–83.

Pathan member of a people of NW Pakistan and Afghanistan, numbering about 14 million (1984). The majority are Sunni Muslims. The Pathans speak Pashto, a member of the Indo-Iranian branch of the Indo-European family.

The Pathans comprise distinct groups, some living as nomads with herds of goats and camels, while others are farmers. Formerly a constant threat to the British Raj, the Pakistani

Pathans are now claiming independence, with the Afghani Pathans, in their own state of Pakhtoonistan, although this has not yet been recognized.

Pathé Charles 1863–1957. French film pioneer who began his career selling projectors in 1896 and with the profits formed Pathé Frères with his brothers. In 1901 he embarked on film production and by 1908 had become the world's biggest producer, with branches worldwide. He also developed an early color process and established a weekly newsreel, *Pathé Journal*. World War I disrupted his enterprises and by 1918 he was gradually forced out of business by foreign competition.

pathogen (Greek "disease producing") in medicine, a bacterium or virus that causes disease. Most pathogens are ⬡parasites, and the diseases they cause are incidental to their search for food or shelter inside the host. Nonparasitic organisms, such as soil bacteria or those living in the human gut and feeding on waste foodstuffs, can also become pathogenic to a person whose immune system or liver is damaged. The larger parasites that can cause disease, such as nematode worms, are not usually described as pathogens.

pathology medical specialty concerned with the study of disease processes and how these provoke structural and functional changes in the body and its tissues.

Patmos Greek island in the Aegean, one of the Dodecanese; the chief town is Hora. St John is said to have written the New Testament Book of Revelation while in exile here.

Patna capital of Bihar state, India, on the River Ganges; population (1981) 916,000. It has remains of a hall built by the emperor Asoka in the 3rd century BC.

Paton Alan 1903–1988. South African writer. His novel *Cry, the Beloved Country* 1948 focused on racial inequality in South Africa. Later books include the study *Land and People of South Africa* 1956, *The Long View* 1968, and his autobiography *Towards the Mountain* 1980.
Born in Pietermaritzburg, he became a schoolmaster and in 1935 the principal of a reformatory near Johannesburg, which he ran along enlightened lines.

Patou Jean 1880–1936. French clothes designer who opened a fashion house 1919. He was an overnight success, and his swimsuits and innovative designs became popular in the 1920s. He dominated both the couture and the ready-to-wear sectors of the fashion world until his death, and had a great influence on the designers he employed, many of whom went on to make names for themselves.
He created the perfume Joy 1926.

Patras (Greek *Pátrai*) industrial city (hydro-electric installations, textiles, paper) in the NW Peloponnese, Greece, on the Gulf of Patras; population (1981) 141,500. The ancient Patrai is the only one of the 12 cities of ⬡Achaea to survive.

patriarch (Greek "ruler of a family") in the Old Testament, one of the ancestors of the human race, and especially those of the ancient Hebrews, from Adam to Abraham, Isaac, Jacob, and his sons (who became patriarchs of the Hebrew tribes). In the Eastern Orthodox Church, the term refers to the leader of a national church.

patrician member of a privileged class in ancient Rome, descended from the original citizens. After the 4th century BC the rights formerly exercised by the patricians alone were made available to the ordinary people, the plebeians, and patrician descent became only a matter of prestige.

Patrick, St 389–c. 461. Patron saint of Ireland. Born in Britain, probably in S Wales, he was carried off by pirates to six years' slavery in Antrim, Ireland, before escaping either to Britain or Gaul—his poor Latin suggests the former—to train as a missionary. He is variously said to have landed again in Ireland 432 or 456, and his work was a vital factor in the spread of Christian influence there. His symbols are snakes and shamrocks; feast day March 17.

Patriot missile ground-to-air medium-range missile system used in air defense. It has high-altitude coverage, electronic jamming capability, and excellent mobility. US Patriot missiles were tested in battle against ⬡Scud missiles fired by the Iraqis in the 1991 Gulf War.
The Patriot missile was developed in the US during the late 1970s. It entered service with NATO in West Germany 1985.

patronage power to give a favored appointment to an office or position in politics, business, or the church; or ⬡sponsorship of the arts. Patronage was for centuries bestowed mainly by individuals (in Europe often royal or noble) or by the church. In the 20th century, patrons have tended to be political parties, the state, and—in the arts—private industry and foundations.

Patton George (Smith) 1885–1945. US general in World War II, known as "Old Blood and Guts." He was appointed to command the 2nd Armored Division 1940 and became commanding general of the First Armored Corps 1941. In 1942 he led the Western Task Force that landed at Casablanca, Morocco. After commanding the 7th Army, he led the 3rd Army across France and into Germany, and in 1945 took over the 15th Army.
Patton was an outspoken advocate of mobility and armor. He played a central role in stopping the German counteroffensive at the Battle of the ⬡Bulge Dec 1944–Jan 1945.

Pau industrial city (electrochemical and metallurgical products) and resort, capital of Pyrénées-Atlantiques *département* in Aquitaine, SW France, near the Spanish border; population (1982) 131,500. It is the center of the ⬡Basque area of France, and the site of fierce guerrilla activity.

Paul Les. Adopted name of Lester Polfuss 1915– . US inventor of the solid-body electric guitar in the early 1940s, and a pioneer of recording techniques including overdubbing and electronic echo. The Gibson Les Paul guitar was first marketed 1952. As a guitarist in the late 1940s and 1950s he recorded with the singer Mary Ford (1928–1977).

Paul 1901–1964. King of the Hellenes (Greece) from 1947, when he succeeded his brother George II. He was the son of Constantine I. In 1938 he married Princess Frederika (1917–), daughter of the Duke of Brunswick.

Paul six popes, including:

Paul VI Giovanni Battista Montini 1897–1978. Pope from 1963. His encyclical *Humanae Vitae/Of Human Life* 1968 reaffirmed the church's traditional teaching on birth control, thus following the minority report of the commission originally appointed by Pope John rather than the majority view.
He was born near Brescia, Italy. He spent more than 25 years in the Secretariat of State under Pius XI and Pius XII before becoming archbishop of Milan in 1954. In 1958 he was created a cardinal by Pope John, and in 1963 he succeeded him as pope, taking the name of Paul as a symbol of ecumenical unity.

Paul I 1754–1801. Tsar of Russia from 1796, in succession to his mother Catherine II. Mentally unstable, he pursued an erratic foreign policy and was assassinated.

Pauli Wolfgang 1900–1958. Austrian physicist who originated the **exclusion principle**: in a given system no two fermions (electrons, protons, neutrons, or other elementary particles of half-integral spin) can be characterized by the same set of ⬡quantum numbers. He also predicted the existence of neutrinos. He was awarded a Nobel Prize 1945 for his work on atomic structure.

Pauling Linus Carl 1901– . US chemist, author of fundamental work on the nature of the chemical bond and on the discovery of the helical structure of many proteins. He also investigated the properties and uses of vitamin C as related to human health. He won the Nobel Prize for Chemistry 1954. An outspoken opponent of nuclear testing, he also received the Nobel Peace Prize in 1962.

Paul, St c. AD 3–c. AD 68. Christian missionary and martyr; in the New Testament, one of the apostles and author of 13 epistles. Originally opposed to Christianity, he took part in the stoning of St Stephen. He is said to have been converted by a vision on the road to Damascus. After his conversion he made great missionary journeys, for example to Philippi and Ephesus, becoming known as the Apostle of the Gentiles (non-Jews). His emblems are a sword and a book; feast day June 29.
The Jewish form of his name is Saul. He was born in Tarsus (now in Turkey), son of well-to-do Pharisees, and had Roman citizenship. On his return to Jerusalem after his missionary journeys, he was arrested, appealed to Caesar, and (as a citizen) was sent to Rome for trial about 57 or 59. After two years in prison, he may have been released before his final arrest and execution under the emperor Nero.
St Paul's theology was rigorous on such questions as sin and atonement, and his views on the role of women were adopted by the Christian church generally.

Pausanias 2nd century AD. Greek geographer, author of a valuably accurate description of Greece compiled from his own travels, *Description of Greece*, also translated as *Itinerary of Greece*.

Pavarotti Luciano 1935– . Italian tenor whose operatic roles have included Rodolfo in *La Bohème*, Cavaradossi in *Tosca*, the Duke of Mantua in *Rigoletto*, and Nemorino in *L'Elisir d'amore*. He gave his first performance in the title role of *Otello* in Chicago 1991.

Pavia, Battle of battle 1525 between France and the Holy Roman Empire. The Hapsburg emperor Charles V defeated and captured Francis I of France; the battle marked the onset of Hapsburg dominance in Italy.

Pavlov Ivan Petrovich 1849–1936. Russian physiologist who studied conditioned reflexes in animals. His work had a great impact on behavioral theory (see ⬡behaviorism) and ⬡learning theory. See also ⬡conditioning. Nobel Prize for Medicine 1904.

Pavlova Anna 1881–1931. Russian dancer. Prima ballerina of the Imperial Ballet from 1906, she left Russia 1913, and went on to become one of the world's most celebrated exponents of Classical ballet. With London as her home, she toured extensively with her own company, influencing dancers worldwide with roles such as Mikhail ◊Fokine's *The Dying Swan* solo 1905.

pawnbroker one who lends money on the security of goods held. The traditional sign of the premises of a pawnbroker is three gold balls, the symbol used in front of the houses of the medieval Lombard merchants of Italy.

pawpaw or *papaw* small tree *Asimina triloba* of the custard-apple family Annonaceae, native to the eastern USA. It bears oblong fruits 5 in/ 13 cm long with yellowish, edible flesh. The name pawpaw is also used for the ◊papaya.

Pawtucket city in NE Rhode Island, on the Blackstone River, NE of Providence. Industries include textiles, thread, machinery, and metal and glass products; population (1990) 72,600. It was the home of the first US water-powered cotton mill 1790.

Pax Roman goddess of peace; her Greek counterpart is ◊Irene.

Pays de la Loire agricultural region of W France, comprising the *départements* of Loire-Atlantique, Maine-et-Loire, Mayenne, Sarthe, and Vendée; capital Nantes; area 12,391 sq mi/ 32,100 sq km; population (1986) 3,018,000. Industries include shipbuilding and wine.

Paz Octavio 1914– . Mexican poet and essayist. His works reflect many influences, including Marxism, surrealism, and Aztec mythology. His long poem *Piedra del sol/Sun Stone* 1957 uses contrasting images, centering upon the Aztec Calendar Stone (representing the Aztec universe), to symbolize the loneliness of individuals and their search for union with others. Nobel Prize for Literature 1990.

PCB abbreviation for ◊*polychlorinated biphenyl*, ◊*printed circuit board*.

PCP abbreviation for **phencyclidine hydrochloride**, a drug popularly known as ◊angel dust.

pea climbing plant *Pisum sativum*, family Leguminosae, with pods of edible seeds, grown since prehistoric times for food. The pea is a popular vegetable and is eaten fresh, canned, dried, or frozen. The sweet pea *Lathyrus odoratus* of the same family is grown for its scented, butterfly-shaped flowers.

Peace river formed in British Columbia, by the union at Finlay Forks of the Finlay and Parsnip rivers and flowing through the Rocky Mountains and across Alberta to join the River Slave just north of Lake Athabasca; length 1,000 mi/ 1,600 km.

Peace Corps US organization of trained men and women, inspired by the British program Voluntary Service Overseas (VSO) and established by President Kennedy 1961. The Peace Corps provides skilled volunteer workers for Third World countries, especially in the fields of teaching, agriculture, and health, for a period of two years.

Living among the country's inhabitants, workers are paid only a small allowance to cover their basic needs and maintain health. Over 130,000 Americans have been involved.

peace movement collective opposition to war. The Western peace movements of the late 20th century can trace their origins to the pacifists of the 19th century and conscientious objectors during World War I. The campaigns after World War II have tended to concentrate on nuclear weapons, but there are numerous organizations devoted to peace, some wholly pacifist, some merely opposed to escalation.

Other organizations are concerned with the future of life on planet Earth and the environment. In the US, opposition to the Vietnam War, which grew from the late 1960s, was the primary post-World War II peace movement. It greatly influenced US politics and society, although Ban the Bomb opposition was older, a post-World War II posture against nuclear weapons.

peach tree *Prunus persica*, family Rosaceae. It has ovate leaves and small, usually pink flowers. The yellowish edible fruits have thick velvety skins; the nectarine is a smooth-skinned variety.

peacock technically, the male of any of various large pheasants. The name is most often used for the common peacock *Pavo cristatus*, a bird of the pheasant family, native to S Asia. It is rather larger than a pheasant. The male has a large fan-shaped tail, brightly colored with blue, green, and purple "eyes" on a chestnut background. The female (peahen) is brown with a small tail.

Peale Charles Willson 1741–1827. American artist, head of a large family of painters. His portraits of leading figures in the Revolutionary War include the earliest known portrait of George Washington, painted in 1772.

Peale was also a naturalist, interested in paleontology and taxidermy, and an inventor. Five of Peale's 17 children also became painters —Titian Peale (1799–1885), animal painter; Rubens Peale (1784–1865), still-life painter; Raphaelle Peale (1774–1825), still-life and portrait painter; Rembrandt Peale (1778–1860), portrait and historical painter; and Franklin Peale (1795–1890), natural history painter. His brother James Peale (1749–1831) and James's daughters were portrait painters and miniaturists.

Peale Norman Vincent 1898– . US religious leader. After serving congregations in Brooklyn 1924–27 and Syracuse 1927–32, he became pastor of the Marble Collegiate Church in New York City. Through his radio program and book *The Art of Living* 1948, Peale became one of the best-known religious figures in the country. His *The Power of Positive Thinking* 1952 became a national bestseller. Peale was elected president of the Reformed Church in America in 1969.

Born in Bowersville, Ohio, Peale was educated at Ohio Wesleyan University and was ordained in the Methodist Episcopal Church in 1922.

peanut or *groundnut* or **monkey nut** South American vinelike annual plant *Arachis hypogaea*, family Leguminosae. After flowering, the flower stalks bend and force the pods into the earth to ripen underground. The nuts are a staple food in many tropical countries and are widely grown in the southern US. They yield a valuable edible oil and are the basis for numerous processed foods.

pear tree *Pyrus communis*, family Rosaceae, native to temperate regions of Eurasia. It has a succulent edible fruit, less hardy than the apple.

pearl shiny, hard, rounded abnormal growth composed of nacre (or mother-of-pearl), a chalky substance. Nacre is secreted by many mollusks, and deposited in thin layers on the inside of the shell around a parasite, a grain of sand, or some other irritant body. After several years of the mantle (the layer of tissue between the shell and the body mass) secreting this nacre, a pearl is formed.

Although commercially valuable pearls are obtained from freshwater mussels and oysters, most precious pearls come from the various species of the family Pteriidae (the pearl oysters) found in tropical waters off N and W Australia, off the Californian coast, in the Persian Gulf, and in the Indian Ocean. Because of their rarity, large mussel pearls of perfect shape are worth more than those from oysters.

Artificial pearls were first cultivated in Japan in 1893. A tiny bead of shell from a clam, plus a small piece of membrane from another pearl oyster's mantle (to stimulate the secretion of nacre) is inserted in oysters kept in cages in the sea for three years, and then the pearls are harvested.

Pearl Harbor an inlet of the Pacific Ocean where the US naval base was situated in Hawaii on Oahu Island. It was the scene of a Japanese surprise air attack on Dec 7, 1941, that brought the US into World War II. It took place while Japanese envoys were holding so-called peace talks in Washington. The local commanders Admiral Kummel and Lieutenant General Short were relieved of their posts and held responsible for the fact that the base, despite warnings, was totally unprepared at the time of the attack. About 3,300 US military personnel were killed, 4 battleships were lost, and a large part of the US Pacific fleet was destroyed or damaged. The Japanese, angered by US embargoes of oil and other war materiel and convinced that US entry into the war was inevitable, opted to strike a major blow in hopes of forcing US concessions. Instead, it galvanized public opinion and raised anti-Japanese sentiment to a fever pitch, with war declared thereafter.

Today it is a submarine base, supply center, and naval shipyard.

Pears Peter 1910–1986. English tenor. A cofounder with Benjamin ◊Britten of the Aldeburgh Festival, he was closely associated with the composer's work and sang the title role in *Peter Grimes*.

Pearse Patrick Henry 1879–1916. Irish poet prominent in the Gaelic revival, a leader of the ◊Easter Rising 1916. Proclaimed president of the provisional government, he was court-martialed and shot after its suppression.

Pearson Drew 1897–1969. US newspaper columnist. Although his frank, anonymously published exposé *Washington Merry-Go-Round* 1931 became a bestseller, he was fired from the *Baltimore Sun* when his authorship became known. In 1932, however, he began openly publishing a syndicated column of the same name, working in conjunction with Robert Allen until 1942. Pearson continued the column alone until his death, after which it was taken over by Jack Anderson (1922–).

Pearson Lester Bowles 1897–1972. Canadian politician, leader of the Liberal Party from 1958, prime minister 1963–68. As foreign minister 1948–57, he represented Canada at the United Nations, playing a key role in settling the ◊Suez Crisis 1956. Nobel Peace Prize 1957.

Pearson served as president of the General Assembly 1952–53 and helped to create the UN Emergency Force (UNEF) that policed Sinai following the Egypt–Israel war of 1956. As prime minister, he led the way to formulating a national medicare (health insurance) law.

Peary Robert Edwin 1856–1920. US polar explorer who, after several unsuccessful attempts, became the first person to reach the North Pole on April 6, 1909. In 1988 an astronomer claimed Peary's measurements were incorrect.

He sailed to Cape Sheridan in the *Roosevelt* with his aide Matthew Henson, and they then made a sled journey to the Pole.

One of his companions on an 1891 voyage was Frederick A Cook who, in 1909, claimed he had reached the North Pole before Peary. Although Cook's claim is generally discredited, it continues to cast a shadow over Peary's achievement.

peasant country-dweller engaged in small-scale farming. A peasant normally owns or rents a small amount of land, aiming to be self-sufficient and to sell surplus supplies locally.

In the UK, the move toward larger farms in the 18th century resulted in the disappearance of the independent peasantry, although small-scale farming survives in smallholdings and Scottish crofts. Landowners in countries such as France, Spain, and Italy showed less direct interest in agriculture, so the tradition of small independent landholding remains a distinctive way of life today. See also ⟡commune.

Peasants' Revolt the rising of the English peasantry in June 1381, the culminative result of economic, social, and political disillusionment. It was sparked off by the imposition of a new poll tax, three times the rates of those imposed in 1377 and 1379. Led by Wat ⟡Tyler and John ⟡Ball, rebels from SE England marched on London and demanded reforms. The revolt was put down by deceit and force by the authorities.

Following the plague of the Black Death, a shortage of agricultural workers led to higher wages. The Statute of Laborers, enacted 1351, attempted to return wages to pre-plague levels. When the third poll tax was enforced 1381, riots broke out all over England, especially in Essex and Kent. Wat Tyler and John Ball emerged as leaders and the rebels went on to London, where they continued plundering, burning John of Gaunt's palace at the Savoy, and taking the prisons at Newgate and Fleet. The young king Richard II attempted to appease the mob, who demanded an end to serfdom and feudalism. The rebels then took the Tower of London and murdered Archbishop Sudbury and Robert Hales. Again the king attempted to make peace at Smithfield, but Tyler was stabbed to death by William Walworth, the Lord Mayor of London. The king made concessions to the rebels, and they dispersed, but the concessions were revoked immediately.

peat fibrous organic substance found in bogs and formed by the incomplete decomposition of plants such as sphagnum moss. N Asia, Finland, Ireland, and other places have large deposits, which have been dried and used as fuel from ancient times. Peat can also be used as a soil additive.

Peat bogs began to be formed when glaciers retreated, about 9,000 years ago. They grow at the rate of only a millimeter a year, and large-scale digging can result in destruction both of the bog and of specialized plants growing there.

Peat bogs allow for excellent preservation of organic materials (wood, leather, plant matter, animals), which usually decompose in archeological sites. Several in Scandinavia have been excavated and have provided data on prehistoric settlements. A number of ancient corpses, some the result of ritual murders, have also been found preserved in peat bogs.

pecan nut-producing ⟡hickory tree *Carya illinoensis* or *C. pecan*, native to central US and N Mexico and now widely cultivated. The tree grows to over 150 ft/45 m, and the edible nuts are smooth-shelled, the kernel resembling a smoothly ovate walnut.

peccary one of two species of the New World genus *Tayassu* of piglike hoofed mammals. A peccary has a gland in the middle of the back which secretes a strong-smelling substance. Peccaries are blackish in color, covered with bristles, and have tusks that point downward. Adults reach a height of 16 in/40 cm, and a weight of 60 lb/25 kg.

Pechora river in N Russia, rising in the N Urals. It transports coal, timber, and furs (June–Sept) to the Barents Sea, 1,125 mi/ 1,800 km to the north.

Peck (Eldred) Gregory 1916– . US film actor specializing in strong, upright characters. His films include *Spellbound* 1945, *Duel in the Sun* 1946, *Gentleman's Agreement* 1947, *To Kill a Mockingbird* 1962, for which he won an Academy Award, and, (cast against type as a Nazi doctor) *The Boys from Brazil* 1974.

Peckinpah Sam 1925–1985. US film director, often of Westerns, usually associated with slow-motion, blood-spurting violence. His best films, such as *The Wild Bunch* 1969, exhibit a thoughtful, if depressing, view of the world and human nature.

Pécs city in SW Hungary, the center of a coal-mining area on the Croatian frontier; population (1988) 182,000. Industries include metal, leather, and wine. The town dates from Roman times and was under Turkish rule 1543–1686.

pectoral in vertebrates, the upper area of the thorax associated with the muscles and bones used in moving the arms or forelimbs. In birds, the *pectoralis major* is the very large muscle used to produce a powerful downbeat of the wing during flight.

pediatrics medical specialty concerned with the care of children.

pedicel the stalk of an individual flower, which attaches to the main floral axis, often developing in the axil of a bract.

pediment in architecture, the triangular part crowning the fronts of buildings in Classical styles. The pediment was a distinctive feature of Greek temples.

pedomorphosis in biology, an alternate term for ⟡neoteny.

Pedro two emperors of Brazil:

Pedro I 1798–1834. Emperor of Brazil 1822–31. The son of John VI of Portugal, he escaped to Brazil on Napoleon's invasion, and was appointed regent 1821. He proclaimed Brazil independent 1822 and was crowned emperor, but abdicated 1831 and returned to Portugal.

Pedro II 1825–1891. Emperor of Brazil 1831–89. He proved an enlightened ruler, but his anti-slavery measures alienated the landowners, who compelled him to abdicate.

Peel Robert 1788–1850. British Conservative politician. As home secretary 1822–27 and

1828–30, he founded the modern police force and in 1829 introduced Roman Catholic emancipation. He was prime minister 1834–35 and 1841–46, when his repeal of the ⟡Corn Laws caused him and his followers to break with the party.

Peenemünde fishing village in Germany, used from 1937 by the Germans to develop the V2 rockets used in World War II.

peer group in the social sciences, people who have a common identity based on such characteristics as similar social status, interests, age, or ethnic group. The concept has proved useful in analyzing the power and influence of co-workers, school friends, and ethnic and religious groups in socialization and social behavior.

Pegasus in astronomy, a constellation of the northern hemisphere, near Cygnus, and represented as the winged horse of Greek mythology.

It is the seventh-largest constellation in the sky, and its main feature is a square outlined by four stars, one of which (Alpherata) is actually part of the adjoining constellation Andromeda. Diagonally across is Markab (or Alpha Pegasus), about 100 light-years distant.

Pegasus in Greek mythology, the winged horse that sprang from the blood of the Gorgon Medusa. He was transformed into a constellation.

Hippocrene, the spring of the Muses on Mount Helicon, is said to have sprung from a blow of his hoof.

pegmatite extremely coarse-grained ⟡igneous rock of any composition found in veins usually associated with large granite masses.

Pei I(eoh) M(ing) 1917– . Chinese-born American architect, noted for innovative modern design and high-technology structures, particularly the use of glass walls. His buildings include the Mile High Center in Denver, the National Airlines terminal (now owned by TWA) at Kennedy Airport in New York City, the John Hancock tower in Boston, the National Gallery extension in Washington, DC, the Bank of China Tower, Hong Kong, and the glass pyramid in front of the Louvre, Paris.

Peiping name (meaning "northern peace") 1928–49 of ⟡Beijing in China.

Peipus, Lake (Estonian *Peipsi*, Russian *Chudskoye*) lake forming the boundary between Estonia and Pskov'oblast, an administrative region of Russia. Alexander Nevski defeated the Teutonic Knights on its frozen surface 1242.

Peirce Charles Sanders 1839–1914. US philosopher and logician, founder of ⟡pragmatism (which he later called pragmaticism), who argued that genuine conceptual distinctions must be correlated with some differences of practical effect. He wrote extensively on the logic of scientific inquiry, suggesting that truth could be conceived of as the object of an ultimate consensus.

Born in Cambridge, Massachusetts, his father Benjamin Peirce was professor of astronomy and mathematics at Harvard University from where Charles graduated in 1863. He went on to spend much of his life in government service, and was an astronomer and physicist before becoming a lecturer 1879–84 at Johns Hopkins University. His works include *How to Make Our Ideas Clear* 1878; his *Collected Papers* were published posthumously 1931–58.

Peking alternative transcription of ⏵Beijing, capital of China.

pekingese breed of long-haired dog with a flat skull and flat face, typically less than 10 in/25 cm tall and weighing less than 11 lb/5 kg.

It was first bred at the Chinese court as the "imperial lion dog." The first specimens brought to the West were those taken during the Opium Wars when the Summer Palace in Beijing was looted 1860.

Peking man Chinese representative of an early species of human, found as fossils, 500,000–750,000 years old, in the cave of Choukoutien 1927 near Beijing (Peking). Peking man used chipped stone tools, hunted game, and used fire. Similar varieties of early human have been found in Java and E Africa. Their classification is disputed: some anthropologists classify them as *Homo erectus*, others as *Homo sapiens pithecanthropus*.

A skull found near Beijing 1927 was sent to the US 1941 but disappeared; others have since been found.

Pelagius 360–420. British theologian. He taught that each person possesses free will (and hence the possibility of salvation), denying Augustine's doctrines of predestination and original sin. Cleared of heresy by a synod in Jerusalem 415, he was later condemned by the pope and the emperor.

pelargonium flowering plant of the genus *Pelargonium* of the geranium family Geraniaceae, grown extensively in gardens, where it is familiarly known as the **geranium**. Ancestors of the garden hybrids came from S Africa.

Pelé Adopted name of Edson Arantes do Nascimento 1940– . Brazilian soccer player. A prolific goal scorer, he appeared in four World Cup competitions 1958–70 and led Brazil to three championships (1958, 1962, 1970).

He spent most of his playing career with the Brazilian team, Santos, before ending it with the New York Cosmos in the US.

Pelée, Mont volcano on the island of Martinique in the West Indies; height 4,428 ft/1,350 m. It destroyed the town of St Pierre during its eruption 1902.

pelican any of a family (Pelecanidae) of large, heavy water birds remarkable for the pouch beneath the bill which is used as a fishing net and temporary store for catches of fish. Some species grow up to 6 ft/1.8 m, and have wingspans of 10 ft/3 m.

They include the American brown pelican *Pelicanus occidentalis*, which is marine, and dives for its food; the pinkish common pelican *P. onocrotalus* of Europe, Asia, and Africa; and the Australian black-backed pelican *P. conspicillatus*. The last two do not dive for food but dip their bills into the water while swimming.

Pelion mountain in Thessaly, Greece, near Mount Ossa; height 5,079 ft/1,548 m. In Greek mythology it was the home of the centaurs, creatures half man and half horse.

pellagra chronic disease of subtropical countries in which the staple food is corn, caused by deficiency of nicotinic acid (one of the B vitamins), which is contained in protein foods, beans and peas, and yeast. Symptoms include digestive disorders, skin eruptions, and mental disturbances.

pellitory-of-the-wall plant *Parietaria judaica* of the nettle family, found growing in cracks in walls and rocks and also on banks, in W and S Europe; it is widely cultivated in gardens. The stems are up to 3 ft/1 m and reddish, the leaves lance-shaped, and the greenish male and female flowers are separate but on the same plant.

Peloponnese (Greek *Peloponnesos*) peninsula forming the southern part of Greece; area 8,318 sq mi/21,549 sq km; population (1991) 1,077,000. It is joined to the mainland by the narrow isthmus of Corinth and is divided into the nomes (administrative areas) of Argolis, Arcadia, Achaea, Elis, Corinth, Lakonia, and Messenia, representing its seven ancient states.

Peloponnesian War conflict between Athens and Sparta and their allies, 431–404 BC, originating in suspicions about the "empire-building" ambitions of the Athenian leader Pericles. It was ended by the Spartan general Lysander's capture of the Athenian fleet in 405, and his starving the Athenians into surrender in 404. Sparta's victory meant the destruction of the political power of Athens.

Pelops in Greek mythology, the son of Tantalus, brother of Niobe, and father of Atreus. He gave his name to the southern part of mainland Greece, the Peloponnese.

pelota see ⏵jai alai.

Peltier effect in physics, a change in temperature at the junction of two different metals produced when an electric current flows through them. The extent of the change depends on what the conducting metals are, and the nature of change (rise or fall in temperature) depends on the direction of current flow. It is the reverse of the ⏵Seebeck effect. It is named after the French physicist Jean Charles Peltier (1785–1845) who discovered it 1834.

pelvis in vertebrates, the lower area of the abdomen featuring the bones and muscles used to move the legs or hindlimbs. The **pelvic girdle** is a set of bones that allows movement of the legs in relation to the rest of the body and provides sites for the attachment of relevant muscles.

Pemba coral island in the Indian Ocean, 30 mi/48 km NE of Zanzibar, and forming with it part of Tanzania
area 380 sq mi/984 sq km
capital Chake Chake
products cloves, copra
population (1985) 257,000.

pemmican preparation of dried lean bison or venison pounded into a paste with fat and dried berries and preserved as pressed cakes, once used as a food by Plains Indians. Similar preparations made from beef were used for high-energy rations by early Arctic explorers, and by mountaineers.

PEN abbreviation for *Poets, Playwrights, Editors, Essayists, Novelists*, a literary association established 1921 by C A ("Sappho") Dawson Scott, to promote international understanding among writers.

penance Roman Catholic sacrament, involving confession of sins and receiving absolution, and works performed (or punishment self-inflicted) in atonement for sin. Penance is worked out nowadays in terms of good deeds rather than routine repetition of prayers.

Penang (Malay *Pulau Pinang*) state in W Peninsular Malaysia, formed of Penang Island, Province Wellesley, and the Dindings on the mainland
area 398 sq mi/1,030 sq km
capital Penang (George Town)
population (1990) 1,142,200.
Penang Island was bought by Britain from the ruler of Kedah 1785; Province Wellesley was acquired 1800.

penates the household gods of a Roman family. See ⏵lares and penates.

Penda c. 577–654. King of Mercia, an Anglo-Saxon kingdom in England, from about 632. He raised Mercia to a powerful kingdom, and defeated and killed two Northumbrian kings, Edwin 632 and ⏵Oswald 641. He was killed in battle by Oswy, king of Northumbria.

Penderecki Krzystof 1933– . Polish composer. His expressionist works, such as the *Threnody for the Victims of Hiroshima* 1961 for strings, employ cluster and percussion effects. He later turned to religious subjects and a more orthodox style, as in the *Magnificat* 1974 and the *Polish Requiem* 1980–83. His opera *The Black Mask* 1986 explored a new vein of surreal humor.

Pendleton Act in US history, a civil service reform bill 1883 sponsored by senator George Pendleton (1825–1889) of Ohio that was designed to curb the power of patronage exercised by new administrations over a swelling federal bureaucracy. Initially about 10% of civil service appointments were made subject to competitive examinations administered by an independent Civil Service Commission.

pendulum weight (called a "bob") swinging at the end of a rod or cord. The regularity of a pendulum's swing was used in making the first really accurate clocks in the 17th century. Pendulums can be used for measuring the acceleration due to gravity (an important constant in physics), and in prospecting for oils and minerals.

Specialized pendulums are used to measure velocities (ballistic pendulum) and to demonstrate the Earth's rotation (Foucault's pendulum).

Penelope in Greek legend, the wife of Odysseus, ruler of Ithaca and one of the leaders of the Greek forces in the Trojan War. During his absence after the siege of Troy she kept her many suitors at bay by asking them to wait until she had woven a shroud for her father-in-law, but unraveled her work each night. When Odysseus returned, after 20 years, he killed her suitors.

penguin any of an order (Sphenisciformes) of marine flightless birds, mostly black and white, found in the southern hemisphere. They range in size from 1.6 ft/40 cm to 4 ft/1.2 m tall, and have thick feathers to protect them from the intense cold. They are awkward on land, but their wings have evolved into flippers, making them excellent swimmers. Penguins congregate to breed in "rookeries," and often spend many months incubating their eggs while their mates are out at sea feeding.

Largest is the **emperor penguin** *Aptenodytes forsteri* 4 ft/1.2 m tall, whose single annual egg is brooded by the male in the warmth of a flap of his body skin, so that it rests on his feet. Among the small species is the **jackass penguin** *Spheniscus demerss*, which lays two eggs in a scraped hollow in the ground. Jackass penguins have declined in numbers, at first because of egg-collecting by humans, but more recently owing to overfishing, which deprives them of food, and to oil spills near their breeding colonies.

penicillin any of a group of ▷antibiotic (bacteria killing) compounds obtained from filtrates of molds of the genus *Penicillium* (especially *P. notatum*) or produced synthetically. Penicillin was the first antibiotic to be discovered (by Alexander ▷Fleming); it kills a broad spectrum of bacteria, many of which cause disease in humans.

The use of the original type of penicillin is limited by the increasing resistance of ▷pathogens and by allergic reactions in patients. Since 1941, numerous other antibiotics of the penicillin family have been discovered which are more selective against, or resistant to, specific microorganisms.

peninsula land surrounded on three sides by water but still attached to a larger landmass. Florida is an example.

Peninsular War war 1808–14 caused by the French emperor Napoleon's invasion of Portugal and Spain. British expeditionary forces under Sir Arthur Wellesley (Duke of ▷Wellington), combined with Spanish and Portuguese resistance, succeeded in defeating the French at Vimeiro 1808, Talavera 1809, Salamanca 1812, and Vittoria 1813. The results were inconclusive, and the war was ended by Napoleon's abdication.

penis male reproductive organ, used for internal fertilization; it transfers sperm to the female reproductive tract. In mammals, the penis is made erect by vessels that fill with blood, and in most mammals (but not humans) is stiffened by a bone. It also contains the urethra, through which urine is passed. Snakes and lizards have a paired structure that serves as a penis, other reptiles have a single organ. A few birds, mainly ducks and geese, also have a type of penis, as do snails, barnacles, and some other invertebrates. Many insects have a rigid, nonerectile male organ, usually referred to as an intromittent organ.

Penn Irving 1917– . US fashion, advertising, portrait, editorial, and fine art photographer. In 1948 he took the first of many journeys to Africa and the Far East, resulting in a series of portrait photographs of local people, avoiding sophisticated technique. He was associated for many years with *Vogue* magazine in the US.

Penn William 1644–1718. English Quaker and founder of Pennsylvania, born in London. He joined the Quakers 1667 and was imprisoned several times for his beliefs. In 1681 he obtained a grant of land in America, in settlement of a debt owed by Charles II to his father, on which he established the colony of Pennsylvania as a refuge for the persecuted Quakers. Penn made religious tolerance a cornerstone of his administration of the colony. He maintained good relations with neighboring colonies and with the Indians in the area, but his utopian ideals were not successful for the most part.

In 1697 he presented a plan, never acted upon, for a union among the colonies. In 1701 he established, with his Charter of Privileges, a bicameral legislature as the government for Pennsylvania.

Pennines mountain system, "the backbone of England," broken by a gap through which the River Aire flows to the east and the Ribble to the west; length (Scottish border to the Peaks in Derbyshire) 250 mi/400 km.

Pennsylvania state in NE US: nickname Keystone State
area 45,316 sq mi/117,400 sq km
capital Harrisburg

Pennsylvania

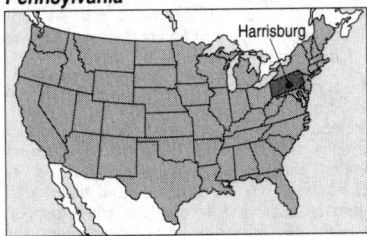
Harrisburg

cities Philadelphia, Pittsburgh, Erie, Allentown, Scranton
features Allegheny mountains; rivers: Ohio, Susquehanna, Delaware; Independence National Historic Park, Philadelphia; Valley Forge National Historic Park; Gettysburg Civil War battlefield; Pennsylvania Dutch country; Poconos resort region
products hay, cereals, mushrooms, cattle, poultry, dairy products, cement, coal, steel, petroleum products, pharmaceuticals, motor vehicles and equipment, electronic components, textiles
population (1990) 11,881,600
famous people Marian Anderson, Andrew Carnegie, Stephen Foster, Benjamin Franklin, Robert Fulton, Martha Graham, George C Marshall, Robert E Peary, Benjamin Rush, Gertrude Stein, John Updike
history disputed by Sweden, the Netherlands, and England early 17th century; granted to Quaker William ▷Penn 1682 by English King Charles II, after the 1664 capture of New Netherlands. The Declaration of Independence was proclaimed in Philadelphia, and many important Revolutionary War battles were fought here 1777–78. One of the original thirteen states, Pennsylvania was a leader in both agriculture and industry. The Battle of Gettysburg 1863 was a turning point in the Civil War for the Union cause. Until 1920, Pennsylvania was dominant in oil, coal, iron, steel, and textile production, but it already was losing its industrial lead when the Great Depression struck; by 1933, 37% of the work force was unemployed. Some areas never fully recovered, and the state now looks to agriculture, service-related industries, trade, and tourism for economic growth.

Pennsylvanian US term for the upper ▷Carboniferous period of geological time, named after the US state.

pennyroyal European perennial plant *Mentha pulegium* of the mint family, with oblong leaves and whorls of purplish flowers. It is found growing in wet places on sandy soil.

A similar North American mint *Hedeoma pulegioides* that yields an aromatic oil is also called pennyroyal.

Pensacola port in NW Florida, on the Gulf of Mexico, with a large naval air-training station; industries include chemicals, synthetic fibers, and paper; population (1990) 58,200.

The University of West Florida is here. Pensacola was founded by the Spanish 1696, passed to the British 1763, and returned to the Spanish again in the early 1780s. It was seized by US forces in 1814 and 1818 and was formally ceded with the rest of Florida in 1821. Union forces gained control of the city in 1862, during the Civil War.

pension a payment, not wages, made to a person (or his/her family) after fulfillment of certain conditions of service; an organized retirement plan. Pension plans vary widely, with some pensions calculated at a specified percentage of a worker's income, payable annually after retirement. Others provide lump-sum savings available for withdrawal at age 65. Employers sometimes match employee contributions; some plans are strictly employee contributions plus interest. Some plans are mandatory, others voluntary.

The most significant provider of retirement income in the US is the Social Security Administration, funded through nonvoluntary contributions assessed on both employers and employees. Unions make employer contributions to pension plans an important element of their contract negotiations, and accumulated pension funds have become important sources of investment capital. Under federal tax regulations, individuals can deposit specified maximum amounts into personal retirement funds, have their income tax liability reduced by that amount as a deduction, and have taxes on the fund's interest deferred until they withdraw the money at or after retirement.

pentadactyl limb typical limb of the mammals, birds, reptiles, and amphibians. These vertebrates (animals with backbone) are all descended from primitive amphibians whose immediate ancestors were fleshy-finned fish. The limb which evolved in those amphibians had three parts: a "hand/foot" with five digits (fingers/toes), a lower limb containing two bones, and an upper limb containing one bone.

This basic pattern has persisted in all the terrestrial vertebrates, and those aquatic vertebrates (such as seals) which are descended from them. Natural selection has modified the pattern to fit different ways of life. In flying animals (birds and bats) it is greatly altered and in some vertebrates, such as whales and snakes, the limbs are greatly reduced or lost. Pentadactyl limbs of different species are an example of ▷homologous organs.

Pentagon the headquarters of the US Department of Defense, Arlington, Virginia. One of the world's largest office buildings (five-sided with a pentagonal central court), it houses the administrative and command headquarters for the US armed forces and has become synonymous with the military establishment bureaucracy.

Pentagon Papers Case US Supreme Court decision (*New York Times* v *US*; *US* v *Washington Post*) 1971 dealing with the right of the federal government to enjoin the publication of sensitive or classified material. The federal government filed the suit against the *Times* and the *Post* to discontinue publication of portions of "The Pentagon Papers," a set of classified documents about US involvement in Vietnam. The government argued that the threat to national security warranted the infringement on First-Amendment rights. The Court ruled 6 to 3 to dismiss the government's suit, judging any suppression of the press, without proof of actual damage to national security, to be a violation of the First Amendment.

pentanol $C_5H_{11}OH$ (common name **amyl alcohol**) clear, colorless, oily liquid, usually having a characteristic choking odor. It is obtained by the fermentation of starches and from the distillation of petroleum.

Pentateuch Greek (and Christian) name for the first five books of the Bible, ascribed to Moses, and called the **Torah** by Jews.

pentathlon five-sport competition. Pentathlon consists of former military training pursuits:

swimming, fencing, running, horsemanship, and shooting. Formerly a five-event track and field competition for women, it was superseded by the seven-event heptathlon 1981.

Pentecost in Judaism, the festival of *Shavuot*, celebrated on the 50th day after ⟡Passover in commemoration of the giving of the Ten Commandments to Moses on Mount Sinai, and the end of the grain harvest; in the Christian church, Pentecost is the day on which the apostles experienced inspiration of the Holy Spirit, commemorated on Whit Sunday.

Pentecostal movement Christian revivalist movement originating in the US 1906. Spiritual renewal is sought through baptism by the Holy Spirit, as experienced by the apostles on the first Pentecost. It represented a reaction against the rigid theology and formal worship of the traditional churches. Glossolalia, or speaking in tongues, often occurs. Pentecostalists believe in the literal word of the Bible and faith healing. They disapprove of alcohol, tobacco, dancing, the theater, gambling, and so on. It is an intensely missionary faith, and recruitment in person and on television has been very rapid since the 1960s: worldwide membership is more than 20 million, and it is the world's fastest growing sector of Christianity.

The Pentecostal movement dates from April 4, 1906, when members of the congregation of the Azusa Street Mission in Los Angeles experienced "baptism in the Spirit." Its appeal was to the poor and those alienated by the formalism and modernist theology of established denominations. It combined a highly emotional, informal approach to worship with an ethical emphasis on sobriety and hard work, and it became a way for poor and marginal groups to improve their economic and social status while retaining their religious faith.

The movement grew rapidly in the South and in impoverished urban areas, meanwhile dividing into dozens of small, contentious sects separated by doctrine and by such practices as faith healing. In the 1950s, faith healing, represented most prominently by Oral Roberts, was at its peak among Pentecostalists. After the 1960s, prosperity through faith became a dominant theme, taken up by Roberts and other television evangelists. But all the Pentecostal sects—ranging from the largest, the Assemblies of God, to small storefront churches—shared a rapturous, ecstatic tone that continued to have a powerful appeal in the US, Latin America, and Africa. The movement in Europe, after rapid growth in the early 20th century, had stabilized by mid-century. A similar movement within the Roman Catholic Church, the charismatic movement, won large numbers of followers from the 1960s.

peony any perennial plant of the genus *Paeonia*, family Paeoniaceae, remarkable for their brilliant flowers. Most popular are the common peony *P. officinalis*, the white peony *P. lactiflora*, and the taller tree peony *P. suffruticosa*.

Peoria city in central Illinois, on the Illinois River; a transport, mining, and agricultural center; population (1990) 113,500. Fort Crève Coeur was built here by the French explorer La Salle 1680 and became a trading center. The first US settlers arrived 1818, and the town was known as Fort Clark until 1825.

Pepin the Short c. 714–c. 768. King of the Franks from 751. The son of Charles Martel, he acted as ⟡Mayor of the Palace to the last Merovingian king, Childeric III, deposed him and assumed the royal title himself, founding the ⟡Carolingian dynasty. He was ⟡Charlemagne's father.

pepper climbing plant *Piper nigrum* native to the E Indies, of the Old World pepper family Piperaceae. When gathered green, the berries are crushed to release the seeds for the spice called black pepper. When the berries are ripe, the seeds are removed and their outer skin is discarded, to produce white pepper. Chilipepper, cayenne or red pepper and the sweet peppers used as a vegetable come from ⟡capsicums native to the New World.

peppermint perennial herb *Mentha piperita* of the mint family, native to Europe, with ovate, aromatic leaves and purple flowers. Oil of peppermint is used in medicine and confectionery.

pepsin enzyme that breaks down proteins during digestion. It requires a strongly acidic environment and is found in the stomach.

peptide molecule comprising two or more ⟡amino acid molecules (not necessarily different) joined by **peptide bonds**, whereby the acid group of one acid is linked to the amino group of the other (–CO.NH). The number of amino acid molecules in the peptide is indicated by referring to it as a di-, tri-, or polypeptide (two, three, or many amino acids).

Proteins are built up of interacting polypeptide chains with various types of bonds occurring between the chains. Incomplete hydrolysis (splitting up) of a protein yields a mixture of peptides, examination of which helps to determine the sequence in which the amino acids occur within the protein.

Pepys Samuel 1633–1703. English diarist. His diary 1659–69 was a unique record of both the daily life of the period and the intimate feelings of the man. Written in shorthand, it was not deciphered until 1825. Pepys was imprisoned 1679 in the Tower of London on suspicion of being connected with the Popish Plot (see Titus ⟡Oates).

Pepys was born in London, entered the navy office 1660, and was secretary to the Admiralty 1672–79.

Perak state of W Peninsular Malaysia; capital Ipoh; area 8,106 sq mi/21,000 sq km; population (1990) 2,222,200. It produces tin and rubber. The government is a sultanate. The other principal town is Taiping.

perborate any salt formed by the action of hydrogen peroxide on borates. Perborates contain the radical BO_3.

percentage way of representing a number as a ⟡fraction of 100. Thus 45 percent (45%) equals 45/100, and 45% of 20 is 45/100 × 20 = 9.

In general, if a quantity x changes to y, the percentage change is $100(x-y)/x$. Thus, if the number of people in a room changes from 40 to 50, the percentage increase is $(100 \times 10)/40 = 25\%$. To express a fraction as a percentage, its denominator must first be converted to 100—for example, 1/8 = 12.5/100 = 12.5%. The use of percentages often makes it easier to compare fractions that do not have a common denominator.

The percentage sign is thought to have been derived as an economy measure when recording in the old counting houses; writing in the numeric symbol for 25/100 of a cargo would take two lines of parchment, and hence the "100" denominator was put alongside the 25 and rearranged to "%."

Perceval Spencer 1762–1812. British Tory politician. He became chancellor of the Exchequer 1807 and prime minister 1809. He was shot in the lobby of the House of Commons 1812 by a merchant who blamed government measures for his bankruptcy.

perch any of the largest order of spiny-finned bony fishes, the Perciformes, with some 8,000 species. This order includes the sea basses, cichlids, damselfishes, mullets, barracudas, wrasses, and gobies. Perches of the freshwater genus *Perca* are found in Europe, Asia, and North America. They have varied shapes and are usually a greenish color. They are very prolific, spawning when about three years old, and have voracious appetites.

The American yellow perch *P. flavescens*, to 12 in/30 cm, is abundant in lakes and streams, feeding on insects and other fishes.

percussion instrument musical instrument played by being struck with the hand or a beater. Percussion instruments can be divided into those that can be tuned to produce a sound of definite pitch, such as the kettledrum, tubular bells, glockenspiel, and xylophone and those without pitch, including bass drum, tambourine, triangle, cymbals, and castanets.

The **kettledrum** is a hemispherical bowl of metal with a membrane stretched across the top, tuned by screwtaps around the rim; **tubular bells** are suspended on a frame; the **glockenspiel** (German "bell play") is a small keyboard of steel bars; similar to the glockenspiel is the **xylophone** which has wooden rather than metal bars.

The **snare drum** has a membrane across both ends, and a "snare" that rattles against the underside when the drum is beaten, while the **bass drum** produces the lowest sound in the orchestra; the **tambourine** has a wooden hoop with a membrane stretched across it, and has metal jingles inserted in the sides; a **triangle** is formed from a suspended triangular-shaped steel bar, played by striking it with a separate bar of steel—the sound produced can by clearly perceived even when played against a full orchestra; **cymbals** are two brass dishes struck together; **castanets** are two hollow shells of wood struck together; and the **gong** is a suspended disk of metal struck with a soft hammer.

Percy Henry "Hotspur" 1364–1403. English soldier, son of the 1st Earl of Northumberland. In repelling a border raid, he defeated the Scots at Homildon Hill in Durham 1402. He was killed at the battle of Shrewsbury while in revolt against Henry IV.

Perelman S(idney) J(oseph) 1904–1979. US humorist. His work was often published in *The New Yorker* magazine, and he wrote film scripts for the Marx Brothers. He shared an Academy Award for the script of *Around the World in 80 Days* 1956.

He was born in New York.

perennating organ in plants, that part of a ⟡biennial plant or herbaceous perennial that allows it to survive the winter; usually a root, tuber, rhizome, bulb, or corm.

perennial plant plant that lives for more than two years. Herbaceous perennials have aerial stems and leaves that die each autumn. They survive the winter by means of an underground storage (perennating) organ, such as a bulb or rhizome. Trees and shrubs or woody perennials have stems that persist above ground throughout the year, and may be either ◊deciduous or ◊evergreen. See also ◊annual plant, ◊biennial plant.

Peres Shimon 1923– . Israeli socialist politician, prime minister 1984–86. Peres was prime minister, then foreign minister, under a power-sharing agreement with the leader of the Consolidation Party (Likud), Yitzhak ◊Shamir. From 1989 to 1990 he was finance minister in a new Labor–Likud coalition.

Peres emigrated from Poland to Palestine 1934, but was educated in the US. In 1959 he was elected to the Knesset (Israeli parliament). He was leader of the Labor Party 1977–1992, when he was replaced by Yitzhak Rabin.

perestroika (Russian "restructuring") in Soviet politics, the wide-ranging economic and political reforms initiated from 1985 by Mikhail Gorbachev, finally leading to the demise of the Soviet Union. Originally, in the economic sphere, *perestroika* was conceived as involving "intensive development" concentrating on automation and improved labor efficiency. It evolved to attend increasingly to market indicators and incentives ("market socialism") and the gradual dismantling of the Stalinist central-planning system, with decision-taking being devolved to self-financing enterprises.

Pérez de Cuéllar Javier 1920– . Peruvian diplomat, secretary-general of the United Nations 1982–91. He raised the standing of the UN by his successful diplomacy in ending the Iran–Iraq War 1988 and securing the independence of Namibia 1989.

A delegate to the first UN General Assembly 1946–47, he subsequently held several ambassadorial posts. He was unable to resolve the Gulf conflict resulting from Iraq's invasion of Kuwait 1990 before combat against Iran by the UN coalition began Jan 1991, but later in 1991 he negotiated the release of Western hostages held in Beirut.

Pérez Galdós Benito 1843–1920. Spanish novelist, born in the Canary Islands. His works include the 46 historical novels in the cycle *Episodios nacionales* and the 21-novel cycle *Novelas españolas contemporáneas*, which includes *Doña Perfecta* 1876 and the epic *Fortunata y Jacinta* 1886–87, his masterpiece. In scale he has been compared to the French writer Honoré de Balzac and the English novelist Charles Dickens.

performance art staged artistic events, sometimes including music, painting, and sculpture. The events, which originated in the 1950s, are akin to happenings but less spontaneous.

perfume fragrant essence used to scent the body, cosmetics, and candles. More than 100 natural aromatic chemicals may be blended from a range of 60,000 flowers, leaves, fruits, seeds, woods, barks, resins, and roots, combined with natural animal fixatives and various synthetics. Favored ingredients include ◊balsam, ◊civet (from the African civet cat) hyacinth, jasmine, lily of the valley, musk (from the ◊musk deer), orange blossom, rose, and tuberose.

Culture of the cells of fragrant plants, on membranes that are constantly bathed in a solution to carry the essential oils away for separation, is now being adopted to reduce costs.

Perga ruined city of Pamphylia, 10 mi/16 km NE of Adalia, Turkey, noted for its local cult of Artemis. It was visited by the apostle Paul.

Pergamum ancient Greek city in W Asia Minor, which became the capital of an independent kingdom 283 BC. As the ally of Rome it achieved great political importance in the 2nd century BC, and became a center of art and culture. Close to its site is the modern Turkish town of Bergama.

peri in Persian myth, a beautiful, harmless being, ranking between angels and evil spirits. Peris were ruled by Eblis, greatest of evil spirits.

Peri Jacopo 1561–1633. Italian composer who served the Medici family, the rulers of Florence. His experimental melodic opera *Euridice* 1600 established the opera form and influenced Monteverdi. His first opera, *Dafne* 1597, is now lost.

perianth in botany, a collective term for the outer whorls of the ◊flower, which protect the reproductive parts during development. In most ◊dicotyledons the perianth is composed of two distinct whorls, the calyx of ◊sepals and the corolla of ◊petals, whereas in many ◊monocotyledons the sepals and petals are indistinguishable and the segments of the perianth are then known individually as tepals.

periastron in astronomy, the point at which an object traveling in an elliptical orbit around a star is at its closest to the star; the point at which it is furthest is known as the apastron.

pericarp wall of a ◊fruit. It encloses the seeds and is derived from the ◊ovary wall. In fruits such as the acorn, the pericarp becomes dry and hard, forming a shell around the seed. In fleshy fruits the pericarp is typically made up of three distinct layers. The *epicarp*, or *exocarp*, forms the tough outer skin of the fruit, while the *mesocarp* is often fleshy and forms the middle layers. The innermost layer or *endocarp*, which surrounds the seeds, may be membranous or thick and hard, as in the ◊drupe (stone) of cherries, plums, and apricots.

Pericles c. 490–429 BC. Athenian politician who dominated the city's affairs from 461 BC (as leader of the democratic party), and under whom Greek culture reached its height. He created a confederation of cities under the leadership of Athens, but the disasters of the ◊Peloponnesian War led to his overthrow 430 BC. Although quickly reinstated, he died soon after.

peridot pale-green, transparent gem variety of the mineral ◊olivine. Peridot is an ultrabasic (silica-poor) ◊igneous rock that consists almost entirely of olivine.

peridotite rock consisting largely of the mineral olivine; pyroxene and other minerals may also be present. Peridotite is an ultrabasic rock containing less than 45% silica by weight. It is believed to be one of the rock types making up the Earth's upper mantle, and is sometimes brought from the depths to the surface by major movements, or as inclusions in lavas.

perigee the point at which an object, traveling in an elliptical orbit around the Earth, is at its closest to the Earth. The point at which it is furthest from the Earth is the apogee.

Périgueux capital of Dordogne *département*, Aquitaine, France, on the River Isle, 79 mi/127 km ENE of Bordeaux; trading center for wine and truffles; population (1982) 35,392. The Byzantine cathedral dates from 984.

perihelion the point at which an object, traveling in an elliptical orbit around the Sun, is at its closest to the Sun. The point at which it is furthest from the Sun is the aphelion.

Perim island in the strait of Bab-el-Mandeb, the southern entrance to the Red Sea; part of Yemen; area 5 sq mi/13 sq km.

period another name for menstruation; see ◊menstrual cycle.

period in physics, the time taken for one complete cycle of a repeated sequence of events. For example, the time taken for a pendulum to swing from side to side and back again is the period of the pendulum.

period punctuation mark (.). The term "period" is universally understood in English and is the preferred usage in North America; "full stop" is the preferred term in the UK. The period has two functions: to mark the end of a sentence and to indicate that a word has been abbreviated. It is also used in mathematics to indicate decimals and is then called a point.

periodic table of the elements classification of the elements to reflect the periodic law, namely that the properties of the chemical elements recur periodically when the elements are arranged in increasing order of their ◊atomic number and are shown in related groups. Today's arrangement is by atomic numbers as devised by Moseley in 1913–14; the original tables were set up by atomic weights (masses), first proposed by Newlands in 1863 and expanded on by Mendeleyev and Meyer in 1869. There are similarities in the chemical properties of the elements in each of the main vertical groups and a gradation of properties along the horizontal periods. The periods correspond to the filling of successive electron shells, and the groups correspond to the number of valence electrons.

The continuous sequence of elements divides into seven periods and nine groups. The members of a group, and the subgroups (a) and (b) into which each group is divided, show similar chemical properties. The Roman numeral at the top of each group is equal to a valence (the minimum, as in group I, or the maximum, as in group VII) of the elements it contains. *See p. 816 and p. 817.*

periodontal disease formerly known as *pyorrhoea*, disease of the gums and bone supporting the teeth, caused by the accumulation of plaque and microorganisms; the gums recede, and the teeth eventually become loose and may drop out unless treatment is sought.

peripheral device in computing, any item of equipment attached to and controlled by a computer. Peripherals are typically for input from and output to the user (for example, a keyboard or printer), storing data (for example, a disk drive), communications (such as a modem), or for performing physical tasks (such as a robot).

periscope optical instrument designed for observation from a concealed position such as from a submerged submarine. In its basic form it consists of a tube with parallel mirrors at each end, inclined at 45° to its axis. The periscope attained prominence in naval and military operations of World War I.

peristalsis wavelike contractions, produced by the contraction of smooth muscle, that pass along tubular organs, such as the intestines. The same term describes the wavelike motion of earthworms and other invertebrates, in which part of the body contracts as another part elongates.

peritoneum transparent tissue lining the abdominal cavity and curving around all the visceral organs of vertebrates.

periwinkle in botany, any of several trailing blue-flowered evergreen plants of the genus *Vinca* of the dogbane family Apocynaceae. They range in length from 8 in/20 cm to 3 ft/1 m.

The related Madagascar periwinkle *Catharanthus roseus* produces chemicals that inhibit the division of cells and are used to treat leukemia.

periwinkle in zoology, any marine snail of the family Littorinidae, found on the shores of Europe and E North America. Periwinkles have a conical spiral shell, and feed on algae.

perjury the offense of deliberately making a false statement on ▷oath (or ▷affirmation) when appearing as a witness in legal proceedings, on a point material to the question at issue. In Britain and the US it is punishable by a fine, imprisonment, or both.

Perkins Anthony 1932–1992. US film actor who played the mother-fixated psychopath Norman Bates in Alfred Hitchcock's *Psycho* 1960 and *Psycho II* 1982. He played shy but subtle roles in *Friendly Persuasion* 1956, *The Trial* 1962, and *The Champagne Murders* 1967. He also appeared on the stage in London and New York.

Perkins Frances 1882–1965. US public official. Holding a succession of posts in state regulatory agencies, Perkins became a reformer of labor standards and served on the State Industrial Board 1923–29. Perkins was appointed New York State's industrial commissioner 1929 and became the first female cabinet officer when she served as secretary of labor under F D Roosevelt 1933–45. Under Truman she was a member of the federal civil service commission 1946–53.

Born in Boston and educated at Mount Holyoke, Perkins worked at Hull House in Chicago before receiving a master's degree in economics from Columbia University 1910.

Perlis border state of Peninsular Malaysia, NW Malaysia; capital Kangar; area 309 sq mi/ 800 sq km; population (1990) 187,700. It produces rubber, rice, coconuts, and tin. Perlis is ruled by a raja. It was transferred by Siam to Britain 1909.

Perls Laura (born Lore Posner) 1906–1990. German-born US psychotherapist who, together with her husband, Fritz, helped develop the ▷gestalt method of psychotherapy. The gestalt treatment relies on a wide range of techniques to treat emotional illness, including some derived from theater and dance movement. Perls and her husband founded the New York Institute for Gestalt Therapy 1952.

Perm industrial city (shipbuilding, oil refining, aircraft, chemicals, lumber mills), and capital of Perm region, N Russia, on the Kama near the Ural mountains; population (1987) 1,075,000. It was called Molotov 1940–57.

permafrost condition in which a deep layer of soil does not thaw out during the summer but remains at below 32°F/0°C for at least two years, despite thawing of the soil above. It is claimed that 26% of the world's land surface is permafrost.

Permafrost gives rise to a poorly drained form of grassland typical of N Canada, Siberia, and Alaska known as ▷tundra.

Permian period of geological time 290–245 million years ago, the last period of the Paleozoic era. Its end was marked by a

significant change in marine life, including the extinction of many corals and trilobites. Deserts were widespread, and terrestrial amphibians and mammallike reptiles flourished. Cone-bearing plants (gymnosperms) came to prominence.

permutation in mathematics, a specified arrangement of a group of objects. It is the arrangement of a distinct objects taken b at a time in all possible orders. It is given by $a!/(a-b)!$, where "!" stands for ▷factorial. For example, the number of permutations of four letters taken from any group of six different letters is $6!/2! = (1 \times 2 \times 3 \times 4 \times 5 \times 6)/(1 \times 2) = 360$. The theoretical number of four-letter "words" that can be made from an alphabet of 26 letters is $26!/22! = 358,800$.

Pernambuco state of NE Brazil, on the Atlantic
area 37,946 sq mi/98,281 sq km
capital Recife (former name Pernambuco)
features highlands; the coast is low and humid
population (1985) 6,776,000.

Perón (María Estela) Isabel (born Martínez) 1931– . President of Argentina 1974–76, and third wife of Juan Perón. She succeeded him after he died in office, but labor unrest, inflation, and political violence pushed the country to the brink of chaos. Accused of corruption, she was held under house arrest for five years. She went into exile in Spain.

Peron Juan Domingo 1895–1974. President of Argentina 1946–55 and 1973–74. A professional

army officer, Perón took part in the right-wing military coup that toppled Argentina's government in 1943.

As secretary of labor and social welfare in the new government, he developed a pro-labor program that won him the loyalty of the *descamisados* "shirtless ones." With their support, and the aid of his actress wife, Eva ▷Perón, he was elected president in 1946. With Argentinian beef and wheat in high demand in the years following World War II, Perón was able to improve the country's economy substantially, but his increasingly dictatorial methods caused him to lose the support of the Roman Catholic Church. The death of his popular wife 1952 diminished his support among the workers, and in 1955 he was ousted by the military. Perón returned to Argentina 1973 and was elected president again; his third wife, Isabel Martinez de Perón, became vice-president. Upon his death in 1974, she assumed the presidency but was soon ousted by the military.

Perón Maria Eva (Evita) Duarte de 1919–1952. Argentinian populist leader, born in Buenos Aires. A successful film actress, she married Juan ▷Perón in 1945. When he became president the following year, she became his chief adviser and the unofficial minister of health and labor, devoting herself to helping the poor, improving education, and achieving women's suffrage. She was politically astute and sought the vice presidency in 1951 but was opposed by the army and withdrew. After her death from

periodic table of the elements *The periodic table of the elements arranges the elements into horizontal rows (called periods) and vertical columns (called groups) according to their atomic numbers.*

cancer in 1952, Juan's political strength began to decline.

perpendicular in mathematics, at a right angle; also, a line at right angles to another or to a plane. For a pair of skew lines (lines in three dimensions that do not meet), there is just one common perpendicular, which is at right angles to both lines; the nearest points on the two lines are the feet of this perpendicular.

perpetual motion the idea that a machine can be designed and constructed in such a way that, once started, it will continue in motion indefinitely without requiring any further input of energy (motive power). Such a device contradicts the two laws of thermodynamics that state that (1) energy can neither be created nor destroyed (the law of conservation of energy) and (2) heat cannot by itself flow from a cooler to a hotter object. As a result, all practical (real) machines require a continuous supply of energy, and no heat engine is able to convert all the heat into useful work.

Perpignan market town (olives, fruit, wine), resort, and capital of the Pyrénées-Orientales *département* of France, just off the Mediterranean coast, near the Spanish border; population (1982) 138,000. Overlooking Perpignan is the castle of the counts of Roussillon.

Perrault Charles 1628–1703. French author of the fairy tales *Contes de ma mère l'oye/Mother Goose's Fairy Tales* 1697, which include "Sleeping Beauty," "Little Red Riding Hood," "Blue Beard," "Puss in Boots," and "Cinderella."

Perrin Jean 1870–1942. French physicist who produced the crucial evidence that finally established the atomic nature of matter. Assuming the atomic hypothesis, Perrin demonstrated how the phenomenon of ◊Brownian movement could be used to derive precise values for ◊Avogadro's number. He was awarded the 1926 Nobel Prize for Physics.

perry fermented alcoholic beverage similar to hard cider, but made from pears, produced mainly in Normandy and the English West Country.

Perry Matthew Calbraith 1794–1858. US naval officer, commander of the expedition of 1853 that reopened communication between Japan and the outside world after 250 years' isolation. A show of evident military superiority, the use of steamships (thought by the Japanese to be floating volcanoes), and an exhibition of US technical superiority enabled him to negotiate the Treaty of Kanagawa 1854, granting the US trading rights with Japan.

Born in Newport, Rhode Island, he fought in the War of 1812 and the Mexican War 1847. In the early 1800s he helped to found the African state of Liberia for free US blacks, and in the 1830s and 1840s he developed an engineering corps for the US navy. He was the younger brother of Oliver Hazard ◊Perry.

Perry Oliver Hazard 1785–1819. US naval officer. During the War of 1812 he played a decisive role in securing American control of Lake Erie. Ordered there in 1813, he supervised the construction of a small battle fleet

and was responsible for the decisive victory over the British at the Battle of Put-in-Bay and participated in the Battle of the Thames.

Born in South Kingston, Rhode Island, Perry began his naval career 1799 as a midshipman and saw action in the Tripolitan War. He died of fever while on a cruise to South America.

Perse Saint-John. Adopted name of Alexis Saint-Léger 1887–1975. French poet and diplomat, a US citizen from 1940. His first book of verse, *Eloges* 1911, reflects the ambience of the West Indies, where he was born and raised. His later works include *Anabase* 1924, an epic poem translated by T S Eliot in 1930. He was awarded a Nobel Prize in 1960.

Entering the foreign service in 1914, he was secretary-general 1933–40. He then emigrated permanently to the US, and was deprived of French citizenship by the Vichy government.

Persephone Greek goddess (Roman Proserpina), the daughter of Zeus and Demeter. She was carried off to the underworld as the bride of Pluto, who later agreed that she should spend six months of the year with her mother. The myth symbolizes the growth and decay of vegetation and the changing seasons.

Persepolis ancient capital of the Persian Empire, 40 mi/65 km NE of Shiraz. It was burned down after its capture in 331 BC by Alexander the Great.

Perseus in Greek mythology, son of Zeus and Danaë. He slew Medusa, the ◊Gorgon, and cut off her head, which he set in his shield, rescued ◊Andromeda, and became king of Tiryns.

Perseus in astronomy, a constellation of the northern hemisphere, near Cassiopeia, and represented as the mythological hero. The eye of the decapitated Gorgon, Medusa, is identified with the variable star Algol. Perseus lies in the Milky Way and contains the Double Cluster, a twin cluster of stars. Every August the Perseid meteor shower radiates from its northern part.

Pershing John Joseph 1860–1948. US general, who commanded the American Expeditionary Force sent to France 1917–18 during World War I. He was responsible for more than 2 million men and fought successfully to keep them a separate unit.

Born in Laclede, Missouri, Pershing graduated from West Point 1886 and served in the Spanish-American War 1898, the Philippines 1899–1903, and Mexico 1916–17. His distinguished service as commander of the American Expeditionary Forces in France earned him a newly created rank, general of the armies. His memoirs, *My Experiences in the World War* 1931, earned him a Pulitzer prize in history 1932.

Persia, ancient kingdom in SW Asia. The early Persians were a nomadic Aryan people who migrated through the Caucasus to the Iranian plateau.

7th century BC The Persians were established in the present region of Fars, which then belonged to the Assyrians.

550 BC Cyrus the Great overthrew the empire of the Medes, to whom the Persians had been subject, and founded the Persian Empire.

539 BC Having conquered all Anatolia, Cyrus added Babylonia (including Syria and Palestine) to his empire.

529–485 BC Darius I organized an efficient centralized system of administration and extended Persian rule east into Afghanistan and

					VII	2 Helium **He** 4.00260
		III	IV	V	VI	
		5 Boron **B** 10.81	6 Carbon **C** 12.011	7 Nitrogen **N** 14.0067	8 Oxygen **O** 15.9994	9 Fluorine **F** 18.99840	10 Neon **Ne** 20.179
		13 Aluminium **Al** 26.98154	14 Silicon **Si** 28.086	15 Phosphorus **P** 30.97376P	16 Sulphur **S** 32.06	17 Chlorine **Cl** 35.453	18 Argon **Ar** 39.948

28 Nickel **Ni** 58.70	29 Copper **Cu** 63.546	30 Zinc **Zn** 65.38	31 Gallium **Ga** 69.72	32 Germanium **Ge** 72.59	33 Arsenic **As** 74.9216	34 Selenium **Se** 78.96	35 Bromine **Br** 79.904	36 Krypton **Kr** 83.80
46 Palladium **Pd** 106.4	47 Silver **Ag** 107.868	48 Cadmium **Cd** 112.40	49 Indium **In** 114.82	50 Tin **Sn** 118.69	51 Antimony **Sb** 121.75	52 Tellurium **Te** 127.75	53 Iodine **I** 126.9045	54 Xenon **Xe** 131.30
78 Platinum **Pt** 195.09	79 Gold **Au** 196.9665	80 Mercury **Hg** 200.59	81 Thallium **Tl** 204.37	82 Lead **Pb** 207.37	83 Bismuth **Bi** 207.2	84 Polonium **Po** 210	85 Astatine **At** 211	86 Radon **Rn** 222.0176

63 Europium **Eu** 151.96	64 Gadolinium **Gd** 157.25	65 Terbium **Tb** 158.9254	66 Dysprosium **Dy** 162.50	67 Holmium **Ho** 164.9304	68 Erbium **Er** 167.26	69 Thulium **Tm** 168.9342	70 Ytterbium **Yb** 173.04	71 Lutetium **Lu** 174.97
95 Americium **Am** 243.0614	96 Curium **Cm** 247.0703	97 Berkelium **Bk** 247.0703	98 Californium **Cf** 251.0786	99 Einsteinium **Es** 252.0828	100 Fermium **Fm** 257.0951	101 Mendelevium **Me** 258.0986	102 Nobelium **No** 259.1009	103 Lawrencium **Lr** 260.1054

NW India and as far north as the Danube, but the empire was weakened by internal dynastic struggles.

499–449 BC The Persian Wars with Greece ended Persian domination of the ancient world.

331 BC Alexander the Great drove the Persians under Darius III (died 330 BC) into retreat at Arbela on the Tigris, marking the end of the Persian Empire and the beginning of the Hellenistic period under the Seleucids.

AD 226 The Sassanian Empire was established in Persia and annexed Parthia.

637 Arabs took the capital, Ctesiphon, and introduced Islam in place of Zoroastrianism. For modern history see ▷Iran.

Persian inhabitant of or native to Persia, now Iran, and referring to the culture and the language (see also ▷Persian language). The Persians are descended from central Asians of S Russia (▷Aryans), who migrated south into the region about 2000 BC.

Persian art see ▷ancient art: art of early civilizations.

Persian Gulf or *Arabian Gulf* large shallow inlet of the Arabian Sea; area 90,000 sq mi/233,000 sq km. It divides the Arabian peninsula from Iran and is linked by the Strait of Hormuz and the Gulf of Oman to the Arabian Sea. Oil-fields surround it in the Gulf States of Bahrain, Iran, Iraq, Kuwait, Oman, Qatar, Saudi Arabia, and the United Arab Emirates.

Persian language member of the Indo-Iranian branch of the Indo-European language family and the official language of the state once known as Persia but now called Iran. Persian is known to its own speakers as *Farsi*, the language of the province of Fars (Persia proper). It is written in a modified Arabic script, from right to left, and has a large mixture of Arabic religious, philosophical, and technical vocabulary.

Persian literature before the Arab conquest Persian literature is represented by the sacred books of ▷Zoroastrianism known as the *Avesta* and later translated into Pahlavi, in which language there also appeared various secular writings. After the conquest the use of Arabic became widespread. The Persian language was revived during the 9th century, and the following centuries saw a succession of brilliant poets, including the epic writer Firdawsi, the didactic S'adi (1184–1291), the mystic Rumi (1207–1273), the lyrical Háfiz, and Jami, who combined the gifts of his predecessors and is considered the last of the Classical poets. Omar Khayyam, who is well known outside Iran, is considered less important there. In the 16th and 17th centuries many Persian writers worked in India, still using Classical forms and themes, and it was not until the revolutionary movements and contact with the West during the 20th century that Persian literature developed further.

Persian Wars series of conflicts between Greece and Persia 499–449 BC. The eventual victory of Greece marked the end of Persian domination of the ancient world and the beginning of Greek supremacy.

499 BC Revolt of the Ionian Greeks against Persian rule.

490 BC Darius I of Persia defeated at Marathon.

480 BC Xerxes I victorious at Thermopylae (narrow pass from Thessaly to Locris, which Leonidas, King of Sparta, and 1,000 men defended to the death against the Persians);

Athens was captured, but the Greek navy was victorious at ▷Salamis.

479 BC Greeks under Spartan general Pausanias (died *c.* 470) victorious at Plataea, driving the Persians from the country.

persimmon any tree of the genus *Diospyros* of the ebony family Ebenaceae, especially the common persimmon *D. virginiana* of the southeastern US. Up to 60 ft/19 m high, the persimmon has alternate oval leaves and yellow-green unisexual flowers. The small, sweet, orange fruits are edible.

The Japanese persimmon *D. kaki* has larger fruits and is widely cultivated.

personal computer (PC) another name for ▷microcomputer. The term is also used, more specifically, to mean the IBM Personal Computer and computers based on it.

The first IBM PC was introduced in 1981; it had 64 kilobytes of random access memory (RAM) and one floppy-disk drive. It was followed in 1983 by the XT (with a hard-disk drive) and in 1984 by the AT (based on a more powerful ▷microprocessor). Many manufacturers have copied the basic design, which is now regarded as a standard for business microcomputers. Computers designed to function like an IBM PC are called **IBM-compatible computers**.

personality individual's characteristic way of behaving across a wide range of situations. Two broad dimensions of personality are ▷extroversion and ▷neuroticism. A number of more specific personal traits have also been described, including ▷psychopathy (antisocial behavior).

personification figure of speech (poetic or imaginative expression) in which animals, plants, objects, and ideas are treated as if they were human or alive ("Clouds chased each other across the face of the Moon;" "Nature smiled on their work and gave it her blessing;" "The future beckoned eagerly to them").

perspiration excretion of water and dissolved substances from the ▷sweat glands of the skin of mammals. Perspiration has two main functions: body cooling by the evaporation of water from the skin surface, and excretion of waste products such as salts.

Perth industrial town in Tayside, E Scotland, on the River Tay; population (1981) 42,000. It was the capital of Scotland from the 12th century until James I of Scotland was assassinated here 1437.

Perth capital of Western Australia, with its port at nearby Fremantle on the Swan River; population (1990) 1,190,100. Products include textiles, cement, furniture, and vehicles. It was founded 1829 and is the commercial and cultural center of the state.

Peru country in South America, on the Pacific, bounded N by Ecuador and Colombia, E by Brazil and Bolivia, and S by Chile.

government The 1980 constitution provides for a president who is head of both state and government, elected by universal suffrage for a five-year term, and governing with an appointed council of ministers.

The two-chamber legislature, the National Congress, comprises a 60-member Senate and a 180-member Chamber of Deputies, also popularly elected for five years. Senators are elected on a national basis, but members of the Chamber are elected, through a system of proportional representation, from local constituencies.

history For early history, see ▷American Indian. The ▷Chimu culture flourished from about 1200 and was gradually superseded by the ▷Inca empire, building on 800 years of Andean civilization and covering a large part of South America. Civil war had weakened the Incas when the conquistador ▷Pizarro arrived from Spain 1531 and began raiding, looting, and enslaving the people. He executed the last of the Inca emperors, Atahualpa, 1533. Before Pizarro's assassination 1541, Spanish rule was firmly established.

independence A native revolt 1780 failed, and during the successful rebellions by the European settlers in other Spanish possessions in South America 1810–22, Peru remained the Spanish government's headquarters; it was the last to achieve independence 1824. It attempted union with Bolivia 1836–39. It fought a naval war against Spain 1864–66, and in the ▷Pacific War against Chile 1879–83 over the nitrate fields of the Atacama Desert, Peru was defeated and lost three provinces (one, Tacna, was returned 1929). Other boundary disputes were settled by arbitration 1902 with Bolivia, 1927 with Colombia, and 1942 with Ecuador. Peru declared war on Germany and Japan Feb 1945.

dictatorships Peru was ruled by right-wing dictatorships from the mid-1920s until 1945, when free elections returned. Although Peru's oldest political organization (the American Popular Revolutionary Alliance (APRA)), was the largest party in Congress, it was constantly thwarted by smaller conservative groups, anxious to protect their business interests. APRA was founded in the 1920s to fight imperialism throughout South America, but Peru was the only country where it became established.

military rule In 1948 a group of army officers led by General Manuel Odría ousted the elected government, temporarily banned APRA, and installed a military junta. Odría became president 1950 and remained in power until 1956. In 1963 military rule ended, and Fernando Belaúnde Terry, the joint candidate of the Popular Action (AP) and Christian Democrats (PDC) parties, won the presidency, while APRA took the largest share of the Chamber of Deputies seats.

After economic problems and industrial unrest, Belaúnde was deposed in a bloodless coup 1968, and the army returned to power led by General Velasco Alvarado. Velasco introduced land reform, with private estates being turned into cooperative farms, but he failed to return any land to Indian peasant communities, and the Maoist guerrillas of Sendero Luminoso ("Shining Path") became increasingly active in the Indian region of S Peru.

economic and social crisis Another bloodless coup, 1975, brought in General Morales Bermúdez. He called elections for the presidency and both chambers of Congress 1980, and Belaúnde was reelected. Belaúnde embarked on a program of agrarian and industrial reform, but at the end of his presidency, in 1985, the country was again in a state of economic and social crisis. His constitutionally elected successor was the young Social Democrat Alan García Pérez, who embarked on a program to cleanse the army and police of the old guard. By 1986 about 1,400 had elected to retire. After trying to expand the economy with price and exchange controls, in 1987 he announced his intention to nationalize the banks and insurance companies but delayed the move, after a vigorous campaign against the proposal.

Peru
Republic of (*República del Perú*)

area 496,216 sq mi/1,285,200 sq km
capital Lima, including port of Callao
cities Arequipa, Iquitos, Chiclayo, Trujillo
physical Andes mountains NW–SE cover 27% of Peru, separating Amazon river-basin jungle in NE from coastal plain in W; desert along coast N–S
environment an estimated 3,000 out of the 3,100 sq mi/8,000 sq km of coastal lands under irrigation are either waterlogged or suffering from saline water. Only half the population have access to clean drinking water
features Lake Titicaca; Atacama Desert; Nazca lines, monuments of Machu Picchu, Chan Chan, Charín de Huantar
head of state and government Alberto Fujimori from 1990
political system democratic republic
political parties American Popular Revolutionary Alliance (APRA), moderate, left-wing; United Left (IU), left-wing; Change 90, centrist
exports coca, coffee, alpaca, llama and vicuña wool, fish meal, lead (largest producer in South America), copper, iron, oil
currency new sol
population (1990 est) 21,904,000 (46% Indian, mainly Quechua and Aymara; 43%

mixed Spanish–Indian descent); growth rate 2.6% p.a.
life expectancy men 61, women 66
languages Spanish 68%, Quechua 27% (both official), Aymara 3%
religion Roman Catholic 90%
literacy men 91%, women 78% (1985 est)
GNP $19.6 bn (1988); $940 per head (1984)
chronology
1824 Independence achieved from Spain.
1849–74 Some 80,000–100,000 Chinese laborers arrived in Peru to fill menial jobs such as collecting guano.
1902 Boundary dispute with Bolivia settled.
1927 Boundary dispute with Colombia settled.
1942 Boundary dispute with Ecuador settled.
1948 Army coup, led by General Manuel Odría, installed a military government.
1963 Return to civilian rule, with Fernando Belaúnde Terry as president.
1968 Return of military government in a bloodless coup by General Juan Velasco Alvarado.
1975 Velasco replaced, in a bloodless coup, by General Morales Bermúdez.
1980 Return to civilian rule, with Fernando Belaúnde as president.
1981 Boundary dispute with Ecuador renewed.
1985 Belaúnde succeeded by Social Democrat Alan García Pérez.
1987 President García delayed the nationalization of Peru's banks after a vigorous campaign against the proposal.
1988 García pressured to seek help from the International Monetary Fund.
1989 Mario Vargas Llosa entered presidential race; his Democratic Front won municipal elections Nov.
1990 Alberto Fujimori defeated Vargas Llosa in presidential elections. Assassination attempt on president failed.
1992 April: Fujimori sided with army to avert coup, announcing crackdown on rebels and drug traffickers. USA suspended humanitarian aid. Sendero Luminoso ("Shining Path") terrorists continued campaign of violence.
May: Fujimori promised return to democracy.
Sept: Sendero Luminoso leader, Abimael Guzman Reynoso, arrested; extremist attacks stepped up. Oct: Reynoso received life sentence.

In 1989 the International Development Bank suspended credit to Peru because it was six months behind in debt payments. The annual inflation rate to April was 4,329%. García Pérez declared his support for the Sandinista government in Nicaragua and criticized US policy throughout Latin America. The party of García Pérez, constitutionally barred from seeking reelection, saw its popularity slip in the Nov 1989 municipal elections. Novelist Mario Vargas Llosa, the candidate of the center-right Democratic Front coalition, was long considered the favorite to succeed García Pérez. However, Alberto Fujimori, the son of Japanese immigrants and leader of a new party, Change 90, forced a run-off in April elections. A political novice, Fujimori won a substantial victory in June. Soon after taking office he instituted a drastic economic adjustment program in an attempt to halt Peru's inflation and to pay foreign debt. In Aug 1990 an attempt to assassinate the president, by means of an automobile filled with dynamite ramming the presidential palace, failed.
opposition to Fujimori With mounting opposition to the government and fears of a military

coup, Fujimori allied himself April 1992 with the army, suspended the assembly, and sacked half of the country's top judges, declaring them to be corrupt. The move, which he announced as a crackdown on rebel leaders and drug traffickers, brought international criticism (including a suspension of US humanitarian aid) and a challenge from his deputy, Maximo San Roman, who branded him a dictator. Fujimori said he would return to democratic rule within a year.
rebel leader arrested Shining Path terrorists stepped up their campaign in response to crackdown, with renewed attacks on property in Lima reported July 1992. In Sept police arrested Shining Path leader Abimael Guzman Reynoso, along with several other high-ranking members of the group. All received life sentences Oct; terrorist attacks intensified in response. *See illustration box.*

Peru Current formerly known as *Humboldt Current* cold ocean ◊current flowing north from the Antarctic along the west coast of South America to S Ecuador, then west. It reduces the coastal temperature, making the

west slopes of the Andes arid because winds are already chilled and dry when they meet the coast.

Perugia capital of Umbria, Italy, 1,700 ft/520 m above the River Tiber, about 85 mi/137 km N of Rome; population (1988) 148,000. Its industries include textiles, liqueurs, and chocolate. One of the 12 cities of the ancient country of Etruria, it surrendered to Rome 309 BC. There is a university, founded 1276; a municipal palace, built 1281; and a 15th-century cathedral.

Perugino Pietro. Original name of Pietro Vannucci 1446–1523. Italian painter, active chiefly in Perugia. He taught Raphael who absorbed his soft and graceful figure style. Perugino produced paintings for the lower walls of the Sistine Chapel of the Vatican 1481 and in 1500 decorated the Sala del Cambio in Perugia.

Perutz Max 1914– . Austrian-born British biochemist who shared the 1962 Nobel Prize for Chemistry with John Kendrew for work on the structure of the haemoglobin molecule.
Perutz moved to Britain in 1936 to work with John Bernal (1901–1971) at Cambridge University. After internment in Canada as an alien during World War II he returned to Cambridge and completed his research in 1959.

Pescadores (Chinese *Penghu*) group of about 60 islands off Taiwan, of which they form a dependency; area 50 sq mi/130 sq km.

Peshawar capital of North-West Frontier Province, Pakistan, 11 mi/18 km E of the Khyber Pass; population (1981) 555,000. Products include textiles, leather, and copper.

pessary medical device designed to be inserted into the vagina either to support a displaced womb or as a contraceptive. The word is also used for a vaginal suppository used for administering drugs locally, made from glycerol or oil of theobromine, which melts within the vagina to release the contained substance—for example, a contraceptive, antibiotic, or antifungal agent.

Pessoa Fernando 1888–1935. Portuguese poet. Born in Lisbon, he was brought up in South Africa and was bilingual in English and Portuguese. His verse is considered to be the finest written in Portuguese this century. He wrote under three assumed names, which he called "heteronyms"—Alvaro de Campos, Ricardo Reis, and Alberto Caeiro—for each of which he invented a biography.

pest in biology, any insect, fungus, rodent, or other living organism that has a harmful effect on human beings, other than those that directly cause human diseases. Most pests damage crops or livestock, but the term also covers those that damage buildings, destroy food stores, and spread disease.

Pestalozzi Johann Heinrich 1746–1827. Swiss educator who advocated the French philosopher Jean-Jacques Rousseau's "natural" principles (of natural development and the power of example), and described his own theories in *Wie Gertrude ihre Kinder lehrt/ How Gertrude Teaches her Children* 1801. He stressed the importance of mother and home in a child's education.

pesticide any chemical used in farming, gardening or indoors to combat pests. Pesticides are of three main types: *insecticides* (to kill insects), *fungicides* (to kill fungal diseases), and *herbicides* (to kill plants, mainly those considered weeds). The safest pesticides are those made from plants, such as the insecticides pyrethrum and derris. Pesticides cause a number of pollution problems through spray drift onto surrounding areas, direct contamination of users or the public, and as residues on food.

More potent are synthetic products, such as chlorinated hydrocarbons. These products, including DDT and dieldrin, are highly toxic to wildlife and human beings, so their use is now restricted by law in some areas and is declining. Safer pesticides such as malathion are based on organic phosphorus compounds, but they still present hazards to health. The aid organization Oxfam estimates that pesticides cause about 10,000 deaths worldwide every year.

Pesticides were used to deforest SE Asia during the Vietnam War, causing death and destruction to the area's ecology and lasting health and agricultural problems.

In 1991 Central America was the world's highest consumer of pesticides per head of the population.

pet animal kept for companionship and occasionally for status. Research suggests that interaction with a pet induces relaxation (slower heart rate and lower blood pressure). In 16th–17th century Europe, keeping animals in this way was thought suggestive of witchcraft.

Pétain Henri Philippe 1856–1951. French general and right-wing politician. His defense of Verdun 1916 during World War I made him a national hero. In World War II he became chief of state June 1940 and signed an armistice with Germany. Removing the seat of government to Vichy, a health resort in central France, he established an authoritarian regime. He was imprisoned after the war.

With the Allied invasion he was taken to Germany, but returned 1945 and was sentenced to death for treason, the sentence being commuted to life imprisonment.

petal part of a flower whose function is to attract pollinators such as insects or birds. Petals are frequently large and brightly colored and may also be scented. Some have a nectary at the base and markings on the petal surface, known as honey guides, to direct pollinators to the source of the nectar. In wind-pollinated plants, however, the petals are usually small and insignificant, and sometimes absent altogether. Petals are derived from modified leaves, and are known collectively as a corolla.

Some insect-pollinated plants also have inconspicuous petals, with large colorful ⟂bracts (leaflike structures) or ⟂sepals taking over their role, or strong scents that attract pollinators such as flies.

Petaluma city in NW California, N of San Francisco, on the Petaluma River. It is an agricultural center for poultry and dairy products; population (1990) 43,200.

Peter Laurence J 1910–1990. Canadian writer and teacher, author (with Raymond Hull) of *The Peter Principle* 1969, in which he outlined the theory that people tend to be promoted into positions for which they are incompetent.

Peter three tsars of Russia:

Peter I *the Great* 1672–1725. Tsar of Russia from 1682 on the death of his brother Tsar Feodor. He assumed control of the government 1689. He attempted to reorganize the country on Western lines; the army was modernized, a fleet was built, the administrative and legal systems were remodeled, education was encouraged, and the church was brought under

state control. On the Baltic coast, where he had conquered territory from Sweden, Peter built his new capital, St Petersburg.

After a successful campaign against the Ottoman Empire 1696, he visited Holland and Britain to study Western techniques, and worked in Dutch and English shipyards. In order to secure an outlet to the Baltic, Peter undertook a war with Sweden 1700–21, which resulted in the acquisition of Estonia and parts of Latvia and Finland. A war with Persia 1722–23 added Baku to Russia.

Peter II 1715–1730. Tsar of Russia from 1727. Son of Peter the Great, he had been passed over in favor of Catherine I 1725 but succeeded her 1727. He died of smallpox.

Peter III 1728–1762. Tsar of Russia 1762. Weak-minded son of Peter I's eldest daughter, Anne, he was adopted 1741 by his aunt ⟂Elizabeth, Empress of Russia, and at her command married the future Catherine II 1745. He was deposed in favor of his wife and probably murdered by her lover, Alexius Orlov.

Peter I 1844–1921. King of Serbia from 1903. He was the son of Prince Alexander Karageorgevich and was elected king when the last Obrenovich king was murdered 1903. He took part in the retreat of the Serbian army 1915, and in 1918 was proclaimed first king of the Serbs, Croats, and Slovenes (renamed Yugoslavia in 1921).

Peter II 1923–1970. King of Yugoslavia 1934–45. He succeeded his father, Alexander I, and assumed the royal power after the overthrow of the regency 1941. He escaped to the UK after the German invasion, and married Princess Alexandra of Greece 1944. He was dethroned 1945 when Marshal Tito came to power and the Soviet-backed federal republic was formed.

Peterborough city in Cambridgeshire, England, noted for its 12th-century cathedral; population (1991) 148,800, one of the fastest growing cities in Europe. It has an advanced electronics industry. Nearby Flag Fen disclosed 1985 a well-preserved Bronze Age settlement of 660 BC.

Peterborough was designated a new town 1967.

Peterloo massacre the events in St Peter's Fields, Manchester, England, Aug 16, 1819, when an open-air meeting in support of parliamentary reform was charged by yeomanry and hussars. Eleven people were killed and 500 wounded. The name was given in analogy with the Battle of Waterloo.

Peter Pan or *The Boy Who Wouldn't Grow Up* play for children by James ⟂Barrie, first performed in 1904. Peter Pan, an orphan with magical powers, arrives in the night nursery of the Darling children, Wendy, John, and Michael. He teaches them to fly and introduces them to the Never Never Land inhabited by fantastic characters, including the fairy Tinkerbell, the Lost Boys, and the pirate Captain Hook. The play was followed by a story, *Peter Pan in Kensington Gardens* 1906, and a book of the play 1911.

Peter Rabbit full title *The Tale of Peter Rabbit* first of the children's stories written and illustrated by English author Beatrix ⟂Potter, published in 1900.

Peter, St Christian martyr, the author of two epistles in the New Testament and leader of the apostles. He is regarded as the first bishop of Rome, whose mantle the pope inherits. His

real name was Simon, but he was nicknamed Kephas ("Peter," from the Greek for "rock") by Jesus, as being the rock upon which he would build his church. His emblem is two keys; feast day June 29.

Originally a fisherman of Capernaum, on the Sea of Galilee, Peter may have been a follower of John the Baptist, and was the first to acknowledge Jesus as the Messiah. Tradition has it that he later settled in Rome; he was martyred during the reign of the emperor Nero, perhaps by crucifixion. Bones excavated from under the Basilica of St Peter's in the Vatican 1968 were accepted as those of St Peter by Pope Paul VI.

Petersburg city in SE Virginia, on the Appomattox River, S of Richmond. Industries include tobacco products, textiles, leather products, boat building, and chemicals; population (1990) 38,400. It was the site of Fort Henry 1646, as well as of Revolutionary War and Civil War battles.

Peter's pence in the Roman Catholic Church, a voluntary annual contribution to papal administrative costs; during the 10th–16th centuries it was a compulsory levy of one penny per household.

petiole in botany, the stalk attaching the leaf blade, or ⟂lamina, to the stem. Typically it is continuous with the midrib of the leaf and attached to the base of the lamina, but occasionally it is attached to the lower surface of the lamina, as in the nasturtium (a peltate leaf). Petioles that are flattened and leaflike are termed phyllodes. Leaves that lack a petiole are said to be sessile.

Petipa Marius 1818–1910. French choreographer who created some of the most important ballets in the Classical repertory. For the Imperial Ballet in Russia he created masterpieces such as *La Bayadère* 1877, *The Sleeping Beauty* 1890, *Swan Lake* 1895 (with Ivanov), and *Raymonda* 1898.

petit point or *tent stitch* short, slanting embroidery stitch used on open-net canvas for upholstery and cushions to form a solid background. Petit point embroidery was common in the 18th century.

Petőfi Sándor 1823–1849. Hungarian nationalist poet. He published his first volume of poems 1844. He expressed his revolutionary ideas in the semi autobiographical poem "The Apostle," and died fighting the Austrians in the battle of Segesvár.

Petra (Arabic *Wadi Musa*) ancient city carved out of the red rock at a site in Jordan, on the eastern slopes of the Wadi el Araba, 56 mi/90 km S of the Dead Sea. An Edomite stronghold and capital of the Nabataeans in the 2nd century, it was captured by the Roman emperor Trajan 106 and destroyed by the Arabs in the 7th century. It was forgotten in Europe until 1812 when the Swiss traveler Jacob Burckhardt (1818–1897) came across it.

Petrarch (Italian *Petrarca*) Francesco 1304–1374. Italian poet, born in Arezzo, a devotee of the Classical tradition. His *Il Canzoniere* is composed of sonnets in praise of his idealized love, "Laura," whom he first saw 1327 (she was a married woman and refused to become his mistress).

From 1337 he often stayed in secluded study at his home at Vaucluse, near Avignon, then the residence of the popes. Petrarch, eager to restore the glories of Rome, wanted to return the papacy there. He was a friend of the poet Giovanni Boccaccio, and supported the political reformer Cola di Rienzi's attempt to establish a republic 1347.

petrel any of various families of seabirds, including the worldwide *storm petrels* (family Procellariidae), which include the smallest seabirds (some only 5 in/13 cm long), and the *diving petrels* (family Pelecanoididae) of the southern hemisphere, which feed by diving underwater and are characterized by having nostril tubes. They include ◊fulmars and ◊shearwaters.

Most familiar is Wilson's storm petrel *Oceanites oceanicus*, which breeds in the southern hemisphere and migrates to the N Atlantic in winter. Seldom coming to land except to breed, Wilson's storm petrels lay a single egg in holes among the rocks. They are 7 in/18 cm long and sooty black with a white rump band.

Like other ground-nesting or burrow-nesting seabirds, petrels are vulnerable to predators such as rats that take eggs and nestlings. Several island species are in danger of extinction, including the Bermuda petrel *Pterodroma cahow* and the Freira petrel of Madeira *P. madeira*.

Petrie (William Matthew) Flinders 1853–1942. English archeologist who excavated sites in Egypt (the pyramids at Gîza, the temple at Tanis, the Greek city of Naucratis in the Nile delta, Tell el Amarna, Naquada, Abydos, and Memphis) and Palestine from 1880.

petrochemical chemical derived from the processing of petroleum (crude oil). *Petrochemical industries* are those that obtain their raw materials from the processing of petroleum.

petrodollars in economics, dollar earnings of nations that make up the ◊Organization of Petroleum-Exporting Countries (OPEC).

Petrograd former name (1914–24) of St Petersburg, city in Russia.

petroleum or *crude oil* natural mineral oil, a thick greenish-brown flammable liquid found underground in permeable rocks. Petroleum consists of hydrocarbons mixed with oxygen, sulfur, nitrogen, and other elements in varying proportions. It is thought to be derived from ancient organic material that has been converted by, first, bacterial action, then heat and pressure (but its origin may be chemical also). From crude petroleum, various products are made by distillation and other processes; for example, fuel oil, gasoline, kerosene, diesel, lubricating oil, paraffin wax, and petroleum jelly.

The organic material in petroleum was laid down millions of years ago (hence it is known as a fossil fuel). Petroleum is often found as large lakes floating on water but under a layer of natural gas (mainly methane), in anticlines and other traps below impervious rock layers. Oil may flow naturally from wells under gas pressure from above or water pressure from below, causing it to rise up the borehole, but many oil wells require pumping to bring the oil to the surface.

The occurrence of petroleum was known in ancient times, and it was used medicinally by American Indians, but the exploitation of oil fields began with the first commercial well in Pennsylvania 1859.

The US led in production until the 1960s, when the Middle East outproduced other areas, their immense reserves leading to a worldwide dependence on cheap oil for transport and industry. In 1961 the Organization of the Petroleum Exporting Countries (OPEC) was established to avoid exploitation of member countries; after OPEC's price rises in 1973, the International Energy Agency (IEA) was established 1974 to protect the interests of oil-consuming countries. New technologies were introduced to pump oil from offshore and from the Arctic (the Alaska pipeline) in an effort to avoid a monopoly by OPEC.

Petroleum products and chemicals are used in large quantities in the manufacture of detergents, artificial fibers, plastics, insecticides, fertilizers, pharmaceuticals, toiletries, and synthetic rubber. Aviation fuel is a volatile form of gasoline.

The burning of petroleum fuel is one cause of air pollution. The transport of oil can lead to major catastrophes—for example, the *Torrey Canyon* tanker lost off SW England 1967, which led to an agreement by the international oil companies 1968 to pay compensation for massive shore pollution. The 1989 oil spill in Alaska from the *Exxon Valdez* damaged the area's fragile environment, despite clean-up efforts. Drilling for oil involves the risks of accidental spillage and drilling-rig accidents. The problems associated with oil have led to the various ◊alternative energy technologies.

A new kind of bacterium was developed during the 1970s in the US, capable of "eating" oil as a means of countering oil spills. Its creation gave rise to the so-called Frankenstein law (a ruling that allowed new forms of life created in laboratories to be patented).

petrology branch of geology that deals with the study of rocks, their mineral compositions, and their origins.

Petronius Gaius, known as *Petronius Arbiter*, died *c.* AD 66. Roman author of the licentious romance *Satyricon*. He was a companion of the emperor Nero and supervisor of his pleasures.

pewter any of various alloys of mostly tin with varying amounts of lead, copper, or antimony. Pewter has been known for centuries and was once widely used for domestic utensils but is now used mainly for ornamental ware.

peyote spineless cactus *Lophophora williamsii* of N Mexico and the southwestern US. It has white or pink flowers. Its buttonlike tops contain the hallucinogen **mescaline**, which is used by American Indians in religious ceremonies.

pH scale from 0 to 14 for measuring acidity or alkalinity. A pH of 7.0 indicates neutrality, below 7 is acid, while above 7 is alkaline. Strong acids, such as those used in car batteries, have a pH of about 2; strong alkalis such as sodium hydroxide are pH 13.

Acidic fruits such as citrus fruits are about pH 4. Fertile soils have a pH of about 6.5 to 7.0, while weak alkalis such as soap are 9 to 10.

The pH value of a solution equals the negative logarithm of the concentration of hydrogen ions.

Phaedra in Greek mythology, a Cretan, daughter of Minos and Pasiphae, married to Theseus of Athens. Her adulterous passion for her stepson, Hippolytus, led to her death. The story is told in plays by Euripides, Seneca, and Racine.

Phaethon in Greek mythology, the son of Helios, the Sun god, who was allowed for one day to drive the chariot of the Sun. Losing control of the horses, he almost set the Earth on fire and was killed by Zeus with a thunderbolt.

phage another name for a ◊bacteriophage, a virus that attacks bacteria.

phagocyte type of ◊white blood cell, or leukocyte, that can engulf a bacterium or other invading microorganism. Phagocytes are found in blood, lymph, and other body tissues, where they also ingest foreign matter and dead tissue. A ◊macrophage differs in size and life span.

Phalangist member of a Lebanese military organization (*Phalanges Libanaises*), since 1958 the political and military force of the ◊Maronite Church in Lebanon.

The Phalanges Libanaises was founded 1936 by Pierre Gemayel after seeing the discipline and authoritarianism of Nazi Germany. Its initial aim was to protect the Maronite position in Lebanon; in 1958 it entered the political arena to oppose growing Arab nationalism.

petroleum: chronology

1859	Edwin Drake drilled the world's first successful oil well in Titusville, Pennsylvania, to a depth of 70 ft/18 m.
1865	The first oil pipeline, 32,000 ft/9,750 m long, was constructed at Oil Creek, Pennsylvania, to carry oil from well to nearby coalfield.
1896	The first offshore wells were drilled from piers off the California coast.
1899	The first gravity meter was produced.
1914	Reginald Fessenden patented the seismograph.
1939	The aircraft-borne magnetometer was developed to measure magnetism of rocks.
1966	Oil was discovered beneath the North Sea.
1967	The worst oil spill in British waters from the *Torrey Canyon*, which struck rocks at Lands End. Over 108,000 metric tons of oil were spilled.
1974	The world's deepest oil well, 31,441 ft/10,941 m, was drilled in Oklahoma.
1979	The oil rig *Ixtoc I* in the Gulf of Mexico accidentally released 545,000 metric tons of oil into the sea. The slick spread for 400 miles. Later the same year, the worst tanker spillage occurred. Two tankers, the *Atlantic Empress* and the *Aegean Captain*, collided off the island of Tobago, in the Caribbean Sea. More than 230,000 metric tons of oil were spilled.
1984	An exploratory well was drilled off the coast of New England, in water of depth 6,942 ft/2,116 m—a world record.
1988	The Piper Alpha drilling rig in the North Sea caught fire in July, killing 167 people.
1989	The worst spill in American waters occurred when 55,000 metric tons of oil escaped from the *Exxon Valdez* off the Alaskan coast, near Prince William Sound.
1991	The worst spill to date was a consequence of the Gulf War when Iraqi forces opened the pipeline into the Persian Gulf and coalition forces caused further damage during Operation Desert Storm.

Phalaris 570–554 BC. Tyrant of the Greek colony of Acragas (Agrigento) in Sicily. He is said to have built a hollow bronze bull in which his victims were roasted alive. He was killed in a people's revolt.

The *Letters of Phalaris* attributed to him were proved by the British scholar Richard Bentley to be a forgery of the 2nd century AD.

phalarope any of a genus *Phalaropus* of small, elegant shorebirds in the sandpiper family (Scolopacidae). They have the habit of spinning in the water to stir up insect larvae. They are native to North America, the UK, and the polar regions of Europe.

The male phalarope is courted by the female and hatches the eggs. The female is always larger and more colorful.

The red-necked phalarope *P. lobatus*, gray *P. fulicarius*, and Wilson's phalarope *P. tricolor* can be found in North America.

phallus model of the male sexual organ, used as a fertility symbol in ancient Greece, Rome, Anatolia, India, and many other parts of the world. In Hinduism it is called the *lingam*, and is used as the chief symbolical representation of the deity Shiva.

phanerogam obsolete term for a plant that bears flowers or cones and reproduces by means of seeds, that is an ⟡angiosperm and ⟡gymnosperm, or a ⟡seed plant. Plants such as mosses, fungi, and ferns were known as *cryptogams*.

Phanerozoic (Greek *phanero* "visible") eon in Earth history, consisting of the most recent 570 million years. It comprises the Paleozoic, Mesozoic, and Cenozoic eras. The vast majority of fossils come from this eon, owing to the evolution of hard shells and internal skeletons. The name means "interval of well-displayed life."

Pharaoh Hebrew form of the Egyptian royal title Per-'o. This term, meaning "great house," was originally applied to the royal household, and after about 950 BC to the king.

Pharisee (Hebrew "separatist") member of an ancient Hebrew political party and sect of Judaism that formed in Roman-occupied Palestine in the 2nd century BC in protest against all movements favoring Hellenization. The Pharisees were the party of the common man, standing for rabbi, prayer, and synagogue. They were opposed by the aristocratic Sadducees.

The Pharisees rejected political action, and in the 1st century AD one group of their followers, the Zealots, broke away to pursue a nationalist policy. After the fall of Jerusalem and the destruction of the Temple AD 70, Pharisee ideas became the basis of orthodox Judaism as the people were dispersed throughout the W Roman empire.

pharmacology study of the origins, applications, and effects of chemical substances on living organisms. Products of the pharmaceutical industry range from aspirin to anticancer agents.

A wide range of resources has been investigated in the search for new and better drugs (human and plant molecular biology, newly discovered soil-grown molds, genetically engineered compounds, and monoclonal antibiotics).

pharynx interior of the throat, the cavity at the back of the mouth. Its walls are made of muscle strengthened with a fibrous layer and lined with mucous membrane. The internal nostrils lead backward into the pharynx, which continues downward into the esophagus and (through the epiglottis) into the windpipe. On each side, a Eustachian tube enters the pharynx from the middle ear cavity.

The upper part (nasopharynx) is an airway, but the remainder is a passage for food. Inflammation of the pharynx is named pharyngitis.

phase in physics, a stage in an oscillatory motion, such as a wave motion: two waves are in phase when their peaks and their troughs coincide. Otherwise, there is a *phase difference*, which has consequences in ⟡interference phenomena and ⟡alternating current electricity.

phase see ⟡Moon.

PhD abbreviation for the degree of *Doctor of Philosophy*.

pheasant any of various large, colorful Asiatic fowls of the family Phasianidae, which also includes grouse, quail, and turkey. The plumage of the male Eurasian ring-necked or common pheasant *Phasianus colchicus* is richly tinted with brownish-green, yellow, and red markings, but the female is a camouflaged brownish color. The nest is made on the ground. The male is polygamous.

According to legend, the Eurasian common pheasant was introduced from Asia to Europe by the Argonauts, who brought it from the banks of the River Phasis. It has also been introduced to North America.

Among the more exotically beautiful pheasants of other genera, often kept as ornamental birds, are the golden pheasant *Chrysolophus pictus* from China and the argus pheasant *Argusianus argus* of Malaysia, which has metallic spots or "eyes" on the wings.

phencyclidine hydrochloride (PCP) technical name for ⟡angel dust.

phenol member of a group of aromatic chemical compounds with weakly acidic properties, which are characterized by a hydroxyl (OH) group attached directly to an aromatic ring. The simplest of the phenols, derived from benzene, is also known as phenol and has the formula C_6H_5OH. It is sometimes called *carbolic acid* and can be extracted from coal tar.

Pure phenol consists of colorless, needle-shaped crystals, which take up moisture from the atmosphere. It has a strong and characteristic smell and was once used as an antiseptic. It is, however, toxic by absorption through the skin.

phenomena in philosophy, a technical term used in Immanuel ⟡Kant's philosophy, describing things as they appear to us, rather than as they are in themselves.

phenomenalism philosophical position that argues that statements about objects can be reduced to statements about what is perceived or perceivable. Thus English philosopher John Stuart Mill defined material objects as "permanent possibilities of sensation." Phenomenalism is closely connected with certain forms of ⟡empiricism.

phenomenology the philosophical perspective, founded by the German philosopher Edmund ⟡Husserl, that concentrates on phenomena as objects of perception (rather than as facts or occurrences that exist independently) in attempting to examine the ways people think about and interpret the world around them. It has been practiced by the philosophers Martin Heidegger, Jean-Paul Sartre, and Maurice Merleau-Ponty.

In contrast to positivism or "scientific" philosophy, phenomenology sees reality as essentially relative and subjective, and uses such tools as ethnomethodology and symbolic interactionism to focus on the structure of everyday life.

phenotype in genetics, visible traits, those actually displayed by an organism. The phenotype is not a direct reflection of the ⟡genotype because some alleles are masked by the presence of other, dominant alleles (see ⟡dominance). The phenotype is further modified by the effects of the environment (for example, poor nutrition stunts growth).

phenylketonuria genetic condition in which the liver of a child cannot control the level of phenylalanine (an ⟡amino acid derived from protein food) in the bloodstream in the normal way by excretion in the urine. It is controlled by special diet. Untreated, it causes severe mental handicap.

pheromone chemical signal (such as an odor) that is emitted by one animal and affects the behavior of others. Pheromones are used by many animal species to attract mates.

Phidias mid-5th century BC. Greek Classical sculptor. He supervised the sculptural program for the Parthenon (most of it is preserved in the British Museum, London, and known as the *Elgin marbles*). He also executed the colossal statue of Zeus at Olympia, one of the Seven Wonders of the World.

He was a friend of the political leader Pericles, who made him superintendent of public works in Athens.

Philadelphia industrial city and the world's largest freshwater port, on the Delaware River at the junction of the Schuylkill River, in Pennsylvania; population (1990) 1,585,600, metropolitan area 5,899,300. Products include refined oil, chemicals, textiles, processed food, printing and publishing, and transportation equipment. It is also a major port of entry and a financial, corporate, and research center. The University of Pennsylvania, the Franklin Institute, and Temple University are here, and the Philadelphia Orchestra and Museum of Art are among the nation's finest. Independence National Historic Park contains Independence Hall (1732–59), where the Declaration of Independence was adopted 1776, and the Liberty Bell.

Founded 1682 by William Penn as the "city of brotherly love," its religious tolerance caused it to become the most populous city in the Thirteen Colonies; it was the first capital of the US (before New York and Washington, DC). The Constitution was drafted here 1787. Benjamin Franklin lived and published here. By 1850 Philadelphia had more than 500,000 inhabitants. The Centennial Exposition, the first US international trade fair (world's fair), was held here 1876. Philadelphia reached a peak population of 2.1 million in 1950. Despite urban decay and substantial outmigration of people and industry since, it is the center of a large metropolitan area that extends into New Jersey and Delaware.

Philae island in the Nile, Egypt, above the first rapids, famed for the beauty of its temple of Isis (founded about 350 BC and in use until the 6th century AD). In 1977 the temple was re-erected on the nearby island of Agilkia above the flooding caused by the Aswan Dam.

philately the collection and study of postage stamps. It originated as a hobby in France about 1860.

Many countries earn extra revenue and cater to the philatelist by issuing sets of stamps to commemorate special events, anniversaries, and so on. There are many specialized fields of collection, from particular countries to specimens that have some defect; for example, contemporary issues that accidentally remain unperforated.

Philby Kim (Harold) 1912–1988. British intelligence officer from 1940 and Soviet agent from 1933. He was liaison officer in Washington 1949–51, when he was confirmed to be a double agent and asked to resign. Named in 1963 as having warned Guy Burgess and Donald Maclean (similarly double agents) that their activities were known, he fled to the USSR and became a Soviet citizen and general in the KGB. A fourth member of the ring was Anthony Blunt.

Philip "King." Name given to Metacomet c. 1639–1676. Wampanoag leader. In 1662, after the death of his father and elder brother, Metacomet assumed power and was called "King Philip" by the English colonists. Growing tension over Indian v settlers' land rights led to Philip's arrest and the disarming of his people 1671. The full-scale hostilities that broke out 1675, known as King Philip's War, culminated with Philip's defeat and murder 1676. Although costly to the English, it ended Indian resistance in New England.

Born in Rhode Island, Metacomet was the son of Wampanoag chieftain Massasoit.

Philip Duke of Edinburgh 1921– . Prince of the UK, husband of Elizabeth II, a grandson of George I of Greece and a great-great-grandson of Queen Victoria. He was born in Corfu, Greece but brought up in England.

A naturalized British subject, taking the surname Mountbatten, he married Princess Elizabeth (from 1952 Queen Elizabeth II) in 1947, having the previous day received the title Duke of Edinburgh.

Philip six kings of France, including:

Philip II (Philip Augustus) 1165–1223. King of France from 1180. As part of his efforts to establish a strong monarchy and evict the English from their French possessions, he waged war in turn against the English kings Henry II, Richard I (with whom he also went on the Third Crusade), and John (against whom he won the decisive battle of Bouvines in Flanders 1214).

Philip IV *the Fair* 1268–1314. King of France from 1285. He engaged in a feud with Pope Boniface VIII and made him a prisoner 1303. Clement V (1264–1314), elected pope through Philip's influence 1305, moved the papal seat to Avignon 1309 and collaborated with Philip to suppress the ⬦Templars, a powerful order of knights. Philip allied with the Scots against England and invaded Flanders.

Philip VI 1293–1350. King of France from 1328, first of the house of Valois, elected by the barons on the death of his cousin, Charles IV. His claim was challenged by Edward III of England, who defeated him at Crécy 1346.

Philip II of Macedon 382–336 BC. King of ⬦Macedonia from 359 BC. He seized the throne from his nephew, for whom he was regent, conquered the Greek city-states, and formed

them into a league whose forces could be united against Persia. He was assassinated while he was planning this expedition, and was succeeded by his son ⬦Alexander the Great.

Philip's tomb was discovered at Vergina, N Greece, in 1978.

Philip five kings of Spain, including:

Philip I *the Handsome* 1478–1506. King of Castile from 1504, through his marriage 1496 to Joanna the Mad (1479–1555). He was the son of the Holy Roman emperor Maximilian I.

Philip II 1527–1598. King of Spain from 1556. He was born at Valladolid, the son of the Hapsburg emperor Charles V, and in 1554 married Queen Mary of England. On his father's abdication 1556 he inherited Spain, the Netherlands, and the Spanish possessions in Italy and the Americas, and in 1580 he annexed Portugal. His intolerance and lack of understanding of the Netherlanders drove them into revolt. Political and religious differences combined to involve him in war with England and, after 1589, with France. The defeat of the ⬦Spanish Armada (the fleet sent to invade England in 1588) marked the beginning of the decline of Spanish power.

Philip V 1683–1746. King of Spain from 1700. A grandson of Louis XIV of France, he was the first Bourbon king of Spain. He was not recognized by the major European powers until 1713. See ⬦Spanish Succession, War of the.

Philip Neri, St 1515–1595. Italian Roman Catholic priest who organized the Congregation of the Oratory (see ⬦Oratorian). He built the oratory over the church of St Jerome, Rome, where prayer meetings were held and scenes from the Bible performed with music, originating the musical form ⬦oratorio. Feast day May 26.

Philippi ancient city of Macedonia founded by Philip of Macedon 358 BC. Near Philippi, Mark Antony and Augustus defeated Brutus and Cassius 42 BC. It was the first European town where St Paul preached, founding the congregation to which he addressed the Epistle to the Philippians (about AD 53).

Philippines country in SE Asia, on an archipelago of more than 7,000 islands W of the Pacific Ocean and S of the SE Asian mainland.

government The constitution was approved by plebiscite Feb 1987. It provides for a US-style executive president who is elected for a non-renewable six-year term and a two-chamber legislature or congress: a 24-member Senate and 250-member House of Representatives, with similar respective powers to their counterparts in the US. Senators are elected in national-level contests for six-year terms (a maximum of two consecutive terms). Representatives serve three-year terms (up to a maximum of three consecutive), with 200 being directly elected at the district level and up to a further 50 being appointed by the president from lists of "minority groups." The president appoints an executive cabinet, but, as in the US, while being unable directly to introduce legislation, may impose vetoes on congressional bills that can only be overridden by two-thirds majorities in each chamber. There is also a "Bill of Rights" and a 15-member Supreme Court.

history The people of the Philippine islands probably came from the ⬦Malay Peninsula. They were seminomadic and lived by hunting and fishing when the first Europeans, ⬦Magellan's crew, arrived 1521, followed by conquering Spanish forces 1565. Roman Catholicism was introduced during the reign

of ⬦Philip II (after whom the islands were named), replacing Islam, which had been spread by Arab traders and missionaries.

During the 19th century there was a series of armed nationalist revolts. In 1898 the US sank the Spanish Armada in Manila Bay. Philippine nationalists proclaimed their independence, but were put down by US forces who killed 200,000 Filipinos (one-fifth of the population), most of them civilians; 4,000 US soldiers also died before the war ended in 1901. The revolts continued after the islands were ceded by Spain to the US 1898, and increasing self-government was granted 1916 and 1935.

republic The Philippines were occupied by Japan 1942–45, before becoming a fully independent republic 1946. A succession of presidents drawn from the islands' wealthy estate-owning elite followed, doing little to improve the lot of the peasants.

In 1965 President Diosdado Macapagal was defeated by Ferdinand ⬦Marcos, the leader of the Nationalist Party. Marcos initiated rapid economic development and some land reform. He was reelected 1969, but encountered growing opposition from communist insurgents and Muslim separatists in the south. A high rate of population growth aggravated poverty and unemployment.

martial law Some months before his second term was completed, Marcos declared martial law 1972, suspended the constitution, and began to rule by decree. Intermittent referenda allowed him to retain power. Marcos's authoritarian leadership was criticized for corruption, and in 1977 the opposition leader, Benigno Aquino, was jailed under sentence of death for alleged subversion. In 1978 martial law was relaxed, the 1972 ban on political parties was lifted, and elections for an interim national assembly were held, resulting in an overwhelming victory for Marcos.

partial return to democracy In 1981 martial law was lifted completely, and hundreds of political prisoners released. Marcos then won approval, by referendum, for a partial return to democratic government with himself as president, working with a prime minister and executive council. Political and economic conditions deteriorated, communist-guerrilla insurgency escalated, unemployment climbed to over 30% and the national debt increased. In 1983 Benigno Aquino, returning from self-imposed exile in the US, was shot dead on his arrival at Manila airport. Marcos was widely suspected of involvement in a conspiracy to murder Aquino.

National assembly elections were held 1984, and although the government party stayed in power, the opposition registered significant gains. Then early in 1986 the main anti-Marcos movement, United Nationalist Democratic Organization (UNIDO), chose Corazón ⬦Aquino, Benigno's widow, despite her political inexperience, to contest new presidential elections that Marcos had been persuaded to hold as a means of maintaining vital US economic and diplomatic support.The campaign resulted in over 100 deaths, and large-scale electoral fraud was witnessed by international observers. The national assembly declared Marcos the winner, a result disputed by an independent electoral watchdog.

"people's power" Corazón Aquino began a non-violent protest, termed "people's power," which gathered massive popular support, backed by the Roman Catholic Church; President Marcos came under strong international pressure, particularly from the US, to step

Philippines
Republic of the (*Republika ng Pilipinas***)**

area 115,800 sq mi/300,000 sq km
capital Manila (on Luzon)
cities Quezon City (Luzon), Zamboanga (Mindanao); ports Cebu, Davao (on Mindanao), and Iloilo
physical comprises over 7,000 islands; volcanic mountain ranges traverse main chain N–S; 50% still forested. The largest islands are Luzon 41,754 sq mi/108,172 sq km and Mindanao 36,372 sq mi/94,227 sq km; others include Samar, Negros, Palawan, Panay, Mindoro, Leyte, Cebu, and the Sulu group
environment cleared for timber, tannin, and the creation of fish ponds, the mangrove forest was reduced from an area of 1,930 sq mi/5,000 sq km to 146 sq mi/380 sq km between 1920 and 1988
features Luzon, site of Clark Field, US air base used as a logistical base in Vietnam War; Subic Bay, US naval base; Pinatubo volcano (5,770 ft/1,759 m); Mindanao has active volcano Apo (9,690 ft/2,954 m) and mountainous rainforest
head of state and government Fidel Ramos from 1992
political system emergent democracy
political parties People's Power, including the PDP–Laban Party and the Liberal Party, centrist pro-Aquino; Nationalist Party, Union for National Action (UNA), and Grand Alliance for Democracy (GAD), conservative

opposition groupings; Mindanao Alliance, island-based decentralist body
exports sugar, copra (world's largest producer) and coconut oil, timber, copper concentrates, electronics, clothing
currency peso
population (1990 est) 66,647,000 (93% Malaysian); growth rate 2.4% p.a.
life expectancy men 63, women 69 (1989)
languages Tagalog (Filipino, official); English and Spanish
religion Roman Catholic 84%, Protestant 9%, Muslim 5%
literacy 88% (1989)
GNP $38.2 bn; $667 per head (1988)
chronology
1542 Named the Philippines (Filipinas) by Spanish explorers.
1565 Conquered by Spain.
1898 Ceded to the US after Spanish–American War.
1935 Granted internal self-government.
1942–45 Occupied by Japan.
1946 Independence achieved from USA.
1965 Ferdinand Marcos elected president.
1983 Opposition leader Benigno Aquino murdered by military guard.
1986 Marcos overthrown by Corazón Aquino's People's Power movement.
1987 "Freedom constitution" adopted, giving Aquino mandate to rule until June 1992; People's Power won majority in congressional elections. Attempted right-wing coup suppressed. Communist guerrillas active. Government in rightward swing.
1988 Land Reform Act gave favorable compensation to large estate-holders.
1989 Referendum on southern autonomy failed; Marcos died in exile; Aquino refused his burial in Philippines. Sixth coup attempt suppressed with US aid; Aquino declared state of emergency.
1990 Seventh coup attempt survived by President Aquino.
1991 June: eruption of Mount Pinatubo, hundreds killed. USA agreed to give up Clark Field airbase but keep Subic Bay naval base for ten more years. Sept: Philippines Senate voted to urge withdrawal of all US forces. US renewal of Subic Bay lease rejected. Nov: Imelda Marcos returned.
1992 Fidel Ramos elected to replace Aquino.

powers to impose order. The death of Marcos in exile Sept 28, 1989 provoked rallies of supporters demanding that his body be returned from Hawaii to the Philippines, a demand that Aquino refused. President Aquino survived another coup attempt Oct 1990.

Mount Pinatubo eruption At least 343 people were killed and 100,000–200,000 made homeless when the Mount Pinatubo volcano, dormant for 600 years and situated 56 mi/90 km NW of Manila, erupted June 1991. The US Clark Field and Subic Bay military bases, 9 and 25 mi/15 and 40 km away, had to be evacuated, and much rice-growing land was covered in up to 10 ft/3 m of volcanic ash.

US military bases The Philippines' Senate voted Sept 1991 to reject a renewal of the US lease for its Subic Bay Naval Base. Renewal of the lease would have given the Philippines over $2 billion in aid over a ten-year period and the provision of up to 45,000 jobs. Although Aquino supported renewal of the lease, opposition was overwhelming. Critics of the base claimed that its existence contravened a clause in the constitution which banned nuclear weapons.

In Nov 1991 Imelda Marcos returned to the Philippines after almost six years in exile. She immediately posted bail against seven charges of tax evasion, and subsequently declared herself a presidential candidate.

Ramos elected president In Jan 1992 President Aquino confirmed that she would not contest the presidential elections. The elections took place in May, and in June Fidel Ramos was announced as Aquino's successor. *See illustration box.*

Philip, St 1st century AD. In the New Testament, one of the 12 apostles. He was an inhabitant of Bethsaida (N Israel), and is said to have worked as a missionary in Anatolia. Feast day May 3.

Philip the Good 1396–1467. Duke of Burgundy from 1419. He engaged in the Hundred Years' War as an ally of England until he made peace with the French at the Council of Arras 1435. He made the Netherlands a center of art and learning.

Philistine member of a seafaring people of non-Semitic origin who founded city-states on the Palestinian coastal plain in the 12th century BC, adopting a Semitic language and religion. They were at war with the Israelites in the 11th–10th centuries BC and were largely absorbed into the kingdom of Israel under King David, about 1000 BC.

Phillips Wendell 1811–1884. US reformer. Born in Boston and educated at Harvard, Phillips was admitted to the bar 1834. After attending the World Anti-Slavery Convention in London 1840, he became an outspoken abolitionist. A widely traveled lecturer, Phillips espoused a variety of social causes in addition to abolitionism, including feminism, prohibition, labor unionization, and improved treatment of American Indians.

Critical of the Mexican War and the conduct of the American Civil War by Lincoln, Phillips was a reform candidate for governor of Massachusetts 1870.

Phillips curve graph showing the relationship between percentage changes in wages and unemployment, and indicating that wages rise faster during periods of low unemployment as employers compete for labor. The implication is that the dual objectives of low unemployment and low inflation are inconsistent. The concept has been widely questioned since the early

down. The army, led by Chief of Staff Lt Gen Fidel Ramos and Defense Minister Juan Enrile, declared its support for Aquino, and Marcos left for exile in Hawaii.

On assuming the presidency, Corazón Aquino dissolved the pro-Marcos national assembly. She proceeded to govern in a conciliatory fashion, working with a coalition cabinet team comprising opposition politicians and senior military figures. She freed 500 political prisoners and granted an amnesty to the New People's Army (NPA) communist guerrillas in an effort to end the 17-year-old insurgency and introduced a major rural-employment economic program, with land reforms opposed by property owners.

freedom constitution The new administration endured a series of attempted coups by pro-Marcos supporters and faced serious opposition from Juan Enrile, dismissed Nov 1986. In Feb 1987 a new "freedom constitution" was overwhelmingly approved in a national plebiscite. This gave Aquino a mandate to rule as president until June 30, 1992. In the

subsequent congressional elections, Aquino's People's Power coalition won over 90% of the elected seats. However, in Aug 1987 the government was rocked by a coup attempt led by Col Gregorio "Gringo" Honasan, an army officer closely linked with Enrile, which claimed 53 lives. In response, Aquino effected a major cabinet reshuffle that signaled a shift to the right in the government's policy, with tougher measures being instituted toward the NPA and the Land Reform Act 1988 being diluted. Aquino endured a further reverse Nov 1989 when a regional referendum proposing the merging of the 13 southern provinces, including ◊Mindanao, into an "autonomous region" was rejected. This initiative had been made in an attempt to end 20 years of Muslim separatist struggle.

relations with US US economic and military aid to the Philippines between 1985 and 1989 was approximately $1.5 billion. In Dec 1989 US air support was provided to help foil a further Honasan-planned coup attempt. Aquino declared a state of emergency, giving her broad

1960s because of the apparent instability of the wages/unemployment relationship. It was developed by the British economist A(lban) W(illiam) Phillips (1914–1975), who plotted graphically wage and unemployment changes between 1861 and 1957.

Philoctetes in Greek mythology, a hero in the Trojan War who killed the Trojan prince Paris.

Philo Judaeus lived 1st century AD. Jewish philosopher of Alexandria who in AD 40 undertook a mission to Caligula to protest against the emperor's claim to divine honors. In his writings Philo Judaeus attempts to reconcile Judaism with Platonic and Stoic ideas.

philology (Greek "love of language") in historical ◊linguistics, the study of the development of languages. It is also an obsolete term for the study of literature.

In this sense the scholars of Alexandria, who edited the Greek epics of Homer, were philologists. The Renaissance gave great impetus to this kind of study. Dutch scholars took the lead in the 17th century while Richard Bentley made significant contributions in England. *Comparative philology* arose at the beginning of the 19th century from the study of Sanskrit, under Franz Bopp's (1791–1867) leadership. It was originally mainly concerned with the ◊Indo-European languages, while the Romantic movement greatly inspired the establishment of national philology throughout Europe and Asia.

philosophy (Greek "love of wisdom") branch of learning that includes metaphysics (the nature of being), epistemology (theory of knowledge), logic (study of valid inference), ethics, and aesthetics. Philosophy is concerned with fundamental problems—including the nature of mind and matter, perception, self, free will, causation, time and space, and the existence of moral judgments—which cannot be resolved by a specific method.

Oldest of all philosophical systems is the Vedic system from about 2500 BC, but, like many other Eastern systems, it rests on a primarily mystic basis. The first scientific system originated in Greece in the 6th century BC with the Milesian school (Thales, Anaximander, Anaximenes). Both they and later pre-Socratics (Pythagoras, Xenophon, Parmenides, Zeno of Elea, Empedocles, Anaxagoras, Heraclitus, Democritus) were lively theorists, and ideas such as atomism, developed by Democritus, occur in later schemes of thought. Originally, philosophy included all intellectual endeavor, but over time traditional branches of philosophy have acquired their own status as separate areas of study. In the 5th century Socrates, foremost among the teachers known as the Sophists, laid the foundation of ethics; Plato evolved a system of universal ideas; Aristotle developed logic. Later schools include Epicureanism (Epicurus), stoicism (Zeno) and skepticism (Pyrrho); the eclectics—not a school, they selected what appealed to them from various systems (Cicero and Seneca); and the Neoplatonists, infusing a mystic element into the system of Plato (Philo, Plotinus and, as disciple, Julian the Apostate). The close of the Athenian schools of philosophy by Justinian AD 529 marks the end of ancient philosophy, though many of its teachers moved eastward; Greek thought emerges in Muslim philosophers as Avicenna and Averroes, and the Jewish Maimonides. For the West the work of Aristotle was transmitted through Boethius. Study by medieval scholastic philosophers, mainly concerned with

the reconciliation of ancient philosophy with Christian belief, began in the 9th century with John Scotus Erigena and includes Anselm, Abelard, Albertus Magnus, Thomas Aquinas, his opponent Duns Scotus, and William of Occam.

In the 17th century Descartes, with his rationalist determination to doubt and faith in mathematical proof, marks the beginning of contemporary philosophy, and was followed by Spinoza, Leibniz, and Hobbes. The empiricists, principally an 18th-century English school (Locke, Berkeley, Hume), turned instead to physics as indicating what can be known and how, and led up to the transcendental criticism of Kant. In the early 19th century Classical German idealism (Fichte, Schelling, Hegel) repudiated Kant's limitation of human knowledge; in France Comte developed the positivist thought that attracted Mill and Spencer. Notable also in the 19th century are the pessimistic atheism of Schopenhauer; the dialectical materialism of Marx and Engels; the work of Nietzsche and Kierkegaard, which led toward 20th-century existentialism; the pragmatism of

philosophy: the great philosophers

name	dates
Heraclitus	c. 544–483 BC
Parmenides	c. 510–c. 450 BC
Socrates	469–399 BC
Plato	428–347 BC
Aristotle	384–322 BC
Epicurus	341–270 BC
Lucretius	c. 99–55 BC
Plotinus	AD 205–270
Augustine	354–430
Aquinas	c. 1225–1274
Duns Scotus	c. 1266–1308
William of Occam	c. 1285–1349
Nicholas of Cusa	1401–1464
Giordano Bruno	1548–1600
Bacon	1561–1626
Hobbes	1588–1679
Descartes	1596–1650
Pascal	1623–1662
Spinoza	1632–1677
Locke	1632–1704
Leibniz	1646–1716
Vico	1668–1744
Berkeley	1685–1753
Hume	1711–1776
Rousseau	1712–1778
Diderot	1713–1784
Kant	1724–1804
Fichte	1762–1814
Hegel	1770–1831
Schelling	1775–1854
Schopenhauer	1788–1860
Comte	1798–1857
Mill	1806–1873
Kierkegaard	1813–1855
Marx	1818–1883
Dilthey	1833–1911
Pierce	1839–1914
Nietzsche	1844–1900
Bergson	1859–1941
Husserl	1859–1938
Russell	1872–1970
Lukács	1885–1971
Wittgenstein	1889–1951
Heidegger	1889–1976
Gadamer	1900–
Sartre	1905–1980
Merleau Ponty	1908–1961
Quine	1908–
Foucault	1926–1984

James and Dewey; and the absolute idealism at the turn of the century of the neo-Hegelians (Bradley, Royce).

Among 20th-century movements are the logical positivism of the Vienna Circle (Carnap, Popper, Ayer); the creative evolution of Bergson; neo-Thomism, the revival of the medieval philosophy of Aquinas (Maritain); existentialism (Heidegger, Jaspers, Sartre); the phenomenology of Husserl, who influenced Ryle; and realism (Russell, Moore, Broad, Wittgenstein). Twentieth-century philosophers have paid great attention to the nature and limits of language, in particular in relation to the language used to formulate philosophical problems. They are inclined to think of philosophy as an investigation of the fundamental assumptions that govern our ways of understanding and acting in the world.

phlebitis inflammation of a vein. It is sometimes associated with blockage by a blood clot (◊thrombosis), in which case it is more accurately described as thrombophlebitis.

Phlebitis may occur as a result of the hormonal changes associated with pregnancy, or due to long-term use of contraceptive pills, or following prolonged immobility (which is why patients are mobilized as soon as possible after surgery). If a major vein is involved, nearly always in a leg, the part beyond the blockage swells and may remain engorged for weeks. It is very painful. Treatment is with ◊anticoagulant drugs and sometimes surgery.

phloem tissue found in vascular plants whose main function is to conduct sugars and other food materials from the leaves, where they are produced, to all other parts of the plant.

Phloem is composed of sieve elements and their associated companion cells, together with some ◊sclerenchyma and ◊parenchyma cell types. Sieve elements are long, thin-walled cells joined end to end, forming sieve tubes; large pores in the end walls allow the continuous passage of nutrients. Phloem is usually found in association with ◊xylem, the water-conducting tissue, but unlike the latter it is a living tissue.

phlogiston hypothetical substance formerly believed to have been produced during combustion. The term was invented by the German chemist Georg Stahl. The phlogiston theory was replaced by the theory of oxygen gain and loss, first enunciated by the French chemist Antoine Lavoisier.

phlox any plant of the genus *Phlox*, native to North America and Siberia. Phloxes are small with alternate leaves and showy white, pink, red, or purple flowers.

Woodland phlox *P. divaricata* is native to central US.

Phnom Penh capital of Cambodia, on the Mekong River, 130 mi/210 km NW of Saigon; population (1989) 800,000. Industries include textiles and food-processing.

On April 17, 1975 the entire population (about 3 million) was forcibly evacuated by the Khmer Rouge communist movement; survivors later returned.

phobia excessive irrational fear of an object or situation—for example, agoraphobia (fear of open spaces and crowded places), acrophobia (fear of heights), claustrophobia (fear of enclosed places). Behavior therapy is one form of treatment.

Phobos one of the two moons of Mars, discovered 1877 by the US astronomer Asaph Hall

(1829–1907). It is an irregularly shaped lump of rock, cratered by ▷meteorite impacts. Phobos is $17 \times 13 \times 12$ mi/$27 \times 22 \times 19$ km across, and orbits Mars every 0.32 days at a distance of 5,840 mi/9,400 km from the planet's center. It is thought to be an asteroid captured by Mars' gravity.

Phoenicia ancient Greek name for N ▷Canaan on the E coast of the Mediterranean. The Phoenicians lived about 1200–332 BC. Seafaring traders and artisans, they are said to have circumnavigated Africa and established colonies in Cyprus, N Africa (for example, Carthage), Malta, Sicily, and Spain. Their cities (Tyre, Sidon, and Byblos were the main ones) were independent states ruled by hereditary kings but dominated by merchant ruling classes. The fall of Tyre to Alexander the Great ended the separate history of Phoenicia.

The Phoenicians occupied the seaboard of Lebanon and Syria, north of Mount Carmel. Their exports included Tyrian purple dye and cloth, furniture (from the timber of Lebanon), and jewelry. Documents found 1929 at Ugarit on the Syrian coast give much information on their civilization; their deities included ▷Baal, Astarte or ▷Ishtar, and ▷Moloch. Competition from the colonies combined with attacks by the Sea Peoples, the Assyrians, and the Greeks on the cities in Phoenicia led to their ultimate decline.

phoenix mythical Egyptian bird that burned itself to death on a pyre every 500 years and rose rejuvenated from the ashes.

Phoenix capital of Arizona; industrial city (steel, aluminum, electrical goods, food processing) and tourist center on the Salt River; population (1990) 983,400.

Settled 1868, Phoenix became the territorial capital 1889. The completion of a dam 1912 provided the water and power needed for economic development. Tremendous growth, beginning in the 1940s, has transformed Phoenix from what was largely a health resort and retirement community into a major economic center.

Phoenix Islands group of eight islands in the South Pacific, included in Kiribati; total land area 11 sq mi/18 sq km; population (1990) 45. Drought has rendered them all uninhabitable.

phon unit of loudness, equal to the value in decibels of an equally loud tone with frequency 1,000 Hz. The higher the frequency, the louder a noise sounds for the same decibel value; thus an 80-decibel tone with a frequency of 20 Hz sounds as loud as 20 decibels at 1,000 Hz, and the phon value of both tones is 20. An aircraft engine has a loudness of around 140 phons.

phonetics identification, description, and classification of sounds used in articulate speech. These sounds are codified in the International Phonetic Alphabet (a highly modified version of the English/Roman alphabet).

A **phoneme** is the range of sound that can be substituted without change of meaning in the words of a particular language; for example, *r* and *l* form a single phoneme in Japanese but are two distinct phonemes in English. The study of phonemes is called phonemics, a branch of linguistics.

phonograph alternate name for ▷record player.

phony war the period in World War II between Oct 1939, when the Germans had occupied Poland, and April 1940, when the invasions

of Denmark and Norway took place. During this time there were few signs of hostilities in Western Europe; indeed, Hitler made some attempts to arrange a peace settlement with Britain and France.

phosphate salt or ester of ▷phosphoric acid. Incomplete neutralization of phosphoric acid gives rise to acid phosphates (see ▷acid salts and ▷buffer). Phosphates are used as fertilizers, and are required for the development of healthy root systems. They are involved in many biochemical processes, often as part of complex molecules, such as ▷ATP.

phospholipid any ▷lipid consisting of a glycerol backbone, a phosphate group, and two long chains. Phospholipids are found everywhere in living systems as the basis for biological membranes.

One of the long chains tends to be hydrophobic and the other hydrophilic (that is, they interrelate with water in opposite ways). This means that phospholipids will line up the same way round when in solution.

phosphor any substance that is phosphorescent, that is, gives out visible light when it is illuminated by a beam of electrons or ultraviolet light. The television screen is coated on the inside with phosphors that glow when beams of electrons strike them. Fluorescent lamp tubes are also phosphor-coated. Phosphors are also used in Day-Glo paints, and as optical brighteners in detergents.

phosphorescence in physics, the emission of light by certain substances after they have absorbed energy, whether from visible light, other electromagnetic radiation such as ultraviolet rays or X-rays, or cathode rays (a beam of electrons). When the stimulating energy is removed phosphorescence ceases, although it may persist for a short time after (unlike ▷fluorescence, which stops immediately).

phosphoric acid acid derived from phosphorus and oxygen. Its commonest form (H_3PO_4) is also known as orthophosphoric acid, and is produced by the action of phosphorus pentoxide (P_2O_5) on water. It is used in rust removers and for rust-proofing iron and steel.

phosphorus (Greek *phosphoros* "bearer of light") highly reactive, nonmetallic element, symbol P, atomic number 15, atomic weight 30.9738. It occurs in nature as phosphates (commonly in the form of the mineral ▷apatite), and is essential to plant and animal life. Compounds of phosphorus are used in fertilizers, various organic chemicals, for matches and fireworks, and in glass and steel.

Phosphorus was first identified 1674 by German alchemist Hennig Brand (c. 1630–?), who prepared it from urine. The element has three allotropic forms: a black powder; a white-yellow, waxy solid that ignites spontaneously in air to form the poisonous gas phosphorus pentoxide; and a red-brown powder that neither ignites spontaneously nor is poisonous.

photocell or **photoelectric cell** device for measuring or detecting light or other electromagnetic radiation, since its electrical state is altered by the effect of light. In a **photoemissive** cell, the radiation causes electrons to be emitted and a current to flow (▷photoelectric effect); a **photovoltaic** cell causes an ▷electromotive force to be generated in the presence of light across the boundary of two substances. A **photoconductive** cell, which contains a semiconductor, increases its conductivity when exposed to electromagnetic radiation.

Photocells are used for photographers' exposure meters, burglar and fire alarms, automatic doors, and in solar energy arrays.

photochemical reaction any chemical reaction in which light is produced or light initiates the reaction. Light can initiate reactions by exciting atoms or molecules and making them more reactive: the light energy becomes converted to chemical energy. Many photochemical reactions set up a ▷chain reaction and produce ▷free radicals.

This type of reaction is seen in the bleaching of dyes or the yellowing of paper by sunlight. It is harnessed by plants in ▷photosynthesis and by humans in ▷photography. Chemical reactions that produce light are most commonly seen when materials are burned. Light-emitting reactions are used by living organisms in ▷bioluminescence. One photochemical reaction is the action of sunlight on car exhaust fumes, which results in the production of ▷ozone. Some large cities, such as Los Angeles, and Santiago, Chile, now suffer serious pollution due to photochemical smog.

photocopier machine that uses some form of photographic process to reproduce copies of documents or illustrations. Most modern photocopiers, as pioneered by the Xerox Corporation, use electrostatic photocopying, or ▷xerography ("dry writing"). This employs a drum coated with a light-sensitive material such as selenium, which holds a pattern of static electricity charges corresponding to the dark areas of an image projected onto the drum by a lens. Finely divided pigment (toner) of opposite electric charge sticks to the charged areas of the drum and is transferred to a sheet of paper, which is heated briefly to melt the toner and stick it to the paper.

Additional functions of photocopiers include enlargement and reduction, copying on both sides of the sheet of paper, copying in color, collating, and stapling.

photoelectric effect in physics, the emission of ▷electrons from a substance (usually a metallic surface) when it is struck by ▷photons (quanta of electromagnetic radiation), usually those of visible light or ultraviolet radiation.

photography process for reproducing images on sensitized materials by various forms of radiant energy, including visible light, ultraviolet, infrared, X-rays, atomic radiations, and electron beams.

The most familiar photographic process depends upon the fact that certain silver compounds (called ▷halides) are sensitive to light. A photographic film is coated with these compounds and, in a camera, is exposed to light. An image, or picture, of the scene before the camera is formed on the film because the silver halides become activated (light-altered) where light falls but not where light does not fall. The image is made visible by the process of ▷developing, made permanent by fixing, and, finally, is usually printed on paper. Motion-picture photography uses a camera that exposes a roll of film to a rapid succession of views that, when developed, are projected in equally rapid succession to provide a moving image.

photogravure ▷printing process that uses a plate prepared photographically, covered with a pattern of recessed cells in which the ink is held. See ▷gravure.

photometer instrument that measures luminous intensity, usually by comparing relative intensities from different sources. Bunsen's grease-spot photometer 1844 compares the *photography: chronology*

1515	Leonardo da Vinci described the camera obscura.
1750	The painter Canaletto used a camera obscura as an aid to his painting in Venice.
1790	Thomas Wedgwood in England made photograms -placing objects on leather, sensitized using silver nitrate.
1826	Nicephore Niépce (1765–1833), a French doctor, produced the world's first photograph from nature on pewter plates with a camera obscura and an eight-hour exposure.
1835	Niépce and L J M Daguerre produced the first Daguerreotype camera photograph.
1839	Daguerre was awarded an annuity by the French government and his process given to the world.
1840	Invention of the Petzval lens, which reduced exposure time by 90%. Herschel discovered sodium thiosulfate as a fixer for silver halides.
1841	Fox Talbot's calotype process was patented—the first multicopy method of photography using a negative/positive process, sensitized with silver iodide.
1844	Fox Talbot published the first photographic book, *The Pencil of Nature*.
1845	Hill and Adamson began to use calotypes for portraits in Edinburgh.
1851	Fox Talbot used a one-thousandth of a second exposure to demonstrate high-speed photography. Invention of the wet-collodion-on-glass process and the waxed-paper negative. Photographs were displayed at the Great Exhibition in London.
1852	The London Society of Arts exhibited 779 photographs.
1855	Roger Fenton made documentary photographs of the Crimean War from a specially constructed wagon with portable darkroom.
1859	Nadar in Paris took photographs underground using battery-powered arc lights.
1860	Queen Victoria was photographed by Mayall. Abraham Lincoln was photographed by Matthew Brady, who subsequently documented the civil war.
1861	The single-lens reflex plate camera was patented by Thomas Sutton. The principles of three-color photography were demonstrated by J C Maxwell.
1862	Nadar took aerial photographs over Paris.
1870	Julia Margaret Cameron used long lenses for her distinctive portraits.
1871	Gelatin-silver bromide was developed.
1878	In the US Edweard Muybridge analyzed the movements of animals through sequential photographs, using a series of cameras.
1879	The photogravure process was invented.
1880	A silver bromide emulsion was fixed with hypo. Photographs were first reproduced in newspapers in New York using the half-tone engraving process. The first twin-lens reflex camera was produced in London. Gelatin-silver chloride paper was introduced.
1884	George Eastman produced flexible negative film.
1889	The Eastman Company in the US produced the Kodak No 1 camera and roll film, facilitating universal, hand-held snapshots.
1891	The first telephoto lens was introduced. The interference process of color photography was developed by the French doctor Gabriel Lippmann.
1897	The first issue of Alfred Stieglitz's *Camera Notes* was published in the US.
1902	In Germany, Deckel invented a prototype leaf shutter and Zeiss introduced the Tessar lens.
1904	The autochrome color process was patented by the Lumière brothers.
1905	Alfred Stieglitz opened the gallery "291" in New York promoting photography. Lewis Hine used photography to expose the exploitation of children in American factories, causing protective laws to be passed.
1907	The autochrome process began to be factory-produced.
1914	Oskar Barnack designed a prototype Leica camera for Leitz in Germany.
1924	Leitz launched the first 35 mm camera, the Leica, delayed because of World War I. It became very popular with photojournalists because it was quiet, small, dependable, and had a range of lenses and accessories.
1929	Rolleiflex produced a twin-lens reflex camera in Germany.
1935	In the US, Mannes and Godowsky invented Kodachrome transparency film, which produced sharp images and rich color quality. Electronic flash was invented in the US. Social documentary photography received wide attention through the photographs of Dorothea Lange, Margaret Bourke-White, Arthur Rothstein, Walker Evans, and others taken for the Farm Security Administration of the plight of the poor tenant farmers.
1936	*Life* magazine, significant for its photojournalism, was first published in the US.
1938	*Picture Post* magazine was introduced in the UK.
1940	Multigrade enlarging paper by Ilford was made available in the UK.
1942	Kodacolor negative film was introduced.
1945	The zone system of exposure estimation was published in the book *Exposure Record* by Ansel Adams.
1947	Polaroid black-and-white instant process film was invented by Dr Edwin Land, who set up the Polaroid corporation in Boston, Massachusetts. The principles of holography were demonstrated in England by Dennis Gabor.
1955	Kodak introduced Tri-X, a black-and-white 200 ASA film.
1959	The zoom lens was invented by the Austrian firm of Voigtlander.
1960	The laser was invented in the US, making holography possible. Polacolor, a self-processing color film, was introduced by Polaroid, using a 60-second color film and dye diffusion technique.
1963	Cibachrome, paper and chemicals for printing directly from transparencies, was made available by Ciba-Geigy of Switzerland. One of the most permanent processes, it is marketed throughout the world.
1966	The International Center of Photography was established in New York.
1969	Photographs were taken on the Moon by US astronauts.
1970	A charge-coupled device was invented at Bell Laboratories in New Jersey, to record very faint images (for example, in astronomy). *Rencontres Internationales de la Photographie*, the annual summer festival of photography with workshops, was founded in Arles, France.
1971	Opening of the Photographers' Gallery, London, and the Photo Archive of the Bibliothèque Nationale, Paris.
1972	The SX70 system, a single-lens reflex camera with instant prints, was produced by Polaroid.
1975	The Center for Creative Photography was established at the University of Arizona.
1980	Ansel Adams sold an original print, *Moonrise: Hernandez*, for $45,000, a record price, in the US. *Voyager 1* sent photographs of Saturn back to Earth across space.
1983	The National Museum of Photography, Film and Television opened in Bradford, England.
1985	The Minolta Corporation in Japan introduced the Minolta 7000—the world's first body-integral autofocus single-lens reflex camera.
1988	The electronic camera, which stores pictures on magnetic disk instead of on film, was introduced in Japan.
1990	Kodak introduced PhotoCD which converts 35 mm camera pictures (on film) into digital form and stores them on compact disk (CD) for viewing on TV.

intensity of a light source with a known source by each illuminating one half of a translucent area. Modern photometers use ▷photocells, as in a photographer's exposure meter. A photomultiplier can also be used as a photometer.

photomultiplier instrument that detects low levels of electromagnetic radiation (usually visible light or ▷infrared radiation) and amplifies it to produce a detectable signal.

One type resembles a ▷photocell with an additional series of coated ▷electrodes (dynodes) between the ▷cathode and ▷anode. Radiation striking the cathode releases electrons (primary emission) which hit the first dynode, producing yet more electrons (▷secondary emission), which strike the second dynode. Eventually this produces a measurable signal up to 100 million times larger than the original signal by the time it leaves the anode. Similar devices, called image intensifiers, are used in television camera tubes that "see" in the dark.

photon in physics, the ▷elementary particle or "package" (quantum) of energy in which light and other forms of electromagnetic radiation are emitted. The photon has both particle and wave properties; it has no charge, is considered massless but possesses momentum and energy. It is one of the ▷gauge bosons, a particle that cannot be subdivided, and is the carrier of the ▷electromagnetic force, one of the fundamental forces of nature.

According to ▷quantum theory the energy of a photon is given by the formula $E = hf$, where h is Planck's constant and f is the frequency of the radiation emitted.

photoperiodism biological mechanism that determines the timing of certain activities by responding to changes in day length. The flowering of many plants is initiated in this way. Photoperiodism in plants is regulated by a light-sensitive pigment, *phytochrome*. The breeding seasons of many temperate-zone animals are also triggered by increasing or declining day length, as part of their ▷biorhythms.

Autumn-flowering plants (for example, chrysanthemum and soybean) and autumn-breeding mammals (such as goats and deer) require days that are shorter than a critical length; spring-flowering and spring-breeding ones (such as radish and lettuce, and birds) are triggered by longer days.

photosphere visible surface of the Sun, which emits light and heat. About 200 mi/300 km deep, it consists of incandescent gas at a temperature of 5,800K (9,980°F/5,530°C).

Rising cells of hot gas produce a mottling of the photosphere known as *granulation*, each granule being about 620 mi/1,000 km in diameter. The photosphere is often marked by large, dark patches called ▷sunspots.

photosynthesis process by which green plants trap light energy and use it to drive a series of chemical reactions, leading to the formation of carbohydrates. All animals ultimately depend on photosynthesis because it is the method by which the basic food (sugar) is created. For photosynthesis to occur, the plant must possess ▷chlorophyll and must have a supply of carbon dioxide and water. Actively photosynthesizing green plants store excess sugar as starch (this can be tested for in the laboratory using iodine).

The chemical reactions of photosynthesis occur in two stages. During the *light reaction* sunlight is used to split water (H_2O) into

oxygen (O_2), protons (hydrogen ions, H^+), and electrons, and oxygen is given off as a by-product. In the second stage *dark reaction*, for which sunlight is not required, the protons and electrons are used to convert carbon dioxide (CO_2) into carbohydrates ($C_m(H_2O)_n$). Photosynthesis depends on the ability of chlorophyll to capture the energy of sunlight and to use it to split water molecules.

Other pigments, such as ▷carotenoids, are also involved in capturing light energy and passing it on to chlorophyll. Photosynthesis by cyanobacteria was responsible for the appearance of oxygen in the Earth's atmosphere 2 billion years ago, and photosynthesis by plants maintains the oxygen level today.

phototropism movement of part of a plant toward or away from a source of light. Leaves are positively phototropic, detecting the source of light and orientating themselves to receive the maximum amount.

phrase-structure grammar theory of language structure that proposes that a given language has several different potential sentence patterns, consisting of various sorts of phrases, which can be expanded in various ways.

For example, the sentence "The girl opened the door" contains a noun phrase, *the girl*, and a verb phrase, *opened the door*; the verb phrase can be further analyzed into a verb, *opened*, and a noun phrase, *the door*; and so on.

phrenology study of the shape and protuberances of the skull, based on the (now discredited) theory of the Viennese physician Dr Franz Josef Gall that such features revealed measurable psychological and intellectual traits.

Phrygia former kingdom of W Asia covering the Anatolian plateau. It was inhabited in ancient times by an Indo-European people and achieved great prosperity in the 8th century BC under a line of kings bearing in turn the names Gordius and Midas, but then fell under Lydian rule. From Phrygia the cult of the Earth goddess Cybele was introduced into Greece and Rome.

Phyfe Duncan c. 1768–1854. Scottish-born US furniture maker. He established his own workshop in New York City 1792, where he gained a national reputation for his expensive and finely-worked furniture. Although derived from earlier English and Greco-Roman designs, the Phyfe style was distinctive in its simplicity of line with elaborate ornamentation and carving. In 1837 Phyfe brought his sons into the business, reorganizing his firm as Duncan Phyfe and Sons.

Phyfe immigrated with his family to America 1784. He settled in Albany, New York, and learned the cabinetmaker's trade. He remained active until his retirement in 1847.

phylacteries in Judaism, another name for ▷tefillin.

phyllite ▷metamorphic rock produced under increasing temperature and pressure, in which mica crystals are aligned so that the rock splits along their plane of orientation, the resulting break being shiny and smooth. It is intermediate between slate and schist.

phyllotaxis the arrangement of leaves on a plant stem. Leaves are nearly always arranged in a regular pattern and in the majority of plants they are inserted singly, either in a *spiral* arrangement up the stem, or on *alternate* sides. Other principal forms are opposite

leaves, where two arise from the same node, and whorled, where three or more arise from the same node.

phylloxera any of a family (Phylloxeridae) of small plant-sucking insects (order Homoptera) that attack the leaves and roots of some plants.

The species *Phylloxera vitifolia*, a native of North America, attacks grapevines, laying its eggs under the bark. European vines are markedly susceptible and many French vineyards suffered from the arrival of the pest in Europe in the 19th century; most European vines are now grafted on to rootstock of the American vine, which is not as susceptible to the disease. Phylloxera insects (hemipterans) may be destroyed by spraying with carbon disulfide or petroleum.

phylogeny historical sequence of changes that occurs in a given species during the course of its evolution. It was once erroneously associated with ontogeny (the process of development of a living organism).

phylum (plural *phyla*) major grouping in biological classification. Mammals, birds, reptiles, amphibians, fishes, and tunicates belong to the phylum Chordata; the phylum Molluska consists of snails, slugs, mussels, clams, squid, and octopuses; the phylum Porifera contains sponges; and the phylum Echinodermata includes sea stars, sea urchins, and sea cucumbers. Among plants there are between four and nine phyla (or divisions) depending on the classification used. Related phyla are grouped together in a ▷kingdom; phyla are subdivided into ▷classes.

physical change in chemistry, a type of change that does not produce a new chemical substance, does not involve large energy changes, and that can be easily reversed (the opposite of a ▷chemical change). Boiling and melting are examples of physical change.

physical chemistry branch of chemistry concerned with examining the relationships between the chemical compositions of substances and the physical properties that they display. Most chemical reactions exhibit some physical phenomenon (change of state, temperature, pressure, or volume, or the use or production of electricity), and the measurement and study of such phenomena has led to many chemical theories and laws.

physics branch of science concerned with the laws that govern the structure of the universe, and the forms of matter and energy and their interactions. For convenience, physics is often divided into branches such as nuclear physics, particle physics, solid- and liquid-state physics, electricity, electronics, magnetism, optics, acoustics, heat, and thermodynamics. Before this century, physics was known as *natural philosophy*.

physiological psychology aspect of ▷experimental psychology.

physiology branch of biology that deals with the functioning of living animals, as opposed to anatomy, which studies their structures.

physiotherapy treatment of injury and disease by physical means such as exercise, heat, manipulation, massage, and electrical stimulation.

Piacenza industrial city (agricultural machinery, textiles, pottery) in Emilia-Romagna, N Italy, on the River Po 40 mi/65 km SE of Milan; population (1988) 105,000. The Roman

physics: chronology

*c.*400BC	The first "atomic" theory was put forward by Democritus.
c. 250	Archimedes' principle of buoyancy was established.
45	The Julian calendar as used in most Western countries was introduced.
AD 1600	Magnetism was described by William Gilbert.
c. 1610	The principle of falling bodies descending to earth at the same speed was established by Galileo.
1642	The principles of hydraulics were put forward by Blaise Pascal.
1643	The mercury barometer was invented by Evangelista Torricelli.
1656	The pendulum clock was invented by Christiaan Huygens.
1662	Boyle's law concerning the behavior of gases was established by Robert Boyle.
c. 1665	Isaac Newton put forward the law of gravity, stating that the Earth exerts a constant force on falling bodies.
1690	The wave theory of light was propounded by Christiaan Huygens.
1704	The corpuscular theory of light was put forward by Isaac Newton.
1714	The mercury thermometer was invented by Daniel Fahrenheit.
1764	Specific and latent heats were described by Joseph Black.
1771	The link between nerve action and electricity was discovered by Luigi Galvani.
c. 1787	Charles's law relating the pressure, volume, and temperature of a gas was established by Jacques Charles.
1795	The metric system was adopted in France.
1798	The link between heat and friction was discovered by Benjamin Rumford.
1800	Alessandro Volta invented the Voltaic cell.
1801	Interference of light was discovered by Thomas Young.
1808	The "modern" atomic theory was propounded by John Dalton.
1811	Avogadro's hypothesis relating volumes and numbers of molecules of gases was proposed by Amedeo Avogadro.
1815	Refraction of light was explained by Augustin Fresnel.
1819	The discovery of electromagnetism was made by Hans Oersted.
1821	The dynamo principle was described by Michael Faraday; the thermocouple was discovered by Thomas Seebeck.
1822	The laws of electrodynamics were established by André Ampère.
1824	Thermodynamics as a branch of physics was proposed by Sadi Carnot.
1827	Ohm's law of electrical resistance was established by Georg Ohm; Brownian motion resulting from molecular vibrations was observed by Robert Brown.
1829	The law of gaseous diffusion was established by Thomas Graham.
1831	Electromagnetic induction was discovered by Faraday.
1834	Faraday discovered self-induction.
1842	The principle of conservation of energy was observed by Julius von Mayer.
c. 1847	The mechanical equivalent of heat was described by James Joule.
1849	A measurement of speed of light was put forward by French physicist Armand Fizeau (1819–1896).
1873	Light was conceived as electromagnetic radiation by James Maxwell.
1877	A theory of sound as vibrations in an elastic medium was propounded by John Rayleigh.
1887	The existence of radio waves was predicted by Heinrich Hertz.
1895	X-rays were discovered by Wilhelm Röntgen.
1896	The discovery of radioactivity was made by Antoine Becquerel.
1897	Joseph Thomson discovered the electron.
1899	Ernest Rutherford discovered alpha and beta rays.
1900	Quantum theory was propounded by Max Planck; the discovery of gamma rays was made by French physicist Paul-Ulrich Villard (1860–1934).
1904	The theory of radioactivity was put forward by Rutherford and Frederick Soddy.
1905	Albert Einstein propounded his special theory of relativity.
1908	The Geiger counter was invented by Hans Geiger and Rutherford.
1911	The discovery of the atomic nucleus was made by Rutherford.
1913	The orbiting electron atomic theory was propounded by Danish physicist Niels Bohr.
1915	X-ray crystallography was discovered by William and Lawrence Bragg.
1916	Einstein put forward his general theory of relativity; mass spectrography was discovered by William Aston.
1926	Wave mechanics was introduced by Erwin Schrödinger.
1927	The uncertainty principle of atomic physics was established by Werner Heisenberg.
1931	The cyclotron was developed by Ernest Lawrence.
1932	The discovery of the neutron was made by James Chadwick; the electron microscope was developed by Vladimir Zworykin.
1933	The positron, the antiparticle of the electron, was discovered by Carl Anderson.
1934	Artificial radioactivity was developed by Frédéric and Irène Joliot-Curie.
1939	The discovery of nuclear fission was made by Otto Hahn and Fritz Strassmann (1902–).
1942	The first controlled nuclear chain reaction was achieved by Enrico Fermi.
1956	The neutrino, an elementary particle, was discovered by Clyde Cowan and Fred Reines.
1960	The Mössbauer effect of atom emissions was discovered by Rudolf Mössbauer; the first maser was developed by US physicist Theodore Maiman (1927–).
1963	Maiman developed the first laser.
1964	Murray Gell-Mann and George Zweig discovered the quark.
1971	The theory of superconductivity was announced, where electrical resistance in some metals vanishes above absolute zero.
1973	The discovery of pulsars was made by Antony Hewish.
1979	The discovery of the asymmetry of elementary particles was made by US physicists James W Cronin and Val L Fitch.
1982	The discovery of processes involved in the evolution of stars was made by Subrahmanyan Chandrasekhar and William Fowler.
1983	Evidence of the existence of weakons (W and Z particles) was confirmed at CERN, validating the link between the weak nuclear force and the electromagnetic force.
1986	The first high-temperature superconductor was discovered, able to conduct electricity without resistance at a temperature of 35K.
1989	Stanley Pons and Martin Fleischmann claimed to have achieved nuclear fusion at room temperature and pressure (cold fusion). CERN's Large Electron–Positron Collider (LEP), a particle accelerator with a circumference of 16.8 mi/27 km, came into operation.
1991	LEP experiments demonstrated the existence of three generations of elementary particles, each with two quarks and two leptons.
1992	Japanese researchers developed a material that becomes superconducting at –153°F/–103°C (about 80°F/456°C warmer than the previous record).

Placentia, Piacenza dates from 218BC and has a 12th-century cathedral.

Piaf Edith. Adopted name of Edith Gassion 1915–1963. French singer and songwriter, a cabaret singer in Paris from the late 1930s. She is remembered for the defiant song "Je ne regrette rien/I Regret Nothing" and "La Vie en rose" 1946.

Piaget Jean 1896–1980. Swiss psychologist distinguished by his studies of child development in relation to thought processes, and concepts of space, time, causality, and objectivity.

Piaget believed this was a vital framework for studying human intelligence and he stressed the interaction of biological and environmental factors.

piano or **pianoforte** stringed musical instrument, played by felt-covered hammers activated from a keyboard, and capable of soft (piano) or loud (forte) tones, hence its name. The first piano was constructed 1704 and introduced 1709 by Bartolommeo Cristofori, a harpsichord-maker of Padua. It uses a clever mechanism to make the keyboard touch-sensitive. Extensively developed during the 18th century, the piano attracted admiration among many composers, although it was not until 1768 that Johann Christian Bach gave one of the first public recitals on the instrument.

Further improvements in the keyboard action and tone by makers such as Broadwood, Erard, and Graf, together with a rapid expansion of published music by Haydn, Beethoven, Schubert, and others, led to the development of the powerfully resonant concert grand piano and the mass production of smaller upright pianos for the home.

The **player piano** is designed to reproduce key-actions recorded on a perforated paper roll. The concert **Duo-Art** reproducing piano encoded more detailed information, to the extent that audiences were unable to distinguish a live performance from a reproduced performance.

Piano Renzo 1939– . Italian architect who designed (with Richard Rogers) the Pompidou Center, Paris, completed 1977. Among his other buildings are the Kansai Airport, Osaka, Japan and a sports stadium in Bari, Italy, both using new materials and making imaginative use of civil-engineering techniques.

Picardy (French *Picardie*) region of N France, including Aisne, Oise, and Somme *départements*
area 7,488 sq mi/19,400 sq km
population (1986) 1,774,000
products chemicals and metals
history in the 13th century the name Picardy was used to describe the feudal smallholdings north of Paris added to the French crown by Philip II. During the Hundred Years' War the area was hotly contested by France and England, but it was eventually occupied by Louis XI in 1477. Picardy once more became a major battlefield in World War I.

picaresque (Spanish *pícaro* "rogue") in literature, a genre of novels that takes for its heroes rogues and villains, telling their story in a series of loosely linked episodes. Examples include Daniel Defoe's *Moll Flanders*, Henry Fielding's *Tom Jones*, and Mark Twain's *Huckleberry Finn*.

Picasso Pablo 1881–1973. Spanish artist, active chiefly in France, one of the most inventive and prolific talents in 20th-century art. His Blue Period 1901–04 and Rose Period 1905–06 preceded the revolutionary *Les Demoiselles d'Avignon* 1907 (Metropolitan Museum of Art, New York), which paved the way for Cubism. In the early 1920s he was considered a leader of the Surrealist movement. In the 1930s his work included metal sculpture, book illustration, and the mural *Guernica* 1937 (Casón del Buen Retiro, Madrid), a comment on the bombing of civilians in the Spanish Civil War. He continued to paint into his eighties.

Picasso was born in Málaga, son of an art teacher, José Ruiz Blasco, and an Andalusian mother, Maria Picasso López; he stopped using the name Ruiz in 1898. He was a mature artist at the age of 10, and at 16 was holding his first exhibition. In 1900 he made an initial visit to Paris, where he was to settle. From 1946 he lived mainly in the south of France where, in addition to painting, he experimented with ceramics, sculpture, sets for ballet (for example *Parade* in 1917 for Diaghilev), book illustrations (such as Ovid's *Metamorphoses*), and portraits (Stravinsky, Valéry, and others).

Piccard Auguste 1884–1962. Swiss scientist. In 1931–32, he and his twin brother, **Jean Félix** (1884–1963), made ascents to 55,000 ft/17,000 m in a balloon of his own design, resulting in useful discoveries concerning stratospheric phenomena such as ◊cosmic radiation. He also built and used, with his son **Jacques Ernest** (1922–), bathyscaphes for research under the sea.

piccolo woodwind instrument, the smallest member of the ◊flute family.

picketing gathering of workers and their labor-union representatives to try to persuade others to support them in an industrial dispute. They often carry signs attached to pickets, hence the term.

Pickett George Edward 1825–1875. US military leader. At the outbreak of the American Civil War, he joined the Confederate army, rising to the rank of brigadier general 1862. Although he saw action in many battles, he is best remembered for leading the bloody, doomed "Pickett's Charge" at Gettysburg 1863. After the war Pickett declined further military appointments and retired to private life.

Born in Richmond, Virginia, Pickett graduated from West Point 1846 and was commended for bravery during the Mexican War. After service in Texas 1849–55, he was transferred to the Pacific Northwest.

Pickford Mary. Adopted name of Gladys Mary Smith 1893–1979. Canadian-born US actress. The first star of the silent screen, she was known as "America's Sweetheart," and played innocent ingenue roles into her thirties. She and her second husband (from 1920), Douglas ◊Fairbanks, Sr, were known as "the world's sweethearts." With her husband and Charlie ◊Chaplin, she founded United Artists studio 1919. For many years she was the wealthiest and most influential woman in Hollywood.

Her films include *Rebecca of Sunnybrook Farm* 1917, *Pollyanna* 1920, *Little Lord Fauntleroy* 1921, and *Coquette* 1929, her first talkie (Academy Award). She was presented a special Academy Award 1976.

Pico della Mirandola Count Giovanni 1463–1494. Italian mystic philosopher. Born at Mirandola, of which his father was prince, he studied Hebrew, Chaldean, and Arabic, showing particular interest in the Jewish and theosophical system, the ◊kabbala. His attempt to reconcile the religious base of Christianity, Islam, and the ancient world earned Pope Alexander VI's disapproval.

Pict Roman term for a member of the peoples of N Scotland, possibly meaning "painted" (tattooed). Of pre-Celtic origin, and speaking a non-Celtic language, the Picts are thought to have inhabited much of England before the arrival of the Celtic Britons. They were united with the Celtic Scots under the rule of Kenneth MacAlpin 844.

PID (abbreviation for *pelvic inflammatory disease*) serious gynecological condition characterized by lower abdominal pain, malaise, and fever; menstruation may be disrupted; infertility may result. Treatment is with antibiotics. The incidence of the disease is twice as high in women using intrauterine contraceptive devices (IUDs).

PID is potentially life-threatening, and, while mild episodes usually respond to antibiotics, surgery may be necessary in cases of severe or recurrent pelvic infection. The bacterium *Chlamydia trachomatis* (see ◊chlamydia) has been implicated in a high proportion of cases. The condition is increasingly common.

pidgin language any of various trade jargons, contact languages, or ◊lingua francas arising in ports and markets where people of different linguistic backgrounds meet for commercial and other purposes. Usually a pidgin language is a rough blend of the vocabulary of one (often dominant) language with the syntax or grammar of one or more other (often dependent) groups. Pidgin English in various parts of the world, *français petit negre*, and Bazaar Hindi or Hindustani are examples of pidgins that have served long-term purposes to the extent of being acquired by children as one of their everyday languages. At this point they become ◊Creole languages.

Pidgin English originally referred to the trade jargon developed between the British and the Chinese in the 19th century (*pidgin* is believed to have been a Chinese pronunciation of the English word *business*). There have been many forms of pidgin English, often with common elements because of the wide range of contacts made by commercial shipping. The original pidgin English of the Chinese ports combined words of English with a rough-and-ready Chinese grammatical structure. Melanesian pidgin English (also known as Tok Pisin) combines English and the syntax of local Melanesian languages. For example, the English pronoun "we" becomes both *yumi* (you and me) and *mifela* (me and fellow, excluding you).

Generally, a pidgin language comes into existence to answer short-term needs—for example, the Korean Bamboo English used during the Korean War. Unless there is a reason for extending the life of such a hybrid form (in the case of Korean Bamboo English combining elements of English, Korean, and Japanese), it will fade away when the need passes.

Piedmont (Italian *Piemonte*) region of N Italy, bordering Switzerland on the N and France on the W, and surrounded, except on the E, by the Alps and the Apennines; area 9,804 sq mi/25,400 sq km; population (1990) 4,356,200. Its capital is Turin, and towns include Alessandria, Asti, Vercelli, and Novara. It also includes the fertile Po river valley. Products include fruit, grain, cattle, automobiles, and textiles. The movement for the unification of Italy started in the 19th century in Piedmont, under the house of Savoy.

pier structure built out into the sea from the coastline for use as a landing place or promenade.

Pierce Franklin 1804–1869. 14th president of the US. He served in the New Hampshire state legislature 1829–33, the US House of Representatives 1833–37, and the US Senate 1837–42. Pierce subsequently returned to New Hampshire, serving briefly as US attorney and seeing action in the Mexican War. Chosen as a compromise candidate of the Democratic party, he was elected president 1852. Despite his expansionist foreign policy, North–South tensions grew more intense, and Pierce was denied renomination 1856.

Born in Hillsboro, New Hampshire, Pierce was admitted to the bar 1827.

Piercy Marge 1937– . US poet and novelist. Her fiction looks at the fringes of American social life and the world of the liberated woman. Her novels include the utopian *Woman on the Edge of Time* 1979, *Fly Away Home* 1984, and *Summer People* 1989.

Piero della Francesca c. 1420–1492. Italian painter, active in Arezzo and Urbino; one of the major artists of the 15th century. His work has a solemn stillness and unusually solid figures, luminous color, and compositional harmony. It includes a fresco series, *The Legend of the True Cross* (S Francesco, Arezzo), begun about 1452. Piero wrote two treatises, one on mathematics, one on the laws of perspective in painting.

Piero di Cosimo c. 1462–1521. Italian painter, known for his inventive pictures of mythological subjects, often featuring fauns and centaurs. He also painted religious subjects and portraits.

Pierre capital of South Dakota, located in the central part of the state, on the Missouri River, near the geographical center of North America. Industries include tourism and grain and dairy products; population (1990) 12,900. As Fort Pierre in the early 1800s, it served as a fur-trading post; in the late 1800s it was a supply center for gold miners.

Pietermaritzburg industrial city (footwear, furniture, aluminum, rubber, brewing), and capital, from 1842, of Natal, South Africa; population (1985) 192,400. Founded 1838 by Boer trekkers from the Cape, it was named after their leaders, Piet Retief and Gert Maritz, who were killed by the Zulus.

Pietism religious movement within Lutheranism in the 17th century which emphasized spiritual and devotional faith rather than theology and dogma. It was founded by Philipp Jakob Spener (1635–1705), a minister in Frankfurt, Germany, who emphasized devotional meetings for "groups of the Elect" rather than biblical learning; he wrote the *Pia Desideria* 1675. The movement was for many years associated with the University of Halle (founded 1694), Germany.

pietra dura (Italian "hard stone") Italian technique of inlaying furniture with semiprecious stones, such as agate or quartz, in a variety of colors, to create pictures or patterns.

piezoelectric effect property of some crystals (for example, quartz) to develop an electromotive force or voltage across opposite faces when subjected to a mechanical strain, and, conversely, to expand or contract in size when subjected to an electromotive force. Piezoelectric crystal ◊oscillators are used as frequency standards (for example, replacing balance wheels in watches), and for producing ◊ultrasound.

The crystals are also used in phonograph pickups, transducers in ultrasonics, and certain gas lighters.

pig any even-toed hoofed mammal of the family Suidae. They are omnivorous, and have simple, non-ruminating stomachs and thick hides. The Middle Eastern **wild boar** *Sus scrofa* is the ancestor of domesticated breeds; it is 4.5 ft/1.5 m long and 3 ft/1 m high, with formidable tusks, but not naturally aggressive.

Wild pigs include the ◊*babirusa* and the ◊*wart hog*. The farming of domesticated pigs was practiced during the Neolithic in the Middle East and China at least 11,000 years ago and the pig was a common farm animal in ancient Greece and Rome. Over 400 breeds evolved over the centuries, many of which have all but disappeared in more recent times with the development of intensive rearing systems; however, different environments and requirements have ensured the continuation of a variety of types. The Berkshire, Chester White, Poland, China, Saddleback, Yorkshire, Duroc, and Razorback are the main surviving breeds. Modern indoor rearing methods favor the large white breeds, such as the Chester White and the originally Swedish Landrace, over colored varieties, which tend to be hardier and can survive better outdoors. Since 1960, hybrid pigs, produced by crossing two or more breeds, have become popular for their heavy but lean carcasses.

pigeon any bird of the family Columbidae, sometimes also called doves, distinguished by their large crops, which, becoming glandular in the breeding season, secrete a milky fluid ("pigeon's milk") that aids digestion of food for the young. They are found worldwide.

There are many species: domesticated varieties (including the city pigeon) derive from the Eurasian rock dove *Columba livia*. New World species include the mourning-doves, which live much of the time on the ground. The fruit pigeons of Australasia and the Malay regions are beautifully colored. In the US, there were once millions of passenger pigeons *Ectopistes migratorius*, but they have been extinct since 1914.

pigeon hawk another name for the merlin, a small ◊falcon.

pig iron or **cast iron** the quality of iron produced in a ◊blast furnace. It contains around 4% carbon plus some other impurities.

pika or **mouse-hare** any small mammal of the family Ochotonidae, belonging to the order Lagomorpha (rabbits and hares). The single genus *Ochotona* contains about 15 species, most of which live in mountainous regions of Asia, although two species are native to North America.

Pikas have short, rounded ears, and most species are about 8 in/20 cm long, with grayish-brown fur and no visible tail. Their warning call is a sharp whistle. They are vegetarian and in late summer cut grasses and other plants and place them in piles to dry as hay, which is then stored for the winter.

pike any of a family Esocidae in the order Salmoniformes, of slender, freshwater bony fishes with narrow pointed heads and sharp, pointed teeth. The northern pike *Esox lucius*, of North America and Eurasia, may reach 7 ft/ 2.2 m and 20 lb/9 kg.

Other kinds of pike include muskellunges, up to 7 ft/2.2 m long, and the smaller pickerels, both in the genus *Esox*.

Pike Zebulon Montgomery 1779–1813. US explorer and military leader. In 1805 he was sent by the governor of the Louisiana Territory to explore the source of the Mississippi River. In 1806 he was sent to explore the Arkansas River and to contest Spanish presence in the area. After crossing Colorado and failing to reach the summit of the peak later named after him, he was captured by the Spanish, who released him 1807. Pike was later promoted to brigadier general and was killed in action in the War of 1812.

Born in Lamberton, New Jersey, Pike joined the army at age 15 and served in the Department of the West.

pikeperch any of various freshwater members of the perch family, resembling pikes, especially the walleye *Stizostedion vitreum*, common in Europe, W Asia, and North America. It reaches over 3 ft/1 m.

Pikes Peak mountain in the Rampart of the Rocky Mountains, Colorado; height 14,110 ft/ 4,300 m. It has commanding views, reachable by cog railroad and road. Pikes Peak was discovered 1806 by Zebulon Pike and first scaled 1820.

Pilate Pontius early 1st century AD. Roman procurator of Judea AD 26–36. The New Testament Gospels describe his reluctant ordering of Jesus' crucifixion.

Pilate was unsympathetic to the Jews; his actions several times provoked riots, and in AD 36 he was recalled to Rome to account for the brutal suppression of a Samaritan revolt. The Greek historian Eusebius says he committed suicide after Jesus' crucifixion.

pilchard any of various small, oily members of the herring family, Clupeidae, especially the commercial sardine of Europe *Sardina pilchardus*, and the California sardine *Sardinops sagax*.

pilgrimage journey to sacred places inspired by religious devotion. For Hindus, the holy places include Varanasi and the purifying River Ganges; for Buddhists, the places connected with the crises of Buddha's career; for the ancient Greeks, the shrines at Delphi and Ephesus among others; for Jews, the sanctuary at Jerusalem; and for Muslims, Mecca.

Among Christians, pilgrimages were common by the 2nd century, and as a direct result of the growing frequency and numbers of pilgrimages there arose numerous hospices catering to pilgrims, the religious orders of knighthood, and the Crusades. The great centers of Christian pilgrimages have been, or still are, Jerusalem, Rome, the tomb of St James of Compostela in Spain, the shrine of Becket in Canterbury, England, and the holy places at La Salette and Lourdes in France.

Pilgrimage of Grace rebellion against Henry VIII of England 1536–37, originating in Yorkshire and Lincolnshire. The uprising was directed against the policies of the monarch (such as the dissolution of the monasteries and the effects of the enclosure of common land).

Pilgrims the emigrants who sailed from Plymouth, England, in the *Mayflower* on Sept 16, 1620, to found the first colony in New England at New Plymouth, Massachusetts.

Of the 102 passengers, about a third were English Puritan refugees escaping religious persecution from Anglican England.

First known as Separatists, they were led by William Brewster, a wealthy layman, and William Bradford and had lived in Holland for ten years. The voyagers had called themselves "Saints," the term "Pilgrim" not being applied to them until the 19th century. The Pilgrims originally set sail for Virginia in the *Mayflower* and *Speedwell* from Southampton on Aug 5, 1620, but had to put into Dartmouth when the latter needed repair. Bad weather then drove them into Plymouth Sound where the *Speedwell* was abandoned. After two months of sailing, they landed at Cape Cod in December and decided to stay, moving on to find Plymouth harbor and founding the Massachusetts colony. Considerable religious conflict had erupted between the 35 Puritans and the other, largely Anglican, passengers. Open mutiny was averted by the Mayflower Compact, which established the rights of the non-Puritans. About half their number died over the winter before they received help from the Indians; the survivors celebrated ⬦Thanksgiving in the fall of 1621.

The voyage was duplicated in 1957 with *Mayflower II*, a reproduction presented by Britain and now at Plymouth, Massachusetts.

Pilgrim's Progress allegory by John Bunyan, published 1678–84, that describes the journey through life to the Celestial City of a man called Christian. On his way through the Slough of Despond, the House Beautiful, Vanity Fair, Doubting Castle, and other landmarks, he meets a number of allegorical figures.

This work was often the only other book an American pioneer family owned and read, besides the Bible.

Pill, the commonly used term for the contraceptive pill, based on female hormones. The combined pill, which contains estrogen and progesterone, stops the production of eggs, and makes the mucus produced by the cervix hostile to sperm. It is the most effective form of contraception apart from sterilization, being more than 99% effective.

The **minipill** or progesterone-only pill prevents implantation of a fertilized egg into the wall of the uterus. The minipill has a slightly higher failure rate, especially if not taken at the same time each day, but has fewer side effects and is considered safer for long-term use. Possible side effects of the Pill include migraine or headache and high blood pressure. More seriously, estrogen-containing pills can slightly increase the risk of a clot forming in the blood vessels. This risk is increased in women over 35 if they smoke. Controversy surrounds other possible health effects of taking the Pill. The evidence for a link with cancer is slight (and the Pill may protect women from some forms of cancer). Once a woman ceases to take it, there is an increase in the chance of conceiving identical twins.

pillory instrument of punishment consisting of a wooden frame set on a post, with holes in which the prisoner's head and hands were secured. Bystanders threw whatever was available at the miscreant.

Similar to the ⬦stocks, its use for punishing petty offenders ended in the US in Delaware 1905.

Pilobolous Dance Theater US modern-dance troupe whose members collectively choreograph surreal body-sculptures with a mixture of dance, gymnastics and mime. It is whimsically named after a light-sensitive fungus.

pilotfish small marine fish *Naucrates ductor* of the family Carangidae, which also includes pompanos. It hides below sharks, turtles, or boats, using the shade as a base from which to prey on smaller fish. It is found in all warm oceans and grows to about 1.2 ft/36 cm.

Piłsudski Józef (Klemens) 1867–1935. Polish nationalist politician, dictator from 1926. Born in Russian Poland, he founded the Polish Socialist Party 1892 and was twice imprisoned for anti-Russian activities. During World War I he commanded a Polish force to fight for Germany but fell under suspicion of intriguing with the Allies and was imprisoned by the Germans 1917–18. When Poland became independent 1919, he was elected chief of state, and led an unsuccessful Polish attack on the USSR 1920. He retired 1923, but in 1926 led a military coup that established his dictatorship until his death.

Piltdown man fossil skull fragments "discovered" by Charles Dawson at Piltdown, E Sussex, England, in 1913, and believed to be the earliest European human remains until proved a hoax in 1953 (the jaw was that of an orangutan).

pimento or **allspice** tree found in tropical parts of the New World. The dried fruits of the species *Pimenta dioica* are used as a spice. Also, a sweet variety of ⬦capsicum pepper (more correctly spelled **pimiento**).

pimpernel any plant of the genus *Anagallis* of the primrose family Primulaceae comprising about 30 species mostly native to W Europe. The European scarlet pimpernel *A. arvensis* grows in cornfields, the flowers opening only in full sunshine. It is naturalized in North America.

PIN (acronym for **personal identification number**) in banking, a unique number used as a password to establish the identity of a customer using an automatic cash dispenser. The PIN is normally encoded into the magnetic strip of the customer's bank card and is known only to the customer and to the bank's computer. Before a cash dispenser will issue money or information, the customer must insert the card into a slot in the machine (so that the PIN can be read from the magnetic strip) and enter the PIN correctly at a keyboard. This effectively prevents stolen cards from being used to obtain money from cash dispensers.

Pinatubo, Mount active volcano on Luzon Island, the Philippines, 55 mi/88 km N of Manila. Dormant for 600 years, it erupted June 1991, killing 343 people and leaving as many as 200,000 homeless. Surrounding rice fields were covered with 10 ft/3 m of volcanic ash and the large volume of volcanic material released into the atmosphere was expected to affect the global climate.

The huge US Clark Air Force Base, a total loss, was abandoned.

Pincus Gregory Goodwin 1903–1967. US biologist who, together with Min Chueh Chang (1908–) and John Rock (1890–1984), developed the contraceptive pill in the 1950s.

As a result of studying the physiology of reproduction, Pincus conceived the idea of using synthetic ⬦hormones to mimic the condition of pregnancy in women. This effectively prevents impregnation.

Pindar *c.* 552–442 BC. Greek poet, born near Thebes. He is renowned for his choral lyrics, the "Pindaric odes," written in honor of the victors of athletic games.

Pindling Lynden (Oscar) 1930– . Bahamian prime minister 1967–92. After studying law in London, he returned to the island to join the newly formed Progressive Liberal Party and then became the first black prime minister of the Bahamas.

Pindus Mountains (Greek **Pindhos Oros**) range in NW Greece and Albania, between Epirus and Thessaly; highest point Smolikas, 8,638 ft/2,633 m.

pine any coniferous tree of the genus *Pinus*, family Pinaceae. There are 70–100 species, of which about 35 are native to North America. These are generally divided into two groupings: the soft pines and the hard pines. The former have needles in bundles of five and stalked cones without prickles; for example, eastern white pine *P. strobus*. Hard pines usually have needles in bundles of two or three and prickly cones; for example, jack pine *P. banksiana*. The oldest living species is probably the bristlecone pine *P. aristata*, native to California, of which some specimens are said to be 4,600 years old.

pineal body or **pineal gland** a cone-shaped outgrowth of the vertebrate brain. In some lower vertebrates, it develops a rudimentary lens and retina, which show it to be derived from an eye, or pair of eyes, situated on the top of the head in ancestral vertebrates. In fishes that can change color to match the background, the pineal perceives the light level and controls the color change. In birds, the pineal detects changes in daylight and stimulates breeding behavior as spring approaches. Mammals also have a pineal gland, but it is located deeper within the brain. It secretes a hormonelike substance, melatonin, thought to influence rhythms of activity. In humans, it is a small piece of tissue attached to the posterior wall of the third ventricle of the brain.

pineapple plant *Ananas comosus* of the bromeliad family, native to South and Central America, but now cultivated in many other tropical areas, such as Hawaii and Queensland, Australia. The mauvish flowers are produced in the second year, and subsequently consolidate with their bracts into a fleshy fruit.

For export to world markets the fruits are cut unripe and lack the sweet juiciness typical of the canned pineapple (usually the smoother-skinned Cayenne variety), which is allowed to mature fully.

Pine Bluff city in SE Arkansas, on the Arkansas River, SE of Little Rock, seat of Jefferson county. Industries include paper, cotton, grain, and furniture; population (1990) 57,100.

Pinero Arthur Wing 1855–1934. British dramatist. A leading exponent of the "well-made" play, he enjoyed great contemporary success with his farces, beginning with *The Magistrate* 1885. More substantial social drama followed with *The Second Mrs Tanqueray* 1893, and comedies including *Trelawny of the "Wells"* 1898.

pine siskin streaked, tan, black, and yellow ⬦finch *Carduelis pinus* of North America, about 5 in/12 cm long.

pink any annual or perennial plant of the genus *Dianthus* of the family Carophyllaceae. The stems have characteristically swollen nodes, and the flowers range in color from white through pink to purple. Members of the pink family include carnations, sweet williams, and baby's breath *Gypsophila paniculata*.

Deptford pink *D. armeria*, with deep pink flowers with pale dots, is native to Europe and naturalized in the US.

Pinkerton Allan 1819–1884. US detective, born in Glasgow, Scotland. He founded Pinkerton's National Detective Agency 1852 and built up the federal secret service from the espionage system he developed during the American Civil War. He thwarted an early assassination plot against Abraham ▷Lincoln and compiled the nation's most complete files on criminal activity. His agency became increasingly involved in the suppression of labor unrest. His men fought brutal battles against striking steelworkers 1892 and the ▷Molly Maguires.

Pink Floyd British psychedelic rock group, formed 1965. The original members were Syd Barrett (1946–), Roger Waters (1944–), Richard Wright (1945–), and Nick Mason (1945–). Their albums include *The Dark Side of the Moon* 1973 and *The Wall* 1979, with its spin-off film starring Bob Geldof.

pinna in botany, the primary division of a pinnate leaf.

pinnate leaf leaf that is divided up into many small leaflets, arranged in rows along either side of a midrib, as in ash trees (*Fraxinus*). It is a type of compound leaf. Each leaflet is known as a *pinna*, and where the pinnae are themselves divided, the secondary divisions are known as pinnules.

Pinocchio fantasy for children by Carlo Collodi, published in Italy 1883 and in an English translation 1892. It tells the story of a wooden puppet that comes to life and assumes the characteristics of a human boy. Pinocchio's nose grows longer every time he tells a lie. A Walt Disney cartoon film, based on Collodi's story, was released in 1940 and brought the character to a wider audience.

Pinochet (Ugarte) Augusto 1915– . Military ruler of Chile from 1973, when a coup backed by the US Central Intelligence Agency ousted and killed President Salvador Allende. Pinochet took over the presidency and governed ruthlessly, crushing all opposition. He was voted out of power when general elections were held in Dec 1989 but remains head of the armed forces until 1997.

In 1990 Pinochet's attempt to reassert political influence was firmly censured by President Patricio Aylwin.

pint liquid or dry measure of volume or capacity. A liquid pint is equal to 16 fluid ounces or half a liquid quart (0.473 liter), while a dry pint is equal to half a dry quart (0.551 liter).

The British and Canadian imperial pint equals 0.568 liter.

Pinter Harold 1930– . English dramatist, originally an actor. He specializes in the tragicomedy of the breakdown of communication, broadly in the tradition of the Theater of the ▷Absurd—for example, *The Birthday Party* 1958 and *The Caretaker* 1960. Later plays include *The Homecoming* 1965, *Old Times* 1971, *Betrayal* 1978, and *Mountain Language* 1988.

Pinturicchio (or *Pintoricchio*) pseudonym of Bernardino di Betto *c.* 1454–1513. Italian painter, active in Rome, Perugia, and Siena.

His chief works are the frescoes in the Borgia Apartments in the Vatican, painted in the 1490s, and in the Piccolomini Library of Siena Cathedral, 1503–08. He is thought to have assisted ▷Perugino in decorating the Sistine Chapel, Rome.

pinworm ▷nematode worm *Enterobius vermicularis*, an intestinal parasite of humans.

Pinyin Chinese phonetic alphabet approved 1956 by the People's Republic of China, and used since 1979 in transcribing all names of people and places from Chinese ideograms into other languages using the English/Roman alphabet. For example, the former transcription Chou En-lai becomes Zhou Enlai, Hua Kuo-feng became Hua Guofeng, Teng Hsiao-ping became Deng Xiaoping, Peking became Beijing.

pion or *pi meson* in physics, any of three ▷mesons (positive, negative, neutral) that play a role in binding together the neutrons and protons in the nucleus of an atom. They belong to the ▷hadron class of ▷elementary particles.

The mass of a positive or negative pion is 273 times that of an electron; the mass of a neutral pion is 264 times that of an electron.

Pioneer probe any of a series of US solar-system space probes 1958–78. The probes *Pioneer 4–9* went into solar orbit to monitor the Sun's activity during the 1960s and early 1970s. *Pioneer 5*, launched 1960, was the first of a series to study the solar wind between the planets. *Pioneer 10*, launched March 1972, was the first probe to reach Jupiter (Dec 1973) and to leave the Solar System 1983. *Pioneer 11*, launched April 1973, passed Jupiter Dec 1974, and was the first probe to reach Saturn (Sept 1979), before also leaving the Solar System.

Pioneer 10 and *11* carry plaques containing messages from Earth in case they are found by other civilizations among the stars. Pioneer Venus probes were launched May and Aug 1978. One orbited Venus, and the other dropped three probes onto the surface. In early 1990 *Pioneer 10* was 4.4 billion mi/7.1 billion km from the Sun. Both it and *Pioneer 11* were still returning data measurements of starlight intensity to Earth.

Pioneer 1, 2, and *3*, launched 1958, were intended Moon probes, but *Pioneer 2*'s launch failed, and *1* and *3* failed to reach their target, although they did measure the ▷Van Allen radiation belts. *Pioneer 4* began to orbit the Sun after passing the Moon.

Pioneer 6 (1965), *7* (1966), *8* (1967), and *9* (1968) monitored solar activity.

pioneer species in ecology, those species that are the first to colonize and thrive in new areas. Coal tips, recently cleared woodland, and new roadsides are areas where pioneer species will quickly appear. As the habitat matures other species take over, a process known as *succession*.

pipefish any of various long-snouted, thin, pipelike marine fishes in the same family (Syngnathidae) as seahorses. The great pipefish *S. acus* grows up to 1.6 ft/50 cm, and the male has a brood pouch for eggs and developing young.

pipit any of various sparrow-sized ground-dwelling songbirds of the genus *Anthus* of the family Motacillidae, which also includes wagtails.

The North American water pipit *A. spinoletta* lives near water in fields and on beaches. It is brown and tan with a slender bill.

piracy the taking of a ship, aircraft, or any of its contents, from lawful ownership, punishable under international law by the court of any country where the pirate may be found or taken. When the craft is taken over to alter its destination, or its passengers held to ransom, the term is ▷hijacking. Piracy is also used to describe infringement of ▷copyright.

Algiers (see ▷corsairs), the West Indies (see ▷buccaneers), the coast of Trucial Oman (the Pirate Coast), Chinese and Malay waters, and such hideouts as Lundy Island, SW England, were pirate haunts for many years. Between the 16th and 18th centuries, the Barbary states of N Africa (Morocco, Algiers, Tunis, and Tripoli) were called the Pirate States. Modern communications and the complexities of supplying and servicing modern vessels tend to eliminate piracy or confine it to the immediate vicinity of a harbor; it is still common in South America and SE Asian waters.

The US sent a fleet to fight the Barbary pirates 1800–15, its first overseas naval and marine war, which was successfully concluded when Capt S ▷Decatur forced the dey of Algiers to cease the practice of holding US sailors hostage until tribute was paid.

Piraeus port of both ancient and modern Athens and main port of Greece, on the Gulf of Aegina; population (1981) 196,400. Constructed as the port of Athens about 493 BC, it was linked with that city by the Long Walls about 460 BC. After the destruction of Athens by Sulla 86 BC, Piraeus declined. Modern Piraeus is an industrial suburb of Athens.

Pirandello Luigi 1867–1936. Italian writer. His plays include *La morsa/The Vice* 1912, *Sei personaggi in cerca d'autore/Six Characters in Search of an Author* 1921, and *Enrico IV/Henry IV* 1922. The themes and treatment of his plays anticipated the work of Brecht, O'Neill, Anouilh, and Genet. Nobel Prize 1934.

Piranesi Giambattista 1720–1778. Italian architect, most significant for his powerful etchings of Roman antiquities and as a theorist of architecture, advocating imaginative use of Roman models. Only one of his designs was built, Sta Maria del Priorato, Rome.

piranha any South American freshwater fish of the genus *Serrusalmus*, in the same order as cichlids. They can grow to 2 ft/60 cm long, and have razor-sharp teeth; some species may rapidly devour animals, especially if attracted by blood.

pirouette in dance, a movement comprising a complete turn of the body on one leg with the other raised.

Pisa city in Tuscany, Italy; population (1988) 104,000. It has an 11th–12th-century cathedral. Its famous campanile, the Leaning Tower of Pisa (repaired 1990), is 180 ft/55 m high and about 16.5 ft/5 m out of perpendicular. It has foundations only about 10 ft/3 m deep.

Pisa was a maritime republic in the 11th–12th centuries. The university dates from 1338. The scientist Galileo was born here.

Pisanello nickname of Antonio Pisano *c.* 1395–1455. Italian artist active in Verona, Venice, Naples, Rome, and elsewhere. His panel paintings reveal a rich International Gothic style. He was also an outstanding portrait medalist. His frescoes in the Palazzo Ducale in Mantua were rediscovered after World War II.

Pisces zodiac constellation, mainly in the northern hemisphere between Aries and

Aquarius, near Pegasus. It is represented by two fish tied together by their tails. The Circlet, a delicate ring of stars, marks the head of the western fish in Pisces. The constellation contains the **vernal equinox**, the point at which the Sun's path around the sky (the **ecliptic**) crosses the celestial equator. The Sun reaches this point around March 21 each year as it passes through Pisces from mid-March to late April. In astrology, the dates for Pisces are between about Feb 19 and March 20 (see ⇨precession).

Piscis Austrinus or **Southern Fish** constellation of the southern hemisphere near Capricornus. Its brightest star is ⇨Fomalhaut.

Pisistratus c. 605–527 BC. Athenian politician. Although of noble family, he assumed the leadership of the peasant party, and seized power 561 BC. He was twice expelled, but recovered power from 541 BC until his death. Ruling as a dictator under constitutional forms, he was the first to have the Homeric poems written down, and founded Greek drama by introducing the Dionysiac peasant festivals into Athens.

Pissarro Camille 1831–1903. French Impressionist painter, born in the West Indies. He went to Paris in 1855, met Jean-Baptiste-Camille Corot, then Claude Monet, and became a leading member of the Impressionists. He experimented with various styles, including ⇨Pointillism, in the 1880s.

His son **Lucien Pissarro** (1863–1944) worked in the same style for a time.

pistachio deciduous Eurasian tree *Pistacia vera* of the cashew family Anacardiaceae, with green nuts, which are eaten salted or used to enhance and flavor foods.

pistil general term for the female part of a flower, either referring to one single ⇨carpel or a group of several fused carpels.

pistol any small ⇨firearm designed to be fired with one hand. Pistols were in use from the early 15th century.

The problem of firing more than once without reloading was tackled by using many combinations of multiple barrels, both stationary and revolving. A breech-loading, multichambered revolver of as early as 1650 still survives; the first practical solution, however, was Samuel Colt's six-gun 1847. Behind a single barrel, a short six-chambered cylinder was rotated by cocking the hammer and a fresh round of ammunition brought into firing position. The automatic pistol, operated by gas or recoil, was introduced in Germany in the 1890s. Both revolvers and automatics remain in widespread military use.

piston barrel-shaped device used in reciprocating engines (steam, gasoline, diesel oil) to harness power. Pistons are driven up and down in cylinders by expanding steam or hot gases. They pass on their motion via a connecting rod and crank to a crankshaft, which turns the driving wheels. In a pump or compressor, the role of the piston is reversed, being used to move gases and liquids. See also ⇨internal-combustion engine.

Piston Walter (Hamor) 1894–1976. US composer and teacher. He wrote a number of textbooks, including *Harmony* 1941 and *Orchestration* 1955. His Neo-Classical works include eight symphonies, a number of concertos, chamber music, the orchestral suite *Three New England Sketches* 1959, and the ballet *The Incredible Flautist* 1938.

He was well regarded as a teacher; his pupils included Leonard Bernstein. He taught at Harvard University 1944–60.

pit bull terrier or **American pit bull terrier** variety of dog that was developed in the US solely as a fighting dog. It usually measures about 20 in/50 cm at the shoulder and weighs roughly 50 lb/23 kg, but there are no established criteria since it is not recognized as a breed by either the American or British Kennel Clubs. Selective breeding for physical strength and aggression has created a dog unsuitable for life in the modern community.

Pitcairn Islands British colony in Polynesia, 3,300 mi/5,300 km NE of New Zealand
area 10 sq mi/27 sq km
capital Adamstown
features includes the uninhabited Henderson Islands, an unspoiled coral atoll with a rare ecology, and tiny Ducie and Oeno islands, annexed by Britain 1902
products fruit and souvenirs to passing ships
population (1990) 52
language English
government the governor is the British high commissioner in New Zealand
history first settled 1790 by nine mutineers from the British ship the *Bounty* together with some Tahitians, their occupation remaining unknown until 1808.

pitch in chemistry, a black, sticky substance, hard when cold, but liquid when hot, used for waterproofing, roofing, and paving. It is made by the destructive distillation of wood or coal tar, and has been used since antiquity for caulking wooden ships.

pitch in music, the position of a note in the scale, dependent on the frequency of the predominant sound wave. In **standard pitch**, A above middle C has a frequency of 440 Hz. **Perfect pitch** is an ability to name or reproduce any note heard or asked for; it does not necessarily imply high musical ability.

pitch in mechanics, the distance between the adjacent threads of a screw or bolt. When a screw is turned through one full turn it moves up or down a distance equal to the pitch of its thread. A screw thread is a simple type of machine, acting like a rolled-up inclined plane as may be illustrated by rolling up a paper ramp or long triangle around a pencil. A screw has a ⇨mechanical advantage greater than one.

pitchblende or **uraninite** brownish-black mineral, the major constituent of uranium ore, consisting mainly of uranium oxide (UO_2). It also contains some lead (the final, stable product of uranium decay) and variable amounts of most of the naturally occurring radioactive elements, which are products of either the decay or the fissioning of uranium isotopes. The uranium yield is 50–80%; it is also a source of radium, polonium, and actinium. Pitchblende was first studied by Pierre and Marie ⇨Curie, who found radium and polonium in its residues in 1898.

Pitcher Molly. Nickname of Mary ⇨McCauley.

pitcher plant any of various insectivorous plants of the family Sarraceniaceae, especially the genera *Nepenthes* and *Sarracenia*, the leaves of which are shaped like a pitcher and filled with a fluid that traps and digests insects.

Pitman Isaac 1813–1897. English teacher and inventor of Pitman's shorthand. He studied Samuel Taylor's scheme for shorthand writing,

and in 1837 published his own system, *Stenographic Soundhand*, fast, accurate, and adapted for use in many languages.

Pitot tube instrument that measures fluid (gas and liquid) flow. It is used to measure the speed of aircraft, and works by sensing pressure differences in different directions in the airstream. It was invented in the 1730s by the French scientist Henri Pitot (1695–1771).

The Pitot tube is a small, L-shaped tube that is inserted vertically into a flowing fluid with its open end facing upstream, thus measuring the total pressure of the fluid and indirectly the velocity of its flow.

Pitt William, **the Elder**, 1st Earl of Chatham 1708–1778. British Whig politician, "the Great Commoner." As paymaster of the forces 1746–55, he broke with tradition by refusing to enrich himself; he was dismissed for attacking the Duke of Newcastle, the prime minister. He served effectively as prime minister in coalition governments 1756–61 (successfully conducting the Seven Years' War) and 1766–68.

Entering Parliament 1735, Pitt led the Patriot faction opposed to the Whig prime minister Walpole and attacked Walpole's successor, Carteret, for his conduct of the War of the Austrian Succession. He championed the Americans against the king, though rejecting independence, and collapsed during his last speech in the House of Lords—opposing the withdrawal of British troops—and died a month later.

Pitt William, **the Younger** 1759–1806. British Tory prime minister 1783–1801 and 1804–06. He raised the importance of the House of Commons, clamped down on corruption, carried out fiscal reforms, and effected the union with Ireland. He attempted to keep Britain at peace but underestimated the importance of the French Revolution and became embroiled in wars with France from 1793; he died on hearing of Napoleon's victory at Austerlitz.

Son of William Pitt the Elder, he entered Cambridge University at the age of 14 and Parliament at 22. He was the Whig prime minister William Shelburne's chancellor of the Exchequer 1782–83, and with the support of the Tories and king's friends became Britain's youngest prime minister 1783.

pitta genus of tropical songless bird of order Passeriformes, genus *Pitta*, forming the family Pillidae. Some 20 species are native to SE Asia, W Africa, and Australia. They have round bodies, big heads, and are often brightly colored. They live on the ground and in low undergrowth, and can run from danger.

Pittsburgh industrial city (machinery, chemicals) in the US and the nation's largest inland port, where the Allegheny and Monongahela rivers join to form the Ohio River in Pennsylvania; population (1990) 369,900, metropolitan area 2,242,800.

Established by the French as Fort Duquesne 1750, the site was taken by the British 1758 and renamed Fort Pitt. The main growth of the city's great iron and steel industry came after 1850.

Educational institutions include the University of Pittsburgh and Carnegie-Mellon University. Once a smoky, smoggy, steelmaking city, Pittsburgh was transformed by urban redevelopment from the 1960s and the demise of heavy industry into chiefly a corporate service center.

Pittsfield city in W central Massachusetts on the Housatonic River, just E of the New York border. Industries include electronics and tourism; population (1990) 48,600. Herman Melville wrote *Moby Dick* at his home here.

pituitary gland major ⟂endocrine gland of vertebrates, situated in the center of the brain. The anterior lobe secretes hormones, some of which control the activities of other glands (thyroid, gonads, and adrenal cortex); others are direct-acting hormones affecting milk secretion and controlling growth. Secretions of the posterior lobe control body water balance and contraction of the uterus. The posterior lobe is regulated by nerves from the ⟂hypothalamus, and thus forms a link between the nervous and hormonal systems.

Piura capital of the department of the same name in the arid NW of Peru, situated on the Piura River, 100 mi/160 km SW of Punta Pariñas; population (1981) 186,000. It is the westernmost point in South America and was founded 1532 by the Spanish conquistadors left behind by Francisco Pizarro. Cotton is grown in the surrounding area.

Pius 12 popes, including:

Pius IV 1499–1565. Pope from 1559, of the ⟂Medici family. He reassembled the Council of Trent (see Counter-Reformation under ⟂Reformation) and completed its work 1563.

Pius V 1504–1572. Pope from 1566. He excommunicated Elizabeth I of England, and organized the expedition against the Turks that won the victory of ⟂Lepanto.

Pius VI (Giovanni Angelo Braschi) 1717–1799. Pope from 1775. He strongly opposed the French Revolution, and died a prisoner in French hands.

Pius VII 1742–1823. Pope from 1800. He concluded a concordat (papal agreement) with France 1801 and took part in Napoleon's coronation, but relations became strained. Napoleon annexed the papal states, and Pius was imprisoned 1809–14. After his return to Rome 1814, he revived the Jesuit order.

Pius IX 1792–1878. Pope from 1846. He never accepted the incorporation of the Papal States and of Rome in the kingdom of Italy. He proclaimed the dogmas of the Immaculate Conception of the Virgin 1854 and papal infallibility 1870; his pontificate was the longest in history.

Pius X (Giuseppe Melchiore Sarto) 1835–1914. Pope from 1903, canonized 1954. He condemned ⟂Modernism in a manifesto 1907.

Pius XI (Achille Ratti) 1857–1939. Pope from 1922. He signed the concordat (papal agreement) with Mussolini 1929.

Pius XII (Eugenio Pacelli) 1876–1958. Pope from 1939. He was conservative in doctrine and politics, and condemned ⟂Modernism. He proclaimed the dogma of the bodily assumption of the Virgin Mary 1950 and in 1951 restated the doctrine (strongly criticized by many) that the life of an infant must not be sacrificed to save a mother in labor. He was criticized for failing to speak out against atrocities committed by the Germans during World War II and has been accused of collusion with the Nazis.

pixel (abbreviation for *picture element*) single dot on a computer screen. All screen images are made up of a collection of pixels, with each pixel being either off (dark) or on (illuminated, possibly in color). The number of pixels available determines the screen's resolution. Typical resolutions of microcomputer screens vary from 320×200 pixels to 640×480 pixels, but screens with over $1,000 \times 1,000$ pixels are now quite common for high-quality graphic (pictorial) displays.

The number of bits (binary digits) used to represent each pixel determines how many colors it can display: a two-bit pixel can have four colors; an eight-bit (one-byte) pixel can have 256 colors. The higher the resolution of a screen and the more colors it is capable of displaying, the more memory will be needed in order to store that screen's contents.

Pizarro Francisco *c.* 1475–1541. Spanish conqueror of the Inca empire of Peru. Born in Spain, Pizarro traveled to the West Indies, where he met ⟂Balboa and served as his lieutenant on the expedition that crossed Panama and resulted in their sighting of the Pacific Ocean 1513. While living in Panama, Pizarro heard of a wealthy Indian empire to the south, and beginning 1524 he explored the NW coast of South America, searching for gold and other riches. In 1531, with the permission of the king of Spain, he and 180 followers armed with cannon defeated the Inca king Atahualpa, later murdering him even though he gave them the large quantities of gold and silver they demanded. Pizarro founded Lima as the capital of Peru 1535. A feud then began among the Spanish leaders, and Pizarro was assassinated.

pizzicato (Italian "pinched") in music, an instruction to pluck a bowed stringed instrument (such as the violin) with the fingers.

placebo (Latin "I will please") any harmless substance, often called a "sugar pill," that has no chemotherapeutic value and yet produces physiological changes.

The use of placebos in medicine is limited to drug trials, where a placebo is given alongside the substance being tested, to compare effects. The "placebo effect," first named in 1945, demonstrates the control "mind" exerts over "matter," including causing changes in blood pressure, perceived pain, and rates of healing. Recent research finds the release of certain neurotransmitting substances in the production of the placebo effect.

placenta organ that attaches the developing ⟂embryo or ⟂fetus to the ⟂uterus in placental mammals (mammals other than marsupials, platypuses, and echidnas). Composed of maternal and embryonic tissue, it links the blood supply of the embryo to the blood supply of the mother, allowing the exchange of oxygen, nutrients, and waste products. The two blood systems are not in direct contact, but are separated by thin membranes, with materials diffusing across from one system to the other. The placenta also produces hormones that maintain and regulate pregnancy. It is shed as part of the afterbirth.

It is now understood that a variety of materials, including drugs and viruses, can pass across the placental membrane. HIV, the infection agent that causes ⟂AIDS, can be transmitted in this way.

The tissue in plants that joins the ovary to the ovules is also called a placenta.

placer deposit detrital concentration of an economically important mineral, such as gold, but also other minerals such as cassiterite, chromite, and platinum metals. The mineral grains become concentrated during transport by water or wind because they are more dense than other detrital minerals such as quartz, and (like quartz) they are relatively resistant to chemical breakdown. Examples are the Witwatersrand gold deposits of South Africa, which are gold- and uranium-bearing conglomerates laid down by ancient rivers, and the placer tin deposits of the Malay Peninsula.

plague disease transmitted by fleas (carried by the black rat) which infect the sufferer with the bacillus *Pasteurella pestis*. An early symptom is swelling of lymph nodes, usually in the armpit and groin; such swellings are called "buboes," hence **bubonic** plague. It causes virulent blood poisoning and the death rate is high.

Other and even more virulent forms of plague are **septicaemic** and **pneumonic**; the latter was fatal before the introduction of sulfa drugs and antibiotics. Outbreaks of plague still occur, mostly in poor countries, but never to the extent seen in the late Middle Ages. After the ⟂Black Death in the 14th century, plague remained endemic for the next three centuries, the most notorious outbreak being the Great Plague of London in 1665, when about 100,000 of the 400,000 inhabitants died.

plaice any of various flatfishes of the flounder group, especially the genera *Pleuronectes* and *Hippoglossoides*. The American plaice *H. platessoides* grows to 2.5 ft/80 cm, and is valuable commercially.

plain or **grassland** land, usually flat, upon which grass predominates. The plains cover large areas of the Earth's surface, especially between the deserts of the tropics and the rainforests of the equator, and have rain in one season only. In such regions the climate belts move north and south during the year, bringing rainforest conditions at one time and desert conditions at another. Examples include the North European Plain, the High Plains of the US and Canada, and the Russian Plain also known as the steppe.

Plains Indian member of any of the North American Indian peoples of the Great Plains, which extend over 2,000 mi/3,000 km from Alberta to Texas. The Plains Indians were drawn from diverse linguistic stocks fringing the Plains but shared many cultural traits, especially the nomadic hunting of bison herds once horses became available in the 18th century. The various groups include Blackfoot, Cheyenne, Comanche, Pawnee, and the Dakota or Sioux.

plainsong ancient chant of the Christian church first codified by Ambrose, bishop of Milan, and then by Pope Gregory in the 6th century. See ⟂Gregorian chant.

Planck Max 1858–1947. German physicist who framed the quantum theory 1900. His research into the manner in which heated bodies radiate energy led him to report that energy is emitted only in indivisible amounts, called quanta, the magnitudes of which are proportional to the frequency of the radiation. His discovery ran counter to Classical physics and is held to have marked the commencement of the modern science. Nobel Prize for Physics 1918.

Planck's constant in physics, a fundamental constant (symbol h) that is the energy of one quantum of electromagnetic radiation (the smallest possible "packet" of energy; see ⟂quantum theory) divided by the frequency of its radiation. Its value is 6.626196×10^{-34} joule seconds.

planet large celestial body in orbit around a star, composed of rock, metal, or gas. There are nine planets in the Solar System: Mercury, Venus, Earth, Mars, Jupiter, Saturn, Neptune, Uranus, and Pluto. The inner four, called the **terrestrial planets**, are small and rocky, and include the planet Earth. The outer planets, with the exception of Pluto, are called the giant planets, large balls of rock, liquid, and gas; the largest is Jupiter, which contains more than twice as much mass as all the other planets combined. Planets do not produce light, but reflect the light of their parent star.

planetarium complex optical projection device by means of which the motions of stars and planets are reproduced on a domed ceiling representing the sky.

Also, a building housing such a device, usually with auditoriums and scheduled lectures. About 60 such planetariums exist in the US.

planetary nebula shell of gas thrown off by a star at the end of its life. Planetary nebulae have nothing to do with planets. They were named by William Herschel, who thought their rounded shape resembled the disk of a planet. After a star such as the Sun has expanded to become a ⟩red giant, its outer layers are ejected into space to form a planetary nebula, leaving the core as a ⟩white dwarf at the center.

planetesimal body of rock in space, smaller than a planet, attracted to other such bodies during planet formation. According to modern solar nebula theory, the Sun and the planets are thought to have formed from a rotating dust cloud generated by a supernova explosion. On condensation, this cloud formed a central sun and a rotating disk, the material of which separated into rings of dust grains that began to stick together. Larger and larger clumps formed in each ring and eventually collected into bodies the size of present-day asteroids, called planetesimals. After numerous collisions, these bodies eventually formed the nucleus of the various planets of our Solar System.

A once-popular theory, called the planetesimal theory, held that planetesimals were formed from giant tongues of solar material torn from a preexisting sun by the gravitational attraction of a passing star. These planetesimals then ended up in orbits around the leftover sun in the plane of the passing star. As in the modern theory, the planetesimals then collided and coalesced into the present planets.

planimeter simple integrating instrument for measuring the area of a regular or irregular plane surface. It consists of two hinged arms: one is kept fixed and the other is traced around the boundary of the area. This actuates a small graduated wheel; the area is calculated from the wheel's change in position.

plankton small, often microscopic, forms of plant and animal life that live in the upper layers of fresh and salt water, and are an important source of food for larger animals. Marine plankton is concentrated in areas where rising currents bring mineral salts to the surface.

plant organism that carries out ⟩photosynthesis, has cellulose cell walls and complex cells, and is immobile. A few parasitic plants have lost the ability to photosynthesize but are still considered to be plants.

Plants are autotrophs, that is, they make carbohydrates from water and carbon dioxide, and are the primary producers in all food chains, so that all animal life is dependent on them. They play a vital part in the carbon cycle, removing carbon dioxide from the atmosphere and generating oxygen. The study of plants is known as botany.

Many of the lower plants (the algae and bryophytes) consist of a simple body, or thallus, on which the organs of reproduction are borne. Simplest of all are the threadlike algae, for example *Spirogyra*, which consist of a chain of cells. The seaweeds (algae) and mosses and liverworts (bryophytes) represent a further development, with simple, multicellular bodies that have specially modified areas in which the reproductive organs are carried. Higher in the morphological scale are the ferns, club mosses, and horsetails (pteridophytes). Ferns produce leaflike fronds bearing sporangia on their undersurface in which the spores are carried. The spores are freed and germinate to produce small independent bodies carrying the sexual organs; thus the fern, like other pteridophytes and some seaweeds, has two quite separate generations in its life cycle (see ⟩alternation of generations).

The pteridophytes have special supportive water-conducting tissues, which identify them as vascular plants, a group which includes all seed plants, that is the gymnosperms (conifers, yews, cycads, and ginkgos) and the angiosperms (flowering plants).

The seed plants are the largest group, and structurally the most complex. They are usually divided into three parts: root, stem, and leaves. Stems grow above or below ground. Their cellular structure is designed to carry water and salts from the roots to the leaves in the ⟩xylem, and sugars from the leaves to the roots in the ⟩phloem. The leaves manufacture the food of the plant by means of photosynthesis, which occurs in the ⟩chloroplasts they contain. Flowers and cones are modified leaves arranged in groups, enclosing the reproductive organs from which the fruits and seeds result.

Plantagenet English royal house, reigning 1154–1399, whose name comes from the nickname of Geoffrey, Count of Anjou (1113–1151), father of Henry II, who often wore in his hat a sprig of broom, *planta genista*. In the 1450s, Richard, Duke of York, took "Plantagenet" as a surname to emphasize his superior claim to the throne over Henry VI's.

plantain any plant of the genus *Plantago*, family Plantaginaceae. The great plantain *P. major* has oval leaves, grooved stalks, and spikes of green flowers with purple anthers followed by seeds, which are used in bird food.

The most common introduced species is *P. lanceolata*, native to Europe and Asia and a widespread weed in Australia, Europe, and America. Many other species are troublesome weeds. A type of ⟩banana is also known as plantain.

plantation large farm or estate where commercial production of one crop—such as rubber (in Malaysia), palm oil (in Nigeria), or tea (in Sri Lanka)—is carried out. Plantations are usually owned by large companies, often ⟩multinational corporations, and run by an estate manager. Many plantations were established in countries under colonial rule, using slave labor.

plant classification taxonomy or classification of plants. Originally the plant kingdom included bacteria, diatoms, dinoflagellates, fungi, and slime molds, but these are not now thought of as plants. The groups that are always classified as plants are the bryophytes (mosses and liverworts), pteridophytes (ferns, horsetails, and club mosses), gymnosperms (conifers, yews, cycads, and ginkgos), and angiosperms (flowering plants). The angiosperms are split into monocotyledons (for example, orchids, grasses, lilies) and dicotyledons (for example, oak, buttercup, geranium, and daisy).

The basis of plant classification was established by the Swedish naturalist Carolus ⟩Linnaeus. Among the angiosperms, it is largely based on the number and arrangement of the flower parts.

The unicellular algae, such as *Chlamydomonas*, are often now put with the protists (single-celled organisms) instead of the plants. Some classification schemes even classify the multicellular algae (seaweeds and freshwater weeds) in a new kingdom, the Protoctista, along with the protists.

plant hormone substance produced by a plant that has a marked effect on its growth, flowering, leaf fall, fruit ripening, or some other process. Examples include ⟩auxin, ⟩gibberellin, ⟩ethylene, and ⟩cytokinin.

planets

planet	main constituents	atmosphere	average distance from Sun in millions of km	time for one orbit in Earth-years	diameter in thousands of km	average density if density of water is 1 unit
Mercury	rocky, ferrous	–	58	0.241	4.88	5.4
Venus	rocky, ferrous	carbon dioxide	108	0.615	12.10	5.2
Earth	rocky, ferrous	nitrogen, oxygen	150	1.00	12.76	5.5
Mars	rocky	carbon dioxide	228	1.88	6.78	3.9
Jupiter	liquid hydrogen, helium	–	778	11.86	142.80	1.3
Saturn	hydrogen, helium	–	1,427	29.46	120.00	0.7
Uranus	icy, hydrogen, helium	hydrogen, helium	2,870	84.00	50.80	1.3
Neptune	icy, hydrogen, helium	hydrogen, helium	4,497	164.80	48.60	1.8
Pluto	icy, rocky	methane	5,900	248.50	2.25	about 2

Unlike animal hormones, these substances are not produced by a particular area of the plant body, and they may be less specific in their effects. It has therefore been suggested that they should not be described as hormones at all.

plaque any abnormal deposit on a body surface, especially the thin, transparent film of sticky protein (called mucin) and bacteria on tooth surfaces. If not removed, this film forms tartar (calculus), promotes tooth decay, and leads to gum disease. Another form of plaque is a deposit of fatty or fibrous material in the walls of blood vessels that can block blood flow or break free to form blood clots.

plasma in biology, the liquid part of the ⟡blood.

plasma in physics, an ionized gas produced at extremely high temperatures, as in the Sun and other stars, which contains positive and negative charges in approximately equal numbers. It is a good electrical conductor. In thermonuclear reactions the plasma produced is confined through the use of magnetic fields.

plasmapheresis removal from the body of large quantities of blood, which is then divided into its components (plasma and blood cells) by centrifugal force in a continuous-flow cell separator. Once separated, the elements of the blood are isolated and available for specific treatment. Restored blood is then returned to the venous system of the patient. Sometimes, donated blood is used.

plasmid small, mobile piece of ⟡DNA found in bacteria and used in ⟡genetic engineering. Plasmids are separate from the bacterial chromosome but still multiply during cell growth. Their size ranges from 3% to 20% of the size of the chromosome. There is usually only one copy of a single plasmid per cell, but occasionally several are found. Some plasmids carry "fertility genes" that enable them to move from one bacterium to another and transfer genetic information between strains. Plasmid genes determine a wide variety of bacterial properties including resistance to antibiotics and the ability to produce toxins.

Plassey, Battle of victory in India June 23, 1757, for the British under Robert ⟡Clive, which brought Bengal under British rule.

plaster of Paris form of calcium sulfate, obtained from gypsum; it is mixed with water for making casts and molds.

plastic any of the stable synthetic materials that are fluid at some stage in their manufacture, when they can be shaped, and that later set to rigid or semirigid solids. Plastics today are chiefly derived from petroleum. Most are polymers, made up of long chains of identical molecules.

Processed by extrusion, injection-molding, vacuum-forming and compression, plastics emerge in consistencies ranging from hard and inflexible to soft and rubbery. They replace an increasing number of natural substances, being lightweight, easy to clean, durable, and capable of being rendered very strong—for example, by the addition of carbon fibers—for building aircraft and other engineering projects.

Thermoplastics soften when warmed, then reharden as they cool. Examples of thermoplastics include polystyrene, a clear plastic used in kitchen utensils or (when expanded into a "foam" by gas injection) in insulation and ceiling tiles; polyethylene (polyethene), used for containers and wrapping; and polyvinyl chloride (PVC), used for drainpipes, floor tiles, audio disks, shoes, and handbags.

Thermosets remain rigid once set, and do not soften when warmed. They include bakelite, used in electrical insulation and telephone receivers; epoxy resins, used in paints and varnishes, to laminate wood, and as adhesives; polyesters, used in synthetic textile fibers and, with fiberglass reinforcement, in car bodies and boat hulls; and polyurethane, prepared in liquid form as a paint or varnish, and in foam form for upholstery and in lining materials (where it may be a fire hazard). One group of plastics, the silicones, are chemically inert, have good electrical properties, and repel water. Silicones find use in silicone rubber, paints, electrical insulation materials, laminates, waterproofing for walls, stain-resistant textiles, and cosmetics.

Shape-memory polymers are plastics that can be crumpled or flattened and will resume their original shape when heated. They include trans-polyisoprene and polynorbornene. The initial shape is determined by heating the polymer to over 95°F/35°C and pouring it into a metal mold. The shape can be altered with boiling water and the substance solidifies again when its temperature falls below 95°F/35°C.

Biodegradable plastics are increasingly in demand: Biopol was developed in 1990. Soil microorganisms are used to build the plastic in their cells from carbon dioxide and water (it constitutes 80% of their cell tissue). The unused parts of the microorganism are dissolved away by heating in water. The discarded plastic can be placed in landfill sites where it breaks back down into carbon dioxide and water. It costs three to five times as much as ordinary plastics to produce.

plastic surgery branch of surgery concerned with the repair of congenital disfigurement and the reconstruction of tissues damaged by disease or injury; and *cosmetic surgery* undergone for reasons of vanity to conform to some aesthetic norm or counter the effects of aging; for example, the removal of bags under the eyes or a double chin.

plastid general name for a cell ⟡organelle of plants that is enclosed by a double membrane and contains a series of internal membranes and vesicles. Plastids contain ⟡DNA and are produced by division of existing plastids. They can be classified into two main groups: the *chromoplasts*, which contain pigments such as carotenes and chlorophyll, and the *leucoplasts*, which are colorless; however, the distinction between the two is not always clear-cut.

⟡Chloroplasts are the major type of chromoplast. They contain chlorophyll, are responsible for the green coloration of most plants, and perform ⟡photosynthesis. Other chromoplasts give flower petals and fruits their distinctive color. Leucoplasts are food-storage bodies and include amyloplasts, found in the roots of many plants, which store large amounts of starch.

Plata, Río de la or *River Plate* estuary in South America into which the rivers Paraná and Uruguay flow; length 200 mi/320 km and width up to 150 mi/240 km. The basin drains much of Argentina, Bolivia, Brazil, Uruguay, and Paraguay, which all cooperate in its development.

Plataea, Battle of battle 479 BC, in which the Greeks defeated the Persians during the ⟡Persian Wars.

plateau elevated area of fairly flat land, or a mountainous region in which the peaks are at the same height. An *intermontane plateau* is one surrounded by mountains. A *piedmont plateau* is one that lies between the mountains and low-lying land. A *continental plateau* rises abruptly from low-lying lands or the sea.

platelet tiny "cell" found in the blood, which helps it to clot. Platelets are not true cells, but membrane-bound cell fragments that bud off from large cells in the bone marrow.

plate tectonics concept that attributes ⟡continental drift and ⟡seafloor spreading to the continual formation and destruction of the outermost layer of the Earth. This layer is seen as consisting of major and minor plates, curved to the planet's spherical shape and with a jigsaw fit to one another. Convection currents within the Earth's mantle produce upwellings of new material along joint lines at the surface, forming ridges (for example, the ⟡Mid-Atlantic Ridge). The new material extends the plates, and these move away from the ridges. Where two plates collide, one overrides the other and the lower is absorbed back into the mantle. These ⟡subduction zones occur in the ocean trenches.

The moving plates consist of the Earth's crust and the topmost solid layer of mantle, together called the lithosphere. The plates move on a mobile layer of the mantle called the asthenosphere. Some plates carry only ocean crust, others also carry continental crust. Only ocean crust is formed at mid-ocean ridges. The continents take little part in the generation and destruction of the plate material and are carried along passively on the moving plates.

The concept of continental drift was first put forward in 1915 by the German geophysicist Alfred Wegener; plate tectonics was formulated by Canadian geophysicist J Tuzo Wilson 1965 and has gained widespread acceptance among earth scientists.

Plath Sylvia 1932–1963. US poet and novelist whose powerful, highly personal poems, often expressing a sense of desolation, are distinguished by their intensity and sharp imagery. Her *Collected Poems* 1981 was awarded a Pulitzer Prize. Her autobiographical novel *The Bell Jar* 1961 deals with the events surrounding a young woman's emotional breakdown.

Plath was born in Boston, Massachusetts, attended Smith College and was awarded a Fulbright scholarship to study at Cambridge University, England, where she met the poet Ted Hughes, whom she married 1956; they separated in 1962. She committed suicide while living in London. Collections of her poems include *The Colossus* 1960 and *Ariel* 1965, published after her death.

platinum (Spanish *platina* "little silver" (*plata* "silver")) heavy, soft, silver-white, malleable and ductile, metallic element, symbol Pt, atomic number 78, atomic weight 195.09. It is the first of a group of six metallic elements (platinum, osmium, iridium, rhodium, ruthenium, and palladium) that possess similar traits, such as resistance to tarnish, corrosion, and attack by acid, and that often occur as free metals (⟡native metals). They often occur in natural alloys with each other, the commonest of which is osmiridium. Both pure and as an alloy, platinum is used in dentistry, jewelry, and as a catalyst.

Plato *c.* 428–347 BC. Greek philosopher, pupil of Socrates, teacher of Aristotle, and founder of the Academy school of philosophy. He was the author of philosophical dialogues on such topics as metaphysics, ethics, and politics. Central to his teachings is the notion of Forms, which are located outside the everyday world—timeless, motionless, and absolutely real.

Plato's philosophy has influenced Christianity and European culture, directly and through Augustine, the Florentine Platonists during the Renaissance, and countless others.

Born of a noble family, he entered politics on the aristocratic side, and in philosophy became a follower of Socrates. He traveled widely after Socrates' death, and founded the educational establishment, the Academy, in order to train a new ruling class.

Of his work, some 30 dialogues survive, intended for performance either to his pupils or to the public. The principal figure in these ethical and philosophical debates is Socrates and the early ones employ the Socratic method, in which he asks questions and traps the students into contradicting themselves; for example, *Iron*, on poetry. Other dialogues include the *Symposium*, on love, *Phaedo*, on immortality, and *Apology and Crito*, on Socrates' trial and death. It is impossible to say whether Plato's Socrates is a faithful representative of the real man or an articulation of Plato's own thought. Plato's philosophy rejects scientific rationalism (establishing facts through experiment) in favor of arguments, because mind, not matter, is fundamental, and material objects are merely imperfect copies of abstract and eternal "ideas." His political philosophy is expounded in two treatises, *The Republic* and *The Laws*, both of which describe ideal states. Platonic love is inspired by a person's best qualities and seeks their development.

platoon in the army, the smallest infantry subunit. It contains 30–40 soldiers and is commanded by a lieutenant or second lieutenant. There are three or four platoons in a company.

platypus monotreme, or egg-laying, mammal *Ornithorhynchus anatinus*, found in Tasmania and E Australia. Semiaquatic, it has small eyes and no external ears, and jaws resembling a duck's beak. It lives in long burrows along river banks, where it lays two eggs in a rough nest. It feeds on water worms and insects, and when full-grown is 2 ft/60 cm long.

Plautus *c.* 254–184 BC. Roman dramatist, born in Umbria, who settled in Rome and worked in a bakery before achieving success as a dramatist. He wrote at least 56 comedies, freely adapted from Greek originals, of which 20 survive. Shakespeare based *The Comedy of Errors* on his *Menaechmi*.

playa temporary lake in a region of interior drainage. Such lakes are common features in arid desert basins fed by intermittent streams. The streams bring dissolved salts to the lakes, and when the lakes shrink during dry spells, the salts precipitate as evaporite deposits.

Player Gary 1935– . South African golfer who won major championships in three decades and the first British Open 1959. A match-play specialist, he won the world title five times.

His total of nine "majors" is the fourth (equal) best of all time. He is renowned for wearing all-black outfits. In the 1980s he was a successful Seniors player.

playing cards a set of small pieces of card with different markings, used in playing games. A standard set consists of a "deck" of 52 cards divided into four suits: hearts, clubs, diamonds, and spades. Within each suit there are 13 cards: nine are numbered (two through to ten), three are called face, picture (or court) cards (jack, queen, and king), and one is called the ace.

Playing cards probably originated in China or India, and first appeared in Europe in 14th-century Italy as the 78 cards (22 emblematic, including "the hanged man," and 56 numerals) of the ◊tarot cards, used both for gaming and in fortune-telling. However, in the 15th century they were reduced to the standard pack of 52 for most games, which include bridge, whist, poker, rummy, and cribbage.

pleadings in law, documents exchanged between the parties to court actions, which set out the facts that form the basis of the case they intend to present in court, and (where relevant) stating what damages or other remedy they are claiming.

plebeian member of the unprivileged class in ancient Rome, composed of aliens, freed slaves, and their descendants. During the 5th–4th centuries BC, plebeians waged a long struggle to win political and social equality with the patricians, eventually securing admission to the offices formerly reserved for patricians.

plebiscite referendum or direct vote by all the electors of a country or district on a specific question. Since the 18th century plebiscites have been employed on many occasions to decide to what country a particular area should belong; for example, in Upper Silesia and elsewhere after World War I, and in the Saar 1935.

Pléiade, La group of seven poets in 16th-century France, led by Pierre Ronsard, who were inspired by Classical models to improve French verse. Their name is derived from the seven stars of the Pleiades group.

Pleiades in astronomy, a star cluster about 400 light-years away in the constellation Taurus, representing the Seven Sisters of Greek mythology. Its brightest stars (highly luminous, blue-white giants only a few million years old) are visible to the naked eye, but there are many fainter ones.

The stars of the Pleiades are still surrounded by traces of the reflection ◊nebula from which they formed, visible on long-exposure photographs.

Pleiades in Greek mythology, the seven daughters of the giant Atlas who asked to be changed into a cluster of stars to escape the pursuit of the hunter Orion.

pleiotropy process whereby a given gene influences several different observed characteristics of an organism.

Pleistocene first epoch of the Quaternary period of geological time, beginning 1.8 million years ago and ending 10,000 years ago.

TF	Tropical fresh water
F	Fresh water
T	Tropical salt water
S	Salt water in Summer
W	Salt water in Winter
WNA	Winter in North Atlantic
LR	Lloyd's Register

Plimsoll line

Glaciers were abundant during the ice age of this period, and humans evolved into modern *Homo sapiens sapiens* about 100,000 years ago.

Plekhanov Georgi Valentinovich 1857–1918. Russian Marxist revolutionary and theorist, founder of the ◊Menshevik party. He led the first populist demonstration in St Petersburg, became a Marxist and, with Lenin, edited the newspaper *Iskra* (spark). In 1903 his opposition to Lenin led to the Bolshevik–Menshevik split.

After the Bolshevik victory he lived in Finland.

plesiosaur prehistoric carnivorous marine reptile of the Jurassic and Cretaceous periods, which reached a length of 36 ft/12 m, and had a long neck and paddlelike limbs. The pliosaurs evolved from the plesiosaurs.

Plessy v Ferguson US Supreme Court decision 1896 dealing with state-imposed segregation laws. Homer Plessy brought this case to the Supreme Court to test Louisiana segregation laws after he was arrested for refusing to leave a whites-only train car. He argued that such discrimination was prohibited by the 13th and 14th Amendments, which granted equal protection under the law. The Court ruled 8 to 1 against Plessy, holding that the 13th Amendment only prohibited slavery and that the 14th Amendment guaranteed only political but not social rights. The Court accepted a doctrine of separate but equal accommodations, a standard for segregation maintained until 1954 (see ◊Brown v Board of Education).

pleurisy inflammation of the pleura, the thin, secretory membrane that covers the lungs and lines the space in which they rest. Pleurisy is nearly always due to bacterial or viral infection, which can be treated with antibiotics. It renders breathing painful.

Normally the two lung surfaces move easily on one another, lubricated by small quantities of fluid. When the pleura is inflamed, the surfaces may dry up or stick together, making breathing difficult and painful. Alternatively, a large volume of fluid may collect in the pleural cavity, the space between the two surfaces, and pus (in this case called empyema) may accumulate. Pleurisy occurs in pneumonia and tuberculosis, but may also be a consequence of scarlet fever or rheumatism.

Plexiglas trademark for a clear, lightweight, tough plastic first produced in the US 1930.

Its chemical name is polymethylmethacrylate (PMMA).

Plimsoll line loading mark painted on the hull of merchant ships, first suggested by English social reformer Samuel Plimsoll (1824–1898). It shows the depth to which a vessel may be safely (and legally) loaded.

Pliny the Elder (Gaius Plinius Secundus) *c.* AD 23–79. Roman scientist and historian; only his works on astronomy, geography, and natural history survive. He was killed in an eruption of Vesuvius, the volcano near Naples.

Pliny the Younger (Gaius Plinius Caecilius Secundus) *c.* AD 61–113. Roman administrator, nephew of Pliny the Elder, whose correspondence is of great interest. Among his surviving letters are those describing the eruption of Vesuvius, his uncle's death, and his correspondence with the emperor ⟡Trajan.

Pliocene ("almost recent") fifth and last epoch of the Tertiary period of geological time, 5–1.8 million years ago. The earliest hominid, the humanlike ape "australopithecines," evolved in Africa.

See also ⟡human species.

pliosaur prehistoric carnivorous marine reptile, descended from the plesiosaurs, but with a shorter neck, and longer head and jaws. It was approximately 15 ft/5 m long. In 1989 the skeleton of one of a previously unknown species was discovered in northern Queensland, Australia. A hundred million years ago, it lived in the sea which once covered the Great Artesian Basin.

PLO abbreviation for ⟡*Palestine Liberation Organization*.

Ploeşti industrial city (textiles, paper, petrochemicals; oil center) in SE Romania; population (1985) 234,000.

plotter or *graph plotter* device that draws pictures or diagrams under computer control. Plotters are often used for producing business charts, architectural plans, and engineering drawings. *Flatbed plotters* move a pen up and down across a flat drawing surface, whereas *roller plotters* roll the drawing paper past the pen as it moves from side to side.

Plovdiv industrial city (textiles, chemicals, leather, tobacco) in Bulgaria, on the River Maritsa; population (1990) 379,100. Conquered by Philip of Macedon in the 4th century BC, it was known as *Philippopolis* ("Philip's city").

plover any shore bird of the family Charadriidae, found worldwide. Plovers are usually black or brown above, and white below, and have short bills. The largest of the ringed plovers is the killdeer *Charadrius vociferus*, so called because of its cry.

The semipalmated plover *C. semipalmatus* reaches 7 in/18 cm, has a black neck ring, and is common on beaches and lakeshores.

plow the most important agricultural implement used for tilling the soil. The plow dates from about 3500 BC, when oxen were used to pull a simple wooden blade, or ard. In about 500 BC the iron share came into use.

By about AD 1000 horses as well as oxen were being used to pull wheeled plows, equipped with a plowshare for cutting a furrow, a blade for forming the walls of the furrow (called a colter), and a moldboard to turn a furrow. In the 18th century an innovation introduced by Robert Ransome (1753–1830) led to a reduction in the number of animals used to draw a plow: from an 8–12 oxer, or 6 horses, to a 2- or 4-horse plow. Steam plows came into use in some areas in the 1860s, superseded half a century later by tractor-drawn plows. The present plow consists of many "bottoms," each comprising a curved plowshare and angled moldboard. The bottom is designed so that it slices into the ground and turns the soil over.

plum tree *Prunus domestica*, bearing edible fruits that are smooth-skinned with a flat kernel. There are many varieties, including the Victoria, czar, egg-plum, greengage, and damson; the sloe *P. spinosa* is closely related. Dried plums are known as prunes.

plumule part of a seed embryo that develops into the shoot, bearing the first true leaves of the plant.

plur. in grammar, the abbreviation for *plural*.

pluralism in political science, the view that decision-making in contemporary liberal democracies is the outcome of competition among several interest groups in a political system characterized by free elections, representative institutions, and open access to the organs of power. This concept is opposed by corporatism and other approaches that perceive power to be centralized in the state and its principal elites (the Establishment).

pluralism in philosophy, the belief that reality consists of several different elements, not just two—matter and mind—as in ⟡dualism.

Plutarch *c.* AD 46–120. Greek biographer whose *Parallel Lives* has the life stories of pairs of Greek and Roman soldiers and politicians, followed by comparisons between the two. Thomas North's 1579 translation inspired Shakespeare's Roman plays.

Plutarch was born in Chaeronea. He lectured on philosophy in Rome and was appointed procurator of Greece by Emperor Hadrian.

Pluto in astronomy, the smallest and, usually, outermost planet of the Solar System. The existence of Pluto was predicted by calculation by Percival Lowell and the planet was located by Clyde ⟡Tombaugh 1930. It orbits the Sun every 248.5 years at an average distance of 3.6 billion mi/5.8 billion km. Its highly elliptical orbit occasionally takes it within the orbit of Neptune, as in 1979–99. Pluto has a diameter of about 1,400 mi/2,300 km, and a mass about 0.002 of that of Earth. It is of low density, composed of rock and ice, with frozen methane on its surface and a thin atmosphere.

Charon, Pluto's moon, was discovered 1978, revolving around Pluto with the same period as Pluto's rotation, remaining over the same point on Pluto's surface and showing the same face. The pair may be a double planet system.

Pluto in Greek mythology, the lord of the underworld (Roman Dis). He was the brother of Zeus and Poseidon.

plutonic rock igneous rock derived from magma that has cooled and solidified deep in the crust of the Earth; granites and gabbros are examples of plutonic rocks.

plutonium silvery-white, radioactive, metallic element of the ⟡actinide series, symbol Pu, atomic number 94, atomic weight 239.13. It occurs in nature in minute quantities in ⟡pitchblende and other ores, but is produced in quantity only synthetically. It has six allotropic forms (see ⟡allotropy) and is one of three fissile elements (elements capable of splitting into other elements—the others are thorium and uranium). The element has awkward physical properties and is the most toxic substance known.

Its fissile isotope Pu-239 is usually made in ⟡breeder reactors by bombarding uranium-238 with neutrons. Because Pu-239 is so easily synthesized from abundant uranium, it has been produced in large quantities (hundreds of thousands of pounds) by the weapons industry. It has a long half-life (24,000 years) during which time it remains highly toxic. It is dangerous to handle, difficult to store, and impossible to dispose of—it has become a human-made menace of global proportions. It was first produced in 1940 by Glenn Seaborg and his team at the University of Calilfornia at Berkeley, by bombarding uranium with deuterons; this was the second transuranic element synthesized (after neptunium). It was named by them for the planet Pluto, since it comes after neptunium as the planet Pluto comes after Neptune.

Plymouth city and seaport in Devon, England, at the mouth of the River Plym, with dockyard, barracks, and a naval base at Devonport; population (1981) 244,000.

The city rises north of the Hoe headland where tradition has it that Francis ⟡Drake played bowls before leaving to fight the Spanish Armada. The navigator John Hawkins, Drake, and the *Mayflower* ⟡Pilgrims sailed from Plymouth Sound. The city center was reconstructed after heavy bombing in World War II.

plywood manufactured panel of wood widely used in building. It consists of several thin sheets, or plies, of wood, glued together with the grain (direction of the wood fibers) of one sheet at right angles to the grain of the adjacent plies. This construction gives plywood equal strength in every direction.

PM abbreviation for *prime minister*.

p.m. or *P.M.* abbreviation for *post meridiem* (Latin "after noon").

pneumatic drill drill operated by compressed air, used in mining and tunneling, for drilling shot holes (for explosives), and in road repairs for breaking up pavements. It contains an air-operated piston that delivers hammer blows to the drill bit many times a second. The French engineer Germain Sommeiller (1815–1871) developed the pneumatic drill 1861 for tunneling in the Alps.

pneumatophore erect root that rises up above the soil or water and promotes ⟡gas exchange. Pneumatophores, or breathing roots, are formed by certain swamp-dwelling trees, such as mangroves, since there is little oxygen available to the roots in waterlogged conditions. They have numerous pores or ⟡lenticels over their surface, allowing gas exchange.

pneumectomy surgical removal of all or part of the lung.

pneumoconiosis disease of the lungs caused by dust, especially from coal, asbestos, or silica. Inhaled particles make the lungs gradually fibrous and the victim has difficulty breathing.

pneumonia inflammation of the lungs, generally due to bacterial or viral infection but also to particulate matter or gases. It is characterized by a buildup of fluid in the alveoli, the clustered air sacs (at the end of the air passages) where oxygen exchange takes place.

Symptoms include fever and pain in the chest. With widespread availability of antibiotics, infectious pneumonia is much less common than it was. However, it remains a dire threat to patients whose immune systems are suppressed (including transplant recipients and AIDS and cancer victims) and to those who are critically ill or injured. Pneumocystis pneumonia is a leading cause of death in AIDS.

pneumothorax the presence of air in the pleural cavity, between a lung and the chest wall. It may be due to a penetrating injury of the lung or to lung disease, or it may arise without apparent cause. Prevented from expanding normally, the lung is liable to collapse.

Pnom Penh alternate form of ⬦Phnom Penh, capital of Cambodia.

Po longest river in Italy, flowing from the Cottian Alps to the Adriatic; length 415 mi/ 668 km. Its valley is fertile and contains natural gas. The river is heavily polluted with nitrates, phosphates, and arsenic.

PO abbreviation for *Post Office*.

Pobeda, Pik highest peak in the ⬦Tian Shan mountain range on the Kyrgyz–Chinese border, at 24,406 ft/7,439 m.

Pocahontas *c.* 1595–1617. American Indian woman alleged to have saved the life of English colonist John Smith when he was captured by her father, Powhatan. Pocahontas was kidnapped 1613 by an Englishman, Samuel Argall, and she later married colonist John Rolfe (1585–1622) and was entertained as a princess at the English Court. Her marriage and conversion to Christianity brought about a period of peaceful relations between Indians and settlers, but she died of smallpox after her return to Virginia.

pochard any of various diving ducks found in Europe and North America, especially the genus *Aythya*.

In North America, the canvasback *A. valisineria*, the redhead *A. americana*, the ring-necked *A. collaris*, and two species of scaup, *A. marila* and *A. affinis*, are pochards.

Po Chü-i alternative transliteration of ⬦Bo Zhu Yi, Chinese poet.

pod in botany, a type of fruit that is characteristic of legumes (plants belonging to the Leguminosae family), such as peas and beans. It develops from a single ⬦carpel and splits down both sides when ripe to release the seeds.

In certain species the seeds may be ejected explosively due to uneven drying of the fruit wall, which sets up tensions within the fruit. In agriculture, the name "legume" is used for the crops of the pea and bean family. "Grain legume" refers to those that are grown mainly for their dried seeds, such as lentils, chick peas, and soybeans.

podiatry the medical profession that deals with the specialized care of feet. Some podiatric treatments involve the use of orthopedic devices to correct fallen arches or improve improper positioning of feet during walking.

podzol or *podsol* type of light-colored soil found predominantly under coniferous forests and moorlands in cool regions where rainfall exceeds evaporation. The constant downward movement of water leaches nutrients from the upper layers, making podzols poor agricultural soils.

The leaching of minerals such as iron, lime, and alumina leads to the formation of a bleached zone, often also depleted of clay. These minerals can accumulate lower down

the soil profile to form a hard, impermeable layer that restricts the drainage of water through the soil.

Poe Edgar Allan 1809–1849. US writer and poet. His short stories are renowned for their horrific atmosphere, as in "The Fall of the House of Usher" 1839 and "The Masque of the Red Death" 1842, and for their acute reasoning (ratiocination), as in "The Gold Bug" 1843 and "The Murders in the Rue Morgue" 1841 (in which the investigators Legrand and Dupin anticipate Conan Doyle's Sherlock Holmes). His poems include "The Raven" 1845.

His novel, *The Narrative of Arthur Gordon Pym of Nantucket* 1838, has attracted critical attention.

Born in Boston, he was orphaned 1811 and taken in by the wealthy Allan family of Richmond, Virginia. He was, however, disowned by the Allans when he was expelled from both the University of Virginia and West Point. Poe joined the army but was court-martialed for neglect of duty. Although he already had published *Tammerlane and Other Poems* 1827, *Al Aaraaf* 1829, and *Poems* 1831, he failed to earn a living by writing. He became editor of the *Southern Literary Messenger* in Richmond. In 1847 his wife died, an event he commemorated in his poem "Annabel Lee." He became an alcoholic and exhausted himself, dying at age 40. Poe was the first US poet to become internationally known and admired. His verse, of haunting lyric beauty, in, for example, "Ulalume" 1847 and "The Bells" 1849, influenced the French Symbolists.

poet laureate poet of the British royal household, so called because of the laurel wreath awarded to eminent poets in the Greco-Roman world.

Early poets with unofficial status were Geoffrey Chaucer, John Skelton, Edmund Spenser, Samuel Daniel, and Ben Jonson. Ted Hughes was appointed poet laureate in 1984.

Other modern-day poet laureates include Wordsworth, Tennyson, Cecil Day Lewis, and John Betjeman.

poetry the imaginative expression of emotion, thought, or narrative, frequently in metrical form and often using figurative language. Poetry has traditionally been distinguished from prose (ordinary written language) by rhyme or the rhythmical arrangement of words (meter), although the distinction is not always clear-cut. A distinction is made between lyrical, or songlike, poetry (sonnet, ode, elegy, pastoral), and narrative, or story-telling, poetry (ballad, lay, epic).

Poetic form has also been used as a vehicle for satire, parody, and expositions of philosophical, religious, and practical subjects.

Poetry: A Magazine of Verse influential US literary magazine. One of the first "little magazines" of the early 20th century, and still published today, it was founded in Chicago 1912 by Harriet Monroe (1860–1936) with the poet Ezra Pound as foreign editor. It introduced many major modern poets, including T S Eliot, Wallace Stevens, William Carlos Williams, Marianne Moore, and Carl Sandburg, and it printed the manifesto of Imagism.

pogrom (Russian "destruction") unprovoked violent attack on an ethnic group, particularly Jews, carried out with official sanction. The Russian pogroms against Jews began 1881, after the assassination of Tsar Alexander II, and again in 1903–06; persecution of the Jews

remained constant until the Russian Revolution. Later there were pogroms in E Europe, especially in Poland after 1918, and in Germany under Hitler (see ⬦Holocaust).

poikilothermy the condition in which an animal's body temperature is largely dependent on the temperature of the air or water in which it lives. It is characteristic of all animals except birds and mammals, which maintain their body temperatures by ⬦homeothermy (they are "warm-blooded").

Poikilotherms have behavioral means of temperature control; they can warm themselves up by basking in the sun, or shivering, and can cool themselves down by sheltering from the sun under a rock or by bathing in water.

Poikilotherms are often referred to as "coldblooded animals," but this is not really correct: their internal temperatures, regulated by behavioral means, are often as high as those of birds and mammals during the times they need to be active for feeding and reproductive purposes, and may be higher, for example in very hot climates. The main difference is that their body temperatures fluctuate more than those of homeotherms.

Poincaré Jules Henri 1854–1912. French mathematician who developed the theory of differential equations and was a pioneer in ⬦relativity theory. He suggested that Isaac Newton's laws for the behavior of the universe could be the exception rather than the rule. However, the calculation was so complex and time-consuming that he never managed to realize its full implication.

He also published the first paper devoted entirely to ⬦topology (the branch of geometry that deals with the unchanged properties of figures).

Poincaré Raymond Nicolas Landry 1860–1934. French politician, prime minister 1912–13, president 1913–20, and again prime minister 1922–24 (when he ordered the occupation of the Ruhr, Germany) and 1926–29.

Poindexter John Marlan 1936– . US rear admiral and Republican government official. In 1981 he joined the Reagan administration's National Security Council (NSC) and became national security adviser 1985. As a result of the ⬦Irangate scandal, Poindexter was forced to resign 1986, along with his assistant, Oliver North.

A doctor in nuclear physics, Poindexter served in the US Navy, rising to become deputy head of naval educational training 1978–81. From 1983 he worked closely with the NSC head, Robert McFarlane, and took over when McFarlane left Dec 1985. Poindexter retired from the navy Dec 1987, and was found guilty on all counts April 1990, but his convictions were overturned on appeal Nov 1991.

poinsettia or ***Christmas flower*** winter-flowering shrub *Euphorbia pulcherrima*, with large red leaves encircling small greenish-yellow flowers. It is native to Mexico and tropical America and is a popular houseplant in North America and Europe.

pointe (French "toe of shoe") in dance, the tip of the toe. A dancer *sur les pointes* is dancing on her toes in blocked shoes, as popularized by the Italian dancer Marie ⬦Taglioni 1832.

Pointe-Noire chief port of the Congo, formerly (1950–58) the capital; population (1984) 297,000. Industries include oil refining and shipbuilding.

pointer breed of dog, often white mixed with black, tan, or dark brown, about 2 ft/60 cm tall, and weighing 62 lb/28 kg.

Pointers were bred to scent the position of game and indicate it by standing, nose pointed toward it, often with one forefoot raised, in silence.

Pointillism technique in oil painting developed in the 1880s by the Neo-Impressionist Georges Seurat. He used small dabs of pure color laid side by side to create an impression of shimmering light when viewed from a distance.

pointillism in music, a form of 1950s ⟡serialism in which melody and harmony are replaced by complexes of isolated tones.

point of sale in business premises, the point where a sale is transacted—for example, a supermarket checkout. In conjunction with electronic funds transfer, point of sale is part of the terminology of "cashless shopping," enabling buyers to transfer funds directly from their bank accounts to the shop's.

poise unit (symbol P) of dynamic ⟡viscosity (the property of liquids that determines how readily they flow). It is equal to one dyne-second per square centimeter. For most liquids the centipoise (one hundredth of a poise) is used. Water at 68°F/20°C has a viscosity of 1.002 centipoise.

Poiseuille's formula in physics, a relationship describing the rate of flow of a fluid through a narrow tube. For a capillary (very narrow) tube of length l and radius r with a pressure difference p between its ends, and a liquid of ⟡viscosity η, the velocity of flow expressed as the volume per second is $\pi p r^4/8l\,\eta$. The formula was devised 1843 by French physicist Jean Louis Poiseuille (1799–1869).

poison or **toxin** any chemical substance that, when introduced into or applied to the body, is capable of injuring health or destroying life. The liver removes some poisons from the blood. The majority of poisons may be divided into **corrosives**, such as sulfuric, nitric, and hydrochloric acids; **irritants**, including arsenic and copper sulfate; **narcotics** such as opium, and carbon monoxide; and **narcotico-irritants** from any substances of plant origin including carbolic acid and tobacco.

Corrosives all burn and destroy the parts of the body with which they come into contact; irritants have an irritating effect on the stomach and bowels; narcotics affect the brainstem and spinal cord, inducing a stupor; and narcotico-irritants can cause intense irritations and finally act as narcotics.

In noncorrosive poisoning every effort is made to remove the poison from the system as soon as possible—usually by vomiting induced by an emetic. For some corrosive and irritant poisons there are chemical antidotes, but for recently developed poisons (for example, the herbicide paraquat) that produce proliferative changes in the system, there is no antidote. Drugs (legal and illegal), including nicotine and alcohol, are toxins to the human body.

In most countries the sale of poisons, as such, is carefully controlled by law and, in general, only qualified and registered pharmacists and medical practitioners may dispense them; however, industrial and agricultural poisons are dumped into our waters and onto our lands, entering the food chain, and poisoning us and our planet.

poison ivy North American plant *Rhus radicans* of the cashew family, having leaves composed of three leaflets, yellowish flowers, and ivory-colored, berrylike fruit. The leaves are variable and may be dull or shiny, leathery or thin, toothed or smooth-edged. It can grow as an erect shrub, trailing vine, or climber. All parts of the plant contain a heavy, nonvolatile oil that causes inflammation of the skin with itching rash, blisters, and/or swelling in susceptible persons. Numerous birds feed on the berries.

poison oak any of several North American subspecies of poison ivy *Rhus radicans*. Poison oak always grows as an erect shrub (to 10 in/25 cm tall) with three-parted leaves that are usually blunt-tipped and hairy on both sides. The irritating effects to humans are similar to those of poison ivy.

poison pill in business, a tactic to avoid hostile takeover by making the target unattractive. For example, a company may give a certain class of stockholders the right to have their shares redeemed at a very good price in the event of the company being taken over, thus involving the potential predator in considerable extra cost.

poison sumac shrub or small tree *Rhus vernix* of the cashew family that thrives in a swampy habitat. Its large leaves are composed of 7–13 pointed leaflets, and it bears clusters of white globular fruit. All its parts contain a dangerous skin irritant more virulent than that of poison ivy or poison oak.

Poisson Siméon Denis 1781–1840. French applied mathematician. In probability theory he formulated the **Poisson distribution**, which is widely used in probability calculations. He published four treatises and several hundred papers on aspects of physics, including mechanics, heat, electricity and magnetism, elasticity, and astronomy.

Poitier Sidney 1924– . US actor and film director, Hollywood's first black star. His films as an actor include *Something of Value* 1957, *Lilies of the Field* 1963, and *In the Heat of the Night* 1967, and as director *Stir Crazy* 1980.

Poitiers capital of Poitou-Charentes, W France; population (1982) 103,200; products include chemicals and clothing. The Merovingian king Clovis defeated the Visigoths under Alaric here 507; ⟡Charles Martel stemmed the Saracen advance 732, and ⟡Edward the Black Prince of England defeated the French 1356.

Poitou-Charentes region of W central France, comprising the *départements* of Charente, Charente-Maritime, Deux-Sèvres, and Vienne

capital Poitiers

area 9,959 sq mi/25,800 sq km

population (1986) 1,584,000

products dairy products, wheat, chemicals, metal goods; brandy is made at Cognac

history once part of the Roman province of Aquitaine, this region was captured by the Visigoths in the 5th century and taken by the Franks AD 507. The area was contested by the English and French until the end of the Hundred Years' War in 1453, when it was incorporated into France by Charles II.

poker card game of US origin, in which two to eight people play (usually for stakes) and try to obtain a "hand" of five cards ranking higher than those of their opponents. The best scoring hand wins the "pot."

Standard kinds of poker are five-card draw and stud. In draw poker, players receive five cards face down and then, after a round of betting, may "discard" up to three cards and "draw" replacement cards from the cards not dealt, in an attempt to improve their hands. A final round of betting follows. In stud, players receive one card (five-card stud) or two cards (seven-card stud) face down. Betting is done round by round as the remaining cards are dealt face up; players surmise the odds by viewing the exposed cards. The value of hands, in ascending order, is as follows: high card, one pair, two pairs, three-of-a-kind, straight (five cards in consecutive numerical order), flush (five cards of the same suit), full-house (three-of-a-kind plus 1 pair), four-of-a-kind, straight flush (5 cards of the same suit in consecutive order). Many variations exist; sometimes "wild cards" (such as deuces or one-eyed jacks) are designated.

pokeweed tall North American herbaceous plant *Phytolacca americana* of the family Phytolaccaceae. It has pale greenish flowers and purple berries, the seeds of which are poisonous. North American Indians used the juice of the berries for staining.

Poland country in E Europe, bounded N by the Baltic Sea, E by Lithuania, Belarus, and Ukraine, S by Czechoslovakia, and W by Germany.

government Under the revised constitution adopted 1990–91, Poland has a two-chamber legislature, comprising a 460-member lower assembly, the Sejm (parliament), and a 100-member upper chamber, the Senate. Deputies are elected for four-year terms by means of proportional representation at the district, county, and national levels in free, multiparty contests. The Sejm passes bills, adopts the state budget and economic plan, and appoints a 24-member executive council of ministers, headed by a chair, or prime minister. The Senate has the power of veto in specified areas, which can be overridden by a two-thirds Sejm vote. The president is directly elected for a maximum of two consecutive five-year term in a two-round majority contest. He has responsibility for military and foreign affairs and has the authority to appoint the prime minister, dissolve parliament, call referenda, veto bills, and impose martial law. There are 49 provinces under appointed governors and 2,348 elected local councils.

history In the 10th century the Polish tribes were first united under one Christian ruler, Mieczyslaw. Mongols devastated the country 1241, and thereafter German and Jewish refugees were encouraged to settle among the ⟡Slav population. The first parliament met 1331, and Casimir the Great (1333–1370) raised the country to a high level of prosperity. Under the Jagiellonian dynasty (1386–1572) Poland became a great power, the largest country in Europe when it was united with Lithuania (1569–1776). Elected kings followed the death of the last Jagiello, a reactionary nobility wielded much power, and Poland's strength declined. But Stephen Báthory defeated Ivan the Terrible of Russia 1581, and in 1683 John III Sobieski forced the Turks to raise their siege of Vienna. In the mid-17th century a war against Russia, Sweden, and Brandenburg ended in the complete defeat of Poland, from which it was never allowed to recover.

Wars with the ⟡Ottoman Empire, dissension among the nobles, quarrels at the election of every king, the continuance of serfdom, and the persecution of Protestants and Greek Orthodox Catholics laid the country open to interference by Austria, Russia, and Prussia, ending with partition 1772, and again 1793, when Prussia and Russia seized further areas. A patriotic uprising led by Tadeusz Kościusko was defeated, and Russia, Austria, and Prussia occupied the rest of the country 1795. The Congress of ¢Vienna rearranged the division 1815 and reconstituted the Russian portion as a kingdom under the tsar. Uprisings 1830 and 1863 led to intensified repression and an increased attempt to Russify the population.

independent republic Poland was revived as an independent republic 1918 under the leadership of Józef Piłsudski, who took advantage of the USSR's internal upheaval to advance into Lithuania and the Ukraine before the Polish troops were driven back by the Red Army. Poland and the USSR then agreed on a frontier east of the ¢Curzon Line.

Politically, the initial post-independence years were characterized by instability, 14 multiparty coalition governments holding power 1918–26. Piłsudski seized complete power in a coup and proceeded to govern in an increasingly authoritarian manner until his death in 1935. He was succeeded by a military regime headed by Edward Śmigły-Rydz.

World War II In April 1939 the UK and France concluded a pact with Poland to render military aid if it was attacked, and at the beginning of Sept Germany invaded (see ¢World War II). During the war, western Poland was incorporated into the Nazi Reich, while the remainder, after a brief Soviet occupation of the east (1940–41), was treated as a colony. The country endured the full brunt of Nazi barbarism: a third of the educated elite were "liquidated"

and, in all, 6 million Poles lost their lives, half of them Jews slaughtered in concentration camps.

people's republic A treaty between Poland and the USSR Aug 1945 (ratified 1946) established Poland's eastern frontier at the Curzon Line. Poland lost 70,000 sq mi/181,350 sq km in the east to the USSR but gained 39,000 sq mi/101,000 sq km in the west from Germany. After elections, a "people's republic" was established 1947, and Poland joined ¢Comecon 1949 and the ¢Warsaw Pact 1955, remaining under close Soviet supervision, with the Soviet marshal Rokossovsky serving as minister for war 1949–56. A harsh Stalinist form of rule was instituted under the leadership of Bolesław Bierut (1892–1956), involving rural collectivization, the persecution of Catholic Church opposition, and the arrest of Cardinal Stefan Wyszyński 1953.

civil unrest In 1956, serious strikes and riots, leading to 53 deaths, broke out in Poznań in opposition to Soviet "exploitation" and food shortages. The more pragmatic Władysław Gomułka took over as leader of the Polish United Workers' Party (PUWP) (Communist Party), reintroduced private farming, and released Cardinal Wyszyński.

A further outbreak of strikes and rioting in Gdańsk, Gdynia, and Szczecin 1970 followed sudden food-price rises. This led to Gomułka's replacement as PUWP leader by the Silesia party boss Edward ¢Gierek, whose program aimed at raising living standards and consumer-goods production. The country's foreign debt grew, and food prices again triggered strikes and demonstrations 1976. Opposition to the Gierek regime, which was accused of corruption, mounted 1979 after a visit to his homeland by the recently elected Pope ¢John Paul II.

rise of Solidarity Strikes in Warsaw 1980, following a poor harvest and meat-price increases, rapidly spread across the country. The government attempted to appease workers by entering into pay negotiations with unofficial strike committees, but at the Gdańsk shipyards demands emerged for permission to form free, independent labor unions. The government conceded the right to strike, and in Gdańsk 1980 the ¢Solidarity (Solidarność) union was formed under the leadership of Lech ¢Walesa. In 1980 the ailing Gierek was replaced as PUWP leader by Stanisław Kania, but unrest continued as the 10-million-member Solidarity campaigned for a five-day working week and established a rural section.

martial law With food shortages mounting and PUWP control slipping, Kania was replaced as PUWP leader 1981 by the prime minister, General Wojciech ¢Jaruzelski; the Soviet army was active on Poland's borders; and martial law was imposed Dec 1981. Trade-union activity was banned, the leaders of Solidarity arrested, a night curfew imposed, and the Military Council of National Salvation established, headed by Jaruzelski. Five months of severe repression ensued, resulting in 15 deaths and 10,000 arrests. The US imposed economic sanctions.

In June 1982, curfew restrictions were eased, prompting further serious rioting in Aug. In Nov Walesa was released, and in Dec 1982 martial law was suspended (lifted 1983). The pope visited Poland 1983 and called for conciliation. The authorities responded by dissolving the Military Council and granting an amnesty to political prisoners and activists. In 1984, 35,000 prisoners and detainees were released on the

Poland
Republic of (*Polska Rzeczpospolita*)

area 49,325 sq mi/127,886 sq km
capital Warsaw
cities Łódź, Kraków, Wrocław, Poznań, Katowice, Bydgoszcz, Lublin; ports Gdańsk, Szczecin, Gdynia
physical part of the great plain of Europe; Vistula, Oder, and Neisse rivers; Sudeten, Tatra, and Carpathian mountains on S frontier
environment atmospheric pollution derived from coal (producing 90% of the country's electricity), toxic waste from industry, and lack of sewage treatment have resulted in the designation of 27 ecologically endangered areas. Half the country's lakes have been seriously contaminated and three-quarters of its drinking water does not meet official health standards
features last wild European bison (only in protected herds)
head of state Lech Walesa from 1990
head of government Hanna Suchocka from 1992
political system emergent democratic republic
political parties Democratic Union, centrist, ex-Solidarity; Democratic Left Alliance, ex-communist; Center Alliance, right-of-center, Walesa-linked; Social Democratic Party of the Polish Republic, 1990 successor to Polish United Workers' Party (PUWP), social democratic; Union of Social Democrats, radical breakaway from PUWP formed 1990; Solidarność (Solidarity) Parliamentary Club (OKP), anticommunist coalition
exports coal, softwood timber, chemicals, machinery, ships, vehicles, meat, copper

(Europe's largest producer)
currency zloty
population (1990 est) 38,363,000; growth rate 0.6% p.a.
life expectancy men 66, women 74 (1989)
languages Polish (official), German
religion Roman Catholic 95%
literacy 98% (1989)
GNP $276 billion (1988); $2,000 per head (1986)
chronology
1918 Poland revived as independent republic.
1939 German invasion and occupation.
1944 Germans driven out by Soviet forces.
1945 Polish boundaries redrawn at Potsdam Conference.
1947 Communist people's republic proclaimed.
1956 Poznań riots. Gomułka installed as Polish United Workers' Party (PUWP) leader.
1970 Gomułka replaced by Gierek after Gdańsk riots.
1980 Solidarity emerged as a free labor union following Gdańsk disturbances.
1981 Martial law imposed by General Jaruzelski.
1983 Martial law ended.
1984 Amnesty for political prisoners.
1985 Zbigniew Messner became prime minister.
1987 Referendum on economic reform rejected.
1988 Solidarity-led strikes and demonstrations called off after pay increases. Messner resigned; replaced by the reformist Mieczysław F Rakowski.
1989 Solidarity relegalized. April: new "socialist pluralist" constitution formed. June: widespread success for Solidarity in assembly elections, the first open elections in 40 years. July: Jaruzelski elected president. Sept: "Grand coalition," first non-Communist government since World War II formed; economic restructuring undertaken on free-market lines; W Europe and US create $1 billion aid package.
1990 Jan: PUWP dissolved; replaced by Social Democratic Party and breakaway Union of Social Democrats. Lech Walesa elected president; Dec: prime minister Mazowiecki resigned.
1991 Oct: Multiparty general election produced inconclusive result. Five-party center-right coalition formed under Jan Olszewski. Treaty signed agreeing complete withdrawal of Soviet troops.
1992 June: Olszewski ousted on vote of no confidence; succeeded by Waldemar Pawlak. July: Hanna Suchocka replaced Pawlak as Poland's first woman prime minister.

40th anniversary of the People's Republic, and the US relaxed its economic sanctions.

slow improvements The Jaruzelski administration pursued pragmatic reform, including liberalization of the electoral system. Conditions remained tense, however, strained by the continued ban on Solidarity; and by a threat (withdrawn 1986) to try Walesa for slandering state electoral officials. Economic conditions and farm output slowly improved, but Poland's foreign debt remained huge. During 1988 the nation's shipyards, coalmines, ports, and steelworks were paralyzed by a wave of Solidarity-led strikes for higher wages to offset the effect of recent price rises. With its economic strategy in tatters, the government of prime minister Zbigniew Messner resigned, being replaced Dec 1988 by a new administration headed by the reformist communist Mieczyslaw F Rakowski, and the PUWP's politburo was infused with a new clutch of technocrats.

socialist pluralism After six weeks of PUWP–Solidarity–church negotiations, a historic accord was reached April 1989 under whose terms Solidarity was relegalized, the formation of opposition political associations tolerated, legal rights conferred on the Catholic church, the state's media monopoly lifted, and a new "socialist pluralist" constitution drafted. In the subsequent national assembly elections, held June 1989, Solidarity captured all but one of the Sejm and Senate seats for which they were entitled to contest; 253 (55%) of the Sejm's seats had been reserved for contests between candidates from the Patriotic Movement for National Rebirth (PRON), the PUWP broad front organization; 46 (10%) for nationalist dignitaries; and the remaining 161 (35%) for non-PRON candidates. Jaruzelski was elected president by parliament July 1989.

"grand coalition" In Sept 1989 a "grand coalition" was formed with Tadeusz ◊Mazowiecki, editor of Solidarity's newspaper, who became prime minister. Jaruzelski continued as president, and was reelected in July. The new government, which attracted generous financial aid from Western powers, proceeded to dismantle the command economy and encourage the private sector. A tough austerity program approved by the International Monetary Fund (IMF) was also instituted to solve the problem of hyperinflation, which ran at 550% in 1989.

In Jan 1990 the PUWP voted to disband and re-formed as the Social Democracy Party. In April 1990 the Sejm voted to restore May 3 (the anniversary of the creation of the 1791 constitution) as national day and to cancel the July 22 (anniversary of the 1944 Lublin Manifesto establishing communist rule) as a national vacation. Censorship was abolished in April. During 1990 living standards in Poland fell by 40%. Unemployment rose to over 1 million. In July 1990, 40 members of the 259-strong Solidarity caucus, under the leadership of Zbigniew Bujak and Wladyslaw Frasyniuk, established the Citizens' Movement–Democratic Action Party (ROAD) to provide a credible alternative to the Walesa-oriented Solidarity Center Alliance (SCA) established in May.

presidential elections Walesa accused the government of delaying political and economic reform and forcing workers to bear the brunt of the austerity program. In July 100 SCA deputies and senators petitioned Jaruzelski to stand down to make way for Walesa. In Sept the Sejm passed a bill establishing a presidential term of five years. In the first round of presidential

elections, held Nov 25, 1990, the rupture within Solidarity was exposed by both Prime Minister Mazowiecki and Lech Walesa contesting for the position. Having run a populist campaign, Walesa topped the poll with a 40% vote share, and Mazowiecki, defending an unpopular government, finished in third position, with 18% of the vote, behind Stanislaw Tymiński, a previously obscure, right-wing, returned emigré Canadian entrepreneur, who captured 23% of the vote. In the second round, held Dec 9, Walesa defeated Tymiński.

Walesa elected president In Dec 1990 the defeated Mazowiecki resigned as prime minister and the newly elected Walesa resigned the Solidarity chair and was sworn in as president. He chose for prime minister an economist and former Solidarity activist, Jan Krzysztof Bielecki (1951–), and the new government included the IMF-backed finance minister Leszek Balcerowicz and other ministers from the outgoing administration.

They pledged to consolidate the free market they had introduced, and the first privatization share sales were held Jan 1991, with mixed success.

Poland's relations with the USSR deteriorated in early 1991 over the issue of Soviet troop withdrawals: there were some 50,000 stationed on Polish territory, and the Poles wanted them to leave by the end of the year, coinciding with withdrawals from Hungary and Czechoslovakia. Told that it would take three years, Walesa refused to allow Soviet troops to pass through Poland on their way back to the USSR.

new political parties Three new political parties were formed March–April 1991. The Center Alliance is a right-of-center, Christian Democratic grouping supported by Walesa and the Polish episcopate. It favors a modern market economy and a strong independent state, and claims 20,000 members. The Democratic Social Movement is a successor to ROAD. Led by Zbingniew Bujak, it appealed to workers and farmers, called for complete separation of church and state and was viewed as the chief future electoral rival of the SCA. Party X was formed by Stanislaw Tymiński, the Dec 1990 presidential contender.

public discontent The IMF approved further major loans April 1991 in support of the Polish government's economic reform program. However, there was growing public discontent at the decline in living standards brought about by currency reform and the deepening recession. This led to industrial unrest as unemployment reached 1.5 million (8.4% of the working population) by June 1991. In the same month a treaty of good-neighborliness and friendly cooperation was signed with Germany, confirming the Oder–Neisse border and recognizing the rights of the 500,000-strong German minority in Poland to their own culture, language, and religion.

Bielecki offered his resignation at the end of Aug 1991, complaining that he no longer enjoyed the support of a Sejm that still contained many communists. Parliament refused to accept either the resignation or the government's crucial proposed budget cuts. President Walesa urged it to confer emergency powers to enable the government to rule by decree until the general election. However, this plea was rejected, creating an impasse, although Bielecki agreed to stay as prime minister until the elections.

first multiparty election The Oct 1991 general election was Poland's first post-communist,

fully free, multiparty contest. No dominant party emerged from the voting, and Walesa proposed that he should combine the positions of president and prime minister for two years, heading a "national unity" grand coalition government. However, this failed to gain broad support. An attempt was then made to construct a left-of-center coalition led by Broneslaw Geremek. This foundered, and in Dec 1991 Walesa reluctantly allowed Jan Olszewski, a former Solidarity defense lawyer and a representative of the Center Alliance, to set about forming a five-party, center-right coalition government. This government pledged to pursue a more gradual approach to market-orientated reform and, in particular, to slow down the privatization program by concentrating instead on helping ailing state industries. In Oct 1991 a treaty was signed with the Soviet Union providing for the withdrawal of all Soviet combat troops by Nov 15, 1992 and the remainder by the end of 1993.

In April 1992 Walesa called for greater powers as president. In June Olszewski was ousted on a vote of no confidence; Waldemar Pawlak succeeded him but proved unable to hold together a workable coalition. In July Walesa nominated Hanna Suchocka as Pawlak's successor and Poland's first woman premier.

economic problems At the close of 1991 Poland's foreign debt stood at US $42 billion. GNP fell during 1990 and 1991 by 12% and 17% respectively and employment rose to more than 11%, with more than two million out of work. However, the annual rate of inflation fell from 684% in early 1990 to 60% at the end of 1991. *See illustration box.*

Polanski Roman 1933– . Polish film director, born in Paris. His films include *Repulsion* 1965, *Cul de Sac* 1966, *Rosemary's Baby* 1968, *Tess* 1979, *Frantic* 1988, and *Bitter Moon* 1992.

He suffered a traumatic childhood in Nazi-occupied Poland, and later his wife, actress Sharon Tate, was the victim of murder by the Charles Manson "family." He left the US for Europe and his tragic personal life is reflected in a fascination with horror and violence in his work.

polar coordinates in mathematics, a way of defining the position of a point in terms of its distance r from a fixed point (the origin) and its angle θ to a fixed line or axis. The coordinates of the point are (r,θ).

Often the angle is measured in ◊radians, rather than degrees. The system is useful for defining positions on a plane in programming the operations of, for example, computer-controlled cloth- and metal-cutting machines.

Polaris or *Pole Star* or *North Star* the bright star closest to the north celestial pole, and the brightest star in the constellation Ursa Minor. Its position is indicated by the "pointers" in Ursa Major. Polaris is a yellow ◊supergiant about 500 light-years away.

It currently lies within 1° of the north celestial pole; ◊precession (Earth's axial wobble) will bring Polaris closest to the celestial pole (less than 0.5° away) about AD 2100. It is also known as *Alpha Ursae Minoris*.

polarized light type of light that can be regarded as electromagnetic vibrations taking place in one particular plane as opposed to ordinary light where the vibrations occur at right angles to the line of propagation but in different planes. Polarized light is used to test the strength of sugar solutions, to measure stresses in transparent materials, and to prevent glare.

Ordinary light may be plane-polarized by reflection from a polished surface or by passing it through a Nicol prism or a synthetic polarizing film such as Polaroid.

Polaroid camera instant-picture camera, invented by Edwin Land in the US 1947. The original camera produced black-and-white prints in about one minute. Modern cameras can produce black-and-white prints in a few seconds, and color prints in less than a minute. An advanced model has automatic focusing and exposure. It ejects a piece of film on paper immediately after the picture has been taken.

The film consists of layers of emulsion and color dyes together with a pod of chemical developer. When the film is ejected the pod bursts and processing occurs in the light, producing a paper-backed print.

polar reversal changeover in polarity of the Earth's magnetic poles. Studies of the magnetism retained in rocks at the time of their formation have shown that in the past the Earth's north magnetic pole repeatedly became the south magnetic pole, and vice versa.

Polar reversal seems to be relatively frequent, taking place three or four times every million years. The last occasion was 700,000 years ago. Distinctive sequences of magnetic reversals are used in dating rock formations. Movements of the Earth's molten core are thought to be responsible for both the Earth's magnetic field and its reversal.

polder area of flat reclaimed land that used to be covered by a river, lake, or the sea. Polders have been artificially drained and protected from flooding by building dykes. They are common in the Netherlands, where the total land area has been increased by nearly one-fifth since AD 1200. Such schemes as the Zuider Zee project have provided some of the best agricultural land in the country.

pole either of the geographic north and south points of the axis about which the Earth rotates. The magnetic poles are the points toward which a freely suspended magnetic needle will point; however, they vary continually.

In 1985 the magnetic north pole was some 218 mi/350 km NW of Resolute Bay, Northwest Territories. It moves northward about 6 mi/10 km each year, although it can vary in a day about 50 mi/80 km from its average position. It is relocated every decade in order to update navigational charts. It is thought that periodic changes in the Earth's core cause a reversal of the magnetic poles (see ▷polar reversal, ▷magnetic field). Many animals, including migrating birds and fish, are believed to orientate themselves partly using the Earth's magnetic field. A permanent scientific base collects data at the South Pole.

Pole person of Polish culture from Poland and the surrounding area. There are 37–40 million speakers of Polish (including some in the US), a Slavic language belonging to the Indo-European family. The Poles are predominantly Roman Catholic, though there is an Orthodox Church minority. They are known for their distinctive cooking, folk festivals, and folk arts.

polecat Old World weasel *Mustela putorius* with a brown back and dark belly and two yellow face patches. The body is about 20 in/50 cm long and it has a strong smell from anal

gland secretions. It is native to Asia, Europe, and N Africa. In North America, ▷skunks are sometimes called polecats. A ferret is a domesticated polecat.

Pole Star ▷Polaris, the northern pole star. There is no bright star near the southern celestial pole.

police civil law-and-order force. In the US, law enforcement is the responsibility of municipal and state government except for violations of specific federal laws or cases in which state borders have been crossed. Unlike many countries, there is no national police force. The ▷Federal Bureau of Investigation assists state and local law-enforcement authorities.

The exercise of police power in the US is restricted and controlled in order to protect civil rights. Recent US Supreme Court decisions have relaxed some guidelines for searches.

poliomyelitis or *polio* acute viral infection of the central nervous system affecting nerves that activate muscles. The disease used to be known as infantile paralysis since children were most often affected. The polio virus is a common one, and mostly its effects are confined to the throat and intestine, as in flu or a mild digestive upset. There may also be muscle stiffness in the neck and back. Paralysis is seen in about 1% of cases, and the disease is life-threatening only if the muscles of the throat and chest are affected. Cases of this kind, once entombed in an "iron lung," are today maintained on a respirator. Two kinds of vaccine are available, one injected (see ▷Salk) and one given by mouth.

Polish Corridor strip of land designated under the Treaty of ▷Versailles 1919 to give Poland access to the Baltic. It cut off East Prussia from the rest of Germany. When Poland took over the southern part of East Prussia 1945, it was absorbed.

Polish language member of the Slavonic branch of the Indo-European language family, spoken mainly in Poland. Polish is written in the Roman and not the Cyrillic alphabet and its standard form is based on the dialect of Poznań in W Poland.

Politburo contraction of "political bureau," the executive committee (known as the Presidium 1952–66) of the Supreme Soviet in the USSR, which laid down party policy. It consisted of about 12 voting and 6 candidate (nonvoting) members.

political action committee (PAC) in the US, any organization that raises funds for political candidates and in return seeks to commit them to a particular policy. PACs also spend money on changing public opinion. In 1990, there were about 3,500 PACs, controlling some 25% of all funds spent in elections for ▷Congress. Donations to candidates amounted to $358.1 million, the largest PACs being the National Association of Realtors and the American Medical Association.

political correctness (PC) shorthand term for a set of liberal attitudes about education and society, and the terminology associated with them. To be politically correct is to be sensitive to unconscious racism and sexism and to display environmental awareness. However, the real or alleged enforcement of PC speech codes ("people of color" instead of "colored people," "differently abled" instead of "disabled," and so on) at more than 130 US universities by 1991 attracted derision and was criticized as a form of thought-policing.

political party association of like-minded people organized with the purpose of seeking and exercising political power. A party can be distinguished from an interest or ▷pressure group which seeks to influence governments rather than aspire to office, although some pressure groups, such as the Green movement, have over time transformed themselves into political parties.

Although politics, as an activity, has been practiced for thousands of years, political parties seem to have been largely a product of the 19th century. Although the US constitution contains no reference to parties, the Republican and Democratic parties became essential elements of the political system, reflecting the country's history and social and economic structure. The one-party state, in which party and state institutions became enmeshed, was the distinguishing feature of the political system established in Russia by Lenin (and later Stalin) after World War I.

Polk James Knox 1795–1849. 11th president of the US 1845–49, a Democrat, born in North Carolina. He allowed Texas admission to the Union, and forced the war on Mexico that resulted in the annexation of California and New Mexico.

Polk was an associate of Andrew ▷Jackson, who influenced his strongly expansionist policies. A believer in ▷Manifest Destiny, Polk pursued war with Mexico but avoided armed conflict with Britain over the Oregon–Canada boundary.

polka folk dance in lively two-four time. The basic step is a hop followed by three short steps. The polka originated in Bohemia and spread with German immigrants to the US, becoming a style of Texas country music.

pollack marine fish *Pollachius virens* of the cod family, growing to 2.5 ft/75 cm, and found close to the shore on both sides of the N Atlantic.

Pollaiuolo Antonio *c.* 1432–1498 and Piero *c.* 1441–1496. Italian artists, active in Florence. Both brothers were painters, sculptors, goldsmiths, engravers, and designers. Antonio is said to have been the first Renaissance artist to make a serious study of anatomy. The *Martyrdom of St Sebastian* 1475 (National Gallery, London) is considered a joint work.

pollen the grains of ▷seed plants that contain the male gametes. In ▷angiosperms (flowering plants) pollen is produced within ▷anthers; in most ▷gymnosperms (cone-bearing plants) it is produced in male cones. A pollen grain is typically yellow and, when mature, has a hard outer wall. Pollen of insect-pollinated plants (see ▷pollination) is often sticky and spiny and larger than the smooth, light grains produced by wind-pollinated species.

The outer wall of pollen grains from both insect-pollinated and wind-pollinated plants is often elaborately sculptured with ridges or spines so distinctive that individual species or genera of plants can be recognized from their pollen. Since pollen is extremely resistant to decay, useful information on the vegetation of earlier times can be gained from the study of fossil pollen. The study of pollen grains is known as palynology.

pollen tube outgrowth from a pollen grain that grows toward the ▷ovule, following germination of the grain on the ▷stigma. In ▷angiosperms (flowering plants) the pollen tube reaches the ovule by growing down through the ◊style, carrying the male gametes inside. The gametes are discharged into the ovule and one fertilizes the egg cell.

pollination the process by which pollen is transferred from one plant to another. The male ◊gametes are contained in pollen grains, which must be transferred from the anther to the stigma in ◊angiosperms (flowering plants), and from the male cone to the female cone in ◊gymnosperms (cone-bearing plants). Fertilization (not the same as pollination) occurs after the growth of the pollen tube to the ovary. Self-pollination occurs when pollen is transferred to a stigma of the same flower, or to another flower on the same plant; cross-pollination occurs when pollen is transferred to another plant. This involves external pollen-carrying agents, such as wind (see ◊anemophily), water, insects, birds (see ◊ornithophily), bats, and other small mammals.

Animal pollinators carry the pollen on their bodies and are attracted to the flower by scent, or by the sight of the petals. Most flowers are adapted for pollination by one particular agent only. Those that rely on animals generally produce nectar, a sugary liquid, or surplus pollen, or both, on which the pollinator feeds. Thus the relationship between pollinator and plant is an example of mutualism, in which both benefit. However, in some plants the pollinator receives no benefit (as in ◊pseudocopulation), while in others, nectar may be removed by animals that do not effect pollination.

pollinium group of pollen grains that is transported as a single unit during pollination. Pollinia are common in orchids.

Pollock Jackson 1912–1956. US painter, a pioneer of Abstract Expressionism and the foremost exponent of the technique of ◊action painting, a style he developed around 1946.

In the early 1940s Pollock moved from a vivid Expressionist style, influenced by Mexican muralists such as Siqueiros and by Surrealism, toward a semiabstract style. The paintings of this period are colorful and vigorous, using jumbled signs or symbols like enigmatic graffiti. He moved on to the more violently expressive abstract style, placing large canvases on the studio floor and dripping or hurling his paint on them. He was soon recognized as the leading Abstract Expressionist and continued to develop his style, producing even larger canvases in the 1950s.

Pollock v Farmer's Loan and Trust Co US Supreme Court decision 1895 dealing with the right of Congress to levy a federal income tax. The Gorman Tariff Act 1894 imposed a 2% tax on all annual incomes over $4,000. The ensuing protests, including the test case, focused on three aspects of the tax: (1) it taxed income on state and municipal bonds, an infringement on states' rights; (2) it taxed income on land and private property, making it a direct tax not apportioned among the states according to population; and (3) it exempted certain people on the basis of personal income. The Court found 5 to 4 that these constitutional violations made the tax impermissible. This decision was rendered irrelevant in 1913 by the 16th Amendment, which empowered Congress to enact income taxes.

poll tax tax levied on every individual, without reference to his or her income or property. Being simple to administer, it was among the earliest sorts of tax (introduced in England 1377), but because of its indiscriminate nature (it is a regressive tax, in that it falls proportionately more heavily on poorer people) it has often proved unpopular.

In the US, the tax was widely used as a means of disenfranchising poor blacks in southern states. It was made unconstitutional under the 24th Amendment 1964 for federal elections and 1966 for state races.

pollution the harmful effect on the environment of by-products of human activity, principally industrial and agricultural processes—for example, noise, smoke, car emissions, chemical and radioactive effluents in air, seas, and rivers, pesticides, radiation, sewage (see ◊sewage disposal), and household waste. Pollution contributes to the ◊greenhouse effect.

Pollution control involves higher production costs for the industries concerned, but failure to implement adequate controls may result in irreversible environmental damage and an increase in the incidence of diseases such as cancer. See also ◊nuclear safety.

Natural disasters may also cause pollution; volcanic eruptions, for example, cause ash to be ejected into the atmosphere and deposited on land surfaces.

Pollux in Greek mythology, the twin brother of Castor (see ◊Castor and Pollux).

Pollux or **Beta Geminorum** the brightest star in the constellation Gemini (the twins), and the 17th brightest star in the sky. Pollux is a yellowish star with a true luminosity 45 times that of the Sun. It is 35 light-years away.

polo stick-and-ball game played between two teams of four on horseback. It originated in Iran, spread to India and was first played in England 1869. Polo is played on the largest field of any game, measuring up to 300 yd/274 m by 200 yd/182 m. A small solid ball is struck with the side of a long-handled mallet through goals at each end of the field. A typical match lasts about an hour, and is divided into "chukkas" of 7.5 minutes each. No pony is expected to play more than two chukkas in the course of a day.

Polo Marco 1254–1324. Venetian traveler and writer. He traveled overland to China 1271–75, and served the emperor Kublai Khan until he returned to Europe by sea 1292–95. He was captured while fighting for Venice against Genoa, and, while in prison 1296–98, dictated an account of his travels.

After his father (Niccolo) and uncle (Maffeo) returned from a trading journey to China 1260–69, Marco began his own trip overland to China. Once there, he learned Mongolian and served the emperor Kublai Khan, returning nearly 20 years later by sea to his native country. His accounts of his travels remained the primary source of information about the Far East until the 19th century.

polonaise Polish dance in stately three-four time, that was common in 18th-century Europe. The Polish composer Frédéric Chopin developed the polonaise as a pianistic form.

polonium radioactive, metallic element, symbol Po, atomic number 84, atomic weight 210. Polonium occurs in nature in small amounts and was isolated from ◊pitchblende. It is the element having the largest number of isotopes (27) and is 5,000 times as radioactive as radium, liberating considerable amounts of heat. It was the first element to have its radioactive properties recognized and investigated.

Polonium was isolated in 1898 from pitchblende residues analyzed by Pierre and Marie ◊Curie, and named after Marie Curie's native Poland.

Pol Pot (also known as **Saloth Sar**, **Tol Saut**, and **Pol Porth**) 1925– . Cambodian politician and leader of the Khmer Rouge communist movement that overthrew the government 1975. After widespread atrocities against the civilian population, his regime was deposed by a Vietnamese invasion 1979. Pol Pot continued to help lead the Khmer Rouge until their withdrawal in 1989.

Pol Pot was a member of the anti-French resistance under Ho Chi Minh in the 1940s. In 1975 he proclaimed Democratic Kampuchea with himself as premier. His policies were to evacuate cities and put people to work in the countryside. The Khmer Rouge also carried out a systematic extermination of the Western-influenced educated and middle classes (1–4 million). In 1989 Pol Pot officially resigned from his last position within the Khmer Rouge (although many analysts contend that he continued to exert firm control over the organization).

Poltava industrial city (machinery, foodstuffs, clothing) in Ukraine, capital of Poltava region, on the River Vorskla; population (1987) 309,000. Peter the Great defeated Charles XII of Sweden here 1709.

poltergeist (German "noisy ghost") unexplained phenomenon that invisibly moves objects or hurls them about, starts fires, or causes other mischief.

polyandry system whereby a woman is expected to have more than one husband at the same time. It is found in Tibet and certain parts of India, where polyandry takes the form of the marriage of one woman to several brothers, as a means of keeping intact a family's heritage and property. Although it is found in other areas, in practice, it is neither expected nor normative behavior (see ◊norm).

polyanthus cultivated variety of ◊primrose, with multiple flowers on one stalk, bred in a variety of colors.

Polybius c. 201–120 BC. Greek politician and historian. He was involved with the ◊Achaean League against the Romans and, following the defeat of the Macedonians at Pydna in 168 BC, he was taken as a political hostage to Rome. He returned to Greece in 151 and was present at the capture of Carthage by his friend Scipio in 146. His history of Rome in 40 books, covering the years 220–146, has largely disappeared.

Polycarp, St c. 69–c. 155. Christian martyr allegedly converted by St John the Evangelist. As bishop of Smyrna (modern Izmir, Turkey), he carried on a vigorous struggle against various heresies for over 40 years. He was burned alive at a public festival; feast day Jan 26.

polychlorinated biphenyl (PCB) any of a group of chlorinated isomers of biphenyl $(C_6H_5)_2$. They are dangerous industrial chemicals, valuable for their fire-resisting qualities. They constitute an environmental hazard because of their persistent toxicity. Since 1973 their use has been limited by international agreement.

polyester synthetic resin formed by the ◊condensation of polyhydric alcohols (alcohols containing more than one hydroxyl group) with dibasic acids (acids containing two replaceable hydrogen atoms). Polyesters are thermosetting ◊plastics, used in making synthetic fibers, such as Dacron and Terylene, and

	number of sides	sum of interior angles (degrees)
triangle	3	180
quadrilateral	4	360
pentagon	5	540
hexagon	6	720
heptagon	7	900
octagon	8	1,080
decagon	10	1,440
duodecagon	12	1,800
icosagon	20	3,240

polygon

constructional plastics. With fiberglass added as reinforcement, polyesters are used in car bodies and boat hulls.

polyethylene or ***polyethene*** polymer of the gas ethylene (technically called ethene, C_2H_4). It is a tough, white, translucent, waxy thermoplastic (which means it can be repeatedly softened by heating). It is used for packaging, bottles, toys, electric cable, pipes and tubing.

Polyethylene is produced in two forms: low-density polyethylene, made by high-pressure polymerization of ethylene gas, and high-density polyethylene, which is made at lower pressure by using catalysts. This form, first made by German chemist Karl Ziegler, is more rigid at low temperatures and softer at higher temperatures than the low-density type.

polygamy the practice of having more than one spouse at the same time. It is found among many peoples. Normally it has been confined to the wealthy and to chiefs and nobles who can support several women and their offspring, as among ancient Egyptians, Teutons, Irish, and Slavs. Islam limits the number of legal wives a man may have to four. Certain Christian sects—for example, the Anabaptists of Münster, Germany, and the Mormons—have practiced polygamy because it was the norm in the Old Testament.

When the norm is for one husband and several wives, it is called polygyny; for one wife and several husbands, ▷polyandry. The most common expectation (although not necessarily the reality) was for polygyny. Polyandry was a very rare form of marriage, expected only where maintaining spare property or family heritage was important to the survival of the culture.

polygon in geometry, a plane (two-dimensional) figure with three or more straight-line sides. Common polygons have names which define the number of sides (for example, triangle, quadrilateral, pentagon).

These are all convex polygons, having no interior angle greater than 180°. The sum of the internal angles of a polygon having n sides is given by the formula $(2n - 4) \times 90°$; therefore, the more sides a polygon has, the larger the sum of its internal angles and, in the case of a convex polygon, the more closely it approximates to a circle.

polygraph technical name for a ▷lie detector.

polyhedron in geometry, a solid figure with four or more plane faces. The more faces there are on a polyhedron, the more closely it approximates to a sphere. Knowledge of the properties of polyhedra is needed in crystallography and stereochemistry to determine the shapes of crystals and molecules.

There are only five types of regular polyhedron (with all faces the same size and shape), as was deduced by early Greek mathematicians; they are the tetrahedron (four

equilateral triangular faces), cube (six square faces), octahedron (eight equilateral triangles), dodecahedron (12 regular pentagons) and icosahedron (20 equilateral triangles).

polymer compound made up of a large long-chain or branching matrix composed of many repeated simple units (**monomers**). There are many polymers, both natural (cellulose, chitin, lignin) and synthetic (polyethylene and nylon, types of plastic). Synthetic polymers belong to two groups: thermosoftening and thermosetting (see ▷plastic).

The size of the polymer matrix is determined by the amount of monomer used; it therefore does not form a molecule of constant molecular size or mass.

polymerization chemical union of two or more (usually small) molecules of the same kind to form a new compound. ***Addition polymerization*** produces simple multiples of the same compound. ***Condensation polymerization*** joins molecules together with the elimination of water or another small molecule.

Addition polymerization uses only a single monomer (basic molecule); condensation polymerization may involve two or more different monomers (**co-polymerization**).

polymorphism in genetics, the coexistence of several distinctly different types in a ▷population (groups of animals of one species). Examples include the different blood groups in humans and different color forms in some butterflies.

polymorphism in minerology, the ability of a substance to adopt different internal structures and external forms, in response to different conditions of temperature and/or pressure. For example, diamond and graphite are both forms of the element carbon, but they have very different properties and appearance.

Silica (SiO_2) also has several polymorphs, including quartz, tridymite, cristobalite, and stisthovite (the latter a very high-pressure form found in meteoritic impact craters).

Polynesia islands of Oceania E of 170° E latitude, including Hawaii, Kiribati, Tuvalu, Fiji, Tonga, Tokelau, Samoa, Cook Islands, and French Polynesia.

Polynesian a member of any of the seafaring peoples of Polynesia. They migrated by canoe from S Asia in about 2000 BC, peopling the islands of the S Pacific for about 2,000 years, and settling Hawaii last, from Tahiti. The Polynesian languages belong to the Oceanic branch of the Austronesian family.

Polynesian languages see ▷Malayo-Polynesian languages.

Polynices in Greek mythology, son of ▷Oedipus and Jocasta. Denied his share in the kingship of Thebes by his brother Eteocles, he induced his father-in-law, Adrastus of Argos, to lead the expedition of the ▷Seven against Thebes, in which he and his brother died by each other's hands.

polynomial in mathematics, an algebraic expression that has one or more ▷variables (denoted by letters). A polynomial of degree one, that is, whose highest ▷power of x is 1, as in $2x + 1$, is called a linear polynomial; $3x^2 + 2x + 1$ is quadratic; $4x^3 + 3x^2 + 2x + 1$ is cubic.

polyp or ***polypus*** small "stalked" benign tumor, most usually found on mucous membrane of the nose or bowels. Intestinal polyps are usually removed, since some have been found to be precursors of cancer.

polypeptide long-chain ▷peptide.

Polyphemus in Greek mythology, a Cyclops (a one-eyed giant) who imprisons ▷Odysseus and his companions in his cave on their homeward journey, and is finally blinded by them before they escape. His story forms the subject of Book Eleven of ▷Homer's *Odyssey*.

polyphony music combining two or more "voices" or parts, each with an individual melody.

polyploid in genetics, possessing three or more sets of chromosomes in cases where the normal complement is two sets (▷diploid). Polyploidy arises spontaneously and is common in plants (mainly among flowering plants), but rare in animals. Many crop plants are natural polyploids, including wheat, which has four sets of chromosomes per cell (durum wheat) or six sets (common wheat). Plant breeders can induce the formation of polyploids by treatment with a chemical, colchicine.

Matings between polyploid individuals and normal diploid ones are invariably sterile. Hence, an individual that develops polyploidy through a genetic aberration can initially only reproduce vegetatively, by parthenogenesis, or by self-fertilization (modes of reproduction that are common only among plants). Once a polyploid population is established, however, the members can reproduce sexually.

polysaccharide long-chain ▷carbohydrate made up of hundreds or thousands of linked simple sugars (monosaccharides) such as glucose and closely related molecules.

The polysaccharides are natural polymers. They either act as energy-rich food stores in plants (starch) and animals (glycogen), or have structural roles in the plant cell wall (cellulose, pectin) or the tough outer skeleton of insects and similar creatures (chitin). See also ▷carbohydrate.

polystyrene type of ▷plastic used in kitchen utensils or, in an expanded form, in insulation and ceiling tiles.

polytheism the worship of many gods, as opposed to monotheism (belief in one god). Examples are the religions of ancient Egypt,

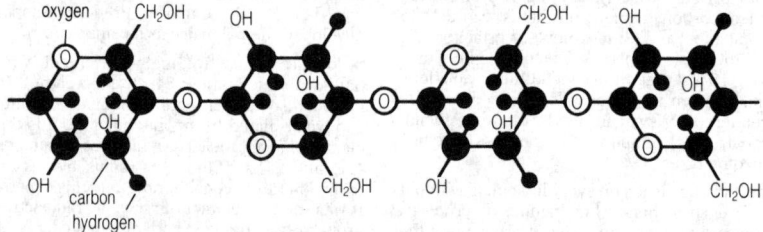

polysaccharide *A typical polysaccharide molecule, glycogen (animal starch), is formed from linked glucose ($C_6H_{12}O_6$) molecules.*

Babylon, Greece, Rome, Mexico, and modern Hinduism.

polytonality in music, the simultaneous use of more than one ▷key. A combination of two keys is bitonality.

polyunsaturate type of ▷fat or oil containing a high proportion of triglyceride molecules whose ▷fatty-acid chains contain several double bonds. By contrast, the fatty-acid chains of the triglycerides in saturated fats (such as lard) contain only single bonds. Medical evidence suggests that polyunsaturated fats, used widely in margarines and cooking fats, are less likely to contribute to cardiovascular disease than saturated fats, but there is also some evidence that they may have adverse effects on health.

The more double bonds the fatty-acid chains contain, the lower the melting point of the fat. Unsaturated chains with several double bonds produce oils, such as vegetable and fish oils, which are liquids at room temperature. Saturated fats, with no double bonds, are solids at room temperature. The polyunsaturated fats used for margarines are produced by taking a vegetable or fish oil and turning some of the double bonds to single bonds, so that the product is semisolid at room temperature. This is done by bubbling hydrogen through the oil in the presence of a catalyst, such as platinum. The catalyst is later removed.

Monounsaturated oils, such as olive oil, whose fatty-acid chains contain a single double bond, are probably healthier than either saturated or polyunsaturated fats. Butter contains both saturated and unsaturated fats, together with ▷cholesterol, which also plays a role in heart disease.

polyurethane polymer made from the monomer urethane. It is a thermoset ▷plastic, used in liquid form as a paint or varnish, and in foam form for upholstery and in lining materials (where it may be a fire hazard).

polyvinyl chloride (PVC) a type of ▷plastic used for drainpipes, floor tiles, audio discs, shoes and handbags.

pome type of ▷pseudocarp, or false fruit, typical of certain plants belonging to the Rosaceae family. The outer skin and fleshy tissues are developed from the ▷receptacle (the enlarged end of the flower stalk) after fertilization, and the five ▷carpels (the true fruit) form the pome's core, which surrounds the seeds. Examples of pomes are apples, pears, and quinces.

pomegranate deciduous shrub or small tree *Punica granatum*, family Punicaceae, native to SW Asia but cultivated widely in tropical and subtropical areas. The round, leathery, reddishyellow fruit contains numerous seeds that can be eaten fresh or made into wine.

Pomerania (Polish *Pomorze*, German *Pommern*) region along the southern shore of the Baltic Sea, including the island of Rügen, divided between Poland and (west of the Oder–Neisse line) East Germany 1945–90, and the Federal Republic of Germany after reunification 1990. The chief port is Gdańsk. It was formerly a province of Germany.

An independent Slavic duchy in the 11th century, Pomerania was taken by Poland in the 12th century and divided into the principalities of West Pomerania and East Pomerania (or Pomerelia). West Pomerania became part of the Holy Roman Empire, while East Pomerania remained part of Poland until 1772, when it was ceded to Prussia.

pomeranian small breed of dog, about 6 in/15 cm high, weighing about 6.5 lb/3 kg. It has long straight hair with a neck frill, and the tail is carried over the back.

Pompadour Jeanne Antoinette Poisson, Marquise de Pompadour 1721–1764. Mistress of ▷Louis XV of France from 1744, born in Paris. She largely dictated the government's ill-fated policy of reversing France's anti-Austrian policy for an anti-Prussian one. She acted as the patron of the Enlightenment philosophers Voltaire and Diderot.

Pompano Beach city in SE Florida, N of Fort Lauderdale, on the Atlantic Ocean. Tourism and fruit processing are important to the economy; population (1990) 72,400.

Pompeii ancient city in Italy, near the volcano ▷Vesuvius, 13 mi/21 km SE of Naples. In AD 63 an earthquake destroyed much of the city, which had been a Roman port and pleasure resort; it was completely buried beneath volcanic ash when Vesuvius erupted AD 79. Over 2,000 people were killed. Pompeii was rediscovered 1748 and the systematic excavation begun 1763 still continues.

Pompey the Great (Gnaeus Pompeius Magnus) 106–48 BC. Roman soldier and politician, consul 70–60 BC. From 60 BC to 53 BC, he was a member of the First Triumvirate with Julius ▷Caesar and Marcus Lucius ▷Crassus, but took the opposite side in the civil war from 49 BC.

Originally a supporter of Lucius Cornelius ▷Sulla and the aristocratic party, Pompey joined the democrats when he became consul with Crassus in 70 BC. He defeated ▷Mithridates VI Eupator of Pontus, and annexed Syria and Palestine. He married Caesar's daughter Julia (died 54 BC) in 59 BC. When the Triumvirate broke down after 53 BC, Pompey returned to the aristocratic party. On the outbreak of civil war 49 BC he withdrew to Greece, was defeated by Caesar at Pharsalus 48 BC, and was murdered in Egypt.

Pompidou Georges 1911–1974. French conservative politician, president 1969–74. He negotiated a settlement with the Algerians 1961 and, as prime minister 1962–68, with the students in the revolt of May 1968.

An adviser on General de Gaulle's staff 1944–46, Pompidou held administrative posts until he became director-general of the French House of Rothschild 1954, and even then continued in close association with de Gaulle, helping to draft the constitution of the Fifth Republic 1958–59. He was elected to the presidency on de Gaulle's resignation.

Ponce major city and industrial port (iron, textiles, sugar, rum) in S Puerto Rico, population (1980) 161,739.

The Catholic University of Puerto Rico is here. The settlement, established in the late 17th century, was named after the Spanish explorer Juan Ponce de León.

Ponce de León Juan 1460–1521. Spanish explorer who discovered Florida. He sailed on Columbus's second voyage to the Americas 1493 and settled in the colony on Hispaniola, later conquering Puerto Rico 1508–09 and becoming its governor. In 1513, while searching for the legendary "fountain of youth," he discovered Florida, exploring much of its east coast and part of the west coast. Ponce de León returned to Florida 1521 and was wounded in a battle with Indians. He died soon after in Cuba.

Pondicherry Union Territory of SE India; area 185 sq mi/480 sq km; population (1991) 789,400. Its capital is Pondicherry, and products include rice, peanuts, cotton, and sugar. Pondicherry was founded by the French 1674 and changed hands several times among the French, Dutch, and British before being returned to France 1814 at the close of the Napoleonic Wars. Together with Karaikal, Yanam, and Mahé (on the Malabar Coast) it formed a French colony until 1954 when all were transferred to the government of India; since 1962 they have formed the Union Territory of Pondicherry. Languages spoken include French, English, Tamil, Telegu, and Malayalam.

pondweed any aquatic plant of the genus *Potamogeton* that either floats on the water or is submerged. The leaves of floating pondweeds are broad and leathery, whereas leaves of the submerged forms are narrower and translucent; the flowers grow in green spikes.

Pontiac city in Michigan, 24 mi/38 km NW of Detroit; population (1990) 71,200; noted for automobile manufacturing.

Pontiac c. 1720–1769. North American Indian, chief of the Ottawa from 1755. Allied with the French during the French and Indian War, Pontiac was hunted by the British after the French withdrawal. He led the "Conspiracy of Pontiac" 1763–64 in an attempt to resist British persecution. He achieved remarkable success against overwhelming odds but eventually signed a peace treaty 1766.

Born near Detroit, Pontiac was murdered by a Peoria Indian in Illinois at the instigation of a British trader.

Pontine Marshes formerly malarial marshes in the Lazio region of Italy, near the coast 25 mi/40 km SE of Rome. Roman attempts to drain them were unsuccessful, and it was not until 1926, under Mussolini's administration, that they were brought into cultivation. Products include cereals, fruit and wine, and sugar beet.

Pontormo Jacopo Carucci 1494–1557. Italian painter, active in Florence. He developed a dramatic Mannerist style, with lurid colors.

Pontus kingdom of NE Asia Minor on the Black Sea from about 300–65 BC when its greatest ruler, Mithridates VI Eupator (132–63 BC), was defeated by the Roman general ▷Pompey.

pony small horse under 4.5 ft/1.47 m (14.2 hands) shoulder height. Although of Celtic origin, all the pony breeds have been crossed with thoroughbred and Arab stock, except for the smallest—the hardy Shetland, which is less than 42 in/105 cm shoulder height.

Pony Express, the in the US, a system of mail-carrying by relays of horse-riders that operated in the years 1860–61 between St Joseph, Missouri, and Sacramento, California, a distance of about 1,800 mi/2,896 km.

The Pony Express was a private venture by a company called Russell, Majors, and Waddell. 157 stations were set up along the route and the riders, who included William Cody, (Buffalo Bill), needed several changes of horses between each station.

poodle breed of dog, including standard (above 15 in/38 cm at shoulder), miniature (below 15 in/38 cm), and toy (below 11 in/28 cm) varieties. The long, curly coat, usually cut into an elaborate style, is often either black or white, although grays and browns are also bred.

The poodle probably originated in Russia, was naturalized in Germany, where it was used for retrieving ducks, and gained its name (from the German *pudeln*, "to splash"), and became a luxury dog in France.

pool or *pocket billiards* game derived from ⟩billiards and played in many different forms. Originally popular in the US, it is now also played in Europe.

It is played with balls of different colors, each of which is numbered. The neutral ball (black) is the number eight ball. The most popular form of pool is *eight-ball pool* in which players have to sink all their own balls before the opponent, and then must sink the eight-ball to win the game. Other forms include sinking balls in numerical order (rotation), or sinking a designated ball into a designated pocket (straight pool).

Pop Iggy. Adopted name of James Newell Osterberg 1947– . US rock singer and songwriter, initially known as *Iggy Stooge*, lead singer with a seminal garage band called the Stooges (1967–74), whose self-destructive proto-punk performances became legendary. His solo career began with *The Idiot* 1977 and *Lust for Life* 1977, composed and produced by David Bowie, who also contributed to *Blah, Blah, Blah* 1986.

Pop art movement of young artists in the mid-1950s and 1960s, reacting against the elitism of abstract art. Pop art used popular imagery drawn from advertising, comic strips, film, and television. It originated in Britain 1956 with Richard Hamilton, Peter Blake (1932–), and others, and broke through in the US with the paintings of flags and numbers by Jasper Johns 1958 and Andy Warhol's first series of soup cans 1962.

Pop art was so named by the British critic Lawrence Alloway (1926–). Richard Hamilton described it in 1957 as "popular, transient, expendable, low-cost, mass-produced, young, witty, sexy, gimmicky, glamorous, and big business." The artists often used repeating images and quoted from others' work. Among them were Roy Lichtenstein and Claes Oldenburg.

pope the bishop of Rome, head of the Roman Catholic Church, which claims he is the spiritual descendant of St Peter. Elected by the Sacred College of Cardinals, a pope dates his pontificate from his coronation with the tiara, or triple crown, at St Peter's Basilica, Rome. The pope had great political power in Europe from the early Middle Ages until the Reformation.

history
11th–13th centuries The papacy enjoyed its greatest temporal power under Gregory VII and Innocent III.
1309–78 The papacy came under French control (headquarters Avignon rather than Rome), "the Babylonian Captivity."
1378–1417 The "Great Schism" followed, with rival popes in Avignon and Rome.
16th century Papal political power further declined with the withdrawal of allegiance by the Protestant states at the Reformation.
1870 The Papal States in central Italy, which had been under the pope's direct rule from 756, merged with the newly united Italian state. At the Vatican Council the doctrine of papal infallibility was proclaimed.
1929 The Lateran Treaty recognized papal territorial sovereignty, even in Italy, only within the Vatican City.

1978 John Paul II became the first non-Italian pope since 1542.

Popé Pueblo leader. Born in the Tewa Pueblo, Popé was a leader of native resistance to Spanish political control and missionary activity in the New Mexico–Arizona area. Establishing his residence in Taos (in present-day New Mexico) in the 1670s, he began to plot a general uprising against the Spanish authorities. In August 1680 the Pueblo rose simultaneously throughout the area, forcing the Spanish to abandon Santa Fe and flee to El Paso. Popé held control of the area until his death, restoring the traditional ways of life. However, raids by Ute and Apache and severe drought led to the Spanish reconquest of the area 1692.

Pope Alexander 1688–1744. English poet and satirist. He established his reputation with the precocious *Pastorals* 1709 and *Essay on Criticism* 1711, which were followed by a parody of the heroic epic *The Rape of the Lock* 1712–14 and "Eloisa to Abelard" 1717. Other works include a highly Neo-Classical translation of Homer's *Iliad* and *Odyssey* 1715–26.

Pope had a biting wit, which he expressed in the form of heroic couplets. As a Catholic, he was subject to discrimination, and he was embittered by a deformity of the spine. His edition of Shakespeare attracted scholarly ridicule, for which he revenged himself by a satire on scholarly dullness, the *Dunciad* 1728. His philosophy, including *An Essay on Man* 1733–34 and *Moral Essays* 1731–35, was influenced by the politician and philosopher Henry Bolingbroke. His finest mature productions are his *Imitations of the Satires of Horace* 1733–38 and his personal letters. Among his friends were the writers Swift, Arbuthnot, and Gay. His line "A little learning is a dangerous thing" is often misquoted.

Popeye cartoon character created 1929 by US cartoonist Elzie Crisler Segar. Popeye made his first appearance in a newspaper strip as a feisty, pipe-smoking, spinach-eating sailor, whose motto was "I yam what I yam!" Between 1933 and 1957, more than 200 animated Popeye cartoons were made. Lanky-legged, button-nosed Olive Oyl, his girlfriend, and their adventurous baby boy, Swee'pea, made later appearances. The 1980 film *Popeye* brought real actors to the cartoon story.

poplar deciduous tree of the genus *Populus*, or cottonwood trees of the willow family Salicaceae. When ripe, the feathery seeds borne on elongated clusters are blown far and wide by the wind. Balsam poplar *P. balsamifera* and eastern cottonwood *P. deltoides* are native to North America. Eurasian white poplar *P. alba* and Lombardy poplar *P. nigra* are grown widely as ornamentals. Aspens belong to the same genus.

poplin strong fabric, originally with a warp of silk and a weft of worsted, but now usually made from cotton, in a plain weave with a finely ribbed surface.

pop music or *popular music* any contemporary music not classifiable as jazz or Classical. Pop became distinct from folk music with the advent of sound-recording techniques, and has incorporated blues, country and western, and music-hall elements; electronic amplification and other technological innovations have played a large part in the creation of new styles. The traditional format is a song of roughly three minutes with verse, chorus, and middle eight bars.

1910s The singer Al Jolson was one of the first recording stars. Ragtime was still popular.
1920s In the US Paul Whiteman and his orchestra played jazz that could be danced to, the country singer Jimmie Rodgers (1897–1933) reached a new record-buying public, the blues was burgeoning; in the UK popular singers included Al Bowlly (1899–1941, born in Mozambique).
1930s Crooner Bing Crosby and vocal groups such as the Andrews Sisters were the alternatives to swing bands.
1940s *Rhythm and blues* evolved in the US while Frank Sinatra was a teen idol and Glenn Miller played dance music; the UK preferred such singers as Vera Lynn.
1950s In the US *doo-wop* group vocalizing preceded *rockabilly* and the rise of *rock and roll* (Elvis Presley, Chuck Berry). British pop records were often cover versions of US originals.
1960s The Beatles and the *Mersey beat* transcended UK borders, followed by the Rolling Stones, *hard rock* (the Who, Led Zeppelin), and *art rock* (Genesis, Yes). In the US *surf music* (group harmony vocals or fast, loud, guitar-based instrumentals) preceded *Motown*, *folk rock* (the Byrds, Bob Dylan), and *blues rock* (Jimi Hendrix, Janis Joplin). *Psychedelic rock* evolved from 1966 on both sides of the Atlantic (the Doors, Pink Floyd, Jefferson Airplane).
1970s The first half of the decade produced *glitter rock* (David Bowie), *heavy metal*, and *disco* (dance music with a very emphatic, mechanical beat); in the UK also *pub rock* (a return to basics, focusing on live performance); *reggae* spread from Jamaica. From 1976 *punk* was ascendant; the US term *New Wave* encompassed bands not entirely within the punk idiom (Talking Heads, Elvis Costello).
1980s Punk continued as *hardcore* or mutated into *gothic*; dance music developed regional US variants: *hip-hop* (New York), *go-go* (Washington, DC), and *house* (Chicago). Live audiences grew, leading to anthemic *stadium rock* (U2, Bruce Springsteen) and increasingly elaborate stage performances (Michael Jackson, Prince, Madonna). An interest in *world music* sparked new fusions.
1990s *Rap*, hard rock, and heavy metal predominated in the US at the start of the decade; on the UK *indie* scene, dance music (Happy Mondays, Inspiral Carpets) and a new wave of guitar groups (Ride, Lush) drew on the psychedelic era.

These songs are usually performed live and recorded for broadcast or home play as singles, albums, or music videos. An enormous industry has grown around the pop music field, worldwide, which dominates radio and has great influences on the young and contemporary life.

Popocatépetl (Aztec "smoking mountain") volcano in central Mexico, 30 mi/50 km SE of Mexico City; 17,526 ft/5,340 m. It last erupted 1920.

Popper Karl (Raimund) 1902– . Austrian philosopher of science. His theory of falsificationism says that although scientific generalizations cannot be conclusively verified, they can be conclusively falsified by a counterinstance; therefore, science is not certain knowledge but a series of "conjectures and refutations," approaching, though never reaching, a definitive truth. For Popper, psychoanalysis and Marxism are unfalsifiable and therefore unscientific.

His major work on the philosophy of science is *The Logic of Scientific Discovery* 1935. Other works include *The Poverty of Historicism* 1957 (about the philosophy of social science), *Conjectures and Refutations* 1963, and *Objective Knowledge* 1972.

poppy any plant of the genus *Papaver*, family Papaveraceae, that bears brightly colored, often dark-centered, flowers and yields a milky sap. Species include the crimson European field poppy *P. rhoeas* and the Asian ▷opium poppies. Closely related are the California poppy *Eschscholtzia californica* and the yellow horned or sea poppy *Glaucium flavum*.

population in biology and ecology, a group of animals of one species, living in a certain area and able to interbreed; the members of a given species in a ▷community of living things.

population the number of people inhabiting a country, region, area, or town. Population statistics are derived from many sources; for example, through the registration of births and deaths, and from censuses of the population. The first US census was taken in 1790; other national censuses were taken in 1800 and 1801 and provided population statistics for Italy, Spain, the UK, and Ireland, and the cities of London, Paris, Vienna, and Berlin.

Since that time a growing number of countries have taken regular censuses, often at ten-yearly intervals, including Austria (1821 onwards), France (1821), China (1851), Russia (1861), Japan (1871) and India (1901). Although censuses are approximately accurate for advanced industrial countries, this may not be the case with developing countries. In May 1991, the UN Population Fund (UNFPA) warned that the world's population was growing much faster than predicted, by 250,000 a day, and was expected to reach 5.4 billion in mid-1991, 6.4 billion in 2001, and 10.2 billion in 2060.

Serious population studies date from the later 18th century; for example, Thomas Malthus's *Essay on the Principle of Population*, first published in 1798.

population control measures taken by some governments to limit the growth of their countries' populations by trying to reduce ▷birth rates. Propaganda, freely available contraception, and tax disincentives for large families are some of the measures that have been tried.

The population-control policies introduced by the Chinese government are the best known. In 1979 the government introduced a "one-child policy" that encouraged ▷family planning and penalized couples who have more than one child. It has been only partially successful since it has been difficult to administer, especially in rural areas, and has in some cases led to the killing of girls in favor of sons as heirs.

population cycle in biology, regular fluctuations in the size of a population, as seen in lemmings, for example. Such cycles are often caused by density-dependent mortality: high mortality due to overcrowding causes a sudden decline in the population, which then gradually builds up again. Population cycles may also result from an interaction between a predator and its prey.

population explosion the rapid and dramatic rise in world population that has occurred over the last few hundred years. Between 1959 and 1990, the world's population increased from 2.5 billion to over 5 billion people. It is estimated

that it will be at least 6 billion by the end of the century. Most of this growth is now taking place in the ▷developing world, where rates of natural increase are much higher than in developed countries. Concern that this might lead to ▷overpopulation has led some countries to adopt ▷population-control policies.

population genetics the branch of genetics that studies the way in which the frequencies of different ▷alleles (alternate forms of a gene) in populations of organisms change, as a result of natural selection and other processes.

Populism in US history, a late 19th-century political movement that developed out of farmers' protests against economic hardship. The Populist, or People's, Party was founded 1892 and ran several presidential candidates. It failed, however, to reverse increasing industrialization and the relative decline of agriculture in the US.

porcupine any ▷rodent with quills on its body, belonging to either of two families: Old World porcupines (family Hystricidae), terrestrial in habit and having long black-and-white quills; or New World porcupines (family Erethizontidae), tree-dwelling, with prehensile tails and much shorter quills.

porcupine fish another name for the ▷puffer fish.

Porgy and Bess classic US folk opera written in 1935 by George and Ira Gershwin, based on the novel *Porgy* 1925 by DuBose Heyward, a story of the black residents of Catfish Row in Charleston, South Carolina.

pornography obscene literature, pictures, photos, or films considered to be of no artistic merit and intended only to arouse sexual desire. Standards of what is obscene and whether a particular work has artistic value are subjective, hence there is often difficulty in determining whether a work violates the ▷obscenity laws. Opponents of pornography claim that it is harmful and incites violence to women and children. Others oppose its censorship claiming that it is impossible to distinguish pornography from art.

porphyria group of genetic disorders caused by an enzyme defect. Porphyria affects the digestive tract, causing abdominal distress; the nervous system, causing psychotic disorder, epilepsy, and weakness; the circulatory system, causing high blood pressure; and the skin, causing extreme sensitivity to light. No specific treatments exist.

In porphyria the body accumulates and excretes (rather than utilizes) one or more porphyrins, the pigments that combine with iron to form part of the oxygen-carrying proteins hemoglobin and myoglobin. It is known as the "royal disease" because sufferers included Mary Queen of Scots, James I, and (disputedly) George III.

porphyry any ▷igneous rock containing large crystals in a finer matrix.

porpoise any small whale of the family Delphinidae that, unlike dolphins, have blunt snouts without beaks. Common porpoises of the genus *Phocaena* can grow to 6 ft/1.8 m long; they feed on fish and crustaceans.

Porsche Ferdinand 1875–1951. German automotive engineer. The Volkswagen (German "people's car") was a product of the 1930s that became an international success (as the Beetle) in the 1950s–1970s. He also designed the original Porsche sports automobiles.

port sweet red, tawny, or white dessert wine, fortified with brandy, made from grapes grown in the Douro basin of Portugal and exported from Oporto, hence the name.

port point where goods are loaded or unloaded from a water-based to a land-based form of transport. Most ports are coastal, though inland ports on rivers also exist. Ports often have specialized equipment to handle cargo in large quantities.

Historically, ports have been important ▷growth poles from which the transport networks of many colonial and trading countries developed, as in Nigeria. Ports with deep-water berths can accommodate large modern shipping; for example, the port of Rotterdam. See also ▷airport.

Port Arthur industrial deepwater port (oil refining, shipbuilding, brass, chemicals) in Texas, 15 mi/24 km SE of Beaumont; population (1990) 58,700. Founded 1895, it gained importance with the discovery of petroleum near Beaumont in 1901.

Port Arthur former name (until 1905) of the port and naval base of Lüshun in NE China, now part of Lüdz.

Port-au-Prince capital and industrial port (sugar, rum, textiles, plastics) of Haiti; population (1982) 763,000.

Porter Cole (Albert) 1891–1964. US composer and lyricist of witty musical comedies. His shows include *The Gay Divorcee* 1932, *Anything Goes* 1934, *Kiss Me, Kate* 1948, and *Silk Stockings* 1955. He also wrote movie musicals, such as *Born to Dance* 1936 and *High Society* 1956.

Born in Indiana of an affluent family, Porter attended Yale and Harvard universities, then did military service during World War I. He became a member of the fashionable set in Europe during the 1920s and established himself with the revue *Paris* 1928. His clever, sophisticated lyrics and appealing melodies have made many of his songs standards, including "Night and Day," "I Get a Kick Out of You," "Begin the Beguine," "My Heart Belongs to Daddy," and "You're the Top."

Porter Edwin Stanton 1869–1941. US director, a pioneer of silent films. His 1903 film *The Great Train Robbery* lasted an unprecedented 12 minutes and contained an early use of the close-up. More concerned with the technical than the artistic side of his films, which include *The Teddy Bears* 1907 and *The Final Pardon* 1912, Porter abandoned filmmaking 1916.

Porter George 1920– . English chemist. From 1949 he and Ronald Norrish (1897–1978) developed the technique by which flashes of high energy are used to bring about and study extremely fast chemical reactions. He shared the 1967 Nobel Prize for Chemistry with Norrish and German chemist Manfred Eigen.

Porter Katherine Anne 1890–1980. US writer. She published three volumes of short stories (*Flowing Judas* 1930, *Pale Horse, Pale Rider* 1939, and *The Leaning Tower* 1944); a collection of essays, *The Days Before* 1952; and the allegorical novel *Ship of Fools* 1962 (made into a film 1965). Her *Collected Short Stories* 1965 won a Pulitzer Prize.

Born in Indian Creek, Texas, Porter began her writing career after high school, working on newspapers and as a freelance, and lived in Mexico and then in Europe. Her short stories are notable for a depth and complexity usually found only in novels. Her correspondence is collected in *Letters of Katherine Anne Porter* 1990.

Porter Rodney Robert 1917–1985. British biochemist. In 1962 Porter proposed a structure for human ◊immunoglobulin in which the molecule was seen as consisting of four chains. Porter was awarded, with Gerald Edelman, the 1972 Nobel Prize for Medicine.

Porter William Sydney. Adopted name "O Henry." 1862–1910. US author. Born in Greensboro, North Carolina, Porter left home at an early age. Settling in Texas, he was convicted of embezzlement 1899 and served several years in prison. It was then that he began to write short stories under the distinctive adopted name "O Henry." After his release 1902, he moved to New York City, where he contributed stories, many with surprise endings, to the *New York World*. Among the published collections of O Henry's most famous stories are *The Four Million* (including "The Gift of the Magi") 1906, *The Voice of the City* 1908, and *Rolling Stones* 1913.

Porterville city in S central California, N of Bakersfield. Industries include citrus fruits and olive oil; population (1990) 29,600.

Port Harcourt port (trading in coal, palm oil, and groundnuts) and capital of Rivers state in SE Nigeria, on the River Bonny in the Niger delta; population (1983) 296,200. It is also an industrial center producing refined mineral oil, sheet aluminum, tires, and paints.

Portland industrial port (aluminum, paper, timber, lumber machinery, electronics) and capital of Multnomah County, NW Oregon; on the Columbia River, 108 mi/173 km from the sea, at its confluence with the Willamette River; population (1990) 437,300.

Portland industrial port and largest city of Maine, on Casco Bay, SE of Sebago Lake; population (1990) 64,400.

The University of Southern Maine is here. Portland was first settled in 1632. The home of the poet Henry Wadsworth Longfellow, who was born here, is now a museum.

Portland William Henry Cavendish Bentinck, 3rd Duke of Portland 1738–1809. British politician, originally a Whig, who in 1783 became nominal prime minister in the Fox–North coalition government. During the French Revolution he joined the Tories, and was prime minister 1807–09.

Port Louis capital of Mauritius, on the island's NW coast; population (1987) 139,000. Exports include sugar, textiles, watches, and electronic goods.

Port Moresby capital and port of Papua New Guinea on the S coast of New Guinea; population (1987) 152,000.

Porto (English *Oporto*) industrial city (textiles, leather, pottery) in Portugal, on the River Douro, 3 mi/5 km from its mouth; population (1984) 327,000. It exports port.

It is the second largest city in Portugal and has a 12th-century cathedral.

Pôrto Alegre port and capital of Rio Grande do Sul state, S Brazil; population (1991) 1,254,600. It is a freshwater port for oceangoing vessels and is Brazil's major commercial center.

Port-of-Spain port and capital of Trinidad and Tobago, on Trinidad; population (1988) 58,000.

Porto Novo capital of Benin, W Africa; population (1982) 208,258. It was a former Portuguese center for the slave and tobacco trade with Brazil and became a French protectorate 1863.

Port Royal former capital of Jamaica, at the entrance to Kingston harbor.

Port Said port in Egypt, on reclaimed land at the northern end of the ◊Suez Canal; population (1983) 364,000. During the 1967 Arab–Israeli war the city was damaged and the canal blocked; Port Said was evacuated by 1969 but by 1975 had been largely reconstructed.

Portsmouth city and naval port in Hampshire, England, opposite the Isle of Wight; population (1991) 174,700. The naval dockyard was closed 1981 although some naval facilities remain.

It was already a port in the days of King Alfred, but in 1194 Richard I recognized its strategic importance and created a settlement on Portsea Island. The Tudor warship *Mary Rose* and Admiral Horatio Nelson's flagship, HMS *Victory*, are exhibited here. The novelist Charles Dickens was born in the Portsmouth suburb of Landport.

Portsmouth port in Rockingham county, SE New Hampshire, on the estuary of the Piscataqua River; the state's only seaport; population (1990) 25,900.

The nearby US Navy Yard (on Seavy's Island) dates from the 1790s and specializes in submarine construction and maintenance. Founded in 1623, Portsmouth was the state capital 1679–1775. The John Paul Jones House is here. The treaty ending the Russo-Japanese War was signed here 1905.

Portsmouth port and independent city in SE Virginia, on the Elizabeth River, seat of a US navy yard and training center; population (1990) 103,900. Manufactured goods include electronic equipment, chemicals, clothing, and processed food.

Portsmouth was a British naval base during the American Revolution. During the Civil War the Confederacy briefly held the naval shipyard here and converted the scuttled steamship USS *Merrimack* into the ironclad warship *Virginia*. It engaged the Union's *Monitor* March 9, 1862, in Hampton Roads in the first naval battle between ironclad vessels.

Portugal country in SW Europe, on the Atlantic Ocean, bounded N and E by Spain.

government The 1976 constitution, revised 1982, provides for a president, elected by universal suffrage for a five-year term, and a single-chamber 250-member assembly, similarly elected and serving a four-year term. The president, an active politician rather than a figurehead, appoints a prime minister who chooses the council of ministers, responsible to the assembly. A council of state, chaired by the president, acts as a supreme national advisory body.

history Portugal originated in the 11th century as a country subject to ◊León, while the south was ruled by the ◊Moors. It became an independent monarchy in the reign of Afonso I (1128–1185), who captured Lisbon 1147. Afonso III (1248–1279) expelled the Moors. During the 13th century the Cortes, an assembly representing nobles, clergy, and cities, began to meet and secured control of taxation. A commercial treaty with England was signed 1294, and an alliance established 1373. During the 15th century Portuguese mariners explored the African coast, opened the sea route to India (Vasco da Gama, 1497–98), and reached Brazil (Cabral, 1500), and colonists followed in the 16th century.

In 1580 Philip II of Spain seized the crown. The Portuguese rebelled against Spanish rule 1640, placed the house of Braganza on the throne, and after a long war forced Spain to recognize their independence 1668. Portugal

fought as the ally of Britain in the War of the ◊Spanish Succession. France invaded Portugal 1807–11 (see ◊Peninsular War). A strong democratic movement developed, and after a civil war 1828–34, constitutional government was established.

republic Carlos I was assassinated 1908; his son Manuel II was driven from the country by a revolution 1910, and a republic was proclaimed. Portugal remained economically weak and corrupt until the start of the dictatorship of Dr António de Oliveira ◊Salazar, prime minister from 1928. Social conditions were improved at the cost of personal liberties. Salazar was succeeded as prime minister 1968 by Dr Marcello Caetano, who proved unable to liberalize the political system or deal with the costly wars in Portugal's colonies of Angola and Mozambique.

military coup Criticisms of his administration led to a military coup April 1974 to "save the nation from government." The Junta of National Salvation was set up, headed by General António Ribeiro de Spínola. He became president a month later, with a military colleague replacing the civilian prime minister. The new president promised liberal reforms, but after disagreements within the Junta, Spínola resigned Sept 1974 and was replaced by General Francisco da Costa Gomes. In 1975 there was a swing to the left among the military and President Gomes narrowly avoided a communist coup by collaborating with the leader of the moderate Socialist Party (PS), Mario ◊Soares.

free elections In 1976 Portugal's first free assembly elections in 50 years were held. The PS won 36% of the vote, and Soares formed a minority government. The army chief, General António Ramalho ◊Eanes, won the presidency, with the support of center and left-of-center parties. After surviving precariously for over two years, Soares resigned 1978. A period of political instability followed, with five prime ministers in two and a half years, until, in Dec 1980, President Eanes invited Dr Francisco Balsemão, a cofounder of the Social Democratic Party (PSD), to form a center-party coalition.

Portugal: former colonies

name	colonized	independent
Brazil	1500	1822
Uruguay	1680	1828
Goa, Daman, and Diu (Portuguese India)	1505–10	1961
Guinea-Bissau	1446	1974
Cape Verde	c. 1462	1975
São Tomé e Príncipe	c. 1485	1975
Mozambique	1505	1975
East Timor	1520	1975
Angola	1575	1975

new constitution Dr Balsemão survived many challenges to his leadership, and in 1982 the assembly approved his draft of a new constitution, which would reduce the powers of the president and move the country to a fully civilian government. In 1983 Soares entered a coalition with the PSD, whose leader was now the former finance minister, Professor Aníbal Cavaco Silva. In 1985 the PS–PSD coalition broke up, and a premature general election was called; Cavaco Silva formed a minority government. He has increased economic growth and raised living standards, and favors a free market and privatization.

civilian president In the 1986 presidential election Soares became Portugal's first civilian president for 60 years. He promised an open and cooperative presidency. Portugal entered the European Community 1986 and is a member of NATO. In July 1987 the Social Democrats won an absolute majority in parliament, with the PRD and Communists both losing seats. In June 1989 the parliament approved a series of measures that denationalized major industries and renounced the socialist economy. In Jan 1991, Soares was reelected to a five-year term, while in the Oct 1991 general election the PSD were reelected with a slightly reduced majority.

Portuguese inhabitant of Portugal. The Portuguese have a mixed cultural heritage that can be traced back to the Lusitanian Celts who were defeated by the Romans about 140 BC. In the 5th century AD the Suebi, a Germanic group, overran the Iberian peninsula, and were later subdued by the Visigoths. In the 8th century AD S Portugal was invaded by the Moors. The Portuguese are predominantly Roman Catholic.

Portuguese East Africa former name of ⟁Mozambique.

Portuguese Guinea former name of ⟁Guinea-Bissau in W Africa.

Portuguese language member of the Romance branch of the Indo-European language family; spoken by 120–135 million people worldwide, it is the national language of Portugal, closely related to Spanish and strongly influenced by Arabic. Portuguese is also spoken in Brazil, Angola, Mozambique, and other former Portuguese colonies.

Portuguese literature under Provençal influence, medieval Portuguese literature produced popular ballads and troubadour songs. The Renaissance provided a stimulus for the outstanding work of the dramatist Gil Vicente and of the lyric and epic poet Camöens. In the 17th and 18th centuries there was a decline toward mere formality, but the *Letters of a Portuguese Nun*, attributed to Marianna Alcoforado, were a poignant exception and found echoes in the modern revolutionary period. No single figure has achieved international acclaim among the varied writers of the 19th and 20th centuries, although there is a lively tradition of writing in Brazil, and Angola developed its own school of Portuguese-African poetry.

Portuguese man-of-war any of a genus *Physalia* of phylum *Coelenterata* (see ⟁coelenterate). They live in the sea, in colonies, and have a large air-filled bladder (or "float") on top and numerous hanging tentacles made up of feeding, stinging, and reproductive individuals. The float can be 1 ft/30 cm long.

Portuguese West Africa former name of ⟁Angola.

Poseidon Greek god (Roman *Neptune*), the brother of Zeus and Pluto. The brothers dethroned their father, Cronus, and divided his realm, Poseidon taking the sea; he was also worshiped as god of earthquakes. His son was the merman sea god ⟁Triton.

currency escudo
population (1990 est) 10,528,000; growth rate 0.5% p.a.
life expectancy men 71, women 78 (1989)
language Portuguese
religion Roman Catholic 97%
literacy men 89%, women 80% (1985)
GNP $33.5 bn (1987); $2,970 per head (1986)
chronology
1928–68 Military dictatorship under António de Oliveira Salazar.
1968 Salazar succeeded by Marcello Caetano.
1974 Caetano removed in military coup led by General António Ribeiro de Spínola. Spínola replaced by General Francisco da Costa Gomes.
1975 African colonies became independent.
1976 New constitution, providing for return to civilian rule, adopted. Minority government appointed, led by Socialist Party leader Mario Soares.
1978 Soares resigned.
1980 Francisco Balsemão formed center-party coalition after two years of political instability.
1982 Draft of new constitution approved, reducing powers of presidency.
1983 Center-left coalition government formed.
1985 Aníbal Cavaco Silva became prime minister.
1986 Mario Soares elected first civilian president in 60 years. Portugal joined European Community.
1988 Portugal joined Western European Union.
1989 Constitution amended to allow major state enterprises to be denationalized.
1991 Mario Soares reelected president; Social Democrats (PSD) majority slightly reduced in assembly elections.

positivism theory that confines genuine knowledge within the bounds of science and observation. The theory is associated with the French philosopher Auguste Comte and ⟁empiricism. *Logical positivism* developed in the 1920s. It rejected any metaphysical world beyond everyday science and common sense, and confined statements to those of formal logic or mathematics.

On the basis of positivism, Comte constructed his "Religion of Humanity," in which the object of adoration was the Great Being, that is, the personification of humanity as a whole. Logical positivism influenced, and became more widely known through, the work of A J Ayer and the Vienna Circle.

positron in physics, the antiparticle of the electron; an ⟁elementary particle having the same magnitude of mass and charge as an electron but exhibiting a positive charge. The positron was discovered in 1932 by US physicist Carl Anderson at Caltech, its existence having been predicted by the British physicist Paul Dirac 1928.

possum another name for the ⟁opossum, a marsupial animal with a prehensile tail found in North, Central and South America. The name is also used for many of the smaller marsupials found in Australia.

postcard card with space for a written message that can be sent through the mail without an envelope. The postcard's inventor was Emmanual Hermann, of Vienna, who in 1869 proposed a "postal telegram," sent at a lower fee than a normal letter with an envelope. The first picture postcard was produced 1894.

poster advertising announcement for public display, often illustrated, first produced in France during the mid-19th century, when color ⟁lithography printing came into its own. Poster artists include Jules Chéret, John Millais, Henri de Toulouse-Lautrec, and Charles Dana Gibson. Poster art flourished again in the 1960s, with an emphasis on psychedelic art and artists such as Rick Griffin (1944–1991), Peter Max, and Stanley Mouse (1921–) in the US and Michael English (1942–) and Martin Sharp in Britain.

Post-Impressionism various styles of painting that followed ⟁Impressionism in the 1880s and 1890s. The term was first used by the British critic Roger Fry in 1911 to describe the works of Paul Cézanne, Vincent van Gogh, and Paul Gauguin. These painters moved away from the spontaneity of Impressionism, attempting to give their work more serious meaning and permanence.

Postmodernism late 20th-century movement in the arts and architecture that rejects the preoccupation of ⟁Modernism and ⟁Functionalism with pure form and technique rather than content. Postmodern designers use an amalgam of style elements from the past, such as the Classical and the Baroque, and apply them to spare modern forms. Their slightly off-key familiarity creates a more immediate appeal than the austerities of Modernism.

post-mortem (Latin "after death") alternate name for ⟁autopsy.

potash general name for any potassium-containing mineral, most often applied to potassium carbonate (K_2CO_3) or potassium hydroxide (KOH). Potassium carbonate, originally made by roasting plants to ashes in earthenware pots, is commercially produced from the mineral sylvite (potassium chloride,

Portugal
Republic of (*República Portuguesa*)

area 35,521 sq mi/92,000 sq km (including the Azores and Madeira)
capital Lisbon
cities Coimbra; ports Porto, Setúbal
physical mountainous in N, plains in S
features rivers Minho, Douro, Tagus (Tejo), Guadiana; Serra da Estrêla mountains
head of state Mario Alberto Nobre Lopes Soares from 1986
head of government Aníbal Cavaco Silva from 1985
political system democratic republic
political parties Social Democratic Party (PSD), moderate, left-of-center; Socialist Party (PS), progressive socialist; Democratic Renewal Party (PRD), center-left; Democratic Social Center Party (CDS), moderate, left of center
exports wine, olive oil, resin, cork, sardines, textiles, clothing, pottery, pulpwood

KCl) and is used mainly in making artificial fertilizers, glass, and soap.

The potassium content of soils and fertilizers is also commonly expressed as potash, although in this case it usually refers to potassium oxide (K_2O).

potassium (Dutch *potassa* "potash") soft, waxlike, silver-white, metallic element, symbol K (Latin *kalium*), atomic number 19, atomic weight 39.0983. It is one of the ◊alkali metals and has a very low density—it floats on water, and is the second lightest metal (after lithium). It oxidizes rapidly when exposed to air and reacts violently with water. Of great abundance in the Earth's crust, it is widely distributed with other elements and found in salt and mineral deposits in the form of potassium aluminum silicates.

Potassium, with sodium, plays a role in the transmission of impulses by nerve cells, and so is essential for animals; it is also required by plants for growth. The element was discovered and named in 1807 by English chemist Humphry Davy, who isolated it from potash in the first instance of a metal being isolated by electric current.

potato perennial plant *Solanum tuberosum*, family Solanaceae, with edible tuberous roots that are rich in starch. Used by the Andean Indians for at least 2,000 years before the Spanish Conquest, the potato was introduced to Europe by the mid-16th century, and reputedly to England by the explorer Walter Raleigh.

In Ireland, the potato famine in 1845, caused by a parasitic fungus, resulted in many thousands of deaths from starvation, and led to large-scale emigration to the US.

See also *sweet potato* under ◊yam.

Potemkin Grigory Aleksandrovich, Prince Potemkin 1739–1791. Russian politician. He entered the army and attracted the notice of Catherine II, whose friendship he kept throughout his life. He was an active administrator who reformed the army, built the Black Sea Fleet, conquered the Crimea, developed S Russia, and founded the Kherson arsenal 1788 (the first Russian naval base on the Black Sea).

potential difference (pd) measure of the electrical potential energy converted to another form for every unit charge moving between two points in an electric circuit (see ◊potential, electric). The unit of potential difference is the volt.

potential, electric in physics, the relative electrical state of an object. A charged conductor, for example, has a higher potential than the Earth, whose potential is taken by convention to be zero. An electric ◊cell (battery) has a potential in relation to emf (◊electromotive force), which can make current flow in an external circuit. The difference in potential between two points—the **potential difference**—is expressed in ◊volts; that is, a 12 V battery has a potential difference of 12 volts between its negative and positive terminals.

potential energy ◊energy possessed by an object by virtue of its relative position or state (for example, as in a compressed spring). It is contrasted with kinetic energy, the form of energy possessed by moving bodies.

potentiometer in physics, an electrical ◊resistor that can be divided so as to compare, measure, or control voltages. In radio circuits, any rotary variable resistance (such as volume control) is referred to as a potentiometer.

A simple type of potentiometer consists of a length of uniform resistance wire (about 3 ft/ 1 m long) carrying a constant current provided by a battery connected across the ends of the wire. The source of potential difference (voltage) to be measured is connected (to oppose the cell) between one end of the wire, through a ◊galvanometer (instrument for measuring small currents), to a contact free to slide along the wire. The sliding contact is moved until the galvanometer shows no deflection. The ratio of the length of potentiometer wire in the galvanometer circuit to the total length of wire is then equal to the ratio of the unknown potential difference to that of the battery.

Potomac river in W Virginia, Virginia, and Maryland states, rising in the Allegheny mountains, and flowing SE through Washington, DC, into Chesapeake Bay. It is formed by the junction of the N Potomac, about 95 mi/153 km long, and S Potomac, about 130 mi/209 km long, and is itself 285 mi/459 km long.

Large ships can sail upstream as far as Washington. The Potomac is of little economic importance, but historic sites such as Mount Vernon, the home of George Washington, are on its banks.

Potosí town in SW Bolivia; on the Cerro de Potosí slopes at 13,189 ft/4,020 m; it is one of the highest towns in the world; population (1988) 114,100. Silver, tin, lead, and copper are mined here. It was founded by Spaniards 1545; during the 17th and 18th centuries it was the chief silver-mining town and foremost city in South America.

potpourri mixture of dried flowers and leaves—for example, rose petals, lavender—and verbena, and spices, used to scent the air.

Also a medley, anthology, or random mixture.

Potsdam capital of the state of Brandenburg, Germany, on the River Havel SW of Berlin
population (1986) 140,000
products textiles, pharmaceuticals, and electrical goods
history a leading garrison and Prussian military center, Potsdam was restored to its position of capital of Brandenburg with the reunification of Germany 1990. The New Palace 1763–70 and Sans Souci were both built by Frederick the Great, and Hitler's Third Reich was proclaimed in the garrison church on March 21, 1933. The Potsdam Conference took place here.

Potsdam Conference conference held in Potsdam, Germany, July 17–Aug 2, 1945 between representatives of the US, the UK, and the USSR. They established the political and economic principles governing the treatment of Germany in the initial period of Allied control at the end of World War II, and sent an ultimatum to Japan demanding unconditional surrender on pain of utter destruction.

pottery and porcelain ◊ceramics in domestic and ornamental use including:
earthenware made of porous clay and fired, whether unglazed (when it remains porous, for example, flowerpots, winecoolers) or glazed (most tableware);
stoneware made of non-porous clay with a high silica content, fired at high temperature, which is very hard; *bone china* (softpaste) semiporcelain made of 5% bone ash and ◊kaolinite; first made in the West in imitation of Chinese porcelain;
porcelain (hardpaste) characterized by its hardness, ringing sound when struck, translucence, and shining finish, like that of a cowrie

shell (Italian *porcellana*); made of kaolin and petuntse (fusible ◊feldspar consisting chiefly of silicates reduced to a fine, white powder); first developed in China. Porcelain is high-fired at 2,552°F/1,400°C.

potto arboreal, nocturnal, African prosimian primate *Perodicticus potto* belonging to the ◊loris family. It has a thick body, strong limbs, and grasping feet and hands, and grows to 16 in/40 cm long, with horny spines along its backbone, which it uses in self-defense. It climbs slowly, and eats insects, snails, fruit, and leaves.

Poughkeepsie city in SE New York, on the Hudson River, N of New York City. Industries include chemicals, ball bearings, and cough drops. Vassar College is here; population (1990) 28,900. Settled by the Dutch 1687, it served as the temporary capital of New York 1717.

Poulenc Francis (Jean Marcel) 1899–1963. French composer and pianist. A self-taught composer of witty and irreverent music, he was a member of the group of French composers known as ◊Les Six. Among his many works are the operas *Les Mamelles de Tirésias* 1947, and *Dialogues des Carmélites* 1957, and the ballet *Les Biches* 1923.

poultry domestic birds such as chickens, turkeys, ducks, and geese. They were domesticated for meat and eggs by early farmers in China, Europe, Egypt, and the Americas. Chickens were domesticated from the SE Asian jungle fowl *Gallus gallus* and then raised in the East as well as the West. Turkeys are New World birds, domesticated in ancient Mexico. Geese and ducks were domesticated in Egypt, China, and Europe.

Good egg-laying breeds of chicken are Leghorns, Minorcas, and Anconas; varieties most suitable for eating are Dorkings, Australorps, Brahmas, and Cornish; those useful for both purposes are Orpingtons, Rhode Island Reds, Wyandottes, Plymouth Rocks, and Jersey White Giants. Most farm poultry are hybrids, selectively crossbred for certain characteristics, including feathers and down. Since World War II, the development of battery-produced eggs and the intensive breeding of broiler fowls and turkeys has roused a public outcry against "factory" methods of farming. The birds are often kept constantly in small cages, have their beaks and claws removed to prevent them from pecking their neighbors, and are given feed containing growth hormones and antibacterial drugs, which eventually make their way up the food chain to humans. Factory farming has led to a growing interest in deep-litter and free-range systems, although these account for only a small percentage of total production.

pound British standard monetary unit, issued as a gold sovereign before 1914, as a note 1914–83, and as a circular yellow metal-alloy coin from 1983. The pound is also the name given to the unit of currency in Egypt, Lebanon, Malta, Sudan, and Syria.

pound imperial unit (symbol lb) of mass equal to 16 ounces (7,000 grains) avoirdupois, or 12 ounces (5,760 grains) troy; the metric equivalents are 0.45 kg and 0.37 kg respectively. It derives from the Roman *libra*, which weighed 0.327 kg.

Pound Ezra 1885–1972. US poet who lived in London from 1908. His *Personae* and *Exultations* 1909 established the principles of ◊Imagism. His largest work was the series of *Cantos* 1925–69 (intended to number 100), which attempted a massive reappraisal of history.

In Paris 1921–25, he was a friend of the writers Gertrude Stein and Ernest Hemingway. He then settled in Rapallo, Italy. His anti-Semitism and sympathy with the fascist dictator Mussolini led him to broadcast from Italy in World War II, and he was arrested by US troops 1945. Found unfit to stand trial, he was confined in a mental hospital until 1958.

His first completely modern poem was "Hugh Selwyn Mauberley" 1920. He also wrote versions of Old English, Provençal, Chinese, ancient Egyptian, and other verse.

poundal imperial unit (abbreviation pdl) of force, now replaced in the SI system by the ⇨newton. One poundal equals 0.1383 newtons.

It is defined as the force necessary to accelerate a mass of one pound by one foot per second per second.

Poussin Nicolas 1594–1665. French painter, active chiefly in Rome; court painter to Louis XIII 1640–43. He was one of France's foremost landscape painters in the 17th century. He painted mythological and literary scenes in a strongly Classical style; for example, *Rape of the Sabine Women* about 1636–37 (Metropolitan Museum of Art, New York).

Poussin went to Rome 1624 and studied Roman sculpture in the studio of the Italian Baroque painter and architect ⇨Domenichino. His style reflects painstaking preparation: he made small wax models of the figures in his paintings, experimenting with different compositions and lighting. Color was subordinate to line.

poverty condition that exists when the basic needs of human beings (shelter, food, and clothing) are not being met. Many different definitions of poverty exist, since there is little agreement on the standard of living considered to be the minimum adequate level (known as the *poverty level*) by the majority of people.

In many countries, poverty is common and persistent, being reflected in poor nutrition, low life expectancy, and high levels of infant mortality. It may result from a country's complete lack of resources, and an inability to achieve economic development.

powder metallurgy method of shaping heat-resistant metals such as tungsten. Metal is pressed into a mold in powdered form and then sintered (heated to very high temperatures).

Powell Adam Clayton, Jr 1908–1972. US political leader. As pastor of the Abyssinian Baptist Church in New York City, he became a leader of New York's black community and was elected to the city council 1941. He was elected to the US Congress 1944 and later became chairman of the House Education and Labor Committee. Due to charges of corruption, Powell was not allowed to take his seat in Congress 1967. Reelected 1968, he won back his seniority by a 1969 decision of the US Supreme Court.

Born in New Haven, Connecticut, and educated at Colgate University, Powell received a doctorate from Shaw University 1938.

Powell Anthony (Dymoke) 1905– . English novelist who wrote the series of 12 volumes *A Dance to the Music of Time* 1951–75 that begins shortly after World War I and chronicles a period of 50 years in the lives of Nicholas Jenkins and his circle of upper-class friends.

Powell Cecil Frank 1903–1969. English physicist. From the 1930s he and his team at Bristol

University investigated the charged subatomic particles in cosmic radiation by using photographic emulsions carried in weather balloons. This led to his discovery of the pion (pi meson) 1946, a particle whose existence had been predicted by the Japanese physicist Hideki Yukawa 1935. Powell was awarded a Nobel Prize in 1950.

Powell Colin (Luther) 1937– . US general, chair of the Joint Chiefs of Staff from 1989 and, as such, responsible for the overall administration of the Allied forces in Saudi Arabia during the ⇨Gulf War 1991. A Vietnam War veteran, he first worked in government 1972 and was national security adviser 1987–89.

Powell was born in New York, the son of Jamaican immigrants; he joined the army in the 1950s, was sent to Vietnam 1962 and volunteered to return 1968. He worked for Caspar ⇨Weinberger and Frank ⇨Carlucci at the Office of Management and Budget 1972, before being posted to Korea 1973. He returned to Washington as assistant to Carlucci at the Defense Department 1981–83 and as adviser to Weinberger 1983–86 and was promoted to general. After a year in West Germany he was recalled to Washington following the ⇨Irangate scandal, first as assistant to Carlucci and then replacing him as national security adviser. In 1989 he was made a four-star general and chair of the Joint Chiefs of Staff.

Powell Lewis Stanley 1907– . US jurist and associate justice of the US Supreme Court 1971–87. A conservative, Powell voted to restrict Fifth Amendment guarantees against self-incrimination and for capital punishment. In *United States* v *Nixon* 1974, he sided with the majority in limiting executive privilege. In *Regents of the University of California* v *Bakke* 1978, he joined the majority in rejecting racial quotas as a basis for admission to an educational program.

Born in Suffolk, Virginia, Powell received his undergraduate and law degrees from Washington and Lee universities and an MA in law from Harvard. Powell practiced in Virginia, becoming president of the American Bar Association 1964–65 and president of the American College of Trial Lawyers 1968–69. President Nixon appointed Powell to the Supreme Court 1971. He retired 1987 for health reasons.

Powell William 1892–1984. US film actor who costarred with Myrna Loy in the *Thin Man* series 1934–47. He also played suave leading roles in *My Man Godfrey* 1936, *Life with Father* 1947, and *Mister Roberts* 1955.

He retired 1955.

power in mathematics, that which is represented by an ⇨exponent or index, denoted by a superior small numeral. A number or symbol raised to the power of 2—that is, multiplied by itself—is said to be squared (for example, 3^2, x^2), and when raised to the power of 3, it is said to be cubed (for example, 2^3, y^3).

power in physics, the rate of doing work or consuming energy. It is measured in watts (joules per second) or other units of work per unit time.

power of attorney in law, legal authority to act on behalf of another, for a specific transaction, or for a particular period.

Powys county in central Wales
area 1,961 sq mi/5,080 sq km
cities Llandrindod Wells (administrative headquarters)
features Brecon Beacons National Park; Black Mountains; rivers: Wye, Severn, which

both rise on Plynlimon in Dyfed; Lake Vyrnwy, artificial reservoir supplying Liverpool and Birmingham, alternative technology center near Machynlleth
products agriculture, dairy cattle, sheep
population (1991) 116,500
language 20% Welsh, English

Poznań (German *Posen*) industrial city (machinery, aircraft, beer) in W Poland; population (1985) 553,000. Founded 970, it was settled by German immigrants 1253 and passed to Prussia 1793; it was restored to Poland 1919.

pp abbreviation for *per procurationem* (Latin "by proxy"); in music, *pianissimo* (Italian "very softly").

PR abbreviation for *public relations*; *proportional representation*; *Puerto Rico*.

Prado Spanish art gallery (*Réal Museo de Pintura del Prado*/Royal Picture Gallery of the Prado) containing the national collection of pictures; founded by Charles III in 1785.

praemunire three English acts of Parliament passed 1353, 1365, and 1393, aimed to prevent appeal to the pope against the power of the king, and therefore an early demonstration of independence from Rome. The statutes were opposed by English bishops.

praetor in ancient Rome, a magistrate, elected annually, who assisted the ⇨consuls (the chief magistrates) and presided over the civil courts. After a year in office, a praetor would act as a provincial governor for a further year. The number of praetors was finally increased to eight.

pragmatism philosophical tradition that interprets truth in terms of the practical effects of what is believed and, in particular, the usefulness of these effects. The US philosopher Charles ⇨Peirce is often accounted the founder of pragmatism; it was further advanced by William James.

Prague (Czech *Praha*) city and capital of the Czech Republic on the River Vltava; population (1991) 1,212,000. Industries include automobiles, aircraft, chemicals, paper and printing, clothing, brewing, and food processing. It became the capital 1918.

Prague Spring the 1968 program of liberalization, begun under a new Communist Party leader in Czechoslovakia. In Aug 1968 Soviet tanks invaded Czechoslovakia and entered the capital Prague to put down the liberalization movement initiated by the prime minister Alexander Dubček, who had earlier sought to assure the Soviets that his planned reforms would not threaten socialism. Dubček was arrested but released soon afterwards. Most of the Prague Spring reforms were reversed.

Praha Czech name for Prague.

Praia port and capital of the Republic of Cape Verde, on the island of São Tiago (Santiago); population (1980) 37,500. Industries include fishing and shipping.

prairie dog any of the North American genus *Cynomys* of burrowing rodents in the squirrel family (Sciuridae). They grow to 12 in/30 cm, plus a short 3 in/8 cm tail. Their "towns" can contain up to several thousand individuals. Their barking cry has given them their name. Persecution by ranchers has brought most of the five species close to extinction.

Prakrit general name for the ancient Indo-European dialects of N India, contrasted with the sacred Classical language Sanskrit. The word is itself Sanskrit, meaning "natural," as opposed to *Sanskrit*, which means "perfected." The Prakrits are considered to be the ancestors of such modern N Indian languages as Hindi, Punjabi, and Bengali.

praseodymium (Greek *praseo* "leek-green" + *dymium*) silver-white, malleable, metallic element of the ◊lanthanide series, symbol Pr, atomic number 59, atomic weight 140.907. It occurs in nature in the minerals monzanite and bastnasite, and its green salts are used to color glass and ceramics. It was named in 1885 by Austrian chemist Carl von Welsbach (1858–1929).

He fractionated it from dydymium (originally thought to be an element but actually a mixture of rare-earth metals consisting largely of neodymium, praseodymium, and cerium), and named it for its green salts and spectroscopic line.

prawn any of various ◊shrimps of the suborder Natantia ("swimming"), of the crustacean order Decapoda, as contrasted with lobsters and crayfishes, which are able to "walk." Species called prawns are generally larger than species called shrimps.

Praxiteles mid-4th century BC. Greek sculptor, active in Athens. His *Aphrodite of Knidos* about 350 BC (known through Roman copies) is thought to have initiated the tradition of life-size freestanding female nudes in Greek sculpture.

prayer address to divine power, ranging from a magical formula to attain a desired end, to selfless communication in meditation. Within Christianity the Catholic and Orthodox churches sanction prayer to the Virgin Mary, angels, and saints as intercessors, whereas Protestantism limits prayer to God alone.

preadaptation in biology, the fortuitous possession of a character that allows an organism to exploit a new situation. In many cases, the character evolves to solve a particular problem that a species encounters in its preferred habitat, but once evolved may allow the organism to exploit an entirely different situation. The ability to extract oxygen directly from the air evolved in some early fishes, probably in response to life in stagnant, deoxygenated pools; this later made it possible for their descendants to spend time on land, so giving rise eventually to the air-breathing amphibians.

Precambrian in geology, the time from the formation of Earth (4.6 billion years ago) up to 570 million years ago. Its boundary with the succeeding Cambrian period marks the time when animals first developed hard outer parts (exoskeletons) and so left abundant fossil remains. It comprises about 85% of geological time and is divided into two periods: the Archaean and the Proterozoic.

precession slow wobble of the Earth on its axis, like that of a spinning top. The gravitational pulls of the Sun and Moon on the Earth's equatorial bulge cause the Earth's axis to trace out a circle on the sky every 25,800 years. The position of the celestial poles (see ◊celestial sphere) is constantly changing owing to precession, as are the positions of the equinoxes (the points at which the celestial equator intersects the Sun's path around the sky). The **precession of the equinoxes** means that there is a gradual westward drift in the ecliptic—the path that the Sun appears to follow—and in the coordinates of objects on the celestial sphere.

This is why the dates of the astrological signs of the zodiac no longer correspond to the times of year when the Sun actually passes through the constellations. For example, the Sun passes through Leo from mid-Aug to mid-Sept, but the astrological dates for Leo are between about July 23 and Aug 22.

precipitation meteorological term for water that falls to the Earth from the atmosphere. It includes rain, snow, sleet, hail, dew, and frost.

precipitation in chemistry, the formation of a suspension of solid, insoluble particles in a liquid as a result of a reaction within the liquid between two or more soluble substances. If the particles settle, they form a *precipitate*; if the particles are very small and remain in suspension, they form a *colloidal precipitate* (see ◊colloid).

predestination in Christian theology, the doctrine asserting that God has determined all events beforehand, including the ultimate salvation or damnation of the individual human soul; see ◊free will.

pref. abbreviation for *prefix*.

prefix letter or group of letters that can be added to the beginning of a word to make a new word. For example, *over*time, *out*rage, *non*sense.

pregnancy in humans, the period during which an embryo grows within the womb. It begins at conception and ends at birth, and the normal length is 40 weeks. Menstruation usually stops on conception. About one in five pregnancies fails, but most of these failures occur very early on, so the woman may notice only that her period is late. After the second month, the breasts become tense and tender, and the areas round the nipples become darker. Enlargement of the uterus can be felt at about the end of the third month, and thereafter the abdomen enlarges progressively. Pregnancy in animals is called ◊gestation.

Occasionally the fertilized egg implants not in the womb but in the ◊Fallopian tube (the tube between the ovary and the uterus), leading to an ectopic ("out of place") pregnancy. This will cause the woman severe abdominal pain and vaginal bleeding. If the growing fetus ruptures the tube, life-threatening shock may ensue.

prehistoric art art of prehistoric cultures; see ◊ancient art.

prehistoric life the diverse organisms that inhabited Earth from the origin of life about 3.5 billion years ago to the time when humans began to keep written records, about 3500 BC. During the course of evolution, new forms of life developed and many other forms, such as the dinosaurs, became extinct. Prehistoric life evolved over this vast timespan from simple bacterialike cells in the oceans to algae and protozoans and complex multicellar forms such as worms, mollusks, crustaceans, fishes, insects, land plants, amphibians, reptiles, birds, and mammals. On a geological timescale human beings evolved relatively recently, about 4 million years ago, although the exact dating is a matter of some debate. See also ◊geological time.

prehistory human cultures before the use of writing. A classification system was devised 1816 by Danish archeologist Christian Thomsen, based on the predominant materials used by early humans for tools and weapons: ◊Stone Age, ◊Bronze Age, ◊Iron Age.

Stone Age Stone, mainly flint, was predominant. The Stone Age is divided into:

Old Stone Age (Paleolithic) 3,500,000–5000 BC. Tools were chipped into shape by early humans, or hominids, from Africa, Asia, the Middle East, and Europe as well as later Neanderthal and Cro-Magnon people; the only domesticated animals were dogs. Some Asians crossed the Bering land bridge to inhabit the Americas. Cave paintings were produced 20,000–8,000 years ago in many parts of the world; for example, Altamira, Spain; Lascaux, France; central Sahara; India; and Australia. *Middle Stone Age* (Mesolithic) and *New Stone Age* (Neolithic). Stone and bone tools were ground and polished as well as chipped. In Neolithic times, agriculture and the domestication of goats, sheep, and cattle began. Stone Age cultures survived in the Americas, Asia, Africa, Oceania, and Australia until the 19th and 20th centuries.

Bronze Age Bronze tools and weapons began approximately 6000 BC in the Far East, and continued in the Middle East until about 1200 BC; in Britain this period lasted from about 2000 to 500 BC. The heroes of the Greek poet Homer lived in the Bronze Age.

Iron Age Iron was hardened (alloyed) by the addition of carbon, so that it superseded bronze for tools and weapons; in the Old World generally from about 1000 BC.

prelude in music, a composition intended as the preface to further music, to set a mood for a stage work, as in Wagner's *Lohengrin*; as used by Chopin, a short piano work.

premenstrual syndrome (PMS) a hormonal condition comprising a number of physical and emotional features that occur cyclically before menstruation, and which disappear with its onset. Symptoms include mood changes, breast tenderness, a feeling of bloatedness, and headache.

Preminger Otto (Ludwig) 1906–1986. Austrian-born US film producer, director, and actor. He directed *Margin for Error* 1942, *Laura* 1944, *The Moon Is Blue* 1953, *The Man with the Golden Arm* 1955, *Anatomy of a Murder* 1959, *Skidoo!* 1968, and *Rosebud* 1974. His films are characterized by an intricate technique of storytelling and a masterly use of the wide screen and the traveling camera.

Born in Vienna, Preminger went to the US 1935.

premolar in mammals, one of the large teeth toward the back of the mouth. In herbivores they are adapted for grinding. In carnivores they may be carnassials. Premolars are present in milk ◊dentition as well as permanent dentition.

Premonstratensian Roman Catholic monastic order founded 1120 by St Norbert (*c.* 1080–1134), a German bishop, at Prémontré, N France. Members were known as White Canons. The rule was a stricter version of that of the St Augustine Canons.

Prendergast Maurice 1859–1924. US painter who created a decorative watercolor style, using small translucent pools of color, inspired by the Impressionists.

He studied in Paris in the 1890s and was influenced by the ◊Nabis painters Pierre Bonnard and Edouard Vuillard. In 1898 he visited Italy. His *Umbrellas in the Rain, Venice* 1899 (Museum of Fine Arts, Boston) is typical of his work.

preparatory school private high school that prepares students for entrance to a college or university.

preposition in grammar, a ⊃part of speech coming before a noun or a pronoun to show a location (*in, on*), time (*during*), or some other relationship (for example, figurative relationships in phrases like "*by heart*" or "*on time*").

In the sentence "Put the book *on* the table," *on* is a preposition governing the noun "table" and relates the verb "put" to the phrase "the table," indicating where the book should go. Some words of English that are often prepositional in function may, however, be used adverbially, as in the sentences "He picked the book *up*" and "He picked *up* the book," in which the ordering is different but the meaning the same. In such cases *up* is called an **adverbial particle** and the form *pick up* is a **phrasal verb**.

Pre-Raphaelite Brotherhood (PRB) group of British painters 1848–53; Dante Gabriel Rossetti, John Everett Millais, and Holman Hunt were founding members. They aimed to paint serious subjects, to study nature closely, and to shun the influence of the styles of painters after Raphael. Their subjects were mainly biblical and literary, painted with obsessive naturalism. Artists associated with the group include Edward Burne-Jones and William Morris.

Presbyterianism system of Christian Protestant church government, expounded during the Reformation by John Calvin in Geneva, which gives its name to the established church of Scotland and is also practiced in the US, England, the Netherlands, Switzerland, and elsewhere. There is no compulsory form of worship, and each congregation is governed by presbyters or elders (clerical or lay), who are of equal rank. Congregations are grouped in presbyteries, synods, and general assemblies.

Presbyterianism came to the American colonies in the 17th century with Scottish and northern Irish immigrants. The main body is the Presbyterian Church in the US, with more than 3 million members. Other groups include the Orthodox Presbyterian Church, the Bible Presbyterian Church, and the Associate Reformed Presbyterian Church. In Canada, most Presbyterians united with Congregationalists and Methodists in 1925 to form the United Church of Canada.

prescription in medicine, an order written in a recognized form by a practitioner of medicine, dentistry, or veterinary surgery to a pharmacist for a preparation of medications to be used in treatment.

By tradition it used to be written in Latin, except for the directions addressed to the patient. It consists of (1) the superscription *recipe* ("take"), contracted to Rx; (2) the inscription or body, containing the names and quantities of the drugs to be dispensed; (3) the subscription, or directions to the pharmacist; (4) the signature, followed by directions to the patient; and (5) the patient's name, the date, and the practitioner's name.

preservative substance (⊃additive) added to a food in order to inhibit the growth of bacteria, yeasts, mold, and other microorganisms, and therefore extend its shelf-life. The term sometimes refers to ⊃antioxidants (substances added to oils and fats to prevent their becoming rancid) as well. All preservatives are potentially damaging to health if eaten in sufficient quantity. Both the amount used, and the foods in which they can be used, are restricted by law.

Alternatives to preservatives include faster turnover of food stocks, refrigeration, better hygiene in preparation, sterilization and pasteurization (see ⊃food technology).

president in government, the usual title of the head of state in a republic; the power of the office may range from diplomatic figurehead to the actual head of the government. For presidents of the US, who head the executive branch and its agencies, see ⊃United States and entries by name.

Presley Elvis (Aron) 1935–1977. US singer and guitarist, the most influential performer of the rock-and-roll era. With his recordings for Sun Records in Memphis, Tennessee, 1954–55 and early hits such as "Heartbreak Hotel," "Hound Dog," and "Love Me Tender," all 1956, he created an individual vocal style, influenced by Southern blues, gospel music, country music, and rhythm and blues. His records continued to sell in their millions into the 1990s.

Presley was born in Tupelo, Mississippi. In the mid-1950s he met Colonel Tom Parker, who would manage his career for his entire life. In addition to selling millions of records, Presley acted in 33 motion pictures and made numerous television appearances. From the late 1960s, he took a Las Vegas-based touring act on the road. He died at Graceland, his mansion in Memphis, in 1977, the victim of drug dependence.

Pressburg German name of ⊃Bratislava, city in Czechoslovakia.

press gang method used to recruit soldiers and sailors into the British armed forces in the 18th and early 19th centuries. In effect it was a form of kidnapping carried out by the services or their agents, often with the aid of armed men. This was similar to the practice of "shanghaiing" sailors for duty in the merchant marine, especially in the Far East.

pressure in physics, the force acting normally (at right angles) to a body per unit surface area. The SI unit of pressure is the pascal (newton per square meter), equal to 0.01 millibars. In a fluid (liquid or gas), pressure increases with depth. At the edge of Earth's atmosphere, pressure is zero, whereas at sea level atmospheric pressure due to the weight of the air above is about 100 kilopascals (1,013 millibars or 1 atmosphere). Pressure is commonly measured by means of a barometer, manometer, or Bourdon gauge.

Pressure at a depth h in a fluid of density d is equal to hdg, where g is the acceleration due to gravity.

pressure cooker closed pot in which food is cooked in water under pressure, where water boils at a higher temperature than normal boiling point (212°F/100°C) and therefore cooks food quickly. The modern pressure cooker has a quick-sealing lid and a safety valve that can be adjusted to vary the steam pressure inside.

The French scientist Denis Papin invented the pressure cooker in England in 1679.

pressure group or *interest group* or *lobby* association that puts pressure on governments or parties to ensure laws and treatment favorable to its own interest. Pressure groups have played an increasingly prominent role in contemporary Western democracies. In general they fall into two types: groups concerned with a single issue, such as nuclear disarmament, and groups attempting to promote their own interest, such as oil producers.

Prester John legendary Christian prince. During the 12th and 13th centuries, Prester John was believed to be the ruler of a powerful empire in Asia. From the 14th to the 16th century, he was generally believed to be the king of Abyssinia (now Ethiopia) in N E Africa.

pretender claimant to a throne. In British history, the term is widely used to describe the Old Pretender (⊃James Edward Stuart) and the Young Pretender (⊃Charles Edward Stuart).

Pretoria administrative capital of the Republic of South Africa from 1910 and capital of Transvaal province from 1860; population (1985) 741,300. Industries include engineering, chemicals, iron, and steel. Founded 1855, it was named after Boer leader Andries Pretorius (1799–1853).

Previn André (George) 1929– . US conductor and composer, born in Berlin. After a period working as a composer and arranger in the US film industry, he concentrated on conducting. He was principal conductor of the London Symphony Orchestra 1968–79. He was appointed music director of Britain's Royal Philharmonic Orchestra 1985 (a post he relinquished the following year, staying on as principal conductor), and of the Los Angeles Philharmonic in 1986.

He has done much on television and on stage to popularize Classical music.

Prévost d'Exiles Antoine François 1697–1763. French novelist, known as Abbé Prévost, who combined a military career with his life as a monk. His *Manon Lescaut* 1731 inspired operas by Massenet and Puccini.

Priam in Greek mythology, the last king of Troy. He was killed by Pyrrhus, son of Achilles, when the Greeks entered the city of Troy concealed in a huge wooden horse which the Trojans believed to be a gift to the city.

Priapus Greek god of fertility, son of Dionysus and Aphrodite, represented as grotesquely ugly, with an exaggerated phallus. He was also a god of gardens, where his image was frequently used as a scarecrow.

Pribilof Islands group of four islands in the Bering Sea, of volcanic origin, 200 mi/320 km SW of Bristol Bay, Alaska. Named after Gerasim Pribilof, who reached them in 1786, they were sold by Russia to the US in 1867 with Alaska, of which they form part. They were made a fur-seal reservation in 1868.

Price Leontyne 1927– . US opera singer. She made her professional debut on Broadway 1952 and was cast by Ira Gershwin to sing one of the lead roles in his revival of *Porgy and Bess* 1952–54. Through concert and television performances, Price gained a national reputation and made her operatic debut in San Francisco 1957. She appeared at La Scala in Milan 1959 and became a regular member of the Metropolitan Opera in New York 1961.

Born in Laurel, Mississippi, and educated at Central State College in Ohio, Price was trained as a soprano at the Juilliard School of Music in New York.

Price Vincent 1911– . US actor who made his film debut in 1938 after a stage career. He is remembered for *Laura* 1944 and *Leave Her To Heaven* 1945 before becoming a star of horror films, including *Dragonwick* 1946, *House of Wax* 1953, the cult favorite *The Tingler* 1959, *The Fall of the House of Usher* 1960, and five more Roger Corman "campy" horrors through 1964. He is noted for hosting TV's *Mystery* series.

prickly heat acute skin condition characterized by small white or red itchy blisters (miliaria), resulting from inflammation of the sweat glands in conditions of heat and humidity.

prickly pear cactus of the genus *Opuntia*, native to Central and South America, mainly Mexico and Chile, but naturalized in S Europe, N Africa, and Australia, where it is a pest. The common prickly pear *Opuntia vulgaris* is low-growing, with flat, oval, stem joints, bright-yellow flowers, and prickly, oval fruit; the flesh and seeds of the peeled fruit have a pleasant taste.

Pride and Prejudice novel by Jane Austen, published in 1813. Mr and Mrs Bennet, whose property is due to pass to a male cousin, William Collins, are anxious to secure good marriage settlements for their five daughters. Central to the story is the romance between the witty Elizabeth Bennet and the proud Mr Darcy.

Pride's purge the removal of about 100 Royalists and Presbyterians of the English House of Commons from Parliament by a detachment of soldiers led by Col Thomas Pride (died 1658) in 1648. They were accused of negotiating with Charles I and were seen as unreliable by the army. The remaining members were termed the ◇Rump and voted in favor of the king's trial.

Pride acted as one of the judges at the trial and also signed the king's death warrant. He opposed the plan to make Cromwell king.

Priestley J(ohn) B(oynton) 1894–1984. English novelist and playwright. His first success was a novel about traveling theater, *The Good Companions* 1929. He followed it with a realist novel about London life, *Angel Pavement* 1930. As a playwright he was often preoccupied with theories of time, as in *An Inspector Calls* 1945.

Priestley had a gift for family comedy, for example the play *When We Are Married* 1938. He was also known for his wartime broadcasts and literary criticism, such as *Literature and Western Man* 1960. Later novels include *Lost Empires* 1965 and *The Image Men* 1968.

Priestley Joseph 1733–1804. English chemist and Unitarian minister who identified oxygen 1774. In 1791 his chapel and house were sacked by a mob because of his support for the French Revolution. He emigrated to the US 1794.

Prigg v Pennsylvania US Supreme Court decision 1842 dealing with state and federal legislation about the removal of escaped slaves from "free" states. When Prigg, sent to recapture an escaped Maryland slave, was arrested for kidnapping under a Pennsylvania "personal liberty" law that prevented forcible seizure and removal of former slaves, he sued Pennsylvania in the US Supreme Court. The Court ruled the Pennsylvania law unconstitutional, upholding the federal Fugitive Slave Act and granting Congress absolute power over legislation about fugitive slaves. Many Northern states responded by passing laws that prohibited state officials from cooperating with the federal removal of runaways.

Prigogine Ilya 1917– . Russian-born Belgian chemist who, as a highly original theoretician, has made major contributions to the field of ◇thermodynamics for which work he was awarded the 1977 Nobel Prize for Physics. Earlier theories had considered systems at or about equilibrium. Prigogine began to study "dissipative" or non-equilibrium structures frequently found in biological and chemical reactions.

primary in presidential election campaigns in the US, a statewide election to decide the candidates for the two main parties. Held in 35 states, primaries begin with New Hampshire in Feb and continue until June; they operate under varying complex rules.

Generally speaking, the number of votes received by a candidate governs the number of delegates who will vote for that person at the national conventions in July/Aug, when the final choice of candidate for both Democratic and Republican parties is made. Some delegates remain loyal to the last ballot, others make deals to benefit the state or local situation as the field of candidates narrows.

primary sexual characteristic the endocrine gland producing maleness and femaleness. In males it is the testis and in females the ovary.

primate in zoology, any member of the order of mammals that includes monkeys, apes, and humans (together called **anthropoids**, as well as lemurs, bushbabies, lorises, and tarsiers, together called **prosimians**). Generally, they have forward-directed eyes, gripping hands and feet, opposable thumbs, and big toes. They tend to have nails rather than claws, with gripping pads on the ends of the digits, all adaptations to the arboreal, climbing mode of life.

primate in the Christian church, the official title of an archbishop.

prime minister or **premier** head of a parliamentary government, usually the leader of the largest party. In countries with an executive president, the prime minister is of lesser standing, whereas in those with dual executives, such as France, power is shared with the president.

The first prime minister in Britain is usually considered to have been Robert ◇Walpole, but the office was not officially recognized until 1905. In some countries, such as Australia, a distinction is drawn between the prime minister of the whole country and the premier of an individual state.

prime number a number that can be divided only by 1 or itself; that is, having no other factors. There is an infinite number of primes, the first ten of which are 2, 3, 5, 7, 11, 13, 17, 19, 23, and 29 (by definition, the number 1 is excluded from the set of prime numbers). The number 2 is the only even prime because all other even numbers have 2 as a factor.

Over the centuries mathematicians have sought general methods (algorithms) for calculating primes, from ◇Eratosthenes' sieve to programs on powerful computers.

In 1989 researchers at Amdahl Corporation, Sunnyvale, California, calculated the largest known prime number. It has 65,087 digits, and is more than a trillion trillion trillion times as large as the previous record holder. It took over a year of computation to locate the number and prove it was a prime.

prime rate the interest rate charged by commercial banks to their best customers. It is the lowest interest or base rate on which other rates are calculated according to the risk involved. Only borrowers who have the highest credit rating qualify for the prime rate.

Primitivism the influence on modern art (Kirchner, Modigliani, Picasso, and others) of the aboriginal cultures of Africa, Australia, the Americas, and also of Western folk art.

Primo de Rivera Miguel 1870–1930. Spanish soldier and politician, dictator from 1923 as

prime ministers of Britain

Sir Robert Walpole	(Whig)	1721
Earl of Wilmington	(Whig)	1742
Henry Pelham	(Whig)	1743
Duke of Newcastle	(Whig)	1754
Duke of Devonshire	(Whig)	1756
Duke of Newcastle	(Whig)	1757
Earl of Bute	(Tory)	1762
George Grenville	(Whig)	1763
Marquess of Rockingham	(Whig)	1765
Duke of Grafton	(Whig)	1766
Lord North	(Tory)	1770
Marquess of Rockingham	(Whig)	1782
Earl of Shelbourne	(Whig)	1782
William Pitt	(Tory)	1783
Duke of Portland	(Coalition)	1783
Henry Addington	(Tory)	1801
William Pitt	(Tory)	1804
Lord Grenville	(Whig)	1806
Duke of Portland	(Tory)	1807
Spencer Percival	(Tory)	1809
Earl of Liverpool	(Tory)	1812
George Canning	(Tory)	1827
Viscount Goderich	(Tory)	1827
Duke of Wellington	(Tory)	1828
Earl Grey	(Whig)	1830
Viscount Melbourne	(Whig)	1834
Sir Robert Peel	(Conservative)	1834
Viscount Melbourne	(Whig)	1835
Sir Robert Peel	(Conservative)	1841
Lord J Russell	(Liberal)	1846
Earl of Derby	(Conservative)	1852
Lord Aberdeen	(Peelite)	1852
Viscount Palmerston	(Liberal)	1855
Earl of Derby	(Conservative)	1858
Viscount Palmerston	(Liberal)	1859
Lord J Russell	(Liberal)	1865
Earl of Derby	(Conservative)	1866
Benjamin Disraeli	(Conservative)	1868
W E Gladstone	(Liberal)	1886
Benjamin Disraeli	(Conservative)	1874
W E Gladstone	(Liberal)	1880
Marquess of Salisbury	(Conservative)	1885
W E Gladstone	(Liberal)	1886
Marquess of Salisbury	(Conservative)	1886
W E Gladstone	(Liberal)	1892
Earl of Roseberry	(Liberal)	1894
Marquess of Salisbury	(Conservative)	1895
Sir H Campbell-Bannerman	(Liberal)	1905
H H Asquith	(Liberal)	1908
H H Asquith	(Coalition)	1915
D Lloyd George	(Coalition)	1916
A Bonar Law	(Conservative)	1922
Stanley Baldwin	(Conservative)	1923
Ramsay MacDonald	(Labour)	1924
Stanley Baldwin	(Conservative)	1924
Ramsay MacDonald	(Labour)	1929
Ramsay MacDonald	(National)	1931
Stanley Baldwin	(National)	1935
N Chamberlain	(National)	1937
Sir Winston Churchill	(Coalition)	1940
Clement Attlee	(Labour)	1945
Sir Winston Churchill	(Conservative)	1951
Sir Anthony Eden	(Conservative)	1955
Harold Macmillan	(Conservative)	1957
Sir Alec Douglas-Home	(Conservative)	1963
Harold Wilson	(Labour)	1964
Edward Heath	(Conservative)	1970
Harold Wilson	(Labour)	1974
James Callaghan	(Labour)	1976
Margaret Thatcher	(Conservative)	1979
John Major	(Conservative)	1990

well as premier from 1925. He was captain-general of Catalonia when he led a coup against the ineffective monarchy and became virtual dictator of Spain with the support of Alfonso XIII. He resigned 1930.

Primorye territory of Russia, SE Siberia, on the Sea of Japan; area 64,079 sq mi/165,900 sq km; population (1985) 2,136,000; capital Vladivostok. Timber and coal are produced.

primrose any plant of the genus *Primula*, family Primulaceae, with showy five-lobed flowers. The common primrose *P. vulgaris* is a woodland plant, native to Europe, bearing pale yellow flowers in spring.

prince royal or noble title. In Rome and medieval Italy it was used as the title of certain officials, for example, *princeps senatus* (Latin "leader of the Senate"). The title was granted to the king's sons in 15th-century France, and in England from Henry VII's time.

Prince Hal (Harold) 1928– . US director of musicals such as *Cabaret* 1968 and *Follies* 1971 on Broadway in New York, and *Evita* 1978 and *Sweeney Todd* 1980 in London's West End.

Prince Adopted name of Prince Rogers Nelson 1960– . US pop musician who composes, arranges, and produces his own records and often plays all the instruments. His albums, including *1999* 1982 and *Purple Rain* 1984, contain elements of rock, funk, and jazz. His stage shows are energetic and extravagant.

His band, the Revolution, broke up after four years in 1986. His hits include "Little Red Corvette" from *1999*, "Kiss" from *Parade* 1986, and "Sign O' The Times" from the album of the same name 1987. He has also starred in several films, including *Graffiti Bridge* 1990. His hometown of Minneapolis, Minnesota, has become a center for recording as a result of his success.

Prince Edward Island province of E Canada
area 2,200 sq mi/5,700 sq km
capital Charlottetown
features named after Prince Edward of Kent, father of Queen Victoria; Prince Edward Island National Park; Summerside Lobster Carnival
products potatoes, dairy products, lobsters, oysters, farm vehicles
population (1991) 129,900
history first recorded visit by Cartier 1534, who called it Isle St-Jean; settled by French; taken by British 1758; annexed to Nova Scotia 1763; separate colony 1769; settled by Scottish 1803; joined Confederation 1873.

In the late 1980s, there was controversy about whether to build a bridge to the mainland.

Princeton borough in Mercer County, W central New Jersey, 50 mi/80 km SW of

Prince Edward Island

printed circuit board *A typical microcomputer printed circuit board, or PCB.*

New York; population (1990) 13,200. It is the seat of Princeton University, founded 1746 at Elizabethtown and moved to Princeton 1756.

It is the site of an important Revolutionary War battle 1777.

Prince William Sound channel in the Gulf of Alaska, extending 125 mi/200 km NW from Kayak Island. In March 1989 the oil tanker *Exxon Valdez* ran aground here, spilling 12 million gallons of crude oil in what was then reckoned to be the world's greatest oil-pollution disaster.

printed circuit board (PCB) electrical circuit created by laying (printing) "tracks" of a conductor such as copper on one or both sides of an insulating board. The PCB was invented in 1936 by Austrian scientist Paul Eisler, and was first used on a large scale in 1948.

Components such as integrated circuits (chips), resistors and capacitors can be soldered to the surface of the board (surface-mounted) or, more commonly, attached by inserting their connecting pins or wires into holes drilled in the board.

printer in computing, an output device for producing printed copies of text or graphics. Types include the *daisywheel printer*, which produces good-quality text but no graphics; the *dot-matrix printer*, which produces text and graphics by printing a pattern of small dots; the *ink-jet printer*, which creates text and graphics by spraying a fine jet of quick-drying ink onto the paper; and the ◊*laser printer*, which uses electrostatic technology very similar to that used by a photocopier to produce high-quality text and graphics.

Printers may be classified as *impact printers* (such as daisywheel and dot-matrix printers), which form characters by striking an inked ribbon against the paper, and *nonimpact printers* (such as ink-jet and laser printers), which use a variety of techniques to produce characters without physical impact on the paper.

A further classification is based on the basic unit of printing, and categorizes printers as character printers, line printers, or page printers, according to whether they print one character, one line of characters, or a complete page at a time.

printing reproduction of text or illustrative material on paper, as in books or newspapers, or on an increasing variety of materials; for example, on plastic containers. The first printing used woodblocks, followed by carved wood type or molded metal type and hand-operated presses. Modern printing is effected by electronically controlled machinery. Current printing processes include electronic phototypesetting with ◊offset printing, and ◊gravure print.

In China the art of printing from a single wooden block was known by the 6th century AD, and movable type was being used by the 11th century. In Europe printing was unknown for another three centuries, and it was only in the 15th century that movable type was reinvented, traditionally by Johannes ◊Gutenberg in Germany. William ◊Caxton introduced printing to England. There was no further substantial advance until, in the 19th century, steam power replaced hand-operation of printing presses, making possible long

printing *The offset litho process, in which the printing plate is wrapped around a cylinder.*

"runs;" hand-composition of type (each tiny metal letter was taken from the case and placed individually in the narrow stick that carried one line of text) was replaced by machines operated by a keyboard.

Linotype, a hot-metal process (it produced a line of type in a solid slug) used in newspapers, magazines, and books, was invented by Ottmar Mergenthaler 1886 and commonly used until the 1980s. The **Monotype**, used in bookwork (it produced a series of individual characters, which could be hand-corrected), was invented by Tolbert Lanston (1844–1913) in the US 1889. Important as these developments were, they represented no fundamental change but simply a faster method of carrying out the same basic typesetting operations. The actual printing process still involved pressing the inked type on to paper, by ◊**letterpress**.

In the 1960s this form of printing began to face increasing competition from ◊**offset printing**, a method that prints from an inked flat surface, and from the ◊**gravure** method (used for high-circulation magazines), which uses recessed plates.

The introduction of electronic phototypesetting machines, also in the 1960s, allowed the entire process of setting and correction to be done in the same way that a typist operates, thus eliminating the hot-metal composing room (with its hazardous fumes, lead scraps, and noise) and leaving only the making of plates and the running of the presses to be done traditionally. By the 1970s some final steps were taken to plateless printing, using various processes, such as a computer-controlled laser beam, or continuous jets of ink acoustically broken up into tiny equal-sized drops, which are electrostatically charged under computer control.

printmaking creating a picture or design by printing from a plate (block, stone, or sheet) that holds ink or color. The oldest form of print is the woodcut, common in medieval Europe, followed by line ◊engraving (from the 15th century), and ◊etching (from the 17th); colored woodblock prints flourished in Japan from the 18th century. ◊Lithography was invented 1796.

The German artist Dürer created outstanding woodcuts and line engravings, and the Dutch painter Rembrandt was one of the first major artists to produce etchings.

prion exceptionally small microorganism, a hundred times smaller than a virus. Composed of protein, and without any detectable amount of nucleic acid (genetic material), it is thought to cause diseases such as scrapie in sheep, and certain degenerative diseases of the nervous system in humans. How it can operate without nucleic acid is not yet known.

Researchers at the University of California 1982 first identified prions in living tissue.

Pripet (Russian **Pripyat**) river in E Europe, a tributary of the river Dnieper, which it joins 50 mi/80 km above Kiev, Ukraine, after a course of about 500 mi/800 km. The **Pripet marshes** near Pinsk were of strategic importance in both world wars.

prism in mathematics, a solid figure whose cross section is constant in planes drawn perpendicular to its axis. A cube, for example, is a rectangular prism with all faces (bases and sides) the same shape and size.

prism in optics, a triangular block of transparent material (plastic, glass, silica) commonly used to "bend" a ray of light or split a beam into its spectral colors. Prisms are used as mirrors to define the optical path in binoculars, camera viewfinders, and periscopes.

prison place of confinement for those accused of and/or convicted of contravening the law; after conviction most jurisdictions claim to aim at rehabilitation and deterrence as well as punishment. For major crimes, life imprisonment or death may be the sentence. Parole and probation programs exist, and "work-release" furlough programs allow convicts to work outside the prison or make family visits during their sentences.

The prison population in the US rose dramatically in the 1980s as stronger drug laws were passed and longer sentences imposed in that area. One result has been massive overcrowding, and several states are under court order not to exceed a specified number of prisoners. In some cases this means that a current prisoner must be released, often after serving only a fraction of the sentence, to make room for a new arrival. The US prison population is about 500,000.

Development of US prisons Loss of liberty was seen from the beginning as a punishment in the US. Prior to the late 18th century, prisons were viewed as a temporary restriction before exile, execution, or flogging was imposed as punishment. The US Constitution prohibited "cruel or unusual punishment," ending many of these methods of punishment; the isolated prison then came to be viewed as an institution in which discipline might be instilled and temptation removed. The system developed 1817 in Auburn, New York (to confine prisoners at night but require them to work during the day), was widely emulated because the use of prisoner labor reduced the costs, and, it was hoped, inculcated respect for authority.

The modern system pursues rehabilitation as its goal by providing work (for pay), training, education, counseling, and the prospect of early release through the parole and probation systems. However, the high recidivism rates suggest that these programs do little to counter the background causes of criminal behavior.

Pritchett V(ictor) S(awdon) 1900– . English short-story writer, novelist, and critic, with an often witty and satirical style. His short stories were gathered in *Collected Stories* 1982 and *More Collected Stories* 1983. His critical works include *The Living Novel* 1946 and biographies of the Russian writers Turgenev 1977 and Chekov 1988.

privacy the right of the individual to be free from secret surveillance (by scientific devices or other means) and from the disclosure to unauthorized persons of personal data, as accumulated in computer data banks. Always an issue complicated by considerations of state security, public welfare (in the case of criminal activity), and other factors, it has been rendered more complex by present-day technology.

computer data All Western countries now have computerized-data protection. In the US the Privacy Act 1974 requires that there should be no secret data banks and that agencies handling data must ensure their reliability and prevent misuse (information gained for one purpose must not be used for another). The public must be able to find out what is recorded and how it is used, and be able to correct it. Under the Freedom of Information Act 1967, citizens and organizations have the right to examine unclassified files.

private enterprise sector of the economy in which economic activity is initiated through private capital and pursued for private profit. It is distinguished from ◊public spending, although public funds are often funneled into private enterprises, as with defense contractors or infrastructure development (public works contractors).

privateer privately owned and armed ship commissioned by a state to attack enemy vessels. The crews of such ships were, in effect, legalized pirates; they were not paid but received a share of the spoils. Privateering existed from ancient times until the 19th century, when it was declared illegal by the Declaration of Paris 1856.

privatization policy or process of selling or transferring state-owned or public assets and services (notably nationalized industries) to private investors. Privatization of services involves the government contracting private firms to supply services previously supplied by public authorities.

The proponents of privatization argue that the public benefits from theoretically greater efficiency from firms already in the competitive market, and the release of resources for more appropriate use by government. Those against privatization believe that it transfers a country's assets from all the people to a controlling minority, that public utilities such as gas and water become private monopolies, and that a profit-making state-owned company raises revenue for the government.

The trend has grown worldwide, since inefficient state-run enterprises with little accountability required ever-larger subsidies. Governments in the US, the UK, France, Japan, and Italy have pursued the policy, as have a number of developing states that seek to stimulate economic activity. Poland and other East European states are moving away from the Communist system of state-run enterprises toward a free-market economy, in hopes of producing more and higher quality goods and services. See also ◊deregulation, ◊monetarism.

privet any evergreen shrub of the genus *Ligustrum* of the olive family Oleaceae, with dark green leaves, including the European common privet *L. vulgare*, with white flowers and black berries, naturalized in North America, and the native North American California privet *L. ovalifolium*, also known as hedge privet.

Privy Council council composed originally of the chief royal officials of the Norman kings in Britain; under the Tudors and early Stuarts it became the chief governing body. It was replaced from 1688 by the ⟡cabinet, originally a committee of the council, and the council itself now retains only formal powers in issuing royal proclamations and orders-in-council. Cabinet ministers are automatically members, and it is presided over by the Lord President of the Council.

Prix Goncourt French literary prize for fiction, given by the Académie Goncourt (founded by Edmond de ⟡Goncourt 1903).

probability likelihood, or chance, that an event will occur, often expressed as odds, or in mathematics, numerically as a fraction or decimal. In general, the probability that *n* particular events will happen out of a total of *m* possible events is n/m. A certainty has a probability of 1; an impossibility has a probability of 0. Empirical probability is defined as the number of successful events divided by the total possible number of events.

In tossing a coin, the chance that it will land "heads" is the same as the chance that it will land "tails," that is, 1 to 1 or even; mathematically, this probability is expressed as 1/2 or 0.5. The odds against any chosen number coming up on the roll of a fair die are 6 to 1; the probability is 1/6 or 0.1666... . If two dice are rolled there are $6 \times 6 = 36$ different possible combinations. The probability of a double (two numbers the same) is 6/36 or 1/6 since there are six doubles in the 36 events: (1,1), (2,2), (3,3), (4,4), (5,5), and (6,6).

Probability theory was developed by the French mathematicians Blaise Pascal and Pierre de Fermat in the 17th century, initially in response to a request to calculate the odds of being dealt various hands at cards. Today probability plays a major part in the mathematics of atomic theory and finds application in insurance and statistical studies.

probate system for the administration of inheritance. Generally the function of probate (sometimes surrogate's) courts, probate determines the validity of wills, and the the satisfaction of requirements of inheritance law. In the cases of persons dying without wills (intestacy), probate courts appoint administrators of estates.

probation in law, the placing of offenders under supervision of probation officers in the community, as an alternative to prison.

procedure in computing, a small part of a computer program that performs a specific task, such as clearing the screen or sorting a file. A *procedural language*, such as BASIC, is one in which the programmer describes a task in terms of how it is to be done, as opposed to a *declarative language*, such as PROLOG, in which it is described in terms of the required result. See ⟡programming.

Careful use of procedures is an element of ⟡structured programming. In some programming languages there is an overlap between procedures, ⟡functions, and subroutines.

processing cycle in computing, the sequence of steps performed repeatedly by a computer in the execution of a program. The computer's CPU (central processing unit) continuously works through a loop, involving fetching a program instruction from memory, fetching any data it needs, operating on the data, and storing the result in the memory, before fetching another program instruction.

processor in computing, another name for the ⟡central processing unit or ⟡microprocessor of a computer.

proconsul Roman ⟡consul (chief magistrate) who went on to govern a province when his term as consul ended.

Proconsul prehistoric ape skull found on Rusinga Island in Lake Victoria (Nyanza), E Africa, by Mary ⟡Leakey. It is believed to be 20 million years old.

Procrustes (Greek "the stretcher") in Greek mythology, a robber who tied his victims to a bed; if they were too tall for it, he cut off the ends of their legs, and if they were too short, he stretched them.

Procyon or *Alpha Canis Minoris* brightest star in the constellation Canis Minor and the eighth brightest star in the sky. Procyon is a white star 11.4 light-years from Earth, with a mass of 1.7 Suns. It has a ⟡white dwarf companion that orbits it every 40 years.

producer price index (PPI) measure of price changes. In 1978 the US government revised its reporting of wholesale price indexes to reflect separate price changes at three stages of the production process. Crude materials, intermediate goods, and finished goods were indexed separately, and each of these is a PPI. The finished goods index, the most cited PPI, and the ⟡consumer price index are the two most common measures of inflation and cost of living.

productivity in economics, the output produced by a given quantity of labor, usually measured as output per person employed in the firm, industry, sector, or economy concerned. Productivity is determined by the quality and quantity of the fixed ⟡capital used by labor, and the effort of the workers concerned.

The level of productivity is a major determinant of cost-efficiency: higher productivity tends to reduce average costs of production. Increases in productivity in a whole economy are a major determinant of economic growth. It is important to distinguish between the rate of growth of productivity and the level of productivity, since at lower levels of productivity, higher rates of productivity growth may be achieved.

productivity, biological in an ecosystem, the amount of material in the food chain produced by the primary producers (plants) that is available for consumption by animals. Plants turn carbon dioxide and water into sugars and other complex carbon compounds by means of photosynthesis. Their net productivity is defined as the quantity of carbon compounds formed, less the quantity used up by the respiration of the plant itself.

profit-sharing system whereby an employer pays workers a share of the company's profits, which is often a percentage based on annual salary and invested by the employer in a retirement plan operated or overseen by the employer. It may be paid as cash or shares of stock in the firm. It originated in France in the early 19th century and was widely practiced for a time within the cooperative movement.

progesterone ⟡steroid hormone that occurs in vertebrates. In mammals, it regulates the menstrual cycle and pregnancy. Progesterone is secreted by the corpus luteum (the ruptured Graafian follicle of a discharged ovum).

programming writing instructions in a programming language for the control of a computer. *Applications programming* is for end-user programs, such as accounts programs or word-processing packages. *Systems programming* is for operating systems and the like, which are concerned more with the internal workings of the computer.

There are several programming styles:
procedural programming, in which programs are written as lists of instructions for the computer to obey in sequence, is by far the most popular. It is the "natural" style, closely matching the computer's own sequential operation;
declarative programming, as used in the programming language PROLOG, does not describe how to solve a problem, but rather describes the logical structure of the problem. Running such a program is more like proving an assertion than following a procedure;
functional programming is a style based largely on the definition of functions. There are very few functional programming languages, HOPE and ML being the most widely used, though many more conventional languages (for example C) make extensive use of functions;
object-oriented programming, the most recently developed style, involves viewing a program as a collection of objects that behave in certain ways when they are passed certain "messages." For example, an object might be defined to represent a table of figures, which will be displayed on screen when a "display" message is received.

programming language in computing, a special notation in which instructions for controlling a computer are written. Programming languages are designed to be easy for people to write and read, but must be capable of being mechanically translated (by a ⟡compiler or an ⟡interpreter) into the ⟡machine code that the computer can execute.

program music music that tells a story, depicts a scene or painting, or illustrates a literary or philosophical idea, such as Richard Strauss's *Don Juan*.

program trading in finance, buying and selling a group of shares using a computer program to generate orders automatically whenever there is an appreciable movement in prices.

One form in use in the US in 1989 was *index arbitrage*, in which a program traded automatically whenever there was a difference between New York and Chicago prices of an equivalent number of shares. Program trading comprised some 14% of daily trading on the New York Stock Exchange by volume in Sept 1989, but was widely criticized for lessening market stability. It has been blamed, among other factors, for the Stock Market crashes of 1987 and 1989.

progression sequence of numbers each formed by a specific relationship to its predecessor. An *arithmetic progression* has numbers that increase or decrease by a common sum or difference (for example, 2, 4, 6, 8); a *geometric progression* has numbers each bearing a fixed ratio to its predecessor (for example, 3, 6, 12, 24); and a *harmonic progression* has numbers whose ⟡reciprocals are in arithmetical progression, for example 1, 1/2, 1/3, 1/4.

progressive education teaching methods that take as their starting point children's own aptitudes and interests, and encourage them to follow their own investigations and lines of inquiry.

Progressivism in US history, the name of both a reform movement and a political party, active in the two decades before World War I. Mainly middle-class and urban-based, Progressives secured legislation at national, state, and local levels to improve the democratic system, working conditions, and welfare provision.

Prohibition in US history, the period 1920–33 when the 18th Amendment to the US Constitution was in force, and the manufacture, transportation, and sale of intoxicating liquors were illegal. It represented the culmination of a long campaign by Populists, Progressives, temperance societies, and the Anti-Saloon League. This led to ◊bootlegging (the illegal distribution of liquor, often illicitly distilled), widespread disdain for the law, speakeasies, and greatly increased organized crime activity, especially in Chicago and towns near the Canadian border. Public opinion insisted on repeal 1933.

The 18th Amendment was enforced by the Volstead Act 1919. Prohibition was repealed by the 21st Amendment 1933.

projector any apparatus that projects a picture on to a screen. In a *slide projector*, a lamp shines a light through the photographic slide or transparency, and a projection ◊lens throws an enlarged image of the slide onto the screen. A *film projector* has similar optics, but incorporates a mechanism that holds the film still while light is transmitted through each frame (picture). A shutter covers the film when it moves between frames.

prokaryote in biology, an organism whose cells lack organelles (specialized segregated structures such as nuclei, mitochondria, and chloroplasts). Prokaryote DNA is not arranged in chromosomes but forms a coiled structure called a *nucleoid*. The prokaryotes comprise only the *bacteria* and *cyanobacteria* (see ◊blue-green algae); all other organisms are eukaryotes.

Prokhorov Aleksandr 1916– . Russian physicist whose fundamental work on microwaves in 1955 led to the construction of the first practical ◊maser (the microwave equivalent of the laser) by Charles ◊Townes, for which they shared the 1964 Nobel Prize for Physics.

Prokofiev Sergey (Sergeyevich) 1891–1953. Soviet composer. His music includes operas such as *The Love for Three Oranges* 1921; ballets for Sergei ◊Diaghilev, including *Romeo and Juliet* 1935; seven symphonies including the *Classical Symphony* 1916–17; music for films; piano and violin concertos; songs and cantatas (for example, that composed for the 30th anniversary of the October Revolution); and *Peter and the Wolf* 1936.

Prokofiev was essentially a classicist in his use of form, but his extensive and varied output demonstrates great lyricism, humor, and skill. Born near Ekaterinoslav, he studied at St Petersburg under Nikolay Rimsky-Korsakov and achieved fame as a pianist. He left Russia in 1918 and lived for some time in the US and in Paris, but returned in 1927 and again in 1935.

prolapse displacement of an organ due to the effects of strain in weakening the supporting tissues. The term is most often used with regard to the rectum (due to chronic bowel problems) or the uterus (following several pregnancies).

proletariat in Marxist theory, those classes in society that possess no property, and therefore depend on the sale of their labor or expertise (as opposed to the capitalists or bourgeoisie, who own the means of production,

and the petty bourgeoisie, or working small-property owners). They are usually divided into the industrial, agricultural, and intellectual proletariat.

The term is derived from Latin *proletarii*, "the class possessing no property," whose contribution to the state was considered to be their offspring, *proles*.

PROLOG (abbreviation for *programming in logic*) high-level computer-programming language based on logic. Invented in 1971 at the University of Marseille, France, it did not achieve widespread use until more than ten years later. It is used mainly for ◊artificial-intelligence programming.

PROM (acronym for *programmable read-only memory*) in computing, a memory device in the form of an integrated circuit (chip) that can be programed after manufacture to hold information permanently. PROM chips are empty of information when manufactured, unlike ROM (read-only memory) chips, which have information built into them. Other memory devices are ◊EPROM (erasable programmable read-only memory) and ◊RAM (random-access memory).

Prometheus in Greek mythology, a ◊Titan who stole fire from heaven for the human race. In revenge, Zeus had him chained to a rock where an eagle came each day to feast on his liver, which grew back each night, until he was rescued by the hero ◊Heracles.

promethium radioactive, metallic element of the ◊lanthanide series, symbol Pm, atomic number 61, atomic weight 145. It occurs in nature only in minute amounts, produced as a fission product/by-product of uranium in ◊pitchblende and other uranium ores; for a long time it was considered not to occur in nature. The longest-lived isotope has a half-life of slightly more than 20 years.

Promethium is synthesized by neutron bombardment of neodymium, and is a product of the fission of uranium, thorium, or plutonium; it can be isolated in large amounts from the fission-product debris of uranium fuel in nuclear reactors. It is used in phosphorescent paints and as an X-ray source.

It was named in 1949 after the Greek Titan Prometheus by G M Coryell for the element isolated by US physicists J A Marinsky and L E Glendenin.

prominence bright cloud of gas projecting from the Sun into space 60,000 mi/100,000 km or more. *Quiescent prominences* last for months, and are held in place by magnetic fields in the Sun's corona. *Surge prominences* shoot gas into space at speeds of 600 mps/1,000 kps. *Loop prominences* are gases falling back to the Sun's surface after a solar ◊flare.

promissory note written promise to pay on demand, or at a fixed future time, a specific sum of money to a named person or bearer. Like a check, it is negotiable if endorsed by the payee. A commercial paper is a form of promissory note that can be bought and sold. These forms of payment are usually issued by large corporations at times when credit is otherwise difficult to obtain. It is often those who are inferior credit risks who are asked to sign promissory notes.

pronghorn ruminant mammal *Antilocapra americana* constituting the family Antilocapridae, native to the western USA. It is not a true antelope. It is light brown and

about 3 ft/1 m high. It sheds its horns annually and can reach speeds of 60 mph/100 kph. The loss of prairies to agriculture, combined with excessive hunting, has brought this unique animal close to extinction.

pronoun in grammar, a part of speech that is used in place of a noun, usually to save repetition of the noun (for example "The people arrived around nine o'clock. *They* behaved as though we were expecting *them*").

They, *them*, *he*, and *she* are *personal pronouns* (representing people); *this/these*, and *that/those* are *demonstrative pronouns* (demonstrating or pointing to something: "*this* book and not *that* book." Words like *that* and *who* can be *relative pronouns* in sentences like "She said *that* she was coming" and "Tell me *who* did it" relating one clause to another), and *myself* and *himself* are *reflexive pronouns* (reflecting back to a person, as in "He did it *himself*").

pronunciation the way in which words are rendered into human speech sounds; either a language as a whole ("French pronunciation") or a particular word or name ("what is the pronunciation of *allophony*?"). The pronunciation of languages forms the academic subject of ◊*phonetics*.

propaganda systematic spreading (propagation) of information or disinformation, usually to promote a religious or political doctrine with the intention of instilling particular attitudes or responses. Examples of the use of propaganda are the racial doctrines put forth by Nazism in World War II, and some of the ideas and strategies propagated by the US and the USSR during the ◊Cold War (1945–90).

In the US in the 1980s, the term "public diplomacy" was introduced. Government-sponsored reports and articles were presented to the media as independent sources, especially on the subject of Central America.

There are various forms of propaganda: black propaganda (a pack of lies), gray propaganda (half-truths and distortions), and white propaganda (the truth).

propane C_3H_8 gaseous hydrocarbon of the ◊alkane series, found in petroleum and used as fuel.

propanol or *propyl alcohol* third member of the homologous series of ◊alcohols. Propanol is usually a mixture of two isomeric compounds (see ◊isomer): propan-1-ol ($CH_3CH_2CH_2OH$) and propan-2-ol ($CH_3CHOHCH_3$). Both are colorless liquids that can be mixed with water and are used in perfumery.

propanone CH_3COCH_3 (common name *acetone*) colorless flammable liquid used extensively as a solvent, as in nail-varnish remover. It boils at 133.7°F/56.5°C, mixes with water in all proportions, and has a characteristic odor.

propellant substance burned in a rocket for propulsion. Two propellants are used: oxidizer and fuel are stored in separate tanks and pumped independently into the combustion chamber. Liquid oxygen (oxidizer) and liquid hydrogen (fuel) are common propellants, used, for example, in the space-shuttle main engines. The explosive charge that propels a projectile from a gun is also called a propellant.

propeller screwlike device used to propel some ships and airplanes. A propeller has a number of curved blades that describe a helical path as they rotate with the hub, and accelerate fluid (liquid or gas) backward during rotation. Reaction to this backward movement of fluid sets up a propulsive thrust forward. The marine screw propeller was developed by Francis Pettit Smith in the UK and Swedish-born John Ericson in the US and was first used 1839.

The airscrew is used to propel piston or turboprop ◊airplanes.

propene $CH_3CH:CH_2$ (common name *propylene*) second member of the alkene series of hydrocarbons. A colorless, flammable gas, it is widely used by industry to make organic chemicals, including polypropylene plastics.

propenoic acid $H_2C:CHCOOH$ (common name *acrylic acid*) acid obtained from the aldehyde propenal (acrolein) derived from glycerol or fats. Glasslike thermoplastic resins are made by polymerizing ◊esters of propenoic acid or methyl propenoic acid and used for transparent components, lenses, and dentures. Other acrylic compounds are used for adhesives, artificial fibers, and artists' acrylic paint.

proper motion gradual change in the position of a star that results from its motion in orbit around our galaxy, the Milky Way. Proper motions are slight and undetectable to the naked eye, but can be accurately measured on telescopic photographs taken many years apart. Barnard's Star is the star with the largest proper motion, 10.3 arc seconds per year.

Propertius Sextus *c.* 47–15 BC. Roman elegiac poet, a member of Maecenas' circle, who wrote of his love for his mistress "Cynthia."

property the right to title and to control the use of a thing (such as land, a building, a work of art, or a computer program). In US law, a distinction is made between real property, which involves a degree of geographical fixity, and personal property, which does not. Property is never absolute, since any society places limits on an individual's property (such as the right to transfer that property to another). Different societies have held widely varying interpretations of the nature of property and the extent of the rights of the owner to that property.

prophet person thought to speak from divine inspiration or one who foretells the future. In the Bible, the chief prophets were Elijah, Amos, Hosea, and Isaiah. In Islam, ◊Mohammed is believed to be the last and greatest of a long line of prophets beginning with Adam and including Moses and Jesus.

In the Bible, one of the succession of saints and seers who preached and prophesied in the Hebrew kingdoms in Palestine from the 8th century BC until the suppression of Jewish independence in 586 BC, and possibly later. The prophetic books of the Old Testament constitute a division of the Hebrew Bible.

prophylaxis any measure taken to prevent disease, including exercise and ◊vaccination. Prophylactic (preventive) medicine is an aspect of public-health provision that is receiving increasing attention.

proportion two variable quantities x and y are proportional if, for all values of x, $y = kx$, where k is a constant. This means that if x increases, y increases in a linear fashion.

A graph of x against y would be a straight line passing through the origin (the point $x = 0$, $y = 0$). y is inversely proportional to x if the graph of y against $1/x$ is a straight line through the origin. The corresponding equation is $y = k/x$. Many laws of science relate quantities that are proportional (for example, ◊Boyle's law).

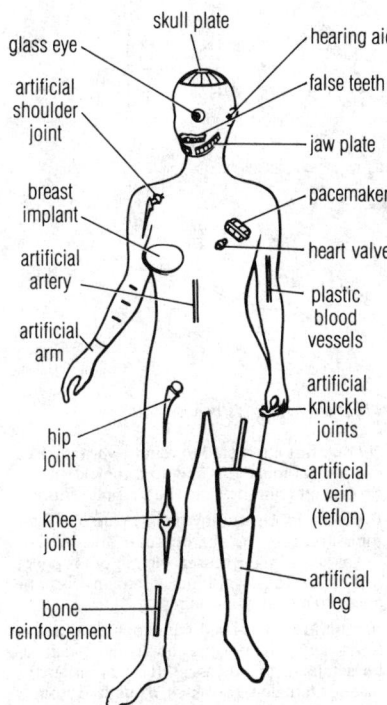

prosthesis An artificial body part used to replace one that is defective or absent.

prop root or *stilt root* modified root that grows from the lower part of a stem or trunk down to the ground, providing a plant with extra support. Prop roots are common on some woody plants, such as mangroves, and also occur on a few herbaceous plants, such as corn. *Buttress roots* are a type of prop root found at the base of tree trunks, extended and flattened along the upper edge to form massive triangular buttresses; they are common on tropical trees.

propyl alcohol common name for ◊propanol.

propylene common name for ◊propene.

prose spoken or written language without metrical regularity; in literature, prose corresponds more closely to the patterns of everyday speech than ◊poetry. In modern literature, the distinction between verse and prose is not always clear cut.

In Western literature prose was traditionally used for what is today called nonfiction—that is, history, biography, essays, and so on—while verse was used for imaginative literature. Prose came into its own as a vehicle for fiction with the rise of the ◊novel in the 18th century.

Proserpina Roman equivalent of ◊Persephone, goddess of the underworld.

prostaglandin any of a group of complex fatty acids that act as messenger substances between cells. Effects include stimulating the contraction of smooth muscle (for example, of the womb during birth), regulating the production of stomach acid, and modifying hormonal activity. In excess, prostaglandins may produce inflammatory disorders such as arthritis. Synthetic prostaglandins are used to induce labor in humans and domestic animals.

The analgesic actions of substances such as aspirin are due to inhibition of prostaglandin synthesis.

prostate gland gland surrounding and opening into the ◊urethra at the base of the ◊bladder in male mammals.

The prostate gland produces an alkaline fluid that is released during ejaculation; this fluid activates sperm, and prevents their clumping together. In humans, the prostate often enlarges and obstructs the urethra; this is treated by prostatectomy.

prosthesis replacement of a body part with an artificial substitute. Prostheses include artificial limbs, hearing aids, false teeth and eyes, and for the heart, a ◊pacemaker and plastic heart valves and blood vessels.

Prostheses in the form of artificial limbs, such as wooden legs and metal hooks for hands, have been used for centuries, although artificial limbs are now more natural-looking and comfortable to wear. The comparatively new field of ◊bionics has developed myoelectric, or bionic, arms, which are electronically operated and worked by minute electrical impulses from body muscles.

prostitution receipt of money for sexual acts. Society's attitude toward prostitution varies according to place and period. In some countries, tolerance is combined with licensing of brothels and health checks of the prostitutes (both male and female).

In the US, laws vary from state to state, with Nevada having legalized prostitution. Where it remains illegal, it is often associated with drug abuse, street crime, and exploitation of children, and many communities expend large resources in an effort to control it.

protactinium (Latin *proto* "before" + actinium) silver-gray, radioactive, metallic element of the ◊actinide series, symbol Pa, atomic number 91, atomic weight 231.036. It occurs in nature in very small quantities, in ◊pitchblende and other uranium ores. It has 14 known isotopes; the longest-lived, Pa-231, has a half-life of 32,480 years.

The element was discovered in 1913 (Pa-234, with a half-life of only 1.2 minutes) as a product of uranium decay by Kasimir Fajans and O Göhring; other isotopes were found in later years and the name was officially adopted in 1949, although it had been in use since 1918.

protandry in a flower, the state where the male reproductive organs reach maturity before those of the female. This is a common method of avoiding self-fertilization. See also ◊protogyny.

protease general term for an enzyme capable of splitting proteins. Examples include pepsin, found in the stomach, and trypsin, found in the small intestine.

protectionism in economics, the imposition of heavy duties or import quotas by a government as a means of discouraging the import of foreign goods likely to compete with domestic products. Price controls, quota systems, and the reduction of surpluses are among the measures taken for agricultural products in the European Community (see ◊agriculture). The opposite practice is ◊free trade.

protectorate formerly in international law, a small state under the direct or indirect control of a larger one. The 20th-century equivalent was a ◊Trust Territory. In English history the rule of Oliver and Richard ◊Cromwell 1653–59 is referred to as *the Protectorate*.

protein complex, biologically important substance composed of amino acids joined by amino acids, where R is one of many possible side chains

peptide
bond

protein *A protein molecule is a long chain of amino acids linked by peptide bonds.*

peptide bonds. Other types of bond, such as sulfur–sulfur bonds, hydrogen bonds, and cation bridges between acid sites, are responsible for creating the protein's characteristic three-dimensional structure, which may be fibrous, globular, or pleated.

Proteins are essential to all living organisms. As **enzymes** they regulate all aspects of metabolism. Structural proteins such as **keratin** and **collagen** make up the skin, claws, bones, tendons, and ligaments; **muscle** proteins produce movement; **haemoglobin** transports oxygen; and **membrane** proteins regulate the movement of substances into and out of cells.

For humans, protein is an essential part of the diet (60 g per day is required), and is found in greatest quantity in soybeans and other grain legumes, meat, eggs, and cheese. Protein provides 4 kcal of energy per gram.

protein synthesis manufacture, within the cytoplasm of the cell, of the ◊proteins an organism needs. The building blocks of proteins are ◊amino acids, of which there are 20 types. The pattern in which the amino acids are linked decides what kind of protein is produced. In turn it is the genetic code, contained within ◊DNA, that determines the precise order in which the amino acids are linked up during protein manufacture. Interestingly, DNA is found only in the nucleus, yet protein synthesis only occurs in the cytoplasm. The information necessary for making the proteins is carried from the nucleus to the cytoplasm by another nucleic acid, ◊RNA.

pro tem abbreviation for *pro tempore* (Latin "for the time being").

Proterozoic period of geological time, 2.5 billion to 570 million years ago, the second division of the Precambrian era. It is defined as the time of simple life, since many rocks dating from this eon show traces of biological activity, and some contain the fossils of bacteria and algae.

Protestantism one of the main divisions of Christianity, which emerged from Roman Catholicism at the ◊Reformation. The chief Protestant denominations are the Episcopalian (Anglican Communion in the UK), Baptists, Christian Scientists, Congregationalists (United Church of Christ), Lutherans, Methodists, Pentecostals, and Presbyterians, with a total membership in about 300 million.

Protestantism takes its name from the protest of Luther and his supporters at the Diet of Spires 1529 against the decision to reaffirm the edict of the Diet of Worms against the Reformation. The ecumenical movement of the 20th century has attempted to reunite various Protestant denominations and, to some extent, the Protestant churches and the Catholic church.

Proteus in Greek mythology, an old man, the warden of the sea beasts of the sea god Poseidon, who possessed the gift of prophecy and could transform himself into any form he chose to evade questioning.

prothallus short-lived gametophyte of many ferns and other ◊pteridophytes (such as horsetails or clubmosses). It bears either the male or female sex organs, or both. Typically it is a small, green, flattened structure that is anchored in the soil by several ◊rhizoids (slender, hairlike structures, acting as roots) and needs damp conditions to survive. The reproductive organs are borne on the lower surface close to the soil. See also ◊alternation of generations.

protist in biology, a single-celled organism which has a eukaryotic cell, but which is not member of the plant, fungal, or animal kingdoms. The main protists are ◊protozoa.

Single-celled photosynthetic organisms, such as diatoms and dinoflagellates, are classified as protists or algae. Recently the term has also been used for members of the kingdom Protista, which features in certain five-kingdom classifications of the living world. This kingdom may include slime molds, all algae (seaweeds as well as unicellular forms), and protozoa.

protocol in computing, an agreed set of standards for the transfer of data between different devices. They cover transmission speed, format of data, and the signals required to synchronize the transfer. See also ◊interface.

protogyny in a flower, the state where the female reproductive organs reach maturity before those of the male. Like protandry, in which the male organs reach maturity first, this is a method of avoiding self-fertilization, but it is much less common.

proton positively charged ◊elementary particle, a constituent of the nucleus of all atoms. It belongs to the ◊baryon group of ◊hadrons and is composed of two up quarks and one down quark. A proton is extremely long-lived, with a life span of at least 10^{32} years. It carries a unit positive charge equal to the negative charge of an ◊electron. Its mass is almost 1,836 times that of an electron, or 1.673×10^{-24} g. The number of protons in the atom of an ◊element is equal to the atomic number of that element.

protonema young ◊gametophyte of a moss, which develops from a germinating spore (see ◊alternation of generations). Typically it is a green, branched, threadlike structure that grows over the soil surface bearing several buds that develop into the characteristic adult moss plants.

proton number alternate name for ◊atomic number.

protoplasm contents of a living cell. Strictly speaking it includes all the discrete structures (organelles) in a cell, but it is often used simply to mean the jellylike material in which these float. The contents of a cell outside the nucleus are called ◊cytoplasm.

protozoan any of a group of single-celled, mainly heterotrophic organisms without rigid cell walls. Some, such as amebas, ingest other cells, but most are ◊saprotrophs or parasites. They all require a fluid environment, and include ciliates, flagellates, rhizopods, and sporozoans.

protractor instrument used to measure a flat ◊angle.

Proudhon Pierre Joseph 1809–1865. French anarchist, born in Besançon. He sat in the Constituent Assembly of 1848, was imprisoned for three years, and had to go into exile in Brussels. He published *Qu'est-ce que la propriété/ What is Property?* 1840 and *Philosophie de la misère/Philosophy of Poverty* 1846; the former contains the dictum "property is theft."

Proust Marcel 1871–1922. French novelist and critic. His immense autobiographical work *A la Recherche du temps perdu/Remembrance of Things Past* 1913–27, consisting of a series of novels, is the expression of his childhood memories coaxed from his subconscious; it is also a precise reflection of life in France at the end of the 19th century.

Born at Auteuil, Proust was a delicate, asthmatic child; until he was 35 he moved in the fashionable circles of Parisian society, but after the death of his parents 1904–05 he went into seclusion in a cork-lined room in his Paris apartment, and devoted the rest of his life to writing his masterpiece.

Prout William 1785–1850. British physician and chemist. In 1815 Prout published his hypothesis that the atomic weight of every atom is an exact and integral multiple of the hydrogen atom. The discovery of isotopes (atoms of the same element that have different masses) in the 20th century bore out his idea.

Provençal language member of the Romance branch of the Indo-European language family, spoken in and around Provence in SE France. It is now regarded as a dialect or patois.

During the Middle Ages Provençal was in competition with French and was the language of the troubadours. It had a strong literary influence on such neighboring languages as Italian, Spanish, and Portuguese. Since the 19th century, attempts have been made to revive it as a literary language.

Provençal literature Provençal literature originated in the 10th century and flowered in the 12th century with the work of the ◊troubadours, poet-musicians of the 12th–13th centuries. After the decline of the troubadours in the 13th century, Provençal disappeared as a literary medium from the 14th until the 19th centuries, when Jacques Jasmin (1798–1864) and others paved the way for the Félibrige group of poets, of whom the greatest are Joseph Roumanille (1818–1891), Frédéric Mistral (1830–1914), and Félix Gras (1844-1901).

Provence-Alpes-Côte d'Azur region of SE France, comprising the *départements* of Alpes-de-Haute-Provence, Hautes-Alpes, Alpes-Maritimes, Bouches-du-Rhône, Var, and Vaucluse; area 12,120 sq mi/31,400 sq km; capital Marseille; population (1986) 4,059,000. The *Côte d'Azur*, on the Mediterranean, is a tourist center. Provence was an independent kingdom in the 10th century, and the area still has its own language, Provençal.

Proverbs book of the Old Testament traditionally ascribed to the Hebrew king ◊Solomon. The Proverbs form a series of maxims on moral and ethical matters.

Providence industrial seaport (jewelry, silverware, textiles and textile machinery, watches, chemicals, meatpacking) and capital of Rhode Island, on Narragansett Bay and the Providence River, 27 mi/43 km from the Atlantic; population (1990) 160,700.

Educational institutions include Brown University and the Rhode Island School of Design. Providence was founded 1636 by Roger Williams, who had been banished from Plymouth colony for his religious beliefs. By the early 18th century the community was thriving as a port for West Indian trade. It was an important base for American and French troops in the American Revolution.

Provincetown Players group of US actors, producers, and playwrights formed 1915 in Provincetown, Cape Cod, Massachusetts; they later moved to New York. Mounting new plays by Eugene O'Neill, Theodore Dreiser, e e cummings, and others, they opened the door to US experimental theater.

Provisions of Oxford provisions issued by Henry III of England 1258 under pressure from Simon de Montfort and the baronial opposition. They provided for the establishment of a baronial council to run the government, carry out reforms, and keep a check on royal power.

provitamin any precursor substance of a vitamin. Provitamins are injested substances that become converted to active vitamins within the organism. One example is ergosterol (provitamin D_2), which through the action of sunlight is converted to calciferol (vitamin D_2); another example is B-carotene, which is hydrolyzed in the liver to vitamin A.

Provo city in N central Utah, on the Provo River, SE of Salt Lake City; seat of Utah county. Industries include iron and steel, food processing, and electronics. Brigham Young University is here; population (1990) 86,800.

Proxima Centauri the closest star to the Sun, 4.2 light-years away. It is a faint ◊red dwarf, visible only with a telescope, and is a member of the Alpha Centauri triple-star system.

It is called Proxima because it is about 0.1 light-years closer to us than its two partners.

proxy in law, a person authorized to stand in another's place; also the document conferring this right. The term usually refers to voting at meetings, but marriages by proxy are possible.

Prudhoe Bay a bay of the Arctic Ocean on the N coast (North Slope) of Alaska. An immense oil strike in the area in 1968 led to the construction of the 789-mi/1,270-km Trans-Alaska Pipeline, completed 1977, that carries oil from Prudhoe Bay to Valdez, on the S coast of Alaska. Almost 20% of US oil comes from the North Slope fields, although production has slowed.

Prud'hon Pierre 1758–1823. French Romantic painter. He became drawing instructor and court painter to the emperor Napoleon's wives.

After winning the Prix de Rome 1784, Prud'hon visited Italy but, unlike his contemporary Jacques Louis David, he was unaffected by the Neo-Classical vogue; his style is indebted to the Italian painter Antonio ◊Correggio.

Prunus genus of trees of the northern hemisphere, family Rosaceae, producing fruit with a fleshy, edible pericarp (outer wall). The genus includes plums, cherries, peaches, apricots, and also almonds.

Prussia N German state 1618–1945 on the Baltic coast. It was an independent kingdom until 1867, when it became, under Otto von ◊Bismarck, the military power of the North German Confederation and part of the German Empire 1871 under the Prussian king Wilhelm I. West Prussia became part of Poland under the Treaty of ◊Versailles, and East Prussia was largely incorporated into the USSR after 1945.

1618 Formed by the union of ◊Brandenburg and the duchy of Prussia (established 1525).
1640–88 The country's military power was founded by Frederick William, the "Great Elector."
1701 Prussia became a kingdom under Frederick I.
1713–40 Frederick William I expanded the army.
1740–86 Silesia, East Frisia, and West Prussia were annexed by ◊Frederick II the Great.
1806 Frederick William III was defeated at Jena by Napoleon Bonaparte.
1815 After the Congress of Vienna Prussia regained its lost territories and also acquired lands in the Rhineland and Saxony.
1848 Bismarck suppressed the ◊revolutions of 1848.
1864 War with Denmark resulted in the acquisition of Schleswig and Holstein.
1866 After the defeat of Austria, Prussia formed the North German Confederation with the territories of Hanover, Nassau, Frankfurt-am-Main, and Hesse-Cassel.
1871 After Prussia's victory in the Franco-Prussian War, the German Empire was proclaimed, under Bismarck's chancellorship, for Wilhelm I.
1918 Prussia became a republic after World War I.
1932 Prussia lost its local independence in Hitler's Germany and came under the control of the Reich.
1946 After World War II the Allies abolished Prussia altogether, dividing its territories among East and West Germany, Poland, and the USSR.

prussic acid former name for ◊hydrocyanic acid.

PS abbreviation for *post scriptum* (Latin "after writing").

psalm sacred poem or song of praise. The Book of Psalms in the Old Testament is divided into five books containing 150 psalms. They are traditionally ascribed to David, the second king of Israel.

pseudocarp fruitlike structure that incorporates tissue that is not derived from the ovary wall. The additional tissues may be derived from floral parts such as the ◊receptacle and ◊calyx. For example, the colored, fleshy part of a strawberry develops from the receptacle and the true fruits are small ◊achenes—the "pips" embedded in its outer surface. Rose hips are a type of pseudocarp that consists of a hollow, fleshy receptacle containing a number of

achenes within. Different types of pseudocarp include pineapples, figs, apples, and pears.

A *coenocarpium* is a fleshy, multiple pseudocarp derived from an ◊inflorescence rather than a single flower. The pineapple has a thickened central axis surrounded by fleshy tissues derived from the receptacles and floral parts of many flowers. A fig is a type of pseudocarp called a *syconium*, formed from a hollow receptacle with small flowers attached to the inner wall. After fertilization the ovaries of the female flowers develop into one-seeded achenes. Apples and pears are ◊pomes, another type of pseudocarp.

pseudocopulation attempted copulation by a male insect with a flower. It results in ◊pollination of the flower and is common in the orchid family, where the flowers of many species resemble a particular species of female bee. When a male bee attempts to mate with a flower, the pollinia (groups of pollen grains) stick to its body. They are transferred to the stigma of another flower when the insect attempts copulation again.

pseudomorph mineral that has replaced another *in situ* and has retained the external crystal shape of the original mineral.

psi in parapsychology, a hypothetical faculty common to humans and other animals said to be responsible for extra-sensory perception (ESP) and telekinesis.

Psilocybe genus of mushroom with hallucinogenic properties, including the Mexican sacred mushroom *P. mexicana*, which contains compounds with effects similar to LSD (lysergic acid diethylamide, a hallucinogen). A related species *P. semilanceata* is found in N Europe.

psittacosis infectious acute or chronic disease, contracted by humans from birds (especially parrots), which may result in pneumonia. It is caused by a bacterium (*Chlamydia psittaci*, see ◊chlamydia) and treated with tetracycline.

psoriasis chronic, recurring skin disease characterized by raised, red, scaly patches, usually on the scalp, back, arms, and/or legs. Tar preparations, steroid creams, and ultraviolet light are used to treat it, and sometimes it disappears spontaneously. Psoriasis may be accompanied by a form of arthritis (inflammation of the joints).

Psyche late Greek personification of the soul as a winged girl or young woman. The goddess Aphrodite was so jealous of Psyche's beauty that she ordered her son Eros, the god of love, to make Psyche fall in love with the worst of men. Instead, he fell in love with her herself.

psychedelic drug any drug that produces hallucinations or altered states of consciousness. Such sensory experiences may be in the auditory, visual, tactile, olfactory, or gustatory fields or in any combination. Among drugs known to have psychedelic effects are LSD (lysergic acid diethylamine), mescaline, and, to a mild degree, marijuana, along with a number of other plant-derived or synthetically prepared substances.

Most of these drugs are known to cause temporary or recurring psychotic episodes.

psychedelic rock or *acid rock* pop music that usually involves advanced electronic equipment for both light and sound. The free-form improvisations and light shows that appeared about 1966, attempting to suggest or improve on mind-altering drug experiences, had by the 1980s evolved into stadium performances with lasers and other special effects.

The swirling organ riffs and multilayered guitar-and-feedback washes in 1980s and 1990s indie rock derive from 1960s psychedelic rock.

psychiatry branch of medicine dealing with the diagnosis and treatment of mental disorder, normally divided into the areas of **neurotic conditions** including anxiety, depression, and hysteria and *psychotic* disorders such as schizophrenia. Psychiatric treatment consists of analysis, drugs, or electroconvulsive therapy.

In practice there is considerable overlap between psychiatry and clinical ⟡psychology, the fundamental difference being that psychiatrists are trained medical doctors (holding an MD degree) and may therefore prescribe drugs, whereas psychologists may hold a PhD but do not need a medical qualification to practice. See also ⟡psychoanalysis.

psychic person allegedly possessed of parapsychological, or paranormal, powers.

psychoanalysis theory and treatment method for neuroses, developed by Sigmund ⟡Freud. The main treatment method involves the free association of ideas, and their interpretation by patient and analyst. It is typically prolonged and expensive and its effectiveness has been disputed.

Psychoanalysis emphasizes that the impact of early childhood sexuality and experiences, stored in the unconscious can lead to the development of adult emotional problems. Treatment involves recognizing these long-buried events in order to relieve actual pressure. Modern approaches, drawing from Freud's ideas, tend to be briefer and more problem-focused.

psychology systematic study of human and animal behavior. The first psychology laboratory was founded 1879 by Wilhelm ⟡Wundt at Leipzig, Germany. The subject includes diverse areas of study and application, among them the roles of instinct, heredity, environment, and culture; the processes of sensation, perception, learning and memory; the bases of motivation and emotion; and the functioning of thought, intelligence, and language. Significant psychologists have included Gustav Fechner (1801–1887) founder of psychophysics; Wolfgang Köhler (1887–1967), one of the ⟡gestalt or "whole" psychologists; Sigmund Freud and his associates Carl Jung, Alfred Adler, and Hermann Rorschach (1884-1922); William James, Jean Piaget; Carl Rogers; Hans Eysenck; J B Watson, and B F Skinner.

Experimental psychology emphasizes the application of rigorous and objective scientific methods to the study of a wide range of mental processes and behavior, whereas social psychology concerns the study of individuals within their social environment; for example, within groups and organizations. This has led to the development of related fields such as ⟡occupational psychology, which studies human behavior at work, and ⟡educational psychology. *Clinical psychology* concerns the understanding and treatment of mental health disorders, such as anxiety, phobias, or depression; treatment may include behavior therapy, cognitive therapy, counseling, psychoanalysis, or some combination of these.

Modern studies have been diverse, for example the psychological causes of obesity; the nature of religious experience; and the

underachievement of women seen as resulting from social pressures. Other related subjects are the nature of sleep and dreams, and the possible extensions of the senses, which leads to the more contentious ground of ⟡parapsychology.

psychometrics measurement of mental processes. This includes intelligence and aptitude testing to help in job selection and in the clinical assessment of cognitive deficiencies resulting from brain damage.

psychopathy personality disorder characterized by chronic antisocial behavior (violating the rights of others, often violently) and an absence of feelings of guilt about the behavior.

Because the term has been misused to refer to any severe mental disorder, many psychologists now prefer the term "antisocial personality disorder."

psychosis or *psychotic disorder* general term for a serious mental disorder where the individual commonly loses contact with reality and may experience hallucinations (seeing or hearing things that do not exist) or delusions (fixed false beliefs). For example, in a paranoid psychosis, an individual may believe that others are plotting against him or her. A major type of psychosis is ⟡schizophrenia (which may be biochemically induced).

psychosomatic a physical symptom or disease, thought to arise from emotional or mental factors.

The term "psychosomatic" has been applied to many conditions, including asthma, migraine, hypertension, and peptic ulcers. Whereas it is unlikely that these and other conditions are wholly due to psychological factors, emotional states such as anxiety or depression do have a distinct influence on the frequency and severity of illness.

psychosurgery operation to achieve some mental effect. For example, **lobotomy** is the separation of the white fibers in the prefrontal lobe of the brain, as a means of relieving a deep state of anxiety.

It is irreversible and the degree of personality change is not predictable. Some states strictly regulate its use.

psychotherapy treatment approaches for psychological problems involving talking rather than surgery or drugs. Examples include ⟡cognitive therapy and ⟡psychoanalysis.

psychotic disorder another name for ⟡*psychosis*.

pt symbol for ⟡*pint*.

Ptah Egyptian god, the divine potter, a personification of the creative force. He was worshiped at ⟡Memphis, and was often portrayed as a mummified man. He was said to be the father of ⟡Imhotep, the physician and architect.

ptarmigan any of a genus (Lagopus) of hardy, northern ground-dwelling birds (family Phasianidae, which also includes ⟡grouse), with feathered legs and feet.

The willow ptarmigan *L. lagopus*, found in bushes and heather in northern parts of North America, Europe, and Asia, grows to 15 in/38 cm and turns white in the winter.

pteridophyte simple type of ⟡vascular plant. The pteridophytes comprise four classes: the Psilosida, including the most primitive vascular plants, found mainly in the tropics; the Lycopsida, including the club mosses; the Sphenopsida, including the horsetails; and the Pteropsida, including the ferns. They do not produce seeds.

They are mainly terrestrial, non-flowering plants characterized by the presence of a vascular system; the possession of true stems, roots, and leaves; and by a marked ⟡alternation of generations, with the sporophyte forming the dominant generation in the life cycle. The pteridophytes formed a large and dominant flora during the Carboniferous period, but many are now known only from fossils.

pterodactyl genus of ⟡pterosaur.

pterosaur extinct flying reptile of the order Pterosauria, existing in the Mesozoic age. They ranged from starling size to a 40 ft/12 m wingspan. Some had horns on their heads that, when in flight, made a whistling to roaring sound.

Pterosaurs were formerly assumed to be smooth-skinned gliders, but recent discoveries

psychology: chronology

1890	William James published the first comprehensive psychology text, *Principles of Psychology*.
1895	Freud's first book on psychoanalysis was published.
1896	The first clinical psychology clinic was founded by Witner at the University of Pennsylvania.
1897	Wilhelm Wundt founded the first psychological laboratory in Leipzig.
1903	Ivan Pavlov reported his early study on conditioned reflexes in animals.
1905	Alfred Binet and Théodore Simon developed the first effective intelligence test.
1908	A first textbook of social psychology was published by William McDougall.
1913	John B Watson published *Behaviorism*, which laid the basis for the school and doctrine of that name.
1926	Jean Piaget presented his first book on child development.
1947	Hans Eysenck published *Dimensions of Personality*, a large-scale study of neuroticism and extraversion.
1953	B F Skinner's *Science of Human Behaviour*, a text of operant conditioning, was published.
1957	Noam Chomsky's *Syntactic Structures*, which stimulated the development of psycholinguistics, the study of language processes, was published.
1963	Milgram's studies of compliance with authority indicated conditions under which individuals behave cruelly to others when instructed to do so.
1967	Neisser's *Cognitive Psychology* marked renewed interest in the study of cognition after years in which behaviorism had been dominant.
1972	Newell and Simon simulated human problem-solving abilities by computer; an example of artificial intelligence.
1989	Jeffrey Masson attacked the fundamental principles of Freudian analytic psychotherapy in his book *Against Therapy*.

show that at least some were furry, probably warm-blooded, and may have had muscle fibers and blood vessels on their wings, stiffened by moving the hind legs, thus allowing controlled and strong flapping flight.

PTO abbreviation for *please turn over*.

Ptolemy (Claudius Ptolemaeus) *c.* 100–AD 170. Egyptian astronomer and geographer who worked in Alexandria. His *Almagest* developed the theory that Earth is the center of the universe, with the Sun, Moon, and stars revolving around it. In 1543 the Polish astronomer ◊Copernicus proposed an alternative to the *Ptolemaic system*. Ptolemy's *Geography* was a standard source of information until the 16th century.

Ptolemy dynasty of kings of Macedonian origin who ruled Egypt over a period of 300 years; they included:

Ptolemy I *c.* 367–283 BC. Ruler of Egypt from 323 BC, king from 304. He was one of ◊Alexander the Great's generals, and possibly his half brother (and married his lover, ◊Thaïs). He established the library in Alexandria.

Ptolemy XIII 63–47 BC. Joint ruler of Egypt with his sister-wife Cleopatra; she put him to death.

ptomaine any of a group of toxic chemical substances (alkaloids) produced as a result of decomposition by bacterial action on proteins.

Ptomaine is not the relevant factor in "food poisoning," which is usually caused by bacteria of the genus *Salmonella*.

puberty stage in human development when the individual becomes sexually mature. It may occur from the age of ten upward. The sexual organs take on their adult form and pubic hair grows. In girls, menstruation begins, and the breasts develop; in boys, the voice breaks and becomes deeper, and facial hair develops.

pubes lowest part of the front of the human trunk, the region where the external generative organs are situated. The underlying bony structure, the pubic arch, is formed by the union in the midline of the two pubic bones, which are the front portions of the hip bones. In women this is more prominent than in men, to allow more room for the passage of the child's head at birth, and it carries a pad of fat and connective tissue, the *mons veneris* (mountain of Venus), for its protection.

public corporation management and administrative structure, similar to a private ◊corporation, established to run state-owned or nationalized enterprises. They are governed by a board of directors, although some level of government is either the sole or controlling stockholder.

Distinct from a publicly held corporation in the US, where shares are sold to the public, then traded in one of the stock markets, public corporations decline in number as the trend toward ◊privatization grows.

public school in the US and many English-speaking countries, "public" schools are maintained by the state, and "private" schools are independent institutions, supported by fees. In England, public schools are fee-paying independent schools.

Since the founding of the nation, universal public education has become an important tradition in the US, and school attendance is compulsory to age 16. Public schools serve as the major method of socialization for immigrants. Since the 1960s, increasing numbers of middle-class whites have withdrawn their

children from urban public school systems, choosing private and parochial (church-run) alternatives, thus compromising public education in the process.

public spending expenditure by government, covering the military, health, education, infrastructure, development projects, and the cost of servicing overseas borrowing.

A principal source of revenue to cover public expenditure is taxation. Most countries present their plans for spending in their annual budgets.

publishing production of books for sale. The publisher arranges for the commissioning, editing, printing, binding, warehousing, and distribution of books to booksellers or book clubs. Although all rights in a book may be purchased by the publisher for a single outright fee, it is more usual that a fixed royalty is paid to the author on every copy sold, in return for the exclusive right to publish in an agreed territory.

Puccini Giacomo (Antonio Domenico Michele Secondo Maria) 1858–1924. Italian opera composer whose music shows a strong gift for melody and dramatic effect and whose operas combine exotic plots with elements of *verismo* (realism). They include *Manon Lescaut* 1893, *La Bohème* 1896, *Tosca* 1900, *Madame Butterfly* 1904, and the unfinished *Turandot* 1926.

Puebla (de Zaragoza) industrial city (textiles, sugar refining, metallurgy, hand-crafted pottery and tiles) and capital of Puebla state, S central Mexico; population (1986) 1,218,000. Founded 1535 as *Pueblo de los Angeles*, it was later renamed after General de Zaragoza, who defeated the French here 1862.

Pueblo US intelligence vessel captured by the North Koreans Jan 1968, allegedly within their territorial waters. The crew, but not the ship, were released Dec 1968. A naval court recommended no disciplinary action.

Pueblo city in S central Colorado, on the Arkansas River, SE of Colorado Springs. Industries include steel, coal, lumber, and livestock and other agricultural products; population (1990) 98,600.

Pueblo Indian (Spanish *pueblos*, villages) generic name for a member of any of the farming groups of the SW US and N Mexico, living in communal villages of flat-topped adobe or stone structures arranged in terraces. Surviving groups include the Hopi and the Zuni.

puerperal fever infection of the genital tract of the mother after childbirth, due to lack of aseptic conditions. Formerly often fatal, it is now rare and treated with antibiotics.

Puerto Rico the Commonwealth of, island of the West Indies (from 1898 to 1932, Porto Rico)
area 3,475 sq mi/9,000 sq km
capital San Juan
cities ports: Mayagüez, Ponce
features Old San Juan; nightclubs and casinos; rain forest of El Yunque; colonial-style San German; Arecibo Observatory
products apparel, textiles, pharmaceuticals, petroleum products, rum, refined sugar, coffee, computers, instruments, office machines, cattle, hogs, milk, cement
currency US dollar
population (1990) 3,522,000
language Spanish and English (official)
religion Roman Catholic

government under the constitution of 1952, similar to that of the US, with a governor elected for four years and a legislative assembly with a senate and house of representatives
famous people Roberto Clemente, José Ferrer, Eugenio María de Hostos, Raul Julia, Rita Moreno, Luis Muñoz Marin
history visited 1493 by Columbus; annexed by Spain 1509; ceded to the US after the ◊Spanish-American War 1898; achieved commonwealth status with local self-government 1952.

This was confirmed in preference to independence by a referendum 1967, but there is both an independence movement and one preferring incorporation as a state of the US. Although legislation in favor of a further referendum was proposed and discussed 1990–91, it was later shelved.

puff adder variety of ◊adder, a poisonous snake.

puffball globulous fruiting body of certain fungi (see ◊fungus) that cracks with maturity, releasing the enclosed spores in the form of a brown powder; for example, the common puffball *Lycoperdon perlatum*.

puffer fish fish of the family Tetraodontidae. As a means of defense it inflates its body with air or water until it becomes spherical and the skin spines become erect. Puffer fish are mainly found in warm waters, where they feed on mollusks, crustaceans, and coral.

They vary in size, up to 20 in/50 cm long. The skin of some puffer fish is poisonous (25 times more toxic than cyanide). In Japan, where they are called *fugu*, they are prized as a delicacy after the poison has been removed. Nevertheless, the death of about 100 diners is recorded each year.

puffin any of various sea birds of the genus *Fratercula* of the ◊auk family, found in the N Atlantic and Pacific. The puffin is about 14 in/35 cm long, with a white face and front, red legs, and a large deep bill, very brightly colored in summer. Having short wings and webbed feet, puffins are poor fliers but excellent swimmers. They nest in rock crevices, or make burrows, and lay a single egg.

pug breed of small dog with short wrinkled face, chunky body, and tail curled over the hip. It weighs 13–18 lb/6–8 kg.

Puget Sound inlet of the Pacific Ocean on the W coast of Washington State.

Puglia (English *Apulia*) region of Italy, the south estern "heel;" area 7,450 sq mi/19,300 sq km; capital Bari; population (1990) 4,081,500. Products include wheat, grapes, almonds, olives, and vegetables. The main industrial center is Taranto.

P'u-i (or *Pu-Yi*) Henry 1906–1967. Last emperor of China (as Hsuan Tung) from 1908 until his deposition 1912; he was restored for a week 1917. After his deposition he chose to be called Henry. He was president 1932–34 and emperor 1934–45 of the Japanese puppet state of Manchukuo (see ◊Manchuria).

Captured by Soviet troops, he was returned to China 1949 and put on trial in the new People's Republic of China 1950. Pardoned by Mao Zedong 1959, he became a worker in a botanical garden in Beijing.

Pula commercial and naval port in W Croatia, on the Adriatic coast; population (1981) 77,278. A Roman naval base, *Colonia Pietas Julia*, it was seized by Venice in 1148, passed to Austria

Pulitzer Prize for fiction

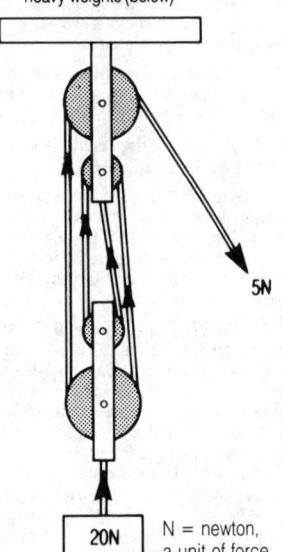

simple pulley (above)
pulley system used for
heavy weights (below)

N = newton,
a unit of force

pulley *The mechanical advantage of a pulley increases with the number of rope strands.*

1815, to Italy 1919, to Yugoslavia 1947, and in 1991 became part of independent Croatia.

Pulaski Casimir 1747–1779. Polish patriot and military leader in the American Revolution. After participating in the unsuccessful Polish defense against the Russian invasion 1770–72, he went into exile and was hired by Silas Deane and Benjamin Franklin to aid the American Revolutionary War effort. Arriving in America 1777, Pulaski was placed in command of the Continental cavalry. He spent the winter of 1777–78 at Valley Forge and after a personal dispute with General Anthony Wayne, was given an independent cavalry command. Pulaski died in action in the siege of Savannah.

Born in Padolia, Poland, Pulaski embarked on a military career early in life.

Pulitzer Joseph 1847–1911. Hungarian-born US newspaper publisher. He acquired *The World* 1883 in New York City and, as a publisher, his format set the style for the modern newspaper. After his death, funds provided in his will established 1912 the school of journalism at Columbia University and the annual Pulitzer Prizes in journalism, literature, and music (from 1917).

Pulitzer came to the US 1864 and became a citizen 1867. A Democrat, he merged two St Louis newspapers and published 1878 the successful St Louis *Post-Dispatch*. He made *The World* into a voice of the Democratic Party. During a circulation battle with rival publisher William Randolph ◊Hearst's papers, he and Hearst were accused of resorting to "yellow journalism," or sensationalism.

pulley simple machine consisting of a fixed, grooved wheel, sometimes in a block, around which a rope or chain can be run. A simple pulley serves only to change the direction of the applied effort (as in a simple hoist for raising loads). The use of more than one pulley results in a mechanical advantage, so that a given effort can raise a heavier load.

The mechanical advantage depends on the arrangement of the pulleys. For instance, a block and tackle arrangement with three ropes supporting the load will lift it with one-third of the effort needed to lift it directly (if friction is ignored), giving a mechanical advantage of 3.

Pullman George 1831–1901. US engineer who developed the Pullman railroad car. In an attempt to improve the standard of comfort of rail travel, he built his first Pioneer Sleeping Car 1863. He formed the Pullman Palace Car Company 1867 and in 1881 the town of Pullman, Illinois, was built for his workers.

pulsar celestial source that emits pulses of energy at regular intervals, ranging from a few seconds to a few thousandths of a second. Pulsars were discovered 1967, and are thought to be rapidly rotating ◊neutron stars, which flash at radio and other wavelengths as they spin. Over 400 radio pulsars are known in our Galaxy, although a million or so may exist.

Pulsars gradually slow down as they get older, and eventually the flashes fade. The most rapid pulsar ever discovered is the neutron star left behind by Supernova SN 1987A, which is spinning at 1,968 revolutions per second, or one-third of the speed of light (measured 1989). Two pulsars, one in the ◊Crab nebula and one in the constellation ◊Vela, give out flashes of visible light. **X-ray pulsars** are caused by hot gas falling on to a spinning neutron star in a binary star system. Pulsars were discovered at the Mullard Radio Astronomy Observatory, Cambridge, England, by Jocelyn

Bell (now ◊Burnell), a member of a team under Antony ◊Hewish.

pulse crop such as peas and beans. Pulses are grown primarily for their seeds, which provide a concentrated source of vegetable protein, and make a vital contribution to human diets in poor countries where meat is scarce, and among vegetarians. Soya beans are the major temperate protein crop in the West; most are used for oil production or for animal feed. In Asia, most are processed into soy milk and beancurd. Groundnuts dominate pulse production in the tropical world and are generally consumed as human food.

Pulses play a useful role in ◊crop rotation as they help to raise soil nitrogen levels as well as acting as break crops. In the mid-1980s, world production was about 50 million tons a year.

pulse impulse transmitted by the heartbeat throughout the arterial systems of vertebrates. When the heart muscle contracts, it forces blood into the ◊aorta (the chief artery). Because the arteries are elastic, the sudden rise of pressure causes a throb or sudden swelling through them. The actual flow of the blood is about 2 ft/60 cm a second in humans. The pulse rate is generally about 70 per minute. The pulse can be felt where an artery is near the surface, for example in the wrist or the neck.

pulse-code modulation (PCM) method of converting a continuous electrical signal (such as that produced by a microphone) into a series of pulses (a digital signal) for transmission along a telephone line.

In a process called ◊digital sampling, the continuous signal is sampled thousands of times a second and each part of the signal is given a number related to its strength when sampled. The numbers are then converted into binary code and transmitted as a series of pulses. At the receiving end the process is reversed. The advantages of the system arise because noise (static) on the line can easily be distinguished from the signal and removed; hence it is possible to send error-free messages. This has led to increasing use of the system in telephone, telegraph, and computer systems since its adoption in the 1960s. It is well suited to transmission along ◊optical fibres.

pulsed high frequency (PHF) instrumental application of high-frequency radio waves in short bursts to damaged tissue to relieve pain, reduce bruising and swelling, and speed healing.

puma also called **cougar** or **mountain lion** large wild cat *Felis concolor* found in North and South America. Tawny-coated, it is 4.5 ft/1.5 m long with a 3 ft/1 m tail. Cougars live alone, with each male occupying a distinct territory; they eat deer, rodents, and cattle. They have been hunted nearly to extinction.

pumice light volcanic rock produced by the frothing action of expanding gases during the solidification of lava. It has the texture of a hard sponge and is used as an abrasive.

pump any device for moving liquids and gases, or compressing gases. Some pumps, such as the traditional **lift pump** used to raise water from wells, work by a reciprocating (up-and-down) action. Movement of a piston in a cylinder with a one-way valve creates a partial vacuum in the cylinder, thereby sucking water into it.

Gear pumps, used to pump oil in a car's lubrication system, have two meshing gears that rotate inside a housing, and the teeth move the oil. **Rotary pumps** contain a rotor with vanes projecting from it inside a casing, sweeping the oil round as they move.

pumped storage hydroelectric plant that uses surplus electricity to pump water back into a high-level reservoir. In normal working conditions the water flows from this reservoir through the ◊turbines to generate power for feeding into the grid. At times of low power demand, electricity is taken from the grid to turn the turbines into pumps that then pump the water back again. This ensures that there is always a maximum "head" of water in the reservoir to give the maximum output when required.

pumpkin gourd *Cucurbita pepo* of the family Cucurbitaceae. The large, spherical fruit has a thick, orange rind, pulpy flesh, and many seeds.

pun figure of speech, a play on words, or double meaning that is technically known as *paronomasia* (Greek "adapted meaning"). Double meaning can be accidental, often resulting from homonymy, or the multiple meaning of words; puns, however, are deliberate, intended as jokes or as clever and compact remarks.

punched card in computing, an early form of data storage and input, now almost obsolete. The 80-column card widely used in the 1960s and 1970s was a thin card, measuring 7.5 in × 3.33 in/190 mm × 84 mm, holding up to 80 characters of data encoded as small rectangular holes.

The punched card was invented by Joseph-Marie Jacquard (1752–1834) in about 1801 to control weaving looms. The first data-processing machine using punched cards was developed by Herman ◊Hollerith in the 1880s for the US census.

punctuated equilibrium model evolutionary theory developed by Niles Eldridge and Stephen Jay Gould 1972 to explain discontinuities in the fossil record. It claims that periods of rapid change alternate with periods of relative stability (stasis), and that the appearance of new lineages is a separate process from the gradual evolution of adaptive changes within a species.

The pattern of stasis and more rapid change is now widely accepted, but the second part of the theory remains unsubstantiated.

punctuation system of conventional signs (punctuation marks) and spaces by means of which written and printed language is organized in order to be as readable, clear, and logical as possible.

It contributes to the effective layout of visual language; if a work is not adequately punctuated, there may be problems of ambiguity and unclear association among words. Conventions of punctuation differ from language to language, and there are preferred styles in the punctuation of a language like English. Some people prefer a fuller use of punctuation, while others punctuate lightly; comparably, the use of punctuation will vary according to the kind of passage being produced: a personal letter, a newspaper article, and a technical report are all laid out and punctuated in distinctive ways.

The standard punctuation marks and conventions are the ◊period, ◊comma, ◊colon, ◊semicolon, exclamation point, ◊question mark, ◊apostrophe, ◊asterisk, ◊hyphen, and parenthesis (including dashes, brackets, and the use of parenthetical commas).

Pune formerly **Poona** city in Maharashtra, India; population (1985) 1,685,000. Products include chemicals, rice, sugar, cotton, paper, and jewelry.

Punic (Latin *Punicus* "a Phoenician") relating to ◊Carthage, ancient city in N Africa founded by the Phoenicians.

Punic Wars three wars between ◊Rome and ◊Carthage:
First 264–241 BC, resulted in the defeat of the Carthaginians under ◊Hamilcar Barca and the cession of Sicily to Rome
Second 218–201 BC, Hannibal invaded Italy, defeated the Romans under ◊Fabius Maximus at Cannae, but was finally defeated by ◊Scipio Africanus Major at Zama (now in Algeria)
Third 149–146 BC, ended in the destruction of Carthage, and its possessions becoming the Roman province of Africa.

Punjab (Sanskrit "five rivers:" the Indus tributaries Jhelum, Chenab, Ravi, Beas, and Sutlej) former state of British India, now divided between India and Pakistan. Punjab was annexed by Britain 1849, after the Sikh Wars 1845–46 and 1848–49, and formed into a province with its capital at Lahore. Under the British, W Punjab was extensively irrigated, and land was granted to Indians who had served in the British army.

Punjab state of NW India
area 19,454 sq mi/50,400 sq km
capital Chandigarh
cities Amritsar
features mainly agricultural, crops chiefly under irrigation; longest life expectancy rates in India (59 for women, 64 for men); Harappa has ruins from the ◊Indus Valley civilization 2500 to 1600 BC
population (1991) 20,190,800
language Punjabi
religion 60% Sikh, 30% Hindu; there is friction between the two groups.

Punjab state of NE Pakistan
area 79,263 sq mi/205,344 sq km
capital Laho re
features wheat cultivation (by irrigation)
population (1981) 47,292,000
language Punjabi, Urdu
religion Muslim.

Punjabi member of the majority ethnic group living in the Punjab. Approximately 37 million live in the Pakistan half of Punjab, while another 14 million live on the Indian side of the border. In addition to Sikhs, there are Rajputs in Punjab, some of whom have adopted Islam. The Punjabi language belongs to the Indo-Iranian branch of the Indo-European family. It is considered by some to be a variety of Hindi, by others to be a distinct language.

punk movement of disaffected youth of the late l970s, manifesting itself in fashions and music designed to shock or intimidate. **Punk rock** began in the UK and stressed aggressive performance within a three-chord, three-minute format, as exemplified by the Sex Pistols.

Ostensibly a rejection of everything that had gone before, punk rock drew on more than a decade of US garage bands; reggae and rockabilly were also important influences on, for example, the Clash (1976–83), the most successful British punk band. The punk movement brought more women into rock (for example, the Slits 1977–82) and was antiracist and anti establishment. The musical limitations imposed by its tenets of amateurism and provoking outrage contributed to the decline of punk rock, but aspects live on in hardcore punk.

Punta Arenas (Spanish "sandy point," former name **Magallanes**) seaport (trading in meat, wool, and oil), in Chile, capital of Magallanes province, on Magellan Strait, southernmost town on the American mainland; population (1990) 120,000.

pupa nonfeeding, largely immobile stage of some insect life cycles, in which larval tissues are broken down, and adult tissues and structures are formed.

In many insects, the pupa is *exarate*, with the appendages (legs, antennae, wings) visible outside the pupal case; in butterflies and moths, it is called a chrysalis, and is *obtect*, with the appendages developing inside the case.

puppet figure manipulated on a small stage, usually by an unseen operator. The earliest known puppets are from 10th-century BC China. The types include *finger* or *glove puppets* (such as Punch); *string marionettes* (which reached a high artistic level in ancient Burma and Sri Lanka and in Italian princely courts from the 16th to 18th centuries, and for which the composer Franz Joseph Haydn wrote his operetta *Dido* 1778); *shadow silhouettes* (operated by rods and seen on a lit screen, as in Java); and *bunraku* (devised in Osaka, Japan), in which three or four black-clad operators on stage may combine to work each puppet about 3 ft/1 m high.

During the 16th and 17th centuries puppet shows became popular with European aristocracy and puppets were extensively used as vehicles for caricature and satire until the 19th century, when they were offered as amusements for children in parks. In the 1920s Russian puppeteer Sergei Obraztsov founded the Puppet Theater in Moscow. Later in the 20th century interest was revived by television; for example, *The Muppet Show* in the 1970s.

In the US, Bill Baird has created more than 2,000 puppets, many for film and television. He worked with Orson Welles, Ziegfeld, at the 1939 and 1965 New York world's fairs, for Radio City Music Hall, and for US State Department tours of India and the USSR. He opened a puppet theater in New York's Greenwich Village 1967.

Purana one of a number of sacred Hindu writings dealing with ancient times and events, and dating from the 4th century AD onwards. The 18 main texts include the *Vishnu Purāna* and *Bhāgavata*, which encourage devotion to Vishnu, above all in his incarnation as Krishna.

Purcell Henry 1659–1695. English Baroque composer. His work can be highly expressive, for example, the opera *Dido and Aeneas* 1689 and music for Dryden's *King Arthur* 1691 and for *The Fairy Queen* 1692. He wrote more than 500 works, ranging from secular operas and incidental music for plays to cantatas and church music.

purchasing-power parity system for comparing standards of living between different countries. Comparing the gross domestic product of different countries involves first converting them to a common currency (usually US dollars or pounds sterling), a conversion which is subject to large fluctuations with variations in exchange rates. Purchasing-power parity aims to overcome this by measuring how much money in the currency of those countries is required to buy a comparable range of goods and services.

purdah (Persian and Hindu "curtain") seclusion of women practiced by some Islamic and Hindu peoples. It had begun to disappear with the adoption of Western culture, but the fundamentalism of the 1980s revived it; for example, the wearing of the ⮕chador (an all-enveloping black mantle) in Iran.

The Koran actually requests only "modesty" in dress.

Pure Land Buddhism dominant form of Buddhism in China and Japan. It emphasizes faith in and love of Buddha, in particular Amitābha (Amida in Japan, Amituofo in China), the ideal "Buddha of boundless light," who has vowed that all believers who call on his name will be reborn in his Pure Land, or Western Paradise. This also applies to women, who had been debarred from attaining salvation through monastic life. There are over 16 million Pure Land Buddhists in Japan.

Amidism developed in China in the 3rd century, where the Pure Land school was, according to tradition, founded by the monk Hui Yuan (334–417); it spread in Japan from the 10th century. The basic teachings are found in the *Sukhāvati vyūha/Pure Land Sūtra*. The prayer *Namu Amida Butsu* or *Nembutsu* was in some sects repeated for several hours a day. The *True Pure Land* school (Jōdo Shinshū), founded by the Japanese monk Shinran (1173–1262), held that a single, sincere invocation was enough and rejected monastic discipline and the worship of all other Buddhas; this has become the largest school.

purgative or *laxative* in medicine, any preparation to ease or accelerate the emptying of the bowels, such as Epsom salts, senna, or castor oil. With a diet containing enough fiber, such aids should not normally be necessary.

purgatory in Roman Catholic belief, a purificatory state or place where the souls of those who have died in a state of grace can expiate their venial sins, with a limited amount of suffering.

purge removal (for example, from a political party) of suspected opponents or persons regarded as undesirable (often by violent means). In 1934 the Nazis carried out a purge of their party and a number of party leaders were executed for an alleged plot against Adolf Hitler. During the 1930s purges were conducted in the USSR under Joseph Stalin, carried out by the secret police against political opponents, Communist Party members, minorities, civil servants, and large sections of the armed forces' officer corps. Some 10 million people were executed or deported to labor camps from 1934 to 1938.

Later purges include Communist purges in Hungary 1949, Czechoslovakia 1951, and China 1955.

Purim Jewish festival celebrated in Feb or March (the 14th of Adar in the Jewish calendar), commemorating ⮕Esther, who saved the Jews from destruction in 473 BC during the Persian occupation.

The festival includes a complete reading of the Book of Esther (the megilla) in the synagogue, during which the listeners respond with stamping, whistling, and hissing to the names of the evil characters.

Puritan from 1564, a member of the Church of England who wished to eliminate Roman Catholic survivals in church ritual, or substitute a presbyterian for an episcopal form of church government. The term also covers the separatists who withdrew from the church altogether.

The Puritans were characterized by a strong conviction of human sinfulness and the wrath of God and by a devotion to plain living and hard work. The Puritan immigrants who settled in New England in the 17th century, most of them Congregationalists and Presbyterians, had a profound, formative influence on American culture, political institutions, and education. See also ⮕Congregationalism.

purpura condition marked by purplish patches on the skin or mucous membranes due to localized spontaneous bleeding. It may be harmless, as sometimes with the elderly, or linked with disease, allergy, or drug reactions.

pus yellowish liquid that forms in the body as a result of bacterial attack; it includes white blood cells (leukocytes) "killed in battle" with the bacteria, plasma, and broken-down tissue cells. An enclosed collection of pus is called an abscess.

Pusan or *Busan* chief industrial port (textiles, rubber, salt, fishing) of South Korea; population (1985) 3,797,600. It was invaded by the Japanese 1592 and opened to foreign trade 1883.

Pushkin town NW of St Petersburg, Russia; population 80,000. Founded by Peter the Great as Tsarskoe Selo ("tsar's village") 1708, it has a number of imperial summer palaces, restored after German troops devastated the town 1941–44. In the 1920s it was renamed Detskoe Selo ("children's village"), but since 1937 it has been known as Pushkin, after the poet Aleksandr Pushkin, who was educated at the school that is now a museum commemorating him.

Pushkin Aleksandr 1799–1837. Russian poet and writer. His works include the novel in verse *Eugene Onegin* 1823–31 and the tragic drama *Boris Godunov* 1825. Pushkin's range was wide, and his willingness to experiment freed later Russian writers from many of the archaic conventions of the literature of his time.

Pushkin was born in Moscow. He was exiled 1820 for his political verse and in 1824 was in trouble for his atheistic opinions. He wrote ballads such as *The Gypsies* 1827, and the prose pieces *The Captain's Daughter* 1836 and *The Queen of Spades* 1834. He was mortally wounded in a duel with his brother-in-law.

Pushtu another name for the ⮕Pashto language of Afghanistan and N Pakistan.

putrefaction decomposition of organic matter by microorganisms.

putsch Swiss German term for a violent seizure of political power, such as Adolf Hitler and Erich von Ludendorff's abortive beerhall putsch Nov 1923, which attempted to overthrow the Bavarian government.

Puttnam David (Terence) 1941– . English film producer who played a major role in reviving the British film industry internationally in the 1980s. Films include *Chariots of Fire* 1981, *The Killing Fields* 1984 (both of which won several Academy Awards), and *Memphis Belle* 1990.

Puvis de Chavannes Pierre Cécile 1824–1898. French Symbolist painter. His major works are vast decorative schemes, mainly on mythological and allegorical subjects, for public buildings such as the Panthéon and Hôtel de Ville in Paris. His work influenced Paul Gauguin.

The Boston Public Library, Massachusetts, also has his murals. His *Poor Fisherman* 1881 (Louvre, Paris) was a much admired smaller Symbolist work.

Pu-Yi alternative transliteration of the name of the last Chinese emperor, Henry ⮕P'u-i.

PVC abbreviation for *polyvinylchloride*, a type of ⮕plastic derived from vinyl chloride (CH_2:CHCl).

pyelitis inflammation of the renal pelvis, the central part of the kidney where urine accumulates before discharge. It is caused by bacterial infection and is more common in women than in men.

Pygmalion in Greek legend, a king of Cyprus who fell in love with an ivory statue he had carved. When Aphrodite brought it to life as a woman, Galatea, he married her.

Pygmy (sometimes *Negrillo*) member of any of several groups of small-statured, dark-skinned peoples of the rainforests of equatorial Africa. They were probably the aboriginal inhabitants of the region, before the arrival of farming peoples from elsewhere. They live nomadically in small groups, as hunter-gatherers; they also trade with other, settled people in the area.

Pym John 1584–1643. English Parliamentarian, largely responsible for the ⮕petition of right 1628. As leader of the Puritan opposition in the ⮕Long Parliament from 1640, he moved the impeachment of Charles I's advisers the Earl of Strafford and William Laud, drew up the ⮕Grand Remonstrance, and was the chief of five members of Parliament Charles I wanted arrested 1642. The five hid themselves and then emerged triumphant when the king left London.

Pynchon Thomas 1937– . US novelist who created a bizarre, labyrinthine world in his books, the first of which was *V* 1963. *Gravity's Rainbow* 1973 represents a major achievement in 20th-century literature, with its fantastic imagery and esoteric language, drawn from mathematics and science.

Born in Glen Cove, New York, Pynchon graduated from Cornell University. His other works include *The Crying of Lot 49* 1966 and *Vineland* 1990. He also published short stories in *Slow Learner* 1984.

Pyongyang capital and industrial city (coal, iron, steel, textiles, chemicals) of North Korea; population (1984) 2,640,000.

pyorrhoea former name for gum disease, now known as ⮕periodontal disease.

pyramid in geometry, a solid figure with triangular side-faces meeting at a common vertex (point) and with a ⮕polygon as its base. The volume V of a pyramid is given by $V = \frac{1}{3}Bh$, where B is the area of the base and h is the perpendicular height.

Pyramids are generally classified by their bases. For example, the Egyptian pyramids have square bases, and are therefore called square pyramids. Triangular pyramids are also known as tetrahedra ("four sides").

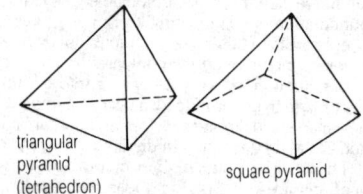

triangular pyramid (tetrahedron)   square pyramid

pyramid

pyramid four-sided building with triangular sides. They were used in ancient Egypt to enclose a royal tomb; for example, the Great Pyramid of Khufu/Cheops at Giza, near Cairo, 755 ft/230 m square and 481 ft/147 m high. In Babylon and Assyria broadly stepped pyramids (ziggurats) were used as the base for a shrine to a god: the Tower of ◊Babel was probably one of these.

Truncated pyramidal temple mounds were also built by the ancient Mexican and Peruvian civilizations, for example, at Teotihuacan and Cholula, near Mexico City, which is the world's largest in ground area (990 ft/300 m base, 195 ft/60 m high). Some New World pyramids were also used as royal tombs, for example, at the Mayan ceremonial center of Palenque.

pyramid of numbers in ecology, a diagram that shows how many plants and animals there are at different levels in a ◊food chain.

There are always far fewer individuals at the bottom of the chain than at the top because only about 10% of the food an animal eats is turned into flesh, so the amount of food flowing through the chain drops at each step. In a pyramid of numbers, the primary producers (usually plants) are represented at the bottom by a broad band, the plant-eaters are shown above by a narrower band, and the animals that prey on them by a narrower band still. At the top of the pyramid are the "top carnivores" such as lions and sharks, which are present in the smallest number.

Pyramus and Thisbe legendary Babylonian lovers whose story was retold by ◊Ovid. Pursued by a lioness, Thisbe lost her veil, and when Pyramus arrived at their meeting place, he found it bloodstained. Assuming Thisbe was dead, he stabbed himself, and she, on finding his body, killed herself. In Shakespeare's *A Midsummer Night's Dream*, the "rude mechanicals" perform the story as a farce for the nobles.

Pyrenees (French *Pyrénées*; Spanish *Pirineos*) mountain range in SW Europe between France and Spain; length about 270 mi/435 km; highest peak Aneto (French Néthon) 11,172 ft/3,404 m. ◊Andorra is entirely within the range. Hydroelectric power has encouraged industrial development in the foothills.

pyrethrum popular name for some flowers of the genus *Chrysanthemum*, family Compositae. The ornamental species *C. coccineum*, and hybrids derived from it, are commonly grown in gardens. Pyrethrum powder, made from the dried flower heads of some species, is a powerful contact pesticide for aphids and mosquitoes.

pyridine C_5H_5N a heterocyclic compound (see ◊cyclic compounds). It is a liquid with a sickly smell that occurs in coal tar. It is soluble in water, acts as a strong ◊base, and is used as a solvent, mainly in the manufacture of plastics.

$$a^2 = b^2 + c^2$$

Pythagorean theorem *The Pythagorean theorem for right-angled triangles is likely to have been known long before the time of Pythagoras.*

pyridoxine or *vitamin B6* $C_8H_{11}NO_3$ member of the ◊vitamin B complex. There is no clearly identifiable disease associated with deficiency but its absence from the diet can give rise to malfunction of the central nervous system and general skin disorders. Good sources are liver, meat, milk, and cereal grains. Related compounds may also show vitamin B6 activity.

pyrite common iron ore, iron sulfide FeS_2; also called *fool's gold* because of its yellow metallic luster. Pyrite has a hardness of 6–6.5 on the Mohs' scale. It is used in the production of sulfuric acid.

pyroclastic in geology, pertaining to fragments of solidified volcanic magma, ranging in size from fine ash to large boulders, that are extruded during an explosive volcanic eruption; also the rocks that are formed by consolidation of such material. Pyroclastic rocks include tuff (ash deposit) and agglomerate (volcanic breccia).

pyrogallol $C_6H_3OH_3$ (technical name *trihydroxybenzene*) derivative of benzene, prepared from gallic acid. It is used in gas analysis for the measurement of oxygen because its alkaline solution turns black as it rapidly absorbs oxygen. It is also used as a developer in photography.

pyrometer instrument used for measuring high temperatures.

pyroxene any one of a group of minerals, silicates of calcium, iron, and magnesium with a general formula X,YSi_2O_6, found in igneous and metamorphic rocks. The internal structure is based on single chains of silicon and oxygen. Diopside (X = Ca, Y = Mg) and augite (X = Ca, Y = Mg,Fe,Al) are common pyroxenes.

Jadeite (Na,Al,Si_2O_6), which is considered the more valuable form of jade, is also a pyroxene.

Pyrrho *c.* 360–*c.* 270 BC. Greek philosopher, founder of ◊Scepticism, who maintained that since certainty was impossible, peace of mind lay in renouncing all claims to knowledge.

Pyrrhus *c.* 318–272 BC. King of ◊Epirus, Greece, from 307, who invaded Italy 280, as an ally of the Tarentines against Rome. He twice defeated the Romans but with such heavy losses that a *Pyrrhic victory* has come to mean a victory not worth winning. He returned to Greece 275 after his defeat at Beneventum, and was killed in a riot in Argos.

Pythagoras *c.* 580–500 BC. Greek mathematician and philosopher who formulated the Pythagorean theorem.

Much of his work concerned numbers, to which he assigned mystical properties. For example, he classified numbers into triangular ones (1, 3, 6, 10,...), which can be represented as a triangular array, and square ones (1, 4, 9, 16,...), which form squares. He also observed that any two adjacent triangular numbers add to a square number (for example, 1 + 3 = 4; 3 + 6 = 9; 6 + 10 = 16;...).

Pythagoras was the founder of a politically influential religious brotherhood in Croton, S Italy (suppressed in the 5th century). Its tenets included the immortality and ◊transmigration of the soul.

Pythagorean theorem in geometry, a theorem stating that in a right triangle, the square of the hypotenuse (the longest side) is equal to the sum of the squares of the other two sides (legs). If the hypotenuse is *c* units long and the lengths of the legs are *a* and *b*, then $c^2 = a^2 + b^2$.

The theorem provides a way of calculating the length of any side of a triangle if the lengths of the other two sides are known. It is also used to determine certain trigonometrical relationships such as $\sin^2\theta + \cos^2\theta = 1$.

Pythagorus of Rhegium 5th century BC. Greek sculptor. He was born on the island of Samos and settled in Rhegium (Reggio di Calabria), Italy. He made statues of athletes and is said to have surpassed his contemporary Myron in this field.

Pytheas 4th century BC. Greek navigator from Marseille who explored the coast of W Europe at least as far north as Denmark, sailed around Britain, and reached what he called Thule, the most northern place known (possibly the Shetlands).

Pythian Games ancient Greek festival in honor of the sun god Apollo, celebrated near Delphi every four years.

python any constricting snake of the Old World subfamily Pythoninae of the family Boidae, which also includes ◊boas and the ◊anaconda. Pythons are found in the tropics of Africa, Asia, and Australia. Unlike boas, they lay eggs rather than produce living young. Some species are small, but the reticulated python *Python reticulatus* of SE Asia can grow to 33 ft/10 m.

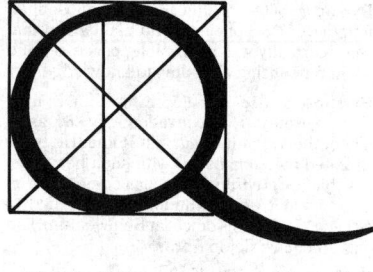

Q 17th letter of the English alphabet, representing *koppa* of the earliest Greek alphabet. In Latin, as in English, it is always followed by *u*, though not in transliterations from Arabic.

Qaboos bin Said 1940– . Sultan of Oman, the 14th descendant of the Albusaid family. Opposed to the conservative views of his father, he overthrew him 1970 in a bloodless coup and assumed the sultanship. Since then he has followed more liberal and expansionist policies, while maintaining his country's position of international nonalignment.

Qaddafi alternate form of ▷Khaddhafi, Libyan leader.

Qadisiya, Battle of battle fought in S Iraq 637. A Muslim Arab force defeated a larger Zoroastrian Persian army and ended the ▷Sassanian Empire. The defeat is still resented in Iran, where Muslim Arab nationalism threatens to break up the Iranian state.

qat shrub *Catha edulis* of the staff-tree family Celastraceae. The leaves are chewed as a mild narcotic in some Arab countries. Its use was banned in Somalia 1983.

Qatar country in the Middle East, occupying Qatar peninsula in the Arabian Gulf, bounded SW by Saudi Arabia and S by United Arab Emirates.

government A provisional constitution adopted 1970 confirmed Qatar as an absolute monarchy, with the emir holding all executive and legislative powers. The emir appoints and heads a council of ministers. An advisory council of 30 was established 1972, with limited powers to question ministers. There are no political parties.

history For early history, see ▷Arabia. Qatar, which used to be under ▷Bahrain's control, has had a treaty with Britain since 1868. It was part of the ▷Ottoman Empire from 1872 until World War I. The British government gave formal recognition 1916 to Sheik Abdullah al-Thani as Qatar's ruler, guaranteeing protection in return for an influence over the country's external affairs.

In 1968 Britain announced its intention of withdrawing its forces from the Persian Gulf area by 1981, and Qatar, having failed in an attempt to form an association with other Gulf states, became fully independent Sept 1, 1971. A new treaty of friendship with the UK replaced the former protectorate.

after independence In 1972, while the emir, Sheik Ahmad, was out of the country, his cousin, the crown prince, Sheik Khalifa, led a bloodless coup; already prime minister, he declared himself also emir. He embarked on an ambitious program of social and economic reform, curbing the extravagances of the royal family. Qatar has good relations with most of its neighbors and is regarded as one of the more stable and moderate Arab states, although it devotes more than 43% of GNP to defense. Development programs are hampered by a lack of skilled workers. In the 1991 ▷Gulf War, Qatar's forces fought with the UN coalition against the Iraqi occupiers of Kuwait.*See illustration box.*

Qattara Depression tract of the Western Desert, Egypt, up to 400 ft/125 m below sea level; area 7,500 sq mi/20,000 sq km. Its very soft sand makes it virtually impassable to vehicles, and it protected the left flank of the Allied armies before and during the battle of ▷Alamein 1942.

QED abbreviation for *quod erat demonstrandum* (Latin "which was to be proved"), added at the end of a geometry proof.

qiblah direction in which Muslims face to pray: the direction of Mecca. In every mosque this is marked by a niche (mihrab) in the wall.

Qin dynasty Chinese imperial dynasty 221–206 BC. ▷Shi Huangdi was its most renowned emperor. The Great Wall of China was built at this time.

Qingdao or *Tsingtao* industrial port (brewing) and summer resort in Shandong province, E China; population (1984) 1,229,500.

Qinghai or *Tsinghai* province of NW China
area 278,306 sq mi/721,000 sq km
capital Xining
features mainly desert, with nomadic herders
products oil, livestock, medical products
population (1990) 4,457,000; minorities include 900,000 Tibetans (mostly nomadic herders); Tibetan nationalists regard the province as being under colonial rule.

Qisarya Mediterranean port N of Tel Aviv-Jaffa, Israel; there are underwater remains of Herod the Great's port of Caesarea.

Qom or *Qum* holy city of Shiite Muslims, in central Iran, 90 mi/145 km S of Tehran; population (1986) 551,000. The Islamic academy of Madresseh Faizieh 1920 became the headquarters of Ayatollah ▷Khomeini.

quadrathon sports event in which the competitors must swim two miles, walk 30 miles, cycle 100 miles, and run 26.2 miles (a marathon) within 22 hours.

quadratic equation in mathematics, a polynomial equation of second degree (that is, an equation containing as its highest power the square of a variable, such as x^2). The general formula of such equations is $ax^2 + bx + c = 0$, in which a, b, and c are real numbers, and only the coefficient a cannot equal 0. In ▷coordinate geometry, a quadratic function represents a ▷parabola.

Some quadratic equations can be solved by factorization, or the values of x can be found by using the formula for the general solution
$$x = [-b \pm \sqrt{(b^2 - 4ac)}]/2a.$$
Depending on the value of the discriminant $b^2 - 4ac$, a quadratic equation has two real, two equal, or two complex roots (solutions). When $b^2 - 4ac > 0$, there are two distinct real roots. When $b^2 - 4ac = 0$, there are two equal real roots. When $b^2 - 4ac < 0$, there are two distinct complex roots.

quadrille square dance for four or more couples, or the music for the dance, which alternates between two and four beats in a bar.

quadrivium in medieval education, the four advanced liberal arts (arithmetic, geometry, astronomy, and music) which were studied after mastery of the trivium (grammar, rhetoric, and logic).

Quadruple Alliance in European history, three military alliances of four nations:
the Quadruple Alliance 1718 Austria, Britain, France, and the United Provinces (Netherlands) joined forces to prevent Spain from annexing Sardinia and Sicily;
the Quadruple Alliance 1813 Austria, Britain, Prussia, and Russia allied to defeat the

Qatar
State of (*Dawlat Qatar*)

area 4,402 sq mi/11,400 sq km
capital (and chief port) Doha
town Dukhan, center of oil production
physical mostly flat desert with salt flats in S
features negligible rain and surface water; only 3% is fertile, but irrigation allows self-sufficiency in fruit and vegetables; extensive oil discoveries since World War II
head of state and government Sheik Khalifa bin Hamad al-Thani from 1972
political system absolute monarchy
political parties none
exports oil, natural gas, petrochemicals, fertilizers, iron, steel
currency riyal
population (1990 est) 498,000 (half in Doha; Arab 40%, Indian 18%, Pakistani 18%); growth rate 3.7% p.a.
life expectancy men 68, women 72 (1989)
languages Arabic (official), English
religion Sunni Muslim 95%
literacy 60% (1987)
GNP $5.9 bn (1983); $35,000 per head
chronology
1916 Qatar became a British protectorate.
1970 Constitution adopted, confirming the emirate as an absolute monarchy.
1971 Independence achieved from Britain.
1972 Emir Sheik Ahmad replaced in bloodless coup by his cousin, Crown Prince Sheik Khalifa.
1991 Forces joined UN coalition in Gulf War against Iraq.

French emperor Napoleon; renewed 1815 and 1818. See Congress of ▷Vienna.

the Quadruple Alliance 1834 Britain, France, Portugal, and Spain guaranteed the constitutional monarchies of Spain and Portugal against rebels in the Carlist War.

quaestor Roman magistrate whose duties were mainly concerned with public finances. The quaestors originated as assistants to the consuls. Both urban and military quaestors existed, the latter being attached to the commanding generals in the provinces.

quagga South African zebra that became extinct in the 1880s. It was brown, with a white tail and legs, and unlike surviving zebra species, had stripes only on its head, neck, and forequarters.

Quai d'Orsay part of the left bank of the river Seine in Paris, where the French Foreign Office and other government buildings are situated. The name has become synonymous with the Foreign Office itself.

quail any of several genera of small ground-dwelling birds of the family Phasianidae, which also includes grouse, pheasants, bobwhites, and prairie chickens.

The California quail *Callipepla californiensis* is one of five species of quail native to North America.

Quaker popular name, originally derogatory, for a member of the Society of ▷Friends.

qualitative analysis in chemistry, a procedure for determining the identity of the component(s) of a single substance or mixture. A series of simple reactions and tests can be carried out on a compound to determine the elements present.

Quant Mary 1934– . British fashion designer who popularized the miniskirt in the UK. Her Chelsea boutique, Bazaar, revolutionized women's clothing and makeup in the "swinging London" of the 1960s. In the 1970s she extended into cosmetics and textile design.

quantitative analysis in chemistry, a procedure for determining the precise amount of a known component present in a single substance or mixture. A known amount of the substance is subjected to particular procedures. *Gravimetric analysis* determines the mass of each constituent present; *volumetric analysis* determines the concentration of a solution by *titration* against a solution of known concentration.

quantity theory of money economic theory claiming that an increase in the amount of money in circulation causes a proportionate increase in prices.

The theory dates from the 17th century and was elaborated by the US economist Irving Fisher (1867–1947). Supported and developed by Milton Friedman, it forms the theoretical basis of ▷monetarism.

Quantrill William Clarke 1837–1865. US proslavery outlaw who became leader of an irregular unit on the Confederate side in the American Civil War. Frank and Jesse ▷James were members of his gang (called Quantrill's Raiders).

quantum chromodynamics (QCD) in physics, a theory describing the interactions of quarks, the elementary particles that make up all hadrons (subatomic particles such as protons and neutrons). In quantum chromodynamics, quarks are considered to interact by exchanging particles called gluons, which carry the strong nuclear force, and whose role is to "glue" quarks together. The mathematics involved in the theory is complex, and although a number of successful predictions have been made, as yet the theory does not compare in accuracy with ▷quantum electrodynamics, upon which it is modeled. See ▷elementary particles and ▷forces, fundamental.

quantum electrodynamics (QED) in physics, a theory describing the interaction of charged subatomic particles within electric and magnetic fields. It combines quantum theory and relativity, and considers charged particles to interact by the exchange of photons. QED is remarkable for the accuracy of its predictions—for example, it has been used to calculate the value of some physical quantities to an accuracy of ten decimal places, a feat equivalent to calculating the distance between New York and Los Angeles to within the thickness of a hair. The theory was developed by US physicists Richard Feynman and Julian Schwinger, and by Japanese physicist Sin-Itiro Tomonaga 1948.

quantum mechanics branch of physics dealing with the interaction of ▷matter and ▷radiation, the structure of the ▷atom, the motion of atomic particles, and with related phenomena (see ▷elementary particle and ▷quantum theory).

quantum number in physics, one of a set of four numbers that uniquely characterize an ▷electron and its state in an ▷atom. The *principal quantum number* n defines the electron's main energy level. The *orbital quantum number* l relates to its angular momentum. The *magnetic quantum number* m describes the energies of electrons in a magnetic field. The *spin quantum number* m_s gives the spin direction of the electron.

The principal quantum number, defining the electron's energy level, corresponds to shells (energy levels) also known by their spectroscopic designations K, L, M, and so on. The orbital quantum number gives rise to a series of subshells designated s, p, d, f, and so on, of slightly different energy levels. The magnetic quantum number allows further subdivision of the subshells (making three subdivisions p_x, p_y, and p_z in the p subshell, for example, of the same energy level). No two electrons in an atom can have the same set of quantum numbers (the ▷Pauli exclusion principle).

quantum theory or *quantum mechanics* in physics, the theory that ▷energy does not have a continuous range of values, but is, instead, absorbed or radiated discontinuously, in multiples of definite, indivisible units called quanta. Just as earlier theory showed how light, generally seen as a wave motion, could also in some ways be seen as composed of discrete particles (▷photons), quantum theory shows how atomic particles such as electrons may also be seen as having wavelike properties. Quantum theory is the basis of particle physics, modern theoretical chemistry, and the solid-state physics that describes the behavior of the silicon chips used in computers.

The theory began with the work of Max Planck 1900 on radiated energy, and was extended by Einstein to electromagnetic radiation generally, including light. Niels Bohr used it to explain the ▷spectrum of light emitted by excited hydrogen atoms. Later work by Schrödinger, Heisenberg, Dirac, and others elaborated the theory to what is called quantum mechanics (or wave mechanics).

quarantine (from French *quarantaine* "40 days") any period for which people, animals, plants, or vessels may be detained in isolation when suspected of carrying contagious disease.

quark in physics, the ▷elementary particle that is the fundamental constituent of all hadrons (baryons, such as neutrons and protons, and mesons). There are six types, or "flavors": up, down, top, bottom, strange, and charm, each of which has three varieties, or "colors": red, yellow, and blue (visual color is not meant, although the analogy is useful in many ways). To each quark there is an antiparticle, called an antiquark.

quart a unit of liquid or dry measure of volume or capacity. One liquid quart is equal to one-fourth of a gallon, or two pints, or 32 fluid ounces (0.946 liters), while a dry quart is equal to one-eighth of a peck, or two dry pints (1.101 liters).

The British and Canadian imperial quart equals two imperial pints or 1.136 liters.

quartz crystalline form of ▷silica SiO_2, one of the most abundant minerals of the Earth's crust (12% by volume). Quartz occurs in many different kinds of rock, including sandstone and granite. It ranks 7 on the Mohs' scale of hardness and is resistant to chemical or mechanical breakdown. Quartzes vary according to the size and purity of their crystals. Crystals of pure quartz are coarse, colorless, and transparent, and this form is usually called rock crystal. Impure colored varieties, often used as gemstones, include ▷agate, citrine quartz, and ▷amethyst. Quartz is used in ornamental work and industry, where its reaction to electricity makes it valuable in electronic instruments (see ▷piezoelectric effect). Quartz can also be made synthetically.

Crystals that would take millions of years to form naturally can now be "grown" in pressure vessels to a standard that allows them to be used in optical and scientific instruments and in electronics, such as quartz wristwatches.

quartzite ▷metamorphic rock consisting of pure quartz sandstone that has recrystallized under increasing heat and pressure.

quasar (from *quas*i-stell*ar* object or QSO) one of the most distant extragalactic objects known, discovered 1964–65. Quasars appear starlike, but each emits more energy than 100 giant galaxies. They are thought to be at the center of galaxies, their brilliance emanating from the stars and gas falling toward an immense ▷black hole at their nucleus.

Quasar light shows a large ▷red shift, indicating that they are very young. Some quasars emit radio waves (see ▷radio astronomy), which is how they were first identified 1963, but most are radio-quiet. About 3,000 are now known in a compact region of space, hence the suggestion that they spiral toward a massive black hole. The furthest are over 10 billion light-years away.

quasi-atom particle assemblage resembling an atom, in which particles not normally found in atoms become bound together for a brief period. Quasi-atoms are generally unstable structures, either because they are subject to matter-antimatter annihilation (positronium), or because one or more of their constituents is unstable (muonium).

Quasimodo Salvatore 1901–1968. Italian poet. His first book *Acque e terre/Waters and Land*

Québec

Québec

appeared 1930. Later books, including *Nuove poesie/New Poetry* 1942 and *Il falso e vero verde/ The False and True Green* 1956, reflect a growing preoccupation with the political and social problems of his time. Nobel Prize 1959.

quassia any tropical American tree of the genus *Quassia*, family Simaroubaceae, with a bitter bark and wood. The heartwood of *Q. amara* is a source of quassiin, an infusion of which was formerly used as a tonic; it is now used in insecticides.

The quassia family includes the Asian ailanthus *Ailanthus altissima*, also called the tree of heaven.

Quaternary period of geological time that began about 1.64 million years ago and is still in process. It is divided into the ⟡Pleistocene and ⟡Holocene epochs.

Quatre Bras, Battle of battle fought June 16, 1815 during the Napoleonic Wars, in which the British commander Wellington defeated French forces under Marshal Ney. It is named after a hamlet in Brabant, Belgium, 20 mi/ 32 km SE of Brussels.

Quayle (J) Dan(forth) 1947– . US Republican politician, vice-president 1989–93. A congressman from Indiana 1977–81, he became a senator 1981.

Born into a rich and powerful Indianapolis newspaper-owning family, Quayle was admitted to the Indiana bar 1974, and was elected to the House of Representatives 1976 and to the Senate 1980. When George Bush ran for president 1988, he selected Quayle as his running mate, admiring his conservative views and believing that Quayle could deliver the youth vote. This choice encountered heavy criticism because of Quayle's limited political experience. As Bush's vice-president, Dan Quayle attracted criticism for, among other things, his enlistment in the 1960s in the Indiana National Guard, which meant that he was not sent overseas during the Vietnam War.

Que. abbreviation for *Québec*.

Quebec capital and industrial port (textiles, leather, timber, paper, printing, and publishing) of Québec province, on the St Lawrence River; population (1986) 165,000, metropolitan area 603,000.

The city was founded by the French explorer Samuel de ⟡Champlain 1608, and was a French colony 1608–1763. The British, under General ⟡Wolfe, captured Quebec 1759 after a battle on the nearby Plains of Abraham; both Wolfe and the French commander ⟡Montcalm were killed. Quebec is a center of French culture, and there are two universities, Laval 1663 (oldest in North America) and Québec

1969. Its picturesque old town survives below the citadel about 360 ft/110 m above the St Lawrence River.

Québec province of E Canada
area 594,710 sq mi/1,540,700 sq km
capital Quebec
cities Montreal, Laval, Sherbrooke, Verdun, Hull, Trois-Rivières
features immense water-power resources (for example, the James Bay project)
products iron, copper, gold, zinc, cereals, potatoes, paper, textiles, fish, maple syrup (70% of world's output)
population (1991) 6,811,800
language French (the only official language since 1974, although 17% speak English). Language laws 1989 prohibit the use of English on street signs
history known as New France 1534–1763; captured by the British and became province of Québec 1763–90, Lower Canada 1791–1846 East 1846–67; one of the original provinces 1867. Nationalist feelings 1960s (despite existing safeguards for Québec's French-derived civil law, customs, religion, and language) were encouraged by French president de Gaulle's exclamation "*Vive le Québec libre/ Long live free Québec*" on a visit to the province, and led to the foundation of the Parti Québecois by René Lévesque 1968. The Québec Liberation Front (FLQ) separatists had conducted a bombing campaign in the 1960s and fermented an uprising 1970; Parti Québecois won power 1976; a referendum on "sovereignty-association" (separation) was defeated 1980. In 1982, when Canada severed its last legal ties with the UK, Québec opposed the new Constitution Act as denying the province's claim to an absolute veto over constitutional change. Robert Bourassa and Liberals returned to power 1985 and enacted restrictive English-language legislation. The right of veto was proposed for all provinces of Canada 1987, but the agreement failed to be ratified by its 1990 deadline and support for independence grew. The Parti Québecois was defeated by the Liberal Party 1989.

Québec Conference two conferences of Allied leaders in the city of Québec during World War II. The *first conference* 1943 approved British admiral Mountbatten as supreme Allied commander in SE Asia and made plans for the invasion of France, for which US general Eisenhower was to be supreme commander. The *second conference* Sept 1944 adopted plans for intensified air attacks on Germany, created a unified strategy against Japan, and established a postwar policy for a defeated Germany.

quebracho any of several South American trees, genus *Schinopsis*, of the cashew family Anacardiaceae, with very hard wood, chiefly the red quebracho *S. lorentzii*, used in tanning.

Quechua or *Quichua* or *Kechua* member of the largest group of South American Indians. The Quechua live in the Andean region. Their ancestors included the Inca, who established the Quechua language in the region. Quechua is the second official language of Peru and is widely spoken as a lingua franca in Ecuador, Bolivia, Columbia, Argentina, and Chile; it belongs to the Andean-Equatorial family.

Queen Anne style decorative art in England 1700–20, characterized by plain, simple lines, mainly in silver and furniture.

Queen Charlotte Islands archipelago about 100 mi/160 km off the coast of ⟡British

Columbia, W Canada, of which it forms part; area 3,780 sq mi/9,790 sq km; population 2,500. Graham and Moresby are the largest of about 150 islands. There are timber and fishing industries.

Queen Maud Land region of Antarctica W of Enderby Land, claimed by Norway since 1939.

Queens mainly residential borough and county at the W end of Long Island, New York City; population (1990) 1,951,600.

It has sports arenas (Shea Stadium, Forest Hills Tennis Club, and the National Tennis Center at Flushing Meadows), a botanical garden, a museum, and several branches of the City University of New York. Both La Guardia and Kennedy airports are here.

Queensberry John Sholto Douglas, 8th Marquess of Queensberry 1844–1900. British patron of boxing. In 1867 he formulated the *Queensberry Rules*, which form the basis of today's boxing rules.

Queensland state in NE Australia
area 666,699 sq mi/1,727,200 sq km
capital Brisbane
cities Townsville, Toowoomba, Cairns
features Great Dividing Range, including Mount Bartle Frere 5,438 ft/1,657 m; Great Barrier Reef (collection of coral reefs and islands about 1,250 mi/2,000 km long, off the E coast); Gold Coast, 20 mi/32 km long, S of Brisbane; Mount Isa mining area; Sunshine Coast, a 100-km/60-mi stretch of coast N of Brisbane, between Rainbow Beach and Bribie Island, including the resorts of Noosa Heads, Coolum Beach, and Caloundra
products sugar, pineapples, beef, cotton, wool, tobacco, copper, gold, silver, lead, zinc, coal, nickel, bauxite, uranium, natural gas
population (1987) 2,650,000
history part of New South Wales until 1859, when it became self-governing. In 1989 the ruling National Party was defeated after 32 years in power and replaced by the Labor Party.

Quemoy island off the SE coast of China, and administered, along with the island of Matsu, by Taiwan. Quemoy: area 50 sq mi/130 sq km; population (1982) 57,847. Matsu: 17 sq mi/ 44 sq km; population (1982) 11,000. China claims Quemoy; the US supported Taiwan until 1979, eight years after Taiwan had ceased to be a member of the United Nations. Since 1986 the Taiwanese government has encouraged the growth of tourism on Quemoy. When the islands were shelled from the mainland 1960, the US declared they would be defended if attacked.

question mark punctuation mark (?) used to indicate inquiry or doubt. When indicating inquiry, it is placed at the end of a *direct question* ("Who is coming?") but never at the end of an *indirect question* ("He asked us who was coming"). When indicating doubt, it usually appears between brackets, to show that a writer or editor is puzzled or uncertain about quoted text.

quetzal long-tailed Central American bird *Pharomachus mocinno* of the ⟡trogon family. The male is brightly colored, with green, red, blue, and white feathers, and is about 4.3 ft/ 1.3 m long including tail. The female is smaller and lacks the tail and plumage.

The quetzal eats fruit, insects, and small frogs and lizards. It is the national emblem of Guatemala, and was considered sacred by the Mayans and the Aztecs. The quetzal's forest habitat is rapidly being destroyed, and hunting of birds for trophies or souvenirs also threatens its survival.

Quetzalcoatl in pre-Columbian cultures of Central America, a feathered serpent god of air and water. In his human form, he was said to have been fair-skinned and bearded and to have reigned on Earth during a golden age. He disappeared across the eastern sea, with a promise to return; the Spanish conquistador Hernán ⊳Cortés exploited the coincidence of description when he invaded. Ruins of Quetzalcoatl's temples survive in various ancient Mesoamerican ceremonial centers, including the one at Teotihuacán in Mexico. (See also ⊳Aztec, ⊳Mayan, and ⊳Toltec civilizations).

Quevedo y Villegas Francisco Gómez de 1580–1645. Spanish novelist and satirist. His picaresque novel *La vida del buscón/The Life of a Scoundrel* 1626 follows the tradition of the roguish hero who has a series of adventures. *Sueños/Visions* 1627 is a brilliant series of satirical portraits of contemporary society.

Quezon City former capital of the Philippines 1948–76, NE part of metropolitan ⊳Manila (the present capital), on Luzon Island; population (1990) 1,166,800. It was named after the Philippines' first president, Manuel Luis Quezon (1878–1944).

Qufu or *Chufu* town in Shandong province, China; population 27,000. It is the birthplace of Kong Zi (⊳Confucius) and the site of the Great Temple of Confucius.

quietism a religious attitude, displayed periodically in the history of Christianity, consisting of passive contemplation and meditation to achieve union with God. The founder of modern quietism was the Spanish priest ⊳Molinos who published a *Guida Spirituale/Spiritual Guide* 1675.

quilt padded bed cover or the method used to make padded covers or clothing. The padded effect is achieved by sewing a layer of down, cotton, wool, or other stuffing between two outer pieces of material; patterned sewing is used (often diamond shapes or floral motifs).

Quilts have been made in the home for centuries throughout Europe, the East, and more recently the US. They are sometimes decorated with patchwork or embroidery.

In the US, group or family efforts resulted in quilting bees, where several people sewed and visited on certain days to finish the project (wedding, baby) and to have company in a vast, relatively unpopulated colonial farming region.

Quimby Fred (erick) 1886–1965. US film producer, head of MGM's short films department 1926–56. Among the cartoons produced by this department were the *Tom and Jerry* series and those directed by Tex ⊳Avery.

quince small tree *Cydonia oblonga*, family Rosaceae, native to W Asia. The bitter, yellow, pear-shaped fruit is used in preserves. Flowering quinces, genus *Chaenomeles*, are cultivated for their flowers.

Quincy Josiah 1772–1864. US public official. Embarking on a political career as a staunch Federalist, he served in the US House of Representatives 1805–13, opposing the trade policies of the Jefferson administration and its acquisition of the Louisiana Territory. As an opponent of US involvement in the War of 1812, he resigned from Congress and returned to Boston, where he was mayor 1823–28.

Born in Braintree, Massachusetts, Quincy was educated at Harvard and admitted to the bar 1793. Quincy also served as president of Harvard 1829–45 and wrote a number of historical works.

Quine Willard Van Orman 1908– . US philosopher and logician. In *Two Dogmas of Empiricism* 1951 he argued against the analytic/synthetic distinction. In *Word and Object* 1960 he put forward the thesis of radical untranslatability, the view that a sentence can always be regarded as referring to many different things.

Born in Akron, Ohio, he graduated from Oberlin College and Harvard University. He was professor of philosophy at Harvard from 1936. He also wrote *Philosophy of Logic* 1970.

quinine antimalarial drug extracted from the bark of the cinchona tree. Peruvian Indians taught French missionaries how to use the bark in 1630, but quinine was not isolated until 1820. It is a bitter alkaloid $C_{20}H_{24}N_2O_2$.

Other drugs against malaria have since been developed with fewer side effects, but quinine derivatives are still valuable in the treatment of unusually resistant strains.

Quinn Anthony 1915– . Mexican-born US actor, in films from 1935. Famous for the title role in *Zorba the Greek* 1964, he later played variations on this larger-than-life character. Other films include Fellini's *La Strada* 1954.

Quinquagesima (Latin "fiftieth") in the Christian church calendar, the Sunday before Lent and 50 days before Easter.

Quintana Roo state in SE Mexico, on the east of the ⊳Yucatán peninsula; population (1989) 414,300. There are Maya remains at Tulum; Cancun is a major resort and free port.

Quintero Serafin Alvárez and Joaquin Alvarez. Spanish dramatists; see ⊳Alvárez Quintero.

Quintilian (Marcus Fabius Quintilianus) *c.* AD 35–95. Roman rhetorician. He was born at Calgurris, Spain, taught rhetoric in Rome from AD 68, and composed the *Institutio Oratoria/The Education of an Orator*, in which he advocated a simple and sincere style of public speaking.

quipu (Quechua "knot") device used by the ⊳Incas of ancient Peru to record numerical information, consisting of a set of knotted cords of one or several colors. Among its applications was the recording of granary and warehouse stores.

Quirinal one of the seven hills on which ancient Rome was built. Its summit is occupied by

a palace built 1574 as a summer residence for the pope and occupied 1870–1946 by the kings of Italy. The name Quirinal is derived from that of Quirinus, local god of the ⊳Sabines.

Quisling Vidkun 1887–1945. Norwegian politician. Leader from 1933 of the Norwegian Fascist Party, he aided the Nazi invasion of Norway 1940 by delaying mobilization and urging non-resistance. He was made premier by Hitler 1942, and was arrested and shot as a traitor by the Norwegians 1945. His name became a generic term for a traitor who aids an occupying force.

Quito capital and industrial city (textiles, chemicals, leather, gold, silver) of Ecuador, about 9,850 ft/3,000 m above sea level; population (1986) 1,093,300. It was an ancient settlement, taken by the Incas about 1470 and by the Spanish 1534. It has a temperate climate all year round.

Quixote, Don novel by the Spanish writer ⊳Cervantes; see ⊳Don Quixote de la Mancha.

Qum alternate spelling of ⊳Qom, city of Iran.

Qumran or *Khirbet Qumran* archeological site in Jordan, excavated from 1951, in the foothills NW of the Dead Sea. Originally an Iron Age fort (6th century BC), it was occupied in the late 2nd century BC by a monastic community, the ⊳Essenes, until the buildings were burned by Romans AD 68. The monastery library once contained the ⊳Dead Sea Scrolls, which had been hidden in caves for safekeeping and were discovered 1947.

quoits game in which a rubber, rope, or metal ring (quoit) is thrown at a peg (hob) from a point 54 ft/16.5 m away. The player whose quoit lands nearest the hob, within a circle 3 ft/1 m in diameter, gains one point. A quoit that encircles the hob is called a ringer and is worth two points.

quorum minimum number of members required to be present for the proceedings of an assembly to be valid. The actual number of people required for a quorum may vary.

quota in international trade, a limitation on the quantities exported or imported. Restrictions may be imposed forcibly or voluntarily. The justification of quotas include protection of a home industry from an influx of cheap goods, prevention of a heavy outflow of goods (usually raw materials) because there are insufficient numbers to meet domestic demand, allowance for a new industry to develop before it is exposed to competition, or prevention of a decline in the world price of a particular commodity.

quo vadis? (Latin) where are you going?

qv abbreviation for *quod vide* (Latin "which see").

QwaQwa black homeland of South Africa that achieved self-governing status 1974; population (1985) 181,600.

R 18th letter of the English alphabet, corresponding to the Semitic *resh* and Greek *rho* (P, ρ). A liquid, pronounced with the tip of the tongue on the palate, it is sometimes trilled by vibration of the tongue, especially in Scotland, but in S England and in the US from the middle Atlantic states to the South, *r* is often weak when used medially and silent finally.

Rabat capital of Morocco, industrial port (cotton textiles, carpets, leather goods) on the Atlantic coast, 110 mi/177 km W of Fez; population (1982) 519,000, Rabat-Salé 842,000. It is named after its original *ribat* or fortified monastery.

Rabaul largest port (trading in copra and cocoa) of Papua New Guinea, on the volcanic island of New Britain, SW Pacific; population (1980) 14,954. It was destroyed by Allied bombing after its occupation by the Japanese in 1942, but was rebuilt.

rabbi in Judaism, the chief religious leader of a synagogue or the spiritual leader (not a hereditary high priest) of a Jewish congregation; also, a scholar of Judaic law and ritual from the 1st century AD.

rabbit any of several genera of hopping mammals of the order Lagomorpha, which together with ◊hares constitute the family Leporidae. Rabbits differ from hares in bearing naked, helpless young and in occupying burrows.

The Old World rabbit (*Oryctolagus cuniculus*), originally from S Europe and N Africa, has now been introduced worldwide. It is bred for meat and for its fur, which is usually treated to resemble more expensive furs. It lives in interconnected burrows called "warrens," unlike cottontails (genus *Sylvilagus*), of which 13 species are native to North and South America.

Rabelais François 1495–1553. French satirist, monk, and physician whose name has become synonymous with bawdy humor. He was educated in the Renaissance humanist tradition and was the author of satirical allegories, including *La Vie inestimable de Gargantua/The Inestimable Life of Gargantua* 1535 and *Faits et dits héroïques du grand Pantagruel/Heroic Deeds and Sayings of the Great Pantagruel* 1533, about two giants (father and son).

Rabi Isidor Isaac 1898–1988. Russian-born US physicist who developed techniques to measure accurately the strength of the weak magnetic fields generated when charged elementary particles, such as the electron, spin about their axes. The work won him the 1944 Nobel Prize for Physics.

rabies or *hydrophobia* disease of the central nervous system that can afflict all warm-blooded creatures. It is almost invariably fatal once symptoms have developed. Its transmission to humans is generally by a bite from an infected dog.

After an incubation period, which may vary from ten days to more than a year, symptoms of fever, muscle spasm, and delirium develop. As the disease progresses, the mere sight of water is enough to provoke convulsions and paralysis. Death is usual within four or five days from the onset of symptoms. Injections of rabies vaccine and antiserum may save those bitten by a rabid animal from developing the disease. Louis ◊Pasteur was the first to produce a preventive vaccine, and the Pasteur Institute was founded to treat the disease. As a control measure for foxes and other wild animals, vaccination (by bait) is recommended. In France, foxes are now vaccinated against rabies with capsules distributed by helicopter.

Rabin Yitzhak 1922– . Israeli Labor politician, prime minister 1974–77 and from 1992. Rabin was minister for defense under the conservative Likud coalition government 1984–90. His policy of favoring Palestinian self-government in the occupied territories contributed to the success of the center-left party in the 1992 elections.

Rabuka Sitiveni 1948– . Fijian soldier and politician, prime minister from 1992. When the 1987 elections in Fiji produced an Indian-dominated government, Rabuka staged two successive coups (the first short-lived). Within months of the second, he stepped down, allowing a civilian government to take over. In May 1992 he was nominated as the new Fijian premier.

raccoon any of several New World species of carnivorous mammals of the genus *Procyon*, in the family Procyonidae. The common raccoon *P. lotor* is about 2 ft/60 cm long, with a gray-brown body, a black-and-white ringed tail, and a black "mask" around its eyes. The crab-eating raccoon *P. cancrivorus* of South America is slightly smaller and has shorter fur.

race in anthropology, the term applied to the varieties of modern humans, *Homo sapiens sapiens*, having clusters of distinctive physical traits in common. The three major varieties are ◊Caucasoid, ◊Mongoloid, and ◊Negroid. During the last 60,000 years, migrations and interbreeding have caused a range of variations to exist today, not distinct or "pure" races (which can exist only under conditions of isolation).

Rachel in the Old Testament, the favorite wife of ◊Jacob, and mother of ◊Joseph and Benjamin.

Rachmaninov Sergei (Vasilevich) 1873–1943. Russian composer, conductor, and pianist. After the 1917 Revolution he went to the US. His dramatically emotional Romantic music has a strong melodic basis and includes operas, such as *Francesca da Rimini* 1906, three symphonies, four piano concertos, piano pieces, and songs. Among his other works are the *Prelude in C-Sharp Minor* 1882 and *Rhapsody on a Theme of Paganini* 1934 for piano and orchestra.

Racine city and port of entry in SW Wisconsin on the Root River where it flows into Lake Michigan. Industries include automotive parts, farm machinery, and wax products; population (1990) 84,300.

Racine Jean 1639–1699. French dramatist and exponent of the Classical tragedy in French drama. His subjects came from Greek mythology and he observed the rules of Classical Greek drama. Most of his tragedies have women in the title role, for example *Andromaque* 1667, *Iphigénie* 1674, and *Phèdre* 1677.

An orphan, Racine was educated by Jansenists at Port Royal (see ◊Jansenism), but later moved away from an ecclesiastical career to success and patronage at court. His ingratiating flattery won him the success he craved in 1677 when he was appointed royal historiographer. After the failure of *Phèdre* in the theater he no longer wrote for the secular stage, but influenced by Madame de ◊Maintenon wrote two religious dramas, *Esther* 1689 and *Athalie* 1691, which achieved posthumous success.

racism belief in, or set of implicit assumptions about, the superiority of one's own ◊race or ethnic group, often accompanied by prejudice against members of an ethnic group different from one's own. Racism may be used to justify ◊discrimination, verbal or physical abuse, or even genocide, as in Nazi Germany, or as practiced by European settlers against American Indians in both North and South America.

Many social scientists believe that even where there is no overt discrimination, racism exists as an unconscious attitude in many individuals and societies, based on a ◊stereotype or preconceived idea about different ethnic groups, which is damaging to individuals (both perpetrators and victims) and to society as a whole. See also ◊ethnicity.

rackets or *racquets* indoor game played on an enclosed court. Although first played in the Middle Ages, rackets developed in the 18th century and was played against the walls of London buildings. It is considered the forerunner of many racket and ball games, particularly ◊squash.

rad unit of absorbed radiation dose, now replaced in the SI system by the gray (one rad equals 0.01 gray), but still commonly used. It is defined as the dose when one kilogram of matter absorbs 0.01 joule of radiation energy (formerly, as the dose when one gram absorbs 100 ergs).

radar (acronym for *radio direction and ranging*) device for locating objects in space, direction finding, and navigation by means of transmitted and reflected high-frequency radio waves.

The direction of an object is ascertained by transmitting a beam of short-wavelength (½–40 in/(1–100 cm), short-pulse radio waves, and picking up the reflected beam. Distance is determined by timing the journey of the radio waves (traveling at the speed of light) to the object and back again. Radar is also used to detect objects underground, for example service pipes, and in archeology. Contours of remains of ancient buildings can be detected down to 66 ft/20 m below ground.

Radar is essential to navigation in darkness, cloud, and fog, and is widely used in warfare to detect enemy aircraft and missiles. To avoid detection, various devices, such as modified shapes (to reduce their radar cross-section), radar-absorbent paints and electronic jamming are used. To pinpoint small targets

⟁laser "radar" instead of microwaves, has been developed. Chains of ground radar stations are used to warn of enemy attack—for example, North Warning System 1985, consisting of 52 stations across the Canadian Arctic and N Alaska. Radar is also used in ⟁meteorology and ⟁astronomy.

radar astronomy bouncing of radio waves off objects in the Solar System, with reception and analysis of the "echoes." Radar contact with the Moon was first made 1945 and with Venus 1961. The travel time for radio reflections allows the distances of objects to be determined accurately. Analysis of the reflected beam reveals the rotation period and allows the object's surface to be mapped. The rotation periods of Venus and Mercury were first determined by radar. Radar maps of Venus were obtained first by Earth-based radar and subsequently by orbiting space probes.

Radha in the Hindu epic ⟁*Mahābhārata*, the wife of a cowherd who leaves her husband for love of Krishna (an incarnation of the god Vishnu). Her devotion to Krishna is seen by the mystical *bhakti* movement as the ideal of the love between humans and God.

radial circuit circuit used in household electric wiring in which all electrical appliances are connected to cables that radiate out from the main supply point or fuse box. In more modern systems, the appliances are connected in a ring, or ⟁ring circuit, with each end of the ring connected to the fuse box.

radian SI unit (symbol rad) of plane angles, an alternative unit to the ⟁degree. It is the angle at the center of a circle when the center is joined to the two ends of an arc (part of the circumference) equal in length to the radius of the circle. There are 2π (approximately 6.284) radians in a full circle (360°).

One radian is approximately 57°, and 1° is $\pi/180$ or approximately 0.0175 radians. Radians are commonly used to specify angles in ⟁polar coordinates.

radiation in physics, emission of radiant ⟁energy as particles or waves—for example, heat, light, alpha particles, and beta particles (see ⟁electromagnetic waves and ⟁radioactivity). See also ⟁atomic radiation.

radiation biology study of how living things are affected by radioactive (ionizing) emissions (see ⟁radioactivity) and by electromagnetic (nonionizing) radiation (⟁electromagnetic waves). Both are potentially harmful and can cause mutations as well as leukemia and other cancers; even low levels of radioactivity are very dangerous. Both are, however, used therapeutically, for example to treat cancer, when the radiation dose is very carefully controlled (⟁*radiotherapy* or X-ray therapy).

Radioactive emissions are more harmful. Exposure to high levels produces radiation burns and radiation sickness, plus genetic damage (resulting in birth defects) and cancers in the longer term. Exposure to low-level ionizing radiation can also cause genetic damage and cancers, particularly leukemia.

Electromagnetic radiation is usually harmful only if exposure is to high-energy emissions, for example close to powerful radio transmitters or near radar-wave sources. Such exposure can cause organ damage, cataracts, loss of hearing, leukemia and other cancers, or premature aging. It may also affect the nervous system and brain, distorting their electrical nerve signals and leading

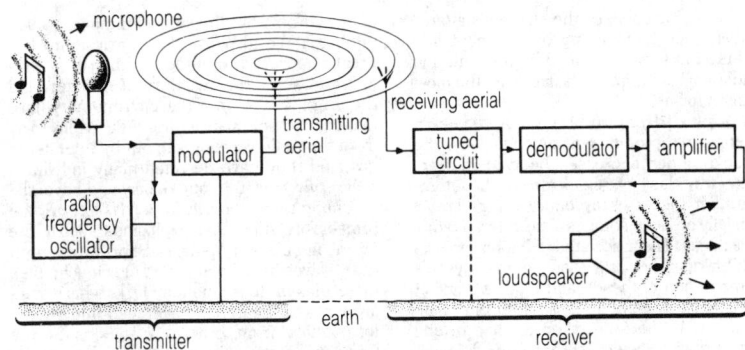

to depression, disorientation, headaches, and other symptoms. Individual sensitivity varies and some people are affected by electrical equipment such as televisions, computers, and refrigerators.

Background radiation is the natural radiation produced by cosmic rays and radioactive rocks such as granite. Readings of background radiation must be taken into account when calculating any effect produced by nuclear accidents or contamination from power stations.

radiation sickness sickness resulting from exposure to radiation, including X-rays, gamma rays, neutrons, and other nuclear radiation, as from weapons and fallout. Such radiation ionizes atoms in the body and causes nausea, vomiting, diarrhea, and other symptoms. The body cells themselves may be damaged even by very small doses, causing ⟁leukemia; genetic changes may be induced in the germ plasm, causing infants to be born damaged or mutated.

radiation units units of measurement for radioactivity and radiation doses. Continued use of the units introduced earlier this century (the curie, rad, rem, and roentgen) has been approved while the derived SI units (becquerel, gray, sievert, and coulomb) become familiar. One curie equals 3.7×10^{-10} becquerels (activity); one rad equals 10^{-2} gray (absorbed dose); one rem equals 10^{-2} sievert (dose equivalent); one roentgen equals 2.58×10^{-4} coulomb/kg (exposure to ionizing radiation).

The average radiation exposure per person per year in the US is one millisievert (0.1 rem), of which 50% is derived from naturally occurring radon.

radical in chemistry, a group of atoms forming part of a molecule, which acts as a unit and takes part in chemical reactions without disintegration, yet often cannot exist alone; for example, the methyl radical $-CH_3$, or the carboxyl radical $-COOH$.

radical in politics, anyone with opinions more extreme than the main current of a country's major political party or parties. It is more often applied to those with left-wing opinions, although the radical right also exists.

Radical in Britain, supporter of parliamentary reform before the Reform Bill 1832. As a group the Radicals later became the progressive wing of the Liberal Party. During the 1860s (led by Cobden, Bright, and J S Mill) they campaigned for extension of the franchise, free trade, and ⟁laissez faire, but after 1870, under the leadership of Joseph Chamberlain and Charles Dilke,

they adopted a republican and semisocialist program. With the growth of ⟁socialism in the later 19th century, Radicalism ceased to exist as an organized movement.

radicle part of a plant embryo that develops into the primary root. Usually it emerges from the seed before the embryonic shoot, or ⟁plumule, its tip protected by a root cap, or calyptra, as it pushes through the soil. The radicle may form the basis of the entire root system, or it may be replaced by adventitious roots (positioned on the stem).

radio transmission and reception of radio waves. In radio transmission a microphone converts ⟁sound waves (pressure variations in the air) into ⟁electromagnetic waves that are then picked up by a receiving aerial and fed to a loudspeaker, which converts them back into sound waves.

The theory of electromagnetic waves was first developed by James Clerk ⟁Maxwell 1864, given practical confirmation in the laboratory 1888 by Heinrich ⟁Hertz, and put to practical use by ⟁Marconi, who in 1901 achieved reception of a signal in Newfoundland transmitted from Cornwall, England.

To carry the transmitted electrical signal, an ⟁oscillator produces a carrier wave of high frequency; different stations are allocated different transmitting carrier frequencies. A modulator superimposes the audiofrequency signal on the carrier. There are two main ways of doing this: amplitude modulation (AM), used for long- and medium-wave broadcasts, in which the strength of the carrier is made to fluctuate in time with the audio signal; and frequency modulation (FM), as used for VHF broadcasts, in which the frequency of the carrier is made to fluctuate. The transmitting aerial emits the modulated electromagnetic waves, which travel outwards from it.

In radio reception a receiving aerial picks up minute voltages in response to the waves sent out by a transmitter. A tuned circuit selects a particular frequency, usually by means of a variable ⟁capacitor connected across a coil of wire. A demodulator disentangles the audio signal from the carrier, which is now discarded, having served its purpose. An amplifier boosts the audio signal for feeding to the loudspeaker. In a superheterodyne receiver, the incoming signal is mixed with an internally generated signal of fixed frequency so that the amplifier circuits can operate near their optimum frequency.

radioactive decay process of continuous disintegration undergone by the nuclei of radioactive elements, such as radium and various isotopes of uranium and the transuranic elements. This changes the element's atomic number, thus transmuting one element into another, and is accompanied by the emission of radiation. Alpha and beta decay are the most common forms.

In **alpha decay** (the loss of a helium nucleus—two protons and two neutrons) the atomic number decreases by two; in **beta decay** (the loss of an electron) the atomic number increases by one. Certain lighter artificially created isotopes also undergo radioactive decay. The associated radiation consists of alpha rays, beta rays, or gamma rays (or a combination of these), and it takes place at a constant rate expressed as a specific half-life, which is the time taken for half of any mass of that particular isotope to decay completely. Less commonly occurring decay forms include heavy-ion emission, electron capture, and spontaneous fission (in each of these the atomic number decreases).

The original nuclide is known as the parent substance, and the product is a daughter nuclide (which may or may not be radioactive). The final product in all modes of decay is a stable element.

radioactive tracer any of various radioactive ♢isotopes used in labeled compounds; see ♢tracer.

radioactive waste any waste that emits radiation in excess of the background level. See ♢nuclear waste.

radioactivity spontaneous alteration of the nuclei of radioactive atoms, accompanied by the emission of radiation. It is the property exhibited by the radioactive ♢isotopes of stable elements and all isotopes of radioactive elements, and can be either natural or induced. See ♢radioactive decay.

Radioactivity establishes an equilibrium in parts of the nuclei of unstable radioactive substances, ultimately to form a stable arrangement of nucleons (protons and neutrons); that is, a non-radioactive (stable) element. This is most frequently accomplished by the emission of ♢alpha particles (helium nuclei); ♢beta particles (electrons and positrons); or ♢gamma radiation (electromagnetic waves of very high frequency). It takes place either directly, through a one-step decay, or indirectly, through a number of decays that transmute one element into another. This is called a decay series or chain, and sometimes produces an element more radioactive than its predecessor.

The instability of the particle arrangements in the nucleus of a radioactive atom (the ratio of neutrons to protons and/or the total number of both) determines the lengths of the ♢half-lives of the isotopes of that atom, which can range from fractions of a second to billions of years. All isotopes of atomic weight 210 and greater are radioactive. Alpha, beta, and gamma radiation are ionizing in their effect and are therefore dangerous to body tissues, especially if a radioactive substance is ingested or inhaled.

radio astronomy study of radio waves emitted naturally by objects in space, by means of a ♢radio telescope. Radio emission comes from hot gases (**thermal radiation**); electrons spiraling in magnetic fields (**synchrotron radiation**); and specific wavelengths (**lines**) emitted by atoms and molecules in space, such as the 21-cm/8-in line emitted by hydrogen gas.

Radio astronomy began 1932 when Karl ♢Jansky detected radio waves from the center of our Galaxy, but the subject did not develop until after World War II. Radio astronomy has greatly improved our understanding of the evolution of stars, the structure of galaxies, and the origin of the universe. Astronomers have mapped the spiral structure of the Milky Way from the radio waves given out by interstellar gas, and they have detected many individual radio sources within our Galaxy and beyond.

Among radio sources in our Galaxy are the remains of ♢supernova explosions, such as the ♢Crab nebula and ♢pulsars. Short-wavelength radio waves have been detected from complex molecules in dense clouds of gas where stars are forming. Searches have been undertaken for signals from other civilizations in the Galaxy, so far without success.

Strong sources of radio waves beyond our Galaxy include ♢radio galaxies and ♢quasars. Their existence far off in the universe demonstrates how the universe has evolved with time. Radio astronomers have also detected weak **background radiation** thought to be from the ♢Big Bang explosion that marked the birth of the universe.

radiocarbon dating or **carbon dating** method of dating organic materials (for example, bone or wood), used in archeology. Plants take up carbon dioxide gas from the atmosphere and incorporate it into their tissues, and some of that carbon dioxide contains the radioactive isotope of carbon, carbon-14. This decays at a known rate (half of it decays every 5,730 years); the time elapsed since the plant died can therefore be measured in a laboratory. Animals take carbon-14 into their bodies from eating plant tissues and their remains can be similarly dated. After 120,000 years so little carbon-14 is left that no measure is possible (see ♢half-life).

Radiocarbon dating was first developed by Willard ♢Libby, a US chemist, in 1949. The method yields reliable ages back to about 50,000 years, but its results require correction since Libby's assumption that the concentration of carbon-14 in the atmosphere was constant through time has subsequently been proved wrong. Radiocarbon dates from tree rings (see ♢dendrochronology) showed that material before 1000 BC had been exposed to greater concentrations of carbon-14. Now radiocarbon dates are calibrated against calendar dates obtained from tree rings, or, for earlier periods, against uranium/thorium dates obtained from coral. The carbon-14 content is determined by counting β particles with either a proportional gas or a liquid scintillation counter for a period of time. A new advance, AMS (accelerator mass spectrometry), requires only tiny samples, and counts the atoms of carbon-14 directly, disregarding their decay.

radio, cellular portable telephone system; see ♢cellular phone.

radiochemistry chemical study of radioactive isotopes and their compounds (whether produced from naturally radioactive or irradiated materials) and their use in the study of other chemical processes.

When such isotopes are used in labeled compounds, they enable the biochemical and physiological functioning of parts of the living body to be observed. They can help in the testing of new drugs, showing where the drug goes in the body and how long it stays there. They are also useful in diagnosis—for example cancer, fetal abnormalities, and heart disease.

radio frequencies and wavelengths classification of, see ♢electromagnetic waves.

radio galaxy galaxy that is a strong source of electromagnetic waves of radio wavelengths. All galaxies, including our own, emit some radio waves, but radio galaxies are up to a million times more powerful.

In many cases the strongest radio emission comes not from the visible galaxy but from two clouds, invisible through an optical telescope, that can extend for millions of light-years either side of the galaxy. This double structure at radio wavelengths is also shown by some ♢quasars, suggesting a close relationship between the two types of object. In both cases, the source of energy is thought to be a massive black hole at the center. Some radio galaxies are thought to result from two galaxies in collision or recently merged.

radiography branch of science concerned with the use of radiation (particularly ♢X-rays) to produce images on photographic film or fluorescent screens. X-rays penetrate matter according to its nature, density, and thickness. In doing so they can cast shadows on photographic film, producing a radiograph. Radiography is widely used in medicine for examining bones and tissues and in industry for examining solid materials; for example, to check welded seams in pipelines.

radioisotope (contraction of **radioactive ♢isotope**) in physics, a naturally occurring or synthetic radioactive form of an element. Most radioisotopes are made by bombarding a stable element with neutrons in the core of a nuclear reactor. The radiations given off by radioisotopes are easy to detect (hence their use as ♢tracers), can in some instances penetrate substantial thicknesses of materials, and have profound effects (such as genetic ♢mutation) on living matter. Although dangerous, radioisotopes are used in the fields of medicine, industry, agriculture, and research.

Most natural isotopes of atomic mass below 208 are not radioactive. Those from 210 and up are all radioactive.

radioisotope scanning use of radioactive materials (radioisotopes or radionuclides) to pinpoint disease. It reveals the size and shape of the target organ and whether any part of it is failing to take up radioactive material, usually an indication of disease.

The specialty known as nuclear medicine makes use of the affinity of different chemical elements for certain parts of the body. Iodine, for instance, always makes its way to the thyroid gland. After being made radioactive, these materials can be given by mouth or injected, and then traced on scanners working on the Geiger-counter principle. The diagnostic record gained from radioisotope scanning is known as a **scintigram**.

radiometric dating method of dating rock by assessing the amount of ♢radioactive decay of naturally occurring ♢isotopes. The dating of rocks may be based on the gradual decay of uranium into lead. The ratio of the amounts of "parent" to "daughter" isotopes in a sample gives a measure of the time it has been decaying, that is, of its age. Different elements and isotopes are used depending on the isotopes present and the age of the rocks to be dated. Once-living matter can often be dated by ♢radiocarbon dating, employing the half-life of the isotope carbon-14, which is naturally present in organic tissue.

radiosonde balloon carrying a compact package of meteorological instruments and a radio transmitter, used to "sound," or measure, conditions in the atmosphere. The instruments measure temperature, pressure, and humidity, and the information gathered is transmitted back to observers on the ground. A radar target is often attached, allowing the balloon to be tracked.

radio telescope instrument for detecting radio waves from the universe in ◊radio astronomy. Radio telescopes usually consist of a metal bowl that collects and focuses radio waves the way a concave mirror collects and focuses light waves. Radio telescopes are much larger than optical telescopes, because the wavelengths they are detecting are much longer than the wavelength of light. The largest single dish is 1,000 ft/305 m across, at Arecibo, Puerto Rico.

A large dish such as that at ◊Jodrell Bank, England, can see the radio sky less clearly than a small optical telescope sees the visible sky. **Interferometry** is a technique in which the output from two dishes is combined to give better resolution of detail than with a single dish. **Very long baseline interferometry** (VBLI) uses radio telescopes spread across the world to resolve minute details of radio sources.

In **aperture synthesis**, several dishes are linked together to simulate the performance of a very large single dish. This technique was pioneered by Martin ◊Ryle at Cambridge, England, site of a radio telescope consisting of eight dishes in a line 3 mi/5 km long. The Very Large Array in New Mexico consists of 27 dishes arranged in a Y-shape, which simulates the performance of a single dish 17 mi/27 km in diameter. Other radio telescopes are shaped like long troughs, and some consist of simple rod-shaped aerials.

radiotherapy treatment of disease by ◊radiation from X-ray machines or radioactive sources. Radiation, which reduces the activity of dividing cells, is of special value for its effect on malignant tissues, certain nonmalignant tumors, and some diseases of the skin.

Generally speaking, the rays of the diagnostic X-ray machine are not penetrating enough to be efficient in treatment, so for this purpose more powerful machines are required, operating from 10,000 to over 30 million volts. The lower-voltage machines are similar to conventional X-ray machines; the higher-voltage ones may be of special design; for example, linear accelerators and betatrons. Modern radiotherapy is associated with fewer side effects than formerly, but radiotherapy to the head can cause temporary hair loss, and if the treatment involves the gut, diarrhea and vomiting may occur. Much radiation now given uses synthesized ◊radioisotopes. Radioactive cobalt is the most useful, since it produces gamma rays, which are highly penetrating, and it is used instead of very high-energy X-rays.

radio wave electromagnetic wave possessing a long wavelength (ranging from about 10^{-3} to 10^4 m) and a low frequency (from about 10^5 to 10^{11} Hz). Included in the radio-wave part of the spectrum are ◊microwaves, used for both communications and for cooking; ultra high- and very high-frequency waves, used for television and FM (◊frequency modulation) radio communications; and short, medium, and long waves, used for AM (◊amplitude modulation) radio communications. Radio waves that are used for communications have all been modulated (see ◊modulation) to carry information. Stars emit radio waves, which may be detected and studied using ◊radio telescopes.

radish annual herb *Raphanus sativus*, family

Cruciferae. It is native to Europe and Asia, and cultivated for its fleshy, pungent, edible root, which is usually reddish but sometimes white or black.

radium (Latin *radius* "ray") white, radioactive, metallic element, symbol Ra, atomic number 88, atomic weight 226.02. It is one of the ◊alkaline earth elements, found in nature in ◊pitchblende and other uranium ores. Of the 16 isotopes, the commonest, Ra-226, has a half-life of 1.622 years. The element was discovered and named in 1898 by Pierre and Marie ◊Curie, who were investigating the residues of pitchblende.

Radium decays in successive steps to produce radon (a gas), polonium, and finally a stable isotope of lead. The isotope Ra-223 decays through the uncommon mode of heavy-ion emission, giving off carbon-14 and transmuting directly to lead. Because radium luminesces, it was formerly used in paints that glowed in the dark; when the hazards of radioactivity became known its use was abandoned, but factory and dump sites remain contaminated and many former workers and neighbors contracted fatal cancers.

radius in biology, one of the two bones in the lower forearm of tetrapod (four-limbed) vertebrates.

radon colorless, odorless, gaseous, radioactive, nonmetallic element, symbol Rn, atomic number 86, atomic weight 222. It is grouped with the ◊inert gases and was formerly considered non-reactive, but is now known to form some compounds with fluorine. Of the 20 known isotopes, only three occur in nature; the longest half-life is 3.82 days.

Radon is the densest gas known and occurs in small amounts in spring water, streams, and the air, being formed from the natural radioactive decay of radium. Ernest Rutherford discovered the isotope Rn-220 in 1899, and Friedrich Dorn (1848–1916) in 1900; after several other chemists discovered additional isotopes, William Ramsay and R W Whytlaw-Gray isolated the element, which they named niton in 1908. The name radon was adopted in the 1920s.

Raeder Erich 1876–1960. German admiral. Chief of Staff in World War I, he became head of the navy 1928, but was dismissed by Hitler in 1943 because of his failure to prevent Allied Arctic convoys from reaching the USSR. Sentenced to life imprisonment at the Nuremberg trials of war criminals, he was released 1955 on grounds of ill health.

RAF abbreviation for ◊*Royal Air Force*.

Rafelson Bob (Robert) 1934– . US film director who gained critical acclaim for his second film, *Five Easy Pieces* 1971. His films include *The King of Marvin Gardens* 1972, *Stay Hungry* 1976, and *The Postman Always Rings Twice* 1981.

Raffles Thomas Stamford 1781–1826. British colonial administrator, born in Jamaica. He served in the British East India Company, took part in the capture of Java from the Dutch 1811, and while governor of Sumatra 1818–23 was responsible for the acquisition and founding of Singapore 1819.

rafflesia or **stinking corpse lily** any parasitic plant without stems of the genus *Rafflesia*, family Rafflesiaceae, native to Malaysia, Indonesia, and Thailand. There are 14 species, several of which are endangered by logging of the forests

where they grow; the fruit is used locally for medicine. The largest flowers in the world are produced by *R. arnoldiana*. About 3 ft/1 m across, they exude a smell of rotting flesh, which attracts flies to pollinate them.

Rafsanjani Hojatoleslam Ali Akbar Hashemi 1934– . Iranian politician and cleric, president from 1989. When his former teacher Ayatollah ◊Khomeini returned after the revolution of 1979–80, Rafsanjani became the speaker of the Iranian parliament and, after Khomeini's death, state president and effective political leader.

Rafsanjani was born near Kerman, SE Iran, to a family of pistachio farmers. At 14 he went to study Islamic jurisprudence with Khomeini in the to Shiites holy city of Qom and qualified as an *alim* (Islamic teacher). During the period 1964–78, he acquired considerable wealth through his construction business but kept in touch with his exiled mentor and was repeatedly imprisoned for fundamentalist political activity. His attitude became more moderate in the 1980s.

Raft George 1895–1980. US film actor, usually cast as a sharp-eyed gangster (as in *Scarface* 1932). His later work included a cameo in *Some Like It Hot* 1959.

raga (Sanskrit *rāga* "tone" or "color") in Indian music, a scale of notes and style of ornament for music associated with a particular mood or time of day; the equivalent term in rhythm is **tala**. A choice of raga and tala forms the basis of improvised music; however, a written composition may also be based on (and called) a raga.

Raglan FitzRoy James Henry Somerset, 1st Baron Raglan 1788–1855. English general. He took part in the Peninsular War under Wellington, and lost his right arm at Waterloo. He commanded the British forces in the Crimean War from 1854. The **raglan sleeve**, cut right up to the neckline with no shoulder seam, is named after him.

Ragnarök or (German) **Götterdämmerung** in Norse mythology, the ultimate cataclysmic battle between gods and forces of evil, from which a new order will come.

ragtime syncopated music ("ragged time") in 2/4 rhythm, usually played on piano. It developed in the US among black musicians in the late 19th century; it was influenced by folk tradition, minstrel shows, and marching bands, and was later incorporated into jazz. Scott ◊Joplin was a leading writer of ragtime pieces, called "rags."

Ragusa Italian name (until 1918) for the Croatian town of ◊Dubrovnik. Its English name was **Arrogosa**, from which the word "argosy" is derived, because of the town's fame for its trading fleets while under Turkish rule in the 16th century.

ragwort any of several European perennial plants of the genus *Senecio*, family Compositae, usually with yellow-rayed flower heads; some are poisonous.

Golden ragwort or groundsel *S. aureus* is native to S US.

Rahman Sheik Mujibur 1921–1975. Bangladeshi Nationalist politician, president 1975. He was arrested several times for campaigning for the autonomy of East Pakistan. He won the elections 1970 as leader of the Awami League but was again arrested when negotiations with the Pakistan government broke down. After the civil war 1971, he became prime minister of the newly independent Bangladesh. He was presidential dictator Jan–Aug 1975, when he was assassinated.

Rahman Tunku Abdul 1903–1990. Malaysian politician, first prime minister of independent Malaya 1957–63 and of Malaysia 1963–70.

Born at Kuala Keda, the son of the sultan and his sixth wife, a Thai princess, the Tunku studied law in England. After returning to Malaya he founded the Alliance Party 1952. The party was successful in the 1955 elections, and the Tunku became prime minister of Malaya on gaining independence 1957, continuing when Malaya became part of Malaysia 1963. His achievement was to bring together the Malay, Chinese, and Indian peoples within the Alliance Party, but in the 1960s he was accused of showing bias toward Malays. Ethnic riots followed in Kuala Lumpur 1969 and, after many attempts to restore better relations, the Tunku retired 1970. In his later years he voiced criticism of the authoritarian leadership of Mahathir bin Mohamad.

raï Algerian pop music developed in the 1970s from the Bedouin song form *melhoun*, using synthesizers and electronic drums. Singers often take the name Cheb or Cheba ("young"); Cheb Khaled is an example.

rail any wading bird of the family Rallidae, including the rails proper (genus *Rallus*), coots, moorhens, and gallinules. Rails have dark plumage, a short neck and wings, and long legs. They are 4–18 in/10–45 cm long.

Many oceanic islands have their own species of rail, often flightless, such as the Guam rail *R. owstoni* and Auckland Island rail *R. muelleri*. Several of these species have declined sharply, usually because of introduced predators such as rats and cats.

railroad method of transport in which trains convey passengers and goods along a twin rail track (at first made of wood but later of iron or steel with ties wedging them apart and relatively parallel). Following the work of English steam pioneers such as James Watt (1736–1819), George ♢Stephenson built the first public steam railroad, from Stockton to Darlington, 1825. This heralded extensive railroad building in Britain, continental Europe, and North America, providing a fast and economical means of transport and communication. After World War II, steam engines were replaced by electric and diesel engines. At the same time, the growth of road building, air services, and car ownership destroyed the supremacy of the railroads.

In North America the growth of railroads, such as the Union Pacific, during the 19th century made shipping from the central and western territories economical and helped the North to win the American Civil War. Railroads were extended into Asia, the Middle East, Africa, and Latin America in the late 19th century and were used for troop and supply transport in both world wars.

With the increasing use of automobiles and truck freight lines after World War II, the demise of steam, rising costs on the railroads meant higher fares, fewer passengers, and declining freight traffic. By 1970 many train services in the US had been discontinued or were under threat of extinction. Short-run commuter services survived and economical train trips are being reestablished to help counter automotive pollution. High-speed trains, developed in the 1970s, continue to serve passenger

railroads: chronology

1500s	Tramways—wooden tracks along which trolleys ran—were in use in mines.
1789	Flanged wheels running on cast-iron rails were first introduced; automobiles were still horse-drawn.
1804	Richard Trevithick built the first steam locomotive, and ran it on the track at the Pen-y-darren ironworks in South Wales.
1825	George Stephenson in England built the first public railroad to carry steam trains—the Stockton and Darlington line—using his engine *Locomotion*.
1829	Stephenson designed his locomotive *Rocket*.
1830	Stephenson completed the Liverpool and Manchester Railway, the first passenger steam line. The first US-built locomotive, *Best Friend of Charleston*, went into service on the South Carolina Railroad.
1835	Germany pioneered steam railroads in Europe, using *Der Adler*, a locomotive built by Stephenson.
1863	Robert Fairlie, a Scot, patented a locomotive with pivoting driving bogies, allowing tight curves in the track (this was later applied in the Garratt locomotives). London opened the world's first underground railroad, powered by steam.
1869	The first US transcontinental railroad was completed at Promontory, Utah, when the Union Pacific and the Central Pacific railroads met. George Westinghouse of the US invented the compressed-air brake.
1879	Werner von Siemens demonstrated an electric train in Germany. Volk's Electric Railway along the Brighton seafront in England was the world's first public electric railroad.
1883	Charles Lartigue built the first monorail, in Ireland.
1885	The trans-Canada continental railroad was completed, from Montréal in the east to Port Moody, British Columbia, in the west.
1890	The first electric underground railroad opened in London.
1901	The world's longest-established monorail, the Wuppertal Schwebebahn, went into service in Germany.
1912	The first diesel locomotive took to the rails in Germany.
1938	The British steam locomotive *Mallard* set a steam-rail speed record of 126 mph/203 kph.
1941	Swiss Federal Railways introduced a gas-turbine locomotive.
1964	Japan National Railways inaugurated the 320 mi/515 km New Tokaido line between Osaka and Tokyo, on which the 130 mph/210 kph "bullet" trains run.
1973	British Rail's High Speed Train (HST) set a diesel-rail speed record of 142 mph/229 kph.
1979	Japan National Railways' maglev test vehicle ML-500 attained a speed of 321 mph/517 kph.
1981	France's Train à Grande Vitesse (TGV) superfast trains began operation between Paris and Lyons, regularly attaining a peak speed of 168 mph/270 kph.
1987	British Rail set a new diesel-traction speed record of 148.5 mph/238.9 kph, on a test run between Darlington and York; France and the UK began work on the Channel Tunnel, a railroad link connecting the two countries, running beneath the English Channel.
1988	The West German Intercity Experimental train reached 252 mph/405 kph on a test run between Würzburg and Fulda.
1990	A new rail-speed record of 320 mph/515 kph was established by a French TGV train, on a stretch of line between Tours and Paris.
1991	The British and French twin tunnels met 14 mi/23 km out to sea to form the Channel Tunnel.

needs between large urban centers. Elsewhere in the world superfast trains running on specially built tracks, such as the Shinkansen (Japan) and ♢TGV (France) networks, are important to public transportation.

rain form of ♢precipitation in which separate drops of water fall to the Earth's surface from clouds. The drops are formed by the accumulation of fine droplets that condense from water vapor in the air. The condensation is usually brought about by rising and subsequent cooling of air.

Rain can form in three main ways—frontal (or cyclonic) rainfall, orographic (or relief) rainfall, and convectional rainfall.

Frontal rainfall takes place at the boundary, or ♢front, between a mass of warm air from the tropics and a mass of cold air from the poles. The water vapor in the warm air is chilled and condenses to form clouds and rain.

Orographic rainfall occurs when an airstream is forced to rise over a mountain range. The air becomes cooled and precipitation takes place. In the UK, the Pennine hills, which extend southward from Northumbria to Derbyshire in N England, interrupt the path of the prevailing southwesterly winds, causing orographic rainfall. Their presence is partly responsible for the west of the UK being wetter than the east. The orographic effect can sometimes occur in large cities, when air rises over tall buildings.

Convectional rainfall, associated with hot climates, is brought about by rising and abrupt cooling of air that has been warmed by the extreme heat of the ground surface. The water vapor carried by the air condenses and so rain falls heavily. Convectional rainfall is usually accompanied by a thunderstorm.

rainbow arch in the sky displaying the seven colors of the ♢spectrum in bands. It is formed by the refraction, reflection, and dispersion of the Sun's rays through rain or mist. Its cause was discovered by ♢Theodoric of Freiburg in the 14th century.

rainbow coalition or *rainbow alliance* in politics, from the mid-1980s, a loose, left-of-center alliance of people from several different sections of society that are traditionally politically underrepresented, such as nonwhite ethnic groups. Its aims include promoting minority rights and equal opportunities.

"Rainbow" is a translation of French *Arc-en-Ciel*, a name brought into prominence by the Rev Jesse Jackson's campaign seeking to represent an alliance of nonwhite political groupings.

rainforest dense forest found on or near the ⏻equator where the climate is hot and wet. Over half the tropical rainforests are in Central and South America, the rest in SE Asia and Africa. They provide the bulk of the oxygen needed for plant and animal respiration. Tropical rainforest once covered 14% of the Earth's land surface. Although by 1991 over 50% of the world's rainforest had been removed, they still comprise about 50% of all growing wood on the planet, and harbor at least 40% of the Earth's species (plants and animals). Rainforests are being destroyed at an increasing rate as their valuable timber is harvested and land cleared for agriculture, causing problems of ⏻deforestation, ⏻soil erosion, flooding, extinction of species, and displacement of tribal people.

Rainforests can be divided into the following kinds: tropical, montane, upper montane or cloud, mangrove, and subtropical. They are characterized by a great diversity of species, usually of tall broad-leafed evergreen trees, with many climbing vines and ferns, some of which are a main source of raw materials for medicines. A tropical forest, if properly preserved, can yield medicinal plants, oils (from cedar, juniper, cinnamon, sandalwood), spices, gums, resins (used in inks, lacquers, linoleum), tanning and dyeing materials, forage for animals, beverages, poisons, green manure, rubber, and animal products (feathers, hides, honey).

Rainforests comprise some of the most complex and diverse ecosystems on the planet and help to regulate global weather patterns. When deforestation occurs, the microclimate of the mature forest disappears; soil erosion and flooding become major problems since rainforests protect the shallow tropical soils.

Clearing of the rainforests may lead to a global warming of the atmosphere, and contribute to the ⏻greenhouse effect. Deforestation also causes the salt level in the ground to rise to the surface, making the land unsuitable for farming or ranching.

Rainier III 1923– . Prince of Monaco from 1949. He was married to the US film actress Grace Kelly.

Rainier, Mount mountain in the ⏻Cascade Range, Washington State; 14,415 ft/4,392 m, crowned by 14 glaciers and carrying dense forests on its slopes. It is a quiescent volcano. Mount Rainier national park was dedicated 1899.

Rais Gilles de 1404–1440. French marshal who fought alongside Joan of Arc. In 1440 he was hanged for the torture and murder of 140 children, but the court proceedings were irregular. He is the historical basis of the ⏻Bluebeard character.

raisin dried grape, used for eating, baking, and for confectionary. The chief kinds are the seedless raisin, the sultana, and the currant. The main producers are the Mediterranean area, California, Mexico, and Australia.

Grapes may be dried in the sun or artificially, using hot air. The darker color of the dried fruit comes from the caramelization of natural sugars during the drying process. Drying reduces

grapes to 25% of their original weight, while retaining almost all the nutritional value of the fresh fruit.

Rajasthan state of NW India
area 132,089 sq mi/342,200 sq km
capital Jaipur
features includes the larger part of the Thar Desert, where India's first nuclear test was carried out; in the SW is the Ranthambhor wildlife reserve, formerly the private hunting ground of the maharajahs of Jaipur, and rich in tiger, deer, antelope, wild boar, crocodile, and sloth bear
products oilseed, cotton, sugar, asbestos, copper, textiles, cement, glass
population (1991) 43,880,600
languages Rajasthani, Hindi
religions 90% Hindu, 3% Muslim
history formed 1948; enlarged 1956.

Rajput member of a Hindu people, predominantly soldiers and landowners, widespread over N India. The Rajput states of NW India are now merged in Rajasthan. The Rana family (ruling aristocracy of Nepal until 1951) was also Rajput. Rajastani languages belong to the Indo-Iranian branch of the Indo-European family.

raku soft, freely hand-modeled earthenware pottery fired at low temperature and partly covered with lead glaze. *Raku* ware was first made in the late 16th century in Kyoto, Japan.

Raku ware was used exclusively for the tea ceremony. The bowls are usually black but sometimes red or white. The style has been widely imitated in Japan and adopted by Western potters. The name is also applied to a method of firing pots used extensively in Japan since the 18th century, and more recently in the US and Britain.

Raleigh industrial city (food processing, electrical machinery, textiles) and capital of North Carolina; population (1990) 208,000.

It benefits from the nearby presence of the Research Triangle Park, a regional research and manufacturing center for high-technology products. Educational institutions include North Carolina State University. The present site was named for Sir Walter Raleigh, selected to be the state capital 1788, and laid out 1792.

Raleigh or **Ralegh** Walter *c.* 1552–1618. English adventurer. He made colonizing and exploring voyages to North America 1584–87 and South America 1595, and naval attacks on Spanish ports. His aggressive actions against Spanish interests brought him into conflict with the pacific James I.

Raleigh was knighted 1584, and made several attempts 1584–87 to establish a colony in "Virginia" (now ⏻North Carolina). In 1595 he led an expedition to South America (described in his *Discoverie of Guiana* 1596) and distinguished himself in expeditions against Spain in Cádiz 1596 and the Azores 1597. After James I's accession 1603 he was condemned to death on a charge of conspiracy, but was reprieved and imprisoned in the Tower of London, where he wrote his unfinished *History of the World*. Released 1616 to lead a gold-seeking expedition to the Orinoco River in South America, which failed disastrously, he was beheaded on his return under his former sentence.

Raleigh, Fort site of the first English settlement in America, at the N end of Roanoke Island, North Carolina, to which in 1585 Walter Raleigh sent 108 colonists from Plymouth, England, under his cousin Richard Grenville.

In 1586 Francis Drake took the dissatisfied survivors back to England. The outline fortifications are preserved.

RAM (acronym for *random-access memory*) in computing, a memory device in the form of a collection of integrated circuits (chips), frequently used in microcomputers. Unlike ⏻ROM (read-only memory) chips, RAM chips can be both read from and written to by the computer, but their contents are lost when the power is switched off. Microcomputers of the 1990s may have 10–20 megabytes of RAM.

Rama incarnation of ⏻Vishnu, the supreme spirit of Hinduism. He is the hero of the epic poem the ⏻*Rāmāyana*, and he is regarded as an example of morality and virtue.

Ramadan in the Muslim ⏻calendar, the ninth month of the year. Throughout Ramadan a strict fast is observed during the hours of daylight; Muslims are encouraged to read the whole Koran in commemoration of the Night of Power (which falls during the month) when, it is believed, Mohammed first received his revelations from the angel Gabriel.

Ramakrishna 1834–1886. Hindu sage, teacher, and mystic (one dedicated to achieving oneness with or a direct experience of God or some force beyond the normal world). Ramakrishna claimed that mystical experience was the ultimate aim of religions, and that all religions which led to this goal were equally valid.

Raman Venkata 1888–1970. Indian physicist who in 1928 discovered what became known as the *Raman effect*: the scattering of monochromatic (single-wavelength) light when passed through a transparent substance. Awarded a Nobel Prize in 1930, in 1948 he became director of the Raman Research Institute and national research professor of physics.

Ramat Gan industrial city (textiles, food processing) in W Israel, NE of Tel Aviv; population (1987) 116,000. It was established 1921.

Rāmāyana Sanskrit epic of *c.* 300 BC, in which Rama (an incarnation of the god Vishnu) and his friend Hanuman (the monkey chieftain) strive to recover Rama's wife, Sita, abducted by the demon king Ravana.

Rambert Marie. Adopted name of Cyvia Rambam 1888–1982. British ballet dancer and teacher born in Poland, who became a British citizen 1918. One of the major innovative and influential figures in modern ballet, she was with the Diaghilev ballet 1912–13, opened the Rambert School 1920, and in 1926 founded the *Ballet Rambert* which she directed. It became a modern dance company from 1966 with Norman Morrice as director, and was renamed the Rambert Dance Company 1987.

Rambouillet Catherine de Vivonne, Marquise de Rambouillet 1588–1665. French society hostess, whose salon at the Hôtel de Rambouillet in Paris included the philosopher Descartes, and the writers La Rochefoucauld and Madame de Sévigné. The salon was ridiculed by the dramatist Molière in his *Les Précieuses ridicules* 1659.

Ram Das 1534–1581. Indian religious leader, fourth guru (teacher) of Sikhism 1574–81, who founded the Sikh holy city of Amritsar.

Rameau Jean-Philippe 1683–1764. French organist and composer. He wrote *Treatise on Harmony* 1722 and his varied works include keyboard and vocal music and many operas, such as *Castor and Pollux* 1737.

Rameses alternate spelling of ⍌Ramses, name of kings of ancient Egypt.

Ramillies, Battle of battle in which British commander Marlborough defeated the French May 23, 1706, during the War of the ⍌Spanish Succession, at a village in Brabant, Belgium, 13 mi/21 km N of Namur.

ramjet simple jet engine (see under ⍌jet propulsion) used in some guided missiles. It only comes into operation at high speeds. Air is then "rammed" into the combustion chamber, into which fuel is sprayed and ignited.

Rampling Charlotte 1945– . British actress whose films include *Georgy Girl* 1966, *The Damned* 1969, and *The Night Porter/Il Portiere di Notti* 1974.

Ramsay William 1852–1916. Scottish chemist who, with Lord Rayleigh, discovered argon 1894. In 1895 Ramsay produced helium and in 1898, in cooperation with Morris Travers, identified neon, krypton, and xenon. In 1903, with Frederick Soddy, he noted the transmutation of radium into helium, which led to the discovery of the density and atomic weight of radium. Nobel Prize 1904.

Ramses or **Rameses** 11 kings of ancient Egypt, including:

Ramses II or **Rameses II** king of Egypt about 1304–1236 BC, the son of Seti I. He campaigned successfully against the Hittites, and built two rock temples at ⍌Abu Simbel in Upper Egypt.

Ramses III or **Rameses III** king of Egypt about 1200–1168 BC. He won a naval victory over the Philistines and other Middle Eastern peoples, and asserted his control over Palestine.

Rance river in Brittany, NW France, flowing into the English Channel between Dinard and St Malo, where a dam built 1960–67 (with a lock for ships) uses the 13-m/44-ft tides to feed the world's first successful tidal power station.

Rand shortened form of ⍌Witwatersrand, a mountain ridge in Transvaal, South Africa.

Rand Ayn. Adopted name of Alice Rosenbaum 1905–1982. Russian-born US novelist. Her novel *The Fountainhead* 1943 (made into a film 1949), describing an idealistic architect who destroys his project rather than see it altered, displays her persuasive blend of vehement anticommunism and fervent philosophy of individual enterprise.

Her allegorical novel *Atlas Shrugged* 1957 was also a bestseller. Her beliefs won her a cult following.

Born and educated in St Petersburg, she came to the US 1926 and settled in Chicago. She became a US citizen 1931. Rand worked as a script writer in Hollywood and edited *The Objectivist*, a magazine that promoted Objectivism, her theory of self-interest and laissez-faire capitalism that is presented in her novels. Her other works include *We, the Living* 1936, *The Virtue of Selfishness* 1965, *Capitalism* 1966, *The New Left* 1971, and *Philosophy: Who Needs It?* 1982.

Rand Sally (Helen Gould Beck) 1904–1979. US exotic dancer. During the 1930s she worked as an exotic dancer in Chicago, developing her trademark nude dance routine to Chopin and Debussy, featuring the coy use of huge ostrich fans.

Born in Hickory County, Missouri, Rand joined the circus in her teenage years as an acrobat, later moving to Hollywood where she played supporting roles in a number of silent films. Her appearances at the 1933 Chicago Exposition and at later fairs and expositions across the country made her a popular favorite. Rand played a featured role in a 1965 burlesque revival on Broadway and continued to dance until 1978.

Randolph Asa Philip 1889–1979. US labor and civil rights leader. Devoting himself to the cause of unionization, especially among black Americans, he founded the periodical *Messenger* 1917. After successfully organizing railroad workers, he served as the president of the Brotherhood of Sleeping Car Porters 1925–68. Named a vice-president of the American Federation of Labor and Congress of Industrial Organizations (AFL-CIO) 1957, Randolph was one of the organizers of the 1963 civil rights march on Washington.

Born in Crescent City, Florida, Randolph was educated at the City College of New York and became involved in labor-organizing activities while still in college.

random number one of a series of numbers having no detectable pattern. Random numbers are used in ⍌computer simulation and ⍌computer games. It is impossible for an ordinary computer to generate true random numbers, but various techniques are available for obtaining pseudo-random numbers—close enough to true randomness for most purposes.

rangefinder instrument for determining the range or distance of an object from the observer; used to focus a camera or to sight a gun accurately. A *rangefinder camera* has a rotating mirror or prism that alters the image seen through the viewfinder, and a secondary window. When the two images are brought together into one, the lens is sharply focussed.

Rangoon former name (until 1989) of ⍌Yangon, capital of Myanmar (Burma).

Ranjit Singh 1780–1839. Indian maharajah. He succeeded his father as a minor Sikh leader 1792, and created a Sikh army that conquered Kashmir and the Punjab. In alliance with the British, he established himself as "Lion of the Punjab," ruler of the strongest of the independent Indian states.

Ranke Leopold von 1795–1886. German historian whose quest for objectivity in history had great impact on the discipline. His attempts to explain "how it really was" dominated both German and outside historical thought until 1914 and beyond. His *Weltgeschichte/World History* (nine volumes 1881–88) exemplified his ideas.

Ransom John Crowe 1888–1974. US poet and critic. He published his romantic but antirhetorical verse in, for example, *Poems About God* 1919, *Chills and Fever* 1924, and *Selected Verse* 1947.

He was born in Tennessee, and was a leader of the Southern literary movement that followed World War I. As a critic and teacher he was a powerful figure in the New Criticism movement, which shaped much literary theory from the 1940s to the 1960s.

At Kenyon College, where he taught from 1937 to 1958, he founded the respected literary magazine *The Kenyon Review*.

Ransome Robert 1753–1830. English ironfounder and agricultural engineer, whose business earned a worldwide reputation in the 19th and 20th centuries. He introduced factory methods for the production of an improved range of plows from 1789. The firm remained at the forefront of advances in agricultural mechanization in connection with steam engines, threshing machines, and lawnmowers.

Rantoul city in E Illinois, S of Chicago. It is a trading center for agricultural products. Manufactures include electronic equipment and motorcycle parts; population (1990) 17,200.

Rao P(amulaparti) V(enkata) Narasimha 1921– . Indian politician, see ⍌Narasimah Rao.

Raoult François 1830–1901. French chemist. In 1882, while working at the University of Grenoble, Raoult formulated one of the basic laws of chemistry. *Raoult's law* enables the molecular weight of a substance to be determined by noting how much of it is required to depress the freezing point of a solvent by a certain amount.

Rapallo port and winter resort in Liguria, NW Italy, 15 mi/24 km SE of Genoa on the Gulf of Rapallo; population (1981) 29,300. Treaties were signed here 1920 (settling the common frontiers of Italy and Yugoslavia) and 1922 (cancelling German and Russian counterclaims for indemnities for World War I). German soldiers were also permitted to train in the USSR, in defiance of the Treaty of ⍌Versailles.

Rapa Nui another name for ⍌Easter Island, an island in the Pacific.

rape in botany, two plant species of the mustard family Cruciferae, *Brassica rapa* and *B. napus*, grown for their seeds, which yield a pungent edible oil. The common turnip is a variety of the former, and the rutabaga turnip of the latter.

rape in law, sexual intercourse without the consent of the subject. Most cases of rape are of women by men. In Islamic law a rape accusation requires the support of four independent male witnesses.

Some jurisdictions allow charges of rape to be brought against husbands replacing older legal doctrine asserting a wife's duty to submit to sex with her spouse. Sexual intercourse with a minor, not necessarily involving penetration, is defined as statutory rape (see ⍌child abuse).

Raphael Sanzio (Raffaello Sanzio) 1483–1520. Italian painter, one of the greatest of the High Renaissance, active in Perugia, Florence, and Rome (from 1508), where he painted frescoes in the Vatican and for secular patrons. His religious and mythological scenes are harmoniously composed; his portraits enhance the character of his sitters and express dignity. Many of his designs were engraved. Much of his later work was the product of his studio.

Raphael was born in Urbino, the son of Giovanni Santi (died 1494), a court painter. In 1499 he went to Perugia, where he worked with ⍌Perugino, whose graceful style is reflected in Raphael's *Marriage of the Virgin* (Brera, Milan). This work also shows his early concern for harmonious disposition of figures in the pictorial space. In Florence 1504–08 he studied the works of Leonardo da Vinci, Michelangelo, Masaccio, and Fra Bartolommeo. His paintings of this period include the *Ansidei Madonna* (National Gallery, London).

Pope Julius II commissioned him to decorate the papal apartments (the Stanze) in the Vatican. In Raphael's first fresco series there, *The School of Athens* 1509 is a complex but classically composed grouping of Greek philosophers and mathematicians, centered on the figures of Plato and Aristotle. A second series of frescoes, 1511–14, includes the dramatic and richly colored *Mass of Bolsena*.

Raphael was increasingly flooded with commissions. Within the next few years he produced mythological frescoes in the Villa Farnesina in Rome (1511–12), cartoons for tapestries for the Sistine Chapel, Vatican (Victoria and Albert Museum, London), and the *Sistine Madonna* about 1512 (Gemäldegalerie, Dresden, Germany), and portraits, for example of Baldassare Castiglione about 1515 (Louvre, Paris). One of his pupils was ⟡Giulio Romano.

Rapid Deployment Force former name (until 1983) of US ⟡Central Command, a military strike force.

rap music rapid, rhythmic chant over a prerecorded repetitive backing track. Rap emerged in New York 1979 as part of the ⟡hip-hop culture, although the macho, swaggering lyrics that initially predominated have roots in ritual boasts and insults. Different styles were flourishing by the 1990s, such as jazz rap, funk rap, and reggae rap.

"The Message" 1982, by Grandmaster Flash and the Furious Five, was the first rap record to expand the content, and female rappers (the Cookie Crew, Yo Yo, and others) have countered the sexism. A school of "conscious rappers" extolling peaceful coexistence, spearheaded by the Jungle Brothers, appeared in the US in the late 1980s. But harsh propaganda for violence and misogyny continued with groups like NWA and 2 Live Crew, who caused a furor over censorship in the US in 1990.

rare-earth element alternate name for ⟡lanthanide.

Ras el Khaimah or *Ra's al Khaymah* emirate on the Persian Gulf; area 652 sq mi/1,690 sq km; population (1980) 73,700. Products include oil, pharmaceuticals, and cement. It is one of the seven members of the ⟡United Arab Emirates.

raspberry prickly cane plant of the genus *Rubus* of the Rosaceae family, native to Eurasia and North America, with white flowers followed by red fruits. These are eaten fresh and used for jam and wine.

Rasputin (Russian "dissolute") Grigory Efimovich 1871–1916. Siberian Eastern Orthodox mystic who acquired influence over the tsarina ⟡Alexandra, wife of ⟡Nicholas II, and was able to make political and ecclesiastical appointments. His abuse of power and notorious debauchery (reputedly including the tsarina) led to his murder by a group of nobles.

Rasputin, the illiterate son of a peasant, began as a wandering "holy man." Through the tsarina's faith in his power to ease her son's suffering from haemophilia, he became a favorite at the court, where he instigated wild parties under the slogan "Sin that you may obtain forgiveness." A larger-than-life character, he even proved hard to kill: when poison had no effect, his assassins shot him and dumped him in the river Neva.

Rastafarianism religion originating in the West Indies, based on the ideas of Marcus ⟡Garvey, who called on black people to return to Africa and set up a black-governed country there. When Haile Selassie (*Ras Tafari*, "Lion of Judah") was crowned emperor of Ethiopia 1930, this was seen as a fulfillment of prophecy and some Rastafarians acknowledged him as an incarnation of God (*Jah*), others as a prophet. The use of ganja (marijuana) is a sacrament.

There are no churches. There were about one million Rastafarians by 1990.

Rastafarians identify themselves with the Chosen People, the Israelites, of the Bible. Ethiopia is seen as the promised land, while all countries outside Africa are *Babylon*, the place of exile. Many Rastafarians do not cut their hair, because of Biblical injunctions against this, but wear it instead in long dreadlocks, often covered in woolen hats in the Rastafarian colors of red, green, and gold. Food laws are very strict: for example, no pork or shellfish, no salt, milk, or coffee.

Rastatt, Treaty of in 1714, agreement signed by Austria and France that supplemented the Treaty of ⟡Utrecht and helped to end the War of the ⟡Spanish Succession.

rat any of numerous long-tailed ⟡rodents (especially of the families Muridae and Cricetidae) larger than mice and usually with scaly, naked tails. The genus *Rattus* in the family Muridae includes the rats found in human housing.

The **brown rat** *R. norvegicus* is about 8 in/20 cm long with a tail of almost equal length. It is believed to have originated in central Asia, and is now found worldwide after being transported from Europe by ships. The **black rat** *R. rattus*, responsible for the ⟡plague, is smaller than the brown rat, but has larger ears and a longer, more pointed snout. It does not interbreed with brown rats. The **pack rat** or **wood rat**, genus *Neotoma*, is common throughout North America and there are seven different species. Their dens, made of partly eaten plants, dung, and miscellaneous objects, are known as middens and can be up to 6.5 ft/2 m across and 8–12 in/20–30 cm high. The rats' crystallized urine preserves the midden, in some cases for up to 40,000 years.

Rathbone (Philip St John) Basil 1892–1967. South African-born British character actor, a specialist in villains. He also played Sherlock Holmes (the fictional detective created by Arthur Conan Doyle) in several films. He worked mainly in Hollywood, in such films as *The Adventures of Robin Hood* 1938 and *The Hound of the Baskervilles* 1939.

Rathenau Walther 1867–1922. German politician. He was a leading industrialist and was appointed economic director during World War I, developing a system of economic planning in combination with capitalism. After the war he founded the Democratic Party, and became foreign minister 1922. The same year he signed the Rapallo Treaty of Friendship with the USSR, cancelling German and Soviet counterclaims for indemnities for World War I, and soon after was assassinated by right-wing fanatics.

Rathlin island off the N Irish coast, in Antrim; St Columba founded a church here in the 6th century, and in 1306 Robert Bruce hid there after his defeat by the English at Methven.

ratio measure of the relative size of two quantities or of two measurements (in similar units), expressed as a proportion. For example, the ratio of vowels to consonants in the alphabet is 5:21; the ratio of 500 m to 2 km is 500:2,000, or 1:4.

rationalism in theology, the belief that human reason rather than divine revelation is the correct means of ascertaining truth and regulating behavior. In philosophy, rationalism takes the view that self-evident propositions deduced by reason are the sole basis of all knowledge (disregarding experience of the senses). It is usually contrasted with ⟡empiricism, which argues that all knowledge must ultimately be derived from the senses.

Following the work of the philosophers Descartes and Spinoza, rationalism was developed by Leibnitz and Kant, through whom it influenced 19th-century idealism and 20th-century analytic philosophy.

rationalized units units for which the defining equations conform to the geometry of the system. Equations involving circular symmetry contain the factor 2π; those involving spherical symmetry 4π. ⟡SI units are rationalized.

rational number in mathematics, any number that can be expressed as an exact fraction (with a denominator not equal to 0), that is, as $a \div b$ where a and b are integers. For example, 2, $\frac{1}{4}$, $\frac{15}{4}$, $-\frac{3}{5}$ are all rational numbers, whereas π (which represents the constant 3.141592...) is not. Numbers such as π are called ⟡irrational numbers.

ratite flightless bird with a breastbone without the keel to which flight muscles are attached. Examples are ostrich, rhea, emu, cassowary, and kiwi.

rat-tail or **grenadier** any fish of the family Macrouridae of deep-sea bony fishes. They have stout heads and bodies, and long tapering tails. They are common in deep waters on the continental slopes. Some species have a light-emitting organ in front of the anus.

Also known as rat-tails are some of the ⟡chimaeras.

Rattigan Terence 1911–77. English playwright. His play *Ross* 1960 was based on the character of T E Lawrence (Lawrence of Arabia).

rattlesnake any of various New World pit ⟡vipers of the genera *Crotalus* and *Sistrurus* (the massasaugas and pygmy rattlers), distinguished by horny flat segments of the tail, which rattle when vibrated as a warning to attackers. They can grow to 8 ft/2.5 m long. The venom injected by some rattlesnakes can be fatal.

There are 31 species distributed from S Canada to central South America. The eastern diamondback (*C. adamanteus*), 2.8–8 ft/0.9–2.5 m long, is at home in the flat pinelands of the southern USA.

Raunkiaer system method of classification devised by the Danish ecologist Christen Raunkiaer (1860–1938) whereby plants are divided into groups according to the position of their perennating (overwintering) buds in relation to the soil surface. For example, plants in cold areas, such as the tundra, generally have their buds protected below ground, whereas in hot, tropical areas they are above ground and freely exposed. This scheme is useful for comparing vegetation types in different parts of the world.

The main divisions are **phanerophytes** with buds situated well above the ground; **chamaephytes** with buds borne within 10 in/25 cm of the soil surface; **hemicryptophytes** with buds at or immediately below the soil surface; and **cryptophytes** with their buds either beneath the soil (**geophyte**) or below water (**hydrophyte**).

Rauschenberg Robert 1925– . US Pop artist, a creator of happenings (art in live performance) and incongruous multimedia works such as *Monogram* 1959 (Moderna Museet,

Stockholm), an automobile tire around the body of a stuffed goat daubed with paint. In the 1960s he returned to painting and used the silk-screen printing process to transfer images to canvas. He also made collages.

His works are spontaneous and use images and objects from everyday life.

Ravel (Joseph) Maurice 1875–1937. French composer. His work is characterized by its sensuousness, unresolved dissonances, and "tone color." Examples are the piano pieces *Pavane pour une infante défunte* 1899 and *Jeux d'eau* 1901, and the ballets *Daphnis et Chloë* 1912 and *Boléro* 1928.

raven any of several large ♢crows (genus *Corvus*). The common raven *C. corax* is about 2 ft/60 cm long, and has black, lustrous plumage. It is a scavenger, and is found only in the northern hemisphere.

Ravens are traditionally associated with death, probably from their practice of gathering in large numbers around a carcass, despite being a normally solitary species.

Raven, The US poem, written 1845 by Edgar Allan Poe, about a bereaved poet haunted by a raven that sonorously warns "Nevermore."

Ravenna historical city and industrial port (petrochemical works) in Emilia-Romagna, Italy; population (1988) 136,000. It lies in a marshy plain and is known for its Byzantine churches with superb mosaics.

history Ravenna was a Roman port and naval station. It was capital of the W Roman emperors 404–93, of ♢Theodoric the Great 493–526, and later of the Byzantine exarchs (bishops) 539–750. The British poet Byron lived for some months in Ravenna, home of Countess Guiccioli, during the years 1819–21.

Rawalpindi city in Punjab province, Pakistan, in the foothills of the Himalayas; population (1981) 928,400. Industries include oil refining, iron, chemicals, and furniture.

Rawlinson Henry Creswicke 1810–1895. English orientalist and political agent in Baghdad in the Ottoman Empire from 1844. He deciphered the Babylonian cuneiform and Old Persian scripts of ♢Darius I's trilingual inscription at Behistun, Persia, and published a *History of Assyria* 1852.

Rawls John 1921– . US philosopher. In *A Theory of Justice* 1971, he revived the concept of the ♢social contract and its enforcement by civil disobedience.

Born in Baltimore, Maryland, Rawls taught at Princeton, Cornell, Massachusetts Institute of Technology, and Harvard.

ray any of several orders (especially Ragiformes) of cartilaginous fishes with a flattened body, winglike pectoral fins, and a whiplike tail.

Species include the stingray, for example the Southern stingray *Dasyatis americana*, which has a serrated, poisonous spine on the tail, and the ♢torpedo fish.

Ray John 1627–1705. English naturalist who devised a classification system accounting for nearly 18,000 plant species. It was the first system to divide flowering plants into ♢monocotyledons and ♢dicotyledons, with additional divisions made on the basis of leaf and flower characters and fruit types.

Ray Nicholas. Adopted name of Raymond Nicholas Kienzle 1911–1979. US film director, critically acclaimed for his socially aware dramas such as *Rebel Without a Cause* 1955. His films include *In a Lonely Place* 1950, *Johnny Guitar* 1954, and *55 Days at Peking* 1963.

Ray Satyajit 1921–1992. Indian film director, internationally known for his trilogy of life in his native Bengal: *Pather Panchali, Unvanquished*, and *The World of Apu* 1955–59. Later films include *The Music Room* 1963, *Charulata* 1964, *The Chess Players* 1977, and *The Home and the World* 1984.

Rayburn Samuel Taliaferro 1882–1961. US political leader. After serving in the Texas state legislature 1907–12, he was elected to the US Congress as a Democrat 1912. Rayburn's tenure in the House 1912–61 was the longest on record. A supporter of the New Deal, he was elected majority leader 1937 and speaker 1940. With the exception of two terms, he served as speaker until his death. A leader of the Democratic party, Rayburn chaired the national conventions in 1948, 1952, and 1956.

Born in Roane County, Tennessee, and raised in Texas, Rayburn received a law degree from the University of Texas 1908.

Rayleigh John W Strutt, 3rd Baron 1842–1919. British physicist who wrote the standard *Treatise on Sound*, experimented in optics and microscopy, and, with William Ramsay, discovered argon. Nobel Prize 1904.

Raynaud's disease chronic condition in which the blood supply to the extremities is reduced by periodic spasm of the blood vessels on exposure to cold. It is most often seen in young women.

Attacks are usually brought on by cold or by emotional factors. Typically, the hands and/or feet take on a corpselike pallor, changing to blue as the circulation begins to return; initial numbness is replaced by a tingling or burning sensation. Drugs may be necessary to control the condition, particularly in severe cases where there is risk of gangrene.

rayon any of various shiny textile fibers and fabrics made from ♢cellulose. It is produced by pressing whatever cellulose solution is used through very small holes and solidifying the resulting filaments. A common type is ♢viscose, which consists of regenerated filaments of pure cellulose. Acetate and triacetate are kinds of rayon consisting of filaments of cellulose acetate and triacetate.

Rayon was originally made in the 1930s from the Douglas fir tree.

rays original name for radiation of all types, such as ♢X-rays and gamma rays.

razor sharpened metallic blade used to remove facial or body hair. Razors were known in the Bronze Age. The safety razor was patented by William Henson in 1847; a disposable version was produced at the start of the 20th century. The earliest electric razors date from the 1920s.

razorbill North Atlantic sea bird *Alca torda* of the auk family, which breeds on cliffs and migrates south in winter. It has a curved beak and is black above and white below. It uses its wings as paddles when diving. Razorbills are common off Newfoundland.

re abbreviation for Latin "with regard to."

reaction in chemistry, the coming together of two or more atoms, ions, or molecules with the result that a chemical change takes place. The nature of the reaction is portrayed by a chemical equation.

reaction principle principle stated by ♢Newton as his third law of motion: to every action, there is an equal and opposite reaction.

In other words, a force acting in one direction is always accompanied by an equal force acting in the opposite direction. This explains how rocket and ♢jet propulsion works and why a gun recoils after firing.

Reader's Digest magazine founded 1922 in the US to publish condensed articles and books, usually uplifting and conservative, along with in-house features. It has editions in many languages and until the mid-1980s was the largest-circulation magazine in the world.

Reading industrial city (textiles, special steels) in E Pennsylvania; population (1990) 78,400.

Reading was laid out in 1748 and was an early iron- and steelmaking center, connected by canal and rail to nearby anthracite mines.

Reagan Ronald (Wilson) 1911– . 40th president of the US 1981–89, a Republican. He was governor of California 1966–74, and a former Hollywood actor. Reagan was a hawkish and popular president. He adopted an aggressive policy in Central America, attempting to overthrow the government of Nicaragua, and invading ♢Grenada 1983. In 1987, ♢Irangate was investigated by the Tower Commission; Reagan admitted that US–Iran negotiations had become an "arms for hostages deal," but denied knowledge of resultant funds being illegally sent to the Contras in Nicaragua. He increased military spending (sending the national budget deficit to record levels), cut social programs, introduced deregulation of domestic markets, and cut taxes. His ♢Strategic Defense Initiative, announced 1983, proved controversial owing to the cost and unfeasibility. He was succeeded by George ♢Bush.

Reagan was born in Tampico, Illinois, the son of a shoe salesman who was bankrupted during the Depression. He became a Hollywood actor 1937 and appeared in 50 films, including *Bedtime for Bonzo* 1951 and *The Killers* 1964. As president of the Screen Actors' Guild 1947–52, he became a conservative, critical of the bureaucratic stifling of free enterprise, and named names before the House Un-American Activities Committee. He joined the Republican Party 1962, and his term as governor of California was marked by battles against students. Having lost the Republican presidential nomination 1968 and 1976 to Nixon and Ford respectively, Reagan won it 1980 and defeated President Carter. He was wounded in an assassination attempt 1981. The invasion of Grenada, following a coup there, generated a revival of national patriotism, and Reagan was reelected by a landslide 1984. His insistence on militarizing space through the Strategic Defense Initiative, popularly called Star Wars, prevented a disarmament agreement when he met the Soviet leader ♢Gorbachev 1985 and 1986, but a 4% reduction in nuclear weapons was agreed 1987. In 1986, he ordered the bombing of Tripoli, Libya, in alleged retaliation for the killing of a US soldier in Berlin by a guerrilla group.

realism in medieval philosophy, the theory that "universals" have existence, not simply as names for entities but as entities in their own right. It is thus opposed to ♢nominalism. In contemporary philosophy, the term stands for the doctrine that there is an intuitively appreciated reality apart from what is presented to the consciousness. It is opposed to ♢idealism.

Realist philosophers include C D Broad and (although their views were later modified)

Bertrand Russell and G E Moore; Wittgenstein was a significant later influence.

Realism in the arts and literature, an unadorned, naturalistic approach to the subject matter. The term **Realism** may also refer to a movement in mid-19th-century European art, a reaction against Romantic and Classical idealization and a rejection of conventional academic subjects, such as mythology, history, and sublime landscapes.

The painters Courbet and Daumier represent 19th-century Realism in France: both chose to paint scenes from contemporary life, using their art to expose injustice in society. Courbet shocked the public by exhibiting large canvases that depicted ordinary people.

real number in mathematics, any of the ▷rational numbers (which include the integers) or ▷irrational numbers. Real numbers exclude ▷imaginary numbers, found in ▷complex numbers of the general form $a + bi$ where $i = \sqrt{-1}$, although these do include a real component a.

realpolitik (German *Realpolitik* "politics of realism") the pragmatic pursuit of self-interest and power, backed up by force when convenient. The term was coined 1853 to describe ▷Bismarck's policies in Prussia during the 1848 revolutions.

real presence or *transubstantiation* in Christianity, the belief that there are present in the properly consecrated Eucharist the body and blood of Jesus. It is held by Roman Catholics, and in some sense by Anglo-Catholics.

real-time system in computing, a program that responds to events in the world as they happen, as, for example, an automatic-pilot program in an aircraft must respond instantly in order to correct deviations from its course. Process control, robotics, games, and many military applications are examples of real-time systems.

Réaumur René Antoine Ferchault de 1683–1757. French scientist. His work on metallurgy *L'Arte de convertir le fer forge en acier* 1722 described how to convert iron into steel and stimulated the development of the French steel industry. He produced a six-volume work 1734–42 on entomology, *L'Histoire des insectes/History of Insects*, which threw much new light on the social insects. He also contributed to other areas of science.

recall process by which voters can demand the removal from office of elected officials, as in some states of the US.

receiver in law, a person appointed by a court to collect and manage the assets of an individual, company, or partnership in serious financial difficulties. In the case of bankruptcy, the assets may be sold and distributed by a receiver to creditors.

In France, a receiver is known as a syndic, and in Germany as an administrator.

receptacle the enlarged end of a flower stalk to which the floral parts are attached. Normally the receptacle is rounded, but in some plants it is flattened or cup-shaped. The term is also used for the region on that part of some seaweeds which becomes swollen at certain times of the year and bears the reproductive organs.

recession in economics, a fall in business activity lasting more than a few months, causing stagnation in a country's output.

The average decline has been about 10% although some recessions, such as 1981–82, can be longer and more severe.

recessive gene in genetics, an ▷allele (alternate form of a gene) that will show in the ▷phenotype (observed characteristics of an organism) only if its partner allele on the paired chromosome is similarly recessive. Such an allele will not show if its partner is dominant, that is if the organism is ▷heterozygous for a particular characteristic. Alleles for blue eyes in humans, and for shortness in pea plants are recessive. Most mutant alleles are recessive and therefore are only rarely expressed (see ▷haemophilia and ▷sickle cell disease).

Recife industrial seaport (cotton textiles, sugar refining, fruit canning, flour milling) and naval base in Brazil; capital of Pernambuco state, at the mouth of the river Capibaribe; population (1991) 1,335,700. It was founded 1504.

reciprocal in mathematics, the result of dividing a given quantity into 1. Thus the reciprocal of 2 is 1/2; of 2/3 is 3/2; of x^2 is $1/x^2$ or x^{-2}. Reciprocals are used to replace division by multiplication, since multiplying by the reciprocal of a number is the same as dividing by that number.

recitative in opera, on-pitch speechlike declamation used in narrative episodes.

recombination in genetics, any process that recombines, or "shuffles," the genetic material, thus increasing genetic variation in the offspring. The two main processes of recombination both occur during meiosis (reduction division of cells). One is ▷*crossing over*, in which chromosome pairs exchange segments; the other is the random reassortment of chromosomes that occurs when each gamete (sperm or egg) receives only one of each chromosome pair.

Reconstruction in US history, the period 1865–77 after the Civil War during which the nation was reunited under the federal government after the defeat of the Southern Confederacy.

Amendments to the US constitution, and to Southern state constitutions, conferred equal civil and political rights on blacks, although many Southern states, still opposed to these radical Republican measures, still practiced discrimination and segregation. During Reconstruction, industrial and commercial projects restored the economy of the South but failed to ensure racial equality, and the former slaves remained, in most cases, landless laborers, although emancipated slaves were assisted in finding work, shelter, and lost relatives through federal agencies. Reconstruction also resulted in an influx of Northern profiteers known as ▷carpetbaggers. Both the imposition of outside authority and the equal status conferred on former slaves combined to make Southerners bitterly resentful. Although Radical Republicans sought punitive measures against the South, they were restrained by President Abraham ▷Lincoln. When President Andrew ▷Johnson refused to agree to their program, the Radicals contrived to bring about his impeachment, failing by one vote to convict him.

recorder in music, a pure-toned instrument of the ▷woodwind family, in which the single reed is integrated with the mouthpiece. Recorders are played in a consort (ensemble) of matching tone and comprise sopranino, descant, treble, tenor, and bass.

The descant, adopted into the orchestra, was gradually superseded by the flute, but was revived as a school music instrument. The

full consort has since been reestablished for performing early music.

recording the process of storing information, or the information store itself. Sounds and pictures can be stored on disks or tape. The phonograph record or ▷compact disc stores music or speech as a spiral groove on a plastic disk and the sounds are reproduced by a record player. In tape recording, sounds are stored as a magnetic pattern on plastic tape. The best-quality reproduction is achieved using digital audio tape.

In *digital recording* the signals picked up by the microphone are converted into precise numerical values by computer. These values, which represent the original sound wave form, are recorded on tape or compact disc. When it is played back by ▷laser, the exact values are retrieved. When the signal is fed via an amplifier to a loudspeaker, sound waves exactly like the original ones are recreated. Pictures can be recorded on magnetic tape in a similar way by using a ▷video tape recorder. The video equivalent of a compact disc is the video disc.

record player device for reproducing recorded sound stored as a spiral groove on a vinyl disk. A motor-driven turntable rotates the record at a constant speed, and a stylus or needle on the head of a pick-up is made to vibrate by the undulations in the record groove. These vibrations are then converted to electrical signals by a ▷transducer in the head (often a ▷piezoelectric effect crystal). After amplification, the signals pass to one or more loudspeakers, which convert them into sound. Alternate formats are ▷compact disc and ▷tape recording, magnetic.

The pioneers of the record player were Thomas ▷Edison, with his ▷phonograph, and Emile Berliner (1851–1929), who invented the predecessor of the vinyl record 1896. More recent developments are stereophonic sound and digital recording on compact disc.

Recruit scandal in Japanese politics, the revelation 1988 that a number of politicians and business leaders had profited from insider trading. It led to the resignation of several cabinet ministers, including Prime Minister Takeshita, whose closest aide committed suicide, and to the arrest of 20 people.

Recruit is an information-publishing conglomerate with property and telecommunications interests. 17 senior politicians and 150 business leaders and other prominent individuals were offered bargain-priced shares in Cosmos, a Recruit subsidiary, a month before they were listed for public sale in 1986. Share prices rose sharply after their public offering, and stockholders made, on average, tax-free profits of 66 million yen. Another 30 MPs, mostly involved in education and labor matters, accepted favors from Recruit. Politicians of all the major parties were tainted by the scandal, notably the ruling Liberal Democratic Party. The leader of the Democratic Socialist Party was forced to resign. Recruit's founder and managing director were among those charged with bribery. Another Recruit executive was caught trying to bribe an MP to stop the inquiry.

rectangle quadrilateral (four-sided plane figure) with opposite sides equal and parallel and with each interior angle a right angle (90°). Its area A is the product of the length l and width w; that is, $A = l \times w$. A rectangle with all four sides equal is a ▷square.

A rectangle is a special case of a ⊘parallelogram. The diagonals of a rectangle are equal and bisect each other.

rectifier in electrical engineering, a device used for obtaining one-directional current (DC) from an alternating source of supply (AC). Types include plate rectifiers, thermionic ⊘diodes, and ⊘semiconductor diodes.

rectum lowest part of the digestive tract of animals, which stores feces prior to elimination (defecation).

recursion in computing and mathematics, a technique whereby a ⊘function or ⊘procedure calls itself into use in order to enable a complex problem to be broken down into simpler steps. For example, a function that finds the factorial of a number n (calculates the product of all the whole numbers between 1 and n) would obtain its result by multiplying n by the factorial of $n - 1$.

recycling processing of industrial and household waste (such as paper, glass, and some metals and plastics) so that it can be reused. This saves expenditure on scarce raw materials, slows down the depletion of ⊘nonrenewable resources, and helps to reduce pollution.

red informal term for a leftist, revolutionary, or communist, which originated in the 19th century in the form "red republican," meaning a republican who favored a social as well as a political revolution, generally by armed violence. Red is the color adopted by socialist and communist parties.

To be soft on these political philosophies, one is thereby tainted "pink."

Red (1) River, W tributary of the ⊘Mississippi River 1,018 mi/1,638 km long; so called because of the reddish soil sediment it carries. The stretch that forms the Texas—Oklahoma border is called Tornado Alley because of the storms caused by the collision in spring of warm air from the Gulf of Mexico with cold fronts from the N. The largest city on the river is Shreveport, Louisiana. (2) River, the Red River of the North, about 545 mi/877 km long, runs from North Dakota into Manitoba, and through Winnipeg, emptying into Lake Winnipeg. The fertile soil of the river valley produces large yields of wheat and other crops.

Red and the Black, The French *Le Rouge et le noir* novel by Stendhal, published 1830. Julien Sorel, a carpenter's son, pursues social advancement by dishonorable means. Marriage to a marquis' daughter, a title, and an army commission are within his grasp when revelation of his murky past by a former lover destroys him.

Red Army name of the army of the USSR until 1946; later known as the *Soviet Army*. It developed from the Red Guards, volunteers who carried out the Bolshevik revolution, and received its name because it fought under the ⊘red flag. The Chinese revolutionary army was also called the Red Army.

Red Badge of Courage, The classic US novel of the American Civil War published 1895 by Stephen Crane; the story of the youth Henry Fleming, his cowardice, courage, and final sense of personal victory.

red blood cell or **erythrocyte** the most common type of blood cell, responsible for transporting oxygen around the body. It contains haemoglobin, which combines with oxygen from the lungs to form oxyhaemoglobin.

When transported to the tissues, these cells are able to release the oxygen because the oxyhaemoglobin splits into its original constituents.

Mammalian erythrocytes are disc-shaped with a depression in the center and no nucleus; they are manufactured in the bone marrow and, in humans, last for only four months before being destroyed in the liver and spleen. Those of other vertebrates are oval and nucleated.

Red Brigades (Italian *Brigate rosse*) extreme left-wing guerrilla groups active in Italy during the 1970s and early 1980s. They were implicated in many kidnappings and killings, some later attributed to right-wing *agents provocateurs*, including that of Christian Democrat leader Aldo Moro 1978.

Red Cloud (Sioux name **Mahpiua Luta**) 1822–1909. Sioux leader. Paramount chief of the Oglala Sioux from 1860, he led the armed resistance to the advance of white settlers along the Bozeman Trail.

Red Cloud was born in the area of modern Nebraska. In 1869 he signed the Fort Laramie Treaty and led his followers to the Red Cloud Agency in Nebraska. They moved to the Pine Ridge Agency in South Dakota 1878. Taking no part in the 1876 war that culminated in the Battle of the Little Bighorn, Red Cloud remained an advocate of accommodation with the US government.

Red Cross international relief agency founded by the Geneva Convention 1864 at the instigation of the Swiss doctor Henri ⊘Dunant to assist the wounded and prisoners in war. Its symbol is a symmetrical red cross on a white ground. In addition to dealing with associated problems of war, such as refugees and the care of the disabled, the Red Cross is increasingly concerned with victims of natural disasters—floods, earthquakes, epidemics, and accidents.

Prompted by war horrors described by Dunant, the Geneva Convention laid down principles to ensure the safety of ambulances, hospitals, stores, and personnel distinguished by the Red Cross emblem. The Muslim equivalent is the **Red Crescent**.

The US National Red Cross was founded 1881.

redcurrant in botany, type of ⊘currant.

Redding Otis 1941–1967. US soul singer and songwriter. He had a number of hits in the mid-1960s such as "My Girl" 1965, "Respect" 1967, and "(Sittin' on the) Dock of the Bay" 1968, released after his death in a plane crash.

red dwarf any star that is cool, faint, and small (about one-tenth the mass and diameter of the Sun). Red dwarfs burn slowly, and have estimated lifetimes of 100 billion years. They may be the most abundant type of star, but are difficult to see because they are so faint. Two of the closest stars to the Sun, ⊘Proxima Centauri and ⊘Barnard's Star, are red dwarfs.

Redford (Charles) Robert 1937– . US actor and film director. His first starring role was in *Barefoot In The Park* 1967, followed by *Butch Cassidy and the Sundance Kid* 1969, and *The Sting* 1973 (both with Paul ⊘Newman).

His other films as an actor include *The Way We Were* 1973, *All the President's Men* 1976, *Out of Africa* 1985, *Havana* 1991, *Sneakers* 1992, and *A River Runs Through It* 1992. He directed *Ordinary People* 1980 and

The Milagro Beanfield War 1988, and established the Sundance Institute in Utah for the development of theatrical talent.

red giant any large bright star with a cool surface. It is thought to represent a late stage in the evolution of a star like the Sun, as it runs out of hydrogen fuel at its center. Red giants have diameters between 10 and 100 times that of the Sun. They are very bright because they are so large, although their surface temperature is lower than that of the Sun, about 2,000–3,000K (3,000°–5,000°F/1,700°–2,700°C).

Redgrave Michael 1908–1985. British actor. His stage roles included Hamlet and Lear (Shakespeare), Uncle Vanya (Chekhov), and the schoolmaster in Rattigan's *The Browning Version* (filmed 1951). On screen he appeared in *The Lady Vanishes* 1938, *The Importance of Being Earnest* 1952, and *Goodbye Mr Chips* 1959. He was the father of Vanessa and Lynn Redgrave, both actresses.

Redgrave Vanessa 1937– . British actress. She has played Shakespeare's Lady Macbeth and Cleopatra on the stage, and Olga in Chekhov's *Three Sisters* 1990. She won an Academy Award for the title role in the film *Julia* 1976; other films include *Howards End* 1992. She is active in left-wing politics.

Red Guard school and college student, wearing red armbands, active in the ⊘Cultural Revolution in China 1966–69. The armed workers who took part in the ⊘Russian Revolution of 1917 were also called Red Guards.

red-hot poker any plant of the African genus *Kniphofia*, family Liliaceae, in particular *K. uvaria*, with a flame-colored spike of flowers.

Redon Odilon 1840–1916. French Symbolist painter and graphic artist. He used fantastic symbols and images, sometimes mythological. From the 1890s he painted still lifes and landscapes. His work was much admired by the Surrealists.

Redon initially worked mostly in black and white, producing charcoal drawings and lithographs, but from 1890, in oils and pastels, he used color in a way that recalled the Impressionists. The head of Orpheus is a recurring motif in his work.

Redon made his reputation as a Symbolist in Paris around 1880.

Redoubt, Mount active volcanic peak rising to 10,197 ft/3,140 m, W of Cook inlet in S Alaska. There were eruptions in 1966 and 1989.

red pepper red fruit of various ⊘capsicums.

Red River river in N Vietnam, 310 mi/500 km long, that flows into the Gulf of Tonkin. Its extensive delta is a main center of population.

Red Scare in US history, campaign against radicals and dissenters which took place in the aftermath of World War I and the Russian Revolution, during a period of labor disorders in the US. A wave of strikes in 1919 was seen as a prelude to revolution and violently suppressed. Thousands of people were arrested on suspicion, and communists were banned from entry to the country.

Some labor organizations, notably the ⊘Industrial Workers of the World, had advocated violence, and there were anarchist bombing incidents. Soon all socialists were perceived as threats to the state. J Edgar ⊘Hoover was enlisted to track subversives, and a nationwide roundup of suspects on Jan 2, 1920 led to 556 deportations. Many of the left-wing leaders were immigrants, and fear of foreigners played a large part in the Red Scare. It was after this that the system of immigration quotas was established.

Red Sea submerged section of the ◊Great Rift Valley (1,200 mi/2,000 km long and up to 200 mi/320 km wide). Egypt, Sudan, and Ethiopia (in Africa) and Saudi Arabia (Asia) are on its shores.

red shift in astronomy, the lengthening of the wavelengths of light from an object as a result of the object's motion away from us. It is an example of the ◊Doppler effect. The red shift in light from galaxies is evidence that the universe is expanding.

Lengthening of wavelengths causes the light to move or shift toward the red end of the ◊spectrum, hence the name. The amount of red shift can be measured by the displacement of lines in an object's spectrum. By measuring the amount of red shift in light from stars and galaxies, astronomers can tell how quickly these objects are moving away from us. A strong gravitational field can also produce a red shift in light; this is termed *gravitational red shift*.

redstart any of several New World wood warblers (family Parulidae), especially the American redstart *Setophaga ruticulla*. The male is black and orange with white underparts. Old World redstarts are small thrushes with a reddish tail, belonging to the genus *Phoenicurus*.

Redstone rocket short-range US military missile, modified for use as a space launcher. Redstone rockets launched the first two flights of the ◊Mercury project. A modified Redstone, *Juno 1*, launched the first US satellite, *Explorer 1*, in 1958.

red tape derogatory term for bureaucratic methods, derived from the fastening of departmental bundles of documents in Britain.

Red Terror term used by opponents to describe the Bolshevik seizure and retention of power in Russia after Oct 1917.

redwood giant coniferous tree, one of the two types of ◊sequoia.

reed any of various perennial tall, slender grasses of wet or marshy environments; in particular, species of the genera *Phragmites* and *Arundo*; also the stalk of any of these plants. The common reed *P. australis* attains a height of 10 ft/3 m, having stiff, erect leaves and straight stems bearing a plume of purplish flowers.

Reed Carol 1906–1976. British film producer and director, an influential figure in the British film industry of the 1940s. His films include *Odd Man Out* 1947, *The Fallen Idol* and *The Third Man* both 1950, *Our Man in Havana* 1959, and the Academy Award-winning musical *Oliver!* 1968.

Reed Ishmael 1938– . US novelist. His experimental, parodic, satirical novels exploit traditions taken from jazz and voodoo, and include *The Free-Lance Pallbearers* 1967, *Mumbo Jumbo* 1972, and *Reckless Eyeballing* 1986.

Reed John 1887–1920. US journalist and author. As a supporter of the Bolsheviks, Reed published his account of the Russian Revolution in *Ten Days that Shook the World* 1919. Later indicted in the US for sedition, Reed fled to the Soviet Union, where he died in exile.

Born in Portland, Oregon, and educated at Harvard, Reed began his journalism career on the staff of the *American Magazine* 1911. Becoming involved in radical politics, he joined the staff of *Masses* 1913. He later published his accounts of overseas conflicts in *Insurgent Mexico* 1914 and *The War in Eastern Europe* 1916.

Reed Lou 1942– . US rock singer, songwriter, and guitarist; former member (1965–70) of the New York avant-garde group *the Velvet Underground*, perhaps the most influential band of the period. His solo work deals largely with urban alienation and angst, and includes the albums *Berlin* 1973, *New York* 1989, and *Magic and Loss* 1991.

Reed Oliver 1938– . British actor, nephew of the director Carol Reed. He appeared in such films as *Women in Love* 1969, *The Devils* 1971, and *Castaway* 1987.

Reed Walter 1851–1902. US physician and medical researcher. His 1898 research into the causes and transmission of typhoid fever brought about significant control of the disease in army camps. Reed's greatest work was carried out 1900–01 in Cuba, where a yellow-fever epidemic was ravaging US troops. His breakthrough isolation of the aedes mosquito as the sole carrier of yellow fever led to the eradication of the deadly disease.

Born in Belroi, Virginia, Reed received an MD degree from the University of Virginia 1869. He joined the Army Medical Corps 1875, served as an army surgeon in Arizona 1876–89 and Baltimore 1890–93, and was professor at the Army Medical College 1893–1902.

reel in cinema, plastic or metal spool used for winding and storing film. As the size of reels became standardized it came to refer to the running time of the film: a standard 35-mm reel holds 900 ft/313 m of film, which runs for ten minutes when projected at 24 frames per second; hence a "two-reeler" was a film lasting 20 minutes. Today's projectors, however, hold bigger reels.

reeve in Anglo-Saxon England, an official charged with the administration of a shire or burgh, fulfilling functions similar to those of the later sheriff. After the Norman Conquest, the term tended to be restricted to the person elected by the villeins to oversee the work of the manor and to communicate with the manorial lord.

referee in science, one who reads and comments on a scientific paper before its publication, normally a scientist of at least equal standing to the author(s).

referee a quasi-judicial officer appointed by a court to take testimony or hear specified types of cases. These officials are sometimes called masters.

referendum procedure whereby a decision on proposed legislation is referred to the electorate for settlement by direct vote of all the people. It is most frequently employed in Switzerland, the first country to use it, but has become increasingly widespread. In 1992 several European countries (Ireland, Denmark, France) held referenda on whether or not to ratify the Maastricht Treaty on closer European economic and political union.

A referendum was held in the UK for the first time 1975 on the issue of membership in the European Community. Critics argue that referenda undermine parliamentary authority, but they do allow the elector to participate directly in decision-making. Similar devices

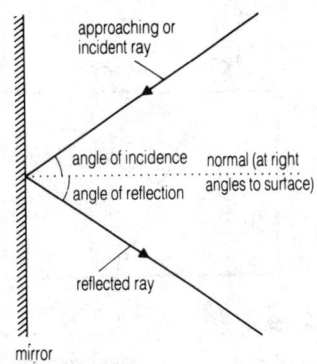

reflection *The law of reflection: the angle of incidence of a light beam equals the angle of reflection of the beam.*

are the ◊recall, whereby voters are given the opportunity of demanding the dismissal from office of officials, and the *initiative* (see ◊initiative, referendum and).

refining any process that purifies or converts something into a more useful form. Metals usually need refining after they have been extracted from their ores by such processes as smelting. Petroleum, or crude oil, needs refining before it can be used; the process involves fractional ◊distillation, the separation of the substance into separate components or "fractions."

Electrolytic metal-refining methods use the principle of ◊electrolysis to obtain pure metals. When refining petroleum, or crude oil, further refinery processes after fractionation convert the heavier fractions into more useful lighter products. The most important of these processes is ◊cracking; others include ◊polymerization, hydrogenation, and reforming.

reflection the throwing back or deflection of waves, such as ◊light or ◊sound waves, when they hit a surface. The *law of reflection* states that the angle of incidence (the angle between the ray and a perpendicular line drawn to the surface) is equal to the angle of reflection (the angle between the reflected ray and a perpendicular to the surface).

reflex in animals, a very rapid automatic response to a particular stimulus. It is controlled by the ◊nervous system. A reflex involves only a few nerve cells, unlike the slower but more complex responses produced by the many processing nerve cells of the brain.

A *simple reflex* is entirely automatic and involves no learning. Examples of such reflexes include the sudden withdrawal of a hand in response to a painful stimulus, or the jerking of a leg when its kneecap is tapped. Sensory cells (receptors) in the knee send signals to the spinal cord along a sensory nerve cell. Within the spine a *reflex arc* switches the signals straight back to the muscles of the leg (effectors) via an intermediate nerve cell and then a motor nerve cell; contraction of the leg occurs, and the leg kicks upward. Only three nerve cells are involved, and the brain is only aware of the response after it has taken place. Such reflex arcs are particularly common in lower animals, and have a high survival value, enabling organisms to take rapid action to avoid potential danger. In higher animals (those with a well-developed ◊central nervous system) the simple reflex can be modified by the involvement of the

refraction

brain—for instance, humans can override the automatic reflex to withdraw a hand from a source of pain.

A *conditioned reflex* involves the modification of a reflex action in response to experience (learning). A stimulus that produces a simple reflex response becomes linked with another, possibly unrelated, stimulus. For example, a dog may salivate (a reflex action) when it sees its owner remove a can-opener from a drawer because it has learned to associate that stimulus with the stimulus of being fed.

reflex camera camera that uses a mirror and prisms to reflect light passing through the lens into the viewfinder, showing the photographer the exact scene that is being shot. When the shutter button is released the mirror springs out of the way, allowing light to reach the film. The most common type is the single-lens reflex (⯌SLR) camera. The twin-lens reflex (⯌TLR) camera has two lenses: one has a mirror for viewing, the other is used for exposing the film.

Reformation religious and political movement in 16th-century Europe to reform the Roman Catholic Church, which led to the establishment of Protestant churches. Anticipated from the 12th century by the Waldenses, Lollards, and Hussites, it was set off by German priest Martin ⯌Luther 1517, and became effective when the absolute monarchies gave it support by challenging the political power of the papacy and confiscating church wealth.

1517 Martin Luther's protest against the sale of ⯌indulgences began the Reformation in Europe.
1519 Ulrich ⯌Zwingli led the Reformation in Switzerland.
1529 The term "Protestant" was first used.
1533 Henry VIII renounced papal supremacy and proclaimed himself head of the Church of England.
1541 The French theologian John ⯌Calvin established Presbyterianism in Geneva, Switzerland.
1559 The Protestant John ⯌Knox returned from exile to found the Church of Scotland.
1545–1563 The *Counter-Reformation* was initiated by the Roman Catholic Church at the *Council of Trent*. It aimed at reforming abuses and regaining the lost ground by using moral persuasion and extending the Spanish Inquisition to other countries.
1648 By the end of the Thirty Years' War, the present European alignment had been reached, with the separation of Catholic and Protestant churches.

refraction the bending of a wave of light, heat, or sound when it passes from one medium to another. Refraction occurs because waves travel at different velocities in different media.

refractive index measure of the refraction of

a ray of light as it passes from one transparent medium to another. If the angle of incidence is i and the angle of refraction is r, the refractive index $n = \sin i / \sin r$. It is also equal to the speed of light in the first medium divided by the speed of light in the second, and it varies with the wavelength of the light.

refractory (of a material) able to resist high temperature, for example ⯌ceramics made from clay, minerals, or other earthy materials. Furnaces are lined with refractory materials such as silica and dolomite.

Alumina (aluminum oxide) is an excellent refractory, often used for the bodies of spark plugs. Titanium and tungsten are often called refractory metals because they are temperature resistant. ⯌Cermets are refractory materials made up of ceramics and metals.

refrigeration use of technology to transfer heat from cold to warm, against the normal temperature gradient, so that a body can remain substantially colder than its surroundings. Refrigeration equipment is used for the chilling and deep-freezing of food in ⯌food technology, and in air conditioners and industrial processes.

Refrigeration is commonly achieved by a vapor-compression cycle, in which a suitable chemical (the refrigerant) travels through a long circuit of tubing, during which it changes from a vapor to a liquid and back again. A compression chamber makes it condense, and thus give out heat. In another part of the circuit, called the evaporator coils, the pressure is much lower, so the refrigerant evaporates, absorbing heat as it does so. The evaporation process takes place near the central part of the refrigerator, which therefore becomes colder, while the compression process takes place near a ventilation grille, transferring the heat to the air outside. The most commonly used refrigerants in modern systems were ⯌chlorofluorocarbons, but these are now being replaced by coolants that do not damage the ozone layer.

refugee person fleeing from oppressive or dangerous conditions (such as political, religious, or military persecution) and seeking refuge in a foreign country. In 1991 there were an estimated 17 million refugees worldwide, whose resettlement and welfare were the responsibility of the United Nations High Commission for Refugees (UNHCR). An estimated average of 3,000 people a day become refugees.

refrigeration *In a refrigerator, a fluid called the refrigerant is pumped around a circuit of tubing which wraps around the freezer compartment and forms the radiator coil at the rear.*

The term was originally applied to the French Huguenots who came to England after toleration of Protestantism was withdrawn with the revocation of the Edict of Nantes in 1685. Major refugee movements in 20th-century Europe include: Jews from the ⯌pogroms of Russia 1881–1914 and again after the Revolution; White Russians from the USSR after 1917; Jews from Germany and other Nazi-dominated countries 1933–45; the displaced people of World War II; and from 1991 victims of the the civil wars in Croatia and Bosnia-Herzegovina.

Many Chinese fled the mainland after the communist revolution of 1949, especially to Taiwan and Hong Kong; many Latin Americans fled from Cuba, Colombia, Brazil, Chile, Argentina, and Central America when new governments took power; and many ⯌boat people left Vietnam after the victory of the North over the South. Refugee movements created by natural disasters and famine have been widespread, most notably in Ethiopia and Sudan, where civil war has also contributed. Between 1985 and 1989 the number of refugees doubled worldwide, and the Gulf War 1991 created 1.5 million refugees, though many were later able to return to their homes.

In 1990 the largest single refugee groupings were: Afghans (about 6 million, temporarily settled in Iran and Pakistan); Ethiopians (1.3 million, mostly Eritreans who have moved to Sudan); Mozambicans (1.2 million, displaced mostly to Malawi); Iraqis (600,000, predominantly Kurds who have settled in Iran); Somalis (400,000); Sudanese (400,000); Sri Lankan Tamils (300,000, who have fled to India); and Cambodians (300,000, who live in refugee camps in Thailand). UNHCR's budget was $550 million in 1990.

A distinction is usually made by Western nations between "political" refugees and so-called "economic" refugees, who are said to be escaping from poverty rather than persecution, particularly when the refugees come from low-income countries. The latter group often become illegal immigrants; see ⯌immigration and emigration. International law recognizes the right of the persecuted to seek asylum but does not oblige states to provide it. Only 0.17% of W Europe's population are refugees.

Internally displaced people, who have been forced to leave their homes but not crossed their country's borders, are not recognized as refugees; they are estimated to number over 30 million (1991).

Regan Donald 1918– . US Republican political adviser to Ronald ⯌Reagan. He was secretary of the Treasury 1981–85, and chief of White House staff 1985–87, when he was forced to resign because of widespread belief in his complicity in the ⯌Irangate scandal.

regelation phenomenon in which water refreezes to ice after it has been melted by pressure at a temperature below the freezing point of water. Pressure makes an ice skate, for example, form a film of water that freezes once again after the skater has passed.

Regency in Britain, the years 1811–20 during which ⯌George IV (then Prince of Wales) acted as regent for his father ⯌George III.

Regency style style of architecture and interior furnishings popular in England during the late 18th and early 19th centuries. The style is characterized by its restrained simplicity and its imitation of ancient Classical elements, often Greek.

regeneration in biology, regrowth of a new

organ or tissue after the loss or removal of the original. It is common in plants, where a new individual can often be produced from a "cutting" of the original. In animals, regeneration of major structures is limited to lower organisms; certain lizards can regrow their tails if these are lost, and new flatworms can grow from a tiny fragment of an old one. In mammals, regeneration is limited to the repair of tissue in wound healing and the regrowth of peripheral nerves following damage.

Regensburg (English **Ratisbon**) city in Bavaria, Germany, on the river Danube at its confluence with the Regen, 63 mi/100 km NE of Munich; population (1988) 124,000. It has many medieval buildings, including a Gothic cathedral 1275–1530.

history Regensburg stands on the site of a Celtic settlement dating from 500 BC. It became the Roman *Castra Regina* AD 179, the capital of the Eastern Frankish Empire, a free city 1245, and seat of the German *Diet* (parliament) 16th century–1806. It was included in Bavaria 1810.

regent person who carries out the duties of a sovereign during the sovereign's minority, incapacity, or lengthy absence from the country. In England since the time of Henry VIII, Parliament has always appointed a regent or council of regency when necessary.

Regents of the University of California v Bakke a US Supreme Court decision 1978 dealing with "benign discrimination" in publicly funded schools. The case was a challenge to an affirmative-action program designed to remedy racial inequality in the University of California Medical School. Bakke, a white applicant denied admission to the school, sued the university on grounds of racial discrimination. He argued that his rejection was the result of a policy that accepted minority applicants at lower standards than those set for nonminorities. The Court sustained Bakke's complaint, ruling that any institution, regardless of motive, that discriminated solely because of race was in violation of the Civil Rights Act of 1964.

reggae predominant form of West Indian popular music of the 1970s and 1980s, characterized by a heavily accented offbeat and a thick bass line. The lyrics often refer to ⟳Rastafarianism. Musicians include Bob Marley, Lee "Scratch" Perry (1940– , performer and producer), and the group Black Uhuru (1974–). Reggae is also played in the UK, South Africa, and elsewhere.

There are several reggae styles. The practice of issuing singles with, on the B-side, a *dub* version, or stripped-down instrumental remix, was designed for use in clubs, where disk jockeys who added a spoken vocal part became known as *toasters*; they in turn released records. A fast reggae-rap style called *ragga* emerged in the early 1990s.

Reggio di Calabria industrial center (farm machinery, olive oil, perfume) of Calabria, S Italy; population (1988) 179,000. It was founded by Greeks about 720 BC.

Regina industrial city (oil refining, cement, steel, farm machinery, fertilizers), and capital of Saskatchewan; population (1986) 175,000. It was founded 1882 as *Pile O'Bones*, and renamed in honor of Queen Victoria of England.

register in computing, a memory location that can be accessed rapidly; it is often built into the computer's central processing unit. Some registers are reserved for special tasks—for example, an *instruction register* is used to hold the machine-code command that the computer is currently executing, while a *sequence-control register* keeps track of the next command to be executed. Other registers are used for holding frequently used data and for storing intermediate results.

Regulus or **Alpha Leonis** the brightest star in the constellation Leo, and the 21st brightest star in the sky. Regulus has a true luminosity 100 times that of the Sun, and is 69 light-years from Earth.

Rehnquist William Hubbs 1924– . US jurist; associate justice 1971–86 and chief justice 1986– of the US Supreme Court. As chief justice, he wrote the majority opinion for such cases as *Morrison* v *Olson* 1988, in which the Court ruled that a special court can appoint special prosecutors to investigate crimes by high-ranking government officials, and *Hustler* v *Falwell* 1988, in which the Court ruled that public figures cannot be compensated for stress caused by parody that cannot possibly be taken seriously. Rehnquist dissented in *Texas* v *Johnson* 1989, in which the Court ruled that the burning of the US flag in protest is protected by individual rights set forth in the First Amendment. In 1990 Rehnquist dissented on the Court's ruling that it is unconstitutional for states to have the right to require a teenager to notify her parents before having an abortion.

Born in Milwaukee, Wisconsin, he graduated from Stanford University and the Stanford Law School. Rehnquist served as clerk to US Supreme Court Justice Robert Jackson before entering private practice in Phoenix, Arizona. He became active in Republican politics. In 1968 Rehnquist was appointed by President Nixon as an assistant US attorney general and in 1971 to the Supreme Court. As an associate justice, Rehnquist argued in dissent for the death penalty in *Furman* v *Georgia* 1972, and again in dissent, against the right to abortion in *Roe* v *Wade* 1973. Writing for the majority, Rehnquist held in *Rostken* v *Goldberg* 1981 that it is constitutional to exclude women for registering for the draft. He was appointed chief justice by President Reagan.

Rehoboam king of Judah about 932–915 BC, son of Solomon. Under his rule the Jewish nation split into the two kingdoms of *Israel* and *Judah*. Ten of the tribes revolted against him and took Jeroboam as their ruler, leaving Rehoboam only the tribes of Judah and Benjamin.

Reich (German "empire") three periods in European history. The First Reich was the Holy Roman Empire 962–1806, the Second Reich the German Empire 1871–1918, and the ⟳Third Reich Nazi Germany 1933–45.

Reich Wilhelm 1897–1957. Austrian doctor, who emigrated to the US 1939. He combined ⟳Marxism and ⟳psychoanalysis to advocate the positive effects of directed sexual energies and sexual freedom. His works include *Die Sexuelle Revolution/The Sexual Revolution* 1936–45 and *Die Funktion des Orgasmus/The Function of the Orgasm* 1948.

He held the view that neuroses were the result of repressed sexual energy that could be released only through orgasm. He extended Freud's hypothesis that sexuality determines personality, and concluded that orgastically potent individuals will spontaneously seek to do what is good and right.

Reichstag German parliament building and lower legislative house during the German Empire 1871–1918 and Weimar Republic 1919–33.

Reichstag Fire burning of the German parliament building in Berlin Feb 27, 1933, less than a month after the Nazi leader Hitler became chancellor. The fire was used as a justification for the suspension of many constitutional guarantees and also as an excuse to attack the communists. There is still debate over whether the Nazis were involved in this crime, of which they were the main beneficiaries.

Although three Bulgarians (⟳Dimitrov, Popov, and Tanev) and a German, Torgler, were all indicted and tried in Leipzig, only a Dutch communist, Marinus van der Lubbe, was convicted, after being found at the scene of the crime and confessing.

Reichstein Tadeus 1897– . Swiss biochemist who investigated the chemical activity of the adrenal glands. By 1946 Reichstein had identified a large number of steroids secreted by the adrenal cortex, some of which would later be used in the treatment of ⟳Addison's disease. Reichstein shared the 1950 Nobel physiology or medicine prize with Edward ⟳Kendall and Philip Hench (1896–1965).

reification alleged social process whereby relations between human beings are transformed into impersonal relations between things. Georg Lukács, in *History and Class Consciousness* 1923, analyzes this process as characteristic of capitalist society. Later Marxists have developed this analysis, thus extending Marx's early critique of alienation in the *Paris Manuscripts* 1844.

Reims (English **Rheims**) capital of Champagne-Ardenne region, France; population (1982) 199,000. It is the center of the champagne industry and has textile industries as well. It was known in Roman times as *Durocorturum*. From 987 all but six French kings were crowned here. Ceded to England 1420 under the Treaty of Troyes, it was retaken by Joan of Arc, who had Charles VII consecrated in the 13th-century cathedral. In World War II, the German High Command formally surrendered here to US general Eisenhower May 7, 1945.

reincarnation belief that after death the human soul or the spirit of a plant or animal may live again in another human or animal. It is part of the teachings of many religions and philosophies, for example ancient Egyptian and Greek (the philosophies of Pythagoras and Plato), Buddhism, Hinduism, Jainism, certain Christian heresies (such as the Cathars), and theosophy. It is also referred to as *transmigration* or metempsychosis.

reindeer or *caribou* deer *Rangifer tarandus* of Arctic and subarctic regions, common to North America and Eurasia. About 4 ft/120 cm at the shoulder, it has a thick, brownish coat and broad hooves well adapted to travel over snow. It is the only deer in which both sexes have antlers; these can grow to 5 ft/150 cm long, and are shed in winter.

The Old World reindeer have been domesticated by the Lapps of Scandinavia for centuries. There are two types of North American caribou: the large woodland caribou of the more southerly regions, and the barren-ground caribou of the far north. Reindeer migrate south in winter, moving in large herds. They eat grass, small plants, and lichens.

Reinhardt Max 1873–1943. Austrian producer and director, whose Expressionist style was predominant in German theater and film during the 1920s and 1930s. Directors such as Murnau and Lubitsch and actors such as Dietrich worked with him. He co-directed the US film *A Midsummer Night's Dream* 1935.

In 1920 Reinhardt founded the Salzburg Festival. When the Nazis came to power, he lost his theaters and, after touring Europe as a guest director, went to the US, where he produced and directed. He founded an acting school and theater workshop in Hollywood.

Reisz Karel 1926– . Czech film director, originally a writer and film critic, who lived in Britain from 1938, and later in the US. His first feature film, *Saturday Night and Sunday Morning* 1960, was a critical and commercial success. His other films include *Morgan* 1966, *The French Lieutenant's Woman* 1981, and *Sweet Dreams* 1986.

relational database ⟡database in which data are viewed as a collection of linked tables. It is the most popular of the three basic database models, the others being **network** and **hierarchical**.

Its theoretical concepts were developed by E F Codd in the early 1970s.

relative atomic mass alternate name for ⟡atomic weight.

relative density or **specific gravity** the density (at 68°F/20°C) of a solid or liquid relative to (divided by) the maximum density of water (at 39.2°F/4°C). The relative density of a gas is its density divided by the density of hydrogen (or sometimes dry air) at the same temperature and pressure.

relative humidity the concentration of water vapor in the air. It is expressed as the percentage that its moisture content represents of the maximum amount that the air could contain at the same temperature and pressure. The higher the temperature the more water vapor the air can hold.

relativism philosophical position that denies the possibility of objective truth independent of some specific social or historical context or conceptual framework.

relativity in physics, the theory of the relative rather than absolute character of motion and mass, and the interdependence of matter, time, and space, as developed by Albert ⟡Einstein in two phases:

special theory (1905) Starting with the premises that (1) the laws of nature are the same for all observers in unaccelerated motion, and (2) the speed of light is independent of the motion of its source, Einstein postulated that the time interval between two events was longer for an observer in whose frame of reference the events occur in different places than for the observer for whom they occur at the same place.

general theory of relativity (1915) The geometrical properties of space-time were to be conceived as modified locally by the presence of a body with mass. A planet's orbit around the Sun (as observed in three-dimensional space) arises from its natural trajectory in modified space-time; there is no need to invoke, as Isaac Newton did, a force of ⟡gravity coming from the Sun and acting on the planet. Einstein's theory predicted slight differences in the orbits of the planets from Newton's theory, which were observable in the case of Mercury. The new theory also said light rays should bend when they pass by a massive object, owing to the object's effect on local space-time. The predicted bending of starlight was observed during the eclipse of the Sun 1919, when light from distant stars passing close to the Sun was not masked by sunlight.

Einstein showed that for consistency with premises (1) and (2), the principles of dynamics as established by Newton needed modification; the most celebrated new result was the equation $E = mc^2$, which expresses an equivalence between mass (*m*) and ⟡energy (*E*), *c* being the speed of light in a vacuum. Although since modified in detail, general relativity remains central to modern ⟡astrophysics and ⟡cosmology; it predicts, for example, the possibility of ⟡black holes. General relativity theory was inspired by the simple idea that it is impossible in a small region to distinguish between acceleration and gravitation effects (as in a lift one feels heavier when the lift accelerates upward), but the mathematical development of the idea is formidable. Such is not the case for the special theory, which a nonexpert can follow up to $E = mc^2$ and beyond.

relay in electrical engineering, an electromagnetic switch. A small current passing through a coil of wire wound around an iron core attracts an ⟡armature whose movement closes a pair of sprung contacts to complete a secondary circuit, which may carry a large current or activate other devices. The solid-state equivalent is a thyristor switching device.

relay neuron nerve cell in the spinal cord, connecting motor neurons to sensory neurons. Relay neurons allow information to pass straight through the spinal cord, bypassing the brain. In humans such reflex actions, which are extremely rapid, cause the sudden removal of a limb from a painful stimulus.

relic part of some divine or saintly person, or something closely associated with them. Christian examples include the arm of St Teresa of Avila, the blood of St Januarius, and the ⟡True Cross. Buddhist relics include the funeral ashes of the historic Buddha, placed in a number of stupas or burial mounds.

In medieval times relics were fiercely fought for, and there were a vast number of fakes. The cult was condemned by Protestant reformers but upheld by the Roman Catholic Church at the Council of Trent in the mid-16th century. Parallel nonreligious examples of the phenomenon include the display of the preserved body of Lenin in Moscow, Russia.

relief in architecture, carved figures and other forms that project from the background. The Italian terms *basso-rilievo* (low relief), *mezzo-rilievo* (middle relief), and *alto-rilievo* (high relief) are used according to the extent to which the sculpture projects. The French term *bas-relief* is commonly used to mean low relief.

religion (Latin *religare* "to bind"; perhaps humans to God) code of belief or philosophy, which often involves the worship of a ⟡God or gods. Belief in a supernatural power is not essential (absent in, for example, Buddhism and Confucianism), but faithful adherence is usually considered to be rewarded, for example, by escape from human existence (Buddhism), by a future existence (Christianity, Islam), or by worldly benefit (Sōka Gakkai Buddhism). Among the chief religions are:

ancient and pantheist religions of Babylonia, Assyria, Egypt, Greece, and Rome;

oriental Hinduism, Buddhism, Jainism, Parseeism, Confucianism, Taoism, and Shinto;

"religions of a book" Judaism, Christianity (the principal divisions are Roman Catholic, Eastern Orthodox, and Protestant), and Islam (the principal divisions are Sunni and Shiite); **combined derivation** such as Baha'ism, the Unification Church, and Mormonism.

Comparative religion studies the various faiths impartially, but often with the hope of finding common ground, to solve the practical problems of competing claims of unique truth or inspiration. The earliest known attempt at a philosophy of religious beliefs is contained in fragments written by Xenophanes in Greece 6th century BC, and later Herodotus and Aristotle contributed to the study. In 17th-century China, Jesuit theologians conducted comparative studies. Towards the end of the 18th century English missionary schools in Calcutta compared the Bible with sacred Indian texts. The work of Charles Darwin in natural history and the growth of anthropology stimulated fresh investigation of religious beliefs; work by the Sanskrit scholar Max Müller (1823–1900), the Scottish anthropologist James Frazer, the German sociologist Max Weber, and the Romanian scholar Mircea Eliade has formed the basis for modern comparative religion.

religious education the formal teaching of religion in schools.

In the US, religious education is prohibited in public (state-maintained) schools because of the separation of church and state guaranteed under the First Amendment to the Constitution; however, the study of comparative religion is permitted, since it is theoretical and secular information, not sacred matter. Private parochial schools offer both state-approved courses and religious instruction.

REM US four-piece rock group formed 1980 in Georgia. Their songs are characterized by melodic bass lines, driving guitar, and evocative lyrics partly buried in the mix. Albums include *Reckoning* 1984, *Green* 1988, and the mass-market breakthrough *Out of Time* 1991.

rem acronym of *roentgen equivalent man* SI unit of radiation dose equivalent.

Some types of radiation do more damage than others for the same absorbed dose; the equivalent dose in rems is equal to the dose in rads multiplied by the relative biological effectiveness. One rem is approximately equivalent to the biological effect produced by one roentgen of X-ray or gamma-ray radiation. Humans can absorb up to 25 rems without immediate ill effects; 100 rems may produce radiation sickness; and more than 800 rems causes death.

Remarque Erich Maria 1898–1970. German novelist, a soldier in World War I, whose *All Quiet on the Western Front* 1929, one of the first antiwar novels, led to his being deprived of German nationality. He lived in Switzerland 1929–39, and then in the US.

Rembrandt Harmensz van Rijn 1606–1669. Dutch painter and etcher, one of the most prolific and significant artists in Europe of the 17th century. Between 1629 and 1669 he painted some 60 penetrating self-portraits. He also painted religious subjects, and produced about 300 etchings and over 1,000 drawings. His group portraits include *The Anatomy Lesson of Dr Tulp* 1632 (Mauritshuis, The Hague) and *The Night Watch* 1642 (Rijksmuseum, Amsterdam).

After studying in Leiden and for a few months in Amsterdam (with a history painter),

Rembrandt began his career 1625 in Leiden, where his work reflected knowledge of ⟳Elsheimer and ⟳Caravaggio, among others. He settled permanently in Amsterdam 1631 and obtained many commissions for portraits from wealthy merchants. The *Self-Portrait with Saskia* (his wife, Saskia van Uylenburgh) about 1634 (Gemäldegalerie, Dresden, Germany) displays their prosperity in warm tones and rich, glittering textiles.

Saskia died 1642, and that year Rembrandt's fortunes began to decline (he eventually became bankrupt 1656). His work became more somber and had deeper emotional content, and his portraits were increasingly melancholy: for example, *Jan Six* 1654 (Six Collection, Amsterdam). From 1660 onward he lived with Hendrickje Stoffels, but he outlived her, and in 1668 his only surviving child, Titus, died too.

Rembrandt had many pupils, including Gerard Dou and Carel Fabritius.

Remington Eliphalet 1793–1861. US inventor, gunsmith, and arms manufacturer (with his father) of the firm that bears his name. He supplied the US army with rifles in the Mexican War, then in 1856 the firm expanded into the manufacture of agricultural implements. His son Philo continued the expansion.

Remington Frederic 1861–1909. US artist and illustrator best known for his paintings, sculptures, and sketches of scenes of the American West, which he recorded during several trips to the region.

Born in Canton, New York, he trained at the Yale School of Fine Arts and at the Art Students League in New York City. He illustrated for Harper publications and other periodicals and for Theodore Roosevelt's *Ranch Life and the Hunting Trail* 1888. Remington wrote and illustrated *Pony Tracks* 1895, *Crooked Trails* 1898, and *John Ermine of Yellowstone* 1902. A correspondent for the Hearst syndicate during the Spanish–American War, he came home to paint and sculpt. The Remington Museum was established in Ogdensburg, New York, near his family's home.

Remington Philo 1816–1889. US inventor and businessman, son of Eliphalet. He ran the arms business during the Civil War, when the firm had government contracts and later supplied several European armies with his new breech-loading rifles. In 1873 he became interested in the manufacture of typewriters, the first being demonstrated at the Centennial Exhibition in Philadelphia. By 1878, he produced the first typewriter with a shift key, which provided lower case as well as upper case letters. In 1879 his firm began making sewing machines.

remora any of a family of warm-water fishes that have an adhesive disk on the head, by which they attach themselves to whales, sharks, and turtles. These provide the remora with shelter and transport, as well as food in the form of parasites on the host's skin.

remotely piloted vehicle (RPV) crewless mini-aircraft used for military surveillance and to select targets in battle. RPVs barely show up on radar, so they can fly over a battlefield without being shot down, and they are equipped to transmit TV images to an operator on the ground. RPVs were used by Israeli forces in 1982 in Lebanon and by the Allies in the 1991 Gulf War. The US system is called Aquila and the British system Phoenix.

remote sensing gathering and recording information from a distance. Space probes have sent back photographs and data about planets as distant as Neptune. In archeology, surface survey techniques provide information without disturbing subsurface deposits.

Satellites such as *Landsat* have surveyed all the Earth's surface from orbit. Computer processing of data obtained by their scanning instruments, and the application of so-called false colors (generated by the computer), have made it possible to reveal surface features invisible in ordinary light. This has proved valuable in agriculture, forestry, and urban planning, and has led to the discovery of new deposits of minerals.

REM sleep (acronym for *rapid-eye-movement* sleep) phase of sleep that recurs several times nightly in humans and is associated with dreaming. The eyes flicker quickly beneath closed lids.

Remus in Roman mythology, the brother of ⟳Romulus.

Renaissance period and intellectual movement in European cultural history that is traditionally seen as ending the Middle Ages and beginning modern times. The Renaissance started in Italy in the 14th century and flourished in W Europe until about the 17th century.

The aim of Renaissance education was to produce the "complete human being" (**Renaissance man**), conversant in the humanities, mathematics and science (including their application in war), the arts and crafts, and athletics and sport; to enlarge the bounds of learning and geographical knowledge; to encourage the growth of skepticism and free thought, and the study and imitation of Greek and Latin literature and art. The revival of interest in Classical Greek and Roman culture inspired artists such as Leonardo da Vinci, Michelangelo, and Dürer, architects such as Brunelleschi and Alberti, writers such as Petrarch and Boccaccio. Scientists and explorers proliferated as well.

The beginning of the Italian Renaissance is usually dated in the 14th century with the writers Petrarch and Boccaccio. The invention of printing (mid-15th century) and geographical discoveries helped spread the new spirit. Exploration by Europeans opened Africa, Asia, and the New World to trade, colonization, and imperialism. Biblical criticism by the Dutch humanist Erasmus and others contributed to the Reformation, but the Counter-Reformation almost extinguished the movement in 16th-century Italy. In the visual arts Renaissance painting and sculpture later moved toward ⟳Mannerism.

Figures of the Renaissance include the politician Machiavelli, the poets Ariosto and Tasso, the philosopher Bruno, the physicist Galileo, and the artists Michelangelo, Cellini, and Raphael in Italy; the writers Rabelais and Montaigne in France, Cervantes in Spain, and Camoëns in Portugal; the astronomer Copernicus in Poland; and the politicians More and Bacon, and the writers Sidney, Marlowe, and Shakespeare in England.

The term "Renaissance," to describe the period of time, was first used in the 18th century.

Renaissance art movement in European art of the 15th and 16th centuries. It began in Florence, Italy, with the rise of a spirit of humanism and a new appreciation of the Classical past. In painting and sculpture this led to greater naturalism and interest in anatomy and perspective. Renaissance art peaked around 1500 with the careers of Leonardo da Vinci, Raphael, Michelangelo, and Titian in Italy and Dürer in Germany.

The Renaissance was heralded by the work of the early 14th-century painter Giotto in Florence, and in the early 15th century a handful of outstanding innovative artists emerged there: Masaccio in painting, Donatello in sculpture, and Brunelleschi in architecture. At the same time the humanist philosopher, artist, and writer Alberti recorded many of the new ideas in his treatises on painting, sculpture, and architecture. These ideas soon became widespread in Italy, and many new centers of patronage formed. In the 16th century Rome superseded Florence as the chief center of activity and innovation, and it became the capital of the High Renaissance.

In northern Europe the Renaissance spirit is apparent in the painting of the van Eyck brothers in the early 15th century. Later, Dürer demonstrated a scientific and inquiring mind and, after his travels in Italy, brought many Renaissance ideas back to Germany. Hans Holbein the Younger brought some of the concerns of Renaissance art to England in the 16th century, but it was not until the 17th century that English taste was significantly affected.

René France-Albert 1935– . Seychelles left-wing politician, the country's first prime minister after independence and president from 1977 after a coup. He has followed a nonnuclear policy of nonalignment.

renewable energy power from any source that replenishes itself. Most renewable systems rely on ⟳solar energy directly or through the weather cycle as ⟳wave power, ⟳hydro-electric power, or wind power via ⟳wind turbines, or solar energy collected by plants (alcohol fuels, for example). In addition, the gravitational force of the Moon can be harnessed through ⟳tidal power stations, and the heat trapped in the center of the Earth is used via ⟳geothermal energy systems.

renewable resource natural resource that is replaced by natural processes in a reasonable amount of time. Soil, water, forests, plants, and animals are all renewable resources as long as they are properly conserved. Solar, wind, wave, and geothermal energies are based on renewable resources.

Reni Guido 1575–1642. Italian painter, active in Bologna and Rome (about 1600–14), whose work includes the fresco *Phoebus and the Hours Preceded by Aurora* 1613 (Casino Rospigliosi, Rome). His workshop in Bologna produced numerous religious images, including Madonnas.

Rennes industrial city (oil refining, chemicals, electronics, cars) and capital of Ille-et-Vilaine *département*, W France, at the confluence of the Ille and Vilaine, 35 mi/56 km SE of St Malo; population (1982) 234,000. It was the old capital of Brittany.

rennet extract, traditionally obtained from a calf's stomach, that contains the enzyme rennin, used to coagulate milk in the cheesemaking process. The enzyme can now be chemically produced.

Reno city in Nevada, known for gambling and easy divorces; population (1990) 133,900.

Products include building materials and electronic equipment. The University of Nevada-Reno is here. Reno was settled 1858 and grew quickly with the discovery nearby of the Comstock Lode, a large gold and silver deposit. The transcontinental railroad reached Reno 1868.

Renoir Jean 1894–1979. French director whose films, characterized by their humanism and naturalistic technique, include *Boudu sauvé des eaux/Boudu Saved from Drowning* 1932, *La grande Illusion* 1937, and *La Règle du jeu/The Rules of the Game* 1939. In 1975 he received an honorary Academy Award for his life's work. He was the son of the painter Pierre-Auguste Renoir.

Renoir Pierre-Auguste 1841–1919. French Impressionist painter. He met Monet and Sisley in the early 1860s, and together they formed the nucleus of the Impressionist movement. He developed a lively, colorful painting style with feathery brushwork and painted many voluptuous female nudes, such as *The Bathers* about 1884–87 (Philadelphia Museum of Art). In his later years he turned to sculpture.

Born in Limoges, Renoir trained as a porcelain painter. He joined an academic studio 1861, and the first strong influences on his style were the Rococo artists Boucher and Watteau and the Realist Courbet. In the late 1860s Impressionism made its impact and Renoir began to work outdoors. Painting with Monet, he produced many pictures of people at leisure by the river Seine. From 1879 he made several journeys abroad, to N Africa, the Channel Islands, Italy, and later to Britain, the Netherlands, Spain, and Germany. After his Italian visit of 1881 he moved toward a more Classical structure in his work, notably in *Les Parapluies/Umbrellas* about 1881–84 (National Gallery, London). In 1906 he settled in the south of France. Many of his sculptures are monumental female nudes not unlike those of ⬦Maillol.

reparation compensation paid by countries that start wars in which they are defeated, as by Germany in both world wars. Iraq is required to pay reparations, under the terms of a United Nations resolution, after its defeat in the 1991 Gulf War.

replication in biology, production of copies of the genetic material DNA; it occurs during cell division (⬦mitosis and ⬦meiosis). Most mutations are caused by mistakes during replication.

repoussé relief decoration on metal, especially silver, brass, and copper, produced by hammering from the underside so that the decoration projects. It is the opposite of ⬦chasing.

The technique was among the first to be developed by ancient metalworkers. Exceptionally fine examples are the Vapheio Cup made in Crete around 1500 BC (National Museum, Athens) and the Scythian animal reliefs of around 600–500 BC (Hermitage, Leningrad).

repression in psychology, unconscious process said to protect a person from ideas, impulses, or memories that would threaten emotional stability were they to become conscious. See also ⬦censor.

reprieve legal temporary suspension of the execution of a sentence of a criminal court. It is usually associated with the death penalty. It is distinct from a pardon (extinguishing the sentence) and commutation (alteration) of a sentence (for example, from death to life imprisonment).

reproduction in biology, process by which a living organism produces other organisms similar to itself. There are two kinds: ⬦asexual reproduction and ⬦sexual reproduction.

reproduction rate or *fecundity* in ecology, the rate at which a population or species reproduces itself.

reptile any member of a class (Reptilia) of vertebrates. Unlike amphibians, reptiles have hard-shelled, yolk-filled eggs that are laid on land and from which fully formed young are born. Some snakes and lizards retain their eggs and give birth to live young. Reptiles are coldblooded, produced from eggs, and the skin is usually covered with scales. The metabolism is slow, and in some cases (certain large snakes) intervals between meals may be months. Reptiles date back over 300 million years.

Many extinct forms are known, including the orders Pterosauria, Plesiosauria, Ichthyosauria, and Dinosauria. The chief living orders are the Chelonia (tortoises and turtles), Crocodilia (alligators and crocodiles), and Squamata, divided into three suborders: Lacertilia (lizards), Ophidia or Serpentes (snakes), and Amphisbaenia (worm lizards). The order Rhynchocephalia has one surviving species, the lizardlike tuatara of New Zealand.

republic country where the head of state is not a monarch, either hereditary or elected, but usually a president whose role may or may not include political functions.

Republic, The treatise by the Greek philosopher Plato in which the voice of ⬦Socrates is used to describe the ideal state, where the cultivation of truth, beauty, and goodness achieves perfection.

Republican Party one of the US's two main political parties, formed 1854. It is considered more conservative than the Democratic Party, favoring capital and big business and opposing state subvention and federal controls. In the late 20th century most presidents have come from the Republican Party, but in Congress Republicans have been outnumbered.

The party was founded by a coalition of ⬦slavery opponents, who elected their first president, Abraham ⬦Lincoln, in 1860. The early Republican Party supported protective tariffs and favored genuine settlers (homesteaders) over land speculators. Toward the end of the century the Republican Party was identified with US imperialism and industrial expansion. With few intermissions, the Republican Party controlled Congress from the 1860s until defeated by the New Deal Democrats 1932.

Conservative tendencies and an antagonism of the legislature to the executive came to the fore after Lincoln's assassination, when Andrew Johnson, his Democratic and Southern successor, was impeached (although not convicted), and General ⬦Grant was elected to the presidency 1868 and 1872. In the bitter period following the Civil War the party was divided into those who considered the South a beaten nation and those who wished to reintegrate the South into the country as a whole, but Grant carried through a liberal Reconstruction policy in the South.

The party became divided during Theodore ⬦Roosevelt's attempts at regulation and control of big business, and in forming the short-lived Progressive Party 1912, Roosevelt effectively removed the liberal influence from the Republican Party.

The Republican Party remained in eclipse until the election of ⬦Eisenhower 1952, more his personal triumph than that of the party, whose control of Congress was soon lost and not regained by the next Republican president, ⬦Nixon, 1968. Both Nixon and his successor, ⬦Ford, pursued active foreign policies; the latter was defeated by ⬦Carter in the presidential election 1976.

However, the party enjoyed landslide presidential victories for ⬦Reagan and also carried the Senate 1980–86. ⬦Bush won the 1988 presidential election but faced a Democratic Senate and House of Representatives, and in 1992 lost the presidency to the Democrat Bill Clinton.

requiem in the Roman Catholic Church, a mass for the dead. Musical settings include those by Palestrina, Mozart, Berlioz, and Verdi.

research the primary activity in science, a combination of theory and experimentation directed toward finding scientific explanations of phenomena. It is commonly classified into two types: *pure research*, involving theories with little apparent relevance to human concerns; and *applied research*, concerned with finding solutions to problems of social importance—for instance in medicine and engineering. The two types are linked in that theories developed from pure research may eventually be found to be of great value to society.

Scientific research is most often funded by government and industry, and so a nation's wealth and priorities are likely to have a strong influence on the kind of work undertaken.

In 1989 the European Community (EC) Council adopted a revised program on research and technological development for the period 1990–94, requiring a total Community finance of 5,700 million ⬦ECUs, to be apportioned as follows: information and communications technology 2,221 million; industrial and materials technologies 888 million; life sciences and technologies 741 million; energy 814 million; human capacity and mobility 518 million; environment 518 million.

reserve currency in economics, a country's holding of internationally acceptable means of payment (major foreign currencies or gold); central banks also hold the ultimate reserve of money for their domestic banking sector. On the asset side of company balance sheets, undistributed profits are listed as reserves.

residue in chemistry, a substance or mixture of substances remaining in the original container after the removal of one or more components by a separation process.

The nonvolatile substance left in a container after ⬦evaporation of liquid, the solid left behind after removal of liquid by filtration, and the substances left in a distillation flask after removal of components by ⬦distillation, are all residues.

resin substance exuded from pines, firs, and other trees in gummy drops that harden in air. Varnishes are common products of the hard resins, and ointments come from the soft resins.

Rosin is the solid residue of distilled turpentine, a soft resin. The name "resin" is also given to many synthetic products manufactured by polymerization; they are used in adhesives, plastics, and varnishes.

resistance in physics, that property of a substance that restricts the flow of electricity through it, associated with the conversion of electrical energy to heat; also the magnitude of this property. Resistance depends on many factors, such as the nature of the material, its temperature, dimensions, and thermal properties; degree of impurity; the nature and state of illumination of the surface; and the frequency and magnitude of the current. The SI unit of resistance is the ohm.

resistance movement opposition movement in a country occupied by an enemy or colonial power, especially in the 20th century; for example, the French resistance to Nazism in World War II.

During World War II, resistance in E Europe took the form of ◊guerrilla warfare, for example in Yugoslavia, Greece, Poland, and by ◊*partisan* bands behind the German lines in the USSR. In more industrialized countries, such as France (where the underground movement was called the **maquis**), Belgium, and Czechoslovakia, sabotage in factories and on the railroads, propaganda, and the assassination of Germans and collaborators were the main priorities.

After World War II resistance movements grew in Palestine, South America, and European colonial possessions in Africa and Asia, aimed at unsettling established regimes.

resistor in physics, any component in an electrical circuit used to introduce ◊resistance to a current. Resistors are often made from wire-wound coils or pieces of carbon. ◊Rheostats and ◊potentiometers are variable resistors.

Resnais Alain 1922– . French film director whose work is characterized by the themes of memory and unconventional concepts of time. His films include *Hiroshima, mon amour* 1959, *L'Année dernière à Marienbad/Last Year at Marienbad* 1961, and *Providence* 1977.

resonance rapid and uncontrolled increase in the size of a vibration when the vibrating object is subject to a force varying at its ◊natural frequency. In a trombone, for example, the length of the air column in the instrument is adjusted until it resonates with the note being sounded. Resonance effects are also produced by many electrical circuits. Tuning a radio, for example, is done by adjusting the natural frequency of the receiver circuit until it coincides with the frequency of the radio waves falling on the aerial.

Resonance has many physical applications. Children use it to increase the size of the movement on a swing, by giving a push at the same point during each swing. Soldiers marching across a bridge in step could cause the bridge to vibrate violently if the frequency of their steps coincided with its natural frequency. Resonance was the cause of the collapse of the Tacoma Narrows bridge in 1940, when the frequency of the wind coincided with the natural frequency of the bridge.

resources materials that can be used to satisfy human needs. Because human needs are diverse and extend from basic physical requirements, such as food and shelter, to ill-defined aesthetic needs, resources encompass a vast range of items. The intellectual resources of a society—its ideas and technologies—determine which aspects of the environment meet that society's needs, and therefore become resources. For example, in the 19th century, uranium was used only in the manufacture of colored glass. Today, with the advent of nuclear technology, it is a military and energy resource. Resources are often categorized into **human resources**, such as labor, supplies, and skills, and **natural resources**, such as climate, fossil fuels, and water. Natural resources are divided into ◊nonrenewable resources and ◊renewable resources.

Nonrenewable resources include minerals such as coal, copper ores, and diamonds, which exist in strictly limited quantities. Once consumed they will not be replenished within the time span of human history. In contrast, water supplies, timber, food crops, and similar resources can, if managed properly, provide a steady yield virtually forever; they are therefore replenishable or renewable resources. Inappropriate use of renewable resources can lead to their destruction, as for example the cutting down of rainforests, with secondary effects, such as the decrease in oxygen and the increase in carbon dioxide and the ensuing ◊greenhouse effect. Some renewable resources, such as wind or solar energy, are continuous; supply is largely independent of people's actions.

Demands for resources made by rich nations are causing concern that the present and future demands of industrial societies cannot be sustained for more than a century or two, and that this will be at the expense of the Third World and the global environment. Other authorities believe that new technologies will emerge, enabling resources that are now of little importance to replace those being exhausted.

respiration biochemical process whereby food molecules are progressively broken down (oxidized) to release energy in the form of ◊ATP. In most organisms this requires oxygen, but in some bacteria the oxidant is the nitrate or sulfate ion instead. In all higher organisms, respiration occurs in the ◊mitochondria. Respiration is also used to mean breathing, although this is more accurately described as a form of ◊gas exchange.

respiratory distress syndrome (RDS) formerly **hyaline membrane disease** condition in which a newborn baby's lungs are insufficiently expanded to permit adequate oxygenation. Premature babies are most at risk. Such babies survive with the aid of intravenous fluids and oxygen, sometimes with assisted ventilation.

Normal inflation of the lungs requires the presence of a substance called surfactant to reduce the surface tension of the alveoli (air sacs) in the lungs. In premature babies, surfactant is deficient and the lungs become hard and glassy. As a result, the breathing is rapid, labored, and shallow, and there is the likelihood of ◊asphyxia. A synthetic replacement for surfactant has now been developed.

response time in computing, the delay between entering a command and seeing its effect.

rest mass in physics, the mass of a body when its velocity is zero. For subatomic particles, it is their mass at rest or at velocities considerably below that of light. According to the theory of ◊relativity, at very high velocities, there is a relativistic effect that increases the mass of the particle.

Restoration in English history, the period when the monarchy, in the person of Charles II, was reestablished after the English Civil War and the fall of the ◊Protectorate 1660.

Restoration comedy style of English theater, dating from the Restoration. It witnessed the first appearance of women on the English stage, most notably in the "breeches part," specially created in order to costume the actress in male attire, thus revealing her figure to its best advantage. The genre placed much emphasis on sexual antics. Examples include Wycherley's *The Country Wife* 1675, Congreve's *The Way of the World* 1700, and Farquhar's *The Beaux' Stratagem* 1707.

restriction enzyme bacterial ◊enzyme that breaks a chain of ◊DNA into two pieces at a specific point; used in ◊genetic engineering. The point along the DNA chain at which the enzyme can work is restricted to places where a specific sequence of base pairs occurs. Different restriction enzymes will break a DNA chain at different points. The overlap between the fragments is used in determining the sequence of base pairs in the DNA chain.

restrictive trade practices agreements between people in a particular trade or business that keep the cost of goods or services artificially high (for example, an agreement to restrict output) or provide barriers to outsiders entering the trade or business. Often, these practices are illegal.

resurrection in Christian, Jewish, and Muslim belief, the rising from the dead that all souls will experience at the Last Judgment. The Resurrection also refers to Jesus rising from the dead on the third day after his crucifixion, a belief central to Christianity and celebrated at Easter.

resuscitation steps taken to revive anyone on the brink of death. The most successful technique for life-threatening emergencies, such as electrocution, near-drowning, or heart attack, is mouth-to-mouth resuscitation. Medical and paramedical staff are trained in cardiopulmonary resuscitation: the use of specialized equipment and techniques to attempt to restart the breathing and/or heartbeat and stabilize the patient long enough for more definitive treatment.

retail sale of goods and services to a consumer. The retailer is the last link in the distribution chain. A retailer's purchases are usually made from a wholesaler.

The large range of retail outlets include vending machines, street peddlers, specialized shops, department stores, supermarkets, and cooperative stores. These are supplemented by auctions, door-to-door selling, telephone selling, and mail order.

retail price index (RPI) indicator of variations in the ◊cost of living, superseded in the US by the ◊consumer price index.

retina light-sensitive area at the back of the ◊eye connected to the brain by the optic nerve. It has several layers and in humans contains over a million rods and cones, sensory cells capable of converting light into nervous messages that pass down the optic nerve to the brain.

The **rod cells**, about 120 million in each eye, are distributed throughout the retina. They are sensitive to low levels of light, but do not provide detailed or sharp images, nor can they detect color. The **cone cells**, about 6 million in number, are mostly concentrated in a central region of the retina called the **fovea**, and provide both detailed and color vision. The cones of the human eye contain three visual pigments, each of which responds to a different primary color (red, green, or blue). The brain can interpret the varying signal levels from the three types of cone as any of the different colors of the visible spectrum.

The image actually falling on the retina is

highly distorted; research into the eye and the optic centers within the brain has shown that this poor quality image is processed to improve its quality. The retina can become separated from the wall of the eyeball as a result of a trauma, such as a boxing injury. It can be reattached by being "welded" into place by a laser.

retriever any of several breeds of hunting dogs, often used as guide dogs for the blind. The commonest breeds are the *Labrador retriever*, large, smooth-coated, and usually black or yellow; and the *golden retriever*, with either flat or wavy coat. They can grow to 2 ft/ 60 cm high and weigh 90 lb/40 kg.

Retrievers were originally developed for retrieving birds and other small game. Their gentle, even-tempered nature makes them popular companion dogs, and Labradors are also used in police work.

retrovirus any of a family (*Retroviridae*) of ▷viruses containing the genetic material ▷RNA rather than the more usual ▷DNA.

For the virus to express itself and multiply within an infected cell, its RNA must be converted to DNA. It does this by using a built-in enzyme known as reverse transcriptase (since the transfer of genetic information from DNA to RNA is known as ▷transcription, and retroviruses do the reverse of this). Retroviruses include those causing ▷AIDS and some forms of leukemia. See ▷immunity.

Réunion French island of the Mascarenes group, in the Indian Ocean, 400 mi/650 km E of Madagascar and 110 mi/180 km SW of Mauritius
area 970 sq mi/2,512 sq km
capital St Denis
physical forested, rising in Piton de Neiges to 10,072 ft/3,069 m
features administers five uninhabited islands, also claimed by Madagascar
products sugar, corn, vanilla, tobacco, rum
population (1987) 565,000
history explored by Portuguese (the first European visitors) 1513; annexed by Louis XIII of France 1642; overseas *département* of France 1946; overseas region 1972.

Reuter Paul Julius, Baron de 1816–1899. German founder of the international news agency *Reuters*. He began a continental pigeon post 1849, and in 1851 set up a news agency in London. In 1858 he persuaded the press to use his news telegrams, and the service became worldwide. Reuters became a public company 1984.

Revelation last book of the New Testament, traditionally attributed to the author of the Gospel of St John but now generally held to be the work of another writer. It describes a vision of the end of the world, of the Last Judgment, and of a new heaven and earth ruled by God from Jerusalem.

revenue sharing in the US, federal aid to state and local government allocated under the State and Local Fiscal Assistance Act 1972.

Revere Paul 1735–1818. American revolutionary, a Boston silversmith, who carried the news of the approach of British troops to Lexington and Concord (see ▷American Revolution) on the night of April 18, 1775. On the next morning the first shots of the Revolution were fired at Lexington. Longfellow's poem "The Midnight Ride of Paul Revere" commemorates the event.

Revere, who took part in the ▷Boston Tea Party, was a courier for the Continental Congress, often riding from Boston to Philadelphia. In early 1775 he alerted rebels in New Hampshire that the British were transporting supplies from Fort William and Mary. The New Hampshire militiamen captured quantities of munitions that proved decisive at the Battle of Bunker Hill. Revere was active throughout the Revolution and printed the first continental money.

reverse osmosis the movement of solvent (liquid) through a semipermeable membrane from a more concentrated solution to a more dilute solution. The solvent's direction of movement is opposite to that which it would experience during ▷osmosis, and is achieved by applying an external pressure to the solution on the more concentrated side of the membrane. The technique is used in desalination plants, when water (the solvent) passes from brine (a salt solution) into fresh water via a semipermeable filtering device.

reverse takeover in business, a ▷takeover where a company sells itself to another (a ▷white knight) to avoid being the target of a purchase by an unwelcome predator.

revisionism political theory derived from Marxism that moderates one or more of the basic tenets of Marx, and is hence condemned by orthodox Marxists.

The first noted Marxist revisionist was Eduard Bernstein, who in Germany in the 1890s questioned the inevitability of a breakdown in capitalism. After World War II the term became widely used by established communist parties, both in E Europe and Asia, to condemn movements (whether more or less radical) that threatened the official party policy.

revolution any rapid, theoretical, violent change in the political, social, or economic structure of society. It is usually applied to political change: examples include the American Revolution, where the colonists broke free from their colonial ties and established a sovereign, independent nation; the French Revolution, where an absolute monarchy was overthrown by opposition from inside the country and a popular uprising; and the Russian Revolution, where a repressive monarchy was overthrown by those seeking to institute widespread social and economic changes based on a socialist model. While political revolutions are often associated with violence, other types of change have just as much impact on society. Most notable is the Industrial Revolution of the mid-18th century. In the 1970s and 1980s a high-tech revolution could be identified, based on the increasing use of computers. In 1989–90 the Eastern Bloc nations demonstrated against and voted out communists, in many cases creating a prodemocracy revolution.

Revolutionary Wars series of wars 1791–1802 between France and the combined armies of England, Austria, Prussia, and others during the period of the French Revolution, and on ▷Napoleon's ambition to conquer Europe.
1791 Emperor ▷Leopold II and Frederick William II of Prussia issued the *Declaration of Pillnitz* inviting the European powers to restore the French king Louis XVI to power.
1792 France declared war on Austria, which formed a coalition with Prussia, Sardinia, and (from 1793) Britain, Spain, and the Netherlands; victories for France at ▷Valmy and Jemappes.
1793 French reverses until the reorganization by Lazare ▷Carnot.

1795 Prussia, the Netherlands, and Spain made peace with France.
1796 Sardinia forced to make peace by the Italian campaign of ▷Napoleon I, then a commander.
1797 Austria compelled to make peace with France under the Treaty of ▷Campo-Formio.
1798 Napoleon's fleet, after its capture of Malta, was defeated by the British admiral ▷Nelson in Egypt at the Battle of the Nile (Aboukir Bay), and Napoleon had to return to France without his army; William Pitt the Younger, Britain's prime minister, organized a new coalition with Russia, Austria, Naples, Portugal, and Turkey.
1798–99 The coalition mounted its major campaign in Italy (under the Russian field marshal ▷Suvorov), but dissension led to the withdrawal of Russia.
1799 Napoleon, on his return from Egypt, reorganized the French army.
1800 June 14 Austrian army defeated by Napoleon at Marengo in NW Italy and again on Dec 3 (by Gen ▷Moreau) at Hohenlinden near Munich; the coalition collapses.
1802 *Treaty of Amiens* truce between France and Britain, followed by the ▷Napoleonic Wars.

revolutions of 1848 series of revolts in various parts of Europe against monarchical rule. While some of the revolutionaries had republican ideas, many more were motivated by economic grievances. The revolution began in France with the overthrow of Louis Philippe and then spread to Italy, the Austrian Empire, and Germany, where the short-lived ▷Frankfurt Parliament put forward ideas about political unity in Germany. None of the revolutions enjoyed any lasting success, and most were violently suppressed within a few months.

Some concessions were made to both liberal and nationalist movements, and 1848 is regarded as ending the conservative domination of ▷Metternich.

revue stage presentation involving short satirical and topical items in the form of songs, sketches, and monologues; it originated in the late 19th century.

Turn-of-the-century revues were spectacular entertainments, but the "intimate revue" became increasingly popular, employing writers such as Noël ▷Coward.

Reye's syndrome rare disorder of the metabolism causing fatty infiltration of the liver and ▷encephalitis. It occurs mainly in children and has been linked with aspirin therapy, although its cause is still uncertain. The mortality rate is 50%.

Reykjavik capital (from 1918) and chief port of Iceland, on the SW coast; population (1988) 93,000. Fish processing is the main industry. Reykjavik is heated by underground mains fed by volcanic springs. It was a seat of Danish administration from 1801 to 1918.

Reynaud Paul 1878–1966. French prime minister in World War II, who succeeded Edouard Daladier in March 1940 but resigned in June after the German breakthrough. He was imprisoned by the Germans until 1945, and again held government offices after the war.

Reynolds Burt 1936– . US film actor and director who excels in adventure films and comedies. He is known for doing his own stunts, since he started as a stuntman. His films include *Deliverance* 1972, the cult film *White Lightning* 1973, *Hustle* 1975, and *City Heat*

1984. He also appeared in 1991 as the lead in the television comedy series *Evening Shade*.

Reynolds Joshua 1723–1792. English portrait painter, active in London from 1752. He became the first president of the Royal Academy 1768. His portraits display a facility for striking and characterful compositions in a consciously grand manner. He often borrowed Classical poses, for example *Mrs Siddons as the Tragic Muse* 1784 (San Marino, California).

Reynolds was apprenticed to the portrait painter Thomas Hudson (1701–79). From 1743 he practiced in Plymouth and London and 1749–52 completed his studies in Rome and Venice, concentrating on the antique and the High Renaissance masters. After his return to London he became the leading portraitist of his day with pictures such as *Admiral Keppel* 1753–54 (National Maritime Museum, London).

RGB (abbreviation of *red–green–blue*) method of connecting a color screen to a computer, involving three separate signals: red, green, and blue. All the colors displayed by the screen can be made up from these three component colors.

Rhadamanthys in Greek mythology, son of ◊Zeus and ◊Europa, ruler of ◊Elysium, and with ◊Minos and Aeacus judge of the dead.

rhapsody in music, instrumental ◊fantasia, often based on folk melodies, such as Lizst's *Hungarian Rhapsodies* 1853–54.

In ancient Greece, *rhapsodes* were a class of reciters of epic poems, especially those of ◊Homer, who performed at festivals. The title means "stitchers of songs."

rhe unit of fluidity equal to the reciprocal of the ◊poise.

rhea one of two flightless birds of the family Rheidae. The common rhea *Rhea americana* is 5 ft/1.5 m high and is distributed widely in South America. The smaller Darwin's rhea *Pterocnemia pennata* occurs only in the south of South America. They differ from the ostrich in their smaller size and in having a feathered neck and head, three-toed feet, and no plumelike tail feathers.

Rhea in Greek mythology, a fertility goddess, one of the Titans, wife of Cronus and mother of several gods, including Zeus.

Rhee Syngman 1875–1965. Korean right-wing politician. A rebel under Chinese and Japanese

rheostat *Rheostat used in a circuit to dim a bulb.*

rule, he became president of South Korea from 1948 until riots forced him to resign and leave the country 1960.

Rheims English version of ◊Reims, city in France.

Rheinland-Pfalz German name for the ◊Rhineland-Palatinate region of Germany.

rhenium (Latin *Rhenus* "Rhine") heavy, silver-white, metallic element, symbol Re, atomic number 75, atomic weight 186.2. It has chemical properties similar to those of manganese and a very high melting point (5,756°F/3,180°C), which makes it valuable as an ingredient in alloys.

It was identified and named in 1925 by German chemists W Noddack (1893–1960), I Tacke, and O Berg from the Latin name for the Rhine river.

rheostat in physics, a variable ◊resistor, usually consisting of a high-resistance wire-wound coil with a sliding contact. It is used to vary electrical resistance without interrupting the current (for example, when dimming lights). The circular type in electronics (which can be used, for example, as the volume control of an amplifier) is also known as a ◊potentiometer.

rhesus factor ◊protein on the surface of red blood cells of humans, which is involved in the rhesus blood group system. Most individuals possess the main rhesus factor (Rh+), but those without this factor (Rh–) produce ◊antibodies if they come into contact with it. The name comes from rhesus monkeys, in whose blood rhesus factors were first found.

If an Rh—mother carries an Rh+ fetus, she may produce antibodies if fetal blood crosses the ◊placenta. This is not normally a problem with the first infant because antibodies are only produced slowly. However, the antibodies continue to build up after birth, and a second Rh+ child may be attacked by antibodies passing from mother to fetus, causing the child to contract anemia, heart failure, or brain damage. In such cases, the blood of the infant has to be changed for Rh–blood. Alternatively, the problem can be alleviated by giving the mother anti-Rh globulin just after the first pregnancy, preventing the formation of antibodies.

rhesus monkey macaque monkey *Macaca mulatta* found in N India and SE Asia. It has a pinkish face, red buttocks, and long, straight, brown-gray hair. It can grow up to 2 ft/60 cm long, with a 8 in/20 cm tail.

rhetoric (Greek *rhetor* "orator") traditionally, the art of public speaking and debate. Rhetorical skills are valued in such occupations as politics, teaching, law, religion, and broadcasting.

Accomplished rhetoricians need not be sincere in what they say; they should, however, be effective, or at least entertaining. Nowadays, "rhetoric" is often a pejorative term (for example, "Cut the rhetoric and tell us what you really think").

rhetorical question question, often used by public speakers and debaters, that either does not require an answer or for which the speaker intends to provide his or her own answer ("Where else in the world can we find such brave young men as these?").

rheumatic fever or *acute rheumatism* acute or chronic illness characterized by fever and painful swelling of joints. Some victims also experience involuntary movements of the limbs and head, a form of ◊chorea.

Rheumatic fever, which strikes mainly children and young adults, is always preceded by

a streptococcal infection such as ◊scarlet fever or a severe sore throat, usually occurring a couple of weeks beforehand. It is treated with bed rest, antibiotics, and painkillers. The most important complication of rheumatic fever is damage to the heart valve, producing rheumatic heart disease, which may lead to disability and death.

rheumatism nontechnical term for a variety of ailments associated with inflammation and stiffness of the joints and muscles.

Rhine (German *Rhein*, French *Rhin*) European river rising in Switzerland and reaching the North Sea via Germany and the Netherlands; length 820 mi/1,320 km. Tributaries include the Moselle and the Ruhr. The Rhine is linked with the Mediterranean by the Rhine–Rhône Waterway, and with the Black Sea by the Rhine–Main–Danube Waterway. It is the longest, and the dirtiest, river in Europe.

The river was severely polluted by a chemical factory fire 1986, as a result of which 30 tonnes of pesticides entered the river, rendering it lifeless for 60–120 mi/100–200 km. The governments of the five countries through which the Rhine flows announced a major clean-up campaign in 1987.

The *Lorelei* is a rock in the river in Rhineland-Palatinate, Germany, with a remarkable echo; the German poet Brentano gave currency to the legend of a siren who lured sailors to death with her song, also the subject of a poem by Heinrich Heine.

Rhine Joseph Banks 1895–1980. US parapsychologist. His work at Duke University, North Carolina, involving controlled laboratory experiments in ◊parapsychology, including telepathy, clairvoyance, precognition, and psychokinesis, described in *Extra-Sensory Perception* 1934, made ESP a common term.

Rhineland former province of Prussia, ceded in 1815. Its unchallenged annexation by Nazi Germany 1936 was a harbinger of World War II.

Under the terms of the Treaty of Versailles 1919, following World War I, the Rhineland was to be occupied by Allied forces for 15 years, with a permanent demilitarized zone. Demilitarization was reaffirmed by the Treaties of Locarno, but German foreign minister Gustav Stresemann achieved the removal of the British forces 1926 and French forces 1930. Both treaties were violated when Adolf Hitler's troops marched into the demilitarized zone of the Rhineland 1936. Britain and France merely protested, and it remained under German occupation. It was the scene of heavy fighting 1944, and was recaptured by US troops 1945, becoming one of the largest states of West Germany after the end of the war.

Rhineland-Palatinate (German *Rheinland-Pfalz*) administrative region (German *Land*) of Germany
area 7,643 sq mi/19,800 sq km
capital Mainz
cities Ludwigshafen, Koblenz, Trier, Worms
physical wooded mountain country, river valleys of Rhine and Moselle
products wine (75% of German output), tobacco, chemicals, machinery, leather goods, pottery
population (1992) 3,702,000
history formed 1946 of the Rhenish ◊Palatinate and parts of Hessen, Rhine province, and Hessen-Nassau.

rhinoceros odd-toed hoofed mammal of the family Rhinocerotidae. The one-horned Indian rhinoceros *Rhinoceros unicornis* is up to 6 ft/ 2 m high at the shoulder, with a tubercled skin, folded into shieldlike pieces; the African rhinoceroses are smooth-skinned and two-horned. All are endangered.

The African black rhinoceros *Diceros bicornis* is 5 ft/1.5 m high, with a prehensile upper lip for feeding on shrubs; the broad-lipped or "white" rhinoceros *Ceratotherium simum* is actually slaty-gray, with a squarish mouth for browsing grass. They are solitary and vegetarian, with poor eyesight but excellent hearing and smell. Needless slaughter has led to the near extinction of all species of rhinoceros, particularly the Sumatran rhinoceros and Javan rhinoceros.

An extinct hornless species, the baluchithere (genus *Baluchitherium*), reached 15 ft/4.5 m.

rhizoid hairlike outgrowth found on the ⬦gametophyte generation of ferns, mosses and liverworts. Rhizoids anchor the plant to the substrate and can absorb water and nutrients. They may be composed of many cells, as in mosses, where they are usually brownish, or may be unicellular, as in liverworts, where they are usually colorless. Rhizoids fulfill the same functions as the ⬦roots of higher plants but are simpler in construction.

rhizome or ⬦**rootstock** horizontal underground plant stem. It is a ⬦perennating organ in some species, where it is generally thick and fleshy, while in other species it is mainly a means of ⬦vegetative reproduction, and is therefore long and slender, with buds all along it that send up new plants. The potato is a rhizome that has two distinct parts, the tuber being the swollen end of a long, cordlike rhizome.

rhm (abbreviation of **roentgen–hour–meter**) the unit of effective strength of a radioactive source that produces gamma rays. It is used for substances for which it is difficult to establish radioactive disintegration rates.

Rhode Island (officially Rhode Island and Providence Plantations) state in NE US; the smallest state of the US; nickname Ocean State
area 1,197 sq mi/3,100 sq km
capital Providence
cities Cranston, Woonsocket
population (1990) 1,003,464
features Narragansett Bay, with America's Cup yacht races; mansions of Newport; Block Island; Brown University; Rhode Island School of Design; University of Rhode Island
products poultry (Rhode Island Reds), jewelry, silverware, textiles, machinery, primary metals, rubber products, submarine assembly

Rhode Island

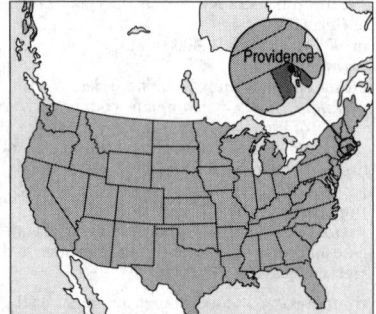

Providence

famous people George M Cohan, Anne Hutchinson, Matthew C Perry, Oliver Hazard Perry, Gilbert Stuart, Roger Williams
history founded 1636 by Roger Williams, exiled from Massachusetts Bay colony for religious dissent; one of the original thirteen states and still the smallest one in area. The principle trends in the 19th century were industrialization, immigration, and urbanization. Rhode Island is the most industrialized state, and it suffers from high unemployment, low-wage manufacturing industries, and susceptibility to recessions.

Rhodes (Greek *Ródhos*) Greek island, largest of the Dodecanese, in the E Aegean Sea
area 545 sq mi/1,412 sq km
capital Rhodes
products grapes, olives
population (1981) 88,000
history settled by Greeks about 1000 BC; the ⬦Colossus of Rhodes (fell 224 BC), was one of the ⬦Seven Wonders of the World; held by the Knights Hospitallers of St John 1306–1522; taken from Turkish rule by the Italian occupation 1912; ceded to Greece 1947.

Rhodes Cecil (John) 1853–1902. South African politician, born in the UK, prime minister of Cape Colony 1890–96. Aiming at the formation of a South African federation and the creation of a block of British territory from the Cape to Cairo, he was responsible for the annexation of Bechuanaland (now Botswana) in 1885. He formed the British South Africa Company in 1889, which occupied Mashonaland and Matabeleland, thus forming **Rhodesia** (now Zambia and Zimbabwe).

The **Rhodes scholarships** were founded at Oxford University, UK, under his will, for students from the Commonwealth, the US, and Germany.

Rhodesia former name of ⬦Zambia (Northern Rhodesia) and ⬦Zimbabwe (Southern Rhodesia).

rhodium (Greek *rhodon* "rose") hard, silver-white, metallic element, symbol Rh, atomic number 45, atomic weight 102.905. It is one of the so-called platinum group of metals and is resistant to tarnish, corrosion, and acid. It occurs as a free metal in the natural alloy osmiridium and is used in jewelry, electroplating, and thermocouples.

Rhodium was discovered in 1803 by English chemist William Wollaston (1766–1828) and named in 1804 for the red color of its salts in solution.

rhododendron any of numerous shrubs of the genus *Rhododendron* of the heath family Ericaceae. Most species are evergreen. The leaves are usually dark and leathery, and the large racemes of flowers occur in all colors except blue. They thrive on acid soils. ⬦Azaleas belong to the same genus.

Rhodope Mountains range of mountains on the frontier between Greece and Bulgaria, rising to 9,497 ft/2,925 m at Musala.

rhombus in geometry, an equilateral (all sides equal) ⬦parallelogram. Its diagonals bisect each other at right angles, and its area is half the product of the lengths of the two diagonals. A rhombus whose internal angles are 90° is called a ⬦square.

Rhône river of S Europe; length 500 mi/810 km. It rises in Switzerland and flows through Lake Geneva to Lyon in France, where at its confluence with the Saône the upper limit

of navigation is reached. The river turns due south, passes Vienne and Avignon, and takes in the Isère and other tributaries. Near Arles it divides into the **Grand** and **Petit Rhône**, flowing respectively SE and SW into the Mediterranean W of Marseille.

Here it forms a two-armed delta; the area between the tributaries is the marshy region known as the ⬦Camargue. The Rhône is harnessed for hydroelectric power, the chief dam being at Genissiat in Ain *département*, constructed 1938–48. Between Vienne and Avignon the Rhône flows through a major wine-producing area.

Rhône-Alpes region of E France in the upper reaches of the Rhône; area 16,868 sq mi/ 43,700 sq km; population (1992) 5,344,000. It consists of the *départements* of Ain, Ardèche, Drôme, Isère, Loire, Rhône, Savoie, and Haute-Savoie. The chief town is Lyon. There are several notable wine-producing areas, including Chenas, Fleurie, and Beaujolais. Industrial products include chemicals, textiles, and motor vehicles.

rhubarb perennial plant *Rheum rhaponticum* of the buckwheat family Polygonaceae, grown for its pink, edible leaf stalks. The leaves contain oxalic acid, and are poisonous. There are also wild rhubarbs native to Europe and Asia.

rhyme identity of sound, usually in the endings of lines of verse, such as *wing* and *sing*. Avoided in Japanese, it is a common literary device in other Asian and European languages. Rhyme first appeared in Europe in late Latin poetry but was not used in Classical Latin or Greek.

rhyolite ⬦igneous rock, the fine-grained volcanic (extrusive) equivalent of granite.

Rhys Jean 1894–1979. British novelist, born in Dominica. Her works include *Wide Sargasso Sea* 1966, a recreation, set in a Caribbean island, of the life of the mad wife of Rochester from Charlotte Brontë's *Jane Eyre*.

rhythm and blues (R & B) US popular music of the 1940s–60s, which drew on swing and jump-jazz rhythms and blues vocals, and was a progenitor of rock and roll. It diversified into soul, funk, and other styles. R & B artists include Bo Diddley (1928–), Jackie Wilson (1934–84), and Etta James (*c.* 1938–).

rhythm method method of natural contraception that works by avoiding intercourse when the woman is producing egg cells (ovulating). The time of ovulation can be worked out by the calendar (counting days from the last period), by temperature changes, or by inspection of the cervical mucus. All these methods are unreliable because it is possible for ovulation to occur at any stage of the menstrual cycle.

RI abbreviation for the state of ⬦**Rhode Island**.

ria long narrow sea inlet, usually branching and surrounded by hills. A ria is deeper and wider toward its mouth, unlike a ⬦fjord. It is formed by the flooding of a river valley due to either a rise in sea level or a lowering of a landmass.

rib long, usually curved bone that extends laterally from the ⬦spine in vertebrates. Most fishes and many reptiles have ribs along most of the spine, but in mammals they are found only in the chest area. In humans, there are 12 pairs of ribs. The ribs protect the lungs and heart, and allow the chest to expand and contract easily.

At the rear, each pair is joined to one of the

vertebrae of the spine. The upper seven are joined by ⬦cartilage directly to the breast bone (sternum). The next three are joined by cartilage to the end of the rib above. The last two ("floating ribs") are not attached at the front.

Ribbentrop Joachim von 1893–1946. German Nazi politician and diplomat, foreign minister 1938–45, during which time he negotiated the Non-Aggression Pact between Germany and the USSR. He was tried at Nuremberg as a war criminal 1946 and hanged.

Ribbentrop was born in the Rhineland. Awarded the Iron Cross in World War I, he became a wine merchant in 1919. He joined the Nazi party 1932 and acted as Hitler's adviser on foreign affairs; he was German ambassador to Britain 1936–38. A political lightweight, he was useful to Hitler since he posed no threat.

Ribbentrop–Molotov pact another name for the ⬦Hitler–Stalin pact.

Ribera José (Jusepe) de 1591–1652. Spanish painter, active in Italy from 1616 under the patronage of the viceroys of Naples. His early work shows the impact of Caravaggio, but his colors gradually lightened. He painted many full-length saints and mythological figures and genre scenes, which he produced without preliminary drawing.

riboflavin or **vitamin B₂** ⬦vitamin of the B complex whose absence in the diet causes stunted growth.

ribonucleic acid full name of ⬦RNA.

ribosome in biology, the protein-making machinery of the cell. Ribosomes are located on the endoplasmic reticulum (ER) of eukaryotic cells, and are made of proteins and a special type of ⬦RNA, ribosomal RNA. They receive messenger RNA (copied from the ⬦DNA) and ⬦amino acids, and "translate" the messenger RNA by using its chemically coded instructions to link amino acids in a specific order, to make a strand of a particular protein.

Ricardo David 1772–1823. English economist, author of *Principles of Political Economy* 1817. Among his discoveries were the principle of ⬦comparative advantage (that countries can benefit by specializing in goods they produce efficiently and trading internationally to buy others), and the law of diminishing returns (that continued increments of capital and labor applied to a given quantity of land will eventually show a declining rate of increase in output).

rice principal cereal of the wet regions of the tropics; derived from grass of the species *Oryza sativa*, probably native to India and SE Asia. It is unique among cereal crops in that it is grown standing in water. The yield is very large, and rice is said to be the staple food of one-third of the world population.

cultivation Rice takes 150–200 days to mature in warm, wet conditions. During its growing period, it needs to be flooded either by the heavy monsoon rains or by adequate irrigation. This restricts the cultivation of swamp rice, the usual kind, to level land and terraces. A poorer variety, known as hill rice, is grown on hillsides. Outside Asia, there is some rice production in the Po valley of Italy, and in the US in Louisiana, the Carolinas, and California.

nutrition Rice contains 8–9% protein. Brown, or unhusked, rice has valuable B-vitamins that are lost in husking or polishing. Most of the the rice eaten in the world is, however, sold in polished form.

history Rice has been cultivated since prehistoric days in the East. New varieties with greatly increased protein content have been developed by gamma radiation for commercial cultivation, and yields are higher than ever before (see ⬦green revolution).

by-products Rice husks when burned provide a ⬦silica ash that, mixed with lime, produces an excellent cement.

Rice Elmer 1892–1967. US playwright. His works include *The Adding Machine* 1923 and *Street Scene* 1929, which won a Pulitzer Prize and was made into an opera by Kurt Weill. Many of his plays deal with such economic and political issues as the Depression (*We, the People* 1933) and racism (*American Landscape* 1939).

Rice Grantland 1880–1954. US sports journalist. Born in Murfreesboro, Tennessee, and educated at Vanderbilt University, Rice joined the staff of the *Nashville News* 1901. Gaining a reputation for vivid sports writing, he was hired by the *New York Mail* 1911 and worked for the *New York Herald Tribune* 1914–30. Rice succeeded Walter Camp in selecting the annual All-America football team.

After 1930 he wrote the column "The Sportlight," which set the standard for modern sports journalism. His autobiography, *The Tumult and the Shouting*, was published 1954.

Rich Adrienne 1929– . US radical feminist poet, writer, and critic. Her poetry is both subjective and political, concerned with female consciousness, peace, and gay rights. Her works include *On Lies, Secrets and Silence* 1979 and *The Fact of a Doorframe: Poems, 1950–84* 1984.

In the 1960s her poetry was closely involved with the student and antiwar movements in the US but since then she has concentrated on women's issues. In 1974, when given the National Book Award, she declined to accept it as an individual, but with Alice Walker and Audrey Rich accepted it on behalf of all women.

Richard three kings of England:

Richard I *the Lion-Heart* (French *Coeur-de-Lion*) 1157–1199. King of England from 1189, who spent all but six months of his reign abroad. He was the third son of Henry II, against whom he twice rebelled. In the third ⬦Crusade 1191–92 he won victories at Cyprus, Acre, and Arsuf (against ⬦Saladin), but failed to recover Jerusalem. While returning overland he was captured by the Duke of Austria, who handed him over to the emperor Henry VI, and he was held prisoner until a large ransom was raised. He then returned briefly to England, where his brother John I had been ruling in his stead. His later years were spent in warfare in France, where he was killed.

Richard II 1367–1400. King of England from 1377, effectively from 1389, son of Edward the Black Prince. He reigned in conflict with Parliament; they executed some of his associates 1388, and he executed some of the opposing barons 1397, whereupon he made himself absolute. Two years later, forced to abdicate in favor of ⬦Henry IV, he was jailed and probably assassinated.

In 1399 his cousin Henry Bolingbroke, Duke of Hereford (later Henry IV), returned from exile to lead a revolt; Richard II was deposed by Parliament and imprisoned in Pontefract Castle, where he died mysteriously.

Richard III 1452–1485. King of England from 1483. The son of Richard, Duke of York, he was created Duke of Gloucester by his brother Edward IV, and distinguished himself in the Wars of the ⬦Roses. On Edward's death 1483 he became protector to his nephew Edward V, and soon secured the crown for himself on the plea that Edward IV's sons were illegitimate. He proved a capable ruler, but the suspicion that he had murdered Edward V and his brother undermined his popularity. In 1485 Henry, Earl of Richmond (later ⬦Henry VII), raised a rebellion, and Richard III was defeated and killed at ⬦Bosworth.

Richards Theodore 1868–1928. US chemist. Working at Harvard University, Boston, for much of his career, Richards concentrated on determining as accurately as possible the atomic weights of a large number of elements. Nobel Prize 1914.

Richardson Henry Hobson 1838–1886. American architect, distinguished for his revival of ⬦Romanesque style. He designed churches, university buildings, homes, railroad stations, and town libraries. He had a stong influence on Louis ⬦Sullivan.

His buildings include Sever Hall and Austin Hall at Harvard University, and the monumental Marshall Field Wholesale Building, Chicago. His best-known work is Trinity Church in Copley Square, Boston.

Richardson Owen Willans 1879–1959. British physicist. He studied the emission of electricity from hot bodies, giving the name ⬦thermionics to the subject. At Cambridge University, he worked under J J ⬦Thomson in the Cavendish Laboratory. Nobel Prize 1928.

Richardson Ralph (David) 1902–1983. English actor. He played many stage parts, including Falstaff (Shakespeare), Peer Gynt (Ibsen), and Cyrano de Bergerac (Rostand). He shared the management of the Old Vic theater with Laurence Olivier 1944–50. In later years he revealed himself as an accomplished deadpan comic.

Richardson Samuel 1689–1761. English novelist, one of the founders of the modern novel. *Pamela* 1740–41, written in the form of a series of letters and containing much dramatic conversation, was sensationally popular all across Europe, and was followed by *Clarissa* 1747–48 and *Sir Charles Grandison* 1753–54.

Richardson Tony 1928–1991. English director and producer. With George Devine he established the English Stage Company 1955 at the Royal Court Theater, with productions such as *Look Back in Anger* 1956. His films include *Saturday Night and Sunday Morning* 1960, *A Taste of Honey* 1961, *Tom Jones* 1963, and *Joseph Andrews* 1977.

Richelieu Armand Jean du Plessis de 1585–1642. French cardinal and politician, chief minister from 1624. He aimed to make the monarchy absolute; he ruthlessly crushed opposition by the nobility and destroyed the political power of the ⬦Huguenots, while leaving them religious freedom. Abroad, he sought to establish French supremacy by breaking the power of the Hapsburgs; he therefore supported the Swedish king Gustavus Adolphus and the German Protestant princes against Austria and in 1635 brought France into the Thirty Years' War.

Born in Paris of a noble family, he entered the church and was created bishop of Luçon 1606 and a cardinal 1622. Through the influence of ⬦Marie de' Medici he became ⬦Louis XIII's chief minister 1624, a position

Richter scale

magnitude	relative amount of energy released	examples
1		
2		
3		
4	1	Carlisle, England, 1979
5	30	San Francisco and New England, 1979
		Wrexham, Wales, 1990
6	100	San Fernando, California, 1971
7	30,000	Chimbote, Peru, 1970
		San Francisco, 1989
8	1,000,000	Gansu, China, 1920
		San Francisco, 1906
		Alaska, 1964

he retained until his death. His secretary Père Joseph was the original Grey Eminence.

Richland city in SE Washington, on the Columbia river, NW of Walla Walla. It is a center for research for the US Department of Energy and a major producer of plutonium for nuclear weapons; population (1990) 33,300. It grew as a residential community for employees of the Hanford Engineer Works that helped to develop the atomic bomb from 1943.

Richler Mordecai 1931– . Canadian novelist, born in Montreal. His novels, written in a witty, acerbic style, include *The Apprenticeship of Duddy Kravitz* 1959 and *St Urbain's Horseman* 1971. Later works include *Joshua Then and Now* 1980 and *Home Sweet Home* 1984.

Richmond industrial city and port on the James River and capital of Virginia; population (1990) 219,000. It is a major tobacco market and distribution, commercial, and financial center of the surrounding region. Its diversified manufactures include tobacco products, chemicals, paper and printing, and textiles. Educational institutions include the University of Richmond and Virginia Commonwealth University. The Museum of the Confederacy and Edgar Allan Poe Museum are here, as are the former homes of John Marshall and Robert E Lee and the graves of James Madison and Jefferson Davis. The first permanent colonial American settlement was established 1637. Richmond was the capital of the Confederacy 1861–65, and several Civil War battles were fought nearby.

Richter Burton 1931– . US high-energy physicist who, in the 1960s, designed the Stanford Positron Accelerating Ring (SPEAR). In 1974 Richter used SPEAR to produce a new particle, a hadeon, composed of a charmed quark and a charmed antiquark. The charmed quark had been first postulated by Sheldon ◁Glashow in 1964. Richter shared the 1976 Nobel Physics Prize with Samuel ◁Ting.

Richter Charles Francis 1900–1985. US seismologist, deviser of the ◁Richter scale used to measure the strength of the waves from earthquakes.

Richter scale scale based on measurement of seismic waves, used to determine the magnitude of an ◁earthquake at its epicenter. The magnitude of an earthquake differs from its intensity, measured by the ◁Mercalli scale, which is subjective and varies from place to place for the same earthquake. The scale is named after US seismologist Charles Richter.

An earthquake's magnitude is a function of the total amount of energy released, and

each point on the Richter scale represents a tenfold increase in energy over the previous point. The greatest earthquake ever recorded, in 1920 in Gansu, China, measured 8.6 on the Richter scale.

Richthofen Manfred, Freiherr von (the "Red Baron") 1892–1918. German aviator. In World War I he commanded the 11th Chasing Squadron, known as **Richthofen's Flying Circus**, and shot down 80 aircraft before being killed in action.

ricin extremely toxic extract from the seeds of the ◁castor-oil plant. When combined with ◁monoclonal antibodies, ricin can attack cancer cells, particularly in the treatment of lymphoma and leukemia.

Ricin was used to assassinate the Bulgarian dissident Georgi Markov in London 1978.

Rickenbacker Edward Vernon 1890–1973. US race-car driver, aviator, and airline executive. Returning to private business after World War I, he founded the Rickenbacker Motor Co 1921, but dissolved it and purchased Eastern Airlines 1938 (which he ran as president to 1959; chairman of the board to 1963). He left briefly to serve as an adviser to the War Department during World War II; he took on special missions and ditched his plane in the Pacific, drifting for 23 days before rescue.

Born in Columbus, Ohio, Rickenbacker became a race-car driver in his teenage years. By 1917 he had established a land speed record of 134 mph/216 kph. At the outbreak of World War I, he joined the army and was chosen for pilot's training in France.

As a member of the 94th Aero Pursuit Squadron, Rickenbacker gained fame as an air ace, downing 26 German aircraft in four months.

rickets defective growth of bone in children due to an insufficiency of calcium deposits. The bones, which do not harden adequately, are bent out of shape. It is usually caused by a lack of vitamin D and insufficient exposure to sunlight. Renal rickets, also a condition of malformed bone, is associated with kidney disease.

Rickey Branch Wesley 1881–1965. US baseball executive. As president of the Brooklyn Dodgers 1942–50, he made baseball history by signing Jackie Robinson, the first black American to play in the major leagues.

Born in Stockdale, Ohio, Rickey received a law degree from the University of Michigan 1911. Always active in athletics, he signed as a catcher with the St Louis Browns 1905–06. After playing with the New York Yankees 1907, he retired as a player. In 1913 he accepted a managerial job with the Browns and four years

later became president of the St Louis Cardinals, the team he managed 1919–25. With the Cardinals, Rickey pioneered the minor-league system of developing talent.

Rickover Hyman George 1900–1986. Russian-born US naval officer. During World War II, Rickover worked on the atomic bomb project, headed the navy's nuclear reactor division, and served on the Atomic Energy Commission. He was responsible for the development of the first nuclear submarine, the *Nautilus*, 1954. He was promoted to the rank of admiral 1973. After retiring 1982, he became an outspoken critic of the dangers of nuclear research and development and the waste in military contracts.

Rickover immigrated to the US with his family 1906 and graduated from the US Naval Academy 1922. After further studies in engineering, he became a specialist in the electrical division of the Bureau of Ships.

Riefenstahl Leni 1902– . German filmmaker. Her film of the Nazi rallies at Nuremberg, *Triumph des Willens/Triumph of the Will* 1934, vividly illustrated Hitler's charismatic appeal but tainted her career. After World War II her work was blacklisted by the Allies until 1952.

Volumes of her still photographs include *The Last of the Nuba* 1973 and *Mein Afrika/My Africa* 1982.

She trained as a dancer, appearing in films in the 1920s, but in the early 1930s formed her own production company, and directed and starred in *Das blaue Licht/The Blue Light* 1932. She also made a two-part documentary of the 1936 Berlin Olympics.

Riel Louis 1844–1885. French-Canadian rebel, a champion of the Métis (an Indian-French people); he established a provisional government in Winnipeg in an unsuccessful revolt 1869–70 and was hanged for treason after leading a second revolt in Saskatchewan 1885.

Riemann Georg Friedrich Bernhard 1826–1866. German mathematician whose system of non-Euclidean geometry, thought at the time to be a mere mathematical curiosity, was used by Einstein to develop his general theory of ◁relativity.

Riesman David 1909– . US sociologist, author of *The Lonely Crowd: A Study of the Changing American Character* 1950. He made a distinction among "inner-directed," "tradition-directed," and "other-directed" societies, the first using individual internal values, the second using established tradition, and the third, other people's expectations, to develop cohesiveness and conformity within a society.

Rietvelt Gerrit Thomas 1888–1964. Dutch architect, an exponent of De ◁Stijl. He designed the Schreder House at Utrecht 1924; he is also well known for colorful, minimalist chair design.

Rif, Er mountain range about 180 mi/290 km long on the Mediterranean seaboard of Morocco.

Riff member of a ◁Berber people of N Morocco, who under ◁Abd el-Krim long resisted the Spanish and French.

rifle ◁firearm that has spiral grooves (rifling) in its barrel. When a bullet is fired, the rifling makes it spin, thereby improving accuracy. Rifles were first introduced in the late 18th century.

rift valley valley formed by the subsidence of

a block of the Earth's ⋄crust between two or more parallel ⋄faults. Rift valleys are steep-sided and form where the crust is being pulled apart, as at ⋄ocean ridges, or in the Great Rift Valley of E Africa.

Rift Valley, Great volcanic valley formed 10–20 million years ago by a crack in the Earth's crust and running about 5,000 mi/8,000 km from the Jordan Valley through the Red Sea to central Mozambique in SE Africa. It is marked by a series of lakes, including Lake Turkana (formerly Lake Rudolf), and volcanoes, such as Mount Kilimanjaro.

At some points its traces have been lost by erosion, but elsewhere, as in S Kenya, cliffs rise thousands of feet.

Rift Valley fever virus disease originating south of the Sahara. Hosted by sheep and cattle, it is spread by mosquitoes to humans, and a virulent strain reached Egypt 1977.

Riga capital and port of Latvia; population (1987) 900,000. A member of the ⋄Hanseatic League from 1282, Riga has belonged in turn to Poland 1582, Sweden 1621, and Russia 1710. It was the capital of independent Latvia 1918–40 and was occupied by Germany 1941–44, before being annexed by the USSR. It again became independent Latvia's capital 1991.

Rigel or *Beta Orionis* brightest star in the constellation Orion. It is a blue-white supergiant, with an estimated diameter 50 times that of the Sun. It is 900 light-years from Earth, and is about 100,000 times more luminous than our Sun. It is the seventh brightest star in the sky.

Rigg Diana 1938– . English actress. Her stage roles include Héloïse in *Abelard and Héloïse* 1970, and television roles include Emma Peel in *The Avengers* 1965–67 and Lady Deadlock in *Bleak House* 1985. She became the hostess for *Mystery Theater* on US public television 1989.

right ascension in astronomy, the coordinate on the ⋄celestial sphere that corresponds to longitude on the surface of the Earth. It is measured in hours, minutes, and seconds eastward from the point where the Sun's path, the ecliptic, once a year intersects the celestial equator; this point is called the **vernal equinox**.

right-hand rule in physics, a memory aid used to recall the relative directions of motion, magnetic field, and current in an electric generator. It was devised by English physicist John Fleming. See ⋄Fleming's rules.

right of way the right to pass over land belonging to another. Other rights of way are licenses (where personal permission is given) and ⋄easements.

Rights of Man and the Citizen, Declaration of the historic French document. According to the statement of the French National Assembly 1789, these rights include representation in the legislature; equality before the law; equality of opportunity; freedom from arbitrary imprisonment; freedom of speech and religion; taxation in proportion to ability to pay; and security of property. In 1946 were added equal rights for women; right to work, join a union, and strike; leisure, social security, and support in old age; and free education.

right triangle triangle in which one of the angles is a right angle (90°). It is the basic form of triangle for defining trigonometrical ratios (for example, sine, cosine, and tangent) and for which the ⋄Pythagorean theorem holds true. The longest side of a right triangle is called the hypotenuse.

Its area is equal to half the product of the lengths of the two shorter sides. A triangle constructed with its hypotenuse as the diameter of a circle with its opposite ⋄vertex on the circumference is a right triangle. This is a fundamental theorem in geometry, first credited to the Greek mathematician Thales about 580 BC.

right wing the more conservative or reactionary section of a political party or spectrum. It originated in the French national assembly 1789, where the nobles sat in the place of honor on the president's right, whereas the commons were on his left (hence ⋄left wing).

rigor medical term for shivering or rigidity. *Rigor mortis* is the stiffness that ensues in a corpse soon after death, owing to the coagulation of muscle proteins.

Rig-Veda oldest of the ⋄Vedas, the chief sacred writings of Hinduism. It consists of hymns to the Aryan gods, such as Indra, and to nature gods.

Riis Jacob August 1849–1914. Danish-born US journalist, photographer, and reformer. As police reporter for the *New York Evening Sun* 1888–99, he was exposed to the grim realities of urban life, and his photographic exposé of conditions in the New York slums, *How the Other Half Lives* 1890, made the American public aware of the poverty in its own midst.

Riis immigrated to the US 1870. After working at a succession of jobs, he was hired as a reporter for the *New York Tribune* 1877. As a social crusader, Riis later established a settlement house, named for him, in New York City. His autobiography, *The Making of an American*, appeared 1901.

Rijeka (Italian *Fiume*) industrial port (oil refining, distilling, paper, tobacco, chemicals) in Croatia; population (1983) 193,044. It has changed hands many times and, after being seized by the Italian nationalist Gabriele ⋄d'Annunzio 1919, was annexed by Italy 1924. It was ceded back to Yugoslavia 1949; in 1991 it became part of newly independent Croatia.

Riley James Whitcomb 1849–1916. US poet. His first collection of poems, *The Old Swimmin' Hole*, was published 1883. His later collections include *Rhymes of Childhood* 1890, *Poems Here at Home* 1893, and *Home Folks* 1900.

Born in Greenfield, Indiana, Riley had little formal education and worked at a series of odd jobs before becoming the editor of a local newspaper. In 1877 he began to contribute light verse to the *Indianapolis Journal*. His use of the Midwestern vernacular and familiar themes earned him the unofficial title "The Hoosier Poet."

Rilke Rainer Maria 1875–1926. Austrian writer. His prose works include the semiautobiographical *Die Aufzeichnungen des Malte Laurids Brigge/Notebook of Malte Laurids Brigge* 1910. His verse is characterized by a form of mystic pantheism that seeks to achieve a state of ecstasy in which existence can be apprehended as a whole.

Rimbaud (Jean Nicolas) Arthur 1854–1891. French Symbolist poet. His verse was chiefly written before the age of 20, notably *Les Illuminations* published 1886. From 1871 he lived with ⋄Verlaine.

Rimini industrial port (pasta, footwear, textiles, furniture) and vacation resort in Emilia-Romagna, Italy; population (1988) 131,000.

history Its name in Roman times was *Ariminum*, and it was the terminus of the

Flaminian Way from Rome. In World War II it formed the eastern strongpoint of the German "Gothic" defense line and was badly damaged in the severe fighting Sept 1944, when it was taken by the Allies.

Rimsky-Korsakov Nikolay Andreyevich 1844–1908. Russian composer. He used Russian folk idiom and rhythms in his Romantic compositions and published a text on orchestration. His operas include *The Maid of Pskov* 1873, *The Snow Maiden* 1882, *Mozart and Salieri* 1898, and *The Golden Cockerel* 1907, a satirical attack on despotism that was banned until 1909.

Other works include the symphonic poem *Sadko* 1867, the program symphony *Antar* 1869, and the symphonic suite *Scheherazade* 1888. He also completed works by other composers, for example, ⋄Mussorgsky's *Boris Godunov*.

rinderpest acute viral disease of cattle (sometimes also of sheep and goats) characterized by fever and bloody diarrhea, due to inflammation of the intestines. It can be fatal. Almost eliminated in the 1960s, it revived in Africa in the 1980s.

ring a circlet, usually of precious metal, sometimes set with gems, worn on a finger as a decoration or token. The origin of the wedding ring is uncertain, but betrothal rings were bestowed in Roman times. Rings were used for money in ancient Egypt and elsewhere. Their connection with the church still survives in instances such as the English coronation.

Ringling Charles 1863–1926. US circus promoter. With its three rings and large cast, the Ringlings' circus was touted as the "Greatest Show on Earth," the byword still most associated with the modern Ringling Brothers and Barnum and Bailey Circus.

Born in McGregor, Iowa, Ringling started a vaudeville act in 1882 with his brothers, John, Albert, Otto, and Alfred. The touring act eventually became a small circus and grew more popular after the purchase of an elephant in 1888. With Charles as business manager, the Ringling Brothers Circus toured widely. In 1907 they acquired the largest of their competitors, the Barnum and Bailey Circus, and established winter quarters in Sarasota, Florida.

ringworm any of various contagious skin infections due to related kinds of fungus, usually resulting in circular, itchy, discolored patches covered with scales or blisters. The scalp and feet (athlete's foot) are generally involved. Treatment is with ⋄antifungal preparations.

Rinzai (Chinese *Lin-ch'i*) school of Zen Buddhism introduced to Japan from China in the 12th century by the monk Eisai and others. It emphasizes rigorous monastic discipline and sudden enlightenment by meditation on a *kōan* (paradoxical question).

Rio de Janeiro port and resort in E Brazil; population (1991) 5,487,300. The name (Portuguese "river of January") commemorates the arrival of Portuguese explorers Jan 1, 1502, but there is in fact no river. Sugar Loaf Mountain stands at the entrance to the harbor. Rio was the capital of Brazil 1763–1960.

Some colonial churches and other buildings survive; there are modern boulevards, including the Avenida Rio Branco, and Copacabana is a luxurious beachside suburb. The city is the capital of the state of Rio de Janeiro, which has a population of 13,267,100 (1987 est).

Río de Oro former district in the S of the province of Spanish Sahara. See ⟡Western Sahara.

Rio Grande river rising in the Rocky Mountains in S Colorado, and flowing S to the Gulf of Mexico, where it is reduced to a trickle by irrigation demands on its upper reaches; length 1,900 mi/3,050 km. Its last 1,500 mi/2,400 km form the US—Mexican border (Mexican name *Río Bravo del Norte*).

Rio Grande do Norte state of NE Brazil; capital Natal; area 20,460 sq mi/53,000 sq km; population (1990) 2,522,700.

Río Muni the mainland portion of ⟡Equatorial Guinea.

Río Negro river in South America, rising in E Colombia and joining the Amazon at Manáus, Brazil; length 1,400 mi/2,250 km.

Riopelle Jean Paul 1923– . Canadian artist, active in Paris from 1946. In the 1950s he developed an Abstract Expressionist style and produced colorful impasto (with paint applied in a thick mass) paintings and sculptures. His *Encounter* 1956 (Wallraf-Richartz Museum, Cologne, Germany) is a typically rough-textured canvas.

RIP abbreviation for *requiescat in pace* (Latin "may he/she rest in peace").

Ripley Robert LeRoy 1893–1949. US cartoonist, creator of the syndicated column "Believe It or Not!," a highly popular compendium of bizarre facts.

Born in Santa Rosa, California, Ripley began cartooning as a teenager and was hired by the sports department of the *San Francisco Bulletin* 1910. In 1913 he became a sports cartoonist for the *New York Globe* and later began to present sports records in the series called "Believe It or Not!" Moving from sports to all kinds of oddities and obscure facts, Ripley took his column to the *New York Evening Post* in 1923 and later to national syndication. Through radio and film appearances and continued syndication, Ripley became a national celebrity and master of the bizarre.

ripple tank in physics, shallow water-filled tray used to demonstrate various properties of waves, such as reflection, refraction, diffraction, and interference, by programming and manipulating their movement.

Rip Van Winkle legendary character created by Washington Irving in his 1819 tale of a man who falls into a magical 20-year sleep, and wakes to find he has slumbered through the Revolutionary War.

RISC (acronym for *reduced instruction-set computer*) in computing, a microprocessor (processor on a single chip) that carries out fewer instructions than other microprocessors in common use in the 1990s. Because of the low number of ⟡machine-code instructions, the processor carries out those instructions very quickly.

Risorgimento movement for Italian national unity and independence from 1815. Leading figures in the movement included ⟡Cavour, ⟡Mazzini, and ⟡Garibaldi. Uprisings 1848–49 failed, but with help from France in a war against Austria—to oust it from Italian provinces in the north—an Italian kingdom was founded 1861. Unification was finally completed with the addition of Venetia 1866 and the Papal States 1870.

Ritter Tex (Woodward Maurice) 1905–1974.

US singer and actor, popular as a singing cowboy in B-films in the 1930s and 1940s (*Arizona Trail* 1943). He sang the title song to *High Noon* 1952.

ritualization in ethology, a stereotype that occurs in certain behavior patterns when these are incorporated into displays. For example, the exaggerated and stylized head toss of the goldeneye drake during courtship is a ritualization of the bathing movement used to wet the feathers; its duration and form have become fixed. Ritualization may make displays clearly recognizable, so ensuring that individuals mate only with members of their own species.

river long water course that flows down a slope along a channel. It originates at a point called its *source*, and enters a sea or lake at its *mouth*. Along its length it may be joined by smaller rivers called *tributaries*. A river and its tributaries are contained within a ⟡drainage basin.

Rivera Diego 1886–1957. Mexican painter, active in Europe until 1921. He received many

major rivers

name and location	mi	km
Nile (NE Africa)	4,160	6,695
Amazon (South America)	4,080	6,570
Chang Jiang (China)	3,900	6,300
Mississippi–Missouri (US)	3,740	6,020
Ob–Irtysh (China/Kazakhstan /Russia)	3,480	5,600
Huang He (China)	3,395	5,464
Paraná (Brazil)	2,800	4,500
Zaïre (Africa)	2,800	4,500
Mekong (Asia)	2,750	4,425
Amur (Asia)	2,744	4,416
Lena (Russia)	2,730	4,400
Mackenzie (Canada)	2,635	4,241
Niger (Africa)	2,600	4,185
Yenisei (Russia)	2,550	4,100
Mississippi (US)	2,350	3,780
Murray–Darling (Australia)	2,330	3,750
Missouri (US)	2,328	3,725
Volga (Russia)	2,290	3,685
Euphrates (Iraq)	2,240	3,600
Madeira (Brazil)	2,013	3,240
São Francisco (Brazil)	1,988	3,199
Yukon (US/Canada)	1,979	3,185
Indus (Tibet/Pakistan)	1,975	3,180
Syrdar'ya (Kazakhstan)	1,913	3,078
Rio Grande (US/Mexico)	1,900	3,050
Purus (Brazil)	1,860	2,993
Danube (Europe)	1,776	2,858
Brahmaputra (Asia)	1,770	2,850
Japurá (Brazil)	1,750	2,816
Salween (Myanmar/China)	1,740	2,800
Tocantins (Brazil)	1,677	2,699
Zambezi (Africa)	1,650	2,650
Paraguay (Paraguay)	1,610	2,591
Nelson–Saskatchewan (Canada)	1,600	2,570
Orinoco (Venezuela)	1,600	2,600
Amu Darya (Tajikistan/Turkmenistan/ Uzbekistan)	1,578	2,540
Ural (Russia/Kazakhstan)	1,575	2,534
Kolyma (Russia)	1,562	2,513
Ganges (India/Bangladesh)	1,560	2,510
Orinoco (Venezuela)	1,490	2,400

public commissions for murals exalting the Mexican revolution. A vast cycle on historical themes (National Palace, Mexico City) was begun 1929. In the 1930s he visited the US and with Ben Shahn produced murals for the Rockefeller Center, New York (later overpainted because he included a portrait of Lenin).

Rivera Primo de. Spanish politician; see ⟡Primo de Rivera.

river blindness another name for ⟡onchocerciasis, a disease prevalent in Third World countries.

Riverside city in California, on the Santa Ana River E of Los Angeles; population (1990) 226,500. Founded 1870. It is the center of a citrus-growing district and has a citrus research station; the seedless orange was developed at Riverside 1873.

The research station, now part of the University of California–Riverside, saved the state's orange trees from obliteration by a virus in the 1940s. Manufactured products include irrigation and electronic equipment, aircraft engines, paper products, and plastics. A land-development company purchased the site and laid out the community 1870.

riveting method of joining metal plates. A hot metal pin called a rivet, which has a head at one end, is inserted into matching holes in two overlapping plates, then the other end is struck and formed into another head, holding the plates tight. Riveting is used in building construction, boilermaking, and shipbuilding.

Riviera the Mediterranean coast of France and Italy from Marseille to La Spezia.

The most exclusive section, with the finest climate, is the Côte d'Azur, Menton–St Tropez, which includes Monaco.

Riyadh (Arabic *Ar Riyād*) capital of Saudi Arabia and of the Central Province, formerly the sultanate of Nejd, in an oasis, connected by rail with Dammam on the Arabian Gulf; population (1986) 1,500,000.

Outside the city are date gardens irrigated from deep wells. There is a large royal palace and an Islamic university 1950.

Rizzio David 1533–1566. Italian adventurer at the court of Mary Queen of Scots. After her marriage to ⟡Darnley, Rizzio's influence over her incited her husband's jealousy, and he was murdered by Darnley and his friends.

RNA *ribonucleic acid* nucleic acid involved in the process of translating ⟡DNA, the genetic material, into proteins. It is usually single-stranded, unlike the double-stranded DNA, and consists of a large number of nucleotides strung together, each of which comprises the sugar ribose, a phosphate group, and one of four bases (uracil, cytosine, adenine, or guanine). RNA is copied from DNA by the assemblage of free nucleotides against an unwound portion (a single strand) of the DNA, with DNA serving as the template. In this process, uracil (instead of the thymine in DNA) is paired with adenine, and guanine with cytosine, forming ⟡base pairs that then separate. The RNA then travels to the ribosomes where it serves to assemble proteins from free amino acids. In a few viruses, such as ⟡retroviruses, RNA is the only hereditary material.

RNA occurs in three major forms, each with a different function in the synthesis of protein molecules. *Messenger RNA* (mRNA) acts as the template for protein synthesis. Each codon (a set of three bases) on the RNA molecule is matched up with the corresponding amino acid, in accordance with the ♢genetic code. This process (translation) takes place in the ribosomes, which are made up of proteins and *ribosomal RNA* (rRNA). *Transfer RNA* (tRNA) is responsible for combining with specific amino acids, and then matching up a special "anticodon" sequence of its own with a codon on the mRNA. This is how the genetic code is translated into proteins.

roach any freshwater fish of the Eurasian genus *Rutilus*, of the carp family, especially *R. rutilus* of N Europe. It is dark green above, whitish below, with reddish lower fins; it grows to 1.2 ft/35 cm.

Roach Hal 1892–1992. US film producer, usually of comedies, who was active from the 1910s to the 1940s. He worked with ♢Laurel and Hardy, and also produced films for Harold Lloyd and Charley Chase. His work includes *The Music Box* 1932, *Way Out West* 1936, and *Of Mice and Men* 1939.

road specially constructed route for wheeled vehicles to travel on. Reinforced tracks became necessary with the invention of wheeled vehicles in about 3000 BC and most ancient civilizations had some form of road network. The Romans developed engineering techniques that were not equaled for another 1,400 years.

Until the late 18th century most European roads were haphazardly maintained, making winter travel difficult. In the UK the turnpike system of collecting tolls created some improvement. The Scottish engineers Thomas Telford and John ♢McAdam introduced sophisticated construction methods in the early 19th century. Recent developments have included durable surface compounds and machinery for rapid ground preparation.

In the US, the first roads were paved in colonial times, first with logs (corduroy roads), later with cobblestones and Belgian building blocks or brick, depending on the region. With the advent of motor vehicles, roads were constructed to reduce time spent draining, fixing flat tires, and seeking services; highways, parkways, freeways, and interstates now offer multilane, landscaped roads, with service areas at roadside, including motels, restaurants, and service stations.

roadrunner crested North American ground-dwelling bird *Geococcyx californianus* of the ♢cuckoo family, found in the SW US and Mexico. It can run at a speed of 15 mph/25 kph.

Roanoke (American Indian "shell money") industrial city (railroad repairs, chemicals, steel goods, furniture, textiles) in Virginia, on the Roanoke River; population (1980) 100,500. Founded in 1834 as *Big Lick*, it was a small village until 1881 when the repair shops of the Virginia Railway were set up here, after which it developed rapidly.

Robbe-Grillet Alain 1922– . French writer, the leading theorist of *le nouveau roman* ("the new novel"), for example his own *Les Gommes/ The Erasers* 1953, *La Jalousie/Jealousy* 1957, and *Dans le labyrinthe/In the Labyrinth* 1959, which concentrates on the detailed description of physical objects. He also wrote the script for the film *L'Année dernière à Marienbad/Last Year in Marienbad* 1961.

robbery in law, a variety of ♢theft: stealing from a person, using force, or the threat of force, to intimidate the victim.

Robbia, della Italian family of sculptors and architects, active in Florence. *Luca della Robbia* (1400–1482) created a number of major works in Florence, notably the marble *cantoria* (singing gallery) in the cathedral 1431–38 (Museo del Duomo), with lively groups of choristers. Luca also developed a characteristic style of glazed terracotta work.

Robbins Jerome 1918– . US dancer and choreographer, codirector of the New York City Ballet 1969–83 (with George Balanchine). His ballets are internationally renowned and he is considered the greatest US-born ballet choreographer. He also choreographed the musicals *The King and I* 1951, *West Side Story* 1957, and *Fiddler on the Roof* 1964.

First a chorus boy on Broadway, then a soloist with the newly formed American Ballet Theater 1941–46, Robbins was associate director of the New York City Ballet 1949–59. His first ballet, *Fancy Free* 1940, was a great success (and was adapted with Leonard Bernstein into the musical *On the Town* 1944). Other Robbins ballets include *Dancers at a Gathering* 1969, *The Goldberg Variations* 1971, and *Glass Pieces* 1983 (based on W H Auden's poem).

Robert two dukes of Normandy, including:

Robert II *c.* 1054–1134. Eldest son of ♢William I (the Conqueror), succeeding him as Duke of Normandy (but not on the English throne) 1087. His brother ♢William II ascended the English throne, and they warred until 1096, after which Robert took part in the First Crusade. When his other brother ♢Henry I claimed the English throne 1100, Robert contested the claim and invaded England unsuccessfully 1101. Henry invaded Normandy 1106, and captured Robert, who remained a prisoner in England until his death.

Robert three kings of Scotland:

Robert I *Robert the Bruce* 1274–1329. King of Scotland from 1306, and grandson of Robert de ♢Bruce. He shared in the national uprising led by William Wallace, and, after Wallace's execution 1305, rose once more against Edward I of England, and was crowned at Scone 1306. He defeated Edward II at ♢Bannockburn 1314. In 1328 the treaty of Northampton recognized Scotland's independence and Robert as king.

Robert II 1316–1390. King of Scotland from 1371. He was the son of Walter (1293–1326), steward of Scotland, who married Marjory, daughter of Robert I. He was the first king of the house of Stuart.

Robert III *c.* 1340–1406. King of Scotland from 1390, son of Robert II. He was unable to control the nobles, and the government fell largely into the hands of his brother, Robert, Duke of Albany (c. 1340–1420).

Robeson Paul 1898–1976. US bass singer and actor. He graduated from Columbia University as a lawyer, but limited opportunities for blacks led him instead to the stage. He appeared in *The Emperor Jones* 1924 and *Showboat* 1928, in which he sang "Ol' Man River." He played *Othello* in 1930, and his films include *Sanders of the River* 1935 and *King Solomon's Mines* 1937. An ardent advocate of black rights, he had his passport withdrawn 1950–58 because of his association with left-wing movements. He then left the US to live in England.

Robespierre Maximilien François Marie Isidore de 1758–1794. French politician in the ♢French Revolution. As leader of the ♢Jacobins in the National Convention, he supported the execution of Louis XVI and the overthrow of the right-wing republican Girondins, and in July 1793 was elected to the Committee of Public Safety. A year later he was guillotined; many believe that he was a scapegoat for the Reign of ♢Terror since he ordered only 72 executions personally.

Robespierre, a lawyer, was elected to the National Assembly of 1789–91. His defense of democratic principles made him popular in Paris, while his disinterestedness won him the nickname of "the Incorruptible." His zeal for social reform and his attacks on the excesses of the extremists made him enemies on both right and left; a conspiracy was formed against him, and in July 1794 he was overthrown and executed by those who actually perpetrated the Reign of Terror.

robin one of two songbirds of the thrush family. (1) North American thrush, the robin *Turdus migratorius*, 10 in/25 cm long, gray-brown with brick-red underparts. (2) Eurasian and African thrush *Erithacus rubecula*, 5 in/13 cm long, olive brown above with a red breast. Some Australian songbirds

Robin Hood legendary English outlaw and champion of the poor against the rich. He is said to have lived in Sherwood Forest, Nottinghamshire, during the reign of Richard I (1189–99). He feuded with the sheriff of Nottingham, accompanied by Maid Marian and a band of followers known as his "merry men." He appears in ballads from the 13th century, but his first datable appearance is in Langland's *Piers Plowman* about 1377.

Robinson Edward G. Adopted name of Emanuel Goldenberg 1893–1973. US film actor, born in Romania, who emigrated with his family to the US 1903. He was noted for his gangster roles, such as *Little Caesar* 1930.

He also performed in dramatic and comedy roles in film and on the stage, and was a great art collector. He wrote two autobiographical volumes, *My Father, My Son* 1958 and *All My Yesterdays* 1973. His other films include *Dr Ehrlich's Magic Bullet* 1940, *Double Indemnity* 1944, *The Ten Commandments* 1956, and *Soylent Green* 1973.

Robinson Edwin Arlington 1869–1935. US poet. His verse, dealing mainly with psychological themes in a narrative style, is collected in volumes such as *The Children of the Night* 1897, which established his reputation. He was awarded three Pulitzer Prizes in poetry: *Collected Poems* 1922, *The Man Who Died Twice* 1925, and *Tristram* 1928.

Well-known poems include "Richard Cory" and "Miniver Cheevy." He also published a series of long narrative poems based on Arthurian legends.

Robinson Jackie (Jack Roosevelt) 1919–1972. US baseball player, the first black to play in the major leagues.

Born in Cairo, Georgia, Robinson attended the University of California at Los Angeles (UCLA) and joined the Kansas City Monarchs of the Negro National League 1945. He came to the attention of Branch ♢Rickey and was signed by a Brooklyn Dodgers minor league team. Robinson became the first black American in the major leagues 1947, playing second base for the Brooklyn Dodgers and winning rookie of the year honors. In 1949 he was the National League's batting champion and was voted the league's most valuable player. He had a career batting average of .311. After retirement as a player 1956, Robinson served as the New York governor's special assistant for

hydraulic lines

hydraulic piston

hinge

claw

stand

steering mechanism

connecting wire

robot pen-tracer ('turtle')

pen

case

wheels   electric motor

robot *Two simple robots.*

community affairs 1966–68. He was elected to the Baseball Hall of Fame 1962.

Robinson Mary 1944– . Irish Labour politician, president from 1990. She became a professor of law at 25. A strong supporter of women's rights, she has campaigned for the liberalization of Ireland's laws prohibiting divorce and abortion.

Robinson was born in County Mayo and educated at Trinity College, Dublin, and Harvard University. As a member of the Labour Party, she tried unsuccessfully to enter the Dáil (parliament) in 1990, and then surprisingly won the presidency of her country, defeating the Fianna Fáil frontrunner Brian Lenihan.

Robinson Robert 1886–1975. English chemist, Nobel Prize-winner 1947 for his research in organic chemistry on the structure of many natural products, including flower pigments and alkaloids. He formulated the electronic theory now used in organic chemistry.

Robinson Smokey (William) 1940– . US singer, songwriter, and record producer, associated with ♢Motown records from its conception. He was lead singer of the Miracles 1957–72 (hits include "Shop Around" 1961, "The Tears of a Clown" 1970) and his solo hits include "Cruisin'" 1979 and "Being With You" 1981. His light tenor voice and wordplay characterize his work.

Robinson Sugar Ray. Adopted name of Walker Smith 1920–1989. US boxer, world welterweight champion 1945–51; he defended his title five times. Defeating Jake LaMotta 1951, he took the middleweight title. He lost the title six times and won it seven times. He retired at the age of 45.

Robinson Crusoe *The Life and strange and surprising Adventures of Robinson Crusoe* novel by Daniel Defoe, published 1719, in which the hero is shipwrecked on an island and survives for years by his own ingenuity until rescued; the plot was based on the adventures of Alexander ♢Selkirk. The book had many imitators and is the first major English novel.

robot any machine controlled by electronic chip or computer that can be programmed to do work (robotics, as opposed to mechanical

work, called automation). The most common types are robotic "arms"; when fixed to the floor or a workbench, they perform functions such as paint spraying or assembling parts in factories. Others include radio-directed or computer-controlled vehicles for carrying materials, and a miscellany of devices from cruise missiles and deep-sea and space-exploration craft to robotic toys.

Records of mechanical people and animals of all sizes go back more than 2,000 years. However, it was only with the incorporation of the computer that the true robot could be built. A robot that plays guitar, and a cello, violin, and recorder robot ensemble, were marketed by a Japanese company 1989.

Rob Roy nickname of Robert MacGregor 1671–1734. Scottish Highland ♢Jacobite outlaw. After losing his estates, he lived by cattle theft and extortion. Captured, he was sentenced to transportation but pardoned 1727. He is a central character in Walter Scott's historical novel *Rob Roy* 1817.

Rocard Michel 1930– . French socialist politician, prime minister 1988–91. A former radical, he joined the Socialist Party (PS) 1973, emerging as leader of its moderate social-democratic wing. He held ministerial office under President François Mitterrand 1981–85.

Rochelle, La see ♢La Rochelle, port in W France.

Rochester industrial city in New York, on the Genesee River S of Lake Ontario; population (1990) 231,600. Its manufactured products include photographic equipment and optical and other precision instruments. It was the birthplace of the Xerox copier, and the world headquarters of the Eastman Kodak Company are here.

The University of Rochester campus is in the suburbs, but Rochester is the home of the famed Eastman School of Music. The International Museum of Photography is at the George Eastman House.

Permanent settlement began 1812, and growth was spurred by the completion of the Erie Canal 1825. During the mid-19th century, Rochester was a focus for abolitionism and women's rights; Susan B Anthony and Frederick Douglass lived here.

Rochester commercial center with dairy and food-processing industries in Minnesota; population (1990) 70,745. Rochester is the home of the noted Mayo Clinic, part of a medical center established 1889.

The University of Minnesota medical school and the Mayo medical school are also here. The community was settled 1854 and named for Rochester, New York.

rochet in the Christian church, vestment worn mainly by Catholic and Anglican bishops and abbots. The Catholic rochet reaches to the knee, while the Anglican rochet is ankle length.

rock constituent of the Earth's crust, composed of mineral particles and/or materials of organic origin consolidated into a hard mass as ♢igneous rocks, ♢sedimentary rocks, or ♢metamorphic rocks.

rock and roll pop music born of a fusion of rhythm and blues and country and western and based on electric guitar and drums. In the mid-1950s, with the advent of Elvis Presley, it became the heartbeat of teenage rebellion in the West and also had considerable impact on other parts of the world. It found perhaps its

purest form in late-1950s *rockabilly*, the style of white Southerners in the US; the blanket term "rock" later came to comprise a multitude of styles.

The term rock and roll was popularized by US disk jockey Alan Freed (1922–1965) beginning in 1951 on radio and in stage shows hosted by him.

rock climbing sport originally an integral part of mountaineering. It began as a form of training for Alpine expeditions and is now divided into three categories: the **outcrop climb** for climbs of up to 100 ft/30 m; the **crag climb** on cliffs of 100–1,000 ft/30–300 m, and the **big wall climb**, which is the nearest thing to Alpine climbing, but without the hazards of snow and ice.

Rockefeller John D(avison) 1839–1937. US industrialist, founder of the Standard Oil Company of Ohio 1870 (which achieved monopolistic control of 90% of US refineries). He also founded the philanthropic Rockefeller Foundation 1913, to which his son John D Rockefeller, Jr (1874–1960) devoted his life.

Born in Richford, New York, Rockefeller was brought up in Cleveland, Ohio, and after high school worked as a bookkeeper. By 1867, after oil was discovered in the US (in Pennsylvania), he and his produce-market partners went into the business of refining kerosene. From this company grew Standard Oil, which by 1911 had ruthlessly created a monopoly on US oil refining and distribution. It was broken up by a US Supreme Court ruling into smaller companies. Rockefeller then formed the General Education Board and the Rockefeller Foundation, philanthropic organizations that fostered educational programs in the South and at the University of Chicago and that funded medical research at the Rockefeller Institute in New York City.

rocket projectile driven by the reaction of gases produced by a fast-burning fuel. Unlike jet engines, which are also reaction engines, modern rockets carry their own oxygen supply to burn their fuel and do not require any surrounding atmosphere. For warfare, rocket heads carry an explosive device.

Rockets have been valued as fireworks over the last seven centuries, but their intensive development as a means of propulsion to high altitudes, carrying payloads, started only in the interwar years with the state-supported work in Germany (primarily by Werner ♢von Braun) and of R H Goddard (1882–1945) in the US. Being the only form of propulsion available that can function in a vacuum, rockets are essential to exploration in outer space. ♢Multistage rockets have to be used, consisting of a number of rockets joined together.

Two main kinds of rocket are used: one burns liquid propellants, the other solid propellants. The fireworks rocket uses gunpowder as a solid propellant. The ♢space shuttle's solid rocket boosters use a mixture of powdered aluminum in a synthetic rubber binder. Most rockets, however, have liquid propellants, which are more powerful and easier to control. Liquid hydrogen and kerosene are common fuels, while liquid oxygen is the most common oxygen provider, or oxidizer. One of the biggest rockets ever built, the Saturn V moon rocket, was a three-stage design, standing 365 ft/111 m high, weighed more than 3,000 tons/2,700 metric tons on the launch pad, developed a takeoff thrust of some 7.5 million lb/3.4 million kg, and could place almost 150 tons/140 metric tons into low Earth orbit. In the early 1990s, the most powerful rocket system was the Soviet Energia, capable of placing 110 tons/100 metric tons into low Earth orbit. The US space shuttle can put only 26 tons/24 metric tons into orbit. See ⟡nuclear warfare and ⟡missile.

Rockford city in N Illinois, on the Rock river, NW of Chicago. Industries include automotive parts, furniture, machine tools, and food products; population (1990) 139,400.

Rock Hill city in N central South Carolina, S of Charlotte, North Carolina. Industries include chemicals, textiles, and paper products; population (1990) 41,600.

Rockingham Charles Watson Wentworth, 2nd Marquess of Rockingham 1730–1782. British Whig politician, prime minister 1765–66 and 1782 (when he died in office); he supported the American claim to independence.

Rock Island city in NW Illinois, on the Mississippi river, W of Chicago. Industries include rubber and electronics. A US government arsenal is located here; population (1990) 40,600.

Rockne Knute Kenneth 1888–1931. Norwegian-born US football coach. His greatest contribution to football was the extensive use of sophisticated formations and the forward pass.

Rockne immigrated with his family to the US 1893. As a student at Notre Dame University 1910–14, he was a star football player and became the school's head football coach 1918. Serving in that position until his death, Rockne established an unparalleled lifetime record of 105 wins, 12 losses, and 5 ties—with 5 undefeated, untied seasons. His book *Coaching, the Way of the Winner* was published 1925. His memoirs, *Autobiography*, appeared 1931.

rock opera musical using pop elements, such as Andrew ⟡Lloyd Webber's *Jesus Christ Superstar* 1970.

Rockwell Norman 1894–1978. US painter and illustrator who designed magazine covers, mainly for *The Saturday Evening Post*, and cartoons portraying American life.

His whimsical view of the ordinary activities of the nation at work and at play earned him huge popularity.

Rocky Mountains or *Rockies* largest North American mountain system. They extend from the junction with the Mexican plateau, N through the W central states of the US, through Canada to the Alaskan border, and then form part of the Continental Divide, which separates rivers draining into the Atlantic or Arctic oceans from those flowing toward the Pacific Ocean. Mount Elbert is the highest peak, 14,433 ft/4,400 m. Some geographers consider the Yukon and Alaska ranges as part of the system, making the highest point Mount Mckinley (Denali) 20,320 ft/6,194 m.

Many large rivers rise in the Rocky Mountains, including the Missouri. Rocky Mountain National Park 1915 in Colorado has more than 107 named peaks over 10,000 ft/3,350 m. Because of the rugged terrain, the Rocky Mountains are sparsely populated. The mountains' chief economic asset is their minerals, including coal, petroleum, natural gas, copper, and gold. Lumbering is found in the N Rockies, and cattle and sheep are raised. The Rockies have US and Canadian national parks that attract many tourists.

Rococo movement in the arts and architecture in 18th-century Europe, tending toward lightness, elegance, delicacy, and decorative charm. The term "Rococo" refers to *rocaille* (rock-or shell-work), a style of interior decoration based on S-curves and scroll-like forms. Watteau's paintings and Sèvres porcelain belong to the French Rococo vogue. In the 1730s the movement became widespread in Europe, notably in the churches and palaces of S Germany and Austria.

Other Rococo features include the use of fantastic ornament, such as Grotesque and chinoiserie, and pretty, naturalistic details. Architectural and decorative ensembles, such as the Amalienburg pavilion at Nymphenburg near Munich, Germany, and the Hôtel de Soubise pavilion in Paris, exemplify the movement. The painters Boucher and Fragonard both painted typically decorative Rococo panels for Parisian *hôtels* (town houses).

rodent any mammal of the worldwide order Rodentia, making up nearly half of all mammal species. Besides ordinary "cheek teeth," they have a single front pair of incisor teeth in both upper and lower jaw, which continue to grow as they are worn down.

They are often subdivided into three suborders: Sciuromorpha, including primitive rodents, with squirrels as modern representatives; Myomorpha, rats and mice and their relatives; and Hystricomorpha, including the Old World and New World porcupines and guinea pigs.

They are often subdivided into three suborders: Sciuromorpha, including primitive rodents, with the squirrels as modern representatives; Caviomorpha, including all the South American rodents, of which the guinea pig is representative; and Myomorpha, rats and mice and their relatives.

rodeo originally a practical means of rounding up cattle in North America. It is now a professional sport in the US and Canada. Ranching skills such as bronco busting, bull riding, steer wrestling, and calf roping are all rodeo events. Because rodeo livestock is valuable, rules for its handling are laid out by the American Humane Association, yet criticism has been leveled at rodeos for cruel treatment of their animals.

Leading professionals earn in excess of $200,000 a season, and a world championship exists. One of the most widely known rodeo shows is the Calgary Stampede in Alberta. In Australia, amateur rodeos are held.

Rodgers Richard (Charles) 1902–1979. US composer. He collaborated with librettist Lorenz Hart (1895–1943) on songs such as "Blue Moon" 1934 and musicals such as *On Your Toes* 1936, and with Oscar Hammerstein II (1895–1960) wrote musicals such as *Oklahoma!* 1943, *South Pacific* 1949, *The King and I* 1951, and *The Sound of Music* 1959.

Rodin Auguste 1840–1917. French sculptor, often considered the greatest of his day. Through his work he freed sculpture from the idealizing conventions of the time by his realistic treatment of the human figure, introducing a new boldness of style and expression. Examples are *Le Penseur/The Thinker* 1880, *Le Baiser/The Kiss* 1886 (marble version in the Louvre, Paris), and *Les Bourgeois de Calais/The Burghers of Calais* 1884–86 (copy in Embankment Gardens, Westminster, London).

Rodin started as a mason, began to study in museums, and in 1875 visited Italy, where he was inspired by the work of Michelangelo. His early statue *Bronze Age* 1877 was criticized for its total naturalism and accuracy. In 1880 he began the monumental bronze *Gates of Hell* for the Ecole des Arts Décoratifs in Paris (inspired by Ghiberti's bronze gates in Florence), a project that occupied him for many years and was unfinished at his death. Many of the figures designed for the gate became independent sculptures. During the 1890s he received two notable commissions, for statues of the writers *Balzac* 1897 (Musée Rodin, Paris) and *Hugo*. He also produced many drawings.

Rodney George Brydges Rodney, Baron Rodney 1718–1792. British admiral. In 1762 he captured Martinique, St Lucia, and Grenada from the French. In 1780 he relieved Gibraltar by defeating a Spanish squadron off Cape St Vincent. In 1782 he crushed the French fleet under Count de Grasse off Dominica, for which he was raised to the peerage.

roebuck male of the Eurasian roe ⟡deer.

roentgen or *röntgen* unit (symbol R) of radiation exposure, used for X- and gamma rays. It is defined in terms of the number of ions produced in one cubic centimeter of air by the radiation. Exposure to 1,000 roentgens gives rise to an absorbed dose of about 870 rads (8.7 grays), which is a dose equivalent of 870 rems (8.7 sieverts).

Roethke Theodore 1908–1963. US poet. His father owned a large nursery business, and the greenhouses and plants of his childhood provide the detail and imagery for much of his lyrical, personal, and visionary poetry. Collections include *Open House* 1941, *The Lost Son* 1948, *The Waking* 1953 (Pulitzer Prize), and the posthumous *Collected Poems* 1968.

Roe v Wade US Supreme Court decision 1973 dealing with the constitutionality of state antiabortion laws. The case challenged a Texas statute prohibiting the abortion of pregnancies that did not threaten the mother's life. The Court struck down the Texas law, ruling that state prohibition of abortion is unconstitutional on two grounds: (1) women are guaranteed the right to privacy by the 14th Amendment, and (2) unborn fetuses are not persons with the right to equal protection of the law. The highly controversial ruling limited state regulation to the prohibition of third-trimester abortions.

Rogers Carl 1902–1987. US psychologist who developed the client-centered approach to counseling and psychotherapy. This stressed the importance of clients making their own decisions and developing their own potential (self-actualization).

He emphasized the value of genuine interest on the part of a therapist who is also accepting and empathetic. Rogers's views became widely employed.

Rogers Ginger. Adopted name of Virginia Katherine McMath 1911– . US actress, dancer, and singer. She worked from the 1930s to the 1950s, often starring with Fred Astaire in such films as *Top Hat* 1935 and *Swing Time* 1936. Her later work includes *Bachelor Mother* 1939 and *Kitty Foyle* 1940.

Rogers Roy. Adopted name of Leonard Slye 1912– . US actor who moved to Hollywood from radio. He was a singing cowboy of the 1930s and 1940s, one of the Sons of the Pioneers. His first Roy Rogers film was *Under*

Western Stars 1938, and he became "King of the Cowboys." He married his costar Dale Evans (who played in 20 of his films) in 1947. He played outside his own films in *Lake Placid Serenade* 1944, *Son of Paleface* 1952, *Alias Jesse James* 1959, and *Mackintosh and TJ* 1975.

Rogers Will (William Penn Adair) 1879–1935. US humorist. Born in Oologah Indian Territory (now Oklahoma), Rogers ended his formal education 1898 to work as a cowboy in Texas. He later traveled widely, performing in Wild West shows from 1902. In 1905 Rogers started his own vaudeville act of rope twirling and humorous banter. After beginning a Broadway career in 1915, which included Ziegfeld's Follies (1916–18, 1922, 1924–25), he moved to California to appear in motion pictures. From 1922 he wrote a humor column for *The New York Times*, and his wry comments on current affairs won him national popularity. Rogers was killed in a plane crash in Alaska with famed pilot Wiley Post.

Among his numerous books are *The Cowboy Philosopher on Prohibition* 1919 and *Ether and Me* 1929. *A Connecticut Yankee* 1931 and *State Fair* 1933 were two of his most popular films.

Roget Peter Mark 1779–1869. English physician, one of the founders of the University of London, and author of a *Thesaurus of English Words and Phrases* 1852, a text constantly revised and still in print, offering synonyms.

Röhm Ernst 1887–1934. German leader of the Nazi Brownshirts, the SA (⟡Sturmabteilung). On the pretext of an intended SA *Putsch* (uprising) by the Brownshirts, the Nazis had some hundred of them, including Röhm, killed June 29–30 , 1934. The event is known as the Night of the Long Knives.

Rohmer Eric. Adopted name of Jean-Marie Maurice Scherer 1920– . French film director and writer, formerly a critic and television-documentary director. Part of the French New Wave, his films are often concerned with the psychology of self-deception. They include *Ma Nuit chez Maud/My Night at Maud's* 1969, *Le Genou de Claire/Claire's Knee* 1970, and *Die Marquise von O/The Marquise of O* 1976.

Roh Tae-woo 1932– . South Korean right-wing politician and general. He held ministerial office from 1981 under President Chun, and became chair of the ruling Democratic Justice Party 1985. He was elected president 1987, amid allegations of fraud and despite being connected with the massacre of about 2,000 antigovernment demonstrators 1980.

Roland French hero whose real and legendary deeds of valor and chivalry inspired many medieval and later romances, including the 11th-century *Chanson de Roland* and Ariosto's *Orlando Furioso*. A knight of ⟡Charlemagne, Roland was killed in 778 with his friend Oliver and the 12 peers of France at Roncesvalles (in the Pyrenees) by Basques. He headed the rearguard during Charlemagne's retreat from his invasion of Spain.

Roland de la Platière Jeanne Manon (born Philipon) 1754–1793. French intellectual politician whose salon from 1789 was a focus of democratic discussion. Her ideas were influential after her husband Jean Marie Roland de la Platière (1734–1793) became minister of the interior 1792. As a supporter of the ⟡Girondin party, opposed to Robespierre and Danton, she was condemned to the guillotine 1793 without being allowed to speak in her own defense. While in prison she wrote *Mémoires*.

role in the social sciences, the part(s) a person plays in society, either in helping the social system to work or in fulfilling social responsibilities toward others. *Role play* refers to the way in which children learn adult roles by acting them out in play (mothers and fathers, cops and robbers). Everyone has a number of roles to play in a society: for example, a woman may be an employee, mother, and wife at the same time.

Sociologists distinguish between formal roles, such as those of a doctor or politician, and informal roles, such as those of mother or husband, which are based on personal relationships. Social roles involve mutual expectations: a doctor can fulfill that role only if the patients play their part; a father requires the support of his children. They also distinguish between ascribed roles (those we are born with) and achieved roles (those we attain).

Role conflict arises where two or more of a person's roles are seen as incompatible; for example, a woman who is a daughter to a sick mother and mother to a sick husband or child.

roller any brightly colored bird of the Old World family Coraciidae, resembling crows but in the same order as kingfishers and hornbills. Rollers grow up to 13 in/32 cm long. The name is derived from the habit of some species of rolling over in flight.

Rolling Stones, the British band formed 1962, once notorious as the "bad boys" of rock. Original members were Mick Jagger (1943–), Keith Richards (1943–), Brian Jones (1942–1969), Bill Wyman (1936–), Charlie Watts (1941–), and the pianist Ian Stewart (1938–1985). A rock-and-roll institution, the Rolling Stones were still performing and recording in the 1990s.

The Stones' earthy sound was based on rhythm and blues, and their rebel image was contrasted with the supposed wholesomeness of the early Beatles. Classic early hits include "Satisfaction" 1965 and "Jumpin' Jack Flash" 1968. The albums from *Beggar's Banquet* 1968 to *Exile on Main Street* 1972 have been rated among their best work; others include *Some Girls* 1978 and *Steel Wheels* 1989.

Rollins Sonny (Theodore Walter) 1930– . US tenor saxophonist and jazz composer. A leader of the hard-bop school, he is known for the intensity and bravado of his music and for his skillful improvisation.

Rollo First duke of Normandy *c.* 860–932. Viking leader. He left Norway about 875 and marauded, sailing up the Seine to Rouen. He besieged Paris 886, and in 912 was baptized and granted the province of Normandy by Charles III of France. He was its duke until his retirement to a monastery 927. He was an ancestor of William the Conqueror.

Rolls Charles Stewart 1877–1910. British engineer who joined with Henry ⟡Royce in 1905 to design and produce automobiles.

Rolls had trained as a mechanical engineer and worked in railroad production and as an automobile dealer before joining up with Royce. Before the business could flourish he died in a flying accident.

Rolls-Royce industrial company manufacturing automobiles and airplane engines, founded 1906 by Henry ⟡Royce and Charles Rolls. The Silver Ghost car model was designed 1906, and produced until 1925, when the Phantom was introduced. In 1914, Royce designed the Eagle aircraft engine, used extensively in World War I. Royce also designed the Merlin engine, used in Spitfires and Hurricanes in World War II. Jet engines followed, and became an important part of the company.

ROM (acronym for *read-only memory*) in computing, a memory device in the form of a collection of integrated circuits (chips), frequently used in microcomputers. ROM chips are loaded with data and programs during manufacture and, unlike ⟡RAM (random-access memory) chips, can subsequently only be read, not written to, by computer. However, the contents of the chips are not lost when the power is switched off, as happens in RAM.

ROM is used to form a computer's permanent store of vital information, or of programs that must be readily available but protected from accidental or deliberate change by a user. For example, a microcomputer ⟡operating system is often held in ROM memory.

Romagna area of Italy on the Adriatic coast, under papal rule 1278–1860 and now part of the region of ⟡Emilia-Romagna.

Romains Jules. Adopted name of Louis Farigoule 1885–1972. French novelist, playwright, and poet. His plays include the farce *Knock, ou le triomphe de la médecine/Dr Knock* 1923 and *Donogoo* 1930, and his novels include *Mort de quelqu'un/Death of a Nobody* 1911, *Les Copains/The Boys in the Back Room* 1913, and *Les Hommes de bonne volonté/Men of Good Will* (27 volumes) 1932–47.

Roman art sculpture and painting of ancient Rome, from the 4th century BC to the fall of the empire. Much Roman art was intended for public education, notably the sculpted triumphal arches and giant columns, such as *Trajan's Column* AD 106–113, and portrait sculptures of soldiers, politicians, and emperors. Surviving mural paintings (in Pompeii, Rome, and Ostia) and mosaic decorations show Greek influence. Roman art was to prove a lasting inspiration in the West.

Realistic *portrait sculpture* was an original development by the Romans. A cult of heroes began and in public places official statues were erected of generals, rulers, and philosophers. The portrait bust developed as a new art form from about 75 BC; these were serious, factual portraits of men to whose wisdom and authority, the busts implied, their subject nations should reasonably submit. Strict realism in portraiture gave way to a certain amount of Greek-style idealization in the propaganda statues of the emperors, befitting their semidivine status.

Narrative relief sculpture also flourished in Rome, linked to the need to commemorate publicly the military victories of their heroes. These appeared on monumental altars, triumphal arches, and giant columns such as *Trajan's Column*, where his battles are recorded in relief like a cartoon strip winding its way around the column for about 655 ft/200 m. Gods and allegorical figures featured with Rome's heroes on narrative relief sculptures, such as those on Augustus's giant altar to peace, the *Ara Pacis* 13–9 BC.

Very little *Roman painting* has survived; much of what has is due to the volcanic eruption of Mount Vesuvius in AD 79 that buried the southern Italian towns of Pompeii and Herculaneum under ash, thus preserving the lively and impressionistic wall paintings that decorated the villas of an art-loving elite. Common motifs were illusion and still life. A type of interior decoration known as *Grotesque*, rediscovered in Rome during the Renaissance, combined swirling plant motifs, strange animals, and tiny fanciful scenes. Grotesque was much used in later decorative schemes to quote the Classical period.

The art of **mosaic** was found throughout the Roman Empire. It was introduced from Greece and used for floors as well as walls and vaults, in *trompe l'oeil* (illusionary) effects, geometric patterns, and scenes from daily life and mythology.

Roman Britain period in British history from the mid-1st century BC to the mid-4th century AD. England was rapidly Romanized, but north of York fewer remains of Roman civilization have been found. Roman towns include London, York, Chester, St Albans, Colchester, Lincoln, Gloucester, and Bath. The most enduring mark of the occupation was the system of military roads radiating from London.

Roman relations with Britain began with Caesar's invasions of 55 and 54 BC, but the actual conquest was not begun until AD 43. After several unsuccessful attempts to conquer Scotland the northern frontier was fixed at ◊Hadrian's Wall. During the 4th century Britain was raided by the Saxons, Picts, and Scots. The Roman armies were withdrawn 407 but there were partial reoccupations 417–c. 427 and c. 450.

Roman Catholicism one of the main divisions of the Christian religion, separate from the Eastern Orthodox Church from 1054, and headed by the pope. For history and beliefs, see ◊Christianity. Membership is about 585 million worldwide, concentrated in S Europe, Latin America, and the Philippines.

The Protestant churches separated from the Catholic with the Reformation in the 16th century, to which the Counter-Reformation was the Catholic response. An attempt to update Catholic doctrines in the late 19th century was condemned by Pope Pius X in 1907, and more recent moves have been rejected by John Paul II.

doctrine The focus of liturgical life is the Mass or Eucharist, and attendance is obligatory on Sundays and Feasts of Obligation such as Christmas or Easter. The Roman Catholic differs from the other Christian churches in that it acknowledges the supreme jurisdiction of the pope, infallible when he speaks *ex cathedra* ("from the throne"); in the doctrine of the Immaculate Conception (which states that the Virgin Mary, the mother of Jesus, was conceived without the original sin with which all other human beings are born); and in according a special place to the Virgin Mary.

organization Since the Second Vatican Council 1962–66, major changes have taken place. They include the use of vernacular or everyday language instead of Latin in the liturgy, and increased freedom among the religious and lay orders. The pope has an episcopal synod of 200 bishops elected by local hierarchies to collaborate in the government of the church. The priesthood is celibate and there is a strong emphasis on the monastic orders.

romance in literature, tales of love and adventure, in verse or prose, that became popular in France about 1200 and spread throughout Europe. There were Arthurian romances about the legendary King Arthur and his knights, and romances based on the adventures of Charlemagne and on Classical themes. In the 20th century the term "romantic novel" is often used disparagingly, to imply a contrast with a realist novel.

The term gradually came to mean any fiction

Romania

area 91,699 sq mi/237,500 sq km
capital Bucharest
cities Braşov, Timişoara, Cluj-Napoca, Iaşi; ports Galaţi, Constanta, Brăila
physical mountains surrounding a plateau, with river plains S and E
environment although sulfur-dioxide levels are low, only 20% of the country's rivers can provide drinkable water
features Carpathian Mountains, Transylvanian Alps; river Danube; Black Sea coast; mineral springs
head of state Ion Iliescu from 1989
head of government Theodor Stolojan from 1991
political system emergent democratic republic
political parties National Salvation Front (NSF), reform socialist; Civic Alliance (CA), right-of-center; Convention for Democracy, umbrella organization for right-of-center National Liberal Party (NLP) and ethnic-Hungarian Magyar Democratic Union (UDM)
exports petroleum products and oil field equipment, electrical goods, automobiles, cereals
currency leu
population (1990 est) 23,269,000 (Romanians 89%, Hungarians 7.9%, Germans 1.6%); growth rate 0.5% p.a.
life expectancy men 67, women 73 (1989)
languages Romanian (official), Hungarian, German
media television is state-run; there are an estimated 900 newspapers and magazines, but only the progovernment papers have adequate distribution and printing facilities
religion Romanian Orthodox 80%, Roman Catholic 6%
literacy 98% (1988)
GNP $151 bn (1988); $6,400 per head
chronology
1944 Pro-Nazi Antonescu government overthrown.
1945 Communist-dominated government appointed.
1947 Boundaries redrawn. King Michael abdicated and People's Republic proclaimed.
1949 New Soviet-style constitution adopted. Joined Comecon.
1952 Second new Soviet-style constitution.
1955 Romania joined Warsaw Pact.
1958 Soviet occupation forces removed.
1965 New constitution adopted.
1974 Ceauşescu created president.
1985–86 Winters of austerity and power cuts.
1987 Workers demonstrated against austerity program.
1988–89 Relations with Hungary deteriorated over "systematization program."
1989 Announcement that all foreign debt paid off. Razing of villages and building of monuments to Ceauşescu; Communist orthodoxy reaffirmed; demonstrations violently suppressed; massacre in Timisoara; army joined uprising; heavy fighting; bloody overthrow of Ceauşescu regime in "Christmas Revolution"; Ceauşescu and wife tried and executed; estimated 10,000 dead in civil warfare; power assumed by new military-dissident-reform communist National Salvation Front, headed by Ion Iliescu.
1990 Securitate replaced by new Romanian Intelligence Service (RIS); religious practices resumed; mounting strikes and protests against effects of market economy.
1991 April: treaty on cooperation and good neighborliness signed with USSR. Aug: privatization law passed. Sept: prime minister Petre Roman resigned following riots, succeeded by Theodor Stolojan heading a new cross-party coalition government. Dec: new constitution endorsed by referendum.
1992 President Iliescu reelected in presidential runoff.

remote from the conditions and concerns of everyday life. In this sense, romance is a broad term which can include or overlap with such genres as the ◊historical novel or ◊fantasy fiction.

Romance languages branch of Indo-European languages descended from the Latin of the Roman Empire ("popular" or "vulgar" as opposed to "Classical" Latin). The present-day Romance languages with national status are French, Italian, Portuguese, Romanian, and Spanish.

Romansch (or Rhaeto-Romanic) is a minority language of Switzerland and one of the four official languages of the country, while Catalan and Gallego (or Galician) in Spain, Provençal in France, and Friulian and Sardinian in Italy are recognized as distinct languages with strong regional and/or literary traditions of their own.

Roman Empire from 27 BC to the 5th century AD; see ◊Rome, ancient.

Romanesque style of W European ◊architecture of the 8th to 12th centuries, marked by rounded arches, solid volumes, and emphasis on perpendicular elements. In England the style is known as Norman architecture.

Romanesque art a style of ◊medieval art.

Romania country in SE Europe, bounded N and E by Ukraine, E by Moldova, SE by the Black Sea, S by Bulgaria, SW by Yugoslavia, and NW by Hungary.

government Under the 1991 constitution, Romania has a two-chamber legislature, comprising a 260-member lower chamber, the Chamber of Deputies, in which additional seats are set aside for minorities, and a 130-member upper chamber, the Senate. Both are elected for four-year terms by means of proportional representation in multiparty contests. An executive president, who appoints the prime minister, is directly elected for a four-year term in a two-round majority contest.

history The earliest known inhabitants merged with invaders from ◊Thrace. Ancient Rome made it the province of Dacia; the poet Ovid was one of the settlers, and the people and language were Romanized. After the withdrawal of the Romans AD 275, Romania was occupied by ⟳Goths, and during the 6th–12th centuries was overrun by ⟳Huns, Bulgars, ⟳Slavs, and other invaders. The principalities of Wallachia in the south, and Moldavia in the east, dating from the 14th century, fell to the ⟳Ottoman Empire in the 15th and 16th centuries.

Turkish rule was exchanged for Russian protection 1829–56. In 1859 Moldavia and Wallachia elected Prince Alexander Cuza, under whom they were united as Romania from 1861. He was deposed 1866 and Prince Charles of ⟳Hohenzollern-Sigmaringen elected. After the Russo-Turkish war 1877–78, in which Romania sided with Russia, the great powers recognized Romania's independence, and in 1881 Prince Charles became King Carol I.

after independence Romania fought against Bulgaria in the Second ⟳Balkan War 1913 and annexed S ⟳Dobruja. It entered World War I on the Allied side 1916, was occupied by the Germans 1917–18, but received Bessarabia from Russia and ⟳Bukovina and ⟳Transylvania from the dismembered Hapsburg empire under the 1918 peace settlement, thus emerging as the largest state in the Balkans. During the late 1930s, to counter the growing popularity of the fascist ⟳Iron Guard movement, ⟳Carol II abolished the democratic constitution of 1923 and established his own dictatorship.

World War II In 1940 he was forced to surrender Bessarabia and N Bukovina to the USSR, N Transylvania to Hungary, and S Dobruja to Bulgaria, and abdicated when Romania was occupied by Germany in Aug. Power was assumed by Ion Antonescu (1882–1946, ruling in the name of Carol's son King ⟳Michael), who signed the ⟳Axis Pact Nov 1940 and declared war on the USSR June 1941. In Aug 1944, with the Red Army on Romania's borders, King Michael supported the ousting of the Antonescu government by a coalition of left and center parties, including the Communists. Romania subsequently joined the war against Germany and in the Paris peace treaties 1947 recovered Transylvania but lost Bessarabia and N Bukovina to the USSR (they were included in Moldavia and the Ukraine) and S Dobruja to Bulgaria.

republic In the elections 1946 a Communist-led coalition achieved a majority and proceeded to force King Michael to abdicate. The new Romanian People's Republic was proclaimed Dec 1947 and dominated by the Romanian Communist Party, then termed the Romanian Workers' Party (RWP). Soviet-style constitutions were adopted 1948 and 1952; Romania joined ⟳Comecon 1949 and co-signed the ⟳Warsaw Pact 1955; and a program of nationalization and agricultural collectivization was launched. After a rapid purge of opposition leaders, the RWP became firmly established in power, enabling Soviet occupation forces to leave the country 1958.

Ceauşescu era The dominant political personality 1945–65 was RWP leader and state president Gheorghe ⟳Gheorghiu-Dej. He was succeeded by Nicolae ⟳Ceauşescu, who placed greater emphasis on national autonomy and proclaimed Romania a socialist republic. Under Ceauşescu, Romania adopted a foreign-policy line independent of the USSR, condemned the 1968 invasion of Czechoslovakia, and refused to participate directly in Warsaw Pact maneuvers or allow Russian troops to enter the country. Ceauşescu called for multilateral nuclear disarmament and the creation of a Balkan nuclear-weapons-

free zone and maintained warm relations with China. He was created president 1974.

austerity programme At home, the secret police (Securitate) maintained a tight Stalinist rein on dissident activities, while a Ceauşescu personality cult was propagated, with almost 40 members of the president's extended family, including his wife Elena and son Nicu, occupying senior party and state positions. Economic difficulties mounted as Ceauşescu, pledging himself to repay the country's accumulated foreign debt (achieved 1989), embarked on an austerity program. This led to food shortages and widespread power cuts in the winters from 1985 onwards; the army occupied power plants and brutally crushed workers' demonstrations in ⟳Braşov 1987.

"systematization plan" After a referendum 1986, military spending was cut by 5%. Ceauşescu was reelected general secretary of the Romanian Communist Party (RCP) and state president 1984–85 and again 1989. From 1985 he refused to follow the ⟳Gorbachev path of political and economic reform, even calling in the spring of 1989 for Warsaw Pact nations to intervene to prevent the opposition Solidarity movement from assuming power in Poland. The country's relations with neighboring Hungary also reached crisis point 1988–89 as a result of a Ceauşescu "systematization plan" to demolish 7,000 villages and replace them with 500 agro-industrial complexes, in the process forcibly resettling and assimilating Transylvania-based ethnic Hungarians.

overthrow of Ceauşescu The unexpected overthrow of the Ceauşescu regime began Dec 1989. It was sparked off by the government's plans to exile a dissident Protestant pastor, László Tökes (1952–), to a remote village. Ethnic Hungarians and Romanians joined forces in the city of Timişoara to form an anti-Ceauşescu protest movement. Hundreds of demonstrators were killed in the state's subsequent crackdown on Dec 17. Four days later, an officially sponsored rally in Bucharest backfired when the crowd chanted anti-Ceauşescu slogans. Divisions between the military and Securitate rapidly emerged and on Dec 22 the army Chief of Staff, General Stefan Gusa, turned against the president and called on his soldiers to "defend the uprising." Ceauşescu attempted to flee, but was caught and summarily tried and executed on Christmas Day.

National Salvation Front Battles between Ceauşescu-loyal Securitate members and the army ensued in Bucharest, with several thousand being killed, but the army seizing the upper hand. A National Salvation Front was established, embracing former dissident intellectuals, reform communists, and military leaders. At its head was Ion Iliescu, a Moscow-trained communist, while Petre Roman (1947–), an engineer without political experience, was appointed prime minister. The Front's council proceeded to relegalize the formation of alternative political parties and draft a new constitution. Faced with grave economic problems, it initiated a ban on the export of foodstuffs, the abandonment of Ceauşescu's "systematization program," the dissolution of the Securitate, the abolition of the RCP's leading role, and the relegalization of small-plot farming and abortion (all contraception had been banned by Ceauşescu).

market economy In April 1990 a new Romanian Intelligence Service, accountable to parliament, was set up to replace the disbanded Securitate. The government legalized the Eastern Orthodox Church and the

Vatican reestablished diplomatic relations. In May 1990 Ion Iliescu won the country's first free elections since World War II. However, his victory heightened tension between Romanians and the Hungarian ethnic minority in Transylvania. Moving toward a legal market economy, the government cut subsidies, the leu was devalued, and prices allowed to float. Industrial exports slumped and strikes and protests increased until the government agreed to postpone its price-liberalization program. Refugees continued to leave the country and there were demonstrations against the government during Dec 1990 and Jan 1991, especially in Timişoara and Bucharest.

The second stage of price liberalization commenced April 1991, despite labor-union protests against the sharply rising cost of living and level of unemployment (over one million). At the same time the leu was devalued by 72% to meet the loan conditions set by the IMF and as a step toward internal convertibility by 1992. In the same month a new treaty on cooperation and good-neighborliness was signed with the USSR, which obliged the two states "not to take part in any type of alliance directed against either of them."

In Aug 1991 President Iliescu signed a law to allow for the privatization of all state enterprises except utilities. In Nov 1991 the leu was made internally convertible. Prices rose 400% during 1991 and hundreds of thousands were on short-time work. GNP fell during 1991 to 12%.

In late Sept 1991 prime minister Petre Roman resigned after three days of riots in Bucharest by thousands of striking miners, protesting against soaring prices and a fall in their living standards. Theodor Stolojan, the finance minister and a proponent of accelerated price liberalization, was appointed prime minister and he formed a new, cross-party, coalition government in Oct 1991. He promised to remain politically neutral and vowed not to run in the 1992 elections.

new constitution A national referendum Dec 1991 overwhelmingly endorsed a new constitution which guaranteed pluralism, human rights, and a free market. This cleared the path for a general election in 1992, which Iliescu won in a presidential runoff in Oct despite more than 3 million votes being declared invalid. *See illustration box.*

Romanian person of Romanian culture from Romania, Yugoslavia, Moldova, and the surrounding area. There are 20–25 million speakers of the Romanian language.

Historically the Romanians were known as Vlachs (German: "foreigner"). The religion of the Romanians is predominantly Romanian Orthodox, though there is a Greek Orthodox minority.

Romanian language member of the Romance branch of the Indo-European language family, spoken in Romania, Macedonia, Albania, and parts of N Greece. It has been strongly influenced by the Slavonic languages and by Greek. The Cyrillic alphabet was used until the 19th century, when a variant of the Roman alphabet was adopted.

Roman law legal system of ancient Rome that is now the basis of ⟳civil law, one of the main European legal systems.

It originated under the republic, was developed under the empire, and continued in use in the Byzantine Empire until 1453. The first codification was that of the 12 Tables (450 BC), of which only fragments survive. Roman law assumed its final form in the codification of Justinian AD 528–34. An outstanding feature of Roman law was its system of international law (*jus gentium*), applied in disputes between Romans and foreigners or provincials, or between provincials of different states.

Roman numerals ancient European number system using symbols different from Arabic numerals (the ordinary numbers 1, 2, 3, 4, 5, and so on). The seven key symbols in Roman numerals, as represented today, are I (1), V (5), X (10), L (50), C (100), D (500) and M (1,000). There is no zero, and therefore no place-value as is fundamental to the Arabic system. The first ten Roman numerals are I, II, III, IV (or IIII), V, VI, VII, VIII, IX, and X. When a Roman symbol is preceded by a symbol of equal or greater value, the values of the symbols are added (XVI = 16). When a symbol is preceded by a symbol of less value, the values are subtracted (XL = 40). A horizontal bar over a symbol indicates a multiple of 1,000 ($\bar{X}$ = 10,000). Although addition and subtraction are fairly straightforward using Roman numerals, the absence of a zero makes other arithmetic calculations (such as multiplication) clumsy and difficult.

Although their role in mathematics is long obsolete, Roman numerals continue to enjoy a limited use as inscribed figures (for example, on timepiece faces, in the pagination of some written material, or as dates on buildings or motion pictures).

Romano Giulio. See ▷Giulio Romano, Italian painter and architect.

Romanov dynasty rulers of Russia from 1613 to the ▷Russian Revolution 1917. Under the Romanovs, Russia developed into an absolutist empire.

The first tsar was Michael; his most famous successors were ▷Peter the Great, ▷Catherine the Great, ▷Alexander I, ▷Nicholas I, and Alexander II. See also Russia: history.

Roman religion religious system that retained early elements of animism (with reverence for stones and trees) and totemism (see ▷Romulus and Remus), and had a strong domestic base in the *lares* and *penates*, the cult of Janus and Vesta. It also had a main pantheon of gods derivative from the Greek one, which included Jupiter and Juno, Mars and Venus, Minerva, Diana, Ceres, and many lesser deities.

The deification of dead emperors served a political purpose and also retained the idea of family—that is, that those who had served the national family in life continued to care, as did one's ancestors, after their death. By the time of the empire, the educated classes tended toward Stoicism or Skepticism, but the following of mystery cults, especially within the army (see ▷Isis and Mithraism under ▷Mithras), proved a strong rival to early Christianity.

Romansch member of the Romance branch of the Indo-European language family, spoken by some 50,000 people in the eastern cantons of Switzerland. It was accorded official status 1937 alongside French, German, and Italian. It is also known among scholars as Rhaeto-Romanic.

Romanticism in literature, music, and art, a style that emphasizes the imagination, emotions, and creativity of the individual artist. The term is often used to characterize the culture of 19th-century Europe, as contrasted with 18th-century ▷Classicism.

Inspired by social change and revolution (US, French) and reacting against the Classical restraint of the Augustan age and the ▷Enlightenment, the Romantics asserted the importance of how the individual feels about the world, natural and supernatural. The French painter Delacroix is often cited as the quintessential Romantic artist. Many of the later Romantics were strong nationalists, for example Pushkin, Wagner, Verdi, Chopin.

In art, nostalgia for an imagined idyllic past and reverence for natural beauty were constant themes, inspiring paintings of grandiose landscapes, atmospheric ruins, historical scenes, portraits of legendary heroes, and so forth. Caspar David Friedrich in Germany and J M W Turner in England were outstanding landscape painters, while Henry Fuseli and William Blake represent a mystical and fantastic trend. The Romantic mood ranged from profound despair to dashing bravado.

Romanticism in music, term that generally refers to a preoccupation with the expression of emotion and with nature and folk history as a source of inspiration. Often linked with nationalistic feelings, the Romantic movement reached its height in the late 19th century, as in the works of Schumann and Wagner.

Romany a nomadic Caucasoid people, also called ▷Gypsy (a corruption of "Egyptian," since they were erroneously thought to come from Egypt). They are now believed to have originated in NW India, and live throughout the world. The Romany language (spoken in different dialects in every country where Gypsies live) is a member of the Indo-European family. In the 14th century they settled in the Balkan peninsula, spread over Germany, Italy, and France, and arrived in England about 1500. During World War II, Nazi Germany tried to exterminate them, along with Jews, Slavs, and political prisoners (see ▷concentration camp).

Rome city in central New York, on the Mohawk river, NW of Albany. Industries include copper and brass products, paint, and household appliances; population (1990) 44,400. Construction of the Erie Canal began here 1817.

Rome (Italian **Roma**) capital of Italy and of Lazio region, on the River Tiber, 17 mi/27 km from the Tyrrhenian Sea; population (1987) 2,817,000. Rome has few industries but is an important cultural, road, and rail center. A large section of the population finds employment in government offices. Remains of the ancient city include the Forum, Colosseum, and Pantheon. *history* (For early history see ▷Rome, ancient.) After the deposition of the last emperor, Romulus Augustulus, 476, the papacy became the real ruler of Rome and from the 8th century was recognized as such. As a result of the French Revolution, Rome temporarily became a republic 1798–99, and was annexed to the French Empire 1808–14, until the pope returned on Napoleon's fall. During the 1848–49 revolution, a republic was established under Mazzini's leadership, but, in spite of Garibaldi's defense, was overthrown by French troops. In 1870 Rome became the capital of Italy, the pope retiring into the Vatican until 1929 when the Vatican City was recognized as a sovereign state. The occupation of Rome by the Fascists 1922 marked the beginning of Mussolini's rule, but in 1943 Rome was occupied by Germany and then captured by the Allies 1944.

features E of the river are the seven hills on which Rome was originally built (Quirinal, Aventine, Caelian, Esquiline, Viminal, Palatine, and Capitol); to the W are the popular quarter of Trastevere, the more modern residential quarters of the Prati, and the Vatican. Among Rome's buildings are Castel Sant' Angelo (the mausoleum of the emperor Hadrian) and baths of Caracalla. Among the Renaissance palaces are the Lateran, Quirinal (with the Trevi fountain nearby), Colonna, Borghese, Barberini, and Farnese. There are a number of churches of different periods; San Paolo was founded by the emperor Constantine on St Paul's grave. The house where the English poet Keats died is near the Piazza di Spagna, known for the Spanish Steps.

Rome, ancient civilization based in Rome, which lasted for about 800 years. Traditionally founded 753 BC, Rome became a republic 510 BC. From then, its history is one of almost continual expansion until the murder of Julius ▷Caesar and foundation of the empire under ▷Augustus and his successors. At its peak under ▷Trajan, the Roman Empire stretched from Britain to Mesopotamia and the Caspian Sea. A long train of emperors ruling by virtue of military, rather than civil, power marked the beginning of Rome's long decline; under ▷Diocletian, the empire was divided into two parts—East and West—although temporarily reunited under ▷Constantine, the first emperor formally to adopt Christianity. The end of the Roman Empire is generally dated by the sack of Rome by the Goths AD 410, or by the deposition of the last emperor in the west AD 476. The Eastern Empire continued until 1453 at ▷Constantinople.

The civilization of ancient Rome occupied first the Italian peninsula, then most of Europe, the Middle East, and North Africa. It influenced the whole of western Europe throughout the Middle Ages, the Renaissance, and beyond, in the fields of art and architecture, literature, law, and engineering, and through continued use by scholars of its language, ▷Latin.

735 BC According to tradition Rome was founded.

510 The Etruscan dynasty of the Tarquins was expelled, and a republic was established, governed by two consuls, elected annually by the popular assembly, and a council of elders or Senate. The concentration of power in the hands of the aristocracy aroused the opposition of the plebeian masses.

390 Rome sacked by the Gauls.

367 The plebeians secured the right to elect tribunes, the codification of the laws, and the right to marry patricians; it was enacted that one consul must be a plebeian.

338 The cities of Latium formed into a league under Roman control.

343–290 The Etruscans to the north and the Samnites to the southeast were subdued during the 5th–4th centuries.

280–272 The Greek cities of the south were conquered.

264–241 First Punic War, ending in a Roman victory and the annexation of Sicily.

238 Sardinia was seized from Carthage and became a Roman province.

226–222 Roman conquest of Cisalpine Gaul (Lombardy); conflict with Carthage, which was attempting to conquer Sicily.

218 Hannibal invaded Italy and won a brilliant series of victories.

202 Victory over Hannibal at Zama, followed by its conversion into a Roman province.

146 After a revolt, Greece became in effect a Roman province. In the same year Carthage was annexed. On the death of the king of

Pergamum, Rome succeeded to his kingdom in Asia Minor.

133 Tiberius Gracchus put forward proposals for agrarian reforms and was murdered by the senatorial party.

123 Tiberius' policy was taken up by his brother Gaius Gracchus, who was likewise murdered.

109–106 The leadership of the democrats passed to Marius.

91–88 Social War: a revolt of the Italian cities compelled Rome to grant citizenship to all Italians.

87–84 While Sulla was repelling an invasion of Greece by Mithridates, Marius seized power.

82 On his return Sulla established a dictatorship and ruled by terror.

70 His changes were reversed by Pompey and Crassus.

66–62 Defeat of Mithridates and annexation of Syria and the rest of Asia Minor.

60 Pompey formed an alliance with the democratic leaders Crassus and Caesar.

51 Gaul conquered by Caesar as far as the Rhine.

49 Caesar's return to Italy (crossing the ⟩Rubicon) led to civil war between Caesar and Pompey.

48 Defeat of Pompey at Pharsalus.

44 Caesar's dictatorship ended by his assassination.

32 The empire divided between Caesar's nephew Octavian in the west and Antony in the east; war between them.

31 Defeat of Antony at ⟩Actium.

30 With the deaths of Antony and Cleopatra, Egypt was annexed.

27 Octavian took the name Augustus; he was by now absolute ruler, although in title only *princeps (first citizen)*.

AD 43 Augustus made the Rhine and the Danube the frontiers of the empire; Claudius added Britain.

96–180 Under the Flavian emperors Nerva, Trajan, Hadrian, Antoninus Pius, and Marcus Aurelius Antoninus the empire enjoyed a golden age.

115 Trajan conquered Macedonia; peak of Roman territorial expansion.

180 Death of Marcus Aurelius Antoninus was followed by a century of war and disorder; a succession of generals was placed on the throne by their armies.

284–305 Diocletian reorganized the empire as a centralized autocracy.

324–337 Constantine I realized the political value of Christianity and became a convert.

364 Constantine removed the capital to Constantinople, and the empire was divided.

410 The Goths overran Greece and Italy, sacked Rome, and finally settled in Spain. The Vandals conquered Italy.

451–452 The Huns raided Gaul and Italy.

476 The last Western emperor was deposed.

Romeo and Juliet romantic tragedy by William Shakespeare, first performed 1594–95. The play is concerned with the doomed love of teenagers Romeo and Juliet, victims of the bitter enmity between their respective families in Verona.

Rome, Sack of AD 410. The invasion and capture of the city of Rome by the Goths, generally accepted as marking the effective end of the Roman Empire.

Rome, Treaties of two international agreements signed March 25, 1957 by Belgium,

France, West Germany, Italy, Luxembourg, and the Netherlands, which established the European Economic Community (⟩European Community) and the European Atomic Energy Commission (EURATOM).

The terms of the economic treaty, which came into effect Jan 1, 1958, provided for economic cooperation, reduction (and eventual removal) of customs barriers, and the free movement of capital, goods, and labor between the member countries, together with common agricultural and trading policies. Subsequent new members of the European Community have been obliged to accept these terms.

Rommel Erwin 1891–1944. German field marshal. He served in World War I, and in World War II he played an important part in the invasions of central Europe and France. He was commander of the N African offensive from 1941 (when he was nicknamed "Desert Fox") until defeated in the Battles of El ⟩Alamein.

Rommel was commander in chief for a short time against the Allies in Europe 1944 but (as a sympathizer with the ⟩Stauffenberg plot against Hitler) was forced to commit suicide.

Romney George 1734–1802. English portrait painter, active in London from 1762. He became, with Gainsborough and Reynolds, one of the most successful portrait painters of the late 18th century. He painted several portraits of Lady Hamilton, Admiral Nelson's mistress.

Romulus in Roman mythology, legendary founder and first king of Rome, the son of Mars and Rhea Silvia, daughter of Numitor, king of Alba Longa. Romulus and his twin brother Remus were thrown into the Tiber by their great-uncle Amulius, who had deposed Numitor, but were suckled by a she-wolf and rescued by a shepherd. On reaching adulthood they killed Amulius and founded Rome.

Having murdered Remus, Romulus reigned alone until he disappeared in a storm; he was thereafter worshiped as a god under the name of Quirinus.

Romulus Augustulus born *c.* AD 461. Last Roman emperor in the West. He was made emperor by his father Orestes, a soldier, about 475 but was compelled to abdicate 476 by Odoacer, leader of the barbarian mercenaries, who nicknamed him Augustulus. Orestes was executed and Romulus Augustulus confined to a Neapolitan villa.

Roncesvalles village of N Spain, in the Pyrenees 5 mi/8 km S of the French border, the scene of the defeat of the rearguard of Charlemagne's army under ⟩Roland, who with the 12 peers of France was killed 778.

rondo form of instrumental music in which the principal section returns like a refrain. Rondo form is often used for the last movement of a sonata or concerto.

Rondônia state in NW Brazil; the center of Amazonian tin and gold mining and of experiments in agricultural colonization; area 93,876 sq mi/243,044 sq km; population (1991) 1,373,700. Known as the Federal Territory of *Guaporé* until 1956, it became a state 1981.

Ronsard Pierre de 1524–1585. French poet, leader of the ⟩Pléiade group of poets. Under the patronage of Charles IX, he published original verse in a lightly sensitive style, including odes and love sonnets, such as *Odes* 1550, *Les Amours/Lovers* 1552–53, and the "Marie" cycle, *Continuation des amours/Lovers Continued* 1555–56.

röntgen alternate spelling for ⟩roentgen, unit of X- and gamma-ray exposure.

Röntgen (or **Roentgen**) Wilhelm Konrad 1845–1923. German physicist who discovered X-rays 1895. While investigating the passage of electricity through gases, he noticed the ⟩fluorescence of a barium platinocyanide screen. This radiation passed through some substances opaque to light, and affected photographic plates. Developments from this discovery have revolutionized medical diagnosis.

He received a Nobel Prize 1901. The unit of electromagnetic radiation (X-ray) is named roentgen or röntgen (r) after him.

rood alternate name for the cross of Christ, often applied to the large crucifix placed on a beam or screen at the entrance to the chancel of a church.

rook gregarious European ⟩crow *Corvus frugilegus*. The plumage is black and lustrous and the face bare; a rook can grow to 18 in/ 45 cm long. Rooks nest in colonies at the tops of trees.

Roosevelt (Anna) Eleanor 1884–1962. US social worker, lecturer and First Lady; her newspaper column "My Day" was widely syndicated. She was a delegate to the UN general assembly and chair of the UN commission on human rights 1946–51. She helped to draw up the Declaration of Human Rights at the UN 1945. Within the Democratic Party she formed the left-wing Americans for Democratic Action group 1947. She was married to President Franklin Roosevelt.

The niece of Theodore ⟩Roosevelt, she was educated in Europe. Following her husband's death 1945, she continued to work on civil rights for US blacks and for human rights worldwide.

Roosevelt Franklin D(elano) 1882–1945. 32nd president of the US 1933–45, a Democrat. He served as governor of New York 1929–33. Becoming president during the ⟩Depression, he launched the ⟩*New Deal* economic and social reform program, which made him popular with the people. After the outbreak of World War II he introduced ⟩lend-lease for the supply of war materials and services to the Allies and drew up the ⟩Atlantic Charter of solidarity. Once the US had entered the war 1941, he spent much time in meetings with Allied leaders (see ⟩Québec, ⟩Tehran, and ⟩Yalta conferences).

Born in Hyde Park, New York, of a wealthy family, Roosevelt was educated in Europe and at Harvard and Columbia universities, and became a lawyer. In 1910 he was elected to the New York state senate. He held the assistant secretaryship of the navy in Wilson's administrations 1913–21, and did much to increase the efficiency of the navy during World War I. He suffered from polio from 1921 but returned to politics, winning the governorship of New York State in 1929.

When he first became president 1933, Roosevelt inculcated a new spirit of hope by his skillful "fireside chats" on the radio and his inaugural-address statement: "The only thing we have to fear is fear itself." Surrounding himself by a "Brain Trust" of experts, he immediately launched his reform program. Banks were reopened, federal credit was restored, the gold standard was abandoned, and the dollar devalued. During the first hundred days of his administration, major legislation to facilitate industrial and agricultural recovery was enacted. In 1935 he introduced the Utilities Act, directed against abuses in the large holding companies, and the Social Security Act, providing for disability and retirement insurance. The presidential election 1936 was won entirely on the record of the New Deal. During 1935–36 Roosevelt was involved in a conflict over the composition of the Supreme Court, following its nullification of major New Deal measures as unconstitutional. In 1938 he introduced measures for farm relief and the improvement of working conditions.

In his foreign policy, Roosevelt endeavored to use his influence to restrain Axis aggression, and to establish "good neighbor" relations with other countries in the Americas. Soon after the outbreak of war, he launched a vast rearmament program, introduced conscription, and provided for the supply of armaments to the Allies on a "cash-and-carry" basis. In spite of strong isolationist opposition, he broke a longstanding precedent in running for a third term; he was reelected 1940. He announced that the US would become the "arsenal of democracy." Roosevelt was eager for US entry into the war on behalf of the Allies. In addition to his revulsion for Hitler, he wanted to establish the US as a world power, filling the vacuum he expected to be left by the breakup of the British Empire. He was restrained by isolationist forces in Congress, and some argued that he welcomed the Japanese attack on Pearl Harbor.

The slaughter at Pearl Harbor Dec 7, 1941 incited public opinion, and the US entered the war. From this point on, Roosevelt concerned himself solely with the conduct of the war. He participated in the Washington 1942 and Casablanca 1943 conferences to plan the Mediterranean assault, and the conferences in Québec, Cairo, and Tehran 1943, and Yalta 1945, at which the final preparations were made for the Allied victory. He was reelected for a fourth term 1944, but died 1945.

Roosevelt Theodore 1858–1919. 26th president of the US 1901–09, a Republican. After serving as governor of New York 1898–1900 he became vice-president to ◊McKinley, whom he succeeded as president on McKinley's assassination 1901. He campaigned against the great trusts (associations of enterprises that reduce competition), while carrying on a jingoist foreign policy designed to enforce US supremacy over Latin America.

Roosevelt, born in New York, was elected to the state legislature 1881. He was assistant secretary of the Navy 1897–98, and during the Spanish–American War 1898 commanded a volunteer force of "rough riders." At age 42, Roosevelt was the youngest person to become president of the US. (John F Kennedy was the youngest person to be *elected* president). In office he became more liberal. He tackled business monopolies, initiated measures for the conservation of national resources, and introduced the Pure Food and Drug Act. He won the Nobel Peace Prize 1906 for his part in ending the Russo-Japanese war. Alienated after his retirement by the conservatism of his successor Taft, Roosevelt formed the Progressive or "Bull Moose" Party. As their candidate he unsuccessfully ran for the presidency 1912. During World War I he strongly advocated US intervention.

root the part of a plant that is usually underground, and whose primary functions are anchorage and the absorption of water and dissolved mineral salts. Roots usually grow downward and toward water (that is, they are positively geotropic and hydrotropic; see ◊tropism). Plants such as epiphytic orchids, which grow above ground, produce aerial roots that absorb moisture from the atmosphere. Others, such as ivy, have climbing roots arising from the stems, which serve to attach the plant to trees and walls.

The absorptive area of roots is greatly increased by the numerous, slender root hairs formed near the tips. A calyptra, or root cap, protects the tip of the root from abrasion as it grows through the soil.

Symbiotic associations occur between the roots of certain plants, such as clover, and various bacteria that fix nitrogen from the air (see ◊nitrogen fixation). Other modifications of roots include ◊contractile roots, ◊pneumatophores, ◊taproots, and ◊prop roots.

root of an equation, a value that makes the equation true. For example, $x = 0$ and $x = 5$ are roots of the equation $x^2 - 5x = 0$.

root crop plant cultivated for its swollen edible root (which may or may not be a true root). Potatoes are the major temperate root crop; the major tropical root crops are cassava, yams, and sweet potatoes. Together they are second in importance only to cereals as human food. Roots have a high carbohydrate content, but their protein content rarely exceeds 2%. Consequently, communities relying almost exclusively upon roots may suffer from protein deficiency. Food production for a given area from roots is greater than from cereals.

In the mid-1980s, world production of potatoes, cassava, and yams was just under 600 million tonnes. Potatoes are the major temperate root crop; the major tropical root crops are cassava (a shrub that produces starchy tubers), yams, and sweet potatoes. Root crops are also used as animal feed, and may be processed to produce starch, glue, and alcohol. Sugar beet has largely replaced sugar cane as a source of sugar in Europe.

root hair tubular outgrowth from a cell on the surface of a plant root. It is a delicate structure, which survives for a few days only and does not develop into a root. New root hairs are continually being formed near the root tip to replace the ones that are lost. The majority of land plants possess root hairs, which greatly increase the surface area available for the absorption of water and mineral salts from the soil. The layer of the root's epidermis that produces root hairs is known as the *piliferous layer*.

root-mean-square (RMS) in mathematics, value obtained by taking the ◊square root of the mean of the squares of a set of values; for example the RMS value of four quantities a, b, c, and d is $\sqrt{[(a^2 + b^2 + c^2 + d^2)/4]}$.

For an alternating current (AC), the RMS value is equal to the peak value divided by the square root of 2.

roots music term originally denoting ◊reggae, later encompassing any music indigenous to a particular culture.

rope stout cordage with circumference over 1 in/2.5 cm. Rope is made similarly to thread or twine, by twisting yarns together to form strands, which are then in turn twisted around one another in the direction opposite to that of the yarns. Although ◊hemp is still used to make rope, nylon is increasingly used.

Roquefort a strong, blue-veined cheese made from sheep's milk and matured in damp mountain caves. It is named after the village of Roquefort-sur-Soulzon in Aveyron *département*, France. One of the oldest cheeses, it was known to the Romans.

rorqual any of a family (Balaenopteridae) of baleen whales, especially the genus *Balaenoptera*, which includes the blue whale *B. musculus*, the largest of all animals, measuring 100 ft/30 m and more. The common rorqual or fin whale *B. physalus* is slate-colored and not quite so long.

The sei whale *B. borealis*, the minke whale *B. acutorostrata*, Bryde's whale *B. edeni*, and the humpbacked whale *Megaptera novaeangliae* also belong to this family. All are long-bodied whales with pleated throats.

Rorschach test in psychology, method of diagnosis involving the use of inkblot patterns that subjects are asked to interpret, to help indicate personality type, degree of intelligence, and emotional stability. It was invented by the Swiss psychiatrist Hermann Rorschach (1884–1922).

Rosario industrial river port (sugar refining, meat packing, maté processing) in Argentina, 175 mi/280 km NW of Buenos Aires, on the river Paraná; population (1991) 1,078,400. It was founded 1725.

rosary string of beads used in a number of religions, including Buddhism, Christianity, and Islam. The term also refers to a form of prayer used by Catholics, consisting of 150 Ave Marias or Hail Marys and 15 Paternosters and Glorias, or to a string of 165 beads for keeping count of these prayers; it is linked with the adoration of the Virgin Mary.

ROSAT joint US/German/UK satellite launched 1990 to study cosmic sources of X-rays and extremely short ultraviolet wavelengths, named after Wilhelm Röntgen, the discoverer of X-rays.

Roscellinus Johannes *c.* 1050–*c.* 1122. Philosopher regarded as the founder of ◊scholasticism because of his defense of ◊nominalism (the idea that classes of things are simply names and have no objective reality) against ◊Anselm.

Roscommon (originally Ros-Comain, "wood around a monastery") county of the Republic of Ireland in the province of Connacht
area 950 sq mi/2,460 sq km
cities county town Roscommon
physical bounded on the E by the river Shannon; lakes: Gara, Key, Allen; rich pastures
features remains of a castle put up in the 13th century by English settlers
population (1991) 51,900.

rose any shrub or climber of the genus *Rosa*, family Rosaceae, with prickly stems and fragrant flowers in many different colors. Numerous cultivated forms have been derived from the Eurasian sweetbrier or eglantine *R. rubiginosa* and dogrose *R. canina*. There are many climbing varieties, but the forms more commonly cultivated are bush roses and standards (cultivated roses grafted on to a briar stem).

Roseau formerly **Charlotte Town** capital of ◊Dominica, West Indies; population (1981) 20,000.

Rosebery Archibald Philip Primrose, 5th Earl of Rosebery 1847–1929. British Liberal politician. He was foreign secretary 1886 and 1892–94, when he succeeded Gladstone as prime minister, but his government survived less than a year. After 1896 his imperialist views gradually placed him further from the mainstream of the Liberal Party.

rosemary evergreen shrub *Rosmarinus*

officinalis of the mint family Labiatae, native to the Mediterranean and W Asia, with small, scented leaves. It is widely cultivated as a culinary herb and for the aromatic oil extracted from the clusters of pale blue or purple flowers.

Rosenberg Alfred 1893–1946. German politician, born in Tallinn, Estonia. He became the chief Nazi ideologist and was minister for eastern occupied territories 1941–44. He was tried at ¢Nuremberg 1946 as a war criminal and hanged.

Rosenberg Julius 1918–53 and Ethel Greenglass 1915–53 US married couple, convicted of being leaders of a nuclear-espionage ring passing information from Ethel's brother via courier to the USSR. The Rosenbergs were executed after much public controversy and demonstration. They were the only Americans executed for espionage during peacetime.

Both were born in New York City; Julius owned a radio repair shop and was a member of the Communist Party. Despite an offer of clemency from the government, they both maintained their innocence right up to their executions. Other implicated Party members received long prison terms. The ¢Cold War atmosphere was one of widespread fear of the Soviet Union, and several major spy scandals had occurred at this time. The death penalty was ruled as justified because of the danger to the US from their actions. Recently published journals kept by ¢Khrushchev further implicate the Rosenbergs.

Roses, Wars of the civil wars in England 1455–85 between the houses of ¢Lancaster (badge, red rose) and ¢York (badge, white rose), both of whom claimed the throne through descent from the sons of Edward III. As a result of ¢Henry VI's lapse into insanity, Richard, Duke of York, was installed as protector of the realm. Upon his recovery, Henry forced York to take up arms in self-defense.

1455 Opened with battle of St Albans May 22, a Yorkist victory (¢Henry VI made prisoner).
1459–61 War renewed until ¢Edward IV, having become king, confirmed his position by a victory at Towton March 29, 1461.
1470 ¢Warwick (who had helped Edward to the throne) allied instead with Henry VI's queen, ¢Margaret of Anjou; Henry VI restored to the throne.
1471 Edward returned, defeated Warwick at Barnet April 14 and Margaret at Tewkesbury May 4, her son killed, and her forces destroyed. Henry VI was murdered in the Tower of London.
1485 Yorkist regime ended with the defeat of ¢Richard III by the future ¢Henry VII at ¢Bosworth Aug 22.

The name Wars of the Roses was given in the 19th century by novelist Walter Scott.

Rosetta Stone slab of basalt with inscriptions from 197 BC, found near the town of Rosetta, Egypt, 1799. Giving the same text in three versions—Greek, hieroglyphic, and demotic script—it became the key to deciphering other Egyptian inscriptions.

Discovered during the French Revolutionary Wars by one of Napoleon's officers in the town now called Rashid, in the Nile delta, the Rosetta Stone was captured by the British 1801, and placed in the British Museum 1802. Demotic is a cursive script (for quick writing) derived from Egyptian hieratic, which in turn is a more easily written form of hieroglyphic.

Rosh Hashanah two-day holiday that marks the start of the Jewish New Year (first new

moon after the autumn equinox), traditionally announced by blowing a ram's horn (a ¢shofar).

Rosicrucians group of early 17th-century philosophers who claimed occult powers and employed the terminology of ¢alchemy to expound their mystical doctrines (said to derive from ¢Paracelsus). The name comes from books published in 1614 and 1615, attributed to Christian Rosenkreutz ("rosy cross"), most probably an adopted name but allegedly a writer living around 1460. Several societies have been founded in Britain and the US that claim to be their successors, such as the Rosicrucian Fraternity (1614 in Germany, 1861 in the US).

Ross Betsy 1752–1836. American seamstress remembered as the maker of the first US flag. Despite little historical substantiation, it is believed by many that the familiar red and white stripes with white stars on a field of blue was Ross's original concept.

Born Elizabeth Griscom in Philadelphia to a devout Quaker family, she married upholsterer John Ross 1773. Upon his death 1776, she took over his business. According to popular legend, Ross was approached in June 1776 by family acquaintance George Washington to create an official flag for the new nation. Becoming famous after the war, she continued in the upholstery business until her retirement 1827.

Ross James Clark 1800–1862. English explorer who discovered the magnetic North Pole 1831. He also went to the Antarctic 1839; Ross Island, Ross Sea, and Ross Dependency are named after him.

Ross Ronald 1857–1932. British physician and bacteriologist, born in India. From 1881 to 1899 he served in the Indian medical service, and during 1895–98 identified mosquitoes of the genus *Anopheles* as being responsible for the spread of malaria. Nobel Prize 1902.

Ross Dependency all the Antarctic islands and territories between 160° E and 150° W longitude and S of 60° S latitude; it includes Edward VII Land, Ross Sea and its islands, and parts of Victoria Land.
area 173,700 sq mi/450,000 sq km
features the **Ross Ice Shelf** (or Ross Barrier), a permanent layer of ice across the Ross Sea about 1,400 ft/425 m thick
population a few scientific bases with about 250 staff members, 12 of whom are present during winter
history given to New Zealand 1923. It is probable that marine organisms beneath the ice shelf had been undisturbed from the Pleistocene period until drillings were made 1976.

Rossellini Roberto 1906–1977. Italian film director. His World War II trilogy, *Roma città aperta/Rome, Open City* 1945, *Paisà/Paisan* 1946, and *Germania anno zero/Germany Year Zero* 1947, reflects his humanism, and is considered a landmark of European cinema.

In 1949 he made *Stromboli*, followed by other films in which his wife Ingrid Bergman appeared. After their divorce he made *General della Rovere* 1959 and embarked on television work including a feature-length film for French TV, *La Prise de Pouvoir par Louis XIV/The Rise of Louis XIV* 1966.

Rossetti Christina (Georgina) 1830–1894. English poet, sister of Dante Gabriel Rossetti and a devout High Anglican (see ¢Oxford movement). Her verse includes *Goblin Market*

and Other Poems 1862 and expresses unfulfilled spiritual yearning and frustrated love. She was a skillful technician and made use of irregular rhyme and line length.

Rossetti Dante Gabriel 1828–1882. British painter and poet, a founding member of the ¢*Pre-Raphaelite Brotherhood* (PRB) in 1848. As well as romantic medieval scenes, he produced many idealized portraits of women. His verse includes "The Blessed Damozel" 1850. His sister was the poet Christina Rossetti.

Rossetti was a friend of the critic ¢Ruskin, who helped establish his reputation as a painter, and of William Morris and his wife Jane, who became Rosetti's lover and the subject of much of his work.

Rossini Gioacchino (Antonio) 1792–1868. Italian composer. His first success was the opera *Tancredi* 1813. In 1816 his "opera buffa" *Il barbiere di Siviglia/The Barber of Seville* was produced in Rome. During 1815–23 he produced 20 operas, and created (with ¢Donizetti and ¢Bellini) the 19th-century Italian operatic style.

After *Guillaume Tell/William Tell* 1829, Rossini gave up writing opera and his later years were spent in Bologna and Paris. Among the works of this period are the *Stabat Mater* 1842 and the piano music arranged for ballet by Respighi as *La Boutique fantasque/The Fantastic Toyshop* 1919.

Ross Island two islands in Antarctica:
Ross Island in Weddell Sea, discovered 1903 by the Swedish explorer Nordenskjöld, area about 1,500 sq mi/3,885 sq km;
Ross Island in Ross Sea, discovered 1841 by the British explorer James Ross, area about 2,500 sq mi/6,475 sq km, with the research stations Scott Base (New Zealand) and McMurdo (US). Mount Erebus (12,520 ft/3,794 m) is the world's southernmost active volcano; its lake of molten lava may provide a window on the ¢magma beneath the Earth's crust that fuels volcanoes.

Ross Sea Antarctic inlet of the S Pacific. See also ¢Ross Dependency and ¢Ross Island.

Rostand Edmond 1869–1918. French dramatist, who wrote *Cyrano de Bergerac* 1897 and *L'Aiglon* 1900 (based on the life of Napoleon III), in which Sarah Bernhardt played the leading role.

Rostock industrial port (electronics, fish processing, ship repair) in the state of Mecklenburg-West Pomerania, Germany, on the river Warnow 8 mi/13 km S of the Baltic; population (1990) 250,000.

Founded 1189, in the 14th century Rostock became a powerful member of the ¢Hanseatic League. It was rebuilt in the 1950s and was capital of an East German district of the same name 1952–90.

Rostov-on-Don industrial port (shipbuilding, tobacco, automobiles, locomotives, textiles) in SW Russia, capital of Rostov region, on the river Don, 14 mi/23 km E of the Sea of Azov; population (1987) 1,004,000. Rostov dates from 1761 and is linked by river and canal with Volgograd on the Volga.

Rostropovich Mstislav 1927– . Russian cellist and conductor, deprived of Soviet citizenship 1978 because of his sympathies with political dissidents. Prokofiev, Shostakovich, Khachaturian, and Britten wrote pieces for him. Since 1977 he has directed the National Symphony Orchestra, Washington, DC.

Rotary Club philanthropic society of business and professional people; founded by US lawyer Paul Harris (1878–1947) in Chicago 1905. It is now international, with some 750,000 members.

Roth Philip 1933– . US novelist whose portrayals of 20th-century Jewish-American life include *Goodbye Columbus* 1959 and *Portnoy's Complaint* 1969. Psychosexual themes are prominent in his work.

Roth's series of semiautobiographical novels about a writer, Nathan Zuckerman, includes *The Ghost Writer* 1979, *Zuckerman Unbound* 1981, *The Anatomy Lesson* 1984, and *The Counterlife* 1987. *Patrimony* 1991 concerned his father's death.

Rothko Mark 1903–1970. Russian-born US painter, an Abstract Expressionist and a pioneer of **Colour Field** painting (abstract, dominated by areas of unmodulated, strong color). Rothko produced several series of paintings in the 1950s and 1960s, including one at Harvard University; one in the Tate Gallery, London; and one for a chapel in Houston, Texas, 1967–69.

He received his only training at New York City's Art Students League. During the 1930s he painted for the Federal Arts Project and, with Adolph Gottlieb, founded the expressionist group The Ten.

After his suicide 1970, his estate, consisting primarily of a huge number of his paintings, became the subject of a long legal battle.

Rothschild European family active in the financial world for two centuries. *Mayer Anselm* (1744–1812) set up as a moneylender in Frankfurt-am-Main, Germany, and business houses were established throughout Europe by his ten children.

Nathan Mayer (1777–1836) settled in England, and his grandson *Nathaniel* (1840–1915) was created a baron in 1885. *Lionel Walter* (1868–1937) succeeded his father as 2nd Baron Rothschild and was an eminent naturalist. His daughter *Miriam* (1908–) is an entomologist, renowned for her studies of fleas. The 2nd baron's nephew, *Nathaniel* (1910–1990), 3rd Baron Rothschild, was a scientist. During World War II he worked in British military intelligence. He was head of the central policy-review staff in the Cabinet Office (the "think tank" set up by Edward Heath) 1970–74. Of the French branch, Baron *Eric de Rothschild* (1940–) owns Château Lafite and Baron *Philippe de Rothschild* (1902–) owns Château Mouton-Rothschild, both leading red Bordeaux-producing properties in Pauillac, SW France.

rotifer any of the tiny invertebrates, also called "wheel animalcules," of the phylum Rotifera. Mainly freshwater, some marine, rotifers have a ring of ⮡cilia that carries food to the mouth and also provides propulsion. They are the smallest of multicellular animals; few reach 0.02 in/0.05 cm.

Rotterdam industrial port (brewing, distilling, shipbuilding, sugar and petroleum refining, margarine, tobacco) in the Netherlands and one of the foremost ocean cargo ports in the world, in the Rhine-Maas delta, linked by canal 1866–90 with the North Sea; population (1991) 582,266.

Rotterdam dates from the 12th century or earlier, but the center was destroyed by German air attack 1940, and rebuilt; its notable art collections were saved. The philosopher Erasmus was born here.

Rottweiler breed of dog originally developed in Rottweil, Germany, as a herding and guard dog, and subsequently used as a police dog. Powerfully built, the dog is about 25–27 in/63–66 cm high at the shoulder, black with tan markings, a short coat and docked tail.

Rouault Georges 1871–1958. French painter, etcher, illustrator, and designer. Early in his career he was associated with the ⮡Fauves but created his own style using heavy, dark colors and bold brushwork. His subjects included sad clowns, prostitutes, and evil lawyers; from about 1940 he painted mainly religious works.

Rouen industrial port (cotton textiles, electronics, distilling, oil refining) on the river Seine, in Seine-Maritime *département*, central N France; population (1988) 102,000.

history Rouen was capital of ⮡Normandy from 912. Lost by King ⮡John 1204, it returned briefly to English possession 1419–49; Joan of Arc was burned in the square 1431. The novelist Flaubert was born here, and the hospital where his father was chief surgeon is now a Flaubert museum.

Rouget de Lisle Claude-Joseph 1760–1836. French army officer who composed, while in Strasbourg 1792, the "Marseillaise," the French national anthem.

roughage alternative term for dietary ⮡fiber, material of plant origin that cannot be digested by enzymes normally present in the human ⮡gut.

roulette game of chance in which the players bet on a ball landing in the correct segment (numbered 0–36 and alternately colored red and black) on a rotating wheel.

Bets can be made on a single number, double numbers, 3, 4, 6, 8, 12, or 24 numbers. Naturally the odds are reduced the more numbers are selected. Bets can also be made on the number being odd or even, between 1 and 18 or 19 and 36, or being red or black; the odds are even in each of those cases. The advantage is with the banker, however, because the 0 (zero) gives all stakes to the bank unless a player bets on 0. The play is under the control of a croupier.

Roundhead member of the Parliamentary party during the English Civil War 1640–60, opposing the royalist Cavaliers. The term referred to the short hair then worn only by men of the lower classes.

Rousseau Henri "Le Douanier" 1844–1910. French painter, a self-taught naive artist. His subjects included scenes of the Parisian suburbs and exotic junglescapes, painted with painstaking detail; for example, *Surprised! Tropical Storm with a Tiger* 1891 (National Gallery, London).

Rousseau served in the army for some years, then became a toll collector (hence *Le Douanier*, "the customs official"), and finally took up full-time painting in 1885. He exhibited at the Salon des Indépendants from 1886 to 1910 and was associated with the group led by Picasso and the poet Apollinaire, but his position was unique. As a naive and pompous person, he was considered ridiculous, yet admired for his inimitable style.

Rousseau Jean-Jacques 1712–1778. French social philosopher and writer whose *Du Contrat social/Social Contract* 1762, emphasizing the rights of the people over those of the government, was a significant influence on the French Revolution. In the novel *Emile* 1762 he outlined a new theory of education.

Rousseau was born in Geneva, Switzerland. *Discourses on the Origins of Inequality* 1754 made his name: he denounced civilized society and postulated the paradox of the superiority of the "⮡noble savage." *Social Contract* stated that a government could be legitimately overthrown if it failed to express the general will of the people. *Emile* was written as an example of how to elicit the unspoiled nature and abilities of children, based on natural development and the power of example.

Rousseau's ideas were condemned by philosophers, the clergy, and the public, and he lived in exile in England for a year, being helped by Scottish philosopher David Hume until they fell out. He was a contributor to the *Encyclopédie* and also wrote operas. *Confessions*, published posthumously 1782, was a frank account of his occasionally immoral life and was a founding work of autobiography.

Rousseau (Etienne-Pierre) Théodore 1812–1867. French landscape painter of the ⮡Barbizon School. Born in Paris, he came under the influence of the British landscape painters Constable and Bonington, sketched from nature in many parts of France, and settled in Barbizon in 1848.

Rovaniemi capital of Lappi province, N Finland, and chief town of Finnish Lapland, situated just south of the Arctic Circle; population (1990) 33,500. After World War II the town was rebuilt by the architect Alvar Aalto, who laid out the main streets in the form of a reindeer's antlers.

rowan another name for the European ⮡mountain ash tree.

rowing propulsion of a boat by oars, either by one rower with two oars (sculling) or by crews (two, four, or eight persons) with one oar each, often with a coxswain. Major events include the world championship, first held in 1962 for men and 1974 for women, and the Boat Race between Britain's Oxford and Cambridge universities, first held in 1829.

Doggett's Coat and Badge 1715, begun for Thames watermen and also the first English race, still survives. Rowing as a sport began with the English Leander Club 1817, followed by the Castle Garden boat club, 1834.

In the US the Harvard–Yale boat race is held on the Thames at New London, Connecticut, and National Championships are held annually.

Rowling Wallace "Bill" 1927– . New Zealand Labor politician, party leader 1969–75, prime minister 1974–75.

Rowse A(lfred) L(eslie) 1903– . English popular historian. He published a biography of Shakespeare 1963, and in 1973 controversially identified the "Dark Lady" of Shakespeare's sonnets as Emilia Lanier, half-Italian daughter of a court musician, with whom the Bard is alleged to have had an affair 1593–95.

Royal Ballet title under which the British Sadler's Wells Ballet (at Covent Garden), Sadler's Wells Theater Ballet, and the Sadler's Wells Ballet School were incorporated 1956.

Royal Botanic Gardens, Kew botanic gardens in Richmond, Surrey, England, popularly known as ⮡Kew Gardens.

Royal Canadian Mounted Police (RCMP) Canadian national police force, known as the ⮡Mounties.

Royal Greenwich Observatory the national astronomical observatory of the UK, founded

1675 at Greenwich, E London, England, to provide navigational information for sailors. After World War II it was moved to Herstmonceux Castle, Sussex; in 1990 it was transferred to Cambridge. It also operates telescopes on La Palma in the Canary Islands, including the 4.2-m/165-in William Herschel Telescope, commissioned 1987.

The observatory was founded by King Charles II. The eminence of its work resulted in Greenwich Time and the Greenwich Meridian being adopted as international standards of reference 1884.

Royal Shakespeare Company (RSC) British professional theater company that performs Shakespearean and other plays. It was founded 1961 from the company at the Shakespeare Memorial Theater 1932 (now the Royal Shakespeare Theater) in Stratford-upon-Avon, Warwickshire, England.

Royal Society oldest and premier scientific society in Britain, originating 1645 and chartered 1660; Christopher ◊Wren and Isaac ◊Newton were prominent early members. Its Scottish equivalent is the Royal Society of Edinburgh 1783.

royalty in law, payment to the owner for rights to use or exploit literary or artistic copyrights and patent rights in new inventions of all kinds.

Oil, gas, and other mineral deposits are also subject to royalty payments.

Royce (Frederick) Henry 1863–1933. British engineer, who so impressed Charles ◊Rolls by the car he built for his own personal use 1904 that ◊Rolls-Royce Ltd was formed 1906 to produce automobiles and engines.

Royce Josiah 1855–1916. US idealist philosopher who in *The Conception of God* 1895 and *The Conception of Immortality* 1900 interpreted Christianity in philosophical terms.

Born in Grass Valley, California, Royce taught at the University of California and Harvard University. His philosophy saw God as cosmic purpose, which man embraces.

RPI abbreviation for *retail price index*; see ◊cost of living.

rpm abbreviation for *revolutions per minute*.

RSFSR abbreviation for *Russian Soviet Federal Socialist Republic*, the largest republic of the former Soviet Union; renamed the ◊Russian Federation 1991.

RSVP abbreviation for *répondez s'il vous plaît* (French "please reply").

Ruanda part of the former Belgian territory of Ruanda-Urundi until it achieved independence as ◊Rwanda, country in central Africa.

Rub' al Khali (Arabic "empty quarter") vast sandy desert in S Saudi Arabia; area 250,000 sq mi/650,000 sq km. The British explorer Bertram Thomas (1892–1950) was the first European to cross it 1930–31.

rubber coagulated latex of a variety of plants, mainly from the New World. Most important is Para rubber, which derives from the tree *Hevea brasiliensis* of the spurge family. It was introduced from Brazil to SE Asia, where most of the world supply is now produced, the chief exporters being Peninsular Malaysia, Indonesia, Sri Lanka, Cambodia, Thailand, Sarawak, and Brunei. At about seven years the tree, which may grow to 60 ft/20 m, is ready for "tapping." Small incisions are made in the trunk and the latex drips into collecting cups. In pure form, rubber is white and has the formula $(C_5H_8)n$.

Other sources of rubber are the Russian dandelion *Taraxacum koksagyz*, which grows in temperate climates and can yield about 100 lb/45 kg of rubber per ton of roots, and guayule *Parthenium argentatum*, a small shrub of the Compositae family, which grows in SW US and Mexico.

Early uses of rubber were limited by its tendency to soften on hot days and harden on colder ones, a tendency that was eliminated by Charles Goodyear's invention of ◊vulcanization 1839.

In the 20th century, world production of rubber has increased a hundredfold, and World War II stimulated the production of synthetic rubber to replace the supplies from Malaysian sources overrun by the Japanese. There are an infinite variety of synthetic rubbers adapted to special purposes, but economically foremost is SBR (styrene-butadiene rubber). Cheaper than natural rubber, it is preferable for some purposes; for example, on car tires, where its higher abrasion-resistance is useful, and it is either blended with natural rubber or used alone for industrial molding and extrusions, shoe soles, hoses, and latex foam.

rubber plant Asiatic tree *Ficus elastica* of the mulberry family Moraceae, native to Asia and N Africa, producing latex in its stem. It has shiny, leathery, oval leaves, and young specimens are grown as house plants.

rubella technical term for ◊German measles.

Rubens Peter Paul 1577–1640. Flemish painter, who brought the exuberance of Italian Baroque to N Europe, creating, with an army of assistants, innumerable religious and allegorical paintings for churches and palaces. These show mastery of drama in large compositions, and love of rich color. He also painted portraits and, in his last years, landscapes.

Rubens entered the Antwerp painters' guild 1598 and went to Italy in 1600, studying artists of the High Renaissance. In 1603 he visited Spain and in Madrid painted many portraits of the Spanish nobility. From 1604 to 1608 he was in Italy again, and in 1609 he settled in Antwerp and was appointed court painter to the archduke Albert and his wife Isabella. His *Raising of the Cross* 1610 and *Descent from the Cross* 1611–14, both in Antwerp Cathedral, show his brilliant painterly style. He went to France 1620, commissioned by the regent Marie de' Medici to produce a cycle of 21 enormous canvases allegorizing her life (Louvre, Paris). In 1628 he again went to Madrid, where he met the painter Velázquez. In 1629–30 he was in London as diplomatic envoy to Charles I, and painted the ceiling of the Banqueting House in Whitehall.

Rubens's portraits range from intimate pictures of his second wife, such as *Hélène Fourment in a Fur Wrap* about 1638 (Kunsthistorisches Museum, Vienna), to dozens of portraits of royalty.

Rubicon ancient name of the small river flowing into the Adriatic which, under the Roman Republic, marked the boundary between Italy proper and Cisalpine Gaul. When ◊Caesar led his army across it 49 BC he therefore declared war on the republic; hence to "cross the Rubicon" means to take an irrevocable step.

The Rubicon is believed to be the present-day *Fiumicino*, which rises in the Etruscan Apennines 10 mi/16 km WNW of San Marino and enters the Adriatic 10 mi/16 km NW of Rimini.

rubidium (Latin *rubidus* "red") soft, silver-white, metallic element, symbol Rb, atomic number 37, atomic weight 85.47. It is one of the ◊alkali metals, ignites spontaneously in air, and reacts violently with water. It is used in photoelectric cells and vacuum-tube filaments.

Rubidium was discovered spectroscopically by Robert Bunsen and Gustav Kirchhoff in 1861, and named for the red lines in its spectrum.

Rubik Erno 1944– . Hungarian architect who invented the **Rubik cube**, a multicolored puzzle that can be manipulated and rearranged in only one correct way, but about 43 trillion wrong ones. Intended to help his students understand three-dimensional design, it became a fad that swept around the world.

Rubinstein Artur 1887–1982. Polish-born US pianist. He studied in Warsaw and Berlin and for 85 of his 95 years appeared with the world's major symphony orchestras, specializing in the music of Mozart, Chopin, Debussy, and the Spanish composers.

He appeared in the US in 1906 and 1919, but it was not until a concert at Carnegie Hall 1937 that he was hailed as a genius in the US. He and his family emigrated to the US in the 1940s, and he became a citizen in 1946. Considered by many to be the greatest 20th-century piano virtuoso, he played with an intellectual and commanding tone, appeared in films, and made many distinctive recordings.

Rubinstein Helena 1882–1965. Polish-born cosmetics tycoon, who emigrated to Australia 1902, where she started a cosmetics business. She moved to Europe 1904 and later to the US, opening salons in London, Paris, and New York.

Rublev (Rublyov) Andrei *c.* 1360–1430. Russian icon painter. Only one documented work of his survives, the *Holy Trinity* about 1411 (Tretyakov Gallery, Moscow). This shows a basically Byzantine style, but with a gentler expression.

ruby the red transparent gem variety of the mineral ◊corundum Al_2O_3, aluminum oxide. Small amounts of chromium oxide, Cr_2O_3, substituting for aluminum oxide, give ruby its color. Natural rubies are found mainly in Myanmar (Burma), but rubies can also be produced artificially and such synthetic stones are used in ◊lasers.

rudd freshwater fish *Scardinius erythrophthalmus*, a type of minnow, belonging to the carp family Cypridae, common in lakes and slow rivers of Europe; now introduced in the US. Brownish green above and silvery below, with red fins and golden eyes, it can reach a length of 1.5 ft/45 cm and a weight of 2.2 lb/1 kg.

Rude François 1784–1855. French Romantic sculptor. He produced the low-relief scene on the Arc de Triomphe, Paris, showing the capped figure of Liberty leading the revolutionaries (1833, known as *The Volunteers of 1792* or *The Marseillaise*).

Rudolf, Lake former name of Lake ◊Turkana in E Africa.

Rudolph 1858–1889. Crown prince of Austria, the only son of Emperor Franz Joseph. From an early age he showed progressive views that brought him into conflict with his father. He conceived and helped to write a history of the Austro-Hungarian Empire. In 1881, he married Princess Stephanie of Belgium, and they had one daughter, Elizabeth. In 1889 he and his mistress, Baroness Marie Vetsera, were found shot in his hunting lodge at Mayerling, near Vienna. The official verdict was suicide, although there were rumors that it was perpetrated by Jesuits, Hungarian nobles, or the baroness's husband.

Rudolph two Holy Roman emperors:

Rudolph I 1218–1291. Holy Roman emperor from 1273. Originally count of Hapsburg, the was the first Hapsburg emperor and expanded his dynasty by investing his sons with the duchies of Austria and Styria.

Rudolph II 1552–1612. Holy Roman emperor from 1576, when he succeeded his father Maximilian II. His policies led to unrest in Hungary and Bohemia, which led to the surrender of Hungary to his brother Matthias 1608 and religious freedom for Bohemia.

rue shrubby perennial herb *Ruta graveolens*, family Rutaceae, native to S Europe and temperate Asia. It bears clusters of yellow flowers. An oil extracted from the strongly scented, blue-green leaves is used in perfumery.

ruff bird *Philomachus pugnax* of the sandpiper family Scolopacidae. The name is taken from the frill of erectile feathers developed in the breeding season around the neck of the male. The ruff is found across N Europe and Asia, and migrates south in winter. It is a casual migrant throughout North America.

Rugby market town and railroad junction in Warwickshire, England; population (1981) 59,500. Rugby School 1567 established its reputation under Thomas Arnold. Rugby football originated here.

rugby contact sport that originated at the Rugby boys' school, England, 1823, when a boy picked up the ball and ran with it while playing soccer. Rugby is played with an oval ball. It is now played in two forms: Rugby League (for professionals) and Rugby Union (for amateurs).

Rügen a Baltic island in the state of Mecklenburg-West Pomerania, Germany; area 358 sq mi/927 sq km. It is a vacation center, linked by causeway to the mainland; chief town Bergen, main port Sassnitz. As well as tourism there are agriculture and fishing, and chalk is mined. Rügen was annexed by Denmark 1168, Pomerania 1325, Sweden 1648, and Prussia 1815.

Ruhr river in Germany; it rises in the Rothaargebirge and flows W to join the Rhine at Duisburg. The *Ruhr valley* (142 mi/228 km), a metropolitan industrial area (petrochemicals, automobiles; iron and steel at Duisburg and Dortmund) was formerly a coal-mining center.

The area was occupied by French and Belgian troops 1923–25 in an unsuccessful attempt to force Germany to pay reparations laid down in the Treaty of Versailles. During World War II the Ruhr district was severely bombed. Allied control of the area from 1945 came to an end with the setting-up of the European Coal and Steel Community 1952.

rule of law doctrine that no individual, however powerful, is above the law. The principle had a significant influence on attempts to restrain the arbitrary use of power by rulers and on the growth of legally enforceable human rights in many Western countries. It is often used as a justification for separating legislative from judicial power.

Rum or *Rhum* island of the Inner Hebrides,

Highland Region, Scotland, area 42 sq mi/110 sq km, a nature preserve from 1957. Askival is 2,658 ft/810 m high.

Rumania alternate spelling of ⬦Romania.

ruminant any even-toed hoofed mammal with a rumen, the "first stomach" of its complex digestive system. Plant food is stored and fermented before being brought back to the mouth for chewing (chewing the cud) and then is swallowed to the next stomach. Ruminants include cattle, antelopes, goats, deer, and giraffes, all with a four-chambered stomach. Camels are also ruminants, but they have a three-chambered stomach.

rummy card game in which the players score by obtaining cards either of the same denomination or in sequence in the same suit. It probably derives from mah-jongg.

Rump, the English parliament formed between Dec 1648 and Nov 1653 after ⬦Pride's purge of the ⬦Long Parliament to ensure a majority in favor of trying Charles I. It was dismissed 1653 by Cromwell, who replaced it with the so-called Barebones Parliament (named after one of its members, Praise-God Barbon).

Reinstated after the Protectorate ended 1659 and the full membership in the Long Parliament restored 1660, the Rump dissolved itself shortly afterwards and was replaced by the Convention Parliament, which brought about the restoration of the monarchy.

Rundstedt Karl Rudolf Gerd von 1875–1953. German field marshal in World War II. Largely responsible for the German breakthrough in France 1940, he was defeated on the Ukrainian front 1941. As commander in chief in France from 1942, he resisted the Allied invasion 1944 and in Dec launched the temporarily successful Ardennes offensive.

rune character in the oldest Germanic script, chiefly adapted from the Latin alphabet, the earliest examples being from the 3rd century, and found in Denmark. Runes were scratched on wood, metal, stone, or bone.

runner in botany, aerial stem that produces new plants; also called a ⬦*stolon*.

Runnymede meadow on the south bank of the river Thames near Egham, Surrey, England, where on June 15, 1215 King John put his seal to the ⬦Magna Carta.

Runyon (Alfred) Damon 1884–1946. US journalist, primarily a sports reporter, whose short stories in *Guys and Dolls* 1932 deal wryly with the seamier side of New York City life in his own invented jargon.

He reached the height of his popularity in the 1930s, writing a syndicated newspaper feature, "As I See It."

Rupert Prince 1619–1682. English Royalist general and admiral, born in Prague, son of the Elector Palatine Frederick V (1596–1632) and James I's daughter Elizabeth. Defeated by Cromwell at ⬦Marston Moor and ⬦Naseby in the Civil War, he commanded a privateering fleet 1649–52, until routed by Admiral Robert Blake, and, returning after the Restoration, was a distinguished admiral in the Dutch Wars. He founded the ⬦Hudson's Bay Company.

Rupert's Land area of N Canada, of which Prince ⬦Rupert was the first governor. Granted to the ⬦Hudson's Bay Company 1670, it was later split among Québec, Ontario, Manitoba, and the Northwest Territories.

rupture in medicine, another name for ⬦hernia.

rush any grasslike plant of the genus *Juncus*, family Juncaceae, found in wet places in cold and temperate regions. The round stems and flexible leaves of some species have been used for making mats and baskets since ancient times.

Rush Benjamin 1745–1813. US physician and public official. Committed to the cause of the American Revolution, he was a signer of the Declaration of Independence and was named surgeon general of the Continental army 1777.

Born in Bayberry, Pennsylvania, Rush was educated at the College of New Jersey and received his MD degree from the University of Edinburgh 1768. His involvement in agitation against Washington's leadership led to his resignation. After the war, Rush served on the medical faculty of the University of Pennsylvania 1780–97 and was active in public-health programs. From 1797 to his death he was treasurer of the US Mint.

Rushdie (Ahmed) Salman 1947– . British writer, born in India of a Muslim family. His novel *The Satanic Verses* 1988 (the title refers to verses deleted from the Koran) offended many Muslims with alleged blasphemy. In 1989 the Ayatollah Khomeini of Iran called for Rushdie and his publishers to be killed.

Rushdie was born in Bombay and later lived in Pakistan before moving to the UK. His earlier novels in the magic-realist style include *Midnight's Children* 1981, which deals with India from the date of independence and won the Booker Prize, and *Shame* 1983, set in an imaginary parallel of Pakistan. The furor caused by the publication of *The Satanic Verses* led to the withdrawal of British diplomats from Iran. In India and elsewhere, people were killed in demonstrations against the book and Rushdie was forced to go into hiding. *Haroun and the Sea of Stories*, a children's book, was published 1990.

Rushmore, Mount mountain in the Black Hills, South Dakota; height 6,203 ft/1,890 m. On its granite face are carved giant portrait heads of presidents Washington, Jefferson, Lincoln, and Theodore Roosevelt. The sculptor was Gutzon ⬦Borglum.

Rusk Dean 1909– . US Democrat politician. He was secretary of state to presidents J F Kennedy and L B Johnson 1961–69, and became unpopular through his involvement with the ⬦Vietnam War.

During World War II he fought in Burma (now Myanmar) and China and became deputy Chief of Staff of US forces. After the war he served in the Department of State, and as assistant secretary of state for Far Eastern affairs was prominent in ⬦Korean War negotiations.

Ruskin John 1819–1900. English art critic and social critic. He published five volumes of *Modern Painters* 1843–60 and *The Seven Lamps of Architecture* 1849, in which he stated his philosophy of art. His writings hastened the appreciation of painters considered unorthodox at the time, such as J M W ⬦Turner and the ⬦Pre-Raphaelite Brotherhood. His later writings were concerned with social and economic problems.

Born in London, the only child of a prosperous wine-merchant, Ruskin was able to travel widely and was educated at Oxford. In 1848 he married Euphemia "Effie" Chalmers Gray, but six years later the marriage was annulled.

In *The Stones of Venice* 1851–53, he drew moral lessons from architectural history. From 1860 he devoted himself to social and economic problems, in which he adopted an individual and radical outlook exalting the "craftsman." He became increasingly isolated in his views. To this period belong a series of lectures and pamphlets (*Unto this Last* 1860, *Sesame and Lilies* 1865 on the duties of men and women, *The Crown of Wild Olive* 1866).

Russell Bertrand (Arthur William), 3rd Earl Russell 1872–1970. English philosopher and mathematician who contributed to the development of modern mathematical logic and wrote about social issues. His works include *Principia Mathematica* 1910–13 (with A N ⬎Whitehead), in which he attempted to show that mathematics could be reduced to a branch of logic; *The Problems of Philosophy* 1912; and *A History of Western Philosophy* 1946. He was an outspoken liberal pacifist.

The grandson of Prime Minister John Russell, he was educated at Trinity College, Cambridge, where he specialized in mathematics and became a lecturer 1895. Russell's pacifist attitude in World War I lost him the lectureship, and he was imprisoned for six months for an article he wrote in a pacifist journal. His *Introduction to Mathematical Philosophy* 1919 was written in prison. He and his wife ran a progressive school 1927–32. After visits to the USSR and China, he went to the US 1938 and taught at many universities. In 1940, a US court disqualified him from teaching at City College of New York because of his liberal moral views. He later returned to England and was a fellow of Trinity College. He was a life-long pacifist except during World War II. From 1949 he advocated nuclear disarmament and until 1963 was on the Committee of 100, an offshoot of the Campaign for Nuclear Disarmament.

Among his other works are *Principles of Mathematics* 1903, *Principles of Social Reconstruction* 1917, *Marriage and Morals* 1929, *An Enquiry into Meaning and Truth* 1940, *New Hopes for a Changing World* 1951, and *Autobiography* 1967–69.

Russell Charles Taze 1852–1916. US founder of the ⬎Jehovah's Witness sect 1872. Born in Pittsburgh, Russell, a successful businessman, began studying the Bible after encountering some Adventists and becoming convinced that Christ's return was imminent. On the basis of his studies he came to believe that Christ's "invisible return" had taken place in 1874 and that in 1914 a series of apocalyptic events would culminate in Christ's thousand-year reign on Earth. In 1879 he founded the journal that became *The Watchtower*, which spread his ideas. The movement under his leadership survived the failure of his prophecies in 1914, and it continued to grow rapidly after his death.

Russell Jane 1921– . US actress who was discovered by producer Howard Hughes. Her first film, *The Outlaw* 1943, was not properly released for several years because of censorship problems. Other films include *The Paleface* 1948, *Gentlemen Prefer Blondes* 1953, and *The Revolt of Mamie Stover* 1957. She retired 1970.

Russell John, 1st Earl Russell 1792–1878. British Liberal politician, son of the 6th Duke of Bedford. He entered the House of Commons 1813 and supported Catholic emancipation and the Reform Bill. He held cabinet posts 1830–41, became prime minister 1846–52, and was again a cabinet minister until becoming prime minister again 1865–66. He retired after the defeat of his Reform Bill 1866.

Russell Ken 1927– . English film director whose work includes *Women in Love* 1969, *The*

Russian rulers 1547–1917

House of Rurik	
Ivan "the Terrible"	1547–84
Theodore I	1584–98
Irina	1598
House of Godunov	
Boris Godunov	1598–1605
Theodore II	1605
usurpers	
Dimitri III	1605–06
Basil IV	1606–10
interregnum 1610–13	
House of Romanov	
Michael Romanov	1613–45
Alexis	1645–76
Theodore III	1676–82
Peter I "Peter the Great" and Ivan V (brothers)	1682–96
Peter I, as tsar	1689–1721
Peter I, as emperor	1721–25
Catherine I	1725–27
Peter II	1727–30
Anna Ivanovna	1730–40
Ivan VI	1740–41
Elizabeth	1741–62
Peter III	1762
Catherine II "Catherine the Great"	1762–96
Paul I	1796–1801
Alexander I	1801–25
Nicholas I	1825–55
Alexander II	1855–81
Alexander III	1881–94
Nicholas II	1894–1917

Devils 1971, and *Gothic* 1986. He has made television documentaries of the lives of the composers Elgar, Delius, and Richard Strauss.

Russia originally the name of the pre-revolutionary Russian Empire (until 1917), now accurately restricted to the ⬎Russian Federation.

Russia: history
the southern steppes of Russia were originally inhabited by nomadic peoples, and the northern forests by Slavonic peoples who slowly spread southward.

9th–10th centuries Viking chieftains established their own rule in Novgorod, Kiev, and other cities.
10th–12th centuries Kiev temporarily united the Russian peoples into an empire. Christianity was introduced from Constantinople 988.
13th century The Mongols (the Golden Horde) overran the southern steppes 1223, compelling the Russian princes to pay tribute.
14th century Byelorussia and Ukraine came under Polish rule.
1462–1505 Ivan III ("the Great"), prince of Moscow, threw off the Mongol yoke and united the northwest.
1547–84 Ivan IV ("the Terrible") assumed the title of tsar and conquered Kazan and Astrakhan. During his reign the colonization of Siberia began.
1613 The first Romanov tsar, Michael, was elected after a period of chaos.
1667 Following a Cossack revolt, E Ukraine was reunited with Russia.
1682–1725 Peter I ("the Great") modernized the bureaucracy and army. He founded a navy and a new capital, St Petersburg; introduced Western education; and wrested the Baltic seaboard from Sweden. By 1700 the colonization of Siberia had reached the Pacific.

1762–96 Catherine II ("the Great") annexed the Crimea and part of Poland and recovered W Ukraine and White Russia.
1798–1814 Russia intervened in the Revolutionary and Napoleonic Wars (1798–1801, 1805–07) and after repelling Napoleon's invasion, took part in his overthrow (1812–14).
1827–29 War with Turkey resulted from Russian attempts to dominate the Balkans.
1853–56 The Crimean War.
1858–60 The treaties of Aigun 1858 and Peking 1860 were imposed on China, annexing territories north of the Amur and east of the Ussuri rivers.
1861 Serfdom was abolished (on terms unfavorable to the peasants). A rapid growth of industry followed, a working-class movement developed, and revolutionary ideas spread, culminating in the assassination of Alexander II 1881.
1877–78 Balkan war with Turkey.
1898 The Social Democratic Party was founded.
1904–05 The occupation of Manchuria resulted in war with Japan (see ⬎Russo-Japanese War).
1905 A revolution, although suppressed, compelled the tsar to accept a parliament (the Duma) with limited powers.
1914 Russo-German rivalries in the Balkans, which had brought Russia into an alliance with France 1895 and Britain 1907, were one of the causes of the outbreak of World War I.
1917 During World War I, the ⬎Russian Revolution began.
For subsequent history until 1991, see ⬎Union of Soviet Socialist Republics.

Russian member of the majority ethnic group living in Russia. Russians are also often the largest minority in neighboring republics. The Russian language is a member of the East Slavonic branch of the Indo-European language family and was the official language of the USSR, with 130–150 million speakers. It is written in the Cyrillic alphabet. The ancestors of the Russians migrated from central Europe between the 6th and 8th centuries AD.

The people of Russia proper have traditionally referred to their language as Great Russian, in contrast with Ukrainian (which they call Little Russian) and the language of Byelorussia (White Russian). Ukrainians have traditionally objected to this usage, arguing that theirs is a distinct language. Even before the 1917 revolution, Russian language and culture was imposed on the country's minorities; this was to some extent reversed in the face of growing nationalist feeling in many of the republics of the USSR and subsequently of the Russian Federation.

Russian art painting and other products of the visual arts from pre-1917 Russia; later applied to art from the USSR. From the 10th to the 17th century Russian art was dominated by the Eastern Orthodox Church and was influenced by various styles of Byzantine art. Painters such as Andrei Rublev produced icons, images of holy figures that were often considered precious. By the 17th century European influence had grown strong and in the 18th century the tsars imported European sculptors and painters. Early Russian Modernism 1910–30 anticipated Western trends but was then suppressed in favor of art geared to the sentimental glorification of workers.

Russian Far East geographical, not administrative, division of Asiatic Russia, on the

Russian Federation formerly (until 1991) **Russian Soviet Federal Socialist Republic**

area 6,591,100 sq mi/17,075,500 sq km
capital Moscow
cities St Petersburg (Leningrad), Nizhni-Novgorod (Gorky), Rostov-on-Don, Samara (Kuibyshev), Tver (Kalinin), Volgograd, Vyatka (Kirov), Ekaterinburg (Sverdlovsk)
physical fertile Black Earth district; extensive forests; the Ural Mountains with large mineral resources
features the heavily industrialized area around Moscow; Siberia; includes 16 autonomous republics (capitals in brackets): Bashkir (Ufa); Buryat (Ulan-Ude); Checheno-Ingush (Grozny); Chuvash (Cheboksary); Dagestan (Makhachkala); Kabardino-Balkar (Nalchik); Kalmyk (Elista); Karelia (Petrozavodsk); Komi (Syktyvkar); Mari (Yoshkar-Ola); Mordovia (Saransk); Vladikavkaz (formerly Ordzhonikidze); Tatarstan (Kazan); Tuva (Kizyl); Udmurt (Izhevsk); Yakut (Yakutsk)
head of state and government Boris Yeltsin from 1990/91
political system emergent democracy
political parties Democratic Russia, liberal-radical, pro-Yeltsin; Congress of Civil and Patriotic Groups (CCDG), right-wing; Civic Union, right-of-center; Nashi (Ours), far-right, Russian imperialist coalition; Communist (Bolshevik) Party, Stalinist-communist
products iron ore, coal, oil, gold, platinum, and other minerals, agricultural produce
currency ruble
population (1990) 148,000,000 (82% Russian, Tatar 4%, Ukrainian 3%, Chuvash 1%)
language Great Russian
religion traditionally Russian Orthodox
chronology
1945 Became a founding member of United Nations.
1988 Aug: Democratic Union formed in Moscow as political party opposed to totalitarianism. Oct: Russian language demonstrations in Leningrad and Tsarist flag raised.
1989 March: Boris Yeltsin elected to USSR Congress of People's Deputies. Sept: conservative-nationalist Russian United Workers' Front established in Sverdlovsk.
1990 May: anticommunist May Day protests in Red Square, Moscow; Yeltsin narrowly elected RSFSR president by Russian parliament. June: economic and political sovereignty declared; Ivan Silaev became Russian prime minister. July: Yeltsin resigned his party membership. Aug: Tatarstan declared sovereignty. Dec: rationing introduced in some cities; private land ownership allowed.
1991 March: Yeltsin secured the support of Congress of Peoples' Deputies for direct election of an executive president. June: Yeltsin elected president under a liberal-radical banner. July: Yeltsin issued a sweeping decree to remove Communist Party cells from workplaces; sovereignty of the Baltic republics recognized by the republic. Aug: Yeltsin stood out against abortive anti-Gorbachev coup, emerging as key power-broker within Soviet Union. Nov: Yeltsin named as prime minister; CPSU and Russian Communist Party banned; Yeltsin's goverment gained control of Russia's economic assets and armed forces. Dec: Yeltsin negotiated formation of new confedaral Commonwealth of Independent States (CIS); admitted into United Nations (UN); Russian independence recognized by US and European Community (EC).
1992 Jan: admitted into Conference on Security and Cooperation in Europe (CSCE); assumed former USSR's permanent seat on UN Security Council; prices freed. Feb: demonstrations in Moscow and other cities as living standards plummet. June: Yeltsin-Bush summit meeting; Yeltsin proposed further major reductions in strategic nuclear weapons. March: 18 out of 20 republics signed treaty agreeing to remain within loose Russian Federation; Tatarstan and Checheno-Ingush refused to sign. Aug: agreement with Ukraine on joint control of Black Sea fleet.

Pacific coast. It includes the Amur, Lower Amur, Kamchatka, and Sakhalin regions, and Khabarovsk and Maritime territories.

Russian Federation or **Russia** country in N Asia and E Europe, bounded N by the Arctic Ocean, E by the Bering Sea and the Sea of Okhotsk, W by Norway, Finland, the Baltic States, Belarus, and Ukraine, and S by China, Mongolia, Georgia, Azerbaijan, and Kazakhstan.
government From 1990 the Russian Federation has had a two-tier legislative structure, consisting of a 1,068-member directly elected Congress of People's Deputies and a two-chamber standing Russian parliament (supreme soviet) elected by the Congress from among its members. Congress deputies are elected by a majority system, and there is a second ballot runoff race in contests in which there is no clear first-round majority. The executive state president is directly elected, enjoys substantial decree powers, and may also hold the portfolio of prime minister. There is an elected vice-president. A constitutional court was established 1991 to supervise Russian laws and treaties with foreign states, and to examine territorial disputes.
history For pre-1990 history see ⇨*Russia, history and* ⇨*Union of Soviet Socialist Republics.* The Russian Federation declared its economic and political sovereignty in June 1990 and began to challenge Soviet authority. The republic held back revenue from the center, embarked on a strategy of market reform, and established its own independent security and communications structures.
Commonwealth of Independent States formed After the defeat of the coup attempt against Soviet president Gorbachev Aug 1991, the Russian Federation, led by Boris Yeltsin, Russia's first ever popularly elected leader, moved swiftly to break the political-institutional structures that had held together the USSR, in particular the Communist Party of the Soviet Union (CPSU). Russia sought to maintain some sort of confederal structure in order that economic ties might continue and territorial disputes be avoided, but was wary of Gorbachev's plan for a reorganized federation. Instead, after Ukraine's independence referendum on Dec 1, 1991, Russia proposed the ⇨Commonwealth of Independent States (CIS). The US officially acknowledged Russia's independence in the same month and accorded it diplomatic recognition, as did the European Community, and admission to the United Nations was granted.
the newly independent republic The Russian Federation contains almost half the population of the former USSR and around 70% of its agricultural and industrial output. It is a vast federation, spanning 11 time zones, stretching 2,000 mi/3,000 km from the Arctic Ocean to China and containing 16 "autonomous republics," five "autonomous regions," and ten "autonomous districts," each catering to a distinct non-Russian ethnic group, including Tatars, Chechens, Chuvash, Dagestanis, Buryats, Yakuts, Kalmyks, and Chuchi, and each with its own parliament and laws. After 1990 many of these made sovereignty or independence declarations, most conspicuously the oil-rich and predominantly Muslim Tataria (Tatarstan), where Russia's largest ethnic minority resides, gas-rich Bashkir, Siberian Yakutia, and Checheno-Ingush in the SW, which made integration into the new federation difficult despite Russia's pledge to concede considerable autonomy. The Russian Federation also faced the threat of territorial claims and border conflicts with neighboring republics.

The new Russian Federation, despite the weakness of its economy, remained a "great power." It inherited much of the former USSR's strategic and diplomatic assets, including a permanent seat on the United Nations Security Council (taken up 1992), embassies overseas, and a considerable conventional and nuclear military arsenal. It was admitted into the ⇨Conference on Security and Cooperation (CSCE) in Europe Jan 1992.

Despite growing internal frictions, a federal treaty between Yeltsin and the leaders of 18 of Russia's 20 main political subdivisions was signed in March 1992 giving regional governments broad autonomy within a loose Russian Federation. Checheno-Ingush and Tatarstan refused to sign, the latter voting in a referendum for sovereignty within Russia, a move opposed by Yeltsin.
economic problems Russia's immediate concern was the rapid deterioration in living standards and shortages of food and consumer goods as a result of loosening price restraints and the restructuring of commerce, the military sector, and industry. In Jan 1992 nearly a dozen cities were rocked by rioting consumers protesting over the lifting of price controls. International efforts to stabilize the economy included a $1 billion loan from the International Monetary Fund (IMF) in Aug and the offer Sept 1992 of more than $1 billion in food aid from the US.
arms control The first official Russian-American summit held in June 1992 resulted in Yeltsin and Bush agreeing on a major reduction in strategic nuclear weapons. The pact would leave the two powers with less than one-half of the warheads they would have retained under

the 1991 START agreement. In Aug 1992 an agreement was reached for joint control of the disputed Black Sea fleet by Russia and the Ukraine until 1995, after which time it would be divided between the two countries. The pact effectively removed the fleet from the command of the CIS. *See illustration box.*

Russian literature literary works produced in Russia and later in the USSR. The earliest known works are sermons and chronicles and the unique prose poem "Tale of the Armament of Igor," belonging to the period in the 11th and 12th centuries when the center of literary culture was Kiev. By the close of the 14th century leadership had passed to Moscow, which was isolated from developments in the West until the 18th century; in this period are the political letters of Ivan the Terrible; the religious writings of the priest Avvakum (1620–1681), who was the first to use vernacular Slavonic (rather than the elaborate Church Slavonic language) in literature; and traditional oral folk poems dealing with legendary and historical heroes, which were collected in the 18th and 19th centuries.

Modern Russian literature begins with Mikhail Lomonosov (1711–1765) who fused elements of Church Slavonic with colloquial Russian to create an effective written medium. Among the earlier writers, working directly under French influence, were the fabulist Ivan Krylov (1768–1844) and the historian Nikolai Karamzin (1765–1826). In the 19th century poetry reached its greatest heights with Alexander Pushkin and the tempestuously Byronic Mikhail Lermontov, while prose was dominated by Nikolai Gogol. Typifying the intellectual unrest of the mid-19th century are the works of the prose writer Alexander Herzen, known for his memoirs.

The golden age of the 19th-century Russian novel produced works by literary giants such as Ivan Turgenev, Ivan Goncharov, Fyodor Dostoievsky, and Leo Tolstoy. In their wake came Nikolai Leskov (1831–1895), the morbid Vsevolod Garshin (1855–1888), and Vladimir Korolenko (1853–1921), and in drama the innovative genius of Anton Chekhov. Maxim Gorky rose above the pervasive pessimism of the 1880s and found followers in Alexander Kuprin (1870–1938) and Ivan Bunin; in contrast are the depressingly negative Leonid Andreyev and Mikhail Artsybashev. To the more mystic school of thought belong the novelist Dmitri Merezhkovsky (1865–1941) and the poet and philosopher Vladimir Soloviev (1853–1900), who molded the thought of the Symbolist poet Alexander Blok.

Many writers left the country at the time of the Revolution, but in the 1920s two groups emerged: the militantly socialist LEF (Left Front of the Arts) led by the Futurist Mayakovsky, and the fellow-travelers of NEP (New Economic Policy) including Boris Pilnyak (1894–1938), Boris Pasternak, Alexei Tolstoy, and Ehrenburg. Literary standards reached a low ebb during the first five-year plan (1928–32), when facts were compulsorily falsified in the effort to fortify socialism, but the novelist Sholokhov and poets Mandelshtam, Akhmatova, and Nikolai Tikhonov were notable in this period. More freedom was allowed by the subsequent Realism movement, seen for example in the works of Simonov and the poet Alexander Tvardovsky (1910–1971).

During World War II censorship was again severe until the thaw after Stalin's death—when Vladimir Dudintsev published his *Not by Bread Alone* 1956—but was then soon renewed. Landmark events were the controversy over the award of a Nobel Prize to Pasternak, the public statements by the poet Yevtushenko, and the imprisonment in 1966 of the novelists Andrei Sinyavsky (1926–) and Yuli Daniel (1926–) for smuggling their works abroad for publication. Other writers fled the country, such as Anatoly Kuznetsov (1929–), whose novel *The Fire* 1969 obliquely criticized the regime, and Solzhenitsyn, who found a different kind of disillusionment in the West. To evade censorship writers have also resorted to allegory, as in for example Vasili Aksyonov's *The Steel Bird* 1979, which grotesquely satirizes dictatorship. Among those apart from all politics was the nonsense-verse writer Kornei Chukovsky. The intellectual and cultural thaw under President Gorbachev heralded an era of literary revaluation as well as fresh discoveries of writers from the 1930s onwards.

Russian Orthodox Church another name for the ⟡Orthodox Church.

Russian Revolution two revolutions of Feb and Oct 1917 (Julian ⟡calendar) that began with the overthrow of the Romanov dynasty and ended with the establishment of a communist soviet (council) state, the Union of Soviet Socialist Republics (USSR).

The *February Revolution* (March by the Western calendar) arose because of food and fuel shortages, the ongoing repressiveness of the tsarist government, and military incompetence in World War I. Riots in Petrograd (as St Petersburg was named 1914–24) led to the abdication of Tsar Nicholas II and the formation of a provisional government under Prince Lvov. They had little support as troops, communications, and transport were controlled by the Petrograd workers' and soldiers' council. ⟡Lenin returned to Russia in April as head of the ⟡Bolsheviks. Kerensky replaced Lvov as head of government in July. During this period, the Bolsheviks gained control of the soviets and advocated land reform (under the slogan "All power to the Soviets") and an end to their involvement in World War I.

The *October Revolution* was a coup on the night of Oct 25–26 (Nov 6–7) Western calendar). Bolshevik workers and sailors seized the government buildings and the Winter Palace, Petrograd. The second All-Russian Congress of Soviets, which met the following day, proclaimed itself the new government of Russia, and Lenin became leader. Bolsheviks soon took control of the cities, established worker control in factories, and nationalized the banks. The ⟡Cheka (secret police) was set up to silence the opposition. The government concluded peace with Germany early in 1918 through the Treaty of ⟡Brest-Litovsk, but civil war broke out in that year when anti-Bolshevik elements within the army attempted to seize power. The war lasted until 1922, when the Red Army, organized by ⟡Trotsky, finally overcame "White" (Tsarist) opposition, but with huge losses, after which communist control was complete. Some 2 million refugees fled during these years.

Russian Soviet Federal Socialist Republic (RSFSR) former name (until 1991) of the ⟡Russian Federation.

Russo-Japanese War war between Russia and Japan 1904–05, which arose from conflicting ambitions in Korea and ⟡Manchuria, specifically, the Russian occupation of Port Arthur (modern Dalian) 1896 and of the Amur province 1900. Japan successfully besieged Port Arthur May 1904–Jan 1905, took Mukden (modern Shenyang) Feb 29–March 10, and on May 27 defeated the Russian Baltic fleet, which had sailed halfway around the world to Tsushima Strait. A peace was signed Aug 23, 1905. Russia surrendered its lease on Port Arthur, ceded S Sakhalin to Japan, evacuated Manchuria, and recognized Japan's interests in Korea.

russula any fungus of the genus *Russula*, comprising many species. They are medium to large mushrooms with flattened caps, and many are brightly colored.

R. emetica is a common species found in damp places under conifers. Up to 3.5 in/9 cm across, the cap is scarlet, fading to cherry, and the gills are white. This toadstool tastes acrid and causes vomiting eaten raw, but some russulas are edible.

rust in botany, common name for the minute parasitic fungi of the order Uredinales, which appear on the leaves of their hosts as orange-red spots, later becoming darker. The commonest is the wheat rust *Puccinia graminis*.

rutabaga (or *swede*) annual or biennial plant *Brassica napus*, widely cultivated for its edible root, which is yellow, purple, or white. It is similar in taste to the turnip *Brassica rapa* but has more carbohydrates and sugars, is firmer fleshed, and longer keeping.

Ruth in the Old Testament, Moabite (see ⟡Moab) ancestor of David (king of Israel) by her second marriage to Boaz. When her first husband died, she preferred to stay with her mother-in-law, Naomi, rather than return to her own people.

Ruth Babe (George Herman) 1895–1948. US baseball player, regarded by many as the greatest of all time. He played in ten ⟡World Series and hit 714 home runs, a record that stood from 1935 to 1974 and led to the nickname "Sultan of Swat."

Ruth started playing 1914 as a pitcher-outfielder for the Boston Braves before moving to the Boston Red Sox later that year. He joined the New York Yankees 1920 and became one of the best hitters in the game. He hit 60 home runs in the 1927 season (a record beaten 1961 by Roger Maris). He is still the holder of the record for most bases in a season: 457 in 1921. Yankee Stadium is known as "the house that Ruth built" because of the money he brought into the club.

CAREER HIGHLIGHTS

games: 2,503
runs: 2,174
home runs: 714
average: .342
World Series wins: 1915–16, 1918, 1923, 1927–28, 1932

Ruthenia or *Carpathian Ukraine* region of central Europe, on the southern slopes of the Carpathian Mountains, home of the Ruthenes or Russniaks. Dominated by Hungary from the 10th century, it was part of Austria-Hungary until World War I. Divided between Czechoslovakia, Poland, and Romania 1918, it was independent for a single day in 1938, immediately occupied by Hungary, captured by the USSR 1944, and 1945–47 became incorporated into Ukraine Republic, USSR. Ukraine became an independent republic 1991.

ruthenium hard, brittle, silver-white, metallic element, symbol Ru, atomic number 44, atomic weight 101.07. It is one of the so-called platinum group of metals; it occurs in platinum ores as a free metal and in the natural alloy osmiridium. It is used as a hardener in alloys and as a catalyst; its compounds are used as coloring agents in glass and ceramics.

It was discovered in 1827 by Estonian chemist G W Osann, who produced it in impure form from residues of platinum ores, and named after 1828 for its place of discovery, the Ural mountains in Ruthenia (now part of the Ukraine). Pure ruthenium was isolated in 1845 by K K Klaus.

Rutherford Ernest 1871–1937. New Zealand physicist, a pioneer of modern atomic science. His main research was in the field of radioactivity, and he discovered alpha, beta, and gamma rays. He named the nucleus, and was the first to recognize the nuclear nature of the atom. Nobel Prize 1908.

Rutherford Margaret 1892–1972. English film and theater actress who specialized in formidable yet jovially eccentric roles.

One of the great character actresses, she became mildly successful in the mid-1930s but went on to her greatest success when she played Agatha Christie's Miss Marple, with her husband, actor Stringer Davis, in four films in the early 1960s and won an Academy Award for her role in *The VIPs* 1963.

She was also seen in *Blithe Spirit* 1945, *Passport to Pimlico* 1949, *Mouse on the Moon* 1943, and Orson Welles's *Chimes at Midnight* 1966.

rutherfordium name proposed by US scientists for the element currently known as ⊅unnilquadium (atomic number 104), to honor New Zealand physicist Ernest Rutherford.

rutile TiO_2, titanium oxide, a naturally occurring ore of titanium. It is usually reddish brown to black, with a very bright (adamantine) surface luster. It crystallizes in the tetragonal system. Rutile is common in a wide range of igneous and metamorphic rocks and also occurs concentrated in sands; the coastal sands of E and W Australia are a major source. It is also used as a pigment that gives a brilliant white to paint, paper, and plastics.

Rutledge Wiley Blount, Jr 1894–1949. US jurist and associate justice of the US Supreme Court 1943–49. He was known as a liberal, often dissenting from conservative Court decisions, such as in *Wolf v Colorado* 1949, which allowed illegally obtained evidence to be used against a defendant in state courts.

Born in Cloverport, Kentucky, Rutledge studied law at the University of Colorado and was admitted to the bar 1922. He became a teacher of law at the University of Colorado 1924–26, Washington University 1926–35, and the State University of Iowa 1935–39. In 1939 he was appointed judge of the US Court of Appeals for the District of Columbia. President F D Roosevelt appointed him to the Court 1943.

Ruwenzori mountain range on the frontier between Zaire and Uganda, rising to 16,794 ft/5,119 m at Mount Stanley.

Ruyter Michael Adrianszoon de 1607–1676. Dutch admiral who led his country's fleet in the wars against England. On June 1–4, 1666 he forced the British fleet under Rupert and Albemarle to retire into the Thames, but on July 25 was heavily defeated off the North Foreland, Kent. In 1667 he sailed up the Medway, burning three men-of-war at Chatham, and capturing others.

Ruzicka Leopold Stephen 1887–1976. Swiss chemist who began research on natural compounds such as musk and civet secretions. In the 1930s he investigated sex hormones, and in 1934 succeeded in extracting the male hormone androsterone from 7,000 gallons/31,815 liters of urine and synthesizing it. Born in Croatia, Ruzicka settled in Switzerland in 1929. Ruzicka shared the 1939 Nobel Chemistry Prize with Butenandt.

Rwanda landlocked country in central Africa, bounded N by Uganda, E by Tanzania, S by Burundi, and W by Zaire.
government The 1978 constitution provides for a president and a single-chamber legislature, the National Development Council, all elected by universal adult suffrage for a five-year term. The president appoints and leads a council of ministers.

Rwanda is a one-party state, the sole legal party being the National Revolutionary Movement for Development (MRND), whose leader is the president.
history For early history, see ⊅Africa. The population comprises two ethnic groups: the Hutu majority were dominated by the Tutsi minority; there is also a pygmy minority, the Twa.

Rwanda was linked to the neighboring state of Burundi, 1891–1919, within the empire of German East Africa, then under Belgian administration as a League of Nations mandate, and then as a United Nations trust territory.

In 1961 the monarchy was abolished, and Ruanda, as it was then called, became a republic. It achieved full independence 1962 as Rwanda, with Grégoire Kayibanda as its first president. Fighting broke out 1959 between the Hutu and the Tutsi, resulting in the loss of some 20,000 lives before an uneasy peace was agreed 1965.
after independence Kayibanda was reelected president 1969, but by the end of 1972 the civil warfare had resumed, and in 1973 the head of the National Guard, Maj Gen Juvenal Habyarimana, led a bloodless coup, ousting Kayibanda and establishing a military government. Meetings of the legislature were suspended, and the MRND was formed as the only legally permitted political organization. A referendum held at the end of 1978 approved a new constitution, but military rule continued until 1980, when civilian rule was adopted. In Oct 1990, in response to an attack by the Rwandan Patriotic Army, the government promised to reform the constitution after an invasion from Uganda of Tutsi refugees was contained. An agreement was signed Sept 1992 with the Rwanda Patriotic Front (FPR) to end the rebel war that had begun 1990. *See illustration box.*

Ryan Robert 1909–1973. US theater and film actor who was equally impressive in leading and character roles.

His films include *Woman on the Beach* 1947, *The Set-Up* and *Caught* both 1949, *Billy Budd* 1962, and *The Wild Bunch* 1969.

Ryazan industrial city (agricultural machinery, leather, shoes) dating from the 13th century, capital of Ryazan region, W Russia, on the river Oka SE of Moscow; population (1987) 508,000.

Ryder Albert Pinkham 1847–1917. US painter who developed one of the most original styles of his time. He painted with broad strokes that tended to simplify form and used yellowish colors that gave his works an eerie, haunted quality. His works are poetic, romantic, and filled with unreality; *Death on a Pale Horse* 1910 (Cleveland Museum of Art) is typical.

Born in New Bedford, Massachusetts, he was self-taught and, as time passed, became more and more a recluse.

Ryder Cup golf tournament for professional

Rwanda
Republic of (*Republika y'u Rwanda*)

area 10,173 sq mi/26,338 sq km
capital Kigali
cities Butare, Ruhengeri
physical high savanna and hills, with volcanic mountains in NW
features part of lake Kivu; highest peak Mount Karisimbi 14,792 ft/4,507 m; Kagera River (whose headwaters are the source of the Nile) and National Park
head of state and government Maj Gen Juvenal Habyarimana from 1973
political system one-party military republic
political party National Revolutionary Movement for Development (MRND), nationalist, socialist
exports coffee, tea, pyrethrum
currency franc
population (1990 est) 7,603,000 (Hutu 90%, Tutsi 9%, Twa 1%); growth rate 3.3% p.a.
life expectancy men 49, women 53 (1989)
languages Kinyarwanda, French (official); Kiswahili
religion Roman Catholic 54%, animist 23%, Protestant 12%, Muslim 9%
literacy men 50% (1989)
GNP $2.3 bn (1987); $323 per head (1986)
chronology
1916 Belgian troops occupied Rwanda; League of Nations mandated Rwanda and Burundi to Belgium as Territory of Ruanda-Urundi.
1959 Interethnic warfare between Hutu and Tutsi.
1962 Independence from Belgium achieved, with Grégoire Kayibanda as president.
1972 Renewal of interethnic fighting.
1973 Kayibanda ousted in a military coup led by Maj Gen Juvenal Habyarimana.
1978 New constitution approved; Rwanda remained a military-controlled state.
1980 Civilian rule adopted.
1988 Refugees from Burundi massacres streamed into Rwanda.
1990 Government attacked by Rwandan Patriotic Front (FPR), a Tutsi military-political organization based in Uganda. Constitutional reforms promised.
1992 Peace accord with Rwandan Patriotic Front.

men's teams from the US and Europe. It is played every two years, and the match is made up of a series of singles, foursomes, and fourballs played over three days.

Named after entrepreneur Samuel Ryder, who donated the trophy 1927, the tournament is played alternately in the US and Great Britain. The match was between the US and Great Britain 1927–71; US v Great Britain and Ireland 1973–77, and US v Europe from 1979.

Ryder Cup: recent winners

USA 1927, 1931, 1935, 1937, 1947, 1949, 1951, 1953, 1955, 1959, 1961, 1963, 1965, 1967, 1971, 1973, 1975, 1977, 1979, 1981, 1983, 1991
Great Britain 1929, 1933, 1957
Europe 1985, 1987
drawn: 1969, 1989

rye cereal *Secale cereale* grown extensively in N Europe and other temperate regions. The flour is used to make dark-colored ("black") breads. Rye is grown mainly as a forage crop, but the grain is also used to make whiskey and breakfast cereals.

rye-grass any perennial, wiry grass of the genus *Lolium*, especially *L. perenne*, common in pastures and waste places. It grows up to 24 in/ 60 cm high, flowers in midsummer, and sends up abundant nutritious leaves, good for cattle. It is a Eurasian genus but has been introduced to Australia and North America.

Rye House Plot conspiracy 1683 by English Whig extremists against Charles II for his Roman Catholic leanings. They intended to murder Charles and his brother James, Duke of York, at Rye House, Hoddesdon, Hertfordshire, but the plot was betrayed. The Duke of ◇Monmouth was involved, and alleged conspirators, including Lord William ◇Russell and Algernon Sidney (1622–1683) were executed for complicity.

Ryle Gilbert 1900–1976. British philosopher. His *The Concept of Mind* 1949 set out to show that the distinction between an inner and an outer world in philosophy and psychology cannot be sustained. He ridiculed the mind–body dualism of ◇Descartes as the doctrine of "the Ghost in the Machine."

Ryle Martin 1918–1984. English radio-astronomer. At the Mullard Radio Astronomy Observatory, Cambridge, he developed the technique of sky-mapping using "aperture synthesis," combining smaller dish aerials to give the characteristics of one large one. His work on the distribution of radio sources in the universe brought confirmation of the ◇Big Bang theory. He won, with Antony ◇Hewish, the Nobel Prize for Physics 1974.

Ryukyu Islands southernmost island group of Japan, stretching toward Taiwan and including Okinawa, Miyako, and Ishigaki
area 870 sq mi/2,254 sq km
capital Naha, on Okinawa
features 73 islands, some uninhabited; subject to typhoons
products sugar, pineapples, fish
population (1985) 1,179,000
history originally an independent kingdom; ruled by China from the late 14th century until seized by Japan 1609 and controlled by the Satsuma feudal lords until 1868, when the Japanese government took over. Chinese claims to the islands were relinquished 1895. In World War II the islands were taken by USA 1945 (see under ◇Okinawa); northernmost group, Oshima, restored to Japan 1953, the rest 1972.

Ryzhkov Nikolai Ivanovich 1929– . Soviet Communist politician. He held governmental and party posts from 1975 before being brought into the Politburo and serving as prime minister 1985–90 under Gorbachev. A low-profile technocrat, Ryzhkov was the author of unpopular economic reforms.

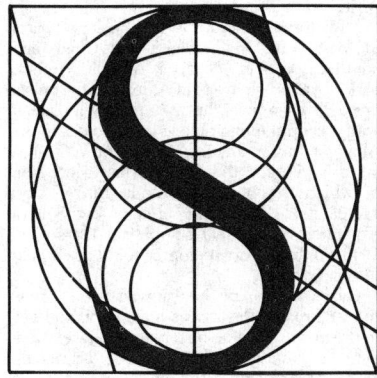

S 19th letter in the English alphabet, and its principal sibilant. It represents an alveolar fricative, either voiceless s (*sing*) or voiced z (*roses*).

S abbreviation for *south*.

Saar (French *Sarre*) river in W Europe; it rises in the Vosges mountains in France, and flows 149 mi/240 km N to join the river Moselle in Germany. Its valley has many vineyards.

Saarinen Eero 1910–1961. Finnish-born US architect. Son of Eliel ⟡Saarinen. He is known for a wide range of innovative modern designs using a variety of creative shapes for buildings. His works include the TWA terminal at Kennedy Airport in New York City; Dulles Airport outside Washington DC; the General Motors Technical Center in Warren, Michigan; the Thomas J Watson Research Center in Yorktown, New York; Ezra Stiles and Morse colleges and the ice-hockey rink at Yale University; Kresge Auditorium at the Massachusetts Institute of Technology; and US embassies in London and Oslo.

Saarinen Eliel 1873–1950. Finnish-born US architect and founder of the Finnish Romantic school. His most famous European work is the Helsinki railroad station. In the US he is particularly remembered for his designs for Cranbrook School in Bloomfield Hills, Michigan, and Christ Church in Minneapolis.

Saarland (French *Sarre*) *Land* (state) of Germany
area 992 sq mi/2,570 sq km
capital Saarbrücken
features one-third forest; crossed northwest to south by the river Saar
products cereals and other crops; cattle, pigs, poultry. Former flourishing coal and steel industries survive only by government subsidy
population (1988) 1,034,000
history in 1919, the Saar district was administered by France under the auspices of the League of Nations; a plebiscite returned it to Germany 1935; Hitler gave it the name Saarbrücken. Part of the French zone of occupation 1945, it was included in the economic union with France 1947. It was returned to Germany 1957.

Sabah self-governing state of the federation of Malaysia, occupying NE Borneo, forming (with Sarawak) East Malaysia

area 28,415 sq mi/73,613 sq km
capital Kota Kinabalu (formerly Jesselton)
physical chiefly mountainous (highest peak Mount Kinabalu 13,450 ft/4,098 m) and forested
products hardwoods (25% of the world's supplies), rubber, fish, cocoa, palm oil, copper, copra, and hemp
population (1990) 1,470,200, of which the Kadazans form the largest ethnic group at 30%; also included are 250,000 immigrants from Indonesia and the Philippines
languages Malay (official) and English
religion Sunni Muslim and Christian (the Kadazans, among whom there is unrest about increasing Muslim dominance)
government consists of a constitutional head of state with a chief minister, cabinet, and legislative assembly
history In 1877–78 the Sultan of Sulu made concessions to the North Borneo Company, which was eventually consolidated with Labuan as a British colony 1946, and became the state of Sabah within Malaysia 1963. The Philippines advanced territorial claims on Sabah 1962 and 1968 on the grounds that the original cession by the Sultan was illegal, Spain having then been sovereign in the area.

Sabah Sheik Jabir al Ahmadal Jabir al-1928– . Emir of Kuwait from 1977. He suspended the national assembly 1986, after mounting parliamentary criticism, ruling in a feudal, paternalistic manner. On the invasion of Kuwait by Iraq 1990 he fled to Saudi Arabia, returning to Kuwait in March 1991.

Sabatier Paul 1854–1951. French chemist. He found in 1897 that if a mixture of ethylene and hydrogen was passed over a column of heated nickel, the ethylene changed into ethane. Further work revealed that nickel could be used to catalyze numerous chemical reactions. Sabatier shared the 1912 Nobel Prize for Chemistry with François ⟡Grignard.

Sabbatarianism belief held by some Protestant Christians in the strict observance of the Sabbath, Sunday, following the fourth commandment of the ⟡Bible. It began in the 17th century.

Sabbatarianism has taken various forms, including an insistence on the Sabbath lasting a full 24 hours; prohibiting sports and games and the buying and selling of goods on the Sabbath; and ignoring public holidays when they fall on a Sunday.

Sabbath (Hebrew *shābath*, "to rest") the seventh day of the week, commanded by God in the Old Testament as a sacred day of rest; in Judaism, from sunset Friday to sunset Saturday; in Christianity, Sunday (or, in some sects, Saturday).

sabin unit of sound absorption, used in acoustical engineering. One sabin is the absorption of one square foot (0.093 square meter) of a perfectly absorbing surface (such as an open window).

Sabin Albert 1906– . Polish-born US microbiologist whose involvement in the antipolio campaigns led to the development of a new, highly effective, live vaccine. The earlier vaccine, developed by the physicist Jonas ⟡Salk, was based on heat-killed viruses. Sabin was convinced that a live form would be longer-lasting and more effective, and he succeeded in weakening the virus so that it lost its virulence. The vaccine can be given by mouth.

Sabine member of an ancient people of central Italy, conquered by the Romans and amalgamated with them in the 3rd century BC. The so-called **rape of the Sabine women**—a mythical attempt by ⟡Romulus in the early days of Rome to carry off the Sabine women to colonize the new city—is frequently depicted in art.

sabka flat shoreline zone in arid regions above the high-water mark in which the sediments are heavily laden with ⟡evaporites. These occur in the form of nodules, crusts, and crystalline deposits of halite, anhydrite, and gypsum, as well as mineral grains of various sorts. Some of the evaporites form from rapid evaporation of marine waters soaking through from the bordering tidal flats, but some can be derived also from sediment-laden continental waters coming down from adjoining highlands.

Sabkas are common features along the Persian Gulf. Former sabka environments can be deduced from the sedimentary record of much of the oil-rich Permian Basin of Texas, as an ancient sea moved back and forth across the continent.

sable marten *Martes zibellina*, about 20 in/50 cm long and usually brown. It is native to N Eurasian forests, but now found mainly in E Siberia. The sable has diminished in numbers because of its valuable fur, which has long attracted hunters. Conservation measures and sable farming have been introduced to save it from extinction.

saccharide another name for a ⟡sugar molecule.

saccharin or *ortho-sulpho benzimide* $C_7H_5NO_3S$ sweet, white, crystalline solid derived from coal tar and substituted for sugar. Since 1977 it has been regarded as potentially carcinogenic. Its use is not universally permitted and it has been largely replaced by other sweetening agents.

Sacco-Vanzetti case murder trial in Massachusetts, 1920–21. Italian immigrants Nicola Sacco (1891–1927) and Bartolomeo Vanzetti (1888–1927) were convicted of murder during an alleged robbery. The conviction was upheld on appeal, with application for retrial denied. Prolonged controversy delayed execution until 1927. In 1977 the verdict was declared unjust (by Massachusetts governor Michael Dukakis) because of the judge's prejudice against the accuseds' anarchist views.

The two accused men were philosophical anarchists who had evaded the draft in World War I. Protests were made from many quarters arguing that the two were victims of the ⟡Red Scare. Modern ballistics evidence suggests that one of the fatal shots was fired from Sacco's gun, but the judge's prejudice against the defendants' political views raised questions about the fairness of the trial. The case was extremely divisive at the time.

Sacher-Masoch Leopold von 1836–1895. Austrian novelist. His books dealt with the sexual pleasure of having pain inflicted on oneself, hence ⟡masochism.

sackbut musical instrument of the ⟡brass family, a form of trombone, common from the 14th century.

Sackville-West Vita (Victoria) 1892–1962. British poet and novelist, wife of Harold Nicolson from 1913; *Portrait of a Marriage* 1973 by their son Nigel Nicolson described their married life. Her novels include *The Edwardians* 1930 and *All Passion Spent* 1931;

she also wrote the pastoral poem *The Land* 1926. The fine gardens around her home at Sissinghurst, Kent, were created by her.

sacrament in Christian usage, observances forming the visible sign of inward grace. In the Roman Catholic Church there are seven sacraments: baptism, Holy Communion (Eucharist or mass), confirmation, rite of reconciliation (confession and penance), holy orders, matrimony, and the anointing of the sick.

Sacramento industrial port and capital (since 1854) of California, 80 mi/130 km NE of San Francisco; population (1990) 369,400, metropolitan area 1,481,100. It stands on the Sacramento River, which flows 382 mi/615 km through Sacramento Valley to San Francisco Bay. Industries include the manufacture of detergents and jet aircraft and food processing, including almonds, peaches, and pears. It was founded as **Fort Sutter** 1848 on land bought by John Sutter 1839. Its old town has been restored. A deepwater port channel to San Francisco Bay was completed 1963.

sacred cow any person, institution, or custom that is considered above criticism. The term comes from the Hindu belief that cows are sacred and must not be killed.

Sadat Anwar 1918–1981. Egyptian politician. Succeeding ◊Nasser as president 1970, he restored morale by his handling of the Egyptian campaign in the 1973 war against Israel. In 1974 his plan for economic, social, and political reform to transform Egypt was unanimously adopted in a referendum. In 1977 he visited Israel to reconcile the two countries, and shared the Nobel Peace Prize with Israeli prime minister Menachem Begin 1978. He was assassinated by Islamic fundamentalists.

Sadducee (Hebrew "righteous") member of the ancient Hebrew political party and sect of ◊Judaism that formed in pre-Roman Palestine in the first century BC. They were the group of priestly aristocrats in Jerusalem until the final destruction of the Temple AD 70.

They opposed the ◊Pharisees and favored Hellenization. They stood for the hereditary high priesthood, the Temple, and sacrifice. Sadducees denied the immortality of the soul and the existence of angels, and maintained the religious law in all its strictness. Many of their ideas and practices resurfaced in medieval Jewish sects after Pharisee ideas dominated the dispersed Jews of the western Roman empire.

Sade Donatien Alphonse François, Comte de, known as the **Marquis de Sade** 1740–1814. French author who was imprisoned for sexual offenses and finally committed to an asylum. He wrote plays and novels dealing explicitly with a variety of sexual practices, including ◊sadism.

S'adi or **Saadi**. Adopted name of Sheik Moslih Addin *c.* 1184–*c.* 1291. Persian poet, author of *Bustan/Tree-garden* and *Gulistan/ Flower-garden*.

sadism tendency to derive pleasure (usually sexual) from inflicting physical or mental pain on others. The term is derived from the Marquis de ◊Sade.

Sadowa, Battle of or **Battle of Königgrätz** Prussian victory over the Austrian army 8 mi/ 13 km NW of Hradec Kralove (German Königgrätz) July 3, 1866, ending the ◊Seven Weeks' War. It confirmed Prussian hegemony over the German states and led to the formation of the North German Confederation 1867. It is named after the nearby village of Sadowa (Czech Sadová) in Czechoslovakia.

safflower Asian plant *Carthamus tinctorius*, family Compositae. It is thistlelike, and widely grown for the oil from its seeds, which is used in cooking, margarine, and paints and varnishes; the seed residue is used as cattle feed.

saffron plant *Crocus sativus* of the iris family, probably native to SW Asia, and formerly widely cultivated in Europe; also the dried orange-yellow ◊stigmas of its purple flowers, used for coloring and flavoring.

saga prose narrative written down in the 11th– 13th centuries in Norway and Iceland. The sagas range from family chronicles, such as the *Landnamabok* of Ari (1067–1148), to legendary and anonymous works such as the *Njala* saga.

Other sagas include the *Heimskringla* of Snorri Sturluson celebrating Norwegian kings (1178–1241), the *Sturlunga* of Sturla Thordsson (1214–1284), and the legendary and anonymous *Laxdaela* and *Grettla* sagas.

Sagan Carl 1934– . US physicist and astronomer, renowned for his popular science writings and broadcasts. His books include *Cosmic Connection: An Extraterrestrial Perspective* 1973; *Broca's Brain: Reflections on the Romance of Science* 1979; *Cosmos* 1980, based on his television series of that name; and the science-fiction novel *Contact* 1985.

Sagan became professor of astronomy and space science at Cornell University, New York, in 1970. His research concerned the chemistry and physics of planetary atmospheres, the origin of life on Earth, the probable climatic effects of nuclear war, and the possibility of life on other planets.

Sagan Françoise 1935– . French novelist. Her studies of love relationships include *Bonjour Tristesse/Hello Sadness* 1954, *Un Certain Sourire/A Certain Smile* 1956, and *Aimez-vous Brahms?/Do You Like Brahms?* 1959.

sage perennial herb *Salvia officinalis* with gray-green aromatic leaves used for flavoring. It grows up to 20 in/50 cm high and has bluish-lilac or pink flowers.

Saginaw city and port in E Michigan on the Saginaw river, near Lake Huron, NW of Flint. Industries include automotive parts, metal products, salt, coal, and sugar beets; population (1990) 69,500. Saginaw was a lumber center until the late 19th century.

Sagittarius zodiac constellation in the southern hemisphere, represented as a centaur aiming a bow and arrow at neighboring Scorpius. The Sun passes through Sagittarius from mid-Dec to mid-Jan, including the winter solstice, when it is farthest south of the equator. The constellation contains many nebulae and ◊globular clusters, and open ◊star clusters. Kaus Australis and Nunki are its brightest stars. The center of our Galaxy, the Milky Way, is marked by the radio source Sagittarius A. In astrology, the dates for Sagittarius are between about Nov 22 and Dec 21 (see ◊precession).

sago starchy material obtained from the pith of the sago palm *Metroxylon sagu*. It forms a nutritious food and is used for manufacturing glucose and sizing textiles.

Saguenay river in Québec, used for hydroelectric power as it flows from Lac St Jean SE to the St Lawrence estuary; length 475 mi/ 765 km.

Sahara largest desert in the world, occupying 2,100,000 sq mi/5,500,000 sq km of N

Africa from the Atlantic to the Nile, covering: W Egypt; part of W Sudan; large parts of Mauritania, Mali, Niger, and Chad; and southern parts of Morocco, Algeria, Tunisia, and Libya. Small areas in Algeria and Tunisia are below sea level, but it is mainly a plateau with a central mountain system, including the Ahaggar Mountains in Algeria, the Aïr Massif in Niger, and the Tibesti Massif in Chad, of which the highest peak is Emi Koussi 11,208 ft/3,415 m. The area of the Sahara expanded by 251,000 sq mi/650,000 sq km 1940–90, but reforestation is being attempted in certain areas.

Oases punctuate the caravan routes, now modern roads. Resources include oil and gas in the north. Satellite observations have established a pattern below the surface of dried-up rivers that existed 2 million years ago. Cave paintings confirm that 4,000 years ago running rivers and animal life existed. Satellite photos taken during the 1980s have revealed that the Sahara expands and contracts from one year to another depending on rainfall; that is, there is no continuous expansion, as had been feared.

Sahel (Arabic *sahil* "coast") marginal area to the south of the Sahara, from Senegal to Somalia, where the desert is gradually encroaching. The desertification is partly due to climatic change but has also been caused by the pressures of a rapidly expanding population, which have led to overgrazing and the destruction of trees and scrub for fuelwood. In recent years many famines have taken place in the area.

Saida (ancient **Sidon**) port in Lebanon; population (1980) 24,740. It stands at the end of the Trans-Arabian oil pipeline from Saudi Arabia. Sidon was the chief city of ◊Phoenicia, a bitter rival of Tyre about 1400–701 BC, when it was conquered by ◊Sennacherib. Later a Roman city, it was taken by the Arabs AD 637 and fought over during the Crusades.

saiga antelope *Saiga tartarica* of E European and W Asian steppes and deserts. Buff-colored, whitish in winter, it stands 30 in/75 cm at the shoulder, with a body about 5 ft/1.5 m long. Its nose is unusually large and swollen, an adaptation which may help warm and moisten the air inhaled, and keep out the desert dust. The saiga can run at 50 mph/80 kph.

Only the male has horns, which are straight and up to 1 ft/30 cm long. Once a vanishing species but now protected, the saiga has returned to some areas, and herds of thousands migrate with the changing seasons.

Saigon former name (until 1976) of ◊Ho Chi Minh City, Vietnam.

sailing pleasure cruising or racing a small and light vessel, whether sailing or power-driven. At the Olympic Games, seven categories exist: Soling, Flying Dutchman, Star, Finn, Tornado, 470, and Windglider or ◊windsurfing (boardsailing), which was introduced at the 1984 Los Angeles games. All these Olympic categories are sail-driven. The Finn and Windglider are solos events; the Soling class is for three-person crews; all other classes are for crews of two.

saint holy man or woman respected for their wisdom, spirituality, and dedication to their faith. Within the Roman Catholic church a saint is officially recognized through ◊canonization by the pope. Many saints are associated with miracles and canonization usually occurs after a thorough investigation of the lives and miracles attributed to them. In the Orthodox church saints are recognized by the patriarch and Holy Synod after recommendation by local churches. The term is also used in Buddhism for individuals who have led a virtuous and holy life, such as Kūkai (775–835), founder of the Japanese Shingon sect of Buddhism. For individual saints, see under forename, for example ⫶Paul, St.

The lives of thousands of Catholic saints have been collected by the Bollandists, a group of Belgian Jesuits. In 1970 Pope Paul VI revised the calendar of saints' days: excluded were Barbara, Catherine, Christopher, and Ursula (as probably nonexistent); optional veneration might be given to George, Januarius, Nicholas (Santa Claus), and Vitus; insertions for obligatory veneration include St Thomas More and the Uganda martyrs.

St Augustine port and vacation resort in Florida; population (1990) 11,700. Founded by the Spanish 1565, and the oldest permanent settlement in the US, it was burned by the English sea captain ⫶Drake 1586 and ceded to the US 1821. It includes the oldest house (late 16th century) and oldest masonry fort (Castillo de San Marcos 1672) in the continental US.

St Bartholomew, Massacre of slaughter of ⫶Huguenots (Protestants) in Paris, Aug 24–Sept 17, 1572, and until Oct 3 in the provinces. About 25,000 people are believed to have been killed. When ⫶Catherine de' Medici's plot to have Admiral ⫶Coligny assassinated failed, she resolved to have all the Huguenot leaders killed, persuading her son Charles IX it was in the interest of public safety.

Catherine received congratulations from all the Catholic powers, and the pope ordered a medal to be struck.

St Christopher (St Kitts)–Nevis
Federation of

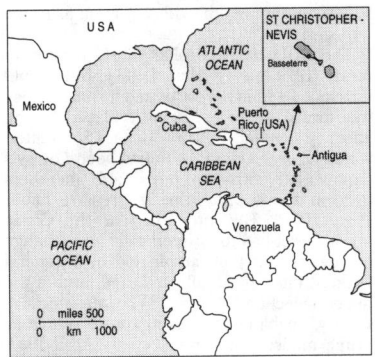

area 104 sq mi/269 sq km (St Christopher 68 sq mi/176 sq km, Nevis 36 sq mi/93 sq km)
capital Basseterre (on St Christopher)
cities Charlestown (largest on Nevis)
physical both islands are volcanic
features fertile plains on coast; black beaches
head of state Elizabeth II from 1983 represented by governor-general
head of government Kennedy Simmonds from 1980
political system federal constitutional monarchy
political parties People's Action Movement (PAM), center-right; Nevis Reformation Party (NRP), Nevis-separatist; Labor Party, moderate, left-of-center **exports** sugar,

molasses, electronics, clothing
currency E Caribbean dollar
population (1990 est) 45,800; growth rate 0.2% p.a.
life expectancy men 69/women 72
language English
media no daily newspaper; two weekly papers, published by the governing and opposition party respectively—both receive advertising support from the government
religion Anglican 36%, Methodist 32%, other protestant 8%, Roman Catholic 10% (1985 est)
literacy 90% (1987)
GNP $40 million (1983); $870 per head
chronology
1871–1956 Part of the Leeward Islands Federation.
1958–62 Part of the Federation of the West Indies.
1967 St Christopher, Nevis, and Anguilla achieved internal self-government, within the British Commonwealth, with Robert Bradshaw, Labor Party leader, as prime minister.
1971 Anguilla returned to being a British dependency.
1978 Bradshaw died; succeeded by Paul Southwell.
1979 Southwell died; succeeded by Lee L Moore.
1980 Coalition government led by Kennedy Simmonds.
1983 Full independence achieved within the Commonwealth.
1984 Coalition government reelected.
1989 Prime Minister Simmonds won a third successive term.

St Bernard breed of large, heavily built dog 30 in/70 cm high at the shoulder, weight about 150 lb/70 kg. They have pendulous ears and lips, large feet, and drooping lower eyelids. They are usually orange and white.

They are named after the Augustinian monks of Grand St Bernard Hospice, Switzerland, who kept them for finding lost travelers in the Alps and to act as guides.

St Bernard Passes the (*Great St Bernard Pass* and *Little St Bernard Pass*) passes through the ⫶Alps.

St Christopher (St Kitts)–Nevis country in the West Indies, in the E Caribbean Sea, part of the Leeward Islands.
government The islands of St Christopher (often called St Kitts) and Nevis form a federal state within the British ⫶Commonwealth. The constitution dates from independence 1983. The governor-general is the formal head of state, representing the British monarch, and appoints the prime minister and cabinet, who are drawn from and responsible to the assembly.

There is a single-chamber national assembly of 14 members, 11 elected by universal suffrage and three appointed by the governor-general, two on the advice of the prime minister and one on the advice of the leader of the opposition.

Nevis Island has its own assembly of five elected and three nominated members, a prime minister and cabinet, and a deputy governor-general. It has the option to secede in certain conditions.
history The original ⫶American Indian inhabitants were Caribs. St Christopher (then called Liamuiga) and Nevis were named by

Christopher ⫶Columbus 1493. St Christopher became Britain's first West Indian colony 1623, and Nevis was settled soon afterwards. France also claimed ownership until 1713. Sugar plantations were worked by slaves.

The islands were part of the Leeward Islands Federation 1871–1956 and a single colony with the British Virgin Islands until 1960. In 1967 St Christopher, Nevis, and Anguilla attained internal self-government within the Commonwealth as associated states, and Robert Bradshaw, leader of the Labor Party, became the first prime minister. In 1970 the Nevis Reformation Party (NRP) was formed, calling for separation for Nevis, and the following year Anguilla, disagreeing with the government in St Christopher, chose to return to being a British dependency.

Bradshaw died 1978 and was succeeded by his deputy, Paul Southwell. He died the following year, to be replaced by Lee L Moore. The 1980 general election produced a hung assembly, and, although Labor won more than 50% of the popular vote, a People's Action Party (PAM)–NRP coalition government was formed, with the PAM leader, Dr Kennedy Simmonds, as prime minister.
independence On Sept 1, 1983 St Christopher and Nevis became independent. In the 1984 general election the PAM–NRP coalition was decisively returned to office. In the 1989 general election, PAM won 6 of the 11 elective seats in the national assembly and Dr Kennedy Simmonds continued in office. *See illustration box.*

St-Denis industrial town, a northern suburb of Paris, France; population (1983) 96,000. ⫶Abelard was a monk at the 12th-century Gothic abbey, which contains many tombs of French kings.

St Elias Mountains mountain range on the Alaska–Canada border. Its highest peak, Mount Logan 19,850 ft/6,050 m, is Canada's highest mountain.

St Elmo's fire bluish, flamelike electrical discharge that sometimes occurs above ships' masts and other pointed objects or about aircraft in stormy weather. Although high voltage, it is low current and therefore harmless. St Elmo (or St Erasmus) is the patron saint of sailors.

Saint-Etienne city in S central France, capital of Loire *département*, Rhônes-Alpes region; population (1982) 317,000. Industries include the manufacture of aircraft engines, electronics, and chemicals, and it is the site of a school of mining, established 1816.

Saint-Exupéry Antoine de 1900–1944. French author who wrote the autobiographical *Vol de nuit/Night Flight* 1931 and *Terre des hommes/Wind, Sand, and Stars* 1939. His children's book *Le Petit Prince/The Little Prince* 1943 is also an adult allegory.

Saint-Gaudens Augustus 1848–1907. Irishborn US sculptor, one of the leading Neo-Classical sculptors of his time. His monuments include the *Admiral Farragut* 1877 in Madison Square Park and the giant nude *Diana* that topped Stanford ⫶White's Madison Square Garden, both in New York City, and the *Adams Memorial* 1891 in Rock Creek Cemetery, Washington, DC.

He was brought to the US as an infant, trained as a cameo cutter, studied at the National Academy of Design, and from 1867 traveled widely in Europe. After studying at the Ecole des Beaux-Arts in Paris, he returned to the US;

established studios in New York City 1876 and Cornish, New Hampshire, 1885; and worked with the nation's major architects to produce public monuments. He also designed bronze medals, plaques, portrait tablets, and low reliefs. He was commissioned 1905 by President T Roosevelt to redesign US gold coinage; the 1907 double eagle ($20) was the only design approved before his death.

St George's port and capital of ▷Grenada; population (1986) 7,500, urban area 29,000.

St Germain-en-Laye, Treaty of 1919 treaty condemning the war between Austria and the Allies, signed at St Germain-en-Laye, a town 13 mi/21 km W of Paris. Representatives of the US signed it, but because the US Senate failed to ratify the Treaty of ▷Versailles, the Treaty of St Germain was not submitted to it. The US made a separate peace with Austria in 1921.

St Gotthard Pass pass through the Swiss ▷Alps, at an altitude of 6,500 ft/2,000 m. A rail tunnel is planned, running 30 mi/48 km through the St Gotthard massif, to be built 1990–2010.

St Helena British island in the S Atlantic, 1,200 mi/1,900 km W of Africa, area 47 sq mi/122 sq km; population (1987) 5,600. Its capital is Jamestown, and it exports fish and timber. Ascension and Tristan da Cunha are dependencies.

St Helena became a British possession 1673, and a colony 1834. Napoleon died in exile here 1821.

St Helens, Mount volcanic mountain in Washington State. When it erupted 1980 after being quiescent since 1857, it devastated an area of 230 sq mi/600 sq km and its height was reduced from 9,682 ft/2,950 m to 8,402 ft/2,560 m.

St Helier resort and capital of Jersey, Channel Islands; population (1981) 25,700. The "States of Jersey," the island legislature, sits here in the *salle des états.*

Saint John largest city of New Brunswick, on the Saint John River; population (1986) 121,000. It is a fishing port and has shipbuilding, timber, fish-processing, petroleum, refining, and textile industries. Founded by the French as **Saint-Jean** 1635, it was taken by the British 1758.

After the American Revolution, several thousand Loyalists from the US settled here 1783, and it was the first Canadian city to be incorporated 1785.

St John, Order of (full title **Knights Hospitallers of St John of Jerusalem**) oldest order of Christian chivalry, named after the hospital at Jerusalem founded about 1048 by merchants of Amalfi for pilgrims, whose travel routes the knights defended from the Muslims. Today there are about 8,000 knights (male and female), and the Grand Master is the world's highest ranking Roman Catholic lay person.

On being forced to leave Palestine, the knights went to Cyprus 1291, to Rhodes 1309, and to Malta (granted to them by Emperor Charles V) 1530. Expelled by Napoleon (on his way to Egypt) 1798, they established their headquarters in Rome (Palazzo di Malta).

St John's capital and chief port of Newfoundland; population (1986) 96,000, urban area 162,000. The main industry is fish processing; other products include textiles, fishing equipment, furniture, and machinery.

It was founded by English navigator Humphrey ▷Gilbert 1582. The inventor Marconi's first transatlantic radio message

was received on Signal Hill 1901. Memorial University was founded 1925.

St John's port and capital of Antigua and Barbuda, on Antigua; population (1982) 30,000.

Saint-Just Louis Antoine Léon Florelle de 1767–1794. French revolutionary. A close associate of ▷Robespierre, he became a member of the Committee of Public Safety 1793, and was guillotined with Robespierre.

Elected to the National Convention in 1792, he was its youngest member at 25 and immediately made his mark by a radical speech condemning King Louis XVI ("one cannot reign without guilt"). His later actions confirm the tone of his book *The Spirit of the Revolution* 1791 in which he showed his distrust of the masses and his advocacy of repression. On his appointment to the Committee of Public Safety he was able to carry out his theories by condemning "not merely traitors, but the indifferent," including Danton and Lavoisier, although his own death was to follow within weeks.

St Kitts–Nevis contracted form of ▷St Christopher–Nevis.

Saint-Laurent Yves (Henri Donat Mathieu) 1936– . French fashion designer who has had an exceptional influence on fashion in the second half of the 20th century. He began working for Christian ▷Dior 1955 and succeeded him as designer on Dior's death 1957. He established his own label 1962 and went on to create the first "power-dressing" looks for men and women: classical, stylish city clothes.

In 1966 Saint Laurent established a chain of boutiques called Rive Gauche selling his ready-to-wear line. By the 1970s he had popularized a style of women's day wear that was inspired by conventionally "masculine" garments such as blazers, trousers, and shirts. He launched a menswear collection in 1974.

St Lawrence river in E North America. From ports on the ▷Great Lakes it forms, with linking canals (which also give great hydroelectric capacity to the river), the St Lawrence Seaway for oceangoing ships, ending in the Gulf of St Lawrence. It is 745 mi/1,200 km long and is icebound annually for four months.

The river's source is Lake Ontario. In its upper course the St Lawrence includes the scenic Thousand Islands and forms the border between the Canadian province of Ontario and the US state of New York. It then enters the province of Québec and flows past Montréal and the city of Québec. Below the latter, it broadens to a maximum width of 90 mi/145 km when it empties into the Gulf of St Lawrence, an arm of the Atlantic Ocean. French explorer Jacques Cartier discovered the river 1535, and the first permanent colonial settlement (city of Québec) was established 1608 by Samuel de Champlain.

St-Lô market town in Normandy, France, on the river Vire; population (1982) 24,800. In World War II it was almost entirely destroyed July 10–18, 1944, when US forces captured it from the Germans.

St Louis city in Missouri, on the Mississippi River; population (1990) 396,700, metropolitan area 2,444,100. Its industries include aerospace equipment, aircraft, vehicles, chemicals, electrical goods, steel, food processing, and beer. Its central US location makes it a warehousing and distribution center and a hub of rail, truck, and airline transportation. St Louis and Washington universities are here, and the University of Missouri has a campus in the city.

Founded as a French trading post 1764, it passed to the US 1803 under the ▷Louisiana Purchase. The Gateway Arch 1965 is a memorial by Eliel Saarinen to the pioneers of the West. A world's fair and the Olympic Games were held in the city 1904. After 1950, St Louis lost much of its population to the suburbs, and large areas fell into decay; redevelopment revived the center city in the late 1970s.

St Lucia country in the West Indies, in the E Caribbean Sea, one of the Windward Islands.

government The constitution dates from independence 1979. The governor-general is the formal head of state, representing the British monarch. The governor-general appoints a prime minister and cabinet, drawn from and responsible to the House of Assembly.

There is a two-chamber parliament comprising the Senate, of 11 appointed members, and the House of Assembly, of 17 members, elected from single-member constituencies by universal suffrage. Six senators are appointed by the governor-general on the advice of the prime minister, three on the advice of the leader of the opposition, and two after wider consultation. Parliament has a life of five years.

history The original inhabitants were Carib Indians. ▷Columbus arrived 1502. The island was settled by the French 1635, who introduced ▷slavery, and ceded to Britain 1803. It became a crown colony 1814.

independence St Lucia was a colony within the Windward Islands federal system until 1960, and acquired internal self-government 1967 as a West Indies associated state. The leader of the United Workers' Party (UWP), John Compton, became prime minister. In 1975 the associated states agreed to seek independence separately, and in Feb 1979, after prolonged negotiations, St Lucia achieved full independence within the British ▷Commonwealth, with Compton as prime minister.

The St Lucia Labor Party (SLP) came to power 1979 led by Allan Louisy, but a split developed within the party, and in 1981 Louisy was forced to resign, being replaced by the attorney general, Winston Cenac. Soon afterwards George Odlum, who had been Louisy's deputy, left with two other SLP members to form a new party, the Progressive Labor Party (PLP). For the next year the Cenac government had to fight off calls for a change of government that culminated in a general strike. Cenac eventually resigned, and in the general election 1982 the UWP won a decisive victory, enabling John Compton to return as prime minister. In new elections April 1987, Compton's UWP was only narrowly returned by a 9:8 majority over the SLP.

In Sept 1991 representatives of Dominica, St Lucia, St Vincent and the Grenadines, and Grenada proposed that integration with the Windward Islands would benefit the islands politically and economically. Integration would be based on a federal state system, with an elected, executive president and a two-chamber assembly.

In the April 1992 general election the UWP won its fourth consecutive victory. *See illustration box.*

St-Malo seaport and resort in the Ille-et-Vilaine *département*, W France, on the Rance estuary; population (1985) 47,500. It took its name from the Welshman Maclou, who was bishop here in about 640.

St Lucia

area 238 sq mi/617 sq km
capital Castries
cities Vieux-Fort, Soufrière
physical mountainous island with fertile valleys; mainly tropical forest
features volcanic peaks; Gros and Petit Pitons
head of state Elizabeth II from 1979 represented by governor-general
head of government John Compton from 1982
political system constitutional monarchy
political parties United Workers' Party (UWP), moderate, left-of-center; St Lucia Labor Party (SLP), moderate, left-of-center; Progressive Labor Party (PLP), moderate, left-of-center **exports** coconut oil, bananas, cocoa, copra
currency E Caribbean dollar
population (1990 est) 153,000; growth rate 2.8% p.a.
life expectancy men 68, women 73 (1989)
languages English; French patois
media two independent biweekly newspapers
religion Roman Catholic 90%
literacy 78% (1989)
GNP $166 million; $1,370 per head (1987)
chronology
1814 Became a British crown colony following Treaty of Paris.
1967 Acquired internal self-government as a West Indies associated state.
1979 Independence achieved from Britain within the Commonwealth, with John Compton, leader of the United Workers' Party (UWP), as prime minister. Allan Louisy, leader of the St Lucia Labor Party (SLP), replaced Compton as prime minister.
1981 Louisy resigned; replaced by Winston Cenac.
1982 Compton returned to power at the head of a UWP government.
1987 Compton reelected with reduced majority.
1991 Integration with Windward Islands proposed.
1992 UWP won general election.

St Moritz winter sports center in SE Switzerland; it contains the Cresta Run (built 1885) for toboggans, bobsleds, and luges. It was the site of the Winter Olympics 1928 and 1948.

St Paul capital and industrial city of Minnesota, adjacent to ⟡Minneapolis; population (1990) 272,200. Industries include electronics, publishing and printing, chemicals, refined petroleum, machinery, and processed food.

Educational institutions include Hamline University and Macalester College. The city is noted for its annual Winter Carnival and the St Paul Chamber Orchestra. French explorer Father Louis Hennepin visited the area 1680, but the first settlers did not arrive until 1838. St Paul became the territorial capital 1849. The first railroad reached here 1862.

St Paul's Cathedral cathedral church of the City of London, and the largest Protestant church in England. A Norman building, which had replaced the original Saxon church, was burned down in the Great Fire 1666; the present cathedral, designed by Christopher ⟡Wren, was built 1675–1710.

St Petersburg capital of the St Petersburg region, Russia, at the head of the Gulf of Finland; population (1987) 4,948,000. Industries include shipbuilding, machinery, chemicals, and textiles. It was renamed *Petrograd* 1914 and was called *Leningrad* from 1924 until 1991, when its original name was restored.

features St Petersburg is notable for its wide boulevards and the scale of its architecture. Most of its fine baroque and Classical buildings of the 18th and early 19th centuries survived World War II. Museums include the Winter Palace, occupied by the tsars until 1917, the Hermitage, the Russian Museum (formerly Michael Palace), and St Isaac's Cathedral. The oldest building in St Petersburg is the fortress of St Peter and St Paul, on an island in the Neva, now a political prison.

St Petersburg became a seaport when it was linked with the Baltic by a ship canal built 1875–93. It is also linked by canal and river with the Caspian and Black seas, and in 1975 a seaway connection was completed via lakes Onega and Ladoga with the White Sea near Belomorsk, allowing naval forces to reach the Barents Sea free of NATO surveillance.

St Petersburg is split up by the mouths of the Neva, which connects it with Lake Ladoga. The site is low and swampy, and the climate severe. The university was founded 1819.

history capital of the Russian Empire 1709–1918, it was founded as an outlet to the Baltic 1703 by Peter the Great, who took up residence there 1712. St Petersburg was the center of all the main revolutionary movements from the Decembrist revolt 1825 up to the 1917 revolution.

During the German invasion in World War II the city withstood siege and bombardment Sept 1941–Jan 1944. Over 100,000 bombs were dropped by the Luftwaffe, and 150,000–200,000 shells were fired, but most deaths (estimate 1 million) resulted from famine and the cold. Soviet counter attacks began 1943, but the siege was not completely lifted until Jan 1944.

In June 1991, the city's electors voted by 55% to 43% to restore the Tsarist (1703–1914) designation, St Petersburg. This vote received parliamentary sanction in Sept 1991. In the previous month, the city's mayor, Anatoly Sobchak, and thousands of citizens had resisted an attempted coup to oust Soviet leader Gorbachev.

St Petersburg seaside resort and industrial city (space technology), W Florida; population (1990) 238,600. It is across Tampa Bay from ⟡Tampa.

Besides aerospace and electronic equipment, the city produces boats and processed seafood. It is also a major tourist and retirement center. St Petersburg was platted 1884 and grew as a resort with the arrival of the railroad in the late 1880s.

St Pierre and Miquelon territorial dependency of France, eight small islands off the S coast of Newfoundland

area St Pierre group 10 sq mi/26 sq km; Miquelon-Langlade group 83 sq mi/216 sq km
capital St Pierre
features the last surviving remnant of France's North American empire
products fish
currency French franc
population (1987) 6,300
language French
religion Roman Catholic
government French-appointed commissioner and elected local council; one representative in the National Assembly in France
history settled 17th century by Breton and Basque fisherfolk; French territory 1816–1976; overseas *département* until 1985; violent protests 1989 when France tried to impose its claim to a 200-mi/320-km fishing zone around the islands; Canada maintains that there is only a 12-mi/19-km zone.

St-Quentin town on the river Somme, Picardie, N France; population (1985) 69,000. It was the site of a Prussian defeat of the French 1871 and was almost obliterated in World War I. It is linked by canal to the industrial centers of Belgium and Germany. Its traditional textile production has been replaced by chemicals and metalworks.

Saint-Saëns (Charles) Camille 1835–1921. French composer, pianist and organist. Among his many lyrical Romantic pieces are concertos, the symphonic poem *Danse macabre* 1875, the opera *Samson et Dalila* 1877, and the orchestral *Carnaval des animaux/Carnival of the Animals* 1886.

Saint-Simon Claude Henri, Comte de 1760–1825. French socialist who fought in the American Revolution and was imprisoned during the French Revolution. He advocated an atheist society ruled by technicians and industrialists in *Du Système industrielle/The Industrial System* 1821.

Saint-Simon Louis de Rouvroy, Duc de 1675–1755. French soldier, courtier, and politician whose *Mémoires* 1691–1723 are unrivaled as a description of the French court.

St-Tropez resort and fishing port on the French Côte d'Azur; population (1985) 6,250. It became popular as a resort in the 1960s.

St Valentine's Day Massacre the murder in Chicago of seven unarmed members of the "Bugs" Moran gang on Feb 14, 1929 by members of Al Capone's gang disguised as policemen. The killings testified to the intensity of gangland warfare for the control of the trade in illicit liquor during ⟡Prohibition.

St Vincent and the Grenadines country in the West Indies, in the E Caribbean Sea, part of the Windward Islands.

government The constitution dates from independence 1979. The head of state is a resident governor-general representing the British monarch. The governor-general appoints a prime minister and cabinet, drawn from and responsible to the assembly.

There is a single-chamber legislature, the House of Assembly, with 19 members, of which 13 are elected by universal suffrage, 4 appointed by the governor-general on the advice of the prime minister, and 2 on the advice of the

St Vincent and the Grenadines

area 150 sq mi/388 sq km, including islets of the Northern Grenadines 17 sq mi/43 sq km
capital Kingstown
cities Georgetown, Chateaubelair
physical volcanic mountains, thickly forested
features Mustique, one of the Grenadines, a vacation resort; Soufrière volcano
head of state Elizabeth II from 1979 represented by governor-general
head of government James Mitchell from 1984

political system constitutional monarchy
political parties New Democratic Party (NDP), moderate, left-of-center; St Vincent Labor Party (SVLP), moderate, left-of-center
exports bananas, taros, sweet potatoes, arrowroot, copra
currency E Caribbean dollar
population (1990 est) 106,000; growth rate –4% p.a.
life expectancy men 69, women 74 (1989)
languages English; French patois
media government-owned radio station; two privately owned weekly newspapers, subject to government pressure
religion 47% Anglican, 28% Methodist, 13% Roman Catholic
literacy 85% (1989)
GNP $188 million; $1,070 per head (1987)
chronology
1783 Became a British crown colony.
1958–62 Part of the West Indies Federation.
1969 Achieved internal self-government.
1979 Achieved full independence from Britain within the Commonwealth, with Milton Cato as prime minister.
1984 James Mitchell replaced Cato as prime minister.
1989 Mitchell decisively reelected.
1991 Integration with Windward Islands proposed.

leader of the opposition. The assembly has a life of five years.

history The original inhabitants were Carib Indians. ▷Columbus landed on St Vincent 1498. Claimed and settled by Britain and France, with African labor (see ▷slavery), the islands were ceded to Britain 1783.

independence Collectively known as St Vincent, the islands of St Vincent and the islets of the northern Grenadines were part of the West Indies Federation until 1962 and acquired internal self-government 1969 as an associated state. They achieved full independence, within the ▷British Commonwealth, as St Vincent and the Grenadines, Oct 1979.

Until the 1980s two parties dominated politics in the islands, the St Vincent Labor Party (SVLP) and the People's Political Party (PPP). Milton Cato, SVLP leader, was prime minister at independence but his leadership was challenged 1981 when a decline in the economy and his attempts to introduce new industrial-relations legislation resulted in a general strike. Cato survived mainly because of divisions in the opposition parties, and in 1984 the centrist New Democratic Party (NDP), led by an SVLP defector and former prime minister, James Mitchell, won a surprising victory. He was reelected 1989, his party winning all the assembly seats.

In Sept 1991 representatives of Dominica, St Lucia, St Vincent and the Grenadines, and Grenada proposed that integration with the Windward Islands would benefit the islands politically and economically. Integration would be based on a federal state system, with an elected, executive president and a two-chamber assembly. *See illustration box.*

St Vitus's dance former name for ▷chorea, a nervous disorder. St Vitus, martyred under the Roman emperor Diocletian, was the patron saint of dancers.

sake Japanese wine made from rice. It is usually served heated but may also be drunk at room temperature. There are both dry and sweet types. Sake contains 14%–18% alcohol.

The starch in the rice is converted to glucose by enzymes produced by a mold of the genus *Aspergillus*, and then fermented. Two-thirds of Japanese sake is made with the same strain of rice; variations in taste and quality depend on the water and on how highly polished the rice is. Sake is aged for up to a year, traditionally in cedar barrels but oak is also used. *Mirin* is a sweet spirit derived from sake and used chiefly in cooking.

Sakhalin (Japanese *Karafuto*) island in the Pacific, N of Japan, that since 1947, with the Kurils, forms a region of Russia; capital Yuzhno-Sakhalinsk (Japanese *Toyohara*); area 28,564 sq mi/74,000 sq km; population (1981) 650,000, including aboriginal ▷Ainu and Gilyaks. There are two parallel mountain ranges, rising to over 5,000 ft/1,525 m, which extend throughout its length, 600 mi/965 km.

The economy is based on dairy farming, leguminous crops, oats, barley, and sugar beet. In the milder south, there is also timber, rice, wheat, fish, some oil, and coal. The island was settled by both Russians and Japanese from the 17th century. In 1875 the south was ceded by Japan to Russia, but Japan regained it 1905, only to cede it again 1945. It has a missile base.

Sakharov Andrei Dmitrievich 1921–1989. Soviet physicist, known both as the "father of the Soviet H-bomb" and as an outspoken human-rights campaigner. In 1948 he joined Igor Tamm in developing the hydrogen bomb; he later protested against Soviet nuclear tests and was a founder of the Soviet Human Rights Committee, winning the Nobel Peace Prize 1975. In 1980 he was sent to internal exile in Gorky (now Nizhni-Novgorod) for criticizing Soviet action in Afghanistan. At the end of 1986 he was allowed to return to Moscow and resume his place in the Soviet Academy of Sciences.

He was elected to the Congress of the USSR People's Deputies (CUPD) 1989, where he emerged as leader of its radical reform grouping prior to his death later the same year.

Saki adopted name of H(ugh) H(ector) Munro 1870–1916. Burmese-born British writer of ingeniously witty and bizarre short stories, often with surprise endings. He also wrote two novels, *The Unbearable Bassington* 1912 and *When William Came* 1913.

Sakkara or *Saqqara* village in Egypt, 10 mi/16 km S of Cairo, with 20 pyramids, of which the oldest (third dynasty) is the "Step Pyramid" designed by ▷Imhotep, whose own tomb here was the nucleus of the Aesklepieion, a center of healing in the ancient world.

Saladin or *Sala-ud-din* 1138–1193. Born a Kurd, sultan of Egypt from 1175, in succession to the Atabeg of Mosul, on whose behalf he conquered Egypt 1164–74. He subsequently conquered Syria 1174–87 and precipitated the third ▷Crusade by his recovery of Jerusalem from the Christians 1187. Renowned for knightly courtesy, Saladin made peace with Richard I of England 1192.

Salado two rivers of Argentina, both rising in the Andes, and about 1,000 mi/1,600 km long. *Salado del Norte*, or *Juramento*, flows from the Andes to join the Paraná; the *Salado del Sud*, or *Desaguadero*, joins the Colorado and flows into the Atlantic S of Bahía Blanca.

Salamanca city in Castilla-León, W Spain, on the river Tormes, 162 mi/260 km NW of Madrid; population (1986) 167,000. It produces pharmaceuticals and wool. Its university was founded about 1230. It has a superbly designed square, the Plaza Mayor.

Salamanca, Battle of victory of the British commander Wellington over the French army in the ▷Peninsular War, July 22, 1812.

salamander any tailed amphibian of the order *Urodela*. They are sometimes confused with lizards, but unlike lizards they have no scales or claws. Salamanders have smooth or warty moist skin. The order includes some 300 species, arranged in nine families, found mainly in the northern hemisphere. Salamanders include hellbenders, mudpuppies, waterdogs, sirens, mole salamanders, newts, and lungless salamanders (dusky, woodland, and spring salamanders).

Salamis island off Piraeus, the port of ▷Athens, Greece; area 39 sq mi/101 sq km; population (1981) 19,000. The town of Salamis, on the west coast, is a naval station.

Salamis ancient city on the east coast of Cyprus, the capital under the early Ptolemies until its harbor silted up about 200 BC, when it was succeeded by Paphos in the southwest.

Salamis, Battle of naval battle off the coast of the island of Salamis in which the Greeks defeated the Persians 480 BC.

sal ammoniac former name for ▷ammonium chloride.

salat the daily prayers that are one of the Five Pillars of ▷Islam.

Muslims are required to pray five times a day, the first prayer being before dawn and the last after dusk. Prayer must be preceded by ritual washing and may be said in any clean place, facing the direction of Mecca. The prayers, which are recited in Arabic, follow a fixed series of words and movements.

Salazar Antonio de Oliveira 1889–1970. Portuguese prime minister 1932–68 who exercised a virtual dictatorship. During World War II he maintained Portuguese neutrality but fought long colonial wars in Africa (Angola and

Mozambique) that impeded his country's economic development as well as that of the colonies.

A corporative constitution on the Italian model was introduced 1933, and until 1945 Salazar's National Union, founded 1930, remained the only legal party. Salazar was also foreign minister 1936–47.

Salem city and manufacturing center in Massachusetts, 15 mi/24 km NE of Boston; population (1990) 38,100.

Leather goods, electrical equipment, and machinery are manufactured here. Points of interest include Salem Maritime National Historic Site, the birthplace of Nathaniel Hawthorne, and the House of the Seven Gables 1668 that gave rise to his novel of the same name. Salem was settled 1626 and was the site of witchcraft trials 1692 that resulted in the execution of about 20 people.

Salem city in NW Oregon, settled about 1840 and made state capital 1859; population (1980) 89,200. It processes timber into wood products and has a prosperous fruit-and vegetable-canning industry.

Williamette University is here. Salem was established by Methodist missionaries 1840–41 and became the territorial capital 1851.

Salerno port in Campania, SW Italy, 30 mi/ 48 km SE of Naples; population (1988) 154,000. It was founded by the Romans about 194 BC, destroyed by Charlemagne, and sacked by Holy Roman Emperor Henry VI 1194. The temple ruins of the ancient Greek city of ♢**Paestum**, with some of the earliest Greek paintings known, are nearby. Salerno has had a university (1150–1817, revived 1944) and medical school since medieval times.

Salic law a law adopted in the Middle Ages by several European royal houses, excluding women from succession to the throne. The name derives mistakenly from the Salian or northern division of the Franks, who supposedly practiced it.

salicylic acid HOC_6H_4COOH the active chemical constituent of aspirin, an analgesic drug. The acid and its salts (salicylates) occur naturally in many plants; concentrated sources include willow bark and oil of wintergreen.

When purified, salicylic acid is a white solid that crystallizes into prismatic needles at 318°F/159°C. It is used as an antiseptic, in food preparation and dyestuffs, and in the preparation of aspirin.

Salieri Antonio 1750–1825. Italian composer. He taught Beethoven, Schubert, and Liszt, and was the musical rival of Mozart, whom it has been suggested, without proof, that he poisoned, at the emperor's court in Vienna, where he held the position of court composer.

Salinas city in W central California, S of San Jose. Fruits and vegetables, such as lettuce, are the economy's mainstay; population (1990) 108,800.

Salinas de Gortiari Carlos 1948– . Mexican politician, president from 1988, a member of the dominant Institutional Revolutionary Party (PRI).

Educated in Mexico and the US, he taught at Harvard and in Mexico before joining the government in 1971 and thereafter held a number of posts, mostly in the economic sphere, including finance minister. He narrowly won the 1988 presidential election, despite allegations of fraud.

Salinger J(erome) D(avid) 1919– . US writer, author of the classic novel of mid-20th-

century adolescence *The Catcher in the Rye* 1951. He also wrote short stories about a Jewish family named Glass, including *Franny and Zooey* 1961.

Born in New York City, Salinger studied writing at Columbia University. In the late 1940s, he established an association with *The New Yorker*, which published most of his short stories. After *The Catcher in the Rye* became a classic, particularly among college students, he moved to New Hampshire, became increasingly reclusive, and published nothing after the mid-1960s. He also wrote *Nine Stories* 1953 and *Raise High the Roof Beam, Carpenters* and *Seymour: An Introduction* 1963.

Salisbury city and market town in Wiltshire, England, 84 mi/135 km SW of London; population (1981) 35,355. Salisbury is an agricultural center, and industries include brewing and carpet manufacture (in nearby Wilton). The cathedral of St Mary, built 1220–66, is an example of Early English architecture; its decorated spire 404 ft/123 m is the highest in England; its clock (1386) is one of the oldest still working. The cathedral library contains one of only four copies of the *Magna Carta*.

Another name for it is **New Sarum**, Sarum being a medieval Latin corruption of the ancient Romano-British name Sorbiodonum. **Old Sarum**, on a 300-ft/90-m hill to the north, was deserted when New Sarum was founded 1220 but was later again inhabited; it was brought within the town boundary 1953.

Salisbury former name (until 1980) of ♢Harare, capital of Zimbabwe.

Salisbury Robert Arthur James Gascoyne-Cecil, 5th Marquess of Salisbury 1893–1972. British Conservative politician. He was Dominions secretary 1940–42 and 1943–45, colonial secretary 1942, Lord Privy Seal 1942–43 and 1951–52, and Lord President of the Council 1952–57.

saliva in vertebrates, a secretion from the salivary glands that aids the swallowing and digestion of food in the mouth. In mammals, it contains the enzyme amylase, which converts starch to sugar. The salivary glands of mosquitoes and other blood-sucking insects produce ♢anticoagulants.

Salk Jonas Edward 1914– . US physician and microbiologist. In 1954 he developed the original vaccine that led to virtual eradication of paralytic ♢poliomyelitis in industrialized countries. He was director of the Salk Institute for Biological Studies, University of California, San Diego, 1963–75.

Sallust Gaius Sallustius Crispus 86–*c*. 34 BC. Roman historian, a supporter of Julius Caesar. He wrote accounts of Catiline's conspiracy and the Jugurthine War in an epigrammatic style.

salmon any of the various bony fishes of the family Salmonidae. More specifically the name is applied to several species of game fishes of the genera Salmo and Oncorhynchus of North America and Eurasia that mature in the ocean but, to spawn, return to the freshwater streams where they were born. Their normal color is silvery with a few dark spots, but the color changes at the spawning season.

The spawning season is between Sept and Jan, although they occasionally spawn at other times. The orange eggs, about 0.25 in/6 mm in diameter, are laid on the river bed, fertilized by the male, and then covered with gravel by the female. The incubation period is from five weeks to five months. The young hatched fish

are known as **alevins**, and when they begin feeding they are called **parr**. At about two years old, the coat becomes silvery, and they are then **smolts**. Depending on the species, they may spend up to four years at sea before returning to their home streams to spawn (at this stage called **grilse**), often overcoming great obstacles to get there and die.

Salmon are increasingly "farmed" in cages, and "ranched" (selectively bred, hatched, and fed before release to the sea). Stocking rivers indiscriminately with hatchery fish may destroy the precision of their homing instinct by interbreeding between those originating in different rivers.

Salmonella very varied group of bacteria. They can be divided into three broad groups. One of these causes typhoid and paratyphoid fevers, while a second group causes salmonella ♢food poisoning, which is characterized by stomach pains, vomiting, diarrhea, and headache. It can be fatal in elderly people, but others usually recover in a few days without antibiotics. Most cases are caused by contaminated animal products, especially poultry meat.

Human carriers of the disease may be well themselves but pass the bacteria on to others through unhygienic preparation of food. Domestic pets can also carry the bacteria while appearing healthy.

Salome 1st century AD. In the New Testament, granddaughter of the king of Judea, Herod the Great. Rewarded for her skill in dancing, she requested the head of John the Baptist from her stepfather ♢Herod Antipas.

Salomon Haym *c*. 1740–1785. Polish-born American financier. Salomon traveled extensively throughout Europe before settling permanently in New York 1772. As a successful merchant and supporter of American independence, he undertook the provisioning of Continental troops at the outbreak of the Revolutionary War. He was arrested briefly by the British as a spy 1776, and in 1778 he was captured and sentenced to death. After escaping, Salomon offered his financial services to the Continental Congress. From 1778 to 1782 he raised large public subscriptions for the continuance of the war.

salon (French "drawing room") meeting place provided by a wealthy host or hostess for writers, artists, and musicians. The term was first used in 17th-century Paris to describe the gatherings of artists and intellectuals in the houses of rich and cultured ladies. The tradition of the "literary hostess" has continued in Europe and the US.

Salonika English name for ♢Thessaloniki, port in Greece.

salsa Latin big-band dance music popularized by Puerto Ricans in New York City in the 1980s and by, among others, the Panamanian singer Rubén Blades (1948–).

salsify or **vegetable oyster** hardy biennial *Tragopogon porrifolius*, family Compositae. Its white fleshy roots and spring shoots are cooked and eaten.

salt in chemistry, any compound formed from an acid and a base through the replacement of all or part of the hydrogen in the acid by a metal or electropositive radical. **Common salt** is sodium chloride (see ♢salt, common).

A salt may be produced by chemical reaction between an acid and a base, or by the displacement of hydrogen from an acid by a metal (see ♢displacement activity). As a solid, the ions normally adopt a regular arrangement to form crystals. Some salts only form stable crystals as hydrates (when combined with water). Most inorganic salts readily dissolve in water to give an electrolyte (a solution that conducts electricity).

SALT abbreviation for ◊*Strategic Arms Limitation Talks*, a series of US–Soviet negotiations 1969–79.

saltation (Latin *saltare* "to leap") in biology, the idea that an abrupt genetic change can occur in an individual, which then gives rise to a new species. The idea has now been largely discredited, although the appearance of ◊polyploid individuals can be considered an example.

salt, common or *sodium chloride* NaCl white crystalline solid, found dissolved in sea water and as rock salt (halite) in large deposits and salt domes. Common salt is used extensively in the food industry as a preservative and for flavoring, and in the chemical industry in the making of chlorine and sodium.

While common salt is an essential part of our diet, some medical experts believe that excess salt can lead to high blood pressure and increased risk of heart attacks.

Salt has historically been considered a sustaining substance, often taking on religious significance in ancient cultures. Roman soldiers were paid part of their wages as salt allowance (Latin *salerium argentinium*), hence the term "salary."

Salt Lake City capital of Utah, on the river Jordan, 11 mi/18 km SE of the Great Salt Lake; population (1990) 159,900.

Founded 1847, it is the headquarters of the Church of Jesus Christ of Latter-Day Saints (Mormon Church). The Mormon Tabernacle, Mormon Temple, and University of Utah are here. Products include refined petroleum, metal goods, processed food, and textiles; nearby mining adds to the city's economy. Salt Lake City became the territorial capital 1856.

salt marsh wetland with halophytic vegetation (tolerant to sea water). Salt marshes develop around estuaries and on the sheltered side of sand and shingle spits. Salt marshes usually have a network of creeks and drainage channels by which tidal waters enter and leave the marsh.

Salton Sea brine lake in SE California, area 250 sq mi/650 sq km, accidentally created in the early 20th century during irrigation works from the Colorado River. It is used to generate electricity; see ◊solar ponds.

saltpeter former name for potassium nitrate (KNO₃), the compound used in making gunpowder (from about 1500). It occurs naturally, being deposited during dry periods in places with warm climates, such as India.

saluki breed of dog resembling the grayhound. It is about 26 in/65 cm high and has a silky coat, which is usually fawn, cream, or white.

It is descended from the hound of the African desert Bedouins.

Salvador port and naval base in Bahia state, NE Brazil, on the inner side of a peninsula separating Todos Santos Bay from the Atlantic; population (1991) 2,075,400. Products include cocoa, tobacco, and sugar. Founded 1510, it was the capital of Brazil 1549–1763.

Salvador, El republic in Central America; see ◊El Salvador.

salvage saving or rescue, either as a whole or in part, of any property threatened with

destruction, especially at sea. The term is used more specifically for compensation payable to those who, by voluntary effort, have saved a ship and/or its cargo and passengers from complete loss through shipwreck, fire, or enemy action.

Salvarsan historical proprietary name for arsphenamine (technical name 3,3-diamino-4,4-dihydroxyarsenobenzene dichloride), the first specific antibacterial agent, discovered by Paul Ehrlich in 1909. Because of its destructive effect on *Spirochaeta pallida*, it was used in the treatment of syphilis before the development of antibiotics.

Salvation Army Christian evangelical, social-service, and social-reform organization, originating 1865 in London, with the work of William ◊Booth. It has military titles for its officials, is renowned for its brass bands, and it publishes the weekly journal *War Cry*. Originally called the Christian Revival Association, it has been known since 1878 as the Salvation Army. It provides food-and-shelter missions for social derelicts and runs "thrift shops," selling second-hand merchandise to raise funds.

It was established in the US 1880 and in Canada 1881 and has conducted missionary work throughout the world. The American Rescue Workers split off from the organization in 1884, and the Volunteers of America withdrew in 1894 after disputes over organizational structure and autonomy. Doctrine and ritual have never been primary concerns of the Salvation Army, which devotes itself to preaching redemption from a sinful life. It currently has about 300,000 US members.

sal volatile another name for ◊smelling salts.

Salween river rising in E Tibet and flowing 1,740 mi/2,800 km through Myanmar (Burma) to the Andaman Sea; it has many rapids.

Salyut (Russian "salute") series of seven space stations launched by the USSR 1971–82. Salyut was cylindrical in shape, 50 ft/15 m long, and weighed 21 tons. It housed two or three cosmonauts at a time, for missions lasting up to eight months.

Salyut 1 was launched April 19, 1971. It was occupied for 23 days in June 1971 by a crew of three, who died during their return to Earth when their ◊Soyuz ferry craft depressurized. *Salyut 2*, in 1973, broke up in orbit before occupation. The first fully successful Salyut mission was a 14-day visit to *Salyut 3* in July 1974. In 1984–85 a team of three cosmonauts endured a record 237-day flight in *Salyut 7*. In 1986, the Salyut series was superseded by ◊*Mir*, an improved design capable of being enlarged by additional modules sent up from Earth.

Salzburg capital of the state of Salzburg, W Austria, on the river Salzach, in W Austria; population (1981) 139,400. The city is dominated by the Hohensalzburg fortress. It is the seat of an archbishopric founded by St Boniface about 700 and has a 17th-century cathedral. Industries include stock rearing, dairy farming, forestry, and tourism.

It is the birthplace of the composer Wolfgang Amadeus Mozart and an annual music festival has been held here since 1920.

Salzburg federal province of Austria; area 2,779 sq mi/7,200 sq km; population (1987) 462,000. Its capital is Salzburg.

samara in botany, a winged fruit, a type of ◊achene.

Samara capital of Kuibyshev region, W central Russia, and port at the junction of the rivers

Samara and Volga, situated in the center of the fertile middle Volga plain; industries include aircraft, locomotives, cables, synthetic rubber, textiles, fertilizers, petroleum refining, and quarrying; population (1987) 1,280,000. From 1935–91 it was called *Kuibyshev*, reverting to its former name Jan 1991.

The city was provisional capital of the USSR 1941–43.

Samaria region of ancient Israel. The town of Samaria (now Sebastiyeh) on the west bank of the river Jordan was the capital of Israel in the 10th–8th centuries BC. It was renamed Sebarte in the 1st century BC by the Roman administrator Herod the Great. Extensive remains have been excavated.

Samaritan member or descendant of the colonists forced to settle in Samaria (now N Israel) by the Assyrians after their occupation of the ancient kingdom of Israel 722 BC. Samaritans adopted a form of Judaism, but adopted only the Pentateuch, the five books of Moses of the Old Testament, and regarded their temple on Mount Gerizim as the true sanctuary.

They remained a conservative, separate people and declined under Muslim rule, with only a few hundred, in a small community at Nablus, surviving today.

samarium hard, brittle, gray-white, metallic element of the ◊lanthanide series, symbol Sm, atomic number 62, atomic weight 150.4. It is widely distributed in nature and is obtained commercially from the minerals monzanite and bastnasite. It is used only occasionally in industry, mainly as a catalyst in organic reactions. Samarium was discovered by spectroscopic analysis of the mineral samarskite and named in 1879 by French chemist Paul Lecoq de Boisbaudran (1838–1912) after its source.

Samarkand city in E Uzbekistan, capital of Samarkand region, near the river Zerafshan, 135 mi/217 km E of Bukhara; population (1987) 388,000. Industries include cotton-ginning, silk manufacture, and engineering.

Samarkand was the capital of the empire of ◊Tamerlane, the 14th-century Mongol ruler, who is buried here, and was once a major city on the ◊Silk Road. It was occupied by the Russians in 1868 but remained a center of Muslim culture until the Russian Revolution.

Samarra ancient town in Iraq, on the river Tigris, 65 mi/105 km NW of Baghdad; population (1970) 62,000. Founded 836 by the Abbasid Caliph Motassim, it was the Abbasid capital until 876 and is a place of pilgrimage for ◊Shiite Muslims. It is the site of a poison-gas plant.

samba Latin American ballroom dance; the music for this. Samba originated in Brazil and became popular in the West in the 1940s. There are several different samba rhythms; the *bossa nova* is a samba-jazz fusion.

samizdat (Russian "self-published") in the USSR and eastern Europe before the 1989 uprisings, written material circulated underground to evade state censorship; for example, reviews of Solzhenitzyn's banned novel *August 1914* 1972.

Samoa volcanic island chain in the SW Pacific. It is divided into Western Samoa and American Samoa.

Samoa, American group of islands 2,610 mi/4,200 km S of Hawaii, administered by the US

area 77 sq mi/200 sq km
capital Fagatogo on Tutuila

Samoa, Western
Independent State of (*Samoa i Sisifo*)

area 1,093 sq mi/2,830 sq km
capital Apia (on Upolu island)
physical comprises South Pacific islands of Savai'i and Upolu, with two smaller tropical islands and islets; mountain ranges on main islands
features lava flows on Savai'i
head of state King Malietoa Tanumafili II from 1962
head of government Tofilau Eti Alesana from 1988
political system liberal democracy
political parties Human Rights Protection Party (HRPP), led by Tofilau Eti Alesana; the Va'ai Kolone Group (VKG); Christian Democratic Party (CDP), led by Tupua Tamasese

Efi. All "parties" are personality-based groupings
exports coconut oil, copra, cocoa, fruit juice, cigarettes, timber
currency talà
population (1989) 169,000; growth rate 1.1% p.a.
life expectancy men 64, women 69 (1989)
languages English, Samoan (official)
religion Protestant 70%, Roman Catholic 20%
literacy 90% (1989)
GNP $110 million (1987); $520 per head
chronology
1899–1914 German protectorate.
1920–61 Administered by New Zealand.
1959 Local government elected.
1961 Referendum favored independence.
1962 Independence achieved within the Commonwealth, with Fiame Mata Afa Mulinu'u as prime minister.
1975 Mata Afa died.
1976 Tupuola Taisi Efi became first nonroyal prime minister.
1982 Va'ai Kolone became prime minister; replaced by Tupuola Efi. Assembly failed to approve budget; Tupuola Efi resigned; replaced by Tofilau Eti Alesana.
1985 Tofilau Eti resigned; head of state invited Va'ai Kolone to lead the government.
1988 Elections produced a hung parliament, with first Tupuola Efi as prime minister and then Tofilau Eti Alesana.
1990 Universal adult suffrage introduced.
1991 Tofilau Eti Alesana reelected. Fiame Naome became first woman in cabinet.

features five volcanic islands, including Tutuila, Tau, and Swain's Island, and two coral atolls. National park (1988) includes prehistoric village of Saua, virgin rainforest, flying foxes
exports canned tuna, handicrafts
currency US dollar
population (1990) 46,800
language Samoan and English
religion Christian
government as a non-self-governing territory of the US, under Governor A P Lutali, it is constitutionally an unincorporated territory of the US, administered by the Department of the Interior
history the islands were acquired by the US in Dec 1899 by agreement with Britain and Germany under the Treaty of Berlin. A constitution was adopted 1960 and revised 1967.

Samoa, Western country in the SW Pacific Ocean, in ⟡Polynesia, NE of Fiji.
government Western Samoa is an independent state within the British ⟡Commonwealth. The 1962 constitution provides for a parliamentary system of government, with a constitutional head of state, a single-chamber legislative assembly, and a prime minister and cabinet drawn from and responsible to the assembly. The head of state is normally elected by the assembly for a five-year term, but the present holder of the office has been elected for life. The head of state appoints the prime minister and cabinet on the basis of assembly support.

The assembly (Fono) has 47 members, including 45 Samoans, who are elected by clan chiefs (holders of Matai titles) in 41 territorial constituencies, and two, usually European, members who are elected by voters of European descent. The assembly has a life of three years.

history The original inhabitants were Polynesians, and the first Europeans to reach the island group of Samoa, 1722, were Dutch. In the 19th century, Germany, the UK, and the US had conflicting interests in the islands and administered them jointly 1889–99, when they were divided into American ⟡Samoa and Western Samoa. Western Samoa was a German colony until World War I and from 1920 was administered by New Zealand, first as a League of Nations mandate and from 1946 as a United Nations trust territory.
independence Western Samoa was granted internal self-government gradually until it achieved full independence, within the Commonwealth, Jan 1, 1962. The office of head of state was held jointly by two traditional rulers, but on the death of one of them, the other, Malietoa Tanumafili II, became the sole head of state for life. The prime minister at the time of independence was Fiame Mata Afa Mulinu'u. He lost power 1970 but regained it 1973 and held office until his death 1975. In 1976 the first prime minister who was not of royal blood was elected, Tupuola Taisi Efi.

In 1979 the opposition politicians came together to form the Human Rights Protection Party (HRPP) which won the 1982 election, Va'ai Kolone becoming prime minister. Later that year he was replaced by Tupuola Efi. Efi resigned a few months later when his budget was not approved and was replaced by the new HRPP leader, Tofilau Eti Alesana. The HRPP won a decisive victory Feb 1985, and Tofilau Eti Alesana continued as prime minister. At the end of the year he resigned and Va'ai Kolone returned to lead a government of independents and members of Tupuola Taisi Efi's (now known as Tupua Tamasese Efi) newly formed Christian Democratic Party (CDP). The general election Feb 1988 produced a hung parliament with Tofilau Eti Alesana emerging

as premier. Following the introduction of universal adult suffrage 1990, Tofilau Eti Alesana was returned for a further three-year term in the April 1991 general election, and Va'ai Kolone resumed leadership of the opposition. Tofilau Eti Alesana made wholesale changes to his cabinet May 1991, bringing in Fiame Naomi as the first woman to serve in a Western Samoan cabinet. *See illustration box.*

Samos Greek island in the Aegean Sea, off the W coast of Turkey; area 184 sq mi/476 sq km; capital Limén Vathéos; population (1981) 31,600. Mountainous but fertile, it produces wine and olive oil. The mathematician Pythagoras was born here. The town of Teganion is on the site of the ancient city of Samos, which was destroyed by Darius I of Persia.

samoyed breed of dog, originating in Siberia. It weighs about 60 lb/25 kg and is 23 in/58 cm tall. It resembles a ⟡chow chow, but has a more pointed face and a white or cream coat.

samphire or *glasswort* or *sea asparagus* perennial plant *Crithmum maritimum* found on sea cliffs in Europe. The aromatic leaves are fleshy and sharply pointed; the flowers grow in yellow-green umbels. It is used in salads, or pickled.

Samson 11th century BC. In the Old Testament, a hero of Israel. He was renowned for exploits of strength against the Philistines, which ended when his lover Delilah cut off his hair, the source of his strength, as told in the Book of Judges.

Samuel 11th–10 centuries BC. In the Old Testament, the last of the judges who ruled the ancient Hebrews before their adoption of a monarchy, and the first of the prophets; the two books bearing his name cover the story of Samuel and the reigns of kings Saul and David.

Samuelson Paul 1915– . US economist. He became professor at the Massachusetts Institute of Technology 1940 and was awarded a Nobel Prize 1970 for his application of scientific analysis to economic theory. His books include *Economics* 1948, a classic textbook, and *Linear Programming and Economic Analysis* 1958.

samurai member of the military caste in Japan from the mid-12th century until 1869, when the feudal system was abolished and all samurai pensioned off by the government. A samurai was an armed retainer of a *daimyō* (large landowner) with specific duties and privileges and a strict code of honor. A *rōnin* was a samurai without feudal allegiance.

From the 16th century, commoners were not allowed to carry swords, whereas samurai had two swords, and the higher class of samurai were permitted to fight on horseback. It is estimated that 8% of the population belonged to samurai families. A financial depression from about 1700 caused serious hardship to the samurai, beginning a gradual disintegration of their traditions and prestige, accelerated by the fall of the Tokugawa shogunate 1868, in which they had assisted. Under the new Meiji emperor they were stripped of their role, and many rebelled. Their last uprising was the **Satsuma Rebellion** 1877–78, in which 40,000 samurai took part.

San'a capital of Yemen, SW Arabia, 200 mi/320 km N of Aden; population (1986) 427,000. A walled city, with fine mosques and traditional architecture, it is rapidly being modernized.

San Andreas fault geological fault line stretching for 700 mi/1,125 km in a NW–SE direction through the state of California.

Two sections of the Earth's crust meet at the San Andreas fault, and friction is created as the coastal Pacific plate moves northwest, rubbing against the American continental plate, which is moving slowly southeast. The relative movement is only about 2 in/5 cm a year, which means that Los Angeles will reach San Francisco's latitude in 10 million years. The friction caused by this tectonic movement gives rise to periodic ◊earthquakes.

San Angelo city in W central Texas, where the North and Middle Concho rivers meet, SW of Abilene. Industries include wool, food processing, oil, livestock, and clay products; population (1990) 84,500.

San Antonio city in S Texas; population (1990) 936,000. It is a commercial and financial center; industries include aircraft maintenance, oil refining, and meat packing.

Of great economic importance are Fort Sam Houston, four Air Force bases, South Texas Medical Center, and the Southwest Research Center, all within city limits. Educational institutions include Trinity University and the University of Texas at San Antonio. Points of interest include 18th-century Spanish missions and the Alamo, the Texan-occupied mission-fortress stormed in 1836 by Mexican troops who massacred the entire garrison. A Spanish mission and fort were established here on an Indian site 1718, and a community was laid out 1731. It passed from Spanish to Mexican rule 1821, to the Texas republic 1836, and to the US 1845.

San Bernardino city in California, 50 mi/80 km E of Los Angeles; population (1980) 164,200, metropolitan area 703,000.

Manufactured products include processed food, steel, and aerospace and electronic equipment. Norton Air Force Base is just outside the city. San Bernardino was named by Spanish missionaries who arrived 1810. A group of Mormons platted the community in the 1850s.

San Cristóbal capital of Tachira state, W Venezuela, near the Colombian border; population (1989) 355,900. It was founded by Spanish settlers 1561 and stands on the ◊Pan-American Highway.

sanction economic or military measure taken by a state or number of states to enforce international law. The first use of sanctions was the attempted economic boycott of Italy (1935–36) during the Abyssinian War by the League of Nations.

Other examples of sanctions are the economic boycott of Rhodesia, after its unilateral declaration of independence 1965, by the United Nations; the call for measures against South Africa on human-rights grounds by the UN and other organizations from 1985; and the economic boycott of Iraq 1990 in protest over its invasion of Kuwait, following resolutions passed by the UN.

Sanctorius Sanctorius 1561–1636. Italian physiologist who pioneered the study of ◊metabolism and invented the clinical thermometer and a device for measuring pulse rate.

Sanctorius introduced quantitative methods into medicine. For 30 years he weighed both himself and his food, drink, and waste products. He determined that over half of normal weight loss is due to "insensible perspiration."

sanctuary (Latin *sanctuarium* "sacred place") the holiest area of a place of worship; also, a place of refuge from persecution or prosecution, usually in or near a place of worship. The custom of offering sanctuary in specific places goes back to ancient times and was widespread in Europe in the Middle Ages.

The ancient Hebrews established six separate towns of refuge, and the Greek temple of Diana at Ephesus provided sanctuary within a radius of two stadia (about 475 yd/434 m). In Roman temples the sanctuary was the *cella* (inner room), in which stood the statue of the god worshiped there.

In the Middle Ages criminals or the hunted could take refuge for 40 days, then opt for safe passage out of the country.

sand loose grains of rock, sized 0.0008–0.0800 in/0.02–2.00 mm in diameter, consisting chiefly of ◊quartz, but owing their varying color to mixtures of other minerals. Sand is used in cement-making, as an abrasive, in glass-making, and for other purposes.

Sands are classified into marine, freshwater, glacial, and terrestrial. Some "light" soils contain up to 50% sand. Sands may eventually consolidate into ◊sandstone.

Sand George. Adopted name of Amandine Aurore Lucie Dupin 1804–1876. French author whose prolific literary output was often autobiographical. In 1831 she left her husband after nine years of marriage and, while living in Paris as a writer, had love affairs with Alfred de ◊Musset, ◊Chopin, and others. Her first novel *Indiana* 1832 was a plea for women's right to independence.

Her other novels include *La mare au diable/The Devil's Pool* 1846 and *La petite Fadette/The Little Fairy* 1848. In 1848 she retired to the château of Nohant, in central France.

sandalwood fragrant heartwood of any of certain Asiatic and Australian trees of the genus *Santalum*, family Santalaceae, used for ornamental carving, in perfume, and burned as incense.

sandbar ridge of sand built up by the currents across the mouth of a river or bay. A sandbar may be entirely underwater or it may form an elongated island that breaks the surface. A sandbar stretching out from a headland is a *sand spit*.

Sandburg Carl August 1878–1967. US poet. He worked as a farm laborer and a bricklayer, and his poetry celebrates ordinary life in the US, as in *Chicago Poems* 1916, *The People, Yes* 1936, and *Complete Poems* 1951 (Pulitzer Prize). In free verse, it is reminiscent of Walt Whitman's poetry. Sandburg also wrote a monumental biography of Abraham Lincoln, *Abraham Lincoln: The Prairie Years* 1926 (two volumes) and *Abraham Lincoln: The War Years* 1939 (four volumes; Pulitzer Prize). *Always the Young Strangers* 1953 is his autobiography.

Born in Galesburg, Illinois, where a Lincoln-Douglas debate had taken place 1858, Sandburg left school after the eighth grade to work. After serving in the Spanish-American War, he briefly attended college but never graduated. *The American Songbag* 1927 is his collection of folk ballads and songs assembled during his travels around the US 1902–04. He also wrote *Smoke and Steel* 1920, *Slabs of the Sunburnt West* 1922, *Mary Lincoln, Wife and Widow* 1932, and *Storm Over the Land* 1942. Sandburg's children's books include *Rootabaga Stories* 1922.

sandgrouse any bird of the family Pteroclidae. They look like long-tailed grouse, but are actually closely related to pigeons. They live in warm, dry areas of Europe, Asia,

and Africa and have long wings, short legs, and thick skin.

Sandgrouse may travel long distances to water to drink, and some carry water back to their young by soaking the breast feathers.

sand hopper or *beachflea* any of various small crustaceans belonging to the order Amphipeda, with laterally compressed bodies, that live in beach sand and jump like fleas. The eastern sand hopper *Orchestia agilis* of North America is about 0.5 in/1.3 cm long.

San Diego city and military and naval base in California; population (1990) 1,110,600, metropolitan area 2,498,000. It is an important Pacific Ocean fishing port. Manufacturing includes aerospace and electronic equipment, metal fabrication, printing and publishing, seafood canning, and shipbuilding.

The US Navy's largest operational complex is here. Educational institutions include the Salk Institute of Biological Studies, San Diego State University, the University of San Diego, and the University of California at San Diego, which includes the Scripps Institute of Oceanography in neighboring La Jolla. Attractions include the San Diego Zoo and Sea World. A 16-mi/26-km transit line opened 1981 connects to Tijuana, Mexico. San Diego's excellent deepwater harbor was discovered by Portuguese explorer Juan Rodriquez Cabrillo 1542. A Spanish mission and fort were established 1769. It passed to the US 1846 in the Mexican War. The coming of the railroad in 1884 began a period of rapid growth, particularly after 1940, with the establishment of military installations and defense-related industries.

Sandinista member of the socialist movement that carried out the ◊Nicaraguan Revolution.

sandpiper any of various shorebirds belonging to the family Scolopacidae, which includes godwits, ◊curlews, and ◊snipes.

Other members of the family include yellowlegs, tattlers, and dowitchers. The purple sandpiper *Calidris maritima* of E North America 9 in/23 cm long, has buff and brown plumage, orange-yellow legs, and a long, slender bill.

sandstone ◊sedimentary rocks formed from the consolidation of sand, with sand-sized grains (0.0025–0.08 in/0.0625–2 mm) in a matrix or cement. The principal component is quartz. Sandstones are classified according to the matrix or cement material (whether derived from clay or silt; for example, as calcareous sandstone, ferruginous sandstone, siliceous sandstone).

Sandwich resort and market town in Kent, England; population (1981) 4,184. It has many medieval buildings and was one of the ◊Cinque Ports, but recession of the sea has left the harbor useless since the 16th century.

Sandwich John Montagu, 4th Earl of Sandwich 1718–1792. British politician. He was an inept First Lord of the Admiralty 1771–82 during the American Revolution, and his corrupt practices were blamed for the British navy's inadequacies.

The Sandwich Islands (Hawaii) were named after him, as are sandwiches, which he invented so that he could eat without leaving the gaming table.

Sandwich Islands former name of ◊Hawaii, a group of islands in the Pacific.

San Francisco chief Pacific port of the US, in California; population (1990) 724,000, metropolitan area of San Francisco and Oakland

3,686,600. The city stands on a peninsula, south of the Golden Gate 1937, the world's second longest single-span bridge, 4,200 ft/ 1,280 m. The strait gives access to San Francisco Bay. Manufactured goods include textiles, fabricated metal products, electrical equipment, petroleum products, chemicals, and pharmaceuticals.

San Francisco is also a financial, trade, corporate, and diversified service center, and tourism is important to its economy as well. Points of interest include Chinatown, Fisherman's Wharf, Nob and Telegraph hills, and Golden Gate Park. Educational institutions include San Francisco State University, the University of San Francisco, and the University of California at San Francisco. It is also connected by bridge to Berkeley, with the University of California at Berkeley campus.

history In 1578 Sir Francis Drake's flagship, the *Golden Hind*, stopped near San Francisco on its voyage around the world. A Spanish fort and mission were established 1776. The original Spanish village was called Yerba Buena; its name was changed to San Francisco in 1846. In the same year the town was occupied during the war with Mexico. When gold was discovered in 1848 its population increased from about 800 to about 25,000 in two years. In 1906 the city was almost destroyed by an earthquake and subsequent fire that killed 452 people. It was the site of the drawing up of the United Nations Charter 1945 and of the signing of the peace treaty between the Allied nations and Japan 1951. Another earthquake rocked the city 1989.

San Francisco conference conference attended by representatives from 50 nations who had declared war on Germany before March 1, 1945; held in San Francisco, California. The conference drew up the United Nations Charter, which was signed June 26, 1945.

Sanger Frederick 1918–   . English biochemist, the winner of two Nobel Prizes for Chemistry: one for his clarifying the structure of insulin, and the other, with two US scientists, for his work on the chemical structure of genes.

Sanger Margaret Higgins 1883–1966. US health reformer and crusader for birth control. In 1914 she founded the National Birth Control League and in 1917 was sent briefly to prison for opening in 1916 a public birth-control clinic in Brooklyn.

Born in Corning, New York, Sanger received nursing degrees from White Plains Hospital and the Manhattan Eye and Ear Clinic. As a nurse, she saw the deaths and deformity caused by self-induced abortions and became committed to providing health and birth-control education to the poor. She founded and presided over the American Birth Control League 1921–28, the organization that later became the Planned Parenthood Federation of America, and the International Planned Parenthood Federation 1952. Her *Autobiography* appeared 1938.

Sanhedrin (2nd century BC–1st century AD) ancient supreme court in Jerusalem headed by the Jewish high priest. Its functions were judicial, administrative, and religious.

The Great Sanhedrin was purely religious and continued on in Europe until *c.* 450 as the rabbinic patriarchate.

San José capital of Costa Rica; population (1989) 284,600. Products include coffee, cocoa, and sugar cane. Founded 1737; capital since 1823.

San José city in Santa Clara Valley, California; population (1990) 782,200. It is the center of "Silicon Valley," the site of many high-technology electronic firms turning out semiconductors and other computer components. There are also electrical, aerospace, missile, rubber, metal, and machine industries, and it is a commercial and transportation center for orchard crops and wines produced in the area.

San Jose State University is here, and the Lick Observatory is on nearby Mount Hamilton. San Jose was founded as California's first nonmilitary settlement in 1777 and served as the state capital 1849–51. The population increased more than sixfold between 1950 and 1980 as it was transformed from an agricultural to an industrial center.

San Juan capital of Puerto Rico; population (1990) 437,750. It is a port and industrial city. Products include chemicals, pharmaceuticals, machine tools, electronic equipment, textiles, plastics, and rum.

The main campus of the University of Puerto Rico is here. San Juan was settled 1521 and remained under Spanish rule until 1898, when the island was ceded to the US.

San Luis Potosí silver-mining city and capital of San Luis Potosi state, central Mexico; population (1986) 602,000. Founded 1586 as a Franciscan mission, it became the colonial administrative headquarters and has fine buildings of the period.

San Marino small landlocked country within NE Italy.

government San Marino has no formal constitution. The single-chamber Great and General Council has 60 members, elected by universal suffrage for a five-year term. The council elects two of its members, one representing the capital and one the country, to serve a six-month period as captains-regent. Together they share the duties of head of state and head of government. They preside over a cabinet of ten, elected by the Council for a five-year term, called the Congress of State.

The country is divided into nine "castles," which correspond to the original nine parishes of the republic. Each castle is governed by a

castle captain and an auxiliary council, both serving a one-year term.

history San Marino claims to be the world's oldest republic, founded by St Marinus in the 4th century; it is the only city-state to remain after the unification of Italy in the 19th century. It has had a treaty of friendship with Italy since 1862. Women had no vote until 1960.

San Marino's multiparty system mirrors that of the larger country that surrounds it. Since about 1950 it has been governed by a series of left-wing coalitions; the "grand coalition," comprising the Communists (PCS), and Christian Democrats (PDCS), was formed July 1986. At the May 1988 council election the PDCS secured 27 seats and the PCS 18, while the opposition Socialist Unionist Party (PSU) captured 8 and the Socialist Party (PPS) 7 seats. San Marino became a member of the United Nations 1992. *See illustration box.*

San Martín José de 1778–1850. South American revolutionary leader. He served in the Spanish army during the Peninsular War, but after 1812 he devoted himself to the South American struggle for independence, playing a large part in the liberation of Argentina, Chile, and Peru from Spanish rule.

Born in Argentina, he was educated in Spain and served in the Spanish army for more than 20 years. In 1812 he returned to Argentina to fight for South American independence from Spain. In 1817 he and Bernardo O'Higgins led an army across the snow-covered Andes and attacked Spanish forces in Chile, liberating that country the following year. He helped liberate Peru 1821 and assumed the title "Protector of Peru" but resigned the following year and returned to Argentina. He went into exile in Europe 1824.

sannyasin in Hinduism, a person who has renounced worldly goods to live a life of asceticism and seek *moksha*, or liberation from reincarnation, through meditation and prayer.

San Pedro Sula main industrial and commercial city in NW Honduras, the second-largest city in the country; population (1989) 300,900. It trades in bananas, coffee, sugar, and timber and manufactures textiles, plastics, furniture, and cement.

San Marino
Republic of (*Repubblica di San Marino*)

area 24 sq mi/61 sq km
capital San Marino
cities Serravalle (industrial center)
physical on the slope of Mount Titano
features surrounded by Italian territory; one

of the world's smallest states
head of state and government two captains regent, elected for a six-month period
political system direct democracy
political parties San Marino Christian Democrat Party (PDCS), right-of-center; Democratic Progressive Party (PDP), Socialist Unity Party (PSU), and Socialist Party (PSS), all three left-of-center **exports** wine, ceramics, paint, chemicals, building stone
currency Italian lira
population (1990 est) 23,000; growth rate 0.1% p.a.
life expectancy men 70, women 77
language Italian
religion Roman Catholic 95%
literacy 97% (1987)
chronology
1862 Treaty with Italy signed; independence recognized under Italy's protection.
1947–86 Governed by a series of left-wing and center-left coalitions.
1986 Formation of Communist and Christian Democrat "grand coalition."
1992 Joined the United Nations (UN).

San Salvador capital of El Salvador 30 mi/ 48 km from the Pacific, at the foot of San Salvador volcano (8,360 ft/2,548 m); population (1984) 453,000. Industries include food processing and textiles. Since its foundation 1525, it has suffered from several earthquakes.

sans-culotte (French "without knee breeches") in the French Revolution, a member of the working classes, who wore trousers, as opposed to the aristocracy and bourgeoisie, who wore knee breeches.

San Sebastián port and resort in the Basque Country, Spain; population (1986) 180,000. It was formerly the summer residence of the Spanish court.

Sanskrit the dominant Classical language of the Indian subcontinent, a member of the Indo-Iranian group of the Indo-European language family, and the sacred language of Hinduism. The oldest form of Sanskrit is *Vedic*, the variety used in the *Vedas* and *Upanishads* (about 1500–700 BC).

Classical Sanskrit was systematized by Panini and other grammarians in the latter part of the 1st millennium BC and became fixed as the spoken and written language of culture, philosophy, mathematics, law, and medicine. It is written in Devanagari script and is the language of the two great Hindu epics, the *Mahābhārata* and the *Rāmāyana*, as well as many other Classical and later works. Sanskrit vocabulary has not only influenced the languages of India, Thailand, and Indonesia, but has also enriched several European languages, including English, with borrowed words as well as etymological bases.

Santa Ana commercial city in NW El Salvador, the second largest city in the country; population (1980) 205,000. It trades in coffee and sugar.

Santa Ana periodic warm Californian ▷wind.

Santa Anna Antonio López de 1795–1876. Mexican revolutionary who became general and dictator of Mexico for most of the years between 1824 and 1855. He led the attack on the ▷Alamo fort in Texas 1836.

A leader in achieving Mexican independence from Spain 1821, he led revolts against Emperor Agustín and two presidents, becoming president himself in 1833 and later assuming dictatorial powers. When the people of Texas, then part of Mexico, revolted against the Santa Anna government, he led the forces that captured the Alamo in San Antonio 1836 but was wounded and captured later that year. Released after agreeing to independence for Texas, he returned to Mexico, where he regained political power. Defeated by US forces during the Mexican War 1846–48, Santa Anna was forced into exile, but he seized power again 1853, ruling as a dictator until he was forced from power for the last time 1855. For most of the next 20 years he lived in exile but returned to Mexico shortly before his death.

Santa Barbara oceanside city in S California; population (1990) 85,571. It is the site of a campus of the University of California. The Santa Ynez mountains are to the N. Manufactures include aircraft and aerospace equipment, precision instruments, and electronic components, but the city is better known for its wealthy residents and as a resort. A Spanish presidio and a mission (still in use) were built here in the 1780s, and the first American settler arrived 1816.

Santa Claus the American name, derived from the Dutch, for St Nicholas. He is depicted as a fat, jolly old man with a long white beard, dressed in boots and a red hat and suit trimmed with white fur. He lives with Mrs Claus and his toy-making elves at the North Pole, and on Christmas Eve he travels in an airborne sleigh, drawn by eight reindeer, to deliver presents to good children, who are fast asleep when Santa arrives. The most popular legends claim that Santa lands his sleigh on rooftops, secretly entering homes through the chimney.

Santa Cruz city in W central California at the N end of Monterey Bay, SW of San Jose. A division of the University of California is here. Industries include tourism, food processing, fishing, and electronics; population (1990) 49,000.

Santa Cruz de la Sierra capital of Santa Cruz department in E Bolivia, the second-largest city in the country; population (1988) 615,100. Sugar cane and cattle were the base of local industry until newly discovered oil and natural gas led to phenomenal growth.

Santa Cruz de Tenerife capital of Tenerife and of the Canary Islands; population (1991) 192,000. It is a fueling port and cable center. Industry also includes oil refining, pharmaceuticals, and trade in fruit. Santa Cruz was bombarded by the British admirals Blake 1657 and Nelson 1797 (the action in which he lost his arm).

Santa Fé capital of Santa Fé province, Argentina, on the Salado River 95 mi/153 km N of Rosario; population (1980) 287,000. It has shipyards and exports timber, cattle, and wool. It was founded 1573, and the 1853 constitution was adopted here.

Santa Fe capital of New Mexico, on the Santa Fe River, 40 mi/65 km W of Las Vegas; population (1990) 55,900, many Spanish-speaking. A number of buildings date from the Spanish period, including a palace 1609–10; the cathedral 1869 is on the site of a monastery built 1622. Santa Fe produces American Indian jewelry and textiles; its chief industry is tourism.

It is home to many artists and is noted for theater and opera. Santa Fe was founded 1610; it passed to Mexico 1821 and to the US 1846, during the Mexican War. It became the territorial capital 1851.

Santa Fe Trail US trade route 1821–80 from Independence, Missouri, to Santa Fe, New Mexico.

Established by trader William Becknell, the trail passed through Raton Pass and between tributaries of the Kansas and Arkansas rivers. Later, to allow the passage of wheeled wagons, Becknell turned south and headed across the Cimarron Desert. This reduced the journey by 100 mi/160 km but increased the hardship and danger of Indian attack. The trade along the trail expanded to nearly 5,000 wagons carrying millions of dollars' worth of goods each year. It was rendered obsolete in 1880 when railroad lines were extended to Santa Fe.

Santa Maria city in SW California, NW of Santa Barbara. Industries include oil, food processing, and dairy products; population (1990) 61,284.

Santa Rosa city in NW California, N of San Francisco. Industries include wine, fruit, chemicals, and clothing; population (1990) 113,300.

Santayana George 1863–1952. Spanish-born US philosopher and critic. He developed his philosophy based on naturalism and taught that everything has a natural basis.

Born in Madrid, Santayana grew up in Spain and the US and graduated from Harvard University. He taught at Harvard 1889–1912. His books include *The Life of Reason* 1905–06, *Skepticism and Animal Faith* 1923, *The Realm of Truth* 1937, *Background of My Life* 1945; volumes of poetry; and the best-selling novel *The Last Puritan* 1935.

Santiago capital of Chile; population (1990) 4,385,500. Industries include textiles, chemicals, and food processing. It was founded 1541 and is famous for its broad avenues.

Santiago de Compostela city in Galicia, Spain; population (1991) 105,500. The 11th-century cathedral was reputedly built over the grave of Sant Iago el Mayor (St ▷James the Great), patron saint of Spain, and was one of the most popular places for medieval pilgrimage.

Santiago de los Caballeros second largest city in the Dominican Republic; population (1982) 395,000. It is a trading and processing center for sugar, coffee, and cacao.

Santo Domingo capital and chief sea port of the Dominican Republic; population (1982) 1,600,000. Founded 1496 by Bartolomeo, brother of Christopher Columbus, it is the oldest colonial city in the Americas. Its cathedral was built 1515–40.

Sānusī Sidi Mohammed ibn 'Ali as- *c.* 1787–1859. Algerian-born Muslim religious reformer. He preached a return to the puritanism of early Islam and met with much success in Libya, where he founded the sect named after him.

Saône river in E France, rising in the Vosges mountains and flowing 300 mi/480 km to join the Rhône at Lyon.

São Paulo city in Brazil, 45 mi/72 km NW of its port Santos; population (1991) 9,700,100, metropolitan area 15,280,000. It is 3,000 ft/ 900 m above sea level, and 2°S of the Tropic of Capricorn. It is South America's leading industrial city, producing electronics, steel, and chemicals; it has meatpacking plants and is the center of Brazil's coffee trade. It originated as a Jesuit mission in 1554.

São Tomé port and capital of São Tomé e Príncipe, on São Tomé island, Gulf of Guinea; population (1984) 35,000.

São Tomé e Príncipe country in the Gulf of Guinea, off the coast of W Africa.

government The 1982 constitution describes the Movement for the Liberation of São Tomé e Príncipe (MLSTP) as the leading political force in the nation and the National People's Assembly as the supreme organ of the state. It has 40 members, all MLSTP nominees, elected by people's district assemblies for a five-year term. The president is also nominated by the MLSTP and elected for a five-year term by popular vote.

history The islands were uninhabited until the arrival of the Portuguese 1471, who brought convicts and exiled Jews to work on sugar plantations. Later ▷slavery became the main trade, and in the 19th century forced labor was used on coffee and cocoa plantations.

independence As a Portuguese colony, São Tomé e Príncipe acquired internal self-government 1973. After the military coup in Portugal 1974, the new government in Lisbon formally recognized the liberation movement, MLSTP, led by Dr Manuel Pinto da Costa, as the sole representative of the people of the islands and granted full independence July 1975. Dr da

São Tomé e Príncipe
Democratic Republic of

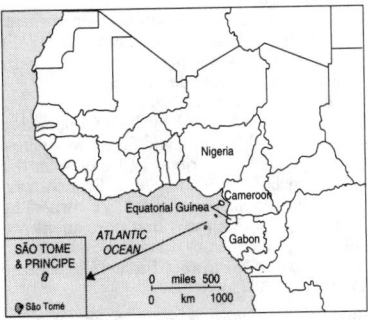

area 386 sq mi/1,000 sq km
capital São Tomé
cities Santo Antonio, Santa Cruz
physical comprises two main islands and several smaller ones, all volcanic; thickly forested and fertile
head of state and government Miguel Trovoada from 1991
political system emergent democratic republic

political parties Movement for the Liberation of São Tomé e Príncipe (MLSTP), nationalist socialist; Democratic Convergence Party–Reflection Group (PCD–EMO), center-left
exports cocoa, copra, coffee, palm oil and kernels
currency dobra
population (1990 est) 125,000; growth rate 2.5% p.a.
life expectancy men 62, women 62
languages Portuguese (official), Fang (Bantu)
religion Roman Catholic 80%, animist
literacy men 73%, women 42% (1981)
GNP $32 million (1987); $384 per head (1986)
chronology
1471 Discovered by Portuguese.
1522–1973 A province of Portugal.
1973 Achieved internal self-government.
1975 Independence achieved from Portugal, with Manuel Pinto da Costa as president.
1984 Formally declared a nonaligned state.
1987 Constitution amended.
1988 Unsuccessful coup attempt against da Costa.
1990 New constitution approved.
1991 First multiparty elections held; Miguel Trovoada replaced Pinto da Costa.

Costa became the first president, and in Dec a national people's assembly was elected. During the first few years of his presidency there were several unsuccessful attempts to depose him, and small opposition groups still operate from outside the country, mainly from Lisbon. *international links* With a worsening economy, da Costa began to reassess his country's international links, which had made it too dependent on the Eastern bloc and, in consequence, isolated from the West. In 1984 he proclaimed that in future São Tomé e Príncipe would adhere to the policy of the ◊nonaligned movement, and the number of Angolan, Cuban, and Soviet advisers in the country was sharply reduced. Gradually São Tomé e Príncipe has turned toward nearby African states such as Gabon, Cameroon, and Equatorial Guinea, as well as maintaining its links with Lisbon. In 1987 the constitution was amended, making the president subject to election by popular vote, and in March 1988 an attempted coup against him was foiled. In Sept 1990 a new constitution, introducing multiparty politics, was approved by referendum. In Jan 1991 multiparty elections were held for the assembly, resulting in the party losing its majority. In March the country's first free election led to the election of Miguel Trovoada after President Manuel Pinto da Costa withdrew. *See illustration box.*

sap the fluids that circulate through ◊vascular plants, especially woody ones. Sap carries water and food to plant tissues. Sap contains alkaloids, protein, and starch; it can be milky (as in rubber trees), resinous (as in pines), or syrupy (as in maples).

saponification in chemistry, the ◊hydrolysis (splitting) of an ◊ester by treatment with a strong alkali, resulting in the liberation of the alcohol from which the ester had been derived and a salt of the constituent fatty acid. The process is used in the manufacture of soap.

sapphire deep-blue, transparent gem variety of the mineral ◊corundum Al₂O₃, aluminum oxide. Small amounts of iron and titanium give it its color. A corundum gem of any color except red (which is a ruby) can be called a sapphire; for example, yellow sapphire.

Sappho *c.* 612–580 BC. Greek lyric poet, friend of the poet ◊Alcaeus and leader of a female literary coterie at Mytilene (now *Lesvos*, hence ◊lesbianism). Legend says she committed suicide when her love for the boatman Phaon was unrequited. Only fragments of her poems have survived.

Sapporo capital of ◊Hokkaido, Japan; population (1989) 1,637,000. Industries include rubber and food processing. It is a winter sports center and was the site of the 1972 Winter Olympics. Giant figures are sculpted in ice at the annual snow festival.

The university was founded 1876 as the Sapporo Agricultural College.

saprophyte in botany, an obsolete term for a ◊saprotroph, an organism that lives in dead or decaying matter.

saprotroph (formerly *saprophyte*) organism that feeds on the excrement or the dead bodies or tissues of others. They include most fungi (the rest being parasites); many bacteria and protozoa; animals such as dung beetles and vultures; and a few unusual plants, including several orchids. Saprotrophs cannot make food for themselves, so they are a type of ◊heterotroph. They are useful scavengers, and in sewage farms and refuse dumps break down organic matter into nutrients easily assimilable by green plants.

Saracen ancient Greek and Roman term for an Arab, used in the Middle Ages by Europeans for all Muslims. The equivalent term used in Spain was ◊Moor.

Saragossa English spelling of ◊Zaragoza, city in Aragon, Spain.

Sarajevo capital of ◊Bosnia-Herzegovina; population (1982) 449,000. Industries include engineering, brewing, chemicals, carpets, and ceramics. It was the site of the 1984 Winter Olympics. From Jan 1992 the city was the subject of attacks from Serb militia units opposed to Bosnia-Herzegovina's moves toward independence, and following EC recognition of the republic's independence in April, the city was under constant siege. Fighting intensifed in July with fresh Serb offensives endangering a mounting UN effort to deliver relief supplies.

A Bosnian, Gavrilo Princip, assassinated Archduke ◊Franz Ferdinand here 1914, thereby precipitating World War I.

Sarasota city in SW Florida, on the Gulf of Mexico, S of Tampa. It is a resort town specializing in food processing and electronics research. It is the winter home of Ringling Brothers and Barnum and Bailey Circus; population (1990) 51,000.

Saratoga Springs city and spa in New York State; population (1990) 25,000. In 1777 the British general John ◊Burgoyne was defeated in two engagements nearby during the American Revolution.

Horse racing is popular during the summer.

Saratov industrial port (chemicals, oil refining) on the river Volga in W central Russia; population (1987) 918,000. It was established in the 1590s as a fortress to protect the Volga trade route.

Sarawak state of Malaysia, on the NW corner of the island of Borneo
area 48,018 sq mi/124,400 sq km
capital Kuching
products it has a tropical climate and produces timber, oil, rice, pepper, rubber, and coconuts
population (1991) 1,669,000; 24 ethnic groups make up almost half this number
physical mountainous; the rainforest, which may be 10 million years old, contains several thousand tree species. A third of all its plant species are endemic to Borneo. 30% of the forest was cut down 1963–89; timber expected to run out 1995–2001
history Sarawak was granted by the Sultan of Brunei to James Brooke 1841, who became "Rajah of Sarawak." It was a British protectorate from 1888 until captured by the Japanese in World War II. It was a crown colony from 1946 until 1963, when it became part of Malaysia.

sarcoma malignant ◊tumour arising from the fat, muscles, bones, cartilage, or blood and lymph vessels and connective tissues. Sarcomas are much less common than ◊carcinomas.

sardine common name for various small fishes (◊pilchards) in the herring family.

Sardinia (Italian *Sardegna*) mountainous island, special autonomous region of Italy; area 9,303 sq mi/24,100 sq km; population (1990) 1,664,400. Its capital is Cagliari, and it exports cork and petrochemicals. It is the second-largest Mediterranean island and includes Costa Smeralda (Emerald Coast) tourist area in the northeast and *nuraghi* (fortified Bronze Age dwellings). After centuries of foreign rule, it became linked 1720 with Piedmont, and this dual kingdom became the basis of a united Italy 1861.

Sarenzen Gene 1902– . US golfer. He won the first of his two US open titles in 1922 at the age of 20 and a couple of months later added the US PGA title, which he retained the following year. He won the British Open in 1932 and the Masters in 1935, when he became the first person to complete a "set" of major titles.

Sargasso Sea part of the N Atlantic (between 40° and 80°W and 25° and 30°N) left static by circling ocean currents, and covered with floating weed *Sargassum natans.*

Sargent John Singer 1856–1925. US portrait painter. Born in Florence of American parents, he studied there and in Paris, then settled in London around 1885. He was a fashionable and prolific painter.

Sargent left Paris after a scandal concerning his décolleté portrait *Madame Gautreau* 1884. Later subjects included the actress Ellen Terry, President Theodore Roosevelt, and the writer Robert Louis Stevenson. He also painted watercolor landscapes and murals.

Sargon two Mesopotamian kings:

Sargon I king of Akkad *c.* 2334–2279 BC, and founder of the first Babylonian empire. Like Moses, he was said to have been found floating in a cradle on the local river, in his case the Euphrates.

Sargon II died 705 BC. King of Assyria from 722 BC, who assumed the name of his predecessor. To keep conquered peoples from rising against him, he had whole populations moved from their homelands, including the Israelites from Samaria.

Sark one of the ◊Channel Islands , 6 mi/ 10 km E of Guernsey; area 2 sq mi/5 sq km; there is no town or village. It is divided into Great and Little Sark, linked by an isthmus, and is of great natural beauty. The Seigneurie of Sark was established by Elizabeth I, the ruler being known as Seigneur/Dame, and has its own parliament, the Chief Pleas. There is no income tax, and automobiles are forbidden; immigration is controlled.

Sarmatian member of an Indo-European nomadic people who, from the 3rd century BC, slowly ousted the ◊Scythians from present-day Ukraine. They had given way to the ◊Goths by the 3rd century AD.

Sarney (Costa) José 1930– . Brazilian politician, member of the center-left Democratic Movement (PMDB), president 1985–90.

Sarney was elected vice-president 1985 and within months, on the death of President Neves, became head of state. Despite earlier involvement with the repressive military regime, he and his party won a convincing victory in the 1986 general election. In Dec 1989, Ferdinando Collor de Mello of the Party for National Reconstruction was elected to succeed Sarney in March 1990.

Sarnoff David 1891–1971. Russian-born US broadcasting pioneer. Sarnoff immigrated with his family to New York 1900. After studying electrical engineering at the Pratt Institute, he was hired by the Marconi Wireless Co 1906. At first a telegraph operator, Sarnoff rose to become commercial manager of the company when it was taken over by the Radio Corporation of America (RCA) 1919. He was named general manager of RCA 1921 and founded the first radio network, the National Broadcasting Co (NBC), as a broadcast subsidiary 1926. Named RCA president 1930 and board chairman 1947, Sarnoff was an early promoter of television broadcasting during the 1940s and the first to manufacture color sets and to transmit color programs in the 1950s.

Saroyan William 1908–1981. US author. He wrote short stories, such as "The Daring Young Man on the Flying Trapeze" 1934, idealizing the hopes and sentiments of the "little man." His plays include *The Time of Your Life* (Pulitzer prize; refused) 1939, about eccentricity; *My Heart's in the Highlands* 1939; and *Talking to You* 1962.

Saskatchewan

Regina

Born in Fresno, California, Saroyan also wrote *The Human Comedy* 1942 and *One Day in the Afternoon of the World* 1964, both novels, and the novella *Boys and Girls Together* 1963. Other plays include *Love's Old Sweet Song* 1941 and *The Beautiful People* 1941. He also wrote autobiographical works, including *The Bicycle Rider in Beverly Hills* 1952 and *Here Comes, There Goes, You Know Who* 1961.

Sarraute Nathalie 1920– . Russian-born French novelist whose books include *Portrait d'un inconnu/Portrait of a Man Unknown* 1948, *Les Fruits d'or/The Golden Fruits* 1964, and *Vous les entendez?/Do You Hear Them?* 1972. An exponent of the ◊nouveau roman, Sarraute bypasses plot, character, and style for the half-conscious interaction of minds.

sarsaparilla drink prepared from the long twisted roots of several plants in the genus *Smilax* (family Liliaceae), native to Central and South America; it is used as a tonic.

Sartre Jean-Paul 1905–1980. French author and philosopher, a leading proponent of ◊existentialism. He published his first novel, *La Nausée/Nausea*, 1937, followed by the trilogy *Les Chemins de la Liberté/Roads to Freedom* 1944–45 and many plays, including *Huis Clos/ In Camera* 1944. *L'Etre et le néant/Being and Nothingness* 1943, his first major philosophical work, sets out a radical doctrine of human freedom. In the later work *Critique de la raison dialectique/Critique of Dialectical Reason* 1960 he tried to produce a fusion of existentialism and Marxism.

Sartre was born in Paris, and was the long-time companion of the feminist writer Simone de Beauvoir. During World War II he was a prisoner for nine months, and on his return from Germany joined the Resistance. As a founder of existentialism, he edited its journal *Les Temps modernes/Modern Times*, and expressed its tenets in his novels and plays. According to Sartre, people's awareness of their own freedom takes the form of anxiety, and they therefore attempt to flee from this awareness into what he terms *mauvaise foi* ("bad faith"); this is the theory he put forward in *L'Etre et le néant/Being and Nothingness*. In *Crime passionel/Crime of Passion* 1948 he attacked aspects of communism while remaining generally sympathetic. In his later work Sartre became more sensitive to the social constraints on people's actions. He refused the Nobel Prize for Literature 1964 for "personal reasons," but allegedly changed his mind later, saying he wanted it for the money.

Sask. abbreviation for ◊*Saskatchewan*.

Saskatchewan (Cree *Kis-is-ska-tche-wan* "swift flowing") province of W Canada
area 251,788 sq mi/652,300 sq km
capital Regina

cities Saskatoon, Moose Jaw, Prince Albert
physical prairies in the south; to the north, forests, lakes, and subarctic tundra; Prince Albert National Park
products more than 60% of Canada's wheat; oil, natural gas, uranium, zinc, potash (world's largest reserves), copper, helium (the only western reserves outside the US)
population (1991) 995,300
history once inhabited by Indians speaking Athabaskan, Algonquin, and Sioux languages, who depended on caribou and moose in the north and buffalo in the south. French trading posts established about 1750; owned by Hudson's Bay Company, first permanent settlement 1774; ceded to Canadian government 1870 as part of Northwest Territories; became a province 1905.

Saskatoon largest city in Saskatchewan; population (1986) 177,641. Industries include cement, oil refining, chemicals, metal goods, and processed foods. The University of Saskatchewan is here. Saskatoon was settled 1882.

Sassanian Empire Persian empire founded AD 224 by Ardashir, a chieftain in the area of what is now Fars, in Iran, who had taken over ◊Parthia; it was named after his grandfather, Sasan. The capital was Ctesiphon, near modern ◊Baghdad, Iraq. After a rapid period of expansion, when it contested supremacy with Rome, it was destroyed in 637 by Muslim Arabs at the Battle of ◊Qadisiya.

Sassau-Nguesso Denis 1943– . Congolese socialist politician, president 1979–92. He progressively consolidated his position within the ruling left-wing Congolese Labor Party (PCT), at the same time as improving relations with France and the US. In 1990, in response to public pressure, he agreed that the PCT should abandon Marxism-Leninism and that a multiparty system should be introduced.

Sassoon Siegfried 1886–1967. English writer, author of the autobiography *Memoirs of a Foxhunting Man* 1928. His *War Poems* 1919 express the disillusionment of his generation.

Educated at Cambridge, Sassoon enlisted in the army 1915, serving in France and Palestine. He published many volumes of poetry and three volumes of childhood autobiography, *The Old Century and Seven More Years* 1938, *The Weald of Youth* 1942, and *Siegfried's Journey* 1945. He wrote a biography of the novelist George Meredith 1948 and published *Collected Poems* in 1961.

Satan a name for the ◊devil.

satellite any small body that orbits a larger one, either natural or artificial. Natural satellites that orbit planets are called moons. The first *artificial satellite*, Sputnik 1, was launched into orbit around the Earth by the USSR 1957. Artificial satellites are used for scientific purposes, communications, weather forecasting, and military applications. The largest artificial satellites can be seen by the naked eye.

At any time, there are several thousand artificial satellites orbiting the Earth, including active satellites, satellites that have ended their working lives, and discarded sections of rockets. Artificial satellites eventually reenter the Earth's atmosphere. Usually they burn up by friction, but sometimes debris falls to the Earth's surface, as with ◊Skylab and Salyut 7. The US launched 23 nuclear-powered satellites 1961–77, of which four malfunctioned.

The ♢Strategic Defense Initiative (Star Wars) program proposes sending as many as 100 nuclear reactors into space. From 1965, the USSR launched 39 nuclear reactors on orbiting satellites, of which six malfunctioned.

More than 70,000 pieces of space junk, ranging from disabled satellites to tiny metal fragments, are careering around the Earth. The amount of waste is likely to increase, as the waste particles in orbit are continually colliding and fragmenting further.

satellite applications the uses to which artificial satellites are put. These include:
scientific experiments and observation Many astronomical observations are best taken above the disturbing effect of the atmosphere. Satellite observations have been carried out by *IRAS* (*Infrared Astronomical Satellite*, 1983) which made a complete infrared survey of the skies, and *Solar Max* 1980, which observed solar flares. The *Hipparcos* satellite, launched 1989, is expected to measure the positions of the stars with unprecedented accuracy. Medical experiments have been carried out aboard crewed satellites, such as the Soviet *Mir* and the US *Skylab*.
reconnaissance and mapping applications Apart from military use and routine mapmaking, the US *Landsat*, the French *SPOT*, and equivalent USSR satellites have provided much useful information about water sources and drainage, vegetation, land use, geological structures, oil and mineral locations, and snow and ice.
weather monitoring The US NOAA series of satellites, and others launched by the European space agency, Japan, and India, provide continuous worldwide observation of the atmosphere.
navigation The US Global Positioning System, when complete in 1993, will feature 24 Navstar satellites that will enable users (including walkers and motorists) to find their position to within 328 ft/100 m. The US military will be able to make full use of the system, obtaining accuracy to within 4 ft 6ins/1.5 m. The Transit system, launched in the 1960s, with 12 satellites in orbit, locates users to within 328 ft/100 m.
communications A complete worldwide communications network is now provided by satellites such as the US-run ♢Intelsat system.

satellite television transmission of broadcast signals through artificial communications satellites. Mainly positioned in ♢geostationary orbit, satellites have been used since the 1960s to relay television pictures around the world. Higher-power satellites have more recently been developed to broadcast signals to cable systems or directly to people's homes.

Satie Erik (Alfred Leslie) 1866–1925. French composer. His piano pieces, such as *Gymnopédies* 1888, often combine wit and melancholy. His orchestral works include *Parade* 1917, among whose sound effects is a typewriter. He was the mentor of the group of composers known as ♢*Les Six*.

satire poem or piece of prose that uses wit, humor, or irony, often through ♢allegory or extended metaphor, to ridicule human pretensions or expose social evils. Satire is related to ♢parody in its intention to mock, but satire tends to be more subtle and to mock an attitude or a belief, whereas parody tends to mock a particular work (such as a poem) by imitating its style, often with purely comic intent.

The Roman poets Juvenal and Horace wrote *Satires*, and the form became popular in Europe in the 17th and 18th centuries, used by Voltaire in France and by Alexander Pope and Jonathan Swift in England. Both satire and parody are designed to appeal to the intellect rather than the emotions and both, to be effective, require a knowledge of the original attitude, person, or work that is being mocked (although much satire, such as *Gulliver's Travels* by Swift, can also be enjoyed simply on a literal level).

Satō Eisaku 1901–1975. Japanese conservative politician, prime minister 1964–72. He ran against Hayato Ikeda (1899–1965) for the Liberal Democratic Party leadership and succeeded him as prime minister, pledged to a more independent foreign policy. He shared a Nobel Prize for Peace in 1974 for his rejection of nuclear weapons. His brother **Nobosuke Kishi** (1896–1987) was prime minister of Japan 1957–60.

satrap title of a provincial governor in ancient Persia. Under Darius I, the Persian Empire was divided between some 20 satraps, each owing allegiance only to the king.

satsuma small, hardy, loose-skinned orange *Citrus reticulata* of the tangerine family, originally from Japan. It withstands cold conditions well.

saturated fatty acid ♢fatty acid in which there are no double bonds in the hydrocarbon chain.

saturated solution in physics, a solution obtained when a solvent (liquid) can dissolve no more of a solute (usually a solid) at a particular temperature. Normally, a slight fall in temperature causes some of the solute to crystallize out of solution. If this does not happen the phenomenon is called supercooling, and the solution is said to be **supersaturated**.

Saturday Evening Post popular US magazine founded in Philadelphia 1821, specializing in family reading and known for its folksy Norman Rockwell covers. Its contributors included Edgar Allan Poe and Harriet Beecher Stowe.

It was transformed into a modern magazine by G H Lorimer and remodeled again in the 1960s.

Saturn in astronomy, the second-largest planet in the Solar System, sixth from the Sun, and encircled by bright and easily visible equatorial rings. Viewed through a telescope it is ochre. Saturn orbits the Sun every 29.46 years at an average distance of 886,700,000 mi/1,427,000,000 km. Its equatorial diameter is 75,000 mi/120,000 km, but its polar diameter is 7,450 mi/12,000 km smaller, a result of its fast rotation and low density, the lowest of any planet.

Saturn spins on its axis every 10 hours 14 minutes at its equator, slowing to 10 hours 40 minutes at high latitudes. Its mass is 95 times that of Earth, and its magnetic field 1,000 times stronger. Saturn is believed to have a small core of rock and iron, encased in ice and topped by a deep layer of liquid hydrogen. There are over 20 known moons, its largest being ♢Titan. The rings visible from Earth begin about 9,000 mi/14,000 km from the planet's cloudtops and extend out to about 47,000 mi/76,000 km. Made of small chunks of ice and rock (averaging 3 ft/1 m across), they are 170,000 mi/275,000 km rim to rim, but only 300 ft/100 m thick. The Voyager probes

showed that the rings actually consist of thousands of closely spaced ringlets, looking like the grooves in a phonograph record.

Like Jupiter, Saturn's visible surface consists of swirling clouds, probably made of frozen ammonia at a temperature of –274°F/–170°C, although the markings in the clouds are not as prominent as Jupiter's. The space probes *Voyager 1* and *2* found winds reaching 1,100 mph/1,800 kph. The Voyagers photographed numerous small moons orbiting Saturn, taking the total to 21–23, more than for any other planet. The largest moon, Titan, has a dense atmosphere.

From Earth, Saturn's rings appear to be divided into three main sections. Ring A, the outermost, is separated from ring B, the brightest, by the Cassini division (named after its discoverer ♢Cassini), 2,000 mi/3,000 km wide; the inner, transparent ring C is called the Crepe Ring. Each ringlet of the rings is made of a swarm of icy particles like snowballs, a few fractions of an inch to a few yards in diameter. Outside the A ring is the narrow and faint F ring, which the Voyagers showed to be twisted or braided. The rings of Saturn could be the remains of a shattered moon, or they may always have existed in their present form.

Saturn in Roman mythology, the god of agriculture (Greek **Kronos**), whose period of rule was the ancient Golden Age. He was dethroned by his sons Jupiter, Neptune, and Pluto. At his festival, the Saturnalia in Dec, gifts were exchanged, and slaves were briefly treated as their masters' equals.

Saturn rocket a family of large US rockets, developed by Wernher von Braun for the ♢Apollo project. The two-stage *Saturn IB* was used for launching *Apollo* spacecraft into orbit around the Earth. The three-stage *Saturn V* sent *Apollo* spacecraft to the Moon, and launched the ♢Skylab space station. The lift-off thrust of a *Saturn V* was 3,850 tons. After *Apollo* and *Skylab*, the Saturn rockets were retired in favor of the ♢Space Shuttle.

satyagraha (Sanskrit "insistence on truth") nonviolent resistance to British rule in India, as employed by Mahatma ♢Gandhi from 1918 to press for political reform; the idea owes much to the Russian writer Leo ♢Tolstoy.

satyr in Greek mythology, a lustful, drunken woodland creature characterized by pointed ears, two horns on the forehead, and a tail. Satyrs attended the god of wine, ♢Dionysus. Roman writers confused satyrs with goat-footed fauns.

Saudi Arabia country on the Arabian peninsula, stretching from the Red Sea in the W to the Arabian Gulf in the E, bounded N by Jordan, Iraq, and Kuwait; E by Qatar and United Arab Emirates; SE by Oman; and S by Yemen.

government Saudi Arabia is an absolute monarchy with no written constitution, no legislature, and no political parties. The king rules, in accordance with Islamic law, by decree. He appoints and heads a council of ministers, whose decisions are the result of a majority vote but always subject to the ultimate sanction of the king.

history For early history, see ♢Arabia. The sultanate of Nejd in the interior came under Turkish rule in the 18th century. Present-day Saudi Arabia is almost entirely the creation of King Ibn Saud who, after the dissolution of the ♢Ottoman Empire 1918, fought rival Arab rulers until, in 1926, he had established himself as the undisputed king of the Hejaz and sultan of Nejd. In 1932 Nejd and Hejaz became the United Kingdom of Saudi Arabia.

economic prosperity Oil was discovered in the 1930s, commercially exploited from the 1940s, and became the basis of the country's prosperity. Ibn Saud died 1953 and was succeeded by his eldest son, Saud. During King Saud's reign relations between Saudi Arabia and Egypt became strained, and in 1964 he abdicated in favor of his brother Faisal. Under King Faisal, Saudi Arabia became a leader among Arab oil producers.

In 1975 Faisal was assassinated and his half brother, Khalid, succeeded him. Khalid was in failing health and increasingly relied on his brother Fahd to perform the duties of government. King Khalid died 1982 and was succeeded by Fahd.

Middle East affairs Saudi Arabia has drawn up proposals for a permanent settlement of the Arab–Israeli dispute. It gave financial support to Iraq in its war with Iran. The ⟡Iran–Iraq War also prompted Saudi Arabia to buy advanced missiles from the US. Islamic fundamentalists staged demonstrations in ⟡Mecca 1979 and 1987, leading to violence and worsening relations with Iran. In 1989 Saudi Arabia assumed a leading role in the search for a settlement of the Lebanese civil war, hosting a constitutional convention of Lebanese legislators in Taif.

On Aug 2, 1990 Iraq invaded and occupied neighboring Kuwait, threatening the security of Saudi Arabia. King Fahd turned to the US and UK for protection and a massive buildup of ground and air strength began, alongside Saudi Arabia's own forces, culminating in the ⟡Gulf War 1991 and Iraq's forced withdrawal from Kuwait. In return, King Fahd agreed to increase his oil output to offset the loss of Kuwaiti and Iraqi production, and to pay a substantial part of the cost of maintaining US and British forces. During the Gulf War, Saudi Arabia served as the staging ground for the air and ground assaults on Iraqi forces. The country was hit by Iraqi missile strikes but suffered no serious damage. In May 1991 religious leaders demanded the creation of a "consultative council" to assist in the government of the kingdom, as proposed by King Fahd a month earlier. In Nov 1991, Saudi Arabia was one of the main participants in the historic Middle East peace conference in Spain. The formation of a "consultative council" March 1992, as a move toward more representative government, was viewed with cynicism by some observers. *See illustration box.*

Saul in the Old Testament, the first king of Israel. He was anointed by Samuel and warred successfully against the neighboring Ammonites and Philistines, but fell from God's favor in his battle against the Amalekites. He became jealous and suspicious of David and turned against him and Samuel. After being wounded in battle with the Philistines, in which his three sons died, he committed suicide.

Sault Ste Marie twin industrial ports on the Canadian/US border, one in Ontario and one in Michigan; population (1981) 82,902 and (1990) 14,700, respectively. They stand at the falls (French *sault*) in St Mary's River, which links Lakes Superior and Huron. The falls are bypassed by canals. Industries include steel, pulp, and agricultural trade.

Saudi Arabia
Kingdom of (*al-Mamlaka al-'Arabiya as-Sa'udiya*)

area 849,400 sq mi/2,200,518 sq km
capital Riyadh
cities Mecca, Medina, Taif; ports Jidda, Dammam
physical desert, sloping to the Persian Gulf from a height of 9,000 ft/2,750 m in the W
environment oil pollution caused by the Gulf War 1990–91 has affected 285 mi/460 km of the Saudi coastline, threatening desalination plants and damaging the wildlife of saltmarshes, mangrove forest, and mudflats
features Nafud Desert in N and the Rub'al Khali (Empty Quarter) in S, area 250,000 sq mi/650,000 sq km; with a ban on women drivers, there are an estimated 300,000 chauffeurs
head of state and government King Fahd

Ibn Abdul Aziz from 1982
political system absolute monarchy
political parties none
exports oil, petroleum products
currency rial
population (1990 est) 16,758,000 (16% nomadic); growth rate 3.1% p.a.
life expectancy men 64, women 67 (1989)
language Arabic
religion Sunni Muslim; there is a Shiite minority
literacy men 34%, women 12% (1980 est)
GNP $70 bn (1988); $6,170 per head (1988)
chronology
1926–32 Territories united and kingdom established.
1953 King Ibn Saud died and was succeeded by his eldest son, Saud.
1964 King Saud forced to abdicate; succeeded by his brother, Faisal.
1975 King Faisal assassinated; succeeded by his half brother, Khalid.
1982 King Khalid died; succeeded by his brother, Crown Prince Fahd.
1987 Rioting by Iranian pilgrims caused 400 deaths in Mecca; diplomatic relations with Iran severed.
1990 Iraqi troops invaded and annexed Kuwait and massed on Saudi Arabian border. King Fahd called for help from US and UK forces.
1991 King Fahd provided military and financial assistance in Gulf War. Calls from religious leaders for "consultative assembly" to assist in government of kingdom. Saudi Arabia attended Middle East peace conference.
1992 Formation of a "consultative council" seen as possible move toward representative government.

sauna bath causing perspiration by means of dry heat. It consists of a small room in which the temperature is raised to about 200°F/90°C. The bather typically stays in it for only a few minutes and then follows it with a cold shower or swim. Saunas are popular in health clubs and sports centers.

The sauna derives from a Finnish dry-heat bath in which small quantities of steam can be produced by throwing cold water over hot stones; this is traditionally followed by a beating of the skin with birch twigs to stimulate the circulation, and a plunge into a lake or snow outdoors.

Saunders Clarence 1881–1953. US retailer who opened the first self-service supermarket, Piggly-Wiggly, in Memphis, Tennessee, 1919.

Saussure Ferdinand de 1857–1913. Swiss language scholar, a pioneer of modern linguistics and the originator of the concept of ⟡structuralism as used in linguistics, anthropology, and literary theory.

He taught at the universities of Paris and Geneva. His early work, on the Indo-European language family, led to a major treatise on its vowel system. He is best known for *Cours de linguistique générale/Course in General Linguistics* 1916, a posthumous work derived mainly from his lecture notes by his students Charles Bally and Albert Séchehaye. Saussurean concepts include: (1) language seen as both a unified and shared social system (*langue*) and as individual and idiosyncratic speech (*parole*); (2) language described in **synchronic** terms (as a system at a particular time) and in **diachronic** terms (as changing through time).

Sauternes sweet white table wine produced in the Gironde *département*, SW France. It takes its name from the village of Sauternes.

Savage Michael Joseph 1872–1940. New Zealand Labor politician. As prime minister 1935–40, he introduced much social-security legislation.

savanna or *savannah* extensive open tropical grasslands, with scattered trees and shrubs. Savannas cover large areas of Africa, North and South America, and N Australia.

The name was originally given by Spaniards to the treeless plains of the tropical South American prairies. Most of North America's savannas have been built over.

Savannah city and port of Georgia, 18 mi/29 km from the mouth of the Savannah River; population (1990) 137,600. Founded 1733, Savannah was the first city in the US to be laid out in geometrically regular blocks.

Manufactures include paper products, aircraft, transportation equipment, chemicals, and food products. The *Savannah*, the first steam-powered ship to cross the Atlantic, was built here; most of the 25-day journey, in 1819, was made under sail. The first nuclear-powered merchant ship, launched by the US 1959, was given the same name. Founded by James Oglethorpe in 1733, Savannah is the oldest settlement in Georgia and was its capital 1754–86. World cotton prices were set by the exchange here from the late 18th century until 1895.

Savery Thomas *c.* 1650–1715. British engineer who invented the steam-driven water pump, precursor of the steam engine, 1696.

The pump used a boiler to raise steam, which was condensed (in a separate condenser) by an external spray of cold water. The partial vacuum created sucked water up a pipe from the mine shaft; steam pressure was then used to force the water away, after which the cycle was repeated. Savery patented his invention 1698.

Savimbi Jonas 1934– . Angolan soldier and right-wing revolutionary, founder and leader of the National Union for the Total Independence of Angola (UNITA). From 1975 UNITA under Savimbi's leadership tried to overthrow the government. An agreement between the two parties was reached May 1991, but fighting broke out again following elections Sept 1992.

savings the amount of current income that is not spent on consumption. Distinct from ⟡investments, which are considered expenditures for the production of goods for future consumption, savings usually takes the form of bank time deposits. The savings rate depends on many factors, such as interest rates, inflation rates, unemployment rates, and expectations for future earnings.

savings and loan association (**S&L**) a co-operative, mutual, savings organization that sells stock to its members. Created primarily to finance home mortgages, S&Ls at one time provided 40% of the funds for home purchases. From 1986, an industry-wide crisis developed when, in some parts of the US, declining real estate values and rising unemployment reduced the value of investments and the ability of borrowers to repay loans. For the first time, mergers were permitted across state lines in hopes that the healthier institutions could assume the debt of the weaker, but losses mounted. The Federal Home Loan Board (FHLB) and the Federal Savings and Loan Insurance Corporation (FSLIC) were unable to reverse the tide or cover the losses. By 1989 the losses were enormous, and a federal bailout pledging more than $100 billion in taxpayer funds was negotiated.

Savonarola Girolamo 1452–1498. Italian reformer, a Dominican friar and an eloquent preacher. His crusade against political and religious corruption won him popular support, and in 1494 he led a revolt in Florence that expelled the ruling Medici family and established a democratic republic. His denunciations of Pope ⟡Alexander VI led to his excommunication in 1497, and in 1498 he was arrested, tortured, hanged, and burned for heresy.

Savoy area of France between the Alps, Lake Geneva, and the river Rhône. A medieval duchy, it was made into the *départements* of Savoie and Haute-Savoie, in the Rhône-Alpes region.
history Savoy was a duchy from the 14th century, with the capital Chambéry. In 1720 it became a province of the kingdom of Sardinia which, with Nice, was ceded to France in 1860 by Victor Emmanuel II (king of Italy from 1861) in return for French assistance in driving the Austrians from Italy.

Sawchuk Terry (Terrance Gordon) 1929–1970. Canadian ice-hockey player, often considered the greatest goaltender of all time. He played for Detroit, Boston, Toronto, Los Angeles, and New York Rangers 1950–67, and holds the National Hockey League (NHL) record of 103 shut-outs (games in which he did not concede a goal).

sawfish any fish of an order *Pristiformes* of large, sharklike ⟡rays, characterized by a flat, sawlike snout edged with teeth. The common sawfish *P. pectinatus*, also called the smalltooth, is more than 19 ft/6 m long. It has

some 24 teeth along an elongated snout (6 ft/ 2 m) that can be used as a weapon.

sawfly any of several families of insects of the order Hymenoptera, related to bees, wasps, and ants, but lacking a "waist" on the body. The egg-laying tube (ovipositor) of the female is surrounded by a pair of sawlike organs, which it uses to make a slit in a plant stem to lay its eggs. Horntails are closely related.

Saxe-Coburg-Gotha Saxon duchy. Albert, the Prince Consort of Britain's Queen Victoria, was a son of the 1st Duke, Ernest I (1784–1844), who was succeeded by Albert's elder brother, Ernest II (1818–1893). It remained the name of the British royal house until 1917, when it was changed to Windsor.

saxhorn family of brass musical instruments played with valves, invented by the Belgian Adolphe Sax (1814–1894) in 1845.

saxifrage any plant of the genus *Saxifraga*, family Saxifragaceae, occurring in rocky, mountainous, and alpine situations in the northern hemisphere. They are low plants with groups of small white, pink, or yellow flowers.
Early saxifrage *S. virginiensis* is native to North America.

Saxon member of a Teutonic people who invaded Britain in the early Middle Ages; see ⟡Anglo-Saxon.

Saxony (German *Sachsen*) administrative *Land* (state) of Germany
area 6,580 sq mi/17,036 sq km
capital Dresden
cities Leipzig, Chemnitz, Zwickau
physical on the plain of the river Elbe north of the Erzgebirge mountain range
products electronics, textiles, vehicles, machinery, chemicals, coal
population (1990) 5,000,000
history conquered by Charlemagne 792, Saxony became a powerful medieval German duchy. The electors of Saxony were also kings of Poland 1697–1763. Saxony was part of East Germany 1946–90, forming a region with Anhalt.
Saxony takes its name from the early Saxon inhabitants whose territories originally reached as far west as the Rhine. The duchy of Saxony was divided 1260 but reconstituted in 1424 when a new electorate embracing Thuringia, Meissen, and Wittenberg was formed. The northern part of Saxony became a province of Prussia 1815, its king having sided with Napoleon. In 1946 Saxony was joined with Anhalt as a region of East Germany and in 1952 it was split into the districts of Leipzig, Dresden, and Chemnitz (later named Karl-Marx-Stadt). The state of Saxony was restored 1990 following German reunification and the abolition of the former East German districts.

Saxony-Anhalt administrative *Land* (state) of Germany
area 10,000 sq mi/20,450 sq km
capital Magdeburg
cities Halle, Dessau
products chemicals, electronics, rolling stock, footwear, cereals, vegetables
population (1990) 3,000,000
history Anhalt became a duchy 1863 and a member of the North German Confederation 1866. Between 1946 and 1990 it was joined to the former Prussian province of Saxony as a region of East Germany.
The territory of Anhalt, named after the medieval castle of Anhalt, was divided and reunited many times before becoming a duchy.

In 1952, as part of the East German region of Saxony-Anhalt, it was divided into the districts of Halle and Magdeburg. After the reunification of Germany in 1990, Saxony-Anhalt was reconstituted as one of the five new *Länder* of the Federal Republic.

saxophone large family of wind instruments combining woodwind and brass features, the single reed of the clarinet and the wide bore of the bugle. Patented in 1846 by Adolphe Sax (1814–1894), a Belgian instrument maker, the saxophone is a lively and versatile instrument that has played a prominent part in the history of jazz. Four of the original eight sizes remain in common use: soprano, alto, tenor, and baritone. The soprano is usually straight, the others curved back at the mouthpiece end, and with an upturned bell.

Sayan Mountains range in E Siberian Russia, on the Mongolian border; the highest peak is Munku Sardik 11,451 ft/3,489 m. The mountains have coal, gold, silver, graphite, and lead resources.

Sayers Dorothy L(eigh) 1893–1957. English writer of crime novels featuring detective Lord Peter Wimsey and heroine Harriet Vane, including *Strong Poison* 1930, *The Nine Tailors* 1934, and *Gaudy Night* 1935. She also wrote religious plays for radio, and translations of Dante.

Say's law in economics, the "law of markets" formulated by Jean-Baptiste Say (1767–1832) to the effect that supply creates its own demand and that resources can never be underused.
Widely accepted by Classical economists, the "law" was regarded as erroneous by J M Keynes in his analysis of the depression in Britain during the 1920s and 1930s.

sc. abbreviation for *scilicet* (Latin "let it be understood").

SC abbreviation for the state of ⟡**South Carolina**.

scabies contagious infection of the skin caused by the parasitic itch mite *Sarcoptes scaboi*, which burrows under the skin to deposit eggs. Treatment is by antiparasitic creams and lotions.

scabious any plant of the Eurasian genus *Scabiosa* of the teasel family Dipsacaceae, with many small, usually blue, flowers borne in a single head on a tall stalk. The small scabious *S. columbaria* and the Mediterranean sweet scabious *S. atropurpurea* are often cultivated.

Scafell Pike highest mountain in England, 3,210 ft/978 m. It is in Cumbria in the Lake District and is separated from Scafell (3,164 ft/964 m) by a ridge called Mickledore.

scalar quantity in mathematics and science, a quantity that has magnitude but no direction, as distinct from a ⟡vector quantity, which has a direction as well as a magnitude. Temperature, mass, and volume are scalar quantities.

scalawag or *scallywag* in US history, a derogatory term for white Southerners who, during and after the Civil War of 1861–65, supported the Republican Party, and black emancipation and enfranchisement.
The reforms instituted by the scalawags were widely resented in the South, and their influence diminished with the rise of the Democratic party in the South.

scale in music, a sequence of pitches that establishes a key, and in some respects the character of a composition. A scale is defined by its starting note and may be *major* or

minor depending on the order of intervals. A **chromatic** scale is the full range of 12 notes: it has no key because there is no fixed starting point.

A **whole-tone** scale is a six-note scale and is also indeterminate in key: only two are possible. A **diatonic** scale has seven notes, a **pentatonic** scale has five.

scale insect any small plant-sucking insect (order *Homoptera*) of the superfamily Cocceidea. Some species are major pests—for example, the citrus mealy bug (genus *Pseudococcus*), which attacks citrus fruits in North America. The female is often wingless and legless, attached to a plant by the head and with the body covered with a waxy scale. The rare males are winged.

Scalia Antonin 1936– . US jurist and associate justice of the US Supreme Court 1986– . He concurred with the majority opinion of the court in *Texas v Johnson* 1989, that ruled constitutional the burning of the US flag in protest. He dissented in *Edwards v Aguillard* 1987 when the Court ruled that states may not mandate the teaching of the theory of creationism to counteract the teaching of the theory of evolution.

Born in Trenton, New Jersey, he graduated from Georgetown University and the Harvard University Law School. After practicing law in Cleveland, Scalia accepted a teaching position at the University of Virginia Law School in 1967. From 1971 he worked as a lawyer in the executive branch of the federal government, ultimately becoming assistant attorney general 1974, where he advised the Gerald Ford White House in the Watergate scandal. He later became professor of law at the University of Chicago, where he was known for his support of economic deregulation and judicial restraint. In 1982 President Reagan appointed Scalia to the US Court of Appeals for the District of Columbia. On the court, Scalia favored judicial restraint, circumscription of freedom of the press, and strong federal executive powers, especially in foreign policy areas. President Reagan appointed Scalia to the Supreme Court 1986.

scallop any marine bivalve ▷mollusk of the family Pectinidae, with a fan-shaped shell. There are two "ears" extending from the socketlike hinge. Scallops use water-jet propulsion to move through the water to escape predators such as starfish. The giant Pacific scallop found from Alaska to California can reach 8 in/20 cm width.

scaly anteater another name for the ▷pangolin.

Scandinavia peninsula in NW Europe, comprising Norway and Sweden; politically and culturally it also includes Denmark, Iceland, the Faroe Islands and Finland.

Scandinavian inhabitant of or native to Scandinavia (Denmark, Norway, Sweden, Iceland, and, often, Finland); also referring to the languages and cultures. The Scandinavian languages, including Faroese, belong to the Indo-European family.

scandium silver-white, metallic element of the ▷lanthanide series, symbol Sc, atomic number 21, atomic weight 44.956. Its compounds are found widely distributed in nature, but only in minute amounts. The metal has little industrial importance.

Scandium is relatively more abundant in the Sun and other stars than on Earth. Scandium oxide (scandia) is used as a catalyst,

in making crucibles and other ceramic parts, and scandium sulfate (in very dilute aqueous solution) is used in agriculture to improve seed germination.

The element was discovered and named in 1879 by Swedish chemist Lars Nilson (1840–99), for Latin *Scandia*, because it occurs in the Scandinavian mineral euxenite, on which he worked.

scanner device, usually electronic, used to sense and reproduce an image. Magnetic resonance imaging was being used in 1990 to tell stale food from fresh: the image of a fresh vegetable is different from that of one frozen and thawed.

scanning in medicine, the noninvasive examination of body organs to detect abnormalities of structure or function. Detectable waves—for example, ▷ultrasound, magnetic, or ▷X-rays—are passed through the part to be scanned. Their absorption pattern is recorded, analyzed by computer, and displayed pictorially on a screen.

scanning tunnelling microscope (STM) microscope that produces a magnified image by moving a tiny tungsten probe across the surface of the specimen. The tip of the probe is so fine that it may consist of a single atom, and it moves so close to the specimen surface that electrons jump (or tunnel) across the gap between the tip and the surface.

The magnitude of the electron flow (current) depends on the distance from the tip to the surface, and so by measuring the current, the contours of the surface can be determined. These can be used to form an image on a computer screen of the surface, with individual atoms resolved.

Scapa Flow expanse of sea in the Orkney Islands, Scotland, until 1957 a base of the Royal Navy. It was the main base of the Grand Fleet during World War I and in 1919 was the scene of the scuttling of 71 surrendered German warships.

scapolite group of white or grayish minerals, silicates of sodium, aluminum, and calcium, common in metamorphosed limestones and forming at high temperatures and pressures.

scapula or **shoulder blade** large bone forming part of the pectoral girdle, assisting in the articulation of the arm with the chest region. Its flattened shape allows a large region for the attachment of muscles.

scarab any of a family Scarabaeidae of beetles, often brilliantly colored, and including ▷cockchafers, June beetles, and dung beetles. The *Scarabeus sacer* was revered by the ancient Egyptians as the symbol of resurrection.

Scarlatti (Giuseppe) Domenico 1685–1757. Italian composer, eldest son of Alessandro ▷Scarlatti, who lived most of his life in Portugal and Spain in the service of the Queen of Spain. He wrote highly original harpsichord sonatas.

Scarlatti (Pietro) Alessandro (Gaspare) 1660–1725. Italian Baroque composer, Master of the Chapel at the court of Naples, who developed the opera form. He composed more than 100 operas, including *Tigrane* 1715, as well as church music and oratorios.

scarlet fever or **scarlatina** acute infectious disease, especially of children, caused by the bacterium *Streptococcus pyogenes*. It is marked by a sore throat and a bright red rash spreading from the upper to the lower part of the body. The rash is followed by the skin peeling in flakes. It is treated with antibiotics.

scarp and dip in geology, the two slopes formed when a sedimentary bed outcrops as a landscape feature. The scarp is the slope that cuts across the bedding plane; the dip is the opposite slope which follows the bedding plane. The scarp is usually steep, while the dip is a gentle slope.

scatter diagram or **scattergram** a diagram whose purpose is to establish whether or not a connection or ▷correlation exists between two variables, for example between life expectancy and GNP. Each observation is marked with a dot in a position that shows the value of both variables. The pattern of dots is then examined to see if they show any underlying trend by means of a **best-fit line** (a straight line drawn so that its distance from the various points is as short as possible).

scent gland gland that opens onto the outer surface of animals, producing odorous compounds that are used for communicating between members of the same species (▷pheromones), or for discouraging predators.

Schechter v US a US Supreme Court decision 1935 dealing with the constitutionality of New Deal legislation over labor standards and trade practices. Found guilty under the National Industrial Recovery Act 1933 of violating minimum-wage and maximum-hours regulations, Schechter, a New York poultry dealer, appealed his case to the US Supreme Court. He argued that since he was a local dealer operating an exclusively intrastate trade, the case was outside federal jurisdiction. The Court found that Schechter's trade had no direct effect on interstate commerce and was therefore not subject to Congressional regulation. This was a serious blow to New Deal recovery policies.

Scheele Karl Wilhelm 1742–1786. Swedish chemist and pharmacist. In the book *Experiments on Air and Fire* 1777, he argued that the atmosphere was composed of two gases. One, which supported combustion (oxygen), he called "fire air," and the other, which inhibited combustion (nitrogen), he called "vitiated air." He thus anticipated Joseph ▷Priestley's discovery of oxygen by two years.

Scheherazade the storyteller in the ▷*Arabian Nights*.

Schelling Friedrich Wilhelm Joseph 1775–1854. German philosopher who began as a follower of Fichte, but moved away from subjective ▷idealism, which treats the external world as essentially immaterial, toward a "philosophy of identity" (*Identitätsphilosophie*), in which subject and object are seen as united in the absolute. His early philosophy influenced ▷Hegel, but his later work criticizes Hegel, arguing that being necessarily precedes thought.

Schenck v US a US Supreme Court decision 1919 dealing with Congress's power to revoke First-Amendment rights. Schenck, an outspoken antidraft activist, was convicted of providing aid and comfort to the enemy, in violation of the Espionage Act 1917. The Court unanimously upheld his conviction, ruling that Congress was obligated to interfere with the freedom of speech when it presented a "clear and present danger" to the well-being of the society.

Schenectady industrial city on the Mohawk River, New York State; population (1990) 65,600. It dates from 1662 and has long been noted as a producer of electrical goods.

Scherchen Hermann 1891–1966. German conductor. He collaborated with ▷Schoenberg, and in 1919 founded the journal *Melos* to promote contemporary music. He moved to Switzerland in 1933, and was active as a conductor and teacher. He wrote two texts, *Handbook of Conducting* and *The Nature of Music*. During the 1950s he founded a music publishing house, Ars Viva Verlag, and an electronic studio at Gravesano.

scherzo (Italian "joke") in music, a lively piece, usually in rapid triple (3/4) time; often used for the third movement of a symphony, sonata, or quartet.

Schiaparelli Giovanni (Virginio) 1835–1910. Italian astronomer who discovered the so-called "Martian canals." He studied ancient and medieval astronomy, discovered the asteroid 69 (Hesperia) April 1861, observed double stars, and revealed the connection between comets and meteors. In 1877 he was the first to draw attention to the linear markings on Mars, which gave rise to the "Martian canal" controversy. These markings are now known to be optical effects and not real lines.

Schick test injection of a small quantity of diphtheria toxin to ascertain whether or not a person is immune to the disease. If there is no immunity, a local inflammation develops.

Schiele Egon 1890–1918. Austrian Expressionist artist. Originally a landscape painter, he was strongly influenced by Art Nouveau and developed a contorted linear style. His subject matter included portraits and nudes. In 1911 he was arrested for alleged obscenity.

Schiller Johann Christoph Friedrich von 1759–1805. German dramatist, poet, and historian. He wrote *Sturm und Drang* ("storm and stress") verse and plays, including the dramatic trilogy *Wallenstein* 1798–99. Much of his work concerns the aspirations for political freedom and the avoidance of mediocrity.

He was a qualified surgeon, but after the success of the play *Die Räuber/The Robbers* 1781, he devoted himself to literature and completed his tragedies *Die Verschwörung des Fiesko zu Genua/ Fiesco, or, the Genoese Conspiracy* and *Kabale und Liebe/Love and Intrigue* 1783. Moving to Weimar in 1787, he wrote his more mature blank-verse drama *Don Carlos* and the hymn "An die Freude/Ode to Joy," later used by ▷Beethoven in his ninth symphony. As professor of history at Jena from 1789 he completed a history of the Thirty Years' War and developed a close friendship with ▷Goethe after early antagonism. His essays on aesthetics include the piece of literary criticism *Über naive und sentimentalische Dichtung/Naive and Sentimental Poetry*. Schiller became the foremost German dramatist with his classic dramas *Wallenstein*, *Maria Stuart* 1800, *Die Jungfrau von Orleans/The Maid of Orleans* 1801, and *Wilhelm Tell/William Tell* 1804.

schipperke (Dutch "little boatman" from its use on canal barges) breed of tailless watchdog, bred in Belgium. It has black fur and erect ears, is about 1 ft/30 cm high, and weighs about 16 lb/7 kg.

schism formal split over a doctrinal difference between religious believers, as in the ▷Great Schism in the Roman Catholic Church; over the doctrine of papal infallibility, as with the Old Catholics in 1879; and over the use of the Latin Tridentine mass 1988.

schist ▷metamorphic rock containing ▷mica or another platy or elongate mineral, whose crystals are aligned to give a foliation (planar texture) known as schistosity. Schist may contain additional minerals such as ▷garnet.

schistosomiasis another name for ▷bilharzia.

schizocarp dry ▷fruit that develops from two or more carpels and splits, when mature, to form separate one-seeded units known as mericarps.

The mericarps may be dehiscent, splitting open to release the seed when ripe, as in *Geranium*, or indehiscent, remaining closed once mature, as in mallow *Malva* and plants of the Umbelliferae family, such as the carrot *Daucus carota* and parsnip *Pastinaca sativa*.

schizophrenia mental disorder, a psychosis of unknown origin, which can lead to profound changes in personality and behavior including paranoia and hallucinations. Contrary to popular belief, it does not involve a split personality. Modern treatment approaches include drugs, family therapy, stress reduction, and rehabilitation.

Schizophrenia implies a severe divorce from reality in the patient's thinking. Although the exact cause is unknown, circumstantial evidence points to an overactivity in the brain of those nerve cells that have dopamine as their transmitter substance. Drugs that interfere with the action of dopamine, such as chlorpromazine, may be of benefit.

Schlegel August Wilhelm von 1767–1845. German Romantic author, translator of Shakespeare, whose *Über dramatische Kunst und Literatur/Lectures on Dramatic Art and Literature* 1809–11 broke down the formalism of the old Classical criteria of literary composition. Friedrich von Schlegel was his brother.

Schlegel Friedrich von 1772–1829. German critic who (with his brother August) was a founder of the Romantic movement, and a pioneer in the comparative study of languages.

Schlesinger Arthur Meier, Jr 1917– . US historian. His first book, *The Age of Jackson*, won a Pulitzer Prize 1945. After being named to the Harvard faculty 1946, he became active in Democratic politics, serving as a speechwriter in the presidential campaigns of Adlai Stevenson 1956 and John Kennedy 1960. Schlesinger was presidential assistant for Latin American Affairs 1961–64 and in 1967 became a professor at the City College of New York.

Born in Columbus, Ohio, the son of a prominent historian, Schlesinger was educated at Harvard and served as an intelligence officer during World War II.

Schlesinger John 1926– . English film and television director who was responsible for such British films as *Billy Liar* 1963 and *Darling* 1965. His first US film, *Midnight Cowboy* 1969, was a big commercial success and was followed by *Sunday, Bloody Sunday* 1971, *Marathon Man* 1976, and *Yanks* 1979.

Schleswig-Holstein *Land* (state) of Germany
area 6,060 sq mi/15,700 sq km
capital Kiel
cities Lübeck, Flensburg, Schleswig
features river Elbe, Kiel Canal, Heligoland
products shipbuilding, mechanical and electrical engineering, food processing
population (1988) 2,613,000
religion 87% Protestant; 6% Catholic
history Schleswig (Danish *Slesvig*) and Holstein were two duchies held by the kings of Denmark from 1460, but were not part of the kingdom; a number of the inhabitants were German, and Holstein was a member of the Confederation of the Rhine formed 1815. Possession of the duchies had long been disputed by Prussia, and when Frederick VII of Denmark died without an heir 1863, Prussia, supported by Austria, fought and defeated the Danes 1864, and in 1866 annexed the two duchies. A plebiscite held 1920 gave the northern part of Schleswig to Denmark, which made it the province of Haderslev and Aabenraa; the rest, with Holstein, remained part of Germany.

Schlieffen Plan military plan produced Dec 1905 by German chief of general staff, General Count Alfred von Schlieffen (1833–1913), that formed the basis of German military planning before World War I, and inspired Hitler's plans for the conquest of Europe in World War II. It involved a simultaneous attack on Russia and France, the object being to defeat France quickly and then deploy all available resources against the Russians.

Schliemann Heinrich 1822–1890. German archeologist. He earned a fortune in business, retiring in 1863 to pursue his lifelong ambition to discover a historical basis for Homer's *Iliad*. In 1871 he began excavating at Hissarlik, Turkey, a site which yielded the ruins of nine consecutive cities and was indeed the site of Troy. His later excavations were at Mycenae 1874–76, where he discovered the ruins of the ▷Mycenaean civilization.

Schluter Poul Holmskov 1929– . Danish right-wing politician, leader of the Conservative People's Party (KF) from 1974 and prime minister from 1982. Having joined the KF in his youth, he trained as a lawyer and then entered the Danish parliament (Folketing) in 1964. His center-right coalition survived the 1990 election and was reconstituted, with Liberal support.

Schmidt Helmut 1918– . German socialist politician, member of the Social Democratic Party (SPD), chancellor of West Germany 1974–83. As chancellor, Schmidt introduced social reforms and continued Brandt's policy of ▷Ostpolitik. With the French president Giscard d'Estaing, he instigated annual world and European economic summits. He was a firm supporter of ▷NATO and of the deployment of US nuclear missiles in West Germany during the early 1980s.

Schmidt was elected to the Bundestag (federal parliament) in 1953. He was interior minister 1961–65, defense minister 1969–72, and finance minister 1972–74. He became federal chancellor (prime minister) on Willy ▷Brandt's resignation in 1974. Reelected 1980, he was defeated in the Bundestag in 1982 following the switch of allegiance by the SPD's coalition allies, the Free Democratic Party. Schmidt retired from federal politics at the general election of 1983, having encountered growing opposition from the SPD's left wing, who opposed his stance on military and economic issues.

Schmidt-Rottluff Karl 1884–1974. German Expressionist painter and printmaker, a founding member of the movement Die ▷Brücke in Dresden 1905, active in Berlin from 1911. Inspired by Vincent van Gogh and ▷Fauvism, he developed a vigorous style of brushwork and a bold palette. He painted portraits and landscapes and produced numerous woodcuts and lithographs.

Schnabel Artur 1882–1951. Austrian pianist, teacher, and composer. He taught music at the

Berlin State Academy 1925–30, but settled in the US in 1939, where he composed symphonies and piano works. He excelled at playing Beethoven and trained many pianists.

Schoenberg Arnold (Franz Walter) 1874–1951. Austro-Hungarian composer, a US citizen from 1941. After Romantic early works such as *Verklärte Nacht/Transfigured Night* 1899 and the *Gurrelieder/Songs of Gurra* 1900–11, he experimented with �Datonality (absence of key), producing works such as *Pierrot Lunaire* 1912 for chamber ensemble and voice, before developing the 12-tone system of musical composition. This was further developed by his pupils Alban ⟩Berg and Anton Webern.

After World War I he wrote several Neo-Classical works for chamber ensembles. He taught at the Berlin State Academy 1925–33. Driven from Germany by the Nazis, he settled in the US 1933, where he influenced music scoring for films. Later works include the opera *Moses und Aron* 1932–51.

scholasticism the theological and philosophical systems that were studied in both Christian and Judaic schools in Europe in the medieval period. Scholasticism sought to integrate biblical teaching with Platonic and Aristotelian philosophy.

John Scotus (Erigena) is regarded as the founder, but the succession of "schoolmen," as scholastic philosophers were called, opened with Roscellinus at the end of the 11th century, when as a supporter of nominalism he was countered by Anselm, the champion of realism. The controversy over ⟨Duniversals thus begun continued for several centuries. William of Champeaux, Abelard, the English monk Alexander of Hales (died 1222), Albertus Magnus, and Peter Lombard played prominent parts, but more significant were Thomas Aquinas, whose writings became the Classical textbooks of Catholic doctrine, and the Franciscan Duns Scotus. In the late 12th century the Spanish philosopher Moses Maimonides published a work that helped to introduce Europe to an integrated approach to Aristotle. The last major scholastic philosopher was William of Occam, who, in the first half of the 14th century, restated ⟩nominalism.

In the 20th century there has been a revival of interest in scholasticism, in the writings of Jacques Maritian (1882–1973) and other Catholic scholars.

school in education, an institution where instruction takes place. Some are accredited.

School District of Abington Township v Schempp a US Supreme Court decision 1963 dealing with mandatory religious worship in public schools. The case challenged the constitutionality of an Abington, Pennsylvania, statute that forced students to recite Bible verses and the Lord's Prayer in school. The Court ruled that such practice violated First-Amendment measures against establishing an official religion. Since the statute had no secular legislative purpose, it was declared invalid.

Schopenhauer Arthur 1788–1860. German philosopher whose *The World as Will and Idea* 1818 expounded an atheistic and pessimistic world view: an irrational will is considered as the inner principle of the world, producing an ever-frustrated cycle of desire, of which the only escape is aesthetic contemplation or absorption into nothingness.

This theory struck a responsive chord in the philosopher Nietzsche, the composer Wagner,

the German novelist Thomas Mann, and the English writer Thomas Hardy.

Schrödinger Erwin 1887–1961. Austrian physicist who advanced the study of wave mechanics (see ⟩quantum theory). Born in Vienna, he became senior professor at the Dublin Institute for Advanced Studies 1940. He shared (with Paul Dirac) a Nobel Prize 1933.

Schubert Franz (Peter) 1797–1828. Austrian composer. His ten symphonies include the incomplete eighth in B minor (the "Unfinished") and the "Great" in C major. He wrote chamber and piano music, including the "Trout Quintet," and over 600 lieder (songs) combining the Romantic expression of emotion with pure melody. They include the cycles *Die schöne Müllerin/The Beautiful Maid of the Mill* 1823 and *Die Winterreise/The Winter Journey* 1827.

Schulz Charles Monroe 1922– . US cartoonist. His idea for the "Peanuts" cartoon strip was accepted by United Features Syndicate 1950. As the characters Snoopy, Charlie Brown, Lucy, and Linus became famous throughout the country, Schulz further promoted them through merchandise lines and television specials. In 1967 a musical based on the "Peanuts" characters, *You're a Good Man, Charlie Brown*, played on Broadway.

Born in Minneapolis, Minnesota, Schulz gained his only formal training through a correspondence course with the Minneapolis Art Institute. He joined the staff of the *St Paul Pioneer Press* 1948.

Schumacher Fritz (Ernst Friedrich) 1911–1977. German economist who believed that the increasing size of institutions, coupled with unchecked economic growth, created a range of social and environmental problems. He argued his case in books like *Small is Beautiful* 1973, and tested it practically through establishing the ⟩Intermediate Technology Development Group.

Schuman Robert 1886–1963. French politician. He was prime minister 1947–48, and as foreign minister 1948–53 he proposed in May 1950 a common market for coal and steel (the **Schuman Plan**), which was established as the European Coal and Steel Community 1952, the basis of the European Community.

Schumann Clara (Josephine) (born Wieck) 1819–1896. German pianist. She married Robert ⟩Schumann in 1840 (her father had been his piano teacher). During his life and after his death she was devoted to popularizing his work, appearing frequently in European concert halls.

Schumann Robert Alexander 1810–1856. German Romantic composer. His songs and short piano pieces show simplicity combined with an ability to portray mood and emotion. Among his compositions are four symphonies, a violin concerto, a piano concerto, sonatas, and song cycles, such as *Dichterliebe/Poet's Love* 1840. Mendelssohn championed many of his works.

Schumpeter Joseph A(lois) 1883–1950. US economist and sociologist. In *Capitalism, Socialism and Democracy* 1942 he contended that Western capitalism, impelled by its very success, was evolving into a form of socialism because firms would become increasingly large and their managements increasingly divorced from ownership, while social trends were undermining the traditional motives for entrepreneurial accumulation of wealth.

Schumpeter was born in Moravia, now the Czech Republic, and migrated to the US 1932.

He was deeply interested in mathematics, and he took part in the founding of the Econometric Society 1930. His writings established him as an authority on economic theory as well as the history of economic thought. Among other standard reference works, he wrote the *History of Economic Analysis* 1954, published posthumously.

Schurz Carl 1829–1906. German-born US editor and political leader. Named US minister to Spain 1861–62, he returned to see action as a staff officer in the American Civil War. After working briefly as editor of the *Detroit Post* 1866, he moved to St Louis and was elected to the US Senate, where he sat 1869–75. After serving as secretary of the interior under President Hayes 1877–81, Schurz became editor of the *New York Evening Post* 1881–83. A harsh critic of government corruption, he was president of the National Civil Service Reform League 1892–1901.

Schurz came to the US 1852, studied law, and was admitted to the Wisconsin bar 1859.

Schuschnigg Kurt von 1897–1977. Austrian chancellor 1934–38, in succession to ⟩Dollfuss. He tried in vain to prevent Nazi annexation (*Anschluss*) but in Feb 1938 he was forced to accept a Nazi minister of the interior, and a month later Austria was occupied and annexed by Germany. He was imprisoned in Germany until 1945, when he went to the US; he returned to Austria 1967.

Schuyler Philip John 1733–1804. American public official. Born in Albany, New York, Schuyler inherited extensive real estate holdings in the Mohawk Valley. After service in the French and Indian War, he was elected to the provincial assembly 1768 and was a member of the Continental Congress 1775–77. At the outbreak of the American Revolution, he was named general in command of the Department of New York. Replaced in 1777, he returned to the Continental Congress 1778–81. A supporter of the US Constitution, Schuyler became one of New York's first US senators 1789–91 and later served 1797–98.

Schwarzenegger Arnold 1947– . Austrian-born US film actor, one of the biggest box-office attractions of the late 1980s and early 1990s. He starred in sword-and-sorcery films such as *Conan the Barbarian* 1982 and later graduated to large-scale budget action movies such as *Terminator* 1984, *Predator* 1987, and *Terminator II* 1991.

Schwarzenegger began his career as a bodybuilder and won numerous medals including the 1969 Mr Universe competition. He came to the attention of Hollywood in *Pumping Iron* 1977, a documentary about body-building. He was cast in a series of roles which made much of his physique and little of his character, thus overcoming fears over the apparent obstacle of his Austrian accent. The power of his onscreen personality soon enabled him to play a variety of roles, including a comic role in *Twins* 1989. His other films include *Raw Deal* 1986, *Total Recall* 1990, and *Kindergarten Cop* 1991.

Schwarzkopf (H) Norman (nicknamed "Stormin' Norman") 1934– . US general who was supreme commander of the Allied forces in the ⟩Gulf War 1991. He planned and executed a blitzkrieg campaign, "Desert Storm," sustaining remarkably few casualties in the liberation of Kuwait. He was a battalion commander in the Vietnam War and deputy commander of the 1983 US invasion of Grenada.

A graduate of the military academy at West Point, Schwarzkopf obtained a master's degree in guided-missile engineering. He became an infantryman and later a paratrooper, and did two tours of service in Vietnam. Maintaining the 28-member Arab-Western military coalition against Iraq 1991 extended his diplomatic skills, and his success in the Gulf War made him a popular hero in the US. He retired from the army Aug 1991 and published his autobiography, *It Doesn't Take A Hero* 1992.

Schwarzkopf Elisabeth 1915– . German soprano, known for her dramatic interpretation of operatic roles, such as Elvira in *Don Giovanni* and the Marschallin in *Der Rosenkavalier*, as well as songs.

Schwarzwald German name for the ⟡Black Forest, coniferous forest in Germany.

Schweitzer Albert 1875–1965. French Protestant theologian, organist, and missionary surgeon. He founded the hospital at Lambaréné in Gabon in 1913, giving organ recitals to support his work there. He wrote a life of Bach and *Von reimarus zu Wrede/The Quest for the Historical Jesus* 1906 and was awarded the Nobel Peace Prize in 1952 for his teaching of "reverence for life."

Schwinger Julian 1918– . US quantum physicist. His research concerned the behavior of charged particles in electrical fields. This work, expressed entirely through mathematics, combines elements from quantum theory and relativity theory. Schwinger shared the Nobel Prize for Physics 1963 with Richard ⟡Feynman and Sin-Itiro Tomonaga (1906–1979).

Described as the "physicist in knee pants," he entered college in New York at the age of 15, transferred to Columbia University and graduated at 17. At the age of 29 he became Harvard University's youngest full professor.

Schwitters Kurt 1887–1948. German artist, a member of the ⟡Dada movement. He moved to Norway in 1937 and to England in 1940. From 1918 he developed a variation on collage, using discarded rubbish such as buttons and bus tickets to create pictures and structures.

He called these art works *Merz*, and produced a magazine of the same name from 1923. Later he created *Merzbau*, extensive constructions of wood and scrap, most of which were destroyed.

Schwyz capital of Schwyz canton, Switzerland; population (1990) 12,700. Schwyz was one of the three original cantons of the Swiss Confederation 1291, which gave its name to the whole country about 1450.

sciatica persistent pain in the leg, along the sciatic nerve and its branches. Causes of sciatica include inflammation of the nerve or pressure on, or inflammation of, a nerve root leading out of the lower spine.

science (Latin *scientia* "knowledge") any systematic field of study or body of knowledge that aims, through experiment, observation, and deduction, to produce reliable explanation of phenomena, with reference to the material and physical world.

Activities such as healing, star-watching, and engineering have been practiced in many societies since ancient times. Pure science, especially physics (formerly called natural philosophy), had traditionally been the main area of study for philosophers. The European scientific revolution between about 1650 and 1800 replaced speculative philosophy with a new

combination of observation, experimentation, and rationality.

Today, scientific research involves an interaction among tradition, experiment and observation, and deduction. The subject area called *philosophy of science* investigates the nature of this complex interaction, and the extent of its ability to gain access to the truth about the material world. It has long been recognized that induction from observation cannot give explanations based on logic. In the 20th century Karl ⟡Popper has described ⟡scientific method as a rigorous experimental testing of a scientist's ideas or hypotheses (see ⟡hypothesis). The origin and role of these ideas, and their interdependence with observation, have been examined, for example, by the US thinker Thomas S ⟡Kuhn, who places them in a historical and sociological setting. The *sociology of science* investigates how scientific theories and laws are produced, and questions the possibility of objectivity in any scientific endeavor. One controversial point of view is the replacement of scientific realism with scientific relativism, as proposed by Paul K ⟡Feyerabend. Questions concerning the proper use of science and the role of science education are also restructuring this field of study.

Science is divided into separate areas of study, such as astronomy, biology, geology, chemistry, physics, and mathematics, although more recently attempts have been made to combine traditionally separate disciplines under such headings as ⟡life sciences and ⟡earth sciences. These areas are usually jointly referred to as the *natural sciences*. Physics and chemistry are sometimes separated out and called the physical sciences, with mathematics left in a category of its own. The application of science for practical purposes is called *technology*. *Social science* is the systematic study of human behavior, and includes such areas as anthropology, economics, psychology, and sociology. One area of contemporary debate is whether the social-science disciplines are actually sciences; that is, whether the study of human beings is capable of scientific precision or prediction in the same way as natural science is seen to be.

science fiction or *speculative fiction* (also known as *SF* or *sci-fi*) genre of fiction and film with an imaginary scientific, technological, or futuristic basis. It is sometimes held to have its roots in the works of Mary Shelley, notably *Frankenstein* 1818. Often taking its ideas and concerns from current ideas in science and the social sciences, science fiction aims to shake up standard perceptions of reality.

SF works often deal with alternative realities, future histories, robots, aliens, utopias and dystopias (often satiric), space and time travel, natural or human-made disasters, and psychic powers. Early practitioners were Jules Verne and H G Wells. In the 20th century the US pulp-magazine tradition of SF produced such writers as Arthur C Clarke, Isaac Asimov, Robert Heinlein, and Frank Herbert; a consensus of "pure storytelling" and traditional values was disrupted by writers associated with the British magazine *New Worlds* (Brian Aldiss, Michael Moorcock, J G Ballard) and by younger US writers (Joanna Russ, Ursula Le Guin, Thomas Disch, Gene Wolfe) who used the form for serious literary purposes and for political and sexual radicalism. Thriving SF traditions, only partly influenced by the Anglo-American one, exist in France, Germany, and

E Europe. In the 1980s the cyberpunk school spread from the US, spearheaded by William Gibson and Bruce Sterling (1954–).

Science-fiction writers include James Tiptree Jr (Alice Sheldon 1915–1987), Philip K Dick, John Brunner (1934– , UK), Samuel Delany (1942–), Stanislaw Lem (1921– , Poland), Boris and Arkady Strugatsky (1931– and 1925–1991, USSR), Harlan Ellison (1934–), Damon Knight (1922–), John Campbell (1910–1971), and Frederik Pohl (1919–)—the last four all US editors and anthologists.

Many mainstream writers have written SF, including Aldous Huxley (*Brave New World* 1932), George Orwell (*Nineteen Eighty-Four* 1949), and Doris Lessing (series of five books *Canopus in Argos: Archives* 1979–83).

science park site near a university on which high-technology industrial businesses are housed, so that they can benefit from the research expertise of the university's scientists. Science parks originated in the US in the 1950s.

scientific law in science, principles that are taken to be universally applicable.

Laws (for instance, ⟡Boyle's law and ⟡Newton's laws of motion) form the basic theoretical structure of the physical sciences, so that the rejection of a law by the scientific community is an almost inconceivable event. On occasion a law may be modified, as was the case when Einstein showed that Newton's laws of motion do not apply to objects traveling at speeds close to that of light.

scientific method in science, the belief that experimentation and observation, properly understood and applied, can avoid the influence of cultural and social values and so build up a picture of a reality independent of the observer.

Improved techniques and mechanical devices, which improve the reliability of measurements, may seem to support this theory; but the realization that observations of subatomic particles influence their behavior has undermined the view that objectivity is possible in science (see ⟡uncertainty principle).

Scientology (Latin *scire* "to know" and Greek *logos* "branch of learning") "applied religious philosophy" based on ⟡dianetics, founded in California in 1954 by L Ron ⟡Hubbard as the *Church of Scientology*. It claims to "increase man's spiritual awareness," but its methods of recruiting and retaining converts have been criticized. Its headquarters from 1959 have been in Sussex, England.

scilla any bulbous plant of the genus *Scilla*, family Liliaceae, bearing blue, pink, or white flowers, and including the spring squill *S. verna*.

Scilly Islands group of 140 islands and islets lying 25 mi/40 km SW of Land's End, England; administered by the Duchy of Cornwall; area 6.3 sq mi/16 sq km; population (1981) 1,850. The five inhabited islands are *St Mary's*, the largest, on which is Hugh Town, capital of the Scillies; *Tresco*, the second largest, with subtropical gardens; *St Martin's*, noted for beautiful shells; *St Agnes*; and *Bryher*.

Products include vegetables and flowers, and tourism is important. The islands have remains of Bronze Age settlements.

scintillation counter instrument for measuring very low levels of radiation. The radiation strikes a scintillator (a device that emits a unit of light when a charged elementary particle collides with it), whose light output is "amplified" by a ◊photomultiplier; the current pulses of its output are in turn counted or added by a scaler to give a numerical reading.

Scipio Africanus Major 237–c. 183 BC. Roman general. He defeated the Carthaginians in Spain 210–206, invaded Africa 204, and defeated Hannibal at Zama 202.

Scipio Africanus Minor c. 185–129 BC. Roman general, the adopted grandson of Scipio Africanus Major, also known as **Scipio Aemilianus**. He destroyed Carthage 146, and subdued Spain 134. He was opposed to his brothers-in-law, the Gracchi (see ◊Gracchus), and his wife is thought to have taken part in his murder.

Scipio Publius Cornelius died 211 BC. Roman general, father of Scipio Africanus Major. Elected consul 218, during the 2nd Punic War, he was defeated by Hannibal at Ticinus and killed by the Carthaginians in Spain.

SCLC abbreviation for US civil-rights organization ◊**Southern Christian Leadership Conference**.

sclerenchyma plant tissue whose function is to strengthen and support, composed of thick-walled cells that are heavily lignified (toughened). On maturity the cell inside dies, and only the cell walls remain.

Sclerenchyma may be made up of one or two types of cells: **sclereids**, occurring singly or in small clusters, are often found in the hard shells of fruits and in seed coats, bark, and the stem cortex; **fibers**, frequently grouped in bundles, are elongated cells, often with pointed ends, associated with the vascular tissue (◊xylem and ◊phloem) of the plant.

Some fibers provide useful materials, such as flax from *Linum usitatissimum* and hemp from *Cannabis sativa*.

sclerosis any abnormal hardening of body tissues or parts, especially the nervous system or walls of the arteries. See ◊multiple sclerosis and ◊atherosclerosis.

scoliosis lateral curvature of the spine. Correction by operations to insert bone grafts (thus creating a straight but rigid spine) has been replaced by insertion of an electronic stimulative device in the lower back to contract the muscles adequately.

Scopes monkey trial trial held in Dayton, Tennessee, 1925. John T Scopes, a science teacher at the high school, was accused of teaching, contrary to a law of the state, Darwin's theory of evolution. He was fined $100, but this was waived on a technical point. The defense counsel was Clarence Darrow and the prosecutor William Jennings Bryan.

scopolamine trade name for ◊hyoscine, a sedative drug.

scorched earth in warfare, the policy of burning and destroying everything that might be of use to an invading army, especially the crops in the fields. It was used to great effect in Russia in 1812 against the invasion of the French emperor Napoleon and again during World War II to hinder the advance of German forces in 1941.

scorpion any arachnid of the order Scorpiones. Common in the tropics and subtropics, scorpions have large pincers and long tails ending in upcurved poisonous stings, though the venom is not usually fatal to a healthy adult human. Some species reach 10 in/25 cm. They produce live young rather than eggs, and hunt chiefly by night.

scorpion fly any insect of the order Mecoptera. They have a characteristic downturned beak with jaws at the tip, and many males have a scorpionlike upturned tail, giving them their common name. Most feed on insects or carrion. They are an ancient group with relatively few living representatives.

Scorpius zodiacal constellation in the southern hemisphere between Libra and Sagittarius, represented as a scorpion. The Sun passes briefly through Scorpius in the last week of Nov. The heart of the scorpion is marked by the red supergiant star Antares. Scorpius contains rich Milky Way star fields, plus the strongest ◊X-ray source in the sky, Scorpius X-1. In astrology, the dates for Scorpius are between about Oct 24 and Nov 21 (see ◊precession).

Scorsese Martin 1942– . US director, screenwriter, and producer whose films concentrate on complex characterization and the themes of alienation and guilt. Drawing from his Italian-American Catholic background, his work often deals with sin and redemption, such as in his first major film, *Boxcar Bertha* 1972. His influential, passionate, and forceful movies includes *Mean Streets* 1973, *Taxi Driver* 1976, *Raging Bull* 1980, *The Last Temptation of Christ* 1988, *GoodFellas* 1990, and *Cape Fear* 1991.

Scot inhabitant of Scotland, part of Britain; or person of Scottish descent. Originally the Scots were a Celtic (Gaelic) people of N Ireland who migrated to Scotland in the 5th century.

Scotland the northernmost part of Britain, formerly an independent country, now part of the UK
area 30,297 sq mi/78,470 sq km
capital Edinburgh
cities Glasgow, Dundee, Aberdeen
features the Highlands in the north (with the Grampian Mountains); central Lowlands, including valleys of the Clyde and Forth, with most of the country's population and industries; Southern Uplands (including the Lammermuir Hills); and islands of the Orkneys, Shetlands, and Western Isles; the world's greatest concentration of nuclear weapons are at the UK and US bases on the Clyde, near Glasgow; 8,000-year-old pinewood forests once covered 3,706,500 acres/1,500,000 hectares, now reduced to 30,900 acres/12,500 hectares
industry electronics, marine and aircraft engines, oil, natural gas, chemicals, textiles, clothing, printing, paper, food processing, tourism
currency pound sterling
population (1987) 5,113,000
language English; Gaelic spoken by 1.3%, mainly in the Highlands
religion Presbyterian (Church of Scotland), Roman Catholic
famous people Robert Bruce, Walter Scott, Robert Burns, Robert Louis Stevenson, Adam Smith
government Scotland sends 72 members to the UK Parliament at Westminster. Local government is on similar lines to that of England, but there is a differing legal system. There is a movement for an independent or devolved Scottish assembly.

Scotland: history for early history, see also ◊Britain, ancient; ◊Celt; ◊Pict.
4th century BC Celts reached British Isles.
1st century AD Picts prevented Romans from penetrating far into Scotland.
5th–6th centuries Christianity introduced from Ireland.

9th century Kenneth MacAlpin united kingdoms of Scotland.
946 Malcolm I conquered Strathclyde.
1015 Malcolm II conquered Lothian.
1263 Defeat of Haakon, king of Norway, at Battle of Largs.
1266 Scotland gained Hebrides from Norway at Treaty of Perth.
1292 Scottish throne granted by Edward I (attempting to annex Scotland) to John Baliol.
1297 Defeat of England at Stirling Bridge by William Wallace.
1314 Robert Bruce defeated English at Bannockburn.
1328 Scottish independence recognized by England.
1371 First Stuart king, Robert II.
1513 James IV killed at Battle of Flodden.
1540s–1550s John Knox introduced Calvinism to Scotland.
1565 Mary Queen of Scots married Darnley.
1567 Darnley murdered.
1568 Mary fled to England.
1578 James VI took over government.
1587 Mary beheaded.
1592 Presbyterianism established.
1603 James VI became James I of England.
1638 Scottish rebellion against England.
1643 Solemn League and Covenant.
1651–1660 Cromwell conquered Scotland.
1679 Covenanters defeated at Bothwell Brig.
1689 Jacobite forces defeated the army of William III at Killiecrankie, but rebellion collapsed soon after.
1692 Massacre of Glencoe.
1707 Act of Union with England.
1715, 1745 Failed Jacobite risings against England.
18th and 19th centuries Highland clearances: tenant farmers evicted to make way for sheep.
1945 First Scottish Nationalist member of Parliament elected.
1979 Referendum on Scottish directly elected assembly failed.
1989 Local rates replaced by "poll tax" despite wide opposition.
1990 350,000 warrants issued by March for nonpayment of poll tax.

Scots language the form of the English language as traditionally spoken and written in Scotland, regarded by some scholars as a distinct language. Scots derives from the Northumbrian dialect of Anglo-Saxon or Old English, and has been a literary language since the 14th century.

It is also known as **Inglis** (now archaic, and a variant of "English"), ◊**Lallans** ("Lowlands"), **Lowland Scots** (in contrast with the Gaelic of the Highlands and Islands), and "**the Doric**" (as a rustic language in contrast with the "Attic" or "Athenian" language of Edinburgh's literati, especially in the 18th century). It is also often referred to as Broad Scots in contrast to the anglicized language of the middle classes.

Scots has been spoken in SE Scotland since the 7th century. During the Middle Ages it spread to the far north, blending with the Norn dialects of Orkney and Shetland (once distinct varieties of Norse). Scots has a wide range of poetry, ballads, and prose records, including two national epic poems: Barbor's *Bruce* and Blind Harry's *Wallace*. With the transfer of the court to England upon the Union of the Crowns in 1603 and the dissemination of the King James Bible, Scots ceased to be a national and court language, but has retained its vitality among the general population and in various literary and linguistic revivals.

Words originating in Scots that are now widely used in English include *bonnie* (= good-looking), *glamour*, *raid*, and *wee* (= small). In Scotland a wide range of traditional Scots usage intermixes with standard English.

Scott George C(ampbell) 1927– . US actor who played mostly tough, authoritarian film roles. His work includes *Dr Strangelove* 1964, *Patton* 1970, *The Hospital* 1971, and *Firestarter* 1984.

Scott Paul (Mark) 1920–1978. English novelist, author of *The Raj Quartet* consisting of *The Jewel in the Crown* 1966, *The Day of the Scorpion* 1968, *The Towers of Silence* 1972, and *A Division of the Spoils* 1975, dealing with the British Raj in India. Other novels include *Staying On* 1977.

Scott Randolph. Adopted name of Randolph Crane 1903–1987. US actor. He began his career in romantic films before becoming one of Hollywood's Western stars in the 1930s. His films include *Roberta* 1934, *Jesse James* 1939, and *Ride the High Country* 1962.

Scott Ridley 1939– . English director and producer of some of the most visually spectacular and influential films of the 1980s and 1990s, such as *Alien* 1979, *Blade Runner* 1982, and *1492 -The Search for Paradise* 1992. Criticized for sacrificing storyline and character development in favor of ornate sets, Scott replied with *Thelma and Louise* 1991, a carefully wrought story of female bonding and adventure.

Having started as a set designer, Scott graduated to directing episodes of the television series *Z Cars* before leaving the BBC in 1967. He completed his first film *The Duellists* in 1977. Among his other films are *Legend* 1985, *Someone to Watch Over Me* 1987, and *Black Rain* 1989.

Scott Robert Falcon (known as *Scott of the Antarctic*) 1868–1912. English explorer who commanded two Antarctic expeditions, 1901–04 and 1910–12. On Jan 18, 1912 he reached the South Pole, shortly after Norwegian Roald ◊Amundsen, but on the return journey he and his companions died in a blizzard only a few miles from their base camp. His journal was recovered and published in 1913.

Scott Walter 1771–1832. Scottish novelist and poet. His first works were translations of German ballads, followed by poems such as "The Lady of the Lake" 1810 and "Lord of the Isles" 1815. He gained a European reputation for his historical novels such as *Heart of Midlothian* 1818, *Ivanhoe* 1819, and *The Fair Maid of Perth* 1828. His last years were marked by frantic writing to pay off his debts, after the bankruptcy of his publishing company in 1826.

Scott Winfield 1786–1866. US military leader. During the Mexican War he led the capture of Veracruz and Mexico City. An unsuccessful Whig candidate for president 1852, Scott was still head of the army at the outbreak of the Civil War but retired from active service 1861.

Born in Petersburg, Virginia, Scott attended the College of William and Mary and began his military career 1807. As a colonel in the War of 1812, he won distinction at the battles of Chippewa and Lundy's Lane. Promoted to brigadier general, he saw action in the Black Hawk 1832 and Seminole 1835–37 wars. In 1841 he became general in chief of the army.

Scottish Gaelic literature the earliest examples of Scottish Gaelic prose belong to the period 1000–1150, but the most significant early original composition is the history of the MacDonalds in the Red and Black Books at Clanranald. The first printed book in Scottish Gaelic was a translation of Knox's Prayer Book in 1567. Prose Gaelic is at its best in the folk tales, proverbs, and essays by writers such as Norman MacLeod in the 19th and Donald Lamont in the 20th century. Scottish Gaelic poetry falls into two main categories. The older, syllabic verse was composed by professional bards. The chief sources of our knowledge of this are the Book of the Dean of Lismore (16th century), which is also the main early source for the Ossianic ballads; the panegyrics in the Books of Clanranald; and the Fernaig manuscript.

Modern Scottish Gaelic stressed poetry began in the 17th century but reached its zenith during the Jacobite period with Alexander MacDonald, Duncan Macintyre, Rob Donn, and Dugald Buchanan. Only William Livingstone (1808–1870) kept alive the old nationalistic spirit in the 19th century. During and after World War II a new school emerged, including Somhairle MacGilleathain, George Campbell-Hay, and Ruaraidh MacThómais.

Scout member of a worldwide youth organization that emphasizes character, citizenship, and outdoor life. It was founded (as the Boy Scouts) in England 1908 by Robert ◊Baden-Powell. His book *Scouting for Boys* 1908 led to the incorporation in the UK of the Boy Scout Association by royal charter in 1912.

The Boy Scouts of America was founded on the Baden-Powell model in 1910. There are about 3.5 million Boy Scouts in the US. Girl Scouts of the US was founded 1912, following the same model. There are about 2 million Girl Scouts, including Brownies (aged 6–8), Juniors (aged 9–11), Cadettes (12–14), and Seniors (14–17).

Scrabble trademark of a board game for two to four players, based on the crossword puzzle, in which lettered tiles of varying point values are used to form words. International competitions are held.

Scranton industrial city on the Lackawanna River, Pennsylvania; population (1990) 81,800. Anthracite coal is mined nearby, but production has declined sharply, and the city now manufactures such products as electronic equipment, fabricated metal, clothing, plastic goods, and printed materials.

The University of Scranton is here. Scranton was settled 1771 but developed chiefly with the erection of anthracite-fired furnaces 1840.

scrapie fatal disease of sheep and goats that attacks the central nervous system, causing deterioration of the brain cells. It is believed to be caused by a submicroscopic organism known as a prion and may be related to ◊bovine spongiform encephalopathy, the disease of cattle known as "mad cow disease."

screamer any South American marsh-dwelling bird of the family Anhimidae; there are only three species, all in the genus *Anhima*. They are about 30 in/80 cm long, with short curved beaks, long toes, dark plumage, spurs on the fronts of the wings, and a crest or horn on the head.

Screamers wade in wet forests and marshes, although their feet are scarcely webbed. They are related to ducks and are placed in the same order, the Anseriformes.

scree pile of rubble and sediment that forms an ascending slope at the foot of a mountain range or cliff.

The rock fragments that form scree are usually slide rock or pieces broken off by frost action. As fragments are loosened, they clatter downward in a series of free falls, bounces, and slides. With time, the rock waste builds in a heap or sheet of rubble that may eventually bury even the upper cliffs, and the growth of the scree then stops. Usually, however, erosional forces decompose the rock waste so that the scree stays restricted to lower slopes.

screening or *health screening* the systematic search for evidence of a disease, or of conditions that may precede it, in people who are not suffering from any symptoms. The aim of screening is to try to limit ill health from diseases that are difficult to prevent and might otherwise go undetected. Examples are hypothyroidism and phenylketonuria, for which all newborn babies in Western countries are screened; breast cancer (◊mammography) and cervical cancer; and stroke, for which high blood pressure is a known risk factor.

The criteria for a successful screening program are that the disease should be important and treatable, the population at risk identifiable, the screening test acceptable, accurate, and cheap, and that the results of screening should justify the costs involved.

screw in construction, cylindrical or tapering piece of metal or plastic (or formerly wood) with a helical groove cut into it. Each turn of a screw moves it forward or backward by a distance equal to the pitch (the spacing between neighboring threads).

Its mechanical advantage equals $2 \; r/P$, where P is the pitch and r is the radius of the thread. Thus the mechanical advantage of a tapering wood screw, for example, increases as it is rotated into the wood.

The thread is comparable to an inclined plane (wedge) wrapped around a cylinder or cone.

Scriabin Alexander (Nikolayevich) 1872–1915. Russian composer and pianist born in Moscow, whose powerfully emotional piano works—tone poems, such as *Prometheus* 1911, and symphonies, such as *Divine Poem* 1903—employed unusual harmonies to express his musical feelings.

Scribe member of an ancient Jewish group of Biblical scholars, both priests and laypersons, who studied the books of Moses and sat in the ◊Sanhedrin (supreme court). In the New Testament they are associated with the ◊Pharisees. Later, they are the copyists of Hebrew scripture.

Scripps James Edmund 1835–1906. US newspaper publisher who established the *Detroit Evening News* 1873, and who in 1880 with his younger brother Edward (1854–1926) created the first US national newspaper chain.

Born in London, Scripps began his newspaper career in Chicago 1857. He later moved to Michigan and became part owner of the *Detroit Daily Advertiser* in the early 1860s. Together with his brother he founded the *Cleveland Press* 1878, and two years later they created a national chain by purchasing the *St Louis Evening Chronicle* and the *Cincinnati Post*. Scripps was also active in Republican politics.

scrofula tuberculosis of the lymph glands, especially of the neck, marked by enlargement, oozing, and scar formation. Treatment is with antibiotics and surgery. Scrofula is uncommon outside the Third World.

scrub bird one of two Australian birds of the genus *Atrichornis*, order Passeriformes. Both are about 7 in/18 cm long, rather wrenlike but long-tailed. Scrub birds are good mimics.

The noisy scrub bird *Atrichornis clamosus* was feared to be extinct, but has been rediscovered, although numbers are still low. The other species is the rufous scrub bird *A. rufescens*.

scuba acronym for *self-contained underwater breathing apparatus*, another name for ⯎aqualung.

Scud Soviet-produced surface-to-surface ⯎missile that can be armed with a nuclear, chemical, or conventional warhead. The *Scud-B*, deployed on a mobile launcher, was the version most commonly used by the Iraqi army in the Gulf War 1991. It is a relatively inaccurate weapon.

The Scud-B has a range of 180 mi/300 km; modified by the Iraqi army into the **al-Hussayn**, it was capable of projecting a smaller payload (about 1,100 lb/500 kg) for a distance of up to 400 mi/650 km, and was used during the Gulf War to hit Israel and Saudi Arabia.

Scullin James Henry 1876–1953. Australian Labor politician. He was leader of the Federal Parliamentary Labor Party 1928–35, and prime minister and minister of industry 1929–31.

sculpture the artistic shaping in relief or in the round of materials such as wood, stone, metal, and, more recently, plastic and other synthetics. The earliest sculptures are Paleolithic stone, bone, and ivory carvings. All ancient civilizations, including the Assyrian, Egyptian, Indian, Chinese, and Mayan, have left examples of sculpture. Traditional European sculpture descends from that of Greece, Rome, and Renaissance Italy. The indigenous tradition of sculpture in Africa (see ⯎African art), South America, and the Caribbean has inspired much contemporary sculpture.

In the 20th century Alexander ⯎Calder invented the *mobile*, in which the suspended components move spontaneously with the currents of air. An extension is the *structure vivante*, in which a mechanism produces a prearranged pattern produced by magnets, lenses, bubbles, and so on, accompanied by sound; leading exponents are Bury, Soto, and Takis. Another development has been the sculpture garden; for example, Hakore open-air museum in Japan and the Grizedale Forest sculpture project in the Lake District, England.

Major Western sculptors include:

ancient Greek Phidias, Praxiteles
Renaissance Donatello, Verrochio, della Robbia, Michelangelo
Baroque Giovanni Bernini, Etienne-Maurice Falconet, Jean-Antoine Houdon, Grinling Gibbons
Neo-Classical Antonio Canova, John Flaxman
20th-century American Jacques Lipchitz, Alexander Calder, David Smith
20th-century British Jacob Epstein, Henry Moore, Barbara Hepworth, Reg Butler, Anthony Caro
20th-century European Jean Arp, Henri Gaudier-Brzeska, Auguste Rodin, Aristide Maillol, Pablo Picasso, Ivan Meštrović, Constantin Brancusi, Marino Marini, Alberto Giacometti, Naum Gabo, and Neizvestny.

scurvy disease caused by deficiency of vitamin C (ascorbic acid), which is contained in fresh vegetables and fruit. The signs are weakness and aching joints and muscles, progressing to bleeding of the gums and then other organs, and drying-up of the skin and hair. Treatment is by giving the vitamin.

scurvy grass plant *Cochlearia officinalis* of the crucifer family, growing on salt marshes and banks by the sea in the northern hemisphere. Shoots may grow low, or more erect up to 20 in/50 cm, with rather fleshy heart-shaped leaves; flowers are white or mauve and four-petaled. The edible, sharp-tasting leaves are a good source of vitamin C and were formerly eaten by sailors as a cure for scurvy.

scutage in medieval Europe, a feudal tax imposed on knights as a substitute for military service. It developed from fines for non-attendance at musters under the Carolingians, but in England by the 12th century it had become a purely fiscal measure designed to raise money to finance mercenary armies, reflecting the decline in the military significance of feudalism.

Scylla and Charybdis in Classical mythology, a sea monster and a whirlpool, between which Odysseus had to sail. Later writers located them in the Straits of Messina, between Sicily and Italy.

scythe harvesting tool with long wooden handle and sharp, curving blade. It is similar to a ⯎sickle. The scythe was in common use in the Middle East and Europe from the dawn of agriculture until the early 20th century, by which time it had generally been replaced by machinery.

Until the beginning of the 19th century, the scythe was used in the hayfield for cutting grass, but thereafter was applied to cereal crops as well, because it was capable of a faster work rate than the sickle. One person could mow 1 acre/0.4 hectares of wheat in a day with a scythe. Next came a team of workers to gather and bind the crop into sheaves and stand them in groups, or stooks, across the field.

Scythia region north of the Black Sea between the Carpathian mountains and the river Don, inhabited by the Scythians 7th–1st centuries BC. From the middle of the 4th century, they were slowly superseded by the Sarmatians. The Scythians produced ornaments and vases in gold and electrum with animal decoration. Although there is no surviving written work, there are spectacular archeological remains, including vast royal burial mounds which often contain horse skeletons.

SD abbreviation for the state of ⯎*South Dakota*.

SDI abbreviation for ⯎*Strategic Defense Initiative*.

sea anemone invertebrate marine animal of the phylum Cnidaria with a tubelike body attached by the base to a rock or shell. The other end has an open "mouth" surrounded by stinging tentacles, which capture crustaceans and other small organisms. Many sea anemones are beautifully colored, especially those in tropical waters.

sea bass any marine fish of the family Serranidae, of perchlike appearance. Striped bass *Roccus saxatilis* of the E North American coast, is the best known.

Seaborg Glenn Theodore 1912– . US nuclear chemist associated with the preparation and synthesis of all the ⯎transuranic elements with atomic numbers 94–105 at the Lawrence Radiation Laboratory, University of California at Berkeley. With Edwin M McMillan he produced plutonium in 1940, for which both shared the 1951 Nobel Prize for Chemistry.

During World War II he worked on the development of the first nuclear weapon, then served as chair of the US Atomic Energy Commission 1961–71. For his leadership in the development of nuclear chemistry and atomic energy, he received the 1959 Enrico Fermi award.

sea cucumber any echinoderm of the class Holothuroidea with a cylindrical body that is tough-skinned, knobbed, or spiny. The body may be several feet in length. Sea cucumbers are sometimes called "cotton-spinners" from the sticky filaments they eject from the anus in self-defense.

seafloor spreading growth of the ocean ⯎crust outwards (sideways) from ocean ridges. The concept of seafloor spreading has been combined with that of continental drift and incorporated into ⯎plate tectonics.

Seafloor spreading was proposed by US geologist Harry Hess (1906–1969) in 1962, based on his observations of ocean ridges and the relative youth of all ocean beds. In 1963, British geophysicists Fred Vine and Drummond Matthews observed that the floor of the Atlantic Ocean was made up of rocks that could be arranged in strips, each strip being magnetized either normally or reversely (due to changes in the Earth's polarity when the North Pole becomes the South Pole and vice versa, termed ⯎polar reversal). These strips were parallel and formed identical patterns on both sides of the ocean ridge. The inference was that each strip was formed at some stage in geological time when the magnetic field was polarized in a certain way. The seafloor magnetic-reversal patterns could be matched to dated magnetic reversals found in terrestrial rock. It could then be shown that new rock forms continuously and spreads away from the ocean ridges, with the oldest rock located farthest away from the midline. The observation was made independently in 1963 by Canadian geologist Lawrence Morley, studying an ocean ridge in the Pacific near Vancouver Island.

seagull see ⯎gull.

sea horse any marine fish of several related genera, especially *Hippocampus*, of the family Syngnathidae, which includes the ⯎pipefishes. The body is small and compressed and covered with bony plates raised into tubercles or spines. The tail is prehensile, and the tubular mouth sucks in small shellfish and larvae as food. The head and foreparts, usually carried upright, resemble those of a horse.

Unusually for fish, sea horses have a relatively long courtship, from 3–7 days. The female deposits her eggs, from dozens to hundreds, in a special pouch in the male and the male later releases and rears the young fish.

seakale perennial plant *Crambe maritima* of the family Cruciferae. In Europe the young shoots are cultivated as a vegetable.

seal aquatic carnivorous mammal of the families Otariidae and Phocidae (sometimes placed in a separate order, the Pinnipedia). The eared seals or sea lions (Otariidae) have small external ears, unlike the true seals (Phocidae). Seals have a streamlined body with thick blubber for insulation, and front and hind flippers. They feed on fish, squid, or crustaceans, and are commonly found in Arctic and Antarctic seas, but also in Mediterranean, Caribbean, and Hawaiian waters.

In true seals, the hind flippers provide the thrust for swimming, but they cannot be brought under the body for walking on land. Among eared seals (and walruses), the front flippers are the most important for swimming and the hind flippers can be brought forward under the body for walking.

True seals include the common or harbor seal *Phoca ritulina*, found in coastal regions over much of the northern hemisphere. The largest seal is the southern elephant seal *Mirounga leonina*, which can be 20 ft/6 m long and weigh 4.5 tons; the smallest is the Baikal seal *Pusa sibirica*, only 4 ft/1.2 m long and the only seal to live entirely in fresh water. Eared seals include ◊sea lions and fur seals.

The rarest seals are the monk seals, the only species to live in warmer waters. The Caribbean monk seal *Monachus tropicalis* may already be extinct, and the Mediterranean *M. monachus* and Hawaiian *M. schauinslandi* species are both endangered, mainly owing to disturbance by humans. For seal hunting, see ◊sealing.

seal mark or impression made in a block of wax to authenticate letters and documents. Seals were used in ancient China and are still used in China, Korea, and Japan.

sea lily any ◊echinoderm of the class Crinoidea. In most, the rayed, cuplike body is borne on a sessile stalk (permanently attached to a rock) and has feathery arms in multiples of five encircling the mouth. However, some sea lilies are free-swimming and unattached.

sealing the hunting of seals. Seals are killed for their meat, blubber, and their skins, which are sold as fine furs. Conservationists have campaigned to stop the killing of seals for fur, with some success.

sea lion any of several genera of ◊seals of the family Otariidae (eared seals), which also includes the fur seals. These streamlined animals have large fore flippers which they use to row themselves through the water. The hind flippers can be turned beneath the body to walk on land.

There are two species of sea lion in the northern hemisphere, and three in the south. They feed on fish, squid, and crustaceans. Steller's sea lion *Eumetopias jubatus* lives in the N Pacific, large numbers breeding on the Aleutian Islands. Males may be up to 11 ft/3.4 m long, with a thick neck with a characteristic mane, and weigh up to one ton. Females are one-third the weight. The Californian sea lion *Zalophus californianus* only reaches 7 ft/2.3 m, and is the species most often seen in zoos and as a "performing seal."

Sealyham breed of terrier dog, named after the place in Pembrokeshire, Wales, where it originated in the 19th century as a cross of the Welsh and Jack Russell terriers. It reaches a height of 12 in/30 cm.

sea mouse any of a genus *Aphrodite* of large marine ◊annelid worms (polychaetes), with oval bodies covered in bristles and usually found on muddy sea floors.

seaplane airplane capable of taking off from, and landing on, water. There are two major types, floatplanes and flying boats. The floatplane is similar to an ordinary airplane but has floats in place of wheels; the flying boat has a broad hull shaped like a boat and may also have floats attached to the wing tips.

Seaplanes depend on smooth water for a good landing, and since World War II few have been built, although the first successful international airlines, such as Pan Am, relied on a fleet of flying boats in the 1920s and 1930s.

The seaplane was invented by Glenn ◊Curtiss.

searching in computing, extracting a specific item from a large body of data, such as a file or table. The method used depends on how the data are organized. For example, a binary search, which requires the data to be in sequence, involves first deciding which half of the data contains the required item, then which quarter, then which eighth, and so on until the item is found.

sea robin any of a family (Triglidae) of spine-finned coastal fishes, especially the slender sea robin *Prionotus scitulus* of the Gulf and SE North American coast. They have large heads and creep along the sea bottom by means of three fingerlike appendages detached from the pectoral fins.

Seaside city in W central California, on the S shore of Monterey Bay, S of San Francisco. Industries include fruit processing; population (1990) 38,900.

sea slug any of an order (Nudibranchia) of marine gastropod mollusks in which the shell is reduced or absent. The order includes some very colorful forms, especially in the tropics. They are largely carnivorous, feeding on hydroids and ◊sponges.

Most are under 1 in/2.5 cm long, and live on the sea bottom or on vegetation, although some live in open waters. Tentacles on the back help take in oxygen.

season period of the year having a characteristic climate. The change in seasons is mainly due to the change in attitude of the Earth's axis in relation to the Sun, and hence the position of the Sun in the sky at a particular place. In temperate latitudes four seasons are recognized: spring, summer, autumn (fall), and winter. Tropical regions have two seasons—the wet and the dry. Monsoon areas around the Indian Ocean have three seasons: the cold, the hot, and the rainy.

The northern temperate latitudes have summer when the southern temperate latitudes have winter, and vice versa. During winter, the Sun is low in the sky and has less heating effect because of the oblique angle of incidence and because the sunlight has further to travel through the atmosphere. The differences between the seasons are more marked inland than near the coast, where the sea has a moderating effect on temperatures. In polar regions the change between summer and winter is abrupt; spring and autumn are hardly perceivable. In tropical regions, the belt of rain associated with the trade winds moves north and south with the Sun, as do the dry conditions associated with the belts of high pressure near the tropics. The monsoon's three seasons result from the influence of the Indian Ocean on the surrounding land mass of Asia in that area.

seasonal adjustment in statistics, an adjustment of figures designed to take into account influences that are purely seasonal, and relevant only for a short time. The resulting figures are then thought to reflect long-term trends more accurately.

seasonal affective disorder (SAD) recurrent depression characterized by an increased incidence at a particular time of year. One type of seasonal affective disorder increases in incidence in autumn and winter, and is associated with increased sleeping and appetite.

It has been suggested that seasonal affective disorder may be caused by a change in the release of melatonin, a hormone secreted in response to the diurnal variation in light and dark.

seasonal unemployment unemployment arising from the seasonal nature of some economic activities. An example is agriculture, which uses a smaller labor force in winter.

Seasonal employment can be created, however, as in the example of the retail sector in Western countries over the Christmas period.

sea squirt or **tunicate** any solitary or colonial-dwelling saclike ◊chordate of the class Ascidiacea. A pouch-shaped animal attached to a rock or other base, it draws in food-carrying water through one siphon and expels it through another after straining it through numerous gill slits. The young are free-swimming tadpole-shaped organisms, which, unlike the adults, have a ◊notochord.

Sea squirts have transparent or translucent tunics made of cellulose. They vary in size from a few millimeters to 12 in/30 cm in length and are cylindrical, circular, or irregular in shape.

SEATO abbreviation for ◊*Southeast Asia Treaty Organization.*

Seattle port (grain, timber, fruit, fish) of the state of Washington, situated between Puget Sound and Lake Washington; population (1990) 516,300, metropolitan area (with Everett) 2,559,200. It is a center for the manufacture of jet aircraft (Boeing), and also has shipbuilding, food processing, and paper industries.

There are two universities, Washington (1861) and Seattle (1891). First settled 1852,

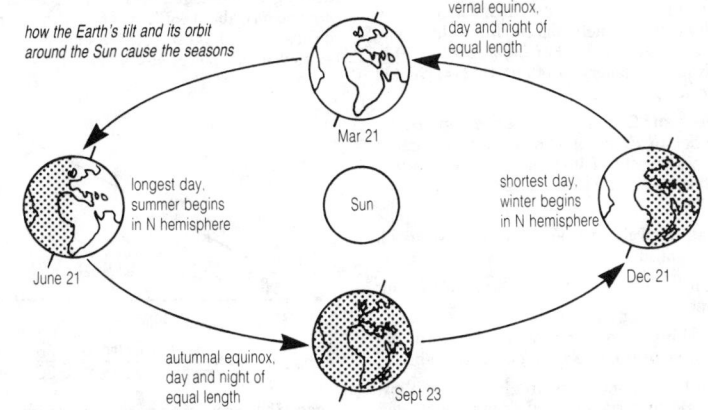

how the Earth's tilt and its orbit around the Sun cause the seasons

vernal equinox, day and night of equal length

Mar 21

Sun

longest day, summer begins in N hemisphere

June 21

shortest day, winter begins in N hemisphere

Dec 21

autumnal equinox, day and night of equal length

Sept 23

season *The cause of the seasons.*

as the nearest port for Alaska, Seattle grew in the late 19th century with the arrival of a transcontinental railroad 1884 and the Klondike gold rush of the 1890s. Since World War II the economy has been dominated by the aerospace industry. The 606-ft/185-m-high Space Needle was erected for the 1962 world's fair.

sea turtle any of various marine species of ▷turtles, some of which grow up to a length of up to 8 ft/2.5 m. They are excellent swimmers, having legs that are modified to oarlike flippers but make them awkward on land. The shell is more streamlined and lighter than that of other turtles. They often travel long distances to lay their eggs on the beaches where they were born.

Species include the green turtle *Chelonia mydas*; the loggerhead *Caretta caretta*; the giant leatherback *Dermochelys coriacea* which can weigh half a ton; and the hawksbill *Eretmochelys imbricata*. Like many species of turtle, the hawksbill is now endangered, mainly through being hunted for its shell, which provides "tortoiseshell." Other turtles have suffered through destruction of their breeding sites (often for tourist developments) and egg-collecting.

sea urchin any of various orders of the class Echinoidea among the ▷echinoderms. They all have a globular body enclosed with plates of lime and covered with spines. Sometimes the spines are anchoring organs, and they also assist in locomotion. Sea urchins feed on seaweed and the animals frequenting them, and some are edible.

seaweed any of a vast collection of marine and freshwater, simple, multicellular plant forms belonging to the ▷algae and found growing from about high-water mark to depths of 300–600 ft/100–200 m. Some have holdfasts, stalks, and fronds, sometimes with air bladders to keep them afloat, and are green, blue-green, red, or brown.

Many have traditionally been gathered for food, such as purple laver *Porphyra umbilicalis*, green laver *Ulva lactuca*, and carragheen moss *Chondrus crispus*. From the 1960s, seaweeds have been farmed, and the alginates extracted are used in convenience foods, ice cream, and animal feed, as well as in toothpaste, soap, and the manufacture of iodine and glass.

Sebastiano del Piombo c. 1485–1547. Italian painter, born in Venice, one of the great painters of the High Renaissance. Sebastiano was a pupil of ▷Giorgione and developed a similar style of painting. In 1511 he moved to Rome, where his friendship with Michelangelo (and rivalry with Raphael) inspired him to his greatest works, such as *The Raising of Lazarus* 1517–19 (National Gallery, London). He also painted powerful portraits.

Sebastian, St Roman soldier, traditionally a member of Emperor Diocletian's bodyguard until his Christian faith was discovered. He was martyred by being shot with arrows. Feast day Jan 20.

Sebastopol alternate spelling of ▷Sevastopol, port in Ukraine.

sec or **s** abbreviation for *second*, a unit of time.

SEC abbreviation for ▷*Securities and Exchange Commission*, US government body.

secant in trigonometry, the function of a given angle in a right-angled triangle, obtained by dividing the length of the hypotenuse (the longest side) by the length of the side adjacent to the angle. It is the ▷reciprocal of the ▷cosine (sec = 1/cos).

secession (Latin *secessio*) in politics, the withdrawal from a federation of states by one or more of its members, as in the secession of the Confederate states from the Union in the US 1860.

second basic ▷SI unit (symbol sec or s) of time, one-sixtieth of a minute. It is defined as the duration of 9,192,631,770 cycles of regulation (periods of the radiation corresponding to the transition between two hyperfine levels of the ground state) of the cesium-133 isotope. In mathematics, the second is a unit (symbol ″) of angular measurement, equaling one-sixtieth of a minute, which in turn is one-sixtieth of a degree.

secondary emission in physics, an emission of electrons from the surface of certain substances when they are struck by high-speed electrons or other particles from an external source. See also ▷photomultiplier.

secondary growth or *secondary thickening* increase in diameter of the roots and stems of certain plants (notably shrubs and trees) that results from the production of new cells by the ▷cambium. It provides the plant with additional mechanical support and new conducting cells, the secondary ▷xylem and ▷phloem. Secondary growth is generally confined to ▷gymnosperms and, among the ▷angiosperms, to the dicotyledons. With just a few exceptions, the monocotyledons (grasses, lilies) exhibit only primary growth, resulting from cell division at the apical ▷meristems.

secondary market market for resale of purchase or shares, bonds, and commodities outside of organized stock exchanges and primary markets.

secondary sexual characteristic in biology, an external feature of an organism that is characteristic of its gender (male or female), but not the reproductive organs themselves. They include facial hair in men and breasts in women, combs in roosters, brightly colored plumage in many male birds, and manes in male lions. In many cases, they are involved in displays and contests for mates and have evolved by ▷sexual selection. Their development is stimulated by sex hormones.

Second World War alternate name for ▷World War II, 1939–45.

secretary bird ground-hunting, long-legged, mainly gray-plumaged bird of prey *Sagittarius serpentarius*, about 4 ft/1.2 m tall, with an erectile head crest. It is protected in southern Africa because it eats poisonous snakes.

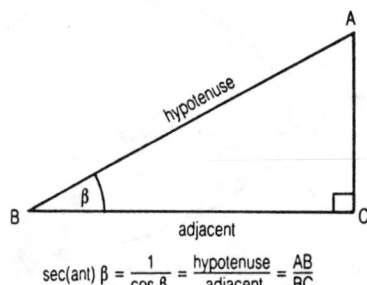

$$\sec(\text{ant})\,\beta = \frac{1}{\cos\beta} = \frac{\text{hypotenuse}}{\text{adjacent}} = \frac{AB}{BC}$$

secant *The secant of an angle is a function used in the mathematical study of the triangle.*

It gets its name from the fact that its head crest supposedly looks like a pen behind a clerk's ear. It is the only member of its family Sagittaridae, in the same order (Falconiformes) as vultures, eagles, and hawks.

secretary of state the title of the cabinet official with responsibility for conducting the foreign affairs of the US. It is the senior cabinet post and is fourth in line of succession to the presidency in the event of death or incapacitation.

secretin ▷hormone produced by the small intestine of vertebrates that stimulates the production of digestive secretions by the pancreas and liver.

secretion in biology, any substance (normally a fluid) produced by a cell or specialized gland, for example, sweat, saliva, enzymes, and hormones. The process whereby the substance is discharged from the cell is also known as secretion.

secret police any state security force that operates internally, against political dissenters or subversives; for example, the US ▷Federal Bureau of Investigation and the UK ▷Special Branch.

Secret Service any government ▷intelligence organization. The US Secret Service is a law-enforcement unit of the Treasury Department. It is charged with combating counterfeiters and has responsibility for protecting the president and other senior members of the government.

sect small ideological group, usually religious in nature, that may have moved away from a main group, often claiming a monopoly of access to truth or salvation. Sects are usually highly exclusive. They demand strict conformity, total commitment to their code of behavior, and complete personal involvement, sometimes to the point of rejecting mainstream society altogether in terms of attachments, names, possessions, and family.

Most sects are short-lived, either because their appeal dies out and their members return to mainstream society, or because their appeal spreads and they become part of mainstream society (for example, Christianity began as a small sect in Roman-ruled Palestine).

sector theory model of urban land use in which the various land-use zones are shaped like wedges radiating from the central business district. According to sector theory, the highest prices for land are found along transport routes (especially roads), and once an area has gained a reputation for a particular type of land use (such as industry), it will attract the same land users as the city expands outwards over time.

secularization the process through which religious thinking, practice, and institutions lose their religious and/or social significance. The concept is based on the theory, held by some sociologists, that as societies become industrialized their religious morals, values, and institutions give way to secular ones and some religious traits become common secular practices.

Securities and Exchange Commission (*SEC*) official US agency created 1934, under Joseph P ▷Kennedy, to ensure full disclosure to the investing public and protection against malpractice in the securities (stocks and bonds) and financial markets (such as ▷insider trading).

The SEC, created in the wake of the 1929 stock market crash, operates under several major statutes. The Securities Act of 1933 is concerned with the accuracy of registration statements, made when a firm goes public and stock is offered for sale. The Securities Exchange Act of 1934 regulates trading in securities after they have been issued. The Investment Company Act 1940 regulates mutual funds, and the Investment Advisors Act of 1940 registers investment advisors. The SEC is also an impartial advisor to federal courts in bankruptcy cases involving publicly held corporations. Since 1988, the SEC has been authorized to pay bounties for information leading to conviction of inside traders.

Sedan town on the river Meuse, in Ardennes *département*, NE France; population (1982) 24,535. Industries include textiles and dyestuffs; the town's prosperity dates from the 16th–17th centuries, when it was a ◊Huguenot center. In 1870 Sedan was the scene of Napoleon III's surrender to Germany during the ◊Franco-Prussian War. It was the focal point of the German advance into France 1940.

sedan chair enclosed chair for one passenger carried on poles by two or more bearers. Introduced into England by Sir Sanders Dunscombe in 1634, by the 18th century it was the equivalent of a one-person taxi. The name derives from S Italy rather than from the French town of Sedan.

sedative any medication with the effect of lessening nervousness, excitement, or irritation. Sedatives will induce sleep in larger doses. Examples are ◊barbiturates, ◊narcotics, and ◊benzodiazepines.

Seddon Richard John 1845–1906. New Zealand Liberal politician, prime minister 1893–1906.

seder meal that forms part of the Jewish festival of Passover, which celebrates the ◊Exodus.

sedge any perennial grasslike plant of the family Cyperaceae, especially the genus *Carex*, usually with three-cornered solid stems, common in low water or on wet and marshy ground.

sediment any loose material that has "settled"—deposited from suspension in water, ice, or air, generally as the water current or wind speed decreases. Typical sediments are, in order of increasing coarseness, clay, mud, silt, sand, gravel, pebbles, cobbles, and boulders.

Sediments differ from sedimentary rocks in which deposits are fused together in a solid mass of rock by a process called ◊diagenesis. Pebbles are cemented into ◊conglomerates; sands become sandstones; muds become mudstones or shales; peat is transformed into coal.

sedimentary rock rock formed by the accumulation and cementation of deposits that have been laid down by water, wind, ice, or gravity. Sedimentary rocks cover more than two-thirds of the Earth's surface and comprise three major categories: *clastic*, *chemically precipitated*, and *organic*. Clastic sediments are the largest group and are composed of fragments of pre-existing rocks; they include clays, sands, and gravels. Chemical precipitates include limestones such as chalk, and evaporated deposits such as gypsum and halite (rock salt). Coal, oil shale, and limestone made of fossil material are examples of organic sedimentary rocks.

Most sedimentary rocks show distinct layering (stratification), caused by alterations in composition or by changes in rock type. These strata may become folded or fractured by the movement of the Earth's crust, a process known as *deformation*.

sedition the stirring up of discontent, resistance, or rebellion against the government in power.

Seebeck effect in physics, the generation of a voltage in a circuit containing two different metals, or semiconductors, by keeping the junctions between them at different temperatures. Discovered by the German physicist Thomas Seebeck (1770–1831), it is also called the thermoelectric effect, and is the basis of the ◊thermocouple. It is the opposite of the ◊Peltier effect (in which current flow causes a temperature difference between the junctions of different metals).

seed the reproductive structure of higher plants (◊angiosperms and ◊gymnosperms). It develops from a fertilized ovule and consists of an embryo and a food store, surrounded and protected by an outer seed coat, called the testa. The food store is contained either in a specialized nutritive tissue, the ◊endosperm, or in the ◊cotyledons of the embryo itself. In angiosperms the seed is enclosed within a ◊fruit, whereas in gymnosperms it is usually naked and unprotected, once shed from the female cone. Following ◊germination the seed develops into a new plant.

Seeds may be dispersed from the parent plant in a number of different ways. Agents of dispersal include animals, as with ◊burrs and fleshy edible fruits, and wind, where the seed or fruit may be winged or plumed. Water can disperse seeds or fruits that float, and various mechanical devices may eject seeds from the fruit, as in some pods or leguminous plants (see ◊legume).

There may be a delay in the germination of some seeds to ensure that growth occurs under favorable conditions (see ◊after-ripening, ◊dormancy). Most seeds remain viable for at least 15 years if dried to about 5% water and kept at –20°C, although 20% of them will not survive this process.

seed drill machine for sowing cereals and other seeds, developed by Jethro ◊Tull in England 1701, although simple seeding devices were known in Babylon 2000 BC.

The seed is stored in a hopper and delivered by tubes into furrows in the ground. The furrows are made by a set of blades, or colters, attached to the front of the drill. A ◊harrow is drawn behind the drill to cover up the seeds.

seed plant any seed-bearing plant; also known as a *spermatophyte*. The seed plants are subdivided into two classes, the ◊angiosperms, or flowering plants, and the ◊gymnosperms, principally the cycads and conifers. Together, they comprise the major types of vegetation found on land.

Angiosperms are the largest, most advanced, and most successful group of plants at the present time, occupying a highly diverse range of habitats. There are estimated to be about 250,000 different species. Gymnosperms differ from angiosperms in their ovules which are borne unprotected (not within an ◊ovary) on the scales of their cones. The arrangement of the reproductive organs, and their more simplified internal tissue structure, also distinguishes them from the flowering plants. In contrast to the gymnosperms, the ovules of angiosperms are enclosed within an ovary and many species have developed highly specialized reproductive structures associated with ◊pollination by insects, birds, or bats.

Seeger Pete 1919– . US folk singer and songwriter of antiwar protest songs, such as "Where Have All The Flowers Gone?" 1956 and "If I Had A Hammer" 1949.

Seeger was active in left-wing politics from the late 1930s and was a victim of the witch-hunt of Senator Joe ◊McCarthy in the 1950s. As a member of the vocal group *the Weavers* 1948–58, he popularized songs of diverse ethnic origin and had several hits.

Seeland German form of ◊Sjælland, the main island of Denmark.

Seferis George. Assumed name of Georgios Seferiades 1900–1971. Greek poet and diplomat. Ambassador to Lebanon 1953–57 and to the UK 1957–62, when he helped to resolve the Cyprus crisis. He published his first volume of lyrics 1931 and his *Collected Poems* 1950. Nobel Prize 1963.

Segovia town in Castilla-León, central Spain; population (1991) 58,000. Thread, fertilizer, and chemicals are produced. It has a Roman aqueduct with 118 arches in current use, and the Moorish ◊alcázar (fortress) was the palace of the monarchs of Castile. Isabella of Castile was crowned here 1474.

Segovia Andrés 1893–1987. Spanish virtuoso guitarist, for whom works were composed by Manuel de ◊Falla, Heitor ◊Villa-Lobos, and others.

Segrè Emilio 1905–1989. Italian physicist settled in the US, who in 1955 discovered the antiproton, a new form of ◊antimatter. He shared the 1959 Nobel Prize for Physics with Owen Chamberlain. Segrè had earlier discovered the first synthetic element, technetium (atomic number 43), in 1937.

Seifert Jaroslav 1901–1986. Czech poet who won state prizes under the communists, but became an original member of the Charter 77 human-rights movement. His works include *Mozart in Prague* 1970 and *Umbrella from Piccadilly* 1978. Nobel Prize 1984.

Seikan Tunnel the world's largest underwater tunnel, opened 1988, linking the Japanese islands of Hokkaido and Honshu, which are separated by the Tsungaru Strait; length 32.3 mi/51.7 km.

Seine French river rising on the Langres plateau NW of Dijon, and flowing 472 mi/774 km in a NW direction to join the English Channel near Le Havre, passing through Paris and Rouen.

seismology study of earthquakes and how their shock waves travel through the Earth. By examining the global pattern of waves produced by an earthquake, seismologists can deduce the nature of the materials through which they have passed. This leads to an understanding of the Earth's internal structure.

On a smaller scale artificial earthquake waves, generated by explosions or mechanical vibrators, can be used to search for subsurface features in, for example, oil or mineral exploration. Earthquake waves from underground nuclear explosions can be distinguished from natural waves by their shorter wavelength and higher frequency.

Sekondi-Takoradi seaport of Ghana; population (1982) 123,700. The old port was founded by the Dutch. Takoradi has an artificial harbor, opened 1928, and railroad engineering, boat building, and cigarette manufacturing industries.

Selangor state of the Federation of Malaysia; area 3,071 sq mi/7,956 sq km; population (1990) 1,978,000. It was under British protection from 1874 and was a federated state 1895–1946. The capital was transferred to Shah Alam from Kuala Lumpur 1973. Klang is the seat of the sultan and a center for rubber-growing and tin-mining; Port Klang (formerly Port Keland and, in 1971, Port Swettenham) exports tin.

Selective Service Cases several US Supreme Court cases (including *Arver* v *US* 1918) dealing with the right of Congress to enact a mandatory military service law during wartime. The Court voted unanimously to uphold the Selective Service Law, the World War I conscription act. The decision was based on a judgment that the right to establish a military draft is implied in the Constitution in Congress's authority to declare war and maintain an army.

Selene in Greek mythology, the goddess of the Moon. She was the daughter of Titan, and the sister of Helios and Eos. In later times she was identified with ⟡Artemis.

selenium (Greek *Selene* "Moon") gray, nonmetallic element, symbol Se, atomic number 34, atomic weight 78.96. It belongs to the sulfur group and occurs in several allotropic forms that differ in their physical and chemical properties. It is an essential trace element in human nutrition. Obtained from many sulfide ores and selenides, it is used as a red coloring for glass and enamel.

Because its electrical conductivity varies with the intensity of light, selenium is used extensively in photoelectric devices. It was discovered 1817 by Swedish chemist Jöns Berzelius and named after the Moon because its properties follow those of tellurium, whose name derives from Latin *Tellus* "Earth."

Seles Monica 1973– . Yugoslavian lawn-tennis player who won her first Grand Slam title, the French Open, at the age of 16. She dominated the major events in 1991 but withdrew from Wimbledon and consequently missed the chance to achieve the Grand Slam. In 1991 she became the youngest woman player ever to achieve number-one ranking.

CAREER HIGHLIGHTS

US Open
singles: 1991, 1992
French Open
singles: 1990–92
Australian Open
singles: 1991–93

Seleucus I Nicator *c.* 358–280 BC. Macedonian general under Alexander the Great and founder of the *Seleucid Empire*. After Alexander's death 323 BC, Seleucus became governor and then (312 BC) ruler of Babylonia, founding the city of Seleucia on the river Tigris. He conquered Syria and had himself crowned king 306 BC, but his expansionist policies brought him into conflict with the Ptolemies of Egypt, and he was assassinated by Ptolemy Ceraunus. He was succeeded by his son Antiochus I.

self-induction or *self-inductance* in physics, the creation of a counter emf (⟡electromotive force) in a coil because of variations in the current flowing through it.

Seljuk Empire empire of the Turkish people (converted to Islam during the 7th century)

under the leadership of the invading Tatars or Seljuk Turks. The Seljuk Empire 1055–1243 included all Anatolia and most of Syria. It was succeeded by the ⟡Ottoman Empire.

Selkirk Alexander 1676–1721. Scottish sailor marooned 1704–09 in the Juan Fernández Islands in the S Pacific. His story inspired Daniel Defoe to write *Robinson Crusoe*.

Sellers Peter 1925–1980. English comedian and film actor. He made his name in the madcap British radio program *The Goon Show* 1949–60; his films include *The Ladykillers* 1955, *I'm All Right Jack* 1960, *Dr Strangelove* 1964, five *Pink Panther* films 1964–78 (as the bumbling Inspector Clouseau), and *Being There* 1979.

selva equatorial rainforest, such as that in the Amazon basin in South America.

Selznick David O(liver) 1902–1965. US film producer whose early work includes *King Kong, Dinner at Eight*, and *Little Women* all 1933. His independent company, Selznick International (1935–40), made such lavish films as *Gone With the Wind* 1939, *Rebecca* 1940, and *Duel in the Sun* 1946.

He had under contract Alfred Hitchcock and Ingrid Bergman who together made several films. He launched the careers of director George Cukor and actors Katharine Hepburn, Fred Astaire, Gregory Peck, and Joan Fontaine.

semantics branch of ⟡linguistics dealing with the meaning of words.

semaphore visual signaling code in which the relative positions of two moveable pointers or hand-held flags stand for different letters or numbers. The system is used by ships at sea and for railroad signals.

Semarang port in N Java, Indonesia; population (1980) 1,027,000. There is a shipbuilding industry, and exports include coffee, teak, sugar, tobacco, kapok, and petroleum from nearby oil fields.

Semele in Greek mythology, mother of Dionysus by Zeus. At Hera's suggestion she demanded that Zeus should appear to her in all his glory, but when he did so she was consumed by lightning.

semelparity in biology, the occurrence of a single act of reproduction during an organism's lifetime. Most semelparous species produce very large numbers of offspring when they do reproduce, and normally die soon afterwards. Examples include the Pacific salmon and the pine looper moth. Many plants are semelparous, or ⟡monocarpic. Repeated reproduction is called ⟡iteroparity.

semen see ⟡sperm.

Semenov Nikoly 1896–1986. Russian physical chemist who made significant contributions to the study of chemical chain reactions. Working mainly in Leningrad at the Institute for Chemical Physics, in 1956 he became the first Russian to gain the Nobel Prize for Chemistry, which he shared with Cyril ⟡Hinshelwood.

semicircular canal one of three looped tubes that form part of the labyrinth in the inner ⟡ear. They are filled with fluid and detect changes in the position of the head, contributing to the sense of balance.

semicolon punctuation mark (;) with a function halfway between the separation of sentence from sentence by means of a period, or full stop, and the gentler separation provided

by a comma. It also helps separate items in a complex list: "pens, pencils, and paper; staples, such as rice and beans; tools, various; and rope."

Rather than the abrupt "We saw Mark last night. It was good to see him again," and the casual (and often condemned) "We saw Mark last night, it was good to see him again," the semicolon reflects a link in a two-part statement and is considered good style: *We saw Mark last night; it was good to see him again*. In such cases an alternative is to use a comma followed by *and* or *but*.

semiconductor crystalline material with an electrical conductivity between that of metals (good) and insulators (poor). The conductivity of semiconductors can usually be improved by minute additions of different substances or by other factors. Silicon, for example, has poor conductivity at low temperatures, but this is improved by the application of light, heat, or voltage; hence silicon is used in transistors, rectifiers, and integrated circuits (silicon chips).

semiology or *semiotics* the study of the function of signs and symbols in human communication, both in language and by various nonlinguistic means. Beginning with the notion of the Swiss linguist Ferdinand de ⟡Saussure that no word or other sign (*signifier*) is intrinsically linked with its meaning (*signified*), it was developed as a scientific discipline, especially by Claude ⟡Lévi-Strauss and Roland ⟡Barthes.

Semiotics has combined with structuralism in order to explore the "production" of meaning in language and other sign systems and has emphasized the conventional nature of this production.

semiotics synonym for ⟡semiology.

Semiramis lived *c.* 800 BC. Assyrian queen, later identified with the chief Assyrian goddess ⟡Ishtar.

Semite member of any of the peoples of the Middle East originally speaking a Semitic language, and traditionally said to be descended from Shem, a son of Noah in the Bible. Ancient Semitic peoples include the Hebrews, Ammonites, Moabites, Edomites, Babylonians, Assyrians, Chaldaeans, Phoenicians, and Canaanites. The Semitic peoples founded the monotheistic religions of Judaism, Christianity, and Islam.

They speak languages of the Hamito-Semitic branch of the Afro-Asiatic family.

Semitic languages branch of the ⟡Hamito-Semitic language.

Semmes Raphael 1809–1877. American naval officer. Semmes joined the US Navy 1826 and rose to the rank of lieutenant 1836. After seeing action in the Mexican War, he was promoted to commander 1851. At the outbreak of the Civil War, he joined the Confederate navy and attacked Union shipping in the Atlantic. He was placed in command of the Confederate cruiser *Alabama* 1862, losing the ship in a battle with the USS *Kearsarge* in the English Channel 1864.

Semmes was born in Charles County, Maryland. He studied law and practiced as a lawyer after fighting in the Mexican War. After the Civil War he was imprisoned briefly and thereafter practiced law again. He also edited the *Memphis Daily Bulletin*.

Senanayake Don Stephen 1884–1952. First prime minister of independent Sri Lanka (formerly Ceylon) 1947–52.

Senanayake Dudley 1911–1973. Prime minister of Sri Lanka 1952–53, 1960, and 1965–70; son of Don Senanayake.

senate in ancient Rome, the "council of elders." Originally consisting of the heads of patrician families, it was recruited from ex-magistrates and persons who had rendered notable public service, but was periodically purged by the censors. Although nominally advisory, it controlled finance and foreign policy.

The US Senate consists of 100 members, two from each state, elected for a six-year term. The term also refers to the upper house of the Canadian parliament and to the upper chambers of Italy and France. It is also given to the governing bodies in some universities, for example, the Faculty Senate.

Sendai city in Tōhoku region, NE Honshu, Japan; population (1989) 889,100. Industries include metal goods (a metal museum was established 1975), electronics, metal goods, textiles, pottery, and food processing. It was a feudal castle town from the 16th century.

Sendak Maurice 1928– . US writer and book illustrator, whose children's books with their deliberately arch illustrations include *Where the Wild Things Are* 1963, *In the Night Kitchen* 1970, and *Outside Over There* 1981.

Born in Brooklyn, New York, he attended the Art Students League and illustrated books for other authors. *Kenny's Window* 1956 was the first book that he both wrote and illustrated. *Very Far Away* 1957 and *The Sign on Rosie's Door* 1960 soon followed. He also designed several works for the stage, including an operatic version of *Where the Wild Things Are* and a production of Mozart's *Magic Flute*.

Sendero Luminoso (Shining Path) Maoist guerrilla group active in Peru, formed 1980 to overthrow the government. Until 1988 its activity was confined to rural areas. By June 1988 an estimated 9,000 people had been killed in the insurgency, about half of them guerrillas. In 1992 attacks intensified in response to a government crackdown.

The guerrillas have been known to attack projects supported by aid agencies, accusing the workers and peasants involved of cooperating with neocolonialists. In 1992 they stepped up their campaign in response to a crackdown imposed by Peruvian president Fujimori with the support of the military. The arrest of their leader, Abimael Guzman Reynoso (1934–), in Sept, along with other leading members of the group, led to an intensification of attacks. Reynoso, known as Presidente Gonzalo, was sentenced to life imprisonment in Oct, as were those arrested alongside him.

Seneca Lucius Annaeus *c.* 4 BC–AD 65. Roman Stoic playwright, author of essays and nine tragedies. He was tutor to the future emperor Nero but lost favor after the latter's accession to the throne and was ordered to commit suicide. His tragedies were accepted as Classical models by 16th-century dramatists.

Seneca Falls Convention in US history, a meeting in New York State July 1848 of women campaigning for greater rights. A Declaration of Sentiments, paraphrasing the US Declaration of Independence, called for female suffrage, equal educational and employment opportunities, and more legal rights.

Senegal river in W Africa, formed by the confluence of the Bafing and Bakhoy rivers and flowing 700 mi/1,125 km NW and W to join the Atlantic near St Louis, Senegal. In 1968 the Organization of Riparian States of the River Senegal (Guinea, Mali, Mauritania, and Senegal) was formed to develop the river valley, including a dam for hydroelectric power and irrigation at Joina Falls in Mali; its headquarters is in Dakar. The river gives its name to the Republic of Senegal.

Senegal country in W Africa, on the Atlantic Ocean, bounded N by Mauritania, E by Mali, S by Guinea and Guinea-Bissau, and enclosing Gambia on three sides.

government The constitution of 1963, amended, provides for a single-chamber legislature, the 120-member national assembly, and a president who is head of both state and government. The assembly and president are elected at the same time by universal suffrage to serve a five-year term. The president appoints and leads a council of ministers. Senegal's ten regions enjoy a high degree of autonomy, each having its own appointed governor and elected assembly and controlling a separate budget.

history For early history, see ◊Africa. Portuguese explorers arrived in the 15th century, and French settlers in the 17th. Senegal had a French governor from 1854, became part of ◊French West Africa 1895, and a territory 1902.

independence Senegal became an independent republic Sept 1960, with Léopold Sédar ◊Senghor, leader of the Senegalese Progressive Union (UPS), as its first president. Senghor was also prime minister 1962–70. The UPS was the only legal party from 1966 until in Dec 1976 it was reconstituted as the Senegalese Socialist Party (PS) and two opposition parties were legally registered. In 1978 Senghor was decisively reelected.

Senghor retired at the end of 1980 and was succeeded by Abdou Diouf, who declared an amnesty for political offenders and permitted more parties to register. In the 1983 elections the PS won 111 of the assembly seats and the main opposition, the Senegalese Democratic Party (PDS), eight seats. Later that year Diouf tightened control of his party and the government, abolishing the post of prime minister. This met open, sometimes violent, opposition, but he and the PS remained firmly in power.

Senegambia confederation In 1980 Senegal sent troops to Gambia to protect it against a suspected Libyan invasion, and it intervened again 1981 to thwart an attempted coup. As the two countries came closer together, they agreed on an eventual merger, and the confederation of Senegambia came into being Feb 1982. Senegal has always maintained close links with France, allowing it to retain military bases. In the Feb 1988 elections Diouf was reelected president with 73% of the vote, but his ruling party had a slightly reduced majority in the national assembly. In April 1989 border disputes led to a severance of diplomatic relations with neighboring Mauritania, with more than 450 people killed during violent clashes between Senegalese and Mauritanians. Over 50,000 people were repatriated from both countries May 1989. In Aug 1989 formal recognition was given of the ending of the unsuccessful federation of Senegambia.

Constitutional changes were proposed Sept 1991, including the reduction of the voting age from 21 to 18 and the limitation of the presidential mandate to two terms. Diplomatic relations

Senegal
Republic of (*République du Sénégal*)

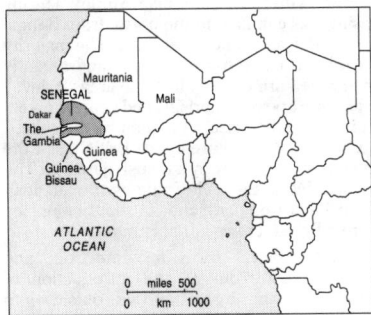

area 75,753 sq mi/196,200 sq km
capital (and chief port) Dakar
cities Thiès, Kaolack
physical plains rising to hills in SE; swamp and tropical forest in SW
features river Senegal; Gambia forms an enclave within Senegal
head of state and government Abdou Diouf from 1981
political system emergent socialist democratic republic
political parties Senegalese Socialist Party (PS), democratic socialist; Senegalese Democratic Party (PDS), left-of-center
exports peanuts, cotton, fish, phosphates
currency franc CFA
population (1990 est) 7,740,000; growth rate 3.1% p.a.
life expectancy men 51, women 54 (1989)

languages French (official); African dialects are spoken
religion Muslim 80%, Roman Catholic 10%, animist
literacy men 37%, women 19% (1985 est)
GNP $2 bn (1987); $380 per head (1984)
chronology
1659 Became a French colony.
1854–65 Interior occupied by French.
1902 Became a territory of French West Africa.
1959 Formed the Federation of Mali with French Sudan.
1960 Independence achieved from France, but withdrew from the federation. Léopold Sédar Senghor, leader of the Senegalese Progressive Union (UPS), became president.
1966 UPS declared the only legal party.
1974 Pluralist system reestablished.
1976 UPS reconstituted as Senegalese Socialist Party (PS). Prime Minister Abdou Diouf nominated as Senghor's successor.
1980 Senghor resigned; succeeded by Diouf. Troops sent to defend Gambia.
1981 Military help again sent to Gambia.
1982 Confederation of Senegambia came into effect.
1983 Diouf reelected. Post of prime minister abolished.
1988 Diouf decisively reelected.
1989 Violent clashes between Senegalese and Mauritanians in Dakar and Nouakchott killed more than 450 people; over 50,000 people repatriated from both countries. Senegambia federation abandoned.
1991 Constitutional changes outlined.
1992 Diplomatic links with Mauritania reestablished.

with Mauritania, severed 1989, were restored April 1992. *See illustration box.*

senescence in biology, the deterioration in physical and reproductive capacities associated with old age. See ◊aging.

Senghor Léopold (Sédar) 1906– . Senegalese politician and writer, first president of independent Senegal 1960–80. He was Senegalese deputy to the French National Assembly 1946–58, and founder of the Senegalese Progressive Union. He was also a well-known poet and a founder of *négritude*, a black literary and philosophical movement.

senile dementia ◊dementia associated with old age, often caused by ◊Alzheimer's disease.

Sennacherib died 681 BC. King of Assyria from 705 BC. Son of ◊Sargon II, he rebuilt the city of Nineveh on a grand scale, sacked Babylon 689, and defeated ◊Hezekiah, king of Judah, but failed to take Jerusalem. He was assassinated by his sons, and one of them, Esarhaddon, succeeded him.

Sennett Mack. Adopted name of Michael Sinnott 1880–1960. Canadian-born US film director. Born in Richmond, Québec, Sennett moved to New York 1904, where he began to perform in vaudeville. After working as an actor in Biograph Studio films under D W Griffith 1908–11, he founded his own film production company, the Keystone Company 1911. As director, Sennett made hundreds of short slapstick comedies, cast Charles ◊Chaplin in his first feature film (*Tillie's Punctured Romance* 1914), and started the career of Gloria Swanson. In the following years, Sennett developed the slapstick style of comedy, featuring the first flying custard pie and his Keystone Kops. Before his career ended, with the advent of sound films, he had directed most of Hollywood's major silent film stars. His studio closed 1933.

sense organ any organ that an animal uses to gain information about its surroundings. All sense organs have specialized receptors (such as light receptors in an eye) and some means of translating their response into a nerve impulse that travels to the brain. The main human sense organs are the eye, which detects light and color (different wavelengths of light); the ear, which detects sound (vibrations of the air) and gravity; the nose, which detects some of the chemical molecules in the air; and the tongue, which detects some of the chemicals in food, giving a sense of taste. There are also many small sense organs in the skin, including pain sensors, temperature sensors, and pressure sensors, contributing to our sense of touch.

Research suggests that our noses may also be sensitive to magnetic forces, giving us an innate "sense of direction." This sense is well developed in other animals, as are a variety of senses that we do not share. Some animals can detect small electric discharges, underwater vibrations, minute vibrations of the ground, or sounds that are below (infrasound) or above (ultrasound) our range of hearing. Sensitivity to light varies greatly. Most mammals cannot distinguish different colors, whereas some birds can detect the polarization of light. Many insects can see light in the ultraviolet range, which is beyond our spectrum, while snakes can form images of infrared radiation (radiant heat). In many animals, light is also detected by another organ, the pineal gland, which "sees" light filtering through the skull, and measures the length of the day to keep track of the seasons.

Seoul or *Sŏul* capital of South ◊Korea (Republic of Korea), near the Han River, and with its chief port at Inchon; population (1985) 10,627,800. Industries include engineering, textiles, food processing, electrical and electronic equipment, chemicals, and machinery.

It was the capital of Korea 1392–1910, and has universities and a 14th-century palace. It was the site of the 1988 Summer Olympics.

sepal part of a flower, usually green, that surrounds and protects the flower in bud. The sepals are derived from modified leaves, and collectively known as the ◊calyx.

In some plants, such as the marsh marigold *Caltha palustris*, where true ◊petals are absent, the sepals are brightly colored and petallike, taking over the role of attracting insect pollinators to the flower.

separation of powers an approach to limiting the powers of government by separating governmental functions into the executive, legislative, and judiciary. The concept has its fullest practical expression in the the US constitution (see ◊federalism).

Sephardi (plural *Sephardim*) Jew descended from those expelled from Spain and Portugal in the 15th century, or from those forcibly converted during the Inquisition to Christianity (Marranos). Many settled in N Africa and in the Mediterranean countries, as well as in the Netherlands, England, and Dutch colonies in the New World. Sephardim speak Ladino, a 15th-century Romance dialect, as well as the language of their nation.

Sepoy Indian soldier in the service of the British or Indian army in the days of British rule in India. The Indian Mutiny 1857–58 was thus also known as the ◊Sepoy Rebellion or Mutiny.

Sepoy Rebellion revolt 1857–58 of Indian soldiers (Sepoys) against the British in India; also known as the Sepoy, or Indian, Mutiny. The uprising was confined to the north, from Bengal to the Punjab, and central India. The majority of support came from the army and recently dethroned princes, but in some areas it developed into a peasant uprising and general revolt. It included the seizure of Delhi by the rebels, its siege and recapture by the British, and the defense of Lucknow by a British garrison. The mutiny led to the end of rule by the ◊British East India Company and its replacement by direct British crown administration.

sepsis general term for infection; any poisoned state due to the introduction of disease-causing organisms from outside into the bloodstream.

septicemia technical term for ◊blood poisoning.

septic shock life-threatening fall in blood pressure caused by blood poisoning (septicemia). Toxins produced by bacteria infecting the blood induce a widespread dilation of the blood vessels throughout the body, and it is this that causes the patient's collapse (see ◊shock). Septic shock can occur following bowel surgery, after a penetrating wound to the abdomen, or as a consequence of infection of the urinary tract. It is usually treated in an intensive care unit and has a high mortality rate.

Septuagesima in the Christian church calendar, the third Sunday before Lent; the 70th day before Easter.

Septuagint (Latin *septuagint*, seventy) the oldest Greek version of the Old Testament or Hebrew Bible, traditionally made by 70 scholars.

seq. abbreviation for *sequentes* (Latin "the following").

sequoia two species of conifer in the redwood family Taxodiaceae, native to western US. The redwood *Sequoia sempervirens* is a long-lived timber tree, and one specimen, the Howard Libbey Redwood, is the world's tallest tree at 361 ft/110 m, with a circumference of 44 ft/13.4 m. The giant sequoia *Sequoiadendron giganteum* reaches up to 100 ft/30 m in circumference at the base, and grows almost as tall as the redwood. It is also (except for the bristlecone pine) the oldest living tree, some specimens being estimated at over 3,500 years of age.

Sequoya George Guess 1770–1843. American Indian scholar and leader. After serving with the US army in the Creek War 1813–14, he made a study of his own Cherokee language and created a syllabary which was approved by the Cherokee council 1821. This helped thousands of Indians toward literacy and resulted in the publication of books and newspapers in their own language.

Sequoya went on to write down ancient tribal history. In later life he became political representative of the Western tribes in Washington, negotiating for the Indians when the US government forced resettlement in Indian territory in the 1830s.

A type of giant redwood tree, the ◊sequoia, is named after him, as is a national park in California.

Serang alternate form of ◊Ceram, an Indonesian island.

seraph (plural *seraphim*) in Christian and Judaic belief, an ◊angel of the highest order. They are mentioned in the book of Isaiah in the Old Testament.

Serapis ancient Graeco-Egyptian god, a combination of Apis and Osiris, invented by the Ptolemies; his finest temple was the Serapeum in Alexandria.

Serb member of Yugoslavia's largest ethnic group, found mainly in Serbia, but also in the neighboring independent republics of Bosnia-Herzegovina and Croatia. Their language, generally recognized to be the same as Croat and hence known as Serbo-Croatian, belongs to the Slavic branch of the Indo-European family. It has more than 17 million speakers.

The Serbs are predominantly Greek Orthodox Christians and write in a Cyrillic script. Although they are closely related linguistically to the Croats, there are cultural differences and long-standing enmities, which resurfaced with the outbreak of civil war 1991. In the province of Kosovo, the Serbs are in conflict with Yugoslavian Albanians, who comprise the majority.

Serbia (Serbo-Croatian *Srbija*) constituent republic of Yugoslavia, which includes Kosovo and Vojvodina
area 34,122 sq mi/88,400 sq km
capital Belgrade
physical fertile Danube plains in the north, mountainous in the south
features includes the autonomous provinces of ◊Kosovo, capital Priština, of which the predominantly Albanian population demands unification with Albania, and ◊*Vojvodina*, capital Novi Sad, largest town Subotica, with a predominantly Serbian population

population (1986) 9,660,000
language the Serbian variant of Serbo-Croatian
religion Serbian Orthodox
history The Serbs settled in the Balkans in the 7th century and became Christians in the 9th century. They were united as one kingdom about 1169; the Serbian hero Stephan Dushan (1331–1355) founded an empire covering most of the Balkans. After their defeat at Kosovo 1389 they came under the domination of the Turks, who annexed Serbia 1459. Uprisings 1804–16, led by Kara George and Milosh Obrenovich, forced the Turks to recognize Serbia as an autonomous principality under Milosh. The assassination of Kara George on Obrenovich's orders gave rise to a long feud between the two houses. After a war with Turkey 1876–78, Serbia became an independent kingdom. On the assassination of the last Obrenovich 1903 the Karageorgevich dynasty came to the throne.

The two Balkan Wars 1912–13 greatly enlarged Serbia's territory at the expense of Turkey and Bulgaria. Serbia's designs on Bosnia and Herzegovina, backed by Russia, led to friction with Austria, culminating in the outbreak of war 1914. Serbia was overrun 1915–16 and was occupied until 1918, when it became the nucleus of the new kingdom of the Serbs, Croats, and Slovenes, and subsequently ◊Yugoslavia. Rivalry between Croats and Serbs continued within the republic. During World War II Serbia was under a puppet government set up by the Germans; after the war it became a constituent republic of Yugoslavia.

From 1986 Slobodan Milosević as Serbian party chief and president waged a populist campaign to end the autonomous status of the provinces of Kosovo and Vojvodina. Despite a violent Albanian backlash in Kosovo 1989–90 and growing pressure in Croatia and Slovenia to break away from the federation, Serbia formally annexed Kosovo Sept 1990. Milosević was reelected by a landslide majority Dec 1990, but in March 1991 there were anticommunist and anti-Milosević riots in Belgrade. The 1991 civil war in Yugoslavia arose from the Milosević nationalist government attempting the forcible annexation of Serb-dominated regions in Croatia, making use of the largely Serbian federal army. In Oct 1991 Milosević renounced territorial claims on Croatia pressured by threats of European Community (EC) and United Nations (UN) sanctions, but the fighting continued until a cease-fire was agreed Jan 1992. EC recognition of Slovenia's and Croatia's independence in Jan 1992 and Bosnia-Herzegovina's in April left Serbia dominating a greatly reduced "rump" Yugoslavia. A successor Yugoslavia, announced by Serbia and Montenegro April 1992, was rejected by the US and EC because of concerns over serious human rights violations in Kosovo and Serbia's continued attempted partition of Bosnia-Herzegovina. In March 1992, and again in June, thousands of Serbs marched through Belgrade, demanding the ousting of President Milosević and an end to the war in Bosnia-Herzegovina.

sere plant ◊succession developing in a particular habitat. A *lithosere* is a succession starting on the surface of bare rock. A *hydrosere* is a succession in shallow freshwater, beginning with planktonic vegetation and the growth of pondweeds and other aquatic plants, and ending with the development of swamp. A *plagiosere* is the sequence of communities that follows the clearing of the existing vegetation.

serenade musical piece for chamber orchestra or wind instruments in several movements, originally intended for evening entertainment, such as Mozart's *Eine kleine Nachtmusik/A Little Night Music*.

serfdom the legal and economic status of peasants under ◊feudalism. Serfs could not be sold like slaves, but they were not free to leave their master's estate without his permission. They had to work the lord's land without pay for a number of days every week and pay a percentage of their produce to the lord every year. They also served as soldiers in the event of conflict. Serfs also had to perform extra labor at harvest time and other busy seasons; in return they were allowed to cultivate a portion of the estate for their own benefit.

In England serfdom died out between the 14th and 17th centuries, but it lasted in France until 1789, in Russia until 1861, and in most other European countries until the early 19th century.

Sergius, St of Radonezh 1314–1392. Patron saint of Russia, who founded the Eastern Orthodox monastery of the Blessed Trinity near Moscow 1334. Mediator among Russian feudal princes, he inspired the victory of Dmitri, Grand Duke of Moscow, over the Tatar khan Mamai at Kulikovo, on the upper Don, 1380.

serialism in music, an alternate name for the ◊twelve-tone system of composition.

It usually refers to post-1950 compositions in which further aspects such as dynamics, durations, and attacks are brought under serial control. These other series may consist of fewer than 12 degrees while some pitch series can go higher.

series circuit electrical circuit in which the components are connected end to end, so that the current flows through them all one after the other.

Serkin Rudolf 1903–1991. Austrian-born US pianist and teacher, in the US from 1939, remembered for the quality and sonority of his energetic interpretations of works by J S Bach and Viennese classics. He founded, with German violinist Adolf Busch, the Marlboro Festival for chamber music in Vermont, and served as its director from 1952 until his death.

Serkin first appeared at the age of 12 with the Vienna Symphony. He played with the New York Philharmonic orchestra in Switzerland 1936. Emigrating to the US, he joined the piano faculty of the Curtis Institute in Philadelphia, where he taught until 1975, serving as director from 1968 to 1975.

Serlio Sebastiano 1475–1554. Italian architect and painter, author of *L'Architettura* 1537–51, which set down practical rules for the use of the Classical orders, and was used by architects of the Neo-Classical style throughout Europe.

Serpens constellation of the equatorial region of the sky, represented as a serpent coiled around the body of Ophiuchus. It is the only constellation divided into two halves: *Serpens Caput*, the head (on one side of Ophiuchus), and *Serpens Cauda*, the tail (on the other side). Its main feature is the Eagle nebula.

serpentine group of minerals, hydrous magnesium silicate, $Mg_3Si_2O_5(OH)_4$, occurring in soft ◊metamorphic rocks and usually dark green. The fibrous form *chrysolite* is a source of ◊asbestos; other forms are *antigorite, talc, and meerschaum.* Serpentine minerals are formed by hydration of ultrabasic rocks during metamorphism. Rare snake-patterned forms are used in ornamental carving.

Serpent Mound earthwork built by Hopewell Indians 2nd–1st centuries BC in Ohio. It is 1,330 ft/405 m long, 4 ft/1.3 m high, and about 19 ft/6 m across and may have been constructed in the shape of a snake for religious purposes.

Serpent Mound is in a state park in Adams County, Ohio.

Serra Junipero 1713–1784. Spanish missionary and explorer of California, where he founded several missions.

Born in Majorca, Spain, Serra joined the Franciscan order 1730. After receiving a doctorate in theology, he served on the faculty of the University of Palma 1743–49. Pursuing a missionary career, he arrived in Mexico City 1750. Having served in Querétaro 1750–58, he was transferred to Baja California with the expulsion of the Jesuits from Mexico 1767. Two years later he led a missionary expedition to Alta California and spent the remainder of his life establishing missions throughout the region.

serum clear fluid that remains after blood clots. It is blood plasma with the anticoagulant proteins removed, and contains ◊antibodies and other proteins, as well as the fats and sugars of the blood. It can be produced synthetically, and is used to protect against disease.

serval African wild cat *Felis serval*. It is a slender, long-limbed cat, about 3 ft/1 m long, with a yellowish-brown, black-spotted coat. It has large, sensitive ears, with which it locates its prey, mainly birds and rodents.

Servan-Schreiber Jean Jacques 1924– . French Radical politician, and founder of the magazine *L'Express* 1953. His *Le Défi americain* 1967 maintained that US economic and technological dominance would be challenged only by a united left-wing Europe. He was president of the Radical Party 1971–75 and 1977–79.

Servetus Michael (Miguel Serveto) 1511–1553. Spanish Christian Anabaptist theologian and physician. He was a pioneer in the study of the circulation of the blood and found that it circulates to the lungs from the right chamber of the heart. He was burned alive by the church reformer Calvin in Geneva, Switzerland, for publishing attacks on the doctrine of the Trinity.

service industry commercial activity that provides and charges for various services to customers (as opposed to manufacturing or supplying goods), such as restaurants, the tourist industry, cleaning, hotels, and the retail trade (shops and supermarkets).

With the decline in the manufacturing sector in many Western countries, service industries have become major employers of labor.

service tree deciduous Eurasian tree *Sorbus domestica* of the rose family Rosaceae, with alternate pinnate leaves, white flowers, and small, edible, oval fruit. The European wild service tree *Sorbus torminalis* has oblong rather than pointed leaflets. It is related to the ◊mountain ash.

servomechanism automatic control system used in aircraft, motor automobiles, and other complex machines. A specific input, such as moving a lever or joystick, causes a specific output, such as feeding current to an electric motor that moves, for example, the rudder of the aircraft. At the same time, the position of the rudder is detected and fed back to the central control, so that small adjustments can continually be made to maintain the desired course.

sesame annual plant *Sesamum indicum* of the family Pedaliaceae, probably native to SE Asia. It produces oily seeds used for food and soap making.

sessile in botany, a leaf, flower, or fruit that lacks a stalk and sits directly on the stem, as with the acorns of the California white oak *Quercus lobata*. In zoology, it is an animal that normally stays in the same place, such as a barnacle or mussel. The term is also applied to the eyes of crustaceans when these lack stalks and sit directly on the head.

Sessions Roger (Huntington) 1896–1985. US composer whose Modernist, dissonant works include *The Black Maskers* incidental music 1923, eight symphonies, and *Concerto for Orchestra* 1971. He was instrumental in increasing the understanding and appreciation of modern music.

Born in Brooklyn, New York, he attended Harvard and Yale, then studied under Ernest Bloch. He became a leading teacher of composition, serving on the faculties of Boston University, Princeton University, the University of California at Berkeley, and the Juilliard School of Music.

set or *class* in mathematics, any collection of defined things (elements), provided the elements are distinct and that there is a rule to decide whether an element is a member of a set. It is usually denoted by a capital letter and indicated by curly brackets { }.

For example, L may represent the set that consists of all the letters of the alphabet. The symbol $\in$ stands for "is a member of"; thus $p \in L$ means that p belongs to the set consisting of all letters, and $4 \in L$ means that 4 does not belong to the set consisting of all letters.

There are various types of sets. A *finite set* has a limited number of members, such as the letters of the alphabet; an *infinite set* has an unlimited number of members, such as all whole numbers; an *empty* or *null set* has no members, such as the number of people who have swum across the Atlantic Ocean, written

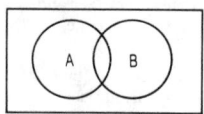

A and B are overlapping sets

A and B are disjoint sets

A is the subset of B

set Venn diagram showing the various relationships between sets A and B.

as {} or ∅; a *single-element set* has only one member, such as days of the week beginning with M, written as {Monday}. *Equal sets* have the same members; for example, if W = {days of the week} and S = {Sunday, Monday, Tuesday, Wednesday, Thursday, Friday, Saturday}, it can be said that $W = S$. Sets with the same number of members are *equivalent sets*. Sets with some members in common are *intersecting sets*; for example, if R = {red playing cards} and F = {face cards}, then R and F share the members that are red face cards. Sets with no members in common are *disjoint sets*, such as {minerals} and {vegetables}. Sets contained within others are *subsets*; for example, {vowels} is a subset of {letters of the alphabet}. Sets and their interrelationships are often illustrated by a ⟩Venn diagram.

Set in Egyptian mythology, the god of night, the desert, and of all evils. He was the murderer of ⟩Osiris, portrayed as a grotesque animal.

Seton Ernest Thompson (born Ernest Seton Thompson) 1860–1946. Canadian author and naturalist, born in England. He illustrated his own books with drawings of animals. He was the founder of the Woodcraft Folk youth movement, a non-religious alternative to the scouting movement.

Seton St Elizabeth Ann Bayley 1774–1821. US religious leader and social benefactor. A convert to Roman Catholicism, she founded schools for the poor. Known as "Mother Seton," she was proclaimed the first American saint 1975.

Born in New York, Seton was devoted to the service of the poor and established the Society for the Relief of Poor Widows with Small Children 1797. After a trip to Italy and the death of her first husband, she joined the Roman Catholic Church 1805. In 1809, with her own funds, she established a Catholic elementary school in Baltimore. Soon afterward becoming a nun, she formed the Sisters of St Joseph and founded St Joseph's College for Women 1809.

setter any of various breeds of gun dog, about 2.2 ft/66 cm high and weighing about 55 lb/25 kg. They have a long, smooth coat, feathered tails, and spaniellike faces. They are called "setters" because they were trained in crouching or "setting" on the sight of game to be pursued.

The Irish setter is a rich red, the English setter is usually white with black, tan, or liver markings, and the Gordon setter is black and brown.

Settlement, Act of in Britain, a law passed 1701 during the reign of King William III, designed to ensure a Protestant succession to the throne by excluding the Roman Catholic descendants of James II in favor of the Protestant House of Hanover. Elizabeth II still reigns under this act.

settlement out of court a compromise reached between the parties to a legal dispute. Most civil legal actions are settled out of court, reducing legal costs and avoiding the uncertainty of the outcome of a trial.

Seurat Georges 1859–1891. French artist. He originated, with Paul Signac, the Neo-Impressionist technique of ⟩*Pointillism* (painting with small dabs rather than long brushstrokes). Examples of his work are *Bathers at Asnières* 1884 (National Gallery, London) and *Sunday on the Island of La Grande Jatte* 1886 (Art Institute of Chicago).

Seurat also departed from Impressionism by evolving a more formal type of composition based on the Classical proportions of the

⟩golden section, rather than aiming to capture fleeting moments of light and movement.

Seuss, Dr see ⟩Geisel, Theodore Seuss.

Sevastopol or *Sebastopol* Black Sea port, resort, and fortress in the Crimea, Ukraine; population (1987) 350,000. It was the base of the former Soviet Black Sea fleet. It also has shipyards and a wine-making industry. Founded by Catherine II 1784, it was successfully besieged by the English and French in the Crimean War (Oct 1854–Sept 1855), and in World War II by the Germans (Nov 1941–July 1942), but was retaken by Soviet forces 1944.

Seven against Thebes in Greek mythology, the attack of seven captains led by Adrastus, king of Argos, on the seven gates of ancient Thebes, prompted by the rivalry between the two sons of Oedipus, ⟩Polynices and ⟩Eteocles, for the kingship of Thebes. The subject of tragedies by ⟩Aeschylus and ⟩Euripides (*The Phoenician Women*), and of the epic *Thebaid* by the Roman poet Statius, it forms the background to other Greek tragedies by ⟩Sophocles (*Antigone, Oedipus at Colonus*) and Euripides (*Suppliant Women*).

seven deadly sins in Christian theology, anger, avarice, envy, gluttony, lust, pride, and sloth.

Seventh-Day Adventist or ⟩*Adventist* member of the Protestant religious sect of the same name. It originated in the US in the fervent expectation of Christ's Second Coming, or advent, that swept across New York State following William Miller's prophecy that Christ would return on Oct 22, 1844. When this failed to come to pass, a number of Millerites, as his followers were called, reinterpreted his prophetic speculations and continued to maintain that the millennium was imminent. Adventists observe Saturday as the Sabbath and emphasize healing and diet; many are vegetarians. The sect has about 500,000 members in the US.

The chief author of what became Seventh-Day Adventist doctrine was Ellen G White, and the sect considers her works canonical. She held that Christ's judgment of humanity had begun in 1844 and would continue in preparation for his return and thousand-year reign on Earth.

Seven Weeks' War war 1866 between Austria and Prussia, engineered by the German chancellor ⟩Bismarck. It was nominally over the possession of ⟩Schleswig-Holstein, but it was actually to confirm Prussia's superseding Austria as the leading German state. The Battle of ⟩Sadowa was the culmination of General von ⟩Moltke's victories.

Seven Wonders of the World in antiquity, the pyramids of Egypt, the hanging gardens of Babylon, the temple of Artemis at Ephesus, the statue of Zeus at Olympia, the mausoleum at Halicarnassus, the Colossus of Rhodes, and the Pharos (lighthouse) at Alexandria.

Seven Years' War (in North America known as the *French and Indian War*) war 1756–63 arising from the conflict between Austria and Prussia, and between France and Britain over colonial supremacy. Britain and Prussia defeated France, Austria, Spain, and Russia; Britain gained control of India and many of France's colonies, including Canada. Spain ceded Florida to Britain in exchange for Cuba. Fighting against great odds, Prussia was eventually successful in becoming established as one of the great European powers. The war ended with the Treaty of Paris 1763, signed by Britain, France, and Spain.

severe combined immune deficiency (SCID) rare condition in which a baby is born without the body's normal defenses against infection. The child must be kept within a transparent plastic tent until a matched donor can provide a bone-marrow transplant (bone marrow is the source of disease-fighting cells in the body).

Severn river of Wales and England, rising on the NE side of Plynlimmon, N Wales, and flowing 210 mi/338 km through Shrewsbury, Worcester, and Gloucester to the Bristol Channel. The *Severn bore* is a tidal wave up to 6 ft/ 2 m high.

S England and S Wales are linked near Chepstow by a rail tunnel 1873–85 over the Severn, and a road bridge 1966.

Severus Lucius Septimus 146–211. Roman emperor. He held a command on the Danube when in 193 the emperor Pertinax was murdered. Proclaimed emperor by his troops, Severus proved an able administrator. He was born in N Africa, and was the only African to become emperor. He died at York while campaigning in Britain against the Caledonians.

Severus of Antioch 467–538. Christian bishop, one of the originators of the Monophysite heresy. As patriarch of Antioch (from 512), Severus was the leader of opposition to the Council of Chalcedon 451, an attempt to unite factions of the early church, by insisting that Christ existed in one nature only. He was condemned by the emperor Justin I in 518, and left Antioch for Alexandria, never to return.

Seville (Spanish *Sevilla*) city in Andalusia, Spain, on the Guadalquivir River, 60 mi/ 96 km N of Cadiz; population (1991) 683,500. Products include machinery, spirits, porcelain, pharmaceuticals, silk, and tobacco.

Formerly the center of a Moorish kingdom, it has a 12th-century alcazar, or fortified palace, and a 15th–16th-century Gothic cathedral. Seville was the birthplace of the artists Murillo and Velázquez. Expo 92 celebrated the 500th anniversary of the discovery of the New World.

Sèvres fine porcelain produced at a factory in Sèvres, France, now a Paris suburb, since the early 18th century. It is characterized by the use of intensely colored backgrounds (such as pink and royal blue), against which flowers are painted in elaborately embellished frames, often in gold.

It became popular after the firm's patronage by Louis XV's mistress, Madame de ⬦Pompadour. The state porcelain factory was established in the park of ⬦St-Cloud 1756, and it is also the site of a national museum of ceramics.

Sèvres, Treaty of the last of the treaties that ended World War I. Negotiated between the Allied powers and the Ottoman Empire, it was finalized Aug 1920 but never ratified by the Turkish government.

The treaty reduced the size of Turkey by making concessions to the Greeks, Kurds, and Armenians, as well as ending Turkish control of Arab lands. Its terms were rejected by the newly created nationalist government and the treaty was never ratified. It was superseded by the Treaty of ⬦Lausanne in 1923.

sewage disposal the disposal of human excreta and other waterborne waste products

from houses, streets, and factories. Conveyed through sewers to sewage plants, sewage has to undergo a series of treatments to be acceptable for discharge into rivers or the sea, according to various local laws and ordinances. Raw sewage, or sewage that has not been treated adequately, is one serious source of water pollution and a cause of ⬦eutrophication.

In the industrialized countries of the West, most industries are responsible for disposing of their own wastes. Government agencies establish industrial waste-disposal standards. In most countries, sewage plants for residential areas are the responsibility of local authorities. The solid waste (sludge) may be spread over fields as a fertilizer or, in a few countries, dumped at sea. A significant proportion of bathing beaches in densely populated regions have unacceptably high bacterial content, largely as a result of untreated sewage being discharged into rivers and the sea.

The use of raw sewage as a fertilizer (long practiced in China) has the drawback that disease-causing microorganisms can survive in the soil and be transferred to people or animals by consumption of subsequent crops. Sewage sludge is safer, but may contain dangerous levels of heavy metals and other industrial contaminants.

Seward William Henry 1801–1872. US public official. A lawyer, he was elected to the New York state senate 1830 and served as governor 1838–42 and US senator 1849–61. An active abolitionist, Seward became a leader of the Republican party and was appointed secretary of state by Lincoln. Although seriously wounded in the 1865 assassination plot against Lincoln, Seward continued to serve as secretary of state under Andrew Johnson, purchasing Alaska from Russia 1867 for $7.2 million.

Born in Florida, New York, Seward was educated at Union College and was admitted to the bar 1822.

sewing machine apparatus for the mechanical sewing of cloth, leather, and other materials by a needle, powered by hand, treadle, or belted electric motor. The popular lockstitch machine, using a double thread, was invented independently in the US by both Walter Hunt 1834 and Elias ⬦Howe 1846. Howe's machine was the basis of the machine patented 1851 by Isaac ⬦Singer.

In modern microprocessor-controlled sewing machines, as many as 25 different stitching patterns can be selected by push button.

sex determination process by which the sex of an organism is determined. In many species, the sex of an individual is dictated by the two sex chromosomes (X and Y) it receives from its parents. In mammals, some plants, and a few insects, males are XY, and females XX; in birds, reptiles, some amphibians, and butterflies the reverse is the case. In bees and wasps, males are produced from unfertilized eggs, females from fertilized eggs. Environmental factors can affect some fish and reptiles, such as turtles, where sex is influenced by the temperature at which the eggs develop.

Many fish have a very flexible system of sex determination, which can be affected by external factors. For example, most members of the sea-bass family start as females and later reverse their sex, depending on the local sex ratio, to become males.

sexism belief in (or set of implicit assumptions about) the superiority of one's own sex, often accompanied by a ⬦stereotype or preconceived idea about the opposite sex. Sexism

may also be accompanied by ⬦discrimination on the basis of sex, generally as practiced by men against women.

The term, coined by analogy with racism, was first used in the 1960s by feminist writers to describe language or behavior that implied women's inferiority. Examples include the contentious use of male pronouns to describe both men and women, and the assumption that some jobs are typically performed only by one sex.

sex linkage in genetics, the tendency for certain characteristics to occur exclusively, or predominantly, in one sex only. Human examples include red-green color blindness and haemophilia, both found predominantly in males. In both cases, these characteristics are recessive (see ⬦recessive gene) and are determined by genes on the ⬦X chromosome.

Since females possess two X chromosomes, any such recessive ⬦allele on one of them is likely to be masked by the corresponding allele on the other. In males (who have only one X chromosome paired with a largely inert ⬦Y chromosome) any gene on the X chromosome will automatically be expressed. Color blindness and haemophilia can appear in females, but only if they are ⬦homozygous for these traits, due to inbreeding, for example.

Sex Pistols, the UK punk rock group (1975–78) that became notorious under the guidance of their manager, Malcolm McLaren (1946–). The first singles, "Anarchy in the UK" 1976 and "God Save the Queen" 1977, unbridled attacks on contemporary Britain, made the Pistols into figures the media loved to hate.

The original line-up was Johnny Rotten (real name John Lydon, 1956–), vocals; Steve Jones (1955–), guitar; Glen Matlock (1956–), bass; and Paul Cook (1956–), drums. Their best-known member, Sid Vicious (real name John Ritchie, 1957–1979), joined in 1977. They released one album, *Never Mind the Bollocks, Here's the Sex Pistols* 1977.

sextant navigational instrument for determining latitude by measuring the angle between some heavenly body and the horizon. It was invented by John Hadley (1682–1744) in 1730 and can be used only in clear weather.

When the horizon is viewed through the right-hand side *horizon glass*, which is partly clear and partly mirrored, the light from a star can be seen at the same time in the mirrored left-hand side by adjusting an *index mirror*. The angle of the star to the horizon can then be read on a calibrated scale.

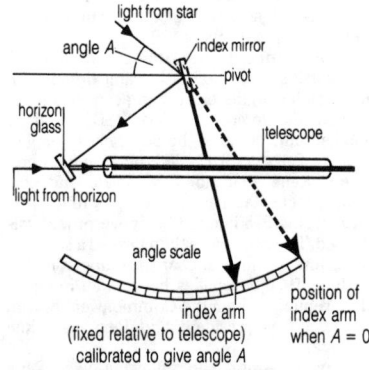

sextant *The geometry of the sextant.*

Sexton Anne 1928–1974. US poet. She studied with Robert Lowell and wrote similarly confessional poetry, as in *To Bedlam and Part Way Back* 1960 and *All My Pretty Ones* 1962. She committed suicide, and her *Complete Poems* appeared posthumously 1981.

sexual reproduction reproductive process in organisms that requires the union, or ◊fertilization, of gametes (such as eggs and sperm). These are usually produced by two different individuals, although self-fertilization occurs in a few ◊hermaphrodites such as tapeworms. Most organisms other than bacteria and cyanobacteria (◊blue-green algae) show some sort of sexual process. Except in some lower organisms, the gametes are of two distinct types called eggs and sperm. The organisms producing the eggs are called females, and those producing the sperm, males. The fusion of a male and female gamete produces a *zygote*, from which a new individual develops.

The alternatives to sexual reproduction are binary fission, budding, vegetative reproduction, parthenogenesis, and spore formation.

sexual selection process similar to ◊natural selection but relating exclusively to success in finding a mate for the purpose of sexual reproduction and producing offspring. Sexual selection occurs when one sex (usually but not always the female) invests more effort in producing young than the other. Members of the other sex compete for access to this limited resource (usually males competing for the chance to mate with females).

Sexual selection often favors features that increase a male's attractiveness to females (such as the pheasant's tail) or enable males to fight with one another (such as a deer's antlers). More subtly, it can produce hormonal effects by which the male makes the female unreceptive to other males, causes the abortion of fetuses already conceived, or removes the sperm of males who have already mated with a female.

Seychelles country in the Indian Ocean, off E Africa, N of Madagascar.
government Seychelles is a republic within the British ◊Commonwealth. The constitution of 1979 makes Seychelles a one-party state. The president, who is head of both state and government, and the single-chamber legislature, the national assembly, both serve a five-year term. The president and 23 of the 25 assembly members are elected by universal suffrage, and 2 are appointed by the president.
history For early history, see ◊Africa. The islands were probably visited by the Portuguese about 1500 and became a French colony 1744. Seychelles was ceded to Britain by France 1814 and was ruled as part of ◊Mauritius until it became a crown colony 1903.
independence In the 1960s several political parties were formed, campaigning for independence, the most significant being the Seychelles Democratic Party (SDP), led by James Mancham, and the Seychelles People's United Party (SPUP), led by France-Albert René. René demanded complete independence, while Mancham favored integration with Britain. The 1975 internal self-government was agreed. The two parties then formed a coalition government with Mancham as prime minister. In June 1976 Seychelles became an independent republic within the Commonwealth, with Mancham as president and René as prime minister.
one-party state The following year René staged an armed coup while Mancham was

attending a Commonwealth conference in London, and declared himself president. After a brief suspension of the constitution, a new one was adopted, creating a one-party state, with the SPUP being renamed the Seychelles People's Progressive Front (SPPF). René, as the only candidate, was formally elected president 1979 and then reelected 1984 and 1989. There have been several unsuccessful attempts to overthrow him, the last reported 1987.
moves toward democracy In Dec 1991 President René promised that he would introduce multiparty democracy and this promise was subsequently endorsed by the SPPF.
René followed a policy of the ◊nonaligned movement and prohibited the use of port facilities to vessels carrying nuclear weapons. He maintained close links with Tanzania, which provided military support. The demise of the Soviet Union and the consequential loss of economic support considerably weakened René's position.
In April 1992 James Mancham, the country's former president, returned from exile in Britain announcing that he hoped to contest the presidency. In July a 20-member commission was elected to produce a new, democratic constitution. *See illustration box.*

Seyfert galaxy galaxy whose small, bright center is caused by hot gas moving at high speed around a massive central object, possibly a ◊black hole. Almost all Seyferts are spiral galaxies. They seem to be closely related to ◊quasars, but are about 100 times fainter. They are named after their discoverer Carl Seyfert (1911–1960).

Seymour Jane c. 1509–1537. Third wife of Henry VIII, whom she married in 1536. She died soon after the birth of her son Edward VI.

Seymour Lynn 1939– . Canadian ballerina of rare dramatic talent. She was principal dancer of the Royal Ballet from 1959 and artistic

director of the Munich State Opera Ballet 1978–80.

Sfax (Arabic *Safaqis*) port and second largest city in Tunisia; population (1984) 232,000. It is the capital of Sfax district, on the Gulf of Gabès, and lies about 150 mi/240 km SE of Tunis. Products include leather, soap, and carpets; there are also salt works and phosphate workings nearby. Exports include phosphates, olive oil, dates, almonds, esparto grass, and sponges.

Sforza Italian family that ruled the duchy of Milan 1450–99, 1512–15, and 1522–35. Its court was a center of Renaissance culture and its rulers prominent patrons of the arts.

The family's original name was Attendoli but it took the name Sforza (Italian "force") in the early 13th century. Francesco Sforza (1401–66) obtained Milan by marriage to a Visconti in 1441; then his son Galeazzo (1444–76) ruled and became a patron of the arts. After his assassination, his brother Ludovico (1451–1508) seized power, made Milan one of the most powerful Italian states, and became a great patron of artists, especially ◊Leonardo da Vinci. He was ousted by Louis XII of France 1499, restored 1512–15, then ousted again. His son Francesco (1495–1535) was reestablished 1522 by Emperor Charles V. Francesco had no male heirs, and Milan passed to Charles 1535.

SFSR abbreviation for *Soviet Federal Socialist Republic*, administrative subdivision of the former USSR.

's-Gravenhage Dutch name for The ◊Hague.

Shaanxi or *Shensi* province of NW China
area 75,579 sq mi/195,800 sq km
capital Xian
physical mountains; Huang He valley, one of the earliest settled areas of China
products iron, steel, mining, textiles, fruit, tea, rice, wheat
population (1990) 32,882,000.

Seychelles
Republic of

area 175 sq mi/453 sq km
capital Victoria (on Mahé island)
cities Cascade, Port Glaud, Misere
physical comprises two distinct island groups, one concentrated, the other widely scattered, totaling over 100 islands and islets
features Aldabra atoll, containing world's largest tropical lagoon; the unique "double coconut" (*coco de mer*); tourism is important
head of state and government France-Albert René from 1977
political system one-party socialist republic
political party Seychelles People's Progressive Front (SPPF), nationalist socialist

exports copra, cinnamon
currency Seychelles rupee
population (1990) 71,000; growth rate 2.2% p.a.
life expectancy 66 years (1988)
languages Creole (Asian, African, European mixture) 95%, English, French (all official)
religion Roman Catholic 90%
literacy 80% (1989)
GNP $175 million; $2,600 per head (1987)
chronology
1744 Became a French colony.
1794 Captured by British.
1814 Ceded by France to Britain; incorporated as a dependency of Mauritius.
1903 Became a separate British colony.
1975 Internal self-government agreed.
1976 Independence achieved from Britain as a republic within the Commonwealth, with James Mancham as president.
1977 Albert René ousted Mancham in an armed coup and took over presidency.
1979 New constitution adopted; Seychelles People's Progressive Front (SPPF) sole legal party.
1981 Attempted coup by South African mercenaries thwarted.
1984 René reelected.
1987 Coup attempt foiled.
1989 René reelected.
1991 Multiparty politics promised.
1992 Mancham returned from exile. Constitutional commission elected.

Shaba formerly (until 1972) *Katanga*. Region of Zaire; area 191,828 sq mi/496,965 sq km; population (1984) 3,874,000. Its main town is ⊅Lubumbashi, formerly Elisabethville.

shackle obsolete unit of length, used at sea for measuring cable or chain. One shackle is 15 fathoms (90 ft/27 m).

Shackleton Ernest 1874–1922. Irish Antarctic explorer. In 1907–09, he commanded an expedition that reached 88° 23′ S latitude, located the magnetic South Pole, and climbed Mount ⊅Erebus.

He was a member of Scott's Antarctic expedition 1901–04, and also commanded the expedition 1914–16 to cross the Antarctic, when he had to abandon his ship, the *Endurance*, crushed in the ice of the Weddell Sea. He died on board the *Quest* on his fourth expedition 1921–22 to the Antarctic.

shad any of several marine fishes, especially the genus *Alosa*, the largest (2 ft/60 cm long and 6 lb/2.7 kg in weight) of the herring family (Clupeidae). They migrate in shoals to breed in rivers.

The American shad *A. sapidissima*, once common along the Atlantic coast, was badly affected by stream pollution but is now making a comeback. It was successfully introduced along the Pacific in 1870. The gizzard shad *Dorosoma cepedianum* has been widely introduced into fresh waters of the US as food for other fishes.

shadoof or **shaduf** machine for lifting water, consisting typically of a long, pivoted wooden pole acting as a lever, with a weight at one end. The other end is positioned over a well, for example. The shadoof was in use in ancient Egypt and is still used in Arab countries today.

SHAEF (abbreviation for *Supreme Headquarters Allied Expeditionary Force*) World War II military center established Feb 15, 1944 in London, where final plans were made for the Allied invasion of Europe (under US general Eisenhower).

Shaffer Peter 1926– . English playwright. His plays include *Five Finger Exercise* 1958, the historical epic *The Royal Hunt of the Sun* 1964, *Equus* 1973, and *Amadeus* 1979 about the composer Mozart.

Shaftesbury Anthony Ashley Cooper, 1st Earl of Shaftesbury 1621–1683. English politician, a supporter of the Restoration of the monarchy. He became Lord Chancellor in 1672, but went into opposition in 1673 and began to organize the ⊅Whig Party. He headed the Whigs' demand for the exclusion of the future James II from the succession, secured the passing of the Habeas Corpus Act 1679, then, when accused of treason 1681, fled to Holland.

Shaftesbury Anthony Ashley Cooper, 7th Earl of Shaftesbury 1801–1885. British Tory politician. He strongly supported the Ten Hours Act of 1847 and other factory legislation, including the 1842 act forbidding the employment of women and children underground in mines. He was also associated with the movement to provide free education for the poor.

shag common name for the double-crested ⊅cormorant *Phalacrocorax auritis*.

shah (more formally, **shahanshah** "king of kings") traditional title of ancient Persian rulers, and also of those of the recent ⊅Pahlavi dynasty in Iran.

Shah Jahan 1592–1666. Mogul emperor of India 1628–58. During his reign the ⊅Taj

Mahal and the Pearl Mosque at Agra were built. From 1658 he was a prisoner of his son Aurangzeb.

Shahn Ben 1898–1969. Lithuanian-born US artist. Social Realist painter whose work included drawings and paintings on the ⊅Dreyfus case and the ⊅Sacco-Vanzetti case in which two Italian anarchists were accused of murders. He painted murals for the Rockefeller Center, New York (with the Mexican artist Diego Rivera), and the Federal Security Building, Washington, 1940–42.

Shaka or **Chaka** c. 1787–1828. Zulu chief who formed a Zulu empire in SE Africa. He seized power from his half brother 1816 and then embarked on a bloody military campaign to unite the Zulu clans. He was assassinated by his two half brothers.

Shaker popular name for a member of the Christian sect of the United Society of Believers in Christ's Second Appearing (and an offshoot of the ⊅Quakers). This was founded by James and Jane Wardley in England about 1747 and taken to North America 1774 by Ann Lee (1736–84), the wife of a Manchester blacksmith, known as Mother Ann. She founded a colony in New York, and eventually 18 colonies existed in several states. Separation from the world in self-regulating farm communities, prescribed modes of simple dress and living conditions, celibacy, and faith healing characterized their way of life. The name was applied because of their ecstatic trembling and shaking during worship.

Mrs Lee held that God had appeared in his masculine aspect as Jesus and would appear a second time in a female aspect, which her followers identified with her. She held that sex is inherently sinful, and Shakers were forbidden to marry. New members were supplied to the colonies through conversion and adopting orphans, but by the 20th century their numbers steadily declined, and today there are only a few Shakers left. Shaker design became renowned for pleasing but austere simplicity.

Shakespeare William 1564–1616. English dramatist and poet. Established in London by 1589 as an actor and a playwright, he was England's unrivaled dramatist until his death, and is considered the greatest English playwright. His plays, written in blank verse, can be broadly divided into lyric plays, including ⊅*Romeo and Juliet* and *A Midsummer Night's Dream*; comedies, including *The Comedy of Errors*, *As You Like It*, *Much Ado About Nothing*, and *Measure For Measure*; historical plays, such as *Henry VI* (in three parts), *Richard III*, and *Henry IV* (in two parts), which often showed cynical political wisdom; and tragedies, such as ⊅*Hamlet*, ⊅*Macbeth*, and ⊅*King Lear*. He also wrote numerous sonnets.

Born in Stratford-on-Avon, the son of a wool dealer, he was educated at the grammar school, and in 1582 married Anne Hathaway. They had a daughter, Susanna, in 1583, and twins Hamnet (died 1596) and Judith in 1595. Early plays, written around 1589–93, were the tragedy *Titus Andronicus*; the comedies *The Comedy of Errors*, *The Taming of the Shrew*, and *The Two Gentlemen of Verona*; the three parts of *Henry VI*; and *Richard III*. About 1593 he came under the patronage of the Earl of ⊅Southampton, to whom he dedicated his long poems *Venus and Adonis* 1593 and *The Rape of Lucrece* 1594; he also wrote for him the comedy *Love's Labour's Lost*, satirizing ⊅Raleigh's circle, and seems to have dedicated to him his

sonnets written around 1593–96, in which the mysterious "Dark Lady" appears.

From 1594 Shakespeare was a member of the Chamberlain's (later the King's) company of players, and had no rival as a dramatist, writing, for example, the lyric plays *Romeo and Juliet*, *A Midsummer Night's Dream*, and *Richard II* 1594–95, followed by *King John* and *The Merchant of Venice* in 1596. The Falstaff plays of 1597–99—*Henry IV* (parts I and II), *Henry V*, and *The Merry Wives of Windsor* (said to have been written at the request of Elizabeth I)—brought his fame to its height. He wrote *Julius Caesar* 1599. The period ended with the lyrically witty *Much Ado about Nothing*, *As You Like It*, and *Twelfth Night*, about 1598–1601.

With *Hamlet* begins the period of the great tragedies, 1601–08: *Othello*, *Macbeth*, *King Lear*, *Timon of Athens*, *Antony and Cleopatra*, and *Coriolanus*. This "darker" period is also reflected in the comedies *Troilus and Cressida*, *All's Well that Ends Well*, and *Measure for Measure* around 1601–04.

It is thought that Shakespeare was only part author of *Pericles*, which is grouped with the other plays of around 1608–11—*Cymbeline*, *The Winter's Tale*, and *The Tempest*—as the mature romance or "reconciliation" plays of the end of his career. During 1613 it is thought that Shakespeare collaborated with John Fletcher on *Henry VIII* and *Two Noble Kinsmen*. He had already retired to Stratford in about 1610, where he died on April 23, 1616.

shale fine-grained and finely layered ⊅sedimentary rock composed of silt and clay, usually formed in lowland areas. It is a weak rock, splitting easily along bedding planes to form thin, even slabs (by contrast, mudstone splits into irregular flakes). Oil shale contains kerogen, a solid bituminous material that yields ⊅petroleum when heated.

shallot small onion *Allium ascalonicum* in which bulbs are clustered like garlic; used for cooking and in pickles.

Shalmaneser five Assyrian kings, including:

Shalmaneser III king of Assyria 859–824 BC who pursued an aggressive policy and brought Babylon and Israel under the domination of Assyria.

shaman (Tungu *samân*) ritual leader who acts as intermediary between society and the supernatural world in many indigenous cultures of Asia, Africa, and the Americas. Also known as a *medicine man*, *seer*, or *sorcerer*, the shaman is expected to use special powers to cure illness and control good and evil spirits. The term is used for any tribal sorcerer or medicine man regardless of geography.

Shamans also use local medicines and curative techniques. Scientists and pharmaceutical companies have begun to take an interest in traditional knowledge systems, which puts the intellectual rights of shamans at issue.

Shamir Yitzhak 1915– . Polish-born Israeli right-wing politician; prime minister 1983–84 and 1986–92; leader of the Likud (Consolidation Party). He was foreign minister under Menachem Begin 1980–83, and again foreign minister in the ⊅Peres unity government 1984–86.

In Oct 1986, he and Peres exchanged positions, Shamir becoming prime minister and Peres taking over as foreign minister. Shamir was reelected 1989 and formed a new coalition government with Peres; this broke up 1990 and Shamir then formed a government without

Labor membership and with religious support. He was a leader of the ▷Stern Gang of guerrillas (1940–48) during the British mandate rule of Palestine.

shamrock several trifoliate plants of the family Leguminosae, including clovers. St Patrick is said to have used one to illustrate the doctrine of the Holy Trinity, and it was made the national badge of Ireland.

Shan member of a people of the mountainous borderlands separating Thailand, Myanmar (Burma), and China. They are related to the Laos and Thais, and their language belongs to the Sino-Tibetan family.

Shandong or **Shantung** province of NE China
area 59,174 sq mi/153,300 sq km
capital Jinan
cities ports: Yantai, Weihai, Qingdao, Shigiusuo
features crossed by the Huang He River and the ▷Grand Canal; Shandong Peninsula
products cereals, cotton, wild silk, varied minerals
population (1990) 84,393,000.

Shanghai port on the Huang-pu and Wusong rivers, Jiangsu province, China, 15 mi/24 km from the Chang Jiang estuary; population (1986) 6,980,000, the largest city in China. The municipality of Shanghai has an area of 2,239 sq mi/5,800 sq km and a population of 13,342,000. Industries include textiles, paper, chemicals, steel, agricultural machinery, precision instruments, shipbuilding, flour and vegetable-oil milling, and oil refining. It handles about 50% of China's imports and exports.

Shanghai is reckoned to be the most densely populated area in the world, with an average of 65 sq ft/6 sq m of living space and 2.6 sq yd/2.2 sq m of road per person.
features Notable buildings include the Jade Buddha Temple 1882, the former home of the revolutionary ▷Sun Yat-sen, the house where the First National Congress of the Communist Party of China met secretly in 1921, and the house, museum, and tomb of the writer Lu Xun.
history Shanghai was a city from 1360 but became significant only after 1842, when the treaty of Nanking opened it to foreign trade. In the 1920s, about 40,000 foreigners lived in Shanghai, more than 2% of the total population; in 1925 the electorate consisted of 2,742 voters, of which 1,000 were British. The Municipal Council issued a de facto unilateral declaration of independence 1925. The international settlement then developed, which remained the commercial center of the city after the departure of European interests 1943–46.

Shankar Ravi 1920– . Indian composer and musician. A virtuoso of the ▷sitar, he has composed film music and founded music schools in Bombay and Los Angeles.

Shankara 799–833. Hindu philosopher who wrote commentaries on some of the major Hindu scriptures, as well as hymns and essays on religious ideas. Shankara was responsible for the final form of the Advaita Vedanta school of Hindu philosophy, which teaches that Brahman, the supreme being, is all that exists in the universe, everything else is illusion. Shankara was fiercely opposed to Buddhism and may have influenced its decline in India.

Shannon longest river in Ireland, rising in County Cavan and flowing 240 mi/386 km

through loughs Allen and Ree and past Athlone, to reach the Atlantic through a wide estuary below Limerick. It is also the greatest source of electric power in the republic, with hydroelectric installations at and above Ardnacrusha, 3 mi/5 km N of Limerick.

Shannon Claude Elwood 1916– . US mathematician whose paper *The Mathematical Theory of Communication* 1948 marks the beginning of the science of information theory. He argued that information data and ▷entropy are analogous, and obtained a quantitative measure of the amount of information in a given message.

He wrote the first effective program for a chess-playing computer.

Shansi alternative transliteration of the Chinese province of ▷Shanxi.

Shantung alternative transliteration of the Chinese province of ▷Shandong.

Shanxi or **Shansi** province of NE China
area 60,641 sq mi/157,100 sq km
capital Taiyuan
features a drought-ridden plateau, partly surrounded by the ▷Great Wall of China
products coal, iron, fruit
population (1990) 28,759,000
history saw the outbreak of the Boxer Rebellion 1900.

SHAPE acronym for **Supreme Headquarters Allied Powers Europe**, situated near Mons, Belgium, and the headquarters of NATO's Supreme Allied Commander Europe (SACEUR).

Shapiro Karl 1913– . US poet whose work includes the striking *V Letter* 1945, written after service in World War II.

He was born in Baltimore. Later volumes of poetry include *Poems of a Jew* 1958. He has also written numerous critical works.

Shapley Harlow 1885–1972. US astronomer, whose study of ▷globular clusters showed that they were arranged in a halo around the Galaxy, and that the Galaxy was much larger than previously thought. He realized that the Sun was not at the center of the Galaxy as then assumed, but two-thirds of the way out to the rim.

Shapley joined the Mount Wilson Observatory, California, 1914.

sharecropping farming someone else's land, where the farmer gives the landowner a proportion of the crop instead of money. This system of rent payment was common in the US, especially the South, until after World War II. It is still common in parts of the developing world; for example, in India. Often the farmer is left with such a small share of the crop that he or she is doomed to poverty.

Shari'a the law of ▷Islam believed by Muslims to be based on divine revelation, and drawn from a number of sources, including the Koran, the Hadith, and the consensus of the Muslim community. Under this law, **qisās**, or retribution, allows a family to exact equal punishment on an accused; **diyat**, or blood money, is payable to a dead person's family as compensation.

From the latter part of the 19th century, the role of the Shari'a courts in the majority of Muslim countries began to be taken over by secular courts, and the Shari'a to be largely restricted to family law. Modifications of Koranic maxims have resulted from the introduction of Western law; for example, compensation can now be

claimed only after a conviction by a criminal court.

Sharif Omar. Adopted name of Michael Shalhoub 1932– . Egyptian-born actor (of Lebanese parents), who was Egypt's top male star before breaking into international films after his successful appearance in *Lawrence of Arabia* 1962.

His films include *Dr Zhivago* 1965, *Funny Girl* 1968, and *Funny Lady* 1975.

Sharjah or **Shariqah** third largest of the seven member states of the ▷United Arab Emirates, situated on the Arabian Gulf NE of Dubai; area 1,004 sq mi/2,600 sq km; population (1985) 269,000. Since 1952 it has included the small state of Kalba. In 1974 oil was discovered offshore. Industries include ship repair, cement, paint, and metal products.

shark any member of various orders of cartilaginous fishes (class Chondrichthyes), found throughout the oceans of the world. There are about 400 known species of shark. They have tough, usually gray, skin covered in denticles (small toothlike scales). A shark's streamlined body has side pectoral fins, a high dorsal fin, and a forked tail with a large upper lobe. Five open gill slits are visible on each side of the generally pointed head. Most sharks are fish-eaters, and a few will attack humans. They range from several feet in length to the great **white shark** *Carcharodon carcharias*, 30 ft/9 m long, and the harmless plankton-feeding **whale shark** *Rhincodon typus*, over 50 ft/15 m in length.

Relatively few attacks on humans lead to fatalities, and research suggests that the attacking sharks are not searching for food, but attempting to repel perceived rivals from their territory. Game fishing for "sport," the eradication of sharks in swimming and recreation areas, and their industrial exploitation as a source of leather, oil, and protein have reduced their numbers. Some species, such as the great white shark, the tiger shark, and the hammerhead, are now endangered and their killing has been banned in US waters since July 1991. Other species will be protected by catch quotas.

Sharon coastal plain in Israel between Haifa and Tel Aviv, and a sub-district of Central district; area 134 sq mi/348 sq km; population (1983) 190,400. It has been noted since ancient times for its fertility.

Sharon city in W Pennsylvania on the Shenango river, N of Pittsburgh, near the Ohio border. Industries include steel products and electronics; population (1990) 17,500.

Sharpeville black township in South Africa, 40 mi/65 km S of Johannesburg and N of Vereeniging; 69 people were killed here when police fired on a crowd of antiapartheid demonstrators March 21, 1960.

Shasta, Mount dormant volcano rising to a height of 14,162 ft/4,317 m in the Cascade Range, N California.

Shastri Lal Bahadur 1904–1966. Indian politician, prime minister 1964–66. He campaigned for national integration, and secured a declaration of peace with Pakistan at the Tashkent peace conference 1966.

Before independence, he was imprisoned several times for civil disobedience. Because of his small stature, he was known as "the Sparrow."

Adopting a firm stand against Pakistani attempts to capture Kashmir 1965, he persuaded

Pakistan's leader, Ayaub Khan, to sign a declaration agreeing never to use force again, and died of a heart attack shortly after the agreement was signed.

Shatt-al-Arab (Persian *Arvand*) the waterway formed by the confluence of the rivers ⬦Euphrates and ⬦Tigris; length 120 mi/190 km to the Persian Gulf. Basra, Khorramshahr, and Abadan stand on it.

Its lower reaches form a border of disputed demarcation between Iran and Iraq. In 1975 the two countries agreed on the deepest water line as the frontier, but Iraq repudiated this 1980; the dispute was a factor in the Iran–Iraq war 1980–88.

Shaw George Bernard 1856–1950. Irish dramatist. He was also a critic and novelist, and an early member of the socialist ⬦Fabian Society. His plays combine comedy with political, philosophical, and polemic aspects, aiming to make an impact on his audience's social conscience as well as their emotions. They include *Arms and the Man* 1894, *Devil's Disciple* 1897, *Man and Superman* 1905, *Pygmalion* 1913, and *St Joan* 1924. Nobel Prize 1925.

Born in Dublin, the son of a civil servant, Shaw went to London in 1876, where he became a brilliant debater and supporter of the Fabians, and worked as a music and drama critic. He wrote five unsuccessful novels before his first play, *Widowers' Houses*, was produced 1892. Attacking slum landlords, it allied him with the realistic, political, and polemical movement in the theater, pointing to people's responsibility to improve themselves and their social environment.

The volume *Plays: Pleasant and Unpleasant* 1898 also included *The Philanderer, Mrs Warren's Profession*, dealing with prostitution and banned until 1902; and *Arms and the Man* about war. *Three Plays for Puritans* 1901 contained *The Devil's Disciple, Caesar and Cleopatra* (a companion piece to Shakespeare's *Antony and Cleopatra*), and *Captain Brassbound's Conversion*, written for the actress Ellen ⬦Terry. *Man and Superman* 1903 expounds his ideas of evolution by following the character of Don Juan into hell for a debate with the devil.

The "antiromantic" comedy *Pygmalion*, first performed 1913, was written for the actress Mrs Patrick Campbell (and later converted to a musical as *My Fair Lady*). Later plays included *Heartbreak House* 1917, *Back to Methuselah* 1921, and the historical *St Joan* 1924.

Altogether Shaw wrote more than 50 plays and became a byword for wit. His theories were further explained in the voluminous prefaces to the plays, and in books such as *The Intelligent Woman's Guide to Socialism and Capitalism* 1928. He was also an unsuccessful advocate of spelling reform and a prolific letter-writer.

shawm in music, an early form of oboe. Similar instruments survive in the Middle East and India.

Shays Daniel *c.* 1747–1825. American political agitator who led a revolt of impoverished farmers demanding government aid.

Born in W Massachusetts, Shays served in the 5th Massachusetts Regiment during the American Revolution, seeing action at the battles of Bunker Hill, Ticonderoga, and Saratoga. Returning to civilian life 1780, Shays led an armed uprising of hard-pressed farmers 1786 against the refusal of the state government to offer economic relief. Shays' Rebellion was suppressed 1787 by a Massachusetts militia force, but its effect within the state was to turn public attention to the plight of the western farmers, and on a national level it underlined the need for a stronger central government. Shays was pardoned 1788.

Shearer (Edith) Norma 1900–1983. Canadian-born US actress who starred in silent films and in talkies such as *Private Lives* 1931, *Romeo and Juliet* 1936, *Marie Antoinette* 1938, and *The Women* 1939. She was married to MGM executive Irving Thalberg and retired after *Her Cardboard Lover* 1942.

shearwater any sea bird of the genus *Puffinus*, in the same family (Procellariidae) as the diving ⬦petrels.

The sooty shearwater *P. griseus* is common on both North Atlantic coasts.

Sheba ancient name for S ⬦Yemen (Sha'abijah). It was once renowned for gold and spices. According to the Old Testament, its queen visited Solomon; until 1975 the Ethiopian royal house traced its descent from their union.

Sheboygan city in E Wisconsin, on Lake Michigan, N of Milwaukee. Industries include wood, food, plastic, and enamel products; population (1990) 50,000.

Shechem ancient town in Palestine, capital of Samaria. In the Old Testament, it is the traditional burial place of Joseph; nearby is Jacob's well. Shechem was destroyed about AD 67 by the Roman emperor Vespasian; on its site stands Nablus (a corruption of Neapolis) built by the Roman emperor ⬦Hadrian.

Sheeler Charles 1883–1965. US painter. He is best known for his paintings of factories and urban landscapes (for example, *American Landscape* 1930).

Born in Philadelphia, he was associated with precisionism, a movement that used sharply defined shapes to represent objects. His style was to photograph his subjects before painting them.

sheep any of several ruminant, even-toed, hoofed mammals of the family Bovidae. Wild species survive in the uplands of central and eastern Asia, N Africa, southern Europe and North America. The domesticated breeds are all classified as *Ovis aries*. Various breeds of sheep are reared worldwide for meat, wool, milk, and cheese, and for rotation on arable land to maintain its fertility.

Domestic sheep are descended from wild sheep of the Neolithic Middle East. The original species may be extinct but was probably closely related to the surviving mouflon *O. musimom* of Sardinia and Corsica. Only a small proportion of European and North American breeds are still in full commercial use. Among those, the Rambouillet breed is used extensively in the US for its fine wool, and the Columbia is a popular meat-producing breed.

sheepdog any of several breeds of dog, bred originally for herding sheep. The Old English sheepdog is gray or blue-gray, with white markings, and is about 22 in/56 cm tall at the shoulder. The Shetland sheepdog is much smaller, 14 in/36 cm tall, and shaped more like a long-coated collie. The dog now most commonly used by shepherds and farmers to tend sheep is the border collie.

Sheffield industrial city on the river Don, South Yorkshire, England; population (1991 est) 499,700. From the 12th century, iron smelting was the chief industry, and by the 14th century, Sheffield cutlery, silverware, and plate were made. During the Industrial Revolution the iron and steel industries developed rapidly. It now produces alloys and special steels, cutlery of all kinds, permanent magnets, drills, and precision tools. Other industries include electroplating, type-founding, and the manufacture of optical glass.

sheik leader or chief of an Arab family or village.

Shelburne William Petty FitzMaurice, 2nd Earl of Shelburne 1737–1805. British Whig politician. He was an opponent of George III's American policy, and as prime minister in 1783, he concluded peace with the United States of America.

shelduck duck *Tadorna tadorna* with a dark-green head and red bill, with the rest of the plumage strikingly marked in black, white, and chestnut. Widely distributed in Europe and Asia, it lays 10–12 white eggs in rabbit burrows on sandy coasts, and is usually seen on estuary mudflats.

shelf sea relatively shallow sea, usually no deeper than 650 ft/200 m, overlying the continental shelf around the coastlines. Most fishing and marine mineral exploitations are carried out in shelf seas.

shellac resin derived from secretions of the ⬦lac insect.

Shelley Mary Wollstonecraft 1797–1851. English writer, the daughter of Mary Wollstonecraft and William Godwin. In 1814 she eloped with the poet Percy Bysshe Shelley, whom she married in 1816. Her novels include ⬦*Frankenstein* 1818, *The Last Man* 1826, and *Valperga* 1823.

Shelley Percy Bysshe 1792–1822. English lyric poet, a leading figure in the Romantic movement. Expelled from Oxford University for atheism, he fought all his life against religion and for political freedom. This is reflected in his early poems such as *Queen Mab* 1813. He later wrote tragedies including *The Cenci* 1818, lyric dramas such as *Prometheus Unbound* 1820, and lyrical poems such as "Ode to the West Wind." He drowned while sailing in Italy.

Born near Horsham, Sussex, he was educated at Eton public school and University College, Oxford, where his collaboration in a pamphlet *The Necessity of Atheism* 1811 caused his expulsion. While living in London he fell in love with 16-year-old Harriet Westbrook, whom he married 1811. He visited Ireland and Wales, writing pamphlets defending vegetarianism and political freedom, and in 1813 published privately *Queen Mab*, a poem with political freedom as its theme. Meanwhile he had become estranged from his wife and in 1814 left England with Mary Wollstonecraft Godwin, whom he married after Harriet drowned herself 1816. *Alastor*, written 1815, was followed by the epic *The Revolt of Islam*, and by 1818 Shelley was living in Italy. Here he produced the tragedy *The Cenci*; the satire on Wordsworth, *Peter Bell the Third* 1819; and the lyric drama *Prometheus Unbound* 1820. Other works of the period are "Ode to the West Wind" 1819; "The Cloud" and "The Skylark," both 1820; "The Sensitive Plant" and "The Witch of Atlas"; "Epipsychidion" and, on the death of the poet Keats, "Adonais" 1821; the lyric drama *Hellas* 1822; and the prose *Defence of Poetry* 1821. In July 1822 Shelley was drowned while sailing near Viareggio, and his ashes were buried in Rome.

shellfish popular name for mollusks and crustaceans, including the whelk and periwinkle, mussel, oyster, lobster, crab, and shrimp.

shell shock or *combat neurosis* or *battle fatigue* any of the various forms of mental disorder that affect soldiers exposed to heavy explosions or extreme ▷stress. Shell shock was first diagnosed during World War I.

Following the Vietnam War, many veterans were found to be suffering from post traumatic shock syndrome, in which recurring "flashbacks" to combat experiences torment the sufferer.

Shema in Judaism, prayer from the Torah, recited by orthodox men every morning and evening, which affirms the special relationship of the Jews with God.

It begins with the Hebrew for "Hear, O Israel, the Lord our God, the Lord is One."

Shenandoah river in Virginia, 55 mi/89 km long, a tributary of the Potomac, which it joins at Harper's Ferry, West Virginia.

The river is not navigable, but it has several hydroelectric facilities, and the Shenandoah valley is one of the nation's main apple-growing regions. In the Civil War, the Union general Philip Sheridan laid waste to the valley 1864–65.

Shensi alternative transcription of the Chinese province of ▷Shanxi.

Shenyang industrial city and capital of Liaoning province, China; population (1990) 4,500,000. It was the capital of the Manchu emperors 1644–1912; their tombs are nearby.

Historically known as *Mukden*, it was taken from Russian occupation by the Japanese in the Battle of Mukden Feb 20–March 10, 1905, and was again taken by the Japanese 1931.

Shenzen special economic zone established in 1980 opposite Hong Kong on the coast of Guangdong province, S China. Its status provided much of the driving force of its spectacular development in the 1980s when its population rose from 20,000 in 1980 to 600,000 in 1989. Part of the population is "rotated": newcomers from other provinces return to their homes after a few years spent learning foreign business techniques.

Shepard Alan Bartlett, Jr 1923– . US astronaut. He undertook the first manned US space flight, the suborbital *Mercury-Redstone 3* mission on board the *Freedom 7* capsule May 1961, and commanded the *Apollo 14* lunar landing mission 1971. Born in East Derry, New Hampshire, he graduated 1944 from the US Naval Academy at Annapolis and served as a fighter pilot, test pilot, and aircraft readiness officer for the Atlantic fleet before becoming an astronaut.

Shepard Sam 1943– . US dramatist and actor. His work combines colloquial American dialogue with striking visual imagery, and includes *The Tooth of Crime* 1972 and *Buried Child* 1978, for which he won a Pulitzer Prize. *Seduced* 1979 is based on the life of the recluse Howard Hughes. He has acted in a number of films, including *The Right Stuff* 1983, *Fool for Love* 1986, based on his play of the same name, and *Steel Magnolias* 1989.

shepherd's purse annual plant *Capsella bursa-pastoris* of the Cruciferae family, distributed worldwide in temperate zones. It is a persistent weed with white flowers followed by heart-shaped, seed-containing pouches from which its name derives.

Sheraton Thomas *c.* 1751–1806. English designer of elegant inlaid furniture. He was influenced by his predecessors ▷Hepplewhite and ▷Chippendale.

Sheridan Philip Henry 1831–1888. Union general in the American ▷Civil War. Recognizing Sheridan's aggressive spirit, General Ulysses S ▷Grant gave him command of his cavalry in 1864, and soon after of the Army of the Shenandoah Valley, Virginia. Sheridan laid waste to the valley, cutting off grain supplies to the Confederate armies. In the final stage of the war, Sheridan forced General Robert E ▷Lee to retreat to Appomattox and surrender.

Born in Albany, New York, Sheridan graduated from West Point 1853. Following the war, Sheridan led troops at the Mexican border and hastened the collapse of the regime of Emperor Maximilian. Sheridan served as military governor of Texas and Louisiana during ▷Reconstruction; his policies were so harsh that he was removed by President Andrew ▷Johnson. He was made general in chief of the US army 1883–88.

Sheridan Richard Brinsley 1751–1816. Irish dramatist and politician, born in Dublin. His social comedies include *The Rivals* 1775, celebrated for the character of Mrs Malaprop, *The School for Scandal* 1777, and *The Critic* 1779. In 1776 he became lessee of the Drury Lane Theater. He became a member of Parliament in 1780.

sheriff (Old English *scīr* "shire", *gerēfa* "reeve") in the US, in all states but Rhode Island, the chief elected officer of a county law-enforcement agency, usually responsible for enforcement in unincorporated areas of the county and for the operation of the jail. The sheriff is also the officer of the local court who serves papers and enforces court orders.

Sherman city in NE Texas, N of Dallas. It is a processing and shipping center for agricultural products; textiles, electronics, and machinery are manufactured; population (1990) 31,600.

Sherman Roger 1721–1793. American public official; signer of the Declaration of Independence, Articles of Confederation, and Constitution. After service in Connecticut's provincial legislature, he became superior court judge 1766–85. A supporter of American independence, he was a member of the Continental Congress 1774–81 and 1783–84. As a delegate to the Constitutional Convention 1787, he introduced the "Connecticut Compromise" that provided for a bicameral federal legislature. Sherman served in the US House of Representatives 1789–91 and Senate 1791–93.

Born in Newton, Massachusetts, Sherman moved to Connecticut 1743. He later studied law and was admitted to the bar 1754.

Sherman William Tecumseh 1820–1891. Union general in the American ▷Civil War. In 1864 he captured and burned Atlanta; continued his march eastward, to the sea, laying Georgia waste; and then drove the Confederates northward. He was US Army chief of staff 1869–83.

Born in Lancaster, Ohio, Sherman graduated from West Point 1840. He served in the Mexican War and then became a banker. Early in the Civil War he served at the First Battle of Bull Run 1861 and Shiloh 1862. He replaced General U S ▷Grant as commander of the West 1864 and launched his Georgia campaign. Despite the ruthlessness of his campaign to capture Atlanta and the widespread destruction he inflicted as he marched to the sea, he

was conciliatory in victory, offering terms that had to be repudiated by President A Johnson. Following the war, there was a move to nominate Sherman for president, but he announced that he would not run if nominated and would not serve if elected. He succeeded Grant as commander of the army 1869.

Sherman Anti-Trust Act in US history, an act of Congress 1890, named after senator John Sherman (1823–1900) of Ohio, designed to prevent powerful corporations from monopolizing industries and restraining trade for their own benefit. Relatively few prosecutions of such trusts were successful under the act.

Sherpa member of a people in NE Nepal related to the Tibetans and renowned for their mountaineering skill. They frequently work as support staff and guides for climbing expeditions. A Sherpa, Tensing Norgay, was one of the first two people to climb to the summit of Everest.

Sherrington Charles Scott 1857–1952. English neurophysiologist who studied the structure and function of the nervous system. *The Integrative Action of the Nervous System* 1906 formulated the principles of reflex action. Nobel Prize for Medicine (with E D ▷Adrian) 1932.

Sherwood Robert 1896–1955. US dramatist. His plays include *The Petrified Forest* 1934, *Idiot's Delight* 1936, *Abe Lincoln in Illinois* 1938, and *There Shall Be No Night* 1940. For each of the last three he received a Pulitzer prize.

Sherwood worked as a magazine editor during the 1920s. Later he became Franklin Roosevelt's speechwriter and adviser and held various political offices. After World War II he produced little important theatrical material except for the Academy Award-winning film *The Best Years of Our Lives* 1946.

Sherwood Forest hilly stretch of parkland in W Nottinghamshire, England, area about 200 sq mi/520 sq km. Formerly a royal forest, it is associated with the legendary outlaw ▷Robin Hood.

Shetland Islands islands off the north coast of Scotland, beyond the Orkneys
area 541 sq mi/1,400 sq km
cities Lerwick (administrative headquarters), on Mainland, largest of 19 inhabited islands
physical over 100 islands including Muckle Flugga (latitude 60° 51′ N) the northernmost of the British Isles
products processed fish, handknits from Fair Isle and Unst, miniature ponies. Europe's largest oil port is Sullom Voe, Mainland
population (1987) 22,000
language dialect derived from Norse, the islands having been a Norse dependency until 1472.

Shevardnadze Edvard 1928– . Georgian politician, Soviet foreign minister 1985–91, head of state of Georgia from 1992. A supporter of ▷Gorbachev, he was first secretary of the Georgian Communist Party from 1972 and an advocate of economic reform. In 1985 he became a member of the Politburo, working for détente and disarmament. In July 1991, he resigned from the Communist Party (CPSU) and, along with other reformers and leading democrats, established the Democratic Reform Movement. In March 1992 he was chosen as chair of Georgia's ruling military council, and in Oct elected speaker of parliament.

On Dec 20, 1990, he dramatically resigned as foreign minister as a measure of protest against what he viewed as the onset of a dictatorship in the USSR, as reactionary forces, particularly within the military, regained the ascendancy. Following the abortive anti-Gorbachev coup Aug 1991 (in which he stood alongside Boris ◊Yeltsin) and the dissolution of the CPSU, the Democratic Reform Party stood out as a key force in the "new politics" of Russia and the USSR. Shevardnadze turned down an offer from President Gorbachev to join the post-coup Soviet security council, but subsequently agreed to join Gorbachev's advisory council. In March 1992, following the ousting of President Gamsakhurdia, he was chosen as chair of Georgia's ruling State Council, and in the first parliamentary elections Oct was elected speaker of parliament (equivalent to president), with 90% of the vote.

SHF in physics, the abbreviation for *super-high ◊frequency*.

Shidehara Kijuro 1872–1951. Japanese politician and diplomat, prime minister 1945–46. As foreign minister 1924–27 and 1929–31, he promoted conciliation with China, and economic rather than military expansion. After a brief period as prime minister 1945–46, he became speaker of the Japanese Diet (parliament) 1946–51.

shield in geology, alternate name for ◊craton, the ancient core of a continent.

shield in technology, any material used to reduce the amount of radiation (electrostatic, electromagnetic, heat, nuclear) reaching from one region of space to another, or any material used as a protection against falling debris, as in tunneling. Electrical conductors are used for electrostatic shields, soft iron for electromagnetic shields, and poor conductors of heat for heat shields. Heavy materials such as lead and concrete are used for protection against X-rays and nuclear radiation. See also ◊heat shield.

Shihchiachuang alternative transliteration of the city of ◊Shijiazhuang in China.

Shi Huangdi or *Shih Huang Ti* 259–210 BC. Emperor of China who succeeded to the throne of the state of Qin in 246 BC and reunited China as an empire by 228 BC. He burned almost all existing books in 213 BC to destroy ties with the past; rebuilt the ◊Great Wall of China; and was buried at Xian in a tomb complex guarded by 10,000 life-size terracotta warriors (excavated by archeologists in the 1980s).

He had so overextended his power that the dynasty and the empire collapsed with the death of his weak successor in 207 BC.

Shiite or *Shiah* member of a sect of Islam who believe that ◊Ali was ◊Mohammed's first true successor. They are doctrinally opposed to the Sunni Muslims. They developed their own law differing only in minor directions, such as inheritance and the status of women. Holy men have greater authority in the Shiite sect than in the Sunni sect. They are prominent in Iran, the Lebanon, and Indo-Pakistan, and are also found in Iraq and Bahrain.

Shijiazhuang or *Shihchiachuang* city and major railroad junction in Hebei province, China; population (1989) 1,300,000. Industries include textiles, chemicals, printing, and light engineering.

Shikoku smallest of the four main islands of Japan, S of Honshu, E of Kyushu; area 7,257 sq mi/18,800 sq km; population (1986) 4,226,000; chief town Matsuyama. Products include rice, wheat, soybeans, sugar cane, orchard fruits, salt, and copper.

It has a mild climate, and annual rainfall in the south can reach 105 in/266 cm. The highest point is Mount Ishizuchi (6,498 ft/ 1,980 m). A suspension bridge links Shikoku to Awajishima Island over the Naruto whirlpool in the ◊Seto Naikai (Inland Sea).

shingles common name for ◊herpes zoster, a disease characterized by infection of sensory nerves, with pain and eruption of blisters along the course of the affected nerves.

Shinto (Chinese *shin tao* "way of the gods") the indigenous religion of Japan. It combines an empathetic oneness with natural forces and loyalty to the reigning dynasty as descendants of the Sun goddess, Amaterasu-Omikami. Traditional Shinto followers stressed obedience and devotion to the emperor, and an aggressive nationalistic aspect was developed by the Meiji rulers. Today Shinto has discarded these aspects.

Shinto is the Chinese transliteration of Japanese *Kami-no-Michi*. Shinto ceremonies appeal to the kami, the mysterious forces of nature manifest in topographical features such as mountains, trees, stones, springs, and caves. Shinto focuses on purity, devotion, and sincerity; aberrations can be cleansed through purification rituals. In addition, purification procedures make the worshiper presentable and acceptable when making requests before the kami.

Shinto's holiest shrine is at Ise, near Kyoto, where in the temple of the Sun goddess is preserved the mirror that she is supposed to have given to Jimmu, the legendary first emperor, in the 7th century BC. Sectarian Shinto consists of 130 sects; the sects are officially recognized but not state-supported (as was state Shinto until its disestablishment after World War II and Emperor Hirohito's disavowal of his divinity 1946).

There is no Shinto philosophical literature, though there are texts on mythologies, ceremonial and administrative procedures, religious laws, and chronicles of ruling families and temple construction.

ship large seagoing vessel. The Greeks, Phoenicians, Romans, and Vikings used ships extensively for trade, exploration, and warfare. The 14th century was the era of European exploration by sailing ship, largely aided by the invention of the compass. In the 15th century Britain's Royal Navy was first formed, but in the 16th–19th centuries Spanish and Dutch fleets dominated the shipping lanes of both the Atlantic and Pacific. The ultimate sailing ships, the fast US and British tea clippers, were built in the 19th century. Also in the 19th century, iron was first used for some shipbuilding instead of wood. Steam-propelled ships of the late 19th century were followed by compound engine and turbine-propelled vessels from the early 20th century.

The Greeks and Phoenicians built wooden ships, propelled by oar or sail. The Romans and Carthaginians built war galleys equipped with rams and several tiers of rowers. The oak ships of the Vikings were built for rough seas and propelled by oars and sail. The Crusader fleet of Richard the Lion-Hearted was largely of sail. The invention of the compass in the 14th century led to exploration by sailing ship, especially by the Portuguese, resulting in the discovery of "new worlds." In the 15th century Henry VIII built the *Great Harry*, the first double-decked English warship. In the 16th century ships were short and high-sterned, and despite Pett's

three-decker in the 17th century, English ships did not bear comparison with the Spanish and Dutch until the early 19th century. In the 1840s iron began replacing wood in shipbuilding, pioneered by Brunel's *Great Britain* 1845.

The US and Britain experimented with steam propulsion as the 19th century opened. The paddle-wheel-propelled *Comet* appeared 1812, the Canadian *Royal William* crossed the Atlantic 1833, and the English *Great Western* steamed from Bristol to New York 1838. Pettit Smith first used the screw propeller in the *Archimedes* 1839, and after 1850 the paddle wheel was used mainly on inland waterways, especially the great rivers of the Americas. The introduction of the compound engine and turbine (the latter 1902) completed the revolution in propulsion until the advent of nuclear-powered vessels after World War II, chiefly submarines (which are considered boats, not ships).

More recently ◊hovercraft and ◊hydrofoil boats have been developed for specialized purposes, particularly as short-distance ferries. Sailing ships in automated form for cargo purposes, and ◊maglev ships, were in development in the early 1990s.

Shiraz ancient walled city of S Iran, the capital of Fars province; population (1986) 848,000. It is known for its wines, carpets, and silverwork and for its many mosques.

shire administrative area formed in Britain for the purpose of raising taxes in Anglo-Saxon times. By AD 1000 most of southern England had been divided into shires with fortified strongholds at their centers. The Midland counties of England are still known as *the Shires*; for example Derbyshire, Nottinghamshire, and Staffordshire.

Shirer William L(awrence) 1904– . US journalist and historian. From 1937 to 1941, Shirer worked with E R ◊Murrow covering the events leading up to the outbreak of World War II for the Columbia Broadcasting System (CBS). He remained a columnist and commentator for CBS until 1947 and for the Mutual Broadcasting System 1947–49. His best-known book is *The Rise and Fall of the Third Reich* 1960. Other works include *The Nightmare Years: 1930–1940* 1984.

Born in Chicago, Shirer was educated at Coe College and joined the Paris bureau of the *Chicago Tribune* 1926. Traveling widely throughout Europe, he joined the Paris staff of the *New York Herald Tribune* 1934.

Shiva alternate spelling of ◊Siva, Hindu god.

Shkodër (Italian *Scutari*) town on the river Bojana, NW Albania, SE of Lake Shkodër, 12 mi/19 km from the Adriatic; population (1983) 71,000. Products include woolens and cement. During World War I it was occupied by Austria 1916–18, and during World War II by Italy.

shock in medicine, circulatory failure marked by a sudden fall of blood pressure and resulting in pallor, sweating, fast (but weak) pulse, and sometimes complete collapse. Causes include disease, injury, and psychological trauma.

In shock, the blood pressure falls below that necessary to supply the tissues of the body, especially the brain. Treatment depends on the cause. Rest is needed, and, in the case of severe blood loss, restoration of the normal circulating volume.

Shockley William 1910–1989. US physicist and amateur geneticist who worked with John

Bardeen and Walter Brattain on the invention of the ◊transistor. They were jointly awarded a Nobel Prize 1956. During the 1970s Shockley was criticized for his claim that blacks were genetically inferior to whites in terms of intelligence.

He donated his sperm to the bank in S California established by the plastic-lens millionaire Robert Graham for the passing on of the genetic code of geniuses.

shoebill or **whale-headed stork** large, gray, long-legged, swamp-dwelling African bird *Balaeniceps rex*. Up to 5 ft/1.5 m tall, it has a large wide beak 8 in/20 cm long, with which it scoops fish, mollusks, reptiles, and carrion out of the mud.

Shoemaker Willie (William Lee) 1931– . US jockey 1949–90. He rode 8,833 winners from 40,351 mounts and his earnings exceeded $123 million. He retired Feb 1990 after finishing fourth on Patchy Groundfog at Santa Anita, California.

He was the leading US jockey 10 times. After his retirement he became a successful trainer before an automobile accident 1991 left him paralyzed. Standing 4 ft 11 in/1.5 m tall, he weighed about 95 lb/43 kg.

CAREER HIGHLIGHTS

US Triple Crown
wins:
Kentucky Derby: 1955, 1959, 1965, 1986
Preakness Stakes: 1963, 1967
Belmont Stakes: 1957, 1959, 1962, 1967, 1975
Leading US money winner: 1951, 1953–54, 1958–64

shofar in Judaism, a ram's horn blown in the synagogue as a call to repentance at the new-year festivals of Rosh Hashanah and Yom Kippur.

shogun in Japanese history, title of a series of military dictators 1192–1867 who relegated the emperor's role to that of figurehead. Technically an imperial appointment, the office was treated as hereditary and was held by the Minamoto clan 1192–1219, by the Ashikaga 1336–1573, and by the Tokugawa 1603–1867. The shogun held legislative, judicial, and executive power.

The emperor had been a national and religious figurehead rather than a direct ruler since the rise of the Fujiwara clan in the 9th century, but the exercise of power had been by officials of the court rather than of the army. The title of *seii-tai-shōgun*, "barbarian-subduing commander," first given 794 to one of the imperial guards appointed to lead an expedition against the Ainu people, had before 1192 entailed only temporary military command. The *bakufu* (shogunate), the administrative structure set up by the first Minamoto shogun, gradually extended its area of operations to all aspects of government. Mirroring the workings of the imperial court, the *bakufu* would sometimes function without the active participation of the current shogun.

The abdication of the last shogun in 1867 was the result of a power struggle between court and *bakufu* factions that followed the arrival of the representatives of foreign powers in the 1850s, ending Japan's centuries of isolation.

Sholes Christopher Latham 1819–1890. American printer and newspaper editor who, in 1867, invented the first practicable typewriter in association with Carlos Glidden and Samuel Soulé. In 1873, they sold their patents to ◊Remington & Sons, a firm of gunsmiths in

New York, who developed and sold the machine commercially. In 1878 Sholes developed a shift-key mechanism that made it possible to touch-type.

Sholokhov Mikhail Aleksandrovich 1905–1984. Soviet novelist. His *And Quiet Flows the Don* 1926–40 depicts the Don Cossacks through World War I and the Russian Revolution. Nobel Prize 1965.

Shona member of a Bantu-speaking people of southern Africa, comprising approximately 80% of the population of Zimbabwe. They also occupy the land between the Save and Pungure rivers in Mozambique, and smaller groups are found in South Africa, Botswana, and Zambia. The Shona are mainly farmers, living in scattered villages. The Shona language belongs to the Niger-Congo family.

shoot in botany, the parts of a ◊vascular plant growing above ground, comprising a stem bearing leaves, buds, and flowers. The shoot develops from the ◊plumule of the embryo.

shooting star another name for a ◊meteor.

short circuit direct connection between two points in an electrical circuit. Its relatively low resistance means that a large current flows through it, bypassing the rest of the circuit, and this may cause the circuit to overheat dangerously.

shorthand any system of rapid writing, such as the abbreviations practiced by the Greeks and Romans. The first perfecter of an entirely phonetic system was Isaac ◊Pitman, by which system speeds of about 300 words a minute are said to be attainable.

The earliest recorded instance of shorthand being used is the system used by the historian Xenophon to write the memoirs of Socrates. The art of shorthand died out in the Middle Ages because of its imagined associations with witchcraft. It was revived in the 16th century when Timothy Bright (1551–1615) published his *Characterie: An Arte of Shorte, Swifte, and Secrete Writing by Character* 1588. The earliest shorthand system to be based on the alphabet was that of John Willis published 1603. Later alphabetic systems in England were devised by Thomas Shelton (1601–1650) in 1630 (used by the diarist Pepys) and Thomas Burney 1750, used by novelist Charles Dickens as a reporter. In the US, the most popular system is that of Irish-born John Robert Gregg (1867–1948) 1888.

Stenotype machines, using selective keyboards enabling several word contractions to be printed at a time, are equally speedy and accurate. Abbreviations used can be transferred by the operator to a television screen, enabling the deaf to follow the spoken word.

Short Parliament the English Parliament that was summoned by Charles I on April 13, 1640 to raise funds for his war against the Scots. It was succeeded later in the year by the ◊Long Parliament.

When it became clear that the parliament opposed the war and would not grant him any money, he dissolved it May 5 and arrested some of its leaders.

short story short work of prose fiction, which typically either sets up and resolves a single narrative point or depicts a mood or an atmosphere. Noted short-story writers include Anton Chekhov, Rudyard Kipling, Guy de Maupassant, Saki, Jorge Luis Borges, Edgar Allan Poe, and Ernest Hemingway.

Shostakovich Dmitry (Dmitriyevich) 1906–1975. Soviet composer. His music is tonal, expressive, and sometimes highly dramatic; it was not always to official Soviet taste. He wrote 15 symphonies, chamber music, ballets, and operas, the latter including *Lady Macbeth of Mtsensk* 1934, which was suppressed as "too divorced from the proletariat," but revived as *Katerina Izmaylova* 1963.

shot put in track and field, the sport of throwing (or putting) overhand from the shoulder a metal ball (or shot). Standard shot weights are 16 lb/7.26 kg for men and 8.8 lb/4 kg for women.

shoveler fresh-water duck *Anas clypeata*, so named after its long and broad flattened beak. Spending the summer in N Europe or North America, it winters further south.

The male has a green head, white and brown body plumage, and can grow up to 20 in/50 cm long. The female is speckled brown.

show trial public and well-reported trial of people accused of crimes against the state. In the USSR in the 1930s and 1940s, Stalin carried out show trials against economic saboteurs, Communist Party members, army officers, and even members of the Bolshevik leadership.

Andrei Vyshinksy was the Soviet prosecutor for many of the most notorious show trials of the 1930s.

Shrapnel Henry 1761–1842. British army officer who invented shells containing bullets, to increase the spread of casualties, first used 1804; hence the word **shrapnel** to describe shell fragments.

Shreveport port on the Red River, Louisiana; population (1990) 198,600. Industries include oil, natural gas, steel, telephone equipment, glass, and timber. It was founded 1836 and named after Henry Shreve, a riverboat captain who cleared a giant logjam.

The discovery of oil nearby 1906 stimulated economic growth.

shrew insectivorous mammal of the family Soricidae, found in Eurasia and the Americas. It is mouselike, but with a long nose and pointed teeth. Its high metabolic rate means that it must eat almost constantly. The common shrew *Sorex araneus* is about 3 in/7.5 cm long.

The pigmy shrew *Sorex minutus* is only about 2 in/5 cm long.

Shrewsbury market town on the river Severn, Shropshire, England; population (1991) 90,900. It is the administrative headquarters of the county. To the east is the site of the Roman city of Viroconium (larger than Pompeii). In the 5th century, as **Pengwern**, Shrewsbury was capital of the kingdom of Powys, which later became part of Mercia. In the battle of Shrewsbury 1403, Henry IV defeated the rebels led by Hotspur (Sir Henry ◊Percy).

The city declined an invitation in 1539, at the dissolution of the monasteries, to become a cathedral city.

shrike "butcher-bird" of the family Laniidae, of which there are over 70 species, living mostly in Africa, but also in Eurasia and North America. They often impale insects and small vertebrates on thorns. They can grow to 14 in/35 cm long, and have gray, black, or brown plumage.

shrimp crustacean related to the ◊prawn. It has a cylindrical, semitransparent body, with ten jointed legs. Some shrimps grow as large as 10 in/25 cm long.

The European common shrimp *Crangon vulgaris* is greenish, translucent, has its first pair of legs ending in pincers, possesses no rostrum (the beaklike structure which extends forward from the head in some crustaceans), and has comparatively shorter antennae than the prawn.

Shropshire county in W England. Sometimes abbreviated to *Salop*, it was officially known by this name from 1974 until local protest reversed the decision 1980
area 1,347 sq mi/3,490 sq km
cities Shrewsbury (administrative headquarters), Telford, Oswestry, Ludlow
physical bisected, on the Welsh border, NW to SE by the river Severn; Ellesmere, the largest of several lakes; the Clee Hills rise to about 1,800 ft/610 m in the SW
features Ironbridge Gorge open-air museum of industrial archeology, with the Iron Bridge 1779
products chiefly agricultural: sheep and cattle
population (1991) 401,600
famous people Charles Darwin, Wilfred Owen, Gordon Richards.
history Shropshire became a county in the 10th century, as part of the kingdom of Mercia in its defense against the Danes. During the Middle Ages, it was part of the Welsh Marches and saw much conflict between the lords of the Marches and the Welsh.

shroud of Turin Christian relic; see ♢Turin shroud.

Shrove Tuesday in the Christian calendar, the day before the beginning of Lent. It is also known as *Mardi Gras*.

shrub perennial woody plant that typically produces several separate stems, at or near ground level, rather than the single trunk of most trees. A shrub is usually smaller than a tree, but there is no clear distinction between large shrubs and small trees.

Shultz George P 1920– . US Republican politician, economics adviser to President ♢Reagan 1980–82, and secretary of state 1982–89. Shultz taught as a labor economist at the University of Chicago before serving in the 1968–74 ♢Nixon administration, including secretary of labor 1969–70 and secretary of the Treasury 1972–74.
As State Department secretary, he was in charge of the formulation of US foreign policy. He was pragmatic and moderate, against the opposition of Defense Secretary Caspar ♢Weinberger.

Shute Nevil. Adopted name of Nevil Shute Norway 1899–1960. English novelist. Among his books are *A Town Like Alice* 1949 and *On the Beach* 1957.

shuttle diplomacy in international relations, the efforts of an independent mediator to achieve a compromise solution between belligerent parties, traveling back and forth from one to the other.
The term came into use in the 1970s. In 1990–91 shuttle diplomacy was practiced by US secretary of state James Baker in the period leading up to, and following, the ♢Gulf War.

SI abbreviation for *Système International [d'Unités]* (French "International System [of Metric Units]"); see ♢SI units.

Siachen Glacier Himalayan glacier at an altitude of 17,000 ft/5,236 m in the Karakoram mountains of N Kashmir. Occupied by Indian forces 1984, the glacier has been the focal point of a territorial dispute between India and Pakistan since independence 1947.

sial in geochemistry and geophysics, the substance of the Earth's continental ♢crust, as distinct from the ♢sima of the ocean crust. The name is derived from *si*lica and *al*umina, its two main chemical constituents.

siamang the largest ♢gibbon *Symphalangus syndactylus*, native to Malaysia and Sumatra. Siamangs have a large throat pouch to amplify the voice, making the territorial "song" extremely loud.
They are black-haired, up to 3 ft/90 cm tall, with very long arms (a span of 5 ft/150 cm).

Sian alternative transliteration of ♢Xian, China.

Sibelius Jean (Christian) 1865–1957. Finnish composer. His works include nationalistic symphonic poems such as *En saga* 1893 and *Finlandia* 1900, a violin concerto 1904, and seven symphonies.
He studied the violin and composition at Helsinki and went on to Berlin and Vienna. In 1940 he abruptly ceased composing and spent the rest of his life as a recluse.

Siberia Asian region of Russia, extending from the Urals to the Pacific
area 4,650,000 sq mi/12,050,000 sq km
cities Novosibirsk, Omsk, Krasnoyarsk, Irkutsk
features long and extremely cold winters
products hydroelectric power from rivers Lena, Ob, and Yenisei; forestry; mineral resources, including gold, diamonds, oil, natural gas, iron, copper, nickel, cobalt
history overrun by Russia in the 17th century, Siberia was used from the 18th century to exile political and criminal prisoners. The first **Trans-Siberian Railway** 1892–1905 from St Petersburg (via Omsk, Novosibirsk, Irkutsk, and Khabarovsk) to Vladivostok, approximately 5,400 mi/8,700 km, began to open it up. A popular front was formed 1988, campaigning for ecological and political reform.

Sibyl in Roman mythology, priestess of Apollo. She offered to sell ♢Tarquinius Superbus, nine collections of prophecies, the *Sibylline Books*, but the price was too high. When she had destroyed all but three, he bought those for the identical price, and these were kept for consultation in emergency at Rome.

sic (Latin "thus," "so") sometimes found in brackets within a printed quotation to show that an apparent error is in the original.

Sichuan or *Szechwan* province of central China
area 219,634 sq mi/569,000 sq km
capital Chengdu
cities Chongqing
features surrounded by mountains, it was the headquarters of the Nationalist government 1937–45, and China's nuclear research centers are here. It is China's most populous administrative area
products rice, coal, oil, natural gas
population (1990) 107,218,000.

Sicily (Italian *Sicilia*) largest Mediterranean island, an autonomous region of Italy; area 9,920 sq mi/25,700 sq km; population (1990) 5,196,800. Its capital is Palermo, and towns include the ports of Catania, Messina, Syracuse, and Marsala. It exports Marsala wine, olives, citrus, refined oil and petrochemicals, pharmaceuticals, potash, asphalt, and marble. The autonomous region of Sicily also includes the islands of ♢Lipari, Egadi, Ustica, and ♢Pantelleria. Etna, 10,906 ft/3,323 m high, is the highest volcano in Europe; its last major eruption was in 1971.
Conquered by most of the major powers of the ancient world, Sicily flourished under the Greeks who colonized the island during the 8th–5th centuries BC. It was invaded by Carthage and became part of the Roman empire 241 BC–AD 476. In the Middle Ages it was ruled successively by the Arabs; the Normans 1059–1194, who established the **Kingdom of the Two Sicilies** (that is, Sicily and the southern part of Italy); the German emperors; and then the Angevins, until the popular revolt known as the **Sicilian Vespers** 1282. Spanish rule was invited and continued in varying forms, with a temporary displacement of the Spanish Bourbons by Napoleon, until ♢Garibaldi's invasion 1860 resulted in the two Sicilies being united with Italy 1861.

sickle harvesting tool of ancient origin characterized by a curving blade with serrated cutting edge and short wooden handle. It was widely used in the Middle East and Europe for cutting wheat, barley, and oats from about 10,000 BC to the 19th century.

sickle-cell disease hereditary chronic blood disorder common among people of black African descent; also found in the E Mediterranean, parts of the Persian Gulf, and in NE India. It is characterized by distortion and fragility of the red blood cells, which are lost too rapidly from the circulation. This often results in ♢anemia.
People with this disease have abnormal red blood cells (sickle cells), containing a defective ♢hemoglobin. The presence of sickle cells in the blood, with or without accompanying anemia, is called *sicklemia*. It confers a degree of protection against ♢malaria because fewer normal red blood cells are available to the parasites for infection.

sidereal period the orbital period of a planet around the Sun, or a moon around a planet, with reference to a background star. The sidereal period of a planet is in effect a "year." A ♢synodic period is a full circle as seen from Earth.

sidewinder rattlesnake *Crotalus cerastes* that lives in the deserts of the SW US and Mexico, and moves by throwing its coils into a sideways "jump" across the sand. It can grow up to 30 in/75 cm long.

Sidi-Bel-Abbès trading city in Algeria; population (1983) 187,000. Because of its strategic position, it was the headquarters of the French Foreign Legion until 1962.

Sidon alternate name for ♢Saida, Lebanon.

SIDS acronym for *sudden infant death syndrome*, the technical name for ♢crib death.

Siegel Don(ald) 1912–1991. US film director of thrillers, Westerns, and police dramas. Two of his low-budget features, the prison film *Riot in Cell Block 11* 1954 and the science-fiction story *Invasion of the Body Snatchers* 1956, were widely recognized for transcending their lack of resources. Siegel moved on to bigger budgets, but retained his taut, acerbic view of life in such films as the Clint Eastwood vehicles *Coogan's Bluff* 1969 and *Dirty Harry* 1971.

Siegfried or *Sigurd* legendary Germanic hero. It is uncertain whether his story has a historical basis, but it was current about

Sierra Leone
Republic of

area 27,710 sq mi/71,740 sq km
capital Freetown
cities Koidu, Bo, Kenema, Makeni
physical mountains in E; hills and forest; coastal mangrove swamps
features hot and humid climate (138 in/3,500 mm rainfall p.a.)
head of state and government military council headed by Capt Valentine Strasser from 1992
political system transitional
political parties All People's Congress (APC), moderate socialist; United Front of Political Movements (UNIFORM), center-left
exports palm kernels, cocoa, coffee, ginger, diamonds, bauxite, rutile
currency leone
population (1990 est) 4,168,000; growth rate 2.5% p.a.
life expectancy men 41, women 47 (1989)

languages English (official), local languages
media no daily newspapers; 13 weekly papers, of which 11 are independent but only one achieves sales of over 5,000 copies
religion animist 52%, Muslim 39%, Protestant 6%, Roman Catholic 2% (1980 est)
literacy men 38%, women 21% (1985 est)
GNP $965 million (1987); $320 per head (1984)
chronology
1808 Became a British colony.
1896 Hinterland declared a British protectorate.
1961 Independence achieved from Britain within the Commonwealth, with Milton Margai, leader of Sierra Leone People's Party (SLPP), as prime minister.
1964 Milton succeeded by his half brother, Albert Margai.
1967 Election results disputed by army, who set up a National Reformation Council and forced the governor-general to leave.
1968 Army revolt made Siaka Stevens, leader of the All People's Congress (APC), prime minister.
1971 New constitution adopted, making Sierra Leone a republic, with Stevens as president.
1978 APC declared only legal party. Stevens sworn in for another seven-year term.
1985 Stevens retired; succeeded by Maj Gen Joseph Momoh.
1989 Attempted coup against President Momoh foiled.
1991 Referendum endorsed multiparty politics.
1992 Military take-over; President Momoh fled. National Provisional Ruling Council (NPRC) established under Capt Valentine Strasser.

Sierra Leone country in W Africa, on the Atlantic Ocean, bounded N and E by Guinea and SE by Liberia.

government The 1978 constitution makes Sierra Leone a one-party state. The constitution also provides for a president, who is head of both state and government, and a single-chamber legislature, the House of Representatives. The house has 127 members, 105 elected for five years by universal suffrage, 12 paramount chiefs, one for each district, and 10 additional members appointed by the president. The president, who is also leader and secretary-general of the All People's Congress (APC), is endorsed by the party as the sole candidate and then popularly elected for a seven-year term. The president appoints a cabinet and two vice-presidents.

history For early history, see ⏵Africa. Freetown, the capital, was founded by Britain 1787 for homeless Africans rescued from ⏵slavery. Sierra Leone became a British colony 1808.

independence Sierra Leone achieved full independence as a constitutional monarchy within the British ⏵Commonwealth 1961, with Sir Milton Margai, leader of the Sierra Leone People's Party (SLPP), as prime minister. He died 1964 and was succeeded by his half brother, Dr Albert Margai. The 1967 general election was won by the APC, led by Dr Siaka Stevens, but the result was disputed by the army, which assumed control and forced the governor-general to leave the country.

one-party state In 1968 another army revolt brought back Stevens as prime minister, and in 1971, after the constitution had been changed to make Sierra Leone a republic, he became

president. He was reelected 1976, and the APC, having won the 1977 general election by a big margin, began to demand the creation of a one-party state. To this end, a new constitution was approved by referendum 1978, and Stevens was sworn in as president.

Stevens did not run 1985, and the APC endorsed the commander of the army, Maj Gen Joseph Momoh, as the sole candidate for the party leadership and presidency. Momoh appointed a civilian cabinet and dissociated himself from the policies of his predecessor, who had been criticized for failing to prevent corruption within his administration. The last elections for the House of Representatives were held May 1982 but annulled because of alleged irregularities. It was reported Oct 1989 that an attempted coup against the government had been put down. In Aug 1991 a move toward multiparty politics was approved by referendum. Subsequently six political parties decided to combine to form the United Front of Political Movements (UNIFORM). The parties are the National Action Party (NAP), Sierra Leone People's Party (SLPP), Democratic People's Party (DPP), National Democratic Alliance (NDA), National Democratic Party (NDP), and the Civic Development Education Movement (CDM).

In April 1992 the army took over the government and President Momoh fled to neighboring Guinea. An interim National Provisional Ruling Council (NPRC) was set up, led by Capt Valentine Strasser, that consisted of eighteen army officers and four civilians. Capt Strasser pledged to restore civilian rule and multiparty politics. *See illustration box.*

Sierra Madre chief mountain system of Mexico, consisting of three ranges, enclosing the central plateau of the country; highest point Pico de Orizaba 18,700 ft/5,700 m. The Sierra Madre del Sur ("of the south") runs along the SW Pacific coast.

Sierra Nevada mountain range of S Spain; highest point Mulhacén 11,425 ft/3,481 m.

Sierra Nevada mountain range in E California; highest point Mount Whitney 14,500 ft/4,418 m. The Sierra Nevada includes the King's Canyon, Sequoia, and Yosemite Valley national parks.

About 400 mi/640 km in length, the Sierra Nevada separates California from the rest of the continent. In 1848 settlers found gold in its western foothills, touching off the great 1849 gold rush. Silver mines have been opened on its east side.

sievert SI unit (symbol Sv) of radiation dose equivalent. It replaces the rem (1 Sv equals 100 rem). Some types of radiation do more damage than others for the same absorbed dose—for example, the same absorbed dose of alpha radiation causes 20 times as much biological damage as the same dose of beta radiation. The equivalent dose in sieverts is equal to the absorbed dose of radiation in rays multiplied by the relative biological effectiveness. Humans can absorb up to 0.25 Sv without immediate ill effects; 1 Sv may produce radiation sickness; and more than 8 Sv causes death.

Sieyes Emmanuel-Joseph 1748–1836. French cleric and constitutional theorist who led the bourgeois attack on royal and aristocratic privilege in the ⏵States General (parliament) 1788–89. Active in the early years of the French Revolution, he later retired from politics, but re-emerged as an organizer of the coup that brought Napoleon I to power in 1799.

AD 700. A version of the story is in the German ⏵Nibelungenlied/Song of the Nibelung. In the poems of the Norse Elder ⏵Edda and in the prose Völsunga Saga, Siegfried appears under the name of Sigurd.

Siegfried Line in World War I, a defensive line established 1918 by the Germans in France; in World War II, the Allies' name for the West Wall, a German defensive line established along its western frontier, from the Netherlands to Switzerland.

siemens SI unit (symbol S) of electrical conductance, the reciprocal of the ⏵impedance of an electrical circuit. One siemens equals one ampere per volt. It was formerly called the mho or reciprocal ohm.

Siemens German industrial empire created by four brothers. The eldest, **Ernst Werner von Siemens** (1812–1892), founded the original electrical firm of Siemens und Halske 1847 and made many advances in telegraphy. **William (Karl Wilhelm)** (1823–1883) moved to England; he perfected the open-hearth production of steel, pioneered the development of the electric locomotive and the laying of transoceanic cables, and improved the electric generator.

Siena city in Tuscany, Italy; population (1985) 60,670. Founded by the Etruscans, it has medieval architecture by Pisano and Donatello, including a 13th-century Gothic cathedral, and many examples of the Sienese school of painting that flourished from the 13th to the 16th centuries. The *Palio* ("banner," in reference to the prize) is a dramatic and dangerous horse race in the main square, held annually since the Middle Ages.

sight the detection of light by an ⇨eye, which can form images of the outside world.

Sigismund 1368–1437. Holy Roman emperor from 1411. He convened and presided over the council of Constance 1414–18, where he promised protection to the religious reformer ⇨Huss, but imprisoned him after his condemnation for heresy and acquiesced in his burning. King of Bohemia from 1419, he led the military campaign against the ⇨Hussites.

Sigma Octantis the star closest to the south celestial pole (see ⇨celestial sphere), in effect the southern equivalent of ⇨Polaris, although far less conspicuous. Situated just less than 1° from the south celestial pole in the constellation Octans, Sigma Octantis is 120 light-years away.

Signac Paul 1863–1935. French artist. In 1884 he joined with Georges Seurat in founding the Salon des Artistes Indépendants and developing the technique of ⇨Pointillism.

signal any sign, gesture, sound, or action that conveys information. Examples include the use of flags (⇨semaphore), light (traffic and railroad signals), radio telephony, radio telegraphy (⇨Morse code), and electricity (telecommunications and computer networks).

The International Code of Signals used by shipping was drawn up by an international committee and published 1931. The codes and abbreviations used by aircraft are dealt with by the International Civil Aviation Organization, established 1944.

Sigurd in Norse mythology, a hero who appears in both the *Nibelungenlied/Song of the Nibelung (under his German name of Siegfried) and the* ⇨*Edda.*

Sihanouk Norodom 1922– . Cambodian politician, king 1941–55, prime minister 1955–70, when his government was overthrown by a military coup led by Lon Nol. With Pol Pot's resistance front, he overthrew Lon Nol 1975 and again became prime minister 1975–76, when he was forced to resign by the ⇨Khmer Rouge. He returned from exile Nov 1991 under the auspices of a United Nations-brokered peace settlement to head the Supreme National Council, a new coalition comprising all Cambodia's warring factions, including the Khmer Rouge.

Sikhism religion professed by 14 million Indians, living mainly in the Punjab. Sikhism was founded by Nanak (1469–c. 1539). Sikhs believe in a single God who is the immortal creator of the universe and who has never been incarnate in any form, and in the equality of all human beings; Sikhism is strongly opposed to caste divisions.

Their holy book is the *Guru Granth Sahib.* Guru Gobind Singh (1666–1708) instituted the *Khanda-di-Pahul,* the baptism of the sword, and established the Khalsa ("pure"), the company of the faithful. The Khalsa wear the five Ks: *kes,* long hair; *kangha,* a comb; *kirpan,* a sword; *kachh,* short trousers; and *kara,* a steel bracelet. Sikh men take the last name "Singh" ("lion") and women "Kaur" ("princess").

beliefs Human beings can make themselves ready to find God by prayer and meditation but can achieve closeness to God only as a result of God's *nadar* (grace). Sikhs believe in ⇨reincarnation and that the ten human gurus were teachers through whom the spirit of Guru Nanak was passed on to live today in the *Guru Granth Sahib* and the Khalsa.

practice Sikhs do not have a specific holy day, but hold their main services on the day of rest of the country in which they are living. Daily prayer is important in Sikhism, and the gurdwara functions as a social as well as religious center; it contains a kitchen, the *langar,* where all, male and female, Sikh and non-Sikh, may eat together as equals. Sikh women take the same role as men in religious observances, for example, in reading from the *Guru Granth Sahib* at the gurdwara. Festivals in honor of the ten human gurus include a complete reading of the *Guru Granth Sahib*; Sikhs also celebrate at the time of some of the major Hindu festivals, but their emphasis is on aspects of Sikh belief and the example of the gurus. Sikhs avoid the use of all nonmedicinal drugs and, in particular, tobacco.

history On Nanak's death he was followed as guru by a succession of leaders who converted the Sikhs (the word means "disciple") into a military confraternity which established itself as a political power. The last of the gurus, Guru Gobind Singh (1666–1708), instituted the *Khanda-di-Pahul* and established the Khalsa. Gobind Singh was assassinated by a Muslim 1708, and since then the *Guru Granth Sahib* has taken the place of a leader.

Upon the partition of India many Sikhs migrated from W to E Punjab, and in 1966 the efforts of Sant Fateh Singh (*c.* 1911–72) led to the creation of a Sikh state within India by partition of the Punjab. However, the Akali separatist movement agitates for a completely independent Sikh state, Khalistan, and a revival of fundamentalist belief, and was headed from 1978 by Sant Jarnail Singh Bhindranwale (1947–84), killed in the siege of the Golden Temple, ⇨Amritsar. In retaliation for this, the Indian prime minister Indira Gandhi was assassinated in Oct of the same year by her Sikh bodyguards. Heavy rioting followed, in which 1,000 Sikhs were killed. Mrs Gandhi's successor, Rajiv Gandhi, reached an agreement for the election of a popular government in the Punjab and for state representatives to the Indian parliament with the moderate Sikh leader Sant Harchand Singh Longowal, who was himself killed 1985 by Sikh extremists.

Sikh Wars two wars in India between the Sikhs and the British:
The *First Sikh War 1845–46* followed an invasion of British India by Punjabi Sikhs. The Sikhs were defeated and part of their territory annexed.
The *Second Sikh War 1848–49* arose from a Sikh revolt in Multan. They were defeated, and the British annexed the Punjab.

Si-Kiang alternative transliteration of ⇨Xi Jiang, Chinese river.

Sikkim or *Denjong* state of NE India; formerly a protected state, it was absorbed by India 1975, the monarchy being abolished. China does not recognize India's sovereignty
area 2,818 sq mi/7,300 sq km
capital Gangtok
features Mount Kangchenjunga; wildlife including birds, butterflies, and orchids
products rice, grain, tea, fruit, soybeans, carpets, cigarettes, lead, zinc, copper
population (1991) 403,600
language Bhutia, Lepecha, Khaskura (Nepali)—all official
religion Mahayana Buddhism, Hinduism
history ruled by the Namgyol dynasty from the 14th century to 1975, when the last chogyal, or king, was deposed. Allied to Britain in 1886,

Sikkim became a protectorate of India 1950 and a state of India 1975.

Sikorski Wladyslaw 1881–1943. Polish general and politician; prime minister 1922–23, and 1939–43 of the Polish government in exile in London during World War II. He was killed in an airplane crash near Gibraltar in controversial circumstances.

Sikorsky Igor 1889–1972. Ukrainian-born US engineer who built the first successful helicopter. He emigrated to the US 1918, where he first constructed multi-engined flying boats. His first helicopter (the VS300) flew 1939 and a commercial version (the R3) went into production 1943.

silage fodder preserved through controlled fermentation in a ⇨silo, an airtight structure that presses green crops. It is used as a winter feed for livestock. The term also refers to stacked crops that may be preserved indefinitely.

Silenus in Greek mythology, the son of Hermes, or Pan, and companion of ⇨Dionysus. He is portrayed as a jovial old man, usually drunk.

Silesia region of Europe that has long been disputed because of its geographical position, mineral resources, and industrial potential; now in Poland and Czechoslovakia. Dispute began in the 17th century with claims on the area by both Austria and Prussia. It was seized by Prussia's Frederick the Great, which started the War of the ⇨Austrian Succession; this was finally recognized by Austria 1763, after the Seven Years' War. After World War I, it was divided in 1919 among newly formed Czechoslovakia, revived Poland, and Germany, which retained the largest part. In 1945, after World War II, all German Silesia east of the Oder-Neisse line was transferred to Polish administration; about 10 million inhabitants of German origin, both there and in Czechoslovak Silesia, were expelled.

The chief towns (with their German names) are: Wroclaw (Breslau), Katowice (Kattowitz), Zabrze (Hindenburg), Chorzow (Königshütte), Gliwice (Gleiwitz), and Bytom (Beuthen) in Poland, and Opava (Troppau) in Czechoslovakia.

silhouette profile or shadow portrait filled in with black or a dark color. A common pictorial technique in Europe in the late 18th and early 19th centuries, it was named after Etienne de Silhouette (1709–1767), a French finance minister who made paper cut-outs as a hobby.

silica silicon dioxide, SiO_2, the composition of the most common mineral group, of which the most familiar form is quartz. Other silica forms are ⇨chalcedony, chert, opal, tridymite, and cristobalite.

Chalcedony includes some semiprecious forms: gem varieties include agate, onyx, sardonyx, carnelian, and tiger's eye.

silicate one of a group of minerals containing silicon and oxygen in tetrahedral units of SiO_4, bound together in various ways to form specific structural types. Silicates are the chief rock-forming minerals. Most rocks are composed, wholly or in part, of silicates (the main exception being limestones). Common natural silicates are sands (common sand is the oxide of silicon known as silica). Glass is a manufactured complex polysilicate material in which other elements (boron in borosilicate glass) have been incorporated.

Generally, additional cations are present in the structure, especially Al^{3+}, Fe^{2+}, Mg^{2+}, Ca^{2+}, Na^+, K^+, but quartz and other polymorphs of SiO_2 are also considered to be silicates; stishorite (a high pressure form of SiO_2) is a rare exception to the usual tetrahedral coordination of silica and oxygen.

In **orthosilicates**, the oxygens are all ionically bonded to cations such as Mg^{2+} or Fe^{2+} (as olivines), and are not shared between tetrahedra. All other silicate structures involve some degree of oxygen sharing between adjacent tetrahedra. For example, beryl is a **ring silicate** based on tetrahedra linked by sharing oxygens to form a circle. Pyroxenes are single **chain silicates**, with chains of linked tetrahedra extending in one direction through the structure; amphiboles are similar but have double chains if tetrahedra. In micas, which are **sheet silicates**, the tetrahedra are joined to form continuous sheets that are stacked upon one another. **Framework silicates**, such as feldspars and quartz, are based on three-dimensional frameworks of tetrahedra in which all oxygens are shared.

silicon (Latin *silicium* "silica") brittle, nonmetallic element, symbol Si, atomic number 14, atomic weight 28.086. It is the second most abundant element (after oxygen) in the Earth's crust and occurs in amorphous and crystalline forms. In nature it is found only in combination with other elements, chiefly with oxygen in silica (silicon dioxide, SiO_2) and the silicates. These form the mineral ▷quartz, which makes up most sands, gravels, and beaches.

Pottery glazes and glassmaking are based on the use of silica sands and date from prehistory. Today the crystalline form of silicon is used as a deoxidizing and hardening agent in steel, and has become the basis of the electronics industry because of its ▷semiconductor properties, being used to make "silicon chips" for microprocessors.

The element was isolated by Swedish chemist Jöns Berzelius in 1823, having been named in 1817 by Scottish chemist Thomas Thomson by analogy with boron and carbon because of its chemical resemblance to these elements.

silicon chip ▷integrated circuit with microscopically small electrical components on a piece of silicon crystal only a few millimeters square.

One may contain more than a million components. A chip is mounted in a rectangular plastic package and linked via gold wires to metal pins, so that it can be connected to a printed circuit board for use in electronic devices, such as computers, calculators, television sets, car dashboards, and domestic appliances.

In 1991 IBM launched the world's fastest high-capacity memory computer chip. SRAM (static random-access memory) can send or receive 8 billion ▷bits of information per second. It "reads" and "writes" data to its circuits at the same time, instead of in separate processes as other chips do.

Silicon Valley nickname given to Santa Clara County, California, since the 1950s the site of many high-technology electronic firms, whose prosperity is based on the silicon chip.

silicosis chronic disease of miners and stone cutters who inhale ▷silica dust, which makes the lung tissues fibrous and less capable of aerating the blood. It is a form of ▷pneumoconiosis.

silk fine soft thread produced by the larva of the ▷silkworm moth when making its cocoon.

It is soaked, carefully unwrapped, and used in the manufacture of textiles. The introduction of synthetics originally harmed the silk industry, but rising standards of living have produced an increased demand for real silk. It is manufactured in China, India, Japan, and Thailand.

Silk Road ancient and medieval overland route of about 4,000 mi/6,400 km by which silk was brought from China to Europe in return for trade goods; it ran west via the Gobi Desert, Samarkand, and Antioch to Mediterranean ports in Greece, Italy, the Middle East, and Egypt.

silk-screen printing or **serigraphy** method of ▷printing based on stencils. It can be used to print on most surfaces, including paper, plastic, cloth, and wood. An impermeable stencil (either paper or photographic) is attached to a finely meshed silk screen that has been stretched on a wooden frame, so that the ink passes through to the area beneath only where the image is required. The design can also be painted directly on the screen with varnish. A series of screens can be used to add successive layers of color to the design.

The process was developed in the early 20th century for commercial use and adopted by many artists from the 1930s onwards.

silkworm usually the larva of the **common silkworm moth** *Bombyx mori*. After hatching from the egg and maturing on the leaves of white mulberry trees (or a synthetic substitute), it spins a protective cocoon of fine silk thread 900 ft/275 m long. To keep the thread intact, the moth is killed before emerging from the cocoon, and several threads are combined to form the commercial silk thread woven into textiles.

Other moths produce different fibers, such as **tussah** from *Antheraea mylitta*. The raising of silkworms is called **sericulture** and began in China about 2000 BC. Chromosome engineering and artificial selection practiced in Japan have led to the development of different types of silkworm for different fibers.

sillimanite aluminum silicate, Al_2SiO_5, a mineral that occurs either as white to brownish prismatic crystals or as minute white fibers. It is an indicator of high temperature conditions in metamorphic rocks formed from clay sediments. Andalusite, kyanite, and sillimanite are all polymorphs of Al_2SiO_5.

Sillitoe Alan 1928– . English novelist who wrote *Saturday Night and Sunday Morning* 1958, about a working-class man in Nottingham, Sillitoe's hometown. He also wrote *The Loneliness of the Long Distance Runner* 1959, *Life Goes On* 1985, many other novels, and poems, plays, and children's books.

Sills Beverly. Adopted name of Belle Silverman 1929– . US coloratura soprano. She was a child radio star who became one of the world's most dramatically gifted opera singers, making her debut at 17 in Philadelphia. She joined the New York City Opera 1955. She appeared at such European opera houses as La Scala, Milan 1969, and Covent Garden, London 1970. Her Metropolitan Opera debut was in 1975; in 1979 she became director of the New York City Opera, announcing her retirement in 1988. She wrote an autobiography, *Bubbles*, 1976.

silo in farming, an airtight tower in which ▷silage is made by the fermentation of freshly cut grass and other forage crops. In military

technology, a silo is an underground chamber for housing and launching a ballistic missile.

Silone Ignazio. Adopted name of Secondo Tranquilli 1900–1978. Italian novelist. His novel *Fontamara* 1933 deals with the hopes and disillusionment of a peasant village from a socialist viewpoint. His other works include *Una manciata di more/A Handful of Blackberries* 1952.

Silurian period of geological time 438–408 million years ago, the third period of the Paleozoic era. Silurian sediments are mostly marine and consist of shales and limestone. Luxuriant reefs were built by corallike organisms. The first land plants began to evolve during this period, and there were many ostracoderms (armored jawless fishes). The first jawed fishes (called acanthodians) also appeared.

Silvanus Roman woodland deity identified in later times with ▷Pan.

silver white, lustrous, extremely malleable and ductile, metallic element, symbol Ag (from Latin *argentum*), atomic number 47, atomic weight 107.868. It occurs in nature in ores and as a free metal; the chief ores are sulfides, from which the metal is extracted by smelting with lead. It is one of the best metallic conductors of both heat and electricity; its most useful compounds are the chloride and bromide, which darken on exposure to light and are the basis of photographic emulsions.

Silver is used ornamentally, for jewelry and tableware, for coinage, in electroplating, electrical contacts, and dentistry, and as a solder. It has been mined since prehistory; its name is an ancient non-Indo-European one, *silubr*, borrowed by the Germanic branch as *silber*.

silver age period of Latin literature after the death of ▷Augustus, with a florid and rhetorical writing style; authors included Seneca, Juvenal, and Suetonius.

silverberry a North American shrub *Eleagnus commutata* of the oleaster family, having twigs marked with brown and silver scales and bearing silvery yellow, fragrant flowers. The silvery berrylike fruits are edible.

silverfish wingless insect, a type of ▷bristletail.

sima in geochemistry and geophysics, the substance of the Earth's oceanic ▷crust, as distinct from the ▷sial of the continental crust. The name is derived from *si*lica and *ma*gnesia, its two main chemical constituents.

Simenon Georges 1903–1989. Belgian crime writer. Initially a pulp fiction writer, in 1931 he created Inspector Maigret of the Paris Sûreté who appeared in a series of detective novels.

Simeon Stylites, St *c.* 390–459. Syrian Christian ascetic who practiced his ideal of self-denial by living for 37 years on a platform on top of a high pillar. Feast day Jan 5.

simile (Latin "likeness") an expression in speech that in English uses the conjunctions *like* and *as* to express comparisons ("run like the devil"; "as deaf as a post"). It is sometimes confused with ▷metaphor.

Simla capital of Himachal Pradesh state, India, 7,500 ft/2,300 m above sea level, population (1980) 70,604. It was the summer administrative capital of British India 1864–1947.

Simmons Jean 1929– . English actress who worked mainly in Hollywood. She starred in the films *Black Narcissus* 1947, *Guys and Dolls* 1955, and *Spartacus* 1960.

Simon Claude 1913– . French novelist. Originally an artist, he abandoned "time structure" in such novels as *La Route de Flandres/ The Flanders Road* 1960, *Le Palace* 1962, and *Histoire* 1967. His later novels include *Les Géorgiques* 1981 and *L'Acacia* 1989. Nobel Prize 1985.

Simon Herbert 1916– . US social scientist. He researched decision making in business corporations and argued that maximum profit was seldom the chief motive. He attempted to examine the psychological factors involved in decision making and created the concept of "satisfying behavior" as motivation for some decisions. He also was deeply involved in the effort to create artificial intelligence technology capable of analyzing the factors that influence human problem-solving processes. He was awarded the Nobel Prize for Economics 1978.

Simon (Marvin) Neil 1927– . US playwright. His stage plays (which were made into films) include the wryly comic *Barefoot in the Park* 1963, *The Odd Couple* 1965, and *The Sunshine Boys* 1972, and the more serious, autobiographical trilogy *Brighton Beach Memoirs* 1983, *Biloxi Blues* 1985, and *Broadway Bound* 1986. He has also written screenplays and co-written musicals.

The musicals include *Sweet Charity* 1966, *Promises, Promises* 1968, and *They're Playing Our Song* 1978.

His play *Jake's Women* 1992 featured extensive interior monologs.

Simon Paul 1942– . US pop singer and songwriter. In a folk-rock duo with Art Garfunkel (1942–), he had such hits as "Mrs Robinson" 1968 and "Bridge Over Troubled Water" 1970. Simon's solo work includes the critically acclaimed album *Graceland* 1986, for which he drew on Cajun and African music, and *The Rhythm of the Saints* 1990.

Simone Martini. Sienese painter; see ⟁Martini, Simone.

simony in the Christian church, the buying and selling of church preferments, now usually regarded as a sin.

The term is derived from **Simon Magus** (Acts 8) who offered money to the Apostles for the power of the Holy Ghost.

simple harmonic motion (SHM) oscillatory or vibrational motion in which an object (or point) moves so that its acceleration toward a central point is proportional to its distance from it. A simple example is a pendulum, which also demonstrates another feature of SHM, that the maximum deflection is the same on each side of the central point.

A graph of the varying distance with respect to time is a sine curve, a characteristic of the oscillating current or voltage of an alternating current (AC), which is another example of SHM.

Simplon (Italian *Sempione*) Alpine pass Switzerland–Italy. The road was built by Napoleon 1800–05, and the Simplon Tunnel 1906, 12.3 mi/19.8 km, is one of Europe's longest.

Simpson Wallis Warfield, Duchess of Windsor 1896–1986. US socialite, twice divorced. She married ⟁Edward VIII 1937, who abdicated in order to marry her. He was given the title Duke of Windsor by his brother, George VI, who succeeded him.

Simpson Desert desert area in Australia, chiefly in Northern Territory; area 56,000 sq mi/145,000 sq km. It was named after a president of the South Australian Geographical Society who financed its exploration.

simultaneous equations in mathematics, one of two or more algebraic equations that contain two or more unknown quantities that may have a unique solution. For example, in the case of two linear equations with two unknown variables, such as (i) $x + 3y = 6$ and (ii) $3y - 2x = 4$, the solution will be those unique values of x and y that are valid for both equations. Linear simultaneous equations can be solved by using algebraic manipulation to eliminate one of the variables, ⟁coordinate geometry, or matrices (see ⟁matrix).

For example, by using algebra, both sides of equation (i) could be multiplied by 2, which gives $2x + 6y = 12$. This can be added to equation (ii) to get $9y = 16$, which is easily solved: $y = 16/9$. The variable x can now be found by inserting the known y value into either original equation and solving for x. Another method is by plotting the equations on a graph, because the two equations represent straight lines in co-ordinate geometry and the coordinates of their point of intersection are the values of x and y that are true for both of them. A third method of solving linear simultaneous equations involves manipulating matrices. If the equations represent either two parallel lines or the same line, then there will be no solutions or an infinity of solutions respectively.

sin transgression of the will of God or the gods, as revealed in the moral code laid down by a particular religion. In Roman Catholic theology, a distinction is made between **mortal sins**, which, if unforgiven, result in damnation, and **venial sins**, which are less serious. In Islam, the one unforgivable sin is **shirk**, denial that Allah is the only god.

In Christian belief, humanity is in a state of *original sin* and therefore in need of redemption through the crucifixion of Jesus. The sacrament of ⟁penance is seen as an earthly means of atonement for sin.

Sinai Egyptian peninsula, at the head of the Red Sea; area 25,000 sq mi/65,000 sq km. Resources include oil, natural gas, manganese, and coal; irrigation water from the river Nile is carried under the Suez Canal.

Sinai was occupied by Israel 1967–82. After the Battle of Sinai 1973, Israel began a gradual withdrawal from the area, under the disengagement agreement 1975, and the Camp David peace treaty 1979 and restored the whole of Sinai to Egyptian control by April 1982.

Sinai, Battle of battle Oct 6–24, 1973 during the Yom Kippur War between Israel and Egypt. It was one of the longest tank battles in history. Israeli troops crossed the Suez canal Oct 16, cutting off the Egyptian 3rd Army.

Sinai, Mount (Arabic *Gebel Mûsa*) mountain near the tip of the Sinai Peninsula; height 7,500 ft/2,285 m. According to the Old Testament this is where ⟁Moses received the Ten Commandments from God.

Sinan 1489–1588. Ottoman architect, chief architect from 1538 to Suleiman the Magnificent. Among the hundreds of buildings he designed are the Suleimaniye in Istanbul, a mosque complex, and the Topkapi Saray, palace of the sultan (now a museum).

Sinatra Frank (Francis Albert) 1915– . US singer and film actor. Celebrated for his phrasing and emotion, especially on love ballads, he

is particularly associated with the song "My Way." His films from 1941 include *From Here to Eternity* 1953 (Academy Award) and *Guys and Dolls* 1955.

In the 1940s he sang such songs as "Night and Day" and "You'd Be So Nice to Come Home To" with Harry James's and Tommy Dorsey's bands; many of his later recordings were made with arranger Nelson Riddle (1921–1985). After a slump in his career, he established himself as an actor. His later career includes film, television, and club appearances, and setting up a record company, Reprise, 1960.

From 1943 to 1945, he was a soloist on "Your Hit Parade," earning even wider popularity.

Sinclair Upton 1878–1968. US novelist. His concern for social reforms is reflected in *The Jungle* 1906, an important example of naturalistic writing, which exposed the horrors of the Chicago meatpacking industry and led to a change in food-processing laws; *Boston* 1928; and his Lanny Budd series 1940–53, including *Dragon's Teeth* 1942, which won a Pulitzer Prize.

He was a committed Socialist who was actively involved in politics.

Sind province of SE Pakistan, mainly in the Indus delta
area 54,393 sq mi/140,914 sq km
capital and chief seaport Karachi
population (1981) 19,029,000
language 60% Sindi; others include Urdu, Punjabi, Baluchi, Pashto
features Sukkur Barrage, which enables water from the Indus River to be used for irrigation
history annexed 1843, it became a province of British India, and part of Pakistan on independence. There is agitation for its creation as a separate state, Sindhudesh.

Sindhi member of the majority ethnic group living in the Pakistani province of Sind. The Sindhi language is spoken by about 15 million people. Since the partition of India and Pakistan 1947, large numbers of Urdu-speaking refugees have moved into the region from India, especially into the capital, Karachi.

Sinding Christian (August) 1856–1941. Norwegian composer. His works include four symphonies, piano pieces (including *Rustle of Spring*), and songs. His brothers Otto (1842–1909) and Stephan (1846–1922) were painter and sculptor, respectively.

sine in trigonometry, a function of an angle in a right triangle which is defined as the ratio of the length of the side opposite the angle to the length of the hypotenuse (the longest side).

Various properties in physics vary sinusoidally; that is, they can be represented diagrammatically by a sine wave (a graph obtained by plotting values of angles against the values of their sines). Examples include ⟁simple harmonic motion, such as the way alternating current (AC) electricity varies with time. *See diagram on p. 962.*

sinfonietta orchestral work that is of a shorter, lighter nature than a ⟁symphony. Also the name for a small-scale orchestra specializing in such works.

Singapore (Sanskrit *Singa pura* "city of the lion") country in SE Asia, off the tip of the Malay Peninsula.
government Singapore has a single-tier system of government. The constitution of 1965, amended 1991, provides for a one-chamber

Singapore
Republic of

area 240 sq mi/622 sq km
capital Singapore City
cities Jurong, Changi
physical comprises Singapore Island, low and flat, and 57 small islands
features Singapore Island is joined to the mainland by causeway across Strait of Johore; temperature range 69°–93°F/21°–34°C
head of state Wee Kim Wee from 1985
head of government Goh Chok Tong from 1990
political system liberal democracy with strict limits on dissent
political parties People's Action Party (PAP), conservative; Workers' Party (WP), socialist; Singapore Democratic Party (SDP), liberal pluralist
exports electronics, petroleum products, rubber, machinery, vehicles
currency Singapore dollar
population (1990 est) 2,703,000 (Chinese 75%, Malay 14%, Tamil 7%); growth rate 1.2% p.a.
life expectancy men 71, women 77 (1989)
languages Malay (national tongue), Chinese, Tamil, English (all official)
religion Buddhist, Taoist, Muslim, Hindu, Christian
literacy men 93%, women 79% (1985 est)
GDP $19.9 bn (1987); $7,616 per head
chronology
1819 Singapore leased to British East India Company.
1858 Placed under crown rule.
1942 Invaded and occupied by Japan.
1945 Japanese removed by British forces.
1959 Independence achieved from Britain; Lee Kuan Yew became prime minister.
1963 Joined new Federation of Malaysia.
1965 Left federation to become an independent republic.
1984 Opposition made advances in parliamentary elections.
1986 Opposition leader convicted of perjury and prohibited from running for election.
1988 Ruling conservative party elected to all but one of available assembly seats; increasingly authoritarian rule.
1990 Lee Kuan Yew resigned as prime minister; replaced by Goh Chok Tong.
1991 People's Action Party (PAP) and Goh Chok Tong reelected.

parliament, whose 81 members are elected for five-year terms by universal suffrage from single-member constituencies on a winner-take-all basis. Parliament debates and votes on legislation. Executive power is held by a prime minister and cabinet drawn from the majority party within parliament, and by a president with powers over financial matters and senior military and government appointments.

history For early history, see ◊Malaysia. Singapore was leased as a trading post 1819 from the sultan of Johore by the British East India Company at a time when it was a swampy jungle. It passed to the crown 1858 and formed part of the ◊Straits Settlements 1867–1942.

During World War II, Singapore functioned as a vital British military base in the Far East. Designed to be invulnerable to naval attack, it was invaded by land and occupied by Japan Feb 1942—Sept 1945. Singapore became a separate British crown colony 1946 and fully self-governing, with Lee Kuan Yew as prime minister, from 1959. It joined the Federation of Malaysia 1963 but seceded 1965, alleging discrimination against the federation's Chinese members. A new independent republic of Singapore, within the British ◊Commonwealth, was thus formed Sept 1965.

rapid development The new republic's internal political affairs were dominated by Prime Minister Lee Kuan Yew's People's Action Party (PAP), which gained a monopoly of all parliamentary seats in the elections between 1968 and 1980. Under Lee's stewardship, Singapore has developed rapidly as a commercial and financial entrepôt and as a center for new export industries. Today its inhabitants enjoy the highest standard of living in Asia outside Japan and Brunei.

During the early 1980s, as the pace of economic growth briefly slowed, opposition to the Lee regime began to surface, with support for the PAP falling from 76% to 63% in the Dec 1984 election and two opposition deputies winning parliamentary seats for the first time. Lee responded by taking a firmer line against dissent, with J B Jeyaretnam, the Workers' Party leader, being conveniently found guilty of perjury Nov 1986 and deprived of his parliamentary seat. Support for the PAP held steady, at 62%, in the Sept 1988 election and the opposition won only one seat. Plans were unveiled to create a new position of elected executive president. In Nov 1990 Lee resigned, handing over to his deputy, Goh Chok Tong, but remaining a senior member of the cabinet. The PAP was returned to power with 61% of the vote in the general election held, ahead of schedule, Aug 1991.

foreign policy Singapore allied itself closely with the US 1965–74. Since the mid-1970s, however, it has pursued a neutralist foreign policy and improved its relations with China. It is a member of ◊ASEAN. *See illustration box.*

Singapore City capital of Singapore, on the SE coast of the island of Singapore; population (1980) 2,413,945. It is an oil refining center and port.

Singer Isaac Bashevis 1904–1991. Polish-born US novelist and short-story writer, in the US from 1935. His works, written in Yiddish, often portray traditional Jewish life in Poland and the US, and the loneliness of old age. They include *The Family Moskat* 1950 and *Gimpel the Fool and Other Stories* 1957. Nobel Prize 1978.

Written in an often magical storytelling style, his works combine a deep psychological insight with dramatic and visual impact. Many of his novels were written for serialization in New York Yiddish newspapers. Among his works are *The Slave* 1960, *Shosha* 1978, *Old Love* 1979, *Lost in America* 1981, *The Image and Other Stories* 1985, and *The Death of Methuselah* 1988. He also wrote plays and books for children.

He fled Nazi-dominated Europe and became a US citizen 1942.

Singer Isaac Merit 1811–1875. US inventor of domestic and industrial sewing machines. Within a few years of opening his first factory 1851, he became the world's largest manufacturer (despite charges of patent infringement by Elias ◊Howe), and by the late 1860s more than 100,000 Singer sewing machines were in use in the US alone.

To make his machines available to the widest market, Singer became the first manufacturer to offer attractive installment credit terms.

Singh Vishwanath Pratap 1931– . Indian politician, prime minister 1989–90. As a member of the Congress (I) Party, he held ministerial posts under Indira Gandhi and Rajiv Gandhi, and from 1984 led an anticorruption drive. When he unearthed an arms-sales scandal 1988, he was ousted from the government and party and formed a broad-based opposition alliance, the ◊*Janata Dal*, which won the Nov 1989 election. Mounting caste and communal conflict split the Janata Dal and forced him out of office Nov 1990.

Singh, Gobind see ◊Gobind Singh, Sikh guru.

Note: BÔP₄ = 180° − BÔP₁   ⇒ sin BÔP₄ = sin BÔP₁
BÔP₃ = 180° − BÔP₂   & sin BÔP₃ = sin BÔP₂

sine *(left)* The sine of an angle; *(right)* constructing a sine wave.

single-party state another name for ▷one-party state.

single-sideband transmission radio-wave transmission using either the frequency band above the carrier wave frequency, or below, instead of both (as now).

Sing Sing name until 1901 of the village of *Ossining*, New York, with a state prison of that name from 1825 to 1969, when it was renamed the Ossining State Correctional Facility.

singularity in astrophysics, the point at the center of a ▷black hole at which it is predicted that the infinite gravitational forces will compress the infalling mass of the collapsing star to infinite density. It is a point in space-time at which the known laws of physics break down. It is also thought, in the ▷Big Bang theory of the origin of the universe, to be the point from which the expansion of the universe began.

Sinhalese member of the majority ethnic group of Sri Lanka (70% of the population). Sinhalese is the official language of Sri Lanka; it belongs to the Indo-Iranian branch of the Indo-European family, and is written in a script derived from the Indian Pali form. The Sinhalese are Buddhists. Since 1971 they have been involved in a violent struggle with the Tamil minority, who are seeking independence.

Sinkiang-Uighur alternative transliteration of ▷Xinjiang Uygur, autonomous region of NW China.

Sinn Féin ("We ourselves") Irish nationalist party founded by Arthur Griffith (1872–1922) in 1905; in 1917 Eamon ▷de Valera became its president. It is the political wing of the Irish Republican Army, and is similarly split between comparative moderates and extremists. In 1985 it gained representation in 17 out of 26 district councils in Northern Ireland.

Sino-Japanese Wars two wars waged by Japan against China 1894–95 and 1931–45 to expand to the mainland. Territory gained in the First Sino-Japanese War (Korea) and in the 1930s (Manchuria, Shanghai) was returned at the end of World War II.

First Sino-Japanese War 1894–95. Under the treaty of Shimonoseki, Japan secured the "independence" of Korea, cession of Taiwan and the nearby Pescadores Islands, and the Liaodong peninsula (for a naval base). France, Germany, and Russia pressured Japan into returning the last-named, which Russia occupied 1896 to establish Port Arthur (now Lüda); this led to the Russo-Japanese War 1904–05.

Second Sino-Japanese War 1931–45.
1931–32 The Japanese occupied Manchuria, which they formed into the puppet state of Manchukuo. They also attacked Shanghai, and moved into NE China.
1937 Chinese leaders Chiang Kai-shek and Mao Zedong allied to fight the Japanese; war was renewed as the Japanese overran NE China and seized Shanghai and Nanjing.
1938 Japanese capture of Wuhan and Guangzhou was followed by the transfer of the Chinese capital to Chongqing; a period of stalemate followed.
1941 Japanese attack on the US (see ▷ Pearl Harbor) led to the extension of lend-lease aid to China and US entry into war against Japan and its allies.
1944 A Japanese offensive threatened Chongqing.
1945 The Chinese received the Japanese surrender at Nanjing in Sept, after the Allies had concluded World War II.

Sino-Tibetan languages group of languages spoken in SE Asia. This group covers a large area, and includes Chinese and Burmese, both of which have numerous dialects. Some classifications include the Tai group of languages (including Thai and Lao) in the Sino-Tibetan family.

sinusitis painful inflammation of one of the sinuses, or air spaces, that surround the nasal passages. Most cases clear with antibiotics and nasal decongestants, but some require surgical drainage.

Sinusitis most frequently involves the maxillary sinuses, within the cheek bones, producing pain around the eyes, toothache, and a nasal discharge.

Sioux (or *Dakota*) a member of a group of North American ▷Plains Indians, now living on reservations in South Dakota and Nebraska, and among the general public. Their language belongs to the Macro-Siouan family.

When gold was discovered in their treaty territory, the US sent in troops to remove them 1876. Under chiefs Crazy Horse and Sitting Bull they defeated General George Custer at Little Bighorn, Montana; as a result, Congress abrogated the Fort Laramie Treaty of 1868 (which had given the Sioux a large area in the Black Hills of Dakota). Gold, uranium, coal, oil, and natural gas have been found there since, and the Sioux pressed for and were awarded $160 million compensation 1980.

Sioux City city in NW Iowa, on the Missouri river, near Iowa's border with Nebraska and South Dakota. Industries include food processing, fabricated metals, fertilizer, and meatpacking. It is the head of navigation for the Missouri river; population (1990) 80,500.

Sioux Falls largest city in South Dakota; population (1990) 100,800. Its industry (electrical goods and agricultural machinery) is powered by the Big Sioux River over the Sioux Falls 100 ft/30 m.

Large stockyards, slaughterhouses, and meatpacking plants are also here. Sioux Falls was founded 1856 but was abandoned during the Sioux Indian uprising of 1862. It was re-settled with the establishment of Fort Dakota here 1865.

siphon tube in the form of an inverted U with unequal arms. When it is filled with liquid and the shorter arm is placed in a tank or reservoir, liquid flows out of the longer arm provided that its exit is below the level of the surface of the liquid in the tank.

It works on the principle that the pressure at the liquid surface is atmospheric pressure, whereas at the lower end of the longer arm it is less than atmospheric pressure, causing flow to occur.

siphonogamy plant reproduction in which a pollen tube grows to enable male gametes to pass to the ovary without leaving the protection of the plant. Siphonogamous reproduction is found in all angiosperms and most gymnosperms, and has enabled these plants to reduce their dependency on wet conditions for reproduction, unlike the zoidogamous plants (see ▷zoidogamy).

siren in Greek mythology, a sea nymph who lured sailors to their deaths along rocky coasts by her singing. ▷Odysseus, in order to hear the sirens safely, tied himself to the mast of his ship and stuffed his crew's ears with wax.

Sirius or *Dog Star* or *Alpha Canis Majoris* the brightest star in the sky, 8.6 light-years from Earth in the constellation Canis Major. Sirius is a white star with a mass 2.3 times that of the Sun, a diameter 1.8 times that of the Sun, and a luminosity of 23 Suns. It is orbited every 50 years by a white dwarf, Sirius B, also known as the Pup.

sirocco hot, normally dry and dust-laden wind that blows from the deserts of N Africa across the Mediterranean into S Europe. It occurs mainly in the spring. The name "sirocco" is also applied to any hot oppressive wind.

Sirte, Gulf of gulf off the coast of Libya, on which Benghazi stands. Access to the gulf waters has been a cause of dispute between Libya and the US.

sisal strong fiber made from various species of ▷agave, such as *Agave sisalina*.

Sisley Alfred 1839–1899. French Impressionist painter whose landscapes include views of Port-Marly and the river Seine, painted during floods in 1876.

Sisley studied in an academic studio in Paris, where he met Monet and Renoir. They took part in the First Impressionist Exhibition 1874. Unlike most other Impressionists, Sisley developed his style slowly and surely, without obvious changes.

Sistine Chapel chapel in the Vatican, Rome, begun under Pope Sixtus IV in 1473 by Giovanni del Dolci, and decorated by (among others) Michelangelo. It houses the conclave that meets to select a new pope.

Built to the proportions of Solomon's temple in the Old Testament (its height one-half and its width one-third of its length), it has frescoes on the walls (emphasizing the authority and legality of the papacy) by ▷Botticelli, ▷Ghirlandaio, and, on the altar wall and ceiling, ▷Michelangelo.

Sisulu Walter 1912– . South African civil-rights activist, one of the first full-time secretary-generals of the African National Congress (ANC), in 1964, with Nelson Mandela. He was imprisoned following the 1964 Rivonia Trial for opposition to the apartheid system and released, at the age of 77, as a gesture of reform by President F W ▷de Klerk 1989. In 1991, when Mandela became ANC president, Sisulu became his deputy.

Sisyphus in Greek mythology, king of Corinth who, after his evil life, was condemned in the underworld to roll a huge stone uphill, which always fell back before he could reach the top.

Sita in Hinduism, the wife of Rama, an avatar (manifestation) of the god Vishnu; a character in the ▷*Rāmāyaṇa* epic, characterized by chastity and kindness.

sitar Indian stringed instrument. It has a pear-shaped body, long neck, and an additional gourd resonator at the opposite end. A principal solo instrument, it has seven metal strings extending over movable frets and two concealed strings that provide a continuous singing drone.

sitatunga herbivorous antelope *Tragelaphus spekei* found in several swamp regions in Central Africa. Its hooves are long and splayed to help progress on soft surfaces. It grows to about 4 ft/1.2 m high at the shoulder; the male has thick horns up to 3 ft/90 cm long.

Males are dark grayish-brown, females and young are chestnut, all with whitish markings on the rather shaggy fur.

Sitting Bull *c.* 1834–1893. North American Indian chief who agreed to ▷Sioux resettlement 1868. When the treaty was broken by the US, he led the Sioux against Lieutenant Colonel ⟩Custer at the Battle of the ⟩Little Bighorn 1876.

He was pursued by the US Army and forced to flee to Canada. He was allowed to return 1881, and he toured in the Wild West show of "Buffalo Bill" ⟩Cody. He settled on a Dakota reservation and was killed during his arrest on suspicion of involvement in Indian agitations.

situationism in ethics, the doctrine that any action may be good or bad depending on its context or situation. Situationists argue that no moral rule can apply in all situations and that what may be wrong in most cases may be right if the end is sufficiently good. In general, situationists believe moral attitudes are more important than moral rules.

One of the central books of situationism was Joseph Fletcher's *Situation Ethics* 1966. Situationism has been most influential in Christian moral theology, where its proponents have argued that an intensely thankful and loving attitude will result in good actions.

Sitwell Edith 1887–1964. English poet whose series of poems *Façade* was performed as recitations to the specially written music of William ⟩Walton from 1923.

Sitwell Sacheverell 1897–1988. English poet and art critic. His work includes *Southern Baroque Art* 1924 and *British Architects and Craftsmen* 1945; poetry; and prose miscellanies such as *Of Sacred and Profane Love* 1940 and *Splendour and Miseries* 1943.

SI units (French *Système International d'Unités*) standard system of scientific units used by scientists worldwide. Originally proposed in 1960, it replaces the m.k.s., c.g.s., and f.p.s. systems. It is based on seven basic units: the meter (m) for length, kilogram (kg) for weight, second (s) for time, ampere (A) for electrical current, kelvin (K) for temperature, mole (mol) for amount of substance, and candela (cd) for luminosity.

Siva or *Shiva* in Hinduism, the third chief god (with Brahma and Vishnu). As Mahadeva (great lord), he is the creator, symbolized by the phallic *lingam*, who restores what as Mahakala he destroys. He is often sculpted as Nataraja, performing his fruitful cosmic dance. His consort or female principle (*sakti*) is Parvati, otherwise known as Durga or Kali.

Six-Day War another name for the third ⟩Arab-Israeli War.

Six, Les group of French 20th-century composers; see ⟩Les Six.

Sixtus five popes, including:

Sixtus IV 1414–1484. Pope from 1471. He built the Sistine Chapel in the Vatican, which is named after him.

Sixtus V 1521–1590. Pope from 1585. He supported the Spanish Armada against Britain and the Catholic League against Henry IV of France.

SJ abbreviation for *Society of Jesus* (see ⟩Jesuits).

Sjælland or *Zealand* the main island of Denmark, on which Copenhagen is situated; area 2,700 sq mi/7,000 sq km; population (1970) 2,130,000. It is low-lying with an irregular coastline. The chief industry is dairy farming.

Skagerrak arm of the North Sea between the S coast of Norway and the N coast of Denmark. In May 1916 it was the scene of the Battle of ⟩Jutland.

Skåne or *Scania* area of S Sweden. It is a densely populated and fertile agricultural region, comprising the counties of Malmöhus and Kristianstad. Malmö and Hälsingborg are leading centers. It was under Danish rule until ceded to Sweden 1658.

skate any of several species of flatfish of the ray group. The common skate *Raja batis* is up to 6 ft/1.8 m long and grayish, with black specks. Its egg cases ("mermaids' purses") are often washed ashore by the tide.

skateboard single flexible board mounted on wheels and steerable by weight positioning. As a land alternative to surfing, skateboards developed in California in the 1960s and became a worldwide craze in the 1970s. Skateboarding is practiced in urban environments and has enjoyed a revival since the late 1980s.

skating self-propulsion on ice by means of bladed skates, or on other surfaces by skates with small rollers (wheels of wood, metal, or plastic). The chief competitive ice-skating events are figure skating, for singles or pairs, ice-dancing, and simple speed skating. The first world ice-skating championships were held in 1896.

Ice-skating became possible as a world sport from the opening of the first artificial ice rink in London, England, 1876. Figure skating includes both compulsory figures and freestyle combinations to music; ice-dancing has developed into a choreographed combination of ballet and popular dance movements welded to an artistic whole, as exemplified by John Curry and the team of Jayne Torvill and Christopher Dean.

The roller skate was the invention of James L Plympton, who opened the first rink in Newport, Rhode Island, 1866; events are as for ice-skating with European and world championships.

skeleton the rigid or semirigid framework that supports an animal's body, protects its internal organs, and provides anchorage points for its muscles. The skeleton may be composed of bone and cartilage (vertebrates), chitin (arthropods), calcium carbonate (mollusks and other invertebrates), or silica (many protists).

It may be internal, forming an ⟩endoskeleton, or external, forming an ⟩exoskeleton. Another type of skeleton, found in invertebrates such as earthworms, is the **hydrostatic skeleton**. This gains partial rigidity from fluid enclosed within a body cavity. Because the fluid cannot be compressed, contraction of one part of the body results in extension of another part, giving peristaltic motion.

skepticism ancient philosophical view that absolute knowledge of things is ultimately unobtainable, hence the only proper attitude is to suspend judgment. Its origins lay in the teachings of the Greek philosopher Pyrrho, who maintained that peace of mind lay in renouncing all claims to knowledge.

It was taken up in a less extreme form by the Greek ⟩Academy in the 3rd and 2nd centuries BC. Academic skeptics claimed that although truth is finally unknowable, a balance of probabilities can be used for coming to decisions. The most radical form of skepticism is known as ⟩solipsism, which maintains that the self is the only thing that can be known to exist.

skiing self-propulsion on snow by means of elongated runners (skis) for the feet, slightly bent upward at the tip. It is a popular recreational sport, as cross-country ski touring or

as downhill runs on mountain trails; events include downhill; slalom, in which a series of turns between flags have to be negotiated; cross-country racing; and ski jumping, when jumps of over 490 ft/150 m are achieved from ramps up to 295 ft/90 m high. Speed-skiing uses skis approximately one-third longer and wider than normal with which speeds of up to 125 mph/200 kph have been recorded. Recently, **snowboarding** (or monoboarding), the use of a single, very broad ski, similar to a surf board, used with the feet facing the front and placed together, has become increasingly popular.

Skiing was known as a means of transportation across snow in N Europe and Asia from about 3000 BC, but developed into a sport when innovations in ski design made it possible to maneuver more accurately, around 1896. Ski resorts then began as a winter vacation business in Europe and the US, but not until the 1970s did skiing become a recreation for any but the wealthy or those who lived in ski conditions. The Alpine World Cup was first held 1967.

skin the covering of the body of a vertebrate. In mammals, the outer layer (epidermis) is dead and protective, and its cells are constantly being rubbed away and replaced from below. The lower layer (dermis) contains blood vessels, nerves, hair roots, and sweat and sebaceous glands, and is supported by a network of fibrous and elastic cells.

Skin grafting is the repair of injured skin by placing pieces of skin, taken from elsewhere on the body, over the injured area. The field of medicine dealing with skin is called dermatology.

skink lizard of the family Scincidae, a large family of about 700 species found throughout the tropics and subtropics. The body is usually long and the legs are reduced. Some skinks are legless and rather snakelike. Many are good burrowers, or can "swim" through sand, like the *sandfish* genus *Scincus* of N Africa. Some skinks lay eggs, others bear live young.

Skinks include the **three-toed skink** *Chalcides chalcides* of S Europe and NW Africa, up to 16 in/40 cm long, of which half is tail, and the **stump-tailed skink** *Tiligua rugosus* of Australia, which stores fat in its triangular tail, looks the same at either end, and feeds on fruit as well as small animals.

Skinner B(urrhus) F(rederic) 1903–1990. US psychologist, a radical behaviorist who rejected mental concepts, seeing the organism as a "black box" where internal processes are not significant in predicting behavior. He studied operant conditioning and maintained that behavior is shaped and maintained by its consequences.

His text *The Behavior of Organisms* 1938 set forth his argument that a certain behavior may be obtained by positive reinforcement or eliminated by withholding reinforcement. He applied his conditioning technique to education—pioneering programmed learning—and to clinical work with psychotic patients. He devised a teaching machine to reinforce learning by reward.

Skopje capital and industrial city of Macedonia, Yugoslavia; population (1981) 506,547. Industries include iron, steel, chromium mining, and food processing.

It stands on the site of an ancient town destroyed by an earthquake in the 5th century and was taken in the 13th century by the Serbian king Milutin, who made it his capital. Again

crab
(carapace and
exoskeleton)

stag beetle
(exoskeleton)

gorilla

fish (perch)

skeleton *The skeleton gives the body of an animal support and protection.*

destroyed by an earthquake 1963, Skopje was rebuilt on a safer site nearby. It is an Islamic center.

skua dark-colored gull-like seabird living in Arctic and Antarctic waters. Skuas can grow up to 2 ft/60 cm long and are good fliers. They are aggressive scavengers, and seldom fish for themselves but force gulls to disgorge their catch, and also eat chicks of other birds.

The largest species is the great skua *Stercorarius skua* of the N Atlantic, 2 ft/60 cm long and dark brown on the upper parts.

skull in vertebrates, the collection of flat and irregularly shaped bones (or cartilage) that enclose the brain and the organs of sight, hearing, and smell, and provide support for the jaws. In mammals, the skull consists of 22 bones joined by sutures. The floor of the skull is pierced by

a large hole for the spinal cord and a number of smaller apertures through which other nerves and blood vessels pass.

The bones of the face include the upper jaw, enclose the sinuses, and form the framework for the nose, eyes, and roof of the mouth cavity. The lower jaw is hinged to the middle of the skull at its lower edge. The opening to the middle ear is located near the jaw hinge. The plate at the back of the head is jointed at its lower edge with the upper section of the spine. Inside, the skull has various shallow cavities into which fit different parts of the brain.

The human skull has evolved from robust to gracile in the past 5.5 milion years; it exhibits ⟡neoteny (infantilism), whereby the youthful features of ancient ⟡human species are retained in the adult skulls of modern humans—probably to make room for the evolving and enlarging brain.

skunk North American mammal of the weasel family. The common skunk *Mephitis mephitis* has a long, arched body, short legs, a bushy tail, and black fur with white streaks on the back. In self-defense, it discharges a foul-smelling fluid.

skunk cabbage either of two disagreeably smelling North American plants of the arum family Araceae: *Symplocarpus foetidus*, of the E, growing in wet soils and having large, cabbagelike leaves and a fleshy blunt spike of tiny flowers in a purple, hooded sheath; or *Lysichiton americanum* of the W, having similar appearance except that the sheath enclosing a more elongated flower spike is yellow.

skydiving sport of freefalling from an aircraft at a height of up to 3,650m/12,000 ft, performing aerobatics, and opening a parachute when 2,000 ft/600 m from the ground.

Skye largest island of the Inner Hebrides, Scotland; area 672 sq mi/1,740 sq km; population (1987) 8,100. It is separated from the mainland by the Sound of Sleat. The chief port is Portree. The economy is based on crofting, tourism, and livestock.

Skylab US space station, launched May 14, 1973, made from the adapted upper stage of a Saturn V rocket. At 82.5 tons/75 tonnes, it was the heaviest object ever put into space, and was 84 ft/25.6 m long. *Skylab* contained a workshop for carrying out experiments in weightlessness, an observatory for monitoring the Sun, and cameras for photographing the Earth's surface.

Damaged during launch, it had to be repaired by the first crew of astronauts. Three crews, each of three astronauts, occupied *Skylab* for periods of up to 84 days, at that time a record duration for human spaceflight. *Skylab* finally fell to Earth on July 11, 1979, dropping debris on Western Australia.

skylark a type of ⟡lark.

Skyros or *Skiros* Greek island, the largest of the northern ⟡Sporades; area 81 sq mi/210 sq km; population (1981) 2,750. It is known for its furniture and weaving. The English poet Rupert Brooke is buried here.

skyscraper building so tall that it appears to "scrape the sky," developed 1868 in New York, where land prices were high and the geology allowed such methods of construction. Skyscrapers are now found in cities throughout the world. The world's tallest free-standing structure is the CN (Canadian National) Tower, Toronto, 1,821 ft/555 m.

meters

600
500
400
300
200
100
0

| Nat West tower, London | Eiffel tower, Paris | John Hancock building Chicago | Empire State building New York | World Trade Center, New York | Sears tower Chicago | Canadian National tower, Toronto |

skyscraper *The CN Tower in Toronto is the world's tallest free-standing structure at 1,821 ft/555 m.*

In Manhattan, New York, are the Empire State Building (1931), 102 stories and 1,250 ft/381 m high, and the twin towers of the World Trade Center 1,361 ft/415 m, but these are surpassed by the Sears Tower (1973) 1,454 ft/443 m in Chicago. Chicago was the home of the first skyscraper, the Home Insurance Building (1885), which was built ten stories high with an iron and steel frame. A rigid steel frame is the key to skyscraper construction, taking all the building loads. The walls simply "hang" from the frame (curtain walling), and they can thus be made from relatively flimsy materials such as glass and aluminum.

Skyscrapers were made possible by the invention of elevators in the 1950s; the introduction of metal-frame construction in Chicago in the 1880s allowed for advances, and skyscrapers are now found in cities throughout the world.

slag in chemistry, the molten mass of impurities that is produced in the smelting or refining of metals.

The slag produced in the manufacture of iron in a ◊blast furnace floats on the surface above the molten iron. It contains mostly silicates, phosphates, and sulfates of calcium. When cooled, the solid is broken up and used as a core material in the foundations of roads and buildings.

slaked lime $Ca(OH)_2$ (technical name **calcium hydroxide**) substance produced by adding water to quicklime (calcium oxide, CaO). Much heat is given out and the solid crumbles as it absorbs water. A solution of slaked lime is called limewater.

slang extremely informal language usage that often serves to promote a feeling of group membership. It is not usually accepted in formal speech or writing and includes expressions that may be impolite or taboo in conventional terms.

Forms of slang develop among particular groups, for example soldiers, teenagers, and criminals, and are often extended into more general use because social conditions make them fashionable or people have grown accustomed to using them. Some types of slang are highly transient; others may last across generations and gain currency in the standard language. Because slang is often vivid, suggestive, and linked with subjects such as defecation, urination, sex, blasphemy, drink, and drugs, many people find it offensive. It is, however, pervasive in its influence.

slash and burn simple agricultural method whereby natural vegetation is cut and burned, and the clearing then farmed for a few years until the soil loses its fertility, whereupon farmers move on and leave the area to regrow. Although this is possible with a small, widely dispersed population, it becomes unsustainable with more people and is now a form of ◊deforestation.

slate fine-grained, usually gray metamorphic rock that splits readily into thin slabs along its ◊cleavage plane. It is the metamorphic equivalent of ◊shale.

Slate is highly resistant to atmospheric conditions and can be used for writing on with chalk (actually gypsum). Quarrying slate takes such skill and time that it is now seldom used except for roof and sill material except in restoring historic buildings.

Slater Samuel 1768–1835. British-born US industrialist, whose business acumen as a mill owner and banker made him a central figure in the New England textile industry.

Slater was trained in machinery manufacture and worked as a mechanical supervisor in a textile mill. Immigrating to the US 1789 with detailed knowledge of British industrial technology, he was quickly hired by several American machine manufacturing firms. In 1791 he supervised the construction of a mill, based on the design of the English model, in Providence, Rhode Island, and eventually established his own manufacturing company 1798.

Slaughterhouse Cases two related US Supreme Court cases (*The Butchers' Benevolent Association of New Orleans* v *The Crescent City Livestock Landing and Slaughter Co; Esteban* v *Louisiana*) 1873 brought against the Louisiana legislature for its law granting one slaughterhouse exclusive rights to operate in New Orleans. The suits claimed that this monopoly was in violation of the privileges and immunities clause of the 14th Amendment because it prevented citizens from pursuing the professions of their choice. The Court upheld the Louisiana monopoly statute by 5 to 4, implementing a narrow interpretation of the 14th Amendment that left the protection of most civil rights to state governments.

Slav member of an Indo-European people in central and E Europe, the Balkans, and parts of N Asia, speaking closely related Slavonic languages. The ancestors of the Slavs are believed to have included the ◊Sarmatians and Scythians (see ◊Scythia). Moving west from Central Asia, they settled in E and SE Europe during the 2nd and 3rd millennia BC.

The present Slavonic nations emerged around the 5th and 6th centuries AD. By the 7th century they were the predominant population of E and SE Europe. During the 9th century they adopted Christianity,

slavery the enforced servitude of one person (a slave) to another or one group to another. A slave has no personal rights and is the property of another person through birth, purchase, or capture. Slavery goes back to prehistoric times but declined in Europe after the fall of the Roman Empire. During the imperialism of Spain, Portugal, and Britain in the 16th–18th centuries and in the American South in the 17th–19th centuries, slavery became a mainstay of an agricultural factory economy, with millions of Africans sold to work on plantations in North and South America. Millions more died in the process, but the profits from this trade were enormous. Slavery was abolished in the British Empire 1833 and in the US at the end of the Civil War 1863–65, but continues illegally in some countries.

Chattel slavery involves outright ownership of the slave by a master, but there are forms of partial slavery where an individual is tied to the land, or to another person, by legal obligations, as in ◊serfdom.

As a social and economic institution, slavery originated in the times when humans adopted sedentary farming methods of subsistence rather than more mobile forms of hunting and gathering. It was known in Shang dynasty China (c. 1600–1100 BC) and ancient Egypt, and is recorded in the Babylonian code of Hammurabi (c. 1750 BC), the Sanskrit Laws of Manu (c. 600 BC), and the Bible. Slave labor became commonplace in ancient Greece and Rome, when it was used to cultivate large estates and to meet the demand for personal servants in the towns. Slaves were created through the capture of enemies, through birth to slave parents, through sale into slavery by free parents, and as a means of punishment.

After the fall of the Roman Empire in the 5th century, slavery persisted in Arab lands and in central Europe, where many Slavs were captured and taken as slaves to Germany (hence the derivation of the word). Historically, slave-owning societies included the Ottoman Empire, the Crimean Khanate, the Inca Empire (Peru), and the Sokoto Caliphate, the Hausa (Nigeria). Central Asians such as the Mongols, Kazakhs, and various Turkic groups also kept slaves, as did some Native American peoples (such as Comanche and Creek). In Spain and Portugal, where the reconquest of the peninsula from the Moors in the 15th century created an acute shortage of labor, captured Muslims were enslaved. They were soon followed by slaves from Africa, imported by the Portuguese prince Henry the Navigator after 1444. Slaves were used for a wide range of tasks, and a regular trade in slaves was established between the Guinea Coast and the slave markets of the Iberian peninsula.

Slavery became of major economic importance after the 16th century with the European conquest of South and Central America. Needing a labor force but finding the indigenous inhabitants unwilling or unable to cooperate, the Spanish and Portuguese conquerors used ever-increasing numbers of slaves drawn from Africa. These slaves had a great impact on the sugar and coffee plantations. A lucrative triangular trade was established with alcohol, firearms, and textiles being shipped from Europe to be traded for slaves in Africa. The slaves would then be shipped to South or Central America where they would be traded for staples such as molasses and later raw cotton. In 1619 the first black slaves landed in an English colony in North America (Virginia).

The vast profits became a major element in the British economy and the West Indian trade in general. It has been estimated that the British slave trade alone shipped 2 million slaves from Africa to the West Indies between 1680 and 1786. The total slave trade to the Americas in the single year of 1790 may have exceeded 70,000. According to another estimate, during the nearly 400 years of the slave trade, a total of 15 million slaves were delivered to buyers and some 40 million Africans lost their lives in the notorious "middle passage."

Anti-slavery movements and changes in the political and economic structure of Europe helped to bring about the abolition of slavery in most of Europe during the later 18th and early 19th century, followed by abolition in overseas territories somewhat later.

Only in the Southern states of the US did slavery persist as a major, if not essential, component of the economy—providing the labor force for the cotton and other plantations. While the Northern states abolished slavery in the 1787–1804 period, the Southern states insisted on protecting the institution. Slavery became an issue in the economic struggles between Southern plantation owners and Northern industrialists in the first half of the 19th century, a struggle that culminated in the American Civil War.

Despite the common perception to the contrary, the war was not fought primarily on the slavery issue. Abraham Lincoln, however, saw the political advantages of promising freedom for Southern slaves, and the Emancipation Proclamation was enacted in 1863. This was reinforced after the war by the 13th, 14th, and 15th amendments to the US constitution (1865, 1868, and 1870), which abolished slavery altogether and guaranteed citizenship and civil rights to former slaves. Apart from the moral issues, there has also been a good deal of debate on the economic efficiency of slavery as a system of production in the US. It has been argued that plantation owners might have been better off employing labor, although the effect of emancipating vast numbers of slaves could, and did, have enormous political and social repercussions in the Reconstruction period following the Civil War.

Although outlawed in most countries, various forms of slavery continue to exist—as evidenced by the steps taken by international organizations such as the League of Nations between the world wars and the United Nations since 1945 to curb such practices.

Slavonic or **Slavic language** branch of the Indo-European family spoken in central and E Europe, the Balkans, and parts of N Asia. The family comprises the southern group

Slavery: The Triangular Trade

slavery

(Serbo-Croatian, Slovenian, and Macedonian in Yugoslavia, and Bulgarian in Bulgaria); the western group (Czech and Slovak in Czechoslovakia, Sorbian in Germany, and Polish and its related dialects); and the eastern group (Russian, Ukrainian, and Byelorussian in the former USSR).

There is such a high degree of uniformity among the Slavic languages that scholars speak of a "dialect continuum" in which the users of one variety understand fairly well much of what is said in other varieties. Some Slavic languages, like Polish, are written in the Roman alphabet while others, like Russian, use the Cyrillic alphabet.

Slavophile intellectual and political group in 19th-century Russia that promoted the idea of an Eastern orientation for the empire in opposition to those who wanted the country to adopt Western methods and ideas of development.

SLBM abbreviation for **submarine-launched ballistic missile**; see ◊nuclear warfare.

sleep state of reduced awareness and activity that occurs at regular intervals in most mammals and birds, though there is considerable variation in the amount of time spent sleeping. Sleep differs from hibernation in that it occurs daily rather than seasonally, and involves less drastic reductions in metabolism. The function of sleep is unclear. People deprived of sleep become irritable, uncoordinated, forgetful, hallucinatory, and even psychotic.

In humans, sleep is linked with hormone levels and specific brain electrical activity, including delta waves, quite different from the brain's waking activity. REM (rapid eye movement) phases, associated with dreams, occur at regular intervals during sleep, when the eyes move rapidly beneath closed lids.

Species that do not have distinct periods of sleep (most invertebrates and fishes, for example) have short intervals of reduced activity throughout a given 24-hour period.

Extensive periods of sleep may have developed to make animals inconspicuous at times when they would be vulnerable to predators.

sleeping pill any pill or capsule that contains a drug (especially one of the ◊barbiturates) that induces sleep; in small doses, such drugs may relieve anxiety.

sleeping sickness or **trypanosomiasis** infectious disease of tropical Africa. Early symptoms include fever, headache, and chills, followed by ◊anemia and joint pains. Later, the disease attacks the central nervous system, causing drowsiness, lethargy, and, if left untreated, death. Sleeping sickness is caused by either of two ◊trypanosomes, *Trypanosoma gambiense* or *T. rhodiense*. Control is by eradication of the tsetse fly, which transmits the disease to humans.

A viral infection of the brain, ◊encephalitis, is also sometimes called sleeping sickness; sleeping sickness in cattle is called nagana; see also ◊trypanosomiasis.

sleet precipitation consisting of a mixture of water and ice.

Technically, it refers to precipitation in the form of ice pellets smaller than 0.2 in/5 mm. The icy coating when rain freezes on trees and streets is also called sleet.

Slidell John 1793–1871. American public official and diplomat. He was US senator from Louisiana until the outbreak of the Civil War, when he resigned and joined the Confederacy. He was captured and imprisoned by the US navy, and went to Europe on his release.

Born in New York and educated at Columbia University, Slidell moved to New Orleans 1819 and was admitted to the bar. He served as district attorney 1829–33 and US congressman 1843–45. He was named minister to Mexico by President Polk 1845–48 and later served in the US Senate 1853–61. Resigning at the outbreak of the Civil War, he was named Confederate representative to France and was taken prisoner on the high seas by the US Navy. Released 1862, Slidell remained in exile in France after the war but died on the British Isle of Wight.

slide rule mathematical instrument with pairs of logarithmic sliding scales, used for rapid calculations, including multiplication, division, and the extraction of square roots. It has been largely superseded by the electronic calculator.

It was invented 1622 by the English mathematician William Oughtred. A later version was devised by the French army officer Amédée Mannheim (1831–1906).

Sligo county in the province of Connacht, Republic of Ireland, situated on the Atlantic coast of NW Ireland; area 695 sq mi/1,800 sq km; population (1991) 54,700. The county town is Sligo; there is livestock and dairy farming.

Slim William Joseph, 1st Viscount 1891–1970. British field marshal in World War II. He commanded the 1st Burma Corps 1942–45, stemming the Japanese invasion of India, and then forcing them out of Burma (now Myanmar). He was governor-general of Australia 1953–60.

slime mold an extraordinary organism that shows some features of ◊fungus and some of ◊protozoa. Slime molds are not closely related to any other group, although they are often classed, for convenience, with the fungi.

Cellular slime molds go through a phase of living as single cells, looking like amebas, and feed by engulfing the bacteria found in rotting wood, dung, or damp soil. When a food supply is exhausted, up to 100,000 of these amebas form into a colony resembling a single sluglike animal and migrate to a fresh source of bacteria. The colony then takes on the aspect of a fungus, and forms long-stalked fruiting bodies which release spores. These germinate to release amebas, which repeat the life cycle.

Plasmodial slime molds have a more complex life cycle involving sexual reproduction. They form a slimy mass of protoplasm with no internal cell walls, which slowly spreads over the bark or branches of trees.

Sloan John 1871–1951. US painter. He was encouraged to paint by Robert ◊Henri, with whom he later organized "The Eight," a group of realists who were against academic standards. He moved to New York 1904 and helped to organize the avant-garde Armory Show 1913. He was president of the Society of Independent Artists 1918–44 and taught at the Art Students League 1916–37. His paintings of working-class urban life pioneered the field of American realism.

Born in Lock Haven, Pennsylvania, he started as a newspaper illustrator for several Philadelphia newspapers.

sloth South American mammal, about 2.5 ft/70 cm long, of the order Edentata. Sloths are grayish brown and have small rounded heads, rudimentary tails, and prolonged forelimbs.

Slovenia
Republic of

area 7,817 sq mi/20,251 sq km
capital Ljubljana
cities Maribor, Kranj, Celji; chief port: Koper
physical mountainous; rivers: Sava, Drava
head of state Milan Kucan from 1990
head of overnment Janez Drnovsek from 1992
political system emergent democracy
political parties Democratic Opposition of Slovenia (DEMOS), six-party, right-of-center coalition; Party of Democratic Reform, reform-communist
products grain, sugarbeet, livestock, timber, cotton and woolen textiles, steel, vehicles
currency tolar
population (1990) 2,000,000 (91% Slovene, 3% Croat, 2% Serb)
languages Slovene, resembling Serbo-Croat,

Each foot has long curved claws adapted to clinging upside down from trees. They are vegetarian.

Species include the *three-toed sloth* or *ai Bradypus tridactylus*, and the *two-toed sloth Choloepus didactylus* of northern South America.

Slovakia one of the two republics forming the Federative Republic of ◊Czechoslovakia. It was settled in the 5th–6th centuries by Slavs; occupied by the Magyars in the 10th century; part of the kingdom of Hungary until 1918, when it became a province of Czechoslovakia. Slovakia was a puppet state under German domination 1939–45, and was abolished as an administrative division in 1949. Its capital and chief town is Bratislava.

Slovene member of the Slavic people of Slovenia and parts of the Austrian Alpine provinces of Styria and Carinthia. There are 1.5–2 million speakers of Slovene, a language belonging to the South Slavonic branch of the Indo-European family. The Slovenes use the Roman alphabet and the majority belong to the Roman Catholic Church.

Slovenia or *Slovenija* country in S central Europe, bounded N by Austria, E by Hungary, W by Italy, and S by Croatia.

government There is a three-chamber parliament and an executive president directly elected for a four-year term. Election contests are based on a majority system, and there is a second-round "runoff" race if no candidate secures a majority of the vote in the first round.

history Settled by the Slovenes in the 6th century, the region came under Frankish rule 788, and then under Hungarian domination 907–

written in Roman characters
religion Roman Catholic
chronology
1918 United with Serbia and Croatia.
1929 The kingdom of Serbs, Croats, and Slovenes took the name of Yugoslavia.
1945 Became a constituent republic of Yugoslav Socialist Federal Republic.
mid-1980s The Slovenian Communist Party liberalized itself and agreed to free elections. The Yugoslav counterintelligence (KOV) began repression.
1989 Jan: Social Democratic Alliance of Slovenia launched as first political organization independent of Communist Party. Sept: constitution changed to allow secession from federation.
1990 Feb: Slovene League of Communists, renamed as the Party of Democratic Reform, severed its links with the Yugoslav League of Communists. April: nationalist DEMOS coalition secured victory in first multiparty parliamentary elections; Milan Kucan became president. July: sovereignty declared. Dec: independence overwhelmingly approved in referendum.
1991 June: independence declared; 100 killed after federal army intervened; cease-fire brokered by European Community (EC). July: cease-fire agreed between federal troops and nationalists. Oct: withdrawal of Yugoslav National Army (JNA) completed.
1992 Jan: European Community recognized Slovenia's independence. April: Janez Drnovsek appointed prime minister designate; independence recognized by US. May: admitted into United Nations (UN) and Conference on Security and Cooperation in Europe (CSCE).

55. It was controlled by the Hapsburgs from 1335. It formed part of the Austrian crownlands of Carniola, Styria, and Carinthia prior to its incorporation 1918 into the kingdom of the Serbs, Croats, and Slovenes, which became part of Yugoslavia 1928. Unlike neighboring Croatia, there were few Slovenian demands for autonomy during the 1930s. During World War II the region was occupied by Germany and Italy; it was made a constituent republic within the Yugoslav Socialist Federal Republic in Nov 1945. It was the most economically advanced and politically liberal republic within the federation, helping to subsidize the poorer republics. *nationalist unrest* From the 1980s there was economic decline and increasing nationalist unrest. The leadership of the ruling Slovene League of Communists (LCS) responded by pressing for greater autonomy within the federation to enable the republic to pursue a strategy of economic liberalization and political pluralism. In 1989 opposition parties were legalized and a free, multiparty election was held in April 1990. Despite renaming themselves the Party of Democratic Reform (PDR) and adopting a social democratic program, the communists were convincingly defeated by the six-party Democratic Opposition of Slovenia (DEMOS), a nationalist, center-right coalition, which campaigned for independence within a year. However, the PDR's reformist leader was popularly elected state president, renouncing his party membership once installed in office. The new government promoted the formation of a new loose Yugoslav confederation, but this was resisted by Serbia.

secession from Yugoslavia With overwhelming support given to a referendum on independence held in Dec 1990, plans were made for secession. An independent army, the Slovenian Territorial Defense Force, was established in the spring of 1991. Following the announcement on May 8, 1991 that secession of both Slovenia and Croatia from the federation would take place on June 26, 1991, more than 100 were killed in clashes around newly established Slovene border posts. The European Community (EC) brokered a cease-fire, based upon a three-month suspension of Slovenia's declaration of independence and the withdrawal of the Yugoslav National Army (JNA) from the republic. This was successfully implemented as the focus of the Serb-dominated JNA's activity switched to Croatia, with its much larger Serb minority. On Dec 23, 1991 Slovenia adopted a new constitution. Slovenia, whose independence was formally recognized by the European Community (EC) and the US Jan 1992, joined the UN in May 1992. In April, Yugoslavia's formation of a new federated republic excluded Slovenia, thereby acknowledging its independence. *See illustration box.*

slow-worm harmless species of lizard *Anguis fragilis*, once common in Europe, now a protected species in Britain. Superficially resembling a snake, it is distinguished by its small mouth and movable eyelids. It is about 1 ft/30 cm long, and eats worms and slugs.

SLR abbreviation for *single-lens reflex*, a type of ⟂camera in which the image can be seen through the lens before a picture is taken.

A small mirror directs light entering the lens to the viewfinder. When a picture is taken the mirror moves rapidly aside to allow the light to reach the film. The SLR allows different lenses, such as close-up or zoom lenses, to be used because the photographer can see exactly what is being focused on.

slug air-breathing gastropod related to the snails, but with absent or much reduced shell.

slug obsolete unit of mass, equal to 32.17 lb/14.6 kg. It is the mass that will have an acceleration of one foot per second when under a force of one pound weight.

small arms one of the two main divisions of firearms: guns that can be carried by hand. The first small arms were portable handguns in use in the late 14th century, supported on the ground and ignited by hand. Today's small arms range from breech-loading single-shot rifles and shotguns to sophisticated automatic and semiautomatic weapons. In 1980, there were 11,522 deaths in the US caused by hand-held guns; in the UK, there were 8. From 1988 guns accounted for more deaths among teenage US males than all other causes put together.

The matchlock, which evolved during the 15th century, used a match of tow and saltpeter gripped by an S-shaped lever, which was rocked toward the touch hole with one finger, enabling the gun to be held, aimed, and fired in much the same way as today. Front and back sights, followed by a curved stock that could be held against the shoulder (in the hackbut or Hookgun), gave increased precision. The difficulty of keeping a match alight in wet weather was overcome by the introduction of the wheel lock, in about 1515, in which a shower of sparks was produced by a spring-drawn steel wheel struck by iron pyrites. This cumbersome and expensive mechanism evolved into the simpler flintlock in about 1625, operated by flint striking steel and in general use for 200 years

until a dramatic advance, the "percussion cap," invented in 1810 by a sport-loving Scottish cleric, Alexander Forsyth (1769–1843), removed the need for external igniters. From then on, weapons were fired by a small explosive detonator placed behind or within the base of the bullet, struck by a built-in hammer.

The principles of rifling, breech-loading, and the repeater, although known since the 16th century, were not successfully exploited until the 19th century. It was known that imparting a spin made the bullet's flight truer, but the difficulty of making the bullet bite the grooves had until then prevented the use of rifling. The Baker rifle, issued to the British Rifle Brigade in 1800, was loaded from the front of the barrel (muzzle) and had a mallet for hammering the bullets into the grooves.

The first breechloader was von Dreyse's "needle gun," issued to the Prussian army in 1842, in which the detonator was incorporated with the cartridge. By 1870 breech-loading was in general use, being quicker, and sweeping the barrel out after each firing. An early rifle with bolt action was the Lee-Metford 1888, followed by the Lee-Enfield, both having a magazine beneath the breech, containing a number of cartridges. A modified model is still used by the British army. US developments favored the repeater (such as the Winchester) in which the fired case was extracted and ejected, the hammer cocked, and a new charge inserted into the chamber, all by one reciprocation of a finger lever. In the semiautomatic, part of the explosion energy performs the same operations: the Garand, long used by the US army, is of this type. Completely automatic weapons were adopted during World War II. Improvements since then have concentrated on making weapons lighter and faster-firing, as with the M-16, extensively used by US troops in the Vietnam War.

small claims court in the US, a court that deals with small civil claims, using a simple procedure, often without attorney intervention.

smallpox acute, highly contagious viral disease, marked by aches, fever, vomiting, and skin eruptions leaving pitted scars. Widespread vaccination programs have almost eradicated this often fatal disease.

It was endemic in Europe until the development of vaccination by Edward ⟂Jenner about 1800, and remained so in Asia, where a virulent form of the disease (variola major) entailed a fatality rate of 30% until the World Health Organization campaign from 1967, which resulted in its virtual eradication by 1980. The virus now survives chiefly in storage in various research institutes.

smart card plastic card with an embedded microprocessor and memory. It can store, for example, personal data, identification, and bank-account details, to enable it to be used as a credit or debit card. The card can be loaded with credits, which are then spent electronically, and reloaded as needed. Possible other uses range from hotel door "keys" to passports.

The smart card was invented by French journalist Juan Moreno in 1974. By the year 2000 it will be possible to make cards with as much computing power as the leading personal computers of 1990.

smell sense that responds to chemical molecules in the air. It works by having receptors for particular chemical groups, into which the airborne chemicals must fit to trigger a message to the brain.

A sense of smell is used to detect food and to communicate with other animals (see ⟂pheromone and ⟂scent gland). Aquatic animals can sense chemicals in water, but whether this sense should be described as "smell" or "taste" is debatable. See also ⟂nose.

smelling salts or *sal volatile* a mixture of ammonium carbonate, bicarbonate, and carbamate together with other strong-smelling substances, formerly used as a restorative for dizziness or fainting.

smelt small fish, usually marine, although some species are freshwater. They occur in Europe and North America. The most common European smelt is the sparling *Osmerus eperlanus.*

Smersh formerly the main administration of counterintelligence in the USSR, established 1942; a subsection of the ⟂KGB.

Smetana Bedřich 1824–1884. Czech composer whose music has a distinct national character, as in, for example, the operas *The Bartered Bride* 1866 and *Dalibor* 1868, and the symphonic suite *My Country* 1875–80. He conducted the National Theater of Prague 1866–74.

Smith Adam 1723–1790. Scottish economist, often regarded as the founder of political economy. His *The Wealth of Nations* 1776 defined national wealth in terms of labor. The cause of wealth is explained by the division of labor—dividing a production process into several repetitive operations, each carried out by different workers. Smith advocated the free working of individual enterprise, and the necessity of "free trade."

He was born in Kirkcaldy, and was professor of moral philosophy at Glasgow 1752–63. He published *Theory of Moral Sentiments* 1759.

Smith Al (Alfred Emanuel) 1873–1944. US political leader who served four terms as governor of New York but was unsuccessful as a candidate for the presidency.

Born in New York, Smith left school in his teens and became involved in local Democratic politics. After serving in the New York state assembly 1905–15 he became New York County sheriff 1915–17. In 1918 he was elected governor of New York. He was defeated for reelection 1920 but was victorious in 1922, 1924, and 1926. In 1928 he became the first Roman Catholic to receive a presidential nomination. In his lively, yet unsuccessful, campaign against Herbert Hoover he was called "The Happy Warrior."

Smith Bessie 1894–1937. US jazz and blues singer, born in Chattanooga, Tennessee. Known as the "Empress of the Blues," she established herself in the 1920s after she was discovered by Columbia Records. She madee over 150 recordings accompanied by such greats as Louis Armstrong and Benny Goodman.

Her popularity waned in the Depression and she died after an auto accident.

Smith David 1906–1965. US sculptor and painter, whose work made a lasting impact on sculpture after World War II. He trained as a steel welder in an automobile factory. His pieces are large openwork metal abstracts.

Smith turned first to painting and then, about 1930, to sculpture. Using welded steel, he created abstract structures influenced by the metal sculptures of Picasso. In the 1940s and 1950s he developed a more linear style.

The *Cubi* series of totemlike abstracts, some of them painted, was designed to be placed in the open air.

Smith Ian (Douglas) 1919– . Rhodesian politician. He was a founder of the Rhodesian Front 1962 and prime minister 1964–79. In 1965 he made a unilateral declaration of Rhodesia's independence and, despite United Nations sanctions, maintained his regime with tenacity. In 1979 he was succeeded as prime minister by Bishop Abel Muzorewa, when the country was renamed Zimbabwe. He was suspended from the Zimbabwe parliament April 1987 and resigned in May as head of the white opposition party.

Smith John 1580–1631. English colonist. After an adventurous early life he took part in the colonization of Virginia, acting as president of the North American colony 1608–09. He explored New England in 1614, which he named, and published pamphlets on America and an autobiography. His trade with the Indians may have kept the colonists alive in the early years.

During an expedition among the American Indians he was captured, and his life is said to have been saved by the intervention of the chief's daughter ▷Pocahontas.

Smith Joseph 1805–1844. US founder of the ▷Mormon religious sect.

Born in Vermont, he received his first religious call in 1820, and in 1827 claimed to have been granted the revelation of the *Book of Mormon* (an ancient American prophet), inscribed on gold plates and concealed a thousand years before in a hill near Palmyra, New York. He founded the Church of Jesus Christ of Latter-day Saints in Fayette, New York, 1830. The headquarters of the church was moved to Kirkland, Ohio, 1831; to Missouri 1838; and to Nauvoo, Illinois, 1840. Smith began the construction of a Mormon temple at Nauvoo, organized a private army to defend the sect from its enemies, and declared his candidacy for president. Hostility to Smith intensified when rumors that he had taken several wives began to circulate; Smith publicly opposed polygamy and acknowledged only one wife. He was jailed after some of his followers destroyed the printing press of a newspaper that had attacked him, and a mob stormed the jail and killed him. Historians still differ on whether Smith practiced polygamy; some have concluded that he secretly married more than 20 women. Some of his followers who accompanied Brigham ▷Young to Salt Lake City openly espoused polygamy; those who organized a separate branch in Missouri, headed by Smith's son, strongly opposed it. Smith's chief works are *Doctrines and Covenants* and *Pearl of Great Price*.

Smith Maggie (Margaret Natalie) 1934– . English actress, notable for her commanding presence, fluting voice, and throwaway lines. Her films include *The Prime of Miss Jean Brodie* 1969 (Academy Award), *California Suite* 1978, *A Private Function* 1984, and *A Room with a View* 1986.

Smith William 1769–1839. British geologist, the founder of stratigraphy. Working as a canal engineer, he observed while supervising excavations that different beds of rock could be identified by their fossils, and so established the basis of ▷stratigraphy. He also produced the first geological maps of England and Wales.

Smithson James 1765–1829. British chemist and mineralogist. The *Smithsonian Institution* in Washington, DC, was established in

1846 as "an establishment for the increase and diffusion of knowledge," following his bequest of $100,000 for this purpose.

Branches of the institution include research laboratories, collections, and exhibits in a wide range of fields in the arts and sciences. It sponsors scientific expeditions and publishes the results.

smoker or **hydrothermal vent** crack in the ocean floor, associated with an ▷ocean ridge, through which hot, mineral-rich ground water erupts into the sea, forming thick clouds of suspended material. The clouds may be dark or light, depending on the mineral content, thus producing "white smokers" or "black smokers."

Sea water percolating through the sediments and crust is heated in the active area beneath and dissolves minerals from the hot rocks. As the charged water is returned to the ocean, the sudden cooling causes these minerals to precipitate from solution, so forming the suspension. The chemical-rich water around a smoker gives rise to colonies of bacteria, and these form the basis of food chains that can be sustained without sunlight and photosynthesis. Strange animals that live in such regions include huge tube worms 6 ft/2 m long, giant clams, and species of crab, anemone, and shrimp found nowhere else.

smoking inhaling the fumes from burning substances, generally ▷tobacco in the form of ▷cigarettes. The practice can be habit-forming and is dangerous to health, since carbon monoxide and other toxic materials result from the combustion process. A direct link between lung cancer and tobacco smoking was established 1950; the habit is also linked to respiratory and coronary heart diseases. In the West, smoking is now forbidden in many public places because even *passive smoking*—breathing in fumes from other people's cigarettes—can be harmful.

Some illegal drugs, such as ▷crack and ▷opium, are also smoked.

Smolensk city on the river Dnieper, W Russia; population (1987) 338,000. Industries include textiles, distilling, and flour milling. It was founded 882 as the chief town of a Slavic tribe and was captured by Napoleon 1812. German troops took the city 1941, and it was liberated by Soviet forces 1943. Nearby is ▷Katyn Forest.

smuggling the illegal import or export of prohibited goods or the evasion of customs duties on dutiable goods. Smuggling has a long tradition in most border and coastal regions; goods smuggled include tobacco, spirits, diamonds, gold, and illegal drugs.

Restrictions on imports, originally a means of preventing debasement of coinage (for example, in 14th-century England), were later used for raising revenue, mainly on luxury goods, and led to a flourishing period of smuggling during the 18th century in such goods as wine, brandy, tea, tobacco, and lace.

The smuggling of illegal substances such as cocaine and marijuana into the US from Mexico and various South American countries is a serious problem today.

smut in botany, any parasitic ▷fungus of the order Ustilaginales, which infects flowering plants, particularly cereal grasses.

Smuts Jan Christian 1870–1950. South African politician and soldier; prime minister 1919–24 and 1939–48. He supported the Allies in both

world wars and was a member of the British imperial war cabinet 1917–18.

During the Second ▷South African War (1899–1902) Smuts commanded the Boer forces in his native Cape Colony. He subsequently worked for reconciliation between the Boers and the British. On the establishment of the Union of South Africa, he became minister of the interior 1910–12 and defense minister 1910–20. During World War I he commanded the South African forces in E Africa 1916–17. He was prime minister 1919–24 and minister of justice 1933–39; on the outbreak of World War II he succeeded General Hertzog as premier. He was made a field marshal in 1941.

Smyrna former name of the Turkish port of ▷Izmir.

snail air-breathing gastropod mollusk with a spiral shell. There are thousands of species, on land and in water. The typical snails of the genus *Helix* have two species in Europe. The common garden snail *H. aspersa* is very destructive to plants.

The Roman snail *Helix pomatia* is "corralled" for the gourmet food market. Overcollection has depleted the population. The French eat as much as 11 lb/5 kg of snails per capita each year.

snake reptile of the suborder Serpentes of the order Squamata, which also includes lizards. Snakes are characterized by an elongated limbless body, possibly evolved because of subterranean ancestors. One of the striking internal modifications is the absence or greatly reduced size of the left lung. The skin is covered in scales, which are markedly wider underneath where they form. There are 3,000 species found in the tropical and temperate zones, but none in New Zealand, Ireland, Iceland, and near the poles. Only three species are found in Britain: the adder, smooth snake, and grass snake.

In all except a few species, scales are an essential aid to locomotion. A snake is helpless on glass where scales can effect no "grip" on the surface; progression may be undulant, "concertina," or creeping, or a combination of these. Detailed vision is limited at a distance, though movement is immediately seen; hearing is restricted to ground vibrations (sound waves are not perceived); the sense of touch is acute; besides the sense of smell through the nasal passages, the flickering tongue picks up airborne particles which are then passed to special organs in the mouth for investigation; and some (rattlesnakes) have a cavity between eye and nostril which is sensitive to infrared rays (useful in locating warm-blooded prey in the dark). All snakes are carnivorous, and often camouflaged for better concealment in hunting as well as for their own protection. Some are oviparous and others ovoviviparous, that is, the eggs are retained in the oviducts until development is complete; in both cases the young are immediately self-sufficient.

The majority of snakes belong to the Colubridae, chiefly harmless, such as the common grass snake of Europe, but including the deadly African boomslang *Dispholidus typus*.

The venomous families include the Elapidae, comprising the true ▷cobras, the New World coral snakes, and the Australian taipan, copperhead, and death adder; the Viperidae (see ▷viper); and the Hydrophiidae, aquatic seasnakes. Antisera against snakebite (made from the venom) are expensive to prepare and store, and specific to one snake species, so that experiments have been made with more widely valid treatment, for example, trypsin, a powerful protein-degrading enzyme, effective against the cobra/mamba group.

Among the more primitive snakes are the Boidae, which still show links with the lizards and include the boa constrictor, anaconda, and python. These kill by constriction but their victims are usually comparatively small animals.

Snake tributary of the Columbia River, in NW US; length 1,038 mi/1,670 km. It flows 40 mi/65 km through Hell's Canyon, one of the deepest gorges in the world.

Extensive irrigation in S Idaho makes possible the farmland that grows Idaho potatoes and other crops.

snapdragon perennial herbaceous plant of the genus *Antirrhinum*, family Scrophulariaceae, with spikes of brightly colored two-lipped flowers.

Snell Willebrord 1581–1626. Dutch mathematician and physicist who devised the basic law of refraction, known as *Snell's law*, in 1621. This states that the ratio between the sine of the angle of incidence and the sine of the angle of refraction is constant.

snipe European marsh bird of the family Scolopacidae, order Charadriiformes; species include common snipe *Gallinago gallinago* and the rare great snipe *G. media*, of which the males hold spring gatherings to show their prowess. It is closely related to the ◊woodcock.

snooker indoor game derived from ◊billiards (via ◊pool). It is played with 22 balls: 15 red, one each of yellow, green, brown, blue, pink, and black, and one white cueball. Red balls are worth one point when sunk, while the colored balls have ascending values from two points for the yellow to seven points for the black. The world professional championship was first held in 1927. The world amateur championship was first held 1963.

The game, invented 1875 by British officers serving in India, did not gain popularity among the British until the 1920s. Since then it has grown to become one of the biggest television sports in the UK, and it is gaining in popularity across Europe, the Far East, and the US.

snoring loud noise during sleep made by vibration of the soft palate (the rear part of the roof of the mouth), caused by streams of air entering the nose and mouth at the same time. It is most common when the nose is partially blocked.

It is common in men, but women and children also snore.

snow precipitation in the form of soft, white, crystalline flakes caused by the condensation in air of excess water vapor below freezing point. Light reflecting in the crystals, which have a basic hexagonal (six-sided) geometry, gives snow its white appearance.

Snow C(harles) P(ercy), Baron Snow 1905–1980. English novelist and physicist. He held government scientific posts in World War II and 1964–66. His sequence of novels *Strangers and Brothers* 1940–64 portrayed English life from 1920 onwards. His *Two Cultures* (Cambridge Rede lecture 1959) discussed the absence of communication between literary and scientific intellectuals in the West, and added the phrase "the two cultures" to the language.

Snowdon Anthony Armstrong-Jones, Earl of Snowdon 1930– . English portrait photographer. In 1960 he married Princess Margaret; they were divorced 1978.

Snowdon (Welsh *Y Wyddfa*) highest mountain in Wales, 3,560 ft/1,085 m above sea level. It consists of a cluster of five peaks. At the foot of Snowdon are the Llanberis, Aberglaslyn, and Rhyd-ddu passes. A rack railroad ascends to the summit from Llanberis. *Snowdonia*, the surrounding mountain range, was made a national park 1951. It covers 845 sq mi/2,188 sq km of mountain, lakes, and forest land.

snowdrop bulbous plant *Galanthus nivalis*, family Amaryllidaceae, native to Europe, with white, bell-shaped flowers, tinged with green, in early spring.

snow leopard a type of ◊leopard.

"Snow White" traditional European fairy tale. Snow White is a beautiful princess persecuted by her jealous stepmother. Taking refuge in a remote cottage inhabited by seven dwarfs, she is tricked by the disguised queen into eating a poisoned apple. She is woken from apparent death by a prince.

Snowy Mountains range in the Australian Alps, chiefly in New South Wales, near which the Snowy River rises; both river and mountains are known for a hydroelectric and irrigation system.

snuff finely powdered ◊tobacco for sniffing up the nostrils (or sometimes chewed or rubbed on the gums) as a stimulant or sedative. Snuff taking was common in 17th-century England and the Netherlands, and spread in the 18th century to other parts of Europe, but was largely superseded by cigarette smoking.

soap mixture of the sodium salts of various ◊fatty acids: palmitic, stearic, and oleic acid. It is made by the action of sodium hydroxide (caustic soda) or potassium hydroxide (caustic potash) on fats of animal or vegetable origin. Soap makes grease and dirt disperse in water in a similar manner to a ◊detergent.

Soap was mentioned by Galen in the 2nd century for washing the body, although the Romans seem to have washed with a mixture of sand and oil. Soap was manufactured in Britain from the 14th century, but better-quality soap was imported from Castile or Venice. The Soapmakers' Company, London, was incorporated 1638. Soap was taxed in England from the time of Cromwell in the 17th century to 1853.

soap opera television or radio melodrama. It originated in the US as a series of daytime programs sponsored by soap-powder and detergent manufacturers.

The popularity of the genre has led to soap operas being shown at peak viewing times in many languages and countries.

soapstone compact, massive form of impure ◊talc.

Soares Mario 1924– . Portuguese socialist politician, president from 1986. Exiled 1970, he returned to Portugal 1974, and, as leader of the Portuguese Socialist Party, was prime minister 1976–78. He resigned as party leader 1980, but in 1986 he was elected Portugal's first socialist president.

Sobieski John. Alternative name for ◊John III, king of Poland.

soccer or *football* ball game originating in the UK, popular in Europe, the Middle East, and North and South America. It is played between two teams each of 11 players, on a field 100–130

yd/90–120 m long and 50–100 yd/45–90 m wide, with a spherical, inflated (traditionally leather) ball, circumference 27 in/0.69 m. The object of the game is to send the ball with the feet or head into the opponents' goal, an area 8 yd/7.31 m wide and 8 ft/2.44 m high.

A team is broadly divided into defense (the goalkeeper and defenders), midfield (whose players collect the ball from the defense and distribute it to the attackers), and attack (forward or strikers). The number of players assigned to each role varies according to the tactics adopted, but a typical formation is 4–4–2 (four defenders, excluding goalkeeper, four midfield, and two forward).

The field has a halfway line marked with a center circle, two penalty areas, and two goal areas. Corner kicks are taken from the nearest 1 yd/1 m area at each corner of the field, when the ball goes behind the goal-line off a defender. A ball kicked over the sidelines is thrown in by one of the opposing side. Only the goalkeeper is allowed to touch the ball with the hands and only then in an assigned penalty area. For major offenses committed within the defenders' penalty area, a penalty kick may be awarded by the referee to the attacking team. This is taken 12 yd/11 m from the goal center, with only the goalkeeper inside the area and standing still on the goal-line.

The game is started from the center spot. At the adult level, it is played for two periods of 45 minutes each, the teams changing ends at half-time; for younger players the games are shorter. The game is controlled by a referee; two linesmen bring rule infringements to the referee's attention.

Played in England from the 14th century, soccer developed in the 19th century and the first set of rules were drawn up at Cambridge University 1848. The modern game is played in the UK according to the rules laid down by the Football Association, founded 1863. There are slight differences in the rules of the sport's world governing body, Fédération Internationale de Football Association (FIFA, 1904), whose rules are followed in the US. FIFA organizes the competitions for the World Cup, held every four years from 1930.

World Cup

recent winners
1974 West Germany
1978 Argentina
1982 Italy
1986 Argentina
1990 West Germany

Social and Liberal Democrats official name for the British political party formed 1988 from the former Liberal Party and most of the Social Democratic Party. The common name for the party is the *Liberal Democrats*.

social behavior in zoology, behavior concerned with altering the behavior of other individuals of the same species. Social behavior allows animals to live harmoniously in groups by establishing hierarchies of dominance to discourage disabling fighting. It may be aggressive or submissive (for example, cowering and other signals of appeasement), or designed to establish bonds (such as social grooming or preening).

The social behavior of mammals and birds is generally more complex than that of lower organisms, and involves relationships with individually recognized animals. Thus, courtship displays allow individuals to choose appropriate mates and form the bonds necessary for successful reproduction. In the social systems of bees, wasps, ants, and termites, an individual's status and relationships with others are largely determined by its biological form, as a member of a caste of workers, soldiers, or reproductives; see ⟡eusociality.

social contract the idea that government authority derives originally from an agreement between ruler and ruled in which the former agrees to provide order in return for obedience from the latter. It has been used to support both absolutism (⟡Hobbes) and democracy (⟡Locke, ⟡Rousseau).

social credit theory, put forward by Canadian C H Douglas (1879–1952), that economic crises are caused by bank control of money, which leads to shortage of purchasing power. His remedy was payment of a "social dividend." There have been provincial social-credit governments in Canada, but the central government has always vetoed the plan.

social democracy political ideology or belief in the gradual evolution of a democratic ⟡socialism within existing political structures. The earliest was the German Sozialdemokratische Partei (SPD), today one of the two main German parties, created in 1875 from August Bebel's earlier German Social Democratic Workers' Party, founded 1869. Parties along the lines of the German model were founded in the last two decades of the 19th century in a number of countries, including Austria, Belgium, the Netherlands, Hungary, Poland, and Russia. The British Labour Party is in the social democratic tradition.

Social Democratic Party (SDP) British centrist political party 1981–90, formed by members of Parliament who resigned from the Labour Party. The 1983 and 1987 general elections were fought in alliance with the Liberal Party as the *Liberal/SDP Alliance*. A merger of the two parties was voted for by the SDP 1987, and the new party became the ⟡Social and Liberal Democrats, leaving a rump SDP that folded 1990.

social history branch of history that documents the living and working conditions of people rather than affairs of state. In recent years television programs, books, and museums have helped to give social history a wide appeal.

History became a serious branch of study in the 18th century, but was confined to ancient civilizations and to recent political and religious history. Only in the early 20th century did historians begin to study how people lived and worked in the past.

socialism movement aiming to establish a classless society by substituting public for private ownership of the means of production, distribution, and exchange. The term has been used to describe positions as widely apart as anarchism and social democracy. Socialist ideas appeared in Classical times; in early Christianity; among later Christian sects such as the ⟡Anabaptists and ⟡Diggers; and, in the 18th and early 19th centuries, were put forward as systematic political aims by Jean-Jacques Rousseau, Claude Saint-Simon, François Fourier, and Robert Owen, among others. See also Karl ⟡Marx and Friedrich ⟡Engels.

The late 19th and early 20th centuries saw a division between those who reacted against Marxism leading to social-democratic parties and those who emphasized the original revolutionary significance of Marx's teachings.

Weakened by these divisions, the second ⟡International (founded in 1889) collapsed in 1914, right-wing socialists in all countries supporting participation in World War I while the left opposed it. The Russian Revolution took socialism from the sphere of theory to that of practice, and was followed in 1919 by the foundation of the Third International, which completed the division between right and left. This lack of unity, in spite of the temporary successes of the popular fronts in France and Spain in 1936–38, facilitated the rise of fascism and Nazism.

After World War II socialist and communist parties tended to formal union in Eastern Europe, although the rigid communist control that ensued was later modified in some respects in, for example, Poland, Romania, and Yugoslavia. Subsequent tendencies to broaden communism were suppressed in Hungary (1956) and Czechoslovakia (1968). In 1989, however, revolutionary change throughout Eastern Europe ended this rigid control; this was followed in 1991 by the disbanding of the Soviet Communist Party and the ensuing disintegration of the Soviet Union. In Western Europe a communist takeover of the Portuguese revolution failed 1975–76, and elsewhere, as in France under François Mitterrand, attempts at socialist-communist cooperation petered out. Most countries in W Europe have a strong socialist party; for example, in Germany the Social Democratic Party and in Britain the ⟡Labour Party.

Socialist Realism artistic doctrine set up by the USSR during the 1930s setting out the optimistic, socialist terms in which society should be portrayed in works of art—in music and the visual arts as well as writing.

The policy was used as a form of censorship of artists whose work, it was felt, did not follow the approved Stalinist party line, or was too "Modern." The policy was relaxed after Stalin's death, but remained somewhat in force despite the changes engendered by the Soviet era of *glasnost* at the end of the 1980s. Artists whose work was censured in this way included the composer Shostakovich and the writers Solzhenitsyn and Sholokhov.

socialization process, beginning in childhood, by which a person becomes a member of a society, learning its norms, customs, laws, and ways of living. The main agents of socialization are the family, school, peer groups, work, religion, and the mass media. The main methods of socialization are direct instruction, rewards and punishment, imitation, experimentation, role play, and interaction.

Some agents of socialization, such as the family and the peer group, may conflict with each other, offering alternative goals, values, and styles of behavior. Socialization is of particular interest to psychologists, anthropologists, and sociologists, but there are diverse opinions about its methods and effects.

social mobility movement of groups and individuals up and down the social scale in a classed society. The extent or range of social mobility varies in different societies. Individual social mobility may occur through education, marriage, talent, and so on; group mobility usually occurs through change in the occupational structure caused by new technological or economic developments.

The caste system of India and the feudalism of medieval Europe are cited as examples of closed societies, where little social mobility

was possible; the class system of Western industrial societies is considered relatively open and flexible.

Social Realism in painting, art that realistically depicts subjects of social concern, such as poverty and deprivation. The French artist Courbet provides a 19th-century example of the genre. Subsequently, in the US, the Ashcan school and Ben Shahn are among those described as Social Realists.

social science the group of academic disciplines that investigate how and why people behave the way they do, as individuals and in groups. The term originated with the 19th-century French thinker Auguste ⟡Comte. The academic social sciences are generally listed as sociology, economics, anthropology, political science, and psychology.

Western thought about society has been influenced by the ideas and insights of such great theorists as Plato, Aristotle, Machiavelli, Rousseau, Hobbes, and Locke. The study of society, however, can be traced to the great intellectual period of the 18th century called the Enlightenment, and to the industrial and political revolutions of the 18th and 19th centuries, to the moral philosophy of ⟡positivism. Comte attempted to establish the study of society as a scientific discipline, capable of precision and prediction in the same way as natural science, but it overlaps extensively with such subject areas as history, geography, law, philosophy, and even biology. Although some thinkers—such as Marx—have attempted to synthesize the study of society within one theory, none has yet achieved what Einstein did for physics or Charles Darwin for biology. A current debate is whether the study of people can or should be a science.

social security state provision of financial aid to alleviate poverty and to provide income to retired persons and disabled workers. The term "social security" was first applied officially in the US, in the Social Security Act 1935. The term usually refers specifically to old-age pensions, which have a contributory element, unlike "welfare." The federal government is responsible for social security (medicare, retirement, survivors', and disability insurance); unemployment insurance is covered by a joint federal-state system for industrial workers, few in agriculture are covered; and welfare benefits are the responsibility of individual states, with some federal assistance. The program is an important source of income for the growing population of retired Americans. Politically sacrosanct, the benefits pose a growing burden for the working-age population.

The concept of such payments developed in the late 19th century in Europe—for example, compulsory social insurance in Germany from 1883. In the US the program was developed as part of the effort to cope with the effects of the ⟡Depression from 1929, when large numbers of Americans were without income.

society the organization of people into communities or groups. Social science, in particular sociology, is the study of human behavior in a social context. Various aspects of society are discussed under ⟡class, ⟡community, ⟡culture, ⟡kinship, ⟡norms, ⟡role, ⟡socialization, and ⟡status.

Society Islands (French *Archipel de la Société*) archipelago in ⟡French Polynesia, divided into Windward Islands and Leeward Islands; area 650 sq mi/1,685 sq km; population (1983) 142,000. The administrative headquarters is Papeete on ⟡Tahiti. The

Windward Islands (French *Îles du Vent*) have an area of 460 sq mi/1,200 sq km and a population (1983) of 123,000. They comprise Tahiti, Moorea (area 51 sq mi/132 sq km; population 7,000), Maio (or Tubuai Manu; 3.5 sq mi/9 sq km; population 200), and the smaller Tetiaroa and Mehetia. The *Leeward Islands* (French *Îles sous le Vent*) have an area of 156 sq mi/404 sq km and a population of 19,000. They comprise the volcanic islands of Raiatea (including the main town of Uturoa), Huahine, Bora-Bora, Maupiti, Tahaa, and four small atolls. Claimed by France 1768, the group became a French protectorate 1843 and a colony 1880.

sociology the systematic study of society, in particular of social order and social change, social conflict, and social problems. It studies institutions such as the family, law, and the church, as well as concepts such as norm, role, and culture. Sociology attempts to study people in their social environment according to certain underlying moral, philosophical, and political codes of behavior.

Sociology today reflects a variety of perspectives and traditions. Its focus tends to be on contemporary industrial society, sometimes comparing it with preindustrial society, and occasionally drawing on such related disciplines as history, geography, politics, economics, psychology, and anthropology. Its concerns range from theories of social order and change to detailed analyses of small groups, individuals, and the routines of daily life. The relation between theory and method is one part of the current debate about whether sociology is or should be a science, and whether it can or should be free of ideology.

Socotra Yemeni island in the Indian Ocean; capital Tamridah; area 1,351 sq mi/ 3,500 sq km. Under British protection from 1886, it became part of South Yemen 1967.

Socrates *c.* 469–399 BC. Athenian philosopher. He wrote nothing but was immortalized in the dialogues of his pupil Plato. In his desire to combat the skepticism of the ◇sophists, Socrates asserted the possibility of genuine knowledge. In ethics, he put forward the view that the good person never knowingly does wrong. True knowledge emerges through dialogue and systematic questioning and an abandoning of uncritical claims to knowledge.

The effect of Socrates' teaching was disruptive since he opposed tyranny. Accused in 399 on charges of impiety and corruption of youth, he was condemned by the Athenian authorities to die by drinking hemlock.

Socratic method method of teaching used by Socrates, in which he aimed to guide pupils to clear thinking on ethics and politics by asking questions and then exposing their inconsistencies in cross-examination. This method was effective against the ◇sophists.

soda ash former name for sodium carbonate (Na_2CO_3).

soda lime powdery mixture of calcium hydroxide and sodium hydroxide or potassium hydroxide, used in medicine and as a drying agent.

Soddy Frederick 1877–1956. English physical chemist who pioneered research into atomic disintegration and coined the term ◇isotope. He was awarded a Nobel Prize 1921 for investigating the origin and nature of isotopes.

sodium soft, waxlike, silver-white, metallic element, symbol Na (from Latin *natrium*), atomic number 11, atomic weight 22.898. It is one of the ◇alkali metals and has a very low density, being light enough to float on water. It is the sixth most abundant element (the fourth most abundant metal) in the Earth's crust. Sodium is highly reactive, oxidizing rapidly when exposed to air and reacting violently with water. Its most familiar compound is sodium chloride (common salt), which occurs naturally in the oceans and in salt deposits left by dried-up ancient seas.

Other sodium compounds are of great industrial importance and thousands of tons are manufactured annually. Sodium functions with potassium on the cellular level to make possible neuronal transmission, and so it is an essential nutrient for animals. It was named in 1807 by Humphry Davy, because he isolated it from caustic soda (sodium hydroxide).

sodium chloride or *common salt* or *table salt* NaCl white, crystalline compound found widely in nature. It is a typical ionic solid with a high melting point (1,474°F/801°C); it is soluble in water, insoluble in organic solvents, and is a strong electrolyte when molten or in aqueous solution. Found in concentrated deposits, it is widely used in the food industry as a flavoring and preservative, and in the chemical industry in the manufacture of sodium, chlorine, and sodium carbonate.

sodium hydroxide or *caustic soda* NaOH the commonest ◇alkali. The solid and the solution are corrosive. It is used to neutralize acids, in the manufacture of soap and in oven cleaners, for example. Sodium hydroxide is prepared industrially from sodium chloride by the electrolysis of concentrated brine.

Sodom and Gomorrah two ancient cities in the Dead Sea area of the Middle East, recorded in the Old Testament (Genesis) as being destroyed by fire and brimstone for their wickedness.

Sofia or *Sofiya* capital of Bulgaria since 1878; population (1990) 1,220,900. Industries include textiles, rubber, machinery, and electrical equipment. It lies at the foot of the Vitosha Mountains.

softball bat-and-ball game similar to ◇baseball. Among the differences between the two sports are playing-field dimensions and equipment specifications; softball diamonds are smaller overall. The distance between bases is 60 ft/18.3 m; pitchers stand 46 ft/14 m from home plate; and the softball itself (which is about as hard as a baseball) is approximately 12 in/30.5 cm in circumference (a baseball is about 9 in/23 cm). In proportional terms of weight to size, a soft ball is lighter than a baseball and therefore, when pitched or batted, generally will not attain the speed and distance of a well-hit baseball. Softball bats can be no longer than 34 in/86.4 cm.

A regulation softball game is seven innings (for baseball it is nine), but actual play (rules, actions, and objectives) is so alike in both games that the technical differences cannot disguise the fact that softball is the legitimate offspring of baseball. The one element of play that is significantly distinct, however, is the execution of the pitch; a legally delivered softball must be thrown underhand. Pitching defines the two styles of softball play: fast pitch and slow pitch. Of the nearly 175,000 teams registered with the US Amateur Softball Association, more than 80% play slow-pitch softball.

The slow-pitch game customarily is played with 10-player teams, the tenth being a fourth outfielder or a "short fielder" (covering the area between infield and outfield). The arc of a slow-pitched ball must be not less than 3 ft/ 0.9 m, and the ball must cross home plate in a downward motion. Both bunting and base stealing are illegal in slow-pitch games. Some slow-pitch teams use a ball that is as large as 16 in/40.6 cm in circumference. Bunting and stealing are allowed in fast-pitch games, but it is never legal in softball for a runner to get a "jump" on a steal by leaving the base before the ball is pitched.

soft currency vulnerable currency that tends to fall in value on foreign-exchange markets because of political or economic uncertainty. Governments are unwilling to hold soft currencies in their foreign-exchange reserves, preferring strong or hard currencies, which are easily convertible.

software in computing, a collection of programs and procedures for making a computer perform a specific task, as opposed to ◇hardware, the physical components of a computer system. Software is created by programmers and is either distributed on a suitable medium, such as the ◇floppy disk, or built into the computer in the form of firmware. Examples of software include ◇operating systems, ◇compilers, and application programs, such as payrolls. No computer can function without some form of software.

softwood any coniferous tree, or the wood from it. In general this type of wood is softer and easier to work, but in some cases less durable, than wood from flowering (or angiosperm) trees.

soil loose covering of broken rocky material and decaying organic matter overlying the bedrock of the Earth's surface. Various types of soil develop under different conditions: deep soils form in warm wet climates and in valleys; shallow soils form in cool dry areas and on slopes. *Pedology*, the study of soil, is significant because of the relative importance of different soil types to agriculture.

The organic content of soil is widely variable, ranging from zero in some desert soils to almost 100% in peats.

soil creep gradual movement of soil down a slope. As each soil particle is dislodged by a raindrop it moves slightly further downhill. This eventually results in a mass downward movement of soil on the slope.

Evidence of soil creep includes the formation of terracettes (steplike ridges along the hillside), leaning walls and telegraph poles, and trees that grow in a curve to counteract progressive leaning.

soil erosion the wearing away and redistribution of the Earth's soil layer. It is caused by the action of water, wind, and ice, and also by improper methods of ◇agriculture. If unchecked, soil erosion results in the formation of deserts. It has been estimated that 20% of the world's cultivated topsoil was lost between 1950 and 1990.

If the rate of erosion exceeds the rate of soil formation (from rock), then the land will decline and eventually become infertile. The removal of forests or other vegetation often leads to serious soil erosion, because plant roots bind soil, and without them the soil is free to wash or blow away, as in the American ◇dust bowl. The effect is worse on hillsides, and there has been devastating loss of soil where forests have been cleared from mountainsides, as in

Madagascar. Improved agricultural practices are needed to combat soil erosion. Windbreaks, such as hedges or strips planted with coarse grass, are valuable. Organic farming can reduce soil erosion by as much as 75%.

soil mechanics branch of engineering that studies the nature and properties of the soil. Soil is investigated during construction work to ensure that it has the mechanical properties necessary to support the foundations of dams, bridges, and roads.

Soissons market town in Picardie region, N France; population (1982) 32,000. The chief industry is metallurgy. In 486 the Frankish king ⟡Clovis defeated the Gallo-Romans here, ending their rule in France.

Sokoto state in Nigeria, established 1976; capital Sokoto; area 39,565 sq mi/102,500 sq km; population (1984) 7,609,000. It was a ⟡Fula sultanate from the 16th century until occupied by the British 1903.

solan goose another name for the ⟡gannet.

solar energy energy derived from the Sun's radiation. The amount of energy falling on just 0.3861 sq mi/1 sq km is about 4,000 megawatts, enough to heat and light a small town. In one second the Sun gives off 13 million times more energy than all the electricity used in the US in one year. *Solar heaters* have industrial or domestic uses. They usually consist of a black (heat-absorbing) panel containing pipes through which air or water, heated by the Sun, is circulated, either by thermal ⟡convection or by a pump.

Solar energy may also be harnessed indirectly using *solar cells* (photovoltaic cells) made of panels of ⟡semiconductor material (usually silicon), which generate electricity when illuminated by sunlight. Although it is difficult to generate a high output from solar energy compared to sources such as nuclear or fossil fuels, it is a major nonpolluting and renewable energy source used as far north as Scandinavia as well as in the SW US and in Mediterranean countries.

A solar furnace, such as that built in 1970 at Odeillo in the French Pyrénées, has thousands of mirrors to focus the Sun's rays; it produces uncontaminated intensive heat for industrial and scientific or experimental purposes. Advanced schemes have been proposed that would use giant solar reflectors in space to harness ⟡solar energy and beam it down to Earth in the form of ⟡microwaves. Despite their low running costs, their high installation cost and low power output have meant that solar cells have found few applications outside space probes and artificial satellites. Solar heating is, however, widely used for domestic purposes in many parts of the world.

solar pond natural or artificial "pond," such as the Dead Sea, in which salt becomes more soluble in the Sun's heat. Water at the bottom becomes saltier and hotter, and is insulated by the less salty water layer at the top. Temperatures at the bottom reach about 212°F/100°C and can be used to generate electricity.

solar radiation radiation given off by the Sun, consisting mainly of visible light, ⟡ultraviolet radiation, and ⟡infrared radiation, although the whole spectrum of ⟡electromagnetic waves is present, from radio waves to X-rays. High-energy charged particles such as electrons are also emitted, especially from solar ⟡flares. When these reach the Earth, they cause magnetic storms (disruptions of the Earth's magnetic field), which interfere with radio communications.

Solar System the Sun and all the bodies orbiting it: the nine planets (Mercury, Venus, Earth, Mars, Jupiter, Saturn, Uranus, Neptune, and Pluto), their moons, the asteroids, and the comets. It is thought to have formed from a cloud of gas and dust in space about 4.6 billion years ago. The Sun contains 99% of the mass of the Solar System. The edge of the Solar System is not clearly defined, marked only by the limit of the Sun's gravitational influence, which extends about 1.5 light-years, almost halfway to the nearest star, Alpha Centauri, 4.3 light-years away.

solar wind stream of atomic particles, mostly protons and electrons, from the Sun's corona, flowing outwards at speeds of between 200 mps/300 kps and 600 mps/1,000 kps.

The fastest streams come from "holes" in the Sun's corona that lie over areas where no surface activity occurs. The solar wind pushes the gas of comets' tails away from the Sun, and "gusts" in the solar wind cause geomagnetic disturbances and auroras on Earth.

solder any of various alloys used when melted for joining metals such as copper, its common alloys (brass and bronze), and tin-plated steel, as used for making food cans.

Soft solders (usually alloys of tin and lead, sometimes with added antimony) melt at low temperatures (about 392°F/200°C), and are widely used in the electrical industry for joining copper wires. Hard (or brazing) solders, such as silver solder (an alloy of copper, silver, and zinc), melt at much higher temperatures and form a much stronger joint.

A necessary preliminary to making any solder joint is thorough cleaning of the surfaces of the metal to be joined (to remove oxide) and the use of a flux (to prevent the heat applied to melt the solder from reoxidizing the metal).

sole flatfish found in temperate and tropical waters. The **common sole** *Solea solea*, also called **Dover sole**, is found in the southern seas of NW Europe. Up to 20 in/50 cm long, it is a prized food fish, as is the **sand** or **French sole** *Pegusa lascaris* further south.

solenodon rare insectivorous shrewlike mammal, genus *Solenodon*. There are two species, one each on Cuba and Hispaniola, and they are threatened with extinction owing to introduced predators. They are about 1 ft/30 cm long with a 10 in/25 cm tail, slow-moving, and produce venomous saliva.

solenoid coil of wire, usually cylindrical, in which a magnetic field is created by passing an electric current through it (see ⟡electromagnet). This field can be used to move an iron rod placed on its axis. Mechanical valves attached to the rod can be operated by switching the current on or off, so converting electrical energy into mechanical energy. Solenoids are used to relay energy from the battery of a car to the starter motor by means of the ignition switch.

sole proprietorship or *sole trader* one person who runs a business, receiving all profits and responsible for all liabilities. Most small businesses are headed by sole proprietors.

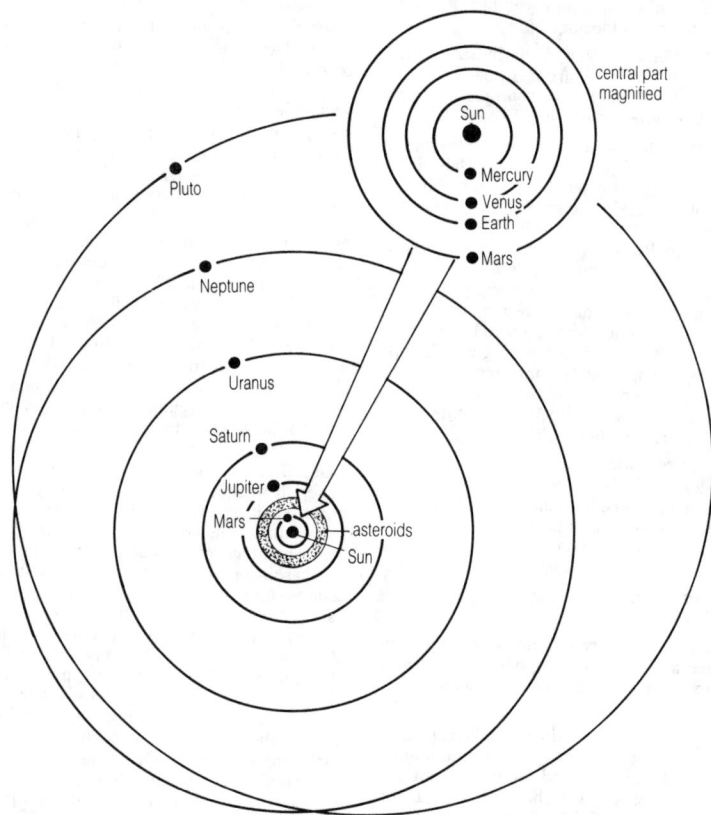

Solar System *If the Sun were the size of a basketball, the planet closest to the Sun, Mercury, would be the size of a mustard seed 48 ft/15 m from the Sun.*

Solferino, Battle of Napoleon III's victory over the Austrians 1859 at a village near Verona, N Italy, 5 mi/8 km S of Lake Garda.

solicitor general the second-ranking member of the US Department of Justice, charged with representing the federal government before the US Supreme Court, and any other courts, and who must approve any appeal the federal government might take to an apellate court.

solid in physics, a state of matter that holds its own shape (as opposed to a liquid, which takes up the shape of its container, or a gas, which totally fills its container). According to ◊kinetic theory, the atoms or molecules in a solid are not free to move but merely vibrate about fixed positions, such as those in crystal lattices.

Solidarity (Polish *Solidarność*) national confederation of independent labor unions in Poland, formed under the leadership of Lech ◊Walesa Sept 1980. An illegal organization from 1981 to 1989, it was then elected to head the Polish government. Divisions soon emerged in the leadership. Solidarity had 2.8 million members in 1991. Solidarity emerged from a summer of industrial disputes caused by the Polish government's attempts to raise food prices. The strikers created a labor-union movement independent of the Communist Party, and protracted negotiations with the government led to recognition of Solidarity in exchange for an acceptance of the leading role of the Communist Party in Poland. Continuing unrest and divisions in Solidarity's leadership led to the declaration of martial law in Dec 1981; the union was banned and its leaders were arrested. Walesa was released Dec 1982, and Solidarity continued to function as an underground organization. It was legalized again April 1989 following a further wave of strikes under its direction and round-table talks with the government. In the elections of June 1989 it won almost every seat open to it, and became the senior partner in a "grand coalition" government formed Sept 1989 with Tadeusz ◊Mazowiecki as prime minister. In Dec 1990, after a damaging break with Mazowiecki, Walesa became Poland's president. Walesa left the confederation, and by mid-1991 Solidarity found itself opposing some of its former leader's economic policies and with diminished national influence.

Solidarity's achievements inspired the successful "people power" movements in other E European countries during 1989, as well as the formation of more independent labor unions in the USSR.

solid-state circuit electronic circuit where all the components (resistors, capacitors, transistors, and diodes) and interconnections are made at the same time, and by the same processes, in or on one piece of single-crystal silicon. The small size of this construction accounts for its use in electronics for space vehicles and aircraft.

solipsism in philosophy, a view that maintains that the self is the only thing that can be known to exist. It is an extreme form of ◊scepticism. The solipsist sees himself or herself as the only individual in existence, assuming other people to be a reflection of his or her own consciousness.

soliton non-linear solitary wave that maintains its shape and velocity, and does not widen and disperse in the normal way. Such behavior is characteristic of the waves of ◊energy that constitute the particles of atomic physics, and the mathematical equations that sum

up the behavior of solitons are being used to further research in nuclear fusion and superconductivity.

It is so named after a solitary wave seen on a canal by Scottish engineer John Scott Russell (1808–1882), who raced after it on his horse.

Solomon *c.* 974–*c.* 937 BC. In the Old Testament, third king of Israel, son of David by Bathsheba. During a peaceful reign, he was famed for his wisdom and his alliances with Egypt and Phoenicia. The much later biblical Proverbs, Ecclesiastes, and Song of Songs are attributed to him. He built the temple in Jerusalem with the aid of heavy taxation and forced labor, resulting in the revolt of N Israel.

Solomon Islands country in the SW Pacific Ocean, E of New Guinea, comprising many hundreds of islands, the largest of which is Guadalcanal.

government The constitution dates from 1978 and creates a constitutional monarchy within the British ◊Commonwealth, with a resident governor-general representing the UK monarch as head of state. There is a single-chamber legislature, the National Parliament, with 38 members elected by universal suffrage for a four-year term. The governor-general appoints a prime minister and cabinet drawn from and collectively responsible to the parliament.

history The islands were inhabited by Melanesians, and were sighted by a 1568 expedition from Peru led by the Spanish navigator Alvaro de Mendaña. They became a British protectorate in the 1890s.

independence The Solomon Islands acquired internal self-government 1976, with Peter Kenilorea, leader of the Solomon Islands United Party (SIUPA), as chief minister. He

became prime minister when they achieved full independence within the Commonwealth 1978. In 1981 he was replaced by Solomon Mamaloni of the People's Progressive Party. Kenilorea had been unable to devolve power to the regions while preserving the unity of the state, but Mamaloni created five ministerial posts specifically for provincial affairs.

In the 1984 general election SIUPA won 13 seats and the opposition, now the People's Alliance Party (PAP), 12. Sir Peter Kenilorea, as he had become, returned to office at the head of a coalition government. He immediately abolished the five provincial ministries. Kenilorea, after narrowly surviving a series of no-confidence motions, resigned again as prime minister Dec 1986, following allegations that he had accepted US $47,000 of French aid to repair cyclone damage to his home village in Malaita province. Kenilorea remained in the cabinet of his successor, Ezekiel Alebua, a fellow SIUPA member, and became deputy prime minister from Feb 1988. In the general election of Feb 1989 support for the SIUPA halved to six seats and the PAP, led by Mamaloni, re-emerged, with 14 seats, as the dominant party. Mamaloni formed a coalition government which included members of the opposition. The coalition government promised to reform the constitution so as to establish a republic and also to reduce the influence of "foreign aid personnel." In Oct 1990 Mamaloni resigned as leader of the ruling PAP after receiving a vote of no confidence. He continued as head of government and as a result both the PAP and the opposition parties splintered into personality-based factions.

foreign relations In its external relations, the Solomon Islands, under the SIUPA

Solomon Islands

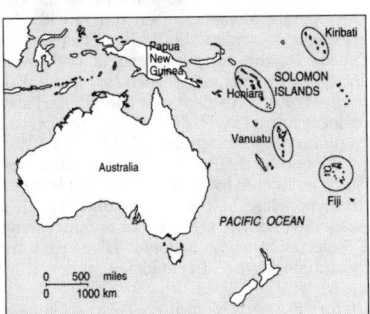

area 10,656 sq mi/27,600 sq km
capital Honiara (on Guadalcanal)
cities Gizo, Yandina
physical comprises all but the northernmost islands (which belong to Papua New Guinea) of a Melanesian archipelago stretching nearly 900 mi/1,500 km. The largest is Guadalcanal (area 2,510 sq mi/6,500 sq km); others are Malaita, San Cristobal, New Georgia, Santa Isabel, Choiseul; mainly mountainous and forested
features rivers ideal for hydroelectric power
head of state Elizabeth II represented by governor-general
head of government Solomon Mamaloni from 1989
political system constitutional monarchy
political parties People's Alliance Party (PAP), center-left; Solomon Islands United

Party (SIUPA), right-of-center
exports fish products, palm oil, copra, cocoa, timber
currency Solomon Island dollar
population (1990 est) 314,000 (Melanesian 95%, Polynesian 4%); growth rate 3.9% p.a.
life expectancy men 66, women 71
languages English (official); there are some 120 Melanesian dialects
religion Anglican 34%, Roman Catholic 19%, South Sea Evangelical 17%
literacy 60% (1989)
GNP $141 million; $420 per head (1987)
chronology
1893 Solomon Islands placed under British protection.
1978 Independence achieved from Britain within the Commonwealth, with Peter Kenilorea as prime minister.
1981 Solomon Mamaloni replaced Kenilorea as prime minister.
1984 Kenilorea returned to power, heading a coalition government.
1986 Kenilorea resigned after allegations of corruption; replaced by his deputy, Ezekiel Alebua.
1988 Kenilorea elected deputy prime minister. Joined Vanuatu and Papua New Guinea to form the Spearhead Group, aiming to preserve Melanesian cultural traditions and secure independence for the French territory of New Caledonia.
1989 Solomon Mamaloni (People's Action Party) elected prime minister; formed PAP-dominated coalition.
1990 Mamaloni resigned as PAP party leader, but continued as head of national unity government.

administrations, has pursued a moderate pro-Western course. However, during the 1981–84 Mamaloni administration, relations with the US were strained by the government's refusal to allow nuclear-powered warships within the islands' territorial waters. In pursuit of a new, broader "Pacific strategy," the Solomon Islands joined Papua New Guinea and Vanuatu in forming the Spearhead Group, March 1988, with the aim of preserving Melanesian cultural traditions and securing independence for the French dependency of New Caledonia. *See illustration box.*

Solomon's seal any perennial plant of the genus *Polygonatum* of the lily family Liliaceae, native to Europe and found growing in moist, shady woodland areas. They have bell-like white or greenish-white flowers drooping from the leaf axils of arching stems, followed by blue or black berries.

Great Solomon's seal *P. commutatum* is native to E North America.

Solon *c.* 638–558 BC. Athenian statesman. As one of the chief magistrates about 594 BC, he carried out the revision of the constitution that laid the foundations of Athenian democracy.

Solti Georg 1912– . Hungarian-born British conductor. He was music director at the Royal Opera House, Covent Garden, London, 1961–71, and became director of the Chicago Symphony Orchestra 1969. He was also principal conductor of the London Philharmonic Orchestra 1979–83.

solubility in physics, a measure of the amount of solute (usually a solid or gas) that will dissolve in a given amount of solvent (usually a liquid) at a particular temperature. Solubility may be expressed as grams of solute per 100 grams of solvent or, for a gas, in parts per million (ppm) of solvent.

solution two or more substances mixed to form a single, homogenous phase. One of the substances is the *solvent* and the others (*solutes*) are said to be dissolved in it.

The constituents of a solution may be solid, liquid, or gaseous. The solvent is normally the substance that is present in greatest quantity; however, if one of the constituents is a liquid this is considered to be the solvent even if it is not the major substance.

Solvay process industrial process for the manufacture of sodium carbonate.

It is a multistage process in which carbon dioxide is generated from limestone and passed through ⬦brine saturated with ammonia. Sodium hydrogen carbonate is isolated and heated to yield sodium carbonate. All intermediate by-products are recycled so that the only ultimate by-product is calcium chloride.

solvent substance, usually a liquid, that will dissolve another substance (see ⬦solution). Although the commonest solvent is water, in popular use the term refers to low-boiling-point organic liquids, which are harmful if used in a confined space. They can give rise to respiratory problems, liver damage, and neurological complaints.

Typical organic solvents are petroleum distillates (in glues), xylol (in paints), alcohols (for synthetic and natural resins such as shellac), esters (in lacquers, including nail polish), ketones (in cellulose lacquers and resins), and chlorinated hydrocarbons (as paint stripper and dry-cleaning fluids). The fumes of some solvents, when inhaled (⬦glue-sniffing), affect mood and perception. In addition to damaging the brain and lungs, repeated inhalation of solvent from a plastic bag can cause death by asphyxia.

Solzhenitsyn Alexander (Isayevich) 1918– . Soviet novelist, a US citizen from 1974. He was in prison and exile 1945–57 for anti-Stalinist comments. Much of his writing is semiautobiographical and highly critical of the system, including *One Day in the Life of Ivan Denisovich* 1962, which deals with the labor camps under Stalin, and *The Gulag Archipelago* 1973, an exposé of the whole Soviet labor-camp network. This led to his expulsion from the USSR 1974.

He was awarded a Nobel Prize in 1970. Other works include *The First Circle* and *Cancer Ward*, both 1968. His autobiography, *The Oak and the Calf*, appeared 1980. He has adopted a Christian position, and his criticism of Western materialism is also stringent.

soma intoxicating drink made from the fermented sap of the *Asclepias acida* plant, used in Indian religious ritual as a sacrifice to the gods. As *haoma*, its consumption also constituted the central rite in Zoroastrian ritual. Some have argued that the plant was in fact a hallucogenic mushroom.

Somali member of a group of E African peoples from the Horn of Africa. Although the majority of Somalis live in the Somali Republic, there are minorities in Ethiopia and Kenya. Their Cushitic language belongs to the Hamitic branch of the Afro-Asiatic family.

Somalia country in NE Africa (the Horn of Africa), on the Indian Ocean, bounded NW by Djibouti, W by Ethiopia, and SW by Kenya.

government The 1979 constitution defines Somalia as a Socialist state with power in the hands of the Somali Revolutionary Socialist Party (SRSP). The party and the state system operate alongside each other, with the president bestriding both. The president is chosen by the party as head of both state and government and is secretary-general of the party and president of its politburo. Party policy is formulated by the 51-member central committee, operating through 13 bureaus and sanctioned by the Politburo. A council of ministers, appointed by the president, implements these policies. In the 177-member People's Assembly, six are presidential nominees and 171 elected by secret ballot for a five-year term from a single list of candidates approved by the party.

history For early history, see ⬦Africa. Somalia developed around Arab trading posts that grew into sultanates. A British protectorate of Somaliland was established 1884–87, and Somalia, an Italian protectorate, 1889. The latter was a colony from 1927 and incorporated into Italian East Africa 1936; it came under British military rule 1941–50, when as a United Nations trusteeship it was again administered by Italy.

independence Somalia became a fully independent republic 1960 through a merger of the two former colonial territories. Since then, Somalia has been involved in disputes with its neighbors because of its insistence on the right of all Somalis to self-determination, wherever they have settled. This has frequently applied to those living in the Ogaden district of Ethiopia and in NE Kenya. A dispute over the border with Kenya resulted in a break in diplomatic relations with Britain 1963–68. The dispute with Ethiopia led to an eight-month war 1978, in which Somalia was defeated by Ethiopian troops assisted by Soviet and Cuban weapons and advisers. Some 1.5 million refugees entered Somalia, and guerrilla fighting continued in Ogaden until its secession 1991. There was a rapprochement with Kenya 1984 and, in 1986, the first meeting for ten years between the Somali and Ethiopian leaders.

The first president of Somalia was Aden Abdullah Osman, who was succeeded 1967 by Dr Abdirashid Ali Shermarke of the Somali Youth League (SYL), which had become the dominant political party. In Oct 1969, President Shermarke was assassinated, and the army seized power under Maj Gen Mohamed Siad Barre. He suspended the 1960 constitution, dissolved the national assembly, banned all political parties, and formed a military government. In 1970 he declared Somalia a socialist state.

one-party state In 1976, the junta transferred power to the newly created SRSP, and three years later the constitution for a one-party state was adopted. Over the next few years Barre consolidated his position by increasing the influence of his own clan and reducing that of his northern rival, despite often violent opposition.

opposition and repression In 1982 the antigovernment Somali National Movement (SNM) was formed. Oppressive countermeasures by the government led to an estimated 50,000–60,000 civilian deaths by 1990 and 400,000 refugees fleeing to Ethiopia. All post was censored in the north, identity cards were necessary for travel within the country, and contact with foreigners was discouraged.

Barre was reelected Jan 1987, although the Somali National Movement had taken control of large parts of the north and east of the country. In riots June 1989 an estimated 400 people were killed by government troops; the government claimed only 24 people died. Government soldiers, pursuing refugees believed to be SNM rebels, crossed into Kenya Sept 1989 and killed four Kenyan policemen. Kenya threatened reprisals even as Prime Minister Samantar announced the release of all political prisoners. He ruled out talks with the SNM.

rebel coup In Oct 1990 the government announced that it would hold a referendum, within 12 months, for greater liberalization, including electoral reform. In Jan 1991 President Barre survived an attempted coup but fled the capital as rebels captured it. They promised free elections. After discussions with different political and social groups, Ali Mahdi Mohammed was named president. The secession of NE Somalia, as the Somaliland Republic, was announced May 1991. A cease-fire signed June 1991 between four rival Somali factions (United Somali Congress (USC), Somali Salvation Democratic Front (SSDF), Somali Patriotic Movement (SPM), and Somali Democratic Movement (SDM)), failed to hold. In Sept 1991 the outbreak of severe fighting with many casualties was reported in Mogadishu, the capital. The fighting continued in the succeeding months and 20,000 people were reported to have been killed or injured by the year's end.

It was revealed April 1992 that Mohamed Siad Barre had given up his attempt to return to power and had taken his family and the remnants of his army into exile in Kenya.

famine The widespread famine of 1992, caused in most part by the civil war, was estimated by the International Red Cross to have affected more than a fourth of Somalia's six million people. In order to alleviate this disaster, the US organized its largest relief

Somalia
Somali Democratic Republic (*Jamhuriyadda Dimugradiga Somaliya*)

area 246,220 sq mi/637,700 sq km
capital Mogadishu
cities Hargeisa, Kismayu, port Berbera
physical mainly flat, with hills in N
environment destruction of trees for fuel and by grazing livestock has led to an increase in desert area
features occupies a strategic location on the Horn of Africa
head of state and government Ali Mahdi Mohammed from 1991
political system one-party socialist republic
political party Somali Revolutionary Socialist Party (SRSP), nationalist, socialist
exports livestock, skins, hides, bananas, fruit
currency Somali shilling
population (1990 est) 8,415,000 (including 350,000 refugees from Ethiopia and 50,000 in Djibouti); growth rate 3.1% p.a.
life expectancy men 53, women 53 (1989)
languages Somali, Arabic (both official), Italian, English
religion Sunni Muslim 99%
literacy 40% (1986)
GNP $1.5 bn; $290 per head (1987)
chronology
1884–87 British protectorate of Somaliland established.
1889 Italian protectorate of Somalia established.
1960 Independence achieved from Italy and Britain.
1963 Border dispute with Kenya; diplomatic relations with the UK broken.
1968 Diplomatic relations with the UK restored.
1969 Army coup led by Maj Gen Mohamed Siad Barre; constitution suspended, Supreme Revolutionary Council set up; name changed to Somali Democratic Republic.
1978 Defeated in eight-month war with Ethiopia. Armed insurrection began in north.
1979 New constitution for socialist one-party state adopted.
1982 Antigovernment Somali National Movement formed. Oppressive countermeasures by government.
1987 Barre reelected president.
1989 Dissatisfaction with government and increased guerrilla activity in north.
1990 Civil war intensified. Constitutional reforms promised.
1991 Mogadishu captured by rebels; Barre fled; Ali Mahdi Mohammed named president; free elections promised. Secession of NE Somalia, as the Somaliland Republic, announced. Cease-fire signed, but later collapsed. Thousands of casualties as a result of heavy fighting in capital.
1992 Relief efforts to ward off impending famine severely hindered by unstable political situation; relief convoys hijacked by "war lords." Dec: UN peacekeeping troops sent in to protect relief operations.

operation to Africa in August. Other western nations also contributed to the airlift and the UN sent additional troops to guard the food shipments. Relief efforts were hampered by the continued unstable political situation; amidst fighting among the clans, UN peacekeeping troops, initially mainly from the United States, ensured that aid eventually reached the worst areas Dec 1992. US troops helped to pacify the country in early 1992. *See illustration box.*

Somaliland region of Somali-speaking peoples in E Africa including the former British Somaliland Protectorate (established 1887) and Italian Somaliland (made a colony 1927, conquered by Britain 1941 and administered by Britain until 1950)—which both became independent 1960 as the Somali Democratic Republic, the official name for ¢Somalia—and former French Somaliland, which was established 1892, became known as the Territory of the Afars and Issas 1967, and became independent as ¢Djibouti 1977.

Somerset county in SW England
area 1,336 sq mi/3,460 sq km
cities administrative headquarters Taunton; Wells, Bridgwater, Glastonbury, Yeovil
physical rivers Avon, Parret, and Exe; marshy coastline on the Bristol Channel; Mendip Hills (including Cheddar Gorge and Wookey Hole, a series of limestone caves where Old Stone Age flint implements and bones of extinct animals have been found); the Quantock Hills; Exmoor
products engineering, dairy products, cider, Exmoor ponies
population (1991) 459,100
famous people Ernest Bevin, Henry Fielding, John Pym.

Somerset Edward Seymour, 1st Duke of Somerset *c.* 1506–1552. English politician. Created Earl of Hertford after Henry VIII's marriage to his sister Jane, he became Duke of Somerset and protector (regent) for Edward VI in 1547. His attempt to check enclosure (the transfer of land from common to private ownership) offended landowners and his moderation in religion upset the Protestants, and he was beheaded on a fake treason charge in 1552.

Somme, Battle of the Allied offensive in World War I July–Nov 1916 at Beaumont-Hamel-Chaulnes, on the river Somme in N France, during which severe losses were suffered by both sides. It was planned by the Marshal of France, Joseph Joffre, and UK commander in chief Douglas Haig; the Allies lost over 600,000 soldiers and advanced 20 mi/ 32 km. It was the first battle in which tanks were used. The German offensive around St Quentin March–April 1918 is sometimes called the Second Battle of the Somme.

Somoza Anastasio 1896–1956. Nicaraguan soldier and politician. As head of the Nicaraguan army, he deposed President Juan Bautista Sacasa, his uncle, 1936 and assumed the presidency the following year, ruling as a dictator until his assassination 1956. During his rule, Somoza exiled most of his political foes and amassed a fortune. He was succeeded by

his sons Luis Somoza Debayle (1922–67), who was president 1957–63, and Anastasio Somoza Debayle (1925–80), who ruled 1963–79, when he was overthrown by the leftist Sandinista rebels (he, too, was later assassinated).

Somoza Debayle Anastasio 1925–1980. Nicaraguan soldier and politician, president 1967–72 and 1974–79. The second son of Anastasio Somoza García, he succeeded his brother Luis Somoza Debayle (1922–1967; president 1956–63) as president of Nicaragua in 1967, to head an even more oppressive regime. He was removed by Sandinista guerrillas in 1979, and assassinated in Paraguay 1980.

sonar (acronym for *sound navigation and ranging*) method of locating underwater objects by the reflection of ultrasonic waves. The time taken for an acoustic beam to travel to the object and back to the source enables the distance to be found since the velocity of sound in water is known. Sonar devices, or *echo sounders*, were developed 1920.

The process is similar to that used in ¢radar. During World War I and after, the Allies developed and perfected an apparatus for detecting the presence of enemy U-boats beneath the sea surface by the use of ultrasonic echoes. It was named ASDIC (from antisubmarine detection investigation committee), but in 1963 the name was changed to sonar.

sonata (Italian "sounded") piece of instrumental music written for a soloist or a small ensemble and consisting of a series of related movements.

sonata form in music, the structure of a movement, typically involving division into exposition, development, and recapitulation sections. It is the framework for much Classical music, including sonatas, ¢symphonies, and ¢concertos.

Sondheim Stephen (Joshua) 1930– . US composer and lyricist. He wrote the lyrics of Leonard Bernstein's *West Side Story* 1957 and composed witty and sophisticated musicals, including *A Little Night Music* 1973, *Pacific Overtures* 1976, *Sweeney Todd* 1979, *Into the Woods* 1987, and *Sunday in the Park with George* 1989.

sone unit of subjective loudness. A tone of 40 decibels above the threshold of hearing with a frequency of 1,000 hertz is defined as one sone; any sound that seems twice as loud as this has a value of two sones, and so on. A loudness of one sone corresponds to 40 ¢phons.

son et lumière (French "sound and light") outdoor night-time dramatization of the history of a notable building, monument, town, and so on, using theatrical lighting effects, sound effects, music, and narration; invented by Paul Robert Houdin, curator of the Château de Chambord, France.

song composition for one or more singers, often with instrumental accompaniment, such as madrigals and chansons. Common forms include folk song and ballad. The term "song" is used for secular music, whereas motet and cantata tend to be forms of sacred music.

song cycle sequence of songs related in mood and sung as a group, used by romantic composers such as Franz Schubert, Robert Schumann, and Hugo Wolf.

Songhai Empire former kingdom of NW Africa, founded in the 8th century, which developed into a powerful Muslim empire under the rule of Sonni Ali (reigned 1464–92). It superseded the ¢Mali Empire and extended its territory, occupying an area that included parts of present-day Guinea, Burkina Faso, Senegal, Gambia, Mali, Mauritania, Niger, and Nigeria. In 1591 it was invaded and overthrown by Morocco.

"Song of Myself" the longest poem in Walt Whitman's ▷Leaves of Grass, relating the poet, the "single separate person," to the democratic "en masse." It was regularly revised from its original form of 1855 to incorporate new experiences and "cosmic sensations."

sonic boom noise like a thunderclap that occurs when an aircraft passes through the ▷sound barrier, or begins to travel faster than the speed of sound. It happens when the cone-shaped shock wave caused by the plane touches the ground.

sonnet fourteen-line poem of Italian origin introduced to England by Thomas ▷Wyatt in the form used by Petrarch (rhyming *abba abba cdcdcd* or *cdecde*) and followed by Milton and Wordsworth; Shakespeare used the form *abab cdcd efef gg*.

sonoluminescence emission of light by a liquid that is subjected to high-frequency sound waves. The rapid changes of pressure induced by the sound cause minute bubbles to form in the liquid, which then collapse. Light is emitted at the final stage of the collapse, probably because it squeezes and heats gas inside the bubbles.

Sons of Liberty in American colonial history, the name adopted by those colonists opposing the ▷Stamp Act of 1765. Merchants, lawyers, farmers, artisans, and laborers joined what was an early instance of concerted resistance to British rule, causing the repeal of the act in March 1766.

Sontag Susan 1933– . US critic, novelist, and screenwriter. Her novel *The Benefactor* appeared in 1963, and she established herself as a critic with the influential cultural essays of *Against Interpretation* 1966 and *Styles of Radical Will* 1969. More recent studies, showing the influence of French structuralism, are *On Photography* 1976 and the powerful *Illness as Metaphor* 1978 and *Aids and its Metaphors* 1989.

Soochow alternative transliteration of the Chinese city of ▷Suzhou.

Soong Ching-ling 1890–1981. Chinese politician, wife of the ▷Guomindang Nationalist leader founder ▷Sun Yat-sen; she remained a prominent figure in Chinese politics after his death, being a vice chair of the People's Republic of China from 1959.

Sophia Electress of Hanover 1630–1714. Twelfth child of Frederick V, elector palatine of the Rhine and king of Bohemia, and Elizabeth, daughter of James I of England. She married the elector of Hanover in 1658. Widowed in 1698, she was recognized in the succession to the English throne in 1701, and when Queen Anne died without issue in 1714, her son George I founded the Hanoverian dynasty.

sophist (Greek "wise man") one of a group of 5th-century BC lecturers on culture, rhetoric, and politics. Skeptical about the possibility of achieving genuine knowledge, they applied bogus reasoning and were concerned with winning arguments rather than establishing the truth. ▷Plato regarded them as dishonest and **sophistry** came to mean fallacious reasoning.

Sophocles 495–406 BC. Greek dramatist who, with Aeschylus and Euripides, is one of the

three great tragedians. He modified the form of tragedy by introducing a third actor and developing stage scenery. He wrote some 120 plays, of which seven tragedies survive. These are *Antigone* 441 BC, *Oedipus Tyrannus*, *Electra*, *Ajax*, *Trachiniae*, *Philoctetes* 409 BC, and *Oedipus at Colonus* 401 BC.

Sophocles lived in Athens when the city was ruled by Pericles, a period of great prosperity. His many friends included the historian Herodotus. In his tragedies, human will plays a greater part than that of the gods, as in the plays of Aeschylus, and his characters are generally heroic. This is perhaps what he meant when he said of Euripides "He paints men as they are" and of himself "I paint men as they ought to be." A large fragment of his satyric play (a tragedy treated in a grotesquely comic fashion) *Ichneutae* also survives.

Sopwith Thomas Octave Murdoch 1888–1989. English designer of the Sopwith Camel biplane, used in World War I, and joint developer of the Hawker Hurricane fighter plane used in World War II.

sorbic acid $CH_3CH:CHCH:CHCOOH$ tasteless acid found in the fruit of the mountain ash (genus *Sorbus*) and prepared synthetically. It is widely used in the preservation of food—for example, cider, wine, soft drinks, animal feeds, bread, and cheese.

Sorbonne common name for the University of Paris, originally a theological institute founded 1253 by Robert de Sorbon, chaplain to Louis IX.

Richelieu ordered the reconstruction of the buildings in 1626, which were again rebuilt 1885. In 1808, the Sorbonne became the seat of the Académie of Paris and of the University of Paris. It is the most prestigious French university.

Sorbus genus of deciduous trees and shrubs of the northern hemisphere, family Rosaceae, including American and Eurasian ▷mountain ash species; the latter include ▷whitebeam and ▷service tree.

Sorel Georges 1847–1922. French philosopher who believed that socialism could only come about through a general strike; his theory of the need for a "myth" to sway the body of the people was used by fascists.

sorghum or **great millet** or **Guinea corn** any cereal grass of the genus *Sorghum*, native to Africa but cultivated widely in India, China, the US, and S Europe. The seeds are used for making bread. ▷Durra is a member of the genus.

sorrel (Old French *sur* "sour") any of several plants of the genus *Rumex* of the buckwheat family Polygonaceae. *R. acetosa* is grown for its bitter salad leaves.

Sorrento town on the Gulf of Naples, SW Italy; population (1981) 17,301. It has been a vacation resort since Roman times.

sorting arranging data in sequence. When sorting a collection, or file, of data made up of several different ▷fields, one must be chosen as the **key field** used to establish the correct sequence. For example, the data in a company's mailing list might include fields for each customer's first names, surname, address, and telephone number. For most purposes the company would wish the records to be sorted alphabetically by surname; therefore, the surname field would be chosen as the key field.

The choice of sorting method involves a compromise between running time, memory usage, and complexity. Those used include **selection sorting**, in which the smallest item is found and exchanged with the first item, the second smallest exchanged with the second item, and so on; **bubble sorting**, in which adjacent items are continually exchanged until the data are in sequence; and **insertion sorting**, in which each item is placed in the correct position and subsequent items moved down to make a place for it.

sorus in ferns, a group of sporangia, the reproductive structures that produce ▷spores. They occur on the lower surface of fern fronds.

SOS internationally recognized distress signal, using letters of the ▷Morse code (...—...).

Sōseki Natsume, adopted name of Natsume Kinnosuke 1867–1916. Japanese novelist whose works are deep psychological studies of urban intellectual lives. Strongly influenced by English literature, his later works are somewhat reminiscent of Henry James; for example, the unfinished *Meian/Light and Darkness* 1916. Sōseki is regarded as one of Japan's greatest writers.

Sōseki was born in Tokyo and studied English literature there and (1900–03) in the UK. He became well known with his debut novel, *Wagahai wa neko de aru/I Am a Cat* 1905, followed by the humorous *Botchan* 1906, but found a more serious, sensitive style in his many later novels, such as *Sore kara/And Then* 1909. He also studied Classical Chinese literature and Zen Buddhism and wrote on literary theory.

Sotho member of a large ethnic group in southern Africa, numbering about 7 million (1987) and living mainly in Botswana, Lesotho, and South Africa. The Sotho are predominantly farmers, living in small village groups. They speak a variety of closely related languages belonging to the Bantu branch of the Niger-Congo family. With English, Sotho is the official language of Lesotho.

soul according to many religions, the intangible and immortal part of a human being that survives the death of the physical body.

Judaism, Christianity, and Islam all teach that at the end of the world each soul will be judged and assigned to heaven or hell on its merits. According to orthodox Jewish doctrine, most souls first spend time in purgatory to be purged of their sins, and are then removed to paradise. In Christianity the soul is that part of the person that can be redeemed from sin through divine grace. In other religions, such as Hinduism, the soul is thought to undergo ▷reincarnation until the individual reaches enlightenment and is freed from the cycle of rebirth. According to the teachings of Buddhism, no permanent self or soul exists.

In his 1990 New Year's message, the Pope appeared to agree that animals have souls by stating, "animals possess a soul and that man must love and feel solidarity with our smaller brethren." This statement is still a source of considerable debate within the Roman Catholic Church.

soul music emotionally intense style of ▷rhythm and blues sung by, among others, Sam Cooke (1931–1964), Aretha Franklin (1942–), and Al Green (1946–). A synthesis of blues, gospel music, and jazz, it emerged in the 1950s. Sometimes all popular music made by African-Americans is labeled soul music.

Soult Nicolas Jean de Dieu 1769–1851. Marshal of France. He held commands in Spain in the Peninsular War, where he sacked the port of Santander 1808, and was Chief of Staff at the Battle of ◊Waterloo. He was war minister 1830–40.

sound physiological sensation received by the ear, originating in a vibration (pressure variation in the air) that communicates itself to the air, and travels in every direction, spreading out as an expanding sphere. All sound waves in air travel with a speed dependent on the temperature; under ordinary conditions, this is about 1,070 ft/330 m per second. The pitch of the sound depends on the number of vibrations imposed on the air per second, but the speed is unaffected. The loudness of a sound is dependent primarily on the amplitude of the vibration of the air.

The lowest note audible to a human being has a frequency of about 20 ◊hertz (vibrations per second), and the highest one of about 15,000 Hz; the lower limit of this range varies little with the person's age, but the upper range falls steadily from adolescence onwards.

Sound, the strait dividing SW Sweden from Denmark and linking the Kattegat and the Baltic; length 70 mi/113 km; width between 3–37 mi/5–60 km.

sound barrier concept that the speed of sound, or sonic speed (about 760 mph/1,220 kph at sea level), constitutes a speed limit to flight through the atmosphere, since a badly designed aircraft suffers severe buffeting at near sonic speed owing to the formation of shock waves. US test pilot Chuck Yeager first flew through the "barrier" in 1947 in a Bell X-1 rocket plane. Now, by careful design, such aircraft as Concorde can fly at supersonic speed with ease, though they create in their wake a ◊sonic boom.

sound synthesis the generation of sound (usually music) by electronic ◊synthesizer.

soundtrack band at one side of a cine film on which the accompanying sound is recorded. Usually it takes the form of an optical track (a pattern of light and shade). The pattern is produced on the film when signals from the recording microphone are made to vary the intensity of a light beam. During playback, a light is shone through the track on to a photocell, which converts the pattern of light falling on it into appropriate electrical signals. These signals are then fed to loudspeakers to recreate the original sounds.

Souphanouvong Prince 1912– . Laotian politician, president 1975–86. After an abortive revolt against French rule in 1945, he led the guerrilla organization Pathet Lao, and in 1975 became the first president of the Republic of Laos.

source language in computing, the language in which a program is written, as opposed to ◊machine code, which is the form in which the program's instructions are carried out by the computer. Source languages are classified as either ◊high-level languages or ◊low-level languages, according to whether each notation in the source language stands for many or only one instruction in machine code.

Programs in high-level languages are translated into machine code by either a ◊compiler or an ◊interpreter program. Low-level programs are translated into machine code by means of an ◊assembler program. The program, before translation, is called the **source program**; after translation into machine code it is called the **object program**.

Sousa John Philip 1854–1932. US bandmaster and composer of marches, such as "The Stars and Stripes Forever!" 1897.

He became known as a brilliant bandmaster during his tenure as leader of the Marine Band 1880–92. He went on to form the Sousa Band 1892 and toured internationally with this group until his death. In addition to about 140 stirring marches, he composed operettas, symphonic poems, suites, waltzes, and songs.

sousaphone large bass ◊tuba designed to wrap round the player in a circle and having a forward-facing bell. The form was suggested by US bandmaster John Sousa. Today they are largely fabricated in lightweight fiberglass.

Souter David Hackett 1939– . US jurist and associate justice of the US Supreme Court 1990– .

Born in Melrose, Massachusetts, he graduated from Harvard College, received a Rhodes scholarship to Oxford University, and graduated from the Harvard Law School. After private practice in New Hampshire, Souter served as state assistant and deputy attorney general before being appointed state attorney general 1976. He became a judge on the state trial court 1978 and was named to the state supreme court 1983. He was appointed by President Bush to the US Court of Appeals for the First Circuit 1990 and to the Supreme Court later in 1990.

South Africa country on the southern tip of Africa, bounded N by Namibia, Botswana, and Zimbabwe and NE by Mozambique and Swaziland.

government The 1984 constitution is based on racial discrimination. The legislature and government are dominated by the descendants of Europeans, termed whites in the context of ◊apartheid. There is only conditional participation in government for nonwhites, in the form of coloreds, or persons of mixed European and African descent, and Asians. Black Africans are completely unrepresented at national level.

The three-chamber parliament consists of the House of Assembly, for whites; the House of Representatives, for coloreds; and the House of Delegates, for Indians. The House of Assembly has 178 members, 166 elected by universal white suffrage, 4 nominated by the president on the basis of one for each province, and 8 elected by the 166. The House of Representatives has 85 members, 80 elected by universal colored suffrage, 2 nominated by the president and 3 elected by the 80. The House of Delegates has 45 members, 40 elected by universal Indian suffrage, 2 nominated by the president, and 3 elected by the 40 directly elected members. Each house is responsible for its "own affairs," meaning matters affecting only whites, coloreds, or Indians, as the case may be. General legislation applying to all races, including black Africans, has to be approved by all three houses and the president. Members of all three houses serve a five-year term.

The state president, who combines the roles of head of both state and government, is elected for the duration of Parliament by an 88-member electoral college: 50 from the House of Assembly, 25 from the House of Representatives, and 13 from the House of Delegates. The president appoints and presides over a cabinet dominated by whites and is advised by an appointed council of 60 members: 20 from the House of Assembly, 10 from the House of Representatives, 5 from the House of Delegates, and 25 chosen by the president. There are also three advisory ministers' councils: one for the whole country, one for the colored community, and one for the Indians. Each of South Africa's four provinces has an adminstrator, appointed by the president, and an elected provincial council.

history For early history, see ◊Africa. The area was originally inhabited by Kung and Khoikhoi. Bantu-speaking peoples, including Sotho, Swazi, Xhosa, and Zulu, settled there before the 17th century. The Cape of Good Hope was rounded by Bartolomeu Diaz 1488; the coast of Natal was sighted by Vasco da Gama 1497. The Dutch East India Company founded Cape Town 1652 as a port of call on the way to the Indies. Occupied by Britain 1795 and 1806, Cape Town and the hinterland were purchased by Britain 1814 for £6 million. Britons also settled in Natal, on the coast near Durban, 1824. In 1836 some 10,000 Dutch, wishing to escape from British rule, set out north on the Great Trek and founded the republic of Transvaal and the Orange Free State; they also settled in N Natal, which became part of Cape Colony 1844 and a separate colony 1856. The Orange Free State was annexed by Britain 1848 but became independent 1854.

Boer War The discovery of diamonds at Kimberley, Cape Colony, 1867, and of gold in Transvaal 1886, attracted prospectors, who came into conflict with the Dutch farmers, the ◊Boers. Britain attempted to occupy Transvaal 1877–81 but withdrew after a severe defeat at Majuba in the first of the ◊South African Wars. Denial of citizenship rights to the migrant miners (*uitlanders*) in Transvaal, and the imperialist ambitions of Cecil ◊Rhodes and others, led to the Jameson Raid (see L S ◊Jameson) and the Boer War 1899–1902.

Union of South Africa In 1910 the Union of South Africa was formed, comprising the provinces of Cape of Good Hope, Natal, Orange Free State, and Transvaal. A Boer rebellion on the outbreak of World War I was speedily crushed by Jan ◊Smuts. South Africa occupied German SW Africa (now Namibia). Between the wars the union was alternately governed by the republican nationalists under James ◊Hertzog and the South African Party under Smuts, who supported the Commonwealth connection. Hertzog wanted South Africa to be neutral in World War II, but Smuts took over as premier, and South African troops fought with the Allies.

introduction of apartheid The National Party (NP) came to power 1948 and has ruled South Africa ever since. Its leader, Daniel Malan, initiated the policy of apartheid, attempting to justify it as "separate but equal" development. In fact, all but the white minority are denied a voice in the nation's affairs. In the 1950s the ◊African National Congress (ANC) led a campaign of civil disobedience until it and other similar movements were declared illegal 1960, and in 1964 the ANC leader Nelson Mandela was sentenced to life imprisonment for alleged sabotage. He became a central symbol of black opposition to the apartheid regime, remaining in prison until 1990.

"homelands" established Malan was succeeded 1958 by Hendrik Verwoerd (1901–66), who withdrew from the Commonwealth rather than abandon apartheid, and the Union became the Republic of South Africa 1961.

South Africa
Republic of (*Republiek van Suid-Afrika*)

area 472,148 sq mi/1,223,181 sq km (includes Walvis Bay and independent black homelands)
capital and port Cape Town (legislative), Pretoria (administrative), Bloemfontein (judicial)
cities Johannesburg; ports Durban, Port Elizabeth, East London
physical southern end of large plateau, fringed by mountains and lowland coastal margin
territories Marion Island and Prince Edward Island in the Antarctic
features Drakensberg Mountains, Table Mountain; Limpopo and Orange rivers; the Veld and the Karoo; part of Kalahari Desert; Kruger National Park
head of state and government F W de Klerk from 1989
political system racist, nationalist republic, restricted democracy
political parties White: National Party (NP), right of center, racist; Conservative Party of South Africa (CPSA), extreme right, racist; Democratic Party (DP), left of center, multiracial. Colored: Labor Party of South Africa, left of center; People's Congress Party, right of center. Indian: National People's Party, right of center; Solidarity Party, left of center **exports** corn, sugar, fruit, wool, gold (world's largest producer), platinum, diamonds, uranium, iron and steel, copper; mining and minerals are largest export industry, followed by arms manufacturing
currency rand
population (1990 est) 39,550,000 (73% black: Zulu, Xhosa, Sotho, Tswana; 18% white; 3% mixed, 3% Asian); growth rate 2.5% p.a.
life expectancy whites 71, Asians 67, blacks 58
language Afrikaans and English (both official), Bantu
religion Dutch Reformed Church 40%, Anglican 11%, Roman Catholic 8%, other Christian 25%, Hindu, Muslim
literacy whites 99%, Asians 69%, blacks 50% (1989)

GNP $81 bn; $1,890 per head (1987)
chronology
1910 Union of South Africa formed from two British colonies and two Boer republics.
1912 African National Congress (ANC) formed.
1948 Apartheid system of racial discrimination initiated by Daniel Malan, leader of National Party (NP).
1955 Freedom Charter adopted by ANC.
1958 Malan succeeded as prime minister by Hendrik Verwoerd.
1960 ANC banned.
1961 South Africa withdrew from Commonwealth and became a republic.
1962 ANC leader Nelson Mandela jailed.
1964 Mandela, Walter Sisulu, Govan Mbeki, and five other ANC leaders sentenced to life imprisonment.
1966 Verwoerd assassinated; succeeded by B J Vorster.
1976 Soweto uprising.
1977 Death in custody of Pan African Congress activist Steve Biko.
1978 Vorster resigned and was replaced by Pieter W Botha.
1984 New constitution adopted, giving segregated representation to Coloreds and Asians and making Botha president. Non-aggression pact with Mozambique signed but not observed.
1985 Growth of violence in black townships.
1986 Commonwealth agreed on limited sanctions. US Congress voted to impose sanctions. Some major multinational companies closed down their South African operations.
1987 Government formally acknowledged the presence of its military forces in Angola.
1988 Botha announced "limited constitutional reforms." South Africa agreed to withdraw from Angola and recognize Namibia's independence as part of regional peace accord.
1989 Botha gave up NP leadership and state presidency. F W de Klerk became president. ANC activists released; beaches and public facilities desegregated. Elections held in Namibia to create independence government.
1990 ANC ban lifted; Nelson Mandela released from prison. NP membership opened to all races. Oliver Tambo returned. Daily average of 35 murders and homicides recorded.
1991 Mandela and Zulu leader Buthelezi urged end to fighting between ANC and Inkatha. Mandela elected ANC president. Revelations of government support for Inkatha threatened ANC cooperation. De Klerk announced repeal of remaining apartheid laws. South Africa readmitted to international sport. US lifted sanctions. PAC and Buthelezi withdrew from negotiations over new constitution.
1992 Constitution leading to all-races majority rule approved by whites-only referendum. Massacre of civilians at Boipathong township near Johannesburg threatened constitutional talks. Sept: talks resumed after a four-month hiatus. Oct: special session of parliament discussed interim government.

followed the news of the death in detention of the black community leader Steve Biko 1977.
constitutional reform In 1978 Vorster resigned and was succeeded by Pieter W ⟩Botha. He embarked on constitutional reform to involve coloreds and Asians, but not blacks, in the governmental process. This led to a clash within the NP, and in March 1982 Dr Adries Treurnicht, leader of the hard-line (*verkrampte*) wing, and 15 other extremists were expelled. They later formed a new party, the Conservative Party of South Africa (CPSA). Although there were considerable doubts about Botha's proposals in the colored and Indian communities as well as among the whites, they were approved by 66% of the voters in an all-white referendum and came into effect Sept 1984. In 1985 a number of apartheid laws were amended or repealed, including the ban on sexual relations or marriage between people of different races and the ban on mixed racial membership in political parties, but the underlying inequalities in the system remained and dissatisfaction of the black community grew. In the 1986 cabinet of 21, including Botha, there were 19 whites, 1 colored, and 1 Indian. The National Party continued to increase its majority at each election, with the white opposition parties failing to unseat the NP. Both the Conservative Party (CP) and the Democratic Party (DP) made gains in the Sept 1989 elections, with the ruling NP losing one-fourth of its seats. Its new total was only nine seats more than was required for a majority, its worst electoral showing since coming to power 1948.
state of emergency In May 1986 South Africa attacked what it claimed to be guerrilla strongholds in Botswana, Zambia, and Zimbabwe. The exiled ANC leader Oliver ⟩Tambo was receiving increasing moral support in meetings with politicians throughout the world, and Winnie ⟩Mandela, during her husband's continuing imprisonment, was "banned" repeatedly for condemning the system publicly. Nonviolent resistance was advocated by Bishop ⟩Tutu, the ⟩Inkatha movement, and others. A state of emergency was declared June 1986, a few days before the tenth anniversary of the first ⟩Soweto uprising, marked by a strike in which millions of blacks participated. Serious rioting broke out in the townships and was met with police violence, causing hundreds of deaths. Between 1980 and 1990 some 1,070 people were judicially executed.
sanctions imposed Abroad, calls for economic sanctions against South Africa grew during 1985 and 1986. At the Heads of Commonwealth conference 1985 the Eminent Persons' Group (EPG) of Commonwealth politicians was conceived to investigate the likelihood of change in South Africa without sanctions. In July 1986 the EPG reported that there were no signs of genuine liberalization. Reluctantly, Britain's prime minister, Margaret Thatcher, agreed to limited measures. Some Commonwealth countries, notably Australia and Canada, took additional independent action. The US Congress eventually forced President Reagan to move in the same direction. Between 1988 and 1990 economic sanctions cost the South African treasury more than $4 billion in lost revenue. The decisions by individual multinational companies to close down their South African operations (see ⟩disinvestment) may, in the long term, have the greatest effect.
promise of reform At the end of 1988 South Africa signed a peace agreement with Angola and Cuba, which included the acceptance of Namibia's independence, and in 1989, under

Verwoerd was assassinated 1966, but his successor, B J ⟩Vorster, pursued the same policy. Pass laws restricting the movement of blacks within the country had been introduced, causing international outrage, and ten "homelands" (Bantustans; see ⟩Black National State)

were established to contain particular ethnic groups. By the 1980s thousands of the apartheid regime's opponents had been imprisoned without trial and more than 3,000,000 people had been forcibly resettled in black townships. International condemnation of police brutality

UN supervision, free elections took place there. In Feb 1989 state president Botha suffered a stroke that forced him to give up the NP leadership and later the presidency. He was succeeded in both roles by F W de Klerk, who promised major constitutional reforms. Meanwhile the nonracialist Democratic Party was launched, advocating universal adult suffrage, and made significant progress in the Sept 1989 whites-only assembly elections. Despite de Klerk's release of the veteran ANC activist, Walter Sisulu, and some of his colleagues Oct 1989, the new president's promises of political reform were treated with skepticism by the opposition until he announced the lifting of the ban on the ANC, followed by the release of Mandela Feb 11, 1990. In Sept President de Klerk declared membership in the National Party open to all races. In Dec ANC president Tambo returned triumphantly and in Jan 1991 after a meeting between Nelson Mandela and Zulu leader Chief Buthelezi both urged their followers to end attacks on one other. Mandela was subsequently elected ANC president, but revelations of government financial support and police funding for Inkatha political activities, for example to counter the ANC and foment division among blacks, threatened ANC cooperation.

abandonment of apartheid announced In Feb 1991 President de Klerk announced the intended repeal of all remaining apartheid laws. In March he announced legislation to abolish all racial controls on land ownership, enabling all South Africans to purchase land anywhere. In June 1991 all the remaining racially discriminating laws were repealed. As a result the US lifted its trade and investment sanctions against South Africa in July and the country was readmitted to international sports by the International Olympic Committee. In Sept, President de Klerk announced a draft constitution, giving black people the franchise but providing strong safeguards for the white minority. It was immediately criticized by the ANC because it served to perpetuate the white hegemony. However, the ANC agreed to negotiate and it joined with the Pan-Africanist Congress (PAC) to form a united front against the government. In Dec, however, PAC withdrew, claiming that the planning of the negotiations was undemocratic. Chief Buthelezi also withdrew, but Inkatha remained. A whites-only referendum held March 1992 gave de Klerk a clear mandate to proceed with plans for the new constitution which would end white minority rule.

massacre at Boipathong More than 40 blacks were killed in the black township of Boipathong by Inkatha, aided and abetted by police forces June 1992. The ANC called a halt to the constitutional talks, but they were resumed in Sept, and parliament held a special session in Oct to discuss plans for an interim government. *See illustration box.*

South African literature the founder of South African literature in English was Thomas Pringle (1789–1834), who published lyric poetry and the prose *Narrative of a Residence in South Africa*. More recent poets are Roy Campbell and Francis C Slater (1876–1959). The first work of South African fiction to receive attention outside the country was Olive Schreiner's *Story of an African Farm* 1833; later writers include Sarah Gertrude Millin, Pauline Smith (1882–1959), William Plomer (1903–1973), Laurens van der Post, Alan Paton, Nadine Gordimer (winner of the Nobel Prize

for Literature 1991), and playwright Athol Fugard (1932–).

Original writing in ⊳Afrikaans developed rapidly after the South African War, and includes works by the lyricists C Louis Leipoldt (1880–1947), Jan Celliers (1865–1940), and Eugène Marais (1871–1936); the satirical sketch and story writer C J Langenhoven; and the student of wildlife "Sangiro" (A A Peinhar), author of *The Adventures of a Lion Family*, which became popular in English translation. In more recent years the intellectual barriers imposed by South Africa's isolation have prevented its writers from becoming more widely known, but there has been much spirited work, including that of the novelists André P Brink (1935–) and Etienne Leroux (1922–), and the poet Ingrid Jonker (1933–1965).

Notable works by black writers include the autobiographical *Down Second Avenue* 1959, by Ezekiel Mphahlele (1919–); and the drama *The Rhythm of Violence* 1964, by Lewis Nkosi (1936–).

South African Wars two wars between the Boers (settlers of Dutch origin) and the British; essentially fought for the gold and diamonds of the Transvaal.

The **War of 1881** was triggered by the attempt of the Boers of the ⊳Transvaal to reassert the independence surrendered 1877 in return for British aid against African peoples. The British were defeated at Majuba, and the Transvaal again became independent.

The **War of 1899–1902**, also known as the **Boer War**, was preceded by the armed Jameson Raid into the Boer Transvaal; a failed attempt, inspired by the Cape Colony prime minister Rhodes, to precipitate a revolt against Kruger, the Transvaal president. The *uitlanders* (non-Boer immigrants) were still not given the vote by the Boers, negotiations failed, and the Boers invaded British territory, besieging Ladysmith, Mafeking (now Mafikeng), and Kimberley. The war ended with the Peace of Vereeniging following the Boer defeat.

South America fourth largest of the continents, nearly twice as large as Europe, extending S from ⊳Central America.

area 6,893,429 sq mi/17,854,000 sq km

largest cities (over 3.5 million inhabitants) Buenos Aires, São Paulo, Rio de Janeiro, Bogotá, Santiago, Lima, Caracas

features Andes in the W; Brazilian and Guiana highlands; central plains from the Orinoco basin to Patagonia; Parana-Paraguay-Uruguay system flowing to form the La Plata estuary; Amazon river basin, with its remaining great forests and their rich fauna and flora

products coffee; cocoa; sugar; bananas; oranges; wine; meat and fish products; cotton; wool; handicrafts; minerals incuding oil, silver, iron ore, copper

population (1985) 263,300,000: originally ⊳American Indians, who survive chiefly in Bolivia, Peru, and Ecuador and are increasing in number. In addition there are many mestizo (people of mixed Spanish or Portuguese and Indian ancestry) elsewhere; many people originally from Europe, largely Spanish, Italian, and Portuguese; and many of African descent, originally imported as slaves

language Spanish, Portuguese (chief language in Brazil), many Indian languages

religion Roman Catholic, Indian beliefs

history (for the ancient and later American Indian cultures, see ⊳American Indian):

16th century arrival of Europeans, with the Spanish (⊳Pizarro) and Portuguese conquest;

the American Indians were mainly killed, assimilated, or, where considered unsuitable for slave labor, replaced by imported slaves from Africa.

18th century Revolt of ⊳Túpac Amaru.

19th century Napoleon's toppling of the Spanish throne opened the way for the liberation of its colonies (led by ⊳Bolívar and ⊳San Martín). Brazil became independent peacefully. Large-scale European immigration took place (Hispanic, Italian, and German). Interstate wars took a heavy toll—for example, the Paraguay War (see under ⊳Paraguay) and ⊳Pacific War.

20th century Rapid industrialization and high population growth. In the 1980s heavy indebtedness incurred to fund economic expansion led to an inability to meet interest payments in the world slump.

1946–55 Perón president in Argentina.

1952 Revolution in Bolivia limits large landowners, nationalizes tin mines.

1970–73 Elected socialist regime under Salvador Allende in Chile, ended in military coup.

1982 Falklands War between the UK and Argentina.

1985 Brazil inaugurates first civilian president since 1964.

1989 Democratic transition of power in Argentina. Initial steps taken toward reestablishment of relations with Britain.

Southampton port in Hampshire, S England; population (1981) 204,604. Industries include engineering, chemicals, plastics, flour-milling, and tobacco; it is also a passenger and container port.

The *Mayflower* set sail from here en route to North America in 1620, as did the *Titanic* on its fateful maiden voyage in 1912. There is a university, established 1952.

South Arabia, Federation of former grouping (1959–67) of Arab emirates and sheikdoms, joined by ⊳Aden 1963. The western part of the area was claimed by ⊳Yemen, and sporadic fighting and terrorism from 1964 led to British withdrawal 1967 and the proclamation of the Republic of South Yemen.

South Asia Regional Cooperation Committee (SARCC) organization established 1983 by India, Pakistan, Bangladesh, Nepal, Sri Lanka, Bhutan, and the Maldives to cover agriculture, telecommunications, health, population, sports, art, and culture.

South Australia state of the Commonwealth of Australia

area 379,824 sq mi/984,000 sq km

capital Adelaide (chief port)

cities Whyalla, Mount Gambier

features Murray Valley irrigated area, including wine-growing Barossa Valley; lakes: ⊳Eyre, Torrens; mountains: Mount Lofty, Musgrave, Flinders; parts of the ⊳Nullarbor Plain, and Great Victoria and Simpson deserts; experimental rocket range in the arid north at Woomera

products meat and wool (80% of area cattle and sheep grazing), wines and spirits, dried and canned fruit, iron (Middleback Range), coal (Leigh Creek), copper, uranium (Roxby Downs), oil and natural gas in the northeast, lead, zinc, iron, opals, household and electrical goods, vehicles

population (1987) 1,388,000; 1% Aborigines

history possibly known to the Dutch in the 16th century; surveyed by Dutch navigator Abel Tasman 1644; first European settlement

South Carolina

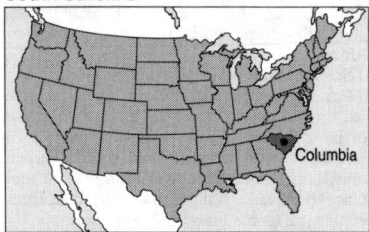

1834; province 1836; state 1901. In 1963 British nuclear tests were made at Maralinga, in which Aborigines were said to have died.

South Bend city on the St Joseph River, N Indiana; population (1990) 105,500. Industries include the manufacture of agricultural machinery, automobiles, and aircraft equipment.

The University of Notre Dame is on the outskirts. The community developed around a fur-trading post established 1823.

South Carolina state in SE US; nickname Palmetto State
area 31,112 sq mi/80,600 sq km
capital Columbia
cities Charleston, Greenville-Spartanburg
population (1990) 3,486,700
features large areas of woodland; subtropical climate in coastal areas; antebellum Charleston; Myrtle Beach and Hilton Head Island ocean resorts
products tobacco, soybeans, lumber, textiles, clothing, paper, wood pulp, chemicals, nonelectrical machinery, primary and fabricated metals
famous people John C Calhoun, "Dizzy" Gillespie, DuBose Heyward, Francis Marion, John B Watson
history explored first by De Gordillo for Spain 1521; Charles I gave the area (known as Carolina) to Robert Heath (1575–1649) in 1629, and the first English settlement was in 1670 at Albemarle Point, but poor conditions drove the settlers to Charles Town (now Charleston). South Carolina, one of the original thirteen states, was the first state to secede from the Union 1860, and the first battle of the Civil War took place at Fort Sumter in Charleston Harbor, April 12, 1861. Union troops caused widespread destruction in the closing months of the war 1865, including the burning of Columbia. Under Reconstruction, the state was readmitted to the Union 1868, and federal troops left 1877. Tenant farming, or sharecropping, replaced plantation slave labor and, beginning around 1890, tobacco and soybeans replaced rice and cotton as the main crops. Textiles became the state's leading industry after 1900. After 1954, desegregation proceeded very slowly but peaceably. In 1989 Hurricane Hugo devastated coastal areas in the state.

South Dakota state of the US; nickname Coyote or Sunshine State
area 77,123 sq mi/199,800 sq km
capital Pierre
cities Sioux Falls, Rapid City, Aberdeen
physical Great Plains; Black Hills (which include granite Mount Rushmore, on whose face giant relief portrait heads of former presidents Washington, Jefferson, Lincoln, and T Roosevelt are carved); Badlands
products cereals, hay, livestock, gold (second-largest US producer), meat products
population (1990) 696,000

famous people Crazy Horse, Sitting Bull, Ernest O Lawrence
history first explored 1743 by Verendrye for France; claimed by France 18th century; passed to the US as part of the Louisiana Purchase 1803; explored by Lewis and Clark 1804–06; first permanent settlement, Fort Pierre 1817, reached by first Missouri River steamboat 1831. A gold rush brought thousands of prospectors and settlers to the Black Hills by railroad 1873–74, and South Dakota became a state 1889. In the 20th century, dam construction along the Missouri river, rural electrification, and reclamation of arid land helped raise the standard of living, but economic opportunities remain limited.

Southeast Asia Treaty Organization (SEATO) collective military system 1954–77 established by Australia, France, New Zealand, Pakistan, the Philippines, Thailand, the UK, and the US, with Vietnam, Cambodia, and Laos as protocol states. After the Vietnam War, SEATO was phased out.

Southern African Development Coordination Conference (SADCC) organization of countries in the region working together to reduce their economic dependence on South Africa. It was established 1980 and focuses on transport and communications, energy, mining, and industrial production. The member states are Angola, Botswana, Lesotho, Malawi, Mozambique, Namibia, Swaziland, Tanzania, Zambia, and Zimbabwe; headquarters in Gaborone, Botswana.

Heads of state and government hold annual meetings and SADCC ministers meet at least twice a year to formulate plans. **Southern and Antarctic Territories** French overseas territory created 1955. It comprises the islands of *St Paul* and *Amsterdam* (26 sq mi/67 sq km); the *Kerguelen* and *Crozet* Islands (2,901 sq mi/7,515 sq km); and *Adélie Land* on Antarctica (165,500 sq mi/432,000 sq km). All are uninhabited, except for research stations.

Southern Christian Leadership Conference (SCLC) US civil rights organization founded 1957 by Martin Luther ◊King, Jr, and led by him until his assassination 1968. It advocated nonviolence and passive resistance, and it sponsored the 1963 march on Washington, DC that focused national attention on the civil rights movement. Its nonviolent philosophy was increasingly challenged by militants in the civil rights movement, and it lost its central position in the movement. The Rev Jesse ◊Jackson began his association with the civil rights movement when King was at the SCLC.

Southern Cone Common Market free-trade zone among Brazil, Argentina, Uruguay, and Paraguay, agreed March 1991 for complete implementation by Jan 1995. It allows for a steady reduction of customs tariffs between members. Established by the Treaty of Asunción, it has headquarters in Montevideo.

Southern Cross popular name for the constellation ◊Crux.

southern lights common name for the ◊aurora australis, colored light in southern skies.

Southern US fiction part of a long tradition of fiction and *belles lettres* in the US South since Edgar Allan Poe, often distinctively different from other US fiction. In the 20th century, a remarkable literary revival began, exemplified by the work of Ellen Glasgow and William Faulkner, dealing with the experience of a

South Dakota

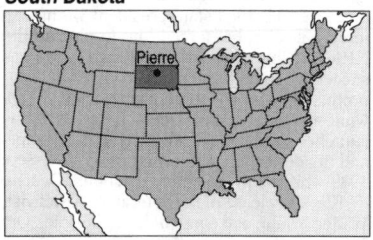

defeated agrarian region with proud traditions. Among 20th-century writers are Thomas Wolfe, Robert Penn Warren, Katherine Anne Porter, Eudora Welty, William Styron, and Margaret Mitchell, author of *Gone With the Wind* 1936. The Southern Gothic school includes Flannery O'Connor and Carson McCullers.

Writers of the 19th century include William Gilmore Simms, Joel Chandler Harris, and George Washington Cable.

South Georgia island in the S Atlantic, a British crown colony administered with the South Sandwich Islands; area 1,450 sq mi/3,757 sq km. South Georgia lies 800 mi/1,300 km SE of the Falkland Islands, of which it was a dependency until 1985. The British Antarctic Survey has a station on nearby Bird Island.

South Georgia was visited by Captain James Cook 1775. The explorer Edward Shackleton is buried there. The chief settlement, Grytviken, was established as a whaling station 1904 and abandoned 1966; it was reoccupied by a small military garrison after the Falklands War 1982.

South Glamorgan (Welsh *De Morgannwg*) county in S Wales
area 162 sq mi/420 sq km
cities Cardiff (administrative headquarters), Barry, Penarth
features fertile Vale of Glamorgan; Welsh Folk Museum at St Fagans, near Cardiff
products dairy farming, industry (steel, plastics, engineering) in the Cardiff area
population (1991) 383,300
language English; 6% are Welsh-speaking
famous people Sarah Siddons, Shirley Bassey, R S Thomas

South Holland (Dutch *Zuid-Holland*) low-lying coastal province of the Netherlands
area 1,123 sq mi/2,910 sq km
population (1991) 3,245,300
capital The Hague
cities Rotterdam, Dordrecht, Leiden, Delft, Gouda
products bulbs, horticulture, livestock, dairy products, chemicals, textiles
history once part of the former county of Holland, which was divided into two provinces 1840.

South Korea see ◊Korea, South.

South Orkney Islands group of barren, uninhabited islands in ◊British Antarctic Territory, SE of Cape Horn; area 240 sq mi/622 sq km. They were discovered by the naval explorer Capt George Powell 1821. Argentina, which lays claim to the islands, maintained a scientific station there 1976–82.

South Pacific Commission (SPC) organization to promote economic and social cooperation in the region, established 1947. Its members include most of the sovereign and dependent states in the South Pacific, plus

France, the UK, and the US; headquarters in Nouméa, New Caledonia.

South Sandwich Islands actively volcanic uninhabited British Dependent Territory; area 130 sq mi/337 sq km. Along with ◊South Georgia, 470 mi/750 km to the NW, it is administered from the Falkland Islands. They were claimed by Capt Cook 1775 and named after his patron John Montagu, the 4th Earl of Sandwich. The islands were annexed by the UK 1908 and 1917. They were first formally claimed by Argentina 1948. In Dec 1976, 50 Argentine "scientists" landed on Southern Thule and were removed June 1982. There is an ice-free port off Cumberland Bay. Over 21 million penguins breed on Zavadovski Island.

South Sea Bubble financial crisis in Britain in 1720. The South Sea Company, founded 1711, which had a monopoly of trade with South America, offered in 1719 to take over more than half the national debt in return for further concessions. Its 100 shares rapidly rose to 1,000, and an orgy of speculation followed. When the "bubble" burst, thousands were ruined. The discovery that cabinet ministers had been guilty of corruption led to a political crisis.

South Shetland Islands archipelago of 12 uninhabited islands in the South Atlantic, forming part of ◊British Antarctic Territory; area 1,785 sq mi/4,622 sq km.

South, the historically, the states of the US bounded on the N by the ◊Mason–Dixon Line, the Ohio River, and the E and N borders of Missouri, with an agrarian economy based on plantations worked by slaves, and which seceded from the Union 1861, beginning the American Civil War, as the ◊Confederacy. The term is now loosely applied in a geographical and cultural sense, with Texas often regarded as part of the Southwest rather than the South.

By its broadest definition, the South consists of 16 states (including Texas and Oklahoma) and the District of Columbia, with an area of 898,575 sq mi/2,327,309 sq km. Houston is the largest city.

South West Africa former name (until 1968) of ◊Namibia.

South Yorkshire metropolitan county of England, created 1976, originally administered by an elected council; its powers reverted to district councils from 1986
area 602 sq mi/1,560 sq km
cities Barnsley, Sheffield, Doncaster
features river Don; part of Peak District National Park
products metal work, coal, dairy, sheep, arable farming
population (1991) 1,269,300
famous people Ian Botham, Arthur Scargill.

Soutine Chaim 1894–1943. Lithuanian-born French Expressionist artist. He painted landscapes and portraits, including many of painters active in Paris in the 1920s and 1930s. He had a distorted style, using thick application of paint (impasto) and brilliant colors.

sovereignty absolute authority within a given territory. The possession of sovereignty is taken to be the distinguishing feature of the state, as against other forms of community. The term has an internal aspect, in that it refers to the ultimate source of authority within a state, such as a parliament or monarch, and an external aspect, where it denotes the independence of the state from any outside authority.

soviet (Russian "council") originally a strike committee elected by Russian workers in the 1905 revolution; in 1917 these were set up by peasants, soldiers, and factory workers. The soviets sent delegates to the All-Russian Congress of Soviets to represent their opinions to a future government. They were later taken over by the ◊Bolsheviks.

Soviet Central Asia former name (until 1991) of the ◊Central Asian Republics.

Soviet Far East former name (until 1991) of geographical division of Asiatic Russia, now known as ◊Russian Far East.

Soviet Union alternate name for the former ◊Union of Soviet Socialist Republics (USSR).

sovkhoz Soviet state-owned farm where the workers were state employees (such farms are still widespread in ex-Soviet republics). The sovkhoz differs from the **kolkhoz** where the farm is run by a collective (see ◊collective farm).

Soweto (abbreviation for *South West Township*) racially segregated urban settlement in South Africa, SW of Johannesburg; population (1983) 915,872. It has experienced civil unrest because of the ◊apartheid regime.

It began as a shanty town in the 1930s and is now the largest black city in South Africa, but until 1976 its population could have status only as temporary residents, serving as a work force for Johannesburg. There were serious riots in June 1976, sparked by a ruling that Afrikaans be used in African schools there. Reforms followed, but riots flared up again in 1985 and have continued into the 1990s.

soybean leguminous plant *Glycine max*, native to E Asia, in particular Japan and China. Originally grown as a forage crop, it is increasingly used for human consumption in cooking oils and margarine, as a flour, soy milk, soy sauce, or processed into tofu, miso, or textured vegetable protein.

Soyinka Wole 1934– . Nigerian author who was a political prisoner in Nigeria 1967–69. His works include the play *The Lion and the Jewel* 1963; his prison memoirs *The Man Died* 1972; *Aké, The Years of Childhood* 1982, an autobiography, and *Isara*, a fictionalized memoir 1989. He was the first African to receive the Nobel Prize for Literature, in 1986.

Soyuz (Russian "union") Soviet series of spacecraft, capable of carrying up to three cosmonauts. Soyuz spacecraft consist of three parts: a rear section containing engines; the central crew compartment; and a forward compartment that gives additional room for working and living space. They are now used for ferrying crews up to space stations, though they were originally used for independent space flight.

Soyuz 1 crashed on its first flight April 1967, killing the lone pilot, Vladimir Komarov. Yet in 1968 *Soyuz 3* had the first manned rendezvous and possible docking by a cosmonaut; in 1969 *Soyuz 6* had three spacecraft and seven men put into Earth orbit simultaneously for the first time; and in 1971 *Soyuz 11* linked up with the first space station, *Salyut 1*, although three cosmonauts died on reentry due to loss of pressure in the spacecraft.

Spa town in Liège province, Belgium; population (1991) 10,100. A health resort since the 14th century for its mineral springs, it has given its name to similar centers elsewhere; see ◊spa town.

Spaak Paul-Henri 1899–1972. Belgian socialist politician. From 1936 to 1966 he held office almost continuously as foreign minister or prime minister. He was an ardent advocate of international peace.

space the void that exists beyond Earth's atmosphere. Above 75 mi/120 km, very little atmosphere remains, so objects can continue to move quickly without extra energy. The space between the planets is not entirely empty, but filled with the tenuous gas of the ◊solar wind as well as dust specks.

The space between stars is also filled with thin gas and dust. Evidence also exists for highly rarefied gas in the space between clusters of galaxies, and for that between individual galaxies.

Spacek Sissy (Mary Elizabeth) 1949– . US film actress who starred in *Badlands* 1973 and *Carrie* 1976, in which she played a repressed telekinetic teenager. Other films include *Coal Miner's Daughter* 1979 and *Missing* 1982.

Spacelab small space station built by the European Space Agency, carried in the cargo bay of the US space shuttle, in which it remains throughout each flight, returning to Earth with the shuttle. Spacelab consists of a pressurized module in which astronauts can work, and a series of pallets, open to the vacuum of space, on which equipment is mounted.

Spacelab is used for astronomy, Earth observation, and experiments utilizing the conditions of weightlessness and vacuum in orbit. The pressurized module can be flown with or without pallets, or the pallets can be flown on their own, in which case the astronauts remain in the shuttle's own crew compartment. All the sections of Spacelab can be reused many times. The first Spacelab mission, consisting of a pressurized module and pallets, lasted ten days Nov–Dec 1983.

space probe any instrumented object sent beyond Earth to collect data from other parts of the Solar System and from deep space. The first probe was the Soviet *Lunik 1*, which flew past the Moon 1959. The first successful planetary probe was the US *Mariner 2*, which flew past Venus 1962, using ◊transfer orbit. The first space probe to leave the Solar System was *Pioneer 10* 1983. Space probes include *Giotto*, the ◊Moon probes, and the Mariner, Pioneer, Viking, and Voyager series. Japan launched its first space probe 1990.

space shuttle reusable crewed spacecraft. The first was launched April 12, 1981 by the US. It was developed by NASA to reduce the cost of using space for commercial, scientific, and military purposes. After leaving its payload in space, the space-shuttle orbiter can be flown back to Earth to land on a runway, and is then available for reuse.

Four orbiters were built: *Columbia*, *Challenger*, *Discovery*, and *Atlantis*. *Challenger* was destroyed in a midair explosion just over a minute after its tenth launch Jan 28, 1986, killing all seven crew members, the result of a failure in one of the solid rocket boosters. Flights resumed with redesigned boosters in Sept 1988. A replacement orbiter, *Endeavor*, was built. At the end of the 1980s, an average of $375 million had been spent on each space-shuttle mission.

The USSR produced a shuttle of similar size and appearance to the US one. The first Soviet shuttle, *Buran*, was launched without a crew by the Energia rocket Nov 15, 1988. In Japan, development of a crewless shuttle began 1986.

The space shuttle orbiter, the part that goes into space, is 122 ft/37.2 m long and weighs

75 tons. Although most of its cargoes will be unmanned, two to eight crew members may occupy the orbiter's nose section for up to 30 days. In its cargo bay the orbiter can carry up to 32 tons of satellites, scientific equipment, ▷Spacelab, or military payloads. At launch, the shuttle's three main engines are fed with liquid fuel from a cylindrical tank attached to the orbiter; this tank is discarded shortly before the shuttle reaches orbit. Two additional solid-fuel boosters provide the main thrust for launch, but are jettisoned after two minutes.

space sickness or **space adaptation syndrome** feeling of nausea, sometimes accompanied by vomiting, experienced by about 40% of all astronauts during their first few days in space. It is akin to travel sickness, and is thought to be caused by confusion of the body's balancing mechanism, located in the inner ear, by weightlessness. The sensation passes after a few days as the body adapts.

space station any large structure designed for human occupation in space for extended periods of time. Space stations are used for carrying out astronomical observations and surveys of Earth, as well as for biological studies and the processing of materials in weightlessness. The first space station was ▷*Salyut 1*, and the US has launched ▷*Skylab*.

NASA plans to build a larger space station, to be called *Freedom*, in orbit during the 1990s, in cooperation with other countries, including the European Space Agency, which is building a module called *Columbus*, and Japan, also building a module.

space suit protective suit worn by astronauts and cosmonauts in space. It provides an insulated, air-conditioned cocoon in which people can live and work for hours at a time while outside the spacecraft. Inside the suit is a cooling garment that keeps the body at a comfortable temperature even during vigorous work. The suit provides air to breathe, and removes exhaled carbon dioxide and moisture. The suit's outer layers insulate the occupant from the extremes of hot and cold in space (−240°F/−150°C in the shade to +350°F/+180°C in sunlight), and from the impact of small meteorites. Some space suits have a jet-propelled backpack, which the wearer can use to move about.

space-time in physics, combination of space and time used in the theory of ▷relativity. When developing relativity, Einstein showed that time was in many respects like an extra dimension (or direction) to space. Space and time can thus be considered as entwined into a single entity, rather than two separate things.

Space-time is considered to have four dimensions: three of space and one of time. In relativity theory, events are described as occurring at points in space-time. The **general theory of relativity** describes how space-time is distorted by the presence of material bodies, an effect that we observe as gravity.

spadix in botany, an ▷inflorescence consisting of a long, fleshy axis bearing many small, stalkless flowers. It is partially enclosed by a large bract or ▷spathe. A spadix is characteristic of plants belonging to the family Araceae, including the arum lily *Zantedeschia aethiopica*.

Spain country in SW Europe, on the Iberian Peninsula between the Atlantic Ocean and the Mediterranean Sea, bounded N by France and W by Portugal.

government The 1978 constitution puts a hereditary monarch as formal head of state. The monarch appoints a prime minister, called president of government, and a council of ministers, all responsible to the national assembly, Las Cortes Generales. The Cortes consists of two chambers, the chamber of deputies, with 350 members, and the senate, with 208. Deputies are elected by universal suffrage through a system of proportional representation, and 208 of the senators are directly elected to represent the whole country and 49 to represent the regions. All serve a four-year term.

Spain has developed a regional self-government whereby each of the 50 provinces has its own council (Diputación Provincial) and civil governor. The devolution process was extended 1979 when 17 autonomous communities were approved, each with a parliament elected for a four-year term.

history Pre-Roman Spain was inhabited by Iberians, Basques, Celts, and Celtiberians. Greece and Phoenicia established colonies on the coast from the 7th century BC; Carthage dominated from the 5th century, trying to found an empire in the southeast. This was conquered by ancient Rome about 200 BC, and after a long struggle all Spain was absorbed into the Roman Empire. At the invitation of Rome the Visigoths (see ▷Goths) set up a kingdom in Spain from the beginning of the 5th century AD until the invasion by the ▷Moors 711. Christian resistance held out in the north, and by 1250 they had reconquered all Spain except ▷Granada. During this struggle a number of small kingdoms were formed, all of which by the 13th century had been absorbed by ▷Castile and ▷Aragon. The marriage of ▷Ferdinand of Aragon to Isabella of Castile 1469 united their domains on their accession 1479. The conquest of Granada 1492 completed the unification of Spain.

world power Under Ferdinand and Isabella, Charles I (see ▷Charles V of the Holy Roman Empire), and Philip II, Spain became one of the greatest powers in the world. The discoveries of Columbus, made on behalf of Spain, were followed by the conquest of most of Central and South America. Naples and Sicily were annexed 1503, Milan 1535, Portugal 1580, and Charles I inherited the Netherlands, but with the revolt in the Netherlands and the defeat of the Armada 1588, Spain's power began to decline. The loss of civil and religious freedom, constant wars, inflation, a corrupt bureaucracy, and the expulsion of the Jews and Moors undermined the economy. By the peace of Utrecht that concluded the War of the ▷Spanish Succession 1713, Spain lost Naples, Sicily, Milan, Gibraltar, and its last possessions in the Netherlands.

wars and revolutions The 18th century saw reforms and economic progress, but Spain became involved in the ▷Revolutionary and ▷Napoleonic wars, first as the ally, then as the opponent of France. France occupied Spain 1808 and was expelled with British assistance 1814. Throughout the 19th century conflict raged between monarchists and liberals; revolutions and civil wars took place 1820–23, 1833–39, and 1868, besides many minor revolts, and a republic was temporarily established 1873–74. Spain lost its American colonies between 1810 and 1830 and after the ▷Spanish-American War 1898 ceded Cuba and the Philippines to the US.

Spanish Civil War Republicanism, socialism, and anarchism grew after 1900; ▷Primo de Rivera's dictatorship 1923–30 failed to preserve

the monarchy under ▷Alfonso XIII, and in 1931 a republic was established. In 1936 the Popular Front, a center-left alliance, took office and introduced agrarian and other reforms that aroused the opposition of the landlords and the Catholic church. A military rebellion led by General Francisco ▷Franco resulted in the Spanish ▷Civil War 1936–39. Franco, who was supported by the German Nazis and Italian Fascists, won the war, establishing a military dictatorship.

monarchy restored In 1947 Franco allowed the revival of a legislature with limited powers and announced that after his death the monarchy would be restored, naming the grandson of the last monarch, Prince Juan Carlos de Bourbon, as his successor. Franco died 1975, and King Juan Carlos became head of state. There followed a slow but steady progress to democratic government, with the new constitution endorsed by referendum 1978.

regional demands and right-wing threat Spain faced two main internal problems, the demands for independence by regional extremists and the possibility of a right-wing military coup. The aims of the ruling Democratic Center Party (UCD), led by Adolfo Suárez, included a devolution of power to the regions (Basque, Catalonia, and eventually Andalusia), entry into the North Atlantic Treaty Organization (NATO), and membership in the European Economic Community. In 1981 Suárez suddenly resigned and was succeeded by his deputy, Leopoldo Calvo Sotelo. He was immediately confronted with an attempted army coup in Madrid, while at the same time the military commander of Valencia declared a state of emergency there and sent tanks out on the streets. Both uprisings failed, and the two leaders were tried and imprisoned. Sotelo's decision to take Spain into NATO was widely criticized, and he was forced to call a general election Oct 1982. The result was a sweeping victory for the Socialist Workers' Party (PSOE), led by Felipe González. The Basque separatist organization, ETA, had stepped up its campaign for independence with widespread terrorist activity, spreading in 1985 to the Mediterranean vacation resorts and threatening Spain's lucrative tourist industry.

González administration The PSOE had fought the 1982 election on a policy of taking Spain out of NATO and carrying out extensive nationalization. Once in office, however, González showed himself to be a pragmatist. His nationalization program was highly selective, and he left the decision on NATO to a referendum. In Jan 1986 Spain became a full member of the European Community, and in March the referendum showed popular support for remaining in NATO. In the July 1986 election González returned for another term as prime minister. In Nov 1988 Spain, with Portugal, became a member of the ▷Western European Union. In the Nov 1989 general election the PSOE won only 175 seats in the 350-member national assembly but retained power under Prime Minister González. Major tax reforms were passed 1991 in an effort to help the nation's struggling economy. The 1992 Summer Olympic Games were held in Barcelona. *See illustration box.*

Spandau suburb of Berlin, Germany. The chief war criminals condemned at the Nuremberg Trials 1946 were imprisoned in the fortress there. The last of them was the Nazi leader Rudolf Hess, and the prison was demolished after his death 1987.

Spain
(*España*)

area 194,960 sq mi/504,750 sq km
capital Madrid
cities Zaragoza, Seville, Murcia, Córdoba; ports Barcelona, Valencia, Cartagena, Málaga, Cádiz, Vigo, Santander, Bilbao
physical central plateau with mountain ranges; lowlands in S
territories Balearic and Canary Islands; in N Africa: Ceuta, Melilla, Alhucemas, Chafarinas Is, Peñón de Vélez
features rivers Ebro, Douro, Tagus, Guadiana, Guadalquivir; Iberian Plateau (Meseta); Pyrenees, Cantabrian Mountains, Andalusian Mountains, Sierra Nevada
head of state King Juan Carlos I from 1975
head of government Felipe González Márquez from 1982
political system constitutional monarchy
political parties Socialist Workers' Party (PSOE), democratic socialist; Popular Alliance (AP), center-right; Christian Democrats (DC), centrist; Liberal Party (PL), left-of-center
exports citrus fruits, grapes, pomegranates, vegetables, wine, sherry, olive oil, canned fruit and fish, iron ore, cork, vehicles, textiles, petroleum products, leather goods, ceramics
currency peseta
population (1990 est) 39,623,000; growth rate 0.2% p.a.
life expectancy men 74, women 80 (1989)
language Spanish (Castilian, official), Basque, Catalan, Galician, Valencian, Majorcan
religion Roman Catholic 99%
literacy 97% (1989)
GNP $288 bn (1987); $4,490 per head (1984)
chronology
1936–39 Civil war; General Francisco Franco became head of state and government; fascist party Falange declared only legal political organization.
1947 General Franco announced restoration of the monarchy after his death, with Prince Juan Carlos as his successor.
1975 Franco died; succeeded as head of state by King Juan Carlos I.
1978 New constitution adopted with Adolfo Suárez, leader of the Democratic Center Party, as prime minister.
1981 Suárez resigned; succeeded by Leopoldo Calvo Sotelo. Attempted military coup thwarted.
1982 Socialist Workers' Party (PSOE), led by Felipe González, won a sweeping electoral victory. Basque separatist organization (ETA) stepped up its guerrilla campaign.
1985 ETA's campaign spread to vacation resorts.
1986 Referendum confirmed NATO membership. Spain joined the European Economic Community.
1988 Spain joined the Western European Union.
1989 PSOE lost seats to hold only parity after general election. Talks between government and ETA collapsed and truce ended.
1992 Summer Olympic Games held in Barcelona.

spaniel any of several breeds of dog, characterized by large, drooping ears and a wavy, long, silky coat. The *Sussex spaniel* is believed to be the oldest variety, weighs 45 lb/ 20 kg, is 15 in/40 cm tall, and is a golden liver color.

The *springer* (English and Welsh), about 45 lb/20 kg and 20 in/50 cm tall, is so called because of its use for "springing" game. The *cocker* (English and American) is smaller (25 lb/12 kg, 15 in/40 cm tall), and of various colors.

Spanish an inhabitant of Spain or a person of Spanish descent, as well as the culture and Romance language of such persons. The standard Spanish language, Castilian, originated in the kingdoms of Castile and Aragon (Catalan and Basque languages are also spoken in Spain).

Spanish-American War brief war 1898 between Spain and the US over Spanish rule in Cuba and the Philippines; the complete defeat of Spain made the US a colonial power. The Treaty of Paris ceded the Philippines, Guam, and Puerto Rico to the US; Cuba became independent. The US paid $20 million to Spain. Thus ended Spain's colonial presence in the Americas.

The war began in Cuba when the US battleship *Maine* was blown up in Havana harbor, allegedly by the Spanish. Other engagements included the Battle of Manila Bay, in which Commander George Dewey's navy destroyed the Spanish fleet in the Philippines; and the taking of the Cuban port cities of El Caney and San Juan Heights (in which Theodore Roosevelt's regiment, the Rough Riders, was involved), destroying the Spanish fleet there.

Spanish architecture the architecture of Spain has been influenced by both Classical and Islamic traditions. Styles include **Roman** (3rd–5th century); **Asturian** (9th century), taking its name from the district in NW Spain which was unconquered by the Moors; **Mozarabic** (9th–11th centuries), a style of Spanish Christian architecture, showing the influence of Islamic architecture; **Romanesque** (11th and 12th centuries); **Gothic** (13th–16th centuries); **Renaissance** (15th–17th centuries), which is based on Italian models; **Baroque** (17th–18th centuries), a style which reached its peak in the fantastic designs of Churriguera and his followers; **Neo-Classical** (18th and 19th centuries); and **Modern** Oscar Niemeyer and Antonio ▷Gaudí.

Spanish Armada fleet sent by Philip II of Spain against England in 1588. Consisting of 130 ships, it sailed from Lisbon and carried on a running fight up the Channel with the English fleet of 197 small ships under Howard of Effingham and Francis ▷Drake. The Armada anchored off Calais but fireships forced it to put to sea, and a general action followed off Gravelines. What remained of the Armada escaped around the N of Scotland and W of Ireland, suffering many losses by storm and shipwreck on the way. Only about half the original fleet returned to Spain.

Spanish art painting and sculpture of Spain:
painting
late 15th–16th centuries Italian and Flemish influences contributed to Spanish Renaissance painting. The painters of this period include Bartolomé Bermejo (1440–1495), Alonzo Sánchez Coello (1515–1590), Luis de Vargas (1502–1568), Francisco de Herrera the Elder, Juan de Juanes (1523–1579), Juan Navarrete (1526–1579), Luis de Morales (1509–1586), and El Greco.
17th century The leading Spanish artist was Velázquez.
18th century Goya was to exert a great influence on European art of the following century.
20th century Painters include the Cubist Juan Gris, the Surrealists Joan Miró and Salvador Dali, and Pablo Picasso, widely regarded as the most innovative painter of the century.
sculpture Spanish sculptors include Berruguete (c. 1488–1561), El Greco, Montañes (1568–1649), Alonso Cano (1601–1667), Julio González (1876–1942), and Pablo Picasso.

Spanish Civil War 1936–39. See ▷Civil War, Spanish.

Spanish fly alternate name for a European blister ▷beetle *Lytta vesicatoria*, once used in powdered form as a dangerous diuretic and supposed aphrodisiac.

Spanish Guinea former name of the Republic of ▷Equatorial Guinea.

Spanish language member of the Romance branch of the Indo-European language family, traditionally known as Castilian and originally spoken only in NE Spain. As the language of the court, it has been the standard and literary language of the Spanish state since the 13th century. It is now a world language, spoken in Mexico and all South and Central American countries (except Brazil, Guyana, Suriname, and French Guiana) as well as in the Philippines, Cuba, Puerto Rico, and much of the US.

Castilian Spanish has never succeeded in supplanting such regional languages as Basque, Gallego or Galician, and Catalan. Because of the long Muslim dominance of the S Iberian peninsula, Spanish has been considerably influenced by Arabic. Words in English of Spanish origin include *bronco, cargo, galleon, mosquito, ranch,* and *sherry.*

Spanish literature of the Classical Spanish epics, the 12th-century *El cantar de Mio Cid* is the only complete example. The founder of Castilian prose was King Alfonso X, El Sabio (the Wise), who also wrote lyric poetry in the Galician dialect. The first true poet was the 14th-century satirist Juan Ruiz (c. 1283–1350), archpriest of Hita. To the 15th century belong the Marquis of Santillana (Iñigo López de Mendoza), poet, critic, and collector of proverbs; chivalric romances, such as the *Amadis de Gaula*; ballads dealing with the struggle against the Moors; and the *Celestina*, a novel in dramatic form. The flowering of verse drama began with Lope de Rueda (died 1565), and reached its height with Lope de Vega and Calderón de la Barca.

In poetry the golden age of the 15th–16th

centuries produced the lyrical Garcilaso de la Vega; the patriotic Fernando de Herrera (1534–1597); the mystics Santa Teresa and Luis de León; the elaborate style of Luis de Góngora (1561–1627), who popularized the decadent "gongorism"; and the biting satire of Francisco de Quevedo. In fiction there developed the pastoral romance, for example Jorge de Montemayor's *Diana*; the picaresque novel, established by the anonymous *Lazarillo del Tormes*; and the work of Cervantes.

In the 18th century the Benedictine Benito J Feijoo introduced scientific thought to Spain, and French influence emerged in the comedies of Leandro F de Moratín (1760–1828) and others. Typical of the romantic era were the poets and dramatists Angel de Saavedra (Duque de Rivas) (1791–1865) and José Zorilla (1817–1893), and the lyricist José de Espronceda (1810–1842). Among 19th-century novelists were Pedro de Alarcón (1833–1891), Emilia, condesa de Pardo Bazán (1852–1921), and Vicente Blasco Ibáñez (1867–1928); a 19th-century dramatist is José Echegaray (1832–1916).

The "Generation of 1898" included the philosophers Miguel de Unamuno (1864–1936) and José Ortega y Gasset (1883–1955); the novelist Pío Baroja (1872–1956); the prose writer Azorín (José Martínez Ruiz, 1874–1967); and the Nobel Prize-winning poet Juan Ramón Jiménez (1881–1958). The next generation included novelist Camilo José Cela (1916–); the poets Antonio Machado (1875–1939), Rafael Alberti (1902–), Luis Cernuda (1902–1963), and the Nobel Prize-winner Vincente Aleixandre (1898–1984); and the dramatists Jacinto Benavente (1866–1954), the brothers Quintero, and—the most striking—Federico García Lorca. The Civil War and the strict censorship of the Franco government disrupted mid-20th-century literary life, but later names include the novelists Rafael Sánchez Ferlosio (1927–) and Juan Goytisolo (1931–); and the poets Blas de Otero (1916–) and José Hierro (1922–).

Spanish Main common name for the Caribbean in the 16th–17th centuries, but more properly the South American mainland between the river Orinoco and Panama.

Spanish Sahara former name for ▷Western Sahara.

Spanish Succession, War of the war 1701–14 of Britain, Austria, the Netherlands, Portugal, and Denmark (the Allies) against France, Spain, and Bavaria. It was caused by Louis XIV's acceptance of the Spanish throne on behalf of his grandson, Philip V of Spain, in defiance of the Partition Treaty of 1700, under which it would have passed to Archduke Charles of Austria (later Holy Roman emperor Charles VI).

Peace was made by the Treaties of Utrecht 1713 and Rastatt 1714. Philip V was recognized as king of Spain, thus founding the Spanish branch of the Bourbon dynasty. Britain received Gibraltar, Minorca, and Nova Scotia; and Austria received Belgium, Milan, and Naples.

Spanish Town town in Middlesex county, Jamaica; population (1982) 89,000. Founded by Diego Columbus about 1525, it was the capital of Jamaica 1535–1871.

Spark Muriel 1918– . Scottish novelist. She is a Catholic convert, and her enigmatic satires include: *The Ballad of Peckham Rye* 1960, *The Prime of Miss Jean Brodie* 1961, *The Only Problem* 1984, and *Symposium* 1990.

spark chamber electronic device for recording tracks of charged subatomic ▷particles, decay products, and rays. In combination with a stack of photographic plates, a spark chamber enables the point where an interaction has taken place to be located, to within a cubic centimeter. At its simplest, it consists of two smooth threadlike ▷electrodes that are positioned 0.5–1 in/1–2 cm apart, the space between being filled by an inert gas such as neon. Sparks jump through the gas along the ionized path created by the radiation.

spark plug plug that produces an electric spark in the cylinder of a gasoline engine to ignite the fuel mixture. It consists essentially of two electrodes insulated from one another. High-voltage (18,000 V) electricity is fed to a central electrode via the distributor. At the base of the electrode, inside the cylinder, the electricity jumps to another electrode earthed to the engine body, creating a spark. See also ▷ignition coil.

sparrow any of a family (Passeridae) of small Old World birds of the order Passeriformes with short, thick bills, including the now worldwide house or English sparrow *Passer domesticus*. Many numbers of the New World family Emberizidae, which includes ▷warblers, orioles, and buntings are also called sparrows; for example, the North American song sparrow *Melospize melodia*.

sparrow hawk alternate (but no longer correct) name for the American ▷kestrel. The name now only refers to a small woodland ▷hawk *Accipiter nisus* found in Eurasia and N Africa. It has a long tail and short wings. The male grows to 11 in/28 cm long, and the female 15 in/38 cm. It hunts small birds.

Sparta ancient Greek city-state in the S Peloponnese (near Sparte), developed from Dorian settlements in the 10th century BC. The Spartans, known for their military discipline and austerity, took part in the Persian and Peloponnesian wars.

The Dorians formed the ruling race in Sparta, the original inhabitants being divided into *perioeci* (tributaries without political rights) and helots or serfs. The state was ruled by two hereditary kings, and under the constitution attributed to Lycurgus all citizens were trained for war from childhood. As a result, the Spartans became proverbial for their indifference to pain or death, their contempt for luxury and the arts, and their harsh treatment of the helots. They distinguished themselves in the ▷Persian and ▷Peloponnesian wars, but defeat by the Thebans in 371 BC marked the start of their decline. The ancient city was destroyed by the Visigoths in AD 396.

Spartacist member of a group of left-wing radicals in Germany at the end of World War I, founders of the ***Spartacus League***, which became the German Communist Party in 1919. The league participated in the Berlin workers' revolt of Jan 1919, which was suppressed by the Freikorps on the orders of the socialist government. The agitation ended with the murder of Spartacist leaders Karl ▷Liebknecht and Rosa ▷Luxemburg.

Spartacus Thracian gladiator who in 73 BC led a revolt of gladiators and slaves in Capua, near Naples. He was eventually caught by Roman general ▷Crassus and crucified.

Spartanburg city in NW South Carolina, NW of Columbia. In the foothills of the Blue Ridge Mountains, it is an agricultural center. Its industries include food products, furniture, textiles, paper, and plumbing supplies; population (1990) 43,500.

spastic person with ▷cerebral palsy. The term is also applied generally to limbs with impaired movement, stiffness, and resistance to passive movement, and to any body part (such as the colon) affected with spasm.

spathe in flowers, the single large bract surrounding the type of inflorescence known as a ▷spadix. It is sometimes brightly colored and petallike, as in the brilliant scarlet spathe of the flamingo plant *Anthurium andreanum* from South America; this serves to attract insects.

spa town town with a spring, the water of which, it is claimed, has the power to cure illness and restore health. Spa treatment involves drinking and bathing in the naturally mineralized spring water.

The name derives from the Belgian town of Spa, whose mineral springs have attracted patients since the 14th century. The earliest spas date from Roman times.

speakeasy bar that illegally sold alcoholic beverages during the ▷Prohibition period (1920–33) in the US. The term is probably derived from the need to speak quickly or quietly to the doorkeeper in order to gain admission.

speaker presiding officer in the US House of Representatives. The speaker is second in line of succession to the presidency in the event of death or incapacitation.

spearmint perennial herb *Mentha spicata* of the mint family Labiatae, with aromatic leaves and spikes of purple flowers, used for flavoring food.

special drawing right (SDR) the right of a member state of the ▷International Monetary Fund to apply for money to finance its balance of payments deficit. Originally, the SDR was linked to gold and the US dollar. After 1974 SDRs were defined in terms of a "basket" of the 16 currencies of countries doing 1% or more of the world's trade. In 1981 the SDR was simplified to a weighted average of US dollars, French francs, German marks, Japanese yen, and UK pounds sterling.

special education education, often in separate "special schools," for children with specific physical or mental problems or disabilities.

In the US, the federal department of education has been leading the recent movement toward "mainstreaming," which calls for the integration of students with special needs into the normal school system whenever practical.

speciation emergence of a new species during evolutionary history. One cause of speciation is the geographical separation of populations of the parent species, followed by reproductive isolation and selection for different environments so that they no longer produce viable offspring when they interbreed. Other causes are ▷assortative mating and the establishment of a ▷polyploid population.

species in biology, a distinguishable group of organisms that resemble each other or consist of a few distinctive types (as in ▷polymorphism), and that can all interbreed to produce fertile offspring. Species are the lowest level in the system of biological classification.

Related species are grouped together in a genus. Within a species there are usually two or more separate ▷populations, which may in time become distinctive enough to be designated subspecies or varieties, and could eventually give rise to new species through ⟡speciation. Around 1.4 million species have been identified so far, of which 750,000 are insects, 250,000 are plants, and 41,000 are vertebrates. In tropical regions there are roughly two species for each temperate-zone species. It is estimated that one species becomes extinct every day through habitat destruction.

specific gravity alternative term for ⟡relative density.

specific heat capacity in physics, quantity of heat required to raise unit mass (1 kg) of a substance by one ⟡kelvin (1°C). The unit of specific heat capacity in the SI system is the ⟡joule per kilogram kelvin (J kg^{-1} K^{-1}).

speckle interferometry technique whereby large telescopes can achieve high resolution of astronomical objects despite the adverse effects of the atmosphere through which light from the object under study must pass. It involves the taking of large numbers of images, each under high magnification and with short exposure times. The pictures are then combined to form the final picture. The technique was introduced by the French astronomer Antoine Labeyrie 1970.

spectroscopy the study of spectra (obtained by the use of an optical instrument called a spectroscope) associated with atoms or molecules in solid, liquid, or gaseous phase. Spectroscopy can be used to identify unknown compounds and is an invaluable tool to scientists, industry (for example, pharmaceuticals for purity checks), and medical workers.

Emission spectroscopy is the study of the characteristic series of sharp lines in the spectrum produced when an ⟡element is heated. Thus an unknown mixture can be analyzed for its component elements. Related is absorption spectroscopy, dealing with atoms and molecules as they absorb energy in a characteristic way. Again, dark lines can be used for analysis. More detailed structural information can be obtained using infrared spectroscopy (concerned with molecular vibrations) or nuclear magnetic resonance (NMR) spectroscopy (concerned with interactions between adjacent atomic nuclei).

spectrum (plural **spectra**) in physics, an arrangement of frequencies or wavelengths when electromagnetic radiations are separated into their constituent parts. Visible light is part of the ⟡electromagnetic spectrum and most sources emit waves over a range of wavelengths that can be broken up or "dispersed"; white light can be separated into red, orange, yellow, green, blue, indigo, and violet. The visible spectrum was first studied by Isaac ⟡Newton, who showed in 1672 how white light could be broken up into different colors.

speculum (plural **specula**) medical instrument to aid examination of an opening into the body; for example, the nose or vagina. The speculum allows the opening to be widened, permitting the passage of instruments. Many specula also have built-in lights to illuminate the cavity being examined.

The earliest recorded vaginal speculum was used by Greek physician Archigenes in the 2nd century AD.

speech recognition or **voice input** in computing, any technique by which a computer can understand ordinary speech. Spoken words are divided into "frames," each lasting about one-thirtieth of a second, which are converted to a wave form. These are then compared with a series of stored frames to determine the most likely word. Research into speech recognition started in 1938, but the technology did not become sufficiently developed for commercial applications until the late 1980s.

There are three types: **separate word recognition** for distinguishing up to several hundred separately spoken words; **connected speech recognition** for speech in which there is a short pause between words; and **continuous speech recognition** for normal but carefully articulated speech.

speech synthesis or **voice output** computer-based technology for generating speech. A speech synthesizer is controlled by a computer, which supplies strings of codes representing basic speech sounds (phonemes); together these make up words. Speech-synthesis applications include children's toys, car and aircraft warning systems, and talking books for the blind.

speed the rate at which an object moves. The constant speed v of an object may be calculated by dividing the distance s it has traveled by the time t taken to do so, and may be expressed as:
$$v = s/t$$
The usual units of speed are meters per second or kilometers per hour.

Speed is a scalar quantity in which direction of motion is unimportant (unlike the vector quantity ⟡velocity, in which both magnitude and direction must be taken into consideration). See also ⟡distance-time graph.

speed of light speed at which light and other ⟡electromagnetic waves travel through empty space. Its value is 186,281 mi/299,792,458 m per second. The speed of light is the highest speed possible, according to the theory of ⟡relativity, and its value is independent of the motion of its source and of the observer. It is impossible to accelerate any material body to this speed because it would require an infinite amount of energy.

speed of sound speed at which sound travels through a medium, such as air or water. In air at a temperature of 32°F/0°C, the speed of sound is 1,087 ft/331 m per second. At higher temperatures, the speed of sound is greater; at 64°F/18°C it is 1,123 ft/342 m per second. It is greater in liquids and solids; for example, in water it is around 4,724 ft/1,440 m per second, depending on the temperature.

speedometer instrument attached to the transmission of a vehicle by a flexible drive shaft, which indicates the speed of the vehicle in miles or kilometers per hour on a dial easily visible to the driver.

speedwell any flowering plant of the genus *Veronica* of the snapdragon family Scrophulariaceae. Of the many wild species, most are low-growing with small, bluish flowers.

Brookline speedwell *V. americana* grows in marshes all across North America.

Speer Albert 1905–1981. German architect and minister in the Nazi government during World War II. Commissioned by Hitler, Speer, like his counterparts in Fascist Italy, chose an overblown Classicism to glorify the state, as, for example, in his plan for the Berlin and Nuremberg Party Congress Grounds 1934.

Speke John Hanning 1827–1864. British explorer. He joined British traveler Richard ⟡Burton on an African expedition in which they reached Lake Tanganyika 1858; Speke became the first European to see Lake ⟡Victoria.

speleology scientific study of caves, their origin, development, physical structure, flora, fauna, folklore, exploration, mapping, photography, cave-diving, and rescue work. **Potholing**, which involves following the course of underground rivers or streams, has become a popular sport.

Speleology first developed in France in the late 19th century, where the Société de Spéléologie was founded in 1895.

Spencer Herbert 1820–1903. British philosopher. He wrote *Social Statics* 1851, expounding his *laissez-faire* views on social and political problems, *Principles of Psychology* 1855, and *Education* 1861. In 1862 he began his ten-volume *System of Synthetic Philosophy*, in which he extended Charles ⟡Darwin's theory of evolution to the entire field of human knowledge. The chief of the ten volumes are *First Principles* 1862 and *Principles* of biology, sociology, and ethics. Other works are *The Study of Sociology, Man v. the State, Essays*, and an autobiography.

Spender Stephen (Harold) 1909– . English poet and critic. His earlier poetry has a left-wing political content, as in *Twenty Poems* 1930, *Vienna* 1934, *The Still Centre* 1939, and *Poems of Dedication* 1946. Other works include the verse drama *Trial of a Judge* 1938, the autobiography *World within World* 1951, and translations. His *Journals 1939–83* were published 1985.

Spengler Oswald 1880–1936. German philosopher whose *Decline of the West* 1918 argued that civilizations go through natural cycles of growth and decay. He was admired by the Nazis.

Spenser Edmund *c.* 1552–1599. English poet, who has been called the "poet's poet" because of his rich imagery and command of versification. His major work is the moral allegory *The Faerie Queene*, of which six books survive (three published 1590 and three 1596). Other books include *The Shepheard's Calendar* 1579, *Astrophel* 1586, the love sonnets *Amoretti* and the *Epithalamion* 1595.

Born in London and educated at Cambridge University, in 1580 he became secretary to the Lord Deputy in Ireland and at Kilcolman Castle completed the first three books of *The Faerie Queene*. In 1598 Kilcolman Castle was burned down by rebels, and Spenser with his family narrowly escaped. He died in London, and was buried in Westminster Abbey.

sperm or **semen** the fluid containing the male ⟡gametes (sperm cells) of animals. Usually, each sperm cell has a head capsule containing a nucleus, a middle portion containing ⟡mitochondria (which provide energy), and a long tail (flagellum).

In most animals, sperm cells (sometimes called "sperm" for short) are motile, and are propelled by a long flagellum, but in some (such as crabs and lobsters) they are nonmotile. The term is sometimes used for the motile male gametes (⟡antherozoids) of lower plants.

spermaceti glistening waxlike substance, not a true oil, contained in the cells of the huge, almost rectangular "case" in the head of the sperm whale, amounting to about 3 tons/2.8 tonnes. It rapidly changes in density with variations in temperature. It was formerly used in lubricants and cosmetics, but in 1980 a blend of fatty acids and esters from tallow and coconut oil was developed as a substitute.

spermatophore small, nutrient-rich packet of ⬦sperm produced in invertebrates, newts, and cephalopods.

spermatophyte in botany, another name for a ⬦seed plant.

spermicide any cream, jelly, pessary, or other preparation that kills the ⬦sperm cells in semen. Spermicides are used for contraceptive purposes, usually in combination with a ⬦condom or ⬦diaphragm. Sponges impregnated with spermicide have been developed but are not yet in widespread use. Spermicide used alone is only 75% effective in preventing pregnancy.

Sperry Elmer Ambrose 1860–1930. US engineer who developed various devices using ⬦gyroscopes, such as gyrostabilizers (for ships and torpedoes) and gyro-controlled autopilots.

sphere in mathematics, a perfectly round solid with all points on its surface the same distance from the center. This distance is the radius of the sphere. For a sphere of radius r, the volume $V = 4/3\pi r^3$ and the surface area $A = 4\pi^2$.

The Earth is a sphere that is slightly flattened at its north and south poles.

sphincter ring of muscle found at various points in the alimentary canal, which contracts and relaxes to control the movement of food. The *pyloric sphincter*, at the base of the stomach, controls the release of the gastric contents into the duodenum. After release the sphincter contracts, closing off the stomach.

Sphinx mythological creature, represented in Egyptian, Assyrian, and Greek art as a lion with a human head. In Greek myth the Sphinx was female and killed travelers who failed to answer a riddle; she killed herself when ⬦Oedipus gave the right answer.

sphygmomanometer instrument for measuring blood pressure. Consisting of an inflatable arm cuff joined by a rubber tube to a pressure-recording device (often a column-of-mercury scale), it is used, together with a stethoscope, to measure arterial blood pressure.

Spica or *Alpha Virginis* the brightest star in the constellation Virgo and the 16th brightest star in the sky. Spica has a true luminosity of over 1,500 times that of the Sun, and is 140 light-years from Earth. It is also a spectroscopic ⬦binary star, the components of which orbit each other every four days.

spice any aromatic vegetable substance used as a condiment and for flavoring food. Spices are mostly obtained from tropical plants, and include pepper, nutmeg, ginger, and cinnamon. They have little food value but increase the appetite and may facilitate digestion.

spicebush aromatic E North American shrub *Lindera benzoin* of the laurel family Lauraceae, with leathery, elliptical leaves. Its red, aromatic berries can be dried and crushed for use as a spice and its leaves for tea.

Spice Islands former name of the ⬦Moluccas, a group of islands in the Malay Archipelago.

spicules, solar in astronomy, short-lived jets of hot gas in the upper ⬦chromosphere of the Sun. Spiky in appearance, they move at high velocities along lines of magnetic force to which they owe their shape, and last for a few minutes each. Spicules appear to disperse material into the ⬦corona.

spider any arachnid (eight-legged animal) of the order Araneae. There are about 30,000 known species. Unlike insects, the head and breast are merged to form the cephalothorax, connected to the abdomen by a characteristic narrow waist. There are eight legs, and usually eight simple eyes. On the undersurface of the abdomen are spinnerets, usually six, which exude a viscid fluid. This hardens on exposure to the air to form silky threads, used to make silken egg cases, silk-lined tunnels, or various kinds of webs and snares for catching prey that is then wrapped. The fangs of spiders inject substances to subdue and digest prey, the juices of which are then sucked into the stomach by the spider.

Spiders are found everywhere in the world except Antarctica. Species of interest include the zebra spider *Salticus scenicus*, a longer-sighted species which stalks its prey and has pads on its feet which enable it to walk even on glass; the poisonous ⬦tarantula and ⬦black widow; the cross spider *Araneus diadematus*, which spins webs of remarkable beauty; the only aquatic species of spider, the water spider *Argyroneta aquatica*, which fills a "diving bell" home with air trapped on the hairs of the body; and the largest members of the group, the *bird-eating spider* genus *Mygale* of South America, with a body about 2.4–3.5 in/6–9 cm long and a leg-span of 1 ft/30 cm. Spider venom is a powerful toxin which paralyses its prey.

spider plant African plant of the genus *Chlorophytum* of the lily family. Two species, *C. comosum* and *C. elatum*, are popular house plants. They have long narrow variegated leaves and produce flowering shoots from which the new plants grow. The flowers are small and white. Spider plants absorb toxins from the air and therefore have a purifying action on the local atmosphere.

Spielberg Steven 1947– . US film director, writer, and producer. His highly successful films, including *Jaws* 1975, *Close Encounters of the Third Kind* 1977, *Raiders of the Lost Ark* 1981, and *ET* 1982 have given popular cinema a new "respectable" appeal. He also directed *Indiana Jones and the Temple of Doom* 1984, *The Color Purple* 1985, *Empire of the Sun* 1987, and *Indiana Jones and the Last Crusade* 1989.

spikelet in botany, one of the units of a grass ⬦inflorescence. It comprises a slender axis on which one or more flowers are borne.

Each individual flower or floret has a pair of scalelike bracts, the glumes, and is enclosed by a membranous lemma and a thin, narrow palea, which may be extended into a long, slender bristle, or *awn*.

spikenard Himalayan plant *Nardostachys jatamansi* of the valerian family Valerianaceae; its underground stems give a perfume used in Eastern aromatic oils. Also, a North American plant *Aralia racemosa* of the ginseng family, with fragrant roots.

Spillane Mickey (Frank Morrison) 1918– . US crime novelist who began by writing for pulp magazines and became known for violent and sexually explicit crime novels featuring his "one-man police force" hero Mike Hammer; for example, *Vengeance is Mine* 1950 and *The Long Wait* 1951.

His other works include *I, The Jury* 1947, *Day of the Guns* 1964, and *The Delta Factor* 1968. Some were made into films during the era of ⬦film noir, and a TV series was based on Mike Hammer. He also wrote *Kiss Me, Deadly* 1952, *The Death Dealers* 1965, *Survival . . . Zero* 1970, *The Last Cop Out* 1973, and *The Day the Sea Rolled Back* 1979.

spin in physics, the intrinsic angular momentum of a subatomic particle, nucleus, atom, or molecule, which continues to exist even when the particle comes to rest. A particle in a specific energy state has a particular spin, just as it has a particular electric charge and mass. According to quantum theory, this is restricted to discrete and indivisible values, specified by a spin quantum number. Because of its spin, a charged particle acts as a small magnet and is affected by magnetic fields.

spina bifida congenital defect in which part of the spinal cord and its membranes are exposed, due to incomplete development of the spine (vertebral column).

Spina bifida, usually present in the lower back, varies in severity. The most seriously affected babies may be paralyzed below the waist. There is also a risk of mental retardation and death from hydrocephalus, which is often associated. Surgery is performed to close the spinal lesion shortly after birth, but this does not usually cure the disabilities caused by the condition. **spinach** annual plant *Spinacia oleracea* of the goosefoot family Chenopodiaceae. It is native to Asia and widely cultivated for its leaves, which are eaten as a vegetable.

spinal cord major component of the ⬦central nervous system in vertebrates.

It is a thick cord of nerve tissue enclosed by dorsal extensions from each vertebra along the spinal column. It runs from the medulla oblongata of the brain all the way down the back.

spinal tap another term for ⬦lumbar puncture, a medical test.

spine the backbone of vertebrates. It consists of separate disk-shaped bony units (vertebrae), processes that enclose and protect the spinal cord. The spine connects with the skull, ribs, back muscles, and pelvis.

In humans, there are seven cervical *vertebrae* in the neck; 12 thoracic in the upper trunk; five lumbar in the lower back; the sacrum (consisting of five vertebrae fused together, joined to the hipbones); and the coccyx (four vertebrae, fused into a tailbone). The human spine has four curves (front to rear), which allow for the increased size of the chest and pelvic cavities, and for a degree of spring so as to minimize jolting of the internal organs.

spinel any of a group of "mixed oxide" minerals consisting mainly of the oxides of magnesium and aluminum, $MgAl_2O_4$ and $FeAl_2O_4$. Spinels crystallize in the cubic system, forming octahedral crystals. They are found in high-temperature igneous and metamorphic rocks. The aluminum oxide spinel contains gem varieties, such as the ruby spinels of Sri Lanka and Myanmar (Burma).

spinet plucking-action keyboard instrument, similar to a ⬦harpsichord but smaller, which has only one string for each note.

spinning art of drawing out and twisting fibers (originally wool or flax) into a long thread, or yarn, by hand or machine. Synthetic fibers are extruded as a liquid through the holes of a spinneret.

Spinning was originally done by hand, then with the spinning wheel, and in about 1767 in England James ⬦Hargreaves built the *spinning jenny*, a machine that could spin 8, then 16, bobbins at once. Later, Samuel ⬦Crompton's *spinning mule* 1779 had a moving carriage carrying the spindles and is still in use today.

Also used is the ring-spinning frame introduced in the US in 1828 where sets of rollers moving at various speeds draw out finer and finer thread, which is twisted and wound onto rotating bobbins.

Originally, some 9,000 years ago, spinning was done by hand using a distaff (a cleft stick holding a bundle of fibers) and a weighted spindle, which was spun to twist the thread. In the 1300s the spinning wheel came to Europe, though it had been in use earlier in the East. It provided a way of turning the spindle mechanically. By the next century, the wheel was both spinning and winding the yarn onto a bobbin, but further mechanical development did not occur until the 18th century.

Spinoza Benedict or Baruch 1632–1677. Dutch philosopher who believed in a rationalistic pantheism that owed much to Descartes' mathematical appreciation of the universe. Mind and matter are two modes of an infinite substance that he called God or Nature, good and evil being relative. He was a determinist, believing that human action was motivated by self-preservation.

Ethics 1677 is his main work. *A Treatise on Religious and Political Philosophy* 1670 was the only one of his works published during his life, and was attacked by Christians. He was excommunicated by the Jewish community in Amsterdam on charges of heretical thought and practice 1656. He was a lens-grinder by trade.

spiny anteater alternate name for ◊echidna.

spiracle in insects, the opening of a ◊trachea, through which oxygen enters the body and carbon dioxide is expelled. In cartilaginous fishes (sharks and rays), the same name is given to a circular opening that marks the remains of the first gill slit.

In tetrapod vertebrates, the spiracle of early fishes has evolved into the Eustachian tube, which connects the middle ear cavity with the pharynx.

spiral a plane curve formed by a point winding round a fixed point from which it distances itself at regular intervals, for example the spiral traced by a flat coil of rope. Various kinds of spirals can be generated mathematically—for example, an equiangular or logarithmic spiral (in which a tangent at any point on the curve always makes the same angle with it) and an ◊involute. Spirals also occur in nature as a normal consequence of accelerating growth, such as the spiral shape of the shells of snails and some other mollusks.

spiritualism belief in the survival of the human personality and in communication between the living and those who have "passed on." The spiritualist movement originated in the US in 1848. Adherents to this religious denomination practice *mediumship*, which claims to allow clairvoyant knowledge of distant events and spirit healing. The writer Arthur Conan Doyle and the Victorian prime minister Gladstone were converts.

spit sandbar (sand ridge) projecting into a body of water and growing out from land, deposited by a current carrying material from one direction to another across the mouth of an inlet.

Spitsbergen main island in the Norwegian archipelago of ◊Svalbard.

spittle alternate name for ◊saliva.

spittlebug alternate name for ◊froghopper.

Spitz Mark Andrew 1950– . US swimmer. He won a record seven gold medals at the 1972 Olympic Games, all in world record times.

He won 11 Olympic medals in total (four in 1968) and set 26 world records between 1967 and 1972. His attempt to qualify for the 1992 Olympics failed.

spleen organ in vertebrates, part of the lymphatic system, which helps to process ◊lymphocytes. It also regulates the number of red blood cells in circulation by destroying old cells, and stores iron. It is situated behind the stomach.

splenectomy surgical removal of the ◊spleen. It may be necessary following injury to the spleen, or when it becomes involved in leukemia or lymphoma.

Split (Italian *Spalato*) port in Croatia, on the Adriatic; population (1981) 236,000. Industries include engineering, cement, and textiles, and it is also a tourist resort. Split was bombed during 1991 as part of Yugoslavia's blockade of the Croatian coast.

The Roman emperor Diocletian retired here in 305.

Spock Benjamin McLane 1903– . US pediatrician and writer on child care. His *Common Sense Book of Baby and Child Care* 1946 urged less rigidity in bringing up children than had been advised by previous generations of writers on the subject, but this was misunderstood as advocating permissiveness. He was also active in the peace movement, especially during the Vietnam War.

In his later work he stressed that his common-sense approach had not implied rejecting all discipline, but that his main aim was to give parents the confidence to trust their own judgment rather than rely on books by experts who did not know a particular child.

spoils system in the US, the granting of offices and favors among the supporters of a party in office. The spoils system, a type of ◊patronage, was used by President Jefferson and was enlarged in scope by the 1820 Tenure of Office Act, which gave the president and Senate the power to reappoint posts that were the gift of the government after each four-year election. The practice remained common in the 20th century in US local government.

The term is derived from a speech after an election victory by Secretary of State William Marcy: "To the victor belong the spoils of the enemy."

The system reached a peak under the presidency of Ulysses S Grant (1869–77). In the 20th century, civil-service posts in large cities were often filled on the recommendation of newly elected political leaders. The system was epitomized by the Democratic Party "machine" of Richard Daley (1902–76), mayor of Chicago 1955–76.

Spokane city on the Spokane River, E Washington; population (1990) 177,200. It is situated in a mining, timber, and rich agricultural area, and is the seat of Gonzaga University 1887.

Spokane was incorporated 1881 and was the site of Expo '74 (International Exposition of Environment).

Spoleto town in Umbria, central Italy; population (1985) 37,000. There is an annual opera and drama festival established by Gian Carlo ◊Menotti. It was a papal possession 1220–1860 and has Roman remains and medieval churches.

sponge any saclike simple invertebrate of the phylum Porifera, usually marine. A sponge has a hollow body, its cavity lined by cells bearing flagellae, whose whiplike movements keep water circulating, bringing in a stream of food particles. The body walls are strengthened with protein (as in the bath sponge) or small spikes of silica, or a framework of calcium carbonate.

sponsorship form of advertising in sports, music, broadcasting, and the arts. Sponsorship became a major source of finance for sport in the 1970s, and takes several forms. Many companies sponsor sporting events, while others give money to individuals who wear the company's logo or motifs while performing. Concerts are also commonly sponsored by advertisers, although some performers refuse in principle to endorse a product in this way. Art exhibitions are often sponsored by large companies, a form of corporate funding for tax deductions.

In the US, radio broadcasts were sponsored by consumer goods and television services companies; this continued as television programs became the prime mode of home entertainment. The object for sponsors, often, is a "name" association with a particular show, event, or personality, thus enhancing product image.

spontaneous generation or *abiogenesis* erroneous belief that living organisms can arise spontaneously from non-living matter. This survived until the mid-19th century, when the French chemist Louis Pasteur demonstrated that a nutrient broth would not generate microorganisms if it was adequately sterilized. The theory of ◊biogenesis holds that spontaneous generation cannot now occur; it is thought, however, to have played an essential role in the origin of ◊life on this planet 4 billion years ago.

spoonbill any of several large wading birds of the Ibis family (Threskiornithidae), characterized by a long, flat bill, dilated at the tip in the shape of a spoon. Spoonbills are white or pink, and up to 3 ft/90 cm tall.

The roseate spoonbill *Ajaia ajaja* of North and South America is found in shallow open water, which it sifts for food.

spoonerism exchange of elements in a flow of words. Usually a slip of the tongue, a spoonerism can also be contrived for comic effect (for example "a troop of Boy Scouts" becoming "a scoop of Boy Trouts"). William Spooner (1844–1930) gave his name to the phenomenon.

Sporades Greek island group in the Aegean Sea. The chief island of the **Northern Sporades** is ◊Skyros. The **Southern Sporades** are more usually referred to as the ◊Dodecanese.

sporangium structure in which ◊spores are produced.

spore small reproductive or resting body, usually consisting of just one cell. Unlike a ◊gamete, it does not need to fuse with another cell in order to develop into a new organism. Spores are produced by the lower plants, most fungi, some bacteria, and certain protozoa. They are generally light and easily dispersed by wind movements.

Plant spores are haploid and are produced by the sporophyte, following ◊meiosis; see ◊alternation of generations.

sporophyte diploid spore-producing generation in the life cycle of a plant that undergoes ◊alternation of generations.

sport activity pursued for exercise or pleasure, performed individually or in a group, often involving the testing of physical capabilities and usually taking the form of a competitive game.

Many sports can be traced to ancient Egyptian or Greek times. Coursing was believed to have taken place in Egypt in 3000 BC, using Saluki dogs. Wrestling took place in what is now Iraq more than 4,000 years ago; a form of hockey was played in Egypt about 2050 BC; and falconry, boxing, track and field athletics, and fencing all existed more than 4,000 years ago.

The real development of the majority of sports as competitions, rather than pastimes, was in the 18th and 19th centuries, when sports such as baseball, soccer, cricket, rugby, golf, tennis, and many more became increasingly popular. The traditional sports have changed very little over the years but televised events have led to more and more competitions within each sport.

SPQR abbreviation for *Senatus Populusque Romanus*, Latin "the Senate and the Roman People."

Spratly Islands (Chinese *Nanshan Islands*) group of small islands, coral reefs, and sandbars dispersed over a distance of 600 mi/965 km in the South China Sea. Used as a submarine base by the Japanese during World War II, the islands are claimed in whole or part by the People's Republic of China, Taiwan, Malaysia, Vietnam (which calls the islands *Truong Sa*), and the Philippines (which calls them *Kalayaan*). The islands are of strategic importance, commanding the sea passage from Japan to Singapore, and in 1976 oil was discovered.

spreadsheet in computing, a program that mimics a sheet of ruled paper, divided into columns and rows. The user enters values in the sheet, then instructs the program to perform some operation on them, such as totaling a column or finding the average of a series of numbers. Highly complex numerical analyses may be built up from these simple steps.

Spreadsheets are widely used in business for forecasting and financial control. The first spreadsheet program, VisiCalc, appeared in 1979. The best known include Lotus 1–2–3 and Excel.

spring device, usually a metal coil, that returns to its original shape after being stretched or compressed. Springs are used in some machines (such as clocks) to store energy, which can be released at a controlled rate. In other machines (such as engines) they are used to close valves.

In vehicle-suspension systems, springs are used to cushion passengers from road shocks. These springs are used in conjunction with shock absorbers to limit their amount of travel. In bedding and upholstered furniture springs add comfort.

spring in geology, a natural flow of water from the ground, formed at the point of intersection of the water table and the ground's surface. The source of water is rain that has percolated through the overlying rocks. During its underground passage, the water may have dissolved mineral substances that may then be precipitated at the spring (hence, a mineral spring).

A spring may be continuous or intermittent and depends on the position of the water table and the topography.

springbok South African antelope *Antidorcas marsupialis* about 30 in/80 cm at the shoulder,

with head and body 4 ft/1.3 m long. It may leap 10 ft/3 m or more in the air when startled or playing, and has a fold of skin along the middle of the back which is raised to a crest in alarm. Springboks once migrated in herds of over a million, but are now found only in small numbers where protected.

Springdale city in NW Arkansas, NW of Little Rock. Industries include food and livestock processing; population (1990) 29,900.

Springfield capital and agricultural and mining center of Illinois; population (1990) 105,200. President Abraham Lincoln was born and is buried here.

Lincoln lived and practiced law in Springfield from 1837 until he became president 1861. His home and tomb are historic sites. Sangamon State University is here. Springfield was settled 1818 and became the state capital 1837.

Springfield city in Massachusetts; population (1990) 157,000. It was the site (1794–1968) of the US arsenal and armory, known for the Springfield rifle.

Basketball originated here 1891, and points of interest include the National Basketball Hall of Fame. The community dates from 1636.

Springfield city and agricultural center in Missouri; population (1990) 140,500. Industries include electronic equipment and processed food.

The city is also a tourist center for the Ozark Mountains and the home of Southwest Missouri State University. Springfield was settled 1829.

Springfield city in W Oregon on the Willamette river, E of Eugene. Industries include lumber, animal feeds, and agricultural products; population (1990) 45,000.

Springsteen Bruce 1949– . US rock singer, songwriter, and guitarist, born in New Jersey. His music combines melodies in traditional rock/pop idiom and reflective lyrics about working-class life and the pursuit of the American Dream on albums such as *Born to Run* 1975, *Born in the USA* 1984, and the 1992 dual releases *Human Touch* and *Lucky Town*.

Springsteen began his early career in the late 1960s playing small East Coast clubs, where he earned a cult following. In concerts with the E Street Band, playing long ambitious sets, his performance is electrifying. "The Boss" won many new fans in the mid-1980s performing in a series of sold-out concerts across the US.

sprite in computing, a graphics object made up of a pattern of ⊃pixels (picture elements) defined by a computer programmer. Some ⊃high-level languages and ⊃applications programs contain routines that allow a user to define the shape, colors, and other characteristics of individual graphics objects. These objects can then be manipulated and combined to produce animated games or graphic screen displays.

spruce coniferous tree of the genus *Picea* of the pine family, found over much of the northern hemisphere. Pyramidal in shape, spruces have rigid, prickly needles and drooping, leathery cones. Some are important forestry trees, such as sitka spruce *P. sitchensis*, native to W North America, and the Norway spruce *P. abies*, now planted widely in North America.

Spurs, Battle of the victory 1513 over the French at Guinegate, NW France, by Henry VII of England; the name emphasizes the speed of the French retreat.

Sputnik (Russian "fellow traveler") series of ten Soviet Earth-orbiting satellites. *Sputnik 1* was the first artificial satellite, launched Oct 4, 1957. It weighed 185 lb/84 kg, with a 23 in/58 cm diameter, and carried only a simple radio transmitter which allowed scientists to track it as it orbited Earth. It burned up in the atmosphere 92 days later. Sputniks were superseded in the early 1960s by the Cosmos series.

Sputnik 2, launched Nov 3, 1957, weighed about 1,100 lb/500 kg including the dog Laika, the first living creature in space. Unfortunately, there was no way to return the dog to Earth, and it died in space. Later Sputniks were test flights of the ⊃Vostok spacecraft.

sq abbreviation for *square* (measure).

SQL (abbreviation of *structured query language*) high-level computer language designed for use with ⊃relational databases. Although it can be used by programmers in the same way as other languages, it is often used as a means for programs to communicate with each other. Typically, one program (called the "client") uses SQL to request data from a database "server."

Although originally developed by IBM, SQL is now widely used on many types of computer. SQL obtained approval from ANSI in 1986.

Squanto *c.* 1580–1622. Pawtuxet ally of the Plymouth colonists. Also known as Tisquantum, he was born in SE New England and kidnapped and taken to England 1605 by the English explorer George Weymouth. After residing in England and providing Fernando Gorges with information on the native peoples of New England, he returned there 1619 as a guide for Capt John Slaine. With his own tribe wiped out by an epidemic, Squanto settled among the Wampanoag. After serving as interpreter for Wampanoag chief Massasoit in his dealings with the Pilgrims, Squanto eventually settled in Plymouth, living there until his death.

square in geometry, a quadrilateral (four-sided) plane figure with all sides equal and each angle a right angle. Its diagonals bisect each other at right angles. The area A of a square is the length l of one side multiplied by itself ($A = l \times l$).

Also, any quantity multiplied by itself is termed a square, represented by an ⊃exponent of power 2; for example, $4 \times 4 = 4^2 = 16$ and $6.8 \times 6.8 = 6.8^2 = 46.24$.

An algebraic term is squared by doubling its exponent and squaring its coefficient if it has one; for example, $(x^2)^2 = x^4$ and $(6y^3)^2 = 36y^6$. A number that has a whole number as its ⊃square root is known as a *perfect square*; for example, 25, 144, and 54,756 are perfect squares (with roots of 5, 12, and 234, respectively).

square root in mathematics, a number that when squared (multiplied by itself) equals a given number. For example, the square root of 25 (written $\sqrt{25}$) is ± 5, because $5 \times 5 = 25$, and $(-5) \times (-5) = 25$. As an ⊃exponent, a square root is represented by 1/2, for example, $16^{1/2} = 4$.

Negative numbers (less than 0) do not have square roots that are ⊃real numbers. Their roots are represented by ⊃complex numbers, in which the square root of –1 is given the symbol i (that is, $\pm\ i^2 = -1$). Thus the square root of –4 is $\sqrt{[(-1) \times 4]} = \sqrt{-1} \times \sqrt{4} = 2i$.

squash racket-and-ball game usually played by two people on an enclosed court, derived from ⊃rackets. Squash became a popular sport in the 1970s and then a fitness craze as well as a competitive sport. There are two forms of squash: the American form, which is played in North and some South American countries, and the English, which is played mainly in Europe and Commonwealth countries such as Pakistan, Australia, and New Zealand.

In singles squash under the American rules, the court is 32 ft/10 m long and 18 ft 6 in/5.6 m wide. The front and side walls are 16 ft/4.9 m high and the back wall is 6 ft 6 in/2 m high. In doubles it measures 25 ft/7.6 m by 45 ft/13.7 m.

In English singles, the court is 21 ft/6.4 m wide and 32 ft/10 m long. The front wall is 15 ft/5 m high, and the back wall is 7 ft/2.1m high. The side walls slant down from 15 ft at the front to 7 ft at the back. Doubles squash is played by two teams of two players each on a larger court.

Players use rackets and a small rubber ball which, in the English form, is softer than that used in the American sport. The ball is hit against a wall (the front wall) and when serving, must be above a line about 6 ft/1.83 m high. Thereafter the ball must be hit alternately against the front wall, within certain limitations, but rebounds off the other three walls are permitted. The object is to win points by playing shots the opponent cannot return to the wall.

squill bulb-forming perennial plant of the genus *Scilla*, family Liliaceae, found growing in dry places near the sea in W Europe. Cultivated species usually bear blue flowers either singly or in clusters at the top of the stem.

squint or *strabismus* common condition in which one eye deviates in any direction. A squint may be convergent (with the bad eye turned inward), divergent (outward), or, in rare cases, vertical. A convergent squint is also called *cross-eye*.

There are two types of squint: *paralytic*, arising from disease or damage involving the extraocular muscles or their nerve supply; and *nonparalytic*, which may be inherited or due to some refractive error within the eye. Nonparalytic (or concomitant) squint is the typical condition seen in small children. It is treated by corrective glasses, exercises for the eye muscles, or surgery.

squirrel rodent of the family Sciuridae. Squirrels are found worldwide except for Australia, Madagascar, and polar regions. Some are tree dwellers; these generally have bushy tails, and some, with membranes between their legs, are called ◊flying squirrels. Others are terrestrial, generally burrowing forms called ground squirrels; these include chipmunks, gophers, marmots, and prairie dogs.

The small red squirrel *Tamia sciurus* grows to 14 in/35 cm including the tail, of Alaska, the Rocky Mountains, and NE US, builds large tree nests and accumulates the cones of spruce and other conifers for winter use. The larger eastern gray squirrel *Sciurus carolinensis* of E North America grows to 20 in/50 cm including tail, stores nuts and acorns, and is a common sight in city parks and suburbs.

Sri Lanka island in the Indian Ocean, off the SE coast of India.

government Under the 1978 constitution, the head of state and chief executive is the president, directly elected by universal suffrage for six-year terms. A two-term limit applies and voting is by the single transferable vote system. The president appoints and dismisses cabinet ministers, including the prime minister, and may hold selected portfolios and dissolve parliament. Parliament, which is known as the

National State Assembly, is a single-chamber body with supreme legislative authority. There are 168 members, directly elected by a complex system of proportional representation for six-year terms. A two-thirds parliamentary majority is required to alter the constitution.

history The aboriginal people, the Vedda, were conquered about 550 BC by the Sinhalese from N India under their first king, Vijaya. In the 3rd century BC the island became a world center of Buddhism. The spice trade brought Arabs, who called the island Serendip, and Europeans, who called it Ceylon. Portugal established settlements 1505, taken over by the Netherlands 1658 and by Britain 1796. Ceylon was ceded to Britain 1802 and became a crown colony.

Sinhalese/Tamil conflict Under British rule Tamils from S India (Hindus who had been settled in the north and east for centuries) took up English education and progressed rapidly in administrative careers. Many more Tamils immigrated to work on the tea and rubber plantations developed in central Sri Lanka. Conflicts between the Sinhalese majority and the Tamils surfaced during the 1920s as nationalist politics developed. In 1931, universal suffrage was introduced for an elected legislature and executive council in which power was shared with the British, and in Feb 1948 independence was achieved.

Sri Lanka
Democratic Socialist Republic of
(*Prajathanrika Samajawadi Janarajaya Sri Lanka*) (until 1972 **Ceylon**)

area 25,328 sq mi/65,600 sq km
capital (and chief port) Colombo
cities Kandy; ports Jaffna, Galle, Negombo, Trincomalee
physical flat in N and around the coast; hills and mountains in S and central interior
features Adam's Peak (7,538 ft/2,243 m); ruined cities of Anuradhapura, Polonnaruwa
head of state Ranasinghe Premadasa from 1989
head of government Dingiri Banda Wijetunge from 1989
political system liberal democratic republic
political parties United National Party (UNP), right-of-center; Sri Lanka Freedom Party (SLFP), left-of-center; Democratic United National Front (DUNF), center-left; Tamil United Liberation Front (TULF), Tamil autonomy; Eelam People's Revolutionary Liberation Front (EPLRF), Indian-backed

dominion status Between 1948 and 1972, Sri Lanka remained a dominion within the British Commonwealth with a titular governor-general. The United National Party (UNP), led consecutively by Don and Dudley ◊Senanayake, held power until 1956, when the radical socialist and more narrowly Sinhalese Sri Lanka Freedom Party (SLFP), led by Solomon ◊Bandaranaike, gained electoral victory and established Sinhalese rather than English as the official language to be used for entrance to universities and the civil service. This precipitated Tamil riots, culminating in the prime minister's assassination Sept 1959. Bandaranaike's widow, Sirimavo, became prime minister and held office until 1977, except for UNP interludes 1960 and 1965–70. She implemented a radical economic program of nationalization and land reform, a pro-Sinhalese educational and employment policy, and an independent military policy based on that of the ◊nonaligned movement.

Tamil separatist movement In 1972 the Senate upper chamber was abolished, and the new national name Sri Lanka ("Resplendent Island") adopted. Economic conditions deteriorated, while Tamil complaints of discrimination bred a separatist movement calling for the creation of an independent Tamil state (Eelam) in the north and east. The Tamil United Liberation Front (TULF) coalition was

Tamil-secessionist "Tamil Tigers"
exports tea, rubber, coconut products, graphite, sapphires, rubies, other gemstones
currency Sri Lanka rupee
population (1990 est) 17,135,000 (Sinhalese 74%, Tamils 17%, Moors 7%); growth rate 1.8% p.a.
life expectancy men 67, women 72 (1989)
languages Sinhala, Tamil, English
religion Buddhist 69%, Hindu 15%, Muslim 8%, Christian 7%
literacy 87% (1988)
GNP $7.2 bn; $400 per head (1988)
chronology
1802 Ceylon became a British colony.
1948 Ceylon achieved independence from Britain within the Commonwealth.
1956 Sinhala established as the official language.
1959 Prime Minister Solomon Bandaranaike assassinated.
1972 Socialist Republic of Sri Lanka proclaimed.
1978 Presidential constitution adopted by new Jayawardene government.
1983 Tamil guerrilla violence escalated; state of emergency imposed.
1987 President Jayawardene and Indian prime minister Rajiv Gandhi signed Colombo Accord. Violence continued despite cease-fire policed by Indian troops.
1988 Left-wing guerrillas campaigned against Indo-Sri Lankan peace pact. Prime Minister Ranasinghe Premadasa elected president.
1989 Premadasa became president; D B Wijetunge, prime minister. Leaders of the TULF and terrorist People's Liberation Front assassinated.
1990 Indian peacekeeping force withdrawn. Violence continued.
1991 March: defense minister, Ranjan Wijeratne, assassinated; Sri Lankan army killed 2,552 Tamil Tigers at Elephant Pass. October: impeachment motion against President Premadasa failed. Dec: new party, the Democratic United National Front, formed by former members of UNP.

formed 1976 to campaign for this goal and emerged as the second-largest party in parliament from the elections July 1977, easily won by the UNP led by Junius Jayawardene. The new government remodeled the 1972 constitution and introduced a new freer-market economic program, which recorded initial success. In Oct 1980 Sirimavo Bandaranaike was deprived of her civil rights for six years for alleged abuses of power. The guerrilla activities of the Liberation Tigers of Tamil Eelam (LTTE) in the north and east provoked the frequent imposition of a state of emergency. In 1982 Jayawardene was reelected president, and the life of parliament was prolonged by referendum.

civil war The violence escalated 1983, causing the deaths of over 400 people, mainly Tamils in the Jaffna area. This prompted legislation outlawing separatist organizations, including the TULF. The near civil war has cost thousands of lives and blighted the country's economy; the tourist industry has collapsed, foreign investment dried up, and aid donors have become reluctant to prop up a government seemingly bent on imposing a military solution.

Colombo Accord All-party talks with Indian mediation repeatedly failed to solve the Tamil dispute, but in July 1987, amid protest riots, President Jayawardene and the Indian prime minister Rajiv Gandhi signed a peace pact. It proposed to make Tamil and English official languages, create a semi autonomous homeland for the Tamils in the north and east, recognize the Tigers (once disarmed) as their representatives, and hold a referendum 1988 in the eastern province, which has pockets of Sinhalese and 32% Muslims. To police this agreement, a 7,000-strong Indian peacekeeping force (IPKF) was despatched to the Tiger-controlled Jaffna area. The Tamil Tigers put down their weapons and agreed to talks with the Sri Lankan government April 1989.

This employment of Indian troops served to fan unrest among the Sinhala community, who viewed the July 1987 Colombo Accord as a sellout to Tamil interests. Protest riots erupted in the south and senior UNP politicians, including President Jayawardene, were targeted for assassination by the resurfaced Sinhala-Marxist People's Liberation Front (JVP). In the north, the IPKF failed to capture the Tigers' leader Velupillai Prabhakaran, who continued to wage a guerrilla war from fresh bases in the rural east.

reconciliation attempts Prime Minister Ranasinghe Premadasa ran for the governing party in the presidential election of Dec 1989 and defeated the SLFP's Sirimavo Bandaranaike, who called for the immediate withdrawal of the IPKF in a campaign that was marred by JVP-induced violence. In the elections that followed in Feb 1989 the UNP secured a narrow overall majority. After the election, finance minister D B Wijetunge was appointed prime minister and proceeded, with President Premadasa, to work for national reconciliation. Round-table negotiations were held with Tiger leaders June 1989 and India withdrew its troops March 1990. Despite these moves the civil war, with its two fronts in the north and south, continued, with the death toll exceeding 1,000 a month, and around 100 people a week being detained under the emergency laws. At the end of July 1991 President Premadasa suspended parliament for a month after an impeachment motion was brought

against him, alleging 24 cases of gross abuse of power, corruption, and illegal family deals. Members of the UNP apparently supported the motion. It is believed that they seek a national referendum to abandon the executive presidency, which they see as having concentrated too much power in Premadasa's hands, and restore parliamentary power. In Aug 1991 the Sri Lankan army secured a major victory against the Tamil Tigers at Elephant Pass, the gateway between the Tigers' stronghold of Jaffna peninsula and the Sri Lankan mainland, killing 2,552 Tiger guerrillas for the loss of 153 soldiers. There was some evidence that the Tamil Tigers were disintegrating but there remained an average of 150 people killed per day in interethnic violence. In Dec 1991 eight former members of the UNP joined a new party, the Democratic United National Front (DUNF). The dissidents pledged to fight for the democratic ideals upon which the UNP was founded.

Sri Lanka is a member of the Commonwealth and ◊nonaligned movement and joined the South Asian Association for Regional Cooperation 1985. *See illustration box.*

Srinagar summer capital of the state of ◊Jammu and Kashmir, India; population (1981) 520,000. It is a beautiful resort, intersected by waterways, and has carpet, papier mâché, and leather industries.

SS Nazi elite corps (German *Schutz-Staffel* "protective squadron") established 1925. Under ◊Himmler its 500,000 membership included the full-time **Waffen-SS** (armed SS), which fought in World War II, and spare-time members. The SS performed state police duties and was brutal in its treatment of the Jews and others in the concentration camps and occupied territories. It was condemned at the Nuremberg Trials of war criminals.

stability in physics, how difficult it is to move an object from a position of ◊equilibrium. A stable object returns to its rest position after being shifted slightly; an unstable object topples or falls when shifted slightly.

stabilizer one of a pair of fins fitted to the sides of a ship, especially one governed automatically by a ◊gyroscope mechanism, designed to reduce side-to-side rolling of the ship in rough weather.

stadholder or **stadtholder** leader of the United Provinces of the Netherlands from the 15th to the 18th century.

Originally provincial leaders appointed by the central government, stadholders were subsequently elected in the newly independent Dutch republic. For much of their existence they competed with the States General (parliament) for control of the country. The stadholders later became dominated by the house of ◊Orange-Nassau. In 1747 the office became hereditary, but was abolished in 1795.

Staël Anne Louise Germaine Necker, Madame de 1766–1817. French author, daughter of the financier ◊Necker. She wrote semiautobiographical novels such as *Delphine* 1802 and *Corinne* 1807, and the critical work *De l'Allemagne* 1810, on German literature. She was banished from Paris by Napoleon in 1803 because of her advocacy of political freedom.

Staffordshire county in W central England
area 1,050 sq mi/2,720 sq km
cities Stafford (administrative headquarters), Stoke-on-Trent
features largely flat, comprising the Vale of Trent and its tributaries; Cannock Chase;

Keele University 1962; Staffordshire bull terriers
products coal in the north; china and earthenware in the Potteries and the upper Trent basin
population (1991) 1,020,300
famous people Arnold Bennett, Peter de Wint, Robert Peel.

stagflation economic condition (experienced in the US in the 1970s) in which rapid inflation is accompanied by stagnating, even declining, output and by increasing unemployment. It is a recently coined term to explain a condition that violates many of the suppositions of Classical economics. Under the Carter administration, interest rates skyrocketed, prices rose dramatically, and a deep recession occurred. The increase in ◊OPEC petroleum prices was a major contributing factor.

Stahl Georg Ernst 1660–1734. German chemist who produced a fallacious theory of combustion. He was professor of medicine at Halle, and physician to the king of Prussia. He argued that objects burn because they contain a combustible substance, phlogiston. Substances rich in phlogiston, such as wood, burn almost completely away. Metals, which are low in phlogiston, burn less well. Chemists spent much of the 18th century evaluating Stahl's theories before these were finally proved false by Antoine ◊Lavoisier.

stained glass colored pieces of glass that are joined by lead strips to form a pictorial window design.

The art is said to have originated in the Middle East. At first only one monumental figure was represented on each window, but by the middle of the 12th century, incidents in the life of Jesus or of one of the saints were commonly depicted. Fine examples of medieval stained glass are to be found in the cathedrals of Canterbury, Lincoln, Chartres, Cologne, and Rouen. More recent designers include William ◊Morris, Edward ◊Burne-Jones, and Marc ◊Chagall. Since World War II the use of thick, faceted glass joined by cement (common in the 6th century) has been revived.

stainless steel widely used ◊alloy of iron, chromium, and nickel that resists rusting. Its chromium content also gives it a high tensile strength. It is used for cutlery and kitchen fittings. Stainless steel was first produced in the UK 1913 and in Germany 1914.

stalactite and stalagmite cave structures formed by the deposition of calcite dissolved in ground water. **Stalactites** grow downward from the roofs or walls and can be icicle-shaped, straw-shaped, curtain-shaped, or formed as terraces. **Stalagmites** grow upward from the cave floor and can be conical, fir-cone-shaped, or resemble a stack of saucers. Growing stalactites and stalagmites may meet to form a continuous column from floor to ceiling.

Stalactites are formed when ground water, hanging as a drip, loses a proportion of its carbon dioxide into the air of the cave. This reduces the amount of calcite that can be held in solution, and a small trace of calcite is deposited. Successive drips build up the stalactite over many years. In stalagmite formation the calcite comes out of the solution because of agitation—the shock of a drop of water hitting the floor is sufficient to remove some calcite from the drop. The different shapes result from the splashing of the falling water.

Stalin Joseph. Adopted name (Russian "steel") of Joseph Vissarionovich Djugashvili 1879–1953. Soviet politician. A member of the October Revolution Committee 1917, Stalin became general secretary of the Communist Party 1922. After ◊Lenin's death 1924, Stalin sought to create "socialism in one country" and clashed with ◊Trotsky, who denied the possibility of socialism inside Russia until revolution had occurred in W Europe. Stalin won this ideological struggle by 1927, and a series of five-year plans was launched to collectivize industry and agriculture from 1928. All opposition was eliminated in the Great Purge 1936–38. During World War II, Stalin intervened in the military direction of the campaigns against Nazi Germany. His role was denounced after his death by Khrushchev and other members of the Soviet regime.

Born in Georgia, the son of a shoemaker, Stalin was educated for the priesthood but was expelled from his seminary for Marxist propaganda. He became a member of the Social Democratic Party 1898, and joined Lenin and the Bolsheviks 1903. He was repeatedly exiled to Siberia 1903–13. He then became a member of the Communist Party's ◊Politburo, and sat on the October Revolution committee. Stalin rapidly consolidated a powerful following (including Molotov); in 1921 he became commissar for nationalities in the Soviet government, responsible for the decree granting equal rights to all peoples of the Russian Empire, and was appointed general secretary of the Communist Party 1922. As dictator in the 1930s, he disposed of all real and imagined enemies. In recent years increasing evidence has been uncovered revealing Stalin's anti-Semitism, for example, the execution of 19 Jewish activists in 1952 for a "Zionist conspiracy."

Stalingrad former name (1925–61) of the Russian city of ◊Volgograd.

Stalinsk former name (1932–61) of ◊Novokuznetsk, city in Russia.

Stallone Sylvester 1946– . US film actor, a bit player who rocketed to fame as the boxer in *Rocky* 1976 and its sequels. Other films include the *Rambo* series.

Stamboul old part of the Turkish city of ◊Istanbul, the area formerly occupied by ◊Byzantium.

stamen male reproductive organ of a flower. The stamens are collectively referred to as the ◊androecium. A typical stamen consists of a stalk, or filament, with an anther, the pollen-bearing organ, at its apex, but in some primitive plants, such as *Magnolia*, the stamen may not be markedly differentiated.

The number and position of the stamens are significant in the classification of flowering plants. Generally the more advanced plant families have fewer stamens, but they are often positioned more effectively so that the likelihood of successful pollination is not reduced.

Stamford city in SW Connecticut, on Long Island Sound, NE of New York City. Industries include computers, hardware, rubber, plastics, and pharmaceuticals; population (1990) 108,000.

Stamp Act UK act of Parliament in 1765 that sought to raise enough money from the American colonies to cover the cost of their defense. Refusal to use the required tax stamps and a blockade of British merchant shipping in the colonies forced repeal of the act the following year. It was a precursor of the ◊American Revolution.

The act provoked vandalism and looting in America, and the ***Stamp Act Congress*** in Oct of that year (the first intercolonial congress) declared the act unconstitutional, with the slogan "No taxation without representation," because the colonies were not represented in the British Parliament.

standard atmosphere alternative term for ◊atmosphere, a unit of pressure.

standard deviation in statistics, a measure of the spread of data. The deviation (difference) of each of the data items from the mean is found, and their values squared. The mean value of these squares is then calculated. The standard deviation is the square root of this mean.

To simplify the calculations, the formula used for a sample standard deviation s is

$$s = \sqrt{\Sigma[(x_i - \bar{x})^2 \div (n-1)]}$$

where x_i is a particular value of the n pieces of data, and $\bar{x}$ is the sample mean. For example, to find the standard deviation of the ages of a group of eight people in a room, the mean is first found (in this case by adding all the ages together and dividing the total by 8), and deviations between all the individual ages and the mean calculated. Thus, if the ages of the eight people are 14, 14.5, 15, 15.5, 16, 17, 19, and 21, the mean age is $132 \div 8 = 16.5$. The deviations between the individual ages and this mean age are –2.5, –2.0, –1.5, –1.0, –0.5, +0.5, +2.5 and +4.5. These values are then squared to give 6.25, 4.00, 2.25, 1.00, 0.25, 0.25, 6.25, and 20.25, with a mean value of $40.5 \div 8 = 5.0625$. The square root of this figure is 2.25, which is the standard deviation in years.

standard form method of writing numbers often used by scientists, particularly for very large or very small numbers. The numbers are written with one digit before the decimal point and multiplied by a power of 10. The number of digits given after the decimal point depends on the accuracy required. For example, the ◊speed of light is 1.8628×10^5 mi/2.9979 $\times 10^8$ m per second.

standard gravity acceleration due to gravity, generally taken as 32.38204 ft/9.81274 m per second per second.

standard illuminant any of three standard light intensities, A, B, and C, used for illumination when phenomena involving color are measured. A is the light from a filament at 2,848 K (4,667°F/2,575°C), B is noon sunlight, and C is normal daylight. B and C are defined with respect to A. Standardization is necessary because colors appear different when viewed in different lights.

standard model in physics, the modern theory of ◊elementary particles and their interactions. According to the standard model, elementary particles are classified as leptons (light particles, such as electrons), hadrons (particles, such as neutrons and protons, that are formed from quarks), and gauge bosons. Leptons and hadrons interact by exchanging gauge bosons, each of which is responsible for a different fundamental force: photons mediate the electromagnetic force, which affects all charged particles; gluons mediate the strong nuclear force, which affects quarks; gravitons mediate the force of gravity; and the weakons (intermediate vector bosons) mediate the weak nuclear force. See also ◊quantum electrodynamics and ◊quantum chromodynamics.

standard of living in economics, the measure of consumption and welfare of a country, community, class, or person. Individual standard-of-living expectations are heavily influenced by the income and consumption of other people in similar jobs.

Universal measures of standards of living cannot be applied to individuals. National income and gross national product, which measure a country's wealth, do not take into account unpaid work (housework and family labor) or quality of life and do not show the distribution of wealth or reflect the particular national or individual aspirations, duties, or responsibilities, which differ widely from person to person, class to class, and country to country.

Standard Oil Co of New Jersey et al v US US Supreme Court decision 1911 dealing with the dissolution of unreasonable corporate monopolies. The Standard Oil Co, ordered to dissolve after being convicted of an attempt to eliminate free competition in the industry, appealed to the Supreme Court. The Court upheld the conviction formulating a new subjective definition of an illegal trust as "an unreasonable attempt" to restrain competition in trade.

standard temperature and pressure (STP) in chemistry, a standard set of conditions for experimental measurements, to enable comparisons to be made between sets of results. Standard temperature is 0°C and standard pressure 1 atmosphere (101,325 Pa).

standard time alternate name for ◊zone standard time.

standard volume in physics, the volume occupied by one kilogram molecule (the molecular mass in kilograms) of any gas at standard temperature and pressure. Its value is approx 22.414 cubic meters.

standing crop in ecology, the total number of individuals of a given species alive in a particular area at any moment. It is sometimes measured as the weight (or ◊biomass) of a given species in a sample section.

standing wave in physics, a wave in which the positions of ◊nodes (positions of zero vibration) and antinodes (positions of maximum vibration) do not move. Standing waves result when two similar waves travel in opposite directions through the same space.

For example, when a sound wave is reflected back along its own path, as when a stretched string is plucked, a standing wave is formed. In this case the antinode remains fixed at the center and the nodes are at the two ends. Water and ◊electromagnetic waves can form standing waves in the same way.

Standish Miles *c.* 1584–1656. Colonial American military leader. Meeting the Puritan Separatists who were about to embark for America, he agreed to serve as their military adviser. Arriving in New England, Standish led negotiations with the Wampanoag and supervised the Plymouth colonists' military training. After returning to England in 1625 to obtain a charter for Plymouth Colony, he became one of its chief investors 1627. He later established the nearby town of Duxbury and settled there 1637.

Born in Lancashire, England, Standish began his military career as a mercenary in the Dutch rebellion against the Spanish. Although one of the most influential figures in colonial New England, Standish is best remembered through Longfellow's *The Courtship of Miles Standish*, a narrative poem presumably more fictitious than historical.

Stanford Leland 1824–1893. US public official and railroad developer. Settling in California 1856, he became a successful merchant in Sacramento and was elected governor 1861. In the same year, he became president of the Central Pacific Railroad and exerted his political influence to gain government concessions for its transcontinental route. Stanford was one of the founders of the Southern Pacific Railroad 1870. He later served in the US Senate 1885–93 and endowed Stanford University.

Born in Watervliet, New York, Stanford was educated at Cazenovia Seminary and was admitted to the bar 1848.

Stanislavsky Konstantin Sergeivich 1863–1938. Russian actor, director, and teacher of acting. He rejected the declamatory style of acting in favor of a more realistic approach, concentrating on the psychological basis for the development of character. The ▷Actors Studio is based on this approach.

Stanley town on E Falkland, capital of the ▷Falkland Islands; population (1986) 1,200. After changing its name only once between 1843 and 1982, it was renamed five times in the space of six weeks during the Falklands War April–June 1982.

Stanley Henry Morton. Adopted name of John Rowlands 1841–1904. Welsh-born US explorer and journalist who made four expeditions to Africa. He and David ▷Livingstone met at Ujiji 1871 and explored Lake Tanganyika. He traced the course of the river Zaïre (Congo) to the sea 1874–77, established the Congo Free State (Zaire) 1879–84, and charted much of the interior 1887–89.

Stanley worked his passage over to America when he was 18. He fought on both sides in the US Civil War. He worked for the *New York Herald* from 1867, and in 1871 he was sent by the editor James Gordon Bennett (1795–1872) to find the ailing Livingstone, which he did on Nov 10. From Africa he returned to the UK and was elected to Parliament 1895.

Stanley Wendell 1904–1971. US biochemist who crystallized the tobacco mosaic virus (TMV) in 1935. He demonstrated that, despite its crystalline state, TMV remained infectious. Together with John Northrop and James Sumner, Stanley received the 1946 Nobel Prize for Chemistry.

Stanley Cup North American ▷ice hockey playoffs held at the end of the regular season in the National Hockey League (NHL). It was inaugurated 1917 and named after Lord Stanley of Preston, former governor-general of Canada.

Stanleyville former name (until 1966) of the Zairean port of ▷Kisangani.

Stanton Edwin McMasters 1814–1869. US public official; secretary of war 1862–68. A lawyer and a Democrat, he was appointed US attorney general by President Buchanan 1860 and then secretary of war by Republican president Lincoln 1862.

Born in Steubenville, Ohio, Stanton attended Kenyon College, was admitted to the bar 1836, and gained a reputation as a skilled lawyer. As secretary of war he was an effective, if autocratic administrator. Although retained in office by Andrew Johnson, Stanton eventually broke with him over Reconstruction policies and was

forced to resign 1868. He was named to the US Supreme Court 1869 by Grant but died before taking office.

Stanton Elizabeth Cady 1815–1902. US feminist who, with Susan B ▷Anthony, founded the National Woman Suffrage Association 1869, the first women's movement in the US and was its first president. She and Anthony wrote and compiled the *History of Women's Suffrage* 1881–86. Stanton also worked for the abolition of slavery.

She organized the International Council of Women in Washington, DC. Her publications include *Degradation of Disenfranchisement* and *Solitude of Self* 1892, and in 1885 and 1898 she published a two-part feminist critique of the Bible: *The Woman's Bible*.

Stanwyck Barbara. Adopted name of Ruby Stevens 1907–1990. US film actress, equally at home in comedy or melodrama. Her films include *Stella Dallas* 1937, *Double Indemnity* 1944, and *Executive Suite* 1954.

stanza (Italian "resting or stopping place") group of lines in a poem. Each stanza has a set, repeatable pattern of meter and rhyme, and is normally divided from the following stanza by a blank line.

staple in medieval Europe, a riverside town where merchants had to offer their wares for sale before proceeding to their destination, a practice that constituted a form of toll; such towns were particularly common on the Rhine.

In English usage, it referred to a town appointed as the exclusive market for a particular commodity, especially wool. The wool staple was established by the English crown in Calais 1353. This form of monopoly trading was abandoned 1617.

star luminous globe of gas, producing its own heat and light by nuclear reactions. Stars are born from ▷nebulae, and consist mostly of hydrogen and helium gases. Surface temperatures range from 3,600°F/2,000°C to above 54,000°F/30,000°C and the corresponding colors range from red to blue-white. The brightest stars have the highest masses, 100 times that of the Sun, and emit as much light as millions of suns: they live for less than a million years before exploding as ▷supernovae. The faintest stars are the ▷red dwarfs, less than one-thousandth the brightness of the Sun.

The smallest mass possible for a star is about 8% that of the Sun (80 times the mass of the planet Jupiter), otherwise nuclear reactions do not occur. Objects with less than this critical mass shine only dimly, and are termed *brown dwarfs*. There is no firm distinction between a small brown dwarf and a large planet, like Jupiter. Towards the end of its life, a star like the Sun swells up into a ▷red giant, before losing its outer layers as a ▷planetary nebula, and finally shrinking to become a ▷white dwarf. For most of a star's life, energy is produced by the fusion of hydrogen into helium at its center. See also ▷binary star, ▷Hertzsprung–Russell diagram, ▷supergiant, ▷variable star.

starch widely distributed, high-molecular-mass ▷carbohydrate, produced by plants as a food store; main dietary sources are cereals, legumes, and tubers, including potatoes. It consists of varying proportions of two ▷glucose polymers (▷polysaccharides): straight-chain (amylose) and branched (amylopectin) molecules.

Purified starch is a white powder used to stiffen textiles and paper and as a raw material

for making various chemicals. It is used in the food industry as a thickening agent. Chemical treatment of starch gives rise to a range of "modified starches" with varying properties. Hydrolysis (splitting) of starch by acid or enzymes generates a variety of "glucose syrups" or "liquid glucose" for use in the food industry. Complete hydrolysis of starch with acid generates the ▷monosaccharide glucose only. Incomplete hydrolysis or enzymic hydrolysis yields a mixture of glucose, maltose and non-hydrol fractions called "dextrins."

Star Chamber in English history, a civil and criminal court, named after the star-shaped ceiling decoration of the room in the Palace of Westminster, London, where its first meetings were held. Created in 1487 by Henry VII, the Star Chamber comprised some 20 or 30 judges. It was abolished 1641 by the ▷Long Parliament.

The Star Chamber became notorious under Charles I for judgments favorable to the king and to Archbishop ▷Laud (for example, the branding on both cheeks of William Prynne in 1637 for seditious libel). Under the Thatcher government 1979–90 the term was revived for private ministerial meetings at which disputes between the Treasury and high-spending departments were resolved.

star cluster group of related stars, usually held together by gravity. Members of a star cluster are thought to form together from one large cloud of gas in space. *Open clusters* such as the Pleiades contain from a dozen to many hundreds of young stars, loosely scattered over several light-years. ▷Globular clusters are larger and much more densely packed, containing perhaps 100,000 old stars.

starfish or *seastar* any ▷echinoderm of the subclass Asteroidea with arms radiating from a central body. Usually there are five arms, but some species have more. They are covered with spines and small pincerlike organs. There are also a number of small tubular processes on the skin surface that assist in locomotion and respiration. Starfish are predators, and vary in size from 0.5 in/1.2 cm to 3 ft/90 cm.

Some species use their suckered tube feet to pull open the shells of bivalve molluscs, then evert their stomach to surround and digest the animal inside. The poisonous and predatory crown-of-thorns of the Pacific is very destructive to coral and severely damaged Australia's Great Barrier Reef when it multiplied prolifically in the 1960–70s, but by 1990 it had itself practically disappeared, perhaps because of attack by parasites.

Stark Johannes 1874–1957. German physicist. In 1902 he predicted, correctly, that high-velocity rays of positive ions (canal rays) would demonstrate the ▷Doppler effect, and in 1913 showed that a strong electric field can alter the wavelength of light emitted by atoms (the *Stark effect*). He was awarded the Nobel Prize for Physics 1919.

starling any member of a large widespread Old World family (Sturnidae) of chunky, dark, generally gregarious birds of the order Passeriformes. The European starling *Sturnus vulgaris*, common in N Eurasia, has been naturalized in North America from the late 19th century. The black, speckled plumage is glossed with green and purple. Its own call is a bright whistle, but it is a mimic of the songs of other birds. It is about 8 in/20 cm long.

Strikingly gregarious in feeding, flight, and roosting, it often becomes a pest in large cities, where it becomes attached to certain buildings as "dormitories," returning each night from omnivorous foraging in the countryside. If disturbed, starlings have been known to lay eggs in the nests of other birds before starting a new nest with their mate elsewhere.

Star of David or *Magen David* six-pointed star (made with two equilateral triangles), a symbol of Judaism since the 17th century. It is the central motif on the flag of Israel, and, since 1897, the emblem of Zionism.

START acronym for ◊*Strategic Arms Reduction Talks*.

Star Wars popular term for the ◊Strategic Defense Initiative announced by US president Reagan in 1983.

state territory that forms its own domestic and foreign policy, acting through laws that are typically decided by a government and carried out, by force if necessary, by agents of that government. It can be argued that growth of regional international bodies such as the European Community means that states no longer enjoy absolute sovereignty.

Although most states are members of the United Nations, this is not a completely reliable criterion: some are not members by choice, like Switzerland; some have been deliberately excluded, like Taiwan; and some are members but do not enjoy complete national sovereignty. The classic definition of a state is given by R M MacIver (*The Modern State* 1926): "An association which, acting through law as promulgated by a government endowed to this end with coercive power, maintains within a community territorially demarcated the universal external conditions of social order." There are four essential elements in this definition: that people have formed an association to create and preserve social order; that the community comprising the state is clearly defined in territorial terms; that the government representing the people acts according to promulgated laws; and that it has power to enforce these laws.

Today, the state is seen as the nation state so that any community that has absolute sovereignty over a specific area is a state. Thus the so-called states of the US, which are to some degree subject to the will of the federal government, are not states in international terms, nor are colonial or similar possessions, which, too, are subject to an overriding authority.

state change in science, a change in the physical state (solid, liquid, or gas) of a material. For instance, melting, boiling, and evaporation, and their opposites (solidification and condensation) are changes of state.

These changes require energy in the form of heat, called ◊latent heat, even though the temperature of the material does not change during the transition between states.

State Department (Department of State) US government department responsible for ◊foreign relations, headed by the ◊secretary of state, the senior cabinet officer of the executive branch.

Staten Island island in New York harbor, part of New York City, comprising the county of Richmond and, since 1975, the borough of Staten Island; area 60 sq mi/155 sq km.

Staten Island is the city borough with the smallest population. Although mainly residential, it has oil refineries, docks, diversified manufactures, city garbage dumps, and the new nuclear home port of the US Navy. It is

linked to Manhattan by ferry, to Brooklyn by the Verrazano-Narrows Bridge, and to New Jersey by the Outerbridge Crossing. Colonial settlement began 1661 by the Dutch; it passed to the English 1664 and became part of the city 1898. Residents petitioned 1989 and voted 1990 to take a step toward separation from New York City, since they feel they are exploited by but inadequately serviced by the city.

States General former French parliament that consisted of three estates: nobility, clergy, and commons. First summoned 1302, it declined in importance as the power of the crown grew. It was not called at all 1614–1789 when the crown needed to institute fiscal reforms to avoid financial collapse. Once called, the demands made by the States General formed the first phase in the ◊French Revolution. States General is also the name of the Dutch parliament.

states of matter forms (solid, liquid, or gas) in which material can exist. Whether a material is solid, liquid, or gas depends on its temperature and the pressure on it. The transition between states takes place at definite temperatures, called melting point and boiling point.

◊Kinetic theory describes how the state of a material depends on the movement and arrangement of its atoms or molecules. A hot ionized gas or ◊plasma is often called the fourth state of matter, but liquid crystals, ◊colloids, and glass also have a claim to this title.

static electricity ◊electric charge that is stationary, usually acquired by a body by means of electrostatic induction or friction. Rubbing different materials can produce static electricity, as seen in the sparks produced on combing one's hair or removing a nylon shirt. In some processes static electricity is useful, as in paint spraying where the parts to be sprayed are charged with electricity of opposite polarity to that on the paint droplets, and in ◊xerography.

statics branch of mechanics concerned with the behavior of bodies at rest and forces in equilibrium, and distinguished from ◊dynamics.

stations of the Cross in the Christian church, a series of 14 crosses, usually each with a picture or image, depicting the 14 stages in Jesus' journey to the Crucifixion.

statistical mechanics branch of physics in which the properties of large collections of particles are predicted by considering the motions of the constituent particles.

statistics branch of mathematics concerned with the collection and interpretation of data. For example, to determine the ◊mean age of the children in a school, a statistically acceptable answer might be obtained by calculating an average based on the ages of a representative sample, consisting, for example, of a random tenth of the pupils from each class. ◊Probability is the branch of statistics dealing with predictions of events.

status in the social sciences, an individual's social position, or the esteem in which he or she is held by others in society. Both within and between most occupations or social positions there is a status hierarchy. *Status symbols*, such as insignia of office or an expensive car, often accompany high status.

The two forms of social prestige may be separate or interlinked. Formal social status is attached to a certain social position, occupation, role, or office. Informal social status is

based on an individual's own personal talents, skills, or personality. Sociologists distinguish between *ascribed status*, which is bestowed by birth, and *achieved status*, the result of one's own efforts.

The German sociologist Max Weber analyzed social stratification in terms of three separate but interlinked dimensions: class, status, and power. Status is seen as a key influence on human behavior, on the way people evaluate themselves and others.

Staudinger Hermann 1881–1965. German organic chemist, founder of macromolecular chemistry, who carried out pioneering research into the structure of albumen and cellulose. Nobel Prize 1953.

Stauffenberg Claus von 1907–1944. German colonel in World War II who, in a conspiracy to assassinate Hitler, planted a bomb in the dictator's headquarters conference room in the Wolf's Lair at Rastenburg, East Prussia, July 20, 1944. Hitler was merely injured, and Stauffenberg and 200 others were later executed by the Nazi regime.

staurolite silicate mineral, $(Fe,Mg)_2(Al,Fe)_9Si_4O_{20}(OH)_2$. It forms brown crystals that may be twinned in the form of a cross. It is a useful indicator of medium grade (moderate temperature and pressure) in metamorphic rocks formed from clay sediments.

Stavropol territory of the Russian Federation, lying N of the Caucasus Mountains; area 31,128 sq mi/80,600 sq km; population (1985) 2,715,000. The capital is Stavropol. Irrigated land produces grain and sheep are also reared. There are natural gas deposits.

STD abbreviation for *sexually transmitted disease*, a term encompassing not only traditional ◊venereal disease, but also a growing list of conditions, such as ◊AIDS and scabies, which are known to be spread by sexual contact. Other diseases that are sexual in origin include viral ◊hepatitis and cancer of the cervix.

steady-state theory theory that the universe appears the same wherever (and whenever) viewed. This seems to be refuted by the existence of ◊cosmic background radiation.

The theory was proposed 1948 by Hermann ◊Bondi, Thomas Gold (1920–), and Fred ◊Hoyle.

stealth technology methods used to make an aircraft as invisible as possible, primarily to radar detection but also to detection by visual means and heat sensors. This is achieved by a combination of aircraft-design elements: smoothing off all radar-reflecting sharp edges; covering the aircraft with radar-absorbent materials; fitting engine coverings that hide the exhaust and heat signatures of the aircraft; and other, secret technologies.

The US F-117A stealth fighter-bomber was used successfully during the 1991 Gulf War to attack targets in Baghdad completely undetected. The B-2 bomber, a larger, projected stealth aircraft, may be too expensive to put into production.

steam in chemistry, a dry, invisible gas formed by vaporizing water. The visible cloud that normally forms in the air when water is vaporized is due to minute suspended water particles. Steam is widely used in chemical and other industrial processes and for the generation of power.

steam engine engine that uses the power of steam to produce useful work. It was the principal power source during the British Industrial Revolution in the 18th century. The first successful steam engine was built 1712 by Thomas Newcomen, and it was developed further by James Watt from 1769 and by Richard Trevithick, whose high-pressure steam engine 1802 led to the development of the steam locomotive.

In Newcomen's engine, steam was admitted to a cylinder as a piston moved up, and was then condensed by a spray of water, allowing air pressure to force the piston downward. James Watt improved Newcomen's engine in 1769 by condensing the steam outside the cylinder (thus saving energy formerly used to reheat the cylinder) and by using steam to force the piston upward. Watt also introduced the *double-acting engine*, in which steam is alternately sent to each end of the cylinder. The *compound engine* (1781) uses the exhaust from one cylinder to drive the piston of another. A later development was the steam ▷turbine, still used today to power ships and generators in power stations. In other contexts, the steam engine was superseded by the ▷internal-combustion engine.

stearic acid $CH_3(CH_2)_{16}COOH$ saturated long-chain ▷fatty acid, soluble in alcohol and ether but not in water. It is found in many fats and oils, and is used to make soap and candles and as a lubricant. The salts of stearic acid are called stearates.

steel alloy or mixture of iron and up to 1.7% carbon, sometimes with other elements, such as manganese, phosphorus, sulfur, and silicon. The US, Russia, Ukraine, and Japan are the main steel producers. Steel has innumerable uses, including ship and automobile manufacture, skyscraper frames, and machinery of all kinds.

Steels with only small amounts of other metals are called *carbon steels*. These steels are far stronger than pure iron, with properties varying with the composition. *Alloy steels* contain greater amounts of other metals. Low-alloy steels have less than 5% of the alloying material; high-alloy steels have more. Low-alloy steels containing up to 5% silicon with relatively little carbon have a high electrical resistance and are used in power transformers and motor or generator cores, for example. *Stainless steel* is a high-alloy steel containing at least 11% chromium. Steels with up to 20% tungsten are very hard and are used in high-speed cutting tools. About 50% of the world's steel is now made from scrap.

Steel is produced by removing impurities, such as carbon, from raw or pig iron, produced by a ▷blast furnace. The main industrial process is the ▷*basic-oxygen process*, in which molten pig iron and scrap steel is placed in a container lined with heat-resistant, alkaline (basic) bricks. A pipe or lance is lowered near to the surface of the molten metal and pure oxygen blown through it at high pressure. The surface of the metal is disturbed by the blast and the impurities are oxidized (burned out). The *open-hearth process* is an older steelmaking method in which molten iron and limestone are placed in a shallow bowl or hearth (see ▷open-hearth furnace). Burning oil or gas is blown over the surface of the metal, and the impurities are oxidized. High-quality steel is made in an *electric furnace*. A large electric current flows through electrodes in the furnace, melting a charge of scrap steel and iron. The quality of the steel produced can be controlled precisely because the temperature

of the furnace can be maintained exactly and there are no combustion by-products to contaminate the steel. Electric furnaces are also used to refine steel, producing the extra-pure steels used, for example, in the petrochemical industry.

The steel produced is cast into ingots, which can be worked when hot by hammering (forging) or pressing between rollers to produce sheet steel. Alternatively, the **continuous-cast process**, in which the molten metal is fed into an open-ended mold cooled by water, produces an unbroken slab of steel.

steel band musical ensemble common in the West Indies, consisting mostly of percussion instruments made from oil drums that give a sweet, metallic ringing tone.

Steele Richard 1672–1729. Irish essayist who founded the journal *The Tatler* 1709–11, in which Joseph ▷Addison collaborated. They continued their joint work in *The Spectator*, also founded by Steele, 1711–12, and *The Guardian* 1713. He also wrote plays, such as *The Conscious Lovers* 1722.

Steen Jan 1626–1679. Dutch painter. Born in Leiden, he was also active in The Hague, Delft, and Haarlem. He painted humorous everyday scenes, mainly set in taverns or bourgeois households, as well as portraits and landscapes.

Stefan–Boltzmann constant in physics, a constant relating the energy emitted by a black body (a hypothetical body that absorbs or emits all the energy falling on it) to its temperature. Its value is 5.6697×10^{-8} W m^{-2} K^{-4}.

Stefan–Boltzmann law in physics, a law that relates the energy, E, radiated away from a perfect emitter (a ▷black body), to the temperature, T, of that body. It has the form $M = \sigma T^4$, where M is the energy radiated per unit area per second, T is the temperature, and σ is the **Stefan–Boltzmann constant**. Its value is 5.6697×10^{-8} W m^{-2} K^{-4}. The law was derived by Austrian physicists Joseph Stefan and Ludwig Boltzmann.

Steffens Lincoln 1866–1936. US journalist. Born in San Francisco and educated at Berkeley, Steffens joined the staff of the *New York Evening Post* 1892. An expert in financial affairs, Steffens served as editor of the *New York Commercial Advertiser* 1897–1901 and later joined the staff of *McClure's Magazine*. Intent on exposing corruption and fraud in high places, he joined forces with writers Ida Tarbell and Ray Stannard Baker and initiated the style of investigative journalism since known as "muckraking." Steffens later covered the Mexican Revolution and befriended Lenin. His *Autobiography* appeared 1931.

Steichen Edward 1897–1973. Luxembourg-born US photographer, who with Alfred ▷Stieglitz helped to establish photography as an art form. His style evolved during his career from painterly impressionism to realism.

During World War I he helped to develop aerial photography, and in World War II he directed US naval-combat photography. He turned to fashion and advertising 1923–38, working mainly for *Vogue* and *Vanity Fair* magazines. He was in charge of the Museum of Modern Art's photography collection 1947–62, where in 1955 he organized the renowned "Family of Man" exhibition.

Steiger Rod(ney Stephen) 1925– . US character actor of the ▷Method school. His work

includes *On the Waterfront* 1954, *In the Heat of the Night* 1967, and the title role in *W C Fields and Me* 1976.

Stein Gertrude 1874–1946. US writer who influenced authors Ernest ▷Hemingway, Sherwood ▷Anderson, and F Scott ▷Fitzgerald with her conversational tone, cinematic technique, use of repetition, and absence of punctuation: devices intended to convey immediacy and realism. Her work includes the self-portrait *The Autobiography of Alice B Toklas* 1933.

Born in Allegheny, Pennsylvania, Stein went to Paris 1903 after medical school at Johns Hopkins University and lived there, writing and collecting art, for the rest of her life. She settled in with her brother, also a patron of the arts, and a companion/secretary, Alice B Toklas (1877–1967), and in her home she held court to a "lost generation" of expatriate US writers and modern artists (Picasso, Matisse, Braque, Gris). She also wrote *The Making of Americans* 1906–11, *Composition as Explanation* 1926, *Tender Buttons* 1941, *Mrs. Reynolds* 1952, and the operas (with composer Virgil Thomson) *Four Saints in Three Acts* 1929 and *The Mother of Us All* 1947. A tour of the US 1934 resulted in *Everybody's Autobiography* 1937.

Steinbeck John (Ernst) 1902–1968. US novelist. His realist novels, such as *In Dubious Battle* 1936, *Of Mice and Men* 1937, and *The Grapes of Wrath* 1939 (Pulitzer Prize 1940), portray agricultural life in his native California, where migrant farm laborers from the Oklahoma dust bowl struggled to survive. Nobel Prize 1962.

Born in Salinas, California, Steinbeck worked as a laborer to support his writing career, and his experiences supplied him with authentic material for his books. He first achieved success with *Tortilla Flat* 1935, a humorous study of the lives of Monterey *paisanos* (farmers). His early naturalist works are his most critically acclaimed. Later books include *Cannery Row* 1944, *The Wayward Bus* 1947, *East of Eden* 1952, *Once There Was a War* 1958, *The Winter of Our Discontent* 1961, and *Travels with Charley* 1962. He also wrote screenplays for films, notably *Viva Zapata!* 1952. His best-known short story is the fable "The Pearl."

Steinberg Saul 1914– . Romanian-born US artist. He was educated at the University of Bucharest and received his doctorate in architecture from the Reggio Politecnico in Milan 1940. Embarking on a career as a painter and cartoonist, he immigrated to the US 1942. After service as an American intelligence officer in Italy during World War II, Steinberg became a regular cover illustrator for the *New Yorker*. Collections of his paintings, cartoons, and murals were exhibited at galleries throughout the country. He was inducted into the National Institute of Arts and Letters 1968.

Steinem Gloria 1934– . US journalist and liberal feminist who emerged as a leading figure in the US women's movement in the late 1960s. She was also involved in radical protest campaigns against racism and the Vietnam War. She cofounded the Women's Action Alliance 1970 and *Ms* magazine. In 1983 a collection of her articles was published as *Outrageous Acts and Everyday Rebellions*.

Steiner Max(imilian Raoul) 1888–1971. Austrian composer of accomplished film music, in the US from 1914.

He composed his first film score in 1929 and produced some of motion pictures' finest music, including the scores to *King Kong* 1933, *Gone With the Wind* 1939, and *Casablanca* 1942.

Steiner Rudolf 1861–1925. Austrian philosopher, originally a theosophist (see ◊Blavatsky), who developed his own mystic and spiritual teaching, anthroposophy, designed to develop the whole human being. A number of Steiner schools follow a curriculum laid down by him with a strong emphasis on the arts, although the schools also include the possibilities for pupils to take state exams.

Steinmetz Charles 1865–1923. US engineer who formulated the *Steinmetz hysteresis law* in 1891, which describes the dissipation of energy that occurs when a system is subject to an alternating magnetic force.

He worked on the design of alternating current transmission and from 1894 to his death served as consulting engineer to General Electric.

Stella Frank 1936–   . US painter, a pioneer of the hard-edged geometric trend in abstract art that followed Abstract Expressionism. From around 1960 he also experimented with the shape of his canvases.

Stella Joseph 1877–1946. Italian-born US painter. He painted cubistic and futuristic views of New York City, such as his *Brooklyn Bridge* 1919–20 and *New York Interpreted* 1920–22. Stella's works are mostly mechanical and urban scenes, although his later paintings include tropical landscapes.

stem main supporting axis of a plant that bears the leaves, buds, and reproductive structures; it may be simple or branched. The plant stem usually grows above ground, although some grow underground, including ◊rhizomes, ◊corms, and ◊tubers. Stems contain a continuous vascular system that conducts water and food to and from all parts of the plant.

The point on a stem from which a leaf or leaves arise is called a node, and the space between two successive nodes is the internode. In some plants, the stem is highly modified; for example, it may form a leaflike ◊cladode or it may be twining (as in many climbing plants), or fleshy and swollen to store water (as in cacti and other succulents). In plants exhibiting ◊secondary growth, the stem may become woody, forming a main trunk, as in trees, or a number of branches from ground level, as in shrubs.

Stendhal adopted name of Marie Henri Beyle 1783–1842. French novelist. His novels *Le Rouge et le noir/The* ◊*Red and the Black* 1830 and *La Chartreuse de Parme/The Charterhouse of Parma* 1839 were pioneering works in their treatment of disguise and hypocrisy; a review of the latter by fellow novelist ◊Balzac in 1840 furthered Stendhal's reputation.

Stendhal was born in Grenoble. He served in Napoleon's armies and took part in the ill-fated Russian campaign. Failing in his hopes of becoming a prefect, he lived in Italy from 1814 until suspicion of espionage drove him back to Paris in 1821, where he lived by literary hackwork. From 1830 he was a member of the consular service, spending his leaves in Paris.

Stephen c. 1097–1154. King of England from 1135. A grandson of William I, he was elected king 1135, although he had previously recognized Henry I's daughter ◊Matilda as heiress to the throne. Matilda landed in England 1139, and civil war disrupted the country until 1153, when Stephen acknowledged Matilda's son, Henry II, as his own heir.

Stephen I, St 975–1038. King of Hungary from 997, when he succeeded his father. He completed the conversion of Hungary to Christianity and was canonized in 1803.

Stephens Alexander Hamilton 1812–1883. American public official. As one of the leaders of the Whig party in the US House of Representatives 1843–59, Stephens, from Georgia, opposed the Mexican War and remained a strong defender of slavery. In 1861 he was chosen vice-president of the Confederacy. Arrested and briefly imprisoned at the end of the Civil War, he served again as US congressman 1872–82 and as Georgia governor 1882–83.

Born in Taliaferro County, Georgia, Stephens was educated at the University of Georgia and was admitted to the bar 1834. He served in the Georgia state legislature 1836–41.

Stephen, St died c. AD 35. The first Christian martyr; he was stoned to death. Feast day Dec 26.

Stephenson George 1781–1848. English engineer who built the first successful steam locomotive, and who also invented a safety lamp in 1815. He was appointed engineer of the Stockton and Darlington Railway, the world's first public railroad, in 1821, and of the Liverpool and Manchester Railway in 1826. In 1829 he won a £500 prize with his locomotive *Rocket*.

Stephenson Robert 1803–1859. English civil engineer who constructed railroad bridges such as the high-level bridge at Newcastle upon Tyne, England, and the Menai and Conway tubular bridges in Wales. He was the son of George Stephenson.

steppe the temperate grasslands of Europe and Asia. Sometimes the term refers to other temperate grasslands and semiarid desert edges.

steradian SI unit (symbol sr) of measure of solid (three-dimensional) angles, the three-dimensional equivalent of the ◊radian. One steradian is the angle at the center of a sphere when an area on the surface of the sphere equal to the square of the sphere's radius is joined to the center.

stereophonic sound system of sound reproduction using two complementary channels leading to two loudspeakers, which gives a more natural depth to the sound. Stereo recording began with the introduction of two-track magnetic tape in the 1950s. See ◊hi-fi.

stereotype (Greek "fixed impression") in sociology, a fixed, exaggerated, and preconceived description about a certain type of person, group, or society. It is based on prejudice rather than fact, but by repetition and with time, stereotypes become fixed in people's minds, resistant to change or factual evidence to the contrary.

The term, originally used for a method of duplicate printing, was adopted in a social sense by the US journalist Walter Lippman in 1922. Stereotypes can prove dangerous when used to justify persecution and discrimination. Some sociologists believe that stereotyping reflects a power structure in which one group in society uses labeling to keep another group "in its place."

sterilization any surgical operation to terminate the possibility of reproduction. In women, this is normally achieved by sealing or tying off the ◊Fallopian tubes (tubal ligation) so that fertilization can no longer take place. In men, the transmission of sperm is blocked by ◊vasectomy.

Sterilization is a safe alternative to ◊contraception and may be encouraged by governments to limit population growth or as part of a selective-breeding policy (see ◊eugenics).

sterilization the killing or removal of living organisms such as bacteria and fungi. A sterile environment is necessary in medicine, food processing, and some scientific experiments. Methods include heat treatment (such as boiling), the use of chemicals (such as disinfectants), irradiation with gamma rays, and filtration. See also ◊asepsis.

sterling silver ◊alloy containing 925 parts of silver and 75 parts of copper. The copper hardens the silver, making it more useful.

Stern Otto 1888–1969. German physicist. Stern studied with Einstein in Prague and Zürich, where he became a lecturer in 1914. After World War I he demonstrated by means of the *Stern–Gerlach apparatus* that elementary particles have wavelike properties as well as the properties of matter that had been demonstrated. He left Germany for the US in 1933. He was awarded the Nobel Prize for Physics in 1943.

Sternberg Josef von 1894–1969. Austrian film director, in the US from childhood. He is best remembered for his seven films with Marlene Dietrich, including *The Blue Angel/Der blaue Engel* 1930, *Blonde Venus* 1932, and *The Devil Is a Woman* 1935, all of which are marked by his expressive use of light and shadow.

Sterne Laurence 1713–1768. Irish writer, creator of the comic antihero Tristram Shandy. *The Life and Opinions of Tristram Shandy, Gent* 1760–67, an eccentrically whimsical and bawdy novel, foreshadowed many of the techniques and devices of 20th-century novelists, including James Joyce. His other works include *A Sentimental Journey through France and Italy* 1768.

Stern Gang formal name *Fighters for the Freedom of Israel* Zionist guerrilla group founded 1940 by Abraham Stern (1907–1942). The group carried out anti-British attacks during the UK mandate rule in Palestine, both on individuals and on strategic targets. Stern was killed by British forces in 1942, but the group survived until 1948, when it was outlawed with the creation of the independent state of Israel.

steroid in biology, any of a group of cyclic, unsaturated alcohols (lipids without fatty acid components), which, like sterols, have a complex molecular structure consisting of four carbon rings. Steroids include the sex hormones, such as ◊testosterone, the corticosteroid hormones produced by the ◊adrenal gland, bile acids, and ◊cholesterol. The term is commonly used to refer to ◊anabolic steroid.

sterol any of a group of solid, cyclic, unsaturated alcohols, with a complex structure that includes four carbon rings; cholesterol is an example. Steroids are derived from sterols.

stethoscope instrument used to ascertain the condition of the heart and lungs by listening to their action. It consists of two earpieces connected by flexible tubes to a small plate that is placed against the body. It was invented in 1819 in France by René Théophile Hyacinthe ◊Laënnec.

Stettin German name for the Polish city of ◊Szczecin.

Steuben Friedrich Wilhelm von, Baron 1730–1794. Prussian military leader in the American Revolution. Seeking employment as an officer in the American Revolution, Steuben left Europe and joined Washington at Valley Forge 1778. Named inspector general of the Continental army, he was placed in charge of training and compiled a manual of military regulations. He later saw action in the South and was present at Yorktown.

Born in Prussia, Steuben began his military career in the Seven Years' War. After leaving active duty 1763, he was a functionary in the court of Hohenzollern-Hechingen 1764–75 and was made a baron.

Steubenville city in E Ohio, on the Ohio River, S of Youngstown, near the West Virginia border. Industries include steel, coal, paper, and chemicals; population (1990) 22,100. Originally **Fort Steuben**, it was built 1786 to protect government land agents from the Indians.

Stevens George 1904–1975. US film director who began as a director of photography. He made such films as *Swing Time* 1936 and *Gunga Din* 1939, and his reputation grew steadily, as did the length of his films. His later work included *A Place in the Sun* 1951, *Shane* 1953, and *Giant* 1956.

Stevens John Paul 1920– . US jurist and associate justice of the US Supreme Court from 1975. He was a moderate whose opinions and dissents were wide ranging. He argued for Congressional authority to regulate wages in *National League of Cities* v *Usery* 1976, that the death penalty is not by definition cruel and unusual punishment in *Jurek* v *Texas* 1976, and held, in a dissent, that minority contracting guarantees are unconstitutional in *Fullilove* v *Klutznick* 1980. He also argued that a state cannot require the teaching of creationism to counteract the teaching of evolution in *Edwards* v *Aguillard* 1987 and that the burning of the US flag in protest is unconstitutional in *Texas* v *Johnson*.

Born in Chicago, Illinois, he graduated from the University of Chicago and Northwestern University Law School and served as clerk to US Supreme Court Justice Wiley Rutledge. After entering private practice, Stevens also taught at Chicago and Northwestern before being appointed judge of the US Court of Appeals for the Seventh Circuit. President Ford appointed him to the Supreme Court in 1975.

Stevens Wallace 1879–1955. US poet. An insurance company executive, he was not recognized as a major poet until late in life. His volumes of poetry include *Harmonium* 1923, *The Man with the Blue Guitar* 1937, and *Transport to Summer* 1947. *The Necessary Angel* 1951 is a collection of essays. An elegant and philosophical poet, he won the Pulitzer Prize 1954 for his *Collected Poems*.

Stevenson Adlai 1900–1965. US Democratic politician. He is best known as the losing Democratic nominee in two presidential elections against Dwight ⟩Eisenhower 1952 and 1956. He served in the F D ⟩Roosevelt administration in the 1930s and 1940s and became a successful reform-minded governor of Illinois 1949–52. He was named ambassador to the UN by John ⟩Kennedy 1961.

Born in Los Angeles, California, Stevenson graduated from Princeton University and Northwestern Law School 1926. He practiced law in Chicago, where he became active on the Council on Foreign Relations and the Committee to Defend America by Aiding the Allies.

Stevenson Robert Louis 1850–1894. Scottish novelist and poet, author of the adventure novel *Treasure Island* 1883. Later works included the novels *Kidnapped* 1886, *The Master of Ballantrae* 1889, *Dr Jekyll and Mr Hyde* 1886, and the anthology *A Child's Garden of Verses* 1885.

Stevenson was born in Edinburgh. He studied at the university there and qualified as a lawyer, but never practiced. Early works include *An Island Voyage* 1878 and *Travels with a Donkey* 1879. In 1879 he met the American Fanny Osbourne in France and followed her to the US, where they married in 1880. In the same year they returned to Britain, and he subsequently published a volume of stories, *The New Arabian Nights* 1882, and essays; for example, *Virginibus Puerisque* 1881 and *Familiar Studies of Men and Books* 1882. The humorous *The Wrong Box* 1889 and the novels *The Wrecker* 1892 and *The Ebb-tide* 1894 were written in collaboration with his stepson, Lloyd Osbourne (1868–1920). In 1890 he settled at Vailima, in Samoa, where he sought a cure for his tuberculosis.

Stewart James 1908– . US actor. He made his Broadway debut in 1932 and soon after worked in Hollywood. Speaking with a soft drawl, he specialized in the role of the stubbornly honest, ordinary American in such films as *Mr Smith Goes to Washington* 1939, *The Philadelphia Story* 1940 (Academy Award), *It's a Wonderful Life* 1946, *Harvey* 1950, *The Man from Laramie* 1955, and *The FBI Story* 1959. His films with director Alfred ⟩Hitchcock include *Rope* 1948, *Rear Window* 1954, *The Man Who Knew Too Much* 1956, and *Vertigo* 1958.

Born in Indiana, Pennsylvania, he was an air force pilot in World War II.

Stewart Potter 1915–1985. US jurist and associate justice of the US Supreme Court 1958–81. Seen as a moderate, he is known for opinions upholding civil rights for minorities and for opinions on criminal procedure. In writing the majority opinion in *Elkins* v *United States* 1960, he stated the Court's prohibition of the use of evidence illegally obtained by state officials in federal criminal trials. He dissented in both *Escabedo* v *Illinois* 1964 and *Miranda* v *Arizona*, which gave defendants expanded procedural rights, and in *In re Gault* 1967, which gave juveniles due process rights. In other cases he ruled for defendants' rights.

Born in Chicago, Illinois, Stevens graduated from Yale and Yale Law School and entered private practice in New York City and Cincinnati, Ohio. He was appointed judge of the US Court of Appeals for the Sixth Circuit 1954. In 1958 President Eisenhower appointed him to the Supreme Court.

Stewart Island volcanic island divided from South Island, New Zealand, by the Foveaux Strait; area 676 sq mi/1,750 sq km; population (1981) 600. Industries include farming, fishing, and granite quarrying. Oban is the main settlement.

stickleback any fish of the family Gasterosteidae, found in marine and fresh waters of the northern hemisphere. It has a long body that can grow to 7 in/18 cm. The spines along a stickleback's back take the place of the first dorsal fin, and can be raised to make the fish difficult to eat for predators. The male builds a nest for the female's eggs, which he then guards.

The common three-spined stickleback, *Gasterosteus aculeatus*, up to 4 in/10 cm, is found in freshwater habitats and also in brackish estuaries.

Stieglitz Alfred 1864–1946. US photographer who was mainly responsible for the recognition of photography as an art form. After forming the multimedia Photo-Secession Group at 291 Fifth Avenue, New York, with Edward ⟩Steichen, he began the magazine *Camera Work* 1902–17. Through exhibitions, competitions, and publication at his galleries, he helped establish a photographic esthetic.

He was also instrumental in promoting modern art, both by European and American artists. He was the first exhibitor to show such painters and sculptors as Picasso, Cézanne, Rodin, Matisse, Brancusi, and Georgia O'Keeffe, who became his wife 1924. His cloud series, the portraits of O'Keeffe, and his studies of New York City, are his most famous works.

stigma in a flower, the surface at the tip of a ⟩carpel that receives the ⟩pollen. It often has short outgrowths, flaps, or hairs to trap pollen and may produce a sticky secretion to which the grains adhere.

stigmata impressions or marks corresponding to the five wounds Jesus received at his crucifixion, which are said to have appeared spontaneously on St Francis and other saints.

Stijl, De (Dutch "the style") group of 20th-century Dutch artists and architects led by ⟩Mondrian from 1917. They believed in the concept of the "designer"; that all life, work, and leisure should be surrounded by art; and that everything functional should also be aesthetic. The group had a strong influence on the ⟩Bauhaus school.

The name came from a magazine, *De Stijl*, founded 1917 by Mondrian and Theo van Doesburg (1883–1931).

Stilicho Flavius AD 359–408. Roman general, of ⟩Vandal origin, who campaigned successfully against the Visigoths and Ostrogoths. He virtually ruled the western empire as guardian of Honorius (son of ⟩Theodosius I) but was executed on the orders of Honorius when he was suspected of wanting to make his own son successor to another son of Theodosius in the eastern empire.

Stilwell Joseph Warren 1883–1946. US general, nicknamed "Vinegar Joe." In 1942 he became US military representative in China, when he commanded the Chinese forces cooperating with the British (with whom he quarreled) in Burma (now Myanmar); he later commanded all US forces in the Chinese, Burmese, and Indian theaters until recalled to the US 1944 after differences over nationalist policy with ⟩Chiang Kai-shek. Stilwell sought engagement of 30 divisions of Chinese nationalist troops in battle against the Japanese. Chiang Kai-shek refused, preferring to reserve his forces for use against the Chinese Communists in the anticipated Chinese civil war. At Chiang's insistence, President F D ⟩Roosevelt recalled Stilwell, giving him command of the US 10th Army on the Japanese island of Okinawa.

Born in Palatka, Florida, Stilwell graduated from West Point 1904.

Stimson Henry Lewis 1867–1950. US politician. He was war secretary in Taft's cabinet 1911–13, Hoover's secretary of state 1929–33, and war secretary 1940–45.

stimulant any drug that acts on the brain to increase alertness and activity; for example, ⟩amphetamine. When given to children, stimulants may have a paradoxical, calming effect. Stimulants cause liver damage, are habit-forming, have limited therapeutic value, and are now prescribed only to treat ⟡narcolepsy and to reduce the appetite in dieting.

Sting adopted name of Gordon Sumner 1951– . English pop singer, songwriter, actor, and bass player. As a member of the trio *the Police* 1977–83, he had UK number-one hits with "Message in a Bottle" 1979, "Walking on the Moon" 1979, and "Every Breath You Take" 1983. In his solo career he has drawn on a variety of musical influences in such albums as the jazz-based *The Dream of Blue Turtles* 1985, the eclectic *Nothing But the Sun ...* 1989, and *Soul Cages* 1991.

stinkhorn any foul-smelling fungus of the European genus *Phallus*, especially *P. impudicus*; they first appear on the surface as white balls.

stinkwood any of various trees with unpleasant-smelling wood. The S African tree *Ocotea bullata*, family Lauraceae, has offensive-smelling wood when newly felled, but fine, durable timber used for furniture. Another stinkwood is *Gustavia augusta* from tropical America.

stipule outgrowth arising from the base of a leaf or leaf stalk in certain plants. Stipules usually occur in pairs or fused into a single semicircular structure.

They may have a leaflike appearance, as in rose plants *Rosa*; be spiny, as in black locust *Robinia pseudoacacia*; or look like small scales. In some species they are large and contribute significantly to the photosynthetic area, as in the garden pea *Pisum sativum*.

Stirling administrative headquarters of Central Region, Scotland, on the river Forth; population (1981) 39,000. Industries include the manufacture of agricultural machinery, textiles, and carpets. The castle, which guarded a key crossing of the river, predates the 12th century and was long a Scottish royal residence. William Wallace won a victory at Stirling bridge 1297. Edward II of England (in raising a Scottish siege of the town) went into battle at Bannockburn 1314 and was defeated by Robert I (the Bruce).

St Joseph city in NW Missouri, on the Missouri River, NW of Kansas City. Industries include food processing, dairy products, metal products, concrete, and steel; population (1980) 76,691. In the mid-1800s, it served as the eastern terminus for the Pony Express.

stoat another name for the ⟡ermine or short-tailed weasel *Mustela erminea*, used for Old World members of this northern hemisphere species.

stock in the US, each share of stock represents proportional ownership in a corporation. Once offered by a corporation going public, stock can be bought and sold on a ⟡stock exchange, but the corporation has no obligation to buy it back. Sold to raise capital, stock gives the holder specified rights, including the right to examine the books and the right to vote for the directors. Dividends can be paid, in cash or in stock, when the corporation declares a profit.

stock in botany, any of several herbaceous plants of the genus *Matthiola* of the Crucifer family, commonly grown as garden ornamentals. Many cultivated varieties, including simple-stemmed, queen's, and ten-week, have been derived from the wild stock *M. incana*; *M. bicornis* becomes aromatic at night and is known as night-scented (or evening) stock.

stock-car racing sport popular in the US. Stock cars are high-powered sports cars that race on specially built tracks at distances up to 400–500 mi/640–800 km. The sport is governed in the US by the National Association for Stock Car Auto Racing (NASCAR) founded 1947.

stock exchange institution for the buying and selling of stock in publicly held corporations. An exchange trades in stocks that are already issued. Trading is done only by members who have purchased or inherited a "seat" on the exchange. They can act as brokers for nonmembers, on a commission basis, or as floor brokers, acting for other members. Registered traders have no contact with the public but trade only their private accounts. The world's largest exchanges are in New York, London, and Tokyo, and stock prices are watched carefully as indicators of confidence in the economy.

Stockhausen Karlheinz 1928– . German composer of avant-garde music who has continued to explore new musical sounds and compositional techniques since the 1950s. His major works include *Gesang der Jünglinge* 1956 and *Kontakte* 1960 (electronic music); and *Sirius* 1977.

Since 1977 all his works have been part of *Licht*, a cycle of seven musical ceremonies intended for performance on the evenings of a week. He has completed *Donnerstag* 1980, *Samstag* 1984, *Montag* 1988, and *Dienstag* 1992.

Stockholm capital and industrial port of Sweden; population (1990) 674,500. It is built on a number of islands. Industries include engineering, brewing, electrical goods, paper, textiles, and pottery.

A network of bridges links the islands and the mainland; an underground railroad was completed 1957. The 18th-century royal palace stands on the site of the 13th-century fortress that defended the trading settlements of Lake Mälar, around which the town first developed. The old town is well preserved and has a church 1264. The town hall was designed by Ragnar Östberg 1923. Most of Sweden's educational institutions are in Stockholm (including the ⟡Nobel Institute). The warship *Wasa* (built for King Gustavus Adolphus, 75 yd/69 m long and 57 yd/52 m high, which sank in the harbor 1628, was raised in 1961 and is preserved in a museum.

Stock Market Crash, 1929 Wall Street crash, 1929 a panic in the US following an artificial stock market boom 1927–29 fed by speculation of shares bought on 10% margin. On Oct 24, 1929, 13 million shares changed hands, with further selling on Oct 28, and the disposal of 16 million shares on Oct 29. Many stockholders were ruined, banks and businesses failed, and unemployment rose to approximately 17 million during the Great Depression 1929–40 that ensued.

stock rights issue in finance, new shares offered to existing stockholders to raise new capital. Stockholders receive a discount on the market price while the company benefits from not having the costs of a relaunch of the new issue.

The amount of shares offered depends on the capital the company needs. In a "one for one rights issue," a stockholder is offered one share for each that he or she already holds. For companies this is the least expensive way of raising more capital.

stocks wooden frame with holes used in Europe and the US until the 19th century to confine the legs and sometimes the arms of minor offenders, and expose them to public humiliation. The ⟡pillory had a similar purpose.

Stockton industrial river port (agricultural machinery, food processing) on the San Joaquin River in California; population (1990) 210,900.

The University of the Pacific is here. Stockton was founded in the late 1840s as a supply center for the California gold rush. The deep-water channel to San Francisco Bay was completed 1933.

stoicism (Greek *stoa* "porch") Greek school of philosophy, founded about 300 BC by Zeno of Citium. The stoics were pantheistic materialists who believed that happiness lay in accepting the law of the universe. They emphasized human brotherhood, denounced slavery, and were internationalist. The name is derived from the porch on which Zeno taught.

In the 3rd and 2nd centuries BC, stoics took a prominent part in Greek and Roman revolutionary movements. After the 1st century BC stoicism became the philosophy of the Roman ruling class and lost its revolutionary significance; outstanding stoics of this period were Seneca, Epictetus, and Marcus Aurelius Antoninus.

Stoke-on-Trent city in Staffordshire, England, on the river Trent; population (1991) 244,800. It is the heart of the ⟡Potteries and a major ceramic center. Other industries include steel, chemicals, engineering machinery, paper, rubber, and coal.

Stoke was formed 1910 from Burslem, Hanley, Longton, Stoke-upon-Trent, Fenton, and Tunstall. The ceramics factories of ⟡Wedgwood are here.

Stoker Bram (Abraham) 1847–1912. Irish novelist, actor, theater manager, and author. His novel ⟡*Dracula* 1897 crystallized most aspects of the traditional vampire legend and became the source for all subsequent fiction and films on the subject.

stokes unit (symbol St) of kinematic viscosity (a liquid's resistance to flow).

Liquids with higher kinematic viscosity have higher turbulence than those with low kinematic viscosity. It is found by dividing the dynamic viscosity in ⟡poise by the density of the liquid.

Stokes George Gabriel 1819–1903. Irish physicist. During the late 1840s, he studied the ⟡viscosity (resistance to relative motion) of fluids. This culminated in **Stokes' law**, $F = 6\pi\varepsilon rv$, which applies to a force acting on a sphere falling through a liquid, where ε is the liquid's viscosity and r and v are the radius and velocity of the sphere.

Stokowski Leopold 1882–1977. US conductor, born in London. An outstanding experimentalist, he introduced modern music (for example, Mahler's Eighth Symphony) to the US; appeared in several films; and conducted the music for Walt Disney's animated film *Fantasia* 1940.

He led the Philadelphia Orchestra 1912–38, established the All-American Youth Orchestra, and gave low-priced concerts at the New York City Center.

STOL (acronym for *short takeoff and landing*) aircraft fitted with special devices on the wings (such as sucking flaps) that increase aerodynamic lift at low speeds. Small passenger and freight STOL craft may become common with the demand for small airports, especially in difficult terrain.

stolon in botany, a type of �ârunner.

stoma (plural **stomata**) in botany, a pore in the epidermis of a plant. Each stoma is surrounded by a pair of guard cells that are crescent-shaped when the stoma is open but can collapse to an oval shape, thus closing off the opening between them. Stomata allow the exchange of carbon dioxide and oxygen (needed for ⟨photosynthesis and ⟨respiration) between the internal tissues of the plant and the outside atmosphere. They are also the main route by which water is lost from the plant, and they can be closed to conserve water, the movements being controlled by changes in turgidity of the guard cells.

Stomata occur in large numbers on the aerial parts of a plant, and on the undersurface of leaves, where there may be as many as 300,000 per square inch.

stomach the first cavity in the digestive system of animals. In mammals it is a bag of muscle situated just below the diaphragm. Food enters it from the esophagus, is digested by the acid and ⟨enzymes secreted by the stomach lining, and then passes into the duodenum. Some plant-eating mammals have multichambered stomachs that harbor bacteria in one of the chambers to assist in the digestion of ⟨cellulose. The gizzard is part of the stomach in birds.

Stone Harlan Fiske 1872–1946. US jurist; associate justice 1925–41 and chief justice 1941–46 of the US Supreme Court. During World War II he authored opinions favoring federal war powers and regulation of aliens.

Born in Chesterfield, New Hampshire, Stone graduated from Amherst College and Columbia University School of Law. He practiced in New York City and taught at Columbia, serving as dean of the law school 1910–23. President Coolidge appointed Stone US attorney general 1924 and to the US Supreme Court 1925. As an associate justice, Stone favored judicial restraint, the making of decisions on constitutional rather than personal grounds. He dissented from numerous conservative decisions opposing President F D Roosevelt's New Deal legislation. He supported voting rights and use of the Constitution's commerce clause to justify federal legislation regulating interstate commerce. In 1941 Roosevelt appointed Stone chief justice.

Stone Lucy 1818–1893. US feminist orator and editor. Married to the radical Henry Blackwell in 1855, she gained wide publicity when, after a mutual declaration rejecting the legal superiority of the man in marriage, she chose to retain her own surname despite her marriage. The term "Lucy Stoner" was coined to mean a woman who advocated doing the same.

In the 1860s she helped to establish the American Woman Suffrage Association and founded and edited the Boston *Woman's Journal*, a suffragist paper that was later edited by her daughter Alice Stone Blackwell (1857–1950).

stone plural **stone** British unit (symbol st) of mass (chiefly used to express body mass) equal to 14 pounds avoirdupois (6.35 kg).

Stone Robert 1937– . US novelist and journalist. His *Dog Soldiers* 1974 is a classic novel about the moral destructiveness of the Vietnam War. *A Flag for Sunrise* 1982 similarly explores the political and moral consequences of US

intervention in a corrupt South American republic. Among his other works is *Children of Light* 1986.

Stone Age the developmental stage of humans in ⟨prehistory before the use of metals, when tools and weapons were made chiefly of stone, especially flint. The Stone Age is subdivided into the Old or Paleolithic, the Middle or Mesolithic, and the New or Neolithic. The people of the Old Stone Age were hunters and gatherers, whereas the Neolithic people took the first steps in agriculture, the domestication of animals, weaving, and pottery.

stonechat small insectivorous ⟨thrush *Saxicola torquata* frequently found in Eurasia and Africa on open land with bushes. The male has a black head and throat, tawny breast, and dark back; the female is browner.

stonecrop any of several plants of the genus *Sedum* of the orpine family Crassulaceae, a succulent herb with fleshy leaves and clusters of starlike flowers. Stonecrops are characteristic of dry, rocky places and some grow on walls.

stonefish any of a family (Synanceiidae) of tropical marine bony fishes with venomous spines and bodies resembling encrusted rocks.

stonefly any insect of the order Plecoptera, with a long tail and antennae and two pairs of membranous wings. Stoneflies live near fresh water. There are over 1,300 species.

The aquatic larvae live mainly in streams with stony bottoms.

Stonehenge megalithic monument dating from about 2800 BC on Salisbury Plain, Wiltshire, England. It consisted originally of a circle of 30 upright stones, their tops linked by lintel stones to form a continuous circle about 100 ft/30 m across. Within the circle was a horseshoe arrangement of five trilithons (two uprights plus a lintel, set as five separate entities), and a so-called "altar stone"—an upright pillar—on the axis of the horseshoe at the open, NE end, which faces in the direction of the rising sun. It has been suggested that it served as an observatory.

stoneware very hard opaque pottery made of nonporous clay with feldspar and a high silica content, fired at high temperature.

Stoppard Tom 1937– . Czechoslovak-born British playwright whose works use wit and wordplay to explore logical and philosophical ideas. His play *Rosencrantz and Guildenstern are Dead* 1966 was followed by comedies including *The Real Inspector Hound* 1968, *Jumpers* 1972, *Travesties* 1974, *Dirty Linen* 1976, *The Real Thing* 1982, and *Hapgood* 1988. He has also written for radio, television, and the cinema.

store or **shop** a building or part of a building used for the retail sale of goods. Roman *stoae* were market stalls enclosed by an arcaded walkway; stores changed little from ancient times until the latter part of the 19th century, when concentration of population and greater availability of manufactured goods gave rise to the department store, in effect a number of small specialty shops under one roof, and to the chain store and the supermarket.

With the spread of chain stores to several cities, all having the same ownership, the relationship between retailers and manufacturers changed. Direct links with factories bypassed middlemen (wholesalers) and lowered costs, in some cases forcing small independent stores to focus on narrow specialties not otherwise

available. In the 1970s in the US, to coincide with the population shift out of urban centers, enclosed shopping malls of up to 250 specialty stores, anchored by at least one large department store, were constructed in many suburban areas. These "controlled shopping environments" have music, free parking, movie theaters, restaurants, and, in some instances, even child-care facilities. The idea has been adopted in the UK and elsewhere, although resistance is rising from those who wish to preserve the viability of downtown (urban center) areas.

stork any of a family (Ciconiidea) of long-legged, long-necked wading birds with long, powerful wings, and long bills used for spearing prey. Some species grow up to 5 ft/1.5 m tall.

Species include the Eurasian **white stork** *Ciconia ciconia*, which is encouraged to build on rooftops as a luck and fertility symbol; and the *jabiru Jabiru mycteria* of the Americas. Up to 5 ft/1.5 m high, it is white plumaged, with a black and red head.

Storting the Norwegian parliament, which consists of 150 representatives, elected every four years.

Story Joseph 1779–1845. US jurist and associate justice of the US Supreme Court 1811–45. On the Court he wrote several decisions defining the role of federal courts in admiralty law. The most notable was *United States* v *Schooner Amistad* 1841, in which the Court ordered black slaves who had seized a slaving ship repatriated to Africa. He also wrote the Court's decision in *Martin* v *Hunter's Lessee* 1816, which established the Court as final arbiter of constitutional issues. He was also a member of the Court when it decided *Dartmouth College* v *Woodward* 1819 and *McCulloch* v *Maryland* 1819, enhancing Congressional authority over states' rights. Story became professor of law at Harvard 1829–45 in addition to his court duties.

Born in Marblehead, Massachusetts, Story was a graduate of Harvard College and practiced law in Massachusetts. He served in the Massachusetts legislature 1805–08 and the US House of Representatives 1808–09, before returning to the Massachusetts legislature, of which he became speaker 1811. President Madison appointed Story to the Supreme Court 1811.

Stowe Harriet Beecher 1811–1896. US suffragist, abolitionist, and author of the antislavery novel *Uncle Tom's Cabin*, first published serially 1851–52. The inspiration came to her in a vision in 1848, and the book brought immediate success.

Stowe was a daughter of Congregationalist minister Lyman ⟨Beecher and in 1836 married C E Stowe, a professor of theology. Her book was radical in its time and did much to spread antislavery sentiment, but in the 20th century was criticized for sentimentality and racism.

She also published other works from 1856, including the New England novels *The Minister's Wooing* 1859 and *Old-Town Folks* 1869, as well as essays and religious poems.

strabismus technical term for a ⟨squint.

Strabo *c.* 63 BC–AD 24. Greek geographer and historian who traveled widely to collect first-hand material for his *Geography*.

Strachey (Giles) Lytton 1880–1932. English critic and biographer, a member of the ⟨Bloomsbury Group of writers and artists. He wrote *Landmarks in French Literature* 1912.

The mocking and witty treatment of Cardinal Manning, Florence Nightingale, Thomas Arnold, and General Gordon in *Eminent Victorians* 1918 won him recognition. His biography of *Queen Victoria* 1921 was more affectionate.

Stradivari Antonio (Latin form *Stradivarius*) 1644–1737. Italian stringed instrument maker, generally considered the greatest of all violin makers. He was born in Cremona and studied there with Niccolo ▷Amati. He produced more than 1,100 instruments from his family workshops, over 600 of which survive. The secret of his mastery is said to be in the varnish but is probably a combination of fine proportioning and aging.

Straits Settlements former province of the ▷British East India Company 1826–58, a British crown colony 1867–1946; it comprised Singapore, Malacca, Penang, Cocos Islands, Christmas Island, and Labuan.

Strasberg Lee 1902–1982. US actor and artistic director of the ▷Actors Studio from 1948, who developed Method acting from ▷Stanislavsky's system; pupils have included Marlon Brando, Paul Newman, Julie Harris, Kim Hunter, Geraldine Page, Al Pacino, and Robert de Niro.

In 1931 Strasberg was one of the founders of the Group Theater, with Harold Clurman and Cheryl Crawford. It became known for its experimental plays, such as *Men in White* 1934 (Pulitzer Prize). He founded the Lee Strasberg Institute of Theater 1969. Strasberg made his film acting debut in *The Godfather II* 1974. He is the father of the actress Susan Strasberg.

Strasbourg city on the River Ill, in Bas-Rhin *département*, capital of Alsace, France; population (1982) 373,000. Industries include car manufacture, tobacco, printing and publishing, and preserves. The ▷Council of Europe meets here, and sessions of the European Parliament alternate between Strasbourg and Luxembourg.

Seized by France 1681, it was surrendered to Germany 1870–1919 and 1940–44. It has a 13th-century cathedral.

strata (singular *stratum*) layers or ▷beds of ▷sedimentary rock.

Strategic Air Command (SAC) the headquarters commanding all US land-based strategic missile and bomber forces. It is located in Colorado in an underground complex with an instant communications link to the president of the US.

Strategic Arms Limitation Talks (SALT) series of US-Soviet discussions aimed at reducing the rate of nuclear-arms buildup. (See also ▷disarmament.) The talks, delayed by the Soviet invasion of Czechoslovakia 1968, began in 1969 between US president Lyndon Johnson and Soviet leader Brezhnev. Neither the SALT I accord (effective 1972–77) nor SALT II called for reductions in nuclear weaponry, merely a limit on the expansion of these forces. SALT II was mainly negotiated by US president Ford before 1976 and signed by Soviet leader Brezhnev and President Carter in Vienna in 1979l. It was never fully ratified because of the Soviet occupation of Afghanistan, although the terms of the accord were respected by both sides until President ▷Reagan exceeded its limitations during his second term 1985–89. SALT talks were superseded by START (Strategic Arms Reduction Talks) negotiations under Reagan, and the first significant reductions began under Soviet President Gorbachev.

Strategic Arms Reduction Talks (START) a phase in US-Soviet peace discussions. START began with talks in Geneva 1983, leading to the signing of the ▷Intermediate Nuclear Forces Treaty (INF) 1987. In 1989 proposals for reductions in conventional weapons were added to the agenda. As the Cold War drew to a close from 1989, the two nations moved rapidly toward total agreement, and in July 1991 the START treaty was signed in Moscow. See also ▷disarmament.

Strategic Defense Initiative (SDI) also called *Star Wars* attempt by the US to develop a defense system against incoming nuclear missiles, based in part outside the Earth's atmosphere. It was announced by President Reagan in March 1983, and the research had by 1990 cost over $16.5 billion. In 1988, the joint Chiefs of Staff announced that they expected to be able to intercept no more than 30% of incoming missiles. Some scientists maintain that the system is basically unworkable.

Stratford port and industrial town in SW Ontario; population (1981) 26,000. It is the site of a Shakespeare festival.

Stratford-upon-Avon market town on the river Avon, in Warwickshire, England; population (1981) 21,000. It is the birthplace of William ▷Shakespeare.

The Royal Shakespeare Theater 1932 replaced an earlier building 1877–79 that burned down in 1926. Shakespeare's birthplace contains relics of his life and times. His grave is in the parish church; his wife Anne Hathaway's cottage is nearby. It receives 2.5 million tourists a year.

Strathclyde region of Scotland
area 5,367 sq mi/13,900 sq km
cities Glasgow (administrative headquarters), Paisley, Greenock, Kilmarnock, Clydebank, Hamilton, Coatbridge, Prestwick
features includes some of Inner ▷Hebrides; river Clyde; part of Loch Lomond; Glencoe, site of the massacre of the Macdonald clan; Breadalbane; islands: Arran, Bute, Mull
products dairy, pig, and poultry products; shipbuilding; engineering; coal from Ayr and Lanark; oil-related services
population (1991) 2,218,200, half the population of Scotland
famous people William Burrell, James Keir Hardie, David Livingstone.

stratigraphy branch of geology that deals with the sequence of formation of ▷sedimentary rock layers and the conditions under which they were formed. Its basis was developed by William ▷Smith, a British canal engineer.

Stratigraphy involves both the investigation of sedimentary structures to determine ancient geographies and environments, and the study of fossils for identifying and dating particular beds of rock.

Stratigraphy is a also a vital tool in the interpretation of archeological excavations. The basic principle of superimposition establishes that upper layers or deposits have accumulated later in time than lower ones, thus providing a relative chronology for the levels and the artifacts within them.

stratosphere that part of the atmosphere 6–25 mi/10–40 km from Earth, where the temperature slowly rises from a low of –67°F/–55°C to around 32°F/0°C. The air is rarefied and at around 15 mi/25 km much ▷ozone is concentrated.

Strauss Johann (Baptist) 1825–1899. Austrian conductor and composer, the son of composer Johann Strauss (1804–1849). In 1872 he gave up conducting and wrote operettas, such as *Die Fledermaus* 1874, and numerous waltzes, such as *The Blue Danube* and *Tales from the Vienna Woods*, which gained him the title "the Waltz King."

Strauss Richard (Georg) 1864–1949. German composer and conductor. He followed the German Romantic tradition but had a strongly personal style, characterized by his bold, colorful orchestration. He first wrote tone poems such as *Don Juan* 1889, *Till Eulenspiegel's Merry Pranks* 1895, and *Also sprach Zarathustra* 1896. He then moved on to opera with *Salome* 1905 and *Elektra* 1909, both of which have elements of polytonality. He reverted to a more traditional style with *Der Rosenkavalier* 1911.

He spent his final years in the US, teaching and composing at the Eastman School of Music in New York.

Stravinsky Igor 1882–1971. Russian composer, later of French (1934) and US (1945) nationality. He studied under ▷Rimsky-Korsakov and wrote the music for the Diaghilev ballets *The Firebird* 1910, *Petrushka* 1911, and *The Rite of Spring* 1913 (controversial at the time for their unorthodox rhythms and harmonies). His versatile work ranges from his Neo-Classical ballet *Pulcinella* 1920 to the choral-orchestral *Symphony of Psalms* 1930. He later made use of serial techniques in such works as the *Canticum Sacrum* 1955 and the ballet *Agon* 1953–57.

strawberry low-growing perennial plant of the genus *Fragaria*, family Rosaceae, widely cultivated for its red, fleshy fruits, which are rich in vitamin C. Wild strawberry *F. virginiana* has small aromatic fruits and grows over much of the eastern half of North America. Cultivated strawberries are hybrids between North American wild species and European species.

streamlining shaping a body so that it offers the least resistance when traveling through a medium such as air or water. Aircraft, for example, must be carefully streamlined to reduce air resistance, or ▷drag.

High-speed aircraft must have swept-back wings, supersonic craft a sharp nose and narrow body.

stream of consciousness narrative technique in which a writer presents directly the uninterrupted flow of a character's thoughts, impressions, and feelings, without the conventional devices of dialogue and description. It first came to be widely used in the early 20th century. Leading exponents have included the novelists Virginia Woolf, James Joyce, and William Faulkner.

Molly Bloom's soliloquy in Joyce's *Ulysses* is a good example of the technique. The English writer Dorothy Richardson (1873–1957) is said to have originated the technique in her novel sequence *Pilgrimage*, the first volume of which was published 1915 and the last posthumously. The term "stream of consciousness" was introduced by the philosopher William James in 1890.

Streep Meryl 1949– . US actress known for her strong character roles. She became a leading star of the 1980s, winning numerous awards. Her films include *The Deer Hunter* 1978, *Kramer vs Kramer* 1979 (Academy Award), *The French Lieutenant's Woman* 1980, *Sophie's Choice* 1982 (Academy Award), *Out of Africa* 1985, *Ironweed* 1988, *A Cry in the Dark* 1989, and the comedy *Death Becomes Her* 1992 .

streetcar or **trolley** transport system, widespread in the US and Europe from the late 19th to the mid-20th century, where wheeled vehicles ran on parallel rails.

It originated in British collieries in the 18th century, and the earliest passenger system was in New York City, 1832. They were powered either by electric conductor rails below ground or conductor arms connected to overhead wires. They were designed for urban and interurban service and vast networks ran from city to city, especially in the NE US, where they ran more often to small towns than did the railroads.

Greater flexibility was achieved with trolley buses, similarly powered by conductor arms overhead but without tracks. In the 1930s–1960s most were retired. In the 1980s both streetcars and trolley buses were in some areas being revived. Both vehicles have the advantage of being nonpolluting to the local environment, since they produce no exhaust gases. However, electricity *is* polluting at the source.

Streisand Barbra (Barbara Joan) 1942– . US singer and actress who became a film star in *Funny Girl* 1968. Her subsequent films include *What's Up Doc?* 1972, *The Way We Were* 1973, and *A Star Is Born* 1979. She directed, scripted, composed, and starred in *Yentl* 1983 and *Prince of Tides* 1991.

streptomycin antibiotic drug discovered in 1944, used to treat tuberculosis, influenzal meningitis, and other infections, some of which are unaffected by ⟡penicillin.

Streptomycin is derived from a soil bacterium *Streptomyces griseus* or synthesized.

stress in psychology, any event or situation that makes demands on a person's mental or emotional resources. Stress can be caused by overwork, anxiety about exams, money, or job security, unemployment, bereavement, poor relationships, marriage breakdown, sexual difficulties, poor living or working conditions, and constant exposure to loud noise.

Many changes that are apparently "for the better," such as being promoted at work, going to a new school, moving to a new house, and getting married, are also a source of stress. Stress can cause, or aggravate, physical illnesses, among them psoriasis, eczema, asthma, stomach and mouth ulcers. Apart from removing the source of stress, acquiring some control over it and learning to relax when possible are the best treatments.

stress and strain in the science of materials, measures of the deforming force applied to a body (stress) and of the resulting change in its shape (strain). For a perfectly elastic material, stress is proportional to strain (⟡Hooke's law).

stride piano jazz piano style alternating left-hand chords with single bass notes; it was popularized in the 1930s by such musicians as Fats ⟡Waller.

stridulatory organs in insects, organs that produce sound when rubbed together. Crickets rub their wings together, but grasshoppers rub a hind leg against a wing. Stridulation is thought to be used for attracting mates, but may also serve to mark territory.

Temperatures can be determined from the stridulations of crickets: adding 40 to the number of chirps counted in 15 seconds gives the approximate temperature in Fahrenheit.

strike stoppage of work by employees (with picketing), often as members of a labor union,

to obtain or resist change in wages, hours, or conditions. A "lockout" is a weapon of an employer to thwart or enforce such change by preventing employees from working. Another measure is "work to rule," when production is virtually brought to a halt by strict observance of union rules.

Strikes may be "official" (union-authorized) or "wildcat" (undertaken spontaneously) and may be accompanied by a sit-in or work-in, the one being worker occupation of a factory and the other continuation of work in a plant the employer wishes to close. In a "sympathetic" strike, action is in support of other workers on strike elsewhere, possibly in a different industry. See also ⟡industrial relations.

Strindberg August 1849–1912. Swedish playwright and novelist. His plays, influential in the development of dramatic technique, are in a variety of styles including historical plays, symbolic dramas (the two-part *Dödsdansen/The Dance of Death* 1901) and "chamber plays" such as *Spöksonaten/The Ghost [Spook] Sonata* 1907. *Fadren/The Father* 1887 and *Fröken Julie/Miss Julie* 1888 are among his works.

Born in Stockholm, he lived mainly abroad after 1883, having been unsuccessfully prosecuted for blasphemy in 1884 following publication of his short stories *Giftas/Marrying*. His life was stormy and his work has been criticized for its hostile attitude to women, but he is regarded as one of Sweden's greatest writers.

stringed instrument musical instrument that produces a sound by making a stretched string vibrate. Today the strings are made of gut, metal, and Pearlon (a plastic). Types of stringed instruments include: **bowed** violin family, viol family; **plucked** guitar, ukelele, lute, sitar, harp, banjo, lyre; **plucked mechanically** harpsichord; **struck mechanically** piano, clavichord; **hammered** dulcimer.

string quartet ⟡chamber music ensemble consisting of first and second violins, viola, and cello. The 18th-century successor to the domestic viol consort, the string quartet with its stronger and more rustic tone formed the basis of the symphony orchestra. Important composers for the string quartet include Haydn (more than 80 string quartets), Mozart (27), Schubert (20), Beethoven (17), Dvořák (8), and Bartók (6).

String-quartet music evolved from the decorative but essentially vocal style of viol music into a vigorously instrumental style exploiting the instruments' full expressive potential. The older hierarchy of solo and accompanying voices also changed to a concertante style offering solo opportunities for each player, a trend accelerated by the adoption of shriller metal strings in the 19th century.

strip mining or **open-pit mining** mining from the surface rather than by tunneling underground. Coal, iron ore, and phosphates are often extracted by strip mining. Often the mineral deposit is covered by soil, which must first be stripped off, usually by large machines such as walking draglines and bucket-wheel excavators. The ore deposit is then broken up by explosives and collected from the surface.

One of the largest excavations in the world has been made by open-pit mining at the Bingham Canyon copper mine in Utah, measuring 2,590 ft/790 m deep and 2.3 mi/3.7 km across.

strobilus in botany, a reproductive structure found in most ⟡gymnosperms and some

⟡pteridophytes, notably the club mosses. In conifers the strobilus is commonly known as a ⟡cone.

stroboscope instrument for studying continuous periodic motion by using light flashing at the same frequency as that of the motion; for example, rotating machinery can be optically "stopped" by illuminating it with a stroboscope flashing at the exact rate of rotation.

Stroessner Alfredo 1912– . Military leader and president of Paraguay 1954–89. As head of the armed forces from 1951, he seized power in a coup in 1954 sponsored by the right-wing ruling Colorado Party. Accused by his opponents of harsh repression, his regime spent heavily on the military to preserve his authority. Despite criticisms of his government's civil-rights record, he was reelected seven times and remained in office until ousted in an army-led coup 1989.

Stroheim Erich von. Assumed name of Erich Oswald Stroheim 1885–1957. Austrian actor and director, in Hollywood from 1914. He was successful as an actor in villainous roles, but his career as a director was wrecked by his extravagance (*Greed* 1923) and he returned to acting in such international films as *La Grande Illusion* 1937 and *Sunset Boulevard* 1950.

He also directed *Queen Kelly* 1928 (unfinished).

stroke or **cerebrovascular accident** or **apoplexy** interruption of the blood supply to part of the brain due to a sudden bleed in the brain (cerebral haemhorrhage) or ⟡embolism or ⟡thrombosis. Strokes vary in severity from producing almost no symptoms to proving rapidly fatal. In between are those (often recurring) that leave a wide range of impaired function, depending on the size and location of the event.

Strokes involving the right side of the brain, for example, produce weakness of the left side of the body. Some affect speech. Transient ischemic attacks, or "mini-strokes," with effects lasting only briefly (less than 24 hours), require investigation to try to forestall the possibility of a subsequent full-blown stroke.

The disease of the arteries that predisposes to stroke is ⟡atherosclerosis. High blood pressure (⟡hypertension) is also a precipitating factor. Strokes can sometimes be prevented by surgery (as in the case of some ⟡aneurysms), or by use of ⟡anticoagulant drugs or vitamin E or daily aspirin to minimize the risk of stroke due to blood clots.

Stromboli Italian island in the Tyrrhenian Sea, one of the ⟡Lipari Islands; area 5 sq mi/12 sq km. It has an active volcano, 3,039 ft/926 m high. The island produces Malmsey wine and capers.

strong nuclear force one of the four ⟡fundamental forces of nature, the other three being the electromagnetic force, gravity, and the weak nuclear force. The strong nuclear force was first described by Japanese physicist Hideki Yukawa 1935. It is the strongest of all the forces, acts only over very small distances within the nucleus of the atom (10^{-13} cm), and is responsible for binding together ⟡quarks to form ⟡hadrons, and for binding together protons and neutrons in the atomic nucleus. The particle that is the carrier of the strong force is the ⟡gluon, of which there are eight kinds, each with zero mass and zero charge.

strontium soft, ductile, pale-yellow, metallic element, symbol Sr, atomic number 38, atomic weight 87.62. It is one of the ◊alkaline-earth metals, widely distributed in small quantities only as a sulfate or carbonate. Strontium salts burn with a red flame and are used in fireworks and signal flares.

The radioactive isotopes Sr-89 and Sr-90 (half-life 25 years) are some of the most dangerous products of the nuclear industry; they are fission products in nuclear explosions and in the reactors of nuclear power plants. Strontium is chemically similar to calcium and deposits in bones and other tissues, where the radioactivity is damaging. The element was named in 1808 by English chemist Humphry Davy, who isolated it by electrolysis, after Strontian, a mining location in Scotland where it was first found.

strophanthus any tropical plant of the genus *Strophanthus* of the dogbane family Apocynaceae, native to Africa and Asia. Seeds of the handsome climber *S. gratus* yield a poison, strophantin, used on arrows in hunting, and in medicine as a heart stimulant.

structuralism 20th-century philosophical movement that has influenced such areas as linguistics, anthropology, and literary criticism. Inspired by the work of the Swiss linguist Ferdinand de Saussure, structuralists believe that objects should be analyzed as systems of relations, rather than as positive entities.

Saussure proposed that language is a system of arbitrary signs, meaning that there is no intrinsic link between the "signifier" (the sound or mark) and the "signified" (the concept it represents). Hence any linguistic term can only be defined by its differences from other terms. His ideas were taken further by Roman Jakobson (1896–1982) and the Prague school of linguistics, and were extended into a general method for the social sciences by the French anthropologist Claude Lévi-Strauss. The French writer Roland Barthes took the lead in applying the ideas of structuralism to literary criticism, arguing that the critic should identify the structures within a text that determine its possible meanings, independently of any reference to the real. This approach is radicalized in Barthes' later work and in the practice of "deconstruction," pioneered by the French philosopher Jacques Derrida (1930–). Here the text comes to be viewed as a "decentered" play of structures, lacking any ultimately determinable meaning.

structured programming in computing, the process of writing a program in small, independent parts. This makes it easier to control a program's development and to design and test its individual component parts. Structured programs are built up from units called *modules*, which normally correspond to single ◊procedures or ◊functions. Some programming languages, such as PASCAL and Modula-2, are better suited to structured programming than others.

strychnine $C_{21}H_{22}O_2N_2$ bitter-tasting, poisonous alkaloid. It is a poison that causes violent muscular spasms, and is usually obtained by powdering the seeds of plants of the genus *Strychnos* (for example *S. nux vomica*). Curare is a related drug.

Stuart Gilbert Charles 1755–1828. American artist. He became a protégé of the American painter Benjamin ◊West in London 1776–82. Gaining fame as one of the foremost portraiturists in England, he worked in Ireland 1787–93 and eventually returned to the US, setting up a studio in Philadelphia 1794.

Stuart, best known for his portraits of George Washington, lived in Washington, DC 1803–05, producing portraits of various prominent public figures. He resided in Boston from 1805 until his death.

Stuart was born in North Kingstown, Rhode Island, and trained by the Scottish painter Cosmo Alexander.

Stuart or *Stewart* royal family who inherited the Scottish throne in 1371 and the English throne in 1603.

Stubbs George 1724–1806. English artist, known for paintings of horses. After the publication of his book of engravings *The Anatomy of the Horse* 1766, he was widely commissioned as an animal painter.

Stubbs began his career as a portrait painter and medical illustrator in Liverpool. In 1754 he went to Rome, continuing to study nature and anatomy. Before settling in London in the 1760s he rented a farm and carried out a series of dissections of horses, which resulted in his book of engravings. The dramatic *Lion Attacking a Horse* 1770 (Yale University Art Gallery, New Haven, Connecticut) and the peaceful *Reapers* 1786 (Tate Gallery, London) show the variety of mood in his painting.

Students for a Democratic Society (SDS) US student movement, founded 1962, which steered a middle line between Marxism and orthodox left-wing politics; its members opposed racism and imperialism. At its peak it had some 100,000 members. In 1968 they were split by the hard-line Weatherman faction, which aimed for violent revolution and control from above.

sturgeon any of a family (Acipenseridae) of large, primitive, bony fishes with five rows of bony plates, small sucking mouths, and chin barbels used for exploring the bottom of the water for prey.

The beluga sturgeon *Huso huso* of the Caspian Sea can reach a length of 25 ft/8 m and weigh 3,300 lb/1,500 kg.

North American species include the Atlantic sturgeon *Acipenser oxyrhynchus*, over 10 ft/3 m long.

Sturluson Snorri 1179–1241. Icelandic author of the Old Norse poems called ◊Eddas and the *Heimskringla*, a saga chronicle of Norwegian kings until 1177.

Sturmabteilung (SA) German terrorist militia, also known as *Brownshirts*, of the ◊Nazi Party, established 1921 under the leadership of Ernst ◊Röhm, in charge of physical training and political indoctrination.

Sturm und Drang (German "storm and stress") German early Romantic movement in literature and music, from about 1775, concerned with the depiction of extravagant passions. Writers associated with the movement include Herder, Goethe, and Schiller. The name is taken from a play by Friedrich von Klinger 1776.

Stuttgart capital of Baden-Württemberg, Germany; population (1988) 565,000. Industries include publishing and the manufacture of vehicles and electrical goods.

It is the headquarters of US European Command (Eucom). The philosopher Hegel was born here.

Stuyvesant Peter 1610–1672. Dutch colonial leader. Named governor of Curacao 1643, he lost his right leg in a battle on nearby St Maarten. He was appointed director general

of New Netherland 1646 and arrived there the following year. He reorganized the administration of the colony and established a permanent boundary with Connecticut by the Treaty of Hartford 1650. Forced to surrender the colony to the British 1664, Stuyvesant remained there for the rest of his life.

Born in Holland, Stuyvesant first worked as an official of the Dutch West India Company.

style in flowers, the part of the ◊carpel bearing the ◊stigma at its tip. In some flowers it is very short or completely lacking, while in others it may be long and slender, positioning the stigma in the most effective place to receive the pollen.

Usually the style withers after fertilization but in certain species, such as rock clematis *Clematis verticillaris*, it develops into a long feathery plume that aids dispersal of the fruit.

Styria (German *Steiermark*) Alpine province of SE Austria; area 6,330 sq mi/16,400 sq km; population (1987) 1,181,000. Its capital is Graz, and its industries include iron, steel, lignite, vehicles, electrical goods, and engineering. An independent state from 1056 until it passed to the ◊Habsburgs in the 13th century, it was annexed by Germany in 1938.

Styx in Greek mythology, the river surrounding the underworld.

subatomic particle any of the subdivisions of the atom, including those ◊elementary particles that combine to form all ◊matter. See also ◊particle physics.

subduction zone region where two plates of the Earth's rigid lithosphere collide, and one plate descends below the other into the semiliquid asthenosphere. Subduction occurs along ocean trenches, most of which encircle the Pacific Ocean; portions of the ocean plate slide beneath other plates carrying continents.

Ocean trenches are usually associated with volcanic ◊island arcs and deep-focus earthquakes (more than 185 mi/300 km below the surface), both the result of disturbances caused by the plate subduction. The Aleutian Trench bordering Alaska is an example of an active subduction zone, which has produced the Aleutian Island arc.

sublimation in chemistry, the conversion of a solid to vapor without passing through the liquid phase.

Some substances that do not sublime at atmospheric pressure can be made to do so at low pressures. This is the principle of freeze-drying, during which ice sublimes at low pressure.

subliminal message any message delivered beneath the human conscious threshold of perception. It may be visual (words or images flashed between the frames of a cinema or TV film), or aural (a radio message broadcast constantly at very low volume).

Attempts to use subliminal perception in advertising have raised public fears of manipulation; there is little evidence to show that such messages are effective.

submarine vessel capable of traveling and functioning under water, used in research and military operations. The first underwater boat was constructed for James I of England by the Dutch scientist Cornelius van Drebbel (1572–1633) in 1620. In the 1760s, the American David Bushnell (1742–1824) designed a submarine called *Turtle* for attacking British ships, and in 1800, Robert Fulton designed a submarine called *Nautilus* for Napoleon for the same purpose. John P Holland, an Irish emigrant to the US, designed a submarine about 1875, which was used by both the US and the British navies at the turn of the century. A naval submarine, or submersible torpedo boat, the *Gymnote*, was launched by France 1888. The conventional submarine of World War I was driven by diesel engine on the surface and by battery-powered electric motors underwater. The diesel engine also drove a generator that produced electricity to charge the batteries. In both world wars submarines, from the oceangoing to the midget type, played a vital role. The first nuclear-powered submarine, the *Nautilus*, was launched by the US 1954. In oceanography, salvage, and pipe-laying, smaller submarines called submersibles are used.

submersible vessel designed to operate under water, especially a small submarine used by engineers and research scientists as a ferry craft to support diving operations. The most advanced submersibles are the so-called lockout type, which have two compartments: one for the pilot, the other to carry divers. The diving compartment is pressurized and provides access to the sea.

subpoena (Latin "under penalty") in law, an order requiring someone who might not otherwise come forward of his or her own volition to give evidence before a court or judicial official at a specific time and place. A witness who fails to comply with a subpoena is in ▷contempt of court.

subsidy government payment or concession granted to a state or private company, or an individual. A subsidy may be provided to keep prices down, to stimulate the market for a particular product, or because it is perceived to be in the public interest.

The payment of subsidies may distort the market, create shortages, reduce efficiency, or waste resources that could be used more beneficially elsewhere. Export subsidies are usually condemned because they represent unfair competition.

Many countries provide subsidies for transport systems and public utilities such as water, gas, and electricity supplies. Subsidies are also given for art, science, and religion when they cannot be self-supporting to the standards perceived desirable.

subsistence farming farming when the produce is enough to feed only the farmer and

family and there is no surplus to sell.

substrate in biochemistry, a compound or mixture of compounds acted on by an enzyme. The term also refers to a substance such as ▷agar that provides the nutrients for the metabolism of microorganisms. Since the enzyme systems of microorganisms regulate their metabolism, the essential meaning is the same.

subway or **underground** rail service that runs underground. The first underground line in the world was in London. Opened 1863, it was essentially a roofed-in trench. The London Underground is still the longest, with over 250 mi/400 km of routes. Many major cities throughout the world have extensive systems; New York's subway system and Moscow's each handle millions of passengers a day.

succession in ecology, a series of changes that occur in the structure and composition of the vegetation in a given area from the time it is first colonized by plants (**primary succession**), or after it has been disturbed by fire, flood, or clearing (**secondary succession**).

If allowed to proceed undisturbed, succession leads naturally to a stable ▷climax community (for example, oak and hickory forest or savannah grassland) that is determined by the climate and soil characteristics of the area.

Succot or **Sukkoth** in Judaism, a harvest festival celebrated in Oct, also known as the **Feast of Booths**, which commemorates the time when the Israelites lived in the wilderness during the ▷Exodus from Egypt. As a reminder of the shelters used in the wilderness, huts are built and used for eating and sleeping during the seven days of the festival.

succubus a female spirit; see ▷incubus.

succulent plant thick, fleshy plant that stores water in its tissues; for example, cacti and stonecrops *Sedum*. Succulents live either in areas where water is very scarce, such as deserts, or in places where it is not easily obtainable because of the high concentrations of salts in the soil, as in salt marshes. Many desert plants are ▷xerophytes.

sucker fish another name for ▷remora.

suckering in plants, reproduction by new shoots (suckers) arising from an existing root system rather than from seed. Plants that produce suckers include elm, dandelion, and members of the rose family.

sucrase enzyme capable of digesting sucrose

into its constituent molecules of glucose and fructose.

In mammals this action takes place within the wall of the intestine, the products of the reaction being liberated into the lumen. This is an example of intracellular digestion.

Sucre legal capital and judicial seat of Bolivia; population (1988) 95,600. It stands on the central plateau at an altitude of 9,320 ft/2,840 m.

The city was founded in 1538, its cathedral dates from 1553, and the University of San Francisco Xavier 1624 is probably the oldest in South America. The first revolt against Spanish rule in South America began here May 25, 1809.

Sucre Antonio José de 1795–1830. South American revolutionary leader. As chief lieutenant of Simón ▷Bolivar, he won several battles in freeing the colonies of Ecuador and Bolivia from Spanish rule, and in 1826 became president of Bolivia. After a mutiny by the army and invasion by Peru, he resigned in 1828 and was assassinated in 1830 on his way to join Bolivar.

sucrose or *cane sugar* or *beet sugar* $C_{12}H_{22}O_{11}$ a sugar found in the pith of sugar cane and in sugar beets. It is popularly known as ▷sugar.

Sucrose is a disaccharide sugar, each of its molecules being made up of two simple sugar (monosaccharide) units: glucose and fructose.

Sudan country in NE Africa, bounded N by Egypt, NE by the Red Sea, E by Ethiopia, S by Kenya, Uganda, and Zaire, W by the Central African Republic and Chad, and NW by Libya. It is the largest country in Africa.

government After a military coup April 1985 a transitional constitution was introduced, providing for a 264-member legislative assembly, a supreme council under a president, and a council of ministers led by a prime minister. The assembly is charged with the task of producing a new constitution and, after a further transitional period, of declaring itself a parliament, subject to election every four years.

history In ancient times, the region was known as ▷Nubia and was taken over by the kingdoms of Upper and Lower Egypt. The Nubians were later converted to Coptic Christianity in the 6th century and to Islam in the 15th century when Arabs invaded. Sudan was again ruled by Egypt from 1820. A revolt began 1881, led by a sheik who took the title of ▷Mahdi and captured ▷Khartoum 1885. It was subdued by an Anglo-Egyptian army under Lord ▷Kitchener 1896–98 and administered as an Anglo-Egyptian condominium from 1899.

independent republic The Sudan, as it was called, achieved independence as a republic 1956. Two years later a coup ousted the civil administration, and a military government was set up; in 1964 this was overthrown and civilian rule was reinstated. Five years later the army returned in a coup led by Col Gaafar Mohammed Nimeri. All political bodies were abolished, the Revolutionary Command Council (RCC) set up, and the country's name changed to the Democratic Republic of Sudan. Close links were soon established with Egypt, and in 1970 an agreement in principle was reached for eventual union. In 1972 this should have become, with the addition of Syria, the Federation of Arab Republics, but internal opposition blocked both developments. In 1971 a new constitution was adopted, Nimeri confirmed as president, and the Sudanese Socialist Union (SSU) declared the only party.

regional problems The most serious prob-

maneuvering motor   viewing port   access hatch   diver's compartment   main propeller

manipulator arm   crew compartment   air cylinders   battery compartment   diver's hatch

submersible *A crewed submersible or small submarine.*

lem confronting Nimeri was open aggression between the Muslim north and the chiefly Christian south, which had started as long ago as 1955. At a conference in Addis Ababa 1972 he granted the three southern provinces a considerable degree of autonomy, but fighting continued. Nimeri had come to power in a left-wing revolution but soon turned to the West, and the US, for support. By 1974 he had established a national assembly, but his position still relied on army backing. In 1983 he was reelected for a third term, but his regional problems persisted. By sending more troops south against the Sudan People's Liberation Army he alienated the north and then caused considerable resentment in the south by replacing the penal code with strict Islamic law. His economic policies contributed to the widespread unrest.

military takeover In March 1985 a general strike was provoked by a sharp devaluation of the Sudanese pound and an increase in bread prices. Nimeri was in the US when army mutiny threatened. One of his supporters, General Swar al-Dahab, took over in a bloodless coup. He set up a transitional military council and

held elections for a legislative assembly April 1986, contested by more than 40 parties, the three most significant being the New National Umma Party (NNUP), which won 99 seats; the Democratic Unionist Party (DUP), 63 seats; and the National Islamic Front, 51 seats. A coalition government was formed, with Ahmed Ali El-Mirghani (DUP) as president of the Supreme Council and Sadiq al-Mahdi (NNUP) as prime minister. Strikes and shortages persisted, with inflation running at about 100% and the highest national debt in Africa, and in July 1987 a state of emergency was declared. In Oct 1987 the prime minister announced the breakup of the government of national unity and the formation of a new coalition. In Dec 1988 the signing of a peace agreement with the Sudan People's Liberation Movement (SPLM), led by John Garang, threatened to split the coalition government and eventually led to a military takeover by General Ahmed el-Bashir July 1989. El-Bashir established a 15-man revolutionary council with himself as head of state and government. Just weeks before the successful coup, the military foiled the second attempt in six months to restore former

strongman, Gaafar Nimeri, to power. Bashir's government arrested al-Mahdi and announced that its first priority was to bring an end to the six-year war between the Muslim north and the Christian and animist south. A major government against the south 1992 brought the rebels near defeat. Food shortages and starvation remained a severe problem throughout the country 1992. In 1992 the dinar replaced the Sudanese pound. *See illustration box.*

Sudbury city in Ontario; population (1986) 149,000. A buried meteorite there yields 90% of the world's nickel.

sudden infant death syndrome (SIDS) in medicine, the technical term for ▷crib death.

Sudetenland mountainous region of N Czechoslovakia, annexed by Germany under the ▷Munich Agreement 1938; it was returned to Czechoslovakia 1945.

Suetonius (Gaius Suetonius Tranquillus) *c.* AD 69–140. Roman historian, author of *Lives of the Caesars* (Julius Caesar to Domitian).

Suez (Arabic *El Suweis*) port at the Red Sea terminus of the Suez Canal; population (1985) 254,000. Industries include oil refining and the manufacture of fertilizers. It was reconstructed after the ▷Arab-Israeli Wars in 1979.

Suez Canal artificial waterway, 100 mi/160 km long, from Port Said to Suez, linking the Mediterranean and Red seas, separating Africa from Asia, and providing the shortest eastward sea route from Europe. It was opened 1869, nationalized 1956, blocked by Egypt during the Arab-Israeli war 1967, and not re-opened until 1975.

The French Suez Canal Company was formed 1858 to execute the scheme of Ferdinand de Lesseps. The canal was opened 1869, and in 1875 British prime minister ▷Disraeli acquired a major stockholding for Britain from the khedive of Egypt. The 1888 Convention of Constantinople opened it to all nations. The Suez Canal was admininstered by a company with offices in Paris controlled by a council of 33 (10 of them British) until 1956 when it was forcibly nationalized by President ▷Nasser of Egypt. The new Damietta port complex on the Mediterranean at the mouth of the canal was inaugurated 1986. The port is designed to handle 16 million tons of cargo.

Suez Crisis military confrontation Oct–Dec 1956 following the nationalization of the Suez Canal by President Nasser of Egypt. In an attempt to reassert international control of the canal, Israel launched an attack, after which British and French troops landed. Widespread international censure (Soviet protest, US non-support, and considerable domestic opposition) forced the withdrawal of British and French troops. The crisis resulted in the resignation of British prime minister Eden. British, French, and Australian relations with the US were greatly strained during this period.

Sudan

Democratic Republic of (*Jamhuryat es-Sudan*)

area 967,489 sq mi/2,505,800 sq km
capital Khartoum
cities Omdurman, Juba, Wadi Medani, al-Obeid, Kassala, Atbara, al-Qadarif, Kosti; chief port Port Sudan
physical fertile valley of river Nile separates Libyan Desert in W from high rocky Nubian Desert in E
environment the building of the Jonglei Canal to supply water to N Sudan and Egypt threatens the grasslands of S Sudan
features Sudd swamp; largest country in Africa
head of state and government General Omar Hassan Ahmed el-Bashir from 1989
political system military republic
political parties New National Umma Party (NNUP), Islamic, nationalist; Democratic Unionist Party (DUP), moderate, nationalist; National Islamic Front, Islamic, nationalist
exports cotton, gum arabic, sesame seed, peanuts, sorghum
currency dinar
population (1990 est) 25,164,000; growth rate 2.9% p.a.
life expectancy men 51, women 55 (1989)
languages Arabic 51% (official), local languages
religion Sunni Muslim 73%, animist 18%, Christian 9% (in south)
literacy 30% (1986)

GNP $8.5 bn (1988); $330 per head (1988)
chronology
1820 Sudan ruled by Egypt.
1885 Revolt led to capture of Khartoum by self-proclaimed Mahdi.
1896–98 Anglo-Egyptian offensive led by Lord Kitchener subdued revolt.
1899 Sudan administered as an Anglo-Egyptian condominium.
1955 Civil war between Muslim north and non-Muslim south broke out.
1956 Sudan achieved independence from Britain and Egypt as a republic.
1958 Military coup replaced civilian government with Supreme Council of the Armed Forces.
1964 Civilian rule reinstated.
1969 Coup led by Col Gaafar Mohammed Nimeri established Revolutionary Command Council (RCC); name changed to Democratic Republic of Sudan.
1970 Union with Egypt agreed in principle.
1971 New constitution adopted; Nimeri confirmed as president; Sudanese Socialist Union (SSU) declared only legal party.
1972 Proposed Federation of Arab Republics, comprising Sudan, Egypt, and Syria, abandoned. Addis Ababa conference proposed autonomy for southern provinces.
1974 National assembly established.
1983 Nimeri reelected. *Shari'a* (Islamic law) introduced.
1985 Nimeri deposed in a bloodless coup led by General Swar al-Dahab; transitional military council set up. State of emergency declared.
1986 More than 40 political parties fought general election; coalition government formed.
1987 Virtual civil war with Sudan People's Liberation Movement (SPLM).
1988 Al-Mahdi formed a new coalition. Another flare-up of civil war between north and south created tens of thousands of refugees. Floods made 1.5 million people homeless. Peace pact signed with SPLM.
1989 Sadiq al-Mahdi overthrown in coup led by General Omar Hassan Ahmed el-Bashir.
1990 Civil war continued with new SPLM offensive.
1991 Federal system introduced, with division of country into nine states.
1992 Dinar replaced Sudanese pound.

suffix letter or group of letters added to the end of a word in order to form a new word. For example, the suffix *-ist* can be added to *sex* to form the word *sexist*.

Suffolk county of E England
area 1,467 sq mi/3,800 sq km
cities Ipswich (administrative headquarters), Bury St Edmunds, Lowestoft, Felixstowe
physical low undulating surface and flat coastline; rivers: Waveney, Alde, Deben, Orwell, Stour; part of the Norfolk Broads
features Minsmere marshland bird reserve, near Aldeburgh; site of ▷Sutton Hoo (7th-cen-

tury ship-burial); site of Sizewell B, Britain's first pressurized-water nuclear reactor plant (under construction)

products cereals, sugar beet, working horses (Suffolk punches), fertilizers, agricultural machinery

population (1991) 629,900

famous people John Constable, Thomas Gainsborough, Elizabeth Garrett Anderson, Benjamin Britten, George Crabbe.

suffragist a woman fighting for the right to vote. In the US, the suffragist movement officially began at the ⟂Seneca Falls Convention 1848. Elizabeth Cady ⟂Stanton and Susan B ⟂Anthony founded the National Woman Suffrage Association 1869. At about the same time, Lucy ⟂Stone formed the American Woman Suffrage Association. The two groups merged 1890 as the National American Woman Suffrage Association. The perseverance of this group and others led to the ratification of the 19th Amendment 1920, which gave US women the right to vote.

Sufism mystical movement of ⟂Islam that originated in the 8th century. Sufis believe that deep intuition is the only real guide to knowledge. The movement has a strong strain of asceticism. The name derives from Arabic *suf*, a rough woolen robe worn as an indication of disregard for material things. There are a number of groups or brotherhoods within Sufism, each with its own method of meditative practice, one of which is the whirling dance of the ⟂dervishes.

Sufism was originally influenced by the ascetics of the early Christian church, but later developed within the structure of orthodox Islam.

sugar any sweet, soluble crystalline carbohydrate, either a monosaccharide or disaccharide. The major sources are tropical sugar cane *Saccharum officinarum*, which accounts for about two-thirds of production, and temperate sugar beet *Beta vulgaris*. ⟂Honey also contains sugars.

Cane, which is a grass, usually yields over 9 tons of sugar per acre per year; sugar beet rarely exceeds 3 tons per acre per year. Beet sugar is more expensive to produce, but is often subsidized by European governments wishing to support the agricultural sector and avoid over-dependence on the volatile world sugar market. Minor quantities of sugar are produced from the sap of maple trees, and from sorghum and date palms. Sugar is a major source of energy, but also contributes to tooth decay.

Monosaccharides are the simplest sugars; examples include fructose and glucose, both obtained from fruit and honey. Disaccharides are sugars which, when hydrolyzed by dilute acids, give two of either the same or different simple sugars (monosaccharides). Examples are sucrose from sugar cane and sugar beet, which breaks down to glucose and fructose. Polysaccharides, such as starch and cellulose, hydrolyze to many simple sugars. Sucrose is produced commercially from sugar cane by crushing the stem. Molasses is the uncrystallized syrup drained from the crystallized sugar, then refined by stages to "pure" whiteness. Fermented unrefined molasses produces rum. Highly refined forms of sugar include cube, granulated, confectioner's, and icing.

Sugar is also produced from sugar beet; the pulp remaining from the process is used as cattle feed. The fibrous residue of sugar cane, called bagasse, is used in the manufacture of

paper, cattle feed, and fuel; and new types of cane are being bred for low sugar and high fuel production.

history

c. 700 BC sugar first refined in India

c. 650 BC first bee husbandry in the Mediterranean and Mexico, for honey

c. 1300 sugar industry spread from Arab countries to Spain (Italy main trader) and to Latin America by the Spanish (16th–17th centuries)

1319 first record of sugar in England

18th century rise in European consumption

late 18th century Margraf isolated sugar in beet

1885 beet and cane sugar trade.

sugar maple E North American ⟂maple tree *Acer saccharum*.

Suger *c.* 1081–1151. French historian and politician, regent of France during the Second Crusade. In 1122 he was elected abbot of St Denis, Paris, and was counselor to, and biographer of, Louis VI and Louis VII. He began the reconstruction of St Denis as the first large-scale Gothic building.

Suharto Raden 1921– . Indonesian politician and general. He ousted Sukarno to become president 1967. He ended confrontation with Malaysia, invaded East Timor 1975, and reached a cooperation agreement with Papua New Guinea 1979. His authoritarian rule has met with domestic opposition from the left. He was reelected 1973, 1978, 1983, and 1988.

suicide the act of killing oneself intentionally; a person who does this.

It is often considered a crime in law, with consequences for a suicide's estate, or criminal prosecution for unsuccessful attempt. It is also a crime in terms of some religious laws. Aiding and abetting another's suicide is often considered illegal. Survivors of joint suicides may be charged with manslaughter. In some cultures, suicide is considered honorable behavior, such as suicide in ancient Rome, historic ⟂hara-kiri in Japan, or historic suttee in India.

suite in music, formerly a grouping of old dance forms; later the term came to be used to describe a set of instrumental pieces, sometimes assembled from a stage work, such as Tchaikovsky's *Nutcracker Suite* 1891–92.

Sukarno Achmed 1901–1970. Indonesian nationalist, president 1945–67. During World War II he cooperated in the local administration set up by the Japanese, replacing Dutch rule. After the war he became the first president of the new Indonesian republic, becoming president-for-life in 1966; he was ousted by ⟂Suharto.

Sulawesi formerly *Celebes* island in E Indonesia, one of the Sunda Islands; area (with dependent islands) 73,000 sq mi/ 190,000 sq km; population (1980) 10,410,000. It is mountainous and forested and produces copra and nickel.

Suleiman or *Solyman* 1494–1566. Ottoman sultan from 1520, known as **the Magnificent** and **the Lawgiver**. Under his rule, the Ottoman Empire flourished and reached its largest extent. He made conquests in the Balkans, the Mediterranean, Persia, and N Africa, but was defeated at Vienna in 1529 and Valletta (on Malta) in 1565. He was a patron of the arts, a poet, and an administrator.

Suleiman captured Belgrade in 1521, the Mediterranean island of Rhodes in 1522, defeated the Hungarians at Mohács in 1526, and

was halted in his advance into Europe only by his failure to take Vienna, capital of the Austro-Hungarian Empire, after a siege Sept–Oct 1529. In 1534 he turned more successfully against Persia, and then in campaigns against the Arab world took almost all of N Africa and the Red Sea port of Aden. Only the Knights of Malta inflicted severe defeat on both his army and fleet when he tried to take Valletta in 1565.

sulfate SO_4^{2-} salt or ester derived from sulfuric acid. Most sulfates are water soluble (the exceptions are lead, calcium, strontium, and barium sulfates), and require a very high temperature to decompose them.

The commonest sulfates seen in the laboratory are copper(II) sulfate ($CuSO_4$), iron(II) sulfate ($FeSO_4$), and aluminum sulfate ($Al_2(SO_4)_3$). The ion is detected in solution by using barium chloride or barium nitrate to precipitate the insoluble sulfate.

sulfide compound of sulfur and another element in which sulfur is the more electronegative element (see ⟂electronegativity). Sulfides occur in a number of minerals. Some of the more volatile sulfides have extremely unpleasant odors (hydrogen sulfide smells of bad eggs).

sulfite SO_3^{2-} salt or ester derived from sulfurous acid.

sulfonamide any of a group of compounds containing the chemical group sulfonamide (SO_2NH_2) or its derivatives, which were, and still are in some cases, used to treat bacterial diseases. Sulfadiazine ($C_{10}H_{10}N_4O_2S$) is an example.

Sulfonamide was the first commercially available antibacterial drug, the forerunner of a range of similar drugs. Toxicity and increasing resistance have limited their use chiefly to the treatment of urinary-tract infection.

sulfur brittle, pale-yellow, nonmetallic element, symbol S, atomic number 16, atomic weight 32.064. It occurs in three allotropic forms: two crystalline (rhombic and monoclinic) and one amorphous. It burns in air with a blue flame and a stifling odor; it is insoluble in water but soluble in carbon disulfide. It is found abundantly in volcanic regions and occurs in nature in combination with metals and other substances, as well as a free, brittle, crystalline solid.

Sulfur is a constituent of proteins. Its greatest industrial use is in the commercial preparation of sulfuric acid to treat phosphate rock in producing fertilizers. It is also used in making paper, matches, gunpowder and fireworks, in vulcanizing rubber, and in medicines and insecticides. It has been known since ancient times and was called *sulphur*, later *sulfur*, in Latin.

sulfur dioxide SO_2 a pungent gas, produced by burning sulfur in air or oxygen.

It is used widely for disinfecting food vessels and equipment, and as a preservative in some food products. It occurs in industrial flue gases and is a major cause of ⟂acid rain.

sulfuric acid H_2SO_4 (also called oil of vitriol) dense, oily, colorless liquid that gives out heat when added to water. It is used extensively in the chemical industry, gasoline refining, and in manufacturing fertilizers, detergents, explosives, and dyes.

sulfurous acid H_2SO_3 solution of sulfur dioxide (SO_2) in water. It is a weak acid.

Sulla Lucius Cornelius 138–78 BC. Roman general and politician, a leader of the senatorial party. Forcibly suppressing the democrats in 88 BC, he departed for a successful campaign against ◊Mithridates VI of Pontus. The democrats seized power in his absence, but on his return Sulla captured Rome and massacred all opponents. The reforms he introduced as dictator, which strengthened the Senate, were backward-looking and short-lived. He retired 79 BC.

Sullivan Arthur (Seymour) 1842–1900. English composer who wrote operettas in collaboration with William Gilbert, including *HMS Pinafore* 1878, *The Pirates of Penzance* 1879, and *The Mikado* 1885. Their partnership broke down in 1896. Sullivan also composed serious instrumental, choral, and operatic works—for example, the opera *Ivanhoe* 1890—which he valued more highly than the operettas.

Sullivan John L(awrence) 1858–1918. US prizefighter. He won the heavyweight championship from Paddy Ryan 1882 and in the following years toured widely throughout the US and British Isles. In 1892 Sullivan lost his title to James "Gentleman Jim" Corbett in the first championship bout held according to the Marquis of Queensbury rules. After his retirement from the ring, Sullivan became a popular vaudevillian and was a saloonkeeper in New York.

Born in Boston, Sullivan briefly attended Boston College before beginning a professional boxing career.

Sullivan Louis Henry 1856–1924. US architect, a leader of the Chicago school of architects and an early developer of the ◊skyscraper. His skyscrapers include the Wainwright Building, St Louis, 1890 and the Guaranty Building, Buffalo, 1894. He was the teacher of Frank Lloyd ◊Wright.

Other notable works include the Chicago Auditorium and the Carson Pirie and Scott department store, Chicago.

Sully Maximilien de Béthune, Duc de Sully 1560–1641. French politician, who served with the Protestant ◊Huguenots in the wars of religion, and, as Henry IV's superintendent of finances 1598–1611, aided French recovery.

Sully-Prudhomme Armand 1839–1907. French poet who wrote philosophical verse including *Les Solitudes/Solitude* 1869, *La Justice/Justice* 1878, and *Le Bonheur/Happiness* 1888. He was awarded the Nobel Prize for Literature 1901.

Sulu Archipelago group of about 870 islands off SW Mindanao in the Philippines, between the Sulawesi and Sulu seas; area 1,042 sq mi/2,700 sq km; population (1989) 12,507,700. The capital is Jolo, on the island (the largest) of the same name. Until 1940 the islands were an autonomous sultanate.

sumac any bush or tree of the genus *Rhus* of the cashew family, having pinnate compound leaves and clusters of small reddish fruits. Staghorn sumac *Rhus typhina*, growing to 36 ft/11 m tall, is common in North America. Included too are several poisonous plants (sometimes referred to collectively as the genus *Toxicodendron*), such as ◊poison ivy, ◊poison sumac, and certain Japanese sumacs.

Sumatra or *Sumatera* second largest island of Indonesia, one of the Sunda Islands; area 182,800 sq mi/473,600 sq km; population (1989) 36,882,000. East of a longitudinal volcanic mountain range is a wide plain; both are heavily forested. Products include rubber, rice, tobacco, tea, timber, tin, and petroleum.

Northern Sumatra is rapidly being industrialized, and the Asakan River (rising in Lake Toba) was dammed for power 1974. The main towns are Palembang, Padang, and Benkuelen.

A Hindu empire was founded in the 8th century, but Islam was introduced by Arab traders from the 13th century and by the 16th century was adopted throughout the island.

Sumerian civilization the world's earliest ◊civilization, dated about 3500 BC, and located at the confluence of the Tigris and Euphrates rivers in lower Mesopotamia (present-day Iraq). It was a city-state with priests as secular rulers. Sumerian culture was based on the taxation of the surplus produced by agricultural villagers to support the urban ruling class and its public-works program, which included state-controlled irrigation. Cities included ◊Lagash, Eridu, and ◊Ur. Trade with Egypt and the Indus Valley led to the formation of the ancient Egyptian civilization and the ◊Indus Valley civilization. **summit** or *summit conference* meeting of heads of government to discuss common interests, especially the US-Soviet summits 1959–90, of which there were 15. The term was first used during World War II, and the ◊Yalta Conference and ◊Potsdam Conference 1945 were summits that did much to determine the political structure of the postwar world. Later summits have been of varying importance, partly as public-relations exercises.

summons in law, a court order officially delivered, requiring someone to appear in court on a certain date.

Sumner Charles 1811–1874. US political leader. He taught at Harvard, lectured on abolitionism and pacifism, and was elected to the US Senate as a FreeSoil Democrat 1852. For his fierce opposition to any compromise on the issue of slavery, Sumner was badly beaten by South Carolina congressman Preston Brooks 1856. Although long an invalid, he was a Republican leader in Congress during the Civil War. A supporter of Radical Reconstruction, he opposed Grant's renomination 1872.

Born in Boston and educated at Harvard, Sumner was admitted to the bar 1833. He traveled in Europe before teaching at Harvard.

Sumner James 1887–1955. US biochemist. In 1926 he succeeded in crystallizing the enzyme urease and demonstrating its protein nature. For this work Sumner shared the 1946 Nobel Prize for Chemistry with John Northrop and Wendell Stanley.

sumo wrestling national sport of Japan. Fighters of larger than average size (rarely less than 285 lb/130 kg) try to push, pull, or throw each other out of a circular ring.

Fighters follow a traditional diet and eat a great deal to build up body weight. In the ring, they try to get their center of gravity as low to the ground as possible. Championships, lasting up to 15 days each, are held six times a year in Japan; millions of fans watch the contests live and on television. Sumo wrestling originated as a religious ritual performed at Shinto shrines. In the 17th and 18th centuries it evolved into a popular spectator sport.

sumptuary law any law restraining excessive individual consumption, such as expenditure on food and dress, or attempting to control religious or moral conduct.

The Romans had several sumptuary laws; for example, the *lex Orchia* in 181 BC limited the number of dishes at a feast. In England sumptuary laws were introduced by Edward III and Henry VII.

Sun the ◊star at the center of the Solar System. Its diameter is 865,000 mi/1,392,000 km; its temperature at the surface is about 5,800K (9,980°F/5,530°C), and at the center 15,000,000K (27,000,000°F/15,000,000°C). It is composed of about 70% hydrogen and 30% helium, with other elements making up less than 1%. The Sun's energy is generated by nuclear fusion reactions that turn hydrogen into helium at its center. The gas core is far denser than mercury or lead on Earth. The Sun is about 4.7 billion years old, with a predicted lifetime of 10 billion years.

At the end of its life, it will expand to become a ◊red giant the size of Mars's orbit, then shrink to become a ◊white dwarf. The Sun spins on its axis every 25 days near its equator, but more slowly toward its poles. Its rotation can be followed by watching the passage of dark ◊sunspots across its disk. Sometimes bright eruptions called ◊flares occur near sunspots. Above the Sun's ◊photosphere lies a layer of thinner gas called the ◊chromosphere, visible only by means of special instruments or at eclipses. Tongues of gas called ◊prominences extend from the chromosphere into the corona, a halo of hot, tenuous gas surrounding the Sun. Gas boiling from the corona streams outwards through the Solar System, forming the ◊solar wind. Activity on the Sun, including sunspots, flares, and prominences, waxes and wanes during the *solar cycle*, which peaks every 11 years or so. The unmanned space probe *Pioneer 9* achieved solar orbit in 1968, and reported data on solar radiation.

Sunbelt popular name for the southern and southwestern continental US because of the warm climate. The Sunbelt is growing much faster in population than the northern US, with a steady migration of retirees and high-tech and service industries. The 20 states that, roughly, comprise the Sunbelt have a population of more than 110 million. The largest city in the Sunbelt is Los Angeles.

Sun City alternate name for ◊Mmabatho, resort in Bophuthatswana, South Africa.

Sunda Islands islands west of the Moluccas, in the Malay Archipelago, the greater number belonging to Indonesia. They are so named because they lie largely on the Indonesian extension of the Sunda continental shelf. The *Greater Sundas* include Borneo, Java (including the small island of Madura), Sumatra, Sulawesi, and Belitung. The *Lesser Sundas* (Indonesian *Nusa Tenggara*) are all Indonesian and include Bali, Lombok, Flores, Sumba, Sumbawa, and Timor.

sun dance religious ceremony performed by certain ◊Plains Indians at the time of the summer solstice.

Sundanese member of the second largest ethnic group in the Republic of Indonesia. There are more than 20 million speakers of Sundanese, a member of the western branch of the Austronesian family. Like their neighbors, the Javanese, the Sundanese are predominantly Muslim. They are known for their performing arts, especially *jaipongan* dance traditions, and distinctive batik fabrics.

Sunday first day of the week; in Christianity, Sunday is set aside for worship in commemoration of Jesus' resurrection, and in predominantly Christian societies banks, offices, and many shops are generally closed. It replaced the Jewish ⟡Sabbath, or day of rest, observed on Saturday.

"Blue laws," which restricted commercial activities, entertainment, and the purveying of alcoholic beverages on Sunday, have been repealed in many parts of the US since the 1950s.

sundew any insectivorous plant of the genus *Drosera*, family Droseraceae, with viscid hairs on the leaves for catching prey.

sundial instrument measuring time by means of a shadow cast by the Sun. Almost completely superseded by the proliferation of clocks, it survives ornamentally in gardens. The dial is marked with the hours at graduated distances, and a style or gnomon (parallel to Earth's axis and pointing to the north) casts the shadow.

sunfish any of various small members of the North American family (Centrarchidae) of freshwater bony fishes with compressed, almost circular bodies ranging from 6 in/ 15 cm to 12 in/30 cm and including bluegills, pumpkinseeds, rock bass, and crappies. The considerably larger basses also belong to this family. Ocean sunfishes of the family Molidae have disk-shaped, abruptly truncated bodies. The 10 ft/3 m species *Mola mola* is found worldwide.

sunflower tall plant of the genus *Helianthus*, family Compositae. The common sunflower *H. annuus*, probably native to Mexico, grows to 15 ft/4.5 m in favorable conditions. It is commercially cultivated in central Europe, the US, Russia, Ukraine, and Australia for the oil-bearing seeds that follow the yellow-petalled flowers.

Sunni member of the larger of the two main sects of ⟡Islam, with about 680 million adherents. Sunni Muslims believe that the first three caliphs were all legitimate successors of the prophet Mohammed, and that guidance on belief and life should come from the Koran and the Hadith, and from the Shari'a, not from a human authority or spiritual leader. Imams in Sunni Islam are educated lay teachers of the faith and prayer leaders. The name derives from the *Sunna*, Arabic "code of behavior," the body of traditional law evolved from the teaching and acts of Mohammed.

sunspot dark patch on the surface of the Sun, actually an area of cooler gas, thought to be caused by strong magnetic fields that block the outward flow of heat to the Sun's surface. Sunspots consist of a dark central **umbra**, about 4,000K (6,700°F/3,700°C), and a lighter surrounding **penumbra**, about 5,500K (9,400°F/ 5,200°C). They last from several days to over a month, ranging in size from 1,250 mi/2,000 km to groups stretching for over 62,000 mi/ 100,000 km. The number of sunspots visible at a given time varies from none to over 100 in a cycle averaging 11 years.

sunstroke or **heat stroke** rise in body temperature caused by excessive exposure to heat. Mild sunstroke is experienced as feverish lassitude, sometimes with simple fainting; recovery is prompt following rest and replenishment of salt lost in sweat. Severe sunstroke causes collapse akin to that see in acute ⟡shock, and is potentially lethal without prompt treatment of cooling the body carefully and giving fluids to relieve dehydration.

In severe sunstroke the brain swells, resulting in confusion of thought, the body becomes feverish and dehydrated, blood circulation

slows, and organs, such as the kidneys, fail to function. Coma may ensue, and possibly cardiac arrest.

Sun Yat-sen or **Sun Zhong Shan** 1867–1925. Chinese revolutionary leader, founder of the ⟡Guomindang (Nationalist party) 1894, and provisional president of the Republic of China 1912 after playing a vital part in deposing the emperor. He was president of a breakaway government from 1921.

Sun Yat-sen was the son of a Christian farmer. After many years in exile he returned to China during the 1911 revolution that overthrew the Manchu dynasty and was provisional president of the republic in 1912. In an effort to bring unity to China, he soon resigned in favor of the military leader Yuan Shih-k'ai. As a result of Yuan's increasingly dictatorial methods, Sun established an independent republic in S China based in Canton 1921. He was criticized for lack of organizational ability, but his "three people's principles" of nationalism, democracy, and social reform are accepted by both the Nationalists and the Chinese Communists.

superactinide any of a theoretical series of superheavy, radioactive elements, starting with atomic number 113, that extend beyond the ⟡transactinide series in the periodic table. They do not occur in nature and none has yet been synthesized.

It is postulated that this series has a group of elements that have half-lives longer than those of the transactinide series. This group, centered on element 114, is referred to as the "island of stability," based on the nucleon arrangement. The longer half-lives will, it is hoped, allow enough time for their chemical and physical properties to be studied when they have been synthesized.

Super Bowl US professional championship, inaugurated 1966. It is the annual end-of-season contest between the American Football Conference (AFC) and the National Football Conference (NFC) champions. See ⟡football.

supercomputer the fastest, most powerful type of computer, capable of performing its basic operations in picoseconds (trillionths of a second), rather than nanoseconds (billionths of a second), like most other computers.

To achieve these extraordinary speeds, supercomputers use several processors working together and techniques such as cooling processors down to nearly ⟡absolute zero temperature, so that their components conduct electricity many times faster than normal.

superconductivity in physics, increase in electrical conductivity at low temperatures. The resistance of some metals and metallic compounds decreases uniformly with decreasing temperature until at a critical temperature (the superconducting point), within a few degrees of absolute zero (0 K/−459.67°F/ −273.16°C), the resistance suddenly falls to zero. The phenomenon was discovered by Dutch scientist Heike Kamerlingh-Onnes (1853–1926) in 1911.

In this superconducting state, an electric current will continue indefinitely after the magnetic field has been removed, provided that the material remains below the superconducting point. In 1986 IBM researchers achieved superconductivity with some ceramics at −405°F/−243°C; Paul Chu at the University of Houston, Texas, achieved superconductivity at −290°F/−179°C, a temperature that can be sustained using liquid nitrogen.

Some metals, such as platinum and copper, do not become superconductive; as the temperature decreases, their resistance decreases to a certain point but then rises again. Superconductivity can be nullified by the application of a large magnetic field. Superconductivity has been produced in a synthetic organic conductor that would operate at much higher temperatures, thus cutting costs.

supercooling in physics, the lowering in temperature of a ⟡saturated solution without crystallization taking place, forming a supersaturated solution. Usually crystallization rapidly follows the introduction of a small (seed) crystal or agitation of the supercooled solution.

superego in Freudian psychology, the element of the human mind concerned with the ideal, responsible for ethics and self-imposed standards of behavior. It is characterized as a form of conscience, restraining the ⟡ego, and responsible for feelings of guilt when the moral code is broken.

supergiant the largest and most luminous type of star known, with a diameter of up to 1,000 times that of the Sun and absolute magnitudes of between −5 and −9.

Superior, Lake largest and deepest of the Great Lakes and the largest freshwater lake in the world; area about 31,700 sq mi/ 82,100 sq km. It is bordered by the Canadian province of Ontario and the US states of Minnesota, Wisconsin, and Michigan. As the westernmost of the Great Lakes, Superior is at the western end of the St Lawrence Seaway. Duluth, Minnesota, is the largest US city on its shores, and with its sister city, Superior, Wisconsin, it is the busiest Great Lakes port, shipping grain and iron ore to the US and Europe. Also on Lake Superior is Canada's busiest Great Lakes port, Thunder Bay, Ontario, shipping coal and grain chiefly to points in E Canada.

superior planet planet that is farther away from the Sun than the Earth is: that is, Mars, Jupiter, Saturn, Uranus, Neptune, and Pluto.

Superman the first comic-strip superhero, created 1938 in the US by writer Jerome Siegel and artist Joseph Shuster, later featured in films, television, and other media. In the German philosopher ⟡Nietzsche's work, his ideal future human being was the *Übermensch*, or Superman.

supermarket large self-service store selling food and household goods. The first, Piggly-Wiggly, was introduced by US retailer Clarence Saunders in Memphis, Tennessee, 1919.

Supermarkets have a high turnover and are therefore able to buy goods in bulk. This cuts down the unit cost and, in turn, the price, which further encourages custom. Cut-price supermarkets have in some places led to the closure of small local shops.

supernova the explosive death of a star, which temporarily attains a brightness of 100 million Suns or more, so that it can shine as brilliantly as a small galaxy for a few days or weeks. Very approximately, it is thought that a supernova explodes in a large galaxy about once every 100 years. Many supernovae remain undetected because of obscuring by interstellar dust—astronomers estimate some 50%.

Type I supernovae are thought to occur in ⟡binary star systems in which gas from one star falls on to a ⏴white dwarf, causing it to explode. **Type II** supernovae occur in stars ten or more times as massive as the Sun, which suffer runaway internal nuclear reactions at the ends of their lives, leading to explosions. These are thought to leave behind ⏴neutron stars and ⏴black holes. Gas ejected by such an explosion causes an expanding radio source, such as the ⏴Crab nebula. Supernovae are thought to be the main source of elements heavier than hydrogen and helium.

The first supernova recorded (although not identified as such at the time) was in 185 in China. The last supernova seen in our Galaxy was in 1604, but many others have been seen since in other galaxies. In 1987 a supernova visible to the unaided eye occurred in the Large ⏴Magellanic Cloud, a small neighboring galaxy. Eta Carinae, an unusual star in the constellation Carina in the southern hemisphere, may become a supernova in a few hundred years.

The name "supernova" was coined by US astronomers Fritz Zwicky and Walter Baade in 1934. Zwicky was also responsible for the division into types I and II.

superpower term used to describe the US and the USSR from the end of World War II 1945, when they emerged as significantly stronger than all other countries.

supersaturation in chemistry, the state of a solution that has a higher concentration of solute than would normally be obtained in a ⏴saturated solution.

Many solutes have a higher ⏴solubility at high temperatures. If a hot saturated solution is cooled slowly, sometimes the excess solute does not come out of solution. This is an unstable situation and the introduction of a small solid particle will encourage the release of excess solute.

supersonic speed speed greater than that at which sound travels, measured in ⏴Mach numbers. In dry air at 32°F/0°C, sound travels at about 727 mph/1,170 kph, but decreases with altitude until, at 39,000 ft/12,000 m, it is only 658 mph/1,060 kph.

When an aircraft passes the ⏴sound barrier, shock waves are built up that give rise to ⏴sonic boom, often heard at ground level. US pilot Captain Charles Yeager was the first to achieve supersonic flight, in a Bell VS-1 rocket plane on Oct 14, 1947.

Superstring Theory in physics and astronomy, the theory that attempts to link the four ⏴fundamental forces. It postulates that each force emerged separately during the expansion of the very early universe from the ⏴Big Bang. It also postulates viewing matter as tiny vibrating strings instead of particles within a universe of more than the currently known four dimensions. Continuing research pursues a model based on a ten-dimensional universe, present at ⏴singularity. At the Big Bang, the ten dimensions split into two components, with four dimensions expanded into the current observable universe while the other six dimensions contracted to a point in space.

supersymmetry in physics, a theory that relates the two classes of elementary particle, the ⏴fermions and the ⏴bosons. According to supersymmetry, each fermion particle has a boson partner particle, and vice versa. It has not been possible to marry up all the known fermions with the known bosons, and so the theory postulates the existence of other, as yet undiscovered fermions, such as the photinos

(partners of the photons), gluinos (partners of the gluons), and gravitinos (partners of the gravitons). Using these ideas, it has become possible to develop a theory of gravity—called supergravity—that extends Einstein's work and considers the gravitational, nuclear, and electromagnetic forces to be manifestations of an underlying superforce. Supersymmetry has been incorporated into the ⏴superstring theory, and appears to be a crucial ingredient in the "theory of everything" sought by scientists.

supply in economics, the production of goods or services for a market in anticipation of an expected ⏴demand. There is no guarantee that supply will match actual demand.

supply and demand one of the fundamental approaches to economics, which examines and compares the supply of a good with its demand (usually in the form of a graph of supply and demand curves plotted against price). For a typical good, the supply curve is upward-sloping (the higher the price, the more the manufacturer is willing to sell), while the demand curve is downward-sloping (the cheaper the good, the more demand there is for it). The point where the curves intersect is the equilibrium price at which supply equals demand.

supply-side economics school of economic thought advocating government policies that allow market forces to operate freely, such as privatization, cuts in public spending and income tax, reductions in labor-union power, and cuts in the ratio of unemployment benefits to wages. Supply-side economics developed as part of the monetarist (see ⏴monetarism) critique of ⏴Keynesian economics.

Supply-siders argue that increases in government expenditure to stiumlate demand and reduce unemployment, advocated by Keynesians, are ineffective in the long term because intervention distorts market forces and creates inefficiencies that prevent the "supply side" of the economy from responding to increases in demand. Critics, however, argue that failure of supply to respond to increases in demand may result from the failure of market forces to take account of ⏴social costs and benefits. This may require increased public spending on infrastructure, training, and research and development. It is also suggested that such policies create a more uneven distribution of income and wealth, as happened in the US and the UK in the 1980s.

suprarenal gland alternate name for the ⏴adrenal gland.

Supremacy, Acts of two UK acts of Parliament 1534 and 1559, which established Henry VIII and Elizabeth I respectively as head of the English church in place of the pope.

Suprematism Russian abstract-art movement developed about 1913 by Kasimir ⏴Malevich. The Suprematist paintings gradually became more severe, until in 1918 they reached a climax with the *White on White* series showing white geometrical shapes on a white ground.

Suprematism was inspired in part by Futurist and Cubist ideas. Early paintings such as *Black Square* 1915 (Russian Museum, St Petersburg) used purely geometrical shapes in bold dynamic compositions. The aims of the movement were expressed by Malevich as "the supremacy of pure feeling or perception in the pictorial arts—the expression of non-objectivity."

Supreme Court highest US judicial tribunal, composed since 1869 of a chief justice (William

Rehnquist from 1986) and eight associate justices. Appointments are made for life by the president, with the advice and consent of the Senate, and justices can be removed only by impeachment.

The US Supreme Court hears appeals from decisions of the US Court of Appeals and from the state supreme courts. It also adjudicates questions of constitutional propriety and conflicts between the executive and legislative branches of the federal government. See also individual biographies and court decisions.

Supremes, the US vocal group, pioneers of the Motown sound, formed 1959 in Detroit. Beginning in 1962, the group was a trio comprising, initially, Diana Ross (1944–), Mary Wilson (1944–), and Florence Ballard (1943–1976). The most successful female group of the 1960s, they had a string of pop hits beginning with "Where Did Our Love Go?" 1964 and "Baby Love" 1964. Diana Ross left to pursue a solo career 1969.

Surabaya port on the island of Java, Indonesia; population (1980) 2,028,000. It has oil refineries and shipyards and is a naval base.

surd an expression containing the root of an ⏴irrational number that can never be exactly expressed—for example, √3 = 1.732050808... .

surface-area-to-volume ratio the ratio of an animal's surface area (the area covered by its skin) to its total volume. This is high for small animals, but low for large animals such as elephants.

The ratio is important for endothermic (warm-blooded) animals because the amount of heat lost by the body is proportional to its surface area, whereas the amount generated is proportional to its volume. Very small birds and mammals, such as hummingbirds and shrews, lose a lot of heat and need a high intake of food to maintain their body temperature. Elephants, on the other hand, are in danger of overheating, which is why they have no fur.

surface tension in physics, the property that causes the surface of a liquid to behave as if it were covered with a weak elastic skin; this is why a needle can float on water. It is caused by the exposed surface's tendency to contract to the smallest possible area because of unequal cohesive forces between ⏴molecules at the surface. Allied phenomena include the formation of droplets, the concave profile of a meniscus, and the ⏴capillary action by which water soaks into a sponge.

surfing sport of riding on the crest of large waves while standing on a narrow, keeled surfboard, usually of light synthetic material such as fiberglass, about 6 ft/1.8 m long (or about 8–9 ft/2.4–7 m known as the Malibu), as first developed in Hawaii and Australia. ⏴Windsurfing is a recent development.

surgeon fish any fish of the tropical marine family Acanthuridae. It has a flat body up to 20 in/50 cm long, is brightly colored, and has a movable spine on each side of the tail that can be used as a weapon.

surgery in medicine, originally the removal of diseased parts or foreign substances from the body through cutting and other manual operations. It now includes such techniques as beamed high-energy ultrasonic waves, binocular magnifiers for microsurgery, and lasers.

Circumstances permitting, surgery is carried out under sterile conditions using an ⏴anesthetic. There are many specialized fields, including cardiac (heart), orthopedic (bones and joints), ophthalmic (eye), neuro (brain and nerves), thoracic (chest), renal (kidney), and fetal (the developing embryo) surgery; other specialties include ⟳microsurgery, cosmetic and ⟳plastic surgery, and ⟳transplant surgery.   Historically, surgery for abscesses, amputation, dental problems, trepanning, and childbirth was practiced by the ancient civilizations of both the Old World and the New World. During the Middle Ages, Arabic surgeons passed their techniques on to Europe, where, during the Renaissance, anatomy and physiology were pursued. By the 19th century, anesthetics and Joseph ⟳Lister's discovery of antiseptics became the basis for successful surgical practices. The 20th century's use of antibiotics and blood ⟳transfusions has made surgery less dangerous.

Suriname country on the N coast of South America, bounded W by French Guiana, S by Brazil, E by Guyana, and N by the Atlantic Ocean.

government The constitution was suspended 1980, and in 1982 an interim president took office as head of state, with ultimate power held by the army through its commander in chief who is also chair of the Supreme Council, the country's controlling group. A nominated 31-member national assembly was established Jan 1985, consisting of 14 military, 11 labor union, and 6 business nominees. It was given 27 months in which to prepare a new constitution.

Suriname
Republic of (*Republiek Suriname*)

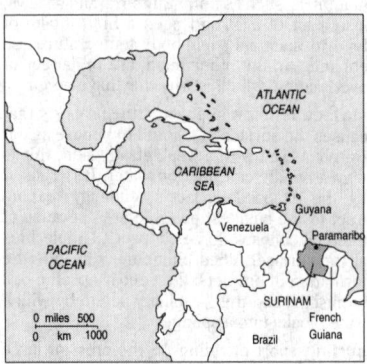

area 63,243 sq mi/163,820 sq km
capital Paramaribo
cities Nieuw Nickerie, Brokopondo, Nieuw Amsterdam
physical hilly and forested, with flat and narrow coastal plain
features Suriname River
head of state and government Ronald Venetiaan from 1991
political system emergent democratic republic
political parties Party for National Unity and Solidarity (KTPI)*, Indonesian, left-of-center; Suriname National Party (NPS)*, Creole, left-of-center; Progressive Reform Party (VHP)*, Indian, left-of-center; New Front For Democracy (NF)
*members of Front for Democracy and Development (FDD)
exports alumina, aluminum, bauxite, rice,

---

history For early history, see ⟳American Indian, ⟳South America. Founded as a colony by the English 1650, Suriname became Dutch 1667. In 1954, as Dutch Guiana, it was made an equal member of the Kingdom of the Netherlands, with internal self-government. Full independence was achieved 1975, with Dr Johan Ferrier as president and Henck Arron, leader of the Suriname National Party (NPS), as prime minister.

military coup In 1980 Arron's government was overthrown in an army coup, but President Ferrier refused to recognize the military regime and appointed Dr Henk Chin A Sen, of the Nationalist Republican Party, to head a civilian administration. Five months later the army staged another coup, and President Ferrier was replaced by Dr Chin A Sen. The new president announced details of a draft constitution that would reduce the army's role in government, whereupon the army, led by Lt Col Desi Bouterse, dismissed Dr Chin A Sen and set up the Revolutionary People's Front.

instability There followed months of confusion in which a state of siege and then martial law were imposed. From Feb 1980 to Jan 1983 there were six attempted coups by different army groups. Because of the chaos and killings of opposition leaders, Netherlands and US aid was stopped, and Bouterse turned to Libya and Cuba for assistance. The partnership between the army, the labor unions, and business, which had operated since 1981, broke up 1985, and Bouterse turned to the traditional parties that had operated before the 1980 coup: the

timber
currency Suriname guilder
population (1990 est) 408,000 (Hindu 37%, Creole 31%, Javanese 15%); growth rate 1.1% p.a.
life expectancy men 66, women 71 (1989)
languages Dutch (official), Sranan (Creole), English, others
religion Christian 30%, Hindu 27%, Muslim 20%
literacy 65% (1989)
GNP $1.1 bn (1987); $2,920 per head (1985)
chronology
1667 Became a Dutch colony.
1954 Achieved internal self-government as Dutch Guiana.
1975 Independence achieved from the Netherlands, with Dr Johan Ferrier as president and Henck Arron as prime minister; 40% of the population emigrated to the Netherlands.
1980 Arron's government overthrown in army coup; Ferrier refused to recognize military regime; appointed Dr Henk Chin A Sen to lead civilian administration. Army replaced Ferrier with Dr Chin A Sen.
1982 Army, led by Lt Col Desi Bouterse, seized power, setting up a Revolutionary People's Front.
1985 Ban on political activities lifted.
1986 Antigovernment rebels brought economic chaos to Suriname.
1987 New constitution approved.
1988 Ramsewak Shankar elected president.
1989 Bouterse rejected peace accord reached by President Shankar with guerrilla insurgents, vowed to continue fighting.
1990 Shankar deposed in army coup.
1991 Johan Kraag became interim president. New Front for Democracy won assembly majority. Ronald Venetiaan elected president.
1992 Peace accord with guerrilla groups.

NPS, the left-wing Indian Progressive Reform Party (VHP), and the Indonesian Party for National Unity and Solidarity (KTPI). The ban on political activity was lifted, and leaders of the three main parties were invited to take seats on the Supreme Council, with Wym Udenhout as prime minister. The Nov 1987 election was won by the three-party Front for Democracy and Development (FDD) and Ramsewak Shankar was elected president of the national assembly. In March 1989 a new constitution was approved prior to an election in Nov.

A bloody coup by the army Dec 1990 removed President Shankar, Bouterse denying any involvement. In Jan 1991 the assembly elected Johan Kraag as caretaker president. In national elections held May 1991 the New Front for Democracy (NF) won 29 seats in the 51-seat National Assembly. Ronald Venetiaan was elected president in Sept. In Aug 1992 the government reached an agreement with the two largest guerrilla groups, the Surinamese Liberation Army and the Tucayana Amazonas, to end hostilities. *See illustration box.*

Surrealism movement in art, literature, and film that developed out of ⟳Dada around 1922. Led by André ⟳Breton, who produced the *Surrealist Manifesto* 1924, the Surrealists were inspired by the thoughts and visions of the subconscious mind. They explored varied styles and techniques, and the movement became the dominant force in Western art between World Wars I and II.

Surrealism followed the Freudian theory of the unconscious. In art it encompassed André ⟳Masson's automatic drawings, paintings based on emotive semiabstract forms (Ernst, Miró, Tanguy), and dreamlike images painted in a realistic style (Dalí, Magritte). The poets Aragon and Eluard and the film-maker Buñuel were also part of the movement.

Surrey county in S England
area 641 sq mi/1,660 sq km
cities Kingston upon Thames (administrative headquarters), Guildford, Woking
features rivers: Thames, Mole, Wey; hills: Box and Leith; North Downs; Runnymede, Thameside site of the signing of Magna Carta; Yehudi Menuhin School; Kew Palace and Royal Botanic Gardens; in 1989 it was the most affluent county in Britain—average income 40% above national average
products vegetables, agricultural products, service industries
population (1991) 997,000
famous people Eric Clapton, John Galsworthy, Aldous Huxley, Laurence Olivier.

surrogacy practice whereby a woman is sought, and usually paid, to bear a child for an infertile couple or a single parent.

Surtsey volcanic island 12 mi/20 km SW of Heimaey in the Westman Islands of Iceland. The island was created by an underwater volcanic eruption in Nov 1963.

surveying the accurate measuring of the Earth's crust, or land features or buildings. It is used to establish boundaries, and to evaluate the topography for engineering work. The measurements used are both linear and angular, and geometry and trigonometry are applied in the calculations.

Sūrya in Hindu mythology, the sun god, son of the sky god Indra. His daughter, also named Sūrya, is a female personification of the Sun.

suslik small Eurasian ground ⟳squirrel *Citellus citellus*.

Susquehanna river rising in central New York State, and flowing 444 mi/715 km to Chesapeake Bay. It is used for hydroelectric power. On the strength of its musical name, Samuel ⟡Coleridge planned to establish a communal settlement here with his fellow poet Robert Southey.

Sussex former county of England, on the south coast, now divided into ⟡East Sussex and ⟡West Sussex.

According to tradition, the Saxon Ella landed here 477, defeated the inhabitants, and founded the kingdom of the South Saxons, which was absorbed by Wessex 825.

sustained-yield cropping in ecology, the removal of surplus individuals from a ⟡population of organisms so that the population maintains a constant size. This usually requires selective removal of animals of all ages and both sexes to ensure a balanced population structure. Taking too many individuals can result in a population decline, as in overfishing.

Excessive cropping of young females may lead to fewer births in following years, and a fall in population size. Appropriate cropping frequencies can be determined from an analysis of a ⟡life table.

Sutherland Donald 1934– . Canadian-born US film actor who usually appears in offbeat roles. He starred in *M.A.S.H.* 1970, and his subsequent films include *Klute* 1971, *Don't Look Now* 1973, and *Revolution* 1986. He is the father of actor Kiefer Sutherland.

Sutherland Earl Wilbur Jr 1915–1974. US physiologist, discoverer of cyclic AMP, a chemical "messenger" made by a special enzyme in the wall of living cells. Many hormones operate by means of this messenger. He was awarded the Nobel Prize for Medicine 1971.

Sutherland Joan 1926– . Australian soprano. She went to England in 1951, where she made her debut the next year in *The Magic Flute*; later roles included *Lucia di Lammermoor*, Donna Anna in *Don Giovanni*, and Desdemona in *Otello*. She retired from the stage in 1990.

She usually performed under the baton of her husband, conductor Richard Bonynge.

sūtra in Buddhism, discourse attributed to the historical Buddha. In Hinduism, the term generally describes any sayings that contain moral instruction.

suttee Hindu custom whereby a widow committed suicide by joining her husband's funeral pyre, often under public and family pressure. Banned in the 17th century by the Mogul emperors, the custom continued even after it was made illegal under British rule 1829. There continue to be sporadic revivals.

Sutton Hoo archeological site in Suffolk, England, where in 1939 a Saxon ship burial was excavated. It is the funeral monument of Raedwald, King of the East Angles, who died about 624 or 625. The jewelry, armor, and weapons discovered were placed in the British Museum, London.

suture any thread or wire used in surgery to stitch together the edges of a wound or incision. Also, the stitch itself.

Suu Kyi Aung San 1945– . Myanmar (Burmese) politician and human rights campaigner, leader of the National League for Democracy (NLD), the main opposition to the military junta. When the NLD won the 1990 elections, the junta refused to surrender power, and placed Suu Kyi under house arrest. She

was awarded the Nobel Peace Prize 1991 in recognition of her "non-violent struggle for democracy and human rights" in Myanmar. She is the daughter of former Burmese premier ⟡Aung San.

Suva capital and industrial port of Fiji, on Viti Levu; population (1981) 68,000. It produces soap and coconut oil.

Suzhou or **Soochow**, formerly **Wuhsien** 1912–49; city south of the Yangtze river delta and east of the ⟡Grand Canal, in Jiangsu province, China; population (1983) 670,000. It has embroidery and jade-carving traditions and Shizilin and Zhuozheng gardens. The city dates from about 1000 BC, and the name Suzhou from the 7th century AD; it was reputedly visited by the Venetian Marco ⟡Polo.

Suzuki Zenkō 1911– . Japanese politician. Originally a socialist member of the Diet in 1947, he became a conservative (Liberal Democrat) in 1949, and was prime minister 1980–82.

Svalbard Norwegian archipelago in the Arctic Ocean. The main island is Spitsbergen; other islands include North East Land, Edge Island, Barents Island, and Prince Charles Foreland.
area 23,938 sq mi/62,000 sq km
cities Longyearbyen on Spitsbergen
features weather and research stations. Wildlife includes walrus and polar bear; fossil palms show that it was in the tropics 40 million years ago
products coal, phosphates, asbestos, iron ore, and galena—all mined by Russia, Kazakhstan, and Norway
population (1982) 4,000; 62% Russian, 36% Norwegian
history under the **Svalbard Treaty** 1925, Norway has sovereignty, but allows free scientific and economic access to others.

Svedberg Theodor 1884–1971. Swedish chemist. In 1924 he constructed the first ultracentrifuge, a machine that allowed the rapid separation of particles by mass. He was awarded the Nobel Prize for Chemistry 1926.

Svengali person who molds another into a performer and masterminds his or her career. The original Svengali was a character in the novel *Trilby* 1894 by George ⟡Du Maurier.

Svetambara ("white-clad") sect of Jain monks (see ⟡Jainism) who wear white loincloths, as opposed to the Digambaras sect which believes that total nudity is correct for the Jain monk.

Swabia (German *Schwaben*) historic region of SW Germany, an independent duchy in the Middle Ages. It includes Augsburg and Ulm and forms part of the *Länder* (states) of Baden-Württemberg, Bavaria, and Hessen.

Swahili (Arabic *sawahil* "coasts") language belonging to the Bantu branch of the Niger-Congo family, widely used in east and central Africa. Swahili originated on the E African coast as a *lingua franca* used among traders, and contains many Arabic loan words. It is an official language in Kenya and Tanzania.

The name Swahili is also used for a member of an African people using the language, especially someone living in Zanzibar and adjoining coastal areas of Kenya and Tanzania. The Swahili are not an isolated group, but are part of a mixed coastal society engaged in fishing and trading.

swallow any bird of the family Hirundinidae of small, insect-eating birds in the order

Passeriformes, with long, narrow wings and deeply forked tails. Swallows feed while flying.

Species include the barn swallow *Hirundo rustica* and the purple martin *Progne subis*.

swami title of respect for a Hindu teacher.

swamp permanently or periodically water-logged tract of wet, spongy land, often overgrown with plants.

swan any of several large, long-necked, aquatic, web-footed birds of the family Anatidae, which also includes ducks and geese.

Species include the Old World mute swan *Cygnus olor*, with all-white plumage, now introduced in parks worldwide, and the **black swan** of Australia, *Cygnus atratus*. The North American **trumpeter swan** *Cygnus buccinator* is the largest, with a wingspan of 8 ft/2.4 m. This species was nearly extinct by 1900, and although numbers have recovered, it is still endangered. Pairing is generally for life, and the young are called cygnets.

Swann v Charlotte-Mecklenburg Board of Education US Supreme Court decision 1971 dealing with methods of court-ordered desegregation in public schools. The Court unanimously upheld a district court order implementing its own desegregation plan after the school board's proved unsatisfactory. Among the methods judged legitimate in the forced desegregation of delinquent school systems were busing, racial quotas, and the rearrangement of school districts.

Swanson Gloria. Adopted name of Gloria Josephine Mae Svenson 1897–1983. US actress, a star of silent films who influenced American tastes and fashion for more than 20 years. She retired in 1932 but made several major comebacks. Her work includes *Sadie Thompson* 1928, *Queen Kelly* 1928 (unfinished), and *Sunset Boulevard* 1950.

She was second only to Mary Pickford in fame and in 1926 she formed her own production company with Joseph Kennedy as her financial backer.

SWAPO (*South West Africa People's Organization*) organization formed 1959 in South West Africa (now ⟡Namibia) to oppose South African rule. SWAPO guerrillas, led by Sam Nujoma, began attacking with support from Angola. In 1966 SWAPO was recognized by the United Nations as the legitimate government of Namibia, and won the first independent election 1989.

swastika (Sanskrit *svastika*) cross in which the bars are extended at right angles in the same clockwise or counterclockwise direction. An ancient good-luck symbol in both the New and the Old World an Aryan and Buddhist mystic sign, it was adopted by Hitler as the emblem of the Nazi Party and incorporated into the German national flag 1935–45.

Swazi member of the majority group of people in Swaziland. The Swazi are primarily engaged in cultivating and raising livestock, but many work in industries in South Africa. The Swazi language belongs to the Bantu branch of the Niger-Congo family.

Swazi kingdom S African kingdom, established by Sobhuza I (died 1839), and named after his successor Mswati (ruled 1840–75).

Swaziland country in SE Africa, bounded E by Mozambique and SE, S, W, and N by South Africa.

government Swaziland is a monarchy within the British ⟡Commonwealth. Under the 1978 constitution the monarch is head of both

1012 sweat gland

Swaziland
Kingdom of (*Umbuso weSwatini*)

area 6,716 sq mi/17,400 sq km
capital Mbabane
cities Manzini, Big Bend
physical central valley; mountains in W (Highveld); plateau in E (Lowveld and Lubombo plateau)
features landlocked enclave between South Africa and Mozambique
head of state and government King Mswati III from 1986
political system near-absolute monarchy
political party Imbokodvo National Movement (INM), nationalist monarchist
exports sugar, canned fruit, wood pulp, asbestos
currency lilangeni
population (1990 est) 779,000; growth rate 3% p.a. **life expectancy** men 47, women 54 (1989)
language Swazi 90%, English (both official)
religion Christian 57%, animist
literacy men 70%, women 66% (1985 est)
GNP $539 million; $750 per head (1987)
chronology
1903 Swaziland became a special High Commission territory.
1967 Achieved internal self-government.
1968 Independence achieved from Britain, within the Commonwealth, as the Kingdom of Swaziland, with King Sobhuza II as head of state.
1973 The king suspended the constitution and assumed absolute powers.
1978 New constitution adopted.
1982 King Sobhuza died; his place was taken by one of his wives, Dzeliwe, until his son, Prince Makhosetive, reached the age of 21.
1983 Queen Dzeliwe ousted by another wife, Ntombi.
1984 After royal power struggle, it was announced that the crown prince would become king at 18.
1986 Crown prince formally invested as King Mswati III.
1987 Power struggle developed between advisory council Liqoqo and Queen Ntombi over accession of king. Mswati dissolved parliament; new government elected with Sotsha Dlamini as prime minister.
1991 Calls for democratic reform.

state and government, and chooses the prime minister and cabinet. There is a two-chamber legislature, the Libandla, consisting of a 20-member senate and a 50-member house of assembly. Ten senators are appointed by the sovereign and ten elected by and from an 80-member electoral college, made up of two representatives from each of the country's 40 chieftancies (Tinkhundla). Forty of the house of assembly deputies are also elected by the electoral college, with the remaining ten appointed by the monarch.

history For early history, see ▷South Africa. The region's original autonomy was guaranteed by Britain and the Transvaal, and Swaziland became a special High Commission territory 1903. The South African government repeatedly asked for Swaziland to be placed under its jurisdiction, but this call was resisted by the British government as well as the people of Swaziland. In 1967 the country achieved internal self-government and in 1968 full independence within the Commonwealth, with King Sobhuza II as head of state. In 1973 the king suspended the constitution and assumed absolute powers. In 1978 the new constitution was announced.

power struggles over accession King Sobhuza died 1982, and the role of head of state passed to the queen mother, Dzeliwe, until the king's heir, Prince Makhosetive, should reach the age of 21 in 1989, but a power struggle developed within the royal family. Queen Dzeliwe was ousted by another of King Sobhuza's wives, Ntombi, who became queen regent Oct 1983, and in April 1986 the crown prince was formally invested as King Mswati III. He has a supreme advisory body, the Liqoqo, all of whose 11 members are appointed by him. By June 1987 a power struggle had developed between the Liqoqo and Queen Ntombi over the accession of her son Mswati III. He dissolved parliament and a new government was elected in the same year, with Sotsha Dlamini as prime minister. Following demands for greater freedom and complaints of government hostility toward labor unions, King Mswati called for the creation of an *indaba* (popular parliament) Aug 1990, in which people's views could be expressed. There were doubts about whether this was a genuine move toward democratic reform. There was agitation for further democratic reforms Oct 1991. *See illustration box.*

sweat gland ▷gland within the skin of mammals that produces surface perspiration. In primates, sweat glands are distributed over the whole body, but in most other mammals they are more localized; for example, in cats and dogs, they are restricted to the feet and around the face.

In humans, sweat glands occur in larger numbers in the male than the female.

sweatshop workshop or factory where employees work long hours under substandard conditions for low wages. Exploitation of labor in this way is associated with unscrupulous employers, who often employ illegal immigrants or children in their labor force.

At the turn of the century women were employed on a large scale since they would work for less money than men. Such exploitation led to the rise of labor unions and the labor movement.

Sweatt v Painter US Supreme Court decision 1950 dealing with racial discrimination in publicly funded schools. Herman Sweatt, a black prospective law student, filed the suit against administrators of the University of Texas after being denied admission because of his race. The defendants argued that a separate law school for blacks was soon to be opened. The Court maintained the separate but equal doctrine but ruled that the black law school was decidedly inferior to the white one. The university was found guilty of violating the equal protection clause of the 14th Amendment.

Sweden country in N Europe, bounded W by Norway, NE by Finland and the Gulf of Bothnia, SE by the Baltic Sea, and SW by the Kattegat.

government Sweden has a hereditary monarch as formal head of state and a popularly elected government. The constitution from 1809, amended several times, is based on four fundamental laws: the Instrument of Government Act, the Act of Succession, the Freedom of the Press Act, and the Riksdag Act. The Riksdag is a single-chamber parliament of 349 members, elected by universal suffrage, through a system of proportional representation, for a three-year term.

The prime minister is nominated by the speaker of the Riksdag and confirmed by a vote of the whole house. The prime minister chooses a cabinet, and all are then responsible to the Riksdag. The king or queen now has a purely formal role; the normal duties of a constitutional monarch, such as dissolving parliament and deciding who should be asked to form an administration, are undertaken by the speaker.

history S Sweden has been inhabited since about 6000 BC. The Swedish Vikings in AD 800–1060 sailed mainly to the east and founded the principality of ▷Novgorod. In the mid-12th century the Swedes in the north were united with the Goths in the south and accepted Christianity. A series of crusades from the 12th to the 14th centuries brought Finland under Swedish rule. Sweden, Norway, and Denmark were united under a Danish dynasty 1397–1520. ▷Gustavus Vasa was subsequently elected king of Sweden. The Vasa line ruled until 1818, when the French marshal Bernadotte established the present dynasty.

Sweden's territorial ambitions led to warfare in Europe from the 16th to the 18th centuries (see ▷Gustavus Adolphus, ▷Thirty Years' War, ▷Charles X, ▷Charles XII) which left the country impoverished. Science and culture flourished under Gustavus III 1771–91. Sweden lost Finland to Russia 1809 but seized Norway 1814, a union dissolved 1905.

Sweden has a long tradition of neutrality and political stability, and a highly developed social welfare system. The office of ombudsman is a Swedish invention, and Sweden was one of the first countries to adopt a system of open government.

constitutional reform The Social Democratic Labor Party (SAP) was continuously in power 1951–76, usually in coalition. In 1969 Olof Palme became prime minister. He carried out two major reforms of the constitution, reducing the chambers in parliament from two to one 1971 and in 1975 removing the last of the monarch's constitutional powers. In the general election 1976 he was defeated over the issue of the level of taxation needed to fund the welfare system.

Thorbjörn Fälldin, leader of the Center Party, formed a center-right coalition government. The Fälldin administration fell 1978 over its wish to follow a non-nuclear energy policy, and was replaced by a minority Liberal government. Fälldin returned 1979, heading another

Sweden
Kingdom of (*Konungariket Sverige*)

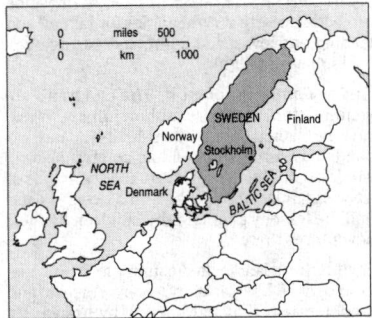

area 173,745 sq mi/450,000 sq km
capital Stockholm
cities Göteborg, Malmö, Uppsala, Norrköping, Västerås
physical mountains in W; plains in S; thickly forested; more than 20,000 islands off the Stockholm coast
environment of the country's 90,000 lakes, 20,000 are affected by acid rain; 4,000 are so severely acidified that no fish are thought to survive in them
features lakes, including Vänern, Vättern, Mälaren, Hjälmaren; islands of Öland and Gotland; wild elk
head of state King Carl XVI Gustaf from 1973
head of government Carl Bildt from 1991
political system constitutional monarchy
political parties Social Democratic Labor party (SAP), moderate, left-of-center; Moderate Party, right-of-center; Liberal Party, center-left; Center Party, centrist; Christian Democratic Party, Christian, centrist; Left (Communist) Party, European, Marxist; Green, ecological
exports aircraft, vehicles, ballbearings, drills, missiles, electronics, petrochemicals, textiles, furnishings, ornamental glass, paper,

iron and steel
currency krona
population (1990 est) 8,407,000 (including 17,000 Saami (Lapps) and 1.2 million postwar immigrants from Finland, Turkey, Yugoslavia, Greece, Iran, other Nordic countries); growth rate 0.1% p.a.
life expectancy men 74, women 81 (1989)
languages Swedish; there are Finnish- and Saami-speaking minorities
religion Lutheran (official) 95%
literacy 99% (1989)
GNP $179 bn; $11,783 per head (1989)
chronology
12th century United as an independent nation.
1397–1520 Under Danish rule.
1914–45 Neutral in both world wars.
1951–76 Social Democratic Labor Party (SAP) in power.
1969 Olof Palme became SAP leader and prime minister.
1971 Constitution amended, creating a single-chamber Riksdag, the governing body.
1975 Monarch's last constitutional powers removed.
1976 Thorbjörn Fälldin, leader of the Center Party, became prime minister, heading center-right coalition.
1982 SAP, led by Palme, returned to power.
1985 SAP formed minority government, with Communist support.
1986 Olof Palme murdered. Ingvar Carlsson became prime minister and SAP party leader.
1988 SAP reelected with reduced majority; Green Party gained representation in Riksdag.
1990 SAP government resigned. Sweden to apply for European Community (EC) membership.
1991 Formal application for EC membership submitted. Election defeat for SAP; coalition government formed; Carl Bildt became new prime minister.
1992 Agreement between SAP and conservative parties to solve economic problems.

coalition, and in a referendum the following year there was a narrow majority in favor of continuing with a limited nuclear-energy program.
relations with the USSR Fälldin remained in power until 1982, when the Social Democrats, with Olof Palme, returned with a minority government. Palme was soon faced with deteriorating relations with the USSR, arising from suspected violation of Swedish territorial waters by Soviet submarines. The situation had improved substantially by 1985. After the general election in that year, Palme's party had 159 Riksdag seats, and he was able to continue with Communist support. In Feb 1986, Olof Palme was murdered by an unknown assailant. Palme's deputy, Ingvar Carlsson, took over as prime minister and leader of the SAP.

In the Sept 1988 general election Carlsson and the SAP were reelected with a reduced majority. The Green Party won enough votes to gain representation in the Riksdag. In Feb 1990, with mounting opposition to its economic policies, the government resigned, leaving Carlsson as a caretaker prime minister. In Dec 1990 the Riksdag supported the government's decision to apply for European Community membership. Elections in Sept 1991 led to the defeat of Carlsson's government. He was succeeded as prime minister by Carl Bildt who led a minority coalition comprising the

Moderate Party (M), the Liberals (Fp), the Center Party (C), and the Christian Democratic Community Party (KdS). In Sept 1992 it was announced that an unprecedented agreement between the conservative parties and Social Democrats had been reached to work together to attack the country's economic problems. *See illustration box.*

Swedenborg Emanuel 1688–1772. Swedish theologian and philosopher. He trained as a scientist, but from 1747 concentrated on scriptural study, and in *Divine Love and Wisdom* 1763 concluded that the Last Judgment had taken place in 1757, and that the **New Church**, of which he was the prophet, had now been inaugurated. His writings are the scriptures of the sect popularly known as Swedenborgians, and his works are kept in circulation by the Swedenborg Society, London.

Swedish art painting and sculpture of Sweden. A geometrically stylized dragon ornament characterized Swedish art and crafts before and during the Viking period. Bright and cheerful folk art flourished in church and secular decorations from the Middle Ages into the 19th century. Although the main movements in European art have successively taken hold in Sweden, artists have repeatedly returned to a national tradition.

5000–500 BC Animal pictures carved in or

painted on rock can be found in central Sweden.
500 BC–11th century AD Bronze and gold jewelry; memorial stones carved with runes and ornaments.
12th–16th centuries Woven tapestries show the geometrically stylized animals that also occur in jewelry and carvings. Churches were decorated with lively, richly ornamented frescoes. Wooden sculptures were initially stiff and solemn, later more realistic and expressive.
17th century Sculptors and portrait painters who had studied Italian Baroque were patronized by Sweden's rulers.
18th century Swedish Rococo was more restrained than its French models; chinoiserie was popular because of Swedish trade with the Far East. Alexander Roslin (1718–1793) was one of several portrait painters who continued their careers in France. Rococo was supplanted toward the end of the century by a light Neo-Classical style known as Gustavian. The sculptor J T Sergel based his strong, sensual work on studies of ancient art in Rome.
19th century Academic history painting was superseded by the work of artists influenced by the French Impressionists and by the nationalist spirit current in many countries. The watercolor interiors by Carl Larsson (1853–1919) of his home were very popular. Anders Zorn (1860–1920) loved color and nudes. Bruno Liljefors (1860–1939) specialized in paintings of animals.
early 20th century The Romantic nationalist Jugend style can be seen in the monumental sculptures of Carl Milles (1875–1955) throughout Sweden and in the US. Albert Engström (1869–1940) was a prolific illustrator and cartoonist. Nils von Dardel (1888–1943) was an early Surrealist painter.
late 20th century Figurative art predominated, ranging from the dreamlike, symbolic paintings of Lena Cronqvist, Åsa Moberg, and others to the realistic still-life graphics of Philip von Schantz (1928–).

Swedish language member of the Germanic branch of the Indo-European language family, spoken in Sweden and Finland and closely related to Danish and Norwegian.

sweet cicely plant *Myrrhis odorata* of the carrot family Umbelliferae, native to S Europe; the root is eaten as a vegetable, and the aniseed-flavored leaves are used in salads.

Also, one of several North American plants (genus *Osmorhiza*) of the same family with clusters of small white flowers.

sweet pea plant of the ⟩pea family.

sweet potato tropical American plant *Ipomoea batatas* of the morning-glory family Convolvulaceae; the white-orange tuberous root is used as a source of starch and alcohol and eaten as a vegetable.

sweet william biennial to perennial plant *Dianthus barbatus* of the pink family Caryophyllaceae, native to S Europe. It is grown for its fragrant red, white, and pink flowers.

Sweyn I died 1014. King of Denmark from about 986, nicknamed "Forkbeard." He raided England, finally conquered it in 1013, and styled himself king, but his early death led to the return of ⟩Ethelred II.

swift any fast-flying, short-legged bird of the family Apodidae, of which there are about 75 species, found largely in the tropics. They are 4–11 in/9–23 cm long, with brown or gray plumage, long, pointed wings, and usually a forked tail. They are capable of flying 70 mph/110 kph.

The chimney swift *Chaetura pelagica*, which breeds in North America, is 5.5 in/13 cm long, with a cigar-shaped body and a short, stubby, superficially unforked tail.

Swift Jonathan 1667–1745. Irish satirist and Anglican cleric, author of *Gulliver's Travels* 1726, an allegory describing travel to lands inhabited by giants, miniature people, and intelligent horses. Other works include *The Tale of a Tub* 1704, attacking corruption in religion and learning; contributions to the Tory paper *The Examiner*, of which he was editor 1710–11; the satirical *A Modest Proposal* 1729, which suggested that children of the poor should be eaten; and many essays and pamphlets.

Swift, born in Dublin, became secretary to the diplomat William Temple (1628–1699) at Moor Park, Surrey, where his friendship with the child "Stella" (Hester Johnson 1681–1728) began in 1689. Returning to Ireland, he was ordained in the Church of England 1694, and in 1699 was made a prebendary of St Patrick's, Dublin. In 1710 he became a Tory pamphleteer, and obtained the deanery of St Patrick in 1713. His *Journal to Stella* is a series of letters, 1710–13, in which he described his life in London. "Stella" remained the love of his life, but "Vanessa" (Esther Vanhomrigh 1690–1723), a Dublin woman who had fallen in love with him, jealously wrote to her rival in 1723 and so shattered his relationship with both women. From about 1738 his mind began to fail.

Swift and Co v US US Supreme Court decision 1905 dealing with federal regulation of local business transactions. When the meatpacking industry colluded to fix the price of fresh meat in Chicago, the federal government issued an injunction against price fixing. The beef trust appealed, arguing that local commerce was outside of federal jurisdiction. The Court upheld the injunction, ruling that, since the local transaction affected businesses that participated in interstate trade, the federal government had the power to regulate it.

swim bladder thin-walled, air-filled sac found between the gut and the spine in bony fishes. Air enters the bladder from the gut or from surrounding capillaries (see ⏃capillary), and changes of air pressure within the bladder maintain buoyancy whatever the water depth.   In evolutionary terms, the swim bladder of higher fishes is a derivative of the lungs present in all primitive fishes (not just lungfishes).

swimming self-propulsion of the body through water. As a competitive sport there are four strokes: crawl, breaststroke, backstroke, and butterfly. (In freestyle events, the crawl is usually used, since it is the "fastest" stroke for most swimmers; but any stroke may be used.) Distances of races vary from 25 yards up to the mile or more. Swimming meets are held in pools and at beach clubs (for the events longer than the mile).

Swimming has been known since ancient times, in the training of Greek and Roman warriors. Competitive swimming is known to have taken place in Japan 36 BC, and became compulsory in schools there in 1603. Fear of infection prevented Europeans from swimming during the Middle Ages, but during the late 19th century swimming pools with chlorine as a disinfectant began to be built at major schools

and universities. By the early 20th century in the US, public pools were features of parks and clubs, and swimming, diving, and water polo were part of the sports revival that gave pleasure to the leisured classes. Swimming has become a popular pastime and competitive sport for age-grade, school, amateur, and senior contestants in all parts of the US.

⏃Synchronized swimming is a form of "ballet" performed in and under water. Underwater swimming developed with the invention of such equipment as flippers, snorkel, and self-contained underwater breathing apparatus (scuba). See also ⏃diving. Swimming has been included in the Olympic Games since 1896 for men and 1912 for women. The world championships were introduced in 1973, later held in 1975 and 1978 and every four years since.

Swinburne Algernon Charles 1837–1909. English poet. He attracted attention with the choruses of his Greek-style tragedy *Atalanta in Calydon* 1865, but he and ⏃Rossetti were attacked in 1871 as leaders of "the fleshly school of poetry," and the revolutionary politics of *Songs before Sunrise* 1871 alienated others.

swine flu virulent, highly contagious form of influenza, infecting pigs and communicable to people.

swine vesicular disease virus disease (porcine enterovirus) closely resembling foot and mouth disease, and communicable to humans. It may have originated in the infection of pigs by a virus that causes flulike symptoms in people.

swing music jazz style popular in the 1930s–40s, a big-band dance music with a simple harmonic base of varying tempo from the rhythm section (percussion, guitar, piano), harmonic brass and woodwind sections (sometimes strings), and superimposed solo melodic line from, for example, trumpet, clarinet, or saxophone. Exponents included Benny Goodman, Duke Ellington, and Glenn Miller, who introduced jazz to a mass white audience.

swing wing correctly *variable-geometry wing* aircraft wing that can be moved during flight to provide a suitable configuration for either low-speed or high-speed flight. The British engineer Barnes ⏃Wallis developed the idea of the swing wing, first used on the US-

forms delta wing with tailplane

fully extended position (low speed)

swept-back position (high-speed)

swing wing *The swing-wing fighter aircraft forms a delta shape for supersonic flight.*

built Northrop X-4, and since used in several aircraft, including the US F-111, F-114, and the B-1, the European Tornado, and several Soviet-built aircraft. These craft have their wings projecting nearly at right angles for takeoff and landing and low-speed flight, and swung back for high-speed flight.

Swiss Family Robinson, The children's adventure story by Swiss author Johann Wyss, first published in German 1812–13 and expanded by subsequent editors and translators. Modeled on Defoe's *Robinson Crusoe*, it tells of a Swiss family shipwrecked on a desert island and the lessons taught to the children by their adventures there.

Switzerland landlocked country in W Europe, bounded N by Germany, E by Austria and Liechtenstein, S by Italy, and W by France.
government Switzerland is a federation of 20 cantons and six half-cantons (canton is the name for a political division, derived from Old French). The constitution dates from 1874 and provides for a two-chamber federal assembly, consisting of the National Council and the Council of States. The National Council has 200 members, elected by universal suffrage, through a system of proportional representation, for a four-year term. The Council of States has 46 members, each canton electing two representatives and each half-canton one. Members of the Council of States are elected for three or four years, depending on the constitutions of the individual cantons.

The federal government is in the hands of the Federal Council, consisting of seven members elected for a four-year term by the assembly, each heading a specific federal department. The federal assembly also appoints one member to act as federal head of state and head of government for a year, the term of office beginning on Jan 1. The federal government is allocated specific powers by the constitution with the remaining powers left with the cantons, each having its own constitution, assembly, and government. At a level below the cantons are more than 3,000 communes, whose populations range from fewer than 20 to 350,000. Direct democracy is encouraged through communal assemblies and referenda.
history The region was settled by peoples that the Romans called Helvetians or Transalpine Gauls, and it became a province of the Roman Empire after Julius Caesar's conquest. In 1291 the cantons of Schwyz, Uri, and Lower Unterwalden formed the Everlasting League to defend their liberties against their ⏃Habsburg overlords. More towns and districts joined them, and there were 13 cantons by 1513. The Reformation was accepted during 1523–29 by Zürich, Berne, and Basel, but the rural cantons remained Catholic. Switzerland gradually won more freedom from Hapsburg control until its complete independence was recognized by the Treaty of ⏃Westphalia 1648.
democratic federation A peasant uprising 1653 was suppressed. A French invasion 1798 established the Helvetic Republic with a centralized government; this was modified by Napoleon's Act of Mediation 1803, which made Switzerland a democratic federation. The Congress of ⏃Vienna 1815 guaranteed Swiss neutrality, and Switzerland received Geneva and other territories, increasing the number of cantons to 22. After a civil war between the Sonderbund (a union of the Catholic cantons Lucerne, Zug, Freiburg, and Valais) and the Liberals, a revised federal constitution,

Switzerland
Swiss Confederation (German **Schweiz**, French **Suisse**, Romansch **Svizzera**)

area 15,946 sq mi/41,300 sq km
capital Bern
cities Zürich, Geneva, Lausanne; river port Basel (on the Rhine)
physical most mountainous country in Europe (Alps and Jura mountains); highest peak Dufourspitze 15,203 ft/4,634 m in Apennines
environment an estimated 43% of coniferous trees, particularly in the central alpine region, have been killed by acid rain, 90% of which comes from other countries. Over 50% of bird species are classified as threatened
features winter sports area of the upper valley of the river Inn (Engadine); lakes Maggiore, Lucerne, Geneva, Constance
head of state and government René Felber from 1992

government federal democratic republic
political parties Radical Democratic Party (FDP), radical, center-left; Social Democratic Party (SPS), moderate, left-of-center; Christian Democratic Party (PDC), Christian, moderate, centrist; People's Party (SVP), center-left; Liberal Party (PLS), federalist, center-left; Green Party, ecological
exports electrical goods, chemicals, pharmaceuticals, watches, precision instruments, confectionery
currency Swiss franc
population (1990 est) 6,628,000; growth rate 0.2% p.a.
life expectancy men 74, women 82 (1989)
languages German 65%, French 18%, Italian 12%, Romansch 1% (all official)
religion Roman Catholic 50%, Protestant 48%
literacy 99% (1989)
GNP $111 bn (1988); $26,309 per head (1987)
chronology
1648 Became independent of the Holy Roman Empire.
1798–1815 Helvetic Republic established by French revolutionary armies.
1847 Civil war resulted in greater centralization.
1874 Principle of the referendum introduced.
1971 Women given the vote in federal elections.
1984 First female cabinet minister appointed.
1986 Referendum rejected proposal for membership in United Nations.
1989 Referendum supported abolition of citizen army and military service requirements.
1991 18-year-olds allowed to vote for first time in national elections. Four-party coalition remained in power.
1992 René Felber elected president with Adolf Ogi as vice-president. Decision to apply for full European Community (EC) membership.

giving the central government wide powers, was introduced 1848; a further revision 1874 increased its powers and introduced the principle of the referendum.
international role Switzerland, for centuries a neutral country, has been the base for many international organizations and the host of many international peace conferences. A referendum 1986 rejected the advice of the government and came out overwhelmingly against membership in the United Nations. Its domestic politics have been characterized by coalition governments and a stability that has enabled it to become one of the world's richest countries (per person).

After the Oct 1987 election, the four-party coalition continued in power, although there was a significant increase in the number of seats held by the Green Party. In 1989, a referendum found widespread dissatisfaction with the national militia and military service requirements. In Aug 1991 the country celebrated its 700th anniversary. The Oct 1991 national elections, in which 18-year-olds were allowed to vote for the first time, saw little change in the resulting seat distribution, with the four-party coalition retaining control. In Jan 1992 René Felber became president and Adolf Ogi vice-president. Switzerland decided to apply for full membership in the European Community. *See illustration box.*

swordfish marine bony fish *Xiphias gladius*, the only member of its family (Xiphiidae), characterized by a long swordlike beak protruding from the upper jaw. It may reach 15 ft/4.5 m in length and weigh 1,000 lb/450 kg.

sycamore or *plane tree* any of several Eurasian trees of the genus *Platanus* of the family Plantanaceae. Species include the oriental plane tree *P. orientalis*, a favorite of the Greeks and Romans; the American sycamore *P. occidentalis* of the eastern US; and the Arizona sycamore *P. Wrightii*. All species have pendulous burrlike fruits and some grow to 100 ft/30 m high.

Sydenham Thomas 1624–1689. English physician, the first person to describe measles and to recommend the use of quinine for relieving symptoms of malaria. His original reputation as "the English Hippocrates" rested upon his belief that careful observation is more useful than speculation. His *Observationes medicae* was published in 1676.

Sydney capital and port of New South Wales, Australia; population (1990) 3,656,900. Industries include engineering, oil refining, electronics, scientific equipment, chemicals, clothing, and furniture. It is a financial center, and has three universities. The 19th-century Museum of Applied Arts and Sciences is the most popular museum in Australia.

Originally a British penal colony 1788, Sydney developed rapidly following the discovery of gold in the surrounding area. The main streets still follow the lines of the original wagon tracks, and the Regency Bligh House survives. Modern landmarks are the harbor bridge (single span 1,652 ft/503.5 m) 1923–

32, Opera House 1959–73, and Center Point Tower 1980.

Sydow Max (Carl Adolf) von 1929– . Swedish actor associated with the director Ingmar Bergman. He made his US debut as Jesus in *The Greatest Story Ever Told* 1965. His other films include *The Seventh Seal* 1957, *The Exorcist* 1973, and *Hannah and Her Sisters* 1985.

syenite gray, crystalline, plutonic (intrusive) ◊igneous rock, consisting of feldspar and hornblende; other minerals may also be present, including small amounts of quartz.

syllogism set of philosophical statements devised by Aristotle in his work on logic. It establishes the conditions under which a valid conclusion follows or does not follow by deduction from given premises. The following is an example of a valid syllogism: "All men are mortal, Socrates is a man, therefore Socrates is mortal."

Sylvanus in Roman mythology, another version of ◊Silvanus.

symbiosis any relationship between two organisms of different species, where both partners benefit from the association. A well-known example is the pollination relationship between insects and flowers, where the insects feed on nectar and carry pollen from one flower to another. This kind of relationship is better known as ◊mutualism. Strictly speaking, symbiosis refers to continuous, intimate contact between mutually benefiting species, such as the fungus and alga in ◊lichen.

symbol in general, something that stands for something else. A symbol may be an aesthetic device or a sign used to convey information visually, thus saving time, eliminating language barriers, or overcoming illiteracy.

Symbols are used in art, mathematics, music, and literature; for practical use in science and medicine; for road signs; and as warnings—for example, a skull and crossbones to indicate dangerous contents.

symbolic interactionism sociological method, founded by the US pragmatist George Mead, that studies the behavior of individuals and small groups through observation and description, viewing people's appearance, gestures, and language as symbols they use to interact with others in social situations. In contrast to theories such as Marxism or functionalism that attempt to analyze society as a whole through economic or political systems, it takes a perspective of society from within, as created by people themselves.

symbolic processor computer purpose-built to run so-called symbol-manipulation programs rather than programs involving a great deal of numerical computation. They exist principally for the ◊artificial intelligence language ◊LISP, although some have also been built to run ◊PROLOG.

symbolism in the arts, the use of symbols as a device for concentrating or intensifying meaning. In particular, the term is used for a late 19th-century movement in French poetry, associated with Verlaine, Mallarmé, and Rimbaud, who used words for their symbolic rather than concrete meaning.

Symbolism movement in late 19th-century painting that emerged in France inspired by the trend in poetry. The subjects were often mythological, mystical, or fantastic. Gustave Moreau was a leading Symbolist painter.

Other Symbolist painters included Puvis de Chavannes and Odilon Redon in France,

Arnold Böcklin in Switzerland, and Edward Burne-Jones in the UK. Statuesque female figures were often used to embody qualities or emotions.

symmetry exact likeness in shape about a given line (axis), point, or plane. A figure has symmetry if one half can be rotated or reflected onto the other. In a wider sense, symmetry exits if a change in the system leaves the essential features of the system unchanged; for example, reversing the sign of electric charges does not change the electrical behavior of an arrangement of charges.

symphonic poem in music, a term originated by Franz Liszt for his 13 one-movement orchestral works that interpret a story from literature or history, also used by many other composers. Richard Strauss preferred the title "tone poem."

symphony musical composition for orchestra, traditionally in four separate but closely related movements. It developed from the smaller ⟡sonata form, the Italian overture, and the dance suite of the 18th century.

Haydn established the mature form of the symphony, written in slow, minuet, and allegro movements. Mozart and Beethoven (who replaced the ⟡minuet with the scherzo) expanded the form, which has been developed further by successive composers: Brahms, Tchaikovsky, Bruckner, Dvořák, Mahler, Sibelius, Vaughan Williams, Walter Piston, Prokofiev, Carl Nielsen, Shostakovich, Stravinsky, and Aaron Copland.

synagogue Jewish place of worship, also called a temple by the non-Orthodox. As an institution it dates from the destruction of the Temple in Jerusalem AD 70, although it had been developing from the time of the Babylonian Exile as a substitute for the Temple. In antiquity it was a public meeting hall where the Torah was also read, but today it is used primarily for prayer and services. A service requires a quorum (*minyan*) of ten adult Jewish men.

In addition to the ark (the sacred ornamented enclosure that holds the Torah scrolls) the synagogue contains a raised platform (*bimah*) from which the service is conducted, with seats for the hereditary high priests. The rest of the congregation sits or stands facing it. Two tablets above the ark are inscribed with the Ten Commandments. In Orthodox synagogues women sit apart from the men.

synapse junction between two ⟡nerve cells, or between a nerve cell and a muscle (a neuromuscular junction), across which a nerve impulse is transmitted. The two cells are separated by a narrow gap called the **synaptic cleft**. The gap is bridged by a chemical ⟡neurotransmitter, released by the nerve impulse.

The threadlike extension, or ⟡axon, of the transmitting nerve cell has a slightly swollen terminal point, the **synaptic knob**. This forms one half of the synaptic junction and houses membrane-bound vesicles, which contain a chemical neurotransmitter. When nerve impulses reach the knob, the vesicles release the transmitter and this flows across the gap and binds itself to special receptors on the receiving cell's membrane. If the receiving cell is a nerve cell, the other half of the synaptic junction will be one or more extensions called ⟡dendrites; these will be stimulated by the neurotransmitter to set up an impulse, which will then be conducted along the length of the

nerve cell and on to its own axons. If the receiving cell is a muscle cell, it will be stimulated by the neurotransmitter to contract.

Synapsida group of mammallike reptiles living 315–195 million years ago, whose fossil record is largely complete, and who were for a while the dominant land animals, before being replaced by the dinosaurs. The true mammals are their descendants.

synchronized swimming swimming discipline that demands artistry as opposed to speed. Competitors, either individual (solo) or in pairs, perform rhythmic routines to music, which include difficult but graceful movements called "stunts," similar to diving positions. Points are awarded for interpretation and style, and stunt performance (multiplied by a degree of difficulty scale as in ⟡diving). It was introduced into the Olympic swimming program in 1984.

synchrotron another name for a particle ⟡accelerator.

syncline geological term for a fold in the rocks of the Earth's crust in which the layers or ⟡beds dip inwards, thus forming a troughlike structure with a sag in the middle. The opposite structure, with the beds arching upward, is an ⟡anticline.

syncopation in music, the deliberate upsetting of rhythm by shifting the accent to a beat that is normally unaccented.

syncope medical term for any temporary loss of consciousness, as in ⟡fainting.

syndicalism (French *syndicat* "labor union") political movement in 19th-century Europe that rejected parliamentary activity in favor of direct action, culminating in a revolutionary general strike to secure worker ownership and control of industry. After 1918 syndicalism was absorbed in communism, although it continued to have an independent existence in Spain until the late 1930s.

The idea originated under Robert ⟡Owen's influence in the 1830s, acquired its name and its more violent aspects in France from the philosopher Georges ⟡Sorel, and also reached the US (see ⟡Industrial Workers of the World).

syndrome in medicine, a set of signs and symptoms that always occur together, thus characterizing a particular condition or disorder.

synecdoche (Greek "accepted together") figure of speech that uses either the part to represent the whole ("There were some *new faces* at the meeting," rather than *new people*), or the whole to stand for the part ("The West Indies beat England at cricket," rather than naming the national teams in question).

synergy (Greek "combined action") in architecture, the augmented strength of systems, where the strength of a wall is greater than the added total of its individual units.

synergy in medicine, the "cooperative" action of two or more drugs, muscles, or organs; applied especially to drugs whose combined action is more powerful than their simple effects added together.

Synge J(ohn) M(illington) 1871–1909. Irish playwright, a leading figure in the Irish dramatic revival of the early 20th century. His six plays reflect the speech patterns of the Aran Islands and W Ireland. They include *In the Shadow of the Glen* 1903, *Riders to the Sea* 1904, and *The Playboy of the Western World* 1907, which caused riots at the Abbey Theater, Dublin, when first performed.

Synge Richard 1914– . British biochemist who investigated paper ⟡chromatography (a means of separating mixtures). By 1940 techniques of chromatography for separating proteins had been devised. Still lacking were comparable techniques for distinguishing the amino acids that constituted the proteins. By 1944, Synge and his colleague Archer Martin had worked out a procedure, known as ascending chromatography, which filled this gap and won them the 1952 Nobel Prize for Chemistry.

synodic period the time taken for a planet or moon to return to the same position in its orbit as seen from the Earth; that is, from one ⟡opposition to the next. It differs from the ⟡sidereal period because the Earth is moving in orbit around the Sun.

synonymy near or identical meaning between or among words. There are very few strict synonyms in any language, although there may be many near-synonyms, depending upon the contexts in which the words are used. Thus *brotherly* and *fraternal* are synonyms in English, but a *brotherhood* is not the same as a *fraternity*. People talk about the brotherhood of man but seldom if ever about the "fraternity of man." *Brotherhood* and *fraternity* are not therefore strictly synonymous.

synovial fluid viscous yellow fluid that bathes movable joints between the bones of vertebrates. It nourishes and lubricates the ⟡cartilage at the end of each bone.

Synovial fluid is secreted by a membrane that links movably jointed bones. The same kind of fluid is found in bursae, the membranous sacs that buffer some joints, such as in the shoulder and hip region.

synovitis inflammation of the membranous lining of a joint, or of a tendon sheath, caused by injury or infection.

synthesis in chemistry, the formation of a substance or compound from more elementary compounds. The synthesis of a drug can involve several stages from the initial material to the final product; the complexity of these stages is a major factor in the cost of production.

synthesizer device that uses electrical components to produce sounds. In *preset synthesizers*, the sound of various instruments is produced by a built-in computer-type memory. In *programmable synthesizers* any number of new instrumental or other sounds may be produced at the will of the performer. *Speech synthesizers* can break down speech into 128 basic elements (allophones), which are then combined into words and sentences, as in the voices of electronic teaching aids.

In preset synthesizers the memory triggers all the control settings required to produce the sound of a trumpet or violin. For example, the "sawtooth" sound wave produced by a violin is artificially produced by an electrical tone generator, or oscillator, and then fed into an electrical filter set to have the resonances characteristic of a violin body. The first electronic sound synthesizer was developed 1964 by US engineer Robert Moog (1934–). Synthesizers are played via a keyboard. A drum machine is a specialized form of synthesizer.

synthetic any material made from chemicals. Since the 1900s, more and more of the materials used in everyday life are synthetics, including plastics (polythene, polystyrene), ⟡synthetic fibers (nylon, acrylics, polyesters), synthetic resins, and synthetic rubber. Most naturally occurring organic substances are now made synthetically, especially pharmaceuticals.

synthetic in philosophy, a term employed by ⬦Kant to describe a judgment in which the predicate is not contained within the subject; for example, "The flower is blue" is synthetic, since every flower is not blue. It is the converse of ⬦analytic.

synthetic fiber fiber made by chemical processes, unknown in nature. There are two kinds. One is made from natural materials that have been chemically processed in some way; ⬦rayon, for example, is made by processing the cellulose in wood pulp. The other type is the true synthetic fiber, made entirely from chemicals. ⬦Nylon was the original synthetic fiber, made from chemicals obtained from petroleum (crude oil).

Fibers are drawn out into long threads or filaments, usually by so-called spinning methods, melting or dissolving the parent material and then forcing it through the holes of a perforated plate, or spinneret.

syphilis venereal disease caused by the spiral-shaped bacterium (spirochete) *Treponema pallidum*. Untreated, it runs its course in three stages over many years, often starting with a painless hard sore, or chancre, developing within a month on the area of infection (usually the genitals). The second stage, months later, is a rash with arthritis, hepatitis, and/or meningitis. The third stage, years later, leads eventually to paralysis, blindness, insanity, and death. The Wassermann test is a diagnostic blood test for syphilis.

With widespread availability of antibiotics, syphilis is now increasingly cured in the industrialized world, at least to the extent that the final stage of the disease is rare. The risk remains that the disease may go undiagnosed or that it may be transmitted by a pregnant woman to her fetus. It has been implicated in the onset of ⬦AIDS symptoms.

Syracuse industrial city on Lake Onondaga, in New York State; population (1990) 163,900. Industries include the manufacture of electrical and other machinery, paper, and food processing. There are canal links with the ⬦Great Lakes, and the Hudson and St Lawrence rivers.

synthetic *The manufacture of nylon fiber.*

nylon chips —
manufacture of nylon, a synthetic fiber
furnace — molten nylon
spinneret —
cool air →
→ steam
— nylon yarn

Syria
Syrian Arab Republic (*al-Jamhuriya al-Arabya as-Suriya*)

area 71,506 sq mi/185,200 sq km
capital Damascus
cities Aleppo, Homs, Hama; chief port Latakia
physical mountains alternate with fertile plains and desert areas; Euphrates River
features Mount Hermon, Golan Heights; crusader castles (including Krak des Chevaliers); Phoenician city sites (Ugarit), ruins of ancient Palmyra
head of state and government Hafez al-Assad from 1971
political system socialist republic
political parties National Progressive Front (NPF), pro-Arab, socialist; Communist Action Party, socialist
exports cotton, cereals, oil, phosphates, tobacco
currency Syrian pound
population (1990 est) 12,471,000; growth rate 3.5% p.a.
life expectancy men 67, women 69 (1989)
languages Arabic 89% (official), Kurdish 6%, Armenian 3%
religion Sunni Muslim 74%; ruling minority

Alawite, and other Islamic sects 16%; Christian 10%
literacy men 76%, women 43% (1985 est)
GNP $17 bn (1986); $702 per head
chronology
1946 Achieved full independence from France.
1958 Merged with Egypt to form the United Arab Republic (UAR).
1961 UAR disintegrated.
1967 Six-Day War resulted in the loss of territory to Israel.
1970–71 Syria supported Palestinian guerrillas against Jordanian troops.
1971 Following a bloodless coup, Hafez al-Assad became president.
1973 Israel consolidated its control of the Golan Heights after the Yom Kippur War.
1976 Substantial numbers of troops committed to the civil war in Lebanon.
1978 Assad reelected.
1981–82 Further military engagements in Lebanon.
1982 Islamic militant uprising suppressed; 5,000 dead.
1984 Presidents Assad and Gemayel approved plans for government of national unity in Lebanon.
1985 Assad secured the release of 39 US hostages held in an aircraft hijacked by extremist Shiite group, Hezbollah. Assad reelected.
1987 Improved relations with US and attempts to secure the release of Western hostages in Lebanon.
1989 Diplomatic relations with Morocco restored. Continued fighting in Lebanon; Syrian forces reinforced in Lebanon; diplomatic relations with Egypt restored.
1990 Diplomatic relations with Britain restored.
1991 Syria fought against Iraq in Gulf War. President Assad agreed to US Middle East peace plan. Assad reelected as president.
1992 Middle East peace talks continued; some restrictions on Syrian Jews lifted. Syrian troops continued to occup Lebanon.

Syracuse University is here. Syracuse was settled in the 1780s on the site of a former Iroquois capital and developed as a salt-mining center.

Syracuse (Italian *Siracusa*) industrial port (chemicals, salt) in E Sicily; population (1988) 124,000. It has a cathedral and remains of temples, aqueducts, catacombs, and an amphitheater. Founded 734 BC by the Corinthians, it became a center of Greek culture under the elder and younger ⬦Dionysius. After a three-year siege it was taken by Rome 212 BC. In AD 878 it was destroyed by the Arabs, and the rebuilt town came under Norman rule in the 11th century.

Syria country in W Asia, on the Mediterranean Sea, bounded N by Turkey, E by Iraq, S by Jordan, and SW by Israel and Lebanon.
government The 1973 constitution provides for a president, elected by universal adult suffrage for a seven-year term, who appoints and governs with the help of a prime minister and a council of ministers. There is a single-chamber legislature, the 195-member Majlis al-Sha'ab, also elected by universal adult suffrage.
history Ancient Syria was inhabited by various small kingdoms that fought against Israel and were subdued by the Assyrians. It was subsequently occupied by Babylonia, Persia,

and Macedonia but gained prominence under Seleucus Nicator, founder of ⬦Antioch 300 BC, and ⬦Antiochus the Great. After forming part of the Roman and Byzantine empires, it was conquered by the Saracens 636. During the Middle Ages, Syria was the scene of many battles between Muslims and European Crusaders.

Syria was part of the ⬦Ottoman Empire 1516–1918. It was occupied by British and French troops 1918–19 and in 1920 placed under French mandate. Syria became independent 1946 and three years later came under military rule.
military coup In 1958 Syria merged with Egypt to become the United Arab Republic (UAR), but after an army coup 1961 Syria seceded, and the independent Syrian Arab Republic was established. In 1963 a government was formed, mainly from members of the Arab Socialist Renaissance (Ba'ath) Party, but three years later the army removed it. In 1970 the moderate wing of the Ba'ath Party, led by Lt Gen Hafez al-Assad, secured power in a bloodless coup, and in the following year Assad was elected president. He also became head of government, secretary-general of the Ba'ath Arab Socialist Party, and president of the National Progressive Front (NPF), an umbrella organization for the five main socialist parties. Syria

is therefore in reality, if not in a strictly legal sense, a one-party state.

Middle East affairs Externally Syria has played a leading role in Middle East affairs. In the Six-Day War 1967 it lost territory to Israel, and after the Yom Kippur War 1973 Israel formally annexed the Golan Heights, which had previously been part of Syria. During 1976 Assad increasingly intervened in the civil war in Lebanon, eventually committing some 50,000 troops to the operations. Relations between Syria and Egypt cooled after President Sadat's Israel peace initiative 1977 and the subsequent ▷Camp David agreements. Assad consistently opposed US-sponsored peace moves in Lebanon, arguing that they infringed upon Lebanese sovereignty. He also questioned Yassir Arafat's leadership of the Palestine Liberation Organization (PLO) and supported opposition to him.

leaning toward the West In 1984 President Assad and the Lebanese president Amin Gemayel approved plans for a government of national unity in Lebanon, which would give equal representation to Muslims and Christians, and secured the reluctant agreement of Nabih Berri of the Shiite Amal Militia and Walid Jumblatt, leader of the ▷Druse. Fighting still continued, and Assad's credibility suffered, but in 1985 his authority proved sufficient to secure the release of 39 US hostages from an aircraft hijacked by the extremist Shiite group Hezbollah. In Nov 1986 Britain broke off diplomatic relations after claiming to have proof of Syrian involvement in international terrorism, when a Syrian citizen attempted to blow up an Israeli plane at Heathrow, London. In July 1987 Syria instigated a crackdown on the pro-Iranian Hezbollah party.

Syria has been leaning to the West, its policies in Lebanon in direct conflict with Iran's dream of an Islamic republic, and its crumbling economy has been promised Arab aid if Damascus switches allegiance. In June 1987, following a private visit by former US president Jimmy ▷Carter, Syria's relations with the US began to improve, and efforts were made to arrange the release of Western hostages in Lebanon, a process that continued through 1991. After Iraq's invasion of Kuwait Aug 1990, Syria sided with other Arab states and the UN coalition against Iraq, contributing troops for the ▷Gulf War. In Nov 1990 full diplomatic relations with Britain were resumed, and in 1991 President Assad agreed to a US Middle East peace plan. In Dec Assad was reelected, unopposed, for a fourth term. As Middle East peace talks continued, some restrictions on Syrian Jews were lifted. Syrian troops continued to occupy Lebanon. *See illustration box.*

Syriac language ancient Semitic language, originally the Aramaic dialect spoken in and around Edessa (now in Turkey) and widely used in W Asia from about 700 BC to AD 700. From the 3rd to 7th centuries it was a Christian liturgical and literary language.

syringa common, but incorrect, name for the ▷mock orange *Philadelphus*. The genus *Syringa* includes ▷lilac *Syringa vulgaris*, and is not related to mock orange.

Système International d'Unités official French name for ▷SI units.

systemic in medicine, relating to or affecting the body as a whole. A systemic disease is one where the effects are present throughout the body, as opposed to local disease, such as ▷conjunctivitis, which is confined to one part.

systems analysis in computing, the investigation of a business activity or clerical procedure, with a view to deciding if and how it can be computerized. The analyst discusses the existing procedures with the people involved, observes the flow of data through the business, and draws up an outline specification of the required computer system.

Systems in use in the 1990s include Yourdon, SSADM, and Soft Systems Methodology.

systems design in computing, the detailed design of an ▷applications package. The designer breaks the system down into component programs, and designs the required input forms, screen layouts, and printouts. Systems design forms a link between systems analysis and ▷programming.

Szczecin (German *Stettin*) industrial (shipbuilding, fish processing, synthetic fibers, tools, iron) port on the river Oder, in NW Poland; population (1990) 413,400.

A Hanseatic port (see ▷Hanseatic League) from 1278, it was Swedish from 1648 until 1720, when it was taken by Prussia. It was Germany's chief Baltic port until captured by the Russians in 1945, and came under Polish administration. Catherine the Great of Russia was born here.

Szechwan alternate spelling for the central Chinese province of ▷Sichuan.

Szent-Györgyi Albert 1893–1986. Hungarian-born US biochemist who isolated vitamin C and studied the chemistry of muscular activity. He was awarded the Nobel Prize for Medicine 1937.

Szilard Leo 1898–1964. Hungarian-born US physicist who, in 1934, was one of the first scientists to realize that nuclear fission, or atom splitting, could lead to a chain reaction releasing enormous amounts of instantaneous energy. He emigrated to the US in 1938 and there influenced ▷Einstein to advise President Roosevelt to begin the nuclear arms program. After World War II he turned his attention to the newly emerging field of molecular biology.

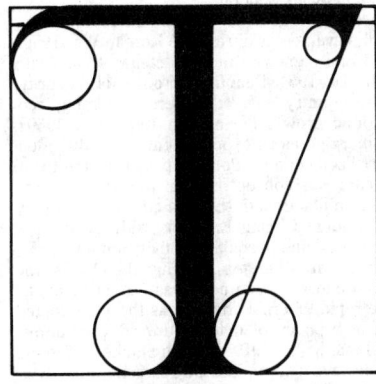

T 20th letter of the English alphabet, whose sound is usually a voiceless alveolar plosive. The earliest form was X, which the Phoenicians called *tau*, a cross or sign, but in the Greek alphabet (still called *tau*) its form was T, τ.

Tabah or *Taba* small area of disputed territory, 0.6 mi/1 km long, between Eilat (Israel) to the east and the Sinai Desert (Egypt) to the west on the Red Sea. Under an Anglo-Egyptian-Turkish agreement 1906, the border ran through Tabah; under a British survey of 1915 headed by T E Lawrence (of Arabia), who made "adjustments" allegedly under British government orders, it runs to the east. Taken by Israel 1967, Tabah was returned to Egypt 1989.

Table Bay inlet on the SW coast of the Cape of Good Hope, South Africa, on which Cape Town stands. It is overlooked by *Table Mountain* (highest point Maclear's Beacon 3,568 ft/1,087 m), the cloud that often hangs above it being known as the "tablecloth."

table tennis or *ping pong* indoor game played on a rectangular table by two or four players. It was developed in Britain about 1880 and derived from lawn tennis. World championships were first held 1926.

Play takes place on a table measuring 9 ft/2.74 m long by 5 ft/1.52 m wide. Across the middle is a 15.25-cm/6-in-high net over which the ball must be hit. The players use small, wooden paddles covered in sponge or rubber. A feature of the game is the amount of spin put on the small plastic ball. Points are scored by forcing the opponent(s) into an error. The first to score 21 wins the game. Volleying is not allowed. A match may consist of three or five games. In doubles play, the players must hit the ball in strict rotation.

taboo (Polynesian *tabu*, "forbidden") prohibition applied to magical and religious objects. In psychology and the social sciences the term refers to practices that are generally prohibited because of religious or social pressures; for example, ◊incest is forbidden in most societies.

Tabriz city in NW Iran; industries include metal casting, carpets, cotton, and silk textiles; population (1986) 972,000.

Tacitus Publius Cornelius *c.* AD 55–*c.* 120. Roman historian. A public orator in Rome, he was consul under Nerva 97–98 and proconsul of Asia 112–113. He wrote histories of the Roman Empire, *Annales* and *Historiae*, covering the years AD 14–68 and 69–97 respectively. He also wrote a *Life of Agricola* 97 (he married Agricola's daughter in 77) and a description of the German tribes, *Germania* 98.

Tacoma port in Washington State, on Puget Sound, 25 mi/40 km south of Seattle; population (1990) 176,700. It is a lumber and shipping center, with fishing and boat-building industries. Manufactures include primary metals, wood and paper products, chemicals, and processed foods. Founded 1868, the city developed after being chosen as the terminus of the North Pacific Railroad 1873.

Educational institutions include the University of Puget Sound and Pacific Lutheran University.

Taegu largest inland city of South Korea after Seoul; population (1990) 2,228,800.

Taejon (Korean "large rice paddy") capital of South Chungchong province, central South Korea; population (1990) 1,062,100. Korea's tallest standing Buddha and oldest wooden building are found NE of the city at Popchusa in the Mount Songnisan National Park.

tae kwon do one of the Korean ◊martial arts similar to ◊karate, which includes punching and kicking. It was included in the 1988 Olympic Games as a demonstration sport.

taffeta (Persian "spun") light, plain-weave fabric with a high luster, originally silk but today also manufactured from artificial fibers.

Taft Robert Alphonso 1889–1953. US right-wing Republican senator from 1939, and a candidate for the presidential nomination 1940, 1944, 1948, and 1952. He sponsored the Taft–Hartley Labor Act 1947, restricting union power. He was the son of President William Taft.

Taft was born in Cincinnati, Ohio. Known as "Mr Republican," he was the standard-bearer of the conservative wing of the Republican Party, and he was lost in the liberal tide that swept the US during the 1930s. He was further isolated by his resistance to US involvement against Nazi Germany, a view he held as late as 1943.

Taft William Howard 1857–1930. 27th president of the US 1909–13, a Republican. He was secretary of war 1904–08 in Theodore Roosevelt's administration, but as president his conservatism provoked Roosevelt to stand against him in the 1912 election. Taft served as chief justice of the Supreme Court 1921–30.

Born in Cincinnati, Ohio, Taft graduated from Yale University and Cincinnati Law School. His first interest was always the judiciary, although he accepted a post as governor of the Philippines and took responsibility for the construction of the ◊Panama Canal. His single term as president was characterized by struggles against progressives, although he prosecuted more trusts than had his predecessor. As chief justice of the Supreme Court, he supported a minimum wage.

Tagalog member of the majority ethnic group living around Manila on the island of Luzon, in the Philippines, and numbering about 10 million (1988). The Tagalog live by fishing and trading. In its standardized form, known as Pilipino, Tagalog is the official language of the Philippines, and belongs to the Western branch of the Austronesian family. The Tagalogs' religion is a mixture of animism, Christianity, and Islam.

Tagliacozzi Gaspare 1546–1599. Italian surgeon who pioneered plastic surgery. He was the first to repair noses lost in duels or through ◊syphilis. He also repaired ears. His method involved taking flaps of skin from the arm and grafting them into place.

Taglioni Marie 1804–1884. Italian dancer. A ballerina of ethereal style and exceptional lightness, she was the first to use ◊pointe work, or dancing on the toes, as an expressive part of ballet rather than as sheer technique. She created many roles, including the title role in *La Sylphide* 1832, first performed at the Paris Opéra, and choreographed by her father *Filippo* (1771–1871).

Tagore Rabindranath 1861–1941. Bengali Indian writer, born in Calcutta, who translated into English his own verse *Gitanjali* ("song offerings") 1912 and his verse play *Chitra* 1896. Nobel Prize for Literature 1913.

An ardent nationalist and advocate of social reform, he resigned his knighthood as a gesture of protest against British repression in India.

Tagus (Spanish *Tajo*, Portuguese *Tejo*) river rising in Aragon, Spain, and reaching the Atlantic at Lisbon, Portugal; length 626 mi/1,007 km. At Lisbon it is crossed by the April 25 (formerly Salazar) Bridge, so named in honor of the 1974 revolution. The *Tagus-Segura* irrigation scheme serves the rainless Murcia/Alicante region for early fruit and vegetable growing.

Tahiti largest of the Society Islands, in ◊French Polynesia; area 402 sq mi/1,042 sq km; population (1983) 116,000. Its capital is Papeete. Tahiti was visited by Captain James ◊Cook 1769 and by Admiral ◊Bligh of the *Bounty* 1788. It came under French control 1843 and became a colony 1880.

Tai member of any of the groups of SE Asian peoples who speak Tai languages, all of which belong to the Sino-Tibetan language family. There are over 60 million speakers, the majority of whom live in Thailand. Tai peoples are also found in SW China, NW Myanmar (Burma), Laos, and N Vietnam.

T'ai Chi series of 108 complex, slow-motion movements, each named (for example, the White Crane Spreads Its Wings) and designed to ensure effective circulation of the *chi*, or intrinsic energy of the universe, through the mind and body. It derives partly from the Shaolin ◊martial arts of China and partly from ◊Taoism.

taiga or *boreal forest* Russian name for the forest zone south of the ◊tundra, found across the northern hemisphere. Here, dense forests of conifers (spruces and hemlocks), birches, and poplars occupy glaciated regions punctuated with cold lakes, streams, bogs, and marshes. Winters are prolonged and very cold, but the summer is warm enough to promote dense growth.

The varied fauna and flora are in delicate balance because the conditions of life are so precarious. This ecology is threatened by mining, forestry, and pipeline construction.

Taine Hippolyte Adolphe 1828–1893. French critic and historian. He analyzed literary works as products of period and environment, as in *Histoire de la littérature anglaise/History of English Literature* 1863 and *Philosophie de l'art/Philosophy of Art* 1865–69.

taipan species of small-headed cobra *Oxyuranus scutellatus* found in NE Australia

Taiwan
Republic of China (*Chung Hua Min Kuo*)

area 13,965 sq mi/36,179 sq km
capital Taipei
cities ports Kaohsiung, Keelung
physical island (formerly Formosa) off
People's Republic of China; mountainous,
with lowlands in W
environment industrialization has taken its
toll: an estimated 30% of the annual rice crop
is dangerously contaminated with mercury,
cadmium, and other heavy metals
features Penghu (Pescadores), Jinmen
(Quemoy), Mazu (Matsu) islands
head of state Lee Teng-hui from 1988
head of government Hau Pei-tsun from 1990
political system emergent democracy
political parties Nationalist Party of China
(Kuomintang: KMT), anticommunist, Chinese nationalist; Democratic Progressive
Party (DPP), centrist-pluralist, pro-self-
determination grouping; Workers' Party
(Kuntang), left-of-center
exports textiles, steel, plastics, electronics,
foodstuffs

currency New Taiwan dollar
population (1990) 20,454,000 (84%
Taiwanese, 14% mainlanders); growth rate
1.4% p.a.
life expectancy men 70, women 75 (1986)
language Mandarin Chinese (official); Taiwan,
Hakka dialects
religion officially atheist; Taoist, Confucian,
Buddhist, Christian
literacy 90% (1988)
GNP $119.1 bn; $6,200 per head (1988)
chronology
1683 Taiwan (Formosa) annexed by China.
1895 Ceded to Japan.
1945 Recovered by China.
1949 Flight of Nationalist government to
Taiwan after Chinese communist revolution.
1954 US-Taiwanese mutual defense treaty.
1971 Expulsion from United Nations.
1972 Commencement of legislature elections.
1975 President Chiang Kai-shek died;
replaced as Kuomintang leader by his son,
Chiang Ching-kuo.
1979 US severed diplomatic relations and
annulled 1954 security pact.
1986 Democratic Progressive Party (DPP)
formed as opposition to the nationalist
Kuomintang.
1987 Martial law lifted; opposition parties
legalized; press restrictions lifted.
1988 President Chiang Ching-kuo died;
replaced by Taiwanese-born Lee Teng-hui.
1989 Kuomintang (KMT) won assembly
elections.
1990 Formal move toward normalization of
relations with China. Hau Pei-tsun became
prime minister.
1991 President Lee Teng-hui declared end
to state of civil war with China. Constitution
amended. KMT won landslide victory in
assembly elections.
1992 Diplomatic relations with South Korea
broken.

1971, when they were expelled and replaced by
the People's Republic.
economic growth Taiwan was protected by
US naval forces during the Korean War 1950–
53 and signed a mutual defense treaty with
the US 1954. Benefiting from such security,
the country enjoyed a period of rapid economic growth during the 1950s and 1960s,
emerging as an export-oriented, newly industrialized country. Political power during these
years was concentrated in the hands of the
Kuomintang and the armed forces led by
President Chiang Kai-shek, with martial law
imposed and opposition activity outlawed.
external changes During the 1970s the
Taiwanese government was forced to adjust
to rapid external changes as the US adopted
a new policy of détente toward Communist
China. In Jan 1979 this culminated in the full
normalization of Sino-US relations, the severing of Taiwanese-US diplomatic contacts, and
the annulment of the US's 1954 security pact.
Other Western nations followed suit in ending
diplomatic relations with Taiwan during the
1970s and early 1980s.
democratization and "Taiwanization"
These developments, coupled with
generational change within the Kuomintang,
prompted a slow review of Taiwanese policies,
both domestic and external. Chiang Kai-shek
died in April 1975 and his son Chiang Ching-
kuo (1910–1988) became party chair and, from
1978, state president. Under his stewardship,
a program of gradual democratization and
"Taiwanization" was adopted, with elections
being held for "vacated seats" within the
national assembly and Legislative Yuan and
native Taiwanese being more rapidly inducted
into the Kuomintang. In the Dec 1986 elections a formal opposition party, the Democratic
Progressive Party (DPP), led by Chiang Peng-
chien, was tolerated and captured 22% of the
vote to the Kuomintang's 69%. In July 1987 martial law was lifted and replaced with a national
security law under which demonstrations and
the formation of opposition parties were legalized, provided they forswore communism, and
press restrictions were lifted.
accelerating reform President Chiang was
succeeded on his death by Lee Teng-hui,
the Taiwanese-born vice-president from 1984.
The new president accelerated the pace of
reform. Many "old guard" figures were retired 1988–89 and a plan for phasing out by
1992, through voluntary retirement, up to 200
mainland constituencies and replacing them
with Taiwanese deputies was approved. In
the Dec 1989 Legislative Yuan elections the
Kuomintang's vote share fell to 59% and the
DPP increased its number of seats from 12 to
21. In Sept 1990, on the death of a 95-year-old
legislator, the "ancient guard" Chinese-born
Kuomintang members became a minority within Taiwan's parliament and their influence
rapidly declined.
relations with China normalized On May
1, 1991 President Lee Teng-hui officially declared an end to the 42 years of "civil war"
("Period of Communist Rebellion") between
the Kuomintang government of the Republic
of China (Taiwan) and the People's Republic
of China. For the first time, the existence of
a Communist Party-led government in Beijing
was officially recognized and on April 28,
1991 the first formal Taiwanese delegation
visited Beijing. The country's constitution was
amended April 1991 in readiness for the
election of a new, islander-dominated national
assembly.

and New Guinea. It is about 10 ft/3 m long, and
has a brown back and yellow belly. Its venom
is fatal within minutes.

Taipei or *Taibei* capital and commercial center of Taiwan; industries include electronics,
plastics, textiles, and machinery; population
(1990) 2,719,700. The National Palace Museum 1965 houses the world's greatest
collection of Chinese art, taken there from the
mainland 1948.

Taira or *Heike* in Japanese history, a military
clan prominent in the 10th–12th centuries and
dominant at court 1159–85. Their destruction
by their rivals, the ♢Minamoto, 1185 is the subject of the 13th-century literary classic *Heike
Monogatari/The Tale of the Heike*.

Taiwan country in E Asia, officially the Republic of China, occupying the island of Taiwan
between the E China Sea and the S China
Sea, separated from the coast of China by the
Formosa Strait.
government The 325-member national assembly (Kuo-Min Ta-Hui) elects the president
and vice-president and has power to amend the
constitution of 1947. Until the 1991 elections,
its membership was dominated by veterans
who, originally elected from mainland China in
1947, were allowed to retain their seats as "life
members" after their constituencies fell under
communist Chinese control 1949.
  Taiwan's president, elected for a six-year
term, is head of state and commander-in-chief
of the armed forces, and promulgates laws. The

president works with a cabinet, the Executive
Yuan, headed by a prime minister, responsible
to a single-chamber legislature, the Legislative
Yuan. The Legislative Yuan comprises 125
members, Before 1972, it was dominated by
mainlander "life members." Now, however, all
its deputies have been elected in Taiwan. Three
Control, Judicial, and Examination Yuans also
exist, with the tasks of investigating the work
of the executive, interpreting the constitution,
and overseeing entrance examinations for
public offices.
history Taiwan, then known as Formosa ("the
beautiful"), was settled by ♢China from the
15th century, briefly occupied by the Dutch
during the mid-17th century, and annexed
by the Manchu dynasty 1683. It was ceded
to Japan under the terms of the Treaty of
Shimonoseki after the 1895 Sino-Japanese war
and not regained by China until the Japanese
surrender Aug 1945.
Chinese nationalist government In Dec
1949 Taiwan became the refuge for the Chinese nationalist government forces of ♢Chiang
Kai-shek which were compelled to evacuate
the mainland after their defeat by the communist troops of Mao Zedong. Chiang and his
nationalist followers dominated the island and
maintained an army of 600,000 in the hope of
reconquering the mainland, over which they
still claimed sovereignty. They continued to be
recognized by the US as the legitimate government of China, and occupied China's United
Nations and Security Council seats until Oct

Tajikistan
Republic of

area 55,251 sq mi/143,100 sq km
capital Dushanbe
cities Khodzhent (formerly Leninabad), Kurgan-Tyube, Kulyab
physical mountainous, more than half of its territory lying above 10,000 ft/3,000 m; huge mountain glaciers which are the source of many rapid rivers
features Pik Kommuniza (Communism Peak); health resorts and mineral springs
head of state to be elected
head of government Akbar Mizoyev from 1992
political system socialist pluralist

political parties Socialist (formerly Communist) Party of Tajikistan (SPT); Democratic Party; Islamic Revival Party
products fruit, cereals, cotton, cattle, sheep, silks, carpets, coal, lead, zinc, chemicals, oil, gas
population (1990) 5,300,000 (63% Tajik, 24% Uzbek, 8% Russian, 1% Tatar, 1% Kyrgyz, 1% Ukrainian)
language Tajik, similar to Farsi (Persian)
religion Sunni Muslim
chronology
1921 Part of Turkestan Soviet Socialist Autonomous Republic.
1929 Became a constituent republic of USSR.
1990 Ethnic Tajik/Armenian conflict in Dushanbe resulted in rioting against Communist Party of Tajikistan (TCP); state of emergency and curfew imposed.
1991 Jan: curfew lifted in Dushanbe. March: maintenance of Union endorsed in referendum. Aug: President Makhkamov forced to resign after failed anti-Gorbachev coup; TCP broke links with Moscow. Sept: declared independence; Nabiyev elected president; TCP renamed Socialist Party of Tajikistan (SPT); state of emergency declared. Dec: joined new Commonwealth of Independent States (CIS).
1992 Jan: admitted into Conference for Security and Cooperation in Europe (CSCE). Nabiyev temporarily ousted; state of emergency lifted. Feb: joined the Muslim Economic Cooperation Organization (ECO). March: admitted into United Nations (UN); US diplomatic recognition achieved. May: coalition government formed. Sept: Nabiyev forced to resign.

calls for independence rejected In Oct 1991 the opposition party, DPP, introduced a new clause into its charter which advocated Taiwanese independence and called for a plebiscite on the issue, despite the fact that calling for independence remained a seditious offense.

At the end of 1991 the 566 last remaining "life members" formally resigned from their legislative posts. In Dec 1991 a new national assembly was elected and became the first to be controlled by Taiwan-elected members. The KMT won a landslide victory when it captured 71% of the vote and 254 of the 325 seats at stake, thus securing the required majority to push through fundamental reform of the constitution. The DPP was clearly damaged by its technically illegal pro-independence stance; the Taiwanese remained concerned that a declaration of independence might prompt invasion by mainland China or an uprising by internal factional divisions.

Following the diplomatic pact between China and South Korea signed Aug 1992, Taiwan severed relations with the latter. South Africa was left as the only major country with full diplomatic links with Taiwan. *See illustration box.*

Taiyuan capital of Shanxi province, on the river Fen He, NE China; industries include iron, steel, agricultural machinery, and textiles; population (1989) 1,900,000. It is a walled city, founded in the 5th century AD, and is the seat of Shanxi University.

Tajik or *Tadzhik* speaker of any of the Tajiki dialects that belong to the Iranian branch of the Indo-European family. The Tajiks have long been associated with neighboring Turkic

peoples and their language contains Altaic loan words. The Tajiks inhabit Tajikistan, parts of Uzbekistan, and Afghanistan.

Tajikistan formerly (until 1991) *Tadzhikistan*, country in central Asia, bounded N by Kyrgyzstan and Uzbekistan, E by China, and S by Afghanistan and Pakistan.
government There is a 230-member legislature, the supreme soviet (parliament), to which deputies are elected by a majority system, and a second ballot "runoff" race in contests in which there is no clear first-round majority. From the majority grouping within the supreme soviet, a prime minister (chairman of the cabinet of ministers) is drawn. The state president is directly elected.
history The Tajiks are descended from the Mongol invaders who swept across Asia from the 13th century. Conquered by Tsarist Russia 1877–1900, and formed 1924 from the Tajik areas of Bokhara and Turkestan, it became a constituent republic of the Soviet Union 1929. Its people speak a Persian language.
growth of nationalism From the late 1980s there was a resurgence in Tajik consciousness. In 1989 a Rastakhiz ("Revival") Popular Front was established and during 1990 there were serious inter-ethnic clashes in Dushanbe.
independence declared The Communist Party of Tajikistan (CPT), led by the conservative Kakhar Makhkamov, initially supported the Aug 1991 anti-Gorbachev attempted coup in Moscow. However, after prodemocracy demonstrations in Dushanbe and a vote of no confidence, Makhkamov was forced to resign on Aug 31, 1991. Under acting president Kadreddin Aslonov, a declaration of independence was made on Sept 9, 1991, and the

activities of the CPT, now renamed the Socialist Party of Tajikistan (SPT), were banned on September 22. A day later, at a special session of the supreme soviet, this ban was overturned. Aslonov was replaced as president by Rakhman Nabiyev, the former Brezhnev-appointed CPT leader who had been removed by Mikhail ▷Gorbachev in 1985, and a three-month state of emergency was imposed. However, after more than a week of popular protest, hunger strikes, and civil disobedience, orchestrated by the opposition Union of Democratic Forces, Nabiyev agreed to resuspend the SPT, lift the state of emergency, legalize the opposition parties, step down as president, and hold direct elections on Nov 24, 1991. Nabiyev comfortably secured election, capturing 58% of the vote. However, the opposition, and outside observers, claimed that voting had been rigged.
CIS membership Tajikistan joined the ▷Commonwealth of Independent States (CIS) in Dec 1991. It was admitted into the ▷Conference on Security and Cooperation in Europe (CSCE) in Jan 1992 and, two months later, became a member of the United Nations (UN). In Feb Tajikistan joined the Economic Cooperation Organization (ECO) founded by Iran, Pakistan, and Turkey 1975, which aimed to reduce customs tariffs and eventually form a customs union. US diplomatic recognition was also given at this time. In May 1992, because of public unrest, President Nabiyev was forced into a coalition with opposition leaders and in Sept he was forced to resign.

Taj Mahal white marble mausoleum built 1630–53 on the river Jumna near Agra, India. Erected by Shah Jahan to the memory of his favorite wife, it is a celebrated example of Indo-Islamic architecture, the fusion of Muslim and Hindu styles.

It took 20,000 workers to build the Taj Mahal, which has a central dome and minarets on each corner. Every façade is inlaid with semiprecious stones. Ransacked in the 18th century, it was restored in the early 20th century and is a symbol of India to the world.

Tajo Spanish name for the river ▷Tagus.

takahe flightless bird *Porphyrio mantelli* of the rail family, native to New Zealand. It is about 2 ft/60 cm tall, with blue and green plumage and a red beak. The takahe was thought to have become extinct at the end of the 19th century, but in 1948 small numbers were rediscovered in the tussock grass of a mountain valley on South Island.

takeover in business, the acquisition by one company of a sufficient number of shares in another company to have effective control of that company—usually 51%, although a controlling stake may be as little as 30%.

Takeovers may be agreed or contested; methods employed include the ▷*dawn raid*, and methods of avoiding an unwelcome takeover include ▷*reverse takeover*, ▷*poison pills*, or inviting a ▷*white knight* to make a takeover bid.

Takeshita Noboru 1924– . Japanese right-wing politician. Elected to parliament as a Liberal Democratic Party (LDP) deputy 1958, he became president of the LDP and prime minister Oct 1987. He and members of his administration were shown in the ▷Recruit scandal to have been involved in insider-trading and he resigned April 1989.

Talbot William Henry Fox 1800–1877. English pioneer of photography. He invented the paper-based ▷calotype process, the first negative/positive method. Talbot made photograms several years before Louis Daguerre's invention was announced.

talc $Mg_3Si_4O_{10}(OH)_2$, mineral, hydrous magnesium silicate. It occurs in tabular crystals, but the massive impure form, known as *steatite* or *soapstone*, is more common. It is formed by the alteration of magnesium compounds and usually found in metamorphic rocks. Talc is very soft, ranked 1 on the Mohs' scale of hardness. It is used in powdered form in cosmetics, lubricants, and as an additive in paper manufacture.

French chalk and potstone are varieties of talc. Soapstone has a greasy feel to it, and is used for carvings such as Inuit sculptures.

Talien part of the port of ▷Lüda, China.

Talking Heads US New Wave rock group formed 1975 in New York; disbanded 1991. Their nervy minimalist music was inspired by African rhythms; albums include *More Songs About Buildings and Food* 1978, *Little Creatures* 1985, and *Naked* 1988.

Tallahassee (Cree Indian "old town") capital of Florida; an agricultural and lumbering center; population (1990) 124,800. The Spanish explorer Hernando de Soto (1496–1542) founded an Indian settlement here 1539, and the site was chosen as the Florida territorial capital 1821.

During the Civil War, Tallahassee was the only Confederate capital east of the Mississippi River not captured by Union troops, and the city still has many pre–Civil War mansions.

Florida Agricultural and Mechanical University and Florida State University are here.

Talleyrand Charles Maurice de Talleyrand-Périgord 1754–1838. French politician and diplomat. As bishop of Autun 1789–91 he supported moderate reform during the ▷French Revolution, was excommunicated by the pope, and fled to the US during the Reign of Terror (persecution of antirevolutionaries). He returned and became foreign minister under the Directory 1797–99 and under Napoleon 1799–1807. He represented France at the Congress of ▷Vienna 1814–15.

Tallinn (German *Reval*) naval port and capital of Estonia; industries include electrical and oil-drilling machinery, textiles, and paper; population (1987) 478,000. Founded 1219, it was a member of the ▷Hanseatic League; it passed to Sweden 1561 and to Russia 1750. Vyshgorod castle (13th century) and other medieval buildings remain. It is a yachting center.

Talmud the two most important works of post-Biblical Jewish literature. The Babylonian and the Palestinian (or Jerusalem) Talmud provide a compilation of ancient Jewish law and tradition. The Babylonian Talmud was edited at the end of the 5th century AD and is the more authoritative version for later Judaism; both Talmuds are written in a mix of Hebrew and Aramaic. They contain the commentary (*gemara*) on the ▷Mishna (early rabbinical commentaries compiled about AD 200), and the material can be generally divided into *halakhah*, consisting of legal and ritual matters, and *haggadah*, concerned with ethical, theological, and folklorist matters.

talus the pile of rubble and sediment that forms an ascending slope at the foot of a mountain range or cliff.

The rock fragments that form a talus are usually slide rock or pieces broken off by frost action. As fragments are loosened they clatter downward in a series of free falls, bounces, and slides. With time, the rock waste builds in a heap or sheet of rubble that may eventually bury even the upper cliffs, and the growth of the talus then stops. Usually, however, erosional forces decompose the rock waste so that a talus stays restricted to lower slopes.

tamandua tree-living toothless anteater *Tamandua tetradactyla* found in tropical forests and tree savanna from S Mexico to Brazil. About 1.8 ft/56 cm long with a prehensile tail of equal length, it has strong foreclaws with which it can break into nests of tree ants and termites, which it licks up with its narrow tongue.

Tamar in the Old Testament, the sister of ▷Absalom. She was raped by her half brother Amnon, who was then killed by Absalom.

tamarack coniferous tree *Larix laricina*, native to boggy soils in North America, where it is used for timber. It is a type of larch.

tamarind evergreen tropical tree *Tamarindus indica*, family Leguminosae, native to the Old World, with pinnate leaves and reddish-yellow flowers, followed by pods. The pulp surrounding the seeds is used medicinally and as a flavoring.

tamarisk any small tree or shrub of the genus *Tamarix*, flourishing in warm, salty, desert regions of Europe and Asia where no other vegetation is found. The common tamarisk *T. gallica* has scalelike leaves and spikes of very small, pink flowers.

Tambo Oliver 1917– . South African nationalist politician, in exile 1960–90, president of the African National Congress (ANC) 1977–91. Because of poor health, he was given the honorary post of national chair July 1991, and Nelson ▷Mandela resumed the ANC presidency.

tambourine musical percussion instrument of ancient origin, almost unchanged since Roman times, consisting of a shallow drum with a single skin and loosely set jingles in the rim that increase its effect.

Tamerlane or *Tamburlaine* or *Timur i Leng* 1336–1405. Mongol ruler of ▷Samarkand from 1369 who conquered Persia, Azerbaijan, Armenia, and Georgia. He defeated the ▷Golden Horde 1395, sacked Delhi 1398, invaded Syria and Anatolia, and captured the Ottoman sultan in Ankara 1402; he died invading China.

Tamil member of the majority ethnic group living in the Indian state of Tamil Nadu (formerly Madras). Tamils also live in S India, N Sri Lanka, Malaysia, Singapore, and South Africa, totaling 35–55 million worldwide. Tamil belongs to the Dravidian family of languages; written records in Tamil date from the 3rd century BC. The 3 million Tamils in Sri Lanka are predominantly Hindu, although some are Muslims, unlike the Sinhalese majority, who are mainly Buddhist. The *Tamil Tigers*, most prominent of the various Tamil groupings, are attempting to create a separate homeland in N Sri Lanka through both political and military means.

The Dravidian ancestors of the Tamils settled in S India well before the arrival of the Aryans from the NW. Although they share the Hindu religion with their northern neighbors, the Tamils retain a distinct culture. They possess an ancient literary tradition and have developed their own court arts. The majority of Tamils are farmers, cultivating rice in irrigated fields. They are also known for their handicrafts, including pottery. During the 19th century the British encouraged Tamils to move to work on plantations in Sri Lanka, where there was already a Tamil population, and Malaysia. In both countries many Tamils have gained access to higher education and sought employment in government service and the professions.

Tamil Nadu formerly (until 1968) *Madras State* state of SE India
area 50,219 sq mi/130,100 sq km
capital Madras
products mainly industrial: cotton, textiles, silk, electrical machinery, tractors, rubber, sugar refining
population (1991) 55,638,300
language Tamil
history the present state was formed 1956. Tamil Nadu comprises part of the former British Madras presidency (later province) formed from areas taken from France and Tipu Sahib, the sultan of Mysore, in the 18th century, which became a state of the Republic of India 1950. The northeast was detached to form Andhra Pradesh 1953; in 1956 other areas went to Kerala and Mysore (now Karnataka), and the Laccadive Islands (now Lakshadweep) became a separate Union Territory.

Taming of the Shrew, The comedy by William Shakespeare, first performed 1593–94. Bianca, who has many suitors, must not marry until her elder sister Katherina (the shrew) has done so. Petruchio agrees to woo Katherina so that his friend Hortensio may marry Bianca. Petruchio succeeds in "taming" Katherina but Bianca marries another.

Tammany Hall Democratic Party organization in New York. It originated 1789 as the Society of St Tammany, named after an American Indian chief. It was dominant from 1800 until the 1930s and gained a reputation for corruption and rule by bosses; its domination was broken by Mayor ▷La Guardia in the 1930s and Mayor Koch in the 1970s.

Tammuz in Sumerian legend, a vegetation god, who died at midsummer and was brought back from the underworld in spring by his lover Ishtar. His cult spread over Babylonia, Syria, Phoenicia, and Palestine. In Greek mythology Tammuz appears as ▷Adonis.

Tampa port and resort on Tampa Bay in W Florida; industries include fruit and vegetable canning, shipbuilding, and the manufacture of fertilizers, clothing, beer, and cigars; population (1990) 280,000.

Tampa was settled 1823, and a fort was built the next year that was taken from Confederate forces by Union troops in the Civil War.

The University of South Florida and Busch Gardens are here. Economic growth was spurred in the 1880s by the discovery of phosphates in the area, the arrival of the railroad, and the establishment of a cigar-making industry.

Tampere (Swedish *Tammerfors*) city in SW Finland; industries include textiles, paper, footwear, and turbines; population (1990) 172,600, metropolitan area 258,000. It is the second largest city in Finland.

Tampico port on the Rio Pánuco, 6 mi/10 km from the Gulf of Mexico, in Tamaulipas state, Mexico; industries include oil refining and fishing; population (1980) 268,000.

$$\tan(\text{gent}) \ \beta = \frac{\sin \beta}{\cos \beta} = \frac{\text{opposite}}{\text{adjacent}} = \frac{AC}{BC}$$

tangent *The tangent of an angle is a mathematical function used in the study of right triangles.*

Tana lake in Ethiopia, 5,900 ft/1,800 m above sea level; area 1,390 sq mi/3,600 sq km. It is the source of the Blue Nile.

tanager any of various New World passerine birds, of the family Emberizidae, which also includes blackbirds, orioles, and grackles (or crow blackbirds). Tanagers that breed in N America all belong to the genus *Piranga* and include the scarlet tanager *P. olivacea*, about 7 in/18 cm long. There are about 230 species in forests of Central and South America; all males are brilliantly colored.

Tanaka Kakuei 1918– . Japanese right-wing politician, leader of the dominant Liberal Democratic Party (LDP) and prime minister 1972–74. In 1976 he was charged with corruption and resigned from the LDP but remained a powerful faction leader.

In the Diet (Japanese parliament) from 1947, Tanaka was minister of finance 1962–65 and of international trade and industry 1971–72, before becoming LDP leader. In 1974 he had to resign the premiership because of allegations of corruption and 1976 he was arrested for accepting bribes from the Lockheed Corporation while premier. He was found guilty 1983, but remained in the Diet as an independent deputy pending appeal. He was also implicated in the 1988–89 ◊Recruit scandal of insider trading.

Tananarive former name for ◊Antananarivo, capital of Madagascar.

Taney Roger Brooke 1777–1864. US lawyer and chief justice of the US. In 1835 he succeeded John Marshall as chief justice of the US Supreme Court. In 1857 he ruled in the Dred Scott case that Congress had no right to ban slavery in the territories, a decision that gravely aggravated sectional tensions.

Born in Calvert County, Maryland, Taney was educated at Dickinson College and became a lawyer 1799. He served as a Maryland state senator 1816–21, state attorney general 1827–31, President Jackson's attorney general 1831, and US secretary of the treasury 1833–35.

Tanganyika former British colony in E Africa, which now forms the mainland of ◊Tanzania.

Tanganyika, Lake lake 2,534 ft/772 m above sea level in the Great Rift Valley, E Africa, with Zaire to the W, Zambia to the S, and Tanzania and Burundi to the E. It is about 400 mi/645 km long, with an area of about 12,000 sq mi/31,000 sq km, and is the deepest lake (4,710 ft/1,435 m) in Africa. The mountains around its shores rise to about 8,860 ft/2,700 m. The chief ports are Bujumbura (Burundi), Kigoma (Tanzania), and Kalémié (Zaire).

Tange Kenzo 1913– . Japanese architect. His works include the National Gymnasium,

Tokyo, for the 1964 Olympics, and the city of Abuja, planned to replace Lagos as the capital of Nigeria.

tangent in geometry, a straight line that touches a curve and has the same ◊gradient as the curve at the point of contact. At a maximum or minimum, the tangent to a curve has zero gradient. Also, in trigonometry, a function of an acute angle in a right-angled triangle, defined as the ratio of the length of the side opposite the angle to the length of the side adjacent to it; a way of expressing the slope of a line.

tangerine small ◊orange *Citrus reticulata.*

Tangier or *Tangiers* or *Tanger* port in N Morocco, on the Strait of Gibraltar; population (1982) 436,227. It was a Phoenician trading center in the 15th century BC. Captured by the Portuguese 1471, it passed to England 1662 as part of the dowry of Catherine of Braganza, but was abandoned 1684, and later became a lair of ◊Barbary Coast pirates. From 1923 Tangier and a small surrounding enclave became an international zone, administered by Spain 1940–45. In 1956 it was transferred to independent Morocco and became a free port 1962.

tango couples dance of Latin-American origin or the music for it. The dance consists of two long sliding steps followed by three short steps and stylized body positions.

Tangshan industrial city in Hebei province, China; population (1986) 1,390,000. Almost destroyed by an earthquake 1976, with 200,000 killed, it was rebuilt on a new site, coal seams being opened up under the old city.

Tanguy Yves 1900–1955. French Surrealist painter who lived in the US from 1939. His inventive canvases feature semiabstract creatures in a barren landscape.

Tanguy was first inspired to paint by de ◊Chirico's work and in 1925 he joined the Surrealist movement. He soon developed his characteristic style with bizarre, slender forms in a typically Surrealist wasteland.

Tanizaki Jun-ichirō 1886–1965. Japanese novelist. His works include a version of ◊Murasaki's *The Tale of Genji* 1939–41, *The Makioka Sisters* in three volumes 1943–48, and *The Key* 1956.

His work matured when he moved from Tokyo after the 1923 earthquake to the Kyoto-Osaka region, where ancient tradition is stronger.

tank armored fighting vehicle that runs on tracks and is fitted with weapons systems capable of defeating other tanks and destroying life and property. The term was originally a code name for the first effective tracked and armored fighting vehicle, invented by the British soldier and scholar Ernest Swinton, and used in the battle of the Somme 1916.

A tank consists of a body or hull of thick steel, on which are mounted machine guns and a larger gun. The hull contains the crew (usually consisting of a commander, driver, and one or two soldiers), engine, radio, fuel tanks, and ammunition. The tank travels on caterpillar tracks that enable it to cross rough ground and debris. It is known today as an MBT (main battle tank).

Tannenberg, Battle of two battles, named after a village now in N Poland:
1410 the Poles and Lithuanians defeated the Teutonic Knights, establishing Poland as a major power;

1914 during World War I, when Tannenberg was part of East Prussia, ◊Hindenburg defeated the Russians.

tannic acid or *tannin* $C_{14}H_{10}O_9$ yellow astringent substance, composed of several ◊phenol rings, occurring in the bark, wood, roots, fruits, and galls (growths) of certain trees, such as the oak. It precipitates gelatin to give an insoluble compound, used in the manufacture of leather from hides (tanning).

tanning treating animal skins to preserve them and make them into leather. In vegetable tanning, the prepared skins are soaked in tannic acid. Chrome tanning, which is much quicker, uses solutions of chromium salts.

tansy perennial herb *Tanacetum vulgare*, family Compositae, native to Europe. The yellow flower heads grow in clusters on stalks up to 4 ft/120 cm tall, and the aromatic leaves are used in cooking.

tantalum hard, ductile, lustrous, gray-white, metallic element, symbol Ta, atomic number 73, atomic weight 180.948. It occurs with niobium in tantalite and other minerals. It can be drawn into wire with a very high melting point and great tenacity, useful for lamp filaments subject to vibration. It is also used in alloys, for corrosion-resistant laboratory apparatus and chemical equipment, as a catalyst in manufacturing synthetic rubber, in tools and instruments, and in rectifiers and capacitors.

It was discovered and named 1802 by Swedish chemist Anders Ekeberg (1767–1813) after the mythological Greek character Tantalus.

Tantalus in Greek mythology, a king whose crimes were punished in ◊Tartarus (a part of the underworld) by the provision of food and drink he could not reach.

Tantrism forms of Hinduism and Buddhism that emphasize the division of the universe into male and female forces that maintain its unity by their interaction; this gives women equal status with men. Tantric Hinduism is associated with magical and sexual yoga practices that imitate the union of Siva and Sakti, as described in religious books known as the *Tantras*. In Buddhism, the *Tantras* are texts attributed to the Buddha, describing methods of attaining enlightenment.

Tantric Buddhism, practiced in medieval India, depended on the tuition of teachers and the use of yoga, mantras, and meditation to enable its followers to master themselves and gain oneness with the universe.

Tanzania country in E Africa, bounded N by Uganda and Kenya; S by Mozambique, Malawi, and Zambia; W by Zaire, Burundi, and Rwanda; and E by the Indian Ocean.
government The 1977 constitution made Tanzania a one-party socialist republic with the Revolutionary Party of Tanzania (CCM). The president is chosen by the party to serve a maximum of two five-year terms. The president appoints two vice-presidents from members of the National Assembly, and if the president comes from the mainland, the first vice-president must come from Zanzibar. The second vice-president is termed prime minister. The president also appoints and presides over a cabinet.

The single-chamber National Assembly has 243 members: 118 directly elected by universal suffrage for the mainland, 50 for the islands of Zanzibar and Pemba, 25 regional commissioners, 15 nominated by the president and 35 indirectly elected, to represent specific sections, including women and party organizations.

history For early history, see ⏵Africa. Zanzibar was under Portuguese control during the 16th–17th centuries. In 1822 it was united with the nearby island of Pemba. It was a British protectorate 1890–1963, when it became an independent sultanate; an uprising followed, and the sultan was overthrown 1964.

independence Tanganyika was a German colony 1884–1914, until conquered by Britain during World War I; it was a British League of Nations mandate 1920–46 and came under United Nations (UN) trusteeship 1946–62. It achieved full independence within the British ⏵Commonwealth, 1961, with Julius ⏵Nyerere as prime minister. He gave up the post some six weeks after independence to devote himself to the development of the Tanganyika African National Union (TANU), but in Dec 1962, when Tanganyika became a republic, he returned to become the nation's first president.

United Republic of Tanzania Tanzania was founded by the union of Tanganyika and Zanzibar April 1964. Nyerere became president of the new United Republic of Tanzania and dominated the nation's politics for the next 20 years, being reelected 1965, 1970, 1975, and 1980. Known throughout Tanzania as Mwalimu ("teacher"), he established himself as a Christian socialist who attempted to put into practice a philosophy that he believed

would secure his country's future. He committed himself in the Arusha Declaration of 1967 (the name comes from the N Tanzanian town where he made his historic statement) to building a socialist state for the millions of poor peasants through a series of village cooperatives (*ujamas*). Nyerere became one of Africa's most respected politicians. In the final years of his presidency economic pressures, domestic and international, forced him to compromise his ideals and accept a more capitalistic society than he would have wished, but his achievements have included the best public health service on the African continent, according to UN officials, and a universal primary school system.

foreign relations Relations between Tanzania and its neighbors have been variable. The East Africa Community (EAC) of Tanzania, Kenya, and Uganda, formed 1967, broke up 1977, and relations between Tanzania and the more capitalistic Kenya became uneasy. In 1979 Nyerere sent troops to support the Uganda National Liberation Front in its bid to overthrow President Idi Amin. This enhanced Nyerere's reputation but damaged his country's economy. Tanzania also supported the liberation movements in Mozambique and Rhodesia.

In 1977 TANU and the Afro-Shirazi Party of Zanzibar merged to become the Revolutionary Party of Tanzania (CCM), and this was made the only legal political organization. Nyerere

retired from the presidency at the end of 1985 but remained as CCM chair. The president of Zanzibar, Ali Hassan Mwinyi, was adopted as the sole presidential candidate by the CCM congress Dec 1985. In May 1990 Julius Nyerere announced his retirement as party chair and in Aug 1990 he was replaced by President Mwinyi.

end of one-party rule In Feb 1992 the governing CCM party endorsed a proposal to introduce multiparty politics; Mwinyi's government had tolerated the formation of at least five opposition groups since 1991. Also in Feb, it was announced that the East Africa co-operation agreement with Kenya and Uganda would be revived. *See illustration box.*

Taoism Chinese philosophical system, traditionally founded by the Chinese philosopher Lao Zi 6th century BC. He is also attributed authorship of the scriptures, *Tao Te Ching*, although these were apparently compiled 3rd century BC. The "tao" or "way" denotes the hidden principle of the universe, and less stress is laid on good deeds than on harmonious interaction with the environment, which automatically ensures right behavior. The magical side of Taoism is illustrated by the *I Ching* or *Book of Changes*, a book of divination.

beliefs The universe is believed to be kept in balance by the opposing forces of yin and yang that operate in dynamic tension between themselves. Yin is female and watery: the force in the moon and rain which reaches its peak in the winter; yang is masculine and solid: the force in the sun and earth which reaches its peak in the summer. The interaction of yin and yang is believed to shape all life.

This magical, ritualistic aspect of Taoism developed from the 2nd century AD and was largely responsible for its popular growth; it stresses physical immortality, and this was attempted by means ranging from dietary regulation and fasting to alchemy. By the 3rd century, worship of gods had begun to appear, including that of the stove god Tsao Chun. From the 4th century, rivalry between Taoists and Mahāyāna Buddhists was strong in China, leading to persecution of one religion by the other; this was resolved by mutual assimilation, and Taoism developed monastic communities similar to those of the Buddhists.

Taoist texts record the tradition of mental and physical discipline, and methods to use in healing, exorcism, and the quest for immortality. The second major work is that of Zhuangzi (*c.* 389–286 BC), *The Way of Zhuangzi*.

tap dancing rapid step dance, derived from clog dancing. Its main characteristic is the tapping of toes and heels accentuated by steel taps affixed to the shoes. It was popularized in vaudeville and in 1930s films by such dancers as Fred Astaire and Bill "Bojangles" Robinson (1878–1949).

tape recording, magnetic method of recording electric signals on a layer of iron oxide, or other magnetic material, coating a thin plastic tape. The electrical signals from the microphone are fed to the electromagnetic recording head, which magnetizes the tape in accordance with the frequency and amplitude of the original signal. The impulses may be audio (for sound recording), video (for television), or data (for computer). For playback, the tape is passed over the same, or another, head to convert magnetic into electrical signals, which are then amplified for reproduction. Tapes are easily demagnetized (erased) for reuse, and come in cassette, cartridge, or reel form.

Tanzania
United Republic of (*Jamhuri ya Muungano wa Tanzania*)

area 364,865 sq mi/945,000 sq km
capital Dodoma (since 1983)
cities Zanzibar Town, Mwanza; chief port and former capital Dar es Salaam
physical central plateau; lakes in N and W; coastal plains; lakes Victoria, Tanganyika, and Niasa
environment the black rhino faces extinction as a result of poaching
features comprises islands of Zanzibar and Pemba; Mount Kilimanjaro, 19,340 ft/5,895 m, the highest peak in Africa; Serengeti National Park, Olduvai Gorge; Ngorongoro Crater, 9 mi/14.5 km across, 2,500 ft/762 m deep
head of state and government Ali Hassan Mwinyi from 1985
political system one-party socialist republic
political party Revolutionary Party of Tanzania (CCM), African, socialist
exports coffee, cotton, sisal, cloves, tea,

tobacco, cashew nuts, diamonds
currency Tanzanian shilling
population (1990 est) 26,070,000; growth rate 3.5% p.a.
life expectancy men 49, women 54 (1989)
languages Kiswahili, English (both official)
religion Muslim 35%, Christian 35%, traditional 30%
literacy 85% (1987)
GNP $4.9 bn; $258 per head (1987)
chronology
16th–17th centuries Zanzibar under Portuguese control.
1890–1963 Zanzibar became a British protectorate.
1920–46 Tanganyika administered as a British League of Nations mandate.
1946–62 Tanganyika came under United Nations (UN) trusteeship.
1961 Tanganyika achieved independence from Britain, within the Commonwealth, with Julius Nyerere as prime minister.
1962 Tanganyika became a republic with Nyerere as president.
1964 Tanganyika and Zanzibar became the United Republic of Tanzania with Nyerere as president.
1967 East African Community (EAC) formed. Arusha Declaration.
1977 Revolutionary Party of Tanzania (CCM) proclaimed the only legal party. EAC dissolved.
1978 Ugandan forces repulsed after crossing into Tanzania.
1979 Tanzanian troops sent to Uganda to help overthrow the president, Idi Amin.
1985 Nyerere retired from presidency but stayed on as CCM leader; Ali Hassan Mwinyi became president.
1990 Nyerere surrendered CCM leadership; replaced by President Mwinyi.
1992 CCM agreed to abolish one-party rule. East African cooperation pact with Kenya and Uganda to be reestablished.

tapestry ornamental woven textile used for wall hangings, furniture, and curtains. The tapestry design is threaded into the warp with various shades of yarn. The great European centers of tapestry weaving were in Belgium, France, and England. The ⟡Bayeux Tapestry is an embroidery rather than a true tapestry.

Tapestries have been woven for centuries in many countries, and during the Middle Ages the art was practiced in monasteries. European tapestries of the 13th century frequently featured oriental designs brought back by the Crusaders. The ⟡Gobelins tapestry factory of Paris was made a royal establishment in the 17th century. In England, William Morris established the Merton Abbey looms in the late 19th century. Other designers have included the painters Raphael, Rubens, and Burne-Jones.

tapeworm any of various parasitic flatworms of the class Cestoda. They lack digestive and sense organs, can reach 50 ft/15 m in length, and attach themselves to the host's intestines by means of hooks and suckers. Tapeworms are made up of hundreds of individual segments, each of which develops into a functional hermaphroditic reproductive unit capable of producing numerous eggs. The larvae of tapeworms usually reach humans in imperfectly cooked meat or fish, causing anemia and intestinal disorders.

tapioca granular starch used in cooking, produced from the ⟡cassava root.

tapir any of the odd-toed hoofed mammals (perissodactyls) of the single genus *Tapirus*, now constituting the family Tapiridae. There are four species living in the American and Malaysian tropics. They reach 3 ft/1 m at the shoulder and weigh up to 770 lb/350 kg. Their survival is in danger because of destruction of the forests.

The Malaysian tapir *T. indicus* is black with a large white patch on the back and hindquarters. The three South American species are dark to reddish brown.

Their general body form is rounded in back and tapering up front, with a short tail and a short trunk.

taproot in botany, a single, robust, main ⟡root that is derived from the embryonic root, or ⟡radicle, and grows vertically downward, often to considerable depth. Taproots are often modified for food storage and are common in biennial plants such as the carrot *Daucus carota*, where they act as ⟡perennating organs.

tar dark brown or black viscous liquid obtained by the destructive distillation of coal, shale, and wood. Tars consist of a mixture of hydrocarbons, acids, and bases. ⟡Creosote and ⟡paraffin are produced from wood tar. See also ⟡coal tar.

Tara Hill ancient religious and political center in County Meath, S Ireland. It was the site of a palace and coronation place of many Irish kings, abandoned in the 6th century. St ⟡Patrick preached here.

tarantella peasant dance of southern Italy; also a piece of music composed for, or in the rhythm of, this dance, in fast six-eight time.

Taranto naval base and port in Puglia region, SE Italy; population (1988) 245,000. It is an important commercial center, and its steelworks are part of the new industrial complex of S Italy. It was the site of the ancient Greek *Tarentum*, founded in the 8th century BC by ⟡Sparta, and was captured by the Romans 272 BC.

tarantula wolf spider *Lycosa tarantula* with a 1 in/2.5 cm body. It spins no web, relying on its speed in hunting to catch its prey. The name "tarantula" is also used for any of the numerous large, hairy spiders of the family Theraphosidae, with large poison fangs, native to the SW US and tropical America.

In the Middle Ages, the wolf spider's bite was thought to cause hysterical ailments for which dancing was the cure, hence the dance named "tarantella."

Tarawa port and capital of Kiribati; population (1990) 28,800.

Tarbell Ida Minerva 1857–1944. US journalist whose exposés of corruption in high places made her one of the most prominent "muckrakers" in the US. She was an editor and contributor to *McClure's Magazine* 1894–1906. Her book *The History of the Standard Oil Company* 1904 sparked antitrust reform. From 1906 to 1915 she joined Lincoln Steffens and Ray Stannard Baker on the staff of the *American Magazine*.

Tarbell was born in Erie County, Pennsylvania, educated at Allegheny College and the Sorbonne, Paris, and became an editor of the *Chautauquan* 1883. Her autobiography, *All in a Day's Work*, appeared 1939.

tare alternative common name for ⟡vetch.

tariff tax or duty placed on goods when they are imported into a country or trading bloc (such as the European Community) from outside. The aim of tariffs is to reduce imports by making them more expensive. Organizations such as the EC, the European Free Trade Association (EFTA), and the General Agreement on Tariffs and Trade (GATT) have worked toward mutual lowering of tariffs among countries.

Tariffs have generally been used by governments to protect home industries from lower-priced foreign goods, and have been opposed by supporters of free trade. For a tariff to be successful, it must not provoke retaliatory tariffs from other countries.

Tarim Basin (Chinese *Tarim Pendi*) internal drainage area in Xinjiang Uygur province, NW China, between the Tien Shan and Kunlun mountains; area about 350,000 sq mi/ 900,000 sq km. It is crossed by the river Tarim He and includes the lake of Lop Nur. The Taklimakan desert lies to the south of the Tarim He.

Tarkington Booth 1869–1946. US novelist, born in Indiana, author of *Monsieur Beaucaire* 1900 and novels of the Midwest, such as *The Magnificent Ambersons* 1918 (filmed 1941 by Orson Welles). His novels for young people, which include *Penrod* 1914, are classics. He was among the best-selling authors of the early 20th century.

taro or *eddo* plant *Colocasia esculenta* of the arum family Araceae, native to tropical Asia; the tubers are edible and are the source of Polynesian poi (a fermented food).

tarot cards fortune-telling aid consisting of 78 cards: the *minor arcana* in four suits (resembling playing cards) and the *major arcana*, 22 cards with densely symbolic illustrations that have links with astrology and the ⟡Kabbala.

history The earliest known reference to tarot cards is from 1392. The pack is of unknown (probably medieval) origin and may have been designed in Europe in the early 14th century as a repository of Gnostic ideas then being suppressed by the Christian church. Since the

18th century the tarot has interested occult scholars.

tarpon large silver-sided fish *Tarpon atlanticus* of the family Megalopidae. It reaches 6 ft/2 m and may weigh 300 lb/135 kg. It lives in warm W Atlantic waters.

Tarquinius Superbus lived 5th century BC. Last king of Rome 534–510 BC. He abolished certain rights of Romans, and made the city powerful. He was deposed when his son Sextus raped ⟡Lucretia.

tarragon perennial bushy herb *Artemisia dracunculus* of the daisy family Compositae, native to the Old World, growing to 5 ft/1.5 m, with narrow leaves and small green-white flower heads arranged in groups. Tarragon contains an aromatic oil; its leaves are used to flavor salads, pickles, and tartar sauce. It is closely related to wormwood.

Tarshish city mentioned in the Old Testament, probably the Phoenician settlement of Tartessus in Spain.

tarsier any of three species of the prosimian primates, genus *Tarsius*, of the East Indies and the Philippines. These survivors of early primates are about the size of a rat with thick, light-brown fur, very large eyes, and long feet and hands. They are nocturnal, arboreal, and eat insects and lizards.

Tarsus city in İçel province, SE Turkey, on the river Pamuk; population (1980) 121,000. Formerly the capital of the Roman province of Cilicia, it was the birthplace of St ⟡Paul.

tartan woolen cloth woven in specific checked patterns individual to Scottish clans, with stripes of different widths and colors crisscrossing on a colored background; used in making skirts, kilts, trousers, and other articles of clothing.

Developed in the 17th century, tartan was banned after the 1745 ⟡Jacobite rebellion, and not legalized again until 1782.

tartaric acid $HCOO(CHOH)_2COOH$ organic acid present in vegetable tissues and fruit juices in the form of salts of potassium, calcium, and magnesium. It is used in carbonated drinks and baking powders.

Tartarus in Greek mythology, a part of ⟡Hades, the underworld, where the wicked were punished.

Tartini Giuseppe 1692–1770. Italian composer and violinist. In 1728 he founded a school of violin playing in Padua. A leading exponent of violin technique, he composed the *Devil's Trill* sonata, about 1714.

Tarzan fictitious hero inhabiting the African rainforest, created by US writer Edgar Rice ⟡Burroughs in *Tarzan of the Apes* 1914, with numerous sequels. He and his partner Jane have featured in films, comic strips, and television series.

Tarzan, raised by apes from infancy, is in fact a British peer, Lord Greystoke. He has enormous physical strength and the ability to communicate with animals. Jane Porter, an American, falls in love with him while on safari and elects to stay.

Tasaday member of an indigenous people of the rainforests of Mindanao in the ⟡Philippines, contacted in the 1960s. Some anthropologists doubt their claim to leading a hunter-gatherer way of life.

Tashkent capital of Uzbekistan; population (1990) 2,100,000. Industries include the manufacture of mining machinery, chemicals, textiles, and leather goods. Founded in the 7th century, it was taken by the Turks in the 12th century and captured by Tamerlane 1361. In 1865 it was taken by the Russians. It was severely damaged by an earthquake 1966.

A temporary truce between Pakistan and India over ◊Kashmir was established at the **Declaration of Tashkent** 1966.

Tasman Abel Janszoon 1603–1659. Dutch navigator. In 1642, he was the first European to see Tasmania. He also made the first European sightings of New Zealand, Tonga, and Fiji.

Tasmania former name (1642–1856) **Van Diemen's Land** island off the south coast of Australia; a state of the Commonwealth of Australia;
area 26,171 sq mi/67,800 sq km
capital Hobart
cities Launceston (chief port)
features an island state (including small islands in the Bass Strait, and Macquarie Island); Franklin River, a wilderness area saved from a hydroelectric scheme 1983, which also has a prehistoric site; unique fauna including the Tasmanian devil
products wool, dairy products, apples and other fruit, timber, iron, tin, coal, copper, silver
population (1987) 448,000
history the first European to visit here was Abel Tasman 1642; the last of the Tasmanian Aboriginals died 1876. Tasmania joined the Australian Commonwealth as a state 1901.

Tasmanian devil carnivorous marsupial *Sarcophilus harrisii*, in the same family (Dasyuridae) as native "cats." It is about 2.1 ft/ 65 cm long with a 10 in/25 cm bushy tail. It has a large head, strong teeth, and is blackish with white patches on the chest and hind parts. It is nocturnal, carnivorous, and can be ferocious when cornered. It has recently become extinct in Australia and survives only in remote parts of Tasmania.

Tasmanian wolf or **thylacine** carnivorous marsupial *Thylacinus cynocephalus*, in the family Dasyuridae. It is doglike in appearance and can be nearly 6 ft/2 m from nose to tail tip. It was hunted to probable extinction in the 1930s, but there are still occasional unconfirmed reports of sightings.

The dingo exterminated the Tasmanian wolf on the Australian mainland.

Tasman Sea part of the ◊Pacific Ocean between SE Australia and NW New Zealand. It is named after the Dutch explorer Abel Tasman.

Tass acronym **Telegrafnoye Agentstvo Sovyetskovo Soyuza**, the international news agency of the former Soviet Union. In Jan 1992 the creation of a replacement body, the Russian Information Telegraph Agency (RITA), was announced, although the name TASS was to be retained for the domestic wire service within the Commonwealth of Independent States.

Tasso Torquato 1544–1595. Italian poet, author of the romantic epic poem of the First Crusade *Gerusalemme Liberata/Jerusalem Delivered* 1574, followed by the *Gerusalemme Conquistata/Jerusalem Conquered*, written during the period from 1576 when he was mentally unstable.

taste sense that detects some of the chemical constituents of food. The human ◊tongue can distinguish only four basic tastes (sweet, sour, bitter, and salty) but it is supplemented by the nose's sense of smell. What we refer to as taste is really a composite sense made up of both taste and smell.

Tatar or **Tartar** member of a Turkic people, the descendants of the mixed Mongol and Turkic followers of ◊Genghis Khan, called the Golden Horde because of the wealth they gained by plunder. The vast Tatar state was conquered by Russia 1552. The Tatars now live mainly in the Russian autonomous republic of Tatarstan, W Siberia, Turkmenistan, and Uzbekistan (where they were deported from the Crimea 1944). There are over 5 million speakers of the Tatar language, which belongs to the Turkic branch of the Altaic family. The Tatar people are mainly Muslim, although some have converted to the Orthodox Church.

Tatarstan formerly **Tatar Autonomous Republic** autonomous republic of E Russia;
area 26,250 sq mi/68,000 sq km
capital Kazan
products oil, chemicals, textiles, timber
population (1986) 3,537,000 (48% Tatar, 43% Russian)
history a territory of Volga-Kama Bulgar state from the 10th century when Islam was introduced; conquered by the Mongols 1236; capital of the powerful Khanate of Kazan until conquered by Russia 1552; an autonomous republic from 1920. In recent years the republic (mainly Muslim and an important industrial and oil-producing area) has seen moves toward increased autonomy. In Aug 1990 the republic's assembly upgraded Tatarstan to full republic status, proclaiming its economic and political "sovereignty," and in April 1991 there were popular demonstrations in support of this action. In June 1991 it refused to participate in the Russian presidential election, and in March 1992 declined to be party to a federal treaty, signed in Moscow by 18 of Russia's other 20 main political subdivisions. A referendum March 21, 1992 favored Tatarstan becoming a sovereign state within Russia.

Tate Gallery art gallery (British art from late 16th century, and international from 1810) in London. Endowed by the sugar merchant Henry Tate (1819–1899), it was opened 1897.

Tatlin Vladimir 1885–1953. Russian artist, cofounder of ◊**Constructivism**. After encountering Cubism in Paris 1913 he evolved his first Constructivist works, using raw materials such as tin, glass, plaster, and wood to create abstract sculptures that he suspended in the air.

Tatra Mountains range in central Europe, extending for about 40 mi/65 km along the Polish-Czechoslovakian border; the highest part of the central ◊Carpathian Mountains.

tatting lacework in cotton, made since medieval times by knotting and looping a single thread with a small shuttle.

Tatum Art(hur) 1910–1956. US jazz pianist who, in the 1930s, worked mainly as a soloist. Tatum is considered among the most technically brilliant of jazz pianists and his technique and chromatic harmonies influenced many musicians, such as Oscar Peterson (1925–). He improvised with the guitarist Tiny Grimes (1916–) in a trio from 1943.

Tatum Edward Lawrie 1909–1975. US microbiologist. For his work on biochemical genetics, he shared the 1958 Nobel Prize for Medicine with George Beadle and Joshua Lederberg.

Taube Henry 1915– . US chemist who established the basis of inorganic chemistry through his study of the loss or gain of electrons by atoms during chemical reactions.

He was awarded a Nobel Prize in chemistry 1983 for his work on electron transference between molecules in chemical reactions.

Tau Ceti one of the nearest stars visible to the naked eye, 11.9 light-years from Earth in the constellation Cetus. It has a diameter slightly less than that of the Sun, and an actual luminosity of about 45% of the Sun's. Its similarity to the Sun is sufficient to suggest that Tau Ceti may possess a planetary system, although observations have yet to reveal evidence of this.

Taurus zodiacal constellation in the northern hemisphere near Orion, represented as a bull. The Sun passes through Taurus from mid-May to late June. Its brightest star is Aldebaran, seen as the bull's red eye. Taurus contains the Hyades and Pleiades open ◊star clusters, and the Crab nebula. In astrology, the dates for Taurus are between about April 20 and May 20 (see ◊precession).

Taurus Mountains (Turkish **Toros Dağlari**) mountain range in S Turkey, forming the southern edge of the Anatolian plateau and rising to over 12,000 ft/3,656 m.

Taussig Helen Brooke 1898–1986. US cardiologist who developed surgery for "blue" babies. Such babies never fully develop the shunting mechanism in the circulatory system that allows blood to be oxygenated in the lungs before passing to the rest of the body. The babies are born chronically short of oxygen and usually do not survive without surgery.

tautology repetition of the same thing in different words, or the ungrammatical use of unnecessary words: for example, it is tautologous to say that something is *most unique*, since something unique cannot, by definition, be comparative.

taxation the raising of money from individuals and organizations by state and local governments, to pay for the goods and services they provide. Taxation can be direct (a deduction from income) or indirect (added to the purchase price of goods or services—that is, a tax on consumption).

The most common form of indirect taxation in the US is the sales tax, applied to the purchase price of items. The most common form of direct taxation is the income tax, withheld from paychecks and imposed by most of the states as well as the federal government.

Taxation can be an important economic and social policy tool. By themselves, taxes would reduce economic activity by taking money out of circulation. The benefit of taxes, then, depends on the use to which the funds are put. A redistribution of resources takes place when funds collected from taxpayers are used to pay contractors to build housing or provide food or education for the poor. The tax structure helps determine the distribution of resources. For example, progressive taxes take an increasing percentage of income as it rises; proportional tax rates take the same percentage of income across all levels; and regressive rates take a higher percentage as income is reduced. Direct taxes tend to be proportional or progressive, whereas indirect taxes are generally regressive, since they take a higher percentage of income from the poor.

Taxes have important social as well as economic purposes. High excise taxes, applied to specific commodities, can be used either to raise tax revenues or to try to discourage consumption of those items, examples being cigarettes, liquor, gasoline, and luxury items. In some states following the Civil War, poll taxes were used to disenfranchise poor blacks who could not afford to pay them. Corporate taxes must find a delicate balance, since rates that are too high can drive businesses from one state to another or, in extreme instances, force them to relocate in another country, or cease operating entirely.

During the Reagan administrations, it was argued by supply-side economists that reductions in tax rates would actually produce increased revenues by stimulating a growth in overall economic activity. Conversely, it was held that increased tax rates would yield decreased revenue by discouraging growth. Federal taxation was simplified and rates reduced by Congress to some of the lowest rates among industrialized nations 1987.

tax deductible any item that may be offset against tax liability, such as the cost of an automobile when it is required as an integral part of a job, is termed "tax deductible."

tax haven country or state where taxes are much lower than elsewhere. It is often used by companies of another country that register in the tax haven to avoid tax. Any business transacted is treated as completely confidential. Tax havens include the Channel Islands, Switzerland, Bermuda, the Bahamas, and Liberia.

taxis (plural *taxes*) or *tactic movement* in botany, the movement of a single cell, such as a bacterium, protozoan, single-celled alga, or gamete, in response to an external stimulus. A movement directed toward the stimulus is described as positive taxis, and away from it as negative taxis. The alga *Chlamydomonas*, for example, demonstrates positive *phototaxis* by swimming toward a light source to increase the rate of photosynthesis. *Chemotaxis* is a response to a chemical stimulus, as seen in many bacteria that move toward higher concentrations of nutrients.

Taxodium tree genus of the redwood family (Taxodiaceae). Also called ▷wormwood.

taxonomy another name for the ▷classification of living organisms.

tax shelter investment opportunity designed to reduce the tax burden on an individual or group of individuals but at the same time to stimulate finance in the direction of a particular location or activity. Such shelters might be tax exempt or lightly taxed securities in government or a local authority, or forestry or energy projects.

Tay longest river in Scotland; length 118 mi/189 km. Rising in NW Central region, it flows NE through Loch Tay, then E and SE past Perth to the Firth of Tay, crossed at Dundee by the Tay Bridge, before joining the North Sea. The Tay has salmon fisheries; its main tributaries are the Tummel, Isla, and Earn.

Taylor Elizabeth 1932– . English-born US actress. Noted for both her beauty and acting skill, her films include *Lassie Come Home* 1942, *National Velvet* 1944, *Father of the Bride* 1950, *Giant* 1956, *Raintree County* 1957, *Cat on a Hot Tin Roof* 1958, *Butterfield 8* 1960 (Academy Award), *Cleopatra* 1963, and *Who's Afraid of Virginia Woolf?* 1966 (Academy Award). She appeared on Broadway in *The Little Foxes* 1981.

Her eight husbands included the actors Michael Wilding, Eddie Fisher, and Richard ▷Burton (twice).

Taylor Frederick Winslow 1856–1915. US engineer and management consultant, the founder of scientific management. His ideas, published in *Principles of Scientific Management* 1911, were based on the breakdown of work to the simplest tasks, the separation of planning from execution of tasks, and the introduction of time-and-motion studies. His methods were clearly expressed in assembly-line factories, but have been criticized for degrading and alienating workers and producing managerial dictatorship.

Taylor Zachary 1784–1850. 12th president of the US 1849–50. A veteran of the War of 1812 and a hero of the Mexican War (1846–48), he was nominated for the presidency by the Whigs in 1848 and was elected, but died less than one and a half years into his term. He was succeeded by Vice President Millard Fillmore.

Taylor was born in Virginia but grew up in frontier Kentucky. He began 40 years of army service in 1808 and played a key role in Fort Harrison's defense during the War of 1812. Most of his military career was spent on the frontier, and he distinguished himself in campaigns against the Indians. In the Seminole Wars in Florida his successes led to his promotion to brigadier general and command of the Florida department (1838–40). By now known by his nickname "Old Rough and Ready," Taylor won his greatest fame in the Mexican War. While commander of the US forces occupying the recently annexed Texas, he opposed Mexican forces on President Polk's orders.

In spring 1846, Taylor advanced into Mexico and almost immediately won several battles and a promotion to major general. By fall he had taken Monterrey and in Feb 1847 defeated Santa Anna at Buena Vista.

Having defeated his opponents Lewis Cass and Martin van Buren for the presidency, Taylor found his short term in office dominated by controversies over the slavery issue, with Taylor supporting the antislavery elements that were pushing for the admission to the Union of more free states. Taylor died unexpectedly of cholera while the Compromise of 1850 was being shaped.

Tay-Sachs disease inherited disorder, due to a defective gene, causing an enzyme deficiency that leads to blindness, retardation, and death in childhood. Because of their enforced isolation and inbreeding during hundreds of years, it is most common in people of E European Jewish descent.

Tayside region of Scotland
area 2,973 sq mi/7,700 sq km
cities Dundee (administrative headquarters), Perth, Arbroath, Forfar
features river Tay; Grampian Mountains; Lochs Tay and Rannoch; hills: Ochil and Sidlaw; vales of the North and South Esk
products beef and dairy products, soft fruit from the fertile Carse of Gowrie (SW of Dundee)
population (1991) 385,300
famous people J M Barrie, John Buchan, Princess Margaret.

TB abbreviation for the infectious disease ▷tuberculosis.

Tbilisi formerly *Tiflis* capital of the Republic of Georgia; industries include textiles, machinery, ceramics, and tobacco; population (1987) 1,194,000. Dating from the 5th century, it is a center of Georgian culture, with fine medieval churches. Anti-Russian demonstrations were quashed here by troops 1981

and 1989; the latter clash followed rejected demands for autonomy from the Abkhazia enclave, and resulted in 19 or more deaths from poison gas (containing chloroacetophenone) and 100 injured. In Dec 1991 at least 50 people were killed as well-armed opposition forces attempted to overthrow President Gamsakhurdia, eventually forcing him to flee.

T cell or *T lymphocyte* immune cell (see ▷immunity and ▷lymphocyte) that plays several roles in the body's defenses. T cells are so called because they mature in the ▷thymus.

There are three main types of T cells: T helper cells (Th cells), which allow other immune cells to go into action; T suppressor cells (Ts cells), which stop specific immune reactions from occurring; and T cytotoxic cells (Tc cells), which kill cells that are cancerous or infected with viruses. Like ▷B cells, to which they are related, T cells have surface receptors that make them specific for particular antigens.

Tchaikovsky Pyotr Il'yich 1840–1893. Russian composer. His strong sense of melody, personal expression, and brilliant orchestration are clear throughout his many Romantic works, which include six symphonies, three piano concertos, a violin concerto, operas (for example, *Eugene Onegin* 1879), ballets (for example, *The Nutcracker* 1892), orchestral fantasies (for example, *Romeo and Juliet* 1870), and chamber and vocal music.

Professor of harmony at Moscow 1865, he later met ▷Balakirev, becoming involved with the nationalist movement in music. He was the first Russian composer to establish a reputation with Western audiences.

He was invited to conduct the opening night program at Carnegie Hall, in New York City, 1891.

tea evergreen shrub *Camellia sinensis*, family Theaceae, of which the fermented, dried leaves are infused to make a beverage of the same name. Known in China as early as 2737 BC, tea was first brought to Europe AD 1610 and rapidly became a fashionable drink. In 1823 it was found growing wild in N India, and plantations were later established in Assam and Sri Lanka; producers today include Africa, South America, Georgia, Azerbaijan, Indonesia, and Iran.

Growing naturally to 40 ft/12 m, the tea plant is restricted in cultivation to bushes 4 ft/1.5 m high. The young shoots and leaves are picked every five years. After 24 hours spread on shelves in withering lofts, they are broken up by rolling machines to release the essential oils, and then left to ferment. This process is halted by passing the leaves through ovens where moisture is removed and the blackish-brown *black tea* emerges ready for sifting into various grades. *Green tea* is steamed and quickly dried before fermentation, remaining partly green in color.

Tea was not in use in England until 1657. It remained expensive as long as cargoes had to be brought from China in sailing ships, the fast tea clippers. Methods of consumption vary: in Japan special teahouses and an elaborate tea ceremony have evolved and in Tibet hard slabs of compressed tea are used as money before being finally brewed.

In the US, tea with lemon and honey is a cold remedy, but iced tea has become a year-round soft drink, sold in cans like colas. After the American Revolution, the new US citizens turned away from tea (as being British) and imported ▷coffee instead. Only after 200 years did tea revive its popularity in the US.

teak tropical Asian timber tree *Tectona grandis*, family Verbenaceae, with yellowish wood used in furniture and shipbuilding.

teal any of various small, short-necked dabbling ducks of the genus *Anas*. The drakes generally have a bright head and wing markings. The green-winged teal *A. crecca* is about 14 in/35 cm long.

Teapot Dome Scandal US political scandal that revealed the corruption of President ◊Harding's administration. It centered on the leasing of naval oil reserves 1921 at Teapot Dome, Wyoming, without competitive bidding, as a result of bribing the secretary of the interior, Albert B Fall (1861–1944). Fall was tried and imprisoned 1929.

A Senate investigation revealed that Fall had accepted gifts and loans totaling $400,000. The US Supreme Court nullified the leases 1927. The two oil-company executives involved were acquitted on technicalities, but one of them, Harry Sinclair, was later imprisoned for jury tampering and contempt of the Senate.

tear gas any of various volatile gases that produce irritation and tearing of the eyes, used by police against crowds and used in chemical warfare. The gas is delivered in pressurized, liquid-filled canisters or grenades, thrown by hand or launched from a specially adapted rifle. Gases (such as Mace) cause violent coughing and blinding tears, which pass when the victim breathes fresh air, and there are no lasting effects. Blister gases (such as mustard gas) and nerve gases are more harmful and may cause permanent injury or death.

teasel erect, prickly, biennial herb *Dipsacus fullonum*, family Dipsacaceae, native to Eurasia. The dry, spiny seed heads were once used industrially to tease, or raise the nap of, cloth.

Tebaldi Renata 1922– . Italian dramatic soprano, renowned for the controlled purity of her voice and for her roles in ◊Puccini operas.

technetium (Greek *technetos* "artificial") silver-gray, radioactive, metallic element, symbol Tc, atomic number 43, atomic weight 98.906. It occurs in nature only in extremely minute amounts, produced as a fission product from uranium in ◊pitchblende and other uranium ores. Its longest-lived isotope, Tc-99, has a half-life of 216,000 years. It is a superconductor and is used as a hardener in steel alloys and as a medical tracer.

It was synthesized 1937 (named 1947) by Italian physicists Carlo Perrier and Emilio Segrè, who bombarded molybdenum with deuterons, looking to fill a missing spot in the ◊periodic table of the elements (at that time it was considered not to occur in nature). It was later isolated in large amounts from the fission-product debris of uranium fuel in nuclear reactors.

Technicolor trade name for a film color process using three separate negatives of blue, green, and red images. It was invented by Daniel F Comstock and Herbert T Kalmus in the US 1922. Originally, Technicolor was a two-color process in which superimposed red and green images were projected on to the screen by a special projector. This initial version proved expensive and imperfect, but when the three-color process was introduced 1932, the system was widely adopted, culminating in its use in *The Wizard of Oz* and *Gone With the Wind*, both 1939. Technicolor remains the most commonly used color process for cinematography.

technology the use of tools, power, and materials, generally for the purposes of production. Almost every human process for getting food and shelter depends on complex technological systems, which have been developed over a 5-million-year period. Significant milestones include the advent of the ◊steam engine 1712, the introduction of ◊electricity and the ◊internal-combustion engine in the mid-1800s, and recent developments in ◊communications, ◊electronics, and the nuclear and space industries. The *advanced technology* (highly automated and specialized) on which modern industrialized society depends is frequently contrasted with the *low technology* (labor-intensive and unspecialized) that characterizes some developing countries. ◊*Intermediate technology* is an attempt to adapt scientifically advanced inventions to less developed areas by using local materials and methods of manufacture.

power In human prehistory, the only power available was muscle power, augmented by primitive tools, such as the wedge or lever. The domestication of animals about 8500 BC and invention of the wheel about 300 BC paved the way for the water mill (1st century BC) and later the windmill (12th century AD). Not until 1712 did an alternative source of power appear in the form of the first working steam engine, constructed by Thomas Newcomen; subsequent modifications improved its design. Michael Faraday's demonstration of the dynamo 1831 revealed the potential of the electrical motor, and in 1876 the German scientist Nicholas Otto introduced the four-stroke cycle used in the modern internal-combustion engine. The 1940s saw the explosion of the first atomic bomb and the subsequent development of the nuclear power industry. Latterly concern over the use of nonrenewable power sources and the ◊pollution caused by the burning of fossil fuels has caused technologists to turn increasingly to exploring renewable sources of energy, in particular ◊solar energy, wind energy, and wave power.

materials The earliest materials used by humans were wood, bone, horn, shell, and stone. Metals were rare and/or difficult to obtain, although forms of bronze and iron were in use from 6000 BC and 1000 BC respectively. The introduction of the blast furnace in the 15th century enabled cast iron to be extracted, but this process remained expensive until Abraham Darby substituted coke for charcoal 1709, thus ensuring a plentiful supply of cheap iron at the start of the Industrial Revolution. Rubber, glass, leather, paper, bricks, and porcelain underwent similar processes of trial and error before becoming readily available. From the mid-1800s, entirely new materials, synthetics, appeared. First dyes, then plastic and the more versatile celluloid, and later drugs were synthesized, a process continuing into the 1980s with the growth of ◊genetic engineering, which enabled the production of synthetic insulin and growth hormones.

production The utilization of power sources and materials for production frequently lagged behind their initial discovery. The ◊lathe, known in antiquity in the form of a pole powered by a foot treadle, was not fully developed until the 18th century when it was used to produce objects of great precision, ranging from astronomical instruments to mass-produced screws. The realization that gears, cranks, cams, and wheels could operate in harmony to perform complex motion made ◊mechanization possible. Early attempts at ◊automation

include James Watt's introduction of the fly-ball governor into the steam engine 1769 to regulate the machine's steam supply automatically, and Joseph Marie Jacquard's demonstration 1804 of how looms could be controlled automatically by punched cards. The first moving assembly line appeared 1870 in meatpacking factories in Chicago, transferring to the motor industry 1913. With the perfection of the programmable electronic computer in the 1960s, the way lay open for fully automatic plants. The 1960s–90s saw extensive developments in the electronic and microelectronic industries (initially in the West but latterly Japan and the Pacific region have become primary producers) and in the field of communications.

tectonics in geology, the study of the movements of rocks on the Earth's surface. On a small scale tectonics involves the formation of ◊folds and ◊faults, but on a large scale ◊plate tectonics deals with the movement of the Earth's surface as a whole.

Tecumseh 1768–1813. North American Indian chief of the Shawnee. He attempted to unite the Indian peoples from Canada to Florida against the encroachment of white settlers, but the defeat of his brother Tenskwatawa, popularly known as "the Prophet," at the battle of Tippecanoe in Nov 1811 by then-governor of the Indiana Territory W H ◊Harrison, largely destroyed the confederacy built by Tecumseh. He allied himself with the British in the War of 1812, during which he helped take Detroit, fomented the Creek War 1813 in the South, and led an invasion of Ohio. He was killed in Canada at the Battle of the Thames 1813, a battle won by Harrison, who would campaign for the presidency 1840 largely on the strength of his military exploits against Tecumseh.

Tedder Arthur William, 1st Baron Tedder 1890–1967. UK marshal of the Royal Air Force in World War II. As deputy supreme commander under US general Eisenhower 1943–45, he was largely responsible for the initial success of the 1944 Normandy landings.

Teesside industrial area at the mouth of the river Tees, Cleveland, NE England; population (1981) 382,700. Industries include high technology, capital-intensive steelmaking, chemicals, an oil-fuel terminal, and the main North Sea natural-gas terminal. Middlesbrough is a large port.

tefillin or *phylacteries* in Judaism, two small leather boxes containing scrolls from the Torah, that are strapped to the left arm and forehead by Jewish men for daily prayer.

Teflon trade name for polytetrafluoroethene (PTFE), a tough, waxlike, heat-resistant plastic used for coating nonstick cookware and in gaskets and bearings.

Tegucigalpa capital of Honduras; industries include textiles and food-processing; population (1989) 608,000. It was founded 1524 as a gold- and silver-mining center.

Tehran capital of Iran; industries include textiles, chemicals, engineering, and tobacco; population (1986) 6,043,000. It was founded in the 12th century and made the capital 1788 by Mohammed Shah. Much of the city was rebuilt in the 1920s and 1930s. Tehran is the site of the Gulistan Palace (the former royal residence).

Tehran Conference conference held 1943 in Tehran, Iran, the first meeting of World War II Allied leaders Churchill, Roosevelt, and Stalin.

The chief subject discussed was coordination of Allied strategy in W and E Europe.

Teilhard de Chardin Pierre 1881–1955. French Jesuit theologian, paleontologist, and philosopher. He developed a creative synthesis of nature and religion, based on his field-work and fossil studies. Publication of his *Le Phénomène humain/The Phenomenon of Man*, written 1938–40, was delayed (due to his unorthodox views) until after his death by the embargo of his superiors. He saw humanity as being in a constant process of evolution, moving toward a perfect spiritual state.

Tej Bahadur 1621–1675. Indian religious leader, ninth guru (teacher) of Sikhism 1664–75, executed for refusing to renounce his faith.

Te Kanawa Kiri 1944– . New Zealand soprano. Te Kanawa's first major role was the Countess in Mozart's *The Marriage of Figaro* at Covent Garden, London, 1971. Her voice combines the purity and intensity of the upper range with an extended lower range of great richness and resonance. Apart from Classical roles, she has also featured popular music in her repertoire, such as the 1984 recording of Leonard Bernstein's *West Side Story*.

tektite (from Greek *tektos* "molten") small, rounded glassy stone, found in certain regions of the Earth, such as Australasia. Tektites are probably the scattered drops of molten rock thrown out by the impact of a large ◊meteorite.

Tel Aviv officially *Tel Aviv–Jaffa* city in Israel, on the Mediterranean Sea; industries include textiles, chemicals, sugar, printing, and publishing; population (1987) 320,000. Tel Aviv was founded 1909 as a Jewish residential area in the Arab town of Jaffa, with which it was combined 1949; their ports were superseded 1965 by Ashdod to the south.

telecommunications communications over a distance, generally by electronic means. Long-distance voice communication was pioneered 1876 by Alexander Graham Bell, when he invented the telephone as a result of Faraday's discovery of electromagnetism. Today it is possible to communicate with most countries by telephone cable, or by satellite or microwave link, with over 100,000 simultaneous conversations and several television channels being carried by the latest satellites. ◊Integrated-Services Digital Network (ISDN) makes videophones and high-quality fax possible; the world's first large-scale center of ISDN began operating in Japan 1988. The chief method of relaying long-distance calls on land is microwave radio transmission.

The first mechanical telecommunications systems were ◊semaphore and heliograph (using flashes of sunlight), invented in the mid-19th century, but the forerunner of the present telecommunications age was the electric telegraph. The earliest practicable telegraph instrument was invented by W F Cooke and Charles Wheatstone in Britain 1837 and used by railroad companies. In the US, Samuel Morse invented a signaling code, ◊Morse code, which is still used, and a recording telegraph, first used commercially between England and France 1851. As a result of ◊Hertz's discoveries using electromagnetic waves, ◊Marconi pioneered a "wireless" telegraph, ancestor of the radio. He established wireless communication between England and France 1899 and across the Atlantic 1901. The modern telegraph uses teleprinters to send coded messages along telecommunications lines. Telegraphs are keyboard-operated machines that transmit a five-unit Baudot code (see ◊baud). The receiving teleprinter automatically prints the received message.

The drawback to long-distance voice communication via microwave radio transmission is that the transmissions follow a straight line from tower to tower, so that over the sea the system becomes impracticable. A solution was put forward 1945 by the science-fiction writer Arthur C Clarke, when he proposed a system of communications satellites in an orbit 22,300 mi/35,900 km above the equator, where they would circle the Earth in exactly 24 hours, and thus appear fixed in the sky. Such a system is now in operation internationally, by ◊Intelsat. The satellites are called geostationary satellites (syncoms). The first to be successfully launched, by Delta rocket from Cape Canaveral, was *Syncom 2* in July 1963. Many such satellites are now in use, concentrated over heavy traffic areas such as the Atlantic, Indian, and Pacific oceans. Telegraphy, telephony, and television transmissions are carried simultaneously by high-frequency radio waves. They are beamed to the satellites from large dish antennae or Earth stations, which connect with international networks. Recent advances include the use of fiber-optic cables consisting of fine fiberglasss for telephone lines instead of the usual copper cables. The telecommunications signals are transmitted along the fibers on pulses of laser light. ISDN is a system that transmits voice and image data on a single transmission line by changing them into digital signals,

telegraphy transmission of coded messages along wires by means of electrical signals. The first modern form of telecommunication, it now uses printers for the transmission and receipt of messages. Telex is an international telegraphy network.

Overland cables were developed in the 1830s, but early attempts at underwater telegraphy were largely unsuccessful until the discovery of the insulating gum ◊gutta-percha 1843 enabled a cable to be laid across the English Channel 1851. *Duplex telegraph* was invented in the 1870s, enabling messages to be sent in both directions simultaneously. Early telegraphs were mainly owned by the UK: 72% of all submarine cables were British-owned 1900.

Telemachus in Greek mythology, son of ◊Odysseus and ◊Penelope. He attempts to control the conduct of his mother's suitors in Homer's *Odyssey* while his father is believed dead, but on Odysseus' return helps him to kill them, with the support of the goddess ◊Athena.

telemetry measurement at a distance, in particular the systems by which information is obtained and sent back by instruments on board a spacecraft. See ◊remote sensing.

telepathy "the communication of impressions of any kind from one mind to another, independently of the recognized channels of sense," as defined by F W H Myers (1843–1901), cofounder 1882 of the Psychical Research Society, who coined the term.

telephone instrument for communicating by voice over long distances, invented by Alexander Graham ◊Bell 1876. The transmitter (mouthpiece) consists of a carbon microphone, with a diaphragm that vibrates when a person speaks into it. The diaphragm vibrations compress grains of carbon to a greater or lesser extent, altering their resistance to an electric current passing through them. This sets up variable electrical signals, which travel along the telephone lines to the receiver of the person being called. There they cause the magnetism of an electromagnet to vary, making a diaphragm above the electromagnet vibrate and give out sound waves, which mirror those that entered the mouthpiece originally. *See illustration on p. 1030.*

telephoto lens photographic lens of longer focal length than normal that takes a very narrow view and gives a large image through a combination of telescopic and ordinary photographic lenses.

teleprinter or *teletypewriter* transmitting and receiving device used in telecommunications to handle coded messages. Teleprinters are automatic typewriters keyed telegraphically to convert typed words into electrical signals (using a 5-unit Baudot code, see ◊baud) at the

satellite ground station antenna

satellite communications signals

microwave relay towers

relayed signal

international exchange

national exchange

broadcasting station

telecommunications *The international telecommunications system relies on microwave and satellite links for long-distance international calls.*

telephone *Sound vibrations are converted to an electric signal and back again.*

transmitting end, and signals into typed words at the receiving end.

telescope optical instrument that magnifies images of faint and distant objects; any device for collecting and focusing light and other forms of electromagnetic radiation. It is a major research tool in astronomy and is used to sight over land and sea; small telescopes can be attached to cameras and rifles. A telescope with a large aperture, or opening, can distinguish finer detail and fainter objects than one with a small aperture. The *refracting telescope* uses lenses, and the *reflecting telescope* uses mirrors. A third type, the *catadioptric telescope*, with a combination of lenses and mirrors, is used increasingly. See also ◊radio telescope.

In a refractor, light is collected by a ◊lens called the *object glass* or *objective*, which focuses light down a tube, forming an image magnified by an *eyepiece*. Invention of the refractor is attributed to a Dutch optician, Hans ◊Lippershey 1608. The largest refracting telescope in the world, at ◊Yerkes Observatory, Wisconsin, has an aperture of 40 in/102 cm.

In a reflector, light is collected and focused by a concave mirror. The first reflector was built about 1670 by Isaac ◊Newton. Large mirrors are cheaper to make and easier to mount than large lenses, so all the largest telescopes are reflectors. The largest reflector with a single mirror, 236 in/6 m, is at Zelenchukskaya, Russia. Telescopes with larger apertures composed of numerous smaller segments are being built, such as the Keck Telescope on ◊Mauna Kea. A *multiple-mirror telescope* was installed on Mount Hopkins, Arizona 1979. It consists of six mirrors of 72 in/1.8 m aperture, which perform like a single 176 in/4.5 m mirror. *Schmidt telescopes* are used for taking wide-field photographs of the sky. They have a main mirror plus a thin lens at the front of the tube to increase the field of view.

Large telescopes can now be placed in orbit above the distorting effects of the Earth's atmosphere. Telescopes in space have been used to study infrared, ultraviolet, and X-ray radiation that does not penetrate the atmosphere but carries much information about the births, lives, and deaths of stars and galaxies. The 95-in/2.4-m Hubble Space Telescope, launched 1990, can see the sky more clearly than can any telescope on Earth, despite an optical defect that impairs its performance.

televangelist in North America, a fundamentalist Christian minister, often of a Pentecostal church, who hosts a television show and solicits donations from viewers. Well-known

telescope *Three kinds of telescope.*

televangelists include Jim Bakker, convicted 1989 of fraudulent misuse of donations, and Jimmy Swaggart.

television (TV) reproduction at a distance by radio waves of visual images. For transmission, a television camera converts the pattern of light it takes in into a pattern of electrical charges. This is scanned line by line by a beam of electrons from an electron gun, resulting in variable electrical signals that represent the visual picture. These vision signals are combined with a radio carrier wave and broadcast as magnetic waves. The TV aerial picks up the wave and feeds it to the receiver (TV set). This separates out the vision signals, which pass to a cathode-ray tube. The vision signals control the strength of a beam of electrons from an electron gun, aimed at the screen and making it glow more or less brightly. At the same time the beam is made to scan across the screen line by line, mirroring the action of the gun in the TV camera. The result is a recreation of the pattern of light that entered the camera. Thirty pictures are built up each second with interlaced scanning in North America (25 in Europe), with a total of 525 lines in North America and Japan (625 lines in Europe).

television channels In addition to transmissions received by all viewers, the 1970s and 1980s saw the growth of pay-television cable networks, which are received only by subscribers, and of devices, such as those used in the Qube system (US), which allow the viewers' opinions to be transmitted instantaneously to the studio via a response button, so that, for example, a home viewing audience can vote in a talent competition. The number of program channels continues to increase, following the introduction of satellite-beamed TV signals.

Further use of TV sets has been brought about by ◊videotex and the use of video recorders to tape programs for playback later or to play prerecorded videocassettes, and by their use as computer screens and for security systems. Extended-definition television gives a clear enlargement from a microscopic camera and was first used 1989 in neurosurgery to enable medical students to watch brain operations.

history In 1873 it was realized that, since the electrical properties of the nonmetallic chemical element selenium vary according to the amount of light to which it is exposed, light could be converted into electrical impulses, making it possible to transmit such impulses over a distance and then reconvert them into light. The chief difficulty was seen to be the "splitting of the picture" so that the infinite variety of light and shade values might be transmitted and reproduced. In 1908 Campbell-Swinton pointed out that cathode-ray tubes would best effect transmission and reception. Mechanical devices were used at the first practical demonstration of television, given by J L Baird in London Jan 27, 1926, and cathode-ray tubes were used experimentally in the UK from 1934.

color television Baird gave a demonstration of color TV in London 1928, but it was not until Dec 1953 that the first successful system was adopted for broadcasting, in the US. This is called the NTSC system, since it was developed by the National Television System Committee, and variations of it have been developed in Europe; for example, SECAM (sequential and memory) in France and PAL (phase alternation by line) in West Germany. The three differ only in the way color signals are prepared for transmission. When there was no agreement on a universal European system 1964, in 1967 the UK, West Germany, the Netherlands, and Switzerland adopted PAL while France and the USSR adopted SECAM. In 1989 the European Community agreed to harmonize TV channels from 1991, allowing any station to show programs anywhere in the EC.

The method of color reproduction is related to that used in color photography and printing. It uses the principle that any colors can be made by mixing the primary colors red, green, and blue in appropriate proportions. In color television the receiver reproduces only three basic colors: red, green, and blue. The effect of yellow, for example, is reproduced by combining equal amounts of red and green light, while white is formed by a mixture of all three basic colors. Signals indicate the amounts of red, green, and blue light to be generated at the receiver.

To transmit each of these three signals in the same way as the single brightness signal in black and white television would need three times the normal band width and reduce the number of possible stations and programs to one-third of that possible with monochrome television. The three signals are therefore coded into one complex signal, which is transmitted as a more or less normal black and white signal and produces a satisfactory—or compatible—picture on black and white receivers. A fraction of each primary red, green, and blue signal is added together to produce the normal brightness, or luminance, signal. The minimum of extra coloring information is then sent by a special subcarrier signal, which is superimposed on the brightness signal. This extra coloring information corresponds to the hue and saturation of the transmitted color, but without any of the fine detail of the picture. The impression of sharpness is conveyed only by the brightness signal, the coloring being added as a broad color wash. The various color systems differ only in the way in which the coloring information is sent on the subcarrier signal.

The color receiver has to amplify the complex signal and decode it back to the basic red, green, and blue signals; these primary signals are then applied to a color cathode-ray tube. The color display tube is the heart of any color receiver. Many designs of color picture tubes have been invented; the most successful of these is known as the "shadow mask tube." It operates on similar electronic principles to the black and white television picture tube, but the screen is composed of a fine mosaic of over one million dots arranged in an orderly fashion. One-third of the dots glow red when bombarded by electrons, one-third glow green, and one-third blue. There are three sources of electrons, respectively modulated by the red, green, and blue signals. The tube is arranged so that the shadow mask allows only the red signals to hit red dots, the green signals to hit green dots, and the blue signals to hit blue dots. The glowing dots are so small that from a normal viewing distance the colors merge into one another and a picture with a full range of colors is seen.

high-definition television (HDTV) This system offers a significantly greater number of scanning lines, and therefore a clearer picture, than the 525/625 lines of established television systems. In 1989 the Japanese broadcasting station NHK and a consortium of manufacturers launched the Hi-Vision HDTV system, with 1,125 lines and a wide-screen format. The

Eureka research project has gathered together 30 European electronics companies, research laboratories, and broadcasting authorities to provide a common 1,250-line system for Europe by 1993.

In the US, TV technology was pioneered by David ◊Sarnoff and US physicist Lee De Forest (1873-1961) and sets became available in the 1930s. However, few performances were televised until the late 1940s, when local and network shows were scheduled in major cities and, by coaxial cable, across the nation. Live performances gave way to videotaped shows by the late 1950s, and color sets became popular from the 1960s. Cable networks expanded during the 1980s.

Tell Wilhelm (William) legendary 14th-century Swiss archer, said to have refused to salute the Hapsburg badge at Altdorf on Lake Lucerne. Sentenced to shoot an apple from his son's head, he did so, then shot the tyrannical Austrian ruler Gessler, symbolizing his people's refusal to submit to external authority.

The first written account of the legend dates from 1474, the period of the wars of the Swiss against Charles the Bold of Burgundy; but the story of a man showing his skill with the crossbow in such a way is much earlier. The legend has been used for plays (by Schiller, 1804) and an opera (by Rossini, 1829), as well as in filmed versions.

Tell el Amarna site of the ancient Egyptian capital ◊Akhetaton. The ◊Amarna tablets were found there.

Teller Edward 1908– . Hungarian-born US physicist. Born in Budapest, Teller received his PhD from the University of Leipzig 1930. After a period of research at Göttingen 1931–33 and with Niels Bohr in 1934, he immigrated to the US and became a faculty member of George Washington University 1935. Teller joined the staff of Columbia University 1941 and the University of Chicago 1942 to work with Enrico Fermi on atomic fission. From 1941 to 1945 he was also a member of the Manhattan Project, which developed the first atomic bombs. In 1946 Teller was appointed professor at the University of Chicago and played a central role in the development and testing of the first hydrogen bomb 1952.

From 1958 to 1975 he was associated with the Lawrence Livermore laboratories (for radiation and weapons research) at the University of California at Berkeley. One of the most controversial of nuclear scientists, he advocated the nuclear weapons buildup for supremacy over the USSR, including weapons in space (SDI or "Star Wars"), and opposed all test-ban treaties.

tellurium (Latin *Tellus* "Earth") silver-white, semimetallic (◊metalloid) element, symbol Te, atomic number 52, atomic weight 127.60. Chemically it is similar to sulfur and selenium, and it is considered as one of the sulfur group. It occurs naturally in telluride minerals, and is used in coloring glass blue–brown, in the electrolytic refining of zinc, in electronics, and as a catalyst in refining petroleum.

It was discovered by Austrian mineralogist Franz Müller (1740–1825) 1782, and named 1798 by German chemist Martin Klaproth.

Telstar US communications satellite, launched July 10, 1962, which relayed the first live television transmissions between the US and Europe. *Telstar* orbited the Earth in 158 minutes, and so had to be tracked by ground stations, unlike the geostationary satellites of today.

Telugu language spoken in SE India. It is the official language of Andhra Pradesh, and is also spoken in Malaysia, giving a total number of speakers of around 50 million. Written records in Telugu date from the 7th century AD. Telugu belongs to the Dravidian family.

Tema port in Ghana; population (1982) 324,000. It has the largest artificial harbor in Africa, opened 1962, as well as oil refineries and a fishing industry.

temp. abbreviation for *temperature*; *temporary*.

tempera painting medium in which powdered pigments are bound together, usually with egg yolk and water. A form of tempera was used in ancient Egypt, and egg tempera was the foremost medium for panel painting in late medieval and early Renaissance Europe. It was gradually superseded by oils from the late 15th century onwards.

temperament in music, a system of tuning the pitches of a mode or scale; in folk music to preserve its emotional or ritual meaning, in Western music to allow maximum flexibility for changing key. J S Bach wrote *The Well-Tempered Clavier* to demonstrate the superiority of this system of tuning.

temperature state of hotness or coldness of a body, and the condition that determines whether or not it will transfer heat to, or receive heat from, another body according to the laws of ◊thermodynamics. It is measured in degrees Celsius (before 1948 called centigrade), kelvin, or Fahrenheit.

The normal temperature of the human body is about 98.4°F/36.9°C. Variation by more than a degree or so indicates ill-health, a rise signifying excessive activity (usually due to infection), and a decrease signifying deficient heat production (usually due to lessened vitality).

temperature regulation the ability of an organism to control its internal body temperature; in warm-blooded animals this is known as ◊homeothermy.

Although some plants have evolved ways of resisting extremes of temperature, sophisticated mechanisms for maintaining the correct temperature are found in multicellular animals. Such mechanisms may be behavioral, as when a lizard moves into the shade in order to cool down, or internal, as in mammals and birds, where temperature is regulated by the ◊medulla.

tempering heat treatment for improving the properties of metals, often used for steel alloys. The metal is heated to a certain temperature and then cooled suddenly in a water or oil bath.

Tempest, The romantic drama by William Shakespeare, first performed 1611–12. Prospero, usurped as duke of Milan by his brother Antonio, lives on a remote island with his daughter Miranda and Caliban, a deformed creature. Prospero uses magic to shipwreck Antonio and his party on the island and, with the help of the spirit Ariel, regains his dukedom.

Templar member of a Christian military order, founded in Jerusalem 1119, the **Knights of the Temple of Solomon**. The knights took vows of poverty, chastity, and obedience and devoted themselves to the recovery of Palestine from the Muslims.

They played an important part in the Crusades of the 12th and 13th centuries. The enormous wealth of the order aroused the envy of Philip IV of France, who arranged for charges of heresy to be brought against its members 1307, and the order was suppressed 1308–12.

Temple industrial city (building materials, steel, furniture, railroad supplies) in central Texas, S of Waco; population (1990) 46,100.

Temple of Jerusalem the center of Jewish national worship in both ancient and modern days. The Western or Wailing Wall is the surviving part of the western wall of the platform of the enclosure of the Temple. Solomon built the Temple c. 950 BC but it was destroyed by Nebuchadnezzer in 586 BC. It was rebuilt in the late 6th century BC, restored by the ⏵Maccabees and later by Herod the Great, but destroyed by the Romans in AD 70. Since then, Jews have come here to pray, to mourn their dispersion and the loss of their homeland.

The Mosque of Omar now stands on the site. Under Jordanian rule Jews had no access, but Israel retook this part of the city during the 1967 war.

Temple Shirley 1928– . US actress who became the most successful child star of the 1930s. The charming, curly-haired, dimpled tot's films include *Bright Eyes* 1934, in which she sang "On the Good Ship Lollipop;" *Little Miss Marker* 1934; *The Little Colonel* 1935; *Captain January* 1936; *Heidi* 1937; and *The Little Princess* 1939.

As Shirley Temple Black, she was active in the Republican Party and diplomatic affairs. She was a delegate to the United Nations 1969–70, US chief of protocol 1976–77, and ambassador to Ghana and Czechoslovakia.

tempo (Italian "time") in music, the speed at which a piece is played.

tenant farming system whereby farmers rent their holdings from a landowner in return for the use of agricultural land.

tench European freshwater bony fish *Tinca tinca*, a member of the carp family, now established in North America. It is about 18 in/45 cm long, weighing 4.5 lb/2 kg, colored olive green above and gray beneath. The scales are small and there is a barbel at each side of the mouth.

Ten Commandments in the Old Testament, the laws given by God to the Hebrew leader Moses on Mt Sinai, engraved on two tablets of stone. They are: to have no other gods besides Jehovah; to make no idols; not to misuse the name of God; to keep the sabbath holy; to honor one's parents; not to commit murder, adultery, or theft; not to give false evidence; not to be covetous. They form the basis of Jewish and Christian moral codes; the "tablets of the Law" given to Moses are also mentioned in the Koran. The giving of the Ten Commandments is celebrated in the Jewish festival of *Shavuot* (see ⏵Pentecost).

tendon or *sinew* cord of tough, fibrous connective tissue that joins muscle to bone in vertebrates. Tendons are largely composed of the protein collagen, and because of their inelasticity are very efficient at transforming muscle power into movement.

tendril in botany, a slender, threadlike structure that supports a climbing plant by coiling around suitable supports, such as the stems and branches of other plants. It may be a modified stem, leaf, leaflet, flower, leaf stalk, or stipule (a small appendage on either side of the leaf stalk), and may be simple or branched.

The tendrils of Virginia creeper *Parthenocissus quinquefolia* are modified flower heads with suckerlike pads at the end that stick to walls, while those of the grapevine *Vitis* grow away from the light and thus enter dark crevices where they expand to anchor the plant firmly.

Tenerife largest of the ⏵Canary Islands, Spain; area 795 sq mi/2,060 sq km; population (1981) 557,000. *Santa Cruz* is the main town, and *Pico de Teide* is an active volcano.

Teng Hsiao-ping alternate spelling of ⏵Deng Xiaoping, Chinese politician.

Teniers family of Flemish painters, active in Antwerp. *David Teniers the Younger* (David II, 1610–1690) became court painter to Archduke Leopold William, governor of the Netherlands, in Brussels. He painted scenes of peasant life.

As curator of the archduke's art collection, David Teniers made many copies of the pictures and a collection of engravings, *Theatrum Pictorium* 1660. His peasant scenes are humorous and full of vitality, inspired by Brouwer. His father, *David Teniers the Elder* (David I, 1582–1649), painted religious pictures.

Tennessee state in E central US; nickname Volunteer State;
area 42,151 sq mi/109,200 sq km
capital Nashville
cities Memphis, Knoxville, Chattanooga, Clarksville
features Tennessee Valley Authority; Great Smoky Mountains National Park; Grand Old Opry, Nashville; Beale Street Historic District and Graceland, estate of Elvis Presley, Memphis; research centers, including Oak Ridge National Laboratory;
products cereals, cotton, tobacco, soybeans, livestock, timber, coal, zinc, copper, chemicals
population (1990) 4,877,200
famous people Davy Crockett, David Farragut, W C Handy, Cordell Hull, Andrew Jackson, Andrew Johnson, Dolly Parton, John Crowe Ransom, Bessie Smith
history first settled by Europeans 1757; became a state 1796. Tennessee was deeply divided in the Civil War and was a major war theater, with the battles of Shiloh, Murfreesboro, Chattanooga, and Nashville among those fought in the state.

Tennessee was explored by De Soto for Spain 1521, La Salle for France in the 1670s, and Virginia colonists James Needham and Gabriel Arthur for England in the 1680s. After England obtained the region as settlement of the French and Indian War 1763, it was occupied by settlers from Virginia and the Carolinas. After the Civil War, with Tennessean Andrew Johnson in the White House, it was the only former Confederate state not to have a military government imposed during Reconstruction. Coal and iron deposits attracted Northern capital, and by the early 1880s, flour, wool, and paper mills

Tennessee

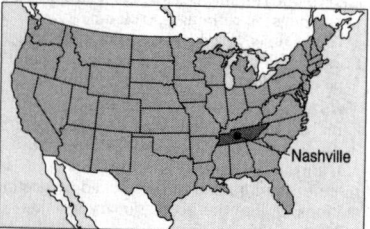

Nashville

were established in all the urban areas. Both prohibitionism and religious fundamentalism were strong; in 1925 the ⏵Scopes monkey trial was held in Dayton, and the law against the teaching of the theory of evolution in public schools was not repealed until 1967. The 1930s brought large-scale development in the form of the federal Tennessee Valley Authority and prepared the state for the industrialization that followed World War II.

Tennessee Valley Authority (TVA) US government corporation founded 1933 to develop the Tennessee river basin (an area of some 40,000 sq mi/104,000 sq km) by building hydroelectric power stations, producing and distributing fertilizers, and similar activities. The TVA was one of President F D Roosevelt's ⏵New Deal measures, promoting economic growth by government investment.

Its two major functions were to control the destructive flooding that had long plagued the valley and to provide employment in a 7-state area hard hit by the ⏵Depression. There were 32 major dams incorporated into a massive river-control system that also provided electric power for a wide region. Today about half of TVA's electrical output is devoted to defense installations surrounding the generating plants. The TVA has undertaken reforestation projects and agricultural research.

tennis racket and ball game invented toward the end of the 19th century. It was introduced by Major Clopton Wingfield at a Christmas party at Nantclwyn, Wales, in 1873. His game was then called "Sphairistike." It derived from ⏵court tennis. Although played on different surfaces (grass, wood, shale, clay, concrete), it is sometimes called "lawn tennis."

The aim of the two or four players is to strike the ball into the prescribed area of the court, with oval-headed rackets (strung with gut or nylon), in such a way that it cannot be returned. The game is won by those first winning four points (called 15, 30, 40, game), unless both sides reach 40 (deuce), when two consecutive points are needed to win. A set is won by winning six games with a margin of two over opponents, although a tie-break system operates, that is, at six games to each side (or in some cases eight), except in the final set. Major events include the ⏵*Davis Cup*, first contested in 1900 for international men's competition; the annual All England Tennis Club championships (originating 1877), an open event for players of both sexes at Wimbledon; and the US, French and Australian Opens.

tennis: recent winners

Wimbledon championships
men's singles
1983 John McEnroe *(US)*
1984 John McEnroe *(US)*
1985 Boris Becker *(West Germany)*
1986 Boris Becker *(West Germany)*
1987 Pat Cash *(Australia)*
1988 Stefan Edberg *(Sweden)*
1989 Boris Becker *(West Germany)*
1990 Stefan Edberg *(Sweden)*
1991 Michael Stich *(Germany)*
1992 Andre Agassi *(US)*
women's singles
1983 Martina Navratilova *(US)*
1984 Martina Navratilova *(US)*
1985 Martina Navratilova *(US)*
1986 Martina Navratilova *(US)*
1987 Martina Navratilova *(US)*
1988 Steffi Graf *(West Germany)*

1989 Steffi Graf *(West Germany)*
1990 Martina Navratilova *(US)*
1991 Steffi Graf *(Germany)*
1992 Steffi Graf *(Germany)*
US Open
men's singles
1983 Jimmy Connors *(US)*
1984 John McEnroe *(US)*
1985 Ivan Lendl *(Czechoslovakia)*
1986 Ivan Lendl *(Czechoslovakia)*
1987 Ivan Lendl *(Czechoslovakia)*
1988 Mats Wilander *(Sweden)*
1989 Boris Becker *(West Germany)*
1990 Pete Sampras *(US)*
1991 Stefan Edberg *(Sweden)*
1992 Stefan Edberg *(Sweden)*
women's singles
1983 Martina Navratilova *(US)*
1984 Martina Navratilova *(US)*
1985 Hana Mandlikova *(Czechoslovakia)*
1986 Martina Navratilova *(US)*
1987 Martina Navratilova *(US)*
1988 Steffi Graf *(West Germany)*
1989 Steffi Graf *(West Germany)*
1990 Gabriela Sabatini *(Argentina)*
1991 Monica Seles *(Yugoslavia)*
1992 Monica Seles *(Yugoslavia)*
French Open
men's singles
1983 Yannick Noah *(France)*
1984 Ivan Lendl *(Czechoslovakia)*
1985 Mats Wilander *(Sweden)*
1986 Ivan Lendl *(Czechoslovakia)*
1987 Ivan Lendl *(Czechoslovakia)*
1988 Mats Wilander *(Sweden)*
1989 Michael Craig *(US)*
1990 Andres Gomez *(Ecuador)*
1991 Jim Courier *(US)*
1992 Jim Courier *(US)*
women's singles
1983 Chris Evert-Lloyd *(US)*
1984 Martina Navratilova *(US)*
1985 Chris Evert-Lloyd *(US)*
1986 Chris Evert-Lloyd *(US)*
1987 Steffi Graf *(West Germany)*
1988 Steffi Graf *(West Germany)*
1989 Arantxa Sanchez Vicario *(Spain)*
1990 Monica Seles *(Yugoslavia)*
1991 Monica Seles *(Yugoslavia)*
1992 Monica Seles *(Yugoslavia)*
Australian Open
men's singles
1984 Mats Wilander *(Sweden)*
1985 Stefan Edberg *(Sweden)*
1986 *not held*
1987 Stefan Edberg *(Sweden)*
1988 Mats Wilander *(Sweden)*
1989 Ivan Lendl *(Czechoslovakia)*
1990 Ivan Lendl *(Czechoslovakia)*
1991 Boris Becker *(Germany)*
1992 Jim Courier *(US)*
1993 Jim Courier *(US)*
women's singles
1984 Chris Evert-Lloyd *(US)*
1985 Martina Navratilova *(US)*
1986 *not held*
1987 Hana Mandlikova *(Czechoslovakia)*
1988 Steffi Graf *(West Germany)*
1989 Steffi Graf *(West Germany)*
1990 Steffi Graf *(West Germany)*
1991 Monica Seles *(Yugoslavia)*
1992 Monica Seles *(Yugoslavia)*
1993 Monica Seles *(Yugoslavia)*

Tennstedt Klaus 1926– . German conductor, musical director of the London Philharmonic Orchestra 1983–87. He excelled at interpreting works by Mozart, Beethoven, Bruckner, and Mahler.

Tennyson Alfred, 1st Baron Tennyson 1809–1892. English poet, poet laureate 1850–92, whose verse has a majestic, musical quality. His works include "The Lady of Shalott," "The Lotus Eaters," "Ulysses," "Break, Break, Break," "The Charge of the Light Brigade;" the longer narratives *Locksley Hall* 1832 and *Maud* 1855; the elegy *In Memoriam* 1850; and a long series of poems on the Arthurian legends *The Idylls of the King* 1857–85.

Tennyson was born at Somersby, Lincolnshire. The death of A H Hallam (a close friend during his years at Cambridge) 1833 prompted the elegiac *In Memoriam*, unpublished until 1850, the year in which he succeeded Wordsworth as poet laureate and married Emily Sellwood.

tenure employment terms and conditions. Security of tenure is often granted to the judiciary, civil servants, educators, and others in public office, where impartiality and freedom from political control are considered necessary.

The length of tenure depends on the service involved, and termination of it would only occur in exceptional cases, such as serious misconduct.

Tenzing Norgay known as *Sherpa Tenzing* 1914–1986. Nepalese mountaineer. In 1953 he was the first, with Edmund Hillary, to reach the summit of Mount Everest.

He had previously made 19 Himalayan expeditions as a porter. He subsequently became a director of the Himalayan Mountaineering Institute, Darjeeling.

Teotihuacán huge ancient city in central Mexico, a religious center of Mesoamerican civilization that was inhabited by many cultures from 6000 BC on. It is one of the best-excavated archeological sites in Mexico.

tequila Mexican alcoholic liquor distilled from the ◊agave plant. It is named after the place, near Guadalajara, where the conquistadors first developed it from Aztec *pulque*, which would keep for only a day.

teratogen any nongenetic agent that can induce deformities in the fetus if absorbed by the mother during pregnancy. Teratogens include some drugs (notably alcohol and ◊thalidomide), other chemicals, certain disease organisms, and radioactivity.

terbium soft, silver-gray, metallic element of the ◊lanthanide series, symbol Tb, atomic number 81, atomic weight 158.925. It occurs in gadolinite and other ores, with yttrium and ytterbium, and is used in lasers, semiconductors, and television tubes. It was named in 1843 by Swedish chemist Carl Mosander (1797–1858) for the town of Ytterby, Sweden, where it was first found.

Terbrugghen Hendrik 1588–1629. Dutch painter, a leader of the *Utrecht school* with Honthorst. He visited Rome around 1604 and was inspired by Caravaggio's work. He painted religious subjects and genre (everyday) scenes.

Terence (Publius Terentius Afer) 190–159 BC. Roman dramatist, born in Carthage and taken as a slave to Rome, where he was freed and came under ◊Scipio Africanus Minor's patronage. His surviving six comedies (including *The Eunuch* 161 BC) are subtly characterized and based on Greek models.

Terengganu alternate spelling of ◊Trengganu, state in Peninsular Malaysia.

Teresa Mother. Born Agnes Bojaxhiu 1910– . Roman Catholic nun. She was born in Skopje, Albania, and at 18 entered a Calcutta convent and became a teacher. In 1948 she became an Indian citizen and founded the Missionaries of Charity, an order for men and women based in Calcutta that helps abandoned children and the dying. Nobel Peace Prize 1979.

Teresa, St 1515–1582. Spanish mystic who founded an order of nuns 1562. She was subject to fainting fits, during which she saw visions. She wrote *The Way to Perfection* 1583 and an autobiography, *Life of the Mother Theresa of Jesus*, 1611. In 1622 she was canonized, and in 1970 was made the first female Doctor of the Church. She was born in Avila.

Tereshkova Valentina Vladimirovna 1937– . Soviet cosmonaut, the first woman to fly in space. In June 1963 she made a three-day flight in *Vostok 6*, orbiting the Earth 48 times.

term in architecture, a pillar in the form of a pedestal supporting the bust of a human or animal figure. Such objects derive from Roman boundary marks sacred to *Terminus*, the god of boundaries.

terminal in computing, a device consisting of a keyboard and display screen (◊VDT)—or, in older systems, a teleprinter—to enable the operator to communicate with the computer. The terminal may be physically attached to the computer or linked to it by a telephone line (remote terminal). A "dumb" terminal has no processor of its own, whereas an "intelligent" terminal has its own processor and takes some of the processing load away from the main computer.

termite any member of the insect order Isoptera. Termites are soft-bodied social insects living in large colonies which include one or more queens (of relatively enormous size and producing an egg every two seconds), much smaller kings, and still smaller soldiers, workers, and immature forms. Termites build galleried nests of soil particles that may be 20 ft/6 m high.

One group, the Macrotermitinae, constructs fungus gardens from its own feces by infecting them with a special fungus that digests the feces and renders them edible. Termites may dispose of a fourth of the vegetation litter of an area, and their fondness for wood (as in houses and other buildings) brings them into conflict with humans. The wood is broken down in their stomachs by numerous microorganisms living in ◊symbiosis with their hosts. Some species construct adjustable air vents in their nests, and one species moistens the inside of the nest with water to keep it cool.

tern any of various lightly built seabirds placed in the same family (Laridae) as gulls and characterized by pointed wings and bill and usually a forked tail. Terns plunge-dive after aquatic prey. They are 8–20 in/20–50 cm long, and usually colored in combinations of white and black.

The *common tern* *Sterna hirundo* has white underparts, gray upper wings, and a black crown on its head. The *Arctic tern* *Sterna paradisea* migrates from northern parts of Greenland, North America, and Europe to the Antarctic.

Terpsichore in Greek mythology, the ◊Muse of dance and choral song.

terracotta (Italian "baked earth") brownish-red baked clay, usually unglazed, used in building, sculpture, and pottery. The term is specifically applied to small figures or figurines, such as those found at Tanagra. Excavations at Xian, China, have revealed life-size terracotta figures of the army of the Emperor Shi Huangdi dating from the 3rd century BC.

terrapin general name for any turtle that frequents fresh or brackish water. The name is sometimes specifically used for the tidewater diamondback terrapins (genus *Malaclemys*) of E North America.

Terre Haute city in W Indiana, on the Wabash River; industries (plastics, chemicals, glass); population (1990) 57,500. Terre Haute was laid out 1816.

Points of interest include the birthplace of author Theodore Dreiser and the home of labor leader Eugene V Debs. Indiana State University is here.

terrier any of various breeds of highly intelligent, active dogs. They are usually small. Types include the bull, cairn, fox, Irish, Scottish, Sealyham, Skye, and Yorkshire terriers. They were originally bred for hunting rabbits and following quarry such as foxes down into burrows.

The small Parson Jack Russell terrier was recognized by the Kennel Club 1990 as a variant of the fox terrier.

territorial behavior in biology, any behavior that serves to exclude other members of the same species from a fixed area or ▷territory. It may involve aggressively driving out intruders, marking the boundary (with dung piles or secretions from special scent glands), conspicuous visual displays, characteristic songs, or loud calls.

territorial waters area of sea over which the adjoining coastal state claims territorial rights. This is most commonly a distance of 12 nautical mi/22.2 km from the coast, but, increasingly, states claim fishing and other rights up to 200 mi/370 km.

territory in animal behavior, a fixed area from which an animal or group of animals excludes other members of the same species. Animals may hold territories for many different reasons; for example, to provide a constant food supply, to monopolize potential mates, or to ensure access to refuges or nest sites. The size of a territory depends in part on its function: some nesting and mating territories may be only a few square yards, whereas feeding territories may be as large as hundreds of square miles.

terrorism systematic violence in the furtherance of political aims, often by small ▷guerrilla groups.

Terror, Reign of period of the ▷French Revolution when the Jacobins were in power (Oct 1793–July 1794) under ▷Robespierre and instituted mass persecution of their opponents. About 1,400 were executed, mainly by guillotine, until public indignation rose and Robespierre was overthrown in July 1794.

Terry Alfred Howe 1827–1890. US military leader. He served with distinction in the Civil War as colonel of the 2nd Connecticut militia and was promoted to brigadier general 1865. After the war he was placed in command of the Department of Dakota and also served in the Department of the South 1869–72. He was George ▷Custer's commander in the 1876 Sioux War, later negotiated with Sitting Bull, and supervised the opening of the Northern Plains.

Terry was born in Hartford, Connecticut, educated at Yale University, and became a lawyer 1849.

Terry Ellen 1847–1928. British actress, leading lady to Henry ▷Irving from 1878. She excelled in Shakespearean roles, such as Ophelia in *Hamlet*. She had a correspondence with the playwright G B Shaw.

Terry-Thomas Adopted name of Thomas Terry Hoar Stevens 1911–1990. British film comedy actor who portrayed upper-class English fools and cads in such films as *I'm All Right Jack* 1959, *It's a Mad, Mad, Mad, Mad World* 1963, and *How to Murder Your Wife* 1965.

tertiary in the Roman Catholic Church, a member of a "third order" (see under ▷holy orders); a lay person who, while marrying and following a normal employment, attempts to live in accordance with a modified version of the rule of one of the religious orders. The first such order was founded by St ▷Francis 1221.

Tertiary period of geological time 65–1.64 million years ago, divided into five epochs: Paleocene, Eocene, Oligocene, Miocene, and Pliocene. During the Tertiary, mammals took over all the ecological niches left vacant by the extinction of the dinosaurs, and became the prevalent land animals. The continents took on their present positions, and climatic and vegetation zones as we know them became established. Within the geological time column the Tertiary follows the Cretaceous period and is succeeded by the Quaternary period.

Tertullian Quintus Septimius Florens AD 155–222. Carthaginian Father of the Church, the first major Christian writer in Latin; he became a leading exponent of ▷Montanism.

terza rima poetical meter used in Dante's *Divine Comedy*, consisting of three-line stanzas in which the second line rhymes with the first and third of the following stanza. The English poet Shelley's "Ode to the West Wind" is another example.

tesla SI unit (symbol T) of ▷magnetic flux density. One tesla represents a flux density of one ▷weber per square meter, or 10^4 ▷gauss. It is named after the Croatian engineer Nikola Tesla.

Tesla Nikola 1856–1943. Croatian electrical engineer who emigrated to the US 1884. He invented fluorescent lighting, the Tesla induction motor, and the Tesla coil, and developed the ▷alternating current (AC) electrical supply system.

Test Act act of Parliament passed in England 1673, more than 100 years after similar legislation in Scotland, requiring holders of public office to renounce the doctrine of ▷transubstantiation and take the sacrament in an Anglican church, thus excluding Catholics, Nonconformists, and non-Christians from office. Its clauses were repealed 1828–29. Scottish tests were abolished 1889. In Ireland the Test Act was introduced 1704 and English legislation on oaths of allegiance and religious declarations were made valid there 1782. All these provisions were abolished 1871.

Test Ban Treaty agreement signed by the US, the USSR, and the UK Aug 5, 1963 contracting to test nuclear weapons only underground. In the following two years 90 other nations signed the treaty, the only major nonsignatories being France and China, which continued underwater and ground-level tests.

testis (plural *testes*) the organ that produces ▷sperm in male (and hermaphrodite) animals. In vertebrates it is one of a pair of oval structures that are usually internal, but in mammals

(other than elephants and marine mammals), the paired testes (or testicles) descend from the body cavity during development, to hang outside the abdomen in a scrotal sac.

testosterone in vertebrates, hormone secreted chiefly by the testes, but also by the ovaries and the cortex of the adrenal glands. It promotes the development of secondary sexual characteristics in males. In animals with a breeding season, the onset of breeding behavior is accompanied by a rise in the level of testosterone in the blood.

Synthetic or animal testosterone is used to treat inadequate development of male characteristics or (illegally) to aid athletes' muscular development. Like other sex hormones, testosterone is a ▷steroid.

tetanus or *lockjaw* acute disease caused by the toxin of the bacillus *Clostridium tetani*, which usually enters the body through a wound. The bacterium is chiefly found in richly manured soil. Untreated, in seven to ten days tetanus produces muscular spasm and rigidity of the jaw spreading to the other muscles, convulsions, and death. There is a vaccine, and the disease may be treatable with tetanus antitoxin and antibiotics.

Tethys in Greek mythology, one of the ▷Titans, the wife of the god ▷Oceanus.

Tethys Sea sea that once separated ▷Laurasia from ▷Gondwanaland; roughly corresponding to the present-day Mediterranean.

Tet Offensive in the Vietnam War, a prolonged attack mounted by the Vietcong against Saigon (now Ho Chi Minh City) and other South Vietnamese cities and hamlets beginning Jan 30, 1968. Although the Vietcong were finally forced to withdraw, the Tet Offensive brought into question the ability of the South Vietnamese army and their US allies to win the war and added fuel to the antiwar movement in both the US and Australia.

Some 84,000 communist Vietcong took part in the offensive, with 32,000 being killed by mid-Feb. The fighting in Saigon was especially fierce, and in Hue, which the Vietcong controlled for almost a month, 3,000 civilians were executed. The US Marine base at Khe San was besieged for almost three months, and although the Vietcong were finally repulsed with heavy losses, the US later abandoned the base.

tetra any of various brightly colored tropical freshwater bony fishes of the family Characidae, formerly placed in the genus *Tetragonopterus*. Tetras are found mainly in tropical South America, and also in Africa.

tetracycline one of a group of antibiotic substances having in common the four-ring structure of chlortetracycline, the first member of the group to be isolated. They are prepared synthetically or obtained from certain bacteria of the genus *Streptomyces*. They are broad-spectrum antibiotics, effective against a wide range of disease-causing bacteria.

tetrahedron (plural *tetrahedra*) in geometry, a solid figure (▷polyhedron) with four triangular faces; that is, a ▷pyramid on a triangular base. A regular tetrahedron has equilateral triangles as its faces.

In chemistry and crystallography, tetrahedra describe the shapes of some molecules and crystals; for example, the carbon atoms in a crystal of diamond are arranged in space as a set of interconnected regular tetrahedra.

tetrapod (Latin "four-legged") type of ▷vertebrate. The group includes mammals, birds, reptiles, and amphibians. Birds are included because they evolved from four-legged ancestors, the forelimbs having become modified to form wings. Even snakes are tetrapods, because they are descended from four-legged reptiles.

Teutonic Knight member of a German Christian military order, the *Knights of the Teutonic Order*, founded 1190 by Hermann of Salza in Palestine. They crusaded against the pagan Prussians and Lithuanians from 1228 and controlled Prussia until the 16th century. Their capital was Marienburg (now Malbork, Poland).

The Teutonic Knights were originally members of the German aristocracy who founded an order of hospitallers in Acre 1190 and became a military order 1198. They wore white robes with black crosses. They were based in Palestine until 1268 when they were expelled by the Mamelukes (rulers of Egypt), after which they concentrated on taking Roman Catholicism into E Europe under the control of the pope. They were prevented from expanding into Russia by ◊Alexander Nevski at the battle of Lake Peipus 1243, but they ruthlessly colonized Prussia 1226–83. By the 15th century, pressure from neighboring powers and the decline of the crusader ideal led to their containment within E Prussia. Their influence ended 1525 when their grand master Albert of Brandenburg was converted to Lutheranism and declared Prussia to be a secular duchy.

Texarkana twin cities that straddle the Texas–Arkansas border; industries include furniture, lumber, cotton, and sand and gravel; population (1990) 22,600 (Texas), 31,700 (Arkansas).

Texas state in SW US; nickname Lone Star State
area 266,803 sq mi/691,200 sq km
capital Austin
cities Houston, Dallas-Fort Worth, San Antonio, El Paso, Corpus Christi, Lubbock
features rivers: Rio Grande, Red; arid Staked Plains, reclaimed by irrigation; the Great Plains; Gulf Coast resorts; the Lyndon B Johnson Space Center, Houston; Alamo, San Antonio; Big Bend and Guadalupe Mountains national parks
products rice, cotton, sorghum, wheat, hay, livestock, shrimp, meat products, lumber, wood and paper products, petroleum (nearly one-third of US production), natural gas, sulfur, salt, uranium, chemicals, petrochemicals, nonelectrical machinery, fabricated metal

tetrahedron *A regular tetrahedron is a pyramid on a triangular base with all its sides equal in length.*

Texas

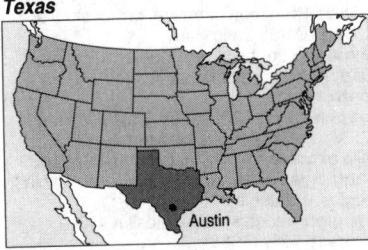

Austin

products, transportation equipment, electric and electronic equipment
population (1990) 16,986,500
famous people James Bowie, George Bush, Buddy Holly, Sam Houston, Howard Hughes, Lyndon Johnson, Janis Joplin, Katherine Anne Porter, Tina Turner
history settled by the Spanish 1682; part of Mexico 1821–36; Santa Anna massacred the Alamo garrison 1836, but was defeated by Sam Houston at San Jacinto the same year; Texas became an independent republic 1836–45, with Houston as president; in 1845 it became a state of the US. Texas is the only state in the US to have previously been an independent republic.

The Texas region was explored by Cabeza de Vaca and Coronado in the 16th and 17th centuries, and Spaniards settled at Ysleta (near El Paso) 1682. Americans led by Stephen Austin settled along the Brazos River from 1821.

Texas joined the Confederacy in the Civil War but saw little fighting and rejoined the Union 1870. The economy flourished with the development of the cattle industry; in 1901 oil was struck, leading to the development of the petroleum and petrochemical industries. Aircraft and other high technology contributed to the industrialization of Texas during and after World War II.

Texas City city in SE Texas, on Galveston Bay, SE of Houston; industries include tin, chemicals, oil, and grains; population (1990) 40,800.

Texas v White a US Supreme Court decision 1869 that dealt with the legal status of Confederate and Reconstruction governments. The provisional Reconstruction government of Texas sued for the return of property sold by the Confederate government during the Civil War. The case raised the question of which, if either, of the two governments was the valid, legal representative of Texas with the power to control state finances. The Court ruled that since secession was unconstitutional the Confederate state government had never existed as a legal body. It therefore had no right to dispose of state property. The Court also ruled that the provisional postwar government was a valid legal state government with the right to sue in the name of the people of Texas.

Texel or *Tessel* largest and most westerly of the ◊Frisian Islands, in North Holland province, the Netherlands; area 73 sq mi/ 190 sq km; population (1991) 12,700. Den Burg is the chief settlement.

textile (Latin *texere* "to weave") woven fabric; formerly a material woven from natural spun thread, now loosely extended to machine knits and spun-bonded fabrics (in which a web of fiber is created and then fuse-bonded by passing it through controlled heat).
natural Textiles made from natural fibers include cotton, linen, silk, and wool (including angora, llama, and many others). For particular

qualities, such as flame resistance or water and stain repellence, these may be combined with synthetic fibers or treated with various chemicals.
synthetic The first commercial synthetic thread was "artificial silk," or rayon, with filaments made from modified cellulose (wood pulp) and known according to later methods of manufacture as *viscose* (using caustic soda and carbon disulfide) or *acetate* (using acetic acid); the first fully synthetic textile fiber was ◊*nylon* 1937. These, with *acrylics*, such as Orlon, used in knitwear, *polyesters*, such as Terylene, and *spandex* or *elastomeric fibers*, for example Lycra, form the basis of most of today's industry.
geotextiles These are made from plastic and synthetic fibers; either felted for use as filters or stabilizing grids, or woven for strength. They form part of drainage systems, road foundations, and barriers to sea and river defenses against erosion.

TGV *train à grande vitesse* (French "high-speed train") French electrically powered train that provides the world's fastest rail service. Since it began operating 1981, it has carried more than 100 million passengers between Paris and Lyon, at average speeds of 167 mph/268 kph. In 1990 a second service, the Atlantique, was launched, running from Paris to Le Mans and Tours. A third is planned, linking Paris with the Channel Tunnel, Brussels, and Cologne. In 1990, a TGV broke the world speed record, reaching a speed of 320.2 mph/ 515.3 kph (about half that of a passenger jet aircraft) on a stretch of line near Tours.

In its regular service, the TGV covers the 264 mi/425 km distance between Paris and Lyon in two hours.

Thackeray William Makepeace 1811–1863. English novelist and essayist, born in Calcutta, India. He was a regular contributor to *Fraser's Magazine* and *Punch. Vanity Fair* 1847–48 was his first novel, followed by *Pendennis* 1848, *Henry Esmond* 1852 (and its sequel *The Virginians* 1857–59), and *The Newcomes* 1853–55, in which Thackeray's tendency to sentimentality is most marked.

Son of an East India Company official, he was educated at Cambridge. He studied law, and then art in Paris, before ultimately becoming a journalist in London. Other works include *The Book of Snobs* 1848 and the fairy tale *The Rose and the Ring* 1855.

Thailand country in SE Asia on the Gulf of Siam, bounded E by Laos and Cambodia, S by Malaysia, and W by Myanmar (Burma).
government A hereditary monarch is head of state. The 1978 constitution was suspended 1991 and a legislative assembly of up to 300 predominantly military members was appointed to draw up a new constitution. The country is controlled by a military junta called the National Peacekeeping Assembly, with a handpicked civilian administration as a front.

Far-left parties, such as the Communist Party, are outlawed, as are parties that field candidates in fewer than half the nation's constituencies. Effective political power in Thailand remains ultimately with the army leadership.
history Thailand has an ancient civilization, with Bronze Age artifacts from as early as 4000 BC. Siam, as it was called until 1939 (and 1945–49), has been united as a kingdom since 1350; the present dynasty dates from 1782. It was reached by Portuguese traders 1511, followed by the British East India Company and the Dutch in the 17th century. Treaties of

Thailand

Kingdom of (*Prathet Thai* or *Muang-Thai*)

area 198,108 sq mi/513,115 sq km
capital (and chief port) Bangkok
cities Chiangmai, Nakhon Sawan river port
physical mountainous, semiarid plateau in NE, fertile central region, tropical isthmus in S
environment tropical rainforest was reduced to 18% of the land area 1988 (from 93% in 1961); logging was banned by the government 1988
features rivers Chao Phraya, Mekong, Salween; ancient ruins of Sukhothai and Ayurrhaya
head of state King Bhumibol Adulyadej from 1946
head of government Chuan Leekpai from 1992
political system military-controlled emergent democracy
political parties New Aspiration Party; Samakkhi Tham (Justice and Unity) Party, right-of-center, airforce-linked; Palang Dharma, anticorruption; Social Action Party (Kij Sangkhom), right-of-center; Thai Nation (Chart Thai), conservative, pro-business; Liberal Democratic Party
exports rice, textiles, rubber, tin, rubies, sapphires, corn, tapioca
currency baht
population (1990 est) 54,890,000 (Thai 75%, Chinese 14%); growth rate 2% p.a.
life expectancy men 62, women 68 (1989)
languages Thai and Chinese (both official); regional dialects
religion Buddhist 95%, Muslim 4%
literacy 89% (1988)
GNP $52 bn (1988); $771 per head (1988)
chronology
1782 Siam absolutist dynasty commenced.
1896 Anglo-French agreement recognized Siam as independent buffer state.
1932 Constitutional monarchy established.
1939 Name of Thailand adopted.
1941–44 Japanese occupation.
1947 Military seized power in coup.
1972 Withdrawal of Thai troops from South Vietnam.
1973 Military government overthrown.
1976 Military reassumed control.
1980 General Prem Tinsulanonda assumed power.
1983 Civilian government formed; martial law maintained.
1988 Prime Minister Prem resigned; replaced by Chatichai Choonhavan.
1989 Thai pirates continued to murder, pillage, and kidnap Vietnamese "boat people" at sea.
1991 Military seized power in coup. Interim civilian government formed under Anand Panyarachun. 50,000 demonstrated against new military-oriented constitution.
1992 March: general election produced five-party coalition; Narong Wongwan named premier but removed a month later. April: appointment of General Suchinda Kraprayoon as premier provoked widespread riots. May: Suchinda forced to stand down. June: Anand made interim prime minister. Sept: new coalition government led by Chuan Leekpai.

friendship and trade 1826 and 1855 established Britain as the paramount power in the region and opened Siam to foreign commerce. The US presence was especially welcomed, since Americans brought the printing press, small-pox vaccinations, and other medical advances to a country that was fascinated by technology. Anglo-French diplomatic agreements of 1896 and 1904 established Siam as a neutral buffer kingdom between British Burma and French Indochina.

After World War I, a movement for national renaissance developed, which culminated in a coup against the absolute monarch King Prajadhipok and the establishment instead of a constitutional monarchy of an elected, representative system of government 1932. The name of Muang Thai ("land of the free") was adopted 1939. Thailand was occupied by Japan 1941–44. The government collaborated, but there was a guerrilla resistance movement. A period of instability followed the Japanese withdrawal, King Ananda Mahidol was assassinated 1946, and the army assumed power in a coup 1947 led by Field Marshal Pibul Songgram.

military junta rule The army retained control during the next two decades, with the leader of the military junta periodically changed by a series of bloodless coups: Field Marshal Pibul Songgram 1947–57, Field Marshal Sarit Thanarat 1958–63, and General Thanom Kittikachorn 1964–73. The monarch, King ◊Bhumibol Adulyadej, was only a figurehead, and experiments with elected assemblies were undertaken 1957–58 and 1968–71. During this era of junta rule, Thailand allied itself with the US and encountered serious communist guerrilla insurgency along its borders with Laos, Cambodia, and Malaysia. Despite achievements in the economic sphere, the junta was overthrown by violent student riots Oct 1973. A democratic constitution was adopted a year later, and free elections were held 1975 and 1976. A series of coalition governments lacked stability, and the military assumed power again 1976–77, annulling the 1974 constitution.

The army supreme commander, General Kriangsak Chomanan, held power 1977–80 and promulgated a new constitution Dec 1978. This established a mixed civilian and military form of government under the monarch's direction. Having deposed Kriangsak Oct 1980, General Prem Tinsulanonda (1920–) formally relinquished his army office and headed the civilian coalition governments that were formed after the parliamentary elections of April 1983 and July 1986.

rapid economic growth Attempted coups April 1983 and Sept 1985 were easily crushed by Prime Minister Prem, who ruled in a cautious apolitical manner and retained the confidence of the army leadership and the public. Under his stewardship, the country achieved a rapid rate of economic growth, 9%–10% a year, emerging as an export-oriented newly industrializing country. However, during the spring of 1988 divisions began to emerge within the ruling coalition and parliament was dissolved in April of that year. Following the general election July 1988, a six-party coalition, consisting of the Thai Nation, Democratic, Social Action, Citizens', United Democratic, and Muan Chon parties, was formed, which asked Prem to come into parliament and assume its leadership. Prem declined this offer for "personal" reasons and the Thai Nation's leader took over as premier.

In Feb 1991 Chatichai Choonhavan, Thailand's first prime minister in 12 years to be elected rather than appointed, was overthrown in a bloodless coup led by General Sunthorn Kongsompong, the supreme military commander, and army chief General Suchinda Kraprayoon. It was the country's 17th coup or attempted putsch since the abolition of the absolute monarchy 1932. An interim civilian administration was appointed, with Anand Panyarachun as prime minister, subject to the ultimate control of the military junta, which retained direct charge of the defense and interior ministry portfolios.

new constitution A new constitution was endorsed Dec 1991 in spite of protests that it reinforced the power of the military. In the March general election that followed, the three leading pro-military parties secured over half the total seats at stake. Narong Wongwan was named premier of a five-party coalition, but he was replaced a month later by General Suchinda. His appointment sparked huge street demonstrations, forcing him to resign. In May 1992 the ruling coalition agreed to a package of constitutional reforms, including the proviso that the prime minister should not come from the ranks of the military. Anand was made interim prime minister in June. The Sept 1992 general election gave a Democratic coalition 185 seats in the 360-member parliament and Chuan Leekpai became prime minister.

foreign affairs The civil war in Cambodia and Laos, which resulted in the flight of more than 500,000 refugees to Thailand 1975–90, provided justification for continued quasi-military rule and the maintenance of martial law until May 1991, when it was lifted along with the ban on political gatherings and activities imposed Feb 1991. Thailand drew closer to its ◊ASEAN allies, who jointly supported the Cambodian guerrilla resistance to the Vietnamese-imposed government, and its relations improved. Thailand was drawn more deeply into the Cambodian civil war with the shelling July 1989 of a refugee camp in Thailand, but tensions eased after the Cambodian peace agreement 1991. *See illustration box.*

Thaïs 4th century BC. Greek courtesan, mistress of ◊Alexander the Great and later wife of ◊Ptolemy I, king of Egypt. She allegedly instigated the burning of ◊Persepolis.

thalassemia or *Cooley's anemia* any of a group of chronic hereditary blood disorders that are widespread in the Mediterranean countries, Africa, the Far East, and the Middle East. They are characterized by an abnormality of the red blood cells and bone marrow, with enlargement of the spleen. The genes responsible are carried by about 100 million people worldwide.

Thalberg Irving Grant 1899–1936. US film-production executive. At the age of 20 he was head of production at Universal Pictures, and in 1924 he became production supervisor of the newly formed Metro-Goldwyn-Mayer (MGM). He was responsible for such prestige films as *Ben-Hur* 1926 and *Mutiny on the Bounty* 1935. With Louis B Mayer he built up MGM into one of the biggest Hollywood studios of the 1930s.

Born in Brooklyn, New York, Thalberg was hired 1918 as assistant to Carl Laemmle, president of Universal Pictures Corporation in New York. Having moved to Hollywood 1919, Thalberg, "the boy genius," was named head of the studio 1923, leaving to become vice-president in charge of production for MGM the following year. Throughout the rest of his brief career, he displayed an uncanny eye for talent and a consummate skill in business matters. Among his most memorable productions were *Grand Hotel* 1932 and *A Night at the Opera* 1935.

Thales 640–546 BC. Greek philosopher and scientist. He made advances in geometry, predicted an eclipse of the Sun 585 BC, and, as a philosophical materialist, theorized that water was the first principle of all things, that the Earth floated on water, and so proposed an explanation for earthquakes. He lived in Miletus in Asia Minor.

Thalia in Greek mythology, the ⬦Muse of comedy and pastoral poetry.

thalidomide ⬦hypnotic drug developed in the 1950s for use as a sedative. When taken in early pregnancy, it caused malformation of the fetus (such as abnormalities in the limbs) in over 5,000 recognized cases, and the drug was withdrawn.

thallium (Greek *thallos* "young green shoot") soft, bluish-white, malleable, metallic element, symbol Tl, atomic number 81, atomic weight 204.37. It is a poor conductor of electricity. Its compounds are poisonous and are used as insecticides and rodent poisons; some are used in the optical-glass and infrared-glass industries and in photoelectric cells.

Discovered spectroscopically 1861 by its green line, thallium was isolated and named by William Crookes 1861.

thallus any plant body that is not divided into true leaves, stems, and roots. It is often thin and flattened, as in the body of a seaweed, lichen, or liverwort, and the gametophyte generation (⬦prothallus) of a fern.

Some flowering plants (⬦angiosperms) that are adapted to an aquatic way of life may have a very simple plant body which is described as a thallus (for example, duckweed *Lemna*).

Thames river in S England; length 210 mi/338 km. It rises in the Cotswolds above Cirencester and is tidal as far as Teddington. Below London there is protection from flooding by means of the Thames barrier. The headstreams unite at Lechlade.

thanatology study of the psychological aspects of the experiences of death and dying and its application in counseling and assisting the terminally ill. It was pioneered by US psychiatrist Elizabeth Kübler-Ross in the 1970s.

Thanksgiving (Day) national holiday in the US (fourth Thursday in Nov) and Canada (second Monday in Oct), first celebrated by the Pilgrim settlers in Massachusetts after their first harvest 1621.

In the US it was proclaimed a national holiday 1863. Since 1942 it has been celebrated, by act of Congress, on the fourth Thursday in November. The original day of thanksgiving was proclaimed by Massachusetts governor William Bradford after the Pilgrims had survived their first winter, owing largely to help from their Indian ally Massasoit.

Thant, U 1909–1974. Burmese diplomat, secretary-general of the United Nations 1962–71. He helped to resolve the US-Soviet crisis over the Soviet installation of missiles in Cuba, and he made the controversial decision to withdraw the UN peacekeeping force from the Egypt–Israel border 1967 (see ⬦Arab-Israeli Wars).

Thar Desert or **Indian Desert** desert on the borders of ⬦Rajasthan and Pakistan; area about 96,500 sq mi/250,000 sq km.

Tharp Twyla 1942– . US modern dancer and choreographer who has worked with various companies, including the American Ballet Theater. Her works include *Eight Jelly Rolls* 1971, *Deuce Coupe* 1973, and *Push Comes to Shove* 1976.

Thatcher Margaret Hilda (born Roberts), Baroness Thatcher of Kesteven 1925– . British Conservative politician, prime minister 1979–90. She was education minister 1970–74 and Conservative Party leader from 1975. In 1982 she sent British troops to recapture the Falkland Islands from Argentina. She confronted labor-union power during the miners' strike 1984–85, sold off majority stakes in many public utilities to the private sector, and reduced the influence of local government through such measures as the abolition of metropolitan councils, the control of expenditure through "rate-capping," and the introduction of the community charge, or ⬦poll tax, from 1989. In 1990 splits in the cabinet over the issues of Europe and consensus government forced her resignation. An astute Parliamentary tactician, she tolerated little disagreement, either from the opposition or from within her own party.

theater performance by actors for an audience; it may include ⬦drama, dancing, music, ⬦mime, and ⬦puppets. The term is also used for the place or building in which dramatic performances take place. Theater history can be traced to Egyptian religious ritualistic drama as long ago as 3200 BC. The first known European theaters were in Greece from about 600 BC.

history The earliest Greek theaters were open spaces around the altar of Dionysus. The great stone theater at Athens was built about 500 BC, and its semicircular plan provided for an audience of 20,000–30,000 people sitting in tiers on the surrounding slopes; it served as a model for the theaters that were erected in all the main cities of the Graeco-Roman world. After the collapse of the Roman Empire the theaters were deserted. Examples of Roman theaters exist at Orange, France, St Albans, England, and elsewhere.

In medieval times, temporary stages of wood and canvas, one for every scene, were set up side by side in fairgrounds and market squares for the performance of mimes and ⬦miracle plays. Small enclosed theaters were built in the 16th century, for example in Vicenza, Italy (by the architect Palladio). The first London theater was built in Shoreditch 1576 by James ⬦Burbage, who also opened the first covered theater in London, the Blackfriars 1596. His son was responsible for building the ⬦Globe Theatre, the venue for Shakespeare's plays.

In the US the center of commercial theater is New York City, with numerous theaters on or near ⬦Broadway, although Williamsburg, Virginia (1716), and Philadelphia (1766) had the first known American theaters. The "little theaters," off-Broadway, developed to present less commercial productions, often by new playwrights, and of these the first was the Theater Guild (1919); off-off-Broadway then developed as ⬦fringe theater (alternative theater).

In Britain repertory theaters (theaters running a different play every few weeks) proliferated until World War II; for example, the ⬦Old Vic. The ⬦Comédie Française in Paris (founded by Louis XIV 1690 and given a permanent home 1792) was the first national theater. In Britain the National Theatre company was established 1963; other national theaters exist in Stockholm, Moscow, Athens, Copenhagen, Vienna, Warsaw, and elsewhere. Although the repertory movement declined from the 1950s with the spread of cinema and television, a number of regional community theaters developed. Recently established theaters are often associated with a university or are part of a larger cultural center. *See also chronology on p. 1038.*

thebaine $C_{19}H_{21}NO_3$ highly poisonous extract of ⬦opium.

Thebes capital of Boeotia in ancient Greece. In the Peloponnesian War it was allied with Sparta against Athens. For a short time after 371 BC when Thebes defeated Sparta at Leuctra, it was the most powerful state in Greece. Alexander the Great destroyed it 336 BC and although it was restored, it never regained its former power.

Thebes Greek name of an ancient city (*Niut-Ammon*) in Upper Egypt, on the Nile. Probably founded under the first dynasty, it was the center of the worship of Ammon, and the Egyptian capital under the New Kingdom about 1600 BC. Temple ruins survive near the villages of Karnak and Luxor, and in the nearby *Valley of the Kings* are buried the 18th–20th dynasty kings, including Tutankhamen and Amenhotep III.

theft dishonest appropriation of another's property with the intention of depriving him or her of it permanently.

In the US it is an informal name for the crime of ⬦larceny.

theism belief in the existence of gods, but more specifically in that of a single personal God, at once immanent (active) in the created world and transcendent (separate) from it.

Themis in Greek mythology, one of the ⬦Titans, the daughter of Uranus and Gaia. She was the personification of law and order.

Themistocles *c.* 525–*c.* 460 BC. Athenian soldier and politician. Largely through his policies in Athens (creating its navy and strengthening its walls), Greece was saved from Persian conquest. He fought with distinction in the Battle of Salamis 480 BC during the Persian War. About 470 he was accused of embezzlement and conspiracy against Athens, and banished by Spartan influence. He fled to Asia, where Artaxerxes, the Persian king, received him with favor.

Theocritus *c.* 310–*c.* 250 BC. Greek poet whose *Idylls* became models for later pastoral poetry. Probably born in Syracuse, he spent much of his life in Alexandria.

theater: chronology

c. 3200 BC	Beginnings of Egyptian religious drama, essentially ritualistic.
c. 600 BC	Choral performances (dithyrambs) in honor of Dionysus formed the beginnings of Greek tragedy, according to Aristotle.
500–300 BC	Great age of Greek drama which included tragedy, comedy, and satyr plays (grotesque farce).
468 BC	Sophocles' first victory at the Athens festival. His use of a third actor altered the course of the tragic form.
458 BC	Aeschylus' *Oresteia* were first performed.
c. 425–388 BC	Comedies of Aristophanes including *The Birds* 414, *Lysistrata* 411, and *The Frogs* 405. In tragedy the importance of the chorus diminished under Euripides, author of *The Bacchae* 405.
c. 350 BC	Menander's "New Comedy" of social manners developed.
c. 240 BC–AD 500	Emergence of Roman drama, adapted from Greek originals. Plautus, Terence, and Seneca were the main playwrights.
c. AD 375	Kālidāsa's *Sakuntalā* marked the height of Sanskrit drama in India.
c. 1250–1500	European mystery (or miracle) plays flourished, first in the churches, later in marketplaces, and were performed in England by town guilds.
c. 1375	Nō (or Noh) drama developed in Japan.
c. 1495	*Everyman*, the best known of all the morality plays, was first performed.
1500–1600	Italian commedia dell'arte troupes performed popular, improvised comedies; they were to have a large influence on Molière and on English harlequinade and pantomime.
c. 1576	The first English playhouse, The Theatre, was built by James Burbage in London.
1587	Christopher Marlowe's play *Tamburlaine the Great* marked the beginning of the great age of Elizabethan and Jacobean drama in England.
c. 1589	Thomas Kyd's play *Spanish Tragedy* was the first of the "revenge" tragedies.
c. 1590–1612	Shakespeare's greatest plays, including *Hamlet* and *King Lear*, were written.
1614	Lope de Vega's *Fuenteovejuna* marked the Spanish renaissance in drama. Other writers include Calderón de la Barca.
1637	Pierre Corneille's *Le Cid* established Classical tragedy in France.
1642	An act of Parliament closed all English theaters.
1660	With the restoration of Charles II to the English throne, dramatic performances recommenced. The first professional actress appeared as Desdemona in Shakespeare's *Othello*.
1664	Molière's *Tartuffe* was banned for three years by religious factions.
1667	Jean Racine's first success, *Andromaque*, was staged.
1680	The Comédie Française was formed by Louis XIV.
1700	William Congreve, the greatest exponent of Restoration comedy, wrote *The Way of the World*.
1716	The first known American theater was built in Williamsburg, Virginia.
1728	John Gay's *The Beggar's Opera* was first performed.
1737	The Stage Licensing Act in England required all plays to be approved by the Lord Chamberlain before performance.
1747	The actor David Garrick became manager of the Drury Lane Theatre, London.
1773	In England, Oliver Goldsmith's *She Stoops to Conquer* and Richard Sheridan's *The Rivals* 1775 established the "comedy of manners." Goethe's *Götz von Berlichingen* was the first *Sturm und Drang* play (literally, storm and stress).
1830	Victor Hugo's *Hernani* caused riots in Paris. His work marked the beginning of a new Romantic drama, changing the course of French theater.
1878	Henry Irving became actor-manager of the Lyceum with Ellen Terry as leading lady.
1879	Henrik Ibsen's *A Doll's House*, an early example of realism in European theater.
1888	August Strindberg wrote *Miss Julie*.
1893	George Bernard Shaw wrote *Mrs Warren's Profession* (banned until 1902 because it deals with prostitution). Shaw's works brought the new realistic drama to Britain and introduced social and political issues as subjects for the theater.
1895	Oscar Wilde's comedy *The Importance of Being Earnest*. Alfred Jarry's *Ubu Roi*, a forerunner of Surrealism.
1896	The first performance of Anton Chekhov's *The Seagull* failed.
1899	The Abbey Theatre, Dublin, founded by W B Yeats and Lady Gregory, marked the beginning of an Irish dramatic revival.
1904	Chekhov's *The Cherry Orchard*.
1919	The Theater Guild was founded in the US to perform less commercial new plays.
1920	*Beyond the Horizon*, Eugene O'Neill's first play, marked the beginning of serious theater in the US.
1921	Luigi Pirandello's *Six Characters in Search of an Author* introduced themes of the individual and exploration of reality and appearance.
1928	Bertolt Brecht's *Die Dreigroschenoper/The Threepenny Opera* with score by Kurt Weill; other political satires by Karel Čapek and Elmer Rice. In the US Jerome Kern's *Show Boat* with Paul Robeson, and other musical comedies by Cole Porter, Irving Berlin, and George Gershwin, became popular.
1930s	US social-protest plays of Clifford Odets, Lillian Hellman, Thornton Wilder, and William Saroyan.
1935	T S Eliot's *Murder in the Cathedral*.
1935–39	WPA Federal Theater Project in the US.
1943	The first of the musicals, *Oklahoma!*, opened.
1944–45	Jean-Paul Sartre's *Huis Clos/In Camera*; Jean Anouilh's *Antigone*; Arthur Miller's *Death of a Salesman*.
post-1945	Resurgence of German-language theater, including Wolfgang Borchert, Max Frisch, Friedrich Dürrenmatt, and Peter Weiss.
1947	Tennessee Williams's *A Streetcar Named Desire*. First Edinburgh Festival, Scotland, with fringe theater events.
1953	Arthur Miller's *The Crucible* opened in the US; *En attendant Godot/Waiting for Godot* by Samuel Beckett exemplified the Theater of the Absurd.
1956	The English Stage Company was formed at the Royal Court Theater to provide a platform for new dramatists. John Osborne's *Look Back in Anger* was included in its first season.
1957	Leonard Bernstein's *West Side Story* opened in New York.
1960	Harold Pinter's *The Caretaker* was produced in London.
1960s	Off-off-Broadway theater, a more daring and experimental type of drama, began to develop in New York.
1961	The Royal Shakespeare Company was formed in the UK under the directorship of Peter Hall.
1963–64	The UK National Theatre Company was formed at the Old Vic under the directorship of Laurence Olivier.
1967	Success in the US of *Hair*, the first of the "rock" musicals.
1968	Abolition of theater censorship in the UK.
1975	*A Chorus Line*, to become the longest-running musical, opened in New York.
1980	Howard Brenton's *The Romans in Britain* led in the UK to a private prosecution of the director for obscenity.
1989	Discovery of the remains of the 16th-century Rose and Globe theatres, London.
1992	Agatha Christie's *The Mousetrap* entered its 40th year in the West End, London, the longest-running play in the world.

theodolite instrument for the measurement of horizontal and vertical angles, used in surveying. It consists of a small telescope mounted so as to move on two graduated circles, one horizontal and the other vertical, while its axes pass through the center of the circles. See also ◊triangulation.

Theodora 508–548. Byzantine empress from 527. She was originally the mistress of Emperor Justinian before marrying him in 525. She earned a reputation for charity, courage, and championing the rights of women.

The daughter of a bear-keeper, Theodora became an actress and, as mistress and later wife of the emperor, the most influential woman in Europe, since Justinian consulted her on all affairs of state.

Theodoric of Freiburg c. 1250–1310. German scientist and monk. He studied in Paris 1275–77. In his work *De Iride/On the Rainbow* he describes how he used a water-filled sphere to simulate a raindrop, and determined that colors are formed in the raindrops and that light is reflected within the drop and can be reflected again, which explains secondary rainbows.

Theodoric the Great c. 455–526. King of the Ostrogoths from 474 in succession to his father. He invaded Italy 488, overthrew King Odoacer (whom he murdered) and established his own Ostrogothic kingdom there, with its capital in Ravenna. He had no strong successor, and his kingdom eventually became part of the Byzantine Empire of Justinian.

Theodosius I "the Great" c. AD 346–395. Roman emperor AD 388–95. A devout Christian and an adherent of the Nicene creed, he dealt harshly with heretics and in 391 crushed all forms of pagan religion in the empire. He thus founded the orthodox Christian state, acquiring his title. After his reign, the Roman empire was divided into eastern and western halves.

Theodosius II 401–450. Byzantine emperor from 408 who defeated the Persians 421 and 441, and from 441 bought off ◊Attila's Huns with tribute.

theology study of God or gods, either by reasoned deduction from the natural world or through revelation, as in the scriptures of Christianity, Islam, or other religions.

Theophanes the Greek 14th century. Byzantine painter active in Russia. He influenced painting in Novgorod, where his frescoes in Our Savior of the Transfiguration are dated to 1378. He also worked in Moscow with Andrei ◊Rublev.

theory in science, a set of ideas, concepts, principles, or methods used to explain a wide set of observed facts. Among the major theories of science are ◊relativity, ◊quantum theory, ◊evolution, and ◊plate tectonics.

theosophy any religious or philosophical system based on intuitive insight into the nature of the divine, but especially that of the Theosophical Society, founded in New York 1875 by Madame Blavatsky and H S Olcott. It was based on Hindu ideas of ◊karma and ◊reincarnation, with ◊nirvana as the eventual aim.

Theravāda one of the two major forms of ◊Buddhism, common in S Asia (Sri Lanka, Thailand, Cambodia, and Myanmar); the other is the later Mahāyāna.

Thérèse of Lisieux, St 1873–1897. French saint. She was born in Alençon, and entered a Carmelite convent in Lisieux at 15, where her holy life induced her superior to ask her to write her spiritual autobiography. She advocated the "Little Way of Goodness" in small things in everyday life, and became known as the "Little Flower of Jesus." She died of tuberculosis and was canonized 1925.

therm unit of energy defined as 10^5 British thermal units; equivalent to 1.055×10^8 joules. It is no longer in scientific use.

thermal capacity or *heat capacity* the heat energy, C, required to increase the temperature of an object by one degree. It is measured in joules per degree, $J/°C$ or J/K. If an object has mass m and is made of a substance with ◊specific heat capacity c, then $C = mc$.

thermal conductivity in physics, the ability of a substance to conduct heat. Good thermal conductors, like good electrical conductors, are generally materials with many free electrons (such as metals).

Thermal conductivity is expressed in units of joules per second per meter per kelvin ($J\,s^{-1}\,m^{-1}\,K^{-1}$). For a block of material of cross-sectional area a and length l, with temperatures T_1 and T_2 at its end faces, the thermal conductivity λ equals $Hl/at(T_2 - T_1)$, where H is the amount of heat transferred in time t.

thermal expansion in physics, expansion that is due to a rise in temperature. It can be expressed in terms of linear, area, or volume expansion.

The coefficient of linear expansion α is the increase in unit length per degree temperature rise; area, or superficial, expansion β is the increase in unit area per degree; and volume, or cubic, expansion γ is the increase in unit volume per degree. As a close approximation, $\beta = 2\alpha$ and $\gamma = 3\alpha$.

Thermidor 11th month of the French Revolutionary calendar, which gave its name to the period after the fall of the Jacobins and the proscription of Robespierre by the National Convention 9 Thermidor 1794.

thermionics branch of electronics dealing with the emission of electrons from matter under the influence of heat. Thermionics was named by O W ◊Richardson.

thermionic tube an electronic tube, used in telegraphy and telephony and in radio and radar, using space conduction by thermionically emitted electrons from an electrically heated cathode. Classification is into diode, triode, and multielectrode tubes, but in most applications they have been replaced by ◊transistors.

thermite process method used in incendiary devices and welding operations. It uses a powdered mixture of aluminum and (usually) iron oxide, which, when ignited, gives out enormous heat. The oxide is reduced to iron, which is molten at the high temperatures produced. This can be used to make a weld. The process was discovered 1895 by German chemist Hans Goldschmidt (1861–1923).

thermocouple electric temperature-measuring device consisting of a circuit having two wires made of different metals welded together at their ends. A current flows in the circuit when the two junctions are maintained at different temperatures (◊Seebeck effect). The electromotive force generated—measured by a millivoltmeter—is proportional to the temperature difference.

thermodynamics branch of physics dealing with the transformation of heat into and from other forms of energy. It is the basis of the study of the efficient working of engines, such as the steam and internal-combustion engines. The three laws of thermodynamics are (1) energy can be neither created nor destroyed, heat and mechanical work being mutually convertible; (2) it is impossible for an unaided self-acting machine to convey heat from one body to another at a higher temperature; and (3) it is impossible by any procedure, no matter how idealized, to reduce any system to the ◊absolute zero of temperature (0K/–273°C) in a finite number of operations. Put into mathematical form, these laws have widespread applications in physics and chemistry.

thermography photographic recording of heat patterns. It is used medically as an imaging technique to identify "hot spots" in the body —for example, tumors, where cells are more active than usual.

Thermography was developed in the 1970s and 1980s by the military to assist night vision by detecting the body heat of an enemy or the hot engine of a tank. It uses a photographic method (using infrared radiation) called the Aga system.

thermoluminescence release in the form of light of stored energy from a substance heated by ◊irradiation. It occurs with most crystalline substances to some extent. It is used in archeology to date pottery, and by geologists in studying terrestrial rocks and meteorites.

thermometer instrument for measuring temperature. There are many types, designed to measure different temperature ranges to varying degrees of accuracy. Each makes use of a different physical effect of temperature.

Expansion of a liquid is employed in common *liquid-in-glass thermometers*, such as those containing mercury or alcohol. The more accurate *gas thermometer* uses the effect of temperature on the pressure of a gas held at constant volume. A *resistance thermometer* takes advantage of the change in resistance of a conductor (such as a platinum wire) with variation in temperature. Another electrical thermometer is the ◊thermocouple. Mechanically, temperature change can be indicated by the change in curvature of a *bimetallic strip*.

Thermopylae, Battle of battle during the ◊Persian Wars 480 BC when Leonidas, king of Sparta, and 1,000 men defended the pass of Thermopylae to the death against a much greater force of Persians. The pass led from Thessaly to Locris in central Greece.

Thermos originally a trademarked name for a container for keeping things either hot or cold for several hours. It has two silvered glass walls enclosing a vacuum, filled into a metal or plastic outer case. This design reduces the three forms of heat transfer: radiation (prevented by the silvering) and conduction and convection (prevented by the vacuum). A vacuum flask is therefore equally efficient at keeping cold liquids cold, or hot liquids hot. It was invented by James Dewar (1842–1923) about 1872 to store liquefied gases.

thermosphere layer in the Earth's ◊atmosphere above the mesosphere and below the exosphere. Its lower level is about 50 mi/ 80 km above the ground, but its upper level is undefined. The ionosphere is located in the thermosphere. In the thermosphere the temperature rises with increasing height to several thousand degrees Celsius. However, because of the thinness of the air, very little heat is actually present.

Theroux Paul (Edward) 1941– . US novelist and travel writer. His works include the novels *Saint Jack* 1973, *The Mosquito Coast* 1981, *Doctor Slaughter* 1984, and *Chicago Loop* 1990, and accounts of his travels by train *The Great Railway Bazaar* 1975, *The Old Patagonian Express* 1979, *Kingdom by the Sea* 1983, and *Riding the Iron Rooster* 1988.

thesaurus (Greek "treasure") collection of synonyms or words with related meaning. Thesaurus compilers include Francis ⟡Bacon, Comenius (1592–1670), and Peter Mark ⟡Roget, whose work was published 1852.

Theseus legendary hero of ⟡Attica, supposed to have united the states of the area under a constitutional government in Athens. Ariadne, whom he later abandoned on Naxos, helped him find his way through the Labyrinth to kill the ⟡Minotaur. He also fought the Amazons and was one of the ⟡Argonauts.

Thespis 6th century BC. Greek poet, born in Attica, said to have introduced the first actor into plays (previously presented by choruses only), hence the word *thespian* for an actor. He was also said to have invented tragedy and to have introduced the wearing of linen masks.

Thessaloníki (English *Salonika*) port in Macedonia, NE Greece, at the head of the Gulf of Thessaloníki, the second largest city of Greece; population (1981) 706,200. Industries include textiles, shipbuilding, chemicals, brewing, and tanning. It was founded from Corinth by the Romans 315 BC as *Thessalonica* (to whose inhabitants St Paul addressed two epistles), captured by the Saracens AD 904 and by the Turks 1430, and restored to Greece 1912.

Thessaly (Greek *Thessalia*) region of E central Greece, on the Aegean; area 5,367 sq mi/13,904 sq km; population (1991) 731,200. It is a major area of cereal production. It was an independent state in ancient Greece and later formed part of the Roman province of ⟡Macedonia. It was Turkish from the 14th century until incorporated in Greece 1881.

Thetis in Greek mythology, daughter of Nereus, and mother of ⟡Achilles, to whom she brings armor forged by Hephaestus in Homer's *Iliad*. Fated to have a son more powerful than his father, she was married by the gods to a mortal, Peleus.

thiamine or *vitamin B₁* ⟡vitamin of the B complex. Its absence from the diet causes the disease beriberi.

Thibodaux town in SE Louisiana, SW of New Orleans; population (1980) 15,810. It is an agricultural center for sugar, dairy products, vegetables, and cotton.

Thiers Louis Adolphe 1797–1877. French politician and historian, first president of the Third Republic 1871–73. He held cabinet posts under Louis Philippe, led the parliamentary opposition to Napoleon III from 1863, and as head of the provisional government 1871 negotiated peace with Prussia and suppressed the briefly autonomous ⟡Paris Commune.

His economic policies facilitated the nation's recovery after the Franco-Prussian War.

Thimbu or *Thimphu* capital since 1962 of the Himalayan state of Bhutan; population (1987) 15,000.

thing-in-itself (German *Ding-an-sich*) technical term in the philosophy of ⟡Kant, employed

to denote the unknowable source of the sensory component of our experience. Later thinkers, including ⟡Fichte and ⟡Hegel, denied the coherence of this concept.

think tank popular name for research foundations, generally private, that gather experts to study policy questions and make recommendations. There are think tanks representing positions across the political spectrum, and they are sometimes funded according to the viewpoints they represent.

Third Reich (Third Empire) term used by the Nazis to describe Germany during the years of Hitler's dictatorship after 1933. The idea of the Third Reich was based on the existence of two previous German empires, the medieval Holy Roman Empire and the second empire 1871–1918.

The term was coined by the German writer Moeller van den Bruck (1876–1925) in the 1920s.

Third World those countries that are less developed than the industrialized free-market countries of the West (First World) and the industrialized former Communist countries (Second World). Third World countries are the poorest, as measured by their income per head of population, and are concentrated in Asia, Africa, and Latin America.

They are divided into low-income countries, including China and India; middle-income countries, such as Nigeria, Indonesia, and Bolivia; and upper-middle-income countries, such as Brazil, Algeria, and Malaysia. The Third World has 75% of the world's population but consumes only 20% of its resources. In 1990 the average income per head of population in the northern hemisphere was $12,500, which is 18 times higher than that in the southern hemisphere.

Problems associated with developing countries include high population growth and mortality rates; poor educational and health facilities; heavy dependence on agriculture and commodities for which prices and demand fluctuate; high levels of underemployment, and, in some cases, political instability. Third World countries, led by the Arab oil-exporting countries, account for over 75% of all arms imports. The economic performance of developing countries in recent years has been mixed, with sub-Saharan Africa remaining in serious difficulties and others, as in Asia, making significant progress. Failure by many developing countries to meet their enormous foreign debt obligations has led to stringent terms being imposed on loans by industrialized countries, as well as rescheduling of loans (deferring payment).

Thirteen Colonies 13 American colonies that signed the ⟡Declaration of Independence from Britain 1776. Led by George Washington, the Continental Army defeated the British army in the ⟡American Revolution 1776–81 to become the original 13 United States of America: Connecticut, Delaware, Georgia, Maryland, Massachusetts, New Hampshire, New Jersey, New York, North Carolina, Pennsylvania, Rhode Island, South Carolina, and Virginia. They were united first under the Articles of ⟡Confederation and from 1789, the US ⟡constitution.

38th parallel demarcation line between North (People's Democratic Republic of) and South (Republic of) Korea, agreed at the Yalta Conference 1945 and largely unaltered by the Korean War 1950–53.

35 mm width of photographic film, the most popular format for the camera today. The 35-mm camera falls into two categories, the ⟡SLR and the ⟡rangefinder.

Thirty Years' War major war 1618–48 in central Europe. Beginning as a German conflict between Protestants and Catholics, it gradually became transformed into a struggle to determine whether the ruling Austrian Hapsburg family would gain control of all Germany. The war caused serious economic and demographic problems in central Europe.

1618–20 A Bohemian revolt against Austrian rule was defeated. Some Protestant princes continued the struggle against Austria.
1625–27 Denmark entered the war on the Protestant side.
1630 Gustavus Adolphus of Sweden intervened on the Protestant side, overrunning N Germany.
1631 The Catholic commander Tilly stormed Magdeburg.
1632 Tilly was defeated at Breitenfeld and the Lech, and was killed. The German general Wallenstein was defeated at the Battle of Lützen; Gustavus Adolphus was killed.
1634 When the Swedes were defeated at Nördlingen, ⟡Richelieu brought France into the war to inflict several defeats on Austria's Spanish allies. Wallenstein was assassinated.
1648 The *Treaty of Westphalia* gave France S Alsace, and Sweden got certain Baltic provinces, the emperor's authority in Germany becoming only nominal. The mercenary armies of Wallenstein, Tilly, and Mansfeld devastated Germany.

thistle prickly plant of several genera, such as *Carduus*, *Carlina*, <12>Onopordum, and *Cirsium*, in the family Compositae. The stems are spiny, the flower heads purple, white, or yellow and cottony, and the leaves deeply indented with prickly margins. The thistle is the Scottish national emblem.

Thomas Clarence 1948– . US Supreme Court justice (1991–). Born in Savannah, Georgia, he received a law degree from Yale University Law School (1974). President Reagan appointed him head of the civil rights division of the Department of Education 1981 and the head of the Equal Employment Opportunities Commission 1982. Thomas served there until 1990, when President Bush appointed him a justice on the US Court of Appeals. In 1991 he was nominated to the Supreme Court to succeed Thurgood Marshall, and after extremely bitter and sensational confirmation hearings, in which he was accused of sexual harassment by former colleague Anita Hill, Thomas was confirmed by the Senate and took his seat on the Court.

Thomas Dylan (Marlais) 1914–1953. Welsh poet. His poems include the celebration of his 30th birthday "Poem in October" and the evocation of his youth "Fern Hill" 1946. His "play for voices" *Under Milk Wood* 1954 describes with humor and compassion a day in the life of the residents of a small Welsh fishing village, Llareggub. The short stories of *Portrait of the Artist as a Young Dog* 1940 are autobiographical.

Born in Swansea, son of the English teacher at the local grammar school where he was educated, he worked as a reporter on the *South Wales Evening Post*, then settled as a journalist in London and published his first volume *Eighteen Poems* 1934.

Thomas Lowell (Jackson) 1892–1981. US journalist, a radio commentator for the Columbia

Broadcasting System (CBS) 1930–76. Traveling to all World War II theaters of combat and to remote areas of the world, he became one of America's best-known journalists.

Born in Woodington, Ohio, Thomas was educated at Northern Indiana University and the University of Denver and joined the staff of the *Chicago Journal* 1912. After receiving an MA from Princeton 1915, he served as a special observer for President Wilson during World War I. His first-person account of the Arab Revolt was published as *With Lawrence in Arabia* 1924.

Thomas Norman Mattoon 1884–1968. US political leader, six times Socialist candidate for president 1928–48. He was one of the founders of the American Civil Liberties Union 1920 and served as a director of the League for Industrial Democracy 1922–37.

Thomas, born in Marion, Ohio, graduated from Princeton 1905 and after study at the Union Theological Seminary was ordained a Presbyterian minister 1911. As pastor of the East Harlem Church he first confronted the problem of urban poverty and joined the Socialist Party 1918, leaving the ministry for political activism two years later. By 1950, he noted, most of his so-called radical platform had been adopted by the US, such as Social Security and public-health programs. He was a brilliant speaker and published *A Socialist's Faith* 1951.

Thomas Seth 1785–1859. US clock manufacturer. He was born in Wolcott, Connecticut, and trained as a carpenter and cabinetmaker. In 1807 he joined Silas Hoadley and Eli Terry in a partnership in Plymouth, Connecticut, for the production of clocks. Thomas established his own firm 1812 and became enormously successful in the manufacture of affordable shelf clocks. In 1853 the firm was reorganized as the Seth Thomas Clock Company and continued to prosper into the 20th century. Its base of operations, Plymouth Hollow, Connecticut, was renamed Thomaston.

Thomas à Kempis 1380–1471. German Augustinian monk who lived at the monastery of Zwolle. He took his name from his birthplace Kempen; his real surname was Hammerken. His *De Imitatio Christi/Imitation of Christ* is probably the most widely known devotional work ever written.

Thomas Aquinas medieval philosopher; see ◊Aquinas, St Thomas.

Thomas, St in the New Testament, one of the 12 Apostles, said to have preached in S India, hence the ancient churches there were referred to as the "Christians of St Thomas." He is not the author of the Gospel of St Thomas, the Gnostic collection of Jesus' sayings.

Thomism in philosophy, the method and approach of Thomas ◊Aquinas. Neo-Thomists apply this philosophical method to contemporary problems.

Thompson David 1770–1857. Canadian explorer and surveyor who mapped extensive areas of W Canada, including the Columbia River, for the Hudson's Bay Company 1789–1811.

Thompson John Taliaferro 1860–1940. US colonel, inventor of the Thompson submachine gun (see ◊machine gun).

Thomsen Christian (Jürgensen) 1788–1865. Danish archeologist. He devised the classification of prehistoric cultures into Stone Age, Bronze Age, and Iron Age.

Thomson Elihu 1853–1937. US inventor. He founded, with E J Houston (1847–1914), the Thomson-Houston Electric Company 1882, later merging with the Edison Company to form the General Electric Company. He made advances into the nature of the ◊electric arc and invented the first high-frequency ◊dynamo and ◊transformer.

Thomson George Paget 1892–1975. English physicist whose work on ◊interference phenomena in the scattering of electrons by crystals helped to confirm the wavelike nature of particles. He shared a Nobel Prize with C J ◊Davisson 1937.

Thomson J(oseph) J(ohn) 1856–1940. English physicist who discovered the ◊electron. He was responsible for organizing the Cavendish atomic research laboratory at Cambridge University. His work inaugurated the electrical theory of the atom and led to ◊Aston's discovery of ◊isotopes. Nobel Prize 1906.

Thomson Virgil 1896–1989. US composer and critic. He studied in France with Nadia ◊Boulanger 1921–22 and returned to Paris 1925–40, mixing with Gertrude Stein and her circle. He is best known for his opera *Four Saints in Three Acts* 1927–33 to a libretto by Stein, and the film scores *The Plow That Broke the Plains* 1936 and *Louisiana Story* 1948. His music is notable for a refined absence of expression, his criticism for trenchant matter-of-factness, both at odds with the prevailing US musical culture.

Thor in Norse mythology, god of thunder (his hammer), and represented as a man of enormous strength defending humanity against demons. He was the son of Odin and Freya, and Thursday is named after him.

thorax in tetrapod vertebrates, the part of the body containing the heart and lungs, and protected by the rib cage; in arthropods, the middle part of the body, between the head and abdomen.

In mammals the thorax is separated from the abdomen by the muscular diaphragm. In insects the thorax bears the legs and wings. The thorax of spiders and crustaceans is fused with the head, to form the cephalothorax.

Thoreau Henry David 1817–1862. US author and naturalist. His work *Walden, or Life in the Woods* 1854 stimulated the back-to-nature movement, and he completed some 30 volumes based on his daily nature walks. His essay "Civil Disobedience" 1849, prompted by his refusal to pay taxes, advocated peaceful resistance to unjust laws and had a wide impact, even in the 20th century.

Born in Concord, Massachusetts, Thoreau graduated from Harvard University. His friend, transcendentalist Ralph Waldo ◊Emerson, encouraged him to write and offered him land near Walden Pond on which to set up his experiment 1845–47 in living a life close to nature, requiring little manual labor and allowing him time to write. His other works include *A Week on the Concord and Merrimack Rivers* 1849 and, published posthumously, *Excursions* 1863, *The Maine Woods* 1864, *Cape Cod* 1865, and *A Yankee in Canada* 1866.

thorium dark-gray, radioactive, metallic element of the ◊actinide series, symbol Th, atomic number 90, atomic weight 232.038. It occurs throughout the world in small quantities in minerals such as thorite and is widely distributed in monzanite beach sands. It is

one of three fissile elements (the others are uranium and plutonium), and its longest-lived isotope has a half-life of 1.39×10^{10} years. Thorium is used to strengthen alloys. It was discovered by Jöns Berzelius 1828 and was named by him after the Norse god Thor.

thorn apple or *jimson weed* annual plant *Datura stramonium* of the nightshade family, growing to 6 ft/2 m in northern temperate and subtropical areas; native to America and naturalized worldwide. It bears white or violet trumpet-shaped flowers and capsulelike fruit that split to release black seeds. All parts of the plant are poisonous.

The fruit of the ◊hawthorn is also called thorn apple.

Thorndike Edward Lee 1874–1949. US educational psychologist whose experiments in behavior of cats and dogs in a "puzzle box" brought him to the conclusion that learning was improved when it achieved a satisfactory result. He extended this theory to human learning and found that students were encouraged by good results, but that being wrong did not teach them to correct their errors.

thoroughbred horse bred for racing purposes. All racehorses are thoroughbreds, and all male thoroughbreds are direct descendants of one of three stallions imported into Britain during the 17th and 18th centuries: the Darley Arabian, Byerley Turk, and Godolphin Barb.

Thorpe Jim (James Francis) 1888–1953. US athlete. Born in Prague, Oklahoma, Thorpe attended the Carlisle Indian School in Pennsylvania. An outstanding football player, he was named All-American in 1911 and 1912. A member of the 1912 US Olympic Team in Stockholm, Thorpe won gold medals for the decathlon and pentathlon. However, when he admitted to having played semiprofessional baseball, he was forced to return his medals. Thorpe later played major-league baseball 1913–19 and professional football 1917–29. He was posthumously elected to the Football Hall of Fame 1963, and his Olympic medals were restored by the Amateur Athletic Union 1973.

Thoth in Egyptian mythology, god of wisdom and learning. He was represented as a scribe with the head of an ◊ibis, the bird sacred to him.

Thothmes four Egyptian kings of the 18th dynasty, including:

Thothmes I king of Egypt 1540–1501 BC. He founded the Egyptian empire in Syria.

Thothmes III king of Egypt c. 1500–1446 BC. He extended the empire to the river Euphrates, and conquered Nubia. He was a grandson of Thothmes I.

Thousand Islands group of about 1,700 islands in the upper St Lawrence River, on the border between Canada and the US. Most of them are in Ontario; the rest are in the US state of New York. Some are in Canada's St Lawrence Islands National Park; many of the others are privately owned. The largest is Wolfe Island in Ontario, 49 sq mi/127 sq km. The islands are popular summer resorts.

Thrace (Greek *Thráki*) ancient empire (6000 BC–AD 300) in the Balkans, SE Europe, formed by parts of modern Greece and Bulgaria. It was held successively by the Greeks, Persians, Macedonians, and Romans.

The area was divided 1923 into western Thrace (the Greek province of Thráki) and eastern Thrace (European Turkey). The heart of the ancient Thracian Empire was Bulgaria, where since 1945 there have been tomb finds of gold and silver dishes, drinking vessels, and jewelry with animal designs. The legend of ◊Orpheus and the cult of ◊Dionysus were both derived by the Greeks from Thrace. The area was conquered by Persia 6th–5th centuries BC and by Macedonia 4th–2nd centuries BC. From AD 46 it was a Roman province, then part of the Byzantine Empire, and Turkish from the 15th century until 1878; it was then subject to constant dispute until after World War I.

Three Mile Island island in the Shenandoah River near Harrisburg, Pennsylvania, site of a nuclear power station which was put out of action following a major accident March 1979. Opposition to nuclear power in the US was reinforced after this accident and safety standards reassessed.

Three Musketeers, The romance by Alexandre Dumas *père*, published in France 1844–45. D'Artagnan, a poor gentleman, joins forces with three of King Louis XIII's musketeers, Athos, Porthos, and Aramis, in a series of adventures.

Three Rivers English name for the Canadian port of ◊Trois-Rivières.

threshing agricultural process of separating cereal grains from the plant. Traditionally, the work was carried out by hand in winter months using the flail, a jointed beating stick. Today, threshing is done automatically inside the combine harvester at the time of cutting.

From the late 18th century, through the work of Andrew Meikle and others, machine threshing slowly overtook the flail and made rapid progress after 1850.

thrift or **sea pink** any plant of the genus *Armeria*, family Plumbaginaceae. *A. maritima* occurs on seashores and cliffs in Europe. The leaves are small and linear; the dense round heads of pink flowers rise on straight stems.

thrips any of a number of tiny insects of the order Thysanoptera, usually with feathery wings. Many of the 3,000 species live in flowers and suck their juices, causing damage and spreading disease. Others eat fungi, decaying matter, or smaller insects.

throat in human anatomy, the passage that leads from the back of the nose and mouth to the ◊trachea and ◊esophagus. It includes the ◊pharynx and the ◊larynx, the latter being at the top of the trachea. The word "throat" is also used to mean the front part of the neck, both in humans and other vertebrates; for example, in describing the plumage of birds. In engineering, it is any narrowing entry, such as the throat of a carburetor.

thrombosis condition in which a blood clot forms in a vein or artery, causing loss of circulation to the area served by the vessel. If it breaks away, it often travels to the lungs, causing pulmonary embolism.

Thrombosis in veins of the legs is often seen in association with ◊phlebitis, and in arteries with ◊atheroma. Thrombosis increases the risk of heart attack (myocardial ◊infarct) and stroke. It is treated by surgery and/or anticoagulant drugs.

throwing event field event. There are four at most major international track and field meets: ◊discus, ◊hammer, ◊javelin, and ◊shot put.

thrush any bird of the large family Turdidae, order Passeriformes, found worldwide and known for their song. Thrushes are usually brown with speckles of other colors. They are 5–12 in/12–30 cm long.

North American species include the hermit thrush *Catharus guttatus*, a beautiful songster; the wood thrush *Hylocichla mustelina*; and the American robin *Turdus migratorius*. European species include the song thrush *Turdus philomelos*, and the mistle thrush *T. viscivorus*.

thrush infection usually of the mouth (particularly in infants), but also sometimes of the vagina, caused by a yeastlike fungus (genus *Candida*). It is seen as white patches on the mucous membranes.

Thrush, also known as **candidiasis**, may be caused by antibiotics removing natural antifungal agents from the body. It is treated with a further antibiotic.

Thucydides *c.* 455–400 BC. Athenian historian who exercised command in the ◊Peloponnesian War with Sparta 424 with so little success that he was banished until 404. In his *History of the Peloponnesian War*, he attempted a scientific impartiality.

thug originally a member of a Hindu sect who strangled travelers as sacrifices to ◊Kali, the goddess of destruction. The sect was suppressed about 1830.

thulium soft, silver-white, malleable and ductile, metallic element, of the ◊lanthanide series, symbol Tm, atomic number 69, atomic weight 168.94. It is the least abundant of the rare-earth metals, and was first found in gadolinite and various other minerals. It is used in arc lighting.

The X-ray-emitting isotope Tm-170 is used in portable X-ray units. Thulium was named by French chemist Paul Lecoq de Boisbaudran 1886 after the northland, Thule.

Thunder Bay city and port on Lake Superior, Ontario, formed by the union of Port Arthur and its twin city of Fort William to the S; industries include shipbuilding, timber, paper, wood pulp, and export of wheat; population (1986) 122,000.

Thunderbird legendary bird of the North American Indians, the creator of storms. It is said to produce thunder by flapping its wings; lightning by opening and closing its eyes.

Thünen Johann von 1785–1850. German economist and geographer who believed that the success of a state depends on the well-being of its farmers. His book *The Isolated State* 1820, a pioneering study of land use, includes the earliest example of **marginal productivity theory**, a theory that he developed to calculate the natural wage for a farmworker. He has been described as the first modern economist.

Thurber James (Grover) 1894–1961. US humorist. His short stories, written mainly for the *New Yorker* magazine, include "The Secret Life of Walter Mitty" 1932, and his doodle drawings include fanciful impressions of dogs.

Born in Columbus, Ohio, Thurber was partially blind as a result of an accident in childhood; he became totally blind in the last ten years of his life but continued to work. His stories and sketches are collected in *Is Sex Necessary?* (with E B White) 1929, *The Middle-Aged Man on the Flying Trapeze* 1935, *The Last Flower* 1939, and *My World and Welcome to It* 1942. He also wrote adult fairy tales —*Many Moons* 1943, *The Great Quillow* 1944, *The White Deer* 1945, *The 13 Clocks* 1950, and *The Wonderful O* 1957—and a play, *The Male Animal* 1940.

Thuringia administrative *Land* (state) of Germany;

area 5,980 sq mi/15,482 sq km
capital Erfurt
cities Weimar, Gera, Jena, Eisenach
products machine tools, optical instruments, steel, vehicles, ceramics, electronics, glassware, timber
population (1990) 2,500,000
history a historic, densely forested region of Germany that became a province 1918 and a region of East Germany 1946. It was split into the districts of Erfurt, Gera, and Suhl 1952 but reconstituted as a state following German reunification 1990.

Thyestes in Classical mythology, son of ◊Pelops and brother of ◊Atreus. His rivalry with Atreus for the kingship of Mycenae was continued by their sons, Aegisthus and Agamemnon.

thylacine another name for the ◊Tasmanian wolf.

thyme herb, genus *Thymus*, of the mint family Labiatae. Garden thyme *T. vulgaris*, native to the Mediterranean, grows to 1 ft/30 cm high, and has pinkish flowers. Its aromatic leaves are used for seasoning.

thymus organ in vertebrates, situated in the upper chest cavity in humans. The thymus processes ◊lymphocyte cells to produce T-lymphocytes (T denotes "thymus-derived"), which are responsible for binding to specific invading organisms and killing them or rendering them harmless.

The thymus reaches full size at puberty, and shrinks thereafter; the stock of T-lymphocytes is built up early in life, so this function diminishes in adults, but the thymus continues to function as an ◊endocrine gland, producing the hormone thymosin, which stimulates the activity of the T-lymphocytes.

thyristor type of ◊rectifier, an electronic device that conducts electricity in one direction only. The thyristor is composed of layers of ◊semiconductor material sandwiched between two electrodes called the anode and cathode. The current can be switched on by using a third electrode called the gate.

Thyristors are used to control mains-driven motors and in lighting dimmer controls.

thyroid ◊endocrine gland of vertebrates, situated in the neck in front of the trachea. It secretes several hormones, principally thyroxine, an iodine-containing hormone that stimulates growth, metabolism, and other functions of the body. The thyroid gland may be thought of as the regulator gland of the body's metabolic rate. If it is overactive, as in thyrotoxicosis, the sufferer feels hot and sweaty, has an increased heart rate, diarrhea, and weight loss. Conversely, an underactive thyroid leads to myxedema, a condition characterized by sensitivity to the cold, constipation, and weight gain. In infants, an underactive thyroid leads to cretinism, a form of mental retardation.

Tiahuanaco or **Tihuanaco** site of a Peruvian city, S of Lake Titicaca in the Andes, which gave its name to the 8th–14th-century civilization that preceded the Inca and built many of the roads the Inca are credited with building.

Tiananmen Square (Chinese "Square of Heavenly Peace") paved open space in central Beijing (Peking), China, the largest public square in the world (area 0.14 sq mi/ 0.4 sq km). On June 3–4, 1989, more than 1,000 unarmed protesters were killed by government troops in a massacre that crushed China's emerging prodemocracy movement.

Hundreds of thousands of demonstrators had occupied the square from early May, calling for political reform and the resignation of the Communist leadership. They were led by students, 3,000 of whom staged a hunger strike in the square. The massacre that followed was sanctioned by the old guard of leaders, including Deng Xiaoping.

Tianjin or *Tientsin* port and industrial and commercial city in Hubei province, central China; population (1989) 5,620,000. The special municipality of Tianjin has an area of 1,544 sq mi/4,000 sq km and a population (1990) of 8,788,000. Its handmade silk and wool carpets are renowned. Dagan oil field is nearby. Tianjin was opened to foreign trade 1860 and occupied by the Japanese 1937.

Tian Shan (Chinese *Tien Shan*) mountain system in central Asia. *Pik Pobedy* on the Xinjiang-Kyrgyz border is the highest peak at 24,415 ft/7,440 m.

Tiber (Italian *Tevere*) river in Italy on which Rome stands; length from the Apennines to the Tyrrhenian Sea 250 mi/400 km.

Tiberias, Lake or *Sea of Galilee* lake in N Israel, 689 ft/210 m below sea level, into which the ○Jordan flows; area 66 sq mi/170 sq km. The first Israeli ○kibbutz (cooperative settlement) was founded nearby 1909.

Tiberius Claudius Nero 42 BC–AD 37. Roman emperor, the stepson, adopted son, and successor of Augustus from AD 14. A distinguished soldier, he was a conscientious ruler under whom the empire prospered.

Tibet autonomous region of SW China (Pinyin form *Xizang*);
area 471,538 sq mi/1,221,600 sq km
capital Lhasa
features Tibet occupies a barren plateau bounded south and southwest by the Himalayas and north by the Kunlun Mountains, traversed west to east by the Bukamagna, Karakoram, and other mountain ranges, and having an average elevation of 13,000–15,000 ft/4,000–4,500 m. The Sutlej, Brahmaputra, and Indus rivers rise in Tibet, which has numerous lakes, many of which are salty. The ○yak is the main domestic animal.
government Tibet is an autonomous region of China, with its own People's Government and People's Congress. The controlling force in Tibet is the Communist Party of China, represented locally by First Secretary Wu Jinghua from 1985. Tibetan nationalists regard the province as being under colonial rule
products wool, borax, salt, horn, musk, herbs, furs, gold, iron pyrites, lapis lazuli, mercury, textiles, chemicals, agricultural machinery
population (1987) 2,030,000; including 900,000 Tibetans (mostly nomadic herders); many Chinese have settled in Tibet. In 1988 the population of Tibet included 2 million Tibetans and 73,000 Han Chinese; there were 2 million Tibetans in China outside Tibet
religion traditionally Lamaist (a form of Mahāyāna Buddhism)
history Tibet was an independent kingdom from the 5th century AD. It came under nominal Chinese rule about 1700. Independence was regained after a revolt 1912. China regained control 1951 when the historic ruler and religious leader, the ○Dalai Lama, was driven from the country and the monks (who formed 25% of the population) were forced out of the monasteries. Between 1951 and 1959 the Chinese

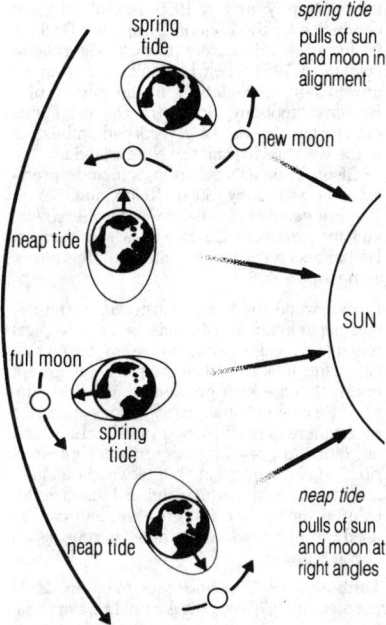

tide *The gravitational pull of the Moon is the main cause of the tides.*

People's Liberation Army (PLA) controlled Tibet, although the Dalai Lama returned as nominal spiritual and temporal head of state. In 1959 a Tibetan uprising spread from bordering regions to Lhasa and was supported by Tibet's local government. The rebellion was suppressed by the PLA, prompting the Dalai Lama and 9,000 Tibetans to flee to India. The Chinese proceeded to dissolve the Tibet local government, abolish serfdom, collectivize agriculture, and suppress ○Lamaism. In 1965 Tibet became an autonomous region of China. Chinese rule continued to be resented, however, and the economy languished.

From 1979, the leadership in Beijing adopted a more liberal and pragmatic policy toward Tibet. Traditional agriculture, livestock, and trading practices were restored (under the 1980 slogan "relax, relax, and relax again"), a number of older political leaders and rebels were rehabilitated or pardoned, and the promotion of local Tibetan cadres was encouraged. In addition, a somewhat more tolerant attitude toward Lamaism has been adopted (temples damaged during the 1965–68 Cultural Revolution are being repaired) and attempts, thus far unsuccessful, have been made to persuade the Dalai Lama to return from exile.

Pro-independence demonstrations erupted in Lhasa in Sept–Oct 1987, repeatedly throughout 1988, and in March 1989 and were forcibly suppressed by Chinese troops. In May and Oct 1988 peacefully demonstrating monks and civilians were shot by police. In 1989 many anti-China demonstrators were shot and all foreigners were expelled. These clashes exhibit the continuing strength of nationalist feeling. The country is of immense strategic importance to China, being the site of 50,000–100,000 troops and a major nuclear missile base at Nagchuka.

Tibetan member of a Mongolian people inhabiting Tibet who practice a form of Mahāyāna Buddhism, introduced in the 7th

century. Since China's Cultural Revolution 1966–68, refugee communities formed in India and Nepal. The Tibetan language belongs to the Sino-Tibetan language family.

tibia the anterior of the pair of bones found between the ankle and the knee. In humans, the tibia is the shinbone.

tick any of an arachnid group (Ixodoidea) of large bloodsucking mites. Many carry and transmit diseases to mammals (including humans) and birds.

tidal wave misleading name for a ○tsunami.

tide rise and fall of sea level due to the gravitational forces of the Moon and Sun. High tide occurs at an average interval of 12 hr 24 min 30 sec. The highest or *spring tides* are at or near new and full Moon; the lowest or *neap tides* when the Moon is in its first or third quarter. Some seas, such as the Mediterranean, have very small tides.

Other factors affecting sea level are (1) a combination of naturally high tides with storm surge, as sometimes happens along the low-lying coasts of Germany and the Netherlands; (2) the water walls created by typhoons and hurricanes, such as often hit Bangladesh; (3) underwater upheavals in the Earth's crust which may cause a ○tsunami; and (4) global temperature change melting the polar ice caps.

Tien Shan Chinese form of ○Tian Shan, mountain system of central Asia.

Tientsin alternate form of ○Tianjin, industrial city in NE China.

Tiepolo Giovanni Battista 1696–1770. Italian painter, born in Venice. He created monumental Rococo decorative schemes in palaces and churches in NE Italy, SW Germany, and Madrid (1762–70). The style is light-hearted, the palette light and warm, and he made great play with illusion.

Tierra del Fuego island group divided between Chile and Argentina. It is separated from the mainland of South America by the Strait of Magellan, and Cape Horn is at the southernmost point. The chief town, Ushuaia, Argentina, is the world's most southerly town. Industries include oil and sheep farming.

To the south of the main island is *Beagle Channel* (named after the ship of the scientist Charles Darwin's voyage), with three islands at the eastern end, finally awarded 1985 to Chile rather than Argentina.

Tiffany Louis Comfort 1848–1933. US artist and glassmaker, son of Charles Louis Tiffany, who founded Tiffany and Company, the New York City jewelers. He produced stained-glass windows, iridescent Favrile (from Latin *faber* "craftsman") glass, and lampshades in the Art Nouveau style. He used glass that contained oxides of iron and other elements to produce rich colors.

In 1881 he founded his own decorating firm. By 1893, he began producing his glass art objects, which remained popular through the 1920s and enjoyed a resurgence of popularity from the 1950s on.

Tiflis former name (until 1936) of the city of ○Tbilisi in Georgia.

tiger largest of the great cats *Panthera tigris*, formerly found in much of central and S Asia but nearing extinction because of hunting and the destruction of its natural habitat. The tiger can grow to 12 ft/3.6 m long and weigh 660 lb/300 kg; it has a yellow-orange coat with black stripes. It is solitary, and feeds on large ruminants. It is a good swimmer.

Human-eating tigers are rare and are the result of weakened powers or shortage of game. The striped markings—black on reddish-fawn—are present from birth, although rare cream or black specimens have been known.

In Sumatra there are about 800 tigers left, and 200 are killed each year by poachers. They are continually losing their jungle habitat: companies plunder the forest for timber and minerals, and then farmers, often transplanted from other parts of Indonesia, move in and take over the land, often ruining it after a few years owing to poor farming practices.

Tigré a people of N Ethiopia. The Tigré language is spoken by about 2.5 million people; it belongs to the SE Semitic branch of the Afro-Asiatic family. *Tigrinya* is a closely related language spoken slightly to the south.

Tigré or *Tigray* region in the northern highlands of Ethiopia; area 25,444 sq mi/65,900 sq km. The chief town is Mekele. The region had an estimated population of 2.4 million in 1984, at a time when drought and famine were driving large numbers of people to fertile land in the south or into neighboring Sudan. Since 1978 a guerrilla group known as the Tigré People's Liberation Front (TPLF) has been fighting for regional autonomy. In 1989 government troops were forced from the province, and the TPLF advanced toward Addis Ababa, playing a key role in the fall of the Ethiopian government in May 1991.

Tigris (Arabic *Shatt Dijla*) river flowing through Turkey and Iraq (see also ♢Mesopotamia), joining the ♢Euphrates above Basra, where it forms the ♢Shatt-al-Arab; length 1,000 mi/1,600 km.

Tijuana city and resort in NW Mexico; population (1990) 742,700; known for horse races and casinos. ♢San Diego adjoins it across the US border.

Tilden Samuel Jones 1814–1886. US Democratic politician, governor of New York 1874–76. As chair of the New York State Democratic committee 1866–74, he campaigned against the Tammany Hall Organization and its leader, William "Boss" Tweed. Tilden was elected governor on a reform ticket 1874. He received the Democratic presidential nomination 1876, and although he received a plurality of popular votes, the 1877 electoral college awarded the majority of electoral votes to Rutherford B Hayes.

Tilden was born in New Lebanon, New York, educated at Yale and New York universities, and became a lawyer 1841.

till or *boulder clay* deposit of clay, mud, gravel, and boulders left by a ♢glacier. It is unsorted, with all sizes of fragments mixed up together, and shows no stratification; that is, it does not form clear layers or ♢beds.

Tillich Paul Johannes 1886–1965. Prussian-born US theologian. In 1929 he was appointed professor of philosophy at the University of Frankfurt, a post from which he was removed by the Nazis. He arrived in the US 1933 and served as professor of theology at the Union Theological Seminary 1933–55, Harvard University 1955–62, and the University of Chicago 1962–65. He is best remembered for his *Systematic Theology* 1951–63.

Tillich received his PhD from the University of Breslau 1911. Ordained a pastor in the Evangelical Lutheran Church 1912, he served as a chaplain during World War I.

Tilson Thomas Michael 1944– . US conductor and pianist, principal guest conductor for the Boston Symphony 1969–74 and principal conductor for the London Symphony Orchestra from 1988. His career took off in storybook fashion in 1969 when he took over from an unwell William Steinberg in the middle of a Boston Symphony Orchestra concert. Since then he has appeared and recorded orchestras in the US, the UK, and the Netherlands.

Tilson Thomas's recordings include premieres of works by Steve Reich and Simon Bainbridge, also pieces by George Gershwin, and the complete Charles Ives symphonies. He has also recorded the complete Beethoven symphonies.

timber wood used in construction, furniture, and paper pulp. Hardwoods include tropical mahogany, teak, ebony, rosewood, temperate oak, elm, beech, and eucalyptus. All except eucalyptus are slow-growing, and world supplies are near exhaustion. Softwoods comprise the conifers (pine, fir, spruce, and larch), which are quick to grow and easy to work but inferior in quality of grain. White woods include ash, birch, and cottonwood; all have light-colored timber, are fast-growing, and can be used through modern methods as veneers on cheaper timber.

Timbuktu or *Tombouctou* town in Mali; population (1976) 20,500. A camel caravan center from the 11th century on the fringe of the Sahara, since 1960 it has been surrounded by the southward movement of the desert, and the former canal link with the river Niger is dry. Products include salt.

time continuous passage of existence, recorded by division into hours, minutes, and seconds. Formerly the measurement of time was based on the Earth's rotation on its axis, but this was found to be irregular. Therefore the second, the standard ♢SI unit of time, was redefined 1956 in terms of the Earth's annual orbit of the Sun, and 1967 in terms of a radiation pattern of the element cesium.

Universal time (UT), based on the Earth's actual rotation, was replaced by coordinated universal time (UTC) 1972, the difference between the two involving the addition (or subtraction) of leap seconds on the last day of June or Dec. National observatories make standard time available in various countries. From 1986 the term Greenwich Mean Time was replaced by UTC. However, the Greenwich meridian, adopted 1884, remains that from which all longitudes are measured, and the world's standard time zones are calculated from it.

time and motion study process of analysis applied to a job or number of jobs to check the efficiency of the work method, equipment used, and the worker. Its findings are used to improve performance.

Time and motion studies were introduced in the US by Frederick Taylor (1856–1915) at the beginning of the 20th century. Since then, the practice has spread throughout the industrialized world.

time-sharing in computing, a way of enabling several users to access the same computer at the same time. The computer rapidly switches between user ♢terminals and programs, allowing each user to work as if he or she had sole use of the system.

Time-sharing was common in the 1960s and 1970s before the spread of cheaper computers.

Timişoara capital of Timiş county, W Romania; population (1985) 319,000. The revolt against the Ceauşescu regime began here in Dec 1989 when demonstrators prevented the arrest and deportation of a popular Protestant minister who was promoting the rights of ethnic Hungarians. This soon led to large prodemocracy rallies.

Timon Athenian of the age of ♢Pericles notorious for his misanthropy, which was reported and elaborated by Classical authors, and became the subject of the play by ♢Shakespeare.

Timor largest and most easterly of the Lesser Sunda Islands, part of Indonesia; area 12,973 sq mi/33,610 sq km. *West Timor* (capital Kupang) was formerly Dutch and was included in Indonesia on independence. *East Timor* (capital Dili), an enclave on the NW coast, and the islands of Atauro and Jaco formed an overseas province of Portugal until it was seized by Indonesia 1975. The annexation is not recognized by the United Nations, and guerrilla warfare by local people seeking independence continues. Since 1975 over 500,000 Timorese have been killed by Indonesian troops or have resettled in West Timor, according to Amnesty International. Products include coffee, corn, rice, and coconuts.

Timothy in the New Testament, companion to St ♢Paul, both on his missionary journeys and in prison. Two of the Pauline epistles are addressed to him.

tin soft, silver-white, malleable and somewhat ductile, metallic element, symbol Sn (from Latin *stannum*), atomic number 50, atomic weight 118.69. Tin exhibits ♢allotropy, having three forms: the familiar lustrous metallic form above 55.8°F/13.2°C; a brittle form above 321.8°F/161°C; and a gray powder form below 55.8°F/13.2°C (commonly called tin pest or tin disease). The metal is quite soft (slightly harder than lead) and can be rolled, pressed, or hammered into extremely thin sheets; it has a low melting point. In nature it occurs rarely as a free metal. It resists corrosion and is therefore used for coating and plating other metals.

Tin and copper smelted together form the oldest desired alloy, bronze; since the Bronze Age (3,500 BC) that alloy has been the basis of both useful and decorative materials. The mines of Cornwall were the principal western source from then until the 19th century, when rich deposits were found in South America, Africa, and SE Asia. Tin is also alloyed with metals other than copper to make solder and pewter. It was recognized as an element by Antoine Lavoisier, but the name is very old and comes from the Germanic form *zinn*.

tinamou any fowllike bird of the South American order Tinamiformes, of which there are some 45 species. They are up to 16 in/40 cm long, and their drab color provides good camouflage. They are excellent runners but poor flyers and are thought to be related to the ratites (flightless birds). Tinamous are mainly vegetarian, but sometimes eat insects. They escape predators by remaining still or by burrowing through dense cover.

Tinbergen Jan 1903–1988. Dutch economist. He shared a Nobel Prize 1969 with Ragnar Frisch for his work on ♢econometrics (the mathematical-statistical expression of economic theory).

Tinbergen Niko(laas) 1907– . Dutch zoologist. He was one of the founders of ♢ethology, the scientific study of animal behavior in natural surroundings. Specializing in the study of instinctive behavior, he shared a Nobel Prize with Konrad ⟳Lorenz and Karl von ⟳Frisch 1973. He is the brother of Jan Tinbergen.

Ting Samuel 1936– . US physicist. In 1974 he and his team at the Brookhaven National Laboratory, New York, detected a new subatomic particle, which he named the J particle. It was found to be identical to the ψ (psi) particle discovered in the same year by Burton ⟳Richter and his team at the Stanford Linear Accelerator Center, California. Ting and Richter shared the Nobel Prize for Physics 1976.

tinnitus in medicine, constant internal sounds, inaudible to others. The phenomenon may originate from noisy conditions (drilling, machinery, or loud music) or from infection of the middle or inner ear. The victim may become overwhelmed by the relentless noise in the head.

In some cases there is a hum at a frequency of about 40 Hz, which resembles that heard by people troubled by environmental ⟳hum but may include whistles and other noises resembling a machine workshop. Being in a place where external noises drown the internal ones gives some relief, and devices may be worn that create pleasant, soothing sounds to override them.

tin ore mineral from which tin is extracted, principally cassiterite, SnO_2. The world's chief producers are Malaysia, Thailand, and Bolivia.

tinplate milled steel coated with tin, the metal used for most "tin" cans. The steel provides the strength, and the tin provides the corrosion resistance, ensuring that the food inside is not contaminated. Tinplate may be made by ⟳electroplating or by dipping in a bath of molten tin.

Tintoretto adopted name of Jacopo Robusti 1518–1594. Italian painter, active in Venice. His dramatic religious paintings are spectacularly lit and full of movement, such as his huge canvases of the lives of Christ and the Virgin in the Scuola di San Rocco, Venice, 1564–88.

Tintoretto was so named because his father was a dyer (*tintore*). He was a student of ⟳Titian and admirer of Michelangelo. *Miracle of St Mark Rescuing a Slave* 1548 (Accademia, Venice) marked the start of his successful career. In the Scuola di San Rocco he created a sequence of heroic scenes with bold gesture and foreshortening, and effects of supernatural light. He also painted canvases for the Doge's Palace.

Tiomkin Dimitri 1899–1979. Russian composer who lived in the US from 1925. From 1930 he wrote Hollywood film scores, including music for *Duel in the Sun* 1946, *The Thing* 1951, and *Rio Bravo* 1959. His score for *High Noon* 1952 won him an Academy Award.

Tipperary county in the Republic of Ireland, province of Munster, divided into north and south regions. *North Tipperary*: administrative headquarters Nenagh; area 772 sq mi/2,000 sq km; population (1991) 57,800. *South Tipperary*: administrative headquarters Clonmel; area 872 sq mi/2,260 sq km; population (1991) 74,800. It includes part of the Golden Vale, a dairy-farming region.

Tippett Michael (Kemp) 1905– . English composer whose works include the operas *The Midsummer Marriage* 1952, *The Knot Garden* 1970, and *New Year* 1989; four symphonies; *Songs for Ariel* 1962; and choral music including *The Mask of Time* 1982.

Tirana or *Tiranë* capital (since 1920) of Albania; population (1990) 210,000. Industries

include metallurgy, cotton textiles, soap, and cigarettes. It was founded in the early 17th century by Turks when part of the Ottoman Empire. Although the city is now largely composed of recent buildings, some older districts and mosques have been preserved.

tire inflatable (pneumatic) rubber casing fitted to the wheel rims of bicycles and motor vehicles. The first pneumatic rubber tire was patented by R W Thompson 1845, but it was John Boyd Dunlop of Belfast who independently reinvented pneumatic tires for use with bicycles 1888–89. ⟳Vulcanization, used in tire manufacture, was invented by Charles ⟳Goodyear in 1844.

Tiresias or *Teiresias* in Greek mythology, a man blinded by the gods and given the ability to predict the future.

According to the poet Ovid, Tiresias once saw two snakes mating, struck at them, and was changed into a woman. Seven years later, in a repetition of the same scene, he reverted back to manhood. Later, he was called upon to settle a dispute between the two gods Zeus and Hera on whether men or women enjoy sex more. He declared for women, and as a result Hera blinded him, but Zeus gave him the gift of foresight.

Tirol federal province of Austria; area 4,864 sq mi/12,600 sq km; population (1989) 619,600. Its capital is Innsbruck, and it produces diesel engines, optical instruments, and hydroelectric power. Tirol was formerly a province (from 1363) of the Austrian Empire, divided 1919 between Austria and Italy (see ⟳Trentino–Alto Adige).

Tirpitz Alfred von 1849–1930. German admiral. As secretary for the navy 1897–1916, he created the German navy and planned the World War I U-boat campaign.

Tiruchirapalli formerly *Trichinopoly* ("town of the sacred rock") city in Tamil Nadu, India; chief industries are cotton textiles, cigars, and gold and silver filigree; population (1981) 362,000. It is a place of pilgrimage and was the capital of Tamil kingdoms during the 10th to 17th centuries.

Tiryns ancient Greek city in the Peloponnese on the plain of Argos, with remains of the ⟳Mycenaean civilization.

Tiselius Arne 1902–1971. Swedish chemist who developed a powerful method of chemical analysis known as ⟳electrophoresis. He applied his new techniques to the analysis of animal proteins. Nobel Prize 1948.

tissue in biology, any kind of cellular fabric that occurs in an organism's body. Several kinds of tissue can usually be distinguished, each consisting of cells of a particular kind bound together by cell walls (in plants) or extracellular matrix (in animals). Thus, nerve and muscle are different kinds of tissue in animals, as are ⟳parenchyma and ⟳sclerenchyma in plants.

tissue culture process by which cells from a plant or animal are removed from the organism and grown under controlled conditions in a sterile medium containing all the necessary nutrients. Tissue culture can provide information on cell growth and differentiation, and is also used in plant propagation and drug production. See also ⟳meristem.

tissue plasminogen activator (tPA) naturally occurring substance in the body tissues that activates the enzyme plasmin, which is able to

dissolve blood clots. Human tPA, produced in bacteria by genetic engineering, has been used to try to dissolve blood clots in the coronary arteries of heart-attack victims. However, tPA is ten times more expensive than streptokinase, and has not been shown to be more effective.

Titan in astronomy, largest moon of the planet Saturn, with a diameter of 3,200 mi/5,150 km and a mean distance from Saturn of 759,000 mi/1,222,000 km. It was discovered 1655 by Christiaan ⟳Huygens, and is the second largest moon in the Solar System (Ganymede, of Jupiter, is larger).

Titan is the only moon in the Solar System with a substantial atmosphere (mostly nitrogen), topped with smoggy orange clouds that obscure the surface, which may be covered with liquid ethane lakes. Its surface atmospheric pressure is greater than Earth's. Radar signals suggest that Titan has dry land as well as oceans (among the planets, only Earth has both in the Solar System).

Titan in Greek mythology, any of the giant children of Uranus and Gaia, who included Cronus, Rhea, Themis (mother of Prometheus and personification of law and order), and Oceanus. Cronus and Rhea were in turn the parents of Zeus, who ousted Cronus as the ruler of the world.

Titanic British passenger liner, supposedly unsinkable, that struck an iceberg and sank off the Grand Banks of Newfoundland on its first voyage April 14–15, 1912; 1,513 lives were lost. In 1985 it was located by robot submarine 2.5 mi/4 km down in an ocean canyon, preserved by the cold environment. In 1987 salvage operations began.

titanium strong, lightweight, silver-gray, metallic element, symbol Ti, atomic number 22, atomic weight 47.90. The ninth most abundant element in the Earth's crust, its compounds occur in practically all igneous rocks and their sedimentary deposits. It is very strong and resistant to corrosion, so it is used in building high-speed aircraft and spacecraft; it is also widely used in making alloys, as it unites with almost every metal except copper and aluminum. Titanium oxide is used in high-grade white pigments.

The element was discovered 1791 by English mineralogist William Gregor (1761–1817) and was named by German chemist Martin Klaproth 1796 after Titan, one of the giants of Greek mythology. It was not obtained in pure form until 1925.

titanium ore any mineral from which titanium is extracted, principally ilmenite ($FeTiO_3$) and rutile (TiO_2). Brazil, India, and Canada are major producers.

Titan rocket family of US space rockets, developed from the Titan intercontinental missile. Two-stage Titan rockets launched the ⟳Gemini crewed missions. More powerful Titans, with additional stages and strap-on boosters, were used to launch spy satellites and space probes, including ⟳Viking and ⟳Voyager.

tithe formerly, payment exacted from the inhabitants of a parish for the maintenance of the church and its incumbent; some religious groups continue the practice by giving 10% of members' incomes to charity.

It was originally the grant of a tenth of all agricultural produce made to priests in Hebrew society. In the Middle Ages the tithe was adopted as a tax in kind paid to the local parish church, usually for the support of the incumbent, and stored in a special tithe ⋄barn; as such, it survived into contemporary times in Europe and Britain. In Protestant countries, these payments were often appropriated by lay landlords.

Titian anglicized form of Tiziano Vecellio c. 1487–1576. Italian painter, active in Venice, one of the greatest artists of the High Renaissance. In 1533 he became court painter to Charles V, Holy Roman emperor, whose son Philip II of Spain later became his patron. Titian's work is richly colored, with inventive composition. He produced a vast number of portraits, religious paintings, and mythological scenes, including *Bacchus and Ariadne* 1520–23, *Venus and Adonis* 1554, and the *Entombment of Christ* 1559.

Titian probably studied with Giovanni ⋄Bellini but also learned much from ⋄Giorgione and seems to have completed some of Giorgione's unfinished works, such as *Noli Me Tangere* (National Gallery, London). His first great painting is the *Assumption of the Virgin* 1518 (Church of the Frari, Venice), typically sublime in mood, with upward-thrusting layers of figures. Three large mythologies painted in the next few years for the d'Estes of Ferrara show yet more brilliant use of color, and numerous statuesque figures suggest the influence of Classical art. By the 1530s Titian's reputation was widespread.

In the 1540s Titian visited Rome to paint the pope; in Augsburg, Germany, 1548–49 and 1550–51 he painted members of the imperial court. In his later years he produced a series of mythologies for Philip II, notably *The Rape of Europa* 1562 (Isabella Stewart Gardner Museum, Boston, Massachusetts). His handling became increasingly free and his palette somber, but his work remained full of drama. He made an impact not just on Venetian painting but on art throughout Europe.

Titicaca lake in the Andes, 12,500 ft/3,810 m above sea level; area 3,200 sq mi/8,300 sq km, the largest lake in South America. It is divided between Bolivia (port at Guaqui) and Peru (ports at Puno and Huancane). It has enormous edible frogs.

titmouse any of a family (Paridae) of small birds of the order Passeriformes, found worldwide except in South America and Australia. There are 65 species, all agile and hardy, and often seen hanging upside down from twigs to feed. In North America many of the species are called chickadees.

North American species include the tufted titmouse *Parus bicolor*, with a gray crest, and the black-capped chickadee *P. atricapillus*.

Tito adopted name of Josip Broz 1892–1980. Yugoslav communist politician, in power from 1945. In World War II he organized the National Liberation Army to carry on guerrilla warfare against the German invasion 1941, and was created marshal 1943. As prime minister 1946–53 and president from 1953, he followed a foreign policy of "positive neutralism."

Born in Croatia, Tito served in the Austrian army during World War I, was captured by the Russians, and fought in the Red Army during the civil wars. Returning to Yugoslavia 1923, he became prominent as a communist and during World War II as ⋄partisan leader against the Nazis. In 1943 he established a provisional government and gained Allied recognition (previously given to the ⋄Chetniks), and with Soviet help proclaimed the federal

republic 1945. As prime minister, he settled the Yugoslav minorities question on a federal basis, and in 1953 took the newly created post of president (for life from 1974). In 1948 he was criticized by the USSR and other communist countries for his successful system of decentralized profit-sharing workers' councils, and became a leader of the ⋄nonaligned movement.

Titus Flavius Sabinus Vespasianus AD 39–81. Roman emperor from AD 79. Eldest son of ⋄Vespasian, he stormed Jerusalem 70 to end the Jewish revolt in Roman Palestine. He completed the Colosseum, and enjoyed a peaceful reign, except for ⋄Agricola's campaigns in Britain.

Titusville town in E Florida, on the Indian River, E of Orlando; population (1990) 39,400. Industries include citrus fruits and sport fishing. The Kennedy Space Center is nearby.

Tivoli town NE of Rome, Italy; population (1981) 52,000. It has remains of Hadrian's villa, with gardens; and the Villa d'Este with Renaissance gardens laid out 1549 for Cardinal Ippolito d'Este.

Tlatelolco, Treaty of international agreement signed 1967 in Tlatelolco, Mexico, prohibiting nuclear weapons in Latin America.

Tlingit member of a North American Indian people of the NW coast, living in S Alaska and N British Columbia. They used to carve wooden poles representing their family crests, showing such animals as the raven, whale, octopus, beaver, bear, wolf, and the mythical "thunderbird." Their language is related to the Athabaskan languages.

TLR camera twin-lens reflex camera that has a viewing lens of the same angle of view and focal length mounted above and parallel to the taking lens.

TM abbreviation for ⋄*transcendental meditation*.

TN abbreviation for the state of ⋄*Tennessee*.

TNT abbreviation for *trinitrotoluene*, $CH_3C_6H_2(NO_2)_3$, a powerful high explosive. It is a yellow solid, prepared in several isomeric forms from ⋄toluene by using sulfuric and nitric acids.

toad any of the more terrestrial warty-skinned members of the tailless amphibians (order Anura). The name commonly refers to members of the genus *Bufo*, family Bufonidae, which are found worldwide, except for the Australian and polar regions.

The American toad *B. americanus* reaches 3.5 in/9 cm and is found from suburban backyards to mountain wilderness throughout the NE US.

toadflax any small W Eurasian plant of the genus *Linaria* of the snapdragon family Scrophulariaceae. Toadflaxes have spurred, two-lipped flowers, commonly purple or yellow, and grow to 8–32 in/20–80 cm tall.

toadstool inedible or poisonous type of ⋄fungus with a fleshy, gilled fruiting body on a stalk.

tobacco any large-leaved plant of the genus *Nicotiana* of the nightshade family Solanaceae, native to tropical parts of the Americas. *N. tabacum* is widely cultivated in warm, dry climates for use in cigars and cigarettes, and in powdered form as snuff.

The leaves are cured, or dried, and matured in storage for two to three years before use.

Introduced to Europe as a medicine in the 16th century, tobacco was recognized from the 1950s as a major health hazard; see ⋄cancer. The leaves also yield the alkaloid nicotine, a colorless oil, one of the most powerful poisons known, and addictive in humans. It is used in insecticides.

Tobago island in the West Indies; part of the republic of ⋄Trinidad and Tobago.

Tobin James 1918– . US Keynesian economist. He was awarded a Nobel Prize 1981 for his "general equilibrium" theory, which states that other criteria than monetary considerations are applied by households and firms when making decisions on consumption and investment. He is critical of monetarists for putting too much emphasis on a single asset—money—and he has analyzed the impact of changes in fiscal or monetary policy on the economy as a whole. He also has examined the process of portfolio selection, considering the trade-off between risk and yield across a broad range of assets.

Born in Champaign, Illinois, Tobin received his undergraduate and graduate degrees from Harvard. He taught at Yale, becoming the Sterling Professor of Economics from 1957. He served on the President's Council of Economic Advisers during President Kennedy's administration. Tobin's works include the three-volume *Essays in Economics* 1971–82 and *The New Economics, One Decade Older* 1974.

toboggan flat-bottomed sled, curved upward and backward at the front, used on snow or ice slopes or banked artificial courses.

Tobruk Libyan port; population (1984) 94,000. Occupied by Italy 1911, it was taken by Britain 1941 during World War II, and unsuccessfully besieged by Axis forces April–Dec 1941. It was captured by Germany June 1942 after the retreat of the main British force to Egypt, and this precipitated the replacement of Auchinleck by Montgomery as British commander.

toccata in music, a display piece for keyboard instruments, such as the organ.

Tocqueville Alexis de 1805–1859. French politician and political scientist, author of the first analytical study of the US constitution, *De la Démocratie en Amérique/Democracy in America* 1835, and of a penetrating description of France before the Revolution, *L'Ancien Régime et la Révolution/The Old Regime and the Revolution* 1856.

Elected to the Chamber of Deputies 1839, Tocqueville became vice-president of the Constituent Assembly and minister of foreign affairs 1849. He retired after Napoleon III's coup 1851.

tofu or *dofu* or *doufu* pressed ⋄soybean curd derived from soy milk. It is a good source of protein and naturally low in fat.

Tofu comes in three varieties: smooth and firm, in small white blocks, used for stir-frying or steaming; as a junketlike solid used in making dips, salad dressings, or ice cream; and hard, fermented, and/or seasoned cakes, which may be sliced and eaten or used in cooking. The flavor is bland, but it combines readily with other ingredients; the fermented and seasoned tofu has the taste and texture of various cheeses.

tog unit of measure of thermal insulation used in the textile trade; a light summer suit provides 1.0 tog.

The tog-value of an object is equal to ten times the temperature difference (in 8°C) between its two surfaces when the flow of heat is equal to one watt per square meter; one tog equals 0.645 ▷clo.

Togliatti or *Tolyatti*, formerly *Stavropol* port on the river Volga, W central Russia; industries include engineering and food processing; population (1989) 630,000. The city was relocated in the 1950s after a flood and renamed after the Italian communist Palmiro Togliatti.

Togliatti Palmiro 1893–1964. Italian politician who was a founding member of the Italian Communist Party 1921 and effectively its leader for almost 40 years from 1926 until his death. In exile 1926–44, he returned after the fall of the Fascist dictator Mussolini to become a member of Badoglio's government and held office until 1946.

Togo country in W Africa, on the Atlantic Ocean, bounded N by Burkina Faso, E by Benin, and W by Ghana.
government The 1979 constitution created a one-party, socialist republic based on the Assembly of the Togolese People (RPT). The president is elected by universal suffrage for a seven-year term and is eligible for reelection. The president is head of both state and government, appointing and presiding over a council of ministers, and is also president of the RPT.

There is a single-chamber legislature, the National Assembly, of 77 members, elected by universal suffrage from a list of RPT nominees and serving for five years.
history For early history, see ▷Africa. Called Togoland, the country was a German protectorate 1885–1914, when it was captured by Anglo-French forces. It was divided between

Britain and France 1922 under a League of Nations mandate and continued under United Nations trusteeship from 1946. In 1956 British Togoland voted for integration with Ghana, where it became Volta region 1957.
independence French Togoland voted to become an autonomous republic within the French union. The new Togolese republic achieved internal self-government 1956 and full independence 1960. Sylvanus Olympio, leader of the United Togolese (UT) party, became president in an unopposed election April 1961. In 1963 Olympio was killed in a military coup and his brother-in-law Nicolas Grunitzky, who had gone into exile, was recalled to become president.
gradual democratization In 1967 Grunitzky was, in turn, deposed in a bloodless military coup, led by Lt Gen Etienne Gnassingbé Eyadéma. The new constitution was suspended; Eyadéma assumed the presidency and banned all political activity. Six years later he founded a new party, the socialist, nationalist RPT, and declared it the only legal political organization. Between 1967 and 1977 there were several attempts to overthrow him but by 1979 Eyadéma felt sufficiently secure to propose a new coalition and embark on a policy of gradual democratization. An attempt to overthrow him Oct 1986, by mercenaries from Burkina Faso and Ghana, was easily thwarted. In 1991, in response to pressure from demonstrators, Eyadéma announced the introduction of a multiparty system. In April he legalized opposition parties, freed political prisoners, and granted amnesty to those implicated in the 1986 attempted coup. In a prodemocracy

conference in August, Eyadéma's presidential power was substantially reduced and an interim government was formed, headed by premier Joseph Kokou Koffigoh. Between Oct and Nov 1991, three attempts by Eyadéma's troops to oust the interim government all failed. In a referendum Sept 1992 there was overwhelming support for a new, multiparty constitution. *See illustration box.*

Tohoku mountainous region of N Honshu island, Japan; population (1988) 9,745,000; area 25,867 sq mi/66,971 sq km. Timber, fruit, fish, and livestock are produced. The chief city is Sendai. Aomori in the NE is linked to Hakodate on the island of Hokkaido by the *Seikan tunnel*, the world's longest underwater tunnel.

Tōjō Hideki 1884–1948. Japanese general and premier 1941–44 during World War II. Promoted to Chief of Staff of Japan's Guangdong army in Manchuria 1937, he served as minister for war 1940–41. He was held responsible for defeats in the Pacific 1944 and forced to resign. After Japan's defeat, he was hanged as a war criminal.

tokamak experimental machine designed by Soviet scientists to investigate controlled nuclear fusion. It consists of a doughnut-shaped chamber surrounded by electromagnets capable of exerting very powerful magnetic fields. The fields are generated to confine a very hot (millions of degrees) ▷plasma of ions and electrons, keeping it away from the chamber walls. See also ▷JET.

Tokay sweet white wine made near the Hungarian town of Tokaj; also the grape from which it is made.

Tokelau formerly *Union Islands* overseas territory of New Zealand, 300 mi/480 km N of Western Samoa, comprising three coral atolls: Atafu, Fakaofo, and Nukunonu; area 4 sq mi/10 sq km; population (1986) 1,700.

Tokugawa military family that controlled Japan as ▷shoguns 1603–1867. *Tokugawa Ieyasu* (1542–1616) was the Japanese general and politician who established the Tokugawa shogunate. The Tokugawa were feudal lords who ruled about one-fourth of Japan.

Tokyo capital of Japan, on Honshu Island; population (1989) 8,099,000, metropolitan area over 12 million. The Sumida River delta separates the city from its suburb of Honjo. It is Japan's main cultural and industrial center (engineering, chemicals, textiles, electrical goods). Founded in the 16th century as *Yedo* (or *Edo*), it was renamed when the emperor moved his court there from Kyoto 1868. An earthquake 1923 killed 58,000 people and destroyed much of the city, which was again severely damaged by Allied bombing in World War II. The subsequent rebuilding has made it into one of the world's most modern cities.

Features include the Imperial Palace, National Diet (parliament), Asakusa Kannon Temple (7th century, rebuilt after World War II), National Theater, National Museum and other art collections, Tokyo University 1877, Tokyo Disneyland, and the National Athletic Stadium.

Toledo city on the river Tagus, Castilla–La Mancha, central Spain; population (1982) 62,000. It was the capital of the Visigoth kingdom 534–711 (see ▷Goth), then became a Moorish city, and was the Castilian capital 1085–1560.

In the 12th century, Toledo had a flourishing steel industry and a school of translators, run

Togo
Republic of (*République Togolaise*)

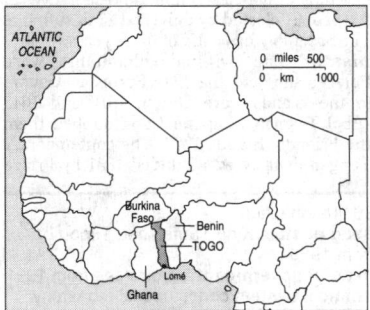

area 21,930 sq mi/56,800 sq km
capital Lomé
cities Sokodé, Kpalimé
physical two savanna plains, divided by range of hills NE–SW; coastal lagoons and marsh
environment the homes of thousands of people in Keto were destroyed by coastal erosion as a result of the building of the Volta dam
features Mono Tableland, Oti Plateau, Oti River
head of state President Eyadéma
head of government Jospeh Kokou Koffigoh from 1991
political system transitional
political parties Rally of the Togolese People (RPT), centrist nationalist; Alliance of Togolese Democrats (ADT), left-of-center; Togolese Movement for Democracy (MDT), left-of-center

exports phosphates, cocoa, coffee, coconuts
currency franc CFA
population (1990 est) 3,566,000; growth rate 3% p.a.
life expectancy men 53, women 57 (1989)
languages French (official), Ewe, Kabre
religion animist 46%, Catholic 28%, Muslim 17%, Protestant 9%
literacy men 53%, women 28% (1985 est)
GNP $1.3 bn (1987); $240 per head (1985)
chronology
1885–1914 Togoland was a German protectorate until captured by Anglo-French forces.
1922 Divided between Britain and France under League of Nations mandate.
1946 Continued under United Nations trusteeship.
1956 British Togoland integrated with Ghana.
1960 French Togoland achieved independence from France as the Republic of Togo with Sylvanus Olympio as head of state.
1963 Olympio killed in a military coup. Nicolas Grunitzky became president.
1967 Grunitzky replaced by Lt Gen Etienne Gnassingbé Eyadéma in bloodless coup.
1973 Assembly of Togolese People (RPT) formed as sole legal political party.
1975 EEC Lomé convention signed in Lomé, establishing trade links with developing countries.
1979 Eyadéma returned in election. Further EEC Lomé convention signed.
1986 Attempted coup failed.
1991 Eyadéma legalized opposition parties. National conference elected Joseph Kokou Koffigoh head of interim government; troops loyal to Eyadéma failed to reinstate him.
1992 Overwhelming referendum support for multiparty politics.

by Archbishop Raymond (1125–1151), writing Latin versions of Arabic philosophical works. The painter El Greco worked here from about 1575 (his house and garden are preserved), and the local landscape is the setting of Cervantes' novel *Don Quixote*.

Toledo port on Lake Erie, Ohio, at the mouth of the Maumee River; industries include food processing and the manufacture of vehicles, electrical goods, and glass; population (1990) 332,900. A French fort was built 1700, but permanent settlement did not begin until after the War of 1812.

The University of Toledo is here.

Tolkien J(ohn) R(onald) R(euel) 1892–1973. English writer who created the fictional world of Middle Earth in *The Hobbit* 1937 and the trilogy *The Lord of the Rings* 1954–55, fantasy novels peopled with hobbits, dwarves, and strange magical creatures. His work developed a cult following in the 1960s and had many imitators. At Oxford University he was professor of Anglo-Saxon 1925–45 and Merton professor of English 1945–59.

Tolstoy Leo Nikolaievich 1828–1910. Russian novelist who wrote ⟡*War and Peace* 1863–69 and ⟡*Anna Karenina* 1873–77. From 1880 Tolstoy underwent a profound spiritual crisis and took up various moral positions, including passive resistance to evil, rejection of authority (religious or civil) and private ownership, and a return to basic mystical Christianity. He was excommunicated by the Orthodox Church, and his later works were banned.

Tolstoy was born of noble family at Yasnaya Polyana, near Tula, and fought in the Crimean War. His first published work was *Childhood* 1852, the first part of the trilogy that was completed with *Boyhood* 1854 and *Youth* 1857. *Tales from Sebastopol* was published 1856; later books include *What I Believe* 1883 and *The Kreutzer Sonata* 1889, and the novel *Resurrection* 1900. His desire to give up his property and live as a peasant disrupted his family life, and he finally fled his home and died of pneumonia at the railroad station in Astapovo.

Toltec member of an ancient American Indian people who ruled much of Mexico in the 10th–12th centuries, with their capital and religious center at Tula, NE of Mexico City. They also constructed a similar city at Chichén Itzá in Yucatán. After the Toltecs' fall in the 13th century, the Aztecs took over much of their former territory, except for the regions regained by the Maya.

toluene or *methyl benzene* $C_6H_5CH_3$ colorless, inflammable liquid, insoluble in water, derived from petroleum. It is used as a solvent, in aircraft fuels, in preparing phenol (carbolic acid, used in making resins for adhesives, pharmaceuticals, and as a disinfectant), and the powerful high explosive ⟡TNT.

tomato annual plant *Lycopersicon esculentum* of the nightshade family Solanaceae, native to South America. It is widely cultivated for the many-seeded red fruit (technically a berry), used in salads and cooking.

Tombaugh Clyde (William) 1906– . US astronomer who discovered the planet ⟡Pluto 1930.

Tombaugh, born in Streator, Illinois, became an assistant at the Lowell Observatory in Flagstaff, Arizona, in 1929, and photographed the sky in search of an undiscovered remote planet as predicted by the observatory's founder, Percival ⟡Lowell. Tombaugh found Pluto

on Feb 18, 1930, from plates taken three weeks earlier. He continued his search for new planets across the entire sky; his failure to find any placed strict limits on the possible existence of planets beyond Pluto.

Tombstone former silver-mining town in the desert of SE Arizona. The gunfight at the OK Corral, with deputy marshal Wyatt Earp, his brothers, and "Doc" Holliday against the Clanton gang, took place here Oct 26, 1881.

Tom Jones, The History of novel by Henry Fielding, published in England 1749. It describes the complicated, and not always reputable, early life of Tom Jones, an orphan, who is good-natured but hot-headed.

tomography the obtaining of plane-section X-ray photographs, which show a "slice" through any object. Crystal detectors and amplifiers can be used that have a sensitivity 100 times greater than X-ray film, and, in conjunction with a computer system, can detect, for example, the difference between a brain tumor and healthy brain tissue.

Godfrey Hounsfield was a leading pioneer in the development of this technique. In modern medical imaging there are several types, such as the ⟡CAT scan (computerized axial tomography).

Tom Sawyer, The Adventures of novel by US author Mark Twain, published 1876. It describes the childhood escapades of Tom Sawyer and his friends Huckleberry Finn and Joe Harper in a small Mississippi community before the Civil War. It and its sequel *The Adventures of Huckleberry Finn* 1885 are remarkable for their rejection of the high moral tone prevalent in 19th-century children's literature.

Tomsk city on the river Tom, W central Siberia; industries include synthetic fibers, timber, distilling, plastics, and electrical motors; population (1987) 489,000. It was formerly a gold-mining town and the administrative center of much of Siberia.

Tom Thumb tiny hero of English folk tale, whose name has often been given to those of small stature, including **Charles Sherwood**

Stratton 1838–1883, nicknamed General Tom Thumb by the circus proprietor P T Barnum.

ton unit (symbol t) of mass. The **short ton**, used in the US and Canada, is 2,000 lb/907 kg. The **long ton**, used in the UK, is 2,240 lb/1,016 kg. The **metric ton** or **tonne** is 2,205 lb/1,000 kg.

In shipping, gross tonnage is calculated in units of volume (called register tons) equal to 100 cubic ft/2.8 cubic m; it measures the total internal volume of a ship. Net register tonnage is the amount of gross tonnage (in register tons) used for carrying cargo or passengers. Displacement tonnage is the weight of the vessel, in terms of the number of long tons of sea water displaced when the ship is loaded to its load line; it is used to describe warships, and one displacement ton equals 35 cubic ft/1 cubic m.

tonality in music, the observance of a key structure; that is, the recognition of the importance of a tonic or key note and of the diatonic scale built upon it. See also ⟡atonality and ⟡polytonality.

tone poem in music, another name for ⟡symphonic poem as used, for example, by Richard Strauss.

Tonga country in the SW Pacific Ocean, in ⟡Polynesia.

government Tonga is an independent hereditary monarchy within the British ⟡Commonwealth. Its constitution dates from 1875 and provides for a monarch who exercises executive power in conjunction with an appointed 10-member Privy Council, which functions as a cabinet and is headed by a prime minister.

There is a single-chamber legislature, the Legislative Assembly, of 29 members, which include the monarch, the Privy Council, nine hereditary nobles, and nine representatives of the people, elected by universal adult suffrage. The assembly has a life of three years.

history The original inhabitants were Polynesians, and the first European visitors to the islands were Dutch, 1616 and 1643 (Abel Tasman). Captain Cook dubbed them the Friendly Islands 1773. The contemporary Tongan dynasty was founded 1831 by Prince

Tonga
Kingdom of (*Pule'anga Fakatu'i 'o Tonga*) or **Friendly Islands**

area 290 sq mi/750 sq km
capital Nuku'alofa (on Tongatapu island)
cities Pangai, Neiafu
physical three groups of islands in SW Pacific, mostly coral formations, but actively volcanic in W
features of 170 islands in the Tonga group,

36 are inhabited
head of state King Taufa'ahau Tupou IV from 1965
head of government Baron Vaea from 1991
political system constitutional monarchy
political parties none
currency Tongan dollar or pa'anga
population (1988) 95,000; growth rate 2.4% p.a.
life expectancy men 69, women 74 (1989)
languages Tongan (official), English
religion Wesleyan 47%, Roman Catholic 14%, Free Church of Tonga 14%, Mormon 9%, Church of Tonga 9%
literacy 93% (1988)
GNP $65 million (1987); $430 per head
chronology
1831 Tongan dynasty founded by Prince Taufa'ahau Tupou.
1900 Became a British protectorate.
1965 Queen Salote died; succeeded by her son, King Taufa'ahau Tupou IV.
1970 Independence achieved from Britain within the Commonwealth.
1990 Three prodemocracy candidates elected. Calls for reform of absolutist power.

Taufa'ahau Tupou, who assumed the designation King George Tupou I when he ascended the throne. He consolidated the kingdom by conquest, encouraged the spread of Christianity, and granted a constitution. Tonga became a British protectorate from 1900, but under the terms of revised treaties of 1958 and 1967 recovered increased control over its internal affairs.

Queen Salote Tupou III died 1965 and was succeeded by her son, Prince Tupouto'a Tungi, who as King Tupou IV led his nation to full independence, within the Commonwealth, 1970.

In the Feb 1990 elections for nine elected representatives of the people in the Legislative Assembly, three prodemocracy candidates were successful. They attempted to secure support for some dilution of the absolute power of the king. *See illustration box.*

tongue in tetrapod vertebrates, a muscular organ usually attached to the floor of the mouth. It has a thick root anchored at the base to a skeletal system (the hyoid apparatus), formed from what were gill supports in fishes. The tongue is covered with a ⟩mucous membrane containing nerves and "taste buds" in mammals. It directs food to the teeth and into the throat for chewing and swallowing. In humans, it is crucial for speech; in other animals, for lapping up water and for grooming. In some animals, such as frogs, it can be flipped forward to catch insects; in others, such as anteaters, it serves to reach for food found in deep holes.

tonka South American tree *Dipteryx odorata*, family Leguminosae. The fruit, a dry fibrous pod, encloses a black aromatic bean used in flavoring, perfumery, and the manufacture of snuff and tobacco.

Tonkin or *Tongking* former region of Vietnam, on the China Sea; area 39,951 sq mi/ 103,500 sq km. Under Chinese rule from 111 BC, Tonkin became independent AD 939 and remained self-governing until the 19th century. A part of French Indochina 1885–1946, capital Hanoi, it was part of North Vietnam from 1954 and was merged into Vietnam after the Vietnam War.

Tonkin Gulf Incident clash that triggered US entry into the Vietnam War in Aug 1964. Two US destroyers (USS *C Turner Joy* and USS *Maddox*) reported that they were fired on by North Vietnamese torpedo boats. It is unclear whether hostile shots were actually fired, but the reported attack was taken as a pretext for making air raids against North Vietnam. On Aug 7 the US Congress passed the **Tonkin Gulf Resolution**, which formed the basis for the considerable increase in US military involvement in the Vietnam War.

The resolution allowed President Johnson to "take all necessary steps, including the use of armed forces" to help SEATO (South-East Asia Treaty Organization) members "defend their freedom." This resolution formed the basis for the considerable increase in US military involvement in the Vietnam War; it was repealed 1970 in the light of evidence that the Johnson administration contrived to deceive Congress about the incident.

Tonkin, Gulf of part of the South China Sea, with oil resources. China and Vietnam disagree over their respective territorial boundaries in the area.

Tonle Sap or *Great Lake* lake on a tributary of the ⟩Mekong River, W Cambodia; area

tooth *Adults have 32 teeth: two incisors, one canine, two premolars, and three molars on each side of each jaw.*

ranging from 1,000 sq mi/2,600 sq km to 2,500 sq mi/6,500 sq km at the height of the monsoon. During the June–Nov wet season it acts as a natural flood reservoir.

Tönnies Ferdinand 1855–1936. German social theorist and philosopher, one of the founders of the sociological tradition of community studies and urban sociology through his key work, ⟩*Gemeinschaft–Gesellschaft* 1887.

tonsils in higher vertebrates, masses of lymphoid tissue situated at the back of the mouth and throat (palatine tonsils), and on the rear surface of the tongue (lingual tonsils). The tonsils contain many ⟩lymphocytes and are part of the body's defense system against infection.

The adenoids are sometimes called pharyngeal tonsils.

tonsure the full or partial shaving of the head as a symbol of entering clerical or monastic orders. Until 1973 in the Roman Catholic Church, the crown was shaved (leaving a surrounding fringe to resemble Jesus' crown of thorns); in the Eastern Orthodox Church the hair is merely shorn close. For Buddhist monks, the entire head is shaved except for a topknot.

Tonton Macoute member of a private army of death squads on Haiti. The Tontons Macoutes were initially organized by François ⟩Duvalier, president of Haiti 1957–71, and continued to terrorize the population under his successor J C Duvalier. It is alleged that the organization continued to operate after Duvalier's exile to France.

Tony award annual award by the League of New York Theaters to playwrights, performers, and technicians in ⟩Broadway plays. It is named after the US actress and producer Antoinette Perry (1888–1946).

tool any implement that gives the user a ⟩mechanical advantage, such as a hammer or a saw;

a **machine tool** is a tool operated by power. Tools are the basis of industrial production; the chief machine tool is the ⟩lathe. The industrial potential of a country is often calculated by the number of machine tools available. Automatic control of machine tools, a milestone in industrial development, is known as ⟩automation, and electronic control is called robotics (see ⟩robot).

tooth in vertebrates, one of a set of hard, bonelike structures in the mouth, used for biting and chewing food, and in defense and aggression. In humans, the first set (20 milk teeth) appear from age six months to two and a half years. The permanent ⟩dentition replaces these from the sixth year onwards, the wisdom teeth (third molars) sometimes not appearing until the age of 25 or 30. Adults have 32 teeth: two incisors, one canine (eye tooth), two premolars, and three molars on each side of each jaw. Each tooth consists of an enamel coat (hardened calcium deposits), dentine (a thick, bonelike layer), and an inner pulp cavity, housing nerves and blood vessels. Mammalian teeth have roots surrounded by cementum, which fuses them into their sockets in the jawbones. The neck of the tooth is covered by the ⟩gum, while the enamel-covered crown protrudes above the gum line.

The chief diseases of teeth are misplacements resulting from defect or disturbance of the tooth-germs before birth, eruption out of their proper places, and caries (decay).

topaz mineral, aluminum fluosilicate, $Al_2SiO_4(F,OH)_2$. It is usually yellow, but pink if it has been heated, and is used as a gemstone when transparent. It ranks 8 on the Mohs' scale of hardness.

tope slender shark *Galeorhinus galeus* ranging through temperate and tropical seas. Dark gray above and white beneath, it reaches 6 ft/ 2 m in length. The young are born well-formed, sometimes 40 at a time.

tope tumulus found in India and SE Asia; a Buddhist monument usually built over a relic of Buddha or his disciples. Topes date from 400– 300 BC including ones at Sanchi, near Bhilsa, central India.

Topeka capital of Kansas; population (1990) 119,900. It is a center for agricultural trade, and its manufactures include processed food, printed materials, and rubber and metal products.

The Menninger Foundation, a noted psychiatric center, is here. The community was platted 1854 and developed as a railroad center. It was made the state capital 1861.

topi or *korrigum* antelope *Damaliscus korrigum* of equatorial Africa, head and body about 5.5 ft/1.7 m long, 3.5 ft/1.1 m high at the shoulder, with a chocolate-brown coat.

topiary clipping of trees and shrubs into ornamental shapes, originated by the Romans in the 1st century and revived in the 16th–17th centuries in formal European and American gardens.

topography the surface shape and aspect of the land, and its study. Topography deals with relief and contours, the distribution of mountains and valleys, the patterns of rivers, and all other features, natural and artificial, that produce the landscape.

topology branch of geometry that deals with those properties of a figure that remain unchanged even when the figure is transformed

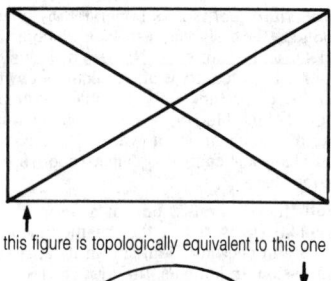

this figure is topologically equivalent to this one

topology *Topology is often called "rubber sheet geometry."*

(bent, stretched)—for example, when a square painted on a rubber sheet is deformed by distorting the sheet. Topology has scientific applications, as in the study of turbulence in flowing fluids. The map of a subway system is an example of the topological representation of a network; connectivity (the way the lines join together) is preserved, but shape and size are not.

The topological theory, proposed 1880, that only four colors are required in order to produce a map in which no two adjoining countries have the same color, inspired extensive research, and was proved 1972 by Kenneth Appel and Wolfgang Haken.

topsoil the upper, cultivated layer of soil, which may vary in depth from 3 to 18 in/8 to 45 cm. It contains organic matter—the decayed remains of vegetation, which plants need for active growth—along with a variety of soil organisms, including earthworms.

Torah in ⏃Judaism, the first five books of the Hebrew Bible (Christian Old Testament). It contains a traditional history of the world from the Creation to the death of Moses; it also includes the Hebrew people's covenant with their one God, rules for religious observance, and guidelines for social conduct, including the Ten Commandments.

Scrolls on which the Torah is hand-written in the original Hebrew are housed in a sacred enclosure, the ark, in every synagogue, and are treated with great respect. Jews believe that by observing the guidelines laid down in the Torah, they fulfill their part of their covenant with God.

Torino Italian name for the city of ⏃Turin.

tornado extremely violent revolving storm with swirling, funnel-shaped clouds, caused by a rising column of warm air propelled by strong wind. A tornado can rise to a great height, but with a diameter of only a few hundred yards or meters or less. Tornadoes move with wind speeds of 100–300 mph/160–480 kph, destroying everything in their path. They are common in the central US and Australia.

Toronto (North American Indian "place of meeting") known until 1834 as **York**. Port

and capital of Ontario, on Lake Ontario; metropolitan population (1985) 3,427,000. It is Canada's main industrial and commercial center (banking, shipbuilding, automobiles, farm machinery, food processing, publishing) and also a cultural center, with theaters and a film industry. A French fort was established 1749, and the site became the provincial capital 1793.

torpedo self-propelled underwater missile, invented 1866 by British engineer Robert ⏃Whitehead. Modern torpedoes are homing missiles; some resemble mines in that they lie on the seabed until activated by the acoustic signal of a passing ship. A television camera enables them to be remotely controlled, and in the final stage of attack they lock on to the radar or sonar signals of the target ship.

torpedo or **electric ray** any species of the order Torpediniformes of mainly tropical rays (cartilaginous fishes), whose electric organs between the pectoral fin and the head can give a powerful shock. They can grow to 6 ft/180 cm in length.

The electric ray *Torpedo nobiliana* is found on both sides of the Atlantic.

torque the turning effect of force on an object. A turbine produces a torque that turns an electricity generator in a power station. Torque is measured by multiplying the force by its perpendicular distance from the turning point.

torque converter device similar to a turbine, filled with oil, used in automatic transmission systems in motor vehicles and locomotives to transmit power (torque) from the engine to the gears.

Torquemada Tomás de 1420–1498. Spanish Dominican monk, confessor to Queen Isabella I. In 1483 he revived the ⏃Inquisition on her behalf, and at least 2,000 "heretics" were burned; Torquemada also expelled the Jews from Spain 1492, with a resultant decline of the economy.

torr unit of pressure equal to 1/760 of an ⏃atmosphere, used mainly in high-vacuum technology.

One torr is equivalent to 133.322 pascals, and for practical purposes is the same as the millimeter of mercury. It is named after Evangelista ⏃Torricelli.

Torreón industrial and agricultural city in Coahuila state, N Mexico, on the river Nazas at an altitude of 3,700 ft/1,127 m; population (1986) 730,000. Before the arrival of the railroad 1907 Torreón was the largest of the three Laguna cotton-district cities (with Gómez Palacio and Ciudad Lerdo). Since then it has developed as a major thoroughfare and commercial center.

Torres-García Joaquim 1874–1949. Uruguayan artist, born in Montevideo. In Paris from 1926, he was influenced by ⏃Mondrian and others and, after going to Madrid in 1932, by Inca, and Nazca pottery. His mature style is based on a grid pattern derived from the aesthetic proportion of the ⏃golden section.

Torres Strait channel separating New Guinea from Australia, with scattered reefs; width 80 mi/130 km. The first European to sail through it was the Spanish navigator Luis Vaez de Torres 1606.

Torricelli Evangelista 1608–1647. Italian physicist and pupil of ⏃Galileo who devised the mercury ⏃barometer.

torsion in physics, the state of strain set up in a twisted material; for example, when a thread,

wire, or rod is twisted, the torsion set up in the material tends to return the material to its original state. The **torsion balance**, a sensitive device for measuring small gravitational or magnetic forces, or electric charges, balances these against the restoring force set up by them in a torsion suspension.

tort in law, a wrongful act for which someone can be sued for damages in a civil court. It includes such acts as libel, trespass, injury done to someone (whether intentionally or by negligence), and inducement to break a contract (although breach of contract itself is not a tort).

In general a tort is distinguished from a crime in that it affects the interests of an individual rather than of society at large, but some crimes can also be torts.

tortoise any member of the family Testudinidae, the land-living members of the order Chelonia, which includes all ⏃turtles, terrestrial or aquatic. The shell of tortoises is generally more domed than that of aquatic turtles; their hind legs are stumpy and columnar; the front legs are often shovel-shaped for digging. Tortoises are herbivorous and occur in the warmer regions of all continents except Australia. Tortoises range in size from 4 in/10 cm to 5 ft/150 cm, and some are known to live for 150 years.

Best-known in the pet trade is the small spur-thighed tortoise *Testudo graeca* found in Asia Minor, the Balkans, and N Africa. The giant species of the Galapagos and Seychelles may reach a length of 5 ft/1.5 m and weigh over 500 lb/225 kg. They can yield about 200 lb/90 kg of meat, hence their almost complete extermination by sailors in passing ships. North American tortoises are represented by four species of gopher tortoises (genus *Gophenus*) living in the SW US and Mexico.

Tortoiseshell is the semitransparent shell of the marine hawksbill turtle.

Tortuga (French *La Tortue* "turtle") island off the N coast of ⏃Haiti; area 69 sq mi/180 sq km. It was a pirate lair during the 17th century.

Tory Party the forerunner of the British ⏃Conservative Party about 1680–1830. It was the party of the squire and parson, as opposed to the Whigs (supported by the trading classes and Nonconformists). The name is still applied colloquially to the Conservative Party. In the US a Tory was an opponent of the break with Britain in the Revolutionary War 1775–83.

Toscana Italian name for the region of ⏃Tuscany.

Toscanini Arturo 1867–1957. Italian conductor. He made La Scala, Milan (where he conducted 1898–1903, 1906–08, and 1921–29), the world's leading opera house. Opposed to the Fascist regime, in 1936 he returned to the US, where he had conducted at the Metropolitan Opera 1908–15. The NBC Symphony Orchestra was formed for him in 1937. He retired in 1954.

total internal reflection the complete reflection of a beam of light that occurs from the surface of an optically "less dense" material. For example, a beam from an underwater light source can be reflected from the surface of the water, rather than escaping through the surface. Total internal reflection can only happen if a light beam hits a surface at an angle greater than the ⏃critical angle for that particular pair of materials.

Total internal reflection is used as a means of reflecting light inside ⏃prisms and ⏃optical fibers. Light is contained inside an optical fiber not by the cladding around it, but by the ability of the internal surface of the glass-fiber core to reflect 100% of the light, thereby keeping it trapped inside the fiber.

totalitarianism government control of all activities within a country, overtly political or otherwise, as in fascist or communist dictatorships. Examples of totalitarian regimes are Italy under Benito ▷Mussolini 1922–45; Germany under Adolph ▷Hitler 1933–45; the USSR under Joseph ▷Stalin from the 1930s until his death in 1953; more recently Romania under Nicolae ▷Ceaușescu 1974–89.

totemism (Algonquin Indian "mark of my family") the belief in individual or clan kinship with an animal, plant, or object. This totem is sacred to those concerned, and they are forbidden to eat or desecrate it; marriage within the clan is usually forbidden. Totemism occurs among Pacific Islanders and Australian Aborigines, and was formerly prevalent throughout Europe, Africa, and Asia. Most North and South American Indian societies had totems as well.

Totem poles are carved by Native Americans of the NW coast of North America and incorporate totem objects (carved and painted) as a symbol of the people or to commemorate the dead.

toucan any South and Central American forest-dwelling bird of the family Ramphastidae. Toucans have very large, brilliantly colored beaks and often handsome plumage. They live in small flocks and eat fruits, seeds, and insects. They nest in holes in trees, where the female lays 2–4 eggs; both parents care for the eggs and young. There are 37 species, ranging from 1 ft/30 cm to 2 ft/60 cm in size.

touch sensation produced by specialized nerve endings in the skin. Some respond to light pressure, others to heavy pressure. Temperature detection may also contribute to the overall sensation of touch. Many animals, such as nocturnal ones, rely on touch more than humans do. Some have specialized organs of touch that project from the body, such as whiskers or antennae.

touch screen in computing, an input device allowing the user to communicate with the computer by touching a display screen with a finger. In this way, the user can point to a required ▷menu option or item of data. Touch screens are used less widely than other pointing devices such as the ▷mouse or ▷joystick.

Typically, the screen is able to detect the touch either because the finger presses against a sensitive membrane or because it interrupts a grid of light beams crossing the screen surface.

touch sensor in a computer-controlled ▷robot, a device used to give the robot a sense of touch, allowing it to manipulate delicate objects or move automatically about a room. Touch sensors provide the feedback necessary for the robot to adjust the force of its movements and the pressure of its grip. The main types include the strain gauge and the microswitch.

Toulon port and capital of Var *département*, SE France, on the Mediterranean Sea, 30 mi/48 km SE of Marseille; population (1983) 410,000. It is the chief Mediterranean naval station of France. Industries include oil refining, chemicals, furniture, and clothing. Toulon was the Roman *Telo Martius* and was made a port

by Henry IV. It was occupied by the British 1793, and Napoleon first distinguished himself in driving them out. In World War II the French fleet was scuttled here to avoid its passing to German control.

Toulouse capital of Haute-Garonne *département*, SW France, on the river Garonne SE of Bordeaux; population (1982) 541,000. The chief industries are textiles and aircraft construction (the supersonic airliner Concorde was built here). Toulouse was the capital of the Visigoths (see ▷Goth) and later of Aquitaine 781–843.

Toulouse has a 12th–13th-century cathedral. The Duke of Wellington repulsed the French marshal Soult at Toulouse 1814 in the ▷Peninsular War.

Toulouse-Lautrec Henri Marie Raymond de 1864–1901. French artist, associated with the Impressionists. He was active in Paris, where he painted entertainers and prostitutes. From 1891 his lithograph posters were a great success.

Toulouse-Lautrec showed an early gift for drawing, to which he turned increasingly after a riding accident at the age of 15 left him with crippled and stunted legs. In 1882 he began to study art in Paris. He admired Goya's etchings and Degas's work, and in the 1880s he met Gauguin and was inspired by Japanese prints. Lautrec became a familiar figure drawing and painting in the dance halls, theaters, cafés, circuses, and brothels. Many of his finished works have the spontaneous character of sketches. He often painted with thinned-out oils on cardboard.

touraco any fruit-eating African bird of the family Musophagidae. They have long tails, erectile crests, and short, rounded wings. The largest are 28 in/70 cm long.

The *white-cheeked touraco Touraco leucotis* resembles a multicolored magpie.

Touraine former province of W central France, now part of the *départements* of Indre-et-Loire and Vienne; capital Tours.

Tour de France French road race for professional cyclists held annually over approximately 3,000 mi/4,800 km of primarily French roads. The race takes about three weeks to complete and the route varies each year, often taking in adjoining countries, but always ending in Paris. A separate stage is held every day, and the overall leader at the end of each stage wears the coveted "yellow jersey" (French *maillot jaune*).

First held in 1903, it is now the most watched sporting event in the world, with more than 10 million spectators. Although it is a race for individuals, sponsored teams of 12 riders take part, each with its own "star" rider whom team members support.

Tour de France: recent winners

1983	Laurent Fignon *(France)*
1984	Laurent Fignon *(France)*
1985	Bernard Hinault *(France)*
1986	Greg LeMond *(US)*
1987	Stephen Roche *(Ireland)*
1988	Pedro Delgado *(Spain)*
1989	Greg LeMond *(US)*
1990	Greg LeMond *(US)*
1991	Miguel Indurain *(Spain)*
1992	Miguel Indurain *(Spain)*

Tourette's syndrome or *Gilles de la Tourette syndrome* rare condition characterized by multiple tics and vocal phenomena such as grunting, snarling, and

obscene speech, named after French physician Georges Gilles de la Tourette (1859–1904). It affects one to five people per 10,000, with males outnumbering females by four to one, and the onset is usually around the age of six. There are no convincing explanations of its cause, and it is usually resistant to treatment.

tourmaline hard, brittle mineral, a complex of various metal silicates, but mainly sodium aluminum borosilicate.

Small tourmalines are found in granites and gneisses. The common varieties range from black (schorl) to pink, and the transparent gemstones may be colorless (achroite), rose pink (rubellite), green (Brazilian emerald), blue (indicolite, verdelite, Brazilian sapphire), or brown (dravite).

Tours industrial (chemicals, textiles, machinery) city and capital of the Indre-et-Loire *département*, W central France, on the river Loire; population (1982) 263,000. It has a 13th–15th-century cathedral. An ancient city and former capital of ▷Touraine, it was the site of the French defeat of the Arabs 732 under ▷Charles Martel. Tours became the French capital for four days during World War II.

Toussaint L'Ouverture Pierre Dominique c. 1743–1803. Haitian revolutionary leader, born a slave. He joined the insurrection of 1791 against the French colonizers and was made governor by the revolutionary French government. He expelled the Spanish and British, but when the French emperor Napoleon reimposed slavery he revolted, was captured, and died in prison in France. In 1983 his remains were returned to Haiti.

Tower John 1925–1991. US Republican politician, a senator from Texas 1961–83. Despite having been a paid arms-industry consultant, he was selected 1989 by President Bush to serve as defense secretary, but the Senate refused to approve the appointment because of Tower's previous heavy drinking.

Tower, in 1961 the first Republican to be elected senator from Texas, emerged as a military expert in the Senate, becoming chair of the Armed Services Committee in 1981. After his retirement from the Senate in 1983, he acted as a consultant to arms manufacturers and chaired the 1986–87 *Tower Commission*, which investigated aspects of the Irangate arms-for-hostages scandal.

Tower of London fortress on the Thames bank to the east of the City. The keep, or White Tower, was built about 1078 by Bishop Gundulf on the site of British and Roman fortifications. It is surrounded by two strong walls and a moat (now dry), and was for centuries a royal residence and the principal state prison.

Today it is a barracks, an armory, and a museum.

Townes Charles 1915– . US physicist who in 1953 designed and constructed the first ▷maser. For this work, he shared the 1964 Nobel Prize with Soviet physicists Nikolai Basov and Aleksandr Prokhorov.

Townshend Charles 1725–1767. British politician, chancellor of the Exchequer 1766–67. The *Townshend Acts*, designed to assert Britain's traditional authority over its colonies, resulted in widespread resistance. Among other things they levied taxes on imports (such as tea, glass, and paper) into the North American colonies. Opposition in the colonies to taxation without representation (see ▷Stamp Act) precipitated the American Revolution.

toxemia condition in which poisons are spread throughout the body by the bloodstream, such as those produced by ◊pathogens or by localized cells in the body.

Toxemia of pregnancy is a potentially serious condition marked by high blood pressure, ◊edema, and sometimes convulsions. Arising from unknown causes, it disappears when pregnancy is over.

toxic poisonous or harmful. Radioactivity, air and water pollutants, and poisons ingested or inhaled—for example, lead from car exhausts, asbestos, and chlorinated solvents are some toxic substances that occur in the environment; generally the effects take some time to become apparent (anything from a few hours to many years). The cumulative effects of toxic waste pose a serious threat to the ecological stability of the planet.

toxicity tests tests carried out on new drugs, cosmetics, food additives, pesticides, and other synthetic chemicals to see whether they are safe for humans to use. They aim to identify potential toxins, carcinogens, teratogens, and mutagens.

Traditionally such tests use live animals such as rats, rabbits, and mice. Animal tests have become a target for criticism by ◊antivivisection groups, and alternatives have been sought. These include tests on human cells cultured in a test tube and on bacteria.

toxic shock syndrome rare condition marked by rapid onset of fever, vomiting, and low blood pressure, sometimes leading to death. It is caused by a toxin of the bacterium *Staphylococcus aureus*, normally harmlessly present in the body, which may accumulate, for example, if a tampon used by a woman during a period remains unchanged beyond four to six hours.

toxin any chemical molecule that can damage the living body. In vertebrates, toxins are broken down by ◊enzyme action, mainly in the liver.

toxocariasis infection of humans by a canine intestinal worm, which results in a swollen liver and sometimes eye damage.

Toynbee Arnold Joseph 1889–1975. English historian whose *A Study of History* 1934–61 was an attempt to discover the laws governing the rise and fall of civilizations.

trace element chemical element necessary for the health of a plant or animal, but only in minute quantities. For example, iodine is needed by the thyroid gland of mammals for making hormones that control growth and body chemistry, and for all metabolic processes.

tracer in science, a small quantity of a radioactive ◊isotope (form of an element) used to follow the path of a chemical reaction or a physical or biological process. The location (and possibly concentration) of the tracer is usually detected by using a Geiger–Muller counter.

For example, the activity of the thyroid gland can be followed by giving the patient an injection containing a small dose of a radioactive isotope of iodine, which is selectively absorbed from the bloodstream by the gland.

trachea tube that forms an airway in air-breathing animals. In land-living ◊vertebrates, including humans, it is also known as the **windpipe** and runs from the larynx to the upper part of the chest. Its diameter is about 0.6 in/1.5 cm

and its length 4 in/10 cm. It is strong and flexible, and reinforced by rings of ◊cartilage. In the upper chest, the trachea branches into two tubes: the left and right bronchi, which enter the lungs. Insects have a branching network of tubes called tracheae, which conduct air from holes (◊spiracles) in the body surface to all the body tissues. The finest branches of the tracheae are called tracheoles.

Some spiders also have tracheae but, unlike insects, they possess gill-like lungs (book lungs) and rely on their circulatory system to transport gases throughout the body.

tracheid cell found in the water-conducting tissue (◊xylem) of many plants, including gymnosperms (conifers) and pteridophytes (ferns). It is long and thin with pointed ends. The cell walls are thickened by ◊lignin, except for numerous small rounded areas, or pits, through which water and dissolved minerals pass from one cell to another. Once mature, the cell itself dies and only its walls remain.

tracheotomy surgical opening in the windpipe (trachea), usually created for the insertion of a tube to enable the patient to breathe. It is done either to bypass the airway impaired by disease or injury, or to safeguard it during surgery or a prolonged period of mechanical ventilation.

trachoma chronic eye infection, resembling severe ◊conjunctivitis. The conjunctiva becomes inflamed, with scarring and formation of pus, and there may be damage to the cornea. It is caused by a viruslike organism (◊chlamydia), and is a disease of dry tropical regions. Although it responds well to antibiotics, numerically it remains the biggest single cause of blindness worldwide.

Tractarianism another name for the ◊Oxford Movement, 19th-century movement for Catholic revival within the Church of England.

tractor in agriculture, a powerful motor vehicle, commonly having large rear wheels or caterpillar tracks, used for pulling farm machinery and loads. It is usually powered by a diesel engine and has a power-takeoff mechanism for driving machinery, and a hydraulic lift for raising and lowering implements.

Tracy Spencer 1900–1967. US actor distinguished for his understated, seemingly effortless, natural performances. His films include *Captains Courageous* 1937 and *Boys' Town* 1938 (for both of which he won Academy Awards), and he starred with Katharine Hepburn in nine films, including *Adam's Rib* 1949 and *Guess Who's Coming to Dinner* 1967, his final appearance.

His other films include *Bad Day at Black Rock* 1955, *The Last Hurrah* 1958, *The Old Man and the Sea* 1958, and *Inherit the Wind* 1960. He was one of Hollywood's most versatile performers.

trademark name or symbol that is distinctive of a marketed product.

The owner may register the mark to prevent its unauthorized use.

tradescantia any plant of the genus *Tradescantia* of the family Commelinaceae, native to North and Central America. The spiderwort *T. virginiana* is a cultivated garden plant; the wandering jew *T. albiflora* is a common house plant, with green oval leaves tinged with pink or purple or silver-striped.

trade wind prevailing wind that blows toward the equator from the northeast and southeast. Trade winds are caused by hot air rising at

the equator and the consequent movement of air from north and south to take its place. The winds are deflected toward the west because of the Earth's west-to-east rotation. The unpredictable calms known as the ◊doldrums lie at their convergence.

The trade-wind belts move north and south about 5° with the seasons. The name is derived from the obsolete expression "to blow *trade*" meaning consistently in a constant direction, which indicates the trade winds' importance to navigation in the days of cargo-carrying sailing ships.

Trafalgar, Battle of battle Oct 21, 1805 in the ◊Napoleonic Wars. The British fleet under Admiral Nelson defeated a Franco-Spanish fleet; Nelson was mortally wounded. The victory laid the foundation for British naval supremacy throughout the 19th century. It is named after Cape Trafalgar, a low headland in SW Spain, near the western entrance to the Straits of Gibraltar.

tragedy in the theater, a play dealing with a serious theme, traditionally one in which a character meets disaster as a result of either personal failings or circumstances beyond his or her control. Historically the Greek view of tragedy, as defined by Aristotle and expressed by the great tragedians Aeschylus, Euripides, and Sophocles, has been predominant in the western tradition. In the 20th century tragedies in the narrow Greek sense of dealing with exalted personages in an elevated manner have virtually died out. Tragedy has been replaced by dramas with "tragic" implications or overtones, as in the work of Ibsen, O'Neill, Tennessee Williams, Pinter, and Osborne, for example, or by the hybrid tragicomedy.

The Greek view of tragedy provided the subject matter for later tragic dramas, but it was the Roman Seneca (whose works were intended to be read rather than acted) who influenced the Elizabethan tragedies of Marlowe and Shakespeare. French Classical tragedy developed under the influence of both Seneca and an interpretation of Aristotle which gave rise to the theory of unities of time, place, and action, as observed by Racine, one of its greatest exponents. In Germany the tragedies of Goethe and Schiller led to the exaggerated ◊melodrama, which replaced pure tragedy. In the 18th century unsuccessful attempts were made to "domesticate" tragedy. In the 20th century "tragedy" has come to refer to dramas with "tragic" implications for individuals or society.

tragicomedy drama that contains elements of tragedy and comedy; for example, Shakespeare's "reconciliation" plays, such as *The Winter's Tale*, which reach a tragic climax but then lighten to a happy conclusion. A tragicomedy is the usual form for plays in the tradition of the Theater of the ◊Absurd, such as Samuel ◊Beckett's *En attendant Godot/Waiting for Godot* 1953 and Tom ◊Stoppard's *Rosencrantz and Guildenstern are Dead* 1967.

tragopan any of several species of bird of the genus *Tragopan*, a short-tailed pheasant living in wet forests along the S Himalayas. Tragopans are brilliantly colored with arrays of spots, long crown feathers and two blue erectile crests. All have been reduced in numbers by destruction of their habitat. The western tragopan is the rarest, as a result of extensive deforestation.

Males inflate colored wattles and throat pouches in their spring courtship displays.

Trajan Marcus Ulpius (Trajanus) AD 52–117. Roman emperor and soldier, born in Seville.

He was adopted as heir by ◊Nerva, whom he succeeded AD 98.

He was a just and conscientious ruler, corresponded with Pliny about the Christians, and conquered Dacia (Romania) 101–07 and much of ◊Parthia. **Trajan's Column**, Rome, commemorates his victories.

trance mental state in which the subject loses the ordinary perceptions of time and space, and even of his or her own body.

In this highly aroused state, often induced by rhythmic music, "speaking in tongues" (glossolalia) may occur (see ◊Pentecostal Movement); this usually consists of the rhythmic repetition of apparently meaningless syllables, with a euphoric return to consciousness. It is also practiced by native American and Australian Aboriginal healers, Afro-Brazilian spirit mediums, and Siberian shamans.

tranquilizer common name for any drug for reducing anxiety or tension (◊anxiolytic), such as ◊benzodiazepines, barbiturates, antidepressants, and beta-blockers. The use of drugs to control anxiety is becoming much less popular, because most of the drugs used are capable of inducing dependence.

transactinide any of a series of nine radioactive, metallic elements with atomic numbers that extend beyond the ◊actinide series, those from 104 (rutherfordium) to 112 (unnamed). They are grouped because of their expected chemical similarities (they are all bivalent), the properties differing only slightly with atomic number. All have ◊half-lives that measure less than two minutes.

Trans-Alaskan Pipeline one of the world's greatest civil engineering projects, the construction of a pipeline to carry petroleum (crude oil) 800 mi/1,285 km from N Alaska to the ice-free port of Valdez. It was completed 1977 after three years' work and much criticism by ecologists.

The engineers had to elevate nearly half the pipeline on supports above ground level to avoid thawing the permafrost (permanently frozen ground), which would have caused much environmental damage. They also had to cross 600 rivers and streams and two mountain ranges, and allow for earthquakes.

Trans-Amazonian Highway or **Trans-amazonica** road in Brazil, linking Recife in the east with the provinces of Rondonia, Amazonas, and Acre in the west.

Transcaucasia geographical region S of the Caucasus, which includes Armenia, Azerbaijan, and Georgia. It formed the **Transcaucasian Republic** 1922, but was broken up 1936 into three separate Soviet republics. All three republics became independent 1991.

transcendentalism philosophy inaugurated in the 18th century by Immanuel Kant and developed in the US in the mid-19th century into a mystical and social doctrine. As opposed to metaphysics in the traditional sense, transcendental philosophy is concerned with the conditions of possibility of experience, rather than the nature of being. It seeks to show the necessary structure of our "point of view" on the world.

Introduced to England, transcendentalism influenced the writers Samuel Coleridge and Thomas Carlyle. In the US it was taken up in New England about 1840–60, influenced by European Romanticism, by Henry Thoreau,

Ralph Waldo Emerson, the feminist Margaret Fuller (1810–1850), and Orestes Brownson, who saw God as immanent in nature and the human soul. Transcendentalism had religious, philosophical, and political implications, shaping American ideals of self-reliance, attitudes toward reform and slavery-abolition, feminism, and various forms of Utopian idealism displayed in the movement's experimental community at Brook Farm near Boston, Massachusetts. Emphasizing the role of the poet and the need for an original US literature, it also had literary consequences, and out of it came Emerson's essays and poems, Jones Very's poetry, Thoreau's *Walden* 1854, and, less directly, the novels and stories of Nathaniel Hawthorne, and Walt Whitman's *Leaves of Grass* 1855.

transcendental meditation (TM) technique of focusing the mind, based in part on Hindu meditation. Meditators are given a mantra (a special word or phrase) to repeat over and over to themselves; such meditation is believed to benefit the practitioner by relieving stress and inducing a feeling of well-being and relaxation. It was introduced to the West by Maharishi Mahesh Yogi and popularized by the Beatles in the late 1960s.

transcription in living cells, the process by which the information for the synthesis of a protein is transferred from the ◊DNA strand on which it is carried to the messenger ◊RNA strand involved in the actual synthesis.

It occurs by the formation of ◊base pairs when a single strand of unwound DNA serves as a template for assembling the complementary nucleotides that make up the new RNA strand.

transducer device that converts one form of energy into another. For example, a thermistor is a transducer that converts heat into an electrical voltage, and an electric motor is a transducer that converts an electrical voltage into mechanical energy. Transducers are important components in many types of sensor, converting the physical quantity to be measured into a proportional voltage signal.

transfer orbit elliptical path followed by a spacecraft moving from one orbit to another, designed to save fuel although at the expense of a longer journey time.

Space probes travel to the planets on transfer orbits. A probe aimed at Venus has to be "slowed down" relative to the Earth, so that it enters an elliptical transfer orbit with its perigee (point of closest approach to the Sun) at the same distance as the orbit of Venus; toward Mars, the vehicle has to be "speeded

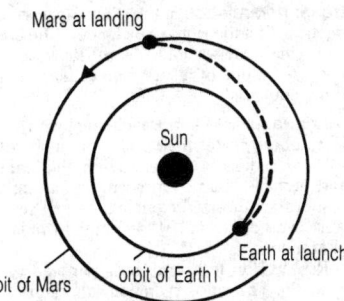

transfer orbit *The transfer orbit used by a spacecraft when traveling from Earth to Mars.*

up" relative to the Earth, so that it reaches its apogee (furthest point from the Sun) at the same distance as the orbit of Mars. **Geostationary transfer orbit** is the highly elliptical path followed by satellites to be placed in ◊geostationary orbit around the Earth (an orbit coincident with Earth's rotation). A small rocket is fired at the transfer orbit's apogee to place the satellite in geostationary orbit.

transformational grammar theory of language structure initiated by Noam ◊Chomsky, which proposes that below the actual phrases and sentences of a language (its **surface structure**) there lies a more basic layer (its **deep structure**), which is processed by various transformational rules when we speak and write.

Below the surface structure "the girl opened the door" would lie the deep structure "the girl open + (past tense) the door." Note that there is usually more than one way in which a deep structure can be realized; in this case, "the door was opened by the girl."

transformer device in which, by electromagnetic induction, an alternating current (AC) of one voltage is transformed to another voltage, without change of ◊frequency. Transformers are widely used in electrical apparatus of all kinds, and in particular in power transmission where high voltages and low currents are utilized.

A transformer has two coils, a primary for the input and a secondary for the output, wound on a common iron core. The ratio of the primary to the secondary voltages (and currents) is directly (and inversely) proportional to the number of turns in the primary and secondary coils.

transfusion intravenous delivery of blood or blood products (plasma, red cells) into a patient's circulation to make up for deficiencies due to disease, injury, or surgical intervention. Cross-matching is carried out to ensure the patient receives the right type of blood. Because of worries about blood-borne disease, self-transfusion with units of blood "donated" over the weeks before an operation is popular.

Blood transfusion, first successfully pioneered in humans 1818, remained highly risky until the discovery of blood groups, by Karl ◊Landsteiner 1900, indicated the need for compatibility of donated blood.

transgenic organism plant, animal, bacterium, or other living organism which has had a foreign gene added to it by means of ◊genetic engineering.

transhumance seasonal movement by pastoral farmers of their livestock between areas of different climate. There are three main forms: in **Alpine** regions, such as Switzerland, cattle are moved to high-level pastures in summer and returned to milder valley pastures in winter; in **Mediterranean** lands, summer heat and drought make it necessary to move cattle to cooler mountain slopes; in **W Africa**, the nomadic herders of the ◊Fulani peoples move cattle south in search of grass and water in the dry season and north in the wet season to avoid the ◊tsetse fly.

transistor solid-state electronic component, made of ◊semiconductor material, with three or more ◊electrodes, that can regulate a current passing through it. A transistor can act as an amplifier, ◊oscillator, photocell, or switch, and (unlike earlier electron tubes) usually operates on a very small amount of power. Transistors commonly consist of a tiny sandwich of ◊germanium or ◊silicon, alternate layers having different electrical properties. A crystal of pure germanium or silicon would act as an insulator (nonconductor).

By introducing impurities in the form of atoms of other materials (for example, boron, arsenic, or indium) in minute amounts, the layers may be made either **n-type**, having an excess of electrons, or **p-type**, having a deficiency of electrons. This enables electrons to flow from one layer to another in one direction only.

Transistors have had a great impact on the electronics industry, and are now made in the thousands of millions each year. They perform many of the same functions as thermionic tubes but have the advantages of greater reliability, long life, compactness, and instantaneous action, no warming-up period being necessary. They are widely used in most electronic equipment, including portable radios and televisions, computers, satellites, and space research, and are the basis of the ◊integrated circuit (silicon chip). They were invented at Bell Telephone Laboratories in the US in 1948 by John ◊Bardeen and ◊Walter Brattain, developing the work of William ◊Shockley.

transit in astronomy, the passage of a smaller object across the visible disk of a larger one. Transits of the inferior planets occur when they pass directly between the Earth and the Sun, and are seen as tiny dark spots against the Sun's disk.

Other forms of transit include the passage of a satellite or its shadow across the disk of Jupiter and the passage of planetary surface features across the central ◊meridian of that planet as seen from Earth. The passage of an object in the sky across the observer's meridian is also known as a transit.

transition metal any of a group of metallic elements that have incomplete inner electron shells and exhibit variable valency—for example, cobalt, copper, iron, and molybdenum. They are excellent conductors of electricity, and generally form highly colored compounds.

Transjordan former name (1923–49) of the Hashemite kingdom of ◊Jordan.

Transkei largest of South Africa's Bantustans, or homelands, extending northeast from the Great Kei River, on the coast of Cape Province, to the border of Natal; area 16,910 sq mi/ 43,808 sq km; population (1985) 3,000,000, including small white and Asian minorities. It became self-governing 1963, and achieved full "independence" 1976. Its capital is Umtata, and it has a port at Mnganzana. It is one of the two homelands of the Xhosa people (the other is Ciskei), and products include livestock, coffee, tea, sugar, corn, and sorghum. It is governed by a military council since a 1987 coup (military leader Maj Gen H B Holomisa from 1987).

translation in living cells, the process by which proteins are synthesized. During translation, the information coded as a sequence of nucleotides in messenger ◊RNA is transformed into a sequence of amino acids in a peptide chain. The process involves the "translation" of the ◊genetic code. See also ◊transcription.

translation in literature, the rendering of words from one language to another. The first recorded named translator was Livius Andronicus, who translated Homer's *Odyssey* from Greek to Latin in 240 BC.

transmigration of souls another name for ◊reincarnation.

transpiration the loss of water from a plant by evaporation. Most water is lost from the leaves through pores known as ◊stomata, whose primary function is to allow ◊gas exchange between the plant's internal tissues and the atmosphere. Transpiration from the leaf surfaces causes a continuous upward flow of water from the roots via the ◊xylem, which is known as the transpiration stream.

A single corn plant has been estimated to transpire 64 gal/245 l of water in one growing season.

transplant in medicine, the transfer of a tissue or organ from one human being to another or from one part of the body to another (skin grafting). In most organ transplants, the operation is for life-saving purposes, though the immune system tends to reject foreign tissue. Careful matching and immunosuppressive drugs must be used, but these are not always successful.

Corneal grafting, which may restore sight to a diseased or damaged eye, was pioneered 1905, and is the oldest successful human transplant procedure. Of the internal organs, kidneys were first transplanted successfully in the early 1950s and are the most readily received by the body. Recent transplant also encompasses hearts, lungs, livers, pancreatic, bone, and bone-marrow tissue. Most transplant material is taken from cadaver donors, usually those suffering death of the ◊brainstem, or from frozen tissue banks. In rare cases, kidneys, corneas, and part of the liver may be obtained from living donors. Besides the shortage of donated material, the main problem facing transplant surgeons is rejection of the donated organ by the new body. The 1990 Nobel Prize for Medicine and Physiology was awarded to two US surgeons, Donnall Thomas and Joseph Murray, for their pioneering work on organ transplant.

transsexual person who identifies himself or herself completely with the opposite sex, believing that the wrong sex was assigned at birth. Unlike **transvestites**, who desire to dress in clothes traditionally worn by the opposite sex; transsexuals think and feel emotionally in a way typically considered appropriate to members of the opposite sex, and may undergo surgery to modify external sexual characteristics.

Trans-Siberian Railway railroad line connecting the cities of European Russia with Omsk, Novosibirsk, Irkutsk, and Khabarovsk, and terminating at Vladivostok on the Pacific. It was built 1891–1905; from Leningrad to Vladivostok is about 5,400 mi/8,700 km. A 1,928-mi/3,102-km northern line was completed 1984 after ten years' work.

transubstantiation in Christian theology, the doctrine that the whole substance of the bread and wine changes into the substance of the body and blood of Jesus when consecrated in the ◊Eucharist.

transuranic any chemical element with atomic number greater than that of uranium (92). All are radioactive. Neptunium, plutonium, and perhaps americium occur in nature; the rest are synthesized elements only. The first were synthesized in 1940, neptunium and then plutonium.

Research in transuranics is pursued mainly at the Lawrence radiation laboratories of the University of California at Berkeley; the Joint Institute for Nuclear Research in Dubna, Russia; and the Institute for Heavy Ion Research in Darmstadt, Germany.

Transvaal province of NE South Africa, bordering Zimbabwe to the north; area 101,325 sq mi/262,499 sq km; population (1985) 7,532,000. Its capital is Pretoria, and towns include Johannesburg, Germiston, Brakpan, Springs, Benoni, Krugersdorp, and Roodepoort. Products include diamonds, coal, iron ore, copper, lead, tin, manganese, meat, corn, tobacco, and fruit. The main rivers are the Vaal and Limpopo with their tributaries. Swaziland forms an enclave on the Natal border. It was settled by *Voortrekkers*, Boers who left Cape Colony in the Great Trek from 1831. Independence was recognized by Britain 1852, until the settlers' difficulties with the conquered Zulus led to British annexation 1877. It was made a British colony after the South African War 1899–1902, and in 1910 became a province of the Union of South Africa.

Transylvania mountainous area of central and NW Romania, bounded to the south by the Transylvanian Alps (an extension of the ◊Carpathian Mountains), formerly a province, with its capital at Cluj. It was part of Hungary from about 1000 until its people voted to unite with Romania 1918. It is the home of the vampire legends.

trapezium in geometry, a four-sided plane figure (quadrilateral) with no two sides parallel.

trapezoid in geometry, a four-sided plane figure (quadrilateral) with only two sides parallel. If the parallel sides have lengths a and b and the perpendicular distance between them is h (the height of the trapezoid), its area $A=1/2h(a+b)$.

An isosceles trapezoid has its sloping sides (legs) equal, is symmetrical about a line drawn through the midpoints of its parallel sides, and has equal base angles.

Trappist member of a Roman Catholic order of monks and nuns, renowned for the strictness of their rule, which includes the maintenance of silence, manual labor, and a vegetarian diet. The order was founded 1664 at La Trappe, in Normandy, France, by Armand de Rancé (1626–1700) as a reformed version of the ◊Cistercian order. In 1792 the monks were expelled (during the French Revolution) but the community remained together until it could return in 1817.

Traven B(en). Adopted name of Herman Feige 1882–1969. German-born US novelist whose true identity was not revealed until 1979. His books include the bestseller *The Death Ship* 1926 and *The Treasure of the Sierra Madre* 1934, which was made into a film starring Humphrey Bogart in 1948.

Born in a part of Germany now in Poland, he was in turn known as the anarchist Maret Rut, Traven Torsvan, and Hollywood scriptwriter Hal Croves. Between the two world wars he lived in obscurity in Mexico and avoided recognition.

Travers Morris William 1872–1961. English chemist who, with William Ramsay, between 1894 and 1908 first identified what were called the ◊inert gases or noble gases: krypton, xenon, and radon.

treadmill wheel turned by foot power (often by a domesticated animal) and used, for instance, to raise water from a well or grind grain.

treason act of betrayal, in particular against the sovereign or the state to which the offender owes allegiance.

In the US, treason is defined in the constitution as the crime of "levying war against [the United States], or adhering to their enemies, giving them aid and comfort." Congress has the power to declare the punishment for treason.

Treasure Island adventure story for children by R L ⟁Stevenson, published in 1883. Jim Hawkins, the story's narrator, sets sail with Squire Trelawney in the *Hispaniola*, armed with a map showing the location of buried treasure. Attempts by the ship's crew of pirates, including Long John Silver, to seize the map are foiled after much fighting and the squire finds the treasure.

treaty written agreement between two or more states. Treaties take effect either immediately on signature or, more often, on ratification. Ratification involves a further exchange of documents and usually takes place after the internal governments have approved the terms of the treaty. Treaties are binding in international law, the rules being laid down in the Vienna Convention on the Law of Treaties 1969.

tree perennial plant with a woody stem, usually a single stem or "trunk," made up of ⟁wood and protected by an outer layer of ⟁bark. It absorbs water through a root system. There is no clear dividing line between ⟁shrubs and trees, but sometimes a minimum height of 20 ft/6 m is used to define a tree.

A treelike form has evolved independently many times in different groups of plants. Among the ⟁angiosperms, or flowering plants, most trees are ⟁dicotyledons. This group includes trees such as oak, beech, ash, chestnut, lime, and maple, and they are often referred to as ⟁broad-leaved trees because their leaves are broader than those of conifers, such as pine and spruce. In temperate regions angiosperm trees are mostly ⟁deciduous (that is, they lose their leaves in winter), but in the tropics most angiosperm trees are evergreen. There are fewer trees among the ⟁monocotyledons, but the palms and bamboos (some of which are treelike) belong to this group. The ⟁gymnosperms include many trees and they are classified into four orders: Cycadales (including cycads and sago palms), Coniferales (the conifers), Ginkgoales (including only one living species, the ginkgo, or maidenhair tree), and Taxales (including yews). Apart from the ginkgo and the larches (conifers), most gymnosperm trees are evergreen. There are also a few living trees in the ⟁pteridophyte group, known as tree ferns. In the swamp forests of the Carboniferous era, 300 million years ago, there were giant treelike horsetails and club mosses in addition to the tree ferns. The world's oldest trees are found in the Pacific forest of North America, some more than 2,000 years old.

trefoil any of several clover plants of the genus *Trifolium* of the pea family Leguminosae, the leaves of which are divided into three leaflets. The name is also used for other plants with leaves divided into three lobes.

Bird's-foot trefoil Lotus corniculatus, also of the pea family, is a low-growing perennial found in grassy places throughout Europe, N Asia, parts of Africa, and Australia. It has five leaflets to each leaf, but the first two are bent back so it appears to have only three. The yellow flowers, often tinged orange or red, are borne in heads with only a few blooms.

trematode parasitic flatworm with an oval non-segmented body, of the class Trematoda, including the ⟁fluke.

Trengganu or *Terengganu* state of E Peninsular Malaysia; capital Kuala Trengganu; area 5,018 sq mi/13,000 sq km; population

(1990) 752,000. Its exports include copra, black pepper, tin, and tungsten; there are also fishing and offshore oil industries.

Trent third-longest river of England; length 170 mi/275 km. Rising in the S Pennines, it flows first south and then northeast through the Midlands to the Humber. It is navigable by barge for nearly 100 mi/160 km.

Trent, Council of conference held 1545–63 by the Roman Catholic Church at Trento, N Italy, initiating the ⟁Counter-Reformation; see also ⟁Reformation.

Trentino–Alto Adige autonomous region of N Italy, comprising the provinces of Bolzano and Trento; *capital* Trento; *chief towns* Trento in the Italian-speaking southern area, and Bolzano-Bozen in the northern German-speaking area of South Tirol (the region was Austrian until ceded to Italy 1919); *area* 5,250 sq mi/13,600 sq km; *population* (1990) 891,400.

Trento capital of Trentino–Alto Adige region, Italy, on the Adige River; population (1988) 101,000. Industries include the manufacture of electrical goods and chemicals. The Council of ⟁Trent was held here 1545–63.

Trenton capital and industrial city (metalworking, ceramics) of New Jersey, on the Delaware River; population (1990) 88,700. It was first settled by Quakers 1679; George Washington defeated the British here 1776. It became the state capital 1790.

trespass going on to the land of another without authority. In law, a landowner has the right to eject a trespasser by the use of reasonable force and can sue for any damage caused.

A trespasser injured on another's land cannot usually recover damages from the landowner unless the latter did him or her some positive injury.

Trevelyan George Macaulay 1876–1962. British historian. Regius professor of history at Cambridge 1927–40, he pioneered the study of social history, as in his *English Social History* 1942.

Trèves French name for ⟁Trier, a city in Germany.

Trevino Lee Buck 1939– . US golfer who won his first major title, the 1968 US Open, as a virtual unknown, and won it again in 1971. He has also won the British Open and US PGA titles twice, and is one of only five players to have won the US Open and British Open in the same year. He played in six Ryder Cup matches and was non-playing captain in 1985.

During the early 1990s he enjoyed great success on the US Senior Tour.

CAREER HIGHLIGHTS

British Open
1971–72
US Open
1968, 1971
US PGA Championship
1974, 1984
Ryder Cup
team: 1969, 1971, 1973, 1975, 1979, 1981

Treviso city in Veneto, NE Italy; population (1981) 88,000. Its industries include the manufacture of machinery and ceramics. The 11th-century cathedral has an altarpiece by Titian.

Trevithick Richard 1771–1833. British engineer, constructor of a steam road locomotive 1801 and the first steam engine to run on rails 1804.

Triad secret society, founded in China as a Buddhist cult AD 36. It became known as the Triad because the triangle played a significant part in the initiation ceremony. Today it is reputed to be involved in organized crime (drugs, gambling, prostitution) among overseas Chinese. Its headquarters are alleged to be in Hong Kong.

In the 18th century the Triad became political, aiming at the overthrow of the Manchu dynasty, and backed the Taiping Rebellion 1851 and Sun Yat-sen's establishment of a republic 1912.

trial by ordeal in the Middle Ages, a test of guilt or innocence by which God's judgment of the case was supposedly revealed through the accused's exposure to fire, water, or blessed bread. The practice originated with the Franks in the 8th century, and survived until the 13th century. In the ordeal by cold water, the accused would be bound and thrown into the water. If he or she sank, it would prove innocence, but if he or she remained alive, it would show guilt.

If the accused ate blessed bread, the theory was that the guilty would not be able to swallow it.

triangle in geometry, a three-sided plane figure, the sum of whose interior angles is 180°. Triangles can be classified by the relative lengths of their sides. A *scalene triangle* has no sides of equal length; an *isosceles triangle* has at least two equal sides; an *equilateral triangle* has three equal sides (and three equal angles of 60°).

Triangles can also be classified by their angle properties: a right triangle has one right (90°) angle; an acute triangle has three acute (less than 90°) angles; an obtuse triangle has one obtuse (greater than 90°) angle; an equiangular triangle has three equal angles. (All equilateral triangles are equiangular, and vice versa.) If the length of one side of a triangle is l and the perpendicular distance from that side to the opposite corner is h (the height or altitude of the triangle), its area $A = \frac{1}{2}$ ($l \times h$). *See illustration on p. 1056.*

triangle of forces method of calculating the force produced by two other forces (the resultant). It is based on the fact that if three forces acting at a point can be represented by the sides of a triangle, the forces are in equilibrium. See ⟁parallelogram of forces.

triangulation technique used in surveying and navigation to determine distances, using the properties of the triangle. To begin, surveyors measure a certain length exactly to provide a base line. From each end of this line they then measure the angle to a distant point, using a ⟁theodolite. They now have a triangle in which they know the length of one side and the two adjacent angles. By simple trigonometry they can work out the lengths of the other two sides.

To make a complete survey of the region, they repeat the process, building on the first triangle.

Trianon two palaces in the park at ⟁Versailles, France: Le Grand Trianon built for Louis XIV, and Le Petit Trianon for Louis XV.

Triassic period of geological time 245–208 million years ago, the first period of the Mesozoic era. The continents were fused together to form the world continent ⟁Pangaea. Triassic sediments contain remains of early dinosaurs and other reptiles now extinct. By late Triassic times, the first mammals had evolved.

triathlon test of stamina involving three sports: swimming 2.4 mi/3.8 km, cycling 112 mi/180 km, and running a marathon 26 mi/42.195 km, each one immediately following the last.

It was first established as a sport in the US 1974. The most celebrated event is the Hawaii Ironman.

Tribal Areas, Federally Administered part of the mountainous frontier of NW Pakistan with Afghanistan, comprising the districts of Malakand, Mohmand, Khyber, Kurram, and Waziristan, administered directly from Islamabad; area 10,507 sq mi/27,219 sq km; population (1985) 2,467,000; chief towns are Wana, Razmak, Miram Shah.

tribal society way of life in which people govern their own affairs as independent local communities of families and clans without central government organizations or states. They are found in parts of SE Asia, New Guinea, South America, and Africa.

As the world economy expands, natural resources belonging to tribal peoples are coveted and exploited for farming or industrial use and the people are frequently dispossessed. Pressure groups such as Survival International and Cultural Survival have been established in some Western countries to support the struggle of tribal peoples for property rights as well as civil rights within the borders of the countries of which they are technically a part.

tribune Roman magistrate of ◊plebeian family, elected annually to defend the interests of the common people; only two were originally

chosen in 494 BC, but there were later ten. They could veto the decisions of any other magistrate.

triceratops any of a genus *Triceratops* of massive, horned dinosaurs of the order Ornithischia. They had three horns and a neck frill and were up to 25 ft/8 m long; they lived in the Cretaceous period.

trichloromethane technical name for ◊chloroform.

tricolor (French *tricouleur*) the French national flag of three vertical bands of red, white, and blue. The red and blue were the colors of Paris and the white represented the royal house of Bourbon. The flag was first adopted on July 17, 1789, three days after the storming of the Bastille during the French Revolution.

tricuspid valve flap of tissue situated on the right side of the ◊heart between the atrium and the ventricle. It prevents blood flowing backward when the ventricle contracts.

As in all valves, its movements are caused by pressure changes during the beat rather than by any intrinsic muscular activity. As the valve snaps shut, a vibration passes through the chest cavity and is detectable as the first sound of the heartbeat.

Trident nuclear missile deployed on certain US nuclear-powered submarines and in the 1990s also being installed on four UK submarines. Each missile has eight warheads (◊MIRVs) and each of the four submarines will have 16 Trident D-5 missiles. The Trident replaced the earlier Polaris and Poseidon missiles.

Trier (French *Trèves*) city in Rhineland-Palatinate, Germany; population (1984) 95,000. Once the capital of the Treveri, a Celto-Germanic tribe, it became known as *Augusta Treverorum* under the Roman emperor Augustus about 15 BC and was the capital of an ecclesiastical principality during the 14th–18th centuries. Karl Marx was born here.

Trieste port on the Adriatic, opposite Venice, in Friuli-Venezia-Giulia, Italy; population (1988) 237,000, including a large Slovene minority. It is the site of the International Center for Theoretical Physics, established 1964.

history Trieste was under Austrian rule from 1382 (apart from Napoleonic occupation 1809–14) until transferred to Italy 1918. It was claimed after World War II by Yugoslavia, and the city and surrounding territory were divided 1954 between Italy and Yugoslavia.

triggerfish any marine bony fish of the family Balistidae, with a laterally compressed body, up to 2 ft/60 cm long, and deep belly. They have small mouths but strong jaws and teeth. The first spine on the dorsal fin locks into an erect position, allowing them to fasten themselves securely in crevices for protection; it can only be moved by depressing the smaller third ("trigger") spine.

There are many species, found mainly in warm waters, and some are very colorful.

trigonometry branch of mathematics that solves problems relating to plane and spherical triangles. Its principles are based on the fixed proportions of sides for a particular angle in a right-angled triangle, the simplest of which are known as the ◊sine, ◊cosine, and ◊tangent (so-called trigonometrical ratios). It is of practical importance in navigation, surveying, and simple harmonic motion in physics.

Invented by ◊Hipparchus, trigonometry was developed by ◊Ptolemy of Alexandria and was known to early Hindu and Arab mathematicians.

triiodomethane technical name for ◊iodoform.

Trilling Lionel 1905–1975. US author and literary critic. His books of criticism include *The Liberal Imagination* 1950, *Beyond Culture* 1965, and *The Experience of Literature* 1967. He also produced annotated editions of the works of Matthew Arnold and John Keats.

Born in New York and educated at Columbia University, Trilling joined the Columbia English Department faculty 1932. He received his PhD 1938 and was appointed professor 1948. He published frequent reviews and essays and was a visiting professor at Oxford 1964–65 and Harvard 1969–70. His novel *The Middle of the Journey* 1947 is based on the character of Whittaker Chambers, who was to be a protagonist of the Alger ◊Hiss case.

trillium any of various perennial herbaceous woodland plants of the genus *Trillium* of the lily family. They have a whorl of three leaves around the erect stem. The single terminal flower has three green sepals and three usually maroon or white petals. The nodding trillium *Trillium cernuum* ranges across most of the eastern half of North America.

trilobite any of a large class (Trilobita) of extinct, marine, invertebrate arthropods of the Paleozoic era, with a flattened, oval body, 0.4–26 in/1–65 cm long. The hard-shelled body was divided by two deep furrows into three lobes.

Some were burrowers, others were swimming and floating forms. Their worldwide

Equilateral triangle: all the sides are the same length; all the angles are equal to 60°

Isosceles triangle: two sides and two angles are the same

Scalene triangle: all the sides and angles are different

Acute-angle triangle: each angle is acute (less than 90°)

Obtuse-angle triangle: one angle is obtuse (more than 90°)

A right-angle triangle has one angle of 90°, the *hypotenuse* is the side opposite the right angle

hypotenuse

Area of triangle = ½lh

Triangles are *congruent* if corresponding sides and corresponding angles are equal

Similar triangles have corresponding angles that are equal; they therefore have the same shape

triangle

distribution, many species, and the immense quantities of their remains make them useful in geologically dating.

Trimurti the Hindu triad of gods, representing the Absolute Spirit in its three aspects: Brahma, personifying creation; Vishnu, preservation; and Siva, destruction.

Trinidad town in Beni region, N Bolivia, near the river Mamoré, 250 mi/400 km NE of La Paz; population (1980) 36,000. It is built on an artificial earth mound, above flood level, the work of a little-known early American Indian people.

Trinidad and Tobago country in the West Indies, off the coast of Venezuela.
government Trinidad and Tobago is an independent republic within the British ♢Commonwealth. The 1976 constitution provides for a president as head of state and a two-chamber parliament, consisting of a senate of 31 members and a house of representatives of 36. The president appoints the prime minister and cabinet, who are collectively responsible to parliament. The president also appoints the senators, 16 on the advice of the prime minister, 6 on the advice of the leader of the opposition, and 9 after wider consultation. The 36 members of the House of Representatives are elected by universal adult suffrage. Parliament has a life of five years.

Tobago was given its own house of assembly 1980. It has 15 members, 12 popularly elected and 3 chosen by the majority party.
history For early history, see ♢American Indian. The islands of Trinidad and Tobago were visited by Columbus 1498. Trinidad was colonized by Spain from 1532 and ceded to Britain 1802, having been captured 1797. Tobago was settled by the Netherlands in the 1630s and subsequently occupied by various countries before being ceded to Britain by France 1814. Trinidad and Tobago were amalgamated 1888 as a British colony.
independence Trinidad and Tobago's first political party, the People's National Movement (PNM), was formed 1956 by Dr Eric Williams, and when the colony achieved internal self-government 1959 he became the first chief minister. Between 1958 and 1961 it was a member of the Federation of the West Indies but withdrew and achieved full independence, within the Commonwealth, 1962, Williams becoming the first prime minister.
republic A new constitution was adopted 1976 that made Trinidad and Tobago a republic. The former governor-general, Ellis Clarke, became the first president and Williams continued as prime minister. Williams died March 1981 without having nominated a successor, and the president appointed George Chambers; the PNM formally adopted him as leader May 1981. The opposition, a moderate left-wing party grouping led by Arthur Robinson, was during the next few years reorganized as the National Alliance for Reconstruction (NAR), until in the 1986 general election it swept the PNM from power and Arthur Robinson became prime minister.

An attempted coup July 1990 resulted in the capture of Prime Minister Robinson by a former policeman, Abu Bakr. In Aug 1990 the rebels surrendered and an injured Robinson was released. Robinson was defeated in the Dec 1991 general election and was succeeded as prime minister by Patrick Manning, leader of the PNM. NAR won only two of the 36 assembly seats, compared with PNM's 21. *See illustration box.*

Trinitarianism belief in the Christian Trinity.

Trinity in Christianity, the union of three persons—Father, Son, and Holy Ghost/Spirit—in one godhead. The precise meaning of the doctrine has been the cause of unending dispute, and was the chief cause of the split between the Eastern Orthodox and Roman Catholic churches. *Trinity Sunday* occurs on the Sunday after Pentecost.

triode three-electrode thermionic tube containing an anode and a cathode (as does a ♢diode) with an additional negatively based control grid. Small variations in voltage on the grid bias result in large variations in the current. The triode was commonly used in amplifiers until largely superseded by the ♢transistor. The tube was invented by the US radio engineer Lee De Forest.

Triple Alliance pact from 1882 among Germany, Austria-Hungary, and Italy to offset the power of Russia and France. It was last renewed 1912, but during World War I Italy's initial neutrality gradually changed and it denounced the alliance 1915. The term also refers to other alliances: 1668—England, Holland, and Sweden; 1717—Britain, Holland, and France (joined 1718 by Austria); 1788—Britain, Prussia, and Holland; 1795—Britain, Russia, and Austria.

Triple Entente alliance of Britain, France, and Russia 1907–17. In 1911 this became a military alliance and formed the basis of the Allied powers in World War I against the Central Powers, Germany and Austria-Hungary.

The failure of the alliance system to create a stable balance of power, coupled with widespread horror of the carnage created by World War I, led to attempts to create international cooperation with the League of Nations.

triple jump field event in track and field comprising a hop, step, and jump sequence from a takeoff board into a sandpit landing area measuring 26.25 ft/8 m (minimum) in length. The takeoff board is usually 42.65 ft/13 m from the landing area. Each competitor has six attempts and the winner is the one with the longest jump.

triploblastic in biology, having a body wall composed of three layers. The outer layer is the *ectoderm*, the middle layer the *mesoderm*, and the inner layer the *endoderm*. This pattern of development is shown by most multicellular animals (including humans).

Tripoli (Arabic *Tarabolus esh-sham*) port in N Lebanon, 40 mi/65 km NE of Beirut; population (1980) 175,000. It stands on the site of the Phoenician city of Oea.

Tripoli (Arabic *Tarabolus al-Gharb*) capital and chief port of Libya, on the Mediterranean; population (1982) 980,000. Products include olive oil, fruit, fish, and textiles.
history Tripoli was founded about the 7th century BC by Phoenicians from Oea (now Tripoli in Lebanon). It was a base for Axis powers during World War II. In 1986 it was bombed by the US Air Force in retaliation for international guerrilla activity.

Tripolitania former province of Libya, stretching from Cyrenaica in the east to Tunisia in

Trinidad and Tobago
Republic of

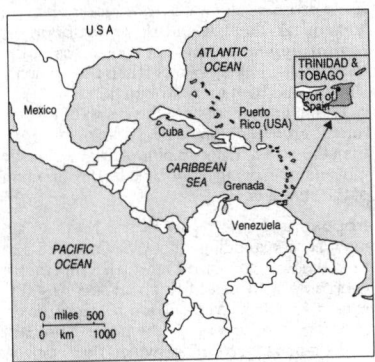

area Trinidad 1,864 sq mi/4,828 sq km and Tobago 116 sq mi/300 sq km
capital Port-of-Spain
cities San Fernando, Arima, Scarborough (Tobago)
physical comprises two main islands and some smaller ones; coastal swamps and hills E–W
features Pitch Lake, a self-renewing source of asphalt used by 16th-century explorer Walter Raleigh to repair his ships
head of state Noor Hassanali from 1987
head of government Patrick Manning from 1991
political system democratic republic
political parties National Alliance for Reconstruction (NAR), nationalist, left-of-center; People's National Movement (PNM), nationalist, moderate, centrist
exports oil, petroleum products, chemicals, sugar, cocoa
currency Trinidad and Tobago dollar
population (1990 est) 1,270,000 (40% African descent, 40% Indian, 16% European, 2% Chinese and others), 1.2 million on Trinidad; growth rate 1.6% p.a.
life expectancy men 68, women 72 (1989)
languages English (official), Hindi, French, Spanish
media freedom of press guaranteed by constitution and upheld by government; there are two independent morning newspapers and several weekly tabloids
religion Roman Catholic 32%, Protestant 29%, Hindu 25%, Muslim 6%
literacy 97% (1988)
GNP $4.5 bn; $3,731 per head (1987)
chronology
1888 Trinidad and Tobago united as a British colony.
1956 People's National Movement (PNM) founded.
1959 Achieved internal self-government, with PNM leader Eric Williams as chief minister.
1962 Independence achieved from Britain, within the Commonwealth, with Williams as prime minister.
1976 Became a republic, with Ellis Clarke as president and Williams as prime minister.
1981 Williams died and was succeeded by George Chambers, with Arthur Robinson as opposition leader.
1986 National Alliance for Reconstruction (NAR), headed by Arthur Robinson, won general election.
1987 Noor Hassanali became president.
1990 Attempted antigovernment coup defeated.
1991 General election saw victory for PNM, with Patrick Manning as prime minister.

the west. Italy captured it from Turkey 1912, and the British captured it from Italy 1942 and controlled it until it was incorporated into the newly independent United Kingdom of Libya, established 1951. In 1963 Tripolitania was subdivided into administrative divisions.

Tripura state of NE India since 1972, formerly a princely state, between Bangladesh and Assam;
area 4,053 sq mi/10,500 sq km
capital Agartala
features agriculture on a rotation system in the rainforest, now being superseded by modern methods
products rice, cotton, tea, sugar cane, steel, jute
population (1991) 2,744,800
language Bengali
religion Hindu.

trireme ancient Greek warship with three banks of oars as well as sails, 115 ft/38 m long. They were used at the battle of Salamis and by the Romans until the 4th century AD.

Tristan hero of Celtic legend who fell in love with Iseult, the bride he was sent to win for his uncle King Mark of Cornwall; the story became part of the Arthurian cycle and is the subject of Wagner's opera *Tristan und Isolde*.

Tristan da Cunha group of islands in the S Atlantic, part of the British dependency of ⇨St Helena;
area 42 sq mi/110 sq km
features comprises four islands: Tristan, Gough, Inaccessible, and Nightingale. Tristan consists of a single volcano 6,761 ft/2,060 m; it is an important meteorological and radio station
government administrator and island council
products crawfish
currency pound sterling
population (1990) 299
language English
history the first European to visit the then uninhabited islands was the Portuguese admiral after whom they are named, in 1506; they were annexed by Britain 1816. Believed to be extinct, the Tristan volcano erupted 1961 and the population was evacuated, but in 1963 they chose to return.

Tristram Shandy novel by Laurence Sterne, published 1759–67. The work, a forerunner of the 20th-century stream-of-consciousness novel, has no coherent plot and uses typographical devices to emphasize the author's disdain for the structured novels of his contemporaries.

triticale cereal crop of recent origin that is a cross between wheat *Triticum* and rye *Secale*. It can produce heavy yields of high-protein grain, principally for use as animal feed.

tritium radioactive isotope of hydrogen, three times as heavy as ordinary hydrogen, consisting of one proton and two neutrons. It has a half-life of 12.5 years.

Triton in Greek mythology, a merman sea god, the son of ⇨Poseidon and the sea goddess Amphitrite. He is traditionally shown blowing on a conch shell.

Triton in astronomy, the largest of Neptune's moons and one of the four largest in the Solar System. It has a diameter of 1,680 mi/2,700 km, and orbits Neptune every 5.88 days in a retrograde (east to west) direction.
It is slightly larger than the planet Pluto, which it is thought to resemble in composition and appearance. Probably Triton was formerly

a separate body like Pluto but was captured by Neptune. Triton was discovered in 1846 by British astronomer William Lassell (1799–1880) only weeks after the discovery of Neptune.
Triton's surface, as revealed by the *Voyager 2* space probe, has a temperature of 38K (–391°F/–235°C), making it the coldest known place in the Solar System. It is covered with frozen nitrogen and methane, some of which evaporates to form a tenuous atmosphere with a pressure only 0.00001 that of the Earth at sea level. Triton has a pink south polar cap, probably colored by the effects of solar radiation on methane ice. Dark streaks on Triton are thought to be formed by geysers of liquid nitrogen.

triumvir one of a group of three administrators sharing power in ancient Rome, as in the *First Triumvirate* 60 BC: Caesar, Pompey, Crassus; and *Second Triumvirate* 43 BC: Augustus, Antony, and Lepidus.

Trivandrum capital of Kerala, SW India; population (1981) 483,000. It has chemical, textile, and rubber industries. Formerly the capital of the princely state of Travancore, it has many palaces, an old fort, and a shrine.

trivium in medieval European education, the three lower liberal arts (grammar, rhetoric, and logic) studied before the ⇨quadrivium.

trogon any species of the order Trogoniformes of tropical birds, up to 1.7 ft/50 cm long, with resplendent plumage, living in the Americas and Afro-Asia. Most striking is the ⇨quetzal.

Trois-Rivières port on the St Lawrence River, Québec; population (1986) 129,000. The chief industry is the production of newsprint. It was founded by ⇨Champlain 1634.

Trojan horse seemingly innocuous but treacherous gift from an enemy. In Greek legend, during the siege of Troy, the Greek army left an enormous wooden horse outside the gate of the city and retreated. When the Trojans had brought it in, Greek soldiers emerged from within the hollow horse and opened the city gates to enable it to be captured.

Trollope Anthony 1815–1882. English novelist who delineated provincial English middle-class society in a series of novels set in or around the imaginary cathedral city of Barchester. *The Warden* 1855 began the series, which includes *Barchester Towers* 1857, *Doctor Thorne* 1858, and *The Last Chronicle of Barset* 1867. His political novels include *Can You Forgive Her?* 1864, *Phineas Finn* 1867–69, and *The Prime Minister* 1875–76.

trombone ⇨brass wind musical instrument developed from the sackbut. It consists of a tube bent double, varied notes being obtained by an inner sliding tube. Usual sizes of trombone are alto, tenor, bass, and contra-bass.

trompe l'oeil (French "deceives the eye") painting that gives a convincing illusion of three-dimensional reality. It has been common in most periods in the West, from Classical Greece through the Renaissance and later.

Trondheim fishing port in Norway; population (1988) 136,000. It has canning, textile, margarine, and soap industries. It was the medieval capital of Norway, and Norwegian kings are crowned in the cathedral.

trophic level in ecology, the position occupied by a species (or group of species) in a ⇨food chain. The main levels are *primary producers* (photosynthetic plants), *primary consumers* (herbivores), *secondary consumers* (carnivores), and *decomposers* (bacteria and fungi).

tropical disease any illness found mainly in hot climates. The most important tropical diseases worldwide are ⇨malaria, ⇨schistosomiasis, ⇨leprosy, and ⇨river blindness. Malaria kills about 1.5 million people each year, and produces chronic anemia and tiredness in 100 times as many, while schistosomiasis is responsible for 1 million deaths a year. All the main tropical diseases are potentially curable, but the facilities for diagnosis and treatment are rarely adequate in the countries where they occur.

tropics the area between the tropics of Cancer and Capricorn, defined by the parallels of latitude approximately 23°30′ N and S of the equator. They are the limits of the area of Earth's surface in which the Sun can be directly overhead. The mean monthly temperature is over 68°F/20°C.

tropine $C_8H_{15}NO$ poisonous crystalline solid formed by the hydrolysis of the ⇨alkaloid atropine.

tropism or *tropic movement* the directional growth of a plant, or part of a plant, in response to an external stimulus such as gravity or light. If the movement is directed toward the stimulus it is described as positive; if away from it, it is negative. *Geotropism* for example, the response of plants to gravity, causes the root (positively geotropic) to grow downward, and the stem (negatively geotropic) to grow upward.
Phototropism occurs in response to light, *hydrotropism* to water, *chemotropism* to a chemical stimulus, and *thigmotropism*, or *haptotropism*, to physical contact, as in the tendrils of climbing plants when they touch a support and then grow around it.
Tropic movements are the result of greater rate of growth on one side of the plant organ than the other. Tropism differs from a ⇨nastic movement in being influenced by the direction of the stimulus.

troposphere lower part of the Earth's ⇨atmosphere extending about 6.5 mi/10.5 km from the Earth's surface, in which temperature decreases with height to about –76°F/–60°C except in local layers of temperature inversion. The *tropopause* is the upper boundary of the troposphere, above which the temperature increases slowly with height within the atmosphere.

Trotsky Leon. Adopted name of Lev Davidovitch Bronstein 1879–1940. Russian revolutionary. He joined the Bolshevik party and took a leading part in the seizure of power 1917 and raising the Red Army that fought the Civil War 1918–20. In the struggle for power that followed ⇨Lenin's death 1924, ⇨Stalin defeated Trotsky, and this and other differences with the Communist Party led to his exile 1929. He settled in Mexico, where he was assassinated with an ice pick at Stalin's instigation. Trotsky believed in world revolution and in permanent revolution, and was an uncompromising, if liberal, idealist.
Trotsky became a Marxist in the 1890s and was imprisoned and exiled for opposition to the tsarist regime. He lived in W Europe from 1902 until the 1905 revolution, when he was again imprisoned but escaped to live in exile

until 1917. Although as a young man Trotsky admired Lenin, when he worked with him organizing the revolution of 1917, he objected to Lenin's dictatorial ways. He was second in command until Lenin's death. Trotsky's later works are critical of the Soviet regime; for example, *The Revolution Betrayed* 1937. His greatest work is his magisterial *History of the Russian Revolution* 1932–33. Official Soviet recognition of responsibility for his assassination through the secret service came in 1989.

Trotskyism form of Marxism advocated by Leon Trotsky. Its central concept is that of *permanent revolution*. In his view a proletarian revolution, leading to a socialist society, could not be achieved in isolation, so it would be necessary to spark off further revolutions throughout Europe and ultimately worldwide. This was in direct opposition to the Stalinist view that socialism should be built and consolidated within individual countries.

Trotskyism developed in an attempt to reconcile Marxist theory with actual conditions in Russia in the early 20th century, but it was never officially accepted within the USSR. Instead found much support worldwide, primarily in Third World countries, and the Fourth ▷International, which Trotsky founded 1937, has sections in over 60 countries.

troubadour one of a group of poet musicians in Provence and S France in the 12th–13th centuries, which included both nobles and wandering minstrels. The troubadours originated a type of lyric poetry devoted to themes of courtly love and the idealization of women and to glorifying the deeds of their patrons, reflecting the chivalric ideals of the period. Little is known of their music, which was passed down orally.

Among the troubadours were Bertran de Born (1140–*c*. 1215), who was mentioned by Dante; Arnaut Daniel; and Bernard de Ventadour. The troubadour tradition spread to other parts of Europe, including northern France (the *trouvères*) and Germany (the Minnesingers).

Troy (Latin *Ilium*) ancient city of Asia Minor, besieged in the ten-year Trojan War (mid-13th century BC), which the poet Homer described in the *Iliad*. The city fell to the Greeks, who first used the stratagem of leaving behind, in a feigned retreat, a large wooden horse containing armed infiltrators to open the gates. Believing it to be a religious offering, the Trojans took it within the walls.

Nine cities found one beneath another at the site Hissarlik, near the Dardanelles, were originally excavated by Heinrich ▷Schliemann from 1874–90. Recent research suggests that the seventh, sacked and burned about 1250 BC, is probably the Homeric Troy, which was succeeded by a shanty town sacked by the ▷Sea Peoples about 780 BC. It has been suggested that Homer's tale of war might have a basis in fact, for example, a conflict arising from trade rivalry (Troy was on a tin trade route), which might have been triggered by such an incident as Paris running off with ▷Helen. The wooden horse may have been a votive offering left behind by the Greeks after ▷Poseidon (whose emblem was a horse) had opened breaches in the city walls for them by an earthquake.

Troy city in E New York, E of Albany on the east bank of the Hudson River; seat of Rensselear County, incorporated 1816; population (1990) 54,300. Industries include apparel, abrasives, metals, paper, car and railroad parts, and processed foods.

A Mohegan Indian fortress, it was explored by Henry Hudson 1609, granted by the Dutch East India Company as a patroonship to Kiliaen Van Rensselaer, and founded as a town 1786. Rensselaer Polytechnic Institute 1824 and Russell Sage College 1916 are here.

Troyes industrial (textiles and food processing) town in Champagne-Ardenne, NE France; population (1982) 65,000. It was the capital of the medieval province of Champagne. The *Treaty of Troyes* 1420 made Henry V of England heir to the French crown.

troy system system of units used for precious metals and gems. The pound troy (0.37 kg) consists of 12 ounces (each of 120 carats) or 5,760 grains (each equal to 65 mg).

Trucial States former name (until 1971) of the ▷United Arab Emirates. It derives from the agreements made with Britain 1820 to ensure a truce in the area and to suppress piracy and slavery.

Trudeau Pierre (Elliott) 1919– . Canadian Liberal politician. He was prime minister 1968–79 and 1980–84. In 1980, having won again by a landslide on a platform opposing Québec separatism, he helped to defeat the Québec independence movement in a referendum. He repatriated the constitution from Britain 1982, but by 1984 had so lost support that he resigned.

Truffaut François 1932–1984. French New Wave film director and actor, formerly a critic. A popular, romantic, and intensely humane filmmaker, he wrote and directed a series of semiautobiographical films starring Jean-Pierre Léaud, beginning with *Les Quatre Cent Coups/The 400 Blows* 1959. His other films include *Jules et Jim* 1961, *Fahrenheit 451* 1966, *L'Enfant sauvage/The Wild Child* 1970, and *La Nuit américaine/Day for Night* 1973 (Academy Award).

His interest in cinema led to a job as film critic for *Cahiers du Cinema* during the 1950s before embarking on his career as director. His later work includes *The Story of Adèle H* 1975 and *The Last Metro* 1980. He was influenced by Alfred Hitchcock, and also drew on Surrealist and comic traditions. He played one of the leading roles in Steven Spielberg's *Close Encounters of the Third Kind* 1977.

truffle subterranean fungus of the order Tuberales. Certain species are valued as edible delicacies; in particular, *Tuber melanosporum*, generally found growing under oak trees. It is native to the Périgord region of France but cultivated in other areas as well. It is rounded, blackish brown, covered with warts externally, and with blackish flesh.

Dogs and pigs are traditionally used to discover truffles, but in 1990 an artificial "nose" developed at the University of Manchester Institute of Science and Technology, England, proved more effective in tests in Bordeaux.

Trujillo Molina Rafael (Leónidas) 1891–1961. Dictator of the Dominican Republic from 1930. As commander of the Dominican Guard, he seized power and established a ruthless dictatorship. He was assassinated.

Truk group of about 55 volcanic islands surrounded by a coral reef in the E Caroline islands of the W Pacific, forming one of the four states of the Federated States of Micronesia. Fish and copra are the main products.

The lagoon area (one of the largest in the world) has an area of 822 sq mi/2,130 sq km.

The main island is Moen. More than 60 ships of the Japanese fleet, destroyed during World War II, lie at the bottom of the lagoon.

Truman Harry S 1884–1972. 33rd president of the US 1945–53, a Democrat. In Jan 1945 he became vice-president to F D Roosevelt, and president when Roosevelt died in April that year. He played an important role at the ▷Potsdam Conference, used ▷atomic bombs against Japan to end World War II, launched the ▷Marshall Plan to restore Western Europe's postwar economy, and nurtured the European Community and NATO (including the rearmament of West Germany). He believed in the ▷United Nations (UN) and when South Korea was invaded by North Korea 1950, had US forces join the UN forces, with General ▷MacArthur at their head. He fired MacArthur 1951 when the general's war policy conflicted with UN aims.

Born in Lamar, Missouri, he was an officer in World War I, was a partner in a clothing store that was bankrupted by the ▷Depression, and ran for various local political offices. He became a senator 1934, was selected as Roosevelt's fourth-term vice-president 1944, succeeded to the presidency 1945, and in 1948 was elected for a second term in an upset victory over Republican Thomas Dewey (1902–71). At home, Truman had difficulty with Congress and with labor groups in converting the economy back to peacetime conditions; he also failed to prevent the Congressional witch hunts on suspected Communists (see ▷Hiss, ▷McCarthy). He enunciated the Truman Doctrine, which called for aid to nations threatened by Communist expansion. His policy of ▷containment of Soviet expansionsim initiated the long ▷cold war with the Soviet Union. Truman retired to Independence, Missouri.

Truman Doctrine US president Harry Truman's 1947 dictum that the US would "support free peoples who are resisting attempted subjugation by armed minorities or by outside pressures." It was used to justify sending a counterinsurgency military mission to Greece after World War II and sending US troops abroad (for example, to Korea).

Trumbull John 1756–1843. American artist. Born in Lebanon, Connecticut, the son of Governor Jonathan Trumbull, he was educated at Harvard and saw action during the Revolutionary War. In 1780 he traveled to England to study art with Benjamin ▷West and was briefly imprisoned for espionage. In 1789 Trumbull returned to the US to work on a series of historical paintings of Revolutionary War scenes; the most famous was his depiction of the signing of the Declaration of Independence. From 1793 to 1804 he undertook diplomatic assignments in England. He later served as president of the American Academy of Fine Arts 1817–36.

trumpet small high-register ▷brass wind instrument; a doubled tube with valves. Before the 19th century, the trumpet had no valves and was restricted to harmonies.

trumpeter any South American bird of the genus *Psophia*, family Psophiidae, up to 20 in/50 cm tall, related to the cranes. Trumpeters have long legs, a short bill, and dark plumage. The name is also applied to the trumpeter ▷swan.

Truong Sa one of the ▷Spratly Islands in the South China Sea.

trust arrangement whereby a person or group of people (the trustee or trustees) hold property for others (the beneficiaries) entitled to the beneficial interest. A trust can be a legal arrangement under which A is empowered to administer property belonging to B for the benefit of C. A and B may be the same person; B and C may not.

A *unit trust* holds and manages a number of marketable securities; by buying a "unit" in such a trust, the purchaser has a proportionate interest in each of the securities so that his or her risk is spread. Nowadays, an investment trust is not a trust, but a public company investing in marketable securities money subscribed by its stockholders who receive dividends from the income earned. A charitable trust, such as the Ford Foundation, administers funds for charitable purposes.

A business trust is formed by linking several companies by transferring shares in them to trustees; or by the creation of a holding company, whose shares are exchanged for those of the separate companies. Competition is thus eliminated, and in the US both types were outlawed by the Sherman Antitrust Act 1890 (first fully enforced by "trust buster" Theodore ◊Roosevelt, as in the breakup of the Standard Oil Company of New Jersey by the Supreme Court 1911).

Trust Territory country or area formerly held under the United Nations trusteeship system to be prepared for independence, either former ◊mandates, territories taken over by the Allies in World War II, or those voluntarily placed under the UN by the administering state.

Truth Sojourner. Adopted name of Isabella Baumfree, later Isabella Van Wagener 1797–1883. US antislavery and women's-suffrage campaigner. Born a slave, she ran away and became involved with religious groups. In 1843 she was "commanded in a vision" to adopt the name Sojourner Truth. She published an autobiography, *The Narrative of Sojourner Truth*, in 1850.

trypanosome any parasitic flagellate protozoan of the genus *Trypanosoma* that lives in the blood of vertebrates, including humans. They often cause serious diseases, called trypanosomiases, such as sleeping sickness or Chagas' disease, and are transmitted by the bite of such insects as tsetse flies or assassin bugs.

trypanosomiasis any of several debilitating long-term diseases caused by a trypanosome (protozoan of the genus *Trypanosoma*). They include sleeping sickness (nagana) in Africa, transmitted by the bites of ◊tsetse flies, and ◊Chagas' disease in the Americas, spread by assassin bugs.

Trypanosomes can live in the bloodstream of humans and other vertebrates. Millions of people are affected in warmer regions of the world; the diseases also affect cattle, horses, and wild animals, which form a reservoir of infection.

tsar the Russian imperial title 1547–1721 (although it continued in popular use to 1917), derived from Latin *caesar*.

tsetse fly any of a number of blood-feeding African flies of the genus *Glossina*, some of which transmit the disease nagana to cattle and sleeping sickness to human beings. Tsetse flies may grow up to 0.6 in/1.5 cm long.

Tsingtao alternative transliteration of ◊Qingdao, port in E China.

Tsiolkovsky Konstantin 1857–1935. Russian scientist. Despite being handicapped by deafness from the age of ten, he developed the theory of space flight, publishing the first practical paper on astronautics 1903, dealing with space travel by rockets using liquid propellants, such as liquid oxygen.

tsunami (Japanese "harbor wave") giant wave generated by an undersea ◊earthquake or other disturbance. In the open ocean it may take the form of several successive waves, traveling at tens of miles/tens of kilometers per hour but with an amplitude (height) of approximately 3 ft/1 m. In the coastal shallows, tsunamis slow down and build up, producing towering waves that can sweep inland and cause great loss of life and property.

Before each wave there may be a sudden, unexpected withdrawal of water from the beach. Used synonymously with tsunami, the popular term "tidal wave" is misleading.

Tsushima Japanese island between Korea and Japan in *Tsushima Strait*; area 271 sq mi/702 sq km. The Russian fleet was destroyed by the Japanese here May 27, 1905 in the ◊Russo-Japanese War, and 12,000 Russians were killed. The chief settlement is Izuhara.

Tswana member of the majority ethnic group living in Botswana. The Tswana are divided into four subgroups: the Bakwena, the Bamangwato, the Bangwaketse, and the Batawana. Traditionally they are rural-dwelling farmers, though many now leave their homes to work as migrant laborers in South African industries. The Tswana language belongs to the Bantu branch of the Niger-Congo family.

Tuamotu Archipelago two parallel ranges of 78 atolls, part of ◊French Polynesia; area 266 sq mi/690 sq km; population (1983) 11,800, including the ◊Gambier Islands to the E. The atolls stretch 1,300 mi/2,100 km N and E of the Society Islands. The administrative headquarters is Apataki. The largest atoll is Rangiroa, the most significant is Hao; they produce pearl shell and copra. Mururoa and Fangataufa atolls to the SE have been a French nuclear test site since 1966. Spanish explorers landed 1606, and the islands were annexed by France 1881.

Tuareg a member of a nomadic Berber people of the west and central Sahara.

tuatara lizardlike reptile *Sphenodon punctatus*, found only on a few islands off New Zealand. It grows up to 2.3 ft/70 cm long, is greenish black, and has a spiny crest down its back. On the top of its head is the ◊pineal body, or so-called "third eye," linked to the brain, which probably acts as a kind of light meter.

It is the sole survivor of the reptilian order Rhynchocephalia. It lays eggs in burrows that it shares with seabirds, and has the longest incubation period of all reptiles (up to 15 months).

tuba large bass ◊brass wind musical instrument of the cornet family. The *Wagner tuba* combines features of the euphonium and french horn.

tube or *electron tube* in electronics, a glass tube containing gas at low pressure, which is used to control the flow of electricity in a circuit. Three or more metal electrodes are inset into the tube. By varying the voltage on one of them, called the grid electrode, the current through the tube can be controlled, and the tube can act as an amplifier. Tubes have been replaced for most applications by ◊transistors. However, they are still used in high-power transmitters and amplifiers, and in some hi-fi systems.

tuber swollen region of an underground stem or root, usually modified for storing food. The potato is a *stem tuber*, as shown by the presence of terminal and lateral buds, the "eyes" of the potato. *Root tubers*, for example dahlias, developed from adventitious roots (growing from the stem, not from other roots) lack these. Both types of tuber can give rise to new individuals and so provide a means of ◊vegetative reproduction.

Unlike a bulb, a tuber persists for one season only; new tubers developing on a plant in the following year are formed in different places. See also ◊rhizome.

tuberculosis (TB) formerly known as *consumption* or *phthisis* infectious disease caused by the bacillus *Mycobacterium tuberculosis*. It takes several forms, of which pulmonary tuberculosis is by far the most common. A vaccine, ◊BCG, was developed around 1920 and the first antituberculosis drug, streptomycin, in 1944.

In pulmonary TB, a patch of inflammation develops in the lung, with formation of an abscess. Often, this heals spontaneously, leaving only scar tissue. The dangers are of rapid spread through both lungs (what used to be called "galloping consumption") or the development of miliary tuberculosis (spreading in the bloodstream to other sites) or tuberculous ◊meningitis. In addition to streptomycin there are two other drugs used to treat TB: rifampicin and isoniazid.

In practice, most people who are infected do not become ill, and, with public-health measures such as screening people for disease (patch tests) and pasteurization of milk, active tuberculosis is rare in the affluent parts of the world, although in the US from 1990 there was a sharp rise in the number of AIDS-related TB cases, with a high proportion of drug-resistant strains of the disease. It is more common in Asians and in those who are ◊immunocompromised. It still threatens, however, where there is malnutrition and overcrowding.

tuberose Mexican flowering plant *Polianthes tuberosa* of the ◊agave family, grown as a sweet-smelling greenhouse plant.

Tubman Harriet Ross 1821–1913. US abolitionist. Born a slave in Maryland, she escaped to Philadelphia (where slavery was outlawed) 1849. She set up the *Underground Railroad*, a secret network of sympathizers, to help slaves escape to the North and Canada. During the American ◊Civil War she spied for the Union army. She spoke against slavery and for women's rights, and founded schools for emancipated slaves after the Civil War.

Tubman William V S 1895–1971. Liberian politician. The descendant of US slaves, he was a lawyer in the US. After his election to the presidency of Liberia 1944 he concentrated on uniting the various ethnic groups. Reelected several times, he died in office of natural causes, despite frequent assassination attempts.

Tubuai Islands or *Austral Islands* chain of volcanic islands and reefs 800 mi/1,300 km long in ◊French Polynesia, S of the Society Islands; area 57 sq mi/148 sq km; population (1983) 6,300. The main settlement is Mataura on Tubuai. They were visited by Captain Cook 1777 and annexed by France 1880.

Tucana constellation of the southern hemisphere, represented as a toucan. It contains the second most prominent ◊globular cluster in the sky, 47 Tucanae, and the Small ◊Magellanic Cloud.

Tucana is one of the 11 constellations named by Johann Bayer (1572–1625) early in the 17th century to complement the 65 constellations delineated in ancient times.

Tucson resort city in the Sonora Desert in SE Arizona; population (1990) 405,400. It stands 2,500 ft/760 m above sea level, and the Santa Catalina Mountains to the NE rise to about 9,000 ft/2,750 m. Industries include aircraft, electronics, and copper smelting. Tucson passed from Mexico to the US 1853 and was the territorial capital 1867–77.

The University of Arizona is here, and Kitt Peak National Observatory is in the area. An Indian village was on the site when a Jesuit mission was founded about 1700. A Spanish fort, and eventually a settlement, grew around the mission. Growth has been rapid since World War II.

Tucumán or *San Miguel de Tucumán* capital of Tucumán province, NW Argentina, on the Rio Sali, in the foothills of the Andes; population (1991) 473,000. Industries include sugar mills and distilleries. Founded 1565, Tucumán was the site of the signing of the Argentine declaration of independence from Spain 1816.

tucu-tuco any member of the genus *Ctenomys*, a burrowing South American rodent about 8 in/20 cm long with a 3 in/7 cm tail. It has a large head, sensitive ears, and enormous incisor teeth.

Tucu-tucos spend most of their time below ground in a burrow system, generally one animal to a burrow. The name tucu-tuco is an attempt to imitate the bubbling call.

Tudjman Franjo 1922–   . Croatian nationalist leader and historian, president from 1990. As leader of the center-right Croatian Democratic Union (HDZ), he led the fight for Croatian independence. During the 1991–92 civil war his troops were hampered by lack of arms and the military superiority of the Serb-dominated federal army, but Croatia's independence was recognized following a successful UN-negotiated cease-fire Jan 1992. Tudjman was reelected Aug 1992.

Tudor dynasty English dynasty 1485–1603, descended from the Welsh Owen Tudor (*c.* 1400–1461), second husband of Catherine of Valois (widow of Henry V of England). Their son Edmund married Margaret Beaufort (1443–1509), the great-granddaughter of ◊John of Gaunt, and was the father of Henry VII, who became king by overthrowing Richard III 1485. The dynasty ended with the death of Elizabeth I 1603.

The Tudors were portrayed in a favorable light in Shakespeare's history plays.

tufa or *travertine* soft, porous, ◊limestone rock, white in color, deposited from solution from carbonate-saturated ground water around hot springs and in caves.

Tu Fu or *Du Fu* 712–770. Chinese poet of the Tang dynasty, with Li Po one of the two greatest Chinese poets. He wrote about the social injustices of his time, peasant suffering, and war, as in *The Army Carts* on conscription, and *The Beauties*, comparing the emperor's wealth with the lot of the poor.

Tukano member of an indigenous South American Indian people of the Vaupés region on the Colombian-Brazilian border, numbering approximately 2,000. An estimated 12,000

speak languages related to Tukano. The other main Tukanoan groups are Bara, Barasana, Cubeo, Desana, and Makuna.

Tula ancient Toltec city in Mexico, 40 mi/65 km NW of Mexico City, which flourished *c.* 750–1168. It had a population of about 40,000. The modern town of Tula de Allende is nearby.

Tulare town in S central California, S of Fresno, in the San Joaquin Valley; population (1990) 33,200. Industries include food processing, wine, and dairy products. Tulare was built 1871 as a division headquarters for the Southern Pacific Railroad.

tulip plant of the genus *Tulipa*, family Liliaceae, usually with single goblet-shaped flowers on the end of an upright stem and leaves of a narrow oval shape with pointed ends. It is widely cultivated as a garden flower.

Tulipa gesnerana, from which most of the garden cultivars have been derived, probably originated in Asia Minor. Quickly adopted in Europe during the 16th century, it became a craze in 17th-century Holland. Today it is commercially cultivated on a large scale in the Netherlands and East Anglia, England.

The *tulip tree* *Liriodendron tulipifera* of the eastern US is a member of the magnolia family, with large, tulip-shaped blooms.

Tull Jethro 1674–1741. English agriculturist who about 1701 developed a drill that enabled seeds to be sown mechanically and spaced so that cultivation between rows was possible in the growth period. His chief work, *Horse-Hoeing Husbandry*, was published 1731.

Tulsa city in NE Oklahoma, on the Arkansas River, NE of Oklahoma City; population (1990) 367,300. It is an oil-producing and aerospace center; other industries include mining, machinery, metals, and cement.

tumor overproduction of cells in a specific area of the body, often leading to a swelling or lump. Tumors are classified as benign or malignant (see ◊cancer).

Benign tumors grow more slowly, do not invade surrounding tissues, do not spread to other parts of the body, and do not usually recur after removal. However, some benign tumors can be dangerous, such as in areas like the brain. The most familiar types of benign tumor are warts on the skin. In some cases, there is no sharp dividing line between benign and malignant tumors.

tuna any of various large marine bony fishes of the mackerel family, especially the genus *Thunnus*, popular as food and game. Albacore *T. alalunga*, bluefin tuna *T. thynnus*, and yellowfin tuna *T. albacores* are commercially important.

Tuna fish gather in shoals and migrate inshore to breed, where they are caught in large numbers. The increasing use by Pacific tuna fishers of enormous driftnets, which kill dolphins, turtles, and other marine creatures as well as catching the fish, has caused protests by environmentalists; tins labeled "dolphin-friendly" contain tuna not caught by driftnets. Thailand is a major tuna-importing and canning country.

Tunbs, the two islands in the Strait of Hormuz, formerly held by Ras al Khaimah and annexed from other Gulf states by Iran 1971; their return to their former owners was an Iraqi aim in the Iran–Iraq War.

tundra region of high latitude almost devoid of trees, resulting from the presence of ◊permafrost. The vegetation consists mostly of

grasses, sedges, heather, mosses, and lichens. Tundra stretches in a continuous belt across N North America and Eurasia.

tung oil oil used in paints and varnishes, obtained from trees of the genus *Aleurites*, family Euphorbiaceae, native to China.

tungsten (Swedish *tung sten* "heavy stone") hard, heavy, gray-white, metallic element, symbol W (from German *Wolfram*), atomic number 74, atomic weight 183.85. It occurs in the minerals wolframite, scheelite, and hubertite. It has the highest melting point of any metal (6,170°F/3,410°C) and is added to steel to make it harder, stronger, and more elastic; its other uses include high-speed cutting tools, electrical elements, and thermionic couplings. Its salts are used in the paint and tanning industries.

Tungsten was first recognized in 1781 by Swedish chemist Karl Scheele in the ore scheelite. It was isolated in 1783 by Spanish chemists Fausto D'Elhuyar (1755–1833) and his brother Juan José (1754–1796).

tungsten ore either of the two main minerals, wolframite $(FeMn)WO_4$ and scheelite, $CaWO_4$, from which tungsten is extracted. Most of the world's tungsten reserves are in China, but the main suppliers are Bolivia, Australia, and the US.

Tunguska Event explosion at Tunguska, central Siberia, Russia, in June 1908, which devastated around 2,500 sq mi/6,500 sq km of forest. It is thought to have been caused by either a cometary nucleus or a fragment of ◊Encke's comet. The magnitude of the explosion was equivalent to an atomic bomb and produced a colossal shock wave; a bright falling object was seen 375 mi/600 km away and was heard up to 625 mi/1,000 km away.

tunicate alternate name for ◊sea squirt.

tuning fork in music, a device for providing a reference pitch. It is made from hardened metal and consists of parallel bars about 3–4 in/10 cm long joined at one end and terminating in a blunt point. When the fork is struck and the point placed on a wooden surface, a pure tone is heard. It was invented in England in 1711.

There are tuning forks for each musical pitch. A is known as "concert pitch," since the instruments of the orchestra and the singers of the chorus are tuned to A above middle C.

Tunis capital and chief port of Tunisia; population (1984) 597,000. Industries include chemicals and textiles. Founded by the Arabs, it was captured by the Turks in 1533, then occupied by the French 1881 and by the Axis powers 1942–43. The ruins of ancient ◊Carthage are to the northeast.

Tunisia country in N Africa, on the Mediterranean Sea, bounded SE by Libya and W by Algeria.

government The constitution was adopted 1959, providing for a president who is both head of state and head of government, elected by universal suffrage for a five-year term and eligible for reelection. The president governs through an appointed council of ministers. There is a single-chamber national assembly of 141 members, elected in the same way and for the same term as the president.

history Founded as ◊Carthage by the Phoenicians in the 8th century BC, Tunisia was under Arab rule from the 7th century AD until it became part of the ◊Ottoman Empire 1574. It harbored the ◊Barbary Coast pirates until the 19th century. It became a French protectorate 1881.

The Destour Socialist Party (PSD), founded 1934 by Habib Bourguiba, led Tunisia's campaign for independence from France. The country achieved internal self-government 1955 and full independence 1956, with Bourguiba as prime minister. A year later the monarchy was abolished, and Tunisia became a republic, with Bourguiba as president. A new constitution was adopted 1959, and the first national assembly elected. Between 1963 and 1981 the PSD was the only legally recognized party, but since then others have been allowed. In Nov 1986 the PSD won all the assembly seats, while other parties boycotted the elections.

foreign affairs President Bourguiba followed a distinctive foreign policy, establishing links with the Western powers, including the US, but joining other Arab states in condemning the US-inspired Egypt–Israel treaty. He allowed the Palestine Liberation Organization (PLO) to use Tunis as its headquarters, and this led to an Israeli attack 1985 that strained relations with the US. Diplomatic links with Libya were severed 1985.

Bourguiba's firm and paternalistic rule, and his long period in Tunisian politics, made him a national legend, evidenced by the elaborate mausoleum that was built in anticipation of his death. However, in Nov 1987 he was deposed and replaced by Zine el-Abidine Ben Ali. In July 1988, a number of significant constitutional changes were announced, presaging a move to more pluralist politics, but in the April 1989 elections the renamed PSD, the Constitutional Democratic Rally (RCD), won all 141 assembly seats. During the Gulf War Jan–Feb 1991 which followed Iraq's invasion of Kuwait, there were anti-US protests in Tunisia.

Ben Ali's active repression of Islamic fundamentalists provoked criticism from Western nations Jan 1992. Hundreds of supporters of the fundamentalist al-Nahda party, whose aim was to turn the country into an Islamic state, were alleged to have been tortured during their detention since 1990. The West saw the crackdown as a major setback in Tunisia's progress toward democracy. *See illustration box.*

tunnel passageway through a mountain, under a body of water, or under ground. Tunnelling is a significant branch of civil engineering in both mining and transport. In the 19th century there were two major advances: the use of compressed air within underwater tunnels to balance the external pressure of water, and the development of the tunnel shield to support the face and assist excavation.

In recent years there have been notable developments in linings (for example, concrete segments and steel liner plates), and in the use of rotary diggers and cutters and explosives.

Major tunnels include:

Orange–Fish River (South Africa) 1975, longest irrigation tunnel, 51 mi/82 km;
Chesapeake Bay Bridge-Tunnel (US) 1963, combined bridge, causeway, and tunnel structure, 17.5 mi/28 km;
St Gotthard (Switzerland–Italy) 1980, longest road tunnel, 10.1 mi/16.3 km;
Seikan (Japan) 1964–85, longest rail tunnel, Honshu–Hokkaido, under Tsugaru Strait, 33.5 mi/53.9 km, 14.5 mi/23.3 km undersea (however, a bullet-train service is no longer economical);
Simplon (Switzerland–Italy) 1906, longest rail tunnel on land, 12.3 mi/19.8 km;
Rogers Pass (Canada) 1989, longest tunnel in the western hemisphere, 22 mi/35 km long, through the Selkirk Mountains, British Columbia.

Plans for the ⟩*Channel tunnel* were approved by the French and British governments in 1986, and work is under way with a schedule for completion in early 1993.

Tunney Gene 1898–1978. US prizefighter. As a professional he won the US light-heavyweight title 1922. He began to fight as a heavyweight in 1924 and was the upset winner over heavyweight champion Jack Dempsey 1926. Tunney retained the title against Dempsey in the famous "Long Count" bout 1927 and retired undefeated 1928.

Tunney, born in New York, attended LaSalle Academy and worked as a steamship clerk 1912–17. As an amateur boxer, he won the US armed-forces championship in Paris 1919. After his retirement from boxing, he became successful in business and published *A Man Must Fight* 1932 and *Arms for Living* 1941.

Túpac Amarú adopted name of José Gabriel Condorcanqui *c.* 1742–1781. Peruvian Indian revolutionary leader, executed for his revolt against Spanish rule 1780; he claimed to be descended from the last chieftain of the Incas.

Tupamaros urban guerrilla movement operating in Uruguay, aimed at creating a Marxist revolution, largely active in the 1960s–70s, named after 18th-century revolutionary Túpac Amarú. It was founded by Raul Sendic (died 1989); he served more than 13 years in prison.

turbine engine in which steam, water, gas, or air (see ⟩windmill) is made to spin a rotating shaft by pushing on angled blades, like a fan. Turbines are among the most powerful machines. Steam turbines are used to drive generators in power stations and ships' propellers; water turbines spin the generators in hydroelectric power plants; and gas turbines (as jet engines; see ⟩jet propulsion) power most aircraft and drive machines in industry.

The high-temperature, high-pressure steam for **steam turbines** is raised in boilers heated by furnaces burning coal, oil, or gas, or by nuclear energy. A steam turbine consists of a shaft, or rotor, which rotates inside a fixed casing (stator). The rotor carries "wheels" consisting of blades, or vanes. The stator has vanes set between the vanes of the rotor, which direct the steam through the rotor vanes at the optimum angle. When steam expands through the turbine, it spins the rotor by ⟩reaction. The steam engine of Hero of Alexandria (130 BC), called the *aeolipile*, was the prototype of this type of turbine, called a **reaction turbine**. Modern development of the reaction turbine is largely due to English engineer Charles Parsons. Less widely used is the **impulse turbine**, patented by Carl Gustaf Patrick de Laval (1845–1913) 1882. It works by directing a jet of steam at blades on a rotor. Similarly there are reaction and impulse water turbines: impulse turbines work on the same principle as the water wheel and consist of sets of buckets arranged around the edge of a wheel; reaction turbines look much like propellers and are fully immersed in the water.

In a **gas turbine** a compressed mixture of air and gas, or vaporized fuel, is ignited, and the hot gases produced expand through the turbine blades, spinning the rotor. In the industrial gas turbine, the rotor shaft drives machines. In the jet engine, the turbine drives the compressor, which supplies the compressed air to the engine, but most of the power developed comes from the jet exhaust in the form of propulsive thrust.

turbocharger turbine-driven device fitted to engines to force more air into the cylinders, producing extra power. The turbocharger consists of a "blower," or compressor, driven by a

---

Tunisia
Tunisian Republic (*al-Jumhuriya at-Tunisiya*)

area 63,378 sq mi/164,150 sq km
capital (and chief port) Tunis
cities ports Sfax, Sousse, Bizerta
physical arable and forested land in N graduates toward desert in S
features fertile island of Jerba, linked to mainland by causeway (identified with island of lotus-eaters); Shott el Jerid salt lakes; holy city of Kairouan, ruins of Carthage
head of state and government Zine el-Abidine Ben Ali from 1987
political system emergent democratic republic
political party Constitutional Democratic Rally (RCD), nationalist, moderate, socialist
exports oil, phosphates, chemicals, textiles, food, olive oil
currency dinar
population (1990 est) 8,094,000; growth rate 2% p.a.
life expectancy men 68, women 71 (1989)
languages Arabic (official), French
media publications must be authorized; the offense of defamation is used to protect members of the government from criticism
religion Sunni Muslim 95%; Jewish, Christian
literacy men 68%, women 41% (1985 est)
GNP $9.6 bn (1987); $1,163 per head (1986)
chronology
1883 Became a French protectorate.
1955 Granted internal self-government.
1956 Independence achieved from France as a monarchy, with Habib Bourguiba as prime minister.
1957 Became a republic with Bourguiba as president.
1975 Bourguiba made president for life.
1985 Diplomatic relations with Libya severed.
1987 Bourguiba removed Prime Minister Rashed Sfar and appointed Zine el-Abidine Ben Ali. Ben Ali declared Bourguiba incompetent and seized power.
1988 Constitutional changes toward democracy announced. Diplomatic relations with Libya restored.
1989 Government party, RDC, won all assembly seats in general election.
1991 Opposition to US actions during the Gulf War. Crackdown on religious fundamentalists.

turbocharger *The turbocharger increases the power of an automobile engine by forcing compressed air into the engine cylinders.*

turbine, which in most units is driven by the exhaust gases leaving the engine.

turbofan jet engine of the type used by most airliners, so called because of its huge front fan. The fan sends air not only into the engine for combustion but also around the engine for additional thrust. This results in a faster and more fuel-efficient propulsive jet (see ◊jet propulsion).

turbojet jet engine that derives its thrust from a jet of hot exhaust gases. Pure turbojets can be very powerful but use a lot of fuel.

A single-shaft turbojet consists of a shaft (rotor) rotating in a casing. At the front is a multiblade compressor, which takes in and compresses air and delivers it to one or more combustion chambers. Fuel (kerosene) is then sprayed in and ignited. The hot gases expand through a nozzle at the rear of the engine after spinning a ◊turbine. The turbine drives the compressor. Reaction to the backward stream of gases produces a forward propulsive thrust.

turboprop jet engine that derives its thrust partly from a jet of exhaust gases, but mainly from a propeller powered by a turbine in the jet exhaust. Turboprops are more economical than turbojets but can be used only at relatively low speeds.

A turboprop typically has a twin-shaft rotor. One shaft carries the compressor and is spun by one turbine, while the other shaft carries a propeller and is spun by a second turbine.

turbot any of various flatfishes of the flounder group prized as food, especially *Scophthalmus maximus* found in European waters. It grows up to 3 ft/1 m long and weighs up to 30 lb/14 kg. It is brownish above and whitish underneath.

Turenne Henry de la Tour d'Auvergne, Vicomte de Turenne 1611–1675. French marshal under Louis XIV, known for his siege technique. He fought for the Protestant alliance during the Thirty Years' War, and on both sides during the wars of the Fronde.

Turgenev Ivan Sergeievich 1818–1883. Russian writer, notable for poetic realism, pessimism, and skill in characterization. His works include the play *A Month in the Country* 1849, and the novels *A Nest of Gentlefolk* 1858, *Fathers and Sons* 1862, and *Virgin Soil* 1877. His series *A Sportsman's Sketches* 1852 criticized serfdom.

Turgot Anne Robert Jacques 1727–1781. French finance minister 1774–76, whose reforming economies led to his dismissal by a hostile aristocracy.

Turin (Italian *Torino*) capital of Piedmont, NW Italy, on the river Po; population (1988) 1,025,000. Industries include iron, steel, automobiles, silk and other textiles, fashion goods, chocolate, and wine. It was the first capital of united Italy 1861–64.

Turin became important after the union of Savoy and Piedmont 1416. There is a university, established 1404, and a 15th-century cathedral. It became the Savoyard capital during the 16th century. In 1706 Prince ◊Eugène defeated a French army besieging the city, thus ensuring the survival of the Savoy duchy.

Turing Alan Mathison 1912–1954. English mathematician and logician. In 1936 he described a "universal computing machine" that could theoretically be programmed to solve any problem capable of solution by a specially designed machine. This concept, now called the *Turing machine*, foreshadowed the digital computer.

During World War II Turing worked on the Ultra project in the team that cracked the German Enigma secret cipher code, and was subsequently involved in the pioneering computer developed at Manchester University from 1948. He is believed to have been the first to suggest the possibility of machine learning and artificial intelligence. His test for distinguishing between real (human) and simulated (computer) thought is known as the *Turing test*: with a person in one room and the machine in another, an interrogator in a third room asks questions of both to try to identify them. When the interrogator cannot distinguish between them by questioning, the machine will have reached a state of humanlike intelligence.

Turin shroud ancient piece of linen bearing the image of a body, claimed to be that of Jesus. Independent tests carried out 1988 by scientists in Switzerland, the US, and the UK showed that the cloth of the shroud dated from between 1260 and 1390. The shroud, property of the pope, is kept in Turin Cathedral, Italy.

Turk member of any of the Turkic-speaking peoples of Asia and Europe, especially the principal ethnic group of Turkey. Turkic languages belong to the Altaic family and include Uzbek, Ottoman, Turkish, Azerbaijani, Turkoman, Tatar, Kirghiz, and Yakut.

Turkana, Lake formerly (to 1979) *Lake Rudolf* lake in the Great Rift Valley, 1,230 ft/375 m above sea level, with its northernmost end in Ethiopia and the rest in Kenya; area 3,475 sq mi/9,000 sq km. It is saline, and shrinking by evaporation. Its shores were an early human hunting ground, and valuable remains have been found that are accurately datable because of undisturbed stratification.

Turkestan area of central Asia divided among Kazakhstan, Kyrgyzstan, Tajikistan, Turkmenistan, Uzbekistan, Afghanistan, and China (part of Xinjiang Uygur).

turkey any of several large game birds of the pheasant family, native to the Americas. The wild turkey *Meleagris galloparvo* reaches a length of 4.3 ft/1.3 m, and is native to North and Central American woodlands. The domesticated turkey derives from the wild species. The ocellated turkey *Agriocharis ocellata* is found in Central America; it has eyespots on the tail.

The domesticated turkey was introduced to Europe in the 16th century. Since World War II, it has been intensively bred, in the same way as the chicken. It is gregarious, except at breeding time.

Turkey country between the Black Sea to the N and the Mediterranean Sea to the S, bounded E by Armenia, Georgia, and Iran, SE by Iraq and Syria, W by Greece and the Aegean Sea, and NW by Bulgaria.

government The constitution of 1982 provides for a single-chamber legislature of 450 members, the National Assembly, and an executive president who is elected by the assembly for a seven-year term. He is obliged to work in conjunction with the prime minister. The assembly is elected by universal suffrage for a five-year term.

history The Turks originally came from Mongolia and spread into Turkestan in the 6th century AD. During the 7th century they adopted Islam. In 1055 the Seljuk Turks secured political control of the caliphate and established an empire in Asia Minor. The Ottoman Turks, driven from central Asia by the Mongols, entered the service of the Seljuks, and Osman I founded a kingdom of his own 1299. Having overrun Asia Minor, the Ottomans began their European conquests by seizing Gallipoli 1354; they captured Constantinople 1453 and by 1480 were masters of the Balkans. By 1550 they had conquered Egypt, Syria, Arabia, Mesopotamia, Tripoli, and most of Hungary; thereafter the empire ceased to expand, although Cyprus was taken 1571 and Crete 1669.

decline of Ottoman Empire The Christian counteroffensive opened 1683 with the defeat of the Turks before Vienna; in 1699 the Turks lost Hungary, and in 1774 Russia ousted them from Moldavia, Wallachia, and the Crimea. In the Balkans there was an unsuccessful revolt in Serbia 1804, but Greece threw off Turkish rule 1821–29. Russia's attempts to exploit this situation were resisted by Britain and France, which in the Crimean War (1854–56) fought on the Turkish side. The Bulgarian uprising of 1876 led to a new war between Turkey and Russia, and by the Treaty of Berlin 1878 Turkey lost Bulgaria, Bosnia, and Herzegovina. A militant nationalist group, the Young Turks, secured the grant of a constitution 1908; Italy took advantage of the ensuing crisis to seize Tripoli 1911–12, while the Balkan states expelled the Turks from Albania and Macedonia 1912–13. Turkey entered World War I on the German side 1914, only to lose Syria, Arabia, Mesopotamia, and its nominal suzerainty in Egypt.

independent republic The Greek occupation of Izmir 1919 provoked the establishment of a nationalist congress with Mustafa Kemal (◊Atatürk) as president. Having defeated Italian and French forces, he expelled the Greeks 1922. Peace was concluded 1923 with the Treaty of ◊Lausanne and Turkey was proclaimed an independent republic with Kemal as its first president. He introduced a policy of westernization and a new legal code. He died 1938, but his People's Party remained in power.

series of governments Turkey's first free elections were held 1950 and won by the Democratic Party (DP), led by Celal Bayar and Adnan Menderes. Bayar became president and Menderes prime minister. In 1960, after a military coup, President Bayar was imprisoned and Menderes executed. A new constitution was adopted 1961 and civilian rule restored, but with the leader of the coup, General Cemal Gürsel, as president. There followed a series of civilian governments, led mainly by the veteran politician Ismet Inonu until 1965, when the Justice Party (JP), led by Suleyman Demirel, came to power. Prompted by strikes and student unrest, the army forced Demirel to resign 1971, and for the next two years the country came under military rule again.

effective partition of Cyprus A civilian government was restored 1973, a coalition led by Bulent Ecevit. The following year Turkey sent troops to Cyprus to protect the Turkish-Cypriot community, resulting in the effective partition of the island. Ecevit's government fell when he refused to annex N Cyprus, and in 1975 Suleyman Demirel returned at the head of a right-wing coalition. Elections held 1977 were inconclusive, and Demirel precariously held on to power until 1978 when Ecevit returned, leading another coalition. He was faced with a deteriorating economy and outbreaks of sectional violence and by 1979 had lost his working majority and resigned.

Turkey
Republic of (*Türkiye Cumhuriyeti*)

area 300,965 sq mi/779,500 sq km
capital Ankara
cities ports Istanbul and Izmir
physical central plateau surrounded by mountains
environment only 0.3% of the country is protected by national parks and reserves compared with a global average of 7% per country
features Bosporus and Dardanelles; Mount Ararat; Taurus Mountains in SW (highest peak Kaldi Dağ, 12,255 ft/3,734 m); sources of rivers Euphrates and Tigris in E; archeological sites include Çatal Hüyük, Ephesus, and Troy; rock villages of Cappadocia; historic towns (Antioch, Iskenderun, Tarsus)
head of state Turgut Özal from 1989
head of government Suleyman Demirel from 1991
political system democratic republic
political parties Motherland Party (ANAP), Islamic, nationalist, right-of-center; Social Democratic Populist Party (SDPP), moderate, left-of-center; True Path Party (TPP), center-right
exports cotton, yarn, hazelnuts, citrus, tobacco, dried fruit, chromium ores
currency Turkish lira
population (1990 est) 56,549,000 (85% Turkish, 12% Kurdish); growth rate 2.1% p.a.
life expectancy men 63, women 66 (1989)

international pressure Demirel returned in Nov, but the violence continued and in Sept l980 the army stepped in and set up a national security council, with Bulent Ulusu as prime minister. Martial law was imposed, political activity suspended, and a harsh regime established. Strong international pressure was put on Turkey to return to a more democratic system of government, and in May 1983 political parties were allowed to operate again. The old parties reformed under new names and in Nov three of them contested the assembly elections: the conservative Motherland Party (ANAP), the Nationalist Democracy Party (MDP), and the Populist Party (SDPP). The ANAP won a large majority and its leader, Turgut Özal, became prime minister. Ethnic Kurds suffer from discrimination; since 1984 there has been guerrilla fighting in ⊃Kurdistan, and a separatist Kurdish Workers' Party (PKK) is active. In 1989 Özal was elected president, with Yildirim Akbulut as prime minister. In 1991 Mesut Yilmaz replaced Akbulut as head of the ANAP and became prime minister.

languages Turkish (official), Kurdish, Arabic
religion Sunni Muslim 98%
literacy men 86%, women 62% (1985)
GNP $62 bn (1987); $1,160 per head (1986)
chronology
1919–22 Turkish War of Independence provoked by Greek occupation of Izmir. Mustafa Kemal (Atatürk), leader of nationalist congress, defeated Italian, British, French, and Greek forces.
1923 Treaty of Lausanne established Turkey as independent republic under Kemal. Westernization began.
1950 First free elections; Adnan Menderes became prime minister.
1960 Menderes executed after military coup by General Cemal Gürsel.
1965 Suleyman Demirel became prime minister.
1971 Army forced Demirel to resign.
1973 Civilian rule returned under Bulent Ecevit.
1974 Turkish troops sent to protect Turkish community in Cyprus.
1975 Demirel returned to head of a right-wing coalition.
1978 Ecevit returned, as head of coalition, in the face of economic difficulties and factional violence.
1979 Demeril returned. Violence grew.
1980 Army took over, and Bulent Ulusu became prime minister. Harsh repression of political activists attracted international criticism.
1982 New constitution adopted.
1983 Ban on political activity lifted. Turgut Özal became prime minister.
1987 Özal maintained majority in general election.
1988 Improved relations and talks with Greece.
1989 Turgut Özal elected president; Yildirim Akbulut became prime minister. Application to join EC rejected.
1991 Mesut Yilmaz became prime minister. Turkey sided with UN coalition against Iraq in Gulf War. Conflict with Kurdish minority continued. Coalition government formed under Suleyman Demirel after inconclusive election result.
1992 Earthquake claimed hundreds of lives.

EC membership refused After World War II Turkey felt itself threatened by the USSR and joined a number of military alliances, including NATO 1952 and the Baghdad Pact 1955, which became the Central Treaty Organization 1959 and was dissolved 1979. Turkey strengthened Western links and by 1987 was making overtures to the European Community. Turkey has long been criticized for the harshness of its penal system and its violations of human rights. Its future role will depend on its willingness and ability to create a more humane and fully democratic system of government, but, despite significant advances since 1983, at the end of 1989 it learned that its application for membership in the European Community had been refused and would not be considered again until at least the mid-1990s. During the 1990–91 Gulf War, Turkey supported the US-led forces, allowing use of vital bases in the country.

Demirel regains premiership Following the inconclusive general election held in Oct 1991, Suleyman Demirel eventually formed a coalition government Nov 1991 with the support of the Social Democratic Populist Party. Demirel became premier for the seventh time.

earthquake causes chaos Two earthquakes March 1992 killed hundreds of people and destroyed numerous buildings, bridges, and roads. The worst-hit areas centered around Tunceli and Erzincan. *See illustration box.*

turkish bath bathing that involves exposure to warm air and steam, followed by massage and coldwater immersion. Originating from Roman and East Indian traditions, the concept was introduced to Western Europe by the Crusaders but only became popular when hot water could be supplied in sufficient quantities.

Turkish language language of central and W Asia, the national language of Turkey. It belongs to the Altaic language family. Varieties of Turkish are spoken in NW Iran and several of the Central Asian Republics, and all have been influenced by Arabic and Persian. Originally written in Arabic script, it has been written within Turkey in a variant of the Roman alphabet since 1928.

Words of Turkish origin in English include *divan, coffee, cossack, horde, kiosk,* and *yoghourt/yogurt.*

Turkish literature for centuries Turkish literature was based on Persian models, but under ⊃Suleiman the Great (1494–1566) the Golden Age began, of which the poet Fuzuli (died 1563) is the great exemplar, and continued in the following century with the great poet satirist Nefi of Erzerum (died 1635) and others. During the 19th century westernization overtook Turkish literature, as in the use of French models by Ibrahim Shinasi Effendi (1826–1871), poet and prose writer. Effendi was cofounder of the New School with Mehmed Namik Kemal (1840–1880), poet and author of the revolutionary play *Vatan/The Fatherland,* which led to his exile by the sultan. Unlike these, the poet Tevfik Fikret (1867–1915) turned rather to Persian and Arabic than to native sources for his vocabulary. The poet Mehmed Akif (1873–1936) was the author of the words of the Turkish national anthem, and the work of the contemporary poet and novelist Yashar Kemal (1923–) describes the hard life of the peasant (*Memed, My Hawk* 1955 and *The Wind from the Plain* 1961).

Turkmenistan country in central Asia, bounded N by Kazakhstan and Uzbekistan, W by the Caspian Sea, and S by Iran and Afghanistan.

government There is a 330-member legislature, the supreme soviet, to which deputies are elected by a majority system, and a second ballot "runoff" race in contests in which there is no clear first-round majority. From the majority grouping within the supreme soviet, a prime minister (chairman of the cabinet of minsters) is drawn. The state president is directly elected.

history The principal Turkmen tribes are the Tekkes of Merv and Attok, the Ersaris, the Yomuds, and the Gokluns, all speaking varieties of a Turkic language and descended from the Mongol invaders who swept across Asia in the 13th century. Conquered by Tsarist Russia 1877–1900, the region became part of the Turkestan Soviet Socialist Autonomous Republic 1921, and a constituent republic of the USSR 1925. The Soviet-built Kara Kum canal brought millions of acres of desert to life, although living standards remained very low.

independence achieved Turkmenistan's nationalist movement was more muted than in other former Soviet Central Asian republics. In Aug 1990 Turkmenistan's supreme soviet declared its "sovereignty"; however, in the March 1991 USSR constitutional referendum the population voted to maintain the Union, and the anti-Gorbachev attempted coup in Moscow in Aug 1991 was initially supported by President Niyazov. However, in the Oct 1991 referendum there was an overwhelming (94%) vote in favor of independence, duly declared.

Turkmenistan joined the ◊Commonwealth of Independent States (CIS) in Dec 1991. It was admitted into the ◊Conference on Security and Cooperation in Europe (CSCE) in Jan 1992 and into the United Nations March 1992. In the same month US diplomatic recognition was achieved. In Feb Turkmenistan had joined the Economic Cooperation Organization (ECO), founded by Iran, Pakistan, and Turkey 1975, which aimed to reduce customs tariffs and eventually form a customs union. A new constitution was introduced May 1992 but the republic's political system remained dominated by communists.

Turkoman or **Turkmen** member of a Turkic-speaking people living in Turkmenistan to the E of the Caspian Sea, around the Kara Kum desert, and along the borders of Afghanistan and Iran. Their language belongs to the Turkic branch of the Altaic family.

Turks and Caicos Islands British crown colony in the West Indies, the SE archipelago of the Bahamas;
area 166 sq mi/430 sq km
capital Cockburn Town on Grand Turk
features a group of some 30 islands, of which six are inhabited. The largest is the uninhabited **Grand Caicos**; others include **Grand Turk** (population 3,100), **South Caicos** (1,400), **Middle Caicos** (400), **North Caicos** (1,300), **Providenciales** (1,000), and **Salt Cay** (300); since 1982 the Turks and Caicos have developed as a tax haven
government governor, with executive and legislative councils (chief minister from 1987 Michael John Bradley, Progressive National Party)
exports crayfish and conch (flesh and shell)
currency US dollar
population (1980) 7,500, 90% of African descent
language English, French Creole
religion Christian
history secured by Britain 1766 against French and Spanish claims, the islands were a Jamaican dependency 1873–1962, and in 1976 attained internal self-government.

Turku (Swedish **Åbo**) port in SW Finland, near the mouth of the river Aura, on the Gulf of Bothnia; population (1990) 159,200. Industries include shipbuilding, engineering, textiles, and food processing. It was the capital of Finland until 1812.

turmeric perennial plant *Curcuma longa* of the ginger family, native to India and the East Indies; also the ground powder from its tuberous rhizomes, used in curries to give a yellow color, and as a dyestuff.

Turner Frederick Jackson 1861–1932. US historian, professor at Harvard University 1910–24. He emphasized the significance of the frontier in US historical development, attributing the distinctive character of US society to the influence of changing frontiers over three centuries of westward expansion.

Turner John Napier 1929– . Canadian Liberal politician, prime minister 1984. He was elected to the House of Commons 1962 and served in the cabinet of Pierre Trudeau until resigning 1975. He succeeded Trudeau as party leader and prime minister 1984, but lost the 1984 and 1988 elections. Turner resigned as leader 1989, and returned to his law practice. He was replaced as Liberal Party chief by Herbert Gray in Feb 1990.

Turner Joseph Mallord William 1775–1851. English landscape painter. He traveled widely in Europe, and his landscapes became increasingly Romantic, with the subject often transformed in scale and flooded with brilliant, hazy light. Many later works anticipate Impressionism; for example, *Rain, Steam and Speed* 1844 (National Gallery, London).

A precocious talent, Turner went to the Royal Academy schools in 1789. In 1792 he made the first of several European tours, from which numerous watercolor sketches survive. His early oil paintings show Dutch influence, but by the 1800s he had begun to paint landscapes in the grand manner, reflecting the style of artists such as ◊Claude Lorrain.

Many of Turner's most dramatic works are set in Europe or at sea; for example, *Shipwreck* 1805, *Snowstorm: Hannibal Crossing the Alps* 1812 (both Tate Gallery, London), and *The Slave Ship* 1839 (Museum of Fine Arts, Boston, Massachusetts).

Turner Lana (Julia Jean Mildred Frances) 1920– . US actress who appeared in melodramatic films of the 1940s and 1950s such as *Peyton Place* 1957. Her other films include *The Postman Always Rings Twice* 1946, *The Three Musketeers* 1948, and *Imitation of Life* 1959.

Her debut was in *They Won't Forget* 1937, after her legendary "discovery" at a Hollywood soda fountain at the age of 16. By the mid-1940s she was a star, and she proved her acting ability in *The Bad and the Beautiful* 1952. In the 1960s, she starred in glossy Douglas Sirk and Ross Hunter productions.

Turner Nat 1800–1831. US slave, who led 60 slaves in the most serious US slave revolt—the Southampton Insurrection of 1831—to capture an armory in Southampton County, Virginia. Before he and 16 of the others were hanged, at least 55 people throughout the region, 24 of them children, had been killed. He thought himself divinely appointed to lead the slaves to freedom. He eluded capture for 6 weeks following the uprising, which so alarmed slave owners that repressive measures forbidding the educating of any blacks were swiftly enacted. Widespread torture and execution followed as owners exacted retribution, and the abolition movement in the South was abandoned.

Turkmenistan
Republic of

area 188,406 sq mi/488,100 sq km
capital Ashkhabad
cities Chardzhov, Mary (Merv), Nebit-Dag, Krasnovodsk
physical some 90% of land is desert including the Kara Kum "Black Sands" desert (area 120,000 sq mi/310,800 sq km)
features on the edge of the Kara Kum desert is the Altyn Depe, "golden hill," site of a ruined city with a ziggurat, or stepped pyramid; river Amu Darya; rich deposits of petroleum, natural gas, sulfur, and other industrial raw materials
head of state Saparmurad Niyazov from 1991
head of government Khan Akhmedov from 1989
political system socialist pluralist
products silk, karakul, sheep, astrakhan fur, carpets, chemicals, rich deposits of petroleum, natural gas, sulfur, and other industrial raw materials
population (1990) 3,600,000 (72% Turkmen, 10% Russian, 9% Uzbek, 3% Kazakh, 1% Ukrainian)
language West Turkic, closely related to Turkish
religion Sunni Muslim
chronology
1921 Part of Turkestan Soviet Socialist Autonomous Republic.
1925 Became a constituent republic of USSR.
1990 Aug: economic and political sovereignty declared.
1991 Jan: Communist Party leader Niyazov became state president. March: endorsed maintenance of the Union in USSR referendum. Aug: President Niyazov initially supported attempted anti-Gorbachev; Oct: independence declared. Dec: joined new Commonwealth of Independent States (CIS).
1992 Jan: admitted into Conference for Security and Cooperation in Europe (CSCE). Feb: joined the Muslim Economic Cooperation Organization (ECO). March: admitted into United Nations (UN); US diplomatic recognition achieved. May: new constitution adopted.

Turner Robert Edward III "Ted" 1938– . US businessman and sportsman who developed a conglomerate that includes WTBS, a sports and entertainment cable television channel; CNN, a cable television news network; MGM/UA Entertainment Company; the Atlanta Braves baseball team; and the Atlanta Hawks basketball team.

Born in Cincinnati, Ohio, Turner attended Brown University but left 1960 to work for the family-owned billboard advertising company, which he headed after his father's suicide 1963. Turner won yachting's America's Cup 1977 and was the prime promoter of the Goodwill Games, first held in Moscow 1986. He is married to actress Jane Fonda.

Turner Tina. Adopted name of Annie Mae Bullock 1938– . US rhythm-and-blues singer who recorded 1960–76 with her husband *Ike Turner* (1931–), including *River Deep, Mountain High* 1966, produced by Phil ▷Spector. She achieved success in the 1980s as a solo artist, recording such albums as *Private Dancer* 1984, and as a live performer.

turnip biennial plant *Brassica rapa* cultivated in temperate regions for its edible white- or yellow-fleshed root and the young leaves, which are used as a green vegetable. Closely allied to it is the ▷swede *Brassica napus*.

turnstone any of a genus *Arenaria* of small wading shorebirds, especially the ruddy turnstone *A. interpres*, which breeds in the Arctic and migrates to the southern hemisphere. It is seen on rocky beaches, turning over stones for small crustaceans and insects.

It is about 9 in/23 cm long, has a summer plumage of black and chestnut above, white below, and is duller in winter.

turpentine solution of resins distilled from the sap of conifers, used in varnish and as a paint solvent but now largely replaced by ▷white spirit.

Turpin Ben 1874–1940. US comedian, a star of silent films. Cross-eyes were his hallmark, and a taste for parodying his fellow actors. His work includes *The Shriek of Araby* 1923, *A Harem Knight* 1926, and *Broke in China* 1927.

Turpin Dick 1706–1739. English highwayman. The son of an innkeeper, he turned to highway robbery, cattle-thieving, and smuggling, and was hanged at York.

turquoise mineral, hydrous basic copper aluminum phosphate. Blue-green, blue, or green, it is a gemstone. Turquoise is found in Iran, Turkestan, Mexico, and southwestern US.

turtle any member of the reptilian order Chelonia, characterized by a horn-covered bony shell consisting of an upper and lower portion joined along the sides. The main divisions are the hidden-necked turtles (Cryptodira) that withdraw their heads in an S-shaped vertical curve and the side-necked turtles (Pleurodira) that withdraw their heads in a horizontal, sideways curve. See also ▷terrapin, ▷tortoise, and ▷sea turtle.

Tuscaloosa city in W central Alabama, on the Black Warrior River, SW of Birmingham; industries include chemicals, tires, paper, and lumber; population (1990) 77,800. It was originally founded by Creek Indians 1809.

The University of Alabama 1831 is here.

Tuscan in Classical architecture, one of the five ▷orders (types of ▷column).

Tuscany (Italian *Toscana*) region of central Italy; area 8,878 sq mi/23,000 sq km; population (1990) 3,562,500. Its capital is Florence, and towns include Pisa, Livorno, and Siena. The area is mainly agricultural, with many vineyards, such as in the Chianti hills; it also has lignite and iron mines and marble quarries. The Tuscan dialect has been adopted as the standard form of Italian. Tuscany was formerly the Roman *Etruria*, and inhabited by Etruscans around 500 BC. In medieval times the area was divided into small states, united under Florentine rule during the 15th–16th centuries. It became part of united Italy 1861.

Tussaud Madame (Anne Marie Grosholtz) 1761–1850. French wax-modeler. In 1802 she established an exhibition of wax models of celebrities in London. It was destroyed by fire 1925, but reopened 1928.

Born in Strasbourg, she went to Paris 1766 to live with her wax-modeler uncle, Philippe Curtius, whom she soon surpassed in technique. During the French Revolution they were forced to take death masks of many victims and leaders (some still exist in the Chamber of Horrors).

Tutankhamen king of Egypt of the 18th dynasty, about 1360–1350 BC. A son of Ikhnaton (also called Amenhotep IV), he was about 11 at his accession. In 1922 his tomb was discovered by the British archeologists Lord Carnarvon and Howard Carter in the Valley of the Kings at Luxor, almost untouched by tomb robbers. The contents included many works of art and his solid-gold coffin, which are now displayed in a Cairo museum.

Tutsi member of a minority ethnic group living in Rwanda and Burundi. Although fewer in number, they have traditionally been politically dominant over the Hutu majority and the Twa (or Pygmies). The Tutsi are traditionally farmers; they also hold virtually all positions of importance in Burundi's government and army. They have carried out massacres in response to Hutu rebellions, notably in 1972 and 1988. In Rwanda the balance of power is more even.

Tutu Desmond (Mpilo) 1931– . South African priest, Anglican archbishop of Cape Town and general secretary of the South African Council of Churches 1979–84. One of the leading figures in the struggle against apartheid in the Republic of South Africa, he was awarded the 1984 Nobel Prize for Peace.

Tuva (Russian *Tuvinskaya*) autonomous republic (administrative unit) of Russia, northwest of Mongolia;
capital Kyzyl
area 65,813 sq mi/170,500 sq km
population (1986) 284,000
features good pasture; gold, asbestos, cobalt
history part of Mongolia until 1911 and declared a Russian protectorate 1914; after the 1917 revolution it became the independent Tannu-Tuva republic 1920, until incorporated in the USSR as an autonomous region 1944. It was made the Tuva Autonomous Republic 1961.

Tuvalu country in the SW Pacific Ocean; formerly (until 1976) the Ellice Islands; part of ▷Polynesia.
government The constitution dates from 1978 when Tuvalu became an independent state within the British ▷Commonwealth, accepting the British monarch as head of state, represented by a resident governor-general, who must be a Tuvaluan citizen and is appointed on the recommendation of the prime minister.

There is a single-chamber parliament of 12 members and a prime minister and cabinet elected by and responsible to it. Members of parliament are elected by universal suffrage for a four-year term. Each of the inhabited atolls of the Tuvalu group has its own elected island council, responsible for local affairs.
history The islands were inhabited by Melanesians, and were invaded and occupied by Samoans during the 16th century. They were first reached by Europeans 1765. During the mid-19th century European slave traders captured indigenous Melanesians for forced labor on plantations in South America. As a result of this, and the importation of European diseases, the population declined from an estimated 20,000 to barely 3,000. Originally known as the Ellice Islands, they were a British protectorate 1892–1915 and part of the Gilbert

Tuvalu
South West Pacific State of (formerly Ellice Islands)

area 9.5 sq mi/25 sq km
capital Funafuti
physical nine low coral atolls forming a chain of 650 mi/579 km in the SW Pacific
features maximum height above sea level 20 ft/6 m; coconut palms are main vegetation
head of state Elizabeth II from 1978 represented by governor-general

head of government Bikenibeu Paeniu from 1989
political system liberal democracy
political parties none; members are elected to parliament as independents
exports copra, handicrafts, stamps
currency Australian dollar
population (1990 est) 9,000 (Polynesian 96%); growth rate 3.4% p.a.
life expectancy 60 men, 63 women (1989)
languages Tuvaluan, English
religion Christian (Protestant)
literacy 96% (1985)
GDP (1983) $711 per head
chronology
1892 Became a British protectorate forming part of the Gilbert and Ellice Islands group.
1916 The islands acquired colonial status.
1975 The Ellice Islands were separated from the Gilbert Islands.
1978 Independence achieved from Britain within the Commonwealth with Toaripi Lauti as prime minister.
1981 Dr Tomasi Puapua replaced Lauti as premier.
1986 Islanders rejected proposal for republican status.
1989 Bikenibeu Paeniu elected new prime minister.

and Ellice Islands colony 1915–75, when they became a separate British colony.

special member of Commonwealth In 1978 the Ellice Islands became fully independent within the Commonwealth, reverting to their old name of Tuvalu, meaning "eight standing together" (there are nine, but one is very small). Because of its small size, Tuvalu is a "special member" of the Commonwealth and does not have direct representation at meetings of heads of government. Its first prime minister was Toaripi Lauti, replaced 1981 as a result of his alleged involvement in an investment scandal, by Dr Tomasi Puapua, who was reelected 1985. In 1986 a poll was taken to decide whether Tuvalu should remain a constitutional monarchy or become a republic. Only one atoll favored republican status. Following new elections Sept 1989, Puapua was replaced as prime minister by Bikenibeu Paeniu, whose new administration pledged to reduce the country's dependence on foreign aid, which contributes more than a fourth of gross domestic product. *See illustration box.*

TVP (abbreviation for *texturized vegetable protein*) meat substitute usually made from soybeans. In manufacture, the soybean solids (what remains after oil has been removed) are ground finely and mixed with a binder to form a sticky mixture. This is forced through a spinneret and extruded into fibers, which are treated with salts and flavorings, wound into hanks, and then chopped up to resemble meat chunks.

Twa member of an ethnic group comprising 1% of the populations of Burundi and Rwanda. The Twa are the aboriginal inhabitants of the region. They are a pygmoid people, and live as nomadic hunter-gatherers in the forests.

Twain Mark. Adopted name of Samuel Langhorne Clemens 1835–1910. US writer. He established his reputation with the comic masterpiece *The Innocents Abroad* 1869 and two classic American novels, in dialect, *The Adventures of Tom Sawyer* 1876 and *The Adventures of Huckleberry Finn* 1885. He also wrote satire, as in *A Connecticut Yankee at King Arthur's Court* 1889.

Born in Florida, Missouri, Twain grew up along the Mississippi River in Hannibal, Missouri, the setting for many of his major works, and was employed as a riverboat pilot before he moved west; taking a job as a journalist, he began to write. The tale "The Celebrated Jumping Frog of Calaveras County" was his first success. After a trip by boat to Palestine, he wrote *The Innocents Abroad*. As his writing career blossomed, he also became a lecturer very much in demand. By 1870 he married, and a few years later he and his wife settled in Hartford, Connecticut.

Huckleberry Finn is Twain's masterpiece, for its use of the vernacular, vivid characterization and descriptions, and its theme, underlying the humor, of man's inhumanity to man. He also wrote *Roughing It* 1872, *The Gilded Age* 1873, *Old Times on the Mississippi* 1875, *The Prince and the Pauper* 1882, *Life on the Mississippi* 1883, *Pudd'nhead Wilson* 1894, and *Personal Recollections of Joan of Arc* 1896. His later works, such as *The Mysterious Stranger*, unpublished until 1916, are less humorous and more pessimistic. He is recognized as one of America's finest and most characteristic writers.

tweed cloth made of woolen yarn, usually of several shades, but in its original form without a regular pattern and woven on a hand loom in the more remote parts of Ireland, Wales, and Scotland.

Harris tweed is made on the island of Harris in the Outer Hebrides; it is highly durable and largely weatherproof. Nowadays, tweed is often machine-woven, patterned, and processed.

Tweed William Marcy ("Boss") 1823–1878. US politician who emerged as the leader of Tammany Hall (a New York City Democratic club, founded 1789) and was elected to the city board of supervisors 1856. In various municipal offices, and from 1867 in the state senate, Tweed, by then a master of graft, controlled government spending and accumulated a fortune estimated at somewhere between $45 million and $200 million. He was convicted of forgery and larceny in 1873.

Born in New York City, Tweed worked briefly as a clerk in his father's brush factory. Becoming involved in municipal politics, he served as an alderman 1852–56 and in the US House of Representatives 1853–55. Arrested on charges of forgery and larceny, Tweed was convicted and sentenced to prison 1873–75. Shortly thereafter he was rearrested and jailed, but in Dec 1875 he escaped to Spain via Cuba. His anonymity in Spain was subverted by a Thomas ◊Nast cartoon, from which Tweed was recognized and sent back to New York, where he died in prison.

Twelfth Night comedy by William Shakespeare, first performed 1601–02. The plot builds on misunderstandings and mistaken identities, leading to the successful romantic unions of Viola and her twin brother Sebastian with Duke Orsino and Olivia respectively, and the downfall of Olivia's steward Malvolio.

Twelver member of a Shiite Muslim sect who believes that the 12th imam (Islamic leader) did not die, but is waiting to return toward the end of the world as the Mahdi, the "rightly guided one," to establish a reign of peace and justice on Earth.

twelve-tone system or **twelve-note system** system of musical composition in which the 12 notes of the chromatic scale are arranged in a particular order, called a "series" or "tone-row." A work using the system consists of restatements of the series in any of its formations. Arnold ◊Schoenberg and Anton ◊Webern were exponents of this technique.

twin one of two young produced from a single pregnancy. Human twins may be genetically identical, having been formed from a single fertilized egg that splits into two cells, both of which became implanted. Nonidentical twins are formed when two eggs are fertilized at the same time.

two-stroke cycle operating cycle for internal combustion piston engines. The engine cycle is completed after just two strokes (movement up or down) of the piston, which distinguishes it from the more common ◊four-stroke cycle. Power mowers and lightweight motorcycles use two-stroke gasoline engines, which are cheaper and simpler than four-strokes.

Most marine diesel engines are also two-strokes. In a typical two-stroke motorcycle engine, fuel mixture is drawn into the crankcase as the piston moves up on its first stroke to compress the mixture above it. Then the compressed mixture is ignited, and hot gases are produced, which drive the piston down on its second stroke. As it moves down, it uncovers an opening (port) that allows the fresh fuel mixture in the crankcase to flow into the combustion space above the piston. At the same time, the exhaust gases leave through another port.

TX abbreviation for the state of ◊*Texas*.

Tyche personification of Chance in Classical Greek thought, whose cult developed in the Hellenistic and Roman periods, when it was identified with that of the Roman ◊Fortuna.

Tyler city in NE Texas, SE of Dallas; industries include oil, roses, vegetables, furniture, and plastics; population (1990) 75,508.

Tyler John 1790–1862. 10th president of the US 1841–45, succeeding Benjamin ◊Harrison, who died after only one month in office. Tyler was the first US vice-president to succeed to the presidency. Because he was not in favor of many of the Whig Party's policies, he was constantly at odds with the cabinet and Congress, until elections forced the Whigs from power and enabled Tyler to reorganize his cabinet. His government negotiated the Webster–Ashburton Treaty, which settled the Maine–New Brunswick boundary dispute in Canada 1842 and annexed Texas 1845.

Tyler, a lawyer, served in the US House of Representatives 1817–21 and in the Senate 1827–36, representing his home state of Virginia, of which he was governor 1825–27.

Tyler Wat died 1381. English leader of the ◊Peasants' Revolt of 1381. He was probably born in Kent or Essex, and may have served in the French wars. After taking Canterbury he led the peasant army to Blackheath and occupied London. At Mile End King Richard II met the rebels and promised to redress their grievances, which included the imposition of a poll tax. At a further conference at Smithfield, Tyler was murdered.

Tyndale William 1492–1536. English translator of the Bible. The printing of his New Testament (the basis of the King James Version) was begun in Cologne 1525 and, after he had been forced to flee, completed in Worms. He was strangled and burned as a heretic at Vilvorde in Belgium.

Tyndall John 1820–1893. Irish physicist who 1869 studied the scattering of light by invisibly small suspended particles. Known as the *Tyndall effect*, it was first observed with colloidal solutions, in which a beam of light is made visible when it is scattered by minute colloidal particles (whereas a pure solvent does not scatter light). Similar scattering of blue wavelengths of sunlight by particles in the atmosphere makes the sky look blue (beyond the atmosphere, the sky is black).

Tyne and Wear metropolitan county in NE England, created 1974, originally administered by an elected metropolitan council; its powers reverted to district councils 1986;
area 208 sq mi/540 sq km
cities Newcastle-upon-Tyne (administrative headquarters), South Shields, Gateshead, Sunderland
features bisected by the rivers Tyne and Wear; includes part of ◊Hadrian's Wall; Newcastle and Gateshead, linked with each other and with the coast on both sides by the Tyne and Wear Metro (a light railroad using existing suburban lines, extending 34 mi/54 km)
products once a center of heavy industry, it is now being redeveloped and diversified
population (1991) 1,087,000
famous people Thomas Bewick, Robert Stephenson, Harry Patterson ("Jack Higgins").

typeface style of printed lettering. Books, newspapers, and other printed matter display different styles of lettering; each style is named, common examples being Times and ⟡Baskerville. These different "families" of alphabets have been designed over the centuries since printing was invented, and each has distinguishing characteristics. See also ⟡typography.

type metal ⟡alloy of tin, lead, and antimony, for making the metal type used by printers.

typesetting means by which text, or copy, is prepared for ⟡printing, now usually carried out by computer. Text is keyed on a typesetting machine in a similar way to typing. Laser or light impulses are projected on to light-sensitive film that, when developed, can be used to make plates for printing.

typewriter keyboard machine that produces characters on paper. The earliest known typewriter design was patented by Henry Mills in England 1714. However, the first practical typewriter was built 1867 in Milwaukee, Wisconsin, by Christopher Sholes, Carlos Glidden, and Samuel Soulé. By 1873 ⟡Remington and Sons, US gunmakers, produced under contract the first machines for sale and 1878 patented the first with lower-case as well as upper-case (capital) letters.

The first typewriter patented by Sholes included an alphabetical layout of keys, but Remington's first commercial typewriter had the QWERTY keyboard, designed by Sholes to slow down typists who were too fast for their mechanical keyboards. (Other layouts include the Dvorak keyboard developed by John Dvorak 1932, in which the most commonly used letters are evenly distributed between left and right, and under the strongest fingers.) Later developments include tabulators from about 1898, portable machines about 1907, the gradual introduction of electrical operation (allowing increased speed, since the keys are touched, not depressed), proportional spacing 1940, and the rotating typehead with stationary plates 1962. More recent typewriters work electronically, are equipped with a memory, and can be given an interface that enables them to be connected to a computer.

typhoid fever acute infectious disease of the digestive tract, caused by the bacterium *Salmonella typhi*, and usually contracted through a contaminated water supply. It is characterized by bowel haemorrhage and damage to the spleen. Treatment is with antibiotics.

The symptoms begin 10–14 days after ingestion and include fever, headache, cough, constipation, and rash. The combined TAB vaccine protects both against typhoid and the milder, related condition known as *paratyphoid fever*.

typhoon violently revolving storm, a ⟡hurricane in the W Pacific Ocean.

typhus acute infectious disease, often fatal, caused by bacteria transmitted by lice, fleas, mites, and ticks. Symptoms include fever, headache, and rash. Typhus is epidemic among people living in overcrowded conditions. Treatment is by antibiotics.

The microorganisms responsible are of the genus *Rickettsia*, especially *R. prouazekii*. A preventive vaccine exists.

typography design and layout of the printed word. Typography began with the invention of writing and developed as printing spread throughout Europe after the invention of metal moveable type by Johann ⟡Gutenberg about 1440. Hundreds of variations have followed since, but the basic design of the Frenchman Nicholas Jensen (about 1420–80), with a few modifications, is still the ordinary ("roman") type used in printing.

Type sizes are measured in points (there are approximately 2.8 points to the millimeter); the length of a typeset line, called the measure, is measured in pica ems (1 pica em has a width of a little over 0.15 in/4 mm). The space between lines (known as leading) is also measured in points, although new photosetting and computer-assisted setting systems also work in metric sizes.

Ease of reading is sought in text typefaces; ornament is sought in display typefaces.

Tyr in Norse mythology, the god of battles, whom the Anglo-Saxons called Týw, hence "Tuesday."

tyrannosaurus any of a genus *Tyrannosaurus* of gigantic flesh-eating ⟡dinosaurs, order Saurischia, which lived in North America and Asia about 70 million years ago. They had two feet, were up to 50 ft/15 m long, 20 ft/6.5 m tall, weighed 10 tonnes, and had teeth 6 in/15 cm long.

Only a few whole skeletons are known; the most complete was discovered 1989 in Hell Creek, Montana, and will be preserved in the Museum of the Rockies, Bozeman, Montana.

Tyre (Arabic *Sur* or *Soûr*) town in SW Lebanon, about 50 mi/80 km S of Beirut, formerly a port until its harbor silted up; population (1980 est) about 14,000. It stands on the site of the ancient city of the same name, a seaport of ⟡Phoenicia.

history Built on the mainland and two small islands, the city was a commercial center, known for its purple dye. Besieged and captured by Alexander the Great 333–332 BC, it came under Roman rule 64 BC and was taken by Arab forces AD 638. The Crusaders captured it 1124, and it never recovered from the destruction it suffered when retaken by the Arabs 1291. In the 1970s it became a Palestinian guerrilla stronghold and was shelled by Israel 1979.

Tyrol variant spelling of ⟡Tirol, state of Austria.

Tyrone county of Northern Ireland;
area 1,220 sq mi/3,160 sq km
cities Omagh (county town), Dungannon, Strabane, Cookstown
features rivers: Derg, Blackwater, Foyle; Lough Neagh
products mainly agricultural
population (1981) 144,000.

Tyrrhenian Sea arm of the Mediterranean surrounded by mainland Italy, Sicily, Sardinia, Corsica, and the Ligurian Sea. It is connected to the Ionian Sea through the Straits of Messina. Islands include Elba, Ustica, Capri, Stromboli, and the Lipari Islands.

Tyson Mike (Michael Gerald) 1966– . US heavyweight boxer, undisputed world champion from Aug 1987 to Feb 1990. He won the World Boxing Council heavyweight title 1986 when he beat Trevor Berbick to become the youngest world heavyweight champion. He beat James "Bonecrusher" Smith for the World Boxing Association title 1987 and later that year became the first undisputed champion since 1978 when he beat Tony Tucker for the International Boxing Federation title.

He turned professional 1985. Of Tyson's first 25 opponents, 15 were knocked out in the first round. He was undefeated until 1990, when he lost the championship in an upset to James "Buster" Douglas. He was scheduled to fight again for the championship, but was convicted 1992 of rape and imprisoned.

Tyumen oldest town in Siberia, central Russia (founded 1586), on the river Nitsa; industries include oil refining, machine tools, and chemicals; population (1987) 456,000.

Tzu-Hsi alternative transliteration of ⟡Zi Xi, dowager empress of China.

U the 21st letter of the English alphabet, and the 20th in the ancient Roman, in which it was identical with V. U has various sounds, as in the pronunciation of the English words *truth, bull, duke, busy, bury.*

U-2 US military reconnaissance airplane, used in secret flights over the USSR from 1956 to photograph military installations. In 1960 a U-2 was shot down over the USSR and the pilot, Gary Powers, was captured and imprisoned. He was exchanged for a US-held Soviet agent two years later.

The U-2 affair led to the cancellation of a proposed meeting in Moscow between President Eisenhower and Soviet leader Khrushchev, precipitating a greatly increased Soviet arms spending in the 1960s and 1970s. U-2 flights in 1962 revealed the construction of Soviet missile bases in Cuba. Designed by Richard Bissell, the U-2 flew higher (70,000 ft/21,000 m) and further (2,200 mi/3,500 km) than any previous plane.

U2 Irish rock group formed 1977 by singer Bono Vox (born Paul Hewson, 1960–), guitarist Dave "The Edge" Evans (1961–), bassist Adam Clayton (1960–), and drummer Larry Mullen (1961–). The band's albums include *The Unforgettable Fire* 1984, *The Joshua Tree* 1987, and *Achtung Baby* 1992.

uakari any of several rare South American monkeys of the genus *Cacajao*. There are three species. They have bald faces and long fur. About 1.8 ft/55 cm long in head and body, and with a comparatively short 6 in/15 cm tail, they rarely leap, but are good climbers, remaining in the tops of the trees in swampy forests and feeding largely on fruit. The black uakari is in danger of extinction because it is found in such small numbers already, and the forests where it lives are fast being destroyed.

Ubangi-Shari former name for the ▷Central African Republic.

U-boat (German *Unterseeboot* "undersea boat") German submarine. The title was used in both world wars.

Uccello Paolo. Adopted name of Paolo di Dono 1397–1475. Italian painter, active in Florence, one of the first to use perspective. His surviving paintings date from the 1430s onwards. Decorative color and detail dominate his later

pictures. His works include *St George and the Dragon* about 1460 (National Gallery, London).

Uccello is recorded as an apprentice in Lorenzo Ghiberti's workshop in 1407. His fresco *The Deluge* about 1431 (Sta Maria Novella, Florence) shows his concern for pictorial perspective, but in later works this aspect becomes superficial. His three battle scenes painted in the 1450s for the Palazzo Medici, Florence, are now in the Ashmolean Museum, Oxford, the National Gallery, London, and the Louvre, Paris.

Udall Nicholas 1504–1556. English schoolmaster and playwright. He was the author of *Ralph Roister Doister* about 1553, the first known English comedy.

Udmurt (Russian *Udmurtskaya*) autonomous republic in the W Ural foothills, central Russia
area 16,200 sq mi/42,100 sq km
capital Izhevsk
products timber, flax, potatoes, peat, quartz
population (1985) 1,559,000; 58% Russian, 33% Udmurt, 7% Tatar
history conquered in the 15th–16th centuries; constituted the Votyak Autonomous Region 1920; name changed to Udmurt 1932; Autonomous Republic 1934; part of the independent republic of Russia from 1991.

Ufa industrial city (engineering, oil refining, petrochemicals, distilling, timber) and capital of the Bashkir autonomous republic, central Russia, on the river Bielaia, in the W Urals; population (1987) 1,092,000. It was founded by Russia 1574 as a fortress.

Uffizi art gallery in Florence, Italy. Its collection, based on that of the Medici family, is one of the finest in Europe.

Uganda landlocked country in E Africa, bounded N by Sudan, E by Kenya, S by Tanzania and Rwanda, and W by Zaire.
government The 1969 constitution provides for a single-chamber national assembly of 126 elected members and a president who is both head of state and head of government. In 1985 a military coup suspended the constitution and dissolved the national assembly. The National Resistance Council (NRC) is an interim legislative body.
history For early history, see ▷Africa. Uganda was a British protectorate 1894–1962. It became an independent member of the British ▷Commonwealth 1962, with Dr Milton Obote, leader of the Uganda People's Congress (UPC), as prime minister. In 1963 it was proclaimed a federal republic; King Mutesa II became president, ruling through a cabinet. King Mutesa was deposed in a coup 1966, and Obote became executive president. One of his first acts was to end the federal status. After an attempt to assassinate him 1969, Obote banned all opposition and established what was effectively a one-party state.

Uganda
Republic of

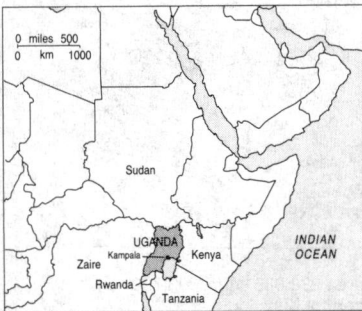

area 91,351 sq mi/236,600 sq km
capital Kampala
cities Jinja, M'Bale, Entebbe, Masaka
physical plateau with mountains in W; forest and grassland; arid in NE
features Ruwenzori Range (Mount Margherita, 16,765 ft/5,110 m); national parks with wildlife (chimpanzees, crocodiles, Nile perch to 160 lb/70 kg); Owen Falls on White Nile where it leaves Lake Victoria; Lake Albert in W
head of state and government Yoweri Museveni from 1986
political system emergent democratic republic
political parties National Resistance Movement (NRM), left-of-center; Democratic Party (DP), center-left; Conservative Party (CP), center-right; Uganda People's Congress (UPC), left-of-center; Uganda Freedom Movement (UFM), left-of-center
exports coffee, cotton, tea, copper
currency Uganda new shilling
population (1990 est) 17,593,000 (largely the Baganda, from whom the country is named; also Langi and Acholi, some surviving

Pygmies); growth rate 3.3% p.a.
life expectancy men 49, women 51 (1989)
languages English (official), Kiswahili, Luganda, and other African languages
religion Roman Catholic 33%, Protestant 33%, Muslim 16%, animist
literacy men 70%, women 45% (1985 est)
GNP $3.6 bn (1987); $220 per head
chronology
1962 Independence achieved from Britain within the Commonwealth with Milton Obote as prime minister.
1963 Proclaimed a federal republic with King Mutesa II as president.
1966 King Mutesa ousted in coup led by Obote, who ended the federal status and became executive president.
1969 All opposition parties banned after assassination attempt on Obote.
1971 Obote overthrown in army coup led by Maj Gen Idi Amin Dada; ruthlessly dictatorial regime established; nearly 49,000 Ugandan Asians expelled; over 300,000 opponents of regime killed.
1978 Amin forced to leave country by opponents backed by Tanzanian troops. Provisional government set up with Yusuf Lule as president. Lule replaced by Godfrey Binaisa.
1978–79 Fighting broke out against Tanzanian troops.
1980 Binaisa overthrown by army. Elections held and Milton Obote returned to power.
1985 After opposition by National Resistance Army (NRA), and indiscipline in army, Obote ousted by Brig Tito Okello; power-sharing agreement entered into with NRA leader Yoweri Museveni.
1986 Agreement ended; Museveni became president, heading broad-based coalition government.
1992 Announcement made that East African cooperation pact with Kenya and Tanzania would be revived.

Idi Amin's regime In 1971 Obote was overthrown in an army coup led by Maj Gen Idi ⇩Amin Dada, who suspended the constitution and all political activity and took legislative and executive powers into his own hands. Obote fled to Tanzania. Amin proceeded to wage what he called an "economic war" against foreign domination, resulting in the mass expulsion of people of Asian ancestry, many of whom settled in Britain. In 1976 Amin claimed that large tracts of Kenya historically belonged to Uganda and accused Kenya of cooperating with the Israeli government in a raid on Entebbe airport to free hostages held in a hijacked aircraft. Relations with Kenya became strained, and diplomatic links with Britain were severed. During the next two years the Amin regime carried out a widespread campaign against any likely opposition, resulting in thousands of deaths and imprisonments. The East African Community (EAC) consisting of Tanzania, Kenya, and Uganda, formed 1967, collapsed 1977.

military coups In 1978, when Amin annexed the Kagera area of Tanzania, near the Uganda border, the Tanzanian president, Julius Nyerere, sent troops to support the Uganda National Liberation Army (UNLA), which had been formed to fight Amin. Within five months Tanzanian troops had entered the Uganda capital, Kampala, forcing Amin to flee, first to Libya and then to Saudi Arabia. A provisional government, drawn from a cross-section of exiled groups, was set up, with Dr Yusuf Lule as president. Two months later Lule was replaced by Godfrey Binaisa who, in turn, was overthrown by the army. A military commission made arrangements for national elections, which were won by the UPC, and Milton Obote came back to power.

Obote's government was soon under pressure from a range of exiled groups operating outside the country and guerrilla forces inside, and he was only kept in office by the presence of Tanzanian troops. When they were withdrawn June 1982 a major offensive was launched against the Obote government by the National Resistance Movement (NRM) and the National Resistance Army (NRA), led by Dr Lule and Yoweri Museveni. By 1985 Obote was unable to control the army, which had been involved in indiscriminate killings, and he was ousted in July in a coup led by Brig Tito Okello. Obote fled to Kenya and then Zambia, where he was given political asylum.

national reconciliation Okello had little more success in controlling the army and, after a brief period of power-sharing with the NRA, fled to Sudan Jan 1986. Museveni was sworn in as president and announced a policy of national reconciliation, promising a return to normal parliamentary government within three to five years. He formed a cabinet in which most of Uganda's political parties were represented, including the NRM, which is the political wing of the NRA, the Democratic Party, the Conservative Party, the UPC, and the Uganda Freedom Movement. He worked at consolidating his hold domestically, reviving the economy, and improving African relations, as in the nonaggression treaty signed with Sudan 1990.

foreign relations In Feb 1992 it was announced that EAC, the East Africa co-operation pact, would be revived. *See illustration box.*

Uganda Martyrs 22 Africans, of whom 12 were boy pages, put to death 1885–87 by King Mwanga of Uganda for refusing to renounce Christianity. They were canonized as the first African saints of the Roman Catholic Church 1964.

Ugarit ancient trading-city kingdom (modern *Ras Shamra*) on the Syrian coast. It was excavated by the French archeologist Claude Schaeffer (1898–1982) from 1929, with finds dating from about 7000 to the 15th–13th centuries BC, including the earliest known alphabet.

ugli fruit trademark for a cultivated Jamaican citrus fruit, a three-way cross between a grapefruit, a tangerine, and an orange. Sweeter than a grapefruit but sharper than a tangerine, with rough skin, it is eaten fresh or used in jams and preserves for a sweet-sour flavor. It is native to the East Indies and its name comes from its misshapen appearance.

UHF (abbreviation for *ultra high frequency*) referring to radio waves of very short wavelength, used, for example, for television broadcasting.

Uigur member of a Turkic people living in NW China and Kazakhstan; they form about 80% of the population of the Chinese province of Xinjiang Uygur. There are about 5 million speakers of Uigur, a language belonging to the Turkic branch of the Altaic family; it is the official language of the province.

The Uigur are known to have lived in the region since the 3rd century AD, and converted to Islam in the 14th century. They have been under Chinese rule since the 17th century. A small number fled to Kazakhstan at that time, and it is from them that the present minority is descended.

Ujung Pandang formerly (until 1973) *Macassar* or *Makassar* chief port (trading in coffee, rubber, copra, and spices) on Sulawesi, Indonesia, with fishing and food-processing industries; population (1980) 709,000. It was established by Dutch traders 1607.

UK abbreviation for the ⇩*United Kingdom*.

Ukraine country in E central Europe, bounded E by Russia, N by Belarus, S by Moldova, Romania, and the Black Sea, and W by Poland, Czechoslovakia, and Hungary.

government There is a 450-member legislature, the supreme soviet, to which deputies are elected by a majority system, and a second ballot "runoff" race in contests in which there is no clear first-round majority. From the majority grouping within the supreme soviet, a prime minister (chairman of the cabinet of ministers) is drawn. The executive state president is directly elected.

history The Ukraine formed the heartland of the medieval state of Kievan Rus

Ukraine

area 233,089 sq mi/603,700 sq km
capital Kiev
cities Kharkov, Donetsk, Odessa, Dnepropetrovsk, Lugansk (Voroshilovgrad), Lviv (Lvov), Mariupol (Zhdanov), Krivoi Rog, Zaporozhye
physical Russian plain: Carpathian and Crimean Mountains; rivers: Dnieper (with the Dnieper dam 1932), Donetz, Bug
features Askaniya-Nova Nature Preserve (established 1921); health spas with mineral springs
head of state Leonid Kravchuk from 1990
head of government Vitold Fokin from 1990
political system emergent democracy
political party Ukrainian People's Movement (Rukh), umbrella nationalist grouping, with three leaders
products grain, coal, oil, various minerals
currency grivna
population (1990) 51,800,000 (73% Ukrainian, 22% Russian, 1% Byelorussian, 1% Russian-speaking Jews; some 1.5 million have emigrated to the US, 750,000 to Canada)
language Ukrainian (Slavonic), with a literature that goes back to the Middle Ages
famous people Ivan Kotlyarevsky and Taras

Shevchenko
religion traditionally Ukrainian Orthodox; also Ukrainian Catholic
chronology
1918 Independent People's Republic proclaimed.
1920 Conquered by Soviet Red Army.
1921 Poland alloted charge of W Ukraine.
1932–33 Famine caused the deaths of more than 7.5 million people.
1939 W Ukraine occupied by Red Army.
1941–44 Under Nazi control; Jews massacred at Babi Yar; more than five million Ukrainians and Ukrainian Jews deported and exterminated.
1944 Soviet control reestablished.
1945 Became a founder member of the United Nations.
1946 Ukrainian Uniate Church proscribed and forcibly merged with Russian Orthodox Church.
1986 April: Chernobyl nuclear disaster.
1989 Feb: Ukrainian People's Movement (Rukh) established. Ban on Ukrainian Uniate Church lifted.
1990 July: voted to proclaim sovereignty; Leonid Kravchuk indirectly elected as president; sovereignty declared.
1991 Aug: demonstrations against the abortive anti-Gorbachev coup; independence declared, pending referendum; Communist Party (CP) activities suspended. Oct: voted to create independent army. Dec: Kravchuk popularly elected president; independence overwhelmingly endorsed in referendum; joined new Commonwealth of Independent States (CIS); independence acknowledged by USA and European Community (EC).
1992 Jan: admitted into Conference on Security and Cooperation in Europe (CSCE); pipeline deal with Iran to end dependence on Russian oil; prices freed. Feb: prices "temporarily" re-regulated. March: agreed tactical arms-shipments to Russia suspended. May: Crimean sovereignty declared, but subsequently rescinded. Aug: joint control of Black Sea fleet agreed upon with Russia.

which emerged in the 9th century. Uniting Ukrainians, Russians (Muscovites), and Belorussians, it became the leading power in eastern Europe, before being destroyed by Mongol invasion in the 13th century. Christianity was adopted from Byzantium 988. It came under Catholic Polish rule from the 14th century, with the peasantry reduced to serfdom. In 1648 there was a revolt against Polish oppression led by Cossacks, composed originally of runaway serfs, and a militarist state was established by hetman (elected leader) Bohdan Khmelnytsky (d. 1657). East and West Ukraine were partitioned between Muscovy and Poland in 1667.

Tsarist rule Under Tsar ▷Peter I the publication of Ukrainian books was banned in 1720 and serfdom was introduced into E Ukraine ("Little Russia") in 1783. In the late 18th century, Russia also secured control over all of W Ukraine, except Galicia, which was annexed by Austria in 1772. The 19th century witnessed a Ukrainian cultural revival and the establishment of secret nationalist organizations, especially in Galicia. During the late 19th and early 20th centuries there was rapid economic development and urbanization, but under the late Tsars suppression of Ukraininan culture and "Russification" intensified.

World War I and II After the overthrow of the Tsar, an independent Ukrainian People's Republic was proclaimed in 1918, which allied itself with the ▷Central Powers. The Germans installed a conservative hetman regime, which was popularly overthrown at the close of World War I. After two years of civil war, W Ukraine (Galicia-Volhymia) was transferred to Polish rule, while the remainder came under Soviet control, becoming a constituent republic of the USSR in 1922. In the mid-1920s a conciliatory policy of Ukrainization was pursued; however, during the 1930s there was a mass purge of intellectuals, kulks ("rich farmers") and the destruction of the Ukrainian Orthodox Church. During the "collectivization famine" of 1932–33 at least 7 million peasants died. Polish-controlled W Ukraine was occupied by the Red Army from Sept 1939 until the Nazi German invasion of the USSR in June 1941, followed by mass deportations and exterminations of more than 5 million Ukrainians and Ukrainian Jews. In 1944 Moscow ordered the deportation en masse to Central Asia of Crimean Tatars, who were accused of collaboration.

Sovietization After World War II, Soviet-ruled Ukraine was enlarged to include territories formerly under Polish (W Ukraine), Czechoslovak (Transcarpathian Ukraine), and Romanian (N Bukovina and part of Bessarabia) control and became a founding member of the ▷United Nations. W Ukraine remained the site of partisan resistance by the Ukrainian Insurgent Army (UPA) until the early 1950s and, as part of a "sovietization" campaign, there were mass arrests and deportations to Siberia of 500,000 people and inward migration of Russians. The Uniate Church was forcibly merged with the Russian Orthodox Church in 1946. After Stalin's death in 1953, Ukraine was treated in a more conciliatory fashion by Nikita ▷Khrushchev, who had been Ukrainian Communist Party (UCP) leader 1938–47. In Feb 1954, to "celebrate" the 300th anniversary of Slavic "fraternal union," Crimea was transferred back to Ukraine's jurisdiction and in the 1960s there was a Ukrainian literary revival and growth of the dissident movement. In 1972–73 a crackdown on dissent was launched and the Brezhnevite Vladimir Shcherbitsky replaced

the more liberal Petro Shelest as UCP leader. However, from the mid-1970s Helsinki Monitoring Groups became active and the Uniate Church continued to operate underground in W Ukraine. In the wake of the ▷Chernobyl incident in 1986 a popular environmentalist movement, Green World, emerged in Ukraine.

nationalism intensifies Emboldened by ▷glasnost, nationalist and proreform demonstrations increased, led by the People's Movement of Ukraine for Restructuring ("Rukh"), established Feb 1989. Shcherbitsky was ousted as CP leader Sept 1989, the Uniate Church was allowed to re-register Dec 1989, and in the March 1990 republic supreme soviet election, "reform communist" and Rukh candidates in the Democratic Bloc polled strongly in a number of areas. In all, the Democratic Bloc won 170 of the 450 supreme soviet seats and in July 1990 the new parliament declared the republic's economic and political sovereignty. Ukrainian nationalist sentiment accelerated from the spring of 1991, when striking miners called for the resignation of the Soviet president, Mikhail ▷Gorbachev. In May 1991, the republic's supreme soviet agreed to hold a referendum on independence later in the year.

declaration of independence Ukraine's president, Leonid Kravchuk, was slow to condemn the Aug 1991 anti-Gorbachev attempted coup in Moscow, which had provoked a series of Rukh-led prodemocracy rallies in Lviv (Lvov). However, after the coup's failure, Kravchuk swiftly donned nationalist colors, banning the UCP and declaring the republic's provisional independence on Sept 24, 1991, pending the referendum. There was a resounding (90%) vote in favor of independence in the Dec 1, 1991 plebiscite and, simultaneously, Kravchuk was popularly elected president, capturing 61% of the vote.

CIS membership Ukraine joined the ▷Commonwealth of Independent States (CIS), formed Dec 1991, and its independence was immediately recognized by Canada, home to around 1,000,000 Ukrainians, as well as by Ukraine's central European neighbors. In the same month its independence was recognized by the US, and by the European Community (EC). In Jan 1992, Ukraine was admitted into the ▷Conference on Security and Cooperation in Europe (CSCE).

economic reforms A program of market-centerd economic reform and privatization was launched, with prices freed Jan 1992 but "temporarily" re-regulated Feb. A pipeline deal completed with Iran helped to reduce Ukraine's dependence on Russia for oil. Coupons were introduced as a secondary currency to the ruble, pending the creation of an independent currency, the grivna. However, the continued strength of ex-communist apparatchiks threatened to frustrate the program.

military reorganization Ukraine inherited a substantial nuclear arsenal, but pledged to become a nuclear-free state by 1994, while establishing an independent 200,000–400,000-strong army. In March it suspended tactical-arms shipments to Russia, claiming that there was no assurance that Russia was dismantling them. Post-independence quarrels with Russia over the division of military forces continued; agreement was reached Aug 1992 on joint control of the Black Sea fleet until 1995, after which time it would probably be divided between the two countries.

Crimean demands for recognition The Crimea, which, despite the return of 150,000

Tatars since 1989, is 70% Russian, declared its independence Sept 1991 but confirmed that it would remain part of the Ukraine. In May 1992 a declaration of sovereignty was made but subsequently rescinded after Ukraine threatened to use "all available means" to prevent the republic's secession. *See illustration box.*

Ukrainian member of the majority ethnic group living in Ukraine; there are minorities in Siberian Russia, Kazakhstan, Poland, Czechoslovakia, and Romania. There are 40–45 million speakers of Ukrainian, a member of the East Slavonic branch of the Indo-European family, closely related to Russian. Ukrainian-speaking communities are also found in Canada and the US.

The word "Ukraine" is derived from a Slav word meaning "borderland," and historically the region was ruled by Russians and Poles. It is sometimes referred to by Russians as Little Russia, although this is a description that Ukrainians generally do not find appropriate. In the Ukraine there are distinct Ukrainian communities in the west (Lemky), east (Verkhovyntsi), north (Volhynians), and southwest (Hutusuls).

ukulele type of small four-stringed ▷guitar.

Ulaanbaatar or *Ulan Bator*; formerly (until 1924) *Urga* capital of the Mongolian Republic; a trading center producing carpets, textiles, vodka; population (1991) 575,000.

Ulam Stanislaw Marcin 1909–1985. Polish-born US mathematician. He was a member of the Manhattan Project that produced the first atomic bomb 1943–45, and from 1946 collaborated with Edward ▷Teller on the design of the hydrogen bomb, solving the problem of how to ignite the bomb. All previous designs had collapsed.

Ulbricht Walter 1893–1973. East German communist politician, in power 1960–71. He lived in exile in the USSR during Hitler's rule 1933–45. A Stalinist, he became first secretary of the Socialist Unity Party in East Germany 1950 and (as chair of the Council of State from 1960) was instrumental in the building of the Berlin Wall 1961. He established East Germany's economy and recognition outside the Eastern European bloc.

ulcer any persistent breach in a body surface (skin or mucous membrane). It may be caused by infection, irritation, or tumor. Common ulcers include stomach, peptic, mouth (aphthous), intestinal (see ▷colitis), and varicose.

The disintegration of tissue is often accompanied by the discharge of pus and blood. Bleeding stomach ulcers can be repaired without an operation by the use of endoscopy: a flexible fiber-optic tube is passed into the stomach and under direct vision a remote-controlled stitching machine sews up the ulcer.

Ullmann Liv 1939– . Norwegian actress notable for her work with the Swedish director Ingmar Bergman. Her films include *Persona* 1966, *Pope Joan* 1972 (the title role), and *Autumn Sonata* 1978.

Ulm industrial city (vehicles, agricultural machinery, precision instruments, textiles) in Baden-Württemberg, Germany, on the river Danube; population (1988) 101,000. Its Gothic cathedral with the highest stone spire ever built (528 ft/161 m) escaped damage in World War II when two-thirds of Ulm was destroyed. It was a free imperial city from the 14th century to 1802. Albert Einstein was born here.

ulna one of the two bones found in the lower limb of the tetrapod (four-limbed) vertebrate.

Ulster former kingdom in Northern Ireland, annexed by England 1461, from Jacobean times a center of English, and later Scottish, settlement on land confiscated from its owners; divided 1921 into Northern Ireland (counties Antrim, Armagh, Down, Fermanagh, Londonderry, and Tyrone) and the Republic of Ireland (counties Cavan, Donegal, and Monaghan).

ultrabasic in geology, an igneous rock with a lower silica content than basic rocks (less than 45% silica).

Ultramontanism (Latin "beyond the mountains," that is, the Alps) in the Roman Catholic Church, the tenets of an Italian movement that stresses papal authority rather than nationalism in the church.

ultrasonics study and application of the sound and vibrations produced by ultrasonic pressure waves (see ⟡ultrasound).

ultrasound pressure waves similar in nature to sound waves but occurring at frequencies above 20,000 Hz (cycles per second), the approximate upper limit of human hearing (15–16 Hz is the lower limit). ⟡Ultrasonics is concerned with the study and practical application of these phenomena.

The earliest practical application was to detect submarines during World War I, but recently the field of ultrasonics has greatly expanded. Frequencies above 80,000 Hz have been used to produce echoes as a means of measuring the depth of the sea or to detect flaws in metal, and in medicine, high-frequency pressure waves are used to investigate various body organs. High-power ultrasound has been used with focusing arrangements to destroy deep-lying tissue in the body, and extremely high frequencies of 1,000 MHz (megahertz) or more are used in ultrasonic microscopes.

ultrasound scanning or **ultrasonography** in medicine, the use of ultrasonic pressure waves to create a diagnostic image. It is a safe, noninvasive technique that often eliminates the need for exploratory surgery.

The sound waves transmitted through the body are absorbed and reflected to different degrees by different body tissues.

By recording the "echoes," a picture of the various structures being scanned can be built up. Free of the risks of ionizing radiation (see ⟡radioactivity), unlike X-rays and ⟡CAT scan, ultrasound scanning is especially valuable in obstetrics, where it has revolutionized fetal evaluation and diagnosis.

ultraviolet astronomy study of cosmic ultraviolet emissions using artificial satellites. The US has launched a series of satellites for this purpose, receiving the first useful data 1968. Only a tiny percentage of solar ultraviolet radiation penetrates the atmosphere, this being the less dangerous longer-wavelength ultraviolet. The dangerous shorter-wavelength radiation is absorbed by gases in the ozone layer high in the Earth's upper atmosphere.

The US Orbiting Astronomical Observatory (OAO) satellites provided scientists with a great deal of information regarding cosmic ultraviolet emissions. *OAO-1*, launched 1966, failed after only three days, although *OAO-2*, put into orbit 1968, operated for four years instead of the intended one year, and carried out the first ultraviolet observations of a supernova and also of Uranus. *OAO-3 (Copernicus),*

launched 1972, continued transmissions into the 1980s and discovered many new ultraviolet sources. The *International Ultraviolet Explorer (IUE)*, launched Jan 1978 and still operating in the early 1990s, observed all the main objects in the Solar System (including Halley's comet), stars, galaxies, and the interstellar medium.

ultraviolet radiation light rays invisible to the human eye, of wavelengths from about 4×10^{-4} to 5×10^{-6} millimeters (where the ⟡X-ray range begins). Physiologically, they are important but also dangerous, causing the formation of vitamin D in the skin and producing sunburn in excess. They are strongly germicidal and may be produced artificially by mercury vapor and arc lamps for therapeutic use.

Much of ultraviolet radiation may be detected with ordinary photographic plates or films. It can also be studied by its fluorescent effect on certain materials. The desert iguana, *Disposaurus dorsalis*, uses it to locate the boundaries of its territory and to find food.

Ulysses Roman name for ⟡Odysseus, Greek mythological hero.

Ulysses novel by James Joyce, published 1922. It employs ⟡stream of consciousness, linguistic experimentation, and parody to describe in enormous detail a single day (June 16, 1904) in the life of its characters in Dublin.

It was first published in Paris but, because of obscenity prosecutions, not until 1933 in the US.

Ulysses space probe to study the Sun's poles, launched 1990 by a US space shuttle. It is a joint project by NASA and the European Space Agency. The gravity of Jupiter will swing *Ulysses* on to a path that loops it first under the Sun's south pole and then over the north pole to study the Sun and solar wind at latitudes not observable from the Earth.

Umar 2nd caliph (head) of Islam, a strong disciplinarian. Under his rule Islam spread to Egypt and Persia. He was assassinated in Medina.

Umayyad alternate spelling of ⟡Omayyad dynasty.

Umberto two kings of Italy:

Umberto I 1844–1900. King of Italy from 1878, who joined the Triple Alliance 1882 with Germany and Austria-Hungary; his colonial ventures included the defeat at Aduwa, Abyssinia, 1896. He was assassinated by an anarchist.

Umberto II 1904–1983. Last king of Italy 1946. On the abdication of his father, Victor Emmanuel III, he ruled May 9–June 13, 1946, when he had to abdicate because a referendum established a republic. He retired to Portugal.

umbilical cord connection between the ⟡embryo and the ⟡placenta of placental mammals. It has one vein and two arteries, transporting oxygen and nutrients to the developing young, and removing waste products. At birth, the connection between the young and the placenta is no longer necessary. The umbilical cord drops off or is severed, leaving a scar called the navel.

umbrella portable protection against the rain (when used in the sun it is usually called a parasol or sunshade). In use in China for more than a thousand years, umbrellas were also held over the rulers of ancient Egypt and Assyria as symbols of power and had a similar significance for Aztec and African

rulers and dignitaries of the Roman Catholic Church.

umbrella bird bird of tropical South and Central America, family Contingidae. The Amazonian species *Cephalopterus ornatus* has an inflatable wattle at the neck to amplify its humming call, and in display elevates a long crest (4 in/12 cm) lying above the bill so that it rises umbrellalike above the head. These features are less noticeable in the female, which is brownish, whereas the male is blue-black.

Umbria mountainous region of Italy in the central Apennines, including the provinces of Perugia and Terni; area 3,281 sq mi/ 8,500 sq km; population (1990) 822,700. Its capital is Perugia, and the river Tiber rises in the region. Industries include wine, grain, olives, tobacco, textiles, chemicals, and metalworking. This is the home of the Umbrian school of artists, including Raphael.

Umm al Qaiwain one of the ⟡United Arab Emirates.

Umtali former name (until 1982) for the town of ⟡Mutare in Zimbabwe.

UN abbreviation for the ⟡*United Nations*.

Unamuno Miguel de 1864–1936. Spanish writer of Basque origin, exiled 1924–30 for criticism of the military directorate of ⟡Primo de Rivera. His works include mystic poems and the study *Del sentimiento trágico de la vida/The Tragic Sense of Life* 1913, about the conflict of reason and belief in religion.

uncertainty principle or **indeterminacy principle** in quantum mechanics, the principle that it is meaningless to speak of a particle's position, momentum, or other parameters, except as results of measurements; measuring, however, involves an interaction (such as a ⟡photon of light bouncing off the particle under scrutiny), which must disturb the particle, though the disturbance is noticeable only at an atomic scale. The principle implies that one cannot, even in theory, predict the moment-to-moment behavior of such a system.

It was established by Werner ⟡Heisenberg, and gave a theoretical limit to the precision with which a particle's momentum and position can be measured simultaneously: the more accurately the one is determined, the more uncertainty there is in the other.

Uncle Remus US folk tales by Joel Chandler Harris of Brer Rabbit, Brer Fox, and others, taken from black plantation legends in the 1870s and 1880s, and part of the tradition of US Southern humor.

Uncle Sam nickname for the US government. It was coined during the War of 1812 by opponents of US policy. It was probably derived from the initials "US" placed on government property.

Uncle Tom's Cabin best-selling US novel by Harriet Beecher Stowe, written 1851–52. A sentimental but powerful portrayal of the cruelties of slave life on Southern plantations, it promoted the call for abolition. The heroically loyal slave Uncle Tom has in the 20th century become a byword for black subservience.

uncommitted logic array (ULA) or *gate array* in computing, a type of semicustomized integrated circuit in which the logic gates are laid down to a general-purpose design but are not connected to each other. The interconnections can then be set in place according to the requirements of individual manufacturers. Producing ULAs may be cheaper than using a large number of TTL (⟩transistor–transistor logic) chips or commissioning a fully customized chip.

unconformity in geology, a break in the sequence of ⟩sedimentary rocks. It is usually seen as an eroded surface, with the ⟩beds above and below lying at different angles. An unconformity represents an ancient land surface, where exposed rocks were worn down by erosion and later covered in a renewed cycle of deposition.

unconscious in psychoanalysis, part of the personality of which the individual is unaware, and which contains impulses or urges that are held back, or repressed, from conscious awareness.

UNCTAD acronym for *United Nations Commission on Trade and Development*.

underground economy unofficial economy of a country, which includes undeclared earnings from a second job ("moonlighting") and enjoyment of undervalued goods and services (such as company "perks"), designed for tax evasion purposes. In industrialized countries, it has been estimated to equal about 10% of ⟩gross domestic product.

Underground Railroad in US history, a network established in the North before the ⟩American Civil War to provide sanctuary and assistance for escaped black slaves. Safe houses, transport facilities, and "conductors" existed to lead the slaves to safety in the North and Canada, although the number of fugitives who secured their freedom by these means may have been exaggerated.

Undset Sigrid 1882–1949. Norwegian novelist, author of *Kristin Lavransdatter* 1920–22, a strongly Catholic novel set in the 14th century. She was awarded the Nobel Prize for Literature 1928.

unemployment lack of paid employment. The unemployed are usually defined as those out of work who are available for and actively seeking work. Unemployment is measured either as a total or as a percentage of those who are available for work, known as the working population or labor force. Periods of widespread unemployment in Europe and the US in the 20th century include 1929–1930s, and the years since the mid-1970s.

Unemployment is, generally, subdivided into *frictional unemployment*, the inevitable temporary unemployment of those moving from one job to another; *cyclical unemployment*, caused by a downswing in the business cycle; *seasonal unemployment*, in an area where there is high demand only during vacation periods, for example; and *structural unemployment*, where changing technology or other long-term change in the economy results in large numbers without work.

Many Third World countries suffer from severe unemployment and underemployment; the problem is exacerbated by rapid growth of population and lack of skills. In industrialized countries, unemployment has been a phenomenon since the mid-1970s, when the rise in world oil prices caused a downturn in economic activity, and greater use of high technology has improved output without the need for more jobs. The average unemployment rate in industrialized countries (the members of the Organization for Economic Cooperation and Development) rose to 11% in 1987 compared with only 3% in 1970, with some countries, such as Spain and Ireland, suffering around 20%. There continues to be a great deal of youth unemployment despite government training and job creation schemes. In the US the official unemployment rate was 5.3% in 1989, but it is estimated that 20% to 25% of those who want employment cannot find any (and have never had a job or are out of work longer than unemployment compensation is paid, so are not counted by labor statisticians). In China, nearly a fourth of the urban labor force is unemployed.

UNESCO (acronym for *United Nations Educational, Scientific, and Cultural Organization*) agency of the UN, established 1946, with its headquarters in Paris. The US, contributor of 25% of its budget, withdrew 1984 on grounds of its "overpoliticization and mismanagement," and Britain followed 1985.

Ungaretti Giuseppe 1888–1970. Italian poet who lived in France and Brazil. His lyrics show a cosmopolitan independence from Italian poetic tradition. His poems, such as the *Allegria di naufragi/Joy of Shipwrecks* 1919, are of great simplicity.

Ungava district in N Québec and Labrador, E of Hudson Bay; area 351,780 sq mi/911,110 sq km. It has large deposits of iron ore.

ungulate general name for any hoofed mammal. Included are the odd-toed ungulates (perissodactyls) and the even-toed ungulates (artiodactyls), along with subungulates such as elephants.

UNHCR abbreviation for *United Nations High Commission for Refugees*.

Uniate Church any of the ⟩Orthodox churches that accept the Catholic faith and the supremacy of the pope, and are in full communion with the Roman Catholic Church, but retain their own liturgy and separate organization.

In Ukraine, despite being proscribed 1946–89, the Uniate Church claimed some 4.5 million adherents when it was once again officially recognized. Its rehabilitation was marked by the return of its spiritual leader, Cardinal Miroslav Lubachivsky, to take up residence in Lvov in W Ukraine after 52 years' exile in Rome.

UNICEF acronym for *United Nations International Children's Emergency Fund*.

unicellular organism animal or plant consisting of a single cell. Most are invisible without a microscope but a few, such as the giant ⟩ameba, may be visible to the naked eye. The main groups of unicellular organisms are bacteria, protozoa, unicellular algae, and unicellular fungi or yeasts.

Some become disease-causing agents, ⟩pathogens.

unicorn mythical animal referred to by Classical writers, said to live in India and resembling a horse, but with one spiraled horn growing from the forehead.

It was especially important in medieval Christian symbolism and lore.

unidentified flying object or *UFO* any light or object seen in the sky whose immediate identity is not apparent. Despite unsubstantiated claims, there is no evidence that UFOs are alien spacecraft. On investigation, the vast majority of sightings turn out to have been of natural or identifiable objects, notably bright stars and planets, meteors, aircraft, and satellites, or to have been perpetrated by pranksters. The term *flying saucer* was coined in 1947 and has been in use since.

Unification Church or *Moonies* church founded in Korea 1954 by the Reverend Sun Myung ⟩Moon. The number of members (often called "moonies") is about 200,000 worldwide. The theology unites Christian and Taoist ideas and is based on Moon's book *Divine Principle*, which teaches that the original purpose of creation was to set up a perfect family, in a perfect relationship with God.

unified field theory in physics, the theory that attempts to explain the four fundamental forces (strong nuclear, weak nuclear, electromagnetic, and gravity) in terms of a single unified force (see ⟩particle physics).

Research was begun by Albert Einstein and, by 1971, a theory developed by Steven Weinberg, Sheldon Glashow, Abdus Salam, and others, had demonstrated the link between the weak and electromagnetic forces. The next stage is to develop a theory (called the ⟩grand unified theory, or GUT) that combines the strong nuclear force with the electroweak force. The final stage will be to incorporate gravity into the scheme. Work on the ⟩SuperstringTheory indicates that this may be the ultimate "theory of everything."

uniformitarianism in geology, the principle that processes that can be seen to occur on the Earth's surface today are the same as those that have occurred throughout geological time. For example, desert sandstones containing sand-dune structures must have been formed under conditions similar to those present in deserts today. The principle was formulated by James ⟩Hutton and expounded by Charles ⟩Lyell.

Unilateral Declaration of Independence (UDI) unnegotiated severing of relations with a colonial power; especially, the declaration made by Ian Smith's Rhodesian Front government Nov 11, 1965, announcing the independence of Rhodesia (now Zimbabwe) from Britain.

unilateralism in politics, support for *unilateral nuclear disarmament*: scrapping a country's nuclear weapons without waiting for other countries to agree to do so at the same time.

Union, Act of 1707 Act of Parliament that brought about the union of England and Scotland; that of 1801 united England and Ireland. The latter was revoked when the Irish Free State was constituted 1922.

Union of Soviet Socialist Republics (USSR) former country in N Asia and E Europe that reverted to independent states following the resignation of Mikhail Gorbachev 1991; see ⟩Armenia, ⟩Azerbaijan, ⟩Belarus, ⟩Estonia, ⟩Georgia, ⟩Kazakhstan, ⟩Kyrgyzstan, ⟩Latvia, ⟩Lithuania, ⟩Moldova, ⟩Russian Federation, ⟩Tajikistan, ⟩Turkmenistan, ⟩Ukraine, and ⟩Uzbekistan.

history For history before 1922, see ⟩Russia: history. The Union of Soviet Socialist Republics was formed 1922, and a constitution adopted 1923. Lenin, who had led the new regime, died 1924, and an internal party controversy broke out between the communist leaders Stalin and Trotsky over the future of socialism and the necessity of world revolution.

Stalin's socialism Trotsky was expelled 1927, and Stalin's policy of socialism in one country adopted. During the first two five-year plans 1928–39, heavy and light industries were developed, and agriculture collectivized. The country was transformed as industry grew at an annual (official) rate of 16% with, as a consequence, the size of the manual work force quadrupling and the urban population doubling. However, the social cost was enormous, with millions dying in the Ukraine and Kazakhstan famine of 1932–34, as well as in the political purges and liquidations launched during the 1920s and 1930s. Leading party figures, including Nikolai Bulkharin, Lev Kamenev, and Grigory Zinoviev were victims of these "show trial" purges. In the process, the Soviet political system was deformed, as inner-party democracy gave way to autocracy based around a Stalinist personality cult.

From 1933 the USSR put forward a policy of collective resistance to aggression. In 1939 it concluded a nonaggression pact with Germany, and Poland was invaded and divided between them. The USSR invaded Finland 1939 but signed a brief peace 1940. For events 1941–45, see ⟩World War II. Some 25 million Russians perished during this "Great Patriotic War."

Cold War During the immediate postwar years the USSR concentrated on consolidating its empire in Eastern Europe and on providing indirect support to anticolonial movements in the Far East. Relations with the West, particularly the US, sharply deteriorated. On the death of Stalin in March 1953, a collective leadership, including Nikita Khrushchev (CPSU first or general secretary 1953–64), Georgi Malenkov (prime minister 1953–55), Nikolai Bulganin (prime minister 1955–58), Vyacheslav Molotov (foreign minister 1953–56), and Lazar Kaganovich, assumed power. They combined to remove the secret-police chief Lavrenti Beria in Dec 1953, and introduced a new legal code that regularized the political system. Strong differences emerged within the collective leadership over future political and economic reform, and a fierce succession struggle developed.

Khrushchev's "liberalization policy" Khrushchev emerged dominant from this contest, ousting Malenkov, Molotov, and Kaganovich (the "antiparty" group) June 1957 and Bulganin June 1958 to combine the posts of prime minister and party first secretary. At the 1961 Party Congress, Khrushchev introduced a new party program for rapid agricultural, industrial, and technological development to enable the USSR to move ahead of the US in economic terms by 1980 and attain full communism. He launched a "virgin lands" cultivation campaign in Kazakhstan, increased rural incentives, and decentralized industrial management through the creation of new regional economic councils (*sovnarkhozy*). In addition, Khrushchev introduced radical party rule changes, sanctioned a cultural thaw, and devised the principle of "peaceful coexistence" with the West to divert resources from the military sector. These reforms enjoyed initial success; having exploded its first hydrogen bomb 1953 and launched a space satellite (Sputnik I) 1957, the USSR emerged as a serious technological rival to the US. But Khrushchev's liberalization policy and his denunciation of the errors and crimes of the Stalin era at the Feb 1956 Party Congress had serious repercussions among the USSR's satellites—a nationalist revolt in Hungary and a breach in relations with Yugoslavia and China—while his administrative reforms were fiercely opposed by senior party and state officials. After a series of poor harvests in overcropped Kazakhstan and the ⟩Cuban missile crisis 1962, these opponents succeeded in ousting Khrushchev at the Central Committee meeting Oct 1964.

A new and conservative collective leadership, based around the figures of Leonid Brezhnev (CPSU general secretary 1964–82), Alexei Kosygin (prime minister 1964–80), Nikolai Podgorny (state president 1965–77), and Mikhail Suslov (ideology secretary 1964–82), assumed power and immediately abandoned Khrushchev's *sovnarkhozy* and party reforms and reimposed strict censorship in the cultural sphere. Priority was now given to the expansion and modernization of the Soviet armed forces, including the creation of a naval force with global reach. This, coupled with the Warsaw Pact invasion of Czechoslovakia 1968, resulted in a renewal of the ⟩Cold War 1964–70.

the Brezhnev doctrine During the later 1960s, Leonid Brezhnev emerged as the dominant figure. He governed in a cautious and consensual manner and brought into the Politburo leaders from all the significant centers of power, including the ⟩KGB (Yuri Andropov), the army (Marshal Andrei Grechko), and the diplomatic service (Andrei Gromyko). Working with Prime Minister Kosygin, Brezhnev introduced a series of minor economic reforms and gave new priority to agricultural and consumer-goods production. He oversaw the framing of a new constitution 1977 where the limits for internal dissent were clearly set out and the "Brezhnev doctrine" was also promulgated 1968, establishing the power of the USSR to intervene to "preserve socialism" in E Europe as it did in Czechoslovakia.

era of détente Brezhnev, who became the new state president May 1977, emerged as an international figure during the 1970s, frequently meeting Western leaders during a new era of détente. The landmarks of this period were the SALT I and SALT II Soviet-US arms-limitation agreements of 1972 and 1979 (see ⟩Strategic Arms Limitation Talks) and the Helsinki Accord 1975, which brought Western recognition of the postwar division of Eastern Europe. Another cultural thaw resulted in the emergence of a vocal dissident movement. The political and military influence of the USSR was extended into Africa with the establishment of new communist governments in Mozambique 1974, Angola and Ethiopia 1975, and South Yemen 1978. The détente era was brought to an end by the Soviet invasion of Afghanistan in Dec 1979 and the Polish crisis 1980–81. The final years of the Brezhnev administration were ones of hardening policy, mounting corruption, and economic stagnation.

Andropov and Chernenko Yuri Andropov, the former KGB chief, was elected CPSU leader on Brezhnev's death Nov 1982 and began energetically to introduce a series of radical economic reforms aimed at streamlining and decentralizing the planning system and inculcating greater labor discipline. Andropov also launched a campaign against corrupt and complacent party and state bureaucrats. These measures had a perceptible impact on the Soviet economy during 1983, but when Andropov died Feb 1984 he was succeeded by the cautious and elderly Brezhnev supporter Konstantin Chernenko. Chernenko held power as a stop-gap leader for 13 months, his sole initiative being a renewed search for détente with the US that was rejected by the hard-line Reagan administration.

Gorbachev's "market socialism" On Chernenko's death in March 1985, power was transferred to a new generation led by Mikhail Gorbachev, at 54 the CPSU's youngest leader since Stalin. Gorbachev introduced a number

of reforms. He began to free farmers and factory managers from bureaucratic interference and to increase material incentives in a "market socialist" manner. Working with Ideology Secretary Yegor Ligachev and Prime Minister Nikolai Ryzhkov, he restructured party and state bureaucracies and replaced cautious Brezhnevites with ambitious technocrats. Ligachev soon became the leading voice for the conservative wing of the Politburo and was increasingly considered an obstacle to Gorbachev's policies of *glasnost* ("openness"). Ligachev was demoted to the agriculture portfolio, and he was openly ridiculed and accused of corruption. Gorbachev made explicit his renunciation of the "Brezhnev doctrine" 1989.

These changes were not lost on the opposition leaders in the Baltic republics or on Communist deputies in the newly assertive Soviet Parliament. Lithuania declared it would permit free elections, then the Lithuanian Communist Party declared its independence from Moscow. By Jan 1990, Gorbachev was faced with growing calls for secession from the Soviet Union, and he had been forced to reconsider his earlier opposition to a multiparty system in the USSR itself. He also was provoked to declare a state of emergency and despatch troops to quell warfare between Armenians and Azerbaijanis, fighting each other for religious and territorial reasons.

détente initiative Working with Foreign Secretary Edvard Shevardnadze, Gorbachev made skillful use of the foreign media to put the case against space weapons and nuclear testing. He met US president Reagan in Geneva and Reykjavik in Nov 1985 and Oct 1986 and, at the Washington summit of Dec 1987, he concluded a treaty designed to eliminate medium-range Intermediate Nuclear Forces (INF) from European soil. This treaty was ratified at the Moscow summit of May–June 1988. As part of the new détente initiative, the USSR also withdrew all its troops from Afghanistan in Feb 1989 and made broad cutbacks in the size of its conventional forces 1989–90.

glasnost and perestroika Gorbachev pressed for an acceleration (*uskoreniye*) of his domestic, economic, and political program of restructuring (*perestroika*) from 1987, but faced growing opposition both from conservatives grouped around Ligachev and radicals led by Boris Yeltsin. Gorbachev's *glasnost* policy helped fan growing nationalist demands for secession among the republics of the Baltic and Transcaucasia. To add momentum to the reform process, in June 1988 Gorbachev convened a special 4,991 member All-Union Party Conference, the first since 1941. At this meeting a radical constitutional overhaul was approved. A new "super-legislature," the Congress of the USSR People's Deputies (CUPD), was created, from which a full-time working parliament was subsequently to be elected, headed by a state president with increased powers. The members of this CUPD were to be chosen in competition with one another. The authority of the local soviets was enhanced and their structures made more democratic, while, in the economic sphere, it was agreed to reintroduce private leasehold farming, reform the price system, and allow part-time private enterprise in the service and small-scale industry sectors.

"socialist pluralism" The June 1988 reforms constituted the most fundamental reordering of the Soviet policy since the "Stalinist departure" of 1928, entailing the creation of a new type of "socialist democracy," as well as a new mixed economic system. The CUPD elections of March–April 1989 showed clear opposition to conservative *apparatchiks*. In May 1989, the CUPD elected Gorbachev as its chair, and thus as state president. During 1989 this movement toward "socialist pluralism" was furthered by Gorbachev's abandonment of the ◊Brezhnev Doctrine and his sanctioning of the establishment of noncommunist and "reform communist" governments elsewhere in Eastern Europe. This led to the ruling regimes of Poland, Czechoslovakia, and Romania being overthrown in a wave of "people's power." Responding to these developments in Feb 1990, the CPSU Central Committee agreed to create a new directly elected state executive presidency on US and French models. In March 1990 the Soviet Parliament authorized private ownership of the means of production, forbidden since the 1920s. Further constitutional amendments made 1990 supported the right of self-determination, including secession of republics, and ended the CPSU's monopoly of power.

popular discontent The Gorbachev reform program showed signs of running out of control 1989–90 as a result both of growing nationalist tensions (which in April 1989 and Jan 1990 had prompted the despatch of troops to the Caucasus region) and mounting popular discontent over the failure of *perestroika* to improve living standards.

end of Cold War In their Dec 1989 summit meeting in Malta, Gorbachev and US president Bush declared an end to the Cold War, opening the possibility of most-favored-nation trading status with the US, membership in ◊General Agreement on Tariffs and Trade (GATT), and an influx of Western investment. A Gorbachev trip to Canada and the US followed May–June 1990 and a ◊Conference on Security and Cooperation in Europe (CSCE) in Paris Nov 1990.

moves toward independence in the republics Throughout 1990 the political and economic situation deteriorated. In pluralist elections held at local and republic levels, anticommunist, nationalist, and radical deputies polled strongly, particularly in the Baltic republics and cities. Their new governments issued declarations of republican sovereignty and, in the case of the Baltics, independence. These Moscow refused to recognize, and imposed a temporary economic blockade on Lithuania. As the year progressed, a "war of laws" developed between the center and the republics, who kept back funds (leading to a worsening federal budget deficit), and the system of central economic planning and resource distribution began to break down. As a consequence, with crime and labor unrest also increasing, the USSR's national income fell by at least 4% during 1990 and was to decline by a further 15% during 1991. Indeed, despite a bumper, but ill-collected, harvest, mounting food shortages led to rationing and an emergency international airlift of food aid during the winter of 1990–91.

break-up of the CPSU The CPSU also began to fracture during 1990 as a result of nationalist challenges within the republics and divisions among conservatives (grouped in the Soyuz and Communists for Russia bodies), liberals (Communists for Democracy), and radicals (Democratic Platform) over the direction and pace of economic and political reform. A split was formalized at the 28th CPSU Congress July 1990, when Boris Yeltsin, the new indirectly elected president of the RSFSR, and

Gavriil Popov and Anatoly Sobchak, radical mayors of Moscow and Leningrad, resigned their party membership. Earlier, in the RSFSR, a new Russian Communist Party had been formed.

Gorbachev's swing to the right In Dec 1990, concerned at the gathering pace of economic and political disintegration and ethnic strife, Gorbachev persuaded the Soviet parliament to vote him increased emergency presidential powers and approve a new federalized political structure. Subsequently, under pressure from the Soyuz group, the military, and the KGB, a clear rightward shift in policy became apparent.

proposed new union treaty From the spring of 1991, after his proposal to preserve the USSR as a "renewed federation of equal sovereign republics" secured public approval in a unionwide referendum (though boycotted by six republics), Gorbachev again attempted to reconstruct a center-left reform alliance with liberals and radicals. In April 1991 a pact aimed at achieving stable relations between the federal and republican governments and concerned with economic reform (price liberalization, progressive privatization, and the control of political strikes) was signed by the presidents of nine republics; the Baltic States, Armenia, Georgia, and Moldova refused to sign. Two months later, the draft of a new Union Treaty, entailing a much greater devolution of authority and the establishment of a new two-chamber federal legislature and a directly elected executive president, was also approved by nine republics. In July 1991 Gorbachev's standing was further enhanced by his attendance, as an invited guest, at the Group of Seven (G7) summit of the leaders of the chief industrialized Western countries, held in London, and the signing, in Moscow, of a Strategic Arms Reduction Treaty (START), to reduce the number of US and Soviet long-range nuclear missiles. At home, however, Boris Yeltsin, who was popularly elected as the RSFR's president June 1991, pressed for even greater reform and in July 1991 Communist Party cells were banned from operating in factories, farms, and government offices in the Russian Republic. In the same month a Democratic Reform Movement was formed by Eduard Shevardnadze, Alexander Yakovlev, and the mayors of Moscow and Leningrad, Anatoly Sobchak and Gavriil Popov.

abortive anti-Gorbachev coup These liberal-radical initiatives raised disquiet among CPSU conservatives and in June 1991 Prime Minister Pavlov unsuccessfully attempted to persuade the Soviet parliament to vote him extra powers. Two months later, on Monday Aug 19, 1991, a day before the new union treaty was to be signed, an attempted coup was launched by a reactionary alliance of leaders of the Communist Party *apparatchiki*, the military-industrial complex, the KGB, and the armed forces. It was declared in the early hours of the morning that President Gorbachev was ill and that Vice President Gennady Yanayev would take over as president, as part of an eight-person emergency committee, which also included Prime Minister Pavlov, Defense Minister Dmitri Yazov, KGB Chief Vladimir Kryuchkov, and Interior Minister Boris Pugo. The committee assumed control over radio and television, banned demonstrations and all but eight newspapers, imposed a curfew, and sent tanks into Moscow. They failed, however, to arrest the Russian president Boris Yeltsin, who defiantly stood out as head of a democratic "opposi-

tion state" based at the Russian Parliament, the so-called "White House," where external telephone links remained in operation. Yeltsin called for a general strike and the reinstatement of President Gorbachev. On Wednesday morning, having failed to wrest control of the "White House" and win either international or unionwide acknowledgment of the change of regime, and having endured large demonstrations in Moscow, St Petersburg (formerly Leningrad), Kishinev (Moldova), and Lvov (Ukraine) on Tuesday, the coup disintegrated. The junta's leaders were arrested and in the early hours of Thursday Aug 22 President Gorbachev, fully reinstated, arrived back in Moscow. There were 15 fatalities during the crisis.

aftermath of the coup In the wake of the failed coup, established communist structures, as well as the union itself, rapidly disintegrated, faced by a popular backlash which resulted in such icons of communism as the Felix Dzerzhinsky statue outside the KGB headquarters in Moscow being toppled and the Red Flag burned, being replaced by traditional, in some cases tsarist, symbols. President Gorbachev initially misjudged the changed mood, intimating his continued faith in the popularly discredited Communist Party and seeking to keep to a minimum of changes in personnel and institutions. However, forced by pressure exerted by the public and by Boris Yeltsin, whose stature both at home and abroad had been hugely enhanced, a succession of far-reaching reforms were instituted which effectively sounded the death knell of Soviet communism and resulted in the fracturing of the union and its subsequent refounding on a much changed and truncated basis.

The new union cabinet was effectively selected by Yeltsin and staffed largely with radical democrats from the Russian Republic—the Russian prime minister Ivan Silaev became the Soviet prime minister. Yeltsin also declared himself to have assumed charge of the armed forces within the Russian Republic and, at a heated session of the Russian Parliament, pressurized President Gorbachev into signing a decree suspending the activities of the Russian Communist Party. In addition, a new Russian national guard was established and control assumed over all economic assets in the republic. Recognizing the changed realities, Gorbachev announced Aug 24, 1991 that he was immediately resigning as general secretary of the Communist Party of the Soviet Union and ordered its Central Committee to dissolve itself.

republics declare independence The attempted coup also speeded up the movement toward dissolution of the Soviet Union. During the coup, when Red Army tanks were sent into their capitals with orders to seize radio and television stations, the Estonian and Latvian parliaments followed the earlier example of Lithuania and declared independence. After the coup the largely conservative-communist controlled republics of Azerbaijan, Belarus, and Uzbekistan, as well as the key republic of Ukraine, also joined the Baltics, Georgia, Moldova, and Armenia in declaring their independence. Their governments acted partly in the hope of shoring up their authority and privileges and partly because they feared Russian domination of the existing USSR and possible future territorial disputes.

new union treaty signed At an emergency session of the Congress of People's Deputies, the union was partially salvaged through the negotiation of a new union treaty in which each republic was to be allowed to decide its own terms of association, with much greater power being devolved from the center in what represented a new loose confederation, or "Union of Sovereign States," though with the armed forces retained under a single military command. Ten republics—the three Baltics, Georgia, and Moldova being the exceptions—declared a willingness to sign this agreement. The Congress also voted Sept 5, 1991 to establish a new system of government in which it would be abolished and its powers would be assumed by a revamped, two-chamber supreme soviet, with its upper chamber chosen by the republics and its decisions ratified by the latter; a state council (government), comprising President Gorbachev and the heads of the ten republics; and an interrepublican economic committee with equal representation from all 15 republics and chaired by Ivan Silaev. It also acknowledged the rights of republics to secede, opening the way Sept 6, 1991 for President Gorbachev to formally recognize the independence of the Baltic states by decree.

decentralization and new realities The possibility of forging a new, decentralized union receded as 1991 progressed. Concerned at the accumulation of political and economic authority by Russia, several of the republics began to seek full independence so as to escape Russian domination, refusing to sign new economic and political agreements. Although a declaration of intent to maintain a "common economic zone" of interrepublican free trade and to uphold existing factory ties was initialled Oct 1991, along with a civic and interethnic accord, the republics proved unable to agree on specific details of a proposed new economic and political union. As a consequence, President Gorbachev occupied the position of a figurehead leader, possessing little real authority, although his position was slightly strengthened by the return of Shevardnadze to head the foreign relations ministry Nov 1991. Instead, the preeminent leader in the former USSR, governing significantly from the former office of the CPSU Politburo, was Russia's president, Boris Yeltsin. In Nov 1991 the Russian Republic took over control of the Soviet money supply and exchange rate, and began implementing a market-centered economic reform program. On Nov 14 preliminary agreement was reached on the formation of a new "Union of Sovereign States," but in a subsequent meeting on Nov 25 the republican delegations that attended refused to initial the treaty.

The growing power of the individual republics became apparent in late Nov when the Group of Seven (G7) industrial countries reached a Soviet debt-deferral agreement with the USSR and included eight of the republics as signatories. On Dec 8, 1991 the most powerful of the republics –Russia, Belarus, and Ukraine—agreed to form the ◊Commonwealth of Independent States (CIS), a development denounced by Gorbachev. By mid-Dec, the five Central Asian republics (Kazakhstan, Kyrgyzstan, Tajikistan, Turkmenistan, and Uzbekistan) had announced that they would join the CIS, and Gorbachev had agreed on a transfer of power from the centralized government to the CIS. The remaining republics (Armenia, Azerbaijan, and Moldova) except Georgia, torn by civil war, joined the others in signing agreements on Dec 21 to establish the commonwealth, formally designated

an alliance of independent states. The formal dissolution of the USSR came on Dec 25 when Gorbachev resigned as president.

history
1917 Revolution: provisional democratic government established by Mensheviks. Communist takeover by Bolsheviks under Lenin.
1922 Soviet Union established.
1924 Death of Lenin.
1928 Stalin emerged as absolute ruler after ousting Trotsky.
1930s Purges of Stalin's opponents took place.
1939 Nonaggression pact signed with Germany.
1941–45 Great Patriotic War against Germany.
1949 Comecon created.
1953 Stalin died. Beria removed. "Collective leadership" in power.
1955 Warsaw Pact created.
1956 Khrushchev made February "secret speech." Hungarian uprising.
1957–58 Ousting of "antiparty" group and Bulganin.
1960 Sino-Soviet rift.
1962 Cuban missile crisis.
1964 Khrushchev ousted by new "collective leadership."
1968 Czechoslovakia invaded.
1969 Sino-Soviet border war.
1972 Salt I arms-limitation agreed with US.
1977 Brezhnev elected president.
1979 Salt II. Soviet invasion of Afghanistan.
1980 Kosygin replaced as prime minister by Tikhonov.
1980–81 Polish crisis.
1982 Deaths of Suslov and Brezhnev. Andropov became Communist Party leader.
1984 Chernenko succeeded Andropov.
1985 Gorbachev succeeded Chernenko and introduced wide-ranging reforms. Gromyko appointed president.
1986 Gorbachev's power consolidated at 27th Party Congress. Chernobyl nuclear disaster.
1987 USSR and US agreed to scrap intermediate-range nuclear missiles. Boris Yeltsin, Moscow party chief, dismissed for criticizing slow pace of reform.
1988 Nationalists challenged in Kazakhstan, Baltic republics, Armenia, and Azerbaijan. Earthquake killed thousands in Armenia. Constitution radically overhauled; private sector encouraged at Special All-Union Party Conference. Gorbachev replaced Gromyko as head of state.
1989 Troops withdrew from Afghanistan. General election held, with candidate choice for new congress of People's eputies. Nationalist riots in Georgia. 74 members of (25%) CPSU Central Committee removed. Gorbachev elected state president; conservative communist regimes in Eastern Europe overthrown. Relations with Chinese normalized. Lithuania allowed multiparty elections. Gorbachev and US president Bush declared end of Cold War; Gorbachev renounced "Brezhnev doctrine;" Soviet Union admitted invasion of Afghanistan and intervention in Czechoslovakia to have been mistakes; Gorbachev opposed calls to modify Soviet constitution; economic problems mounted; Lithuanian Communist Party declared independence from Moscow.
1990 Troops sent to Azerbaijan during civil war with Armenia. CPSU Central Committee agreed to end one-party rule. Increased powers voted to state president by CUPD. Gorbachev opposed independence of Baltic republics;

sanctions imposed on Lithuania; elections showed strength of liberal Communists. Boris Yeltsin elected president of Russian republic by RSFSR parliament and left the Communist Party. Summit meeting with President Bush. supreme soviet passed law allowing freedom of religious expression, ending official atheism.
1991 Plan to preserve USSR as "renewed federation of equal sovereign republics" approved in unionwide referendum, though boycotted by six republics. April: cooperation pact signed by Gorbachev and presidents of nine republics. June: Yeltsin elected president of Russian Republic in direct, popular election and issued decree banning Communist Party cells in the RSFSR. Shevardnadze left CPSU and, with other liberal reformers, formed Democratic Reform Movement. New Union treaty approved by nine republics. July: START treaty signed with US. Gorbachev addressed G7 leaders and obtained promise of technical help from West. Aug: coup by hard-line communists, led by Yanayev and Pavlov, removed Gorbachev from power; Gorbachev restored but position greatly undermined by Yeltsin who initiated a rapid dissolution of communist rule, the KGB, and all existing communist structures. In wake of failed coup several republics declared independence. Sept: independence of the republics of Latvia, Lithuania, and Estonia formally and internationally acknowledged. In following months remaining republics seceded piecemeal. Nov: Efforts to form a new "Union of Sovereign States" failed. Dec: Gorbachev resigned; new federated arrangement emerged, the Commonwealth of Independent States (CIS); Soviet parliament voted USSR out of existence.

unit standard quantity in relation to which other quantities are measured. There have been many systems of units. Some ancient units, such as the day, the foot, and the pound, are still in use. ◊SI units, the latest version of the metric system, are widely used in science.

UNITA (acronym for *União Nacional para a Independencia Total de Angola*/National Union for the Total Independence of Angola) Angolan nationalist movement backed by South Africa, which continued to wage guerrilla warfare against the ruling MPLA regime after the latter gained control of the country in 1976. The UNITA leader Jonas ◊Savimbi founded the movement 1966. A peace agreement ending the civil war between MPLA–PT and UNITA was signed May 1991, but fighting broke out again Sept 1992 after Savimbi disputed an election victory for the ruling party. UNITA forces rapidly took control of more than half the country, including northern diamond areas.

Unitarianism a Christian denomination that rejects the orthodox doctrine of the Trinity and gives a preeminent position to Jesus as a religious teacher, while denying his deity. Unitarians believe in individual conscience and reason as a guide to right action, rejecting the doctrines of original sin, the atonement, and eternal punishment. See also ◊Arianism.

Unitarianism arose independently in the 16th century in Poland, where its chief exponent was Faustus Socinus (1539–1604), and in the Transylvanian region of Hungary and Romania. During the 17th century a number of English writers began to accept Jesus' humanity while denying the doctrine of the Trinity. The movement grew amid the ◊rationalism of the 18th century, and the first Unitarian

United Arab Emirates

(UAE) (*Ittihad al-Imarat al-Arabiyah*) federation of the emirates of Abu Dhabi, Ajman, Dubai, Fujairah, Ras al Khaimah, Sharjah, Umm al Qaiwain

total area 32,292 sq mi/83,657 sq km
capital Abu Dhabi
cities (chief port) Dubai
physical desert and flat coastal plain; mountains in E
features linked by dependence on oil revenues
head of state and of government Sheik Sultan Zayed bin al-Nahayan of Abu Dhabi from 1971
political system absolutism
political parties none
exports oil, natural gas, fish, dates
currency UAE dirham
population (1990 est) 2,250,000 (10% nomadic); growth rate 6.1% p.a.
life expectancy men 68, women 72 (1989)
languages Arabic (official), Farsi, Hindi, Urdu, English
religion Muslim 96%, Christian, Hindu
literacy 68% (1989)
GNP $22 bn (1987); $11,900 per head
chronology
1952 Trucial Council established.
1971 Federation of Arab Emirates formed; later dissolved. Six Trucial States formed United Arab Emirates, with ruler of Abu Dhabi, Sheik Zayed, as president.
1972 The seventh state joined.
1976 Sheik Zayed threatened to relinquish presidency unless progress toward centralization became more rapid.
1985 Diplomatic and economic links with USSR and China established.
1987 Diplomatic relations with Egypt restored.
1990–91 Iraqi invasion of Kuwait opposed; UAE fights with UN coalition.
1991 Bank of Commerce and Credit International (BCCI), controlled by Abu Dhabi's ruler, collapsed.

(BCCI) had serious implications for the UAE because Abu Dhabi's ruler held a controlling interest in the bank. In Feb 1992 the Abu Dhabi government agreed to pay a sum amounting to $2.2 billion to creditors and depositors of the former BCCI.

Supreme Council of Rulers:
Abu Dhabi Sheik Sultan Zayed bin al-Nahayan, president (1966);
Ajman Sheik Humaid bin Rashid al-Nuami (1981);
Dubai Sheik Maktoum bin Rashid al-Maktoum (1990);
Fujairah Sheik Hamad bin Mohammed al-Sharqi (1974);
Ras al Khaimah Sheik Saqr bin Mohammed al-Quasimi (1948);
Sharjah Sheik Sultan bin Mohammed al-Quasimi (1972);
Umm al Qaiwain Sheik Rashid bin Ahmad al-Mu'alla (1981). *See illustration box.*

United Arab Republic union formed 1958, broken 1961, between ⟡Egypt and ⟡Syria. Egypt continued to use the name after the breach until 1971.

United Artists (UA) Hollywood film production, releasing, and distribution company formed 1919 by silent-screen stars Charles Chaplin, Mary Pickford, and Douglas Fairbanks, and director D W Griffith, in order to take control of their artistic and financial affairs.

United Australia Party Australian political party formed by Joseph ⟡Lyons 1931 from the right-wing Nationalist Party. It was led by Robert Menzies after the death of Lyons. Considered to have become too dominated by financial interests, it lost heavily to the Labor Party 1943, and was reorganized as the ⟡Liberal Party 1944.

United Irishmen society formed 1791 to campaign for parliamentary reform in Ireland. It later became a secret revolutionary group.
Inspired by the republican ideals of the French Revolution, the United Irishmen was initially a debating society, calling for reforms such as the right of Catholics to vote in Irish elections, but after an attempt to suppress it in 1793, the organization became secret, looking to France for military aid. An attempted insurrection 1798 was quickly defeated and the leaders captured.

United Kingdom (UK) country in NW Europe off the coast of France, consisting of England, Scotland, Wales, and Northern Ireland.
government The UK is a constitutional monarchy with parliamentary government. There is no written constitution. Cabinet government, which is at the heart of the system, is founded on rigid convention, and the relationship between the monarch as head of state and the prime minister as head of government is similarly based. Parliament is sovereign, in that it is free to make and unmake any laws that it chooses, and the government is subject to the laws that Parliament makes, as interpreted by the courts.
Parliament has two legislative and debating chambers, the House of Lords and the House of Commons. The House of Lords has three main kinds of members: those who are there by accident of birth, the hereditary peers; those who are there because of some office they hold; and those who are appointed to serve for life, the life peers. There are nearly 800 hereditary peers. Among those sitting by virtue of their position are 2 archbishops and

chapel was established in London 1774. American Unitarianism emerged as a secession movement from the Congregational Church in New England. Its most eloquent spokesman was William Ellery Channing (1780–1842). The transcendentalism of ⟡Emerson and ⟡Thoreau was a major influence on American Unitarianism. In the 20th century, Unitarianism became identified closely with a liberal political stance and the cause of world peace, and its specific Christian affinities have been replaced gradually by a rational commitment to the moral and spiritual progress of humanity. The chief Unitarian body in the US is the Unitarian Universalist Association, formed 1961 by the merger of the American Unitarian Association and the Universalist Church.

Unitas John Constantine 1933– . US football player. Born in Pittsburgh, Unitas was a football star for the University of Louisville and was drafted by the Pittsburgh Steelers of the National Football League (NFL) 1955. Released after a single season, he was signed by the Baltimore Colts 1956. As Colt quarterback for 17 seasons, Unitas led the team to 5 NFL championship titles in the years 1958–71. Following his release from the Colts, Unitas played for the San Diego Chargers 1973. One of the greatest passers in the history of the game, he was elected to the Football Hall of Fame 1979.

United Arab Emirates federation in SW Asia, on the Arabian Gulf, bounded NW by Qatar, SW by Saudi Arabia, and SE by Oman.
government A provisional constitution for the United Arab Emirates (UAE) has been in effect since Dec 1971 and provides a federal structure for a union of seven sheikdoms. The highest authority is the Supreme Council of Rulers, which includes all seven sheiks. Each is a hereditary emir and an absolute monarch in his own country. The council elects two of its members to be president and vice-president of the federal state for a five-year term. The

president then appoints a prime minister and council of ministers.
There is a federal national council of 40 members appointed by the emirates for a two-year term, and this operates as a consultative assembly. There are no political parties.
history For early history, see ⟡Arabia. In 1952 the seven sheikdoms of Abu Dhabi, Ajman, Dubai, Fujairah, Ras al Khaimah, Sharjah, and Umm al Qaiwain set up, on British advice, the Trucial Council, consisting of all seven rulers, with a view to eventually establishing a federation. In the 1960s the Trucial States, as they were known, became very wealthy through the exploitation of oil deposits.
The whole area was under British protection, but in 1968 the British government announced that it was withdrawing its forces within three years. The seven Trucial States, with Bahrain and Qatar, formed the Federation of Arab Emirates, which was intended to become a federal state, but in 1971 Bahrain and Qatar seceded to become independent nations. Six of the Trucial States then combined to form the United Arab Emirates. The remaining sheikdom, Ras al Khaimah, joined Feb 1972. Sheik Sultan Zayed bin al-Nahayan, the ruler of Abu Dhabi, became the first president.
In 1976 Sheik Zayed, disappointed with the slow progress toward centralization, was persuaded to accept another term as president only with assurances that the federal government would be given more control over such activities as defense and internal security. In recent years the United Arab Emirates has played an increasingly prominent role in Middle East affairs, and in 1985 it established diplomatic and economic links with the USSR and China.
In 1990–91, the UAE opposed Iraq's invasion of Kuwait and contributed troops and economic support to the UN coalition that defeated Iraq in the ⟡Gulf War. The international financial scandal surrounding the 1991 collapse of the ⟡Bank of Commerce and Credit International

United Kingdom
of Great Britain and Northern Ireland (UK)

area 94,247 sq mi/244,100 sq km
capital London
cities Birmingham, Glasgow, Leeds, Sheffield, Liverpool, Manchester, Edinburgh, Bradford, Bristol, Belfast, Newcastle-upon-Tyne, Cardiff
physical became separated from European continent about 6000 BC; rolling landscape, increasingly mountainous toward the N, with Grampian Mountains in Scotland, Pennines in N England, Cambrian Mountains in Wales; rivers include Thames, Severn, and Spey
territories Anguilla, Bermuda, British Antarctic Territory, British Indian Ocean Territory, British Virgin Islands, Cayman Islands, Falkland Islands, Gibraltar, Hong Kong (until 1997), Montserrat, Pitcairn Islands, St Helena and Dependencies (Ascension, Tristan da Cunha), Turks and Caicos Islands
environment an estimated 67% (the highest percentage in Europe) of forests have been damaged by acid rain
features milder climate than N Europe because of Gulf Stream; considerable rainfall. Nowhere more than 74.5 mi/120 km from sea; indented coastline, various small islands
head of state Elizabeth II from 1952
head of government John Major from 1990
political system liberal democracy
political parties Conservative and Unionist Party, right-of-center; Labour Party, moderate, left-of-center; Social and Liberal Democrats, center-left; Scottish National Party (SNP), Scottish nationalist; Plaid Cymru (Welsh Nationalist Party), Welsh nationalist; Official Ulster Unionist Party (OUP), Northern Ireland moderate right-of-center; Democratic Unionist Party (DUP), Northern Ireland, right-of-center; Social Democratic Labour Party

(SDLP), Northern Ireland, moderate, left-of-center; Ulster People's Unionist Party (UPUP), Northern Ireland, militant right-of-center; Sinn Féin, Northern Ireland, pro-united Ireland; Green Party, ecological
exports cereals, rape, sugar beet, potatoes, meat and meat products, poultry, dairy products, electronic and telecommunications equipment, engineering equipment and scientific instruments, oil and gas, petrochemicals, pharmaceuticals, fertilizers, film and television programs, aircraft
currency pound sterling
population (1990 est) 57,121,000 (81.5% English, 9.6% Scottish, 1.9% Welsh, 2.4% Irish, 1.8% Ulster); growth rate 0.1% p.a.
religion Christian (55% Protestant, 10% Roman Catholic); Muslim, Jewish, Hindu, Sikh
life expectancy men 72, women 78 (1989)
languages English, Welsh, Gaelic
literacy 99% (1989)
GNP $758 bn; $13,329 per head (1988)
chronology
1707 Act of Union between England and Scotland under Queen Anne.
1721 Robert Walpole unofficially first prime minister, under George I.
1783 Loss of North American colonies that form US; Canada retained.
1801 Act of Ireland united Britain and Ireland.
1819 Peterloo massacre: cavalry charged a meeting of supporters of parliamentary reform.
1832 Great Reform Bill became law, shifting political power from upper to middle class.
1838 Chartist working-class movement formed.
1846 Corn Laws repealed by Robert Peel.
1851 Great Exhibition in London.
1867 Second Reform Bill, extending the franchise, introduced by Disraeli and passed.
1906 Liberal victory; program of social reform.
1911 Powers of House of Lords curbed.
1914 Irish Home Rule Bill introduced.
1914–18 World War I.
1916 Lloyd George became prime minister.
1920 Home Rule Act incorporated NE of Ireland (Ulster) into the United Kingdom of Great Britain and Northern Ireland.
1921 Ireland, except for Ulster, became a dominion (Irish Free State, later Eire, 1937).
1924 First Labour government led by Ramsay MacDonald.
1926 General Strike.
1931 Coalition government; unemployment reached 3 million.
1939 World War II began.
1940 Winston Churchill became head of coalition government.
1945 Labour government under Clement Attlee; welfare state established.

1951 Conservatives under Winston Churchill defeated Labour.
1956 Suez Crisis.
1964 Labour victory under Harold Wilson.
1970 Conservatives under Edward Heath defeated Labour.
1972 Parliament prorogued in Northern Ireland; direct rule from Westminster began.
1973 UK joined European Economic Community.
1974 Three-day week, coal strike; Wilson replaced Heath.
1976 James Callaghan replaced Wilson as prime minister.
1977 Liberal–Labour pact.
1979 Victory for Conservatives under Margaret Thatcher.
1981 Formation of Social Democratic Party (SDP). Riots occurred in inner cities.
1982 Unemployment over 3 million. Falklands War.
1983 Thatcher reelected.
1984–85 Coal strike, the longest in British history.
1986 Abolition of metropolitan counties.
1987 Thatcher reelected for third term.
1988 Liberals and most of SDP merged into the Social and Liberal Democrats, leaving a splinter SDP. Inflation and interest rates rose.
1989 The Green Party polled 2 million votes in the European elections.
1990 Riots as poll tax introduced in England. Troops sent to the Persian Gulf following Iraq's invasion of Kuwait. British hostages held in Iraq, later released. Britain joined European exchange rate mechanism (ERM). Thatcher replaced by John Major as Conservative leader and prime minister.
1991 British troops took part in US-led war against Iraq under United Nations umbrella. Support was given to the USSR during the dissolution of communism and the restoration of independence to the republics. John Major visited Beijing to sign agreement with China on new Hong Kong airport. At home, Britain suffered severe economic recession and rising unemployment.
1992 Economic recession continued. April: Conservative Party, led by John Major, won fourth consecutive general election, but with reduced majority. Neil Kinnock resigned. July: John Smith became new Labour leader. Sept: sterling devalued and UK withdrawn from ERM. Oct: drastic coal-mine closure program encountered massive public opposition; subsequently reviewed. Major's popularity at unprecedentedly low rating. Nov: government motion in favor of ratification of Maastricht Treaty narrowly passed. Revelations of past arms sales to Iraq implicated senior government figures.

24 bishops of the Church of England and 9 senior judges, known as the law lords. The appointed life peers include about 65 women, or peeresses. The House of Commons has 650 members, elected by universal adult suffrage from single-member geographical constituencies, each constituency containing, on average, about 65,000 electors.

Although the House of Lords is termed the upper house, its powers, in relation to those of the Commons, have been steadily reduced so that now it has no control over financial legislation and merely a delaying power, of a year, over other bills. Before an act of Parliament becomes law it must pass through a five-stage process in each chamber—first reading, sec-

ond reading, committee stage, report stage, and third reading—and then receive the formal royal assent. Bills, other than financial ones, can be introduced in either house, but most begin in the Commons.

The monarch appoints as prime minister the leader of the party with most support in the House of Commons and he or she, in turn, chooses and presides over a cabinet. The voting system, which does not include any form of proportional representation, favors two-party politics, and both chambers of Parliament are physically designed to accommodate two parties, the ruling party sitting on one side of the presiding Speaker and the opposition on the other. The party with the second largest num-

ber of seats in the Commons is recognized as the official opposition, and its leader is paid a salary out of public funds and provided with an office within the Palace of Westminster, as the Houses of Parliament are called.

history For early history, see ⊳Britain, ancient; ⊳England: history; ⊳Scotland: history; ⊳Wales: history; ⊳Ireland: history. The term "United Kingdom" became official 1801, but was in use from 1707, when the Act of Union combined Scotland and England into the United Kingdom of Great Britain. Cabinet government developed under Robert Walpole, in practice the first prime minister (1721–42). Two ⊳Jacobite rebellions sought to restore the Stuarts to the throne until the Battle of ◊Culloden 1746, after which the Scottish Highlanders were brutally suppressed. The American colonies that became the US were lost in the ◊American Revolution.

The Act of Ireland 1801 united Britain and Ireland. This was the time of the ◊Industrial Revolution, the mechanization of production that shifted the balance of political power from the landowner to the industrial capitalist and created an exploited urban working class. In protest, the ◊Luddites destroyed machinery. Agricultural enclosures were driving the small farmers off the land. The alliance of the industrialists with the Whigs produced a new party, the Liberals, with an ideology of ◊free trade and nonintervention in economic affairs. In 1832 they carried a Reform Bill transferring political power from the aristocracy to the middle classes and for the next 40 years the Liberal Party was a major force. The working classes, who had no vote, created their own organizations in the labor unions and ◊Chartism; their attempts to seek parliamentary reform were brutally suppressed (at the ◊Peterloo massacre 1819). The Conservative prime minister Robert Peel introduced a number of domestic reforms, including the repeal of the Corn Laws 1846.

After 1875 the UK's industrial monopoly was challenged by Germany and the US. To seek new markets and sources of raw materials, the Conservatives under Disraeli launched the UK on a career of imperialist expansion in Egypt, South Africa, and elsewhere. Canada, Australia, and New Zealand became self-governing dominions.

World War I and the Depression The domestic issues after 1900 were social reform and home rule for Ireland; the Labour Party emerged from an alliance of labor unions and small socialist bodies 1900; the ◊suffragists were active until ◊World War I. After the war a wave of strikes culminated in the general strike 1926; three years later a world economic crisis precipitated the Depression that marked the 1930s and brought to power a coalition government 1931.

The following years were dominated by unemployment, which reached almost 3 million in 1933, and the approach of ◊World War II. The death of George V Jan 1936 brought Edward VIII to the throne, closely followed by the ◊abdication crisis precipitated by his desire to marry US divorcee Wallis Simpson. In Dec 1936, Edward VIII abdicated, and George VI came to the throne.

World War II In 1939 Germany invaded Poland, and Britain entered World War II by declaring war on Germany. In 1940 Winston Churchill became prime minister, leader of the Conservative Party, and head of a coalition government. The country sustained intensive bombardment in the "Battle of Britain" July–Oct 1940, and the "blitz" of night bombing which affected especially London and Coventry. After the defeat of Germany 1945, the Labour Party, led by Clement Attlee, gained power.

reform and renewal In 1945 the UK was still nominally at the head of an empire that covered a fourth of the world's surface and included a fourth of its population, and, although two world wars had gravely weakened it, many of its citizens and some of its politicians still saw it as a world power. The reality of its position soon became apparent when the newly elected Labour government confronted the problems of rebuilding the war-damaged economy. This renewal was greatly helped, as in other W

European countries, by support from the US through the ◊Marshall Plan. Between 1945 and 1951 the Labour government carried out an ambitious program of public ownership and investment and laid the foundations of a national health service and welfare state. During the same period the dismemberment of the British Empire, restyled the British ◊Commonwealth, was begun, a process that was to continue into the 1980s.

Suez Crisis When in 1951 the Conservative Party was returned to power, under Winston Churchill, the essential features of the welfare state and the public sector were retained. In 1955 Churchill, in his 81st year, was succeeded by the foreign secretary, Anthony Eden. In 1956 Eden found himself confronted by the takeover of the Suez Canal by the president of Egypt, Gamal Nasser. Eden's perception of the threat posed by Nasser was not shared by everyone, even within the Conservative Party. The British invasion of Egypt, in conjunction with France and Israel, brought widespread criticism and was abandoned in the face of pressure from the US and the United Nations. Eden resigned, and the Conservatives chose Harold Macmillan as their new leader and prime minister.

European Economic Community By the early 1960s, the economy had improved, living standards had risen, and Prime Minister Harold Macmillan was known as "Supermac." Internationally, he established working relationships with the US presidents Eisenhower and Kennedy. He also did much for the Commonwealth, but he was sufficiently realistic to see that the UK's long-term economic and political future lay in Europe. By the mid-1950s the framework for the European Economic Community (EEC) had been created, with the UK an onlooker rather than a participant. The Conservatives won the 1959 general election with an increased majority, and in 1961 the first serious attempt was made to join the EEC, only to have it blocked by the French president, Charles de Gaulle.

UK's poor economic performance Despite rising living standards, the UK's economic performance was not as successful as that of many of its competitors, such as West Germany and Japan. There was a growing awareness that there was insufficient investment in industry, that young talent was going into the professions or financial institutions rather than manufacturing, and that training was poorly planned and inadequately funded. It was against this background that Macmillan unexpectedly resigned 1963, on the grounds of ill health, and was succeeded by the foreign secretary, Lord Home, who immediately renounced his title to become Alec Douglas-Home.

In the general election 1964 the Labour Party won a slender majority, and its leader, Harold Wilson, became prime minister. The election had been fought on the issue of the economy. Wilson created the Department of Economic Affairs (DEA) to challenge the short-term conservatism of the Treasury, and brought in a leading labor unionist to head a new Department of Technology. In an early general election 1966 Wilson increased his Commons majority, but his promises of fundamental changes in economic planning, industrial investment, and improved work practices were not fulfilled. The DEA was disbanded 1969 and an ambitious plan for the reform of industrial relations was dropped in the face of labor union opposition.

Heath's "counter-revolution" In 1970 the Conservatives returned to power under Edward Heath. He, too, saw institutional change as one way of achieving industrial reform and created two new central departments (Trade and Industry, Environment) and a "think tank" to advise the government on long-term strategy, the Central Policy Review Staff (CPRS). He attempted to change the climate of industrial relations through a long and complicated Industrial Relations Bill. He saw entry into the EEC as the "cold shower of competition" that industry needed, and membership was negotiated 1972.

national miners' strike Heath's "counter-revolution," as he saw it, was frustrated by the labor unions, and the sharp rise in oil prices 1973 forced a U-turn in economic policy. Instead of abandoning "lame ducks" to their fate, he found it necessary to take ailing industrial companies, such as Rolls-Royce, into public ownership. The introduction of a statutory incomes policy precipitated a national miners' strike in the winter of 1973–74 and Heath decided to challenge the unions by holding an early general election 1974. The result was a hung Parliament, with Labour winning the biggest number of seats but no single party having an overall majority. Heath tried briefly to form a coalition with the Liberals and, when this failed, resigned.

Wilson's "social contract" Harold Wilson returned to the premiership, heading a minority government, but in another general election later the same year won enough additional seats to give him a working majority. He had taken over a damaged economy and a nation puzzled and divided by the events of the previous years. He turned to Labour's natural ally and founder, the labor union movement, for support and jointly they agreed on a "social contract:" the government pledged itself to redress the imbalance between management and unions created by the Heath industrial-relations legislation, and the unions promised to cooperate in a voluntary industrial and incomes policy. Wilson met criticism from a growing left-wing movement within his party, impatient for radical change. In March 1976 Wilson, apparently tired and disillusioned, retired in mid-term.

financial crisis Wilson was succeeded by James Callaghan, his senior by some four years. In the other two parties, Heath had unexpectedly been ousted by Margaret Thatcher, and the Liberal Party leader, Jeremy Thorpe, had resigned after a personal scandal and been succeeded by the young Scottish MP David Steel. Callaghan was now leading a divided party and a government with a dwindling parliamentary majority. Later in 1976 an unexpected financial crisis arose from a drop in confidence in the overseas exchange markets, a rapidly falling pound, and a drain on the country's foreign reserves. After considerable debate within the cabinet, both before and afterwards, it was decided to seek help from the International Monetary Fund and submit to its stringent economic policies. Within weeks the crisis was over and within months the economy was showing clear signs of improvement.

"Lib–Lab Pact" In 1977, to shore up his slender parliamentary majority, Callaghan entered into an agreement with the new leader of the Liberal Party, David Steel. Under the "Lib–Lab Pact" Labour pursued moderate, nonconfrontational policies in consultation with the Liberals, who, in turn, voted with the government, and the economy improved

dramatically. The Lib–Lab Pact had effectively finished by the autumn of 1978, and soon the social contract with the unions began to disintegrate. Widespread and damaging strikes in the public sector badly affected essential services during what became known as the "winter of discontent." At the end of March 1979 Callaghan lost a vote of confidence in the House of Commons and was forced into a general election.

Conservatives under Thatcher The Conservatives returned to power under the UK's first woman prime minister, Margaret Thatcher. She inherited a number of inflationary public-sector pay awards that, together with a budget that doubled the rate of value added tax, resulted in a sharp rise in prices and interest rates. The Conservatives were pledged to reduce inflation and did so by mainly monetarist policies, which caused the number of unemployed to rise from 1.3 million to 2 million in the first year. Thatcher had experience in only one government department, and it was nearly two years before she made any major changes to the cabinet she inherited from Heath. In foreign affairs Zimbabwe became independent 1980 after many years, and without the bloodshed many had feared.

creation of SDP Meanwhile, changes were taking place in the other parties. Callaghan resigned the leadership of the Labour Party 1980 and was replaced by the left-winger Michael Foot, and early in 1981 three Labour shadow cabinet members, David Owen, Shirley Williams, and William Rodgers, with the former deputy leader Roy Jenkins (collectively dubbed the "Gang of Four"), broke away to form a new centrist group, the ◊Social Democratic Party (SDP). The new party made an early impression, winning a series of by-elections within months of its creation. From 1983 to 1988 the Liberals and the SDP were linked in an electoral pact, the Alliance. They advocated the introduction of a system of proportional representation, which would ensure a fairer parity between votes gained and seats won.

Falklands War Unemployment continued to rise, passing the 3 million mark Jan 1982, and the Conservatives and their leader were receiving low ratings in the public-opinion polls. An unforeseen event rescued them, the invasion of the Falkland Islands by Argentina. Thatcher's decision to send a battle fleet to recover the islands paid off. The general election 1983 was fought with the euphoria of the Falklands victory still in the air and the Labour Party, under its new leader, divided and unconvincing. The Conservatives had a landslide victory, winning more Commons seats than any party since 1945, although with less than half the popular vote. Thatcher was able to establish her position firmly, replacing most of her original cabinet.

domestic problems The next three years were marked by rising unemployment and growing dissent: a dispute at the government's main intelligence-gathering station, GCHQ; a bitter and protracted miners' strike; increasing violence in Northern Ireland; an attempted assassination of leading members of the Conservative Party during their annual conference; and riots in inner-city areas of London, Bristol, and Liverpool. The government was further embarrassed by its own prosecutions under the Official Secrets Act and the resignations of two prominent cabinet ministers. With the short-term profits from North Sea oil and an ambitious privatization program, the inflation

rate continued to fall and by the winter of 1986–87 the economy was buoyant enough to allow the chancellor of the Exchequer to arrange a preelection spending and credit boom.

party leadership changes Leadership changes took place by 1987 in two of the other parties. Michael Foot was replaced by his Welsh protégé, Neil Kinnock; Roy Jenkins was replaced by David Owen as SDP leader, to be succeeded in turn by Robert MacLennan Sept 1987, when the SDP and Liberal parties voted to initiate talks toward a merger. Despite high unemployment and Thatcher's increasingly authoritarian style of government, the Conservatives were reelected June 1987.

The merger of the Liberal and Social Democratic parties was an acrimonious affair, with the SDP, led by David Owen, refusing to join the merged party and operating as a rival group. Paddy Ashdown emerged as the leader of the new party.

In a cabinet reshuffle July 1989, Geoffrey Howe was replaced as foreign secretary by John Major. In Oct 1989 the chancellor of the Exchequer, Nigel Lawson, resigned because of disagreements with the prime minister, and Major replaced him. Douglas Hurd took over the foreign office. In Dec 1989 Mrs Thatcher won the party leadership election. The government was widely criticized for its decision forcibly to repatriate Vietnamese "boat people" and for the perceived over-liberality of its decision to give UK right of abode to the families of 50,000 "key" Hong Kong citizens, after the transfer of the colony to China 1997. David Owen announced that the SDP would no longer be able to fight in all national constituencies and would only operate as a "guerrilla force." The Green Party polled 2 million votes in the European elections. The Labour Party launched a new policy review.

Thatcher challenged In Sept 1990 the House of Commons was recalled for an emergency debate that endorsed the government's military activities in the Persian Gulf. In Oct the government announced that it was joining the European exchange-rate mechanism (ERM). In Nov the deputy prime minister, Geoffrey Howe, gave a dramatic resignation speech, strongly critical of Thatcher. Michael Heseltine then announced his candidacy for the leadership of the Conservative Party. Having failed to gain a clear victory in the first ballot of the leadership election, Thatcher was eventually persuaded by her colleagues to withdraw from the contest. In the subsequent second ballot Michael Heseltine (131 votes) and Douglas Hurd (56) conceded that John Major (185) had won. He consequently became party leader and prime minister.

Major's leadership Major was initially popular for his consensual style of leadership, but dissatisfaction with the poll tax continued and was seen as the main cause of a 25% swing away from the Conservatives in a March 1991 by-election. Another form of local taxation to replace the poll tax was announced, but did not repair the damage done to the Conservative Party, which sustained heavy losses in the May 1991 local elections. The deterioration of the National Health Service was also an issue. Despite the apparent waning popularity of the Conservative government and almost two years of economic recession, the party won its fourth consecutive victory in the April 1992 general election, with a reduced majority. Neil Kinnock announced his resignation as leader of the Labour Party; John Smith was elected as the new Labour leader July 1992.

financial crisis With a deepening recession and international pressure on the pound, the government was forced to devalue Sept 1992 and leave the Exchange Rate Mechanism (ERM). Further criticism in Oct forced it to fundamentally review its economic strategy.

coal-mine closures In the same month, a drastic coal-mine closure program was announced, involving the loss of 30,000 miners' jobs. The announcement met with such massive public opposition that the the government was forced to backtrack and review its policy. John Major's leadership and the ability of the Conservative government to rule the country were questioned and the party suffered internal division and loss of public respect.

closer European union In November 1992, the government had a narrow majority (3) on ratification of the Maastricht Treaty on closer European economic and political union.

Iraqgate scandal Revelations of British arms sales to Iraq prior to the 1991 Gulf War and the alleged complicity of senior Conservative figures, including John Major, further damaged the government's public image. See illustration box.

United Nations (UN) association of states for international peace, security, and cooperation, with its headquarters in New York. The UN was established 1945 as a successor to the ◊League of Nations, and has played a role in many areas, such as refugees, development assistance, disaster relief, and cultural cooperation. Its total proposed budget for 1992/93 was $2,006 million. Boutros ◊Boutros-Ghali became secretary-general 1992.

Members contribute financially according to their resources, an apportionment being made by the General Assembly, with the addition of voluntary contributions from some governments to the funds of the UN. These finance the program of assistance carried out by the UN intergovernmental agencies, the **United Nations Children's Fund** (UNICEF), the UN refugee organizations, and the **United Nations Special Fund** for developing countries. Total unpaid contributions of about $988 million had by the end of 1991 brought the UN to the brink of insolvency. Fewer than half the members had paid their full contributions. There are six official working languages: English, French, Russian, Spanish, Chinese, and Arabic.

The UN charter was drawn up at the San Francisco Conference 1945, based on proposals drafted at the Dumbarton Oaks conference. The original intention was that the UN's Security Council would preserve the wartime alliance of the US, USSR, and Britain (with France and China also permanent members) in order to maintain the peace. This never happened because of the outbreak of the Cold War.

The influence in the UN, originally with the Allied states of World War II, is now more widely spread. Although part of the value of the UN lies in recognition of member states as sovereign and equal, the rapid increase in membership in minor (in some cases minute) states was causing concern by 1980 (154 members) as lessening the weight of voting decisions. Taiwan, formerly a permanent member of the Security Council, was expelled 1971 on the admission of China. The breakup of the USSR and the increasing recognition of independent states throughout the world resulted in a further increase in UN membership between 1990 and 1992. The Russian Federation took over the Soviet permanent seat on the Security Council.

The US regularly (often alone or nearly so) votes against General Assembly resolutions on aggression, international law, human-rights abuses, and disarmament, and has exercised its veto on the Security Council more times than any other member (the UK is second, France a distant third). The UN suffers from a lack of adequate and independent funds and forces, the latter having been employed with varying success, for example, in Korea, Cyprus, and Sinai, and the intrusion of the Cold War which divided members into adherents of the East or West and the uncommitted. However, as secretary-general 1982–91, Javier Pérez de Cuéllar was responsible for several successful peace initiatives, including the ending of the Iran-Iraq War and the withdrawal of South African and Cuban troops from Angola. The UN also responded promptly to the Iraqi invasion of Kuwait 1990 but was less successful in its efforts to establish a permanent peace in the former republics of Yugoslavia.

The principal UN institutions (all based in New York except the International Court of Justice in The Hague) are:

General Assembly one member from each of 178 member states who meet annually for a session generally lasting from late Sept to the end of the year; it can be summoned at any time for an emergency session. Decisions are made by simple majority voting, but on certain important issues, such as the condemnation of an act by one of its members, a two-thirds majority is needed;

Security Council see ⟡United Nations Security Council;

Economic and Social Council 54 members elected for three years, one-third retiring in rotation; presidency rotating on same system as Security Council. It initiates studies of international economic, social, cultural, educational, health, and related matters, and may make recommendations to the General Assembly. It operates largely through specialized commissions of international experts on economics, transport and communications, human rights, status of women, and so on, as well as regional commissions and hundreds of nongovernmental agencies that have been granted consultative status. It coordinates the activities of the ⟡**Food and Agriculture Organization** (FAO);

Trusteeship Council responsible for overseeing the administration of the UN trust territories. Its members are China, France, the Russian Federation, the UK, and the US. It holds one regular session a year and can meet in special sessions if required;

International Court of Justice 15 independent judges, elected by the Security Council and the General Assembly on the basis of their competence in international law and irrespective of their nationalities, except that no two judges can be nationals of the same state. They serve for nine years and may be immediately reelected. The president and vice-president are elected by the court for three-year terms. Decisions are by majority vote of the judges present, and the president has a casting vote. Only states, not individuals, can be parties to cases before the court. There is no appeal;

Secretariat the chief administrator of the UN is the secretary-general, who has under- and assistant secretaries general and a large international staff. The secretary-general is appointed by the General Assembly for a renewable five-year term.

UN specialized agencies are:

General Agreement on Tariffs and Trade (GATT) established 1948, headquarters in Geneva; reduction of trade barriers, antidumping code, assistance to trade of developing countries;

⟡**International Atomic Energy Agency** (IAEA);

International Bank for Reconstruction and Development (IBRD) popularly known as the ⟡World Bank;

International Civil Aviation Organization (ICAO) established 1947, headquarters in Montreal; safety and efficiency, international facilities and air law;

International Development Association (IDA) administered by the World Bank;

International Finance Corporation (IFC) established 1956; affiliated to the World Bank, it encourages private enterprise in less industrialized countries;

International Fund for Agricultural Development (IFAD) established 1977, headquarters in Rome; additional funds for benefiting the poorest in Third World countries;

⟡**International Labor Organization** (ILO);

International Maritime Organization (IMO) established 1958, headquarters in London; safety at sea, pollution control, abolition of restrictive practices;

⟡**International Monetary Fund** (IMF);

International Telecommunication Union (ITU) established 1934, headquarters in Geneva; allocation of radio frequencies; promotes low tariffs and life-saving measures for, for example, disasters at sea;

United Nations Center for Human Settlements (UNCHS) (Habitat) established 1978, headquarters in Nairobi, Kenya;

United Nations Conference on Trade and Development (UNCTAD) established 1964, headquarters in Geneva;

United Nations Development Program (UNDP) established 1960 to promote higher standards of living in the poorer nations and to try to remedy the economic imbalance between North and South; has 48 members, 15 of them in advanced industrial countries and the rest in varying stages of industrialization; headquarters in New York;

Office of the United Nations Disaster Relief Coordinator (UNDRO) established 1972 to coordinate international relief; headquarters in Geneva;

United Nations Environment Program (UNEP) established 1972 to monitor the state of the environment and promote environmentally sound developments throughout the world; headquarters in Nairobi;

United Nations Educational, Scientific, and Cultural Organization (⟡UNESCO);

United Nations Fund for Population Activities (UNFPA) established 1972 under the umbrella of UNDP, headquarters in New York;

United Nations High Commission for Refugees (UNHCR) established 1951, headquarters in Geneva;

United Nations International Children's Fund (UNICEF) established 1953, headquarters in New York;

United Nations Institute for Training and Research (UNITAR) established 1965, headquarters in New York;

United Nations Research Institute for Social Development (UNRISD) established 1964, headquarters in Geneva;

⟡**Universal Postal Union** (UPU);

World Food Council (WFC) established 1974, headquarters in Rome;

World Food Program (WFP) established 1963 to improve economic and social development through food aid and to provide emergency relief; headquarters in Rome;

⟡**World Health Organization** (WHO);

World Intellectual Property Organization (WIPO) established 1974, headquarters in Geneva; protection of copyright in the arts, science, and industry;

World Meteorological Organization (WMO) established 1951, headquarters in Geneva.

UN membership

country	year of admission	contribution to UN budget (%)
Afghanistan	1946	0.01
Albania	1955	0.01
Algeria	1962	0.16
Angola	1976	0.01
Antigua & Barbuda	1981	0.01
Argentina †	1945	0.57
Armenia	1992	***
Australia †	1945	1.51
Austria	1955	0.75
Azerbaijan	1992	***
Bahamas	1973	0.02
Bahrain	1971	0.03
Bangladesh	1974	0.01
Barbados	1966	0.01
Belarus †	1945	0.31
Belgium †	1945	1.06
Belize	1981	0.01
Benin	1960	0.01
Bhutan	1971	0.01
Bolivia †	1945	0.01
Bosnia-Herzegovina	1992	***
Botswana	1966	0.01
Brazil †	1945	1.59
Brunei	1984	0.03
Bulgaria	1955	0.13
Burkina Faso	1960	0.01
Burundi	1962	0.01
Cambodia	1955	0.01
Cameroon	1960	0.01
Canada †	1945	3.11
Cape Verde	1975	0.01
Central African Republic	1960	0.01
Chad	1960	0.01
Chile †	1945	0.08
China †	1945	0.77
Colombia †	1945	0.13
Comoros	1975	0.01
Congo	1960	0.01
Costa Rica †	1945	0.01
Côte d'Ivoire	1960	0.02
Croatia	1992	***
Cuba †	1945	0.09
Cyprus	1960	0.02
Czechoslovakia †	1945	0.55
Denmark †	1945	0.65
Djibouti	1977	0.01
Dominica	1978	0.01
Dominican Republic †	1945	0.02
Ecuador †	1945	0.03
Egypt †	1945	0.07
El Salvador †	1945	0.01
Equatorial Guinea	1968	0.01
Estonia	1991	***
Ethiopia †	1945	0.01
Fiji	1970	0.01
Finland	1955	0.57
France †	1945	6.00
Gabon	1960	0.02
Gambia	1965	0.01

Georgia	1992	***
Germany **	1973/1990	8.93
Ghana	1957	0.01
Greece †	1945	0.35
Grenada	1974	0.01
Guatemala †	1945	0.02
Guinea	1958	0.01
Guinea-Bissau	1974	0.01
Guyana	1966	0.01
Haiti †	1945	0.01
Honduras †	1945	0.01
Hungary	1955	0.18
Iceland	1946	0.03
India †	1945	0.36
Indonesia	1950	0.16
Iran †	1945	0.77
Iraq †	1945	0.13
Ireland	1955	0.18
Israel	1949	0.23
Italy	1955	4.29
Jamaica	1962	0.01
Japan	1956	12.45
Jordan	1955	0.01
Kazakhstan	1992	***
Kenya	1963	0.01
Kuwait	1963	0.25
Kyrgyzstan	1992	***
Laos	1955	0.01
Latvia	1991	***
Lebanon †	1945	0.01
Lesotho	1966	0.01
Liberia †	1945	0.01
Libya	1955	0.24
Liechtenstein	1990	0.01
Lithuania	1991	***
Luxembourg †	1945	0.06
Madagascar	1960	0.01
Malawi	1964	0.01
Malaysia	1957	0.12
Maldives	1965	0.01
Mali	1960	0.01
Malta	1964	0.01
Marshall Islands	1991	0.01
Mauritania	1961	0.01
Mauritius	1968	0.01
Mexico †	1945	0.88
Micronesia	1991	0.01
Moldova	1992	***
Mongolia	1961	0.01
Morocco	1956	0.03
Mozambique	1975	0.01
Myanmar (Burma)	1948	0.01
Namibia	1990	0.01
Nepal	1955	0.01
Netherlands †	1945	1.50
New Zealand †	1945	0.24
Nicaragua †	1945	0.01
Niger	1960	0.01
Nigeria	1960	0.20
North Korea	1991	0.05
Norway †	1945	0.55
Oman	1971	0.03
Pakistan	1947	0.06
Panama †	1945	0.02
Papua New Guinea	1975	0.01
Paraguay †	1945	0.03
Peru †	1945	0.06
Philippines †	1945	0.07
Poland †	1945	0.47
Portugal	1955	0.20
Qatar	1971	0.05
Romania	1955	0.17
Russian Federation *	1945	9.41
Rwanda	1962	0.01
St Christopher-Nevis	1983	0.01
St Lucia	1979	0.01
St Vincent & Grenadines	1980	0.01
San Marino	1992	***
São Tomé e Principe	1975	0.01
Saudi Arabia †	1945	0.96
Senegal	1960	0.01
Seychelles	1976	0.01
Sierra Leone	1961	0.01
Singapore	1965	0.12
Slovenia	1992	***
Solomon Isles	1978	0.01
Somalia	1960	0.01
South Africa †	1945	0.41
South Korea	1991	0.69
Spain	1955	1.98
Sri Lanka	1955	0.01
Sudan	1956	0.01
Suriname	1975	0.01
Swaziland	1968	0.01
Sweden	1946	1.11
Syria †	1945	0.04
Tajikistan	1992	***
Tanzania	1961	0.01
Thailand	1946	0.11
Togo	1960	0.01
Trinidad & Tobago	1962	0.05
Tunisia	1956	0.03
Turkey †	1945	0.27
Turkmenistan	1992	***
Uganda	1962	0.01
Ukraine †	1945	1.18
United Arab Emirates	1971	0.21
United Kingdom †	1945	5.02
United States of America †	1945	25.00
Uruguay †	1945	0.04
Uzbekistan	1992	***
Vanuatu	1981	0.01
Venezuela †	1945	0.49
Vietnam	1977	0.01
Western Samoa	1976	0.01
Yemen **	1947	0.01
Yugoslavia †	1945	0.42
Zaire	1960	0.01
Zambia	1964	0.01
Zimbabwe	1980	0.02

† founder members
* Became a separate member upon the demise of the USSR which was a founder member 1945
** represented by two countries until unification 1990
*** contributions to be determined

The sovereign countries that are not UN members are Andorra, Kiribati, Monaco, Nauru, Switzerland, Taiwan, Tonga, Tuvalu, and Vatican City.

UN Security Council

permanent members
United States of America
United Kingdom
France
China
Russia

rotating members
(terms end Jan 1994)
Cape Verde
Hungary
Japan
Morocco
Venezuela

United Nations Security Council most powerful body of the UN. It has five permanent members—the US, Russia, the UK, France, and China—which exercise a veto in that their support is requisite for all decisions, plus ten others, elected for two-year terms by a two-thirds vote of the General Assembly; retiring members are not eligible for re-election.

Any UN member may be invited to participate in the Security Council's discussions (though not to vote) if they bear on its interests. The council may undertake investigations into disputes and make recommendations to the parties concerned and may call on all members to take economic or military measures to enforce its decisions; it has at its disposal a Military Staff Committee, composed of the chiefs of staff of the permanent member countries. The presidency of the Security Council is held for a month at a time by a representative of a member state, in English-language alphabetical order.

United Provinces of Central America political union 1823–38 established by the Central American states of Costa Rica, El Salvador, Guatemala, Honduras, and Nicaragua. The union followed the breakup of the Spanish empire and was initially dominated by Guatemala. Its unity was more apparent than real, and the federation fell apart in 1838. Subsequent attempts at reunification foundered.

United States (US) officially *United States of America* (USA), country in North America, extending from the Atlantic Ocean in the east to the Pacific Ocean in the west, bounded north by Canada and south by Mexico, and including the outlying states of Alaska and Hawaii.

government The US is a federal republic comprising 50 states and the District of ▷Columbia. Under the 1787 constitution, which has had 26 amendments, the constituent states are reserved considerable powers of self-government. The federal government concentrated originally on military and foreign affairs and the coordination of interstate concerns, leaving legislation in other spheres to the states, each with its own constitution, elected legislature, governor, supreme court, and local taxation powers. Since the 1930s, however, the federal government has become increasingly active and has therefore impinged upon what were previously state affairs. It has become the principal revenue-raising and spending agency. This activism was criticized during the 1980s, and Republican administrations professed a desire to reverse the process.

The executive, legislative, and judicial branches of the federal government are deliberately separate from each other, working in a system of checks and balances. At the head of the executive branch is a president elected every four years in a national contest by universal adult suffrage but votes are counted at the state level on a winner-take-all basis, with each state (and the District of Columbia) being assigned votes (equivalent to the number of its congressional representatives) in a national electoral college that formally elects the president. The president serves as head of state, of the armed forces, and of the federal civil service. He or she is restricted to a maximum of two terms and, once elected, cannot be removed except through impeachment and subsequent conviction by Congress. The president works with a personally selected (appointed) cabinet team, subject to the Senate's approval, whose members are prohibited from serving in the legislature.

US: presidents and elections

year elected/took office	president	party	losing candidate(s)	party
1789	1. George Washington	Federalist	no opponent	
1792	reelected		no opponent	
1796	2. John Adams	Federalist	Thomas Jefferson	Democrat–Republican
1800	3. Thomas Jefferson	Democrat–Republican	Aaron Burr	Democrat–Republican
1804	reelected		Charles Pinckney	Federalist
1808	4. James Madison	Democrat–Republican	Charles Pinckney	Federalist
1812	reelected		DeWitt Clinton	Federalist
1816	5. James Monroe	Democrat–Republican	Rufus King	Federalist
1820	reelected		John Quincy Adams	Democrat–Republican
1824	6. John Quincy Adams	Democrat–Republican	Andrew Jackson	Democrat–Republican
			Henry Clay	Democrat–Republican
			William H Crawford	Democrat–Republican
1828	7. Andrew Jackson	Democrat	John Quincy Adams	National Republican
1832	reelected		Henry Clay	National Republican
1836	8. Martin Van Buren	Democrat	William Henry Harrison	Whig
1840	9. William Henry Harrison	Whig	Martin Van Buren	Democrat
1841	10. John Tyler[1]	Whig		
1844	11. James K Polk	Democrat	Henry Clay	Whig
1848	12. Zachary Taylor	Whig	Lewis Cass	Democrat
1850	13. Millard Fillmore[2]	Whig		
1852	14. Franklin Pierce	Democrat	Winfield Scott	Whig
1856	15. James Buchanan	Democrat	John C Fremont	Republican
1860	16. Abraham Lincoln	Republican	Stephen Douglas	Democrat
			John Breckinridge	Democrat
			John Bell	Constitutional Union
1864	reelected		George McClellan	Democrat
1865	17. Andrew Johnson[3]	Democrat		
1868	18. Ulysses S Grant	Republican	Horatio Seymour	Democrat
1872	reelected		Horace Greeley	Democrat–Liberal Republican
1876	19. Rutherford B Hayes	Republican	Samuel Tilden	Democrat
1880	20. James A Garfield	Republican	Winfield Hancock	Democrat
1881	21. Chester A Arthur[4]	Republican		
1884	22. Grover Cleveland	Democrat	James Blaine	Republican
1888	23. Benjamin Harrison	Republican	Grover Cleveland	Democrat
1892	24. Grover Cleveland	Democrat	Benjamin Harrison	Republican
			James Weaver	People's
1896	25. William McKinley	Republican	William J Bryan	Democrat–People's
1900	reelected		William J Bryan	Democrat
1901	26. Theodore Roosevelt[5]	Republican		
1904	reelected		Alton B Parker	Democrat
1908	27. William H Taft	Republican	William J Bryan	Democrat
1912	28. Woodrow Wilson	Democrat	Theodore Roosevelt	Progressive
			William H Taft	Republican
1916	reelected		Charles E Hughes	Republican
1920	29. Warren G Harding	Republican	James M Cox	Democrat
1923	30. Calvin Coolidge[6]	Republican		
1924	reelected		John W Davis	Democrat
			Robert M LaFollette	Progressive
1928	31. Herbert Hoover	Republican	Alfred E Smith	Democrat
1932	32. Franklin D Roosevelt	Democrat	Herbert Hoover	Republican
			Norman Thomas	Socialist
1936	reelected		Alfred Landon	Republican
1940	reelected		Wendell Willkie	Republican
1944	reelected		Thomas E Dewey	Republican
1945	33. Harry S Truman[7]	Democrat		
1948	reelected		Thomas E Dewey	Republican
			J Strom Thurmond	States' Rights
			Henry A Wallace	Progressive
1952	34. Dwight D Eisenhower	Republican	Adlai E Stevenson	Democrat
1956	reelected		Adlai E Stevenson	Democrat
1960	35. John F Kennedy	Democrat	Richard M Nixon	Republican
1963	36. Lyndon B Johnson[8]	Democrat		
1964	reelected		Barry M Goldwater	Republican
1968	37. Richard M Nixon	Republican	Hubert H Humphrey	Democrat
			George C Wallace	
1972	reelected		George S McGovern	Democrat
1974	38. Gerald R Ford[9]	Republican		
1976	39. Jimmy Carter	Democrat	Gerald R Ford	Republican
1980	40. Ronald Reagan	Republican	Jimmy Carter	Democrat
			John B Anderson	Independent
1984	reelected		Walter Mondale	Democrat
1988	41. George Bush	Republican	Michael Dukakis	Democrat
1992	42. William Clinton	Democrat	George Bush	Republican

[1] became president on death of Harrison
[2] became president on death of Taylor
[3] became president on assassination of Lincoln
[4] became president on assassination of Garfield
[5] became president on assassination of McKinley
[6] became president on death of Harding
[7] became president on death of F D Roosevelt
[8] became president on assassination of Kennedy
[9] became president on resignation of Nixon

United States
(US)

area 3,618,770 sq mi/9,368,900 sq km
capital Washington, DC
cities New York, Los Angeles, Chicago, Philadelphia, Detroit, San Francisco, Washington, Dallas, San Diego, San Antonio, Houston, Boston, Baltimore, Phoenix, Indianapolis, Memphis, Honolulu, San José
physical topography and vegetation from tropical (Hawaii) to arctic (Alaska); mountain ranges parallel with E and W coasts; the Rocky Mountains separate rivers emptying into the Pacific from those flowing into the Gulf of Mexico; Great Lakes in N; rivers include Hudson, Mississippi, Missouri, Colorado, Columbia, Snake, Rio Grande, Ohio
environment the US produces the world's largest quantity of municipal waste per person (1,900 lb/850 kg) annually
features see individual states
territories the commonwealths of Puerto Rico and Northern Marianas; the federated states of Micronesia; Guam, the US Virgin Islands, American Samoa, Wake Island, Midway Islands, Marshall Islands, Belau, and Johnston and Sand Islands
head of state and government Bill Clinton from 1993
political system liberal democracy
political parties Democratic Party, liberal, center; Republican Party, center-right
currency US dollar
population (1990 est) 250,372,000 (white 80%, black 12%, Asian/Pacific islander 3%, American Indian, Inuit, and Aleut 1%, Hispanic [included in above percentages] 9%); growth rate 0.9% p.a.

life expectancy men 72, women 79 (1989)
languages English, Spanish
religion Christian 86.5% (Roman Catholic 26%, Baptist 19%, Methodist 8%, Lutheran 5%), Jewish 1.8%, Muslim 0.5%, Buddhist and Hindu less than 0.5%
literacy 99% (1989)
GNP $3,855 bn (1983); $13,451 per head
chronology
1776 Declaration of Independence.
1787 US constitution drawn up.
1789 Washington elected as first president.
1803 Louisiana Purchase.
1812–14 War with England, arising from commercial disputes caused by Britain's struggle with Napoleon.
1819 Florida purchased from Spain.
1836 The battle of the Alamo, Texas, won by Mexico.
1841 First wagon train left Missouri for California.
1846 Mormons, under Brigham Young, founded Salt Lake City, Utah.
1846–48 Mexican War resulted in cession to US of Arizona, California, part of Colorado and Wyoming, Nevada, New Mexico, Texas, and Utah.
1848–49 California gold rush.
1860 Lincoln elected president.
1861–65 Civil War between North and South.
1865 Slavery abolished. Lincoln assassinated.
1867 Alaska bought from Russia.
1890 Battle of Wounded Knee, the last major battle between American Indians and US troops.
1898 War with Spain ended with the Spanish cession of Philippines, Puerto Rico, and Guam; it was agreed that Cuba be independent. Hawaii annexed.
1917–18 US entered World War I.
1919–1921 Wilson's 14 Points became base for League of Nations.
1920 Women achieved the vote.
1924 American Indians made citizens by Congress.
1929 Wall Street stock-market crash.
1933 F D Roosevelt's New Deal to alleviate the Depression put into force.
1941–45 The Japanese attack on Pearl Harbor Dec 1941 precipitated US entry into World War II.
1945 US ended war in the Pacific by dropping A-bombs on Hiroshima and Nagasaki, Japan.
1950–53 US involvement in Korean War. McCarthy anticommunist investigations (HUAC) became a "witch hunt."
1954 Civil Rights legislation began with segregation ended in public schools.
1957 Civil Rights bill on voting.
1958 First US satellite in orbit.
1961 Bay of Pigs abortive CIA-backed

invasion of Cuba.
1963 President Kennedy assassinated; L B Johnson assumed the presidency.
1964–68 "Great Society" civil-rights and welfare measures in the Omnibus Civil Rights bill.
1964–75 US involvement in Vietnam War.
1965 US intervention in Dominican Republic.
1969 US astronaut Neil Armstrong was the first human on the Moon.
1973 OPEC oil embargo almost crippled US industry and consumers. Inflation began.
1973–74 Watergate scandal began in effort to reelect Nixon and ended just before impeachment; Nixon resigned as president; replaced by Ford, who pardoned Nixon.
1975 Final US withdrawal from Vietnam.
1979 US–Chinese diplomatic relations normalized.
1979–80 Iranian hostage crisis; relieved by Reagan concessions and released on his inauguration day Jan 1981.
1981 Space shuttle mission was successful.
1983 US invasion of Grenada.
1986 "Irangate" scandal over secret US government arms sales to Iran, with proceeds to antigovernment Contra guerrillas in Nicaragua.
1987 Reagan and Gorbachev (for USSR) signed intermediate-range nuclear forces treaty. Wall Street stock-market crash caused by program trading.
1988 US became world's largest debtor nation, owing $532 billion. George Bush elected president.
1989 Bush met Gorbachev at Malta, end to Cold War declared; large cuts announced for US military; US invaded Panama; Noriega taken into custody.
1990 Bush and Gorbachev met again. Nelson Mandela freed in South Africa, toured US. US troops sent to Middle East following Iraq's invasion of Kuwait.
1991 Jan–Feb: US-led assault by UN coalition drove Iraq from Kuwait in Gulf War. US support was given to the USSR during the dissolution of communism and the recognition of independence of the Baltic republics. July: Strategic Arms Reduction Treaty (START) signed at US–Soviet summit held in Moscow. Nov: Bush co-hosted Middle East peace conference in Spain.
1992 Bush's popularity slumped as economic recession continued. Widespread riots in Los Angeles. Nov: Democrats, led by Bill Clinton, won presidential elections for first time since 1976; independent candidate Ross Perot captured nearly 20% of votes.
1993 Clinton inaugurated; faced budget crisis.

The second branch of government, Congress, the federal legislature, comprises two houses, the 100-member Senate and the 435-member House of Representatives. Senators serve six-year terms, and there are two from each state regardless of its size and population. Every two years a third of the seats come up for election. Representatives are elected from state congressional districts of roughly equal demographic sizes and serve two-year terms.

Congress operates through a system of specialized standing committees in both houses. The Senate is the more powerful chamber of Congress, since its approval is required for key federal appointments and for the ratification of foreign treaties. The president's policy

program needs the approval of Congress, and the president addresses Congress in Jan for an annual "State of the Union" speech and sends periodic "messages" and "recommendations." The success of a president to carry out his or her platform depends on voting support in Congress, bargaining skills, and public support. Proposed legislation, to become law (an Act of Congress), requires the approval of both houses of Congress as well as the signature of the president. If differences exist, "conference committees" are convened to effect compromise agreements. The president can impose a veto, which can be overridden only by two-thirds majorities in both houses. Constitutional amendments require two-thirds

majorities from both houses and the support of three-quarters of the nation's 50 state legislatures.

The third branch of government, the judiciary, headed by the Supreme Court, interprets the written US constitution; its function is to ensure that a correct balance is maintained between federal and state institutions and the executive and legislature and to uphold the constitution, especially the civil rights described in the first ten (the ◊Bill of Rights) and later amendments. The Supreme Court comprises nine judges appointed by the president with the Senate's approval, who serve life terms and can only be removed by impeachment, trial, and conviction by Congress.

The US administers a number of territories, including American Samoa and the US Virgin Islands, which have local legislatures and a governor. These territories, as well as the "self-governing territories" of Puerto Rico and Guam, each send a nonvoting delegate to the US House of Representatives.

The District of Columbia, centered around the city of Washington, DC, is the site of the federal legislature, judiciary, and executive. Since 1971 it has sent one nonvoting delegate to the House and since 1961 its citizens have been able to vote in presidential elections (the District having three votes in the national electoral college).

history For early history, see ⟳American Indian. The Spanish first settled in Florida 1565. The first permanent English settlement was at Jamestown, Virginia, 1607. In 1620

United States of America

state	capital	date of joining the Union
Alabama	Montgomery	1819
Alaska	Juneau	1959
Arizona	Phoenix	1912
Arkansas	Little Rock	1836
California	Sacramento	1850
Colorado	Denver	1876
Connecticut	Hartford	1788
Delaware	Dover	1787
Florida	Tallahassee	1845
Georgia	Atlanta	1788
Hawaii	Honolulu	1959
Idaho	Boise	1890
Illinois	Springfield	1818
Indiana	Indianapolis	1816
Iowa	Des Moines	1846
Kansas	Topeka	1861
Kentucky	Frankfort	1792
Louisiana	Baton Rouge	1812
Maine	Augusta	1820
Maryland	Annapolis	1788
Massachusetts	Boston	1788
Michigan	Lansing	1837
Minnesota	St Paul	1858
Mississippi	Jackson	1817
Missouri	Jefferson City	1821
Montana	Helena	1889
Nebraska	Lincoln	1867
Nevada	Carson City	1864
New Hampshire	Concord	1788
New Jersey	Trenton	1787
New Mexico	Santa Fé	1912
New York	Albany	1788
North Carolina	Raleigh	1789
North Dakota	Bismarck	1889
Ohio	Columbus	1803
Oklahoma	Oklahoma City	1907
Oregon	Salem	1859
Pennsylvania	Harrisburg	1787
Rhode Island	Providence	1790
South Carolina	Columbia	1788
South Dakota	Pierre	1889
Tennessee	Nashville	1796
Texas	Austin	1845
Utah	Salt Lake City	1896
Vermont	Montpelier	1791
Virginia	Richmond	1788
Washington	Olympia	1889
West Virginia	Charleston	1863
Wisconsin	Madison	1848
Wyoming	Cheyenne	1890

English ⟳Pilgrims landed at Plymouth and founded the colony of Massachusetts and, later, Connecticut. English Catholics founded Maryland 1634; English Quakers founded Pennsylvania 1682. A Dutch settlement 1611 on Manhattan Island, named New Amsterdam 1626, was renamed New York after it was taken by England 1664. In the 18th century the English colonies were threatened by French expansion from the Great Lakes to Louisiana until the English won the French and Indian War (in Europe called the Seven Years' War 1756–63).

American Revolution In 1775, following years of increasing tension, the 13 colonies (Connecticut, Delaware, Georgia, Maryland, Massachusetts, New Hampshire, New Jersey, New York, North Carolina, Pennsylvania, Rhode Island, South Carolina, and Virginia) rose against the British government, assembled at the Continental Congress, and fought British troops in Massachusetts, at Lexington and Concord. Meeting in Philadelphia in 1776, they declared themselves to be "free and independent states." Led by General George Washington, they defeated George III's armies in the ⟳American Revolution. By the Treaty of Paris 1783 Britain recognized the independence of the 13 colonies. The constitution came into force 1789. Washington was unanimously elected as the first president.

The ⟳Louisiana territory was bought from Napoleon 1803, and Florida from Spain 1819. Napoleon's trade blockade of British shipping led indirectly to the Anglo-American War 1812–14. Expansion to the west, called ⟳manifest destiny, reached the Pacific, and the Mexican War 1846–48 secured the areas of Arizona, California, part of Colorado and Wyoming, Nevada, Utah, New Mexico, and Texas. ⟳Alaska was purchased from Russia 1867. Hawaii ceded itself to the US 1898.

The American ⟳Civil War 1861–65 put an end to slavery but left ill feeling between north and south. It stimulated additional industrial development in the north, as well as the construction of roads and railroads, which continued until the end of that century.

international involvement Involvement in international affairs really began with the Spanish-American War 1898, which involved the US in Guam, Puerto Rico, and the Philippines. The Panama Canal Zone rights were leased 1903. After trying to maintain an isolationist stance, under President Woodrow Wilson, the US entered ⟳World War I 1917; it was not a party to the Treaty of Versailles but made peace by separate treaties 1921. A period of isolationism followed. The country's economic, industrial, and agricultural expansion was brought to a halt by the stock-market crash 1929, which marked the start of the ⟳Depression. President Franklin Roosevelt's ⟳New Deal 1933 did not solve the problem, and only preparations for ⟳World War II brought full employment. The US did not declare war until Japan attacked ⟳Pearl Harbor on Honolulu Dec 1941.

the Truman doctrine The US, having emerged from the war as a superpower, remained internationalist during the prosperity of the postwar era. Under the presidency of Harry S Truman (Democrat), a doctrine of intervention in support of endangered "free peoples" and of "containing the spread of communism" was devised by secretaries of state George ⟳Marshall and Dean ⟳Acheson. This led to the US's intervention in Greece and support for Nationalist Taiwan 1949 and its

participation in the ⟳Korean War 1950–53. The US, in addition, helped to create new global and regional bodies designed to maintain the peace—the United Nations (UN) 1945, the Organization of American States (OAS) 1948, the North Atlantic Treaty Organization (NATO) 1949, the South-East Asia Treaty Organization (SEATO) 1954—and launched the Marshall Plan 1947 to begin strengthening the capitalist economies of its allies while standing off similar strategies of the USSR-dominated Eastern Bloc. This began the ⟳Cold War. Domestically, President Truman sought to introduce liberal reforms designed at extending civil and welfare rights under the slogan "a fair deal." These measures were blocked by a combination of Southern Democrats and Republicans in Congress. Truman's foreign policy was criticized as being "soft on communism" between 1950 and 1952, as a wave of anti-Soviet hysteria, spearheaded by Senator Joseph McCarthy, swept the nation.

Eisenhower era of growth This rightward shift in the public mood brought Republican victory in the congressional and presidential elections 1952, with popular military commander General Dwight D Eisenhower becoming president. He was reelected by an increased margin Nov 1956. Eisenhower adhered to the Truman–Acheson doctrine of "containment," while at home he pursued a policy of "progressive conservatism" designed to encourage business enterprise. The Eisenhower era was one of growth, involving the migration of southern blacks to the northern industrial cities and rapid expansion in the educational sector. In the southern states, where racial segregation and discrimination were openly practiced, a new civil-rights movement developed under the leadership of Dr Martin Luther King, Jr. Promising a "New Frontier" program of social reform, John F Kennedy (Democrat) won the presidential election Nov 1960 and emerged as an active supporter of civil rights and space exploration and an opponent of communism abroad (see ⟳Bay of Pigs). He was assassinated Nov 1963.

"Great Society" It was left to his vice-president and successor, Lyndon B Johnson, to oversee the passage of additional reforms, called the "Great Society" by Johnson. These measures, which included the Equal Opportunities, Voting Rights, Housing, and Medicare acts, guaranteed blacks their civil rights and extended the reach and responsibilities of the federal government. The black migration to the northern cities went into reverse from 1970, stimulated by new economic opportunity in American sunbelt states, new black political influence, and a feeling of returning to earlier roots.

Vietnam War Abroad, President Johnson escalated US involvement in the ⟳Vietnam War 1964–75, which polarized public opinion and deeply divided the Democratic Party into "hawks and doves." Johnson declined to run for reelection Nov 1968, and his vice-president, Hubert Humphrey, was defeated by Republican Richard Nixon. Working with National Security Adviser Henry ⟳Kissinger, Nixon escalated the Vietnam conflict by invading neighboring Cambodia before he began a gradual disengagement, launching a policy of détente that brought an improvement in relations with the Soviet Union (see ⟳Strategic Arms Limitation Talks) and a visit to Communist China 1973.

Watergate scandal Nixon, faced with a divided opposition led by the liberal George

McGovern, had gained reelection by an over-whelming margin Nov 1972, but during the campaign, Nixon's staff had broken into the Democratic Party's ◊Watergate headquarters. When this and the attempts at cover-up came to light, the scandal forced the resignation of the president Aug 1974, just short of impeachment. Watergate shook the US public's confidence in the Washington establishment. Gerald Ford, who had been appointed vice-president when Spiro Agnew was forced to step down Dec 1973, pardoned Nixon and kept the services of Kissinger and the policy of détente when he became president. He faced a hostile, Democrat-dominated Congress that introduced legislation curbing the unauthorized power of the presidency, attempting to mend fences both at home and abroad. He also had to deal with the economic recession and increased OPEC oil prices that began under Nixon 1973.

Carter presidency Ford ran in the presidential election Nov 1976, but was defeated by Washington outsider and Democrat Jimmy Carter, who promised open and honest government. Carter was a fiscal conservative but social liberal, who sought to extend welfare provision through greater administrative efficiency. He substantially ended the fuel crisis through enforced conservation in the energy bills 1978 and 1980. In foreign relations President Carter emphasized human rights. In the Middle East, he moved close to a peace settlement 1978–79 (see ◊Camp David Agreements) and in Jan 1979 the US's diplomatic relations with Communist China were fully normalized. The Carter presidency was, however, brought down by two foreign-policy crises 1979–80: the fall of the shah of Iran and the Soviet invasion of Afghanistan. The president's leadership style, military economies, and moralistic foreign policy were blamed by the press for weakening US influence abroad. There was a swell of anticommunist feeling and mounting support for a new policy of rearmament and selective interventionism. President Carter responded to this new mood by enunciating the hawkish ◊Carter Doctrine 1980 and supporting a new arms-development program, but his popularity plunged during 1980 as economic recession gripped the country and US embassy staff members were held hostage by Shiite Muslim fundamentalists in Tehran.

Reagan administration The Republican Ronald Reagan benefited from Carter's difficulties and was elected Nov 1980, when the Democrats also lost control of the Senate. The new president had risen to prominence as an effective, television-skilled campaigner. He purported to believe in a return to traditional Christian and family values and promoted a domestic policy of supply-side economics, decentralization, and deregulation. The early years of the Reagan presidency witnessed substantial reductions in taxation, with cutbacks in federal welfare programs that created serious hardships in many sectors as economic recession gripped the nation. Reagan rejected détente and spoke of the USSR as an "evil empire" that needed to be checked by a military buildup and a readiness to employ force. This led to a sharp deterioration in Soviet-US relations, ushering in a new cold war during the Polish crisis 1981. He was reelected on a wave of optimistic patriotism Nov 1984, defeating the Democrat ticket of Walter ◊Mondale and Geraldine ◊Ferraro by a record margin. A radical tax-cutting bill passed in Congress, and

in 1986 a large budget and trade deficit developed (as a spending economy was developed to control Congress). At home and overseas the president faced mounting public opposition to his interventions in Central America. The new Soviet leader Mikhail ◊Gorbachev pressed unsuccessfully for arms reduction during superpower summits at Geneva (Nov 1985) and Reykjavik (Oct 1986), but a further summit Dec 1987, with an agreement to scrap intermediate-range nuclear missiles, appeared to promise a new détente.

Irangate scandal In Nov 1986 the Republican Party lost control of the Senate in the midterm elections, just before the disclosure of a scandal concerning US arms sales to Iran in return for hostages held in Beirut, with the profits illegally diverted to help the Nicaraguan "Contra" (anticommunist) guerrillas. The ◊Irangate scandal briefly dented public confidence in the administration and forced the dismissal and resignation of key cabinet members. During the last two years of his presidency, a more consensual Reagan was on view and, helped by his Dec 1987 arms reduction deal, he left office with much of his popular affection restored.

Bush in power Reagan's popularity transferred itself to Vice President George Bush who, despite selecting the inexperienced Dan Quayle as his running-mate and despite opposition charges that he had been indirectly involved in the Irangate proceedings, defeated the Democrats' candidate Michael Dukakis in the presidential election of Nov 1988. Bush came to power, after six years of economic growth, at a time of uncertainty. Reagan's tax-cutting policy had led to mounting federal trade and budget deficits, which had served to turn the US into a debtor nation for the first time in its history and had precipitated a stock market crash Oct 1987. Retrenchment was thus needed and was concentrated 1989–90 in the military sphere, helped by continuing Soviet moves toward reductions in both conventional and nuclear forces. Domestically, Bush spoke of the need to create a "kinder, gentler nation," and unveiled minor initiatives in the areas of education, drug control, and the environment, where problems had surfaced during the Reagan years. (In 1990, almost 500,000 children were suffering from malnutrition and at least 100,000 people were homeless.) The start of his presidency was marred by the Senate's rejection of his nomination for Defense Secretary, John Tower, following criticisms of Tower's lifestyle and his links to military contractors. With his overthrowing of the corrupt Panamanian leader, General Manuel Noriega, Dec 1989, Bush began to establish his presidency.

In Sept 1990 the Senate confirmed David Souter, a conservative jurist from New Hampshire who had been nominated by President Bush, as a new Supreme Court justice. He replaced Justice William Brennan, a veteran liberal, who resigned in July. Souter's appointment appeared likely to strengthen the conservative majority that had been established within the Court, as did the confirmation in 1991 of Clarence Thomas after long and bitter Congressional hearings.

Gulf War The US responded to Iraq's unprovoked invasion and annexation of Kuwait Aug 2, 1990 by coordinating, in the United Nations, the passage of a series of resolutions demanding Iraq's unconditional withdrawal and imposing comprehensive economic sanctions. By late Nov the US had sent more than 230,000 troops and support personnel to Saudi Arabia

to form the core of a 400,000-strong Western and Arab "desert shield" with the object of defending the Saudi frontier and, if necessary, dislodging Iraq from Kuwait. A further 150,000 US troops were sent early Dec and the ◊Gulf War was fought in Jan–Feb 1991.

US reaction to demise of Soviet Union In July 1991 Bush and Soviet leader Gorbachev held the first superpower summit since the end of the ◊Cold War and signed the long-awaited START treaty (see ◊Strategic Arms Reduction Talks). The US condemned the attempted Moscow coup Aug 1991 which briefly removed Gorbachev and backed Boris ◊Yeltsin's efforts to restore the Soviet president. His reaction to later developments—the resignation of Gorbachev, the demise of the Soviet Union, and the creation of the ◊Commonwealth of Independent States (CIS)—was initially cautious. Having granted recognition to the independence of the Baltic States in Sept 1991, Bush acknowledged the independence of all remaining 12 republics, but proceeded slowly in granting full diplomatic recognition. Bush followed US success in the Gulf War by pushing for and convening a Middle East peace conference in Spain in Nov 1991; other conferences followed 1992. Domestically, the US had less success as the economic recession continued. A trip by Bush to Australia and East Asia to press for trade concessions ended in Japan in Jan 1992 with little progress. Bush's approval rating slumped and he faced increased public criticism. Racial upheaval in Los Angeles and natural disasters in Florida and Hawaii to which the federal government's response was criticized also contributed to decreased popularity.

Clinton takes over presidency Arkansas governor Bill Clinton won the 1992 presidential elections for the Democrats in Nov, having campaigned on a platform of better healthcare, cautious federal intervention to boost the economy, increased protection for the environment, and protection of minority rights. Although he and vice-presidential candidate Al Gore had only a 5% lead over Bush in the popular vote, he won 33 states, plus the District of Columbia, to Bush's 17. The independent candidate, Ross Perot, won nearly 20% of the popular vote but no electoral college votes. His campaign had little effect on the overall result but probably resulted in the winning candidate attracting less than 50% of the vote for the first time since Richard Nixon's 1968 success.

United States: architecture little survives of the earliest native American architecture, although the early settlers in each region recorded the house and village styles of the local Indians. The most notable prehistoric remains are the cliff dwellings in the Southwest. Archeologists have also discovered traces of structures associated with the moundbuilding peoples in the Mississippi river valley. Subsequent architectural forms are those that came with colonizers from European cultures, those adapted to American conditions and social development, and, most recently, those that were developed and innovated by American architects.

16th and 17th centuries Earliest European architectural influences were those of the Spanish colonizers, coming N from their Mexican colony or from early settlements in Florida; most were small or transitory. Spanish influence in the Southwest and California grew through the 19th century and continued in the 20th. The dominant American colonial architecture came to the east coast from 17th-century English immigrants, but also from Dutch, Swedish, and German settlers. Generally, new arrivals attempted to reconstruct the architecture they had known in their home countries, making adaptations to available materials and craftsmanship. Wood tended to be the material of choice in the northern colonies; wood, brick, and stone in the middle colonies; and wood and brick in the southern colonies. The earliest styles were primarily for farm homes and some urban dwellings, churches, and a few public buildings. Houses most often were small, had massive chimney stacks, and were timber-framed with brick, clapboard, or wattle-and-daub walls. Early churches and civic buildings were like large houses rather than imposing edifices. By the end of the century, with more settlers, greater resources, and more skilled builders, more elegant and elaborate examples of Jacobean and Queen Anne style were built, and more imposing public architecture was constructed, such as William and Mary College in Williamsburg, Virginia.

18th century Neo-Classical style dominated and was referred to as Georgian architecture, although designs lagged behind English sources, and the scale of projects was generally modest. No architects set up offices, but itinerant master craftsmen with plan-and-model books, working for educated colonial sponsors, diffused European-style developments along the eastern seaboard. Many fine homes were built, with distinct variations preferred in each of the colonial regions. Many churches and public buildings were influenced by British architect Christopher Wren. As settlement moved inland, the rough-hewn timber or log cabin became an American architectural mainstay. Other, finer, buildings from this period include numerous plantation houses, such as Westover or Carter's Grove in Virginia; Dutch patroon mansions along the Hudson River in New York or in E Pennsylvania; the then Virginia capital of Williamsburg; churches with steeples, such as Old North Church in Boston, Christ Church in Philadelphia, Christ Church in Williamsburg; public buildings, such as the Old State House or Fanueil Hall in Boston, Independence Hall in Philadelphia, or Charles Bulfinch's new State House in Boston; and numerous urban structures.

19th century Early in the century, Neo-Classical patterns were used to design the new republic's buildings, such as the Capitol and the ⊘White House in Washington, DC. The style was given strong inspiration by Thomas Jefferson, especially after his stay in Europe. He introduced and promoted a revival of Renaissance architecture based on Andrea Palladio and otherwise helped define what is now known as Federal-period architecture. His own work is best seen in his Virginia home, Monticello (which started as an 18th-century Georgian project and which he transformed throughout his life); in his design for the Virginia state capitol in Richmond, adapted from the Roman Maison Carré at Nimes, France; and in his harmonious plan for the campus of the University of Virginia at Charlottesville. Other structures from the first half of the century include the Greek-revival work of Charles Bulfinch and Benjamin Latrobe (notably in their work on the US Capitol). After the Civil War, Romanesque forms in stone and brick were promoted by Henry Hobson Richardson. An appreciation for and adaptation of French Renaissance de-

sign emerged, as well as a Romantic revival of Gothic architecture in both domestic and public buildings.

20th century Architecture in the early 20th century often combined the elements of earlier times and cultures; pseudo-English Tudor, French Provincial, and Spanish Mission models were built for residences, but Stanford White's Beaux Arts style dominated office buildings, clubs, mansions, and theaters, such as his Madison Square Garden in New York City. Most dramatically, this was the century of the modern architect, and Americans became internationally famous for innovative and creative design, since the ⊘skyscraper became the fundamental US contribution to world architecture. Spare, functional Modernist form predominated by mid-century, but by the 1980s a return to softening elements was promoted by Postmodernists. Notable 20th-century US architects include Frank Lloyd Wright, Louis Henry Sullivan, Walter Gropius, Ludwig Mies van der Rohe, Eliel and Eero Saarinen, I M Pei, Philip Johnson, Kevin Roche, Minoru Yamasaki, and Edward Durrell Stone.

United States: art painting and sculpture in the US from colonial times to the present. The unspoiled American landscapes romantically depicted in the 18th and 19th centuries gave way to realistic and Modernistic city scenes in the 20th. Modern movements have flourished in the US, among them Abstract Expressionism and Pop art.

colonial The first American-born artist in the European tradition was the portraitist Robert Feke (1705–50). The historical painter Benjamin West, working mainly in England, encouraged the portraitist John Singleton Copley. Charles Willson Peale and Gilbert Stuart, a student of West's, painted the founders of the new nation.

19th century The recording of the Indians' lifeways by George Catlin, the dramatic landscapes of Washington Allston, the nature pictures of Audubon, the seascapes of Winslow Homer, the art of the West of Frederic Remington, the realism of Thomas Eakins, and the Romantic landscapes of the Hudson River school found in the works of such artists as Thomas Cole, Asher B Durand, Martin Johnson Heade, and Frederick Edwin Church represent the vitality of US art in this century. The Impressionist-influenced James Whistler and Mary Cassatt and the society painter John Singer Sargent were active mainly in Europe.

early 20th century The members of the Ashcan school, led by Robert Henri, introduced social realism in art; they depicted slum squalor and city life. The group was actually known as The Eight and also included John Sloan, George Luks, William Glackens, Everett Shinn, Maurice Prendergast, Ernest Lawson, and Arthur B Davies. The controversial New York Armory Show 1913 introduced Europe's most avant-garde styles, Cubism and Futurism; Dada arrived soon after, and New York City vied with Paris as the world capital of art. In the 1930s and 1940s, several major European artists emigrated to the US, notably Max Ernst, Max Beckmann, Piet Mondrian, Hans Hoffmann, and Lyonel Feininger. The giant heads of presidents were carved out of Mount Rushmore by G Borglum.

mid-20th century Abstract Expressionism was practiced by the inventor of action painting, Jackson Pollock, his wife Lee Krasner, and the spiritual Mark Rothko. More politically concerned, Ben Shahn created influential

graphics. The sculptor Alexander Calder invented mobiles.

late 20th century The Pop-art movement, begun in the 1950s with Robert Rauschenberg and Jasper Johns and led by such artists as Andy Warhol, was a reaction against abstract art. It used precise and distorted images from the media, such as advertising, film, television, and comic strips. Andy Warhol painted soup cans 1962; Jasper Johns painted flags and numbers; Roy Lichtenstein used comic-strip characters to depict romance and heroism; Claes Oldenburg made soft sculptures of everyday items, many times their normal size. It led to multimedia works and performance art in the following decades.

By the 1990s, extremely high prices were being paid at auction for works of art by well-known artists; museum facilities were expanded to house donated collections and traveling exhibitions; and the designs for art exhibitions, their catalogs, and posters had become, in some ways, art forms in themselves.

United States: literature early US literature falls into two distinct periods: colonial writing 1620–1776, largely dominated by the Puritans, and post-Revolutionary literature after 1787, when the ideal of US literature developed, and poetry, fiction, and drama began to evolve on national principles.

colonial period 1607–1765 Literature of this period includes travel books and religious verse, but is mainly theological: Roger Williams, Cotton Mather, and Jonathan Edwards were typical Puritan writers. Benjamin Franklin's *Autobiography* is the first work of more than historical interest.

post-Revolutionary period 1785–1820 This period produced much political writing, by Thomas Paine, Thomas Jefferson, and Alexander Hamilton, and one noteworthy poet, Philip Freneau.

early 19th century The influence of English Romantics became evident, notably in the poems of William Cullen Bryant (1794–1878), Washington Irving's tales, Charles Brockden Brown's Gothic fiction, and James Fenimore Cooper's novels of frontier life. During 1830–60 intellectual life was centered in New England, which produced the essayists Ralph Waldo Emerson, Henry Thoreau, and Oliver Wendell Holmes; the poets Henry Wadsworth Longfellow, James Lowell, and John Whittier; and the novelists Nathaniel Hawthorne and Louisa May Alcott. Outside the New England circle were the novelists Edgar Allan Poe and Herman Melville.

post-Civil War period 1865–1900 The disillusionment of this period found expression in the realistic or psychological novel. Ambrose Bierce and Stephen Crane wrote realistic war stories; Mark Twain and Bret Harte dealt with western life; the growth of industrialism led to novels of social realism, notably the works of William Howells and Frank Norris; and Henry James and his disciple Edith Wharton developed the novel of psychological analysis among the well-to-do. The dominant poets were Walt Whitman and Emily Dickinson.

short story This form has attracted many of the major novelists from Hawthorne, Poe, and James onwards, and was popularized as a form by O Henry; writers specializing in it have included Ring Lardner, Katherine Anne Porter, Flannery O'Connor, William Saroyan, Eudora Welty, Grace Paley, and Raymond Carver.

drama The US produced a powerful group of playwrights between the wars, including

Eugene O'Neill, Maxwell Anderson, Lillian Hellman, Elmer Rice, Thornton Wilder, and Clifford Odets. They were followed by Arthur Miller and Tennessee Williams. A later generation now includes Edward Albee, Neil Simon, David Mamet, John Guare, and Sam Shepard.

poetry Poets like Edwin Arlington Robinson, Carl Sandburg, Vachel Lindsay, Robert Frost, and Edna St Vincent Millay extended the poetic tradition of the 19th century, but after the Imagist movement (see ⟡Imagism) of 1912–14 an experimental modern tradition arose with Ezra Pound, T S Eliot, William Carlos Williams, Marianne Moore, "HD" (Hilda Doolittle), and Wallace Stevens. Attempts at writing the modern US epic include Pound's *Cantos*, Hart Crane's *The Bridge*, and William Carlos Williams's *Paterson*. Among the most striking post-World War II poets are Karl Shapiro, Theodore Roethke, Robert Lowell, Charles Olson, Sylvia Plath, Gwendolyn Brooks, Denise Levertov, John Ashbery, A R Ammons, and Allen Ginsberg.

literary criticism Irving Babbitt (1865–1933), George Santayana, H L Mencken, and Edmund Wilson (1895–1972) were dominant figures, followed by Lionel Trilling (1905–75), Van Wyck Brooks, Yvor Winters (1900–68), and John Crowe Ransom, author of *The New Criticism* 1941, which stressed structural and linguistic factors. More recently, US criticism has been influenced by French literary theory and the journalistic criticism of Gore Vidal, Tom Wolfe, George Plimpton, and Susan Sontag.

fiction since 1900 The main trends have been realism, as exemplified in the work of Jack London, Upton Sinclair, and Theodore Dreiser, and modernist experimentation. After World War I, Sherwood Anderson, Sinclair Lewis, Ernest Hemingway, William Faulkner, Thomas Wolfe, F Scott Fitzgerald, John Dos Passos, Henry Miller, and Richard Wright established the main literary directions. Among the internationally known novelists since World War II have been John O'Hara, James Mitchener, Eudora Welty, Truman Capote, J D Salinger, Saul Bellow, John Updike, Norman Mailer, Vladimir Nabokov, Bernard Malamud, Philip Roth, Ralph Ellison, and James Baldwin. Recent US literature increasingly expresses the cultural pluralism, regional variety, and historical and ethnic range of US life. Feminism and minority consciousness have been brought to the fore by authors such as Alice Walker, Toni Morrison, and Maya Angelou.

Best-selling authors of popular fiction include Judith Kravitz, Sidney Sheldon, Anne Rice, and Stephen King.

US v American Tobacco Co a US Supreme Court decision 1911 dealing with the distinction between reasonable and unreasonable formations of trusts. The American Tobacco Co appealed to the Supreme Court after being convicted of monopolistic practices by the federal government. The federal district court had ordered the dissolution of the company, but the Supreme Court revised this decision on the grounds that the attempts to restrain trade had not been unreasonable. The Court ordered that the company be reorganized but not dissolved.

US v Butler a US Supreme Court decision 1936 concerning a New Deal policy of using federal taxing powers to regulate the economy. The challenge was brought against the Agricultural Adjustment Act (AAA), which taxed food processing to pay for farm subsidies, thereby discouraging the planting of certain crops. The Court ruled the AAA invalid on the grounds that it taxed with the purpose of regulating agricultural production.

US v Classic a US Supreme Court decision 1941 dealing with Congress's right to interfere with the operation of state primaries. Convicted of fraud in a Louisiana state primary, Classic appealed on the grounds that primaries, as functions of state political parties, were not subject to government regulation. The Court upheld Classic's conviction, ruling 4 to 3 that the primary had clear impact on the selection of federal representatives. Since Congress had the responsibility to monitor and regulate federal elections, state primaries were judged to be under Congressional authority.

US v Darby Lumber Co a US Supreme Court decision 1941 that decided the issue of federal control of commerce, overturning ⟡*Hammer* v *Dagenhart* 1918. The case dealt with the constitutionality of the Fair Labor Standards Act (FLSA) of 1938, which established maximum hours and minimum wages for workers. The interstate sale of any products manufactured in violation of the standards was strictly prohibited. The Court upheld the FLSA ruling that commerce is an integrated whole, not divisible into state and federal spheres. According to the unanimous decision, it was not the Court's role to judge the motives of Congressional legislation; Congress had the right to regulate national commerce without judicial interference.

US v E C Knight Co a US Supreme Court decision 1895 dealing with the right of the federal government to restrict the formation of corporate monopolies. The American Sugar Co established a 98% monopoly on sugar manufacturing in the US when it purchased the E C Knight Sugar Co, its leading competitor. The Justice Department filed suit against Knight for conspiracy to violate federal antitrust legislation. The Court ruled 8 to 1 that manufacturing was distinct from commerce and therefore outside of federal regulatory jurisdiction. The charges against Knight were dropped, virtually nullifying an important provision of the Sherman Antitrust Act 1890.

US v Gouveja a US Supreme Court decision 1984 dealing with the constitutional right of accused persons to an attorney. The case was brought to appeal the conviction of six prison inmates for a murder committed in the prison. The six argued that their right to counsel had been violated when they were detained without lawyers during the initial investigation. The Court ruled that the right to counsel applies only to "adversarial judicial proceedings," not to preliminary investigations.

US v Nixon a US Supreme Court decision 1974 dealing with the extent to which a US president may exercise executive privilege in a criminal investigation. During the ⟡Watergate investigations, President Nixon cited this privilege in refusing to produce certain tape recordings that had been subpoenaed by Special Prosecutor Jaworski. The Court ruled unanimously that while the president had certain privileges, they were subject to definition by the judiciary, the final interpreters of the Constitution. According to the Court, given the circumstances of the criminal investigation, Jaworski had the power to overrule presidential autonomy, requiring Nixon to yield the tapes.

universal in philosophy, a property that is instantiated by all the individual things of a specific class: for example, all red things instantiate "redness." Many philosophical debates have centered on the status of universals, including the medieval debate between ⟡nominalism and ⟡realism.

universal indicator in chemistry, a mixture of ⟡pH indicators, used to gauge the acidity or alkalinity of a solution. Each component changes color at a different pH value, and so the indicator is capable of displaying a range of colors, according to the pH of the test solution, from red (at pH 1) to purple (at pH 13).

The pH of a substance may be found by adding a few drops of universal indicator and noting the color, or by dipping in an absorbent paper strip that has been impregnated with the indicator.

universal joint flexible coupling used to join rotating shafts; for example, the drive shaft in an automobile. In a typical universal joint the ends of the shafts to be joined end in U-shaped yokes. They dovetail into each other and pivot flexibly about an X-shaped spider. This construction allows side-to-side and up-and-down movement, while still transmitting rotary motion.

Universal Postal Union agency of the United Nations responsible for collaboration of postal services. It was established 1875, and became an agency of the UN in 1947, with headquarters in Berne, Switzerland.

universal time (UT) another name for ⟡Greenwich Mean Time. It is based on the rotation of the Earth, which is not quite constant. Since 1972, UT has been replaced by *coordinated universal time* (UTC), which is based on uniform atomic time; see ⟡time.

universe all of space and its contents, the study of which is called cosmology. The universe is thought to be between 10 billion and 20 billion years old, and is mostly empty space, dotted with ⟡galaxies for as far as telescopes can see. The most distant detected galaxies and ⟡quasars lie 10 billion light-years or more from Earth, and are moving farther apart as the universe expands. Several theories attempt to explain how the universe came into being and evolved, for example, the ⟡Big Bang theory of an expanding universe originating in a single explosive event, and the contradictory ⟡steady-state theory.

Apart from those galaxies within the ⟡Local Group, all the galaxies we see display ⟡red shifts in their spectra, indicating that they are moving away from us. The farther we look into space, the greater are the observed red shifts, which implies that the more distant galaxies are receding at ever greater speeds. This observation led to the theory of an expanding universe, first proposed by Edwin Hubble 1929, and to Hubble's law, which states that the speed with which one galaxy moves away from another is proportional to its distance from it. Current data suggest that the galaxies are moving apart at a rate of 30–60 mps/50–100 kps for every million ⟡parsecs of distance.

university institution of higher learning for those who have completed primary and secondary education.

In the US there are both state universities (funded by the individual states) and private universities. The oldest universities in the US are all private: Harvard 1636, William and Mary 1693, Yale 1701, Pennsylvania 1741, and Princeton 1746. Typically, a university offers advanced degrees in addition to the four-year bachelor's degree; is made up of colleges, such as liberal arts, sciences, law, medicine; and offers special degrees such as divinity, technical, and vocational as well. Recent innovations include universities serving international areas, for example, the Middle East Technical University 1961 in Ankara, Turkey, supported by the United Nations; the United Nations University in Tokyo 1974; and the British Open University 1969, based on a mixed media curriculum.

The first European university was established in the 9th century at Salerno, Italy, and was followed in the 12th century by Bologna in Italy, Paris, Oxford, and Cambridge.

Unix multiuser ⟩operating system designed for minicomputers but becoming increasingly popular on large microcomputers, workstations, and supercomputers. It was developed by Bell Laboratories in the US during the late 1960s, using the programming language ⟩C. It could therefore run on any machine with a C compiler, so ensuring its wide portability. Its wide range of functions and flexibility have made it widely used by universities and in commercial software.

unnilennium synthesized radioactive element of the ⟩transactinide series, symbol Une, atomic number 109, atomic weight 266. It was first produced in 1982 at the Laboratory for Heavy Ion Research in Darmstadt, Germany, by fusing bismuth and iron nuclei; it took a week to obtain a single new, fused nucleus.

The element is (like unnilhexium, uniloctium, unnilpentium, unnilquadium, and unnilseptium) as yet unnamed; temporary identification was assigned until a name is approved by the International Union of Pure and Applied Chemistry.

unnilhexium synthesized radioactive element of the ⟩transactinide series, symbol Unh, atomic number 106, atomic weight 263. It was first synthesized in 1974 by two institutions, each of which claims priority. The University of California at Berkeley bombarded californium with oxygen nuclei to get isotope 263; the Joint Institute for Nuclear Research in Dubna, Russia, bombarded lead with chromium nuclei to obtain isotopes 259 and 260.

unniloctium synthesized, radioactive element of the ⟩transactinide series, symbol Uno, atomic number 108, atomic weight 265. It was first synthesized in 1984 by the Laboratory for Heavy Ion Research in Darmstadt, Germany.

unnilpentium synthesized, radioactive, metallic element of the ⟩transactinide series, symbol Unp, atomic number 105, atomic weight 262. Six isotopes have been synthesized, each with very short (fractions of a second) half-lives. Two institutions claim to have been the first to produce it: the Joint Institute for Nuclear Research in Dubna, Russia, in 1967 (proposed name **nielsbohrium**); and the University of California at Berkeley, who disputed the Soviet claim, in 1970 (proposed name **hahnium**).

unnilquadium synthesized, radioactive, metallic element, the first of the ⟩transactinide series, symbol Unq, atomic number 104, atomic weight 262. It is produced by bombarding californium with carbon nuclei and has ten isotopes, the longest-lived of which, Unq-262, has a half-life of 70 seconds. Two institutions claim to be the first to have synthesized it: the Joint Institute for Nuclear Research in Dubna, Russia, in 1964 (proposed name **kurchatovium**); and the University of California at Berkeley, in 1969 (proposed name **rutherfordium**).

unnilseptium synthesized, radioactive element of the ⟩transactinide series, symbol Uns, atomic number 107, atomic weight 262. It was first synthesized by the Joint Institute for Nuclear Research in Dubna, Russia, in 1976; in 1981 the Laboratory for Heavy Ion Research in Darmstadt, Germany, confirmed its existence.

untouchable or **harijan** member of the lowest Indian ⟩caste, formerly forbidden to be touched by members of the other castes.

Upanishad one of a collection of Hindu sacred treatises, written in Sanskrit, connected with the ⟩Vedas but composed later, about 800–200 BC. Metaphysical and ethical, their doctrine equated the atman (self) with the Brahman (supreme spirit)—*"Tat tvam asi"* ("Thou art that")—and developed the theory of the transmigration of souls.

Updike John (Hoyer) 1932– . US writer. Associated with the *New Yorker* magazine from 1955, he soon established a reputation for polished prose, poetry, and criticism. His novels include *The Poorhouse Fair* 1959, *The Centaur* 1963, *Couples* 1968, *The Witches of Eastwick* 1984, *Roger's Version* 1986, and *S.* 1988, and deal with the tensions and frustrations of contemporary US middle-class life and their effects on love and marriage.

Updike was born in Shillington, Pennsylvania, and graduated from Harvard University. Two characters recur in Updike's novels: the former basketball player "Rabbit" Angstrom, who matures in the series *Rabbit, Run* 1960, *Rabbit Redux* 1971, *Rabbit is Rich* 1981 (Pulitzer prize), and *Rabbit at Rest* 1990; and the novelist Henry Bech, who appears in *Bech: A Book* 1970 and *Bech is Back* 1982.

Other novels by Updike include *Of the Farm* 1965, *A Month of Sundays* 1972, *Marry Me* 1976, and *The Coup* 1978. His short-story collections include *The Same Door* 1959, *Pigeon Feathers* 1962, *Museums and Women* 1972, and *Problems* 1979. His body of work includes essay collections, such as *Hugging the Shore* 1983, and the play *Buchanan Dying* 1974.

Upper Austria (German *Oberösterreich*) mountainous federal province of Austria, drained by the Danube; area 4,632 sq mi/ 12,000 sq km; population (1987) 1,294,000. Its capital is Linz. In addition to wine, sugar beet and grain, there are reserves of oil. Manufactured products include textiles, chemicals, and metal goods.

Upper Volta former name (until 1984) of ⟩Burkina Faso.

Uppsala city in Sweden, NW of Stockholm; population (1990) 167,500. Industries include engineering and pharmaceuticals. The botanist Linnaeus lived here. The university was founded 1477; there are Viking relics and a Gothic cathedral.

Ur ancient city of the ⟩Sumerian civilization, in modern Iraq. Excavations by the British archeologist Leonard Woolley show that it was inhabited 3500 BC. He discovered evidence of a flood that may have inspired the *Epic of* ⟩*Gilgamesh* as well as the biblical account, and remains of ziggurats, or step pyramids, as well as social and cultural materials.

Ural Mountains (Russian *Ural'skiy Khrebet*) mountain system running from the Arctic to the Caspian Sea, traditionally separating Europe from Asia. The highest peak is Naradnaya 6,214 ft/1,894 m. It has vast mineral wealth.

uraninite uranium oxide, UO_2, an ore mineral of uranium, also known as **pitchblende**

when occurring in massive form. It is black or brownish black, very dense, and radioactive. It occurs in veins and as massive crusts, usually associated with granite rocks.

uranium hard, lustrous, silver-white, malleable and ductile, radioactive, metallic element of the ⟩actinide series, symbol U, atomic number 92, atomic weight 238.029. It is the most abundant radioactive element in the Earth's crust, its decay giving rise to essentially all radioactive elements in nature; its final decay product is the stable element lead. Uranium combines readily with most elements to form compounds that are extremely poisonous. The chief ore is ⟩pitchblende, in which the element was discovered by German chemist Martin Klaproth 1789; he named it after the planet Uranus, which had been discovered 1781.

Small amounts of certain compounds containing uranium have been used in the ceramics industry to make orange-yellow glazes and as mordants in dyeing; however, this practice was discontinued when the dangerous effects of radiation became known.

Uranium is one of three fissile elements (the others are thorium and plutonium). It was long considered to be the element with the highest atomic number to occur in nature. The isotopes U-238 and U-235 have been used to help determine the age of the Earth.

Uranium-238, which comprises about 99% of all naturally occurring uranium, has a half-life of 4.51×10^9 years. Because of its abundance, it is the isotope from which fissile plutonium is produced in breeder ⟩nuclear reactors. The fissile isotope U-235 has a half-life of 7.13×10^8 years and comprises about 0.7% of naturally occurring uranium; it is used directly as a fuel for nuclear reactors and in the manufacture of nuclear weapons.

uranium ore material from which uranium is extracted, often a complex mixture of minerals. The main ore is uraninite (or pitchblende) UO_2, which is commonly found with sulfide minerals. The US and South Africa are the main producers in the West.

Uranus in Greek mythology, the primeval sky god. He was responsible for both the sunshine and the rain, and was the son and husband of ⟩Gaia, the goddess of the Earth. Uranus and Gaia were the parents of ⟩Cronus and the ⟩Titans.

Uranus the seventh planet from the Sun, discovered by William ⟩Herschel 1781. It is twice as far out as the sixth planet, Saturn. Uranus has a diameter of 31,600 mi/50,800 km and a mass 14.5 times that of Earth. It orbits the Sun in 84 years at an average distance of 1.8 billion mi/2.9 billion km. The spin axis of Uranus is tilted at 98°, so that one pole points toward the Sun, giving extreme seasons. It has 15 moons, and in 1977 was discovered to have thin rings around its equator.

Uranus has a peculiar magnetic field, whose axis is tilted at 60° to its axis of spin, and is displaced about one-third of the way from the planet's center to its surface. Observations of the magnetic field show that the solid body of the planet rotates every 17.2 hours. Uranus spins from east to west, the opposite of the other planets, with the exception of Venus and possibly Pluto. The rotation rate of the atmosphere varies with latitude, from about 16 hours in mid-southern latitudes to longer than 17 hours at the equator.

Data derived from the space probe *Voyager 1* in 1986 revealed that Uranus is covered with a cloud layer under which a hot ocean of superheated water exists. The pressure caused by the thick atmosphere keeps the water from boiling away and the heat keeps the pressure from solidifying the water. This has led to suggestions that the planet may have formed from the coalescence of comets. Other discoveries were that the pole facing the Sun is no hotter than the pole facing away, and that four known methane clouds in the atmosphere rotate with the planet, not in the expected opposite direction. *Voyager 2* detected ten rings, composed of chunky rock and large ice boulders, around the planet's equator, and found ten small moons in addition to the five visible from Earth. Titania, the largest moon, has a diameter of 1,000 mi/ 1,610 km. The rings are charcoal black, and may be debris of former "moonlets" that have broken up.

Urban six popes, including:

Urban II *c.* 1042–1099. Pope 1088–99. He launched the First ⟁Crusade at the Council of Clermont in France 1095.

Urbana industrial city (food processing, electronics, and metal products) in E central Illinois, E of Springfield; population (1990) 36,300. The University of Illinois 1867 is here.

urbanization process by which the proportion of a population living in or around towns and cities increases through migration as the agricultural population decreases. The growth of urban concentrations in the US and Europe is a relatively recent phenomenon, dating back only about 150 years to the beginning of the Industrial Revolution (although the world's first cities were built more than 5,000 years ago.)

Urbanization has had a major effect on the social structures of industrial societies, affecting not only where people live but how they live, and urban sociology has emerged as a distinct area of study.

urban renewal adaptation of existing buildings and neighborhoods in towns and cities to meet changes in economic, social, and environmental requirements, rather than demolishing them. Since the early 1970s, when it became less expensive to renew than to build, urban renewal has increased.

A major objective is to preserve the historical and cultural character of a locality, but at the same time to improve the environment and meet new demands, such as rapidly increasing automobile traffic.

Urdu language member of the Indo-Iranian branch of the Indo-European language family, related to Hindi and written not in Devanagari but in Arabic script. Urdu is strongly influenced by Farsi (Persian) and Arabic. It is the official language of Pakistan and is used by Muslims in India.

urea CO(NH$_2$)$_2$ waste product formed in the mammalian liver when nitrogen compounds are broken down. It is excreted in urine. When purified, it is a white, crystalline solid. In industry it is used to make urea-formaldehyde plastics (or resins), pharmaceuticals, and fertilizers.

uremia excess of urea (a nitrogenous waste product) in the blood, caused by kidney damage.

ureter tube connecting the kidney to the bladder. Its wall contains fibers of smooth muscle, whose contractions aid the movement of urine out of the kidney.

urethra in mammals, a tube connecting the bladder to the exterior. It carries urine and, in males, semen.

Uruguay
Oriental Republic of (*República Oriental del Uruguay***)**

area 68,031 sq mi/176,200 sq km
capital Montevideo
cities Salto, Paysandú
physical grassy plains (pampas) and low hills
features rivers Negro, Uruguay, Río de la Plata
head of state and government Luis Alberto Lacalle from 1989
political system democratic republic
political parties Colorado Party (PC), progressive, center-left; National (Blanco)
Party (PN), traditionalist, right-of-center; Amplio Front (FA), moderate, left-wing
exports meat and meat products, leather, wool, textiles
currency nuevo peso
population (1990 est) 3,002,000 (Spanish, Italian; mestizo, mulatto, black); growth rate 0.7% p.a.
life expectancy men 68, women 75 (1989)
language Spanish
media the Ministry of Defense controls broadcasting licenses
religion Roman Catholic 66%
literacy 96% (1984)
GNP $7.5 bn; $2,470 per head (1988)
chronology
1825 Independence declared from Brazil.
1836 Civil war.
1930 First constitution adopted.
1966 Blanco party in power, with Jorge Pacheco Areco as president.
1972 Colorado Party returned, with Juan Maria Bordaberry Arocena as president.
1976 Bordaberry deposed by army; Dr Méndez Manfredini became president.
1984 Violent antigovernment protests after ten years of repressive rule.
1985 Agreement reached between the army and political leaders for return to constitutional government. Colorado Party won general election; Dr Julio Maria Sanguinetti became president.
1986 Government of national accord established under President Sanguinetti's leadership.
1989 Luis Alberto Lacalle elected president.

Urey Harold Clayton 1893–1981. US chemist. In 1932 he isolated ⟁heavy water and discovered ⟁deuterium, for which he was awarded the 1934 Nobel Prize for Chemistry.

During World War II he was a member of the Manhattan Project that produced the atomic bomb, but after the war he advocated nuclear disarmament and world government.

uric acid C$_5$H$_4$N$_4$O$_3$ nitrogen-containing waste substance, formed from the breakdown of food and body protein. It is only slightly soluble in water. Uric acid is the normal means by which most land animals that develop in a shell (birds, reptiles, insects, and land gastropods) deposit their waste products. The young are unable to get rid of their excretory products while in the shell and therefore store them in this insoluble form.

Humans and other primates produce some uric acid as well as urea, the normal nitrogen-waste product of mammals, adult amphibians, and many marine fishes. If formed in excess and not excreted, uric acid may be deposited in sharp crystals in the joints and other tissues, causing gout; or it may form stones (calculi) in the kidneys or bladder.

urinary system system of organs that removes nitrogenous waste products and excess water from the bodies of animals. In vertebrates, it consists of a pair of kidneys, which produce urine; ureters, which drain the kidneys; and (in bony fishes, amphibians, some reptiles, and mammals) a bladder, which stores the urine before its discharge. In mammals, the urine is expelled through the urethra; in other vertebrates, the urine drains into a common excretory chamber called a ⟁cloaca, and the urine is not discharged separately.

urine amber-colored fluid made by the kidneys from the blood. It contains excess water, salts, proteins, waste products in the form of urea, a pigment, and some acid.

The kidneys pass it through two fine tubes (ureters) to the bladder, which may act as a reservoir for up to 1.5 pt/0.7 l at a time. In mammals, it then passes into the urethra, which opens to the outside by a sphincter (constricting muscle) under voluntary control. In reptiles and birds, nitrogenous wastes are discharged as an almost solid substance made mostly of ⟁uric acid, rather than urea.

Ursa Major (Latin "Great Bear") the third largest constellation in the sky, in the north polar region. Its seven brightest stars make up the familiar shape of the *Big Dipper*. The second star of the "handle" of the dipper, called Mizar, has a companion star, Alcor. Two stars forming the far side of the "bowl" (one of them, Dubhe, being the constellation's brightest star) act as pointers to the north pole star, Polaris.

Ursa Minor (Latin "Little Bear") constellation in the northern sky. It is shaped like a dipper, with the north pole star Polaris at the end of the handle.

It contains the orange subgiant Kochab, about 95 light-years from Earth.

Ursula, St 4th century AD. English legendary saint, supposed to have been martyred with 11 virgins (misread as 11,000 in the Middle Ages) by the Huns in the Rhineland.

urticaria or *nettle rash* or *hives* irritant skin condition characterized by itching, burning, stinging, and the spontaneous appearance of raised patches of skin. Treatment is usually by antihistamines or steroids taken orally or applied as lotions. Its causes are varied and include allergy and stress.

Uruguay country in South America, on the Atlantic coast, bounded N by Brazil and W by Argentina.

government The 1966 constitution provides for a president who is head of state and head of government, elected by universal suffrage for a five-year term, and a two-chamber legislature, comprising a senate and a federal chamber of deputies. The president is assisted by a vice-president and presides over a council of ministers.

The senate has up to 30 members and the chamber of deputies 99, all elected for a five-year term by universal suffrage through a system of proportional representation. The voting system ensures that there are at least two deputies representing each of the republic's 19 departments.

history For early history, see ⏵American Indian. The area was settled by both Spain 1624 and Portugal 1680, but Spain secured the whole in the 18th century. In 1814 Spanish rule was overthrown under the leadership of José Artigas, dictator until driven out by Brazil 1820. Disputed between Argentina and Brazil 1825–28, Uruguay declared its independence 1825, although it was not recognized by its neighbors until 1853.

The names of Uruguay's two main political parties, the liberal Colorado (the Reds) and the conservative Blanco (the Whites), are derived from the colors of the flags carried in the civil war 1836. From 1951 to 1966 there was a collective leadership called "collegiate government," and then a new constitution was adopted and a single president elected, the Blanco candidate, Jorge Pacheco Areco. His presidency was marked by high inflation, labor unrest, and growing guerrilla activity by the ⏵Tupamaros.

repressive regime In 1972 Pacheco was replaced by the Colorado candidate, Juan Maria Bordaberry Arocena. Within a year the Tupamaros had been crushed, and all other left-wing groups banned. Bordaberry now headed a repressive regime, under which the normal democratic institutions had been dissolved. In 1976 he refused any movement toward constitutional government, was deposed by the army, and Dr Aparicio Méndez Manfredini was made president. Despite promises to return to democratic government, the severe repression continued, and political opponents were imprisoned.

"Program of National Accord" In 1981 the deteriorating economy made the army anxious to return to constitutional government, and a retired general, Gregorio Alvarez Armellino, was appointed president for an interim period. Discussions between the army and the main political parties failed to agree on the form of constitution to be adopted, and civil unrest, in the shape of strikes and demonstrations, grew. By 1984 antigovernment activity had reached a crisis point, and eventually all the main political leaders signed an agreement for a "Program of National Accord." The 1966 constitution, with some modifications, was restored, and in 1985 a general election was held. The Colorado Party won a narrow majority, and its leader, Dr Julio Maria Sanguinetti, became president. The army stepped down, and by 1986 President Sanguinetti was presiding over a government of national accord in which all the main parties—Colorado, Blanco, and the left-wing Broad Front—were represented. In the Nov 1989 elections Luis Alberto Lacalle was narrowly elected president, with 37% of the vote compared with 30% for his Colorado opponent. After his inauguration in 1990, he concentrated his efforts on economic problems but his modernizing programs were hindered by the collapse of the coalition government. In 1992 Lacalle reorganized the cabinet. *See illustration box.*

Urumqi or *Urumchi* industrial city and capital of Xinjiang Uygur autonomous region, China, at the northern foot of the Tian Shan mountains; population (1989) 1,110,000. It produces cotton textiles, cement, chemicals, iron, and steel.

US abbreviation for the *United States of America* (popular and most frequent name used by speakers of American English for the nation).

USA abbreviation (official) for the ⏵*United States of America*; *US Army*.

USDA abbreviation for the *US Department of Agriculture.*

USGS abbreviation for the *US Geological Survey*, part of the department of the interior.

Ushant (French *Ouessant*) French island 11 mi/18 km W of Brittany, area 9 sq mi/15 sq km, off which the British admiral Richard ⏵Howe defeated the French navy 1794 on "the Glorious First of June." The chief town is Lampaul.

USIA abbreviation for *US Information Agency.*

Usküb Turkish name of ⏵Skopje, the capital of Macedonia, Yugoslavia.

US Naval Observatory US government observatory in Washington, DC, which provides the nation's time service and publishes almanacs for navigators, surveyors, and astronomers. It contains a 26-in/66-cm refracting telescope opened 1873. A 61-in/1.55-m reflector for measuring positions of celestial objects was opened 1964 at Flagstaff, Arizona.

USO abbreviation for *United Service Organizations.*

USS abbreviation for *US Ship*.

USSR abbreviation for the former ⏵*Union of Soviet Socialist Republics.*

Ustinov Peter 1921– . English stage and film actor, writer, and director. He won an Academy Award for *Spartacus* 1960. Other film appearances include *Topkapi* 1964, *Death on the Nile* 1978, and *Evil under the Sun* 1981. He published his autobiography *Dear Me* 1983.

Ust-Kamenogorsk river port and chief center of the nuclear industry in Russia, situated in the Altai mountains, on the river Irtysh; population (1987) 321,000.

usury former term for charging interest on a loan of money. In medieval times, usury was held to be a sin, and Christians were forbidden to lend (although not to borrow).

The practice of charging interest is still regarded as usury in some Muslim countries.

UT abbreviation for the state of ⏵*Utah*.

Utagawa Kuniyoshi. Japanese printmaker; see ⏵Kuniyoshi Utagawa.

Utah state in W US; nickname Beehive State/Mormon State
area 84,881 sq mi/219,900 sq km
capital Salt Lake City
cities Provo, Ogden
physical Colorado Plateau to the east, mountains in center, Great Basin to the west, Great Salt Lake
features Great American Desert; Colorado

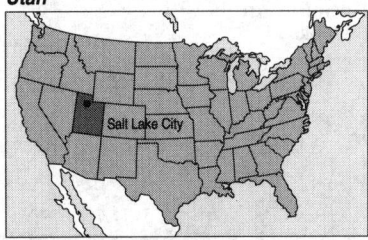

river system; Dinosaur and Rainbow Bridge national monuments; five national parks: the Arches, Bryce Canyon, Canyonlands, Capitol Reef, Zion; auto racing at Bonneville Salt Flats; Mormon temple and tabernacle, Salt Lake City
products wool, gold, silver, copper, coal, salt, steel
population (1990) 1,722,900
famous people Brigham Young
history explored first by Franciscan friars for Spain 1776; Great Salt Lake discovered by US frontier scout Jim Bridger 1824; part of the area ceded by Mexico 1848; developed by Mormons, still by far the largest religious group in the state; territory 1850, but not admitted to statehood until 1896 because of Mormon reluctance to relinquish plural marriage.

The world's largest open-pit copper mine began 1906 at Bingham Canyon. Largely because of the high birth rate, the state's population has more than doubled since World War II.

Utamaro Kitagawa 1753–1806. Japanese artist of the *ukiyo-e* ("floating world") school, who created muted color prints of beautiful women, including informal studies of prostitutes.

His style was distinctive: his subject is often seen close up, sometimes from unusual angles or viewpoints, and he made use of bold curvaceous lines and highly decorative textiles.

uterus hollow muscular organ of female mammals, located between the bladder and rectum, and connected to the Fallopian tubes above and the vagina below. The embryo develops within the uterus, and in placental mammals is attached to it after implantation via the ⏵placenta and umbilical cord. The lining of the uterus changes during the ⏵menstrual cycle. In humans and other higher primates, it is a single structure, but in other mammals it is paired.

The outer wall of the uterus is composed of smooth muscle, capable of powerful contractions (induced by hormones) during childbirth.

U Thant Burmese diplomat; see ⏵Thant, U.

Utica industrial city (engine parts, clothing) in central New York State; population (1990) 68,600. Utica was an important textile center from about 1850 to 1950. The first Woolworth store was opened here 1879.

The settlement 1773 was on the site of an Iroquois center and a British fort.

utilitarianism philosophical theory of ethics outlined by the philosopher Jeremy ⏵Bentham and developed by John Stuart Mill. According to utilitarianism, an action is morally right if it has consequences that lead to happiness, and wrong if it brings about the reverse. Thus society should aim for the greatest happiness of the greatest number.

Utopia (Greek "no place") any ideal state in literature, named after philosopher Thomas More's ideal commonwealth in his book *Utopia* 1516. Other versions include Plato's *Republic*, Francis Bacon's *New Atlantis* 1626, and *City of*

Uzbekistan
Republic of

area 172,741 sq mi/447,400 sq km
capital Tashkent
cities Samarkhand, Bukhara, Namangan
physical oases in the deserts; rivers: Amu
Darya, Syr Darya; Fergana Valley; rich in
mineral deposits
features more than 20 hydroelectric plants;
three natural gas pipelines
head of state Islam Karimov from 1990
head of government Abdul Hashim Mutalov
from 1991
political system socialist pluralist
political parties Uzbekistan Socialist
(formerly Communist) Party, reform-socialist;
Democratic Party, tolerated opposition
products rice, dried fruit, vines (all grown
by irrigation); cotton, silk
population (1990) 20,300,000 (71% Uzbek,
8% Russian, 5% Tajik, 4% Kazakh)
language Uzbek, a Turkic language
religion Sunni Muslim
chronology
1921 Part of Turkestan Soviet Socialist
Autonomous Republic.
1925 Became constituent republic of the
USSR.
1944 Some 160,000 Meskhetian Turks
forcibly transported from their native Georgia
to Uzbekistan by Stalin.
1989 June: Tashlak, Yaipan, and Ferghana
were the scenes of riots in which Meskhetian
Turks were attacked; 70 killed and 850
wounded.
1990 June: economic and political sovereignty
declared.
1991 March: Uzbek supported "renewed
federation" in USSR referendum. Aug: anti-
Gorbachev coup in Moscow initially accepted
by President Karimov; later, Karimov resigned
from Soviet Communist Party (CPSU) Politburo;
Uzbek Communist Party (UCP) broke with
CPSU; prodemocracy rallies dispersed by
militia; independence declared. Dec: joined
new Commonwealth of Independent States
(CIS).
1992 Jan: admitted into Conference on
Security and Cooperation in Europe (CSCE);
violent food riots in Tashkent. March: joined
the United Nations (UN); US diplomatic
recognition achieved.

isters) is drawn. The state president is directly
elected.
history The Turkmen are Turkic-speaking
descendants of the Mongol invaders who
swept across Asia from the 13th century. Part
of ⏵Turkestan, Turkmenistan was conquered
by Tsarist Russia 1865–76, with the emir of
Bukhara becoming a vassal. The Tashkent
soviet gradually extended its power 1917–
24, with the emir of Bukhara deposed 1920.
Uzbekistan became a constituent republic of
the USSR 1925, although guerrilla resistance
continued for a number of years. Some 160,000
Meskhetian Turks were forcibly transported
from their native Georgia to Uzbekistan by
Stalin 1944. After World War II Uzbekistan
became a major cotton-growing region, producing two-thirds of Soviet output. The Uzbek
Communist Party (UCP) leadership, who controlled the republic like a feudal fief, were both
notorious for the extent of their corruption
and for their obedience to Moscow. In return,
Uzbekistan received large subsidies.
growth of nationalism From the late 1980s
there was an upsurge in Islamic consciousness
provoking violent clashes with Meskhetian,
Armenian, and Kyrgyz minority communities,
particularly in the Ferghana Valley, which
had become a hotbed for ⏵Wahabi Islamic
militancy. In Sept 1989 an Uzbek nationalist organization, the Birlik ("Unity") People's
Movement, was formed. The UCP, under the
leadership of Islam Karimov, responded by
declaring the republic's "sovereignty" in June
1990 and replacing Russian administrators
with Uzbeks.
independence recognized President
Karimov did not immediately condemn the
Aug 1991 anti-Gorbachev attempted coup in
Moscow. However, once the coup was defeated, the UCP broke its links with the
Communist Party of the Soviet Union and
on Aug 31, 1991 the republic declared its
independence. Uzbekistan joined the new
⏵Commonwealth of Independent States (CIS)
in Dec 1991. On Dec 29 Karimov was directly
elected president, capturing 86% of the vote.
Uzbekistan was admitted to the ⏵Conference
on Security and Cooperation in Europe (CSCE)
in Jan 1992. In Feb it also joined the Economic
Cooperation Organization (ECO), founded by
Iran, Pakistan, and Turkey 1975, which aimed
to reduce customs tariffs and eventually form
a customs union. Admission to the United Nations was granted March 1992; US diplomatic
recognition was also achieved.

President Karimov embarked on a strategy
of gradualist market-centered economic reform. However, political authoritarianism continued. Communist Party cells were banned
from the armed forces, the police, and civil
service and the UCP changed its designation.
Nevertheless, the former UCP apparatus and
personnel remained very much in control, with
opposition groups either harassed or, in the
case of the Islamic Renaissance Party, banned.
A coalition of clergymen, led by the ⏵mufti
of Tashkent, called for fresh multiparty elections and an end to Communist Party activity.
Ethnic Russians, formerly preponderant in the
industrial work force and bureaucracy, began
to leave the republic, with adverse economic
consequences. In Jan 1992 several people died
in student-led food riots in Tashkent after prices had been liberalized. Aided by an inflow of
funds from Saudi Arabia and despite the secu-
larist stance of President Karimov, a revival of
Islamic teaching and studies commenced. *See
illustration box.*

---

the Sun by the Italian Tommaso Campanella
(1568–1639). Utopias are a common subject in
⏵science fiction.

Utrecht province of the Netherlands lying SE
of Amsterdam, on the Kromme Rijn (Crooked
Rhine)
area 513 sq mi/1,330 sq km
population (1991) 1,026,800
capital Utrecht
cities Amersfoort, Zeist, Nieuwegeun,
Veenendaal
products chemicals, livestock, textiles, electrical goods
history ruled by the bishops of Utrecht in
the Middle Ages, the province was sold to the
emperor Charles V of Spain 1527. It became a
center of Protestant resistance to Spanish rule
and, with the signing of the Treaty of Utrecht,
became one of the seven United Provinces of
the Netherlands 1579.

Utrecht, Treaty of treaty signed 1713 that
ended the War of the ⏵Spanish Succession.
Philip V was recognized as the legitimate king
of Spain, thus founding the Spanish branch of
the Bourbon dynasty and ending the French
king Louis XIV's attempts at expansion; the
Netherlands, Milan, and Naples were ceded to
Austria; Britain gained Gibraltar; the duchy of
Savoy was granted Sicily.

Utrecht, Union of in 1579, the union of
seven provinces of the N Netherlands—Holland, Zeeland, Friesland, Groningen, Utrecht,
Gelderland, and Overijssel—that became the
basis of opposition to the Spanish crown and
the foundation of the present-day Dutch state.

Utrillo Maurice 1883–1955. French artist. He
painted townscapes of his native Paris, many
depicting Montmartre, often from postcard
photographs.

Utrillo was the son of Suzanne Valadan, a
trapeze-performer who was encouraged to become an artist herself after posing as a model
for many painters of the day. His work from
1908–14 is considered his best.

Uttar Pradesh state of N India
area 113,638 sq mi/294,400 sq km
capital Lucknow
cities Kanpur, Varanasi, Agra, Allahabad,
Meerut
features most populous state; Himalayan peak
Nanda Devi 25,655 ft/7,817 m
population (1991) 138,760,400
famous people Indira Gandhi, Ravi Shankar
language Hindi
religion 80% Hindu, 15% Muslim
history formerly the heart of the Mogul
Empire and generating point of the ⏵Sepoy
Rebellion 1857 and subsequent opposition to
British rule; see also the United Provinces of
⏵Agra and ⏵Oudh.

UV in physics, abbreviation for *ultraviolet*.

uvula fleshy flap that hangs at the back of the
throat in humans.

Uzbek member of certain Turkic-speaking
peoples of Uzbekistan (where they form 70% of
the population) and neighboring regions.

Uzbekistan country in central Asia, bounded
N by Kazakhstan and the Aral Sea, E by
Kyrgyzstan and Tajikistan, S by Afghanistan,
and W by Turkmenistan.
government There is a 500-member legislature, the supreme soviet, to which deputies
are elected by a majority system, and a second
ballot "runoff" race in contests in which there
is no clear first-round majority. From the majority grouping within the supreme soviet, a
prime minister (chairman of the cabinet of min-

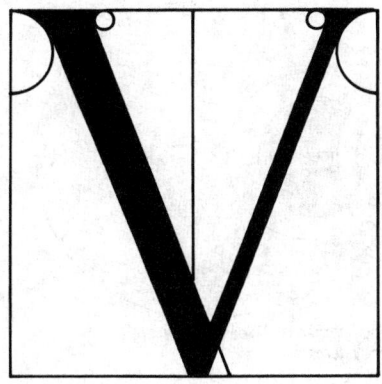

V the 22nd letter of the English alphabet. In sound it is the voiced labiodental fricative. It was not differentiated from U until about the 16th century.

V Roman numeral for *five*; in physics, symbol for *volt*.

v in physics, symbol for *velocity*.

V1, V2 (German *Vergeltungswaffe* "revenge weapons") German flying bombs of World War II, launched against Britain in 1944 and 1945. The V1, also called the doodlebug and buzz bomb, was an uncrewed monoplane carrying a bomb, powered by a simple kind of jet engine called a pulse jet. The V2, a rocket bomb with a preset guidance system, was the first long-range ballistic ◊missile. It was 47 ft/14 m long, carried a 1-ton warhead, and hit its target at a speed of 3,000 mph/5,000 kph.

The V2 was developed by the rocket engineer Wernher ◊von Braun. After the war captured V2 material became the basis of the space race in both the USSR and the US.

VA abbreviation for the state of ◊*Virginia*.

vaccination use of specially modified ◊pathogens (bacteria and viruses) to confer immunity to the diseases with which they are associated. When injected or taken by mouth, a vaccine stimulates the production of antibodies to protect against that particular disease. Vaccination is the oldest form of ◊immunization.

vaccine any preparation of modified viruses or bacteria that is introduced into the body, usually either orally or by a hypodermic syringe, to induce the specific ◊antibody reaction that produces ◊immunity against a particular disease.

In 1796, Edward ◊Jenner was the first to inoculate a child successfully with cowpox virus to produce immunity to smallpox. His method, the application of an infective agent to an abraded skin surface, is still used in smallpox inoculation.

vacuole in biology, a fluid-filled, membrane-bound cavity inside a cell. It may be a reservoir for fluids that the cell will secrete to the outside, or filled with other excretory products or essential nutrients that the cell needs to store. In amebas (single-cell animals), vacuoles are sites for digestion of engulfed food particles. A plant cell usually has a large central vacuole to increase its surface area for food absorption.

vacuum in general, a region completely empty of matter; in physics, any enclosure in which the gas pressure is considerably less than atmospheric pressure (101,325 ◊pascals).

Vaduz capital of the European principality of Liechtenstein; industries include engineering and agricultural trade; population (1984) 5,000.

vagina the front passage in female mammals, linking the uterus to the exterior. It admits the penis during sexual intercourse, and is the birth canal down which the fetus passes during delivery.

vaginismus spasmodic contraction of the entrance to the vagina during attempted intercourse, thus preventing the entrance of the penis. It is usually of psychological origin, although it may be due to inflammation of the vagina, causing a reflex contraction.

Vail Alfred Lewis 1807–1859. US communications pioneer. Having a close association with Samuel ◊Morse in 1837, he developed an improved design for the telegraph mechanism, beginning production of the new model 1838. With Congressional funding for a telegraph line between Washington and Baltimore, Vail renewed his working relationship with Morse 1844.

Vail was born in Morristown, New Jersey, educated at New York University, and worked as a mechanic at his father's iron foundry. Vail's book *The American Electro Magnetic Telegraph* was published 1845, and he retired from business 1849.

Valdemar alternate spelling of ◊Waldemar, name of four kings of Denmark.

Valdivia Pedro de *c.* 1497–1554. Spanish explorer who traveled to Venezuela about 1530 and accompanied Francisco ◊Pizarro on his second expedition to Peru. He then went south into Chile, where he founded the cities of Santiago 1541 and Valdivia 1544. In 1552 he crossed the Andes to explore the Negro River. He was killed by Araucanian Indians.

valence the combining capacity of an ◊atom or ◊radical, determined by the number of electrons that an atom will add, lose, or share when it reacts with another atom. Elements that lose electrons (such as hydrogen and the ◊metals) have a positive valence; those that add electrons (such as oxygen and other nonmetals) have a negative valence.

valence electron in chemistry, an electron in the outermost shell of an ◊atom. It is the valence electrons that are involved in the formation of ionic and covalent bonds (see ◊molecule). The number of electrons in this outermost shell represents the maximum possible valence for many elements and matches the number of the group that the element occupies in the ◊periodic table of the elements.

Valencia industrial city (textiles, leather, sugar) and agricultural center in Carabobo state, N Venezuela, on the Cabriales River; population (1989) 1,227,472. It is 1,569 ft/478 m above sea level and was founded 1555.

Valencia industrial city (wine, fruit, chemicals, textiles, ship repair) in Valencia region, E Spain; population (1991) 777,400. The Community of Valencia, consisting of Alicante, Castellón, and Valencia, has an area of 8,994 sq mi/23,300 sq km and a population of 3,772,000.

Valencia was ruled by El ◊Cid 1094–99, after he recaptured it from the Moors. There is a cathedral of the 13th–15th centuries and a university founded 1500.

Valenciennes industrial town in Nord *département*, NE France, near the Belgian border, once known for its lace; population (1982) 349,500. It became French 1678.

valency shell in chemistry, outermost shell of electrons in an ◊atom. It contains the ◊valence electrons. Elements with four or more electrons in their outermost shell can show variable valency. Chlorine can show valencies of 1, 3, 5, and 7 in different compounds.

Valentine, St according to tradition a bishop of Terni martyred at Rome, now omitted from the calendar of saints' days as probably nonexistent. His festival was Feb 14, but the custom of sending "valentines" to a loved one on that day seems to have arisen because the day accidentally coincided with the Roman mid-February festival of ◊Lupercalia.

valerian perennial plant of either of two genera, *Valeriana* and *Centranthus*, family Valerianaceae, native to the northern hemisphere, with clustered heads of fragrant tubular flowers in red, white, or pink. The root of the common valerian or garden heliotrope *Valeriana officinalis* is used medicinally to relieve flatulence and as a sedative.

Valéry Paul 1871–1945. French poet and mathematician. His poetry includes *La Jeune Parque/The Young Fate* 1917 and *Charmes/Enchantments* 1922.

For most of his adult life (from 1894) he would wake before 5 a.m. and immediately write in his journals, which totaled over 26,000 pages by the time he died. He regarded the journals as his most important writing.

Valhalla in Norse mythology, the hall in ◊Odin's palace where he feasts with the souls of heroes killed in battle.

Valkyrie in Norse mythology, any of the female attendants of ◊Odin. They select the most valiant warriors to die in battle and escort them to Valhalla.

Valladolid industrial town (food processing, vehicles, textiles, engineering), and capital of Valladolid province, Spain; population (1991) 345,300.

It was the capital of Castile and Leon in the 14th–15th centuries, then of Spain until 1560. The Catholic monarchs Ferdinand and Isabella were married at Valladolid 1469. The explorer Columbus died here, and the home of the writer Cervantes is preserved. It has a university founded 1346 and a cathedral 1595.

Vallandigham Clement Laird 1820–1871. US political leader. He served in the Ohio legislature 1845–47 and the US House of Representatives 1858–63. A staunch Democrat, he supported Stephen Douglas for president 1860 and, as leader of the "Copperheads," opposed many of Lincoln's war policies. Defeated for reelection to the House and arrested for sedition 1862, Vallandigham was deported to the Confederacy. Returning to Ohio 1864, he remained a strong foe of the Radical Republicans until his death.

Born in New Lisbon, Ohio, and educated at Washington and Jefferson College, Vallandigham was admitted to the bar 1842.

Valle d'Aosta autonomous region of NW Italy; area 1,274 sq mi/3,300 sq km; population (1990) 116,000, many of whom are French-speaking. It produces wine and livestock. Its capital is Aosta.

Vallee Rudy (Hubert Prior) 1901–1986. US

singer, actor, and bandleader. Establishing a clean-cut, college-boy image, he became one of the most popular crooners of the 1920s. He formed his band the Connecticut Yankees 1928 and hosted a radio program with the theme song "My Time Is Your Time" (recorded 1929). From 1929 he appeared in films and stage musicals.

Vallejo industrial city (fruit and flour processing and petroleum refining) in NW California, on San Pablo Bay, NE of Berkeley; population (1990) 109,200. It served as California's capital 1852–53.

Vallejo Mariano Guadelupe 1808–1890. American military leader in colonial California. Born in Monterey, California, Vallejo chose a military career early in life. A supporter of Mexican independence, he was stationed in Alta California and helped put down an Indian uprising at San Jose 1829. Through the 1830s, Vallejo consistently opposed the rule of autocratic governors sent from Mexico City and in 1838 became the military commander of the province. He was briefly imprisoned during the Bear Flag revolt 1849 but later chose to become a citizen of the state of California, serving as a member of the state senate.

Valletta capital and port of Malta; population (1987) 9,000; urban area 101,000.

It was founded 1566 by the Knights of ⟡St John of Jerusalem and named after their grand master Jean de la Valette (1494–1568), who fended off a Turkish siege May–Sept 1565. The 16th-century palace of the grand masters survives. Malta was formerly a British naval base and came under heavy attack in World War II.

Valley Forge site in Pennsylvania 20 mi/ 32 km NW of Philadelphia, where George Washington's army spent the winter of 1777–78 in great hardship during the ⟡American Revolution. Of the 10,000 men there, 2,500 died of disease and the rest suffered from lack of rations and other supplies; many deserted.

During that winter, Washington introduced Prussian officers who trained the irregulars. The Franco-American alliance 1778 boosted morale and brought new recruits to the army, which emerged from the ordeal to inflict heavy losses on the British.

Valley of Ten Thousand Smokes valley in SW Alaska, on the Alaska Peninsula, where in 1912 Mount Katmai erupted in one of the largest volcanic explosions ever known, though without loss of human life since the area was uninhabited. It was dedicated as the Katmai National Monument 1918. Thousands of fissures on the valley floor continue to emit steam and gases.

Valley of the Kings burial place of ancient kings opposite ⟡Thebes, Egypt, on the left bank of the Nile.

Valois branch of the Capetian dynasty, originally counts of Valois (see Hugh ⟡Capet) in France, members of which occupied the French throne from Philip VI 1328 to Henry III 1589.

Valparaíso industrial port (sugar, refining, textiles, chemicals) in Chile; capital of Valparaíso province, on the Pacific; population (1990) 276,800. Founded 1536, it was occupied by the English naval adventurers ⟡Drake 1578 and Hawkins 1595, pillaged by the Dutch 1600, and bombarded by Spain 1866; it has also suffered from earthquakes.

value-added tax (VAT) tax on goods and

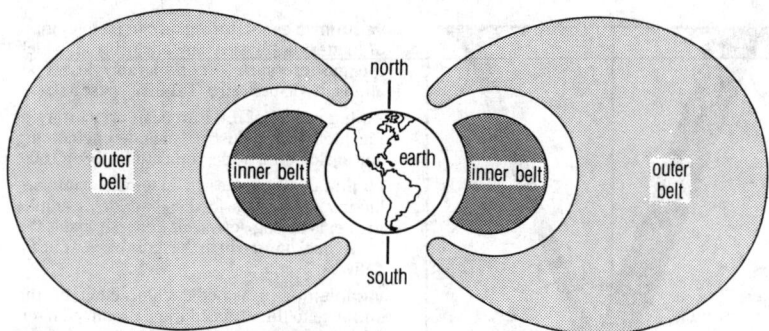

Van Allen radiation belts *The Van Allen belts of trapped charged particles are a hazard to spacecraft, affecting on-board electronics and computer systems.*

services. VAT is imposed by the European Community on member states. The tax varies from state to state. An agreed proportion of the tax money is used to fund the EC.

VAT is applied at each stage of the production of a commodity, and it is charged only on the value added at that stage. It is not levied, unlike sales tax, on the sale of the commodity itself, but at this stage the VAT paid at earlier stages of the commodity's manufacture cannot be reclaimed. In the UK, food, newspapers, and books are exempt from VAT.

valve device that controls the flow of a fluid. Inside a valve, a plug moves to widen or close the opening through which the fluid passes. The valve was invented by US radio engineer Lee de Forest (1873–1961).

Common valves include the cone or needle valve, the globe valve, and butterfly valve, all named after the shape of the plug. Specialized valves include the one-way valve, which permits fluid flow in one direction only, and the safety valve, which cuts off flow under certain conditions.

valve in animals, a structure for controlling the direction of the blood flow. In humans and other vertebrates, the contractions of the beating heart cause the correct blood flow into the arteries because a series of valves prevent back flow. Diseased valves, detected as "heart murmurs," have decreased efficiency. The tendency for low-pressure venous blood to collect at the base of limbs under the influence of gravity is counteracted by a series of small valves within the veins. It was the existence of these valves that prompted the 17th-century physician William Harvey to suggest that the blood circulated around the body.

vampire (Magyar *vampir*) in Hungarian and Slavonic folklore, an "undead" corpse that sleeps by day in its native earth, and by night, often in the form of a bat, sucks the blood of the living. ⟡Dracula is a vampire in popular fiction.

vampire bat any South and Central American bat of the family Desmodontidae, of which there are three species. The ***common vampire*** *Desmodus rotundus* is found from N Mexico to central Argentina; its head and body grow to 3.5 in/9 cm. Vampires feed on the blood of birds and mammals; they slice a piece of skin from a sleeping animal with their sharp incisor teeth and lap up the flowing blood.

Vampires feed on all kinds of mammals including horses, cattle, and occasionally humans. They fly low and settle on the ground before running to a victim. The bite is painless and the loss of blood is small; the victim seldom comes to any harm. Vampire bats are intelligent and among the few mammals to manifest

altruistic behavior (they adopt orphans and help other bats in need).

vanadium silver-white, malleable and ductile, metallic element, symbol V, atomic number 23, atomic weight 50.942. It occurs in certain iron, lead, and uranium ores and is widely distributed in small quantities in igneous and sedimentary rocks. It is used to make steel alloys, to which it adds tensile strength.

Spanish mineralogist Andrés del Rio (1764–1849) and Swedish chemist Nils Sefström (1787–1845) discovered vanadium independently, the former 1801 and the latter 1831. Del Rio named it "erythronium," but was persuaded by other chemists that he had not in fact discovered a new element; Sefström gave it its present name, after the Norse goddess of love and beauty, Vanadis (or Freya).

Van Allen James (Alfred) 1914– . US physicist whose instruments aboard the first US satellite *Explorer 1* 1958 led to the discovery of the Van Allen belts, two zones of intense radiation around the Earth. He pioneered high-altitude research with rockets after World War II.

Born in Mount Pleasant, Iowa, Van Allen received a PhD in physics from the University of Iowa 1939. He studied captured German V2 rockets after World War II, and became professor of physics at the University of Iowa 1951.

Van Allen radiation belts two zones of charged particles around the Earth's magnetosphere, discovered 1958 by US physicist James Van Allen. The atomic particles come from the Earth's upper atmosphere and the ⟡solar wind, and are trapped by the Earth's magnetic field. The inner belt lies 620–3,100 mi/1,000–5,000 km above the equator, and contains ⟡protons and ⟡electrons. The outer belt lies 9,300–15,500 mi/15,000–25,000 km above the equator, but is lower around the magnetic poles. It contains mostly electrons from the solar wind.

Van Buren Martin 1782–1862. Eighth president of the US 1837–41, a Democrat, who had helped establish the ⟡Democratic Party. He was secretary of state 1829–31, minister to Britain 1831–33, vice-president 1833–37, and president during the Panic of 1837, the worst US economic crisis until that time, caused by land speculation in the West. Refusing to intervene, he advocated the establishment of an independent treasury, one not linked to the federal government, worsening the depression and losing the 1840 election.

Born of Dutch ancestry in Kinderhook, New York, Van Buren was a US senator from New York 1821–28, and governor of New York 1829. As president, he attempted to hold the Southern states in the Union by advocating a strict states' rights position on slavery, but his refusal to annex Texas alienated many Southerners. He adhered to Jeffersonian principles of non-intervention in economic affairs. He lost the 1844 Democratic nomination to Polk, and in 1848 ran unsuccessfully for president as a candidate of Free Soil, a small but influential political party opposed to the expansion of slavery in the western territories.

Vance Cyrus 1917– . US Democratic politician, secretary of state 1977–80. He resigned because he did not support President Carter's abortive mission to rescue the US hostages in Iran.

Van Cortlandt Stephanus 1643–1700. Dutch-American colonial official. Born in New Amsterdam (now New York), the son of a prominent family of Dutch settlers, Van Cortlandt became a prosperous merchant and expanded his landholdings after the English conquest of the colony in 1664. A longtime colonel in the provincial militia, he served on the governor's council and in 1677 became the first native-born mayor of New York. He was a local judge 1677–91 and justice of the provincial supreme court 1691–1700.

Vancouver industrial city (oil refining, engineering, shipbuilding, aircraft, timber, pulp and paper, textiles, fisheries) in Canada, its chief Pacific seaport, on the mainland of British Columbia; population (1986) 1,381,000.

Vancouver is situated on Burrard Inlet, at the mouth of the Fraser River. George Vancouver took possession of the site for Britain 1792. It was settled by 1875, under the name of *Granville*, and was renamed when it became a city 1886, having been reached by the Canadian Pacific Railroad. In 1989 it had an ethnic Chinese population of 140,000, and this was rapidly augmented by thousands of immigrants from Hong Kong.

Vancouver city in SW Washington, on the Columbia River, N of Portland, Oregon; a manufacturing and shipping center for agriculture and timber; population (1990) 46,400. It began as a trading post for the Hudson's Bay Company 1825.

Vancouver George *c.* 1758–1798. British navigator who made extensive exploration of the west coast of North America. He accompanied James ◊Cook on two voyages, and served in the West Indies. He also surveyed parts of Australia, New Zealand, Tahiti, and Hawaii.

Vancouver Island island off the west coast of Canada, part of British Columbia
area 12,404 sq mi/32,136 sq km
cities Victoria, Nanaimo, Esquimalt (naval base)
products coal, timber, fish
history visited by British explorer Cook 1778; surveyed 1792 by Captain George Vancouver.

Vandal member of a Germanic people related to the ◊Goths. In the 5th century AD the Vandals moved from N Germany to invade Roman ◊Gaul and Spain, many settling in Andalusia (formerly Vandalitia) and others reaching N Africa 429. They sacked Rome 455 but accepted Roman suzerainty in the 6th century.

van de Graaff Robert Jemison 1901–1967. US physicist who from 1929 developed a high-voltage generator, which in its modern form can produce more than a million volts. It consists of a continuous vertical conveyor belt that carries electrostatic charges (resulting from

van de Graaff *US physicist Robert Jemison van de Graaff developed this high-powered generator that can produce more than a million volts.*

friction) up to a large hollow sphere supported on an insulated stand. The lower end of the belt is earthed, so that charge accumulates on the sphere. The size of the voltage built up in air depends on the radius of the sphere, but can be increased by enclosing the generator in an inert atmosphere, such as nitrogen.

Vandenberg Arthur Hendrick 1884–1951. US public official. Active in Republican state politics, he was named to fill a vacant US Senate seat 1928 and remained in that office for the next 23 years. Although initially an isolationist, Vandenberg supported F D Roosevelt's war policies and was a supporter of the United Nations 1945. He was chair of the Senate Foreign Relations Committee 1946–48.

Born in Grand Rapids, Michigan, Vandenberg briefly attended the University of Michigan Law School, leaving to join the staff of the *Grand Rapids Herald*, of which he became editor 1906.

Vanderbilt Cornelius 1794–1877. US industrialist who made a fortune in steamships and (from the age of 70) by financing railroads. He defeated stock raids and takeover attempts by other financiers in the process of amassing a fortune of more than $100 million. Despite his wealth, he did not engage in any philanthropic activities until near his death, when he gave $1 million to what would become Vanderbilt University. See also Jay ◊Gould.

Born in Port Richmond, New York, Vanderbilt, at the age of 16, began a ferry operation between Staten Island and Manhattan. By 1829, he had established his own steamship line, at first to service local New York and New England ports, and from 1850 to reach California by a shorter route, through Nicaragua. In the 1860s he began to acquire and merge railroad lines in New York and Chicago.

Vanderbilt William Henry 1821–1885. US financier and railroad promoter. Born in New Brunswick, New Jersey, son of financier Cornelius Vanderbilt, he was given control of

the Staten Island Railroad 1857. He was named vice-president of the New York and Harlem Railroad 1864, acquired other railroads, and became president of the New York Central Railroad 1877. As the head of a railroad trust, he was deeply involved in rate fixing and strongly opposed government regulation of the railroad industry. Vanderbilt, famous for his contemptuous phrase "The public be damned," retired in 1883.

Van der Post Laurens (Jan) 1906– . South African writer whose books, many of them autobiographical, reflect his openness to diverse cultures and his belief in the importance of intuition, individualism, and myth in human experience. A formative influence was his time spent with the San Bushmen of the Kalahari while growing up, and whose disappearing culture he recorded in *The Lost World of the Kalahari* 1958, *The Heart of the Hunter* 1961, and *Testament to the Bushmen* 1984.

van der Waals Johannes Diderik 1837–1923. Dutch physicist who was awarded a Nobel Prize 1910 for his theoretical study of gases. He emphasized the forces of attraction and repulsion between atoms and molecules in describing the behavior of real gases, as opposed to the ideal gases dealt with in ◊Boyle's law and ◊Charles's law.

Van Devanter Willis 1859–1941. US Supreme Court justice 1910–37. He was active in Republican politics and served as assistant US attorney general 1897–1903 and federal circuit judge 1903–10. He was appointed to the US Supreme Court by President Taft. A staunch conservative, Van Devanter was a bitter opponent of the New Deal until his retirement.

Van Devanter was born in Marion, Indiana, educated at Asbury University and received a law degree from the University of Cincinnati 1881. Settling in Cheyenne, Wyoming, he served as city attorney 1887–88 and chief justice of the territorial supreme court 1888–90.

Van Diemen's Land former name (1642–1855) of ◊Tasmania, Australia. It was named by Dutch navigator Abel Tasman after the governor-general of the Dutch East Indies, Anthony van ◊Diemen. The name Tasmania was used from the 1840s and became official 1855.

van Dyck Anthony. Flemish painter, see ◊Dyck, Anthony van.

Vane Henry 1613–1662. English politician. In 1640 elected a member of the ◊Long Parliament, he was prominent in the impeachment of Archbishop ◊Laud and in 1643–53 was in effect the civilian head of the Parliamentary government. At the Restoration of the monarchy he was executed.

Vane John 1927– . British pharmacologist who discovered the wide role of prostaglandins in the human body, produced in response to illness and stress. He shared the 1982 Nobel Prize for Medicine with Sune Bergström and Bengt Samuelson of Sweden.

van Eyck Jan. Flemish painter; see ◊Eyck, Jan van.

van Gogh Vincent. Dutch painter; see ◊Gogh, Vincent van.

Vanguard early series of US Earth-orbiting satellites and their associated rocket launcher. *Vanguard 1* was the second US satellite,

Vanuatu
Republic of (*Ripablik Blong Vanuatu***)**

area 5,714 sq mi/14,800 sq km
capital Vila (on Efate)
cities Luganville (on Espíritu Santo)
physical comprises around 70 islands, including Espíritu Santo, Malekula, and Efate; densely forested, mountainous
features three active volcanoes
head of state Fred Timakata from 1989
head of government Maxime Carlot from 1991
political system democratic republic
political parties Union of Moderate Parties (UMP), Francophone centrist; Vanuatu National United Party (VNUP), formed by Walter Lini; Vanua'aku Pati (VP), Anglophone centrist; Melanesian Progressive Party (MPP), Melanesian centrist; Fren Melanesian Party
exports copra, fish, coffee, cocoa
currency vatu
population (1989) 152,000 (90% Melanesian); growth rate 3.3% p.a.
life expectancy men 67, women 71 (1989)
languages Bislama 82%, English, French (all official)
literacy 53%
religion Presbyterian 40%, Roman Catholic 16%, Anglican 14%, animist 15%
GDP $125 million (1987); $927 per head
chronology
1906 Islands jointly administered by France and Britain.
1975 Representative assembly established.
1978 Government of national unity formed, with Father Gerard Leymang as chief minister.
1980 Revolt on the island of Espíritu Santo delayed independence but it was achieved within the Commonwealth, with George Kalkoa (adopted name Sokomanu) as president and Father Walter Lini as prime minister.
1988 Dismissal of Lini by Sokomanu led to Sokomanu's arrest for treason. Lini reinstated.
1989 Sokomanu sentenced to six years' imprisonment; succeeded as president by Fred Timakata.
1991 Lini voted out by party members; replaced by Donald Kalpokas. General election produced UMP–VNUP coalition under Maxime Carlot.

launched March 17, 1958 by the three-stage Vanguard rocket. Tracking of its orbit revealed that Earth is slightly pear-shaped. The series ended Sept 1959 with *Vanguard 3*.

vanilla any climbing orchid of the genus *Vanilla*, native to tropical America but cultivated elsewhere, with fragrant, large, white or yellow flowers. The dried and fermented fruit, or podlike capsules, of *Vanilla planifolia* are the source of the vanilla flavoring used in cooking and baking.

Annual world production of vanilla pods is estimated at 1,500 tons. Vanilla flavoring (**vanillin**) can now be produced artificially from waste sulfite liquor, a by-product of paper pulp-making.

Vanity Fair novel by William Makepeace Thackeray, published in the UK 1847–48. It deals with the contrasting fortunes of the tough orphan Becky Sharp and the soft-hearted, privileged Amelia Sedley, who first meet at Miss Pinkerton's Academy for young ladies.

Van Rensselaer Stephen 1764–1839. American public official and soldier. At the start of the War of 1812, he commanded American forces at New York State's northern border but suffered a serious defeat at Queenstown. Van Rensselaer was a US congressman 1822–29, and as president of the New York Canal Commission 1825–39 he oversaw the construction of the Erie Canal.

Van Rensselaer, born in New York and educated at Harvard, inherited extensive real estate holdings and served in the New York state assembly 1789–91, in the state senate 1791–96, and as a major general in the militia. He founded the Rensselaer Polytechnic Institute 1824.

van't Hoff Jacobus Henricus 1852–1911. Dutch physical chemist. He explained the "asymmetric" carbon atom occurring in optically active compounds. His greatest work—the concept of chemical affinity as

the maximum work obtainable from a reaction—was shown with measurements of osmotic and gas pressures, and reversible electrical cells. He was the first recipient of the Nobel Prize for Chemistry, in 1901.

Vanuatu group of islands in the SW Pacific Ocean, part of ◊Melanesia.
government Vanuatu is an independent republic within the British ◊Commonwealth. The constitution dates from independence 1980. It provides for a president, who is formal head of state, elected for a five-year term by an electoral college consisting of parliament and the presidents of the country's regional councils. Parliament consists of a single chamber of 46 members, elected by universal suffrage, through a system of proportional representation, for a four-year term. From among their members they elect a prime minister who then appoints and presides over a council of ministers.
history Originally settled by Melanesians, the islands were reached from Europe 1606 by the Portuguese navigator Pedro Fernandez de Queiras. Called the New Hebrides, they were jointly administered by France and Britain from 1906. Vanuatu escaped Japanese occupation during World War II.

In the 1970s two political parties were formed, the New Hebrides National Party, supported by British interests, and the Union of New Hebrides Communities, supported by France. Discussions began in London about eventual independence, and they resulted in the election of a representative assembly Nov 1975. Independence was delayed because of objections by the National Party, which had changed its name to the Vanua'aku Party (VP). A government of national unity was formed Dec 1978 with Father Gerard Leymang as chief minister and the VP leader, Father Walter Lini, as his deputy. In 1980 a revolt by French settlers and plantation workers on the island

of Espíritu Santo was put down by British, French, and Papua New Guinean troops.
independence Later in 1980 the New Hebrides became independent, within the Commonwealth, as the Republic of Vanuatu. The first president was George Kalkoa, who adopted the name Sokomanu, and the first prime minister was Father Lini.

Lini pursued a left-of-center, nonaligned foreign policy, which included support for the Kanak separatist movement in New Caledonia. This soured relations with France and provoked mounting opposition within parliament. Despite the VP retaining its majority after the Nov 1987 general election, this opposition continued, prompting Lini in July 1988 to expel from parliament his rival Barak Sope. Lini was then dismissed as prime minister and parliament dissolved by President Sokomanu, who appointed his nephew Sope head of an interim government. However, the Supreme Court ruled these actions unconstitutional and security forces loyal to Lini arrested the president, Sope, and opposition leader Maxime Carlot and reinstated the former prime minister. Fred Timakata, formerly minister of health, was elected president in Jan 1989.

In Aug 1991 the VP voted to replace Lini as its leader, and thus as prime minister, with Donald Kalpokas, a former education and foreign minister and fellow founder of the party. The reason appeared to be opposition to Lini's autocratic leadership style. Lini initially refused to stand down. However, in Sept he agreed to do so, but expected to return as premier after the Nov 1991 general election.
coalition formed In the Dec 1991 general election none of the parties won an overall majority. The Union of Moderate Parties (UMP) and the Vanuatu National United Party (VNUP), formed by Lini, finally agreed to form a coalition government under Maxime Carlot on the understanding that Lini would not be a member of the new government.
role in Pacific region Externally, since independence, Vanuatu has sought to promote greater cooperation among the states of the Pacific region. As part of this strategy, along with Papua New Guinea and the Solomon Islands, it formed, in March 1988, the "Spearhead Group," whose aim is to preserve Melanesian cultural tradition and campaign for New Caledonia's independence. *See illustration box.*

Varanasi or **Benares** holy city of the Hindus in Uttar Pradesh, India, on the river Ganges; population (1981) 794,000. There are 1,500 golden shrines, and a 3 mi/5 km frontage to the Ganges with sacred stairways (*ghats*) for purification by bathing.

At the burning ghats, the ashes of the dead are scattered on the river to ensure a favorable reincarnation.

Varangian member of a widespread Swedish Viking people in E Europe and the Balkans; more particularly a member of the Byzantine imperial guard founded 988 by Vladimir of Kiev (955–1015), which lasted until the fall of Constantinople 1453.

Varèse Edgard 1885–1965. French composer who settled in New York 1916 where he founded the New Symphony Orchestra 1919 to advance the cause of modern music. His work is experimental and often dissonant, combining electronic sounds with orchestral instruments, and includes *Hyperprism* 1923, *Intégrales* 1931, and *Poème Electronique* 1958.

Vargas Getúlio 1883–1954. President of Brazil

1930–45 and 1951–54. He overthrew the republic 1930 and in 1937 set up a totalitarian, profascist state known as the **Estado Novo**. Ousted by a military coup 1945, he returned as president 1951 but, amid mounting opposition and political scandal, committed suicide 1954.

Vargas Llosa Mario 1937– . Peruvian novelist, author of *La ciudad y los perros/The Time of the Hero* 1963 and *La guerra del fin del mundo/ The War at the End of the World* 1982.

As a writer he belongs to the magic realist school. *La tía Julia y el escribidor/ Aunt Julia and the Scriptwriter* 1977 is a humorously autobiographical novel. His other works are *Historia de Mayta/The Real Life of Alejandro Mayta* 1985, an account of an attempted revolution in Peru in 1958, and *The Storyteller* 1990.

In his political career, Vargas Llosa began as a communist and turned to the right; he ran unsuccessfully for the presidency 1990. He has been criticized for being out of touch with Peru's large Quechua Indian community.

variable in mathematics, a changing quantity (one that can take various values), as opposed to a ⟁constant. For example, in the algebraic expression $y = 4x^3 + 2$, the variables are x and y, whereas 4 and 2 are constants.

A variable may be dependent or independent. Thus if y is a ⟁function of x, written $y = f(x)$, such that $y = 4x^3 + 2$, the domain of the function includes all values of the **independent variable** x while the range (or codomain) of the function is defined by the values of the **dependent variable** y.

variable star in astronomy, a star whose brightness changes, either regularly or irregularly, over a period ranging from a few hours to months or even years. The ⟁Cepheid variables regularly expand and contract in size every few days or weeks.

Stars that change in size and brightness at less precise intervals include **long-period variables**, such as the red giant Mira in the constellation Cetus (period about 330 days), and **irregular variables**, such as some red supergiants. **Eruptive variables** emit sudden outbursts of light. Some suffer flares on their surfaces, while others, such as a ⟁nova, result from transfer of gas between a close pair of stars. A ⟁supernova is the explosive death of a star. In an ⟁**eclipsing binary**, the variation is due not to any change in the star itself, but to the periodical eclipse of a star by a close companion.

variations in music, a form based on constant repetition of a simple theme, each new version being elaborated or treated in a different manner. The theme is easily recognizable, either as a popular tune or—as a gesture of respect—as the work of a fellow composer; for example, Brahms honors Bach in the *Variations on the St Antony Chorale*.

varicose veins or **varicosis** condition where the veins become swollen and twisted. The veins of the legs are most often affected; other vulnerable sites include the rectum (⟁hemorrhoids) and testes.

Some people have an inherited tendency to varicose veins, and the condition often appears in pregnant women, but obstructed blood flow is the direct cause. They may cause a dull ache or may be the site for ⟁thrombosis, infection, or ulcers. The affected veins can be injected with a substance that causes them to shrink, or surgery may be needed.

variegation description of plant leaves or stems that exhibit patches of different colors. The term is usually applied to plants that show white, cream, or yellow on their leaves, caused by areas of tissue that lack the green pigment ⟁chlorophyll. Variegated plants are bred for their decorative value, but they are often considerably weaker than the normal, uniformly green plant. Many will not breed true and require ⟁vegetative reproduction.

The term is sometimes applied to abnormal patchy coloring of petals, as in the variegated petals of certain tulips, caused by a virus infection. A mineral deficiency in the soil may also be the cause of variegation.

Varna port in Bulgaria, on an inlet of the Black Sea; population (1990) 320,600. Industries include shipbuilding and the manufacture of chemicals.

Varna was a Greek colony in the 6th century BC and part of the Ottoman Empire 1391–1878; it was renamed **Stalin** 1949–56.

varnish solution of resins or resinous gums dissolved in linseed oil, turpentine, or other solvents, or the synthetic equivalents. It is used to give a shiny, sealed surface to furniture and interior fittings.

Varuna in early Hindu mythology, the sky god and king of the universe.

varve in geology, a pair of thin sedimentary beds, one coarse and one fine, representing a cycle of thaw followed by an interval of freezing, in lakes of glacial regions.

Each couplet thus constitutes the sedimentary record of a year, and by counting varves in glacial lakes a record of absolute time elapsed can be determined. Summer and winter layers often are distinguished also by color, with lighter layers representing summer deposition, and darker layers the result of dark clay settling from water while the lake was frozen.

Vasari Giorgio 1511–1574. Italian art historian, architect, and painter, author of *Lives of the Most Excellent Architects, Painters and Sculptors* 1550 (enlarged and revised 1568), in which he proposed the theory of a Renaissance of the arts beginning with Giotto and culminating with Michelangelo. He designed the Uffizi Palace, Florence.

Vasco da Gama Portuguese navigator; see ⟁Gama.

vascular bundle strand of primary conducting tissue (a "vein") in vascular plants, consisting mainly of water-conducting tissues, metaxylem and protoxylem, which together make up the primary ⟁xylem, and nutrient-conducting tissue, ⟁phloem. It extends from the roots to the stems and leaves. Typically the phloem is situated nearest to the epidermis and the xylem toward the center of the bundle. In plants exhibiting ⟁secondary growth, the xylem and phloem are separated by a thin layer of vascular ⟁cambium, which gives rise to new conducting tissues.

vascular plant plant containing vascular bundles. ⟁Pteridophytes (ferns, horsetails, and club mosses), ⟁gymnosperms (conifers and cycads), and ⟁angiosperms (flowering plants) are all vascular plants.

vas deferens in male vertebrates, a tube conducting sperm from the testis to the urethra. The sperms are carried in a fluid secreted by various glands, and can be transported very rapidly when the smooth muscle in the wall of the vas deferens undergoes rhythmic contraction, as in sexual intercourse.

vasectomy male sterilization; an operation to

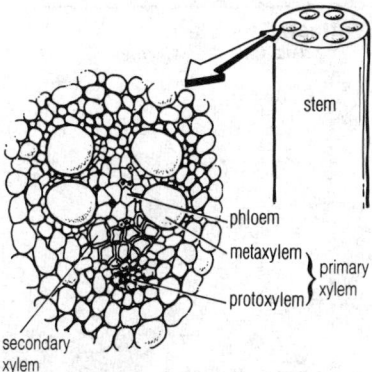

vascular bundle The fluid-carrying tissue of most plants is normally arranged in units called vascular bundles.

cut and tie the ducts (see ⟁vas deferens) that carry sperm from the testes to the penis. Vasectomy does not affect sexual performance, but the semen produced at ejaculation no longer contains sperm.

Some surgical attempts to reopen the duct have been successful, and some have opened spontaneously, thus making conception possible.

vassal in medieval Europe, a person who paid feudal homage to a superior lord (see ⟁feudalism), and who promised military service and advice in return for a grant of land. The term was used from the 9th century.

The relationship of vassalage was the mainstay of the feudal system and declined along with it during the transition to bastard feudalism.

Vassar Matthew 1792–1868. British-born US entrepreneur and educational philanthropist. A proponent of higher education for women, he endowed Vassar Female College in Poughkeepsie, New York, 1861. The school opened 1865 with a full college curriculum and became one of the finest women's educational institutions in the US.

Vassar came to the US with his family 1796. He worked in his father's brewery in Poughkeepsie before establishing his own firm 1811, and successfully expanded his business interests and real-estate investments.

Vatican Bank bank of the Vatican City State, officially known as the Institute of Religious Works (IOR).

In 1982 Roberto Calvi, known as "God's banker" because of his ties with the Vatican, was found hanged under a London bridge shortly before the collapse of the Banco Ambrosiano, the Italian bank of which he was chair. Warrants were issued in Italy against three Vatican Bank executives held responsible for the crash. The warrants were annulled 1987 because the affairs of the Vatican Bank are outside Italian jurisdiction.

Vatican City State sovereign area within the city of Rome, Italy.

government The pope, elected for life by the Sacred College of ⟁Cardinals, is absolute head of state. He appoints a pontifical commission to administer the state's affairs on his behalf and under his direction.

history The pope has traditionally been based in Rome, where the Vatican has been a papal residence since 1377. The Vatican Palace is one of the largest in the world and contains a valuable collection of works of art.

Vatican City State
(*Stato della Città del Vaticano*)

area 109 acres/0.4 sq km
physical forms an enclave in the heart of
Rome, Italy
features Vatican Palace, official residence of the pope; basilica and square of St Peter's; churches in and near Rome, the pope's summer villa at Castel Gandolfo; the world's smallest state
head of state and government John Paul II from 1978
political system absolute Catholicism
currency Vatican City lira; Italian lira
population (1985) 1,000
languages Latin (official), Italian
religion Roman Catholic
chronology
1929 Lateran Treaty recognized sovereignty of the pope.
1947 New Italian constitution confirmed the sovereignty of the Vatican City State.
1978 John Paul II became the first non-Italian pope for more than 400 years.
1985 New concordat signed under which Roman Catholicism ceased to be Italy's state religion.

The Vatican City State came into being through the Lateran Treaty of 1929, under which Italy recognized the sovereignty of the pope over the city of the Vatican. The 1947 Italian constitution reaffirmed the Lateran Treaty, and under its terms, Roman Catholicism became the state religion in Italy, enjoying special privileges. This remained so until, under a new 1984 Concordat (ratified 1985), Catholicism ceased to be the state religion. Karol Wojtyla, formerly archbishop of Krakow in Poland, has been pope since 1978 under the title of ⟡John Paul II. *See illustration box.*

Vatican Council either of two Roman Catholic ecumenical councils called by Pope Pius IX 1869 (which met 1870) and by Pope John XXIII 1959 (which met 1962). These councils deliberated over elements of church policy.

Vauban Sébastien le Prestre de 1633–1707. French marshal and military engineer. In Louis XIV's wars he conducted many sieges and rebuilt many of the fortresses on France's east frontier.

Vaucluse mountain range in SE France, part of the Provence Alps, E of Avignon, rising to 4,075 ft/1,242 m. It gives its name to a *département*. The Italian poet Petrarch lived in the Vale of Vaucluse 1337–53.

vaudeville variety entertainment in theaters, popular in the US from the 1890s to the 1920s. Consisting of 10 to 15 acts, ranging from singers and dancers to magicians, jugglers, acrobats, and comedians, it was the equivalent of the English music hall.

The forerunners of vaudeville, variety shows held in cities and frontier settlements, were often coarse and lewd and intended largely for male audiences. By the 1890s these shows had become suitable family entertainment. Many performers who later became famous for their stage and screen work—George Burns, W C Fields, and Will Rogers, for instance—began their careers as vaudeville artists. Vaudeville declined during the 1930s because of the economic hardships of the Depression and the growth of radio and motion pictures. It all but disappeared by the end of World War II, with the advent of television.

Vaughan Sarah (Lois) 1924–1990. US jazz singer whose voice had a range of nearly three octaves. She began by singing bebop with such musicians as Dizzy Gillespie and later moved effortlessly between jazz and romantic ballads. She toured very widely and had several hit singles, including "Make Yourself Comfortable" 1954, "Mr Wonderful" 1956, and "Broken-Hearted Melody" 1959.

Vaughan Williams Ralph 1872–1958. English composer. His style was tonal and often evocative of the English countryside through the use of folk themes. Among his works are the orchestral *Fantasia on a Theme by Thomas Tallis* 1910; the opera *Sir John in Love* 1929, featuring the Elizabethan song "Greensleeves"; and nine symphonies 1909–57.

VDT abbreviation for ⟡*visual display terminal*.

Veblen Thorstein (Bunde) 1857–1929. US social critic who taught at the University of Chicago 1892–1906 and edited the *Journal of Political Economy* 1892–1905. Veblen's insights on culture and economics were expressed in his books *The Theory of the Leisure Class* 1899 and *The Theory of Business Enterprise* 1904.

vector graphics computer graphics that are stored in the computer memory by using geometric formulas. Vector graphics can be transformed (enlarged, rotated, stretched, and so on) without loss of picture resolution. It is also possible to select and transform any of the components of a vector-graphics display because each is separately defined in the computer memory. In these respects vector graphics are superior to raster graphics. Vector graphics are typically used for drawing applications, allowing the user to create and modify technical diagrams such as designs for houses or automobiles.

vector quantity any physical quantity that has both magnitude and direction (such as the velocity or acceleration of an object) as distinct from ⟡scalar quantity (such as speed, density, or mass), which has magnitude but no direction. A vector is represented either geometrically by an arrow whose length corresponds to its magnitude and points in an appropriate direction, or by a pair of numbers written vertically and placed within brackets (x) (y) (z).

Vectors can be added graphically by constructing a parallelogram of vectors (such as the parallelogram of forces commonly employed in physics and engineering).

If two forces p and q are acting on a body at A, then the parallelogram of forces is drawn to determine the resultant force and direction r. p, q, and r are vectors. In technical writing, a vector is denoted by **bold** type, underlined AB, or overlined AB.

Veda (Sanskrit "divine knowledge") the most sacred of the Hindu scriptures, hymns written in an old form of Sanskrit; the oldest may date from 1500 or 2000 BC. The four main collections are: the *Rigveda* (hymns and praises); *Yajurveda* (prayers and sacrificial formulae); *Sāmaveda* (tunes and chants); and *Atharvaveda*, or Veda of the Atharvans, the officiating priests at the sacrifices.

Vedānta school of Hindu philosophy that developed the teachings of the *Upanishads*. One of its teachers was Śamkara, who lived in S India in the 8th century AD and is generally regarded as a manifestation of Siva. He taught that there is only one reality, Brahman, and that knowledge of Brahman leads finally to *moksha*, or liberation from reincarnation.

Vedda (Sinhalese "hunter") member of the aboriginal peoples of Sri Lanka, who occupied the island before the arrival of the Aryans *c.* 550 BC. Formerly cave-dwelling hunter-gatherers, they have now almost died out or merged with the rest of the population. They speak a Sinhalese language, belonging to the Indo-European family.

They live mainly in the central highlands, and many practice shifting cultivation.

Veeck William Louis, Jr 1914–1986. US baseball executive. In 1941 he bought a minor league baseball team in Milwaukee and pioneered marketing promotions that would later become standard in professional sports. After service in the US Marines during World War II, he became part owner of the Cleveland Indians, helping to guide the team to a World Series victory 1948. As owner of the St Louis Browns 1951–53 and Chicago White Sox 1959–61, he introduced innovations in the sale of television rights and the drafting of amateurs.

Vega or **Alpha Lyrae** brightest star in the constellation Lyra and the fifth brightest star in the sky. It is a blue-white star, 25 light-years from Earth, with a luminosity 50 times that of the Sun.

In 1983 the Infrared Astronomy Satellite (IRAS) discovered a ring of dust around Vega, possibly a disk from which a planetary system is forming.

vegan vegetarian who eats no foods of animal origin whatever, including fish, eggs, and milk.

vegetable any food plant, especially leafy plants (cabbage and lettuce), roots and tubers (carrots, parsnips, and potatoes), legumes (peas, lentils, and beans), and even flowers (cauliflower, broccoli, and artichoke). Tomatoes, peppers, eggplants, and cucumbers are generally regarded as vegetables but are technically fruits. Green leafy vegetables and potatoes are good sources of vitamin C, though much is lost in cooking, and legumes are

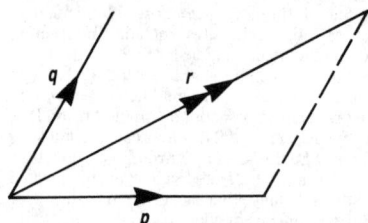

vector quantity *A parallelogram of vectors.*

a main source of protein. Cooking softens vegetables by dissolving pectins and hemicellulose and gelatininzing starch.

vegetarian person who eats only foods obtained without slaughter, for humanitarian, aesthetic, political, or health reasons. ◊Vegans abstain from all foods of animal origin.

vegetative reproduction type of ◊asexual reproduction in plants that relies not on spores, but on multicellular structures formed by the parent plant. Some of the main types are ◊stolons and runners, ◊gemmae, ◊bulbils, sucker shoots produced from roots (such as in the creeping thistle *Cirsium arvense*), ◊tubers, ◊bulbs, ◊corms, and ◊rhizomes. Vegetative reproduction has long been exploited in horticulture and agriculture, with various methods employed to multiply stocks of plants.

Veil Simone 1927– . French politician. A survivor of Hitler's concentration camps, she was minister of health 1974–79 and framed the French abortion bill. She was president of the European Parliament 1979–81.

vein in animals with a circulatory system, any vessel that carries blood from the body to the heart. Veins contain valves that prevent the blood from running back when moving against gravity. They always carry deoxygenated blood, with the exception of the veins leading from the lungs to the heart in birds and mammals, which carry newly oxygenated blood.

The term is also used more loosely for any system of channels that strengthens living tissues and supplies them with nutrients—for example, leaf veins (see ◊vascular bundle), and the veins in insects' wings.

Vela constellation of the southern hemisphere near Carina, represented as the sails of a ship. It contains large wisps of gas—called the Gum nebula after its discoverer, the Australian astronomer Colin Gum (1924–1960)—believed to be the remains of one or more ◊supernovae. Vela also contains the second optical ◊pulsar (a pulsar that flashes at a visible wavelength) to be discovered.

Its four brightest stars are second-magnitude, one of them being Suhail, about 490 light-years from Earth.

Velázquez Diego Rodríguez de Silva y 1599–1660. Spanish painter, born in Seville, the outstanding Spanish artist of the 17th century. In 1623 he became court painter to Philip IV in Madrid, where he produced many portraits of the royal family as well as occasional religious paintings, genre scenes, and other subjects. *Las Meninas/The Ladies-in-Waiting* 1655 (Prado, Madrid) is a complex group portrait that includes a self-portrait, but nevertheless focuses clearly on the doll-like figure of the Infanta Margareta Teresa.

His early work in Seville shows exceptional realism and dignity, delight in capturing a variety of textures, rich use of color, and contrasts of light and shade. In Madrid he was inspired by works by Titian in the royal collection and by Rubens, whom he met in 1628. He was in Italy 1629–31 and 1648–51; on his second visit he painted *Pope Innocent X* (Doria Gallery, Rome).

Velázquez's work includes an outstanding formal history painting, *The Surrender of Breda* 1634–35 (Prado), studies of the male nude, and a reclining female nude, *The Rokeby Venus* about 1648 (National Gallery, London). Around half of the 100 or so paintings known to be by him are owned by the Prado, Madrid.

Velcro (from "velvet" and "crochet") system of

very small hooks and eyes for fastening clothing, developed by Swiss inventor Georges de Mestral (1902–1990) after studying why burrs stuck to his trousers and noting that they were made of thousands of tiny hooks.

Velde, van de family of Dutch artists. Both *Willem van de Velde* the Elder (1611–93) and his son *Willem van de Velde* the Younger (1633–1707) painted sea battles for Charles II and James II (having settled in London 1672). Another son *Adriaen van de Velde* (1636–1672) painted landscapes.

veldt subtropical grassland in South Africa, equivalent to the ◊Pampas of South America.

vellum type of parchment, often rolled in scrolls, made from the skin of a calf, kid, or lamb. It was used from the late Roman Empire and Middle Ages for exceptionally important documents and the finest manuscripts. For example, *Torahs* (the five books of Moses) are always written in Hebrew on parchment. The modern term now describes thick, high-quality paper that resembles fine parchment.

velocity speed of an object in a given direction. Velocity is a ◊vector quantity, since its direction is important as well as its magnitude (or speed).

The velocity at any instant of a particle traveling in a curved path is in the direction of the tangent to the path at the instant considered.

velocity ratio (VR), or *distance ratio* in a machine, the ratio of the distance moved by an effort force to the distance moved by the machine's load in the same time. It follows that the velocities of the effort and the load are in the same ratio. Velocity ratio has no units.

velvet fabric of silk, cotton, nylon, or other textile, with a short, thick pile. Utrecht, Netherlands, and Genoa, Italy, are traditional centers of manufacture. It is woven on a double loom, then cut between the center pile to form velvet nap.

vena cava one of the large, thin-walled veins found just above the ◊heart, formed from the junction of several smaller veins. The *posterior vena cava* receives oxygenated blood returning from the lungs, and empties into the left atrium. The *anterior vena cava* collects deoxygenated blood returning from the rest of the body and passes it into the right side of the heart, from where it will be pumped into the lungs.

Venda ◊Black National State from 1979, near the Zimbabwe border, in South Africa
area 2,510 sq mi/6,500 sq km
capital Thohoyandou
cities MaKearela
features homeland of the Vhavenda people
government military council since a coup 1990 (military leader Ramushwana from 1990)
products coal, copper, graphite, construction stone
population (1980) 343,500
language Luvenda, English.

Vendée, Wars of the in the French Revolution, a series of peasant uprisings against the revolutionary government that began in the Vendée *département*, W France 1793, and spread to other areas of France, lasting until 1795.

vendetta (Italian "vengeance") any prolonged feud, in particular one in which the relatives of a dishonored or murdered person seek revenge on the wrongdoer or members of the family. The tradition is Mediterranean, known in Europe and the US as a way of settling wrongs in

Corsica, Sardinia, and Sicily, as practiced by the ◊Mafia.

Vendôme Louis Joseph, Duc de Vendôme 1654–1712. Marshal of France under Louis XIV, he lost his command after defeat by the British commander Marlborough at Oudenaarde, Belgium, 1708, but achieved successes in the 1710 Spanish campaign during the War of the ◊Spanish Succession.

venereal disease (VD) any disease mainly transmitted by sexual contact, although commonly the term is used specifically for gonorrhea and syphilis, both occurring worldwide, and chancroid ("soft sore") and lymphogranuloma venerum, seen mostly in the tropics. The term *sexually transmitted diseases* (◊STDs) is more often used to encompass a growing list of conditions passed on primarily, but not exclusively, in this way.

Venetia Roman name of that part of NE Italy which later became the republic of Venice, including the Veneto region.

Veneto region of NE Italy, comprising the provinces of Belluno, Padova (Padua), Treviso, Rovigo, Venezia (Venice), and Vicenza; area 7,102 sq mi/18,400 sq km; population (1990) 4,398,100. Its capital is Venice, and towns include Padua, Verona, and Vicenza. The Veneto forms part of the N Italian plain, with the delta of the river Po; it includes part of the Alps and Dolomites, and Lake Garda. Products include cereals, fruit, vegetables, wine, chemicals, ships, and textiles.

Venezia Italian form of ◊Venice, city, port, and naval base on the Adriatic.

Venezuela country in northern South America, on the Caribbean Sea, bounded E by Guyana, S by Brazil, and W by Colombia.
government Venezuela is a federal republic of 20 states, 2 federal territories, and a federal district based on the capital, Caracas. The 1961 constitution provides for a president, who is head of state and head of government, and a two-chamber national congress, consisting of a senate and a chamber of deputies. The president is elected by universal suffrage for a five-year term and may not serve two consecutive terms. The president appoints and presides over a council of ministers.

The senate has 44 members elected by universal suffrage, on the basis of two representatives for each state and two for the federal district, plus any living ex-presidents. The chamber has 196 deputies, also elected by universal suffrage. Both chambers serve five-year terms.

history For early history, see ◊American Indian, ◊South America. Columbus visited Venezuela 1498, and there was a Spanish settlement from 1520. In 1811 a rebellion against Spain began, led by Simón Bolívar, and Venezuela became independent 1830.

After a long history of dictatorial rule, Venezuela adopted a new constitution 1961, and three years later Rómulo Betancourt became the first president to have served a full term of office. He was succeeded by Dr Raúl Leoni 1964 and by Dr Rafael Caldera 1969. The latter did much to bring economic and political stability, although underground abductions and assassinations still occurred. In 1974 Carlos Andrés Pérez, of the Democratic Action Party (AD), became president, and stability increased. In 1979 Dr Luis Herrera, leader of the Social Christian Party (COPEI), was elected.

Venezuela
Republic of (*República de Venezuela*)

area 352,162 sq mi/912,100 sq km
capital Caracas
cities Barquisimeto, Valencia; port Maracaibo
physical Andes Mountains and Lake Maracaibo in NW; central plains (llanos); delta of river Orinoco in E; Guiana Highlands in SE
features Angel Falls, world's highest waterfall
head of state and of government Carlos Andrés Pérez from 1988
government federal democratic republic
political parties Democratic Action Party (AD), moderate, left-of-center; Social Christian Party (COPEI), Christian center-right; Movement toward Socialism (MAS), left-of-center
exports coffee, timber, oil, aluminum, iron ore, petrochemicals

currency bolívar
population (1990 est) 19,753,000 (mestizos 70%, white [Spanish, Portuguese, Italian] 20%, black 9%, amerindian 2%); growth rate 2.8% p.a.
life expectancy men 67, women 73 (1989)
religion Roman Catholic 96%, Protestant 2%
languages Spanish (official), Indian languages 2%
literacy 88% (1989)
GNP $47.3 bn (1988); $2,629 per head (1985)
chronology
1961 New constitution adopted, with Rómulo Betancourt as president.
1964 Dr Raúl Leoni became president.
1969 Dr Rafael Caldera became president.
1974 Carlos Andrés Pérez became president.
1979 Dr Luis Herrera became president.
1984 Dr Jaime Lusinchi became president; social pact established among government, labor unions, and business; national debt rescheduled.
1987 Widespread social unrest triggered by inflation; student demonstrators shot by police.
1988 Carlos Andrés Pérez elected president. Payments suspended on foreign debts (increase due to drop in oil prices).
1989 Economic austerity program enforced by $4.3 billion loan from International Monetary Fund. Price increases triggered riots; 300 people killed. Feb: martial law declared. May: General strike. Elections boycotted by opposition groups.
1991 Protests against austerity program continued.
1992 Two attempted antigovernment coups failed. Pérez promised constitutional changes.

austerity policies Against a background of growing economic problems, the 1984 general election was contested by 20 parties and 13 presidential candidates. It was a bitterly fought campaign and resulted in the election of Dr Jaime Lusinchi as president and a win for the Democratic Action Party (AD) with an absolute majority in congress. President Lusinchi's austere economic policies were unpopular, and he tried to conclude a social pact among the government, labor unions, and business. He reached an agreement with the government's creditor bankers for a rescheduling of Venezuela's large public debt.

In 1988 Venezuela suspended payment on its foreign debt, which had grown due to a drop in oil prices since the 1970s. In Feb 1989, newly elected president Carlos Andrés Pérez instituted price increases and other austerity measures designed to satisfy $4.3 billion loan terms imposed by the International Monetary Fund. Riots followed in which at least 300 people were killed. In May a general strike was declared to protest against the austerity program. Elections held in Dec were boycotted by the main opposition groups.

At a meeting in Caracas in May 1991, the leaders of the Andean Common market countries agreed to create a Latin American free-trade zone.

Throughout 1990 and 1991 dissatisfaction with the austerity plan increased, resulting in more violent demonstrations, especially by students. In Feb 1992 an attempted coup by a group of army officers was foiled by troops loyal to the president, who acted quickly to remove a number of senior commanders. Pressured by mounting public unrest, Pérez promised major constitutional reforms and approval by referendum. Another military coup, also unsuccessful, was attempted in Nov. *See illustration box.*

Venice (Italian *Venezia*) city, port, and naval base, capital of Veneto, Italy, on the Adriatic; population (1990) 79,000. The old city is built on piles on low-lying islands. Apart from tourism (it draws 8 million tourists a year), industries include glass, jewelry, textiles, and lace. Venice was an independent trading republic from the 10th century, ruled by a doge, or chief magistrate, and was one of the centers of the Italian Renaissance.

It is now connected with the mainland and its industrial suburb, Mestre, by road and rail viaduct. The Grand Canal divides the city and is crossed by the Rialto bridge; transport is by traditional gondola or *vaporetto* (water bus).

St Mark's Square has the 11th-century Byzantine cathedral of San Marco, the 9th–16th-century campanile (rebuilt 1902), and the 14th–15th-century Gothic Doge's Palace (linked to the former state prison by the 17th-century Bridge of Sighs). The nearby Lido is a bathing resort. The *Venetian School* of artists includes the Bellinis, Carpaccio, Giorgione, Titian, Tintoretto, and Veronese.

history In 1991 archeologist Ernesto Canal established that the city was founded by the Romans in the 1st century AD; it was previously thought to have been founded by mainlanders fleeing from the Barbarians in AD 421. Venice became a wealthy independent trading republic in the 10th century, stretching by the mid-15th century to the Alps and including Crete. It was governed by an aristocratic oligarchy, the Council of Ten, and a senate, which appointed the doge 697–1797. Venice helped defeat the Ottoman Empire in the naval battle of Lepanto 1571 but the republic was overthrown by Napoleon 1797. It passed to Austria 1815 but finally became part of the kingdom of Italy 1866.

veni, vidi, vici (Latin "I came, I saw, I conquered") Julius ◊Caesar's description of his victory over King Pharnaces II (63–47 BC) at Zela in 47 BC.

Venizelos Eleuthérios 1864–1936. Greek politician born in Crete, leader of the Cretan movement against Turkish rule until the union of the island with Greece in 1905. He later became prime minister of the Greek state on five occasions, 1910–15, 1917–20, 1924, 1928–32, and 1933, before being exiled to France in 1935.

Venn diagram in mathematics, a diagram representing a ◊set or sets and the logical relationships between them. The sets are drawn as circles. An area of overlap between two circles (sets) contains elements that are common to both sets, and thus represents a third set. Circles that do not overlap represent sets with no elements in common (disjoint sets). The method is named after the British logician John Venn (1834–1923).

Vent, Îles du French name for the Windward Islands, part of the ◊Society Islands in ◊French Polynesia. The Leeward Islands are known as the *Îles sous le Vent*.

Ventris Michael (George Francis) 1922–1956. English archeologist. Deciphering Minoan Linear B, the language of the tablets found at Knossos and Pylos, he showed that it was a very early form of Greek, thus revising existing views on early Greek history.

Ventura city in SW California, on the Pacific Ocean, NW of Los Angeles; population (1980) 83,475. Industries include oil and agricultural products, such as citrus fruits and lima beans.

venture capital or *risk capital* financing provided by venture capital companies, individuals, and merchant banks for medium- or long-term business ventures that are not their own and in which there is a strong element of risk.

In recent years, there has been a large growth in the number of companies specializing in providing venture capital.

Venturi Robert 1925– . US architect. He pioneered Postmodernism through his books *Complexity and Contradiction in Architecture* 1967 (Pulitzer Prize 1991) and *Learning from Las Vegas* 1972. In 1986 he was commissioned to design the extension to the National Gallery, London, opened 1991.

He is famous for his slogan "Less is a bore," countering German architect Ludwig Mies van der Rohe's "Less is more."

Venus in Roman mythology, the goddess of love and beauty (Greek ◊Aphrodite). The patrician Romans believed that they were descended from Aeneas, the son of the goddess and Anchises, a shepherd. She was venerated as the guardian of the Roman people.

Venus second planet from the Sun. It orbits the Sun every 225 days at an average distance of 67.2 million mi/108.2 million km and can approach the Earth to within 24 million mi/38 million km, closer than any other planet. Its diameter is 7,500 mi/12,100 km and its mass is 0.82 that of Earth. Venus rotates on its axis more slowly than any other planet, once every 243 days and from east to west, the opposite direction to the other planets (except Uranus and possibly Pluto). Venus is shrouded by clouds of sulfuric acid droplets that sweep across the planet from east to west every four days. The atmosphere is almost entirely carbon dioxide, which traps the Sun's heat by the ⟡greenhouse effect and raises the planet's surface temperature to 900°F/480°C, with an atmospheric pressure of 90 times that at the surface of the Earth.

The surface of Venus consists mainly of plains dotted with deep impact craters. The largest highland area is Aphrodite Terra near the equator, half the size of Africa. The highest mountains are on the N highland region of Ishtar Terra, where the massif of Maxwell Montes rises to 35,000 ft/10,600 m above the average surface level. The highland areas on Venus were formed by volcanoes, which may still be active.

The first artificial object to hit another planet was the Soviet probe *Venera 3*, which crashed on Venus March 1, 1966. Later Venera probes parachuted down through the atmosphere and landed successfully on its surface, analyzing surface material and sending back information and pictures. In Dec 1978 a US ⟡Pioneer Venus probe went into orbit around the planet and mapped most of its surface by radar, which penetrates clouds. A more detailed map was made by the US *Magellan* probe, which went into orbit Aug 1990.

Venus flytrap insectivorous plant *Dionaea muscipula* of the sundew family, native to the SE US; its leaves have two hinged blades that close and entrap insects.

Veracruz port (trading in coffee, tobacco, and vanilla) in E Mexico, on the Gulf of Mexico; population (1980) 305,456. Products include chemicals, sisal, and textiles. It was founded by the Spanish conquistador Cortés as Villa Nueva de la Vera Cruz ("new town of the true cross") on a nearby site 1519 and transferred to its present site 1599.

verb grammatical part of speech for what someone or something does (*to go*), experiences (*to live*), or is (*to be*). Verbs involve the grammatical categories known as number (singular or plural: "He *runs*; they *run*"), voice (active or passive: "She *writes* books; it *is written*"), mood (statements, questions, orders, emphasis, necessity, condition), aspect (completed or continuing action: "She *danced*; she *was dancing*"), and tense (variation according to time: simple present tense, present progressive tense, simple past tense, and so on).

Many verbs are formed from nouns and adjectives by adding affixes (prison: *imprison*; light: *enlighten*; fresh: *freshen up*; pure: *purify*). Some words function as both nouns and verbs (*crack*, *run*), as both adjectives and verbs (*clean*; *ready*), and as nouns, adjectives, and verbs (*fancy*). In the sentences "They *saw* the accident," "She *is working* today," and "He *should have been trying to meet* them," the words in italics are verbs (and, in the last case, two verb groups together); these sentences show just how complex the verbs of English can be.

types of verb
A **transitive** verb takes a direct object ("He *saw* the house").
An **intransitive** verb has no object ("She *laughed*").
An **auxiliary or helping** verb is used to

express tense and/or mood ("He *was* seen"; "They *may* come").
A **modal** verb or **modal auxiliary** generally shows only mood; common modals are *may/might, will/would, can/could, shall/should, must*.
The **infinitive** of the verb usually includes *to* (*to go, to run*, and so on), but may be a bare infinitive (for example, after modals, as in "She may *go*").
A **regular** verb forms tenses in the normal way (*I walk: I walked: I have walked*); irregular verbs do not (*swim: swam: swum; put: put: put*; and so on). Because of their conventional nature, regular verbs are also known as weak verbs, while some irregular verbs are strong verbs with special vowel changes across tenses, as in *swim: swam: swum* and *ride: rode: ridden*.
A **phrasal verb** is a construction in which a particle attaches to a usually single-syllable verb (for example, *put* becoming *put up*, as in "He put up some money for the project," and *put up with*, as in "I can't put up with this nonsense any longer").

verbena any plant of the genus *Verbena*, family Verbenaceae, of about 100 species, mostly found in the American tropics. The leaves are fragrant and the tubular flowers arranged in close spikes in colors ranging from white to rose, violet, and purple. The garden verbena is a hybrid annual.

Vercingetorix Gallic chieftain. Leader of a revolt of all the tribes of Gaul against the Romans 52 BC; he lost, was captured, displayed in Julius Caesar's triumph 46 BC, and later executed. This ended the Gallic resistance to Roman rule.

Verdi Giuseppe (Fortunino Francesco) 1813–1901. Italian opera composer of the Romantic period, who took his native operatic style to new heights of dramatic expression. In 1842 he wrote the opera *Nabucco*, followed by *Ernani* 1844 and *Rigoletto* 1851. Other works include *Il Trovatore* and *La Traviata* both 1853, *Aïda* 1871, and the masterpieces of his old age, *Otello* 1887 and *Falstaff* 1893. His *Requiem* 1874 commemorates Alessandro ⟡Manzoni.

During the mid-1800s, Verdi became a symbol of Italy's fight for independence from Austria, frequently finding himself in conflict with the Austrian authorities, who felt that his operas encouraged Italian nationalism.

verdict in law, a jury's decision, usually a finding of "guilty" or "not guilty."

verdigris green-blue coating of copper ethanoate that forms naturally on copper, bronze, and brass. It is an irritating, greenish, poisonous compound made by treating copper with ethanoic acid, and was formerly used in wood preservatives, antifouling compositions, and green paints.

Verdun fortress town in NE France on the Meuse. During World War I it became the symbol of French resistance, withstanding a German onslaught 1916.

Vergil alternate spelling for ⟡Virgil, Roman poet.

Verlaine Paul 1844–1896. French lyric poet who was influenced by the poets Baudelaire and ⟡Rimbaud. His volumes of verse include *Poèmes saturniens/Saturnine Poems* 1866, *Fêtes galantes/Amorous Entertainments* 1869, and *Romances sans paroles/Songs without Words* 1874. In 1873 he was imprisoned for attempting to shoot Rimbaud. His later works reflect

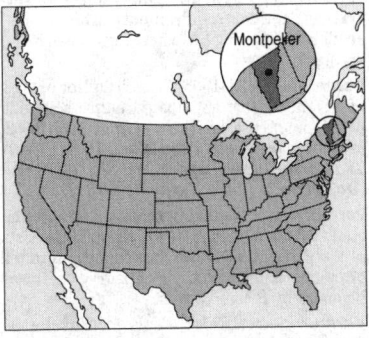
Vermont

his attempts to lead a reformed life. He was acknowledged as leader of the Symbolist poets (see ⟡Symbolism).

Vermeer Jan 1632–1675. Dutch painter, active in Delft. Most of his pictures are ⟡genre scenes, with a limpid clarity and distinct air of stillness, and a harmonious palette often focusing on yellow and blue. He frequently depicted solitary women in domestic settings, as in *The Lacemaker* (Louvre, Paris).

Vermeer is thought to have spent his whole life in Delft. There are only 35 paintings ascribed to him. His work fell into obscurity until the mid- to late 19th century, but he is now ranked as one of the greatest Dutch artists.

Vermont state in NE US; nickname Green Mountain State
area 9,611 sq mi/24,900 sq km
capital Montpelier
cities Burlington, Rutland, Barre
features brilliant autumn foliage and winter sports; Green Mountains; Lake Champlain
products apples, maple syrup, dairy products, kaolinite, granite, marble, slate, business machines, paper and allied products; tourism is important
population (1990) 562,800
famous people Chester A Arthur, Calvin Coolidge, John Dewey
history explored by Champlain from 1609; settled 1724; state 1791.

The first French settlement was at Fort Ste Anne 1666; first English settlers 1724 at Fort Drummer (now Brattleboro). England controlled the area from 1763 after the French and Indian War. The Green Mountain Boys, organized 1764 to protect Vermont from New York's territorial claims, captured Ticonderoga and Crown Point from the British 1775. After the Civil War—in which half the men of military age joined the army, and one in seven lost his life—young people tended to move west, and the state economy stagnated. Tourism now accounts for more than 20% of the gross state product. The "back to the earth" movement has brought new farmers, businesses, and second-home owners to Vermont, so the population and cultural activities grow.

vermouth sweet or dry white wine flavored with bitter herbs and fortified with alcohol. It is made in France, Italy and the US.

vernal equinox spring ⟡equinox.

vernalization the stimulation of flowering by exposure to cold. Certain plants will not flower unless subjected to low temperatures during their development. For example, winter wheat will flower in summer only if planted in the previous autumn. However, by placing partially germinated seeds in low temperatures for several days, the cold requirement can be supplied artificially, allowing the wheat to be sown in the spring.

Verne Jules 1828–1905. French author of tales of adventure that anticipated future scientific developments: *Five Weeks in a Balloon* 1862, *Journey to the Centre of the Earth* 1864, *Twenty Thousand Leagues under the Sea* 1870, and *Around the World in Eighty Days* 1873.

vernier device for taking readings on a graduated scale to a fraction of a division. It consists of a short divided scale that carries an index or pointer and is slid along a main scale. It was invented by Pierre Vernier.

Vernier Pierre 1580–1637. French mathematician who invented a means of making very precise measurements with what is now called the vernier scale. He was a French government official and in 1631 published *La construction, l'usage, et les proprie1tez du quadrant nouveau mathe1matique/The construction, uses and properties of a new mathematical quadrant*, in which he explained his method.

Verona industrial city (printing, paper, plastics, furniture, pasta) in Veneto, Italy, on the Adige; population (1988) 259,000. It also trades in fruit and vegetables.

Its historical sights include one of the largest Roman amphitheaters in the world, Castelvecchio—the 14th-century residence of the Scaligers, the tomb of Juliet, and a 12th-century cathedral.

Veronese Paolo c. 1528–1588. Italian painter, born in Verona, active mainly in Venice (from about 1553). He specialized in grand decorative schemes, such as his ceilings in the Doge's Palace in Venice, with *trompe l'oeil* effects and inventive detail. The subjects are religious, mythological, historical, and allegorical.

Titian was a major influence, but Veronese also knew the work of Giulio Romano and Michelangelo. His decorations in the Villa Barbera at Maser near Vicenza show his skill at illusionism and a typically Venetian rich use of color; they are also characteristically full of inventive fantasy. He took the same approach to religious works, and as a result his *Last Supper* 1573 (Accademia, Venice, renamed *The Feast in the House of Levi*) was the subject of a trial by the Inquisition, since the holy event seems to be almost subordinated by profane details: figures of drunkards, soldiers conversing, dogs, and so on.

Veronica, St woman of Jerusalem who, according to tradition, lent her veil to Jesus to wipe the sweat from his brow on the road to Calvary, whereupon the image of his face was printed upon it. A relic alleged to be the actual veil is preserved in St Peter's, Rome.

Verrocchio Andrea del 1435–1488. Italian painter, sculptor, and goldsmith, born in Florence, where he ran a large workshop and received commissions from the Medici family. The vigorous equestrian statue of *Bartolomeo Colleoni*, begun 1481 (Campo SS Giovanni e Paolo, Venice), was his last work.

Verrocchio was a pupil of ◊Donatello and himself the early teacher of Leonardo da Vinci. In his *Baptism* about 1472 (Uffizi, Florence) Leonardo is said to have painted the kneeling angel shown in profile. Verrocchio's sculptures include a bronze *Christ and St Thomas* 1465 (Orsanmichele, Florence) and *David* 1476 (Bargello, Florence).

Versailles city in N France, capital of Les Yvelines *département*, on the outskirts of Paris; population (1982) 95,240. It grew up around the palace of Louis XV. Within the palace park are two small châteaux, Le Grand and Le Petit ◊Trianon, built for Louis XIV (by Jules-Hardouin ◊Mansart) and Louis XV (by Jacques Gabriel 1698–1782) respectively.

Versailles, Treaty of peace treaty after World War I between the Allies and Germany, signed June 28, 1919. It established the League of Nations. Germany surrendered Alsace-Lorraine to France, and large areas in the east to Poland, and made smaller cessions to Czechoslovakia, Lithuania, Belgium, and Denmark. The Rhineland was demilitarized, German rearmament was restricted, and Germany agreed to pay reparations for war damage. The treaty was never ratified by the US, which made a separate peace with Germany and Austria 1921.

verse arrangement of words in a rhythmic pattern, which may depend on the length of syllables (as in Greek or Latin verse), or on stress, as in English. Classical Greek verse depended upon quantity, a long syllable being regarded as occupying twice the time taken up by a short syllable.

Long and short syllables were combined in *feet*, examples of which are:

dactyl (long, short, short);
spondee (long, long);
anapaest (short, short, long);
iamb (short, long);
trochee (long, short).

Rhyme (repetition of sounds in the endings of words) was introduced to W European verse in late Latin poetry, and *alliteration* (repetition of the same initial letter in successive words) was the dominant feature of Anglo-Saxon poetry. Both these elements helped to make verse easily remembered in the days when it was spoken rather than written.

Form The Spenserian stanza (in which ◊Spenser wrote *The Faerie Queene*) has nine iambic lines rhyming ababbcbcc. In English, the ◊sonnet has 14 lines, generally of ten syllables each; it has several rhyme schemes. *Blank verse*, consisting of unrhymed five-stress lines, as used by Marlowe, Shakespeare, and Milton develops an inner cohesion that replaces the props provided by rhyme and stanza. It became the standard meter for English dramatic and epic poetry. ◊*Free verse*, or *vers libre*, avoids rhyme, stanza form, and any obvious rhythmical basis.

vertebrate any animal with a backbone. The 41,000 species of vertebrates include mammals, birds, reptiles, amphibians, and fishes. They include most of the larger animals, but in terms of numbers of species are only a tiny proportion of the world's animals. The zoological taxonomic group Vertebrata is a subgroup of the ◊phylum Chordata.

vertex (plural *vertices*) in geometry, a point shared by three or more sides of a solid figure; the point farthest from a figure's base; or the point of intersection of two sides of a plane figure or the two rays of an angle.

vertical takeoff and landing craft (VTOL) aircraft that can take off and land vertically. ◊Helicopters, airships, and balloons can do this, as can a few fixed-wing airplanes, like the ◊convertiplane.

vertigo dizziness; a whirling sensation accompanied by a loss of any feeling of contact with the ground. It may be due to temporary disturbance of the sense of balance (as in spinning for too long on one spot), psychological reasons, disease, or intoxication.

Verwoerd Hendrik (Frensch) 1901–1966. South African right-wing Nationalist Party politician, prime minister 1958–66. As minister of native affairs 1950–58, he was the chief promoter of apartheid legislation (segregation by race). He made the country a republic 1961. He was assassinated 1966.

Very Large Array (VLA) largest and most complex single-site radio telescope in the world. It is located on the Plains of San Augustine, 50 mi/80 km west of Socorro, New Mexico. It consists of 27 dish antennae, each 82 ft/25 m in diameter, arranged along three equally spaced arms forming a Y-shaped array. Two of the arms are 13 mi/21 km long, and the third, to the north, is 11.8 mi/19 km long. The dishes are mounted on railroad tracks enabling the configuration and size of the array to be altered as required.

Pairs of dishes can also be used as separate interferometers (see ◊radio telescope), each dish having its own individual receivers that are remotely controlled, enabling many different frequencies to be studied.

There are four standard configurations of antennae ranging from A (the most extended) through B and C to D. In the A configuration the antennae are spread out along the full extent of the arms and the VLA can map small, intense radio sources with high resolution. The smallest configuration, D, uses arms that are just 0.4 mi/0.6 km long for mapping larger sources. Here the resolution is lower, although there is greater sensitivity to fainter, extended fields of radio emission.

Vesalius Andreas 1514–1564. Belgian physician who revolutionized anatomy. His great innovations were to perform postmortem dissections and to make use of illustrations in teaching anatomy.

The dissections (then illegal) enabled him to discover that ◊Galen's system of medicine was based on fundamental anatomical errors. Vesalius's book *De Humani Corporis Fabrica/On The Structure of the Human Body* 1543, together with the major work of the astronomer Copernicus, published in the same year, marked the dawn of modern science.

Vesey Denmark c. 1767–1822. American resistance leader. Probably born on the Caribbean island of St Thomas, he was purchased 1781 by Capt John Vesey and taken to Charleston, South Carolina, 1783. In 1800 Vesey bought his own freedom for $600 and established himself as a carpenter. An outspoken and eloquent critic of the institution of slavery, he was arrested 1822 on suspicion of fomenting a rebellion among local slaves. Although only circumstantial evidence was brought against him in court, Vesey and five other black leaders were hanged.

Vespasian (Titus Flavius Vespasianus) AD 9–79. Roman emperor from AD 69. He was the son of a moneylender, and had a distinguished military career. He was proclaimed emperor by his soldiers while he was campaigning in Palestine. He reorganized the eastern provinces, and was a capable administrator.

vespers seventh of the eight canonical hours in the Catholic Church.

The phrase *Sicilian Vespers* refers to the massacre of the French rulers in Sicily 1282, signaled by vesper bells on Easter Monday.

Vespucci Amerigo 1454–1512. Florentine

merchant. The Americas were named after him as a result of the widespread circulation of his accounts of his explorations. His accounts of the voyage 1499–1501 indicate that he had been to places he could not possibly have reached (the Pacific Ocean, British Columbia, Antarctica).

Vesta in Roman mythology, the goddess of the hearth (Greek *Hestia*). In Rome, the sacred flame in her shrine in the Forum was kept constantly lit by the six *Vestal Virgins*.

vestigial organ in biology, an organ that remains in diminished form after it has ceased to have any significant function in the adult organism. In humans, the appendix is vestigial, having once had a digestive function in our ancestors.

Vesuvius (Italian *Vesuvio*) active volcano SE of Naples, Italy; height 4,190 ft/1,277 m. In 79 BC it destroyed the cities of Pompeii, Herculaneum, and Oplonti.

vetch trailing or climbing plant of any of several genera, family Leguminosae, usually having seed pods and purple, yellow, or white flowers, including the fodder crop alfalfa *Medicago sativa*.

veterinary science the study, prevention, and cure of disease in animals. More generally, it covers animal anatomy, breeding, and relations to humans.

The American Veterinary Medical Association was formed 1883.

veto (Latin "I forbid") exercise by a sovereign, branch of legislature, or other political power, of the right to prevent the enactment or operation of a law, or the taking of some course of action.

Under the US Constitution, the president may veto legislation, although that veto may, in turn, be overruled by a two-thirds majority in Congress. At the United Nations, members of the Security Council can exercise a veto on resolutions.

VHF (abbreviation for *very high frequency*) referring to radio waves that have very short wavelengths (10 m–1 m). They are used for interference-free ⏵FM (frequency-modulated) transmissions. VHF transmitters have a relatively short range because the waves cannot be reflected over the horizon like longer radio waves.

v.i. in grammar, abbreviation for *verb intransitive*.

vibraphone electrically amplified musical percussion instrument resembling a ⏵xylophone but with metal keys. Spinning disks within resonating tubes under each key give the instrument a vibrato sound that can be controlled in speed with a foot pedal.

viburnum any small tree or shrub of the genus *Viburnum* of the honeysuckle family Caprifoliaceae, found in temperate and subtropical regions, including the ⏵wayfaring tree, the laurustinus, and the guelder rose of Europe and Asia, and the North American blackhaws and arrowwoods.

Vichy health resort with thermal springs, known to the Romans, on the river Allier in Allier *département*, central France. During World War II it was the seat of the French general ⏵Pétain's government 1940–44 (known also as the Vichy government), which collaborated with the Nazis.

Vichy government in World War II, the right-wing government of unoccupied France after the country's defeat by the Germans June 1940,

named after the spa town of Vichy, France, where the government was based under Chief of State Pétain until the liberation 1944. *Vichy France* was that part of France not occupied by German troops until Nov 1942. Authoritarian and collaborationist, the Vichy regime cooperated with the Germans even after they had moved to the unoccupied zone Nov 1942. It imprisoned some 135,000 people, interned another 70,000, deported some 76,000 Jews to their deaths, and sent 650,000 French workers to Germany.

Vico Giambattista 1668–1744. Italian philosopher, considered the founder of the modern philosophy of history. He argued that we can understand history more adequately than nature, since it is we who have made it. He believed that the study of language, ritual, and myth was a way of understanding earlier societies. His cyclical theory of history (the birth, development, and decline of human societies) was put forward in *New Science* 1725.

Vico postulated that society passes through a cycle of four phases: the divine, or theocratic, when people are governed by their awe of the supernatural; the aristocratic, or "heroic" (Homer, *Beowulf*); the democratic and individualistic; and chaos, a fall into confusion that startles people back into supernatural reverence. This is expressed in his dictum *verum et factum convertuntur* ("the true and the made are convertible"). His belief that the study of language and rituals was a better way of understanding early societies was a departure from the traditional ways of writing history either as biographies or as preordained God's will. He was born in Naples and was professor of rhetoric there 1698. He became historiographer to the king of Naples 1735.

Victor Emmanuel three kings of Italy, including:

Victor Emmanuel II 1820–1878. First king of united Italy from 1861. He became king of Sardinia on the abdication of his father Charles Albert 1849. In 1855 he allied Sardinia with France and the UK in the Crimean War. In 1859 in alliance with the French he defeated the Austrians and annexed Lombardy. By 1860 most of Italy had come under his rule, and in 1861 he was proclaimed king of Italy. In 1870 he made Rome his capital.

Victor Emmanuel III 1869–1947. King of Italy from the assassination of his father, Umberto I, 1900. He acquiesced in the Fascist regime of Mussolini from 1922 and, after the dictator's fall 1943, relinquished power to his son Umberto II, who cooperated with the Allies. Victor Emmanuel formally abdicated 1946.

Victoria state of SE Australia
area 87,854 sq mi/227,600 sq km
capital Melbourne
cities Geelong, Ballarat, Bendigo
physical part of the Great Dividing Range, running E–W and including the larger part of the Australian Alps; Gippsland lakes; shallow lagoons on the coast; the ⏵mallee shrub region
products sheep, beef cattle, dairy products, tobacco, wheat, vines for wine and dried fruit, orchard fruits, vegetables, gold, brown coal (Latrobe Valley), oil and natural gas (Bass Strait)
population (1987) 4,184,000; 70% in the Melbourne area
history annexed for Britain by Captain Cook 1770; settled in the 1830s; after being part of New South Wales became a separate colony 1851, named after the queen; became a state 1901.

Victoria industrial port (shipbuilding, chemicals, clothing, furniture) on Vancouver Island, capital of British Columbia; population (1986) 66,303.

It was founded as Fort Victoria 1843 by the Hudson's Bay Company. Its university was founded 1964.

Victoria port and capital of the Seychelles, on Mahé island; population (1987) 24,300.

Victoria city in S Texas, on the Guadalupe River, near the Gulf of Mexico; a transportation center for oil, natural gas, chemicals, and dairy products; population (1990) 55,100.

Victoria district of ⏵Hong Kong, rising to 1,800 ft/554 m at Victoria Park.

Victoria 1819–1901. Queen of the UK from 1837, when she succeeded her uncle William IV, and empress of India from 1876. In 1840 she married Prince ⏵Albert of Saxe-Coburg and Gotha. Her relations with her prime ministers ranged from the affectionate (Melbourne and Disraeli) to the stormy (Peel, Palmerston, and Gladstone). Her golden jubilee 1887 and diamond jubilee 1897 marked a waning of republican sentiment, which had developed with her withdrawal from public life on Albert's death 1861.

Only child of Edward, duke of Kent, fourth son of George III, she was born in London. She and Albert had four sons and five daughters. After Albert's death 1861 she lived mainly in retirement. Nevertheless, she kept control of affairs, refusing the prince of Wales (Edward VII) any active role.

Victoria Cross British decoration for conspicuous bravery in wartime, instituted by Queen Victoria 1856.

Victoria Falls or *Mosi-oa-tunya* waterfall on the river Zambezi, on the Zambia–Zimbabwe border. The river is 5,580 ft/1,700 m wide and drops 400 ft/120 m to flow through a gorge, 100 ft/30 m wide.

The falls were named after Queen Victoria by the Scottish explorer Livingstone 1855.

Victoria, Lake or *Victoria Nyanza* largest lake in Africa; area over 26,800 sq mi/69,400 sq km; length 255 mi/410 km. It lies on the equator at an altitude of 3,728 ft/1,136 m, bounded by Uganda, Kenya, and Tanzania. It is a source of the Nile.

The British explorer Speke named it after Queen Victoria 1858.

Victorian the mid- and late-19th century in England, covering the reign of Queen Victoria 1837–1901. Victorian style was often very ornate, markedly so in architecture, and Victorian Gothic drew on the original Gothic architecture of medieval times. It was also an era when increasing mass production by machines threatened the existence of crafts and craft skills.

vicuna ⏵ruminant mammal *Lama vicugna* of the camel family that lives in herds on the Andean plateau. It can run at speeds of 30 mph/50 kph. It has good eyesight, fair hearing, and a poor sense of smell. It was hunted close to extinction for its meat and soft brown fur, which was used in textile manufacture, but the vicuna is now a protected species; populations are increasing thanks to strict conservation measures. It is related to the ⏵alpaca, the ⏵guanaco, and the ⏵llama.

Vidal Gore 1925– . US writer and critic. Much of his fiction deals satirically with history and politics and includes the novels *Myra

Breckinridge 1968, *Burr* 1973, and *Empire* 1987, plays and screenplays, including *Suddenly Last Summer* 1958, and essays, such as *Armageddon?* 1987.

video art art that may combine music, dance, performance, and computer graphics, shown in the video medium. Video artists include the Korean-born US artist Nam June Paik.

video camera or *camcorder* portable television camera that takes moving pictures electronically on magnetic tape. It produces an electrical output signal corresponding to rapid line-by-line scanning of the field of view. The output is recorded on videocassette and is played back on a television screen via a videocassette recorder.

video cassette recorder (VCR) device for recording pictures and sound on cassettes or spools of magnetic tape. The first commercial VCR was launched 1956 for the television broadcasting industry, but from the late 1970s cheaper models developed for home use, to record broadcast programs for future viewing and to view rented or owned videocassettes of commercial films.

Video recording works in the same way as audio ◊tape recording: the picture information is stored as a line of varying magnetism, or track, on a plastic tape covered with magnetic material. The main difficulty—the huge amount of information needed to reproduce a picture—is overcome by arranging the video track diagonally across the tape. During recording, the tape is wrapped around a drum in a spiral fashion. The recording head rotates inside the drum. The combination of the forward motion of the tape and the rotation of the head produces a diagonal track. The audio signal accompanying the video signal is recorded on a separate track along the edge of the tape.

Two videocassette systems were introduced by Japanese firms in the 1970s. The Sony Betamax was considered technically superior, but Matsushita's VHS had larger marketing resources behind it and after some years became the sole system on the market. Super-VHS is an improved version of the VHS system, launched 1989, with higher picture definition and color quality.

video disc disk with pictures and sounds recorded on it, played back by laser. The video disc is a type of ◊compact disc.

The video disc (originated by Scottish inventor John Baird 1928; commercially available from 1978) is chiefly used to provide commercial films for private viewing. Most systems use a 12 in/30 cm rotating vinyl disk coated with a reflective material. Laser scanning recovers picture and sound signals from the surface where they are recorded as a spiral of microscopic pits.

video game electronic game played on a visual-display screen or, by means of special additional or built-in components, on the screen of a television set. The first commercially sold was a simple bat-and-ball game developed in the US 1972, but complex variants are now available in color and with special sound effects.

video tape recorder (VTR) device for recording visuals and sound on spools of magnetic tape. It is used in television broadcasting.

videotex or *videotext* any of various systems in which information (text) is displayed on a television (video) screen. There are two basic systems. In one, information is broadcast using the standard television signals; in the other,

information is relayed to the screen from a central data bank via the telephone network. Both systems require the use of a television receiver with decoding device.

Vidor King 1894–1982. US film director who made such epics as *The Big Parade* 1925 and *Duel in the Sun* 1946. He has been praised as a cinematic innovator, and received an honorary Academy Award 1979. His other films include *The Crowd* 1928 and *Guerra e Pace/War and Peace* 1956.

Vienna (German *Wien*) capital of Austria, on the river Danube at the foot of the Wiener Wald (Vienna Woods); population (1986) 1,481,000. Industries include engineering and the production of electrical goods and precision instruments.

The United Nations city 1979 houses the United Nations Industrial Development Organization (UNIDO) and the International Atomic Energy Agency (IAEA).

features Renaissance and baroque architecture; the Hofburg (former imperial palace); the 18th-century royal palaces of Schönbrunn and Belvedere, with formal gardens; the Steiner house 1910 by Adolf Loos; and several notable collections of paintings. Vienna is known for its theater and opera. Sigmund Freud's home is a museum, and there is a university built in 1365.

history Vienna was the capital of the Austro-Hungarian Empire 1278–1918 and the commercial center of E Europe. The old city walls were replaced by a wide street, the Ringstrasse, 1860. After much destruction in World War II the city was divided into US, British, French, and Soviet occupation zones 1945–55. Vienna is associated with J Strauss waltzes, as well as the music of Haydn, Mozart, Beethoven, and Schubert and the development of atonal music. Also figuring in Vienna's cultural history were the Vienna Sezession group of painters and the philosophical Vienna Circle; psychoanalysis originated here.

Vienna, Congress of international conference held 1814–15 that agreed the settlement of Europe after the Napoleonic Wars. National representatives included the Austrian foreign minister Metternich, Alexander I of Russia, the British foreign secretary Castlereagh and military commander Wellington, and the French politician Talleyrand.

Its final act created a kingdom of the Netherlands, a German confederation of 39 states, Lombardy–Venetia subject to Austria, and the kingdom of Poland. Monarchs were restored in Spain, Naples, Piedmont, Tuscany, and Modena; Louis XVIII was confirmed king of France.

Vientiane (Lao *Vieng Chan*) capital and chief port of Laos on the Mekong River; population (1985) 377,000.

Vietcong (Vietnamese "Vietnamese communists") in the Vietnam War 1954–75, the members of the National Front for the Liberation of South Vietnam, founded 1960, who fought the South Vietnamese and US forces. The name was coined by the South Vietnamese government to differentiate these communist guerrillas from the ◊Vietminh.

Vietminh the Vietnam Independence League, founded 1941 to oppose the Japanese occupation of Indochina and later directed against the French colonial power. The Vietminh were instrumental in achieving Vietnamese independence through military victory at Dien Bien Phu 1954.

Vietnam country in SE Asia, on the South

China Sea, bounded N by China and W by Cambodia and Laos.

government Under the constitution 1980, the highest state authority and sole legislative chamber in Vietnam is the national assembly, composed of 496 members directly elected every five years by universal suffrage. The assembly meets twice a year and elects from its ranks a permanent, 15-member council of state, whose chair acts as state president, to function in its absence. The executive government is the council of ministers, headed by the prime minister, which is responsible to the national assembly.

The dominating force in Vietnam is the Communist Party. It is controlled by a politburo, and is prescribed a "leading role" by the constitution.

history Originally settled by SE Asian hunters and agriculturalists, Vietnam was founded 208 BC in the Red River delta in the north, under Chinese overlordship. Under direct Chinese rule 111 BC–AD 939, it was thereafter at times nominally subject to China. It annexed land to the south and defeated the forces of Kublai Khan 1288. European traders arrived in the 16th century. The country was united under one dynasty 1802.

France conquered Vietnam between 1858–84, and it joined Cambodia, Laos, and Annam as the French colonial possessions of Indochina. French Indochina was occupied by Japan 1940–45.

north/south division ◊Ho Chi Minh, who had built up the Vietminh (Independence) League, overthrew the Japanese-supported regime of Bao Dai, the former emperor of Annam, Sept 1945. French attempts to regain control and restore Bao Dai led to bitter fighting 1946–54, and final defeat of the French at Dien Bien Phu. At the 1954 Geneva Conference the country was divided along the 17th parallel of latitude into Communist North Vietnam, led by Ho Chi Minh, with its capital at Hanoi, and pro-Western South Vietnam, led by Ngo Dinh Diem, with its capital at Saigon.

Vietnam War Within South Vietnam, the Communist guerrilla National Liberation Front, or Vietcong, gained strength, being supplied with military aid by North Vietnam and China. The US gave strong backing to the incumbent government in South Vietnam and became, following the Aug 1964 ◊Tonkin Gulf incident, actively embroiled in the ◊Vietnam War. The years 1964–68 witnessed an escalation in US military involvement to 500,000 troops. From 1969, however, as a result of mounting casualties and domestic opposition, the US gradually began to withdraw its forces and sue for peace. A cease-fire agreement was negotiated Jan 1973 but was breached by the North Vietnamese, who moved south, surrounding and capturing Saigon (renamed Ho Chi Minh City) in April 1975.

socialist republic The Socialist Republic of Vietnam was proclaimed July 1976, and a program to integrate the south was launched. The new republic encountered considerable problems. The economy was in ruins, the two decades of civil war having claimed the lives of more than 2 million; it had maimed 4 million, left more than half the population homeless, and resulted in the destruction of 70% of the country's industrial capacity.

In Dec 1978 Vietnam was at war again, toppling the pro-Chinese Khmer Rouge government in Kampuchea (now Cambodia) led by Pol Pot and installing a puppet administration led by Heng Samrin. A year later, in response to accusations of maltreatment of ethnic Chinese living in Vietnam, China mounted a brief, largely unsuccessful, punitive invasion of North Vietnam Feb 17–March 16, 1979. These actions, coupled with campaigns against private businesses in the south, induced the flight of about 700,000 Chinese and middle-class Vietnamese from the country 1978–79, often by sea (the "boat people"). Economic and diplomatic relations with China were severed as Vietnam became closer to the USSR, being admitted into Comecon June 1978.

economic reform Despite considerable economic aid from the Eastern bloc, Vietnam did not reach its planned growth targets 1976–85. This forced policy adjustments 1979 and 1985. Further economic liberalization followed the death of Le Duan (1907–1986), effective leader since 1969, and the retirement of other prominent "old guard" leaders 1986, including Prime Minister Pham Van Dong and President Truong Chinh. Under the pragmatic lead of Nguyen Van Linh, a "renovation" program was launched. The private marketing of agricultural produce and formation of private businesses were now permitted, agricultural cooperatives were partially dismantled, foreign "joint venture" inward-investment was encouraged, and more than 10,000 political prisoners were released. Economic reform proved most successful in the south. In general, however, the country faced a severe economic crisis from 1988, with inflation, famine conditions in rural areas, and rising urban unemployment inducing a further flight of "boat people" refugees 1989–90, predominantly to Hong Kong. In Dec 1989 the British colony of ⮕Hong Kong began the forced repatriation of some Vietnamese refugees. Earlier in 1989 Vietnam announced the final withdrawal of its troops from Cambodia.

Nguyen Van Linh resigned from his leadership of the Communist Party at the congress held June 1991 and Do Muoi, a supporter of Linh's policies, was elected the party's new general secretary. Vo Van Kiet, a leading advocate of capitalist-style reform, replaced him as prime minister Aug 1991. The new government, anxious to secure foreign economic aid, pledged to improve foreign relations.

improved foreign relations The signing of the Cambodian peace agreement in Oct 1991 helped improve Vietnam's external image. Relations with China were finally normalized—after a 12-year breach—in Nov 1991, when Do Muoi and Vo Van Kiet paid a state visit to Beijing and signed a series of commercial and diplomatic agreements. Commerical links have also been established with a number of ⮕ASEAN states. The US embargo on trade with and investment in Vietnam, first imposed in 1975, remains in force as does the veto on IMF loans, but US relations improved in fall 1992 as Vietnam cooperated with US attempts to investigate status of missing-in-action (MIA) soldiers from Vietnam War. *See illustration box.*

Vietnam
Socialist Republic of (*Công Hòa Xã Hôi Chu Nghĩa Viêt Nam*)

area 127,259 sq mi/329,600 sq km
capital Hanoi
cities ports Ho Chi Minh City (formerly Saigon), Da Nang, Haiphong
physical Red River and Mekong deltas, center of cultivation and population; tropical rainforest; mountainous in N and NW
environment during the Vietnam War an estimated 5.4 million acres/2.2 million hectares of forest were destroyed. The country's National Conservation Strategy is trying to replant 500 million trees each year
features Karst hills of Halong Bay, Cham Towers
head of state Vo Chi Cong from 1987
head of government Vo Van Kiet from 1991
political system communism
political party Communist Party
exports rice, rubber, coal, iron, apatite
currency dong

population (1990 est) 68,488,000 (750,000 refugees, majority ethnic Chinese left 1975–79, some settled in SW China, others fled by sea—the "boat people"—to Hong Kong and elsewhere); growth rate 2.4% p.a.
life expectancy men 62, women 66 (1989)
languages Vietnamese (official), French, English, Khmer, Chinese, local
media independent newspapers prohibited by law 1989; central government approval is required for appointment of editors
religion Buddhist, Taoist, Confucian, Christian
literacy 78% (1989)
GNP $12.6 bn; $180 per head (1987)
chronology
1945 Japanese removed from Vietnam at end of World War II.
1946 Commencement of Vietminh war against French.
1954 France defeated at Dien Bien Phu. Vietnam divided along 17th parallel.
1964 US troops entered Vietnam War.
1973 Paris cease-fire agreement.
1975 Saigon captured by North Vietnam.
1976 Socialist Republic of Vietnam proclaimed.
1978 Admission into Comecon. Vietnamese invasion of Cambodia.
1979 Sino-Vietnamese border war.
1986 Retirement of "old guard" leaders.
1987–88 Over 10,000 political prisoners released.
1988–89 Troop withdrawals from Cambodia continued.
1989 "Boat people" leaving Vietnam murdered and robbed at sea by Thai pirates. Troop withdrawal from Cambodia completed. Hong Kong forcibly repatriated some Vietnamese refugees.
1991 Vo Van Kiet replaced Do Muoi as prime minister. Cambodia peace agreement signed. Relations with China normalized.
1992 Vietnam cooperated with US in search for information on US soldiers missing in action from Vietnam War.

Vietnamese member of the majority group (90%) of peoples inhabiting Vietnam and referring to their language and culture, which is also called Annamese. Although Annamese is an independent language, it has been influenced by Chinese and there are Khmer loan words.

Vietnam War 1954–1975 war between communist North Vietnam and US-backed South Vietnam. Following the division of French Indochina into North and South Vietnam and the Vietnamese defeat of the French 1954, US involvement in Southeast Asia grew through the ⮕SEATO pact. Noncommunist South Vietnam was viewed, in the context of the 1950s and the ⮕cold war, as a bulwark against the spread of communism throughout SE Asia. Advisers and military aid were dispatched to the region at increasing levels because of the so-called domino theory, which contended that the fall of South Vietnam would precipitate the collapse of neighboring states. Corruption and inefficiency within the South Vietnamese government led the US to assume ever greater responsibility for the war effort, until 1 million US combat troops were engaged.

In the US, the draft, the high war casualties, and the undeclared nature of the war resulted in growing domestic resistance, which caused social unrest and forced President Johnson to abandon reelection plans. President Nixon first expanded the war to Laos and Cambodia but finally phased out US involvement; his national security adviser Henry Kissinger negotiated a peace treaty 1973 with North Vietnam, which soon conquered the South and united the nation. Between 1961 and 1975, 56,555 US soldiers were killed; also some 200,000 South Vietnamese soldiers, plus 1 million North Vietnamese soldiers, and 500,000 civilians died.

Although US forces were never militarily defeated, Vietnam was considered a most humiliating political defeat for the US.
1954 Under the Geneva Convention the former French colony of Indochina was divided into the separate states of North and South Vietnam. Within South Vietnam the communist Vietcong, supported by North Vietnam and China, attempted to seize power. The US began to provide military advisers to support the South Vietnamese.
1964 The Tonkin Gulf Incident, when North Vietnamese torpedo boats allegedly attacked two US destroyers, prompted the US to send troops.
1967 Several large-scale invasion attempts by North Vietnam were defeated by indigenous and US forces.
1968 Tet Offensive in South Vietnam; My Lai massacre by US troops.
1973 In the US, the unpopularity of sending troops to an undeclared war led to the start of US withdrawal. A peace treaty was signed between North and South Vietnam.
1975 South Vietnam was invaded by North Vietnam in March.
1976 South Vietnam was annexed by North Vietnam, and the two countries were renamed the Socialist Republic of Vietnam.

Vigée-Lebrun Elisabeth 1755–1842. French portrait painter, trained by her father (a painter in pastels) and Greuze. She became painter to Queen Marie Antoinette in the 1780s (many royal portraits survive).

Vigeland Gustav 1869–1943. Norwegian sculptor. He studied in Oslo and Copenhagen and with ⮕Rodin in Paris 1892. His program of sculpture in Frogner Park, Oslo, conceived 1900, was never finished. The style is heavy and monumental; the sculpted figures and animals enigmatic.

vigilante in US history, originally a member of a "vigilance committee," a self-appointed group to maintain public order in the absence of organized authority.

Early vigilante groups included the "Regulators" in South Carolina in the 1760s and in Pennsylvania 1794 during the Whiskey Rebellion. Many more appeared in the 19th century in frontier towns. Once authorized police forces existed, certain vigilante groups, such as the post-Civil War ◊Ku Klux Klan, operated outside the law, often as perpetrators of mob violence such as lynching.

Vigny Alfred, Comte de 1797–1863. French romantic writer whose works include the historical novel *Cinq-Mars* 1826, the play *Chatterton* 1835, and poetry, for example, *Les Destinées/Destinies* 1864.

Viking or **Norseman** medieval Scandinavian sea warrior. They traded with and raided Europe in the 8th–11th centuries, and often settled there. In France the Vikings were given ◊Normandy. Under Sweyn I they conquered England 1013, and his son Canute was king of England as well as Denmark and Norway. In the east they established the first Russian state and founded ◊Novgorod. They reached the Byzantine Empire in the south, and in the west sailed the seas to Ireland, Iceland, Greenland, and North America; see ◊Eric the Red, Leif ◊Ericsson, ◊Vinland.

In their narrow, shallow-draft, highly maneuverable longships, the Vikings penetrated far inland along rivers. They plundered for gold and land, and the need for organized resistance accelerated the growth of the feudal system. In England and Ireland they were known as "Danes." They created settlements, for example in York, and greatly influenced the development of the English language. The Vikings had a sophisticated literary culture (◊sagas), and an organized system of government with an assembly (thing). As ◊"Normans" they achieved a second conquest of England 1066.

The Swedish *Varangians* were invited to settle differences among the Slav chieftains in Russia 862. The Varangians also formed the imperial guard in Constantinople.

Viking art sculpture and design of the Vikings. Viking artists are known for woodcarving and metalwork and for an intricate interlacing ornament similar to that found in Celtic art. The dragon is a recurring motif.

The burial ship from Oseberg (University Museum, Oslo) is an early example. After the conversion to Christianity in the 10th century, the traditional Viking ornament continued: for example, carvings on the wooden stave churches of Norway, in Borgund and Urnes. Viking art was gradually absorbed into the Romanesque style.

Viking probes two US space probes to Mars, each one consisting of an orbiter and a lander. They were launched Aug 20 and Sept 9, 1975. They transmitted color pictures, and analyzed the soil. No definite signs of life were found.

Viking 1 carried life detection labs and landed on July 20, 1976 for detailed research and photos. Designed to work for 90 days, it operated for six and a half years, going silent Nov 1982. *Viking 2* was similar in setup to *Viking 1*; it landed on Mars Sept 3, 1976 and functioned for three and a half years.

Villa-Lobos Heitor 1887–1959. Brazilian composer. His style was based on folk tunes collected on travels in his country; for example, in the *Bachianas Brasileiras* 1930–44, he treats them in the manner of Bach. His works range from guitar solos to film scores to opera; he produced 2,000 works, including 12 symphonies.

Villehardouin Geoffroy de c. 1160–1213. French historian, the first to write in the French language. He was born near Troyes, and was a leader of the Fourth ◊Crusade, of which his *Conquest of Constantinople* (about 1209) is an account.

villeinage system of serfdom that prevailed in Europe in the Middle Ages. A villein was a peasant who gave dues and services to his lord in exchange for land. In France until the 13th century, "villeins" could refer to rural or urban non-nobles, but after this, it came to mean exclusively rural non-noble freemen. In Norman England, it referred to free peasants of relatively high status.

Their social position declined until, by the early 14th century, their personal and juridicial status was close to that of serfs. After the mid-14th century, as the effects of the Black Death led to a severe labor shortage, their status improved. By the 15th century villeinage had been supplanted by a system of free tenure and labor in England, but it continued in France until 1789.

Villon François 1431–c. 1465. French poet who used satiric humor, pathos, and lyric power in works written in the slang of the time. Among the little of his work that survives, *Petit Testament* 1456 and *Grand Testament* 1461 are prominent (the latter includes the "Ballade des dames du temps jadis/Ballad of the Ladies of Former Times").

Vilnius capital of Lithuania; population (1987) 566,000. Industries include engineering and the manufacture of textiles, chemicals, and foodstuffs.

From a 10th-century settlement, Vilnius became the Lithuanian capital 1323 and a center of Polish and Jewish culture. It was then Polish from 1386 until the Russian annexation 1795. Claimed by both Poland and Lithuania after World War I, it was given to Poland 1921, occupied by the USSR 1939, and immediately transferred to Lithuania. The city was the focal point of Lithuania's agitation for independence from the USSR 1989–91, and became the country's capital when independence was realized 1991.

Vimy Ridge hill in N France, taken in World War I by Canadian troops during the battle of Arras, April 1917, at the cost of 11,285 lives. It is a spur of the ridge of Nôtre Dame de Lorette, 5 mi/8 km NE of Arras.

Vincennes the University of Paris VIII, usually known as Vincennes after the suburb of E Paris where it was founded 1970 (following the 1968 student rebellion) for blue-collar workers. By 1980, it had 32,000 students. In June 1980, it was moved to the industrial suburb of St-Denis.

Vincent de Paul, St c. 1580–1660. French Roman Catholic priest and founder of the two charitable orders of Dazarists 1625 and Sisters of Charity 1634. After being ordained 1600, he was captured by Barbary pirates and held as a slave in Tunis until he escaped 1607. He was canonized 1737; feast day July 19.

vincristine ◊alkaloid extracted from the blue periwinkle plant (*Vinca rosea*). Developed as an anticancer agent, it has revolutionized the treatment of childhood acute leukemias; it is also included in ◊chemotherapy regimens for some lymphomas (cancers arising in the lymph tissues) and lung and breast cancers. Side effects, such as nerve damage and loss of hair, are severe but usually reversible.

vine or **grapevine** any of various climbing woody plants of the genus *Vitis*, family Vitaceae, especially *V. vinifera*, native to Asia Minor and cultivated from antiquity. Its fruit is eaten or made into wine or other fermented drinks; dried fruits of certain varieties are known as raisins and currants. Many other species of climbing plant are also termed vines.

vinegar sour liquid consisting of a 4% solution of acetic acid produced by the oxidation of alcohol, used to flavor food and as a preservative in pickling. **Malt vinegar** is brown and made from malted cereals; **white vinegar** is distilled from it. Other sources of vinegar include cider, wine, and honey. **Balsamic vinegar** is wine vinegar aged in wooden barrels.

Vineland industrial city (foundry products, glassware, chemicals, and vegetables) in SW New Jersey, N of Millville; population (1990) 54,800.

Vinland Norse name for the area of North America, probably the coast of Nova Scotia or New England, which the Norse adventurer and explorer Leif ◊Ericsson visited about 1000. It was named after the wild grapes that grew there and is celebrated in an important Norse saga.

Vinson Frederick Moore 1890–1953. US jurist and chief justice of the US Supreme Court 1946–53. Vinson was known for opinions defending the propriety of wide-ranging federal intervention in social and economic matters. He wrote the decision upholding the contempt convictions of union leader John L Lewis in *United States* v *United Mine Workers* 1947 and a dissent in *Youngstown Sheet and Tube Co* v *Sawyer* 1952, revoking presidential nationalization of the steel industry during the Korean War. He was conservative on issues of national security, most notably in *Rosenberg* v *United States* 1953, denying a stay of execution of convicted spies Ethel and Julius Rosenberg. He supported civil rights, writing the majority opinion in *Shelly* v *Kraemer* 1948, ruling that state courts may not enforce discrimination by private landlords, and *McLaurin* v *Oklahoma State Regents* 1950, attacking the "separate but equal" doctrine.

Vinson, born in Louisa, Kentucky, received his undergraduate and law degrees from Center College and became a lawyer active in Democratic politics, ultimately serving as a member of the US House of Representatives 1924–28 and 1930–38. He was appointed judge of the US Court of Appeals for the District of Columbia 1939. During World War II he was chief judge of the US Emergency Court of Appeals and director of the Office of Economic Stabilization. President Truman appointed Vinson secretary of the Treasury 1945 and chief justice 1946.

Vinson Massif highest point in ◊Antarctica, rising to 16,863 ft/5,140 m in the Ellsworth Mountains.

viol family of bowed stringed instruments prominent in the 16th–18th centuries, before their role was taken by the violins. Developed for close-harmony chamber music, they have a pure and restrained tone. Viols normally have six strings, a flat back, and narrow shoulders.

Members of the family include treble, alto, tenor, bass (or *viola da gamba*), and double bass (or *violone*). The smaller instruments are rested on the knee, not held under the chin. They are tuned in fourths, like a guitar. The only viol to survive in use in the symphony orchestra is the double bass, which was modified to have four strings and no frets.

viola bowed, stringed musical instrument, alto member of the ◊violin family.

violet plant of the genus *Viola*, family Violaceae, with toothed leaves and mauve, blue, or white flowers, such as the Canada violet *V. canadensis* and primrose violet *V. primulifolia* of North America and the sweet violet *V. odorata* of Europe. The pansy is also a kind of violet.

violin bowed, four-stringed musical instrument, the smallest and highest pitched of the violin family. The strings are tuned in fifths (G, D, A, and E), with G as the lowest, tuned below middle C.

The violin had its origins in Italy in a variety of small-sized three- and four-stringed designs during the first third of the 16th century, with the classic form being finalized shortly after about 1535 by the Cremonese master Andrea ◊Amati. Guarneri and Stradivari were apprenticed at the Amati workshop and soon constructed violins based on his pattern. Some of these very violins from the 16th century are still being played, studied, collected, and emulated by luthiers. Today's violin has not changed in form since that time, but in the late 18th century, aspects of the design were modified to produce a bigger sound and greater projection for the concert hall and to allow for evolving virtuoso expression. These include a lengthened fingerboard, an angled neck, and larger-sized basebar and soundpost.

violin family family of bowed stringed instruments developed in Italy during the 17th century, which eventually superseded the viols and formed the basis of the modern orchestra. There are three instruments: violin, viola, and cello (or violoncello); the double bass is descended from the double bass viol (or violone).

violoncello or *cello* bowed, stringed musical instrument, tenor member of the ◊violin family.

VIP abbreviation for *very important person*.

viper any front-fanged venomous snake of the family Viperidae. Vipers range in size from 1 ft/ 30 cm to 10 ft/3 m, and often have diamond or jagged markings. Most give birth to live young.

There are 150 species of viper. The true vipers, subfamily *Viperinae*, abundant in Africa and SW Asia, include the ◊adder *Vipera berus*, the African puff adder *Bitis arietans*, and the horned viper of North Africa *Cerastes cornutus*. The second subfamily *Crotalinae* includes the mostly New World pit vipers, such as ◊rattlesnakes and copperheads of the Americas, which have a heat-sensitive pit between each eye and nostril.

Virgil (Publius Vergilius Maro) 70–19 BC. Roman poet who wrote the *Eclogues* 37 BC, a series of pastoral poems; the *Georgics* 30 BC, four books on the art of farming; and his epic masterpiece, the ◊*Aeneid*.

Virgil, born near Mantua, came of the small farmer class. He was educated in Cremona and Mediolanum (Milan) and studied philosophy and rhetoric in Rome before returning to his

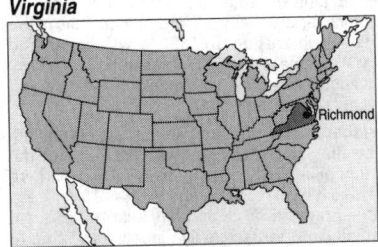

Virginia

farm, where he began the *Eclogues* 43 BC. He wrote the *Georgics* at the suggestion of his patron, Maecenas, to whom he introduced Horace. Virgil devoted the last 11 years of his life to the composition of the *Aeneid*, considered the greatest epic poem in Latin literature and a major influence on later European literature.

virginal in music, a small type of ◊harpsichord.

Virginia state in E US; nickname Old Dominion
area 40,762 sq mi/105,600 sq km
capital Richmond
cities Norfolk, Virginia Beach, Newport News, Hampton, Chesapeake, Portsmouth
features Blue Ridge mountains, which include the Shenandoah National Park; Arlington National Cemetery; Mount Vernon (home of George Washington 1752–99); Monticello (Thomas Jefferson's home near Charlottesville); Stratford Hall (Robert E Lee's birthplace at Lexington); Williamsburg restoration; Jamestown and Yorktown historic sites
products sweet potatoes, corn, tobacco, apples, peanuts, coal, ships, trucks, paper, chemicals, processed food, textiles
population (1990) 6,187,400
famous people Richard E Byrd, Patrick Henry, Meriwether Lewis, William Clark, Edgar Allan Poe, Booker T Washington
history named in honor of Elizabeth I; Jamestown (now in ruins) was the first permanent English settlement in the New World 1607; took a leading part in the American Revolution, and was one of the original Thirteen States; joined the Confederacy in the Civil War.

Virginia Beach resort city in SE Virginia, on Chesapeake Bay, E of Norfolk; population (1990) 393,100. The colonists who settled Jamestown first landed here 1607.

Virginia creeper or *woodbine* E North American climbing vine *Parthenocissus quinquefolia* of the grape family, having tendrils, palmately compound leaves, green flower clusters, and blue berries consumed by numerous birds but inedible to humans.

Virgin Islands group of about 100 small islands, northernmost of the Leeward Islands in the Antilles, West Indies. Tourism is the main industry.

They comprise the **US Virgin Islands** St Thomas (with the capital, Charlotte Amalie), St Croix, St John, and about 50 small islets; area 135 sq mi/350 sq km; population (1990) 101,800; and the **British Virgin Islands** Tortola (with the capital, Road Town), Virgin Gorda, Anegada, and Jost van Dykes, and about 40 islets; area 58 sq mi/150 sq km; population (1987) 13,250.

Christopher Columbus reached these islands 1493. They were divided between Britain and Denmark 1666. Denmark sold its islands

to the US 1917; they form an unincorporated territory, with residents electing a governor and legislature. The British Virgin Islands have partial internal self-government.

Virgo zodiacal constellation, the second largest in the sky. It is represented as a maiden holding an ear of wheat. The Sun passes through Virgo from late Sept to the end of Oct. Virgo's brightest star is the first-magnitude ◊Spica. Virgo contains the nearest large cluster of galaxies to us, 50 million light-years away, consisting of about 3,000 galaxies centered on the giant elliptical galaxy M87. Also in Virgo is the nearest ◊quasar, 3C 273, an estimated 3 billion light-years distant. In astrology, the dates for Virgo are between about Aug 23 and Sept 22 (see ◊precession).

virion the smallest unit of a mature ◊virus.

Virtanen Artturi Ilmari 1895–1973. Finnish chemist who from 1920 made discoveries in agricultural chemistry. Because green fodder tends to ferment and produce a variety of harmful acids, it cannot be preserved for long. Virtanen prevented the process from starting by acidifying the fodder. In this form it lasted longer and remained nutritious. Nobel Prize for Chemistry 1945.

virtual memory in computing, a technique whereby a portion of the computer backing storage, or external, ◊memory is used as an extension of its immediate-access, or internal, memory. The contents of an area of the immediate-access memory are stored on, say, a hard disk while they are not needed, and brought back into main memory when required.

The process, called paging or segmentation, is controlled by the computer ◊operating system and is hidden from the programmer, to whom the computer's internal memory appears larger than it really is. The technique can be successfully implemented only if very fast backing store is available, so that "pages" of memory can be rapidly switched into and out of the immediate-access memory.

virtual reality advanced form of computer simulation, in which a participant has the illusion of being part of an artificial environment. The participant views the environment through two tiny 3-D television screens built into a visor. Sensors detect movements of the participant's head or body, causing the apparent viewing position to change. Gloves (datagloves) fitted with sensors may be worn, which allow the participant seemingly to pick up and move objects in the environment.

The technology is still under development but is expected to have widespread applications; for example, in military and surgical training, architecture, and home entertainment.

virtuoso in music, a performer of unusual interpretive and technical skill.

virus infectious particle consisting of a core of nucleic acid (DNA or RNA) enclosed in a protein shell. Viruses are acellular and able to function and reproduce only if they can invade a living cell to use the cell's system to replicate themselves. In the process they may disrupt or alter the host cell's own DNA. The healthy human body reacts by producing an antiviral protein, ◊interferon, which prevents the infection spreading to adjacent cells.

Many viruses mutate continuously so that the host's body has little chance of developing permanent resistance; others transfer between species, with the new host similarly unable to develop resistance. The viruses that cause ▷AIDS and ▷Lassa fever are both thought to have "jumped" to humans from other mammalian hosts.

Among diseases caused by viruses are canine distemper, chickenpox, common cold, herpes, influenza, rabies, smallpox, yellow fever, AIDS, and many plant diseases. Recent evidence implicates viruses in the development of some forms of cancer (see ▷oncogenes).

Bacteriophages are viruses that infect bacterial cells.

Retroviruses are of special interest because they have an RNA genome and can produce DNA from this RNA by a process called reverse transcription.

Viroids, discovered 1971, are even smaller than viruses; they consist of a single strand of nucleic acid with no protein coat. They may cause stunting in plants and some rare diseases in animals, including humans. It is debatable whether viruses and viroids are truly living organisms, since they are incapable of an independent existence. Outside the cell of another organism they remain completely inert. The origin of viruses is also unclear, but it is believed that they are degenerate forms of life, derived from cellular organisms, or pieces of nucleic acid that have broken away from the genome of some higher organism and taken up a parasitic existence.

Antiviral drugs are difficult to develop because viruses replicate by using the genetic machinery of host cells, so that drugs tend to affect the host cell as well as the virus. Acyclovir (used against the herpes group of diseases) is one of the few drugs so far developed that is successfully selective in its action. It is converted to its active form by an enzyme that is specific to the virus, and it then specifically inhibits viral replication. Some viruses have shown developing resistance to the few antiviral drugs available.

Viruses have recently been found to be very abundant in seas and lakes, with between 5 and 10 million per cubic centimeter of water at most sites tested, but up to 250 million per cubic centimeter in one polluted lake. These viruses infect bacteria and, possibly, single-celled algae. They may play a crucial role in controlling the survival of bacteria and algae in the plankton.

virus in computing, a piece of ▷software that can replicate itself and transfer itself from one computer to another, without the user being aware of it. Some viruses are relatively harmless, but others can damage or destroy data. They are written by anonymous programmers, often maliciously, and are spread along telephone lines or on ▷floppy disks. Antivirus software can be used to detect and destroy well-known viruses, but new viruses continually appear and these may bypass existing antivirus programs.

Visalia city in central California, in the San Joaquin Valley, SE of Fresno; an agricultural center for grapes, citrus fruits, and dairy products; population (1990) 75,600.

Visby historic town and bishopric on the Swedish island of Gotland in the Baltic that became the center of the German ▷Hanseatic League.

It was founded as a Viking trading post on the route from Novgorod to the west. During the 12th and 13th centuries, the Scandinavian population became outnumbered by German colonists, and Visby became the nucleus of the Hanseatic League. In 1361, it was conquered by Waldemar IV. It possesses impressive fortifications, dated from the time of the Hanse, and many Gothic churches.

viscacha Argentinian Pampas and scrubland-dwelling rodent *Lagostomus maximus* of the chinchilla family. It is up to 2.2 ft/70 cm long with a 8 in/20 cm tail, and weighs 15 lb/7 kg. It is gray and black and has a large head and small ears. Viscachas live in warrens of up to 30 individuals. They are nocturnal and feed on grasses, roots, and seeds.

Four species of **Mountain viscachas** genus *Lagidium*, also called Peruvian hares, are smaller and have long ears and tails and are found in rocky places feeding by day on sparse vegetation.

Visconti dukes and rulers of Milan 1277–1447. They originated as north Italian feudal lords who attained dominance over the city as a result of alliance with the Holy Roman emperors. Despite papal opposition, by the mid-14th century they ruled 15 other major towns in northern Italy. The duchy was inherited by the ▷Sforzas 1447.

They had no formal title until Gian Galeazzo (1351–1402) bought the title of duke from Emperor Wenceslas IV (1361–1419). On the death of the last male Visconti, Filippo Maria 1447, the duchy was inherited by his son-in-law, Francesco Sforza.

Visconti Luchino 1906–1976. Italian film, opera, and theater director. The film *Ossessione* 1942 pioneered neorealist cinema despite being subject to censorship problems from the fascist government. His later works include *Rocco and His Brothers* 1960, *The Leopard* 1963, *The Damned* 1969, and *Death in Venice* 1971. His powerful social commentary led to clashes with the Italian government and Roman Catholic Church.

His stage work introduced Tennessee Williams, Arthur Miller, Sartre and Cocteau to Italy.

viscose yellowish, syrupy solution made by treating cellulose with sodium hydroxide and carbon disulfide. The solution is then regenerated as continuous filament for the making of ▷rayon and as cellophane.

viscosity in physics, the resistance of a fluid to flow, caused by its internal friction, which makes it resist flowing past a solid surface or other layers of the fluid. It applies to the motion of an object moving through a fluid as well as the motion of a fluid passing by an object.

Fluids such as pitch, treacle, and heavy oils are highly viscous; for the purposes of calculation, many fluids in physics are considered to be perfect, or nonviscous.

viscount in the UK peerage, the fourth degree of nobility, between earl and baron.

Vishnu in Hinduism, the second in the triad of gods (with Brahma and Siva) representing three aspects of the supreme spirit. He is the **Preserver**, and is believed to have assumed human appearance in nine *avatāra*s, or incarnations, in such forms as Rama and Krishna. His worshipers are the Vaishnavas.

Visigoth member of the western branch of the ▷Goths, an E Germanic people.

vision defect any abnormality of the eye that causes less than perfect sight. In a **nearsighted** eye, the lens is fatter than normal, causing light from distant objects to be focused in front and not on the retina. A person with this complaint, called ▷myopia, cannot see clearly for distances over a few yards, and needs glasses with diverging lenses. **Farsightedness**, also called hypermetropia, is caused by an eye lens thinner than normal that focuses light from distant objects behind the retina. The sufferer cannot see close objects clearly, and needs converging-lens glasses. There are other vision defects, such as ▷color blindness and ▷astigmatism.

vision system computer-based device for interpreting visual signals from a video camera. Computer vision is important in robotics where sensory abilities would considerably increase the flexibility and usefulness of a robot.

Although some vision systems exist for recognizing simple shapes, the technology is still in its infancy.

Vistula Polish **Wisła** river in Poland that rises in the Carpathians and runs SE to the Baltic at Gdańsk; length 677 mi/1,090 km. It is heavily polluted, carrying into the Baltic every year large quantities of industrial and agricultural waste, including phosphorus, oil, nitrogen, mercury, cadmium, and zinc.

visual display terminal computer terminal consisting of a keyboard for input data and a screen for displaying output. The oldest and the most popular type of VDT screen is the ▷cathode-ray tube (CRT), which uses essentially the same technology as a television screen. Other types use plasma display technology and ▷liquid-crystal displays.

vitalism the idea that living organisms derive their characteristic properties from a universal life force. In the present century, this view is associated with the philosopher Henri ▷Bergson.

vitamin any of various chemically unrelated organic compounds that are necessary in small quantities for the normal functioning of the body. Many act as coenzymes, small molecules that enable ▷enzymes to function effectively. They are normally present in adequate amounts in a balanced diet. Deficiency of a vitamin will normally lead to a metabolic disorder ("deficiency disease"), which can be remedied by sufficient intake of the vitamin. They are generally classified as **water-soluble** (B and C) or **fat-soluble** (A, D, E, and K).

Scurvy (the result of vitamin C deficiency) was observed at least 3,500 years ago, and sailors from the 1600s were given fresh sprouting cereals or citrus-fruit juice to prevent or cure it. The concept of scurvy as a deficiency disease, however, caused by the absence of a specific substance, emerged later. In the 1890s a Dutch doctor, Christiaan ▷Eijkman, discovered that he could cure hens suffering from a condition like beriberi by feeding them on whole-grain, rather than polished, rice. In 1912 Casimir Funk, a Polish-born biochemist, had proposed the existence of what he called "vitamines," but it was not fully established until about 1915 that several deficiency diseases were preventable and curable by extracts from certain foods. By then it was known that two groups of factors were involved, one being water-soluble and present, for example, in yeast, rice-polishings, and wheat germ, and the other being fat-soluble and present in egg yolk, butter, and fish-liver oils. The water-soluble substance, known to be effective against beriberi, was named vitamin B. The fat-soluble vitamin complex was at first called vitamin A. As a result of analytical techniques these have been subsequently separated into their various components, and others have been discovered.

vitamin C alternate name for ▷ascorbic acid.

vitreous humor transparent jellylike substance behind the lens of the vertebrate ▷eye. It gives rigidity to the spherical form of the eye and allows light to pass through to the retina.

vitriol any of a number of sulfate salts. Blue, green, and white vitriols are copper, ferrous, and zinc sulfate, respectively. *Oil of vitriol* is sulfuric acid.

Vitruvius (Marcus Vitruvius Pollio) 1st century BC. Roman architect whose ten-volume interpretation of Roman architecture *De architectura* influenced Leon Battista Alberti and Andrea Palladio.

Vitus, St Christian saint, perhaps Sicilian, who was martyred in Rome early in the 4th century. Feast day June 15.

Vivaldi Antonio (Lucio) 1678–1741. Italian Baroque composer, violinist, and conductor. He wrote 23 symphonies, 75 sonatas, over 400 concertos, including the *Four Seasons* (about 1725) for violin and orchestra, over 40 operas, and much sacred music. His work was largely neglected until the 1930s.

Known as the Red Priest, because of his flaming hair color, Vivaldi spent much of his church career teaching music at a girl's orphanage. He wrote for them and for himself.

vivipary in animals, a method of reproduction in which the embryo develops inside the body of the female from which it gains nourishment (in contrast to ▷oviparity and ▷ovoviviparity). Vivipary is best developed in placental mammals, but also occurs in some arthropods, fishes, amphibians, and reptiles that have placentalike structures. In plants, it is the formation of young plantlets or bulbils instead of flowers. The term also describes seeds that germinate prematurely, before falling from the parent plant.

Premature germination is common in mangrove trees, where the seedlings develop sizable spearlike roots before dropping into the swamp below; this prevents their being washed away by the tide.

vivisection literally, cutting into a living animal. Used originally to mean experimental surgery or dissection practiced on a live subject, the term is often used by ▷antivivisection campaigners to include any experiment on animals, surgical or otherwise.

viz abbreviation for *videlicet* (Latin "that is to say," "namely").

Vladimir I St 956–1015. Russian saint, prince of Novgorod, and grand duke of Kiev. Converted to Christianity 988, he married Anna, Christian sister of the Byzantine emperor ▷Basil II, and established the Byzantine rite of Orthodox Christianity as the Russian national faith.

Vladivostok port (naval and commercial) in E Siberian Russia, at the Amur Bay on the Pacific coast; population (1987) 615,000. It is kept open by icebreakers during winter. Industries include shipbuilding and the manufacture of precision instruments.

It was established 1860 as a military port. It is the administrative center of the Far East Science Center 1969, with subsidiaries at Petropavlovsk, Khabarovsk, and Magadan.

Vlaminck Maurice de 1876–1958. French painter who began using brilliant color as an early member of the *Fauves* (see ▷Fauvism),

mainly painting landscapes. He later abandoned Fauve colour. He also wrote poetry, novels, and essays.

Initially he was inspired by van ▷Gogh but by 1908 ▷Cézanne had become the chief influence. Vlaminck was a multitalented eccentric: his pastimes included playing the violin and farming.

VLF in physics, the abbreviation for *very low* ▷*frequency*.

VLSI (abbreviation for *very large-scale integration*) in electronics, the early-1990s level of advanced technology in the microminiaturization of ▷integrated circuits, and an order of magnitude smaller than ▷LSI (large-scale integration).

voc. in grammar, abbreviation for *vocative*.

vocal cords the paired folds, ridges, or cords of tissue within a mammal's larynx, and a bird's syrinx. Air passing over the folds or membranes makes them vibrate, producing sounds. Muscles in the larynx change the pitch of the sounds produced, by adjusting the tension of the vocal cords.

vocational education education relevant to a specific job or career.

Community colleges provide two-year training in the trades as well as secretarial, business, accounting, and other business and job-related studies. Technical colleges may be two-year, four-year, or prestigious advanced degree institutions, such as the Massachusetts Institute of Technology or Rensselaer Polytechnic Institute.

vocative in the grammar of certain inflected languages, for example Latin, the form of a word, especially a name, that is used to indicate that a person or thing is being addressed.

vodka strong colorless alcoholic liquor distilled from rye, potatoes, or barley.

voice sound produced through the mouth and by the passage of air between the ▷vocal cords. In humans the sound is much amplified by the hollow sinuses of the face, and is modified by the movements of the lips, tongue, and cheeks.

voiceprint graph produced by a sound spectograph showing frequency and intensity changes in the human voice when visually recorded. It enables individual speech characteristics to be determined. First used as evidence in criminal trials in the US 1966, voiceprints were banned 1974 by the US Court of Appeal as "not yet sufficiently accepted by scientists."

Voight Jon 1938– . US film actor who starred with Dustin Hoffman in *Midnight Cowboy* 1969. His subsequent films include *Deliverance* 1972, *Coming Home* 1978, and *Runaway Train* 1985.

Vojvodina autonomous area in N Serbia, Yugoslavia; area 8,299 sq mi/21,500 sq km; population (1986) 2,050,000, including 1,110,000 Serbs and 390,000 Hungarians. Its capital is Novi Sad. In Sept 1990 Serbia effectively stripped Vojvodina of its autonomous status, causing antigovernment and anticommunist riots in early 1991.

vol abbreviation for *volume*.

volatile in chemistry, term describing a substance that readily passes from the liquid to the vapor phase. Volatile substances have a high ▷vapor pressure.

volcanic rock ▷igneous rock formed at the surface of the Earth. It is usually fine-grained, unlike the more coarse-grained intrusive (under the surface) types of igneous rocks.

Volcanic rock can be either **lava** (solidified magma) or a **pyroclastic deposit** (fragmentary lava or ash), such as tuff (volcanic ash that has fused to form rock).

Basalt and andesite are the main types of lava. Rhyolite often occurs as a pyroclastic deposit.

volcano vent in the Earth's ▷crust from which molten rock, lava, ashes, and gases are ejected. Usually it is cone-shaped with a pitlike opening at the top called the crater. Some volcanoes, for example, Stromboli and Vesuvius in Italy, eject the material with explosive violence; others, for example on Hawaii, are quiet and the lava simply rises into the crater and flows over the rim.

Volcanoes are closely associated with the movements of lithospheric plates (the top layer of the Earth's structure), particularly around plate boundaries (see ▷plate tectonics). The violent ones are associated with ▷subduction zones and emit a lava that is rich in silica (andesite). The quiet ones are associated with mid-▷ocean ridges or with "hot spots" far from plate-margin activity. These emit a lava that is silica-poor (basalt).

Many volcanoes are submarine and occur along mid-ocean ridges. The chief terrestrial volcanic regions are around the Pacific rim (Cape Horn to Alaska); the central Andes of Chile (with the world's highest volcano, Guallatiri, 19,900 ft/6,060 m); North Island, New Zealand; Hawaii; Japan; and Antarctica. There are about 600 active volcanoes on Earth. Volcanism has helped shape other members of the Solar System, including the Moon, Mars, Venus, and Jupiter's moon Io.

Volcker Paul 1927– . US economist. As chair of the board of governors of the Federal Reserve System 1979–87, he controlled the amount of money in circulation in the US. He was succeeded by Alan Greenspan.

vole any of various rodents of the family Cricetidae, subfamily Microtinae, distributed over Europe, Asia, and North America, and related to hamsters and lemmings. They are characterized by stout bodies and short tails. They have brown or gray fur, and blunt noses, and some species reach a length of 12 in/ 30 cm. They feed on grasses, seeds, aquatic plants, and insects. Many show remarkable fluctuations in numbers over 3–4 year cycles.

The most common genus is *Microtus*, which includes some 45 species distributed across North America and Eurasia.

Volga longest river in Europe; 2,290 mi/3,685 km, 2,200 mi/3,540 km of which are navigable. It drains most of the central and eastern parts of European Russia, rises in the Valdai plateau, and flows into the Caspian Sea 55 mi/88 km below Astrakhan.

Volgograd formerly (until 1925) *Tsaritsyn* and (1925–61) *Stalingrad*. Industrial city (metal goods, machinery, lumber mills, oil refining) in SW Russia, on the river Volga; population (1987) 988,000.

Its successful defense 1942–43 against Germany was a turning point in World War II.

volleyball indoor and outdoor team game played on a court between two teams of six players each. A net is placed across the center of the court, and players hit the ball with their hands over it, the aim being to ground it in the opponents' court.

Originally called Mintonette, the game was invented 1895 by William G Morgan in

Massachusetts, as a rival to the newly developed basketball. The playing area measures 59 ft/18 m by 29 ft 5 in/9 m. The ball, slightly smaller than a basketball, may not be hit more than three times on one team's side of the net. The world championships were first held 1949 for men, and 1952 for women (Olympic winners automatically become world champions).

volt SI unit (symbol V) of electromotive force or electric potential. A small battery usually has a potential of one or two volts; the domestic electricity supply in the US is 110 volts. A high-tension transmission line may carry up to 765,000 volts.

The absolute volt is defined as the potential difference necessary to produce a current of one ampere through an electric circuit with a resistance of one ohm. It can also be defined as the potential difference that requires one joule of work to move a positive charge of one coulomb from the lower to the higher potential. It is named after the Italian scientist Alessandro Volta.

Volta main river in Ghana, about 1,000 mi/1,600 km long, with two main upper branches, the Black and White Volta. It has been dammed to provide power.

Volta Alessandro 1745–1827. Italian physicist who invented the first electric cell (the voltaic pile), the electrophorus (an early electrostatic generator), and an ◊electroscope.

Born in Como, he was a professor there and at Pavia. The ◊volt is named after him.

Voltaire Adopted name of François-Marie Arouet 1694–1778. French writer who believed in ◊deism and devoted himself to tolerance, justice, and humanity. He was threatened with arrest for *Lettres philosophiques sur les Anglais/Philosophical Letters on the English* 1733 (essays in favor of English ways, thought, and political practice) and had to take refuge. Other writings include *Le Siècle de Louis XIV/The Age of Louis XIV* 1751; *Candide* 1759, a parody on ◊Leibniz's "best of all possible worlds;" and *Dictionnaire philosophique* 1764.

Voltaire was born in Paris, the son of a notary, and used his adopted name from 1718. He was twice imprisoned in the Bastille and exiled from Paris 1716–26 for libelous political verse. *Oedipe/Oedipus*, his first essay in tragedy, was staged 1718. While in England 1726–29 he dedicated an epic poem on Henry IV, *La Henriade/The Henriade*, to Queen Caroline, and on returning to France published the successful *Histoire de Charles XII/History of Charles XII* 1731, and produced the play *Zaïre* 1732. He took refuge with his mistress, the Marquise de ◊Châtelet, at Cirey in Champagne, where he wrote the play *Mérope* 1743 and much of *Le Siècle de Louis XIV*. Among his other works are histories of Peter the Great, Louis XV, and India; the satirical tale *Zadig* 1748; *La Pucelle/The Maid* 1755, on Joan of Arc;and the tragedy *Irène* 1778. From 1751 to 1753 he stayed at the court of Frederick II (the Great) of Prussia, who had long been an admirer, but the association ended in deep enmity. From 1754 he established himself near Geneva, and after 1758 at Ferney, just across the French border. His remains were transferred 1791 to the Panthéon in Paris.

voltmeter instrument for measuring potential difference (voltage). It has a high internal resistance (so that it passes only a small current), and is connected in parallel with the component across which potential difference is to be measured. A common type is constructed

from a sensitive current-detecting moving-coil ◊galvanometer placed in series with a high-value resistor (multiplier). To measure an AC (◊alternating current) voltage, the circuit must usually include a rectifier; however, a moving-iron instrument can be used to measure alternating voltages without the need for such a device.

volume in geometry, the space occupied by a three-dimensional solid object. A prism (such as a cube) or a cylinder has a volume equal to the area of the base multiplied by the height. For a pyramid or cone, the volume is equal to one-third of the area of the base multiplied by the perpendicular height. The volume of a sphere is equal to $\frac{4}{3}\pi r^3$, where r is the radius. Volumes of irregular solids may be calculated by the technique of ◊integration.

vomiting expulsion of the contents of the stomach through the mouth. It may have numerous causes, including direct irritation of the stomach, severe pain, dizziness, and emotion. Sustained or repeated vomiting may indicate serious disease, and dangerous loss of water, salt, and acid may result (as in ◊bulimia).

von Braun Wernher 1912–1977. German rocket engineer who developed German military rockets (◊V1 and V2) during World War II and later worked for the space agency ◊NASA in the US.

During the 1940s his research team at Peenemünde on the Baltic coast produced the V1 (flying bomb) and supersonic V2 rockets. In the 1950s von Braun was part of the team that produced rockets for US satellites (the first, *Explorer I*, was launched early 1958) and early space flights by astronauts.

von Karajan Herbert. Austrian conductor. See ◊Karajan, Herbert von.

Vonnegut Kurt, Jr 1922– . US writer whose work generally has surrealistic elements, satire, and fantasy and depicts the flaws of contemporary society. His novel *Slaughterhouse Five* 1969 mixes his World War II experience of the fire-bombing of Dresden, Germany, with a fantasy world on the planet Tralfamadore with the science-fiction element dominated by absurdism and earthly black humor.

Born in Indianapolis, Indiana, Vonnegut graduated from Cornell University and the University of Chicago. In the 1960s and 1970s his work became very popular, particularly among college students. Other novels include *Player Piano* 1952, *The Sirens of Titan* 1958, *Cat's Cradle* 1963, *Breakfast of Champions* 1973, *Slapstick* 1976, *Jailbird* 1979, *Deadeye Dick* 1982, *Galapagos* 1985, and *Hocus Pocus* 1990. His short stories are collected in *Welcome to the Monkey House* 1968. His autobiography was published as *Palm Sunday* 1981.

Von Neumann John 1903–1957. Hungarian-born US scientist and mathematician, known for his pioneering work on computer design. He invented his "rings of operators" (called Von Neumann algebras) in the late 1930s, and also contributed to set theory, games theory, cybernetics (with his theory of self-reproducing automata, called **Von Neumann machines**), and the development of the atomic and hydrogen bombs.

He was born in Budapest and became an assistant professor of physical mathematics at Berlin University before moving to Princeton, in 1929, where he later became professor of mathematics. In the early 1940s he described a design for a stored-program computer.

voodoo set of magical beliefs and practices, followed in some parts of Africa, South America, and the West Indies, especially Haiti. It arose in the 17th century on slave plantations as a combination of Roman Catholicism and W African religious traditions; believers retain membership in the Roman Catholic church. Beliefs include the existence of *loa*, spirits who closely involve themselves in human affairs, and some of whose identities mesh with those of Christian saints. The loa are invoked by the priest (*houngan*) or priestess (*manbo*) at ceremonies, during which members of the congregation become possessed by the spirits and go into a trance.

A voodoo temple (*houmfort*) has a central post from which the loa supposedly descend to "mount" the worshiper. The loa can be identified by the characteristic behavior of the possessed person. Loa include Baron Samedi, who watches over the land of the dead; Erzulie, the black Virgin or Earth goddess; Ogu, a warrior, corresponding to St James the Great; and Legba, the lord of the road and interpreter between humans and spirits, who corresponds to St Anthony the hermit.

Vorarlberg ("in front of the Arlberg") Alpine federal province of W Austria draining into the Rhine and Lake Constance; area 1,004 sq mi/2,600 sq km; population (1987) 314,000. Its capital is Bregenz. Industries include forestry and dairy farming.

Voronezh industrial city (chemicals, construction machinery, electrical equipment) and capital of the Voronezh region of Russia, S of Moscow on the Voronezh River; population (1987) 872,000. There has been a town on the site since the 11th century.

Voroshilov Klement Efremovich 1881–1969. Marshal of the USSR. He joined the Bolsheviks 1903 and was arrested many times and exiled, but escaped. He became a Red Army commander in the civil war 1918–20, a member of the central committee 1921, commissar for war 1925, member of the Politburo 1926, and marshal 1935. He was removed as war commissar 1940 after defeats on the Finland front and failing to raise the German siege of Leningrad. He was a member of the committee for defense 1941–44 and president of the Presidium of the USSR 1953–60.

Voroshilovgrad former name (1935–58; 1970–89) of ◊Lugansk, a city in Ukraine.

Vorster Balthazar Johannes 1915–1983. South African Nationalist politician, prime minister 1966–78, and president 1978–79. During his term as prime minister some elements of apartheid were allowed to lapse, and attempts were made to improve relations with the outside world. He resigned the presidency because of a financial scandal.

Vosges mountain range in E France, rising in the Ballon de Guebwiller to 4,667 ft/1,422 m and forming the western edge of the Rhine rift valley.

Vostok (Russian "east") first Soviet spacecraft, used 1961–63. Vostok was a metal sphere 7.5 ft/2.3 m in diameter, capable of carrying one cosmonaut. It made flights lasting up to five days. *Vostok 1* carried the first person into space, Yuri ◊Gagarin.

vote expression of opinion by ballot, show of hands, or other means. For direct vote, see ◊plebiscite and ◊referendum. In parliamentary elections the results can be calculated in a number of ways.

In the US the voting age is 18. Conditions

of residence vary from state to state and registration is required before election day. Until declared illegal 1965, literacy tests or a ◊poll tax were often used to prevent black people from voting in the South. Voter registration and turnout in the US remains the lowest in the industrialized world. In 1988, 37% of potential voters failed to register and barely 50% voted in the presidential election, so that George Bush became president with the support of only 27% of the people. Voter registration increased in 1992, and record numbers of voters went to the polls.

Voyager probes two US space probes, originally ◊Mariners. *Voyager 1*, launched Sept 5, 1977, passed Jupiter March 1979, and reached Saturn Nov 1980. *Voyager 2* was launched earlier, Aug 20, 1977, on a slower trajectory that took it past Jupiter July 1979, Saturn Aug 1981, Uranus Jan 1986, and Neptune Aug 1989. Like the ◊Pioneer probes, the Voyagers are on their way out of the Solar System. Their tasks now include helping scientists to locate the position of the heliopause, the boundary at which the influence of the Sun gives way to the forces exerted by other stars.

Both Voyagers carry specially coded long-playing records called "Sounds of Earth" for the enlightenment of any other civilizations that might find them.

Voyager 2 was not intended to visit Uranus and Neptune, but scientists were able to reprogram its computer to take it past those planets. *Voyager 2* passed by Neptune at an altitude of 3,000 mi/4,800 km; its radio signals took 4 hours 6 minutes to reach Earth.

VSTOL (abbreviation for *vertical/short takeoff and landing*) aircraft capable of taking off and landing either vertically or using a very short length of runway (see ◊STOL). Vertical takeoff requires a vector-control system that permits the thrust of the aircraft engine to be changed from horizontal to vertical for takeoff and back again to horizontal to permit forward flight. An alternative VSTOL technology developed in the US involves tilting the wings of the aircraft from vertical to horizontal and along with them the aircraft propellers, thus changing from vertical lift to horizontal thrust.

The British Harrier fighter bomber was the first VSTOL aircraft. It is now manufactured under license in the US and provides integral air support for the US Marines. In addition to the UK's Royal Air Force and Royal Navy, the Indian, Spanish, and Italian navies are equipped with the Harrier. It was used in the 1982 Falklands conflict and the 1991 Gulf War.

v.t. in grammar, abbreviation for *verb transitive*.

VT abbreviation for the state of ◊**Vermont**.

Vuillard (Jean) Edouard 1886–1940. French painter and printmaker, a founding member of *les* ◊**Nabis**. His work is mainly decorative, with an emphasis on surface pattern reflecting the influence of Japanese prints. With ◊Bonnard he produced numerous lithographs and paintings of simple domestic interiors, works that are generally categorized as *intimiste*.

Vulcan in Roman mythology, the god of fire and destruction, later identified with the Greek god ◊Hephaestus.

vulcanization technique for hardening rubber by heating and chemically combining it with sulfur. The process also makes the rubber stronger and more elastic. If the sulfur content is increased to as much as 30%, the product is the inelastic solid known as ebonite. More expensive alternatives to sulfur, such as selenium and tellurium, are used to vulcanize rubber for specialized products such as vehicle tires. The process was discovered accidentally by US inventor Charles ◊Goodyear 1839 and patented 1844.

Accelerators can be added to speed the vulcanization process, which takes from a few minutes for small objects to an hour or more for vehicle tires. Molded objects are often shaped and vulcanized simultaneously in heated molds; other objects may be vulcanized in hot water, hot air, or steam.

vulcanology the study of ◊volcanoes and the geological phenomena that cause them.

Vulgate (Latin "common") the Latin translation of the Bible produced by St Jerome in the 4th century.

It is the oldest surviving version of the entire Bible and differs from earlier Latin translations in working from the Hebrew rather than the Greek. In 1546 it was adopted by the Council of Trent as the official Roman Catholic Bible and was later used for official English versions like the Douai.

Vulpecula small constellation in the northern hemisphere of the sky just south of Cygnus, represented as a fox. It contains a major planetary ◊nebula, the Dumbbell, and the first ◊pulsar (pulsating radio source) to be discovered.

vulture any of various carrion-eating birds of prey with naked heads and necks and with keen senses of sight and smell. Vultures are up to 3.3 ft/1 m long, with wingspans of up to 11.5 ft/3.5 m. The plumage is usually dark, and the head brightly colored.

True vultures are placed in the family Accipitridae along with hawks and eagles and are found only in the Old World. American vultures are placed in a family of their own (Cathartidae) and include turkey vultures and ◊condors. The vulture has keen senses of sight and smell. Its eyes are adapted to give an overall view with a magnifying area in the center, enabling it to locate possible food sources and see the exact site in detail.

W the 23rd letter of the English alphabet, representing a labial-velar semivowel: a *u* in consonantal function. It is called double *u* because it was written *uu* or *vv*, which in ligature resulted in *w*. It is not pronounced before *r* (*write*, *wren*) and in cases like *two* and *sword*.

W abbreviation for *west*; in physics, symbol for *watt*.

WA abbreviation for the state of ⟡*Washington*; ⟡*Western Australia*.

Waco city in E central Texas, on the Brazos River, S of Fort Worth; population (1990) 103,600. It is an agricultural shipping center for cotton, grain, and livestock; industries include aircraft parts, glass, cement, tires, and textiles. Baylor University 1845 is here.

wadi in arid regions of the Middle East, a steep-sided valley containing an intermittent stream that flows in the wet season.

wafer in microelectronics, a "superchip" some 3–4 in/8–10 cm in diameter, for which wafer-scale integration (WSI) is used to link the equivalent of many individual ⟡silicon chips, improving reliability, speed, and cooling.

wage and price controls government directives freezing or limiting wages and prices, usually in time of emergency, such as wars or in the event of severe ⟡inflation.

The use of such controls in the US has been relatively rare, the strongest control occurring during World War II. Under President Nixon, wages and prices were frozen for 90 days in 1971. Since then, presidents have preferred to use persuasion rather than impose controls.

Wagner Honus (John Peter) 1874–1955. US baseball player. Born in Mansfield, Pennsylvania, Wagner began his professional baseball career 1895 and was signed as a shortstop by the Louisville club of the National League 1897. He was acquired by the Pittsburgh Pirates 1899 and remained there until his retirement 1917. He was a consistent hitter with an impressive lifetime batting average of .329. In addition to his fielding skills, he was a great runner; his career record of 722 stolen bases won him the nickname "the Flying Dutchman." Wagner was elected to the Baseball Hall of Fame 1936.

Wagner Richard 1813–1883. German opera composer. He revolutionized the 19th-century conception of opera, envisaging it as a wholly new art form in which musical, poetic, and scenic elements should be unified through such devices as the ⟡leitmotif. His operas include *Tannhäuser* 1845, *Lohengrin* 1850, and *Tristan und Isolde* 1865. In 1872 he founded the Festival Theater in Bayreuth; his masterpiece *Der Ring des Nibelungen/The Ring of the Nibelung*, a sequence of four operas, was first performed there in 1876. His last work, *Parsifal*, was produced in 1882.

Wagner's early career was as director of the Magdeburg Theater, where he unsuccessfully produced his first opera *Das Liebesverbot/ Forbidden Love* 1836. He lived in Paris 1839–42 and conducted the Dresden Opera House 1842–48. He fled Germany to escape arrest for his part in the 1848 revolution, but in 1861 he was allowed to return. He won the favor of Ludwig II of Bavaria 1864 and was thus able to set up the Festival Theater in Bayreuth. The Bayreuth tradition was continued by his wife Cosima (Liszt's daughter, whom he married after her divorce from Hans von ⟡Bülow); by his son **Siegfried Wagner** (1869–1930), a composer of operas such as *Der Bärenhäuter*; and by later descendants.

Wagner Robert F(erdinand) 1877–1953. US Democratic senator 1927–49, a leading figure in the development of welfare provision in the US, especially in the ⟡New Deal era. He helped draft much new legislation, including the National Industrial Recovery Act 1933, the Social Security Act 1936, and the National Labor Relations Act 1935, known as the Wagner Act.

Wagner-Jauregg Julius 1857–1940. Austrian neurologist. He received a Nobel Prize in 1927 for his work on the use of induced fevers in treating mental illness.

Wagram, Battle of battle July 1809 when French troops under Emperor Napoleon won an important victory over the Austrian army under Archduke Charles near the village of Wagram, NE of Vienna, Austria. The outcome forced Austria to concede general defeat to the French.

wagtail any slim narrow-billed bird of the genus *Motacilla*, about 7 in/18 cm long, with a characteristic flicking movement of the tail. There are about 30 species, found mostly in Eurasia and Africa.

Wahabi puritanical Saudi Islamic sect founded by Mohammed ibn-Abd-al-Wahab (1703–1792), which regards all other sects as heretical. By the early 20th century it had spread throughout the Arabian peninsula; it still remains the official ideology of the Saudi Arabian kingdom.

Wailing Wall or (in Judaism) *Western Wall* the remaining part of the ⟡Temple in Jerusalem, a sacred site of pilgrimage and prayer for Jews. There they offer prayers either aloud ("wailing") or on pieces of paper placed between the stones of the wall.

Waite Morrison Remick 1816–1888. US lawyer and chief justice of the US from 1874, appointed by President Grant. As chief justice, he presided over constitutional challenges to Reconstruction, but is best remembered for his decisions upholding the right of states to regulate public utilities.

Born in Lyme, Connecticut, and educated at Yale, Waite settled in Ohio, where he was admitted to the bar 1839. After serving in the state legislature 1849–50, he returned to private practice. A staunch Republican, he was named US counsel in the 1871 ⟡Alabama claims case.

Waite Terry (Terence Hardy) 1939– . British religious adviser to the archbishop of Canterbury, then Dr Robert Runcie, 1980–87. As the archbishop's special envoy, Waite disappeared Jan 20, 1987 while engaged in secret negotiations to free European hostages in Beirut, Lebanon. He had been taken hostage by an Islamic group and was released Nov 18, 1991.

Wajda Andrzej 1926– . Polish film and theater director, one of the major figures in postwar European cinema. His films are concerned with the predicament and disillusion of individuals caught up in political events. His works include *Ashes and Diamonds* 1958, *Man of Marble* 1977, *Man of Iron* 1981, *Danton* 1982, and *Korczak* 1990.

He was also mentor to filmmaker Roman Polanski.

Wake Islands small Pacific atoll comprising three islands 2,300 mi/3,700 km W of Hawaii, under US Air Force administration since 1972; area 3 sq mi/8 sq km; population (1980) 300. It was discovered by Captain William Wake 1841, annexed by the US 1898, and uninhabited until 1935 when it was made an air staging point, with a garrison. It was occupied by Japan 1941–45.

Waksman Selman Abraham 1888–1973. US biochemist, born in Ukraine. He coined the word "antibiotic" for bacteria-killing chemicals derived from microorganisms. Waksman was awarded a Nobel Prize in 1952 for the discovery of streptomycin, an antibiotic used against tuberculosis.

Walachia alternate spelling of ⟡Wallachia, part of Romania.

Walcheren island in Zeeland province, the Netherlands, in the estuary of the Scheldt
area 80 sq mi/200 sq km
capital Middelburg
cities Vlissingen (Flushing)
features flat and for the most part below sea level
products dairy, sugar beet, and other root vegetables
history a British force seized Walcheren 1809; after 7,000 of the garrison of 15,000 had died of malaria, the remainder were withdrawn. It was flooded by deliberate breaching of the dykes to drive out the Germans 1944–45, and in 1953 by abnormally high tides.

Walcott Derek 1930– . West Indian poet and playwright. His work fuses Caribbean and European, Classical and contemporary elements, and deals with the divisions within colonial society and his own search for cultural identity. His works include the long poem *Omeros* 1990, and his adaptation for the stage of Homer's *The Odyssey* 1992; his *Collected Poems* were published in 1986. He won the Nobel Prize for Literature 1992.

Walcott was born in St Lucia and was educated at the University of the West Indies. He has taught writing at the Universities of Columbia, Yale, and Harvard. He contributed greatly to the development of an indigenous West Indian theater, and for 25 years ran a theater in Trinidad. Other plays include *Dream on Monkey Mountain* 1970, *O Babylon!* 1978, and *Remembrance* 1980.

Wald George 1906– . US biochemist who explored the chemistry of vision. He found that a crucial role was played by the retinal pigment rhodopsin, derived in part from vitamin A. For this he shared the 1967 Nobel Prize for Physiology or Medicine with Ragnar Granit (1900–) and Haldan Hartline (1903–1983).

Wald Lillian D 1867–1940. US public health administrator and founder of New York City's Henry Street Settlement House 1895. In 1912 she founded the National Organization for Public Health Nursing and was also active in union and antiwar activities.

Waldemar or **Valdemar** four kings of Denmark, including:

Waldemar I *the Great* 1131–1182. King of Denmark from 1157, who defeated rival claimants to the throne and overcame the ◊Wends on the Baltic island of Rügen 1169.

Waldemar II *the Conqueror* 1170–1241. King of Denmark from 1202. He was the second son of Waldemar I and succeeded his brother Canute VI. He gained control of land north of the river Elbe (which he later lost), as well as much of Estonia, and he completed the codification of Danish law.

Waldemar IV 1320–1375. King of Denmark from 1340, responsible for reuniting his country by capturing Skåne (S Sweden) and the island of Gotland 1361. However, the resulting conflict with the ◊Hanseatic League led to defeat by them, and in 1370 he was forced to submit to the Peace of Stralsund.

Waldenses also known as **Waldensians** or **Vaudois** Protestant religious sect, founded *c.* 1170 by Peter Waldo, a merchant of Lyons. They were allied to the ◊Albigenses. They lived in voluntary poverty, refused to take oaths or take part in war, and later rejected the doctrines of transubstantiation, purgatory, and the invocation of saints. Although subjected to persecution until the 17th century, they spread in France, Germany, and Italy, and still survive in Piedmont.

Waldheim Kurt 1918– . Austrian politician and diplomat, president 1986–92. He was secretary-general of the United Nations 1972–81, having been Austria's representative there 1964–68 and 1970–71. He was elected president of Austria despite revelations that during World War II he had been an intelligence officer in an army unit responsible for transporting Jews to death camps. His election therefore led to some diplomatic isolation of Austria, and in 1991 he announced that he would not run for reelection.

Wales (Welsh *Cymru*) Principality of; constituent part of the United Kingdom, in the west between the British Channel and the Irish Sea
area 8,021 sq mi/20,780 sq km
capital Cardiff
cities Swansea, Wrexham, Newport, Carmarthen
features Snowdonia mountains (Snowdon 3,561 ft/1,085 m, the highest point in England and Wales) in the NW and in the SE the Black Mountain, Brecon Beacons, and Black Forest ranges; rivers Severn, Wye, Usk, and Dee
exports traditional industries (coal and steel) have declined, but varied modern and high-technology ventures are being developed. Tourism is important
currency pound sterling
population (1987) 2,836,000
language Welsh 19% (1981), English
religion Nonconformist Protestant denominations; Roman Catholic minority
government returns 38 members to the UK Parliament.
history for ancient history, see also ◊Britain, ancient.
c. 400 BC Wales occupied by Celts from central Europe.

AD 50–60 Wales became part of the Roman Empire.
c. 200 Christianity adopted.
c. 450–600 Wales became the chief Celtic stronghold in the west since the Saxons invaded and settled in S Britain. The Celtic tribes united against England.
8th century Frontier pushed back to ◊Offa's Dyke.
9th–11th centuries Vikings raided the coasts. At this time Wales was divided into small states organized on a clan basis, although princes such as Rhodri (844–878), Howel the Good (*c.* 904–949), and Griffith ap Llewelyn (1039–1063) temporarily united the country.
11th–12th centuries Continual pressure on Wales from the Normans across the English border was resisted, notably by ◊Llewelyn I and II.
1277 Edward I of England accepted as overlord by the Welsh.
1284 Edward I completed the conquest of Wales that had been begun by the Normans.
1294 Revolt against English rule put down by Edward I.
1350–1500 Welsh nationalist uprisings against the English; the most notable was that led by Owen Glendower.
1485 Henry Tudor, a Welshman, became Henry VII of England.
1536–43 Acts of Union united England and Wales after conquest under Henry VIII. Wales sent representatives to the English Parliament; English law was established in Wales; English became the official language.
18th century Evangelical revival made Nonconformism a powerful factor in Welsh life. A strong coal and iron industry developed in the south.
19th century The miners and ironworkers were militant supporters of Chartism, and Wales became a stronghold of labor unionism and socialism.
1893 University of Wales founded.
1920s–30s Wales suffered from industrial depression; unemployment reached 21% 1937, and a considerable exodus of population took place.
post-1945 Growing nationalist movement and a revival of the language, earlier suppressed or discouraged.
1966 Plaid Cymru, the Welsh National Party, returned its first member to Westminster.
1979 Referendum rejected a proposal for limited home rule.
1988 Bombing campaign against estate agents selling Welsh properties to English buyers.
For other history, see also ◊England: history; ◊United Kingdom.

Walesa Lech 1943– . Polish labor-union leader and president of Poland from 1990, founder of ◊Solidarity (Solidarność) in 1980, an organization, independent of the Communist Party, which forced substantial political and economic concessions from the Polish government 1980–81 until being outlawed. He was awarded the Nobel Prize for Peace 1983.

As an electrician at the Lenin shipyard in Gdańsk, Walesa became a labor-union organizer and led a series of strikes that drew wide public support. In Dec 1981 Solidarity was outlawed and Walesa arrested, after the imposition of martial law by the Polish leader Gen Jaruzelski. Walesa, a devout Catholic, was released 1982.

The coalition government elected Sept 1989 was dominated by Solidarity. Rifts appeared,

but Walesa went on to be elected president Dec 1990.

Wales, Prince of title conferred on the eldest son of the UK's sovereign. Prince ◊Charles was invested as 21st prince of Wales at Caernarvon 1969 by his mother, Elizabeth II.

walkabout Australian Aboriginal term for a nomadic ritual return into the bush by an urbanized Aboriginal; also used more casually for any similar excursion.

Walker Alice 1944– . US poet, novelist, critic, and essay writer. She was active in the US civil-rights movement in the 1960s and, as a black woman, wrote about the double burden of racist and sexist oppression that such women bear. Her novel *The Color Purple* 1983 (filmed 1985) won the Pulitzer Prize.

Born in Eatonton, Georgia, she also wrote the novels *The Third Life of Grange Copeland* 1970, *Meridian* 1976, and *The Temple of My Familiar* 1989. Walker's collections of poems include *Once* 1968 and *Revolutionary Petunias* 1973; her short stories and essays are collected in *Love and Trouble: Stories of Black Women* 1973 and *In Search of Our Mothers' Gardens: Womanist Prose* 1983.

Walker Jimmy (James John) 1881–1946. US public official. In 1925 Walker was elected mayor of New York City and in that position became a popular personality, familiarly known to his constituents as "Jimmy." Although Walker made great improvements to the city's infrastructure, he was charged with graft and forced to resign 1932.

Born in New York, Walker attended St Francis Xavier College and was admitted to the bar 1912. Becoming active in Democratic party politics, he served in the state assembly 1909–15 and the state senate 1915–25, where he became a protégé of Al Smith.

Walker William 1824–1860. US adventurer who for a short time established himself as president of a republic in NW Mexico, and was briefly president of Nicaragua 1856–57. He was eventually executed and is now regarded as a symbol of US imperialism in Central America.

wallaby any of various small and medium-sized members of the ◊kangaroo family.

Wallace George Corley 1919– . US politician who was opposed to integration; he was governor of Alabama 1963–67, 1971–79, and 1983–87. He contested the presidency in 1968 as an independent (the American Independent Party) and in 1972 campaigned for the Democratic nomination but was shot at a rally and became partly paralyzed.

Wallace was born in Clio, Alabama, and held various state jobs before being elected to the governorship for the first time. During the 1963 integration of the University of Alabama, he defied a court order and prevented access to black students; he later complied with the order. His wife served as governor 1967–71 when he was ineligible to run for a third consecutive term. Wallace moderated his staunchly antiintegration views and was elected for a fourth term as governor by a populist coalition of blacks and whites 1982. He retired 1987.

Wallace Henry Agard 1888–1965. US editor and public official. Although his father was a prominent Republican, the younger Wallace joined the Democratic party 1928. He was appointed secretary of the treasury by Franklin Roosevelt 1933 and served as vice-president during Roosevelt's third term 1941–45. Wallace later broke with Truman and, after serving as editor of the *New Republic* 1946–47, was the unsuccessful Progressive Party candidate for president 1948.

Born in Adair County, Iowa, Wallace was educated at Iowa State College and in 1910 joined the staff of the family-owned periodical *Wallace's Farmer*.

Wallace Lew(is) 1827–1905. US general and novelist. He served in the Mexican War and the American Civil War and subsequently became governor of New Mexico and minister to Turkey. He was credited with saving Washington, DC, from capture by Confederate forces and served on the tribunal that tried those accused of conspiring to assassinate Abraham ◊Lincoln. He wrote several historical novels, including *The Fair God* 1873 and *Ben Hur* 1880 which was filmed twice, in 1926 and 1959.

Wallachia independent medieval principality, founded 1290, with allegiance to Hungary until 1330 and under Turkish rule 1387–1861, when it was united with the neighboring principality of Moldavia to form Romania.

Wallenberg Raoul 1912–1947. Swedish business executive who attempted to rescue several thousand Jews from German-occupied Budapest 1944, during World War II. He was taken prisoner by the Soviet army 1945 and was never heard from again.

In Hungary he tried to rescue and support Jews in safe houses, and provided them with false papers to save them from deportation to extermination camps. After the arrival of Soviet troops in Budapest, he reported to the Russian commander Jan 1945 and then disappeared. The Soviet government later claimed that he died of a heart attack July 1947. However, rumors persisted into the 1980s that he was alive and held in a Soviet prison camp. In the 1990s the Russians said that he had died as claimed.

Wallenstein Albrecht Eusebius Wenzel von 1583–1634. German general who, until his defeat at Lützen 1632, led the Hapsburg armies in the Thirty Years' War. He was assassinated.

Waller Fats (Thomas Wright) 1904–1943. US jazz pianist and composer with a forceful ◊stride piano style. His songs, many of which have become jazz standards, include "Ain't Misbehavin'" 1929, "Honeysuckle Rose" 1929, and "Viper's Drag" 1934.

An exuberant, humorous performer, Waller toured extensively and appeared in several musical films, including *Stormy Weather* 1943. His first recordings were on piano rolls and in the 1920s he recorded pipe-organ solos. In the 1930s he worked with a small group (as Fats Waller and his Rhythm Boys), before leading a big band 1939–42.

wallflower European perennial garden plant *Cheiranthus cheiri*, family Cruciferae, with fragrant red or yellow flowers in spring.

Wallis Hal (Harold Brent) 1899–1986. US film producer with a keen eye for choosing potential box-office successes. He was chief executive in charge of production at Warner Brothers 1933–44, when he left to establish his own company, Hal Wallis Productions.

Wallis and Futuna two island groups in the SW Pacific, an overseas territory of France; area 143 sq mi/367 sq km; population (1990) 13,700. They produce copra, yams, and bananas. Discovered by European sailors in the 18th century, the islands became a French protectorate 1842 and an overseas territory 1961.

Walloon member of a French-speaking people of SE Belgium and adjacent areas of France. The name "Walloon" is etymologically linked to "Welsh."

Wall Street the financial center of the US on lower Manhattan Island in New York City. It is often synonymous with the New York Stock Exchange, which is housed there. The street was so named because of a stockade erected by the Dutch 1653.

walnut genus *Juglans* of trees of the family Juglandaceae, closely related to hickories. Walnuts have pinnately compound leaves and nuts enclosed in a thick leathery husk. Six species, including the black walnut *J. nigra* and the butternut *J. cinerea*, are native to the US. About 15 other species occur in South America and Eurasia. The English walnut *J. regia*, originally from SE Europe and Asia, is cultivated widely for its nut crop.

Walpole Horace, 4th Earl of Orford 1717–1797. English novelist, letter writer and politician, the son of Robert Walpole. He was a Whig member of Parliament 1741–67. He converted his house at Strawberry Hill, Twickenham (then a separate town SW of London), into a Gothic castle; his *The Castle of Otranto* 1764 established the genre of the Gothic, or "romance of terror," novel. More than 4,000 of his letters have been published.

Walpole Robert, 1st Earl of Orford 1676–1745. British Whig politician, the first "prime minister" as First Lord of the Treasury and chancellor of the Exchequer 1715–17 and 1721–42. He encouraged trade and tried to avoid foreign disputes (until forced into the War of Jenkins's Ear with Spain 1739).

Opponents thought his foreign policies worked to the advantage of France. He held favor with George I and George II, struggling against ◊Jacobite intrigues, and received an earldom when he eventually retired 1742.

Walpurga, St English abbess who preached Christianity in Germany. ***Walpurgis Night***, the night of May 1 (one of her feast days), became associated with witches' sabbaths and other superstitions. Her feast day is Feb 25.

Walras Léon 1834–1910. French economist. In his *Éléments d'économie politique pure* 1874–77 he attempted to develop a unified model for general equilibrium theory (a hypothetical situation in which demand equals supply in all markets). He also originated the theory of diminishing marginal utility of a good (the increased value to a person of consuming more of a product).

walrus Arctic marine carnivorous mammal *Odobenus rosmarus* of the same family (Otariidae) as the eared ◊seals. It can reach 13 ft/4 m in length, and weigh up to 3,000 lb/1,400 kg. It has webbed flippers, a bristly moustache, and large tusks. It is gregarious except at breeding time and feeds mainly on mollusks. It has been hunted close to extinction for its ivory tusks, hide, and blubber. The Alaskan walrus is close to extinction.

Walton Ernest 1903– . Irish physicist who, as a young doctoral student at the Cavendish laboratory in Cambridge, England, collaborated with John ◊Cockcroft on investigating the structure of the atom. In 1932 they succeeded in splitting the atom; for this experiment they shared the 1951 Nobel Prize for Physics.

Walton Izaak 1593–1683. English author of the classic fishing text *Compleat Angler* 1653. He

was born in Stafford and settled in London as an ironmonger. He also wrote short biographies of the poets George Herbert and John Donne and the theologian Richard Hooker.

waltz ballroom dance in three-four time evolved from the Austrian *Ländler* (traditional peasants' country dance) and later made popular by the ◊Strauss family in Vienna.

Walvis Bay chief port serving Namibia, SW Africa; population (1980) 26,000. It has a fishing industry with allied trades. It has been a detached part (area 425 sq mi/1,100 sq km) of Cape Province from 1884 but was administered by South Africa from 1922 until Namibian independence 1990.

The South African and Namibian governments agreed Sept 1991 on joint control of the disputed port of Walvis Bay, pending a final settlement of the future of the disputed territory.

wampum cylindrical beads ground from sea shells, of white and purple, for ceremony, currency, and decoration by North American Indians of the northeastern woodlands.

Wanamaker John 1838–1922. US retailer who developed the modern department store. He established his own firm, John Wanamaker and Company, 1869. Renting an abandoned railroad depot 1876, he merchandised goods in distinct departments; he publicized his stores through extensive advertising.

Wanamaker, born in Philadelphia, worked as a delivery boy and store clerk, founding the dry-goods firm of Brown and Wanamaker with his brother-in-law 1861. A staunch Republican, Wanamaker served as postmaster general in the Benjamin Harrison administration 1889–93.

Wandering Jew in medieval legend, a Jew named Ahasuerus, said to have insulted Jesus on his way to Calvary and to have been condemned to wander the world until the Second Coming.

Wang An 1920–1990. Chinese-born US engineer, founder of Wang Laboratories 1951, one of the world's largest computer companies in the 1970s. He emigrated to the US 1945 and three years later invented the computer memory core, the most common device used for storing computer data before the invention of the integrated circuit (chip).

Wankel engine rotary gasoline engine developed by the German engineer Felix Wankel (1902–) in the 1950s. It operates according to the same stages as the ◊four-stroke gasoline engine cycle, but these stages take place in different sectors of a figure-eight chamber in the space between the chamber walls and a triangular rotor. Power is produced once on every turn of the rotor. The Wankel engine is simpler in construction than the four-stroke piston gasoline engine, and produces rotary power directly (instead of via a crankshaft). Problems with rotor seals have prevented its widespread use.

wapiti alternate name for ◊elk.

war act of force, usually on behalf of the state, intended to compel a declared enemy to obey the will of the other. The aim is to render the opponent incapable of further resistance by destroying its capability and will to bear arms in pursuit of its own aims. War is therefore a continuation of politics carried on with violent and destructive means, as an instrument of policy.

War and Peace novel by Leo Tolstoy, published 1863–69. It chronicles the lives of three noble families in Russia during the Napoleonic Wars and is notable for its complex characters and optimistic tone.

waratah Australian shrub or tree of the family Proteaceae, including the crimson-flowered *Telopea speciosissima*, floral emblem of New South Wales.

War between the States another (usually Southern) name for the American ⟡Civil War.

warbler any of two families of songbirds, order Passeriformes.

American or wood warblers (family Parulidae) are small, insect-eating birds, often brightly colored, such as the yellow warbler, prothonotary warbler, and dozens of others. This group is sometimes placed in the same family (Emberizidae) with sparrows and ⟡orioles. Old World warblers (family Sylviidae) are typically slim and dull-plumaged above, lighter below, insectivorous, and fruit-eating, overwhelmingly represented in Eurasia and Africa. These are sometimes considered a subgroup of the same family (Muscicapidae) that includes thrushes.

Warburg Otto 1878–1976. German biochemist who in 1923 devised a manometer (pressure gauge) sensitive enough to measure oxygen uptake of respiring tissue. By measuring the rate at which cells absorb oxygen under differing conditions, he was able to show that enzymes called cytochromes enable cells to process oxygen. He was awarded the Nobel Prize for Medicine 1931. Warburg also demonstrated that cancerous cells absorb less oxygen than normal cells.

war crime offense (such as murder of a civilian or a prisoner of war) that contravenes the internationally accepted laws governing the conduct of wars, particularly The Hague Convention 1907 and the Geneva Convention 1949. A key principle of the law relating to such crimes is that obedience to the orders of a superior is no defense. In practice, prosecutions are generally brought by the victorious side.

Ward Artemus. Adopted name of Charles Farrar Browne 1834–1867. US humorist who achieved great popularity with comic writings such as *Artemus Ward: His Book* 1862 and *Artemus Ward: His Travels* 1865, and with his deadpan lectures. He influenced Mark Twain.

Ward Montgomery 1843–1913. US retailer who pioneered the mass marketing of clothing and personal items through the mails. Serving the needs of farm families in remote rural areas, Ward constantly expanded his catalog from its inception in 1872. Although he retired from the day-to-day operations of the firm in 1886, the business continued to expand, eventually moving its headquarters to the Ward Tower in Chicago 1900.

Ward, born in Chatham, New Jersey, left school in his teens to become a traveling representative for several Midwestern dry-goods firms.

warfarin poison that induces fatal internal bleeding in rats; neutralized with sodium hydroxide, it is used in medicine as an anticoagulant: it prevents blood clotting by inhibiting the action of vitamin K. It can be taken orally and begins to act several days after the initial dose.

Warfarin is a crystalline powder, $C_{19}H_{16}O_4$. ⟡Heparin may be given in treatment at the same time and discontinued when warfarin

takes effect. It is often given as a preventive measure, to reduce the risk of ⟡thrombosis or ⟡embolism after major surgery.

Warhol Andy. Adopted name of Andrew Warhola 1928–1987. US Pop artist and filmmaker. He made his name in 1962 with paintings of Campbell's soup cans, Coca-Cola bottles, and film stars. In his New York studio, the Factory, he produced series of garish silk-screen prints. His films include the semidocumentary *Chelsea Girls* 1966 and *Trash* 1970.

Warhol was born in Pittsburgh, where he studied art. In the 1950s he became a leading commercial artist in New York. With the breakthrough of Pop art, his bizarre personality and flair for self-publicity made him a household name. He was a pioneer of multimedia events with the Exploding Plastic Inevitable touring show in 1966 featuring the Velvet Underground (see Lou ⟡Reed). In 1968 he was shot and nearly killed by a radical feminist, Valerie Solanas. In the 1970s and 1980s Warhol was primarily a society portraitist, although his activities included a magazine (*Interview*) and a cable TV show.

warlord in China, any of the provincial leaders who took advantage of central government weakness, after the death of the first president of Republican China 1912, to organize their own private armies and fiefdoms. They engaged in civil wars until Chiang Kai-shek's Northern Expedition against them 1926, but they exerted power until the Communists came to power under Mao Zedong 1949.

Warner Robins city in central Georgia, S of Macon; industries include nuts, fruits, and airplane parts; population (1990) 43,700.

warning coloration in biology, an alternative term for ⟡aposematic coloration.

War of 1812 a war between the US and Britain caused by British interference with American trade (shipping) as part of Britain's economic warfare against Napoleonic France. US sailors were impressed from American ships, and a blockade was imposed on US shipping by Britain. Also, British assistance was extended to Indians harassing the NW settlements (see ⟡Tecumseh). President Madison authorized the beginning of hostilities against the British on the high seas and in Canada. US forces failed twice in attempts to invade British-held Canada but achieved important naval victories, while in 1814 British forces occupied Washington, DC, and burned the White House and the Capitol. A treaty signed at Ghent, Belgium, in Dec 1814 ended the conflict. Before news of the treaty reached the US, American troops under Andrew ⟡Jackson defeated the British at New Orleans 1815.

War Powers Act US Congressional legislation passed 1973, over President Nixon's veto, aimed at restricting the president's introduction of US forces into potentially hostile situations without Congressional declaration of war. The measure calls for notification of Congress by the president of plans to dispatch military forces and sets a time limit by which either Congress must approve or the forces must be withdrawn. The act has been considered unconstitutional by each president since its passage, and its provisions generally have been ignored by both Congress and presidents.

warrant officer an officer in the US armed forces who holds office on a warrant rather than a commission. Such officers rank

above noncommissioned officers but below commissioned officers.

Warren industrial city (steel and iron products, tools, and paint) in NE Ohio, on the Mahoning River, NW of Youngstown; population (1990) 50,800.

Warren Earl 1891–1974. US jurist and chief justice of the US Supreme Court 1953–69. He served as governor of California 1943–53. As chief justice, he presided over a moderately liberal court, taking a stand against racial discrimination and ruling that segregation in schools was unconstitutional. He headed the commission that investigated 1963–64 President Kennedy's assassination.

Born in Los Angeles, Warren graduated from the University of California at Berkeley 1914 and practiced law in the San Francisco area. He became active in the Republican party and in 1938 was appointed California's attorney general, which paved the way for the governorship. He was appointed to the Supreme Court by President Eisenhower. His most important ruling was in *Brown v Board of Education* 1954, in which the Court unanimously ruled against segregation in public schools and made it illegal to classify races for discrimination purposes. The Warren Court oversaw the reapportionment by population of many election districts in cases such as *Reynolds v Sims* 1964. Other rulings involved individual rights, especially in criminal procedures, as in *Miranda v Arizona* 1966, which ruled in favor of a defendant being informed of his or her rights at the time of arrest. The Warren Commission 1963–64, appointed by President Johnson, reached the controversial conclusion that no conspiracy was involved in the assassination of President Kennedy. Warren retired from the Court 1969 and was succeeded by Warren Burger.

Warren Joseph 1741–1775. Colonial American physician and revolutionary leader. Born in Roxbury, Massachusetts, and educated at Harvard, Warren established a private medical practice in Boston. With the enactment of the Stamp Act 1765, he became a full-time political activist. As a leader of the Massachusetts opposition to British colonial rule, Warren served in the provincial congress and committee of safety. In April 1775 he sent Paul Revere and William Dawes to warn the countryside of the approach of the British. Appointed major general of the Massachusetts militia, he was killed at the Battle of Bunker Hill.

Warren Robert Penn 1905–1989. US poet and novelist, the only author to receive a Pulitzer prize for both prose and poetry. His novel *All the King's Men* 1946 was modeled on the career of Huey ⟡Long, and he also won Pulitzer prizes for *Promises* 1968 and *Now and Then: Poems* 1976–78. He was the first official US poet laureate 1986–88.

Born in Guthrie, Kentucky, and educated at Vanderbilt University, Warren received an MA degree from Berkeley 1927 and became a leading figure in the Southern literary revival. A faculty member at Vanderbilt 1931–34; Louisiana State University 1934–42; the University of Minnesota 1942–50; and Yale University 1950–56, 1961–73, Warren was a respected critic. Among his collections of poems is *Brother to Dragons* 1953.

Warsaw (Polish *Warszawa*) capital of Poland, on the river Vistula; population (1990) 1,655,700. Industries include engineering, food processing, printing, clothing, and pharmaceuticals.

Founded in the 13th century, it replaced Kraków as capital 1595. Its university was founded 1818. Between the mid-19th century and 1940, a third of the population were Jews. It was taken by the Germans Sept 27, 1939, and 250,000 Poles were killed during two months of street fighting that started Aug 1, 1944. It was finally liberated Jan 17, 1945. The old city was virtually destroyed in World War II but has been reconstructed. Marie Curie was born there.

Warsaw Pact or *Eastern European Mutual Assistance Pact* military alliance 1955–91 between the USSR and East European communist states, originally established as a response to the admission of West Germany into NATO. Its military structures and agreements were dismantled early in 1991; a political organization remained until the alliance was officially dissolved July 1991.

warship fighting ship armed and crewed for war. The supremacy of the battleship at the beginning of the 20th century was rivaled during World War I by the development of ⟡submarine attack, and was rendered obsolescent in World War II with the advent of long-range air attack. Today the largest and most important surface warships are the ⟡aircraft carriers.

wart protuberance composed of a local overgrowth of skin. The common wart (*verruca vulgaris*) is due to a virus infection. It usually disappears spontaneously within two years, but can be treated with peeling applications, burning away (cautery), or freezing (cryosurgery).

wart hog African wild ⟡pig *Phacochoerus aethiopicus*, which has a large head with a bristly mane, fleshy pads beneath the eyes, and four large tusks. It has short legs and can grow to 2.5 ft/80 cm at the shoulder.

Warwick Richard Neville, Earl of Warwick 1428–1471. English politician, called *the Kingmaker*. During the Wars of the ⟡Roses he fought at first on the Yorkist side against the Lancastrians, and was largely responsible for placing Edward IV on the throne. Having quarrelled with him, he restored Henry VI in 1470, but was defeated and killed by Edward at Barnet, Hertfordshire.

Wash, the bay of the North Sea between Norfolk and Lincolnshire, England.

washing soda $Na_2CO_3.10H_2O$ (chemical name *sodium carbonate decahydrate*) substance added to washing water to "soften" it (see ⟡water, hardness of).

Washington state in NW US; nickname Evergreen State/Chinook State
area 68,206 sq mi/176,700 sq km
capital Olympia
cities Seattle, Spokane, Tacoma
features Columbia River; national parks: Olympic (Olympic Mountains), Mount Rainier (Cascade Range), North Cascades; 90 dams
products apples and other fruits, potatoes, livestock, fish, timber, processed food, wood products, paper and allied products, aircraft and aerospace equipment, aluminum
population (1990) 4,866,700; including 1.4% Indians, mainly of the Yakima people
famous people Bing Crosby, Jimi Hendrix, Mary McCarthy, Theodore Roethke
history explored by Spanish, British, and Americans in the 18th century; settled from 1811; became a territory 1853 and a state 1889.
Rival American and British territorial claims threatened war in the early 1840s that was

settled by the Oregon Treaty 1846. The transcontinental railroad arrived 1883. Radical labor activity repressed 1919. The New Deal era brought many public-works projects, and Boeing became the largest employer in World War II. Mount St Helens erupted here 1980, and many in the state are now fighting to close the antiquated and dangerous nuclear plant at Hanford.

Washington Booker T(aliaferro) 1856–1915. US educationist, pioneer in higher education for black people in the South. He was the founder and first principal of Tuskegee Institute, Alabama, in 1881, originally a training college for blacks, which has become a respected academic institution. He maintained that economic independence was the way to achieve social equality.

Washington George 1732–1799. Commander of the American forces during the Revolutionary War and 1st president of the US 1789–97, known as "the father of his country." An experienced soldier, he had fought in campaigns against the French during the French and Indian War. He was elected to the Virginia House of Burgesses 1759 and was a leader of the Virginia militia, gaining valuable exposure to wilderness fighting. As a strong opponent of the British government's policy, he sat in the Continental Congresses of 1774 and 1775, and on the outbreak of the ⟡American Revolution was chosen commander in chief of the Continental army. After many setbacks, he accepted the surrender of British general Cornwallis at Yorktown 1781.

After the war Washington retired to his Virginia estate, Mount Vernon, but in 1787 he reentered politics as president of the Constitutional Convention in Philadelphia and was elected US president 1789. Although he attempted to draw his ministers from all factions, his aristocratic outlook alienated his secretary of state, Thomas Jefferson, with whose resignation in 1793 the two-party system originated. Washington accepted the fiscal policy championed by Alexander ⟡Hamilton and oversaw the payment of the foreign and domestic debt incurred by the new nation. He also shaped the powers of the presidency, assuming some implied powers not specified in the Constitution–among them, the power to create a national bank.

Washington was reelected president 1793 but refused to serve a third term, setting a precedent that was followed until 1940. In his farewell address 1796, he maintained that the US should avoid European quarrels and entangling alliances. He died and was buried at Mount Vernon.

Washington Convention alternate name for ⟡*CITES*, the international agreement that regulates trade in endangered species.

Washington DC (District of Columbia) national capital of the US, on the Potomac River

Washington

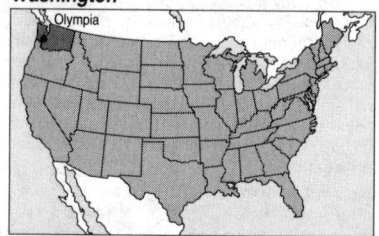

area 69 sq mi/180 sq km
features designed by French engineer Pierre L'Enfant (1754–1825) and completed by Andrew Ellicott and Benjamin Banneker. Among buildings of architectural note are the Capitol, the Pentagon, the White House, the Washington Monument, and the Jefferson and Lincoln memorials. The National Gallery has an outstanding collection of paintings; libraries include the Library of Congress, the National Archives, and the Folger Shakespeare Library. The Smithsonian Institution and its several museums are on the National Mall.
population (1983) 623,000 (metropolitan area, extending outside the District of Columbia, 3,000,000)
history the District of Columbia, initially land ceded from Maryland 1788 and Virginia 1789, was established by an act of Congress 1790–91 and was first used as the seat of Congress Dec 1, 1800. The Virginia portion was returned 1846. The right to vote in national elections was not granted to residents until 1961. Local self-rule began 1975.

wasp any of several families of winged stinging insects of the order Hymenoptera, characterized by a thin stalk between the thorax and the abdomen. Wasps can be social or solitary. Among social wasps, the queens devote themselves to egg laying, the fertilized eggs producing female workers; the males come from unfertilized eggs and have no sting. The larvae are fed on insects, but the mature wasps feed mainly on fruit and sugar. In winter, the fertilized queens hibernate, but the other wasps die.

Paper wasps, family Vespidae, include the common paper wasp *Polistes annularis*, hornets and yellow jackets (both genus *Vespula*). Potter wasps, mason wasps, and mud daubers all use mud with which to construct their nests.

Wassermann August von 1866–1925. German professor of medicine. In 1907 he discovered a diagnostic blood test for ⟡syphilis, known as the *Wassermann reaction*.

waste materials that are no longer needed and are discarded. Examples are household waste, industrial waste (which often contains toxic chemicals), medical waste (which may contain organisms that cause disease), and ⟡nuclear waste (which is radioactive). By ⟡recycling, some materials in waste can be reclaimed for further use. In 1990 the industrialized nations generated 2 billion tons of waste. In the US, 40 tons of solid waste are generated annually per person.

There has been a tendency to increase the amount of waste generated per person in industrialized countries, particularly through the growth in packaging and disposable products, creating a "throwaway society."

waste disposal depositing waste. Methods of waste disposal vary according to the materials in the waste and include incineration, burial at designated sites, and dumping at sea. Organic waste can be treated and reused as fertilizer (see ⟡sewage disposal). ⟡Nuclear waste and toxic waste is usually buried or dumped at sea, although this does not negate the danger.

Waste disposal is an increasing problem in the late 20th century. Environmental groups, such as Greenpeace and Friends of the Earth, are campaigning for more recycling, a change in lifestyle so that less waste (from packaging and containers to nuclear materials) is produced, and safer methods of disposal.

Waste Land, The poem by T S Eliot, first published 1922. It expressed the prevalent mood of depression after World War I and is a key work of Modernism in literature.

watch portable timepiece. In the early 20th century increasing miniaturization, mass production, and, in World War I, the advantages of the wristband led to the watch moving from the pocket to the wrist. Watches were also subsequently made waterproof, antimagnetic, self-winding, and shock-resistant. In 1957 the electric watch was developed, and in the 1970s came the digital watch, which dispensed with all moving parts.

history Traditional mechanical watches with analog dials (hands) are based on the invention by Peter Henlein (1480–1542) of the mainspring as the energy store. By 1675 the invention of the balance spring allowed watches to be made small enough to move from waist to pocket. By the 18th century pocketwatches were accurate, and by the 20th century wristwatches were introduced. In the 1950s battery-run electromagnetic watches were developed; in the 1960s electronic watches were marketed, which use the ¢piezoelectric oscillations of a quartz crystal to mark time and an electronic circuit to drive the hands. In the 1970s quartz watches without moving parts were developed—the solid-state watch with a display of digits. Some include a tiny calculator and such functions as date, alarm, stopwatch, and reminder beeps.

water H_2O liquid without color, taste, or odor. It is an oxide of hydrogen. Water begins to freeze at 0°C or 32°F, and to boil at 100°C or 212°F. When liquid, it is virtually incompressible; frozen, it expands by 1/11 of its volume. At 39.2°F/4°C, one cubic centimeter of water has a mass of one gram; this is its maximum density, forming the unit of specific gravity. It has the highest known specific heat, and acts as an efficient solvent, particularly when hot. Most of the world's water is in the sea; less than 0.01% is fresh water.

Water covers 70% of the Earth's surface and occurs as standing (oceans, lakes) and running (rivers, streams) water, rain, and vapor and supports all forms of Earth's life.

Water makes up 60–70% of the human body or about 42 quarts/40 litres, of which 60% are inside the cells, 40% outside. A loss of 10% of this volume may cause hallucinations; a loss of 20%-25% may cause death. People cannot survive more than five or six days without water or two or three days in a hot environment.

water boatman any water ¢bug of the family Corixidae that feeds on plant debris and algae. It has a flattened body 0.6 in/1.5 cm long, with oarlike legs.

The name is sometimes also used for the backswimmers, genus *Notonecta*, which are superficially similar, but which can fly and which belong to a different family (Notonectidae) of bugs.

water-borne disease disease associated with poor water supply. In the Third World four-fifths of all illness is caused by water-borne diseases, with diarrhea being the leading cause of childhood death. Malaria, carried by mosquitoes dependent on stagnant water for breeding, affects 400 million people every year and kills 5 million. Polluted water is also a problem in industrialized nations, where industrial dumping of chemical, hazardous, and radioactive wastes causes a range of diseases from headache to cancer.

major waterfalls

name and location	total drop	
	ft	m
Angel Falls (Venezuela)	3,212	979
Yosemite Falls (US)	2,425	739
Mardalsfossen-South (Norway)	2,149	655
Tugela Falls (South Africa)	2,014	614
Cuquenan (Venezuela)	2,000	610
Sutherland (South Island, New Zealand)	1,903	580
Takkakaw Falls (Canada)	1,650	503
Ribbon Fall, Yosemite (US)	1,612	491
Great Karamang River Falls (Guyana)	1,600	488
Mardalsfossen-North (Norway)	1,535	468
Della Falls (Canada)	1,443	440
Gavarnie (France)	1,385	422
Skjeggedal (Norway)	1,378	420
Glass Falls (Brazil)	1,325	404
Krimml (Austria)	1,312	400
Trummelbach (Switzerland)	1,312	400
Silver Strand Falls, Yosemite (US)	1,170	357
Wallaman, Stony Creek (Australia)	1,137	346
Wollomombi (Australia)	1,100	335
Cusiana River Falls (Colombia)	984	300
Giessbach (Switzerland)	984	300
Skykkjedalsfossen (Norway)	984	300
Staubbach (Switzerland)	984	300

waterbuck any of several African ¢antelopes of the genus *Kobus* which usually inhabit swampy tracts and reedbeds. They vary in size from 6 ft/1.4 m to 7.25 ft/2.1 m long, are up to 4.5 ft/1.4 m tall at the shoulder, and have long brown fur. The large curved horns, normally carried only by the males, have corrugated surfaces. Some species have white patches on the buttocks. Lechwe, kor, and defassa are alternative names for some of the species.

Waterbury city in W Connecticut, on the Naugatuck River; population (1990) 109,000. Products include clocks, watches, brass and copper ware, and plastics. It was founded 1674.

watercolor painting method of painting with pigments mixed with water, known in China as early as the 3rd century. The art as practiced today began in England in the 18th century with the work of Paul Sandby and was developed by Thomas Girtin and J M W Turner. Other watercolorists were Raoul Dufy, Paul Cézanne, and John Marin. The technique of watercolor painting requires great skill since its transparency rules out overpainting.

Western artists excelling in watercolor painting include J R Cozens, John Sell Cotman, Peter de Wint, John Constable, David Cox, John Singer Sargent, Philip Wilson Steer, Paul Signac, Emil Nolde, Paul Klee, and Paul Nash. Many artists prefer acrylic paint because, as well as drying rapidly, it is easier to handle.

watercress perennial aquatic plant *Nasturtium officinale* of the crucifer family, found in Europe and Asia, and cultivated as a salad crop.

water cycle in ecology, the natural circulation of water through the ¢biosphere. Water is lost from the Earth's surface to the atmosphere either by evaporation from the surface of lakes, rivers, and oceans or through the transpiration of plants. This atmospheric water forms clouds that condense to deposit moisture on the land and sea as rain or snow. The water that collects on land flows to the ocean in streams and rivers.

waterfall cascade of water in a river or stream. It occurs when a river flows over a bed of rock that resists erosion; weaker rocks downstream are worn away, creating a steep, vertical drop and a plunge pool into which the water falls. As the river ages, continuing erosion causes the waterfall to retreat upstream forming a deep valley, or gorge.

water flea any aquatic crustacean in the order Cladocera, of which there are over 400 species. The commonest species is *Daphnia pulex*, used in the pet trade to feed tropical fish.

Waterford port and county town of County Waterford, SE Republic of Ireland, on the Suir; population (1991) 40,300. Handmade Waterford crystal glass (34% lead content instead of the normal 24%) was made here until 1851 and again from 1951.

waterfowl any water bird, but especially any member of the family Anatidae, which consists of ducks, geese, and swans.

Watergate US political scandal, named after the building in Washington, DC, that housed the Democrats' campaign headquarters in the 1972 presidential election. Five men, hired by the Republican Committee to Re-elect the President (CREEP), were caught after breaking into the Watergate with complex electronic surveillance equipment. Investigations revealed that the White House was implicated in the break-in, and that there was a "slush fund," used to finance unethical activities. In Aug 1974, President ¢Nixon was forced by the Supreme Court to surrender to Congress tape recordings of conversations he had held with administration officials, which indicated his complicity in a cover-up. Nixon resigned rather than face impeachment for obstruction of justice and other crimes.

water hyacinth tropical aquatic plant *Eichhornia crassipes* of the pickerelweed family Pontederiaceae. In one growing season 25 plants can produce 2 million new plants. It is liable to choke waterways, depleting the water of nutrients and blocking the sunlight, but can be used as a purifier of sewage-polluted water as well as in making methane gas, compost, concentrated protein, paper, and baskets. Originating in South America, it now grows in more than 50 countries.

water lily aquatic plant of the family Nymphaeaceae. The fleshy roots are embedded in mud and the large round leaves float on the water. The cup-shaped flowers may be white, pink, yellow, or blue.

The white water lily *Nymphaea odorata* is common in E North America as is the yellow-flowered spatterdock *Nuphar advena*. *Victoria regia*, with leaves about 6 ft/2 m in diameter, occurs in South America.

Waterloo, Battle of battle on June 18, 1815 in which British forces commanded by Wellington defeated the French army of Emperor Napoleon near the village of Waterloo, 8 mi/13 km S of Brussels, Belgium. Napoleon found Wellington's army isolated from his allies and began a direct offensive to smash them, but the British held on until joined by the Prussians under General Blücher. Four days later Napoleon abdicated for the second and final time.

Wellington had 68,000 soldiers (of whom 24,000 were British, the remainder being German, Dutch, and Belgian) and Napoleon had 72,000. The French casualties numbered about 37,000, the British 13,000, and the Prussians 7,000.

water meadow irrigated meadow. By flooding the land for part of each year, increased yields of hay are obtained. Water meadows were common in Italy, Switzerland, and England (from 1523) but have now largely disappeared.

watermelon large ⬦melon *Citrullus vulgaris* of the gourd family, native to tropical Africa, with pink, white, or yellow flesh studded with black seeds and a green rind. It is widely cultivated in subtropical regions.

water mill machine that harnesses the energy in flowing water to produce mechanical power, typically for milling (grinding) grain. Water from a stream is directed against the paddles of a water wheel to make it turn. Simple gearing transfers this motion to the millstones. The modern equivalent of the water wheel is the water turbine, used in ⬦hydroelectric power plants.

Although early step wheels were used in ancient China and Egypt, and parts of the Middle East, the familiar vertical water wheel came into widespread use in Roman times. There were two types: **undershot**, in which the wheel simply dipped into the stream, and the more powerful **overshot**, in which the water was directed at the top of the wheel. The Domesday Book records over 7,000 water mills in Britain. Water wheels remained a prime source of mechanical power until the development of a reliable steam engine in the 1700s, not only for milling, but also for metalworking, crushing and grinding operations, and driving machines in the early factories. The two were combined to form paddlewheel steamboats in the 18th century.

water pollution any addition to fresh or sea water that disrupts biological processes or causes a health hazard. Common pollutants include nitrate, pesticides, and sewage (see ⬦sewage disposal), though a huge range of industrial contaminants, such as chemical byproducts and residues created in the manufacture of various goods, also enter water—legally, accidentally, and through illegal dumping.

water polo water sport developed in England 1869, originally called "soccer-in-water." The aim is to score goals, as in soccer, at each end of a swimming pool. It is played by teams of seven on each side (from squads of 13).

An inflated ball is passed among the players, who must swim around the pool without touching the bottom. A goal is scored when the ball is thrown past the goalkeeper and into a net.

water skiing water sport in which a person is towed across water on a ski or skis, wider than those used for skiing on snow, by means of a rope (75 ft/23 m long) attached to a speedboat. Competitions are held for overall performances, slalom, tricks, and jumping.

In 1922, Ralph Samuelson (US) pioneered the sport as it is known today. Its governing body, the Union Internationale de Ski Nautique, was founded 1946. World championships were first held 1949.

water strider any of various insect-eating aquatic ⬦bugs of the family Gerridae that use their long legs to skate along the water surface without breaking through.

water table *The depth of the water table, or level below which rocks are saturated with water, is higher under hills.*

water table the upper level of ground water (water collected underground in porous rocks). Water that is above the water table will drain downward; a spring forms where the water table cuts the surface of the ground. The water table rises and falls in response to rainfall and the rate at which water is extracted, for example, for irrigation.

In many irrigated areas the water table is falling due to the extraction of water. That below N China, for example, is sinking at a rate of 3 ft/1 m a year. Regions with high water tables and dense industrialization have problems with ⬦pollution of the water table. In the US, New Jersey, Florida, and Louisiana have water tables contaminated by both industrial ⬦wastes amd saline seepage from the ocean.

Watson James Dewey 1928– . US biologist whose research on the molecular structure of DNA and the genetic code, in collaboration with Francis ⬦Crick, earned him a shared Nobel Prize in 1962. Based on earlier works, they were able to show that DNA formed a double helix of two spiral strands held together by base pairs.

Watson John Broadus 1878–1958. US psychologist, founder of behaviorism. He rejected introspection (observation by an individual of his or her own mental processes) and regarded psychology as the study of observable behavior, within the scientific tradition.

Watson Tom (Thomas Sturgess) 1949– . US golfer who won the British Open five times (1975, 1977, 1980, 1982, 1983) and by 1990 was ranked third in career earnings in professional golf.

Watson, born in Kansas City, Missouri, joined the professional golfer's tour before his graduation from Stanford University 1971. He won the US Open 1982 and the Masters 1977 and 1981, and led the Professional Golfers Association (PGA) in money earnings 1977–80 and 1984.

CAREER HIGHLIGHTS

US Open
1982
British Open
1975, 1977, 1980, 1982–83
US Masters
1977, 1981
US Ryder Cup team
1977, 1981, 1983, 1989

Watson-Watt Robert Alexander 1892–1973. Scottish physicist who developed a forerunner of ⬦radar. During a long career in government service (1915–52) he proposed in 1935 a method of radiolocation of aircraft—a key factor

in the Allied victory over German aircraft in World War II.

watt SI unit (symbol W) of power (the rate of expenditure or consumption of energy). A light bulb may use 40, 100, or 150 watts of power; an electric heater will use several kilowatts (thousands of watts). The watt is named after the Scottish engineer James Watt.

The absolute watt is defined as the power used when one joule of work is done in one second. In electrical terms, the flow of one ampere of current through a conductor whose ends are at a potential difference of one volt uses one watt of power (watts = volts × amperes).

One watt equals 0.00134 horsepower.

Watt James 1736–1819. Scottish engineer who developed the steam engine. He made Thomas Newcomen's steam engine vastly more efficient by cooling the used steam in a condenser separate from the main cylinder.

Steam engines incorporating governors, sun-and-planet gears, and other devices of his invention were successfully built by him in partnership with English factory owner Matthew Boulton (1728-1809) and were vital to the ⬦Industrial Revolution.

Watteau Jean-Antoine 1684–1721. French Rococo painter. He developed a new category of genre painting known as the *fête galante*, scenes of a kind of aristocratic pastoral fantasy world. One of these pictures, *The Embarkation for Cythera* 1717 (Louvre, Paris), won him membership in the French Academy.

Watteau was born in Valenciennes. At first inspired by Flemish genre painters, he produced tavern and military scenes. His early years in Paris, from 1702, introduced him to fashionable French paintings and in particular to decorative styles and theatrical design. He was also influenced by ⬦Giorgione and ⬦Rubens.

wattle certain species of ⬦acacia in Australia, where their fluffy golden flowers are the national emblem. The leathery leaves, adapted to drought conditions, further avoid loss of water through transpiration by turning their edges to the direct rays of the sun. Wattles are used for tanning and in fencing.

wattle and daub method of constructing walls consisting of upright stakes bound together with withes (strong flexible shoots or twigs, usually of willow), and covered in mud or plaster. This was the usual way of building houses in medieval Europe; it was also the traditional method used in Australia, Africa, the Middle East, and the Far East.

Watts Alan (Witson) 1915–1973. British-born US philosopher. Educated in England, Watts was a longtime student of Eastern religions and published *The Spirit of Zen* 1936. He emigrated to the US 1939, graduated from the Seabury-Weston Theological Seminary, and was ordained in the Episcopal Church 1944. Briefly serving as chaplain at Northwestern University, he moved to California and taught philosophy at the College of the Pacific 1951–57. As a popular lecturer and author, he became a spiritual leader of the "beat generation" of the 1950s. His books include *The Way of Zen* 1957.

Waugh Evelyn (Arthur St John) 1903–1966. English novelist. His social satires include *Decline and Fall* 1928, *Vile Bodies* 1930, and *The Loved One* 1948. A Roman Catholic convert from 1930, he developed a serious concern with religious issues in *Brideshead Revisited*

1945. *The Ordeal of Gilbert Pinfold* 1957 is largely autobiographical.

Wausau industrial city (dairy products, paper products, insurance, chemicals, and plastics) in central Wisconsin, on the Wisconsin River, NW of Green Bay; population (1990) 37,100.

wave in the oceans, a ridge or swell formed by wind or other causes. The power of a wave is determined by the strength of the wind and the distance of open water over which the wind blows (the fetch). Waves are the main agents of ◊coastal erosion and deposition: sweeping away or building up beaches, creating ◊spits and berms (narrow paths or ledges), and wearing down cliffs by their hydraulic action and by the corrasion of the sand and shingle that they carry. A ◊tsunami (misleadingly called a "tidal wave") is formed after a submarine earthquake.

wave in physics, a disturbance consisting of a series of oscillations that propagate through a medium (or space). There are two types: in a *longitudinal wave* (such as a ◊sound wave) the disturbance is parallel to the wave's direction of travel; in a *transverse wave* (such as an ◊electromagnetic wave) it is perpendicular. The medium only vibrates as the wave passes; it does not travel outward from the source with the waves.

A longitudinal wave is characterized by its alternating compressions and rarefactions. In the *compressions* the particles of the medium are pushed together (in a gas the pressure rises); in the *rarefactions* they are pulled apart (in a gas the pressure falls). A transverse wave is characterized by its alternating *crests* and *troughs*. Simple water waves, such as the ripples produced when a stone is dropped into a pond, are transverse waves, as are the waves on a vibrating string.

wavelength the distance between successive crests of a ◊wave. The wavelength of a light wave determines its color; red light has a wavelength of about 700 nanometers, for example. The complete range of wavelengths of electromagnetic waves is called the electromagnetic ◊spectrum.

Wavell Archibald, 1st Earl 1883–1950. British field marshal in World War II. As commander in chief Middle East, he successfully defended Egypt against Italy July 1939. He was transferred as commander in chief India in July 1941, and was viceroy 1943–47.

wax solid fatty substance of animal, vegetable, or mineral origin. Waxes are composed variously of ◊esters, ◊fatty acids, free ◊alcohols, and solid hydrocarbons.
Mineral waxes are obtained from petroleum and vary in hardness from the soft petroleum jelly (or petrolatum) used in ointments to the hard paraffin wax employed for making candles and waxed paper for drinks cartons.
Animal waxes include beeswax, the wool wax lanolin, and spermaceti from sperm-whale oil; they are used mainly in cosmetics, ointments, and polishes. Another animal wax is tallow, a form of suet obtained from cattle and sheep's fat, once widely used to make candles and soap. Sealing wax is made from lac or shellac, a resinous substance obtained from secretions of ◊scale insects.
Vegetable waxes, which usually occur as a waterproof coating on plants that grow in hot, arid regions, include carnauba wax (from the leaves of the carnauba palm) and candelilla wax, both of which are components of hard polishes such as car waxes.

waxbill any of a group of small mainly African seed-eating birds in the family Estrildidae, order Passeriformes, which also includes the grass finches of Australia. Waxbills grow to 6 in/15 cm long, are brown and gray with yellow, red, or brown markings, and have waxy-looking red or pink beaks.

They sometimes raise the young of ◊whydahs, who lay their eggs in waxbill nests.

wax myrtle evergreen bush or tree *Myrica cerifera* of the barberry family, native to SE North America. Its fruit consists of grayish nutlets coated with a wax that is collected for making scented candles; 1 lb/0.5 kg of nutlets immersed in hot water yields about 4 oz/115 g of wax. The fruit is eaten by ground-dwelling birds such as bobwhite and wild turkey.

waxwing any of several fruit-eating birds of the order Passeriformes, family Bombycillidae. They are found in the northern hemisphere. The Bohemian waxwing *B. garrulus* of North America and Eurasia is about 7 in/18 cm long, and is grayish brown above with a reddish-chestnut crest, black streak at the eye, and variegated wings. It undertakes mass migrations in some years.

wayfaring tree European shrub *Viburnum lantana* of the honeysuckle family, with clusters of fragrant white flowers, found on limy soils; naturalized in the NE US.

Wayne Anthony ("Mad Anthony") 1745–1796. American Revolutionary War officer and Indian fighter. He secured a treaty 1795 that made possible the settlement of Ohio and Indiana. He built Fort Wayne, Indiana.

A surveyor and farmer, he was briefly active in politics before the Revolution. He assisted Benedict ◊Arnold in his retreat from Québec, held a variety of increasingly important commands, was with George Washington at Valley Forge 1777–78, took Stony Point, New York, and was then trapped by Cornwallis's superior force at Green Spring, Virginia, but escaped and served under General Greene in Georgia before retiring to farming and business interests. President Washington recalled him 1792 as a major general to command the Army of the West against the Indians.

Wayne John ("Duke"). Adopted name of Marion Morrison 1907–1979. US actor, the archetypal Western hero: plain-speaking, brave, and solitary. His films include *Stagecoach* 1939, *Red River* 1948, *She Wore a Yellow Ribbon* 1949, *The Searchers* 1956, *Rio Bravo* 1959, *The Man Who Shot Liberty Valance* 1962, and *True Grit* 1969 (Academy Award). He was active in conservative politics.

Wayne also appeared in many war films, such as *The Sands of Iwo Jima* 1945, *In Harm's Way* 1965, and *The Green Berets* 1968. His other films include *The Quiet Man* 1952 and *The High and the Mighty* 1954.

weak nuclear force one of the four fundamental forces of nature, the other three being gravity, the electromagnetic force, and the strong nuclear force. It causes radioactive decay and other subatomic reactions. The particles that carry the weak force are called ◊weakons (or intermediate vector bosons) and comprise the positively and negatively charged W particles and the neutral Z particle.

weakon or *intermediate vector boson* in physics, a ◊gauge boson that carries the weak nuclear force, one of the fundamental forces of nature. There are three types of weakon, the positive and negative W particle and the neutral Z particle.

weapon any implement used for attack and defense, from simple clubs, spears, and bows and arrows in prehistoric times to machine guns and nuclear bombs in modern times. The first revolution in warfare came with the invention of ◊gunpowder and the development of cannons and shoulder-held guns. Many other weapons now exist, such as grenades, shells, torpedoes, rockets, and guided missiles. The ultimate in explosive weapons are the atomic (fission) and hydrogen (fusion) bombs. They release the enormous energy produced when atoms split or fuse together (see ◊nuclear warfare). There are also chemical and bacteriological weapons.

Landmarks in the development of weapons:
13th century Gunpowder brought to the West from China (where it was long in use but only for fireworks).
c. 1300 Guns invented by the Arabs, with bamboo muzzles reinforced with iron.
1346 Battle of Crécy in which gunpowder was probably used in battle for the first time.
1376 Explosive shells used in Venice.
17th century Widespread use of guns and cannon in the Thirty Years' War and English Civil War.
1800 Henry Shrapnel invented shrapnel for the British army.
1862 Machine gun invented by Richard Gatling used against American Indians in the US.
1863 TNT discovered by German chemist J Wilbrand.
1867 Dynamite patented by Alfred Nobel.
1915 Poison gas (chlorine) used for the first time by the Germans in World War I.
1916 Tanks used for the first time by the British at Cambrai.
1945 First test explosion and military use of atomic bomb by the US against Japan.
1954–73 Vietnam War, use of chemical warfare (defoliants and other substances) by the US.
1983 Star Wars or Strategic Defense Initiative research announced by the US to develop space laser and particle-beam weapons as a possible future weapons system in space.
1991 "Smart" weapons used by the US and allied powers in the Gulf War; equipped with computers (using techniques such as digitized terrain maps) and laser guidance, they reached their targets with precision accuracy (for example a "smart" bomb destroyed the Ministry of Air Defense in Baghdad by flying into an air shaft).

weasel any of various small, short-legged, lithe carnivorous mammals with bushy tails, especially the genus *Mustela*, found worldwide except Australia. They feed mainly on small rodents although some, like the mink *M. vison*, hunt aquatic prey. Most are 5–10 in/12–25 cm long, excluding tail.

Included are the North American long-tailed weasel, the N hemisphere ermine or stoat, the Eurasian polecat, and the endangered North American black-footed ferret. In cold regions the coat color of several species changes to white during the winter.

weather day-to-day variation of climatic and atmospheric conditions at any one place, or the state of these conditions at a place at any one time. Such conditions include humidity, precipitation, temperature, cloud cover, visibility, and wind. To a meteorologist the term "weather" is limited to the state of the sky, precipitation, and visibility as affected by fog or mist. See ◊meteorology and ◊climate.

Weather forecasts, in which the likely weather is predicted for a particular area, based on meteorological readings, may be short-range (covering a period of one or two days), medium-range (five to seven days), or long-range (a month or so). Readings from a series of scattered recording stations are collected and compiled on a weather map. Such a procedure is called synoptic forecasting. The weather map uses conventional symbols to show the state of the sky, the wind speed and direction, the kind of precipitation, and other details at each gathering station. Points of equal atmospheric pressure are joined by lines called isobars. The trends shown on such a map can be extrapolated to predict what weather is coming.

weathering process by which exposed rocks are broken down by the action of rain, frost, wind, and other elements of the weather. Two types of weathering are recognized: physical and chemical. They usually occur together.
Physical weathering involves such effects as: frost wedging, in which water trapped in a crack in a rock expands on freezing and splits the rock; sand blasting, in which exposed rock faces are worn away by sand particles blown by the wind; and ▷soil creep, in which soil particles gradually move downhill under the influence of gravity.
Chemical weathering is a process by which carbon dioxide in the atmosphere combines with rainwater to produce weak carbonic acid, which may then react with certain minerals in the rocks and break them down. Examples are the solution of caverns in limestone terrains, and the breakdown of feldspars in granite to form kaolinite or kaolin, thus loosening the other minerals present—quartz and mica—which are washed away as sand. Although physical and chemical weathering normally occur together, in some instances it is difficult to determine which type is involved. For example, onion-skin weathering, which produces rounded ▷inselbergs in arid regions, such as Ayers Rock in central Australia, may be caused by the daily physical expansion and contraction of the surface layers of the rock in the heat of the Sun, or by the chemical reaction of the minerals just beneath the surface during the infrequent rains of these areas.

weaver any small bird of the family Ploceidae, order Passeriformes, mostly about 6 in/15 cm long, which includes the house ▷sparrow. The majority of weavers are African, a few Asian. The males use grasses to weave elaborate globular nests in bushes and trees. Males are often more brightly colored than females.
Many kinds are polygamous, so build several nests, and some species build large communal nests with many chambers. One species, the red-billed African quelea *Quelea quelea*, lives and breeds in flocks numbering many thousands of individuals; the flocks migrate to follow food sources. Their destructive power can equal that of locusts.

weaving the production of ▷textile fabric by means of a loom. The basic process is the interlacing at right angles of longitudinal threads (the warp) and horizontal threads (the weft), the latter being carried across from one side of the loom to the other by a type of bobbin called a shuttle.
The technique of weaving has been used all over the world since ancient times and has only fairly recently been mechanized. Hand looms are still used, in many societies: for example,

weaving *The simple handloom.*

in the manufacture of tweeds in the British Isles. They may be horizontal or vertical; industrial looms are generally vertical. In the hand-loom era the ▷Jacquard machine, the last in a series of inventions for producing complicated designs, was perfected in the early 19th century.

Webb (Martha) Beatrice (born Potter) 1858–1943 and Sidney (James), Baron Passfield 1859–1947. English social reformers, writers, and founders of the London School of Economics (LSE) 1895. They were early members of the socialist ▷Fabian Society, and were married in 1892. They argued for social insurance in their minority report (1909) of the Poor Law Commission, and wrote many influential books, including *The History of Trade Unionism* 1894, *English Local Government* 1906–29, and *Soviet Communism* 1935.
Sidney Webb was a member of the Labour Party executive 1915–25, entered Parliament in 1922, and held several government posts.

Webber Andrew Lloyd. English composer of musicals: see ▷Lloyd Webber.

weber SI unit (symbol Wb) of ▷magnetic flux (the magnetic field strength multiplied by the area through which the field passes). One weber equals 10^8 ▷maxwells.
A change of flux at a uniform rate of one weber per second in an electrical coil with one turn produces an electromotive force of one volt in the coil.

Weber Carl Maria Friedrich Ernst von 1786–1826. German composer who established the Romantic school of opera with *Der Freischütz* 1821 and *Euryanthe* 1823. He was kapellmeister (chief conductor) at Breslau 1804–06, Prague 1813–16, and Dresden 1816. He died during a visit to London where he produced his opera *Oberon* 1826, written for the Covent Garden theater.

Weber Ernst Heinrich 1795–1878. German anatomist and physiologist, brother of Wilhelm Weber. He applied hydrodynamics to study blood circulation, and formulated *Weber's law*, relating response to stimulus.
Weber's law (also known as the Weber–Fechner law) states that sensation is proportional to the logarithm of the stimulus. It is the basis of the scales used to measure the loudness of sounds.

Weber Max 1864–1920. German sociologist, one of the founders of modern sociology. He emphasized cultural and political factors as key influences on economic development and individual behavior.
Weber argued for a scientific and value-free approach to research, yet highlighted the importance of meaning and consciousness in understanding social action. His ideas continue to stimulate thought on social stratification, power, organizations, law, and religion.
Key works include *The Protestant Ethic and the Spirit of Capitalism* 1902, *Economy and Society* 1922, *The Methodology of the Social Sciences* 1949, and *The Sociology of Religion* 1920.

Weber Max 1881–1961. Russian-born US painter and sculptor. He immigrated to New York 1891, where he studied painting. Traveling in Europe 1905–09, he was strongly influenced by Parisian avant-garde painters of the Cubist and Futurist schools. He was a prominent figure in importing these styles to the US and also created Futuristic sculpture.

Weber Wilhelm Eduard 1804–1891. German physicist who studied magnetism and electricity, brother of Ernst Weber. Working with Karl Gauss, he made sensitive magnetometers to measure magnetic fields, and instruments to measure direct and alternating currents. He also built an electric telegraph. The SI unit of magnetic flux, the *weber*, is named after him.

Webster Daniel 1782–1852. US politician and orator. He sat in the US House of Representatives 1813–27 and the Senate 1827–41, 1845–50, at first as a ▷Federalist and later as a member of the ▷Whig Party. He was secretary of state 1841–43 and 1850–52, and negotiated the Webster-Ashburton Treaty 1842, which fixed the Maine–Canada boundary. His "seventh of March" speech in the Senate 1850 helped secure a compromise on the slavery issue. He argued that the Congress was powerless under the Constitution to interfere with slavery, and he maintained that the breakup of the Union would produce an even greater evil. He was born in Salisbury, New Hampshire.

Webster John c. 1580–1634. English dramatist who ranks after Shakespeare as the greatest tragedian of his time and is the Jacobean whose plays are most frequently performed today. His two great plays *The White Devil* 1608 and

[Figure labels: roller, warp threads, carding comb, cloth beam, guide rods, lifting shafts, shuttle with bobbin carrying weft thread, treadles]

The Duchess of Malfi 1614 are dark, violent tragedies obsessed with death and decay and infused with poetic brilliance.

Webster Noah 1758–1843. US lexicographer whose books on grammar and spelling and *American Dictionary of the English Language* 1828 standardized US English.

Webster learned 26 languages and began the scientific study of ⟡etymology. Following the American Revolution, he was prompted by patriotic sentiment to create schoolbooks that would impart that sentiment to young students. His *Blue-Backed Speller* sold nearly 100 million copies in a century.

Weddell James 1787–1834. British Antarctic explorer. In 1823, he reached 75°S latitude and 35°W longitude, in the *Weddell Sea*, which is named after him.

Weddell Sea arm of the S Atlantic Ocean that cuts into the Antarctic continent SE of Cape Horn; area 3,000,000 sq mi/8,000,000 sq km. Much of it is covered with thick pack ice for most of the year.

wedge block of triangular cross-section that can be used as a simple machine. An axe is a wedge: it splits wood by redirecting the energy of the downward blow sideways, where it exerts the force needed to split the wood.

Wedgwood Josiah 1730–1795. English pottery manufacturer. He set up business in Staffordshire in the early 1760s to produce his agateware as well as unglazed blue or green stoneware decorated with white Neo-Classical designs, using pigments of his own invention.

weedkiller or *herbicide* chemical that kills some or all plants. Selective herbicides are effective with cereal crops because they kill all broad-leaved plants without affecting grasslike leaves. Those that kill all plants include sodium chlorate and ⟡paraquat; see also ⟡Agent Orange. The widespread use of weedkillers in agriculture has led to a dramatic increase in crop yield but also to pollution of soil and water supplies and killing of birds and small animals, as well as creating a health hazard for humans.

weever fish any of a family (Trachinidae) of marine bony fishes of the perch family, especially the genus *Trachinus*, with poison glands on dorsal fin and gill cover that can give a painful sting. It grows up to 2 in/5 cm long, has eyes near the top of the head, and lives on sandy seabeds.

weevil any of a superfamily (Curculionoidea) of ⟡beetles, usually less than 0.25 in/6 mm long, and with a head prolonged into a downward beak, which is used for boring into plant stems and trees for feeding.

The larvae are usually white and the adults green, black, or brown. The grain weevil *Sitophilus granarius* is a serious pest of stored grain and the boll weevil *Anthonomus grandis* damages cotton crops.

Wegener Alfred Lothar 1880–1930. German meteorologist and geophysicist, whose theory of ⟡continental drift, expounded in *Origin of Continents and Oceans* 1915, was originally known as Wegener's hypothesis. His ideas can now be explained in terms of plate tectonics, the idea that the Earth's crust consists of a number of plates, all moving with respect to one another.

weight the force exerted on an object by ⟡gravity. The weight of an object depends on its mass—the amount of material in it—and the strength of the Earth's gravitational pull, which decreases with height. Consequently, an object weighs less at the top of a mountain than at sea level. On the Moon, an object has only one-sixth of its weight on Earth, because the pull of the Moon's gravity is one-sixth that of the Earth.

weightlessness condition in which there is no gravitational force acting on a body, either because gravitational force is canceled out by equal and opposite acceleration, or because the body is so far outside a planet's gravitational field that it no force is exerted upon it.

weight lifting the sport of lifting the heaviest possible weight above one's head to the satisfaction of judges. In international competitions there are two standard lifts: *snatch* and *jerk*.

In the *snatch*, the bar and weights are lifted from the floor to a position with the arms outstretched and above the head in one continuous movement. The arms must be locked for two seconds for the lift to be good. The *jerk* is a two-movement lift: from the floor to the chest, and from the chest to the outstretched position. The aggregate weight of the two lifts counts. The International Weightlifting Federation was formed 1920, although a world championship was first held 1891. The first women's world championship was held in 1987 in Florida.

Weil Simone 1909–1943. French writer who became a practicing Catholic after a mystical experience in 1938. Apart from essays, her works (advocating political passivity) were posthumously published, including *Waiting for God* 1951, *The Need for Roots* 1952, and *Notebooks* 1956.

Weill Kurt (Julian) 1900–1950. German composer, US citizen from 1943. He wrote chamber and orchestral music and collaborated with Bertolt ⟡Brecht on operas such as *Die Dreigroschenoper/The Threepenny Opera* 1928 and *Aufstieg und Fall der Stadt Mahagonny/The Rise and Fall of the City of Mahagonny* 1930, all attacking social corruption (*Mahagonny* caused a riot at its premiere in Leipzig). He tried to evolve a new form of ⟡music theatre, using subjects with a contemporary relevance and the simplest musical means. In 1935 he left Germany for the US where he wrote a number of successful scores for Broadway, among them the antiwar musical *Johnny Johnson* 1936 (including the often covered "September Song") and *Street Scene* 1947 based on an Elmer Rice play of the Depression.

Weil's disease or *leptospirosis* infectious disease of animals that is occasionally transmitted to human beings, usually by contact with water contaminated with rat urine. It is characterized by acute fever, and infection may spread to the liver, kidneys, and heart.

The usual form occurring in humans is caused by a spiral-shaped bacterium (spirochete) that is a common parasite of rats. The condition responds poorly to antibiotics, and death may result.

Weimar town in the state of Thuringia, Germany, on the river Elm; population (1990) 80,000. Products include farm machinery and textiles. It was the capital of the grand duchy of Saxe-Weimar 1815–1918; in 1919 the German National Assembly drew up the constitution of the new Weimar Republic here. The writers Goethe, Schiller, and Herder and the composer Liszt lived in the town. The former concentration camp of Buchenwald is nearby.

Weimar Republic the constitutional republic in Germany 1919–33, which was crippled by the election of antidemocratic parties to the ⟡Reichstag (parliament), and then subverted by the Nazi leader Hitler after his appointment as chancellor 1933. It took its name from the city where in Feb 1919 a constituent assembly met to draw up a democratic constitution.

Weinberg Steven 1933– . US physicist who in 1967 demonstrated, together with Abdus ⟡Salam, that the weak nuclear force and the electromagnetic force (two of the fundamental forces of nature) are variations of a single underlying force, now called the electroweak force. Weinberg and Salam shared a Nobel Prize with Sheldon ⟡Glashow in 1979.

Weinerg and Salam's theory involved the prediction of a new interaction, the neutral current (discovered in 1973), which required the presence of charm (see ⟡quark).

Weinberger Caspar (Willard) 1917– . US Republican politician. He served under presidents Nixon and Ford, and was Reagan's defense secretary 1981–87.

weir low wall built across a river to raise the water level. The oldest surviving weir in England is at Chester, across the river Dee, dating from around 1100.

Weir Peter 1938– . Australian film director. His films have an atmospheric quality and often contain a strong spiritual element. They include *Picnic at Hanging Rock* 1975, *Witness* 1985, and *The Mosquito Coast* 1986.

Weirton industrial city (coal, steel, chemicals, and cement) in West Virginia, on the Ohio River, W of Pittsburgh; population (1990) 22,100.

Weiser Conrad 1696–1760. Colonial American public official, born in Germany. Weiser immigrated to America 1710, settling in New York's Hudson Valley. Moving to Berks County, Pennsylvania, 1729, Weiser became familiar with the language and customs of the local Iroquois and was frequently used as an official interpreter in government dealings with them. Owing to his efforts, peace conferences were held in Philadelphia in 1731 and 1736.

He later negotiated treaties with the Iroquois to open up western lands to colonial settlement. Weiser served as judge of Berks County 1752–60 and as colonel of the militia.

Weismann August 1834–1914. German biologist. His failing eyesight forced him to turn from microscopy to theoretical work. In 1892 he proposed that changes to the body do not in turn cause an alteration of the genetic material.

This "central dogma" of biology remains of vital importance to biologists supporting the Darwinian theory of evolution. If the genetic material can be altered only by chance mutation and recombination, then the Lamarckian view that acquired bodily changes can subsequently be inherited becomes obsolete.

Weismuller Johnny (Peter John) 1904–1984. US film actor, formerly an Olympic swimmer, who played Tarzan in a long-running series of films for MGM and RKO including *Tarzan the Ape Man* 1932, *Tarzan and His Mate* 1934, and *Tarzan and the Leopard Woman* 1946.

Weizmann Chaim 1874–1952. Zionist leader, the first president of Israel (1948–52), and chemist. Born in Russia, he became a naturalized British subject, and as director of the navy's laboratories 1916–19 discovered a process for manufacturing acetone, a solvent. He conducted the negotiations leading up to the

Balfour Declaration, which favored a Jewish state. He became head of the Hebrew University in Jerusalem, then in 1948 became the first president of the new republic of Israel.

Weizsäcker Richard, Baron von 1920– . German Christian Democrat politician, president from 1984. He began his career as a lawyer and was also active in the German Protestant church and in Christian Democratic Union party politics. He was elected to the West German Bundestag (parliament) 1969 and served as mayor of West Berlin from 1981, before being elected federal president 1984.

Welch Raquel. Adopted name of Raquel Tejada 1940– . US actress, a sex symbol of the 1960s in such films as *One Million Years BC* 1966, *Myra Breckinridge* 1970, and *The Three Musketeers* 1973.

Welch Robert H W, Jr 1899–1985. US anticommunist crusader and business executive. Over the years, he supported conservative political causes and by the 1950s had become an outspoken anticommunist. He founded the magazine *American Opinion* 1956 and organized the John ◊Birch Society 1958. A strong supporter of losing Republican presidential candidate Barry Goldwater in 1964, Welch later became increasingly venomous in his accusations against supposed communist agents and sympathizers.

Born in Chowan County, North Carolina, Welch was educated at the University of North Carolina and joined the family candy business in Boston 1922.

welding joining pieces of metal (or nonmetal) at faces rendered plastic or liquid by heat or pressure (or both). The principal processes today are gas and arc welding, in which the heat from a gas flame or an electric arc melts the faces to be joined. Additional "filler metal" is usually added to the joint.

Forge (or hammer) welding, employed by blacksmiths since early times, was the only method available until the late 19th century. Resistance welding is another electric method in which the weld is formed by a combination of pressure and resistance heating from an electric current. Recent developments include electric-slag, electron-beam, high-energy laser, and the still experimental radio-wave energy-beam welding processes.

Weldon Fay 1931– . British novelist and dramatist whose work deals with feminist themes, often in an ironic or comic manner. Novels include *The Fat Woman's Joke* 1967, *Female Friends* 1975, *Remember Me* 1976, *Puffball* 1980, *The Life and Loves of a She-Devil* 1984 (made into a film with Meryl Streep 1990), and *The Hearts and Lives of Men* 1987. She has also written plays for the stage, radio, and television.

Welensky Roy 1907–1991. Rhodesian politician. He was instrumental in the creation of a federation of North Rhodesia (now Zambia), Southern Rhodesia (now Zimbabwe), and Nyasaland (now Malawi) in 1953 and was prime minister 1956–63, when the federation was disbanded. His Southern Rhodesian Federal Party was defeated by Ian Smith's Rhodesian Front in 1964. In 1965, following Smith's Rhodesian unilateral declaration of Southern Rhodesian independence from Britain, Welensky left politics.

Welland Ship Canal Canadian waterway, part of the ◊St Lawrence Seaway, linking Lake Erie to Lake Ontario.

Welles (George) Orson 1915–1985. US actor and film and theater director, whose first film was *Citizen Kane* 1941, which he produced, directed, and starred in. Using innovative lighting, camera angles and movements, it is a landmark in the history of cinema, yet he subsequently directed very few films in Hollywood. His performances as an actor include the character of Harry Lime in *The Third Man* 1949.

In 1937 he founded the Mercury Theater, New York, with John Houseman, where their repertory productions included a modern-dress version of *Julius Caesar*. Welles's realistic radio broadcast of H G Wells's *The War of the Worlds* 1938 caused panic and fear of Martian invasion in the US. He directed the films *The Magnificent Ambersons* 1942, *The Lady from Shanghai* 1948 with his wife Rita Hayworth, *Touch of Evil* 1958, and *Chimes at Midnight* 1967, a Shakespeare adaptation.

A child prodigy, Welles made his acting debut at 16 in Dublin and toured with Katherine Cornell's company in the US. As his career declined he became a familiar voice and face in US television commercials, and made guest appearances on TV shows.

Welles Gideon 1802–1878. US politician, one of the founders of the Republican Party 1854. Welles was appointed secretary of the navy by President Lincoln 1861 and in that position supervised the expansion of the Union naval forces and advocated the development of ironclads. An opponent of President Grant, he joined the Liberal Republicans 1872.

Born in Glastonbury, Connecticut, and educated at Norwich University, Welles served as editor of the *Hartford Times* 1826–36. As an active Democrat he served in the state legislature 1827–35 and held other state and federal offices before cofounding the Republican Party.

Wellington capital and industrial port (woolen textiles, chemicals, soap, footwear, bricks) of New Zealand in North Island on Cook Strait; population (1989) 324,600. The harbor was sighted by Captain Cook 1773.

Founded 1840 by Edward Gibbon Wakefield as the first settlement of the New Zealand Company, it has been the seat of government since 1865, when it replaced Auckland. Victoria University was founded 1897. A new assembly hall (designed by the British architect Basil Spence and popularly called "the beehive" because of its shape) was opened 1977 alongside the original parliament building.

Wellington Arthur Wellesley, 1st Duke of Wellington 1769–1852. British soldier and Tory politician. As commander in the ◊Peninsular War, he expelled the French from Spain 1814. He defeated Napoleon Bonaparte at Quatre-Bras and Waterloo 1815, and was a member of the Congress of Vienna. As prime minister 1828–30, he was forced to concede Roman Catholic emancipation.

Wells H(erbert) G(eorge) 1866–1946. English writer of "scientific romances" such as *The Time Machine* 1895 and *The War of the Worlds* 1898. His later novels had an antiestablishment, anticonventional humor remarkable in its day, for example *Kipps* 1905 and *Tono-Bungay* 1909. His many other books include *Outline of History* 1920 and *The Shape of Things to Come* 1933, a number of his prophecies from which have since been fulfilled. He also wrote many short stories.

Wells Ida Bell 1862–1931. US journalist and political activist. Born in Holly Springs, Mississippi, Wells was educated in a segregated

school and became a teacher in Memphis, Tennessee. Losing her job in 1891 as the result of a suit she had filed against state segregation laws, she began a career of political activism. Moving to New York City, she joined the staff of *New York Age* and embarked on extensive lecture tours. Bell married and settled in Chicago 1895.

Welsh people of ◊Wales; see also ◊Celts. The term is thought to be derived from an old Germanic term for "foreigner," and so linked to Walloon (Belgium) and Wallachian (Romania). It may also derive from the Latin *Volcae*, the name of a Celtic people of France.

Welsh corgi breed of dog with a foxlike head and pricked ears. The coat is dense, with several varieties of coloring. Corgis are about 1 ft/30 cm at the shoulder, and weigh up to 27 lb/12 kg.

There are two types, the Pembrokeshire and the heavier Cardiganshire. They were originally bred for cattle herding. Their size was an advantage because cattle were unable to bend low enough to gore them.

Welsh language in Welsh **Cymraeg**, member of the Celtic branch of the Indo-European language family, spoken chiefly in the rural north and west of Wales; it is the strongest of the surviving Celtic languages, and in 1981 was spoken by 18.9% of the Welsh population.

Welsh has been in retreat in the face of English expansion since the accession of the Welsh Henry Tudor (as Henry VII) to the throne of England. Modern Welsh, like English, is not a highly inflected language, but British, the Celtic ancestor of Welsh, was, like Latin and Anglo-Saxon, highly inflected. The continuous literature of Welsh, from the 6th century onwards, contains the whole range of change from British to present-day Welsh. Nowadays, few Welsh people speak only Welsh; they are either bilingual or speak only English.

Welsh literature the chief remains of early Welsh literature are contained in the Four Ancient Books of Wales—the *Black Book of Carmarthen*, the *Book of Taliesin*, the *Book of Aneirin*, and the *Red Book of Hergest*—anthologies of prose and verse of the 6th–14th centuries. Characteristic of Welsh poetry is the bardic system, which ensured the continuance of traditional conventions; most celebrated of the 12th-century bards was Cynddelw Brydydd Mawr (active 1155–1200).

The English conquest of 1282 involved the fall of the princes who supported these bards, but after a period of decline a new school arose in South Wales with a new freedom in form and sentiment, the most celebrated poet in the 14th-century being Dafydd ap Gwilym, and in the next century the Classical metrist Dafydd ap Edmwnd (active 1450–1459). With the Reformation biblical translations were undertaken, and Morgan Llwyd (1619–1659) and Ellis Wynne (1671–1734) wrote religious prose. Popular meters resembling those of England developed—for example, the poems of Huw Morys (1622–1709).

In the 18th century the Classical poetic forms revived with Goronwy Owen, and the Eisteddfod (Welsh name for literary festival) movement began: popular measures were used by the hymn-writer William Williams Pantycelyn (1717–1791). The 19th century saw few notable figures save the novelist Daniel Owen (1836–1895), but the foundation of a Welsh university and the work there of John

Morris Jones (1864–1929) produced a 20th-century revival, including T Gwynn Jones (1871–1949), W J Gruffydd (1881–1954), and R Williams Parry (1884–1956). Later writers included the poet J Kitchener Davies (1902–1952), the dramatist and poet Saunders Lewis (1893–1985), and the novelist and short-story writer Kate Roberts (1891–1985). Among writers of the postwar period are the poets Waldo Williams (1904–1971), Euros Bowen (1904–), and Bobi Jones (1929–), and the novelists Islwyn Ffowc Elis (1924–) and Jane Edwards (1938–). Those who have expressed the Welsh spirit in English include the poets Edward Thomas, Vernon Watkins (1906–67), Dylan Thomas, R S Thomas, and Dannie Abse (1923–), and the novelist Emyr Humphreys (1919–).

Welty Eudora 1909– . US novelist and short-story writer, born in Jackson, Mississippi. Her works reflect life in the American South and are notable for their creation of character and accurate rendition of local dialect. Her novels include *Delta Wedding* 1946, *Losing Battles* 1970, and *The Optimist's Daughter* 1972.

The Collected Stories of Eudora Welty appeared in 1980. The autobiographical work *One Writer's Beginnings* 1984 is a warm recounting of the people, places, and incidents that influenced Welty's work.

welwitschia woody plant *Welwitschia mirabilis* of the order Gnetales, found in the deserts of SW Africa. It has a long, water-absorbent taproot and can live for a hundred years.

Wenceslas, St 907–929. Duke of Bohemia who attempted to Christianize his people and was murdered by his brother. He is patron saint of the former Czechoslovakia and the "good King Wenceslas" of a popular carol. Feast day Sept 28.

Wenchow alternative transcription of the Chinese town ▷Wenzhou.

Wends NW Slavonic peoples who settled east of the rivers Elbe and Saale in the 6th–8th centuries. By the 12th century most had been forcibly Christianized and absorbed by invading Germans; a few preserved their identity and survive as the Sorbs of Lusatia (E Germany/Poland).

werewolf in folk belief, a human being either turned by spell into a wolf or having the ability to assume a wolf form. The symptoms of ▷porphyria may have fostered the legends.

Werfel Franz 1890–1945. Austrian poet, dramatist, and novelist, a leading Expressionist. His works include the poems "Der Weltfreund der Gerichtstag"/"The Day of Judgment" 1919; the plays *Juarez und Maximilian* 1924 and *Das Reich Gottes in Böhmen/The Kingdom of God in Bohemia* 1930; and the novels *Verdi* 1924 and *Das Lied von Bernadette/The Song of Bernadette* 1941.

wergild or *wergeld* in Anglo-Saxon and Germanic law during the Middle Ages, the compensation paid by a murderer to the relatives of the victim, its value dependent on the social rank of the deceased. It originated in European tribal society as a substitute for the blood feud (essentially a form of ▷vendetta), and was replaced by punishments imposed by courts of law during the 10th and 11th centuries.

Werner Abraham Gottlob 1750–1815. German geologist, one of the first to classify minerals

systematically. He also developed the later discarded theory of neptunism—that the Earth was initially covered by water, with every mineral in suspension; as the water receded, layers of rocks "crystallized."

Werner Alfred 1866–1919. Swiss chemist. He was awarded a Nobel Prize in 1913 for his work on valency theory, which gave rise to the concept of coordinate bonds and coordination compounds. He demonstrated that different three-dimensional arrangements of atoms in inorganic compounds gives rise to optical isomerism (the rotation of polarized light in opposite directions by molecules that contain the same atoms but are mirror images of each other).

Wesberry v Sanders a US Supreme Court decision 1964 dealing with apportionment of Congressional districts. After a suit against Georgia's apportionment statute was dismissed by the federal circuit court, the case was appealed to the Supreme Court. The Court ruled that all Congressional districts must be equal in size of voting population. The Georgia statute was declared invalid because its unequal apportionment gave greater voting power to residents of certain districts.

Wesley John 1703–1791. English founder of ▷Methodism. When the pulpits of the Church of England were closed to him and his followers, he took the gospel to the people. For 50 years he rode about the country on horseback, preaching daily, largely in the open air. His sermons became the doctrinal standard of the Wesleyan Methodist Church.

Wesley went to Oxford University together with his brother Charles, where their circle was nicknamed Methodists because of their religious observances. He was ordained in the Church of England 1728 and in 1735 he went to the American colony of Georgia as a missionary. On his return he experienced "conversion" 1738, and from being rigidly High Church developed into an ardent Evangelical.

Wessex the kingdom of the West Saxons in Britain, said to have been founded by Cerdic about AD 500, covering present-day Hampshire, Dorset, Wiltshire, Berkshire, Somerset, and Devon. In 829 Egbert established West Saxon supremacy over all England. Thomas ▷Hardy used the term Wessex in his novels for the SW counties of England.

West Benjamin 1738–1820. American Neo-Classical painter, active in London from 1763. He enjoyed the patronage of George III for many years and painted historical pictures.

West was born in Pennsylvania. His *Death of General Wolfe* 1770 (National Gallery, Ottawa) began a vogue for painting recent historical events in contemporary costume. Many early American artists studied with him, including Washington Allston, Gilbert Stuart, and J S Copely.

West Mae 1892–1980. US vaudeville, stage, and film actress. She wrote her own dialogue, setting herself up as a provocative sex symbol and the mistress of verbal innuendo. She appeared on Broadway in *Sex* 1926, *Drag* 1927, and *Diamond Lil* 1928, which was the basis of the film (with Cary Grant) *She Done Him Wrong* 1933. Her other films include *I'm No Angel* 1933, *Going to Town* 1934, *My Little Chickadee* 1944 (with W C Fields), *Myra Breckinridge* 1969, and *Sextette* 1977. Both her plays and her films led to legal battles over censorship.

Two of her often quoted lines are "Come up and see me," and "Beulah, peel me a grape." Her autobiography, *Goodness Had Nothing to Do with It*, was published 1959.

West Nathanael. Adopted name of Nathan Weinstein 1904–1940. US black-humor novelist. His surrealist-influenced novels capture the absurdity and extremity of American life and the dark side of the American dream. *The Day of the Locust* 1939 explores the violent fantasies induced by Hollywood, where West had been a screenwriter.

Miss Lonelyhearts 1933 is about a newspaper advice columnist who feels the misfortunes of his correspondents; *A Cool Million* 1934 satirizes the rags-to-riches dream of success.

West Rebecca. Adopted name of Cicely Isabel Fairfield 1892–1983. British journalist and novelist, an active feminist from 1911. *The Meaning of Treason* 1959 deals with the spies Burgess and Maclean. Her novels have political themes and include *The Fountain Overflows* 1956 and *The Birds Fall Down* 1966.

West African Economic Community international organization established 1975 to end barriers in trade and to achieve cooperation in development. Members include Burkina Faso, Ivory Coast, Mali, Mauritania, Niger, and Senegal; Benin and Togo have observer status.

West, American generally, the region of the US to the west of the Mississippi river from Canada to Mexico. *See chronology on p. 1124.*

West Bank area (2,270 sq mi/5,879 sq km) on the west bank of the river Jordan; population (1988) 866,000. The West Bank was taken by the Jordanian army 1948 at the end of the Arab-Israeli war that followed the creation of the state of Israel, and was captured by Israel during the Six-Day War June 5–10, 1967. The continuing Israeli occupation and settlement of the area has created tensions with the Arab population.

In 1988 King Hussein announced that Jordan was cutting "legal and administrative ties" with the West Bank, leaving responsibility for Arabs in the region to the ▷Palestine Liberation Organization (which was already the position in practice).

West Bengal state of NE India
area 33,929 sq mi/87,900 sq km
capital Calcutta
cities Asansol, Durgarpur
physical occupies the west part of the vast alluvial plain created by the rivers Ganges and Brahmaputra, with the Hooghly River; annual rainfall in excess of 100 in/250 cm
products rice, jute, tea, coal, iron, steel, automobiles, locomotives, aluminum, fertilizers
population (1991) 67,982,700
history created 1947 from the former British province of Bengal, with later territories added: Cooch Behar 1950, Chandernagore 1954, and part of Bihar 1956.

Westerlies prevailing winds from the west that occur in both hemispheres between latitudes of about 35° and 60°. Unlike the ▷trade winds, they are very variable and produce stormy weather.

The Westerlies blow mainly from the SW in the northern hemisphere and the NW in the southern hemisphere, bringing moist weather to the W coast of the landmasses in these latitudes.

western genre of popular fiction and film based on the landscape and settlement of the American West, with emphasis on the conquest of Indian territory. It developed in American ⏵dime novels and ⏵frontier literature. The western became established in written form with such novels as Owen Wister's *The Virginian* 1902 and Zane Grey's *Riders of the Purple Sage* 1912. From the earliest silent films, movies extended the western mythology and, with Italian "spaghetti" westerns and Japanese westerns, established it as an international form.

The romance of the American frontiersman confronting his wilderness was first popularized in James Fenimore ⏵Cooper's *Leatherstocking Tales* 1823–41 and the American hunter stories of Karl May and soon evolved into a national fascination with the West specifically. From the mid-19th century, in stylized form, came frontier tales of cowboy rangers or lawmen portraying good, with Indians, cattle rustlers, or gunmen portraying evil. Most are set vaguely in the post-Civil War era. The characters are sometimes based on real persons, such as Kit Carson, Annie Oakley, Wyatt Earp, and Bat Masterson.

Most westerns are nostalgic, written after the frontier officially closed in 1890. *The Virginian* is the "serious" version of the form, but prolific writers such as Grey; Frederick Faust (Max Brand), who wrote *Destry Rides Again* 1930; and Louis L'Amour, who wrote *Hondo* 1953, developed its pulp possibilities and its place in universal fantasy.

Westerns have provided endless sources for motion pictures, among them *The Great Train Robbery* 1903, *The Covered Wagon* 1923, *Cimarron* 1931, *Stagecoach* 1939, *The Gunfighter* 1950, *High Noon* 1952, *Shane* 1953, *True Grit* 1969, and *Dances with Wolves* 1990. "The Lone Ranger" was a popular serialized western on radio and television. Other western series on television included "Gunsmoke," "Bonanza," "Bat Masterson," and "Wyatt Earp."

Western Australia state of Australia
area 974,843 sq mi/2,525,500 sq km
capital Perth
cities main port Fremantle, Bunbury, Geraldton, Kalgoorlie-Boulder, Albany
features largest state in Australia; Monte Bello Islands; rivers Fitzroy, Fortescue, Gascoyne, Murchison, Swan; NW coast subject to hurricanes (willy-willies); Lasseter's Reef
products wheat, fresh and dried fruit, meat and dairy products, natural gas (NW shelf) and oil (Canning Basin), iron (the Pilbara), copper, nickel, uranium, gold, diamonds
population (1987) 1,478,000
history a short-lived convict settlement at King George Sound 1826; the state founded at Perth 1829 by Captain James Stirling (1791–1865); self-government 1890; state 1901.

Western European Union (WEU) organization established 1955 as a consultative forum for military issues among the W European governments: Belgium, France, the Netherlands, Italy, Luxembourg, the UK, Germany, and (from 1988) Spain and Portugal.

Policy is agreed during meetings of the foreign ministers of the member nations, with administrative work carried out by a permanent secretariat and specialist committees. The WEU is charged under its charter with ensuring close cooperation with NATO. During its early years the WEU supervised the gradual rearmament of West Germany and the transfer of the Saarland back to West German rule 1957. In the early 1990s attempts were made to transform the WEU into a body to coordinate W European security policy either within NATO or within the European Community if the latter were to adopt a common security policy.

Western film genre of films based loosely on the history of the American ⏵West and evolved from the written Western. As a genre, the Western is virtually as old as the cinema. Italian "spaghetti Westerns" and Japanese Westerns established it as an international form. The genre became less popular in the 1970s. There have been only four commercially successful

films since: *Pale Rider* 1985 and *Unforgiven* 1992 (both starring Clint ⏵Eastwood), *Young Guns* 1988 and Oscar-award-winning *Dances with Wolves* 1990.

A memorable early example is *The Great Train Robbery* 1903. The silent era produced such epics as *The Iron Horse* 1924, and the genre remained popular into the coming of sound. The 1930s saw many epics, such as *Union Pacific* 1939, whereas the 1940s often dwelt on specific historical events (including Custer's last stand in *They Died With Their Boots On* 1941). The 1950s brought more realism and serious issues, such as the treatment of the Indians. The Westerns of the 1960s contained an increased amount of violence, partly owing to the influence of the "spaghetti Westerns" (often directed by Sergio ⏵Leone).

Western Isles island area of Scotland, comprising the Outer Hebrides (Lewis, Harris, North and South Uist, and Barra)
area 1,120 sq mi/2,900 sq km
cities Stornoway on Lewis (administrative headquarters)
features divided from the mainland by the Minch channel; Callanish monolithic circles of the Stone Age on Lewis
products Harris tweed, sheep, fish, cattle
population (1991) 29,100
famous people Flora MacDonald.

Western Provinces in Canada, the provinces of ⏵Alberta, ⏵British Columbia, ⏵Manitoba, and ⏵Saskatchewan.

Western Sahara formerly **Spanish Sahara** disputed territory in NW Africa bounded to the N by Morocco, to the W and S by Mauritania, and to the E by the Atlantic Ocean
area 103,011 sq mi/266,800 sq km
capital Ad Dakhla
cities La'Youn, phosphate mining town of Bou Craa
features electrically monitored fortified wall enclosing the phosphate area
exports phosphates
currency dirham
population (1988) 181,400; another estimated 165,000 live in refugee camps near Tindouf, SW Algeria. Ethnic composition: Sawrawis (traditionally nomadic herders)
language Arabic
religion Sunni Muslim
government administered by Morocco
history this 625 mi/1,000-km-long Saharan coastal region, which during the 19th century separated French-dominated Morocco and Mauritania, was designated a Spanish "sphere of influence" 1884 because it lies opposite the Spanish-ruled Canary Islands. On securing its independence 1956, Morocco laid claim to and invaded this "Spanish Sahara" territory, but was repulsed. Moroccan interest was rekindled from 1965, following the discovery of rich phosphate resources at Bou-Craa, and within Spanish Sahara a pro-independence nationalist movement developed, spearheaded by the Popular Front for the Liberation of Saguia al Hamra and Rio de Oro (Polisario), established in 1973.
partition After the death of the Spanish ruler General Franco, Spain withdrew and the territory was partitioned between Morocco and Mauritania. Polisario rejected this partition, declared their own independent Saharan Arab Democratic Republic (SADR), and proceeded to wage a guerrilla war, securing indirect support from Algeria and, later, Libya. By 1979 they had succeeded in their struggle against

chronology: American West

1250	An unidentified epidemic weakened the American Indian civilization.
1550	Horses were introduced by the Spanish. Francisco Coronado made his expedition into the southwest.
1804	Meriwether Lewis and William Clark explored the ⏵Louisiana Purchase lands for President Jefferson.
1805–06	Zebulon Pike (see ⏵Pikes Peak) explorations.
1819	Major Stephen Long, a US government topographical engineer, explored the Great Plains.
1822	The ⏵Santa Fe Trail was established.
1824	The Great Salt Lake was discovered by Jim Bridger, "mountain man," trapper, and guide.
1836	Davy Crockett and other Texans were defeated by Mexicans at the Battle of the ⏵Alamo.
1840–60	The ⏵Oregon Trail was in use.
1846	The Mormon trek was made to Utah under Brigham ⏵Young.
1846–48	The ⏵Mexican War.
1849–56	The ⏵California gold rush.
1860	The Pony Express (St Joseph, Missouri–San Francisco, California) was in operation April 3–Oct 22; it was superseded by the telegraph.
1863	On Jan 1 the first homestead was filed; this was followed by the settlement of the Western Prairies and Great Plains.
1865–90	Wars were fought against the Indians, accompanied by the rapid extermination of the buffalo, upon which much of Great Plains and Indian life depended.
1867–80s	Period of the "cattle kingdom," and cow trails such as the Chisholm Trail from Texas to the railheads at Abilene, Wichita, and Dodge City.
1869	The first transcontinental railroad was completed.
1876	The Battle of the Little Bighorn; see George ⏵Custer and ⏵Plains Indians.
1890	The Battle of ⏵Wounded Knee; official census declaration that the West no longer had a frontier line.

Mauritania, which withdrew from their southern sector and concluded a peace agreement with Polisario, and in 1982 the SADR was accepted as a full member of the ⟡Organization of African Unity. By the end of 1990, 70 countries had granted diplomatic recognition to the SADR.

defensive wall Morocco, which occupied the Mauritanian-evacuated zone, still retained control over the bulk of the territory, including the key towns and phosphate mines, which they protected with an "electronic defensive wall" 2,500 mi/4,000 km long, completed in 1987. From the mid-1980s this wall was gradually extended outwards as Libya and Algeria reduced their support for Polisario and drew closer to Morocco. In 1988, Morocco and the Polisario Front agreed to United Nations-sponsored plans for a cease-fire and a referendum in Western Sahara, based on 1974 voting rolls, to decide the territory's future. However, divisions persisted during 1989 and 1990 over the terms of the referendum and sporadic fighting continued.

Western Samoa see ⟡Samoa, Western.

Western swing big-band, jazz-influenced country music that originated in Texas in the 1930s. A swinging, inventive dance music, with the fiddle a predominant instrument, it was developed by Bob ⟡Wills and his Texas Playboys and remained a strong influence on popular music into the 1950s, with a revival of interest beginning in the early 1970s and still continuing. Other Western swing groups include Milton Brown and his Musical Brownies (1932–36) and Asleep at the Wheel (1969–   ).

West Germany see ⟡Germany, West.

West Indian inhabitant of or native to the West Indies, or person of West Indian descent. The West Indies are culturally heterogeneous; in addition to the indigenous Carib and Arawak Indians, there are peoples of African, European, and Asian descent, as well as peoples of mixed descent.

West Indies archipelago of about 1,200 islands, dividing the Atlantic from the Gulf of Mexico and the Caribbean. The islands are divided into:
Bahamas
Greater Antilles Cuba, Hispaniola (Haiti, Dominican Republic), Jamaica, and Puerto Rico
Lesser Antilles Aruba, Netherlands Antilles, Trinidad and Tobago, the Windward Islands (Grenada, Barbados, St Vincent, St Lucia, Martinique, Dominica, Guadeloupe), the Leeward Islands (Montserrat, Antigua, St Christopher (St Kitts)–Nevis, Barbuda, Anguilla, St Martin, British and US Virgin Islands), and many smaller islands.

West Indies, Federation of the federal union 1958–62 comprising Antigua, Barbados, Dominica, Grenada, Jamaica, Montserrat, St Christopher (St Kitts)–Nevis and Anguilla, St Lucia, St Vincent, and Trinidad and Tobago. This federation came to an end when first Jamaica and then Trinidad and Tobago withdrew.

Westinghouse George 1846–1914. US inventor and manufacturer. The most profitable of his designs was an air brake for railroad automobiles, perfected 1869. Westinghouse later devised a system of railroad signals and an efficient means of distributing natural gas. His greatest success came with the establishment of the Westinghouse Electric Co 1886,

through which he adapted alternating current for domestic and industrial use.

Born in Central Bridge, New York, Westinghouse served in the American Civil War as a teenager. Later working in his father's tool shop, he became an inventor.

West Irian former name of ⟡Irian Jaya.

Westman Islands small group of islands off the south coast of Iceland. In 1973 volcanic eruption caused the population of 5,200 to be temporarily evacuated, and added 1 sq mi/ 2.5 sq km to the islands' area. Heimaey, the largest of the islands, is one of Iceland's chief fishing ports.

Westminster Abbey Gothic church in central London, officially the Collegiate Church of St Peter. It was built 1050–1745 and consecrated under Edward the Confessor 1065. The west towers are by English architect Nicholas Hawksmoor (1661-1736) 1740. Since William I nearly all English monarchs have been crowned in the abbey, and several are buried there; many poets are buried or commemorated there, at Poets' Corner.

The Coronation Chair includes the Stone of Scone, on which Scottish kings were crowned, brought here by Edward I in 1296. Poets' Corner was begun with the burial of ⟡Spenser 1599. Westminster School, a public school with ancient and modern buildings nearby, was once the Abbey School.

Westminster, City of borough of central Greater London, England, on the north bank of the Thames between Kensington and the City of London; population (1991) 181,500. It encompasses Bayswater, Belgravia, Mayfair, Paddington, Pimlico, Soho, St John's Wood, and Westminster.

Westmoreland William (Childs) 1914–   . US military leader who served as commander of US forces in Vietnam 1964–68. He was an aggressive advocate of expanded US military involvement there.

Westmoreland, born in Spartanburg County, South Carolina, was a 1936 graduate of West Point military academy. After service as an artillery officer during World War II, he saw action in the Korean War and served in various administrative capacities at the Pentagon 1953–58. He was superintendent of West Point 1960–63 before being sent to Vietnam, where he was replaced in 1968; he ended his active military career as army chief of staff 1968–72.

Weston Edward 1886–1958. US photographer. A founding member of the "f/64" group (after the smallest lens opening), a school of photography advocating sharp definition. He is noted for the technical mastery, composition, and clarity in his California landscapes, clouds, gourds, cacti, and nude studies.

In his photography, Weston aimed for realism. He never used artificial light and seldom enlarged, cropped, or retouched his negatives. His aesthetic principle dominated American photography for many years.

West Pakistan a province of ⟡Pakistan.

West Palm Beach resort city on the SE coast of Florida, on the lagoon Lake Worth, N of Miami; industries include transistors, aircraft parts, building materials, and citrus fruits; tourism is important to the economy; population (1990) 67,600.

Westphalia independent medieval duchy, incorporated in Prussia by the Congress of Vienna 1815, and made a province 1816 with

Münster as its capital. Since 1946 it has been part of the German *Land* (region) of ⟡North Rhine–Westphalia.

Westphalia, Treaty of agreement 1648 ending the ⟡Thirty Years' War. The peace marked the end of the supremacy of the Holy Roman Empire and the emergence of France as a dominant power. It recognized the sovereignty of the German states, Switzerland, and the Netherlands; Lutherans, Calvinists, and Roman Catholics were given equal rights.

West Point former fort in New York State, on the Hudson River, 50 mi/80 km N of New York City, site of the US Military Academy (commonly referred to as West Point), established 1802. Women were admitted 1976. West Point has been a military post since 1778.

West Sussex county on the south coast of England
area 780 sq mi/2,020 sq km
towns Chichester (administrative headquarters, Crawley, Horsham, Haywards Heath, Shoreham (port); resorts: Worthing, Littlehampton, Bognor Regis
physical the Weald, South Downs; rivers: Arun, West Rother, Adur
population (1987) 700,000

West Virginia state in E central US; nickname Mountain State
area 24,279 sq mi/62,900 sq km
capital Charleston
cities Huntington, Wheeling
physical Allegheny Mountains; Ohio River
features port of Harper's Ferry, restored as when John Brown seized the US armory 1859
products apples, corn, poultry, dairy and meat products, coal, natural gas, oil, chemicals, synthetic fibers, plastics, steel, glass, pottery
population (1990) 1,793,500
famous people Pearl S. Buck, Thomas "Stonewall" Jackson, Walter Reuther, Cyrus Vance
history Moundbuilders in the 6th century; explorers and fur traders 1670s; first settlement at Mill Creek 1731 by Morgan Morgan, who came from Delaware; German settlements 1730s; coal discovered on the Coal River 1742; industrial development early 19th century. On the secession of Virginia from the Union 1861, west Virginians dissented and formed a new state 1863. Industrial expansion was accompanied by labor strife in the early 20th century.

Long one of the poorest parts of the country, West Virginia reached its peak population in 1950. The decline of employment in coal mining and heavy industry has hampered the state's economic life.

West Virginia State Board of Education v Barnette one of the "flag salute" Supreme Court cases 1943 dealing with mandatory recitation of the pledge of allegiance in public school. Barnette issued a legal challenge to a West Virginia statute requiring all public-school children to salute the flag. A Jehovah's

West Virginia

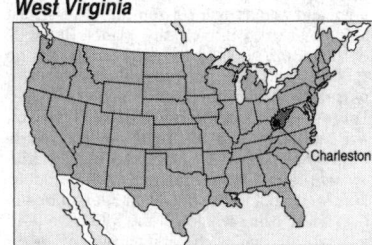

Charleston

Witness, he argued that his child's First-Amendment freedom of religion was being denied, since reciting the pledge was against his religious principles. The Court invalidated the law because it violated First-Amendment rights to freedom of religion, speech, and thought.

weta flightless insect *Deinacrida rugosa*, 3.5 in/8.5 cm long, resembling a large grasshopper, found on offshore islands of New Zealand.

wetland permanently wet land area or habitat. Wetlands include areas of ◊marsh, fen, ◊bog, flood plain, and shallow coastal areas. Wetlands are extremely fertile. They provide warm, sheltered waters for fisheries, lush vegetation for grazing livestock, and an abundance of wildlife. Estuaries and seaweed beds are more than 16 times as productive as the open ocean.

Wexford seaport and county town of Wexford, Republic of Ireland; population (1991) 9,500. Products include textiles, cheese, and agricultural machinery. It was founded by the Danes in the 9th century and devastated by Cromwell 1649.

Weyden Rogier van der *c.* 1399–1464. Netherlandish painter, official painter to the city of Brussels from 1436. He painted portraits and religious subjects, such as *The Last Judgment* about 1450 (Hôtel-Dieu, Beaune). His refined style had considerable impact on Netherlandish painting.

Little is known of his life, and none of his works have been dated, but he was widely admired in his day and his paintings were sent to Italy, Spain, France, and Germany. His *Deposition* before 1443 (Prado, Madrid) shows the influence of Robert ◊Campin.

whale any marine mammal of the order Cetacea, with front limbs modified into flippers and with internal vestiges of hind limbs. The order is divided into the toothed whales (Odontoceti) and the baleen whales (Mysticeti). The toothed whales include ◊dolphins and ◊porpoises, along with large forms such as sperm whales. The baleen whales, with plates of modified mucous membrane called baleen in the mouth, are all large in size and include finback and right whales. There were hundreds of thousands of whales at the beginning of the 20th century, but they have been hunted close to extinction (see ◊whaling).

Whales are extremely intelligent and have a complex communication system, known as "songs." When they surface to breathe, they spout air through the blowhole (single or double nostrils) in the top of the head. Mass strandings where whales swim onto a beach occur occasionally for unknown reasons; it may have something to do with pollution. Group loyalty is strong, and whales may follow a confused leader to disaster.

The **blue whale** *Sibaldus musculus*, one of the finback whales (or rorquals), is 100 ft/31 m long, and weighs over 100 tons. It is the largest animal ever to inhabit the planet. It feeds on plankton, strained through its whalebone "plates." The common **rorqual** *Balaenoptera physalas* is slate-colored, and not quite so large. Largest of the **toothed whales**, which feed on fish and larger animals, is the **sperm whale** *Physeter catodon* (see ◊spermaceti). The **killer whale** is a large member of the dolphin family (Delphinidae), and is often exhibited in oceanaria. Killer whales in the wild have 8–15 special calls, and each family group, or "pod,"

has its own particular dialect: they are the first mammals known to have dialects in the same way as human language. Right whales of the family Ballaenidae have a thick body and an enormous head. They are regarded by whalers as the "right" whale to exploit since they swim slowly and are relatively easy to catch. See also ◊bowhead whale.

whaling the hunting of whales, largely discontinued 1986. Whales are killed for whale oil (made from the thick layer of fat under the skin called "blubber"), used for food and cosmetics; for the large reserve of oil in the head of the sperm whale, used in the leather industry; and for **ambergris**, a waxlike substance from the intestines, used in making perfumes. There are synthetic substitutes for all these products. Whales are also killed for their meat, which is eaten by the Japanese and was used as pet food in the US and Europe.

The International Whaling Commission (IWC), established 1946, failed to enforce quotas on whale killing until world concern about the possible extinction of the whale was mounted in the 1970s. By the end of the 1980s, 90% of blue, fin, humpback, and sperm whales had been wiped out. Low reproduction rates mean that protected species are slow to recover. After 1986 only Iceland, Japan, Norway, and the USSR continued with limited whaling for "scientific purposes," but Japan has been repeatedly implicated in commercial whaling, and pirates also operate. In 1990 the IWC rejected every proposal from Japan, Norway, and the USSR for further scientific whaling. Norway, Greenland, the Faroes, and Iceland formed a breakaway whaling club. In 1991 Japan held a "final" whale feast before conforming to the regulations of the International Whaling Commission.

Wharton Edith (born Jones) 1862–1937. US novelist. Her work, known for its subtlety and form and influenced by her friend Henry James, was mostly set in New York society. It includes *The House of Mirth* 1905, which made her reputation; the grim, uncharacteristic novel of New England *Ethan Frome* 1911; *The Custom of the Country* 1913; and *The Age of Innocence* 1920.

wheat cereal plant derived from the wild *Triticum*, a grass native to the Middle East. It is the chief cereal used in breadmaking and is widely cultivated in temperate climates suited to its growth. Wheat is killed by frost, and damp renders the grain soft, so warm, dry regions produce the most valuable grain.

The main wheat-producing areas of the world are the Ukraine, the prairie states of the US, the Punjab in India, the prairie provinces

of Canada, parts of France, Poland, S Germany, Italy, Argentina, and SE Australia. Flour is milled from the ◊endosperm; the coatings of the grain produce bran. Semolina is also prepared from wheat; it is a by-product from the manufacture of fine flour.

wheatear small (6 in/15 cm long) migratory bird *Oenanthe oenanthe* of the family Muscicapidae, in the order Passeriformes. The family also includes the thrushes. Wheatears are found throughout the Old World and also breed in far northern parts of North America. The plumage is light gray above and white below, with a white patch on the back, a black face-patch, and black and white wings and tail.

Wheeler Mortimer 1890–1976. English archeologist. As director-general of archeology in India in the 1940s he uncovered the ◊Indus Valley civilization. He helped to popularize archeology by his television appearances.

Wheeling city in NW West Virginia, on the Ohio River, SW of Pittsburgh, Pennsylvania; population (1990) 34,900. Industries include coal and natural-gas processing, iron and steel, textiles, glass, pottery, paper, and chemicals. Fort Henry, site of the last battle 1782 of the Revolutionary War, is here.

whelk any of various families of large marine snails with a thick spiral shell, especially the family Buccinidae. Whelks are scavengers, and also eat other shellfish. The largest grow to 16 in/40 cm long. Tropical species, such as the conches, can be very colorful.

The common northern whelk *Buccinum undatum* is widely distributed around the North Sea and the Atlantic.

whey watery by-product of the cheesemaking process, which is drained off after the milk has been heated and ◊rennet (a curdling agent) added to induce its coagulation.

In Scandinavia, especially Norway, whey is turned into cheese, *mysost* and (from goat's whey) *gjetost*. The flavor of whey cheese is sweet from added brown sugar and is an acquired taste.

Whig Party in the UK, predecessor of the Liberal Party. The name was first used of rebel Covenanters (Presbyterian Christians who opposed Charles I's attempt to introduce into Scotland a liturgy on the English model) and then of those who wished to exclude James II from the English succession (as a Roman Catholic). They were in power continuously 1714–60 and pressed for industrial and commercial development, a vigorous foreign policy, and religious toleration. During the French Revolution, the Whigs demanded parliamentary reform in Britain, and from the

■ major areas

wheat *As one of the most important cereals, wheat has been developed in many varieties to suit different growing conditions.*

passing of the Reform Bill in 1832 became known as Liberals.

Whig Party in the US, political party opposed to the autocratic presidency of Andrew Jackson from 1834. The Whig presidents were W H Harrison, Taylor, and Fillmore. The party diverged over the issue of slavery 1852: the Northern Whigs joined the Republican party; the Southern or "Cotton" Whigs joined the Democrats. The title was taken from the British Whig Party which supported Parliament against the king. During the American Revolution, colonial patriots described themselves as Whigs, while those remaining loyal to Britain were known as Tories.

whimbrel ⟩curlew *Numenius phaeopus* with a medium-sized down-curved bill, streaked brown plumage, and striped head. About 1.3 ft/ 40 cm long, it breeds in the Arctic, and winters in Africa, S North America, South America, and S Asia.

whippet breed of dog resembling a small grayhound. It grows to 22 in/56 cm at the shoulder, and 20 lb/9 kg in weight.

The whippet was developed in England for racing. It was probably produced by crossing a terrier and a grayhound.

Whipple Fred Lawrence 1906– . US astronomer whose hypothesis in 1949 that the nucleus of a comet is like a dirty snowball was confirmed 1986 by space-probe studies of ⟩Halley's comet.

Whipple George 1878–1976. US physiologist whose research interest concerned the formation of haemoglobin in the blood. He showed that anemic dogs, kept under restricted diets, responded well to a liver regime, and that their haemoglobin quickly regenerated. This work led to a cure for pernicious anemia. He shared the 1934 Nobel Prize for Medicine with George Minot (1885–1950) and William Murphy (1892–1987).

whippoorwill North American ⟩nightjar *Caprimulgus vociferus*, so called from its cry.

whip snake any of the various species of nonpoisonous slender-bodied tree-dwelling snakes of the New World genus *Masticophis*, family Colubridae, also called **coachwhips**. They are closely allied to members of the genus *Coluber* of SW North America, Eurasia, Australasia, and N Africa, some of which are called whip snakes in the Old World, but racers in North America.

Whip snakes grow to about 5 ft/1.5 m in length, move very quickly, and are partially tree-dwelling. They feed on rodents, small birds, lizards, sucker frogs, and insects. All lay eggs.

whiskey (Gaelic *uisge beatha*, water of life) a strong alcoholic liquor made from a fermented mash of various cereals: Scotch whiskey from malted barley; Irish whiskey usually from barley, and North American whiskey and bourbon from rye and corn. Scotch and other whiskeys are usually blended; pure malt whiskeys are more expensive. Whiskey is generally aged in wooden casks for 4–12 years.

The earliest written record of whiskey comes from Scotland 1494 but the art of distillation is thought to have been known before this time.

whist card game for four, predecessor of ⟩bridge, in which the partners try to win a majority of the 13 tricks (the highest card played being the winner of the trick).

Whistler James Abbott McNeill 1834–1903. US painter and etcher, active in London from 1859. His riverscapes and portraits show subtle composition and color harmonies: for example, *Arrangement in Gray and Black: Portrait of the Painter's Mother* 1871 (Louvre, Paris).

He settled in Chelsea, London, and painted views of the Thames including *Old Battersea Bridge* (*c.* 1872–75) (Tate Gallery, London). In 1877 the art critic John ⟩Ruskin published an article on his *Nocturne in Black and Gold: The Falling Rocket* (now in Detroit) that led to a libel trial in which Whistler was awarded symbolic damages of a farthing (a fourth of an old penny). Whistler described the trial in his book *The Gentle Art of Making Enemies* 1890.

Whistler was born in Lowell, Massachusetts. He originally attended West Point, left after failing a course, and worked as a draftsman. In 1855 he went to Paris where he was associated with the Impressionists.

Whitby, Synod of council summoned by King Oswy of Northumbria 664, which decided to adopt the Roman rather than the Celtic form of Christianity for Britain.

White counterrevolutionary, especially during the Russian civil wars 1917–21. Originally the term described the party opposing the French Revolution, when the royalists used the white lily of the French monarchy as their badge.

White Byron Raymond 1917– . US associate justice of the Supreme Court 1962– . Appointed to the Court by President John F Kennedy, White proved to be a moderate conservative. He usually dissented on the rights of criminals, but upheld the right of accused citizens to trial by jury.

Born in Fort Collins, Colorado, White graduated from the University of Colorado 1938 and played professional football with the Pittsburgh Pirates (now Steelers) 1938. He studied at Oxford as a Rhodes scholar 1939 and entered Yale Law School 1940. At the same time, he played football for the Detroit Lions 1940–41. in 1942, he interrupted his law studies to serve int he US Navy until the end of World War II. White returned to graduate from Yale 1946, after which he served as law clerk 1946–47 to Supreme Court associate justice Fred M Vinson. White practiced law in Denver, Colorado, 1947–60, worked to elect John F Kennedy to the presidency 1960, and served as deputy attorney general 1961–62, before being appointed to the Supreme Court. He was elected to the Football Hall of Fame 1954.

White E(lwyn) B(rooks) 1899–1985. US writer, long associated with *The New Yorker* magazine and renowned for his satire, such as *Is Sex Necessary?* 1929 (with the humorist James Thurber).

With William Strunk, Jr., he published *The Elements of Style* 1935, considered a definitive style manual for the English language. White also wrote children's classics: *Stuart Little* 1945, *Charlotte's Web* 1952, and *The Trumpet of the Swan* 1970.

White Edward Douglass, Jr 1845–1921. US jurist; associate justice 1894–1911 and chief justice 1911–21 of the US Supreme Court. During White's service the Court made important decisions on US economic policy. In *United States v E C Knight and Co* 1895 he joined the majority in weakening the Sherman Antitrust Act by removing manufacture of goods from its purview. In *Standard Oil Co. v United States* 1911 and *United States v American Tobacco Co* the Court created the still-current legal definition of trusts in restraint of trade (see ⟩monopoly). In *McCray v United States* 1904 he wrote the Court's decision expanding federal taxing power. He also participated in several cases that refined US labor policy in civil-rights cases and in the *Selective Draft Law Cases* 1918.

Born in Lafourche Parish, Louisiana, White attended Mount St Mary's College (Maryland), the Jesuit College (New Orleans), and Georgetown University, but left his college studies to serve in the Confederate Army. After the Civil War he studied law at the University of Louisiana Law School in New Orleans; he was admitted to the bar 1868. He entered private practice in his home state and became active in Democratic politics. He was elected to the state senate 1874 and was a justice of the Louisiana supreme court 1878–80. He was elected to the US Senate 1891. In 1893 President Cleveland nominated White to the Supreme Court. President Taft nominated White as chief justice.

White Patrick (Victor Martindale) 1912–1990. Australian writer who did more than any other to put Australian literature on the international map. His partly allegorical novels explore the lives of early settlers in Australia and often deal with misfits or inarticulate people. They include *The Aunt's Story* 1948, *The Tree of Man* 1955, and *Voss* 1957 (based on the ill-fated 19th-century explorer Leichhardt). Nobel Prize for Literature 1973.

White Stanford 1853–1906. US architect. Born in New York City and trained in architecture during an apprenticeship with the firm of Gambril and Richardson, White became one of the most prominent US architects of the 19th century. After a year of study in Europe, he was one of the founders of the architectural firm of McKim, Mead and White 1879. Specializing in the Renaissance style, White designed, among many famous projects, the original Madison Square Garden and the Washington Square Arch, both in New York City. A flamboyant and arrogant personality, he was murdered in the rooftop restaurant of Madison Square Garden by the husband of a former lover.

White T(erence) H(anbury) 1906–1964. English writer who retold the Arthurian legend in four volumes of *The Once and Future King* 1938–58.

whitebait any of the fry (young) of various silvery fishes, especially ⟩herring. It is also the name for a Pacific smelt *Osmerus mordax*.

whitebeam tree *Sorbus aria*, native to S Europe, usually found growing on chalk or limestone. It can reach 60 ft/20 m. It takes its name from the pinnately compound leaves, which have a dense coat of short white hairs on the underside.

It is a type of ⟩mountain ash.

white blood cell or **leucocyte** one of a number of different cells that play a part in the body's defenses and give immunity against disease. Some (⟩phagocytes and ⟩macrophages) engulf invading microorganisms, others kill infected cells, while ⟩lymphocytes produce more specific immune responses. White blood cells are colorless, with clear or granulated cytoplasm, and are capable of independent amoeboid movement. They occur in the blood, ⟩lymph and elsewhere in the body's tissues.

Unlike mammalian red blood cells, they possess a nucleus. Human blood contains about 11,000 leukocytes to the cubic millimeter—about one to every 500 red cells.

White blood cell numbers may be reduced (leucopenia) by starvation, pernicious anemia, and certain infections, such as typhoid and malaria. An increase in their numbers (leukocytosis) is a reaction to normal events such as digestion, exertion, and pregnancy, and to abnormal ones such as loss of blood, cancer, and most infections.

white-collar worker non-manual employee, such as an office worker or manager. With more mechanized production methods, the distinction between white-and blue-collar (manual) workers is becoming increasingly blurred.

white dwarf small, hot ▷star, the last stage in the life of a star such as the Sun. White dwarfs have a mass similar to that of the Sun, but only 1% of the Sun's diameter, similar in size to the Earth. Most have surface temperatures of 14,400°F/8,000°C or more, hotter than the Sun. Yet, being so small, their overall luminosities may be less than 1% of that of the Sun. The Milky Way contains an estimated 50 billion white dwarfs.

White dwarfs consist of degenerate matter in which gravity has packed the protons and electrons together as tightly as is physically possible, so that a spoonful of it weighs several tons. White dwarfs are thought to be the shrunken remains of stars that have exhausted their internal energy supplies. They slowly cool and fade over billions of years.

Whitefield George 1714–1770. British Methodist evangelist. He was a student at Oxford University and took orders in 1738, but was suspended for his unorthodox doctrines and methods. For many years he traveled through Britain and America, and by his preaching contributed greatly to the Great Awakening. He died while visiting New England.

whitefish any of various freshwater fishes, genera *Coregonus* and *Prosopium* of the salmon family, found in lakes and rivers of North America and Eurasia. They include the whitefish *C. clupeaformis* and cisco *C. artedi.*

Whitehead Alfred North 1861–1947. English philosopher and mathematician. In his "theory of organism," he attempted a synthesis of metaphysics and science. His works include *Principia Mathematica* 1910–13 (with Bertrand ▷Russell), *The Concept of Nature* 1920, and *Adventures of Ideas* 1933.

He was professor of applied mathematics at London University 1914–24, and professor of philosophy at Harvard University, 1924–37. Other works include *Principles of Natural Knowledge* 1919, *Science and the Modern World* 1925, and *Process and Reality* 1929.

Whitehorse capital of Yukon Territory; population (1986) 15,199. Whitehorse is on the NW Highway. It replaced Dawson as capital in 1953.

White House official residence of the president of the US, in Washington, DC. It is a plain edifice of sandstone, built in the Italian Renaissance style 1792–99 to the designs of James Hoban, who also restored it after it was burned by the British 1814; it was then painted white to hide the scars.

The structure was completely restored by the Truman administration; the interior was redecorated 1960–63 by First Lady Jacqueline Kennedy. The offices of the president's staff in the White House and nearby buildings are often collectively referred to as "The White House." The president's study and ceremonial office is known from its shape as the Oval Office. The building includes living quarters for the president, the presidential family, and staff and public rooms for dinners, concerts, and receptions. The presidential apartment is separate from the rest of the mansion, which is open to visitors and public tours as a museum. The name White House, first recorded in 1811, is often adapted to refer to other residences of the president; for example, Little White House, at Warm Springs, Georgia, where F D Roosevelt died; Western White House, at San Clemente, California, where Nixon had a home.

white knight in business, a company invited by the target of a takeover bid to make a rival bid. The company invited to bid is usually one that is already on good terms with the target company.

Whiteman Paul 1890–1967. US dance-band and swing-orchestra leader specializing in "symphonic jazz." He commissioned George Gershwin's *Rhapsody in Blue*, conducting its premiere 1924.

whiteout "fog" of grains of dry snow caused by strong winds in temperatures of between 0°F/ −18°C and 30°F/−1°C. The uniform whiteness of the ground and air causes disorientation in humans.

White Russia English translation of ▷Belarus.

White Sea (Russian *Beloye More*) gulf of the Arctic Ocean, on which the port of Archangel stands. There is a warship construction base, including nuclear submarines, at Severodvinsk. The North Dvina and Onega rivers flow into it, and there are canal links with the Baltic, Black, and Caspian seas.

White terror general term used by socialists and Marxists to describe a right-wing counterrevolution: for example, the attempts by the Chinese Guomindang to massacre the communists 1927–31; see ▷White.

whitethroat any of several Old World warblers of the genus *Sylvia*, found in scrub, hedges, and wood clearings of Eurasia in summer, migrating to Africa in winter. They are about 5.5 in/14 cm long.

whiting any of various edible marine bony fishes, especially the silver hake and various kingfishes, genus *Menticirrhus.*

Whitlam Gough (Edward) 1916– . Australian politician, leader of the Labor Party 1967–78 and prime minister 1972–75. He cultivated closer relations with Asia, attempted redistribution of wealth, and raised loans to increase national ownership of industry and resources.

Whitman Walt(er) 1819–1892. US poet who published *Leaves of Grass* 1855, which contains the symbolic "Song of Myself." It used unconventional free verse (with no rhyme or regular rhythm) and scandalized the public by its frank celebration of sexuality.

Born at West Hill (Huntington, Long Island), New York, as a young man Whitman worked as a printer, teacher, and journalist. In 1865 he published *Drum-Taps*, a volume inspired by his work as an army nurse during the Civil War. *Democratic Vistas* 1871 is a collection of his prose pieces. He also wrote an elegy for Abraham Lincoln, "When Lilacs Last in the Dooryard Bloom'd." He preached a particularly American vision of individual freedom and human brotherhood. Such poets as Ezra Pound, Wallace Stevens, and Allen Ginsberg show his influence in their work.

Whitney Eli 1765–1825. US inventor who in 1794 patented the cotton gin, a device for separating cotton fiber from its seeds. Also a manufacturer of firearms, he created a standardization system that was the precursor of the assembly line.

Born in Westborough, Massachusetts, Whitney graduated from Yale 1792. His invention of the cotton gin revolutionized the cotton industry in the South. In a shop in New Haven, Connecticut, he manufactured muskets under a contract from the US government, using power-driven tools to produce interchangeable parts.

Whitney v California a US Supreme Court decision 1927 dealing with state legislation restricting freedom of speech and assembly. Charlotte Whitney had been convicted, under a California law outlawing membership in organizations advocating political or industrial violence, for her activities in the Communist Labor Party. She appealed to the Supreme Court for protection under the First Amendment. The Court upheld the California law, ruling that states were obligated to thwart "all threats to the American form of government, no matter how remote."

Whittier John Greenleaf 1807–1892. US poet who was a powerful opponent of slavery, as shown in the verse *Voices of Freedom* 1846. Among his other works are *Legends of New England in Prose and Verse, Songs of Labor* 1850, and the New England nature poem *Snow-Bound* 1866.

He was also a journalist and humanitarian. Many of his poems have been set to music, and are sung as church hymns.

Whittle Frank 1907– . British engineer who patented the basic design for the turbojet engine 1930. In the Royal Air Force he worked on jet propulsion 1937–46. In May 1941 the Gloster E 28/39 aircraft first flew with the Whittle jet engine. Both the German (first operational jet planes) and the US jet aircraft were built using his principles.

WHO acronym for ▷*World Health Organization.*

Who, the English rock group, formed 1964, with a hard, aggressive sound, high harmonies, and a propensity for destroying their instruments on stage. Their albums include *Tommy* 1969, *Who's Next* 1971, and *Quadrophenia* 1973.

Originally a mod band, the Who comprised Pete Townshend (1945–), guitar and songwriter; Roger Daltrey (1944–), vocals; John Entwistle (1944–), bass; and Keith Moon (1947–1978), drums.

wholesale the business of selling merchandise to anyone other than the final customer. Most manufacturers or producers sell in bulk to a wholesale organization which distributes the smaller quantities required by retail outlets.

whooping cough or *pertussis* acute infectious disease, seen mainly in children, caused by colonization of the air passages by the bacterium *Bordetella pertussis*. There may be catarrh, mild fever, and loss of appetite, but the main symptom is violent coughing, associated with the sharp intake of breath that is the characteristic "whoop," and often followed by vomiting and severe nose bleeds. The cough may persist for weeks.

Although debilitating, the disease is seldom serious in older children, but infants are at risk both from the illness itself and from susceptibility to other conditions, such as ▷pneumonia.

Immunization lessens the incidence and severity of whooping cough.

whydah any of various African birds of the genus *Vidua*, order Passeriformes, of the weaver family. They lay their eggs in the nests of waxbills, which rear the young. Young birds resemble young waxbills, but the adults do not resemble adult waxbills. Males have long tail feathers used in courtship displays.

Whymper Edward 1840–1911. English mountaineer. He made the first ascent of many Alpine peaks, including the Matterhorn 1865, and in the Andes scaled Chimborazo and other mountains.

WI abbreviation for ▷*West Indies*; the state of ▷*Wisconsin*.

Wichita industrial city (oil refining, aircraft, motor vehicles) in S Kansas; population (1990) 304,000. Wichita was founded about 1867.

It became a stopover on the Chisholm cattle-driving trail; when the railroad arrived 1872, the city became a major cattle-shipping point. Petroleum was discovered nearby 1915, and aircraft manufacture began 1920. Wichita State University is here.

Wichita Falls city in N Texas, on the Wichita River, S of the Oklahoma border; population (1990) 96,300. It is an important petroleum-processing center. Other industries include leather goods, textiles, foodstuffs, electronics, and pharmaceutical goods.

wide-angle lens photographic lens of shorter focal length than normal, taking in a wider angle of view.

Widmark Richard 1914– . US actor who made his film debut in *Kiss of Death* 1947 as a psychopath. He subsequently appeared in a great variety of *film noir* roles as well as in *The Alamo* 1960, *Madigan* 1968, and *Coma* 1978.

Wien German name for ▷Vienna, capital of Austria.

Wien Wilhelm 1864–1928. German physicist who studied radiation and established the principle, since known as Wien's law, that the wavelength at which the radiation from an idealized radiating body is most intense is inversely proportional to the body's absolute temperature. (That is, the hotter the body, the shorter the wavelength.) For this and other work on radiation, he was awarded the 1911 Nobel Prize for Physics.

Wiener Norbert 1894–1964. US mathematician. Born in Columbia, Missouri, Wiener was a child prodigy, attending Tufts University at an early age and receiving his PhD from Harvard at age 19. Joining the mathematics faculty at the Massachusetts Institute of Technology 1919, he became one of the pioneers in the development of computer logic. During World War II, Wiener helped to perfect sophisticated weapons guidance systems. Best known for his book *Cybernetics* 1948, he laid the theoretical groundwork for information feedback systems. Two volumes of memoirs were published as *Ex-Prodigy* 1953 and *I Am a Mathematician* 1956.

Wien's law in physics, a law of radiation stating that the wavelength carrying the maximum energy is inversely proportional to the body's absolute temperature: the hotter a body is, the shorter the wavelength. It has the form $\lambda_{max}T =$ constant, where λ_{max} is the wavelength of maximum intensity and T is the temperature. The law is named after German physicist Wilhelm Wien.

Wiesbaden spa town and capital of Hessen, Germany, on the Rhine 12 mi/20 km W of Frankfurt; population (1988) 267,000. Products include cement, plastics, wines, and spirits; most of the German sparkling wine cellars are in this area. Wiesbaden was the capital of the former duchy of Nassau from the 12th century until 1866.

Wiesel Elie 1928– . US academic and human-rights campaigner, born in Romania. He was held in Buchenwald concentration camp during World War II, and has assiduously documented wartime atrocities against the Jews in an effort to alert the world to the dangers of racism and violence. Nobel Peace Prize 1986.

Wiesel sought to remind new generations of the Nazi atrocities so that they might never be repeated. He is considered the most eloquent spokesman of the death-camp survivors.

wig artificial head of hair, either real or synthetic, worn as an adornment, disguise, or to conceal baldness. Wigs were known in the ancient world and have been found on Egyptian mummies. Today they remain part of the uniform of judges, lawyers, and some parliamentary officials in the UK and certain Commonwealth countries.

wigeon either of two species of dabbling duck of genus *Anas*. The American wigeon *A. americana*, about 19 in/48 cm long, is found along both coasts in winter and breeds inland. Males have a white-capped head and a green eye stripe.

The Eurasian wigeon *A. penelope* has a dark head without eye stripe. It is a regular winter visitor along both North American coasts.

Wiggin Kate Douglas 1856–1923. US writer, born in Philadelphia. She was a pioneer in the establishment of kindergartens in the US, and wrote the children's classic *Rebecca of Sunnybrook Farm* 1903 and its sequels.

Wight, Isle of island and county in S England
area 147 sq mi/380 sq km
cities Newport (administrative headquarters), resorts: Ryde, Sandown, Shanklin, Ventnor
features the *Needles*, a group of pointed chalk rocks up to 100 ft/30 m high in the sea to the W; the *Solent*, the sea channel between Hampshire and the island (including the anchorage at *Spithead* opposite Portsmouth, used for naval reviews); *Cowes*, venue of Regatta Week and headquarters of the Royal Yacht Squadron; Osborne House, near Cowes, a home of Queen Victoria, for whom it was built 1845; Farringford, home of Tennyson, near Freshwater
products chiefly agricultural; tourism
population (1991) 126,600
famous people Thomas Arnold, Robert Hooke.
history called *Vectis* ("separate division") by the Romans, who conquered it AD 43. Charles I was imprisoned 1647–48 in Carisbrooke Castle, now ruined.

Wightman Cup annual tennis competition between international women's teams from the US and the UK. The trophy, first contested 1923, was donated by Hazel Hotchkiss Wightman (1886–1974), a former US tennis player who won singles, doubles, and mixed-doubles titles in the US Championships 1909–1911. Because of US domination of the contest it was abandoned 1990, but was reinstated 1991 with the UK side assisted by European players.

Wigner Eugene Paul 1902– . Hungarian-born US physicist who introduced the notion of parity into nuclear physics with the consequence that all nuclear processes should be indistinguishable from their mirror images. For this, and other work on nuclear structure, he shared the 1963 Nobel Prize for Physics with Maria ▷Goeppert-Mayer and Hans Jensen (1906–1973).

Wilberforce William 1759–1833. English reformer who was instrumental in abolishing slavery in the British Empire. He entered Parliament 1780; in 1807 his bill for the abolition of the slave trade was passed, and in 1833, largely through his efforts, slavery was abolished throughout the empire.

Wilde Cornel(ius Louis) 1915–1989. Austrian-born US actor and film director, in the US from 1932. He starred in *A Song to Remember* 1945, and directed *The Naked Prey* 1966 (in which he also acted) and *No Blade of Grass* 1970.

Wilde also starred in *Leave Her to Heaven* 1945 and *Forever Amber* 1947. He produced, directed, and starred (with his wife Jean Wallace) in several films from 1955, including *Storm Fear* 1955, *Maracaibo* 1958, and *Beach Red* 1967. His originality reveals him to be a primitive of the camera, at home in African adventure.

Wilde Oscar (Fingal O'Flahertie Wills) 1854–1900. Irish writer. With his flamboyant style and quotable conversation, he dazzled London society and, on his lecture tour 1882, the US. He published his only novel, *The Picture of Dorian Gray*, 1891, followed by witty plays including *A Woman of No Importance* 1893 and *The Importance of Being Earnest* 1895. In 1895 he was imprisoned for two years for homosexual offenses; he died in exile.

Wilde was born in Dublin and studied at Dublin and Oxford, where he became known as a supporter of the Aesthetic movement ("art for art's sake"). He published *Poems* 1881, and also wrote fairy tales and other stories, criticism, and a long, anarchic political essay, "The Soul of Man Under Socialism" 1891. His elegant social comedies include *Lady Windermere's Fan* 1892 and *An Ideal Husband* 1895. The drama *Salome* 1893, based on the biblical character, was written in French; considered scandalous by the British censor, it was first performed in Paris 1896 with the actress Sarah Bernhardt in the title role.

Among his lovers was Lord Alfred ▷Douglas, whose father provoked Wilde into a lawsuit that led to his social and financial ruin and imprisonment. The long poem *Ballad of Reading Gaol* 1898 and a letter published as *De Profundis* 1905 were written in jail to explain his side of the relationship. After his release from prison 1897, he lived in France and is buried in Paris.

wildebeest another name for ▷gnu.

Wilder Billy 1906– . Austrian-born accomplished US screenwriter and film director, in the US from 1934. He directed and coscripted *Double Indemnity* 1944, *The Lost Weekend* (Academy Award for best director) 1945, *Sunset Boulevard* 1950, *Some Like It Hot* 1959, and the Academy Award-winning *The Apartment* 1960.

He specialized in "smart" romances and worked with Charles Brackett on film scripts such as *Ninotchka* 1939 directed by Lubitsch and produced by Wilder. He won the Thalberg Award 1987.

Wilder Thornton (Niven) 1897–1975. US playwright and novelist. He won Pulitzer prizes for the novel *The Bridge of San Luis Rey* 1927, and for the plays *Our Town* 1938 and *The Skin of Our Teeth* 1942. His farce *The Matchmaker* 1954 was filmed 1958. In 1964 it was adapted into the hit stage musical *Hello, Dolly!*, also made into a film.

His plays are innovative in that they are overtly philosophical, they generally employ no props or scenery, and the characters often directly address the audience.

wilderness area of uncultivated and uninhabited land, which is usually located some distance from towns and cities.

In the US wilderness areas are specially designated by Congress and protected by federal agencies; some are "forever wild."

wild type in genetics, the naturally occurring gene for a particular character that is typical of most individuals of a given species, as distinct from new genes that arise by mutation.

Wilhelm (English *William*) two emperors of Germany:

Wilhelm I 1797–1888. King of Prussia from 1861 and emperor of Germany from 1871; the son of Friedrich Wilhelm III. He served in the Napoleonic Wars 1814–15 and helped to crush the 1848 revolution. After he succeeded his brother Friedrich Wilhelm IV to the throne of Prussia, his policy was largely dictated by his chancellor ◊Bismarck, who secured his proclamation as emperor.

Wilhelm II 1859–1941. Emperor of Germany from 1888, the son of Frederick III and Victoria, daughter of Queen Victoria of Britain. In 1890 he forced Chancellor Bismarck to resign and began to direct foreign policy himself, which proved disastrous. He encouraged warlike policies and built up the German navy. In 1914 he first approved Austria's ultimatum to Serbia and then, when he realized war was inevitable, tried in vain to prevent it. In 1918 he fled to Holland, after Germany's defeat and his abdication.

Wilkes John 1727–1797. British Radical politician, imprisoned for his political views; member of Parliament 1757–64 and from 1774. He championed parliamentary reform, religious toleration, and US independence.

Wilkes, born in Clerkenwell, London, entered Parliament as a Whig 1757. His attacks on the Tory prime minister Bute in his paper *The North Briton* led to his being outlawed 1764; he fled to France, and on his return 1768 was imprisoned. He was four times elected MP for Middlesex, but the Commons refused to admit him and finally declared his opponent elected. This secured him strong working- and middle-class support, and in 1774 he was allowed to take his seat in Parliament.

Wilkes Barre industrial city (furniture, textiles, wire, tobacco products, and heavy machinery) in NE Pennsylvania, on the Susquehanna River, SW of Scranton; population (1990) 47,500.

Wilkins Maurice Hugh Frederick 1916– . New Zealand-born British scientist. In 1962 he shared the Nobel Prize for Medicine with Francis ◊Crick and James ◊Watson for their work on the molecular structure of nucleic acids, particularly ◊DNA, using X-ray diffraction.

will in law, declaration of how a person wishes his or her property to be disposed of after death. It also appoints administrators of the estate (◊executors) and may contain wishes on other matters, such as place of burial or use of organs for transplant. Wills must comply with formal legal requirements of the local jurisdiction.

Willard Frances Elizabeth Caroline 1839–1898. US educator. Born in Churchville, New York, and raised in Wisconsin, Willard was educated at the Northwestern Female College in Evanston, Illinois. After a career as a teacher, she was appointed dean of women at Northwestern University 1873. Becoming increasingly committed to the cause of the prohibition of alcohol, she served as president of the Women's Christian Temperance Union 1879–98. Willard was also elected president of the National Council of Women 1888.

Willem Dutch form of ◊William.

William four kings of England:

William I *the Conqueror* c. 1027–1087. King of England from 1066. He was the illegitimate son of Duke Robert the Devil and succeeded his father as duke of Normandy 1035. Claiming that his relative King Edward the Confessor had bequeathed him the English throne, William invaded the country 1066, defeating ◊Harold II at Hastings, Sussex, and was crowned king of England.

He was crowned in Westminster Abbey on Christmas Day 1066. He completed the establishment of feudalism in England, compiling detailed records of land and property in the Domesday Book, and kept his barons firmly under control. He died in Rouen after a fall from his horse and is buried in Caen, France. He was succeeded by his son William II.

William II *Rufus*, *the Red* c. 1056–1100. King of England from 1087, the third son of William I. He spent most of his reign attempting to capture Normandy from his brother ◊Robert II, duke of Normandy. His extortion of money led his barons to revolt and caused confrontation with Bishop Anselm. He was killed while hunting in the New Forest, Hampshire, and was succeeded by his brother Henry I.

William III *William of Orange* 1650–1702. King of Great Britain and Ireland from 1688, the son of William II of Orange and Mary, daughter of Charles I. He was offered the English crown by the parliamentary opposition to James II. He invaded England 1688 and in 1689 became joint sovereign with his wife, ◊Mary II. He spent much of his reign campaigning, first in Ireland, where he defeated James II at the battle of the Boyne 1690, and later against the French in Flanders. He was succeeded by Mary's sister, Anne.

William IV 1765–1837. King of Great Britain and Ireland from 1830, when he succeeded his brother George IV; third son of George III. He was created duke of Clarence 1789, and married Adelaide of Saxe-Meiningen (1792–1849) 1818. During the Reform Bill crisis he secured its passage by agreeing to create new peers to overcome the hostile majority in the House of Lords. He was succeeded by Victoria.

William three kings of the Netherlands:

William I 1772–1844. King of the Netherlands 1815–40. He lived in exile during the French occupation 1795–1813 and fought against the emperor Napoleon at Jena and Wagram. The Austrian Netherlands were added to his kingdom by the Allies 1815, but secured independence (recognized by the major European states 1839) by the revolution of 1830. William's unpopularity led to his abdication 1840.

William II 1792–1849. King of the Netherlands 1840–49, son of William I. He served with the British army in the Peninsular War and at Waterloo. In 1848 he averted revolution by conceding a liberal constitution.

William III 1817–1890. King of the Netherlands 1849–90, the son of William II. In 1862 he abolished slavery in the Dutch East Indies.

William *the Silent* 1533–1584. Prince of Orange from 1544. Leading a revolt against Spanish rule in the Netherlands from 1573, he briefly succeeded in uniting the Catholic south and Protestant northern provinces, but the former provinces submitted to Spain while the latter formed a federation 1579 which repudiated Spanish suzerainty 1581.

William, brought up at the court of Charles V, was appointed governor of Holland by Philip II of Spain 1559, but joined the revolt of 1572 against Spain's oppressive rule and, as a Protestant from 1573, became the national leader and first ◊stadholder. He was known as "the Silent" because of his absolute discretion. He was assassinated by a Spanish agent.

Williams Roger c. 1603–1683. American colonist, founder of the Rhode Island colony 1636, based on democracy and complete religious freedom. He tried to maintain good relations with the Indians of the region, although he fought against them in the Pequot War and King Philip's War.

He came to America as a Puritan minister in Massachusetts 1631 but was banished from the colony 1635 for his "dangerous opinions;" he deplored theocracy and advocated separation of church and state. He then founded Providence 1636, disavowed Puritanism 1639, and returned to England to secure a patent with full religious freedom for his colony in the face of threats from the Puritans. He subsequently returned to Rhode Island and was the colony's president 1654–57; there he founded the first Baptist Church in America.

Williams Ted (Theodore Samuel) 1918– . US baseball player. Born in San Diego, California, Williams was signed by the Boston Red Sox and made his major league debut 1939. Named rookie of the year, Williams went on to a 19-season career with the Red Sox (interrupted by service in World War II and the Korean War), during which he established a lifetime batting average of .344. He was six times the American League batting champion and twice won the most valuable player award. In 1947 he became only the second player (Rogers ◊Hornsby was first) to twice win the Triple Crown (leading the league in batting, home runs, and runs batted in for a season). Williams retired as a player 1960 and served as manager of the Washington Senators 1969–71 and the Texas Rangers 1972. He was elected to the Baseball Hall of Fame 1966.

Williams Tennessee (Thomas Lanier) 1911–1983. US playwright, born in Mississippi. His work is characterized by fluent dialogue and searching analysis of the psychological deficiencies of his characters. His plays, usually set in the Deep South against a background of decadence and degradation, include *The Glass Menagerie* 1945, *A Streetcar Named Desire* 1947, and *Cat on a Hot Tin Roof* 1955, the last two of which earned Pulitzer Prizes.

Many of his plays have been made into successful theatrical films, several of which were directed memorably by Elia Kazan. His other plays include *Suddenly Last Summer* 1958 and *Sweet Bird of Youth* 1959. After writing *The Night of the Iguana* 1961, also awarded the Pulitzer Prize, he entered a period of ill health, and none of his subsequent plays succeeded. However, his earlier work earned him a reputation as one of America's preeminent playwrights.

Williams William Carlos 1883–1963. US poet. His spare images and language reflect everyday speech. His epic poem *Paterson* 1946–58 celebrates his hometown in New Jersey. *Pictures from Brueghel* 1963 won him, posthumously, a Pulitzer prize. His vast body of prose work includes novels, short stories, and the play *A Dream of Love* 1948. His work had a great impact on younger US poets.

Williamsburg historic city in Virginia; population (1990) 11,500. Founded 1632, capital of the colony of Virginia 1699–1779, much of it has been restored to its 18th-century appearance. The College of William and Mary 1693 is one of the oldest in the US.

Williamsport industrial city (electronics, plastics, metals, lumber, textiles, and aircraft parts) in N central Pennsylvania, on the Susquehanna River, N of Harrisburg; population (1990) 31,900. It is the birthplace 1939 of Little League baseball.

Willkie Wendell Lewis 1892–1944. US politician who was the Republican presidential candidate 1940. After losing to F D Roosevelt, he continued as a leader of the liberal wing of the Republican Party. Becoming committed to the cause of international cooperation, he published *One World* 1942.

Born in Elwood, Indiana, Willkie was educated at Indiana University, and became a lawyer 1916. After service in World War I, he became corporate counsel for a private utility and an outspoken opponent of the economic policies of the New Deal, for which reason he was nominated as the 1940 Republican presidential candidate.

willow any tree or shrub of the genus *Salix*, family Salicaceae. There are over 350 species, mostly in the northern hemisphere, and they flourish in damp places. The leaves are often lance-shaped, and the male and female catkins are found on separate trees.

North American species include black willow *S. nigra* and Pacific willow *S. lasiandra*. The weeping willow *S. babylonica* is a native of China, cultivated worldwide.

willowherb plant of the genus *Epilobium*, a perennial weed. Fireweed *E. angustifolium* is common in woods and waste places, especially after forest fires in areas bordering the Arctic. It grows to 4 ft/1.2 m with long terminal racemes of red or purplish flowers.

Wills Bob (James Robert) 1905–1975. US country fiddle player and composer. As leader of the band known from 1934 as Bob Wills and his Texas Playboys, Wills became a pioneer of ♢Western swing and a big influence on US popular music. "San Antonio Rose" 1938 is his most popular song.

Wills began playing 1920 and went on to do local radio shows, the band being named and renamed after the commercial sponsor's product (for a time they were the Light Crust Doughboys, for example). Their repertory drew on blues, popular ballads, and jazz, as well as country, with much original material.

Wills Helen Newington 1905– . US tennis player. Born in Centerville, California, Wills was educated at the University of California and won her first US women's title 1923 and her first Wimbledon championship 1927. In the course of an unparalleled amateur tennis career, Wills went on to win the US title six more times and Wimbledon seven more times. In addition to many other doubles and singles

titles, Wills won two gold medals in the 1924 Paris Olympics. From 1929 to 1937 she played under her married name, Helen Wills Moody.

Wilmington industrial port and city (chemicals, textiles, shipbuilding, iron and steel goods; headquarters of Du Pont enterprises) in Delaware; population (1990) 71,500. Founded by Swedish settlers as **Fort Christina** 1638, it was taken from the Dutch and renamed by the British 1664.

Wilmington port and industrial city (textiles, tobacco, lumber, and chemicals) in SE North Carolina, on the Cape Fear River, near the Atlantic Ocean; population (1990) 55,500. Tourism is important to the economy.

Wilms' tumour or **nephroblastoma** one of the rare cancers of infancy, arising in the kidneys. Often the only symptom is abdominal swelling. Treatment is by removal of the affected kidney (nephrectomy), followed by radiotherapy and ♢cytotoxic drugs.

Wilson Angus (Frank Johnstone) 1913–1991. English novelist, short-story writer, and biographer, whose acidly humorous books include *Anglo-Saxon Attitudes* 1956 and *The Old Men at the Zoo* 1961. In his detailed portrayal of English society he extracted high comedy from its social and moral grotesqueries.

His nonfiction includes *Emile Zola* 1952, *The World of Charles Dickens* 1970, and *The Strange Ride of Rudyard Kipling* 1977.

Wilson Charles Thomson Rees 1869–1959. British physicist who in 1911 invented the Wilson ♢cloud chamber, an apparatus for studying subatomic particles. He shared a Nobel Prize 1927.

Wilson Edmund 1895–1972. US critic and writer. Perhaps the foremost American social and literary critic of the 20th century, he was an editor of *Vanity Fair* 1920–21, the *New Republic* 1926–31, and *The New Yorker* 1944–48. Among his most influential works are *Axel's Castle* 1931, a survey of symbolism, and *The Wound and the Bow* 1941, a study of the relationship of neurosis to creativity.

Born in Red Bank, New Jersey, Wilson graduated from Princeton 1916. Other works include satirical sketches in *Memoirs of Hecate County* 1946, and two works of social history, *To the Finland Station* 1940, on revolutionary ideology, and *The American Earthquake* 1958, about the Great Depression. He edited his friend F Scott ♢Fitzgerald's posthumous *The Crack-Up* 1956. His *Patriotic Gore* 1962 surveys Civil War literature.

Wilson Edward O 1929– . US zoologist whose books have stimulated interest in biogeography, the study of the distribution of species, and sociobiology, the evolution of behavior. His works include *Sociobiology: The New Synthesis* 1975 and *On Human Nature* 1978.

Wilson (James) Harold, Baron Wilson of Rievaulx 1916– . British Labor politician, party leader from 1963, prime minister 1964–70 and 1974–76. His premiership was dominated by the issue of UK admission to membership in the European Community, the social contract (unofficial agreement with the labor unions), and economic difficulties.

Wilson, born in Huddersfield, West Yorkshire, was president of the Board of Trade 1947–51 (when he resigned because of social-service cuts). In 1963 he succeeded Hugh Gaitskell as Labor leader and became prime minister the following year, increasing his majority 1966. He formed a minority government

Feb 1974 and achieved a majority of three Oct 1974. He resigned 1976 and was succeeded by James Callaghan. He was knighted 1976 and made a peer 1983.

Wilson (Thomas) Woodrow 1856–1924. 28th president of the US 1913–21, a Democrat. He kept the US out of World War I until 1917, and in Jan 1918 issued his "Fourteen Points" as a basis for a just peace settlement. At the peace conference in Paris he secured the inclusion of the ♢League of Nations in individual peace treaties, but these were not ratified by Congress, so the US did not join the League. Nobel Peace Prize 1919.

Wilson, born in Staunton, Virginia, was educated at Princeton University, of which he became president 1902–10. In 1910 he became governor of New Jersey. Elected US president 1912 against Theodore Roosevelt and William Howard Taft, he initiated antitrust legislation and secured valuable economic and social reforms in his progressive "New Freedom" program. Wilson also instituted a federal income tax, the first since the Civil War. He strove to keep the US neutral during World War I, but the unrestricted German U-boat campaign, sensationalized by the sinking of the British liner *Lusitania* (with 128 Americans lost), forced him to declare war 1917. His refusal to compromise on the text of the League of Nations' proposal contributed to its defeat in Congress. In 1919 Wilson suffered a stroke during a nationwide campaign to gain support for the League and retired from public life.

wilting the loss of rigidity (turgor) in plants, caused by a decreasing wall pressure within the cells making up the supportive tissues. Wilting is most obvious in plants that have little or no wood.

Wimbledon English lawn-tennis center used for international championship matches, situated in south London. There are currently 18 courts.

Wimbledon: recent winners
men's singles
1983	John McEnroe *(US)*
1984	John McEnroe *(US)*
1985	Boris Becker *(West Germany)*
1986	Boris Becker *(West Germany)*
1987	Pat Cash *(Australia)*
1988	Stefan Edberg *(Sweden)*
1989	Boris Becker *(West Germany)*
1990	Stefan Edberg *(Sweden)*
1991	Michael Stich *(Germany)*
1992	Andre Agassi *(US)*

women's singles
1983	Martina Navratilova *(US)*
1984	Martina Navratilova *(US)*
1985	Martina Navratilova *(US)*
1986	Martina Navratilova *(US)*
1987	Martina Navratilova *(US)*
1988	Steffi Graf *(West Germany)*
1989	Steffi Graf *(West Germany)*
1990	Martina Navratilova *(US)*
1991	Steffi Graf *(Germany)*
1992	Steffi Graf *(Germany)*

WIMP (acronym for **windows, icons, menus, pointing** device) in computing, another name for ♢graphical user interface (GUI).

Winchell Walter 1897–1972. US journalist, born in New York. He was a columnist for the *New York Mirror* 1929–69, and his bitingly satiric writings were syndicated throughout the US.

Winchester cathedral city and administrative headquarters of Hampshire, on the river

Itchen; population (1984) 93,000. Tourism is important, and there is also light industry. Originally a Roman town, Winchester was the capital of Wessex. Winchester Cathedral is the longest medieval church in Europe and was remodeled from Norman-Romanesque to Perpendicular Gothic under the patronage of William of Wykeham (founder of Winchester College 1382), who is buried there, as are Saxon kings, the English priest St Swithun (bishop of Winchester from 852), and the writers Izaac Walton and Jane Austen.

Winchester drive in computing, a small hard-disk drive commonly used with microcomputers; **Winchester disc** has become synonymous with ◇hard disk.

wind lateral movement of the Earth's atmosphere from high- to low-pressure areas. Although modified by features such as land and water, there is a basic worldwide system of ◇trade winds, ◇Westerlies, ◇monsoons, and others.

A belt of low pressure (the ◇doldrums) lies along the equator. The trade winds blow toward this from the horse latitudes (areas of high pressure at about 30° N and 30° S of the equator), blowing from the NE in the northern hemisphere, and from the SE in the southern. The Westerlies (also from the horse latitudes) blow north of the equator from the SW and south of the equator from the NW.

Cold winds blow outwards from high-pressure areas at the poles. More local effects result from landmasses heating and cooling faster than the adjacent sea, producing onshore winds in the daytime and offshore winds at night.

The ◇monsoon is a seasonal wind of S Asia, blowing from the SW in summer and bringing the rain on which crops depend. It blows from the NE in winter.

Famous or notorious warm winds include the **chinook** of the eastern Rocky Mountains, North America; the **föhn** of Europe's Alpine valleys; the **sirocco** (Italy)/**khamsin** (Egypt)/**sharav** (Israel), spring winds that bring warm air from the Sahara and Arabian deserts across the Mediterranean; and the **Santa Ana**, a periodic warm wind from the inland deserts that strikes the California coast. The dry northerly **bise** (Switzerland) and the **mistral**, which strikes the Mediterranean area of France, are unpleasantly cold winds.

windchill factor or **windchill index** estimate of how much colder it feels when a wind is blowing. It is the sum of the temperature (in °F below zero) and the wind speed (in miles per hour). So for a wind of 15 mph at an air temperature of −5°F, the windchill factor is 20.

wind farm array of windmills or ◇wind turbines used for generating electrical power. A wind farm at Altamont Pass, California, consists of 300 wind turbines, the smallest producing 60 kW and the largest 750 kW of electricity. To produce 1,200 megawatts of electricity (an output comparable with that of a nuclear power station), a wind farm would need to occupy around 140 sq mi/370 sq km.

Denmark has built the world's first offshore wind farm, off Vindeby on Lolland Island in the North Sea.

Windhoek capital of Namibia; population (1988) 115,000. It is just north of the Tropic of Capricorn, 180 mi/290 km from the west coast.

wind instrument musical instrument that uses the performer's breath, sometimes activating a reed or reeds, to make a column

windmill *A simple tower windmill.*

of air vibrate. The pitch of the note is controlled by the length of the column. The main types are ◇woodwind instruments and ◇brass instruments.

windmill mill with sails or vanes that, by the action of wind upon them, drive machinery for grinding corn or pumping water, for example. Wind turbines, designed to use wind power on a large scale, usually have a propeller-type rotor mounted on a tall shell tower. The turbine drives a generator for producing electricity.

Windmills were used in the East in ancient times, and in Europe they were first used in Germany and the Netherlands in the 12th century. The main types of traditional windmill are the **post mill**, which is turned around a post when the direction of the wind changes, and the **tower mill**, which has a revolving turret on top. It usually has a device (fantail) that keeps the sails pointing into the wind. In the US windmills were used by the colonists and later a light type, with steel sails supported on a long steel girder shaft, was introduced for use on farms.

wind power the harnessing of wind energy to produce power. The wind has long been used as a source of energy: sailing ships and windmills are ancient inventions. After the energy crisis of the 1970s ◇wind turbines began to be used to produce electricity on a large scale. By the year 2000, 10% of Denmark's energy is expected to come from wind power.

Windsor industrial lake port (car engines, pharmaceuticals, iron and steel goods, paint, bricks) in Ontario, SE Canada, opposite Detroit, Michigan; population (1986) 254,000. It was founded as a Hudson's Bay Company post 1853.

Windsor, House of official name of the British royal family since 1917, adopted in place of Saxe-Coburg-Gotha. Since 1960 those descendants of Elizabeth II not entitled to the prefix HRH (His/Her Royal Highness) have borne the surname Mountbatten-Windsor.

Windsor town in Berkshire, S England, on the river Thames; population (1981) 28,000. It is the site of Windsor Castle and Eton College (secondary school) 1540 and has a 17th-century guildhall designed by Christopher Wren.

Windsor Duke of. Title of ◇Edward VIII.

windsurfing or **boardsailing** or **sailboarding** water sport combining elements of surfing and sailing, first developed in the US 1968. The windsurfer stands on a board that is propelled and steered by means of a sail attached to a mast that is articulated at the foot. Since 1984 the sport has been included in the Olympic Games as part of the yachting events. From 1992 men and women have to compete in separate categories. There are also annual boardsailing world championships.

wind tunnel test tunnel in which air is blown over, for example, a stationary model aircraft, motor vehicle, or locomotive to simulate the effects of movement. Lift, drag, and airflow patterns are observed by the use of special cameras and sensitive instruments. Wind-tunnel testing assesses aerodynamic design, preparatory to full-scale construction.

wind turbine windmill of advanced aerodynamic design connected to an electricity generator and used in wind-power installations. Wind turbines can be either large propeller-type rotors mounted on a tall tower, or flexible metal strips fixed to a vertical axle at top and bottom. In 1990, over 20,000 wind turbines were in use throughout the world, generating 1,600 megawatts of power.

The world's largest wind turbine is on Hawaii, in the Pacific Ocean. It has two blades 160 ft/50 m long on top of a tower 20 stories high. An example of a propeller turbine is found at Tvind in Denmark and has an output of some 2 megawatts. Other machines use novel rotors, such as the "egg-beater" design developed at Sandia Laboratories in New Mexico.

Windward Islands islands in the path of the prevailing wind, notably: **West Indies** see under ◇Antilles; ◇**Cape Verde Islands**; ◇**French Polynesia** (Tahiti, Moorea, Makatea).

wine alcoholic beverage, usually made from fermented grape pulp, although wines have also traditionally been made from many other fruits such as damsons and elderberries. **Red wine** is the product of the grape with the skin; **white wine** of the inner pulp of the grape. The sugar content is converted to ethyl alcohol by the yeast *Saccharomyces ellipsoideus*, which lives on the skin of the grape. The largest wine-producing countries are Italy, France, Russia, Georgia, Moldova, Armenia, and Spain; others include almost all European countries, Australia, South Africa, the US, and Chile.

For **dry wine** the fermentation is allowed to go on longer than for **sweet** or **medium**; ◇Champagne (sparkling wine from the Champagne region of France) is bottled while still fermenting, but other sparkling wines are artificially carbonated. Some wines are fortified with additional alcohol obtained from various sources, and with preservatives. Some of the latter may cause dangerous side effects (see ◇additive). For this reason, organic wines, containing no preservatives, have recently become popular.

A **vintage wine** is produced during a good year (as regards quality of wine, produced by favorable weather conditions) in

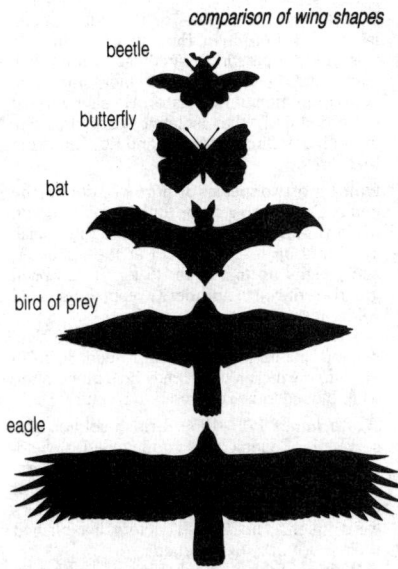

comparison of wing shapes

beetle

butterfly

bat

bird of prey

eagle

wing *Birds can fly because of the specialized shape of their wings: a rounded leading edge, flattened underneath and round on top.*

recognized vineyards of a particular area; France has a guarantee of origin (*appellation controlée*), as do Italy (*Denominazione di Origine Controllata*), Spain (*Denominacion Controllata*), and Germany (a series of graded qualities running from *Qualitätswein* to *Beerenauslese*).

The greatest alcohol concentration that yeasts can tolerate is 16%; most wines have an alcohol content of 10–12%. **Fortified wine** has had alcohol added to bring the content up to about 20%. Such wines keep well because the alcohol kills microorganisms that spoil natural wines. Port, sherry, vermouth, madeira, and Marsala are fortified after fermentation and madeira is then heated gradually.

The yellowish tinge of white wine is caused by tannin contained in the wood of the cask, oxidized while the wine matures. Red wine is mainly made from black grapes, which have a blue-black pigment under the skin that turns red in the presence of acids in the grape juice during pressing. The alcohol in the fermentation dissolves the pigment, which is carried into the wine. Tannin in the skin imparts a bitter taste to the wine.

wing in biology, the modified forelimb of birds and bats, or the membranous outgrowths of the ⟩exoskeleton of insects, which give the power of flight. Birds and bats have two wings. Bird wings have feathers attached to the fused digits ("fingers") and forearm bones, while bat wings consist of skin stretched between the digits. Most insects have four wings, which are strengthened by wing veins.

The wings of butterflies and moths are covered with scales. The hind pair of a fly's wings are modified to form two knoblike balancing organs (halteres).

Winnie-the-Pooh collection of children's stories by British author A A ⟩Milne, published 1926, illustrated by E H Shepard. The stories featured the author's son Christopher Robin, his teddy bear Winnie-the-Pooh, and a group of toy animals, Piglet, Eeyore, Rabbit, Owl, Kanga and Roo, and Tigger. Further stories appeared in *The House at Pooh Corner* 1928.

Winnipeg capital and industrial city (processed foods, textiles, transportation, and transportation equipment) in Manitoba, on the Red River, south of Lake Winnipeg; population (1986) 623,000. Established as Winnipeg 1870 on the site of earlier forts, the city expanded with the arrival of the Canadian Pacific Railroad 1881.

The city annexed several adjacent communities 1972 to become the largest Canadian city W of Toronto. The University of Manitoba and the University of Winnipeg are here.

Winnipeg, Lake lake in S Manitoba, draining much of the Canadian prairies; area 9,460 sq mi/24,500 sq km.

Winston-Salem industrial city (tobacco products, textiles, clothing, and furniture) in N central North Carolina, NE of Charlotte; population (1990) 143,500. Wake Forest University 1834 is here.

wintergreen any of several plants of the genus *Gaultheria* of the heath family Ericaceae, especially *G. procumbens* of NE North America, creeping underground and sending up tiny shoots. Oil of wintergreen, used in treating rheumatism, is extracted from its leaves. Wintergreen is also the name for various plants of the family Pyrolaceae, including the genus *Pyrola* and the green pipsissewa *Chimaphila maculata* of N North America and Eurasia.

Winter Haven city in central Florida, E of Lakeland; a center for citrus-fruit processing and shipping; population (1990) 24,700. Other industries include tourism, cigars, and alcohol.

Winter War the USSR's invasion of Finland Nov 30, 1939–March 12, 1940, also called the Russo-Finnish War.

The USSR set up a Finnish puppet government in E Karelia, but their invasion forces were at first repulsed by the greatly outnumbered Finnish troops under Marshal Mannerheim. In Feb 1940 the Finnish lines were broken by a million-strong Soviet offensive. In the March armistice Finland ceded part of Karelia to the USSR.

Winthrop John 1588–1649. American colonist and first governor of the Massachusetts Bay Colony. A devout Puritan and one of the founders of the Massachusetts Bay Company, he departed for New England with a large group of settlers 1630. He was a founder of the city of Boston the same year.

Born in England and educated at Cambridge, Winthrop studied law at Gray's Inn and became a lawyer 1628. He served as Massachusetts governor or deputy governor until his death. Deeply conservative, he favored the prosecution and banishment of Anne ⟩Hutchinson 1638. His *History of New England from 1630 to 1649* was published 1825.

wire thread of metal, made by drawing a rod through progressively smaller-diameter dies. Fine-gauge wire is used for electrical power transmission; heavier-gauge wire is used to make load-bearing cables.

Gold, silver, and bronze wire has been found in the ruins of Troy and in ancient Egyptian tombs. From early times to the 14th century, wire was made by hammering metal into sheets, cutting thin strips, and making the strips round by hammering them. The Romans made wire by hammering heated metal rods.

Wire drawing was introduced in Germany in the 14th century. In this process, a metal rod is pulled (drawn) through a small hole in a mold (die). Until the 19th century this was done by

hand; now all wire is drawn by machine. Metal rods are pulled through a series of progressively smaller tungsten carbide dies to produce large-diameter wire, and through diamond dies for very fine wire. The die is funnel-shaped, with the opening smaller than the diameter of the rod. The rod, which is pointed at one end, is coated with a lubricant to allow it to slip through the die. Pincers pull the rod through until it can be wound round a drum. The drum then rotates, drawing the wire through the die and winding it into a coil.

There are many kinds of wire for different uses: galvanized wire (coated with zinc), which does not rust; ⟩barbed wire and wire mesh for fencing; and wire cable, made by weaving thin wires into ropes. Needles, pins, nails, and rivets are made from wire.

wireworm the larva of ⟩click beetles.

Wisconsin state in N central US; nickname Badger State
area 56,163 sq mi/145,500 sq km
capital Madison
cities Milwaukee, Green Bay, Racine
features lakes: Superior, Michigan; Mississippi River; Door peninsula
products leading US dairy state; corn, hay, industrial and agricultural machinery, engines and turbines, precision instruments, paper products, automobiles and trucks, plumbing equipment
population (1990) 4,891,800
famous people Edna Ferber, Harry Houdini, Joseph McCarthy, Spencer Tracy, Orson Welles, Thornton Wilder, Frank Lloyd Wright
history explored by Jean Nicolet for France 1634; originally settled near Ashland by the French; passed to Britain 1763; included in US 1783. Wisconsin became a territory 1836 and a state 1848.

Lumbering emerged as a major industry in the late 19th century, and Milwaukee became an industrial center. Germans, Scandinavians, and Poles settled in large numbers. In the early 20th century, Wisconsin pioneered progressive legislation.

Wise Robert 1914– . US film director who began as a film editor. His debut was a horror film, *Curse of the Cat People* 1944; he progressed to such large-scale projects as *The Sound of Music* 1965 and *Star* 1968. His other films include *The Body Snatcher* 1945 and *Star Trek: The Motion Picture* 1979.

Wise Stephen Samuel 1874–1949. Hungarian-born US religious leader. He was ordained as a reform rabbi 1893 and served congregations in New York City 1893–1900 and Portland, Oregon, 1900–07. Returning to New York City 1907, he became rabbi of the Free Synagogue. An ardent Zionist, Wise attended the Versailles Peace Conference and served as president of the American Jewish Congress 1924–49.

Born in Budapest, Wise immigrated to the US with his family 1875. Educated at the City

Wisconsin

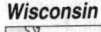

College of New York, he received a PhD from Columbia University 1901. His autobiography, *Challenging Years*, appeared 1949.

wisent another name for the European ⬦bison.

Wister Owen 1860–1938. US novelist who created the genre of the ⬦Western. He was born in Philadelphia, a grandson of the British actress Fanny Kemble, and became known for stories of cowboys, including *The Virginian* 1902. He also wrote *Roosevelt: The Story of a Friendship 1880–1919* 1930, about his relationship with US president Theodore Roosevelt.

wisteria any climbing shrub of the genus *Wisteria*, including *W. sinensis*, of the family Leguminosae, native to eastern US and east Asia. Wisterias have racemes of bluish, white, or pale mauve flowers, and pinnate leaves (leaves on either side of the stem).

Witan or **Witenagemot** council of the Anglo-Saxon kings, the forerunner of Parliament, but including only royal household officials, great landowners, and top churchmen.

witchcraft the alleged possession and exercise of magical powers—***black magic*** if used with evil intent, and ***white magic*** if benign. Its origins lie in traditional beliefs and religions. Practitioners of witchcraft have often had considerable skill in, for example, herbal medicine and traditional remedies; this prompted the World Health Organization in 1976 to recommended the integration of traditional healers into the health teams of African states.

The Christian church persecuted witches in Europe between the 15th and 17th centuries and in North America (see ⬦Salem). The last official execution of a witch in Europe was that of Anna Goddi, hanged in Switzerland in 1782. *Obi* is the witchcraft of black Africa imported to the West Indies, and includes Christian elements; ⬦voodoo is a similar cult.

witch hazel any flowering shrub or small tree of the genus *Hamamelis* of the witch-hazel family, native to North America and E Asia, especially *H. virginiana*. An astringent extract prepared from the bark or leaves is used in medicine as an eye lotion and a liniment.

witch-hunt persecution of minority political opponents or socially nonconformist groups without any regard for their guilt or innocence. Witch-hunts are often accompanied by a degree of public hysteria; for example, the ⬦McCarthy anticommunist hearings during the 1950s in the US.

withholding tax personal income tax on wages, salaries, dividends, or other income that is taxed at source to ensure that it reaches the tax authority. Those not liable to pay the tax can reclaim it by filing a tax return.

witness in law, a person who was present at some event (such as an accident, a crime, or the signing of a document) or has relevant special knowledge (such as a medical expert) and can be called on to give evidence in a court of law.

Wittelsbach Bavarian dynasty, who ruled Bavaria as dukes from 1180, electors from 1623, and kings 1806–1918.

Wittenberg town in the state of Saxony-Anhalt, Germany, on the river Elbe, SW of Berlin; population (1981) 54,000. Wittenberg university was founded 1502, but transferred to Halle 1815. Luther preached in the Stadtkirche (in

which he is buried), nailed his 95 theses to the door of the Schlosskirche 1517, and taught philosophy at the university. The artists Lucas Cranach, father and son, lived here.

Wittgenstein Ludwig 1889–1951. Austrian philosopher. *Tractatus Logico-Philosophicus* 1922 postulated the "picture theory" of language: that words represent things according to social agreement. He subsequently rejected this idea, and developed the idea that usage was more important than convention.

The picture theory said that it must be possible to break down a sentence into "atomic propositions" whose elements stand for elements of the real world. After he rejected this idea, his later philosophy developed a quite different, anthropological view of language: words are used according to different rules in a variety of human activities—different "language games" are played with them. The traditional philosophical problems arise through the assumption that words (like "exist" in the sentence "Physical objects do not really exist") carry a fixed meaning with them, independent of context.

He taught at Cambridge University, England, in the 1930s and 1940s. *Philosophical Investigations* 1953 and *On Certainty* 1969 were published posthumously.

During World War I he fought with the Austro-Hungarian army and was subsequently imprisoned in Italy to Aug 1919.

Witwatersrand or **the Rand** the economic heartland of S Transvaal, South Africa. Its reef, which stretches nearly 60 mi/100 km, produces over half the world's gold. Gold was first found there 1854. The chief city of the region is Johannesburg. Forming a watershed between the Vaal and the Olifant rivers, the Rand comprises a series of parallel ranges which extend 60 mi/100 km E–W and rise to 5,000–6,000 ft/1,525–1,830 m above sea level. Gold occurs in reefs that are mined at depths of up to 10,000 ft/3,050 m.

Wizard of Oz, The Wonderful classic US children's tale of Dorothy's journey by the yellow brick road to an imaginary kingdom, written by L Frank Baum in 1900. It had many sequels and was made into a musical film 1939 with Judy Garland.

woad biennial plant *Isatis tinctoria*, family Cruciferae, native to Europe, with arrow-shaped leaves and clusters of yellow flowers. It was formerly cultivated for a blue dye extracted from its leaves. Ancient Britons used the blue dye as a body paint in battle.

Wodehouse P(elham) G(renville) 1881–1975. English novelist, a US citizen from 1955, whose humorous novels portray the accident-prone world of such characters as the socialite Bertie Wooster and his invaluable and impeccable manservant Jeeves, and Lord Emsworth of Blandings Castle with his prize pig, the Empress of Blandings.

From 1906, Wodehouse also collaborated on the lyrics of Broadway musicals by Jerome Kern, Gershwin, and others. He spent most of his life in the US. Staying in France 1941, during World War II, he was interned by the Germans; he made some humorous broadcasts from Berlin, which were taken amiss in Britain at the time, but he was later exonerated, and was knighted 1975. His work is admired for its style and geniality, and includes *Indiscretions of Archie* 1921, *Uncle Fred in the Springtime* 1939, and *Aunts Aren't Gentlemen* 1974.

Wöhler Friedrich 1800–1882. German chemist, a student of Jöns ⬦Berzelius, who in 1828 was the first person to synthesize an organic compound (⬦urea) from an inorganic compound (ammonium cyanate). He also devised a method 1827 that isolated the metals aluminum, beryllium, yttrium, and titanium from their ores.

wolf any of two species of large wild dogs of the genus *Canis*. The gray or timber wolf *C. lupus*, of North America and Eurasia, is highly social, measures up to 3 ft/90 cm at the shoulder, and weighs up to 100 lb/45 kg. It has been greatly reduced in numbers except for isolated wilderness regions.

The red wolf *C. niger*, generally more slender and smaller (average weight about 35 lb/15 kg) and tawnier in color, may be extinct in the wild. It used to be restricted to S central US.

Wolfe James 1727–1759. British soldier who served in Canada and commanded a victorious expedition against the French general Montcalm in Québec on the Plains of Abraham, during which both commanders were killed. The British victory established their supremacy over Canada.

Wolfe fought at the battles of Dettingen, Falkirk, and ⬦Culloden. With the outbreak of the Seven Years' War (the French and Indian War in North America), he was posted to Canada and played a conspicuous part in the siege of the French stronghold of Louisburg 1758. He was promoted to major general 1759.

Wolfe Thomas 1900–1938. US novelist. He wrote four long and hauntingly powerful autobiographical novels, mostly of the South: *Look Homeward, Angel* 1929, *Of Time and the River* 1935, *The Web and the Rock* 1939, and *You Can't Go Home Again* 1940 (the last two published posthumously).

Born in Asheville, North Carolina, Wolfe studied playwriting at the University of North Carolina and Harvard University. He settled in New York City, with hopes of becoming a playwright. His first novel, *Look Homeward, Angel*, was a realistic, brutal view of the South and Southern family life, the result of six years of work with Scribner's editor Maxwell Perkins. He also wrote *The Story of a Novel* 1936 and the short-story collections *From Death to Morning* 1935 and *The Hills Beyond* 1941.

Wolfe Tom. Adopted name of Thomas Kennerly, Jr 1931– . US journalist and novelist. In the 1960s he was a founder of the "New Journalism," which brought fiction's methods to reportage. Wolfe recorded US mores and fashions in pop-style essays in, for example, *The Kandy-Kolored Tangerine-Flake Streamline Baby* 1965. His sharp social eye is applied to the New York of the 1980s in his novel *The Bonfire of the Vanities* 1988.

Born in Richmond, Virginia, Wolfe graduated from Yale University and worked at newspaper and magazine reporting. He also wrote *The Electric Kool-Aid Acid Test* 1968; *Radical Chic and Mau-Mauing the Flak Catchers* 1970; *The Painted Word* 1975, about art; *The Right Stuff* 1979, about the first US astronauts; and *From Bauhaus to Our House* 1981, about modern architecture. *The Bonfire of the Vanities* was filmed 1990.

wolfram alternate name for ⬦tungsten.

wolframite iron manganese tungstate, $(Fe,Mn)WO_4$, an ore mineral of tungsten. It is dark gray with a submetallic surface luster, and often occurs in hydrothermal veins in association with ores of tin.

Wollaston William 1766–1828. British chemist and physicist. He amassed a large fortune through his discovery in 1804 of how to make malleable platinum. He went on to discover the new elements palladium 1804 and rhodium 1805. He also contributed to optics through the invention of a number of ingenious and still useful measuring instruments.

Wollstonecraft Mary 1759–1797. British feminist, member of a group of radical intellectuals called the English Jacobins, whose book *A Vindication of the Rights of Women* 1792 demanded equal educational opportunities for women. She married William Godwin and died giving birth to a daughter, Mary (later Mary ⌂Shelley).

Wolof member of the majority ethnic group living in Senegal. There is also a Wolof minority in Gambia. There are about 2 million speakers of Wolof, a language belonging to the Niger-Congo family. The Wolof are Muslims.

The Wolof are predominantly arable farmers, and some also raise cattle. Before the French colonized the region in the 19th century, the Wolof were divided into kingdoms; the remnants of this three-tiered social structure comprising aristocracy, artisans, and slaves can still be seen.

Wolsey Thomas *c.* 1475–1530. English cleric and politician. In Henry VIII's service from 1509, he became archbishop of York 1514, cardinal and lord chancellor 1515, and began the dissolution of the monasteries. His reluctance to further Henry's divorce from Catherine of Aragon, partly because of his ambition to be pope, led to his downfall 1529. He was charged with high treason 1530 but died before being tried.

Wolverhampton industrial town (metalworking, chemicals, tires, aircraft, commercial vehicles) in West Midlands, England, 12 mi/20 km NW of Birmingham; population (1991) 239,800.

wolverine largest land member *Gulo gulo* of the weasel family (Mustelidae), found in Europe, Asia, and North America. It is stocky in build, about 3.3 ft/1 m long. Its long, thick fur is dark brown on the back and belly and lighter on the sides. It covers food that it cannot eat with an unpleasant secretion. Destruction of habitat and trapping for its fur have greatly reduced its numbers.

wombat any of a family (Vombatidae) of burrowing, herbivorous marsupials, native to Tasmania and S Australia. They are about 3.3 ft/1 m long, heavy, with a big head, short legs and tail, and coarse fur.

The two living species include the common wombat *Vombatus ursinus* of Tasmania and SE Australia, and *Lasiorhinus latifrons*, the plains wombat of S Australia.

women's movement the campaign for the rights of women, including social, political, and economic equality with men. Early European campaigners of the 17th–19th centuries fought for women's right to own property, to have access to higher education, and to vote (see ⌂suffragist). Once women's suffrage was achieved in the 20th century, the emphasis of the movement shifted to the goals of equal social and economic opportunities for women, including employment. A continuing area of concern in industrialized countries is the contradiction between the now generally accepted principle of equality and the demonstrable inequalities that remain between the sexes in state policies and in everyday life.

Pioneer 19th-century feminists, considered radical for their belief in the equality of the sexes, include Mary Wollstonecraft and Emmeline Pankhurst in the UK, and Susan B Anthony and Elizabeth Cady Stanton in the US. The women's movement gained worldwide impetus after World War II with such theorists as Simone de ⌂Beauvoir, Betty ⌂Friedan, Kate ⌂Millett, Gloria ⌂Steinem, and Germaine ⌂Greer, and the founding of the National Organization of Women (NOW) in New York 1966. From the late 1960s the radical and militant wing of the movement argued that women were oppressed by the male-dominated social structure as a whole, which they saw as pervaded by ⌂sexism, despite legal concessions toward equality of the sexes. In the US the Equal Employment Opportunity Commission, a government agency, was formed 1964 to end discrimination (including sex discrimination) in hiring. The Equal Rights Amendment (ERA), a proposed constitutional amendment prohibiting sex discrimination, was passed by Congress 1972 but failed to be ratified by the necessary majority of 38 states.

Wonder Stevie. Adopted name of Steveland Judkins Morris 1950– . US pop musician, singer, and songwriter, associated with Motown Records. Blind from birth, he had his first hit, "Fingertips," at the age of 12. Later hits, most of which he composed and sang, and on which he also played several instruments, include "My Cherie Amour" 1973, "Master Blaster (Jammin')" 1980, and the album *Innervisions* 1973.

wood the hard tissue beneath the bark of many perennial plants; it is composed of water-conducting cells, or secondary ⌂xylem, and gains its hardness and strength from deposits of ⌂lignin. **Hardwoods**, such as oak, and **softwoods**, such as pine, have commercial value as structural material and for furniture.

The central wood in a branch or stem is known as **heartwood** and is generally darker and harder than the outer wood; it consists only of dead cells. As well as providing structural support, it often contains gums, tannins, or pigments which may impart a characteristic color and increased durability. The surrounding **sapwood** is the functional part of the xylem that conducts water.

The **secondary xylem** is laid down by the vascular ⌂cambium which forms a new layer of wood annually, on the outside of the existing wood and visible as an ⌂annual ring when the tree is felled; see ⌂dendrochronology.

Commercial wood can be divided into two main types: hardwood, containing xylem vessels and obtained from angiosperms (for example, oak) and softwood, containing only ⌂tracheids, obtained from gymnosperms (for example, pine). Although in general softwoods are softer than hardwoods, this is not always the case: balsa, the softest wood known, is a hardwood, while pitch pine, very dense and hard, is a softwood. A superhard wood is produced in wood-plastic combinations (WPC), in which wood is impregnated with liquid plastic (monomer) and the whole is then bombarded with gamma rays to polymerize the plastic.

Wood Grant 1892–1942. US painter based mainly in his native Iowa. Though his work is highly stylized, he struck a note of hard realism in his studies of farmers, such as *American Gothic* 1930 (Art Institute, Chicago).

He also painted landscapes and somewhat humorous scenes: for example, *Daughters of Revolution* 1932 (Cincinnati Art Museum), which satirized membership in patriotic societies.

Wood Natalie. Adopted name of Natasha Gurdin 1938–1981. US film actress who began as a child star. Her films include *Miracle on 34th Street* 1947, *Rebel Without a Cause* 1955, *The Searchers* 1956, and *Bob and Carol and Ted and Alice* 1969.

Other films include *Splendor in the Grass* 1961 and *Gypsy* 1962. She was married to actor Robert Wagner and died by drowning.

woodcarving art form practiced in many parts of the world since prehistoric times: for example, the NW Pacific coast of North America, in the form of totem poles, and W Africa, where there is a long tradition of woodcarving, notably in Nigeria. Woodcarvings survive less often than sculpture in stone or metal because of the comparative fragility of the material.

Ancient woodcarvings have been preserved in hot, dry (Egypt, China) and cool, wet (Scandinavian bogs, estuarine) conditions.

woodcock either of two species of wading birds, genus *Scolopax*, of the family Scolopacidae, which have barred plumage, long bills, and live in wet woodland areas.

The American woodcock *S. minor*, about 11 in/28 cm long, is shortlegged and short-necked, with a long, straight bill. It nests in moist woodlands and thickets throughout E North America. The Eurasian woodcock *S. rusticola*, somewhat larger, is similar in appearance and habits.

woodcut print made by a woodblock in which a picture or design has been cut in relief. The woodcut is the oldest method of ⌂printing, invented in China in the 5th century AD. In the Middle Ages woodcuts became popular in Europe, illustrating early printed books and broadsides.

The German artist Dürer was an early exponent of the technique. Multicolored woodblock prints were developed in Japan in the mid-18th century.

woodland area in which trees grow more or less thickly; generally smaller than a forest. Temperate climates, with four distinct seasons a year, tend to support a mixed woodland habitat, with some conifers but mostly broad-leaved and deciduous trees, shedding their leaves in autumn and regrowing them in spring. In the Mediterranean region and parts of the southern hemisphere, the trees are mostly evergreen.

Temperate woodlands grow in the zone between the cold coniferous forest and the tropical forests of the hotter climates near the equator. They develop in areas where the closeness of the sea keeps the climate mild and moist.

Old woodland can rival tropical rainforest in the number of species it supports, but most of the species are hidden in the soil. A study in Oregon 1991 found that the soil in a single woodland location contained 8,000 arthropod species (such as insects, mites, centipedes, and millipedes), compared with only 143 species of reptile, bird, and mammal in the forest above.

woodlouse any of the several families of mostly terrestrial crustaceans of the order Isopoda (especially the sow bugs, genera *Onisais* and *Porcellio*) that live in damp places under rocks or fallen timber. They have rounded oval, evenly segmented bodies and flat undersides. Some species of sow bugs can roll up when threatened. The pillbugs (family Armadillidiidae) typically roll up. Rock slaters (family Ligiidae) are amphibious on ocean beaches.

woodpecker bird of the family Picidae, which drills holes in trees to obtain insects. There are about 200 species worldwide. The largest of these, the imperial woodpecker *Campephilus imperialis* of Mexico, is very rare and may already be extinct.

North American woodpeckers include four species of sapsuckers (genus *Sphyrapicus*), which drill and then tap holes in trees for sap and the attracted insects. The pileated woodpecker *Dryocopus pileatus* is the largest, about 17 in/43 cm long, with a red crest.

wood pulp wood that has been processed into a pulpy mass of fibers. Its main use is for making paper, but it is also used in making ⟡rayon and other cellulose fibers and plastics.

There are two methods of making wood pulp: mechanical and chemical. In the former, debarked logs are ground with water (to prevent charring) by rotating grindstones; the wood fibers are physically torn apart. In the latter, log chips are digested with chemicals (such as sodium sulfite). The chemicals dissolve the material holding the fibers together.

Woodstock the first free rock festival, held near Bethel, New York State, over three days in Aug 1969. It was attended by 400,000 people, and performers included the Band, Country Joe and the Fish, the Grateful Dead, Jimi Hendrix, Jefferson Airplane, and the Who. The festival was a landmark in the youth culture of the 1960s (see ⟡hippie) and was recorded in the film *Woodstock*.

Woodward Robert 1917–1979. US chemist who worked on synthesizing a large number of complex molecules. These included quinine 1944, cholesterol 1951, chlorophyll 1960, and vitamin B$_{12}$ 1971. Nobel Prize 1965.

Woodward worked throughout his career at Harvard University, Boston.

woodwind musical instrument from which sound is produced by blowing into a tube, causing the air within to vibrate. Woodwind instruments include those, like the flute, originally made of wood but now more commonly of metal. The saxophone, made of metal, is an honorary woodwind because it is related to the clarinet. The oboe, bassoon, flute, and clarinet make up the normal woodwind section of an orchestra.

Woodwind instruments fall into two categories: **reed instruments**, in which air passes via an aperture controlled by a vibrating flexible reed or pair of reeds; and those **without a reed** where air is simply blown into or across a tube. In both cases, different notes are obtained by changing the length of the tube by covering holes along it. Reed instruments include clarinet, oboe (evolved from the medieval shawm and hautboy), cor anglais, saxophone, and bassoon. In recorder, flute, and piccolo, the function of a reed is achieved by design of the mouthpiece.

There is an enormous variety of woodwind instruments throughout the world.

woodworm common name for the larval stage of certain wood-boring beetles. Dead or injured trees are their natural target, but they also attack structural timber and furniture.

Included are the furniture beetle *Anobium punctatum*, which attacks older timber; the powder-post beetle genus *Lyctus*, which attacks

newer timber; the ⟡deathwatch beetle, whose presence always coincides with fungal decay; and wood-boring ⟡weevils. Special wood preservatives have been developed to combat woodworm infestation, which has markedly increased since about 1950.

wool the natural hair covering of the sheep, and also of the llama, angora goat, and some other ⟡mammals. The domestic sheep *Ovis aries* provides the great bulk of the fibers used in (textile) commerce. Lanolin is a by-product.

Sheep have been bred for their wool since ancient times. Hundreds of breeds were developed in the Middle East, Europe, and Britain over the centuries, several dozen of which are still raised for their wool today. Most of the world's finest wool comes from the merino sheep, originally from Spain. In 1797 it was introduced into Australia, which has become the world's largest producer of merino wool; South Africa and South America are also large producers. Wools from crossbred sheep (usually a cross of one of the British breeds with a merino) are produced in New Zealand. Since the 1940s, blendings of wool with synthetic fibers have been developed for textiles.

Woolcott Marion Post 1910–1990. US documentary photographer best known for her work for the Farm Security Administration (with Walker ⟡Evans and Dorothea ⟡Lange), showing the conditions of poor farmers in the late 1930s in Kentucky and the deep South.

Woolf Virginia (born Virginia Stephen) 1882–1941. English novelist and critic. Her first novel, *The Voyage Out* 1915, explored the tensions experienced by women who want marriage and

flute   oboe   bassoon

cor anglais   clarinet

piccolo

woodwind *The instruments in the woodwind section of a modern symphony orchestra have metal keys that are depressed over the holes in the instrument to obtain the different notes.*

a career. In *Mrs Dalloway* 1925 she perfected her "stream of consciousness" technique. Among her later books are *To the Lighthouse* 1927, *Orlando* 1928, and *The Years* 1937, which considers the importance of economic independence for women.

Woollcott Alexander 1887–1943. US theater critic and literary figure. He was *The New York Times*'s theater critic 1914–22, a regular contributor to *The New Yorker* from its inception 1925, and hosted the radio interview program *Town Crier* 1929–42. He appeared on stage in *The Man Who Came to Dinner* 1939 as a character based on himself. Woollcott was a member of the Algonquin Hotel Round Table of wits in New York City, together with Robert Benchley and Dorothy Parker.

Woollcott was born in Phalanx, New Jersey, educated at Hamilton College and joined the staff of the *Times* 1909. Later he worked as a theater critic for the New York *Herald*, *Sun*, and *World*, and wrote several books, including *While Rome Burns* 1934.

Woolley (Charles) Leonard 1880–1960. British archeologist. He excavated at Carchemish in Syria, Tell el Amarna in Egypt, Atchana (the ancient Alalakh) on the Turkish-Syrian border, and Ur in Iraq. He is best remembered for the work on Ur, which he carried out for the British Museum and Pennsylvania University Museum 1922–29. Besides his scholarly excavation reports he published popular accounts of his work—*Ur of the Chaldees* 1929 and *Digging Up the Past* 1930—which helped to promote archeology to a non-specialist audience.

Woolsey Theodore Dwight 1801–1889. US educator. He served as president of Yale 1846–71 and oversaw its expansion into a modern university with specialized departments and graduate degrees. After his retirement as president, Woolsey remained a member of the Yale Corporation 1871–85. Later in life he became increasingly interested in questions of politics and law. He was the author of *Political Science* 1878 and *Communism and Socialism* 1880.

Born in New York and educated at Yale University, Woolsey studied classics in Europe and was appointed to the Yale faculty as a professor of Greek 1831.

Woolworth Frank Winfield 1852–1919. US entrepreneur. He opened his first successful "five and ten cent" store in Lancaster, Pennsylvania, in 1879, and, together with his brother C S Woolworth (1856–1947), built up a chain of similar stores throughout the US, the UK, and Europe.

Woonsocket industrial city (rubber, chemicals, woolen goods) in N Rhode Island, on the Blackstone River, NW of Providence; population (1990) 43,900.

Worcester cathedral city with industries (gloves, shoes, Worcester sauce; Royal Worcester porcelain from 1751) in Hereford and Worcester, W central England, administrative headquarters of the county, on the river Severn; population (1991) 81,000. The cathedral dates from the 13th and 14th centuries. The birthplace of the composer Elgar at nearby Broadheath is a museum. At the **Battle of Worcester** 1651 Cromwell defeated Charles I.

Worcester industrial port (textiles, engineering, printing) in central Massachusetts, on the Blackstone River; population (1990) 169,800. It was permanently settled 1713.

Educational institutions include Clark University and Worcester Polytechnic Institute.

word in computing, a group of bits (binary digits) that a computer's central processing unit treats as a single working unit. The size of a word varies from one computer to another and, in general, increasing the word length leads to a faster and more powerful computer. In the late 1970s and early 1980s, most microcomputers were 8-bit machines. During the 1980s 16-bit microcomputers were introduced and 32-bit microcomputers are now available. Mainframe computers may be 32-bit or 64-bit machines.

word processor in computing, a program that allows the input, amendment, manipulation, storage, and retrieval of text; or a computer system that runs such software. Since word-processing programs became available to microcomputers, the method has been gradually replacing the typewriter for producing letters or other text.

Typical facilities include insert, delete, cut and paste, reformat, search and replace, copy, print, mail merge, and spelling check.

Wordsworth William 1770–1850. English Romantic poet. In 1797 he moved with his sister Dorothy to Somerset to be near ▷Coleridge, collaborating with him on *Lyrical Ballads* 1798 (which included "Tintern Abbey"). From 1799 he lived in the Lake District, and later works include *Poems* 1807 (including "Intimations of Immortality") and *The Prelude* (written by 1805, published 1850). He was appointed poet laureate in 1843.

Wordsworth was born in Cockermouth, Cumbria, and educated at Cambridge University. In 1791 he returned from a visit to France, having fallen in love with Marie-Anne Vallon, who bore him an illegitimate daughter. In 1802 he married Mary Hutchinson. *The Prelude* was written to form part of the autobiographical work *The Recluse*, never completed.

work in physics, a measure of the result of transferring energy from one system to another to cause an object to move. Work should not be confused with ▷energy (the capacity to do work, which is also measured in ▷joules) or with ▷power (the rate of doing work, measured in joules per second).

Work W is equal to the product of the force F used and the distance d moved by the object in the direction of that force ($W = F \times d$). For example, the work done when a force of 10 newtons moves an object 5 meters against some sort of resistance is 50 newton-meters (=50 joules).

Works Progress Administration (WPA, renamed **Works Projects Administration** 1939) in US history, a government initiative to reduce unemployment during the Depression (11 million in 1934). Formed 1935, it provided useful work for 8.5 million people during its eight-year existence, mainly in construction projects, at a total cost of $11 billion, and was discontinued only in 1943 when the change to a war economy eliminated unemployment. The WPA was an integral part of President Roosevelt's ▷New Deal.

World Bank popular name for the *International Bank for Reconstruction and Development* specialized agency of the United Nations that borrows in the commercial market and lends on commercial terms. It was established 1945 under the 1944 Bretton Woods agreement, which also created the International Monetary Fund. The *International Development Association* is an arm of the World Bank.

The World Bank now earns almost as much money from interest and loan repayments as it hands out in new loans every year. Over 60% of the bank's loans go to suppliers outside the borrower countries for such things as consultancy services, oil, and machinery. Control of the bank is vested in a board of executives representing national governments, whose votes are apportioned according to the amount they have funded the bank. Thus the US has nearly 20% of the vote and always appoints the board's president.

In 1989 the World Bank made a net transfer of $42.9 billion to developing countries.

World Council of Churches (WCC) international organization aiming to bring together diverse movements within the Christian church. Established 1945, it has a membership in more than 100 countries and more than 300 churches; headquarters in Geneva, Switzerland.

The supreme governing body, the assembly, meets every seven or eight years to frame policy. A 150-member central committee meets once a year and a 22-member executive committee twice a year.

World Health Organization (WHO) agency of the United Nations established 1946 to prevent the spread of diseases and to eradicate them. It has a staff of about 4,500. Its headquarters are in Geneva, Switzerland.

World Intellectual Property Organization (WIPO) specialist agency of the United Nations established 1974 to coordinate the international protection (initiated by the Paris convention 1883) of inventions, trademarks, and industrial designs, and also literary and artistic works (as initiated by the Berne convention 1886).

World Meteorological Organization agency, part of the United Nations since 1950, that promotes the international exchange of weather information through the establishment of a worldwide network of meteorological stations. It was founded as the International Meteorological Organization 1873, and its headquarters are now in Geneva, Switzerland.

World Series annual ▷baseball competition between the winning teams of the National League (NL) and American League (AL). It is a best-of-seven series played each Oct. The first World Series was played 1903 (as a best-of-nine series): the AL's Boston Pilgrims defeated the NL's Pittsburgh Pirates in eight games.

World War I 1914–1918. War between Central European Powers (Germany, Austria-Hungary, and allies) on one side and the Triple Entente (Britain and the British Empire, France, and Russia) and their allies, including the US (which entered 1917), on the other side. An estimated 10 million lives were lost and twice that number were wounded. It was fought on the eastern and western fronts, in the Middle East, Africa, and at sea. Towards the end of the war Russia withdrew because of the Russian Revolution 1917. The peace treaty of Versailles 1919 was the formal end to the war. *1914 outbreak* On June 28 the heir to the Austrian throne was assassinated in Sarajevo, Serbia; on July 28 Austria declared war on Serbia; as Russia mobilized, Germany declared war on Russia and France, taking a short cut in the west by invading Belgium; on Aug 4 Britain declared war on Germany; dominions within the Empire, including Australia, were automatically involved.

Western Front The German advance reached within a few miles of Paris, but an Allied counterattack at the Marne drove them back to the Aisne River; the opposing lines then settled into trench warfare.

Eastern Front The German commander Hindenburg halted the Russian advance through the Ukraine and across Austria–Hungary at the Battle of Tannenberg in E Prussia.

Africa On Sept 16 all Germany's African colonies were in Allied hands.

Middle East On Nov 1 Turkey entered the war on the side of the Central Powers and soon attacked Russia in the Caucasus Mountains.

1915 Western Front Several offensives on both sides resulted in insignificant gains. At Ypres, Belgium, the Germans used poison gas for the first time.

Eastern Front The German field marshals Mackensen and Hindenburg drove back the Russians and took Poland.

Middle East British attacks against Turkey in Mesopotamia (Iraq), the Dardanelles, and at Gallipoli (where 7,600 Anzacs were killed) were all unsuccessful.

Italy Italy declared war on Austria; Bulgaria joined the Central Powers.

war at sea Germany declared all-out U-boat war, but the sinking of the British ocean liner *Lusitania* (with Americans among the 1,198 lost) led to demands that the US enter the war.

1916 Western Front The German attack at Verdun was countered by the Allies on the river Somme, where tanks were used for the first time.

Eastern Front Romania joined the Allies but was soon overrun by Germany.

Middle East Kut-al-Imara, Iraq, was taken from the British by the Turks.

war at sea The Battle of Jutland between England and Germany, although indecisive, put a stop to further German naval participation in the war.

1917 The US entered the war in April. British and Empire troops launched the third battle at Ypres and by Nov had taken Passchendaele.

1918 Eastern Front On March 3 Soviet Russia signed the Treaty of Brest-Litovsk with Germany, ending Russian participation in the war (the Russian Revolution 1917 led into their civil war 1918–21).

Western Front Germany began a final offensive. In April the Allies appointed the French marshal Foch supreme commander, but by June (when the first US troops went into battle) the Allies had lost all gains since 1915, and the Germans were on the river Marne. The battle at Amiens marked the launch of the victorious Allied offensive.

Italy At Vittorio Veneto the British and Italians finally defeated the Austrians.

German capitulation This began with naval mutinies at Kiel, followed by uprisings in the major cities. Kaiser Wilhelm II abdicated, and on Nov 11 the armistice was signed.

1919 June 18, peace treaty of Versailles. (The US signed a separate peace accord with Germany and Austria 1921.)

World War II 1939–1945. War between Germany, Italy, and Japan (the Axis powers) on one side, and Britain, the Commonwealth, France, the US, the USSR, and China (the Allied powers) on the other. An estimated 55 million lives were lost, 20 million of them citizens of the USSR. The war was fought in the Atlantic and Pacific theaters. In 1945, Germany surrendered (May) but Japan fought on until the US dropped atomic bombs on Hiroshima and Nagasaki (Aug).

1939 Sept German invasion of Poland; Britain and France declared war on Germany; the USSR invaded Poland; fall of Warsaw (Poland divided between Germany and USSR).
Nov The USSR invaded Finland.
1940 March Soviet peace treaty with Finland.
April Germany occupied Denmark, Norway, the Netherlands, Belgium, and Luxembourg. In Britain, a coalition government was formed under Churchill.
May Germany outflanked the defensive French Maginot Line.
May–June Evacuation of 337,131 Allied troops from Dunkirk, France, across the Channel to England.
June Italy declared war on Britain and France; the Germans entered Paris; the French prime minister Pétain signed an armistice with Germany and moved the seat of government to Vichy.
July–Oct Battle of Britain between British and German air forces.
Sept Japanese invasion of French ⟩Indochina.
Oct Abortive Italian invasion of Greece.
1941 April Germany occupied Greece and Yugoslavia.
June Germany invaded the USSR; Finland declared war on the USSR.
July The Germans entered Smolensk, USSR.
Dec The Germans came within 25 mi/40 km of Moscow, with Leningrad (now St Petersburg) under siege. First Soviet counteroffensive. Japan bombed Pearl Harbor, Hawaii, and declared war on the US and Britain. Germany and Italy declared war on the US.
1942 Jan Japanese conquest of the Philippines.
June Naval battle of Midway, the turning point of the Pacific War.
Aug German attack on Stalingrad (now Volgograd), USSR.
Oct–Nov Battle of El Alamein in N Africa, turn of the tide for the Western Allies.
Nov Soviet counteroffensive on Stalingrad.
1943 Jan The Casablanca Conference issued the Allied demand of unconditional surrender; the Germans retreated from Stalingrad.
March The USSR drove the Germans back to the river Donetz.
May End of Axis resistance in N Africa.
July A coup by King Victor Emmanuel and Marshal Badoglio forced Mussolini to resign.
Aug Beginning of the campaign against the Japanese in Burma (now Myanmar); US Marines landed on Guadalcanal, Solomon Islands.
Sept Italy surrendered to the Allies; Mussolini was rescued by the Germans who set up a Republican Fascist government in N Italy; Allied landings at Salerno; the USSR retook Smolensk.
Oct Italy declared war on Germany.
Nov The US Navy defeated the Japanese in the Battle of Guadalcanal.
Nov–Dec The Allied leaders met at the Tehran Conference.
1944 Jan Allied landing in Nazi-occupied Italy: Battle of Anzio.
March End of the German U-boat campaign in the Atlantic.
May Fall of Monte Cassino, S Italy.
June 6 D-day: Allied landings in Nazi-occupied and heavily defended Normandy.
July The bomb plot by German generals against Hitler failed.
Aug Romania joined the Allies.
Sept Battle of Arnhem on the Rhine; Soviet armistice with Finland.

Oct The Yugoslav guerrilla leader Tito and Soviets entered Belgrade.
Dec German counteroffensive, Battle of the Bulge.
1945 Feb The Soviets reached the German border; Yalta conference; Allied bombing campaign over Germany (Dresden destroyed); the US reconquest of the Philippines was completed; the Americans landed on Iwo Jima, south of Japan.
April Hitler committed suicide; Mussolini was captured by Italian partisans and shot.
May German surrender to the Allies.
June US troops completed the conquest of Okinawa (one of the Japanese Ryukyu Islands).
July The Potsdam Conference issued an Allied ultimatum to Japan.
Aug Atom bombs were dropped by the US on Hiroshima and Nagasaki; Japan surrendered.

World Wide Fund for Nature (WWF, formerly the *World Wildlife Fund*) international organization established 1961 to raise funds for conservation by public appeal. Projects include conservation of particular species, for example, the tiger and giant panda, and special areas, such as the Simen Mountains, Ethiopia.

The WWF has been criticized for investing in environmentally destructive companies, but the organization announced that this would cease. In 1990, it had 3.7 million members in 28 countries. Its headquarters are in Gland, Switzerland.

World Wildlife Fund former and US name of the *World Wide Fund for Nature*.

worm any of various elongated limbless invertebrates belonging to several phyla. Worms include the ⟩flatworms, such as ⟩flukes and ⟩tapeworms; the roundworms or ⟩nematodes, such as the eelworm and the hookworm; the marine ribbon worms or nemerteans; and the segmented worms or ⟩annelids.

In 1979, giant sea worms about 10 ft/3 m long, living within tubes created by their own excretions, were discovered in hydrothermal vents 8,000 ft/2,450 m beneath the Pacific NE of the Galápagos Islands.

WORM (acronym for *write once read many* times) in computing, a storage device, similar to ⟩CD-ROM. The computer can write to the disk directly, but cannot later erase or overwrite the same area. WORMs are mainly used for archiving and backup copies.

Worms industrial town in Rhineland-Palatinate, Germany, on the Rhine; population (1984) 73,000. Liebfraumilch wine is produced here. The Protestant reformer Luther appeared before the *Diet* (Assembly) *of Worms* 1521 and was declared an outlaw by the Roman Catholic church.

wormwood any plant of the genus *Artemisia*, family Compositae, especially the aromatic herb *A. absinthium*, the leaves of which are used in ⟩absinthe. ⟩Tarragon is a member of this genus.

Wounded Knee site on the Oglala Sioux Reservation, South Dakota, of a confrontation between the US Army and American Indians. Sitting Bull was killed, supposedly resisting arrest, on Dec 15, 1890, and on Dec 29 a group of Indians involved in the Ghost Dance Movement (aimed at resumption of Indian control of North America with the aid of the spirits of dead braves) were surrounded and 153 killed.

In 1973 the militant American Indian Movement, in the siege of Wounded Knee Feb 27–May 8, held hostages and demanded a government investigation of the Indian treaties.

W particle type of ⟩elementary particle.

wpm abbreviation for *words per minute*.

wrack any of the large brown ⟩seaweeds characteristic of rocky shores. The bladder wrack *Fucus vesiculosus* has narrow, branched fronds up to 3.3 ft/1 m long, with oval air bladders, usually in pairs on either side of the midrib or central vein.

Wrangel Ferdinand Petrovich, Baron von 1794–1870. Russian vice admiral and Arctic explorer, after whom Wrangel Island (Ostrov Vrangelya) in the Soviet Arctic is named.

wrasse any bony fish of the family Labridae, found in temperate and tropical seas. They are slender and often brightly colored, with a single long dorsal fin. They have elaborate courtship rituals, and some species can change their coloring and sex. Species vary in size from 2 in/5 cm to 6.5 ft/2 m.

The hogfish *Labrus maximus*, found along S Atlantic shores of North America, is a fine food fish up to 2 ft/0.6 m long, with rapidly changing reddish colors.

wren any of a family (Troglodytidae) of small birds of order Passeriformes, with slender, slightly curved bills, and uptilted tails.

The house wren of North America *Troglodytes aedon* is common in brush, farmyard, and park.

Wren Christopher 1632–1723. English architect, designer of St Paul's Cathedral, London, built 1675–1710; many London churches including St Bride's, Fleet Street, and St Mary-le-Bow, Cheapside; the Royal Exchange; Marlborough House; and the Sheldonian Theater, Oxford.

Wren studied mathematics, and in 1660 became a professor of astronomy at Oxford University. His opportunity as an architect came after the Great Fire of London 1666. He prepared a plan for rebuilding the city, but it was not adopted. Instead, Wren was commissioned to rebuild 51 City churches and St Paul's Cathedral. The west towers of Westminster Abbey, often attributed to him, were the design of his pupil Nicholas Hawksmoor (1661-1736).

wrestling sport popular in ancient Egypt, Greece, and Rome, and included in the Olympics from 704 BC. The two main modern international styles are *Greco-Roman*, concentrating on above-waist holds, and *freestyle*, which allows the legs to be used to hold or trip; in both the aim is to throw the opponent to the ground.

Many countries have their own forms of wrestling. *Glima* is unique to Iceland; *Kushti* is the national style practiced in Iran; *Schwingen* has been practiced in Switzerland for hundreds of years; and ⟩sumo is the national sport of Japan. World championships for freestyle wrestling have existed since 1951 and since 1921 for Greco-Roman style. Greco-Roman was included in the first Olympic program 1896; freestyle made its debut 1904. Competitors are categorized according to weight: there are ten weight divisions in each style of wrestling.

Wright Frank Lloyd 1869–1959. US architect who rejected Neo-Classicist styles for "organic architecture," in which buildings reflected their natural surroundings. Among his buildings are his Wisconsin home Taliesin East 1925; Falling Water, near Pittsburgh,

Pennsylvania, 1936, a house built straddling a waterfall; and the Guggenheim Museum, New York, 1959.

Wright also designed buildings in Japan from 1915 to 1922, most notably the Imperial Hotel in Tokyo 1922. In 1938 he built his winter home in the Arizona desert, Taliesin West, and established an architectural community there. He always designed the interiors and furnishings for his projects, to create a total environment for his patrons.

Wright was a student of Louis ⍉Sullivan 1888–93. Other Wright buildings include the Robie house 1909 in Chicago; the Johnson Wax Company Administration building, Racine, Wisconsin, 1938, and the company's Laboratory Tower 1949; and the high-rise Price Company Tower, Bartlesville, Oklahoma, 1953.

Wright Orville 1871–1948 and Wilbur 1867–1912. US inventors; brothers who pioneered piloted, powered flight. Inspired by Otto ⍉Lilienthal's gliding, they perfected their piloted glider 1902. In 1903 they built a powered machine, a 12-hp 750-lb/341-kg plane, and became the first to make a successful powered flight, near Kitty Hawk, North Carolina. Orville flew 120 ft/36.6 m in 12 sec; Wilbur, 852 ft/260 m in 59 sec.

Both brothers were born in Dayton, Ohio, and became interested in flight at early ages. They devised a wing-control system and added a rudder and a balancing tail to existing gliders. By 1903 they had built and flown a power-driven plane; they received a patent in 1906 and in 1909 set up the American Wright Corp to produce planes for the War Department. After Wilbur's death Orville did research and served on the National Advisory Committee for Aeronautics 1915–48.

Wright Richard 1908–1960. US novelist. He was one of the first to depict the condition of black people in 20th-century US society with *Native Son* 1940 and the autobiography *Black Boy* 1945.

Between 1932 and 1944 he was active in the Communist Party. Shortly thereafter he became a permanent expatriate in Paris. His other works include *White Man, Listen!* 1957, originally a series of lectures.

Wright Sewall 1889–1988. US geneticist and statistician. During the 1920s he helped modernize Charles ⍉Darwin's theory of evolution, using statistics to model the behavior of populations of genes.

Wright's work on genetic drift centered on a phenomenon occurring in small isolated colonies where the chance disappearance of some types of gene leads to evolution without the influence of natural selection.

writ in law, a document issued by a court requiring performance of certain actions.

Examples include a writ of ⍉habeas corpus, a writ of certiorari by which the US Supreme Court calls up cases from inferior courts for review, or writ of attachment of property in civil litigation.

writing any written form of communication using a set of symbols: see ⍉alphabet, ⍉cuneiform, ⍉hieroglyphic. The last two used ideographs (picture writing) and phonetic word symbols side by side, as does modern Chinese. Syllabic writing, as in Japanese, develops from the continued use of a symbol to represent the sound of a short word. Some 8,000-year-old inscriptions, thought to be pictographs, were found on animal bones and tortoise shells in Henan province, China, at a Neolithic site at Jiahu. They are thought to predate by 2,500 years the oldest known writing (Mesopotamian cuneiform of 3,500 BC).

Wroclaw industrial river port in Poland, on the river Oder; population (1990) 643,200. Under the German name of **Breslau**, it was the capital of former German Silesia. Industries include shipbuilding, engineering, textiles, and electronics.

wrought iron fairly pure iron containing some beads of slag, widely used for construction work before the days of cheap steel. It is strong, tough, and easy to machine. It is made in a puddling furnace, invented by Henry Colt in England 1784. Pig iron is remelted and heated strongly in air with iron ore, burning out the carbon in the metal, leaving relatively pure iron and a slag containing impurities. The resulting pasty metal is then hammered to remove as much of the remaining slag as possible. It is still used in fences and grating.

wt abbreviation for *weight*.

Wuchang former city in China; amalgamated with ⍉Wuhan.

Wuhan river port and capital of Hubei province, China, at the confluence of the Han and Chang Jiang rivers, formed 1950 as one of China's greatest industrial areas by the amalgamation of Hankou, Hanyang, and Wuchang; population (1989) 3,710,000. It produces iron, steel, machine tools, textiles, and fertilizer.

A center of revolt in both the Taiping Rebellion 1851–65 and the 1911 revolution, it had an anti-Mao revolt 1967 during the Cultural Revolution.

Wuhsien alternative transliteration for ⍉Suzhou, a city in China.

Wundt Wilhelm Max 1832–1920. German physiologist who regarded psychology as the study of internal experience or consciousness. His main psychological method was introspection; he also studied sensation, perception of space and time, and reaction times.

Württemberg former kingdom (1805–1918) in SW Germany that joined the German Reich 1870. Its capital was Stuttgart. Divided in 1946 between the administrative West German *Länder* of Württemberg-Baden and Württemberg-Hohenzollern, from 1952 it was part of the *Land* of ⍉Baden-Württemberg.

Wuthering Heights novel by Emily Brontë, published in the UK 1847, that chronicles the tumultuous relationship of Heathcliff and Catherine.

Heathcliff is taken in as a child by the Earnshaw family and forms an intense relationship with Catherine Earnshaw but is cruelly treated by her brother Hindley. Heathcliff flees, believing Catherine has rejected him, but returns after a few years to wreak his revenge. He marries Isabella, sister of Catherine's husband, and when Catherine dies in childbirth, Heathcliff forces her daughter Cathy to marry his son Linton. When Linton dies, Cathy turns to Hindley's son Hareton.

WV abbreviation for the state of ⍉*West Virginia*.

WY abbreviation for the state of ⍉*Wyoming*.

Wyatt Thomas c. 1503–1542. English poet. He was employed on diplomatic missions by Henry VIII, and in 1536 was imprisoned for a time in the Tower of London, suspected of having been the lover of Henry's second wife, Anne Boleyn. In 1541 Wyatt was again imprisoned on charges of treason. With the Earl of Surrey, he pioneered the sonnet in England.

Wycherley William 1640–1710. English Restoration playwright. His first comedy, *Love in a Wood*, won him court favor 1671, and later bawdy works include *The Country Wife* 1675 and *The Plain Dealer* 1676.

Wycliffe John c. 1320–1384. English religious reformer. He attacked abuses in the church, maintaining that the Bible rather than the church was the supreme authority. He criticized such fundamental doctrines as priestly absolution, confession, and indulgences, and set disciples to work on translating the Bible into English. He sent out bands of traveling preachers, but was denounced as a heretic, but died peacefully at Lutterworth.

Wyeth Andrew (Newell) 1917– . US painter. His portraits and landscapes, usually in watercolor or tempera, are naturalistic, minutely detailed, and often have a strong sense of the isolation of the countryside: for example, *Christina's World* 1948 (Museum of Modern Art, New York).

Born in Chadds Ford, Pennsylvania, the son of artist-illustrator N C ⍉Wyeth, he is among the most popular of contemporary US artists. His paintings depict people of the land, especially Wyeth's own surroundings in Chadds Ford and Maine, where his summer home is located. His son James Browning Wyeth (1946–) is also an artist.

Wyeth N(ewel) C(onvers) 1882–1944. US artist, the foremost US illustrator of his time as well as an accomplished muralist. He was born in Needham, Massachusetts, and trained by illustrator Howard Pyle. Wyeth illustrated over 20 children's classics, including *Treasure Island*, *The Adventures of Tom Sawyer*, *Robin Hood*, and *The Yearling*. Among his students were his daughter Henriette and his son Andrew Wyeth.

Wyler William 1902–1981. German-born film director who lived in the US from 1922. He directed *Wuthering Heights* 1939, *Mrs Miniver* 1942, *Ben-Hur* 1959, and *Funny Girl* 1968, among others.

Wyndham John. Adopted name of John Wyndham Parkes Lucas Beynon Harris 1903–1969. English science-fiction writer who wrote *The Day of the Triffids* 1951, *The Chrysalids* 1955, and *The Midwich Cuckoos* 1957. A recurrent theme in his work is people's response to disaster, whether caused by nature, aliens, or human error.

Wynne-Edwards Vera 1906– . English zoologist who argued that animal behavior is often altruistic and that animals will behave for the good of the group, even if this entails individual sacrifice. Her study *Animal Dispersal in Relation to Social Behaviour* was published 1962.

Wyoming state in W US: nickname Equality State
area 97,812 sq mi/253,400 sq km

Wyoming

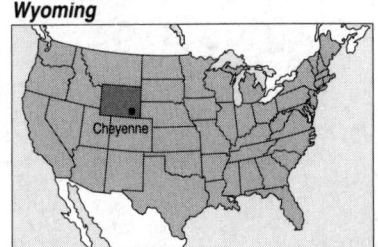

capital Cheyenne

cities Casper, Laramie

features Rocky Mountains; national parks: Yellowstone (including the geyser Old Faithful), Grand Teton

products oil, natural gas, sodium salts, coal, uranium, sheep, beef

population (1990) 453,600

famous people Buffalo Bill Cody, Jackson Pollock

history acquired by US from France as part of the ▷Louisiana Purchase 1803; Fort Laramie, a trading post, settled 1834; granted women the vote 1869; state 1890.

The region was explored 1807 by trapper John Colter, who was the first white to see the Yellowstone area and its geysers and hot springs. The Union Pacific Railroad came through 1867–68; Wyoming then became a territory and passed a pioneering woman's suffrage act. Despite the development of its energy resources, Wyoming remains sparsely settled, with large ranches dotting the arid landscape.

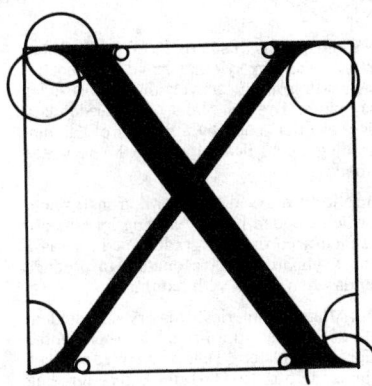

X the 24th letter of the English alphabet, with a sound that can be represented medially by ks and initially by z. It is derived through Latin from the alphabet of W Greece, and was the last letter in the earlier Latin alphabet.

X Roman numeral **ten**; a person or thing unknown.

x in mathematics, an unknown quantity.

xanthophyll yellow pigment in plants that, like ⟲chlorophyll, is responsible for the production of carbohydrates by photosynthesis.

Xavier, St Francis 1506–1552. Spanish Jesuit missionary. He went to the Portuguese colonies in the East Indies, arriving at Goa 1542. He was in Japan 1549–51, establishing a Christian mission that lasted for 100 years. He returned to Goa in 1552, and sailed for China, but died of fever there. He was canonized 1622.

X chromosome larger of the two sex chromosomes, the smaller being the ⟲Y chromosome. These two chromosomes are involved in sex determination. Genes carried on the X chromosome produce the phenomenon of ⟲sex linkage.

xenon (Greek *xenos* "stranger") colorless, odorless, gaseous, non-metallic element, symbol Xe, atomic number 54, atomic weight 131.30. It is grouped with the ⟲inert gases and was long believed not to enter into reactions, but is now known to form some compounds, mostly with fluorine. It is a heavy gas present in very small quantities in the air (about one part in 20 million).

Xenon is used in bubble chambers, light bulbs, vacuum tubes, and lasers. It was discovered in 1898 in a residue from liquid air by William Ramsay and Morris Travers.

Xenophon *c.* 430–354 BC. Greek historian, philosopher, and soldier. He was a disciple of ⟲Socrates (described in Xenophon's *Symposium*). In 401 he joined a Greek mercenary army aiding the Persian prince Cyrus, and on the latter's death took command. His *Anabasis* describes how he led 10,000 Greeks on a 1,000-mi/1,600-km march home across enemy territory. His other works include *Memorabilia* and *Apology*.

xerography dry, electrostatic method of producing images, without the use of negatives or sensitized paper, invented in the US by Chester Carlson 1938 and applied in the Xerox ⟲photocopier. Toner powder is sprayed on paper in highly charged areas and fixed with heat.

xerophyte plant adapted to live in dry conditions. Common adaptations to reduce the rate of ⟲transpiration include a reduction of leaf size, sometimes to spines or scales; a dense covering of hairs over the leaf to trap a layer of moist air (as in edelweiss); and permanently rolled leaves or leaves that roll up in dry weather (as in vinemesquite grass). Many desert cacti are xerophytes.

Xerxes *c.* 519–465 BC. King of Persia from 485 BC when he succeeded his father Darius and continued the Persian invasion of Greece. In 480, at the head of an army of some 400,000 men and supported by a fleet of 800 ships, he crossed the ⟲Hellespont strait (now the Dardanelles) over a bridge of boats. He defeated the Greek fleet at Artemisium and captured and burned Athens, but Themistocles retaliated by annihilating the Persian fleet at Salamis and Xerxes was forced to retreat. He spent his later years working on a grandiose extension of the capital Persepolis and was eventually murdered in a court intrigue.

Xhosa member of a Bantu people of southern Africa, living mainly in the Black National State of ⟲Transkei. Traditionally, the Xhosa were farmers and pastoralists, with a social structure based on a monarchy. Many are now town-dwellers, and provide much of the unskilled labor in South African mines and factories. Their Bantu language belongs to the Niger-Congo family.

Xiamen formerly (until 1979) *Amoy* port on Ku Lang island in Fujian province, SE China; population (1984) 533,000. Industries include textiles, food products, and electronics. It was one of the original five treaty ports used for trade under foreign control 1842–1943 and a special export-trade zone from 1979.

Xian industrial city and capital of Shaanxi province, China; population (1989) 2,710,000. It produces chemicals, electrical equipment, and fertilizers.

It was the capital of China under the Zhou dynasty (1126–255 BC); under the Han dynasty (206 BC–AD 220), when it was called *Changan* ("long peace"); and under the Tang dynasty 618–906, as *Siking* ("western capital"). The Manchus called it *Sian* ("western peace"), now spelled Xian. It reverted to Changan 1913–32, was Siking 1932–43, and again Sian from 1943. It was here that the imperial court retired after the Boxer Rebellion 1900.

Its treasures include the 600-year-old Ming wall; the pottery soldiers buried to protect the tomb of the first Qin emperor, Shi Huangdi; Big Wild Goose Pagoda, one of the oldest in China; and the Great Mosque 742.

Xian Incident kidnapping of the Chinese generalissimo and politician ⟲Chiang Kai-shek Dec 12, 1936, by one of his own generals, to force his cooperation with the Communists against the Japanese invaders.

Xi Jiang or *Si-Kiang* river in China that rises in Yunnan and flows into the South China Sea; length 1,200 mi/1,900 km. Guangzhou lies on the N arm of its delta, and Hong Kong island at its mouth. The name means "west river."

Xingú region in Pará, Brazil, crossed by branches of the Xingu1 River which flows for 1,200 mi/1,900 km to the Amazon Delta. In 1989 Xingú Indians protested at the creation of a vast, intrusive lake for the Babaquara and Kararao dams of the Altamira complex.

Xinhua official Chinese news agency.

Xinjiang Uygur or *Sinkiang Uighur* autonomous region of NW China
area 635,665 sq mi/1,646,800 sq km
capital Urumqi
features largest of Chinese administrative areas; Junggar Pendi (Dzungarian Basin) and Tarim Pendi (Tarim Basin, which includes ⟲Lop Nor, China's nuclear testing ground, although the research centers were moved to the central province of Sichuan 1972) separated by the Tian Shan mountains
products cereals, cotton, fruit in valleys and oases; uranium, coal, iron, copper, tin, oil
population (1990) 15,156,000; the region has 13 recognized ethnic minorities, the largest being 6 million Uigurs (Muslim descendants of Turks)
religion 50% Muslim
history under Manchu rule from the 18th century. Large sections were ceded to Russia 1864 and 1881; China has raised the question of their return and regards the frontier between Xinjiang Uygur and Tajikistan, which runs for 300 mi/480 km, as undemarcated.

Xizang Chinese name for ⟲Tibet, an autonomous region of SW China from 1965.

Xochimilco lake about 7 mi/11 km SE of Mexico City, Mexico, which features floating gardens, all that remains of an ancient water-based agricultural system.

X-ray band of electromagnetic radiation in the wavelength range 10^{-11} to 10^{-9} m (between gamma rays and ultraviolet radiation; see ⟲electromagnetic waves). Applications of X-rays make use of their short wavelength (as in X-ray crystallography) or their penetrating power (as in medical X-rays of internal body tissues). X-rays are dangerous and can cause cancer.

X-rays with short wavelengths pass through most body tissues, although dense areas such as bone prevent their passage, showing up as white areas on X-ray photographs. The X-rays used in ⟲radiotherapy have very short wavelengths that penetrate tissues deeply and destroy them.

X-rays were discovered by Wilhelm Röntgen in 1895 and formerly called roentgen rays. They are produced when high-energy electrons from a heated filament cathode strike the surface of a target (usually made of tungsten) on the face of a massive heat-conducting anode, between which a high alternating voltage (about 100 kV) is applied.

X-ray *An X-ray imager.*

X-ray astronomy detection of X-rays from intensely hot gas in the universe. Such X-rays are prevented from reaching the Earth's surface by the atmosphere, so detectors must be placed in rockets and satellites. The first celestial X-ray source, Scorpius X-1, was discovered by a rocket flight 1962.

Since 1970, special satellites have been orbited to study X-rays from the Sun, stars, and galaxies. Many X-ray sources are believed to be gas falling on to ⊃neutron stars and ⊃black holes.

X-ray diffraction method of studying the atomic and molecular structure of crystalline substances by using ⊃X-rays. X-rays directed at such substances spread out as they pass through the crystals owing to ⊃diffraction (the slight spreading of waves around the edge of an opaque object) of the rays around the atoms. By using measurements of the position and intensity of the diffracted waves, it is possible to calculate the shape and size of the atoms in the crystal. The method has been used to study substances such as ⊃DNA that are found in living material.

X-ray fluorescence spectrometry technique used to determine the major and trace elements in the chemical composition of such materials as ceramics, obsidian, and glass. A sample is bombarded with X-rays, and the wavelengths of the released energy, or fluorescent X-rays, are detected and measured. Different elements have unique wavelengths, and their concentrations can be estimated from the intensity of the released X-rays. This analysis may, for example, help an archeologist in identifying the source of the material.

xylem tissue found in ⊃vascular plants, whose main function is to conduct water and dissolved mineral nutrients from the roots to other parts of the plant. Xylem is composed of a number of different types of cell, and may include long, thin, usually dead cells known as ⊃tracheids; fibers (schlerenchyma); thin-walled ⊃parenchyma cells; and conducting vessels.

In most ⊃angiosperms (flowering plants) water is moved through these vessels. Most ⊃gymnosperms and ⊃pteridophytes lack vessels and depend on tracheids for water conduction.

Non-woody plants contain only primary xylem, derived from the procambium, whereas in trees and shrubs this is replaced for the most part by secondary xylem, formed by ⊃secondary growth from the actively dividing vascular ⊃cambium. The cell walls of the secondary xylem are thickened by a deposit of ⊃lignin, providing mechanical support to the plant; see ⊃wood.

xylophone musical ⊃percussion instrument in which wooden bars of varying lengths are arranged according to graded pitch, or as a piano keyboard, over resonators to produce sounds when struck with hammers.

XYZ Affair in American history, an incident 1797–98 in which the French as represented by foreign minister ⊃Talleyrand were accused of demanding a $250,000 bribe before agreeing to negotiate with US envoys in Paris. The proposed negotiations were part of an attempt to resolve a crisis in Franco-US relations caused by the war in Europe and by French raids on American shipping. Three French agents (referred to by President John Adams 1797 as X, Y, and Z) held secret talks with the envoys over the money. Publicity fueled anti-French feelings in the US and led to increased military spending.

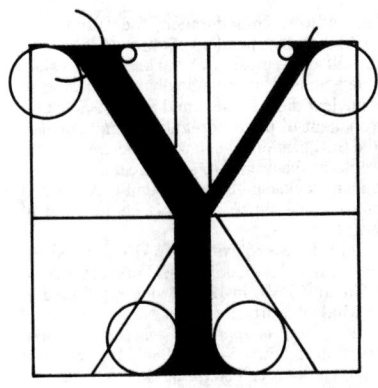

Y 25th letter in the English alphabet, derived through the later Latin alphabet from the Greek letter *upsilon* (Y, υ). In English it represents the same vowel sounds as *i* when used as a vowel (*myth, tryst*), and as a semivowel, phonetic j (*yoke, yacht*), it is a palatal approximant.

Yahya Khan Agha Mohammed 1917–1980. Pakistani president 1969–71. His mishandling of the Bangladesh separatist issue led to civil war, and he was forced to resign.

Yahya Khan fought with the British army in the Middle East during World War II, escaping German capture in Italy. Later, as Pakistan's chief of army general staff, he supported General Ayub Khan's 1958 coup and in 1969 became military ruler. Following defeat by India 1971, he resigned and was under house arrest 1972–75.

yak species of cattle *Bos grunniens*, family Bovidae, which lives in wild herds at high altitudes in Tibet. It stands about 6 ft/2 m at the shoulder and has long shaggy hair on the underparts. It has large, upward-curving horns and humped shoulders. It is in danger of becoming extinct.

In the wild, the yak is brown or black, but the domesticated variety, which is half the size of the wild form, may be white. It is used for milk, meat, leather, and as a beast of burden. The yak is protected from extremes of cold by its thick coat and by the heat produced from the fermentation in progress in its stomach.

Yakima city in S central Washington, on the Yakima River, SE of Seattle. It is an agricultural processing center for sugar beets, apples, hops, and livestock, and produces cider and flour; population (1990) 54,800.

Yakut (Russian *Yakutskaya*) autonomous republic in Siberian Russia
area 1,197,760 sq mi/3,103,000 sq km
capital Yakutsk
features one of world's coldest inhabited places; river Lena
products furs, gold, natural gas, some agriculture in the south
population (1986) 1,009,000; 50% Russians, 37% Yakuts
history the nomadic Yakuts were conquered by Russia 17th century; Yakut was a Soviet republic 1922–91. It remained an autonomous

republic within the Russian Federation after the collapse of the Soviet Union 1991, since when it has agitated for greater independence.

yakuza (Japanese "good for nothing") Japanese gangster. Organized crime in Japan is highly structured, and the various syndicates between them employed some 110,000 people 1989, with a turnover of an estimated 1.5 trillion yen. The *yakuza* are unofficially tolerated and very powerful.

Their main areas of activity are prostitution, pornography, sports, entertainment, and moneylending; they have close links with the construction industry and with some politicians. There is considerable rivalry among gangs. Many *yakuza* have one or more missing fingertips, a self-inflicted ritual injury in atonement for an error.

Yale University US university, founded 1701 in New Haven, Connecticut. It was named after Elihu Yale (1648–1721), born in Boston, Massachusetts, one-time governor of Fort St George, Madras, India.

Yale is considered one of the preeminent US universities, attracting great numbers of foreign students as well as superior US high school graduates. Presidents George Bush and Gerald Ford, among many prominent Americans, attended Yale.

Yalow Rosalyn Sussman 1921– . US physicist who developed radioimmunoassay (RIA), a technique for detecting minute quantities of hormones present in the blood. It can be used to discover a range of hormones produced in the hypothalamic region of the brain. She shared the Nobel Prize for Medicine 1977 with Roger Guillemin (1924–) and Andrew Schally (1926–).

Yalta Conference in 1945, a meeting at which the Allied leaders Churchill (UK), Roosevelt (US), and Stalin (USSR) completed plans for the defeat of Germany in World War II and the foundation of the United Nations. It took place in Yalta, a Soviet vacation resort in the Crimea.

Yalu river forming the N boundary between North Korea and Jilin and Liaoning provinces (Manchuria) in China; length 491 mi/790 km. It is only navigable near the mouth and is frozen from November to March.

yam any climbing plant of the genus *Dioscorea*, family Dioscoreaceae, cultivated in tropical regions; its starchy tubers are eaten as a vegetable. The Mexican yam *D. composita* contains a chemical used in the manufacture of the contraceptive pill.

Yamagata Aritomo 1838–1922. Japanese soldier, politician, and prime minister 1889–93 and 1898. As war minister 1873 and chief of the imperial general staff 1878, he was largely responsible for the modernization of the military system. He returned as chief of staff during the Russo-Japanese War 1904–05 and remained an influential political figure until he was disgraced in 1921 for having meddled in the marriage arrangements of the crown prince.

Yamal Peninsula peninsula in NW Siberian Russia, with gas reserves estimated at 212 trillion cu ft/6 trillion cu m; supplies are piped to W Europe.

Yamamoto Gombei 1852–1933. Japanese admiral and politician. As prime minister 1913–14, he began Japanese expansion into China and initiated political reforms. He became premier again 1923 but resigned the following year.

Yamoussoukro capital of ◊Ivory Coast; population (1986) 120,000. The economy is based on tourism and agricultural trade.

A Roman Catholic basilica (said to be the largest church in the world) was completed 1989.

Yamuna alternate name for the ◊Jumna River in India.

Yanamamo or **Yanomamo** (plural **Yanamami**) a member of a seminomadic South American Indian people, numbering approximately 15,000, who live in S Venezuela and N Brazil. The Yanamamo language belongs to the Macro-Chibcha family. In 1991 Brazil granted them possession of their original land, 58,395 km/36,293 sq mi on its northern border.

Yan'an or **Yenan** industrial city in Shaanxi province, central China; population (1984) 254,000. The ◊Long March ended here Jan 1937, and it was the communist headquarters 1936–47 (the caves in which Mao lived are preserved).

Yangon since 1989 the name for **Rangoon** capital and chief port of Myanmar (Burma) on the Yangon River, 20 mi/32 km from the Indian Ocean; population (1983) 2,459,000. Products include timber, oil, and rice. The city **Dagon** was founded on the site AD 746; it was given the name Rangoon (meaning "end of conflict") by King Alaungpaya 1755.

Yangtze-Kiang alternative transcription of ◊Chang Jiang, the longest river in China.

Yankee initially, a disparaging term for a Dutch freebooter, later applied to English settlers by colonial Dutch in New York. Now it may be a colloquial term for a New Englander, any US northerner (used in the South), or any American (used outside the US).

Yao member of a people living in S China, N Vietnam, N Laos, Thailand, and Myanmar (Burma), and numbering about 4 million (1984). The Yao language may belong to either the Sino-Tibetan or the Thai language family. The Yao incorporate elements of ancestor worship in their animist religion.

The Yao are generally hill-dwelling farmers practicing shifting cultivation, growing rice, vegetables, and also opium poppies. Some are nomadic.

Yaoundé capital of Cameroon, 130 mi/210 km E of the port of Douala; population (1984) 552,000. Industry includes tourism, oil refining, and cigarette manufacturing.

Established by the Germans as a military port 1899, it became capital of French Cameroon 1921.

yapok nocturnal ◊opossum *Chironectes minimus* found in tropical South and Central America. It is about 1.1 ft/33 cm long, with a 1.3 ft/40 cm tail. It has webbed hind feet and thick fur, and is the only aquatic marsupial. The female has a watertight pouch.

yard unit (symbol yd) of length, equivalent to three feet (0.9144 m).

It is sometimes used to denote a cubic yard (0.7646 cubic meters), as of topsoil.

Yaroslavl industrial city (textiles, rubber, paints, commercial vehicles) in W central Russia, capital of Yaroslavl region, on the river Volga 155 mi/250 km NE of Moscow; population (1987) 634,000.

yarrow or **milfoil** perennial herb *Achillea millefolium* of the family Compositae, with feathery, scented leaves and flat-topped clusters of white or pink flowers.

yashmak traditional Muslim face veil, worn by devout Muslim women in the presence of men.

yaws contagious tropical disease common in the West Indies, W Africa, and some Pacific islands, characterized by red, raspberrylike eruptions on the face, toes, and other parts of the body, sometimes followed by lesions of the skin and bones. It is caused by a spirochete (*Treponema pertenue*), a bacterium related to the one that causes ◇syphilis. Treatment is by antibiotics.

yd abbreviation for *yard*.

year unit of time measurement, based on the orbital period of the Earth around the Sun.

The tropical year (also called equinoctal and solar year), from one spring ◇equinox to the next, lasts 365.2422 days. It governs the occurrence of the seasons, and is the period on which the calendar year is based. The sidereal year is the time taken for the Earth to complete one orbit relative to the fixed stars, and lasts 365.2564 days (about 20 minutes longer than a tropical year). The difference is due to the effect of ◇precession, which slowly moves the position of the equinoxes. The anomalistic year is the time taken by any planet in making one complete revolution from perihelion to perihelion; for the Earth this period is about 5 minutes longer than the sidereal year due to the gravitational pull of the other planets. The calendar year consists of 365 days, with an extra day added at the end of Feb each leap year. Leap years occur in every year that is divisible by four, except that a century year is not a leap year unless it is divisible by 400. Hence 1900 was not a leap year, but 2000 will be.

yeast one of various single-celled fungi (especially the genus *Saccharomyces*) that form masses of minute circular or oval cells by budding. When placed in a sugar solution the cells multiply and convert the sugar into alcohol and carbon dioxide. Yeasts are used as fermenting agents in baking, brewing, and the making of wine and spirits. Brewer's yeast *S. cerevisiae* is a rich source of vitamin B.

yeast artificial chromosome (YAC) fragment of ◇DNA from the human genome inserted into a yeast cell. The yeast replicates the fragment along with its own DNA. In this way the fragments are copied to be preserved in a gene library. YACs are characteristically between 250,000 and 1 million base pairs in length. A ◇cosmid works in the same way.

Yeats Jack Butler 1871–1957. Irish painter and illustrator. His vivid scenes of Irish life, for example *Back from the Races* 1925 (Tate Gallery, London), and Celtic mythology reflected a new consciousness of Irish nationalism. He was the brother of the poet W B Yeats.

Yeats W(illiam) B(utler) 1865–1939. Irish poet. He was a leader of the Celtic revival and a founder of the Abbey Theater in Dublin. His early work was romantic and lyrical, as in the poem "The Lake Isle of Innisfree" and plays *The Countess Cathleen* 1892 and *The Land of Heart's Desire* 1894. His later books of poetry include *The Wild Swans at Coole* 1917 and *The Winding Stair* 1929. He was a senator of the Irish Free State 1922–28. Nobel Prize for Literature 1923.

Yeats was born in Dublin. His early poetry, such as *The Wind Among the Reeds* 1899, is romantically and exotically lyrical, and he

drew on Irish legend for his poetic plays, including *Deirdre* 1907, but broke through to a new sharply resilient style with *Responsibilities* 1914. In his personal life there was also a break: the beautiful Maude Gonne, to whom many of his poems had been addressed, refused to marry him, and in 1917 he married Georgie Hyde-Lees, whose work as a medium reinforced his leanings toward mystic symbolism, as in the prose work *A Vision* 1925 and 1937. Among his later volumes of verse are *The Tower* 1928 and *Last Poems and Two Plays* 1939. His other prose works include *Autobiographies* 1926, *Dramatis Personae* 1936, *Letters* 1954, and *Mythologies* 1959.

yellow archangel flowering plant *Lamiastrum galeobdolon* of the mint family Labiatae, found over much of Europe. It grows up to 2 ft/60 cm tall and has nettlelike leaves and whorls of yellow flowers, the lower lips streaked with red in early summer.

yellow fever or *yellow jack* acute tropical viral disease, prevalent in the Caribbean area, Brazil, and on the west coast of Africa. Its symptoms are a high fever and yellowish skin (jaundice, possibly leading to liver failure); the heart and kidneys may also be affected.

Before the arrival of Europeans, yellow fever was not a problem because indigenous people had built up an immunity. The disease was brought under control after the discovery that it is carried by the mosquito *Aëdes aegypti*. The first effective vaccines were produced by Max Theiler (1899–1972) of South Africa, for which he was awarded the 1951 Nobel Prize for Medicine.

yellowhammer Eurasian bird *Emberiza citrinella* of the bunting family Emberizidae. About 6.5 in/16.5 cm long, the male has a yellow head and underside, a chestnut rump, and a brown-streaked back. The female is duller.

The name is sometimes also used for a subspecies of the northern flicker *Colaptes auratus*, a North American woodpecker with a spotted belly and yellow underwings.

Yellowknife capital of Northwest Territories, on the N shore of Great Slave Lake; population (1986) 11,753. It was founded 1935 when gold was discovered in the area and became the capital 1967.

Yellow River English name for the ◇Huang He river, China.

Yellow Sea gulf of the Pacific Ocean between China and Korea; area 180,000 sq mi/ 466,200 sq km. It receives the Huang He (Yellow River) and Chang Jiang.

Yellowstone National Park largest US nature preserve, established 1872, on a broad plateau in the Rocky Mountains, chiefly in NW Wyoming, but also in SW Montana and E Idaho; area 3,469 sq mi/8,983 sq km. The park contains more than 3,000 geysers and hot springs, including periodically erupting Old Faithful. It is one of the world's greatest wildlife refuges. Much of the park was ravaged by forest fires 1988.

John Colter, a trapper, explored the area in 1807.

Yeltsin Boris Nikolayevich 1931– . Russian politician, president of the Russian Soviet Federative Socialist Republic (RSFSR) 1990–91, and president and prime minister of the newly independent Russian Federation from 1991. He directed the Federation's secession from the USSR and the formation of a new,

decentralized confederation, the ◇Commonwealth of Independent States (CIS), with himself as the most powerful leader. He established himself internationally as an advocate of nuclear disarmament and domestically as a proponent of price deregulation and accelerated privatization. Faced with severe economic problems, civil unrest, and threats of a communist backlash, he consistently requested international aid to bring his country out of recession.

Born in Sverdlovsk (now Ekaterinburg), Yelstin joined the Communist Party of the Soviet Union (CPSU) in 1961. Brought to Moscow by Mikhail Gorbachev and Nikolai Ryzhkov in 1985, he was appointed secretary for construction and then, in Dec 1985, Moscow party chief. He was reelected March 1989, and was elected to the Supreme Soviet in May 1989. A supporter of the Baltic states in their calls for greater independence, Yeltsin demanded increasingly more radical economic reform. In 1990 he renounced his CPSU membership and was elected president of the RSFSR, the largest republic of the USSR. Advocating greater autonomy for the constituent republics within a federal USSR, Yeltsin prompted the Russian parliament in June 1990 to pass a decree giving the republic's laws precedence over those passed by the Soviet parliament. In the abortive Aug 1991 coup, Yeltsin supported President Gorbachev. Yelstin was instrumental in the creation of the CIS and combined the offices of Russian president and prime minister to push through an ambitious but unpopular program of price deregulation and accelerated privatization. As the economic situation deteriorated within Russia, his leadership came under increasing challenge, but in April 1992 Yeltsin persuaded 18 of the 20 autonomous republics in the Russian Federation to sign a federative treaty.

Yemen country in SW Asia, bounded N by Saudi Arabia, E by Oman, S by the Gulf of Aden, and W by the Red Sea.

government The unification of North and South Yemen was proclaimed May 1990 with a presidential council formed to oversee a 30-month period of implementation. Many political parties have been legalized or created and, following the approval of a new constitution in May 1991.

history North Yemen was a kingdom in the 2nd millenium BC, followed by successive periods of rule by Egypt, Rome, and Ethiopia. North Yemen adopted Islam 628, formed part of the ◇Ottoman Empire 1538–1630, and was occupied by Turkey in the 19th century.

For the early history of South Yemen, see ◇Arabia.

North Yemen declared a republic The last king of North Yemen, Imam Mohammed, was killed in a military coup 1962. The declaration of the new Yemen Arab Republic (YAR) provoked a civil war between royalist forces, assisted by Saudi Arabia, and republicans, helped by Egypt. By 1967 the republicans, under Marshal Abdullah al-Sallal, had won. Later that year Sallal was deposed while on a foreign visit, and a Republican Council took over.

South Yemen republic founded The People's Democratic Republic of Yemen (South Yemen) was founded 1967 by the union of ◇Aden and the Federation of South Arabia, both of which had been under British rule or protection. Before Britain withdrew, two rival factions fought for power, the Marxist National Liberation Front (NLF) and the Front for the

Liberation of Occupied South Yemen (FLOSY). The NLF eventually won and assumed power as the National Front (NF). On the third anniversary of independence, Nov 1, 1970, the country was renamed the People's Democratic Republic of Yemen, and a provisional Supreme People's Council (SPC) was set up 1971 as the nation's parliament.

The accession of the left-wing NF government caused hundreds of thousands of people to flee to North Yemen, where a more moderate regime was in power. This resulted in clashes between the South Yemen government and mercenaries operating from North Yemen, and war broke out 1971. The Arab League arranged a cease-fire 1972, and the two countries signed an agreement to merge, but the agreement was not honored.

In North Yemen the pro-Saudi Col Ibrahim al-Hamadi seized power 1974, and by 1975 there were rumors of an attempt to restore the monarchy. In 1977 Hamadi was assassinated and Col Ahmed ibn Hussein al-Ghashmi, another member of the Military Command Council which Hamadi had set up 1974, took over. In 1978 a gradual move toward a more constitutional form of government was started, with the appointment of the Constituent People's Assembly, the dissolution of the Military Command Council, and the installation of Ghashmi as president. In 1978 Ghashmi was killed when a bomb exploded in a suitcase carried by an envoy from South Yemen, and Col Ali Abdullah Saleh took over as president.

In the aftermath of Ghashmi's death, the South Yemen president Rubayi Ali was deposed and executed. Two days later the three political parties of South Yemen agreed to merge to form a "Marxist–Leninist vanguard party," the Yemen Socialist Party (YSP), and Abdul Fattah Ismail became its secretary-general. In Dec 1978 Ismail was appointed head of state but four months later resigned and went into exile in the USSR. He was succeeded by Ali Nasser Mohammed.

In 1979 South Yemen's neighbors became concerned when a 20-year Treaty of Friendship and Cooperation was signed, allowing the USSR to station troops in the country, and three years later an aid agreement between the two countries was concluded. A subsequent aid agreement with Kuwait helped to reduce anxieties.

two Yemens at war War broke out again between the two Yemens after the assassination of President Ghashmi of North Yemen. The Arab League again intervened to arrange a cease-fire 1979, and for the second time the two countries agreed to unite. This time definite progress was made so that by 1983 a joint Yemen council was meeting at six-monthly intervals, and in March 1984 a joint committee on foreign policy sat for the first time in Aden. In North Yemen President Saleh was reelected for a further five years 1983, and again 1988, while in South Yemen Ali Nasser Mohammed was reelected secretary-general of the YSP and its political bureau for another five years 1985. He soon began taking steps to remove his opponents, his personal guard killing three bureau members. This led to a short civil war and the dismissal of Ali Nasser from all his posts in the party and the government. A new administration was formed, headed by Haydar Abu Bakr al-Attas, which immediately committed itself to eventual union with North Yemen.

unification A draft constitution of the unified state of Yemen was published Dec 1989 and in Jan 1990 the border between the two countries was opened to allow free movement for all citizens. The unification was proclaimed May 22, with Ali Abdullah Saleh as leader of the new Republic of Yemen and Sana'a as its capital. The new constitution was approved May 1991. *See illustration box.*

Yemen, North former country in SW Asia. It was united with South Yemen 1990 as the Republic of Yemen.

Yemen, South former country in SW Asia. It was united with North Yemen 1990 as the Republic of Yemen.

yen the standard currency of Japan.

Yenan alternative transcription of ◊Yan'an, city in the Chinese province of Shaanxi.

Yenisei river in Asian Russia, rising in the Tuva region and flowing across the Siberian plain into the Arctic Ocean; length 2,550 mi/4,100 km.

Yerevan industrial city (tractor parts, machine tools, chemicals, bricks, bicycles, wine, fruit canning) and capital of Armenia, a few miles N of the Turkish border; population (1987) 1,168,000. It was founded in the 7th century and was alternately Turkish and Persian from the 15th century until ceded to Russia 1828. Armenia became an independent republic 1991.

Its university was founded 1921. The city has seen mounting inter-ethnic violence and Armenian nationalist demonstrations since 1988, fanned by the ◊Nagorno-Karabakh dispute.

Yerkes Observatory astronomical center in Wisconsin, founded by George Hale 1897. It houses the world's largest refracting optical ◊telescope, with a lens of diameter 40 in/102 cm.

yeti Tibetan for the ◊abominable snowman.

Yevtushenko Yevgeny Aleksandrovich 1933– . Soviet poet, born in Siberia. He aroused controversy with his anti-Stalinist "Stalin's Heirs" 1956, published with Khrushchev's support, and "Babi Yar" 1961. His autobiography was published 1963.

yew any evergreen coniferous tree of the genus *Taxus* of the family Taxaceae, native to the northern hemisphere. The leaves and bright red berrylike seeds are poisonous; the wood is hard and close-grained.

The western or Pacific yew *T. brevifolia* is native to North America. English yew *T. baccata* is widely cultivated as an ornamental. The wood was formerly used to make longbows.

Yezidi Islamic sect originating as disciples of

Yemen
Republic of (*al Jamhuriya al Yamaniya*)

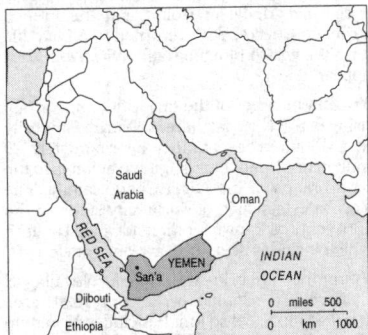

area 205,367 sq mi/531,900 sq km
capital Sana'a
cities Ta'iz; and chief port Aden
physical hot moist coastal plain, rising to plateau and desert
features once known as *Arabia felix* because of its fertility, includes islands of Perim (in strait of Bab-el-Mandeb, at S entrance to Red Sea), Socotra, and Kamaran
head of state and of government Ali Abdullah Saleh from 1990
political system authoritarian republic
political parties Yemen Socialist Party (YSP), Democratic Unionist Party, National Democratic Front, Yemen Reform Group
exports cotton, coffee, grapes, vegetables
currency rial
population (1990 est) 11,000,000; growth rate 2.7% p.a.
life expectancy men 47, women 50
language Arabic
religion Sunni Muslim 63%, Shiite Muslim 37%
literacy men 20%, women 3% (1985 est)
GNP $4.9 bn (1983); $520 per head
chronology
1918 Yemen became independent.
1962 North Yemen declared the Yemen Arab Republic (YAR), with Abdullah al-Sallal as president. Civil war broke out between royalists and republicans.
1967 Civil war ended with the republicans victorious. Sallal deposed and replaced by Republican Council. The People's Republic of South Yemen was formed.
1970 People's Republic of South Yemen renamed People's Democratic Republic of Yemen.
1971–72 War between South Yemen and the YAR; union agreement signed but not kept.
1974 Ibrahim al-Hamadi seized power in North Yemen and Military Command Council set up.
1977 Hamadi assassinated and replaced by Ahmed ibn Hussein al-Ghashmi.
1978 Constituent People's Assembly appointed in North Yemen and Military Command Council dissolved. Ghashmi killed by envoy from South Yemen; succeeded by Ali Abdullah Saleh. War broke out again between the two Yemens. South Yemen president deposed and Yemen Socialist Party (YSP) formed with Abdul Fattah Ismail as secretary-general, later succeeded by Ali Nasser Mohammed.
1979 Cease-fire agreed with commitment to future union.
1983 Saleh elected president of North Yemen for a further five-year term.
1984 Joint committee on foreign policy for the two Yemens met in Aden.
1985 Ali Nasser Mohammed reelected secretary-general of the YSP in South Yemen; removed his opponents. Three bureau members killed.
1986 Civil war in South Yemen; Ali Nasser dismissed. New administration under Haydar Abu Bakr al-Attas.
1988 President Saleh reelected in North Yemen.
1989 Draft constitution for single Yemen state published.
1990 Border between two Yemens opened; countries formally united May 22 as Republic of Yemen.
1991 New constitution approved.

the Sufi saint Sheik Adi ibn Musafir (12th century). The beliefs of its adherents mingle folk traditions with Islam, also incorporating features of Judaism and Christianity (they practice circumcision and baptism), and include a cult of the Fallen Angel who has been reconciled with God. Their chief center is near Mosul, Iraq.

Yezo another name for ⊃Hokkaido, northernmost of the four main islands of Japan.

Yggdrasil in Scandinavian mythology, the world tree, a sacred ash that spans heaven and hell. It is evergreen and tended by the Norns, goddesses of past, present, and future.

Yggdrasil has three roots with a spring under each one. One root covers Nifelheim, the realm of the dead; another runs under Jotunheim, where the giants live; the third under Asgard, home of the gods. By the Norns' well at the third root, the gods regularly gather to confer. Various animals inhabit and feed off the tree.

Yi member of a people living in S China; there are also Yi populations in Laos, Thailand, and Vietnam, totaling about 5.5 million (1987). The Yi are farmers, producing both crops and livestock. Their language belongs to the Sino-Tibetan family; their religion is animist.

Yiddish language member of the west Germanic branch of the Indo-European language family, deriving from 13th–14th-century Rhineland German and spoken by northern, central, and eastern European Jews, who have carried it to Israel, the US, and many other parts of the world. It is written in the Hebrew alphabet and has many dialects reflecting European areas of residence, as well as many borrowed words from Polish, Russian, Lithuanian, and other languages encountered.

In the US, Yiddish has had a powerful impact on English, best heard in the argot of New York City, in the film and stage communities, and in the national media. Such words as *bagel, chutzpah, kibbitz, mench, nosh, schlemiel, schmaltz,* and *schmuck* have entered the American language, but are less used in Britain. The novelist and short-story writer Isaac Bashevis ⊃Singer wrote in Yiddish.

yin and yang Chinese for "dark" and "bright" respectively, referring to the passive (characterized as feminine, negative, intuitive) and active (characterized as masculine, positive, intellectual) principles of nature. Their interaction is believed to maintain equilibrium and harmony in the universe and to be present in all things. In Taoism and Confucianism they are represented by two interlocked curved shapes within a circle, one white, one black, with a spot of the contrasting color within the head of each.

Yippie in the US, a member of the **Youth International Party** (YIP), led by Abbie ⊃Hoffmann and Jerry Rubin (1938–), who mocked the US political process during the 1960s.

Ymir in Scandinavian mythology, the first living being, a giant who grew from melting frost. Among his descendants, the god Odin and his two brothers killed Ymir and created heaven and earth from parts of his body.

yoga (Sanskrit "union") Hindu philosophical system attributed to Patanjali, who lived about 150 BC at Gonda, Uttar Pradesh, India. He preached mystical union with a personal deity through the practice of self-hypnosis and a rising above the senses by abstract meditation,

adoption of special postures, and ascetic practices. As practiced in the West, yoga is more a system of mental and physical exercise, and of induced relaxation as a means of relieving stress.

yogurt also called *yoghurt* or *yoghourt* semisolid curdlike dairy product made from milk fermented with bacteria. It was originally made by nomadic tribes of Central Asia, from mare's milk in leather pouches attached to their saddles. It spread to the Asian and Mediterranean regions, where it is drunk plain, but honey, sugar, and fruit were added in Europe and the US, and the product was made solid and creamy, to be eaten by spoon.

Heat-treated, homogenized milk is inoculated with a culture of *Streptococcus lactis* and *Lactobacillus bulgaricus* in equal amounts, which change the lactose in the milk to lactic acid.

Yogyakarta city in Java, Indonesia, capital 1945–1949; population (1980) 399,000. The Buddhist pyramid shrine to the NW at Borobudur (400 ft/122 m square) was built AD 750–850.

Yokohama Japanese port on Tokyo Bay; population (1989) 3,176,000. Industries include shipbuilding, oil refining, engineering, textiles, glass, and clothing.

In 1859 it was the first Japanese port opened to foreign trade. From then it grew rapidly from a small fishing village to the chief center of trade with Europe and the US. Almost destroyed in an earthquake 1923, it was again rebuilt after World War II.

yolk store of food, mostly in the form of fats and proteins, found in the ⊃eggs of many animals. It provides nourishment for the growing embryo.

yolk sac sac containing the yolk in the egg of most vertebrates. The term is also used for the membranous sac formed below the developing mammalian embryo and connected with the umbilical cord.

Yom Kippur the Jewish Day of ⊃Atonement.

Yom Kippur War the surprise attack on Israel October 1973 by Egypt and Syria; see ⊃Arab-Israeli Wars. It is named after the Jewish national holiday on which it began, the holiest day of the Jewish year.

yoni in Hinduism, an image of the female genitalia as an object of worship, a manifestation of Sakti; the male equivalent is the lingam.

Yonkers city in Westchester County, New York, on the Hudson river, just N of the Bronx, New York City; population (1990) 188,000. Products include machinery, processed foods, chemicals, clothing, and electric and electronic equipment. Yonkers was a Dutch settlement from about 1650.

Sarah Lawrence College is here.

York English dynasty founded by Richard, Duke of York (1411–60). He claimed the throne through his descent from Lionel, Duke of Clarence (1338–1368), third son of Edward III, whereas the reigning monarch, Henry VI of the rival house of Lancaster, was descended from the fourth son. The argument was fought out in the Wars of the ⊃Roses. York was killed at the Battle of Wakefield 1460, but next year his son became King Edward IV, in turn succeeded by his son Edward V and then by his brother Richard III, with whose death at Bosworth the line ended. The Lancastrian victor in that

battle was crowned Henry VII and consolidated his claim by marrying Edward IV's eldest daughter, Elizabeth.

York city in S Pennsylvania, SE of Harrisburg. It is an agricultural processing center for the area and manufactures paper products, building materials, and heavy machinery; population (1990) 42,100. The Articles of Confederation were adopted here during the Continental Congress 1777–78.

York cathedral and industrial city (railroad rolling stock, scientific instruments, sugar, chocolate, and glass) in North Yorkshire, N England
population (1991) 100,600
features The Gothic York Minster, containing medieval stained glass. Much of the 14th-century city wall survives. Jorvik Viking Center, opened 1984 after excavation of a site at Coppergate, contains wooden remains of Viking houses. The National Railway Museum and the 19th-century railroad station; and the university 1963.

York Alvin Cullum "Sergeant" 1887–1964. US war hero. Born in Pall Mall, Tennessee, York was trained as a blacksmith and, although a conscientious objector, was drafted as a private in the 82d Infantry Division in World War I. On Oct 8, 1918, during the Battle of the Argonne Forest, York led a charge against a German position in which he and his comrades captured 132 prisoners and 35 machine guns. Promoted to the rank of sergeant and awarded the Congressional Medal of Honor and the French Croix de Guerre, York returned to private life after the war. A film biography, *Sergeant York*, appeared in 1940.

Yoruba member of the majority ethnic group living in SW Nigeria; there is a Yoruba minority in E Benin. They number approximately 20 million in all, and their language belongs to the Kwa branch of the Niger-Congo family. The Yoruba established powerful city-states in the 15th century, known for their advanced culture which includes sculpture, art, and music.

Yosemite area in the Sierra Nevada, E California, a national park from 1890; area 1,189 sq mi/3,079 sq km. It includes Yosemite Gorge, Yosemite Falls (2,425 ft/739 m in three leaps) with many other lakes and waterfalls, and groves of giant sequoias.

Yoshida Shigeru 1878–1967. Japanese politician who served as prime minister of Occupied Japan for most of the postwar 1946–54 period.

Young Brigham 1801–1877. US ⊃Mormon religious leader, born in Vermont. He joined the Mormon Church, or Church of Jesus Christ of Latter-day Saints, 1832, and three years later was appointed an apostle. After a successful recruiting mission in Liverpool, England, he returned to the US and, as successor of Joseph Smith (who had been murdered), led the Mormon migration to the Great Salt Lake in Utah 1846, founded Salt Lake City, and headed the colony until his death.

Young was preaching in the E US in 1844 when the Mormon prophet and leader Joseph ⊃Smith was murdered in Nauvoo, Illinois, at that time the headquarters of the church. Young returned to Illinois, assumed leadership of most of Smith's distraught followers, and led them away from persecution to a new home near the Great Salt Lake in Utah, establishing a theocratic colony there under his strict and efficient administration. He was appointed governor of Utah territory 1850 and defied federal pressure to repudiate the Mormon practice of polygamy. Young himself had 27 wives and fathered 56 children.

Young Cy (Denton True) 1867–1955. US baseball player. Born in Gilmore, Ohio, Young played for the Cleveland Nationals 1890–98, St Louis Cardinals 1899–1900, Boston Red Sox 1901–08, Cleveland Indians 1909–11, and Boston Braves 1911. As a pitcher of unequaled skill and stamina, Young (nicknamed "Cy" for his "cyclone" pitch) established a lifetime record of 511 victories; 16 times he finished the season with 20 or more wins, 5 times exceeding 30. He was elected to the Baseball Hall of Fame 1937. The Cy Young Award, given annually to the outstanding pitcher in both the American and National leagues, is named after him.

Young John Watts 1930– . US astronaut, the first person to make six space flights. Born in San Francisco, he became a NASA astronaut in 1962 and chief of the Astronaut Office in 1975. His first flight was on *Gemini 3* in 1965, followed by *Gemini 10* in 1966. He flew on *Apollo 10* in 1969 and landed on the Moon with *Apollo 16* in 1972. He was commander of the first flight of the space shuttle *Columbia* in 1981, and commanded the ninth shuttle flight in 1983.

Young Neil 1945– . Canadian rock guitarist, singer, and songwriter, in the US from 1966. His high, plaintive voice and loud, abrasive guitar make his work instantly recognizable, despite abrupt changes of style throughout his career. *Rust Never Sleeps* 1979 and *Arc Weld* 1991 (both with the group Crazy Horse) are among his best work.

Young Thomas 1773–1829. British physicist who revived the wave theory of light and identified the phenomenon of ⟡interference in 1801.

A child prodigy, he had mastered most European languages and many of the Eastern tongues by the age of 20. He had also absorbed the physics of Newton and the chemistry of Lavoisier. He further displayed his versatility by publishing an account of the Rosetta stone; the work played a crucial role in the stone's eventual decipherment by Jean François ⟡Champollion.

Young Ireland Irish nationalist organization, founded 1840 by William Smith O'Brien (1803–1864), who attempted an abortive insurrection of the peasants against the British in Tipperary 1848. O'Brien was sentenced to death, but later pardoned.

Young Italy Italian nationalist organization founded 1831 by Giuseppe ⟡Mazzini while in exile in Marseille. The movement, which was immediately popular, was followed the next year by Young Germany, Young Poland, and similar organizations. All the groups were linked by Mazzini in his Young Europe movement, but none achieved much practical success; attempted uprisings by Young Italy 1834 and 1844 failed miserably. It was superseded in Italy by the ⟡Risorgimento.

Young Men's Christian Association (YMCA) international organization founded 1844 by George Williams (1821–1905) in London and 1851 in the US. It aims at self-improvement—spiritual, intellectual, and physical.

There are about 12 million members in the US in 2,200 groups. YMCAs provide dormitories and rooms for both transients and residents; educational, sports, and civic programs; and recreation facilities for members and for military troops in wartime.

Young Plan scheme devised by US entrepreneur Owen D Young to reschedule German payments of war reparations 1929.

Youngstown industrial city (fabricated metals) in E Ohio, on the Mahoning River; population (1990) 95,700.

Youngstown was laid out 1797, and the city's first steel plant was established 1892, close to coal and iron deposits. Ten thousand workers lost their jobs when three steel plants shut down 1977.

Youngstown Sheet and Tube Co v Sawyer US Supreme Court decision 1952 dealing with the right of the US president to nationalize private industry during wartime. The case arose over President Truman's seizure of steel mills during the Korean War. A crucial part of the war effort, the steel industry had been on the brink of a national strike. The Court ruled that the president's actions were illegal because neither Congressional legislation nor the Constitution had empowered him to intervene in labor disputes or to nationalize property.

Young Turk member of a reformist movement of young army officers in the Ottoman Empire founded 1889. The movement was instrumental in the constitutional changes of 1908 and the abdication of Sultan Abdul-Hamid II 1909. It gained prestige during the Balkan Wars 1912–13 and encouraged Turkish links with the German empire. Its influence diminished after 1918. The term is now used for a member of any radical or rebellious faction within a party or organization.

Young Women's Christian Association *YWCA* organization for the welfare of women and girls, founded London 1855. The first YWCA in the US was formally established 1858 in New York City; another followed in Boston, Massachusetts, 1866. Both were in response to the effects of the Industrial Revolution on women. Its facilities and activities are similar to those of the YMCA.

Yourcenar Marguerite. Adopted name of Marguerite de Crayencour 1903–1987. French writer, born in Belgium. She first gained recognition as a novelist in France in the 1930s with books such as *La Nouvelle Euridyce/The New Euridyce* 1931. Her evocation of past eras and characters, exemplified in *Les Mémoires d'Hadrien/The Memoirs of Hadrian* 1951, brought her acclaim as a historical novelist. In 1939 she settled in the US. In 1980 she became the first woman to be elected to the French Academy.

Ypres (Flemish *Ieper*) Belgian town in W Flanders, 25 mi/40 km S of Ostend, a site of three major battles 1914–17 fought in World War I. The Menin Gate 1927 is a memorial to British soldiers lost in these battles.

Ysselmeer alternate spelling of ⟡IJsselmeer, lake in the Netherlands.

ytterbium soft, lustrous, silvery, malleable, and ductile element of the ⟡lanthanide series, symbol Yb, atomic number 70, atomic weight 173.04. It occurs with (and resembles) yttrium in gadolinite and other minerals, and is used in making steel and other alloys.

In 1878 Swiss chemist Jean-Charles de Marignac gave the name ytterbium (after the Swedish town of Ytterby, near where it was found) to what he believed to be a new element. French chemist Georges Urbain (1872–1938) discovered 1907 that this was in fact a mixture of two elements: ytterbium and lutetium.

yttrium silver-gray, metallic element, symbol Y, atomic number 39, atomic weight 88.905. It is associated with and resembles the ⟡rare-earth elements (⟡lanthanides), occurring in gadolinite, xenotime, and other minerals. It is used in color-television tubes and to reduce steel corrosion.

The name derives from the Swedish town of Ytterby, near where it was first discovered 1788. Swedish chemist Carl Mosander isolated the element 1843.

Yuba City city in N central California, on the Feather River, N of San Francisco. It is an agricultural trading center for nuts, fruits, rice, and dairy products; population (1990) 27,400.

Yucatán peninsula in Central America, divided among Mexico, Belize, and Guatemala; area 70,000 sq mi/180,000 sq km. Tropical crops are grown. It is inhabited by Maya Indians and contains the remains of their civilization.

There are ruins at Chichén Itzá and Uxmal. The Mexican state of Yucatán has an area of 14,823 sq mi/38,402 sq km, and a population (1980) of 1,035,000. Its capital is Mérida.

yucca plant of the genus *Yucca*, family Liliaceae, with over 40 species found in Latin America and southwest US. The leaves are stiff and sword-shaped and the flowers white and bell-shaped.

Yuccas grow in dry soils where nitrate salts, required for protein manufacture, are in short supply. They have therefore evolved the ability to use ammonia, absorbed from animal urine, instead. Feeding extracts of yucca to livestock has been shown to reduce the emission of unpleasant ammoniacal smells from factory farms.

Yugoslavia country in SE Europe, with a SW coastline on the Adriatic Sea, bounded W by Bosnia-Herzegovina, NW by Croatia, E by Romania and Bulgaria, and S by Greece and Albania.

government Under the 1974 constitution, amended 1981, Yugoslavia became a federal republic consisting of six socialist republics (⟡Bosnia-Herzegovina, ⟡Croatia, ⟡Macedonia, ⟡Montenegro, ⟡Serbia, and ⟡Slovenia) and two socialist autonomous provinces (Kosovo and Vojvodina, within Serbia), each with its own assembly. The federal republic itself had a two-chamber legislative assembly comprising the 220-member Federal Chamber and the 88-member Chamber of Republics and Provinces, whose members were indirectly elected every four years, with fixed quotas assigned to the constituent republics and autonomous provinces.

The legislature elected the executive branch of government, which from May 1980 consisted of a nine-member collective presidency, and comprised the head of the Communist Party plus a representative from each republic and province. The presidency's members were appointed for five-year terms, with leadership of the body rotating annually. Day-to-day government administration was carried out by the Federal Executive Council (headed by a president or prime minister), whose members were elected by the legislature for four-year terms.

history Originally inhabited by nomadic peoples from the central Asian plateau, and later by Slavs, the country came under the rule of the Greek and then Roman empires. During the early medieval period the present-day republics of Yugoslavia existed as substantially independent bodies, the most important being the kingdom of Serbia. During the 14th and 15th centuries much of the country was conquered by the Turks and incorporated into the Ottoman Empire, except for mountainous Montenegro, which survived as a sovereign principality, and Croatia and Slovenia in the NW, which formed part of the Austro-Hungarian Hapsburg empire.

Kingdom of the Serbs, Croats, and Slovenes Anti-Ottoman uprisings secured Serbia a measure of autonomy from the early 19th century and full independence from 1878, and the new kingdom proceeded to enlarge its territory, at Turkey and Bulgaria's expense, during the Balkan Wars 1912–13. However, not until the collapse of the Austro-Hungarian empire at the end of World War I were Croatia and Slovenia liberated from foreign control. A new "Kingdom of the Serbs, Croats, and Slovenes" was formed Dec 1918, with the Serbian Peter Karageorgevic at its helm, to which Montenegro acceded following its people's deposition of its own ruler, King Nicholas.

Peter I died 1921 and was succeeded by his son Alexander, who renamed the country Yugoslavia ("nation of the South Slavs") and who, faced with opposition from the Croatians at home and from the Italians abroad, established a military dictatorship 1929. He was assassinated Oct 1934. Alexander's young son ⬦Peter II succeeded, and a regency under the latter's uncle Paul (1893–1976) was set up that came under increasing influence from Germany and Italy. The regency was briefly overthrown by pro-Allied groups March 1941, precipitating an invasion by German troops. Peter II fled, while two guerrilla groups—proroyalist, Serbian-based Chetniks, led by General Draza Mihailovič, and communist partisans, led by Josip Broz (Marshal ⬦Tito)—engaged in resistance activities.

Yugoslav Republic under Tito Tito established a provisional government at liberated Jajce in Bosnia-Herzegovina Nov 1943 and proclaimed the Yugoslav Federal Republic Nov 1945 after the expulsion, with Soviet help, of the remaining German forces. Elections were held, a communist constitution on the Soviet model was introduced, and remaining royalist opposition crushed. Tito broke with Stalin 1948 and, with the constitutional law of 1953, adopted a more liberal and decentralized form of communism centerd around workers'

self-management and the support of private farming. Tito became the dominating force in Yugoslavia and held the newly created post of president from 1953 until his death May 1980.

regional discontent In foreign affairs, the country sought to maintain a balance between East and West and played a leading role in the creation of the ⬦nonaligned movement 1961. Domestically, the nation experienced continuing regional discontent, in particular in Croatia where a violent separatist movement gained ground in the 1970s. To deal with these problems, Tito encouraged further decentralization and devolution of power to the constituent republics. A system of collective leadership and regular rotation of office posts was introduced to prevent the creation of regional cliques. However, the problems of regionalist unrest grew worse during the 1980s, notably in Kosovo, where Albanian and Islamic nationalism respectively were strong.

economic austerity This regionalist discontent was fanned by a decline in living standards from 1980, caused by mounting foreign debt, the service of which absorbed more than 10% of GNP, and a spiraling inflation rate, which reached 200% in 1988 and 700% in 1989. From 1987 to 1988 the federal government under the leadership of Prime Minister Branko Mikulic, a Bosnian, instituted a "market socialist" program of prices and wages decontrol and the greater encouragement of the private sector and foreign "inward investment." The short-term consequence of this restructuring program was a period of increased economic austerity and a rise in the unemployment rate to 15%. Following a wave of strikes and mounting internal disorder, Mikulic was replaced as prime minister Jan 1989 by Ante Marković, a reformist Croatian.

multiparty elections The unity of the ruling Communist Party began to crumble 1988–90 as both personal and ideologically based feuds developed between the leaders of its republican branches. Slobodan Milosević, the hard-line Serbian party chief, waged a populist campaign against Kosovo's and Vojvodina's autonomous status securing their reintegration within Serbia. This led to a violent ethnic Albanian backlash in Kosovo 1989–90 and to growing pressure in more liberal, propluralist Croatia and Slovenia for their republics to break away from the federation. The schism within the Communist Party was confirmed Jan 1990 when its congress had to be abandoned after a walkout by the Slovene delegation. In Sept Kosovo and Vojvodina were effectively stripped of their autonomy when a new multiparty constitution came into effect in Serbia.

In multiparty elections held in Serbia Dec 1990, Slobodan Milosević was elected president and his Serbian Socialist Party (the renamed communists) achieved an assembly majority. In Bosnia-Herzegovina the League of Communists was voted out and the three Muslim, Serb, and Croat nationalist parties formed a coalition. In Macedonia the multiparty election held Nov 1990 resulted in a hung parliament. In Montenegro, the League of Communists held on to power. Concerned at the rising tide of ethnic conflict and political disintegration, Prime Minister Marković founded the Alliance of Reform Forces July 1990 which aimed to preserve Yugoslav unity within a pluralist federation.

Slovenia's call for secession In July 1990 the Slovenian assembly proclaimed full sovereignty and in Feb 1991 called for secession from Yugoslavia.

Yugoslavia

area 34,100 sq mi/88,400 sq km
capital Belgrade
cities Podgorica (Titograd), Kraljevo, Leskovac, Pristina, Novi Sad, Titograd
head of state Dobrica Cosic
head of government Radoje Koutic from Dec 1992
political system socialist pluralist republic
political parties Socialist Party of Serbia, ex-communist; Serbian Renaissance Movement, pro-monarchist; Democratic Party, Serbia-based, liberal, free-market; Montenegro League of Communists; Democratic Coalition of Muslims; Alliance of Reform Forces, Montenegro-based; Internal Macedonian Revolutionary Organization–Democratic Party for Macedonian National Unity (VMRO–DMPNE), Macedonian nationalist; Macedonian League of Communists
exports machinery, electrical goods, chemicals, clothing, tobacco
currency dinar
population (1990) 12,420,000 (53% Serb, 15% Albanian, 11% Macedonian, 5% Montenegrin, 3% Muslim, 2% Croat)
life expectancy men 69, women 75 (1989)
languages Serbian variant of Serbo-Croatian, Macedonian, Slovenian

religion Eastern Orthodox 41% (Serbs), Roman Catholic 12% (Croats), Muslim 3%
literacy 90% (1989)
GNP $154.1 bn; $6,540 per head (1988)
chronology
1918 Creation of Kingdom of the Serbs, Croats, and Slovenes.
1929 Name of Yugoslavia adopted.
1941 Invaded by Germany.
1945 Yugoslav Federal Republic formed under leadership of Tito; communist constitution introduced.
1948 Split with USSR.
1953 Self-management principle enshrined in constitution.
1961 Nonaligned movement formed under Yugoslavia's leadership.
1974 New constitution adopted.
1980 Tito died; collective leadership assumed power.
1987 Threatened use of army to curb unrest.
1988 Economic difficulties: 1,800 strikes, inflation at 250%, 20% unemployment. Ethnic unrest in Montenegro and Vojvodina; party reshuffled and government resigned.
1989 Reformist Croatian Ante Marković became prime minister. 29 died in ethnic riots in Kosovo province, protesting against Serbian attempt to end autonomous status of Kosovo and Vojvodina; state of emergency imposed. May: inflation rose to 490%; tensions with ethnic Albanians rose.
1990 Multiparty systems established in Serbia and Croatia.
1991 June: Slovenia and Croatia declared independence, resulting in clashes between federal and republican armies Slovenia accepted EC-sponsored peace pact. Fighting continued in Croatia; repeated calls for cease-fires failed.
1992 Jan: EC-brokered cease-fire established in Croatia; EC and US recognized Slovenia's and Croatia's independence. Bosnia-Herzegovina and Macedonia declared independence. April: Bosnia-Herzegovina recognized as independent by EC and US amid increasing ethnic hostility; bloody civil war ensued. May: Western ambassadors left Belgrade. Hostilities continued. Sept: United Nations (UN) membership suspended.

Croatian assertion of autonomy In Croatia, ethnic tension between majority Croat and minority Serb populations increased following the election April–May 1990 of a right-wing Croat nationalist government led by Franjo Tudjman. Fearing a resurgence of ethnic persecution, Serbs held, in Aug, an unofficial referendum on the issue of cultural autonomy. In the same month there was an anti-Croat uprising in the Serb-dominated town of Knin in the west. In Feb 1991 the Croatian assembly called for secession from Yugoslavia on the same terms as Slovenia. Serb militants in Krajina in turn demanded secession from Croatia and held a referendum, a week ahead of a referendum on sovereignty throughout Croatia. In Krajina, 90% of electors voted "to remain part of Yugoslavia with Serbia and Montenegro and others who want to preserve Yugoslavia." In Croatia, 93% voted for the republic to become a sovereign and independent country.

In March 1991 there were anticommunist and anti-Milosević riots in Belgrade, spreading to Novi Sad in Vojvodina. On March 15, 1991 the state president, Borisav Jovic, a Serbian, dramatically resigned, after his plan to introduce martial law failed to gain support. There were fears that his departure might presage a military takeover in Yugoslavia. Croatia's representative on the state presidency, Stipe Mesic, a noncommunist committed to the abolition of the federal structure, was formally elected to the collective state presidency June 1991 after three months of political uncertainty. In Bosnia-Herzegovina, there was increasing civil disorder from the spring of 1991.

Slovenia and Croatia declare independence On June 25, 1991 both Slovenia and Croatia issued declarations of independence from Yugoslavia. The lack of recognition from other nations precipitated, from June 1991, bloody military confrontations between the federal army and republican forces. A European Community (EC) delegation of foreign ministers brokered a cease-fire at the end of June but it soon fell apart when the Slovenian parliament overruled the decision of the republic's president, Milan Kucan, to suspend independence for a three-month period. However, threatened with the suspension of EC monetary aid to Yugoslavia it was agreed that the Yugoslav national army would withdraw from Slovenia, which seemed set to secure its independence. But between July and Sept 1991 civil war intensified in ethnically mixed Croatia.

It became uncertain who (politicians or the military) now controlled Yugoslavia at the federal level. Furthermore, the Yugoslav national army had become factionalized, with many units refusing to heed President Mesic's call for a return to barracks.

calls for cease-fire A new cease-fire was ordered by the federal presidency Aug 7, 1991, after the EC, which viewed Serbia as the real aggressor, threatened to apply economic sanctions against the republic. However, the cease-fire again failed to hold and by Sept around a third of Croatia was under Serb control. Oil-rich Croatia responded by imposing an oil supply blockade on Serbia and attacked federal army barracks within the republic. Another EC-brokered cease-fire Sept 2, 1991 collapsed. Both Serbia and Croatia

called for international peacekeeping troops to be deployed and further efforts (including an economic embargo) were made by the EC to achieve a settlement Nov 1991.

other republics call for independence In Aug 1991 Serbia revealed plans to annex the SE part of Bosnia-Herzegovina, causing ethnic clashes within the republic. From Sept 1991 border areas began to fall to the Serbs who established autonomous enclaves. In Oct 1991 the republic's sovereignty was declared but this was resisted by the Serbs. In Macedonia a referendum on independence held Sept 1991 received overwhelming support, despite being boycotted by the Albanian and Serbian minorities. In Kosovo, an unofficial referendum on sovereignty held Sept 1991 received overwhelming support.

collapse of federal government Between Sept and Oct 1991 Croat and Slovene representatives resigned from federal bodies and Bosnian and Macedonian representatives withdrew from the federal presidency. In effect, Serbia was left dominating a "rump" Yugoslavia. On Dec 5, 1991 Stipe Mesic resigned from the presidency, declaring that "Yugoslavia no longer exists." On Dec 20 the federal prime minister, Ante Marković, also resigned.

cease-fire in Croatia In early Jan 1992 a UN peace plan was successfully brokered in Sarajevo which provided for an immediate cease-fire in Croatia. This accord was disregarded by the breakaway Serb leader in Krajina, Milan Babic, but recognized by the main Croatian and Serbian forces. Croatia's and Slovenia's independence was recognized by the EC and the US on Jan 15, 1992.

Bosnia-Herzegovina and Macedonia In Bosnia-Herzegovina, Muslims and Croats held a referendum Feb 1992 and voted overwhelmingly in favor of seeking EC recognition of independence, despite a boycott by the Serbs. Official recognition was granted by the EC and the US in April 1992. Serb opposition to independence continued, with several hundred people killed in violent clashes. Macedonia declared its independence Jan 1992 and immediate recognition was accorded by Bulgaria, but not by Serbia or neighboring Greece. In an unofficial referendum held in the same month, Macedonia's Albanian community voted for autonomy.

Concern for ethnic minorities in Serbia and Serbia's attempted "carve-up" of the newly independent Bosnian republic prompted the EC and the US to deny recognition of a new Yugoslavia, announced by Serbia and Montenegro April 1992. The UN withdrew its ambassadors from Belgrade May 1992 and the US demand for Yugoslavia's expulsion from the ◊Conference on Security and Cooperation in Europe (CSCE) was met July 1992. In Sept Yugoslavia's membership in the UN was suspended because of Serbia's alleged backing of atrocities carried out by Bosnian Serbs against Muslims and Croats, the policy of "ethnic cleansing" carried out by means of enforced evacuations, and the suspected existence of Serbian-run concentration camps in Bosnia. *See illustration box.*

Yugoslav literature Yugoslavian literature evolved from the 9th century translation into Slavonic of the church service books. Its chief

Yukon

glory is folk poetry, in particular the song cycles dealing with the battle of Kosovo and the hero Marko Kraljeviac. After centuries of national repression a revival occurred, notably under Dositej Obradović (1739–1811). Poets of the earlier 19th century include bishop Petar Njegoš (1813–1851), France Prešern (1800–1849), and Ivan Mažuranić (1814–1890). Later, Russian influence predominated. Twentieth-century writers include the novelists Ivan Cankar (1876–1918), Ivo Andrić (1892–1974), and Miroslav Krleža (1893–1981), whose collected works cover 36 volumes, and the poet Oton Župančič (1878–1949).

Yukawa Hideki 1907–1981. Japanese physicist. In 1935 he discovered the strong nuclear force that binds protons and neutrons together in the atomic nucleus, and predicted the existence of the subatomic particle called the ◊meson. He was awarded the Nobel Prize for Physics 1949.

Yukon territory of NW Canada
area 186,631 sq mi/483,500 sq km
capital Whitehorse
cities Dawson, Mayo
features named after its chief river, the Yukon; includes the highest point in Canada, Mount Logan 19,850 ft/6,050 m; Klondike Gold Rush International Historical Park, which extends into Alaska
products gold, silver, lead, zinc, oil, natural gas, coal
population (1991) 26,500
history settlement dates from the gold rush 1896–1910, when 30,000 people moved to the ◊Klondike river valley (silver is now worked there). It became separate from the Northwest Territories 1898, with Dawson as the capital 1898–1951. Construction of the Alcan Highway during World War II helped provide the basis for further development.

Yukon River river in North America, 1,979 mi/3,185 km long, flowing from Lake Tagish in Yukon Territory into Alaska, where it empties into the Bering Sea.

Yungning alternative transcription of ◊Nanning, Chinese port.

Yunnan province of SW China, adjoining Myanmar (Burma), Laos, and Vietnam
area 168,373 sq mi/436,200 sq km
capital Kunming
physical rivers: Chang Jiang, Salween, Mekong; crossed by the Burma Road; mountainous and well forested
products rice, tea, timber, wheat, cotton, rubber, tin, copper, lead, zinc, coal, salt
population (1990) 36,973,000.

Z 26th and last letter in the English and other modern alphabets. Zeta was the 6th in the classical Greek alphabet. It is used initially and medially in many words of Greek or Oriental origin, and many writers employ it in preference to *s* in such words as *baptize* and *organize*, where the suffix is derived originally from the Greek.

Z in physics, the symbol for **impedance** (electricity and magnetism).

Zadar (Italian *Zara*) port and resort in Croatia; population (1981) 116,000. The city was sacked by the army of the Fourth Crusade 1202, which led to the Crusade being excommunicated by Pope Innocent III. It was alternately held and lost by the Venetian republic from the 12th century until its seizure by Austria 1813. It was the capital of Dalmatia 1815–1918 and part of Italy 1920–47, when it became part of Yugoslavia; it is now part of independent Croatia.

Zagreb industrial city (leather, linen, carpets, paper, and electrical goods) and capital of Croatia, on the Sava River; population (1981) 1,174,512. Zagreb was a Roman city (*Aemona*) and has a Gothic cathedral. Its university was founded 1874. The city was bombed Oct 1991 during the Croatian civil war.

Zahir ud-din Mohammed 1483–1530. First Great Mogul of India from 1526, called Babur (Arabic "lion"). He was the great-grandson of the Mongol conqueror Tamerlane and, at the age of 12, succeeded his father, Omar Sheik Mirza, as ruler of Ferghana (Turkestan). In 1526 he defeated the emperor of Delhi at Panipat in the Punjab, captured Delhi and ⟡Agra (the site of the Taj Mahal), and established a dynasty that lasted until 1858.

Zahir Shah Mohammed 1914– . King of Afghanistan 1933–73. Zahir, educated in Kabul and Paris, served in the government 1932–33 before being crowned king. He was overthrown 1973 by a republican coup and went into exile. He became a symbol of national unity for the ⟡Mujaheddin Islamic fundamentalist resistance groups.

In 1991 the Afghan government restored Zahir's citizenship and he prepared to return.

zaibatsu (Japanese "financial clique") Japanese industrial conglomerate (see ⟡cartel).

The old, family-owned Japanese *zaibatsu* had been involved in the military buildup preceding World War II, and, in 1945, after the country's defeat, were broken up by the authorities of the US occupation. Similar conglomerates soon formed in the course of Japan's industrial revival. By the late 1980s there were six *zaibatsu* with 650-member companies between them, employing 6% of the country's work force and controlling 2% of the world economy.

Zaire country in central Africa, bounded W by Congo, N by the Central African Republic and Sudan, E by Uganda, Rwanda, Burundi, and Tanzania, SE by Zambia, and SW by Angola. There is a short coastline on the Atlantic Ocean.

government Zaire was until 1991 a one-party state, based on the Popular Movement of the Revolution (MPR). Under the 1978 constitution, the leader of the MPR is automatically elected president for a nonrenewable seven-year term. The president, head of state and government, appoints and presides over the National Executive Council. There is a single-chamber legislature, the National Legislative Council, whose 210 members are elected by universal suffrage for a five-year term. Ultimate power lies with the MPR, whose highest policy-making body is the 80-member Central Committee, which elects the 14-member Political Bureau.

history The area was originally peopled by central African hunters and agriculturalists. The name Zaire (from *Zadi* "big water") was given by Portuguese explorers who arrived on the country's Atlantic coast in the 15th century. The great medieval kingdom of Kongo, centered on the banks of the Zaïre River, was then in decline, and the subsequent slave trade weakened it further. The interior was not explored by Europeans until the arrival of ⟡Stanley and ⟡Livingstone in the 1870s, partly financed by Leopold II of Belgium, who established the Congo Free State under his personal rule 1885. Local resistance was suppressed, and the inhabitants were exploited. When the atrocious treatment of local labor was made public, Belgium annexed the country as a colony, the Belgian Congo, 1908, and conditions were marginally improved.

independence Zaire was given full independence June 1960 as the Republic of the Congo. The new state was intended to be governed centrally from Leopoldville by President Joseph Kasavubu and Prime Minister Patrice Lumumba, but Moise Tshombe immediately declared the rich mining province of Katanga (renamed Shaba 1972) independent under his leadership. Fighting broke out, which was not quelled by Belgian troops, and the United Nations (UN) Security Council agreed to send a force to restore order and protect lives. Meanwhile, disagreements between Kasavubu and Lumumba on how the crisis should be tackled prompted the Congolese army commander, Col Joseph-Désiré ⟡Mobutu, to step in and temporarily take over the government. Lumumba was imprisoned and later released,

Zaire

Republic of (*République du Zaïre*) (formerly **Congo**)

area 905,366 sq mi/2,344,900 sq km
capital Kinshasa
cities Lubumbashi, Kananga, Kisangani; ports Matadi, Boma
physical Zaïre River basin has tropical rainforest and savanna; mountains in E and W
features lakes Tanganyika, Mobutu Sese Seko, Edward; Ruwenzori mountains
head of state Mobutu Sese Seko Kuku Ngbendu wa Zabanga from 1965
head of government Etienne Tshisekedi from 1992
political system socialist pluralist republic
political parties Popular Movement of the Revolution (MPR), African socialist; numerous new parties registered 1991
exports coffee, copper, cobalt (80% of world output), industrial diamonds, palm oil
currency zaïre
population (1990 est) 35,330,000; growth rate 2.9% p.a.
life expectancy men 51, women 54 (1989)
languages French (official), Swahili, Lingala, other African languages; over 300 dialects
religion Christian 70%, Muslim 10%
literacy men 79%, women 45% (1985 est)
GNP $5 bn (1987); $127 per head
chronology
1908 Congo Free State annexed to Belgium.
1960 Independence achieved from Belgium as Republic of the Congo. Civil war broke out between central government and Katanga province.
1963 Katanga war ended.
1967 New constitution adopted.
1970 Col Mobutu elected president.
1971 Country became the Republic of Zaire.
1972 The Popular Movement of the Revolution (MPR) became the only legal political party. Katanga province renamed Shaba.
1974 Foreign-owned businesses and plantations seized by Mobutu and given in political patronage.
1977 Original owners of confiscated properties invited back. Mobutu reelected; Zairians invaded Shaba province from Angola, repulsed by Belgian paratroopers.
1978 Second unsuccessful invasion from Angola.
1988 Potential rift with Belgium avoided.
1990 Mobutu announced end of ban on multiparty politics, following internal dissent.
1991 Multiparty elections planned for 1992. After antigovernment riots, Mobutu agreed to share power with opposition. Mobutu vowed to remain as president beyond his seven-year term.
1992 Prime Minister Karl-i-bond replaced by Etienne Tshisekedi. Fear of North–South split by followers of Bond.

and five months later power was handed back to Kasavubu. Soon afterwards Lumumba was murdered and the white mercenaries employed by Tshombe were thought to be responsible. The outcry that followed resulted in a new government being formed, with Cyrille Adoula as prime minister.

During the fighting between Tshombe's mercenaries and UN forces the UN secretary-general, Dag ◊Hammarskjöld, flew to Katanga province to mediate and was killed in an airplane crash on the border with Northern Rhodesia. The attempted secession of Katanga was finally stopped 1963 when Tshombe went into exile, taking many of his followers with him to form the Congolese National Liberation Front (FNLC). In July 1964 Tshombe returned from exile, and President Kasavubu appointed him interim prime minister until elections for a new government could be held. In Aug the country was renamed the Democratic Republic of the Congo.

"second republic" A power struggle soon developed between Kasavubu and Tshombe, and again in June, under Mobutu, intervened, establishing a "second republic" Nov 1965. A new constitution was adopted 1967, Tshombe died in captivity 1969, and Mobutu was elected president for a seven-year term 1970. The following year the country became the Republic of Zaire, and the Popular Movement of the Revolution (MPR) was declared the only legal political party 1972. In the same year the president became known as Mobutu Sese Seko.

reform and stability Mobutu, reelected 1977, carried out many political and constitutional reforms. He improved the structure of public administration and brought stability to what had once seemed an ungovernable country, although he faced two revolts in Shaba province. The first in March 1977 was put down with the support of Moroccan forces airlifted to Zaire by France. The second in May 1978 was repulsed by French and Belgian paratroopers. Both invasions were instigated by the Congolese National Liberation Front, operating from bases in Angola. However, the harshness of some of his policies brought international criticism and in 1983 he offered amnesty to all political exiles. Marshal Mobutu, as he was now called, was reelected 1984 for a third term.

After continued pressure, multiparty elections were scheduled for 1992, and by Jan 1991 19 political parties had registered. In Sept 1991, as the country's economy disintegrated and rebellious soldiers and mobs ransacked Zaire's cities, Mobutu agreed to share power and form an emergency government with the opposition. Etienne Tshisekedi of the Democratic Union for Social Progress was appointed prime minister. However, in Oct 1991, after public disagreement, Motubu dismissed Tshisekedi, who then set up an alternative government in opposition to the president. Bernadin Mungul-Diaka was named by Mobutu as the new premier, but he was succeeded in Nov by Jean Nguza Karl-i-Bond. Despite domestic and international opposition to his rule, Mobutu announced Dec 1991 that he intended to remain beyond his seven-year mandate. Creating fears of a North–South split by Bond's followers, in Aug 1992 Tshiksekedi was reinstated as prime minister. *See illustration box.*

Zaïre River formerly (until 1971) *Congo* second longest river in Africa, rising near the Zambia-Zaire border (and known as the *Lualaba River* in the upper reaches) and flowing 2,800 mi/4,500 km to the Atlantic, running in a great curve that crosses the equator

twice, and discharging a volume of water second only to the Amazon. The chief tributaries are the Ubangi, Sangha, and Kasai.

Navigation is interrupted by dangerous rapids up to 100 mi/160 km long, notably from the Zambian border to Bukama; below Kongolo, where the "Gates of Hell" gorge is located; above Kisangani, where the Stanley Falls are situated; and between Kinshasa and Matadi.

Boma is a large port on the estuary; Matadi is a port 50 mi/80 km from the Atlantic, for oceangoing ships; and at Pool Malebo (formerly Stanley Pool), a widening of the river 350 mi/560 km from its mouth which encloses the marshy island of Bamu, are Brazzaville on the western shore and Kinshasa on the southwestern. The Inga dam supplies Matadi and Kinshasa with electricity.

history The mouth of the Zaïre was seen by the Portuguese navigator Diego Cão 1482, but the vast extent of its system became known to Europeans only with the explorations of Livingstone and Stanley.

Zákinthos or *Zante* southernmost of the ◊Ionian Islands, Greece; area 158 sq mi/410 sq km; population (1981) 30,000. Products include olives, currants, grapes, and carpets.

Zama, Battle of battle fought in 202 BC in Numidia (now Algeria), in which the Carthaginians under Hannibal were defeated by the Romans under Scipio, so ending the Second Punic War.

Zambezi river in central and SE Africa; length 1,650 mi/2,650 km from NW Zambia through Mozambique to the Indian Ocean, with a wide delta near Chinde. Major tributaries include the Kafue in Zambia. It is interrupted by rapids, and includes on the Zimbabwe–Zambia border the Victoria Falls (Mosi-oa-tunya) and Kariba

Dam, which forms the reservoir of Lake Kariba with large fisheries.

Zambia landlocked country in S central Africa, bounded N by Zaire and Tanzania, E by Malawi, S by Mozambique, Zimbabwe, Botswana, and Namibia, and W by Angola.

government Zambia is an independent republic within the British ◊Commonwealth. The constitution was adopted 1973 and amended 1990. The state president is elected by universal suffrage for a five-year term, and may be reelected. The president governs with an appointed cabinet and is advised by the House of Chiefs, consisting of chiefs from the country's nine provinces. There is a single-chamber national assembly of 135 members, 125 elected by universal suffrage and 10 nominated by the president. The assembly has a life of five years.

history For early history, see ◊Africa. The country was visited by the Portuguese in the late 18th century and by ◊Livingstone 1851. As Northern Rhodesia it became a British protectorate 1924, together with the former kingdom of Barotseland (now Western Province), taken under British protection at the request of its ruler 1890.

independent republic From 1953 the country, with Southern Rhodesia (now Zimbabwe) and Nyasaland (now Malawi), was part of the Federation of Rhodesia and Nyasaland, dissolved 1963. Northern Rhodesia became the independent Republic of Zambia 1964, within the Commonwealth, with Dr Kenneth ◊Kaunda, leader of the United National Independence Party (UNIP), as its first president. Between 1964 and 1972, when it was declared a one-party state, Zambia was troubled by frequent outbreaks of violence because of disputes within the governing party and conflicts among the country's more than 70 tribes.

Zambia
Republic of

area 290,579 sq mi/752,600 sq km
capital Lusaka
cities Kitwe, Ndola, Kabwe, Chipata, Livingstone
physical forested plateau cut through by rivers
features Zambezi River, Victoria Falls, Kariba Dam
head of state and government Frederick Chiluba from 1991
political system socialist pluralist republic
political parties United National Independence Party (UNIP), African socialist; Movement for Multiparty Democracy (MMD); National Democratic Alliance (Nada)

exports copper, cobalt, zinc, emeralds, tobacco
currency kwacha
population (1990 est) 8,119,000; growth rate 3.3% p.a.
life expectancy men 54, women 57 (1989)
language English (official); Bantu dialects
religion Christian 66%, animist, Hindu, Muslim
literacy 54% (1988)
GNP $2.1 bn (1987); $304 per head (1986)
chronology
1899–1924 As Northern Rhodesia, under administration of the British South Africa Company.
1924 Became a British protectorate.
1964 Independence achieved from Britain, within the Commonwealth, as the Republic of Zambia with Kenneth Kaunda as president.
1972 United National Independence Party (UNIP) declared the only legal party.
1976 Support for the Patriotic Front in Rhodesia declared.
1980 Unsuccessful coup against President Kaunda.
1985 Kaunda elected chair of the African Front Line States.
1987 Kaunda elected chair of the Organization of African Unity (OAU).
1988 Kaunda reelected unopposed for sixth term.
1990 Multiparty system announced for 1991.
1991 Movement for Multiparty Democracy won landslide election victory; Frederick Chiluba became president.
1992 Food and water shortages caused by severe drought.

relations with Rhodesia Zambia was economically dependent on neighboring white-ruled Rhodesia but tolerated liberation groups operating on the border, and relations between the two countries deteriorated. The border was closed 1973, and in 1976 Kaunda declared his support for the Patriotic Front, led by Robert Mugabe and Joshua Nkomo, which was fighting the white regime in Rhodesia. Despite his imposition of strict economic policies, Kaunda was reelected 1983 and again Oct 1988, unopposed, for a sixth consecutive term.

end of Kaunda presidency In 1990, in response to the growing strength of the opposition Movement for Multiparty Democracy (MMD), President Kaunda announced that a multiparty system would be introduced by Oct 1991. The MMD applied for formal registration as a political party and the formation of the National Democratic Alliance (Nada) was announced. Elections were held Oct 1991 and the MMD won an overwhelming victory. Frederick Chiluba was sworn in as Zambia's new president Nov 2, 1991, bringing to an end the 27-year leadership of Kaunda.

drought Zambia was one of the worst hit countries by the drought, the most serious in the 20th century, that plagued Southern Africa in 1992. In March, Mugabe declared the drought a national disaster and appealed for foreign aid. *See illustration box.*

ZANU (acronym for **Zimbabwe African National Union**) political organization founded in 1963 by the Reverend Ndabaningi Sithole and later led by Robert Mugabe. It was banned 1964 by Ian Smith's Rhodesian Front government, against which it conducted a guerrilla war from Zambia until the free elections of 1980, when the ZANU Patriotic Front party, led by Mugabe, won 63% of the vote. In 1987 it merged with ◊ZAPU in preparation for making Zimbabwe a one-party state.

Zanzibar island region of Tanzania
area 640 sq mi/1,658 sq km (50 mi/80 km long)
cities Zanzibar
products cloves, copra
population (1985) 571,000
history settled by Arab traders in the 7th century; became a sultanate; under British protection 1890–1963. Together with the island of Pemba, some nearby islets, and a strip of mainland territory, it became a republic. It merged with Tanganyika as Tanzania 1964.

Zapata Emiliano 1879–1919. Mexican Indian revolutionary leader. He led a revolt against dictator Porfirio Díaz (1830–1915) from 1911 under the slogan "Land and Liberty," to repossess for the indigenous Mexicans the land taken by the Spanish. By 1915 he was driven into retreat, and was assassinated.

Zaporozhye formerly (until 1921) **Aleksandrovsk** industrial city (steel, chemicals, aluminum goods, pig iron, magnesium) in Ukraine, on the river Dnieper; capital of Zaporozhye region and site of the Dnieper Dam; population (1987) 875,000. It was occupied by Germany 1941–43.

Zapotec member of a North American Indian people of S Mexico, now numbering approximately 250,000, living mainly in Oaxaca. The Zapotec language, which belongs to the Oto-Mangean family, has nine dialects. The ancient Zapotec built the ceremonial center of Monte Albán 1000–500 BC; developing one of the classic Mesoamerican civilizations by AD 300, but declined under pressure from the Mixtecs from 900 until the Spanish Conquest 1530s.

ZAPU (acronym for **Zimbabwe African People's Union**) political organization founded by Joshua Nkomo 1961 and banned 1962 by the Rhodesian government. It engaged in a guerrilla war in alliance with ◊ZANU against the Rhodesian regime until late 1979. In the 1980 elections ZAPU was defeated and was then persecuted by the ruling ZANU Patriotic Front party. In 1987 the two parties merged.

Zaragoza (English **Saragossa**) industrial city (iron, steel, chemicals, plastics, canned food, electrical goods) in Aragon, Spain; population (1991) 614,400. The medieval city walls and bridges over the river Ebro survive, and there is a 15th-century university.
history a Celtic settlement known as **Salduba** was captured by the Romans in the 1st century BC; they named it Caesarea Augusta, after their leader; later it was captured by Visigoths and Moors and was taken in 1118 by Alfonso the Warrior, King of Navarre and Aragon, after a nine-month siege. It remained the capital of Aragon until the end of the 15th century. From June 1808 to Feb 1809, in the Peninsular War, it resisted a French siege.

zarzuela (from La Zarzuela, royal country house where it was first developed) Spanish musical theater form combining song, dance, and speech. It originated as an amusement for royalty in the 17th century and found an early exponent in the playwright Calderón. Often satirical, zarzuela gained renewed popularity in the 20th century with the works of Frederico Moreno Tórroba (1891–1982).

Zealand another name for ◊Sjælland, main island of Denmark, and for ◊Zeeland, SW province of the Netherlands.

zebra black and white striped member of the horse genus *Equus* found in Africa; the stripes serve as camouflage or dazzle and confuse predators. It is about 5 ft/1.5 m high at the shoulder, with a stout body and a short, thick mane. Zebras live in family groups and herds on mountains and plains, and can run at up to 40 mph/60 kph. Males are usually solitary.

The **mountain zebra** *E. zebra* was once common in Cape Colony and Natal and still survives in parts of South Africa and Angola. It has long ears and is silvery-white with black or dark brown markings. **Grevy's zebra** *E. grevyi* is much larger, with finer and clearer markings; it inhabits Ethiopia and Somalia. **Burchell's** or the **common zebra** *E. burchelli* is intermediate in size, has white ears, a long mane, and full tail; it roams the plains north of the Orange River in South Africa.

zebu any of a species of ◊cattle *Bos indicus* found domesticated in E Asia, India, and Africa. It is usually light-colored, with large horns and a large fatty hump near the shoulders. It is used for pulling loads, and is held by some Hindus to be sacred. There are about 30 breeds.

Zebus have been crossbred with other species of cattle in hot countries to pass on their qualities of heat tolerance and insect resistance. In the US, they are called Brahman cattle.

Zedekiah last king of Judah 597–586 BC. Placed on the throne by Nebuchadnezzar, he rebelled, was forced to witness his sons' execution, then was blinded and sent to Babylon. The witness to these events was the prophet Jeremiah, who describes them in the Old Testament.

Zeeland province of the SW Netherlands
area 691 sq mi/1,790 sq km
capital Middelburg
cities Vlissingen, Terneuzen, Goes
population (1991) 357,500
products cereals, potatoes
features mostly below sea level, Zeeland is protected by a system of dykes
history disputed by the counts of Flanders and Holland during the Middle Ages, Zeeland was annexed to Holland in 1323 by Count Willam III.

Zeeman Pieter 1865–1943. Dutch physicist who discovered 1896 that when light from certain elements, such as sodium or lithium (when heated), is passed through a spectroscope in the presence of a strong magnetic field, the spectrum splits into a number of distinct lines. His discovery, known as the **Zeeman effect**, won him a share of the 1902 Nobel Prize for Physics.

Zeffirelli Franco 1923– . Italian theater, opera and film director, and stage designer, acclaimed for his stylish designs and lavish productions. His films include *La Traviata* 1983, *Otello* 1986, and *Hamlet* 1990.

zemstvo Russian provincial or district councils established by Tsar Alexander II 1864. They were responsible for local administration until the revolution of 1917.

Zen (abbreviation of Japanese *zenna* "quiet mind concentration") form of ◊Buddhism introduced from India to Japan via China in the 12th century. *Kōan* (paradoxical questions), tea-drinking, and sudden enlightenment are elements of Zen practice. Soto Zen was spread by the priest Dōgen (1200–1253), who emphasized work, practice, discipline, and philosophical questions to discover one's Buddha-nature in the "realization of self.

Zenger John Peter 1697–1746. Colonial American printer and newspaper editor, born in Germany. Zenger immigrated to New York 1710 and was apprenticed to a printer. Establishing his own press 1726, Zenger became active in local political affairs. As editor of the *New York Weekly Journal*, he publicized his opposition to New York governor William Cosby. In 1734 the *Journal*'s virulent antigovernment stance led to Zenger's arrest for seditious libel. Acquitted by a jury in 1735, he published *A Brief Narrative of the Case and Trial of John Peter Zenger* and remained a spokesman for the principle of freedom of the press.

zenith uppermost point of the celestial horizon, immediately above the observer; the ◊nadir is below, diametrically opposite. See ◊celestial sphere.

Zenobia queen of Palmyra AD 266–272. She assumed the crown as regent for her sons, after the death of her husband Odaenathus, and in 272 was defeated at Emesa (now Homs) by Aurelian and taken captive to Rome.

Zeno of Citium c. 335–262 BC. Greek founder of the stoic school of philosophy in Athens, about 300 BC (see ◊stoicism).

Zeno of Elea c. 490–430 BC. Greek philosopher who pointed out several paradoxes that raised "modern" problems of space and time. For example, motion is an illusion, since an arrow in flight must occupy a determinate space at each instant, and therefore must be at rest.

zeolite any of the hydrous aluminum silicates, also containing sodium, calcium, barium, strontium, and potassium, chiefly found in igneous rocks and characterized by a ready loss or gain of water. Zeolites are used as "molecular sieves" to separate mixtures because they are capable of selective absorption. They have a high ion-exchange capacity and can be used to make gasoline, benzene, and toluene from low-grade raw materials, such as coal and methanol.

Zeppelin Ferdinand, Count von Zeppelin 1838–1917. German airship pioneer. On retiring from the army 1891, he devoted himself to the study of aeronautics, and his first airship was built and tested 1900. During World War I a number of Zeppelin airships bombed England. They were also used for luxury passenger transport but the construction of hydrogen-filled airships with rigid keels was abandoned after several disasters in the 1920s and 1930s. Zeppelin also helped to pioneer large multi-engine bomber planes.

Zermatt ski resort in the Valais canton, Switzerland, at the foot of the Matterhorn; population (1985) 3,700.

Zernike Frits 1888–1966. Dutch physicist who developed the phase-contrast microscope 1935. Earlier microscopes allowed many specimens to be examined only after they had been transformed by heavy staining and other treatment. The phase-contrast microscope allowed living cells to be directly observed by making use of the difference in refractive indices between specimens and medium. He was awarded the Nobel Prize for Physics 1953.

zero-based budgeting management technique requiring that no resources for a new period of a program are approved and/or released unless their justification can be demonstrated against alternative options.

Zeus in Greek mythology, chief of the gods (Roman Jupiter). He was the son of Cronus, whom he overthrew; his brothers included Hades and Poseidon, his sisters Demeter and Hera. As the supreme god he dispensed good and evil and was the father and ruler of all humankind. His emblems are the thunderbolt and aegis (shield), representing the thundercloud.

He ate his pregnant first wife Metis (goddess of wisdom), fearing their child (Athena) would be greater than himself. His second wife was Hera, but he also fathered children by other women and goddesses. The offspring, either gods and goddesses or godlike humans, included Apollo, Artemis, Castor and Pollux/Polydeuces, Dionysus, Hebe, Hercules, Hermes, Minos, Perseus, and Persephone.

Zhangjiakou or **Changchiakow** historic town and trade center in Hebei province, China, 100 mi/160 km NW of Beijing, on the Great Wall; population (1980) 1,100,000. Zhangjiakou is on the border of Inner Mongolia (its Mongolian name is **Kalgan**, "gate") and on the road and railroad to Ulaanbaatar in Mongolia. It developed under the Manchu dynasty, and was the center of the tea trade from China to Russia.

Zhao Ziyang 1918– . Chinese politician, prime minister 1980–87 and secretary of the Chinese Communist Party 1987–89. His reforms included self-management and incentives for workers and factories. He lost his secretaryship and other posts after the Tiananmen Square massacre in Beijing June 1989.

Zhejiang or **Chekiang** province of SE China
area 39,295 sq mi/101,800 sq km
capital Hangzhou
features smallest of the Chinese provinces; the base of the Song dynasty 12th–13th centuries; densely populated

products rice, cotton, sugar, jute, corn; timber on the uplands
population (1990) 41,446,000.

Zhelev Zhelyu 1935– . Bulgarian politician, president from 1990. In 1989 he became head of the opposition Democratic Forces coalition. He is a proponent of market-centered economic reform and social peace.

Zhengzhou or **Chengchow** industrial city (light engineering, cotton textiles, foods) and capital (from 1954) of Henan province, China, on the Huang Ho; population (1989) 1,660,000.

In the 1970s the earliest city found in China, from 1500 BC, was excavated near the walls of Zhengzhou. The Shaolin temple, where the martial art of kung fu originated, is nearby.

Zhivkov Todor 1911– . Bulgarian Communist Party leader 1954–89, prime minister 1962–71, president 1971–89. His period in office was one of caution and conservatism. In 1991 he was tried for gross embezzlement.

Zhou Enlai or **Chou En-lai** 1898–1976. Chinese politician. Zhou, a member of the Chinese Communist Party (CCP) from the 1920s, was prime minister 1949–76 and foreign minister 1949–58. He was a moderate Maoist and weathered the Cultural Revolution. He played a key role in foreign affairs.

Born into a declining mandarin gentry family near Shanghai, Zhou studied in Japan and Paris, where he became a founder member of the overseas branch of the CCP. He adhered to the Moscow line of urban-based revolution in China, organizing communist cells in Shanghai and an abortive uprising in Nanchang 1927. In 1935 Zhou supported the election of Mao Zedong as CCP leader and remained a loyal ally during the next 40 years. He served as liaison officer 1937–46 between the CCP and Chiang Kai-shek's nationalist Guomindang government. In 1949 he became prime minister, an office he held until his death Jan 1976.

Zhou, a moderator between the opposing camps of Liu Shaoqi and Mao Zedong, restored orderly progress after the Great Leap Forward (1958–60) and the Cultural Revolution (1966–69), and was the architect of the Four Modernizations program 1975. Abroad, Zhou sought to foster Third World unity at the Bandung Conference 1955, averted an outright border confrontation with the USSR by negotiation with Prime Minister Kosygin 1969, and was the principal advocate of détente with the US during the early 1970s.

Zhu De or **Chu Teh** 1886–1976. Chinese Red Army leader from 1931. He devised the tactic of mobile guerrilla warfare and organized the ⟡Long March to Shaanxi 1934–36. He was made a marshal 1955.

The son of a wealthy Sichuan landlord, Zhu served in the Chinese Imperial Army before supporting Sun Yat-sen in the 1911 revolution. He studied communism in Germany and Paris 1922–25 and joined the Chinese Communist Party (CCP) on his return, becoming commander in chief of the Red Army. Working closely with Mao Zedong, Zhu organized the Red Army's Jiangxi breakout 1931 and led the 18th Route Army during the liberation war 1937–49. He served as head of state (chair of the Standing Committee of the National People's Congress) 1975–76.

Zhukov Georgi Konstantinovich 1896–1974. Marshal of the USSR in World War II and minister of defense 1955–57. As chief of staff from 1941, he defended Moscow 1941, counterattacked at Stalingrad (now

Volgograd) 1942, organized the relief of Leningrad (now St Petersburg) 1943, and led the offensive from the Ukraine March 1944 which ended in the fall of Berlin.

Zhukov joined the Bolsheviks and the Red Army 1918 and led a cavalry regiment in the Civil War 1918–20. His army defeated the Japanese forces in Mongolia 1939. At the end of World War II, he headed the Allied delegation that received the German surrender, and subsequently commanded the Soviet occupation forces in Germany. Under the Khrushchev regime he was denounced 1957 for obstructing party work and encouraging a Zhukov cult, but was restored 1965.

Zia ul-Haq Mohammad 1924–1988. Pakistani general, in power from 1977 until his death, probably an assassination, in an aircraft explosion. He became army chief of staff 1976, led the military coup against Zulfiqar Ali ⟡Bhutto 1977, and became president 1978. Zia introduced a fundamentalist Islamic regime and restricted political activity.

Ziegler Karl 1898–1973. German organic chemist. In 1963 he shared the Nobel Prize for Chemistry with Giulio Natta of Italy for his work on the chemistry and technology of large polymers. He combined simple molecules of the gas ethylene (ethene) into the long-chain plastic polyethylene (polyethene).

ziggurat in ancient Babylonia and Assyria, a step pyramid of sun-baked brick faced with glazed bricks or tiles on which stood a shrine. The Tower of Babel as described in the Bible may have been a ziggurat.

Zimbabwe extensive stone architectural ruins near Victoria in Mashonaland, Zimbabwe. The structure was probably the work of the Shona people who established their rule about AD 1000 and who mined minerals for trading. The word *zimbabwe* means "house of stone" in Shona language. The new state of Zimbabwe took its name from these ruins.

Zimbabwe landlocked country in S central Africa, bounded N by Zambia, E by Mozambique, S by South Africa, and W by Botswana.
government Zimbabwe is an independent republic within the British ⟡Commonwealth. Its constitution dates from 1980 and provides for a president who is formal head of state, a two-chamber parliament consisting of the Senate and the House of Assembly, and a prime minister and cabinet drawn from and responsible to Parliament.

The Senate has 40 members, 24 indirectly elected through an electoral college, 5 elected by Mashona chiefs, 5 chiefs sitting ex officio, and 6 appointed by the president. The House of Assembly has 100 members elected by universal suffrage, through a party list system of proportional representation. Both chambers serve a five-year term and are subject to dissolution within that period. The president is elected by Parliament for a six-year term and in turn appoints the prime minister and cabinet on the basis of parliamentary support.
history For early history, see ⟡Africa. There was a Bantu-speaking civilization in the area before AD 300. By 1200 Mashonaland, now E Zimbabwe, was a major settlement of the Shona people, who had moved in from the north and erected stone buildings. The name Zimbabwe means "stone house" in Bantu. In the 15th century the Shona empire, under Mutota, expanded across Zimbabwe before it fell to the Rozwi, who ruled until the 19th century. Portuguese explorers reached the area in the early 16th century. In 1837 the Matabele,

a Bantu people, in retreat after unsuccessful battles with the ⟩Boers, settled in W Zimbabwe. Mashonaland and ⟩Matabeleland, together with what is now Zambia, were granted to the British South Africa Company 1889, and the whole was named ⟩Rhodesia 1895 in honor of Cecil ⟩Rhodes. King ⟩Lobengula of Matabeleland accepted British protection 1888 but rebelled 1893; he was defeated, but in 1896 after the Jameson Raid (see ⟩ L S Jameson) the Matabele once more unsuccessfully tried to regain their independence. The portion of the area south of the Zambezi River, then known as Southern Rhodesia, became self-governing 1923 and a member of the Federation of Rhodesia and Nyasaland 1953.

African nationalists were campaigning for full democracy, and the African National Congress (ANC), which had been present since 1934, was reconvened 1957 under the leadership of Joshua Nkomo. It was banned 1959, and Nkomo went into exile to become leader of the National Democratic Party (NDP), which had been formed by some ANC members. When the NDP was banned 1961, Nkomo created the Zimbabwe African People's Union (ZAPU); this was banned 1962. In 1963 a splinter group developed from ZAPU, the Zimbabwe African National Union (ZANU), led by the Rev Ndabaningi Sithole, with Robert ⟩Mugabe as its secretary-general.

unilateral declaration of independence After the dissolution of the Federation of Rhodesia and Nyasaland 1963 the leader of the Rhodesian Front party (RF), Winston Field, became the first prime minister of Rhodesia. The RF was a group of white politicians committed to maintaining racial segregation. In April 1964 Field resigned and was replaced by Ian ⟩Smith, who rejected terms for independence proposed by Britain that required clear progress toward majority rule. Four months later ZANU was banned, and Nkomo and Mugabe imprisoned. In Nov 1965, after further British attempts to negotiate a formula for independence, Smith annulled the 1961 constitution and unilaterally announced Rhodesia's independence. Britain broke off diplomatic and trading links and the United Nations initiated economic sanctions, but these were bypassed by many multinational companies. The British prime minister, Harold Wilson, had abortive talks with Smith 1966 and 1968.

disputed independence arrangements In 1969 Rhodesia declared itself a republic and adopted a new constitution, with white majority representation in a two-chamber legislature. Armed South African police at times supported the Smith regime against ZAPU and ZANU guerrillas. In 1972 another draft agreement for independence was rejected by the British government as not acceptable to the Rhodesian people "as a whole." A conference in Geneva 1975 was attended by deputations from the British government, the Smith regime, and the African nationalists, represented by Bishop Abel Muzorewa, president of the African National Council, which had been formed 1971 to oppose the earlier independence arrangements, and Robert Mugabe and Joshua Nkomo, who had been released from detention and had jointly formed the Patriotic Front (PF).

At the beginning of 1979 Smith produced a new "majority rule" constitution, which contained an inbuilt protection for the white minority but which he had managed to get Muzorewa to accept. In June 1979 Bishop Muzorewa was pronounced prime minister of what was to be called Zimbabwe Rhodesia. The new consti-

Zimbabwe
Republic of

area 150,695 sq mi/390,300 sq km
capital Harare
cities Bulawayo, Gweru, Kwekwe, Mutare, Hwange
physical high plateau with central high veld and mountains in E; rivers Zambezi, Limpopo
features Hwange National Park, part of Kalahari Desert; ruins of Great Zimbabwe
head of state and government Robert Mugabe from 1987
political system effectively one-party socialist republic
political party Zimbabwe African National Union–Patriotic Front (ZANU–PF), African socialist
exports tobacco, asbestos, cotton, coffee, gold, silver, copper
currency Zimbabwe dollar
population (1990 est) 10,205,000 (Shona 80%, Ndbele 19%; about 100,000 whites); growth rate 3.5% p.a.
life expectancy men 59, women 63 (1989)
languages English (official), Shona, Sindebele
religion Christian, Muslim, Hindu, animist
literacy men 81%, women 67% (1985 est)
GNP $5.5 bn (1988); $275 per head (1986)
chronology
1889–1923 As Southern Rhodesia, under administration of British South Africa Company.

1923 Became a self-governing British colony.
1961 Zimbabwe African People's Union (ZAPU) formed, with Joshua Nkomo as leader.
1962 ZAPU declared illegal.
1963 Zimbabwe African National Union (ZANU) formed, with Robert Mugabe as secretary-general.
1964 Ian Smith became prime minister. ZANU banned. Nkomo and Mugabe imprisoned.
1965 Smith declared unilateral independence.
1966–68 Abortive talks between Smith and UK prime minister Harold Wilson.
1974 Nkomo and Mugabe released.
1975 Geneva conference set date for constitutional independence.
1979 Smith produced new constitution and established a government with Bishop Abel Muzorewa as prime minister. New government denounced by Nkomo and Mugabe. Conference in London agreed independence arrangements (Lancaster House Agreement).
1980 Independence achieved from Britain, with Robert Mugabe as prime minister.
1981 Rift between Mugabe and Nkomo.
1982 Nkomo dismissed from the cabinet, leaving the country temporarily.
1984 ZANU–PF party congress agreed to create a one-party state in future.
1985 Relations between Mugabe and Nkomo improved. Troops sent to Matabeleland to suppress rumored insurrection; 5,000 civilians killed.
1986 Joint ZANU–PF rally held amid plans for merger.
1987 White-roll seats in the assembly were abolished. President Banana retired; Mugabe combined posts of head of state and prime minister with the title executive president.
1988 Nkomo returned to the cabinet and was appointed vice-president.
1989 Opposition party, the Zimbabwe Unity Movement, formed by Edgar Tekere; draft constitution drawn up, renouncing Marxism–Leninism; ZANU and ZAPU formally merged.
1990 ZANU–PF reelected. State of emergency ended. Opposition to creation of one-party state.
1992 United Front formed to oppose ZANU–PF. March: Mugabe declared dire drought and famine situation a national disaster.

tion was denounced by Mugabe and Nkomo as another attempt by Smith to perpetuate the white domination, and they continued to lead the Zimbabwe African National Liberation Army from bases in neighboring Mozambique. In Aug 1979 the new British prime minister Margaret ⟩Thatcher, under the influence of her foreign secretary Lord Carrington and President Kaunda of Zambia, agreed to the holding of a constitutional conference in London at which all shades of political opinion in Rhodesia would be represented. The conference, Sept 1979, resulted in what became known as the Lancaster House Agreement and paved the way for full independence. A member of the British cabinet, Lord Soames, was sent to Rhodesia as governor-general to arrange a timetable for independence. Economic and trade sanctions were lifted. A small Commonwealth monitoring force supervised the disarming of the thousands of guerrilla fighters who brought their weapons and ammunition from all parts of the country.

independent state achieved A new consti-

tution was adopted, and elections were held, under independent supervision, Feb 1980. They resulted in a decisive win for Robert Mugabe's ZANU–PF party. The new state of Zimbabwe became fully independent April 1980, with the Rev Canaan Banana as president and Robert Mugabe as prime minister. During the next few years a rift developed between Mugabe and Nkomo and between ZANU–PF and ZAPU supporters. Nkomo was accused of trying to undermine Mugabe's administration and was dismissed from the cabinet. Fearing for his safety, he spent some months in the UK. ZAPU was opposed to the 1984 proposal by the ZANU–PF for the eventual creation of a one-party socialist state.

Mugabe's party increased its majority in the 1985 elections with 63 seats against 15 and early in 1986 he announced that the separate seats for the whites in the assembly would be abolished within a year. Relations between the two parties and the two leaders eventually improved and by 1986 discussions of a merger were under way. When President Banana retired 1987, Mugabe combined the posts of head of state and prime minister. In Dec 1989 a draft constitution was drawn up that renounced Marxism–Leninism as the state ideology and created a one-party state, fusing the governing party and opposition groups; the ZANU–PF abandoned its Marxist ideology 1991. A new opposition group headed by former Mugabe ally, Edgar Tekere, was launched 1989, with the intention to challenge the ZANU—PF in the 1990 elections. Tekere announced that his Zimbabwe Unity Movement would advocate capitalism and multiparty democracy. However, the ZANU–PF won a comfortable victory March 1990 and Mugabe was reelected president. The state of emergency, in force since 1965, was ended July 1990. Mugabe's proposals Aug 1990 for a one-party state were strongly opposed. In July 1992 Rev Sithole and Ian Smith formed a United Front to oppose the ZANU–PF.

drought Zimbabwe was one of the worst hit countries by the drought—the most serious in the 20th century—that plagued Southern Africa in 1992. In March Mugabe declared the drought a national disaster and appealed for foreign aid. *See illustration box.*

zinc (Germanic *zint* "point") hard, brittle, bluish-white, metallic element, symbol Zn, atomic number 30, atomic weight 65.37. The principal ore is sphalerite or zinc blende (zinc sulfide, ZnS). Zinc is little affected by air or moisture at ordinary temperatures; its chief uses are in alloys such as brass and in coating metals (for example, galvanized iron). Its compounds include zinc oxide, used in ointments (as an astringent) and cosmetics, paints, glass, and printing ink.

Zinc has been used as a component of brass since the Bronze Age, but it was not recognized as a separate metal until 1746, when it was described by German chemist Andreas Sigismund Marggraf (1709–1782). The name derives from the shape of the crystals on smelting.

zinc ore mineral from which zinc is extracted, principally sphalerite $(Zn,Fe)S$, but also zincite, ZnO_2, and smithsonite, Zn,CO_3, all of which occur in mineralized veins. Ores of lead and zinc often occur together, and are common worldwide; Canada, the US, and Australia are major producers.

Zinnemann Fred(erick) 1907– . Austrian film director, in the US from 1921, latterly in the UK. His films include *High Noon* 1952, *The Nun's Story* 1959, *The Day of the Jackal* 1973, and *Five Days One Summer* 1982.

zinnia any annual plant of the genus *Zinnia*, family Compositae, native to Mexico and South America, notably the cultivated hybrids of *Z. elegans*, with brightly colored, daisylike flowers.

Zinoviev Alexander 1922– . Soviet philosopher whose satire on the USSR, *The Yawning Heights* 1976, led to his exile 1978. *The Reality of Communism* 1984 outlined the argument that communism is the natural consequence of masses of people living under deprived conditions, and thus bound to expand.

Zinoviev Grigory 1883–1936. Russian communist politician whose name was attached to a forgery, the *Zinoviev letter*, inciting Britain's communists to rise, which helped to topple the Labour government 1924.

A prominent Bolshevik, Zinoviev returned to Russia 1917 with Lenin and played a leading part in the Revolution. He became head of the Communist ◊International 1919. As one of the

"Old Bolsheviks," he was seen by Stalin as a threat. He was accused of complicity in the murder of the Bolshevik leader Sergei Kirov 1934, and shot.

Zion Jebusite (Amorites of Canaan) stronghold in Jerusalem captured by King David, and the hill on which he built the Temple, symbol of Jerusalem and of Jewish national life.

Zionism political movement advocating the reestablishment of a Jewish homeland in Palestine, the "promised land" of the Bible, with its capital Jerusalem, the "city of Zion."
1896 As a response to European ◊anti-Semitism, Theodor Herzl published his *Jewish State*, outlining a plan for setting up an autonomous Jewish commonwealth under Ottoman suzerainty.
1897 The World Zionist Congress was established in Basel, Switzerland, with Herzl as its first president. *Hatikva* (The Hope) was adopted as the Zionist anthem, which was the unofficial anthem of Palestine until 1948 when it was sung at the proclamation of the State of Israel on May 14.
1917 The ◊Balfour Declaration was secured from Britain by Chaim Weizmann. It promised the Jews a homeland in Palestine.
1940–48 Jewish settlement in the British mandate of Palestine led to armed conflict between militant Zionists (see ◊Irgun, ◊Stern Gang) and both Palestinian Arabs and the British.
1947 In Nov the United Nations (UN) divided Palestine into Jewish and Arab states, with Jerusalem as an international city.
1948 The Jews in Palestine proclaimed the State of Israel on May 14, but the Arab states rejected both the partition of Palestine and the existence of Israel. The armies of Iraq, Syria, Lebanon, Trans-Jordan, Saudi Arabia, Yemen, and Egypt crossed Israel's borders and attacked en masse but were defeated by the Israeli army (*Haganah*).
1948–73 In addition to constant border sniping and clashes, one or more Arab nations attacked Israel in the on-going ◊Arab–Israeli wars of 1956, 1967, and 1973.
1975 The General Assembly of the UN condemned Zionism as "a form of racism and racial discrimination"; among those voting against the resolution were the US and the members of the European Community.
1991 Attacked during ◊Gulf War by Iraqi missiles and criticized for its stance against Palestinian aspirations, Israel met with Arab nations for the first time in a historic Middle East peace conference held in Spain. The UN General Assembly repealed its 1975 resolution condemning Zionism.

zipper fastening device used in clothing, invented in the US by Whitcomb Judson in 1891, originally for doing up shoes. It has two sets of interlocking teeth, meshed by means of a slide that moves up and down.

zircon zirconium silicate, $ZrSiO_4$, a mineral that occurs in small quantities in a wide range of igneous, sedimentary, and metamorphic rocks. It is very durable and is resistant to erosion and weathering. It is usually colored brown, but can be other colors, and when transparent may be used as a gemstone.

zirconium (Germanic *zircon*, from Persian *zargun* "golden") lustrous, grayish-white, strong, ductile, metallic element, symbol Zr, atomic number 40, atomic weight 91.22. It occurs in nature as the mineral zircon (zirconium

silicate), from which it is obtained commercially. It is used in some ceramics, alloys for wire and filaments, steel manufacture, and nuclear reactors, where its low neutron absorption is advantageous.

It was isolated 1824 by Swedish chemist Jöns Berzelius. The name was proposed by Humphry Davy 1808.

zither a member of a family of musical instruments that have strings attached across a flat sound-board and are plucked, bowed, or struck with a beater, to play a note. Examples are the ◊dulcimer, the Japanese ◊koto, and a 45-stringed folk instrument from Austria and Germany.

zodiac zone of the heavens containing the paths of the Sun, Moon, and planets. When this was devised by the ancient Greeks, only five planets were known, making the zodiac about 16° wide. The stars in it are grouped into 12 signs (constellations), each 30° in extent: Aries, Taurus, Gemini, Cancer, Leo, Virgo, Libra, Scorpius, Sagittarius, Capricornus, Aquarius, and Pisces. Because of the ◊precession of the equinoxes, the current constellations do not cover the same areas of sky as the zodiacal signs of the same name.

zodiacal light cone-shaped light sometimes seen extending from the Sun along the ◊ecliptic, visible after sunset or before sunrise. It is due to thinly spread dust particles in the central plane of the Solar System. It is very faint, and requires a dark, clear sky to be seen.

Zoë *c.* 978–1050. Byzantine empress who ruled from 1028 until 1050. She gained the title by marriage to the heir apparent Romanus III Argyrus, but was reputed to have poisoned him (1034) in order to marry her lover Michael. He died 1041 and Zoë and her sister Theodora were proclaimed joint empresses. Rivalry led to Zoë marrying Constantine IX Monomachus with whom she reigned until her death.

zoetrope optical toy with a series of pictures on the inner surface of a cylinder. When the pictures are rotated and viewed through a slit, it gives the impression of continuous motion.

Zog Ahmed Beg Zogu 1895–1961. King of Albania 1928–39. He became prime minister of Albania 1922, president of the republic 1925, and proclaimed himself king 1928. He was driven out by the Italians 1939 and settled in England.

zoidogamy type of plant reproduction in which male gametes (antherozoids) swim in a film of water to the female gametes. Zoidogamy is found in algae, bryophytes, pteridophytes, and some gymnosperms (others use ◊siphonogamy).

Zola Émile Edouard Charles Antoine 1840–1902. French novelist and social reformer. With *La Fortune des Rougon/The Fortune of the Rougons* 1867 he began a series of some 20 naturalistic novels, portraying the fortunes of a French family under the Second Empire. They include *Le Ventre de Paris/The Underbelly of Paris* 1873, *Nana* 1880, and *La Débâcle/The Debacle* 1892. In 1898 he published *J'accuse/ I Accuse*, a pamphlet indicting the persecutors of ◊Dreyfus, for which he was prosecuted for libel but later pardoned.

Born in Paris, Zola was a journalist and clerk until his *Contes à Ninon/Stories for Ninon* 1864 enabled him to devote himself to literature. Some of the titles in *La Fortune des Rougon* series are *La Faute de l'Abbé Mouret/The Simple Priest* 1875, *L'Assommoir/Drunkard* 1878, *Germinal* 1885, and *La Terre/Earth* 1888. Among later novels are the trilogy *Trois Villes/Three Cities* 1894–98, and *Fécondité/Fecundity* 1899.

Zollverein 19th-century German customs union, begun under Prussian auspices 1828; the union included most German-speaking states except Austria by 1834.

Although designed to remove tariff barriers and facilitate trade within the German confederation, the Zollverein also had a political effect in isolating Austria. The Austrians were committed to trade tariffs to protect their agriculture and industry; thus their inability to join the Zollverein served to increase Prussian power in the confederation.

Zomba former capital of Malawi, 20 mi/32 km W of Lake Shirwa; population (1985) 53,000. It was replaced by Lilongwe as capital 1975 but remains the university town.

zombie corpse believed to be reanimated by a spirit and enslaved. The idea, widespread in Haiti, possibly arose from voodoo priests using the nerve poison tetrodotoxin (from the puffer fish) to produce a semblance of death from which the victim afterwards physically recovers. Those eating incorrectly prepared puffer fish in Japan have been similarly affected.

zone standard time or **standard time** the time in any of the 24 time zones, each an hour apart, into which the Earth is divided. The respective times depend on their distances, east or west of Greenwich, England. In North America the eight zones (Atlantic, Eastern, Central, Mountain, Pacific, Alaska, Hawaii-Aleutian, and Samoa) use the mean solar times of meridians 15° apart, starting with 60° longitude. (See also ▷time.)

zone system in photography, a system of exposure estimation invented by Ansel ▷Adams that groups infinite tonal gradations into ten zones, zone 0 being black and zone 10 white. An ▷f-stop change in exposure is required from zone to zone.

zoo abbreviation for *zoological gardens*, a place where animals are kept in captivity. Originally created purely for visitor entertainment and education, zoos have become major centers for the breeding of endangered species of animals; a 1984 report identified 2,000 vertebrate species in need of such maintenance. The Arabian oryx has already been preserved in this way; it was captured 1962, bred in captivity, and released again in the desert 1972, where it has flourished.

Notable zoos exist in New York, San Diego, Toronto, Chicago, London, Paris, Berlin, Moscow, and Beijing (Peking).

zoology branch of biology concerned with the study of animals. It includes description of present-day animals, the study of evolution of animal forms, anatomy, physiology, embryology, behavior, and geographical distribution.

zoom lens photographic lens that, by variation of focal length, allows speedy transition from long shots to close-ups.

zoonosis any infectious disease that can be transmitted to humans by other vertebrate animals. Probably the most feared example is ▷rabies. The transmitted microorganism sometimes causes disease only in the human host, leaving the animal host unaffected.

Zorach v Clausen US Supreme Court decision 1952 dealing with the inclusion of religious studies in public school education. A New York City program that exempted some public school students from the required curriculum to pursue religious studies elsewhere was challenged as an unconstitutional marriage of church and state. The Court upheld the "release program," ruling that the division between church and state was not meant to be absolute.

Zoroaster or **Zarathustra** 6th century BC. Persian prophet and religious teacher, founder of Zoroastrianism. Zoroaster believed that he had seen God, Ahura Mazda, in a vision. His first vision came at the age of 30 and, after initial rejection and violent attack, he converted King Vishtaspa. Subsequently, his teachings spread rapidly, becoming the official religion of the kingdom. According to tradition, Zoroaster was murdered at the age of 70 while praying at the altar.

Zoroastrianism pre-Islamic Persian religion founded by the Persian prophet Zoroaster in the 6th century BC, and still practiced by the ▷Parsees in India. The **Zend-Avesta** are the sacred scriptures of the faith. The theology is dualistic, **Ahura Mazda** or **Ormuzd** (the good God) being perpetually in conflict with **Ahriman** (the evil God), but the former is assured of eventual victory. There are approximately 100,000 (1991) Zoroastrians worldwide; membership is restricted to those with both parents belonging to the faith.

beliefs Humanity has been given free will to choose between the two powers, thus rendering believers responsible for their fate after death in heaven or hell. Moral and physical purity is central to all aspects of Zoroastrianism *yasna* or worship: since life and work are part of worship, there should be purity of action. Fire is considered sacred, and Ahura Mazda believed to be present when the ritual flame is worshiped at home or in the temple. It is believed that there will be a second universal judgment at *Frashokereti*, a time when the dead will be raised and the world cleansed of unnatural impurity.

The Parsee community in Bombay is now the main center of Zoroastrianism, but since conversion is generally considered impossible, the numbers in India, have been steadily decreasing at the rate of 10% per decade since 1947. Parsee groups, mainly in Delhi and outside India, have been pushing for the acceptance of converts, but the concern of the majority in Bombay is that their religious and cultural heritage will be lost.

Zouave member of a corps of French infantry soldiers, first raised in 1831 from the Zouaoua tribe in Algeria. The term came to be used for soldiers in other corps modeled on the French Zouaves.

Z particle in physics, an ▷elementary particle, one of the weakons responsible for carrying the ▷weak nuclear force.

Zsigmondy Richard 1865–1929. Austrian chemist who devised and built an ultramicroscope in 1903. The microscope's illumination was placed at right angles to the axis. (In a conventional microscope the light source is placed parallel to the instrument's axis.) Zsigmondy's arrangement made it possible to observe gold particles with a diameter of 10-millionth of a millimeter. He received the Nobel Prize for Chemistry 1925.

Zuider Zee former sea inlet in Holland, cut off from the North Sea by the closing of a dyke 1932, much of which has been reclaimed as land. The remaining lake is called the ▷IJsselmeer.

Zulu member of a group of southern African peoples mainly from Natal, South Africa. Their present homeland, KwaZulu, represents the nucleus of the once extensive and militaristic Zulu kingdom. Today many Zulus work in the industrial centers around Johannesburg and Durban. The Zulu language, closely related to Xhosa, belongs to the Bantu branch of the Niger-Congo family.

Zululand region in Natal, South Africa, largely corresponding to the Black National State KwaZulu. It was formerly a province, annexed to Natal 1897.

Zurbarán Francisco de 1598–1664. Spanish painter, based in Seville. He painted religious subjects in a powerful, austere style, often focusing on a single figure in prayer.

Zurbarán used deep contrasts of light and shade to create an intense spirituality in his works and received many commissions from religious orders in Spain and South America. During the 1640s the softer, sweeter style of Murillo displaced Zurbarán's art in public favor in Seville, and in 1658 he moved to Madrid.

Zürich financial center and industrial city (machinery, electrical goods, textiles) on Lake Zürich; capital of Zürich canton and the largest city in Switzerland; population (1990) 341,300.

The university was refounded 1833.

Zweig Stefan 1881–1942. Austrian writer, author of plays, poems, and many biographies of writers (Balzac, Dickens) and historical figures (Marie Antoinette, Mary Stuart). He and his wife, exiles from the Nazis from 1934, despaired at what they saw as the end of civilization and culture and committed suicide in Brazil.

Zwicky Fritz 1898–1974. Bulgarian-born Swiss astronomer who lived in the US from 1925. He was professor of physics at the California Institute of Technology (Caltech) from 1927 until his retirement 1968. In 1934, he predicted the existence of neutron stars and, together with Walter Baade, named supernovae. He discovered 18 supernovae in total, and determined that cosmic rays originated in them.

Zwingli Ulrich 1484–1531. Swiss Protestant, born in St Gallen. He was ordained a Roman Catholic priest 1506, but by 1519 was a Reformer and led the Reformation in Switzerland with his insistence on the sole authority of the Scriptures. He was killed in a skirmish at Kappel during a war against the cantons that had not accepted the Reformation.

Zworykin Vladimir Kosma 1889–1982. Russian-born US electronics engineer, in the US from 1919. He invented a television camera tube and the ▷electron microscope.

zydeco dance music originating in Louisiana, similar to ▷Cajun but more heavily influenced by blues and West Indian music.

Zydeco is fast and bouncy, using instruments like accordions, saxophones, and washboards. It was widely popularized by the singer and accordion player Clifton Chenier (1925–1987).

zygote ▷ovum (egg) after ▷fertilization but before it undergoes cleavage to begin embryonic development.